International
WHO'S WHO
of
Professionals™

Published by

Proud publisher of the following professional reference directories:

International WHO'S WHO of Professionals
International WHO'S WHO of Professional Management
International WHO'S WHO of Entrepreneurs
International WHO'S WHO of Information Technology
WHO'S WHO of Public Service
WHO'S WHO of High School Athletes

414 Bell Fork Road
Jacksonville, North Carolina 28541

ISBN: 1–882952–03–0

International WHO'S WHO of Professionals is published
and distributed annually by:
Gibralter Publishing, Inc.
414 Bell Fork Road, P.O. Box 3002
Jacksonville, NC 28541–3002
Phone: (800) ASK–4–WHO
Fax: (910) 455–1937
E–mail: www.gibralter.com

The annual edition is available to members only for $369.00.
To order a copy, please call Membership Services at (800) ASK–4–WHO
and give the operator the ISBN number above.
A 10% shipping and handling charge will be calculated for U.S. shipments.
International orders must call for exact rates.
North Carolina residents must add appropriate sales tax.

POSTMASTER send address changes to:
International WHO'S WHO of Professionals
C/O Gibralter Publishing, Inc.
414 Bell Fork Road,
Jacksonville, NC 28541–3002

Printed and bound in the United States of America

1996 Edition
Vol. 1, No. 4

International
WHO'S WHO
of
Professionals™

The Ultimate Professional Directory

Disclaimer

This edition was compiled with the assistance of the following individuals at Gibralter Publishing, Inc.:

Edward A. Bohn
Chairman of the Board

Terrence J. Leifheit
President and Chief Executive Officer

Yvonne C. Guy
Director of Marketing

Louann M. Driver
Creative Director

Carrie J. Gillard
Editor

Janet B. Smith
Editorial Assistant

Lisa J. Bowman
Editorial Assistant

International WHO'S WHO *of Professionals*

Published by Gibralter Publishing, Inc.

We would like to gratefully acknowledge the willing participation of our Board of Advisors, whose function is to help us maintain the highest standard of membership and provide us with input regarding world economics, political, industrial and professional issues. Their voluntary efforts and contributions are greatly appreciated.

This Edition was compiled with the assistance of the following accomplished individuals who serve on the International WHO'S WHO of Professionals Board of Advisors:

Pierre E.G. Salinger
Vice Chairman
Burson–Marsteller, Inc.
Washington, DC

Former Chief Foreign Correspondent
ABC News
New York, New York

Former Press Secretary
Presidents Kennedy and Johnson
Washington, DC

Ivana M. Trump
President and Chief Executive Officer
House of Ivana & Ivana Inc.
New York, New York

Past President and Chief Executive Officer
The Plaza Hotel
New York, New York

Past Chief Executive Officer
The Trump's Castle Hotel & Casino
Atlantic City, New Jersey

Tieman Henry Dippel, Jr.
Chairman and President
Brenham Bancshares, Inc.
Brenham, Texas

Chairman and President
Dippel Venture Capital Corporation

Author
The New Legacy

Charles R. Bruce
Vice Chairman of International Marketing
Wendy's International, Inc.
Dublin, Ohio

Chief Charles Adebowale Joshua, Ph.D
President, Board of Trustees, Founder
Bedford–Stuyvesant Mental Health Center
Brooklyn, New York

Executive Director
Central Brooklyn

First American Named To
African Chieftaincy

David G. Nutty
Director of Quality Control/Customer Service, Bankcard Division
First National Bank of Omaha
Omaha, Nebraska

Ramesh C. Pandey, Ph.D.
President and Chief Executive Officer
Xechem, Inc.
New Brunswick, New Jersey

---◆---

Mr. Tieman Henry Dippel, Jr.
Chairman
Brenham Bancshares, Inc.
2211 S. Day Street, Suite 401
Brenham, TX 77833
Fax: Please mail or call.

6059

---◆---

Business Information: Brenham Bancshares, Inc. is a bank holding company. Chairman of the Board and President of Brenham Bancshares, Inc., Chairman of the Board, Brenham National Bank, President and Registered Investment Adviser of Dippel, Winston & Associates, Chairman and President of Dippel Venture Capital Corporation, Partner of Dippel & Alfred Interests, Mr. Dippel is well–known in his community and in the state of Texas as an influential thinker and political independent. Mr. Dippel's knowledge in the four major areas of influence, (politics, economics, media and information), is both comprehensive and far ranging. Tim Richardson, editor of the highly regarded Austin political newsletters Quorum Report, reports, "Tieman Henry Dippel, Jr. is often listed as one of the state's most influential leaders, but his power does not lie in being what one would call 'the networker's networker.'...Far more important, he is a philosophical leader...a political independent who understands the importance of ideas in a state that any presidential candidate must win to have any hope of success. Dippel realizes that we get the government we elect and our level of consciousness and sense of responsibility are the real keys to our future success." His highly acclaimed book, The New Legacy (Taylor Publishing, 1987), has been proclaimed "a map to the future" by Texas Governor Ann Richards, and a "prescription for life and government all wrapped in one" by his friend, Senator Phil Gramm. Fellow Texan Treasury Secretary Lloyd Bentsen comments, "in today's world where roots are often shallow...it is refreshing to find someone who is so firmly grounded in his native heritage." Tim Richardson writes that The New Legacy "could be a singularly influential book to the future of Texas...it is the synergism of the masterful perspective of life, of responsibility, and of history that blend with the vacuum that presently exists in Texas. This book is an inspiration to a sense of destiny because it gives Texans a choice between two futures...increasingly partisan politics and a muddling through, or a vision of Texas being a third coast of thought for a common good with coordinated goals...one of the few recent works that I have seen that has a sense of vision, integrity, and values that could hopefully inspire popular involvement in the process." Mr. Dippel has contributed articles on education, economics, politics, and Texas to many distinguished publications, and has been listed in Who's Who in Finance & Industry (1977/78), Who's Who in American Law (First Edition), and Who's Who in the World (Fifth Edition 1980/81). He has been profiled by Texas Business four times in "The Rising Stars of Texas" (1980), "Who Really Rules Texas" (1983), "Twenty who Hold the Power in Texas" (1986), and "Be the Best" (1987); and twice in Ultra in "Texas CEOs, Young & Powerful" (1984), and "Texas Trailblazers" (1986). Tieman Henry Dippel, Jr. is a distinguished American, and a visionary leader in politics, economics, and the media. Established in 1933, Brenham Bancshares, Inc. employs over 50 people and reports assets in excess of $100 million. **Career Steps:** Chairman of the Board and President, Brenham Bancshares, Inc. (1983–Present); President, Dippel, Winston & Associates (1991–Present); Chairman of the Board and President, Dippel Venture Capital Corporation (1983–Present); Chairman of the Board, Chairman of the Executive Committee, Brenham National Bank (1972–Present); Partner, Dippel & Alfred Interests, Real Estate Development Partnership. **Associations and Accomplishments:** Former President, Texas State Chamber of Commerce; Former Chairman and President, Texas Lyceum Association; Former Chairman, Texans for Quality Education; Former Commissioner and Legislative Chairman, Texas Commission of the Arts; Former President, East Texas Chamber of Commerce; Recipient, John Ben Shepperd Forum "Outstanding Texas Leader" Award (1990); Director and Charter Committee Member, Texas Business Roundtable; Nominating Committee, Texas Research League; Director, Federal Reserve Bank of Dallas–Houston Branch; Executive Committee, Blue Cross and Blue Shield of Texas; Chaired statewide committees of independents for various statewide candidates; Former Director, Covenant House of Texas; Present Director, Caring for Children Foundation; Active in Boy Scouts of America, Eagle Scout with cluster; Methodist Church; University of Texas Centennial Commission; Development Board, University of Texas Health Science Center (Houston). **Education:** University of Texas at Austin, B.B.A. Class Valedictorian (1968); University of Texas at Austin, J.D., Chancellor Society (1971); U.S. Naval Justice School, LTCDR Naval Reserve, Certified Trial & Defense Counsel; Admitted to Practice: United States Supreme Court, United States Tax Court, United States Court of Claims, United States Court of Military Appeals, United States District Court (Western District of Texas), United States Fifth Circuit Court of Appeals, State of Texas Bar; Series 7 Securities License; Real Estate License – Texas; Insurance Licenses – Texas. **Personal:** Son of the late Sheriff and Mrs. Tieman H. Dippel, Sr., of Brenham, Texas. Married to Katherine Wright since 1971. Three children: Margaret, Tieman III, and Elizabeth.

◆

Mr. Pierre E.G. Salinger
Vice Chairman
Burson–Marsteller, Inc.
1850 M Street NW
Washington, DC 20036
(202) 833–4272
Fax: (202) 833–4278
8743

◆

Business Information: Burson–Marsteller, Inc. is the world's leading public relations firm, serving Fortune 500 companies and corporations globally. Established during the 1950's, the Firm has consultants located around the world in over 38 countries. Mr. Salinger is an accessible and articulate spokesman for Burson–Marsteller, Inc. As Vice Chairman, he oversees all global public relations, specializing in the areas of economics and crisis management; and is the general counsel for major corporate clientele. Mr. Salinger began his public life as a musical prodigy at the age of six. He joined the staff of the "San Francisco Chronicle" in 1942 as a reporter, leaving in 1943 for World War II service as a Navy officer, and then returned to the "Chronicle" in 1946 serving as editor. Following this he served as the West Coast editor of "Collier's" magazine. In the Fall of 1956, Pierre went to Seattle and Detroit to investigate The Teamsters Union, led at that time by James Hoffa. "Collier's" folded their business operations in December 1956 before his articles on Teamsters were ever published. This is what led Senator Robert F. Kennedy to contact him, resulting in his serving as investigator for the Senate Labor Rackets Committee. During this time he worked closely with Senator John F. Kennedy, who was also a member of the Investigation Committee. As a result of their close working relationship, Salinger was asked to serve as Kennedy's press aide in his presidential campaign — playing a major role in its success. On November 10, 1960, Salinger was designated by President–elect Kennedy to be his press secretary. Later upon the succession of Lyndon B. Johnson he was appointed in the same role for the duration of his administration. Pierre Salinger has been a major figure in national public life during the past forty years. He served as a U.S. Senator in 1964; and during the period of 1978–1993 was the Chief Foreign Correspondent for ABC News. He writes extensively, is interviewed frequently, and reviews many books. In a recent article in "New Perspectives Quarterly," entitled Cold War Aftershocks, he highlights the new domestic policy and governmental reform needed in the new market democracies of Eastern Europe and the former USSR. **Career Steps:** Vice Chairman, Burson–Marsteller, Inc. (1993–Present); Chief Foreign Correspondent, ABC News (France & United Kingdom) (1978–1993); Editor, L'Express (France) (1973–1978); Press Secretary, President John F. Kennedy and Lyndon B. Johnson (1961–1964); U.S. Senator (1964). **Associations & Accomplishments:** President, Battle of Normandy Foundation; Chief Investigator (1957–1959), Senate Labor Rackets Committee; Vice President, Continental Airlines; World War II Veteran, U.S. Navy (1943–1946). **Education:** University of San Francisco, B.A. (1947) **Personal:** Married to Nicole in 1989. Three children: Suzanne, Stephen, and Gregory.

◆

Edward R. McCarthy, Ph.D.
Director
American Management Association
135 West 50th Street
New York, NY 10020
(212) 903–8358
Fax: (212) 903–9032
8741

◆

Business Information: American Management Association specializes in management education. The Firm produces management seminars and provides customized in–house development and training programs that focus on the clients' internal issues. AMA currently has four centers in the U.S., as well as Europe, the Pacific Rim, Canada and Latin America. As Director, Dr. McCarthy is responsible for curriculum development for public programs and/or designing customized programs and managing relationships with client organizations. Career Steps: Director, American Management Association (1985–Present); Power Sales and Services (1982–1984); Compliance Officer, New York Cotton Exchange (1978–1982); **Education:** Administration and Instructor (1962–1970). **Associations & Accomplishments:** Member, Planning Forum – a professional society for corporate planners; Written two articles in Medeval History. **Education :** City University of New York, Ph.D. (1976); Hunter College, M.A. Degree. **Personal:** Married to Mary Ann in 1982. Dr. McCarthy enjoys hiking, canoeing, cross country skiing, and snowmobiling.

◆

Chief Charles Adebowale Joshua, Ph.D.
President, Board of Trustees, Founder
Bedford–Stuyvesant Mental Health Center
1406 Fulton Street
Brooklyn, NY 11216
(718) 493–6610
Fax: (718) 778–5650

8063

◆

Business Information: Bedford–Stuyvesant Mental Health Center is a full–service provider of mental health, developmentally disabled, drug and alcohol rehabilitation, AIDS, and psychiatric counseling facilities to minority and disadvantaged populace. Chief Joshua, as Founder of the Agency, sets all policies and provides direction in all aspects of its workings. Additionally, for over 20 years, Chief Joshua has been a leader and spokesman for the poor and disadvantaged of Brooklyn as the Executive Director of the Central Brooklyn Coordinating Council, Inc. Representing over 135 social and human service agencies, he has implemented various programs in employment, welfare services, senior citizen services, anti–crime and crime–victim services, children and family services, services for the disabled, mental health, housing and foster child care. As CBCC's leadership for the past three decades, he has struggled relentlessly for social and economic betterment. His work has won him more than 100 awards, and now those services have been recognized abroad. He was the first black American to have an African chieftancy conferred on him and only the fifth person in 150 years to receive the honor. Chief Joshua traveled to the Yoruba town of Oye–Ekiti in Nigeria to receive the title: Balogun Aafin of Oye–Ekiti, which means, Royal Commander of the Palace of Oye–Ekiti. He was also given the middle name Adebowale, meaning the return of the King to his Kingdom, and a rare certificate indicating he comes "from a faraway place." The criteria for his award are "good behavior, proven prowess and influence, success and honesty in one's endeavors, willingness and ability to assist in developing the palace and the town." Formerly chairman of the Caribbean American Chamber of Commerce and Industry, Chief Joshua recognizes the significant role of business in community development and has long and tirelessly advocated and supported community–based small businesses. A dynamic and tireless ball of energy, he is affectionately known to his staff as either "Mr. Perpetual Motion" or the "Mayor of Bed–Stuy". Founded in 1974, Bedford–Stuyvesant Mental Health Center currently employs over 300 administrative staff and medical personnel. It reports assets in excess of $14 million. **Career Steps:** President, Board of Trustees, Founder, Bedford–Stuyvesant Mental Health Center (1974–Present); Executive Director of Central Brooklyn Coordinating Council, Inc. (1973–Present); Project Coordinator, Central Brooklyn Coordinating Council, Inc. (1972–1973); Job Developer, Fort Greene Community Corporation (1972–1973); Housing Appraiser, U.S. Department of Housing and Urban Development (1970–1972); Production Controller, U.S. Army Pictorial Center (1957–1970); Postal Clerk, U.S. Post Office–New York (1956–1957). **Associations and Accomplishments:** National Association for Community Development; National Assocation for Real Estate Brokers; Chairman, Consumer Advisory Council; Chairman, CBCC's City–wide Task Force on Child Abuse & Neglect; Member, Board of Directors, American Red Cross (Brooklyn Branch); Board of Directors, Protestant Board of Guardians; Institute for Urban Design (among over 100 other); Over 100 awards and citations to name a few: Proclamation from New York State Senate, Legislative Resolution #395 Saluting Charles Joshua's Day May 27, 1979; Proclamation from Office of Borough President of Brooklyn declaring Sunday, May 27, 1979 as "Charles Joshua Day" in the Borough of Brooklyn; Certificate of Appreciation: CBCC's Board of Directors, Medgar Evers College, National Democratic Committee, Brooklyn Branch of American Red Cross, President Ronald Reagan, Community Service Award: New York State Assemblyman William Boyland (8/85); Citation–Office of the Borough President of Brooklyn – For Chieftancy in Nigeria – August 15, 1989; Royal Gift presented by the African Peoples Council Inc. – the gift traditionally known as EKPE MASQUELATE is bestowed exclusively to a leader of distinguished nobility. The EKPE MASQUELATE symbolized Law and Order in the Cross River state of Nigeria (7/24/92); Plaque: Most Admired Man of the Decade – American Biographical Institute (July 1992). **Education:** Honorary Professorship, Academia Sciences Humaines Universelles, Paris (July 1993); Honorary Doctorate, London Institute for Applied Research, Commercial Science, Letters, Literature, Fine Arts and Music, Humanities & Law (July 1993); California Western University, B.S./M.B.A. degree Program; International Culteral Diploma of Honor; ABI Fellow, American Biographical Institute; Research Associate, International Biographical Institute Cambridge, England (1992); Installed as Baron – Royal Order Bohemian Crown, (1993); Installed as Knight – "The Order of the Knight Templars of Jerusalem" (August 1993). **Personal:** Married to Anita in 1966. One daughter, Sharon and one grandson.

◆

Ms. Ivana M. Trump

President and Chief Executive Officer
House of Ivana and Ivana, Inc.
725 Fifth Avenue
New York, NY 10022
(212) 319–4500
Fax: Please mail or call

2339

◆

Business Information: Ivana, Inc. manufactures designer clothing, jewelry, and cosmetics. House of Ivana serves as the sales and marketing arm for the worldwide distribution of Ivana, Inc. products through the Home Shopping Network. In 1991, Ivana Trump opened the doors to Ivana, Inc. and in1993, she signed a five–year contract to present an exclusive line of House of Ivana fashions and jewelry on the Home Shopping Network. Her Spring Collection had its debut in 1993 and almost immediately sold out with sales figures topping Home Shopping Club charts. Ivana appears monthly on the Network with her clothing designs, jewelry, and cosmetics, all of which are under the exclusive line of "House of Ivana." As President, Founder, and CEO, Ms. Trump is responsible for all aspects of operations for the House of Ivana and Ivana, Inc. **Career Steps:** A native of Czechoslovakia, Ms. Trump emigrated to Canada in 1972 and worked for many years as a fashion model before moving to the U.S. Ivana served as President and CEO of The Plaza Hotel in New York City (1983–87), one of the world's finest hotels, with a staff of over 1,400 people. She was recognized by her peers as "Hotelier of the Year," by Where Magazine for her work at The Plaza. She was also CEO of The Trump's Castle Hotel & Casino in Atlantic City, with a staff of 4,500 employees, from 1986 to 1990. Under her leadership, Trump's Castle became one of the most profitable casinos in the world. Her first novel, a New York Times best seller, "For Love Alone," was published in hardcover by Pocket Books in1992 and was a CBS "Movie of the Week," in 1994. The response to her novel was so powerful and personal that her next book, entitled "The Best Is Yet To Come," a publication offering advice for the many women who have asked for her help, was published in 1995. Her second novel, "Free to Love," was published in1993. Her books have been overwhelmingly successful around the world and translated into 25 languages in 40 countries. **Associations and Accomplishments:** The New York City Ballet; United Cerebral Palsy; March of Dimes; American Cancer Society; City Meals–on–Wheels; The Fund for Arts and Culture in Central and Eastern Europe; Hiram Walker Foundation; Children's Friends for Life and all charitable AIDS organizations dealing with children with AIDS. **Education:** Ivana Trump was educated in the public schools in Czechoslovakia and received a Masters Degree in Physical Education from Charles University in Prague (1972), where she went on to become a member of the Czechoslovakian Women's Ski Team.

◆

Charles R. Bruce

Vice President of International Marketing
Wendy's International, Inc.
4288 West Dublin Granville Road
Dublin, OH 43017–1442
(614) 764–3067
Fax: (614) 764–3026
EMAIL: See Below

5812

◆

Business Information: Wendy's International, Inc., the world's third largest hamburger restaurant chain, is the franchise headquarters for the Wendy's quick service food chain, started by Dave Thomas in 1969. With twenty years of experience in marketing, Mr. Bruce joined Wendy's International, Inc. as Vice President of International Marketing in 1994. His primary focus is to build Wendy's into a global brand through international marketing efforts. With his extensive international background, fluency in Spanish, and cross–cultural experiences, he is very comfortable working with people from different countries and cultures which has made him successful in his endeavors. Internet users may reach him via: 73041.11 @compuserve.com **Career Steps:** Vice President of International Marketing, Wendy's International, Inc. (1994–Present); Vice President of Marketing, International Pizza Hut Franchise Holders Association, Inc. (1986–1994); International Marketing Manager, The Coleman Co., Inc. (1978–1986). **Education:** Kansas State University, B.A. (1973); Universidad Ibero–Americana – Mexico City, Summer Program; Wichita State University, M.B.A. Program. **Personal:** Married to Kay F. in 1979. One child: Kristen M. Mr. Bruce enjoys international travel (70+ countries), reading, watching football, and sailing.

Mr. David G. Nutty
Director of Customer Service, Bankcard Division
First National Bank of Omaha
One First National Center, 1620 Dodge Street
Omaha, NE 68103
(402) 341–0500 Ext. 6080
Fax: (402) 636–6940

6141

Business Information: First National Bank of Omaha is a financial institution that specializes in banking. Their Bankcard Division is a national issuer of Visa and MasterCard presently serving well over 2.5 million customers. They are the oldest bank West of the Missouri River. In his current capacity, Mr. Nutty serves as the Officer in Charge of Bankcard customer service. He is credited for the implementation of quality control for the Bankcard Division. Established since 1953, The Bankcard Division presently employs 240 people within their customer service departments. **Career Steps:** Supervisor, Auditor (1983–1986), Senior Administrative Assistant (1987–1988), Department Manager, First National Bank of Omaha (1989–1991); Director of Customer Service, Bankcard Division (1991–Present), First National Bank of Omaha; Vice President, Brentwood Bank (1986–1987); Assistant Manager, Household Finance (1981–1983). **Associations and Accomplishments:** (ASQC) American Society for Quality Control. **Education:** Dana College, B.S. Degree (1981); Graduate of the ABA National School of Bankcard Management (1989) **Personal:** Married to Rita for 13 years. Three children: Alyssa, Brianne, and Tyler. Mr. Nutty enjoys music, playing the guitar, and golf.

Ramesh C. Pandey, Ph.D.
President & Chief Executive Officer
Xechem International, Inc.
100 Jersey Avenue, B–310
New Brunswick, NJ 08901
(908) 247–3300
Fax: (908) 247–4090

2834

Business Information: Xechem, Inc., a wholly–owned subsidiary of Xechem International, Inc., specializes in the research, development, and manufacture of pharmaceuticals from plants and fermentation processes. Xechem's facilities are pre–approved under a Master Agreement to bid on National Cancer Institute contracts for the isolation and purification of anti–cancer and anti–AIDS compounds from natural sources for five years. Xechem is currently preparing submissions to the FDA for approval of paclitaxel, a treatment for breast and ovarian cancer. This product is planned to be marketed in 1998. As President and Chief Executive Officer, Dr. Pandey oversees daily operations, serving as administrator and acting as principal scientist for various projects. **Career Steps:** President and Chief Executive Officer, Xechem, Inc. (1990–Present); President and Chief Executive Officer, Xechem International, Inc. (1994–Present); President and Chief Scientist, Xechem – Division of Lyphomed (1983–1990). **Associations and Accomplishments:** American Institute of Chemists; American Chemical Society; American Society of Microbiology; American Society of Mass Spectrometry; American Association of Cancer Research; American Society of Hospital Pharmacists; American Society of Pharmacognosy; Society of Industrial Microbiology; New York Academy of Sciences; Indian Science Congress Association. **Education:** University of Poona–India, Ph.D. (1965); University of Gorakhpur–India, M.Sc.; University of Allahabad–India, B.Sc. **Personal:** Dr. Pandey enjoys photography, table tennis, and collecting stamps and coins.

International WHO'S WHO of Professionals

Welcome to the 4th Edition of International WHO'S WHO of Professionals. This ultimate Professional Directory recognizes the professional and personal accomplishments of successful leaders in the world today.

Viewed by countless elite professionals across the world, this publication introduces members to one another, thus enabling them to further expand their success through networking. According to Pierre E.G. Salinger, Vice Chairman of Burson–Marsteller, Inc., "International WHO'S WHO of Professionals is the most important book for people who want to work around the world and understand the world. We are in a global world now, and WHO'S WHO of Professionals is a global organization which gives you the names of the most significant men and women who are contributing to a rising economy, to a rising social life, to a rising understanding of how the world can be brought back to a world of stability. If you are interested in the world, it is a book you must buy and read."

When you begin networking within this tremendous network resource, you will be in touch with thousands of members worldwide encompassing a broad range of industries, who can help you maintain your level of success and possibly propel you even further. The old addage, "It isn't what you know, but who you know" is true! And we believe it is a combination of both that makes people successful. This benefit of a global audience heightens the importance of being named to International WHO'S WHO of Professionals and further strengthens the networking potential available to those included in the publication.

This unique directory, published annually by Gibralter Publishing, Inc., is dedicated to providing the most up–to–date and complete information available to its members.

This Edition of International WHO'S WHO of Professionals contains biographical entries for more than 11,500 individuals.

The Directory is designed to provide comprehensive biographical information on professionals who have met specific criteria of the International WHO'S WHO of Professionals Board of Advisors.

The biographical information listed has been provided to the Editorial Department of Gibralter Publishing, Inc. by each member.

A professional staff of writers individually created each biographical entry which was approved for accuracy and content by each member.

Each biographical entry consists of the following areas, unless the information was not provided to us by the member:

– Member's Name
– Business Title
– Business Name
– Business Address
– Business Phone, Fax and E–mail Numbers
– Standard Industrial Code
– Business Information
– Career Steps
– Associations & Accomplishments
– Educational
– Personal Information

This simple, easy–to–understand volume is indexed several ways to maximize the networking potential of the members included.

Section 1 is arranged numerically by Standard Industrial Code. Section 2 is an alphabetical index of members by last name. Section 3 is an alphabetical index of members by company name. Section 4 is a geographical index alphabetically by location. Lastly, Section 5 is an alphabetical listing of non–members by last name.

Indexing our network resource in this manner propels this custom publication to the forefront of a diverse industry.

Where else can you interact with so many different professionals from so many areas of expertise? As part of our family, you have access to each one of them.

Each biography is free of confusing codes and jargon. The easy–to–read format enables other recognized and highly accomplished professionals to see not only members names, but a detailed biography listing their history of achievement.

Through direct association with your fellow professionals, you will be able to share experiences and exchange ideas about how to maintain your company's winning edge.

Gibralter Publishing, Inc. urges members of International WHO'S WHO of Professionals to take advantage of the unique networking potential that is available at your fingertips.

The age of high–tech business communications is here, and we at Gibralter Publishing, Inc. want to keep you informed about new trends that will help you remain a competitive force in your industry.

Table of Contents

Volume 1 & 2

Volume 2

Members Indexed Numerically
by
Standard Industrial Code

Section 1

Standard Industrial Code
Table of Contents

0000 – 0999

AGRICULTURE

FORESTRY

and

FISHING

0100 Agricultural Production–Crops

0111 Wheat
0112 Rice
0115 Corn
0116 Soybeans
0119 Cash grains, nec
0131 Cotton
0132 Tobacco
0133 Sugarcane and sugar beets
0134 Irish potatoes
0139 Field crops, except cash grains, nec
0161 Vegetables and melons
0171 Berry crops
0172 Grapes
0173 Tree nuts
0174 Citrus fruits
0175 Deciduous tree fruits
0179 Fruits and tree nuts, nec
0181 Ornamental nursery products
0182 Food crops grown under cover
0191 General farms, primarily crop

Varon Q. Blackburn
Vice President of Human Resources
AgriNorthwest
P.O. Box 2308
TriCities, WA 99302
(509) 783–5421
Fax: (509) 783–5422

0139

Business Information: AgriNorthwest is an agricultural producer of potatoes, sugar beets, corn, sweet corn, onions, and other farm– type produce. As Vice President of Human Resources, Mr. Blackburn is responsible for personnel management, salary/wage oversight, security and safety, and related administrative duties. The Company employs 180 full–time personnel and an average of 600 seasonal employees. **Career Steps:** AgriNorthwest: Vice President of Human Resources (1994–Present), Farm Manager (1990–1994); Association Director/Extension Specialist, Cornell University (1987–1990); Assistant County Supervisor, FMHA (1986). **Associations & Accomplishments:** Board of Directors, Umatilla/Morrow County Farm Bureau; Task Force Member, Association of Washington Business Family Friendly Task Force; Chairman, Oregon State Farm Bureau Water Committee; Chairman, Oregon State University Extension Advisory Committee; Advisory Committee, Columbia Basin College. **Education:** Brigham Young University: M.S. (1982), B.S. in Agricultural Economics. **Personal:** Married to Verena in 1978. Four children: Kara, Shaun, Taryn, and Malissa. Mr. Blackburn enjoys hiking, jogging, fishing, and reading. He is also very active in his community and church organizations.

William W. McClurken
Assistant to President and Chief Information Officer
Abbott–Cobb, Inc.
1251 Northwest 13th Street
Boca Raton, FL 33486–2142
(407) 795–0121
Fax: (407) 393–6738

0161

Business Information: Abbott–Cobb, Inc. is the agro–biotechnology industry specializing in development, marketing and global distribution of hybrid vegetable seed. Abbott–Cobb is the largest independent distributor of hybrid vegetable seed in North America with eight branches throughout the U.S. and two in Mexico. Abbott and Cobb has both research and production strategic alliances throughout the world. Joining Abbott & Cobb as Assistant to President and Chief Information Officer in 1994, Mr. McClurken is responsible for all aspects of the firm's strategic information system including Research and Development, Marketing, and Financial Reporting, as well as

Strategic Planning. **Career Steps:** Assistant to President and Chief Information Officer, Abbott–Cobb, Inc. (1994–Present); Pilot 737, Carnival Airlines (1993–1994); Chief Pilot – Learjet, Jet Flite, Inc. (1990–1993); Adjunct Faculty Member, Florida Atlantic University. **Associations & Accomplishments:** Aircraft Owners & Pilots Association; American Management Association; Children International; Sierra Club. **Education:** Florida Atlantic University, MBA (1994); Franklin and Marshall College, B.A. in Business Management; New York University, International Business Program.

Estefani Chia Pei Liaou
Director of Marketing
Lucky Farms, Inc.
P.O. Box 985
Loma Linda, CA 92354–0985
(909) 799–6688
Fax: (909) 796–6599

0161

Business Information: Lucky Farms, Inc. is an agricultural facility specializing in the production, distribution, and marketing of oriental vegetables. Established in 1983, the Farm employs 800 people, and distributes throughout the United States, Canada, Hawaii, and Great Britain. As Director of Marketing, Ms. Liaou oversees marketing and sales. She is also responsible for recruiting new accounts, customer service trainings, and personnel management. **Career Steps:** Lucky Farms, Inc: Director of Marketing (Present), Sales Manager, Account Executive, Secretary. **Associations & Accomplishments:** Tzu–Chi Free Medical Clinic; Tzu–Chi Volunteer Committee. **Education:** California State, San Bernardino, B.A. (1995). **Personal:** Ms. Pei Liaou enjoys art collecting and creation, music, volunteering at convalescent homes and hospitals.

Melissa A. Lewis
General Manager
Farmer Mac's Berries
180 Berry Patch Road
Hampstead, NC 28443
(910) 270–4618
Fax: (910) 270–4618
Mlewis@nmsu.edu

0171

Business Information: Farmer Mac's Berries is a 10–acre blueberry farm that specializes in the production and wholesale and retail sale of fresh fruits. As General Manager, Ms. Lewis brings several years of accounting and budgeting experience to assist in overseeing all business operations. These responsibilities include marketing, public relations, advertising, personnel matters, sales, purchasing, and accounting. She supervises four permanent and 50 seasonal employees. Internet users can reach her via: Mlewis@nmsu.edu. **Career Steps:** General Manager, Farmer Mac's Berries (1996–Present); Budget Officer, North Carolina State University (1993–1996); Accountant, Hanover Iron Works (1990–1992); Accounting Clerk, CK Supply (1988–1990). **Associations & Accomplishments:** International Food & Business Management Association; Gamma Sigma Delta Honor Society of Agriculture; North Carolina Blueberry Council; National Agricultural Marketing Association; Tru–Blu Cooperative Association; Omicron Delta Epsilon, International Honor Society of Economics; American Agricultural Economics Association. **Education:** New Mexico State University, M.S. (In Progress); North Carolina State University, B.S. (1995). **Personal:** Ms. Lewis enjoys volleyball and soccer.

Mauricio Levy
General Manager
America S.A.
P O Box 2328
La Paz, Bolivia
(591) 231–8748
Fax: (591) 239–1459

0173

Business Information: America S.A., a division of Levy Hermanos, is a producer, processer and exporter of Brazilian nuts to Europe and the United States. Primary customers include Planters and Nabisco. As General Manager, Mr. Levy monitors the day–to–day operations of America S.A. for product quality and quantity. He works closely with other management personnel in the development of budgets, marketing strategies, and sales strategies. Concurrently Mr. Levy serves as Finance Director for Levy Hermanos, Ltda. **Career Steps:** General Manager, America S.A. (1990–Present); Finance Director, Levy Hermanos, Ltda. (1988–Present). **Education:** Cornell University, B.S. (1987). **Personal:** Mr. Levy enjoys cooking, sports, pottery making, and agricultural activities.

Russell D. Caid

Senior Director of Technical Services and Research and Developmen
Chiquita Brands Inc.
35 Marcel Drive
Covington, KY 41017–2327
(513) 784–8031
Fax: (506) 255–3646

0179

Business Information: Chiquita Brands Co. is the world's leading producer and distributor of bananas and other premium fruits and vegetables. Holding various corporate roles for Chiquita since 1978, Mr. Caid was appointed to his current position in 1992. As Director of Technical Services and Research and Development, he oversees all research and development involving disease, pest control, and cultural practices used in banana production. **Career Steps:** Chiquita Brands Inc.: Senior Director of Technical Services and Research and Development (1992–Present); Senior Director – Quality Control (1988–1991); Director of Tropical Research and Investigation (1984–1988); General Manager, Chiriqui Land Co., Pto. Armuelles, Panama (1978–1984). **Associations & Accomplishments:** Entomological Society of America; Horticulture Society of America; Meteorology Society; Council for Agriculture for Science and Technology. **Education:** Oklahoma State University, Master's Degree in Entomology (1955), B.S. (1954); Harvard Business School, Program for Management Development (1976). **Personal:** Married to Ruth LaVerne in 1955. Three children: Steve, Bruce, and Neal. Mr. Caid enjoys gardening, insect collecting, running, and golf.

Irvin C. Chapman
President
Placentia Orchard Company
2962 Airway Avenue
Costa Mesa, CA 92626–6018
(714) 540–1588
Fax: (714) 540–6486

0174

Business Information: The Placentia Orchard Co. is a citrus grower and developer of prime real estate investments, including three golf courses, and numerous office buildings and shopping centers. Established in 1894, Placentia Orchard Company currently employs 150 people. With the same company for 63 years, Mr. Chapman is the President and Chief Executive Officer. As such he is responsible for all aspects of operations, as well as the continued growth and success of the company. **Career Steps:** Placentia Orchard Company: President (1973–Present), Secretary (1955–1973), Ranch Manager (1933–1955). **Associations & Accomplishments:** City of Fullerton: City Council Member (1946–1954), Mayor (1948–1950); National Board YMCA of USA: International Division (1949–1983), Chairman (1970–1977), Member (1963–1983), Vice Chairman (1978–1983); Kiwanis Club: President (1940), Governor – California, Nevada, Hawaii District (1953); Board of Directors, Orange County Fair (1950–1977); Board Member, Office of Criminal Justice, California (1981–Present); Board of Directors, Chapman University (1936–Present). **Education:** Chapman University, A.B. (1933). **Personal:** Married to Edythe in 1976. Two children: Cherie Harrison and Claire Nichols. Mr. Chapman enjoys travel and photography.

C. Curtis Coffey
President
Industria Nacional de Banano, S.A.
AP 6682–1000
San Jose, Costa Rica
(506) 223–4186
Fax: (506) 221–6554

0179

Business Information: Industria Nacional de Banano, S.A. is an independent producer of bananas for export. Comprised of investors and small land owners who split the profits evenly, the Company markets bananas primarily for Standard Fruit Company, a major distributor for Dole Fresh Fruits. Established in 1967, Industria Nacional de Banano, S.A. employs 110 people and has estimated annual revenue in excess of $1 million. As President, Mr. Coffey has full fiscal and operating responsibility, and has over thirty years experience in the agricultural field. Concurrent with his present position, Mr. Coffey is treasurer of Agent Oil Company in Oklahoma, and owns a farm in Kansas. **Career Steps:** President, Industria Nacional de Banano, S.A. (1975–Present); President/General Manager, Inbanano de Bristol S.A. (1991–Present). **Associations & Accomplishments:** Camara Nacional de Bananeros (National Banana Association); National Bridge Association; Caribbean Central American Bridge Association. **Education:** University of Denver, M.B.A. (1963); University of Kansas, B.S. in Business (1951); Certified Public Accountant, State of Idaho (1964). **Personal:** Married to N. Sue in 1951. Three children: M. Lynn Peraza, E. Joan de Leon, and T. Gwyn Coffey. Mr. Coffey enjoys bridge and reading.

Aurelio Tobon Estrada
International Legal and Commercial Director
C.I. Union De Bananeros De Uraba
S.A., Uniban
Calle 52 #47–42 Piso 15
Medellin, AN, Colombia
(574) 511–5540
Fax: (574) 511–8786

0179

Business Information: Uniban is an agro–industrial/marketing company specialized in worldwide distribution of bananas and plantains. Comprised of a 20.000 acres in Colombia and 500 in Costa Rica, distributing products in over 20 countries. Plans for the future include the maintenance of the market shares in the U.S. and the E.U. as well as vigorous penetration to Russia, East European, and Balcan countries. Established in 1965, the Company employs 500 people, and has an estimated annual revenue of $150,000,000. As International Legal and Commercial Director, Mr. Tobon oversees the commercial relationships with clients, handles strategic planning, and provides commercial and legal support for the search and establishment of new markets. He is also responsible for management of international sales, as well as financial aspects derived therefrom. **Career Steps:** Uniban: International Legal and Commercial Director (1995–Present), Mediterranean Route Director (Milan/Athens 1993–1995), Legal Director, Bogota's Electric Bureau (1991–1992); Assistant to the Legal Director, Smit Nederland (Rotterdam 1990); Colombian Representative to the Legal Committee of IMO (London 1990). **Associations & Accomplishments:** Colegio De Abogados Rosaristas (Fellowship of Law Faculty). **Education:** University College, London, LL.M. in International Trade and Maritime Law (1990–1991); Colegio Mayor De Nuestra Senora del Rosario, Bogota, five years of jurisprudence, actually holding a law degree. **Personal:** Married to Lia Cristina Velasquez in 1994. Mr. Tobon speaks fluent English, Italian, and Spanish. Mr. Tobon Estrada enjoys travel, politics, squash, photography, music, and horseback riding.

Diana Jean Blea
Human Resources Manager
Sakata Seed America, Inc.
18095 Serene Drive
Morgan Hill, CA 95037–2833
(408) 778–7758
Fax: (408) 778–7751

0181

Business Information: Sakata Seed America, Inc. is an international producer of flower and vegetable seeds. Established in 1977, the Company employs 100 people and has estimated annual revenue of $53 million. As Human Resources Manager, Ms. Blea oversees all phases of personnel management. She is responsible for recruitment, employee benefits, compensation, and reviews. **Career Steps:** Human Resources Manager, Sakata Seed America, Inc. (1990–Present); Human Resource Manager, Fotomat Corporation (1984–1986); Personnel Manager, M&T Publishing (1982–1984). **Associations & Accomplishments:** Society of Human Resource Management (SHRM); Agricultural Personnel Management Association (APMA); NNA; American Counseling Association (ACA); Single Adoptive Parents of America. **Education:** Liberty University: M.A. (1993), B.S. **Personal:** One child: Allegra Rocio Blea. Ms. Blea enjoys music, travel, and counseling teens in group home.

German Lacoutre
General Manager
Milonga Flowers
Calle 113 #3–54
Bogota, Colombia
(571) 826–1203
Fax: (571) 780–1082

0181

Business Information: Milonga Flowers produces and exports carnations of all colors to the United States and the United Kingdom. Established in 1991, the Company exports over 8 million carnations each year. As General Manager, Mr. Lacoutre oversees the daily operations of the Company from planting through exporting the flowers. **Career Steps:** General Manager, Milonga Flowers (1991–Present). **Associations**

& Accomplishments: Lagartes. **Education:** Business Administration (1987). **Personal:** Mr. Lacoutre enjoys football (soccer), tennis, and golf.

Anne Leventry–Jeffers
Vice President of Human Resources
Bull Horticultural Co.
622 Town Road
West Chicago, IL 60185–2635
(708) 231–3500
Fax: (708) 231–3592

0181

Business Information: Bull Horticultural Co. is a wholesale producer and distributor of horticultural products. Established in 1905, the Company reports annual revenue in excess of $150 million and currently employs 2,500 people. Joining the Company as Vice President of Human Resources in 1994, Ms. Leventry–Jeffers is responsible for all matters involving employees, such as hiring, training, labor relations, and benefits. **Career Steps:** Vice President of Human Resources, Bull Horticultural Co. (1994–Present); Director of Human Resources, PanAmerican Seed Co. (1992–1994); Project Manager, Geo J. Ball, Inc. (1989–1992); Staff Psychologist, Rosalie G. Handler (1985–1988). **Associations & Accomplishments:** Human Resource Management Association of Chicago; Human Resource Executive Roundtable; AMA Chicago Area Training Council; Society for Human Resource Professionals. **Education:** St. Francis College, M.A. (1989); Indiana University of Pennsylvania, M.S. in Clinical Psychology; University of Pittsburgh, B.S. in Psychology. **Personal:** Married to Kenneth in 1979. Ms. Leventry–Jeffers enjoys hiking, music, and spending time with her dogs.

Galo Montano–Perez

General Manager
Diamond Roses S.A.
Suecia No. 277 y Shyris, Edif Suecia 4 To Piso Sur
Quito, Ecuador
(5932) 439835
Fax: (5932) 435939

0181

Business Information: Diamond Roses S.A. is an international exporter, commercializer, and producer of flowers, specifically roses. Sixty percent of the flowers will be exported to the U.S., Europe, and other countries throughout the world. Spending most of his career in public service and industrial development, Mr. Montano–Perez founded Diamond Roses S.A. in 1995. Serving as General Manager, he is responsible for all aspects of operations, including administration, finances, sales, public relations, accounting, marketing, and strategic planning. **Career Steps:** General Manager, Diamond Roses S.A. (1995–Present); Executive Director, Ecuadorian Corporation for Total Quality (1992–1995); President, Corporacion Andina de Fomento (1986–1991); Minister, Ministry of Industries (1978–1982). **Associations & Accomplishments:** Colegio de Ingenieros Quimicos de Pichincha; Former President, Camara de Comercio Ecuatoriano – Americana. **Education:** Escuela Politecnica Nac, Chemical Engineer; University of California – Davis, M.S. **Personal:** Married to Maria Huerta de Montano. Six children: Maria Dolores, Cesar, Galo, Maria Clara, Fatima, and Maria de Lourdes.

Jinga Hydroponic Farms, Ltd.

James N. Walmsley
President
Jinga Hydroponic Farms, Ltd.
1626 West Pike Street
Clarksburg, WV 26301
(304) 623–3267
Fax: (304) 623–9666

0182

Business Information: Jinga Hydroponic Farms, Ltd. specializes in hydroponic farming of crops without the use of soil or chemicals. The Farm was established to aid governments worldwide to help them become self–sufficient and supply food for their citizens without foreign aid. As President and Founder of the Company, Mr. Walmsley is responsible for all aspects of Company operations including new business development, growth and expansion of the Company, and strategic planning. **Career Steps:** President, Jinga Hydroponic Farms, Ltd. (1972–Present); President, Manin International Inc. (1961–1972); Investment Banker, Hornblower & Weeks (1955–1961). **Associations & Accomplishments:** Points of Light Foundation; Children Defense Fund; Who's Who in the World; Who's Who Registry of Global Business Leaders; Royal Horticultural Society, London; American Horticultural

Society; American Security Council; Various professional and civic organizations. **Education:** George Washington University; Loyola University, Business Administration; Northwestern University, Investment Banking. **Personal:** Two children: Kristen V. and Tanya J. Mr. Walmsley enjoys travel and gardening.

Okwokehena (Manny) Wong
Director of Operations
Fully, Inc.
P O Box 55–8126   400 NE 67th Street
Miami, FL 33255–8126
Fax: (305) 758–7074

0182

Business Information: Fully, Inc. is a grower of bean and soy sprouts and a manufacturer of tofu and soy milk. Established in 1978, Fully, Inc. also distributes their products to wholesalers and distributors throughout the United States. As Director of Operations and co–owner, Mr. Wong directs all operations of the company from processing tofu and soy milk to financial decisions to working with distributors. **Career Steps:** Director of Operations, Fully, Inc. (1978–Present); Sales Manager, Charles Kee Realty Company (1976–1978). **Associations & Accomplishments:** Director, International Sprouts Grower Association; Director, Chinese American Chamber of Commerce; Florida Sheriffs Association; National Rifle Association of America. **Education:** Pace University, B.A. (1978). **Personal:** Married to Silvia in 1978. Three children: Olivia, Sabrina, and Marissia. Mr. Wong enjoys woodworking, furniture making, travel, and creative projects.

Stuart Barclay
Founder/General Manager
Seedbiotics
P.O. Box 609   818 Paynter Avenue
Caldwell, ID 83606
(208) 455–0578
Fax: (208) 455–0596

0191

Business Information: Seedbiotics specializes in coating seedlings with a formulation which improves the plant's chances of survival. As General Manager, Mr. Barclay is responsible for supervising employees and managing all daily operations including administration, research, marketing, and production. **Career Steps:** General Manager, Seedbiotics (1989–Present); Celpril Industries, Inc.: Sales Director (1980–1989), Plant Manager (1980–1986); Lieutenant/Aviator, USN. **Associations & Accomplishments:** Rotary, Caldwell Idaho Economic Development Association; St. of Oregon Strategic Water Planning Committee; Director, Oregon Trout. **Education:** California State – Bakersfield, M.B.A. **Personal:** Married to Sandi in 1990. Two children: Margaret and Heather. Mr. Barclay enjoys fly fishing, physical fitness, and golf.

William L. Davey
Owner and President
Davey Farms, Inc.
6020 Silveyville Road, P.O. Box 476
Dixon, CA 95620
(707) 448–4880
Fax: (707) 448–3116

0191

Business Information: Davey Farms, Inc. is a major crop distributor. Cultivated crops include tomatoes, sugar beets, corn, wheat, sunflower seeds, alfalfa, garlic, and carrots. Davey Farms is Campbell Soup's largest producer of tomatoes, and has been for over 30 years. Having been self employed in farming for 50 years, William Davey, with son Walter, owns and runs the farm, including all operational, mechanical, and financial decisions. **Career Steps:** Owner and President, Davey Farms, Inc. (1945–Present). **Personal:** Two children: Walter and Irving. Mr. Davey enjoys travel and fishing.

0200 Agricultural Production–Livestock

0211 Beef cattle feedlots
0212 Beef cattle, except feedlots
0213 Hogs
0214 Sheep and goats
0219 General livestock, NEC
0241 Dairy farms
0251 Broiler, fryer, and roaster chickens
0252 Chicken eggs
0253 Turkeys and turkey eggs
0254 Poultry hatcheries
0259 Poultry and eggs, NEC
0271 Fur–bearing animals and rabbits
0272 Horses and other equines
0273 Animal aquaculture

0279 Animal specialties, NEC
0291 General farms, primarily animal

Phillip M. Kafarakis

Vice President, Sales and Marketing
Jones Dairy Farm
P.O. Box 808
Ft. Atkinson, WI 53538
(414) 563–6800
Fax: (414) 563–6801

0241

Business Information: Jones Dairy Farm, established in 1889, is a privately–held food processing company that produces, sells and internationally exports pork and liver sausage, bacon and ham. As Vice President, Sales and Marketing, Mr. Kafarakis is responsible for the sales, marketing, research and development, and quality control departments. In addition to his duties with Jones Dairy Farm, Mr. Kafarakis presents seminars and speaks on sales motivation and management. **Career Steps:** Vice President, Sales and Marketing, Jones Dairy Farm (1994–Present); District Sales Manager, Kraft Foods (1993–1994); Oscar Mayer Foods: District Sales Planning Manager (1992–1993), Sales Manager (1988–1993). **Associations & Accomplishments:** American Management Association; American Meat Institute; International Deli and Dairy Association; International Foodservice Manufacturing Association. **Education:** Northern Arizona University, B.S.B.A. (1982). **Personal:** Married to Katherine in 1983. Four children: Christopher, Michael, Alex, and Maria. Mr. Kafarakis enjoys reading, public speaking, sports, and family activities.

0700 Agricultural Services

0711 Soil preparation services
0721 Crop planting and protecting
0722 Crop harvesting
0723 Crop preparation services for market
0724 Cotton ginning
0741 Veterinary services for livestock
0742 Veterinary services, specialties
0751 Livestock services, exc. veterinary
0752 Animal specialty services
0761 Farm labor contractors
0762 Farm management services
0781 Landscape counseling and planning
0782 Lawn and garden services
0783 Ornamental shrub and tree services

Dale R. Darling

Agricultural Relations Manager
DuPont Agricultural Products
513 Andover Road
Talleyville, DE 19803–2201
(302) 479–5866
Fax: (302) 479–5866

0721

Business Information: DuPont Agricultural Products is an international manufacturer of crop protection products, specifically for insect, weed and disease management offerings to farmers. Established in the late 1940's, DuPont Agricultural Products reports annual revenue in excess of $2 billion and currently employs 5,000 people. As Agricultural Relations Manager, Mr. Darling is responsible for relationship building activities with national organization leaders to earn preferred supplier status. **Career Steps:** DuPont Agricultural Products: Agricultural Relations Manager (1988–Present), Sales Manager (1987–1988), Regional Marketing Manager (1985–1987), Marketing Services Manager (1983–1985). **Associations & Accomplishments:** National Corn Growers Association; American Soybean Association; National Association of Wheat Growers; Agricultural Retailers Association; National Association of Conservation Districts; American Society of Farm Managers; Conservation Technology Information Center; National Cotton Council; Alpha Zeta; Recipient of DuPont's "Corporate Marketing Excellence" award, DuPont's highest recognition in marketing. **Education:** Texas A & M University: M.S. in Plant Pathology and Plant Virology (1962), B.S. in Plant & Soil Science; Advanced studies in Plant Biochemistry and Physiology, plus research toward Ph.D. **Personal:** Married to Patricia A. (Pat) in 1956. Two children: Michael and Ruth. Mr. Darling enjoys his church, family, agriculture, gardening and his home.

Pamela E. Kidder

Business Analyst
Mycogen Seeds
1562 Taylor Avenue
Marshalltown, IA 50158
(515) 752–4626
Fax: (515) 752–5734
EMail: See Below

0721

Business Information: Mycogen Seeds is a corn and hybrid seed company that sells directly to distributors and farmers. As Business Analyst, Ms. Kidder handles all network information systems, programming, and project development. Internet users can reach her via: Kidder@mycogen.com. **Career Steps:** Business Analyst, Mycogen Seeds (1994–Present); Help Desk Analyst, Iowa State University (1989–1994); Programmer, Gateway Foods (1987–1988). **Associations & Accomplishments:** Treasurer, American Business Womens Association; National Autism Society; Iowa Help Desk Chapter. **Education:** Pennsylvania State University, Computer Science (1987); Iowa State University. **Personal:** Married to Scott T. in 1992. One child: Philip Nazaruk. Ms. Kidder enjoys playing viola and fitness walking.

Jan Coody

Hospital Administrator
Woodland PetCare Center
4720 East 51st
Tulsa, OK 74135–3710
(918) 496–2111
Fax: (918) 496–3445
EMAIL: See Below

0742

Business Information: Woodland Animal Hospital is a full–service, veterinary hospital, providing care of small animals. Services include health care, preventive medicine, surgery, bathing & grooming, adoption services and sales of related products. Established in 1966, Woodland Animal Hospital has six locations in Tulsa, Oklahoma, consisting of 14 veterinary associates and a support staff of 75. As Hospital Administrator, Mrs. Coody is responsible for the management and marketing functions for the Hospital. Internet users can also reach her via: WAMC1@aol **Career Steps:** Hospital Administrator, Woodland Animal Hospital (1978–Present); Administration/Sales, Intercontinental Representative Services (1975–1978). **Associations & Accomplishments:** Veterinary Hospital Managers Association: Vice President, Charter Member; Affection Connection Pet Adoption Center: Board of Directors, Vice President; American Animal Hospitals Association; Charter Member, Management Associates; Volunteer, Metropolitan Tulsa Chamber of Commerce; Miata Club; Contributing Author, "Mastering the Marketplace" by Ross Clark, released January 1996; American Society of Women Accounts: Chapter Development Chairman; National Association of Female Executives. **Education:** Oklahoma City University, M.B.A. (1995); North Texas State University, B.S. (1974). **Personal:** Married to Brad. Two children: Carolyn and Steve. Mrs. Coody enjoys tennis, running, rollerblading and tap dancing.

Ellen S. Harrison, D.V.M.

Chief of Staff
Vetsmart Pet Hospital
597–C East Ordnance Road
Glen Burnie, MD 21060
(410) 863–1100
Fax: (410) 582–9550

0742

Business Information: Vetsmart Pet Hospital, owned and managed by Medical Management International, Inc. (MMI), is a growing concern introducing veterinary medicine to pet owners interested in quality medical care. Primary goals are to make pet health care affordable, to strengthen the value of pets in families, to teach how pet care maximizes lives, and to stop euthanasias by keeping pets healthy. As Chief of Staff at the Glen Burnie, MD Vestmart Pet Hospital, Dr. Harrison is responsible for coordinating staff schedules, staff hiring, training and budget control. She practices as a full time veterinarian in addition to her added responsibilities as hospital team coach and supervisor of overall patient care and services at her location. **Career Steps:** Partner Veterinarian, Vetsmart Pet Hospitals (1995–Present); Associate Veterinarian, South Arundel Veterinary Hospital (Aug., 1995–Oct., 1995); Associate Veterinarian, Erdman Animal Hospital (1993–1995). **Associations & Accomplishments:** American Veterinary Medical Association; Maryland Veterinary Medical Association; Mid Atlantic Avian Veterinary Medical Association; American Ferret Association, former volunteer; Chesapeake Wildlife Sanctuary. **Education:** University of Minnesota, D.V.M. (1991); Washington College, B.S. **Personal:** Dr. Harrison enjoys canoeing, camping, bicycling, and cross country skiing.

Animal Tracks
VETERINARY HOUSE CALLS
Lynn J. Snodgrass, D.V.M.
4500 West 126th Street
Leawood, Kansas 66209

Lynn J. Snodgrass, D.V.M.

Veterinarian
Animal Tracks
4500 West 126th Street
Leawood, KS 66209
(913) 491–5533
Fax: (913) 491–3349

0742

Business Information: Animal Tracks, established in 1993, is a full–service, general veterinary practice providing diagnosis and treatment of domestic and exotic (turtles, lizards, snakes) animals, mostly through housecalls. As Veterinarian, Dr. Snodgrass is responsible for all aspects operations, including medical care of animals. **Career Steps:** Veterinarian, Animal Tracks (1993–Present); Associate Veterinarian, Oak Park Veterinary Clinic (1985–1993); Associate Veterinarian, Leawood Animal Hospital (1984–1985); Registered Nurse, University of California at Irvine (1978–1979). **Associations & Accomplishments:** American Veterinary Medical Association; Kansas Veterinary Medical Association; Kansas City Veterinary Medical Association; Alpha Chi Omega. **Education:** Kansas State Veterinary College, D.V.M. (1984); University of Kansas, B.S. in Nursing, R.N. (1974). **Personal:** Married to Stephen in 1980. Two children: Lance and Jeff. Dr. Snodgrass enjoys sports and flying.

Ronald F. Eustice

Chief Executive Officer
Minnesota Beef Council
2850 Metro Drive, Suite 426
Bloomington, MN 55425
(612) 854–6980
Fax: (612) 854–6906

0751

Business Information: The Minnesota Beef Council, one of 42 state beef councils, primary focus is the representation of beef cattle producers, and the research and overall promotion of the beef industry as a whole. As Chief Executive Officer, Mr. Eustice is responsible for the Council's efficient use of resources. Primary duties involve the oversight of advertising and public relations media, research program implementation, and the overall coordination of public awareness concerning issues related to consumer attitudes toward the beef industry throughout Minnesota. **Career Steps:** Chief Executive Officer, Minnesota Beef Council (1990–Present); Director of International Marketing, Land O' Lakes (1984–1990); Executive Director, Minnesota Holstein Association (1982–1984); Director of International Marketing, American Breeders Service (1978–1984); General Manager, Carnation (1970–1978). **Associations & Accomplishments:** Board and Committee Chair, Partners of the Americas; National Cattlemen's Association; Minnesota Cattlemen's Association; Minnesota Holstein Association; Fluent in four languages; Published in related livestock promotion media and trade journals **Education:** Century University, M.B.A. (1993); University of Minnesota, B.A. (1968). **Personal:** Married to Margaret in 1975. Three children: Kevin, John, and Ann Marie. Mr. Eustice enjoys travel and philately.

Heinz Schmidt, DVM

Assistant Manager
Tiergesundheitsdienst Bayern, Lebensmittelhygiene
Senator–Gerauer–Strasse 23
Poing, Germany D–85586
49–89–9091241
Fax: 49–89–9091202
E MAIL: See Below

0751

Business Information: Tiergesundheitsdienst Bayern, Lebensmittelhygiene provides research and investigation of food and animals for the registration of drugs in Germany, and the FDA in the U.S. As Assistant Manager, Dr. Schmidt is responsible for all administrative duties involving his department, and oversees and performs research. He also instructs courses in chemistry and technology of food of animal origin at Ludwig Maximillian University of Munich, and Technical University of Munich. Internet users can reach him via: Heinz.schmidt@t–online.de. **Career Steps:** Assistant Manager, Tiergesundheitsdienst Bayern, Lebensmittelhygiene (1987–Present); Chief Analyst, Institute of Food Hygiene, University of Munich (1970–1987). **Associations & Accom-**

plishments: Association of German Chemists; German Association of Vet. Medicine; Scientific Committee of Research Association of Food Industry; Member of different working groups of Federal Institute of Health; University Professor of LM University of Munich and Technical University Munich. **Education:** University, Dr.med.vet. (1967); University, Dipl. Chemist; University, Ph.D. **Personal:** Dr. Schmidt enjoys travel and mountain walking.

Bob L. Silveira
International & Western U.S. Sales Manager
Accelerated Genetics
15735 West Perrydale Road
Amity, OR 97101–9519
(503) 843–3129
Fax: (503) 843–2741

0751

Business Information: Accelerated Genetics is a wholesale marketer of livestock genetics (frozen bovine semen) for the dairy and beef industries. Located in the United States, 60% of the Company's business is national and 40% is international. As International & Western U.S. Sales Manager, Mr. Silveira is responsible for the management of all sales activities in the Western U.S. (west of the Rockies) and international countries, in addition to the oversight of a support staff of five and twenty distributors worldwide. He also provides marketing, training, and promotional products to distributors from a remote office in Oregon. **Career Steps:** International & Western U.S. Sales Manager, Accelerated Genetics (1993–Present); Area Sales Representative, U.S. Genes (1991–1993); Progeny Test Coordinator, Golden Genes, Inc. (1990–1991). **Associations & Accomplishments:** Madison (Wisconsin) International Trade Association; National Association of Animal Breeders – International Marketing Committee; Television interview in Bolivia (in Spanish) on genetic trends; Fluent in English, Spanish, and Portuguese.n **Education:** California Polytechnic – San Luis Obispo, B.S. (1989); Merced Community College, A.A. **Personal:** Married to Connie Bispo in 1995. Mr. Silveira enjoys jogging and hiking.

Steven R. Patton

Vice President of the Grain Division
Countrymark Co–op
950 North Meridian Street, 6th Floor
Indianapolis, IN 46204
(317) 685–3334
Fax: (317) 685–3347

0762

Business Information: Countrymark Co–op is a major agricultural supply and grain marketing cooperative. Countrymark Co–op is owned and controlled by over 150 member co–ops, which are, in turn, owned and controlled by their farmer patrons. Member co–ops are located in Indiana, Michigan and Ohio. The company has 22 grain terminals, 9 plant food terminals, 8 feed mills, 6 petroleum terminals, 3 seed corn plants, 2 warehouses, and an oil refinery. Countrymark Co–op's core businesses include crop production, farm energy, grain marketing and livestock nutrition. The company also aggressively seeks out new opportunities that prove beneficial to member co–ops and their farmer patrons. Future plans include expanding more in the turkey, egg, and hog business. Joining Country Mark Co–op as Director of Grain Trading in 1994, Mr. Patton was appointed as Vice President of the Grain Division in 1995. He is responsible for all aspects of grain operations, including export facilities and interior grain handling elevators. **Career Steps:** Country Mark Co–op: Vice President of the Grain Division (1995–Present), Director of Grain Trading (1994–1995); President, Patton & Company (1982–1990). **Associations & Accomplishments:** Experimental Aircraft Association; North America Export Grain Association; National Grain and Feed Association. **Education:** Attended: BGSU (1972); Owens Community College. **Personal:** Two children: Allyson Rae and Joseph Todd. Mr. Patton enjoys owning and piloting aircraft and the outdoors.

Steven Joe Gartman
Virginia Operations Manager
Lasting Impressions, Inc.
7221 Bueleh Street
Alexandria, VA 22315
(703) 924–0798
Fax: (703) 249–2335

0781

Business Information: Lasting Impressions, Inc. is a full service, commercial landscape firm. The Company services apartment complexes, shopping centers, and office buildings. Established in 1983, the company currently employs 78 people and expects to post revenues/sales of over $2 million in 1996. As Virginia Operations Manager, Mr. Gartman handles all operations for the Virginia region. Duties include recruitment, training, and evaluating of staff as well as sale of prod-

ucts and services. Mr. Gartman supervises 45 employees as they maintain the grounds of 52 properties in his region. **Career Steps:** Virginia Operations Manager, Lasting Impressions, Inc. (1987–Present); Track Superintendent, Trinity Meadows (1976–1987). **Associations & Accomplishments:** Hispanic League; Lutheran Social Service. Mr. Gartman has been a guest speaker for the American Quarterhorse Association, colleges, and banquets and has been interviewed for company publications. **Education:** Pima Community College, Business (1993); University of Arizona. **Personal:** Married to Carol in 1988. One child: Donya. Mr. Gartman enjoys boating and his family.

Mike McKeever
President
McKeever Morris Inc.
722 Southwest 2nd Avenue, Suite 400
Portland, OR 97204–3131
(503) 228–7352
Fax: (503) 228–7365
EMAIL: See Below

0781

Business Information: McKeever Morris Inc. is a landscape architectural consulting firm, providing land use planning on all scales (neighborhood, cities, metro), urban design, landscape architecture, and community and public involvement processes. As President, Mr. McKeever is responsible for long range business planning, development, project management, and quality control. Internet users can reach him via: McKeever@Teleport.com **Career Steps:** President, McKeever Morris Inc. (1989–Present); Vice President, The Ben Kendorf Associates (1987–1989); President, Conservation Management Services (1982–1987). **Associations & Accomplishments:** Urban League; Sales Energy Association; American Planning Association; American Institute of Certified Planners; Homebuilders Association. **Education:** University of Oregon, Bachelors (1976). **Personal:** Married to Jeanne in 1990. Five children: Andy, Brian, Dylan, Emily, and Molly.

Dr. Hugh A. Poole
President/Owner
CoHort Associates
3126 Riverview Boulevard West
Bradenton, FL 34205
(941) 745–9939
Fax: (941) 745–9976

0781

Business Information: CoHort Associates is an international horticultural consulting firm specializing in research, development, marketing, and management. As President and Owner, Dr. Poole is responsible for all aspects of company operations, including consulting for the firm's clientele. Established in 1985, CoHort Associates currently employs two professionals. **Career Steps:** President and Owner, CoHort Associates (1985–Present); Director of Research and Development, Speedling, Inc. (1990–Present); Manager, A & L Southern Agricultural Labs (1980–1985). **Associations & Accomplishments:** American Society for Horticultural Sciences; American Society for Agricultural Consultants; Florida Society for Horticultural Sciences; Society of American Florists; Professional Plant Growers Association; American Horticultural Society; American Orchid Society. **Education:** Cornell University, Ph.D. (1974); University of Florida, M.S. in Agriculture (1971); University of Florida, B.S. in Agriculture (1970). **Personal:** Married to Barbara C. Poole in 1969. Two children: Ethan Hugh and Chrysanne Erin Poole. Dr. Poole enjoys hiking, traveling, photography and gardening.

Amelia Primiano

Landscape Maintenance Superintendent
Desert Care Landscaping, Inc.
P. O. Box 60246
Phoenix, AZ 85082–0246
(602) 276–4311
Fax: (602) 276–4383

0781

Business Information: Desert Care Landscaping, Inc. specializes in landscape maintenance, construction, and native tree salvage. Mrs. Primiano joined Desert Care in February of 1995 as Crewleader, moving into her present position as Landscape Maintenance Superintendent later that year. Her responsibilities include multiple property landscape management, multiple crew supervision, cost estimation, and landscape design, renovation, and improvement. Prior to this, she managed the Conrad Schweizer Nurseries on Staten Island, New York. **Career Steps:** Desert Care Landscaping, Inc.: Landscape Maintenance Superintendent (1995–Present), Crewleader (Feb.1995–Oct.1995); Manager, Conrad Schweizer Nurseries (1994–1995); Senior Gardener, Baltimore Zoo (1993–1994); Interior Plant Maintenance Person,

University Flowers and Plants (1991–1992); Teaching Assistant, Floral Design–Virginia Polytechnic Institute (1992–1993), Teaching Assistant, Floral Design – Cornell University (1990–1991). **Associations & Accomplishments:** Association of Zoological Horticulture; Pi Alpha Xi Horticultural Honor Society, Alpha and Kappa Chapters; Staten Island Nursery and Landscape Gardeners Association; Academy Scholarship, Virginia Polytechnic Institute and State University (1992–1993, 1991–1992); Charles A. Ring Award for Academic Excellence; Dean's List, Cornell University; 4H Leadership Certificate of Recognition; Cornell University Alumni Association; American Horticultural Society; Certificate of Training Excellence, Basic Supervision; Frequent Speaker and writer on Horticulture and related subjects. **Education:** Virginia Polytechnic Institute and State University, M.S. in Horticulture (1993); Cornell University, B.S. (1991); Cornell University Minns Garden Internship (1990–1991). **Personal:** Married to Michael Primiano in 1995. Mrs. Primiano enjoys gardening and hiking.

B. Prabhakar Rao, Ph.D. (Sc.)

Partner and General Manager
Akar Technical Services Co., L.L.C.
P.O. Box 14652
Dubai, United Arab Emirates
97–14–359783
Fax: 97–14–359776
EMAIL: See Below

0781

Business Information: Akar Technical Services Co., L.L.C., an affiliate of Al Hareb Group of Companies, is a landscape design and architectural firm, specializing in government projects, private plans, commercial properties, and electro–mechanical industrial projects throughout the United Arab Emirates and Middle East. Future plans include expanding into international tourism, such as waterparks, hotels, zoos, and recreational parks. As Partner and General Manager, Dr. Rao is responsible for the oversight of all aspects of operations, including administration, management, public relations, accounting, and strategic planning. Internet users can also reach him via: bprao@emirates.net.ae **Career Steps:** Partner/General Manager, Akar Technical Services Co., L.L.C. (1994–Present); Manager, Al Manahal Agriculture Tech (1991–1994); Managing Director, Hariyalee (1983–1991). **Associations & Accomplishments:** American Society of Landscape Architects; Published in scientific journals and magazines in India. **Education:** University of Agricultural Science – Blr, India, Ph.D. (1980); Louisiana Tech – Baton Rouge, Landscape Architecture. **Personal:** Married to Rugmani in 1986. Two children: Varun and Aditi. Dr. Rao enjoys making ships–in–bottles.

Kerry L. Rohland

General Manager
Hershey Nursery
25 Northeast Drive
Hershey, PA 17033
(717) 534–3071
Fax: (717) 534–3016

0781

Business Information: Hershey Nursery, a division of Herco, is a residential and commercial landscaper and commercial grounds maintenance company. Hershey Nursery's services cover the areas of Central Pennsylvania (Harrisburg to Lancaster). Established in 1905, Hershey Nursery reports annual revenue of $2.8 million and currently employs 45 people. As General Manager, Mr. Rohland is responsible for all aspects of management operations. **Career Steps:** Hershey Nursery: General Manager (1993–Present), Assistant General Manager and Controller (1992–1993), Controller and Landscape Operations Manager (1988–1992). **Associations & Accomplishments:** Lions Club; Positive Thinkers Club; Past Chairman, United Way. **Education:** Elizabethtown College, B.S. (1977); L.V.C., 18 credits in Accounting and Business. **Personal:** Married to Marcia E. in 1978. Two children: Rachel E. and Allison M.. Mr. Rohland enjoys spending time with his family, travel, golf, music, and collecting sports games.

James W. Ross
Director of Marketing
Automatic Rain Company
P.O. Box 2067
Menlo Park, CA 94026
(415) 329–8344
Fax: (415) 329–9024

0781

Business Information: Automatic Rain Company specializes in providing landscaping, irrigation, and related equipment to companies and individuals involved in the lawn care and landscape business. As Director of Marketing, Mr. Ross oversees strategic and tactical marketing plans and handles applicable administrative duties. **Career Steps:** Director of Marketing, Automatic Rain Company (1993–Present); Director, Sales and Marketing, RCO Parts (1992–1993); Vice President of Operations, Goss–Jewett & Company (1990–1992); Director of Operations, Hydroscape Products (1980–1990). **Associations & Accomplishments:** American Marketing Association; Irrigation Association; California Landscape Contractors Association. **Education:** St. Mary's College, M.B.A. (1996). **Personal:** Married to Laurie in 1982. Two children: Timothy and Patrick. Mr. Ross enjoys fly fishing.

Dominic J. Santosuosso Jr.

Chief Financial Officer
ISS Landscape Management Services, Inc.
5028 Tampa West Boulevard
Tampa, FL 33634–2412
(813) 249–5632
Fax: (813) 249–6908

0781

Business Information: ISS Landscape Management Services, Inc., a wholly–owned subsidiary of New York–based development group ISS, Inc., provides all aspects of landscape contracting for commercial clientele, including office complexes, resort parks and golf courses throughout the U.S. (primarily covering the states of FL, TN, PA, GA and VA). Originally serving as Controller for ISS' Mall Services division since 1991, Dominic Santosuosso was recruited to his current position in February of 1993. Reporting directly to the parent company's Board of Directors, as Chief Financial Officer, he is primarily responsible for the review and assessment of project budget income statements, implementation of collection efforts, and the coordination of the annual budget process. **Career Steps:** Cheif Financial Officer, ISS Landscape Management Services, Inc. (1993–Present); Controller, ISS Mall Services (1991–1993); Controller, Coppinger and Affliates (1988–1989). **Associations & Accomplishments:** SPONSOR: Adopt – A – Highway Clean Up – Tampa, FL; Paint Your Heart Out – Brandon, FL **Education:** University of Tennessee – Chattanooga, M.B.A. (1990); Bentley College: B.S. in Accounting (1983), A.S. in Accounting (1982). **Personal:** Mr. Santosuosso enjoys reading, baseball, basketball, hockey, raquetball, music, darts and the news.

Mickey D. Strauss

President and Chief Executive Officer
American Landscape, Inc.
7949 Deering Avenue
Canoga Park, CA 91304–5009
(818) 999–2041
Fax: (818) 999–2056

0781

Business Information: American Landscape, Inc. provides landscape contract services, including site development and golf course construction. Established in 1973, American Landscape currently employs 300 people and has an estimated annual revenue of $15 million. As President and Chief Executive Officer, Mr. Strauss is responsible for all aspects of operations. Concurrent to his position with American Landscape, Mr. Strauss is also President of two other affiliated companies, American Landscape Maintenance, Inc. and American Wholesale Nurseries, Inc. **Career Steps:** President and Chief Executive Officer, American Landscape, Inc., American Landscape Maintenance, Inc., and American Wholesale Nurseries, Inc. (1973–Present); Vice President, Greenscapes, Inc. (1971–1973); Chief Estimator and Purchasing Agent, Valley Crest Landscape (1967–1971). **Associations & Accomplishments:** Former President, California Landscape Contractors Association (1981); President, California Landscape and Irrigation Council (1995, 1990, 1985); Director: California Green Industry Council, Council for Green Environment, and Los Angeles Green Industry Council; Former Chairman, California Landscape Political Action Committee. **Education:** Pierce College, A.A. (1965). **Personal:** Married to Lucinda in 1968. Two children: Jeffrey Alan and Jason Daniel. Mr. Strauss enjoys boating, water skiing, and horseback riding.

Curt W. Thimm

Vice President and General Manager
E.C. Geiger, Inc.
219 Hendricks Road
Perkiomenville, PA 18074
(215) 256–6511
Fax: (215) 256–6110

0782

Business Information: E.C. Geiger, Inc. is a distributor of greenhouse and nursery supplies through four locations in New York, Pennsylvania and Virginia. Established in 1928, E.C. Geiger, Inc. reports annual revenue of $30 million and currently employs 100 people. Starting as Buyer for Geiger in 1974, Mr. Thimm was promoted to his current position in 1984. As Vice President and General Manager, he is responsible for all aspects of operations for all four locations, including day–to–day operations, administration, finances, sales, public relations, and strategic planning. **Career Steps:** E.C. Geiger, Inc.: Vice President and General Manager (1984–Present), Buyer (1974–1984); Member, U.S. Air Force (1969–1973); Manager, Thimm Brothers, Inc. (1963–1969). **Associations & Accomplishments:** North American Horticultural Suppliers Association; Scotts Distributor Advisory Council; Finance Chair and Sunday School Teacher for his church; Volunteer Umpire, girl's softball team; Leader, Boy Scouts of America. **Education:** West Chester University, no degree – he was drafted in the U.S. Air Force in his senior year (1965–1969). **Personal:** Married to Nancy H. Thimm in 1974. Three children: Becky, Bobby, and Laura. Mr. Thimm enjoys reading, boating, and the theatre.

Steven D. Toeller

General Manager
Trugreen/Chemlawn
461 Enterprise Drive
Westerville, OH 43081
(614) 431–0825
Fax: (614) 431–0155

0782

Business Information: Trugreen/Chemlawn, a subsidairy of Service Master with over 5,700 franchised service stores, specializes in lawn, shrub and tree care. Established in 1969, the Company currently employs 11,000 people and reports annual revenue of $600 million. As General Manager, Mr. Toeller is responsible for all aspects of operations, including a staff of 102 people during peak season. **Career Steps:** Trugreen/Chemlawn: General Manager (1992–Present), Region Manager (1989–1992); Market Manager, Pepisico (1985–1989). **Associations & Accomplishments:** St. Andrews Board (Athletic). **Education:** Southern Methodist University, M.B.A. (1987); Miami University, B.A. in Education. **Personal:** Married to Kathy in 1980. Two children: Nick and Megan. Mr. Toeller enjoys coaching 5th and 6th grade football, baseball, and softball.

Michael J. Barger

Owner and President
Mike's Tree Surgeons, Inc.
263 Park Street
Troy, MI 48083–2726
(810) 588–0202
Fax: (810) 588–4824

0783

Business Information: Mike's Tree Surgeons, Inc. is a major tree, shrub, and landscape maintenance company, providing consulting and advice on urban forestry, as well as pruning, surgery, and management of trees. Establishing Mike's Tree Surgeons in 1984 as Owner and President, Mr. Barger is responsible for all aspects of operations, including sales, employee training, and management of the Company. He also serves as an expert witness when required, and provides professional consulting services (woodlot and specimen tree preservation, tree valuation and appraisal, hazardous tree risk assessment, and plant health care). **Career Steps:** Owner and President, Mike's Tree Surgeons, Inc. (1984–Present); Forestry Worker II, City of Southfield (1981–1984); Tree Trimmer and Spray Technician, Harrison Tree Service (1978–1981). **Associations & Accomplishments:** National Arborist Association; President (1991–1994), Michigan Arborist Association; Proctor (1993), International Society of Arboriculture; Society of Commercial Aborists; Professional Grounds Management Association; American Forestry Association; Michigan Forestry Association; Vice President (1990–1996), Global ReLeaf of Michigan; Builders Association of Michigan; Michigan Forestry and Parks Association; Michigan Turfgrass Association; Michigan Nursery and Landscapers Association, Urban Action Coalition Committee; Metropolitan Detroit Landscapers Association; Profile, Arbor Magazine (1993); Video on Lightning Protection, Independent Protection Company; Green Industry Council; Numerous seminars and workshops on related factors. **Education:** Michigan Technological University, B.S. (1978); I.S.A. Certified Arborist; Michigan Registered Forester; Century 21 Real Estate School (1980). **Personal:** Married to Denise in 1984. Two children: Joseph and Jennifer. Mr. Barger enjoys baseball, hunting, fishing, and golf.

0800 Forestry

0811 Timber tracts
0831 Forest products
0851 Forestry services

Ralph C. Bower, Ph.D.

Manager – Technical Services
MacMillan Bloedel Packaging Inc.
P.O. Box 336
Pine Hill, AL 36769–0336
(334) 963–4391
Fax: (334) 682–4481

0831

Business Information: MacMillan Bloedel Packaging Inc. is a national producer of forestry products (i.e., dimension lumber, plywood, linear board). Joining MacMillan Bloedel Packaging, Inc. in 1985, Ralph Bower was appointed as Manager of Technical Services in 1995. He is responsible for the management of the Technical Department for the Woodlands Division, which includes tree nurseries, tree improvement, GIS, database, safety, scaling for raw and finished materials, etc. **Career Steps:** MacMillan Bloedel Packaging Inc.: Manager Technical Services (1995–Present), Manager, Nursery & Tree Improvement (1988–1995), Research Coordinator (1985–1988). **Associations & Accomplishments:** Society of American Foresters; Alabama Forestry Association. **Education:** Texas A & M, Ph.D. (1977); Southern Illinois University: M.S. (1973), B.S. (1968). **Personal:** Married to Julia in 1968. Two children: John R. and Timothy J.

Kimberly S. Bunting

Corporate Casualty Risk Manager
Georgia Pacific Corporation
P.O. Box 105605
Atlanta, GA 30348–5605
(404) 652–6020
Fax: (404) 583–1438

0831

Business Information: Georgia Pacific Corporation, the leading wholesaler of building supplies in the U.S., is a forest products company, manufacturing paper products and building supplies. Distributing throughout 48 states, excluding Hawaii and Alaska, Georgia Pacific Corporation exports products all over the world. Operating manufacturing plants in the U.S. and Canada, Georgia Pacific reports annual revenue of $13 billion and employs 45,000 people corporate–wide. As Corporate Casualty Risk Manager, Ms. Bunting is responsible for the management of all liability insurance programs including claims, loss prevention, working with the general counsel of the Company using her legal expertise, and supervision of a staff of 10 people. Her greatest achievements include receiving a law degree and a Masters of Business Administration at the same time. **Career Steps:** Georgia Pacific Corporation: Corporate Casualty Risk Manager (1992–Present), Counsel (1992); Litigation and Environmental Counsel, Racetrac Petroleum, Inc. (1990–1992); Attorney, Carter & Ansley (1987–1990); Law Clerk, Honorable Don Langham, Fulton Superior Court (1986–1987) **Associations & Accomplishments:** Georgia Bar Association; American Bar Association; Atlanta Bar Association; Risk & Insurance Management Society. **Education:** Emory University, J.D., M.B.A. (1986); Oglethorpe University, B.A., magna cum laude (1981). **Personal:** Married. One child: daughter.

Dwight W. Guy

Mail Service Coordinator
Georgia Pacific Corporation
P.O. Box 10565
Atlanta, GA 30348–5605
(404) 652–4285
Fax: (404) 230–5646

0831

Business Information: Georgia Pacific Corporation, the leading wholesaler of building supplies in the United States, specializes in the cultivation and field management of timber for the purpose of gathering and producing products. As a forest products company, they manufacture paper products, building supplies, and chemical products to treat wood. Distributing throughout 48 states, Georgia Pacific Corporation also exports products all over the world. Operating manufacturing plants in the U.S. and Canada, Georgia Pacific reports annual revenue of $13 billion and employs 45,000 people corporate–wide. Mr. Guy joined Georgia Pacific as Mail Service Coordinator in 1991 upon his honorable discharge from the U.S. Army where he held the rank of Sergeant. He is presently responsible for overseeing a staff of 35 in the daily operations of shipping, receiving, delivery, and special projects activities. Concurrently, he volunteers his time to various community functions (i.e., Special Olympics, Atlanta Art Festival, Atlanta Fulton County Library). **Career Steps:** Mail Service Coordinator, Georgia Pacific Corporation (1991–Present); U.S. Army: Sergeant, D 1/19, Fort Benning (1989–1991), Sergeant, 2/22 Fort Benning (1986–1989). **Associations & Accomplishments:** Volunteer of the Quarter for Georgia Special Olympics; Volunteer of the Quarter for Atlanta Fulton County Library; Silver Star Volunteer for Georgia Pacific Corporation Olympic Force; Advisory Committee, Harper High Graphic Department; Day Captain, Art Festival Atlanta; Volunteer, High Museum of Art. **Education:** DeVry Institute; Fayetteville State University. **Personal:** Mr. Guy enjoys volunteering for many functions.

James E. Carmichael
Marketing Manager
Afognak Native Corporation
104 Center Street, Suite 201B
Kodiak, AK 99615
(907) 486–5808
Fax: (907) 486–4262
EMail: See Below

0851

Business Information: Afognak Native Corporation specializes in timber and land resource management. The Corporation markets lumber and timber to Asia, selling it for manufacturing purposes. As Marketing Manager, Mr. Carmichael manages the marketing to Asia and negotiates business with various companies. Internet users can reach him via: carjmichj@ptialaska.net. **Career Steps:** Afognak Native Corporation: Marketing Manager (1995–Present), General Manager (1985–1995); Account Executive, Dean Witter Reynolds (1982–1985). **Associations & Accomplishments:** Director, Resource Development Council of Alaska; Director, Alaska Forest Association; Director, Kodiak Outdoor Theater Corporation; Society of American Foresters. **Education:** University of Idaho, B.S. (1966). **Personal:** Married to Margo in 1969. Two children: Andrew and Ryan. Mr. Carmichael enjoys outdoor sports.

Robbie E. Chrishon
Director of Procurement and Property
United States Department of Agriculture Forest Service
1720 Peachtree Road North West, Suite 710 N
Atlanta, GA 30367
(404) 347–2597
Fax: (404) 347–3318

0851

Business Information: United States Department of Agriculture Forest Service is the federal agency charged with enforcing federal laws and regulations regarding government forests and campgrounds. The agency is responsible control of forest fires and the overall ecology of government lands. As Director of Procurement/Property, Ms. Chrishon is charged with the procurement of property and equipment for the Department of Agriculture. Her office is also responsible for the maintenance and upkeep of existing equipment and property. Ms. Chrishon reviews departmental budgets, vendor quotes, and contracts prior to the purchase of new materials. **Career Steps:** United States Department of Agriculture/Forest Service: Director of Procurement/Property (1992–Present), Branch Chief, Procurement/Property (1990–1992), Procurement Analyst, Procurement/Property (1986–1990). **Associations & Accomplishments:** National Forum for Black Public Administrators; Volunteer, Project Atlanta; Southern Christian Leadership Conference; Cobb County National Association for the Advancement of Colored People. **Education:** Harvard University, Senior Executive Fellows Program (1994); North East Louisiana University, B.A. in Business Administration (1972). **Personal:** One child: Kristopher. Ms. Chrishon enjoys reading, walking, needlework, running, and gardening.

Hugues J. Mc Nicoll
General Manager
Centre Sylvicole Forestville
350 Route 138, R.R. 1
Forestville, Quebec G0T 1E0
(418) 587–4353
Fax: (418) 587–4350
EMail: See Below

0851

Business Information: Centre Sylvicole Forestville is a federally–funded organization specializing in the production of forest seedlings, sylvicultural practices, forestry works, and road construction. As General Manager, Mr. Mc Nicoll is responsible for all aspects of Company operations, including research, strategic planning, and administration. Internet users can reach him via: csfinc@quebectel.com. **Career Steps:** General Manager, Centre Sylvicole Forestville (1991–Present); Engineer & Agronomist, Roche Ltee, Groupe–conseil (1985–1991); Research, Universite Laval (1985). **Associations & Accomplishments:** Ordre des Ingenieurs du Quebec; Ordre des Agronomes du Quebec. **Education:** Universite Laval: B.Sc.A. in Engineering (1984), B.Sc.A. in Agronomy (1981); Several courses in continuing education in the field of administration, management, etc.; Speaks French, English, and Spanish. **Personal:** Mr. Mc Nicoll enjoys swimming, reading, and tennis.

Teri A. Perrine
Human Resources Manager
Rayonier – NWFR
3033 Ingram Street
Hoquiam, WA 98550–0200
(360) 538–4583
Fax: (360) 532–5426

0851

Business Information: Rayonier – NWFR is an international forestry management company, involved in the acquisition and harvest management of timberland. Rayonier – NWFR owns and manages land in Northwestern U.S., Russia, China, New Zealand, and Chile, with a manufacturing department that includes mills and logging facilities. Established in 1937, Rayonier – NWFR currently employs 39 people. As Human Resources Manager, Mrs. Perrine oversees all personnel functions to include personnel law compliance, safety, employment, benefit program maintenance, and employee relations. **Career Steps:** Human Resources Manager, Rayonier – NWFR (1995–Present); Human Resource Manager, Evergreen Counseling Center (1990–1995). **Associations & Accomplishments:** Eagles Club; United Way Loaned Executive; American Management Association. **Education:** Eastern Washington University, B.A. in Business (1989). **Personal:** Married to O. Thomas Perrine in 1991. Mrs. Perrine enjoys playing co–ed softball and volleyball, painting, crafts, and music.

James W. (Jim) Stapleton
Deputy Director
USDA Forest Service
P.O. Box 34914
Juneau, AK 99803–4914
(907) 586–7827 (Office Phone)
Fax: (907) 586–7555

0851

Business Information: Established in 1907, the USDA Forest Service, owned by the Federal Government and the United States Department of Agriculture, cares for the land and serves the citizen owners of the Nation's National Forest. Working in administrative engineering roles with various Forest Service divisions since 1972, Jim Stapleton was transferred to the Alaska headquarters in October of 1991. As Deputy Director, he serves as second in command for the oversight and direction of all U.S. Forest Service engineering and aviation activities in the State of Alaska. **Career Steps:** USDA Forest Service: Deputy Director (1991–Present), Forest Engineer (1989–1991), Regional Transportation Engineer (1987–1989), Assistant Forest Engineer (1983–1987), Forest Transportation Engineer (1978–1983), Civil Engineer (1976–1978), Construction Engineer (1972–1976). **Associations & Accomplishments:** American Society of Civil Engineers; American Indian Society of Engineers and Scientists; President, Trout Unlimited – Juneau Chapter. **Education:** University of California – Berkeley, M.S. in Civil Engineering (1977); Oregon Institute of Technology – Klamath Falls, B.T.C.E. (1972). **Personal:** Married to Susan Kay in 1972. One child: Mark Wesley. Mr. Stapleton enjoys hunting and fly fishing.

Steven K. Templin
President
Templin Forestry Inc.
P.O. Box 10
Bentley, LA 71407–0010
(318) 899–3361
Fax: (318) 899–7382

0851

Business Information: Templin Forestry Inc. is a comprehensive forest management service for the public and provides the utmost in modern technology to the owners of private forests by managing timber sales, planting trees, forest analysis, appraisals and long term management. Louisiana Forestry Investments, Inc. is a real estate firm providing buyers and sellers professional representation in buying or selling forested properties. As President, Mr. Templin provides the overall direction and vision for the Company's continued growth, quality delivery to customers, and strategic development. **Career Steps:** President, Templin Forestry Inc. (1983–Present); President and Chief Broker, Louisiana Forestry Investments, Inc. (1984–Present); Administrative Assistant, Davis Forestry Corporation (1979–1983). **Associations & Accomplishments:** Louisiana State Certified General Appraiser; Society of American Foresters: Louisiana Central Chapter Chairman (1986), Louisiana Executive Committee (1986–1993); Louisiana Forestry Association: Area IV Chairman (1989–1993), Board of Directors (1989, 1992, 1993); Association of Consulting Foresters: Louisiana State Chairman (1987–1988), National Public Relations Committee Chairman (1992–Present); Certified Review Appraiser, National Association of Review Appraisers & Mortgage Underwriters; Master Senior Appraiser, National Association of Master Appraisers; Candidate Member, American Society of Farm Managers and Rural Appraisers; Forest Farmers Association; National Woodland Owners Association; Commissioner and Secretary, Grant Parish Planning Commission; Notary Public. **Education:** Northern Arizona University, B.S. in Forestry, summa cum laude (1979); Practicing Foresters Institute (1985). **Personal:** Married to Lorna in 1995. Two children: Kyle and Andrea. Mr. Templin enjoys golf.

0900 Fishing, Hunting, and Trapping

   0912 Finfish
   0913 Shellfish
   0919 Miscellaneous marine products
   0921 Fish hatcheries and preserves
   0971 Hunting, trapping, game propagation

Gerardo Tome
Chief Financial Officer, Director, & Shareholder
Granjas Marinas Bernardo
Edif Los Jarros 301 Boulevard Morazan
Tegucigalpa, Honduras
(504) 32–6005
Fax: (504) 31–5832

0913

Business Information: Granjas Marinas Bernardo is a shrimp farming business specializing in processing, exporting, and marketing shrimp. The Company has recently begun shipping oysters. As Chief Financial Officer, Director, & Shareholder, Mr. Tome is responsible for strategic planning, handling new business development, and marketing. Concurrently, Mr. Tome is the founder of a financial investment corporation and holding company of many subsidiaries. **Career Steps:** Chief Financial Officer, Director, & Shareholder, Granjas Marinas Bernardo (1986–Present). **Education:** The Wharton School, M.B.A. (1988); Yale University (1982). **Personal:** Married to Monique in 1994.

Brian J. Draves
Plant Manager
Clear Springs Foods, Inc.
P O Box 712
Buhl, ID 83316
(208) 543–8816
Fax: (208) 543–4332

0921

Business Information: Clear Springs Foods, Inc. is a vertically integrated trout farm, brood operation, and research and development center. The Company currently has the largest trout farm operation in the United Sates and is branching out into the processing of other food stuffs. Established in 1966, Clear Springs Foods, Inc. has 350 employees and an international client base. As Plant Manager, Mr. Draves handles plant operations for two facilities including processing, sanitation, budgeting, and accounts payable. He is involved in the implementation of new and existing marketing techniques and strategic planning for the Corporation. Mr. Draves was instrumental in organizing the new facility in Buhl, Idaho. **Career Steps:** Plant Manager, Clear Springs Foods, Inc. (1996–Present); Assistant Plant Manager, Van De Kamps (1994–1996); Plant Superintendent, Pet Inc. (1989–1994). **Associations & Accomplishments:** Institute of Food Technologist; Coach Little League Sports; Coach Varsity football; Certified Trainer (Zenger Miller). **Education:** University of Missouri at Columbia, B.S. in Agriculture (1983). **Personal:** Married to Kim in 1985. Mr. Draves enjoys woodworking, sports, boating, hunting, camping, fishing, and coaching football, softball, and soccer.

1000 – 1499

MINING

1000 Metal Mining

1011 Iron ores
1021 Copper ores
1031 Lead and zinc ores
1041 Gold ores
1044 Silver ores
1061 Ferroalloy ores, except vanadium
1081 Metal mining services
1094 Uranium–radium–vanadium ores
1099 Metal ores, NEC

Jonathan H. Holmes
Manager
Inland Steel Mining Co.
5950 Old Highway 53
Virginia, MN 55792–0001
(218) 749–5910
Fax: (218) 749–5256

1011

Business Information: Inland Steel Mining Co., established in 1977, mines and produces taconite ore (a low grade magnetic iron rock) into iron ore pellets, producing 2.8 million gross tons annually. With eighteen years experience in minerals engineering and management, Mr. Holmes joined Inland Steel Mining Co. as Engineer in 1979. Appointed as Manager in 1994, he manages the entire operation, in addition to overseeing all administrative operations for all associates and of a support staff of 362. **Career Steps:** Inland Steel Mining Co.: Manager (1994–Present), Section Manager – Mining (1988–1994), Engineer – Mining (1979–1988); Engineer, Kerr McGee Nuclear Corp. (1978–1979). **Associations & Accomplishments:** Iron Mining Association; Society of Mining Engineers of A.I.M.E. **Education:** University of Minnesota, B.S. in Minerals Engineering (1977). **Personal:** Married to Stacey Hazen in 1987. Two children: Nate and Ben. Mr. Holmes helps his wife race sled dogs.

Craig A. Beasley
Director
Kennecott Utah Copper
P.O. Box 329
Magna, UT 84044–0329
(801) 252–3000 Ext. 3042
Fax: (801) 252–3303

1021

Business Information: Kennecott Utah Cooper specializes in the mining, smelting, and refining of copper, gold, and silver. As Director, Mr. Beasley directs the organizational development, training, and employee communications. Additionally, he is responsible for succession planning, continuing improvement process within his organization, and internal and external communications. **Career Steps:** Kennecott Utah Cooper: Director (1996–Present), Manager of Organization Development (1994–1996); Human Resource Development Consultant, ARCO Coal Company (1992–1994); Principle Consultant, Beasley and Associates (1988–1994). **Associations & Accomplishments:** OD Network; American Society of Training Development; President, Heritage League, 2nd ADA. **Education:** Regis College: M.B.A. (1984), B.S. in Business Administration. **Personal:** Mr. Beasley enjoys motorcycling, fishing, and cooking.

Jim Fuchs, P. Eng.
Superintendent of Engineering
Falconbridge Limited
C/O Fraser Mine
Onaping, Ontario P0M 2R0
(705) 966–3411 Ext. 6165
Fax: Please mail or call

1021

Business Information: Falconbridge Limited is a mining operation specializing in underground and depth mining of nickel, copper, and precious metals. Regional in scope, the Company was established in 1928, employs 2,100 people, and owns several mines within the Ontario area. As Superintendent of Engineering, Mr. Fuchs directs all technical functions at the Fraser/Strathcona complex, in addition to being responsible for for all administrative functions related to his position. **Career Steps:** Superintendent of Engineering, Falconbridge Limited (1996–Present); Professor, Mining Engineering, Laurentian University (1993). **Education:** Laurentian University: M.B.A. (1989), Bachelors in English, B.Sc. in Geology. **Personal:** Married to Monique. Mr. Fuchs enjoys sports, ice hockey, and softball.

Darian Rich
Director of Human Resources
BHP – Nevada Mining
2675 Mineral Drive
Ely, NV 89301
(702) 289–7070
Fax: (702) 289–7079

1021

Business Information: BHP – Nevada Mining is a gold, copper, nickel, and diamond mining company. Additionally, the Company maintains a coal and steel operation in Australia. As Director of Human Resources, Mr. Rich is responsible for designing, developing, and implementing human resource policies, training, safety, and providing strategic direction. **Career Steps:** Director of Human Resources, BHP – Nevada Mining (1994–Present); Manager of Human Resources, Magma Copper Company (1992–1994); Senior Labor Relations Representative, Cadillac Motor Center Division (1989–1992). **Associations & Accomplishments:** Senior Professional in Human Resources, Society for Human Resources; Certified Compensation Professional, American Compensation Association. **Education:** Central Michigan University, M.S. in Administration (1996); Ohio State University, B.S. in Labor and Human Resources (1984). **Personal:** Married to Anita in 1992. Two children: Janine and Autumn. Mr. Rich enjoys single engine flight training, reading, woodworking, and recreational sports.

Jaime Urjel

President
Comsur S.A.
Casilla 4326
La Paz, Bolivia
(591) 236–2080
Fax: (591) 239–1016

1031

Business Information: Comsur S.A. specializes in the operation of mines, primarily zinc, lead and silver. Regional in scope, the Company owns seven mines throughout Bolivia and is in the process of completing construction of a gold mine. Established in 1962, the Company employs 2,000 people. As President, Mr. Urjel oversees all aspects of the Company. His duties include administration, operations, finance and strategic planning. **Career Steps:** Comsur S.A: President (1993–Present), Managing Director (1991–1993), General Manager (1985–1991). **Associations & Accomplishments:** Asociacion Nacional De Mineros Medianos. **Education:** Universidad Mayor De Dan Andres, La Paz, Licensed Electrical Engineer (1973). **Personal:** Married to Cecilia in 1973. Three children: Marcelo, Claudia and Jaime. Mr. Urjel enjoys tennis and racquetball.

Doug Batchelor
General Manager
Kennecott Rawhide Mining Company
P.O. Box 2070
Fallon, NV 89407–2070
(702) 773–2020
Fax: (702) 773–2221

1041

Business Information: Kennecott Rawhide Mining Company specializes in gold heap leach mining, producing 120,000 ounces of gold annually. As General Manager, Mr. Batchelor is the senior officer on–sight, responsible for production and maintaining the objectives of the Company's gold exploration program. **Career Steps:** General Manager, Kennecott Rawhide Mining Company (1995–Present); Palabora Mining Company: Mine Manager (1992–1995), General Superintendent (1991–1992), Mine Superintendent (1988–1990). **Associations & Accomplishments:** Fellow, Institution of Mining and Metallurgy. **Education:** Royal School of Mines, B.S. (1980). **Personal:** Married to Yianna in 1977. Two children: Katerina and Stephanie. Mr. Batchelor enjoys computing.

Louis O. Peloquin
Vice President, General Counsel, Secretary
Golden Star Resources, Ltd.
1700 Lincoln Street, Suite 1950
Denver, CO 80203
(303) 894–4622
Fax: (303) 830–9022

1041

Business Information: Golden Star Resources, Ltd. is a gold and diamond exploration company, holding interests in properties through subsidiaries located in South America and Africa. Established in 1984, Gold Star Resources, Inc. currently employs 450 people. A practicing attorney admitted to practice in domestic and international law since 1987, Mr. Peloquin joined Golden Star Resources, Ltd. in 1993. Serving as Vice President, General Counsel and Secretary, he is responsible for all corporate legal matters, as well as the supervision of all corporate attorneys located in Denver, Colorado (3), Africa (1), French Guyana (1), and Caracas, Venezuela (1). He also negotiates agreements and joint ventures with mining companies, handles acquisitions of new properties, supervises any outside legal counsel needed, and attends all Board meetings. **Career Steps:** Vice President, General Counsel and Secretary, Golden Star Resources, Ltd. (1993–Present); Associate, McCarthy Tetrault (1991–1993); Associate, Shearman & Sterling (1989–1991); Associate, Paul, Weiss, Rifkind, Wharton & Garrison (1988–1989). **Associations & Accomplishments:** American Law Association; New York Bar Association; Denver Bar Association; Quebec Bar Association; Association of American Corporate Counsel; Rocky Mountain Mineral Law Foundation; Published in trade journals. **Education:** New York University Law School, LL.M. (1987); University of Montreal, LL.B. (1984); Laval University, B.B.A. (1980). **Personal:** Married to Carole Plante in 1987. Two children: Louis–Alexandre and Valerie. Mr. Peloquin enjoys golf, skiing, reading, and painting.

Mr. John M. Siriunas
Vice President of Engineering and Principal
NR&J Resource Associates Limited
2803 Hollington Crescent
Mississauga, Ontario L5K 1E8
(905) 823–6928
Fax: (905) 823–6928

1041

Business Information: NR&J Resource Associates Limited is a mineral exploration consulting firm for mine developers in North America. As Vice President of Engineering, and Principal, Mr. Siriunas specializes in geological engineering and mineral mining. Starting with mineral collecting as a hobby, Mr. Siriunas now has investments in Africa and South America, and hopes to grow the business into a worldwide service in the next three to five years. NR&J Resource Associates Limited was established in 1989 by Mr. Siriunas and two partners. **Career Steps:** Vice President, Engineering, and Principal, NR&J Resource Associates Limited (1989–Present); Sole Proprietor, John Siriunas Consulting (1987–1989); Geological Consultant, MPH Consulting Ltd. (1978–1987). **Associations & Accomplishments:** Professional Engineers of Ontario (PEO); Association of Exploration Geochemists; Society for Mining, Metallurgy and Exploration (SME); Published in technical journals. **Education:** University of Toronto, M.A.Sc. (1979); University of Toronto, B.A.Sc. (1976).

Luis F. Uribe Labastida
President of the Board
Compania Minera De Natividad y Anexas S.A.
Colonia Granada Ejercito Nacional 499 Piso 3
Distrito Federal, Mexico
(525) 255–5048
Fax: (525) 255–2474

1041

Business Information: Compania Minera de Natividad y Anexas S.A. is an international gold and silver mining company which sells its products to the Mexican government. Established in 1895, Compania Minera has approximately 20 mines located throughout Mexico. As President of the Board, Mr. Uribe Labastida is responsible for overseeing all operations for the Company. Concurrently, he is the owner and operator of 29 other companies, ranging from mining companies, restaurants, a watch manufacturer and seller (which is the #1 seller of watches in Mexico), a chemical company (the #2 exporter of chemicals to approximately 10 countries), and a plastics company (the #3 exporter of plastics to Central and South America). **Career Steps:** President, Compania Minera De Natividad y Anexas S.A. (1961–Present); Serves as the President of the Board for the following companies: Relojes Exactos S.A. de C.V. (1956–Present), Proquifin S.A. de C.V. (1962–Present), Plasticos Espumados S.A. de C.V. (1964–Present), Bufete Uribe Y Uribe (1939–Present), Grupo Industrial Ubeida S.A. de C.V., Industrial de Espumas Plasticas S.A. de C.V. (1962–Present), Ifusal S.A. de C.V. (1962–Present), Trapla, S.A. de C.V. (1962–Present), Traplausa S.A. de C.V. (1962–Present), Plasticos Urprl S.A. de C.V. (1962–Present), Sinfarmex, S.A. (1964–Present), Helber de Mexico S.A. de C.V. (1964–Present), Laboratorios Galen, S.A. de C.V. (1964–Present), Laboratorios Chemia, S.A. de C.V. (1964–Present), Proguigama S.A. de C.V. (1964–Present), Compania Nacional Relojera S.A. (1966–Present), La Locura Suiza S.A. de C.V. (1966), Mido Swiss, U.S.A. (1966–Present), America Distribuidora y Comercializadora S.A. de C.V. (1980–Present), Crimibe S.A. de C.V. (1980), Cia. Exportadora de Maquila Comexma S.A. de C.V. (1980–Present), Plan Pro Restaurantes S.A. (1982–Present). **Education:** Escuela Libre de Derecho, Lawyer (1938); Colegio Franco Ingles. **Personal:** Married to Cristina de la Mora y Llaca in 1940. Six children: Luis, Carlos, Jaime, Ignacio, Maria Cristina and Enrique Uribe.

James G. Wilson Jr.

Controller
Kinross Delamar Mining Co.
P.O. Box 52
Jordan Valley, OR 97910–0052
(208) 583–2511
Fax: (208) 583–2516

1041

Business Information: Kinross Delamar Mining Co. is a mining and exploration company, involved with base metal and precious metal mining; with current projects primarily focused in gold and silver ore open pit mining operations. International in scope, they currently have 9 locations, with 157 employees at the Jordan Valley site. As Controller, Mr. Wilson oversees all accounting functions, including warehousing and purchasing. Mr. Wilson has over 10 years experience in the mining and petroleum industry. **Career Steps:** Controller, Kinross Delamar Mining Company (1995–Present); Corporate Controller, Kinross Gold U.S.A., Inc. (1993–1995); Corporate Controller, Arava Natural Resources (1991–1993); Mine Controller, U.S. Fuel Company (1989–1991). **Education:** Fort Lewis College, B.A. (1981). **Personal:** Married to Cathie in 1982. Two children: Patrick and Kevin. Mr. Wilson enjoys golf.

Joseph S. Stefanich

Director of Materials
EVTAC Co.
P.O. Box 180
Eveleth, MN 55734
(218) 744–7807
Fax: (218) 744–5841

1081

Business Information: ECTAC Co., owned by Roughe Steel, A–K Steel and Stelco is a national producer of taconise pellets, made by crushing taconite to talcum fineness and separating a rich, black ore, for the automotive industry. As Director of Materials, Mr. Stefanich is responsible for directing all purchasing (fuels and other materials) and material control activities, in addition to overseeing electric power and rail contracts, warehouse and inventory control, and financial matters. **Career Steps:** Eveleth Mines: Director of Materials (1988–Present), Chief Accountant (1977–1988); Manager of International Accounting, Control Data Corporation (1963–1977). **Associations & Accomplishments:** Eveleth Chamber of Commerce; American Management Association; Purchasing Management Association; National Association of Accountants; Author of a cookbook on wild game. **Education:** University of Minnesota, B.A. (1962). **Personal:** Married to Jo Ann in 1960. Three children: Jeff, Steven, and Troy. Mr. Stefanich enjoys hunting, fishing and cooking wild game.

1200 Coal Mining

1221 Bituminous coal and lignite – surface
1222 Bituminous coal – underground
1231 Anthracite mining
1241 Coal mining services

Barbara C. Cole

Senior Tax Manager
A.T. Massey Coal Company, Inc.
P.O. Box 26765
Richmond, VA 23261
(804) 788–1841
Fax: (804) 788–1821

1241

Business Information: A.T. Massey Coal Company, Inc., through its operating subsidiaries, produces high–quality, low sulfur steam coal for the electric generating industry and industrial customers, and metallurgical coal for the steel industry. Massey operates mostly in the Central Appalachia area of West Virginia and Kentucky. Established in 1920, Massey employs 2,500 and has revenues of $850 million. As Senior Tax Manager, Mrs. Cole oversees the Federal and State income tax filings, handles audits for income tax returns and for taxes other than income, such as severance and property taxes, and coordinates research for tax planning, acquisitions and other tax issues. **Career Steps:** Senior Tax Manager, A.T. Massey Coal (1991–Present); Senior Tax Analyst, Deloitte & Touche (1988–1991); Accounting Supervisor, Womack & Burke (1984–1988). **Associations & Accomplishments:** American Institute of Certified Public Accountants; Virginia Society of Certified Public Accountants. **Education:** Virginia Commonwealth University: Bachelors (1981), CPA (1987), Masters in Taxation (In Progress). **Personal:** Married to David Lynn Cole in 1984. Two children: Raven and Ramsey. Mrs. Cole enjoys gardening.

Philip Dinsmoor

Manager of Environmental and Mine Engineering
Amax Coal West, Inc.
P.O. Box 3039
Gillette, WY 82717–3039
(307) 687–3406
Fax: (307) 687–3470

1241

Business Information: Amax Coal West, Inc. is an organization dedicated to the mining of coal in an economical, safe, and environmentally responsible manner. As Manager of Environmental and Mine Engineering, Mr. Dinsmoor leads the department's professional staff in long– and short–term planning, permitting, and compliance. **Career Steps:** Amax Coal West, Inc.: Manager of Environmental and Mine Engineering – Belle Ay Mine (1989–Present), Manager of Environmental and Mine Engineering – Eagle Butte Mine (1988–1989); Manager of Environmental Engineering, Amax Coal Company (1982–1988). **Associations & Accomplishments:** Chairman and Member, Wyoming Air Quality Advisory Board; Wyoming Mining Association Reclamation Committee – Air Subcommittee. **Education:** University of Wisconsin – Madison: M.S. in Landscape Architecture (1977), B.S. in Landscape Architecture (1974); Southern Methodist University (1970–1972). **Personal:** Married to Margot in 1979. Two children: Wesley and Kristen. Mr. Dinsmoor enjoys volleyball, reading, and camping.

Donald Hicks

Vice President
Pacific Canada Resources, Inc.
350 Bay Street, 7th Floor
Toronto, Ontario M5H 2S6
(416) 364–9382
Fax: (416) 368–2579

1241

Business Information: Pacific Canada Resources, Inc. is a Canadian mining company. As Vice President, Mr. Hicks is responsible for corporate development. **Career Steps:** Vice President, Pacific Canada Resources, Inc. (Present). **Associations & Accomplishments:** Law Society of Upper Canada; Canadian Bar Association. Education: School of Law, LL.B. (1985); Queens University: M.B.A. (1981), B.A. (1979).

John A. Stachura Jr.

Vice President
Solar Source Underground L
P.O. Box 325
Monroe City, IN 47557
(812) 743–2015
Fax: (812) 743–2108

1241

Business Information: Solar Source Underground L specializes in the mining of coal for various industries. As Vice President, Mr. Stachura is responsible for all aspects of Company operations, including managing the underground operations. **Career Steps:** Vice President, Solar Source Underground (1993–Present); Superintendent, Black Beauty Coal (1986–1991); Vice President, J&R Coal Company (1978–1984); Foreman, AMAX (1976–1978). **Associations & Accomplishments:** Director, AMBANC; Director, Indiana Mining Board; Elks Club. **Education:** Indiana State University, B.S. in Management (1972). **Personal:** Married to Sara in 1973. Two children: Kristen and Andrew. Mr. Stachura enjoys hunting, fishing, and golf.

1300 Oil and Gas Extraction

1311 Crude petroleum and natural gas
1321 Natural gas liquids
1381 Drilling oil and gas wells
1382 Oil and gas exploration services
1389 Oil and gas field services, NEC

James Barrow

President
Louis A. Pessina Oil and Gas
P.O. Box 79
Grayville, IL 62844–0079
(618) 375–3221
Fax: (618) 375–2509
E–mail: see below

1311

Business Information: Louis A. Pessina Oil and Gas specializes in oil and gas production, exploring and drilling for oil in a 60–mile radius in the Illinois Basin. Established in 1962 and incorporated in 1933, Louis A. Pessina Oil and Gas currently employs 7 people. As President, Mr. Barrow is responsible for all aspects of operations. He can also be reached through the Internet as follows: 75000.2167@compuserv.com **Career Steps:** President, Louis A. Pessina Oil and Gas (Entire Career). **Associations & Accomplishments:** Board of Directors, Illinois Oil and Gas Association; Independent Oil Producers Association; National Rifle Association; Published article in Springfield newspaper. **Education:** Attended Eastern Illinois University, Quincy College and Wabash Valley College. **Personal:** Married to Jane in 1981. Three children: Elizabeth, Alex and Jill. Mr. Barrow enjoys hunting, fishing and politics.

William R. Berls

Purchasing Consultant
Amoco Corporation
200 East Randolph Drive
Chicago, IL 60601
(312) 856–7893
Fax: (312) 856–3060

1311

Business Information: Amoco Corporation is one of the world's largest manufacturers of crude oil and natural gas and a marketer of refined products. The Amoco Energy Trading Corporation is the natural gas marketing arm of the corporation. The Division consists of 247 employees, with Amoco employing 45,000 people worldwide. Serving in various acquisitional management roles for Amoco since 1973, Mr. Berls now concentrates his time as a purchasing consultant — a position he has held since 1990. His primary role in this capacity is to provide the selection, recommendation, and purchase of supplies for all service stations, convenience stores, and fast food equipment and services. **Career Steps:** Amoco Corporation: Purchasing Consultant (1990–Present), Senior Buyer (1982–1990), Supervisor – Distribution (1973–1982). **Education:** Rutgers University, B.S. in Civil Engineering, B.A. in Liberal Arts (1962); Attended: University of Chicago and New York University Graduate Schools. **Personal:** Married to Ellen in 1969. Two children: Eric and Mark. Mr. Berls enjoys international travel (particularly in Europe), music, art, stamp collecting and reading history.

Indranil (Indy) S. Bhosale

Project Engineer
Aeco–Prakla, Schlumberger
1325 South Dairy Ashford
Houston, TX 77077
(713) 596–1882
Fax: (713) 596–1807
EMAIL: See Below

1311

Business Information: Aeco–Prakla, Schlumberger is primarily engaged in the exploration of crude petroleum in more than 100 countries around the world. As Project Engineer, Mr. Bhosale is responsible for UNIX systems administration, analysis, and user support. Internet users can also reach Indy via: bhosale@slb.com **Career Steps:** Project Engineer, Aeco–Prakla, Schlumberger (1996–Present); Systems Manager, Computer Center (1995–1996); Systems Engineer, Computize, Inc. (1994–1995); Systems Manager, Fortune Systems (1992–1994). **Associations & Accomplishments:**

C.N.E.P.A., H.M.M. **Education:** University of Houston, M.S. (1996); University of Poona, Indian, B.E. in Computer Engineering (1990). **Personal:** Married to Veera in 1995. Mr. Bhosale enjoys cultural activities, music, gardening, sports, and working on cars.

Yong Moon Choi, Ph.D.
Executive Director
Yukong, Ltd., R & D in USA
140–A New Dutch Lane
Fairfield, NJ 07004
(201) 227–3939
Fax: (201) 227–4488
E MAIL: See Below

1311

Business Information: Yukong, Ltd., parent company of Yukong, Ltd. Research & Development in the U.S.A. is the leading oil company in Korea with revenue of $8.3 billion. The Company is starting to diversify into the pharmaceutical industry, and for this reason, has opened the research and development facility in New Jersey. As Executive Director, Dr. Choi oversees a staff of 25 employees. He was instrumental in organizing the New Jersey pharmaceutical research and development facility and is responsible for all aspects of its operation. **Career Steps:** Yukong, Ltd., R & D in USA: Executive Director (1996–Present), Director (1993–1995); Section Manager, Carter–Wallace, Inc (1989–1992). **Associations & Accomplishments:** New York Academy of Science; Society for Neuro Science; American Chemical Society; Korean Scientists and Engineers Associate in America, Inc; Expertise in Central Nervous System (CNS) area that ranges from discovery through development and commercialization; Holder of more than 25 patents; Over 30 publications. **Education:** H.C. Brown and R.B. Wetherill Lab; Purdue University, Research Fellow (1978); State University of New York, Ph.D. (1977); Sogang University, B.S. (1973). **Personal:** Married to Hye Kyung Choi in 1980. Two children: Eugene Y. and Brandon J.. Dr. Choi enjoys golf and hiking.

J. David Clyde, M.D.
Medical Director
ARCO International Oil & Gas Company
2300 West Plano Parkway
Plano, TX 75075
(214) 509–3186
Fax: (214) 509–3231

1311

Business Information: ARCO International Oil & Gas Company is one of the leading providers of oil and gas products throughout the world. As Medical Director, Dr. Clyde is responsible for setting up health programs for Company employees worldwide, such as conducting medical evaluations of new sites in order to set up emergency evacuation policies or emergency medical facilities; conducting seminars to teach employees everything from health care to how to effectively parent; and providing instruction on insurance policies. He also works on ways to coordinate programs that will help employees save money or get the most value for their policies and be better health consumers (ask questions, understand policies, etc.). **Career Steps:** Medical Director, ARCO International Oil & Gas Company (1993–Present); Conoco, Inc.: Medical Director, Southern Region (1990–1993), Clinic Medical Director (1988–1990) **Associations & Accomplishments:** American College of Occupational and Environmental Medicine; International Commission on Occupational Health; President–elect, Texas Occupational Medical Association; International Society of Travel Medicine; American Academy of Family Practice. **Education:** Medical University of South Carolina – Charleston, M.D. (1971). **Personal:** Married to Beverly G. in 1968. Dr. Clyde enjoys golf, fishing, and travel.

Randall L. Couch
President, Amoco Energy Trading Corporation
Amoco Corporation
550 Westlake Park Boulevard, Suite 1480W3
Houston, TX 77079
(713) 366–5630
Fax: (713) 366–3285

1311

Business Information: Amoco Corporation is a worldwide producer of crude oil and natural gas and also a marketer of refined products. The Amoco Energy Trading Corporation is the natural gas marketing arm of the corporation. The division has 247 employees; Amoco has over 45,000 employees worldwide. As President, Amoco Energy Trading Corporation, Mr. Couch oversees all North American marketing, transportation and supply of natural gas. **Career Steps:** President, Amoco Energy Trading Corporation, Amoco Corporation (1993–Present); VP–SO, Permian Basin Business Unit, Amoco Production Company (1993); Manager, Salt Lake City Business Unit, Amoco Oil Company (1989–1993); Division Production Manager – Offshore, Gulf of Mexico, Amoco Production Company (1988–1989). **Associations & Accomplishments:** 2nd Vice Chair, Gas Industry Standards Board; Board of Directors, American Gas Cooling Center, Inc.; Steering Committee, Natural Gas Supply Association. Mr. Couch is frequently interviewed by trade journals and newspapers. **Education:** University of Oklahoma, B.S./Che (1975). **Personal:** Married to Sylvia in 1980. Three children: Ryan, Logan and Alexandra. Mr. Couch enjoys golf, tennis and skiing.

Eric R. Graves Sr. A.P.R.
Manager Constituency Affairs
Texaco Incorporated
111 Bagby
Houston, TX 77002
(713) 752–6467
Fax: (713) 752–4130

1311

Business Information: Texaco Incorporated is a major producer and worldwide distributor of petroleum products and technology. As Manager of Constituency Affairs, Mr. Graves is responsible for Texaco's domestic contributions program, constituency development, Houston area community relations, and three national public relations programs. **Career Steps:** Texaco Incorporated: Manager of Constituency Affairs, (1994–Present), Manager of U.S. Public and Government Affairs (1989–1994), Manager of Special Projects (1988–1989), Editorial Services Manager (1987–1988). **Associations & Accomplishments:** Board of Directors and Public Relations Committee, UNCF; Board of Directors and Public Relations Committee of Houston Area Urban League; Leadership Houston Alumni; Leadership Denver Alumni; Houston Business Promise of the Greater Houston Partnership; Accredited Public Relations Practioner PRSA. **Education:** University of Houston, B.A. (1973). **Personal:** Married to Patricia in 1983. Four children: Ashlea, Eric II, Djena and Lisa. Mr. Graves enjoys bridge, chess and writing.

Henry G. Hethcoat
Director of Environmental Services
BP Oil Company
15551 Louisiana Highway 23
Belle Chasse, LA 70037
(504) 656–3225
Fax: (504) 656–3466

1311

Business Information: BP Oil Company specializes in petroleum refining. As Director of Environmental Services, Mr. Hethcoat is responsible for the clean up and prevention of oil spills or anything in the petroleum industry that may harm the environment. **Career Steps:** BP Oil Company: Director of Environmental Services (1991–Present), Supervisor of Environmental Engineering (1988–1991), Supervisor of Laboratory (1984–1988). **Associations & Accomplishments:** Air and Waste Management Association; Water Pollution Control Federation; National Environmental Health Association. **Education:** Tulane University, M.S. (1988); University of New Orleans, B.S. (1970). **Personal:** Married to Ena in 1971. Four children: Ena, Tina, Jenny, and Matthew. Mr. Hethcoat enjoys fishing.

Barbara Hrubetz

Vice President
Hrubetz Oil Company
5949 Sherry Lane, Suite 525
Dallas, TX 75225
(214) 363–7833 Ext.217
Fax: (214) 691–8545

1311

Business Information: Hrubetz Oil Company is a family–owned business which was established in 1980. The Company is involved in the exploration of oil and gas, acquisitions of producing properties and operates several West Texas waterflood projects. Employed with the Company since 1981, Ms. Hrubetz, as Vice President, is responsible for the administration of Corporate operations and financial management, business development, and contract negotiations. She also serves as Chief Executive Officer of a sister company, Hrubetz Environmental Services, Inc. which utilizes a patented technology developed by the company to remediate hydrocarbon contaminated soils. Ms. Hrubetz has traveled extensively in an effort to introduce this new technology to the marketplace. **Career Steps:** Vice President, Hrubetz Oil Company and Hrubetz Operating Company (1981–Present); Chief Executive Officer, Hrubetz Environmental Services, Inc. (1981–Present). **Associations & Accomplishments:** The Dallas Petroleum Club; Director, North Central Texas Regional Advisory Board – Independent Petroleum Association of America; 1995 Regional Chairman, Membership Committee – Independent Petroleum Association of America; Advisory Board to Baylor University's Institute of Family Business; Registered Environmental Property Assessor; American Association of Professional Landmen. **Education:** Southern Methodist University, B.B.A., B.S.in Psychology (1981). **Personal:** Married to J. Lawrence Callaway in 1989. One child: Jennifer.

Robert A. Lane
General Manager, E. & P. Continental Division
Shell Western E&P Inc.
P.O. Box 576
Houston, TX 77001
(713) 544–4300
Fax: (713) 544–2704

1311

Business Information: Shell Western E&P Inc., a division of Shell Oil Company, deals with exploration and production of new oil and gas reserves. The company explores land sites and off–shore sites for possible drilling opportunities. After the gas and oil fields are developed, Shell West begins producing the raw petroleum material that acts as a base for a variety of products. As General Manager, E. & P. Continental Division, Mr. Lane has oversight of all exploration and production activities in the United States, excluding California. He works closely with staff members in the selection of fields to develop. Mr. Lane is involved in contract negotiations/approval regarding mineral rights and production rights. He works with safety inspectors in developing standard for drilling sites and production locations. Mr. Lane is continually planning for expansion and developing new ways to improve production output. **Career Steps:** Shell Oil: General Manager, E. & P. Continental Division, Shell Western E&P Inc. (1993–Present), Shell Oil Liaison – London (1990–1993); General Manager, Production and Engineering, E&P (1989–1993). **Associations & Accomplishments:** Society of Petroleum Engineers; Executive Committee Member, Texas Mid–Continent Oil and Gas Association. **Education:** Iowa State University, B.S. in Chemical Engineering (1968). **Personal:** Married to Jacklyn in 1971. One child: Kristi. Mr. Lane enjoys golf and gardening.

Gary G. Loop
Vice President
ARCO Crude Oil and NGL Marketing
2300 Plano Parkway, Rm PRC–D2602
Plano, TX 75094–0249
(214) 509–3101
Fax: (214) 509–6238

1311

Business Information: ARCO Crude Oil and NGL Marketing is a fully–integrated oil company that markets oil and natural gas liquids to various industries. Established in 1972, ARCO currently employs 25,000 people and Marketing employs 40 people. In various managerial positions with ARCO since 1972, Mr. Loop was appointed to his current position in 1990. As Vice President of Crude Oil and NGL Marketing, he is responsible for marketing domestic crude oil and natural gas liquids. **Career Steps:** Vice President of Crude Oil and NGL Marketing, Arco Crude Oil and NGL Marketing (1990–Present); Arco Crude Oil: Manager of West Coast Crude Oil Marketing (1985–1990), Manager of Crude Supply and Logistics (1980–1984). **Associations & Accomplishments:** Member, New York Mercantile Exchange (NYMEX); Member, NYMEX Marketing Committee. **Education:** California State University at Long Beach, M.B.A. (1978); University of California at Davis, B.S. in Chemical Engineering (1972). **Personal:** Married to Ada C. Loop in 1971. Three children: Kenneth, Jennifer, and Keith. Mr. Loop enjoys fishing and camping.

N. F. McIntyre

Executive Vice President
Petro Canada
150–6TH Ave. S.W., P.O. Box 2844
Calgary, Alberta T2P 3E3
(403) 296–8340
Fax: (403) 296–5776

1311

Business Information: Petro Canada specializes in the production, distribution, sales, and marketing of oil. Mr. McIntyre began his appointment to Petro–Canada Resources in 1982 as Engineering Group Manager. He then progressed into the position of Vice President of Frontier Development. Through the years, he moved his way up the corporate ladder, becoming Senior Vice President of Production, Senior Vice President of the Western Regions, and finally Executive Vice President. In his current capacity, Mr. McIntyre is accountable for the establishment and achievement of all upstream international business objectives of Petro–Canada. As a member of the corporation's Executive Leadership Team, he is also accountable for the effective integration of the planning and execution of upstream business objectives with overall strategies and activities of the corporation. **Career Steps:** Petro Canada: Executive Vice President (1995–Present), President (1991–1995), Senior Vice President, Western Region (1989–1990), Senior Vice President of Production (1988–1989), Vice President of Production (1986–1988), Vice President, Production Development (1985–1986), Vice President, Frontier Development (1983–1985), General Manager, Frontier Development, Offshore Division (1983); Group Manager, Engineering, Offshore Division (1982–1983); Engineer – Onshore/Offshore, Mobil Oil (1967–1982). **Associations & Accomplishments:** Association of Professional Engineers, Geologist, and Geophysicist – Alberta; Canadian Institute of Mining, Metallurgy, and Petroleum; Governor, Canadian Association of Petroleum Producers; Calgary Petroleum Club; Calgary Giencoe Golf & Country Club. **Personal:** Married to Lana Jean in 1967. Two children: Jason Lee and Spencer James.

Mr. Robert A. Piconi

Project Controller
Amoco Corporation
1921 Shellbrook Drive
Huntsville, AL 35806
(205) 340–5206
Fax: (205) 340–5341

1311

Business Information: Amoco Corporation is a global producer and marketer of crude oil, natural gas and refined products. The Amoco Corporation's Chemical Division is the world's largest chemicals manufacturing company (largest manufacturer of PTA – Purified Teraphthalic Acid). As Project Controller, Mr. Piconi financially oversees all chemical expansion projects in North America and Europe. He is currently in the process of starting a joint venture in France for Amoco involving PX (chemical feedstock). **Career Steps:** Project Controller, Amoco Corporation (1991–Present); Financial Advisor, Mobil Oil Company – London (1991); Financial Analyst, Marathon Development Company (1991, 1992). **Associations & Accomplishments:** Financial Management National Honor Society; Board of Directors, Notre Dame Council on International Business Development; Financial Management National Honor Society; Gamma Kappa Alpha, Italian National Honor Society; Christermon Foundation Lifetime Merit Scholar. **Education:** University of Notre Dame, B.B.A. in Finance, magna cum laude (1992); University of Notre Dame, B.A. in Romance Languages and Literature, magna cum laude (1992). **Personal:** Married to Kristina B. in 1993. One child: Roberto Antonio. Mr. Piconi enjoys public speaking, learning and traveling.

Marilyn I. Eckersley

Vice President of Administration
TPC Corporation
200 Westlake Boulevard, Suite 1000
Houston, TX 77079–2655
(713) 597–6219
Fax: (713) 597–6538

1321

Business Information: TPC Corporation is a natural gas company that is engaged in gathering, high–deliverability storage and marketing. Established in 1984, TPC employs 160 people, and has an estimated annual revenue of $312 million. As Vice President of Administration, Ms. Eckersley oversees corporate administration functions which include human resources, asset risk management, office services and management of the MIS department. **Career Steps:** TPC Corporation: Vice President of Administration (1996–Present), Manager of Administration (1994–1996), Manager of Contract Administration (1992–1994), Assistant Controller (1989–1992); Accountant, U.S. Homes. **Associations & Accomplishments:** RIMS. **Education:** State University of New York (SUNY). **Personal:** Married to Bruce in 1984. Ms. Eckersley enjoys snow skiing.

Allan Childs

Regional Operations Director
Champion Technologies, Inc.
11703 FM 307
Midland, TX 79706–5637
(915) 563–0008
Fax: Please mail or call

1381

Business Information: Champion Technologies, Inc., an oil field company, provides different types of chemicals for different situations in the oil field. As Regional Operations Director, Mr. Childs' primary focus is expenses on line items. He has an operations role and is responsible for a large support staff and a fleet of trucks and cars. **Career Steps:** Regional Operations Director, Champion Technologies, Inc. (1984–Present); Childs Corporation (1981–1984); Production Operators (1984–1987). **Associations & Accomplishments:** First Baptist Church, Greenwood. **Education:** Sul Ross State University; Tarleton State. **Personal:** Married to Rita in 1981. One child: Lyndsey. Mr. Childs enjoys team roping, having won several trophies and awards. His daughter, Lyndsey also competes.

Brian Ellis

HSE and Maintenance Manager
Nabors Drilling International
302 The Trails, 200 Dominion Park Drive
Houston, TX 77090–6722
(713) 775–8114
Fax: (713) 775–8114

1381

Business Information: Nabors Drilling International is a drilling contractor specializing in offshore and onshore drilling projects. Established in 1987, Nabors Drilling International currently employs 1,600 people and has an estimated annual revenue of $200 million. As HSE and Maintenance Manager, Mr. Ellis is responsible for all aspects of health, safety and the environment, preventive maintenance, and quality assurance. **Career Steps:** HSE and Maintenance Manager, Nabors Drilling International (1994–Present); Maintenance Manager, Nabors Drilling and Energy Services (1993–1994); Project Engineer, Loffland Brothers (1989–1993). **Associations & Accomplishments:** Institute of Mechanical Engineers, UK; American Society of Safety Engineers; International Association of Drilling Contractors. **Education:** Robert Gordons University, Aberdeen, B.Eng. in Engineering (1989). **Personal:** Mr. Ellis enjoys skiing, scuba diving, computers and travel.

Imam Sayuto

Head of Compensation and Benefits
VICO Indonesia
P.O. Box 2828 Jkt
Jakarta, Indonesia 12940
062021–5236845
Fax: 062021–5236871

1381

Business Information: VICO Indonesia is the largest LNG exporter in the world, exporting primarily to Japan, Korea, and Taiwan. One of the most prominent producers in Indonesia, VICO Indonesia produces approximately 1.6 billion cubic feet of gas per day which is liquified into LNG, thereby contributing approximately 30% of the gas feed. With its head office located in Houston, Texas, VICO Indonesia operates only in Indonesia with 2,000 employees and estimates revenue for 1996 to exceed $1.4 billion. As Head of Compensation and Benefits, Mr. Sayuto oversees all compensation and benefit programs for employees. He is responsible for designing, planning, and implementing compensation concepts, policies, and programs for all employees both Expatriates and National. **Career Steps:** VICO Indonesia: Head of Compensation and Benefits, (1993–Present), Gas Market Analyst (1988–1993), Crude Oil Shipping Coordinator (1982–1986). **Associations & Accomplishments:** American Compensation Association; Society for Human Resources Management; Certified Compensation Professional (CCP). **Education:** The Indonesian Institute for Management Development, M.B.A. (1987); University of Jember, B.Sc. in Economics. **Personal:** Mr. Sayuto enjoys golf and music.

Mr. Fred Callaway

Vice President Corporate
Home Oil Company Limited
1600 Home Oil Tower, 324 8th Avenue SW
Calgary, Alberta T2P 2Z5
(403) 232–7129
Fax: (402) 232–5520

1382

Business Information: Home Oil Company Limited – a public company – is an oil and gas exploration, production and pipeline company, with operations in western Canada and Argentina. As Vice President Corporate, Mr. Callaway is responsible for Executive Compensation as Secretary to the Human Resources Committee. Other responsibilities include information systems, human resources, business development, safety, environment and insurance issues. He is also responsible for building an international oil and gas operation in South America. Established in 1926, Home Oil Company Limited employs a full–time staff of 750 and reports annual revenue in excess of $300 million . **Career Steps:** Vice President Corporate, Home Oil Company Limited (1990–Present); Vice President International, Home Oil Company Limited (1987–1990); Vice President Corporate Affairs, Home Oil Company Limited (1982–1987); General Manager, Corporate Affairs, Hudson's Bay Oil & Gas Co. (1980–1982). **Associations & Accomplishments:** Director, Private Energy Research Association; Director, Heritage Park Society; Alternate Director, Minora Resources NL; Canadian Energy Research Institute; Board of Governors, 45th Oilmen's; Calgary Chamber of Commerce; Calgary Petroleum Club; Calgary Winter Club; Silver Springs Golf & Country Club. **Education:** Chartered Accountant (1962); Banff School of Advanced Management.

Jean–Yves Chatellier, Ph.D.

Advisor
Intevep S.A.
Apdo 76343
Caracas, Venezuela 1070A
(582) 908–6347
Fax: (582) 908–6800
EMAIL: See Below

1382

Business Information: Intevep S.A. is the research lab of P.D.V.S.A., the second largest oil company in the world, specializing in oil exploration and production. The Company performs government research in the hunt for oil reserves and production. Regional in scope, Intevep, S.A. has three oil companies and one research laboratory located within Venezuela. As Advisor, Dr. Chatellier provides advice and consultation to the research laboratory and subsidiaries of Petroleo de Venezuela. Internet users can reach him via: jean@intevep.pdv.com. **Career Steps:** Advisor, Intevep S.A. (1995–Present); Appraisal Project Leader, Brunei Shell Bhd,Sdn. (1993–1995); Responsible for Equity Determination, Shell Expro London (1992–1993). **Associations & Accomplishments:** American Association of Petroleum Geologists (AAPG); Canadian Society of Petroleum Geologists (CSPG); International Association of Sedimentologists (I.A.S.); Society of Economic Paleontologists and Mineralogists (SEPM). **Education:** University of Paris VI, Ph.D. (1984); Calgary, M.Sc. in Sedimentology (1983); Paris, DEA in Structural Geology (1980); Lille, France: Master in Geology (1979), Bachelor in Geology (1977). **Personal:** Married to Monique in 1987. Two children: Michael and Gina. Dr. Chatellier enjoys tennis, table tennis, Telemark, and computers.

William David Collins

Capital Asset Management Business Analyst
Amoco Corporation
15 East 5th Street, P.O. Box 591
Tulsa, OK 74102–0591
(918) 581–3064
Fax: (918) 581–1164

1382

Business Information: Amoco Corporation specializes in oil and gas exploration, production, and sales. Established in 1886, Amoco has estimated annual sales of $30+ billion and employs over 40,000 people. As Capital Asset Management Business Analyst, Mr. Collins oversees specific incomplete wells and appropriations for both domestic and international projects. **Career Steps:** Amoco Corporation: Capital Asset Management Business Analyst (1996–Present), Accountant, Lease Revenue (Jun.1995–Aug.1995); Callidus Technologies: Accounting Assistant to Chief Financial Officer (Jun.1994–Aug.1994), Marketing Assistant to Vice President of Marketing (Jun.1993–Aug.1993). **Associations & Accomplishments:** Past Vice President, State of Missouri Phi Beta Lambda; Esquires Honors Community Service Organization; President Insight Investment Club; Vice President Finance Club; Who's Who in Business (1994–1996); American Scholar U.S. Achievement Academy; National Dean's List; College Republicans; London School of Economics Alumni; The Sorbonne; Consultant for The American Indian College in Phoenix, Arizona. **Education:** Michigan Business School, B.B.A. in Finance (1996); The Alliance Francaise, C.F.F.P.; Evangel

College. **Personal:** Mr. Collins enjoys investment clubs, private flying, travel, soccer, and photography.

Carlos E. Delius

President and General Manager
Occidental Peruana, Inc.
P.O. Box 11174
Bakersfield, CA 93389–1174
011–5114428110
Fax: 011–5114428140
1382

Business Information: Occidental Peruana, Inc. is an oil exploration and production company. Established in 1971, Occidental Peruana, Inc. currently employs 1,000 people. With forty–two years expertise in the petroleum engineering industry, Mr. Delius joined Occidental Peruana in 1990. Serving as President and General Manager, he is responsible for the management of all aspects of Peruvian operations. **Career Steps:** President and General Manager, Occidental Peruana, Inc. (1990–Present); Bolivian Ambassador to the United States, Bolivian Embassy – Washington, D.C. (1988–1989); Vice President Operations, Occidental Petrolera de Argentina (1985–1987). **Associations & Accomplishments:** Society of Petroleum Engineers; National Geographics Society; American Management Association; Professional Engineers of Bolivia – Registration #331. **Education:** University of Oklahoma, B.S. in Petroleum Engineering (1953); University of Piura – Lima, Management and Finance Course of Programa de Alta Direccion. **Personal:** Married to Ninett in 1955. Four children: Carlos, Fernando, Patricia, and Cecilia. Mr. Delius enjoys reading, golf, and tennis.

Mr. David B. DeLozier

Advertising/Market Communications Manager
Energen Corporation
2101 6th Avenue North
Birmingham, AL 35203
(205) 326–2689
Fax: (205) 326–2643
1382

Business Information: Energen Corporation, a diversified energy holding company, specializes in the distribution of natural gas as well as oil and gas exploration and production. Mr. DeLozier joined the company in 1983 upon graduation from college. He currently serves as Advertising/Market Communications Manager, responsible for the planning and direction of consumer campaigns, the direction of ad agency operations, and the production of annual reports . Established in 1852, Energen Corporation presently employs 1,500 people and has an estimated annual revenue in excess of $360 million. **Career Steps:** Advertising/Market Communications Manager, Energen Corporation (1988–Present); Publications Specialist, WUAL – Public Radio (1982–1983); VISA Account Coordinator, First National Bank at Tuscaloosa (1981–1983). **Associations & Accomplishments:** P.R. Committee, Operation New Birmingham; Board Advisor, Birmingham Summerfest; Board Advisor, Birmingham Broadway Series; Media Advisory Board Member, Judson College; National Advertising Committee, American Gas Association; Former officer, Birmingham Ad Club; P.R. Committee, American Red Cross. **Education:** University of Alabama, B.A. Degree (1983); Attended, New York University; Attended, Sanford University; Attended, Germana College.

Keith Ingram Dismuke, Ph.D.

Department Head
Schlumberger–Dowell
5051 South 129th East Avenue
Tulsa, OK 74134
(918) 250–4244
Fax: (918) 250–9323
EMAIL: See Below
1382

Business Information: Schlumberger–Dowell is an international technical company and worldwide leader in oilfield services, measurement and systems, and telecommunications with operations in over 100 countries and 51,000 employees. Schlumberger Oilfield Services in the leading supplier of services and technology to the international petroleum industry. Dowell provides services in three key explorations and production domains: well construction, production, and intervention. Dowell is committed to giving its clients the highest quality fluid engineering and pumping services in the oil and gas industry. Dr. Dismuke is Department Head for Oilfield Chemicals, within the Schlumberger Houston Product Center, a multi–functional engineering, development, and manufacturing group. He leads a group of approximately 90 technical, professional, and contract personnel in the development, commercialization, manufacture, and quality assurance of new stimulation chemical systems. Internet users can reach him via: dismuke@tulsa.dowell.slb.com. **Career Steps:** Department Head, Schlumberger–Dowell (1991–Present); Dow Chemical USA: Research Manager (1989–1991), Research Associate in TS&D (1985–1989), Dow Chemical USA LASTL (1975–1985). **Associations & Accomplishments:** Society of Petroleum Engineers; Technical Association of Pulp and Paper Industry; South Tulsa Baptist Church (Former Chairman of Deacons). **Education:** University of Florida, Ph.D. (1975); Union University, B.S. in Chemistry and Math (1970). **Personal:** Married to Marilyn Lindsey Rose in 1970. Two children: Craig Ian and Leigh Elizabeth.

William R. Dixon

President and Chief Executive Officer
Dixon Exploration, Inc.
2021 Lambert Court
Plano, TX 75075
(214) 691–5200
Fax: (214) 691–0499
1382

Business Information: A successful petroleum exploration businessman for over twenty–five years, William Dixon is the Founder and President of Dixon Exploration, Inc. Founding the Company in 1978, he oversees all business operations and overall planning strategies. He is now currently working under contract with Triton Energy Corporation, serving as Director of Joint Ventures. In this capacity, he is responsible for business development and overall business relationships; searching for possible partner acquisitions to fulfill company projects underway throughout the continental U.S., as well as Alaska sectors. **Career Steps:** President and Chief Executive Officer, Dixon Exploration, Inc. (1978–Present); Director of Joint Ventures, Triton Energy Corporation (1995–Present); Executive Vice President and Chief Operating Officer, Roxy Resources, Inc. (1980–1982); Vice President of Exploration, The Grayrock Corporation (1970–1978). **Associations & Accomplishments:** American Association of Petroleum Geologists; Association of International Petroleum Negotiatures; Independent Petroleum Association of America: Sustained Member and Former Director; Independent Petroleum Association of Mountain States: Sustained Member, Former Executive Vice President; Petroleum Explorration Society of Great Britain; Chairman International Pavilion, 1991 AAPG Convention, Dallas. **Education:** University of Texas, M.A. (1958); Lehigh University, B.A. (1956). **Personal:** Married to Sarah T. in 1963. Three children: Bill, Bret, and Paige. Mr. Dixon enjoys fishing, hunting, sailing, scuba diving, and cross–country skiing.

Craig Dunn

Controller
Dinero, Inc.
P.O. Box 10505, 1004 North Big Spring, Suite 500
Midland, TX 79702
(915) 684–5544
Fax: Please mail or call
1382

Business Information: Dinero, Inc., a wholly–owned subsidiary of the Dinero Group, specializes in oil and gas exploration and production. As Controller, Mr. Dunn is responsible for financial planning, financial reporting, tax planning, and consulting. **Career Steps:** Controller, Dinero, Inc. (1989–Present); Revenue Accounting Manager, Tom Brown, Inc. (1988–1989); Tax Supervisor, Coopers & Lybrand (1987–1988); Tax Supervisor, Enron Corporation (1982–1987). **Associations & Accomplishments:** Permian Basin Petroleum Accountants Society; Texas Society of Certified Public Accountants. **Education:** U.T.P.B., Accounting (1981). **Personal:** One child: Tara Ashley. Mr. Dunn enjoys golf, hunting, fishing, basketball, and softball.

Richard Grimmette

Owner
InterMountain Oil Company
33719 8 Mile Road
Livonia, MI 48152–1294
(810) 476–8171
Fax: Please mail or call
1382

Business Information: InterMountain Oil Company specializes in oil and gas exploration and operation of oil and gas wells. The Company operates fields in Colorado and Nebraska. In the past, the Company has, in the past, operated oil and gas wells in Ohio, Michigan, Louisiana, Kansas, Texas, and New Mexico. As President, Mr. Grimmette is responsible for the choice of oil field locations to drill, supervises drilling, and oversees day–to–day operations. **Career Steps:** President, InterMountain Oil Company (1983–Present); Vice President, Basic Energy (1981–1983); Chairman of Life Sciences Department, Muskegon Community College (1976–1981). **Education:** Western Michigan University: B.S., B.B.A. (1969), Graduate Studies; Eastern Michigan University, M.S. (1971); Petroleum Engineering Educators, Certificate (1982); Schlumberger Education Services (1988); Various other schools operated by the American Association of Petroleum Geologists. **Personal:** Married to Merri Jo Charniga in 1985. Three children: Mark Richard and Karrie Jean by first wife, and Richard Andrew. Mr. Grimmette enjoys hunting both big game and game birds, and fishing.

Mr. Edwin W. Gummett Jr.

Board Chairman
Away Marketing, Inc., Poweram Oil Co., Inc., Centroplex Marketing, Inc.
P.O. Box 7508
Waco, TX 76714
(817) 772–0590
Fax: (817) 772–0993
1382

Business Information: Away Marketing, Inc., Poweram Oil Co., Inc., Centroplex Marketing, Inc. are involved in major oil company distributorships, convenience stores, and commercial real estate build and lease operations. As Board Chairman, Mr. Gummett is the Chief Executive Officer, responsible for overseeing management of all operations for the companies, and concentrates on purchasing, strategic planning, and financing. Established in 1946, Away Marketing, Inc., Poweram Oil Co., Inc., Centroplex Marketing, Inc. employ over 100 people and report combined annual revenue in excess of $25 million. **Career Steps:** Board Chairman, President and Chief Executive Officer, Centroplex Marketing, Inc. (1989– Present); Board Chairman, President and Chief Executive Officer, Away Marketing, Inc. (1974– Present); Board Chairman, President and Chief Executive Officer, Poweram Oil Co., Inc. (1946– Present). **Associations & Accomplishments:** Board Member, Texas Oil Marketers Association; Board Member, Hillcrest Baptist Hospital; First President, EEOAC; Active in Local Baptist Church. **Education:** Baylor University, B.B.A. (1948).

Mr. Edward A. Guthrie Jr.

Vice President of Finance, Chief Financial Officer
Cliffs Drilling Company
1200 Smith Street, Suite 300
Houston, TX 77002
(713) 651–9426
Fax: (713) 951–0649
1382

Business Information: Cliffs Drilling Company specialize in drilling, exploration, and production of oil and oil fields– related engineering services. International in scope, the Company has operations in Mexico, Venezuela and Europe and is currently in the bidding process for projects in the Far East. In his capacity as Vice President of Finance, Mr. Guthrie is responsible for all financial administration to include treasury, accounting, regulatory compliance and corporate strategic plannin g. Established in 1978, Cliffs Drilling Company employs 465 persons and reports annual revenues of $88 million. **Career Steps:** Vice President of Finance and Chief Financial Officer, Cliffs Drilling Company (1992–Present); Vice President and Controller, Cliffs Drilling Company (1991–1992); Controller, Cliffs Drilling Company (1983–1991); Controller, Empire Iron Mining Company (1976–1983). **Associations & Accomplishments:** Director, International Association of Drilling Contractors. **Education:** Case Western Reserve University, M.B.A. (1969).

Dennis L. Hendrix

Manager of Operations
Great Western Drilling
P.O. Box 1659, 700 West Louisiana
Midland, TX 79702
(915) 682–5241
Fax: (915) 684–3702
1382

Business Information: Great Western Drilling is a domestic independent oil and gas exploration and production company. Headquarters and corporate offices are located in Midland, Texas with locations throughout Texas and New Mexico. The Company service area includes seven states: New Mexico, Texas, Colorado, Wyoming, North Dakota, Louisiana, and Oklahoma. Joining Great Western Drilling as Reservoir Engineer in 1992, Mr. Hendrix was appointed as Manager of Operations in 1994. He is responsible for managing and directing all engineering and production activities within the company, including drilling, day–to–day field operations, workovers, environmental compliance, marketing, signing contracts for gas and crude oil projects, obtaining contracts with vendors, legal liability, and the oversight of a staff of 23. **Career Steps:** Great Western Drilling: Manager of Operations (1994–Present), Reservoir Engineer (1992–1994); Production/Reservoir Engineer, Chevron Corporation (1981–1992). **Associations & Accomplishments:** Society of Petroleum Engineers (SPE); New Mexico Oil & Gas Association (NMOGA); Independent Producers Association of America (IPAA); Junior Achievement; United Way; Church groups; Co–authored paper for AAPG (field study) while at Chevron. **Education:** Oklahoma State University, B.S. in Petroleum (1981). **Personal:** Married to Margaret in 1988. One child: Jordyn Elizabeth. Mr. Hendrix enjoys spending time with his family, golf, water skiing, and playing the guitar.

William Dennis Ingram
President
Petroleum Development Company
401 South Boston, Suite 1850
Tulsa, OK 74103
(918) 583–7434
Fax: (918) 583–7451

1382

Business Information: Petroleum Development Company is an oil and gas exploration company. A geologist is sub–contracted to assay prospective drill sites. When gas is found in commercial quantities after drilling and completion of the test-wall, the product is sold to a marketing company for eventual consumer sue. Establishing Petroleum Development Company in 1985, President William Ingram provides the overall executive administration, vision and long–range strategies to keep the company a viable presence in the highly competitive global petroleum and energy arena. **Career Steps:** President, Petroleum Development Company (1985–Present); District Landman, Whitmar Exploration Company (1982–1985). **Education:** University of Central Arkansas, M.B.A. (1981); University of Mississippi, B.A.; University of Mississippi School of Law, no degree. **Personal:** Two children: Mary Elizabeth and Virginia Caroline. Mr. Ingram enjoys fishing.

H. J. Kagie
Vice President – Acquisitions, Engineering & Operations
Ballard & Associates, Inc.
518 17th Street, Suite 400
Denver, CO 80202
(303) 595–8515
Fax: (303) 595–8601

1382

Business Information: Ballard & Associates, Inc. specializes in the exploration and acquisition of oil and gas. As Partner and Vice President of Acquisitions, Engineering and Operations, Mr. Kagie is responsible for all aspects of acquisitions, divestitures, operations, engineering, and the majority of daily business. **Career Steps:** Partner and Vice President of Acquisitions, Engineering and Operations, Ballard & Associates, Inc. (1992–Present); International Negotiator and Engineer, Advantage International, Inc. (1991); Manager of Operations, General Atlantic Resources, Inc. (1989–1990); Operations Engineer, Balcron Oil Company (1987–1988). **Associations & Accomplishments:** Society of Petroleum Engineers; Rocky Mountain Oil and Gas Association. **Education:** University of Wyoming, B.S. in Petroleum Engineering (1978). **Personal:** Married to Janet L. in 1992. One child: Matthew Joseph. Mr. Kagie enjoys golf, backpacking, and fishing.

Mustapha M'Rah, Ph.D.
Exploration Manager
Energy Technology International
P.O. Box 4287
Tulsa, OK 74159
(918) 631–2517
Fax: (918) 744–5694
EMAIL: See Below

1382

Business Information: Energy Technology International is a consulting firm primarily engaged in oil and gas exploration. Established in 1995, the Company is international in scope, providing services in North Africa, the North Sea, and the Middle East. As Exploration Manager, Dr. M'Rah is responsible for overseeing development and exploration, evaluating areas, opening frontiers, and utilizing seismology. He is also fluent in four languages; French, English, German and Arabic. Internet users can reach him via: Goos.Cgb@Vax1/Utulsa.edu. **Career Steps:** Exploration Manager, Energy Technology International (1995–Present); Research Associate, Tulsa University (1995); Senior Staff, Qatar General Petroleum Corporation (1988–1996); Senior Explorator, Phillips Petroleum Company (1978–1987). **Associations & Accomplishments:** Oil and Gas Journal; AAPC; SEG; SEG Tulsa; Was an international basketball player; Presentation on the Straights of Gibralter. **Education:** Ph.D. (1978). **Personal:** Married in 1966. Dr. M'Rah enjoys music and basketball.

Hardy Rose
President and Chief Executive Officer
Geogasco, Inc.
2501 Oak Lawn Avenue, Suite 560
Dallas, TX 75219–4042
(214) 521–5757
Fax: (214) 521–5759

1382

Business Information: Geogasco, Inc. is a domestic oil and gas exploration and production company. Establishing Geogasco, Inc. in 1989, Mr. Rose serves as President and Chief Executive Officer. He is responsible for all aspects of operations, as well as overseeing all administrative operations for associates and a staff of twelve. Concurrent with his position at Geogasco, Inc., he serves as President and Chief Executive Officer of Geonatural Resources, Inc. and The GEO COMPANIES of North America. **Career Steps:** President and Chief Executive Officer, Geogasco, Inc. (1992–Present); President and Chief Executive Officer, The GEO COMPANIES of North America (1994–Present); President and Chief Executive Officer, Geonatural Resources, Inc. (1989–Present); United States Army (1965–1967). **Associations & Accomplishments:** Dallas Geological Society; American Gas Association; Earth Resources Consortium; Natural Gas Vehicle Coalition; Michigan Oil and Gas Association; Natural Resource Council of Texas; North Texas Oil and Gas Association; American Association for Energy Economics; International Association for Energy Economics; Texas Industrial Producers and Royalty Owners Association. **Personal:** Married to Judy Ann in 1983.

William A. Silk Jr.

Vice President
King Ranch Oil & Gas
10055 Grogan's Mill Road
Woodlands, TX 77380
(713) 367–7300
Fax: Please mail or call

1382

Business Information: King Ranch, Inc. is a privately held corporation that was established in 1853. The Company's business is organized into two segments; Agribusiness and Energy. Its energy line, King Ranch Oil & Gas, Inc. is a wholly–owned subsidiary engaged in the business of exploring for oil and gas. Mr. Silk manages a program to find, develop and produce oil and gas which is the Commpany's prime means of creating a profit and providing growth. **Career Steps:** King Ranch Oil & Gas: Vice President (1989–Present), Exploration Advisor (1985–1989); Exploration Geophysicist, Conquest Exploration (1983–1985); The Superior Oil Company (1977–1985). **Associations & Accomplishments:** Society of Exploration Geophysicists; American Association of Petroleum Geologists; Society of Petroleum Engineers; Independent Petroleum Associates of America; American Management Association. **Education:** Colorado School of Mines, B.S. in Geophysical Engineering (1977) **Personal:** Married to Elaine in 1991. Mr. Silk enjoys ocean sailing, golf, tennis and bird hunting.

Mr. Richard (Nick) R. Adams
President and Chief Executive Officer
East Texas Salt Water Disposal Company
1209 Industrial Boulevard, P.O. Box 2459
Kilgore, TX 75662
(903) 984–9216
Fax: (903) 984–6952

1389

Business Information: East Texas Salt Water Disposal Company – a nonprofit company – specializes in the collection, transportation, and disposal of oilfield brine, a by–product of oil well drilling operations. The company handles disposition of approximately 43 million gallons of brine a day, a substance four times saltier than ocean salt water, charging oil producers very reasonable rates. As President and Chief Executive Officer, Mr. Adams is responsible for overseeing all company operations, maintaining company efficiency, establishing policies, and providing guidance to the Board of Directors. Established in 1942, East Texas Salt Water Disposal Company employs a staff of 90 and reports annual revenue of $23 million. **Career Steps:** President and Chief Executive Officer, East Texas Salt Water Disposal Company (1992–Present); Operations Manager, Oryx Energy Company (1988–1992); Various Positions, Sun Company (1970–1988). **Associations & Accomplishments:** Member, Texas Independent Producers & Royalty Owners (TIPRO); Ground Water Protection Council; Society of Petroleum Engineers (SPE); American Management Association (AMA); University of Tulsa Petroleum Engineering Industry Advisory Board. **Education:**

Harvard University, P.M.D. (1984); University of Tulsa, B.S. (1970); Registered Engineer.

Nadia A. Al Kheily
Operations Director
Mohammed Binghalib Energy Enterprises
P.O. Box 7141
Dubai, United Arab Emirates
(971) 4–822825
Fax: (971) 4–823593

1389

Business Information: Mohammed Binghalib Energy Enterprises is recognized as one of several professional companies operating in the field of oil and gas instruments that are supplied to the oil companies. As Operations Director, Ms. Al Kheily is responsible for the direction of daily operations. She is currently implementing a reorganization strategy to convert the company into a manufacturing congolomerate from its present Agent status. **Career Steps:** Operations Director, Mohammed Binghalib Energy Ent. (1991–Present); Auditor Assistant, Price Waterhouse – Dubai (1990–1991). **Education:** Higher Colleges of Technology, Business Administration and Accounting (1991); Golden Gate University. **Personal:** Ms. Al Kheily enjoys travel, swimming, reading, and camping.

Jim D. Callison
Vice President
Schlumberger, Ltd.
1325 South Dairy Ashford
Houston, TX 77077
(713) 368–8661
Fax: (713) 368–8686

1389

Business Information: Schlumberger, Ltd. is an international oil and gas technical services firm for North America, Europe, Venezuela, North Africa, Middle East, and the Far East. Established in 1930, Schlumberger, Ltd. reports annual revenue of $7 billion and currently employs 50,000 people. As Vice President, Mr. Callison is responsible for corporate industry affairs, including negotiations and public relations. He began his career in the oil service industry by taking jobs as a field roustabout and a secondary recovery research assistant. Upon his graduation in 1957, he was employed by Dowell Division of The Dow Chemical Company as a Field Engineer. Dowell Division later became Dowell Schlumberger. For the past 34 years, Mr. Callison has been employed by Dowell Schlumberger/Schlumberger in various technical, marketing, manufacturing and management roles throughout the world. **Career Steps:** Vice President, Schlumberger, Ltd. (1989–Present); Dowell Schlumberger, Inc.: President (1984–1989), Vice President of Europe and Africa (1982–1984); Vice President of Marketing, Dowell Division of The Dow Chemical Co. (1978–1982). **Associations & Accomplishments:** American Petroleum Institute (API) – serves on the Production & Exploration Operating Committee; International Association of Drilling Contractors; Independent Petroleum Association of America; National Ocean Industries Association (NOIA) – Member of The Board of Directors; National Oil–Equipment Manufacturers and Delegates Society; Petroleum Equipment Suppliers Association (PESA) – serves on the Executive Committee; Society of Petroleum Engineering (SPE)–AIME; Spindletop International – Member of The Board of Directors; World Petroleum Congress – Chairman United States National Committee (1994); University of Oklahoma Engineering Board; 25 Year Club of The Petroleum Industry. **Education:** University of Tulsa, B.S. in Petroleum Engineering (1957). **Personal:** Married to Sharon in 1978. Five children: Jimmy, Steve, Ryan, Kathy, Jon and seven grandchildren. Mr. Callison enjoys entertaining, golf, and the sports of bird hunting and fishing.

Sherry L. Galloway
Secretary/Treasurer
O.R.E. Systems
P.O. Box 3677
Farmington, NM 87499
(505) 327–2161 (505) 334–9481
Fax: (505) 326–0866

1389

Business Information: O.R.E. Systems offers services to the oil and gas industries for equipment upkeep (i.e., work over rigs, mechanical failures, and prevention). As Secretary/Treasurer, Ms. Galloway is responsible for Company finances and budgets. She is also County Commissioner for San Juan County, NM, and Internal Auditor for Animas Credit Union. **Career Steps:** Secretary/Treasurer, O.R.E. Systems (1980–Present); County Commissioner, San Juan County (1989–Present); Internal Auditor, Animas Credit Union

(1993–Present). **Associations & Accomplishments:** President, New Mexico Association of Counties; San Juan East Rotary Club; Chairman, San Juan Water Commission; Board of Trustees, Colorado River Water Users Association; Public Utilities Commission for City of Farmington, NM. **Education:** San Juan College, A.A. in History (1989). **Personal:** Married to Zane in 1980. One child: Thomas Eugene. Ms. Galloway enjoys baseball, bowling, and politics.

Michael R. Tyler
Engineer
Fluor Daniel (NPOSR), Inc.
907 North Popular, Suite 100
Casper, WY 82601
(307) 261–5000 Ext. 5704
Fax: (307) 261–5997

1389

Business Information: Fluor Daniel (NPOSR), Inc. is the U.S.'s largest public–owned engineering and construction firm specializing in petrochemical and petroleum facilities, manufacturing plants, hotels, power plants, etc. The Company has 51 offices worldwide. The Rocky Mountain Oilfield Testing Center is operated by Fluor Daniel (NPOSR) Inc., the management and operating contractor for the Department of Energy, and Naval Petroleum Oil Shale Reserves in Colorado, Utah, and Wyoming. As Project Engineer and Training Coordinator, Mr. Tyler is responsible for providing technical evaluation of advanced technology projects, proposals, and development of testing criteria. In addition, he is responsible for providing engineering support and coordinating activities and events for testing Enhanced Oilfield Research and other oilfield processes. The Project Engineer directs the testing projects and authors the results of the test which are presented to industry publications. **Career Steps:** Fluor Daniel (NPOSR), Inc.: Project Engineer and Training Coordinator (1995–present), Field Engineer (1993–1995); Senior Technician (1991–1993); Vice President and General Manager, Michael's Cleaning Service, Inc. (1985–Present); Amoco Production Company (1973–1978): Production Foreman, Field Automation, Roustabout. **Associations & Accomplishments:** Society of Petroleum Engineers; Central Wyoming Homebuilders. **Education:** University of Wyoming, B.S. in Economics (1971); Casper College, A.S. in Business; Parks School of Business, Computer Programming. **Personal:** Married to Kathy in 1973. Two children: Melissa Sue and Aaron Shayne. Mr. Tyler enjoys elk hunting, racquetball, fishing, and walking.

1400 Nonmetallic Minerals, Except Fuels

1411 Dimension stone
1422 Crushed and broken limestone
1423 Crushed and broken granite
1429 Crushed and broken stone, NEC
1442 Construction sand and gravel
1446 Industrial sand
1455 Kaolin and ball clay
1459 Clay and related minerals, NEC
1474 Potash, soda, and borate minerals
1475 Phosphate rock
1479 Chemical and fertilizer mining, NEC
1481 Nonmetallic minerals services
1499 Miscellaneous nonmetallic minerals

Geoffrey V. McAdoo

President
SOLID ROCK Marble & Granite
6411 Ashcroft, Suite A
Houston, TX 77081
(713) 774–7625
Fax: (713) 774–0005

1411

Business Information: SOLID ROCK Marble & Granite is a marble and granite fabricator and installer, serving custom homes and construction industries for luxury residential homes averaging more than $500K. International in scope, SOLID ROCK also contracts in Mexico. Co–founding SOLID ROCK in 1993, President Geoffrey McAdoo provides the overall day–to–day operations administration, focusing on customer service, quality production and corporate strategies. **Career Steps:** President, SOLID ROCK Marble & Granite (1993–Present); Sales Manager, Super Marble (1991–1993); Outside Sales, Hardwood Lumber Company (1986–1991). **Associations & Accomplishments:** Allen Forum; 100 Black Men of Houston. **Education:** Northwest Academy

---

(1981); University of Houston, B.S. in Business and Marketing. **Personal:** Married to Leslie in 1992. Two children: Matthew Allen and Jessica Nicole. Mr. McAdoo enjoys racquetball, golf, working out, and softball.

Waine L. Phillips
Operations Manager
Stone Street Quarries, Inc.
P.O. Box 9246
Ft. Wayne, IN 46899–9246
(219) 639–6511
Fax: (219) 747–4889

1422

Business Information: Stone Street Quarries, Inc. is a locally–owned producer of crushed limestone. As Operations Manager, Mr. Phillips is responsible for all phases of operation, coordinating mechanics and plant support staff, and conducting various administrative functions. **Career Steps:** Operations Manager, Stone Street Quarries, Inc. (1985–Present); Operations Manager, France Stone Company (1965–1985). **Education:** Dale Carnegie Course – Whittenburg University, management training. **Personal:** Married to Cynthia in 1992. Five children: Waine Jr., Dan, Jeff, Mike, and Cheryl. Mr. Phillips enjoys hunting and fishing.

Bobby P. Faulkner
Manager of Business Development and Technology
Svedala, Inc.
20965 Crossroads Circle
Waukesha, WI 53186–4054
(414) 798–6238
Fax: (414) 798–6211

1429

Business Information: Svedala, Inc. specializes in the engineering and design of pyro–processing equipment with twenty–five plants worldwide. As Manager of Business Development and Technology, Mr. Faulkner is responsible for assessment, acquisitions, and internal development. **Career Steps:** Manager of Business Development, Svedala, Inc. (1991–Present); Manager, Pyro Business, Boliden Allis (1989–1991); Assistant Director, Advanced Technologies Center, Allis Chalmers (1974–1989). **Associations & Accomplishments:** Jaycees; Rotary Club; American Institute of Mechanical Engineers. **Education:** Colorado School of Mines, M.S. Met. (1961). **Personal:** Married to Dorothy in 1957. Three children: Bret, Scott, and Nannette. Mr. Faulkner enjoys golf.

Frank Vaughn
Superintendent
Mobile Sand Company
22300 Temescal Canyon Road
Corona, CA 91719–4922
(800) 400–6624
Fax: (909) 277–1837

1442

Business Information: Mobile Sand Company, a division of Standard Concrete Products, is a rock mining operation, providing sand, gravel, top soil, D.G., and base products. Mobile Sand Company serves clientele in Orange, Los Angeles, Riverside, and San Bernardino counties. With twenty–six years experience in the mining industry, Mr. Vaughn joined Mobile Sand Company as Superintendent in 1990. He is responsible for the oversight of operations, including mining the rock from the start to the finished product in the Aggregate Division. **Career Steps:** Superintendent, Mobile Sand Company (1990–Present); Foreman and Dragline Operator, Owl Rock Company (1981–1990); Dragline Operator, Peck RD Gravel (1970–1981). **Education:** Career Management Certificate (1993); USN: Air Conditioning and Refrigeration, Leadership. **Personal:** Mr. Vaughn enjoys restoring old automobiles.

David L. Rose
Secretary/Treasurer
GeoQuest International
350 East Main Street, Suite 6
Gallatin, TN 37066
(615) 451–9672
Fax: (615) 230–9334
EMAIL: See Below

1499

Business Information: GeoQuest International is a regional firm with an international scope. The Company locates and recovers lost treasures, acquires and trades precious minerals and gems, and invests in international mineral mines. As Secretary/Treasurer, Mr. Rose negotiates contracts, has oversight of Company financial matters, and does strategic planning for

---

GeoQuest. He is also the chief scuba diver, infrared photographer, and operates sub–surface radar and other detection instruments used in locating lost items. **Career Steps:** Secretary/Treasurer, GeoQuest International (1996–Present); Director of Surgery, Highland Hospital (1991–1995); President/Chairman/Founder, International Satellite Communication Network (1986–1991). **Associations & Accomplishments:** Chamber of Commerce; National Surgical Assistant Association; Association of Surgical Technologist; National Association of Orthopedic Technologist. **Education:** Volunteer State College, Computer Classes (1994); Cleveland State College, Associate Degree; Certificate – Geophysical Survey Systems; Certificate – Search and Recovery Scuba diver – PADI; Orange County Vocational School, Certificate – Surgical Technology. **Personal:** Married to Kimberly L. in 1992. Two children: Derek and Tyler. Mr. Rose enjoys playing guitar, writing, race car driving, and family activities.

1500 – 1799
CONSTRUCTION

1500 General Building Contractors

1521 Single–family housing construction
1522 Residential construction, NEC
1531 Operative builders
1541 Industrial buildings and warehouses
1542 Nonresidential construction, NEC

Robert E. Brooks
Director of Engineering
Penn Lyon Homes, Inc.
101 Airport Road
Selinsgrove, PA 17870–0027
(717) 374–4004
Fax: (717) 374–8673

1521

Business Information: Penn Lyon Homes, Inc. designs and manufactures modular homes, commercial modular units, office trailers, and custom units, serving a seven state region from Northeastern Virginia to Massachusetts. As Director of Engineering, Mr. Brooks supervises the Engineering Department (including ten CAD operators), coordinating and producing construction documents for commercial, residential, and multi–family divisions, designing and developing new floor plans and elevations. In addition, he oversees all quality control inspectors. **Career Steps:** Director of Engineering, Penn Lyon Homes, Inc. (1993–Present); Manager of Construction, Maurice, Inc. (1990–1993); Project Manager, Union Valley Corporation (1987–1989); Owner/President, Robert Brooks, Builder, Inc. (1985–1987); Product Development Manager, Fuqua Homes, Inc. (1971–1985). **Associations & Accomplishments:** Registered Architect: Texas, Maryland, and Pennsylvania. **Education:** University of Oregon, Bachelor of Architecture (1970). **Personal:** Two children: Timothy and Eric. Mr. Brooks enjoys sailing.

Faythe A. Clemmons
Office Manager
Beems Construction Company, Inc.
2960 Melalevca Drive
West Palm Beach, FL 33406
(407) 641–3511
Fax: (407) 641–3555

1521

Business Information: Beems Construction Company, Inc., a small family–owned general contractor business, specializes in residential remodeling and renovation of Palm Beach estates. As Office Manager, Faythe Clemmons is responsible for all administrative operations, including training and supervision of office staff, directing accounting processes, tax returns, as well as serving as liaison for customer disputes. Concurrently, she owns and operates a private accounting firm — 1 on 1 Administrative Services. **Career Steps:** Office Manager, Beems Construction Company, Inc. (1993–Present); Owner, 1 on 1 Administrative Services (1994–Present). **Associations & Accomplishments:** American Institute of Professional Bookkeepers; National Association of Tax Practitioners; Professional Association of Resume Writers. **Education:** Northwood University: A.A. in Accounting and Business Management, magna cum laude (1994). **Personal:** Ms. Clemmons enjoys Bible educational work.

Frank Dalene

Partner, Chief Executive Officer, and Chief Financial Officer
Telemark Construction, Inc.
P.O. Box 1260
Wainscott, NY 11975
(516) 537–1600
Fax: (516) 537–3951
62foxtrot@hamptons.com

1521

Business Information: Telemark Construction, Inc. is a general contractor of single family luxury homes in the Hamptons of Long Island. The Company has three subsidiaries also involved in the construction industry: Bridgehampton Lumber, Inc. is a regional wholesale distributor of wood products; 367 Butter Lane Cabinetry, Inc. specializes in the manufacture of fine woodworking and customized cabinets; and finally, Dalene Enterprises, Inc. is set up for holding properties. Mr. Dalene is President and Chief Executive Officer of all four companies. He is responsible for the operations of the companies, overseeing the staff, construction, and projects. Internet users can reach him via: 62foxtrot@hamptons.com **Career Steps:** President, Telemark Construction, Inc. (1983–Present); President, 367 Butter Lane Cabinetry, Inc. (1990–Present); President, Bridgehampton Lumber, Inc. (1988–Present); President, Dalene Enterprises, Inc. (1984–Present). **Associations & Accomplishments:** Long Island Builders Institute – East End Association Committee for legislative and legal reform; National Advisory Board for Custom Builder Magazine and CBCE; East Hampton Chamber of Commerce; New York State Builders Association; National Association of Home Builders; National Rifle Association; Airplane Owners and Pilots Association. **Education:** Nyack College, B.A. (1976); Certified Rescue Diver; Certified Pilot – Single Engine Land. **Personal:** Married to Gwendolyn in 1975. Two children: Katherine and Kristofer. Mr. Dalene is a dog fancier and breeder of Rottweilers, and enjoys private piloting, hunting, fishing, scuba diving, and snow boarding.

Frank Keiser

Vice President
Suntree Homes Inc.
13860 Wellington Terrace
West Palm Beach, FL 33414–8588
(407) 795–4141
Fax: (407) 790–8348

1521

Business Information: Suntree Homes Inc. is a residential construction company specializing in single family custom homes. Established in 1989, the Company employs 15 people, and has an estimated annual sales of $9 million. As Vice President, Mr. Keiser is responsible for all aspects of Company operations, including the management of new home construction from obtaining the permit to completion of the project. **Career Steps:** Vice President, Suntree Homes Inc. (1993–Present); Zone Manager, Circle K Corporation (1991–1993); Production Supervisor, Ryland Homes (1989–1991). **Associations & Accomplishments:** Gold Coast Builders Association; Habitat For Humanity; Hurricane Andrew Clean–Up; Hurricane Hugo Clean–Up. **Education:** Westminster College, B.A. (1989); Certified Building Contractor, State of Florida. **Personal:** Married to Elizabeth in 1990. Two children: Katherine and Megan. Mr. Keiser enjoys outdoor activities.

Bill Aardsma, CC Area Manager

Customer Care Area Manager
Pulte Home Corporation
100 Inverness Terrs
Englewood, CO 80112
(303) 649–9222
Fax: Please mail or call

1522

Business Information: Pulte Home Corporation, the largest home builder in the nation, is a major national home builder and residential property development corporation, involved in the financing, marketing and sales of residential homes throughout 40 market areas in the U.S. and Mexico. Established in 1957, Pulte Home Corporation reports annual revenue of $2 billion and currently employs 2,500 people corporate–wide. As Customer Care Area Manager working from the Englewood, Colorado location, Mr. Aardsma serves as liaison between contractors and customers to insure customer satisfaction, including solving problems and overseeing on–site construction on behalf of the customer. **Career Steps:** Customer Care Area Manager, Pulte Home Corporation (1995–Present); TC 4–Technical Coordinator, Aurora Public Schools (1985–1995); Partner, Bill Aardsma Painting (1972–1985). **Associations & Accomplishments:** Impact Team – Hinkley High School; Students–At–Risk Program – Aurora Public Schools; Excelisor Youth Centers; Thirdway Center (co–ed adolescent home); Arapanoe Mental Health Center; Christ Community Church – Sunday School Teacher and Youth Group Leader; American Counseling Association. **Education:** University of Colorado at Denver, M.A. (1993); Metropolitan State College, B.S. in Human Services (1990). **Personal:** Married to Susan in 1978. Three children: Travis, Tara, and Drew. Mr. Aardsma enjoys skiing.

Pedro Archilla

Vice President of Administration and Finance
Mora Development Corporation
P.O. Box 190249
San Juan, Puerto Rico 00919–0249
(809) 781–1233
Fax: (809) 783–4750

1522

Business Information: Mora Development Corporation is one of Puerto Rico's most active developing companies, engaged with its sister companies in construction, real estate, property management and housing development. The Corporation is also responsible for the administration of eleven housing projects (under Section 8 that is supervised by HUD) and an affiliate, Windows Manufacturing Corporation. A highly–experience financial executive with major achievements in operational controls, cash management, MIS, and accounting within a variety of "world–class" business environments, Mr. Archilla joined the Corporation in 1994. Serving as Vice President of Administration and Finance, he is responsible for the oversight of financial planning and control of 28 special partnerships and five corporations with total assets of more than $100 million. **Career Steps:** Vice President of Administration and Finance, Mora Development Corporation (1994–Present); Senior Installation Director, Shared Medical Systems (1986–1994); Audit Supervisor, Diego Perdomo Alvarez, CPA (1978–1986); Chief Financial Officer, Hospital San Rafael, Inc. (1974–1978). **Associations & Accomplishments:** Puerto Rico Manufacturers Association; Deacon (1979–Present), Catholic Church (Working Directly with the Archbishop of San Juan). **Education:** University of Puerto Rico, B.B.A. cum laude in Accounting and Finance (1966); New York University, Cost Accounting for Hospitals; Information Systems at SHS Centers – Malvern, Continued Education. **Personal:** Married to Myrna Rivera in 1966. Four children: Pedro Jose, Francisco Javier, Maria del Carmen, and Jose Antonio. Mr. Archilla enjoys exercising and reading.

Dean H. Campbell

President
Colony Craft Homes, Inc.
282 Grooms Road
Clifton Park, NY 12065
(518) 383–4677
Fax: (518) 383–6599

1522

Business Information: Colony Craft Homes, Inc., established in 1976, is a land and custom residential home construction and development company. Located in two subdivisions in Clifton Park, New York, Colony Craft Homes are priced from $300,000 to $600,000. In 1995, Colony Craft formed Timberwick Consolidated Financial, a factoring brokerage company that purchases debt instruments at discounts. Serving as President and Chief Executive Officer, Mr. Campbell established the Company in 1976. He oversees all administrative operations for associates and a support staff of ten, in addition to the direction of overall management of construction processes. He also purchases land, acquires approvals for loans, meets with clients, and conducts sales. **Career Steps:** President, Colony Craft Homes, Inc. (1976–Present); President, Timberwick Consolidated Financial (Present). **Associations & Accomplishments:** Scuba Instructor, National Association Underwater Instructors; National Association of Entrepreneurs – C.F.S. Designation; National Association of Realtors; National Builders Association. **Education:** Colorado State University, B.A. (1974). **Personal:** Mr. Campbell enjoys scuba diving, skiing, fishing, boating, hunting, and snowmobiling.

Douglass C. Campbell

Vice President of PULTELINC
Pulte Home Corporation
33 Bloomfield Hills Parkway
Bloomfield Hills, MI 48304
(810) 433–4601
Fax: (810) 433–4598

1522

Business Information: Pulte Home Corporation, the second largest home builder in the world, is a major national home builder and residential property development corporation, involved in the financing, marketing and sales of residential homes throughout 40 market areas in the U.S. and Mexico. Established in 1957, Pulte Home Corporation reports annual revenue of $2 billion and currently employs 2,500 corporate–wide. As Vice President of PULTELINC, Mr. Campbell designs and manages the Company's computer operating systems. **Career Steps:** Pulte Home Corporation: Vice President of PULTELINC (1994–Present), Vice President of Construction (1991–1994); Vice President of Operations, Watt Homes – San Diego (1989–1991); Vice President of Construction, Pulte – South Florida Division (1985–1989). **Associations & Accomplishments:** National Association of Home Builders; Michigan Marching Band Alumni. **Education:** University of Michigan, Masters of Music (1961); University of Michigan, Bachelors of Music (1958). **Personal:** Married to Sherry in 1957. Three children: Cynthia, Genifer, and Doug. Mr. Campbell enjoys music, ice hockey, woodworking, and golf.

Greg S. Campbell

Director of Remodel Services
Terwilliger Plaza, Inc.
2545 SW Terwilliger Blvd.
Portland, OR 97201
(503) 299–4616
Fax: (503) 299–4231

1522

Business Information: Terwilliger Plaza, Inc., headquartered in Portland, is a custom designer and remodeler of condominiums in "Type I" high–rise buildings. The Corporation handles approximately 45 projects a year, averaging 10 to 15 at once, including any project having to do with tenant improvements. As Director of Remodel Services, Mr. Campbell is responsible for overseeing of all remodeling projects, as well as meeting with clients and architects, scheduling employees and subcontractors, tracking costs, and meeting budgets. **Career Steps:** Terwilliger Plaza, Inc.: Director of Remodel Services (1995–Present), Remodel Supervisor (1993–1995); Remodel Leadman (1991–1993). **Associations & Accomplishments:** Portland Chamber of Commerce. **Education:** Fred Pryor, Project Management (1996); University of Oregon, Auto CADD, Strong knowledge of Project Management/Software, Accounting Software. **Personal:** Mr. Campbell enjoys computers, skiing, and personal fitness.

Mr. Ray C. Carlson

President
Ray Carlson & Associates, Inc.
411 Russell Avenue
Santa Rosa, CA 95403
(707) 528–7649
Fax: (707) 571–5541

1522

Business Information: Ray Carlson & Associates, Inc. is a land surveying company serving the public and private sector. Surveying and mapping is done for ranches, estates, municipalities, companies, individuals, and consulting engineers using G.P.S. As President, Mr. Carlson is responsible for overseeing company operations, bidding, marketing, networking, and on–site project management. Established in 1976, Ray Carlson & Associates, Inc. employs a professional and diverse administrative staff. **Career Steps:** President, Ray Carlson & Associates, Inc. (1976–Present); Survey Manager, Fred Browne & Associates (1973–1976); Field Survey Supervisor, Robert W. Curtis, Land Surveyor (1969–19 73). **Associations & Accomplishments:** California Land Surveyor's Association; Charter Member, Surveyor's Historical Association; American Congress of Surveying and Mapping; Geyser's Geothermal Association; Santa Rosa Exchange Club; Santa Rosa Chamber of Commerce; Burbank Housing Development Corporation; Habitat for Humanity; Christ Methodist Church; American Forestry Association; Foundation for Prevention of Child Abuse; Kid Street Theatre; The Peoples Foundation. **Education:** Continuing education in both professional and business studies.

Joseph K.C. Chan

Owner
City Gate Development Corporation
2089 36th Avenue East
Vancouver, British Columbia V5P 1C9
(604) 327–0880
Fax: (604) 327–1102

1522

Business Information: City Gate Development Corporation, winner of the British Columbia Housing Award in 1991, builds custom and specialty single–family homes, multi–family condominiums, and commercial structures. Mr. Chan established CGDC in 1989 and now serves as Project Manager, Site Superintendent, and Estimator. He is responsible for personnel decisions, strategic planning, and various administrative functions. **Career Steps:** Owner and Engineer, City Gate Development Corporation (1989–Present); Owner and Manager, CMG Air Products Enterprises, Ltd. (1994–1995); Manager and Partner, HK–Can Development Corporation (1987–1994); Engineer in Training, Yoneda and Associates Ltd. (1984–1985). **Associations & Accomplishments:** Registered Housing Professional; Registered R2000 Builder; Building Board of Appeal – Vancouver, British Columbia; Greater Vancouver Home Builder Association; HRAI Ventilation Installer and Designer. **Education:** University of Western Ontario, B.E.Sc. (1984); Vancouver Community College: Diploma of Electronic Technician, Diploma of Agriculture and Mechanical Drafting. **Personal:** Married to Linda Ho in 1986. Three children: Carmen, Madelon and Garrick. Mr. Chan enjoys computers, electronic devices, building repair, and swimming.

Franklin E. Christian

Owner/Chief Executive Officer
Christian Construction, Inc.
Vega Baja Lakes Calle 4E 26
Vega Baja, Puerto Rico 00693
(787) 855–3055
Fax: (787) 855–3055

1522

Business Information: Christian Construction, Inc. specializes in both general construction and repair work for the commercial and residential industries. As Owner/Chief Executive Officer, Mr. Christian is responsible for all aspects of Company operations, including administration, finance, sales and marketing, and strategic planning. **Career Steps:** Owner/Chief Executive Officer, Christian Construction, Inc. (1989–Present).

David Cool

Project Manager
San Gra Corporation
6755 Manlius Center Road
East Syracuse, NY 13057
(315) 463–2700
Fax: (315) 463–0041

1522

Business Information: San Gra Corporation is a general contracting company located in East Syracuse, New York. The Corporation, established in 1992, currently employs 20 people and posted revenues in excess of $20 million dollars in 1995. As Project Manager, Mr. Cool handles the daily administrative duties of the company and oversees various company projects. **Career Steps:** San Gra Corporation: Project Manager (1995–Present), Controller (1994–1995); Accountant, The Pyramid Company (1985–1994); Accountant, Barrett Paving Company (1983–1985). **Education:** SUNY, at Utica/ Rome, Bachelor's (1977). **Personal:** Married to Sheila in 1987. One child: Brittany. Mr. Cool enjoys sailing.

Cris Driskell

President
Dominion Development Corporation
3190 Northeast Expressway NE, Suite 400
Atlanta, GA 30341
(770) 455–6053
Fax: (770) 455–6941

1522

Business Information: Dominion Development Corporation specializes in apartment construction and development in the southeast part of the United States. The Corporation, which is presently erecting 1800 apartment units, took off immediately upon its inception in 1993. Dominion was recently honored by the National Association of Home Builders with the "Best Luxury Multi–Family Development" award, which is a 'pillar at the industry' award. As President, Mr. Driskell is responsible for all aspects of Company operations, including administration, finance, and strategic planning. **Career Steps:** President, Dominion Development Corporation (1993–Present); Chief Executive Officer, Roberts Properties (1991–1993); Director, Casey–Dotsun (1984–1990). **Associations & Accomplishments:** National Association for Home Builders; Raleigh and Atlanta Chambers of Commerce: TEC. **Education:** Georgia State University, B.S. (1979). **Personal:** Two children: Amy and Alex. Mr. Driskell enjoys racing vintage automobiles.

Scott E. Ellison

Vice President of Construction Operation
Chanen Construction Company, Inc.
P.O. Box 33967
Phoenix, AZ 85067
(602) 266–3600
Fax: (602) 285–9268

1522

Business Information: Chanen Construction Company, Inc. specializes in construction management, general contracting, and design/build. As Vice President of Construction Operations, Mr. Ellison is responsible for the overall operations of the Company, including construction management, operations, and projects, providing executive control, and P&L responsibilities. Mr. Ellison has been involved in projects for the government, airports, schools, institutions, parks, universities, law enforcement, stores, hotels, hospitals, etc. **Career Steps:** Vice President of Construction Operations, Chanen Construction Company (1995–Present); Construction Manager, Centex–Rodgers Construction Company (1983–1995); Chief Operating Officer, Ellison Construction Company (1974–1983). **Associations & Accomplishments:** American Society of Mechanical Engineers; American Concrete Institute; American Society of Plumbing Engineers; American Society of Heating, Refrigeration, and Air Conditioning Engineers; Construction Specification Institute; American Arbitration Association. **Education:** Kennedy Western University, B.S. in Business Administration; California Contractors License #312530. **Personal:** Married to Tina in 1978. Mr. Ellison enjoys travel.

Mr. Greg G. Golden

President
Zedot Construction, Inc.
P.O. Box 846
Wetumpka, AL 36092
(334) 567–2257
Fax: (334) 567–2257

1522

Business Information: Zedot Construction, Inc. is a general contractor specializing in building, renovating residential homes and commercial projects. Established in 1993, the Company currently employs 18 people. As President, Mr. Golden is responsible for all aspects of operations. **Career Steps:** President, Zedot Construction, Inc. (1993–Present); Project Manager, Berger Construction (1991–1993); Project Manager, Torrance Construction (1988–1991). **Associations & Accomplishments:** Auburn Alumni Association; Alabama Home Builders Association; Wetumpka Baptist Church; Builds doll houses for auctions; Christmas in April – Adopt a Child for Christmas; His homes have been published in magazines. **Education:** Auburn University, B.S. in Building Construction (1988). **Personal:** Mr. Golden enjoys snow skiing, scuba diving, weight lifting and swimming.

Emile K. Haddad

Senior Vice President
Bramalea California Inc.
27432 Calle Arroyo
San Juan Capistrano, CA 92675–2747
(714) 488–8850
Fax: (714) 488–8846

1522

Business Information: Bramalea California Inc. is an international land development and homebuilding firm in Canada and the U.S. Joining Bramalea California Inc. as Senior Vice President in 1989, Mr. Haddad directs and oversees all land acquisitions and dispositions, entitlements, engineering, and land development. He also is in charge of all government agency relationships. **Career Steps:** Senior Vice President, Bramalea California Inc. (1989–Present); Vice President, Marlborough Development Corporation (1987–1989); President, Sigma Consultant (1983–1987). **Associations & Accomplishments:** Urban Land Institute (ULI); Building Industry Association (BIA); Registered Civil Engineer – State of California. **Education:** American University – Beirut, Lebanon, B.E. in Civil Engineering (1982); Engineering Contracting License & General Building Contracting License – State of California. **Personal:** Married to Dina since 1986. One child: Serene. Mr. Haddad enjoys golf, soccer, swimming, reading, and following world politics.

William E. Hickman

Vice President of Finance
Universal Constructors, Inc.
2548 Morrison Street
McMinnville, TN 37110
(615) 668–2876
Fax: (615) 668–2142

1522

Business Information: Universal Constructors, Inc. is a general contracting firm concentrating in the construction of multi– family residences, townhouses, apartments, condominiums and Lowe's stores. Established in 1978, Universal Constructors, Inc. reports annual revenue of $126 million and currently employs 260 people. As Vice President of Finance, Mr. Hickman is responsible for all aspects of company finances. Joining the Company in 1994, he was given three years to turn the Company around, succeeding in six months, bringing the Company from $20 million in assets to a total turnaround of $126 million today. **Career Steps:** Vice President of Finance, Universal Constructors, Inc. (1994–Present); Regional Controller, ENSR (1992–1994); Controller, CRS Sirrine, Inc. (1985–1992). **Associations & Accomplishments:** Associated General Contractors; Families in Crisis. **Education:** Columbus College, B.B.A. (1982). **Personal:** Married to Linda in 1989. Two children: Jesse and Jimmie. Mr. Hickman enjoys whitewater rafting, camping, and fishing.

Eddie Martin

President
Tilson Home Corporation
P.O. Box 10100
Houston, TX 77449
(713) 692–5171
Fax: Please mail or call

1522

Business Information: Tilson Home Corporation specializes in home building on scattered lot locations. As President, Mr. Martin provides the overall direction and vision of the company's continued growth and success, quality delivery of products to customers, and business strategic developments. In addition to his responsibilities as the President, Mr. Martin is also an Attorney and a Certified Public Accountant. **Career Steps:** President, Tilson Home Corporation (Present); Chief Operating Officer, Martin Interest Inc. (1982–1989); Senior Tax Accountant, Arthur Andersen & Co. (1979–1982). **Associations & Accomplishments:** Texas Society of Certified Public Accountants; American Institute of Certified Public Accounts; Texas State Bar Association; Greater Houston Homes Association; American Bar Association.

Kelly D. Miller

President
KDM Contracting, Inc.
22032 North 23rd Avenue
Phoenix, AZ 85027–1912
(602) 581–8829
Fax: (602) 581–5174

1522

Business Information: Kelly D. Miller founded KDM Contracting, Inc. in 1985, specializing in residential concrete and home building. As President and Chief of Implementation, he oversees all aspects of operations with a hands–on attitude concerning administrative responsibilities. **Career Steps:** President, KDM Contracting, Inc. (1985–Present); Sales Representative, Colgate–Hoyt (1982–1985). **Associations & Accomplishments:** Board of Directors, Phoenix Homeowners Association; Arizona Concrete Contractors Association. **Education:** University of Idaho, B.S. in Economics (1982); Air Force Academy (1977). **Personal:** Married to Shannon in 1991. One child: Taylor Elaine. Mr. Miller enjoys mountain biking, snow skiing, and outdoor adventures of all types.

Kent Naragon
Director of Purchasing
Sam Rodgers Properties, Inc.
575 Center Road, P.O. Box 1555
Venice, FL 34284
(941) 496–9032
Fax: (941) 496–9285

1522

Business Information: Sam Rodgers Properties, Inc. is a residential construction developer and builder specializing in single–family golf course communities designed for an active retirement lifestyle. As Director of Purchasing, Mr. Naragon is responsible for attaining all necessary supplies for construction and development. He also oversees the design, development, and budgeting process for new production homes. **Career Steps:** Director of Purchasing, Sam Rodgers Enterprises, Inc. (1993–Present); Contract Administrator, Walt Disney World Corporation (1986–1990); Vice President, Purchasing, U.S. Home Corporation (1982–1985). **Education:** Ball State University, B.S. (1971). **Personal:** Mr. Naragon enjoys golf and is active in little league baseball as a manager and umpire.

Kyle Harford Noble
Project Manager & Chief Financial Officer
B.P. Builders, Inc.
P.O. Box 231, 11 Yates Street
Biddeford, ME 04006
(207) 284–4311
Fax: (207) 284–4350

1522

Business Information: B.P. Builders, Inc. is a residential contracting business concentrating on remodeling services. As Project Manager & Chief Financial Officer, Mr. Noble is responsible for managing production and handling daily operations. **Career Steps:** Project Manager, Chief Financial Officer & Part Owner, B.P. Builders, Inc. (1994–Present); Property Manager, Dirigo Management Company (1991–1994); Project Manager, Donalco, Inc. (1990–1991); Project Manager, Roberge Construction (1988–1990). **Associations & Accomplishments:** Firefighter, Biddeford Pool Volunteer Fire Department (1980–Present); Firefighter, Hills Beach Volunteer Fire Department (1983–Present); Trustee, South Congregational Church (1995–Present); Ward 1 Councilor, Biddeford City Council (1986–1991). **Education:** University of Maine – Orono, B.A. in Zoology (1978); Licensed Plumbing Inspector, State of Maine Exam. **Personal:** Married to Diane M. in 1980. Two children: Amanda Leigh and Nicki Beth. Mr. Noble enjoys boating, motorcycling, and camping.

Wendell G. Norris
Owner/General Contractor
Norris Construction Company
534 Winston Road
Clayton, NC 27520
(919) 553–0683 (919) 422–2823
Fax: (919) 553–8014

1522

Business Information: Norris Construction Company serves as a general contractor, specializing in new home construction. As Owner/General Contractor, Mr. Norris is responsible for all aspects of Company operations, including supervision of work sites, employee scheduling, client business, financing, and overseeing all operations. **Career Steps:** Owner/General Contractor, Norris Construction Company (1995–Present); Senior Lab Technical Specialist, IBM (1966–1995); Stock–Produce Manager, Winn–Dixie (1959–1966). **Associations & Accomplishments:** Coach, Clayton Little League; President, C.B. Club. **Education:** Clayton (1959). **Personal:** Married to Faye in 1986. Three children: Joan, Rose, and Wendy. Mr. Norris enjoys horses.

Steve L. Peel
Project Construction Manager
Centex Homes
6702 Lone Oak Boulevard
Naples, FL 33942–6834
(941) 495–7440
Fax: (741) 495–7662

1522

Business Information: Centex Homes designs and constructs single and multi–family residential housing. Joining Centex Homes in 1992 as Field Manager, Mr. Peel was promoted to Project Construction Manager in 1995. He presently oversees four communities of single– and multi–family homes, including supervising construction and support staff and performing various administrative functions. **Career Steps:** Centex Homes: Field Manager (1995–Present), Project Construction Manager (1992–1994). **Education:** University of Florida, B.S. in Building Construction (1992). **Personal:** Married to Kelly C. in 1995. Mr. Peel enjoys fishing.

Robert Porter
President
Beazer Homes Nevada, Inc.
2700 Chandler Avenue, Suite 1A
Las Vegas, NV 89120–4028
(702) 795–2850
Fax: (702) 795–7403

1522

Business Information: Beazer Homes Nevada, Inc. is a homebuilder specializing in residential construction in the Nevada–Las Vegas area. As President, Mr. Porter is responsible for general management and administration of operations, land acquisition, and financial activities. **Career Steps:** President, Beazer Homes Nevada, Inc. (1995–Present); President, Canoa Development; President, Pulte Homes – Arizona; Chief Financial Officer, Mortgage Investors of Washington. **Associations & Accomplishments:** Board of Directors, Goodwill Industries; Board of Directors, Henderson Mental Health Center; Chairman, George Bush for President Campaign. **Education:** Mercer University, B.A. (1970). **Personal:** Married to Cheryl in 1995. Eight children: Tiffany, Kelly, Heather, Courtenay, Palmer, Meagan, Monica, and Kelly. Mr. Porter enjoys golf and sailing He has also written two novels and two screenplays.

James C. Ramirez
Senior Vice President
Fletcher Pacific Construction
707 Richards Street, Suite 400
Honolulu, HI 96813–4623
(808) 533–5000
Fax: (808) 533–5320

1522

Business Information: Fletcher Pacific Construction is a general contracting service, specializing in hotels, condos, offices, retail, renovation, shopping centers, and other such structures. As Senior Vice President, Mr. Ramirez is responsible for all aspects of Company operations, including business development. **Career Steps:** Fletcher Pacific Construction: Senior Vice President/General Manager (4 years), Vice President Operations (6 years), Chief Estimator (3 years). **Associations & Accomplishments:** General Contractors Association; Chamber of Commerce of Hawaii. **Education:** University of Hawaii, B.A. in Civil Engineering. **Personal:** Married to Patricia. Five children: Malia Ramirez, Kaleka Harrison, Gina Vasconcellos, Dino and Jeremy Granito. Mr. Ramirez enjoys tennis, jogging, and spending time with his family.

Gary Rinderle
President
Gary Rinderle Construction
542 33 Road
Clifton, CO 81520–8023
(970) 434–0510
Fax: (970) 434–6510

1522

Business Information: Gary Rinderle Construction is a general contracting firm, providing the initial excavation and clearing for home/residence building and subdivision development, while sub–contracting out the majority of the other aspects. With twenty–nine years experience in the homebuilding industry, Mr. Rinderle established Gary Rinderle Construction in 1990. Serving as President, he is responsible for all aspects of operations, including administration, finances, public relations, accounting, marketing, and strategic planning, as well as serving as General Manager. **Career Steps:** President, Gary Rinderle Construction (1990–Present). **Personal:** Married to Linda in 1966. Mr. Rinderle enjoys hunting, fishing, and travel.

Daniel Mark Roys
Vice President of Construction
Caruso Homes
1662 Village Green
Crofton, MD 21114
(301) 261–0277
Fax: (301) 261–6588

1522

Business Information: Caruso Homes is a builder of single family, townhouse, and custom–built homes. The Company currently builds in six Maryland counties, and is expanding into Virginia. There are plans to possibly expand into other markets, in building related areas. As Vice President of Construction, Mr. Roys is responsible for all field personnel, house development, subcontractor and supplier contact, enforcement,

cad drawings, and custom and singles. **Career Steps:** Caruso Homes: Vice President of Construction (1995–Present), Area Supervisor (1993–1995), Superintendent (1988–1993). **Associations & Accomplishments:** Christmas in April; Waldorf Youth Soccer Coach; OSHA Compliance Course, SMBIA, Builder University; Complete course on Quality, Waste Management Study with NAHB; Member Grace Baptist Church of Bryans Road, Maryland;. **Education:** Salisbury State. **Personal:** Married to Tammy Tara in 1982. One child: Daniel Mark II. Mr. Roys enjoys golf, fishing, and spending time with his family.

Avni Sharma
Vice President and Chief Information Officer
K. Hovnanian Enterprises, Inc.
10 Highway 35
Red Bank, NJ 07701
(908) 747–7800
Fax: (908) 747–6721
EMAIL: See Below

1522

Business Information: K. Hovnanian Enterprises, Inc. is the 10th largest home builder in the nation, developing large residential communities in several states (4,200 homes in FY95 and revenues of $770 million). As Vice President and Chief Information Officer, Mr. Sharma is responsible for all information technology, and software for the Company, in addition to managing a staff of 18 and routine I.S. activities. Internet users can reach him via: Avnis@Aol.com. **Career Steps:** K. Hovnanian Enterprises, Inc.: Vice President and Chief Information Officer (1993–Present), Director of I.S. and Assistant Vice President (1983–1993); Senior Software Specialist, Digital Equipment Corporation (1981–1983); Metal Buildings Engineer, Butler Manufacturing Company – Canada (1974–1981). **Associations & Accomplishments:** Beta Gamma Sigma – National Business School Honor Society; Associaton of Professional Engineers – Ontario, Canada. **Education:** Rutgers University, M.B.A. (1988); Birla Institute of Technology and Science, B.A. in Civil Engineering with honors. **Personal:** Married to Dr. Indu Sharma in 1984. Two children: Anu and Puja. Mr. Sharma enjoys reading, computers, electronic kits, travel, and chess.

Mr. Robert E. Thompson
President/Founder
Thompson Construction of Columbus Inc.
4355N–330W
Columbus, IN 47201
(812) 372–7778
Fax: Please mail or call

1522

Business Information: Thompson Construction of Columbus Inc. is a developer and general contractor specializing in the construction of residential properties and commercial buildings. Established in 1969, the company has estimated annual sales of $5 million. As President, Mr. Thompson is responsible for overseeing all aspects of operations for the company, including finance, administrative proceedings, building plans and designs. **Career Steps:** President/Founder, Thompson Construction of Columbus Inc. (1969–Present); Pastor of the Bethe Holiness Church and builder of its Christian Day School (1968–Present); Administrator, Bethel Holiness Christian School (1974–Present). **Associations & Accomplishments:** Board of Directors and Treasurer, Funds of Missionarys Inc. **Education:** God's Bible School, Cincinnati Ohio, Third year Theology student. **Personal:** Married to Bonnie M. in 1946. Four children: Robert, Jr., Stephen, Vickie and Kevin. Mr. Thompson enjoys outdoor activities.

Theodore M. Visnic
President
Mitchell, Best, & Visnic
1684 East Gude Drive, Suite 301
Rockville, MD 20850–5304
(301) 309–6470
Fax: (301) 309–8820

1522

Business Information: Mitchell, Best, & Visnic — recognized as America's best custom homebuilder (4 years consecutively) — is a small– to medium–volume, custom homebuilding firm, responsible for the construction of over 60 homes to date. Established in 1990, the Firm reports annual revenue in excess of $8 million. With 14 years expertise in the building industry, Mr. Visnic co–founded Mitchell, Best, & Visnic in 1983, serving as Project Manager. Appointed as President in 1990, he is responsible for all aspects of operations. **Career Steps:** Mitchell, Best, & Visnic: President (1990–Present), Project Manager (1983–1990); Project Superintendant, Allan Homes (1981–1983). **Associations & Accomplishments:** Suburban Maryland Building Industry Association; Builder

"20" Club – 20 of the Nation's Best Homebuilders sponsored by the National Association of Homebuilders; Recipient, Builder of the Year Award, Builder's Magazine (1995). **Education:** Attended: University of Maryland (1985). **Personal:** Married to Donna Lee in 1984. Three children: Lauren, Stephen, and Aaron.

Mat Vivona Jr.

President
Father and Son Construction
5032 Rochester Road
Troy, MI 48098
(810) 528–1920
Fax: (810) 528–3275

1522

Business Information: Father and Son Construction is the largest home improvement company in Michigan. The Company's focus and main market is remodeling residential homes, interior and exterior. Mr. Vivona, the son in Father and Son Construction, became President of the Company in 1995, after the death of his father, Mat Vivona, Sr., who started the business from scratch in 1980, making it the number one home improvement company in the state in a mere fifteen years. He is responsible for all aspects of company operations. **Career Steps:** Father and Son Construction: President (1994–Present); Construction Supervisor (1992–96); Architect (1986–92). **Associations & Accomplishments:** National Association of Remodelers, Inc., National Association of Home Builders, Better Business Bureau and Supporter of Friends of the Opera. **Education:** Ferris State University, Business Administration (1992). **Personal:** Mr. Vivona is a Harley Davidson enthusiast and enjoys collecting automobiles.

Gregorio Batista Negron, P.E., GRI

Senior Cost Engineer
Turner Caribe
B5 Camino Alejandrino
Guaynabo, Puerto Rico 00969
(787) 789–4100
Fax: Please mail or call
EMAIL: See Below

1531

Business Information: A subsidiary of Turner Construction Company, one of the largest builders in America, Turner Caribe specializes in the construction of offices and other buildings, while other subsidiaries focus on hospitals and institutions. As Senior Cost Engineer, Mr. Batista Negron is responsible for maintaining the Company's cash flow and providing assistant support. Internet users can reach him via: GBatista@Caribe.net. **Career Steps:** Senior Cost Engineer, Turner Caribe (1991–Present); Surveyor/Engineer, Puerto Rico Highway Authority (1990–1991). **Associations & Accomplishments:** National Association of Realtors; Puerto Rico Association of Realtors; Puerto Rico Board of Professional Engineers; Civil Engineers Institute. **Education:** University of Puerto Rico, B.S. (1991); PROSHA Academy; Cybernetics Institute, Certified Computer Technician; The Realtor's Institute, Graduate/GRI. **Personal:** Married to Wanda in 1991. One child: Geena. Mr. Batista Negron enjoys computers, reading, and the Internet.

Gina M. Caldwell

Finance & Administrative Manager
Carlson Design/Construct Corp.
3200 Park Center Dr., Suite 710
Costa Mesa, CA 92626
(714) 444–9155
Fax: (714) 444–9177

1531

Business Information: Carlson Design/Construct Corp. – Western Division, located in Costa Mesa, California, is a comprehensive firm offering architecture, engineering, process engineering, design/build, construction management and program management. Established in 1945, the Company employs over 200 people. Ms. Caldwell oversees all financial reporting and activities for the Western Division. **Career Steps:** Finance & Administrative Manager, Carlson Design/Construct Corp. (1996–Present); Controller, Magnum Enterprises, Inc. (1993–1996); Director of Accounting, Westport Pacific, Division of HWDC (1990–1993); Accounting Manager, Dutchman Plastering (1986–1992). **Associations & Accomplishments:** Building Industry Association; People Synergistically Involved; Pacesetters Leadership Dynamics. **Education:** Liberty Baptist University. **Personal:** Two children: Kelsey

and Madison. Ms. Caldwell enjoys charity, community functions, theatre, and the arts.

Jerry Dean

President
Miller–Stauch
13000 W. 87th Street, Ste. 110
Lenexa, KS 66215
(913) 599–1040
Fax: (913) 599–2570

1531

Business Information: Miller–Stauch is a family–owned business that provides commercial developing and general contracting on a nationwide basis. As President, Mr. Dean is responsible for coordinating and developing client relations, dealing with long–term lenders, as well as real estate development and acquisitions. **Career Steps:** Miller–Stauch: President (1994–Present), Vice President (1982–94). **Associations & Accomplishments:** Optimist International; Private pilot with multi engine and instrument rating (1982). **Personal:** Married to Dana in 1984. Two children: Megan and Prescott. Mr. Dean enjoys snow skiing, boating, flying, and travel.

H. Ted Dearman

Vice President of Operations and Buildings
W.G. Yates & Sons Construction Company
781 Larson Street
Jackson, MS 39202–3437
(601) 363–9660
Fax: (601) 353–3050

1531

Business Information: W.G. Yates & Sons Construction Company is a multi–faceted company offering services in marine, electrical, roadway and bridge, and heavy concrete utilities construction. The Company also manufactures asphalt, and has five locations across the region. Established in 1963, the Company employs 2,000 people and has an estimated annual revenue of $300 million. As Vice President of Operations and Buildings, Mr. Dearman provides planning for his division, and oversees project completion, bidding, contract negotiation, and contract security. **Career Steps:** Vice President of Operations and Buildings, W.G. Yates & Sons Construction Company (1989–Present); Chief Project Manager, Dunn Construction Company (1984–1989); Plant Manager, Jackson Stone Company (1972–1984). **Associations & Accomplishments:** Mississippi Associated Builders and Contractors: Board of Directors (1984–1995), President (1992), National Board of Directors (1992–1995). **Education:** University of Southern Mississippi, B.S. in Business Administration and Management (1972). **Personal:** Married to Carla Curtis in 1970. Three children: Henry Chase, Caine Newton, and Taylor Woodward. Mr. Dearman enjoys snow skiing.

Ghada Dergham

President and Owner
Advantage Design Custom Homes
76 Court Street, P.O. Box 2529
Plattsburgh, NY 12907–5719
(518) 566–8155
Fax: (518) 566–8166

1531

Business Information: Advantage Design Custom Homes, building ten homes in their first year, is a general construction firm, providing construction of residential homes and steel structures for commercial use, in addition to real estate sales. Advantage Design Custom Homes, the first builder in the area to build with geothermal heating and cooling, serves the tri–county area of Clinton, Essex and Franklin counties. A Licensed Real Estate Broker, Ms. Dergham founded Advantage Design Custom Homes in 1993 and serves as its President and Owner. She is responsible for all aspects of operations, including the direction of building and zoning regulations, managing sales and sales personnel as Sales Manager, overseeing all purchasing activities as Purchasing Agent, and overseeing all construction bids. **Career Steps:** President and Owner, Advantage Design Custom Homes (1993–Present); Commercial Sales Manager, Durhams Exchange, Inc. (1991–1993); Warehouse Manager, C & B Concessions (1988–1991). **Associations & Accomplishments:** Adirondack Builders Association; Membership Committee, Clinton County Board of Realtors; Published in article regarding her geothermal heating and cooling systems. **Education:** Real-

tor Institute Graduate; Attended courses in: Marketing, Architecture, Drafting, and Interior Design. **Personal:** Three children: Cameron, Cayla, and Mila. Ms. Dergham enjoys jet skiing and travel.

Rick Fivekiller

Director of Business Development
Tishman Construction
11400 West Olympic Boulevard, Suite 1500
Los Angeles, CA 90064
(310) 477–7030
Fax: (310) 478–1949

1531

Business Information: Tishman Construction, a division of Tishman Realty and Construction, began operations in 1950 in Los Angeles, California and currently has 48 employees. The Company builds, develops, and manages commercial properties such as hotels, office buildings, entertainment complexes, and retail sites nationwide. As Director of Business Development, Mr. Fivekiller is responsible for the business development, communications, public relations, and marketing for the Western region. **Career Steps:** Director of Business Development, Tishman Construction (1994–Present); Associate Manager/Plant Management and Construction, The New York Public Library (1988–1994); Director of Operations, Risley Childers Anderson (1986–1988); Director of Grants Administration, Western Arkansas Planning and Development (1978–1986). **Associations & Accomplishments:** Board of Directors, ERAS Center, Inc; LA Headquarters Association; Executive Member, Town Hall; Urban Land Institute; Active in political campaigns on the local, state, and national level. **Education:** Graduate Study, New York University; University of Arkansas, Master of Public Administration (1980), B.A. in Political Science (1973). **Personal:** Married to Corinne A. Gillick in 1991. Mr. Fivekiller enjoys travel, running, and weightlifting.

Shaw Flippen

Director of Construction
Gaylord Entertainment Company
One Gaylord Drive
Nashville, TN 37214–1207
(615) 316–6252
Fax: (615) 316–6262

1531

Business Information: Gaylord Entertainment Company is a diversified entertainment and communications company operating in three industry divisions: cable networks, broadcasting, and hospitality and entertainment. Properties include: TNN, CMT, Opryland Hotel and Convention Center, and Opryland Theme Park. As Director of Construction, Mr. Flippen oversees all construction contracts for capital projects and is responsible for administrative and operational duties of the Project Management division based in Nashville. **Career Steps:** Director of Construction, Gaylord Entertainment Company (1988–Present); Director of Construction, LBD Corporation – Austin, Texas (1985–1988). **Associations & Accomplishments:** Auburn University Alumni Association; Historic Richland Neighborhood Association; Sigma Chi Alumni Association. **Education:** Auburn University, B.S. in Construction Management (1985); Nashville State Technical Institute, Real Estate Certificate (1989). **Personal:** Mr. Flippen enjoys historic preservation and renovation.

Karla E. Freeze

Controller
Designtex Enterprises
3030 L.B.J. Freeway, Suite 230 LB4
Dallas, TX 75234
(214) 243–3555
Fax: (214) 241–1811

1531

Business Information: Designtex Enterprises specializes in the construction, design and purchasing of hotels nationwide. With one corporate office, the Company sub–contracts some projects, with the majority of work being done by Company professionals. Established in 1978, the Company employs 65 people, and has estimated annual revenues of $12 million. As Controller, Ms. Freeze oversees all phases of accounting, information systems, personnel, credit, internal control, office operations, and job analysis. **Career Steps:** Designtex Enterprises: Controller (1995–Present), Director of Accounting (1987–1991); Sherwin Williams: Credit Manager (1985–1987), Store Manager (1984–1985). **Associations & Accomplishments:** Institute of Management Accountants; Institute of Internal Auditors. **Education:** Eastern Illinois University, B.S. (1994); Lakeland College, Associates of Science (1993); Bauder College, Associate of Arts (1978). **Personal:** Ms. Freeze enjoys antiquing and camping.

Robert L. Griffin

Vice President
Alpine C.M. Inc.
1111 S. 12th Street
Grand Junction, CO 81501–3820
(970) 245–2505
Fax: (970) 245–2591

1531

Business Information: Alpine C.M. Inc., a full service construction company, provides all aspects of commercial and residential construction and land development throughout the western sector of Colorado. As Vice President, Mr. Griffin oversees all administrative areas of the firm, encompassing the divisions of accounting and computer systems. He also acts on behalf of the President in his absence, and is involved in all business development and strategies. **Career Steps:** Vice President, Alpine C.M. Inc. (1990–Present); Divisional Construction Manager, Trammell Crow Residential (1985–1990); Project Superintendent, Hunt Building Corp. (1981–1985). **Associations & Accomplishments:** President and Board of Directors, Home Builders Association of Northwestern Colorado. **Education:** University of New Mexico, B.S. in Civil Engineering (1981). **Personal:** Married to Martha S. in 1981. Two children: Amber and Dane. Mr. Griffin enjoys mountain biking, snow skiing, horseback riding, and coaching youth baseball, basketball and football.

Lawrence Gruner

National Technical Manager of Geoconstruction
Structural Preservation Systems
3761 Commerce Drive, Suite 414
Baltimore, MD 21227–1644
(410) 247–1016
Fax: (410) 247–1136

1531

Business Information: Structural Preservation Systems, established in 1976, has six offices nationwide for the purpose of geotechnical construction (i.e. tunnels, stabilization of soil, etc.). Headquartered in Baltimore, Maryland and with estimated revenues in excess of $50 million, the company presently employs over 350 people. As National Technical Manager of Geoconstruction, Mr. Gruner is responsible for the technical aspects of contracted projects. Other responsibilities include technical marketing and assisting the construction group on the construction projects. **Career Steps:** National Technical Manager of Geoconstruction, Structural Preservation Systems (1992–Present); North East Regional Manager, Intrustion–Prepakt (1989–1992); Eastern Regional Manager, Raymond International Builders (1976–1989). **Associations & Accomplishments:** American Society of Civil Engineers; ASDSO; DFI. **Education:** Princeton University, A.B. in Geology (1976). **Personal:** Married to Anne in 1981. Two children: Deborah Anne and Robert Lawrence. Mr. Gruner enjoys tennis, swimming, golf, and skiing.

Scott I. Higa

President and Chief Executive Officer
Robert M. Kaya Builders, Inc.
525 Kokea Street, Building B3
Honolulu, HI 96817–4935
(808) 845–6477
Fax: (808) 845–6471

1531

Business Information: Robert M. Kaya Builders, Inc., a third–generation family concern established in 1937, is a general contractor for residential and commercial buildings throughout the Hawaiian islands, focusing on Oahu. Succeeding his father as President and Chief Executive Officer in 1989, Mr. Higa is responsible for all aspects of operations, including administration, finances, public relations, marketing, and strategic planning. **Career Steps:** Robert M. Kaya Builders, Inc.: President and Chief Executive Officer (1989–Present), Executive Vice President (1988–1989), Project Manager (1987–1988); Electrical Engineer, U.S. Navy Public Works Center – SFB (1986–1987). **Associations & Accomplishments:** Phi Kappa Phi; Building Industry Association of Hawaii; General Contractors Association; National Association of Home Builders. **Education:** University of the Pacific, B.S. in Electrical Engineering (1986). **Personal:** Married to Evelyn in 1988. One child: Ashley. Mr. Higa enjoys computers, softball, and golf.

Tari Hoops, CPA

Corporate Controller
J.F. Shea Co. Inc.
655 Brea Canyon Road
Walnut, CA 91789–3010
(909) 594–0987
Fax: Please mail or call

1531

Business Information: J.F. Shea Company, Inc. is a large, privately–held, national real estate and construction company. The Corporation has three primary operating divisions: l) Home Building; 2) Heavy Construction – primarily tunnels; and 3) Commercial Property Development and Management. Established in the late 1800's, J.F. Shea Company, Inc. currently employs 1,400 people. A Certified Public Accountant, Ms. Hoops, joined the Firm as Corporate Controller in 1987. She is responsible for consolidated financial reporting across all major operating entities. **Career Steps:** Corporate Controller, J.F. Shea, Co. Inc. (1987–Present). **Associations & Accomplishments:** American Institute of Certified Public Accountants; California Society of Certified Public Accountants. **Education:** University of California – Los Angeles, M.B.A. (1980), B.A. (1977). **Personal:** Married to Steve Martin in 1985. Two children: Jenna and Scott. Ms. Hoops enjoys hiking, camping, swimming, and spending time with family.

John Jones Jr.

Senior Vice President
Smoot Corporation
907 N. 23rd Street
Columbus, OH 43219
(614) 253–9000
Fax: (614) 253–1504

1531

Business Information: Smoot Corporation is a professional construction management and general contracting company. Focusing primarily on commercial, industrial, education, and corrections contracts, the Company works on approximately twenty different projects at any one time. Comprised of 200 employees, the Company offers clients design build, construction management, and budgetary services, as well as general contracting. As Senior Vice President, Mr. Jones organizes and manages all pre–construction services including planning, scheduling, master pricing development and management, value engineering, establishment of procedures, training, and education. He also designed custom software for the Company to assist in organization and efficiency. **Career Steps:** Senior Vice President, Smoot Corporation (1988–Present); Sherman R. Smoot Company: Vice President (1985), Project Manager (1975). **Associations & Accomplishments:** Society of American Value Engineers; American Management Association; American Society of Professional Estimators; Treasurer, Young Black Professionals; Ordained Minister, Rhema Christian Center; American Concrete Institute; Builders Exchange of Columbus, Ohio. **Education:** Ohio State University, B.A. (1979). **Personal:** Married to Christine in 1987. Mr. Jones enjoys travel and cycling.

Michael K. Matthews

Administrative Vice President
Shawnut Design and Construction
560 Harrison Avenue, Suite 2
Boston, MA 02118–2436
(617) 338–6200
Fax: (617) 338–6699

1531

Business Information: Shawnut Design and Construction is a general contractor, specializing in retail and restaurant construction, and general construction in the health care and educational industries. They also conduct high end quality and fast track jobs (time restricted jobs). Shawnut Design and Construction has two offices (Boston and Washington, D.C.) As Administrative Vice President, Mr. Matthews is responsible for all personnel functions, including hiring, benefits, all MIS and systems, and office and administrative operations. **Career Steps:** Administrative Vice President, Shawnut Design and Construction (1995–Present); Director of Administration, Murphy, Hesse, Toomy and Lehanr (1993–1995); Assistant Executive Director, Hillcrest Education Centers (1988–1993); Program Manager, Generel Electric Corporation (1985–1988). **Associations & Accomplishments:** Association of Northeast Human Resource Directors; University of Massachusetts Alumni Association. **Education:** Western New England College, M.B.A. (1992); University of Massachusetts – Amherst. **Personal:** Married to Michele in 1989. One child: Jacob. Mr. Matthews enjoys golf, swimming and running marathons and triathlons in his leisure time.

Cecil McClary Jr.

President
McClary–Laible, Inc.
634 Hudson Avenue
Rochester, NY 14621–1604
(716) 467–1080
Fax: (716) 467–1085

1531

Business Information: Operating in two counties, McClary–Laible, Inc. is a general contracting residential/commercial construction company and development minority business enterprise. As Founder, President, and Chief Executive Officer with over 30 years experience in construction, Cecil McClary established the business in 1969 and is responsible for financial and quality assurance oversite to ensure his business is successful. **Career Steps:** President, McClary–Laible, Inc. (1969–Present). **Associations & Accomplishments:** U.S. Department of Commerce – Minority Business Development Agency; 1995 Minority Contractor of the Year – New York Region, Rochester Minority Business Development Center; Urban League of Rochester, Minority Business Enterprise. **Education:** Manpower Skills Trades, Certificate (1965). **Personal:** Married to Mary Morris in 1970. Three children: Kenneth, Nkofi, and Natasha. Mr. McClary enjoys basketball, tennis, baseball, and reading.

Matthew D. Miglin

President
Miglin Brothers, Inc.
3490 Valley Road
Basking Ridge, NJ 07902
(800) 835–0000
Fax: (908) 604–0221

1531

Business Information: Miglin Brothers, Inc., a family–owned business, is a commercial remodeling company. Established in 1989 by three brothers, the Company recently merged with Flanagan Drywall Co., another construction company thereby adding one more partner and expanding the business. The Company serves clientele throughout New Jersey and some of Pennsylvania. Co–founding the Corporation in 1989 and serving as its President, Mr. Miglin is responsible for most aspects of operations, including all administration and oversight of all other company functions. **Career Steps:** President and Chief Executive Officer, Miglin Brothers, Inc. (1989–Present); General Partner, Royal Concepts (1995–Present); Supervisor, Westcott Steel (1988–1989). **Associations & Accomplishments:** Marine Corps League; Who's Who Among Business Leaders (1995/1996); Best of Show, Furniture building award (1982); Certified seminar leader with American Seminar Leaders Association. **Education:** The Kings College (1988); Advance Christian Training School Graduate, School of Ministry graduate. **Personal:** Married to Karen M. in 1994. Mr. Miglin enjoys running, reading, and skydiving.

Ron W. Mischnick

President
Walter Mischnick Contractors
1631 Toluca Street
Alliance, NE 69301–2253
(308) 762–1981
Fax: (308) 762–7112

1531

Business Information: Walter Mischnick Contractors is a family–owned general contracting company, serving both residential and commercial clients. Some of their major corporate clientele have included Woolrich, Dayco Corporation and Pepsi–Cola Co. Taking over the direction of the company in 1973, which his father Walter founded in 1949, Ron Mischnick oversees the overall day–to–day operations. His primary functions involve: project bids, contract negotiations, materials procurement, and sub–contractor relations. **Career Steps:** President, Walter Mischnick Contractors (1973–Present). **Associations & Accomplishments:** Lutheran Church Missouri Synod.; Board of Directors, Nebraska Chapter of Associated General Contractors; Board of Adjustment, City of Alliance; Alliance Chamber of Commerce; Box Butte Development Corporation. **Education:** University of Nebraska. **Personal:** Married to Marlene in 1972. Two children: Brian and Eric. Mr. Mischnick enjoys water skiing and collecting "O" gauge electrical trains.

David G. Monroe
Project Manager
Clark Construction Company
3225 W. Saint Joseph Street
Lansing, MI 48907-7287
(517) 224-0325
Fax: (517) 224-0326

1531

Business Information: Clark Construction Company provides general construction and construction management in heavy industrial and institutional/commercial areas. Established in 1946, the Company employs 75 people and has estimated annual revenue of $400 million. As Project Manager, Mr. Monroe oversees the day-to-day operation of the Company, and is responsible for control of projects from inception to completion, including budget development and scheduling. He is also directly responsible for a six-person support staff. **Career Steps:** Project Manager, Clark Construction Company (1990-Present); Project Manager, The Zack Company (1984-1990); Project Manager, Limbach National Construction (1980-1984). **Associations & Accomplishments:** Society of Manufacturing Engineers; American Society of Mechanical Engineers; American Welding Society; American Society of Certified Engineering Technicians; Association of Quality Control Engineers. **Education:** Lake Superior State University, B.S. MET. (1978)p; Michigan Technical University, A.A.S. in Civil Engineering Technology (1972). **Personal:** Married to Laura in 1995. Two children: Robert and Thomas. Mr. Monroe enjoys boating, fishing, and coaching amateur hockey.

Gregory Morris
Chief Financial Officer
Dine Bi Ghan Construction Co., Inc.
392 West Highway 264
St. Michael, AZ 86511
(520) 871-2104
Fax: (520) 871-2104

1531

Business Information: Dine Bi Ghan Construction Co., Inc. is a general contracting and construction company. As Chief Financial Officer, Mr. Morris is responsible for managing and projecting the Company's financial position, including working capital needs, maintaining bank relations, and supervising financial reporting. **Career Steps:** Chief Financial Officer, Dine BI Ghan Construction Co., Inc. (1994-Present); Manager of Project Accounting, ACCI (1993-1994); Project Accountant, OHM Remediation (1992-1993); Project Cost Technician, Riedel Environmental (1989-1991). **Education:** University of Southern Mississippi, General Classes; University of Toledo, Business Classes; Owens College, A.A. in Accounting. **Personal:** Married to Daphney in 1993. Mr. Morris enjoys chess and basketball.

Daniel Paton Sr.
Construction Manager
ITT Community Construction
One Corporate Drive
Palm Coast, FL 32151-0001
(904) 446-6444
Fax: (904) 446-6481

1531

Business Information: ITT Community Construction is a construction business, conducting both industrial and commercial construction. With nineteen years of experience in the construction industry, Mr. Paton joined ITT Community Construction as Construction Manager in 1986. He is responsible for the management of all construction activities, including client relations, troubleshooting, contract work, and bidding processes for jobs. **Career Steps:** Construction Manager, ITT Community Construction (1986-Present); Construction Manager, Calmark – St. Augustine, Florida (1982-1986); Project Manager, Seacoast Construction – Pompano Beach (1979-1982). **Education:** Broward Community College; Palm Beach Community College. **Personal:** Married to Gwynn J. in 1975. Three children: Daniel, Thomas, and Michael. Mr. Paton enjoys fishing, surfing, and boating.

Dean A. Piles
Construction Director
McCarthy Brothers Company
100 Bayview Circle, Suite 3000
Newport Beach, CA 92660
(714) 854-8383
Fax: (714) 854-8398

1531

Business Information: McCarthy Brothers Company is a privately-held General/Engineering Contractor offering a wide range of services from General Contracting, and Construction Management to Design Build concentrating on Health Care, Bio Pharmaceutical, Micro Electronics, Industrial, Research and Academic Facilities, Correctional Institutions, Parking Structures, Bridges, Commercial and Corporate Office, Hotel, Resort, and Retail. Established in 1864, the Company has annual sales in excess of $1 billion and over 860 offices and professional employees. As Construction Director, Mr. Piles oversees multiple construction projects of significant size and type. He is responsible for staff management of estimating, preconstruction services, project documentation, budget control, profit and loss projections, and contracting services. **Career Steps:** McCarthy Brothers Construction: Construction Director (1993-Present), Project Manager (1985-1993); D.L. Withers Construction, Inc.: Vice President Operations (1983-1985), Construction Manager (1982-1983). **Associations & Accomplishments:** Republican National Committee; AGC; CSI; PMI. **Education:** Maricopa Tech, Associate in Construction Technology (1978). **Personal:** Married to Sherry in 1986. Two children: Arthur Ian and Emily Louise. Mr. Piles enjoys golf, sailing, fishing, tennis, and coaching youth soccer and baseball.

Adam B. Roth
President
Briden Enterprises of Virginia, Inc.
2241-N Tacketts Mill Drive
Lakeridge, VA 22192
(703) 497-2532
Fax: (703) 497-0357

1531

Business Information: Briden Enterprises of Virginia, Inc. is a general contract firm, specializing in insurance restoration and repair. New construction projects are also provided by referral for both commercial and residential clients. Established in 1992, Briden Enterprises of Virginia, Inc. reports annual revenue of $2.5 million. As President, Mr. Roth is responsible for all aspects of operations, including serving as General Manager and Personnel Director. **Career Steps:** President, Briden Enterprises of Virginia, Inc. (1992-Present); Regional Manager, Electropace Systems, Inc. (1989-1992); Staff Sergeant, U.S. Air Force (1984-1989). **Education:** University of Georgia, B.S. (1989); Georgia Military College, A.A. in Electronics; Attended several management courses and supervisory seminars over a five-year period. **Personal:** Married to Monique in 1984. Two children: Amanda and Ryan. Mr. Roth enjoys golf, racquetball, woodworking, and fishing.

Gilbert F. Ruizcalderon
Comptroller
Miller & Solomon General Contractor
8491 Northwest 17th Street, Suite L
Miami, FL 33126-1025
(305) 599-2300
Fax: (305) 593-8178
EMAIL: See Below

1531

Business Information: Miller & Solomon General Contractor specializes in general contracting services for commercial, industrial, and residential projects. As Comptroller, Mr. Ruiz-Calderon is responsible for all financial operations, including accounting, payroll, insurance, and bonding. Internet users can reach him via: Gruizcal@aol.com. **Career Steps:** Comptroller, Miller & Solomon General Contractor (1989-Present); Project Controller, Island Developers, Ltd. (1987-1989); Financial Analyst, General Electric Real Estate Equities (1985-1987). **Associations & Accomplishments:** Latin Builders Association; Construction Financial Managers Association; Construction Association of South Florida **tEducation:** Florida International University, B.B.A. (1983). **Personal:** Married to Nury in 1990. Three children: Anthony, Daniel, and David. Mr. Ruizcalderon enjoys sports, fishing, and boating.

Stephen D. Saieed
Vice President and Director
Miller Building Corporation
1410 Commonwealth Drive
Wilmington, NC 28403
(910) 256-2613
Fax: (910) 256-3822

1531

Business Information: Miller Building Corporation, a family held corporation established in 1949 and currently employing 450 people, is a general construction firm. As Vice President and Director of Business Development, Mr. Saieed oversees the development of new client contacts and projects. His duties include obtaining new contracts, reviewing the contracts, and maintaining cost management of new and existing contracts. **Career Steps:** Vice President and Director, Miller Building Corporation (1988-Present); Vice President, Saieed Construction Corporation (1976-1988). **Associations & Accomplishments:** Cape Fear Men's Club; Landfall Country Club. **Education:** Attended, North Carolina State University School of Engineering. **Personal:** Married to Mary in 1989. One child: Stephen. Mr. Saieed enjoys golf, fishing, and travel.

Lee D. Sommerman
Project Manager
Raymond LeChase, Inc.
300 Trolley Boulevard
Rochester, NY 14606
(716) 254-3510
Fax: (716) 254-3871

1531

Business Information: Raymond LeChase, Inc. is a Construction Management and General Construction Firm. The Company's major clients include Eastman Kodak Company, Xerox, Bausch and Lomb, and Blue Cross/Blue Shield. As a Project Manager for the Company's Special Clients Division, Mr. Sommerman oversees projects ranging in value from several thousand to several million dollars. **Career Steps:** Project Manager, Raymond LeChase, Inc. (1995-Present); Estimator, Christa Construction (1993-1995); Superintendent, NPV, Inc. (1991-1993). **Associations & Accomplishments:** American Association of Civil Engineers (AACE); Project Management Institute (PMI); Rochester Memorial Art Gallery. **Education:** Rochester Institute of Technology, B.S. in Civil Engineering (1993); SUNY, Alfred, Architecture (1990). **Personal:** Mr. Sommerman enjoys mountain biking, skiing, and boating.

Carol R. Storey
President
Essex Builders Group
2221 Lee Road, Suite 20
Winter Park, FL 32789
(407) 644-6957
Fax: (407) 628-9916

1531

Business Information: Essex Builders Group is a multi-family residential development and general contracting firm. Specializing in apartment buildings and time share condominiums, the Company provides services state-wide. Established in 1991, the Company employs twelve people, and has an estimated annual revenue of $20 million. As President, Ms. Storey oversees all growth, financial planning and administrative functions of the Company. She is also responsible for public relations, marketing, and risk management. **Career Steps:** President, Essex Builders Group (1996-Present); Vice President (1991-1995). **Education:** Columbia College, B.A. (1968). **Personal:** Married to Edward A. in 1970. Two children: Edward A. III and John Willis Storey. Ms. Storey enjoys tennis and clay work.

Saren Thach
Treasurer
Monarc Incorporated
2781 Hartland Road
Falls Church, VA 22043-3529
(703) 641-8500
Fax: (703) 273-2222

1531

Business Information: Monarc Incorporated is a general contracting and construction company specializing in commercial and residential construction. As Treasurer, Mr. Thach is responsible for all aspects of financial and accounting services. In addition, he serves as a Major in the US Army Reserves. A naturalized citizen, Defense Attache' mobilization designee and founding member of the 1st US Army Reserve Linguist Unit, Mr. Thach returned to his native land in 1992 to lend his Cambodian language skills in the search for missing American servicemen. Mr. Thach is also a real estate Broker and principal of his own Real Estate Firm. **Career Steps:** Treasurer, Monarc Incorporated (1991-Present); Controller, Scott-Long Construction (1983); Senior Auditor, Reznick, Fedder & Silverman, CPA's (1979). **Associations & Accomplishments:** National Association of Realtors, International Real Estate Section; American Institute of Certified Public Accountants; US Army Reserves. **Education:** The American University, M.S. in Taxation (1986); University of Phnom Penh, Cambodia, L.L.B.; Cambodian Royal Military Academy Graduate, Valedictorian. **Personal:** Married to Monida K. in

1983. Four children: Christine, Catherine, Marilyn, and Carolyn. Mr. Thach enjoys reading and parachuting.

Nancy Torres
Administration Manager
Elkin Williams International
800 Robert H. Todd, Suite A1
Santurce, Puerto Rico 00907
(787) 724–8051
Fax: (787) 724–8065

1531

Business Information: Elkin Williams International is a general contracting firm. Established in 1992, the Company employs 25 people. As Administration Manager, Ms. Torres is responsible for all administration duties, purchasing of equipment and materials, and project–related assignments. **Career Steps:** Administration Manager, Elkin Williams International (1994–Present). **Associations & Accomplishments:** National Association for Female Executives (NAFE); American Institute of Professional Bookkeepers (AIPB). **Education:** University of Sagrado Corazon, Accounting (1995). **Personal:** Ms. Torres enjoys open water diving and browsing the Internet.

Michael J. Valentine
President/Founder
DMK Incorporated
5 Corporate Park, Suite 220
Irvine, CA 92714–5113
(714) 474–2412
Fax: (714) 852–1480

1531

Business Information: DMK Incorporated is a general contractor of commercial, retail, restaurant, office, and industrial establishments. As President/Founder, Mr. Valentine is responsible for all aspects of operations, including Company growth and direction, as well as strategic planning. **Career Steps:** President/Founder, DMK Incorporated (1991–Present); Director of Project, Hedley Builders (1990–1991); Project Manager, Century American (1989); Project Manager, Lyle Parks, Jr., Inc. (1984–1989). **Education:** California Polytechnic, San Luis Obispo, B.S. in Construction Management (1986). **Personal:** Married to Kathy in 1980. Three children: Mitchell, Carly, and Alyssa. Mr. Valentine enjoys the keyboard, and arranging and writing songs.

Horacio Villavicencio
• • • ◄━━◉━━► • • •
President
Central de Proyectos SA
Condominio 2000 C Blvd de Los Herves
San Salvador, El Salvador
(503) 226–3440
Fax: (503) 226–0311

1531

Business Information: Central de Proyectos SA is a construction and land development company for apartments, houses, and office complexes. The majority of materials used are imported from the U.S. As President, Mr. Villavicencio is responsible for all aspects of operations, including overseeing all construction and 500 employees. His four sons also work for the Company. **Career Steps:** President, Central de Proyectos Sa (1980–Present); President, Campos Villavicencio (1960–Present); President, Constructora Villavicencio (1970–Present); President, Empress Villavicencio (1980–Present). **Associations & Accomplishments:** Camara Salvadorena de la Construccion; Asociacion Ingenieros y Arquitectos de El Salvador; Fundacion para el Desarrolla de las Comunidades. **Education:** Universidad de El Salvador, Civil Engineer (1967); Busines Administration Incae (1967). **Personal:** Married to Yolanda de Villavicencio in 1966. Five children: Carlos, Eduardo, Enrique, Ana Yolanda, and Guillermo. Mr. Villavicencio enjoys golf, travel, and piloting aircraft.

Jerry D. Walston
President
J.D. Walston and Associates
3105 Central Heights Road
Goldsboro, NC 27534
(919) 778–8513
Fax: (919) 778–1077

1531

Business Information: J.D. Walston and Associates is a residential and commercial construction company specializing in houses, roofing, vinyl siding, drywall, and AC ceilings. As President, Mr. Walston is responsible for all aspects of company operations, including supervision of the roofing crew, framing crew, and commercial crew. Concurrently, Mr. Walston is a Senior Representative for Excell and owns his own real estate business. **Career Steps:** President, J.D. Walston and Associates (1984–Present); Vice President, W.I. Walston (1982–1984). **Associations & Accomplishments:** NABA; WCCC; S.B.4.O.A. **Education:** Attended: E.T. Bedfied

Marvin D. Wilson
Vice President and Chief Executive Officer
Peoples Carpentry, Inc.
408 N. First St.
Ann Arbor, MI 48103
(313) 662–7300
Fax: (313) 662–6369

1531

Business Information: Peoples Carpentry, Inc. is a general contracting and construction management firm, specializing in residential and some commercial remodeling. As Vice President and Chief Executive Officer, Mr. Wilson is responsible for office administration, marketing and sales, as well as overseeing company operations. **Career Steps:** Vice President/CEO, Peoples Carpentry, Inc. (1982–Present); President, Career Paths, Inc. (1994–Present). **Associations & Accomplishments:** First Vice President, Local Home Builders Association. **Education:** Central Michigan University (1971). **Personal:** Married to Leslie in 1978. Three children: Consellow, China, and Blue. Mr. Wilson enjoys music (guitar and vocals) and various sports.

John W. Woods
Controller
American Village Builders, Inc.
4200 West Centre Avenue
Portage, MI 49002–4640
(616) 323–2022
Fax: (616) 323–1899

1531

Business Information: American Village Builders, Inc. is a builder and developer of residential and commercial buildings. Established in 1981, American Village Builders, Inc. currently employs 55 people. As Controller, Mr. Woods is a "hands on" accounting and financial manager responsible for budgeting and forecasting, as well as provides recommendations to homeowners. **Career Steps:** Controller, American Village Builders, Inc. (1994–Present); Certified Public Accountant, Plante & Moran CPA's, LLP (1992–1994); Senior Tax Specialist, KPMG Peat Marwick, LLP (1989–1992); Supervisor, United Parcel Service (1987–1989). **Associations & Accomplishments:** American Institute of Certified Public Accountants; Michigan Association of Certified Public Accountants; Construction Financial Management Association – Southwest Michigan. **Education:** Western Michigan University, B.B.A. (1989). **Personal:** One child: Christopher.

Roy A. Green
• • • ◄━━◉━━► • • •
Resident Civil/Structural Engineer
EMBREE Construction Group, Inc.
6803 Lakewoods Drive, South
Georgetown, TX 78628
(512) 869–2626 Ext. 153
Fax: (512) 869–3442

1541

Business Information: EMBREE Construction Group, Inc. is a national design and building construction firm. The Company designs and builds nationally for Western Auto, Sears, Parts America, NTW Tire Warehouse, Schlotzsky's Delis, and various other business. As Resident Civil/Structural Engineer, Mr. Green is in charge of "value engineering" reviews of EMBREE projects by outside consultants to meet the Company's design criteria. He also performs complete civil and structural design on in–house projects for permit and construction. He works closely with preconstruction, construction, and healthcare division on all problems related to engineering, construction, and field correction. Concurrently, Mr. Green operates his own engineering consulting firm. **Career Steps:** Resident Civil/Structural Engineer, EMBREE Construction Group, Inc. (1995–Present); Project Engineer, Texas National Guard Armory Board (1992–1995); Owner/Manager, Geco Engineering and Design (1979–Present); Resident Civil/Structural Engineer, Austin Independent School District (1984–1989). **Associations & Accomplishments:** American Society of Civil Engineers; National Society of Professional Engineers; Texas Society of Professional Engineers; Formerly on Engineering Team that put Neil Armstrong on the moon (July 1969) (McDonnell–Douglas Astronautics – Subcontractor to NASA); Appointed by National Science Foundation and University of Houston to teach Physics to Junior College Teachers; Taught at University level twice. **Education:** University of Houston, M.S. in Civil Engineering (1972); University of Texas – Austin, B.A. in Physics (1967); Temple Junior College, A.A. in Physics/Engineering (1965). **Personal:** Married to Charu R. in

1971. Two children: Jude Omar and Peyton Elizabeth. Mr. Green enjoys reading, model airplanes, building hot rods, and restoring old cars.

E. Michael Houlihan
Vice President
HS Construction
3401 North Broadway
St. Louis, MO 63147
(314) 621–2222
Fax: (314) 621–8001

1541

Business Information: HS Construction specialized in institutional and industrial construction. As Vice President, Mr. Houlihan is responsible for all aspects of Company operations, including sales and business development. He is currently negotiating a bid for the new Florida training facility for the St. Louis Cardinals. **Career Steps:** Vice President, HS Construction (1988–Present); Vice President, D.I. Tocco & Associates (1983–1988); Project manager, Paric Corporation (1981–1983); Project Engineer, Brunson Construction (1976–1981). **Associations & Accomplishments:** Association of General Contractors; ISFTE. **Education:** University of Illinois, B.L.A. (1973). **Personal:** Single. Three children: Kievin M., Colleen D., and Patricia H.. Mr. Houlihan enjoys scuba diving, golf, art, music, travel, swimming, and spending time with his children.

Manuel Leizan Jr.
• • • ◄━━◉━━► • • •
President and Chief Executive Officer
STATECO P.R., Inc.
Box 153 Senorial Mail Station
Rio Piedras, Puerto Rico 00902–0414
(809) 755–6676
Fax: (809) 755–6770

1541

Business Information: STATECO P.R., INC., a subsidiary of Buildtech Agencies, Inc., is a construction and developing firm providing development, construction and industrial site services for major corporations. Major clientele include Procter & Gamble, Nabisco, and Colgate/Palmolive in Puerto Rico and in the Carribean. STATECO P.R., INC. also has two companies in the U.S., supplying metal building structures to the government and construction companies. Established in 1979, STATECO P.R., INC. reports annual revenue of $9 million and currently employs 116 people. Founding the Company in 1979, Mr. Leizan currently serves as President and Chief Executive Officer and is responsible for all aspects of operations. Concurrent with his position, he also serves on the parent company's Board of Directors as Vice President, setting strategies and development policies. **Career Steps:** President and Chief Executive Officer, STATECO P.R., INC. (1979–Present); Vice President of the Board, Buildtech Agencies, Inc. (1979–Present); General Manager of the Concrete Division, Pavarini Construction Co. (1979). **Associations & Accomplishments:** Director, Cuban American National Foundation, Washington, D.C.; Member, Associated General Contractors of America, S.J. Puerto Rico; Camara Comercio Espana en Puerto Rico, S.J. Puerto Rico; Member, Rio Mar Country Club, S.J. Puerto Rico. **Education:** University of Miami, Engineering (1970). **Personal:** Married to Rosalinda Leizan in 1970. Four children: Annette, Manuel III, Jaime, and Veronica. Mr. Leizan enjoys spending time with his family, boating, golf, antiques, and classic automobiles.

Ronald L. Pelerose
Regional Safety Manager
Marshall Contractors
26 Perimeter Center East, Suite 2690
Atlanta, GA 30346
(770) 392–0932
Fax: (770) 392–0621

1541

Business Information: Marshall Contractors provides construction management personnel who supervise jobs from the design phase through the finished building. The Company specializes in the construction of cleanrooms, labs, fiber–optic facilities, pharmaceutical and bio–technological production facilities, and food processing plants. As Regional Safety Manager, Mr. Pelerose is responsible for writing job–specific safety programs, accident investigation, jobsite inspections, and acting as a liaison between the owners and site management teams. **Career Steps:** Regional Safety Manager, Marshall Contractors (1993–Present); Regional Safety Manager, Green International (1989–1993); Safety Director, Trescon Corporation (1982–1989). **Associations & Accomplishments:** Professional Member, American Society of Safety Engineers; Associated Builders and Contractors of Georgia: Member of Board of Directors, Chairman of CEFGA Safety Committee. **Education:** University of Pittsburgh, B.S. (1974); Georgia Institute of Technology, Continuing Education Programs. **Personal:** Married to Debbie in 1981. Two children: Justin and Adam. Mr. Pelerose enjoys golf, motorcycles, and restoring cars.

Ronald F. Roberts
President
Taggart Brothers, Inc.
P.O. Box 1
Castleton, VT 05735–0001
(802) 468–5797
Fax: (802) 468–5302
1541

Business Information: Taggart Brothers, Inc. is a general contractor, specializing in commercial, industrial and institutional buildings. Joining Taggart Brothers in 1976, Mr. Roberts currently serves as President and General Manager. He is responsible for the oversight of all aspects of the business, including field operations, financial matters, estimations, project management, and sales. **Career Steps:** President, Taggart Brothers, Inc. (1976–Present); General Manager, F. P. Elnicki, Inc. (1976); Estimator and Project Manager, Roy M. Wright, Inc. (1974–1975); Estimator and Project Manager, T. A. Daley & Sons, Inc. (1967–1974); Civil Engineer, City of Springfield, MA (1954–1967). **Associations & Accomplishments:** Associated Builders and Contractors; Rutland Regional Chamber of Commerce. **Education:** Attended: Lowell Tech. (1967–1968). **Personal:** Married to Ann L. in 1957. Five children: Karen, Andrew, Steven, James, and John. Mr. Roberts enjoys sailing, golf, and antiques.

David L. Robison
Division Manager
Swinerton and Walberg Company
1995 Laurelwood Road
Santa Clara, CA 95504
(408) 567–9755
Fax: (408) 567–9754
1541

Business Information: Swinerton and Walberg Company is a commercial, industrial, building contractor specializing in high–rise buildings, airports, clean room, and bio–tech facilities. Comprised of five locations and three subsidiaries, the Company has offices in Los Angeles, San Diego, Denver, San Francisco, and Santa Clara. Established in 1888, Swinerton and Walberg Company employs over 375 people, and has an estimated annual revenue in excess of $500 million. As Division Manager, Mr. Robison is responsible for all supervisory responsibilities. He oversees financial management, handles business operations, and evaluates projects. Additional duties include selection and scheduling of teams, preparing reports for headquarters. **Career Steps:** Division Manager, Swinerton and Walberg Company (1995–Present); Executive Officer of Construction, Teccon Construction, Inc. (1984–1995); Project/Division Manager, S.K. Brown Construction, Inc. (1981–1984); Adjunct Professor, "Clean Room Construction and Design", University of San Jose State. **Associations & Accomplishments:** American Society of Professional Estimators (ASPE); Founding Member #55; Building Owners and Managers Association (BOMA). **Education:** University of Nevada. **Personal:** Married to Kathryn A. in 1992. One child: Taylor M. Mr. Robison enjoys antique Civil War and American Indian artifacts, paintings and historical memorandums, spending time with his family, and going to antique shows with his wife.

Randall B. Roe
Vice Chairman
Burns and Roe Enterprises, Inc.
1400 K Street North West, Suite 910
Washington, DC 20005–2403
(202) 898–1500
Fax: (202) 898–1561
1541

Business Information: Burns and Roe Enterprises is a comprehensive engineering, construction, operations, and maintenance company providing services to private and governmental clients worldwide. The Firm's professional services run the gamut from project inception to operations — including consultation and studies, preliminary engineering, detailed engineering and design, construction management, tests, and start–up services — a recognized leader in new technologies for the efficient and environmentally sound use of fossil fuels, ranking 8th among the Top 20 design firms in the Power Industry. Consultation experience extends to environmental engineering, industrial, commercial, and governmental facilities construction and management, defense and aerospace projects, as well as transportation and infrastructure construction and rehabilitation. Other services provided include construction management, operations and maintenance support, plant support, and information and CAD/CAM services. Mr. Roe has provided executive leadership to international and corpo-

rate business development since joining the company in 1977. Most recently promoted to Vice Chairman in 1995, he is presently responsible for coordinating business development with the private sector, federal agencies, and the United States Congress. **Career Steps:** Burns and Roe Enterprises: Vice Chairman and Director of International and Corporate Development (1995–Present), Corporate Vice President and Director of International and Corporate Development (1979–1995), Assistant to the President and Manager of Proposals (1977–1979). **Associations & Accomplishments:** Nuclear Energy Institute; American Marketing Association; MHD Forum; Alternate Director, National Council on Synthetic Fuels Production; National Energy Resource Organization; National Space Club; Society of American Military Engineers; Washington Business Roundtable; National Press Club; Washington Coal Club; Advisory Council, Korea Economic Institute of America; George Washington University Business Council; Board of Trustees, American Near East Refugee Aid; Board of Trustees, International College of Beirut, Lebanon; Board of Directors, Washington Area Tennis Foundation; Board of Trustees, Washington Opera Company at the Kennedy Center; Board of Governors and Treasurer, Washington International Court Tennis Club; Chairman, Washington Opera Finance Committee (1995–1996); Washington Opera Ball Committee (1994–1996); Founders and Patriots of America; Sons and Daughters of the American Revolution; Board of Trustees, The Grafton School – Winchester, Virginia; Board of Trustees, Meridian International Center; Board of Trustees, Suffield Academy; Honorary Director, Palm Beach Tennis Foundation. **Education:** George Washington University, M.B.A. (1977); Syracuse University, B.S. (1967); Suffield Academy (1963). **Personal:** Married to Marylou in 1971. Mr. Roe enjoys tennis, golf, skiing, bicycling, swimming, equestrian, and skating. He is also an opera enthusiast.

Sharon S. Spurlin
Controller
American Ref–Fuel Company
777 N. Eldridge Parkway
Houston, TX 77079–4425
(713) 584–4658
Fax: (713) 584–4698
1541

Business Information: American Ref–Fuel Company is a construction company, specializing in the construction of waste–to–energy remediation and recycling facilities throughout the East Coast. Established in 1981, American Ref–Fuel Company reports annual revenue of $225 million and currently employs 450 people. As Controller, Mrs. Spurlin is responsible for all aspects of financial activities, including budgeting, cost accounting, and supervision of a staff of 50 people. **Career Steps:** Controller, American Ref–Fuel Company (1994–Present); Audit Manager, Arthur Andersen & Co. (1987–1994). **Associations & Accomplishments:** Texas Society of Certified Public Accountants; Treasurer and Board Member, The Parish School. **Education:** Texas A&M University–Kingsville, B.B.A. (1987). **Personal:** Married to Steve in 1993. One child: Trevor. Mrs. Spurlin enjoys basketball.

Steven Y. Summers, P.E.
Business Unit Manager
James N. Gray Construction Company
250 West Main Street
Lexington, KY 40507
(606) 281–9210
Fax: (606) 252–5300
EMAIL: See Below
1541

Business Information: James N. Gray Construction Company specializes in the design and construction of industrial facilities. Established in 1960, the Company is responsible for such recent projects as the Fruit of the Loom plants in Vidalia, Louisiana, and Campbellsville, Kentucky, as well as developments involving Toyota, Walmart, and the Motor Wheel Corporation. Employing 250 people, the Company has an estimated annual revenue of $175 million. As Business Unit Manager, Mr. Summers is responsible for sales and management of industrial and commercial design/build projects. During the past year he was responsible for the sales and execution of over $50 million dollars worth of design and construction services, accomplished through coordination of leads from the sales department with a core group of 5–6 project and design managers to complete an individual gross margin goal. Internet users can reach him via: Ssummers@jngray.com. **Career Steps:** James N. Gray Construction Company: Business Unit Manager (1995–Present), Senior Project Manager (1985–1995), Project Manager (1982–1985). **Associations & Accomplishments:** Kentucky Society of Professional Engineers; Aircraft Owners and Pilots Association. Licensed as a General Contractor in Florida, North Carolina, South Carolina, Louisiana, Arizona, New Mexico, and California. **Education:** Western Kentucky University, B.S., (cum laude) (1980). **Personal:** Married to Amy in 1985. Two children: Michael and Daniel. Mr. Summers enjoys golf, scuba diving, and flying. He has a commercial pilot license and multi–enginee and instrument ratings.

Lee C. Williams

Owner and Chief Financial Officer
Williams Development & Construction, Inc.
8990 Hempstead Road, Suite 200
Houston, TX 77008
(713) 683–8444
Fax: (713) 680–0204
1541

Business Information: Williams Development & Construction, Inc. is a general construction firm specializing in strictly commercial construction for such companies as Walmart and Albertsons, as well as several school districts. The Company, located in Houston, Texas, and established in 1983, operates throughout the state. As Chief Financial Officer & Owner, Ms. Williams, who took over from her husband Craig in 1987, is responsible for accounts payable and receivable, bonding and insurance requirements, and sub–contractors, as well as overseeing an accounting staff. **Career Steps:** Chief Financial Officer & Owner, Williams Development & Construction, Inc. (1987–Present); Broker – Real Estate, J.B. Goodwin (1982–1987); Securities Assistant, E.F. Hutton (1978–1982). **Associations & Accomplishments:** Construction Financial Management Association; Associated General Contractors; Texas Board of Realtors. **Education:** University of Texas, B.A. (1978). **Personal:** Married to Craig in 1987. Two children: Ashley and Amy. Ms. Williams enjoys boating.

Barry L. Allred
President and Chief Executive Officer
Elkins Constructors, Inc.
4501 Beverly Avenue
Jacksonville, FL 32210
(904) 384–6455
Fax: (904) 387–1303
1542

Business Information: Elkins Constructors, Inc. is a general contracting company specializing in commercial building construction and utility work. Negotiating sixty percent of their work, construction management and design contract work ranges from $1–15 million throughout Florida and Georgia. Established in 1955, Elkins Constructors, Inc. reports annual revenue of $50 million and currently employs 80 people. As President and Chief Executive Officer, Mr. Allred is responsible for all aspects of operations, including administration, sales, personnel supervision, consultation, and management of construction activities. A staff of three vice presidents and a controller report to him. **Career Steps:** President and Chief Executive Officer, Elkins Constructors, Inc. (1984–Present); Vice President, BMW Constructors, Inc. **Associations & Accomplishments:** Rotary International; Associated General Contractors of America; Cornerstone–Jacksonville Chamber of Commerce; Director and Vice Chair, Private Industry Council – Jacksonville; Director and Treasurer, River Region Human Services – Jacksonville. **Education:** Butler University, M.B.A. (1974); University of Evansville, B.S. in Mechanical Engineering (1970). **Personal:** Married to Alice. Mr. Allred enjoys boating in his leisure time.

Dr. Ashvani A. Bhatt
Consulting Engineer
Raytheon Engineers & Constructors
30 South 17th Street, Mail Drop 406
Philadelphia, PA 19103
(215) 422–1693
Fax: (215) 422–4102
1542

Business Information: Raytheon Engineers & Constructors is an international construction and engineering systems consulting firm having diversified divisions as follows: Defense Division — provides systems engineering design of submarine and aircraft integrated systems; and Construction Division — provides all aspects of building/system integration consulting, design and facilities construction for process control to pharmaceutical and food industries worldwide. As Consulting Engineer and a specialist in automation, Dr. Bhatt consults with clients on automation issues, as well as evaluates vendors for contracts. 6,000 professional engineer consultant, administrative and site workers. **Career Steps:** Consulting Engineer, Raytheon Engineers & Constructors, (1993–Present); Manager, Platform, Dow Jones (1992–1993); Director of Application Development, Leeds & Northrup Company (1976–1991). **Associations & Accomplishments:** Institute of Electrical and Electronic Engineers. **Education:** Drexel University, Ph.D. (1976); Drexel University, M.S. (1971). **Personal:** Married to Pravina in 1972. One child: Son. Dr. Bhatt enjoys Golf and bridge.

Edwin J. Brewer
Regional Manager/Secretary
Andrews Construction Services of Florida
311 Altamonte Commerce Boulevard, Suite 1608
Altamonte Springs, FL 32714
(407) 774–5868
Fax: (407) 774–5689

1542

Business Information: Andrews Construction Services of Florida is a general contractor, specializing in insurance reconstruction and health care facility renovation. The Company has experience in rebuilding disaster areas, covering the entire state of Florida. Andrews Construction Services span nationally, with five managing offices and two satellite project sites. Working in management roles for various subsidiary locations of Andrews Construction since 1989, Edwin Brewer was appointed as Regional Manager/Secretary of the Florida office in 1992. He is responsible for creating new businesses and overseeing all operations in Florida, as well as establishing branch offices and strategic planning. **Career Steps:** Andrews Construction Services: Regional Manager/Secretary – Florida (1992–Present); Construction Manager – Atlanta, GA (1990–1992); Estimator/Sales Representative – Charleston, SC (1989–1990). **Associations & Accomplishments:** Florida Home Builders Association; Florida Chamber of Commerce; Member, Church in the Son, Orlando, FL. **Education:** University of Florida, Bachelor of Building Construction (1974). **Personal:** Married to Sharon Lee (Willie) Brewer in 1968. Four children: Paul, Shanan, James, and Kristen.

Richard E. Carrig
President
Carrig & Dancer Enterprises, Inc.
2601–A Mottman Road SW
Tumwater, WA 98512–5648
(360) 753–5905 (800) 547–5831
Fax: (360) 753–5913

1542

Business Information: Carrig & Dancer Enterprises, Inc. is a general construction firm. Established in 1980, Carrig & Dancer Enterprises, Inc. reports annual revenue of $2.5 million and currently employs 32 people. As President, Mr. Carrig is responsible for all aspects of operations. **Career Steps:** President, Carrig & Dancer Enterprises, Inc. (1980–Present); U.S. Air Force: Manager of Combat Mobility, Manager of Military Affiliation Program, and Manager of 62 MAW Affiliation Program. **Associations & Accomplishments:** Blow–In–Blanket Contractor Association; Association of Weatherization Contractors and Suppliers of Washington; Chairman, Yelm, Washington Park Board; Member, Washington State Energy Office Oil Advisory Group; President, AERIE 4144 FOE; Member, Northwest Power Planning Council Conservation Group. **Education:** University of the Air Force (1977); University of Alaska (1960). **Personal:** Married to Gladys M. in 1963. Two children: Charles Steven and Jennifer Lyn. Mr. Carrig enjoys woodworking, fishing, hunting, and civic functions.

Daniel W. Chattin

President and Chief Executive Officer
Chattin Industries
7745 Greenback Lane, Suite 210
Citrus Heights, CA 95610
(916) 726–8416
Fax: (916) 726–2041

1542

Business Information: Chattin Industries is a general contractor and commercial construction contractor for Federal government projects. Founding Chattin Industries as President and Chief Executive Officer in 1992, Mr. Chattin, a 33–year old entrepreneur, is responsible for all aspects of operations, in addition to overseeing all administrative operations for associates and a support staff of 22. **Career Steps:** President and Chief Executive Officer, Chattin Industries (1992–Present); President, Chattin Investments (1989–1992). **Associations & Accomplishments:** Sacramento Chamber of Commerce; Native American Contractors

Association; Northern Sacramento Golf Association; Member of the local country club; Democratic Party; Featured in the Los Angeles Times and the Sacramento Business Journal. **Education:** University of Colorado, B.S. in Political Science (1985). **Personal:** Mr. Chattin enjoys golf and snow skiing.

Charles F. Cogswell
Regional Manager
W.R. Adams Company, Inc.
677 Church Street
Marietta, GA 30060
(770) 793–7740
Fax: (770) 793–7739

1542

Business Information: W.R. Adams Company, Inc. is a program management consulting firm, specializing in large healthcare construction projects and facilities development. National in scope, the Company has locations in Georgia (Rome, Marietta) and Richmond, Virginia. As Regional Manager, Charles Cogswell oversees all projects within W.R. Adams Southwest Region, as well as manages all major hospital construction projects. **Career Steps:** W.R. Adams Company Inc.: Regional Manager (1995–Present), Senior Program Manager (1989–1995); Vice President, Landmark American Corporation (1984–1989); Refining Engineer, Exxon Company USA (1979–1983). **Education:** Vanderbilt University, Bachlor of Engineering, magna cum laude (1979). **Personal:** Married to Tracy in 1995. Two children: Lawson and Hayden. Mr. Cogswell enjoys tennis, biking, running, church, and family.

Duane J. Cook

President
The Southern Group Inc.
P.O. Box 8829
Columbus, MS 39705–8829
(601) 328–0636
Fax: (601) 327–0324

1542

Business Information: The Southern Group Inc. is a general construction company. Established in 1995, the Company contracts throughout Northeast Mississippi and Lokindes County, primarily serving the Columbus, Mississippi metro area. As President, Mr. Cook is responsible for all aspects of operations. **Career Steps:** President, The Southern Group Inc. (1995–Present); Estimator and Project Manager, Phillips Contracting Company, Inc. (1994–1995); Estimator and Project Manager, T.L. Wallace Construction, Inc. (1991–1994). **Associations & Accomplishments:** Associated Builders and Contractors, Inc.; The Exchange Club. **Education:** University of Southern Mississippi, B.S. (1991); Mississippi Gulf Coast Junior College, A.S. **Personal:** Mr. Cook enjoys challenging activities.

Marcus Andrew Cox
Project Manager
Crossland Construction Company
Highway 69, P.O. Box 45
Columbus, KS 66725
(316) 429–1414
Fax: (316) 429–1412

1542

Business Information: Crossland Construction Company is a general contractor specializing in commercial construction projects, including jails, schools, churches, warehouses, and malls. As Project Manager, Mr. Cox is responsible for the coordination of all schedules, material procurement, pay applications, accounting, submittals, and other related activities. **Career Steps:** Crossland Construction Company: Project Manager (1995–Present), Superintendent (1993–1995). **Education:** Oklahoma State University, B.S. in Engineering Technology (1994). **Personal:** Married to Melissa in 1991. Mr. Cox enjoys golf.

Michael H. Curran
Chief Financial Officer
Continental Development Corporation
P.O. Box 916
El Segundo, CA 90245–0916
(310) 640–1520
Fax: (310) 414–9279

1542

Business Information: Continental Development Corporation is a builder of office park developments in California. As Chief Financial Officer, Mr. Curran oversees all day–to–day

operations, focusing on financial reporting and MIS direction. He also serves on the Board of Directors as Treasurer, responsible for all P&L, annual financial reporting and strategies. **Career Steps:** Chief Financial Officer, Continental Development Corporation (1993–Present); Executive Vice President and Chief Financial Officer, Doric Development, Inc. (1990–1993); Executive Vice President and Chief Financial Officer, Real Property Resources, Inc. (1979–1990). **Associations & Accomplishments:** International Council of Shopping Centers; American Management Association; Los Angeles Junior Chamber of Commerce; Cerritos Chamber of Commerce; Sacramento Chamber of Commerce. **Education:** University of Southern California, M.B.A. (1971); Loyola University, B.B.A. in Finance (1970). **Personal:** Married to Vicki Rowland in 1978. Two children: Sean Patrick and Robert Michael. Mr. Curran enjoys martial arts, cycling, squash, and coaching youth basketball.

Walter B. Denmead
Project Executive
Turner Construction Company
353 Sacramento Street
San Francisco, CA 94111
(415) 274–2900
Fax: (415) 989–1370
EMAIL: See Below

1542

Business Information: Turner Construction Company, established in 1902, is a general contracting and construction management firm. The Company specializes in the construction of government buildings, hospitals, institutions, research buildings, and bio pharmaceutical establishments. As Project Executive, Mr. Denmead is responsible for multiple projects, following each from negotiation through final closeout. He works closely with other members of the management staff on developing budgets for projects, submitting information for contract bids, and strategic planning for the future of the company. Other duties include public relations and overseeing the activities of 2,800 employees. Internet users can reach him via: wdenmead@turner.com. **Career Steps:** Turner Construction Company: Project Executive (1986–Present), Project Manager (1979–1986), Project Engineering Support (1965–1974). **Associations & Accomplishments:** International Society of Professional Engineers (ISPE). **Education:** St. Mary's College, M.B.A. (1982); Stevens Institute of Technology, Mechanical Engineer Degree. **Personal:** Married to Ellen in 1966. One child: Kenneth. Mr. Denmead enjoys golf, sewing, weaving, and woodworking.

Pradeep Desai
Executive Vice President of Procurement
A. J. Contracting
15 Fox Run
North Caldwell, NJ 07006
(212) 889–9100
Fax: (201) 228–3894

1542

Business Information: A. J. Contracting is a general contracting firm concentrating in the construction of non–residential buildings. Established in 1917, A. J. Contracting reports annual revenue of $250 million and currently employs 150 people. As Executive Vice President of Procurement, Mr. Desai is responsible for all aspects of company purchasing. **Career Steps:** Executive Vice President of Procurement, A. J. Contracting. **Associations & Accomplishments:** Chairman, Association of Indian in Construction Industry (AICI); Member, American Society of Civil Engineers (ASCE). **Education:** Polytechnic Institute of New York, M.S. (1975), B.S. in Civil Engineering. **Personal:** Married to Rekha in 1973. Two children: daughter, Krupa and son, Tejas. Mr. Desai enjoys golf and music.

Todd A. Engstrom
Vice President of Dobie Operations
American Campus Lifestyles – Dobie Center
2021 Guadalupe
Austin, TX 78705
(512) 505–1000
Fax: (512) 505–0006

1542

Business Information: American Campus Lifestyles specializes in financing, building, and managing on and off campus student housing. A full service organization, the Company provides all amenities including food service areas, study and parking areas. National in scope, the Company actively seeks third party management and building opportunities. Dobie Center is a 27 story private student residence hall serving students of the University of Texas at Austin. The Center offers 947 beds and an integrated retail mall. As Vice President of Dobie Center, Mr. Engstrom is responsible for all areas of operation including directing over 100 employees in the areas of business administration, residence life/student development, food service, maintenance, housekeeping, marketing, leasing, accounting and reporting. Mr. Engstrom has been in the student housing industry for almost 25 years, serving in a variety of positions from student worker to Vice President of Operations, allowing him to have an indepth understanding of management of student housing on every level. His hard work over the years has brought beneficial results to the companies for which he has worked, such as increased occupancy rates and managing large refurbishment programs. **Career Steps:** Vice President of Dobie Center, American Campus Lifestyles (1994–Present); General Manager of Cash Hall, Allen & O'Hara, Inc. (1989–1993); Cardinal Campus Communities: Stadium Club Apts., Director of Operations ; Fontanna Hall, General Manager (1985–1988); Osceola Hall, General Manager (1982–1985); Allen & O'Hara – Summit Hall: Resident Manager (1976–1982), Resident Director (1974–1976), Resident Assistant (1973–1974). **Associations & Accomplishments:** University Area Partners Association; Guadalupe Street Beautification Finance Chairperson; ACUHO; NACUBO. **Education:** West Virginia University: M.B.A. (1982), B.A. in Liberal Arts. **Personal:** Married to Debbie in 1982. Two children: Jason and Brian. Mr. Engstrom enjoys golf, reading, self improvement, and being a good husband and father.

James J. Heinz

President
Heinz–Fischer, Inc.
12961 Maurer Industrial Drive
St. Louis, MO 63127–1515
(314) 842–7010
Fax: (314) 842–2766

1542

Business Information: Heinz–Fischer, Inc. is a general contractor serving clientele in a 300–mile radius, specializing in the construction of cellular tower facilities. With thirteen years expertise in the construction industry, Mr. Heinz co–founded Heinz–Fischer, Inc. as President in 1993. He is responsible for marketing and estimating. In addition, Mr. Heinz oversees all administrative operations for associates and a support staff of 7. **Career Steps:** President, Heinz–Fischer, Inc. (1993–Present); Project Manager, Kozeny–Wagner, Inc. (1984–1993); Project Manager, K&S Associates (1983–1984). **Associations & Accomplishments:** Southern Illinois University – Edwardsville Construction Alumni Society. **Education:** Southern Illinois University – Edwardsville, B.S. in Construction Engineering (1983); Belleville Area College, A.S. in Construction Management (1980). **Personal:** Married to Deborah M. in 1983. Two children: Nick and Jordan. Mr. Heinz enjoys golf and swimming.

Gary S. Jaslovsky

Project Manager
Graycor
One Graycor Dr.
Homewood, IL 60430–4618
(708) 206–0500
Fax: (708) 206–0505

1542

Business Information: Graycor is a construction company consisting of a number of business units including: Commercial and Retail – involved with office space, strip malls, retail stores, etc.; Light Industrial – involved in automotive, healthcare, and pharmaceutical industries; Heavy Industrial – involved in steel mills and power plants. As Project Manager, Mr. Jaslovsky is responsible for the management of projects in the Heavy Industrial Unit, including the power, metal, and other heavy industries. He is the principal interface between the architects, engineering, and construction crews, including having profit and loss accountability of the project, scheduling, and safety regulations. **Career Steps:** Project Manager, Graycor (1991–Present); Project Manager, Ambitech Engineering Corporation (1988–1991); Manager of Projects, FMC Corporation (1979–1988). **Education:** New Jersey Institute of Technology, B.S. in Chemical Engineering (1975). **Personal:** Married to Susan in 1990. Three children: Ryan, Logan, and Erin. Mr. Jaslovsky enjoys golf, home remodeling, carpentry, cabinetry, and fishing.

Vincent G. Johnson

Chief Operating Officer
Riparius Construction, Inc.
215 Cardinal Drive
Shrewsbury, PA 17361
(410) 561–3356
Fax: (410) 561–4565

1542

Business Information: Riparius Construction, Inc. is a general contracting company, specializing in construction management and design building for its own accounts, as well as private accounts from a regional office in Maryland. The Corporation's niche is in the construction of bio–tech pharmaceutical laboratory manufacturing facilities. Major projects have included: Otsuka Pharmaceutical Company, Ltd in Rockville, MD; SmithKline Beecham Diagnostic Laboratories in Owings Mills, MD; Jason Pharmaceuticals in Baltimore, MD; Salisbury District Court/Multi–Service Center and parking structure in Salisbury, MD; and others. With more than thirty years of experience in civil engineering and commercial construction, Mr. Johnson joined Riparius Construction, Inc. as Executive Vice President in 1987 and was appointed as President in 1990. Serving as Chief Operating Officer since 1995, he is responsible for the day–to–day operations of the Company, including profitability, directing all field operations, goal achievement, and ensuring that the construction of high–quality buildings are in compliance with time requirements, budgets, and client's expectations. Mr. Johnson is considered by many of his peers to be a leading authority on the design and construction of sophisticated biotech pharmaceutical manufacturing plants, but he is quick to point out that any successes that he has enjoyed are due to a caring wife, an excellent staff, and God's grace. He claims Philippians 4:13 as his management inspiration. "I can do all things through Christ who strengthens me." **Career Steps:** Riparius Construction, Inc.: Chief Operating Officer (1995–Present), President (1990–1995), Executive Vice President (1987–1990); President, Myers & Chapman (1986–1987); Executive Vice President, McCormick Construction, Inc. (1985–1987). **Associations & Accomplishments:** Shrewsbury Assembly of God Church; Specifications Institute; Who's Who in American Colleges and Universities; Published in Engineering News Record; Member of Promise Keepers, the Christian men's integrity movement; Christian Business Men's Committee; Full Gospel Business Men's Fellowship; He is licensed by the Florida State Commission Industry Licensing Board as a General Contractor; Mr. Johnson is proud that he was nominated and selected by the Department of the Army as a private citizen to attend the annual U.S. War College, Carlisle Barracks, Pennsylvania, conference on National Security. **Education:** C.W. Post College of Long Island University, B.S. in Civil Engineering (1964); The Pennsylvania State University, Graduate School; He has completed the University of Maryland's 4 track Master's Level 2–year program for FDA Regulatory Affairs and current Good Manufacturing Practices (cGMP) for the design and construction of pharmaceutical facilities. **Personal:** Married to Janet Mae in 1954. Five children: Janet, Vincent, Nancy, Gary, and Diane. Mr. Johnson enjoys reading, golf, and spending time with his twelve grandchildren.

Carol S. Libs

President
C.S.L. Enterprises, Inc.
209 Quality Avenue, Suite 9
New Albany, IN 47150–7256
(812) 941–0013
Fax: (812) 941–0014

1542

Business Information: C.S.L. Enterprises, Inc. is a concrete construction and development company for the heavy–highway and commercial markets (i.e., large industrial buildings, schools, and hospitals). With thirty–one years of experience in the construction industry, Ms. Libs has earned the respect as an outstanding professional woman in a man's career. She established C.S.L. Enterprises, Inc. in 1989 and serves as its President and Chief Executive Officer. Ms. Libs is responsible for all aspects of operations, including administration, finances, public relations, accounting, marketing, and strategic planning. **Career Steps:** President, C.S.L. Enterprises, Inc. (1989–Present); Vice President, Arthur M. Libs & Sons, Inc. (1965–1989). **Associations & Accomplishments:** Vice Chair, Floyd Memorial Hospital Foundation Board; President, Floyd County Museum Board; Board of Directors, Southern Indiana Chamber of Commerce; Director, WBE Association of Indiana; Former Director, National Women's Enterprise Association; Recipient, Rising Star Award for small business person by the Chamber of Commerce of Southern Indiana; Active fundraiser for the community. **Education:** Attended Indiana University Southeast. **Personal:** Married to Robert in 1961. Three children: Bobby, Chrys and Robyn. Ms. Libs enjoys golf, tennis, travel, and community service activities.

Mark Liu

Vice President and Principal
Advanced Structures, Inc.
1640 19th Street
Santa Monica, CA 90404
(310) 828–0884
Fax: (310) 828–1504

1542

Business Information: Advanced Structures, Inc. (ASI) is a design, engineering, research and development firm for specialty structures for the construction industry. ASI provides services and technical support, design engineering, construction, consulting, and energy design. "ASI DELIVERS" — and ASI also listened to its clients challenges for innovative solutions to their building problems. Coining the phrase "Inventing the Future of Building", ASI developed a complete systems building process — HyperFrames. Utilizing the HyperFrames system, ASI is able to provide the widest variety of building system solutions in the marketplace, such as space frame structures, long span structures, tensile structures, tension fabric structures, custom space enclosures, monumental skylights, custom curtainwalls, tension–truss glass walls, and domes and shell structures. A designer, project manager and executive with over ten years expertise working with some of the world's leading international architectural design firms, Mark Liu was appointed as Vice President and Principal at ASI in August of 1991. Mr. Liu's current responsibilities include the solidification of new and existing Asian markets and the development of strategic alliances. This led to the Company's first overseas office located in Taipei, Taiwan, established in 1991, to better serve ASI's clients abroad and to create a gateway to Asia. His efforts have resulted in strong sales in the Taiwan market. Projects include the prominent Rapid Transit Stations, and the Park #7 project, located in the heart of Taipei. Born in Taiwan and educated in Hong Kong and the U.S., Mr. Liu's in–depth understanding of the intricate and delicate Asian business cultures provides high level opportunities for ASI. He has consulted with many U.S. firms doing business in Asia and is actively involved with related communities and organizations. Being fluent in both Mandarin and Cantonese, and his earliest work as an architectural designer with several firms in Hong Kong, has helped lay the foundation for ASI's Asian operations. His extensive background includes experience as a senior project manager for a number of sophisticated structures, both in the U.S. and abroad. He has successfully managed a variety of innovative projects incorporating unique structure and cladding systems ranging from space frames to membrane structures. Mark Liu's seasoned management skills were invaluable in his 3–year involvement as the Senior Project Manager on the Biosphere 2 project. His early work as a design specialist included the execution of a number of efficient and cost effective space frame structures for various applications. His strong technical experience provided an ideal background for an increasing involvement in marketing and sales activities. **Career Steps:** Vice President and Principal, Advanced Structures, Inc. (1991–Present); Senior Project Manager, Pearce Structures, Inc. (1985–1991); Designer, Palmer & Turner Architects (1984). **Associations & Accomplishments:** Project Management Institute; Organization of Chinese Americans – Los Angeles Chapter. **Education:** Illinois Institute of Technology, Bachelors of Architecture (1985). **Personal:** Married to Sandra Ahn–Liu in 1994.

Mr. Bruce Lyngaas

Vice President
T&L Omega
3355 West 11th Street
Houston, TX 77008
(713) 863–0000
Fax: (713) 863–101
EMAIL: See Below

1542

Business Information: T & L Omega, a subsidiary of Omega Corporation, is a construction company, providing convenience store construction, petroleum services, and environmental remediation. Joining T&L Omega as Vice President in 1993, Mr. Lyngaas is responsible for quality improvement, operations, sales, electronic laboratory activities, remanufacturing, customer relations, and new business. Internet users can reach him via: BLyngaas@AOL.com **Career Steps:** Vice President, T & L Omega (1993–Present); Service Manager, A.N. Rusche (1987–1993); Owner, Great Western Sign Company (1982–1987). **Associations & Accomplishments:** Petroleum Equipment Institute. **Education:** North Harris County; First Class F.C.C. License to Own and Operate Television and Radio Station **Personal:** Married to Susan F. in 1989. Four children: Christopher, Ellen, Jennifer and Kristi. Mr. Lyngaas enjoys music, electronics and computers.

Robert K. McIntyre

Founder, President and Project Manager
The Mac Group, Inc.
347 New Street
Quakertown, PA 18951
(215) 536–1080
Fax: (215) 536–5786

1542

Business Information: The Mac Group, Inc. is a general mechanical contracting firm for water and wastewater treatment plants throughout the country. Established in 1995, The Mac Group, Inc. reports 1.7 million in contracts and currently employs five people. As Founder, President and Project Manager, Mr. McIntyre is responsible for all aspects of operations. **Career Steps:** Founder, President and Project Manager, The Mac Group, Inc. (1995–Present); Estimator and Project Manager, C & T Associates (1994–1995); Project Manager, M F Ronca & Associates (1992–1994); Estimator, Stone Hill Contracting (1990–1992). **Associations & Accomplishments:** Associated Builders and Contractors; National Utility Contractors Association; Pennsylvania Utility Contractors Association; President and Chairman of Non–Profit, Christian Youth Group – his father is the Pastor, conducts media shows, roller skating parties and contemporary concerts for teens. **Education:** Geneva College, Engineering.

Stephen L. Meranda

Owner/President

Flagship Construction

708 Sherwood Green Court
Mason, OH 45040–2247
(513) 490–4850
Fax: Please mail or call

1542

Business Information: Flagship Construction is a national general contracting and development company, hiring local contractors to design and build restaurants, day care centers, and car washes. As Owner/President, Mr. Meranda is responsible for overseeing daily operations, budgeting, and managing business development and corporate growth. **Career Steps:** Owner/President, Flagship Construction (1992–Present); General Manager/Vice President, Bay Diversified Industries, Inc. (1983–1992); President, Pinnacle Homes, Inc. (1982–1983); General Manager, Vice President, Craftsman Unlimited, Inc. (1978–1981). **Associations & Accomplishments:** National Home Builders Association; Coach, Little League Baseball and Pop Warner Football. **Education:** University of Cincinnati; Several Construction and Business Related Courses. **Personal:** One child: Ryan. Mr. Meranda enjoys scuba diving, golf, sailing, sports, and reading.

G.H. JOHNSON CONSTRUCTION COMPANY

John R. Mohme

Vice President, Estimating

G. H. Johnson Construction Company

5300 West Cypress Street, Suite 261
Tampa, FL 33607–1712
(813) 289–5505
Fax: (813) 289–2817
EMAIL: See Below

1542

Business Information: G. H. Johnson Construction Company is a national, full–service general contracting company, specializing in institutional, commercial, multi–residential, and industrial construction throughout the U.S. Project costs are primarily upper–end, ranging in excess of $20 million, with the Company subcontracting the work and employing engineering and architecture firms for the design work. Known for their quality of work and excellence on each and every aspect, G. H. Johnson has experienced tremendous growth since it was established. With the Company since its inception in 1988, Mr. Mohme serves as Vice President, Estimating and Corporate Qualifier. He is responsible for all aspects of estimating construction projects. Internet users can reach him via: 103404.3623@compuserve.com. **Career Steps:** Vice President, Estimating, G. H. Johnson Construction Company (1988–Present); Chief Estimator and Project Manager, James P. Baldwin, Inc. (1985–1988); Chief Estimator and Project Manager, G. J. Hutton Construction (1983–1985); Senior Estimator, J. Allen Construction (1981–1983). **Associations & Accomplishments:** Sertoma International; Rotary International; Board Member, Secretary (1995), Human Development Center; The Crisis Center. **Education:** University of South Florida, Environmental Engineering (1980); St. Petersburg Junior College, A.A. in Computer Science (1976). **Personal:** Significant Other, Cheryl L. Bradford, RN, CCM. Three children: Susan E. H. Mohme, and Danielle and Brianne Bradford. Mr. Mohme enjoys sculling, cycling, fishing, boating and home remodeling.

Steven R. Myler

Vice President of Field Operations

Myler Company, Inc.

970 North Englewood Drive
Crawfordsville, IN 47933–9725
(317) 362–3353 Ext.112
Fax: (317) 364–8211

1542

Business Information: Myler Company, Inc. is a construction management company specializing in the construction of churches and church affiliated buildings, including religious community schools, gyms, and other necessary church buildings. Currently one of the top nine management companies in the country, with projects in Dallas, Michigan, Pennsylvania, Florida, Alabama, and Concord/Wilmington, North Carolina, the Company plans expansion into North Dakota, following their motto of "Whatever it takes and then some." As Vice President of Field Operations, Mr. Myler oversees all contractors licenses, construction contracts, and manages all superintendents in the various project states. Licensed in six states, he is processing his licensing paperwork in numerous others, and is responsible for all training and personnel management. **Career Steps:** Myler Company, Inc: Vice President of Field Operations (1995–Present), Senior Administrator (193–1995), Field Supervisor (1985–1993). **Associations & Accomplishments:** American Legion; Licensed General Contractor: North Carolina, South Carolina, Virginia, West Virginia, Alabama, and Mississippi. **Personal:** Married to Karen in 1969. Three children: Marilee, Stephanie and Steven and four grandchildren. Mr. Myler enjoys golf, camping, and fishing.

Christopher S. Nolan, CPA

Treasurer and Controller

Damon G. Douglas Company

245 Birchwood Avenue, P. O. Box 1030
Cranford, NJ 07016–1030
(908) 272–0100
Fax: (908) 272–2758
EMAIL: See Below

1542

Business Information: Damon G. Douglas Company is a General Contractor and Construction Management Firm. Established in 1931, the Company conducts business throughout the greater New Jersey and New York areas. A Certified Public Accountant with over eight years in construction financial management and accounting, Christopher Nolan joined Damon G. Douglas in Novermber of 1993. As Treasurer and Controller, he provides the overall executive administration for the areas of MIS, financial reporting and planning, as well as the supervision of clerical and administrative support staff. Internet users can reach him via: DGDCO31@AOL.COM **Career Steps:** Treasurer and Controller, Damon G. Douglas Company (1993–Present); Internal Auditor, Coltec Industries (1991–1993); Senior Accountant, Deloitte and Touche (1987–1991). **Associations & Accomplishments:** Board Member, Construction Financial Management Association; New Jersey State Society of Certified Public Accountants; American Institute of Certified Public Accountants. **Education:** Pace University, B.B.A. in Accounting (1987); Seton Hall University, M.B.A. in Finance (Present). **Personal:** Married to Tracy in 1995. Mr. Nolan enjoys travel, skiing, golf, tennis, and reading.

James R. O'Brien

Vice President

Electronic Environment Corporation

372 University Avenue
Westwood, MA 02090–2311
(617) 461–2600
Fax: (617) 461–1531

1542

Business Information: Electronics Environment Corporation is a designer, builder and servicer of computer rooms, clean rooms, and communications networks in the Northeastern U.S. EEC provides a fleet of 24–hour service vehicles used to maintain temperature control and other maintenance breakdowns. It has also recently formed a national partnership with IBM. Joining Electronics Environment Corporation as Vice President in 1989, Mr. O'Brien is responsible for the supervision of the entire construction staff of project managers and field trades persons. **Career Steps:** Vice President, Electronics Environment Corporation (1989–Present); Senior Project Manager, East Coast Electrical Contractors (1989); Project Manager, Wayne J. Griffin Electric (1984–1988). **Associations & Accomplishments:** T–Ball Coach, Revere Little League; Project Management Institute; Sterling's Who's Who; Commonwealth of Massachusetts; Notary Public. **Education:** Northeast Institute of Industrial Technology, Practical Electricity (1985); Salem State College, A.A. in Accounting and Business Administration; National Burglar and Fire Alarm Association, Burglar and Fire Alarm Technician; State of Massachusetts Master Electrician; Journey Man Electrician; Building Supervisors License; State of Maine and New Hampshire Master Electrician; Fotel Certified Fiber Optics Designer and Installer. **Personal:** Married to Linda in 1980. Two children: John and Derek. Mr. O'Brien enjoys painting, skiing, hiking, karate, and golf.

Jayesh R. Patel

President

Omni Construction Services

P.O. Box 1078
New Castle, DE 19720–7078
(302) 323–1990
Fax: (609) 931–7515

1542

Business Information: Omni Construction Services, established in 1995, is a renovation and construction company for commercial properties, specializing in hotel and motel construction, renovations and sprinkler retrofits. As President, Mr. Patel is responsible for all aspects of operations, including project management. **Career Steps:** President, Omni Construction Services (1995–Present); Turner Construction Co., SPD: Assistant Engineer (1992–1995), Field Engineer (1991–1992); Engineer, Taisei General Constructors – Japan (1989). **Associations & Accomplishments:** American Society of Civil Engineers (ASCE). **Education:** Massachusetts Institute of Technology, M.S. in Civil Engineering (1991); University of Delaware, Bachelors in Civil Engineering and Minor in Biology. **Personal:** Married to Shelpa J. Patel in 1994. Mr. Patel enjoys kayaking, motorcycles, canoeing, and wave running.

Michael D. Phillips

Vice President of Preconstruction

Big D Construction Corporation

4774 S. 1300 W.
Ogden, UT 84405–3621
(801) 392–3200
Fax: (801) 394–3635

1542

Business Information: Big D Construction Corporation is a national commercial contractor specializing in the food processing industries (i.e., dairies, milk plants). Established in 1967 and ranked 98 out of the top 400 contractors, Big D now grosses over $200 million a year. As Vice President of Preconstruction, Mr. Phillips is responsible for business development, finding new clients, estimating costs, and generating working plans for each contract. He joined the company in 1990 as a Senior Estimator and was promoted to his current position in 1992. **Career Steps:** Big D Construction Corporation: Vice President of Preconstruction (1992–Present); Chief Estimator (1991–1992), Senior Estimator (1990–1991); Senior Estimator, Reid & Gary Strickland (1985–1990). **Associations & Accomplishments:** Construction Specification Institute; President, American Society of Professional Engineers. – Salt Lake Chapter; Chairman, Timberline Users Group; Ogden/Weber Chamber of Commerce. **Education:** Fayetteville High School, Diploma (1975). **Personal:** Married to Sandi in 1976. Three children: Austin, Autumn, and Charity. Mr. Phillips enjoys golf and racquetball.

Chris Reynolds

Owner and Vice President

Rey–Bach Inc.

P.O. Box 2333
Sherman, TX 75091
(903) 870–0744
Fax: (903) 870–0938

1542

Business Information: Rey–Bach Inc. is a general contractor for commercial and government building projects. Operating throughout a 100–mile radius of Sherman, Texas, Rey–Bach, Inc. works on approximately 68 projects at a time, primarily in the commercial industry, such as schools and office buildings. The Company primarily conducts renovations and restructuring, but also subcontracts electrical, engineering, and plumbing services. Co–establishing Rey–Bach in 1993, Mr. Reynolds serves as its Owner, Vice President, and one of two partners. He is responsible for all aspects of operations, including bidding and project management functions. **Career Steps:** Owner and Vice President, Rey–Bach Inc. (1993–Present); Owner, Reynolds Custom Homes (1991–1992); Owner, DiamondTree Homes (1989–1990); Manager, United Bilt Homes, Inc. (1983–1989). **Education:** Ouachita Baptist University, B.A. (1983). **Personal:** Married to Judith in 1985. Two children: Jessica and Jordan. Mr. Reynolds enjoys golf and hunting.

Peter Q. Robson

President

Unlimited Construction Services Inc.

P.O. Box 3327
Lihue, HI 96766
(808) 245–7843
Fax: (808) 245–9622

1542

Business Information: Unlimited Construction Services Inc. is a general contracting company specializing in commercial construction. Established in 1990, Unlimited Construction Services, Inc. currently employs 30 people and has an estimated annual revenue of $5 million. As President, Mr. Robson is responsible for all aspects of operations, including business development, administration, project management, and estimates. **Career Steps:** President, Unlimited Construction Services Inc. (Present). **Associations & Accomplishments:** Published in Pacific Business News. **Education:** University of Washington, B.A. (1978). **Personal:** Mr. Robson enjoys riding bicycles, skiing, coaching soccer and being involved in the Cub Scouts.

Jose E. Roque

President
Integral Construction Company, Inc.
4108 Laguna Street
Coral Gables, FL 33146 –140
(305) 446–1707
Fax: (305) 446–1556

1542

Business Information: Geographically covering a range from the Florida Keys to North Palm Beach, Integral Construction Company, Inc. is a commercial and residential general contracting construction company. With an employment of seven and annual sales reaching $6 million, the Company only contracts million dollar projects. As President and Co-Partner, Mr. Jose Roque controls the day–to–day management of Integral Contracting, overseeing estimating, purchasing, and scheduling, with emphasis on new business development. Having a degree in Architecture, he also assists the clientele in layouts, but does not do the actual architectural construction. **Career Steps:** President, Integral Construction Company, Inc. (1994–Present); Managing Member, ICC Commercial, L.C. (1992–1994); Director of Business Development and Senior Project Manager, MK Roark, Inc. (1992). **Associations & Accomplishments:** Building Owners and Managers Association; NAIOP; Childrens Cancer Clinic. **Education:** University of Houston, Texas, B.A. in Architecture (1984); Miami Dade Community College, A.A. (1980). **Personal:** Married to Maria Elena in 1981. Three children: Stephanie Marie, Samantha Helen, and Kyle Joseph. Mr. Roque enjoys basketball, hunting, boating, and the outdoors.

Lemuel Sharp III

President
W.G. Mills, Inc.
3301 Whitfield Ave.
Sarasota, FL 34243
(941) 758–6441
Fax: (941) 753–2235

1542

Business Information: W.G. Mills, Inc. is a Florida–based general contractor/construction management firm, providing diverse services to include multi–family residential, educational facilities, institutional, manufacturing, commercial, and healthcare industries. As President, Mr. Sharp is the major stockholder who oversees key projects on operations level, business development, five branches, and acts as the director of marketing. Mr. Sharp began his career with the company in 1973, six months after the company was established. **Career Steps:** W.G. Mills, Inc.: President (1989–Present), Executive Vice President (1984–1989), Vice President (1980–1984). **Associations & Accomplishments:** State Certified General Contractor; CMAA; Sarasota Chamber of Commerce; Director of Committee of 100; Director, Sarasota Community Blood Bank; Gulfcoast Builders Exchange; Argus Director; Leadership Sarasota; Leadership Manatee; Leadership Southwest Florida; Board of Directors, First Union; University of Florida Advisory Committee; Southern Building Code Congress. **Education:** University of Florida, Bachelor of Building Construction (1972); Licensed Real Estate Sales. **Personal:** Two children: Lindsey and Kendall. Mr. Sharp enjoys golf and tennis.

Johnny Shumate

President
Coalfield Construction Inc.
195 Industrial Park Road
Pikeville, KY 41501
(606) 432–4400
Fax: Please mail or call

1542

Business Information: Coalfield Construction Inc. is a general contracting company. Established in 1993, future goals for the Company include continued expansion throughout the years. After working hard at two jobs for the past 20 years, Mr. Shumate decided to establish Coalfield Construction. In his current capacity as President, Mr. Shumate is responsible for all aspects of operations. He supervises all daily administration, approves bids and contracts, and monitors budgeting and financial matters. Mr. Shumate attributes his success to having the most supportive wife in the world. **Career Steps:** President, Coalfield Construction Inc. (1992–Present). **Personal:** Mr. Shumate, an avid flyer, owns and flys a Cessna 182.

Richard A. Sneed
Executive Vice President
R.J. Griffin & Company, d.b.a. Sebrell/Griffin and Company in North Carolina
5970 Farview Road, Suite 500
Charlotte, NC 28210
(704) 554–0539
Fax: (704) 554–0752

1542

Business Information: R.J. Griffin & Company, d.b.a. Sebrell/Griffin and Company in North Carolina is a general contracting firm, specializing in commercial projects construction to include health care facilities, retail establishments, light industrial buildings, and hotels. Licensed in 27 states, the Company has offices in Atlanta, Georgia (corporate headquarters), Charlotte, North Carolina, and Nashville, Tennessee. Established in 1984, the Company currently employs 70 persons and reports estimated corporate revenue in excess of $100 million. As Executive Vice President, Mr. Sneed is responsible for the administration of all aspects of operations for the Charlotte, North Carolina office. **Career Steps:** Executive Vice President, R.J. Griffin & Company, d.b.a. Sebrell/Griffin and Company in North Carolina (1991–Present); Division Manager – West Coast, R.J. Griffin (1988–1991); Project Manager, Pace Construction Company (1985–1987); Project Manager, McDevitt & Street (1984–1986); Project Coordinator, Gresham & Smith (1979–1983). **Associations & Accomplishments:** Vice President, Home Owners Association. **Education:** University of Tennessee, B.S. in Architecture (1979); Licensed Architect, State of Tennessee (1983). **Personal:** Married since 1981 to Carol S. Sneed. Two children: Laura and Kelsey. Mr. Sneed enjoys golf during his leisure time.

Steve Spain

President
Spain Commercial
11872 Canon Boulevard
Newport News, VA 23606–4227
(804) 873–3577
Fax: (804) 873–8542

1542

Business Information: Spain Commercial, the only Wedge-core Representative in the area, is a general contracting firm, providing commercial work and specializing in hospital construction. Future plans include the expansion of the Company, to include building a 9,000 square foot office building, which is in the construction process. As President, Mr. Spain is responsible for overseeing all operations and handling all estimates and bids. **Career Steps:** President, Spain Commercial (1991–Present); Supervisor, Broccuto Drywall (1984–1991). **Associations & Accomplishments:** Sponsors various activities in the community. **Personal:** Married to Grace M. in 1984. Two children: Ashley and Kayleigh. Mr. Spain enjoys water sports and customizing cars and trucks.

Gilbert P. Thompson Jr.
Vice President and Chief Information Officer
Turner Industries, Ltd.
P.O. Box 2750
Baton Rouge, LA 70821
(504) 922–5048
Fax: (504) 922–5083

1542

Business Information: Turner Industries, Inc. provides industrial construction and maintenance services to businesses. The Corporation has fourteen locations throughout California, Texas, Louisiana, and Alabama. Joining Turner Industries as Vice President and Chief Information Officer in 1993, Mr. Thompson is responsible for leading, directing, and managing technical resources to provide information services to clientele and internal personnel. **Career Steps:** Vice President and Chief Information Officer, Turner Industries, Inc. (1993–Present); Managing Director, Arthur Andersen & Co. (1987–1993). **Associations & Accomplishments:** Board of Directors, Quest – J.D. Edwards User Group; Executive Vice President and Director, Electronic Communications; Advisory Board, MIS Department, Louisiana State University. **Education:** Louisiana State University, B.S. in Accounting (1987). **Personal:** Married to Peggy in 1990. Mr. Thompson enjoys all sports (golf and basketball).

V. Jay Wadman
Founder and Chief Executive Officer
Wadman Corporation
P.O. Box 1458
Ogden, UT 84402–1458
(801) 621–4185
Fax: (801) 621–7232

1542

Business Information: Wadman Corporation is a general building and engineering contractor, concentrating on shopping centers, schools, and government contracts. Established in 1951, Wadman Corporation reports annual revenue of $50 million and currently employs 150 people. As Founder and Chief Executive Officer, Mr. Wadman is responsible for all aspects of operations, including serving as secretary, treasurer, comptroller and chief executive officer. **Career Steps:** Founder and Chief Executive Officer, Wadman Corporation (1951–Present). **Associations & Accomplishments:** Member of the Utah Chapter, Associated Building Contractors; Member, Ogden, Utah Chamber of Commerce; Vice President, American Indian Services – Provo, Utah; Author of two books on his family history (from his grandfather's journey from Liverpool to Utah and his father's journals). **Personal:** Married to June in 1945. Six children: Rick, Larry, Blaine, Grant, David, and Trudi. Mr. Wadman enjoys computers and writing & researching his family history.

Gary F. Watanabe
Vice President
Rojac Construction, Inc.
390 Papa Pl.
Kahului, HI 96732–2425
(808) 871–7079
Fax: (808) 871–4073

1542

Business Information: Rojac Construction, Inc. is a general engineering construction contractor. Beginning his engineering career in 1973, Mr. Watanabe serves as Vice President. He is responsible for all construction operations, with primary duties involving bid estimations, project negotiations, quality service and overall engineering support. **Career Steps:** Vice President, Rojac Construction, Inc. (1995–Present); Vice President – Civil Operations, Fletcher Pacific Construction Company, Inc. (1990–1995); Vice President – Operations, E.E. Black, Ltd. General Contractor (1988–1990); Vice President – Engineering, Hawaii Innovative Engineering, Inc. (1976–1988); Project Engineer, Pacific Construction Company, LTD.,(1973–1976). **Associations & Accomplishments:** National Society of Professional Engineers; Life Member, Amateur Trapshooting Association; Life Member, National Rifle Association; Boy Scouts of America – Cub Scout Pack 68 Webelos Leader; Harley Owners Group. **Education:** Cornell University, Master's Degree in Engineering (1973). **Personal:** Married to Joanne in 1994. Two children: Rhys and Cami. Mr. Watanabe enjoys motorcycling, archery, trapshooting, hunting, skin and scuba diving.

Jim White

Vice President
Environmental Remedies, Inc.
8260 North Highway 35
Alvin, TX 77511–8720
(713) 388–1844
Fax: (713) 388–2261

1542

Business Information: Environmental Remedies, Inc. is a general construction and environmental firm, providing sewer rehabilitation, site work, general contracting, and environmental work. Co–founding Environmental Remedies as Vice President and Partner in 1994, Mr. White is responsible for the overall management, including bidding, estimations, and on-site project supervision. **Career Steps:** Vice President and Partner, Environmental Remedies, Inc. (1994–Present); General Manager, American Egology Corporation (1992–1994); Manager of Operations, Dames & Moore Core Service (1990–1992); General Superintendent, Kinsel Industries (1988–1990). **Associations & Accomplishments:** Alvin Masonic Lodge #762: AF and Galveston Scottish Rite; Associated Builders and Contractors. **Personal:** Married to Becky K. in 1979. Two children: Jessica K. and Jim IV. Mr. White enjoys saltwater fishing, rodeos, and youth organizations.

Thomas H. Wood
President
Branch Construction Company, Inc.
605 Davidson St.
Nashville, TN 37213–1428
(615) 255–7799
Fax: (615) 255–3399

1542

Business Information: Branch Construction Company, Inc., is a general contracting subsidiary of Orion Building Corporation based in Nashville, Tennessee. Branch Construction is a commercial contracting company serving a wide variety of clientele including health care, commercial developers, schools, universities, governmental agencies, and industrial. Branch also has concrete, masonry, and framing divisions which serve other general contractors, as well as self performing on all Branch projects, mainly in the southeastern sector of the U.S. Establishing Branch Construction Company as President in 1994, Mr. Wood is responsible for all aspects of operations, including profits and losses and strategic planning. In addition, he oversees all administrative operations and a support staff of 19. **Career Steps:** President, Branch Construction Company, Inc. (1994–Present); President, THW Management Corporation (1990–1994); Director of Operations, NICO Industries (1987–1990); Project Manager and Estimator, W. E. O'Neill Construction (1985–1987). **Associations & Accomplishments:** Association of General Contractors of America; Association of Builders and Contractors; American Concrete Institute; Secretary, Exchange Club of America. **Education:** Arizona State University, B.S. in Political Science; Arizona State University Graduate School MBA Program. **Personal:** Married to Nancy Carol in 1968. Three children: Barbara, Wendie, and Katherine. Mr. Wood enjoys golf and public speaking.

1600 Heavy Construction, Except Building

1611 Highway and street construction
1622 Bridge, tunnel, and elevated highway
1623 Water, sewer, and utility lines
1629 Heavy construction, NEC

James L. Au
Area Manager
James Julian, Inc.
Route 4, Box 4998
Duncannon, PA 17020–9445
(717) 834–5070
Fax: (717) 834–9575

1611

Business Information: James Julian, Inc., established in 1947, is a construction contract company, specializing in heavy industrial and highway construction. As Area Manager, James Au manages all central and western Pennsylvania operations. His primary duties entail project proposals, bid and contract negotiations, as well as full P&L responsibility for his division. His current focus is on the supervision of Company's $50 million Harrisburg, PA highway reconstruction and widening project. **Career Steps:** Area Manager, James Julian, Inc. (1994–Present); Vice President – Structures Division, HRI, Inc. (1987–1994); Project Manager, General Superintendent, IA Construction (1981–1986). **Associations & Accomplishments:** ASHE, Del Valley, PA Chapter; PE: Pennsylvania, Maryland, Deleware; Associated Pennsylvania Constructors; BPOE, State College, PA. **Education:** Pennsylvania State: B.S.C.E. (1972), Extended Electives in Construction Management, FMI Partnering, and QMI Seminars. **Personal:** Married to Sharon in 1978. Two children: James and John. Mr. Au enjoys baseball, coaching basketball, and golf.

A. D. "Jack" Bailey Jr.
Chief Executive Officer
Triangle Grading & Paving, Inc.
3275 Woodschapel Road
Graham, NC 27253
(910) 376–9837
Fax: (910) 376–8044

1611

Business Information: Triangle Grading & Paving, Inc. is a site contractor, providing concrete and asphalt paving and grading for government contracts, airports, etc., in the Virginia and Carolina areas. Established in 1984, the Company has locations in Graham and Burlington, North Carolina. As Chief Executive Officer, Mr. Bailey is responsible for the day-to-day

operations of the Company, including administration, operations, marketing, and strategic planning. Additionally, he is responsible for providing guidance to employees, overseeing contracts, writing training manuals, and equipment maintenance. He also publishes the Company's newsletter and teaches seminars in construction leadership and training. **Career Steps:** Chief Executive Officer, Triangle Grading & Paving, Inc. (1995–Present); President, Bailey Business Consultants, Inc. (1990–1995); Chairman/Chief Executive Officer, Vidcorp, Inc. (1983–1990); President, United Virginia Development Corporation (1978–1982). **Associations & Accomplishments:** Virginia Road Builders Association: Past Board of Directors, Past District Vice President; Past Board of Directors, Tidewater Business Association; Certified Professional Consultant, Academy of Professional Consultants and Advisors. **Education:** Virginia Polytechnic Institute; North Carolina State. **Personal:** Married to Mary Thomas in 1971. Seven children: Jacqueline, A.D. Jr., Susan, Lynn, Joe, Angela, and Ashley. Mr. Bailey enjoys being active in church seminars throughout the Southeast.

Robert D. Martin
Chairman and Chief Executive Officer
Martin Paving Company
1801 South Nova Road
Daytona Beach, FL 32119–1733
(904) 761–8383
Fax: (904) 756–4326

1611

Business Information: Martin Paving Company, a subsidiary of The Martin Companies, is a family–owned, general contracting company, specializing in highway and heavy construction contracts and providing most phases of horizontal construction (i.e., bridges, highways, roads to airports and subdivisions). Established in 1956, Martin Paving Company currently employs 290 people. A Certified General Contractor and a Certified Highway, Underground Sewer and Water Contractor, Mr. Martin joined his family as Part–Owner in 1972. Appointed as Chairman and Chief Executive Officer in 1980, he is responsible for the oversight of the entire organization, including overall planning and management. **Career Steps:** Chairman and Chief Executive Officer, Martin Paving Company (1972–Present). **Associations & Accomplishments:** Former Chairman (1988–1990), Florida Transportation Builders' Association; President (1993–1995), Florida Asphalt Contractors Association; Board Member, Sun Bank of Volusia County; Former President (1986), Chamber of Commerce of The Daytona Beach and Halifax Area; Board Member, Florida TaxWatch; Board Member, Florida Chamber of Commerce; Board Member, Transportation Road Information Program; Former President (1985), United Way of Volusia County. **Education:** University of Florida, B.S. in Finance (1971). **Personal:** Married to Beverly in 1973. Two children: Julia and Scott. Mr. Martin enjoys golf, football, and basketball.

Starla R. Thurlow, C.P.A.
Controller
Armrel Byrnes Company
11399 Grooms Road
Cincinnati, OH 45242
(513) 489–9400
Fax: (513) 489–1366

1611

Business Information: Armrel Byrnes Company, established during the 1800's, is a major construction holding company. Construction entities consist of the following: Armrel–Byrnes Co. — specializes in underground utilities and highway construction; and Byrnes–Conway Co. — provides utilities construction in a tri–state area. A Certified Public Accountant with over fifteen years expertise in construction and manufacturing accounting, Starla Thurlow joined Armrel–Byrnes in 1992. As Controller/Treasurer, she provides the overall executive administration for all corporate financial aspects. Her major duties entail financial reporting, treasury responsibilities, as well as supervision of all accounting personnel. **Career Steps:** Controller, Armrel Byrnes Company (1993–Present); Controller and Treasurer, Kendrick Brothers Construction Company (1989–1992); Staff Accountant, Farquharson Pointon Pitser (1983–1989); Accounting Department, Savannah Shipyard Company (1980–1983). **Associations & Accomplishments:** American Institute of Certified Public Accountants; Queen City Chief Financial Officers Forum. **Education:** Westminster College, B.S. (1990); University of Utah; Walsh College. **Personal:** Married to Ken R. in 1983. Four children: Anthony, Lori, Stephen, and Mark. Mrs. Thurlow enjoys skiing, sewing, camping, and theater.

N. Wayne Wham Jr.
President and Treasurer
Wham Brothers Construction Company, Inc.
2301 Belhaven Road, P.O. Box 4197
Anderson, SC 29622–4197
(864) 224–3305
Fax: (864) 224–0000

1611

Business Information: Wham Brothers Construction Company, Inc., a family–owned business, performs concrete and asphalt recycling throughout the Southeastern United States along with highway, street, and road construction in South Carolina. The Company operates as WHAM RECYCLING producing construction aggregates from waste concrete and asphalt at the customers site. Wham Brothers Construction Company, Inc. is also involved in land development. With thirty years in the construction industry, Mr. Wham was appointed as President in 1979. Also serving as Treasurer, he is responsible for all aspects of operations, including estimating, purchasing, decision–making, and strategic planning, in addition to overseeing all administrative operations for a support staff of 15. **Career Steps:** Wham Brothers Construction Company, Inc.: President and Treasurer (1979–Present), Supervisor (1969–1979), Forman (1966–1968). **Associations & Accomplishments:** York Rite Bodies; Scottish Rite; Hejaz Shrine Temple; Secretary/Treasurer, Anderson Red Fez Club; Anderson Area Chamber of Commerce; AGC of Carolinas; South Carolina Realtor License. **Education:** Attended: Clemson University. **Personal:** Married to Sylvia Sharpe Wham in 1993. Three children: Christy W. Burnett, Norman W. Wham III (Tripp), and Lexanna R. Jordan. Mr. Wham enjoys white water canoeing and motorcycling.

Bill Wilson Sr.
Risk Manager
Fort Myer Construction Corporation
2237 33rd Street Northeast
Washington, DC 20018
(202) 636–9535
Fax: (202) 635–5564

1611

Business Information: Fort Myer Construction Corporation is a road construction corporation established in 1960, currently employing approximately 500 people. As Risk Manager, Mr. Wilson is responsible for all claim assignments, compensation claims, D.O.T. and OSHA regulations, third party liability payments and the processing of medical billings to three states. **Career Steps:** Risk Manager, Fort Myer Construction Corporation (1990–Present); Safety Director, UFCW Local 400 (1977–1989). **Associations & Accomplishments:** Safety Committee, Board of Directors, Heavy Construction Contractors Association; 1st Vice President, Washington D.C. Area Trucking Association; President, Washington Metropolitan Area Contractors Association; Investor and a collector of authentic Civil War history items. **Education:** Northern Virginia Community College, A.S. in Safety and Health/OSHA 500. **Personal:** Fourteen grandchildren and one great grand child. Mr. Wilson enjoys classical and country music, and watching professional football and college basketball.

Dan L. Baldwin
Project Manager
Kajima Engineering & Construction Company
1635 Argyle Street
Hollywood, CA 90028
(213) 960–1475
Fax: (213) 467–0809

1622

Business Information: Kajima Engineering & Construction Company is a general contracting and engineering company, providing services for general construction projects, buildings, underground subway stations, and tunnel projects. Headquartered in Tokyo, Japan, Kajima Engineering & Construction Company's U.S. subsidiary was established in 1985, currently reporting annual revenue of $300 million, and employing 200 people. With over twenty years expertise in construction engineering management, Mr. Baldwin joined Kajima in 1993. He currently serves as Senior Project Manager, responsible for all construction and engineering activities for the Hollywood & Vine underground subway station, a $50 million project scheduled for completion in four years. **Career Steps:** Project Manager, Kajima Engineering & Construction Company (1993–Present); Project Manager, Plant Construction Company (1990–1993); Project Manager, Robert E. McKee, Inc. (1989–1990). **Associations & Accomplishments:** Associated General Contractors; Certificate of Recognition, City of Los Angeles (1994). **Education:** Texas A&M University, B.S. in Construction Engineering (1976). **Person-

al: Married to Catherine in 1979. Two children: Matt and John. Mr. Baldwin enjoys golf and snow skiing.

Kevin L. Bond
President/Founder
V. J. Enterprises, Inc.
1400 North Mustang Road
Yukon, OK 73099–5105
(405) 350–0282
Fax: (405) 350–0284

1622

Business Information: V. J. Enterprises, Inc. is a construction business specializing in the building of bridges for the State of Oklahoma. As President/Founder, Mr. Bond is responsible for all aspects of Company operations, including the day–to–day operations of the business, administration, strategic planning, public relations, finance, sales, and advertising. **Career Steps:** President/Founder, V. J. Enterprises, Inc. (1985–Present); Foreman, Daryl Bond Construction (1982–1984). **Associations & Accomplishments:** Oklahoma AGC. **Education:** Yukon High School, Diploma (1982). **Personal:** Two children: Keenan and Brady.

Carlos Geraldo C. Magalhaes

Director of Finance
Construtora Oas, Ltda.
Avenue Angelica 2.029–8.0 And.
Sao Paulo, Brazil 01227–200
55–11–236–1475
Fax: 55–11–236–1382

1622

Business Information: Construtora Oas Ltda., established in 1976, is a construction and engineering company. The Company builds roads, bridges, dams, and buildings in Brazil. As Director of Finance, Mr. Magalhaes is responsible for all financial aspects of the Company, including accounting, treasury, and insurance. **Career Steps:** Director of Finance, Construtora Oas Ltda. (1991–Present); Sub–Secretary of Treasury, State of Bahia (1989–1990). President, Companhia de Electricidade do Estado da Bahia (1984–1987). **Education:** Escola de Administracao de Empresas da Bahia, B.A. in Business (1978); Universidade Federal da Bahia, B.S. in Electrical Engineering (1977). **Personal:** Mr. Magalhaes enjoys fine cuisine and wines, and traveling abroad.

Michelle A. Rose

President
Ansley & Sutton Construction Company
8116 Waters Avenue
Savannah, GA 31406
(912) 352–1722
Fax: (912) 352–9372

1622

Business Information: Ansley & Sutton Construction Company is primarily a heavy industrial construction company, providing pile driving, bridges, docks, bulkheads, crane rail, and concrete foundations. Services are provided mainly along the Georgia and South Carolina coast (Brunswick to Hilton Head). Previously owned by Mrs. Rose's father and his partner, Mrs. Rose took over operations of Ansley & Sutton Construction Company in 1992. Serving as President, she is responsible for all aspects of operations, including estimating, accounting, contracts, purchasing, job supervision, insurance, and bonds. Concurrent with her position at Ansley & Sutton, she is part–owner of Ansley Brothers Dockbuilders, Inc., which focuses primarily on residential work. **Career Steps:** Ansley & Sutton Construction Company: President (1992–Present), Corporate Secretary (1983–1992); Field Office Clerk, Batson–Cook Company (1980–1983, 1973–1976) **Associations & Accomplishments:** Associated General Contractors; National Association of Women in Construction. **Education:** Savannah State College, B.B.A. in Accounting (1990). **Personal:** Married to Ronald L. in 1993. Six children: Wayne, David, Julianne, Victoria, Frank, and Frances. Mrs. Rose enjoys auctions, work, and spending time with her children.

Atef M. Sha'aban, P.E.
President
Urban International, Inc.
300 North Third Street
Philadelphia, PA 19106–1193
(215) 922–8080
Fax: (215) 592–1139

1622

Business Information: Urban International, Inc., a subsidiary of Urban Engineers, Inc., is a Philadelphia–based engineering firm which provides highway, bridge and airport design and construction services. Established in 1960, Urban Engineers, Inc. presently employs 320 people and has an estimated annual revenue in excess of $20 million. In his current capacity, Mr. Sha'aban serves as the Principal–in–Charge of the International Design Division. He has been an active member of the international engineering community for 24 years. **Career Steps:** Executive Vice President, Urban Engineers, Inc. (1986–Present); Regional Manager, Team International Saudi Arabia (1980–1986); Assistant District Transportation Engineer, PennDOT, District 6–0 (1976–1980). Mr. Sha'aban's professional engineering career has included managerial responsibility for a number of key transportation projects including IVHS initiatives along the I–476 and I–95 Corridors in the Philadelphia area. He also played a key role in such large–scale transportation planning and design projects that span from introducing the Public Transportation System to the Kingdom of Saudi Arabia, including the Diplomatic Quarters (DQ) in Riyadh; to Interchange 7 Relocation on the New Jersey Turnpike and the I–76 Rehabilitation in Montgomery County, PA, in the United States. **Associations & Accomplishments:** Professional Society of Civil Engineers – Pennsylvania, New Jersey, Delaware, New York; Lebanese Society of Professional Engineers; American Society of Highway Engineers; Intelligent Vehicle Highway System (IVHS) America; Institute of Transportation Engineers; American Task Force for Lebanon; Arab– American Anti Discrimination Committee (ADC). **Education:** Villanova University, Masters of Science in Civil Engineering for both Structures and Transportation–Planning; North Carolina State University, Bachelors Degree in Construction Management. **Personal:** Married since 1970 to Mona. Three children: Sam, Tim, and Shireen. Mr. Sha'aban enjoys scuba diving, soccer, chess, reading, and international cultural events in his leisure time.

Noel Velez

Engineer
Del Valle Group
State Road 865 KM .06 Camp Pamilla Ward
Toa Baja, Puerto Rico 00951
(787) 794–0927
Fax: (787) 794–3434

1622

Business Information: Del Valle Group is a construction company specializing in earthwork, highway construction, bridge construction, and building construction. Established in 1988, the Company has over 500 employees and estimate revenues in excess of $3 million in 1996. As Engineer, Mr. Velez is responsible for compiling data for pre–bid and bid meetings and proposal preparation. Other responsibilities include evaluating and updating the existing computer systems and PC's, estimating costs on civil engineering projects, and conducting site visits on on–going projects. **Career Steps:** Engineer, Del Valle Group (1993–Present). **Associations & Accomplishments:** College of Engineers and Land Surveyors of Puerto Rico: Institute of Civil Engineers of Puerto Rico; Zeta Phi Beta Fraternity. **Education:** University of Puerto Rico, B.S.C.E. (1993).

Steve E. Foutz

Vice–President, Secretary–Treasurer, and General Manager
Foutz & Bursum Construction Company
P.O. Box 307
Farmington, NM 87499–0307
(505) 325–2413
Fax: (505) 326–3213

1623

Business Information: Foutz & Bursum Construction Company specializes in pipeline construction and the installation and maintenance of plants and compressors. After serving in various administrative capacities within the family business, Mr. Foutz was promoted to Vice President and General Manager in 1994, concurrently performing the duties of Secretary–Treasurer. He is currently responsible for contract negotiation, personnel and equipment supervision, and financial management. **Career Steps:** Foutz & Bursum Construction Company:

General Superintendant (1988–1990), Secretary–Treasurer (1990–1994), Vice President, Secretary–Treasurer, and General Manager (1994–Present). **Associations & Accomplishments:** Rocky Mountain Contractors Association. **Education:** Attended, Eastern Arizona (1975). **Personal:** Married to Debbie in 1976. Four children: Steve Jr., Lacie, Crystal and Jessica. Mr. Foutz enjoys fly fishing and rodeos.

Brian L. Ganske
Vice President
Snelson Companies, Inc.
601 West State
Sedro Wolley, WA 98284–0312
(360) 856–6511
Fax: (360) 856–6511

1623

Business Information: Snelson Companies, Inc., founded in 1948 in Sedro Woolley, Washington, is a national general contracting company diversified into various industrial areas including, main line and distribution gas lines, mechanical construction for the pulp industry, refinery maintenance, and refineries. Joining Snelson Companies, Inc. in 1969, Mr. Ganske became one of the Corporate owners in 1990 and was appointed as Vice President in 1991. He is responsible for the administrative aspects of the Corporation. **Career Steps:** Vice President, Snelson Companies, Inc. (1969–Present). **Associations & Accomplishments:** Pipeline Contractors Association; Distribution Contractors Association; Mason's; Scottish Rite; Shriner's; Skagit County Search and Rescue. **Education:** Attended Seminars In: FMI Management, Microsoft Excel, Fowler, President Management Financial Managers. **Personal:** Married to Joanie in 1973. Two children: Sabrina and Nicole. Mr. Ganske enjoys fishing and golf.

W. Mark Gramlich

CEO and Treasurer
Mesa Excavation and Construction
P O Box 250
Riverton, UT 84065
(801) 280–5335
Fax: (801) 280–5431

1623

Business Information: Mesa Excavation and Construction, established in 1993, and currently employing 30 people, does site work for municipalities and custom homebuilders in the western part of the United States. As CEO and Treasurer, Mr. Gramlich oversees the day–to–day operations of the Company. His duties as Treasurer include developing and implementing budgets, payroll, accounting, and tax reporting. Mr. Gramlich works with other members of management on preparing bids for jobs. **Career Steps:** CEO and Treasurer, Mesa Excavation and Construction (1993–Present); Superintendent, Edman Construction (1990–1993); Drilling Foreman, Daves Drilling (1988–1990); Mesa Mining (1982–1988). **Associations & Accomplishments:** Underground Utah Association **Personal:** Married to Dana in 1980. Two children: Kori and Kylee. Mr. Gramlich enjoys boating, snow skiing, softball, and waterskiing.

A. J. Johns

President
A. J. Johns, Inc.
3225 Anniston Road
Jacksonville, FL 32246
(904) 641–2055
Fax: (904) 641–2102

1623

Business Information: A. J. Johns, Inc. is an underground utility contractor, as well as providing services in paving, grading, and clearing of property to private enterprises and municipalities. Established in 1970, A.J. Johns, Inc. reports annual revenue of $10 million and currently employs 125 people. With thirty–eight years expertise in the utility industry, certified in Building Contracting and Underground Utility Contracting, and a Certified Water and Wastewater Plant Operator, Mr. Johns established the Firm in 1970. Serving as President, he supervises and assists operations in nearly all company activities. **Career Steps:** President, A. J. Johns, Inc. (1970–Present); President, Gateway Utility Services (1964–1970); Superintendent, Cedar Hills Utility Company (1957–1964). **Associations & Accomplishments:** President, Utility Operators Association (1966–1967); North Florida Homebuilders Association; National Utility Contractors Association; Board of Directors, Utility Contractors Association (4 years); Chairman of the Board, Christ Bible Church. **Education:** Builders Contractors License; Underground Utility Contractor License; Water and Wastewater Plant Operators License; Various field related courses. **Personal:** Married to Carole in 1961. Two children: Mark and Teresa. Mr. Johns enjoys hunting, snow skiing, and travel.

Robert W. Pine, CPA

Chief Financial Officer
Shanco Corporation
14170 Jetport Loop
Ft. Myers, FL 33013
(315) 252–2844
Fax: (315) 253–8040

1623

Business Information: Shanco Corporation is a cable television and telephone construction contractor. Services provided include daily installation and hookup, as well as upgrades; construction building to cable systems above and below ground – fiber optic from lead to home; and system upgrades – basically upgrading existing systems. Future plans include focusing on construction projects in the Pacific Rim. Co–Founding Shanco Corporation with his partner, Austin Shanfelter in 1985, Mr. Pine currently serves as Chief Financial Officer. He is responsible for the direction and maintenance of the infrastructure of the Company. **Career Steps:** Chief Financial Officer, Shanco Corporation (1995–Present); Partner in Charge, Fagliarone & Associates, CPA's (1990–1995); Partner in Charge, Lyons & Pine, CPA's (1982–1990) **Education:** St. Bonaventure University, B.A. in Accounting (1976); Certified Public Accountant **Personal:** Married to Kim in 1978. Four children: Ryan, Jameson, Taylor and Chelsea. Mr. Pine enjoys all outdoor activities (fishing, hunting, skiing, etc.).

Mr. Alexis Ocasio Agosto, PLS

Project Surveyor
Redondo Construction Corporation
P.O. Box 364185
San Juan, Puerto Rico 00936–4185
(787) 783–1498
Fax: (787) 781–4141
AlexOcasio@AOL.com

1629

Business Information: Redondo Construction Corporation is a general contracting business specializing in heavy construction, marine construction, and precast factory. As Project Surveyor, Mr. Ocasio is responsible for several projects within the Marine Division. He directs several survey crews performing topographic, hydrographic, earthwork, and as–built surveys for the projects. Internet users can also reach him via: AlexOcasio@AOL.com. **Career Steps:** Project Surveyor, Redondo Construction Corporation (1995–Present); Project Surveyor, Miramar Construction Corporation (1993–1995); Project Surveyor, Triangle Engineering Corporation (1990–1993). **Associations & Accomplishments:** Captain, U.S. Army Reserves Corps of Engineers; U.S. Army Achievement Medal; Reserve Officers Association; Phi Eta Mu Fraternity; College of Professional Engineers and Land Surveyors of Puerto Rico; Puerto Rico Institute of Land Surveyors; Puerto Rico Institute of Civil Engineers. **Education:** Polytechnic University of Puerto Rico: B.S. L.S.& M. (1990), Currently studying B.S. in Civil Engineering; U.S. Army Engineer School – Ft. Leonard Wood, MO: Officers Course (1991). **Personal:** Mr. Agosto enjoys scuba diving and is fully bilingual (English and Spanish).

Mr. R. Paul Allio

Chief Administrative Officer
Nicholson Construction Company
3343 Peachtree Road, Suite 920
Atlanta, GA 30326
(404) 442–1801
Fax: (404) 475–8352

1629

Business Information: Nicholson Construction Company is a national geotechnical construction company focusing on sub–terranean construction projects (i.e., sensitive retrofit work with large infrastructures, industrial facilities and bridges). Established in 1955, Nicholson Construction has five offices in the U.S., reports an annual revenue of $55 million and currently employs 125 people. As Chief Administrative Officer, Mr. Allio is responsible for corporate planning, legal, safety, contracts and claims, human resources, MIS and financial matters for all five locations. **Career Steps:** Chief Administrative Officer, Nicholson Construction Company (1992–Present); Director of Corporate Marketing and Planning, Paul C. Rizzo Associates (1990–1992); Vice President, Robert J. Allio & Associates (1980–1990); Teaching Fellow, Harvard University (1984–1988). **Associations & Accomplishments:** The Planning Forum; Strategic Planning Society. **Education:** York University, B.A. (1979); American University; Rensselaer Polytechnic Institute; Harvard University. **Personal:** Married to Beate in 1981. Three children: Chris-

topher, Devon and Nicole. Mr. Allio enjoys judo and tennis and instructing ITF Tae Kwon Do.

Michael A. Kleinhenz

Project Manager
Abel Construction
4600 Robards Lane
Louisville, KY 40218
(502) 451–2235
Fax: (502) 473–7361

1629

Business Information: Abel Construction is a heavy industrial general contractor. The Company has built commercial buildings for various industries, including White Castle, Ashland Oil, Rite Aid, and Ford Motor Company. As Project Manager, Mr. Kleinhenz oversees all projects from the beginning. He handles management, staffing, cost management, designing projects, and business development. **Career Steps:** Project Manager, Abel Construction (1992–Present); Vice President & Project Manager, Ballard Engineering (1990–1992); Partner & Chief Mechanical Engineer, Advanced Consulting Technology (1981–1990); Design Group Leader, Bechtel, Inc. (1977–1981). **Associations & Accomplishments:** American Society of Mechanical Engineers; National Society of Professional Engineers; Kentucky Society of Professional Engineers; Professional Engineers in Construction; Kentucky Industrial Development Council; Kentucky Construction Users Council. **Education:** University of Louisville, B.S. in Physics (1970); Registered Professional Engineer – Kentucky #13067. **Personal:** Married to Adele in 1992. Three children: John, Karey, and Steve. Mr. Kleinhenz enjoys golf, boating, and fishing.

Ms. Marita A. Koller

Accountant
UOP
934 Forest Avenue
Des Plaines, IL 60018
(708) 391–3010
Fax: Please mail or

1629

Business Information: UOP, currently a joint venture of Union Carbide & Allied Cygna, is a designer and servicer of oil refineries. Established in 1909, UOP employs 4,000 people. As Accountant for the Royalty Accounting Department, Ms. Koller is a provider of accounting services. She is currently in the process of computerizing the accounting department. **Career Steps:** Accountant, UOP (1988–Present); Computer Analyst, Baxter Labs (1985–1988); Actuarial Assistant, Towers, Perrin (1980–1985); Congressional Assistant, United States House of Representatives (1977–1980). **Associations & Accomplishments:** League of Women Voters; American Management Association; Association of Certified Public Accountants; Who's Who of American Women; Teaches at local colleges and libraries on personal computers (Oakton College, Des Plaines, IL – Part–time); Presentations at Congress on women's groups; Active in local political campaigns; Taking part of a study out of Harvard, tracking Congressional staff over a three year period. **Education:** American University, M.B.A. (1980); Western Illinois University, B.A.; Studying for C.P.A. **Personal:** Ms. Koller enjoys playing the dulcimer.

William S. Reinhardt

Operations Manager
George C. Halls & Sons, Inc.
60 New County Road, P.O. Box 506
Rockland, ME 04841
(207) 594–4630
Fax: (207) 594–5544
EMAIL: See Below

1629

Business Information: George C. Halls & Sons, Inc. is a heavy construction contractor and construction aggregates supplier, providing services to the State Department of Transportation, local municipalities, the Corps of Engineers, marine industry, private and commercial entities, etc. throughout the State of Maine. A Certified Civil Engineer with thirteen years experience, Mr. Reinhardt joined George C. Halls & Sons, Inc. as Superintendent in 1978. Appointed as Operations Manager and Co–Treasurer in 1993, he is responsible for the management of all operational activities, including equipment purchases, major project bids and schedules, land purchases, and review of the hiring and firing of personnel. Concurrent with his position with the Company, he teaches a part–time senior level course in the Civil Engineering Department at the University of Maine. Internet users can reach him via: 103276,1162@compuserve.com **Career Steps:** George C. Halls & Sons, Inc.: Operations Manager (1993–Present), Superintendent (1978–1981); Visiting Instructor, University of Maine – Civil Engineering Department (1985–Present). **Associations & Accomplishments:** American Society of Civil Engineers; National Society of Professional Engineers; Tau Beta Pi; Chairman, Town of St. George Planning Board.

Education: Massachusettes Institute of Technology, M.S.C.E. (1983); University of Maine, B.S. in Civil Engineering. **Personal:** Married to Lisa A. in 1984. One child: Amelia C. Mr. Reinhardt enjoys camping, hiking, boating, and sailing.

Patrick J. Shields

Vice President
Brown & Brown Inc.
3430 South 38th Street
Phoenix, AZ 85040
(602) 437–0605
Fax: (602) 437–0622

1629

Business Information: Brown & Brown Inc., established in 1946, specializes in industrial and commercial construction, road building, infrastructure, and foundation building. As Vice President, Mr. Shields is responsible for all aspects of Company operations, including sales and operations of the Western Division. **Career Steps:** Vice President, Brown & Brown Inc. (1996–Present); Business Development Manager, Chemical Line Company (1991–1996). **Associations & Accomplishments:** American Society of Chemical Engineers – Local and National; Association of General Contractors – Local and National; American Public Works Association; AAPA; AARA. **Education:** University of Nevada – Reno, Bachelor with emphasis on Environmental (1991). **Personal:** Mr. Shields enjoys golf, basketball, and hiking.

S. Clark Smith

Vice President of Finance
Adams & Smith, Inc.
P.O. Box 70
Orem, UT 84059–0070
(801) 226–4747
Fax: (801) 226–5406

1629

Business Information: Adams & Smith, Inc. is a heavy trades construction contractor, specializing in steel erection and earthquake retrofitting of highways and buildings. As Vice President of Finance, Mr. Smith is responsible for all aspects of company operations, including accounting, payroll and personnel functions. **Career Steps:** Vice President of Finance, Adams & Smith, Inc. (1993–Present); Vice President of Finance, Daw, Inc. (1990–1993); Controller, M.L. Hansen, Inc. (1984–1990); Controller, Terra Tek, Inc. (1972–1980). **Associations & Accomplishments:** Construction Financial Management Association; National Contract Management Association. **Education:** University of Utah: M.B.A. (1972), B.S. in Civil Engineering (1970). **Personal:** Married to Julia in 1968. Four children: Steven, Jason, Jeremy and Jacob. Mr. Smith enjoys music and boating.

Gerry Zurkan

Project Manager
PCL Civil Constructors, Inc.
1620 West Fountain Head Parkway, Suite 290
Tempe, AZ 85282
(619) 523–1081 (602) 829–6333
Fax: (619) 523–1498
EMail: See Below

1629

Business Information: PCL Civil Constructors, Inc. is a general contracting firm, privately–owned with locations throughout the United States. As Project Manager, Mr. Zurkan is responsible for complete construction of light and heavy civil projects. Internet users can reach him via: SAWDAN@AOL. **Career Steps:** Project Manager, PCL Civil Constructors, Inc. (1994–Present); PCL Western – Canada: Project Manager (1991–1995), Estimator/Superintendent (1984–1991). **Associations & Accomplishments:** Cold Regions Engineering and Construction. **Education:** N.A.I.T., Civil Diploma (1986). **Personal:** Married to Jay in 1990. Two children: Sawyer Jane and Daniel. Mr. Zurkan enjoys family, golf, reading, chess, and gardening.

1700 Special Trade Contractors

1794 Excavation work
1795 Wrecking and demolition work
1796 Installing building equipment, NEC
1799 Special trade contractors, NEC

Carlos Armella Jr.

Director
Calef. Y Ventilacion
Prolg. Calle 18 #246
Mexico City, Mexico 01180
(525) 515–5180
Fax: (525) 515–4792

1711

Business Information: Calef. Y Ventaltion is a heating, air conditioning, and ventilation company. Focusing on design installation, commercial systems, and refrigeration (with York American Air/Heat Company and Trane), the Company has three locations in Aquas, Negras, and Cancun, Mexico. Established in 1951, the Company employs 600 people and has an estimated annual revenue of $30 million. As Director, Mr. Armella handles all operational and administrative functions of the Company's three locations. Additional duties include marketing, sales, finance, public relations, and strategic planning. **Career Steps:** Calef. Y Ventilacion: Director (1990–Present), Buyer's Directional (1986–1990), Accounting (1983–1986), Material Handling (1973–1974). **Associations & Accomplishments:** Camara Nacional de La Idustria de la Construccion; Presidente, Associacion Mexicana de Empresas Ramo Instalaciones (Americ); Secretary, Centro Impulsor de la Habitacion (CIHAC). **Education:** University of the Americas, B.A. (1979); Instituto Formacion Tecnica Bancomext; Curso Avanzado Comercio Exterior. **Personal:** Married to Chantal Spitalier in 1977. Four children: Sofia, Valeria, Nathalie, and Mercedes. Mr. Armella enjoys golf and remote control aircraft.

Paul E. Barkman
Director of International Development
Roto – Rooter Corporation
300 Ashworth Road
West Des Moines, IA 50265–3787
(515) 223–1343
Fax: (515) 223–4220

1711

Business Information: Roto – Rooter Corporation is the largest, most well–known plumbing/drain cleaning company in the United States. As Director of International Development, Mr. Barkman is responsible for international expansion and development. **Career Steps:** Director of International Development, Roto – Rooter Corporation (1995–Present); Vice President of Sales & Marketing, George Newman & Co. (1992–1994); President, DuBois International (1986–1992). **Associations & Accomplishments:** Cincinnati Council on World Affairs; World Trade Association; Japan American Society; Southern Ohio District Export Council; Northern Kentucky International; Trade Association; Tokyo American Club; Iowa International Traders. **Education:** Indiana University, M.B.A. (1961); Hanover College, B.A. (1960). **Personal:** Married to Chlois C. in 1970. Two children: Phyllis M. and Tricia A. Mr. Barkman enjoys golf, tennis, and international travel.

Bryan M. Bell
Vice President
Garland Heating & Air
2113 South Garland Avenue
Garland, TX 75041
(214) 278–3506
Fax: (214) 271–6321
EMAIL: See Below

1711

Business Information: Garland Heating & Air, founded in 1952, is a family–owned heating and air conditioning company located in Garland, Texas. Servicing both residential and commercial customers, the Company has a $3.8 million dollar volume. As Vice President, Mr. Bell estimates project management, coordinates billing, oversees payroll, and is network administrator. Internet users can reach him via: bmbell@ix.netcom.com. **Career Steps:** Vice President, Garland Heating & Air (1988–Present). **Education:** University of Texas, Arlington, B.S.M.E. (1988). **Personal:** Married to Priscilla in 1983. Two children: Kaelee and Johnny. Mr. Bell enjoys weightlifting, ministry, computers, and diving.

Thom A. Brazel
Service Manager
McClure Company
2766 West College Avenue, Suite 1
State College, PA 16801
(814) 238–2384
Fax: (814) 238–2386

1711

Business Information: McClure Company, established in 1932, is a mechanical services contractor offering services in heating, air conditioning, and plumbing services. As Service Manager, Mr. Brazel is responsible for the solicitation of new contracts and for the system remodifications on all systems. **Career Steps:** Service Manager, McClure Company (1994–Present); Mechanical Engineer, Phoenix Technical Services (1994). **Associations & Accomplishments:** American Society of Heating, Refrigeration, and Air Conditioning Contractors of America (ASHRAE); American Society of Mechanical Engineering (ASME); Total Quality Council of Central Pennsylvania; Chamber of Business and Industry of Centre County, Pennsylvania; Empire Statesmen Senior Drum and Bugle Corps – 1991 and 1994 World Champions. **Education:** Pennsylvania State University, B.S. M.E. (1993); Edinboro University of Pennsylvania, B.A. Physics. **Personal:** Mr. Brazel enjoys golf, tennis, being a high school marching band instructor, and membership in the Empire Statesmen Senior Drum and Bugle Corps.

Steve (Istvan) Frohling
President
Airflow Testing, Inc.
1379 Dix Road
Lincoln Park, MI 48146–1346
(313) 382–8378
Fax: (313) 382–3183

1711

Business Information: Airflow Testing, Inc. provides testing, balancing, and evaluation of HVAC systems, vibration testing, and hospital/operating room air flow certification. The Company also provides heating and ventilation to many commercial industries, including hospitals and schools, manufacturing, and automobile companies. As President, Mr. Frohling is responsible for all aspects of Company operations, including administration, marketing, and strategic planning. **Career Steps:** President, Airflow Testing, Inc. (1992–Present); Vice President, Aerodynamics Inspecting Company (1968–1992). **Associations & Accomplishments:** Associated Air Balance Council. **Education:** ICS, HVAC Engineering (1979); Eotvos Lorand Technical College, Hungary (1954–1958). **Personal:** Three children: Steve Jr., Peter, and Frank. Mr. Frohling enjoys hunting.

Richard E. (Dick) Gerber
Owner/President
Twin Rivers Plumbing, Inc.
1525 Irving Road
Eugene, OR 97402–9753
(541) 688–1444
Fax: (541) 688–9272

1711

Business Information: Twin Rivers Plumbing, Inc. is a mechanical contractor, accepting 90% new construction contracts and 10% remodeling and repair. Mr. Gerber founded Twin Rivers in 1977, working closely with owners and contractors in construction design and development. His responsibilities as President include various administrative functions, supervision of daily operations, marketing activities, and corporate leadership. **Career Steps:** Owner/President, Twin Rivers Plumbing, Inc. (1977–Present). **Associations & Accomplishments:** President, Mid Oregon PHCC; Board Member, Emerald Empire Late Great Chevys; Board Member, Eugene Builder's Exchange; Eugene Chamber of Commerce; AGC. **Education:** Plumbing Apprenticeship Program – Journeyman Plumber (1969). **Personal:** Married to Sandra in 1965. Two children: Shelley Gerber and Stacie Elder. Mr. Gerber collects classic cars and memorabilia. He also enjoys hunting and fishing.

James Haaf
General Manager
Herb Haaf Heating & Cooling, Inc.
601 Mulberry Street
Jefferson City, MO 65101
(573) 659–8377
Fax: (573) 659–8465
EMAIL: See Below

1711

Business Information: Herb Haaf Heating & Cooling, Inc. is a family–owned contracting company established in 1989, providing sales, service, and installation from two locations in Missouri. As General Manager, Mr. Haaf oversees day–to–day finances, sales, and advertising responsibilities, public relations functions – including television interviews on behalf of the Company – and corporate legislation. In addition, he teaches economics to 8th graders in two counties (more than thirty schools). Internet users can reach him via: Grndsource@aol.com **Career Steps:** General Manager, Herb Haaf Heating & Cooling, Inc. (1989–Present); A.J. Rackers: Project Manager (1987–1989), Warehouse Manager (1985–1989), Installer (1980–1985). **Associations & Accomplishments:** Former President, Missouri Heat Pump Association; Liberty Township Committeeman, Cole County Republican Central Committee. **Education:** Columbia College, B.S. (1990). **Personal:** Married to Kathleen in 1979. Three children: Amanda, Aaron, and Adam. Mr. Haaf enjoys politics, and coaching youth baseball and basketball.

Frederick J. Hutchinson
President
Hutchinson Contracting Company
621 Chapel Avenue
Cherry Hill, NJ 08034
(609) 429–5807
Fax: (609) 429–8911

1711

Business Information: Hutchinson Contracting Company is the parent company of two divisions: Hutchinson Construction Services, a general mechanical contractor; and, Hutchinson Plumbing, Heating, & Cooling, a residential / commercial plumbing, and HVAC contractor. A family–owned business originally founded by three family members in 1948, a partnership was formed in 1983, consisting of a new generation of Hutchinson family members (6 partners). Joining Hutchinson Contracting Company in 1976, Mr. Hutchinson was appointed as President and Chief Executive Officer in 1994. Serving as one of six partners, he is responsible for all aspects of operations, including the coordination of all company activities, sales & marketing, general administration and production efforts. **Career Steps:** Hutchinson Contracting Company: President (1994–Present); Vice President Production and Operations (1988–1994), General Operations Manger (1979–1988), Superintendent (1976–1979). **Associations & Accomplishments:** Better Business Bureau; Chamber of Commerce; Boy Scouts; Little League. **Education:** Spring Garden College, B.A. (1972). **Personal:** Married to M. Katherine in 1981. Two children: Paul C. and Katherine Lynn. Mr. Hutchinson enjoys golf, participating in childrens activities (i.e., coaching), and landscaping.

Kymberly K. Jones
Operations Manager
Stanley Jones Corporation
480–Y Cave Road
Nashville, TN 37210
(615) 889–4551
Fax: (615) 889–4561

1711

Business Information: Founded in 1946, Stanley Jones Corporation is a third generation, mechanical contracting business, serving the Nashville and South Fulton areas. Joining the family–owned business in 1989, Kymberly Jones now holds the title of Operations Manager. Managing operations for the Nashville Branch, her duties include coordination of project selection and bidding, development of new business and the control of personnel administration. Being the third generation of the family business, Ms. Jones is proud to have started as the office manager and to have worked her self up to Operations Manager. **Career Steps:** Stanley Jones Corporation: Operations Manager (1993–Present), Education Director (1993), Marketing Director (1992), Office Manager (1989–1992). **Associations & Accomplishments:** Director (1995–1996), National Association of Women in Construction – Chapter #16; National Association of Female Executives; Associated General Contractors: Middle Tennessee Branch Director (1993–1995), State of Tennessee Branch Director (1993–1995); Middle Tennessee Chapter Director (1994–1996), Associated Builders and Contractors. **Education:** Tennessee State University, M.B.A. in progress; Vanderbilt University, B.S. (1989). **Personal:** Ms. Jones enjoys cooking, sewing, reading and travel.

Farzin Kiani
Project Manager
PSG, Inc.
190 Tafts Avenue
Winthrop, MA 02152–1449
(617) 539–0269
Fax: Please mail or call

1711

Business Information: PSG, Inc. is a contract water and waste water operation and management company. PSG operates waste water plants throughout the United States, specializing in the start up and testing of the plants. As Project Manager, Mr. Kiani coordinates and starts up the equipment for the projects. Additionally, he coordinates the process information control systems and is responsible for the testing of all equipment. **Career Steps:** Project Manager, PSG, Inc. (1993–Present); Project Engineer, BCM, Inc. (1989–1993); Project Engineer, Philadelphia Water Department (1985–1989). **Associations & Accomplishments:** National Society of Professional Engineers; Water Environment Federation; American Board of Certification. **Education:** Villanova University, M.S. in Civil Engineering (1993); Drexel University, B.S. in Chemical Engineering; Professional Engineering Certificate: Massachusetts, Pennsylvania, and New Jersey. **Personal:** Mr. Kiani enjoys skiing, travel, jogging, and playing soccer.

Ronald G. Ledoux
• • • ◦━━◉━━◦ • • •

Senior Exec. Vice President & Chief Operating Officer
J.C. Higgins Corporation
70 Hawes Way
Stoughton, MA 02072
(617) 787–9800
Fax: (617) 344–9283

1711

Business Information: J.C. Higgins Corporation, a wholly-owned subsidiary of Emcor, is the largest mechanical contractor on the East Coast, specializing in commercial and industrial heating, air conditioning, and plumbing. Mr. Ledoux has held various positions with J.C. Higgins, serving as Vice President, Executive Vice President and Construction Manager, and most recently Senior Executive Vice President and Chief Operating Officer since 1995. He is presently responsible for all phases of day–to–day operations, including corporate leadership, purchasing, and cost estimation. **Career Steps:** J.C. Higgins Corporation: Senior Executive Vice President and Chief Operating Officer (1995–Present), Executive Vice President and Construction Manager (1994–1995), Vice President (1992–1994); Vice President, Gibbs McAlister, Inc. (1988–1992). **Associations & Accomplishments:** Director, New England Mechanical Contractors Association; Massachusetts Building Congress; New England Construction Users Council; Zoning Board. **Education:** Roger Williams College, B.S. (1975); Johnson & Whales, B.A.; Wentworth Institute, Associates Degree. **Personal:** Married to Janet in 1973. Two children: Jennifer and Melissa. Mr. Ledoux enjoys golf and boating.

Edward T. Lyons III
Operations Manager
Continental Mechanical Systems
5555 Denver Technological Center
Greenwood Village, CO 80111–3005
(303) 267–0337
Fax: (303) 267–0395

1711

Business Information: Continental Mechanical Systems is a regional plumbing, heating, and air conditioning contractor for commercial and industrial clients. The Company, part of the Benchmark Group, boasts multiple locations west of the Mississippi River. As Operations Manager, Mr. Lyons is responsible for the technicians assigned to his branch office. He assists with project scheduling, equipment purchases, updating training programs for technicians, and developing safety programs. **Career Steps:** Operations Manager, Continental Mechanical Systems (1994–Present); Submarine Officer, U.S. Navy (1989–1994). **Associations & Accomplishments:** United States Naval Reserve. **Education:** United States Merchant Marine Academy. **Personal:** Mr. Lyons enjoys fly fishing, hunting, camping, and woodworking.

Ms. Alice A. Markunas
• • • ◦━━◉━━◦ • • •

President
Piedmont Service Co.
P.O. Box 13705
Durham, NC 27709–3705
(919) 544–9767
Fax: (919) 361–0559

1711

Business Information: Piedmont Service Co. is a HVAC, electrical and plumbing service company providing service to residential and commercial applications. Established in 1993, Piedmont Service Co. currently employs eight people. As President, Ms. Markunas is responsible for managing Company operations. **Career Steps:** President, Piedmont Service Co. (1993–Present); Owner, Pleasure Horse Farm (1993–Present). **Associations & Accomplishments:** Omicron Delta Epsilon – Economic Honor Society. **Education:** North Carolina State University, B.A. in Business Manage-

ment (1993), B.A. in Economics. **Personal:** One child: Robert Morgan. Ms. Markunas enjoys riding and showing horses and golf.

Erik H. Rodriguez
Project Engineer
Lord & Company, Inc.
8811 Sudley Road
Manassas, VA 22110–7232
(703) 631–6843
Fax: (703) 368–8026
EMAIL: See Below

1711

Business Information: Lord & Company, Inc. specializes in building automation, including digital controls for HVAC equipment. As Project Engineer, Mr. Rodriguez is responsible for the design and management of different EMCS, as well as Building Automation Projects. Internet users can reach him via: EHR1@AOL.COM. **Career Steps:** Project Engineer, Lord & Company, Inc. (1990–Present). **Associations & Accomplishments:** Knights of Columbus. **Education:** West Virginia Institute of Technology, B.S.E.E. (1990). **Personal:** Mr. Rodriguez enjoys softball, skiing, tennis, and bike riding.

J. W. Gerald Rupke
General Manager
Wheelabrator EOS Canada, Inc.
1131 Gorham Street, Unit 8
Newmarket, Ontario L3Y 7V1
(905) 853–1223
Fax: (905) 853–8830

1711

Business Information: Wheelabrator EOS Canada, Inc. specializes in contract operations of water and wastewater plants. Established in 1972, the Company employs 550 people and has five locations throughout Canada. As General Manager, Mr. Rupke oversees operations for five wastewater treatment plants, project development, pricing proposals, and management of profit/loss ratios. **Career Steps:** General Manager, Wheelabrator EOS Canada, Inc. (1993–Present); President, Rupke and Associates Limited (1979–1993). **Associations & Accomplishments:** Water Environment Association; American Water Works Association; Professional Engineers of Ontario; Director of Public Traded Company, Akrokeri Ashanti Gold Mines; Chairman of a Private School. **Education:** University of Texas, M.Sc. in Environmental Health (1969); University of Waterloo, B.A.Sc. in Chemical Engineering (1966). **Personal:** Married to Helen in 1966. Four children: Mark, Lisa, Carolyn, and Tracey. Mr. Rupke enjoys gardening, and remodeling an old house for student housing.

David A. Valentine
Director of Safety and Technical Training
Lyons Company, Inc.
308 Samson Street
Glasgow, KY 42141
(502) 651–2733
Fax: (502) 651–6867

1711

Business Information: Lyons Company, Inc. specializes in mechanical contracting, specifically design and construction of building environmental control systems. Regional in scope, the Company has two locations in the Glasgow, Kentucky area. As Director of Safety and Technical Training, Mr. Valentine develops and implements safety programs and presents technical training to employees. He is also responsible for ensuring compliance with all state, federal, and local regulations, performing research, and monitoring employees in the field. **Career Steps:** Director of Safety and Technical Training, Lyons Company, Inc. (1995–Present); Clerk/Safety Officer, James N. Gray Construction (1995); Project Supervisor, Rust Federal Services (1989–1995); Machinist Mate, First Class, United States Navy (1980–1989). **Associations & Accomplishments:** American Society of Safety Engineers; Board of Certified Safety Professionals; American Business of Governmental Industrial Hygienists; Recipient of American Red Cross Lifesaving Award; American Board of Industrial Hygienists. **Education:** Western Kentucky University. **Personal:** Married to Jennifer in 1982. Three children: Jill, Jessica, and Jamie. Mr. Valentine enjoys golf, hunting, and fishing.

Peter Vavrinek
Controller and Treasurer
Campbell, Inc.
255 Grandolph Street
Toledo, OH 43612–1461
(419) 476–4444
Fax: (419) 470–6516

1711

Business Information: Campbell, Inc. is a contracting service company, providing heating, cooling, plumbing, and building automation services to commercial, industrial, and institutional facilities in Northwest Ohio and Southeast Michigan. Campbell, Inc. has two regional locations, one in Toledo, Ohio and one in Ann Arbour, Michigan. As Controller and Treasurer, Mr. Vavrinek is responsible for all aspects of finances, including financial statements, insurance, payroll, union reports, tax returns, and managing a fleet of 34 vehicles, insurance companies, attorneys, and accountants. **Career Steps:** Controller and Treasurer, Campbell, Inc. (1991–Present); Senior Auditor, Ernst & Young (1986–1991); Financial Assistant, Inland Division – General Motors (1984–1986). **Associations & Accomplishments:** Treasurer, Construction Financial Management Association; Ohio Society of Certified Public Accountants; Mechanical Contractors Association; Mechanical Service Contractors Association; Member of The Academy Brass Quintet. **Education:** Adrian College, B.B.A. (1986). **Personal:** One child: Kevin Tyler. Mr. Vavrinek enjoys playing the French horn, exercising, and church activities.

Raymond Warren
Chief Executive Officer
Florida Gold Coast Air and Refrigeration
2440 Southwest 115th Terrace
Davie, FL 33325–4863
(305) 452–5622
Fax: Please mail or call

1711

Business Information: Florida Gold Coast Air and Refrigeration is an international mechanical contracting firm for commercial businesses with seventeen locations in Florida. Prior contracts have been with business in Columbia, El Salvador, Jamaica, and Spain. With eighteen years of experience in the air and refrigeration industry, Mr. Warren joined Florida Gold Coast Air and Refrigeration upon graduation of high school in 1978. Currently serving as Chief Executive Officer, he participates in every aspect of the Company, which includes everything from turning wrenches to strategic planning. He also serves as a Majority Stockholder. **Career Steps:** Chief Executive Officer, Florida Gold Coast Air and Refrigeration (1978–Present).

Nancy R. Cox
President and Owner
Pen Gulf, Inc.
P.O. Box 12916
Pensacola, FL 32576–2916
(904) 433–6302
Fax: (904) 433–1888

1721

Business Information: Pen Gulf, Inc. is an industrial painting contractor, offering the complete range of painting services to corporate and industrial clients throughout an eight state region (Tennessee, Florida, Louisiana, Alabama, Georgia). Services provided include: sandblasting, new construction and general painting projects. As President and Owner, Ms. Cox oversees all aspects of the Company, providing the overall vision and strategies to ensure quality service, customer satisfaction and corporate development. **Career Steps:** Pen Gulf, Inc.: President and Owner (1995–Present), Vice President (1988–1995). **Associations & Accomplishments:** Association of General Contractors; Steel Structures Painting Council; Associated Builders and Contractors of South Alabama. **Education:** University of West Florida, Masters (1984); University of Arkansas, B.S. (1966). **Personal:** Ms. Cox enjoys flower arranging.

T. R. Rudd
• • • ◦━━◉━━◦ • • •

Owner and President
Striping Technology, Inc.
10112 Country Road 489
Tyler, TX 75706
(903) 595–6800
Fax: 903595–6255

1721

Business Information: Striping Technology, Inc. is a highway construction company, providing highway striping (i.e., arrows, turn only arrows, etc.), pavement markings, reflector buttons, etc. for the entire State of Texas. Additional services include installing traffic signals and signs in Northeast Texas. As Owner and President, Mr. Rudd is responsible for all aspects of operations, including administration, finances, sales, public relations, accounting, legal matters, marketing, and strategic planning. **Career Steps:** Owner and President, Striping Technology, Inc. (1991–Present); Owner/President, Traffic Systems, Inc. (1975–1991); Vice–President, Amitech, Inc. (1969–1975). **Associations & Accomplishments:** American Traffic Safety Services (ATSSA)– Director–Texas Division; Associated General Contractors (AGC),–East Texas Area Chairman. **Education:** Texas A&M at Kingsville, B.S. in Chemical Engineering (1961). **Personal:** Married to Linda in 1981. Three children: Brent, Niki and Lana. Mr. Rudd enjoys golf,and hunting.

Ray E. Swope Jr.
Owner, Operator, and President
Artists in Painting and Paperhanging
P.O. Box 91
Womelsdorf, PA 19567
(610) 589–2272
Fax: Please mail or call

1721

Business Information: Artists in Painting and Paperhanging provides painting and paperhanging services for both interior and exterior surfaces. Established in 1952, the Company serves residential and commercial customers. Restoration work, marbleizing, and faux finish work is also available. As Owner and Operator, Mr. Swope oversees and assists in all of the offered services of the Company. He also serves as a decorating consultant and a free lance artist. Mr. Swope tends to all business functions, including finances, budgeting, and personnel. **Career Steps:** Owner and Operator, Artists in Painting and Paperhanging (1982–Present); Ray E. Swope, Sr.: Foreman (1960–1981), Employee (Summers 1952–1959). **Associations & Accomplishments:** President (1969–1971), Vice President (1968–1969), Former Director (1962–1968), Womelsdorf Swimming Pool Association; Womelsdorf Citizens Committee (1962–1994); Den Assistant, Cub Scouts (1970–1972); Zion U.C.C. Youth Fellowship Counselor (1976–1977); Womelsdorf Area Jaycees, Inc.– Junior; Chamber of Commerce: Charter Member (1971), President (1975–1976 and 1978–1979), Chairman of $250,000 Park Improvement Project (1994–1997); National Guild of Professional Paperhangers, Inc.; Central Pennsylvania Guild of Professional Paperhangers; Painting and Decorating Contractors of America; President Elect, Treasure (1994–1996), The Greater Berks County Chapter of Painting and Decorating Contractors of America; New Building Committee, Williamson Lodge No.307 F. & A. M. of Pennsylvania; Scottish Rite Valley of Reading, PA.; Rajah Temple A.A.O.N.M.S. of Reading, PA.; Rajah Temple Antique and Classic Car Club; Antique Automobile Club of America; Reading Company Technical and Historical Society; Womelsdorf Zion U.C.C.; Max W. Scheffer V.F.W. Post; Republican Residential Legion of Merit, Representative of National Committee; National Senatorial Representative; Statue of Liberty, Ellis Island Foundation, Inc.; Outstanding Young Men of America Award (1979); First Place Award, The Painting and Decorating Contractors of America, and the Residential Committee for the Outstanding Presentation of the Company and Improving the Image of the Painting and Decorating Industry (1996); Appointed Jaycee International (JCI) Senator (1976). **Personal:** Married to Geraldine L. in 1986. Two children: Donnie and Elana J. Swope Yeingst. Mr. Swope enjoys art, swimming, and antique toys, trains, and cars.

Ramona E. Alves
President and Chief Executive Officer
CHAT Communications Services
1 Saunders Avenue
San Anselmo, CA 94960–1719
(415) 454–7796
Fax: (415) 453–6179

1731

Business Information: CHAT Communications Services provides the installation of telecommunication equipment for the Pacific Bell Network. Future plans include tripling their growth and diversifying into a full–service engineering firm, both in furnishing and installing communications equipment. Founding CHAT in 1986, as President and Chief Executive Officer, Ms. Alves oversees all aspects of operations, including administration, finances, public relations, accounting, and strategic planning. In addition, she supervises all management associates and a support staff of 64. **Career Steps:** President and Chief Executive Officer, CHAT Communications Services (1986–Present); Installation Technician, AT&T (1978–1985). **Associations & Accomplishments:** Member, Marin County Affirmative Action Committee; Recipient, Outstanding Quality Award from Pacific Bell (1995). **Education:** Sacramento City College, A.A. in Business Management (1978). **Personal:** Ms. Alves enjoys skiing and boating.

D. L. (Augy) Augustine
General Manager
Canter Electric, Inc.
7220 North Market Street
Spokane, WA 99207
(509) 467–6612
Fax: (509) 467–6614

1731

Business Information: Canter Electric, Inc. is a full–service electrical contracting company for the commercial sector, such as grocery stores, manufacturing plants, utility companies, and restaurants. Services include designing of plans, set up lighting, and power distribution. Joining Canter Electric, Inc. as a driver in 1985, Mr. Augustine has worked his way up to his present position as General Manager. He is responsible for the general management of the office, including estimating the values of the job sites, including job costs and time. He also designs lighting and power distribution for the commercial company's service. Career milestones include expanding the Company from six electricians in 1985, to a current 40, while continuing to hire and expand the capacity of the Company. **Career Steps:** General Manager, Canter Electric, Inc. (1985–Present); Ski Shop Manager, Mount Spokane Ski Corporation (1983–1985); Ski Shop Manager, Timberville Lodge (1972–1983). **Associations & Accomplishments:** Local Lions Club; Inland Empire Electrical League. **Personal:** Married to Gwendolyn K. in 1978. Mr. Augustine enjoys skiing, hiking, woodworking, reading, football, and travel.

Beverly A. Bailey
President and Owner
Stronghold Electric
2291 Business Way
Riverside, CA 92501–2246
(909) 684–9303
Fax: (909) 684–9329

1731

Business Information: Stronghold Electric is an electrical contractor partnership, providing electrical services on a contract basis to both commerical and residential clientele. Established in 1991 as a sub–contracting business, the Company receives contracts through private individuals and businesses, as well as serving as a prime contractor for bidding contracts. Co–founding Stronghold Electric in 1991, Ms. Bailey serves as President, Owner, and Majority Shareholder. She is responsible for all aspects of operations, including administration, finances, sales, public relations, accounting, marketing, and strategic planning. **Career Steps:** President and Owner, Stronghold Electric (1991–Present); Construction Lender, Tiffany Mortgage (1989–1991); Owner, Vera Villa Cafe (1982–1985). **Associations & Accomplishments:** Society of American Military Engineers; Women Construction Owners and Executives; Associated Builders and Contractors (ABC); 8(a) Contractor (Small Business Association). **Personal:** Married to Scott in 1981. Three children: Brandon, Kyler, and Alyssa. Ms. Bailey enjoys travel, sports (skiing and bowling), investments, spending time with her family, and church activities.

Maria D. Binkley
• • • ◦ ◉ ◦ • • •

Owner
Binkley Electric–Construction
2636 Carters Gin Road
Toney, AL 35773
(205) 859–0777
Fax: (205) 859–3732

1731

Business Information: Established in 1989, Binkley Electric–Construction is an electrical subcontractor, residential contractor and lease and rental property company. As Owner, Ms. Binkley is responsible for all aspects of company operations, including administration, design, building single family homes, and plaza development for lease spaces. **Career Steps:** Owner, Binkley Electric–Construction (1989–Present). **Associations & Accomplishments:** Huntsville Madison County Builders Association: Board of Directors, Governmental Affair, Charitable, Contributions, Chairperson, Womens Council; Word of Truth World Outreach Church: Minister, Education Department Head; Founder/President, Grace and Power Ministries, Inc. **Personal:** Married to Richard in 1986. Four children: Rachel, Rebekah, Anthony, and Matthew. Ms. Binkley is an author and has recently published "Directing My Day" daily planner.

Justo D. Cerenio
President and Chief Executive Officer
Worldstar Corporation
10217 Cove Ledge Court
Gaithersburg, MD 20879–1057
(301) 517–5669
Fax: (301) 977–5652
EMAIL: See Below

1731

Business Information: Worldstar Corporation installs video–telecommunications equipment for medical applications. Mr. Cerenio founded Worldstar in 1994, managing business development and expansion. Concurrently, he serves as Vice President for International Operations at Vidtel Corporation. Internet users can reach him via: Cerenioj@erols.com **Career Steps:** President and Chief Executive Officer, Worldstar Corporation (1994–Present); Vice President for International Operations, Vidtel Corporation (1995–Present). **Associations & Accomplishments:** American Entrepreneurs Association; American Academy of Medical Administrators. **Education:** Western University, Masters in Hospital Administration (1983). **Personal:** Married to Sonia in 1979. Two children: John and Adrian. Mr. Cerenio enjoys boats and fishing.

Susan L. Clay
General Manager – Network Construction
GTE – California
One GTE Place Ca500nb
Thousand Oaks, CA 91362
(805) 372–6301
Fax: (805) 496–5969

1731

Business Information: GTE Telephone Operations is a world leading telecommunications technology conglomerate. A branch of GTE Telephone, GTE – California, located in southern California, is a 90% digital network and ISDN capable operation serving 3.7 million telecommunication lines. Serving in various managerial roles with GTE–California since 1991, Susan Clay was appointed as General Manager of Network Construction in October of 1994. Primarily responsible for the administration and overall direction of construction activities for GTE–California and OSP Engineering, she also oversees building infrastructure development, as well as ensures quality product output and customer satisfaction. **Career Steps:** GTE – California: General Manager (1994–Present), Acting Vice President/ GM Operations (1993–1994), Director Network Services (1991–1993). **Associations & Accomplishments:** California Utilities Emergency Association. **Education:** Pepperdine University; Redlands University, B.A. (1978). **Personal:** Married to John in 1971. One child: Anne. Mrs. Clay enjoys collecting classic cars and then restoring them.

Dennis Crane
Branch Manager
Sylvania Lighting Services
30675 Huntwood Avenue
Hayward, CA 94544
(510) 487–6008
Fax: (510) 489–4737

1731

Business Information: Sylvania Lighting Services, a division of Osram Sylvania (parent company – Siemens, Inc.), provides ongoing light maintenance to major industries (i.e. Ford, General Motors) and energy conservation and management construction (retrofitting and replacement of older products with new and more cost–efficient products). As Branch Manager, Mr. Crane is responsible for all aspects of operations, including management of daily activities, providing short–term (5 years) planning, and is responsible for the top and bottom line. In addition, he oversees sales personnel, forecasts, Human Resource functions, and controls the budget. **Career Steps:** Branch Manager, Sylvania Lighting Services (1990–Present); President and General Manager, D.B.C., Inc. (1976–1995); Region Manager, JARTRAN Truck Rental (1981–1984). **Associations & Accomplishments:** American Management Association; California Trucking Association; Youth Athletics: Coaching Little League Baseball, PAL Football. **Education:** Univeristy of Wisconsin, B.S. (1968); University of Phoenix, Enrolled in Masters Program; United States Marine Corps, OCS Graduate (1969). **Personal:** Married to Patrica in 1985. Four children: Mika, Jude, Bradley, and Kevin. Mr. Crane enjoys snow and water skiing.

Ray Earle
• • • ◦ ◉ ◦ • • •

Owner/President
Earle Electric, Inc.
89 Jersey Avenue
Port Jervis, NY 12771–2548
(914) 856–3511
Fax: (914) 856–7616

1731

Business Information: Earle Electric, Inc. specializes in electrical consulting, contracting, and wiring. The Company services three states (New Jersey, Pennsylvania, and New York). As Owner/President, Mr. Earle is responsible for all aspects of Company operations, including administration, finance, sales, and strategic planning. **Career Steps:** Owner/President, Earle Electric, Inc. (1987–Present). **Associations & Accomplishments:** Pike County Chamber of Commerce; I.A.E.I.; B.P.O. Elks Lodge #645. **Personal:** Married to Lori in 1973. Five children: Kelly, Ian, Zachary, Tim, and Tristian. Mr. Earle enjoys fishing and jet skiing.

Charles J. Fricke Jr.
Corporate Accountant
Consolidated Electric Centers Engineers
P.O. Box 1528
Dothan, AL 36302
(334) 793–4974
Fax: (334) 793–1266

1731

Business Information: Consolidated Electric Centers Engineers is an electrical contractor, providing industrial, commercial, petrochemical, and residential high–rise electrical construction. Consolidated Electric Centers Engineers is responsible for "handling all electric services from light bulbs to lightning bolts." Joining the Company as Administrative Assistant in 1992, Mr. Fricke was appointed as Corporate Accountant in 1994. He serves as a financial accountant for all internal reporting, cash management, accounts receivable, and monthly/quarterly/annual state and federal filings. He also serves as Accounting Systems Manager. **Career Steps:** Consolidated Electric Centers Engineers: Corporate Accountant (1994–Present), Administrative Assistant (1992–1994); Sales Representative, Montgomery Beverage Company (1990–1991). **Associations & Accomplishments:** Wiregrass Lions Club; Music Ministry – First Presbyterian Church of Dothan. **Education:** Auburn University at Montgomery, B.S. in Business Administration (1993). **Personal:** Married to Alisa M. in 1989. Two children: Elizabeth and Katheryn.

Richard A. Gilman
National Director of Healthcare
Intecom, Inc.
14499 North Dale Mabry Highway, Suite 185 S.
Tampa, FL 33618
(813) 961–4080
Fax: (813) 264–6908
EMAIL: See Below

1731

Business Information: Intecom, Inc. specializes in the manufacture of telecommunications and multi–media networking products primarily, but not exclusively, for hospitals, HMO'S, PPO's, and other healthcare organizations. International in scope, the Company also contracts with the military, prison systems, and private physicians to provide voice/video, data telecommunications, medical solutions, and tele–medicine applications. Established in 1978, the Company employs 650 people, and has an estimated annual revenue of $120 million. As National Director of Healthcare, Mr. Gilman oversees sales activity in the healthcare industry for voice/data networking and tele–medicine. He is responsible for formalizing programs, writing business plans, and coordinating with clinicians and others. Internet users can reach him via: rgilman@intecom.com. **Career Steps:** National Director of Healthcare, Intecom, Inc. (1991–Present); Manager, Informations Systems, Price Waterhouse (1989–1990); Vice President of Marketing and Sales, Wilcom, Inc. (1984–1987); Vice President of Marketing and Sales, Technicom Systems, Inc. **Associations & Accomplishments:** Healthcare Information Management Systems Society (HIMSS); Krewe of Fort Brooke, Tampa; Seishin–Kai International Karate Federation; New Hampshire College Executive Club; New Hampshire College Alumni; New Hampshire Institute of Technology Alumni. **Education:** New Hampshire College, M.B.A. (1980); Newark College of Engineering, B.S.E.E. (1971); New Hampshire Institute of Technology, A.S.E.E. (1969). **Personal:** Married to Paula in 1985. One child: Michael Anderson Gilman. Mr. Gilman enjoys being a second degree black belt–Shotokan, fishing, and boating.

Francis A. Gingras Jr.
President
R. A. Wilson Electrical Contractors, Inc.
61 Depot Street
Dalton, MA 01226–1807
(413) 684–1972
Fax: (413) 684–1860

1731

Business Information: R. A. Wilson Electrical Contractors, Inc. is an electrical contracting corporation, providing services through 95% bid work and 5% in design and services for industrial businesses. With one regional office located in Massa-

chusetts, the Company conducts business throughout Vermont, Massachusetts, Connecticut and New York. Established in 1970, R.A. Wilson Electrical Contractors reports annual revenue of $2.2 million. Joining the business as Electrician in 1988, Mr. Gingras was appointed as President in 1995, after serving the Corporation in various capacities, such as Project Manager and Agent. He is responsible for all aspects of operations, including public relations, marketing, strategic planning, work scheduling, and crew organization. In addition, he oversees all administrative operations for associates and a support staff of 25. **Career Steps:** R. A. Wilson Electrical Contractors, Inc.: President (1995–Present), Agent (1994–1995), Project Manager (1990–1994), Electrician (1988–1990). **Associations & Accomplishments:** Adirondack/Hudson Chapter, International Association of Electrical Inspectors; Associate Member, American Institute of Plant Engineers. **Education:** Hudson Valley Community College, A.S. (1987). **Personal:** Married to Cynthia in 1990. One child: Christopher. Mr. Gingras enjoys family activities and self improvement.

Greg A. Graham
Director of Personnel
Southern Air, Inc.
P.O. Box 4205
Lynchburg, VA 24502
(804) 385–6200
Fax: (804) 385–9081

1731

Business Information: Southern Air, Inc. specializes in mechanical and electrical contracting. As Director of Personnel, Mr. Graham is responsible for the hiring of management and field personnel, development and implementation of training programs, Worker's Compensation, and employee benefits. **Career Steps:** Southern Air, Inc: Director of Personnel (1994–Present), Project Manager (1983–1994), HVAC Designer/Draftsman (1982–1983). **Associations & Accomplishments:** Associate Member, American Society of Heating, Refrigeration, and Air Conditioning Engineers; Certified Master Trainer and Instructor, National Center for Construction Education and Research; Beulah Baptist Church: Deacon, Sunday School Teacher for 5th and 6th Grade Boys, Past Chairman of Budget and Property Committee; United Way Campaign Chairman for Construction Division; Prevention Center for Drug Abuse; United Way Day of Caring Committee; Company Received National Award for Meritorious Achievement presented by U.S. Department of Health and Human Services. **Education:** Virginia Polytechnic Institute, B.S. in Building Construction (1982); Central Virginia Community College, A.A.S. in Drafting and Design Technology (1978); Master Trainer, NCCER Instructor Certification. **Personal:** Married to Leslie Cole in 1984. Three children: Donnie, Haylie Jo, and Jay. Mr. Graham enjoys sports, staying physically fit, and community and church involvement.

Robert Hicks
President and Chief Executive Officer
Hicks Development, Inc.
30D Sanford Avenue
Opelika, AL 36801
(334) 749–4842
Fax: (334) 749–1930

1731

Business Information: Hicks Development, Inc. is a general contractor, specializing in HVAC and electrical work throughout Georgia and Alabama. Future plans include moving into more areas, including the southern parts of Alabama, Georgia, Mississippi, and Florida. Establishing Hicks Development, Inc. in 1990 and serving as President and Chief Executive Officer, Mr. Hicks is responsible for all aspects of operations, including administration, public relations, marketing, and strategic planning. Additional duties include bidding for jobs and serving as Construction Manager. **Career Steps:** President and Chief Executive Officer, Hicks Development, Inc. (1990–Present); President and Chief Executive Officer, Hicks Refrigeration and Service (1976–1990). **Associations & Accomplishments:** Local VFW. **Education:** Opelika Tech. College, A.A. (1976). **Personal:** Married to Kazue in 1957. Four children: Patricia Hicks–Clay, Robert Jr., Gerry R., and Monica Hicks–Crump. Mr. Hicks enjoys fishing and reading.

M. Russ Long
General Manager and Purchasing Agent
Long Industrial Service, Inc.
209 South Hoyle Avenue, P.O. Box 455
Bay Minette, AL 36507–0455
(334) 937–6487
Fax: (334) 937–7671

1731

Business Information: Long Industrial Service, Inc. is a commercial and industrial electrical contractor, with branches in Southern Alabama and Florida. As General Manager and Purchasing Agent, Mr. Long oversees the administrative staff focusing on banking and all financial matters. In addition, he

purchases all miscellaneous material and handles invoices. **Career Steps:** Long Industrial Service, Inc.: General Manager and Purchasing Agent (1995–Present), Project Manager (1993–1995). **Associations & Accomplishments:** Life Member, Auburn University Alumni Association; Centenial Club – Pi Kappa Alpha Alumni; Chamber of Commerce; North Baldwin Recreation. **Education:** Auburn University, B.S. in Management (1991). **Personal:** Married to Elizabeth in 1995. Mr. Long enjoys hunting, water sports, and fundraisers.

Peter Mendoza
• • •━━◉━━• • •

President
MBE Electric, Inc.
P.O. Box 7339
Riverside, CA 92513–7339
(909) 352–2490
Fax: (909) 352–2499

1731

Business Information: MBE Electric, Inc. is an electrical contractor, providing both subcontractural and direct contracting services. Licensed in Southern California, the majority of MBE Electric's business is in government projects and specializing in difficult jobs (i.e., tight schedules, heavily integrated systems, etc.). As one of two founding partners of MBE Electric, Mr. Mendoza currently serves as President of the Company. He is responsible for all aspects of Company operations, including administration, accounting, marketing, public relations, and strategic planning. Career milestones include being involved in the rebuilding of the Santa Monica Freeway after the earthquake – a $14 million contract. **Career Steps:** President, MBE Electric, Inc. (1988–Present); Manager of Street Lighting and TLS Division, VOSCO Corporation (1987–1988); Regional Manager of Public Works Division, Ramor Electric (1986–1987). **Associations & Accomplishments:** National Electrical Contractors Association. **Education:** Cerritos Community College; Fiber Optic Technician/Installer. **Personal:** Mr. Mendoza enjoys recreational vehicles, deep sea fishing, and travel.

Neal G. Myers
• • •━━◉━━• • •

Vice President of Operations
Tele Plus Corporation
140 Western Maryland Parkway
Hagerstown, MD 21740–5197
(301) 797–9500
Fax: (301) 797–1116

1731

Business Information: A regional telecommunications installation and maintenance company, Tele Plus Corporation specializes in the retail and commercial market of business telephone, music and paging systems, serving an area within a 100–mile radius of Hagerstown, MD. Tele Plus operates under three divisions: Voice Products, Premise Distribution Services, and Life Safety. As Vice President of Operations, Neal Myers oversees all operations of the Voice Product Division. His primary duties involve accounting, engineering and all day–to–day operations, including installation, service, personnel and computer maintenance. **Career Steps:** Vice President of Operations, Tele Plus Corporation (1986–Present); Operations Manager, Glessner Communications (1977–1986); Computer Operator, Pentamation Enterprises (1976–1977). **Associations & Accomplishments:** Past Member, International Management Council; Past Member, Local Church Board; Local Pee Wee Football Coach. **Education:** Hagerstown Junior College, currently working towards a management degree. **Personal:** Married to Barbara in 1979. Three children: Matthew, Brett, and Brooke. Mr. Myers enjoys basketball and collecting old oak telephones.

Donald M. Ord
President
Aztec Electric Service
8900–S. Edgeworth Drive
Capital Heights, MD 20743
(301) 324–1200
Fax: Please mail or call

1731

Business Information: Aztec Electric Service is a commercial, industrial, and residential electrical contracting company servicing Maryland, Washington D.C., and Northern Virginia. As President, Mr. Ord is responsible for all aspects of Company operations, including purchasing, project management, and accounting. **Career Steps:** President, Aztec Electric Service (1994–Present); Service Manager, T&H Electric (1983–1994); Electrician, Dyna Electric (1979–1983). **Associations & Accomplishments:** Associated Builders and Contractors. **Education:** JATC; Electric Training Program; 3 Master Electrician Licenses. **Personal:** Mr. Ord enjoys snow skiing and power boating.

Lawson A. Rankin Jr.
Secretary/Treasurer and Chief Financial Officer
Network Construction Services, Inc.
4019 Viewmont Drive
Greensboro, NC 27406
(910) 855-3950
Fax: (910) 292-7560

1731

Business Information: Network Construction Services, Inc. is an engineering and installation service for telecommunications cable, including fiber optic, copper, and coaxial cable. The Company has 49 distribution centers within the U.S., and two international locations. As Secretary/Treasurer and Chief Financial Officer, Mr. Rankin is responsible for the exchange of all financial aspects of the Company, including accounting, human resources, and information systems. **Career Steps:** Secretary/Treasurer and Chief Financial Officer, Network Construction Services, Inc. (1986-Present); Manager of Accounting and Information Systems, Sumitomo Electric Fiber Optics (1989-1993); Manager of Accounting, Northern Telecom (1982-1989); Controller, Business Application Systems (1981-1982). **Associations & Accomplishments:** American Institute of Certified Public Accountants; Construction Financial Management Association; Licensed Certified Public Accountant, State of North Carolina. **Education:** Duke University, M.B.A. (1987); University of North Carolina at Chapel Hill, B.S.B.A. (1977). **Personal:** Married to Gisele Lunsford in 1978. Two children: Lawson Allen III and Kathryn Grace. Mr. Rankin enjoys coaching his son's little league baseball and soccer.

Helen C. Reed
Director of Human Resources
D.C. Electronics
1800 Bering Drive
San Jose, CA 95112-4212
(408) 453-2400
Fax: (408) 453-2970

1731

Business Information: D.C. Electronics is a manufacturer, assembler, and distributor of cable products used for medical, computer, and telecommunication equipment. As Director of Human Resources, Ms. Reed is responsible for directing all personnel administration activities, including payroll, compensation, benefits, recruiting, and employee relations. **Career Steps:** Director of Human Resources, D.C. Electronics (1995-Present); Comp/Benefit Specialist, Net Frame (1992-1995); Human Resources Manager, ICPC (1989-1992). **Associations & Accomplishments:** Society of Human Resources Management; EAC. **Education:** College of Notre Dame, M.P.A. (1993); San Jose State University, B.S. **Personal:** Married to Jim in 1986. Ms. Reed enjoys writing poetry (has been published) and running 10K races.

Karen L. Scalf
Vice President/Secretary/Treasurer
Fast Electrical Contractors
335 Wilhagan Road
Nashville, TN 37217
(800) 297-4812 (615) 360-2300
Fax: (615) 399-1213

1731

Business Information: Fast Electrical Contractors specializes in commercial and industrial electrical construction and installation. As Vice President, Ms. Scalf is responsible for accounts payable, payroll, certified payrolls jobs, and other related activities. **Career Steps:** Vice President, Fast Electrical Contractors (1989-Present); Customer Relations Citation – Data Entry, Smyrna Police Department (1988-1989); Office Manager – Office Service, Hickory Hollow Office Center (1987-1988). **Associations & Accomplishments:** Former Member, National Association of Women in Construction. **Education:** Vocational Interactive Learning Center; Computer Courses. **Personal:** Married to George R. in 1992. One child: Karah Danielle Jackson. Ms. Scalf enjoys gardening, horses, bicycling, and aerobics.

Brenna E. Sharkey
Safety Director
Miller Romanoff Electric
3005 Lamb Avenue
Columbus, OH 43219
(614) 476-6600
Fax: (614) 476-6610

1731

Business Information: Miller Romanoff Electric is an electrical contracting firm providing service to the greater Columbus, Ohio area. As Safety Director, Ms. Sharkey is responsible for safety at twenty five sites. Other responsibilities include CAD (computer-assisted design) operations and design, and oversight of human resources. **Career Steps:** Safety Director, Miller Romanoff Electric (1995-Present); Sears Roebuck and Company: Project Implementor/Coordinator (Jan.1995-Sept.1995), Assistant to Brand Central Manager (1993-1994). **Associations & Accomplishments:** General Member, National Association of Women in Construction. **Education:** Memphis State University, Marketing, B.B.A. (1993). **Personal:** Ms. Sharkey enjoys bike riding and exercising.

Donald J. Spearman
Project Manager
Mitchell Construction Company, Inc.
507 Ocean Blvd.
St. Simons Island, GA 31522
(912) 634-0933
Fax: (912) 634-0155

1731

Business Information: Mitchell Construction Company, Inc. specializes in electrical contracting services for commercial, industrial, traffic signals, roadway lighting and signage, and HUD projects. As Project Manager, Mr. Spearman is responsible for diversified administrative activities, including overseeing all projects and contracts. **Career Steps:** Project Manager, Mitchell Construction Company, Inc. (1994-Present); Owner, Spearman Electric Service, Inc. (1981-1994); Electrical Supervisor, Rich–SeaPak Corporation (1977-1981); Foreman, Davis Electric (1974-1977) **Associations & Accomplishments:** Habitat for Humanity; Southern Baptist Foreign Mission Board Construction Volunteer **Education:** Greenville Technical College, Electronics Engineer (1976); Master Electrician/Electrical Contractor: Georgia, North Carolina, Alabama, Florida, and South Carolina. **Personal:** Married to Bennie Helen in 1974. Four children: Amy, Jessica, Melissa, and Garrison. Mr. Spearman enjoys golf, softball, writing and reading.

John Adam Stewart
Project Manager
Blumenthal and Kahn
10233 South Dolfield Road
Owings Mills, MD 21117-3620
(410) 363-1200
Fax: (410) 363-1215

1731

Business Information: Blumenthal and Kahn provides electrical installation and service for industrial, commercial, utility, and roadway purposes. Established in 1909, the Company currently employs 100 people and maintains annual sales estimated at $15 million. As Project Manager, Mr. Stewart is responsible for estimating projects, negotiating contracts, and managing electrical projects to completion. He also assists in daily Company functions including administration, operations, public relations, marketing, and strategic planning. **Career Steps:** Project Manager, Blumenthal and Kahn (1988-Present); Vice President President, NEA Metals (1990-1991); Project Manager, Blumenthal – Kahn Electric (1985-1990). **Associations & Accomplishments:** United We Stand America; National Rifle Association; MSRPA; Markland; American Homebrewers Association. **Education:** Attended, Essex Community College (1995); Baltimore Gas and Electric Classes; National Electric Code Classes. **Personal:** Mr. Stewart enjoys military history, Zymurgy and custom metal work.

Fernando Luis Sumaza Sr.
President
West Electric Corporation
P.O. Box 3006
Mayaguez, Puerto Rico 00681-3006
(809) 831-1918
Fax: (809) 833-6405

1731

Business Information: West Electric Corporation is an electrical contractor serving clientele throughout the Caribbean Islands. The $7 million corporation has two locations, employing seven engineers and 125 employees. Purchasing the business from his partner in 1969, Mr. Sumaza serves as President, overseeing all corporate operations and all administrative operations for associates and a support staff of 125 people. He has also been the environmental developer for major projects in Cabo Rojo, San Sebastian, Sabana Grande, San German, and Mayaguez, Puerto Rico. **Career Steps:** President, West Electric Corporation (1969-Present); Project Manager, U.S. Naval Station, San Juan, Puerto Rico (1965-1969); Electrical Engineer, Puerto Rico Electric Power Authority, San Juan, Puerto Rico (1962-1963); Military Background: Captain, U.S. Army and National Guard. **Associations & Accomplishments:** Puerto Rico Electrical Contractors Association; Puerto Rico Manufacturers Association; Mayaguez Chamber of Commerce; Institute of Electrical and Electronics Engineers; Puerto Rico Engineers College; Casino de Mayaguez Board; Club Deportivo Del Oeste. **Education:** Mayaguez A&M Puerto Rico, B.S. in Electrical Engineering. **Personal:** Married to Diana Santos in 1980. Five children: Zita Marie, Fernando, Patricio, Diana Marie, and Cristina Marie. Mr. Sumaza enjoys dancing, going to the beach, and walking.

Wilhelm A. Amstutz III
General Manager
Douglas/Gale Insulation
P O Box 25367
Tempe, AZ 85285
(602) 968-7945
Fax: (602) 968-1303

1742

Business Information: Douglas/Gale Insulation, a division of Gale Industries, Inc., is an insulation contractor headquartered in Daytona Beach, Florida. The Company, established in 1974, provides insulation for home and commercial builders, and estimates annual revenue to exceed $15 million. As General Manager, Mr. Amstutz oversees the day–to–day operations of the Tempe, Arizona location. His responsibilities include setting business goals, developing and implementing Facility budgets, and strategic planning for the future. **Career Steps:** General Manager, Douglas/Gale Insulation (1974-Present). **Associations & Accomplishments:** Insulation Contractors Association of America; Associated General Contractors; Home Builders Association of Central Arizona. **Education:** Northern Arizona University. **Personal:** Married to Francene in 1987. Three children: Rebecca, Erin, and Hannah. Mr. Amstutz enjoys deep sea fishing and bicycle riding.

Keith Combee
President
Combee Insulation Company, Inc.
1019 Triangle Street
Lakeland, FL 33805-3523
(941) 682-5783
Fax: (941) 682-7408

1742

Business Information: Mr. Combee established Combee Insulation Company, Inc., a local insulation contracting company, in 1971. As President, he is responsible for overseeing daily operations and performing various administrative functions, as well as hands–on contracting work. **Career Steps:** President, Combee Insulation Company, Inc. (1971-Present). **Associations & Accomplishments:** Lions Club; Independent Contractors Association of America; Chamber of Commerce. **Education:** Troy State University, B.S. (1984). **Personal:** Married to Gerri Gale in 1985. One child: Paige Elizabeth. Mr. Combee enjoys fishing, hunting, and golf.

Austin J. Scanlon III
President and Chief Executive Officer
Austin Scanlon Company
5510–18 North Second Street
Philadelphia, PA 19120
(215) 927-9840
Fax: (215) 927-9843

1742

Business Information: Austin Scanlon Company, is a family-owned, subcontracting firm, specializing in lath, plaster,

steel framing, drywall, acoustical tile, and E.I.F.S. Established in 1926 by Mr. Scanlon's grandfather, the Company reports annual revenue of $2.25 million and currently employs more than 15 people. Joining the Company in 1987, Mr. Scanlon was appointed as President and Chief Executive Officer, responsible for total daily operations, as well as providing estimates, cash maintenance, etc. **Career Steps:** President and Chief Executive Officer, Austin Scanlon Company (1993–Present). **Associations & Accomplishments:** Interior Finish Contractors Association: Vice President, Board of Directors (Since 1992); American Subcontractors Association of Delaware Valley: Former Member of Board of Directors, Sustained Member (Since 1967); Philadelphia Chamber of Commerce; Plasterers Union Local No. 8: President of Joint Apprentice Committee, Trustee. **Education:** Attended: Pennsylvania State (1987). **Personal:** Mr. Scanlon enjoys woodworking, theatre, arts/museums, and vacationing in warm climates.

Maria R. Cornelius

Vice President of Data Processing
Carpenter Contractors of America
941 SW 12th Avenue
Pompano Beach, FL 33069–4610
(305) 781–2660
Fax: (305) 786–9016

1751

Business Information: Carpenter Contractor of America is a carpentry and concrete labor subcontractor and roof and floor truss manufacturer with offices in Florida (Pompano Beach and Winter Haven) and Illinois (Palatine). Established in 1955, Carpenter Contractor of America currently employs 1,200 people. As Vice President of Data Processing, Ms. Cornelius is responsible for all computer systems, data input, data communication and information system personnel. **Career Steps:** Vice President of Data Processing, Carpenter Contractor of America (1988–Present); President, Application Software (1984–1988). **Education:** Florida Atlantic University, B.A.S. (1982). **Personal:** Ms. Cornelius enjoys working out in the gym, jogging and going to see the Miami Dolphins.

Mr. Billy D. Fritsch

Executive Vice President
Carpenter Contractors of America
941 S.W. 12th Avenue
Pompano Beach, FL 33069
(305) 781–2660
Fax: (305) 786–9016

1751

Business Information: Carpenter Contractors of America is a carpentry sub–contractor and truss manufacturer. Established for 39 years, Carpenter Contractors of America presently employs 800 people (Two offices: Chicago and Florida). In his current capacity, Mr. Fritsch is responsible for all financial aspects of the Company. **Career Steps:** Executive Vice President, Carpenter Contractors of America (1979–Present); Staff Accountant, Jonet, Fountain, VandeLoo, et al (1978–1979). **Associations & Accomplishments:** AICPA; Florida Institute of CPA's; Illinois CPA Society; Founding Trustee, Greater Fort Lauderdale Chamber of Commerce; Construction Financial Management Association; (Tax Specialists) Invited to tour China with Citizen Ambassador Program (1988); International Platform Association; Public Speaking. **Education:** Northern Michigan University, B.S. Degree (1978); CPA. **Personal:** Three children: Mackenzie, Billy III, and Jessica.

Mr. John Alan Laurie

Owner and President
Jack Laurie Commercial Floors
1828 South Anthony Boulevard
Ft. Wayne, IN 46803
(219) 745–2161
Fax: (219) 744–5172

1752

Business Information: Jack Laurie Commercial Floors, a family–owned business, is a commercial floor contractor. Established in 1950, the Company reports annual revenue of $2 million and currently employs 15 people. Upon receipt of his Bachelor's Degree in Industrial Management in 1986, his future plans were to work with a big corporation for two to three years and then return to school to earn his master's degree. Immediately following graduation, John fullfilled his goal by being hired by Procter & Gamble in Cincinnati as a Manufacturing Team Manager for Ivory Bar Soap and then into Marketing where he became a Zest Brand Assistant. After two years at Harvard (receiving his Master's degree) and a summer working in Brussels, Belgium, he became National Service Director at Cintas Corporation. Presently serving as Owner and President of a family–owned business, Mr. Laurie is responsible for all aspects of operations, including management of all functional areas, field operations, sales, marketing, finances and administration. **Career Steps:** Owner and President, Jack Laurie Commercial Floors (1994–Present); National Service Director, Cintas Corporation (1992–1995); Manufacturing, Finance & Marketing Manager, Proctor & Gamble Company (1986–1990). **Associations & Accomplishments:** Omicron Delta Kappa (National Leadership Honorary); Phi Eta Sigma (Scholastic Honorary); Distinguished Student Award, Gimlet (Fraternal Leadership Honorary); Purdue Varsity Tennis Team (4–year member); Purdue Student Association – Public Relations; Director, Junior Achievement of Cincinnati; United Way of Greater Cincinnati. **Education:** Harvard Business School, M.B.A. (1990–1992); Purdue University, B.S. in Industrial Management/Industrial Engineering (1986). **Personal:** Mr. Laurie enjoys tennis, basketball, skiing and volleyball.

Lawrence R. Dewine

Vice President
J&B Installations, Inc.
10 Edyth Street
East Rochester, NY 14445
(716) 385–2830
Fax: (716) 385–1675

1761

Business Information: J&B Installations, Inc. specializes in commercial and industrial roofing. Established in 1981, the Company has two locations, employs 50–65 people, and has an estimated annual revenue of $5–6 million. As Vice President, Mr. Dewine oversees and manages daily operations for both locations, including sales and marketing, safety training, and contract negotiations. **Career Steps:** J&B Installations, Inc: Vice President (1990–Present), General Manager (1989–1990); Project Manager, ERC Roofing Corporation (1987–1989); Sales Engineer, Tremco, Inc. (1983–1987). **Associations & Accomplishments:** National Roofing Contractors Association; New York State Roofing Contractors Association; Rochester Builders Exchange; CSI. **Education:** Elmira College, B.S. in Business Administration (1983). **Personal:** Married to Kathaleen in 1981. Three children: Jennifer, Jeffrey, and Marguerite. Mr. Dewine enjoys skiing, golf, boating, and being a CYO basketball coach.

John R. Diehl

President
The Christian Brothers Roofing of Texas, Inc.
1103 South Cedar Ridge Drive
Duncanville, TX 75137
(214) 780–1846
Fax: Please mail or call

1761

Business Information: The Christian Brothers Roofing of Texas, Inc. is a contracting business, specializing in roofing work and repairs. Establishing The Christian Brothers Roofing of Texas, Inc. in 1983, Mr. Diehl serves as President, responsible for all aspects of operations, including administration, management, finances, public relations, and strategic planning. In addition, he oversees all administrative operations for associates and a support staff of 25. **Career Steps:** President, The Christian Brothers Roofing of Texas, Inc. (1983–Present); Road Driver, Yellow Freight; Road Driver, Jones Truck Lines. **Associations & Accomplishments:** National Roofing Contractors Association (NRCA); Texas National Roofing Contractors Association (TNRCA); Homeowners Business Association (HBA). **Personal:** Married to Naomi Ruth in 1963. Three children: Jason, Sherry, and Donna. Mr. Diehl enjoys playing cards.

Daniel Lee Hodge

Controller
Welty Custom Exteriors, Inc.
300 North Bunnell Street
Frankfort, IN 46041–1610
(317) 654–7231
Fax: (317) 659–2984

1761

Business Information: Welty Custom Exteriors, Inc. is a home improvement company, specializing in the manufacture, installation and sales of residential exterior building products. Local in scope, Welty has retail store locations in Frankfort, Kokomo and Indianapolis. As Controller, Dan Hodge is responsible for all financial and sales administration. His primary duties involve: financial statements and reporting, accounts payable/receivable, payroll, as well as marketing strategies and sales marketing strategies and sales support. **Career Steps:** Controller, Welty Custom Exteriors, Inc. (1991–Present); Night Manager, Lees Inn – Lebanon (1987–1990); Night Dispatcher, Circle Van Express (1987). **Associations & Accomplishments:** Treasurer & Deacon, Grace Baptist Church in Lebanon; American Management Association. **Education:** IUPUI: M.A. in Finance (1994), B.A. in Accounting (1990). **Personal:** Married to Pamela in 1993. Three children: Gabrielle, Emily, and Bethany. Mr. Hodge enjoys science fiction.

Dick F. Ward

Vice President
A & W Roofing & Contracting
9391 Davis Avenue, Suite C
Laurel, MD 20723
(301) 317–5706
Fax: (301) 317–5709

1761

Business Information: A & W Roofing & Contracting is a commercial roofing and sheet metal contracting company for government, municipal, hospital, and school contracts. As Vice President, Mr. Ward is responsible for sales, marketing, administrative duties, contract negotiations and estimates, and project management. **Career Steps:** Vice President, A & W Roofing & Contracting (1990–Present); Vice President, Hega Construction (1988–1990); Project Manager, J & R Roofing (1987–1988); Director of Roofing, Meridian Construction (1986–1987). **Associations & Accomplishments:** Board of Directors, Washington Area Roofing Contractors. **Education:** Canton ATC (1977). **Personal:** Married to Cynthia in 1979. One child: Eric. Mr. Ward enjoys swimming, softball, golf, and scuba diving.

Kurt Boski

Operations Manager
Sunshine Masonry, Inc.
11547 Charlie's Terrace
Ft. Myers, FL 33907
(941) 936–6627
Fax: (941) 936–1705
EMAIL: See Below

1771

Business Information: Sunshine Masonry, Inc. is a structural concrete contracting company specializing in building concrete and masonry structures (i.e., buildings, houses, statues, etc.). As Operations Manager, Mr. Boski is responsible for the oversight of all activity, including scheduling manpower for all jobs, reviewing the scope of work for all contracts, and creating contract schedules. He also may be reached through the Internet via: Elbo7@AOL.com **Career Steps:** Operations Manager, Sunshine Masonry, Inc. (1990–Present); President and Owner, K.B. Homes (1987–1989); Field Supervisor, S.K.G. Associates (1982–1986). **Associations & Accomplishments:** American Diabetes Association; West Palm Beach Fishing Club. **Education:** Western Connecticut State University, B.S. in Business (1982). **Personal:** Married to Laurie in 1993. One child: Karissa Lee. Mr. Boski enjoys snow skiing and offshore fishing.

Randall S. Hawkins

General Manager
Conco Companies
510 North Sherman Parkway
Springfield, MO 65802
(417) 862–9336
Fax: (417) 862–9341

1771

Business Information: Conco Companies is a ready–mix concrete and crushed limestone aggregate company. Operations facilities include limestone quarries in Willard, Missouri and ready–mix plants in Willard, Springfield, Republic, Nixa, Hollister, and Branson West, Missouri. With 82 trucks in service, the Company distributes material to general contractors, concrete subcontractors, and homebuilders in Southwestern Missouri. Established in 1948, Conco Companies currently employs 300 people. Mr. Hawkins' background with Conco includes serving as a salesperson for five years, before leaving to establish his own construction business in 1985. Re–joining Conco Companies in 1987 as Marketing Manager, he currently serves as General Manager, responsible for the oversight and direction of all day–to–day activities through plant managers, sales and marketing, and long range planning, growth and expansion of the Company. **Career Steps:** Conco Companies: General Manager (1991–Present), Marketing Manager (1987–1991), Salesperson (1980–1985); Owner and President, Randall S. Hawkins Construction (1985–1987). **Associations & Accomplishments:** First President, Stone County Road Commission; Former President, Kimberling City/Tri Lakes Chamber of Commerce; President and Co–Founder, Tri Lakes Baseball Association (youth sports organization); President and Co–Founder, Concrete Promotional Council of the Ozarks; Board of Governors, Missouri Concrete Association; Treasurer, Springfield Contractors Association; Author of 10 articles published in trade journals. **Education:** Kickapoo High School, 1972 **Personal:** Married to Lisa in 1973. Four children: Jennifer, Leyla, Thomas and Chelsea. Mr. Hawkins enjoys golf, hunting, computer graphics and coaching youth sports.

Janet Kehm

President
H. Kehm Construction of Lincoln, Inc.
6201 Fulton
Lincoln, NE 68507–3222
(402) 464–4919
Fax: (402) 464–4963

1771

Business Information: H. Kehm Construction of Lincoln, Inc. is a concrete contractor, providing all aspects of concrete construction for local municipalities, commercial and industrial businesses through bidding contracts. Construction services include streets, parking lots, and all types of commercial work, as well as offering stamped and colored concrete. Co–Founding the Company in 1980, Janet Kehm serves as its President. She is responsible for all aspects of operations, including the day–to–day operations, office work, and accounting functions, such as bookkeeping and payroll. Her husband, Herman, directs all field operations of the business. **Career Steps:** President, H. Kehm Construction of Lincoln, Inc. (1980–Present); Keypunch/Verifier, Bankers Life Insurance (1967–1970). **Associations & Accomplishments:** Notary Republic – National Notary Association member (1995); National Association for the Self–Employed (1991). **Personal:** Married to Herman J., Jr. in 1967. Three children: Nickole, Amorette, and Teresa. Ms. Kehm enjoys crocheting, needlework, quilting, gardening, and reading.

Lori J. Mason, CPA

Vice President
Atlantic Concrete Forms Inc.
101 Scituate Avenue P.O. Box 8907
Cranston, RI 02920
(401) 942–5544
Fax: (401) 944–8310

1771

Business Information: Atlantic Concrete Forms Inc. is a concrete subcontractor, servicing the State of Rhode Island and Southern Massachusetts in both the residential and commercial markets since 1958. As Vice President, Ms. Mason is responsible for the overall financial operations and day–to–day office management. She also serves as Controller and Chief Financial Officer supervising the daily administration of the Company, as well as serves on the Board of Directors. **Career Steps:** Vice President, Atlantic Concrete Forms Inc. (1986–Present); Senior Accountant, Ernst & Whinney (1986); Senior Accountant, Coopers & Lybrand (1984–1986). **Associations & Accomplishments:** Rhode Island Society of Certified Public Accountants; Commissioner, Rhode Island Ethics Commission. **Education:** Boston College, B.S. in Accounting (1984). **Personal:** One child: Peter F., Jr. Ms. Mason enjoys weightlifting and vocal studies.

Dolores J. Adams

Vice President
Adams Truss, Inc.
12420 Collins Road
Gentry, AR 72734–9375
(800) 228–9221
Fax: (501) 736–2690

1791

Business Information: Adams Truss, Inc., a family–owned and operated company founded by the late Fred Adams, is a national manufacturer of steel building trusses and retailer of building material packages. As Vice President, Ms. Adams is responsible for all aspects of administrative operations for the Company, including payroll, accounts payable and receivable, customer service, etc. Her greatest accomplishment was assisting in the continual success of the Company after the passing of her father, Fred Adams. **Career Steps:** Vice President, Adams Truss, Inc. (1964–Present); Unit Manager/Senior, Unpostables IRS 1970–1975); Cost/Production Clerk, Report Unit IRS (1966–1970); Department Manager, Superior Laundry (1964). **Associations & Accomplishments:** Advocate and Board Member (4 Years), North West Arkansas Rape Crisis Center; National Association of Women in Construction, Served in various offices in North West Arkansas Chapter; Former Church School Board, active in local church in various offices. **Education:** Attended: Union College and University of Arkansas. **Personal:** Ms. Adams enjoys playing the piano, needlework, reading, and working with children.

William B. Gibris

Operations Manager
Steel Fabricators
721 NE 44th Street
Ft. Lauderdale, FL 33334
(954) 772–0440
Fax: (954) 938–7527

1791

Business Information: Steel Fabricators, a division of Canam Steel Corporation, specializes in the fabrication of structural steel buildings and bridges. They also have registered engineers and provide details regarding their structures, the fabrication process, and the erection methods of the buildings and bridges. Mr. Gibris joined Bethlehem Steel Corporation in 1967, serving as Assistant Plant Superintendent. He moved on to become Vice President of Operations at Allied Structural Steel in 1975. In 1989 he became Operations Manager for Steel Fabricator's structural fabrication plant, he presently oversees all shop operations. This includes production, personnel, safety, and strategic planning. In addition, he is responsible in estimating and bidding procedures. **Career Steps:** Steel Fabricators, A Division of Canam Steel Corporation: Operations Manager (1989–Present), Vice President of Operations, Allied Structural Steel (1975–1989), Assistant Plant Superintendent, Bethlehem Steel Corporation (1967–1975). **Associations & Accomplishments:** Vice Chairman, Committee of National Steel Construction Conferences – American Institute of Steel Construction; Executive Committee and First Vice Chair, American Welding Society. **Education:** Northeastern University, B.A. in Civil Engineering (1967); Wentworth Institute, Associate Degree in Civil Engineering (1963). **Personal:** Married to Lynn in 1987. Two children: Laura and Deborah. Mr. Gibris enjoys golf and gardening.

Mr. Donald Edmond Robison

President
Waukegan Steel Sales Inc.
1201 Belvidere St.
Waukegan, IL 60085–6203
(708) 662–2810
Fax: (708) 662–2818

1791

Business Information: Waukegan Steel Sales Inc. specializes in steel fabrication, the erection of steel structures, and miscellaneous iron works. Established in the 1930's, Waukegan Steel currently employs 70 people and has an estimated annual revenue of $8 million. As President and Chief Operating Officer, Mr. Robison is responsible for all aspects of operations. **Career Steps:** President, Waukegan Steel Sales Inc. (1994–Present); Various Positions, Leibovich Brothers (1975–1994); Various Positions, INRYCO (1964–1975). **Associations & Accomplishments:** American Institute of Steel Construction; Construction Fabricators Association. **Education:** Illinois Institute of Technology, B.S. in Engineering Science (1963). **Personal:** Married to Joanne in 1964. Two children: Jody Ann and Donald E. Jr. Mr. Robison enjoys teaching Martial Arts.

Steven D. Zenz

Owner/Chief Financial Officer
South Coast Structural, Inc.
10299 Scribbs Trail, Suite 242
San Diego, CA 92131
(619) 586–0530
Fax: (619) 586–0326
E MAIL: See Below

1791

Business Information: South Coast Structural, Inc., established in 1990, is a structural steel erection company working with field fabricators. The Company estimates revenue of $1.5 million, and presently employs 16 people. As Owner/CFO, Mr. Zenz oversees all Company operations. He is responsible for all contract negotiations, financial decisions, cash management, budgetary concerns, and strategic planning for the future. Mr. Zenz also appears as an expert witness for attorneys engaged in litigation pertaining to construction accidents. Internet users can reach him via: SDZenz@aol.com. **Career Steps:** Owner/Chief Financial Officer, South Coast Structural, Inc. (1991–Present); President/Field Operations Manager, Speed Structural, Inc. (1984–1991); Superintendent, Sierra Steel, Inc. (1979–1984); Project Foreman, Martin iron Works, Inc. (1972–1979). **Associations & Accomplishments:** Associated General Contractors, San Diego; Past President, American Subcontractors Association of California; Co–Chair of Founding Committee and Past President, American Subcontractors Association of San Diego. **Education:** University of Nevada, B.S. (1970). **Personal:** Married to Phyllis in 1981. Four children: Leslie and Amy Jo Zenz and Stacey and Triston Miller. Mr. Zenz enjoys golf, travel, and spending time with his family.

Ronald D. Dodson

Owner
D&W Associates Company Inc.
2091 River Road
Wichita Falls, TX 76304–7262
(817) 322–6095
Fax: (817) 322–2696

1794

Business Information: D&W Associates Company Inc. is a local paving and excavating company serving government, city, and county agencies. As Owner, Mr. Dodson is responsible for all aspects of operations, including management and oversight of projects and employees, in addition to "hands on" activities. **Career Steps:** Owner, D&W Associates Company Inc. (1978–Present); Supervisor, Zack Burkett Company (1972–1976); Supervisor, City of Mineral Wells (1967–1972); Operator, H B Zackery Company (1962–1967). **Associations & Accomplishments:** AGC Texas; IBF Texas; National Right to Work. **Personal:** Married to Pat in 1958. Two children: Cody and Rhonda. Mr. Dodson enjoys travel.

Vickie L. Mansfield

President and Chief Executive Officer
Laser Grading Service, Inc.
1320 Rail Head Boulevard, Suite 5
Naples, FL 33963–8437
(813) 566–1127
Fax: (813) 566–9193

1794

Business Information: Laser Grading Service, Inc., a family–owned business, is a grading and filling sub–contractor, providing dump trucks and land clearing for million dollar homes. Established in 1989, Laser Grading Service, Inc. reports annual revenue of $1 million and currently employs 10 people. As President and Chief Executive Officer, Ms. Mansfield is responsible for all aspects of operations, including accounting and management duties. Her husband serves as Vice President. **Career Steps:** President, Laser Grading Service, Inc. (1989–Present); Field Office Manager, The Hardaway Company (1988–1989); Accounting Manager, Winger, Nadea & Easly (1987–1988); Bookkeeper, Neapolitan Association (1986–1987). **Associations & Accomplishments:** National Association for Female Executives (NAFE); Florida Chamber of Commerce; American Subcontractors Association of Collier County. **Education:** Waukesha Technical Institute, Business Courses; Meno Falls North High School, Graduate (1976). **Personal:** Married to John L. in 1988. Two children: Marissa and Lacy. Ms. Mansfield enjoys dolphin fishing in the Florida Keys, boating, and aerobics.

George J. Radandt

President
F. Radandt Sons Inc.
1800 Johnston Drive
Manitowoc, WI 54220–1333
(414) 682–7758
Fax: (414) 682–6109

1794

Business Information: F. Radandt Sons Inc., a family–owned business established in 1913, is a multi–faceted contract services company. The Company provides a variety of services including: Gravel Production, Excavating, Demolition Trucking, Commercial and Construction Refuse Services. Joining the family business upon completing his military duty in 1968 as a dozer operator in the combat engineers, George Radant was appointed as President in 1982. In this capacity, he is responsible for all operations for the Divisions of Demolition, Excavating and Trucking. **Career Steps:** F. Radandt Sons Inc.: President (1982–Present), Sales (1971–1982), Dispatcher (1968–1971); Combat Engineer, U.S. Army (1965–1968). **Associations & Accomplishments:** Manitowoc County Master Builders; Associated Builders & Contractors; Wisconsin Road Builders; Honorary Member, Wisconsin Concrete Association. **Personal:** Married to Laura Lynn in 1971. Four children: Jason, Brooke, Hilde, and Leslie. Mr. Radandt enjoys woodworking, fishing, and going to old car shows.

Bill Bartlett

• • • ◦ ━━◉━━ ● • • •

President, Chief Executive and Chief Operations Officer

Olshan Demolishing

3575 West 12th Street
Houston, TX 77008–6005
(713) 867–9200
Fax: (713) 867–9215

1795

Business Information: Olshan Demolishing, a wholly–owned subsidiary of NSC Corporation, is a specialty demolitions contractor serving Fortune 500 companies. Established in 1933, it is considered one of the top ten industrial dismantling contractors in the nation. As President, Chief Executive and Chief Operations Officer, Bill Bartlett is responsible for providing executive leadership, carrying out diversified administrative duties, ensuring quality and Company growth, and supervising future expansion plans. **Education:** University of Houston, B.S. (1977). **Personal:** Married to Susan in 1984. Three children: Thomas, Hilary, and Clare. Mr. Bartlett enjoys reading, and playing basketball and football.

Mr. Robert E. Fields

Vice President

D.H. Griffin Wrecking Co., Inc.

4700 Hilltop Road
Greensboro, NC 27407
(910) 855–7030
Fax: (910) 855–9309

1795

Business Information: D.H. Griffin Wrecking Co., Inc. demolishes buildings by means of explosives and conventional demolitions. The Company also operates a 40–acre scrap metal recycling yard, an environmental company, and an asbestos removal company. As Vice President of the Recycling Division, Mr. Fields oversees all aspects of operations for the division, including sales and marketing, and quality control. Established in 1959, D.H. Griffin Wrecking Co., Inc. employs over 500 people and conducts operations worldwide. **Career Steps:** Vice President, D.H. Griffin Wrecking Co., Inc. (1989–Present); Head Purchasing Agent, D.H. Griffin Wrecking Co., Inc. (1972–Present); Military Service, Crew Chief, Vietnam (1969–1972); Head Purchasing Agent, D.H. Griffin Wrecking Co., Inc. (1965–1972). **Associations & Accomplishments:** Institute of Scrap Recycling Industries, Inc. (ISRI); American Demolition Association (ADA); American Ostrich Association. **Education:** Guilford Technical College.

Nancy Cole Allen

• • • ◦ ━━◉━━ ● • • •

Vice President

HTA Enterprises

P.O. Box 58513
Louisville, KY 40268
(502) 933–5900
Fax: (502) 933–0501

1799

Business Information: HTA Enterprises is a subcontracting company, specializing in drilling and blasting, utility construction, site development, and quality control. Jobs are obtained through a bidding process with general contractors, throughout a 100–mile radius of Louisville. Entering the construction industry to earn extra money while attending college, Ms. Allen fell in love with it and has held several construction positions (laborer/operator, driller/blaster, superintendent/foreman) during the past sixteen years. A specialist in construction blasting (her partner's is drilling), she joined HTA Enterprises as Vice President in 1991. She is responsible for the overall management of the Company, including day–to–day operations, estimating and coordinating jobs and processing project billings and pay estimates. **Career Steps:** Vice President, HTA Enterprises (1991–Present); Superintendent/ Foreman, T&C Contracting, Inc. (1987–1991); Driller/Blaster, S&S Piping, Inc. (1986–1987); Laborer/Operator, Skilton Construction, Inc. (1980–1985). **Associations & Accomplishments:** Society of Blasting Engineering – Bluegrass Chapter; National Rifle Association. **Education:** Bellarmine College, Basketball Scholarship, majored in Biology (2 years). **Personal:** Married to Michael in 1994. Two children: Kristie and Donnie. Ms. Allen enjoys participating in sports (softball and basketball), shotgun sports (trap & sporting clays), riding horses, hunting, and fishing.

Pamela C. Berry

Financial Manager

Madison Research Corporation

401 Wynn Drive Northwest
Huntsville, AL 35805
(205) 864–7260
Fax: (205) 864–7288
Email: See Below

1799

Business Information: Madison Research Corporation, headquartered in Huntsville, Alabama, is a government contracting firm specializing in service support, software, drafting, and repairing. The Facility is responsible for the government's small support contract needs. As Financial Manager, Ms. Berry is responsible for handling fiscal matters and performing administrative functions including payroll, proposals, travel, accounts payable, and budgeting. Internet users can reach her via: PBerry@MadisonResearch.com. **Career Steps:** Financial Manager, Madison Research Corporation (1995–Present); Senior Accountant, Computer Sciences Corporation (1994–1995); Lead Accountant, Boeing Information Services (1989–1994); Accountant, UT Health Science Center (1986–1987). **Associations & Accomplishments:** American Society of Women Accountants; Deltec Users Group. **Education:** Wake Forest University, M.B.A. (1989); Birmingham Southern College, B.A. in Accounting (1983). **Personal:** Married to Neal in 1990. Two children: Rebecca and Emily. Ms. Berry enjoys travel and reading.

Marcus L. Eisberner

General Manager

Coastal Container Services

6110 West Marginal Way, SW
Seattle, WA 98106
(206) 764–4500
Fax: (206) 763–6478

1799

Business Information: Coastal Container Services specializes in the repair of marine containers and refrigeration devices, and off dock storage mobile repair. As General Manager, Mr. Eisberner is responsible for all aspects of Company operations, including customer relations, operations, repair, storage, refrigeration maintenance, sales, and trucking. **Career Steps:** Coastal Container Services (1979–Present): General Manager, Sales Manager, Service Manager. **Associations & Accomplishments:** Seattle Transportation Club; Eagles Club. **Education:** Air Cargo/Passenger Service Advanced Course. **Personal:** Mr. Eisberner enjoys golf, softball, fishing, and working out.

Lance G. Fisher

• • • ◦ ━━◉━━ ● • • •

General Manager

Marcor Delmarva

1607 Northwood Drive
Salisbury, MD 21801
(410) 742–6161
Fax: (410) 742–3029

1799

Business Information: Marcor Delmarva is a national environmental remediation contractor for asbestos, lead paint, soils, IAQ, industrial cleaning, etc. Established in 1982, Marcor Delmarva reports annual revenue of $4 million and currently employs 80 people. As General Manager, Mr. Fisher is responsible for all financial decisions of the Company and future direction. **Career Steps:** Marcor Delmarva: General Manager (1994–Present), Project Manager (1989–1994); Industrial Hygienist, A.M.A. (1986–1989). **Associations & Accomplishments:** Beta Beta Beta; Collegiate Scholastic All American College; Salisbury Elks. **Education:** Salisbury State University, B.S. (1987). **Personal:** Married to Carrie in 1992. Mr. Fisher enjoys golf, darts, pool, sports, and tennis.

Arles B. Greene

President

ABG Caulking Contracting, Inc.

P.O. Box 344, 301 South Main Street
Goodlettsville, TN 37070
(615) 859–4935
Fax: (615) 851–7258

1799

Business Information: ABG Caulking Contracting, Inc. is one of the largest caulking and waterproofing companies in the United States. ABG has six offices to serve the Southern States. As President, Mr. Greene is responsible for the Company operations, including administrative finance, sales and marketing. He has his brothers Shannon and Phil along with his sons Scotty and Wesley assisting him on the daily operations. **Career Steps:** President, ABG Caulking Contracting,

Inc. (1971–Present); President, ABG Properties; President, Greene Petroleum. **Associations & Accomplishments:** President, Nashville Contractors Association. **Education:** Carson – Newman, B.S. (1970). **Personal:** Three children: Scott, Wesley, and Shelley. Mr. Greene enjoys fishing and golf.

Miss Bonita J. Hromidko

Secretary/Treasurer

Quality Asphalt Paving, Inc.

240 West 68th Avenue
Anchorage, AK 99518
(907) 522–2211
Fax: (907) 344–5798

1799

Business Information: Quality Asphalt Paving, Inc. (QAP) is a paving construction contractor, specifically for federal and state governmental agencies within the state of Alaska. Miss Hromidko serves as Controller, Office Manager, EEO Officer and Secretary/Treasurer for Quality Asphalt Paving, Inc. In addition, she also serves as a full–charge bookkeeper, Secretary/Treasurer for Hayden & Hayes Construction, Inc. and Aggregate Products, Inc. (subsidiary corporations of QAP), as well as bookkeeper for Hayden & Hayes Company. In her function as Controller for QAP, she reviews and balances the general ledger and prepares accounting documentation for their CPA firm. She handles all billing and collection of receivables, cash flows, union reporting, payroll tax reporting, workmens compensation, EEO reporting, bank reconciliations, year end union and workmens compensation audits. As Office Manager she is responsible for hiring and terminations of staff personnel with accounts payable, payroll, reception, contract document positions; monitoring health insurance, profit sharing, and various other supervisory functions. Her role as EEO Officer requires her attendance at pre– construction conferences for projects awarded, as well as monitoring of the Company's monthly female and minority goals. Duties for AGG-PRO and Hayden & Hayes Construction, Inc. consist of payroll, accounts payable, receivables, general ledger and bank reconciliation. Established in 1970, Quality Asphalt Paving, Inc. employs 180 people. **Career Steps:** Secretary/Treasurer, Quality Asphalt Paving, Inc. (1988–Present and 1981–1986); Owner and President, Sleeping Lady, Inc. (1988–1992); Partner, Double Entry Bookkeeping (1986–1988). **Associations & Accomplishments:** President, Condo Association (1992–Present). **Education:** Bemedji State University; Bagley High School (1968).

Chrisann Karches

President

Southwest Hazard Control, Inc.

5400 W. Massingale Road
Tucson, AZ 85743–9620
(520) 744–1060
Fax: (520) 744–1654

1799

Business Information: Southwest Hazard Control, Inc. is a governmental contractor, specializing in remedial clean–up and assessment of hazardous materials – particularly focusing on asbestos abatement. National in scope, with headquarters in Tucson, Arizona, the Firm also has satellite offices in Phoenix, AZ; Albuquerque, NM; and San Francisco, CA. Joining Southwest Hazard Control in 1983 as Controller, Chrisann Karches was appointed as President in 1995. In this capacity, she provides the overall executive administration, focusing on quality service, contract negotiations, project management, and overall strategies. **Career Steps:** Southwest Hazard Control, Inc.: President (1994–Present), Division Manager (1986–1994), Controller (1983–1986). **Associations & Accomplishments:** SAEMS – EIA. **Education:** University of Arizona, B.S. (1984) **Personal:** Married to Michael Lansky in 1994. Ms. Karches enjoys reading, birding, scuba diving, vacationing and hiking.

Carl J. Ostrom

Plant Manager

MJC, Inc.

2060 Airport Industrial Park Drive
Marietta, GA 30062
(800) 728–1004
Fax: (770) 952–4785

1799

Business Information: MJC, Inc. is an industrial coating and modification plant for HVAC equipment, providing in–plant services not offered by factories. With eighteen years of experience in the HVAC industry, Mr. Ostrom joined MJC, Inc. as Plant Manager. MJC, Inc. was a 400K business at that time, MJC, Inc. is looking at a 4,200K this year. He is responsible for the day–to–day operations for the entire plant, including administration, deadline compliance, and supervision of a staff of 38. **Career Steps:** Plant Manager, MJC, Inc. (1991–Present); Trane Co.: Marketing Specialist (1988–1991), Buyer (1986–1988), Customer Service Supervisor (1981–1986), Factory Cost Auditor (1980–1981), Quality Control Auditor (1978–1980), Shear Line Operator (1973–1978). **Associa-**

tions & Accomplishments: American Society of Heating, Refrigeration, and Air Conditioning Engineers; Published in "Air Conditioning News" (1995). **Education:** Austin Peay State University, B.S. (1979).

Reginald G. Roberson

President
Precision Petroleum, Inc.
1318 18th Avenue
Rockford, IL 61104–5349
(815) 226–8190
Fax: (815) 961–0171

1799

Business Information: Precision Petroleum, Inc. services gas station petroleum equipment. Mr. Roberson established the company in November of 1992, supervising daily operations, sales and marketing, and personnel decisions. In addition to Precision Petroleum, he also serves as President of GFI Services, a petroleum construction company, which he purchased in June of 1995. **Career Steps:** President, Precision Petroleum, Inc. (1992–Present); President, GFI Services (1995–Present); District Manager, Clark Refining Marketing (1993–1992). **Associations & Accomplishments:** Moose Club, Fellowship Degree; Wisconsin Petroleum Equipment; Chicago Oilmens Club; NFIB; Petroleum Equipment Institute; Illinois Petroleum Marketers Association. **Education:** Attended Rock Valley College. **Personal:** Married to Joanne in 1994. One child: Brittany. Mr. Roberson enjoys softball and photography.

Karl J. Schram
Chief Financial Officer
Land Coast Insulation, Inc.
P.O. Box 14110
New Iberia, LA 70562–4110
(318) 367–7741 Ext. 201
Fax: (318) 367–7744
Email: See Below

1799

Business Information: Land Coast Insulation, Inc. is an industrial specialty contractor providing equipment and piping for vessels. As Chief Financial Officer, Mr. Schram is responsible for managing all financial activities, supervising accounting, handling billing and payroll, and maintaining bank relationships. Internet users can reach him via: KarlSchram@aol.com. **Career Steps:** Certified Financial Officer, Land Coast Insulation, Inc. (1995–Present); Internal Auditor, First National Bank of Houma (1992–1993); Partner – CPA, Gus W. Schram, Jr., Ltd. (1978–1989). **Associations & Accomplishments:** Louisiana Society of CPA's; American Institute of CPA's. **Education:** McNeese State University, B.S. in Accounting (1979); Certified Public Accountant (1982). **Personal:** Married to Suzanne in 1993. Two children: Tiffany and Garrett. Mr. Schram enjoys golf, fishing, and hunting.

2000 – 3999
MANUFACTURING

2000 Food and Kindred Products

2011 Meat packing plants
2013 Sausages and other prepared meats
2015 Poultry slaughtering and processing
2021 Creamery butter
2022 Cheese, natural and processed
2023 Dry, condensed, evaporated products
2024 Ice cream and frozen desserts
2026 Fluid milk
2032 Canned specialties
2033 Canned fruits and vegetables
2034 Dehydrated fruits, vegetables, soups
2035 Pickles, sauces, and salad dressings
2037 Frozen fruits and vegetables
2038 Frozen specialties, NEC
2041 Flour and other grain mill products
2043 Cereal breakfast foods
2044 Rice milling
2045 Prepared flour mixes and doughs
2046 Wet corn milling
2047 Dog and cat food
2048 Prepared feeds, NEC

2051 Bread, cake, and related products
2052 Cookies and crackers
2053 Frozen bakery products, except bread
2061 Raw cane sugar
2062 Cane sugar refining
2063 Beet sugar
2064 Candy and other confectionery products
2066 Chocolate and cocoa products
2067 Chewing gum
2068 Salted and roasted nuts and seeds
2074 Cottonseed oil mills
2075 Soybean oil mills
2076 Vegetable oil mills, NEC
2077 Animal and marine fats and oils
2079 Edible fats and oils, NEC
2082 Malt beverages
2083 Malt
2084 Wines, brandy, and brandy spirits
2085 Distilled and blended liquors
2086 Bottled and canned soft drinks
2087 Flavoring extracts and syrups, NEC
2091 Canned and cured fish and seafoods
2092 Fresh or frozen prepared fish
2095 Roasted coffee
2096 Potato chips and similar snacks
2097 Manufactured ice
2098 Macaroni and spaghetti
2099 Food preparations, NEC

William Preston Cox
Vice President and Chief Financial Officer
SMG, Inc.
2890 Chancellor Drive
Crestview Hills, KY 41017
(606) 344–3700
Fax: (513) 871–9141

2011

Business Information: SMG, Inc. is a meat processing and packaging plant, capable of processing over 100 million pounds of meat a year. SMG ships 60 percent of its meat to retail chains, including Food Lion and Acme, and the remainer to food manufacturing conglomerates such as Oscar Mayer and Kraft. Established in 1994, SMG, Inc. currently employs 500 people and has an estimated annual revenue of $160 million. As Vice President and Chief Financial Officer, Mr. Cox is responsible for all aspects of financial operations, including accounting. **Career Steps:** Vice President and Chief Financial Officer, SMG, Inc. (1994–Present); Senior Manager, KPMG, New York (1993–1994, 1986–1990); Senior Manager, KPMG, London, England (1990–1993). **Associations & Accomplishments:** American Institute of Certified Public Accountants; Kentucky Society of Certified Public Accountants. **Education:** University of Kentucky, B.S. (1983). **Personal:** Married. Mr. Cox enjoys family, travel, golf, and horse racing.

Nelson Mamede

Commercial Director
Sadia Concordia, S.A.
Alameda Tocatins 525 Andar 3
Sao Paulo (Alphaville), Brazil 06455–921
55–11–72964485
Fax: 55–11–72964211

2011

Business Information: Sadia Concordia, S.A. is the largest meat processing company in Latin America, serving all of Brazil and exporting to 40 other countries. The Company processes turkey, pork, and chicken for its over 150 thousand clients and supermarkets. With estimated annual export revenue of $500 million, the Company has 25 meat processing plants across Brazil and 5 plants for crushing grain. As Commercial Director, Mr. Mamede handles all supplies and sales of the grains from the crushing plants. He is responsible for the sales of soy bean and oil determination, and oversees all logistics of Sadia Concordia. **Career Steps:** Commercial Director, Sadia Concordia, S.A. (1988–Present); Trading Director, Continental Grain, Inc. (1986–1988); General Manager, Interbras S/A (1978–1986). **Associations & Accomplishments:** Brazilian Association of Agribusiness; Brazilian Association of Seed Crushers; Study Program of Agribusiness – University of Sao Paulo; Brazilian Commodities and Futures Exchange. **Education:** Bennett University, B.Adm. (1974). **Personal:** Married to Cristina in 1977. Two children: Joanna and Pedro. Mr. Mamede enjoys tennis and swimming.

Lee Miles III

Vice President of Retail Sales
Bryan Foods, Inc.
P.O. Box 1177
West Point, MS 39773–1177
(601) 494–3741
Fax: (601) 495–4506

2011

Business Information: Bryan Foods, a division of Sara Lee Corp., is a major manufacturer of processed meat, including hot dogs, smoked sausage, bacon, corn dogs, hams and lunch meat. Established in 1936, Bryan supplies wholesalers and retailers throughout the Southeastern United States. Bryan Foods has production facilities in West Point, MS; Tupelo, MS; and Little Rock, AR. Bryan's corporate office is located in West Point, MS. Bryan employs approximately 2800 people. Mr. Miles is responsible for all aspects of retail sales. This includes a direct sales force of a 120 people, as well as a broker network covering 17 states. **Career Steps:** Bryan Foods: Vice President of Retail Sales (1994–Present), Director of Retail Sales (1993–1994), Regional Manager (1990–1993), District Manager (1986–1990); Manda's Fine Meats: National Sales Manager (1982–1986), District Manager (1980–1982); Sales, Hyde Premium Meats (1975–1980). **Education:** Attended Southeastern Louisiana University. **Personal:** Married to Fern in 1991. Mr. Miles enjoys golf, politics, and reading. Mr. Miles is involved in fund raising activities for the United Way and the Palmer Home for Children.

Flavio R. Schmidt

Director of Administration And System Areas
Sadia Concordia S/A Ind. E. Com.
Alameda Tocantins N 525 – Alphavillo
Barueri SP, Brazil 06455–921
55–11–726–4450
Fax: 55–11–726–4505

2011

Business Information: Sadia Concordia S/A Ind. E. Com. began operations in 1944 and has the leadership of Brazilian slaughter and production of pork, poultry, and turkey. The Sadia Group is among the top five exporters of animal protein and has commercial plants in Milan, Dubai, Tokyo, Buenos Aires, Pequim and Miami. As Director of Administration And System Areas, Mr. Schmidt is responsible for all legal aspects of the operation. He reviews contracts and verifies contract compliance with international regulations. Mr. Schmidt works closely with the accounting departments in the establishment of annual budgets and then monitors all departments for budget compliance. Other duties include development and implementation of information technology systems, public relations, and strategic planning for the future. Internet users can reach him via: rschmidt@sadin.com. **Career Steps:** Sadia Concordia S/A Ind. E. Com.: Director of Administration And System Areas (1994–Present), Vice President of Planning, Control, and Financial Areas (1988–1994), Financial Director (1984–1988). **Associations & Accomplishments:** Fundacao Dom Cabral. **Education:** Universidade do Vale do Rio Dos Sinos, B.A. in Accounting (1978), B.A. in Business Administration (1975); The CIO Workshop Program, BUA (1996); Juse Tos, Seminar for Brazil Top Managerment (1992) Insfade/Fundacao Dom Cabral, IVPGA (1993); **Personal:** Married to Vera Lucia Fontana in 1974. Two children: Alexandre Fontana and Daniel Fontana. Mr. Schmidt enjoys tennis and soccer.

Robert M. Grimes

Director of Sales and Marketing
Lays Fine Foods
P.O. Box 2447
Knoxville, TN 37901–2447
(423) 546–2511
Fax: (423) 546–2130

2013

Business Information: Lays Fine Foods is a national processor and distributor of retail and food service meat products, primarily pork. Joining Lays Fine Foods as Director of Sales and Marketing in 1994, Mr. Grimes directs and manages all facets of sales and marketing, including wholesale, retail, and food service. **Career Steps:** Director of Sales and Marketing, Lays Fine Foods (1994–Present); Brown & Williamson Tobacco Corporation: National Merchandising Manager (1992–1994), Brand Manager of New Products (1991–1992), Brand Manager of Viceroy, GPC (1988–1990). **Associations & Accomplishments:** American Marketing Association; United Methodist Men. **Education:** University of Alabama, B.A. (1996).

Personal: Married to Sheila Spivey Grimes in 1981. Two children: Elizabeth and Sarah. Mr. Grimes enjoys golf, tennis, and being a youth leader.

Jim Schwarz

Sales Manager
Citterio USA Corporation
5115 35th Street
Long Island City, NY 11101–3256
(800) 435–8888
Fax: (718) 937–7138

2013

Business Information: Citterio USA Corporation is a manufacturer, importer, and distributor of Italian specialty meats, including prosciutto (ham), and dry–cured sausages, as well as the importing and selling of Lazzaroni cookies. Clientele include supermarkets, country clubs, higher–end drug stores, and non–food businesses nationwide. With twenty–six years of experience in the food industry (i.e., Nabisco, Keebler, Kellogg, Plumrose USA, Sunshine Biscuits), Mr. Schwarz joined Citterio USA Corporation as Sales Manager in 1995. He is responsible for the total management of sales and marketing activities in the U.S., in addition to overseeing a staff of 8. **Career Steps:** Sales Manager, Citterio USA Corporation (1995–Present); Director of Specialty Foods, Plumrose USA (1985–1995); NE Area Manager, Sunshine Biscuits, Inc. (1982–1985). **Associations & Accomplishments:** Eastern Deli–Dairy Association; New England Deli Dairy Association; Biscuit and Cracker Distributor of America; Promise Keepers. **Education:** Oregon State University, B.S. (1969). **Personal:** Married to Linda in 1976. Four children: Kurtis, Jason, Justin, and Kristen. Mr. Schwarz enjoys hunting, fishing, skiing, church board member, and all sports coach.

Joni M. Wilson

Public Relations Manager
Bryan Foods, Inc.
1 Churchill Road P O Box 1177
West Point, MS 39773
(601) 495–4469
Fax: (601) 495–4509

2013

Business Information: Bryan Foods is the largest pork processor in the country. Specializing in the production of hotdogs, bologna, and related products, the Company has three plants in the U.S., with two in Mississippi. Established in 1936, the Company employs 3,400 people. As Public Relations Manager, Ms. Wilson develops and manages all activities generated to create positive publicity for the Company. He is responsible for sponsorships, marketing programs, promotions, developing web sites, and new product advertising. **Career Steps:** Public Relations Manager, Bryan Foods (1994–Present). **Associations & Accomplishments:** Board Member, Arts Council; United Way Allocations Board. **Education:** Mississippi State University, B.A. (1982); Mississippi for Women, Additional studies in finance and accounting. **Personal:** Ms. Wilson enjoys reading and decorating.

Rick Allred

Plant Manager
Cargill
307 Dogen Place
Ozark, AR 72949–0168
(501) 667–8530
Fax: (501) 667–8521

2015

Business Information: Cargill, the largest employer in Ozark, Arkansas, is an international turkey processing plant, providing company– and private–label whole birds, bone–in breasts, and vacuum–packed parts. Established in 1969, the Ozark, Arkansas plant produces "Honeysuckle White Turkeys" and currently employs 400 people. International in scope, Cargill is headquartered in Minneapolis, Minnesota, employing over 70,000 people in 65 different countries. Joining Cargill in 1976 in the Shipping Department, Mr. Allred was appointed as Plant Manager in 1993. He is responsible for the oversight of plant management, including production, maintenance, refrigeration, wastewater, engineering, safety and projects, budgets, and costs. **Career Steps:** Plant Manager, Cargill (1993–Present); Technical Manager, Cargill–Broilers (1990–1993); Cargill–Turkeys: Quality Assurance Manager (1987–1990), Traffic Coordinator (1984–1987). **Associations & Accomplishments:** Former Member, Jaycees; Amateur Softball Association; Chamber of Commerce. **Education:** Arkansas Tech University, B.S. (1975). **Personal:** Mr. Allred enjoys sports, hunting, and travel.

Mitchell C. Boswell

Division Manager of Developing Markets
Pierce Foods
120 Bellview Avenue
Winchester, VA 22601–3142
(540) 667–7710
Fax: (540) 722–6517

2015

Business Information: Pierce Foods, established in 1951, is a food manufacturer specializing in poultry products. The Company is an innovator and top quality line for further processed chicken. Pierce Foods has one location in Winchester, Virginia and currently employs 800 people. As Division Manager of Developing Markets, Mr. Boswell is required to travel extensively to market products processed by Pierce Foods. He is a major factor in developing markets for new and existing products. Mr. Boswell oversees two managers, one for domestic markets and one for foreign markets. He assists in the recruitment of management staff, evaluates his staff, develops viable budgets for his departments, and public relations. **Career Steps:** Pierce Foods: Division Manager of Developing Markets (1995–Present), National Retail & Convenience Store Division Manager, (1991–1995), and Marketing Coordinator (1984–1991); Commanding Officer – Naval Reserve, Tactical Support Center, United States Naval Reserve (1992–1994). **Associations & Accomplishments:** United States Naval Institute; Naval Reserve Association; United States Naval Academy Alumni Association; United States Naval Academy Athletic Association; Navy Helicopter Association; Association of Naval Aviation; American Legion. **Education:** United States Naval Academy, BS (1974). **Personal:** Married to Cherie in 1974. One child: Tyler Mitchell. Mr. Boswell enjoys running, reading, fishing, and youth sports.

Wang W. Chang

Chief Financial Officer
Perdigao S/A Com. & Ind.
Avenida Escola Politecnica 722 Cep 05349–000
Sao Paulo, Brazil
55–11–268–9184 Ext. 220
Fax: 55–11–869–4436

2015

Business Information: Perdigao S/A is a food processing company specializing in poultry and pork. Established in 1934, they are the 2nd largest food processing company in Brazil, distributing to Asia, Japan, Hong Kong, Singapore, Europe, and the Middle East, expecting $1.1 billion in sales for 1996. International in scope, the Company has 12 plants and 60 units, including slaughter houses, farms, and hatcheries. As Chief Financial Officer, Mr. Chang is responsible for all aspects of company operations (administration, finance, investors relations, accounting, legal, taxes, and strategic planning), and personally oversees the efforts of 200+ employees. **Career Steps:** Chief Financial Officer, Perdigao S/A (1995–Present); Controller, Branco Chase Manhattan S.A. (1992–1995); Treasurer, Chase Manhattan Bank NA–Santiago Branch (1990–1992). **Associations & Accomplishments:** IBEF–Financial Executive Institute. **Education:** PUC–Rio, Master Industrial Engineering (1973); Escola Politecnica–Sao Paulo, Bachelor in Electrical Engineering (1971). **Personal:** One child: Stephanie. Mr. Chang enjoys tennis, golf, site photography and travel.

Dan J. Lightle

Human Resource Safety Manager
Cooper Foods
1 Cooper Farm Drive
St. Henry, OH 45883–9556
(419) 678–4853
Fax: (419) 678–3734

2015

Business Information: Cooper Foods specializes in the process of turkey products to be distributed to various food production industries across the U.S. Holding various managerial roles with Cooper Foods since 1988, Mr. Lightle was appointed to his current position in December of 1994. As Human Resource Safety Manager, he is responsible for ensuring compliance with all OSHA and governmental employee–related regulations, as well as directs all Human Resource functions for the Company. **Career Steps:** Cooper Foods: Human Resource Safety Manager (1994–Present), Superintendent (1990–1994), Supervisor (1988–1990). **Associations & Accomplishments:** Church of the Nazarene; Coach, Little League Baseball. **Education:** Lima Technical College, A.B. (1983); Dale Carnegie and Steven Covey Training Courses. **Personal:** Married to Cheryl in 1983. Two children: Brandon and Abby. Mr. Lightle enjoys bowling, golf, and old cars (Mustangs & T–Birds).

Alfonso Gerardo Moreno Siqueros

Jefe De Compras De Importacion (International Purchasing Rep)
BACHOCO SA DE CV
Ave. Technologico No. 401 Cd. Industrial
Celaya, Gto, Mexico 38010
(52) (461) (16
Fax: (52) (461) (16

2015

Business Information: BACHOCO SA DE CV is a processor of eggs, chicken, pork, and associated by–products. Hated among the Top Ten processing companies in Mexico in 1993, the Company processes 57,000 metric tons of feed per month through six plants, in addition to operating numerous slaughtering/processing facilities and farms. As the International Purchasing Representative, Mr. Moreno Siqueros is responsible for the purchase of processing plant machinery, and a variety of tools and spare parts from more than 80 suppliers in the U.S. and Canada. He also directs the flow of documents necessary to import the merchandise into Mexico (i.e., raw materials). **Career Steps:** International Purchasing Representative, BACHOCO SA DE CV (1991–Present); Jefe De Control De Galidad, BACHOCO SA DE CV (1987–1991). **Associations & Accomplishments:** Importers and Exporters National Association of Mexico; International Trade Reporter. **Education:** International Commerce (1995); Chemist – University Title. **Personal:** Mr. Moreno Siqueros enjoys exercising, reading, painting, and writing.

Ralph E. Nuzzo

Director of Human Resources
Perdue Farm
P.O. Box 1537
Salisbury, MD 21802
(410) 543–3960
Fax: (410) 543–3339

2015

Business Information: Perdue Farm is the second largest poultry processing company in the industry. With eighteen processing plants in the United States, the Company has three joint venture locations in Canada and Mexico. As a part of the food and agricultural industry, Perdue Farm employs over 20,000 people throughout the world. As Director of Human Resources, Mr. Nuzzo is responsible for handling labor disputes, contract negotiations, compensation for employees, and all other human resource functions. He also manages acquisitions, including joint ventures. **Career Steps:** Director of Human Resources, Perdue Farm (1993–Present); Director of Labor Relations, Metz Baking Company (1989–1993); Director of Human Resources – West Coast, Iowa/ Continental Baking Company (1980–1989); Labor Relations/ Human Resource Manager, Ralston – Purina / Continental (1980–1989). **Associations & Accomplishments:** Penn State Alumni; Legislative Committee, National Turkey Federation; Salvation Army; Boy Scouts of America, Order of the Arrow; Fundraising for Coastal Hospice of Salisbury; Human Resource Professionals Organization. **Education:** Penn State University, B.S. (1975); Attended, University of Pittsburgh, M.B.A.; ITT Labor Relations. **Personal:** Married to Penni in 1993. Two children: Carley and Scott. Mr. Nuzzo enjoys coaching football, cooking, golf, and walking.

Gary Thibodeaux

Corporate Fleet Safety Manager
Hudson Foods, Inc.
215 West Poplar Street
Rogers, AR 72756–4556
(501) 631–5200
Fax: (501) 631–5429
EMAIL: See Below

2015

Business Information: Hudson Foods, Inc. is one of the largest food manufacturers and distributors in the world. An international company with locations across the midwest, south, and eastern parts of the U.S., Hudson also maintains offices in Russia and other European countries. Hudson Foods, Inc. also manufactures and distributes other meat products for stores and restaurants (Kentucky Fried Chicken, Boston Chicken, Wal–Mart, Sam's Club, Hooters, etc.). Involved in safety for the past 25 years, and a retired State Trooper, Mr. Thibodeaux joined Hudson Foods, Inc. as Corporate Manager of Hudson Fleet Safety in 1994. He is responsible for the oversight of all programs and regulations for fleet safety in all fleet locations, including DOT regulations, accidents and statistcs, maintaining records, and vehicle safety regulations. Concurrent with his position at Hudson Foods, Inc., he and his wife own and operate a small ranch, where he raises American Paint Horses. **Career Steps:** Corporate Fleet Safety Manager, Hudson Foods, Inc. (1994–Present); Safety Manager, Wal–Mart Stores, Inc. (1986–1994); Safety and Training Manager, Schlumberger Offshore Corporation (1984–1986). **Associations & Accomplishments:** Arkansas Motor Carriers Association: Chairman, Safety Council; National Private

Truck Council: Board Member, Safety Council; American Trucking Association; Safety Council; National Safety Council; Ozark Safety Council; 1994 Arkansas Safety Director of the Year; developed first Driver Fatigue Program in U.S. for Trucking. **Education:** Eastern Kentucky University, B.S. (1972), Graduate work (1973); Southeastern Cristian College, A.A. (1968); North Western Traffic Safety Institute (1980); Louisiana State University, Accident Specialist (1982). **Personal:** Married to Elizabeth Ann in 1968. Three children: Laura, Scott, and Lance. Mr. Thibodeaux enjoys raising horses, rodeos, team penning, basketball and softball.

Scott Etherington

Vice President of Sales
Bel Cheese U.S.A., Inc.
2050 Center Avenue, Suite 250
Ft. Lee, NJ 07024–4996
(201) 592–6601 Ext: 213
Fax: (201) 236–0336

2022

Business Information: Bel Cheese U.S.A., Inc. is the U.S. division of France–based Fromageries Bel, Inc. Established in 1865, Fromageries Bel is an international manufacturer and marketer of cheese products with sales of $1.4 billion. Bel Cheese USA, Inc., established in 1964, reports annual revenue of $70 million. A Senior Executive with a 22–year demonstrated successful track record with two Fortune 50 consumer products companies (KGF–Oscar Mayer/General Foods and Procter & Gamble), Mr. Etherington joined Bel Cheese U.S.A. as Vice President of Sales in 1994. He serves as the company officer of the Refrigerated Dairy division and also as Broker/Distributor of Field Sales for the U.S. office. Reporting directly to the French President of Bel USA, he manages all retail, food service, club, mass merchandise, airline, and private label businesses, in addition to marketing products direct and through a sophisticated broker and distributor field sales network. Managing a senior sales staff of eight Zone/Region Field Sales Managers and a corporate staff of three, he also has nine people directly reporting to him, in addition to over 90 broker/distributor field sales organizations. Key accomplishments include: Increasing sales volume by 20%, utilizing Negotiation & Category Management Skills; Achieving 105% volume goals and 250% profit goals through effective use of Field Sales incentive programs; Achieving two positive years (1994 & 1995) of sales volume for the Company out of past seven years; Reducing slotting by 30% with extensive proactive negotiation training on Zone/Region Field Sales Managers; and, Lowering trade spending by 10% using "fact based" selling techniques and creativity training of Field Sales Managers. **Career Steps:** Vice President of Sales, Bel Cheese U.S.A., Inc. (1994–Present); Vice President of Sales, The Winterbrook Group (1993–1994); Director of Sales, The Dannon Company (1990–1993); J.O.P.S. National Sales Manager, KGF – General Foods/Oscar Mayer (1978–1990). **Associations & Accomplishments:** IDDA; EDDA; NEDDA; IDFA; International Food Service Executives Association; National Food Brokers Association; Indiana University: Life Member, Alumni Foundation; Student Foundation: Life Member, Former Officer; Phi Delta Theta: National Life Member, Indiana Life Member, Former Officer; Mahwah Student Athletic Association: Member, Coach. **Education:** Indiana University, B.S. in Marketing and Advertising (1976). **Personal:** Married to Chris in 1979. Three children: Mark, Jason, and Christopher. Mr. Etherington enjoys family, sports, golf, and stocks & bonds.

Shari L. Gordon

Legal Affairs Manager
Herbalife International
1800 Century Park East
Los Angeles, CA 90067
(310) 410–9600
Fax: (310) 557–3906

2023

Business Information: Herbalife International markets weight control products, nutritional supplements, and personal care products worldwide through a multi–level marketing system. Ms. Gordon joined Herbalife in 1986. She joined the legal department in 1990 and was most recently promoted to Manager in 1993. She is presently responsible for protecting Herbalife trademarks against fraud worldwide and responding to various in–house legal issues. **Career Steps:** Herbalife International: Legal Affairs Manager (1990–Present), Administrative Coordinator (1987–1990); Service Representative, Pacific Telephone (1980–1984). **Associations & Accomplishments:** Los Angeles Paralegal Association; International Trademark Association. **Education:** University of West Los Angeles, B.S. in Paralegal Studies (1992); California State University, Long Beach, B.S. in Business Computer Methods (1985). **Personal:** Married to Mark G. in 1994. Ms. Gordon enjoys social gatherings, music and travel.

Edwin E. Fritz

Vice President, Marketing & Sales
Dippin Dots, Inc.
5101 Charter Oak Drive
Paducah, KY 42001–5209
(502) 443–8994 Ext. 202
Fax: (502) 443–8997

2024

Business Information: Dippin Dots, Inc. is a manufacturer and distributor of frozen beads of ice cream novelty products. The Corporation has over 100 locations in shopping malls throughout the United States and other countries. Dippin Dots, Inc. representatives have appeared on NBC, ABC, and CNN on such shows as the Today Show. As Vice President, Marketing & Sales, Mr. Fritz is in charge of three divisions: domestic dealers, theme and amusement parks, and international dealers. He is involved in developing sales policies and procedures and marketing strategies. Mr. Fritz is in charge of recruiting staff, department budgets, and long range expansion planning. **Career Steps:** Vice President, Marketing & Sales, Dippin Dots, Inc. (1992–Present); Senior Associate, Williams Company (1989–1991); Owner, CEO, Acoustical Instruments (1986–1989). **Associations & Accomplishments:** American Management Association. **Education:** Oklahoma State University, MBA (1972); University of Oklahoma, BBA (1970). **Personal:** Four children: Brad, Alex, Branden, and Jordan. Mr. Fritz enjoys golf and handball.

Mrs. Linda Kerr Kamm

President
Happy & Healthy Products, Inc.
1600 South Dixie Highway, Suite 2AB
Boca Raton, FL 33432
(561) 367–0739
Fax: (561) 368–5267

2024

Business Information: Happy & Healthy Products, Inc. is a specialty wholesale manufacturer and distributor of frozen fruit bars (Fruitfull). Distributing solely to their franchises in over 35 states, the product is then distributed to hospitals, colleges, corporate cafeterias and health clubs across the country. A community–conscious and charitable organization, the Company donates a portion of all Fruitfull sales to the Children's Miracle Network and The Miami Project To Cure Paralysis, an international center for spinal cord injury research. As President, Mrs. Kamm oversees all aspects of operations. Established in 1986, Happy & Healthy Products, Inc. employs 7 people in the Boca Raton headquarters. **Career Steps:** President, Happy & Healthy Products, Inc. (1991–Present); President, Direct Distributors (1983– 1991). **Associations & Accomplishments:** Inc. Magazine finalist for Entrepreneur of the Year (1989). **Education:** University of Georgia, B.A. (1979).

Enrique Salvo–Horvilleur

Co–Owner and Chief Executive Officer
Eskimo Sa
P.O. Box 025640, Nicabx 293
Miami, FL 33102–5640
505–2–660780
Fax: 505–2–663402

2024

Business Information: A family–owned company, distributing to other distributors, wholesalers, and to consumers directly, Eskimo Sa manufactures ice cream, yogurt products and desserts to the Central American market. As Co–Owner and Chief Executive Officer concentrating on the financial and marketing strategies of Eskimo Sa, Enrique Salvo–Horvilleur is responsible for investing in new dessert markets, promoting desserts, and promoting Eskimo's novelty line. **Career Steps:** Co–Owner and Chief Executive Officer, Eskimo Sa (Present); Production Director, Better Bags, Inc. (1989–1990); Co–Owner, Restaurant Investments, Inc. (1988–1989). **Associations & Accomplishments:** Beta Gamma Sigma – University of Notre Dame Chapter; Vice President, Chamber of Industry of Nicaragua; Director, Banco Nicaraguense. **Education:** University of Notre Dame, M.B.A. (1979); Instituto Technologico De Monterrey, Industrial Engineering. **Personal:** Married to Celeste in 1994. Four children: Enrique Javier, Eduardo Martino, Mario Alejandro, and Andrea. Mr. Salvo–Horvilleur enjoys reading and travel.

Leo Mendez

Vice President of Sales and Marketing
Suiza Dairy Corporation
P.O. Box 363207
San Juan, Puerto Rico 00936–3207
(809) 792–7300
Fax: (809) 782–8120

2026

Business Information: Suiza Dairy Corporation is a milk processing plant and frozen food distributing conglomerate. Established in 1942, Suiza Dairy Corporation reports annual revenue of $230 million and currently employs 900 people. Joining Suiza in 1987 as Personnel Manager, he was appointed Vice President in 1992. In this capacity, he is responsible for all sales and marketing strategies, including the supervision of sales representatives. **Career Steps:** Suiza Dairy Corporation: Vice President of Sales and Marketing (1992–Present), Sales Manager (1987–1992), Personnel Manager (prior to 1987). **Associations & Accomplishments:** American Management Association (AMA); National Association of Convenience Stores (NAC); Sales & Marketing Association of San Juan, Inc. (SME); Asociacion de Mercadeo, Industria y Distribucion de Alimentos (MIDA); Deli Bake Association. **Education:** University of Puerto Rico, B.B.A., Major in Accounting and Finance (1965). **Personal:** Married to Noelia Corujo in 1965. Three children: Waleska, Ricky and Neyla. Mr. Mendez enjoys basketball, fishing and jogging.

Luz Alcantara

President
Refresqueria OTOAO, Inc.
PMC B–2 Tabonuco Street, Suite 162
Guaynabo, Puerto Rico 00968–3004
(787) 765–1320
Fax: (787) 765–1320

2033

Business Information: Refresqueria OTOAO, Inc. manufactures and markets seventeen flavors of natural fruit drink in Puerto Rico. As President and Owner since 1974, Ms. Alcantara is responsible for daily operations, staff supervision, client interface, and marketing. **Career Steps:** President, Refresqueria OTOAO, Inc. (1974–Present). **Personal:** Two children: Cecilia and Aida Cuevas. Ms. Alcantara enjoys spending time with her grandson.

Gordon W. Brailsford Jr.

Corporate Engineering Manager
Ocean Spray Cranberries, Inc.
1 Ocean Spray Drive
Middleboro, MA 02349–1000
(508) 946–7428
Fax: (508) 946–7724
EMAIL: See Below

2033

Business Information: Ocean Spray Cranberries, Inc. is a national manufacturer of cranberry juices and other related food products for the food and beverage industry. Established in 1930, Ocean Spray Cranberries, Inc. reports annual revenue in excess of $1.3 billion and currently employs 2,300 people in seven domestic plant facilities. A corporate engineering executive with over ten years expertise, Mr. Brailsford joined Ocean Spray Cranberries, Inc. as Corporate Project Engineer in 1984. Appointed as Corporate Engineering Manager in 1992, he is responsible for all aspects of corporate engineering activities, including the supervision of all engineering support staff. He can also be reached through the Internet via: gbrailsford@oceanspray.com **Career Steps:** Ocean Spray Cranberries, Inc.: Corporate Engineering Manager (1992–Present), Corporate Senior Project Engineer (1988–1992), Corporate Project Engineer (1984–1988). **Associations & Accomplishments:** Kappa Sigma Alumni Association; Instrument Society of America. **Education:** Lesley College, Cambridge, MA, M.S.M (1994); Northeastern University, B.S. MET **Personal:** Married to Linda in 1986. Two children: Brittney and Blake. Mr. Brailsford enjoys computers, photography, travel, home improvement projects, golf and rollerblading.

Abraham M. Joseph, Ph.D.

Executive Vice President
Whitlock Packaging Corporation
1701 South Lee
Ft. Gibson, OK 74434
(918) 478–4300
Fax: (918) 478–2125

2033

Business Information: Whitlock Packaging Corporation (WPC) is one of the largest juice processing and packaging companies with diversified capabilities to pack in cans, glass, plastic, and aseptic brik packs. Customers include Coca-Cola, Nestle, Snapple, Procter & Gamble, Quaker Oats, Dr. Pepper, Fresti, and others. Dr. Joseph is the Executive Vice

President of WPC. As a Food Scientist, he is responsible for plant operations, engineering, quality, logistics, and business development. Established in 1981, WPC presently employs over 500 people and is moving towards multi–plant operations and Coast to Coast. **Career Steps:** Executive Vice President, WPC (1993–Present); Vice President of Manufacturing, WPC (1990– 1993); Vice President of Quality Assurance, WPC (1988–1990); Plant Manager, Nirula Corner House (1984–1988); Food Scientist, Food Science Department of the National Dairy Research Institute (1977–1984). **Associations & Accomplishments:** Institute of Food Technologists (IFT); American Management Association; Association of Statistical Quality Control (ASQC); Published several research papers in International professional journals. **Education:** National Dairy Research Institute (NDRI), Ph.D. in Food and Dairy Science (1982); National Dairy Research Institute (NDRI), M.S. in Food Science; Kerala University, M.S. in Biological Sciences; St. Thomas College, B.S. in Biological Sciences; Additional Training: The Wharton School, University of Pennsylvania – Training in Finance; Michigan State University – Food Protection and Quality Assurance Technology; Executive Enterprises, Inc. – Activity Based Management.

Thomas M. Karwacki

Manager of Supply Chain
Nestle' Beverage

Suffolk, VA
(609) 451–2035 Ext. 211
Fax: (609) 451–1133

2033

Business Information: Nestle' Beverage is a producer of coffee. As Manager of Supply Chain Mr. Karwacki is responsible for production planning, logistics, customer service, distribution and warehousing. **Career Steps:** Manager of Supply Chain, Nestle' Beverage (1996–Present); Director of Purchasing, Minot Food Packers, Inc. (1988–1996); Assistant Director of Corporate Purchasing, Ogden Food Products (Progresso) (1973–1988). **Associations & Accomplishments:** Boy Scouts of America: Scout Master, Assistant Scout Master (11 years). **Education:** Drexel University, B.A. (1972). **Personal:** Married to Mary in 1971. Two children: Thomas Jr. and Jason. Mr. Karwacki enjoys golf, fishing, camping, and skiing.

Dominic Whedbee, OCSO

Director
Trappist Preserves
167 North Spencer Road
Spencer, MA 01562–1233
(508) 885–8740
Fax: (508) 885–8701

2033

Business Information: Trappist Preserves started making preserves over 40 years ago after one of the monks made some jelly from left over erband fruit. Since the monks were not allowed to eat the jelly, the townspeople bought the preserves. The monks decided to help support the monastery by marketing and distributing the preserves. Trappist Preserves soon grew to export to Canada and Japan. The Company currently distributes all over the Eastern United States and as far south as Texas, but they also have contracts in other parts of the nation. The Company is one of the two main supports for the monastery, and all business is located within the enclosure. The preserves themselves are homemade and gourmet, with the same Head Cook preparing the jellies for the past thirty years. The monks cook them early in the morning so as not to interfere with their other duties. As Director of Sales and Marketing, Father Whedbee handles interfacing with brokers and distributors, and is responsible for sales and marketing programs and materials. He is also responsible for the monks in the kitchen and those involved with packing and shipping. **Career Steps:** Director of Sales and Marketing, Trappist Preserves (1990–Present); Subprior/Dean, St. Joseph's Abbey (1988–1990); University Chaplain, Arizona State University (1981–1982); Associate Pastor, St. Dominic's Parish (1977–1980). **Associations & Accomplishments:** International Jelly and Preserves Association; National Association For The Specialty Food Trade; Phi Beta Kappa; Cistercian Order of the Strict Observance. **Education:** Graduate Theological Union, M.Div. (1977); Dominican School of Philosophy & Theology, B.A. in Philosophy; Stanford University, B.A. in Psychology.

Abdullah M. Al Sughayir

General Manager
Al Gassim Dates Factory
P.O. Box 21525
Riyadh, Saudi Arabia 11485
(06) 3321588
Fax: (06) 3320374

2034

Business Information: Al Gassim Dates Factory is a food processing plant, specializing in the cleaning, production, and packaging of 400 varieties of dates, as well as selling and marketing the products. Founding Al Gassim Dates Factory in 1990, Mr. Al Sughayir serves as Owner and General Manager. He is responsible for all aspects of operations, including all strategic planning. **Career Steps:** General Manager, Al Gassim Dates Factory (1990–Present); Secretary General and Investment Manager, King Faisal Foundation (1980–1990); Economist, Ministry of Petroleum (1967–1980). **Education:** Western Michigan University, M.A. in Economics (1977); Riyadh University – Saudi Arabia, B.A. in Economics and Politics (1972); Training: IMI – Boston, Diploma in Marketing (1990). **Personal:** Married to Hessah H. Al Sughayir in 1965. Seven children: Mohamed, Lolwah, Aboulrehman, Nawal, Wafa, Hussein, and Abdulaziz. Mr. Al Sughayir enjoys reading and spending time with his family.

Hector M. Alvarado–Tizol, B.S., D.M.D., J.D., M.B.A.

President and Chief Executive Officer
Productos Mi Viejo Incorporated
P.O. Box 661, Armadeo # 9
Carolina, Puerto Rico 00986–661
(809) 762–5160
Fax: (809) 762–5115

2037

Business Information: Products Mi Viejo Incorporated is a manufacturer of frozen fruits and vegetables. As President and Chief Executive Officer, Dr. Alvarado–Tizol provides the overall vision and strategy for the Company product output, customer satisfaction, and the effective techniques needed to keep the Company a viable presence in the national market. Not only a successful entrepreneur, Dr. Alvarado–Tizos is also a practicing attorney and general dentistry and oral surgeon practitioner. Establishing his private law practice in 1975, he concentrates in the areas of torts and litigation. Opening his oral and maxillofacial surgery clinic in 1984, Dr. Alvarado–Tizol provides treatment and reconstructive surgery for facial deformities resulting from traumatic injuries, as well as genetic malformations and carcinoma–related disorders. He has conducted extensive research on mandibular reconstruction implant techniques for patients with oral carcinoma. **Career Steps:** President and Chief Executive Officer, Productos Mi Viejo Incorporated (1988–Present); Trial Lawyer, Hector M. Alvarado Tizol Law Office (1975–Present); Oral and Maxilofacial Surgeon, Centro de Rehabilitation Bucal (1984–Present). **Associations & Accomplishments:** Lifelong Membership, The Association of Citadel Men; The Best of Who's Who in Puerto Rico (1992–Present); Colegio de Abogados de Puerto Rico; Puerto Rico Society of Oral and Maxillofacial Surgeons: Fomer President, Sustained Member; Colegio de Cirujanos Dentistas de Puerto Rico. **Education:** University of Puerto Rico School of Dentistry, D.M.D. (1961); University of Puerto Rico Medical Center: Oral and Maxillofacial Surgery, Residency Training, (1967); InterAmerican University, J.D. (1974); The Citadel Military College of South Carolina, B.S. (1956); University of Puerto Rico, Graduate School of Business, M.B.A. (1995). **Personal:** Married to Carmen Teresa in 1957. Four children: Maria Victoria, Antonio Ramon, Carmen Teresa, Marta Larissa. Dr. Alvarado–Tizol enjoys baseball and basketball.

Lydia Burgos

Comptroller and Chief of Accounting Department
Procesadora Campofresco, Inc.
Box 755
Santa Isabel, Puerto Rico 00757–0755
(809) 845–4747
Fax: (809) 845–3490

2037

Business Information: Procesadora Campofresco, Inc. is a leading processor, producer and marketer of fruit juices and beverages in Puerto Rico. Brand names include: Caribik Sun, Passionade, Lotus, Campofresco, and Orange Drops, as well as producing (for Procter & Gamble) Sunny Delight and Hawaiian Punch. Established in 1986, Procesadora Campofresco, Inc. reports annual revenue of $15 million and currently employs 62 people. As Comptroller and Chief of Accounting Department, Ms. Burgos is responsible for all aspects of the Company's financing and accounting matters. **Career Steps:** Procesadora Campofresco, Inc.: Comptroller and Chief of Accounting Department (1994–Present), Accounting Manager (1990–1994); Senior Accountant, Jorge Lebron, CPA, local CPA firm (1988–1990). **Education:** University of Puerto Rico, B.B.A. in Accounting (1989), B.A. in Education, Major in Secondary Education in Science. **Personal:** Married to Roberto Rivera in 1982. Four children: Luis Roberto, Arelys, Edgardo, and Mariely. Ms. Burgos enjoys computers, music (playing the guitar), and reading.

Scott Devon

President
Coles Quality Foods, Inc.
1188 Lakeshore Drive
Muskegon, MI 49441
(616) 722–1651
Fax: (616) 726–6687

2038

Business Information: Coles Quality Foods, Inc. specializes in the distribution of frozen foods and wholesale bakery items to grocery stores and restaurants in 35 states. Coles is also a real estate company, with marina and condominum properties. As President, Mr. Devon is responsible for all aspects of Company operations, including administration, finance, sales and marketing, and strategic planning. **Career Steps:** President, Coles Quality Foods, Inc. (1992–Present); President, Saint Honore French Baking (1995–Present). **Associations & Accomplishments:** Trustee, Muskegon Museum of Art, Chairman Development Committee. **Education:** Aquinas College, M.M. (1990); Michigan State University, B.A.; University of London. **Personal:** Married to Terri in 1991. Mr. Devon enjoys poetry, reading, and writing.

Arnold G. Park, U.E.

President & CEO
McCain Foods (Canada)
P.O. Box 97, Main Street
Florenceville, New Brunswick E0J 1K0
(506) 392–5541
Fax: (506) 392–0894

2038

Business Information: McCain Foods (Canada), a division of McCain Food's Limited, is a producer and marketer of frozen food and drinks. Joining McCain Foods, Inc. in Chicago, IL as Director of Marketing in 1989, Mr. Park was appointed as President and Chief Executive Officer of McCain Foods (Canada) in 1996. **Career Steps:** McCain Foods Canada: President and Chief Executive Officer (1996–Present), Executive Vice President (1995–1996), Vice President of Marketing (1993–1995); McCain Foods, Inc.: Vice President of Marketing (1990–1993), Director of Marketing (1989–1990). **Associations & Accomplishments:** Food Institute of Canada; G.P.M.C.; Canadian Frozen Food Association. **Education:** University of Windsor, M.B.A. (1973); Lakehead University, B.A. (1972). **Personal:** Married to Sandra in 1964. Four children: Doug, Stephen, Susan, and Michael. Mr. Park enjoys fishing, reading, and hunting.

Jacinto Alvear

General Manager
Industrial Molinera C.A.
Casilla 644
Guayaquil, Ecuador
(593) 444–7467
Fax: (593) 444–5576

2041

Business Information: Industrial Molinera C.A. is a wheat flour and oatflake company providing and distributing products for Quaker Oats. Headquartered in Ecuador, the Company has four mills located throughout the country. Established in 1961, the Company employs 260 people and has estimated annual revenue of $50 million. As Manager, Mr. Alvear oversees all aspects of Company operations. He is also responsible for all phases of human resources including personnel management and benefits. Additional duties include financing, sales, marketing, production, and logistics. **Career Steps:** Industrial Molinera C.A: Manager (1994–Present), Plant and Operations Manager (1991–1994); Plant and Operations Manager, Fabrica Chocolates La Universal (1986–1989). **Associations & Accomplishments:** Chemical Engineering Association of Ecuador. **Education:** University of Houston, M.Ch.E. (1978); University of Guayaquil, Professional Degree in Chemical Engineering (1975). **Personal:** Married to Sonia Saa V. in 1973. Four children: Lorena, Adriana, Jacinto Jr., and Laila. Mr. Alvear enjoys swimming and reading.

Saragosa Bazan Jr.

President
The Tortilla King Inc.
302 Profit Drive
Victoria, TX 77901-7348
(512) 573-9788
Fax: Please mail or call

2041

Business Information: The Tortilla King Inc. specializes in the manufacture and wholesale market of corn tortillas for retailers and restaurants. Regional in scope, the Company operates one production plant and two distribution centers for market to customers throughout Victoria, Texas and the surrounding 200-mile radius region. As President, Mr. Bazan is responsible for all aspects of operations. Mr. Bazan credits the success of the business to producing a good product, as well as excellent marketing strategies. **Career Steps:** President, The Tortilla King Inc. (1990–Present). **Personal:** Mr. Bazan enjoys owning a ranch and riding in his spare time, as well as spending time with his friends.

Lance E. Broske

Plant Manager
Didion Milling
P.O. Box 495
Cambria, WI 53923-0495
(414) 348-5868
Fax: (414) 348-6203

2041

Business Information: Didion Milling specializes in corn milling and processing. Primarily involved in the grinding of corn for food consumption, the Company sells the processed grit and flour to other companies including Pillsbury, Frito Lay, Stroh's and Haarmann & Reimer. Grinding approximately 13,000 bushels of corn a day, the Company conducts business in Korea and South Africa, in addition to handling government contracts. Established in 1990, the Company employs 35 people, and owns subsidiary grain elevators and a trucking company. As Plant Manager, Mr. Broske oversees all corn operations, maintenance, manages the packing crew, and is responsible for human resources. Additional duties include safety, employee relations, meeting production schedules, and maintaining low production costs. **Career Steps:** Plant Manager, Didion Milling (1995–Present); Lauhoff Grain Company: Packing Supervisor, Corn Mill Supervisor and Scheduling Manager (1989–1995); Technical Writer, Hyster Company (1989–1990); High School Teacher in Education (1985–1988). **Education:** Eastern Illinois University: M.S. in Industrial Technology (1990), B.S. in Technology Education; Kansas State University, Associates of Operative Milling. **Personal:** Married to Kathleen M. in 1990. Mr. Broske enjoys golf, coaching high school sports, Nascar, fishing, camping, running (has run in the Chicago Marathon), and his Golden Retriever, Maze.

Erlito R. Magsadia

Quality Engineer
General Mills
4309 Fruitland Avenue
Los Angeles, CA 90058-3119
(213) 587-8672
Fax: (312) 996-0334

2041

Business Information: General Mills, Inc., established in 1928, is one of the largest flour mills in the United States. As Quality Engineer, Mr. Magsadia is the primary contact in Los Angeles for the Quality and Regulator Operations Laboratory Department. His department is responsible for product testing, plant sanitation, reporting bulk and truck deliveries, monthly warehouse inventory, and daily laboratory reports. Other duties include inspection of incoming products from outside sources, preparation of chemical reagents, and experimental milling of new crops. Currently, Mr. Magsadia manages a departmental staff of 42. **Career Steps:** Quality Engineer, General Mills, Inc. (1980–Present); Assistant Chief Chemist, California (1968–1980); Quality Control Test Baker, Republic Flour Mills (1964–1968); Bleaching Range Supervisor, Floro Textile Mills (1963–1964). **Associations & Accomplishments:** Adamson University Alumni Association; American Association of Cereal Chemists; American Society for Quality Control; American Chemical Society. **Education:** Adamson University, B.S. in Chemistry (1963). **Personal:** Married to Gwendolyn in 1961. Four children: Mariza, Michael,

Matthew, and Mark. Mr. Magsadia enjoys bowling, chess, tennis, and table tennis.

Walter L. Rios, CPA

Financial Controller
Harinas de Puerto Rico, Inc.
BC 15 Calle Laliza
Mayaguez, Puerto Rico 00680-6266
(787) 821-2315
Fax: (787) 821-5544

2041

Business Information: Harinas de Puerto Rico, Inc., established in 1982 and employing 38 people, is a local flour mill, distributing flour and pre-mixes within Puerto Rico and the Dominican Republic. As Financial Controller, Mr. Rios is responsible for all financial business, budgetary concerns and human resources of the Company. The office of the controller is in charge of accounts payable, accounts receivables, cash management, tax planning and reporting, internal controls, budget development and financial analysis/cost and accounting control. **Career Steps:** Financial Controller, Harinas de Puerto Rico, Inc. (1992–Present); International Internal Auditor, Seaboard Corporation (1989–1992); Audit Manager, Rafael Pagan del Toro Company, CPA's (1985–1989). **Associations & Accomplishments:** Puerto Rico Association of Certified Public Accountants. **Education:** University of Puerto Rico at Mayaguez, B.S.B.A. (1985). **Personal:** Married to Ileana Pico in 1987. Three children: Matthew, Andrew, and Samantha. Mr. Rios enjoys basketball, softball, and swimming.

Carol J. Pratt

Manager of Nutrition Marketing
Kellogg Company
1 Kellogg Square
Battle Creek, MI 49017
(616) 961-6921
Fax: Please mail or call

2043

Business Information: Kellogg Company is the leading manufacturer and distributor of breakfast foods, hot and cold cereals, and convenience foods in the world. As Manager of Nutrition Marketing, Ms. Pratt is responsible for the nutritional information on packages and providing nutrition expertise internally and in conjunction with other Kellogg's locations. She additionally handles all levels of management, internal and external personnel, and works with the Grocer Manufacturers of America, FDA, and contemporaries with other companies. **Career Steps:** Manager of Nutrition Marketing, Kellogg Company (1994–Present); Manager of Product Development and Quality, Mrs. Smith's Frozen Foods (1977–1993); Senior Home Economist, Campbell Soup Company (1974–1977). **Associations & Accomplishments:** Chi of Delta Gamma Alumni Association; American Dietetic Association; Cornell University Alumni Association; School of Human Ecology at Cornell Alumni Association. **Education:** Cornell University: M.S. (1974), B.S. (1972). **Personal:** Married to George in 1995. Two children: James and Colin. Ms. Pratt enjoys gardening and reading.

Ruth W. Harris

Human Resources Manager
Pillsbury
7752 Mitchell Road
Eden Prairie, MN 55344
(612) 906-3220
Fax: (612) 975-3680

2045

Business Information: Pillsbury, one of the most popular food companies in the world, provides a wide range of value-added food products, including fresh, frozen, and canned vegetables, side dishes, baking mixtures, prepared dough products, ice cream, frozen yogurt, specialty foods, frozen pizza & pizza snacks, and other desserts and baked goods. As Human Resources Manager, Ms. Harris manages the Human Resource functions, including staffing, training, compensation and benefits, and employee relations. **Career Steps:** Pillsbury: Human Resources Manager (1995–Present), Senior Human Resource Representative (1994–1995); Human Resource Specialist, Pillsbury/GrandMet (1992–1994); Human Resource Staffing Representative, Aetna Health Plans (1991–1992). **Associations & Accomplishments:** TCPA. **Education:** University of Minnesota, M.A.I.R. (1992); Hamline University, B.A. in Psychology and Management (1990). **Personal:** Married to Brian in 1995. Ms. Harris enjoys outdoor activities, reading, and travel.

Carlos Magan

Finance Director
La Saltena S.A.
Acevedo 725
Buenos Aires, Argentina 1414
(541) 777-4585
Fax: Please mail or call

2045

Business Information: La Saltena S.A. is a worldwide producer and distributor of prepared-dough and food products, such as dough used for pasta and pastries. Formerly a family-owned company, La Saltena was acquired by Pillsbury in June 1995. As Finance Director, Mr. Magan is responsible for directing all financial activities, in addition to administrative activities and supervising a support staff of 20. **Career Steps:** Finance Director, La Saltena S.A. (1995–Present); Controller, Krat Suchard Argentina – Philip Morris (1987–1995); Financial Analyst, Molinos Rio de la Plats S.A. (1986–1987). **Associations & Accomplishments:** Instituto Argentino Ejecutivos de Finanzas; Finance Executives Institute of Argentina. **Education:** University of Buenos Aires, Public Accounting (1987); Virginia University – Darden; (1993). **Personal:** Married to Analia in 1993. One child: Agustina. Mr. Magan enjoys sports, particularly tennis and soccer.

H. Richard Farr

General Manager
Farr Feeders
30130 WCR 49
Greeley, CO 80631
(970) 356-6000
Fax: Please mail or call

2048

Business Information: Farr Feeders is a family-owned cattle feeding company, servicing the entire western part of the U.S. A fourth generation of cattle feeders, Mr. Farr was appointed as Vice President upon graduation from college in 1965, advancing to Executive Vice President in 1972. Currently serving as General Manager since 1988, he is responsible for all aspects of management, including daily operations, finances, and overseeing a support staff of 24. **Career Steps:** Farr Feeders: General Manager (1988–Present), Executive Vice President (1972–1988), Vice President (1965–1972). **Associations & Accomplishments:** National Cattlemens Association; National Futures Association; Colorado Cattle Feeders Association; Farm Foundation. **Education:** University of Wyoming, B.S. (1965). **Personal:** Married to Anne D. in 1965. Two children: R.D. Farr and Kristen L. Chandler. Mr. Farr enjoys fly fishing, horseback riding, and travel.

Bruce W. Moechnig

Manager of Feed Technology
MoorMans, Inc.
1000 N. 30th Street
Quincy, IL 62305
(217) 222-7100
Fax: (217) 222-1794
EMAIL: See Below

2048

Business Information: MoorMans Inc. is a major U.S. manufacturer of animal feed products. A research specialist in agricultural production with twenty years expertise, Bruce Moechnig has served as Manager of Feed Technology at MoorMan's since June of 1994. In this capacity, he provides all direction and development in the research of feed processing products. Internet users may reach him via: Moorman4@bcl.net. **Career Steps:** Manager of Feed Technology, MoorMan's Inc. (1994–Present); Cargill Inc.: Feed Technologist – Nutrena Feeds Division (1991–1993), Research Engineer – Central Research Division (1986–1991). **Associations & Accomplishments:** American Society of Agricultural Engineers (ASAE); Institute for Briquetting and Agglomeration (IBA). **Education:** University of Illionis, M.S. in Agricultural Engineering (1977); University of Minnesota, B.S. in Agricultural Engineering; Rochester Community College, A.A. **Personal:** Married to Karen in 1979. Three children: David, Erika, Keith. Mr. Moechnig enjoys vintage tractor restoration and woodworking.

Dov Rine

Vice President
AER Services, Inc.
6315 N. Whipple Street
Chicago, IL 60659
(312) 262-0223
Fax: (312) 262-1677

2048

Business Information: AER Services, Inc., a management company specializing in the Kosher meat industry is the largest company of its kind in the world. Providing assistance and counseling in the production, marketing, and distribution of Kosher meat products, the company has experience with beef, veal, lamb, chicken, and venison. After 25 years as a partnership, the company was incorporated in 1990 and employs 36 people. As Vice President, Mr. Rine coordinates the finance, personnel, productions, and research and development departments. He also troubleshoots Company operations and investigates and negotiates new business. **Career Steps:** Vice President, AER Services, Inc. (1995–Present); Sergeant, Israeli Army (1993–1995); Production Assistant, Bessin Corporation (1989–1992); Vending Machine Repair Technician, Sieco Vending Company (1986–1989). **Associations & Accomplishments:** National Meat Association; United States Tae Kwon Do Union. **Education:** Northeastern University. **Personal:** Married to Debbie in 1995, Mr. Rine has one son, Avremi. Mr. Rine enjoys martial arts, horsemanship, markemanship, and strategic gaming.

Kazuhiro Uozumi

Director of Sales
Heartland Lysine, Inc.
8430 W. Bryn Mawr Avenue, Suite 650
Chicago, IL 60631–3415
(312) 380–7000
Fax: (312) 380–7006
EMAIL: See Below

2048

Business Information: Heartland Lysine, Inc. is a manufacturer and distributor of crystalline amino–acids for feed use. Products are used for livestock, such as pigs and chickens. Marketing both nationwide and to Canada, Heartland is a subsidiary of Ajimomoto Company, Ltd. in Japan. Established in 1986, Heartland Lysine, Inc. reports annual revenue of $50 million and currently employs 86 people. Employed by Ajimomoto Co., Ltd. (the parent company) since 1981, Mr. Uozumi joined Heartland Lysine, Inc. in 1990 as Director of Sales. He is responsible for all aspects of sales and marketing for the Company. He can also be reached through the Internet via: KUOZUMI@AOL.COM **Career Steps:** Director of Sales, Heartland Lysine, Inc. (1990–Present); Sales Manager, Ajinomoto Co., Ltd. – Japan (1981–1990). **Associations & Accomplishments:** American Feed Industry Association; Chicago Feed Club; The Reform of Heisei (based in Japan). **Education:** Tsukuba University, Japan, B.A. (1981). **Personal:** Married to Rika in 1990. One child: Yuma Judy. Mr. Uozumi enjoys skiing, golf and bowling during his leisure time.

Wade Wisdom

Feedmill and Delivery Manager
Plantation Foods
P.O. Box 20788
Waco, TX 76702–0788
(817) 774–9022
Fax: (817) 774–9000

2048

Business Information: Plantation Foods is a milling operation, manufacturing processed feed ingredients into finished turkey feeds for distribution to area turkey farms (approximately 225,000 tons yearly). Joining Plantation Foods as Feedmill and Delivery Manager in 1995, Mr. Wisdom is responsible for the oversight and management of the feed mill facility and the feed transportation. **Career Steps:** Feedmill and Delivery Manager, Plantation Foods (1995–Present); Tyson Foods, Inc.: Mill and Transportation Manager (Oklahoma) (1992–1995), Mill and Transportation Manager (Arkansas) (1975–1992). **Personal:** Married to Paula Elane in 1975. Three children: Megan, Emily, and Carrie. Mr. Wisdom enjoys the outdoors and sports.

Ely Chan–Hosea, CPA

Controller
Hawaii Baking Company, Inc.
98–736 Moanalua Loop
Aiea, HI 96701
(808) 488–6871
Fax: (808) 487–8435

2051

Business Information: Hawaii Baking Company, Inc. d.b.a. Holsum/Oroweat Bakery is one of Hawaii's 250 largest private and public companies. The Bakery produces products under the following labels: Holsum, Oroweat, Pali Ridge, Hearthstone & a number of private labels. As Controller, Ms. Chan–Hosea is responsible for the personnel department, safety & insurance, internal control, Company & computer administration and the Company's financial operations, including audits, taxes, financial statements, budgeting, accounting, and operational analysis. **Career Steps:** Controller, Hawaii Baking Company (1996–Present); Controller, Trade West, Inc. (1992–1995); Management Consultant, Grant Thornton (1991–1992); Senior Accountant, Mukai Fo & Company CPAs (1987–1990). **Associations & Accomplishments:** United Chinese Society; United Chinese Labor Association; Treasurer, AOAO Lele Pono; Hawaii Jaycees. **Education:** Hawaii Pacific University, B.S. in Accounting and Computer Information Systems (1986); University of Hawaii – Manoa, B.B.A. in Business Management (1982). **Personal:** Married to Ainsley K. in 1994. Ms. Chan–Hosea enjoys computers, cooking, and collecting teddy bears.

Joseph M. Cooney

Technologist
Dunkin Donuts
587 Granite Street
Braintree, MA 02184
(617) 961–4000
Fax: (617) 848–5402
EMAIL:See Below

2051

Business Information: Dunkin Donuts, headquartered in Braintree, Massachusetts, is a national fast food breakfast restaurant, specializing in coffee, donuts, muffins, croissants, bagels, breakfast sandwiches, and lunches from locations primarily on the U.S. East Coast (from Maine to Florida). As Technologist, Mr. Cooney is responsible for the development of new bagels and cream cheese varieties, as well as testing and approving the bakery equipment used in all Dunkin Donut shops. Concurrently, he owns Credible Edibles Bakery. Internet users can reach him at Jcooney151@net.com. **Career Steps:** Technologist, Dunkin Donuts; Owner, Credible Edibles Bakery, (1993–Present); Bakery Manager, Purity Supreme (1987–1990). **Associations & Accomplishments:** I.F.T. (Institute of Food Technologists). **Education:** Johnson and Wales, A.S. (1993); Currently taking AIB Correspondence, Science of Baking. **Personal:** Married to Patricia Z. in 1994. One child: Joseph W. Mr. Cooney enjoys biking, snow skiing, water skiing, boating, soccer and basketball.

Claudia T. Goates

President
Express–A–Cake International, Inc.
8776 East Shea Boulevard, Building 3A, Suite 218
Scottsdale, AZ 85260–6629
(602) 996–8635
Fax: (602) 996–8635

2051

Business Information: Express–A–Cake International, Inc. is an international baker and distributor of cakes worldwide for various occasions, such as birthdays and weddings, using the concept of flowers (FTD). The cakes are made and shipped out of California for quality control reasons. Founding Express–A–Cake International as President in 1994, Ms. Goates is responsible for all aspects of operations, including building the team, networking, and setting up the business. **Career Steps:** President, Express–A–Cake International, Inc. (1994–Present); Executive Director, International Association for Families (1990–1994); Owner, Families In Action (1988–1990). **Associations & Accomplishments:** Coordinator and Program Director, International Year of the Family – Salt Lake City, Utah (1994); Coordinator and Program Director for the Huichol Indians of Las Guayabas, Mexico; Utah Syctyvcar, Russia, People–to–People Project; Citation — Awarded by Governor of Utah for exceptional community support against gang violence and other crisis–related community activities. **Education:** University of Utah; Brigham Young University; University of New Mexico. **Personal:** Eight children: Jeanette, Byron, Rebecca Lynn, Alan, Paul, Jon, Kendra and George. Ms. Goates enjoys swimming, skiing, interior decorating, scuba diving, yoga, metaphysics, camping, hiking, travel and the Internet.

Robert E. Smith

Sales Manager
Country Home Bakers
3008 Churchill Drive
Madison, WI 53713–2902
(608) 278–1091
Fax: (608) 278–1091

2051

Business Information: Country Home Bakers is one of the largest suppliers of in–store bakery goods in the world. Country Home Bakers, established in 1912, is a family–owned Company and has locations in the United States and England. As Sales Manager, Mr. Smith manages direct sales and brokered sales for a seven state region. He handles customer service, marketing products and services, coordinates deliveries of products, and assists in developing new products and services. Mr. Smith handles administrative duties for his office and develops budgets for the administrative and sales staff at his facility. **Career Steps:** Sales Manager, Country Home Bakers (1993–Present); General Manager, Ribb Foods (1979–1982); Director, Food – 4 – Less (1987–1991); President, Western Pioneer Foods (1982–1987). **Associations & Accomplishments:** Son's of the American Legion;I.D.D.B.A.; Board of Directors, A.G. St. Louis. **Education:** University of Iowa; University of Denver Colorado. **Personal:** Married to Cindy in 1979. Three children: Jason, Juston, and Jordon. Mr. Smith enjoys golf and sports.

Charles E. Fairbank II

V.P. – Natl. Accts., Channels, Intl & Trade Dvlpmt
Keebler Company
677 Larch
Elmhurst, IL 60126
(708) 833–2900
Fax: Please mail or call

2052

Business Information: The Keebler Company is a worldwide manufacturer and distributor of cookies, crackers and snacks. New varieties are added as developed by research staff and occasionally through recommendations by consumers. Keebler is a wholly–owned subsidiary of United Biscuits (Holdings) PLC. Keebler, the home of Ernie and the Elves is known as the Uncommonly Good Food company with emphasis on quality and taste making Keebler the choice of consumers everywhere. Keebler products can be found across the country in most retail stores. The Keebler Company currently employs 10,500 people and has an estimated annual revenue of $1.7 billion. As Vice President National Accounts, Channels, International and Trade Development, Mr. Fairbank is responsible for the management of revenues, trade marketing and P & L's for national accounts and all trade channels domestically, as well as the total P & L for international markets and specialized trade channels. **Career Steps:** The Keebler Company: Vice President National, Accounts, Channels, International and Trade Development (1992–Present), Group Director of Trade Development (1990–1992), Director of National Accounts (1987–1990). **Associations & Accomplishments:** American Management Association; GSME; Boy Scouts of America; Published contributions to "Brand Week" and Institute for International Research Brand Marketing. **Education:** Texas Tech University, B.B.A. (1973). **Personal:** Married to Becky L. Two children: Charles III (Chet) and Katie. Mr. Fairbank enjoys backpacking, sportfishing and golf.

Sandro Mabel Antonio Scodro

President
Cipa Indl. De Prods Alimentares, Ltda.
Rod. Br. 153–Km.13–Jd. Paraiso
Aparecida De Goiania, Go, Brazil 74984–901
55–62–2836000
Fax: 55–62–2836353

2052

Business Information: Cipa Indl. De Prods Alimentares, Ltda. is a manufacturer of biscuits, cookies, chips, and candy under the brandnames Mabel, Skinny, and Elbes. The Company distributes directly to supermarkets in Brazil and exports items to South America and the United States. As President, Mr. Scodro is responsible for all aspects of Company operations, including administration, sales and marketing, strategic planning, and finances. **Career Steps:** Cipa Indl. De Prods Alimentares, Ltda.: President (1983–Present), Marketing Director (1978–1983), Buyer and Manager (1975–1977). **Education:** University of Ribeirno Preto, B.A. in Business Administration (1981). **Personal:** Married to Claudia M. in 1981. Three children: Camila, Sandro, and Eduardo. Mr. Scodro enjoys tennis and skiing.

Robert L. Suber, Ph.D.

Director of Health and Environmental Sciences
Bowman Gray Technical Center
RJR–Nabisco
950 Reynolds Boulevard, P.O. Box 1487
Winston–Salem, NC 27102
(910) 741–5544
Fax: (910) 741–7472

2052

Business Information: R.J. Reynolds – Nabisco Inc. is a $7.7 billion multinational food and tobacco industry. As Director of Health and Environmental Sciences at RJR's Bowman Gray Technical Center, Dr. Suber is responsible for reviewing all products for food additives, tobacco ingredients and pesticides. Dr. Suber is also responsible for risk assessment, regulatory toxicology and environmental toxicology. **Career Steps:** Bowman Gray Technical Center – RJR – Nabisco: Director of Health and Environmental Sciences (1993–Present), Director of Scientific Affairs (1984–1993); Chief, Clinical Pathology, National Center for Toxicological Research, Food and Drug Administration (1979–1984). **Associations & Accomplishments:** Society of Toxicology; Institute of Food Technology; Society of Regulatory Affairs; Diplomate, American Board of Toxicology; Published numerous scientific papers and book chapters. **Education:** University of Florida: Ph.D. in Toxicology and Clinical Pathology (1979), M.S.

(1975), B.S (1971). **Personal:** Married to Christine in 1972. Two children: R. Lee, Jr. and Alison M. Dr. Suber enjoys fishing, gardening and coaching soccer.

Paul J. Smith

Director of Material Control
Hershey Chocolate
19 East Chocolate Avenue
Hershey, PA 17033–1314
(717) 534–4574
Fax: (717) 534–7207
EMail: See Below

2064

Business Information: Hershey Chocolate is North America's leading manufacturer of chocolate and confectionary products under a variety of brands including Hershey's, Reese's, Peter Paul, Luden's, Kit Kat, 5th Avenue, Twizzlers, and Symphony. Built in the 1800s, Milton S. Hershey began the chocolate factory to embody his dreams and create an enduring legacy. As Director of Material Control, Mr. Smith is responsible for production planning and inventory management for 15 plants in the United States and Canada. Internet users can reach him via: FGHF60A@prodigy.com. **Career Steps:** Hershey Chocolate: Director of Material Control (1988–Present), Manager of Inventory Planning (1980–1988), Industrial Engineer (1976–1980). **Associations & Accomplishments:** Former President, Hershey Kiwanis; Alpha Pi Nu; Tau Beta Pi, Phi Kappa Phi; West Virginia University Industrial and Systems Engineering Advisory Board; Certified Fellow, American Production and Inventory Control Society; Senior Member, Institute of Industrial Engineers. **Education:** West Virginia University, M.S. in Industrial Engineering (1976); Virginia Tech, B.S. in Industrial Engineering and Operations Research (1975); Registered Professional Engineer in Pennsylvania. **Personal:** Married to Alexia Kniska in 1986. Mr. Smith enjoys astronomy, backpacking, and keyboard playing.

Douglas B. Willner

National Training Manager
M & M Mars
800 High Street
Hackettstown, NJ 07840
(908) 850–2742
Fax: (908) 813–4760

2064

Business Information: M & M Mars, established in 1904, is a manufacturer and distributor of confections. Other products include Kal–Kan pet food, Uncle Ben's Rice, Dove Frozen products, and electronics. As National Training Manager, Mr. Willner oversees a staff of 1200 in 40 different training programs. The programs focus on the function of the sales people, how to sell and negotiate, and customer relations. **Career Steps:** M & M Mars: National Training Manager (1994–Present), Sales Operations Manager (1992–1994), Regional Sales Manager (1990–1992), Division Training Manager (1989–1990). **Associations & Accomplishments:** Training Development and Dialogue Group; American Society of Training and Development; Society for Marketing and Sales Training; Washington Township Youth Association. **Education:** University of Connecticut, B.S. (1983). **Personal:** Married to Betsy in 1985. Two children: Lauren and Kaitlyn. Mr. Willner enjoys golf, skiing, and hiking.

Darryl E. Thomas

Administrator
Brazos Valley Geriatric Center
1115 Anderson Street
College Station, TX 77840
(409) 693–1515
Fax: (409) 696–0462
E MAIL: See Below

2069

Business Information: Brazos Valley Geriatric Center is a 136–bed skilled nursing facility offering residential care and therapy to patients. Therapy services include speech, IV, physical, etc. As Administrator, Mr. Thomas oversees the day–to–day operations of the Facility. He is responsible for staff recruitment, training, scheduling, and evaluating. Other duties include marketing services, financial and budgetary concerns, client services, and family counseling. Internet users can reach him via: tntinter@cy–net.net. **Career Steps:** Administrator, Brazos Valley Geriatric Center (1994–Present); Administrator, Leisure Lodge Hearne (1991–1994); Administrator, Canton Nursing Center (1991). **Associations & Accomplishments:** Texas Health Care Association; Texas Board of Licencure for Nursing Facility Administrators. **Education:** Sam Houston State University, B.A. (1990). **Personal:** Married to Lupe in 1989. Two children: Justin and Chelsea. Mr. Thomas enjoys basketball, hunting, and fishing.

Eduardo M.V. Jasson, I.E., M.B.A.

Strategic Planning Manager
Oleaginosa Moreno Hnos. S.A.
Falcon 227 (8000)
Bahia Blanca, Argentina
(54) 91–591333
Fax: (54) 91–591100 (54) 1–7738913
EMAIL: See Below

2076

Business Information: Oleaginosa Moreno Hnos, S.A. is the largest crusher and exporter of sunflower products. The Firm is also developing agro–industrial trading operations for seeds, edible oils, meals, and food processing for consumer markets. The Company has six manufacturing sites and main operations in Latin America, Europe, and Asia. Established in 1906, the Company employs 1,000 people and has an estimated annual revenue of $100 million. As Strategic Planning Manager, Mr. Jasson oversees corporate, business and functional strategies, forecast and budgeting activities, and bench marking processes. Internet users can reach him via: jasson@starnet.net.ar. **Career Steps:** Strategic Planning Manager, Oleaginosa Moreno Hnos. S.A. (1994–Present); Area Manager, Estudio Pena y Asociados (1991–1994); Manufacture–Planning & Control Manager, CALSA (1990–1991); Assistant General Manager, TECNOR – John Brown B.V. (1985–1990). **Associations & Accomplishments:** Planning Forum of U.S.A.; S.N.A.M.E. of the U.S.A. **Education:** Postgraduate studies in International Business Strategy, York University – Canada; N.B.A., I.D.E.A., Argentina (1994); Industrial Engineer, Naval Architect, Bachelor in Engineering, I.T.B.A., Argentina (1987). **Personal:** Mr. Jasson enjoys golf, swimming and listening to musicals.

Ronit Silon

Department General Manager – Marketing
Olivex, Ltd.
P.O.B. 1498
Tel Aviv, Israel 61014
972–3–5604451
Fax: 972–3–5604455

2079

Business Information: Olivex, Ltd. is a producer of edible oil, oilseed, and lechithin. As Department General Manager – Marketing, Ms. Silon is responsible for marketing and business development. She is also the Owner of the Company, one of only 20 women in ownership or management in Israel. **Career Steps:** Department General Manager – Marketing, Olivex, Ltd. (1984–Present); Shareholder & Director, S.R.A. Trade and Investments, Ltd. (1996). **Associations & Accomplishments:** Manufacturers Association of Israel: Member of Presidium, Chairman of Young Generation of Industrialists, Chairman Forum of Women Industrialists. **Education:** Tel Aviv University, M.A. (1980) **Personal:** Married to Igal in 1975. Two children: Roy and Dana. Ms. Silon enjoys skiing, gymnastics, and reading.

Thomas K. Blaedon

Manager of Architectural and Civil Design
Miller Brewing Company
3939 West Highland Boulevard
Milwaukee, WI 53201
(414) 931–3573
Fax: (414) 931–6061

2082

Business Information: Miller Brewing Company is one of the world's largest brewers, producing products for both domestic and international markets. As Manager of Architectural and Civil Design, Thomas Blaedon oversees the work of multiple design consultants relative to civil and architectural disciplines. **Career Steps:** Miller Brewing Company: Manager of Architectural and Civil Design (1974–Present), Senior project Manager (1988–1991), Construction Coordination Engineer (1974–1988) . **Associations & Accomplishments:** Engineers and Scientists of Milwaukee; Project Management Institute; American Society of Civil Engineers; Professional Engineer in the State of Wisconsin. **Education:** Milwaukee School of Engineering, B.S. (1974). **Personal:** Married to Rosemarie in 1974. Three children: Kelly, Lindsey, and Matthew. Mr. Blaedon enjoys golf, fishing, hunting, vacation, and travel.

James E. Collins

Chief Financial Officer
Pete's Brewing Company
514 High Street
Palo Alto, CA 94301
(415) 328–7383
Fax: (800) 200–1767
EMAIL: Jim_Collins@Petes

2082

Business Information: Pete's Brewing Company is the second largest specialty brewing company in the United States. The Company sells their beer under the Pete's Wicked brand name in 49 states, Washington D.C., and the United Kingdom. For the last three years, the Company was named as one of the top 100 fastest growing companies in the world by Inc. Magazine. As Chief Financial Officer, Mr. Collins is responsible for all financial aspects of the Company, as well as operational and strategic development. Internet users can reach him via: Jim.Collins@Petes.com. **Career Steps:** Chief Financial Officer, Pete's Brewing Company (1992–Present), (1989–1990); Manager, Coopers & Lybrand (1990–1992). **Associations & Accomplishments:** American Institute of Certified Public Accountants; California Society of Certified Public Accountants; American Society of Corporate Secretaries. **Education:** University of the Pacific, B.S. (1981). **Personal:** Married to Dorothea McFarland in 1995. One child: Andrew James Collins. Mr. Collins enjoys golf and woodworking.

Jerrel Q. Moore

Safety, Health and Environmental Supervisor
Coors Brewing Company
5151 East Raines Road
Memphis, TN 38118–7026
(901) 375–2847
Fax: (901) 375–2848

2082

Business Information: Coors Brewing Company, founded in 1873, is the third largest brewer in the United States and the eighth largest in the world, producing approximately 20 million barrels (31 gallons each) of beer and other malt beverages annually. Coors uses only the finest ingredients available in an all–natural brewing process to offer a wide range of high–quality beverages. As Safety, Health and Environmental Supervisor, Mr. Moore is responsible for all levels of projects in the anticipation, recognition, evaluation, and control of occupational safety and health hazards. He is involved in developing programs to achieve compliance with safety regulations, improve employee working conditions, and achieve effective loss control. Mr. Moore is also responsible for administering and developing environmental policies, waste management, waste minimization, recycling, environmental remediation, hazardous waste incident, and environmental reporting and compliance. **Career Steps:** Coors Brewing Company: Safety, Health and Environmental Supervisor (1993–Present), Environmental Control Coordinator (1992–1993); Environmental Engineer, State of Tennessee, Department of Environment and Conservation (1989–1992); Construction Engineer, State of Ohio, Department of Transportation (1986–1989). **Associations & Accomplishments:** National Association of Environmental Managers; Alpha Phi Alpha Fraternity; Tennessee State Alumni Association. **Education:** Tennessee State University, B.S. in Industrial Engineering Technology (1986). **Personal:** Married to Deborah in 1992. Two children: Jalen and Jerrel Jr. Mr. Moore enjoys reading, jogging, and sports.

Terrance L. Priest

Corporate Commerce Manager – Logistics
Coors Brewing Company
BC 410 12th & Ford Streets
Golden, CO 80401
(303) 277–5558
Fax: (303) 277–6564

2082

Business Information: Coors Brewing Company, founded in 1873, is the third largest brewer in the United States and the eighth largest in the world, producing approximately 20 million barrels (31 gallons each) of beer and other malt beverages annually. Coors uses only the finest ingredients available in an all–natural brewing process to offer a wide range of high–quality malt beverages. As Corporate Commerce Manager – Logistics, Mr. Priest is responsible for running a competitive business while ensuring that all contracts are legal. **Career Steps:** Corporate Commerce Manager – Logistics, Coors Brewing Company (1982–Present); Corporate Traffic Manager, J. R. Simplot Company (1969–1982); Agent – Telegrapher, Union Pacific Railroad Company (1961–1969). **Associations & Accomplishments:** American Society of Transportation and Logistics: Former National President, Chairman of Board; Society Award for Excellence 1991; Traffic Clubs International: Director, Past President; Former International Director of Education, Delta Nu Alpha International Transportation Fraternity; Alphian of the Year 1986; Board of Governors, National Transportation Library; Circle of Excellence –Council of Logistic Management 1995; Practitioner before the Surface

Transportation Board (ICC); Who's Who in American Business; Sterling's Who's Who; Published in various magazines. **Education:** Boise State University: B.S. (1972), B.A. (1970). **Personal:** Married to Coco in 1971. Two children: Victoria and Samantha. Mr. Priest enjoys fishing, reading, and travel.

Richard Allen Pierce, CPA, CSP, CCP, CMA

Chief Accounting Officer
R. H. Phillips, Inc.
26836 County Road, 12A
Esparto, CA 95627
(916) 662–3215
Fax: (916) 662–2880
EMAIL: See Below

2084

Business Information: One of only four publicly–held wineries, the 21st largest of 800 in California and one of the fastest growing, R. H. Phillips, Inc. produces, bottles, and markets premium varietal wines in all 50 states and five foreign countries. Farming over 1350 acres of wine grapes, R. H. Phillips is a pioneer of Rhone varietals, the largest grower of the Syrah grape in the U.S. and established Dunnigan Hills as a new Viticultural Appellation in 1993. With twenty–one years experience in accounting and a Certified Public Accountant, Mr. Pierce joined R. H. Phillips, Inc. as their Chief Accounting Officer in 1991. He is responsible for all aspects of the Company's accounting and MIS functions, including budgeting, financial reporting and taxes. Among his many accomplishments, Mr. Pierce was instrumental in the planning and implementation of the successful IPO of R. H. Phillips, Inc. in 1994. Internet users can reach him via: AEAA41A@Prodigy.com **Career Steps:** Chief Accounting Officer, R. H. Phillips, Inc. (1991–Present); Owner, A&M Management (1990–1991); Chief Financial Officer, Nevis Industries, Inc. (1987–1990); Chief Financial Officer, Oiltech, Inc. (1982–1987). **Associations & Accomplishments:** Certified Public Accountant; Certified Systems Professional; Certified Computing Professional; Certified Management Accountant; California Society of Certified Public Accountants; Institute of Management Accountants. **Education:** Chico State University, B.S. in Accounting and C.S. (1975). **Personal:** One child: Rachel. Mr. Pierce enjoys fly fishing, reading, and chatting with his friends on the Internet.

James G. Stanley

Vice President of Marketing
Kendall–Jackson Winery
421 Aviation Boulevard
Santa Rosa, CA 95403
(707) 544–4000
Fax: (707) 544–0156

2084

Business Information: Kendall–Jackson Winery, the fastest growing winery in the industry, is a producer of the largest selling, super–premium Chardonnay wines in the country. Kendall–Jackson Winery has a division of subsidiary wineries in the Artisans and Estates portfolio, with 10 wineries located nationally, and vineyards located domestically and internationally. Established in 1983, Kendall–Jackson Winery reports annual revenue of $200 million and currently employs 500 people. As Vice President of Marketing, Mr. Stanley is responsible for the supervision of marketing (brand management), public relations, and hospitality. **Career Steps:** Vice President of Marketing, Kendall–Jackson Winery (1993–Present); Executive Vice President of Sales and Marketing, Sierra On–Line (1992–1993); Director of Marketing, E & J Gallo Winery (1985–1992); General Manager, Crown Zellerbach (1977–1985). **Associations & Accomplishments:** Numerous local civic and athletic associations; Completed 1989 & 1991 Ironman – Kona Hawaii; Selected as one of the Top 100 marketing superstars in Ad Age Magazine (1995). **Education:** University of Michigan, M.B.A. (1967), B.B.A. (1966). **Personal:** Married to Linda in 1968. Two children: Craig and Karyn. Mr. Stanley enjoys Ironman competitions.

Michael Goldberg

Director of Human Resources
Jim Beam Brands Co.
510 Lake Cook Road – Human Resources Department
Deerfield, IL 60015
(847) 948–8888
Fax: (847) 948–0416

2085

Business Information: Jim Beam Brands Co. is an international distiller of alcoholic beverages, specifically whiskey and related products. Established in 1795, the Company has locations throughout the U.S., Canada, Scotland, and Australia. Employing 2,500 people, the Company has an estimated annual revenue of $1.3 billion. As Director of Human Resources, Mr. Goldberg is responsible for employee relations and benefits, personnel management and recruitment, and ensuring training of all employees. **Career Steps:** Jim Beam Brands Co: Director of Human Resources (1996–Present), Manager; Manager, Human Resources, United Stationary Supply Company. **Education:** Roosevelt University, M.A. in Industrial Organizational Psychology (1991); Northern Illinois University, B.S. in Marketing (1983). **Personal:** Married to Joanie in 1995. One child: Derek. Mr. Goldberg enjoys fitness, running, and swimming.

Sharon L. Wayne

Director of Business Services
United Distillers North America, Inc.
6 Landmark Square
Stamford, CT 06901–2704
(203) 967–7741
Fax: (203) 359–7495

2085

Business Information: United Distillers North America, Inc. is a distributor and producer of distilled spirits for United Distillers/Guinness PLC. With parent headquarters located in London, England, United Distillers employs 23,297 people worldwide. Established in 1987, United Distillers North America, Inc. is headquartered in Stamford, CT and reports $7.5 million in the North American Region. As Director of Business Services, Ms. Wayne is responsible for the direction of special projects and the coordination and implementation of all accounting, financing and business system aspects of major projects. **Career Steps:** United Distillers North America, Inc.: Director of Business Services (1995–Present), Director of Accounting (1993–1995), Assistant Controller (1991–1993); Corporate Tax Manager, Glenmore Distilleries (now owned by United Distillers NA) (1979–1991). **Associations & Accomplishments:** Tax Executives Institute: Current Member, Former National Director and Former President. **Education:** University of Louisville: M.B.A. (1982), B.A. in Commerce with honors in Accounting (1977). **Personal:** One child: Christopher Trautwein. Ms. Wayne enjoys golf and basketball.

Catalina del Corral

Senior International Account Executive
The Coca–Cola Company
P.O. Drawer 1734
Atlanta, GA 30301–1734
(404) 676–2448
Fax: (404) 515–3267

2086

Business Information: The Coca–Cola Company is the world's largest beverage company and leading producer and distributor of soft drinks. Established in 1886, The Coca–Cola Company currently employs 30,000 people worldwide and has an estimated annual revenue of $16.2 billion. As Senior International Account Executive, Ms. del Corral is responsible for the management of sales and marketing activities for travel accounts worldwide. **Career Steps:** The Coca–Cola Company: Senior International Account Executive (1994–Present), Principal Business Development Analyst (1991–1994), Principal Accountant of Latin America Financial Services (1989–1991). **Associations & Accomplishments:** Alliance Francaise d'Atlanta; Delta Sigma Pi; Speaks French, Spanish, English and Portuguese. **Education:** University of Georgia: M.B.A. (1984), International Business, B.A. **Personal:** Ms. del Corral enjoys music, geography, tennis, swimming and travel.

Ricardo Leon Delpin

Finance Director
Emb Williamson Balfour SA
Alameda 2222 Casilla 1197
Santiago, Chile
(562) 206–7706
Fax: (562) 206–7721
EMAIL: See Below

2086

Business Information: Emb Williamson Balfour SA, a subsidiary of Inchcape Bottling, is a bottling company for Coca–Cola products and "Vital" (a fruit juice and mineral water product). As Finance Director, Mr. Delpin is responsible for all finances and reports for franchises located throughout Chile, Peru, and Russia. Internet users can reach him via: rleon@ctc_mundo. **Career Steps:** Finance Director, Emb Williamson Balfour SA (1996–Present); Finance Director, Inchape Bottling (1996); Finance Manager, E. Williamson Balfour (1978–1996); Programming Manager, C.A.P. (1968–1978). **Education:** Universidad Concepcion, Engineering (1978). **Personal:** Married to Olga Arias in 1992. Five children: Claudia, Loreto, Ricardo, Juan Pablo, and Ignacio. Mr. Delpin enjoys tennis.

Lilliam Diaz

Manager
Manantial La Montana, Inc.
P.O. Box 521
Saint Just, Puerto Rico 00978–0521
(809) 760–5146
Fax: (809) 748–1968

2086

Business Information: Manantial La Montana, Inc., a family–owned company, is a bottled water plant, processing and distributing bottled water to customers in Puerto Rico. Joining Manantial La Montana as Manager, Ms. Diaz is responsible for general management of the plant, in addition to the oversight of all administrative operations for associates and a support staff of 50. **Career Steps:** Manager, Manantial La Montana, Inc. (1984–Present); Teacher, Colegio Santa Cruz (1979–1984); Teacher, Colegio Maria Auxiliadora (1970–1976). **Associations & Accomplishments:** Asociacion de Productos de Puerto Rico; Camara de Comerciantes Mayoristas; Centro Unido de Detallistas de Puerto Rico. **Education:** University of Phoenix, Masters Degreee (1984); University of Puerto Rico, B.A. (1970). **Personal:** Married to Angel M. Goytia in 1970. Two children: Angel M. and Ricardo. Ms. Diaz enjoys reading, sight seeing, and travel.

Diane Marie Eckland

Senior National Account Executive
The Coca–Cola Company
One Coca–Cola Plaza
Atlanta, GA 30313
(404) 676–2596
Fax: (404) 515–1861

2086

Business Information: Established in 1886, The Coca–Cola Company is a leading international soft drink manufacture and distribution company. Coca–Cola employs 32,500 people and has an annual revenue of $18 billion. As Senior National Account Executive, Ms. Eckland is responsible for sales and marketing, managing three large national accounts, handling negotiations, supervising promotions, and traveling to various sites. **Career Steps:** The Coca–Cola Company: Senior National Account Executive (1996–Present), National Account Executive (1995–1996); Mobil Oil Corporation: Converter Sales Representative (1991–1995), Human Resource Manager (1987–1991). **Associations & Accomplishments:** Atlanta Phoenix Organization; Atlanta Sales & Marketing Executives; Jaycees (1985–1987); Rotary (1988–1990); Coca–Cola Reaching Out. **Education:** University of Massachusetts, M.B.A. (1982); Boston College, B.S. (1980). **Personal:** Ms. Eckland enjoys golf, skiing, and living powerfully in the world.

Marcelo A. Gioffre, Eng., MBA

Logistics Manager
SIRSA
Avellaneda 2254
Buenos Aires, Argentina 1650
(541) 732–5500
Fax: Please mail or call
EMAIL: See Below

2086

Business Information: SIRSA, a former Coca–Cola Bottler, currently provides bottling services to a variety of beverage manufacturers such as RC Cola, Sunkist, Seagrams, etc. The Company also produces concentrated soda and juices for WalMart stores internationally. As Logistics Manager, Mr. Gioffre responsibilities include management of all logistics activities, cost, distribution, and site analysis, and ensuring customer satisfaction and quality service. Internet users can reach him via: magioggre@pinos.com. **Career Steps:** Logistics Manager, SIRSA (1991–Present); Design Engineer, Volvo Car Corporation (1991); Statistics Department Manager, Institute Argentina de Siderurgia (1986–1991). **Associations & Accomplishments:** ARLOG; Asociacia Argentina de Logistca. **Education:** Eseade, M.B.A. (1993); Universidad de Buenos Aires, Electronic Engineering; UCA, Master in Environmental Management. **Personal:** Mr. Gioffre enjoys hockey on skates and time spent with friends.

Pancho D. Hall
General Manager
Pepsi–Cola Company
101 West 48th Street South
Wichita, KS 67217
(316) 529–9709
Fax: (316) 529–9706

2086

Business Information: The Pepsi–Cola Company, Inc. is one of the world's leading producers and marketing distributors of soft drink beverages and consumer food products. The Wichita division currently employs 300 people. As General Manager, Mr. Hall is the executive responsible for the entire geographic territory in the areas of production, distribution and sales, as well as the supervision of all managers. **Career Steps:** Pepsi–Cola Company: General Manager (1995–Present), Director of Marketing Services (1993–1995); A T & T: District Sales Manager (1991–1993), Staff Director (1990–1991). **Associations & Accomplishments:** American Marketing Association; Market Research Association; Board of Riverfeast Events; University of Michigan Alumni Association; University of Chicago Alumni Association. **Education:** University of Chicago, M.B.A. (1989); University of Michigan, M.S. in Mechanical Engineering (1984); General Motors Institute, B.S. in Mechanical Engineering (1983). **Personal:** Married to Kelly in 1989. One child: Ashley. Mr. Hall enjoys golf, football, tennis, basketball and baseball.

Asgarali Khatau
Receiver/Environmental Coordinator
Sweet Ripe Drinks, Ltd.
6745 Invader Crescent
Mississauga, Ontario L5T 2B6
(905) 670–0638 Ext. 239
Fax: (905) 670–0922

2086

Business Information: Sweet Ripe Drinks, Ltd. is the largest Canadian manufacturer of juices and drinks. The Corporation began operations in 1987 and presently has over 350 employees. As Receiving Coordinator, Mr. Khatau is responsible for receiving the merchandise and supplies needed to prepare products for manufacturing. As Environmental Coordinator, he coordinates forklift fleet maintenance, safety compliance, and solid waste management. Concurrently, he assists in the operations at RIN enterprise, a firm dealing with empty steel drums. **Career Steps:** Receiver/Environmental Coordinator, Sweet Ripe Drinks, Ltd. (1989–Present); President/Owner, All Kenya Enterprises (1983–1989); Financial Controller, Severin Hotels, Ltd. (1975–1982); Manager, Uganda Commercial Bank (1967–1975). **Education:** Cambridge Oversees School Certificate (1959). **Personal:** Married to Zarina Dhirani in 1964. Seven children: Mohamed, Hasnain, Sukaina, Zainab, Batul, Sayyeda, and Fatema. Mr. Khatau enjoys swimming, indoor games, and collecting stamps and coins.

Roy G. Layne
Comptroller
Pepsi–Cola of Washington D.C., LP
3900 Penn Belt Place
Forestville, MD 20747
(301) 967–4682
Fax: (301) 967–4620

2086

Business Information: Pepsi–Cola is one of the world's largest beverage and soft drink companies. Established in 1990, Pepsi–Cola of Washington, D.C. is the major distributorship of Pepsi products in the D.C. area. Currently, the Distribution center employs 150 people. As Comptroller, Mr. Layne is responsible for all aspects of finances, including internal and external reporting, cash management, reconciliation, cash projects, accounts payable and receivable, and general ledger entries. Mr. Layne is also responsible for up–dating management and management information systems. **Career Steps:** Comptroller, Pepsi–Cola of Washington D.C. LP (1991–Present); Audit Manager, Coopers & Lybrand, LL.P. (1985–1991). **Associations & Accomplishments:** National Association of Black Accountants; American Institute of Certified Public Accountants; District of Columbia Institute of Certified Public Accountants; Institute of Management Accountants; Chairman, Management Committee of Prince George's Private Industry Council Board of Directors; Grenada Improvement Group; Recipient, C & L Committment Award, Coopers & Lybrand (1990). **Education:** University of District of Columbia, B.B.A., summa cum laude (1985); Certified Public Accountant; Certified Management Accountant. **Personal:** Married to Glennis in 1986. Two children: Danielle & Adrian. Mr. Layne enjoys jogging, soccer, track and field events, and helping young people.

Robert W. McNamara

Vice President and General Manager
Columbine Beverage Company
4301 Broadway
Denver, CO 80216
(303) 294–0315
Fax: (303) 295–1270

2086

Business Information: Columbine Beverage Company, a family–owned business, is a manufacturer and distributor of beverages, primarily soft drinks and private labels to ten states in the Southwestern U.S. Columbine Beverage Company also has a subsidiary specialty food manufacturing entity — Columbine Specialty Products. This division manufactures sauces and cocktail items for the food service industry. Joining Columbine Beverage Company as Vice President of Sales and Marketing in 1990, Mr. McNamara was appointed as Vice President and General Manager in 1995. He is responsible for the oversight of companies, with emphasis on marketing, new accounts, and products. **Career Steps:** Columbine Beverage Company: Vice President and General Manager (1995–Present), Vice President of Sales and Marketing (1990–1995); Captain and Pilot, U.S. Air Force (1981–1990). **Associations & Accomplishments:** Treasurer, Colorado Soft Drink Association; Secretary, Colorado Recycles; Denver Area Manufacturers Reps. **Education:** University of Colorado, Industrial Engineering (1980). **Personal:** Married to Jeanne in 1985. Four children: Michelle, Kyle, Kelly, and Chase. Mr. McNamara enjoys golf, tennis, skiing, and flying.

David Todd Miller
General Manager
Coca–Cola
P O Box 1668
Elkins, WV 26241
(304) 636–3500
Fax: (304) 636–0824

2086

Business Information: Coca–Cola is one of the world's leading producers and marketing distributors of soft drink beverages and consumer food products. As General Manager, Mr. Miller is the executive responsible for production, distribution and sales, and the supervision of all managers within a five–county area. **Career Steps:** General Manager, Coca–Cola (1986–Present). **Associations & Accomplishments:** Chamber of Commerce; Rotary International. **Education:** Fairmont State College **Personal:** Married to Sandy in 1990. Two children: Bianca and Christopher. Mr. Miller enjoys golf, snow skiing, travel with his family, and fishing.

Mr. Rafael Ramos
Director of Manufacturing
Pepsi–Cola International, Latin America Division
1200 North Federal Highway, Suite 401
Boca Raton, FL 33432
(407) 338–6356
Fax: (407) 338–6326

2086

Business Information: Pepsi–Cola International, Latin America Division is responsible for all international operations of Pepsi–Cola Inc., one of the world's largest beverage and soft drink companies. As Director of Manufacturing, Mr. Ramos is responsible for coordination and support of manufacturing and engineering activities, strategic planning, new technologies in Latin America, as well as accounting for about 50% of the international business. He oversees 200 plants in Latin America's five divisions: North Latin America (Central America & Caribbean), Mexico, Venezuela/Columbia, Brazil, and South Latin America (South America). Pepsi–Cola International, Latin America Division employs over 1,500 people and reports annual revenue of $480 million. **Career Steps:** Director of Manufacturing, Pepsi–Cola International, Latin America Division (19920–Present); Plant Manager, Pepsico de Mexico (1990–1992); Field Engineer, Pepsico de Mexico (1987–1990). **Associations & Accomplishments:** American Society for Quality Control; American Production and Inventory Control. **Education:** Tecnologico de Monterrey, M.B.A. (1986); Tecnologico de Monterrey, B.S. in Biochemical Engineering (1983), Certification in Total Quality Management (1990).

Reggie T. Varra
Group Plant Manager
Arrowhead Mountain Spring Water Company
1566 East Washington Boulevard
Los Angeles, CA 90021–3130
(213) 741–0011 Ext: 366
Fax: (213) 748–2561

2086

Business Information: Arrowhead Mountain Spring Water Company is the largest bottled water producer in the United States. Arrowhead is part of the Perrier Group of America, which is owned by Nestles. Joining Arrowhead as Production Manager in 1993, Mr. Varra was promoted to Plant Manager in 1994 over the Los Angeles Plant. In January of 1996 he was promoted to Group Plant Manager for both the Los Angeles and Orange Plants. He oversees both operations with a combined volume of over 12 million cases annually; including quality, profitability, productivity, safety, and utilizations with four other exempts (subordinates). He is also responsible for staffing, strategic planning, budgeting, and capital planning. **Career Steps:** Arrowhead Mountain Spring Water Company: Group Plant Manager (1996–Present), Plant Manager (1994–1996); Production Manager (1993–1994); Production Manager, Pepsi–Cola Company (1991–1993). **Education:** Arizona State University, Mechanical Engineer (1985). **Personal:** Mr. Varra enjoys golf, bowling, physical fitness, travel, and painting.

Gladys E. Arroyo
Operations Secretary
Concentrate Manufacturing Company
P.O. Box 1558
Cidra, Puerto Rico 00739–1558
(787) 739–8411
Fax: (787) 739–4419

2087

Business Information: Concentrate Manufacturing Company specializes in the manufacture of Pepsi–Cola concentrate, which the Company distributes both domestically and internationally. As Operations Secretary, Ms. Arroyo is responsible for diversified administrative activities in the Engineering, Manufacturing, Purchasing, and Logistics divisions. **Career Steps:** Concentrate Manufacturing Company: Operations Secretary (1995–Present), Materials Secretary (1993–1995), Time Keeper (1988–1993). **Associations & Accomplishments:** Lucky Strike Bowling Team. **Education:** Turabo University, Secretarial (1996); Brookdale Community College, Public Relations. **Personal:** Four children: Kalin, Junior, Evelyn, and Lynda. Ms. Arroyo enjoys bowling.

Karen R. Davis
Director of Human Resources
Sahlman Sea Foods, Inc.
1600 Kathleen Road
Lakeland, FL 33805–3435
(941) 687–4411
Fax: (941) 683–7602

2091

Business Information: Sahlman Sea Foods, Inc. is an international seafood processor, maintaining their own ship and truck fleets, processing company, and warehouses. As Director of Human Resources, Ms. Davis coordinates all human relations activities for 600 employees in four different divisions. Her responsibilities include oversight of benefits packages (renewals and budgeting), health and safety (reporting to OSHA), drug testing, security, recruiting and hiring, affirmative action, EEOC, litigation, and retirement. In addition, she coordinates all functions and activities associated with human relations throughout the year. **Career Steps:** Director of Human Resources, Sahlman Sea Foods, Inc. (1988–Present); Employment Specialist, Sun Bank (1985–1988). **Associations & Accomplishments:** Human Resource Professional of the Year (1994); Central Florida Personnel Association: President, Former Vice President of Membership, Legislative Reporter; School Advisory Board; Board Member, New Beginnings. **Education:** Attended: Florida Southern College. **Personal:** Two children: Amber and Vanessa. Ms. Davis enjoys ice skating.

Mary M. Slattery
Vice President of Finance
UniSea, Inc.
15400 North East 90th Street
Redmond, WA 98073–9717
(206) 861–5318
Fax: (206) 882–1660

2092

Business Information: UniSea, Inc. is a manufacturer of seafood and a variety of seafood products for national and international distribution. As Vice President of Finance of UniSea, Inc., and Chief Financial Officer of its subsidiary, UniSea Foods, Inc., Ms. Slattery is responsible for all aspects of financial and accounting for the Companies. **Career Steps:** Vice President of Finance, UniSea, Inc. (1985–Present); Controller, Hagen Corporation (1981–1985); Cost Analyst, Hewlett Packard (1979–1981). **Associations & Accomplishments:** Washington Society of Certified Public Accountants. **Education:** Colorado State University, M.Sc. in Accounting (1976); Illinois Institute of Technology, B.Sc. in Chemical Engineering (1960). **Personal:** Ms. Slattery enjoys dogs, gardening, and hiking.

Darlene M. Barras
Administrative Assistant
American Coffee Company
PO Box 52018
New Orleans, LA 70152
(504) 581–7234
Fax: (504) 581–7518

2095

Business Information: American Coffee Company is a manufacturer of coffee, which also has a collectible line of coffee mugs, tee–shirts, aprons, etc. Additionally, the Company distributes to grocery stores, offices, hotels, restaurants, and gift shops. Mail order service is also available. As Administrative Assistant, Ms. Barras is responsible for diversified administrative activities, including handling insurance issues, all freight traffic, credit checks, collection problems, and assisting the Vice President of Sales with the broker network. **Career Steps:** Administrative Assistant, American Coffee Company (1984–Present). **Associations & Accomplishments:** National Association For Female Executives

Dave Petersen
Director of National Sales
Stewarts Private Blend Foods
4110 Wrightwood Avenue
Chicago, IL 60639–2127
(312) 489–2500
Fax: (312) 489–2148

2095

Business Information: Stewarts Private Blend Foods, a third generation family–owned company, is a manufacturer of gourmet–roasted coffee and tea, specializing in gourmet coffees from around the world. Being and remaining a very reputable company, Stewarts feels there is not as much freshness involved in the distribution of coffee beans, as opposed to vacuum–packed ground coffee. Because of this belief, they have created a "Mini Bin" for specialty coffee roasts. With its main manufacturing plant located in Chicago, Illinois, Stewarts distributes throughout the Mid–West core, (Illinois, Wisconsin, Iowa, Michigan, Ohio, Colorado, North and South Dakota), as well as Pennsylvania, North and South Carolina. Joining Stewarts Private Blend Food as Director of National Sales in 1990, Mr. Petersen oversees all retail sales on a national basis. His position also entails extensive travel throughout the U.S. Career milestones include starting a management program for National Tea Company 30 years ago, and as a result, went into sales and marketing with food brokers, and manufacturers. **Career Steps:** Director of National Sales, Stewarts Private Blend Foods (1990–Present); Retail Sales Manager, L.H. Frohman & Sons, Inc. (1987–1990); Retail Supervisor, Wirth Daniels Corporation (1985–1987); Unit Manager, Key Sales, Inc. (1983–1985). **Associations & Accomplishments:** Merchandising Executives Club; Grocery Manufacturers Sales Executives; Illinois Food Products Club; Wisconsin Grocers Association. **Education:** Monmouth College, B.A. (1963). **Personal:** Married to Karen in 1963. Three children: Dave Jr., Michael, and Matthew. Mr. Petersen enjoys travel and landscape design.

Mr. Jack A. Sprague
Consulting Systems Engineer
Frito–Lay, Inc.
7701 Legacy Drive
Plano, TX 76204
(214) 334–5644
Fax: (214) 334–5090

2096

Business Information: Frito–Lay, Inc. is the world's leading manufacturer and global distributor of snack food products. As a Consulting Systems Engineer at the Plano, Texas facility, Mr. Sprague directs all information systems and advanced planning functions for the company, as well as provides strategic planning and marketing advice. Established in 1937, Frito–Lay, Inc. employs over 35,000 people corporate–wide, and reports annual revenue in excess of $4 billion. **Career Steps:** Consulting Systems Engineer, (1979–Present); Technology Analyst, Hughes Aircraft Company (1977–1979); Senior Programmer, Dynalectron Corporation (1975–1977); Data Center Operations Supervisor, New Mexico State University (1973–1975). **Associations & Accomplishments:** National Association of Rocketry; Dallas Area Rocket Society; National Space Society; Association of Model Aeronautics. **Education:** University of Southern California, M.S. in Computer Science (1979); New Mexico State University (1975).

Michelle A. Wickman, CPA

Department Manager
Frito–Lay, Inc.
P.O. Box 660634
Dallas, TX 75266–0634
(214) 334–7504
Fax: (214) 334–7712

2096

Business Information: Frito–Lay, Inc. is the world's leading manufacturer and global distributor of snack food products. Having served various positions with Frito–Lay since 1991, Michelle Wickman, a Certified Public Accountant, has served in her current role as Department Manager since 1994. She is responsible for three departments of the Frito–Lay operations: Payroll and Benefits; Treasury; and Imaging Technology. **Career Steps:** Frito–Lay, Inc.: Department Manager (1996–Present), Manager, Sales Accounting and Imaging (1994–1996), Accounts Payable Supervisor (1993–1994), Senior Tax Accountant (1991–1993). **Associations & Accomplishments:** Texas State Board of Public Accountancy; Beta Gamma Sigma; National Association for Female Executives; Southern Methodist University Alumni Association. **Education:** Southern Methodist University, M.B.A. (1994); University of Wisconsin, B.A. **Personal:** Married to Don in 1987. Ms. Wickman enjoys biking, rollerblading, and reading.

Shreyas H. Ajmera

President
Seenergy Foods, Inc.
56 Silver Fox Place
Maple, Ontario L6A 1G2
(905) 850–2544
Fax: (905) 850–2081

2099

Business Information: Seenergy Foods, Inc. is a manufacturer of food products, specializing in the production of low cholesterol and low fat foods, such as vegetarian foods. Established in 1994, Seenergy Foods, Inc. currently employs 60 people. As President and Co–Owner, Mr. Ajmera is responsible for all aspects of operations, including international operations with his brother, manufacturing and producing. Career milestones include developing a fully–automated line for bagels, becoming the second largest producer of bagels. **Career Steps:** President, Seenergy Foods, Inc. (1994–Present); Senior Vice President, Dough Delight, Ltd. (1973–1994). **Associations & Accomplishments:** CRFA; Institute of Food Technology (IFT). **Education:** University of Detroit, M.B.A. (1974); University of Bombay, India, B.Sc. **Personal:** Married to Meena in 1979. Two children: Ativ and Samyag. Mr. Ajmera enjoys visiting a variety of restaurants with his family.

Ira A. Haber
Director of Sales
Kraft Foodservice, Inc.
One Parkway North
Deerfield, IL 60015
(708) 405–8561
Fax: (708) 405–8885

2099

Business Information: Kraft Foodservice, Inc. is a national wholesale foodservice distribution company. Kraft Foodservice, Inc. reports annual revenue of $4.2 billion and currently employs 8,000 people. As Director of Sales, Mr. Haber is responsible for directing the sales of 39 distribution centers in the U.S. **Career Steps:** Kraft Foodservice, Inc.: Director of Sales (1993–Present), Vice President of Finance (1991–1993), Controller, Modern Telecommunications (1984–1989); CPA, Coopers & Lybrand (1979–1984). **Associations & Accomplishments:** American Institute of Certified Public Accountants; New York State Society of Certified Public Accountants; Bentley College President's Advisory Council. **Education:** Harvard Business School, M.B.A. (1991); Bentley College, B.S. in Accounting (1979). **Personal:** Married to Joanna C. in 1987. One child: Zachary G.

E. Daniel Karjala
Corporate Training and Development Director
Townsends, Inc.
P.O. Box 468
Millsboro, DE 19966–0468
(302) 934–4041
Fax: (302) 934–3084

2099

Business Information: Townsends, Inc. is an international manufacturer and distributor of prepared foods, such as desserts, poultry and soybean oil. Established in the 1890s, Townsends, Inc. reports annual revenue of $500 million and currently employs 3,800 people corporate–wide. With 12 years expertise in high tech industry, Mr. Karjala joined Townsends, Inc. in 1994. Appointed as Corporate Training and Development Director, he directs management training development, strategy and implementation, and organizational development. He is also responsible for facilitating the Company's desired direction of expansion in revenue and making recommendations in the cultural and management for potential and expected growth. **Career Steps:** Corporate Training and Development Manager, Townsends, Inc. (1994–Present); Senior Corporate Management Consultant, Intergraph Corporation (1991–1994). **Associations & Accomplishments:** American Society for Training and Development; The Heritage Foundation; American Management Association; International Who's Who of Professionals. **Education:** University of Minnesota, B.S. (1980). **Personal:** Married to Kathleen M. in 1978. Two children: Maria K. and Rebekah E. Mr. Karjala enjoys travel, cultural/historical studies, and music.

Abbe Kuhn

Vice President – Research & Development
Celestial Seasonings, Inc.
4600 Sleepytime Drive
Boulder, CO 80301–3284
(303) 581–1238
Fax: (303) 581–1393

2099

Business Information: Celestial Seasonings, Inc., the #1 herbal tea producer in the U.S., is a manufacturer of teas. Products include hot and iced herbal and black teas, caffeinated and non–caffeinated teas, and functional teas. Distributing their products nationally and internationally, Celestial Seasonings, Inc. also owns Botalia, a dietary supplement company. As Vice President of Research & Development, Ms. Kuhn is responsible for overseeing new product development, including cost reductions and product improvement; consumer research; testing; and analytical and quality control services. **Career Steps:** Vice President – Research & Development, Celestial Seasonings, Inc. (1994–Present); Director of Research & Development, A&W Brands (1992–1994); Manager of R&D – North America, Cadbury Beverages (1989–1992) **Associations & Accomplishments:** Institute of Food Technologists; Harbal Research Foundation; American Botanical Council **Education:** Cornell Univeristy, B.S. (1978) **Personal:** Married to Steve in 1993. Ms. Kuhn enjoys skiing, golf and dancing.

H. Darrall Loggins
Senior Buyer
Tetley, Inc.
1267 Cobb Industrial Drive
Marietta, GA 30066
(770) 428–5555
Fax: (770) 422–6839

2099

Business Information: Tetley, Inc. is an international manufacturer and packager of tea and coffee, with locations in the United States, England, Australia, and India. As Senior Buyer, Mr. Loggins is responsible for purchasing for the United States division in tea, packaging, and MRO items totaling $170 million annually. **Career Steps:** Senior Buyer, Tetley, Inc. (1986–Present); Purchasing Director, AVL Scientific (1984–1986); Purchasing Manager, The Heil Company (1982–1986). **Associations & Accomplishments:** American Management Association; National Association of Purchasing Management; Company Coordinator, Aids Walk Atlanta. **Education:** University of Tennessee, B.S. in Business Administration (1982). **Personal:** Mr. Loggins enjoys the outdoors.

J. Manuel Lomas–Purata

Commercial Vice Director
McCormick – PESA S.A. de C.V.
Monterrey No. 420
Mexico City, Mexico 03000
(525) 639–2870
Fax: (525) 639–2936

2099

Business Information: McCormick – PESA S.A. de C.V. is a leading global manufacturer and supplier of ingredients and spices for the food industry. Established in 1945, McCormick – PESA S.A. de C.V. reports annual revenue of $30 million and currently employs 180 people. As Commercial Vice Director, Mr. Lomas–Purata is responsible for a new domestic–approached project related to the meat industry. **Career Steps:** Commercial Vice Director, McCormick – PESA S.A. de C.V. (1995–Present); General Manager, McCormick – PESA – Occidente (1992–1995); Technical Sales, Prov. de Empocadoros S.A. (1991–1992); Plant Manager, RYC Alimentos (1990–1991). **Associations & Accomplishments:** Ateneo Nacional de Artes, Ledron, Ciencia & Tecnologia; Full Scholarship by the Mary Street Jenkins Foundation; Best Student, School of Engineering – Universidad de las Americas–Puebla. **Education:** Universidad de las Americas–Puebla, Food Engineer (1985). **Personal:** Married to Brenda Rocio in 1994. Mr. Lomas–Purata enjoys computers, cooking, biking, reading, and scuba diving.

Alan Michaelson

Director of Sales Training
Sysco Food Service of Los Angeles
20701 Currier Road
Walnut, CA 91789–2904
(909) 595–9595
Fax: (909) 594–9065
EMAIL: See Below

2099

Business Information: Sysco Food Service of Los Angeles is the largest food service distributor in the United States. The Company has recently expanded their client base to include Ontario and British Columbia. Sysco also distributes tableware, equipment, and janitorial supplies to their customers. As Director of Sales Training, Mr. Michaelson oversees the basic and secondary/continuing education of the Marketing Associates. He is also closely involved with the Serving Safe Food program. Internet users can also reach him via: ARM69@IX.NETCOM.COM. **Career Steps:** Director of Sales Training, Sysco Food Services of Los Angeles (1995–Present); Western Regional Sales Manager, American Tombow; National Sales Manager, American International Sales. **Education:** University of Phoenix, B.A. (1991). **Personal:** One child: Ryan. Mr. Michaelson enjoys skiing and volleyball.

Bob O'Connor

Site Controller
Bunge Foods
909 S. Carey Street
Baltimore, MD 21223
(410) 752–0020
Fax: (410) 752–3789

2099

Business Information: Bunge Foods is a food ingredient manufacturer, producing such products as yogurt, fudge, daiquiri mixes, fruit toppers, and desserts. Based in Brazil, the Company has several facilities worldwide. As Site Controller, Mr. O'Connor oversees the administrative and accounting functions for the Baltimore facility. **Career Steps:** Site Controller, Bunge Foods (1995–Present); Staff Auditor, Ernst & Young, LLP (1994–1995); Accounts Payable Clerk, J.G. Edelen Company, Inc. (1991–1993); Junior Accountant, Federal Arnold Express (1990). **Education:** University of Baltimore, B.S. (1993). **Personal:** Married to Donna in 1996. Mr. O'Connor enjoys reading, golf and the expansion of his marketing company, "The Dublin Group".

James Onalfo

Chief Information Officer
Kraft Foods International
250 North Street
White Plains, NY 10625–0001
(914) 335–1198
Fax: (914) 335–7971

2099

Business Information: Kraft Foods International is a worldwide manufacturer and distributor of packaged food products. New varieties are added as developed by research staff and occasionally through recommendations by consumers. Kraft Food products can be found across the country in most retail stores. As Chief Information Officer, Mr. Onalfo is in charge of information systems at the White Plains, New York location. He coordinates with management staff on the development and implementation of workable budgets and strategic plans for the Company. **Career Steps:** Kraft Foods: Chief Information Officer – International (1989–Present), Chief Information Officer – Desserts (1981–1989), Chief Information Officer – Food (1980–1981). **Associations & Accomplishments:** Pooley Consulting Group. **Personal:** Mr. Onalfo enjoys soccer.

James R. Pond Jr.

Vice President
Producers Peanut Company, Inc.
P.O. Box 250, 337 Moore Avenue
Suffolk, VA 23434
(804) 539–7496
Fax: (804) 934–7730

2099

Business Information: Producers Peanut Company, Inc. is a peanut butter manufacturer. Established in 1924, Producers Peanut Company, Inc. currently employs 30 people. In his current capacity, Mr. Pond is responsible for all aspects of company operations, including domestic marketing, corporate costs, international sales, and transportation. **Career Steps:** Vice President, Producers Peanut Company, Inc. (1980–Present); Service Engineer/Marketing, Bendiz Avionics Corporation (1972–1980). **Associations & Accomplishments:** Member, Peanut Butter and Nut Salters Association; Member, Hampton Roads Chamber of Commerce; Member, National Peanut Council; Developed Virginia Finest Specifications for Peanut Butter; Developed all Export Sales of existing company; Speaker at request of the Honorable Norman Sisisky at Agricultural Seminars. **Education:** United Electronics Institute (1972); Broward County Community College. **Personal:** Married to Kathryn in 1972. One child: Jennie. Mr. Pond enjoys fishing, gun collecting, and computing.

Steve C. Selby

Vice President
Waterloo/Small USA
Route 78 East
Swanton, VT 05488
(802) 868–3188
Fax: (802) 868–3180

2099

Business Information: Waterloo/Small USA is a manufacturer and distributor of maple syrup equipment. Ultraport Service Division provides fulfillment services and import and export services. Champlain Dairy Division provides service and supplies of dairy equipment and bomatic equipment. As Vice President, Mr. Selby is responsible for all aspects of Company operations, including administration, sales, employee supervision, and strategic planning. Also, as President of the following companies, Mr. Selby is responsible for all aspects of their operations: Vermont Specialty Equipment Division of Small Bros USA, Inc. (provides distribution of bottling equipment and containers), and Champlain Fulfillment Services Division of Small Bros USA, Inc. (provides credit card processing service). **Career Steps:** Vice President, Waterloo/Small USA (1996–Present); Small Brothers: President – USA (1984–1996), President – Evaporators (1969–1996); President, Selby Investments (1975–1996). **Associations & Accomplishments:** Lions Club; Masons Lodge; Legions. **Education:** McGill University, M.B.A. **Personal:** Two children: Mark and Jodie. Mr. Selby enjoys sailing, hunting, and fishing.

D. L. Peter Shafer

Manager of State Affairs
Grocery Manufacturers of America
241 Ridge Avenue
Baltimore, MD 21286–5433
(202) 337–9400
Fax: (202) 337–4508
EMail: See Below

2099

Business Information: Grocery Manufacturers of America, established in 1908, is a national trade association of Fortune 500 consumer products manufacturers. As Manager of State Affairs, Mr. Shafer is responsible for all strategic and tactical activities in ten New England and Mid–Atlantic states. **Career Steps:** Manager of State Affairs, Grocery Manufacturers of America (1995–Present); Manager of Center for Public Affairs, Public Affairs Council (1990–1995); Manager of Government Markets, United Way of Central Maryland (1988–1990); Private Banking Representative, First National Bank of Maryland (1986–1988). **Associations & Accomplishments:** Atlantic Coast Conference Officials Association; Washington Area Government Affairs Representative; Board of Directors, Johns Hopkins Tutorial Project; State Government Affairs Council; American Society for Quality Control; Omicron Delta Kappa; Kappa Alpha Order Alumni Association. **Education:** University of Maryland, M.G.A. (1994); Washington College,

B.S. in Political Science/Philosophy. **Personal:** Married to Catherine H. in 1991. One child: Reid Pearson. Mr. Shafer enjoys officiating college football and being an author.

Amy Jo Williams

National Events & Travel Manager
Fresh Express, Inc.
1020 Merrill Street
Salinas, CA 93901–4409
(408) 422–5917
Fax: (408) 751–7479

2099

Business Information: Fresh Express, Inc., headquartered in Salinas, CA, is an integral part of three companies under Fresh International, Inc. providing packaged foods and fresh express packaged salads to Taco Bell and Safeway, among others. As National Events & Travel Manager, Ms. Williams manages the travel budget, policy, operations of travel vendors, and convention coordination. **Career Steps:** National Events & Travel Manager, Fresh Express, Inc. (1992–Present); Sales Manager, Brown Palace Hotel – Denver (1991–1992); Sales Manager, Radisson Hotel – Denver (1989–1991). **Associations & Accomplishments:** United Way Marketing Committee; National Business Travel Association; Meeting Planners International; Produce Marketing Association; Exhibitor Board. **Education:** Texas Tech University, Marketing (1987). **Personal:** Ms. Williams enjoys photography, snow skiing, camping, hiking, tennis, and golf.

2100 Tobacco Products

2111 Cigarettes
2121 Cigars
2131 Chewing and smoking tobacco
2141 Tobacco stemming and redrying

Abraham Kovalsi Spitalny

President
Protobaco S.A.
CRA 11 #82–01 P. 6–B
Bogota, Colombia
(571) 621–9088
Fax: (571) 622–4004

2111

Business Information: Protobaco S.A. is a manufacturer of both American blend and black tobacco cigarettes. Brand names of cigarettes include, "Mustang," "President," "Premier," and "Continental," and are available in a variety of flavors. The Company distributes cigarettes throughout Colombia. As President, Mr. Kovalsi Spitalny is responsible for all aspects of Company operations, including day–to–day operations, finances, sales and marketing, and administration. **Career Steps:** Protobaco S.A.: President (1977–Present), Vice President (1971–1977), Plant Manager (1962–1971). **Associations & Accomplishments:** Chairman of the Board, Colegio Colombo Hebreo; Chairman, Keren Hayesod; Member of Several Club in Bogota. **Education:** Rensselaer Polytechnical Institute, Architect (1955). **Personal:** Four children: Helen, Betty Susan, Victor Simon, and Carlos Eduardo. Mr. Kovalsi Spitalny enjoys sports and music.

Pedro A. Trias, C.P.A.

Controller
Congar International Corporation/Division of Consolidated Cigar Corporation
P.O. Box 373100
Cayey, Puerto Rico 00737–3100
(787) 738–2106
Fax: (787) 746–1436

2121

Business Information: Congar International Corporation/Division of Consolidated Cigar Corporation specializes in the manufacture and international distribution of cigars. Established in 1940, the Company employs 750 people, and has an estimated annual revenue of $100 million. As Controller, Mr. Trias oversees all financial aspects of the Company. His responsibilities include forecasting, budgeting, taxes, and accounting. **Career Steps:** Controller, Congar International Corporation/Division of Consolidated Cigar Corporation (1986–Present); Controller, Dorado Hi–Tech (1983); Controller, Pellozzo Iron Works (1977). **Associations & Accomplishments:** American Institute of Certified Public Accountants; Colegio Contadores Publices de Puerto Rico. **Education:** University of Puerto Rico, B.B.A. (1965). **Personal:** Married to Carmen Garcia in 1968. Three children: Pedro Jr., Sandra and Carmen. Mr. Trias enjoys fishing and reading.

Pascal A. Fernandez
Brand Manager
Phillip Morris Inc.
120 Park Avenue
New York, NY 10017–5523
(212) 878–2410
Fax: (212) 922–9426
EMAIL: PASCALFS@AOL.COM

2131

Business Information: Phillip Morris Incorporated is a leading manufacturer and marketer of tobacco products and consumer goods. Joining Phillip Morris–USA in 1991 as Senior Marketing Research Analyst, Mr. Fernandez was appointed to his current role in June of 1995. As Brand Manager, he is responsible for overseeing the development and marketing of new product strategies for Phillip Morris USA. **Career Steps:** Brand Manager, Phillip Morris Incorporated (1995–Present), Assistant Brand Manager (1994), Senior Analyst Marketing Research (1991–1993), Marketing Assistant (1989) **Associations & Accomplishments:** American Marketing Association. **Education:** University Paris Sorbonne: B.S. in Economics, M.S. in Business; University Paris Dauphine, M.S. in Management Information. **Personal:** Married to Jenny in 1993. Mr. Fernandez enjoys travel, tennis, reading books, and being with friends.

Mr. Henry C. Howells IV
Area Vice President
Brown & Williamson Tobacco Corporation
1500 Brown & Williamson Tower
Louisville, KY 40202
(502) 568–7357
Fax: (502) 568–8486

2131

Business Information: Brown & Williamson Tobacco Corporation is a leading manufacturer and marketer of tobacco products; a wholly–owned subsidiary of BAT, based in London, England. BAT owns a variety of tobacco and financial services concerns throughout the world. In his capacity as Area Vice President, Mr. Howells is responsible for the operational management of Southeast United States and the Northern Caribbean, as well as oversee all profit and loss for this territory. Established in 1892, Brown & Williamson Tobacco Corporation employs over 4,500 people company–wide. **Career Steps:** Area Vice President, Brown & Williamson Tobacco Corporation (1994–Present); Regional Vice President – Europe, Brown & Williamson (1992–1994); Director of International Brand Management, Brown & Williamson (1990–1992); Marketing Director, BAT Hong Kong (1988– 1990). **Associations & Accomplishments:** Ohio State University Alumni Association; Board Member, Southern Association of Wholesale Distributors; Lecturer at trade seminars; Interviewed for articles in International trade journal s. **Education:** Ohio State University, M.B.A. (1982); Virginia Polytechnic Institute and State University, B.S. in Finance.

James R. Mortensen
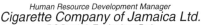
Vice President of Sales for Western Region
Philip Morris U.S.A.
300 North Lake Avenue, Suite 1100
Pasadena, CA 91101–4106
(818) 792–0202
Fax: (818) 356–9870

2131

Business Information: Philip Morris U.S.A., a Fortune 10 company, is the largest manufacturer and marketer of cigarettes in the United States, products such as Marlboro and Virginia Slims. The parent company, Philip Morris International not only owns Philip Morris U.S.A., but it also owns KRAFT Foods and Miller Brewing Company. Joining Philip Morris, U.S.A. in 1989, Mr. Mortensen was appointed as Vice President of Sales for Western Region in 1993. He is responsible for the direction of sales operations in the Western Region of the United States. **Career Steps:** Philip Morris U.S.A.: Vice President of Sales for Western Region (1993–Present), Section Sales Director (1992–1993), Trade Marketing Director (1991–1992). **Education:** University of Buffalo: MBA (1985), B.S. in Business and Finance (1983). **Personal:** Married to Laurie in 1986. Two children: Erik and Dylan. Mr. Mortensen enjoys skiing, rollerblading, tennis, and spending time with family.

Robert D. Stowe
Divisional Vice President, Marketing and Communications
Brown & Williamson Tobacco Corporation
1500 Brown & Williamson Tower, P. O. Box 35090
Louisville, KY 40202
(502) 568–7170
Fax: (502) 568–7027

2131

Business Information: Brown & Williamson Tobacco Company is the third largest tobacco company in the U.S. Wholly owned by British–American Tobacco, Inc. (BAT, Inc.), the Company specializes in the manufacture and distribution of cigarette–grade tobacco. Brands produced include Kool, Capri, Carlton, Viceroy, Misty, GPC, Lucky Strike and Pall Mall. Established in 1893, the Company employs over 5,000 people. As Divisional Vice President, Marketing and Communications, Mr. Stowe oversees all consumer marketing communications, creative development, agency management, sponsorships, promotions and direct mail. Tasked with effectively translating and focusing all brand strategies towards customers, Mr. Stowe is also responsible for creative development and media relations involving the management structure portfolio through which the Company operates. **Career Steps:** Brown & Williamson Tobacco Corporation: Divisional Vice President, Marketing and Communications (1996–Present), Area Vice Director of Sales for the Southeastern U.S. (1995–1996), Director of Human Resources, Marketing and Sales (1993–1995). **Associations & Accomplishments:** Past Member, Board of Directors, Southern Association of Wholesale Distributors; American Management Association; Association of National Advertisers. **Education:** University of Utah: B.S. in Psychology (1981), B.S. in Sociology (1980); Various courses and seminars. **Personal:** Married to Holly Ann, of Salt Lake City, Utah in 1978. Three children: Hailey Quinn, Taylor Paige, and Robert Clinton.

Ashwell Thomas

Human Resource Development Manager
Cigarette Company of Jamaica Ltd.
P.O.Box 100, Twickenham Park
Spanish Town, Jamaica
(809) 984–2826
Fax: (809) 984–6571

2131

Business Information: Established in 1963, Cigarette Company of Jamaica Ltd. is a manufacturer of tobacco products and a member of the Carreras Group of Companies. As Human Resource Development Manager, Mr. Thomas is responsible for planning, directing, and coordinating all human resources policies and programs. **Career Steps:** H.R.D. Manager, Cigarette Company of Jamaica Ltd. (1979–Present); Personnel Officer, Naiser Bauxite Company (1976–1979); Senior Training Officer, Jamaica Industrial Development Corporation (1973–1976). **Associations & Accomplishments:** Society for Human Resource Management; Jamaica Employers Federation; Chairman, Spanish Town Comprehensive High School Board; Jamaica Institute of Management. **Education:** Kensington University: Ph.D. (1996), M.S.C.; University of the West Indies B.A. **Personal:** Married to Audrey in 1975. Three children: Antoinette, Alicia, and Ayania. Mr. Thomas enjoys reading and singing.

2200 Textile Mill Products

2211 Broadwoven fabric mills, cotton
2221 Broadwoven fabric mills, manmade
2231 Broadwoven fabric mills, wool
2241 Narrow fabric mills
2251 Women's hosiery, except socks
2252 Hosiery, NEC
2253 Knit outerwear mills
2254 Knit underwear mills
2257 Weft knit fabric mills
2258 Lace and warp knit fabric mills
2259 Knitting mills, NEC
2261 Finishing plants, cotton
2262 Finishing plants, manmade
2269 Finishing plants, NEC
2273 Carpets and rugs
2281 Yarn spinning mills
2282 Throwing and winding mills
2284 Thread mills
2295 Coated fabrics, not rubberized
2296 Tire cord and fabrics
2297 Nonwoven fabrics

2298 Cordage and twine
2299 Textile goods, NEC

Thomas P. Bruewer
Quality Assurance Mgr, PRECISION Technology Division
Precision Fabrics Group, Inc.
6012 High Point Road
Greensboro, NC 27407
(910) 454–8832
Fax: (910) 454–5660

2221

Business Information: Precision Fabrics Group, Inc. specializes in the design and manufacture of difficult–to–make fine denier filament woven fabrics, and specialized non–woven fabrics. Customers include the medical, aerospace, computer, automotive, home furnishings, filtration, sportswear, and protective apparel industries. Mr. Bruewer is responsible for the quality system necessary to design and manufacture products for the automotive industry (airbags and airbag fabrics). **Career Steps:** Precision Fabrics Group, Inc: Division Quality Assurance Manager (1994–Present), Senior Quality Engineer/ ISO 9000 Coordinator (1991–1994), Plant QA/QE (1990–1991); Electronics Engineer, Naval Avionics Center – Indianapolis (1986–1990). **Associations & Accomplishments:** American Society of Quality Control; Society for Automotive Engineers; North Carolina Zoological Society; National Parks Conservancy Association; Beta Gamma Sigma. **Education:** University of North Carolina – Greensboro, M.B.A. (1990); University of Dayton, Bachelor of Electrical Engineering.

Teryl K. VerPloeg
Director of MIS
Delong Sportswear
733 Broad Street
Grinnell, IA 50112–2227
(515) 236–3106
Fax: (515) 236–3342
EMAIL: tceavp@netins.net

2221

Business Information: Delong Sportswear is a "made to order" manufacturer of outerwear (award jackets, supplex and nylon jackets, and pullovers), team uniforms, and headwear. The Company also silk screens and embroiders the items they produce with team names, logos, etc. A U.S.–based company, Delong Sportswear has locations throughout the country. Employing over 1,000 people, the Company has estimated annual revenue of $65 million. As Director of MIS, Mr. VerPloeg manages a development of six individuals, a support staff of three, and oversees a network of 150 Macintosh computers and a HP3000. Mr. Verploeg has extensive experience in implementing solutions for strategic business problems and objectives associated with controlling costs and achieving the maximum benefit. Internet users can reach him via: tceavp@netins.net. **Career Steps:** Director of MIS, Delong Sportswear (1987–Present); Senior Systems Analyst, Pella Corporation (1974–1987). **Associations & Accomplishments:** Past City Councilman, City of Sully; Secretary, Jasper County Economic Corporation; Lions President, Local Chapter; MacIS. **Education:** Des Moines Area Community College, A.A. (1974). **Personal:** Married to Carol in 1977. Two children: Erin and Amber. Mr. VerPloeg enjoys golf, snow skiing, and AAU coaching.

Ms. Janice W. Vogler
Director of Human Resources
Microfibres, Inc.
3803 Kimwell Drive
Winston–Salem, NC 27103
(910) 768–7312
Fax: (910) 768–7718

2221

Business Information: Microfibres, Inc. is a textile manufacturing company of nylon velvet upholstery for furniture. International in scope, Microfibres, Inc. has over four plants located in Rhode Island, Ontario, Canada, Belgium, and Winston–Salem. In her current capacity, Ms. Vogler is responsible for the administration and oversight of all Human Resources aspects. Established in 1985, Microfibres, Inc. currently employs 380 people in Winston–Salem. **Career Steps:** Director of Human Resources, Microfibres, Inc. (1990–Present); Manager of Benefits and Services, North Carolina Baptist Hospital/Medical Center (1971–1990). **Associations & Accomplishments:** Director and Officer, North Carolina Hospital Personnel Association; Society for Human Resource Management; American Compensation Association; Board of Directors, High Point University Alumni; Membership Committee, United Way (1976–Present); Sun Alliance (Coor. survey of 30+ medical centers); Won 2nd Place in Worker's Compensation Systems. **Education:** High Point University, B.A. in Industrial and Organizational Psychology; University of North Carolina at Greensboro, Business Administration. **Personal:**

Two children: Ian and Phillip. Ms. Vogler enjoys golf, free weights, and traveling.

Steven Frumkin
Vice President
Carleton Woolen Mills
1040 Avenue of The Americas
New York, NY 10018
(212) 391–2555
Fax: (212) 764–8604

2231

Business Information: Carleton Woolen Mills, established in 1950 is a manufacturer of woolen fabrics with three mills in Maine and the executive offices in New York. Carleton Woolen Mills is owned by Allied Textile, a publicly–traded British company and one of the largest modern woolen mills in the world. As Vice President, Mr. Frumkin is responsible for the day–to–day operations of the Company. He is also responsible for all merchandising, quality, and development of new products and technology. Mr. Frumkin's plans for the next few years are to continue to diversify the product mix and to focus on international expansion. In 1994, Mr. Frumkin founded 21st Century Morphology, a firm that markets, sells, distributes, and licenses the use of high technology technical engineering fibers. **Career Steps:** Vice President, Carleton Woolen Mills (1995–Present); President, E.G. Smith/Keepers International (1988–1994); President, Nazzareno Goti, U.S.A. (1984–1988); Vice President, Biltex International, Inc. (1976–1984). **Associations & Accomplishments:** Adjunct Professor, Textile Development and Marketing, Fashion Institute of Technology; Chairman, Executive Board, Textile Veterans Association; Vice President, Board of Education, Pampano Central School District; Zoning Board of Appeals, Village of Montebello; American Arbitration Association. **Education:** Bernard M. Baruch College, M.B.A. (1977); Philadelphia College of Textiles and Science, B.S. (1970). **Personal:** Married to Laura in 1975. Two children: Sarah and Jacob. Mr. Frumkin enjoys rock climbing.

Thomas D. Young, CPA, CMA
Controller
Neuville Industries, Inc.
P.O. Box 286, 9451 Neuville Avenue
Hildebran, NC 28637
(704) 397–5566 Ext. 379
Fax: (704) 397–3248

2252

Business Information: Neuville Industries, Inc. is a manufacturer of both private and brand label men's, ladies', and children's hosiery, including Wrangler, Dickeys, and Keds. As Controller, Mr. Young is responsible for all financial aspects of the Company, including accounting, accounts payable, financial reports, health insurance, payroll, and 401K plans. **Career Steps:** Controller, Neuville Industries, Inc. (1994–Present); Controller, Thorlo, Inc. (1993–1994); Senior Accountant, Deloitte & Touche (1989–1993). **Associations & Accomplishments:** American Institute of Certified Public Accountants; North Carolina Association of Certified Public Accountants; Institute of Management Accountants; Highland Baptists Church. **Education:** Appalachian State University, M.S. in Accounting (1988); Mars Hill College, B.S. in Accounting. **Personal:** Married to Kelly in 1991. Two children: Mallory and Emily. Mr. Young enjoys golf and fishing.

Simon S. Lee
President/Chief Executive Officer
Cititop Inc.
1571 West 132nd Street
Gardena, CA 90249
(310) 324–9294
Fax: (310) 324–9623

2253

Business Information: International in scope, Cititop Inc. is a manufacturer of adult sportswear products, manufacturing both private–label and package branding of golf and polo shirts, crew–neck tee shirts and sweatsuits. Major package brand vendors include J.C. Penny, J. Crew and Calvin Klein. As President and Chief Executive Officer, Mr. Lee oversees all day–to–day operations, with emphasis on marketing, strategic planning and budgets. **Career Steps:** President/Chief Executive Officer, Cititop Inc. (1989–Present); Production Manager, Chalie & Sunny (1981–1989). **Associations & Accomplishments:** U.S. Chamber of Commerce; J.A.H.A.; Published in the "Sun Times" in Los Angeles. **Education:** California Institute of the Arts, BFA (1980). **Personal:** Married

to Yoo–Jung in 1993. Two children: Genos and David. Mr. Lee enjoys golf, playing the guitar, and singing.

/F/R/E/N/C/H/ /R/A/G/S/

Mile J. Rasic
Vice President
Colorknits, Inc., d.b.a. /F/R/E/N/C/H /R/A/G/S
11500 Tennessee Avenue
Los Angeles, CA 90064
(310) 479–5648
Fax: (310) 445–2046
French Rags@aol.com.

2253

Business Information: Colorknits, Inc., dba /F/R/E/N/C/H/R/A/G/S/, is a manufacturer of knitwear mainly for women, including suits, coats, jackets, and sweaters. In order to purchase clothing from the Company, clients must buy from a consultant since clothes are not found in any retail stores. As Vice President, Mr. Rasic is in charge of the entire operation from beginning to end (production process), total production control, and electrical computing programs for knitting machines. Internet users can reach him via: French Rags@aol.com. **Career Steps:** Vice President, Colorknits, Inc., dba /F/R/E/N/C/H/ /R/A/G/S/ (1990–Present); Vice President, Drasin Knitting Mill (1980–1990); Vice President, Merryknits, Inc. (1977–1980); Plant Manager, Neat Fit Knitting Mills (1972–1977). **Associations & Accomplishments:** Chairman, Croatian Democratic Union, Los Angeles Chapter; Croatian National Association. **Education:** East Los Angeles College, A.A. (1976); Textile Engineering. **Personal:** Married to Veronica in 1967. Two children: Mladen Anthony and Milena. Mr. Rasic enjoys bicycles, sports, skiing, tennis, and swimming.

Seth H. Schreiber
Vice President of Manufacturing
A. H. Schreiber Co., Inc.
460 West 34th Street, 10th Floor
New York, NY 10001
(212) 564–2700
Fax: (212) 594–7234

2253

Business Information: A. H. Schreiber Co., Inc., a family–owned business, is an international manufacturer of all types of swimwear. With the head office located in New York, A. H. Schreiber Co., Inc. has locations in Virginia and New York. Established in 1920, A. H. Schreiber Co., Inc. is a privately–held, multi–million dollar corporation and currently employs 500 people. Serving as Vice President of Manufacturing, Mr. Schreiber is responsible for all aspects of domestic and overseas production, including quality issues, new markets and strategies for the manufacture of women's swimwear. **Career Steps:** Vice President of Manufacturing, A. H. Schreiber Co., Inc. (1984–Present). **Education:** City University of New York, B.A. in Economics (1985); Additional years of studies were done abroad. **Personal:** Married to Linda in 1988. Two children. Mr. Schreiber enjoys ice hockey, racquetball, and skiing.

Charles R. Dulaney Jr.
President and Chief Executive Officer
Fashion Fabrics of America, Inc.
1370 Broadway, 9th Floor
New York, NY 10018
(212) 643–0400
Fax: (212) 643–0326

2269

Business Information: Fashion Fabrics of America, Inc., a wholly–owned entity of French–based textile conglomerate DMC, is a manufacturer and distributor of printed cotton and rayon apparel fabrics. The Company operates a manufacturing facility in Orangeburg, SC, as well as sales and creative offices in New York and Los Angeles. As President and Chief Executive Officer, Mr. Dulaney is responsible for all aspects of the company, including administration, operations and strategic planning. He is also a member of the DMC Committee de Direction responsible for the setting of corporate policy and the definition of long range strategic goals. Established in 1989, Fashion Fabrics of America, Inc. employs 235 people. **Career Steps:** President and Chief Executive Officer, Fashion Fabrics of America, Inc. (1994–Present); Regional Director (Asia/Pacific), E.I. Dupont (1989–1993); National Sales Manager, E.I. Dupont (1986–1989). **Education:** Virginia Polytechnic Institute, B.S. in Management (1973). **Personal:** Married to Faith. Two children: Heather and Jessica. Mr. Dulaney enjoys golf and woodworking.

E. David Hobbs
Vice President
Interface, Inc.
P. O. Box 1503
LaGrange, GA 30241–1503
(706) 812–6206
Fax: (706) 885–0050
EMAIL: See Below

2273

Business Information: Interface, Inc. is a recognized leader in the worldwide commercial interiors market. The Company is the world's largest manufacturer of modular carpet and enjoys a position in the forefront of the high quality, designer–oriented segment of the broadloom carpet market. Interface, Inc. is also a leading producer of interior fabrics and upholstery products and provides chemicals used in various rubber and plastic products. There are offices in 195 countries worldwide, and 23 manufacturing locations. As Vice President, Mr. Hobbs is in charge of purchasing, planning and distribution. **Career Steps:** Interface, Inc: Vice President (1994–Present), Director of Customer Service/Planning (1990–1994), Director of Materials Management (1986–1990). **Associations & Accomplishments:** National Association of Purchasing Managers; American Production and Inventory Control Society; American Management Association; Leadership Troup; C.P.M.; C.P.I.M.; Mr. Hobbs is a part–time instructor at La-Grange College. **Personal:** Married to Catherine in 1975. Two children: Tiffany, and Brittany. Mr. Hobbs has a Masters degree in Mathematics, is a Deacon in the Baptist Church, and was an Eagle Scout. He enjoys backpacking, golf, piano, coaching youth sports, and teaching.

Bennie M. Laughter
Vice President and General Counsel
Shaw Industries, Inc.
616 East Walnut Avenue
Dalton, GA 30721
(706) 275–1018
Fax: (706) 275–1442

2273

Business Information: Shaw Industries, Inc. is the world's largest manufacturer of carpeting. Manufacturing plants are located throughout the U.S., United Kingdom, Australia, Mexico, Wales, and Ireland. Established in 1846, Shaw Industries, Inc. reports an annual revenue of $3.0 billion and currently employs more than 24,000 people company–wide. As Vice President and General Counsel, Mr. Laughter serves as Chief Legal Officer and is responsible for all Company legal matters. He is admitted to practice law in District of Columbia, Georgia, Illinois, and North Carolina state courts. Concurrent with his position, he serves as Corporate Secretary and Head of Risk Management Division. **Career Steps:** Vice President and General Counsel, Shaw Industries, Inc. (1986–Present); General Counsel, Estronics, Inc., subsidiary of Beatrice Cos. (1979–1986); Staff Attorney, Esmark, Inc., subsidiary of Beatrice Cos. (1976–1979). **Associations & Accomplishments:** American Bar Association; District of Columbia Bar Association; Georgia Bar Association; Illinois Bar Association; North Carolina Bar Association; B.P.O. Elks; First Baptist Church–Dalton: Deacon, Sunday School Teacher, Royal Ambassadors; Board of Director, Southern Seminary Foundation, Inc.; Former Officer and Director, Carpet Capital Aquatics Club; The Farm Golf Club; UMCH Foster Parent. **Education:** Georgetown University Law Center, J.D. (1976); University of North Carolina, A.B. in English, A.B. with Honors in Political Science (1973). **Personal:** Married to R. Lynette (Dodson) in 1972. Three children: Judson Crandall, Mark Dodson, and Mary Lynette Laughter.

Anthony D. West
Vice President of Operations
Sunrise Carpet Industries
531 Duvall Raod
Chatsworth, GA 30705
(706) 695–9605 Ext. 4206
Fax: (706) 695–9605 Ext. 4433

2273

Business Information: Sunrise Carpet Industries is a manufacturer of carpets. Established in 1976, it is the fifth largest commercial carpet company with international exports. As Vice President of Operations, Mr. West oversees all manufacturing operations, including administrative activities, finance, and strategic planning. **Career Steps:** Vice President of Operations, Sunrise Carpet Industries (1985–Present). **Associations & Accomplishments:** Automation Forum. **Education:** Georgia College, B.S. in Management (1985). **Personal:** Married to Terri in 1994. One child: Alex. Mr. West enjoys sports and politics.

Dan Costant

Executive Vice President
Akzo Nobel Nonwovens Inc.
P O Box 1057
Enka, NC 28728–1057
(704) 665–5070
Fax: (704) 665–5065

2297

Business Information: Akzo Nobel Nonwovens Inc. makes spunbond nonwovens for carpet backing, automotive flooring, bituminized roofing membranes, geosynthetic products. As Executive Vice President, Mr. Costant has total business responsibility over the North Carolina operation, covering NAFTA market. **Career Steps:** Executive Vice President, (1995–Present) Akzo Nobel Nonwovens Inc./U.S.; Technical Director, (1992–1995) Polyenka/Brazil; Plant Manager, (1988–1992) Akzo Carpet Yarn/Netherlands; Chief Engineer, (1984–1988), Enka de Colombia/Colombia; Project Manager, (1975–1983) Methanol Chemie Delfzijl/Netherlands. **Associations & Accomplishments:** In his two previous positions, Mr. Costant developed and implemented turn around programs focusing on Total Quality Management, achieving two ISO–9001 certifications and productivity improvements up to 50%. In Columbia, he developed an engineering department to manage projects up to $80 million. Mr. Costant is fluent in English, Spanish, Dutch, Romanian, Portugese, and is proficient in German. **Education:** Polytechnical Institute of Bucharest, M.Sc. (1970); University of Groningen (Netherlands), two year study in Business Administration and Economics. In addition, he took more than 15 courses in management, strategic planning, total quality, project management, etc. **Personal:** Married to Greet in 1973. Three children: George, Miron, and Ioana. Mr. Costant enjoys tennis, golf, classical music, opera, and reading.

Scott E. Dempsey
Vice President, Marketing and Sales
Lydall Manning NonWovens
P.O. Box 328
Troy, NY 12181–0328
(518) 273–6320
Fax: (518) 273–6361

2297

Business Information: Lydall Manning NonWovens is an international corporation headquartered in Manchester, Connecticut with six other divisions, five of which are located East of the Mississippi River. International locations include production and sales plants in France and a sales plant in Japan. The Corporation specializes in nonwovens for thermal and flame applications. As Vice President, Marketing and Sales, Mr. Dempsey is responsible for devising new and original means of marketing products produced by the corporation. It is his responsibility to expand their client base in order to increase product sales. **Career Steps:** Lydall Manning NonWovens: Vice President, Marketing and Sales (1995–Present), Marketing Manager (1994–1995); Milliken & Company: Business Manager (1992–1994), Product Manager (1990–1992). **Associations & Accomplishments:** I.P.C.; N.F.P.A. **Education:** University of New Hampshire: M.B.A. (1981), B.S. in Mechanical Engineering (1981). **Personal:** Married to Laura in 1987. Two children: Drew, and Grace. Mr. Dempsey enjoys sailing, woodwork, and camping.

Peter P. Gromacki
Business Manager
Technical Fibre Products
RD 1 Box 144
Slate Hill, NY 10973–9767
(914) 355–4190
Fax: (914) 355–4192

2297

Business Information: Technical Fibre Products is a manufacturer and supplier of advanced nonwoven mats formed from carbon, aramid, glass, metal–coated and ceramic fibers. Markets include automotive, commercial, recreational, aerospace and defense. As Business Manager, Mr. Gromacki is responsible for planning marketing strategies and for bringing ideas from inception to commercialization. **Career Steps:** Business Manager, Technical Fibre Products (1991–Present); Market Manager, International Paper (1988–1991). **Associations & Accomplishments:** American Society of Metals; Society of Manufacturing Engineers. **Education:** Long Island University, M.B.A.; State University of New York – Institute of Technology, B.S. **Personal:** Married to Jennifer in 1990. Mr. Gromacki enjoys sailing.

William J. Vogel

Director of Marketing and Sales
Chicopee
317 George Street
New Brunswick, NJ 08901–2008
(908) 524–6260
Fax: (908) 524–6276

2297

Business Information: Chicopee is an international manufacturer of non–woven materials for the healthcare, consumer and industrial markets such as Johnson & Johnson. Established in 1912, Chicopee employs 250 professionals and has an estimated annual revenue of $300 million. As Director of Marketing and Sales, Mr. Vogel is responsible for $50 million in worldwide sales (mostly Asian) and reports directly to the Vice President. He also manages eight associates including three cross functional teams. **Career Steps:** Director of Marketing and Sales, Chicopee (1995–Present); Marketing Specialist, Johnson & Johnson (1991–1995); Sales Manager, L&H Supply, Inc. (1986–1991). **Associations & Accomplishments:** Japan Business Society; American Management Association; Who's Who World Wide of Business Leaders. **Education:** Monmouth University, M.B.A. (1991); Ursnis College: B.S. in Mathematics (1986), M.S. in Accounting. **Personal:** Married to Lynn in 1994. Mr. Vogel enjoys golf, skiing, and volleyball.

Rajeev Agrawal
General Manager
Eternal Glory International, Inc.
5580 Bandini Boulevard
Bell, CA 90201
(213) 262–9972
Fax: (213) 262–2989
EMail: EGLORY333@aol.com

2299

Business Information: Eternal Glory International, Inc. specializes in the manufacture of textiles and garments. Clients include such retail outlets as WalMart and Target. As General Manager, Mr. Agrawal is responsible for all aspects of Company operations, including sales, marketing, and distribution of all orders to the stores. **Career Steps:** General Manager, Eternal Glory International, Inc. (1992–Present); Unit Financial Controller, Hindustan Lever (1988–1992); Finance Manager, ITC, Ltd. (India) Batco Group (1986–1988). **Associations & Accomplishments:** Lok Kalyan Samiti – Voluntary Welfare Organization. **Education:** Institute of Chartered Accountants of India, C.A. (CPA) (1989); Calcutta University – School of Law, LL.B.; Institute of Company Secretaries of India, F.C.S.; Institute of Management Accountants of India, F.C.M.A. **Personal:** Married to Minakshi in 1991. One child: Garima. Mr. Agrawal enjoys reading, writing, and travel.

David L. Crow
Vice President of Administration and Information
Empresas T & M
Independencia 129
Santiago, Dominican Republic
(809) 575–4777
Fax: (809) 575–1232

2299

Business Information: Empresas T & M, located in Santiago, Dominican Republic, is a textile manufacturer for the U.S. market. Products include suits and separates for men's and ladies' apparel. Clients include Liz Claiborne, Stafford, and Haggar. Established in 1964, Empresas T & M reports annual revenue $20MM and currently employs 3,000 people. As Vice President of Administration and Information, Mr. Crow is responsible for all administration, computers, human resources, purchasing, accounting, payroll, plant maintenance, and insurance. Career milestones include bringing American management to Dominican Republic culture. **Career Steps:** Vice President of Administration and Information, Empresas T & M (1985–Present); Systems Analyst, TRW – World Headquarters (1980–1985); Systems Consultant, Decision Sciences, Inc. (1978–1979); Research Assistant, E. L. Crow Consultants, Inc. (1977–1978). **Associations & Accomplishments:** American Chamber of Commerce; Boy Scout Leader. **Education:** Ohio University, M.B.A. (1980); Ohio Wesleyan University, B.A. **Personal:** Married to Carmen R. One child: Eduardo. Mr. Crow enjoys golf and camping.

Kimberly G. Donald
Corporate Human Resources Manager
Mount Vernon Mills, Inc.
1 Insignia Plaza, Suite 700
Greenville, SC 29602
(864) 233–4151
Fax: (864) 370–2315

2299

Business Information: Mount Vernon Mills, Inc. is a textile manufacturing company producing finished upholstery fabric and yarn products. Joining Mount Vernon Mills in 1993, Kim Donald was recently appointed to Corporate Human Resources Manager. She oversees all aspects of human resources operations for 14 locations. **Career Steps:** Mount Vernon Mills, Inc.: Corporate Human Resources Manager (1996–Present), Director of Human Resource Management (1993–1996). **Associations & Accomplishments:** Greenville Area Personnel Association. **Education:** Southern Wesleyan University, B.A. in Human Resource Management (1996). **Personal:** Married to Bryson W. in 1994. Three children: Brittany Elizabeth, Brett Lane, and Jorden Michelle. Ms. Donald enjoys reading, sailing, cooking, and baking.

Dennis L. Lampman

General Manager
Cramer Fabrics
20 Venture Drive
Dover, NH 03820–5912
(603) 742–3838
Fax: (603) 742–5330

2299

Business Information: Cramer Fabrics specializes in the manufacture of industrial fabric and textiles such as sail cloth and filtration fabric. Established in 1993, Cramer Fabrics currently employs 15 people and has an estimated annual revenue of $5 million. As General Manager, Mr. Lampman is responsible for all aspects of operations, from production to finance. **Career Steps:** General Manager, Cramer Fabrics (1993–Present); President, Lampman Management and Consulting (1985–1993); Vice President, Eldorado Woolen Mills, Inc. (1981–1987). **Associations & Accomplishments:** American Society for Testing and Materials. **Education:** California Pacific University: M.B.A. (1988), B.S. in Business Administration (1986). **Personal:** Married to Leslie in 1978. Two children: Lucas and Lindsay. Mr. Lampman enjoys writing.

Geza Victor Maklary
International Sales Manager
Malden Mills Industries
450 7th Avenue, Floor 14
New York, NY 10123–0101
(212) 563–0404
Fax: (212) 564–0914

2299

Business Information: Malden Mills Industries is an international textile business specializing in the manufacturing of fleece 'polartec' fabrics. Established in 1902, Malden Mills Industries reports annual revenue of $400 million and currently employs 3,000 people. As International Sales Manager, Mr. Maklary is responsible for all aspects of European sales and marketing in Southern Europe. **Career Steps:** International Sales Manager, Malden Mills Industries (1989–Present); Import–Export Manager, Marlarex – Belgium (1983–1988). **Education:** European University, Brussels, Belgium, Bachelors (1987).

Howard W. Ward III
Manager, Corporate Management Information Systems
Dan River Inc.
151 Jerry Drive
Danville, VA 24541
(804) 799–7244
Fax: (804) 799–7276
EMAIL: See Below

2299

Business Information: Dan River Inc. manufactures premier home furnishings and apparel textiles (i.e. comforters) to retail entities throughout the U.S. As Manager of Corporate Management Information Systems, Howard Ward is responsible for all financial and materials acquisitions of the Company. Internet users can reach him via: hward3@ns.gamewood.net. **Career Steps:** Manager, Corporate Management Information Systems, Dan River Inc. (1993–Present); Finance Director, City of Ketchikan, Alaska (1988–1991); Director of Accounting and MIS, City of Fredericksburg, Virginia (1983–1987);

Owner, Cambridge Systems, Inc. (1980–1983). **Education:** Averett College, B.S. (1995). **Personal:** Married to Donna in 1970. Two children: Stacey and Jonathan. Mr. Ward enjoys being a church organist and choir director.

Nancy Zarin

President
Belding Hausman Inc.
1430 Broadway
New York, NY 10018
(212) 556–4853
Fax: (212) 556–4884

2299

Business Information: Belding Hausman, Inc. is a manufacturer of textile products, such as home furnishings and fabrics. Established 150 years ago, Belding Hausman, Inc. currently employs 400 people. As President, Ms. Zarin is responsible for all aspects of operations, including administration, finances, sales, public relations, marketing, and strategic planning. **Career Steps:** President, Belding Hausman Inc. (1993–Present); Executive Vice President and Business Manager, The Knoll Group (office furniture company) (1989–1993). **Education:** Sloan School, MIT, M.B.A. in Operations Management (1979); Brandeis University, M.S. in Mathematics; University of Oxford, B.S. in Genetics and Biology.

2300 Apparel and Other Textile Products

2311 Men's and boys' suits and coats
2321 Men's and boys' shirts
2322 Men's and boys' underwear and nightwear
2323 Men's and boys' Neckwear
2325 Men's and boys' trousers and slacks
2326 Men's and boys' work clothing
2329 Men's and boys' clothing, NEC
2331 Women's and misses' blouses and shirts
2335 Women's, juniors', and misses' dresses
2337 Women's and misses' suits and coats
2339 Women's and misses' outerwear, NEC
2341 Women's and children's underwear
2342 Bras, girdles and allied garments
2353 Hats, caps, and millinery
2361 Girls' and children's dresses, blouses
2369 Girls' and children's outerwear, NEC
2371 Fur goods
2381 Fabric dress and work gloves
2384 Robes and dressing gowns
2385 Waterproof outerwear
2386 Leather and sheep–lined clothing
2387 Apparel belts
2389 Apparel and accessories, NEC
2391 Curtains and draperies
2392 Housefurnishings, NEC
2393 Textile bags
2394 Canvas and related products
2395 Pleating and stitching
2396 Automotive and apparel trimmings
2397 Schiffli machine embroideries
2399 Fabricated textile products, NEC

Michael A. Paulin

Controller
Southern Textile Knitters, Inc.
950–A Coleman Drive
Greenwood, SC 29649
(803) 229–3032
Fax: (803) 229–1649

2321

Business Information: Southern Textile Knitters, Inc. is an integrated vertical company that designs, manufactures, distributes and retails boy's and men's knit shirts, domestically and internationally. Established in 1988, Southern Textile Knitters, Inc. currently employs 450 people and has an estimated annual revenue of $25 million. As Controller, Mr. Paulin directs the company's administrative and accounting departments, as well as creates, implements and monitors the company policies and procedures. **Career Steps:** Controller, Southern Textile Knitters, Inc. (1994–Present); Tax Accountant and Business Consultant, Sellars and Bauknight, P.A. (1992–1994);

Tax Accountant, Richard D. Olsen, CPA (1987–1990). **Associations & Accomplishments:** American Institute of Certified Public Accountants; South Carolina Association of Certified Public Accountants; South Carolina Association of P.A.'s; Beta Alpha Psi Accounting Fraternity. **Education:** University of South Carolina – Columbia, B.S. (1992). **Personal:** Married to Sarah Ritter in 1987. Four children: Rebekah, Samuel, Maxmilian, and Hannah. Mr. Paulin enjoys family activities, reading and travel.

David T. Whitaker

Vice President and Assistant General Counsel
Fruit of the Loom
One Fruit of the Loom Drive
Bowling Green, KY 42102–9015
(502) 781–6400
Fax: (502) 781–5762

2322

Business Information: Fruit of the Loom is one of the world's leading manufacturers and distributors of family clothing, particularly undergarments and leisure wear. Brand names manufactured include: Fruit of the Loom, BVD, Wilson, Pro Player, Salem, and Artex. Fruit of the Loom employs over 30,000 people world–wide and has an annual revenue approaching $3 billion. As Vice President and Assistant General Counsel, Mr Whitaker's duties include the supervision of team attorneys coordination of acquisition and licensing and the supervision of complex litigation matters. **Career Steps:** Fruit of the Loom: Vice President and Assistant General Counsel (1992–Present), Attorney (1984–92); Law Clerk, Lucas, Priest, and Owsley (1982–84); Congressional Intern, Sears (Spring of 1981); Reporter and Intern, Associated Press (1979). **Associations & Accomplishments:** Co–Founder and Co–Editor, "The Bar Tab" (local bar association magazine); Former Editor, College Heights "Herald" (Western Kentucky University Student Newspaper). **Education:** University of Kentucky School of Law, J.D. (1984); Western Kentucky University, B.A. **Personal:** Mr. Whitaker enjoys golf, playing the guitar, writing, and reading.

James Bradford

President
Asher–Winer Company, Inc.
1820 Hardeth River Drive
Brentwood, TN 37027
(615) 377–3868
Fax: (615) 370–4543

2325

Business Information: Asher–Winer Company, Inc. is a manufacturer and wholesaler of men's better casual and dress trousers. Established in 1900, Asher–Winer currently employs 210 people and has estimated annual revenue of $14 million. As President, Mr. Bradford is responsible for the management of outside sales staff, sales to key accounts, the purchase and selection of fabrics, and the development of new models and merchandise. **Career Steps:** President, Asher–Winer Company, Inc. (1982–Present); Sales Manager, Xerox Corporation (1968–1981). **Associations & Accomplishments:** Brentwood Tennessee Rotary Club; David Lipscomb University Business Advisory Council; Individualized Apparel Group Management. **Education:** University of North Alabama, B.S. (1965). **Personal:** Married to Brenda G. in 1966. Two children: Bridget and Julie. Mr. Bradford enjoys running, tennis and antique auto restoration.

Henny J. Roeland

Assistant Director of Brandprotection
Levi Strauss & Co.
1155 Battery Street LS7
San Francisco, CA 94111–1230
(415) 544–3496
Fax: (415) 544–7650

2337

Business Information: Levi Strauss & Co. is the world's largest brand–name apparel manufacturer. The Company designs, manufactures and markets branded jeans and casual sportswear for men, women, and youth. Its products are manufactured and sold in numerous countries throughout the world and are primarily marketed under the Levis(R) and Dockers(R) trademarks. Established in 1848 in San Francisco, it's headquarters is still there, with regional headquarters in Brussels and Singapore. As Assistant Director of Brandprotection, Mr Roeland is responsible for ensuring the protection of the Levi's trademarks against fraudulent and illegal use. **Career Steps:** Assistant Director of Brandprotection, Levi Strauss & Co., San Francisco (1995–Present); Assistant Director of Corporate Security Europe, Levi Strauss and Co., Brussels (1988–1995); Senior Investigations Manager, In-

ternational Economic Fraud Department, Ministry of Economics/Justice, The Netherlands (1973–1988). **Associations & Accomplishments:** American Society of Industrial Security; International Anti–Counterfeiting Coalition; World Customs Organization; International Police Association. **Education:** Amsterdam; Business Degree, Law Enforcement, International Law/EEC Regulations. **Personal:** Married to Carin Mourits in 1989. Five children: Marc, Marthyn, Anneke, Marjan and Frank. Mr. Roeland enjoys the outdoors and golf.

Isaac Sutton Tawil

General Manager
Sutton International Sa De Cv
Chabacano 65 F
Mexico City, Mexico
(525) 538–8426
Fax: (525) 741–0354

2329

Business Information: Sutton International Sa De Cv is a manufacturer of infants, toddlers, and childrens shirts, sweat–shirts, and pants. The first to manufacture infant and toddler denim shirts in Mexico, the products are marketed under the brand names "Picadilly", and "Rudo." The Company distributes to discount stores throughout Mexico. As General Manager/Founder, Mr. Sutton Tawil oversees all aspects of the Company, to include administration, operations, finance, sales, public relations, accounting, legal, taxes, marketing, and strategic planning. **Career Steps:** General Manager, Sutton International Sa De Cv (1985–Present). **Education:** Universidad Inter–Americana, Seventh Semester. **Personal:** Mr. Sutton Tawil enjoys being a body–builder and sports fan (soccer, football, and baseball).

Robert M. Spokane

Vice President of Finance
Pennsylvania Fashions Inc.
155 Thorn Hill Road
Warrendale, PA 15086–7527
(412) 776–9780
Fax: (412) 776–4111

2335

Business Information: Pennsylvania Fashions Inc. is a retail clothing chain. Established in 1974, the Company currently temploys 1,200 people and reports estimated annual revenue of $100 million. As Vice President of Finance, Mr. Spokane is responsible for all aspects of finance, including auditing, accounting, payroll and all treasury functions. Mr. Spokane is also responsible for invoice approvals, insurance and health care policies, law suits, leases, financial statements, reports, budgeting, the tax department and internal management. In the retail business for 12 years, Mr. Spokane has enjoyed getting to where he is today. **Career Steps:** Vice President of Finance, Pennsylvania Fashions Inc. (1993–Present); Controller, Scoop, Inc. (1984–1987); Director of Accounting, Eye and Ear Hospital (1983–1984). **Associations & Accomplishments:** American Institute of Certified Public Accountants; Pennsylvania Institute of Certified Public Accountants. **Education:** Pennsylvania State University, B.S. in Accounting (1978). **Personal:** Mr. Spokane enjoys sky diving, and various sports.

Sheryl N. Clough

President/Chief Operating Officer
House of Uniforms
7414 Bellaire Avenue
North Hollywood, CA 91605
(818) 503–0200
Fax: (818) 503–7844

2337

Business Information: House of Uniforms is a designer and manufacturer of custom uniforms for hotels and theme parks. International in scope, some of the Company's major clients are Universal Studios and several major hotel chains. As President/Chief Operating Officer, Ms. Clough oversees every aspect of the Company's operations, including design, sales, purchasing, and other related activities. **Career Steps:** Began working at House of Uniforms in 1973. Promoted to Vice President in 1981. Became President/Chief Operating Officer in 1986. **Associations & Accomplishments:** Network of Executive Women in Business; President, Mothers Club – Marymount High School. **Education:** University of California – Los Angeles, B.A. (1973). **Personal:** Married to Donald in 1976. Two children: Christie and Christopher. Ms. Clough enjoys 100–mile horsedrives, golf, and her job.

Kevin David Rogers
Branch General Manager
G&K Services
1299 Eagan Industrial Road
Eagan, MN 55121
(612) 452–7173
Fax: (612) 452–7267

2337

Business Information: G&K Services provides uniform and textile rentals to business and industry, leasing programs in business for uniforms, clean room garments, flame retardant garments, floor mats, dust mops, shop towels, and linens. As Branch General Manager, Mr. Rogers operates a facility, including a sales, service, office, administrative, warehouse, and shuttle departments. He is additionally responsible for personnel development and corporate training programs. **Career Steps:** G&K Services: Branch General Manager (1995–Present), Branch Manager – Lacrosse (1992–1995), Route Manager – Lacrosse (1991–1992), Sales Representative/Manager Trainee (1989–1991). **Associations & Accomplishments:** Society for the Advancement of Management; Board of Trustees – Secretary, Camp Jim; Program Coordinator, Elk River Jaycees; University Award for Excellence In Leadership; Golden Tribute Sales Achievement; Outstanding College Students in America; Outstanding Young Men in America. **Education:** St. Cloud State University, B.S. in Business Management (1989), minor in Psychology; University of Minnesota; Moody Bible Institute; Inver Hills Community College, A.A.S. (completing M.B.A. degree in Business). **Personal:** Married to Carrie Lee in 1987. Two children: Heather Lee and Brandon. Mr. Rogers enjoys camping, guitar, singing, fishing, racquetball, softball, skiing, and travel.

Edward F. Jankowski
Vice President of Stores
Liz Claiborne, Inc.
1441 Broadway
New York, NY 10018–2002
(212) 626–5408
Fax: (212) 626–5566

2339

Business Information: Liz Claiborne, Inc. is one of the top New York City manufacturers and wholesale designers of women's apparel. Established in 1976, Liz Claiborne Inc. currently employs 3,000 New York City employees. As Vice President of Stores, Mr. Jankowski is responsible for the oversight of all retail divisions and visual presentations throughout all regional stores. **Career Steps:** Vice President of Stores, Liz Claiborne, Inc. (1993–Present); Regional Mgr., Gantos (1989–93); Vice President/Stores, Woman's World (1984–89). **Associations & Accomplishments:** National Retail Foundation. **Education:** Rider University, B.S. in Commerce Marketing/Management (1975). **Personal:** Married to Jamie in 1980. Two children: Ryan and Justin. Mr. Jankowski enjoys travel, golf, and playing sports with his children.

Mr. Joe Phillips
Senior Vice President of Sales
Champion Products
475 Corporate Square Drive
Winston–Salem, NC 27105
(910) 519–5558
Fax: (910) 519–6527

2339

Business Information: Champion Products is a global manufacturer of activewear products, including men's and women's branded and licensed activewear. Their major licenses include the NBA, NFL and Notre Dame. In addition, Champion is an official sponsor of the 1996 Olympics. Champion Products distribute worldwide with a separate European group. Established in 1920, Champion Products currently employs 4,000 people. As Senior Vice President of Sales, Mr. Phillips is responsible for all aspects of operations, including management of two sales divisions, customer service and the Corporate planning functions. **Career Steps:** Senior Vice President of Sales, Champion Products (1992–Present); National Sales Manager, L A Gear (1989–1992); Vice President of Sales, Wilson Sporting Goods (1983–1989). **Education:** George Washington University, B.S. (1973). **Personal:** Married to Elaine in 1978. Three children: Jamie, Alana and Joe. Mr. Phillips enjoys sports.

Mr. Samuel M. Dwek
Vice President
Gelmart Industries, Inc.
112 West 34th Street, 12th Floor
New York, NY 10120
(212) 279–6542
Fax: (212) 279–6331

2341

Business Information: Gelmart Industries, Inc. is a manufacturer and distributor of bras, gloves, scarves and young childrens wear for retail outlets and chain stores. As Vice President of Swimwear, Mr. Dwek runs this division of Gelmart Industries, Inc. Concurrent with his duties at Gelmart, he holds various executive positions at other apparel manufacturing concerns. He is currently the President of Trulo, Inc., a major international manufacturer of swimsuits, producing under such label names as Michael Kors, Valentino and Jerry Hall and distributing in over 22 countries around the world. **Career Steps:** Vice President of Swimwear, Gelmart Industries, Inc. (1994–Present); Consultant/Vice President of Operations, Flyskaters, Inc. (1994–Present); President, Supertech, Inc. (1993–Present); President, Trulo, Inc. (1989–Present). **Associations & Accomplishments:** American Commerce Association; Swimwear Association. **Education:** American College (London), B.A. (1988).

Nelson C. Calcano

Operations Manager
Hanes Panama

San Pedro de Macoris, Dominican Republic
(809) 529–2177
Fax: (809) 529–5450

2342

Business Information: Hanes Panama, a division of Sara Lee Intimates, Sara Lee Corporation, assembles ladies intimate apparel from material and cut–work imported from the United States. As Operations Manager, Mr. Calcano oversees daily operations, supervising product quality control, engineering, and office managers, as well as technicians and controllers. **Career Steps:** Operations Manager, Bali Foundations (1971–Present). **Associations & Accomplishments:** Association of Industries – San Pedro Macoris Free Zone. **Education:** University of Puerto Rico – Mayaguez Campus, B.S. in Industrial Engineering (1970). **Personal:** One child: Jo Ann. Mr. Calcano enjoys reading, movies, and collecting videos.

Deepak D. Chainani
Chief Financial Controller
Kikomo Inc.
275 Hartz Way
Secaucus, NJ 07094
(201) 974–2323 Ext: 430
Fax: (201) 974–2380

2369

Business Information: Kikomo Inc. is a manufacturer of denim sportswear for Junior/children's wear, employing 116 people. As Chief Financial Controller, Mr. Chainani is responsible for all aspects of financial matters, including accounting, budgeting, and bringing operating costs down. **Career Steps:** Chief Financial Controller, Kikomo Inc. (1989–Present); Chief Accountant, LIPFO Company (1982–1989); Cash Manager, Allahbad Bank (1977–1982). **Education:** Master of Commerce degree attained (1980). **Personal:** Married to Neeta in 1994. Mr. Chainani enjoys fishing, reading and listening to soft music in his leisure time.

Daniel Collins
Corporate Sales Representative
Sarah Louise Corporation
162 Margaret Lane, P.O. Box 1436
Hillsborough, NC 27278
(919) 732–1887
Fax: Please mail or call

2369

Business Information: Sarah Louise Corporation is an international manufacturer of exclusive, high–end designer children's clothing. Elite clientele include the Royal Family in England and higher levels in society, such as country club clientele. As Corporate Sales Representative, Mr. Collins is responsible for analyzing and developing new markets for the southeastern United States. **Career Steps:** Corporate Sales Representative, Sarah Louise Corporation (1995–Present); Corporate Sales Executive, ARCH Communications Group (1994–1995); Vice President of Sales and Marketing, AAMOT Information Systems (1990–1994). **Associations & Accomplishments:** Association of Records Managers and Administrators; Association of Information and Image Managers; Hillsborough Youth Athletic Association; American Bowling Congress Association; President's Million Dollar Roundtable Society; Founded his own company; Registered Sales Professional. **Education:** Center for Degree Studies, Business Management (1988); Pillsbury Corporation – Fortune 500, Business Management (1986); Attended over 1,000 hours of seminars and business courses related to business management, sales, marketing, and customer retention. **Personal:** Married to Sohila in 1984. Three children: Nassarin, Joshua, and Chandler. Mr. Collins enjoys spending time with his family, studying positive living, softball, competition bowling, and golf.

J. Carroll Riggan
Manager – Training and Development
Healthtex, Inc.
2303 West Meadowview Road, Suite 200
Greensboro, NC 27407
(910) 316–1192
Fax: (910) 316–1022

2369

Business Information: Healthtex, Inc., a subsidiary of VF Corporation, is an apparel manufacturer, specializing in children's playwear clothing with the Healthtex label. Celebrating their 75th anniversary in 1996, VF Corporation also manufactures Lee jeans (Kansas City, MO), Girbaud jeans (Greensboro, NC), and Wrangler jeans (Greensboro, N.C.) and Bassett–Walker activewear (Martinsville, VA). With twenty–six years of experience in training and human resource development, Mr. Riggan joined Healthtex, Inc. as Manager of Training and Development in 1994. He is responsible for administration and coordination of the entire Corporate Training Program, including conducting training surveys and promoting team management. **Career Steps:** Manager – Training and Development, Healthtex, Inc. (1994–Present); Manager Human Resources Development, Sara Leeknit Products (1988–1994); Regional Training Manager, Lee Apparel Company (VF Corporation) (1985–1988). **Associations & Accomplishments:** American Society for Training & Development; Past President, International Association of Quality Circles; Past Member, Lions Club; Optimist Club; Kiwanis Club; Chairperson of Administrative Board, Leaksville United Methodist Church in Eden, NC. **Education:** Pembroke State University, B.S. in Management (1975); Southwest University, M.S. in Human Resource Management in progress. **Personal:** Married to Jennifer T. in 1968. Three children: Chris, Dawn, and Victoria. Mr. Riggan enjoys being a recording artist and concert performer.

David C. K. Lee
Secretary, Treasurer, and Chief Financial Officer
Island Trading, Inc.
4412 Bluebonnet Drive #101
Stafford, TX 77477–2905
(713) 240–7090
Fax: (713) 240–0222

2381

Business Information: Island Trading, Inc. is an importer and wholesale distributor of industrial safety gloves and accessories to such industrial giants as Chrysler, Ford, and General Electric. As Secretary, Treasurer, and Chief Financial Officer, Mr. Lee is responsible for supervising all major tasks, supplier negotiation, and management decisions. **Career Steps:** Secretary, Treasurer, and Chief Financial Officer, Island Trading, Inc. (1995–Present); Accountant, NCR (HK) Ltd. / AT&T (HK) Ltd. (1964–1995). **Associations & Accomplishments:** Certified Public Accountant; Institute of Financial Accountants of England. **Education:** University of Hong Kong, B.A. (1967). **Personal:** Married to Cathy C. M. Lee in 1968. Two children: Orpheus and Christina. Mr. Lee enjoys travel, collecting stamps and coins.

Edward L. Cole Jr.
Vice President of Sales and Marketing
Rainfair, Inc.
2812 Chicory Road
Racine, WI 53403
(414) 554–7000
Fax: (414) 554–6655

2385

Business Information: Rainfair, Inc. specializes in the manufacture of industrial waterproof, chemical–proof and fire retardant rainwear, insulated clothing, footwear and industrial aprons for industrial, government, military and specialized consumer markets. Rainfair, Inc. manufactures products not only in the U.S. but also in manufacturing facilities around the world. Established in 1881, Rainfair, Inc. currently employs 110 people and has estimated revenue over $10 million. As Vice President, Edward Cole oversees all sales and marketing functions for the Industrial Division including developing and executing the marketing and sales strategies and directing the sales activities of the field sales force. **Career Steps:** Vice President of Sales and Marketing, Rainfair, Inc. (1995–Present); Vice President of Sales and Marketing, Research and Trading Corporation (1992–1995); Vice President of Sales, Tokai Financial Services (1983–1992). **Associations & Accomplishments:** Racine Country Club; Safety Equipment Distributors Association; National Safety Council. **Education:** Western Connecticut State University, B.S. in Business Administration (1976). **Personal:** One child: Edward III. Mr. Cole enjoys golf.

William H. Funkhouser
Management Information Systems Director
Alba Waldensian
P.O. Box 100
Valdese, NC 28690–0100
(704) 879–6513
Fax: (704) 879–1190

2389

Business Information: Alba Waldensian is a diversified manufacturing industry, involved in the manufacture of intimate apparel and specialty medical products. As Management Information Systems Director, Mr. Funkhouser directs and implements all computer applications networks and systems functioning. **Career Steps:** Management Information Systems Director, Alba Waldensian (1994–Present); EDI Project Manager, Guilford Mills Inc. (1988–1994); Programmer Analyst, Florida Informanagement Services (1986–1988); Senior Programmer, Chase Federal Savings and Loan Association (1979–1986). **Associations & Accomplishments:** DPMA of Catawba Valley, NC: Secretary, President; EDI Business Forum – Greensboro, NC. **Education:** High Point College, B.S. in Computer Information Systems (1989); Miami Dade Community College, A.A. in Business Data Processing. **Personal:** Married to Linda in 1982. Two children: Christiaan and Lauren. Mr. Funkhouser enjoys reading, working around the house, and woodworking.

Loretta P. Gragg
Industrial Engineer
Great American Knitting
2621 North Ashe Avenue
Newton, NC 28658–2718
(704) 464–7000
Fax: (704) 464–8494

2389

Business Information: Great American Knitting is a manufacturer and distributor of Gold Toe socks. As Industrial Engineer, Ms. Gragg is responsible for the Industrial Engineering department, including employees, budgeting, operations, and special assignments. **Career Steps:** Industrial Engineer, Great American Knitting (1988–Present); Industrial Engineer, Adams Millis Corporation (1984–1988); Industrial Engineer Technician, Burlington Industries (1973–1983). **Personal:** Two children: Angela and Garrett Brown. Ms. Gragg enjoys spending time with her family.

Frank A. Iannuzzi
National Sales Manager
Russell Corporation
1 Lee Street
Alexander City, AL 35010–1953
(205) 329–5612
Fax: (205) 329–5948

2389

Business Information: Russell Corporation, founded in 1902, is the leading manufacturer of active wear and team uniforms in the U.S. The Corporation has been recognized as one of the most technologically–advanced textile and apparel companies in the world. Mr. Iannuzzi joined Russell Corp. as a Sales Representative in 1989 after completing his M.B.A. program at the University of Alabama at Birmingham. Promoted to Manager of Distributor Sales in 1992, he moved into his present position as National Sales Manager in 1994, overseeing the Jerzees Division. He is responsible for the supervision of three regional managers, thirteen sales representatives, and support staff, as well as personnel motivation, new product and sales tactic development, customer presentations, and regular travel between company locations in Dallas, New York, and Los Angeles. **Career Steps:** Russell Corporation: National Sales Manager (1994–Present), Manager, Distributor Sales (1992–1994), Sales Representative (1989–1992); Director of Tennis, University of Alabama at Birmingham (1987–1989). **Associations & Accomplishments:** American Management Association; St. James Episcopal Church. **Education:** University of Alabama at Birmingham: M.B.A. (1989), B.S. in Marketing (1987). **Personal:** Married to Melany in 1988. Three children: Luke, Nicholas, and Mary Beth. Mr. Iannuzzi enjoys golf, tennis, and fishing.

Alex Koohmarey
Controller
Reebok Apparel San Diego
9401 Waples Street, Suite 100
San Diego, CA 92121–3909
(619) 450–4100 Ext. 312
Fax: (619) 450–4111

2389

Business Information: Reebok is one of the world's leading manufacturers and marketers of athletic footwear and apparel. As Controller, Mr. Koohmarey is responsible for all financial aspects of the Company, including accounting, taxes, financial statements, inventory control and accounts payable. **Career Steps:** Controller, Reebok Apparel San Diego (1986–Present); Controller, Binary Production (1979–1986); Auditor, Pricewater House (1974–1979). **Associations & Accomplishments:** American Production and Inventory Control Society; American Management Association; NAA; Institute of Management Accounts. **Education:** San Diego State University, M.B.A. (1990). **Personal:** Married to Christina in 1991. Two children: Darius and Daniel. Mr. Koohmarey enjoys volleyball and soccer.

Michael Kunde
Project Manager
Starter
370 James Street
New Haven, CT 06513–3051
(203) 781–4041
Fax: (203) 789–2820

2389

Business Information: Starter Apparel Company specializes in the manufacture, distribution and sale of men's, women's and children's sportswear. Famous for their line of professional and college athletic team logo items such as hats, jackets, shorts and tee–shirts, Starter apparel items are sold worldwide. Established in 1972, Starter currently employs 600 people and has an estimated annual revenue of $400 million. As Project Manager, Mr. Kunde is responsible for process management, internal consulting and suggestive improvements. **Career Steps:** Starter: Project Manager (1994–Present), Assistant Vice President of Operations (1991–1994), Staf Accountant (1990–1991). **Associations & Accomplishments:** American Manufacturer's Association. **Education:** Columbia University, M.B.A. (1996); University of Rhode Island, B.S. in Finance (1990). **Personal:** Mr. Kunde enjoys snow skiing.

Mr. David T. Whitaker
Vice President and Assistant General Counsel
Fruit of the Loom
One Fruit of the Loom Drive
Bowling Green, KY 42102–9015
(502) 781–6400
Fax: (502) 781–5762

2389

Business Information: Fruit of the Loom is the world's leading manufacturer and distributor of family clothing, particularly undergarments and leisure wear. Brand names manufactured include: Fruit of the Loom, BVD, Wilson, Pro Player, Salem and Artex. Fruit of the Loom employs over 30,000 people world–wide and has annual revenue in excess of $30 million. As Vice President and Assistant General Counsel, Mr. Whitaker is responsible for the oversight and administration for corporate legal aspects. His duties include the supervison of team attorneys, coordination of acquisition and licensing and the supervision of complex litigation matters. **Career Steps:** Vice President and Assistant General Counsel, Fruit of the Loom (1992–Present); Law Clerk, English, Lucas, Priest and Owsley (1982–1984); Congressional Intern, Sears (Spring of 1981); Reporter and Intern, Associated Press (1979). **Associations & Accomplishments:** Co–Founder and Co–Editor, "The BarTab" (local bar association magazine); Board Member, Big Brothers/Big Sisters Bowling Green, KY Chapter; Former Editor, College Heights "Herald" (Western Kentucky University student newspaper). **Education:** University of Kentucky School of Law, J.D. (1984); Western Kentucky University, B.A. **Personal:** Mr. Whitaker enjoys golf, playing the guitar, writing and reading.

Donna Jo Young
Area Manager
Starter Corporation
4650 East Shelby Drive
Memphis, TN 38118
(901) 367–7580
Fax: (901) 367–7460

2389

Business Information: Starter Corporation specializes in the manufacture, distribution and sale of men's, women's and children's sportswear. Famous for their line of professional and college athletic team logo items such as hats, jackets, shorts and tee–shirts, Starter apparel items are sold worldwide. Established in 1972, Starter currently employs 850 people and has an estimated annual revenue of $450 million. As Area Manager, Ms. Young insures that all products are packed and shipped according to customer routing. She is additionally responsible for customer compliance and satisfaction. **Career Steps:** Outbound Area Manager, Starter Corporation (1990–Present); Machine Adjuster, Pacer's (1988–1990); Breakfast Manager, Hardee's (1985–1988). **Education:** Attended, Pensacola Junior College, Electronic Automotives. **Personal:** Ms. Young enjoys softball and water sports.

Juan Ignacio Vilanova
Human Resources Manager
Textiles San Andres, S.A. De C.V.
Km. 32 Carretera
Santa Ana, El Salvado
(503) 338–4099
Fax: (503) 338–4064

2392

Business Information: Textiles San Andres, S.A. De C.V. is a manufacturer of beach towels, sportswear, loungewear, sleepwear, and other terry cloth products, distributing to retail outlets around the world (Wal–Mart, J.C.Penny, Sears). As Human Resources Manager, Mr. Vilanova is directly responsible for a staff of 25 in processing payroll, developing and implementing policies, hiring and training personnel, overseeing safety and security measures, and facilities maintenance. **Career Steps:** Human Resources Manager, Textiles San Andres, S.A. De C.V. (1995–Present); Human Resources Manager, Kimberly Clark of C.A. (1995); Human Resources Manager, Cessa (1993–1994); Human Resources Manager, UNISOLA (Unilever of C.A.) (1986–1993). **Associations & Accomplishments:** Junior Achievement Association; FI-PRO Association. **Education:** Cornell University, Occupational Safety & Health (1993); UCA – El Salvador, B.S. in Economics; Human Resources Studies; Occupational Safety & Health Studies. **Personal:** Married to Carmen Vargas de Vilanova in 1983. Three children: Virginia Maria, Ana Maria, and Juan Ignacio. Mr. Vilanova enjoys volleyball, chess and soccer.

Nancy W. Webster
Corporate Vice President – Creative Development
Fieldcrest Cannon, Inc.
One Lake Drive
Kannapolis, NC 28081
(704) 939–2168
Fax: (704) 939–2907

2392

Business Information: Fieldcrest Cannon, Inc., one of the leading textile manufacturers in the U.S., is a vertical manufactturer of textiles, including bed and bath products (i.e., blankets, towels, curtains). Clientele include J.C. Pennys, Sears, etc. Established in the late 1800's, Fieldcrest Cannon, Inc. reports annual sales of $1.2 billion and currently employs 16,000 people company–wide. A twenty–year veteran with Fieldcrest Cannon, Inc., Ms. Webster serves as Corporate Vice President of Creative Development. She is responsible for all creative functions inclusive of product design and product development, as well as providing innovative industry leadership. **Career Steps:** Fieldcrest Cannon, Inc.: Corporate Vice President, Creative Development (1994–Present); Vice President, Bed Design & P/D (1993–1994); Vice President, Bed and Bath PD (1988–1993). **Associations & Accomplishments:** Business and Professional Women's Organization – National, State, and Local Member; UNC–G Advisory Board; NCSU Textile Advisory Board; NCSU Foundation Board; Appalachian Graduate Advisory Board; Textile Leader of the Year (1993), first woman to receive; Outstanding Business Woman (1994). **Education:** North Carolina State University, B.S. (1975); New York State University, Fashion Institute of Technology, A.A.S. in Fashion Design; UNC, Young Executives Institute, Certificate. **Personal:** Married to Chris L. Kametches in 1987. Two children: Mark Kametches and Cindy McCrickard. Ms. Webster enjoys music, water sports, snow skiing, boating, travel, and reading.

Coleman Schneider
Chief Executive Officer
AA World Class Corp.
65 Railroad Avenue
Ridgefield, NJ 07657–2130
(201) 313–0022
Fax: (201) 313–0044

2397

Business Information: AA World Class Corp. (a.k.a. – World Class Embroidery) is a major embroidery company providing machine–stitched embroidery services, appliques and patches for commerical businesses and organizations, including the NFL, NBA, NHL, MLB, and over 100 other major licensers. AA World Class Corporation boasts the best quality, fastest delivery and best price in the industry. Established in 1982, AA World Class Embroidery's success stems from years of experience and the ingenuity of its Chief Executive Officer, Coleman Schneider. As Chief Executive Officer, Mr. Schneider is responsible for all aspects of operations. Mr. Schneider began his career in the embroidery business in Hudson County, New Jersey, the hub of embroidery. He started his own manufacturing business with 10 employees in 1947, and over the next few years business was up and down. Mr. Schneider remained steadfast and switched to embroidery design & pattern making in 1951 and gradually expanded to produce 80% of all the embroidery design work in the U.S. By 1960 his one man operation had expanded, grown successfully and was the recipient of two Industry Design Competition awards. In 1968, Mr. Schneider began developing a method of making embroidery tapes by computer, and by 1976 the task was completed. Due to the overwhelming success of the technique Mr. Schneider developed, he published two books which dealt with the transition from mechanical to computerized equipment. A third book was written about computerized machines and pattern making in 1991. All three books were written and published by Mr. Schneider and have been sold in more than 45 countries. In 1983 he created and sold a world–wide newsletter known as the "International Embroidery Newsletter". A 35 minute film "Stitches in Time" was made by Mr. Schneider and was donated to the Schiffli Lace and Embroidery Association, as well as being shown to over a million students throughout the United States. Mr. Schneider has written many articles for leading embroidery magazines and lectures whenever possible. He remains the Chief Executive Officer of one of the largest embroidery companies in the United States. **Career Steps:** Chief Executive Officer, AA World Class Embroidery (1982–Present); Founder and President, All American Emblem (1969–1982); Founder and President, C. Schneider, Designers and Punchers (1951–1968); Pilot (1945); Merchant Marine (1943–1945). **Education:** United States Merchant Marine Academy, Graduate; Rutgers University; Phoenix School of Art; Philadelphia College of Textiles and Science; Taught embroidery design for 4 years at F.I.T. (Fashion Institute of Technology). **Personal:** Married. Mr. Schneider enjoys writing, creative drawing, and sports.

Christina D. Dobleman
Director of Risk Management
Levi Strauss & Company
1155 Battery Street
San Francisco, CA 94111
(415) 544–7141
Fax: (415) 544–1342

2399

Business Information: Levi Strauss & Company is the world's largest brand–name apparel manufacturer. The Company designs, manufactures and markets branded jeans and casual sportswear for men, women, and youth. Its products are manufactured and sold in numerous countries throughout the world, primarily marketed under the Levis(R) and Dockers(R) trademarks. Established in 1848 in San Francisco, it's headquarters is still there, with regional headquarters in Brussels and Singapore. As Director of Risk Management, Ms. Dobleman is responsible for property/casualty, environmental, workers compensation, risk identification, risk assessment, risk mitigation, utilizing insurance, self insurance, and captive approaches to risk financing. She is heavily engaged in managing risk of operations and evaluating products and their potential impacts. **Career Steps:** Levi Strauss & Company: Director of Risk Management (1982–Present), Assistant Director of Risk Management (1978–1982); Risk Analyst, The Clorox Company (1977–1978); Commercial Casualty Underwriter, American International Underwriters (1970–1977). **Associations & Accomplishments:** Former President, Chartered Property and Casualty Underwriter; Chairman of the Board, Insurance Education Association; Board of Directors, Workers Compensation Research Institute. **Education:** American Graduate School of International Management, B.I.M. (1970); North Texas State University, B.B.A. (1969); Chartered Property and Casualty Underwriter (1975). **Personal:** Married to John in 1989. Ms. Dobleman enjoys travel and sports.

Claudia McCotter
President
Sgt. Leisure, Inc.
4602 East Elwood Street, Suite 1
Phoenix, AZ 85040–1960
(602) 966–3533 Ext: 202
Fax: (602) 966–3413

2399

Business Information: Sgt. Leisure, Inc. is a designer, manufacturer, and retailer of exclusive and signature line clothing marketed to resort stores. Products include clothing for men, women, and children. Founding Sgt. Leisure, Inc. as President in 1986, Ms. McCotter is responsible for all aspects of operations, including designing, manufacturing, and sales and marketing. **Career Steps:** President, Sgt. Leisure, Inc. (1986–Present); President, Vackrahus, Inc. (1972–1986). **Associations & Accomplishments:** Young Presidents Organization; Phoenix Art Museum. **Education:** University of Utah. **Personal:** Married to John in 1978. One child: Britni. Ms. McCotter enjoys skiing, watersports, fitness, volunteer work, hiking, and art.

William R. Puckett
Director of Manufacturing
Red Kap Ind.
630 Tynebrae Drive
Franklin, TN 37064–5332
(615) 391–1299
Fax: (615) 791–7935

2399

Business Information: Red Kap Industries is the largest supplier of occupational clothing in the United States. The Company provides clothing to mechanics via rental laundry services, as well as flame retardant clothing and medical attire. As Director of Manufacturing, Mr. Puckett directs the activities of approximately 2,000 associates in seven locations. In his three years at the Company, he has been responsible for a $2 million average annual reduction in operating overhead, a $1 million average annual total direct labor reduction, and many other accomplishments. **Career Steps:** Red Kap Industries: Director of Manufacturing (1993–Present), Manager of Industrial Engineering (1989–1993), Senior Industrial Engineer (1987–1989). **Associations & Accomplishments:** Serves as a Non–Paid Christian Minister. **Education:** Attended: Western Carolina University (1971–1973), JIT Institute of Technology, Philip Crosby Quality College, Bell Advanced Leadership – University of North Carolina – Chapel Hill, Owen Graduate School of Management – Vanderbilt. **Personal:** Married to Peggy in 1973. Three children: Olin, Aaron, and Ashley. Mr. Puckett enjoys fishing, camping, and reading.

Shari Rezi
President & Owner
Rezex Corporation d.b.a. Gellman Industries
1914 Bay Street
Los Angeles, CA 90021–1608
(213) 622–2015
Fax: (213) 622–4572

2399

Business Information: Rezex Corporation d.b.a. Gellman Industries is a textile finishing and laundry company for textile mills and interior designers. As President & Owner, Ms. Rezi is responsible for administrative duties, marketing, finance, strategic planning, public relations, and supervising 53 employees. **Career Steps:** President & Owner, Rezex Corporation d.b.a. Gellman Industries (1981–Present); President & Partner, Mirak Textiles (1988–Present); President, Shamad Collection (1980–1988). **Associations & Accomplishments:** National Association of Women Business Owners; Business Forum; Textile Associate of Los Angeles. **Education:** University of Miami, Bachelors of Business Administration (1973); Published in Top 100 Woman Business Owners by L.A. Business Journal. **Personal:** Two children: Bahaneh

and Kataneh Haydarzadeh. Ms. Rezi enjoys textile design, museum, and travel.

2400 Lumber and Wood Products

Herman E. Baertschiger Jr.
President
H.B. Company
665 Hunt Lane
Grants Pass, OR 97526–9331
(541) 479–8661
Fax: (541) 479–8661

2411

Business Information: H.B. Company is an international timber harvesting (deforestation) company, providing evaluation, marketing and consulting to the timber industry worldwide. H.B. Company also markets its services to sawmills and private timberland owners, offering experienced personnel to perform all aspects of timber harvesting, timberland management, as well as marketing timber worldwide. Some of its major clients are Stone Container, Roseburg Forest Products, Croman Corp. and BIFF of Costa Rica. Founding H.B. Company in 1980 and serving as its Owner, President, and Manager, Mr. Baertschiger is responsible for all aspects of operation, including administration, finances, public relations, management, marketing, and strategic planning. Additionally, he oversees and manages a staff of 20 or more. **Career Steps:** President, H.B. Company (1980–Present). **Associations & Accomplishments:** Oregon Association of Loggers; Chairman, Josephine County Airports; Fluent in English, Spanish and German. **Education:** High School Graduate, three years of higher education; Graduate California Board of Forestry, Timber Operator. **Personal:** Married to Leta in 1987. Two children: Dirk and Tyler. Mr. Baertschiger Jr. is an outdoorsman in the true meaning and a competent pilot that enjoys flying.

Wendell D. Fox
Director of Information Resources
Georgia Pacific
140 Weeping Willow Way
Tyrone, GA 30290–9571
(404) 652–6477
Fax: (770) 486–0347
EMAIL: See Below

2421

Business Information: Georgia Pacific Corporation is one of the largest producers, manufacturers and distributors of softwood and diversified lumber products in the world. A 17–year veteran with Georgia Pacific, Mr. Fox was appointed Director of Information Resources in 1993. In this capacity, he works extensively with clients and various business groups, as well as serves as project leader for infrastructure projects and the supervision of a support staff of 74. He can also be reached through the Internet via: WDFox.GAPAC.com **Career Steps:** Georgia Pacific: Director of Information Resources (1993–Present), Senior Manager — Atlanta Data Center (1992–1993), Manager — IBM Technical Support (1990–1992). **Associations & Accomplishments:** Board of Directors, Ashley County United Way; Data Processing Management Association; Former, Scout Master. **Education:** Shorter College, B.S. in Management Science. **Personal:** Married to Jennifer M. in 1968. One child: Christian. Mr. Fox enjoys outdoor activities.

Matt Hancock
Director of Sawmill Operations
Hancock Lumber
P.O. Box 299
Casco, ME 04015–0299
(207) 627–7600
Fax: (207) 627–4200

2421

Business Information: Hancock Lumber, a sixth generation family–held company since 1849, specializes in the harvest, process and wholesale distribution of eastern white pine lumber. The Company cuts, dries and treats the lumber in two sawmill locations (100 miles apart), after which the lumber is processed into commodity products. Hancock Lumber owns and manages 20,000 acres of timberlands and eight Home Center stores. Joining the family business in 1992, as Director of Sawmill Operations, Matt Hancock is responsible for coordinating communications between sales and production on improvements of capital personnel, as well as directing the operations of both sawmill locations. **Career Steps:** Hancock Lumber: Director of Sawmill Operations (1993–Present), General Manager of Marketing (1992–1993); Captain, High Five America (1991–1992); Matt Hancock's High Intensity International Basketball School (1990–1992). **Associations & Accomplishments:** Pine Species Committee, Northeast Lumber Manufacturers Association; Board of Directors, Maine Forest Products Council; Girl's Basketball Coach, Lake Region High School. **Education:** Colby College, B.S. (1990); Phillips Exeter Academy (1989). **Personal:** Married to Tracy in 1995.

Mr. Henry M. Thomas
Group Manager of the Softwood and Lumber Division
Georgia Pacific Corporation
112 Brentwood Circle
Crossett, AR 71635
(501) 567-5064
Fax: (501) 364-5900

2421

Business Information: Georgia Pacific Corporation is one of the largest producers, manufacturers and distributors of softwood and diversified lumber products in the world. As Group Manager of the Softwood and Lumber Division (Southern Pine Wood and Ply Wood), Mr. Thomas is responsible for the mangement of eleven lumber operational divisions throughout Georgia, Arkansas, South Carolina and North Carolina. His responsibilities include: production, costs, safety, environmental and all other aspects of operations within plant properties. Established in 1927, Georgia Pacific Corporation employs over 1,000 people with annual sales of $444 million. **Career Steps:** Group Manager of the Softwood and Lumber Division, Georgia Pacific Corporation (1981–Present); Assistant Group Manager, Georgia Pacific Corporation (1974–1981); Area Manager, Georgia Pacific Corporation (1973–1974); Manager, Georgia Pacific Corporation (1966–1972). **Associations & Accomplishments:** Board of Governors, Southern Pine Inspection Bureau; American Society of Forestry; Published in many articles in trade journals, including log technical magazines. **Education:** Louisiana Tech, B.S. (1962). **Personal:** Married to Gail Sawyer in 1964. Five children: Joe, Sally T. McLoch, Morgan, Sharon and Karen. Mr. Thomas enjoys golf, hunting and fishing.

C.T. (Chuck) Beatty
Mill Production Manager
Gutchess Lumber Company
P.O. Box 5508
Cortland, NY 13045-5508
(607) 753-1081
Fax: (607) 753-6234

2426

Business Information: Gutchess Lumber Company has been manufacturing hardwood lumber since 1904. As Mill Production Manager, Mr. Beatty manages the Mill Department, overseeing 65 production crew members and supervisors. He maintains accident prevention, quality control, recovery, and production. In addition, he is responsible for all personnel decisions (recruiting, interviewing, hiring, orientation), parts purchasing, and the sale of mill byproducts. **Career Steps:** Mill Production Manager, Gutchess Lumber Company (1988–Present); Lumber Manufacturing Manager, Champion International (1984–1988); St. Regis Paper Company: Sawmill Superintendent (1979–1984), Sawmill Shift Supervisor (1976–1979). **Associations & Accomplishments:** Society for American Foresters; West Coast Dry Kiln Association; Lake Erie & Ontario Sawyers & Filers Association; Former Vice President, International Management Council – Cortland Chapter; University Club – Cortland, New York; Former County Fire District Commisioner – Klickitat County, Washington; Former Certified EMT; Former LCDR., U.S. Naval Reserve. **Education:** State University of New York at Syracuse, M.S. (1977); Syracuse University, M.S. in Resource Management (1976); Iowa State University, B.S. in Forestry Management (1971). **Personal:** Married to Mary L. (Brechwald) Beatty in 1972. Mr. Beatty enjoys skeet shooting, hunting, fishing, golf, and travel.

Larry W. Bybee Jr.
Plant Manager
Federal Door
1101 East Mckinley Avenue
Mishawaka, IN 46545
(219) 256-1411
Fax: Please mail or call

2431

Business Information: Federal Door, located in Mishawaka, Indiana is a manufacturer of interior doors for apartment complexes. The Company is expanding to cabinets and interior trim, and will soon be opening a plant to manufacture windows. As Plant Manager, Mr. Bybee is in charge of plant production, including building doors, loading trucks, shipping and receiving merchandise, and equipment repair. He is responsible for keeping the plant operating in a cost effective manner, but at a high level of production. In the time Mr. Bybee has been with the Company, plant production has increased 180% and job costs have decreased 34%. **Career Steps:** Plant Manager, Federal Door (1996–Present); On Site Supervisor, Briarwood Development (1995–1996); Owner, Bybee Construction (1973–1996). **Associations & Accomplishments:** Vice President, Roseland Park Board; A.B.A.T.E. of Indiana; Fundraiser Volunteer: Roseland Police Department, Park Board, Muscular Dystrophy Association. **Education:** Fred Pryoa Seminars. **Personal:** Married to Gladys Riffel in 1995. Two children: Larry Bybee III, and Jack Riffel. Mr. Bybee enjoys motorcycles, hockey, camping, hunting, and fishing.

Meg Johnson
Design and Sales
DW Industries
9175 North Bradford Street
Portland, OR 97203-2813
(503) 285-0058
Fax: (503) 285-7381
EMAIL: See Below

2434

Business Information: DW Industries designs and manufactures kitchen and bath cabinetry and built–in furniture with two manufacturing plants and numerous sales offices throughout the United States and Canada. A Specialist in Cabinetry and Design, Ms. Johnson has worked in kitchen and bath sales and design for DW Industries since 1990. Internet users can also reach her via: megjohns@europa.com **Career Steps:** Design and Sales, DW Industries (1990–Present); Sales, The Wedding Cottage (1987–1990); Sales, Uieier & Frank (1985–1987). **Associations & Accomplishments:** Northwest Society of Interior Designers; National Kitchen & Bath Association; Historic Preservation Volunteer; Local School Volunteer. **Education:** University of Oregon, B.A.–RL (1976). **Personal:** Two children: Jennifer and Erika. Ms. Johnson enjoys spending time with her family, skiing, golf, and tennis.

Mervin D. Lung
Chairman of the Board
Patrick Industries, Inc.
5020 Lincoln Way East
Mishawaka, IN 46544
(219) 294-7511
Fax: Please mail or call

2434

Business Information: Patrick Industries, Inc., a $365 million dollar company, is a manufacturer of Stylemaster cabinets, doors, and paneling used for the housing industry. Consisting of 40 plants nationwide, Patrick Industries, Inc. has plant locations in Oregon (Portland), California (Sacramento), Arizona (Phoenix), Texas (Waco), Kansas (Wichita), Alabama, Florida, (2) Georgia, North Carolina (Charlotte), Pennsylvania (Lancaster). Patrick Industries was established in 1956. As Chairman of the Board, Mr. Lung **Career Steps:** Chairman of the Board, Patrick Industries, Inc. (1956–Present) **Personal:** Mr. Lung enjoys fishing, boating, visiting home in Michigan, travel, and golf.

G. Douglas Pauley
General Manager
Kitchen & Bath Ideas
One Millrace Dr.
Lynchburg, VA 24502
(804) 385-8200
Fax: (804) 385-8194

2434

Business Information: Kitchen & Bath Ideas, a division of Starmark, is a designer and distributor of cabinetry for the home (e.g., kitchens, baths, bedroom & office furniture). Kitchen & Bath Ideas is national in scope with four locations in the Midwest and one location on the East Coast. As General Manager, Mr. Pauley is responsible for showroom displays, continuing sales, product education, payables, receivables, coordinating service, and installation. In addition, he is responsible for diversified administrative activities, including finance, sales, and marketing. **Career Steps:** General Manager, Kitchen & Bath Ideas (1994–Present); General Manager, Greenwich Kitchens (1991–1994); General Manager, Kitchen Towne (1987–1990); Vice President/Partner, Tidewater Kitchen Distributors, Inc. (1974–1986). **Education:** Old Dominion University (1967). **Personal:** Married to Carol in 1969. One child: Stacey. Mr. Pauley enjoys reading and golf.

Joseph Di Benedetto Sr.
President
DGGR Packaging and Crating Company
1450 South Manhattan Avenue
Fullerton, CA 92631-5222
(714) 635-0055
Fax: (714) 635-0065

2441

Business Information: DGGR Packaging and Crating Company specializes in the manufacture of wooden boxes and crates, corragated cardboard, and foam for packaging and shipping. Major clientele includes Beckman Instruments and Raytheon Company. Established in 1973, DGGR currently employs 15 people and has an estimated annual revenue of $1.5 million. As President, Mr. Di Benedetto is responsible for all aspects of operations, including administration and production. **Career Steps:** President, DGGR Packaging and Crating Company (1970–Present); Owner, Woodspace Industries (1969–1970); President, Di Benedetto Marble Company (1960–1965); Set Engineer, Universal Studios (1963–1969). **Personal:** Married to Caroline in 1955. Two children: Joseph, Jr. and Michael. Mr. Di Benedetto enjoys golf, travel and work. Mr. Di Benedetto has a devoted family. His sons work with him, and he has instilled in them a sense of pride and honesty.

Peter M. Brown
Manager, Administrative Services
Fleetwood Enterprises
3125 Myers Street
Riverside, CA 92503
(909) 351-3616
Fax: (909) 351-3385

2451

Business Information: Fleetwood Enterprises, established in 1949, is the world's largest manufacturer or mobile homes and recreational vehicles. A Fortune 500 Company, Fleetwood Enterprises currently employs over 18,000 people and expect to post sales in excess of $3 billion in 1996. As Manager, Administrative Services, Mr. Brown oversees the activities of a staff of 60 people. He is responsible for office services, graphics, travel, distribution services, disaster preparedness, maintenance and security. Concurrently, he teaches classes at the University of California at Riverside, Riverside Community College, and Ramona High School. **Career Steps:** Manager, Administrative Services, Fleetwood Enterprises (1992–Present); Director, Facilities, Hanna–Barbera Studios (1990–1992); Manager, Administrative Services, Dennison–Avery (1983–1987); Regional Manufacturing Manager, McGraw–Hill (1970–1980). **Associations & Accomplishments:** American Legion; American Society of Industrial Security Specialists; Volunteer Admissions Counselor for University of Rochester. **Education:** University of Rochester, B.A. in Music (1955). **Personal:** Mr. Brown enjoys playing music with local groups, backpacking, and is building a music studio in his spare time.

David Crokie
Director of Manufacturing
New England Homes
270 Ocean Road
Greenland, NH 03840-2442
(603) 436-8830
Fax: (603) 431-8540

2451

Business Information: New England Homes is a manufacturer of modular and panelized homes. Established in 1961, New England Homes currently employ more than 100 people. With more than 12 years expertise in the building industry, Mr. Crokie joined New England Homes in 1995. Currently serving as Director of Manufacturing, he is responsible for all manufacturing related functions. **Career Steps:** Director of Manufacturing, New England Homes (1995–Present); General Manager, Miller Structures, Inc. (1992–1995); Vice President of Manufacturing, Excel Homes (1989–1992). **Associations & Accomplishments:** MENSA; INTERTEL; Former President, Big Brothers; Rotary. **Education:** Ohio State University, B.A. in Industrial Management (1972). **Personal:** Married to Terry in 1977. One son: Kirk. Mr. Crokie enjoys drawing, painting, tennis, golf, fishing, and horseshoes.

Kent W. Sorensen

President

Dessen Homes, Inc.

3400 Columbia Way
Vancouver, WA 98661
(360) 694–2300
Fax: (360) 694–2990

2451

Business Information: Dessen Homes, Inc. is the largest exporter of prefabricated housing in the United States, specializing in pre–cut and partially assembled custom homes. As President and Chief Executive Officer, Mr. Sorensen is responsible for new business development, financial management, and establishing Corporate objectives. **Career Steps:** President and Chief Executive Officer, Dessen Homes, Inc. (1990–Present); Chief Operating Officer, CytoSciences, Inc. (1985–1989); President, Micronetic Laboratories, Inc. (1972–1985). **Associations & Accomplishments:** Distinguished Citizen's Award, City of San Jose, California; Northwest China Council – Portland, Oregon; Japan American Association – Portland, Oregon. **Education:** San Jose State University. **Personal:** Married to Helen in 1985. Six children: Christopher, Sabrina, Shon, Tanton, Tichelle, and Natasha. Mr. Sorensen enjoys photography, gardening, and travel.

Arlend W. Oney

Vice President of Sales Development

Gastineau Log Homes

Old Highway 54
New Bloomfield, MO 65063
(314) 896–5122 Ext. 245
Fax: (314) 896–5510

2452

Business Information: Gastineau Log Homes specializes in the manufacture of fine quality log homes. With 60 dealerships in the United States, Gastineau is unique in the industry for its manufacture of oak and black walnut buildings. In operation since 1977, the Company currently employs 50 people and has an estimated annual revenue of $10 million. As Vice President of Sales Development, Mr. Oney is responsible for the management of the National Dealership Program and all in–house sales departments. Prior to his current position with Gastineau Log Homes, Mr. Oney was a Psychologist and Social Worker. As such, he was directly reponsible for encouraging an adult with an 8th grade education to return to school and complete her GED. Years later, that same woman tracked him down to personally thank him for his support as she had just received her Ph.D. During his years as a high school teacher, Mr. Oney encouraged a very gifted blind student to attend college—this student went on to receive his Ph.D. and was later appointed as President of a University. **Career Steps:** Vice President of Sales Development, Gastineau Log Homes (1984–Present); Regional Supervisor, State of Missouri (1969–1984); Teacher, Monett High School (1963–1969). **Associations & Accomplishments:** National Association of Home Builders; Log Home Council; Building Systems Council; National Budgerigar Association, an association of exotic bird breeders. **Education:** University of Missouri, M.S.W. (1978); Pittsburgh State University, B.S. in Social Science. **Personal:** Married to Lana K. in 1986. Five children: Daniel, Robyn, Brian, Sheila, and Christen. Mr. Oney enjoys raising exotic birds, bowling, hunting, fishing, and softball.

Charles David Smith

Chief Executive Officer and President

SEMO Manufactured Homes and SEMO Properties Ltd.

P.O. Box 243, Highway 25 South
Malden, MO 63863
(314) 276–5700
Fax: (314) 276–2098

2452

Business Information: SEMO Manufactured Homes and SEMO Properties Ltd. specializes in the remanufacture and sale of manufactured homes. The Company also provides such services as financing, insurance, transportation, parts and appraisals. Established in 1974, SEMO currently employs 32 people and has an estimated annual revenue of $2 million. As Chief Executive Officer and President, Mr. Smith provides the overall direction and vision for the company's growth, quality delivery to customers, and strategic development. Mr. Smith is a qualified businessman, honest and concerned about all potentional home buyers, fulfilling the American dream of home ownership. He has sold over 200 units in 1995 and is well on his way to another great year. On an international level, Mr. Smith imports prepared products from overseas manufacturers, and then markets the products throughout the U.S. and foreign sectors. The first to commercially market this unique product, Mr. Smith has coined it as "Mudrunners." **Career Steps:** Chief Executive Officer and President, Semo Manufactured Homes, Semo Properties Ltd. (1974–Present). **Associations & Accomplishments:** Missouri Manufactured Housing Association; Illinois Manufactured Housing Association; National Hot Rod Association; Sponsor, Civic League and Little League Baseball Teams. **Education:** A.D. Banker & Company Insurance, Broker (1995); Fred Prior Resources, Management Certification. **Personal:** Three children: Amanda, Kate, and David. Mr. Smith enjoys auto racing, fishing and old cars.

Mario Vavassori

President

Casema Industria e Comercio Ltda.

KM 56,5 Guaxinduva Rod. D. Pedro I
Bom Jesus Dos Perdoes, Brazil 12950
55–11–402–7612
Fax: 55–11–402–7615
EMAIL: See Below

2452

Business Information: Casema Industria e Comercio Ltda. is a company specializing in general residential construction and the sale of building supplies and related products to contractors and companies in Brazil and more than 40 countries in all five continents. Established in 1982, the Company employs 280 people and has estimated annual revenue of $18 million. As President, Mr. Vavassori oversees all aspects of the Company. His duties include administration, operations, finance, sales, public relations, accounting, marketing, and strategic planning. Internet users can reach him via: casema@sanet.com.br. **Career Steps:** Casema Industria e Comercio Ltda.: President (1984–Present), General Manager (1982–1984), Finance Manager, Grahl S/A (1976–1982). **Associations & Accomplishments:** Rotary International; Associacao Brasileira de Construcao Industrializada (ABCI); Associacao Brasileira dos Productores de Madeira (ABPM). **Education:** Fac. Cien. Economicas Apucarana, Economics, B.Sc. (1973). **Personal:** Married to Heloisa Kissae Akinaga in 1975. Three children: Danilo Akinaga, Hilario Akinaga, and Eduardo Akinaga Vavassori. Mr. Vavassori enjoys playing Boccia, tennis, cards, and reading.

George T. Herczak

President and Chief Executive Officer

A–Zak Wood Specialties, Inc.

8125 Rhodes Avenue
North Hollywood, CA 91605–1340
(818) 768–0799
Fax: (818) 768–9469

2499

Business Information: A–Zak Wood Specialties, Inc. specializes in the manufacture of prefabricated portable playhouses and additional related products such as portable storage sheds, shelves and tables, and recreational vehicle accessories. The Company's signature product is the "Jennifer" playhouse. Based on a prototype of a thirty–year old playhouse built for his granddaughter, Mr. Herczak, the President and Chief Executive Office of the company, has started a business that builds playhouses and other structures as enduring symbols of love and quality. Established in 1984, A–Zak Wood Specialities currently employs 10 people. As President and Chief Executive Officer, Mr. Herczak is responsible for all aspects of operations. A victim of a General Motors plant closure, Mr. Herczak was able to take advantage of the business training programs offered by his former employer, and by using this newly acquired knowledge and the woodworking skills he had been perfecting most of his life, Mr. Herczak has established a successful business and a product that can stand the test of time. **Career Steps:** President and Chief Executive Officer, A–Zak Wood Specialties, Inc. (1984–Present); Team Leader, General Motors Corporation (1964–1996); Assistant Manager, Standard Oil Company (1962–1964). **Associations & Accomplishments:** Elks Lodge #1539, San Fernando, CA; United Auto Worker's Association; American Legion, Post 0581; Veterans of Foreigh Wars, Post 10040; E Clampus Vitus Platrix Chapter #2; 2nd Infantry Division Association; Korean Veterans Association. **Education:** Valley Economic Development Center, Entrepreneur Class (1994); ICS Architect (1965); University of Tennessee (1955–1956); Radio Operator (CW), U.S. Army; General Motors Business School Skill Center, two years. **Personal:** Married to Barbara in 1983. Two children: Mike and Tammy Moody. Mr. Herczak enjoys woodworking, carving, camping, fishing, hunting, and Philanthropy, including support of the Johnny Carpenter's Heaven on Earth Ranch for Handicapped Children.

Henry Jelinek Jr.

President and Chief Executive Officer

Jelinek Cork Corporation

P.O. Box 986
Lockport, NY 14095–0986
(716) 439–4644
Fax: (716) 439–4875
E–mail: see below

2499

Business Information: Jelinek Cork Corporation, established in 1951, is a supplier of stoppers and closures to wineries and distilleries, including stoppers, gaskets, visual aids, acoustical and insulation materials to the automotive, sporting goods, fashion and construction industries. Jelinek imports cork from Portugal, Spain and North Africa. As President and Chief Executive Officer, Mr. Jelinek is responsible for all aspects of operations, including financial decisions and international expansions. He can also be reached through the Internet as follows: jelcork@thenerve.com **Career Steps:** President and Chief Executive Officer, Jelinek Cork Corporation (1972–Present); President and Chief Executive Officer, Jelinek Cork Limited, Oakville, Ontario, Canada (1974–Present); President and Chief Executive Officer, Dodge Cork Canada Ltd. (1981–Present); President and Chief Executive Officer, Korek Jelinek, Czech Republic (1993–Present). **Associations & Accomplishments:** Trustee, Board of Trustees, Marietta College, Marietta, OH; Oakville, Ontario Chamber of Commerce; Participant, Canada–U.S. Business Association; Canadian Affinity Group; Czech–Canadian Chamber of Commerce; Author of "On Thin Ice," Prentice–Hall (1965); Published articles in trade journals; Frequent speaker on the Canadian–U.S. free trade agreement. **Education:** New School of Social Research, New York City, M.A. (1970); Marietta College, B.A. (1968); Swiss Alpine Business School, Business Certification (1965). **Personal:** Married to Cathy in 1970. Three children: Sonny, Keena and Jay. Mr. Jelinek enjoys tennis, wine making, writing and reading.

Nancy T. Krug

Vice President of Manufacturing

Larson – Juhl

3900 Steve Reynolds Boulevard
Norcross, GA 30093
(770) 279–5326
Fax: (770) 279–5297

2499

Business Information: Larson – Juhl is an international manufacturer and distributor of picture frame moulding and supplies for the retail framer. Established in 1894, Larson – Juhl currently employs 2,000 people. As Vice President of Manufacturing, Ms. Krug is responsible for the management of the United States wood and metal moulding plants and the equipment assembly plant. **Career Steps:** Vice President of Manufacturing, Larson – Juhl (1993–Present); E.I. DuPont: Site Manager (1992–1993), Operations Manager (1988–1992); Gemini Consulting (1983–1988); General Public Utilities (1981–1983); AT&T (1980–1981). **Education:** University of Cincinnati: M.B.A. (1980), B.A. in Mathematics; Ohio State University; Rensselaer Polytechnic Institute. **Personal:** Ms. Krug enjoys photography, gardening, amateur art, and overseas travel.

Jean–Pierre R. Libert

General Manager

Hamon Cooling Tower – Mexico Branch

P.O. Box 6830, 245 Highway 22 West
Bridgewater, NJ 08807
(908) 725–3704
Fax: (908) 725–3421

2499

Business Information: Hamon Cooling Tower – Mexico Branch, established in 1994, is a designer and builder of cooling towers for power stations, refineries, chemicals, steel and food industries, HVAC, etc. Future plans include expanding in the North American market and moving into Latin America. An engineering executive with Hamon Corporation in various international subsidiaries since 1979, Mr. Libert now serves as General Manager directing all Mexican operations. Working at the Mexico City office, he can be contacted as follows: Office Phone: 011–525–260–1983 and FAX: 011–525–260–1377. **Career Steps:** General Manager, Hamon Cooling Tower – Mexico Branch (1903–Present); Vice President of Engineering, Hamon Corporation – USA (1985–1993); Application Engineer, Hamon–Sobelco – Belgium (1979–1985). **Associations & Accomplishments:** Cooling Tower Institute – Houston, Texas; Association of the Engineers of Mons Faculty (AIMS), Mons, Belgium; American Concrete Institute – Chicago, Illinois; American Society of Mechanical Engineers; Aircraft Owners & Pilots Association, Frederick, Maryland; Member: Belgium, Luxembourg, and Mexico Chamber of Commerce; Co–author of two articles, presented at the Cooling Tower Institute Conference and published in the proceedings; Fluent in French, Spanish, and English. **Education:** Polytechnical Faculty of Mons, Belgium, M.S. (1978). **Personal:** Married to Dina Amico in 1975. Two children: Julien and Antoine. Mr. Libert enjoys flying, jogging, football, soccer, bicycling, and computers.

Kris L. Moehlman

Administrative Associate to the Vice President of Operations
Cedar Works
19 Cedar Drive
Peebles, OH 45660–9200
(513) 587–2656
Fax: (513) 587–5187

2499

Business Information: Cedar Works is a lumber processing company that manufacturers cedar bird feeders, houses, and mailboxes with posts. As Administrative Associate to the Vice President of Operations, Ms. Moehlman is responsible for diversified administrative activities including reports, graphs, and operations research. **Career Steps:** Cedar Works: Administrative Associate to the Vice President of Operations (1995–Present), Material Traffic Controller (1993–1995), Parts Cutter/Subassembly (1992–1993). **Associations & Accomplishments:** Daughters of the American Revolution; Daughters of 1812. **Education:** Shawnee State University, M.L.T. (1979); Fred Pryor Seminars, continuing education. **Personal:** Two daughters: Ryan and Sara. Ms. Moehlman enjoys counted cross stitch, swimming, gardening, and beadwork.

2500 Furniture and Fixtures

2511 Wood household furniture
2512 Upholstered household furniture
2514 Metal household furniture
2515 Mattresses and bedsprings
2517 Wood TV and radio cabinets
2519 Household furniture, NEC
2521 Wood office furniture
2522 Office furniture, except wood
2531 Public building and related furniture
2541 Wood partitions and fixtures
2542 Partitions and fixtures, except wood
2591 Drapery hardware and blinds and shades
2599 Furniture and fixtures, NEC

Amedeo Arcese
President
C O Arcese Brothers
6124 Shawson Drive
Mississauga, Ontario L5T 1E6
(905) 670–6688
Fax: (905) 670–9089

2511

Business Information: C O Arcese Brothers is an international manufacturer and distributor of dining room and bedroom furniture. Established in 1975, C O Arcese Brothers reports annual revenue of $20 million and currently employs 220 people. As President, Mr. Arcese is responsible for the oversight of all activities, specifically in the designing and planning of business strategies according to market requirements. A native of Ceprano, Italy, Mr. Arcese started his furniture design career during his youth, serving as an apprentice cabinetmaker from the age of 10 through 20 in his homeland. **Career Steps:** President, C O Arcese Brothers (1975–Present); Sample Maker, Emanuel Products (1965–1975). **Personal:** Married to Ezia in 1969. Three children: Antonio, Antonella,

and Alessandro. Mr. Arcese enjoys sports cars, motorcycles, martial arts, skiing, swimming, and trap shooting.

F.J. (Jeff) Brown, CPA
Director of State and Local Taxation
Bassett Furniture Industries, Inc.
P.O. Box 626
Bassett, VA 24055
(540) 629–6000
Fax: (540) 629–6346

2511

Business Information: Bassett Furniture Industries, Inc. is a manufacturer of home furnishings divided into three divisions: Bassett Furniture Industries, a manufacturer of beds and dining room furniture; Bassett Furniture of North Carolina, a manufacturer of upholstered furniture; and Bassett Bedding, manufacturer of mattresses and box springs. As Director of State and Local Taxation, Mr. Brown is responsible for the filing and management of state and local tax matters for the Company. He handles all tax return filings, as well as audits by taxing authorities, and maintains showroom inventory records. **Career Steps:** Director of State and Local Taxation, Bassett Furniture Industries, Inc. (1995–Present); Tax Auditor, Virginia Department of Taxation (1991–1995); Senior Staff CPA, Bostic Tucker & Company (1990–1991); Senior Internal Auditor, Virginia State Board for Community Colleges (1988–1990). **Associations & Accomplishments:** American Institute of Certified Public Accountants; Virginia Society of Certified Public Accountants. **Education:** East Tennessee State University, B.B.A. (1978). **Personal:** Married to Pam in 1980. Two children: Andrew and Jason. Mr. Brown enjoys listening to Bluegrass music and reading.

Craig Smith

President
Harden Manufacturing Corp.
RR 5, Box 289
Haleyville, AL 35565–8940
(205) 486–7872
Fax: (205) 486–6544

2511

Business Information: The Harden Manufacturing Corporation, established in 1972, is a family–owned business specializing in the manufacture of bedroom furniture, occasional tables and cabinet doors; distributing its products to independent representatives, Mom and Pop stores, and retail chain operations. Harden Manufacturing Corporation will ship merchandise anywhere within a 700–mile radius. Starting as a Sales Manager with Harden in 1984, Craig Smith worked his way up the "corporate ladder", appointed President in 1994. **Career Steps:** Harden Manufacturing Corporation: President (1994–Present), Sales Manager (1984–1995); President and Chief Executive Officer, Colby Furniture Company, Hamilton, AL (Present). **Associations & Accomplishments:** Alabama Mobile Home Association; Ducks Unlimited; Arkansas Furniture Association; Southeastern Furniture Association. **Education:** Marion County High School (1984). **Personal:** Married to Deidre in 1987. Two children: Tanner and Dylan. Mr. Smith enjoys golf and duck hunting.

Philippe G. Vallerand

President
Prime Resource Group
11900 Old Baltimore Pike
Beltsville, MD 20705–1288
(800) 206–7909
Fax: (360) 794–5535

2511

Business Information: Prime Resource Group is an international sales, marketing, and development group manufacturing home furnishings for large companies, i.e., WalMart, KMart, Spiegel, and Target. As President, Mr. Vallerand is responsible for developing new products, handling sales, and supervising employees. **Career Steps:** President, Prime Resource Group (1993–Present); Executive Vice President, Source International (1982–1993); Sports Director, Franglo France/England (1980–1982); Sports Director, Club Mediterranee (1978–1980). **Associations & Accomplishments:** American Management Association; Sales & Marketing Executive International; Senior Commander Royal Rangers; Board Member, Assembly of God. **Education:** University of Montreal; University of Sherbrooke; University of Quebec – Montreal; White School of Management – London. **Personal:** Married to Laura. Three children: Harmonie, Jeremy, and Emilie. Mr. Vallerand enjoys skiing and travel.

Scott Holliday
Vice President
Comfort Rest Sleep Products, Inc.
1286 Milledge Road
East Point, GA 30344
(404) 768–1983
Fax: (404) 768–2064

2515

Business Information: Comfort Rest Sleep Products, Inc., a spin–off of Colgate Mattress Company in New York, is a full–line Mattress Manufacturer. Comfort Rest produces products for Holiday Inn Corporate, Rhodes Furniture, Badcock Home-furnishings and many other national and local southeastern area accounts. New to the Atlanta area, Mr. Holiday is responsible for Sales Marketing, customer service, purchasing and design. **Career Steps:** Vice President, Comfort Rest Sleep Products, Inc. (1996–Present); Vice President, Best N' Bedding, Inc. (1993–1996); Vice President and Owner, Carolina Mattress Company (1990–1993); Vice President, Dormir Mattress Co. (1983–1990). **Associations & Accomplishments:** National Home Furnishings Association; National Home Furnishings Reps Association; West Knox Rotary Club; Written Articles for Furniture World Magazine, "Why Not Start in the Middle." and "What Should You Sleep On?" **Education:** Auburn University–Montgomery, Business (1980). **Personal:** Married to Patti in 1991. Two children: Meghan and Garrett. Mr. Holliday enjoys golf, writing, and travel.

Charles H. Frey
Information Systems Manager/Purchasing Agent
Sauder Woodworking Company
502 Middle Street
Archbold, OH 43502
(419) 446–3566
Fax: (419) 446–4900

2519

Business Information: Sauder Woodworking Company is a manufacturer of ready to assemble furniture. As Information Systems Manager/Purchasing Agent, Mr. Frey is responsible for diversified administrative activities, including operations, sales and marketing, public relations, and strategic planning. He is also an AS400 Network Engineer. **Career Steps:** Sauder Woodworking Company: Information Systems Manager/ Purchasing Agent (1994–Present), Information Systems Hardware Technician (1989–1994), Warehouse Manager (1982–1989). **Associations & Accomplishments:** State Teachers Association. **Education:** University of Toledo, Associate (1986). **Personal:** Mr. Frey teaches and enjoys step aerobics.

Jo Nell Haynie
Plant Manager
Berkline
P.O. Box 6003
Morristown, TN 37815
(423) 585–4408
Fax: Please mail or call

2519

Business Information: Berkline is a designer, manufacturer, and distributor of living room furniture, such as sofas, chairs, end tables, coffee tables, etc. worldwide. With twenty–two years of experience in furniture manufacturing, Jo Nell Haynie joined Berkline as Plant Manager in 1990. She is responsible for all aspects of plant operations, including the direction of three different divisions (i.e., serving, filling, CPO) She is also responsible for loading and unloading of materials and plant production. **Career Steps:** Plant Manager, Berkline (1990–Present); Department Manager, Benchcraft (1974–1990). **Personal:** One child: William Paul Jr. Ms. Haynie enjoys crafts and sewing.

Eddie Irizarry

President
Fabrica de Muebles/Mundo de Madera, Inc.
Ave. Pinero 1129
San Juan, Puerto Rico 00920
(809) 731–1569
Fax: (809) 731–2600
EMAIL: See Below

2519

Business Information: Fabrica de Muebles/Mundo de Madera, Inc. is a manufacturer, wholesaler, and retailer of household furniture from two locations in Puerto Rico. In addition to its wholesale distribution, the Company also markets to end users. As President, Mr. Irizarry is responsible for all aspects of operations and management, including finances, marketing, strategic planning, and presiding on all Board meetings.

Concurrent with his executive position, he serves as Vice President of Sun & Sea Marine, a distributor of Rinker & Carver Boats. Internet users can reach him via: Elrizarry. **Career Steps:** President, Fabrica de Muebles/Mundo de Madera, Inc. (1986–Present); President, Irizarry Contruccion (1978–1986); President, Eddie's Electronics (1976–1978); M/Sgt., United States Air Force (1956–1976). **Associations & Accomplishments:** President, Puerto Nuevo Merchant's Association; Director, Furniture Manufacturers Association for Household Furniture; United Retailers Association of Puerto Rico; Scouter and Woodbadger; District 1 Puerto Rico Scout Council. **Education:** Colegio Universitario del Turabo, B.B.A. (1980); MBDC Training by U.S. Department of Commerce; Devry Institute of Technology, A.A. in Electronics; WASE Specialist; Stock Record Specialist; Training Specialist; Works Specialist from United States Air Force. **Personal:** Married to Milagros Suau in 1959. Five children: Eddie, Lourde, Elaine, Lori, and Paul. Mr. Irizarry enjoys photography, boating, fishing, electronics, and scouts.

Sherry H. Qualls

General Manager of Advertising
Armstrong World Industries
150 North Queen Street
Lancaster, PA 17603–3550
(717) 396–4459
Fax: (717) 396–4477

2519

Business Information: Armstrong World Industries is an international manufacturer and distributor of interior finishes and furnishings, including floor coverings and ceilings. Clients include vendors, boutiques, and home furnishing companies. As General Manager of Advertising, Ms. Qualls is responsible for the management of all national advertising functions for residential and commercial floor coverings, in addition to retail advertising, promotions, and overseeing a staff of sixteen. **Career Steps:** General Manager of Advertising, Armstrong World Industries (1987–Present); Senior Accounts Manager, AROCOM Marketing Group (1986–1987); Manager of Advertising, Armstrong WD, Ind. (1980–1986); Assistant Accounts Executive, Perry International (1979–1980). **Associations & Accomplishments:** American Society of Interior Designers (ASID); National Kitchen & Bath Association (NKBA); Virginia Tech Kitchen & Bath Advisory Board Member; Retail Advertising Conference Board. **Education:** Wells College, B.A. (1979). **Personal:** Married to N. Scott in 1983. Two children: Nicole and Brent. Ms. Qualls enjoys sailing, gardening, and skiing.

Mr. Javier R. Aponte

Controller
Simon Drury Limited, Inc.
Amelia Distribution Center, #31 Diana Street
Guaynabo, Puerto Rico 00968–8006
(809) 749–8000
Fax: (809) 749–9800

2521

Business Information: Simon Drury Limited, Inc. specializes in the manufacture and distribution of fine office contract furniture. Established in 1983, Simon Drury Ltd. currently employs 45 people and has an estimated annual revenue of $10 million. As Controller, Mr. Aponte is responsible for all aspects of financial operations, including auditing, supervision, cash management, and investing. Mr. Aponte is also a Certified Public Accountant. **Career Steps:** Controller, Simon Drury Limited, Inc. (1994–Present); Auditor, Coopers & Lybrand (1992–1994); Forensic Auditor, Matson Driscoll & Damico (1989–1992). **Associations & Accomplishments:** Puerto Rico State Society of Certified Public Accountants; American Institute of Certified Public Accountants; Puerto Rico Chamber of Commerce; Vice President, EDP Auditors Association; Published article for newspaper. **Education:** University of Puerto Rico, B.B.A. (1989); Certified Public Accountant. **Personal:** Married to Annette Gonzalez in 1994. One child: Bianca V. Mr. Aponte enjoys boating, and spending time with his family.

Larry J. Knust

General Manager
Harpers
West 1500 Seltice Way
Post Falls, ID 83854
(208) 777–6600
Fax: (208) 777–6603

2521

Business Information: Harpers, a subsidiary of Kimble International, is a manufacturer of office furniture. Product lines include lateral file cabinet systems, office furniture, and chairs, as well as offering services, such as upholstering, stamping, welding, assembly, and wood processing. Kimble, famous for their pianos, consists of many different divisions, including an Electronics Group, Pianos & Organs, Lodging and Office Furniture, Raw Materials Group (own forests), and Home Furniture. Joining Harpers as General Manager of the Metal Office Furniture Manufacturing Division in 1995, Mr. Knust is responsible for the oversight of all operations, including overseeing purchasing, financing, and manufacturing, as well as seeking out new markets. **Career Steps:** General Manager, Harpers (1995–Present); Douglas and Lomason Company: Program Manager (1993–1995), Plant Manager (1990–1993), Manufacturing Manager (1987–1990). **Education:** University of Nebraska – Kearny, B.S. (1984). **Personal:** Married to Karen in 1984. Three children: Kyle, Emily and Kymberly. Mr. Knust enjoys woodworking, collecting antiques and walking.

Michelle T. Vollmer

Quality Programs Coordinator
Kimball International
1600 Royal Street
Jasper, IN 47549
(800) 482–1616
Fax: (812) 482–8980

2521

Business Information: Kimball International is a manufacturer of office furniture lodging and hospitality furniture, and electronics. The Company distributes to various businesses internationally. As Quality Programs Coordinator, Ms. Vollmer coordinates document and data control, internal quality auditing programs, and monitoring the corrective action program. **Career Steps:** Kimball International: Quality Programs Coordinator (1994–Present), Customer Service Coordinator (1992–1994); Citizens National Bank: Discount/Loan Entry (1991–1992), Student Loan Manager (1988–1990). **Associations & Accomplishments:** American Society for Quality Control; Association for Quality and Participation; RAB Lead Auditor Courses and Examination; AQP Basic Facilitation Workshop. **Education:** Certification of Diamontologist and Gemologist. **Personal:** Ms. Vollmer enjoys reading, walking, and music.

Ken J. Hurst

Operations Manager
Kimball Upholstery Products
340 East 11th Avenue
Jasper, IN 47549
(812) 634–3608
Fax: (812) 634–3886

2522

Business Information: Kimball Upholstery Products is a manufacturer of office furniture, healthcare, and hospitality seating. Joining Kimball Upholstery Products in 1989, Mr. Hurst was appointed as Operations Manager in 1995. He is responsible for the oversight of all aspects of business operations. **Career Steps:** Kimball Upholstery Products: Operations Manager (1995–Present), Manufacturing Manager (1991–1995), Production Coordinator (1989–1991). **Associations & Accomplishments:** APICS; CICM; Junior Achievement Volunteer; Member, Local VFD; Licensed High School Basketball Referee. **Personal:** Married to Sharon in 1977. Two children: Lisa and Aaron. Mr. Hurst enjoys hunting.

Pamela E. Witting

Manager of Medical and Wellness Services
Steelcase, Inc. – CM
P.O. Box 1967
Grand Rapids, MI 49501–1967
(616) 246–4005
Fax: (616) 247–2855

2522

Business Information: Steelcase, Inc. – CM is the world's largest manufacturer of office furniture, with 21,000 employees worldwide. As Manager of Medical and Wellness Services, Ms. Witting provides medical treatment and prevention services for employees, families, and retirees. **Career Steps:** Steelcase, Inc. – CM: Manager of Medical and Wellness Services (1995–Present), Manager of Disability Management and Wellness Services (1992–1995), Manager of Wellness Services (1986–1992). **Associations & Accomplishments:** Association for Worksite Health Promotion; National Association of Social Workers; Volunteer, Homeless Youth Program – Advisory Center for Teens; Volunteer, Michigan Special Olympics; Community Wellness Committee, Grand Rapids Chamber of Commerce. **Education:** Western Michigan University: M.S.W. (1996), M.E. (1985); Central Michigan University, B.S. in Physical Education (1980). **Personal:** Ms. Witting enjoys travel, camping, and sailing.

Liz R. Scott

Corporate Director of Health and Safety, Human Resources
Lear Corporation Canada Limited
530 Manitou Drive, P.O. Box 9758
Kitchener, Ontario N2G 4C2
(519) 895–3236
Fax: (519) 895–1608

2531

Business Information: Lear Corporation Canada Limited specializes in the manufacturing of automobile seats and interior automotive parts for direct sale to industry. International in scope, the Company has plants in nine countries, and seven throughout Canada. As Corporate Director of Health and Safety/Human Resources, Ms. Scott is responsible for establishing and directing corporate policy. She has accomplished a significant reduction in disablity and WCB costs since joining Lear. By using a powerful combination of management and leadership skills, she has established a dynamic Human Resources team throughout Lear's Canadian operations. **Career Steps:** Director of Health and Safety/Human Resources, Lear Corporation Canada Limited (1994–Present); Associate Partner, William M. Mercer (1989–1994); Occupational Health, Weston Bakeries (1984–1989); Principal, Industrial Nursing Service (1980–1985). **Associations & Accomplishments:** Automotive Parts Manutacturers Association; Human Resource Development Committee; Past Director of Education an Conference, Ontario Occupational Health Nurses Association; Employer's Occupational Health and Safety Council; Human Resources Professional Association; Resource Line Expert on WCB and Health and Safety. **Education:** D'Youville, M.Sc. (1995).

Gary Geilenfeld

Division Manager
Oklahoma Fixture Company
924 South Hudson Avenue
Tulsa, OK 74112
(918) 834–4666
Fax: (918) 834–6664

2541

Business Information: Oklahoma Fixture Company is a fabricator of custom–designed architectural products, including flat glass and mirror products for designers, contractors, architects, and fixture manufacturers. Oklahoma Fixture Company caters to retailers, banks, and museums. Joining the company in 1973, Mr. Geilenfeld was appointed as Division Manager in 1993. He is responsible for all aspects of plant operations for the division of Glass. **Career Steps:** Oklahoma Fixture Company: Division Manager (1993–Present), Manager of Productivity (1987–1993), Assistant Manager of Production (1975–1987). **Associations & Accomplishments:** Retired 20 years, Fire & Rescue Service; Retired 8 years, Emergency Management Director. **Education:** Tulsa University, working towards M.B.A.; OMA/CJC, Associate of Arts; Oklahoma State University, Fire Academy Professional. **Personal:** Married to Willene in 1995. One child: Valerie. Mr. Geilenfeld enjoys hunting, fishing, and hiking with his wife.

Daniel G. Binetti

Regional Operations Manager
Sandusky Cabinets
P.O. Box 125
Millington, TN 38083–0125
(901) 872–0188
Fax: (901) 873–1239

2542

Business Information: Sandusky Cabinets is a national manufacturer and distributor of steel storage cabinets for major superstores. National in scope, Sandusky Cabinets has three offices located in Ohio, Tennessee, and California. Established in 1947, the Company reports annual revenue of $22 million and currently employs 225 people. With ten years expertise in the manufacturing industry, Mr. Binetti joined the Company in 1994. Serving as Regional Operations Manager, he has complete responsibility for all plant functions and staff. **Career Steps:** Regional Operations Manager, Sandusky Cabinets (1994–Present); Shift Plant Manager, Brockway

Standard, Inc. (1992–1994); Manufacturing Supervisor, Fein Container Corporation (1987–1992); Assistant Plant Manager, Coining Corporation of America (1985–1987). **Education:** Attended: Memphis State University, Bergen Community College; Memphis Vocational and Technical School; Organization Development Services, Management Seminars and Workshops. **Personal:** Mr. Binetti enjoys softball, golf, fishing, and skiing.

Nancy Malone Haist

President
Communication Equipment and Engineering Company
1580 NW 65th Avenue
Plantation, FL 33313–4507
(954) 587–8430
Fax: Please mail or call

2542

Business Information: Communication Equipment and Engineering Company (CEECO) is a telephone manufacturing company specializing in the manufacture of vandal resistant stainless steel public telephones and associated parts (i.e. ADA phones, bar code phones, credit card processing phones, and custom manufacturing). Established in 1930, the Company employs 25 people and has estimated annual revenue of $3 million. As President, Ms. Haist oversees all day–to–day operations. She is responsible for decision making, strategic planning, and administrative functions. **Career Steps:** President, CEECO (1981–Present). **Associations & Accomplishments:** Board of Directors, Telecommunications Industry Association; Presidential Appointments to Small Business Advisory Council Federal Reserve, Atlanta; Women Business Owners Educational Council; Who's Who of Successful American Women; Who's Who of Florida Successful Women; Republican Senatorial Inner Circle; Plantation Chamber of Commerce; Charter Member, U.S. Telecommunications Association; Who's Who in the Republican Party; National Association for Female Executives; Marquis Who's Who Publication Board; Life Member, Republican Presidential Task Force; Board of Governors, Electronics Industry Association; Who's Who of Leading American Executives; Who's Who in Leading American Companies; 2,000 Notable Women; Recipient, South Florida Small Business Pacesetters Award; AT&T Network Systems Excellence Award; Traveled extensively throughout the U.S, Caribbean, and the Orient. **Education:** Florida Real Estate Institute; Licensed Mortgage Broker; Licensed Florida Real Estate Broker. **Personal:** Six children: Penny C. and Jay. Ms. Haist enjoys tennis, golf, being a Harley Davidson biker, swimming, and wildlife.

Richard K. Boyle
Vice President of Retail Sales
Levolor Home Fashions
5603 Tradd Dr.
Greensboro, NC 27455–1261
(910) 881–5848
Fax: (910) 881–5991

2591

Business Information: Levolor Home Fashions, a division of the Newell Company, is the nation's leading manufacturer and global marketer of hard window coverings. Products include mini blinds, vertical blinds and pleated shades. Headquartered in High Point, NC, Levolor distributes products from several locations throughout the U.S., in addition to limited international distribution managed from the office in Canada. As Vice President of Retail Sales, Mr. Boyle is responsible for all aspects of independent sales activities, including administrative duties, marketing, and strategic planning. In addition, he is responsible for the oversight of a staff of special inside managers, 4 regional managers and 37 sales managers. **Career Steps:** Vice President of Retail Sales, Levolor Home Fashions (1995–Present); Del Mar Window Coverings: Vice President of National Accounts (1990–1995), Director of Retail Sales (1988–1990), Regional Manager (1984–1988). **Education:** Duquesne University, B.S. in Marketing (1975). **Personal:** Married to Julie. Mr. Boyle enjoys motorcycling, building custom motorcycles, boating, spending time with his wife, and hiking in the Carolinas.

Daniel G. Daywalt

Vice President of Human Resources
Newell Window Furnishings Company
916 South Arcade Avenue
Freeport, IL 61032–6037
(815) 233–8211
Fax: (815) 233–8357
EMAIL: See Below

2591

Business Information: Newell Window Furnishings Company is a manufacturer of curtain and drapery rods, poles, fixtures, window blinds, shades and accessories. Established in 1921, the Company currently employs 800 professionals and has an estimated annual revenue of $130 million. A human resource management professional for over ten years, Mr. Daywalt serves as Vice President of Human Resources. He is responsible for all aspects of personnel administration and benefits corporate–wide. **Career Steps:** Vice President of Human Resources, Newell Window Furnishing Company (1993–Present); Anchor Hocking Specialty Glass Company – Division of Newell: Vice President of Human Resources (1989–1993), Manager of Human Resources (1987–1989); Manager of Personnel Services, Anchor Hocking Corporation (1987). **Associations & Accomplishments:** Society for Human Resource Management; Board of Directors, Martin Luther King Community Services of Illinois; Co–Chair, Stephenson County Workforce Excellence Council; Mayor, Freeport Education Strategic Planning Committee. **Education:** Youngstown State University, M.B.A. (1986); University of Michigan, B.A. in Economics (1979). **Personal:** Married to Carol L. in 1979. One child: Christopher. Mr. Daywalt enjoys golf and spending time with family.

Mr. John G. Mutimer
Vice President of Contract Division
Levolor
7614 Business Park Drive
Greensboro, NC 27409
(910) 665–2963
Fax: (910) 665–1470

2591

Business Information: Levolor is the nation's leading manufacturer and global marketer of hard window coverings. Products include mini blinds, vertical blinds and pleated shades. In his capacity as Vice President of Contract Division, Mr. Mutimer oversees all operations for the Contract Division. This Division is the marketing control for all commercial customers (650 contractors and dealers nationally). Mr. Mutimer focuses primarily in the administration and direction of marketing, sales, financial, profits, strategic planning, and budgetary aspects. Established in 1907, Levolor employs 2,700 people. **Career Steps:** Vice President of Contract Division, Levolor (1994–Present); Vice President of National Accounts, Newell Window Furnishings (1964–1993); Sales Manager, Heinz (1962–1964). **Associations & Accomplishments:** B.O.M.A.; Published in trade journals. **Education:** Florida Southern, B.S. (1962).

Charles P. Sawyer

Production Manager
Steven Fabrics
1400 Van Buren St., N.E.
Minneapolis, MN 55413–1535
(612) 781–6671
Fax: (612) 781–2135

2591

Business Information: Established in 1946, Steven Fabrics is a wholesale manufacturer of custom window treatments, including blinds and draperies. The Company has a second plant within the same locale responsible for the manufacture of mini–blinds. As Production Manager, Mr. Sawyer is responsible for production, scheduling and delivery, human resources, and quality control. **Career Steps:** Production Manager, Steven Fabrics (1986–Present); Safety Inspector, I.S.A. of North America (1980–1981); Quality Control Manager, Fabric Masters (1978–1980); Field Inspector, Great American Insurance Company (1978). **Associations & Accomplishments:** Product Improvement Advisory Committee, Hunter Douglas Window Fashions; Support/Volunteer, Salvation Army. **Education:** U.W.G.B., B.A. (1977); N.W.T.I., A.S. in Architecture. **Personal:** Mr. Sawyer enjoys cross country skiing, golf, and canoeing.

John S. Crowley
President and Chief Executive Officer
New England Classic Interiors
100 Middle Street
Portland, ME 04101–4100
(207) 879–6006
Fax: (207) 879–6006

2599

Business Information: Distributing their products in North America, Japan and China, New England Classic Interiors is a manufacturer of building products such as interior components, doors, windows and furniture. Founding the Company in 1993, as President and Chief Executive Officer, John Crowley focuses his responsibilities on marketing and new product development. In addition, he also owns a private consulting firm — JSC Group. JSC devises corporate strategy for Fortune 500 companies. **Career Steps:** President and Chief Executive Officer, New England Classic Interiors (1993–Present); President, JSC Group (1990–Present); Senior Research Associate, Massachusettes Institute of Technology (1988–1995); Research and Development Manager, Ryan Homes (1983–1988). **Associations & Accomplishments:** National Association of Home Builders. **Education:** Massachusetts Institute of Technology, M.A. (1982); University of New Hampshire, B.A.. **Personal:** Married to Xiao Yan Zhu in 1994. Mr. Crowley enjoys sailing and skiing.

Paul Darafeev
Chief Executive Officer
Mikhail Darafeev, Inc. (MDI)/Gameroom Gallery
7890 Haven Avenue
Rancho Cucamonga, CA 91730–3051
(818) 960–1871 Ext. 3304
Fax: (909) 987–9911
EMAIL: See Below in text

2599

Business Information: Mikhail Darafeev, Inc. (MDI)/Gameroom Gallery is a manufacturer of gameroom furniture, as well as operating retail stores in California and a new Internet store. Established in 1959, MDI reports annual revenue of $10 million and currently employs 60 people. As Chief Executive Officer, Mr. Darafeev is responsible for developing CD–ROM and virtual catalogs on the Internet, using digital photography and imaging. He can be reached through the Internet as follows: PaulDara@ix.netcom.com **Career Steps:** Chief Executive Officer, Mikhail Darafeev, Inc. (MDI)/Gameroom Gallery (1973–Present). **Associations & Accomplishments:** Technology Chairman, California Furniture Manufacturing Association; Chairman, Christian Coalition at Inland Valley, Pro–Family Voter Registration; Director, New Manna Ministries, California Support Orphanages in Russia; Internet Volunteer for City of Rancho Cucamonga; California and Inland Valley Republican Party. **Education:** University of Phoenix, M.B.A.; Internet On–Line University. **Personal:** Married to Leslie A. in 1981. Two children: Erin and Christopher. Mr. Darafeev enjoys gardening, bass playing, singing, and computers.

Kristina L. Lindsey

President
Kinder Harris, Inc.
203 East 22nd Street
Stuttgart, AR 72160–6726
(501) 673–1518
Fax: (501) 673–4319

2599

Business Information: Kinder Harris, Inc. is a manufacturer, importer, and wholesaler of home accessories to furniture and high–end department stores (i.e., Dillards, Macys). Products include wall (framed) art, decorative accessories, crystal, marble, and portable lamps. Kinder Harris, Inc. also deals with retail stores in Highpoint, North Carolina and export through their international business to South America and limited presence in Europe. With eleven years at Kinder Harris, Inc., Mrs. Lindsey joined the Company in 1984 as a Credit Manager. Currently serving as President, she is responsible for all aspects of operations, including the direction of manufacturing, marketing, and development of high–end accessories, including framed art and lamps. **Career Steps:** Kinder Harris, Inc.: President (1994–Present), Controller (1988–1994), Materials Manager (1986–1988), Credit Manager (1984–1986). **Associations & Accomplishments:** Board of Directors, Local Chapter of American Cancer Society; Alpha Chi Honor Society; New Salem Missionary Baptist Church. **Education:** Southern Arkansas University, B.B.A. (1984). **Personal:** Married to Kelly in 1984. Two children: Eli and Emily. Mrs. Lindsey enjoys singing and spending time with family.

Norbert W. Lyons

Senior Vice President of Sales and Marketing
Syroco, Inc.
175 McClellan Highway
Boston, MA 02128–1146
(617) 561–2200
Fax: Please mail or call

2599

Business Information: The largest resin furniture manufacturer in North America, Syroco, Inc. specializes in the manufacture of aluminum and resin patio furniture and related accessories utilizing the inject molding technique. Syroco, Inc. markets their products nationally and internationally through the use of mass marketing. Recently awarded a Disney contract, Syroco Inc. has been in operation since 1856 and currently employs 700 people. As Senior Vice President of Sales and Marketing, Mr. Lyons is responsible for the management of sales, marketing, and product development, and is personally responsible for 75 percent of the Company's product line. **Career Steps:** Senior Vice President of Sales and Marketing, Syroco, Inc. (1989–Present); Vice President of Sales, EMU, Inc.; Sales Manager, Grosfilley.

J. Mike Patrick

President and Chief Executive Officer
New West
2811 Big Horn Avenue
Cody, WY 82414
(307) 587–2839
Fax: (307) 527–7409
EMAIL: See Below

2599

Business Information: A custom Western furnishing and design firm, New West originated in 1986 at the Patrick Ranch horse barn and has enjoyed phenomenal growth, now occupying a 7,500 square foot shop in Cody. It has furnished homes, resorts, hotels, and showrooms in over forty states and three foreign countries and the New West line is featured in fine stores and galleries throughout the United States. A small, closely–knit team, with nine full–time employees and ten contract artisans, New West draws upon the spirit and creativity of local artisans and craftspeople. The raw materials for most of the New West's products are indigenous to the Rockies. The Company prides itself on unique design meticulously crafted to individual clients' needs. New West has received national and international recognition and has been featured in newspapers and magazines since the Company first made headlines in the New York Times in June of 1989. Mr. Patrick is a fourth generation Wyoming rancher who's native talent for design led to the creation of New West. Inspired by family friend Thomas Molesworth, the famous Western designer, Mr. Patrick began hand–crafting distinctive Western furnishings in the early 1980s. He is now President and Chief Executive Officer of New West, responsible for all aspects of the business. Internet users can reach him via: JMIKE@Tribe.com. **Career Steps:** President and Chief Executive Officer, New West (1988–Present); Construction Foreman, Ishuwooa Construction (1984–1988); Owner/Operator, Patrick Ranch (1976–Present). **Associations & Accomplishments:** President, Corporation for the Northern Rockies; Greater Yellowstone Coalition; Vice President, Northern Wyoming Resource Council; Chairman, Western Design Conference; Vice President, Western Lifestyle and Trade Association; Various publications. **Education:** University of Wyoming (1974). **Personal:** Married to Virginia in 1981. One child: Jim. Mr. Patrick enjoys skiing and golf.

2600 Paper and Allied Products

- 2611 Pulp mills
- 2621 Paper mills
- 2631 Paperboard mills
- 2652 Setup paper board boxes
- 2653 Corrugated and solid fiber boxes
- 2655 Fiber cans, drums and similar products
- 2656 Sanitary food containers
- 2657 Folding paperboard boxes
- 2671 Paper coated and laminated, packaging
- 2672 Paper coated and laminated, NEC
- 2673 Bags: plastics, laminated and coated
- 2674 Bags: uncoated paper and multiwall
- 2675 Die–cut paper and board
- 2676 Sanitary paper products
- 2677 Envelopes
- 2678 Stationery products
- 2679 Converted paper products, NEC

Gary L. Bowen

Executive Vice President
Asia Tech Pulp and Paper Public Co. Ltd.
223 Sumpawuth Rd., 8th Fl., Country Tower Building, Suite 13–20
Bangna, Prakanong, Bangkok, Thailand 10260
(662) 399–4501
Fax: (662) 399–4505

2611

Business Information: Asia Tech Pulp and Paper Public Co., Ltd. was formed to create and operate a new pulp mill in NE Thailand. Asia Tech operates agricultural businesses and a wood processing industry was a logical progression from plantation forestry. Dr. Bowen is responsible for the overall organization and implementation of the project. **Career Steps:** Executive Vice President, Asia Tech Pulp (1995–Present); Dean School of Career Education, University of Alaska SE (1993–1995); Alaska Pulp Corporation: Assistant Mill Manager (1989–1993), Chief Engineer (1987–1989), Project Engineer, (1984–1987). **Associations & Accomplishments:** Member, American Society of Civil Engineers; American Welding Society Certified Welding Inspector, Registered Professional Mechanical Engineer (Washington); Registered Professional Civil Engineer (Alaska); Correspondent and Former Editor Journal of Ferrocement; Lifetime Member Stanford Alumni Association. **Education:** University of Minnesota, Ph.D. in Mechanics of Fluids (1971); Stanford University, M.Sc. in Hydraulic Engineering; University of Alaska, B.Sc. in Civil Engineering. **Personal:** Married to Mary Deborah Modrell in 1965. Two children: Melissa Marie and Jennifer Margaret. Mr. Bowen enjoys sailing.

Richard Lafontaine

Vice President of Human Resources
James Maclaren
C.P. 2100
Buckingham, Quebec J8L 2X3
(819) 986–4331
Fax: (819) 986–5045

2611

Business Information: James Maclaren Industries, Inc. is an important forestry–based company operating in Western Quebec. This dynamic member of Noranda Forest, Inc. employs more than 1,000 workers in plants and mills whose modern production technology is amongst the best in the Canadian forest industry. Maclaren produces newsprint, kraft pulp, and hydroelectricity for Canadian, American and world markets. As Vice President of Human Resources, Mr. Lafontaine is responsible for all aspects of human resources of the Company, including employee benefits, labor relations, compensation, employee relations, training, and payroll. **Career Steps:** James Maclaren: Vice President of Human Resources (1992–Present), Director of Compensation and Employee Benefits (1989–1992); Employee Benefits Administrator, Teleglobe Canada (1981–1988). **Associations & Accomplishments:** Association des Professionnels en Ressources Humaines du Quebec; Ordre des Conseillers en Relations Industrielles; Human Resources Planning Society. **Education:** Universite de Montreal, Master in Industrial Relations (1973); Western Business School, Executive MBA Program. **Personal:** Married to Flor Peralta in 1986. Mr. Lafontaine enjoys sailing, biking, and woodworking.

Sally J. Penley

Director of Communications
Weyerhaeuser Company
33405 8th Avenue South
Federal Way, WA 98003
(206) 924–4471
Fax: (206) 924–3260
EMail: See Below

2611

Business Information: Weyerhaeuser Company is the world's largest private owner of merchantable softwood timber and the largest producer of softwood lumber and market pulp. As Director of Communications, Ms. Penley is responsible for strategic communications for the Company's Timberlands and Wood Products businesses, including issue management, external communications, and other related activities. Internet users can reach her via: penleys@wdni.com. **Career Steps:** Weyerhaeuser Company: Director of Communications (1994–Present), Director of Business Communications (1991–1994); Manager of Design Group (1989–1991). **Associations & Accomplishments:** Public Relations Society of America; Society of Technical Communications; Washington Information Council; Patrons of South Sound Cultural Activities. **Education:** Western Washington University: B.A. in Visual Communications and Secondary Education (1968), Career Executive Program (1986–1989); Center for Creative Leadership (1993); Over 600 hours of Management & Communications. **Personal:** Married to Ron in 1968. Two children: Zak and Parker. Ms. Penley enjoys the fine arts, calligraphy, and skiing.

Jeremy Bazley

Managing Director
J. Bibby Paper, Ltd.
Devon Valley Mill
Hele, Exeter, Devon, England EX5 4PJ
44 392 881731
Fax: 44 392 882297
EMAIL: See below

2621

Business Information: International in scope, J. Bibby Paper is a manufacturer of speciality paper distributed globally from its three main UK–based facilities. In 1995, the Company received the Queen's Award for Environmental Achievement. Currently J. Bibby Paper employs 550 people. As Managing Director, Mr. Bazley is responsible for all aspects of operations of Bibby Paper's three paper mill divisions: Henry Cooke, Oakenholt Mill, and Devon Valley Industries, as well as oversees a wastepaper reclamation operation. He is also a Director of the Bibby Industrial Group. Mr. Bazley has been in manufacturing for 19 years and can be reached through the Internet as follows: jb@jbibby01.2zynet.co.uk **Career Steps:** Managing Director, J. Bibby Paper, Ltd. (1993–Present); Director and General Manager, Devon Valley Industries (1990–1993); Factory Manager, J & J Makin Converting (1988–1990); Works Manager, J & J Makin Disley (1986–1988). **Associations & Accomplishments:** Institute of Directors; Council Member, Paper Federation of Great Britian; Management Board, Pulp and Paper Information Centre; London Business School Alumni Association. **Education:** Plymouth Polytechnic, Diploma in Management Studies (1984); Robert Gordon's Institute of Technology, Aberdeen (1981), Paper and Board Science and Technology; London Business School (1992), Senior Executives Programme. **Personal:** Married to Jane in 1981. Three children: Thomas, Lucy, and Hannah. Mr. Bazley enjoys basketball, cricket, squash, golf, rugby union, and gardening.

Frankie A. Brock

Director of Safety & Security
Alabama River Pulp
P.O. Box 100
Perdue Hill, AL 36470
(334) 743–8589
Fax: (334) 743–8500

2621

Business Information: Alabama River Pulp specializes in chopping and grinding wood pieces into pulp for sale to manufacturers internationally. As Director of Safety & Security, Ms. Brock is responsible for handling administrative duties, managing security, training of employees, supervising 2 illness centers, and measuring the density of pulp in tanks. **Career Steps:** Director of Safety & Security, Alabama River Pulp (1989–Present); Compliance Officer, OSHA (1971–1989); Technical Assistant, NASA, Kennedy Space (1967–1971). **Associations & Accomplishments:** American Society of Safety Engineers; American Management Association; Federal Business Womens Association; Local Emergency Planning Commission; American Meteorological Society; American Business Women of America; Board of Directors, Pulp & Paper Safety Association. **Education:** University of Mobile, B.S.; University of Southern Mississippi, A.A.; Shelton State Fire College – Haz Mat Technician. **Personal:** Ms. Brock enjoys outdoor sports, crafts, piano, flower gardening, and reading.

Wallace D. Cook

Location Training Manager
Champion International Corporation
11611 5th Street
Sheldon, TX 77044
(713) 456–6345
Fax: (713) 456–6508

2621

Business Information: Champion International Corporation manufactures and distributes pulp, paper, and wood products. Joining CIC in 1991, Mr. Cook currently has fourteen years experience in helping organizations improve their effectiveness through high quality technical and organizational development. He has orchestrated more than 45 projects, union and nonunion, performing all phases of industrial competency–based training (CBT) from program design, materials development, and implementation to project management, accounting, and client/vendor interface. As Location Training Manager at CIC since 1993, he is responsible for technical training systems for all employees, including design training and technical training support. **Career Steps:** Champion International Corporation: Location Training Manager – Houston, Texas (1993–Present), Project Training Manager – Canton, North Carolina (1991–1993); Fluor Daniel Corporation: Manager of Training (1983–1991), Project Task Team Leader (1986–1989), Training Specialist/Senior Training Specialist (1983–1986). **Associations & Accomplishments:** American Society for Training and Development; Community Tutor (1991–1993); Tutored Clemson University Athletes (1982–1983). **Education:** Clemson University: M.S. in Industrial Training and Development (1983), B.S. in Industrial

Education/Human Resource Development (1982). **Personal:** Married to Nanelle in 1986. Two children: Necia and Saxon. Mr. Cook enjoys collecting antiques, fishing, and horticulture.

Allen Harrelson
Director of Purchases
Gilman Paper Company
P.O. Box 878
St. Marys, GA 31558–0878
(912) 882–0310
Fax: (912) 882–5528

2621

Business Information: Gilman Paper Company is an international company specializing in paper manufacturing. The Company also operates five sawmills located in Georgia and Florida. As Director of Purchases, Mr. Harrelson is responsible for the purchase and handling of all materials excluding timber for the Saint Marys, GA location. Mr. Harrelson's plans for the next few years are to continue to provide quality service to his customers. **Career Steps:** Gilman Paper Company: Director of Purchases (1981–Present), Assistant Director of Purchases (1972–1981), Storeroom Manager, Converting Division (1962–1972). **Associations & Accomplishments:** President, Osprey Cove Homeowners Association; Chairman/Supervisor Committee, Gilman United Federal Credit Union; District Chairman, Boy Scouts of America–Osprey District; Past District Chairman/Finance Chairman, Osprey District; Founder/Current Chairman, Osprey Cove Golf Tournament; Superintendent, Westside Baptist Sunday School; American Cancer Society; Silver Beaver Award. **Education:** University of Georgia, Executive Development Program. **Personal:** Married to Mary in 1956. Four children: Dottie, Pamila, Melanie, and Jeffery. Mr. Harrelson enjoys golf, fishing, Boy Scout special events, and his 10 grandchildren.

John C. Johnson
Regional Woodlands Manager
Stone Container Corporation
P.O. Box 2565
Panama City, FL 32402–2565
(904) 769–2456
Fax: (904) 769–6818

2621

Business Information: Stone Container Corporation is a global packaging and paper company, manufacturing a multitude of paper products. Headquartered in Chicago, Illinois, Stone Container Corporation's southern woodlands group assists in the management of timberlands for companies and independent land owners. Joining Stone Container Corporation as Regional Woodlands Manager at the Panama City location in 1990, Mr. Johnson is responsible for maintaining wood fiber supply for markets in the area. Traveling extensively to Venezuela on behalf of the corporation, he also oversees all forestry operations for associates and staff. **Career Steps:** Stone Container Corporation: Woodsland Manager – Panama City, Florida (1990–Present), Regional Woodlands Manager – Jacksonville, Florida (1987–1990), Area Woodlands Manager – Hodge, Louisiana (1983–1987); District Forester, Williamette Industries, Inc. (1980–1983); Forester, Vancouver Plywood Inc. (1977–1980); Forest Technician, International Paper (1973–1974). **Associations & Accomplishments:** Florida Forestry Association; Society of American Foresters; Forest Farmers; Alabama Forestry Association; Georgia Forestry Association; Technical Association Pulp & Paper Industries; Bay County School Science Council; Lake City Community College Forest Advisory Board; Deacon, Cook Memorial Baptist Church. **Education:** Louisiana Technological University, B.S. (1977); Emory University, Executive Business Program. **Personal:** Married to Patti W. Johnson in 1978. Three children: Caleb, Katie, and Michael. Mr. Johnson enjoys church activities, spending time with his family, fishing, and golf.

F. J. Pitre
President and Co–Chief Executive Officer
Pine Falls Paper Company
P.O. Box 10
Pine Falls, Manitoba ROE 1MO
(204) 367–5203 (204) 367–5202
Fax: (204) 367–2442

2621

Business Information: Pine Falls Paper Company is an international manufacturer of newsprint paper. Clientele includes major newspaper publishers and commercial printers in the U.S. and Canada's mid–west. The Company is also responsible for the Town's operations which include schools, sports arena, curling clubs, and other facilities. Established in 1994, Pine Falls Paper Company reports annual revenue of $170 million and currently employs 475 people. With twenty–four years expertise in the pulp and paper industry and a Certified Professional Engineer, Mr. Pitre joined Pine Falls Paper Company in 1994. Serving as President and Co–Chief Executive Officer, he is responsible for all aspects of operations and management of the Company, including administration, finances, sales, public relations, accounting, and strategic planning. **Career Steps:** President and Co–Chief Executive Officer, Pine Falls Paper Company (1994–Present); Mill Manager, Abitibi–Price, Inc. (1981–1994); Newsprint Manager, Stora Forest Products (1971–1981). **Associations & Accomplishments:** Professional Engineers of Nova Scotia; Canadian Pulp and Paper Association. **Education:** Technical University of Nova Scotia, Electrical Engineer (1962); St. Francis Xavier Antigonish. **Personal:** Married to Gloria Jean in 1964. Two children: Rene and Andre.

Mr. George A. Pryor
Executive Vice President
Golden Kraft, Inc.
1151 North Tustin Avenue
Anaheim, CA 92807
(714) 632–7100
Fax: (714) 632–6808

2631

Business Information: Golden Kraft, Inc. specializes in the manufacture and regional distribution of corrugated sheet paper to corrugated sheets. At the present time, the Company distributes in Southern California. As Executive Vice President, Mr. Pryor oversees all sales and marketing functions for the Company, as well as serve as Secretary on the Board of Directors. Established in 1982, Golden Kraft, Inc. employs 61 people and has annual revenues in excess of $20 million. **Career Steps:** Executive Vice President, Golden Kraft, Inc. (1982–Present); Vice President and General Manager, Carpentar Offset (1978–1981); Vice President of Sales, Inland Container (1968–1978); Vice President of Sales, Pacific Kraft (1968). **Associations & Accomplishments:** Board of Directors, AICC Western Region. **Education:** Various sales schools.

Jim A. Szaroletta, Ph.D.
Engineering Manager
Menasha Corporation – Paperboard Division
320 North Farmer Street, P.O. Box 155
Otsego, MI 49078
(616) 692–6141
Fax: (616) 692–2060

2653

Business Information: Menasha Corporation – Paperboard Division is a manufacturer of corrugating medium paper for making boxes. Fifteen years of experience in manufacturing – thirteen of those years include management responsibility in both technical and production positions. Dr.Szaroletta joined Menasha Corporation – Paperboard Division as Engineering Manager in 1994. He is responsible for the direction of all engineering activities, including capital budget development and administration. He administers a yearly, non–expansion capital budget averaging $3.5 million, and spends approximately thirty percent of his time on business strategy development and inplementation. A strong advocate of teamwork and developing people, he enjoys giving people the authority to make decisions pertaining to their work. He has created several teams and understands how to make them successful. He is capable of conducting team and facilitator training and has experience in self–directed work teams. Career milestones include the management of organizations of over 100 employees and operating budgets exceeding $20 million; development of a positive working relationship by increasing the union's involvement in decision making – the union participated in the development of training programs and manufacturing vision; implemented Co-Op Engineering Programs; developed and facilitated conferences on leadership and maintenance; and implemented both Computer Maintenance Management Systems (CMMS) and Preventive/Predictive Maintenance Programs. Concurrently, he serves as an Adjunct Professor for LaSalle University and advises six students in their studies. **Career Steps:** Engineering Manager, Menasha Corporation – Paperboard Division (1994–Present); Adjunct Professor, LaSalle University (Present); Scott Paper Company – Foodservice Division: Foodservice Internal Consultant (1993–1994), Manager of Engineering and Technical Services (1991–1993); James River Corporation: Paper Manufacturing Superintendent (1989–1991), Superintendent of Mill Maintenance (1988–1989), Supervisor of Preventive Maintenance (1985–1988), Maintenance Engineer (1983–1985), Project Engineer (1981–1983). **Associations & Accomplishments:** TAPPI; PIMA; Registered Professional Engineer in Wisconsin and Maine; Avid reader of business–related books and periodicals. **Education:** LaSalle University, Ph.D. in Business Management (1994); Washington National University, M.S. in Engineering/Quality Control (1993); Cardinal Stritch College, M.S. in Management (1986); Michigan Technological University, B.S. in Civil Engineering (1981); Completed University of Wisconsin–Madison's Certificate Series in Quality; Attended several management–related conferences and is proficient in several areas, including problem solving, TQM, and team building skills; Completed ISO9000 Internal Auditor Training. **Personal:** Married to Susan in 1984. Two children: Kelsey and Steven. Dr. Szaroletta enjoys home improvement projects, personal fitness, cooking, and cycling.

James T. Temple
Production Manager
Willamette Industries
2900 N. Franklin Road
Indianapolis, IN 46219–1345
(317) 357–2900
Fax: (317) 356–4413

2653

Business Information: Willamette Industries is a leading manufacturer of corrugated shipping containers. With over 15 years in paper and container industry management, Mr. Temple provides the overall day–to–day supervision for the plant, ensuring quality product output, efficient production, as well as serves as liaison in all Union and employee relationships. **Career Steps:** Production Manager, Willamette Industries (1993–Present); Plant Manager, Weyerhaeuser Paper Company (1988–1993); Manufacturing Specialist and Plant Manager, Inland Container (1983–1988). **Associations & Accomplishments:** Technical Association of Pulp & Paper Industry; Optimist International Club. **Education:** American Graduate School of International Management, M.S. (1976); Boston University, B.A. (1974). **Personal:** Married to Rosemarie in 1973. Three children: Justin, Jaime and Jenna. An accomplished musician, he has performed with the New Hampshire Symphonic Orchestra and various bands as a percussionist.

Michael Berg
General Manager
Tetra Pak Inc.
333 West Wacker Drive
Chicago, IL 60606
(614) 785–1818
Fax: (614) 785–1826
EMAIL: See Below

2656

Business Information: Tetra Pak Inc. is the world's leading manufacturer of processing and packing systems utilized for liquid food applications. Privately–owned, customers from the world over range from large dairy operations to major consumer products conglomerates such as Procter & Gamble. A native of Sweden, Michael Berg has served in managerial capacities for Tetra Pak international divisions since 1988. Transferred to the United States in 1991 to serve at Tetra Pak Americas, he was promoted to his current position with Tetra Pak, Inc. in 1994. As General Manager, Mr. Berg oversees regional operations based from the Columbus, Ohio office for the Tetra Pak Group in all U.S. market sectors. Internet users can reach him via: michael.berg@tetrapak.com **Career Steps:** Tetra Pak Inc., General Manager (1994–Present), Marketing Manager, (1992–194); Operations Manager, Tetra Pak Americas (1991–1992); Marketing Services Manager, Tetra Pak International (1988–1991). **Education:** Stockholm School of Economics, M.B.A. (1988); Fluent in English, Swedish and French. **Personal:** Married to Ylva in 1992. Mr. Berg enjoys Scuba diving, skiing, trecking and travel.

Kim Boehm
Commercial Systems Integrator
James River Corporation
451 Harbison Road
Lexington, KY 40511–1059
(606) 259–9107
Fax: (606) 259–9107
EMAIL: See Below

2656

Business Information: James River Corporation is an international manufacturer of paper and plastic cups, food wraps and cartons. Established in 1928, the Company presently employs 10,000 people at 63 locations. As Commercial Systems Integrator, Miss Boehm is responsible for the administration and maintenance of all business computer systems, specifically payroll and financial aspects. Internet users can reach her via: 72652.737@COMPUSERVE.COM **Career Steps:** Commercial Systems Intergrator, James River Corporation (1992–Present); Financial Systems Auditor, Ames Rubber Corporation (1987–1992); Business Systems Programmer/Analyst, Chosen People Ministries (1984–1987). **Associations & Accomplishments:** National Safety Council; Worker and Leader, Youth Ministries; Interex; Vice Chairperson of the Board of Directors, KTNRUG; SIGRUG. **Education:** University of Kentucky, M.S. (1996); Rutgers University, B.S. in Computer Science. **Personal:** Miss Boehm enjoys woodworking, sports, gardening and photography.

Craig A. Erisman
Audit and Finance Manager
Mod–Pac Corporation
1801 Elmwood Avenue
Buffalo, NY 14207–2409
(716) 873–0640
Fax: (716) 873–6008

2656

Business Information: Established in 1886, Mod–Pac Corporation is a manufacturer of folding cartons. As Audit and Finance Manager, Mr. Erisman is responsible for division finances, auditing, telecommunications, systems development, and is the lead ISO 9000 auditor. **Career Steps:** Audit and Finance Manager, Mod–Pac Corporation (1989–Present); Cost Accounting Manager, Trico Products Corporation (1983–1989); Staff Accountant, Marrano Homes (1982–1983). **Associations & Accomplishments:** Technical Association of the Pulp & Paper Industry. **Education:** State University of New York at Buffalo, B.S. in Business Administration (1984). **Personal:** Married to Robin Jean in 1987. Two children: Caitlyn Renee and Nicole Taylor. Mr. Erisman enjoys golf, bowling and travel.

Derrick R. Strand
Audit Manager
Rexam
4201 Congress Street
Charlotte, NC 28209
(704) 551–1559
Fax: (704) 551–1574

2671

Business Information: Rexam is a manufacturer of packaging and laminated and coated products (i.e., boxes for medicine, glass cleaner bottles, potato chip bags). As Audit Manager, Mr. Strand manages the operational reviews, internal audits of the business, coordinates special projects, and does consulting work. **Career Steps:** Audit Manager, Rexam (1994–Present); Senior Auditor, International Paper Company (1994–1995); Senior Auditor, KPMG Peat Marwick (1990–1992). **Associations & Accomplishments:** American Institute of Certified Public Accountants. **Education:** Northern Illinois University, B.S. (1990); Certified Public Accountant (1990). **Personal:** Married to Laura P. in 1995. Mr. Strand enjoys golf, tennis, and volleyball.

Eugene R. Sylva
President
Dimensional Merchandising, Inc.
86 N. Main St.
Wharton, NJ 07885–1607
(201) 328–1600
Fax: Please mail or call

2671

Business Information: Dimensional Merchandising, Inc. is a pharmaceutical and consumer products packaging manufacturer. Major industries served include: Procter & Gamble, Johnson & Johnson, CoverGirl Cosmetics, L'Oreal, Avon, Estee Lauder and Seagrams Beverage Co. As President, Eugene Sylva provides the overall vision and strategies, ensuring product quality output, customer satisfaction and development. **Career Steps:** President, Dimensional Merchandising, Inc. (Present). **Associations & Accomplishments:** Institute of Packaging Professionals; Association of Plastics Engineers; Charter Member, Contract Packaging Association; Board of Trustees, Tri–County Schools; Board, American College of Belgium. **Personal:** Mr. Sylva enjoys spending time with his grandson.

Jeff Semple
President and Chief Executive Officer
Paraco Inc.
1502 12th Street, SW
Canton, OH 44706–1586
(216) 452–4600
Fax: (216) 452–4620

2672

Business Information: Paraco Inc. is a manufacturer and international distributor of coated paper products. As President and Chief Executive Officer, Mr. Semple is responsible for the overall vision and strategies, ensuring quality product output, customer service, and the overall development to keep the Company viable in international and national regions. Concurrent with his duties at Paraco Inc., Mr. Semple also serves as President of Sempec Systems Inc., a flexible packaging manufacturer. **Career Steps:** President and Chief Executive Officer, Paraco Inc. (1989–Present); President and Chief Executive Officer, Sempec Systems Inc. (1987–Present); Sales Representative, Central Coated Products (1985–1987). **Education:** Mount Union College, B.A. (1985). **Personal:** Married to Angela in 1987. Three children: Taylor, Jordan, and Spencer. Mr. Semple enjoys golf and flying.

Edgard R. Rodriguez

President and Owner
Taino Paper Company Inc.
P. O. Box 1047
Bayamon, Puerto Rico 00960–1047
(809) 785–2862
Fax: (809) 740–4080

2674

Business Information: Taino Paper Company Inc. specializes in the manufacture of paper bags, as well as importing plastic bags. The Corporation operates a converting plant and packages its own products. Established in 1984, Taino Paper Company currently employs 40 people and has an estimated annual revenue of $6 million. As President and Owner, Mr. Rodriguez provides the overall direction and vision for the company's continued growth, quality product delivery to customers and strategic development. **Career Steps:** President and Owner, Taino Paper Company Inc. (1984–Present); General Manager, Champion International Corporation (1979–1984); Sales Manager, Pepsi Cola Bottling Company (1974–1979). **Associations & Accomplishments:** Industrial Association of Puerto Rico; Puerto Rico Wholesales Chamber of Commerce. **Education:** World University of Puerto Rico, M.B.A. (1979). **Personal:** Married to Nilda in 1968. Two children: Marisel and Enid. Mr. Rodriguez enjoys tennis and reading.

Dorothy L. Wingert
Department Manager
Stone Container Corporation
610 Third Street
Jonesboro, LA 71251–3317
(318) 259–5411
Fax: (318) 259–5471

2674

Business Information: Stone Container Corporation is a manufacturer of paper grocery store bags and a merchandiser of handle grocery sacks. Joining Stone Container as a Bag Catcher in 1970, Dorothy moved to a Collator Operator in 1974, then to a Clerk in 1980. Supervisor in 1984, she was a Department Manager over the Grocery Department. Then in 1994, she was promoted to Department Manager in Grocer, Sack Line, Hand Sack, Merchandise Line, Bag Finishing, and Paper Finishing the Counter Roll Department. Dorothy Wingert has steadily moved up the corporate ladder, achieving her current position as Department Manager over six departments and ten team leaders. **Career Steps:** Stone Container Corporation: Department Manager (1994–Present), Department Manager – Grocery (1992–1994); Supervisor – Grocery (1988–1992); Department Clerk (1980–1988). **Associations & Accomplishments:** North Hodge Assembly of God Church **Education:** Management Seminar, Dale Caregie Courses; Alabama State Management. **Personal:** Married to John Darrell in 1992. Two children: Michelle and Angie. Three grandchildren: Tiffany, Breanne and Brandon. Ms. Wingert enjoys gospel singing, bowling, and swimming.

Richard Arriaga
Sales Representative
Kimberly Clark
P.O. Box 191859
San Juan, Puerto Rico 00919–1859
(809) 785–3625
Fax: (809) 269–0620

2676

Business Information: Kimberly Clark, a Fortune 100 company, is a leading manufacturer of personal care, consumer tissue, and away from home products. The company's well known products include Huggies, Pull–ups, Good Nites, Kotex, New Freedom, Poise, Depend, Kleenex, Scott Cottonelle, Viva and Job Squad. As Sales Representative, Mr. Arriaga is responsible for negotiating special offers, truckload sales, baby week, and sales by volume. In addition, he is responsible for all major Caribbean accounts with the Company, including Toys "R" Us. **Career Steps:** Kimberly Clark: Key Account (1994–Present), Sales Representative (1992–1994), Merchandiser (1989–1992). **Associations & Accomplishments:** Puerto Rico Tennis Association. **Education:** InterAmerican University **Personal:** Married to Wendy Perry in 1990. Two children: Nicole and Ricardo. Mr. Arriaga enjoys tennis, bicycling, and listening to music.

Philip A. Senn
Plant Manager
Kimberly Clark
2010 N. Rulon White Boulevard
Ogden, UT 84404
(801) 786–2203
Fax: (801) 786–2204

2676

Business Information: Kimberly Clark, a Fortune 100 company, is a leading manufacturer of personal care, consumer tissue, and away from home products. The company's well known products include Huggies, Pull–ups, Good Nites, Kotex, New Freedom, Poise, Depend, Kleenex, Scott Cottonelle, Viva and Job Squad. A management executive with Kimberly Clark since 1987, Mr. Senn was appointed Plant Manager of the Ogden disposable diapers facility in 1992. He provides the overall direction and strategies for the facility. **Career Steps:** Kimberly Clark: Plant Manager (1992–Present), Director of Operations (1990–1992), Operations Manager (1987–1990). **Associations & Accomplishments:** Board Member, United Way of Northern Utah; Board Member, Ogden Applied Technology Center; Chairman of the Board, Ogden Regional Medical Center. **Education:** University of South Carolina, B.S.in Civil Engineering (1976). **Personal:** Married to Karen in 1976. Two children: Danielle and Patrick. Mr. Senn enjoys snow skiing, water skiing, golf, and spending time with his family in various activities.

Kurt E. Braun
General Manager
Niagara Envelope Company
14101 East 3rd Place, Suite A
Aurora, CO 80011–1613
(303) 373–1780
Fax: (303) 745–0129

2677

Business Information: Niagara Envelope Company, a national privately–held company, is the third largest wholesale manufacturer of envelopes in the United States. Mr. Braun served Niagara Envelope as Controller from 1981 to 1989, moving into his present position as General Manager in 1989. He is responsible for overseeing all operations from sales to manufacturing and production for the Denver facility and Seattle warehouse, supervising approximately 90 employees. **Career Steps:** Niagara Envelope Company: General Manager (1989–Present), Controller (1981–1989). **Associations & Accomplishments:** Treasurer, Local SD 14 Credit Union; President, High School Booster Club. **Education:** Fort Hays State College, B.S. (1977). **Personal:** Married to Cynthia in 1978. Two children: Amber and Jeremiah. Mr. Braun enjoys golf.

John R. Foote
National Sales Manager
Southworth Company
P.O. Box 5006
West Springfield, MA 01090–5006
(413) 732–5141
Fax: (413) 732–7118

2678

Business Information: Southworth Company, a privately–held corporation, is a manufacturer of fine paper products and dated goods (calendars) to the office products industry. Products are distributed to retailers, wholesalers, and mass markets. With more than twelve years of experience in sales, Mr. Foote joined Southworth Company as District Sales Manager in 1984. Appointed as National Sales Manager in 1994, he is responsible for the direction of the sales efforts of the Office Products Division and the distribution of products to office supply retailers and wholesalers. **Career Steps:** Southworth Company: National Sales Manager (1994–Present), District Sales Manager (1984–1994); Principal, Knot House Industries (1980–1984). **Associations & Accomplishments:** B.P.I.A.; Beta Sigma Psi National Social Fraternity. **Education:** University of Illinois, B.S. (1972). **Personal:** Married to Susan in 1970. Two children: Brian and Maggie.

Tricia Fitz Gerald Hammer
Director of Marketing
Miami Systems Corporation
10150 Alliance Road
Cincinnati, OH 45242
(513) 793–0110
Fax: (513) 793–1140

2678

Business Information: Miami Systems is a manufacturer of business forms, envelopes, paper roll products, business forms and envelopes for computer software, and variably–imaged direct mail application products. National in scope, Miami Systems has seven plants, and thirty–five office locations, primarily east of the Mississippi. Established in 1926, Miami Systems Corporation reports annual revenue of $130 million, and currently employs 1,100 people. With twenty–two years expertise in the corporate sales industry, Ms. Hammer joined Miami Systems Corporation in 1994. Serving as Director of Marketing, she is responsible for the areas of advertising, public relations, trade show coordination, development of sales literature and videos, and the training of about 120 account executives in sales and sales management skills. She also writes articles for the Corporate monthly newsletter, and Corporate marketing bulletins on sales and marketing strategies. **Career Steps:** Director of Marketing, Miami Systems Corporation (1994–Present); Manager of Training, Bank One, Dayton, N.A. (1987–1994); Manager of Sales Training, Mead Data Central (1983–1987); Sales Training and Sales Development Representative, 3M Co. – Audio Visual Division (1978–1983); National Account Sales Representative, 3M Dealer – Dayton, OH/J.M. Woodhull Inc. (1973–1978). **Associations & Accomplishments:** Junior League of Dayton (1971–1978); Junior League of Minneapolis (1978–1982); American Marketing Association Cincinnati Chapter; American Society of Training and Development: Dayton Chapter, Cincinnati Chapter; U.S. Dressage Federation; American Horse Shows Association; Other Regional & Local Equestrian Associations; Volunteer assistant for the U.S. Team Veterinarians for the 1996 Olympic Equestrian Events; Volunteer for many International Equestrian Events since 1978. **Education:** Sweet Briar College, B.A. (1971). **Personal:** Ms. Hammer enjoys equestrian events (riding, judging, and coaching others), golf, tennis, water skiing, and snow skiing. She also enjoys reading, art history, and classical music.

Antonio Carlos Assumpcao Neto

Finance Director
Dixie Toga South America
Avenue Guido Caloi, 864–Socorro
Sao Paulo, Brazil SP 05802–1
011–55–150314
Fax: 011–55–150361

2679

Business Information: Dixie Toga South America is an international corporation that manufactures flexible and rigid packaging. The product is used by Colgate, Nestle, Unilever and other Brazilian companies. Dixie Toga is a joint venture between C.T.M, a Swiss partnership, and B.M.T. a Brazilian company. As Finance Director, Mr. Assumpcao Neto handles the accounting information systems and is in charge of approximately 70 employees. Mr. Assumpcao Neto's long range plans are to increase the number of joint ventures, increase packaging segments, and develop new technology in the packaging field. **Career Steps:** Dixie Toga South America: Finance Director (1992–Present), Financial Manager (1985–1991), Economic Planning Manager (1980–1984). **Education:** Fudacao Setillo Vangas, Bachelor (1972); Stanford School of Business, Financial Planning Program . **Personal:** Married to Cristina in 1980. Two children: Guillerme and Patricia. Mr. Assumpcao Neto enjoys tennis.

Gregg Krause
Vice President of Sales and Marketing
Central Fiber Corporation
4814 Fiber Lane
Wellsville, KS 66092
(913) 883–4600
Fax: (913) 883–4429

2679

Business Information: Central Fiber Corporation is a manufacturer of products from old newspaper, magazines, and kraft paper. The Corporation creates new products out of old newspapers and has recently developed a landfill cover to be used daily instead of soil. Established in 1983, Central Fiber Corporation reports annual revenue of $8.5 million and currently employs 65 people. With ten years experience in sales and marketing, Mr. Krause joined Central Fiber Corporation in 1991. Serving as Vice President, he is responsible for the sales and marketing activities of environmental products. **Career Steps:** Vice President of Sales and Marketing, Central Fiber Corporation (1991–Present); National Accounts Representative, Farmland Industries (1989–1991); Sales Representative, Rich–Mix Prod. (1985–1989). **Associations & Accomplishments:** Friends of the Zoo; Friends of the Arts; Kansas City Jazz Society; IECA; Kansas Turf Grass Association; Kansas University Alumni Association; HHS Alumni Association. **Education:** University of Kansas, B.S. in Business (1976). **Personal:** One child: Heather. Mr. Krause enjoys golf, and amateur computer programming.

Jose R. Rivera–Casanova
Account Executive
Perfecseal Internacional de Puerto Rico, Inc.
P.O. Box 4851
Carolina, Puerto Rico 00984–4851
(809) 750–8060
Fax: (809) 750–8290

2679

Business Information: Perfecseal Internacional de Puerto Rico, Inc. specializes in the production of medical and pharmaceutical packaging products. Specially–sanitized product lines include: pouches, bags, lids, computer paper and thermal transfer labels. Perfecseal serves clientele throughout Chile, Mexico, Brazil, and Japan. As Account Executive, Mr. Rivera–Casanova coordinates all graphics–related steps, including sales and marketing and new customers. **Career Steps:** Account Executive, Perfecseal Internacional de Puerto Rico, Inc. (1992–Present); Graphics Coordinator, Romallo, Escribano and Engraph (1986–1992); Negative Stripper, Romallo Brothers (1986). **Associations & Accomplishments:** Puerto Rico Sports Officials Association. **Education:** Politechnico College, Draftman (1982). **Personal:** Married to Blanca Cueves in 1993. Mr. Rivera–Casanova enjoys cycling, basketball and computers.

2700 Printing and Publishing

2711 Newspapers
2721 Periodicals
2731 Book publishing
2732 Book printing
2741 Miscellaneous publishing
2752 Commercial printing, lithographic
2754 Commercial printing, gravure
2759 Commercial printing, NEC
2761 Manifold business forms
2771 Greeting cards
2782 Blankbooks and looseleaf binders
2789 Book Binding and related work
2791 Typesetting
2796 Platemaking services

Kevin G. O'Neill

President
Image Axis, Inc.
38 West 21st Street
New York, NY 10010–6906
(212) 989–5000
Fax: (212) 989–1669
EMAIL: See Below

2700

Business Information: Image Axis, Inc. is a magazine and advertising prepress facility, working with Top 10 advertising agencies and magazine publishers in the United States. The Company produces transparencies, color separations, and digitally retouched images. A Co–Founder in 1993, Mr. O'Neill serves as President and Chairman, overseeing corporate expansion, product development, and strategic marketing. Internet users can reach him via: kgo@imageaxis.com. **Career Steps:** President, Image Axis, Inc. (1993–Present); Director, Duggal Color Projects (1987–1992); Manager, H.Y. Photo Service (1985–1987); Assistant Manager, Spectratone Photo Lab (1984–1985). **Associations & Accomplishments:** National Association of Printers and Lithographers; Technology Transfer Society. **Education:** State University of New York; Tulane University. **Personal:** Married to Deborah Cothren O'Neill in 1985. Two children: Alison and Kathleen. Mr. O'Neill enjoys physics, sailing, photography, and the Internet and World Wide Web.

Brian M. Barker
Distribution Manager
Thomson Newspapers, d.b.a. Marion Star
150 Court Street
Marion, OH 43301–1816
(614) 387–5529
Fax: (614) 382–2210
EMAIL: MCI–ID#208–6695

2711

Business Information: Thomson Newspapers, d.b.a. Marion Star is a local newspaper publisher in Marion, Ohio. The paper boasts distribution to approximately 16,500 subscribers. As Distribution Manager, Mr. Barker manages the day–to–day operation of the newspaper, is responsible for the carriers, and ensures timely distribution. **Career Steps:** Distribution Manager, Thomson Newspapers DBA/Marion Star (1996–Present); Distribution Manager, Coshocton Tribune Newspaper (1995–1996); Circulation Manager, Times Recorder Newspaper (1990–1995). **Associations & Accomplishments:** Board Member, United Commercial Travelers; President, Thursday Night Golf League. **Personal:** Married to Cammie in 1990. Two children: Austin Barker and Anissa Larimer. Mr. Barker enjoys softball, golf, and basketball.

Mr. J.W. Andre Bustamante
President
Call and Post
1949 East 105
Cleveland, OH 44106
(216) 791–7600
Fax: (216) 791–6568

2711

Business Information: Call and Post is a weekly newspaper publishing operation, serving the cities of Cleveland, Columbus, Cincinnati, Akron, and Youngstown, Ohio. As President, Mr. Bustamante provides the administration and oversight for overall operations of the Company. Established in 1919, Call and Post employs 55 people and has $3 million in gross annual circulation revenue. **Career Steps:** President, Call and Post (1987–Present); Vice President, Bustamante, Williams, Richard & Smith (1987–Present); Vice President, Bottom Line Productions (1987–Present); Executive Assistant to Chairman, First Bank NA (1987). **Associations & Accomplishments:** Life Member, Presidential Trust; Granville School; Member, NRA; Member, NAACP; University Circle, Inc.; Board of Directors, S.C.L.C.; Republican National Committee; Published in various trade journals. **Education:** Boston University, B.A. (1985).

Maria E. G. Chase
Vice President of Finance
Fox Valley Press, Inc.
P.O. Box 129, 3101 Route 30
Plainfield, IL 60544
(815) 439–5338
Fax: (815) 439–5370

2711

Business Information: Fox Valley Press, Inc. is a newspaper group that publishes four daily and two weekly papers with a circulation of 170,000. The Company is a subsidiary of The Copley Press, Inc. in La Jolla, CA. As Vice President of Finance, Ms. Chase is responsible for directing all financial operations of the Company. **Career Steps:** Fox Valley Press, Inc.: Vice President of Finance (1996–Present), Controller (1994–1996); Audit Senior Manager, Ernst & Young (1979–1994). **Associations & Accomplishments:** American Institute of Certified Public Accountants; Illinois Society of Certified Public Accountants; International Newspaper Financial Executives; National Association of Female Executives. **Education:** Manchester College, B.S. (1979). **Personal:** Married to Mark C. in 1991. Ms. Chase enjoys personal fitness, tennis, and sports.

Nina J. Howard
Advertising Director
Turley Publications
24 Water Street
Palmer, MA 01069–1840
(413) 283–8393
Fax: (413) 289–1977

2711

Business Information: Turley Publications is a family–owned printing and publishing company, producing seven weekly newspapers and one monthly newspaper from four offices. Established in 1962, Turley Publications currently employs 200 people. As Advertising Director, Ms. Howard is responsible for the oversight of all aspects of advertising, including sales, marketing, and administration. **Career Steps:** Advertising Director, Turley Publications (1992–Present); Sales Manager, Bagdon Advertising (1989–1992). **Associations & Accomplishments:** Palmer Downtown Partnership, Inc. (PDP); Board of Directors, Charter Member – Vice President (1993–1994). **Education:** Fisher Junior College, Attends Business Management, Advertising, and Sales Continuing Education courses. **Personal:** Ms. Howard enjoys travel, skiing, reading, and camping.

Carol J. Latham
Owner and Publisher
Montanian Newspaper
P.O. Box 946
Libby, MT 59923–0946
(406) 293–8202
Fax: (406) 293–8202

2711

Business Information: A free, local, weekly newspaper serving Libby, Montana, the Montanian Newspaper is a full–service news release publishing local, state, national and world news, editorials, commentary, classified ads and a cable TV guide. The cost of producing each paper is paid for by all advertising incomes. Owner and Publisher, Carol Latham, performs/oversees all administrative duties in the management of the business and office. Her responsibilities include: personnel administration and benefits, bookkeeping, preparation of subscriber maillist and advertising call list each week, as well as assisting in the distribution of the newspaper. She and her husband, David (serves as Editor), create advertising promotions and sell advertising. **Career Steps:** Owner and Publisher, Montanian Newspaper (1989–Present); Park Ranger and Tour Guide – Libby Dam, U.S. Army Corps of Engineers (1984–1988); Broadcaster and Part Owner, AM Radio Station, Lone Pine, CA (1903–1904); Copywriter and Receptionist, KLCB Radio, Libby, MT (1977–1982). **Associations & Accomplishments:** Libby Chamber of Commerce; Troy Chamber of Commerce; Montana Newspaper Association; Volunteer and professional performer of Vaudeville theatre, Old–Time, and Irish music programs in California, Idaho, and Northwest Montana; Member of Irish Band "Shaughnessy Hill." **Personal:** Married to David in 1982. Three children: Sky Trudo, Kelda Gibbs, and Dolli Baker. Ms. Latham enjoys creating era and ethnic costumes, walking, and entertaining.

Sheri Lynn Lumsden
Personnel Administrator
Durham Herald Company
P.O. Box 2092
Durham, NC 27702
(919) 419–6535
Fax: (919) 419–6895
EMail: See Below

2711

Business Information: Established in 1884, Durham Herald Company is a daily newspaper publishing operation serving individuals and businesses in the Durham, North Carolina area. As Personnel Administrator, Sheri Lynn Lumsden provides the overall administrative direction for Human Resources areas. Her primary responsibilities include: maintenance of all personnel database files, research and development of all reports pertaining to affirmative action, personnel training, and other human resources activities, as well as giving lectures on human resources topics. In addition, Ms. Lumsden serves as the Information Systems Specialist and 401K Specialist. Internet users can reach her via: SLL@HeraldSun.com **Career Steps:** Personnel Administrator, Durham Herald Company (1993–Present); Staffing Coordinator, Monarch Healthcare (1993); Secretary to the President, Monarch Temporary Services (1992–1993). **Associations & Accomplishments:** Triangle Society of Human Resource Management; Alpha Kappa Alpha Sorority, Inc.; Girl Scouts of America – Pines of Carolina Division. **Education:** University of Akron, M.P.A. (1991); North Carolina Central University, B.A. in Public Administration. **Personal:** Ms. Lumsden enjoys going to plays, taking nature walks, movies, and travel.

Barry W. Lyons, CPA
Controller
Concord Monitor
One Monitor Drive
Concord, NH 03302–1177
(603) 224–5301
Fax: Please mail or call

2711

Business Information: Concord Monitor is a newspaper publisher for daily distribution to the Concord, New Hampshire locale. Established in 1900, Concord Monitor currently employs 150 people. A Certified Public Accountant, Mr. Lyons joined The Concord Monitor in 1995. Serving as Controller, he is responsible for all aspects of financial reporting and control as well as various administrative functions. Specific responsibilities include maintaining financial policies and procedures, creation of short and long range operating plans and analysis of operating results and trends. **Career Steps:** Controller, Concord Monitor (1995–Present); Certified Public Accountant, Ernst & Young (1993–1995); Certified Public Accountant, Robert Ercolini & Company (1987–1993); Senior Financial Analyst, Raytheon Company (1984–1987). **Associations & Accomplishments:** American Institute of Certified Public Accountants. **Education:** Boston College, B.S. (1984). **Personal:** Married to Lee Anne in 1988. Two children: Sean and Connor. Mr. Lyons enjoys softball, ice hockey, and chess.

Donna M. Odeen
Agriculture and Feature Reporter
T.R.G.
318 North Main Street
Loyal, WI 54446
(715) 255–8531
Fax: (715) 255–8357

2711

Business Information: T.R.G. is a local Wisconsin newspaper publisher. Having a degree in Agricultural Communications, Donna Odeen serves as the Editor for agricultural interest and feature synopsis report articles. A dedicated community leader, she also served for the past nine years as President of the Wisconsin Jaycees, in addition to extensive sponsorship with local 4–H organizations and other agriculturally–related co–ops. **Career Steps:** Editor – Agriculture and Features, T.R.G. (1991–Present). **Associations & Accomplishments:** President, Wisconsin Jaycees; River Fall Agriculture Alumni Board; 4H Leader; SFA Alumni; Preschool Board. **Education:** University of Wisconsin, Agriculture Communication (1983). **Personal:** Ms. Odeen enjoys spending time with husband and children, crafts, and reading.

Mr. Vicente Pierantoni

President
Periodico El Oriental
Calle Cruz Ortiz Stella #36
Humacao, Puerto Rico 00791
(809) 850–4500
Fax: (809) 852–3405

2711

Business Information: Periodico El Oriental, the third largest paper in Puerto Rico, is a newspaper publisher and distributor, distributed weekly and averaginig 64–72 pages per paper with a circulation of 45,000. Established in 1978, Periodico El Oriental reports annual revenue of $3 million and currently employs 31 people. As President, Mr. Pierantoni is responsible for all aspects of operations and business moves. Concurrent with his position at Periodico El Oriental, he serves as President at Periodico El Opinion (the fourth largest paper in the area, circulation of 15,000) and is the owner of 25% of the printing company stock where his paper is printed. **Career Steps:** President, Periodico El Oriental (1978–Present); President, Periodico El Opinion (1986–Present); Jefe De Circulacion, Periodico El Mundo (1963–1975). **Associations & Accomplishments:** Past President, Lions Club of Apolo Clementina, Guaynabo; Member, Foundation of Culture and Arts of Humacao; Member, Industrial Association of Puerto Rico; Treasurer, Comite Pro Bicentenario Humacao; President, Association of Regular Newspapers of Puerto Rico. **Education:** Catholic University of Puerto Rico, Commercial Administration (1957). **Personal:** Married to Irma de la Torre. Four children: Dr. Vicente, Dr. Miguel A., LCDA. Magda T., and Juan Pierantoni.

Mr. Micheal D. Price
Vice President and Chief Information Officer
Fort Worth Star–Telegram
400 West 7th Street
Ft. Worth, TX 76102
(817) 390–7466
Fax: (817) 390–7270

2711

Business Information: Fort Worth Star–Telegram is a newspaper publishing company, serving the Fort Worth, Texas population. The Star–Telegram has a daily circulation of 250,000 and a Sunday circulation of 350,000. As Vice President, Mr. Price is responsible for the direction and oversight for the departments of Information Services, Technology, and Development. Established in 1906, Fort Worth Star–Telegram employs 1,500 persons. **Career Steps:** Vice President and Chief Information Officer, Fort Worth Star –Telegram (July 1994–Present); Vice President of Operations, Fort Worth Star–Telegram (1993–1994); Pre–Press and Packaging Manager, Fort Worth Star–Telegram (1990–1993). **Associations & Accomplishments:** Fort Worth Chamber of Commerce; South Area Council, Chamber of Commerce; Small Business Solutions Center (Chamber Business Development Group); Executive Board, Board of Managers, East Side YMCA; Leadership Fort Worth. **Education:** Texas Christian University (1975–1979); Howard Payne University; University Texas–Permian Basin; Odessa High School.

Mrs. Beth S. Roddy
Vice President
Harte–Hanks Community Newspaper
801 East Plano Parkway, Suite 100
Plano, TX 75074
(214) 424–6565
Fax: (214) 578–0379

2711

Business Information: Harte–Hanks Community Newspaper is the local publication issued at regular intervals, usually daily or weekly, containing news, comment, features and advertising for the citizens of Plano and surrounding area. Under new ownership since 1984, the Paper currently employs 250 staff members. As Vice President, Mrs. Roddy is responsible for all aspects of adverstising revenue and marketing. **Career Steps:** Harte–Hanks Community Newspaper: Vice President (1995–Present), Advertising Director (1992–1995); Director of Sales, Center Concepts (1990–1992); General Manager, Suburban Publications (1987–1990); Advertising Sales Manager, Dallas Times Herald (1980–1987). **Associations & Accomplishments:** Chamber of Commerce. **Education:** University of Texas – Austin, B.S. in Marketing (1977). **Personal:** Married to Joe in 1981. One child: Allison. Mrs. Roddy enjoys reading and staying involved in community activities.

Caroline S. Sigmon
Marketing Director
Item Osteen Publishing Co., d.b.a. "The Item"
PO Box 1677
Sumter, SC 29151–1677
(803) 775–6331
Fax: (803) 775–1024

2711

Business Information: Item Osteen Publishing Co., d.b.a. "The Item" is a newspaper publishing company. Starting with "The Item" in sales in 1972, Ms. Sigmon was appointed as Marketing Director in 1991. She is responsible for all aspects of operations and management of internal and external marketing activities. **Career Steps:** Item Osteen Publishing Co., d.b.a. "The Item" : Marketing Director (1991–Present); Retail Advertising Manager (1986–1991); Assistant Retail Advertising Manager (1984–1986) **Associations & Accomplishments:** The Greater Sumter Chamber of Commerce; The Form (women's organization); Chair, OctoberFest Southern Style (local Sumter, SC festival); YWCA **Personal:** Married to Harold A. in 1991. Two children: Michael and Theodore Baird.

Thomas M. Stith
Vice President of Distribution
Thomson Newspapers, Inc.
240 Franklin Street SE
Warren, OH 44482–1431
(216) 629–6220
Fax: (216) 841–1721
EMAIL: See Below

2711

Business Information: Tribune Chronical is one of Ohio's leading daily newspaper publishers. A wholly–owned entity of the Thomson Newspaper Group, it has been serving the Warren, Ohio and surrounding counties for 125 years. Working in various roles for Ohio–based newspaper publishers for over ten years, Thomas Stith serves as Vice President of Distribution. He has full responsibility for all distribution efforts covering a six county area. Internet users can reach him via: LEMIEUX180.AOL.COM **Career Steps:** Vice President of Distribution, Thomson Newspapers (1996–Present); Tribune Chronicle: Circulation Director (1990–1995), Circulation Manager (1980–1986); Home Delivery Manager, Youngstown Vindicator (1989–1990); Circulation Manager, Gannett Westchester Newspapers (1986–1988); Circulation Manager, Carlisle Evening Sentinel (1978–1980); District Manager, Ithica Journal (1975–1978). **Associations & Accomplishments:** Sustaining Member, Past Board Member, Ohio Circulation Manager Association; Member, National Newspaper Association; Past President, Secretary, Vice President and Chairman of the Board, Cortland Rotary Club; Rotarian of the Year (1993); Director, Coach, Youngstown Youth Hockey Association; Director, Coach, Lakeview Soccer Association; President, Treasurer, Secretary, Conservation League Inc.; Master Instructor, National Bowhunter Education Foundation; Life Member, North American Hunting Club; Member, National Wild Turkey Federation. **Education:** Lewis Hotel Management School (1973). **Personal:** Married to Mary in 1974. Three children: Karen, Stephanie and Michael. Mr. Stith enjoys all outdoor sports.

Rufus N. Watkins

Editorial Assistant and Senior Copy Clerk
San Francisco Chronicle
2060 O'Farrell Street, #102
San Francisco, CA 94115
(415) 777–7150
Fax: (415) 512–8196

2711

Business Information: The San Francisco Chronicle, in operation since 1865, is one of the Bay Area's daily news publications. As Editorial Assistant and Senior Copy Clerk, Mr. Watkins is responsible for the oversight of content material and information for the publication and printing of the newspaper. **Career Steps:** Editorial Assistant and Senior Copy Clerk, San Francisco Chronicle (1988–Present); San Francisco Junior Chamber of Commerce: Chairman (1991–1994), President (1993–1993). **Associations & Accomplishments:** San Francisco Junior Chamber of Commerce: Chairman of the Board (1991–1994), President (1993–1994), Vice President of Membership (1990–1991), Director of Public Relations (1989 – 1990), Member (Since 1989); Board of Directors, Midtown Park Apartments; Nob Hill Toastmasters: President, Pacific Heights Chapter (1993–1994), Vice President of Membership Development (1993–1994), Treasurer (1993–1994), Secretary (1994), Member (1991–1994), Co–Membership Vice Chair, World Affairs Council of Northern California International Forum (1994–1995); World Affairs Council International Forum: Public Relations Subcommittee, Member of Technology Subcommittee, Logistics Subcommittee, Social Subcommittee, Business and Careers Subcommittee, Donations Subcommittee, Political Subcommittee, Community Service Subcommittee, Arts and Culture Subcommittee; Vice Chair (1994–Present); Commonwealth Club of California; International Platform Association; Saint Ignatious College Prep Alumni Association; Saint Dominic's School Alumni Association; Board of Directors, San Francisco Community Action Network; Party Smart Association; San Francisco Chamber of Commerce; San Francisco Chamber of Commerce Diplomate Corps; Mayor Frank Jordan Transition Team; Mayor Frank Jordan Housing and Economics Development; Citizens Committee on Community Development Advisory Board; Mayor Frank Jordan Community Budget Forum Panel; Election Panel, Robert F. Kennedy Business Democratic Club; Citizens Committee on Community Development; SPECIAL HONORS: Competent Toastmaster Award (1994); California State Junior Chamber of Commerce Presidental Award for Outstanding Performance (1992–1993); Scholar of the Year, San Francisco Police Athletic League (1977); Member of the Month, San Francisco Junior Chamber of Commerce (1989); Top Ten Young San Franciscan Nominee, San Francisco Junior Chamber of Commerce (1991); Presidental Award, San Francisco Junior Chamber of Commerce (1990, 1991); Officer of the Year, San Francisco Junior Chamber of Commerce (1989); Who's Who in the World; Who's Who in the West; Dictionary of International Biography of the 21st Century; Dictionary of International Biography; Outstanding Young Men of America Award; Two Thousand Notable Men of America. **Education:** Baylor University, B.A. in Speech Communications (1987); City College of San Francisco, A.A. in General Education; Saint Ignatius College Preparatory, Diploma. **Personal:** Mr. Watkins enjoys weightlifting, politics, and reading motivational and history books.

Michael W. York

General Sales Manager
THE LEADER Newspaper
801 East Trade Street
Charlotte, NC 28202
(704) 331–4842
Fax: (704) 347–0358

2711

Business Information: THE LEADER Newspaper is the weekly newspaper of Charlotte, North Carolina. THE LEADER, which will celebrate its 25th anniversary in 1997, currently employs 40 people. As General Sales Manager, Mr. York oversees the activities of a 12 person staff. The department handles inside and outside sales, development of new clients, and evaluating advertising opportunities. Mr. York works closely with the Editorial and Production departments to develop new sections and special revenue projects for the paper. Additional responsibilities include staff recruitment, training, evaluating, and counseling. Mr. York has been in the communications field since 1972, when at the age of 15, he became a local radio disk jockey and shortly thereafter, a sports writer for his local paper. **Career Steps:** General Sales Manager, The Leader Newspaper (1996–Present); Regional Sales Manager, Meridian International (1991–1996); Regional Sales, Learfield Communications (1989–1991); TV Magazine Sales Manager, Arkansas Democrat Newspaper (1984–1989). **Associations & Accomplishments:** Received recognition as a top Regional Manager in 1994 for Meridian International and as contributing writer for monthly magazines, and keynote speaker at national and regional meetings for monthly magazines. **Education:** US Air Force Technical School of Communication. **Personal:** Married to Sandi in 1978. Two children: Ryan Michael and Lindsay Nicole. Mr. York enjoys golf, softball, basketball, coaching youth league teams, and spending time with his family.

Gregory S. Krueger

Art Director
Krause Publishing
700 E. State Street
Iola, WI 54945
(715) 445–2214
Fax: Please mail or call

2713

Business Information: Krause Publishing specializes in magazines and books specifically for the outdoor, collectible, and trade industries. Established in 1952, the Company employs 415 people. As Art Director, Mr. Krueger oversees a staff of seven designers, and is responsible for the electronic four–color and photography departments, which will produce at least sixty new book designs this year. **Career Steps:** Art Director, Krause Publishing (1990–Present); Advertising Services Manager, Wausan Daily Herald/Gant Newspapers (1986–1980). **Associations & Accomplishments:** Quark Users International; Scitex Graphic Arts Users Association. **Education:** University of Wisconsin, Stevens Point, B.F.A. (1985). **Personal:** Mr. Krueger enjoys antique toy collecting, computers, and art.

Jeffrey A. Bair

Director of Customer Service
The Sheridan Press
450 Fame Avenue
Hanover, PA 17331–8900
(717) 632–3535
Fax: (717) 633–8900
EMAIL: See Below

2721

Business Information: The Sheridan Press, a full service employee–owned printing company specializing in scientific, technical and medical journals, is a Sheridan Group company, which has locations in Pennsylvania, Michigan, Maryland, and Virginia. Established in 1915, The Sheridan Press employs 380 people, and has an estimated annual revenue of $30 million. As Director of Customer Service, Mr. Bair oversees account management teams and manages subscriber and reprint customer services. Internet users can reach him via: jbair@tsp.sheridan.com. **Career Steps:** The Sheridan Press: Director of Customer Service (present), Director of Publisher Services (1995–1996), Account Manager (1994–1995); R. R. Donnelley & Sons Co.: Customer Service Representative (1989–1994), various conventional and electronic prepress responsibilities (1981–1989). **Associations & Accomplishments:** Phi Beta Kappa,Phi Kappa Phi, Golden Key Honor Society; Penn State Alumni Association; Society of Service Professionals in Printing; Board, Littlestown Chapel; Promise Keepers. **Education:** The Pennsylvania State University, B.A. in Art (1980); graduated highest distinction. **Personal:** Married to Mary in 1983. One child: Josiah David. Mr. Bair enjoys reading, outdoor activities and church–related services.

Cheryl R. Baumgardner

Co–Founder
Singles Profile Magazine, Inc.
8776 E. Shea Boulevard, #B–3A Box 444
Scottsdale, AZ 85260
(602) 341–5455
Fax: (602) 661–1366
EMAIL: singles@getnet.co

2721

Business Information: Singles Profile Magazine, Inc. publishes a monthly magazine for singles in the Arizona area. Distributed in Phoenix, Flagstaff, Tucson, and via the Internet, the magazine focuses primarily on singles worldwide (including photographs). The magazine also features advertising, articles, romance stories, and testimonials of singles who have successfully met through the publication. As Co–Founder, Ms. Baumgardner oversees all aspects of the Company. She started with an idea and through sheer hard work and perseverance, she has made the magazine a huge success. She tnow is responsible for writing articles, compiling the magazine, coordinating advertising, and distribution. Concurrent with her present position, Ms. Baumgardner is a Sales Consultant for U.S. West Communications. She has received numerous commendations for her special customer service. She treats customers the way we would all like to be treated. She also has started Pride Construction, Inc. The Company does land development in Scottsdale. It has grown to 10 times its net worth since 1989 with the help of her Project Manager, Rodger Larsen. **Career Steps:** Co–Founder, Singles Profile Magazine, Inc. (1989–Present); Sales Consultant, U.S. West Communications (1982–Present); President/Owner, Pride Construction, Inc. (1989–Present). **Associations & Accomplishments:** Publisher: Awards for Display Advertising in 1964. **Education:** Certified Medical Biller; Certified Nurses Assistant; Licensed Contractor; ASBI for Data Entry; Achieved Training from U.S. West within the Company; Most of her achievements have been on job learning; Self taught on her home computer with the help of Lowell Stone and Doug Dickson. **Personal:** Born in New Hampshire, moved to Calif., grow up there, moved to Arizona in 1991. Divorced. Very Active. Raised two children Troy and Holly. And now has two beautiful grandchildren Eliya and Nevi. Enjoys traveling, people, and her work. Also loves to cook. Enjoys helping others and does so every chance she gets.

William P. Benjamin

President and Editor
Composite Market Reports
1345 East Main Street, Suite 100
Mesa, AZ 85203
(603) 461–9445
Fax: (602) 461–8177

2721

Business Information: Composite Market Reports is a publisher of monthly newsletters, focusing on the global composites industry (aerospace and nonaerospace). The Company provides a broad perspective on major contracts, events, major programs, and mergers and acquisitions that have a bearing on future business in the composites industry. During the last 26 years of business, the Composite Market Reports has earned the reputation of being the most technically–oriented, informative, and accurate publication of its type. Subscriber list consists of a broad spectrum of the global composites industry, including suppliers of advanced composite materials (fiber, resin & prepeg manufacturers), major airframers, including Boeing, Airbus, McDonnell Douglas, and first and second–tier subcontractors. Over 30% of subscribers are outside of the U.S. Other publications provided readers include quarterly calendars of upcoming meetings and events of interest to those in the advanced composites industry, as well as publishing a number of multiple–client market reports that are sold independently of its newsletters. Publications include: an annual five–year forecast of carbon fiber requirements by the industry, a report called Advanced Composites in the Commercial Jet Transport Industry and another called Opportunities for Advanced Composites in Commercial and Regional Aircraft Interiors. With thirty years in engineering and R&D in the aerospace industry and in marketing composite materials with companies such as Boeing, Northrop, and Fiberite, Mr. Benjamin established Composite Market Reports as President and Editor in 1992. He is responsible for all aspects of operations, including administration, finances, public relations, strategic planning, and editing publications. Well–versed on composite materials and composite manufacturing methods, he has authored a book on plastic tooling which was published by McGraw–Hill in 1972, as well as numerous technical papers and articles. **Career Steps:** President and Editor, Composite Market Reports (1992–Present); Manager of Technical Marketing, ICI Fiberite (1989–1992); Main Technical Manager, Northrop Corporation (1983–1989); Main Research and Development Supervisor, Boeing Commercial Airplanes (1966–1985). **Associations & Accomplishments:** Society of Advanced Materials and Process Engineer; Society of Manufacturing Engineers; Suppliers of Advanced Composites Materials Suppliers. **Education:** University of California – Los Angeles, M.B.A. (1986); Union College, B.S. **Personal:** Married to Cheryl in 1978. Four children: Jennifer, Michelle, Christopher, and Joseph. Mr. Benjamin enjoys fly fishing and leathercraft.

Edgar Theodore Coene, III

Group Publisher
Group C Communications
121 Monmouth Street
Red Bank, NJ 07701
(908) 842–7433 (800) 524–0337
Fax: (908) 758–6634

2721

Business Information: Group C Communications is a Red Bank publisher of business and trade periodicals. Mr. Coene is responsible for the New Jersey Meeting Planning Guide, as well as contract publishing of various state, county, and regional publications including The New Jersey Travel Guide, the Camden County Resource Guide, and The New Jersey State Fish and Wildlife Digests. He is also founder and publisher of Export Connection magazine. As Publisher, Mr. Coene supervises all aspects of creation, production, and advertising sales for the magazines. **Career Steps:** Group C Communications: Group Publisher, (1993–Present), Account Executive (1988–1993); Image Tech: Account Executive (1986–1988). **Associations & Accomplishments:** New York City Traffic Club; Moderator at the International Business Expo Trade Show, New York, New York (1996); Member, Greater Atlantic City Hotel/Motel Association. **Education:** Monmouth University, Graduate Studies in Finance; Wake Forest University, B.A. in Economics. **Personal:** Married to Kimberley in 1996. Mr. Coene enjoys sports (tennis and golf).

Larry Flynt

Chairman of the Board and Owner
L.F.P., Inc.
8484 Wilshire Boulevard, Suite 900
Beverly Hills, CA 90211
(213) 651–5400
Fax: (213) 651–2936

2721

Business Information: L.F.P., Inc. is an international publisher and distributor of over thirty magazines, including music, computer, science fiction, trading cards, boats, tattoos, film and fashion magazines. The founder of Hustler Magazine, Mr. Flynt established L.F.P., Inc. in 1974 and serves as its Owner and Chairman of the Board, responsible for all aspects of operations, in addition to overseeing all administrative operations for associates and a support staff of more than 200. He is also the owner of Flynt Distributing Company (FDC), a distributor of magazines both domestically and internationally. **Career Steps:** Chairman of the Board and Owner, L.F.P., Inc. (1974–Present); Owner, FDC (1977–Present); U.S. Navy (1960–1964). **Associations & Accomplishments:** ACLU; Donates and funds numerous spinal–cord research organizations. **Personal:** Three children: Lisa, Theresa, and Larry Jr. Mr. Flynt enjoys travel and deep sea fishing.

Mrs. Teresa Holleman–Blount

Vice President
Multi Media International, Inc.
3020 Roxburgh Drive
Roswell, GA 30076
(770) 667–0635
Fax: (770) 410–0320

2721

Business Information: Multi Media International, Inc. is involved in the publication of "Atlanta Prime Times", a lifestyle magazine focused on active adults over 40. A free publication, the Company has distributed 50,000 copies in the Atlanta metro area through direct marketing. Established in 1992, the Company employs twenty–three freelance and contract personnel, and has an estimated annual revenue of $200K+. As Vice President, Mrs. Holleman–Blount oversees market development and sales strategy implementation. She is also responsible for budgeting, planning, project management and public relations. **Career Steps:** Vice President, Multi Media International, Inc. (1996–Present); Senior Marketing Manager, CIBA Vision (1983–1995); Senior Sales Representative, Revlon (1981–1983); Assistant Production Manager, Dow Corning Ophthalmics (1979–1981). **Associations & Accomplishments:** Atlanta Chamber of Commerce; Women's Health Care Executives; Volunteer for Atlanta Humane Society. **Education:** Mercer University, M.B.A. (In Progress); Guilford College, B.S. in Sociology (1978). **Personal:** Married to Don in 1993. Mrs. Holleman–Blount enjoys cooking, walking, biking, and travel.

William K. Lavelle

Director of Prepress
TV Guide
100 Matsonford Road, Building 4
Radnor, PA 19088
(610) 293–8541
Fax: (610) 293–6219
EMail: See Below

2721

Business Information: TV Guide is a large publishing company that produces over 129 magazines weekly for distribution nationwide. The Company provides direct distribution to customer's homes and businesses as well as distribution through retailers, including grocery stores and convenience stores. As Director of Prepress, Mr. Lavelle handles all the prepress functions for all TV Guide's 129 magazines. On a weekly basis, he averages about 2,000 negatives converted from digital information, to one piece film and then to offset plates. He also oversees six Production sites in the United States, and a large support staff. **Career Steps:** Director of Prepress, TV Guide (1991–Present); Prepress Superintendent, Hart Graphics (1990–1991); Director of Research and Development, Payne Precision Color (1986–1990). **Associations & Accomplishments:** Printing Industries of America; Technical Association of Graphic Arts; Graphic Arts Association; Research and Engineering Council of the Graphic Arts. **Education:** Rochester Institute of Technology, Completed graduate program of Printing Sciences (1987); Millersville State University, B.S. in Industrial Arts and Visual Communications; Vocational Rehabilitation Therapy, Certificate. **Personal:** Married to Lisa in 1989. Two children: Kathryn Rose and Judith Marie. Mr. Lavelle enjoys golf and spending time with his children.

Anaymir Munoz

President
San Juan City Magazine
P.O. Box 364187
San Juan, Puerto Rico 00936–4187
(809) 782–4200
Fax: (809) 749–8840

2721

Business Information: The San Juan City Magazine is an informative magazine that includes topics from politics to cultural events. Established in 1992, the Magazine currently employs 20 staff members. As President, Ms. Munoz is responsible for all aspects of operations, from sales to distribution. **Career Steps:** President, San Juan City Magazine (1992–Present). **Associations & Accomplishments:** AIHE (business association); Centers Sister Isolina Ferre, Youth Center. **Education:** American University, Human Resource Management (1992). **Personal:** Ms. Munoz enjoys reading, exercise, tennis, and devoting her time to non–profit organizations.

Nicki L. Myhre

Advertising Director
Vintage Guitar, Inc.
P.O. Box 7301
Bismarck, ND 58507–7301
(701) 255–1197
Fax: (701) 255–0250
EMAIL: See Below

2721

Business Information: Vintage Guitar, Inc. publishes a national monthly and quarterly magazine concerned with vintage and classic guitars and other musical equipment. The corporation also produces an annual price guide for vintage guitars and supplemental musical equipment. As Advertising Director, Ms. Myhre handles over 650 advertising accounts for three of the Vintage Guitar publications. With a staff of 11 employees, Ms. Myhre is responsible for selling advertising space in the magazines and the administration and billing of the client accounts. Internet users can reach her via: Nicki@vguitar.com **Career Steps:** Advertising Director, Vintage Guitar (1992–Present). **Associations & Accomplishments:** The Advertising Federation. **Education:** Bismarck State College – Bismarck, ND, General Business (1989). **Personal:** One child: Amber Schaefer. Ms. Myhre enjoys horseback riding and bicycling.

Mr. A. Douglas Peabody

President and Co–Founder
Meighter Communications, L.P.
100 Avenue of the Americas, 7th Floor
New York, NY 10013
(212) 219–7412
Fax: (212) 334–1257

2721

Business Information: As President and Co–Founder of Meighter Communications, L.P., Mr. A. Douglas Peabody is responsible for all aspects of operation for the company.

Eileen S. Robinson, M.S.N., R.N.

Executive Director
Springhouse Corporation
1111 Bethlehem Pike
Spring House, PA 19477–0908
(215) 646–8700 Ext. 304
Fax: (215) 646–0616
EMAIL: See Below

2721

Business Information: Established in 1971, the Springhouse Corporation is engaged in publishing The World's Largest Nursing Journal, six leading nursing journals, and various nursing books. Additionally, they cover healthcare conferences and independent studies. As Executive Director, Ms. Robinson is responsible for conducting continuing education business, conferences, and free standing independent studies on products. She also oversees marketing and promotion copying as well as development and design for her area. Internet users can reach her via: http://www.Springnet.com. **Career Steps:** Springhouse Corporation: Executive Director (1995–Present), Director, Continuing Education (1994–1995), Clinical Editor (1992–1995); Faculty, Chester County Hospital School of Nursing (1988–1992); Adjunct Faculty, Widener University (1983–1988), Clinical Nurse Specialist, Mercy Catholic Medical Center (1982–1988). **Associations & Accomplishments:** American Association of Critical Care Nurses; Sigma Theta Tau International; American Nurses Association; Society of Critical Care Medicine; American Organization of Nurse Executives; Former Volunteer, Women Against Rape; Elementary and Middle School Parent Teacher Organization Volunteer; Published author and recipient of four editorial team awards. **Education:** Widener University: M.S.N. (1982), B.S.N. (1979); Fitzgerald Mercy Hospital School of Nursing, Diploma (1972). **Personal:** Married to James J. Sr. in 1973. Two children: Lyndsay and Jimmy. Ms. Robinson enjoys reading, biking and walking.

Charles E. Smith

Vice President of Sales, Legal Publishing Division
Commerce Clearing House
1801 North Hampton Road, Suite 390
De Soto, TX 75115–2399
(214) 298–6100
Fax: (214) 298–7455

2721

Business Information: Commerce Clearing House is a specialty publisher of documentation for business industries. The Legal Publishing Division is one of 28 divisions and produces documentation for attorneys, accountants, and others associated with the legal field. The Division also prepares electronic daily, weekly, and monthly updates to existing documentation. As Vice President of Sales. Legal Publishing Division, Mr. Smith is accountable for 23 sales associates who cover the Texas, New Mexico, and Oklahoma regions. He is also responsible for all administrative duties associated with the division and assists in the development and implementation of sales strategies. **Career Steps:** Commerce Clearing House: Sales Vice President (1990–Present), Assistant Sales Manager (1988–1990), Sales Associate (1984–1988). **Associations & Accomplishments:** Y.M.C.A.; De Soto Chamber of Commerce. **Education:** Austin College, B.S. (1961). **Personal:** Married to Linda in 1960. Three children: Mark, Chuck, and Michael. Mr. Smith enjoys golf, fishing, travel, camping, and hunting.

Bart Sg. Tubalinal Jr., CPA

President/Publisher
Philippine Time, Inc.
550 North Frontage Road, Suite 2410
Northfield, IL 60089
(847) 446–5158
Fax: (847) 446–5164
EMail: See Below

2721

Business Information: Philippine Time, Inc. is a publisher of American newspapers and magazines for the Philippines. As President/Publisher, Mr. Tubalinal is responsible for the total operations of the Company. Concurrently, Mr. Tubalinal is a Certified Public Accountant and the President of Compuway Accounting Services, Inc. Internet users can reach him via: philtime@aol.com. **Career Steps:** President/Publisher, Philippine Time, Inc. (1991–Present); President, Compuway Accounting Services, Inc. (1988–Present); Planning/Financial Analyst, First Chicago (1986–1994); Assistant Executive Director, Project '80 (1985–1986); Chief Accountant, Van Bergen & Company (1984–1985). **Associations & Accomplishments:** Service Award, Bikol USA; Director, Wednesday Friendship Club of Chicago; President, Novo Ecijanos of the Midwest. **Education:** Keller Graduate School: B.S.C. (1970), attended M.B.A. classes; University of Santo Tomas, law classes. **Personal:** Married to Yoly in 1975. Three children: Bart X., Paul X., and Madelene G. Mr. Tubalinal enjoys bowling, writing, and computer programming.

Murray C. Weil

Publisher and Chief Executive Officer
Los Angeles Computer – Midwest Office
1216 N. LaSalle St.
Chicago, IL 60610
(312) 944–1900
Fax: (312) 280–8327

2721

Business Information: Los Angeles Computer is the fourth largest computer monthly in the world. Main offices are located in Aachen, Germany, Hong Kong, Chicago, New Jersey, and Los Angeles. Publications include "LA Computer Magazine — national edition with a monthly circulation of 500,000; as well as the syndicated television program, Computer Showcase. As Publisher and Chief Executive Officer, Mr. Weil is responsible for company operations, the supervision of 200 employees, as well as serving as publisher to the magazine and television program producer. **Career Steps:** Los Angeles Computer – Midwest Office: Publisher/CEO (1977–Present), Producer (1994–1995), Publisher (1983–1995); Publisher, Chicago Business Review (1977–1983). **Personal:** Mr. Weil enjoys reading, writing, and racing horses.

Venessa C. Williamson
Supervisor
Scholastic, Inc.
555 Broadway
New York, NY 10012
(212) 343–6100
Fax: (212) 343–6737

2731

Business Information: Scholastic, Inc. is a major publisher of childrens books, magazines, software, and television and videos. Products and programs include Charles in Charge, The Indian in the Cupboard, and GooseBumps. Established in 1920, the Company employs 1,000 people and has estimated annual revenue of $100 million. As Supervisor, Ms. Williamson oversees all aspects of the Company. She is responsible for management of the switchboard, support to the telecommunications department, and training of all employees. Additional duties include data entry, maintenance of the telephone log, customer service, and other operational duties. **Career Steps:** Supervisor, Scholastic, Inc. (1990–Present); Tour Guide/Manager Clerk, NBC T.V. (1988–1990). **Associations & Accomplishments:** Black Women in Publishing; Black Filmmaker Foundation (BFF); Latino Coalition; Models Guild Union. **Education:** National Education Center, Licensed Register Medical Assistant. **Personal:** Two children: Charmaine Williamson and Brandon Byrd. Ms. Williamson enjoys modeling, acting, going to concerts, singing, and writing.

Robert S. Acquaye
Vice President and Director of Circulation
Earl G. Graves Publishing Company
130 Fifth Avenue
New York, NY 10011–4306
(212) 886–9568
Fax: (212) 886–9600

2731

Business Information: Earl G. Graves Publishing Company, celebrating 25 years of Black enterprise and Black business achievement, is a publisher of the monthly business magazine, "Black Enterprise," a premier business–service publication targeting African–American entrepreneurs, corporate executives, professionals, and decision–makers. Joining Earl G. Graves Publishing Company as Vice President and Director of Circulation in 1991, Mr. Acquaye is responsible for managing and directing new business strategies, direct response marketing, fulfillment, and newsstand management for the magazine. Mr. Acquaye was responsible for the initiation of an innovative program designed to increase national exposure and to stimulate circulation growth. The program, called Group Initiatives Program, targets professional organizations and has proven quite successful, helping to increase the magazine's subscriber base from 240,000 to the current 300,000. Mr. Acquaye was born in Accra, Ghana and emigrated to the U.S. in 1980. **Career Steps:** Vice President and Director of Circulation, Earl G. Graves Publishing Company (1991–Present); Circulation Director, Medical Economics, RN Magazine (1990–1991); Circulation Director, Fairchild Publications (1984–1989); Staff Analyst, Institutional Investor (1981–1984). **Associations & Accomplishments:** Fulfillment Management Association; Former Board Member, NBCA; National Treasurer and Board Member, NAMD; Bergenfield Volunteer Ambulance Corps.; Board Member, Bergenfield Swim Club. **Education:** Concordia University, B.A. in Economics (1980). **Personal:** Two children: Adrienne and Jason. Mr. Acquaye enjoys tennis and getting involved with children's activities. Mr. Acquaye is also a certified emergency medical technician and volunteers time as a member of the Ambulance Volunteer Corps.

Allen Adcox
Director of Business Support Services
Baptist Sunday School Board
127 9th Avenue, North
Nashville, TN 37234–0195
(615) 251–2616
Fax: (615) 251–3934

2731

Business Information: Baptist Sunday School Board is a religious publisher. As Director of Business Support Services, Mr. Adcox is responsible for financial planning, inventory management, purchasing, and budgeting. **Career Steps:** Baptist Sunday School Board: Director of Business Support Services (1992–Present), Manager of Inventory Management Section (1988–1992), Inventory Specialist (1972–1988), Internal Auditor (1968–1972). **Associations & Accomplishments:** National Association of Purchasing Management. **Education:** Middle Tennessee State University, M.B.A. (1972); Auburn University, B.S. (1968). **Personal:** Married to Katie S. in 1969. Two children: Chris and Sally.

Robert J. Christman
Regional Publisher
Wedding Safari
4691 University Drive, Suite 417
Coral Springs, FL 33067–4620
(954) 755–3400
Fax: (954) 984–0042

2731

Business Information: Wedding Safari is a publisher of 'The Wedding Pages', a 350–page wedding planner for the bride–to–be. Established in 1979, Wedding Safari also publishes an advertising digest for wedding professionals on a local and national level. With an estimated annual revenue in excess of $250,000, the Company is planning for future expansion in the Miami area with the publication of a bridal magazine. As Regional Publisher, Mr. Christman's responsibilities include advertising sales and design, editorial writing and maintaining distribution. **Career Steps:** Regional Publisher, Wedding Safari (1994–Present); President, RJ Merrill Adjusting (1990–1994); Vice President, Escalator Securities (1986–1990). **Associations & Accomplishments:** National Association of Catering Executives; Sterling Who's Who; Cystic Fibrosis Association. **Education:** Queens College, City University of New York (1979–1985). **Personal:** Married to Sharon in 1989. Three children: William, Jennafer, and Dylan. Mr. Christman enjoys karate (black belt).

Dave Christy

President and Chief Operating Officer
Chancellor's
5301 Lakeview Parkway South Drive
Indianapolis, IN 46268
(317) 216–2646
Fax: (317) 216–2650

2731

Business Information: Chancellor's is an educational publication company offering degree programs with coursework through the local university (i.e., CLEP test, ACT, etc.). The Company employs Ph.D.s who conduct research and send test prep to students. The degree programs are fully–accredited (by the agency which accredits Harvard), offering a full range of degrees, including MBA, MSN, AA, BA, BS, BSN, AS, AA, and ASN. As President, Mr. Christy is responsible for all aspects of Company operations, and still makes himself available to speak at numerous seminars. **Career Steps:** President, Chancellor's (1994–Present); National Sales Director, CPRN (1987–1994); Vice President of Sales & Marketing, Overland Express (1982–1987); President, Priority Promotions (1975–1982). **Associations & Accomplishments:** Christian Businessmen; American Management Association; Commercial Pilot; Board Chair CLSI. **Education:** University of California – Los Angeles, Ph.D.; Butler University, M.B.A.; Purdue University, B.S.I.E. **Personal:** Married to Rene in 1987. Four children: Derrick, Andrea, Aaron, and Sarah. Mr. Christy enjoys horses and private piloting.

Candis A. Holloway

Regional Manager, Great Lakes Area
Prentice Hall School Division
108 Wilmot Road, Suite 100
Deerfield, IL 60015–5145
(708) 945–3570
Fax: (708) 945–5987

2731

Business Information: Prentice Hall is an international publishing company. The Prentice Hall School Division specializes in the publishing and printing of secondary school textbooks and teaching aids. Currently the Great Lakes Region employs 23 people and has an estimated annual revenue of $12 million. As Regional Manager, Great Lakes Area, Ms. Holloway is responsible for all aspects of sales and workshops for the region, including Illinois and Michigan. Ms. Holloway has fifteen years teaching experience and extensive knowledge of secondary textbooks. **Career Steps:** Prentice Hall School Division: Regional Manager, Great Lakes Area (1994–Present); Sales Representative (1988–1994); Special Education Consultant, State Department of Education, Oklahoma (1987–1988). **Associations & Accomplishments:** Association of Supervision and Curriculum Instruction; National Council of Teachers of English; International Reading Association. **Education:** University of Central Oklahoma, M.Ed., emphasis in Learning Disabilities (1980); American Management Association, Management Courses (1994); Southwest Oklahoma State University, B.S. in Elementary Education (1970). **Personal:** Ms. Holloway enjoys tennis, playing the piano, and writing poetry.

William C. Korner

President
Rand McNally
8255 Central Park Avenue
Skokie, IL 60076–2908
(847) 329–6241
Fax: (847) 673–0728

2731

Business Information: Rand McNally Book Services is a book and multi–media manufacturing and distribution conglomerate; consisting of four major divisions: Publishing – publishing maps, road atlases, etc.; Ticket – producing airline and mass transit tickets for distribution worldwide; Media Services – producing turnkey packages for software companies and placing the information on CD's or diskettes, then packaging and distributing them worldwide; and Book Services – the largest of the four divisions, produces one half of Rand McNally's revenue. This Division takes contents from publishers, manufacturers books, and distributes to publishers and customers, producing 300 million books per year. Book Services also prints contents in digital form (CD's, diskettes) and packages and distributes them. Joining Rand McNally as President of the Book Services Division in 1991, Mr. Korner oversees all operations, having full responsibility for sales and marketing, finances, manufacturing, human resources, and information technology. In addition, he oversees all administrative operations for associates and a support staff of more than 2,000. **Career Steps:** President, Rand McNalley – Book Services Company (1991–Present); Executive Vice President, Fry Communications (1987–1991); Vice President and General Manager, Crown Zellerbach (1982–1987); President, ABDKK Products Company (1973–1982); Pilot, U.S. Army, U.S. Air Force (1967–1973). **Associations & Accomplishments:** Director, Boot Manufacturers Institute; Daedalians – Military Pilots Association; Military Decorations include: Distinguished Flying Cross, 2 Bronze Stars, 13 Air Medals, Vietnam Medal of Honor, Desert Storm Campaign Medal. **Education:** Pennsylvania State University, B.S. (1967). **Personal:** Married to Alexandria in 1982. Four children: Bill Jr., Jennifer, Shauna, and Haley.

Andrew J. Low
Vice President – International Division
Western Publishing Co. Inc.
850 3rd Avenue
New York, NY 10022–6222
(212) 753–8500
Fax: (212) 753–8562

2731

Business Information: Western Publishing Co. Inc. is a major international printing and publishing company, specializing in children's books, (Golden Books) electronic talking books and puzzles. The Company also provides commercial printing to a variety of customers. As Vice President – International Division, Mr. Low is responsible for all aspects of marketing, advertising, operations management, and product development outside the U.S. **Career Steps:** Vice President, International Division, Western Publishing Co. Inc. (1994–Present); Group Marketing Director, Hallmark – UK (1993–1994); Vice President, Games, Hasbro – Europe (1991–1993); Vice President, Marketing, Tonka – International (1990–1991). **Associations & Accomplishments:** The Marketing Society – UK; The 4I Club – Association with Round Table Britain & Ireland (charitable organization). **Education:** Birmingham University – UK, B.Sc. (1974). **Personal:** Married to Susan in 1981. Two children: Stuart and Jack. Mr. Low enjoys the theatre and sports.

ZondervanPublishingHouse

Jonathan W. Petersen
Director of Strategic Marketing/Corporate Affairs
Zondervan Publishing House
5300 Patterson Avenue, SE
Grand Rapids, MI 49530
(616) 698–3417
Fax: (616) 698–3223
E MAIL: See Below

2731

Business Information: Zondervan Publishing House, a division of Harper Collins Publishers, is an international publisher of Bibles, books, audio, video, software, multimedia, and gift products. This division currently employs over 300 people and projects sales in excess of $100 million in 1996. As Director of Strategic Marketing/Corporate Affairs, Mr. Petersen directs a newly created department responsible for key title promotion, increased author visibility, Internet marketing, segmented marketing, and corporate public relations. He is responsible for the creation of "Zondervan News Service", an e–mail executive summary of current issues and the Zondervan resources that speak to them. Other concerns include strategic planning and execution and travel to expound on current products and services. Concurrently, Mr. Petersen is Chairman of the Corporate Contributions Committee and oversees the Company donation budget to needy civic, cultural, and educational organizations. Internet users may reach Mr. Petersen via: jonathan.petersen@zph.com. **Career Steps:** Zondervan Publishing House: Director of Strategic Marketing/Corporate Affairs (1996–Present), Director of Media Relations/Public Affairs (1986–1996). News Producer & Writer, Freelance (1986–Present); Religion News Editor, United Press International Radio Network (1984–1986). **Associations & Accomplishments:** Religion Newswriters Association; International Association of Business Communicators; Society of Professional Journalists; Radio–Television News Directors Association; Evangelical Press Association; The Religion Publishing Group; Publisher's Publicity Association; Religious Publicist Network. Mr. Petersen has been listed in the following: Sterling's Who's Who (1995); Who's Who Among Young American Professionals; Who's Who of Emerging Leaders in America; Who's Who in Advertising. He has been the recipient of numerous media awards and has had numerous articles published in various trade publications and journals. **Education:** University of Wisconsin, B.A. in Mass Communications – Dean's List (1978); Moody Bible Institute, Diploma in Broadcast Communications (1976). **Personal:** Married to Beth in 1979. Four children: Matthew, Andrew, Sarah, and Rachel. Mr. Petersen enjoys canoeing, shortwave radio, and hiking.

Mrs. Shelia Poling

Vice President
SPC Press/Statistical Process Controls
5908 Toole Drive, Suite C
Knoxville, TN 37919–4172
(615) 584–5005
Fax: (615) 588–9440

2731

Business Information: SPC Press/Statistical Process Controls specializes in quality and productivity improvement publications, products, and seminars. Established since 1982, SPC Press/Statistical Process Controls presently employs 15 people. In her current capacity Mrs. Poling is responsible for marketing, sales, operations, exhibits, advertising, seminar planning, and product development. **Career Steps:** Vice President, SPC Press/Statistical Process Controls (1989–Present); Vice President, Barber Consulting Resources (1987–1989); Vice President, Barber Consulting Resources (1987–1989); Vice President, QualPro, Inc. (1983–1987); Manager, Proffitts Department Store (1979–1983). **Associations & Accomplishments:** American Society for Quality Control; American Marketing Association; Selected Nationally as one of the '94 Meeting Planners to watch in 1994' by Convention South Magazine. **Education:** University of Tennessee, B.S. Degree (1979). **Personal:** Married to Robert in 1979. Mrs. Poling enjoys music, reading and travel in her leisure time.

Jeffrey P. Schullo

Manager of Information Services
Booklet Binding, Inc.
2200 West 16th Street
Broadview, IL 60153–3949
(708) 350–9200
Fax: (708) 350–9480
EMAIL: See Below

2731

Business Information: Booklet Binding, Inc. is a national graphic finishing, binding, data processing, and mailing service. Established in 1976, the Company is based in Chicago with two offices. As Manager of Information Services, Mr. Schullo is responsible for all data processing, network administration, software and hardware administration, and land and cellular phone administration. Internet users can also reach him via: BBIJEF@AOL.COM **Career Steps:** Manager of Information Services, Booklet Binding Inc. (1995–Present); Director of Administration, Hallmark Mailing Services (1992–1995); General Manager, Interstate Mailing Services (1982–1993); Senior Purchasing Agent, McMaster Carr Supply Co. (1980–1981). **Associations & Accomplishments:** Little League Coach (4 years); Den Leader and Cubmaster (3 years). **Education:** Elmhurst College, B.A. (1978). **Personal:** Married to Mary Anne in 1974. Three children: Erin, Phillip and Anne. Mr. Schullo enjoys playing guitar and bass, performing with local contemporary choir.

Jill S. Silverstein

Director of Corporate Training and Development
RIA Group
31 Saint James Avenue, Suite 3B
Boston, MA 02116–4101
(617) 292–8481
Fax: (617) 292–8299
EMAIL:jsilverste@wgl.com

2731

Business Information: RIA Group is a publisher of professional reference materials, serving tax and accounting practitioners from nine national locations. Joining RIA Group as Director of Corporate Training and Development in 1995, Ms. Silverstein is responsible for providing training and development for all employees nationally, in addition to recruiting within the Company. **Career Steps:** Director of Corporate Training and Development, RIA Group (1995–Present); Warren Gorham & Lamont: Director of Corporate Training and Communications (1994–1995), Training Manager (1989–1994); Area Sales Manager, Office Specialists (1988–1989). **Associations & Accomplishments:** American Society for Training and Development (ASTD); ASCD; American Management Association (AMA). **Education:** Boston University: currently working on Ed.D. (1998), Ed.M.; New England Conservatory, Masters of Music; DePaul University, Bachelors of Music. **Personal:** Married to David in 1981. Ms. Silverstein enjoys hiking, canoeing, needlework, and reading.

Craig E. Simmons

Publisher
Haas Publishing Company
4425 Spring Mountain Road, Suite 300
Las Vegas, NV 89102–0145
(702) 736–3943
Fax: (702) 253–5269

2731

Business Information: Haas Publishing Company publishes a free book called "THE APARTMENT GUIDE" (TM) in 23 states with 61 publications. As Publisher, Mr. Simmons is responsible for the entire operation of the Las Vegas office, including sales management, production, distribution, budgets, training, and staff. Further responsibilities include marketing and traffic analysis, occupancy trends and educational seminars for the Las Vegas client base. **Career Steps:** Haas Publishing Company: Publisher – Las Vegas (1995–Present), Publisher – San Diego, Los Angeles (1992–1995), Account Executive/Publisher – Las Vegas (1990–1992); General Manager, Escot Boxing Enterprises (1986–1990). **Associations & Accomplishments:** National Apartment Association; National Suppliers Council; Nevada Apartment Association; Institute of Real Estate Management; Nevada Food Bank; Child Haven; Crisis Committee; Product Service Council. **Education:** Arizona State University, B.A. (1986). **Personal:** Mr. Simmons enjoys all outdoor activities, baseball, volleyball, golf, hiking, skiing, good wine, and fine cigars.

R. Paul Sullivan

Vice President of Editorial Services
Telemedia Communications
300 – 555 West, 12th Avenue
Vancouver, British Columbia V5Z 4L4
(604) 877–4815
Fax: (604) 877–4838
EMAIL: See Below

2731

Business Information: Telemedia Communications is an international distributor of consumer publishing magazines, including Canadian Living, TV Guide, Housemaker's, Harrowsmith Country Life, Equinox, Canadian Select Homes, Vancouver, and Western Living. As Vice President of Editorial Services, Mr. Sullivan is responsible for editorial development, editorial resources for editors of individual magazines, new projects and development, and analytical resources. Internet users can reach him via: psully@aol.com. **Career Steps:** Vice President of Editorial Services, Telemedia Communications (1993–Present); Host, CBC – Vancouver AM Radio (1991–1993); Editor of West Magazine, Globe & Mail (1989–1991). **Associations & Accomplishments:** Board of Director, National Magazine Awards Foundation; Steering Committee, Youth in Dispute Resolution For the 21st Century. **Education:** University of Manitoba, B.A. honors (1971). **Personal:** Married to Elizabeth Jones in 1979. Two children: John and Ann. Mr. Sullivan enjoys running, reading, and golf.

Mr. Andrew R. Vosburgh

Vice President of Operations
Graphic World, Inc.
11687 Adie Road
St. Louis, MO 63043
(314) 567–9854
Fax: (314) 567–7178

2731

Business Information: Graphic World, Inc. is a publishing company specializing in medical, scientific, technical and collegiate book composition and pre–press. In his capacity as Vice President of Operations, Mr. Vosburgh has full profit and loss responsibility, provides sales support, and manages research and development functions. Established in 1974, Graphic World, Inc. employs a staff of 100 and reports annual revenue in excess of $5 million. **Career Steps:** Vice President of Operations, Graphic World, Inc. (1989–Present); Manufacturing Operations Manager, W.A. Krueger Company (1986–1989); Superintendent, Pre–press Operations, W.A. Krueger Company (1984–1986); Systems Manager, W.A. Krueger Company (1979–1983). **Associations & Accomplishments:** President, XyVision Users Group. **Education:** University of Wyoming, B.S. in Physics (1978).

Debra Troglio Waters

Director of Operations
Hambleton Hill Publishing
1501 County Hospital Road
Nashville, TN 37218
(615) 254–2491
Fax: (615) 254–2408

2731

Business Information: Hambleton Hill Publishing specializes in publishing and distribution. The Company started out as a third party logistics company, delivering for publishing companies. The Company then purchased a children's book company named "Ideals Childrens Books," and formed Associated Publishing Group in 1993. As Director of Operations, Ms. Waters is responsible for all aspects of operations, including serving as the customer service and warehouse operations liaison. **Career Steps:** Director of Operations, Hambleton Hill Publishing (1994–Present); Star Song Communications: Director of Operations (1992–1994), Production Manager (1989–1992). **Education:** Indiana State University, B.S. (1988). **Personal:** Married to Richard S. in 1992. One child: Alexandra Elizabeth. Ms. Waters enjoys sign language.

Kevin Lee Green

President
Bertolini Printing Inc.
150 Varick Street
New York, NY 10013–1218
(212) 675–8000
Fax: (212) 255–6933

2732

Business Information: Bertolini Printing Inc., established in 1983, is a provider of electric pre–press, printing, and Internet access (i.e., high quality press runs, brochures, catalogs, and posters) used in advertising and marketing for companies in the regional area. As President and part–owner of Bertolini since 1993, Mr. Green is responsible for all aspects of operations, in addition to overseeing all administrative operations for associates and of a support staff of 35. Concurrent with his executive position at Bertolini Printing, he is Co–owner and President of Big Multi–Media Services and Executive Vice President of CompuTel Network Services. **Career Steps:** President and Part–Owner, Bertolini Printing Inc. (1993–Present); Executive Vice President, CompuTel Network Services (1995–Present); President and Co–Owner, Big Multi–Media Services (1995–Present). **Associations & Accomplishments:** MENSA. **Education:** St. Francis College, B.S. in Biology (1987). **Personal:** Mr. Green is a history buff, especially ancient history. He has a library of over 1,000 history books.

Sharon L. Mitzell

Vice President of Human Resources
York Graphic Services
3600 West Market Street
York, PA 17404–5813
(717) 792–3551
Fax: (717) 792–5616

2732

Business Information: York Graphic Services, an ESOP Company, is a prepress, printing, and publisher of books (i.e., Harcourt, Graw–Hill, McGillion), magazines (i.e., Architectual Magazine), and weekly publications for commercial industries (AT&T, Prudential, Utz Potato Chips, York Wall) and small local companies. Established in 1953, York Graphic Services currently has 400 employees. Starting with the Company as a nightshift proofreader, Ms. Mitzell currently serves as Vice President of Human Resources. She is responsible for all Human Resource functions, including hiring, benefits, employee relations, organizational development, and supervising a staff of six. **Career Steps:** York Graphic Services: Vice President of Human Resources (1993–Present), Director of Employee Relations (1988–1993), Manager of Manufacturing (1986–1988). **Associations & Accomplishments:** Printing Industries of America; Former Board Member, Printing Industries of Maryland (1991–1994); Former Board Member, Friends of The Strand Capitol Performing Arts Center (1993–1995); Board Member, The Visiting Nurse Association of York County (1993–Present); National Association of Printers and Lithographers. **Education:** York College of Pennsylvania, B.A. (1979); Printing Industries of America, completed 2-year Executive Development Program; Attended various classes sponsored by Brigham Young University, Covey Leadership Center, and the Graphic Arts Technical Foundation. **Personal:** Married to Roark M. in 1980. Ms. Mitzell enjoys antiques and going to the theatre and dog shows (owner of a Border collie).

Charles F. Blakeman

Account Executive
Hibbert Group
1601 Park Avenue West
Denver, CO 80216
(303) 297–1601
Fax: (303) 297–0634
E MAIL: See Below

2741

Business Information: Hibbert Group is an international, high technology information fulfillment and distribution concern. The Group serves Fortune 300 companies receiving requests via the internet. Answers are returned via CD Rom, fax, hard copies or on the internet. Over half of the Company business is generated by internet users. The Hibbert Group, established in 1880, currently employs 625 people and has locations in Denver and New Jersey. As Account Executive, Mr. Blakeman is part of the nerve center of the Hibbert Group. His staff obtains new business and maintains current relationships. The new business is acquired by development of new and existing marketing techniques, word of mouth advertising, and cold calling via telemarketing. Mr. Blakeman has eight employees reporting directly to him. Internet users may contact him via: cblakeman@hibbert.com. **Career Steps:** Account Executive, Hibbert Group (1992–Present); President/Owner, Creative Communications Design (1984–1992); President/Owner, Primero/P.A.O. Leather Company (1985–1989); President/Owner, Blakeman Landscape Design and Renovation (1986–1991). **Associations & Accomplishments:** International Customer Service Association; Business Marketing Association; President/Chairman of the Board, Chamber Orchestra of the West; Alpha Sigma Lambda; National Musicians Association; Musician with the Colorado Symphony, Mannheim Steamroller, Colorado Ballet, etc. **Education:** University of Connecticut, B.G.S. (1991); Case Western Reserve; Cleveland Institute of Music; Bowling Green State University; Catholic University of America. **Personal:** Married to Diane in 1976. Three children: Grant Charles, Laura Anne, and Brie Nicole. Mr. Blakeman enjoys classical music, soccer, basketball, running, and leadership consulting.

Gregory A. Brake

Sales Manager
IKON Office Solutions/NightRider
1401 H Street, Lower Level
Washington, DC 20005–2110
(202) 452–8818
Fax: (202) 452–8585

2741

Business Information: IKON–NightRider Legal Document Solutions is the largest Legal Document Services company in the U.S., providing case management to law firms from 77 cities across the country. As a Sales Manager in the Washington, D.C. location for the past 3 years, Mr. Brake has managed the Top Producing Branch every year with sales in excess of $7,200,000 in 1995. He was Sales Manager of the Year in 1995. IKON–NightRider has grown 30% each year since it's inception in 1987. Sales of $150 million were achieved in 1995, and 1996 sales are projected to exceed $220,000,000 with a 10% operating income. Mr. Brake transferred to the Washington, D.C. IKON–Business Solutions Division in March 1995 where he will drive sales in the new Flagship IKON–NightRider Business Document Solutions Division. IKON Business Document Solutions (a Division of ALCO Standard) serves corporations across the country with print on demand services. IKON has a National Network to enable corporations to send digital files for printing virtually anywhere in the country. **Career Steps:** Sales Manager (1993–Present), Account Manager, Night Rider/ALCO Standard (1991–1993); Account Manager, Forman Brothers (1986–1991). **Associations & Accomplishments:** President Neighborhood Homeowners Association; Business Shares Committee, DC Cares; Toast Masters; Rotary; American Society of Training Directors. **Education:** Frostburg State University, B.S. (1986). **Personal:** Married to Eva Galina in 1993. One child: Devon Alexandra. Mr. Brake enjoys being a father, skiing and mountain biking.

Cydney L. Capell

Editor–in–Chief/Marketing Director
Marshall & Swift
911 Wilshire Boulevard, Suite 1600
Los Angeles, CA 90017–3409
(213) 683–9000 Ext. 4725
Fax: (213) 683–9010

2741

Business Information: Marshall & Swift publishes real estate and building cost information to publishers on smaller businesses, and residential housing. International in scope, Marshall & Swift operates two locations in the U.S. and two in Europe. As Editor–in–Chief, Ms. Capell is responsible for directing all trade publications, providing technological support, and working with the Art Department regarding advertisement set–ups. Concurrently, she serves as Director of Marketing, in which she directs all retail marketing activities. **Career Steps:** Editor–in–Chief, Marshall & Swift (1994–Present); Director of Publications, Rauscher, Pierce, Refsnes (1990–1993); Editorial Marketing Director, Technology Based Training (1989–1990); Editor, Foreign Rights, Wordware Publishing (1986–1989). **Associations & Accomplishments:** Women in Communications; MENSA. **Education:** Furman University, B.A. (1977).

Sybilla Green Dorros

Editor
Harvard Family Research Project
632 Washington Street, Apt. G–4
Braintree, MA 02184–5752
(617) 848–3290
Fax: (617) 848–3290
EMail: SYBILLAGD@aol.com.

2741

Business Information: The Harvard Family Research Project (HRFP) produces numerous publications, including "The Evaluation Exchange" – a quarterly, nationally–distributed newsletter. Ms. Dorros edits various HFRP publications and is Editor–in–Chief of the newsletter. She works half–time at Harvard; the rest is spent freelance writing and editing. She began writing when she was asked to write book reviews during her first pregnancy. She has since written and published more than 100 articles in popular magazines and newspapers, including the Asian Wall Street Journal and the Geneva Post; in academic journals; and for a regional news service. In addition, she has written and edited for various international organizations, attended international conferences on complex emergencies as rapporteur, and assisted in the preparation of inter–agency publications (former Yugoslavia and Soviet Union, Somalia) for the Department of the Humanitarian Affairs, United Nations, Geneva in 1992–1993. **Career Steps:** Editor, Harvard Family Research Project (1996–Present); Freelance Writer and Editor (1978–Present); Professor, Asian Studies, Webster University–Geneva Switzerland (1992–1995) and the University of the Philippines (1981–1982); Bookstore Manager, Webster University – Geneva, Switzerland (1987–1992); Regional Coordinator for Asia & the Pacific, Organization Resources Counselors, Inc. (1980–1986). **Associations & Accomplishments:** Written and edited for the World Health Organization (AIDS and Safe Motherhood) (1993–1995), the International Federation of Red Cross and Red Crescent Societies (1994–1995) Management Sciences for Health (1996), and Harvard's Center for Blood Research (1995–1996); Prepared an Annotated Bibliography on Women Workers for ILO (1994); Author of the textbook, "A Lamaze Guide for the Philippines," now in its 3rd edition; Editor of "The Web," Webster University in Geneva's biannual magazine, "The China Reader" and the FOCUS Newsletter – involved in all aspects of production, including graphics and layout; Founded and led two organizations in the Philippines: the Philippine–Association for Childbirth Education (PACE) and the Nursing Mothers' Association of the Philippines (NMAP); Trained expectant parents in over 60 series of childbirth education classes; Developed curriculum and taught courses in Chinese politics; Member of the Board of Directors of the Association for Philippine–China Understanding (1976–1985); Conducted pre–departure orientation seminars for both official Philippine delegations and tour groups going to China; Co–led Webster University's first Business Study Tour to China (1992); She has studied numerous languages, including Flemish, Latin, Italian, and Mandarin Chinese; she is fluent in French. **Education:** Asian Institute of Journalism, Manila, Philippines, Diplomate in Journalism courses (1984–1985); University of Philippines, Ph.D. candidate in Political Science and M.A. in Asian Studies (China), Phi Kappa Phi Honor Society (1976); Sarah Lawrence College, B.A. in International Relations (1967). **Personal:** Three children: Gregory, Christopher, and Samantha. Ms. Dorros enjoys numerous outdoor activities, including hiking and skiing. She is an active member of the Appalachian Mountain Club.

Joanne Dresner

Director of Product Development
Addison Wesley Longman Publishing
10 Bank Street
White Plains, NY 10606
(914) 993–5000
Fax: (914) 997–8115
EMAIL: See Below

2741

Business Information: Addison Wesley Longman Publishing specializes in educational publishing dealing primarily in audios, videos, software, and CD roms. The Company produces "English as a Second Language", and "English as a Foreign Language". As Director of Product Development, Ms. Dresner is responsible for all investments and publishing plan from conception to finished product. Internet users can reach her via: Joanned@aw.com. **Career Steps:** Addison Wesley Longman Publishing: Director of Product Development (1995–Present), Editorial Director (1993–1995), Executive Director (1984–1992), Development Editor (1980–1983). **Associations & Accomplishments:** International Teachers of English to Speakers of Other Languages (TESOL). **Education:** University of Michigan: M.A. in Linguistics (1973), B.A. **Personal:** Married to Jerome Linsner in 1979. Two children: Julia and Theresa. Ms. Dresner enjoys swimming, running, and skiing.

Myron Sachar Einisman

President
OMG/Philanthropy Publications
477 Green Bay Road
Highland Park, IL 60035–4935
(800) 438–3901
Fax: (847) 433–5411

2741

Business Information: OMG/Philanthropy Publications publishes tax–advantaged newsletters for not–for–profit organizations around the United States. As President, Mr. Einisman provides financial management advice to affluent clients, conducts a radio show to promote charitable giving and financial planning, and serves as Senior Writer and Marketer responsible for new business development. **Career Steps:** President, OMG/Philanthropy Publications (1995–Present); Consultant/Owner, Michael Einisman, IDC (1976–1995); Consultant/Principal, Jerold Panas & Partners (1973–1976); Director of Development and Public Relations, United Charities of Chicago (1971–1973); Office of Development and Public Affairs, University of Chicago (1967–1971). **Associations & Accomplishments:** Union League Club of Chicago; Highland Park Country Club; Board of Directors, Apple Tree Theatre; Founding Chairman, University of Chicago Blackfriars/Theatre Alumni Association. **Education:** University of Louisville Law School, J.D. (1966); University of Chicago, Graduate School of Business, Master of Business Administration (1963); University of Chicago, B.A. (1962). **Personal:** Married to Margaret Boland in 1976.

Charles Fazzino

President
Museum Editions Ltd.
32 Relyea Place, Floor 2
New Rochelle, NY 10801–6910
(914) 654–9370
Fax: (914) 654–0622

2741

Business Information: Museum Editions Ltd. specializes in the publishing of artwork (i.e., three dimensional pop art with a clothing line, jewelery line, artwork line). Established in 1993, Museum Editions Ltd. currently employs 60 people and has an estimated annual revenue of $5 million. As President, Mr. Fazzino is responsible for all aspects of operations, including traveling around the world performing one–man shows. **Career Steps:** President, Museum Editions Ltd. (1993–Present); Owner, Charles Fazzino Designs (1980–1993). **Associations & Accomplishments:** Project CCHILD; Finlandia Foundation. **Education:** School of Visual Arts, B.F.A. (1977). **Personal:** Married to Adeline in 1982. One child: Heather. Mr. Fazzino enjoys jogging.

Teresa Hairston

Chief Executive Officer/President
Horizon Concepts
2201 Murfreesboro #C–203
Nashville, TN 37217
(615) 360–9444
Fax: (615) 361–1274
EMail: See Below

2741

Business Information: Horizon Concepts is a marketing, media, and communications company, publishing magazines and newsletters. The Company started out as a full page newsletter called "Score," pertaining to gospel music, heritage, Christian lifestyles, education, and people of the ministry. The name has now changed to "Gospel Today," a large magazine with 50,000 subscribers published 8 times a year. As Chief Executive Officer/President, Ms. Hairston serves as the publisher of the Magazine, responsible for all aspects of administration. Internet users can reach her via: gospel@usit.net. **Career Steps:** Chief Executive Officer/President, Horizon Concepts (1992–Present); Director of A&R and Marketing, Benson Music Company (1991–1992); Director of Promotions, Savoy Records (1987–1991). **Associations & Accomplishments:** Minister of music in churches in the community for over 20 years; Board of Directors, Gospel Music Association; Gospel Music Workshop of America; President, United Gospel Industry Council. **Education:** Southern Illinois University, Master of Music (1982). **Personal:** Three children: Topaz, Tiara, and Roland. Ms. Hairston enjoys spending time with her family.

Scott Hudson Jr.

Creative Director
Headbone Interactive
1520 Bellevue Avenue
Seattle, WA 98122
(206) 323–0073
Fax: (206) 323–0188
EMAIL: See Below

2741

Business Information: Established in 1994, Headbone Interactive is the producer and publisher of interactive media, specializing in children's educational software. As Creative Director, Mr. Hudson is responsible for the writing, editing and production of software programs. He is the designer of "Elroy," an educational children's software program. Internet users can reach him via: Scott&Headbone.com **Career Steps:** Headbone Interactive: Creative Director (1995–Present), Design Director/Producer (1994–1995); Lead Designer, Microsoft Corporation (1993–1994); Owner, Object Durable Design Company (1991–1993). **Associations & Accomplishments:** Computer Game Developers Association; Volunteer, Habitat for Humanity. **Education:** University of Colorado, B.S. (1987). **Personal:** Married to Miranda in 1991. One child: Max. Mr. Hudson enjoys carpentry, rock climbing and spending time with his family.

Thomas G. Hudson

Senior Vice President
McGraw Hill
1221 Avenue of the Americas
New York, NY 10020
(212) 512–3526
Fax: (212) 512–4479

2741

Business Information: McGraw Hill is one of the leading international publishers and information providers. The Company's mission is to educate and inform. Its is primarily a business to business information provider. In addition to the hundreds of books and periodicals published, McGraw provides databases referencing financial statistical information about corporate, industrial and business concerns. This information is compiled and then remarketed in written form to corporate and commercial firms for their use in marketing and research–related projects. As Senior Vice President and general manager, Mr. Hudson is responsible for the administration and oversight of one of McGraw's prized franchises, FW Dodge. Duties include general management, sales, marketing, systems, production, editorial data gathering and business development. As an entrepreneur within the large corporation, Mr. Hudson seeks new business opportunities for his company. In his former position as Vice President at IBM Corporation he was instrumental in the structure and start–up of twelve new businesses. Established in 1888, McGraw Hill employs nearly 14,000 people worldwide with annual sales of nearly $3 billion. The FW Dodge subsidiary employs 1545 people with annual sales in excess of $160 million in the U.S. **Career Steps:** Senior Vice President, McGraw Hill (1993–Present); Vice President, IBM Corporation (1968–1993) **Associations & Accomplishments:** IIA. **Education:** Harvard University, A.M.P. (1990); New York University, M.B.A. in Finance (1974); Notre Dame University, B.S. in Electrical Engineering. **Personal:** Married to Regina in 1968. Four children: Gina, Tom, Anne and Matt. Mr. Hudson enjoys skiing, boating and gardening.

Linda M. Just Isern, Esq.

Managing Director
Michie Butterworth
Cond. El Monte Surth G–714
Hato Rey, Puerto Rico 00918
(809) 721 1340
Fax: (809) 721–1342

2741

Business Information: Michie Butterworth, the official publisher for Supreme and Circuit courts, is a multi–national and international legal publishing and legislative data services company serving the legal community in Puerto Rico. International in scope, Michie Butterworth is headquartered in Virginia, with offices in the U.S., England, Netherlands, and Puerto Rico. Established in 1963, Michie Butterworth reports annual revenue of $1.7 million and currently employs fifteen people. A practicing attorney since 1991, Ms. Just Isern joined Michie Butterworth in 1994. Serving as Managing Director, she is responsible for the management of operations and human resources. **Career Steps:** Managing Director, Michie Butterworth (1994–Present); Senior Legal Editor, Butterworth Legal Publishers (1993–1994); Bilingual Legal Editor, D&S Butterworth Legal Publishers (1992–1993); Adm. Law Judge/Examiner, Department of Consumer Affairs – Puerto Rico (1992). **Associations & Accomplishments:** American Bar Association; Puerto Rico Association; Co–Director, Catholic Young Adults Group, University Gardens. **Education:** University of Puerto Rico Law School, J.D. (1991); University of Maryland, College Park: M.A., B.A. **Personal:** Married to Dr. Ivan E. Montalvo in 1995. Ms. Just Isern enjoys reading, boating, walking, exercising, sewing, arts and crafts, and classical music.

Leslie H. Lazareck

President
Adagio Software, Inc.
2375 East Tropicana Avenue, Suite 322
Las Vegas, NV 89119
(702) 456–4868
Fax: (702) 456–0961

2741

Business Information: Adagio Software, Inc., established in 1993, specializes in the publishing of computer software. As President, Mr. Lazareck is responsible for all aspects of operations, including development and testing, manufacturing, marketing, sales and administration. **Career Steps:** President, Adagio Software, Inc. (1993–Present); President, Blue Sky Software, Inc. (1988–1990); Accounting Systems, IBM (1985–1990); Sales, Southwestern Company (1982–1983). **Associations & Accomplishments:** Active with Blind and Visually Impaired of Nevada; Group Living Well. **Education:** University of Santa Barbara, B.S. in Mechanical Engineering (1985). **Personal:** Mr. Lazareck enjoys tennis, skiing, running, frisbee, travel and being a handiman.

Jill A. Lewis

Vice President of Administration
Graphix Zone, Inc.
42 Corporate Park, Suite 200
Irvine, CA 92714
(714) 833–3838 Ext. 121
Fax: (714) 833–3990

2741

Business Information: Graphix Zone, Inc. is a multi–media publisher specializing in entertainment, television, music and comedy CD ROM's for end–users. Major clientele include large and small companies such as Tower records, and retail chains including K–Mart, Sam's and Target. Established in 1989, Graphix Zone, Inc. currently employs 52 people. As Vice President of Administration, Miss Lewis is responsible for the oversight of the departments of Human Resources, Facilities, and Shipping and Receiving. **Career Steps:** Vice President of Administration, Graphix Zone, Inc. (1995–Present); Vice President of Administration, Introspec Architectural Consultants (1993–1995); Engineering Coordinator, IMPCO Technologies (1991–1992); High School Business Education Teacher, Gordon County Board of Education (1988–1992). **Associations & Accomplishments:** National Educational Association; Professional Human Resources Association. **Education:** University of Georgia, Business Administration (1988). **Personal:** Miss Lewis enjoys reading, golf, snow skiing, tennis, and weight training.

Wayne M. Martin

Chef de Cuisine, Pastry Chef, Consultant
Culinary Information Network
1025 N. Roosevelt Ave.
Loveland, CO 80537–4664
(970) 203–0260
Fax: Please mail or call

2741

Business Information: Culinary Information Network is a culinary communications company providing the creation of recipe books, manuals, and menus for clients. An Executive Chef with over fifteen years expertise, Wayne Martin provides all areas of administration and consultation for his private firm. His duties entail consulting, assistance, and design of restaurants' food and beverage manuals; recipes; signature dishes; point of sales manuals; menus; ads; and profit and loss statements. In addition, he has conducted extensive employee and management training programs and assisted in several restaurant openings by creating full recipes and manuals, including exotic meat. **Career Steps:** Executive Chef/Pastry Chef/Consultant, Culinary Information Network (1995–Present); Kitchen Manager/Assistant Food Operations Director, White Butterbean Restaurant – Orlando, FL (March 1995–June 1995); Head Chef/Kitchen Manager and Trainer, Spragedgies, Italian Kitchen – Orlando, FL (1994–1995); Baker/Trainer, Goodings Grocery Stores, Orlando, FL (June 1994–Oct. 1994); Station Chef–Line/Banquet Cook, Colorado Springs Marriott Hotel – Colorado Springs, CO (1993–1994); Station Chef/Grade Manager/Assistant Baker, Sarasota's – Colorado Springs, CO (1992–1993); Cook–Lead Line and Baker, School House Restaurant – Divide, CO (1991–1993); Head Sous Chef, Colorado Springs Hilton – Colorado Springs, CO (1989–1992); Corporate Head Baker/Sous Chef, Marriott Hotels – South Bend, IN (1988–1989); Director of Work Program Crews, CYC–Camp Benjamin Rosenthall – Eau Claire, MI (Feb. 1988–Oct. 1988); U.S. Army (Dec. 1984–1987); U.S. Marine Corps (May 1984–Dec. 1984). **Associations & Accomplishments:** First Place, South Bend Winter Wonderland Festival, Gingerbread Competition (1988); Volunteer, Colorado Mounted Ranger (Volunteer Police Program). **Education:** Certified Food Handler – Florida; Personal and Career Enhancement Courses: Dale Carnegie; "One Minute Manger"; Kitchen Managers – Spageddies and Brinker International; Nutritional Studies Program. **Personal:** Married to Michele in 1994. Four children: Gregory, Tatiana, Keeano and Zachary. Mr. Martin enjoys studying the culinary arts and collecting cookbooks and magazines from around the world.

Belinda Jean Melanson

International Business Services Manager
Markem Corporation
150 Congress Street
Keene, NH 03431
(603) 357–9403
Fax: (603) 352–0375
EMAIL: See Below

2741

Business Information: Markem Corporation specializes in the manufacture of marking equipment, specifically printed supplies such as data codes, names, and logos for products, including Tylenol. Headquartered in Keene, New hampshire, the Company is a subsidiary of Intel and has fourteen locations throughout the U.S. Established in 1909, the Company employs over 700 people and has estimated annual revenue of $200 million. As International Business Services Manager, Mrs. Melanson oversees all service and traffic. She is responsible for recovery and benefits, and assists in approximately 65% of the Company's market. Internet users can reach her via: Bmelanson@markem.com. **Career Steps:** Markem Corporation: International Business Services Manager (1994–Present), Manufacturing Business Liaison (191–1994); Sales and Store Manager, RV Sales Unlimited (1988–1991); Complex Manager, Pt. Loma Bay Apartments (1986–1988). **Associations & Accomplishments:** International Management Council (IMC); Spanish National Honor Society; Team Captain, United Way; Humane Society. **Education:** Keene State College, Bachelors (1985). **Personal:** Married to Bob in 1985. Mrs. Melanson enjoys being outdoors, volleyball, golf, camping, hiking, riding bikes, rollerblading, and cooking.

Frank G. Milone

Art Director
Warner Brothers Publications
15800 N.W. 48th Avenue
Hialeah, FL 33014–6422
(305) 620–1500 Ext. 118
Fax: (305) 621–0973

2741

Business Information: Warner Brothers Publications is a publisher of popular and educational music, including videos, books, cassettes, and CDs, as well as producing sheet music and children's music. Warner Brothers Publications has two locations (Florida and California). An artist for the past 21 years, Mr. Milone joined Warner Brothers Publication as Art Director in 1995. He is responsible for the creative direction and management of the Art Department, in addition to overseeing a creative staff of 20. Career milestones include creating logos for Metro Zoo, Weeks Air Museum, and Fantasy of Flight. **Career Steps:** Art Director, Warner Brothers Publications (1995–Present); Art Director, Weeks Air Museum (1989–1995); Exhibit Designer, Metro Zoo (1976–1981). **Associations & Accomplishments:** Restoration Volunteer, Weeks Air Museum. **Education:** Florida International Univ., B.FA. (1975). **Personal:** Married to Margaret in 1970. Two children: David and Michelle. Mr. Milone enjoys aircraft restoration, history, and being an active artist (fine arts & graphic arts).

N. Stephan Paterson
Advertising Director
News West Publishing Company
P.O. Box 21209
Bullhead City, AZ 86439–1209
(520) 763–2505
Fax: (520) 763–7820

2741

Business Information: News West Publishing Company a subsidiary for BREHM Communications in San Diego, California, specializes in newspaper and magazine publishing and commercial printing. Printing two community weeklies, two shoppers Casino Entertainment Magazines, and Tri–State Entertainment Weekly, the Company has a circulation of approximately 120,000. As Advertising Director, Mr. Paterson oversees marketing and all aspects of advertising. He is also responsible for sales training, budgeting, promotion, and business development. **Career Steps:** Advertising Director, News West Publishing Company (1993–Present); Co–Op Advertising Director, Journal Register Company (1989–1993); Co–Op Advertising Manager, The Palm Beach Post (1986–1989); Advertising Director, The Deerfield Beach Observer (1982–1986). **Associations & Accomplishments:** Marketing Committee, Arizona Newspaper Association; Co–Op/Vendor Council Member, Newspaper Association of America; Executive Board Member, Bullhead City Chamber of Commerce;. Mohave Mesa Kiwanis. **Education:** Florida Atlantic University, B.A. (1984); Miami Dade Community College, A.A. **Personal:** Married to Debra Lynn in 1981. Two children: Colby Marie and Kelly Nicole. Mr. Paterson enjoys golf, scuba diving, and computers.

Doreen Pomije
Owner and Graphic Designer
Creative Edge
2130 E. Old Shakopee Road, #315
Bloomington, MN 55425
(612) 854–3208 (612) 920–9943
Fax: (612) 920–9930

2741

Business Information: Creative Edge specializes in creating and designing written material such as: newsletters, posters, logos, billboards, business cards, and brochures for clients. As Owner, Doreen is devoted to excellence and coordinates numerous projects with clients. With an eye for design and sensitivity for content and detail, she stays committed to producing quality work on schedule. Concurrent with her present position, she is a representative of Excel Telecommunications and Art Director for Priority Publications, a company which specializes in financial newsletters. Quote from Kathy Cariveau: "Doreen has more positive energy than anyone I have every known. She never gets overwhelmed and always gets things done right. An extremely motivated person and motivates those who work with her." Quotable Quote: "Today is going to be an excellent day in every way." **Career Steps:** Owner, Creative Edge (1986–Present); Representative, Excel Telecommunications (1995–Present); Art Director, Priority Publications (1994–Present); Graphic Designer, Blue Book Publications (1991–1994); Art Coordinator, Ariston Art & Literary Magazine (1990–1991). **Associations & Accomplishments:** Softball Manager, Ladies' Softball Monday Nights; Art Club President (1990–1991); Tau Alpha Kappa; Alpha Lambda Phi. **Education:** College of St. Catherine, B.A. in Studio Art, Minors in Business and Communications (1991). **Personal:** Ms. Pomije enjoys mountain biking, softball, volleyball, camping, and rollerblading in the annual 75–mile marathon for M.S.

Cal Pozo
Vice President of Production
Ppi Entertainment Group
88 Saint Francis Street
Newark, NJ 07105
(201) 344–4214
Fax: Please mail or call

2741

Business Information: Ppi Entertainment Group specializes in the manufacture and distribution of speakers, multi–media games, and educational software for computers. Established in 1940, the Company employs 80 people, and has an estimated annual revenue of $30 million. As Vice President of Production, Mr. Pozo creates, produces, directs, and develops video programs for the home computer market. **Career Steps:** Vice President of Production, Ppi Entertainment Group (1990–Present); Creative Director, Telefitness (1980–1990). **Associations & Accomplishments:** Society of Independent Producers; Writers Guild; ACSM; IDEA. **Education:** New York University, M.S. (1978). **Personal:** Mr. Pozo enjoys cooking."

Thomas N. Rush

Controller
World Service Office, Inc.
19737 Nordhoff Place
Chatsworth, CA 91311–6606
(818) 773–9999
Fax: (818) 700–0700

2741

Business Information: World Service Office, Inc. is an international, self–supported and non–profit organization, which develops, manufactures, prints, and publishes literature regarding narcotics addiction recovery. Literature, such as pamphlets, books, etc. are distributed to members of the Drug Addition Narcotics Anonymous organizations. Services include providing for the development of facilities, editing, computers, and pagemakers for the written word of the recovering addict. International in scope, World Service Office, Inc. has locations in the U.S. (Los Angeles), Belgium (Brussels), and Canada. Future plans include opening facilities in Panama and Australia. A recovered narcotic addict for the past fifteen years, Mr. Rush joined World Service, Inc. as Controller in 1994. He is responsible for all financial matters, including controlling a large volunteer structure of 250 individuals who travel nationally and provide support services to local groups and area committees. **Career Steps:** Controller, World Service Office, Inc. (1994–Present); President/Controller, Van Dyne and Sons Roofing (1979–1992); Marketing Manager, AG Fertilizer (1973–1979). **Associations & Accomplishments:** American Institute of Professional Bookkeepers; Board of Directors (1982–1986), Sparks Community Chamber of Commerce; **Education:** California State University–Sacramento B.A. (1973).

Deana D. Sheriff
Chief Operations Officer
Medical Environment, Inc.
5721 Arapahoe Road, Suite 2B
Boulder, CO 80303–1339
(303) 442–5300
Fax: (303) 440–9897

2741

Business Information: Medical Environment, Inc. is a national publishing company, concentrating on the publishing of OSHA training and compliance information for healthcare facilities. Joining Medical Environment, Inc. as Chief Operations Officer in 1993, Ms. Sheriff oversees all publishing, production, customer service, writing, and marketing operations, as well as producing video training tapes. **Career Steps:** Chief Operations Officer, Medical Environment, Inc. (1993–Present); Manager, A & P Injury Rehabilitation (1992–1993); Office Manager, Keppel Chiropractic (1989–1992); Engineering Coordinator, Solbourne Computer (1987–1989). **Associations & Accomplishments:** Human Factors and Ergonomics Society; Published in the OSHA Update Newsletter. **Education:** University of Denver, B.A. (1987); Parks Junior College, A.S. (1982). **Personal:** Married to Scott in 1984. Ms. Sheriff enjoys surfing the Internet, shooting, bicycling, reading, antiques, and walking.

Ta–Liu Shih
President
World Bliss Publisher
210 South West Clark Street, Apartment A–102
Issaquah, WA 98027–3713
Fax: Please mail or call

2741

Business Information: World Bliss Publisher specializes in the promotion of Buddhism through literary, audio, and video communications worldwide. Offering a newsletter and textbooks in both English and Chinese, the Company plans distribution of the newsletter throughout the world, with the textbooks being sent to select universities nationwide. Established in 1996, the Company presently relies on volunteers. As President, Rev. Shih edits and writes articles about Buddhism and promotes Buddhist practices and orthodox dharmas. She is also responsible for administration, operations, public relations, marketing, and strategic planning, and performs translations of relevant material. A founder and member of the board of directors, she is also responsible for calling meetings and coordinating with supervisory personnel. Rev. Shih would like to donate the achievement to her teacher and master, Rev. Shen–Kai Shin who has been the great guidance in her life. **Career Steps:** President, World Bliss Publisher (1995–Present); Treasurer/Director, B.B.C.C. (1994–1995); Director, JCB Sanger Mission (1993–1994); Secretary/Director, JCB Northridge Mission (1992–1993). **Education:** University of Oregon, B.A.I.B.S. (In Progress); California State, Fresno, and California State, Pomona. **Personal:** Rev. Shih enjoys meditation, sitting, walking, and repenting.

Frank G. Skedel
President and Chief Executive Officer
Ecocenters Corporation
31225 Bainbridge Road
Solon, OH 44139
(216) 498–4900
Fax: (216) 498–4922

2741

Business Information: Ecocenters Corporation is an electronic printing and publishing service bureau. Joining Ecocenters Corporation as President and Chief Executive Officer in 1995, Mr. Skedel is responsible for all aspects of operations, in addition to overseeing all administrative operations for associates and a support staff of 55. **Career Steps:** President and Chief Executive Officer, Ecocenters Corporation (1995–Present); LDI Corporation: Executive Vice President and Chief Financial Officer (1994–1995), Senior Vice President and Treasurer (1990–1994). **Associations & Accomplishments:** March of Dimes (1994–1995); Northern Ohio Chapter Chairman; Chairman, Strategic Planning and Member, Finance Committee; Make–A–Wish Foundation Board and Executive Committee Member (1993); The Executive Committee (1991–1994); Sales and Marketing Executives member; Financial Executives Institute member. **Education:** University of Akron, M.B.A. (1971); Ohio University, B.B.A. in Finance. **Personal:** Married to Susan J. in 1983. Three children: Sheri, Jeff, and Matt. Mr. Skedel enjoys golf and reading.

Miss Julie D. Targos
President and Owner
Nonpareil Communications, Inc. (A Delaware Corporation)
427 Jeffrey
Royal Oak, MI 48073–3336
(810) 288–2180
Fax: Please mail or

2741

Business Information: Nonpareil Communications, Inc. is a full–service advertising firm, providing marketing, publishing, promotion, advertising, and merchandising services for films and film companies. As President and Owner, Miss Targos is responsible for managing all aspects of company operations. The Company is a Delaware Corporation licensed by Lucasfilms, Ltd. on Star Wars posters. Established in 1993, Nonpareil Communications, Inc. employs a full–time professional staff of two and reports annual revenue in excess of $200K. **Career Steps:** President and Owner, Nonpareil Communications, Inc. (A Delaware Corporation) (1994–Present); President and Owner, JDT Associates (Licensed by Paramount on Star Trek:TNG) (1989–1994); Special Projects Coordinator, Marketing Associates, Inc. (1985–1989); Office Manager, Assistant Art Director, G&D Communications, Inc. (1979–1985). **Associations & Accomplishments:** World Trade Club; Women in Communications; Detroit Chamber of Commerce; Dun & Bradstreet; Adcraft Club of Detroit; Who's Who in American Women; Oxford's Who's Who; Who's Who Worldwide; Marketing Research Association; American Advertising Federation; American Marketing Association; Adobe Technology Exchange. **Education:** University of Detroit, Communications (1984); Macomb County Community College (1981).

Dorothy "Dottie" A. Wells

Vice President of Finance and Chief Financial Officer
Lancaster Press, Inc.
3575 Hempland Road
Lancaster, PA 17601–6912
(717) 285–9095
Fax: (717) 285–7261
EMAIL: See Below

2741

Business Information: Lancaster Press, Inc., established in 1877, is a national firm that composes, prints, and electronically distributes scientific, technical, medical, and professional journals. The corporation has two locations and approximately 550 employees. As Vice President of Finance and Chief Financial Officer, Ms. Wells is responsible for all financial aspects of the corporation. Ms. Wells also handles taxes, administration of information technology activities, and administration of reprints. Assuming total responsibility for the Company's operation rather than just the financial responsibilities is Ms. Wells' plan for the future. The secret to success, per Ms. Wells, is to have a strong work ethic and to be consistently fair. Internet users can reach her via: daw@tapsco.com. **Career Steps:** Vice President of Finance and Chief Financial Officer, Lancaster Press, Inc. (1994–Present); President, FSE Holdings, Inc. (1993–Present); Chief Financial Officer/Director Finance, International Envelope Company (1989–1993); Director of Planning, Avery International (1981–1989). **Associations & Accomplishments:** Financial Executives Institute; Board of Trustees, St. Matthews United Methodist Church; Printing Industries Financial Executives; Chester County Aids Support Services; Former AIDS Buddy. **Education:** St. Mary's College, M.B.A. with Honors (1979); University of Maryland, B.S. in Information Systems Management (1969). **Personal:** One child: Michelle McElligott. Ms. Wells enjoys outdoor activities and woodworking.

JoAnn Winstead McPhail

Owner
APT Investments
2608 Stanford Street #A
Houston, TX 77006–2928
(713) 526–9941
Fax: Please mail or call

2741

Business Information: Anna Gold Classics is a publisher of children's audiocassettes for Christian radio broadcast: World Wide Christian Radio, Nashville, TN; KYND–AM, Cypress, TX; KCBT, Dallas, TX; San Angelo, TX; Frederick, OK; KTEK, Houston, TX. As Owner, Ms. Winstead McPhail is responsible for all aspects of company operations, including writing stories, directing readers, recording, music, and working with radio promotion. **Career Steps:** Owner, APT Investments (1994–Present); Owner, Anna Gold Classics (1995–Present); Owner, Golden Galleries (1990–Present). **Associations & Accomplishments:** American Society of Composers; Authors and Publishers/ASCAP; BMI; International Platform Association; National Association for Female Executives; International Society of Poets. **Education:** Attended: Houston Community College, Florida Southern College, and St. Johns River Jr. College. **Personal:** Married to James in 1963. Three children: Angela C. Morris; Dana D. McPhail and Whitney Gold Casso. Ms. Winstead McPhail enjoys sewing, fashion design, stained glass, needle point, furniture restoration and silk screening.

Lisa Wright Theodore

Key Accounts Director
Reed Elsevier/Reed Travel Group
500 Plaza Drive
Secaucus, NJ 07094–3619
(201) 902–1685
Fax: (201) 902–2110

2741

Business Information: Reed Elsevier/Reed Travel Group is the world's largest publisher of travel information. As the Key Accounts Director for the Hotel Marketing Group, Ms. Wright Theodore manages the Company's top revenue–producing key international accounts for the Reed network of fifteen products with a personal portfolio of over $15 million. She is responsible for creating marketing strategies and sales initiatives to meet the unique market challenges and niche opportunities of all HFS hotel brands, Holiday Inn Worldwides, Marriott Hotels, AmeriSuites, Prime Hospitality, and other key accounts. Her products include Hotel Directories and Internet On–Line Directory; these products are used by travel agents, frequent business travelers, and consumers around the world. **Career Steps:** Reed Elsevier/Reed Travel Group: Key Accounts Director of the Hotel Marketing Group (1993–Present), Regional Director, Northeast (1989–1993), Regional Account Manager (1985–1989); Director of Sales, Accor International–Caribbean Division (1983–1985). **Associations & Accomplishments:** Sales and Marketing Executives International (SMEI); American Society of Travel Agents (ASTA); Hospitality Sales and Marketing Association International (HSMAI); Ms. Wright Theodore has received numerous awards including: Effective Key Account Development, #2 Salesperson of the Year, #3 Salesperson of the Year, Regional Director of the Year, Regional Office of the Year. **Education:** Rutgers College/Rutgers University, B.A. (1981). **Personal:** Married to Vassili in 1990. Two children: Stephen and Nicholas. Ms. Wright Theodore enjoys scuba diving, horseback riding, and being the stock selection chairperson of an investment club.

Mr. Joseph C. Mattia

Secretary – Treasurer
Mattia Printing Company, Inc.
29 Park Avenue
Newark, NJ 07104
(201) 482–5130
Fax: (201) 482–3535

2751

Business Information: Mattia Printing Company, Inc. is a family owned commercial printing company founded in 1904 by Mr. Mattia's grandfather. Among their regular printing jobs are the National Enquirer, The Star, Essex County voting ballots and ASA rule books. They perform color, black & white, and computerized printing. As Secretary – Treasurer, Mr. Mattia is the General Manager in charge of Finance, Production, Sales, Purchasing and Personnel. He has a wide knowledge of the business, as he has worked his way through the ranks to his present position. **Career Steps:** Various positions leading to Secretary – Treasurer, Mattia Printing Company, Inc. (1944–Present). **Associations & Accomplishments:** Member, United States Chamber of Commerce; Member, AARP; Member, American Legion; Member, Master Printers; Charter Member, Boy's Club. **Education:** Trade School. **Personal:** Mr. Mattia enjoys antique cars, gourmet cooking, dancing and salt water fishing.

Gary J. Forget

Vice President of Marketing for Canadian Group
Qubecor Printing
275 Wellington Street East
Aurora, Ontario L4G 6J9
(905) 841–4587
Fax: (905) 841–3936
EMAIL: See Below

2752

Business Information: Qubecor Printing is an international printing company specializing in printed materials and related communications products and services. A subsidiary of Quebecor, Inc. in Montreal, the Company is the second largest in the world, and has the status of number one in Europe and Canada, and number two in the U.S. Originally a local newspaper and magazine publisher, the Company diversified in 1965, focusing on printing, and went public in 1992. Employing 23,000 people, Quebecor Printing has an estimated annual revenue of $3 billion. As Vice President of Marketing for Canadian Group, Mr. Forget oversees all aspects of marketing relating to Canada, the U.S. and Europe. He is responsible for writing brochures, attending trade shows, maintaining a low overhead, and handling all public relations. Internet users can reach him via: garyjfor@aol.com. **Career Steps:** Qubecor Printing: Vice President of Marketing for Canadian Group (1994–Present); Group Director/Human Resources (1993–1994); Manager of Human Resources, General Electric Lighting (1989–1993). **Education:** University of Toronto: M.B.A. (1986), B.Sc. With Honors. **Personal:** Married to Susan in 1979. Two children: Lindsay and Jean–Paul.

James S. Gulezian

Senior Human Resources Manager
Safeguard Business Systems
217 Church Road
North Wales, PA 19454
(215) 699–3544
Fax: (215) 699–5291

2752

Business Information: Safeguard Business Systems is a $200 million, privately–held corporation that manufactures standard, semi–custom, and custom one–write checkwriting and recordkeeping systems, continuous forms, and laser checks and forms. The Company provides payroll services, color coded filing systems, and accounting software to clients. As Senior Human Resources Manager, Mr. Gulezian is responsible for approximately 500 employees at four manufacturing locations. Concurrently, Mr. Gulezian is the National Safety Coordinator and has responsibility for all six manufacturing locations as well as five non–manufacturing facilities for a total in excess of 1,000 employees. **Career Steps:** Safeguard Business Systems: Senior Human Resources Manager (1989–Present), National Safety Coordinator (1993–Present); Plant Personnel Manager, Fairchild Weston Systems, Inc. (1984–1989); Manager of Employment/EEO, Infotron Systems Corporation (1983); Manager of Employment, MAI/Sorbus Service Division (1979–1983). **Associations & Accomplishments:** Boy Scouts; Church Board of Trustees; Society of Human Resource Management; Mid–Atlantic Employers Association; National Safety Council; Certified to teach Zenger–Miller courses; Certified to teach WMI Performance Appraisal program; Certified to teach DDI Service Plus program. **Education:** St. Joseph's University, M.B.A. program; Villanova University, B.S. in Business Administration (1975). **Personal:** Married to Elaine in 1982. Two children: Matthew and John. Mr. Gulezian enjoys being a Boy Scout leader.

Brian P. Ilten

Owner/Vice President
Pip Printing
15054 Alondra Boulevard
La Mirada, CA 90638
(714) 522–8680
Fax: (714) 522–0576
EMAIL: See Below

2752

Business Information: Pip Printing is a family–owned business concentrating on business communications including, but not limited to light commercial printing, digital printing, and file transfer. Comprised of two printing franchises, the Company was established in 1968, and employs ten people. As Owner/Vice President, Mr. Ilten oversees all aspects of production, sales, and marketing. He is also responsible for recruitment of new clients and strategic planning. Internet users can reach him via: xplrpip@aol.com. **Career Steps:** Owner/Vice President, Pip Printing (1985–Present). **Associations & Accomplishments:** Past President, La Mirada Chamber of Commerce; Past President, Southern California Pip Owner's Association; Pip Printing Advisory Council; Faith Lutheran Church Elders; Speaker, Rotary Club; **Education:** Cypress College. **Personal:** Married to Susan in 1989. One child: Christian James. Mr. Ilten enjoys church activities, going to Disneyland, and being an avid California Angels fan.

Ms. Linda Moore Linham

Senior Vice President of Marketing and Sales
Renaissance Publishing Company, Inc.
318 East 7th Street
Auburn, IN 46706
(219) 925–1700
Fax: (219) 925–5067

2752

Business Information: Renaissance Publishing Company, Inc. is an establishment primarily engaged in commercial printing, with marketed products including calendars and promotional material. As Senior Vice President of Marketing and Sales, Ms. Moore Linham oversees all sales, customer service, and strategic planning. Established in 1935, Renaissance Publishing Company, Inc. employs 250 people. **Career Steps:** Senior Vice President of Marketing and Sales, Renaissance Publishing Company, Inc. (1995–Present); Vice President Marketing, Renaissance Publishing Company, Inc. (1989–1994); Manager of Marketing Development, Bemrose Group, USA (1987–1989); Regional Sales Manager, Advertising Unlimited (1985–87); Vice President of Sales, Elliot Calendar Company (1975–1985). **Associations & Accomplishments:** Promotional Products Association International; PPAI Educational Program Facilitator/Trainer; Industry speaker on customer service and process management. PPAI Board of Directors (1992–1995), PPAI Strategic Planning Committee (1992–1995), PPAI Technology Committee (1994–1996). Vice Chair of Finance Executive Committee (1994–1995). Volunteer for mentoring programs. Published in trade journals. **Education:** Ohio University, Communications. **Personal:** Married to Stephen V. Linham in 1986. One child: Monica Reed. Ms. Moore Linham enjoys travel and art.

Marie K. Walchalk

Director of Purchasing/Estimating
Press Works, Inc.
1421 West Main Street
Alliance, OH 44601–2153
(330) 823–5699
Fax: Please mail or call

2752

Business Information: Press Works, Inc. provides screen, offset, and Flexo printing. As Director of Purchasing and Estimating, Mrs. Walchalk oversees the purchase of ink, screens, chemicals, paper stock, and office supplies. In addition, she is responsible for estimating and the development of point–of–purchase sign kits. **Career Steps:** Press Works, Inc.: Director of Purchasing/Estimating (1995–Present), Estimator (1995); Sterling, Inc.: Media Buyer (1994), Print Buyer (1990–1994). **Education:** Hammel Business College, Secretarial Skills (1988). **Personal:** Married to Ron in 1990. One child: Ron Jr.

Mrs. Walchalk enjoys fishing and outdoor activities with her son.

Ms. Susan P. Byrd

Vice President of Alliances
Xerox Production Systems
295 Woodcliff Drive
Fairport, NY 14450–4204
(716) 264–2558
Fax: (716) 383–7949
E–mail: See below

2754

Business Information: Xerox Corporation is the world's leading manufacturer and marketer of copiers, facsimile equipment, medical resonant image scanners, personal computers, and related chemical products. Xerox Production Systems, a Division of Xerox, specializes in production printing and publishing. Currently, Xerox employs 90,000 people and has an estimated annual revenue of $15 billion. As Vice President of Alliances, Ms. Byrd is responsible for the operation of the Alliance Program for Xerox production systems, including third party engagements for systems. Ms. Byrd can also be reached through the Internet as follows: SusanByrd@mc.xerox.com **Career Steps:** Vice President of Alliances, Xerox Production Systems (1994–Present); Vice President of Strategy and Development, Xerox Financial Services (1990–1994); Senior Vice President, Mercator Corporation (1984–1990). **Education:** University of Pennsylvania Wharton School of Business, M.B.A. in Finance (1978); Mount Holyoke College, B.A. in Economics (1973). **Personal:** Married to James P., III in 1973. Three children: Ian, Austin and Taylor. Ms. Byrd enjoys skiing, walking, hiking and reading.

DYNOPRESS

Todd R. Amar

Vice President
Dyno Press Inc.
735 Florida Avenue South
Minneapolis, MN 55426–1703
(612) 541–0966
Fax: (612) 541–0878

2759

Business Information: Established in 1972, Dyno Press Inc. specializes in commercial print finishing, including foilstamping, embossing, diecutting, and cosmetic decoration. The Company produces high–quality decorative products for clients such as Levi Strauss, Nike, McDonalds, etc. International in scope, Dyno Press has grown over the last five years by 42 percent annually, increasing the number of employees from 11 to 90. As Vice President and Owner, Mr. Amar provides the overall direction and vision for the company's continued growth, quality delivery to customers, and strategic developments. Concurrent to his position with Dyno Press Inc., Mr. Amar is also the President of RPI Inc., a brokerage company and Vice President of Quality Leather–n–Tag, a screen printing operation. **Career Steps:** Dyno Press Inc.: Vice President (1989–Present), General Manager (1984–1989). **Associations & Accomplishments:** Die Cutting and Die Making Information Network: Foil Stamping and Embossing Association; Institute of Packaged Professionals; International Association of Die Cutting and Die Making; Former Board of Directors, Courage Centers, Minneapolis Crisis Nursing Organization; Published in the International Board Report Magazine. **Education:** University of Minnesota, B.S. (1984). **Personal:** Married to Glenda in 1986. Two children: Jesse and Aaron. Mr. Amar enjoys snow mobile racing, boating, skiing, motorcycling and hunting.

D. Gene Autrey

Director of Sales & Marketing
Knight Graphics
3020 Lincoln Court
Garland, TX 75041
(214) 271–7700
Fax: (214) 503–9149

2759

Business Information: Knight Graphics specializes in commercial printing, including 4–color process, complete printing, and specialty advertising. The Company designs and produces all their own marketing material. In the case of small businesses, the Company will act as an ad agency, as well as a printer. As Director of Sales & Marketing, Mr. Autrey creates marketing niche penetrations and manages sales, marketing, business development, and training. **Career Steps:** Director of Sales & Marketing, Knight Graphics (1989–Present); Vice President of Marketing, Condel, Inc. (1985–1989); Director of Sales and Marketing, Kitchell Contractors of Texas (1981–1985). **Associations & Accomplishments:** Associated General Contractors; Apartment Association of Greater Dallas; Executive Council, Episcopal Diocese of Dallas; Society of Marketing Professional Services. **Education:** University of Texas – Arlington, B.A. in History (1975); Licensed Real Estate Agent – Texas (1986). **Personal:** Married to Janet in 1992. Four children: Shawna, Michele, Dena, and Mark. Mr. Autrey enjoys history, genaeology, reading, and Southwest culture & Art.

Bill Baker

Vice President Courseware
New Horizons Computer Learning Centers Inc.
1231 East Dyer Road, Suite 140
Santa Ana, CA 92705–5606
(714) 438–9421
Fax: (714) 513–7970
EMAIL: See Below

2759

Business Information: New Horizons Computer Learning Centers Inc. is an international publishing company creating courseware for franchises. The Company's mission is to transfer information to computer users. Translated courseware includes Spanish, French, Arabic, and Portugese. New Horizons Computer Learning Center Inc. has offices under the names New Horizons Franchising Inc. and New Horizons Publishing. The Company has over 147 global franchises and have grown rapidly since 1992 when it first franchised. As Vice President Courseware, Mr. Baker oversees the development of courseware. His primary focus is in the area of translations. In addition, he is responsible for sales and marketing. Internet users can reach him via: CSERVE75411,50. **Career Steps:** New Horizons Computer Learning Centers Inc.: Vice President Courseware (1994–Present), Courseware Development Manager (1992–1994); System Manager, Donley Media Group/Hemet News (1990–1992). **Associations & Accomplishments:** Society of Technical Writers; Board of Directors, Kansas Press Association; Ellsworth Chamber of Commerce: President, Board of Directors; President, Kansas Weekly Advertising Managers Association. **Personal:** Mr. Baker enjoys computer software and photography.

Jolene R. Brown

Regional Vice President
Guest Informant
1750 Kalakaua Avenue #212
Honolulu, HI 96826
(808) 944–8036
Fax: (808) 942–2714

2759

Business Information: Guest Informant publishes premier visitor guides in 35 markets in the USA, reaching 40 million visitors annually. As Regional Vice President, Ms. Brown oversees management of the Hawaii Region, concentrating on employee motivation, sales and marketing. Her division is directly responsible for twelve visitor publications in Hawaii. **Career Steps:** Regional Vice President, Guest Informant (1993–Present); Publisher of Catalogs and Tabloids, Honolulu Publishing Company (1987–1992); Publisher of Catalogs and Tabloids, Sturdivant Publishing (1986–1987); President and Publisher, Names N Numbers, Inc. (1972–1986). **Associations & Accomplishments:** Hawaii Hotel Association; The Hawaii Visitors Bureau; Waikiki/Oahu Visitors Association; Honolulu Advertising Federation; Retail Merchants Association; International Council of Shopping Centers. **Education:** Attended: University of Utah (1968); Weber State College (1967). **Personal:** Married to Bruce Brink in 1982. Two children: Michael D. and Douglas J. Ms. Brown enjoys travel, skiing, river rafting, and reading.

Mr. Wayne C. Gerlt

Chairman of the Board and General Counsel
Fepco, Inc.
P.O. Box 559
South Windsor, CT 06074
(203) 644–2565
Fax: (203) 644–2567

2759

Business Information: Fepco, Inc. is a commercial screen printer, specializing in billboards, advertising brochures and banners. Major clients include Toys R Us and Marlboro. As Chairman of the Board and General Counsel, Mr. Gerlt oversees all operational aspects, particularly involved with the strategic growth and development of the Company. A practicing attorney, Mr. Gerlt also has a private practice firm, specializing in civil law and litigation. Areas of specialization include mergers, real estate and banking transactions. He represents wealthy clients, assisting them in land development and acquisitional transactions. Established in 1958, Fepco, Inc. employs 45 people with annual sales of $3.7 million. **Career Steps:** Chairman of the Board and General Counsel, Fepco, Inc. (1958–Present); Attorney, Gerlt Law Offices (1976–Present). **Associations & Accomplishments:** American Bar Association; Connecticut Bar Association; Hartford County Bar Association; Founding Director, Bank of South Windsor; Action in Youth Sports Programs; Former Chairman, Zoning Board of Appeals; Former Town Attorney; Former Treasurer, Connecticut Municipal Attorneys. **Education:** Capital University, J.D. (1975); University of Connecticut, B.A. **Personal:** Married to Elaine in 1970. Three children: Tabetha, Tiffany and Christopher. Mr. Gerlt enjoys golf, water sports, and travel.

Mr. Hugh M. Griffin

Vice President of Sales and Marketing
Stuart F. Cooper Company
1565 East 23rd Street
Los Angeles, CA 90011
(800) 421–8703 Ext. 170
Fax: (213) 747–7141

2759

Business Information: Stuart F. Cooper Company is a full–service international specialty printing and engraving company for professional clientele. In his current capacity, Mr. Griffin is responsible for all sales and marketing functions for the Company to include; new customer development, product development, international growth strategies, public relations, and strategic planning. Established in 1929, Stuart F. Cooper Company employs 280 people. **Career Steps:** Vice President of Sales and Marketing, Stuart F. Cooper Company (1988–Present); Regional Manager, American Bank Stationery (1984–1988); Marketing Director, Encom/Baker International (1982–1984); Vice President of Sales, Petropak/Int'l Projects (1981–1982). **Associations & Accomplishments:** Board of Directors, Engraved Stationery Manufacturers Association; Chairman, Board of Governors, Forty Plus Southern California; Public Relations Director, Neurofibromatosis Foundation – Houston; National Association of Legal Vendors; National Association of Law Firm Marketing; Board of Directors, Broken Bytes; Junior Achievement; Various Youth Sports Organizations. **Education:** Presbyterian College, B.A. (1972); University of Graz, Austria. **Personal:** Married to Maurine in 1974. Three children: David, Scott, and Robert. During his leisure time, he enjoys golf, international business and politics, history, and writing.

Steve G. Haire

Vice President/General Manager
Century Graphics
155 Ida Street
Omaha, NE 68110
(402) 453–1402
Fax: (402) 453–2641

2759

Business Information: Century Graphics specializes in commercial printing, i.e., newspaper inserts, printer inserts, etc. As Vice President/General Manager, Mr. Haire is responsible for overall operational management. **Career Steps:** Vice President/General Manager, Century Graphics (1992–Present); Plant Manager, Rapid Press, Inc (1982–1992); Assistant Pressroom Manager, Hughes Publishing Company (1972–1982). **Associations & Accomplishments:** Craftsman Club of the Midlands; Knights of Columbus. **Education:** Bellevue University, B.S. in Management (1996). **Personal:** Married to Kate in 1975. Three children: Marc, Melissa, and Matt. Mr. Haire enjoys hunting and fishing.

Bill G. Horton Jr

Engineer
CMS Gilbreth Packaging Systems
3300 State Road
Bensalem, PA 19020
(215) 244–2378
Fax: (215) 244–2390

2759

Business Information: CMS Gilbreth Packaging Systems is a manufacturer of tamper evident sleeves, roll fed labels, and label application machinery. Established in 1960, the Company currently employs 300 people. As Engineer, Mr. Horton directs continuous improvement programs and operational research activities. **Career Steps:** Engineer, CMS Gilbreth Packaging Systems (1992–Present); Senior Engineer, QVC Network (1990–1991); Industrial Engineer, UNISYS (1985–1990). **Associations & Accomplishments:** Institute of Industrial Engineers. **Education:** Drexel University, B.S. (1984). **Personal:** Married to Jean in 1992. Three children: Megan, Kristin, and Brooke. Mr. Horton enjoys biking, skiing, reading, and travel.

Mr. Michael Kenner

President
American Printing & Design, Ltd.
3652 Eastham Drive
Culver City, CA 90232
(310) 287–0460
Fax: (310) 287–0109

2759

Business Information: American Printing & Design, Ltd. is a commercial printing and product marketing company, specializing in on–call printing and rush jobs for advertisers and corporations nationwide. As President, Mr. Kenner oversees management of the Company, concentrating on contract negotiations, employee motivation, sales and marketing, investments counselling, and product marketing for equity participation. Established in 1981, American Printing & Design, Ltd. employs a full–time staff of 36 and reports annual sales in excess of $6 million. **Career Steps:** President, American Printing & Design, Ltd. (1981–Present). **Associations & Accomplishments:** Palos Verdes Chamber of Commerce; Advisor, Babytone Corporation; Advisor, Care Card International; Advisor, Bank of San Pedro; Contributor: L.A. Mission, Camp Goodtimes, Special Olympics, City of Hope, Orton Dyslexia Society. **Education:** W.V.I.T., B.S. (1979).

David P. Kerkhoff

Regional Sales Manager
Kinkos Graphic Corporation
1360 Soldiersfield Rd.
Brighton, MA 02135–1099
(617) 782–0919
Fax: (617) 782–1386

2759

Business Information: Kinkos Graphic Corporation provides printing, copying, graphics, and business services to retail and commercial customers. Headquartered in Ventura, California, Kinkos Graphic Corporation has 860 international locations in Japan, Korea, Netherlands, Guam, Canada, and Europe. As Regional Sales Manager, Mr. Kerkhoff oversees all sales and marketing efforts for the outside sales representatives. He is responsible for an annual budget of approximately $7 million, in addition to administrative activities and strategic planning. **Career Steps:** Regional Sales Manager, Kinkos Graphic Corporation (1993–Present); Atlantic Healthcare: Regional Sales Manager (1988–1993), District Sales Manager (1986–1988). **Associations & Accomplishments:** American Management Association; H.I.D.A.; N.A.H.C.E.; Chamber of Commerce; Sigma Nu Fraternity; Christ Church Exeter, Exeter Recreation Coaches Association. **Education:** University of New Hampshire, B.S. (1983). **Personal:** Married to Margaret Ann in 1986. Three children: Jason, Jillian, and Trevor. Mr. Kerkhoff enjoys athletics, coaching, tennis, and reading.

Kevin Leines, C.Q.A.

Quality and Training Director
John and Roberts Company
9687 E. River Road
Coon Rapids, MN 55433
(612) 754–4407
Fax: (612) 755–0394
EMAIL: See Below

2759

Business Information: John and Roberts Company is a general commercial printing company. Family–owned, the Company was established in 1951, employs 320 people and has estimated annual revenue of $52 million. As Quality and Training Director, Mr. Leines oversees system process, manages the team task force, ISO 9000, and is responsible for all training, and application of problem solving tools. Internet users can reach him via: kbrucel@johnroberts.com. **Career Steps:** Quality and Training Director, John and Roberts Company (1994–Present); Director of Total Quality, Printed Medial Services (1990–1994). **Associations & Accomplishments:** American Society for Quality Control; American Management Association; AQP; NAPL; PIM; ASTD. **Education:** Rochester Institute of Technology, M.S. in Printing Technololgy (1990); Moorhead State University, B.S. in Industrial Illustration; North Dakota State University, A.A. in Interior Design. **Personal:** Married to Christina in 1987. Two children: Madeline and Andrew. Mr. Leines enjoys music, singing, basketball, boating, swimming, fishing, and family.

Robert MacDonald

Vice President of Operations
Reprints, Inc.
177 Vallecitos De Oro
San Marcos, CA 92069–1436
(619) 752–9500
Fax: (619) 752–9595

2759

Business Information: Reprints, Inc. is a hi–tech commercial printing corporation, specializing in high quality collateral material (six–color brochures), packaging, and labels. The Company services all industries, focusing on manufacturing companies. As Vice President of Operations, Mr. MacDonald is responsible for designing and directing all manufacturing activities, including personnel, sales and marketing, expansion, equipment acquisition, and implementation. Completely restructuring Reprints upon his appointment in 1993, Mr. MacDonald's leadership has resulted in sales revenue more than doubling. **Career Steps:** Vice President of Operations, Reprints, Inc. (1993–Present); Vice President of Sales/General Manager, Color Litho (1990–1993); Sales Representative, Welsh Graphics (1984–1990); Sales Respresentative, Nevada Web (1981–1984). **Education:** New Mexico State (1975–1978); numerous trade and technical schools and seminars. **Personal:** Mr. MacDonald enjoys yachting, golf, and travel.

Jan V. McCracken

Plant Engineer
R.R. Donnelley & Sons
1145 South Conwell Avenue
Willard, OH 44888
(419) 933–5250
Fax: (419) 933–5480

2759

Business Information: R.R. Donnelley & Sons is the largest commercial printer in the world. Established in 1864, the Company employs over 30,000 people in 80 locations around the world. The Willard, Ohio plant is responsible for printing, binding, and shipping of the Company's customers books. R.R. Donnelley employs 1,800 people at this 1.3 million square foot facility, on 184 acres of land, making it the largest book printing facility in the world. As Plant Engineer, Ms. McCracken oversees the safety and maintenance of all the building equipment and structures. Her duties include: handling of fire safety systems, building, parking lot, and railroad maintenance, roofing, remodeling, new construction, HVA/C, and central pneumatic systems. She is also responsible for sewage and solid waste management, environmental control and filtration, and grounds upkeep. **Career Steps:** Plant Engineer, R.R. Donnelley & Sons (1984–Present); Machine Maintenance Supervisor, U.S. Steel, Lorain Works (1981–1984). **Associations & Accomplishments:** National Cattleman's Association; Ohio Cattleman's Association; Richland County Cattlemen's Association. **Education:** Cleveland State University, B.S.M.E. (1982). **Personal:** Married to Roger Bisel in 1985. Two children: Nichole and Courtney. Ms. McCracken enjoys being active in the BLM Mustang and Wild Burro Adoption Program.

Bonnie L. Mitchell

Human Resource Manager
Carrollton Graphics
707 Canton Road, NW
Carrollton, OH 44615–9447
(330) 627–5511
Fax: (330) 627–7906

2759

Business Information: Carrollton Graphics, one of the primary regional printers serving Eastern United States, is a full–service commercial printing company, offering printing operations from creation to concept through typesetting, color cutting and scanning, press work, binding, and distribution of third class circulars. The largest employer in the rural community of Carrollton, Ohio today, Carrollton Graphics was established as a weekly newspaper in 1906. During the 1950's, it began to change from newspaper publishing to commercial printing and was the first to install a rotary web offset press in Ohio, thereby putting Carrollton on the forefront of the offset revolution and newspaper insert printing. In 1975, the Company name was changed from Carrollton Standard Printing Company to Carrollton Graphics, Inc. and was chartered in the State of Ohio. Joining Carrollton Graphics, Inc. as Pressroom Jogger in 1986, Ms. Mitchell was then promoted to Pressroom Administrative Assistant in 1991. Appointed as Human Resource Manager in 1995, she is responsible for overseeing all personnel matters, including creating new programs and helping department heads with personnel changes. **Career Steps:** Carrollton Graphics: Human Resource Manager (1995–Present), Pressroom Administrative Assistant (1991–1995), Pressroom Jogger (1986–1991); Dietary Assistant, Northwood Hills Healthcare (1985–1986). **Education:** Stark Technical College, A.A.B. (1995). **Personal:** Ms. Mitchell enjoys nature, restoring her farm house, and caring for her animals.

Ned T. Newell

Director
Jones Printing, Inc.
P.O. Box 5129
Chattanooga, TN 37406
(423) 624–3355
Fax: (423) 622–9084

2759

Business Information: Jones Printing, Inc. is a commercial printing company, providing digital communications products (i.e., Internet, WWW, multimedia products, etc.) and printing services throughout 27 states. Services include printing annual reports, sales brochures, etc. for the insurance and cosmetic industries, as well as offering Web pages to their existing clientele at no cost. As Director, Ned Newell is responsible for sales and marketing, recruiting new clientele and marketing the Company throughout the country. **Career Steps:** Director, Jones Printing, Inc. (1990–Present); District Marketing Manager, MCI Telecommunications (1986–1990). **Associations & Accomplishments:** Sponsor: Big Brothers/Big Sisters; United Way. **Education:** University of Georgia, A.B.J. (1989). **Personal:** Mr. Newell enjoys outdoor activities and sailing.

Ralph Oppler

President/Founder
BusinessBuilders Publishing Company, Inc.
39–40 Broadway
Fair Lawn, NJ 07410
(201) 703–1600
Fax: (201) 703–0784

2759

Business Information: BusinessBuilders Publishing Company, Inc. is an advertising sales agency and a publisher of customized real estate buyers guide books and hotel guest room directories. The Company is the number one firm in this industry on the East Coast. As President/Founder, Mr. Oppler is responsible for all aspects of Company operations, including administration, sales and marketing, public relations, finance, and legal matters. **Career Steps:** President/Founder, BusinessBuilders Publishing Company, Inc. (1991–Present); Fund raising Manager, Juvenile Diabetes Foundation (1988–1990); Regional Director, B'nai B'rith International (1978–1987). **Associations & Accomplishments:** Commerce and Industry Association of New Jersey; Fairlawn New Jersey Chamber of Commerce; B'nai B'rith International; B'nai B'rith Leadership Mission to Israel; Sponsor, National A.A.V. Basketball; Recreation Commissioner, Ridgefield, NJ; B'nai B'rith Presidents Club. **Education:** Bryant College (1952). **Personal:** Married to Ruth in 1957. Three children: Charles, Robin, and Stephen. Mr. Oppler enjoys basketball, bowling, and jazz.

Randy L. Schrum

Executive Vice President
Osborn Printing Company
3055 Biglerville Road, P.O. Box 547
Biglerville, PA 17307–0547
(717) 677–8111
Fax: (717) 677–9311

2759

Business Information: Osborn Printing Company is a 75 year old, mid–sized, full–service commercial printing company. Under new ownership starting in 1986 with 9 employees, Osborn Printing has grown to 45 employees and is generating $2.5 million in sales, with plans to open another electronic media division. Assisting the President of Osborn Printing, Mr. Schrum serves as Executive Vice President, and is also producing 55% of sales. In addition, he is responsible for the development of the electronic pre–press department, and the new off–site electronic media division. **Career Steps:** Osborn Printing Company: Executive Vice President (1992–Present), Sales Manager (1989–1992), Management Trainee (1986–1989); Quality Control Technician, C.P. Converters, Inc. (1983–1986). **Associations & Accomplishments:** Treasurer, York Club of Printing House Craftsmen; Outstanding Performance Award, Dale Carnegie. **Personal:** Married to Tammy in 1991. Two children: Kyle and Chloe. Mr. Schrum enjoys downhill skiing, snowmobiling, the outdoors, the beach and spending time with his family.

Gary E. Solomon
Plant Manager
Howard Press
1101 West Elizabeth Avenue
Linden, NJ 07036
(908) 862-3200
Fax: (908) 709-4291

2759

Business Information: Howard Press is an international commercial printing company, specializing in stationary. Clientele include IBM and AT&T. Established in 1974, Howard Press reports annual revenue of $35 million and currently employs 102 people. A Certified Network Engineer in computer networking, Mr. Solomon joined Howard Press in 1994 as Plant Manager. He is responsible for all aspects of plant operations in the Stationary Division. **Career Steps:** Plant Manager, Howard Press (1994-Present); General Manager, Alphagraphics (1989-1994); Owner, Prestige Personals (1982-1989). **Associations & Accomplishments:** Masons; International Thermographers Association; Engravers Association; Computer Network; Auxillary Police Training; Emergency Medical Technician Training. **Education:** West Virginia Institute of Technology, B.A. (1980). **Personal:** Married to Melody in 1988. One child: Meredith. Mr. Solomon enjoys spending time with his family, computers & technology, and the Internet.

Janet A. Spiech
Director of Marketing
Ringier America, Inc.
One Pierce Place
Itasca, IL 60143-1253
(708) 285-6000
Fax: Please mail or call

2759

Business Information: Ringier America, Inc. is a global network of custom information management, printing and distribution of catalogs, inserts, magazines and paperback books. As Director of Marketing since 1995, Ms. Spiech oversees all communications, advertising, and strategic directions. **Career Steps:** Ringier America, Inc.: Director of Marketing (1995-Present), Marketing Manager (1993-1995).

Michael Taylor
Controller
Henry Wurst Inc.
1331 Saline Street
North Kansas City, MO 64116-4410
(816) 842-3113
Fax: (816) 472-6221

2759

Business Information: Established in 1937, Henry Wurst Inc. is a web offset commercial printing company with a market in print catalogs, newspaper inserts, and coupons. Major clients include such names as Domino's Pizza and Sam's Club. As Controller, Mr. Taylor is responsible for all accounting and financial procedures. **Career Steps:** Henry Wurst Inc.: Controller (1995-Present), Assistant Controller (1995); Senior Auditor, Arthur Andersen L.L.P. (1991-1995). **Associations & Accomplishments:** American Institute of Certified Public Accountants; Kansas Society of Certified Public Accountants; Deacon, Leawood Baptist Church; Project Warmth; Habitat For Humanity. **Education:** Wichita State University: Master of Professional Accountancy (1991), B.S. in Accounting (1991). **Personal:** Married to Marcy in 1990. Two children: Ryan and Conner. Mr. Taylor enjoys basketball, softball, sportscard collecting, and reading.

Gerald R. Toates
Operations Manager
Label World, Inc.
29 Jetview Drive
Rochester, NY 14624-4903
(716) 235-0200
Fax: (716) 235-0398

2759

Business Information: Label World, Inc. specializes in the design and development of pressure sensitive labels and four-color processing for any industry. Using Flexagraphic processors, the Company designs, manufactures, markets, and ships the finished products from its Rochester, New York plant. Joining Label World, Inc. as Operations Manager in 1992, Mr. Toates is responsible for the continual education training processes for the Corporation, using his high background of training in the printing field. He is also responsible for the set-up and design of a preventive maintenance program. Along with occasionally operating a press machine, he maintains a one-on-one relationship with all outside venders and the overall day-to-day development of the plant site. **Career Steps:** Operations Manager, Label World, Inc. (1992-Present); Eastman Kodak Company: Production Su-

pervisor (1982-1992), Maintenance Advisor (1972-1982). **Associations & Accomplishments:** Treasurer, Ogden Parma Fire District; Past Commander, United States Power Squadron. **Education:** Rochester Institute of Technology (1974). **Personal:** Married to Jackie in 1968. Three children: Dean, Adam, and Jason. Mr. Toates enjoys boating.

Martin Wickham

Manager, Sales Administration of Eastern Canada
Moore Business Forms & Systems
9999 Cavendish, Suite 300
St. Laurent, Quebec H4M 2X5
(514) 748-8478
Fax: (514) 748-8343

2759

Business Information: Based in Toronto, Moore Business Forms & Systems specializes in the production and sale of electronic and paper-based business forms, communication, and mailing systems in 56 different countries. As Manager of Sales Administration of Eastern Canada, Mr. Wickham is responsible for handling fiscal matters and administrative duties including budgetary concerns, payroll, and purchasing. **Career Steps:** Moore Business Forms & Systems: Manager of Sales Administration of Eastern Canada (1994-Present), Plant Accountant (1991-1994), Administrative Supervisor (1990-1991). **Associations & Accomplishments:** University B.A. in Communications Graduate Association. **Education:** University of Quebec-Montreal, B.A. in Communications (1990). **Personal:** Mr. Wickham enjoys being an all-around sports fan, particularly enjoys baseball.

Carl E. Wolff
Service Representative
Perry Printing Company
PO Box 97
Waterloo, WI 53594
(414) 478-3551
Fax: Please mail or call

2759

Business Information: Perry Printing Company, a Union shop organization, is a full-service commercial graphic printing operation. As Service Representative, Mr. Wolff manages all Union customer accounts. Aside from his duties with Perry Printing, he is an active member of Local 507 of the Graphic Communication International Union serving in executive elected positions since 1993. In his current role as Recording Secretary with GCIU Local 507, he provides general service, records meetings, presides at grievance proceedings, coordinates contracts and other varied administrative duties. **Career Steps:** Service Representative, Perry Printing Company; GCIU, Local 507: Recording Secretary (1993-Present), President (1991-1992), Vice President (1988-1991). **Associations & Accomplishments:** Volunteer at local Fire Department; Delegate – South Central Federation of Labor; President, United Church of Christ, Lowell, WI; Coordinator, St. Jude's Bike-a-Thon; Parade Judge. **Personal:** Married to Terri L. in 1977. Two children: Joshua and Benjamin. Mr. Wolff enjoys hunting, fishing, community services volunteering, carpentry and chess.

William F. Woods Jr

President/Chief Executive Officer
Executive Printing, Inc.
830 Kennesaw Avenue
Marietta, GA 30060
(770) 428-1554
Fax: (770) 421-0112

2759

Business Information: Executive Printing, Inc. is a family-owned, regional, commercial printer. The Company prepares color advertising, corporate communication documentation, letterhead, and business forms. Executive Printing was established in 1975 and currently has 75 employees. As President/CEO, Mr. Woods oversees all operational aspects including sales and technical staff, sub-contractors/associates, strategic planning and customer relations. **Career Steps:** Executive Printing, Inc: President/CEO (1993-Present), President (1986-1993), General Manager (1981-1985), Press Operator (1976-1980). **Associations & Accomplishments:** First Vice Chairman, Printing Industry Association of Georgia; Rotary Club. **Education:** Atlanta Law School, J.D.; University of Georgia, A.B.J. (1981). **Personal:** Married to Carla in 1982. One child: William III.

Linda M. Yarbrough
MIS Director
Buchanan Printing
2330 Jett Street
Farmers Bridge, TX 75234-5760
(214) 241-3311 Ext. 153
Fax: (214) 406-6392
EMAIL: See Below

2759

Business Information: Buchanan Printing specializes in state-wide commercial printing. As MIS Director, Ms. Yarbrough is responsible for all computers, applications, networks, and related activities. Internet users can reach her via: linday@buchpntg.com. **Career Steps:** Buchanan Printing: MIS Director (1996-Present), Accounts Receivable Clerk (1992-1996); Aviation Electrician, U.S. Navy (1987-1990). **Associations & Accomplishments:** Leader of the South Central Users Group for Programmed Solutions; Parent Teachers Association; Supporter of Carrollton Jaguar Semi Pro Football Team. **Education:** University of North Texas; ICS Correspondence School; Upper Iowa University. **Personal:** Married to David Scott in 1990. One child: Jonathan A. Ms. Yarbrough enjoys all sport activities, boating, fishing, and camping.

Dr. Dennis A. Lunder, Ph.D.
Executive Director of Marketing Communications
American Greetings
One American Road
Cleveland, OH 44144-2398
(216) 252-7300 Ext. 1712
Fax: (216) 252-6898
EMAIL: DLunder@aol.com

2771

Business Information: American Greetings has been a leader in the design, manufacturing and marketing of greeting cards and social expression products since 1906 with five regional offices in New Jersey, Texas, Georgia, California, and Chicago, Illinois. As Executive Director of Marketing Communications, Dr. Lunder is responsible for the areas of trade and consumer advertising, business development and planning, sales training and management, sales promotions, event marketing, interactive kiosks, and multimedia productions and communications. Internet users can reach him via: DLunder@aol.com **Career Steps:** American Greetings: Executive Director of Marketing Communications (1993-Present), Director of Sales Personnel and Development (1990-1993), Director of Sales Support, Epson America (1984-1990). **Associations & Accomplishments:** Regional Vice President, Sales Marketing Executives International; Career Advisory Council, Students in Free Enterprise; Job Search of Hudson. **Education:** University of Denver, Ph.D. in Math Education (1978); University of Oklahoma, M.S.; Augustana College, B.S. (1965). **Personal:** Married to Bonnie in 1969. One child: Lisa Marie. Dr. Lunder enjoys tennis, golf, and snow skiing.

Joseph S. Lebb Jr.
Plant Manager
Potter Manufacturing Inc.
1010 Arrowsmith Street
Eugene, OR 97402-9121
(541) 343-4450
Fax: (541) 343-7636

2796

Business Information: Potter Manufacturing Inc. is a manufacturer of screen printed decals, primarily for collegiate, industrial, and commercial use. The Corporation also does die cutting of thermal and steel rolls. As Plant Manager, Mr. Lebb oversees all matters regarding production, policies, materials procurement, and personnel administration. **Career Steps:** Plant Manager, Potter Manufacturing Inc. (1995-Present); Supervisor, TRI-Graphic Inc. (1992-1994); Lead Printer, VCS (1979-1992). **Personal:** Married to Lora in 1985. Three children: Serene, Anna, and Courtney. Mr. Lebb enjoys arts & crafts, woodworking, fishing, and camping.

Rich McGee
Chief Executive Officer
Digital Color Image
5055 Central Highway
Pennsauken, NJ 08109
(609) 662-5532
Fax: (609) 662-0344

2796

Business Information: Digital Color Image, a fully electronic visual communications company, specializes in color separations printing serving the Delaware Valley (Pennsylvania, New Jersey and Delaware), Baltimore, Maryland and Washington, D.C. areas. As Chief Executive Officer, Mr. McGee is responsible for all aspects of operations, including administration, finance, and strategic planning. Established in 1986, Digital

Color Image currently employs 70 people and has annual revenue in excess of $8 million. **Career Steps:** Chief Executive Officer, Digital Color Image (1986–Present); Sales Representative, Lithoprep (1971–1985). **Associations & Accomplishments:** Board Head Committee, International Prepress Association; National Association of Printers & Lithographers; Genesis Counseling Center; Pennsauken High School Foundation. **Education:** LaSalle University, B.S in Marketing (1969). **Personal:** Married to Kelli in 1992. Two children: Megan and Jefferey. Mr. McGee enjoys golf, boating, reading, and watersports.

Michael Southard
Art Director, Vice President of Production Services
CST Entertainment Corporation
5901 Green Valley Circle Suite 400
Culver City, CA 9230–6951
(310) 417–3444
Fax: (310) 417–3500

2796

Business Information: CST Entertainment Corporation creates color effects on commercials and music videos for film and television. CST also specializes in digital ink and paint for animated segments and programs. An artist for over ten years, Michael Southard serves as Art Director and Vice President of Production Services, overseeing the art and marketing departments. He is responsible for creating unique color palets through the SGI computer work–stations with 16 million different colors. Mr. Southard has previously won the "Video of the Year Award" by MTV and the "Monitor Award" on a Janet Jackson video. **Career Steps:** Art Director, Vice President of Production Services, CST Entertainment Corporation (1994–Present); Senior Designer, American Film Technologies (1987–1994); Artist II, Cordura Publications (Mitchell) (1985–1987). **Associations & Accomplishments:** Board Member, AIDS Art Alive; Save Our Heritage Organization. **Education:** University of Massachusetts – Dartmouth, B.F.A. (1984). **Personal:** Mr. Southard enjoys downhill skiing, painting, travel and adventure.

2800 Chemicals and Allied Products

2812 Alkalies and chlorine
2813 Industrial gases
2816 Inorganic pigments
2819 Industrial inorganic chemicals, NEC
2821 Plastics materials and resins
2822 Synthetic rubber
2823 Cellulosic manmade fibers
2824 Organic fibers, noncellulosic
2833 Medicinals and botanicals
2834 Pharmaceutical preparations
2835 Diagnostic substances
2836 Biological products exc. diagnostic
2841 Soap and other detergents
2842 Polishes and sanitation goods
2843 Surface active agents
2844 Toilet preparations
2851 Paints and allied products
2861 Gum and wood chemicals
2865 Cyclic crudes and intermediates
2869 Industrial organic chemicals, NEC
2873 Nitrogenous fertilizers
2874 Phosphatic fertilizers
2875 Fertilizers, mixing only
2879 Agricultural chemicals, NEC
2891 Adhesives and sealants
2892 Explosives
2893 Printing ink
2895 Carbon black
2899 Chemical preparations, NEC

Brian D. Hughes
Worldwide Business Manager
Praxair, Inc.
175 E. Park Drive
Tonawanda, NY 14151
(716) 879–7149
Fax: (716) 879–7047

2813

Business Information: Praxair, Inc. manufacturers and sells a large variety of industrial gases for worldwide industries. As Worldwide Business Manager, Mr. Hughes wears many hats within the Company. He is responsible for recruiting new business, troubleshooting, policy and procedure compliance, and delivery of shipments. **Career Steps:** Praxair, Inc.: Worldwide Business Manager (1995–Present), Asian Business Manager – Asia (1992–1995); Product Manager, Union Carbide Linde

Division (1990–1992). **Education:** Tufts University, B.S. in Chemical Engineering (1982); Northeastern University, graduate Business courses (1982). **Personal:** Married to Kristine in 1980. Three children: Jennifer, Elizabeth, and Catherine. Mr. Hughes enjoys jogging and basketball.

John D. Kronis, Ph.D.
Technology Manager
Degussa Corporation
4 Pearl Court
Allendale, NJ 07401–1611
(201) 818–3700
Fax: (201) 327–7424

2813

Business Information: Degussa Corporation is a wholly–owned subsidiary of Degussa AG, an international leader in the development and manufacture of precious metal, chemical, and pharmaceutical specialties. As part of the Chemical Group, whose primary industries served include feed and animal nutrition, pulp and paper, mining, textiles, agriculture, chemicals and pharmaceuticals, Dr. Kronis is the Technology Manager in the Peroxygen Chemicals Division. He oversees the development and application of peroxygen chemicals, chiefly hydrogen peroxide and formamidine sulfinic acid, in the pulp and paper industry. E–mail: john.kronis@degussa.com. **Career Steps:** Technology Manager (Pulp and Paper), Degussa Corporation (1991–Present); Patent Agent, ICI Canada (1988–1990); Research Scientist, C–I–L, Inc. (1985–1987); Research Associate, Massachusetts Institute of Technology (1983–1985); Post–doctoral Research Associate, Ludwig Institute for Cancer Research (1981–1983). **Associations & Accomplishments:** Technical Association of Pulp and Paper (TAPPI); Canadian Pulp and Paper Association (CPPA); Council for Chemical Research (CCR); Pulp Manufacturers Association (PIMA). **Education:** University of Toronto, Ph.D. (1981).

Terri A. Lastovka, C.P.A., J.D.

Chief Financial Officer
Dar–Tech, Inc.
16485 Rockside Road
Cleveland, OH 44137
(216) 663–7600 Ext. 115
Fax: (216) 663–8007

2816

Business Information: Dar–Tech, Inc. is a primary distributor of specialty chemicals and raw materials for the paint and coating industries. Regional in scope, the Company has markets in Buffalo, Detroit, Louisville, Cincinnati, Pittsburgh, and Cleveland, with an estimated annual revenue of $36 million. As Chief Financial Officer, Ms. Lastovka oversees all monetary functions of the Company, including accounts payable and receivable, budgetary concerns, taxes, finances, and accounting. **Career Steps:** Chief Financial Officer, Dar–Tech, Inc. (1995–Present); Accountant/Consultant, Barnes, Wendling, Cook & O'Conner, Inc. (1990–1995); Field Examiner–ABL, Ameritrust (1989–1990); Staff Accountant, Hausser & Taylor, CPA's (1987–1989). **Associations & Accomplishments:** American Bar Association; Ohio Bar Association; Cleveland Bar Association; American Institute of Certified Public Accountants; Ohio Society of Certified Public Accountants. **Education:** Cleveland Marshall College of Law, J.D. (1995); Kent State University, Bachelor of Business Administration and Accounting (1986); Lorain County Community College, Pre–Business. **Personal:** Ms. Lastovka enjoys skiing and boating.

Ralph Edd Baldock Jr.
Training Manager
Eastman Chemical Company
P.O. Box 1973
Kingsport, TN 37662–5284
(423) 229–3362
Fax: (423) 229–1178

2819

Business Information: Eastman Chemical Company is one of the largest manufacturers of intermediate chemical, fiber, and plastic products in the world. Established in 1925, the company maintains ten facilities in the United States, Europe, South America, and Asia. An Industrial Engineer with 28 years experience, Mr. Baldock has served in various capacities with Eastman since 1977. Promoted to Training Manager in 1995, he is currently responsible for providing training for all maintenance, professional, operational, and technical personnel. **Career Steps:** Eastman Chemical Company: Training Manager (1995–Present), Manager of Management Engineering Services (1990–1995), Project Industrial Engineer (1988–1990). **Associations & Accomplishments:** American Society for Quality Control; Institute of Industrial Engi-

neers; American Society for Training and Development; American Management Association. **Education:** University of Tennessee – Knoxville: M.S. in Engineering Management (1978), B.S. in Industrial Engineering (1968). **Personal:** Married to Peggy in 1969. One child: Mary Elizabeth. Mr. Baldock enjoys sports, gardening, landscaping, and reading history.

Richard G. Barlund
World Wide Logistics Manager
Alcoa Industrial Chemicals
P.O. Box 345
Bauxite, AR 72011–0345
(501) 776–4983
Fax: (501) 776–4970

2819

Business Information: Alcoa's Chemical business originated in 1910, with the Industrial Chemicals group becoming a separate worldwide division in 1979. A 33 year veteran of Alcoa, Mr. Barlund joined the company upon his graduation from the University of Maryland in 1963. After holding a variety of positions at 6 different locations, in 1992 he moved into his present position as Worldwide Logistics Manager. In his current role, he provides strategic logistics direction for the division which include logistics evaluations of new facilities, rate negotiation and outsourcing strategies, as well as the development of pertinent procedures relative to logistics processes. **Career Steps:** Alcoa Industrial Chemicals: World Wide Logistics Manager (1992–Present), Manager of Services, Bauxite Operations (1990–1992). **Associations & Accomplishments:** Council of Logistics Management; Sponsor, Local Association for the Hearing Impaired; Local Port Users Association; NIT. **Education:** University of Maryland, B.S. (1963). **Personal:** Married in 1963. Mr. Barlund enjoys sailing and golf.

James R. Baus
Executive Vice President
Industrial Chemicals Corporation
Firm Delivery
Penuelas, Puerto Rico 00624
(809) 836–1260
Fax: (809) 836–1240

2819

Business Information: Industrial Chemicals Corporation, located in Puerto Rico, manufactures, sells and distributes sulfuric acid and related inorganic chemicals. Clients include pharmaceutical companies, electric power companies, sewer treatment plants, and water treatment plants. As Executive Vice President, Mr. Baus manages the plant, to include personnel, daily production records, troubleshooting, client relations, and accounting consultation. Mr. Baus considers success to be 95% work ethic, pride, and upbringing. The remaining 5% is pure determination and Mr. Baus is determined to become President and owner of Industrial Chemicals. **Career Steps:** Executive Vice President, Industrial Chemicals Corporation (1988–Present); Puerto Rican Aluminum Corporation: Vice President (1990–1992), General Manager (1988–1989); Construction Engineer, Fluor Daniel (1986–1988). **Associations & Accomplishments:** American Waterworks Association; Water Environment Federation. **Education:** Tulane University, B.S. (1986). **Personal:** Mr. Baus enjoys competitive windsurfing, reading, carpentry, and sailing.

William R. Crabtree

Manager
ISP Chemicals Inc.
P.O. Box 37
Calvert City, KY 42029–0037
(502) 395–1240
Fax: (502) 395–1464

2819

Business Information: ISP Chemicals Inc. is a manufacturer and distributor of specialty chemicals. Established in 1956, ISP Chemicals currently employs 560 people. As Manager, Mr. Crabtree is responsible for all aspects of plant production operations (consisting of 4 mini plants), which also includes the utilities area and toll manufacturing functions. **Career Steps:** ISP Chemicals Inc.: Manager of Production, Utilities and Tolling (1994–Present), Manager of Maintenance, Safety & Utilities (1992–1994); Manager of Distribution, Tolling & Safety, GAF/ISP (1987–1992). **Associations & Accomplishments:** Society of Kentucky Colonels. **Education:** Western Kentucky University, B.S. (1965). **Personal:** Married to Beverly. Four children: Paul, Eric, Daron and Brian. Mr. Crabtree enjoys tennis, hiking, hunting, fishing, racquetball, golf, and bridge.

Jal Rustom Dadabhoy
Technical Director
Peroxidos do Brasil Ltda.
Avenida Paulista 2001–15 Andar
Sao Paulo, Brazil 01311–931
55 11 289–0566
Fax: 55 11 287–5427

2819

Business Information: Peroxidos do Brasil Ltda. is the largest Hydrogen Peroxide producer in Latin America and forms part of the Solvy Interox Group, which is the largest hydrogen peroxide proudcer in the world with 17 plants in 15 countries. Peroxidos also produces peracetic acid and commercializes other peroxygen products produced by Solvay Interox. As Technical Director, Mr. Dadabhoy oversees two manufacturing sites in Brazil, all projects involving capital investments, research and development, customer services, and Corporate logistics. **Career Steps:** Peroxidos do Brasil Ltda.: Technical Director (1986–Present); Technical Manager (1983–1986); Works Manager, National Peroxide, Ltd. (1972–1982). **Associations & Accomplishments:** Member of the Hydrogen Peroxide Special Group CEFIC; Indian Institute of Engineers; Indian Institute of Chemical Engineers. **Education:** Indian Institute of Technology, B.Tech (1971). **Personal:** Married to Elizenil de Matos Candido in 1985. Mr. Dadabhoy enjoys reading and cooking.

Michel J. Foure, Ph.D.
Director of Research and Development
Elf Atochem North America, Inc.
P.O. Box 61536
King of Prussia, PA 19406
(610) 878–6790
Fax: (610) 878–6261

2819

Business Information: Elf Atochem North America, Inc. is a manufacturer of specialty chemicals and polymers. Established in 1990, the Company employs 4,800 people, and has an estimated annual revenue of $1.8 billion. As Director of Research and Development, Mr. Foure oversees and implements design and development of new products, and is responsible for quality control, administration, operations, and strategic planning. **Career Steps:** Director of Research and Development, Elf Atochem North America, Inc. (1993–Present); President, Melrablen Company, Holland (1989–1993); M&T Chemicals: Technical Director, France (1988–1989), Director of Research and Development, New Jersey (1985–1988). **Education:** University Wurzburg, Germany, Doctorate (1975); Fairleigh Dickinson University, M.B.A. (1983); Ecole Nationale Superieure de Chimie, France, M.S. in Chemistry. **Personal:** Married to Francoise in 1971. Five children: Laurence, Frederik, Jocelyn, Nathanael, and Sarah–Emily. Dr. Foure enjoys bridge, gardening, and fishing.

Donald G. Harcus
Plant Manager
Faxe Kalk, Inc.
499 Glen Avenue
Johnsonburg, PA 15845
(814) 965–3402
Fax: (814) 965–4517

2819

Business Information: Faxe Kalk, Inc. is a manufacturer of precipitated calcium carbonate man–made limestone which provides services to the paper industry. Headquartered in Atlanta, Georgia, and established in 1994, FAXE Kalk, Inc. employs 10 people. As Plant Manager, Mr. Harcus is responsible for managing the paper machine, the daily reports, maintenance of payrolls, and all purchasing. He also implemented the ISO – 9002 program. Mr. Harcus oversees a staff of 10. **Career Steps:** Plant Manager, FAXE Kalk, Inc. (1994–Present); Senior Project Engineer, Boise Cascade, Canada (1990–1993); Division Engineer, GK Carbonate (1987–1989); Assistant Plant Manager, Continental Lime (1985–1987). **Associations & Accomplishments:** Professional Engineers of Ontario. **Education:** University of Manitoba, B.Sc. in Mechanical Engineering (1973). **Personal:** Married to Barbara in 1980. Two children: Scott and Lindsey. Mr. Harcus enjoys boating and house renovation.

Michael C. Massey
Engineering Manager
Western Environmental Management
911 North Halgueno
Carlsbad, NM 88221–2348
(505) 885–4784
Fax: (505) 885–5349

2819

Business Information: Western Environmental Management designs and constructs sulphur recovery and tail–gas treating plants for the petroleum and petro–chemical industries. As Engineering Manager, Mr. Massey supervises a staff of fifteen in conducting all aspects of engineering/detail design. **Career Steps:** Engineering Manager, Western Environmental Management (1995–Present); Chief Engineer, Pennzoil Company – Sulphur Division (1990–1995); Project Engineer, General Technology Corporation (1987–1990). **Associations & Accomplishments:** American Society of Mechanical Engineers. **Education:** Wichita State University, B.S.M.E. (1986). **Personal:** Married to Daphnie in 1989. One child: Lauren. Mr. Massey enjoys piano, guitar, music composition, and golf.

CALGON CARBON CORPORATION

Jonathan H. Maurer
Vice President of Manufacturing
Calgon Carbon Corporation
P.O. Box 717
Pittsburgh, PA 15230–0717
(412) 787–6789
Fax: (412) 787–4511
EMAIL: see below

2819

Business Information: Calgon Carbon Corporation is a manufacturer of activated carbon products, primarily granular and powder activated carbon. Joining Calgon Carbon in 1991 as Plant Manager for the Big Sandy Plant, Mr. Maurer was appointed to his current position in 1995. As Vice President of Manufacturing, he is responsible for all domestic manufacturing facilities in Kentucky, Mississippi, California, and Pennsylvania. He is also responsible for scheduling, logistics, and purchasing of activated carbon and related systems. Internet users can reach him via: Maurer@calgcarb.com **Career Steps:** Vice President of Manufacturing, Calgon Carbon Corporation (1991–Present); Rod Manufacturing Manager, Bethlehem Steel Corporation(1989–1990); Vice President of Manufacturing, Roessing Bronze Company (1984–1989); Assistant Manager of Coke and Coal Chemicals, LTV Steel Corporation (1977–1984). **Associations & Accomplishments:** Rotary Club: Former President, Former District Rotary Foundation Chairman; Former Board Chairman, Junior Achievement. **Education:** University of Pittsburgh, E.M.B.A. (1987); West Virginia University. **Personal:** Mr. Maurer enjoys basketball and golf.

Ronald C. McBride
Director of Quality
Dexter Electronic Materials
211 Franklin Street
Olean, NY 14760–1211
(716) 372–6300
Fax: (716) 372–6864

2819

Business Information: Dexter Electronic Materials is a manufacturer of epoxy–based moldings and coating encapsulants, and urethane and epoxy liquid encapsulants for the microelectronic, electrical, and electronic markets. As Director of Quality, Mr. McBride is responsible for planning, implementing, and directing state–of–the–art quality techniques and methodologies in functional quality and quality improvement. **Career Steps:** Director of Quality, Dexter Electronic Materials (1994–Present); Director of Quality, Alpha Chemical & Plastic Corporation (1988–1994); Director, Quality Technics (1985–1988). **Associations & Accomplishments:** American Society for Quality Control; American Chemical Society; Toastmasters International; Co–Author of "Team Approach to Problem Solving." **Education:** Heidelberg College, B.S. (1966); Attended, Southern Illinois University. **Personal:** Married to Kate in 1969. Two children: Michael and Andrew. Mr. McBride enjoys tennis, golf, and Nordic Track.

Bernfried A. Messner, Ph.D.
Technical Manager
Stockhausen, Inc.
2408 Doyle Street
Greensboro, NC 27406–2912
(910) 333–7519
Fax: (910) 333–3548

2819

Business Information: Stockhausen, Inc. is a manufacturer of chemicals found in absorbent polymer products such as diapers and sanitary napkins for the hygiene, cable, medical, agricultural applications, and textile industries. As Technical Manager, Mr. Messner is responsible for the direction of all technical duties and projects for the absorbent polymers and textiles divisions. Career milestones include increasing business in the hygiene area by 50% by introducing two new generation polymers, thereby saving and reducing material costs, as well as being very successful in increasing sales in textile auxiliaries. **Career Steps:** Stockhausen, Inc.: Technical Manager (1994–Present), Product Development Manager (1993–1994); Research Chemist, Rohm, GmSH (1991–1992). **Associations & Accomplishments:** American Chemical Society; American Association of Textile Chemists and Colorists. **Education:** University of Freisung – Germany: Ph.D. (1990), Master in Chemistry (1996). **Personal:** Dr. Messner enjoys reading and music.

Christa O. Russell
Manager of Environmental Affairs
Lilly Industries, Inc.
733 South West Street
Indianapolis, IN 46225–1253
(317) 687–6722
Fax: (317) 687–6054

2819

Business Information: Lilly Industries, Inc. is a worldwide manufacturer of industrial coatings for the furniture, boating, farming, and appliance industries. Established in 1865, they are the largest manufacturer of mirror coatings in the world. As Manager of Environmental Affairs, Ms. Russell is responsible for regulating industrial waste materials, including waste water and air emissions, and Superfund compliance in the United States and Canada. She acquires industrial permits, develops environmental reports, and analyzes results. **Career Steps:** Manager of Environmental Affairs, Lilly Industries, Inc. (1991–Present); Indiana Department of Environmental Management: Branch Chief – Technical Support (1990–1991), Branch Chief – Solid Waste (1989–1990). **Associations & Accomplishments:** Air Quality Committee and Water Quality/Waste Management Committee, National Paint and Coatings Association; Environmental Quality Control, Inc. **Education:** University of Missouri, B.S. in Chemical Engineering (1978). **Personal:** Married to Thomas L. in 1989. Three children: Alexander, Emma and Colton. Ms. Russell enjoys landscaping, gardening and sewing.

Rony A. Sanchez–Martinez
Senior Product Development Engineer
Alcoa Industrial Chemicals
4701 Alcoa Road
Bauxite, AR 72011
(501) 776–4903
Fax: (501) 776–4904

2819

Business Information: Alcoa Industrial Chemicals is a primary manufacturer of Alumina and Specialty Chemicals. Products include coarse, fine and submicron particles which are sold into markets such as polymers, papers, ceramics, refractories, dessicants, catalysts, etc. As Senior Product Development Engineer, Mr. Sanchez–Martinez is responsible for the development of new products and processes, assisting with their implementation, and serving as technical resource for designing facilities for them. Additional responsibilities include training process operators, commissioning new equipment, writing ISO operating procedures, and job safety analysis. **Career Steps:** Senior Product Development Engineer, Alcoa Industrial Chemicals (1989–Present); Associate Staff Chemical Engineer, General Electric Corporate Research and Development (1981–1989). **Associations & Accomplishments:** American Institute of Chemical Engineers; American Chemical Society; National Society of Professional Engineers; American Society of Metals International. **Education:** Pratt Institute, B.ChE. (1981). **Personal:** Married to Marie–Sarmy in 1986. Two children: Tatianna and Suzette. Mr. Sanchez–Martinez enjoys performing a yearly presentation of career paths in engineering and science and "hands on science" to high school and grade school students.

Joachim Peter Schulz

Managing Director

Hoechst Consulting, Arabian Gulf Office

P.O. Box 2326
Dubai, United Arab Emirates
971–4–221153
Fax: 971–4–216153

2819

Business Information: Hoechst Consulting, Arabian Gulf Office, is the Dubai branch office of Hoechst AG of Germany, an international manufacturer of industrial and pharmaceutical chemicals. Mr. Schulz has served in several supervisory positions with Hoechst. Promoted to Managing Director of the Dubai branch office in 1991, he is now responsible for overseeing daily operations and administrative functions in Kuwait, United Arab Emirates, Bahrain, Qatar, and Oman. **Career Steps:** Hoechst Consulting: Dubai – Managing Director (1991–Present), Zaire – Managing Director (1983–1990), Industrial Manager (1980–1983). **Education:** Baccalaureate (1961). **Personal:** Married to Amina in 1978. Two children: Bernt Carsten and Armin Christoph. Mr. Schulz enjoys painting, music collecting and swimming.

DU PONT AUTOMOTIVE FINISHES

Enrique Sigas, Esq.

Manager – Automotive Products Department

E.I. DuPont De Nemours & Company, Inc.

P.O. Box 362828
San Juan, Puerto Rico 00936–2828
(809) 793–2959
Fax: (809) 792–9054

2819

Business Information: E.I. DuPont De Nemours & Company, Inc. is a research and technology–based global chemical and energy company offering high–performance products based on chemicals, polymers, fibers and petroleum. Committed to better things for better living, DuPont serves worldwide markets in the aerospace, apparel, automotive, agriculture, construction, packaging, refining and transportation industries. Established in 1802, DuPont currently employs 120,000 people and has an estimated annual revenue of $37 billion corporate–wide. The Puerto Rico site was established in 1940 and has an estimated annual revenue of $7.5 million. Employed with DuPont since 1967, Mr. Sigas has served in a managerial capacity within the Company for the past twenty–five years. Positions have included serving as manager of the San Juan and Ponce branches. Appointed as Manager of the Automotive Products Department in 1982, he is responsible for all operations of the Division, including sales, administration, finances, public relations, accounting, and strategic planning. During his tenure with the Automotive Division, he was the instrumental leader responsible for the Division becoming the top sales generator among DuPont's twenty–six (26) U.S.A. refinish service centers. **Career Steps:** E.I. DuPont De Nemours & Company, Inc.: Manager of the Automotive Products Department – Puerto Rico Office (1982–Present), Manager of the San Juan Area (1982), Manager of the Ponce Area (1978–1982); Manager, Bayamon, Arecibo and Caguas Areas (1971–1978). **Associations & Accomplishments:** American Bar Association; Puerto Rico Bar Association; Federal Bar Association; American Management Association; San Juan Rotary Club; Chamber of Commerce – Puerto Rico; President, Bayamon Exchange Club; President, University of Puerto Rico Alumni Association; President, Inter–American University Alumni Association; Member of the Board of Trustees, Inter–American University of Puerto Rico (1987–Present); President, Lawyers' Graduate Association, Inter–American University of Puerto Rico. **Education:** Inter–American University of Puerto Rico, J.D. (1975); University of Puerto Rico, B.B.A. (1971). **Personal:** Married to Mildred in 1961. Mr. Sigas enjoys traveling, music, reading, and sports.

Jim O. Stokes

Manager of Industrial Relations

UCAR, Inc.

P.O. Box 1001, 65 Canal Bank Street
Welland, Ontario L3B 5R8
(905) 732–6121 Ext.217
Fax: Please mail or call

2819

Business Information: UCAR, Inc. specializes in the manufacturing of carbon and graphite for industrial furnaces. By purchasing coal mixed with pitch as well as petroleum derivatives, the Company uses high temperatures to reprocesses the substances, forming industrial–grade carbon and graphite. International in scope, the Company is headquartered in Connecticut, with branches in West Virginia, Tennessee, Ohio and Canada. Established in 1907, the Company employs 300 people and has an estimated annual revenue of $100 million. As Manager of Industrial Relations, Mr. Stokes deals with labor unions, handles administrative and security contracts and negotiations, and is responsible for personnel management. Additional duties include interpretation of laws governing the processing of necessary substances, and strategic planning. **Career Steps:** Manager of Industrial Relations, Ucar, Inc. (1994–Present); Supervisor, Human Resources, Ucar Carbon, Canada (1990–1994); Union Carbide Consolidated: Environmental Technologist (981–1989), Shift Foreman (1977–1981). **Associations & Accomplishments:** President Human Resource Professionals of Niagara. **Education:** Brock University, B.A. (1992); Canadian Institute of Management (1977). **Personal:** Married to Sandra in 1981. Two children: James and Andrew. Mr. Stokes enjoys motorcycling, travel, hockey, lacrosse, and motor racing.

Janeen N. Wise

Corporate Tax Manager

United Catalysts, Inc.

1227 South 12th Street
Louisville, KY 40210–1570
(502) 634–7387
Fax: (502) 637–8765

2819

Business Information: United Catalysts, Inc. specializes in catalyst manufacturing, clay mining, and processing. As Corporate Tax Manager, Mrs. Wise directs and manages the Company's entire tax function regarding international, state, local, and property. **Career Steps:** Corporate Tax Manager, United Catalysts, Inc. (1988–Present); Corporate Tax Specialist, Island Creek Corporation (1986–1988); Corporate Tax Analyst, Diamond Shamrock Coal Company (1981–1986). **Associations & Accomplishments:** FSC/DISC Tax Association; Tax Executives Institute; Institute Management Accountants; American Cancer Society; March of Dimes Neighborhood Chair. **Education:** Xavier University, M.B.A. (1985); University of Kentucky, B.S. in Accounting; Ivy Tech State College, A.A.S. in Accounting. **Personal:** Married to David R. in 1977. Mrs. Wise enjoys ballroom and country dancing, travel, and water sports.

Scott R. Adams, Esq.

Insurance Counsel

Dow Corning Corporation

2200 West Salzburg Road CO1222
Midland, MI 48686–0994
(517) 496–8512
Fax: (517) 496–1709

2821

Business Information: Dow Corning Corporation is the world's leading manufacturer of silicone and silicone products. Established in 1943, Dow Corning Corporation reports estimated annual revenue of $2 billion and currently employs more than 8,000 people world–wide. A practicing attorney in state and federal courts since 1988, Mr. Adams joined Dow Corning Corporation in 1993. Serving as Insurance Counsel, he provides legal counsel to Dow Corning and world–wide subsidiaries on Risk, Insurance, and Liability matters. **Career Steps:** Insurance Counsel, Dow Corning Corporation (1993–Present); Attorney, Katten, Muchin & Zavis (1990–1993); Attorney, Kilpatrick & Cody (1988–1990). **Associations & Accomplishments:** Risk and Insurance Management Society; Quality Insurance Congress; American Bar Association; Maryland State Bar Association; Chairman, KWELM Reserving Committee; KWELM Creditors' Committee; Creditors' Committee, English and American Insurance Company. **Education:** Brooklyn Law School, J.D. (1988); University of Central Florida: B.A. in Allied Legal Services, B.A. in Public Administration. **Personal:** Married to Kathleen in 1990. One child: Jordan. Mr. Adams enjoys writing.

Mary M. Bolton

Director of Human Resources

Raychem Corporation

8000 Purfoy Road
Fuquay–Varina, NC 27526
(919) 557–8401
Fax: (919) 557–8656

2821

Business Information: Raychem Corporation, an international Fortune 500 company, is a scientific materials laboratory specializing in the testing and production of plastic components (heat–shrinkable plastics products) for industrial, electronics and telecommunications industries. International in scope, Raychem's global reach includes 50 countries. As Director of Human Resources for the Telecommunications Sector in Fuquay Varina, Dr. Bolton is responsible for all aspects of personnel matters, including hiring, payroll, benefits, and administration. In addition, she travels extensively on behalf of the Company. **Career Steps:** Director of Human Resources, Raychem Corporation (1980–Present); Director of Human Resources, Proctor & Gamble (1974–1980). **Associations & Accomplishments:** "Model Inner–City High School Teacher" in Cincinnati, Ohio in the 70's Award; Listed in Who's Who in America; Involved in Black/White community work; "1000,s of Things." **Education:** University of Cincinnati, Doctorate (1974). **Personal:** Married to Charles.

Vince J. DiCecco

Manager of Training and Development

Flexible Products Company

8155 Cobb Center Drive
Kennesaw, GA 30152
(770) 421–3205
Fax: (770) 590–3625
E MAIL: See Below

2821

Business Information: Flexible Products Company, established in 1951, manufactures and distributes specialty chemicals (i.e. plastisol inks and coatings, polyurethane foams, elastomers, etc.) for business and industry. The Company has four domestic and three foreign locations (Canada, Australia, and the Ukraine). As Manager of Training and Development, Mr. DiCecco designs, conducts, and evaluates training and development programs for internal and external needs. Internet users can reach him via: vdicecco@flexpro.com. **Career Steps:** Flexible Products Company: Manager of Training and Development (1995–Present), Marketing Manager (1994–1995); Nalco Chemical Company: Area Sales Manager (1991–1994), Training Specialist (1987–1991). **Associations & Accomplishments:** American Society for Training and Development; American Management Association; Screen Printing and Graphics Imaging Association. **Education:** United States Coast Guard Academy, B.S. (1977); Illinois Benedictine College, Certificate in Management and Organizational Behavior (1989). **Personal:** Married to Karin in 1995. Three children: Dominic, Anthony, and Matteo. Mr. DiCecco enjoys golf, tennis, reading, and computers.

James F. Doose

President

Resin Technology Company

2270 Castle Harbor Place
Ontario, CA 91761–5704
(809) 947–7224
Fax: Please mail or call

2821

Business Information: Resin Technology Company specializes in the manufacture and distribution of polyurethane resin systems for the original equipment manufacturer and construction industry markets. Established in 1982, Resin Technology Company currently employs 17 people and has an estimated annual revenue of $20 million. As President, Mr. Doose provides the overall direction and vision of the Company's continued growth, quality delivery to customers, and strategic development. **Career Steps:** President, Resin Technology Company (1994–Present); Vice President, Foam Resin, Inc.; Technical Director of Polyurethane Division, Reichhold Chemicals. **Associations & Accomplishments:** CSI; SPI; NFIB; NRCA. **Education:** California Polytechnic University, B.S. (1974). **Personal:** Married to Lisa in 1973. Three children: Matthew, Jonathan, and Janelle. Mr. Doose enjoys boating, scuba diving, and fishing.

Mike Hawes

Logistics/Finishing Coordinator

Huntsman Corporation

2701 Range Road
Marysville, MI 48040–2444
(810) 364–1842
Fax: (810) 364–3696

2821

Business Information: Huntsman Corporation is an international company involved in the production of polypropylene. As Logistics/Finishing Coordinator, Mr. Hawes handles both the rail system and warehouse. Rail System duties include scheduling & loading. Warehouse duties include the boxing and bagging of products, and freight and truck loading. Additional activities include, troubleshooting in both areas, as well as transmissions of product types. **Career Steps:** Huntsman Corporation: Logistics/Finishing Coordinator (1996–Present), Logistics Coordinator (1994–1996), Process Technician (1990–1994). **Associations & Accomplishments:** American Legion; United Way CRC. **Personal:** Mr. Hawes enjoys fishing, camping, and getting involved with the local hockey association.

Abhijit M. Joshi
Senior Manufacturing Engineer
Ashland Chemical, Inc.
P O Box 2219
Columbus, OH 43216
(614) 790–4087
Fax: (614) 790–3430

2821

Business Information: Ashland Chemical, Inc., a division of Ashland Oil, produces chemicals for a variety of business applications, markets the products, and distributes them to both wholesale and retail customers. As Senior Manufacturing Engineer, Mr. Joshi is part of the specialty polymers and adhesives division and he deals with solution–based and water–based adhesives. He is primarily responsible for emulsion manufacturing and trouble shooting of other processes. Other duties include small projects, offering technical support to staff and clients, consultation to other divisions, and strategic planning of important issues. **Career Steps:** Senior Manufacturing Engineer, Ashland Chemical, Inc. (1992–Present); Monsanto Company: Research Engineer (1991–1992), Design Engineer (1989–1991). **Associations & Accomplishments:** American Institute of Chemical Engineers; American Chemical Society. **Education:** University of Akron, M.S.Ch.E. (1987); Engineering College (Durjapur, India), Bachelor's Degree in Chemical Engineering. Currently working towards M.B.A. **Personal:** Married to Cindy in 1986. Mr. Joshi enjoys reading mystery novels, hiking, and nature walks.

Lynn Martynowicz–Foxhall
Director of Corporate Purchasing Polymers Worldwide
Huntsman Chemical Corporation
5100 Bainbridge Boulevard
Chesapeake, VA 23320
(804) 494–2594
Fax: (804) 494–2602

2821

Business Information: Huntsman Chemical Corporation is the largest, privately owned manufacturer of raw materials for plastics and chemicals. International in scope, the Company has several divisions with 81 locations in 23 countries. Bringing with her fourteen years of polymer plastics expertise, Dr. Martynowicz–Foxhall joined Huntsman in 1992. Recently appointed as Director of Corporate Purchasing Polymers Worldwide, she is responsible for purchasing raw materials for all ten polymer plants, via negotiating pricing, contracts, global agreements, and various services with major raw material suppliers worldwide. **Career Steps:** Huntsman Chemical Corporation: Director of Corporate Purchasing Polymers Worldwide (1996–Present), Technical Development Manager of North America (1995–1996), Western Accounts Sales & Marketing Manager (1992–1995), Market Manager for Expandable Resins (1990–1992); GE Plastics: Procuct/Process Development Specialist of Marketing/Technology Department (1988–1990), Product Development Scientist of PPO Venture Technology Department (1987–1988); Ph.D. Internship – Polymer R&D Chemist, IBM Corporation (1986); Consultant, Kerr Glass Manufacturing (1984–1986); Consultant, AMP, Inc. (1984–1986); Consultant, Barrier Testing Company (1984–1986); Polymer Chemist, CETA Program (1982). **Associations & Accomplishments:** Review Board, Journal of Cellular Plastics; Society of Plastics Institute: Vice Chairman, Western Expandable Polystyrene Division, Vice President, SPI Arizona Chapter; National Roofing Conference Association; CABO; BOCA; ICBO; SBCCI; Construction Specifiers Institute; ASTM; SPE; ACS; APS; World of Who's Who of Women – Cambridge, England (1992–1993); GE Plastics Best Poster Award (1988); Frequent publications and lecturer at international, national, state and local conference and institutional symposia; Holder of 6 Patents on Expandable Thermoplastic Resin Beads and Polyphenylene Ether; Dr. Martynowics–Foxhall has received the 1996 "Centennial Fellow of the College of Earth and Mineral Science at "The Pennsylvania State University" in recognition for her distinguished achievements among over 12,500 alumni graduates. **Education:** Pennsylvania State University: Ph.D. course work completed in Polymer Science (1986); M.S. in Polymer Science (1985), State University of New York at Fredonia, B.S. in Chemistry and Biology (1983); Certifed Sales Professional: University of Virginia–Richmond (1992). **Personal:** Lynn married Steven in 1995.

Mrs. Melinda S. McWilliams
Senior Electrical Engineer
Solvay Polymers
1230 Battleground Road
Deer Park, TX 77536
(713) 478–3936
Fax: (713) 478–3907

2821

Business Information: Solvay Polymers manufactures polyethylene, polypropylene, and hydrogen peroxide used in the injection mold and automotive industries. In her capacity as an Electrical Engineer, Mrs. McWilliams conducts engineering analysis studies on various plant systems, and does estimate, design, specifications, and constructions supervision of company projects. Established in 1956, Celanese, now Solvay Polymers, employs a full–time staff of 700. **Career Steps:** Solvay Polymers: Senior Electrical Engineer (1996–Present), Electrical Engineer (1993–1996); Electrical Engineer, TCS Design & Management Service (1991–1993); Electrical Engineering Co–op, Oglethorpe Power (1987–1990). **Associations & Accomplishments:** Past Member, Society of Women Engineers; Business and Professional Women's Scholarship. **Education:** Georgia Institute of Technology, B.S. in Electrical Engineering (1991), Minor in Industrial Psychology. **Personal:** Mrs. McWilliams enjoys volleyball in her leisure time.

Nereida Padilla–Colon
Finance Manager
IDI Caribe, Inc.
HC 1 Box 6801
Salinas, Puerto Rico 00751
(787) 853–2186
Fax: (787) 853–2187

2821

Business Information: IDI Caribe, Inc. is a manufacturer of custom thermoset molding compounds, bulk molding compounds, and sheet molding compounds. As Finance Manager, Ms. Padilla–Colon handles Company accounts, payroll accounts, accounts payable and receivable, and department reports. She obtained experience in finance by serving as a reserve member in the U.S. Army in the 338th Finance Co. at Fort Buchana, P.R. Ms. Padilla–Colon then served under the rank of Sergeant in the administrative field for the 941st QM Co. at Juana Diaz USAR Center. **Career Steps:** Finance Manager, IDI Caribe, Inc. (1993–Present); Unit Clerk, US Army Reserve (1986–1990); Customer Service Representative, Communications Authority (1969–1979). **Associations & Accomplishments:** Roslcrusian Order, Member. **Education:** Catholic University, B.B.A. (1992); Caguas City College, Secretary; Finance School – Fort Harrison, IN; Personnel School – GAP, PA & Fort McCoy, WI; Inter–American University, Computer courses (1994); Personnel Administration Advance School (1995); Various seminars and courses. **Personal:** Ms. Padilla–Colon enjoys reading, listening to music, travel, being involved in the coordination and support of the different activities and celebrations of the IDI Caribe, and metahysics.

Ramon L. Reyes
• • • ▬◖◉◗▬ • • •

District Manager
General Polymers
Lot 15, D Street, Amelia Industrial Park
Guaynabo, Puerto Rico 00965
(809) 793–1616
Fax: (809) 793–2907

2821

Business Information: General Polymers, a Division of Ashland Chemicals, is an international manufacturer and distributor of thermoplastic resins. International in scope, General Polymers has twenty–two locations throughout North America (U.S., Puerto Rico, Canada). A Certified Chemical Engineer, Mr. Reyes joined General Polymers as District Manager in 1990. He has complete responsibility for the Puerto Rico office, including overseeing all administrative operations for associates and a support staff of eight. He also serves as Marketing Manager for Ashland Chemicals, opening into new markets and increasing sales. **Career Steps:** District Manager, General Polymers (1990–Present); General Manager, Palmas Plastics (1989–1990); General Manager, Eighth Continent (1988–1989). **Associations & Accomplishments:** Secretary, Society of Plastics Engineers – Puerto Rico Section; American Institute of Chemical Engineers **Education:** University of Puerto Rico, B.S. in Chemical Engineering (1980) **Personal:** Married to Aminta M. Ortiz in 1983. One child: Luis Baysan Reyes. Mr. Reyes enjoys sports, music and reading.

Mario P. Scubla
Vice President of Support Services
Furon Company
29982 Ivy Glenn Drive
Laguna Niguel, CA 92677
(714) 363–6261
Fax: (714) 363–6275
Email: See Below

2821

Business Information: Furon Company is the world's leader in engineered polymer components for the industrial marketplace. The company serves five key markets: electronics, processing industries, captial goods, transportation, and healthcare. As Vice President of Support Services, Mr. Scubla is responsible for the supervision of 160 employees in Information Technology and customer support. Internet users can reach him via: mario.scubla@USA.Furon.com. Established in 1960, Furon Company employs 2,500 people with annual sales of $450 million. **Career Steps:** Vice President of Support Services, Furon Company (1995–Present); Managing Director, Magnetek Italy (1990–1993); Director of Information Systems, Magnatek, Inc. (1986–1990); Director of Information Systems, Smith International (1979–1986). **Education:** Jacksonville State University, B.S. Degree in Math (1963). **Personal:** Married to Kathy in 1974. Two children: Ryan and Kris. Mr. Scubla enjoys sailing and cooking.

John J. Politis
Market Development Specialist
Elf Atochem North America, Inc.
2000 Market Street
Philadelphia, PA 19103–3222
(215) 419–5315
Fax: (215) 419–5305

2822

Business Information: Elf Atochem North America, Inc. is a manufacturer of functional polymers within the polymer and plastic additives group of Elf Atochem North America. As a Market Development Specialist, Mr. Politis is responsible for identifying and promoting new market applications for polybutadiene resin. Established in 1990, Elf Atochem North America, Inc. employs 1,000+ people. **Career Steps:** Market Development Specialist (1994–Present), Product Manager (1989–1994), Elf Atochem North America, Inc.; Technical Sales Representative, Elf Atochem (1989); Technical Sales Representative, Morton International, Ventron Division (1985–1989). **Associations & Accomplishments:** American Chemical Society; Society of Plastics Engineers; Technical Association of the Pulp and Paper Industry. **Education:** University of Massachusetts, M.S. (1984); B.S. (1979). **Personal:** Married to Barbara in 1982. Two children: Jimmy and Michael. Mr. Politis enjoys playing sports and gardening.

Eric Naimark
Plant Manager
Cook Composites & Polymers
340 South Railroad Street
Saukville, WI 53080–2100
(414) 284–5541
Fax: (414) 284–0593

2823

Business Information: Cook Composites & Polymers (CCP) is a manufacturer of resin used in polyester and coatings. CCP has fourteen plant locations throughout the U.S. Joining the Company as Plant Manager in 1992, Mr. Naimark is responsible for all aspects of plant operations, including involvement in community and environmental issues. He also oversees all administrative operations for associates and a support staff of 85. **Career Steps:** Plant Manager, Cook Composites & Polymers (1992–Present). **Education:** Alleghany College, B.S. in Economics (1978). **Personal:** Married to Roberta in 1983. Mr. Naimark enjoys fishing, reading, and exercising.

Fran Ertl, D.V.M.
Vice President
Botanicals International
2550 El Presidio
Long Beach, CA 90810–1113
(310) 637–9566
Fax: (310) 669–8248
EMAIL: See Below

2833

Business Information: Established in 1976, Botanicals International is a bulk manufacturer and distributor of medicinal herbs, spices, and extracts. Bringing with him ten years nutritional expertise, Dr. Fran Ertl was appointed Vice President in 1991. Dr. Ertl is responsible for product development and research, QC, QA, and technical sales, as well as serving as a government and regulatory liaison. Internet users can reach her via: Fertl@botanicals. com **Career Steps:** Vice President, Botanicals International (1991–Present); Technical Director, Omni Pak Industries (1988–1991); Senior Food Technologist, Farmer Brothers Company (1982–1988); Research Assistant, University of California – Davis (1979–1981). **Associations & Accomplishments:** American Herbal Product Association: Board Member and Chairperson of Standardization Committee; American Spice Trade Association: Executive Technical Group, Chairperson of Analytical Group, Chairperson of Volatile Oil Sub–Committee; Association of Official Analytical Chemists; Associate Reference. **Education:** University of Bridgeport, M.S. in Nutrition (1992); University of California – Davis, M.S. in Food Science and Technology (1981); University of Tehran – Iran, D.V.M. (1973). **Personal:** Two children: Tara and Samiy. Dr. Ertl enjoys jogging, meditation, and yoga.

David M. Flowers

Quality Assurance Incoming Inspector and Auditor
Bayer Corporation
P.O. Box 3145
Spokane, WA 99220–3145
(509) 489–5656
Fax: (509) 484–4320
2833

Business Information: Bayer Corporation is a leader in health care, chemicals and imaging technologies – with more than 10,000 products designed to improve the quality of everyday life. As Quality Assurance Incoming Inspector and Auditor for the Allergy Division, Mr. Flowers is responsible for vendor and raw materials audits, ensuring timely development of competitive, high–quality chemistry instrument and reagent systems. Derivative and new platform research projects are managed using a "skill center" concept while product development projects are managed using Product and Cycle–time Excellence (PACE) process, which utilizes cross functional core team methods. His primary focus is to protect a highly profitable >200 million dollar chemistry business via a cross functional core team which is focused on continuous product support and improvement of current products that are developed either internally or licensed from outside. **Career Steps:** Bayer Corporation: Quality Assurance Incoming Inspector and Auditor (1995–Present), Pharmaceutical Specialist (1994–1995). **Associations & Accomplishments:** Spokane Area Chamber of Commerce; Work Force Diversity Committee; Toys for Tots; United Way. **Education:** Eastern Washington University, B.S. in progress. **Personal:** Mr. Flowers enjoys golf, mountain biking and skiing.

Koichi Fujii

Vice President of Operations
Pharmavite Corporation
1150 Aviation Place
San Fernando, CA 91340–1460
(818) 837–3633
Fax: (818) 365–7390
2833

Business Information: Pharmavite Corporation is a manufacturer and distributor of 300 types of vitamins and related products. Established in 1971, the Company employs 770 people and has estimated annual revenue of $270 million. As Vice President of Operations, Mr. Fujii oversees purchasing, logistics, and production engineering. He is also responsible for cost effectiveness and manages profit and loss ratios. **Career Steps:** Vice President of Operations, Pharmavite Corporation (1988–Present); Technical Manager, Europe Office Otsuka Pharmaceutical Company, LTD. (1988); Advisor, Lab Miguel S.A., Spain. **Education:** Chuo University, B.S. (1974). **Personal:** Married to Machiko in 1977. Two children: Yasuhiro and Chihiro. Mr. Fujii enjoys golf, and collecting coins and bills.

Stephen M. Gray

Owner and President
Herbal Pharmaceutical Resource (HPR)
4650 Northgate Boulevard, Suite 130
Sacramento, CA 95834
(916) 927–4372
Fax: (916) 927–4372
2833

Business Information: Herbal Pharmaceutical Resource (HPR) is a research & development and manufacturer of natural medicine products (vitamins) and an international wholesaler and retailer of products to health care professionals and consumers. HPuerto Rico also makes products available as a complimentary handout to health care professionals. Products are also marketed internationally through mail ordering and direct mailings, as well as on the World–Wide WEB. With eighteen years experience in the pharmaceutical industry, Mr. Gray joined Herbal Pharmaceutical Resource in 1995 as Owner and President. He is responsible for directing the nature of the business and overseeing all functions for the professional affairs and corporate development. Career milestones include initiating the marketing of pharmaceuticals through the World Wide Web, which he has taken from inception to reality, seeing the need and market for natural pharmaceuticals. **Career Steps:** Owner and President, Herbal Pharmaceutical Resource (1995–Present); Head Pharmacist, Raleys Drug Chain (1987–1995). **Associations & Accomplishments:** American Pharmaceutical Association; Association of Natural Medicine Pharmacists; Herb Research Foundation; California Pharmacists Association. **Education:** Idaho State University, B.S. (1978). **Personal:** Mr. Gray enjoys outdoor sports, weightlifting & fitness activities, and spiritual development.

Ron E. Ovadia

Technical Director
West Coast Labs
116 East Alondra Boulevard
Gardena, CA 90248
(310) 532–6720
Fax: (310) 532–9736
EMail: See Below
2833

Business Information: West Coast Labs is an international distributor and manufacturer of vitamins and nutritional supplements. As Technical Director, Mr. Ovadia is responsible for formulation, sales, customer service, pricing, and production planning. Internet users can reach him via: ROvadia@aol.com. **Career Steps:** Technical Director, West Coast Labs (1993–Present); Sales, Sportmart Sporting Goods (1991–1993). **Associations & Accomplishments:** Drug, Chemical, and Allied Trade Organization; Pacific Technology Exchange; National Nutritional Foods Association. **Education:** University of California – Irvine, B.S. in Biological Science (1994). **Personal:** Mr. Ovadia enjoys martial arts, weightlifting, hockey, and tennis.

Tang–Sheng Peng, Ph.D.

Laboratory Director
Nature's Herbs, Inc.
600 E. Quality Drive
American Fork, UT 84003
(801) 763–0700
Fax: (801) 763–0789
EMAIL: See Below
2833

Business Information: Nature's Herbs, Inc. creates and produces nutritional supplements, herbal products, and phytomedicines. Comprised of a full research laboratory, and development, production, and marketing departments, the Company was established in 1969 and has estimated annual revenue of $23.5 million. As Laboratory Director, Dr. Peng oversees laboratory organization, performs research and quality assurance analysis. He is also directly responsible for a support staff of fifteen professionals. Internet users can reach him via: ls29360@U.CC.utah.edu. **Career Steps:** Laboratory Director, Nature's Herbs, Inc. (1994–Present); Head Research Associate, University of Utah (1991–1994); Faculty, Zhongshan University, Guangzhou (1984–1986). **Associations & Accomplishments:** American Chemical Society; American Association for the Advancement of Science; American Society of Pharmacognosy; Utah Academy of Sciences. Dr. Peng has published more than 30 research papers in professional journals. **Education:** University of Utah, Ph.D. (1991); University of California, San Diego, M.S. (1988); Zhongshan University: M.S. (1984), B.S. (1982). **Personal:** Married to Fong in 1985. Two children: Kathy and Yinmin. Dr. Peng enjoys medicinal gardening, Tai Chi, hiking, and reading.

Thomas J. Riddle

Operations Manager
Packaging Services, Inc.
P.O. Box 948
Farmington, UT 84025–0617
(801) 451–0120
Fax: (801) 451–0180
2833

Business Information: Packaging Services, Inc. is a manufacturing and packaging corporation, specializing in health supplements. Established in 1992, Packaging Services, Inc. reports annual revenue of $15 million and currently employs 200 people. As Operations Manager, Mr. Riddle is responsible for the operation of the manufacturing and packaging facility. **Career Steps:** Operations Manager, Packaging Services, Inc. (1994–Present); Packaging Manager, General Nutrition Products (1991–1994); Packaging Supervisor, Barr Laboratories (1987–1991); Operations Supervisor, The Dannon Company (1986–1987); Production Supervisor, Revlon Inc. (1985–1986). **Associations & Accomplishments:** Institute of Packaging Professionals (IOPP); American Management Association (AMA). **Education:** Trenton State College, B.S. in Pre–Law and Psychology (1982); The New School of Social Research, Employee Assistance Programs. **Personal:** Mr. Riddle enjoys sports, reading, and chess.

David G. Taylor, Ed.D.

Vice President of Public Affairs and Communications
Ciba–Geigy Corporation
444 Saw Mill River Road
Ardsley, NY 10502
(914) 479–2108
Fax: (914) 479–2179
2833

Business Information: Ciba–Geigy is one of the largest manufacturers of specialty chemicals, pharmaceuticals, and agricultural products. They also set policy and regulations for products affecting the environment. Ciba–Grey presently employs approximately 16,000 people (U.S.) and has an estimated annual revenue of $4.6 billion (U.S.). Dr. Taylor currently serves as a member of the U.S. Corporate Management Committee ad Vice President of Public Affairs and Communications. **Career Steps:** Vice President of Public Affairs and Communications, Ciba–Geigy U.S. Corporation (1993–Present); Head of Corporate Staff, Ciba–Greigy, Japan (1989–1993); Head of International Policies & Issues, Ciba Greigy, Ltd. (1985–1989); Director of Public Policy, Ciba–Greigy Pharmaceuticals, U.S.A. (1981–1985). **Associations & Accomplishments:** Chairman of the Information Committee of the International Medical Benefits Risk Foundation; Member of the President's Council on Sustainable Development Natural Resources Task Force. International Vice President RAD–AR Council, Japan. **Education:** Rutgers University: B.A. (1971), Ed.D. (1975). **Personal:** Married to Keiko Taylor in 1989. Two children: Marisa and Alex.

David G. Taylor, Ed.D.

Vice President of Public Affairs and Communications
Ciba–Geigy Corporation
444 Saw Mill River Road
Ardsley, NY 10502–2699
(914) 479–2108
Fax: (914) 479–2179
2833

Business Information: Ciba–Geigy is one of the largest manufacturers of specialty chemicals, pharmaceuticals, and agricultural products. They also set policy and regulations for products affecting the environment. Ciba–Geigy presently employs approximately 16,000 people (U.S.) and has an estimated annual revenue of $4.6 billion (U.S.). Dr. Taylor currently serves as a member of the U.S. Corporate Management Committee and Vice President of Public Affairs and Communications. **Career Steps:** Vice President of Public Affairs and Communications, Ciba–Geigy U.S. Corporation (1993–Present); Head of Corporate Staff, Ciba–Geigy, Japan (1989–1993); Head of International Policies & Issues, Ciba–Geigy, Ltd. (1985–1989); Director of Public Policy, Ciba–Geigy Pharmaceuticals, U.S.A. (1981–1985). **Associations & Accomplishments:** Chairman of the Information Committee of the International Medical Benefits Risk Foundation; Member of the President's Council on Sustainable Development Natural Resources Task Force. International Vice President RAD–AR Council, Japan. **Education:** Rutgers University, B.A. (1971), Ed.D. (1975). **Personal:** Married to Keiko Taylor in 1989. Two children: Marisa and Alex.

Amilcar Toro

Senior Supervisor
Ortho Biologics, Inc.
P.O. Box 33333
Manati, Puerto Rico 00674
(787) 884–1139
Fax: (787) 748–0106
EMail: See Below
2833

Business Information: Ortho Biologics, Inc., a subsidiary of Johnson & Johnson, manufactures a drug called erythropoeitin, used in kidney dialysis, cancer and AIDS patients, and also before surgery to stimulate production of red blood cells. As Senior Supervisor, Mr. Toro manages and directs the manufacturing purification department. Previous to this work he worked as a Research Associate under noted Biochemist Dr. Efraim Racker at Cornell University, performing cancer research and protein purification work from 1980 to 1983. He later continued research work on membrane phospholipids and sialic acid functions at the University of Puerto Rico School of Medicine from 1983 to 1987. Internet users can reach him via: atoro@obcpr.jnj.com. and tfhome@coqui.net. **Career Steps:** Senior Supervisor, Ortho Biologics, Inc. (1989–Present). **Associations & Accomplishments:** Parenteral Drug Association; American Chemical Society; International Society of Pharmaceutical Engineering; American Society of Quality Control; American Society of Total Productive Maintenance; President and Member Board of Directors, Paseos Homeowners Association. **Education:** Cornell University, B.S. (1980); Attended, University of Puerto Rico – School of Medicine (1987–1989) for an M.S. in Biochemistry. **Personal:** Married to Dr. Maria Flores in 1987. Two children: Gabriel and Paola. Mr. Toro enjoys reading, computers, stamp collecting, and travel.

Leo J. Adalbert

Senior Product Manager
Rhone–Poulenc Rorer Pharmaceuticals, Inc.
304 Missimer Drive
Royersford, PA 19468–2725
(610) 454–3623
Fax: (610) 454–2003

2834

Business Information: Rhone–Poulenc Rorer Pharmaceuticals, Inc. is a leading researcher and developer of biopharmaceuticals. Rhone–Poulenc Rorer employs over 30,000 people globally, with revenue in excess of $4 billion. As Senior Product Manager, Mr. Adalbert is responsible for all marketing, education, and business development in the U.S. for biopharmaceuticals used in the treatment of neurodegenerative diseases (e.g., amyotrophic lateral sclerosis, Huntington's Disease, etc.). **Career Steps:** Senior Product Manager, Rhone–Poulenc Rorer Pharmaceuticals, Inc. (1994–Present); Manager of Market Development, Regeneron Pharmaceuticals, Inc. (1993–1994); Senior Promotion Manager, Marketing Research Analyst, Sales Professional, Merck & Co. (1988–1993). **Associations & Accomplishments:** Special Olympics; Adult Literacy Program Volunteer; Rhodes Scholarship Finalist; Beta Gamma Sigma; Phi Kappa Phi. **Education:** Harvard Business School, M.B.A. (1988); West Virginia University, B.S. in Business Administration, summa cum laude (1983). **Personal:** Married to Renee in 1984. One child: Jenna. Mr. Adalbert enjoys athletics, readings of great philosophers, church activities, and working with underprivileged children.

Cheryl H. Agris

Patent Attorney
Novo Nordisk of North America
102 Iden Avenue
Pelham Manor, NY 10803–2123
(212) 867–0123
Fax: (212) 878–9666

2834

Business Information: Novo Nordisk of North America is a manufacturer of pharmaceuticals, enzymes, and biotechnology, including insulin, human growth hormones, hormone replacement, detergents, and preservatives. As Patent Attorney, Ms. Agris is responsible for contracting with the government in regard to patents and monitoring patents of competitors. **Career Steps:** Patent Attorney, Novo Nordisk of North America (1992–Present); Law Clerk/Patent Agent, Pennie and Edmonds (1988–1992); Research Fellow, Sloan Kettering Institute (1986–1988). **Associations & Accomplishments:** New York Academy of Sciences; American Intellectual Property Law Association; American Bar Association. **Education:** Brooklyn Law School, J.D. (1992); John Hopkins University, Ph.D in Biochemistry (1986); Garchen College, B.A. in Chemistry. **Personal:** Married to Richard Pine in 1985. Ms. Agris enjoys hiking, and scuba diving.

Kathleen A. Allard

Associate Director of Region Operations
Bristol–Myers Squibb
5915 Plantation Drive
Roswell, GA 30075–2867
(404) 231–6400
Fax: (404) 231–6418

2834

Business Information: Bristol–Myers Squibb is one of the world's leading pharmaceutical companies specializing in cardiovascular and oncology drugs – offering cost–effective and disease–oriented patient health care management. Established in 1887, Bristol–Myers Squibb reports annual revenue of $2.2 billion and currently employs 50,000 people corporate–wide. A sales executive with Bristol–Myers Squibb since 1986, Ms. Allard was appointed in her position as Associate Director of Region Operations in January, 1994. She is responsible for the direction of resources, projects, and activities of 14 managers and 186 representatives, as well as P&L for the Southeastern Region of Pharmaceutical Sales Division. **Career Steps:** Bristol–Myers Squibb: Associate Director of Region Operations (1994–Present), Manager of Sales Administration (1993–1994), Manager of Sales Promotions (1990–1992), District Sales Manager (1988–1990), Region Sales Trainer (1988), Sales Representative (1986–1988). **Associations & Accomplishments:** Charter Member, Southeastern Cardiovascular Consortium; Work with The National Council on Alcoholism. **Education:** Syracuse University, B.A. in English and Psychology (1982). **Personal:** Married to Michael in 1987. Two children: Christopher and Natalie. Ms. Allard enjoys tennis, skiing, running, exercise, reading, and music.

Mark W. Ambrose, Ph.D.

Group Leader – In Vitro Testing & Development
Wyeth–Lederle Vaccines and Pediatrics
401 North Middletown Road
Pearl River, NY 10965–1263
(914) 732–4907
Fax: (914) 732–5550

2834

Business Information: Wyeth–Lederle Vaccines and Pediatrics is a biotechnology manufacturer specializing in pediatric vaccines. Established in 1908, the company presently employs 25,000 people. As Quality Control Leader, Dr. Ambrose is responsible for the development and validation of QC release assays for viral and bacterial vaccines. Additionally, he performs research on pediatric products and provides recommendations to the Food & Drug Administration. **Career Steps:** Quality Control Leader, Wyeth–Lederle Vaccines and Pediatrics (1994–Present); Post–doctoral Fellow, University of Texas Medical Branch (1993–1994); Post–doctoral Fellow, St. Jude Research Hospital (1992–1993). **Associations & Accomplishments:** American Society for Microbiology; American Society of Virology; New York Academy of Sciences; American Association for the Advancement of Science; International Society for Vaccines; Parental Drug Association. **Education:** Baylor College of Medicine, Ph.D. (1992); George Mason University, B.S. in Biology. **Personal:** Married to Laor in 1993. Dr. Ambrose enjoys hiking, biking, reading, and gardening.

Sandra A. Anderson

Senior Regulatory Affairs Assistant
Amersham Holdings, Inc.
2636 South Clearbrook Drive
Arlington Heights, IL 60005–4626
(708) 593–6300 Ext: 415
Fax: (708) 437–1699

2834

Business Information: Amersham International, England is the parent company of Amersham Holdings, North America. Amersham is a world leading health science company providing therapeutic and diagnostic radiopharmaceuticals and devices for use in healthcare, life science research, environmental safety and industrial quality assurance. Amersham has developed over 50 years of experience in serving the international community, and currently employs over 700 people. Sandra Anderson joined Amersham Holdings, Inc. in 1990 as Regulatory Affairs Assistant. Currently serving as Senior Regulatory Affairs Assistant, she is responsible for controlling distribution of Investigational New Drugs, ensuring that drugs are not withdrawn from the market by the FDA by submitting all Annual Reports, Periodic Adverse Drug Experience Reports, Drug Master Files, Drug Listings, State Registrations and Renewals, and helping to obtain approval of new drugs. **Career Steps:** Amersham Holdings, Inc.: Senior Regulatory Affairs Assistant (1993–Present), Regulatory Affairs Assistant (1990–1993); E.J. Brach Candy Company: Freight Rate Analyst (1987–1990), Customer Service Correspondent (1986–1987). **Associations & Accomplishments:** Regulatory Affairs Professionals Society; United Way Leadership Award (1993). **Education:** Illinois Wesleyan University, B.A. in Business Administration (1986). **Personal:** Married to Isaac R. in 1991. One child: Raquelle Joye. Mrs. Anderson enjoys track & field, singing, and acting.

Brian E. Andreoli

Director of Tax and Insurance/Tax Counsel
Boehringer Ingelheim Pharmaceuticals, Inc.
900 Ridgebury Road
Ridgefield, CT 06877
(203) 798–4895
Fax: (203) 791–6222

2834

Business Information: Boehringer Ingelheim Pharmaceuticals, Inc., a subsidiary of Boehringer Mannheim Corporation, is a U.S. manufacturer of pharmaceutical products for the health care industry. Established in 1971, Boehringer Ingelheim Pharmaceuticals, Inc. reports annual revenue of $750 million and currently employs 2,200 people. Boehringer Mannheim Corporation, a private company, is an international manufacturer of laboratory equipment, pharmaceuticals, and medical devices for the health care industry. With headquarters located in Germany, subsidiaries are located throughout the world in 140 countries. Established in 1853, Boehringer Mannheim Corporation reports annual revenue of $3.4 billion and currently employs 21,000 people company–wide. Admitted to practice in Connecticut, Massachusetts, and New York state and federal courts, as well as Washington, D.C. state courts, Mr. Andreoli joined the Company as Director of Tax and Insurance and Tax Counsel, upon the conferral of his law degree in 1981. He is responsible for all aspects of legal representation for the Company and North American tax and insurance matters. His experience includes legislation and revision of tax laws. In addition to his admission to the U.S. Court of Appeals (2nd Circuit), U.S. Supreme Court, and U.S. Tax Court, he is also a Certified Public Accountant in the State of New York. **Career Steps:** Director of Tax and Insurance/Tax Counsel, Boehringer Ingelheim Pharmaceuticals, Inc. (1981–Present). **Associations & Accomplishments:** American Bar Association (ABA): State and Local Tax Committee and related affiliated committees; American Institute of Certified Public Accountants (AICPA); International Fiscal Association (IFA) (1995–Present); International Tax Forum (ITF); International Tax Institute, Inc. (ITI); Organization for International Investment (OFII); Pharmaceutical Research & Manufacturers Association (PhRMA): Chairman – State and Local Tax Committee; Tax Executives Institute (TEI) (1983–Present): Chairman – Section 936 Committee; Bar of Admissions: Connecticut (1986), Massachusetts (1982), New York State (1983), Washington, D.C. (1983); Federal Court: Connecticut (1991), Massachusetts (1984), Eastern & Southern Districts of New York (1983); U.S. Court of Appeals – 2nd Circuit (1991); U.S. Supreme Court (1991); U.S. Tax Court (1983); New York CPA (1983). **Education:** University Bridgeport School of Law, LL.M. (1988); New York University Graduate School of Business, M.B.A. (1975); Fordham University School of Law, J.D. (1980); Franklin & Marshall College, B.A. (1973). **Personal:** Married to Marcia in 1976. Three children: Kristen, Rebecca, and Gregory. Mr. Andreoli enjoys tennis and gardening.

Robert M. Atkinson II

Director of Procurement Business Planning
Merck & Company, Inc.
One Merck Drive, P.O. Box 100 WS1E–75
Whitehouse Station, NJ 08889
(908) 423–4473
Fax: (908) 735–1353

2834

Business Information: Merck & Company, Inc. is one of the largest global manufacturers and marketers of pharmaceutical products. As Director of Procurement Business Planning, Dr. Atkinson is responsible for leading a business planning process that results in the achievement of procurement goals. **Career Steps:** Merck & Company, Inc.: Director of Procurement Business Planning (1996–Present), Project Director in Procurement Reengineering (1994–1996); National Account Executive, Merck & Company (1992–1994); Director, Academic Programs, School of Business and Industry, Florida A&M University (1982–1992). **Associations & Accomplishments:** Appointed to the National Commission to study Skills of the American Workforce; Served as 1st Lt., Signal Corps, U.S. Army and received the Bronze Star, Vietnam Campaign Medal and Vietnam Service Medal. **Education:** Carnegie–Mellon University, Ph.D. in Industrial Administration (1976); Carnegie–Mellon University, M.S. in Industrial Administration (1972); Washington University at St. Louis, M.B.A. in Management (1971); Iowa State University, B.S. in Electrical Engineering (1965); Honor Graduate and Distinguished Military Graduate, Signal Corps Officer's Candidate School at Ft. Gordon, GA. **Personal:** Dr. Atkinson enjoys music (jazz organist), sports and computer–related activities.

Sylvia A. Ayler

Patent Attorney
Merck & Company
P.O. Box 2000, Bldg. RY60–30
Rahway, NJ 07065
(908) 594–4909
Fax: (908) 594–4005

2834

Business Information: Merck & Company is a major pharmaceuticals manufacturer, distributing internationally. As a Patent Attorney, Ms. Ayler originates and prosecutes patent applications in the U.S. Patent & Trademark Office, provide patentability and validity opinions regarding patents, address and originate license agreements, and handles other patent related legal matters. Merck & Company employs over 6,000 people. **Career Steps:** Patent Attorney, Merck & Company, (1991–Present); Biochemist, Merck & Company (1987–1991); Chemical Technologist, Exxon (1987); Chemical Technologist, Union Carbide (1985–1987). **Associations & Accomplishments:** American Bar Association; NIAC; Author of "Development of Cross–flow Filtration Processes for the Commercial Scales Isolation of a Bacterial Lipose", [Bio-Process Engineering]. **Education:** Seton Hall Law School, J.D. (1993); Cook College, Rutgers University, B.A. in Biochemistry (1985). **Personal:** Married to Barry Porterfield in 1987. One child: Brysan Tiara Porterfield. Ms. Ayler enjoys reading and aerobic exercise.

John D. Barthel
Director of Management Development
Wyeth–Ayerst Laboratories
150 Radnor Chester Road, Suite C2
Wayne, PA 19087-5252
(610) 902-1225
Fax: (610) 964-3825

2834

Business Information: Wyeth–Ayerst Laboratories, a Division of American Home Products Corporation, is an international pharmaceutical manufacturing and research company. Established in the 1860s, today Wyeth–Ayerst Laboratories reports annual revenue of over $3 billion and currently employs more than 17,000 people company–wide. With 20 years experience in management training, Mr. Barthel joined Wyeth–Ayerst Laboratories in 1986. Currently serving as Director of Management Development, he is responsible for all aspects of domestic sales management development. **Career Steps:** Director of Management Development, Wyeth–Ayerst Laboratories (1986–Present); Manager of Training and Administration, Savage Labs – Houston, TX (1978–1986); Manager of Training, Winthrop Labs – New York, NY (1976–1978). **Associations & Accomplishments:** Former Member – Editorial Committee, National Society Sales Training Executives (NSSTE); Former Member, National Society Pharmaceutical Sales Trainers (NSPST); American Society for Training and Development (ASTD); Course facilitator of parenting classes. **Education:** Villanova University, M.S. in H.O.S. (1995); University of Texas – Austin, B.A. **Personal:** Married to Genevieve. Five children: Kerri, Kristen, Kimberly, Adrienne, and Julia. Mr. Barthel enjoys walking, reading, computers, genealogical research, and travel with his wife.

Anthony (Tony) Blanchet
Director of Human Resources, Canada
Nacan Products, LTD
60 West Drive
Brampton, Ontario L6T 4W7
(905) 454-5492
Fax: (905) 454-4681

2834

Business Information: Nacan Products, LTD specializes in the manufacture of chemical resins, adhesives and starch for food processing and industrial uses. A subsidiary of the U.S.–based company, Natural Starch and Chemical, Nacan Products, LTD has five other locations throughout Canada. Established in 1921, the Company employs 320 people and has estimated annual revenue of $170 million. As Director of Human Resources, Canada, Mr. Blanchet is responsible for coordinating of all human resource functions, including personnel management, training, recruiting, labor relations, compensation and benefits. As Chair of the Quality Improvement Team, Mr. Blanchet coordinates programs that promote education, dedication, and commitment to quality processes. **Career Steps:** Director of Human Resources, Canada/Chairman of the Quality Improvement Team, Nacan Products, LTD (1986–Present); Mediator, Ontario Ministry of Labour (1980–1986); Manager, Employee Relations, University of Guelph (1974–1980); National Representative, Canadian Union of Public Employees (1970–1974). **Associations & Accomplishments:** Ontario Personnel Association. **Education:** Niagara College of Applied Arts, Labour Studies (1972); Canadian Labour College, Certificate in Labour Studies (1972). **Personal:** Mr. Blanchet enjoys charter fishing and power boating.

Sandra Borres Arias
••• ◉ •••

QF & Training Manager
Pfizer Pharmaceuticals, Inc.
P.O. Box 628
Barceloneta, Puerto Rico 00617-0628
(787) 846-4300
Fax: (787) 846-7667

2834

Business Information: Pfizer Pharmaceuticals, Inc. is a subsidiary of Pfizer Inc. engaged in processing and manufacturing pharmaceutical products for human use. As QF Training Manager, Ms. Borres Arias is responsible for ensuring the coordination and facilitation of continuous improvement and training efforts for the whole plant. **Career Steps:** Pfizer Pharmaceuticals, Inc.: QF & Training Manager (1991–Present), Manufacturing Department Manager (1982–1991), Manufacturing Section Manager (1978–1982), Organic Synthesis Project & Process Engineer (1976–1978). **Associations & Accomplishments:** Puerto Rico 2000: (Competitive Team member) and Engineer Association. **Education:** Univ. of Puerto Rico – Mayaguez, Bachelor of Chemical Engineering (1973). **Personal:** Married to Victor Marin in 1995. Ms. Borres Arias enjoys practicing and teaching relaxation methods.

Helene Bourdages
Manager of Human Resources
Sanofi Beaute Canada
6235 Tomken Road
Mississauga, Ontario L5T 1K2
(905) 670-0033
Fax: (905) 670-7476

2834

Business Information: Sanofi Beaute Canada is a manufacturer of pharmaceutical products. As Manager of Human Resources, Ms. Bourdages is responsible for recruiting, payroll, training, employee benefits, appraisals, communications, and specialty in legislation. Ms. Bourdages works directly with the President of the Company. **Career Steps:** Manager of Human Resources, Sanofi Beaute Canada (1995–Present); Director of Human Resources, RONA (Retail) (1995); Manager of Human Resources, Restauronics (1993–1995); Assistant Director of Human Resources, Janpar (1988–1993). **Associations & Accomplishments:** Association of Human Resources Professionals of Quebec. **Education:** University of Montreal, Bachelor's degree (1993). **Personal:** Ms. Bourdages enjoys golf and tennis.

Jorge Braver
President
Elvetium S/A
Avda. del Libertador 4444, Torre 3, Piso 22
Buenos Aires, Argentina 1428
(541) 941-5956
Fax: (541) 941-5980

2834

Business Information: Elvetium S/A, is an international pharmaceutical company/medical specialties laboratory established in 1990, and located in Buenos Aires, Argentina. As President, Mr. Braver is responsible for overseeing the day–to–day operation of the Company, as well as administration, marketing, and strategic planning. **Career Steps:** President, Elvetium S/A, a subsidiary of IVAX Corporation (1990–Present); Director, Beta Laboratory (1983–1990); President / Chief Executive Officer, Magel S.A. (1978–1983); President / Chief Executive Officer (1978–1983). **Associations & Accomplishments:** COOPERALA; Stock Exchange. **Personal:** Married to Magdalena L. De Notta in 1994. Four children: Mariano, Pablo, Alejandro, and Juan. Mr. Braver enjoys chess.

Nelson Alves Brock
••• ◉ •••

President
Labs Wyeth–Whitehall Ltda.
R. Alexandre Dumas, 2.200–8.0
Sao Paulo, Brazil 04717–910
(011) 525.0020
Fax: (011) 541.9005

2834

Business Information: Labs Wyeth–Whitehall Ltda. is a manufacturer of pharmaceuticals, antibiotics, and contraceptives. As President, Mr. Brock is responsible for strategic planning, marketing, daily operations, and financial oversight. **Career Steps:** President, Labs Wyeth–Whitehall Ltda. (1993–Present); Vice President, AHP do Brazil (1992–1993); Chief Financial Officer, Wyeth Brazil (1986–1992); Market Executive, Wyeth South America (1985–1986). **Associations & Accomplishments:** Universidade de Sao Paulo, Ex–Student Association; American Chamber. **Education:** Universidade de Sao Paulo, Economist (1975); Fundacao Getulio Vargas, Business School, University Extension (1985). **Personal:** Married to Iris F. D. Brock. Two children: Jordana Duarte Brock and Ludhiana Duarte Brock. Mr. Brock enjoys tennis, jogging, technical books, and music.

Mr. Ronald A. Caiazza
Assistant Corporate Counsel
Pfizer, Inc.
235 East 42nd Street
New York, NY 10017
(212) 573-1627
Fax: (212) 808-8893

2834

Business Information: Pfizer, Inc. is a multi–billion dollar conglomerate engaged in manufacturing, fabricating and processing drugs in pharmaceutical preparations (prescription and over–the–counter pharmaceuticals and medical devices) for human and veterinary use. As Assistant Corporate Counsel, Mr. Caiazza provides legal counsel to Pfizer's Consumer Health Care Group, responsible for areas regarding regulatory matters, licensing, litigation, labeling, advertising, and other commercial concerns in compliance with the EPA, FDA, and FTC governmental regulatory agencies. **Career Steps:** Assistant Corporate Counsel, Pfizer, Inc. (1990–Present); Litigation Counsel, Pfizer Inc. (1987–1990); Litigation Team Leader, Jacobowitz & Lysaght, Esquires (1986–1987); Attorney of Record, Caiazza & Howard, Esquires (1985–1986). **Associations & Accomplishments:** American Bar Association; New York State Bar Association – food and drug law section; Member of several committees, NDMA; Mr. Caiazza is admitted to practice in New York and is admitted to practice before the federal courts in the Southern and Eastern Districts of New York. **Education:** Pace University School of Law, J.D. (1979); Brooklyn College, B.A. Degree (1976). **Personal:** Mr. Caiazza enjoys cooking, cheese making, wine making, traveling, reading and writing (fiction).

Cristina J. Carlos
Clinical Service Administrator
Pfizer, Inc.
235 East 42nd Street
New York, NY 10017
(212) 573-3447
Fax: (212) 573-1186
EMail: See Below

2834

Business Information: Pfizer, Inc. is a multi–billion dollar conglomerate engaged in manufacturing, fabricating, and processing drugs in pharmaceutical preparations (prescription and over–the counter pharmaceuticals and medical devices) for human and veterinary use. As Clinical Service Administrator, Ms. Carlos is responsible for diversified administrative activities, including clinical operations. Internet users can reach her via: carloc@pfizer.com. **Career Steps:** Clinical Service Administrator, Pfizer, Inc. (1992–Present); Sales Service Coordinator, CBS (1990–1991). **Associations & Accomplishments:** National Association of Women's Health Professionals; Drug Information Association; HBA; AMWA. **Education:** Smith College, B.A. (1989). **Personal:** Ms. Carlos enjoys sailing, scuba diving, skiing, and horseback riding.

Susan P. Cogswell
Director of Shareholder Relations
Genzyme Corporation
1 Kendall Square
Cambridge, MA 02139
(617) 252-7581
Fax: (617) 252-7844
E MAIL: See Below

2834

Business Information: Genzyme Corporation is a biotechnology company focused on developing products and services for major unresolved medical needs. As Director of Shareholder Relations, Ms. Cogswell is the Company liaison to public shareholders. Other duties include oversight of internal stock option/stock purchase programs, two employee stock programs, and an employee stock education program. Internet users can reach her via: cogswell@world.std.com. **Career Steps:** Director of Shareholder Relations, Genzyme Corporation (1990–Present); Manager of Corporate Services, Adams–Russell (1984–1990); Manager of Investors Relations, Unidata Systems (1979–1984). **Associations & Accomplishments:** National Investor Relations Institute; National Association of Stock Plan Professionals; Rotary Club of Cambridge, Massachusetts. **Education:** University of Massachusetts. **Personal:** Three children: Stephen, Karen, and Courtney. Ms. Cogswell enjoys reading, golf, cooking, knitting, and spending time with her grandchild.

Ronald H. Connolly
Pilot Plant Engineer
ESI Lederle
2 Easterbrook Lane
Cherry Hill, NJ 08003
(609) 489-2002
Fax: (609) 489-2050
E MAIL: See Below

2834

Business Information: ESI Lederle, a subsidiary of American Home Products, is the fourth largest generic pharmaceutical manufacturer in the world. As Pilot Plant Engineer, Mr. Connolly develops new generic pharmaceutical formulations in production facilities and manages Project Teams, to develop and launch new generic pharmaceuticals. Additionally, he coordinates technical issues with active ingredient vendors and work validations. Internet users can contact him via: Connollr@labs.wyeth.com. **Career Steps:** Pilot Plant Engineer, ESI Lederle (1994–Present); Associate Scientist/Process Development, Rhone Poulenc Rorer (1991–1994); Process Engineering Assistant, SmithKline Beecham (1989–1990). **Associations & Accomplishments:** International Society for Pharmaceutical Engineering; American Institute of Chemical Engineers; Parenteral Drug Association. **Education:** Drexel university, B.S. in Chemical Engineering (1991). **Personal:** Married to Irene in 1993. Mr. Connolly enjoys tennis, landscaping, playing the saxophone, being a member of a

Church Worship Band, and a member of a Christian Rock Band.

Judith A. Cotton

Human Resources Administrator
Pharmacia & Upjohn, Inc.
7000 Portage Road
Kalamazoo, MI 49001
(616) 833–6132
Fax: (616) 833–5373

2834

Business Information: Pharmacia & Upjohn, Inc. is a pharmaceutical manufacturing company headquartered in London, England, with sales offices and research centers located throughout the world. As Human Resources Administrator, Ms. Cotton administers the Pension and Savings Plans for the Company. In a team–based organization she is responsible for training customer service representatives, managing vendors, problem solving and troubleshooting, systems management and customer consulting services. The reason for her success, per Ms. Cotton, is her determination. **Career Steps:** Upjohn: Human Resources Administrator (1994–Present), Human Resources Technician (1990–1994), Human Resources Representative (1988–1994), Fine Chemicals Office Coordinator (1975–1986), Sales & Marketing Research Secretary (1971–1974). **Associations & Accomplishments:** Girl Scout Leader; Chairperson, Diversity Task Force; Facilitator, Covey Seven Habits of Highly Effective People; Ms. Cotton is a published poet and is currently working on a novel to be published in 1997. **Education:** Kellogg Community College. **Personal:** Three children: Shelby A. Jr., Sherese A., and Jeffrey A. Cotton. Ms. Cotton enjoys being an author and poet. She also provides counseling to troubled youth.

Jose A. Cruz

District Sales Manager
SmithKline Beecham
Call Box 3560
Carolina, Puerto Rico 00984
(787) 752–8000 ext. 534
Fax: (787) 757–8275

2834

Business Information: SmithKline Beecham, formed by a merger of SmithKline Beckman and the Beecham group in July 1989, is considered one of the world's leading companies in healthcare, with ethical pharmaceuticals, over–the–counter medicines, and the largest network of clinical laboratories in North America. SmithKline Beecham Clinical Laboratories provides a broad range of clinical laboratory services to more than 50,000 health care and industry clients. They offer and perform 1,500 different tests on blood, urine, and other body fluids and tissues to provide information for health and well–being. Of increasing prominence is substance abuse testing: SBLC performs more drug testing than anyone else in the industry and was among the first to receive certification from the U.S. Government's National Institute on Drug Abuse (NIDA). Clients include: physicians, hospitals, clinics, dialysis centers, pharmaceutical companies and industry. As District Sales Manager, Mr. Cruz supervises, sets goals, trains and develops sales people, establishes budgets, and handles publicity and advertising. **Career Steps:** SmithKline Beecham: District Sales Manager (1989–Present), Supervisor (1987–1989), Sales Representative (1984–1987). **Education:** Recinto University – Mayaguez, B.S. (1977). **Personal:** Married to Idalni Marrero in 1991. Four children: Melisa, Melanie, Joan Mari, and Mary Jo. Mr. Cruz enjoys tennis, swimming, and reading.

David Cruz Lugo

Manufacturing Business Unit Manager
Warner Lambert, Inc.
P.O. Box 786
Vega Baja, Puerto Rico 00694–0786
(787) 858–2323
Fax: (787) 858–1906

2834

Business Information: Warner Lambert, Inc., headquartered in Morris Plains, New Jersey, is an international manufacturer of ethical pharmaceutical products. Products include Benadryl, Sinutab, Actifed, Listerine, Rolaids, Certs, and Efferdent. Expected to be approved by the FDA by the end of 1996, Warner Lamber, Inc. will have a new product for diabetes called, Razulin. Additional plans for 1996 includes introducing Listerine products to Russia. As Manufacturing Business Unit Manager, Mr. Cruz Lugo is responsible for all manufacturing productions for the Puerto Rico region. He oversees the manufacture and packaging of solid dosage products, as well as planning and engineering services, inventory control, and production. **Career Steps:** Warner Lambert, Inc.: Manufacturing Business Unit Manager (1995–Present), Materials Manager (1994–1995); Pharmaceutical Production Manager, Squibb Manufacturing, Inc. (1971–1994). **Associations & Accomplishments:** Savings and Loan Cooperative La Oriental – Hundero, PR. **Education:** University of Turabo: M.B.A. (1985), B.B.A. **Personal:** Married to Mildred Mauras in 1971. Three children: David, Omar, and Jose. Mr. Cruz Lugo enjoys reading, listening to Latin Jazz and Puerto Rican music, tennis, and golf.

Jack H. Dean, Ph.D.

President – Sanofi Research Division, USA
Sanofi Winthrop, Inc.
9 Great Valley Parkway
Great Valley, PA 19355
(610) 983–5820
Fax: (610) 983–5593

2834

Business Information: Sanofi Winthrop, Inc. is a pharmaceutical research, development and marketing firm concentrating on the development of drugs for cancer, cardiovascular diseases, central nervous systems and thrombosis (clotting). Established in 1974, Sanofi reports annual revenue in excess of $4 billion and currently employs 460 people in the U.S. research division. As President of SRD, Dr. Dean manages the U.S. research division and pre–clinical development worldwide. **Career Steps:** President – Sanofi Research Division, Sanofi Winthrop, Inc. (1994–Present); Executive Vice President of Development, Sterling Winthrop, Inc. (1994); Vice President of Drug Safety, Sterling Winthrop, Inc. (1988–1992); Head of the Department of Molecular Toxicology, Chemical Industry Institute of Toxicology (1981–1988); National Institutes of Health, NIEHS (1979–1981). **Associations & Accomplishments:** President, Society of Toxicology – USA (1995–1996); British Toxicology Society (1990); Treasurer, International Society of Immunopharmacology (1993–1996); American Association of Immunologists (1972–Present); American Association of Advanced Science (1972–Present); First Presbyterian Church; Interviews published in Wall Street Journal and Pennsylvania Inquirer. **Education:** University of Arizona, Ph.D.; California State University at Long Beach, B.S. and M.S. **Personal:** Married to Suellen Dean. Three children: Carl, John and Matthew. Dr. Dean enjoys sailing and travel.

Ana Lourdes del Rio

Sales Manager
Rhone–Poulenc Rorer
Metro Office Park De La Cruz Plaza, Suite 101
Guaynabo, Puerto Rico 00968
(809) 783–6868
Fax: (809) 783–4346

2834

Business Information: Rhone–Poulenc Rorer is the world's leading research development manufacturer of pharmaceuticals and medical/chemical technological products. With nineteen years of experience in pharmacology and a Board–Certified Pharmacist, Ana Lourdes del Rio joined Rhone–Poulenc Rorer as Sales Representative in 1990. She was promoted to sales manager in 1995. She is responsible for the direction of all sales activities in the Puerto Rican markets, including setting objectives with management, developing plan of actions, controlling and setting budgets, and evaluating projects and their results. In addition, she oversees a staff of four area managers, as well as the 28 representatives below them. Concurrently, she writes articles for the College of Pharmacy of Puerto Rico and has taught a group of Pharmacy technicians. **Career Steps:** Rhone–Poulenc Rorer: Sales Manager (1995–Present), Area Manager – Advanced Therapeutics and Oncology Division (1994–1995); First Woman President of the Puerto Rico Board of Pharmacy, Puerto Rico Commonwealth (1990–1995). **Associations & Accomplishments:** National Association of Board of Pharmacy; Puerto Rico Pharmacist Association; American Pharmaceutical Association; National Association of Female Executives; Professional Golf Association; American Society for Pharmacy Law; Arecibos Citizen Pro Art and Culture Association. **Education:** College of Pharmacy – Puerto Rico, B.S. (1977); The Computer Institute of Puerto Rico. **Personal:** Married to Jorge Martinez in 1990. Three children: Vanessa, Rose, and Lourdes. Mrs. del Rio enjoys golf and sewing.

Dr. R. Gordon Douglas

President of Merck Vaccine Division
Merck & Company, Inc.
P.O. Box 100, One Merck Drive
Whitehouse Station, NJ 08889
(908) 423–3234
Fax: (908) 735–1232

2834

Business Information: Merck & Co, Inc. is one of the largest phamaceutical companies in the world. Merck & Co, Inc. has several operating divisions, including the Vaccine Division which specializes in the research, development, manufacture distribution and marketing of vaccines. Attaining his medical degree in 1959, Dr. Douglas joined Merck & Co., Inc. in 1990. As President of the Vaccine Division, he is responsible for all Division operations, primarily focusing in the areas of sales and marketing, research and manufacturing. **Career Steps:** President, Vaccine Division, Merck & Co, Inc. (1990–Present); Chairman, Department of Medicine, New York Hospital – Cornell Medical Center (1982–1990). **Associations & Accomplishments:** National Vaccine Advisory Committee; Association of American Physicians; American Society of Clinical Investigation; American Clinical and Clinitologic Association; Infectious Disease Society of America; Published numerous articles in scientific journals; St. Andrews Society. **Education:** Cornell University Medical College, M.D. (1959); Princeton University, A.B. (1955). **Personal:** Married to Ann in 1956. Three children: Robert G., Timothy S. and Catherine L. Dr. Douglas enjoys sailing and skiing.

Volker Eck, Ph.D.

Research Associate
Schering AG
Muellerstrasse 170–178
Berlin, Germany D–13342
(030) 468–2848
Fax: (030) 461–8027

2834

Business Information: Schering AG is an international pharmaceutical industry conglomerate, specializing in the manufacture, research and development of diagnostics, hormone therapy and dermatology. Current diagnostic research undergoing at Schering AG involves contrast media from x–ray, ultrasound, and enema therapy for cancer and cancer–related disorders for pharmaceutical use. Joining Schering AG as a Research Associate in 1983, Dr. Eck is now responsible for diagnostics in all aspects of administrative functions and quality control of research and development projects, including monitoring the quality of projects and assessing quality for improvement. Prior to joining Schering AG, Dr. Eck was a research staff member with the National Research Foundation. During his tenure there he was involved in electrochemical, physical chemical, and chemical laser research. **Career Steps:** Quality Controller in Research and Development, Schering AG (1983–Present); National Research Foundation (1979–1983). **Associations & Accomplishments:** Presents papers at National and International conferences. **Education:** Free University Berlin, Ph.D. (1983). **Personal:** Dr. Eck enjoys reading, concerts, theaters and sports.

Tyrone V. Edwards

Senior Director – National Accounts Management
Merck & Company, Inc.
222 Las Colins Boulevard West, Suite 1465
Irving, TX 75039
(214) 506–2992
Fax: (214) 506–2961

2834

Business Information: Merck & Company, Inc. specializes in the research, manufacturing, and sales of pharmaceuticals. As Senior Director – National Accounts Management, Mr. Edwards is responsible for sales and contracting in managed care. **Career Steps:** Merck & Company, Inc.: Senior Director – National Accounts Management (1996–Present), Senior Region Director (1993–1995), Senior Customer Manager (1993). **Associations & Accomplishments:** Academy of Managed Care Pharmacy; Harlem YMCA Black Achievers Program. **Education:** North Carolina A&T State University, B.S. (1982). **Personal:** Married to Teresa in 1983. Three children: Linsey, Tyrone, and Kevin.

L. L. Evans

Director of Human Resources
Mallinckrodt Group, Inc.
675 McDonnell Boulevard
St. Louis, MO 63042
(314) 895–2500
Fax: (314) 895–2376

2834

Business Information: Mallinckrodt Group, Inc., established in 1868, is a manufacturer of specialty products for human and animal health care and chemical industries. Specialty medical products include diagnostic imaging, airway management, tracheotomy, and cardiology products. The chemical division manufacturers products used in pharmaceutical production and other specialty uses. The Mallinckrodt Group, Inc. also has a division for the production of veterinary products which are distributed primarily outside of the United States. The Company employs over 10,500 people worldwide and expect to post revenues in excess of $2.0 billion in 1996. As Director of Human Resources, Ms. Evans is responsible for all aspects of human resource activities, including recruiting, salary administration, benefits management, employee relations and safety. She assists in the setting of Company policies for human resource management. **Career Steps:** Mallinckrodt Group, Inc.: Director of Human Resources (1993–Present), Director of Worldwide Compensation (1991–1993); Consultant, McDonnell Douglas Corporation (1988–1991); Manager of Compensation, ConAgra Frozen Foods (1986–1988). **Associations & Accomplishments:** Compensation and Benefits Network of Greater St. Louis; American Compensation Association; Society of Human Resource Management; International Institute, St. Louis. **Education:** University of Akron, M.B.A. (1988); Washington University (St. Louis), M.L.A. **Personal:** Married to Thomas E. Fisher Jr. Ms. Evans enjoys gardening and golf.

George F. Farley

Senior Director of Professional Relations and Drug Plans
Bristol–Myers Squibb – Canada
2365 CH Cote–De–Liesse
St. Laurent, Quebec H4N 2M7
(514) 333–2017
Fax: (514) 333–2024

2834

Business Information: The Pharmaceuticals Division of Bristol–Myers Squibb Canada, is a $200 million subsidiary of Bristol–Myers Squibb, dealing primarily with healthcare in Canada. Its parent company is a world leader in pharmaceutical research, specializing in cardiovascular, psychiatric, anti–infectious and oncology drugs, as well as offering cost–effective, disease–oriented patient health care management. Mr. Farley has served in various supervisory positions with the company, most recently as Senior Director of Professional Relations and Drug Plans since 1992. He is responsible for supervising the reimbursement of drugs, interfacing with medical and pharmaceutical organizations, and coordinating projects for governmental drug formularies and private insurance drug plans. **Career Steps:** Bristol–Myers Squibb, Canada: Senior Director of Professional Relations and Drug Plans (1992–Present), Director of Sales and Marketing Services (1987–1992), Manager of Training and Development (1982–1987). **Associations & Accomplishments:** President, Canadian Society of Industrial Pharmacists (1988–1990); Director, Canadian Pharmaceutical Association (1988–1990); Treasurer, Council for Accreditation of Pharmaceutical Manufacturers Representatives, Canada (1983–1986); National Society of Sales Training Executives (1984–1987); Guest Lecturer: Universite de Montreal, and Concordia University; Several interviews and articles in pharmacy publications. **Education:** Faculty of Pharmacy, B. Pharmacy (1961); Courses in business administration, public relations, sales training and development, drug therapy and management. **Personal:** Married to Marylin in 1961. Mr. Farley enjoys gardening and reading historical novels.

Jere D. Fellman, Ph.D

Director
Neurex Corporation
1474 Lexington Way
Livermore, CA 94550
(415) 853–1500
Fax: (415) 853–1538
EMAIL: See Below

2834

Business Information: Neurex Corporation, established in 1986, is a pharmaceutical laboratory producing medications for use in acute care. The Laboratory primarily produces three types of medications: new analgesics for the treatment of intractable pain; anti–hypertensive medicines for improved treatment of high–blood pressure; and neuro–protective agents for treatment of nerve related injuries and diseases. As Director, Dr. Fellman has oversight of the project managers and the day–to–day operations. He personally directs the SNX–111 Ischemia Program for the development of the drug for indication of head trauma and stroke. Dr. Fellman is concerned with quality control of the various projects in order to obtain true results on drug testings for FDA approval. Internet users can reach him via: fellmann@netcom.com. **Career Steps:** Director, Neurex Corporation (1994–Present); Director of Research, Nycomed (1991–1994); Senior Scientist, Catalytica (1983–1991); Scientist, Dow Chemical (1980–1982). **Associations & Accomplishments:** American Chemical Society. **Education:** Massachusetts Institute of Technology, Ph.D. in Chemistry (1980); University of California at Berkeley, B.S. (1975). **Personal:** Married to Theresa D. in 1977. Two children: Hans J. and Anna Theresa. Dr. Fellman enjoys hiking, woodworking, and scuba diving.

Everett Flanigan, Ph.D.

Director of Research and Development
Armour Pharmaceutical
P.O. Box 511
Kankakee, IL 60901–0511
(815) 935–3102
Fax: (815) 935–3188

2834

Business Information: Armour Pharmaceutical is a developer, manufacturer and marketer of human pharmaceuticals, such as blood proteins and bowel pharmaceuticals. As Director of Research and Development, Dr. Flanigan is responsible for all aspects of research and development. **Career Steps:** Director of Research and Development, Armour Pharmaceutical (1993–Present); Director of Peptide Technology, Armour – RPuerto Rico (1992–1993); Manager of Synthetic Peptides, RPuerto Rico – Kankakee (1987–1992); Principal Scientist, Armour RPuerto Rico (1985–1987). **Associations & Accomplishments:** Chairman, United States Pharmacopia Subcommittee on Biopolymers, Bioproducts and Vaccines (BBV); Member, United States Pharmacopia Committee on Revision (1990–1995 and 1995–2000); Member, American Management Association; Member, National Association for the Advancement of Black Chemists & Chemical Engineers; Member, Board of Directors, United Way; Chairman, Project Discovery. **Education:** Washington University in St. Louis, Ph.D. (1971); Howard University, M.S.; Clark Atlanta University, B.S.; Harvard University, Advanced Certificate. **Personal:** Married to Annette. Four children: Kyle, Ryan, Asa, and Erika.

Donald W. Gaddy II

Midwest Business Unit Manager
Fujisawa U.S.A., Inc.
590 Longhill Road
Gurnee, IL 60031
(847) 263–0488
Fax: (847) 263–9501
EMAIL: See Below

2834

Business Information: Fujisawa U.S.A., Inc. is an international manufacturer of pharmaceuticals catering to a hospital–based clientele. As Midwest Business Unit Manager, Mr. Gaddy is responsible for the direction of all sales and marketing activities within the Midwest region of the U.S., in addition to training support staff. Career highlights include building a successful sales team over a two year time span with no personnel turnover, and continuing to be in the top 10% of the Company sales effort. He may be reached through the Internet via: Gaddy3484@AOL.COM **Career Steps:** Fujisawa U.S.A., Inc.: Midwest Business Unit Manager (1994–Present), Manager, Corporate Marketing (1993–1994), Manager, Sales Training (1991–1993). **Associations & Accomplishments:** National Society of Pharmaceutical Sales; American Society for Training and Development. **Education:** Texas A&M University, B.B.A. (1986); Southern Methodist University, M.B.A. work. **Personal:** Married to Karen in 1992. Mr. Gaddy enjoys golf and travel.

Paul Gilgen, Ph.D.

President of U.S. Vitamins Division
Hoffman – La Roche
45 Eisenhower Drive
Paramus, NJ 07652–1416
(201) 909–8308
Fax: (201) 909–8469

2834

Business Information: Hoffman – La Roche is an international research and development manufacturer and marketer of healthcare pharmaceuticals. Products include bulk vitamins and fine chemicals. Based in Switzerland and established in the 1940's, Hoffman – La Roche reports annual revenue of $700 million and currently employs 1,200 people. An executive with Hoffman–La Roche since 1987, Dr. Gilgen was appointed President of the U.S. Vitamins Division in 1994. In addition to directing all areas of operations for the Vitamin Division, he also serves as Head of Worldwide Technical Operations. **Career Steps:** Hoffman – La Roche: President of U.S. Vitamins Division (1994–Present), Head of Technical Operations Worldwide (1991–1994), Director of Strategic Planning (1987–1990). **Associations & Accomplishments:** United Way; Rotary Club. **Education:** University of Zurich, Ph.D. (1976). **Personal:** Married to Francoise in 1983. Dr. Gilgen enjoys reading, jogging, and tennis.

David I. Goldsmith, M.D.

Corporte Medical Director/Sr. Dir. Prod. Safety Surveillance
Sanofi Winthrop Inc.
90 Park Avenue, 7th Floor
New York, NY 10019
(212) 551–4100
Fax: (212) 551–4907

2834

Business Information: Sanofi Winthrop Inc. is a pharmaceutical manufacturing company, as well as a pre– and post–marketing surveillance research unit. As Corporate Medical Director and Senior Director of Product Safety Surveillance, Dr. Goldsmith is responsible for the management of Product Safety, Professional Services, the Medical Library, databases for ADR's, Product Complaints, Package Insert Consonancy, as well as the Information Service personnel needed to maintain the hardware and software. Dr. Goldsmith is also responsible for the U.S. Product Safety Surveillance Unit, which provides corporate services, including pharmacovigilance and core labelling to the Paris central office for all products developed. Concurrent to his position with Sanofi Winthrop Inc., Dr. Goldsmith is also a Clinical Associate Professor of Pediatrics at the Albert Einstein College of Medicine. **Career Steps:** Corporate Medical Director and Senior Director of Product Safety Surveillance, Sanofi Winthrop Inc. (1994–Present); Sterling Winthrop Inc. (Acquired by Sanofi Winthrop in 1994): Corporate Medical Director and Senior Director of Product Safety Surveillance (1990–1994), Corporate Medical Director and Director of Product Safety Surveillance (1987–1990); Director of International Drug Surveillance, American Cyanamid Company (1983–1987); Director of the Coordinating Center and Associate Director, International Study of Kidney Disease in Children (1980–1983); Pediatric Nephrologist, Albert Einstein College of Medicine (1975–1983); Staff Pediatrician and Pediatric Nephrologist, National Naval Medical Center (1973–1975). **Associations & Accomplishments:** International Society of Pharmacoepidemiology; American Societies of Nephrology and Pediatric Nephrology; International Societies of Nephrology and Pediatric Nephrology; New York Society of Nephrology; American Society of Hypertension; Society for Pediatric Research; New York Academy of Science; Board Certifications: Diplomate, National Board of Medical Examiners (1969), Diplomate, American Board of Pediatrics (1973), Diplomate, Subspecialty Board Pediatric Nephurology (1974); Frequent speaker and lecturer; Numerous published articles and book chapters; Various abstracts and presentations; Dr. Goldsmith is most proud of his position as Chairman of the Pharmaceutical Manufacturers Association's task force for MedWatch from 1992–1994. **Education:** New York Medical College, M.D. (1968); Hofstra University, M.A. in Biology (1963); Washington University, A.B. in Zoology (1962); New York Medical Hospital: Pediatric Internship (1969), Pediatric Resident (1970), Chief Resident, Pediatrics (1971); Fellow, Developmental Renal Physiology and Pediatric Nephrology, Albert Einstein College of Medicine (1973). **Personal:** Dr. Goldsmith enjoys all aspects of the opera.

Madeline Gomez Ramirez, CPA

Senior Accountant
Rhone–Poulenc Rorer Caribbean
P.O. Box 364824
San Juan, Puerto Rico 00936–4824
(787) 783–6868 Ext.5627
Fax: (787) 783–4845

2834

Business Information: Rhone–Poulenc Rorer Caribbean is an establishment primarily engaged in the marketing, sales, and distribution of medicinal products to drug stores, pharmacies, and hospitals. The San Juan division, one of 54 locations worldwide, handles all of Puerto Rico and the Caribbean Islands. Established in 1976, the Company employs 54 people and has an estimated annual revenue of $30,000,000. As Senior Accountant, Miss Gomez Ramirez oversees the finance department. Her duties include accounts payable and receivable, payroll, budgetary concerns, and taxes. **Career Steps:** Rhone Poulenc Rover Caribbean: Senior Accountant (1994–Present), Accountant/LAN Administrator (1992–1994); Accountant and Auditor, B.R. Fernandez, C.P.A. and Associates (1989–1991). **Associations & Accomplishments:** Puerto Rico Society of Certified Public Accountants; American Institute of Certified Public Accountants; Member, Certified Public Accountant Private Industry Committee; Member, Transition Committee of Cond. Plaza Antillana. **Education:** University of Puerto Rico, B.B.A. Magna Cum Laude (1987); M.B.A. in Finance (In Progress); Certified Public Accountant License (1992). **Personal:** Miss Gomez Ramirez enjoys exercising and reading.

Saundra B. Granade

Senior Director
ALPHARMA
7205 Windsor Boulevard
Baltimore, MD 21244–2654
(410) 298–1000 Ext.: 537
Fax: (410) 597–9627

2834

Business Information: ALPHARMA is a national manufacturer of generic pharmaceuticals, marketing its products to the private sector, wholesalers and distributors. As Senior Director of all Q&A activities for the Baltimore, Maryland plant, Saundra Granade ensures compliance of established regulations, insurance market of products, drug applications, and development market of products. **Career Steps:** Senior Director, ALPHARMA (1993–Present); Director Antibody Production, Charles River Lake (1990–1993); Director Analytical Services, Glaxo (1988–1990). **Associations & Accomplishments:** Girl Scout Leader; Parenteral Drug Association. **Education:** Georgia College: M.A. (1980), B.S. **Personal:** Married to Joe A. in 1969. Two children: Tamara Lynn and Louie Adam. Mrs. Granade enjoys art, painting, basketry, and sailing.

Richard Grbic

Controller
Degussa Dental Division
3950 South Clinton Avenue
South Plainfield, NJ 07080–1316
(908) 754–6300 Ext: 350
Fax: (908) 754–6440

2834

Business Information: Degussa Corporation – Dental Division is a wholly–owned entity of the German–based pharmaceutical, chemical, and metal conglomerate Degussa Group. The Dental Division generates over $25 million in sales annually, serves as the distribution arm for the market of dental alloys, equipment and porcelain to dental professionals and laboratories throughout North America. Working as an accounting executive in various divisions of Degussa Corporation since 1987, Richard Grbic was appointed to his current position in May of 1995. As Controller for the Dental Division, he provides the overall executive administration of all internal operations, credit and collections, customer service, and the shipping sectors. **Career Steps:** Degussa Dental Division: Controller (1995–Present), Manager of Accounting (1987–1995); Staff Accountant, Viacom International (1985–1987). **Associations & Accomplishments:** Accounting and Tax Instructor, Hunterdon County Adult Education. **Education:** Pace University: M.B.A. (1989); B.B.A. (1984). **Personal:** Married to Anna in 1986. Mr. Grbic enjoys music and sports.

Colin M. Greene

Vice President of Purchasing
Butler Company
5000 Bradenton Avenue
Dublin, OH 43017–3574
(614) 761–9095
Fax: (614) 761–9842

2834

Business Information: Butler Company is a distributor of wholesale veterinary pharmaceuticals, biologics, and supplies. National in scope, Butler Company has 23 locations in the U.S. Joining Butler Company in 1973, Mr. Green currently serves as Vice President of Purchasing. He is responsible for direct purchasing and inventory control, including finances, strategic planning, formulating policies and providing investment ideas for the purchasing department. **Career Steps:** Vice President of Purchasing, Butler Company (1973–Present). **Associations & Accomplishments:** National Association of Purchasing Managers; American Production and Inventory Control Society; National Rifle Association. **Education:** Ohio State University. **Personal:** Married to Nancy in 1986. Six children: Lorri, Kathleen, Colleen, Theresa, Tami, and Lisa. Mr. Greene enjoys collecting 18th Century Firearms.

Karl R. Hertel

PDM Engineer
Abbott Laboratories
1401 Sheridan Road D719 P13
North Chicago, IL 60064
(847) 937–7379
Fax: (847) 938–8785

2834

Business Information: Abbott Laboratories is a manufacturer of health materials and equipment, including pharmaceuticals, diagnostic, and testing equipment. As PDM Engineer, Mr. Hertel is responsible for systems troubleshooting, vibration analysis, and asset administration. He deals with small project work, assists in technical support, supports chemical operations, and works with small fiber optics, data logging, and ultrasonic equipment. **Career Steps:** PDM Engineer, Abbott Laboratories (1991–Present); Process Engineer, Austin Process (1990–1991); Project/Production Engineer, EPC International (1989–1990); Design Engineer, Envirex (1985–1989). **Associations & Accomplishments:** Eucharistic Ministry at Resurrection Church; Illinois Registered Professional Engineer. **Education:** University of Illinois – Urbana, B.S. in Chemical Engineering (1987); Lewis University, work for M.B.A. **Personal:** Married to Anja in 1989. Three children: Sydney, Alexandra, and Andrew. Mr. Hertel enjoys bicycling, swimming, skiing, running, and home remodeling.

Shane M. Hinze

Chief Executive Officer
Apotheca Inc.
313 Lowrey Drive
Woodbine, IA 51579
(712) 647–3133
Fax: (712) 647–2573

2834

Business Information: Apotheca Inc. is a national distributor and manufacturer of homeopathic and botanical extract pharmaceutical, health & beauty aides products. Founding the company in 1987, as Chief Executive Officer Mr. Hinze provides the overall vision and strategies for the Company's continued development, quality product output, and overall international scope. **Career Steps:** Chief Executive Officer, Apotheca Inc. (1987–Present) **Associations & Accomplishments:** American Association of Homeopathic Pharmacists **Personal:** One child: Zachary. Mr. Hinze enjoys bike racing, reading and outdoors activities.

J. E. Holste, DVM

Associate Director of Contract Research
Merck & Company, Inc.
6498 Jade Road
Fulton, MO 65251–3318
(573) 642–5977
Fax: (573) 642–0365

2834

Business Information: Merck & Company, Inc. is one of the largest global manufacturers and marketers of pharmaceutical products, fabricating and processing drugs in pharmaceutical preparations (prescription and over–the–counter pharmaceuticals and medical devices) for human and veterinary use. As Associate Director of Contract Research, Dr. Holste is responsible for finding qualified investigative experts to comply with the FDA requirements for data on in–house research and development of veterinary pharmaceuticals. In addition, he conducts extensive research, currently developing an anti–parasitic contact serum for dairy cattle. **Career Steps:** Merck & Company, Inc.: Associate Director of Contract Research (1995–Present), Assistant Director (1982–1995); Director of Technical Services, Vigortone Agricultural Products. **Associations & Accomplishments:** American Veterinary Medical Association; Kansas Veterinary Medical Association; American Association of Industrial Veterinarians; American Association of Swine Practitioners. **Education:** Kansas State University: D.V.M. (1970), B.S. **Personal:** Two children: Sarah B. and Joy E. Dr. Holste enjoys fishing and flying.

Vanessa M. Horta

Health and Safety Officer
Labratorio Clinico Caparra
P.O. Box 11560
San Juan, Puerto Rico 00922
(809) 783–3885
Fax: (809) 792–4802

2834

Business Information: Shipping products on the international level, Labratorio Clinico Caparra is a private clinical company manufacturing various types of medicines for hospital and pharmacy use. As Health and Safety Officer, Vanessa Horta is responsible for implementing all federal regulations, including EPA and OSHA rules. **Career Steps:** Labratorio Clinico Caparra: Health and Safety Officer (1994–Present), Medical Technologist (1988–1994), Laboratory Aide (1986–1988). **Associations & Accomplishments:** American Society of Clinical Pathologists; National Safety Council. **Education:** Thomas Jefferson University, Business Management (1986); Chestnut Hill College, B.S **Personal:** Three children: Sarah, Ashley, and Lauren. Ms. Horta enjoys bowling, sewing, and teaching saftey training classes.

Peter T. S. Huang

Vice President and Director
SmithKline Beecham International
1 Franklin Plaza, FP1940
Philadelphia, PA 19101–1514
(215) 751–3048
Fax: (215) 751–5671

2834

Business Information: SmithKline Beecham (SB), formed by a merger of SmithKline Beckman and the Beecham Group in July of 1989, is considered one of the world's leading healthcare companies. SB undertakes the discovery, development, manufacture and marketing of ethical pharmaceuticals, clinical laboratory services, and over–the–counter medicines. The acquisition of Sterling–Winthrop in 1995, made SB the third largest OTC company in the world, number 1 in Europe and the International markets. It is ranked the second largest foreign company in China. SmithKline Beecham set up its International division to meet the healthcare needs of countries outside Europe and North America. Differing patterns of disease are only one factor in an equation which must also take into account differing levels of economical development and a diversity of social, cultural and political conditions. SmithKline Beecham is committed to helping countries around the world fulfill their total healthcare needs from the most basic up to the most sophisticated. Appointed as Vice President for China/Korea operations in February of 1992, Peter Huang has been an instrumental leader in the strategic market development and expansion into the Pacific Rim. **Career Steps:** SmithKline Beecham International: Vice President and Director (1992–Present), Director of China/Korea (1991–1992), Director of China Ops. (1989–1991). **Education:** University of Kansas, M.S. in Business Administration (1978); Wharton Advanced Executive Management. **Personal:** Married to Chieko. Two children: Erica and Kenji. Mr. Huang enjoys golf, tennis, antiques, art, and music.

Susan Irby

Marketing Manager
TL Systems Corporation
8700 Wyoming Avenue North
Minneapolis, MN 55445–1836
(612) 493–6780
Fax: (612) 493–6776

2834

Business Information: TL Systems Corporation, a subsidiary of Robert Bosh Corporation, is a national manufacturer of pharmaceutical processing and packaging equipment (i.e, capsules, vials), used for liquid and dry pharmaceuticals. A $30 million company, TL Systems Corporation produces products for major pharmaceutical companies, and biotechnological, veterinary, and ophthalmic uses. As Marketing Manager, Ms. Irby is responsible for the management of all marketing, advertising, trade shows, research, and product development activities. **Career Steps:** Marketing Manager, TL Systems Corporation (1994–Present); Senior Marketing Analyst, Eaton Corporation (1991–1994); European Manager of Special Projects, Eaton GmbH (1989–1991). **Associations & Accomplishments:** International Society of Pharmaceutical Engineers; Parenteral Drug Association; German American Chamber of Commerce. **Education:** American Graduate School of International Management, M.I.M. (1985); Gustavus Adolphus College, B.A.; Cottey College, A.A. **Personal:** Ms. Irby enjoys volunteering as an educational program and veterinary clinical assistant volunteer.

Jerry W. Irwin

General Manager
Mississippi Chemical Corporation
Highway 49 E
Yazoo City, MS 39194
(601) 746–4131
Fax: (601) 751–2913

2834

Business Information: Mississippi Chemical Corporation is a major manufacturer of fertilizers, and produces and markets all three primary crop nutrients. Nitrogen fertilizer is manufactured at the Yazoo City facility, potash and diammonium phosphate are produced at other locations. As General Manager, Mr. Irwin manages the Yazoo City plant, responsible for maximum production, proper maintenance of the plant, cost–effectiveness of operations, inventory control of product and spare parts, maintenance of work force, and compliance with governmental regulations. **Career Steps:** Mississippi Chemical Corporation: General Manager (1986–Present), Production Manager (1972–1986), Ammonia Plant Superintendent (1971–1972). **Associations & Accomplishments:** American Institute of Chemical Engineers; Mississippi Manufacturers Association – Industrial Training Committee; Chamber of Commerce – Yazoo City, MS; Mississippi State University Alumni. **Education:** Mississippi State University, B.S. (1964). **Personal:** Married to Angela in 1985. Three children: Christy Irwin Walsh, Jerry Jr., and Jason. Mr. Irwin enjoys hunting, fishing, golf, and gardening.

Charles W. Jongeward

•••◄━━◼◉◼━━►•••

Senior Vice President and Chief Operating Officer
Rhone–Poulenc Ag Company
P.O. Box 12014
Research Triangle Park, NC 27709–2014
(919) 549–2341
Fax: (919) 549–3964

2834

Business Information: Rhone–Poulenc Ag Company, a subsidiary of Rhone–Poulenc (the world's leading research development manufacturer of pharmaceuticals and medical/chemical technological products), is a manufacturer of agricultural crop protection products, such as insecticides and herbicides. Research and development of insecticides are conducted in North Carolina and herbicide research and development is done in France. Established in 1986, Rhone–Poulenc Ag Company reports annual revenue in excess of $600 million and currently employs 2,400 people company–wide, including 400 researchers. A ten year veteran with Rhone–Poulenc, Mr. Jongeward joined the Company in 1985 as Director of Divisional Administration and Control. Currently serving as Senior Vice President and Chief Operating Officer of the North America Zone, he is responsible for the supervision and oversight of the U.S., Canada, and Mexico operations. **Career Steps:** Rhone Poulenc Ag Company: Senior Vice President and Chief Operating Officer (1994–Present), Vice President and General Manager (1990–1994), Director of Marketing (1987–1990); Director of Marketing, Rhone Poulenc, Inc. (1985–1987). **Associations & Accomplishments:** Vice Chair, United Way Board for Research Triangle Park; Board Member, American Crop Protection Association; Board Member, Capital Area Soccer Association Women's Division. **Education:** Western Michigan University, B.S. (1975). **Personal:** Married to Elizabeth S. in 1973. Two children: Margaret Ann and Mary Elizabeth. Mr. Jongeward enjoys golf, photography, and watching girl's soccer games.

Dr. Stephen Warren Kaldor

Head of Department
Eli Lilly & Company
Lilly Corporate Center
Indianapolis, IN 46285
(317) 276–4211
Fax: (317) 277–3652
Email: See Below

2834

Business Information: Eli Lilly & Company, established in the late 1800s, is an international manufacturer of pharmaceuticals. The Company employs approximately 730,000 people and posts multi–billion dollar revenues each year. Research and development of new drugs and treatments for humans are of high priority to Eli Lilly & Company, for example, the Company was instrumental in the development of Prozac, a widely–used depression–abatement drug. As Head of Department, Technical Core, Dr. Kaldor directs a group that uses new and existing technology in the development of new drugs for health care practitioners. He monitors the group's production and methods to comply with health and safety regulations, and is involved in Company public relations. Dr. Kaldor frequently speaks with business leaders and the media regarding completed work and in–progress research. His research has been instrumental in the development of a compound treatment for AIDS which has not yet reached Clinical Phase3. Internet users can reach him via: Kaldor_Stephen_W@Lilly.com. **Career Steps:** Eli Lilly & Company: Head of Department (1995–Present), Group Leader, Technology Core (1993–1994), Research Scientist, ID Research (1992–1993). **Associations & Accomplishments:** American Chemical Society; Dr. Kaldor has been quoted in many chemical and engineering magazine articles and conducts lectures daily on a variety of chemical and/or engineering topics. **Education:** Harvard University, Ph.D. (1989); Columbia University/Columbia College, B.A. (1984). **Personal:** Married to Teresa in 1984. One child: Adam. Dr. Kaldor enjoys fishing.

David W. Keiser

Executive Vice President and Chief Operating Officer
Alexion Pharmaceuticals, Inc.
25 Science Park, Suite 360
New Haven, CT 06511–1968
(203) 776–1790
Fax: (203) 776–2089

2834

Business Information: Alexion Pharmaceuticals, Inc. is a biotechnology research and development company, developing biopharmaceutical therapeutics for use in treating various diseases, such as R.A. kidney (lupus), heart attacks, M.S., and diabetes. Established in 1992, Alexion Pharmaceuticals currently employs 47 people. As Executive Vice President and Chief Operating Officer, Mr. Keiser's duties encompass business development, finance, operations, facilities, manufacturing, and project management functions. **Career**

Steps: Executive Vice President and Chief Operating Officer, Alexion Pharmaceuticals, Inc. (1992–Present); Searle: Senior Director of Asia/Pacific Operations (1990–1992), Director of Licensing (1988–1990). **Associations & Accomplishments:** Licensing Executives Society; Director, Madison Chapter of "A Better Chance"; Fluent in German, Swiss dialect, and French. **Education:** Gettysburg College, B.A. (1973). **Personal:** Married to Barbara in 1976. Three children: Stephanie, Amanda, and Joseph. Mr. Keiser enjoys travel, golf, and foreign language studies.

Allison S. Kennington, Ph.D.

Head
Eli Lilly & Company
2001 West Main Street
Greenfield, IN 46140–2714
(317) 277–5306
Fax: (317) 277–4993

2834

Business Information: Eli Lilly & Company is one of the top 10 pharmaceutical manufacturers of prescription veterinary drugs with 40 offices serving more than 100 countries around the world. As Head, Dr. Kennington supervises 50 staff chemists in analytical, metabolism, and formulations development. An expert in residue and food safety, she is responsible for phase three product development and the project registration of drugs. **Career Steps:** Eli Lilly & Company: Head (1995–Present), Senior Scientist (1992–1995); Senior Analytical Chemist, ARCTECH, Inc. (1990–1992). **Associations & Accomplishments:** American Chemical Society; Association of Official Analytical Chemists. **Education:** University of Virginia, Ph.D. (1990); Furman University, B.S. in Chemistry. **Personal:** Married to John Kennington Jr., Ph.D. in 1988. One child: Lauren Amanda. Dr. Kennington enjoys sailing and gardening.

Connie J. Kisinger

Regional Account Manager
Roche Laboratories
6852 Edgevale Road
Kansas City, MO 64113
(816) 523–5521
Fax: (816) 523–5521

2834

Business Information: Roche Laboratories is an international manufacturer and distributor of pharmaceuticals. As Regional Account Manager, Mrs. Kisinger is responsible for troubleshooting key accounts for business units in Kansas, Missouri, and Southern Illinois regions. Key institutional accounts include HMO's. She is also responsible for contracting, value–added programs, and training. **Career Steps:** Roche Laboratories: Regional Account Manager (1995–Present), Division Sales Manager (1991–1994), Sales Representative (1984–1991). **Associations & Accomplishments:** Alumni Member, Tri Delta; Research and Education Board, Missouri Society for Hospital Pharmacists; Christmas in October; Member, St. Agnes Choir; Recipient, President's Achievement Award in 1989 from Roche Laboratories; Recipient, Senior Honor Women Award from college; Intra Collegiate Athletic Board; Young Republican. **Education:** Wichita State University, Bachelor of Health Sciences in Respiratory Therapy (1983); Keller Graduate School of Management, currently pursuing M.B.A. **Personal:** Married to Kirk in 1994. Mrs. Kisinger enjoys skiing, walking, singing, school, and travel.

Hilton J. Klein, V.M.D.

Senior Director of Laboratory Animal Resources
Merck Research Laboratories
W44–2
West Point, PA 19486
(215) 652–6232
Fax: (215) 652–0999
EMAIL: See Below

2834

Business Information: Merck Research Laboratories, a subsidiary of Merck & Company and the second largest pharmaceutical company in the world, is a therapeutic drug development and testing facility. Human and Veterinary pharmaceuticals manufactured include: cardiac medicine, Fosamax (to treat osteoporosis in women), and Ivermectin (veterinary heart guard). Established in the 1930's, Merck Research Laboratories currently employs 53,000 people. Merck & Co. has estimated annual sales of $17 billion. A veterinarian since 1980, Dr. Klein joined Merck Research Laboratories as Associate Director of Laboratory Animal Resources in 1988 and was appointed as Director of Laboratory Animal Resources in 1991. He is responsible for directing all activities of laboratory animal medicine and surgery, as well as conducting biomedical research and development. Internet users can reach Dr. Klein via: klein@merck.com. **Career Steps:** Merck Research Laboratories: Director of Laboratory Animal Resources (1991–1996), Associate Director of Laboratory Animal Resources (1988–1991); Director of Veterinary Science, Whittaker M.A. Bioproducts (1982–1985). **Associations &**

Accomplishments: American College of Laboratory Animal Medicine; American Association Laboratory Animal Science Council; American Association for Accreditation of Laboratory Animal Care; American Society of Laboratory Animal Practitioners; Board of Directors, Pennsylvania Society for Biomedical Research; American Veterinary Medical Association; Board of Directors, Scientists Center for Animal Welfare. **Education:** University of Pennsylvania, V.M.D. (1980); Pennsylvania State University, M.S.; Rutgers University, B.S. **Personal:** Married to Charlotte B. in 1973. Three children: Alyssa, Meghann, and Jacob. Dr. Klein enjoys golf.

Philip G. Koga, Ph.D.

Director of Manufacturing
Cel–Sci Corporation
4820 Seton Drive, Suite C
Baltimore, MD 21215
(410) 358–6866
Fax: (410) 358–1647

2834

Business Information: Cel–Sci Corporation is an international developer and manufacturer of biologicals and pharmaceuticals (vaccines) for diseases, including cancer, AIDS, and Tuberculosis, as well as contract cytokine testing services to corporate, government, and university clients and developing techniques to select the type of immune response. Cel–Sci Corporation has two national locations, one in Alexandria, Virginia and one in Baltimore, Maryland, providing scientific advances around the globe. As Director of Manufacturing, Dr. Koga is responsible for directing the manufacture and distribution of cancer drugs to internal and external customers to include research and development, as well as the oversight of operations at the new subsidiary, PRAL Labs. **Career Steps:** Director of Manufacturing, Cel–Sci Corporation (1994–Present); Program/Marketing Manager and Principal Engineer, Allied–Signal – Bendix, ESD (1987–1994); Group Leader and Physical Scientist, U.S. Army Chemical Research, Development, and Engineering Center (1984–1987); Senior Scientist, Becton–Dickinson and Company (1983–1984). **Associations & Accomplishments:** American Association of Pharmaceutical Scientists; American Society for Microbiology; American Chemical Society; American Association for the Advancement of Science; American Association for Clinical Chemistry; Alpha Chi Sigma, Sigma Xi; Baltimore Council on Foreign Affairs; Johns Hopkins University Immunology Council; U.S. International Delegate for Biological/Chemical Defense; Chairman, NATO Industrial Advisory Group on Biosensors; University of Washington Technical Center Advisory Committee. **Education:** University of California at Berkeley, Ph.D. in Molecular Biology (1978); University of California at Los Angeles, B.S. in Chemistry (1972). **Personal:** Married to Lori A. in 1994. One child: David. Dr. Koga enjoys golf, tennis, racquetball, and squash.

Dr. Robert Krell

Senior Vice President of Research and Development
PANAX Pharmaceutical Company
425 Park Avenue, 27th Floor
New York, NY 10022
(212) 319–8300
Fax: (212) 751–4131

2834

Business Information: PANAX Pharmaceutical Company specializes in pharmaceutical research and development. The Company specialized in plant research, which is specifically targeted toward anti–infective, antifungal, antimicrobial, and anti–inflammatory therapeutic uses. As Senior Vice President of Research and Development, Dr. Krell is responsible for research and development activities in the United States and Russia. **Career Steps:** Senior Vice President of Research and Development, PANAX Pharmaceutical Company (1996–Present); Vice President/General Manager, Biofor, Inc. (1994–1996); Senior Section Manager, Zeneca Pharmaceutical (1980–1994); Senior Scientist, Smith Kline & French (1972–1980). **Associations & Accomplishments:** American Academy of Allergy; American Thoracic Society; American Society of Pharmacology and Experimental Therapeutics; Royal Society of Medicine; New York Academy of Sciences. **Education:** Ohio State University, Ph.D. (1972); University of Toledo, B.S. in Pharmacy. **Personal:** Married to Rebecca in 1966. Two children: Matthew Robert and Melanie Lynn. Dr. Krell enjoys tennis.

Frank J. Kuszpa

Director of Engineering and Technical Services
Bristol–Myers Squibb
5 Research Parkway
Wallingford, CT 06492–7660
(203) 284–7782
Fax: (203) 284–7548

2834

Business Information: Bristol–Myers Squibb is one of the world's leading pharmaceutical companies specializing in cardiovascular and oncology drug research and manufacturing;

offering cost–effective, disease–oriented patient health care management. With twenty–seven years expertise in the mechanical and pharmaceutical engineering industries, Mr. Kuszpa joined Bristol–Myers Squibb as Director of Engineering and Technical Services in 1992. He is responsible for directing all aspects of capital projects for research sites throughout the world. **Career Steps:** Bristol–Myers Squibb: Full Director (1995–Present), Director of Engineering and Technical Services (1992–1995); Assistant Vice President of Operations, University of Hartford (1985–1991); Operations Manager, Facilities Resource Management Company (1980–1985). **Associations & Accomplishments:** Vice President of the New England Chapter, International Society of Pharmaceutical Engineers; American Management Association; American Society of Mechanical Engineers; Published in trade journals and local newpapers on heating and piping; Published a seminar for Physical Plant Administrators, Department of Energy "Dos and Don'ts of Solar Energy." **Education:** University of Hartford, M.B.A. (1988); Rensselaer Polytechnic Institute, M.S. in Mechanical Engineering (1973); Worcester Polytechnic Institute, B.S. in Mechanical Engineering (1968). **Personal:** Married to Helen in 1967. Two children: Michael and John. Mr. Kuszpa enjoys cooking, photography, and working with teenagers.

Athanasios S. Ladas

Director of Product Development

Pfizer, Inc.

400 Webro Road
Parsippany, NJ 07054
(201) 952–7301
Fax: (201) 952–7361
EMail: See Below

2834

Business Information: Pfizer, Inc. is one of the leading manufacturers of pharmaceutical and non–prescription drugs. As Director of Product Development, Mr. Ladas is responsible for diversified administrative activities, including overseeing all new product development. Internet users can reach him via: LadasT@Pfizer.com. **Career Steps:** Pfizer, Inc.: Director of Product Development (1987–Present), Manager of Product Development, Consumer Products Division (1983–1987), Section Manager of Product Development, Consumer Products Division (1976–1983). **Associations & Accomplishments:** American Association for the Advancement of Science; American Chemical Society; New York Academy of Sciences; American Pharmaceutical Association; Pfizer Science and Math Education Intitiative; Board Member, Parsippany Education Foundation; 1995 Parsippany Businessperson of the Year; Former President, Parsippany Soccer Club. **Education:** Brooklyn College: Master of Science (1972), B.S. in Chemistry. **Personal:** Married to Nancy in 1969. Five children: Christina, Cynthia, Vanessa, Stephen, and Andrew. Mr. Ladas enjoys and coaching and playing soccer.

Lora B. Landreth

Quality Control Director

Glaxo Wellcome, Inc.

P.O. Box 1887
Greenville, NC 27835–7027
(919) 707–2138
Fax: (919) 707–7027
EMAIL: See Below

2834

Business Information: Glaxo Wellcome, Inc. is one of the top three pharmaceutical research–based companies in the world, specializing in pharmaceutical research and development, as well as manufacturing and sales. Products manufactured include ointments, creams, liquids, tablets, bulk drugs, and sterile dosage forms. As Quality Control Director, Ms. Landreth is responsible for testing and release of all raw materials, dosage forms, and packaging components. She is also involved in product investigations and FDA audit preparations. Internet users can reach her via: Lora_landreth@us.wfl.com. **Career Steps:** Quality Control Director, Glaxo Wellcome, Inc. (1993–Present); Burroughs Wellcome Company: Quality Control Manager (1994–1995), Quality Control Department Head (1988–1994), Quality Section Head (1983–1988). **Associations & Accomplishments:** American Chemical Society (ACS); American Society for Quality Control (ASQC); Parental Drug Association (PDA); Pharmaceutical Research and Manufacturing Association (PHRMA). **Education:** East Carolina University, B.S. Professional in Chemistry (1974). **Personal:** Married to Charles B. in 1973. Two children: Brian and Kim. Ms. Landreth enjoys reading and puzzles.

Alicia M. Lugo

Technical Training Administrator

Warner Lambert, Inc.

P.O. Box 786
Vega Baja, Puerto Rico 00694–0786
(787) 863–1850
Fax: (787) 863–1266

2834

Business Information: Warner Lambert, Inc., headquartered in Morris Plains, New Jersey, is an international manufacturer of ethical pharmaceutical products. Products include Dilantin Kapseals (TM), Nitrostat, Nearontin, Loestrin, Benadryl, Sinutab, and Listerine. Expected to be approved by the FDA by the end of 1996, Warner–Lambert, Inc. will have a new product for diabetes called Razulin. Additional plans for 1996 include introducing Listerine products to Russia. As Technical Training Administrator, Ms. Lugo oversees all operator technical training design, development, and implementation; handles organizational and career development; department management; and ensures compliance with all regulations. **Career Steps:** Warner Lambert, Inc: Technical Training Administrator (1993–Present), Instructional Designer (1992–1993); School Director, Commercial Banking Institute (1989–1991). **Associations & Accomplishments:** International Society for Performance Improvement (ISPI); American Association for Quality Control (ASQC); American Society of Training and Development (ASTD). **Education:** Inter–American University, M.S. in Counseling Psychology (without thesis) (1987–IP); Puerto Rico University: B.S. in Psychology, B.S. in Medical Science. **Personal:** Ms. Lugo enjoys reading technical, management, development, training, and Spanish literature.

Martha E. Manning, J.D.

Vice President/General Counsel

United States Bioscience, Inc.

1 Tower Bridge, 100 Front Street
Conshohocken, PA 19428
(610) 832–4517
Fax: (610) 832–4595

2834

Business Information: United States Bioscience, Inc. is a pharmaceutical company specializing in the development and commercialization of products for patients with cancer and AIDS. Established in 1987, the Company employs 120 people. As Vice President/General Counsel, Ms. Manning also serves as Secretary of the Corporation and oversees all departments, including homebound patients. **Career Steps:** Vice President./General Counsel, United States Bioscience, Inc. (1993–Present); General Counsel, Wistar Institute (1988–1993); Associate, Morgan, Lewis, & Bockius (1983–1988). **Associations & Accomplishments:** Pennsylvania Bar Association; American Bar Association; Licensing Executives Society; Philadelphia Bar Association. **Education:** University of Pennsylvania, J.D. (1983); University of Massachusetts, B.B.A. (1977). **Personal:** Married to Kevin Gorman in 1983. Six children: Seth, Colin, James, Zachary, Luke, and Marguerite. Ms. Manning enjoys tennis, reading, and spending time with her family.

2834

Atef L. Maquar, M.D.

Vice President

APIC U.S.A. Inc.

825 North Cass Avenue, Suite 102
Westmont, IL 60559
(708) 655–8895
Fax: (708) 655–8897

2834

Business Information: APIC U.S.A. Inc. specializes in the manufacture and distribution of pharmaceuticals and nutracueticals. Established in 1993, APIC, U.S.A. Inc. is a multi–national company with headquarters in Cairo, Egypt. Currently the United States division employs 36 people. As Vice President, Dr. Maquar is the Head of Research and Development, Scientific Affairs, International Trade and Product Development. **Career Steps:** Vice President, APIC U.S.A. Inc. (1993–Present); Senior Medical Advisor, Amoun Pharmaceuticals (1990–1993); Physician (1987–1990). **Education:** Ain Shams Medical School, M.D., M.Sc. (1987). **Personal:** Married to Sonya in 1993. Dr. Maquar enjoys music, soccer, visual arts, and playing the piano.

Daniel C. McIntyre

Director of Regional Remediation

Ciba–Geigy Corporation

P.O. Box 71
Toms River, NJ 08754
(908) 914–2542
Fax: (908) 914–2917

2834

Business Information: Ciba–Geigy Corporation, known as Ciba, is a leading U.S. biological and chemical company, dedicated to fulfilling needs in healthcare, agriculture and industry with innovative products and services. Headquartered in Tarrytown, N.Y., Ciba employs over 15,000 people nationwide. The Company maintains divisional headquarters, production plants, administrative facilities, subsidiaries, regional sales offices and distribution centers throughout the U.S. The Corporation is a wholly–owned subsidiary of Ciba–Geigy Limited, a publicly owned company, headquartered in Basel, Switzerland. The Corporation is the largest Ciba company, generating nearly one–third of worldwide sales. Serving in managerial roles for various Ciba subsidiaries since 1978, Dan McIntyre was appointed to his current position as Director of Regional Remediation in January of 1993. Located at the Toms River, New Jersey facility, he is responsible for the direction and oversight of all remediation activities on 55 company sites with Regions I, II, and III of the U.S. Environmental Protection Agency. **Career Steps:** Ciba–Geigy Corporation: Director of Regional Remediation (1993–Present), Director of Environmental Affairs (1985–93), Plant Manager – St. Gabriel Plant (1978–85). **Associations & Accomplishments:** Chemical Industry Council in New Jersey; National Ground Water Association. **Education:** University of Houston, M.B.A. (1960); University of Illinois, B.S. in Chemical Engineering (1960). **Personal:** Married to Vivian in 1954. Two children: Susan Randal and Dr. Kristi McIntyre. Mr. McIntyre enjoys hunting, fishing and football.

Paul Meade

• • • ◦ ━━◖◎◗━━ • ◦ • • •

Group Director of Business Planning

Glaxo–Wellcome

5 Moore Drive, Dept. of Business Planning
Durham, NC 27709
(919) 248–7966
Fax: (919) 248–7699

2834

Business Information: Glaxo–Wellcome, a subsidiary of Glaxo Inc., is one of the top three pharmaceutical research based companies in the world, specializing in pharmaceutical research and development, as well as manufacturing and sales. Established in 1982 in the U.S., Glaxo Wellcome Inc. currently employs 6,000 professionals. Joining Glaxo Canada as Director of Product Management in 1989, Mr. Meade went on to serving as Director of International Marketing at Glaxo plc (United Kingdom) in 1991. Currently serving as Group Director of Business Planning at Glaxo's subsidiary, Glaxo–Wellcome since 1994, Mr. Meade is responsible for company–wide strategy development for the U.S. While employed at the United Kingdom office, he was responsible for the strategic development and marketing of the largest pharmaceutical drug in the world, Zantac, reaching sales of over $3.5 billion. **Career Steps:** Group Director of Business Planning, Glaxo–Wellcome (1994–Present); Director of International Marketing, Glaxo Plc – UK (1991–1994); Director of Product Management, Glaxo Canada (1989–1991). **Education:** University of Guelph, M.Sc. (1977); Acadia University, B.Sc. (1975). **Personal:** Married to Peg in 1982. Two children: Jeffrey and Samantha. Mr. Meade enjoys golf, tennis, scuba diving, and collecting wine.

Saul Melendez

General Manager

Colorcon Puerto Rico, Inc.

P.O. Box 979
Punta Santiago, Puerto Rico 00741–0979
(787) 852–3815
Fax: (787) 852–0030

2834

Business Information: Colorcon PR, Inc., a subsidiary of Berwin Pharmaceutical, is a bulk chemical manufacturer dedicated to the production of coating solutions for the pharmaceutical industry. Business is conducted with all major pharmaceutical companies, such as Johnson & Johnson and Eli Lilly. As General Manager, Mr. Melendez is responsible for planning, directing, and coordinating all site operations. **Career Steps:** Colorcon PR, Inc.: General Manager (1993–Present),

Manufacturing Manager (1986–1993), Q.C. Manager (1982–1986). **Education:** University of Del Turabo, BBA (1996). **Personal:** Married to Elsie Agosto in 1983. Six children: Saul, Lo Ann, Melvin, Noel, Bernice, and Ivan. Mr. Melendez enjoys reading and bicycling.

Angel B. Mendez, MBA

Financial Controller
Rhone–Poulenc Rorer Caribbean
P.O. Box 364824
San Juan, Puerto Rico 00936–4824
(809) 227–5610
Fax: (809) 783–4346

2834

Business Information: Rhone–Poulenc Rorer Caribbean, a subsidiary of Rhone–Poulenc Rorer, is the world's leading research development manufacturer of pharmaceuticals and medical/chemical technological products. Established in 1980, Rhone–Poulenc Rorer Caribbean reports annual revenue of $40 million and currently employs 53 people. A fourteen–year veteran of the Company, Mr. Mendez has served as Financial Controller since 1981. He is responsible for checking expenditures and finances, as well as regulating and directing financial operations. **Career Steps:** Financial Controller, Rhone–Poulenc Rorer Caribbean (1981–Present). **Associations & Accomplishments:** President, Campaign to raise $1.5 million for a church; Community leader in the neighborhood. **Education:** InterAmerica University, M.B.A. (1986); Universidad Turabo, B.B.A. (1979). **Personal:** Married to Myriam Rodriguez in 1975. Two children: Javier and Orlando. Mr. Mendez enjoys sports.

Leo Grant Michael
Aerospace Industry Manager
Ciba
5121 San Francisco Road West
Los Angeles, CA 90039
(818) 247–6210
Fax: (818) 507–0167

2834

Business Information: Ciba–Geigy Corporation, known as Ciba, is a leading U.S. biological and chemical company, dedicated to fulfilling needs in healthcare, agriculture and industry with innovative products and services. Headquartered in Ardsley, N.Y., Ciba employs over 15,000 people nationwide. The company maintains divisional headquarters, production plants, administrative facilities, subsidiaries, regional sales offices and distribution centers throughout the U.S. The corporation is a wholly–owned subsidiary of Ciba–Geigy Limited, a publicly owned company, headquartered in Basel, Switzerland. The corporation is the largest Ciba company, generating nearly one–third of worldwide sales. As Aerospace Industry Manager, Mr. Michael is responsible for the management of the aerospace adhesives division worldwide in the areas of sales and marketing, research and development, and technical service. The Aerospace Adhesives Division, headquartered in Los Angeles, manufactures formulated epoxy and polyurethane adhesives and resins particularly utilized by the aerospace industry. **Career Steps:** Ciba: Aerospace Industry Manager (1995–Present), Market Development Manager (1994–1995), Regional Sales Manager (1992–1994); Regional Sales Manager, ICI Fiberite (1990–1992). **Associations & Accomplishments:** Association for Professional Model Makers; Society of Manufacturing Engineers; Society for the Advancement of Materials and Process Manufacturing. **Education:** Western Washington University, B.S. (1986). **Personal:** Married to Christine in 1986. Three children: Evan, Samantha and Alexander. Mr. Michael enjoys golf, woodworking, boxing and history.

Debra L. Middleton
Facilities Coordinator & Purchasing
BioCryst Pharmaceuticals, Inc.
2190 Parkway Lake Drive
Birmingham, AL 35244
(205) 444–4600
Fax: (205) 444–4640

2834

Business Information: BioCryst Pharmaceuticals, Inc. is a pharmaceutical company located in Birmingham, Alabama. Established in 1986, the Company currently employs 48 people. As Facilities Coordinator & Purchasing, Ms. Middleton handles the purchasing of materials and equipment for BioCryst. Ms. Middleton also prepares invoices for payment and assists in accounts payable. **Career Steps:** Facilities Coordinator & Purchasing, BioCryst Pharmaceuticals, Inc. (1995–Present); Administrative Assistant to the C.E.O. & Managing Director of Corporate Finance, Needham & Com-

pany, Inc. (1994–1995). **Associations & Accomplishments:** Headed Company United Way Campaign. **Education:** University of Alabama, B.F.A. (1990). **Personal:** Ms. Middleton enjoys singing, plays, and piano.

Tom Millner

Director of Human Resources Planning, Projects and Initiatives
DuPont Merck Pharmaceutical Company
P.O. Box 80024
Wilmington, DE 19880–0024
(302) 992–2230
Fax: (302) 892–8837

2834

Business Information: The DuPont Merck Pharmaceutical Company, a research–based ethical pharmaceutical company, is a joint venture of the E. I. DuPont De Nemours Company and Merck and Company. DuPont Merck develops and markets pharmaceuticals for the treatment of cardiovascular, central nervous system, inflammatory and infectious diseases. The Company's Radiopharmaceuticals Division is the world leader in the field of radio–labeled diagnostic imaging. DuPont Merck has locations in the United States and Puerto Rico, Canada and Europe. Established in 1991, DuPont Merck currently employs 3,900 people. Serving in various managerial roles for DuPont Merck since 1991, Mr. Millner currently serves as Director of Human Resources Planning, Projects and Initiatives, responsible for Human Resources and initiatives that positively impact the overall effectiveness of the organization. **Career Steps:** The DuPont Merck Pharmaceutical Company: Director of Human Resources Planning, Projects and Initiatives (1993–Present), Manager – Management and Employment Development (1992–1993), Manager – Management Development (1991–1992). **Associations & Accomplishments:** ASTD; Society of Human Resources Management; Published ads in the Wall Street Journal, Harvard Business Review and the New York Times. **Education:** University of Pennsylvania, presently attending; Columbia University (1993); University of Bridgeport (1981–1985); Campbell University, B.S. in Biology (1964–1968). **Personal:** Four children: Chad, Ryan, Jahan and Ahsha. Mr. Millner enjoys reading, learning and travel.

Ms. Maida R. Milone
Senior Vice President, General Counsel and Company Secretary
DuPont Merck Pharmaceutical Company
974 Centre Road, WR1023
Wilmington, DE 19807–2802
(302) 892–7725
Fax: (302) 892–8899

2834

Business Information: DuPont Merck Pharmaceutical Company is a worldwide, research–based pharmaceutical company. Formed in 1991 as a partnership between DuPont and Merck & Co., Inc., DuPont Merck is focused on research, development and delivery of pharmaceuticals to treat unmet medical needs in the fight against cardiovascular, central nervous system and inflammatory diseases, cancer and AIDS. As Senior Vice President, General Counsel and Company Secretary, Ms. Milone provides all aspects of legal representation, as well as presides at Partnership Board meetings. The Dupont Merck Pharmaceutical Company employs 3,900 people. **Career Steps:** DuPont Merck Pharmaceutical Company: Senior Vice President, General Counsel and Company Secretary (1994–Present), Vice President and General Counsel (1993–1994), Administrative Director to Company Management Committee (1992–1993), Assistant General Counsel, General Law (1991–1992); Associate General Counsel, Rhone–Poulenc Rorer, Inc. (1990–1991); Assistant General Counsel, Schnader, Harrison, Segal & Lewis, Philadelphia, PA (1984–1988); Law Clerk, Hon. John F. Gerry, Camden, NJ (1982–1984). **Associations & Accomplishments:** Board of Directors, Support Center for Child Advocates. **Education:** The Law School, University of Pennsylvania, J.D. cum laude (1982); University of Pennsylvania, B.A. summa cum laude (1976); Chatham College (1975). **Personal:** Married to Francis M. Milone in 1991. One child: G. Matthew Milone.

Lawrence (Larry) A. Pachla, Ph.D.
Associate Director
Sanofi
1115 Winchester Trail
Downingtown, PA 19335–4014
(610) 889–8794
Fax: Please mail or call

2834

Business Information: Sanofi is a pharmaceutical company, providing developmental research in analytical science, pharmacokinetics and drug metabolism. An esteemed pharmaceutical chemist and research scientist, serving with some of the world's leading biomedical industries, Dr. Pachla serves as Sanofi's Chemistry Division Associate Director. His primary duties involve overseeing analytical chemistry projects, and related budgetary planning and development. **Career Steps:** Associate Director, Sanofi (1989–Present); Assistant Director, Parke Davis (1981–1989); Senior Scientist, McNeil (1978–1981). **Associations & Accomplishments:** American Chemical Society; American Association of Pharmaceutical Scientist; American Pharmaceutical Association. **Education:** Purdue University, Ph.D. (1978); Lawrence Technological University, B.S. **Personal:** Married to Barbara Ann Decast in 1982.

Donald C. Panthen
Network Manager
Pfizer, Inc.
235 East 42nd Street
New York, NY 10017
(212) 573–7452
Fax: (212) 338–1516

2834

Business Information: Pfizer, Inc. is a health care pharmaceutical provider with world headquarters in New York City. As Network Manager, Mr. Panthen is responsible for maintaining computer network servers, implementing changes, and recommending new programs. Responsibilities also include managing over 70 people and insure the functionality of over 5,000 desktop computers. **Career Steps:** Network Manager, Pfizer, Inc. (1994–Present); Ensign, U.S. Navy (Present). **Associations & Accomplishments:** Ensign, U.S. Navy Reserves; New York State Militia; Union League Club; Received two Navy Achievement Medal. **Education:** Pace University, B.B.A. (1989). **Personal:** Married to Carolyn in 1990. One child: Kyle. Mr. Panthen enjoys carpentry.

Dr. James G. Perkins

Vice President of Regulatory Affairs and Quality Assurance
Solvay Pharmaceuticals, Inc.
901 Sawyer Road
Marietta, GA 30062–2224
(770) 578–5509
Fax: (770) 578–5864

2834

Business Information: Solvay Pharmaceuticals, Inc. is a multi–national pharmaceutical company, dealing with therapeutic drugs for the central nervous system, women's health, and gastrointestinal problems. As Vice President of Regulatory Affairs and Quality Assurance, Dr. Perkins investigates adverse reactions to drugs, oversees regulatory compliance, and ensures the quality of the drugs. Additionally, he deals with regulatory affairs and introduction of drugs into the marketplace. **Career Steps:** Vice President of Regulatory Affairs and Quality Assurance, Solvay Pharmaceuticals, Inc. (1994–Present); Vice President of Regulatory Affairs, Hoffmann La Rushe (1993–1994); Department Head of Regulatory Affairs, Burroughs Wellcome (1976–1991). **Associations & Accomplishments:** American Thoracic Society; American Chemical Society; Drug Information Association; United Way Allegations Committee; Scouts Board of Directors; American Association for the Advancement of Science; New York Academy of Science; Rotary; Board of Directors, Essex County Boy Scouts; Community Coordination Committee, Glen Ridge, NJ. **Education:** Indiana University, Ph.D. in Biochemistry (1972), B.S. in Chemistry (1967). **Personal:** Married to Glenda in 1968. One child: Sean. Dr. Perkins enjoys sports, literature, and creative writing.

John C. Petricciani, M.D.

Vice President for Regulatory Affairs
Genetics Institute, Inc.
87 Cambridge Park Drive
Cambridge, MA 02140
(617) 498–8881
Fax: (617) 498–8876

2834

Business Information: Genetics Institute, Inc., the largest biopharmaceutical company in Massachusetts, is involved in the research and development of therapeutic products. As Vice President for Regulatory Affairs, Dr. Petricciani is responsible for regulatory activities with the U.S. Food and Drug Administration and international counterparts. Established in 1981, Genetics Institute, Inc. employs over 1000 people. **Career Steps:** Vice President for Regulatory Affairs, Genetics Institute, Inc. (1992–Present); Vice President for Medical & Regulatory, Pharmaceutical Manufacturers Association (1988–1992); Director, Biologicals, World Health Organization (1985–1987); Director, Biologics, Food and Drug Administration (1983–1984). **Associations & Accomplishments:** AAAS; NYAS; American Medical Association; Published over 100 medical/scientific articles. **Education:** Stanford University, M.D. (1967); University of Nevada, M.S. (1960); Rensselaeur Polytechnical Institute, B.S. (1958).

Ellen L. Potepan

Senior Hospital Business Manager
Bristol Myers Squibb
2767 Thornbrook Road
Ellicott City, MD 21042
(410) 553–1140
Fax: (410) 750–2596
(800) 838–4443 Ext. POTEP

2834

Business Information: Bristol Myers Squibb is a world–wide leader in the pharmaceutical industry, specializing in the research, development, and sales of health care products. As Senior Hospital Business Manager, Ms. Potepan is responsible for the sales of 14 ethical pharmaceutical products within the University of Maryland, and three Maryland–Virginia hospitals in the Maryland area. In addition to her sales responsibilities, she participates in the training and development of new BMS representatives. **Career Steps:** Bristol Myers Squibb: Senior Hospital Business Manager (1994–Present), Hospital Business Manager (1991–1994), Hospital Sales Representative (1989–1991). **Associations & Accomplishments:** Sigma Theta Tau Nursing Honor Society; Bristol's Best Award (1990); Clinton Award (1990); Gold Star Go–Getter Award (1991); ICAAC Award (1992); Pinnacle Award (1994). **Education:** University of Maryland, B.S. in Nursing (1987). **Personal:** Married to Frank III in 1988. Two children: Tyler Logan and Grant Riley. Ms. Potepan enjoys swimming and golf.

Priscilla D. Preston, APR

National Director of Sales & Marketing
Pro Med Pharmacies
1800 South Washington, Suite 101
Amarillo, TX 79102
(806) 379–7126 (800) 879–7775
Fax: (806) 371–0447

2834

Business Information: Pro Med Pharmacies, one of three divisions of Chrysler Management Company, is a mail order pharmacy which markets and sells bronchodilator medications for asthma and chronic obstructive pulmonary diseases. As National Director of Sales & Marketing, Ms. Preston is responsible for all sales, marketing, and public relations for the Company. She handles training and hiring, human resources, and database marketing. **Career Steps:** National Director of Sales & Marketing, Pro Med Pharmacies (1995–Present); Director of Sales & Marketing, Remington Hotel Corporation (1994–1996); Statewide Director of Public Relations, American Heart Association of Colorado (1984–1991); Director of Sales & Marketing, Sheraton Hotel & Towers (1983–1984). **Associations & Accomplishments:** Leadership Amarillo; Denver Woman's Press Club; Board Member, American Cancer Society; Accredited, Public Relations Society of America; National Writers Association. **Education:** Eastern Montana College of Education, B.B.A. in Marketing (1970); Austin School of Massage Therapy, Registered Massage Therapist (1996). **Personal:** Married to Terry Allen McRight in 1996. Ms. Preston enjoys writing, desktop publishing, and tennis.

Carlos M. Quinones

Commercial Director
Glaxo–Wellcome
P O Box 363461
San Juan, Puerto Rico 00936–3461
(809) 250–7580
Fax: (809) 250–6933

2834

Business Information: Glaxo–Wellcome, a subsidiary of Glaxo Inc., is one of the top three pharmaceutical research–based companies in the world, specializing in pharmaceutical research and development, as well as manufacturing and sales. Established in 1982 in the U.S., Glaxo–Wellcome Inc. currently employs 6,000 professionals. As Commercial Director, Mr. Quinones has oversight of all sales and marketing programs for the Puerto Rico operation. He develops and implements new marketing and sales techniques for new and existing products distributed through his location. **Career Steps:** Glaxo–Wellcome: Commercial Director (1995–Present), Director of Sales and Marketing (1991–1995). **Associations & Accomplishments:** American Management Association. **Education:** Century University, B.A. (1980). **Personal:** Four children: Jose Carlos, Glenda Lee, Amaris, and Adriana. Mr. Quinones enjoys golf, playing guitar, playing the piano, and biking.

Mr. Vish G. Raju

President & Chief Executive Officer
Hallmark Pharmaceuticals, Inc.
5 Campus Drive
Somerset, NJ 08873
(908) 563–2245
Fax: (908) 469–2113

2834

Business Information: Hallmark Pharmaceuticals, Inc. specializes in pharmaceutical research and development, as well as manufacturing and sales (solid doses). Established since 1992, Hallmark Pharmaceuticals, Inc. presently employs 36 people. In his current capacity, Mr. Raju is responsible for all aspects of Company operations. **Career Steps:** President & Chief Executive Officer, Hallmark Pharmaceuticals, Inc. (1992– Present); President and Chief Executive Officer, American Therapeutics, Inc. (1990–1991); Vice President & Secretary, American Therapeutics, Inc. (1986–1990). **Education:** Drexel University at Philadelphia, M.B.A. Degree (1985); Annamalai University, Tamil Nadu, India, B.E. Degree in Mechanical Engineering (1970). **Personal:** Married to Rukmini Budharaju in 1970. Three children: Srinivasa, Vijayalakshmi, and Kalyani Budharaju. Mr. Raju enjoys listening to music and reading books in his leisure time.

Joaquim Ramirez Perez

Warehouse and Distribution Supervisor
Laboratorios Lepetit de Mexico
Boulevard Cuernavaca – Cuautla Km. 4.8.
Juitepec, Mexico 62550
(527) 320–9542
Fax: (527) 319–2826

2834

Business Information: Laboratorios Lepetit de Mexico is a pharmaceutical company, in joint venture with an American pharmaceutical company, for the production and distribution of drugs. Working in various research and managerial capacities for Laboratorios Lepetit since 1991, Joaquim Perez was appointed Warehouse and Distribution Supervisor in 1994. In this capacity, he is responsible for the supervision of employees, production forecasts and scheduling, and all distribution activities. **Career Steps:** Laboratorios Lepetit de Mexico: Warehouse and Distribution Supervisor (1994–Present), Production Supervisor (1993–1994), Chemical Analyzer (1991–1993); Engineer in Project, Dow Quimica Mexicana (1990–1991). **Associations & Accomplishments:** Management Center de Mexico, A.C. **Education:** Escuela Superior De Ingenieria Quimica E Industrias Extractivas, Chemical Engineering (1990). **Personal:** Married to Laura E. Garcia Romero in 1993. Mr. Ramirez Perez enjoys swimming and reading.

Jose V. Ramos

Manager, Safety and Loss Prevention Section
Abbott Laboratories
P.O. Box 278
Barceloneta, Puerto Rico 00617
(787) 846–8360
Fax: (809) 846–3625

2834

Business Information: Abbott Laboratories is a world leader in the manufacture and distribution of health care products including pharmaceuticals and antibiotics for diagnostic, agricultural, and veterinary use. As Manager of the Safety and Loss Prevention Section, Mr. Ramos is responsible for the development and implementation of all safety and loss–prevention policies and procedures. **Career Steps:** Manager, Safety and Loss Prevention Section, Abbott Laboratories (1988–Present); Safety and Environmental Manager, Abbott Hospitals, Inc. (1988–1990); Safety and Security Manager, Key Pharmaceuticals (1985–1988); Technical Services Section Manager, Abbott Pharmaceuticals, Inc. (1974–1985). **Associations & Accomplishments:** National Safety Council; National Fire Association; Former President, Home Owners Association – Haciendas la Monserrate; President, Community Awareness and Emergency Response Committee. **Education:** Interamerican University, M.B.A. (1985); University of Puerto Rico, B.S. **Personal:** Married to Mayra V. in 1972. Two children: Jose V. and Mayra Del Carmen Ramos. Mr. Ramos enjoys reading, tennis, softball, swimming, social work in the community, and Little League Baseball.

Henrick S. Rasmussen, M.D., Ph.D.

Vice President of Clinical Research
British Biotech, Inc.
201 Defense Highway, Suite 260
Annapolis, MD 21401–8961
(410) 266–7909
Fax: (410) 266–8032

2834

Business Information: British Biotech, Inc. is the U.S. subsidiary of British Biotech, Plc., which is an evolving biopharmaceutical company, specializing in the discovery and development of new drugs, with specific focus on drugs for cancer and acute care. Trained as a medical doctor and holder of a Ph.D. in Cardiology, Dr. Rasmussen joined British Biotech, Inc. as Vice President of Clinical Research in 1994. He is responsible for the development of the Company's new drugs in North America. Career milestones include research on magnesium in myocardial infarction as well as the development of the new heart drug DOFETILIDE. **Career Steps:** Vice President of Clinical Research, British Biotech, Inc. (1994–Present); Candidate Team Leader/Global Study Director, Cardiovascular Group, Pfizer Central Research (1989–1994). **Associations & Accomplishments:** British Medical Association; European Society for Clinical Investigation; Society of Pharmaceutical Medicine; International Society for Magnesium Research. **Education:** University of Copenhagen: Ph.D./D.M.Sc. (1992), M.D. (1985). **Personal:** Married to Britta in 1981. Three children: Jacob, Camilla, and Ayla. Mr. Rasmussen enjoys reading and sports (tennis, skiing, running).

Barbara A. Reaves

Director of Information Technology
Pfizer, Inc.
400 Webro Road, 3rd Floor
Parsippany, NJ 07054
(212) 573–7011
Fax: (212) 573–7701

2834

Business Information: Pfizer, Inc. is a multi–billion dollar conglomerate engaged in manufacturing, fabricating and processing drugs in pharmaceutical preparations (prescription and over–the–counter pharmaceuticals and medical devices) for human and veterinary use. As Director of Information Technology, Ms. Reaves is responsible for the management, design, implementation of advancing technologies and customer support to solve business problems or support existing business processes. Currently Ms. Reaves is working on the start–up projects and Information Technologies in the Asian, European, and North American regions. **Career Steps:** Director of Information Technology, Pfizer, Inc. (1994–Present); Manager, Andersen Consulting (1992–1994); Principal, P A Consulting Group (1985–1992); Manager, AT&T (1973–1985). **Education:** Rutgers University, B.S. (1973). **Personal:** Married to Terry in 1985. Four children: Jason, Ashley, Brittany, and Christopher. Ms. Reaves enjoys tennis, skiing, and playing bridge.

Carlos A.P. Reis

Finance and Administrative Director
Alteration ISPDO Brazil, Limited
P.O. Box 9693
Sao Paulo, Brazil 01051
55–11–914–3944
Fax: 55–11–914–2771

2834

Business Information: Alteration ISP de Brazil, Limited, is a manufacturer of cosmetic and pharmaceutical products for the personal care market. A subsidiary of G.A.F., a Fortune 500 company, which manufactures building materials, Alteration ISP de Brazil specializes in chemical acetylenes, and currently controls 40% of the pharmaceutical market around the world. With 40 subsidiaries, the Company was established in 1973. As Finance Administration Director, Mr. Reis handles all finances and administration. **Career Steps:** Finance Administration Director, ISPDO Brazil, Limited (1987–Present); Finance and Administration Director, GAF Corporation Brazil Sub (1987–1996); Controller, Warner Lambert Company, Brazil Sub (1973–1986). **Associations & Accomplishments:** American Chamber of Sao Paulo; Sao Paulo's Banker's Association. **Education:** Fundacao Getulio Vargas, Post Graduate, Economist (1982). **Personal:** Married to Anna Tubini in 1972. Three children: Fatima, Elaine, and Daniel. Mr. Reis enjoys being an aero modelist and listening to classic music.

John J. Riefkohl–Vena
Sales Administrator
Cesar Castillo, Inc.
P.O. Box 191149
San Juan, Puerto Rico 00919
(787) 754–8280
Fax: (787) 753–1643

2834

Business Information: Cesar Castillo, Inc. is a manufacturer and distributor of over–the–counter pharmaceuticals for Puerto Rico. As Sales Administrator, Mr. Riefkohl–Vena is responsible for customer service, handling sales, route development, and supervising research and testing. **Career Steps:** Cesar Castillo, Inc.: Sales Administrator (1994–Present), Credit Analist (1993). **Education:** University of Puerto Rico – Bayamon, B.A. in Finance (1993); University of Puerto Rico – Carolina; Associate Degree in Banking, Finance, and Insurance (1990); University of Phoenix, Master Degree in Marketing. **Personal:** Married to Rebecca in 1996. Mr. Riefkohl–Vena enjoys volleyball, chess, and music.

Vilma Rivera Rodriguez, R.Ph.

Pharmacist
Pfizer Corporation
P.O. Box 1859
Carolina, Puerto Rico 00984–1859
(787) 257–5085
Fax: (787) 257–2627

2834

Business Information: Pfizer Corporation is a multi–billion dollar conglomerate engaged in manufacturing, fabricating and processing drugs in pharmaceutical preparations (prescription and over–the–counter pharmaceuticals and medical devices) for human and veterinary use. As Pharmacist, Ms. Rivera Rodriguez is responsible for all importing and exporting of products, warehouse, government bids, prices, and administration of Puerto Rican operations. **Career Steps:** Pharmacist, Pfizer Corporation (1994–Present); Chief Pharmacist, Puerto Rico Drugstores (1992–1994); Chief Pharmacist and Owner, San Jorge Drugstore (1989–1992). **Associations & Accomplishments:** Puerto Rico College of Pharmacists; Puerto Rico Health Professionals; Association of the Mansion Residents. **Education:** Puerto Rico Pharmacy School, Bachelor's Degree (1981). **Personal:** Two children: Miguel A. and Gabriel A. Ms. Rivera Rodriguez enjoys jogging, bicycling, handcrafts, and exercise.

Edwin Rodriguez
Area Sales Manager
Wyeth–Ayerst Laboratories
P.O. Box 362917
San Juan, Puerto Rico 00936–2917
(809) 782–3838
Fax: (809) 783–5215

2834

Business Information: Wyeth–Ayerst Laboratories, a Division of American Home Products Corporation, is an international pharmaceutical manufacturing and research company. The Company promotes pharmaceutical products, specializing in women's health care, cardiovascular, arthritis relief, antibiotics, and managed care. As Area Sales Manager, Mr. Rodriguez handles the Puerto Rican and US Virgin Islands region. He keeps the sales force focused and is responsible for sales and marketing of infant milk and soy baby formulas the region. **Career Steps:** Wyeth–Ayerst Laboratories: Area Sales Manager (1991–Present), Groups Product Manager (1989–1991), Product Manager (1987–1989), District Manager (1980–87), Territory Representative (1974–80). **Education:** University of Puerto Rico, B.A. (1971). **Personal:** Married to Sandra in 1971. Two children: Edwin and Carlos. Mr. Rodriguez enjoys being an amateur radio (Ham) operator, music, and literature.

Joanne Roth, P.E.
Director of Procurement
Hoffmann La Roche, Inc.
340 Kingsland Street
Nutley, NJ 07110
(201) 235–3221
Fax: (201) 235–6847
EMail: See Below

2834

Business Information: Hoffmann La Roche, Inc. is the largest pharmaceutical manufacturer and research company in the nation. As Director of Procurement, Ms. Roth is responsible for procurement of engineering, construction, facilities maintenance, and site services. Additionally, she handles hardware and software purchasing, strategic planning, and purchasing of construction materials. Internet users can reach her via: Joanne_E.Roth@Roche.com. **Career Steps:** Hoffmann La Roche, Inc.: Director of Procurement (1993–Present), Manager of Technical Procurement (1991–1993), Manager of Contract Administration (1989–1991), Principal Project Engineer (1986–1989). **Associations & Accomplishments:** New Jersey Society of Professional Engineers; National Society of Professional Engineers; North Jersey Construction Users Council; Construction Committee of Business Roundtable. **Education:** New Jersey Institute of Technology, M.S. (1993); Newark College of Engineering, B.S. in Chemical Engineering (1967). **Personal:** Married to Robert in 1967. Two children: Robert Charles and Stephanie Mary. Ms. Roth enjoys being a part of the New Jersey State Opera Chorus and the Berkshire Choral Festival.

Peter J. Roylance, M.D.
Executive Medical Director, Human Health Division
Merck & Company, Inc.
8 Magna Drive
Gillette, NJ 07933–1417
(908) 423–7351
Fax: (908) 423–7251 Ext. 141

2834

Business Information: Merck & Company, Inc. specializes in the manufacture of pharmaceuticals. Established in 1891, Merck & Company, Inc. currently employs 23,000 people and has an estimated annual revenue of $14.9 billion. As Executive Medical Director, Human Health Division, Dr. Roylance is responsible for the introduction of new products, international relations and research. **Career Steps:** Executive Medical Director, Human Health Division, Merck & Company, Inc. (1979–Present); Medical Director, MSD Ltd, Hoddesdon, UK (1975–1979); Medical Director, Beecham (1970–1975); Senior Lecturer (Research), Institute of Cancer Research, University of London (1961–1970). **Associations & Accomplishments:** Freeman of the City of London (1974); Clinical Professor of Internal Medicine, Seton Hall University; School of Graduate Medical Education, New Jersey (1991); Life Member, New York Academy of Sciences; American Associationfor the Advancement of Science (1992); Fellow American College of Physicians; Fellow of the Faculty of Pharmaceutical Medicine Royal College of Physicians, UK (1989); Commander of the Venerable Order of St. John; Reserve Decoration for Officers of the Royal Naval Reserve (1977). **Education:** University of Bristol, M.B., Ch.B. (1955) **Personal:** Married to Joan Margaret in 1957. Two children: Katharine Margaret and Wendy Muriel. Roylance enjoys gardening and scuba diving.

Nigel J. Rulewski, M.D.
Vice President–Medical and Regulatory Affairs
Astra USA, Inc.
50 Otis Street
Westborough, MA 01581–4500
(508) 366–1100
Fax: (508) 366–7406

2834

Business Information: Astra USA, Inc. is a pharmaceutical manufacturer, developer and international distributor providing drug development of new chemical entities and generic drugs. Astra USA, Inc. currently employs 600 persons in the Westborough operations. Dr. Rulewski is responsible for the supervision of all drug development planning in the U.S. and handles negotiations with the FDA and other regulatory authorities. **Career Steps:** Vice President–Medical and Regulatory Affairs, Astra USA (1989–Present); Medical Director, Serono (1988–1989); Medical Director–International Operations, Fisons (1985–1988). **Associations & Accomplishments:** Regulatory Affairs Professional Society; Food & Drug Law Institute; Drug Information Association; Association of Medical Directors. **Education:** St. Bartholomews Hospital Medical School, M.B/B.S. (1977); Royal College of Physicians, Post graduate DCH (diploma of child health) DRCOG (diploma of Royal College of Obstetrics and Gynecology). **Personal:** Married to Gina Vild in 1986. Two children: Gillian Victoria and Gareth Victor. Dr. Rulewski enjoys enjoys gardening, reading, and travel during his leisure time.

Robert K. Schultz, Ph.D.
Vice President
Dura Pharmaceuticals, Inc.
5880 Pacific Center Boulevard
San Diego, CA 92121–4204
(619) 457–2553
Fax: (619) 457–3211

2834

Business Information: Dura Pharmaceuticals is a San Diego–based developer and marketer of prescription pharmaceutical products for the treatment of allergies, asthma and related respiratory conditions. Dura's mission is to be the leading niche pharmaceutical and drug delivery company with a focus in the high–growth U.S. respiratory market. The Company is pursuing that goal through two major strategies: (1) acquiring late–stage prescription pharmaceuticals for marketing to high–prescribing respiratory physicians and (2) developing Spiros (TM) a proprietary dry powder pulmonary drug delivery system. Dr. Schultz was recruited by Dura Pharmaceuticals from 3M Pharmaceuticals in 1994, to develop inhalation products using the Spiros inhalation system. Career milestones include responsibility for the development of an alternative propellant meter–dose inhaler during his tenure with 3M. **Career Steps:** Vice President, Dura Pharmaceuticals, Inc. (1994–Present); 3M Pharmaceuticals: Research Specialist and Project Manager (1993–1994), Research Specialist (1990–1993), Senior Pharmacist (1986–1990). **Associations & Accomplishments:** American Association of Pharmaceutical Scientists; 3M Circle of Technical Excellence (1988, 1989, 1993). **Education:** University of Minnesota: Ph.D. (1993), B.S. in Pharmacy (1979). **Personal:** Married to Pat. Three children: Tracy, Mark, and William.

Tamesh C. Singh
Finance Director
Ortho McNeil
P.O. Box 463
Manati, Puerto Rico 00674
(809) 884–1105
Fax: (809) 854–6799

2834

Business Information: Ortho McNeil, a division of Johnson & Johnson, is a manufacturer of pharmaceutical products. The Company is subdivided into three divisions: Pharmaceuticals, Oral Contraceptives and Dermatology Preparations, and Biological Drugs. Established in 1974, Ortho McNeil currently employs 800 people at the Puerto Rico headquarters, and has an estimated annual revenue of $1 billion. As Finance Director, Mr. Singh is responsible for the three Division's financial aspects, as well as forecasting and strategic planning for the Company as a whole. **Career Steps:** Finance Director, Ortho McNeil (1987–Present); Controller and Assistant Treasurer, Baxter–Dade (1979–1987); Cost and Treasury Manager, Abbott Laboratories (1975–1979). **Associations & Accomplishments:** Institute of Management Accountants; British Commonwealth Society; Community Development Committee. **Education:** InterAmerican University of Puerto Rico: M.B.A. (1972), B.A. in Accounting, magna cum laude (1970); University of Minnesota, M.B.A. coursework (1970–1971). **Personal:** Married to Valerie V. in 1962. Five children: Nadiya, Naleena, Nirvana, Nirmala and Narima. Mr. Singh enjoys reading, walking, listening to music and travel.

Robert S.K. Song
Director
Warner Lambert Company
2200 Eglinton Avenue E
Scarborough, Ontario M1L 2N3
(416) 288–2490
Fax: (416) 288–2500

2834

Business Information: Warner Lambert Company is a leading global pharmaceutical and health care development products manufacturer. An expert in logistics management and global competition, Robert Song serves as Director of Warner–Lambert's Canadian division. His duties involve the overall administration of distribution operations and customer service relationships, with the departments of Customer Service, Inventory, EDI, Transportation, Warehousing and Information Technology reporting directly to him. **Career Steps:** Director, Warner Lambert Company (1990–Present); Vice President, Operations, Bausch & Lomb (1983–1986); Vice President, Distribution, Harding Carpet (1980–1983); Manager, Planning and Program, Xerox Canada Inc. (1974–1980). **Associations & Accomplishments:** Canadian Association of Logistics Management; Council of Logistics Management; Canadian Industrial Traffic League; Electronic Data Inter Change Council of Canada; American Management Association; Speaker at many educational institutions, professional seminars and conferences. **Education:** M.B.A. (1970); M.A.

(1969); B.Comm. (1966). **Personal:** Two children: Susie and Jackie Song. Mr. Song enjoys music, reading, travel, and public speaking.

Scott F. Spencer

Managed Healthcare Consultant
Pfizer, Inc., U.S. Pharmaceuticals Group
65 East India Row Unit 10 E
Boston, MA 02110–3390
(617) 720–4987
Fax: (617) 720–5095

2834

Business Information: Pfizer, Inc., U.S. Pharmaceuticals Group is a multi–billion dollar conglomerate engaged in manufacturing, fabricating and processing drugs in pharmaceutical preparations (prescription and over–the counter pharmaceuticals and medical devices) for human and veterinary use. As Managed Healthcare Consultant, Mr. Spencer is responsible for providing customized solutions to the health care needs of customers (managed health plans) by offering expertise in health care interventions, disease management, quality principles, and business management consulting services. **Career Steps:** U.S. Pharmaceuticals Group: Managed Healthcare Consultant, Pfizer, Inc. (1994–Present), Institutional Healthcare Representative (1992–1994), Professional Healthcare Representative (1991–1992). **Associations & Accomplishments:** Leukemia Society of America; Connecticut Business and Industry Association; Massachusetts Society of Healthcare System Pharmacists; American Society of Consultant Pharmacists; Publication: Journal of Professional Services Marketing; Volume 10, Number 1, 1993, by Haworth Press. **Education:** Suffolk University – Boston, MA, M.B.A. (1990); Plymouth State College – Plymouth, NH, B.S. in Business Administration (1983); Dale Carnegie Sales Curriculum and Voluntary Assistant Instructor (1984); Certification: Certified Medical Representative Institute (1995). **Personal:** Mr. Spencer enjoys golf, reading, travel, and running (completed Boston Marathon 1993–1995).

Michael Spino, Pharm.D.

Vice President of Scientific Affairs
Apotex, Inc.
150 Signet Drive
Weston, Ontario M9L 1T9
(416) 749–9300 Ext. 1101
Fax: (416) 749–3234

2834

Business Information: Apotex, Inc. is the largest Canadian–owned pharmaceutical manufacturer. International in scope, the Company has subsidiaries in several countries (U.S., Mexico, Panama, Europe, former East Europe and New Zealand). Established in 1974, Apotex, Inc. currently employs more than 1,500 people. Apotex is also the largest employer in pharmaceutical biotechnology with its three operations in Winnipeg–Apotex Fermentation, Inc., Rh Pharmaceuticals and ApoGen. As Vice President of Scientific Affairs, Dr. Spino is responsible for planning and coordinating research into new investigational drugs and new generic drugs for international development, as well as overseeing all scientific concerns for the Company, nationally and world–wide. Concurrent to his duties at Apotex, Inc., he serves as Professor at the Faculty of Pharmacy, University of Toronto. Dr. Spino's scientific pursuits have been based primarily in the study of drug disposition, mainly in patients with cystic fibrosis. **Career Steps:** Vice President of Scientific Affairs, Apotex, Inc. (1991–Present); Professor, University of Toronto (1974–Present); Director of Pharmacy, Royal Victoria Hospital (1968–1971). **Associations & Accomplishments:** American Assoc. Pharmaceutical Scientists (AAPS); American College of Clinical Pharmacy; American Society of Clinical Pharmacology & Therapeutics (ASCPT); Canadian Pharmaceutical Association (CPhA); Canadian Society for Clinical Pharmacology (CSCP); One of the first persons in Canada to obtain a Pharm.D. **Education:** University of California, Pharm.D. (1973); University of Toronto, B.Sc. in Pharmacy (1967). **Personal:** Married to Olga in 1973. Three children: Tiffany, Kristin and Danielle. Dr. Spino enjoys golf, tennis and squash.

William Leo Sullivan, M.P.H., M.B.A.

Managed Care Specialist
DuPont Merck Pharmaceutical Company
1124 Kaumoku Street
Honolulu, HI 96825
(808) 395–6992
Fax: (808) 395–9502

2834

Business Information: On January 6, 1991, The DuPont Merck Pharmaceutical Company was formed as a joint venture between DuPont and Merck and Co., Inc. DuPont Merck is a research–based pharmaceutical company which develops and markets pharmaceuticals for the treatment of cardiovascular, central nervous system, inflammatory and infectious diseases. The Company also has programs for the treatment of cancer and it's Radiopharmaceuticals Division is the world leader in the field of radio–labeled diagnostic imaging. DuPont Merck is a $1.3 billion company and has locations in the United States, Puerto Rico, Canada and Europe. Currently serving as a Managed Care Specialist, Mr. Sullivan has been involved in setting up anticoagulation management systems in Hawaii's healthcare market. Through these comprehensive programs, medical groups are able to help reduce the incidence of stroke, improve outcomes, and also decrease costs. He has been involved in working with coalitions to improve disease state management while at the same time improving the standards of care. Mr. Sullivan has also been responsible for setting up Treatment Practice Guidelines in the medical community, international medical symposia, and medical studies. He works closely with numerous medical groups, professional associations, and patient support groups. During his tenure with DuPont, he has taken an active role in helping his community, especially with Parkinson's Disease sufferers. Through his work and efforts to initiate more support groups, the number of support groups has grown from one to eight throughout the islands. Mr. Sullivan was also instrumental in securing a national Parkinson's organization to locate a branch in Hawaii. He has organized and held numerous events including annual Parkinson's Disease Symposium (with attendance of 300–500) for patients, family members, and caregivers. These programs have featured local and world renowned neurologists that discuss current treatment of Parkinson's Disease and how to cope with the often–time devastating consequences. He has also been successful in getting the Governor of Hawaii involved by declaring a Proclamation for Hawaii's Parkinson Syndrome Month. Mr. Sullivan has received the Summit Award – DuPont's highest honor – and has received the Outstanding Professional Award from the Hawaii Parkinson Syndrome Organization. He also has been featured in the Pharmaceutical Representative newsmagazine. **Career Steps:** Du Pont Merck: Managed Care Specialist (1994–Present), Sales and Marketing (1990–1994); Director of Cardiac Rehab Services, Straub Clinic and Hospital (1982–1990). **Associations & Accomplishments:** Board of Directors, Hawaii Parkinson's Disease Association; Board of Directors, National Parkinson Foundation – Hawaii Affiliate (1994–Present); Co–Chairman, Hawaii Parkinson's Disease Syndrome Organization (1991–Present); Board of Directors, Epilepsy Foundation of Hawaii (1995–Present); Professional Liaison for Stroke Clubs of Hawaii and American Heart Association – Hawaii Affiliate. **Education:** Chaminade University, M.B.A. (1993); University of Hawaii, M.P.H. (1987); University of Northern Iowa, B.A. **Personal:** Married to Cher in 1990. Mr. Sullivan enjoys athletics, photography, and adventure travel.

D. Taylor, Ed.D.

Vice President of Public Affairs and Communications
Ciba–Geigy Corporation
540 White Plains Road
Tarrytown, NY 10591–5111
(914) 785–2101
Fax: (914) 785–2179

2834

Business Information: Ciba–Geigy Corporation, known as Ciba, is a leading U.S. biological and chemical company, dedicated to fulfilling needs in healthcare, agriculture and industry with innovative products and services. Headquartered in Ardsley, N.Y., Ciba employs over 15,000 people nationwide. The Company maintains divisional headquarters, production plants, administrative facilities, subsidiaries, regional sales offices and distribution centers throughout the U.S. A wholly–owned subsidiary of Ciba–Geigy Limited — a publicly–owned conglomerate, headquartered in Basel, Switzerland — Ciba–Geigy Corporation is the largest Ciba company, generating nearly one–third of worldwide sales. Dr. Taylor is a member of the U.S. Corporate Management Committee and Vice President of Public Affairs and Communications. As Vice President, he strategically leads the Public Affairs & Communications Department, including federal and state government relations, design, internal and external communications. He also serves as Executive Director of the Ciba Educational Foundation. **Career Steps:** Ciba–Geigy Corporation: Vice President of Public Affairs and Communications (1993–Present), Head Corporate Staff of Japan (1989–1993), Head International Policies and Issues of Basel, Switzerland (1985–1989). **Associations & Accomplishments:** Board, Foundation for American Journalism; Co–chairman, Aspen Series on the Environment; President's Council, Sustainable Development Natural Resourses Task Force. **Education:** Rutgers University: Ed.D. (1975), B.A. (1971). **Personal:** Married to Keiko in 1989. Three children: Marissa, Alex, and Alicia. Dr. Taylor enjoys skiing, antique furniture, and hiking.

Ramon A. Torres

Safety Manager
SmithKline Beecham Pharmaceuticals
P.O. Box 6907
Ponce, Puerto Rico 00733–6907
(809) 864–4545
Fax: (809) 864–6450

2834

Business Information: SmithKline Beecham Pharmaceuticals is a manufacturer of bulk pharmaceutical products and chemical compounds. Established in 1977, SmithKline Beecham currently employs 200 people. As Safety Manager, Mr. Torres is responsible for all aspects of safety and security for the chemical plant. In the safety business for 23 years, Mr. Torres is a Certified Hazardous Materials Manager and a Registered Environmental Professional, an important asset to his job. **Career Steps:** Safety Manager, SmithKline Beecham Pharmaceuticals (1977–Present); Safety Supervisor, Procon International, S.A. (1974–1977); Compliance Safety Officer, PROSHO, Puerto Rico (1972–1974). **Associations & Accomplishments:** Chemist Association of Puerto Rico; Registered Environmental Professional; Institute of Hazardous Materials Management; Puerto Rico Accident Prevention Professional Association. **Education:** Pontificial Catholic University of Puerto Rico, B.S. in Chemistry (1971); Oklahoma University, NIOSH, Special Course Safety and Industrial Hygiene (1973); OSHA Compliance Officer Course (1974) **Personal:** Married to Marta M. in 1974. Three children: Ramon Jr., Antonio and Rafael. Mr. Torres enjoys reading and painting with water colors.

Gerardo Turcatti, Ph.D.

Research Scientist
Geneva Bio–Medical Research Institute/Glaxo–Welcome, Research and Development
14 Chemin des Aulx, Case Postale 674
1228 Plan–les Quates, Geneva, Switzerland
4122–706–9836
Fax: 4122–794–6965

2834

Business Information: Geneva Bio–Medical Research Institute is a multidisciplinary research–based institute of the Glaxo–Wellcome pharmaceutical company. Mr. Gerardo Turcatti is a Research Scientist of the Biochemistry Department and specializes in protein structure analysis of cellular membrane receptors that are relevant in human disease. He is responsible for performing experiments and conducting research to assist the company in product development. Internet users can reach him via: GMT4611@GGR.CO.UK **Career Steps:** Research Scientist, Geneva Bio–Medical Research Institute/Glaxo–Wellcome, Research and Development (Present); Glaxo Institute for Molecular Biology: Scientist (1992–Present), Associate Scientist, Head of Analytical Protein Chemistry (1988–1992); Associate Scientist, Biogen S.A., Geneva (1985–1987). **Associations & Accomplishments:** Award for the Best Thesis of the Year (1995). His contribution opens new perspectives for the study of structure and dynamics of proteins inserted in the membrane of living cells important for the pharmaceutical industry. **Education:** Federal Institute of Technology of Lausanne, Ph.D. (1995); University of Geneva: License es Sciences Cliniques (B.S. Equivalent), Diplome d'Ingenieur Chimiste (M.S. Equivalent). **Personal:** Married to Carolina in 1982. Two children: Gabriela and Laura. Dr. Turcatti enjoys contemporary Latin–American literature, cinema and sports.

Leonidas Uzcategui

Director of Treasury
Eli Lilly Export
P.O. Box 192971
San Juan, Puerto Rico 00919–2971
(809) 756–4810
Fax: (809) 756–5900
2834

Business Information: Eli Lilly Export engages in the sales, marketing, and distribution of pharmaceutical and animal health products for Puerto Rico, the Caribbean, Central America, Japan, Korea, and Southeast Asia. As Director of Treasury, Mr. Uzcategui oversees all Accounting and Treasury, customer services, mainly focusing on the export operations part, Management Information Systems, and general services. Additionally he serves as President and Board Member of two affiliated companies. **Career Steps:** Eli Lilly Export: Director of Treasury (1996–Present), Director of Finance (1984–1996), Director of Finance – Elizabeth Arden de Mexico (1981–1983), Administrative Manager – Elizabeth Arden de Puerto Rico (1978–1980); Controller, Able Sales and Subsidiaries; Controller, Condado Holiday Inn and Casino; Audit Supervisor, Laventholl Krekstain Howath and Howath. **Associations & Accomplishments:** Asociacion Analista Financieros de P–Rico; National Association of Accountants; Phi Sigma Alpha. Education: World University, M.S. in Accounting (1980); La Salle University, B.S. Degree in Commerce (1977); Other Courses & Seminars: University of PR, Graduate School of Business, International and Export Business Seminar (1996); Columbia University, Graduate School of Business, Leading and Managing People (1994); Quality for Business Success Institute, Re–Engineering the Corp. (1993); Duke University, Fuqua School of Business, Management Techniques (1993); Dun & Bradstreet Education Services, Credit & Financial Analysis (1987); Briarcliff College, Auditing and Accounting; Eli Lilly & Co., Pricing Workshop (1996), New Managers Program Recruitment Techniques, Tax Seminars. **Personal:** Married to Viola Rodriguez in 1963. Three children: Gisela, Jorge, and Mariela. Mr. Uzcategui enjoys fishing and boating."

Nilda Vazquez

Human Resources Manager
Sartorius Inc.
P.O. Box 6
Yauco, Puerto Rico 00698–0006
(787) 856–5020
Fax: (787) 856–1292
2834

Business Information: Established in Puerto Rico in 1983, the Company has international offices in various parts of Europe, Asia, Canada, California, and corporate offices in New York. As Human Resources Manager, Ms. Vazquez is responsible for human resources department, employee and industrial relations, and in–house legal matters. **Career Steps:** Human Resources Manager, Sartorius Inc. (1994–Present); Part–time Professor, Advanced School of Personnel Administration (1984–Present); Director of Human Resources, The Condado Beach Trio Resort, Casino & Convention Center (1992–1994); Vice President of Human Resources, Damas Hospital (1990–1991); Industrial Relations and Legal Manager, VCS National Packing Company (1989–1990); Director of Human Resources, Sands Hotel & Casino Beach Resort (1987–1989). **Associations & Accomplishments:** Puerto Rico Bar Association; Alumni Association University of Puerto Rico; Society for Human Resource Management; Association of Labor Relations Practitioners; Founder/Director, Anti-discrimination Unit of Puerto Rico Department of Labor; Fiscal Officer, Puerto Rico Women's Conference; Faculty, Preparatory School for Managers and Supervisors. **Education:** University of Puerto Rico School of Law, L.L.B. (1970); University of Puerto Rico, B.A. in Biology and Mathematics. **Personal:** Two children: Oriana and Melina Becerril. Ms. Vazquez enjoys reading, music, and sports.

Angel R. Velez Torres, P.E.

Plant Engineering Manager
Puerto Rico Pharmaceuticals, Inc.
P.O. Box 10000
Guayama, Puerto Rico 00785
(787) 866–1290
Fax: (787) 866–1258
2834

Business Information: IPuerto Rico Pharmaceuticals, Inc., a part of ZENECA Group PLC, is a pharmaceutical chemical plant which manufactures Atenolol and other pharmaceuticals in bulk and distributes them to the U.S., Puerto Rico, and Europe from two locations in Puerto Rico (Carolina & Guayama). As Plant Engineering Manager, Mr. Velez Torres is responsible for organizing, planning, directing, and controlling all plant engineering function activities, as well as managing departmental staff and preparing a control budget for revenue and capital of more than $5 million. **Career Steps:** IPuerto Rico Pharmaceuticals, Inc.: Plant Engineering Manager (1996–Present), Senior Maintenance Engineer (1992–1996); Senior Design Engineer, Phillips GG, Puerto Rico (1985–1988). **Associations & Accomplishments:** ASHRAE; American Welding Society; CIAPuerto Rico – Member of Engineering and Surveyor Association. **Education:** Polytechnic University of Puerto Rico, Masters in Engineering Management (1996); University of Puerto Rico – Mayaguez Campus, B.S. in Mechanical Engineering (1980); Professional Engineer (1989); USAR Captain – Infantry Officer (1990). **Personal:** Married to Shirley Miranda in 1982. Two children: Shirley Anne and Angel R. Velez Miranda. Mr. Velez Torres enjoys table tennis (ping pong) and swimming.

Brenda Martini Wakin

Manager of Customer Marketing
Bristol–Myers Squibb
777 Scuddersmill Road
Plainsboro, NJ 08546
(609) 897–3416
Fax: (609) 897–6655
2834

Business Information: Bristol–Myers Squibb (BMS) is one of the world's leading pharmaceutical companies specializing in cardiovascular and oncology drugs; offering cost–effective, disease–oriented patient health care management. Joining BMS as Senior Territory Manager in 1988, Ms. Wakin has held several positions, including Instructor of Therapeutic Training in 1991 and Assistant Manager of MHC/LTC Training in 1994. Appointed to her current position as Manager of Customer Marketing in 1995, she is responsible for customer marketing for managed care customers, such as initiating strategies to improve profit and customer value, provide a line of products to meet customer needs, and set goals to reach for customers. **Career Steps:** Bristol–Myers Squibb: Manager of Customer Marketing (1995–Present), Assistant Manager of MHC/LTC Training (1994–1995), Instructor Therapeutic Training (1991–1994), Senior Territory Manager (1988–1991). **Associations & Accomplishments:** Female Executives; Pi Beta Phi Sorority; Volunteer, Elderly Groups; Recipient of BMS's Presidential Award for "Work Above & Beyond the Call of Duty," while she was a member of the Pricing and Contracting Task Force. **Education:** Fordham University in New York City: Currently working toward an M.B.A., B.A. (1987). **Personal:** Married to R. Christopher in 1993. Ms. Wakin enjoys skiing, jogging, softball and golf.

Jay Warshell

Systems/Product Engineer
Astra Merck, Inc.
725 Chesterbrook Blvd.
Wayne, PA 19087–5637
(610) 695–1438
Fax: (610) 889–1284
EMAIL: See Below
2834

Business Information: Astra Merck specializes in the development and marketing of pharmaceutical solutions for the gastrointestinal and cardiovascular therapeutic areas. As a Team Leader for the Technology Services Group of the Information Technology Department, Mr. Warshell manages the planning, design, and development of the systems and network infrastructure of the company. Internet users can reach him via: Jay.Warshell@astramerck.com. **Career Steps:** Systems/Product Engineer, Astra Merck, Inc. (1993–Present); Senior Automation Engineer, All–Control Systems, Inc. (1989–1992); Senior Systems Engineer, Computer Task Group, Inc. (1984–1989). **Associations & Accomplishments:** Institute of Electronics and Electrical Engineers. **Education:** Drexel University: M.S.E.E. (1989), B.S.M.E. (1984). **Personal:** Mr. Warshell enjoys researching ancient cultures and scuba diving.

Ludwig J. Weimann, Ph.D.

Senior Research Director
Bertek Incorporated
110 Lake Street
St. Albans, VT 05478–2237
(802) 527–7792
Fax: (802) 527–0486
2834

Business Information: Bertek Incorporated is a manufacturer of pharmaceuticals from three locations. They also manufacture adhesive coatings and printing labels. As Senior Research Director, Dr. Weimann is responsible for the research and development of Transdermal Drug Delivery Systems, in addition to the supervision of a support staff of six. **Career Steps:** Bertek Incorporated: Senior Research Director (1995–Present), Research Director (1980–1995); Consultant, Self Employed (1979–1980). **Associations & Accomplishments:** Controlled Release Society; A.C.S.; A.A.P.S. **Education:** Poznan University, Ph.D. (1970) **Personal:** Married to Maria in 1972. Two children: Jon and Louis. Dr. Weimann enjoys running, biking, swimming and classical music.

Henry A. Weishaar

Divisional Vice President of Human Resources
Abbott Laboratories
200 Abbott Park Road
Abbott Park, IL 60064
(847) 938–8317
Fax: (847) 938–6233
2834

Business Information: Abbott Laboratories is a world leader in the manufacture and distribution of health care products, including pharmaceuticals and antibiotics for diagnostic, agricultural, and veterinary use. Established in 1888, the Company currently has over 50,000 employees worldwide. As Divisional Vice President of Human Resources, Mr. Weishaar is responsible for all aspects of human resource activities, including recruiting, retention, salary administration, benefits management, employee relations and safety. **Career Steps:** Abbott: Divisional Vice President of Human Resources, Hospital Products Division (1992–Present), Divisional Vice President (1985–1992); Vice President of Corporate Human Resources, Imperial Clevite (1980–1985); Director EEO & Labor, American Hospital Supply Corporation (1977–1980). **Associations & Accomplishments:** President, Northern Illinois Council on Alcohol & Substance Abuse Board; Corporate Advisory Board Family Services; Member, St. Therese Medical Center Board of Directors. **Education:** DePaul University, J.D.; Ohio State University, M.S. Degree in Aero Engineering; US Air Force Academy, B.S. Degree in Aero Engineering. **Personal:** Married to Maureen in 1968. Three children: Bridget, Tricia, and Thomas. Mr. Weishaar enjoys golf, reading, physical fitness.

Donald W. Wood, Ph.D.

Chairman and Chief Executive Officer
Freedom Chemical Diamalt
164 Cheshire Way
Naples, FL 33963
49–89–8106–436
Fax: (215) 979–3733
2834

Business Information: Freedom Chemical Diamalt is an international manufacturer of chemical specialties and natural products for the pharmaceuticals industry, food, textiles, leather, paper and construction industries. International in scope, Freedom Chemical Diamalt is located throughout the world with three locations in Germany, one in France, and three in India. Established in 1895, Freedom Chemical Diamalt reports annual revenue of $100 million and currently employs 300 people. As Chairman and Chief Executive Officer, Dr. Wood is responsible for all aspects of operations, including administration, finances, sales, public relations, accounting, marketing, and strategic planning. **Career Steps:** Chairman and Chief Executive Officer, Freedom Chemical Diamalt (1995–Present); President, ARCO Chemical Asia Pacific (1987–1992); Senior Vice President, ARCO Chemical (1978–1987). **Associations & Accomplishments:** American Institute Chemical Engineers; Philadelphia Opera Theater; Inroads. **Education:** University of Illinois, Ph.D. in Chemical Engineering (1951), B.S. (1949), B.A. (1948); Massachusetts Institute of Technology, M.S. (1950). **Personal:** Married to Karin in 1963. Four children: Julia, Nicola, Claudia, and Gregory. Dr. Wood enjoys golf.

Manuel Worcel, M.D.

President/Chief Executive Officer
Nitromed, Inc.
801 Albany Street
Boston, MA 02119–2511
(617) 638–5600
Fax: (607) 638–5601
EMAIL: mworcel@nitromed.c
2834

Business Information: Nitromed, Inc. is a pharmaceutical company specializing in nitric oxide based products for the treatment of cardiovascular, inflammatory, geriotouranary, and respiratory diseases. As President/CEO, Dr. Worcel oversees the day–to–day management of the Company as well as the strategic planning and business development. Internet users can reach him via: Dworcee@nitormed.com. **Career Steps:** President/Chief Executive Officer, Nitromed, Inc. (1993–Present); Vice President of Cardiovascular Research, CIBA, USA (1989–1993); Vice President of Drug Discovery, Roussel Uclaf, France (1982–1988); Director, Cardiovascular Research, Roussel Uclaf, France (1979–1982); Established Investigators (1968–1979), INSERM, France; Fellow, Harvard School of Public Health, Boston, (1967–1968). **Associations & Accomplishments:** American and French Heart Association; American Association for the Advancement of Science; American, French,and British Pharmaceutical Societies. **Education:** Medical School, M.D. Buenos Aires (1960). **Personal:** Married to Marie–Ines Rachmanis in 1961. Five children: Fernando and Alexandre. Daughter–in–law: Isabelle. Granddaughter: Julia, and Marie. Dr. Worcel enjoys music, reading, bicycling, and spending time with family.

Tim C. Birdsall, N.D.

Technical Director
Thorne Research
901 Triangle Drive
Sandpoint, ID 83864–0360
(208) 263–1337
Fax: (208) 265–2488
EMAIL: See Below

2836

Business Information: Thorne Research, established in 1984, is a manufacturer of nutritional supplements. As Technical Director, Dr. Birdsall is responsible for research projects and new product development. Internet users can reach him via: tim@thorne.com. **Career Steps:** Technical Director, Thorne Research (1989–Present); President, Genesis Birth Center (1987–1989); Naturopathic Physician, Kirkland Naturopathic Clinic (1985–1987). **Associations & Accomplishments:** American Association of Naturopathic Physicians; New York Academy of Sciences; American College of Naturopathic Obstetricians; American Association for The Advancement of Science. **Education:** Bastyr University, Doctor of Naturopathic Medicine (1985); Grace College, B.A. (1972). **Personal:** Married to Kathy in 1972. Eight children: Jeremy, Lisa, Aaron, Rebecca, James, John, Andrew, and Addie. Dr. Birdsall enjoys music, skiing, and computers.

John D. Britto

Director of Business Development and Strategic Marketing
Sutton Laboratories
116 Summit Avenue
Chatham, NJ 07928–2727
(201) 701–7250
Fax: (201) 635–1983

2836

Business Information: Sutton Laboratories, established in 1959, is a division of International Specialty Products, and currently employs 50 people, expecting over $50 million dollars in sales in 1996. The Company is a manufacturer of specialty chemicals for the personal care industry. As Director of Business Development and Strategic Marketing, Mr. Britto develops marketing techniques to present new and existing products manufactured by Sutton Laboratories to international consumers, including such companies as Revlon and Procter and Gamble. \ **Career Steps:** Director of Business Development and Strategic Marketing, Sutton Laboratories (1995–Present); International Speciality Products: Business Manager (1992–1995), Product Manager (1991–1992), Account Manager (1986–1991). **Associations & Accomplishments:** Society of Cosmetic Chemists; C–130 pilot in USAF Reserve. **Education:** St. Joseph's University, M.S. in Chemistry (1981); Lehigh University, B.S. in Chemistry (1974). **Personal:** Married to Charlotte in 1973. Eight children: Alicia, Christine, Rebecca, Rachel, Laura, John, Kathering, and Emilie. Mr. Britto enjoys coaching youth sports, football, soccer, reading, travel, and running.

Donald Franklin Gerson, Ph.D.

Director of Vaccine Manufacturing
Wyeth–Lederle Vaccines
401 North Middletown Road
Pearl Run, NY 10965
(914) 732–3501
Fax: (914) 368–8157

2836

Business Information: Wyeth–Lederle Vaccines is the world leader in human vaccines. The Company manufactures some adult vaccines and all children's vaccines, except for DPT and the oral polio vaccine. Wyeth–Lederle Vaccines, established in 1910, currently employs 1500 people and expects to post revenues/sales of over $100 million in 1996. As Director of Vaccine Manufacturing, Dr. Gerson oversees all facets of the manufacturing operation. He is responsible for receiving raw materials, formulation, filling packages, and preparation for shipment. Other duties include public relations and strategic planning for the future. **Career Steps:** Director of Vaccine Manufacturing, Wyeth–Lederle Vaccines (1994–Present); Vice President Research and Development, Apotex Fermentation, Inc. (1992–1994); Assistant Vice President Manufacturing, Connaught Laboratories, Ltd. (1986–1992). **Associations & Accomplishments:** International Society of Pharmaceutical Engineers; American Association for the Advancement of Science; Parental Drug Association; Assistant Scout Master, Boy Scouts of Canada. Dr. Gerson does public speaking and conducts seminars for the Company and universities. **Education:** McGill University, Ph.D. (1972); University of Western Ontario, B.Sc. (1968). **Personal:** Married to Gail in 1980. Three children: Benjamin, Alexander, and Jonas. Dr. Gerson enjoys Boy Scouts.

Michael A. Recny

Director, Biochemical Sciences
Trimeris, Inc.
4727 University Drive
Durham, NC 27707
(919) 419–6050
Fax: (919) 419–1816

2836

Business Information: Trimeris, Inc. is a biotechnology company developing novel anti–veral therapeutic drugs. With thirteen years experience in biotechnology, Dr. Recny joined Trimeris as Director of Biochemical Sciences in 1993. He is responsible for research management encompassing peptide and protein chemistry, biophysical chemistry, assay development, and small molecule screening. He is also the Director for research programs for all therapeutic programs. **Career Steps:** Director, Biochemical Sciences, Trimeris, Inc. (1993–Present); Director, Protein Biochemistry, Procept, Inc. (1988–1993); Senior Fellow, Dana Farber Cancer Institute (1988–1989); Laboratory Head, Genetics Institute, Inc. (1986–1988). **Associations & Accomplishments:** The Protein Society; The American Association for Advancement of Science; Governors Club; The American Society for Biochemstry and Molecular Biology. **Education:** University of Illinois, Ph.D. in Biochemistry (1983); University of Rochester, B.A. in Biochemistry (1979). **Personal:** Married to Catherine Sullivan in 1995.

Dave Toman, Ph.D.

Project Manager
Collagen Corporation
2500 Faber Place
Palo Alto, CA 94303–3329
(415) 856–0200
Fax: (415) 856–0533

2836

Business Information: Collagen Corporation is a manufacturer of biomedical materials, including collagen, for a variety of purposes. As Project Manager, Dr. Toman heads a team of scientists who are focusing on a project dealing with new products. Concurrently, he heads the Molecular Biology Department. **Career Steps:** Project Manager, Collagen Corporation (1993–Present); MD Anderson Cancer Center (1987–1993); Meloy Laboratories (1980–1987). **Education:** George Washington University, Ph.D. (1993); Virginia Tech, M.S. **Personal:** Married to Carol. Dr. Toman enjoys sports, reading, and travel.

Theodore R. Bell

Senior Product Development Engineer
Procter & Gamble
11520 Reed–Hartman Highway
Cincinnati, OH 45209
(513) 626–1388
Fax: (513) 626–4222

2841

Business Information: Procter & Gamble is a major consumer products manufacturer distributing globally. Products include: health and beauty aids; liquid, dry, and flaked soaps; dental care products; household cleaners; and much more. As Senior Product Development Engineer, Mr. Bell is responsible for consumer research project management for Procter & Gamble's laundry and cleaning products division. Established in 1837, Procter & Gamble employs 100,000 people with annual sales of $32 billion. **Career Steps:** Senior Product Development Engineer, Procter & Gamble (1990–Present). **Education:** Princeton University, B.S. Degree in Chemical Engineering (1991). **Personal:** Mr. Bell enjoys martial arts, woodworking, camping, and automobile restoration.

Edward M. Burghard

Director of Marketing
Procter & Gamble
11520 Reed Hartman Highway
Cincinnati, OH 45241
(513) 626–6640
Fax: (513) 626–6482

2841

Business Information: Procter & Gamble, established in 1837, is a manufacturer of consumer goods and health care products. As Director of Marketing, Mr. Burghard is responsible for marketing the Company's pharmaceutical products in North America. **Career Steps:** Procter & Gamble: Director of Marketing, North America (1994–Present), Director of Marketing & Sales, Canada (1992–1994), Associate Director of Marketing, U.S.A. (1990–1992); Brand Manager (1986–1990); Assistant Brand Manager (1983–1986); Manager of Strategic Planning (1981–1983); Sales Administrator (1976–1983). **Associations & Accomplishments:** Future Society; Eagle Scout. **Education:** Syracuse University, M.B.A. (1983); State University of New York, B.A.; Mohawk Valley Community College, A.A.S. **Personal:** Married to Claudia in 1978. Two children: Ryan and Aaron. Mr. Burghard enjoys coaching soccer.

Judith L. Clark, CPA

Controller
Bench Products, Inc.
590 West 6960 St.
Midvale, UT 84047
(801) 561–5655
Fax: (801) 561–9699

2841

Business Information: Bench Products, Inc., established in 1970, is an international manufacturer and distributor of laundry detergent, household cleaning supplies, personal care products, and ice melting products. As Controller, Ms. Clark oversees all financial reporting and budgetary requirements, payroll, and human resource activities. Duties include responsibility for accounts receivable and payable, filing of sales tax information, commission program, treasury and investments, and Company and employee insurance. **Career Steps:** Controller, Bench Products, Inc. (1995–Present); Accountant, Self Employed (1987–1994); Senior Accountant, Booth, Machowicz & Hop, CPA's (1989–1990); Junior Accountant, John s. McCarthy, CPA (1986–1989). **Associations & Accomplishments:** Past Member, American Institute of Certified Public Accountants. **Education:** University of Texas at San Antonio, B.B.A. (1984); San Antonio College, A.A. **Personal:** Four children: Danielle, Kimberly, Cassandra, and Matthew. Ms. Clark enjoys hiking, camping, reading, and needlework.

Robert C. Craig II

Director of Purchasing
Auto Chlor System, Inc.
746 Poplar Avenue
Memphis, TN 38105
(901) 579–2300
Fax: (901) 529–1097

2841

Business Information: Auto Chlor System, Inc. is a manufacturer of chemical detergent cleaning supplies for restaurants, hotels, motels, hospitals, and nursing homes. The Corporation supplies chemical dispensers and dish washers to commercial customers as long as the customer purchases their washing detergents. Established in 1938, Auto Chlor System operates in 38 states and in Canada and posted sales in excess of $100 million dollars in 1995. As Director of Purchasing, Mr. Craig handles all plant operations, negotiates all contracts between clients and Auto Chlor, selects all suppliers, assures quantity and quality of all deliveries, and assures the correctness of price quotes. Mr. Craig works with his department supervisors in the development of a budget each year and works to stay within the budget guidelines. **Career Steps:** Director of Purchasing, Auto Chlor System, Inc. (1981–Present); Plant Manager, Ripley Industries, Inc. (1978–1979); General Manager, Byrd Industries (1974–1978). **Associations & Accomplishments:** Board of Directors, St. Mary's Manassas, Alabama Redevelopment Team: SMART; Advisory Board, City of Memphis Police; National Association of Purchasing Management; Mid–South Minority Purchasing Council; Society of Manufacturing Engineers; Civitan International Valley District: Governor (1995–1996); Lieutenant Governor, Regional Director and Federal Trustee Chair and Secretary; East Memphis Civitan Club; President Elect Director, Photographer, Candy Box Kid; Harwood Center for Handicapped Volunteer and International Special Olympics Volunteer; Committees: Budget and Finance, Outstanding Civitan Award Chair, and Boy Scout Troop 54 Chair; Collierville Civitan Club: past President and Director; Collierville Rotary Club: President Elect, Board of Directors, and Secretary; Committees: Flag Placement Service and Skills for Adolescents at Collierville Middle School. Awards: Valley District Honor Key (1990–1991); Club Honor Key (1989–1990); Civitan International, Distinguished President Award (1983–1984); John Mark Stallings Scholarship Endowment (1993); Celebration of Champions, Baddour Memorial Center; Board of Directors, Emmanuel United Methodist Church; Grand Free Lodge and Accepted Masons of Tennessee; International Supreme Council Order of DeMolay; University of Kansas Alumni Association; Memphis Zoological Society; The Dixon Gallery and Gardens; **Education:** University of Kansas, B.F.A. in Industrial Design (1971). **Personal:** Married to Judith. Five children: Susan, John, Beth, Scott, and Jena and one grandchild.

Ronald G. Graham
Manager of Planning and Analysis
The Dial Corporation
1850 North Central Avenue, MS 2320
Phoenix, AZ 85004–4527
(602) 207–5985
Fax: (602) 207–5665

2841

Business Information: The Dial Corporation, headquartered in Phoenix, Arizona, is an international conglomerate consisting of thirteen companies which participate in a variety of industries such as, consumer products, convention services, airline services, food services management, and travel & leisure services. Entity holdings include: Dobbs International, Aircraft Services International, General Exhibition Services, Brewster Exhibit Group/Giltspur, Premier Cruise Lines, Greyhound Lines of Canada, Greyhound Leisure Services, JetSave, Crystal Holidays, Travelers Express, Restaura, and the Dial Consumer Products Group. As Manager of Planning and Analysis, Mr. Graham reports to the Chairman on the financial condition and key operating issues of the Consumer Products Group. He also provides consulting services to senior management of the Consumer Products Group on operating issue resolution, best practice development, strategic planning, performance measurement, and organizational reengineering. **Career Steps:** Manager of Planning and Analysis, The Dial Corporation (1995–Present); Financial Analyst, Ernest and Julio Gallo Winery (1993–1995); Strategic Analyst, Northwest Airlines (1992–1993); Consultant, Coopers & Lybrand (1991–1992); Marketing Representative, M&I Data Services (1985–1990). **Associations & Accomplishments:** Institute of Management Accountants; Licensed Customs Broker; Ghostwriter for an article in Bank Systems & Equipment, called "Strategic Use of Banking Systems" (1989). **Education:** Northwestern University, M.B.A. (1991); University of Wisconsin, B.B.A. (1984). **Personal:** Mr. Graham enjoys international travel and junior achievement activities.

David C. Kaissling
Operations Manager
Procter & Gamble
P.O. Box 3125
Sherman, TX 75091–3125
(903) 870–1211
Fax: (903) 870–1294

2841

Business Information: Procter & Gamble, a $30 billion corporation, is a Fortune 500 manufacturer and marketer of consumer products globally. Products include: health and beauty aids; liquid, dry, and flaked soaps; dental care products; household cleaners; and much more. Mr. Kaissling started with Procter & Gamble in 1981 and after fourteen months, left to become a Youth Minister for a local church. In 1983, he came back to Procter & Gamble and in 1994 was appointed as Operations Manager for Line operations at the Sherman, Texas plant. In this position, Mr. Kaissling is responsible for the oversight of all line operations for the singles (single–packet coffee) and instant coffee business and a staff of 200 within the Food & Beverage Sector (i.e. coffee, juice, snacks, etc.). **Career Steps:** Procter & Gamble: Operations Manager (1994–Present); Logistics Manager (1993–1994); Personnel Manager (1990–1993). **Associations & Accomplishments:** Deacon, Church of Christ; Former President, Brockville Ontario Chamber of Commerce; Coach, Texoma Soccer Association. **Education:** Zockhurst College, M.B.A. (1991); University of Missouri – Rolla, B.S. in Engineering Management; **Personal:** Married to Kim in 1982. Three children: Julia, Jaclyn, and Andrew. Mr. Kaissling enjoys skiing, scuba diving, soccer, and piloting aircraft (private pilot).

Michael W. Schneider
Plant Manager
Proctor & Gamble
P O Box 2906
Kansas City, KS 66110–2906
(913) 573–0321
Fax: Please mail or call

2841

Business Information: Procter & Gamble, headquartered in Cincinnati, Ohio, is a major consumer products manufacturer distributing globally. Products include health and beauty aids; liquid, dry, and flaked soaps; dental care products; household cleaners; and much more. As Plant Manager, Mr. Schneider is responsible for the oversight of plant management, including production, maintenance, engineering, safety, special projects, budgets, and costs. **Career Steps:** Procter & Gamble: Plant Manager–Kansas City (1994–Present), Plant Manager–Cincinnati (1990–1994), Distribution Operations Manager (1987–1990). **Associations & Accomplishments:** Board of Directors, Wyandotte County United Way. **Educa-**tion: Rose–Holman Institute, B.S. in Mechanical Engineering (1978). **Personal:** Married to Amy in 1978. Two children: Katie and Anna. Mr. Schneider enjoys coaching youth soccer, basketball and softball.

Michael A. Walsh
Research and Development Director
Procter & Gamble
11450 Grooms Road
Cincinnati, OH 45242
(513) 626–3348
Fax: Please mail or call

2841

Business Information: Procter & Gamble, a $30 billion corporation, is a Fortune 500 manufacturer and marketer of consumer products globally. Products include: detergents, soaps, and household cleaners; paper products; health and beauty aides; and many more. With twenty–five years experience in research, development and engineering, Mr. Walsh joined Procter & Gamble in 1973. Appointed as a Research & Development Director in 1992, he has been responsible for managing all research and development activities. Mr. Walsh is currently engaged in materials simplification and standardization, and technical support systems development, a special assignment at the corporate level. Career milestones include creation of a technical center for operations in South America. **Career Steps:** Procter & Gamble: Research and Development Director (1995–Present); Product Development Director – Analgesics & Respiratory Care (1994–1995); Director, International Technology Coordination – Health Care (1992–1994); Product Development Manager – Latin America, Caracas, Venezuela (1985–1989). **Associations & Accomplishments:** Holder of multiple patents in fabric conditioners and juice products. **Education:** Xavier University, M.B.A. (1977); University of Delaware, B.A. & B. in Chemical Engineering (1971).

Mark A. Banghart
Controller/Secretary
Bell Maintenance Products Company
930 East Boot Road
West Chester, PA 19380–4099
(610) 692–5780
Fax: (610) 430–8423

2842

Business Information: Bell Maintenance Products Company is a distributor of sanitary maintenance chemicals and equipment. The Company services schools, restaurants, hotels, hospitals, some government agencies, and cleaning contractors. As Controller/Secretary, Mr. Banghart manages all aspects of computerized accounting and the Information Management Systems. He is also responsible for personnel, benefits administration, network administration, and formatting the financial statements. **Career Steps:** Bell Maintenance Products Company: Controller/Secretary (1993–Present), Inventory Control/Purchaser (1992–1993), Warehouse Manager (1991–1992), Bookkeeper/Office Manager (1984–1986), Salesman (1982–1984). **Associations & Accomplishments:** Chamber of Commerce of Greater West Chester. **Education:** Bucknell University, B.A. (1974). **Personal:** Married to Victoria C. in 1977. Two children: Matthew Ryan and Kyle Steven.

Thomas F. Behrns, CPA

Controller
Lime O Sol
P.O. Box 395
Ashley, IN 46705–0395
(219) 587–9151
Fax: (219) 587–9154

2842

Business Information: Lime O Sol, established in 1946, is a manufacturer of home cleaning products. Products are marketed under the trademark name, "The Works." A Certified Public Accountant since 1983, Mr. Behrns joined the Company as Controller in 1995. He is responsible for managing financial and accounting matters for the Company. **Career Steps:** Controller, Lime O Sol (1995–Present); Controller, Hoosier/Ajax Wire Die (1988–1995); Manager of Budgets and Forecasts, Magnavox Comm. Systems Division (1986–1988). **Associations & Accomplishments:** American Institute of Certified Public Accountants. **Education:** St. Francis College, M.B.A. (1980); Indiana University, B.S. in Accounting (1976); Certified Public Accountant Certification (1983). **Per-**sonal: Married to Jenny in 1979. Two children: Michael and Kellianne. Mr. Behrns enjoys golf, and Indiana University basketball.

M. L. "Rusty" Davis II
Director of Marketing
Automotive Refinish Technologies, Inc.
400 Galleria Officentre, Suite 217
Southfield, MI 48034
(810) 304–5571
Fax: (810) 304–5580

2842

Business Information: Automotive Refinish Technologies, a subsidiary of BASF Corporation, specializes in the acquisition of automotive after–market industries and converts them into wholly–owned distributing outlets in North America. As Director of Marketing, Mr. Davis is responsible for all marketing development and implementation of building staff and development and implementation of soft training. Additionally, he coordinates with the core division soft training and assists in marketing strategies. He also guides and assists the Canadian affiliate in marketing strategies. **Career Steps:** Marketing Director, Automotive Refinish Technologies (1995–Present); Principle, C.E.C., Inc. (1993–1995); Owner, Bartelle II, Inc. (1992–1993); Director of OEM Sales, Sherwin Williams Automotive (1985–1992). **Education:** University of Indianapolis, B.S. (1965). **Personal:** Married to Sandra L. in 1966. Two children: Britt and Nancy. Mr. Davis enjoys golf, reading, workouts, travel, and entertaining.

Richard J. Prutky

President
White House Chemical
455 Trinity Avenue
Mercerville, NJ 08619–2347
(609) 587–6112
Fax: (609) 587–2502

2842

Business Information: White House Chemical is a manufacturer, distributor and service facility for sanitary maintenance and pool/spa supplies and equipment. As President, Mr. Prutky manages all aspects of company operations, concentrating on sales, marketing, and staff training and development. **Career Steps:** White House Chemical: President (1992–Present), Vice President (1986–1992), Sales and Service Representative (1977–1986). **Associations & Accomplishments:** Trustee, New Jersey Sanitary Supply Association; Board of Directors, Pennsylvania/Jersey National Spa and Pool Association; President, Enterprise Volunteer Fire Company. **Education:** NSPI Certified Technician (1996); Dale Carnegie; Pennsylvania Pesticide; Firefighter I; Certified Pool and Spa Operator. **Personal:** One child: Nicholas Michael. Mr. Prutky enjoys camping and firefighting.

Ronald E. Growe Jr.
Senior Project Manager
Colgate Palmolive
PO Box 779
Princeton Junction, NJ 08550–0779
(614) 432–8377
Fax: (212) 310–2103
EMAIL: See Below

2843

Business Information: Colgate Palmolive is one of the world's leading manufacturers and marketers of consumer household and beauty–aid products, with operations in over 170 countries around the world. Joining Colgate Palmolive in 1987 as an operations supervisor, Mr. Growe was appointed to his current role in 1992. As Senior Project Manager, he oversees all U.S. management projects, and has full P&L responsiblity for the capital improvement budget ($30MM annually). He can also be reached through the Internet via: RON_GROWE@COLPAL.COM **Career Steps:** Colgate Palmolive: Senior Project Manager (1992–Present), Operations Supervisor (1987–1992); Project Engineer, Motorola (1985–1987). **Associations & Accomplishments:** American Society of Mechanical Engineers (ASME); EIT – PE Review (May 1996); NMA; Junior Achievement Associate; United Way Volunteer; BPOE – active community service, distributing Christmas baskets to the needy. **Education:** Purdue University, B.S. in Mechanical Engineering (1984); Indiana University, working towards M.B.A. **Personal:** Mr. Growe enjoys golf, travel, and flying (taking courses to receive pilot's certificate).

Richard E. Lepik

Controller
Atotech U.S.A. Inc.
2 Riverview Drive
Somerset, NJ 08873–1150
(908) 302–3520
Fax: (908) 271–8960

2843

Business Information: Atotech U.S.A. Inc., a subsidiary of French–based petroleum conglomerate – Elf–Atochem, is a manufacturer and distributor of specialty chemicals used for plating and surface treatments, as well as a manufacturer and distributor of equipment of electronics. National in scope, Atotech has five locations throughout the U.S. Assisting in the formation of the Company in 1993 and a Certified Public Accountant, Mr. Lepik currently serves as Controller. He is responsible for strategic planning, acquisitions or divestitures, treasury (foreign currencies), financial analysis, directing MIS, re–engineering, management and operational work, and customer service. **Career Steps:** Controller, Atotech U.S.A. Inc. (1993–Present); Auditing Budget Report, Engelhard Corporation (1987–1990); Senior Financial Analyst, Pharmacia, Inc. (1985–1990); Accounting, Ortho Pharmaceutical Division, J&J (1978–1985). **Education:** Seton Hall University, M.B.A. in Marketing and Finance (1982); Certified Public Accountant (1988). **Personal:** Married to Kerry Ann in 1983. One child: Alyssa Liivi. Mr. Lepik enjoys fishing, gardening, and travel.

Terry B. Willis

Director of Food Division
Madison Chemical Company
3141 Clifty Drive
Madison, IN 47250
(812) 273–6000
Fax: (812) 273–6002

2843

Business Information: Madison Chemical Company is a manufacturer of cleaning and sanitizing chemicals for food processors, metal finishing, and paper mill industries. As Director of Food Division, Mr. Willis is responsible for all technical work of the Food Division. He assures that all distribution is going smoothly and all machines are running correctly. **Career Steps:** Director of Food Division, Madison Chemical Company (1979–Present); Project Director, Ichthyological Associates (1975–1978). **Associations & Accomplishments:** Mid–America Food Processors Association; American Meat Institute; Kentucky–Tennessee Meat Processors Association; International Association of Milk, Food, and Environmental Sanitarians. **Education:** Ball State University, M.S. in Environmental Biology (1975); Taylor University B.S. in Biology (1972). **Personal:** Married to Charmane in 1972. Two children: Brooke and Seth. Mr. Willis enjoys street rodding and hunting.

Peter M. Alexander

President and Chief Executive Officer
Tevco, Inc.
110 Pomponio Avenue
South Plainfield, NJ 07080–1900
(908) 754–7306
Fax: (201) 402–6077

2844

Business Information: Tevco, Inc. is a global distributor and contract manufacturer of cosmetics and colored cosmetics, primarily nail polish sold in bulk quantities. Established in 1948, Tevco, Inc. currently employs 60 people and has an estimated annual revenue of $15 million. As President and Chief Executive Officer, Mr. Alexander is responsible for all aspects of operations, including administration, management and strategic planning. **Career Steps:** President and Chief Executive Officer, Tevco, Inc. (1994–Present); President, Dalton and Alexander, Ltd. (1990–1994); President, BH Krueger (1984–1990); Associate, Johnson and Johnson; Associate, Kraft Foods. **Associations & Accomplishments:** Various civic associations; Board of Directors, two New Jersey corporations. **Education:** Columbia University, M.B.A. (1975); Seton Hall University, B.S. (1966). **Personal:** Married to Joanne in 1966. Three children: Stephanie, Susan, and John. Mr. Alexander enjoys softball, cooking, volleyball and rollerblading.

Tina M. Bartucca

Industrial Engineer
Zotos International
300 Forge Avenue
Geneva, NY 14456
(315) 781–9296
Fax: (315) 587–9339

2844

Business Information: Zotos International is a manufacturer of hair care products, specifically perms, hairspray, dyes, shampoos, and conditioners throughout the world. Zotos leads the way with professional products available in over 40 countries. As an Industrial Engineer, Ms. Bartucca observes, records, and analyzes techniques and equipment being used in the production process to see if they can operate more efficiently. She introduces or recommends changes to work methods, safety precautions and organizations of labor to improve and better the ergonomics of the product lines and product packaging. **Career Steps:** Zotos International: Industrial Engineer (1996–Present), Production Supervisor (July 1995–1996). **Associations & Accomplishments:** Safety Committee. **Education:** Rochester Institute of Technology, Bachelor of Science in Marketing (1995); Monroe Community College, Associate's degree in Fashion Buying/Merchandising. **Personal:** Ms. Bartucca enjoys soccer, snowmobiling, water skiing, and boating.

Mrs. Gina R. Boswell

Executive Director, Planning and Development
Estee Lauder Companies
767 Fifth Avenue, 40th Floor
New York, NY 10153
(212) 572–4384
Fax: (212) 527–6633

2844

Business Information: Estee Lauder Companies is one of the world's leading cosmetics companies. As Executive Director, Planning and Development, Mrs. Boswell develops long range business objectives and strategy, and works to improve organizational effectiveness. She also assists the COO in analyzing strategic and operational issues. Established in 1946, Estee Lauder Companies employs 12,000 people. **Career Steps:** Executive Director, Planning and Development, Estee Lauder Companies (1993–Present); Engagement Manager, Marakon Associates (1989–1993); Senior Associate, Arthur Andersen & Co. (1984–1987). **Associations & Accomplishments:** Cosmetic Executive Women; Product Development & Management Association; Advisory Board Member, Stamford Symphony Orchestra. Education: Yale School of Management, Masters in Management – M.B.A. (1989); Boston University, B.S. in Business Administration, summa cum laude (1984); Certified Public Accountant, Commonwealth of Massachusetts. **Personal:** Married to R. Randle Boswell, Jr. in 1992. Mrs. Boswell enjoys piano, Italian and Spanish languages and international travel."

Victor Casale

Managing Director
M.A.C. Cosmetics
200 Bentley Street
Markham, Ontario L3R 3L2
(905) 470–7877
Fax: (416) 488–3794

2844

Business Information: M.A.C. Cosmetics (Make–Up Art Cosmetics, Ltd.), a Canada–based cosmetics company and part of the Estee Lauder cosmetics group, was established in 1984. The first clients M.A.C. recruited were models whose word–of–mouth advertising increased sales until markets were established in department stores such as Saks Fifth Avenue and Henri Bendel's. Today, M.A.C. operates out of more than 100 locations in North America and Europe. The Company feels a deep sense of social consciousness and all products are made cruelty–free and "really clean and natural." In 1993 M.A.C. declared that 100% of the proceeds from the sale of one universally–wearable shade of lipstick, at $11.00 per tube, would be contributed to AIDS charities and research. During the first two years, over $2 million was raised. Since 1995, due to high impact advertising and signing new spokespersons, the total has doubled. In 1994, estimated sales were $78 million, in 1995 sales were in excess of $150 million and in 1996 sales are estimated to be over $300 million. M.A.C. built its business on catering to "all ages, all races, all sexes" and currently offer 130 shades of lipstick and 51 shades of foundation. In 1994 a deal with Estee Lauder was struck whereby the cosmetics would be distributed by Estee Lauder outside the United States. Another twist to this Company's advertising campaign is the models used to publicize their products. M.A.C.'s premiere spokesmodel is a "six–foot seven–inch black man (RuPaul) who dresses as a six–foot seven–inch (without heels) blonde woman." Due to this campaign, the transvestite community worldwide has taken MAC to its heart. Co–spokesperson for the line is a country music personality (k.d. lang) who is well–known for her disdain of the standards and traditions of the genre. Initially, she refused to wear any make–up, due to the cruelty inherent in the research techniques used in make–up production. Upon learning of the "cruelty–free" systems of MAC, she has become one of the most outspoken proponents of the Company. She has also, coincidentally, recently declared her avowed homosexuality. Another whole body of society following a leader to a product, and another coupe for M.A.C. As Managing Director of Development and Operations, Mr. Casale is responsible for the development of new products for M.A.C. Cosmetics. A second year chemistry student when he became chief chemist for M.A.C., Mr. Casale now manages a 400 person research and development department for the Company. As a partner in the Company, he is involved in making decisions regarding public relations, marketing techniques, sales techniques, and strategic planning for the future. **Career Steps:** M.A.C. Cosmetics: Managing Director of Development and Operations (1994–Present), Director of Research and Development/Operations (1986–1994), Chief Chemist (1984–1986). **Associations & Accomplishments:** Society of Cosmetic Chemists. **Education:** University of Toronto, B.Sc. (1986). **Personal:** Married to Julie in 1986. Three children: Christopher, Alex, and Lucas. Mr. Casale enjoys spending time with his family.

Harish M. Dalal

Director of Technology
Tristar Corporation
12500 San Pedro, Suite 500
San Antonio, TX 78216
(210) 402–2224
Fax: (210) 402–2288

2844

Business Information: Tristar Corporation manufactures and develops cosmetics and toiletries. Established in 1992, Tristar Corporation employs 400 professionals and boasts an estimated annual revenue of $50 million. As Director of Technology, Mr. Dalal implements new technological design concepts for product development and packaging. A professional in the field of technology for over a quarter of a century, he holds several patents, one of which was attained in 1985 for the development of a vending machine designed to distribute toiletries. In the future, Mr. Dalal plans to share his expertise through teaching and working on a corporate level as a consultant. **Career Steps:** Director of Technology, Tristar Corporation (1994–Present); President, JHS Ltd. – India (1989–1994); Manager of Materials Group, G.E. Aerospace (1981–1989). **Associations & Accomplishments:** American Society for Metals; San Antonio Manufacturers Association. **Education:** Massachusetts Institute of Technology, Sc.D. (1970). **Personal:** Married to Saryu in 1969. Two children: Renu and Rahul. Mr. Dalal enjoys tennis and reading.

Neville E. Evans, Ph.D.

Vice President of Science & Technology
Dudley Products, Inc.
1080 Old Greensboro Road
Kernersville, NC 27284
(910) 993–8800
Fax: (910) 993–1986

2844

Business Information: Dudley Products, Inc. is an international manufacturer and distributor of hair care and cosmetic products. Established in 1968, Dudley Products, Inc. reports annual revenue of $35 million and currently employs 550 people. As Vice President of Science & Technology, Dr. Evans is responsible for research and development, production, distribution, plant management and international business. **Career Steps:** Vice President of Science & Technology, Dudley Products, Inc. (1992–Present); Director of Science and Technology – International, Soft Sheen Products, Inc. (1984–1992); Manager of Laboratory Services, Clairol, Canada (1978–1984). **Education:** University of Bridgeport, Courses toward M.B.A. (1983); University of Wisconsin, Ph.D.; American Management Association; Executive Management Course. **Personal:** Married to Suzi Lane Evans in 1991. Three children: Kellylee, Christopher, and Larissa. Dr. Evans enjoys reading, travel, nature (ocean, woodlands), peace & quiet, and sports.

Christian M. Gilly

Chief Executive Officer
Guerlain, S.A.
Av Rio San Joaquin 820
Mexico City, Mexico 53390
(525) 395–2742
Fax: (525) 580–0338

2844

Business Information: Guerlain, S.A. is a global company involved in the manufacture of perfume and cosmetics. The Mexico operation is an importer and distributor of Guerlain products (i.e., Shalimar, Jardin de Bagatelle, Samsara, etc.). As Chief Executive Officer, Mr. Gilly is responsible for all aspects of Company operations, including administration, sales and marketing, finances, and strategic planning. **Career**

Steps: Chief Executive Officer, Guerlain, S.A. (1984–Present); Chief Executive Officer, Kenyon & Eckhardt (1979–1984); Vice President/Account Director, Leo Burnett (1974–1978); Marketing and Advertising Assistant Director, Christian Dior (1971–1973). **Education:** E.S.C. Neuchatel – Switzerland, M.B.A. (1963). **Personal:** Married to Marianne in 1969. Two children: Marc and Frederic. Mr. Gilly enjoys tennis and automobiles.

Michael E. Haynes

Construction Manager
Procter and Gamble Cosmetic & Fragrance Products
11050 York Road, M.S. #44
Hunt Valley, MD 21030
(410) 785–4557
Fax: (410) 785–4553

2844

Business Information: Procter and Gamble Cosmetic & Fragrance Products, headquartered in Cincinnati, Ohio, is a major consumer products manufacturer distributing globally. Products include health and beauty aids; liquid, dry, and flaked soaps; dental care products; household cleaners; and much more. As Construction Manager, Mr. Haynes oversees all construction systems, manages staff, and assists with planning of projects, and construction. Additional responsibilities include administration, operations, and finance. **Career Steps:** Procter and Gamble Cosmetic & Fragrance Products: Construction Manager (1995–Present), Senior Project Manager (1993–1995), Project Manager (1989–1993), Associate Project Manager (1987–1989), United States Navy: Construction Manager (1984–1987), Contract Manager (1983–1984), Facilities Program Manager (1981–1983), Assistant Public Works Manager (1979–81). **Associations & Accomplishments:** CHI Epsilon; Beta Gamma Sigma; American Society of Civil Engineers; Society of American Military Engineers; Retired, United States Navy Reserves. **Education:** Loyola College in Maryland, M.B.A. (1993); Virginia Tech, B.S.C.E. (1979). **Personal:** Married to Mary in 1994. Two children: Christina and Samantha. Mr. Haynes enjoys golf, photography and the Parent Teacher Association.

Elias K. Hebeka, Ph.D.

Executive Vice President of Operations Worldwide
Revlon, Inc.
625 Madison Avenue
New York, NY 10022
(212) 527–4972
Fax: (212) 527–4965

2844

Business Information: Revlon, Inc. established by Charles Revlon in 1932, is a leading manufacturer and distributor of cosmetics, toiletries, treatments, implements, and fragrances worldwide. The Corporation has over 10,000 employees and estimates annual sales in excess of $2 billion. As Executive Vice President, Dr. Hebeka is responsible for the worldwide manufacture and distribution of products. He works closely with other members of management on the development of budgets and strategic planning for the future. Other responsibilities include overseeing purchasing, engineering, and package development. **Career Steps:** Executive Vice President, Revlon, Inc. (1993–Present); President and CEO, Liberty Science Center (1993); Corporate Vice President for Operations, Warner Lambert (1979–1993). **Associations & Accomplishments:** American Productivity and Quality Center; American Society for Microbiology. **Education:** Rutgers University, Ph.D. (1963) and M.S. in Bacteriology; University of Cairo, Bachelor's of Pharmacy. **Personal:** Married to Barbara in 1963. Three children: Charles, Michael, and Mark. Dr. Hebeka enjoys golf, reading, travel, and watching television.

Rosendo A. Jimenez

Vice President of Sales/General Manager
Guerlain Puerto Rico, Inc.
P.O. Box 362121
San Juan, Puerto Rico 00936
(787) 783–5820
Fax: (787) 783–5812

2844

Business Information: Guerlain Puerto Rico, Inc. is a cosmetics and fragrance company. The Puerto Rico division imports from France and distributes and sells merchandise to the better department stores. As Vice President of Sales/General Manager, Mr. Jimenez is responsible for all aspects of Company operations, including sales, management, public relations, and marketing. **Career Steps:** Vice President of Sales/General Manager, Guerlain Puerto Rico, Inc. (1979–Present); Sales Manager, Germaine Monteil (1966–1979). **Associations & Accomplishments:** Second Vice President, Puerto Rico Olympic Committee. **Education:** School of Commerce – Cuba, Accounting (1962). **Personal:** Married to Nelsa in 1961. Two children: Rosendo E. and Elizabeth M. Mr. Jimenez enjoys judo (7th Dan and International Referee Classification A).

Lauren S. Kahn

Public Relations Director
J.F. Lazartigue
34 Joyce Road
Hartsdale, NY 10530–2930
(914) 693–5231
Fax: (914) 693–5226
EMail: See Below

2844

Business Information: J.F. Lazartigue is a diagnostic Hair Advisory Center, headquartered in Paris, France. The Company provides hair and scalp analysis, personalized prescriptions and administers hair and scalp treatments. The Company manufactures hair, sun and leg care products. As Public Relations Director, Ms. Kahn is the media contact, as well as marketing and advertising consultant. She oversees all national public relations. Internet users can reach her via: LSTorre@aol.com. **Career Steps:** Public Relations Director, J.F. Lazartigue (1994–Present); Senior Account Executive, Cairns & Associates (1993–1994); Account Executive, Lippe Taylor Public Relations (1992–1993); The Rowland Company (1989–1992). **Education:** State University of New York – Buffalo, B.A. in Communications (1989); Public Relations Certificate. **Personal:** Married to Steve Torre in 1994. One child: Alexandria (5/10/96). Ms. Kahn enjoys cooking, sports, reading, and travel.

Mr. Stuart L. Kantor

Manager of Clinical Research
Estee Lauder, Inc.
125 Pinelawn Road
Melville, NY 11747
(516) 531–1629
Fax: (516) 531–1338

2844

Business Information: Established in 1964, Estee Lauder, Inc. is a manufacturer and distributor of fine cosmetics found in better department stores. As Manager of Clinical Research, Mr. Kantor is responsible for all aspects of the clinical safety testing program and human clinical testing. He utilizes his strong writing skills to produce final claim support documents for legal registration, as well as preparing summaries of safety testing results for all products prior to their release. **Career Steps:** Manager of Clinical Research, Estee Lauder, Inc. (1991–Present); Independent Consultant (1987–1989); Senior Scientist, Richardson–Vicks Inc. (1974–1987). **Education:** Mercy College, B.S. (1976); Westchester Community College, A.A.S. in Medical Laboratory Technology (1973). **Personal:** Mr. Kantor enjoys extensive wine collecting, formal wine tasting, reading historical novels and biographies, ethnic restaurants, including Spanish, Moroccan, Indian, and Vietnamese, and long walks with good company and a good cigar.

Arthur E. Kierstead

Vice President of Worldwide Manufacturing & Technical Operations
JAFRA Cosmetics International
2451 Townsgate Road
Westlake Village, CA 91361
(805) 449–3005
Fax: (805) 449–3254

2844

Business Information: JAFRA Cosmetics International, a wholly–owned division of Gillette — one of the world's leading consumer health and beauty aids conglomerates — is a global marketer and manufacturer of diversified cosmetics lines. As Vice President of Worldwide Manufacturing & Technical Operations, Mr. Kierstead is responsible for worldwide logistics, purchasing, production and inventory control functions. **Career Steps:** Vice President of Worldwide Manufacturing & Technical Operations, JAFRA Cosmetics International (1994–Present); Gillette – Stationery Products: Director of Engineering (1986–1994), Director of Research and Development and Project Management (1977–1986); Gillette – Blades and Razors: Group Manager of New Products (1975–1976), Group Manager of Research and Development (1970–1976). **Associations & Accomplishments:** Army Athletic Association; Golden State Sculpture Association; USTA; SCGA; United States Military Academy – Association of Graduates. **Education:** Northeastern University, M.B.A. (1973); U.S. Military Academy, B.S. in Engineering Sciences (1964). **Personal:** Married to Sally in 1965. He has three sons. Mr. Kierstead enjoys tennis and golf.

Masaki Kondo

President
NOEVIR International Corporation
200 West Grand Avenue
Montvale, NJ 07645
(201) 391–0001 (201) 391–0001
Fax: (201) 391–1740

2844

Business Information: NOEVIR International Corporation is a cosmetics and skin care manufacturer involved in the importing and exporting of its products internationally. Founding NOEVIR in 1992, Masaki Kondo provides the overall corporate vision and strategies, ensuring quality product output and technology development to keep the Company a viable presence in the global cosmetics market. **Career Steps:** President, NOEVIR International Corporation (1992–Present). **Associations & Accomplishments:** Porsche Club. **Education:** Ritsumeikan University, B.A.; London University, Business Degree. **Personal:** Married to Yoko. Two children: Jason and Julie. Mr. Kondo enjoys spending time with his family.

Jose G. Lozano

Vice President of Plant Operations
Cosway Company Inc.
14805 South Maple Avenue
Gardena, CA 90248–1935
(310) 527–9135
Fax: (310) 527–9779

2844

Business Information: Cosway Company Inc. is a diversified chemical compound manufacturer, with products ranging from health and beauty aids additives to toy compounds. One of its major customers is Mattel Toy Company. A nine year veteran with the Company starting as plant manager, Mr. Jose Lozano was promoted to Vice President of Operations in 1992. In this capacity, he is responsible for shipping, receiving, manufacturing, packaging, maintanence engineering and product planning. **Career Steps:** Cosway Company Inc.: Vice President of Plant Operations (1992–Present), Director of Operations (1989–1992), Plant Manager (1986–1989). **Associations & Accomplishments:** Fluent in Italian, English, and Spanish. **Education:** University of California – Los Angeles, Cosmetic Chemistry (1990); Long Beach City College, Petroleum Technology (1984); University of Lima, Industrial Engineering (1979). **Personal:** Two children: Stacy and Joseph. Mr. Lozano enjoys photography, scuba diving, and going to the beach.

Serafin Massol

Operations Director
Avon Products – Puerto Rico
P.O. Box 363774
San Juan, Puerto Rico 00936–3774
(809) 747–6161
Fax: (809) 793–5265

2844

Business Information: Avon Products is the world's leading direct marketing cosmetics conglomerate. National and international operations provide people throughout the world with the beauty, value and fine quality of Avon products. The most modern developmental and manufacturing techniques are utilized to provide representatives with products as up–to–the–minute as possible. All new product formulas are developed by their National Research and Development Laboratories in Suffern, New York. The design of each of their packages is the result of a skilled artistic and creative group. Joining Avon Products – Puerto Rico as Operations Director in 1994, Mr. Massol is responsible for all direction of the Production and Inventory Control, Purchasing, Warehousing, Shipping, Transportation, Quality Assurance, Customer Service, and Safety & Environment Departments. **Career Steps:** Operations Director, Avon Products, Puerto Rico (1994–Present); Director of Finance and Manufacturing, Avon Mirabella, Inc. (1987–1993); Vice President and Managing Director, Beecham de Mexico SA de CV (1981–1987). **Associations & Accomplishments:** Board Member, La Casa de Todos – a non–profit organization that takes care of abused/abandoned children. **Education:** Universidad del Turabo, M.B.A. in Marketing (1995); Catholic University of Puerto Rico, B.B.A. in Accounting (1969); Northwestern University, Audit (1970). **Personal:** Married to Sonia Lugo in 1972. Three children: Serafin, Ana Mercedes, and Sonia Yadira. Mr. Massol enjoys golf and reading.

Anton K. McBurnie

Managing Director and Executive Vice President
Estee Lauder Cosmetics Canada
21 Daffodil Avenue
Thornhill, Ontario L3T 1N2
(416) 363–0449
Fax: Please mail or call

2844

Business Information: Estee Lauder Cosmetics Canada, an international affiliate of Estee Lauder Companies, is one of the world's leading producers of cosmetic products, manufacturing, selling, and marketing a line of prestigious cosmetics and fragrances. Established in 1945, Estee Lauder Companies currently employs 75,000 people Company–wide and 165 people at the Canadian subsidiary. With eight years expertise in the cosmetics industry, Mr. McBurnie joined Estee Lauder Cosmetics Canada in 1992. Serving as Managing Director and Executive Vice President, he is responsible for the P&L of the Canadian affiliate and all aspects of the strategy and development of the business. **Career Steps:** Managing Director and Executive Vice President, Estee Lauder Cosmetics Canada (1992–Present); General Manager, L'Oreal Japan Ltd. – Tokyo (1990–1992); General Manager, Scental (L'Oreal) Ltd. – Hong Kong (1987–1990). **Associations & Accomplishments:** Young Presidents Organizaton, Ontario Chapter; Canadian Cosmetics, Fragrance, and Toiletry Association. **Education:** London Business School, M.B.A. (1983); Exeter University, B.S. in Zoology and Psychology. **Personal:** Married to Bernadette in 1987. Three children: Kyle, Lauren, and Kirsty. Mr. McBurnie enjoys squash, golf, skiing, scuba diving, and video & still photography.

Joan P. Meade

Director, Marketing Research
Takasago International Corporation (U.S.A.)
11 Volvo Drive
Rockleigh, NJ 07647–2507
(201) 767–9001
Fax: (201) 784–7244

2844

Business Information: Takasago International Corporation (U.S.A.) is a leading global creator and manufacturer of fragrances and flavors for consumer products. Takasago is also a supplier of fine chemicals to the pharmaceutical industry utilizing their unique asymmetric synthesis techniques. With parent company operations in Japan being established in 1920, the U.S. subsidiary was incorporated in 1968 and employs over 2,000 personnel worldwide. A consumer foods marketing and research expert, Ms. Meade serves as Director of Takasago's Marketing Research division. Her duties involve the design, development and coordination of domestic and global market research projects. This involves developing questionnaires and test protocols for quantitative and qualitative consumer tests; data analysis; and the presentation of data results to customers. She also provides orientation presentations to international sales and marketing staff personnel, as well as key customers. **Career Steps:** Director, Marketing Research, Takasago International Corporation (1992–Present); KRAFT Foods – Consumer Center: Assistant Manager (1989–1992), Consumer Information Associate (1988–1989). **Associations & Accomplishments:** American Marketing Association; Association for Consumer Research; Received "Best Essay Award" from Takasago's Headquarters in Japan (April 1995). **Education:** Iona College/Hagan School of Business, M.B.A., emphasis in Marketing (1988); Iona College, B.S. in Business Administration (1984). **Personal:** Two children: William A. Jr. and Suzette N. Ms. Meade enjoys travel, dancing, singing in her church choir, reading, table tennis, and going to spectator sports (track & field, baseball, and skating).

Michael Ochoa

Manufacturing Manager
Helene Curtis Industries, Inc.
19161 East Walnut Drive North
City of Industry, CA 91748
(818) 965–3441
Fax: (818) 915–8317

2844

Business Information: Helene Curtis Industries, Inc., an international Fortune 500 company, manufactures personal care products for both consumers and professionals. Product lines include shampoos, conditioners, deodorants, and skin care treatments; as well as manufacturing of the leading professional permanent wave product in the U.S. Established in 1928, Helene Curtis Industries, Inc. reports annual sales in excess of $1 billion and currently employs 1,200 people. As Manufacturing Manager, Mr. Ochoa is responsible for the production of over 75 items timely and efficiently, supervision of 85 employees and management of five departments at the California plant. **Career Steps:** Helene Curtis Industries, Inc.: Manufacturing Manager (1986–Present), Shift Superintendent (1984–1986), Distribution Supervision (1982–1984). **Education:** National University, B.B.A. (1993); Stevens Henager Business College, A.C.S. in Accounting (1981). **Personal:** Married to Carol in 1976. Two teenage sons. Mr. Ochoa enjoys travel, reading, history, and gardening.

Jamezell Sylvain Ottinger

Vice President of North American National Accounts
Sebastian, Inc.
P O Box 746
Monroe, GA 30655–0746
(770) 267–2433
Fax: Please mail or call

2844

Business Information: Sebastian, Inc., established in 1973, is a manufacturer of professional cosmetics and hair care products. As Vice President of North American National Accounts, Mr. Ottinger concentrates on dealing with the large chain accounts throughout North America. **Career Steps:** Vice President of North American National Accounts, Sebastian, Inc. (1994–Present); Director of Sales, Sebastian International (1990–1994); Vice President of Marketing, Lamarick Beauty System (1988–1990); Regional Sales Manager, Redken Inc. (1979–1988). **Education:** Georgia State University, B.A. (1979). **Personal:** Mr. Ottinger enjoys running marathons.

James E. Piechowski

Unit Manager
Helene Curtis
1500 N. Kostner Avenue
Chicago, IL 60651–1610
(312) 292–8664
Fax: (312) 292–8663

2844

Business Information: Helene Curtis is an international Fortune 500 company that manufactures personal care products for both consumers and professionals. Their products include shampoos, conditioners, deodorants and skin care products. They also manufacture the largest professional permanent wave product in the United States. As Unit Manager, Mr. Piechowski manages high speed filling lines in manufacturing, supervises a staff of thirty, oversees the budget, and coordinates all activities of his unit. He is also responsible for introducing the "Merit Pay Program" to the Company in 1995. **Career Steps:** Unit Manager, Helene Curtis (1991–Present); Supervisor, Quill Corporation (1979–1991); Supervisor, Hertz Corporation (1978–1979). **Associations & Accomplishments:** Assistant Scoutmaster, Boy Scouts of America. **Education:** Northwestern University, M.A. (1973); DePaul University, B.A. (1971). **Personal:** Married to Janine in 1972. Three children: Jon, Patricia, and Brian. Mr. Piechowski enjoys hiking, bicycling, backpacking, and gardening.

Louis L. Punto

Manager
R.P. Scherer
2725 Scherer Drive
St. Petersburg, FL 33716
(813) 572–4000
Fax: (813) 572–6037

2844

Business Information: R.P. Scherer is a pharmaceutical company, specializing in gelatin encapsulation for cosmetic industry utilization. With twelve years experience in cosmetic science, Mr. Punto joined R.P. Scherer in 1993. Serving as Manager, he is responsible for directing research and development of products suitable for gelatin encapsulation in topical cosmetics, as well as developing the formulation of the capsules. Established in 1933, R.P. Scherer employs 450 people with annual sales of $600 million. **Career Steps:** Manager, R.P. Scherer (1993–Present); Group Leader, Estee Lauder (1987–1993); Research Chemist, Chesebrough–Pond's (1985–1987); Formulation Chemist, ATI Inc. (1983–1985). **Associations & Accomplishments:** Secretary, Society of Cosmetics' Chemists, Florida Chapter (1994–Present). **Education:** Fordham University, M.S. (1981); College of Mt. St. Vincent – Manhattan College, B.S. (1978). **Personal:** Married to Maryanne in 1987. One child: Steven. Mr. Punto enjoys scuba diving, golf, and working on cars.

Alfred H. Raschdorf Jr.

Supervisor of Maintenance Engineering and Administration
Estee Lauder, Inc.
350 South Service Road
Melville, NY 11747–3233
(516) 454–7173
Fax: (516) 454–7025
EMAIL: See Below

2844

Business Information: Estee Lauder, Inc., the world's 4th largest leading producer of cosmetic products, is a manufacturer, seller, and marketer of a line of prestigious cosmetics, with brand–name product lines to include Aramis, Clinique, Estee Lauder, Prescriptives, Origins, Bobbie Brown, and M.A.C. Products are marketed in over 100 countries from eight manufacturing plants worldwide and by wholly–owned affiliates in 29 countries. As Supervisor of Maintenance Engineering and Administration, Mr. Raschdorf is responsible for taking care of the computerized management system and program databases. His duties include analyzing energy and utilities usage, and Internet users can reach him via: alfred.raschdorf.jr@worldnet.att.net. **Career Steps:** Supervisor of Maintenance Engineering and Administration, Estee Lauder, Inc. (1995–Present); Customer Support Engineer, Parametric Technology Corporation (1994–1995). **Associations & Accomplishments:** Commack Volunteer Ambulance Groups; Association for Facilities Engineering; Cornell Society of Engineers. **Education:** Dowling College, M.B.A.; Cornell University, B.S. (1994). **Personal:** Mr. Raschdorf enjoys kayaking, running, rock climbing, squash, and playing the saxophone.

Stephen Siew

Plant Manager
Westwood Chemical Corporation
46 Tower Drive
Middletown, NY 10940–2023
(914) 692–6721
Fax: (914) 692–5890

2844

Business Information: Westwood Chemical Corporation is an international manufacturer of chemicals, including anti–perspirant active incredients, which are supplied to major cosmetic companies. In addition, water treatment products are also produced and distributed to local municipalities in three states. As Plant Manager, Mr. Siew is responsible for the management of production, shipping & receiving, maintenance, quality control, and Company "bottom–line" profits. Additionally, he is responsible for all safety and security functions. **Career Steps:** Plant Manager, Westwood Chemical Corporation (1988–Present); Packaging Supervisor, Dial Corp. (1993–1994); Production Engineer, Joy Displays, Inc. (1986–1987). **Associations & Accomplishments:** Family of Faith Lutheran Church; Aikido Association; Recipient of three blackbelts, one in Chinese martial arts, one in Ai Kido, and one in Tae Kwon Do; Fluent in English, Chinese, and Malay/Indonesia. **Education:** State University of New York – Buffalo: M.Sc. in Industrial Technology (1988), B.Sc. in Industrial Technology; Jaya Institute of Technology, Associates in Electrical/Electronic Engineering. **Personal:** Married to Debra L. Price in 1988. Two children: Daniel S. and Elizabeth M. Mr. Siew enjoys coin collecting, investing, and martial arts.

Donna Friend Sisson

Owner
Sisson's Health Networking
18375 East County Road 800 N
Kilbourne, IL 62655
(309) 538–9200
Fax: (309) 543–3095

2844

Business Information: Sisson's Health Networking is a marketing company specializing in the distribution of herbs, oils, and related health products. An independent Company, Sisson's Health Networking, established in 1977, provides services to clients nationwide. As Owner, Ms. Sisson is responsible for Company sales and management, oversees contract negotiations with new clients, handles all networking, and is actively involved with consulting. Concurrent with her present position, Ms. Sisson will be opening a bed and breakfast, "Country Inn" in late 1996. **Career Steps:** Owner, Sisson's Health Networking (1977–Present); Elementary School Counselor, Vermont Ipava TableGrove School (1995–1996); Psychology Teacher, Spoon River College (1968–Present); Elementary/Jr./High Counselor, Havana School District (1965–1994). **Associations & Accomplishments:** City Alterman for Havana; American School Counselor Association; Past President, AAUW; Past President, Illinois School Counselor Association; Past President, Delta Kappa Gamma; American Counseling Association; Past President, American Business Women Association; Women in Networking. **Education:** Western Illinois University, M.S. (1970); Mac Murray College, B.S. (1955). **Personal:** Married to Marcus in 1956. Four children: Jeffrey, Jonathan, Janna, and Jennifer (deceased). Ms. Sisson enjoys china painting, reading, and her six grandchildren.

Richard Stanley Sistrunk

Data Processing Technical Operations Manager
Coty, Inc.
P.O. Box 1026
Sanford, NC 27331
(919) 774–8800
Fax: (919) 774–1493
EMAIL: See Below

2844

Business Information: Coty, Inc. manufactures and distributes fragrances, cosmetics, and cologne. Mr. Sistrunk has held various supervisory technical positions with Coty, most recently promoted to Data Processing Technical Operations Manager in 1995. His responsibilities include supervision of all computer resources, including network, mainframe, and midrange platform troubleshooting and maintenance. Internet users can also reach him via: sistrunkr@attmail.com **Career Steps:** Coty, Inc.: Data Processing Technical Operations Manager (1995–Present), Systems Programming Technical Support (1992–1995), Programming and Software Manager (1992). **Associations & Accomplishments:** National Systems Programmers Association. **Education:** Campbell University, B.S. in Math (1971). **Personal:** Married to Jackie T. in 1971. Four children: Amy Noelle, Richard, Jr., Elizabeth Ashley, and Jenny Katherine. Mr. Sistrunk enjoys fishing, hunting, singing, and is a choir director.

Volker Skibbe, Ph.D.

Vice President of Product Development and Quality Assurance
Beiersdorf, Inc.
360 Dr. Martin Luther King Drive
Norwalk, CT 06856
(203) 854–8138
Fax: (203) 854–8165

2844

Business Information: Beiersdorf, Inc. is an international manufacturer and distributor of consumer cosmetic and medical products. With headquarters located in Germany and subsidiaries worldwide, the Corporation sells products in more than 100 countries. Consisting of three divisions: Cosmed, Medical, and Tesa, corporate sales include $4 billion worldwide, with $400 million in the U.S. Five of the subsidiaries are located in the U.S. The Norwalk location manufactures cosmetics and lotions and the North Carolina location manufactures medical devices. As Vice President of Product Development and Quality Assurance, Dr. Skibbe is responsible for all operations concentrating on quality assurance (i.e., chemicals, raw materials, packaging, finished goods) and compliance with test requirements. Additional responsibilities include setting up a proper system for documentation, transferring formulas from Hamburg, Germany to adapt to the U.S. market to meet local regulations, supervision of all clinical testing, and participate in conferences with the CTFA. His greatest accomplishment was the development of Nivea Visage, which was a major strategic move for the Beiersdorf corporation worldwide. Internet users can reach Dr. Skibbe via: 100073.250@compuserve.com **Career Steps:** Beiersdorf, Inc. – U.S.A.: Vice President of Product Development and Quality Assurance (1996–Present), Director of Product Development and Quality Assurance (1994–1995); Beiersdorf, Inc. – Germany: International Marketing Manager (1992–1994), "Leitender Angestellter" – Handlungsvollmacht (1990), Department Head of Product Development Face Care (1989–1992); Beiersdorf Japan: R&D Coordinator (1986–1989), Head – Face Care Laboratory (1985–1989), R&D Training Program (1984–1985). **Associations & Accomplishments:** Dermal Clinical Evaluation Society; Germany D.G.K.; Participant, Cosmetic Toiletry and Fragrance Association (CTFA); Speaker, European Cosmetic Conferences. **Education:** Max–Planck–Institut fur Strahlenchemie: Ph.D., magna cum laude (1985), Masters in Chemistry (1982); Ruhr–Universitat Bochum; Ashridge Management College (1992); Beiersdorf Management Development Programme (1986–1987). **Personal:** Married to Marion in 1980. Three children: Nadine, Michele and Maurice.

ESTĒE LAUDER INTERNATIONAL, INC.

Jeanette S. Wagner

President
Estee Lauder International, Inc.
767 5th Avenue
New York, NY 10153
(212) 572–4730
Fax: (212) 572–5414

2844

Business Information: Estee Lauder International, Inc., established in 1946, is the largest of six divisions within Estee Lauder Companies consisting of 1/2 of the Company and currently employing 12,000 people. Estee Lauder is one of the world's leading producers (the 4th largest) of cosmetic products, with brand–name product lines to include: Aramis, Clinique, Estee Lauder, Prescriptives, Origins, Bobbie Brown, and M.A.C. Products are marketed in over 100 countries from eight manufacturing plants world–wide and by wholly–owned affiliates in 29 countries. As President of the International Division, Ms. Wagner is responsible for all business activities and brands being sold and distributed internationally, excluding the U.S., Canada, and Puerto Rico. Her career has spanned marketing and general management on both domestic and international fronts. Ms. Wagner joined the Estee Lauder Companies as the Vice President and Director of Marketing of the Estee Lauder brand in the International Division, where she revolutionized the process of bringing product to market and exploded the growth of the Lauder brand internationally. Quickly rising to Senior Vice President for both Estee Lauder and Prescriptives International, she was promoted to Corporate Senior Vice President, reporting directly to Leonard Lauder, Chairman and Chief Executive Officer of Estee Lauder Companies. In this role, she worked with Mr. Lauder to help identify the critical issues and develop the strategic plans for the Lauder companies in the years ahead. Following the development of plans for the last decade of the twentieth century, Ms. Wagner was named to her current position as President and Chief Executive Officer of the International Division, now the largest in the Company. In this position, she heads an organization that includes the sales and marketing of the Aramis, Clinique, Estee Lauder, Origins, and Prescriptives brands in over 100 countries, as well as management responsibility for the international distribution of M.A.C. (Make–up Art Cosmetics) and Bobbi Brown Essentials. Under her leadership, new concepts have been developed, including the first free–standing stores for both the Estee Lauder and Clinique brands in the world, located in Eastern Europe and Russia, as well as developing flagship sales environments in five cities in China, and in every major Asia–Pacific country. **Career Steps:** Estee Lauder Inc. (1975–Present): President of the International Division, Corporate Senior Vice President, Senior Vice President, Vice President/Director of Marketing; Editor–in–Chief, The Hearst Corporation; Senior Editor, The Saturday Evening Post. **Associations & Accomplishments:** Vice President, Harvard Business School Club of Greater New York; Founding Member, Harvard Business School Network of Women Alumni; Northwestern Council of One Hundred; Cosmetic Executive Women; President and Chairman of the Board, The Fashion Group International; The Economic Club; Planning Board, American Women's Economic Development Corp.; Asia Society; The China Institute; The Foreign Policy Association; The Japan Society; The Korean Society; The Women's Economic Round Table; The Committee of 200; Advisory Committee on Trade Policy and Negotiations, appointed by President Clinton; Board of Directors and the Audit and Compensation Committees, The American Greetings Corporation, Clevelend, OH; Board of Directors and the Audit and Compensation Committees, The Stride Rite Corporation, Cambridge, MA; Vice President, The Business Council for International Understanding, New York; Chairman, The Fragrance Foundation, New York; The Breast Cancer Research Foundation, New York; The Women's Forum, New York; Awarded the Alumnae Medal, Northwestern University (1995) and the Director's Choice Award, National Womens Economic Alliance Foundation (1995); 1995 Director's Choice Award from the National Womens Economic Alliance Foundation; 1995 Director's Choice Award from the National Womens Economic Alliance Foundation; Cosmetic Executive Woman of the Year 1996. **Education:** Northwestern University, B.S., cum laude; Harvard Business School, Advanced Management Program. **Personal:** Married to Paul A. Wagner, President of NPO Taskforce Inc., a public relations consulting company. Two children: Paula and Paul.

Laura Wagner

Manager of Human Resource Records, Systems & Services
Cheeseborough–Pond's USA
75 Merritt Boulevard
Trumbull, CT 06611–5435
(203) 381–2295
Fax: (203) 381–2509

2844

Business Information: Cheeseborough–Pond's USA is a manufacturer of personal care products (i.e., Close Up toothpaste, Rave, and Ponds). As Manager of Human Resource Records, Systems & Services, Ms. Wagner manages personnel/payroll database, employee services (travel, relocation, service awards, physical exams), and administration of personnel policies. **Career Steps:** Cheeseborough–Pond's USA: Manager of Human Resource Records, Systems & Services (1988–Present), Supervisor of Human Resource Systems and Salary Budgets (1985–1988); Administrator – Division of Pathology and Toxicology, American Health Foundation (1983–1985). **Associations & Accomplishments:** Employee Relocation Council; Connecticut/Westchester Professional Travel Managers Association; International Association for Human Resource Information Management; Presidents Council, Genesys Software Company; Cheeseborough–Pond's 1993 Total Quality Champion; Employee Relocation Council's Outstanding Women in Relocation (1992); Human Resources Team Leader in implementation of HRMS database. **Education:** Pace University, B.S. (1983). **Personal:** Married to Ken in 1988. Two children: Lena Marie and Carol Michelle. Ms. Wagner enjoys being a black belt in Karate.

Kathleen E. Walas

Vice President, U.S. and Global Public Relations
Avon Products, Inc.
9 West 57th Street
New York, NY 10019–2683
(212) 546–7052
Fax: (212) 546–7248

2844

Business Information: Avon Products, Inc. is the world's leading direct selling cosmetics company. National and international operations provide people throughout the world with the beauty, value and fine quality of Avon products. The most modern developmental and manufacturing techniques are utilized to provide sales representatives with products as up–to–the minute as today. All new product formulas are developed by their global research and development laboratories in Suffern, New York. The design of their packages is the result of a skilled artistic and creative group. Established in 1886, Avon Products, Inc. currently employs 32,000 people worldwide. As Vice President, U.S. and Global Public Relations, Ms. Walas is responsible for the development and supervision of public relations strategies for worldwide execution. She also serves as the Company's international beauty and fashion director/spokeswoman for media, sales, and consumer activities. Ms. Walas joined Avon in 1985 after successfully running her own business as a cosmetic industry consultant representing such leaders as Adrien Arpel, Charles of the Ritz, Estee Lauder, Max Factor and Revlon. Among her celebrity clientele were actresses, models and designers, including Faye Dunaway, Mary Tyler Moore, Lauren Hutton, Jill Clayburgh, Kim Alexis, Dorthy Hamill and Adrienne Vittadini. In the beauty business for nearly 20 years and appeared on beauty and fashion segments for the syndicated "You...Video Magazine for Women." Ms. Walas began her Avon career as a product training specialist in the Product Communications area. She held positions within the Public Relations Unit since 1987 which lead to her current position. In 1990, she co–authored "Taking Control of Your Life: The Secrets of a Successful Enterprising Women" and in 1992 she wrote "Real Beauty...Real Women." Ms. Walas has appeared in over 300 television shows around the world. Her creative beauty and lifestyle tips have appeared in numerous magazines including McCall's, Harper's Bazaar, Ladies' Home Journal, New Woman and Cosmopolitan. **Career Steps:** Avon Products, Inc.: Vice President, U.S. and Global Public Relations (1996–Present); Director, Public Relations (1993–1996); Manager of Product Publicity (1990–1993); Product Publicist (1987–1990); Beauty and Training Specialist (1985–1987); Cosmetic Industry Consultant (1979–1985). **Associations & Accomplishments:** Public Affairs Committee, Cosmetic, Toiletry and Fragrance Association; Cosmetic Executive Women; Fashion Group International; New York Women in Communications. **Education:** University of Massachusetts, Amherst. **Personal:** Married. Two Children.

Jules R. Zecchino

Executive Director of Research and Development
Estee Lauder
30 Auryansen Court
Closter, NJ 07624–2847
(516) 531–1651
Fax: (201) 784–7449

2844

Business Information: Estee Lauder, one of the world's leading producers of cosmetic products (the 4th largest), is a manufacturer, seller, and marketer of a line of prestigious cosmetics, with brand–name product lines to include: Aramis, Clinique, Estee Lauder, Prescriptives, Origins, Bobbie Brown, and M.A.C. Products are marketed in over 100 countries from eight manufacturing plants world–wide and by wholly–owned affiliates in 29 countries. With twenty–two years of experience in the research and development of cosmetics, Mr. Zecchino joined Estee Lauder as Executive Director of Research and Development in 1989. He is responsible for the direction of the Formulation Research and Development labs for the products, Estee Lauder and Prescriptives Skin Care, including presenting new technologies, and conducting basic and applied research. He also works with the Marketing Department to set up strategies for product marketing. Career milestones include the formulation of Ceramide for Elizabeth Arden and Fruition for Estee Lauder. **Career Steps:** Executive Director of Research and Development, Estee Lauder (1989–Present); Director Research and Development, Elizabeth Arden, Inc., (1988–1989); Manager, Research and Development, Avon Products, Inc., (1980–1988). **Associations & Accomplishments:** Society of Cosmetic Chemists; Junior Football League Coach. **Education:** University of Bridgeport, B.S. in Chemistry, cum laude, (1978) **Personal:** Married to Mary in 1979. Two children: Alexander J. and Marina R. Mr. Zecchino enjoys golf.

Michael Barto

Director of Sales
Sherwin–Williams Diversified Brands
31500 Solon Road
Solon, OH 44139–3528
(216) 498–6077
Fax: (216) 519–6696

2851

Business Information: Sherwin–Williams Diversified Brands, a division of Sherwin Williams, is a manufacturer and distributor of aerosol coatings (i.e., Krylon) and paint applicators. As Director of Sales, Mr. Barto manages all sales to hardware and craft segments of distribution. **Career Steps:** Sherwin Williams Diversified Brands: Director of Sales (1995–Present), National Sales Manager (1994–1995); National Accounts Manager (1993–1994); Sales Representative, Klesman Associates (1990–1993). **Associations & Accomplishments:** Central States Hardware Association; Circle of Excellence (1994); Champions Club Winner (1995); Vendor of the Year (1994); Vendor of the Year (1995). **Education:** DePaul University, M.B.A. (1994); Northern Illinois University, B.A. (1989). **Personal:** Mr. Barto enjoys waterskiing, golf, and riding motorcycles.

Wayne A. Clanton

President and Chief Executive Officer
Spartan Color Corporation
5803 Northdale Street
Houston, TX 77087–6448
(713) 644–1964
Fax: (713) 644–3469

2851

Business Information: Spartan Color Corporation is a manufacturer of color concentrates for the coatings and plastics industry. With twenty years of sales experience in the color industry and nineteen years experience in marketing, Mr. Clanton joined Spartan Color Corporation as Vice President and Director of Marketing in 1976. Appointed as President and Chief Executive Officer in 1995, he is responsible for all aspects of executive operations, as well as the sales efforts and continuing education of agents throughout the U.S. **Career Steps:** Spartan Color Corporation: President and Chief Executive Officer (1995–Present), Vice President and Marketing Director (1976–1995); Technical Sales Representative, Sun Chemical Corporation (1968–1976); Technical Sales Representative, Inmont Corporation (1955–1968). **Associations & Accomplishments:** Various positions in paint and coatings related associations; Society of Plastic Engineers. **Education:** University of Arkansas at Monticello (UAM), B.S. in Chemistry (1955). **Personal:** Married to Ora K. in 1952. Four children: Timothy D., David A., Mark A., and Mrs. Cathy C. Clanton Reeves, Ph.D. Mr. Clanton enjoys fishing, golf, and gardening.

Antonio Echeverria–Parres

Director General
Empresa AGA, S.A. de C.V.
Km.2.5 Carr. Tepotzotlan Las Cabanan
Tepotzotlan, Mexico 54600
(525) 876–0077
Fax: (525) 876–0077

2851

Business Information: Empresa AGA, S.A. de C.V., a subsidiary of Grupo Comex, is a national manufacturer and international marketer of paint and wall coverings. Future plans include opening markets in Europe. Established in 1976, Empresa AGA currently employs 300 people. As Director General, Mr. Echeverria–Parres is responsible for all aspects of operations of the plant, including strategic planning. **Career Steps:** Director General, Empresa AGA, S.A. de C.V. (1992–Present); Plant Director, Comercial Mex. de Pint. (Comex) (1990–1992); Senior Associate, Booz, Allen & Hamilton (1989–1990); Corporated Planning Manager, Du Pont (1976–1989). **Associations & Accomplishments:** Club de Casa Tiro y Pesca Ferrocarrilero Del Valle de Mexico; Club Casa Blanca San Angel; Club de Golf San Carlos. **Education:** Universidad Iberoamericana, Engineer (1976). **Personal:** Married to Ma. de Los Angeles in 1970. Three children: Jose Antonio, Jose Maria, and Inigo. Mr. Echeverria–Parres enjoys hunting, racqetball, cars, golf, and snowskiing.

Abraham Frem Naranjo

Business Manager
AnylMex S.A. C.V.
Rio Lerma No. 32, Fracc. Ind. Tlaxcolpan
Tlalnepantla Edo. DE, Mexico 54030
5–565–71–65
Fax: 5–565–29–65

2851

Business Information: AnlyMex S.A. C.V. provides the commercialization of textile dyes. Joining AnylMex as a Sales Representative in 1990, Mr. Frem Naranjo was appointed as Business Manager in 1992. He is responsible for all operations and sales for the business. **Career Steps:** AnylMex S.A. C.V.: Business Manager (1992–Present), Sales Representative (1990–1992). **Associations & Accomplishments:** Aniq (Mexican Chemical Industry Association). **Education:** ITAM, M.B.A. (1994); IPN, Chemical Engineer. **Personal:** Married to Berenice Arreola in 1993. One child: Abraham. Mr. Frem Naranjo enjoys tennis, theatre, and spending time with his family.

Herbert Hack

Head of Corporate Marketing
Mann u Hummel, Germany
Hindenburg #45
Ludwigsburg, Germany 71638
49–7141–982220
Fax: 49–7141–982650

2851

Business Information: Mann u Hummel, Germany is a manufacturer of a variety of filters and material handling systems. The Corporate Marketing Department is responsible for all subsidiaries and licenses around the world. The Department is involved in technical service, general management, and controlling the subsidiaries. Mr. Hack, a strategic planning specialist, sets up studies on strategic marketing worldwide. He is responsible for integrating functions from the automobile division, industrial filters division, and various other divisions. **Career Steps:** Mann u Hummel: Head of Corporate Marketing – Germany (1990–Present), Sales Manager of Automotive Division – Germany (1990), Chief Executive Officer – Austria (1980–1990). **Education:** FH – Esslingen, Dipl. GH (1962). **Personal:** Mr. Hack enjoys motorbikes and sailing.

Ronald L. Hayden, P.E.

Industrial Sales Manager
Devoe Coatings Company
2701 South 163rd Street
New Berlin, WI 53151
(414) 789–6950
Fax: (414) 786–0466

2851

Business Information: Devoe Coatings Company, a subsidiary of ICI, is a manufacturer and marketer of high performance coatings (industrial coatings). International in scope, Devoe distributes its products in the U.S.directly from two plant locations in California and New Jersey. Other subsidiaries include Glidden and Fuller–O'Brien. Working in various engineering and managerial roles for Devoe since 1983, Ronald Hayden has held his current position since 1995. As Industrial Sales Manager, he is responsible for the management of the sales and technical services within the mid–central U.S. region. Duties include marketing, hiring, budgeting, and supervision of personnel. **Career Steps:** Devoe Coatings Company: Industrial Sales Manager (1995–Present), District Manager (1988–1995), Senior Corrosion Engineer (1983–1988). **Associations & Accomplishments:** Society of Naval Architects and Marine Engineers; National Association of Corrosion Engineers. **Education:** Ryerson Polytec, B.S. in Civil Engineering (1979); University of Akron, B.S.B.A. in Industrial Management and Economics (1966). **Personal:** Married to Terry in 1979. Mr. Hayden enjoys reading, golf, woodworking, antique collecting and charity work.

Tom Jones

Corporate Environmental Manager
Dunn–Edwards Corporation
4885 East 52nd Place
Los Angeles, CA 90040–2828
(800) 733–3866 Ext. 2240
Fax: (213) 771–4440

2851

Business Information: Dunn–Edwards Corporation is a manufacturer and distributor of fine architectural and industrial finishes throughout the Southwestern United States. Products include paints, lacquers, painting equipment, brushes, and tools. With corporate headquarters located in Los Angeles, California, Dunn–Edwards has forty locations in California, seven in Arizona, and two in Nevada. As Corporate Environmental Manager, Mr. Jones is responsible for ensuring that the Corporation is in environmental compliance with local, state, and federal laws and regulations. **Career Steps:** Dunn Edwards Corporation: Corporate Environmental Manager (1992–Present), Technical Sales Coordinator (1987–1992), Store Sales (1978–1987), Store Driver (1976–1978). **Associations & Accomplishments:** National Fire Protection Association; Certified Incident Commander; Member of California Water Enviroment Association. Featured Speaker at Industrial and Hazardous Waste Conference, February 13, 1996. **Personal:** One child: Devin Jones. Mr. Jones enjoys photography, scuba diving, flying aircraft, and listening to music.

William M. Perry

Plant Manager
Sherwin–Williams Company
11541 South Champlain Avenue
Chicago, IL 60628
(312) 821–3445
Fax: (312) 264–4632

2851

Business Information: Sherwin–Williams Company, a Fortune 200 Company, is a major manufacturer of paint products. A twenty–eight year veteran of Sherwin–Williams, Mr. Perry joined the Company as a Chemist in 1967. In his current role as Plant Manager of the Chicago manufacturing plants, he is responsible for all aspects of management and operations of two plants and their staff. **Career Steps:** Sherwin–Williams Company: Plant Manager (1993–Present), Chemical Coatings Marketing Manager (1991–1993), Plant Manager of Chicago Emulsion (1980–1991); Manager of Production–Resin–Engineering and Quality Assurance, Newark, NJ (1972–1980); Chemist, Morrow, GA Plant (1967–1972). **Associations & Accomplishments:** Calumet Area Industrial Commission; Illinois Manufacturers Association; Chicago Chamber of Commerce. **Education:** Georgia Institute of Technology, B.S. in Chemistry (1967). **Personal:** Married to Midge S. in 1961. Two children: Kelly and Judy. Mr. Perry enjoys scuba diving and flying.

Denver C. Richmond

Regional Sales Manager
Scott Paint Corporation
7839 Fruitville Road
Sarasota, FL 34240
(941) 371–0015
Fax: (941) 378–2887

2851

Business Information: Scott Paint Corporation is a family–owned household paint manufacturer and distributor. Established in 1965, the Corporation currently employs 220 people and has 18 locations on the Florida Gulf Coast. As Regional Sales Manager, Mr. Richmond is in charge of sales and store personnel for his region. He recruits store personnel, evaluates performance, and counsels employees on performance. Mr. Richmond is responsible for developing marketing techniques and strategies for new and existing products in his area. **Career Steps:** Regional Sales Manager, Scott Paint Corporation (1991–Present); Manager, Gulfstream Coatings (1988–1991); Sales Representative, DPI Paints (1983–1988). **Associations & Accomplishments:** Masonic Lodge; Pasco Builders Association; Citrus Builders Association; Hilsboro Builders Association; Kentucky Colonel; N.R.A.; Veterans of Foreign Wars. **Education:** G.M. Management College (1983); Pasco–Hernando Community College, A.S. degree; Management Seminars; Miscellaneous Schools and Locations. **Personal:** Married to Melinda in 1968. One child: Kari Milhollen and two grandsons Mychal and Mitchel. Mr. Richmond enjoys fishing, yard work, and antique shopping with his wife.

Barbara W. Waddell

President
Kansas Paint and Color Co., Inc.
132 North Mosley
Wichita, KS 67202
(316) 264–6353
Fax: (316) 262–7221

2851

Business Information: Kansas Paint and Color Company, Inc. specializes in the manufacture of industrial coatings for original equipment manufacturers and the aircraft industry. Established in 1917, Kansas Paint and Color currently employs 30 people and has an estimated annual revenue of $4 million. As President, Ms. Waddell is responsible for all aspects of operations and sales. **Career Steps:** Kansas Paint and Color Company, Inc.: President (1995–Present), Vice President (1981–1995), Laboratory Assistant (1980–1981), Clerk (1978–1980). **Associations & Accomplishments:** National Paint and Coatings Association; National Federation of Independent Business; U.S. Chamber of Commerce; Kansas Chamber of Commerce; Wichita Junior League; Sustaining Member, Central Christian Church; Domestic Violence Task Force for the City of Wichita; Former Secretary, Meadowlark Pony Club; Train and organize 50 to 100 volunteers twice a year for a United States Combined Training recognized Horse Trial. **Education:** University of Kansas, B.S. (1971). **Personal:** One child: Rebecca L. Ms. Waddell enjoys her daughter, and her daughter's involvement in horses, which has turned her free time into helping to organize horse shows and to promote the sport, especially among youngsters.

David White

Vice President
Cardinal Color, Inc.
50–56 First Avenue
Paterson, NJ 07514–2029
(201) 684–1919
Fax: (201) 684–0865

2851

Business Information: Cardinal Color, Inc. is a manufacturer of color dispersions for the paint, plastics, and ink industries. They also manufacture special dispersions for other industries. Established in 1976, Cardinal Color, Inc. reports annual revenue of $10 million and currently employs 35 people. With 17 years expertise in the paint industry, Mr. White originally joined Cardinal Color in 1985 (working for a year) and returned in 1992 as Vice President. He oversees all aspects of operations of the Research and Quality Control Department, as well as management of the national sales force and conducting sales calls. **Career Steps:** Cardinal Color, Inc.: Vice President (1992–Present), Quality Control Manager (1985–1986); Plant Manager, North American Paint (1986–1992); Production, Hawthorne Paint (1978–1985). **Associations & Accomplishments:** Chairman for Manufacturing Committee, New York Society for Coatings Technology; Pi Kappa Phi Fraternity; Recipient, Bill Harrison Memorial Award; Member, American Institute of Chemical Engineers (AICHE) (1984). **Education:** New Jersey Institute of Technology, B.S. in Chemical Engineering (1984). **Personal:** Mr. White enjoys sports and oil painting.

Patricia S. Barron

Controller
NuTech Environmental Corporation
5350 Washington Street
Denver, CO 80216–1951
(303) 442–5783
Fax: Please mail or call

2869

Business Information: NuTech Environmental Corporation is an innovative vapor phase technologies and systems developer. With the increase in the population density, the lands surrounding the odorous facilities have been developed. This has created the need for effective odor control, which NuTech Environmental Corporation provides. NuTech was incorporated in May of 1982 and is one of a number of affiliated companies owned and operated by the Heller family. Since 1982, NuTech has been working to refine it's vapor phase chemical neutralization process as well as develop a simple and reliable line of economical application equipment. It is their mission to provide practical, cost effective alternatives for low intensity nuisance type odor problems that can be solved without the high expense of conventional wet scrubbing systems. The primary areas where NuTech's products and systems can be used are as follows: collection system pumping stations and vented manholes, small treatment plants headworks, septic receiving areas, large treatment plants headworks, sludge composting and high pH sludge stabilization operations, solid waste recycling operations and as alternative liquids for any existing air scrubbers used in the above areas. As Controller, Ms. Barron is in charge of cash management for the corporation. She manages the daily operations of her department, to include accounting, marketing, personnel concerns, product inventory, purchasing, and equipment production. NuTech's production and sales of equipment has increased 40% over the past three years due to the efforts of Ms. Barrow in these areas. **Career Steps:** Controller, NuTech Environmental Corporation (1993–Present); Vice President, Missouri Holdings Corporation (1990–1993); Executive Director, Hubbard Dianetics Foundation (1986–1989); Head Bookkeeper, Dueck Development (1984–1985). **Education:** Colorado Women's College, Studies in Business and Accounting (1979); Hubbard Management Technology (1986–1989). **Personal:** Married to Robert in 1989. Five children: Timothy, Andrea, Joshua, Anthony, and Samuel. Ms. Barron enjoys sewing and staying active with her children's education and activities.

Ronald Baur, Ph.D.

President
SETA Industrial S/A – Baur–Consult
Rua Sampaio Vidal 235
Sao Paulo, Brazil 01443
(011)282.60.32
Fax: (011)282.60.32

2869

Business Information: SETA Industrial S/A – Baur–Consult maintains facilities engaged in the extraction of tanin powder from trees for use in waterproofing leather. Established in 1941, it is the largest company of its kind in the world, exporting to twenty–five countries worldwide and providing the first environmentally–friendly, natural waterproofing product for leather. As President, Dr. Baur is responsible for daily operations, administrative functions, public relations, personnel coordination, and providing executive leadership. **Career Steps:** President, SETA Industrial S/A – Baur–Consult (1975–Present); Marketing Director, Andritz–Ruthner Ltda. (1975–1980); Marketing Director, Ingersoll–Rand (1968–1975); Technical Director, Manasa–Madeireir Nacional (1965–1975). **Associations & Accomplishments:** Rotary Club; Vdi Verein Deutscher Ingenieure; Terein Deutscher; Papier Ingenieure Kothen–Munchen; Schlaraffia. **Education:** Polytecknikum–Munchen, Dipl.ing. (1952); USP – Sao Paulo, Ph.D. in Philosophy. **Personal:** Married to Anna Maria in 1953. Three children: Mariza, Annaluiza and Myriam. Dr. Baur is a singer, pianist, and director of a sporting club.

Lorin Ben Bradley

Human Resource Manager
A.B.B. Combustion Engineering Nuclear Operations
3300 State Road P.
Hematite, MO 63047
(314) 937–4691 Ext. 423
Fax: (314) 937–7308

2869

Business Information: A.B.B. Combustion Engineering Nuclear Operations is a manufacturer of nuclear fuel, provides power generation and transfer, engineering services, and power plant support. As Human Resource Manager of the Fuel Operations Business Unit, Mr. Bradley handles all employee relations, labor issues, and corporate development. **Career Steps:** Human Resource Manager, A.B.B. Combustion Engineering Nuclear Operations (1994–Present); Staff Human Resource Representative, Appleton Papers, Inc. (1993–1994); Compensation Administrator, Dow Chemical Company (1990–1993). **Associations & Accomplishments:** Society of Human Resource Management; American Management Association; American Society for Training and Development; Associated Industries of Missouri; Boy Scouts of America; Volunteer, YMCA of Jefferson County; United Way Volunteer. **Education:** Michigan State University, M.L.I.R. (1990); Central Michigan University, M.S.A. (1992); Saginaw Valley State University, B.A. (1989); Certified Senior Professional Human Resources (1995). **Personal:** Married to Ginny in 1986. Five children: Meaghan, Kaitlin, Ben, Aaron, and Kirstin. Mr. Bradley enjoys all sports.

Charles (Bill) W. Bray

Senior Cost Engineer
Dow Chemical/Stubbs
400 West Sam Houston Parkway
Houston, TX 77042–1299
(713) 978–2473
Fax: (713) 821–0407
E MAIL: See Below

2869

Business Information: Dow Chemical/Stubbs, a division of Dow Chemical Corporation, is a refinery and petrochemical engineering, construction and manufacturing firm. As Senior Cost Engineer, Mr. Bray has over ten years of experience in the area of controlling, reviewing, and analyzing the flow of funds for each assigned project. Internet users can reach him via: CWB@GNN.COM **Career Steps:** Senior Cost Engineer, Dow Chemical/Stubbs (1996–Present); Senior Projects Controls Manager, Stone & Webster Engineering Company (1992–1996); Senior Project Controls Manager, Jacobs Engineering/Davy McKee (1980–1992). **Associations & Accomplishments:** Treasurer, Sunbury Estates Homeowners Association; Institute of Electronics and Electrical Engineers; ISA: Several Honor Societies. **Education:** University of Houston, Finance (to be completed 1997). **Personal:** Married to Becky in 1984. Two children: Kari and Meghan. Mr. Bray enjoys computers, international finances, and special olympics.

Gustavo Adolfo Cano

Chief Engineer
Quimica Amtex S.A., C.V.
Av. De Las Palmas, #415, Col. Lomas de Chapultepec
Mexico City, Mexico 11000
72–875031
Fax: 72–875229

2869

Business Information: Quimica Amtex S.A., C.V. is a producer and international distributor of carbon methyl cellulose (CMC) used in the manufacture of such consumer food and health products as mayonnaise, toothpaste and petroleum additives. Products are distributed throughout Colombia, Peru and Brazil. Future plans include expanding to England and Japan. Established in 1976, Quimica Amtex S.A., C.V. reports annual revenue of $4 million in U.S. dollars and currently employs 160 people. In his current capacity, Gustavo Cano oversees all operational areas of the Engineering Department and the supervision of maintenance engineers and staff. **Career Steps:** Chief Engineer, Quimica Amtex S.A., C.V. (1992–Present); Administrative Manager, Representaciones COLON (1992); Maintenance Chief, Country Club Medellin (1991–1992); Mechanical/Electrical Chief, Colombian Navy (1985–1990). **Associations & Accomplishments:** Bitacora, Retired Naval Officers Association in Colombia; School of Mechanical and Electrical Engineers of Mexico (CIME). **Education:** Naval School Colombia, Naval Engineer (1985); Bell and Hughes Helicopters Maintenance, Colombian Air Force; Total Productive Maintenance; American Management Association – Mexico. **Personal:** Married to Ana Rocio Arango in 1993. Mr. Cano enjoys music, soccer, and collecting stamps & coins.

Dr. George August Freibott IV

Chief Executive Officer
IOP Technologies, Ltd.
300 South 4th Street, Suite 1111
Las Vegas, NV 89101
(208) 448–2504
Fax: (208) 448–2657

2869

Business Information: IOP Technologies, Ltd. is an international organization of oxidative companies. As Chief Executive Officer, Dr. Freibott provides the overall vision and strategy for the company, ensuring quality product output, customer satisfaction and the effective techniques to keep the company a viable presence in the international market. With over twenty years in the industry, Dr. Freibott is also an esteemed Chemist, Physician and Priest. **Career Steps:** Chief Executive Officer, IOP Technologies, Ltd. (1994–Present); Consultant/Chemist, International Association for Oxygen Therapy (1974–1994); Consultant, American Society of Medical Missionaries (1974–1994). **Associations & Accomplishments:** American Chemical Society; American Society of Metals; American Naturopathic Association; International Tesla Society; International Plateform Association. **Education:** Southern Carter Institute, Paralegal (1993). **Personal:** Seven children: Joel, Solomon, Bethiah, Jessica, Heather, George, and Rachel. Dr. Freibott enjoys material sciences and Bible history.

Richard G. Ivan
Controller and Project Director
Dow Chemical Company
214 West Wackerly Street
Midland, MI 48674
(517) 636–5381
Fax: (517) 638–9805

2869

Business Information: Dow Chemical Company is one of the world's largest chemical manufacturing companies. Among its products are pharmaceuticals, agricultural chemicals, consumer products, and liquid membranes. Dow has 190 locations in the United States, Japan, Canada, Mexico, South America and other areas. Joining Dow Chemical in 1970, Mr. Ivan was appointed as Controller and Project Director in 1993. He is responsible for all financial matters, and direction of projects for the Global Accounting Systems. **Career Steps:** Dow Chemical Company: Controller and Project Director (1993–Present); Project Manager (1989–1993); Division Controller (1985–1989); Various Accounting Assignments – Michigan Division (1970–1985). **Associations & Accomplishments:** America's SAP User Groups; ASUG RW Focus Group. **Education:** University of Michigan, B.B.A. (1970). **Personal:** Married to Sandra in 1969. Three children: Keri, Marnie, and Tim. Mr. Ivan enjoys photography, model trains, and golf.

David L. Moss
Controller
Unichema International
4650 South Racine Avenue
Chicago, IL 60610
(312) 650–7610
Fax: (312) 376–0095

2869

Business Information: Unichema International produces and markets specialty chemicals, including fatty acids, glycerine, and esters. As Controller, Mr. Moss is responsible for handling finances, accounting, and fiscal management activities. **Career Steps:** Controller, Unichema International (1995–Present); Project Management Accountant, Quest International – Chicago (1994–1995); Management Accountant, Quest International – Holland (1993–1994); Management Trainee, Quest International – England (1992–1993). **Associations & Accomplishments:** CIMA. **Education:** University of Virginia, B.S. (1991). **Personal:** Married to Jane Waterman in 1995. Mr. Moss enjoys tennis, golf, skiing, and sailing.

Dennis A. Nadane

Dow North America Supply Chain Manager
Dow Chemical Company
2020 Dow Center
Midland, MI 48674–0001
(517) 636–3915
Fax: (517) 636–4500

2869

Business Information: Dow Chemical Company is one of the world's largest chemical manufacturing companies. Among their products are pharmaceuticals, agricultural chemicals and consumer products. The Company has locations in the United States, Japan, Canada, Mexico, South America and other areas. Established in the 1890's, Dow Chemical reports annual revenue of $20 billion and currently employs 50,000 people. As Dow North America Supply Chain Manager for the Chemicals & Metals Division, Mr. Nadane is responsible for distribution of vinyl chloride monomer, annhydrous hydrochloric acid and aqueous hydrochloric acid throughout the North American region. Joining Dow in 1976 as a chemical engineer, he was appointed to his current position in 1995. **Career Steps:** Dow Chemical Company: Dow North America Supply Chain Manager (1995–Present), Operations Planning Associate (1993–1995), Materials Management Supervisor (1989–1993). **Education:** University of Saskatchewan, Saskatoon, SK., Canada, B.E. in Chemical Engineering (1976). **Personal:** Married to Darlene C. Nadane in 1977. Two children: Alisha Dawn and Amy Alexandra Nadane. Mr. Nadane enjoys golf, fishing, and travel.

Dr. Don O'Shaughnessy
Manager of Product Registration
Terra International
600 Fourth St.
Sioux City, IA 51102–6000
(712) 233–3611
Fax: (712) 233–5506
EMAIL: See Below

2873

Business Information: Terra International, Inc., one of the largest agricultural distributors in the U.S., is an international manufacturer of fertilizer and formulator of pesticides. The Corporation incorporates farm inputs on fertilizers, pesticides, adjuvants, and seeds, in addition to providing precision agriculture/crop consulting. Products are distributed throughout the U.S., Canada, and Mexico. As Manager of Product Registration, Dr. O'Shaughnessy interacts with the EPA, Health Canada, data task forces, and industry associations to ensure regulatory compliance. He may be reached through the Internet via: HiDQE@A0L.COM **Career Steps:** Manager of Product Registration, Terra International (1993–Present); Regulatory Affairs Manager, Zeneca Agro (Canada) (1986–1993); Senior Scientist, Bio–Research Labs, Ltd. (1981–1986); Electron Microscopist, McGill University, Biochemistry (1979–1981); Research Fellow, Experimental Neurosurgery, Montreal Neurological Institute. **Associations & Accomplishments:** Diplomate, American Board of Toxicology; Diplomate, American Board of Forensic Examiners; Society of Toxicology; American Society for Investigative Pathology; Society of Toxicology of Canada; Patron, American Association for the Advancement of Science **Education:** Columbia Pacific University, Ph.D. (1982); McGill University, M.Sc. (1977), B.Sc. (1975) **Personal:** Married to Colette in 1976. Two children: Megan and Breandan. Dr. O'Shaughnessy enjoys collecting and restoring antique fountain pens.

Jo Ann Doherty

Controller
Vigoro Corporation
225 North Michigan Avenue, Suite 2500
Chicago, IL 60601–7601
(312) 819–2031
Fax: (312) 819–2027

2875

Business Information: Vigoro Corporation, a Fortune 500 company, is one of the world's largest manufacturers and distributor of fertilizers and related products. They specialize in industrial sales, export and import wholesale to farmers, and private–label consumer blends. A Certified Public Accountant since 1989, Ms. Doherty joined Vigoro in 1993 as Director of Accounting. Promoted to Controller in April 1996, she is presently responsible for all accounting, financial reporting, and planning for the consolidated company and corporate office. **Career Steps:** Vigoro Corporation: Controller (1996–Present), Director of Accounting (1993–1996); Senior Accountant, Great American Management (1991–1992). **Associations & Accomplishments:** American Institute of Certified Public Accountants; American Management Association; Illinois Certified Public Accountant Society. **Education:** Southern Illinois University at Carbondale: B.S. in Accounting, B.S. in Finance (1987); Certified Public Accountant, Illinois (1989). **Personal:** Married to James P. in 1991. One child: Robert J. Ms. Doherty enjoys spending time with her family.

Carlos Antonio Albert
• • • ◉ • • •

General Manager
ISK Biosciences
Av 9 de Julho, 5617–8 Andar J.D. Paulista
Sao Paulo, Brazil 01407–912
55–11–883–5899
Fax: 55–11–486–0298

2879

Business Information: ISK Biosciences manufactures and distributes agricultural chemicals throughout Latin America. A division of Japan–based Ishihara Sangyo Kaisha, the Brazilian operation began in 1983 and presently employs 30 people. As General Manager, Mr. Albert is responsible for the administration of all Company activities in Brazil, Uruguay, and Paraguay. Other responsibilities include public relations, financial concerns, budgetary matters, and strategic planning for expansion of his region. Before starting work for private companies, Mr. Albert was Head of the Sugarcane Pests and Diseases Control division for the Ministry of Agriculture in Brazil. **Career Steps:** General Manager, ISK Biosciences (1983–Present); Monsanto: Director of Agriculture Division (1969–1982), Latin America Product Development (1974–1978); Regional Manager, GEIGY (1966–1969). **Associations & Accomplishments:** Director, National Crop Protection Association (Brazil); Consulting Committee, Bra-

zilian Crop Protection Industry Syndicate; Sao Paulo Agronomist Association; Former Director, Brazilian Herbicide Society. **Education:** Kansas State University, M.S. (1958); Rural University of Permambuco, B.S. Agricultural Sciences. **Personal:** Married to Cristina in 1976. Four children: Ana Tereza, Silvia Augusta, Henrique, and Lucia Helena. Mr. Albert enjoys reading, theater, volleyball, dogs, and jogging.

William R. Collins
• • • ◄▬ ◉ ▬► • • •

President and Owner
C&S Fertilizer & Chemicals, Inc.
4825 Bourbon Road
Muscotah, KS 66058
(913) 872–3762
Fax: (913) 872–3764

2879

Business Information: C&S Fertilizer & Chemicals, Inc. provides a full scope of agricultural pesticide products and crop fertilization services. As President and Owner, Mr. Collins oversees all operations, providing the overall vision and strategies to ensure quality customer relations and service. **Career Steps:** President and Owner, C&S Fertilizer & Chemicals, Inc. (1993–Present); Operations Manager, Brown County Coop (1967–1993); Manager, Boos Fertilizer & Chemicals (1960–1967). **Associations & Accomplishments:** KFCA; Commissioner City Hiawatha. **Personal:** Married to Mary M. in 1965. Four children: Stacy, Shelly, Tammy, and Billy Jr.. Mr. Collins enjoys fishing, golf, and music.

Margaret C. Gadsby
Director of Scientific and Regulatory Affairs
Agr Evo Canada, Inc.
295 Henderson Drive
Regina, Saskatchewan S4N 6C2
(306) 721–4532
Fax: (306) 721–3555

2879

Business Information: Agr Evo Canada, Inc. researches, develops, and sells crop protection products (i.e. herbicides, insecticides, and fungicides), as well as crop production tools (i.e. herbicide tolerant canola) to agricultural industries and individuals worldwide. The first company in Canada to obtain clearance for the selling of a plant with the novel trait for commercial production, the Company employs 187 people. As Director of Scientific and Regulatory Affairs, Ms. Gadsby is responsible for registration of products in Canada and development of environmental, consumer, and safety data. Additional duties include obtaining proper clearances to market products in Canada, ensuring compliance with federal and government regulations, performing research, and managing consumer and worker safety. Her EMail address is available upon request. **Career Steps:** Agr Evo Canada, Inc: Director of Scientific and Regulatory Affairs (1995–Present), Manager, Scientific and Regulatory Affairs (1992); Manager, Environmental Affairs, Hoechst Canada, Inc. (1990). **Associations & Accomplishments:** Board of Directors, Industrial Biotechnology Association of Canada; Professional Agrologist; Registered In–House Corporate Lobbyist. **Education:** University of British Columbia, M.Sc. (1983); McMaster University, B.Sc. With Honors (1978). **Personal:** Married.

Marisol Chamorro Garcia
Assistant Controller
Ochoa Fertilizer Company, Inc.
269 Calle C Urb Constancia
Ponce, Puerto Rico 00731–6541
(787) 821–2200
Fax: (787) 821–2420

2879

Business Information: Ochoa Fertilizer Company, Inc. is a manufacturer of blended fertilizers for the agricultural industry. The Company is also a distributor of pesticides, wire, and irrigation products. As an Assistant Controller, Ms. Chamorro has oversight of all the accounting department, monthly and year–end financial statement and analysis, cash flow projections, tax issues, internal controls and support to a sister company in Jamaica, as required. **Career Steps:** Assistant Controller, Ochoa Fertilizer Company, Inc. (1995–Present); Auditor, Deloitte & Touche; In Charge Auditor, Castro, Manfredy, Cales & Company. **Associations & Accomplishments:** Certified Public Accountants Association; Ms. Chamorro was nominated to represent Puerto Rico in the National Young Leaders conference in Washington in 1988. **Education:** University of Puerto Rico, B.B.A. Magna Cum Laude (1992); Certified Public Accountant (1994). **Personal:** Married to Eladio Luciano in 1994. Ms. Chamorro enjoys writing essays and short stories.

Mr. Robert H. Lindemann
Western Regional Development Manager
Valent U.S.A. Corporation
7106 North Brawley Avenue
Fresno, CA 93711
(209) 244–3960
Fax: (209) 228–2019

2879

Business Information: Valent U.S.A. Corporation markets and distributes plant protection materials (e.g. insecticides) to dealers and distributors in the U.S. and Mexico. Established in 1989, the corporation currently employs 275 professionals. As Western Development Manager, Mr. Lindemann is responsible for the management and direction of the technical service staff serving in the Western section of the U.S. **Career Steps:** Valent U.S.A. Corporation, Western Development Manager (1994–Present), Field Program Manager (1989–1994); Western Technical Manager, Chevron Chemical Company (1986–1989). **Associations & Accomplishments:** California Weed Society; Western Weed Society; North Central Weed Society; Pacific Branch – Entomological Society of America; Entomological Society of America. **Education:** Rutgers University, M.S. in Crops and Soils (1973); Delaware Valley College, B.S. in Agronomy (1969). **Personal:** Married to Pamela in 1969. Two children: Kurt S. and Chad E.. Mr. Lindemann enjoys gardening, computers and outdoor activities.

Joseph M. Pluskota
Operations Manager
Motomco Ltd.
29 North Fort Harrison Avenue
Clearwater, FL 34165–4016
(800) 237–6843
Fax: (800) 966–2248

2879

Business Information: Motomco Ltd. is a national manufacturer and marketer of Rodenticides under the trade names: Hawk, Tomcat, Rampage, and Eraze. Established in 1982, Motomco LTD markets throughout the continental U.S. as well as their international markets in England and Latin America. As Operations Manager, Mr. Pluskota is responsible for direct marketing, customer service, telemarketing, administration, sales, technical and business presentations, and market research. **Career Steps:** Operations Manager, Motomco Ltd. (1994–Present); Operations Manager, A&M Supply/Vector Industries (1988–1994); United States Coast Guard, Honorable Discharge: Maritime Law Enforcement, Search and Rescue (1982–1986). **Associations & Accomplishments:** American Management Association; Jian Professional Management Association; National Eagle Scout Association of the Boy Scouts of America. **Education:** Marquette University, B.A. in Business Administration (1982). **Personal:** Married to Donna M. in 1991. Mr. Pluskota enjoys the tropical outdoors, dogs, gardening, rehabilitating injured wildlife, remodeling old homes, and spending time with his wife, Donna.

Minoru Takano
• • •━━◖◉◗━━• • •

Finance Director
Iharabras South America Inds. Quims
Avenida Liberdade, 1.701–B1.B
Sorocaba, Brazil
(0152) 25–1744
Fax: (0152) 25–2773

2879

Business Information: Iharabras South America Inds. Quims is a manufacturer and marketer of agricultural pesticides, exporting to Argentina, Uruguay, Chile, Bolivia, Vietnam, and the Far East. As Finance Director, Mr. Takano serves as Controller, managing all financial aspects of daily operations. **Career Steps:** Finance Director, Iharabras South America Inds. Quims (1993–Present); Managing Director, Cooperative Agricola De Cotia (1990–1992); Managing Director, BV Handelmij Bel Agro–Holland (1966–1972). **Associations & Accomplishments:** Economists Society of Sao Paulo; Association of Diplomats of the Guerra Superior School of Sao Paulo; Brazilian Society of Japanese Culture; Society of Nipo–Brazilian Benefits. **Education:** Bachelor of Economics (1964); Future Market of Commodities, Merril Lynch – New York (1974); Marketing and Design of Package, Sao Paulo. **Personal:** Married to Seiko in 1961. Two children: Halley Iuji Takano and Fanny Takano Contart. Mr. Takano enjoys golf, tennis, jogging, reading, and movies. He also speaks English, Spanish, Dutch, Portuguese, and Japanese.

Shari N. Terry
Site Controller
Sandoz Agro Inc.
Route 4 Box 327
Beaumont, TX 77705–9789
(409) 720–5054
Fax: (409) 720–5193

2879

Business Information: Sandoz Agro Inc. is an international manufacturer of agricultural chemicals and herbicides. With more than fifteen years of experience in accounting, Ms. Terry joined Sandoz Agro, Inc. as Site Controller in 1988. She is responsible for the management of all financial and accounting functions at the Beaumont facility. **Career Steps:** Site Controller, Sandoz Agro Inc. (1988–Present); Accounting Manager, M&I Electric Industries (1982–1988); Cost Accountant, Dresser Ideco (1981–1982). **Associations & Accomplishments:** National Association of Female Executives; Phi Kappa Phi Honor Fraternity. **Education:** McNeese State University, B.S. (1979). **Personal:** Married to Stephen in 1994. Ms. Terry enjoys sewing.

Vernon W. Webb
Controller
Bengal Chemical, Inc.
13739 Airline Highway
Baton Rouge, LA 70817–5924
(504) 753–1313
Fax: (504) 753–1464

2879

Business Information: Bengal Chemical, Inc. is a manufacturer of consumer pesticides. With thirteen years experience in auditing, Mr. Webb joined Bengal Chemical, Inc. in 1994. Serving as Controller, he is responsible for all financial operations. **Career Steps:** Controller, Bengal Chemical, Inc. (1994–Present); Internal Audit, Cajun Electric Power (1991–1994); Auditor, Faulk & Winkler (1989–1990); Auditor, Hawthorn, Waymouth & Carroll (1982–1989). **Associations & Accomplishments:** Port Allen Chapter – Rotary International: Sustaining Member, Rotarian of the Year, Former President; Secretary, Lions Club; Charter Member, West Baton Rouge Chamber of Commerce; Cubmaster; LCPA Strategic Planning; Chairman, West Baton Rouge Stadium Committee; Deacon, First Baptist Church Port Allen; Former President, Baton Rouge Kids' Baseball Clinic. **Education:** Southeastern Louisiana University, B.S. (1982). **Personal:** Married to Martha in 1982. Two children: Sam and Rebecca. Mr. Webb enjoys farming and reading.

Mark L. Dodge
Plant Manager
Avery Dennison
250 Chester St.
Painesville, OH 44077–4118
(216) 639–2646
Fax: (216) 639–2683

2891

Business Information: Established in 1935, Avery Dennison is a manufacturer of pressure sensitive adhesive tapes. The Company currently employs 450 people and has estimated annual sales of $115K. Mr. Dodge began his career with Avery Dennison in 1970 upon graduation from high school, and has worked his way through the Company to his current position, Plant Manager. As Plant Manager, Mr. Dodge is responsible for diversified administrative activities and operations, including team meetings, and paper work. **Career Steps:** Avery Dennison: Plant Manger (1992–Present), Production Manager (1989–92), Plant Superintendent (1986–89). **Personal:** Married to Bonita in 1992. Four children: Trisha, Brian, Rusty, and Lisa. Mr. Dodge enjoys softball, golf, bowling, and traveling to Florida or the Bahamas every Spring, and to Las Vegas with his wife every year or two.

Richard E. Hermes Jr.
Vice President/Co–Founder
Tank Seal Technology, Inc.
9710 Windmill Park Lane
Houston, TX 77064
(713) 890–0260
Fax: (713) 890–0271

2891

Business Information: Tank Seal Technology, Inc. is a designer and manufacturer of oil and gas storage tank sealing systems, pipe lines, and refineries. As Vice President/Co–Founder, Mr. Hermes is responsible for all manufacturing and financial aspects of the Company, including production scheduling. **Career Steps:** Plant Manager, RFI Services Corporation (1984–1984); Plant Superintendent, Sapulpa Brick & Tiles Company (1975–1982). **Education:** Oklahoma State University, B.S., B.A. (1974). **Personal:** Married to Denise in

1986. One child: Nicholas. Mr. Hermes enjoys camping and photography.

Tetsuro Maeda
Plant Manager
Three Bond of America, Inc.
20815 Higgins Court
Torrance, CA 90501
(310) 320–3342
Fax: (310) 618–9591

2891

Business Information: Three Bond of America, Inc., an American subsidiary of the Japanese parent company, is an international manufacturer and distributor of glue, such as cyanoacrylate glue (Super or Crazy) which is used primarily in the nail beauty market and supplying sealants (i.e., rubber bonding, industrial strength glue) to various industries. As Plant Manager, Mr. Maeda is responsible for the management of the production area, including scheduling and supervision of purchasing, production cost calculation, etc. **Career Steps:** Three Bond of America, Inc.: Plant Manager (1994–Present), Quality Assurance Manager (1988–1992); Three Bond Co., Ltd. (Japan): Production Control (1993–1994), Technical Quality Control of Promotion (1984–1988). **Education:** Denki–Tsushin Daigaku Institute, B.E. (I.E.) (1983). **Personal:** Married to Yuri in 1993. One child: Kota. Mr. Maeda enjoys golf, windsurfing, and skiing.

Jeanne D. McWhorter
Vice President
Rexam Release
915 Hargar Road, Suite 30
Oak Brook, IL 60521
(708) 574–3400 Ext. 3217
Fax: (708) 586–3200
EMAIL: See Below

2891

Business Information: Rexam Release is a primary manufacturer of release liners (i.e. adhesive type liners on the backs of name tags, game pieces, etc.). With two locations in Oak Brook, Illinois, the Company serves an international market and plans to expand to a new system development for logistics. As Vice President, Ms. McWhorter oversees the daily operations of the Company including public relations and finance, as well as logistics and order fulfillment functions. Internet users can reach her via: Jeanne.D. McWhorter@Rexam.com. **Career Steps:** Vice President, Rexam Release (196–Present); Baxter International: Director of Operations, Senior Purchasing Manager, Inv. Manager–Valulink (1975–1995). **Associations & Accomplishments:** American Management Association; Girl Scouts; United Way. **Education:** University of Wisconsin. **Personal:** Married to Phil in 1976. Two children: Scott and Kelly. Ms. McWhorter enjoys spending time with her family.

H. Michael Simpson
Second Vice President, Corporate Secretary
Fox Industries Inc.
3100 Falls Cliff Road
Baltimore, MD 21211–2756
(410) 243–8856
Fax: (410) 243–2701

2891

Business Information: Fox Industries Inc. is an international manufacturer and distributor of engineered products and services for the construction industry. Product lines include, epoxy compounds, grout, urethanes, concrete admixtures, waterstops, sealants and coatings. As Second Vice President and Corporate Secretary, Mr. Simpson is responsible for contract negotiations and bid proposals for concrete restoration projects, engineering support assistance, writing specs, technical service assistance to customers, and sales. **Career Steps:** Second Vice President, Corporate Secretary, Fox Industries Inc. (1971–Present). **Education:** University of Baltimore, B.A. in History (1972) **Personal:** Married to Janet L. in 1970. Two children: Jennifer and David. Mr. Simpson enjoys golf and coaching youth football, basketball, and baseball.

David T. Snipes
National Sales Manager
Franklin International
2020 Bruck Street
Columbus, OH 43207–2329
(614) 445–1325
Fax: (614) 445–1366

2891

Business Information: Franklin International is a privately–owned international manufacturer of adhesive products. Established in 1935, Franklin International currently employs over 500 people. As National Sales Manager, Mr. Snipes is accountable for a sales territory encompassing the continental United States and Canada. He directly supervises his sales staff and handles all administrative duties/tasks for the industrial adhesive division. Mr. Snipes works with other members of the sales management staff on developing and implementing new sales techniques for the sale of adhesive products. **Career Steps:** Franklin International: National Sales Manager (1992–Present), Territory Manager (1988–1992); Sonoco Products Company: Lumber Sales Representative (1982–1988), Manufacturing Manager (1978–1982). **Associations & Accomplishments:** AFMA; WMMPA. **Education:** Clemson University, B.S. (1977). **Personal:** Married to Kathy in 1974. Two children: Kenny and Matt. Mr. Snipes enjoys golf, running, and reading.

Laura L. Williams, Esquire
Inside Sales Manager
ITW Plexus
30 Endicott Street
Danvers, MA 01923–3712
(800) 851–6692
Fax: (508) 777–7904

2891

Business Information: ITW Plexus is an adhesive manufacturing company. Established in 1980, the Company employs 50 people. As Inside Sales Manager, Ms. Williams manages the domestic and international customer service departments. She is also responsible for drafting of distributor agreements. **Career Steps:** Inside Sales Manager, ITW Plexus (1994–Present). **Education:** Massachusetts School of Law, J.D. (1995). **Personal:** Ms. Williams enjoys hiking, quilting, and music.

William Jeff Jones
General Manager
Inkjet, Inc.
7015 College Boulevard, Suite 725
Overland Park, KS 66211
(913) 491–3087
Fax: (913) 631–8228

2893

Business Information: Inkjet, Inc. specializes in industrial ink manufacturing for printing, silkscreen, and other applications. Established in 1989, the Company employs 100 people. As General Manager, Mr. Jones oversees all sales, marketing and administration, as well as MIS. He is also responsible for meeting with department heads and ensuring inter–department cooperation and efficiency. **Career Steps:** General Manager, Inkjet, Inc. (1993–Present); Regional Manager, Nework Electronics (1990–1993); Branch Manger, Inotek (1987–1990). **Associations & Accomplishments:** Instrument Society of America (ISA); Director, Babe Ruth Baseball; School Site Council Member. **Education:** Mid–American Nazarene M.B.A. (1994); University of Oklahoma, B.S. in Management; Bartlesville Wesleyan. **Personal:** Married to Teresa in 1983. Three children: Jeanna, Matthew, and Jessica. Mr. Jones enjoys golf, fishing, and being a baseball manager for little league.

Michael R. Melick
Process Engineer
Sun Chemical
4502 Chickering Avenue
Cincinnati, OH 45232
(513) 681–5950
Fax: (513) 611–9600

2893

Business Information: Established in 1930, Sun Chemical manufactures specialty pigments and printing inks, and employs 10,000 people. As Process Engineer, Mr. Melick is primarily responsible for research, development, and commercialization of novel manufacturing processes. **Career Steps:** Process Engineer, Sun Chemical (1990–Present); Process Engineer, Fluor Daniel (1985–1990). **Associations & Accomplishments:** American Institute of Chemical Engineers. **Education:** Colorado State University, M.S.C.–Che (1985); Ohio State University: B.S.C–Che (1983), B.S.C–Biochem (1982). **Personal:** Married to Patricia in 1985. Two children: Kenneth and Christina.

Philip G. Bean
Regional Sales Manager
National Chemical
5307 Winthrop Drive
Greensboro, NC 27407–9798
(910) 454–3659
Fax: (910) 454–4392

2899

Business Information: National Chemical, established in 1960 and headquartered in Atlanta, is an international company engaged in the manufacture and distribution of water treatment chemicals for boilers, pressure vessels, cooling systems, and air washers. With locations in Puerto Rico, Louisiana, Texas, Georgia, and North Carolina, National Chemical is able to provide product service to customers and clients worldwide. As Regional Sales Manager, Mr. Bean is responsible for clients in North Carolina, South Carolina, and Georgia. His responsibilities include increasing his client/customer base, recruitment and training of sales staff, equipment testing for clients, and delivering quality products and customer service. **Career Steps:** Regional Sales Manager, National Chemical (1995–Present) and (1978–1989); Director of Sales, RITE Industries (1989–1995). **Associations & Accomplishments:** North and South Carolina Boiler Pressure Association; Association of Water Technologies; North Carolina Hospital Engineers Association; Associated General Contractors of North and South Carolina. **Education:** High Point University, B.S. in Biology (1972). **Personal:** Married to Rita in 1973. Two children: Lindsay and Meredith. Mr. Bean enjoys golf and watching all sports.

David R. Bouchard
Vice President and Flame Retardant Business Unit Leader
Great Lakes Chemical Corporation
P.O. Box 2200
West Lafayette, IN 47906
(317) 497–6359
Fax: (317) 497–0234

2899

Business Information: Great Lakes Chemical Corporation is a major manufacturer and global distributor of specialty chemicals. As Vice President, David R. Bouchard oversees all operations and support staff for the Flame Retardant Business Unit, one of six units at the W. Lafayette, IN plant. **Career Steps:** Vice President and Flame Retardant Business Unit Leader, Great Lakes Chemical Corporation (1982–Present); Vice President, Prochinie International (1979–1982); Product Manager, BASF (1973–1979). **Associations & Accomplishments:** Japan Society of Indiana; Director, Purdue International Management Education Board; American Institute of Chemical Engineers; Chemical Manufacturers Association. **Education:** Purdue University, M.S.I.A. (1985); University of Michigan, B.S.Ch.E. (1967). **Personal:** Married to Judith in 1966. Three children: Eric, Kevin and Craig. Mr. Bouchard enjoys golf and tennis.

Cynthia Bringuier
Supervisor
Standard Abrasives
9351 Deering Avenue
Chatsworth, CA 91311–5858
(818) 718–7070
Fax: (818) 718–2250

2899

Business Information: Standard Abrasives primarily manufactures both coated and non–woven abrasive products for the aerospace and metal working industries. Secondly, Standard Abrasives converts products to finished goods. National in scope, Standard Abrasives has three locations; one in Dayton, Ohio and two in California (one in Chatsworth and one in the desert). As Supervisor, Ms. Bringuier is responsible for the oversight of the Export Department from customer services to sales, including conducting sales trips overseas, in addition to supervising a support staff. **Career Steps:** Supervisor, Standard Abrasives (1987–Present); Sales Assistant, Times Mirror National Marketing (1985–1987); Sales Representative, Dun & Bradstreet (1979–1985); Department Liaison & English Teacher, Dun & Bradstreet, France (1980–1981). **Associations & Accomplishments:** World Trade Center of Orange County; Fluent in Spanish, French, and Italian. **Education:** University of Missouri, M.A. (1976); University of California – Los Angeles, B.A. **Personal:** Married to Jean–Paul in 1979. Three children: Sabrina, Stefan, and Jonathan. Ms. Bringuier enjoys spending time with her children, fine dining with her husband, skiing, travel, and learning foreign languages.

Vanessa L. Brown
Plant Controller
Reichhold Chemicals, Inc.
5980 Arcturus Avenue
Oxnard, CA 93033
(805) 488–0831
Fax: (805) 488–3243

2899

Business Information: Reichhold Chemicals, Inc. (RCI) is a leading manufacturer of polyester resins, adhesive coatings, and emulsion polymers, with approximately $1 billion in annual sales. As a wholly–owned subsidiary of DaiNippon Ink, RCI's products are used in a wide variety of applications – from boat hulls and surfboards to carpet and shower stall enclosures. RCI is comprised of four divisions: Reactive Polymers, Coating Polymers, Emulsion Polymers, and Swift Adhesives, and employs approximately 4,000 people worldwide. RCI is a member in good standing of the Chemical Manufacturers' Association, and actively participates in the CMA's Responsible Care initiatives. Ms. Brown is the Plant Controller for both the Oxnard and Azusa, California, polyester resin manufacturing plants. She is responsible for administering a multi–million dollar budget for both facilities, inclusive of transportation, materials, and capital expenditures. In addition to supervising plant accounting and finance functions, she oversees the human resources function, including hiring, benefits changes, and workers' compensation. **Career Steps:** Plant Controller, Reichhold Chemicals, Inc. (1995–Present); Accounting Manager, Chase Toys, Inc. (1994–1995); Controller, Capstar Hotels, Inc. (1993–1994). **Associations & Accomplishments:** National Association of Female Executives; National Human Resources Association; Employer's Advisory Council, California State Employment Development Department. **Education:** California Polytechnic State University, San Luis Obispo, California, B.A. (1993). **Personal:** Married to Lloyd D. Brown in 1993. Ms. Brown enjoys gardening.

Patrick O. Bruneel
•••━━━◉━━━•••
President
Interflux USA, Inc.
Technology Center, 230 Second Avenue
Waltham, MA 02254
(617) 890–3993
Fax: (617) 890–3994
EMail: See Below

2899

Business Information: Interflux USA, Inc. is a manufacturer of chemistry for the electronics industry, servicing, and consulting "residue–free" soldering technology. As Founder of the No–Residue technology, Mr. Bruneel was recognized by the U.S. Environmental Protection Agency in 1990 as one of the top experts in the world elimination of ozone depletion chemistries. As President, Mr. Bruneel is responsible for all aspects of Company operations, including general management, providing technical advice to their worldwide organization, and administration. In 1994, Mr. Bruneel founded and is currently expanding a similar environmentally–safe company called Ecosol Technologies, Inc. This Company is concerned with environmental issues and is in the process of developing a line of HI–TECH VOC FREE products which brings Ecosol a level further in the technology and environmental awareness. Internet users can reach him via: PATRICKBRUNEEL@MSN.COM. **Career Steps:** President, Interflux USA, Inc. (1992–Present); Technical Director, Interflux Electronics (Belgium) (1988–1992); Head Engineering, Barco Video Systems (Belgium) (1980–1988); Process Engineer, Barco Electronics (Belgium) (1975–1980). **Education:** Electro Mechanical Engineering; Computer Science Engineering. **Personal:** Three children: Benjamin, Mike, and Fanny. Mr. Bruneel enjoys marine aquaria, woodworking, and philosophy.

Mackey L. Cobb
Maintenance Manager
C.H. Patrick & Company Inc.
P.O. Box 2526
Greenville, SC 29602–2526
(864) 244–4831
Fax: (864) 292–0652

2899

Business Information: C.H. Patrick & Company Inc. is a regional company serving the East Coast textile industry. The Company is a manufacturer of chemicals and dyes, and also washes and reconditions drums and bulk tanks for the textile industry. As Maintenance Manager, Mr. Cobb is responsible for all aspects of maintenance in all plant facilities. His duties include equipment upkeep, purchasing of new equipment, re-location and installation of equipment, and coordination with outside contractors. **Career Steps:** Maintenance Manager, C.H. Patrick & Company Inc. (1988–Present); Superintendent/Manager, TMR Mech. Inc. (1982–1988); Mechanical Superintendent, Universal Service Inc. (1968–1982). **Associations & Accomplishments:** Notary of South Carolina; Master Mason; Veterans of Foreign Wars; National Rifle Association (NRA); ILA: South Carolina Sheriffs Association; Youth Instructor, Hunting and Fire Arms Safety; National Fire Protection Association; Shrine Scottish Rite; U.S. Navy (1959–1968); American College of Heraldry; U.S. Navy Divers Association. **Education:** Sumpter Tech., C.E.U.; Clemson University, A.A.; Greenville Tech., A.A.; **Personal:** Married to Virginia C. in 1980. Four children: Bill, Tammy, Rick and Mackey Jr. Mr. Cobb enjoys hunting, fishing, target shooting and carpentry.

Earl Cranor
Director of Operations
Omniglow Corporation
96 Windsor Street
West Springfield, MA 01089–3570
(413) 739–8252
Fax: (413) 739–8432

2899

Business Information: Omniglow Corporation is a manufacturer of chemical lights. International in scope, Omniglow Corporation has six locations throughout the world, including the U.S., China, Korea (Seoul), Japan, England, and Singapore. As Director of Operations, Mr. Cranor is responsible for the management of all manufacturing operations for the Company. **Career Steps:** Director of Operations, Omniglow Corporation (1993–Present); American Cyanamid: Manager of Support Services (1991–1993), Manager of Operations (1989–1991). **Associations & Accomplishments:** Published in the Springfield Journal. **Education:** Auburn University, B.S. in Chemical Engineering (1979). **Personal:** Married to Tina in 1979. Mr. Cranor enjoys reading, teaching and acupuncture.

Mr. Tsuyoshi Fujita
Marketing Coordinator
PPG Canada Inc. (PPG Industries, Inc.)
880 Avonhead Road
Mississauga, Ontario L5J 1K5
(905) 855–5658
Fax: (905) 823–4190 (905) 339–0318

2899

Business Information: PPG Canada Inc. (PPG Industries, Inc.) is a manufacturer and global distributor of chemicals operating through three distinct divisions: Coating & Resins, Glass, and Chemicals. PPG Canada Inc. at the Mississauga, Ontario headquarters, which employs over 370 people, manages all Canadian and some U.S. coating and resins operations of the Corporation. As Marketing Coordinator for PPG Canada, Inc., Mr. Fujita serves as liaison for custom painting and finishing projects, involved mainly with Japanese automobile transplants. **Career Steps:** Marketing Coordinator, PPG Industries, Inc. (PPG Canada Inc.). **Associations & Accomplishments:** Iota Sigma Epsilon **Education:** University of Dallas, M.B.A. in International Management (1994); University of Oregon, B.S. in Management and Marketing; National Ibamaki College of Technology in Japan, A.S. in Mechanical Engineering.

David L. Gray
Plant Engineering Manager
Norit Americas Inc.
Route 3, Box 696
Pryor, OK 74361–9803
(918) 825–8308
Fax: (918) 825–5665

2899

Business Information: Norit Americas Inc. is an international manufacturer of diversified chemical preparations, such as fine and specialty chemicals, petrochemicals, chlorochemicals and plastics. With Norit Americas Inc. parent company headquarters based in France, the Company has three distinct branches; Oil Production and Refinery, Chemical and Pharmaceutical. The Chemical Branch, Norit Americas Inc. has a U.S. subsidiary, Norit Americas Inc. North America, from which basic chemicals is a division, with plants in the states of Washington, Oregon, Wyoming, Texas, South Carolina, Kentucky and Illinois. Globally, Norit Americas Inc. employs over 85,000 people with sales over $35 billion. With fourteen years of experience in engineering, project, and maintenance operations, Mr. Gray joined Norit Americas Inc. activated carbon manufacturing plant in Pryor, Oklahoma as Plant Engineering Manager in 1994. He is responsible for plant maintenance and engineering, as well as the oversight of maintenance storerooms and purchasing activities. **Career Steps:** Plant Engineering Manager, Norit Americas Inc. (1994–Present); Maintenance Superintendent, Arizona Chemical Company

(1992–1994); Maintenance Engineer, Protein Tech. Inc. (1990–1992); Assistant Maintenance Superintendent, Mississippi Power Company (1982–1990). **Associations & Accomplishments:** Vibration Institute; American Society of Mechanical Engineers; HOG. **Education:** University of Mississippi, B.S. in Mechanical Engineering (1982). **Personal:** Married to Sherry in 1990. Mr. Gray enjoys fishing, motorcycle touring and restoring antique cars.

Warren Jones
President
Hi–MAR Specialties, Inc.
1955 Lake Park Drive, Suite 250
Smyrna, GA 30080
(770) 801–6600
Fax: (770) 801–1586

2899

Business Information: Hi–MAR Specialties, Inc., formerly Hickson Specialties, is a chemical manufacturing company that specializes in additives and foam control agents for the paint, pulp and paper, and ink manufacturing industries. As President, Mr. Jones oversees all aspects of the Company and is responsible for the financial health of the Company, international sales, technology, and research and development. **Career Steps:** President, Hickson Specialties (1992–Present); Director of Manufacturing, Rhone Pouleno (1989–1992); Vice President, Production, Colloids, Inc. (1979–1989); Technical Director, S B Penick and Company (1965–1979). **Associations & Accomplishments:** Federation of Coatings Society; Wisconsin Paper Council; DCAT. **Education:** Long Island University, B.S. in Chemistry (1963); Kennedy Western University, Candidate for M.S. in Business. **Personal:** Six children: Warren, Lorri–Ann, Christopher, Richard, Robert, and Patricia. Mr. Jones enjoys fishing, boating, and sports.

Robin G. Klein
Plant Controller
Cabot Corporation
1 Cabot Drive
Waverly, WV 26184–9600
(304) 665–2441
Fax: (304) 665–2259

2899

Business Information: Cabot Corporation is a manufacturer of carbon black, a fine soot, finer and purer than lampblack, formed by the incomplete burning of gas and oil, and used in the manufacture of rubber and printing inks. As Plant Controller, Ms. Klein is responsible for monthly financial closings, accounts payable, purchasing/stores, annual physical inventory, annual budgets, general ledger, cash disbursements, internal controls, special projects, audits, standard cost, tax filings, government reporting, and new system development. **Career Steps:** Cabot Corporation: Plant Controller (1994–Present), Plant Accountant (1992–1994); National Cost Analyst, Moore Business Forms (1991–1992). **Associations & Accomplishments:** Professional Womens Association; Altrusa International; Parkersburg Junior League. **Education:** West Virginia University, Bachelor of Science (1989). **Personal:** Married to Douglas S. in 1995. Ms. Klein enjoys interior decorating, jogging, and golf.

Andrew Liveris
Vice President of Ventures
Dow Chemical, U.S.A.
2040 W.H. Dow Center
Midland, MI 48674
(517) 636–8924
Fax: (517) 636–9714

2899

Business Information: Dow Chemical Company is one of the world's leading chemical manufacturing companies. Among its products are agricultural chemicals, plastics, chemicals and consumer products. The Company has locations in the United States, Japan, Canada, Mexico, South America and other areas. Established in 1897, Dow Chemical currently employs 48,000 people and has an estiamted annual revenue of $20 billion. As Vice President of Ventures, Mr. Liveris is responsible for all aspects of environmental services. **Career Steps:** Dow Chemical, U.S.A.: Vice President of Ventures (1994–Present), General Manager (1993–1994), Business Director (1992–1993); General Manager, Dow Chemical, Thailand (1989–1992). **Associations & Accomplishments:** Institute of Chemical Engineers, UK and Australia. **Education:** University of Queensland, B.S. in Chemical Engineering (1976). **Personal:** Married to Paula in 1983. Three chil-

dren: Nicholas, Alexandra and Anthony. Mr. Liveris enjoys sports and reading.

Robert MacPhail
President and CEO
Prospec Chemicals
34 Clayson Road
North York, Ontario M9M 2G8
(416) 410–0202
Fax: (905) 338–0469

2899

Business Information: Prospec Chemicals, a division of Tennants Consolidated LTD, is a manufacturer of mineral flotation and water treatment chemicals. Established in 1984, Prospec Chemicals employs 60 people. As President and CEO, Mr. MacPhail oversees every aspect of the Company by providing leadership in the Research and Development division and production and sales of the products. **Career Steps:** Prospec Chemicals: President and CEO (1995–Present), Vice President (1994–1995); Manager–Mining Chemicals, Charte Tennant and Company (1992–1994); General Manager, Applied Ore Testing, Inc. (1990–1992). **Associations & Accomplishments:** Association of Professional Engineers of Ontario; Society of Mining Engineers; Canadian Institute of Metallurgists. **Education:** McMaster University, B.Sc. (1978); Waterloo University, B.Sc. in Geology and B.A. in English; Sheridan College, C.E.T. **Personal:** Married to Debra Margaret in 1979. Mr. MacPhail enjoys music and literature.

Robin C. Manastersky
Legal Counsel
BASF Canada, Inc.
345 Calingview Drive
Toronto, Ontario M9W 6N9
(416) 674–2931
Fax: (416) 674–2586

2899

Business Information: BASF Canada, Inc. is a transnational chemical company involved with agriculture (feed and animal nutrition), fibers (carpet), consumer products, and life sciences. As Legal Counsel, Ms. Manastersky handles transactional law, including acquisitions, divestitures, contracts reviews, and litigation. **Career Steps:** Legal Counsel, BASF Canada, Inc. (1995–Present); Associate Lawyer, Pallett Valo (1990–1995); Associate Lawyer, Smith, Lyons (1987–1990). **Associations & Accomplishments:** Canadian Bar Association. **Education:** University of Western Ontario, LL.B. (1985); Queen's University: B.Ed. (1980), B.A. with Honors (1979). **Personal:** Married to Tony in 1980. One child: Taryn Helene.

Alain P. Mari
General Manager – Basic Chemicals Division
Elf Atochem North America, Inc.
2000 Market Street
Philadelphia, PA 19103–3222
(215) 419–7808
Fax: (215) 419–7415

2899

Business Information: Elf Atochem is an international manufacturer of diversified chemical preparations such as fine and specialty chemicals, petrochemicals, chlorochemicals and plastics. With Elf Aquitaine parent company headquarters based in France, the Company has three distinct branches; Oil Production and Refinery, Chemical and Pharmaceutical. The Chemical Branch, Elf Atochem has a U.S. subsidiary, Elf Atochem North America, from which basic chemicals is a division with plants in the states of Washington, Oregon, Wyoming, Texas, South Carolina, Kentucky and Illinois. Globally, Elf Aquitaine employs over 85,000 people with sales over $35 billion. As General Manager for the Chemical Division's Basic Chemicals Branch, Mr. Mari oversees all business aspects for the Branch unit. The Basic Chemicals Branch, with annual sales in excess of $300 million, is responsible for the production of sodium–sulfate, chlor–alkali, sodium chlorate, hydrogen peroxide, ceramics, fluorspar, hydrogen flouride, zinc and barite. **Career Steps:** General Manager, Elf Atochem North America, Inc. (1994–Present); General Manager, Elf Atochem North America, Inc. (1992–1993); Business Manager, Elf Atochem North America, Inc. (1988–1991). **Education:** Mines (France), Engineer (1977). **Personal:** Married to Christine in 1992. One child: Romain. Mr. Mari enjoys hang gliding, sailing and skiing.

Thomas Allen Marr, P.E.
Vice President of Engineering
Osmose Wood Preserving
1142 Anne Street
Griffin, GA 30223–4710
(770) 228–8434
Fax: Please mail or call

2899

Business Information: Osmose Wood Preserving is an international multi–divisional water–borne wood preserving manufacturer, which provides the design, construction and support through engineering and marketing to customer wood preserving plants in the U.S., Canada, and international countries. Products produced with Osmose products include decks, picnic tables, fences, and gazebos. Products produced by Osmose include wood preservatives, colorants, water repellents, stains and coatings, and deck screws. Osmose also produces a T.V. show syndicated as "Backyard America" providing "How–to" programming for home and garden projects. Cypress Gardens of Florida is the shows "Official Gardens". Divisional entities comprise the following: Utility Division – the largest company in the country providing the preservative treatment and repair of telephone and electric poles; Wood Preserving Division – described above; Railroad Division; Marine Division; International Division; and the Canadian Division – operating under the name — Timber Specialists, the largest water–borne wood preservative company in Canada. Serving in managerial capacities for Osmose since 1985, Thomas Marr was appointed as Vice President of Engineering and Environmental Services in 1991. He provides the Engineering and Environmental administrative direction for the Wood Preserving, Canadian and International divisions, as well as managing sales and marketing for the Northern Region of the U.S. as the Regional Sales Manager. **Career Steps:** Osmose Wood Preserving: Vice President of Engineering & Environmental Services, (1991–Present), Regional Sales Manager (1993–Present), Manager of Engineering and Technical Services (1985–1991); Manager of Environmental Engineering, Koppers Company, Inc. (1980–1985). **Associations & Accomplishments:** American Wood Preservers Association; American Wood Preserving Institute; American Society of Mechanical Engineers; Registered Professional Engineers; Arsenical Council, Chemical Manufacturers Association; Author of training manuals for Koppers and Osmose. **Education:** University of Maryland, B.S.M.E. (1973); Dale Carnegie Course. **Personal:** Married to Renee in 1971. Three children: Michelle Tamara, Jenelle Dianne, and Michael Allen Adams. Mr. Marr enjoys skiing, fishing, camping, travel, woodworking, and scuba diving.

Timothy J. McCambridge
Assistant Operations Manager
Hickson Specialties, Inc.
3801 FW Mckinley
Milwaukee, WI 53208
(414) 343–5443
Fax: (414) 342–7871

2899

Business Information: Hickson Specialties, Inc. is a manufacturer of chemicals, defoamers, and anti–foamers for the pulp mill, paper, adhesives, and paint industry. As Assistant Operations Manager, Mr. McCambridge runs the physical plant and warehouse operations, including shipping and handling, and production. **Career Steps:** Assistant Operations Manager, Hickson Specialties, Inc. (1985–Present); Ground Crew/Public Relations, Milwaukee Brewers (1978–1985). **Associations & Accomplishments:** Wisconsin Lake Schooner Education Association. **Education:** Attended, University of Wisconsin – Milwaukee. **Personal:** Two children: Brittany and Timothy II. Mr. McCambridge enjoys piloting, writing, art, cycling, and playing softball.

Edward C. Miller
Owner and General Manager
Xytec Coatings, Inc.
640 8th Street, Apt. 2
Bowling Green, OH 43402–4286
(614) 771–1110
Fax: (614) 771–8092

2899

Business Information: Xytec Coatings, Inc. is an international manufacturer of sputter coating systems, specializing in glass tinting equipment which uses a vacuum instead of applying a film on the glass. Establishing Xytec Coatings, Inc. as Owner and General Manager in 1993, Mr. Miller is responsible for all aspects of operations, including administration, finances, sales, public relations, marketing, strategic planning, proposal writing, and future equipment development. **Career Steps:** Owner and General Manager, Xytec Coatings, Inc. (1993–Present); Regional Manager, Sun Coatings, Inc. (1992–1993); Director of Used Equipment, Royal Tool, Inc. (1990–1992). **Associations & Accomplishments:** Society of Vacuum Coaters; American Vacuum Society; Treasurer, Graduate Business Student Association; Student Senator, Organizational Development Student Network. **Education:**

Bowling Green State University: M.B.A., M.O.D. (1996); Ferris State University, B.S. in Marketing; University of Nantes – France, Studies in European Business and Finance. **Personal:** Mr. Miller enjoys skiing, golf, and travel.

Joseph A. Miller Jr.
Senior Vice President/Chief Technology Officer
DuPont – Central Research & Development
Experimental Station: Building 328 Rm. 411
Wilmington, DE 19880–0328
(302) 695–4673
Fax: (302) 695–9449

2899

Business Information: DuPont is a research and technology–based global chemical and energy company offering high–performance products based on chemicals, polymers, fibers and petroleum. Committed to better things for better living, DuPont serves worldwide markets in the aerospace, apparel, automotive, agriculture, construction, packaging, refining and transportation industries. As Senior Vice President/Chief Technology Officer, Mr. Miller handles all research and development technology activities for the Company. **Career Steps:** DuPont: Senior Vice President/Chief Technology Officer (1994–Present), Vice President of Science and Engineering (1993–1994), Vice President of Polymers (1990–1993). **Associations & Accomplishments:** American Chemical Society; Industrial Research Institute; Fellow, American Association for Advancement of Science; Co–Chair, Committee to Reform Science Education in Delaware; Member of Various Boards of Directors. **Education:** Pennsylvania State University, Ph.D. (1966); Virginia Military Institute, B.S. **Personal:** Married to Katherine in 1967. Three children: Kristin, Allyson, and Sarah. Dr. Miller enjoys fly fishing, and biking.

Dr. Steven Eric Miller
Manager of Technology
Colgate–Palmolive Company
909 River Road
Piscataway, NJ 08855
(908) 878–7438
Fax: Please mail or call

2899

Business Information: Colgate–Palmolive Company is one of the world's leading manufacturers and marketers of consumer household and beauty–aid products, with operations in over 170 countries around the world. As Manager of Technology, Dr. Miller is in charge of basic research and development of several major categories of oral care products. This includes oversight of all researchers in these categories. Dr. Miller assists in scheduling product testing, marketing strategies, and strategic planning for new products. **Career Steps:** Colgate–Palmolive Company: Manager of Technology (1994–Present), Senior Technical Associate (1992–1994), Technical Associate (1989–1992), Senior Research Assistant (1988–1989), Research Scientist (1985–1988). **Associations & Accomplishments:** International Association of Dental Research; American Chemical Society. **Education:** Purdue University, PhD (1984); University of Rhode Island, MS (1980); Florida Institute of Technology, BS (1977) **Personal:** Married to Denise in 1979. Dr. Miller enjoys hunting and making furniture.

Nick Nabours
Supervisor of Professional Employment & College Relations
Eastman Chemical Company
Box 7444
Longview, TX 75607
(903) 237–5007
Fax: (903) 237–6685
EMAIL: See Below

2899

Business Information: Eastman Chemical Company is a global manufacturer of intermediate chemicals and plastics. As Supervisor of Professional Employment & College Relations, Mr. Nabours is responsible for the supervision of staff, as well as maintaining contact and establishing partnerships with schools to enable college graduates to be hired by Eastman Chemical in entry level positions. Concurrent with his position at Eastman Chemical Company, he serves as President of The National Association of Colleges & Employers – an association that has 23 paid staff members. He can also be reached through the Internet as follows: nnabours@eastman.com **Career Steps:** Supervisor of Professional Employment & College Relations, Eastman Chemical Company (1981–Present); Director, Pan American World Airways (1965–1981). **Associations & Accomplishments:** Southwest Association of Colleges & Employers; Rocky Mountain Association of Colleges and Employees; President Longview Arts Council. **Education:** McMurry University, B.A., cum laude (1959). **Personal:** Married to Suzanne S. in 1961. Two children: Melissa Saltman and Ursula Wilmotte. Mr. Nabours

enjoys skiing, gardening, travel, raising and showing Irish Wolfhounds.

Arnold T. Nelson Jr.
Sales and Technical Manager
North Industrial Chemicals
P.O. Box 1904
York, PA 17405
(800) 966–7848
Fax: (717) 846–7350

2899

Business Information: North Industrial Chemicals is a distributor of diversified chemicals, specializing in plating and metal finishing applications. Working in various chemical research and sales positions with North Industrial since 1974, Arnold Nelson was appointed as Sales and Technical Manager in 1989. In this capacity, he provides the overall management of sales and technical functions, including conducting all key finishing and proprietary information. **Career Steps:** North Industrial Chemicals: Sales and Technical Manager (1989–Present), Chemist/Sales (1974–1989); Plant Manager, Guard–All Chemicals (1972–1974). **Associations & Accomplishments:** American Electroplating and Surface Finishing Association; Published in newspapers and purchasing magazines. **Education:** Norwalk State Tech, Chemical Engineer (1972). **Personal:** Married to Tina in 1985. One child: Ashley. Mr. Nelson enjoys golf.

Fernando Ortega
President
Sachs Chemical
P.O. Box 191670
San Juan, Puerto Rico 00919–1670
(809) 720–0470
Fax: (809) 720–0414

2899

Business Information: Sachs Chemical is a major distributor of chemicals and chemical preparations. Established in 1987, Sachs Chemical currently employs 10 people. As President, Mr. Ortega is responsible for all aspects of operations, including administration, sales and marketing. **Career Steps:** President, Sachs Chemical (1980–Present). **Education:** Colegio Marista. **Personal:** Married to Magda Rodriquez in 1987. Three children: Nicole, Camille and Michele. Mr. Ortega enjoys boating and race cars.

Randy J. Pelc
Corporate Facilities Manager
Master Chemical Corporation
P.O. Box 361
Perrysburg, OH 43552–0361
(419) 874–7902
Fax: (419) 874–0684

2899

Business Information: Master Chemical Corporation manufactures metal–working fluids (coolants) for the metal–working industry. Mr. Pelc joined Master Chemical in 1983 as Maintenance Supervisor, promoted to Plant Manager in 1990, and moving into his present position as Corporate Facilities Manager in 1994. He is responsible for maintaining and upgrading all Corporation–owned facilities. **Career Steps:** Master Chemical Corporation: Corporate Facilities Manager (1994–Present), Plant Manager (1990–1994), Maintenance Supervisor (1983–1990); Autobody Repair, Ed Schmidt Pontiac (1977–1983). **Associations & Accomplishments:** American Production and Inventory Control Society, Inc.; The International Society for Measurement and Control; Building Owners Managers Association; Master Chemical Corporation Outstanding Employee (1988). **Personal:** Married to Kim in 1991. Three children: Dodi, Randy Jr., and Dustin. One Grandchild: Andy. Mr. Pelc enjoys customizing cars, bowling, and working on his house.

Richard C. Peterson
Assistant Treasurer
ANGUS Chemical Company
1500 East Lake Cook Road
Buffalo Grove, IL 60089
(708) 215–8600 Ext: 1080
Fax: (708) 808–3707

2899

Business Information: ANGUS Chemical Company — a wholly–owned subsidiary of Alberta Natural Gas (ANG) headquartered in Calgary, Canada — is a worldwide manufacturer of specialty chemicals (nitroparaffins and derivatives) used for pharmaceutical products, paints, coatings, and racing fuel. Established in 1982, ANGUS Chemical Company reports annual revenue of $130 million and currently employs 500 people. A seven–year company veteran, Mr. Peterson joined ANGUS Chemical in 1989. Currently serving as Assistant

Treasurer, he is responsible for the whole realm of banking operations, including credit and collections (domestic and international), cash management, investing, borrowing, Foreign Exchange, and bank relationship management. **Career Steps:** ANGUS Chemical Company: Assistant Treasurer (1994–Present), Manager of Credit and Treasury Services (1992–1994), Assistant Credit Manager (1989–1992); Assistant Credit Manager, Echlin Inc. (1986–1989); Credit and Collection Coordinator, General Electric (1984–1986); Wickes Credit Corporation: Collector (1984), Collection Trainee (1984). **Associations & Accomplishments:** National Association of Credit Management; Treasury Management Association; Certified Credit Executive and Cash Manager; Publication: Credit Risk Scoring System in Credit Research Digest (1994). **Education:** DePaul University, M.B.A. (1983); Dartmouth College, Graduate School of Credit and Financial Management (1993); Northeastern Illinois University, B.A. (1982). **Personal:** Mr. Peterson enjoys fishing, sports, tennis, and basketball.

Margaret A. Savoia

Human Resource Manager
Cabat Corporation
157 Concord Road
Billerica, MA 01821–7001
(508) 670–7054
Fax: (508) 670–7046
EMAIL: See Below

2899

Business Information: Cabot Corporation is an international manufacturer of specialty chemicals, comprised of four distinct businesses within Cabot, Massachusetts. A $2 billion company, Cabot Corporation's headquarters are located in Billerica, Massachusetts. As Human Resource Manager, Ms. Savoia is in charge of all personnel aspects of the Research and Development Division. She handles all personnel functions for her division, including recruiting, promoting and terminating employees, administration of employee benefits programs, and training of new employees. Internet users can also reach her via: Margaret Savoia@cabot–corp.com **Career Steps:** Human Resource Manager, Cabot Corporation (1995–Present); Human Resource Generalist, Data Media Corporation (1990–1992); Human Resource Generalist, Wang Labs (1985–1990). **Associations & Accomplishments:** Boston Human Resources Association; North East Human Resource Association. **Education:** University of New Hampshire, B.A. (1985). **Personal:** Ms. Savoia enjoys sports, running, biking, and tennis.

George W. Schuler

World Wide Business Manager
Akzo Nobel Chemicals, Inc.
5 Livingstone Avenue
Dobbs Ferry, NY 10522
(914) 674–5385
Fax: (914) 693–4487

2899

Business Information: Akzo Nobel Chemicals, Inc., the 9th largest chemical Company in the world, manufactures 5,000 different specialty chemicals (e.g., fire resistant fluid, lube additives, flame retardants, plasticizers, and polymer modifiers). Mr. Schuler served in various supervisory positions with Stauffer Chemical (purchased by Akzo in 1988), most recently promoted to World Wide Business Manager in 1993. He presently supervises operations in the United States, Europe, and Japan, providing strategic direction and overseeing contractual arrangements. **Career Steps:** Akzo Nobel Chemicals, Inc.: World Wide Business Manager (1993–Present), World Wide General Manager of Sulfo and Sulfuric (1989–1993), Business Manager, Intermediates and Amines (1988–1989); Business Manager, Pharmaceutical Intermediates & Specialty Plasticizers, Stauffer Chemical (1985–1988). **Associations & Accomplishments:** Chemist Club. **Education:** University of Connecticut, M.B.A. (1981); Rose–Hulman Institute of Technology – Terre Haute, Indiana, B.S. in Chemical Engineering. **Personal:** Married to Mary in 1973. Three children: Elizabeth, Katherine, and Michelle. Mr. Schuler enjoys golf, fishing, and coaching baseball.

David P. Steinmetz

Supply Chain Consultant
DuPont
26 Basil Court
Hockessin, DE 19707–1334
(302) 999–4765
Fax: (302) 999–4109

2899

Business Information: DuPont is a research and technology–based global chemical and energy company offering high–performance products based on chemicals, polymers, fibers and petroleum. Committed to better things for better living, DuPont serves worldwide markets in the aerospace, apparel, automotive, agriculture, construction, packaging, refining and transportation industries. As Supply Chain Consultant with the Fluoro Products Division, Mr. Steinmetz is Project Manager for global implementation of MRP II, vendor managed inventory and quick response programs. **Career Steps:** DuPont: Supply Chain Consultant (1990–Present), Distribution Manager (1987–1990), Transportation Equipment Manager (1985–1987), Purchasing Agent (1979–1985), Process Engineer (1978–1979). **Associations & Accomplishments:** American Production and Inventory Control Society; Council of Logistics Management. **Education:** Widener University, M.S. in Computer Science (1989); University of Richmond, M.B.A. (1983); Ohio State University, B.S. in Chemical Engineering (1978). **Personal:** Married to Pamela in 1983. One child: Eric.

David Georon Tinkey

Area Manager
BetzDearborn, Inc.
1854 Forsyth Street, Suite #3
Macon, GA 31210
(800) 741–2387
Fax: (912) 746–0234

2899

Business Information: BetzDearborn, Inc. is a $1.2 billion water and process–chemical treatment company serving thousands of industrial, commercial, and institutional establishments in 80 countries on six continents. The Company has four divisions: BetzDearborn Water Management Group, providing water treatment programs; BetzDearborn Paper Process Group, providing process treatment programs to the pulp and paper industry; BetzDearborn Hydrocarbon Process Group, providing process treatment programs to the petroleum refining and petrochemical industries; and BetzDearborn Metals Process Group, providing treatment programs for metals and plastics finishing. As Area Manager, Mr. Tinkey sells and services primarily water treatment chemicals to industry for influent, boiler, cooling, and wastewater systems. His sales and service team serves clients in Central and South Georgia, and North Florida. **Career Steps:** Area Manager, BetzDearborn, Inc. (1995–Present); Betz Entec: Senior Account Manager (1994–1995), Account Manager (1993), Technical Specialist (1991–1992). **Associations & Accomplishments:** First Presbyterian Church: Deacon, held all offices in Sunday School; Former Member, Georgia Rural Water Association; Georgia Municipal Association; Georgia Waste Water and Pollution Control Association; Kappa Alpha Order; Spouse participant, Leadership Georgia (1995); United States Tennis Association. **Education:** Georgia Institute of Technology, B.S. in Industrial Management (1985); Received management and manufacturing training while employed at both Milliken and Harland Company; BetzDearborn: continuing education for chemical and mechanical engineering, customer service, project/financial management, and sales. **Personal:** Married to Stephanie in 1991. One child: Grace Elizabeth. Mr. Tinkey enjoys tennis, fitness, hiking, and participating in church.

James A. Trainham

Technical Director, Dacron
DuPont
Barley Mills Plaza, Building 22, P.O. Box 80022
Wilmington, DE 19880–0022
(302) 992–3898
Fax: (302) 992–2035

2899

Business Information: DuPont is a research and technology–based global chemical and energy company offering high–performance products based on chemicals, polymers, fibers and petroleum. Committed to better things for better living, DuPont serves worldwide markets in the aerospace, apparel, automotive, agriculture, construction, packaging, refining and transportation industries. As Technical Director, Dacron, Mr. Trainham leads or manages all technical aspects of the Dacron Division. He develops and implements sales techniques for new and existing products, develops and implements marketing techniques for products, and works with the research and development teams on the development of new products. Mr. Trainham works closely with other managers on the creation of a workable annual budget and then monitors the department/division figures for compliance. Internet users can also reach him via: trainham@al.esvax.UMC.dupont.com **Career Steps:** DuPont: Technical Director, Dacron (1996–Present), Director, Engineering, Research and Development (1992–1996), Manager, Strategic Process Technology (1988–1992). **Associations & Accomplishments:** American Institute of Chemical Engineering; Electrochemical Society; Council of Chemical Research. Mr. Trainham has had four patents issued, has four which have been accepted, and four are pending as of 1996. **Education:** University of California – Berkeley: Ph.D. (1979), B.S. in Chemical Engineering (1973); University of Wisconsin – Madison, M.S. in Chemical Engineering (1977). **Personal:** Married to Dr. Linda D. Waters in 1980. Dr. Trainham enjoys golf, fly fishing, and skeet shooting.

2900 Petroleum and Coal Products

2911 Petroleum refining
2951 Asphalt paving mixtures and blocks
2952 Asphalt felts and coatings
2992 Lubricating oils and greases
2999 Petroleum and coal products, NEC

Peter J. Barba Jr.

Refinery Manager
Amerada Hess (Port Reading) Corp.
One Hess Plaza
Woodbridge, NJ 07095
(908) 750–7800
Fax: (908) 750–7798
EMAIL: 102013.1261

2911

Business Information: Amerada Hess (Port Reading) Corp. is an integrated petroleum organization established in 1936 with exploration and production locations worldwide and refining facilities in the Northeast and Carribbean. The Amerada Hess (Port Reading) Corp. Refining Facility was established in 1958 and currently operates a 58 MBPD FCC complex which employees 200 people. As Refinery Manager, Mr. Barba has oversight of daily operations. He oversees all matters relating to production, blending, policies, and personnel administration. Mr. Barba is responsible for the business unit's bottom line which includes the development of the facility budget and monitoring expenditures to avoid deficit budget spending. **Career Steps:** Amerada Hess Corporation: Refinery Manager (1992–Present), Corporate Engineering Manager (1985–1992), Various Engineering Management Positions (1977–1985), Process Engineer (1974–1977). **Education:** Newark College of Engineering, BS Chemical Engineering (1974). **Personal:** Married to Karen in 1974. Mr. Barba enjoys raising horses, hunting, fishing, and music.

Clydia J. Cuykendall

General Counsel
Star Enterprise
12700 Northborough Drive
Houston, TX 77067–2508
(713) 874–3820
Fax: (713) 874–7041

2911

Business Information: Star Enterprise, a subsidiary of Texaco, is a national petroleum refining company, encompassing 26 East Coast and Gulf Coast states for domestic clientele. A practicing attorney since 1974, Ms. Cuykendall is admitted to practice in California (1974), Washington (1975), and Texas (1991) state courts. Joining Star Enterprise as General Counsel in 1989, she serves as the Chief Legal Officer responsible for intellectual property management and contracts. Other responsibilities include administration, operations, finances, and strategic planning. **Career Steps:** General Counsel, Star Enterprise (1989–Present); In–house Attorney, Arameo & Affiliates (1979–1988); Associate, Pillsbury, Madison & Sutro (1974–1978). **Associations & Accomplishments:** American Corporate Counsel Association (1989–Present); Board of Directors (1994–Present), Marine Preservation Association; Board of Directors (1992–Present), Business Arts Fund; California State Bar Association (Since 1974); Washington State Bar Association (Since 1975); Texas State Bar Association (Since 1991). **Education:** University of Washington, J.D. (1974); Stanford University, B.S (1971). **Personal:** Ms. Cuykendall enjoys skiing, scuba diving, and golf.

Ms. Margarita D. Gallego

Project Manager
Total Petroleum, Inc.
Total Tower, 900 19th Street
Denver, CO 80202–2523
(303) 291–2275
Fax: (303) 291–2096

2911

Business Information: Total Petroleum, Inc., a petroleum refining and marketing/distribution company, specializes in the production of gasoline, kerosene, distillate fuel oils, residual fuel oils, and lubricants. Established in 1972, the Company employs 6,000 people and has an estimated annual revenue in excess of $2.2 billion. They currently operate four refineries, producing 200,000 barrels per day, as well as 550 company-owned retail stores. As Project Manager, Ms. Gallego is responsible for the management of special projects, focusing on business generation, diversification, and computer applications. **Career Steps:** Project Manager, Total Petroleum, Inc. (1981–Present); LP Modeling Specialist, Total, S.A., Paris, France (1990–1993); Chemical Engineer, Shell Oil Company (1977–1981). **Associations & Accomplishments:** American Institute of Chemical Engineers; Colorado School of Mines Alumni Association. **Education:** Colorado School of Mines, M.S. in Chemical Engineering (1977); Colorado Women's College, B.A. in Chemistry and French. **Personal:** Ms. Gallego enjoys traveling and gardening.

Theo L.K. Lee, Ph.D.
Vice President
Hydrocarbon Technologies, Inc.
1501 New York Avenue
Lawrenceville, NJ 08648–4635
(609) 394–3102
Fax: (609) 394–1278
E/M: hti @ cyberenet.net

2911

Business Information: Hydrocarbon Technologies, Inc. is a process licensing, petrochemical R&D and custom processing pilot facility for oil refining, environmental control, waste, and coal conversion. A professional engineer and internationally registered research scientist, Dr. Theo Lee joined the Company in 1992 as a research associate. Appointed Vice President in April 1995, he has full executive administration over all R&D and technology development. **Career Steps:** Hydrocarbon Technologies: Vice President (1995–Present), President (1995–Present); Research Associate, Hydrocarbon Research, Inc. (1992–1994); Section Manager, Alberta Research Council (1980–1991); Research Associate, New Brunswick Electric Power Commission (1977–1980). **Associations & Accomplishments:** Association of Professional Engineer; Geologists and Geophysicists of Alberta (Canada); American Chemical Society; American Institute of Chemical Engineers; Canadian Chinese National Council. **Education:** University of New Brunswick (Canada), Ph.D. (1977); Tunghai University (Taiwan), B.Sc. (1973). **Personal:** Married to Salina S.C. in 1974. Two children: Patrick C.H. and Christine C.L. Dr. Lee enjoys skiing and soccer.

John Maziuk Jr.
Senior Applications Engineer
Church & Dwight, Inc.
469 North Harrison Street
Perrineville, NJ 08535
(609) 497–7282
Fax: (609) 683–5297
EMail: See Below

2911

Business Information: Church & Dwight, Inc. specializes in the production of sodium, ammonium, and potassium bicarbonates, and production of consumer bicarbonate products. With headquarters in Princeton, NJ, the Company has three locations in the United States, Venezuela, and England, and is world-renowned for their "Arm & Hammer" logo. As Senior Applications Engineer, Mr. Maziuk is responsible for new products and application development. He handles all technical aspects of the Company and oversees two employees. Internet users can reach him via: Maziujo@ChurchDwight.Com. **Career Steps:** Senior Applications Engineer, Church & Dwight, Inc. (1994–Present); Business Director of Specialty Market, Covan, Ltd. (1987–1990); FMC Corporation: Senior Sales Representative (1984–1987), Research Engineer (1976–1984). **Associations & Accomplishments:** American Chemical Society; American Water Works Association. **Education:** Drexel (1978); New Jersey Institute of Technology, B.S.Ch.E. (1976). **Personal:** Married to Deborah in 1969. Three children: Jennifer, Katherine, and David. Mr. Maziuk enjoys being a father, husband, and groundskeeper.

James E. Murphy
Vice President of Finance
United Refining Company
15 Bradley Street, P.O. Box 780
Warren, PA 16365–0780
(814) 726–4674
Fax: (814) 726–4602

2911

Business Information: United Refining Company is a petroleum refining and marketing company providing oil and related products to major wholesale and retail distributors nationwide. Established in 1902, the Company employs 2,800 people and has an estimated annual revenue of $800 million. As Vice President of Finance, Mr. Murphy is responsible for all aspects of his department, including auditing, acquisition and analysis, capital project evaluation, compliance reporting, and bank financing credit line. Additional responsibilities include management of the internal auditing department and the overall supervision of seven employees. **Career Steps:** United Refining Company: Vice President of Finance (1995–Present), Director of Internal Audit (1986–Present); Manager of Financial Accounting (1984–1986). **Associations & Accomplishments:** American Institute of Certified Public Accountant's; Pennsylvania Institute of Certified Public Accountants; Institute of Internal Auditors; Association of Certified Finance Examiners; Certified Public Accountant; Certified Internal Auditor; Certified Financial Executive. **Education:** Gannon University: M.B.A. (1971), B.S. (1973). **Personal:** Married to Christina in 1973. Mr. Murphy enjoys golf, gardening, travel, and Tai Kwon Do.

Sherri K. Razo
Director of Credit
Quaker State Corporation
225 East John Carpenter Freeway
Irving, TX 75062
(214) 868–0400
Fax: (214) 868–0688

2911

Business Information: Quaker State Corporation is one of the leading manufacturers and distributors of automotive oils and lubricants. As Director of Credit, Ms. Razo is responsible for new account approvals and accounts receivable management. **Career Steps:** Director of Credit, Quaker State Corporation (1995–Present); Vice President of Credit Services, Slick 50 Products Corporation (1991–1995); Credit Manager, Beck/Arnley Worldparts Corporation (1988–1991). **Associations & Accomplishments:** National Association of Credit Management; Motor Equipment Manufacturers Association – Volume Retail Group; Tough Love International; Children's and Youth Minister. **Education:** Trevecca Nazarene College, B.S. in Management of Human Resources (1990); Castleton State College. **Personal:** One child: Michael. Ms. Razo enjoys needleworking.

Justin M. Stuhldreher
International Attorney
Amoco Corporation
501 Westlake Park Boulevard (M.C. 5.114)
Houston, TX 77079
(713) 336–3363
Fax: (713) 366–7578

2911

Business Information: AMOCO Corporation is a worldwide producer of crude oil and natural gas and also a marketer of refined products. Established in 1891, AMOCO currently employs 38,000 people and has an estimated annual revenue of $28 billion. As International Attorney, Mr. Stuhldreher renders legal advice and negotiates contracts pertaining to a wide spectrum of the Company's international business activities. **Career Steps:** International Attorney, AMOCO Corporation (1984–Present); Attorney, Gulf Oil Corporation (1978–1984). **Associations & Accomplishments:** American Bar Association; Maritime Law Association; Texas Bar Association; Pennsylvania Bar Association; Beta Gamma Sigma Business Association. **Education:** University of Notre Dame: J.D. (1978), M.B.A. (1978); Villanova University, B.S. (1974). **Personal:** Married to Mary K. in 1975. Four children: Peter, Katie, Amy and Jenny. Mr. Stuhldreher enjoys leisure reading, golf, model building and coaching baseball and basketball.

Jerry E. Throgmorton
Director of Materiel
AMFUEL
P.O. Box 887
Magnolia, AR 71753–0887
(501) 235–7227
Fax: (501) 235–7225

2911

Business Information: AMFUEL is a manufacturer of aircraft, missile, tank, and helicopter fuel cells and bladders. Additionally, they produce coated fabric H2O, fluid, or substance storage containers. As Director of Materiel, Mr. Throgmorton handles procurement, shipping, receiving, inventory control, and property control. **Career Steps:** Director of Materiel, AMFUEL (1995–Present); Manager of Materials, Dynapower/Stratopower (1992–1995); Senior Program Manager, UTC Advanced Systems Division (1982–1992); Lead Senior Quality Assurance Representative, Martin Marietta Aerospace – Michoud division (1980–1982). **Associations & Accomplishments:** American Society for Quality Control; Iota Lambda Sigma Honors Fraternity Industrial Education; Selected "Boss of the Year" in Magnolia, AR. **Education:** Florida Institute of Technology, M.B.A.; Southeast Missouri State University, B.S. in Industrial and Technical Education (1978). **Personal:** One child: Megan. Mr. Throgmorton enjoys Blues music, hunting, drag racing, and engine building.

Steven R. Baer
Environmental Manager
Superior Asphalt Concrete
2000 East Beech Street
Yakima, WA 98901–2147
(509) 248–6823
Fax: (509) 457–8100

2951

Business Information: Superior Asphalt Concrete specializes in the manufacture of asphalt hot mix, used by the Company to pave roads using road builders, rock crushers, and other related materials. As Environmental Manager, Mr. Baer is responsible for quality control, quality assurance, and ensuring day–in and day–out that environmental requirements are being met. **Career Steps:** Environmental Manager, Superior Asphalt Concrete (1991–Present); Operations Manager, Boss & Mayes Testing, Inc. (1986–1992); Laboratory Manager, Chen Northern, Inc. (1978–1986); Engineering Technician, City of Pasco (1975–1978). **Associations & Accomplishments:** Environmental Assessment Association; ASTM; International Registry of Environmental Engineering and Compliance Professionals. **Education:** Columbia Southern University, C.E.C.M. (1992); Environmental Assessment Association, C.E.S. (1995). **Personal:** Married to Leslie in 1980. Four children: Steven T., Tony, Aaron, and Kristopher. Mr. Baer enjoys motorcycles, horses, and ranching.

Robert R. Bartels
Director of Sales & Marketing
IKO
5555 West 65th Street
Chicago, IL 60638
(708) 496–2800
Fax: (219) 922–1604

2952

Business Information: IKO, a privately–held company, is a manufacturer of asphalt roofing shingles for residential construction. International in scope, IKO has nine plants throughout the U.S., Canada, and Europe. Future plans include expanding the U.S. operations. As Director of Sales & Marketing, Mr. Bartels is responsible for the direction of all sales and marketing activities for seven U.S. plants in the Northern Tier of the U.S., as well as directing the activities of seven managers and 40 sales people. In addition, he oversees all sales policies, marketing, and product development. **Career Steps:** Director of Sales & Marketing, IKO (1993–Present); Director of Sales & Marketing, Globe Building Materials (1992); Vice President of Sales, CeloTex Corporation (1971–1991). **Education:** Bowling Green State University, B.S. in Business Administration (1970). **Personal:** Mr. Bartels enjoys spending time with his family, golf, and relaxing.

Michael A. Delgado, PHR

Corporate Human Resource Director
Hollinee Corporation d.b.a. Leatherback Industries
111 Hillcrest Road
Hollister, CA 95023–4920
(408) 636–5042
Fax: (408) 636–5041
Pager # (408) 638–5248

2952

Business Information: Leatherback Industries — one of five wholly–owned subsidiaries of construction materials conglomerate manufacturer Hollinee Corporation — is a manufacturer and international distributor of asphalt roofing materials and fiberglass filter media. Established in 1972, Leatherback Industries reports annual revenue of $128 million and currently employs over 500 people. As Corporate Human Resource Director, Mr. Delgado has overall executive responsibility for all areas of personnel matters, as well as oversees all environmental, health and safety sectors to ensure compliance with governmental regulatory controls. Established in 1972, Hollinee Corporation d.b.a. Leatherback Industries employs 540 people with annual sales of $128 million. **Career Steps:** Corporate Human Resource Director, Hollinee Corporation, d.b.a. Leatherback Industries (1995–Present); Human Resource/Health & Safety Administration, Harte–Hanks Communication (1992–1995); General Manager, Mad–Tech & Associates (1984–1992). **Associations & Accomplishments:** Society of Human Resource Management; American Risk Management; Risk and Insurance Management Association; American Management Association; Morgan Hill Kiwanis; Instruct career planning at intermediate and high school levels. **Education:** University of California: Environmental Safety Resource (1993), B.B.A. (1974); San Jose State University: Occupational Safety on Health Management (1995), Human Resource Development. **Personal:** Married to Hope in 1979. Two children: Justin and Tiffany. Mr. Delgado enjoys reading, coaching Pony League baseball, and instructing classes on career planning at the intermediate and high school levels.

Rear Admiral Robert P. Hickey Jr., U.S.N. (Ret)

Chief Operating Officer
Gardner Asphalt Corporation
4161 East Seventh Avenue
Tampa, FL 33675–5449
(813) 248–2101
Fax: (818) 247–5548

2952

Business Information: Gardner Asphalt Corporation is a national manufacturer of roof coatings and driveway sealants. Established in 1945, Gardner Asphalt Corporation currently employs 350 people. A veteran of thirty–one years of military service (U.S. Navy), Mr. Hickey joined Gardner Asphalt Corporation as Chief Operating Officer in 1995. He is responsible for the oversight of all operations, as well as supervision of a staff of more than 70 people. **Career Steps:** Chief Operating Officer, Gardner Asphalt Corporation (1995–Present); Rear Admiral, United States Navy (1964–1995). **Associations & Accomplishments:** Association of Naval Aviation Society; Tail Hook; Naval Institute; Holder of a pilot's license. **Education:** Holy Cross College, B.A. in Accounting (1964); Harvard University JFK School of Government, International Security Course (1991). **Personal:** Married to Marilyn in 1968. Two children: Robert III and Kristen. Mr. Hickey enjoys sports, boating, snow skiing, travel, and piloting aircraft.

Raymond T. Hyer

Owner, Chairman, and Chief Executive Officer
Gardner Asphalt Corporation
4161 East Seventh Avenue
Tampa, FL 33675
(813) 248–2101
Fax: (813) 247–5548

2952

Business Information: Gardner Asphalt Corporation is a national manufacturer of roof coatings and driveway sealants. Established in 1945, Gardner Asphalt Corporation currently employs 350 people. As Owner, Chairman, and Chief Executive Officer, Mr. Hyer is responsible for all aspects of operations. **Education:** Holly Cross College, B.A. in Accounting (1964); Long Island University, M.B.A. (1966). **Personal:** Married to Kathleen in 1966. Six children: Raymond, Sean, Michael, Bobby, Tim, and Tara.

April E. Josephson

Chief Executive Officer
Ariel Communications Group, Inc.
29851 Avetura, Suite E
Rancho Santa Margarita, CA 92688
(714) 858–1000
Fax: (714) 459–1000
EMAIL: april@ariel.net

2952

Business Information: Ariel Communications Group, Inc., established in 1996, is an Internet provider. As CEO, Ms. Josephson is responsible for all aspects of Corporation operations, including administration, finance, sales, public relations, accounting, legal, taxes, marketing, and strategic planning. **Career Steps:** President, Ariel Communications Group, Inc. (1996); CEO, Environmental Coating Systems (1982–Present). **Associations & Accomplishments:** State Bar of California; Orange County Employer Advisory Council. **Education:** University of Phoenix, M.B.A. (1996); University of San Diego School of Law, J.D. (1984); University of Southern California, A.B. (1981). **Personal:** Married to Don Mathers in 1993. Two children: Stephanie and Jennifer Mathers. Ms. Josephson enjoys Tai–chi chuan.

Gery W. Keith

District Sales Manager
GS Roofing Products
P.O. Box 272580
Tampa, FL 33688
(813) 961–8939
Fax: (813) 961–2395

2952

Business Information: GS Roofing Products is a national manufacturer of roofing materials with over 12 facilities across the country. As District Sales Manager, Mr. Keith is responsible for the southeastern United States, including Florida, Georgia, Alabama, and eastern Tennessee. He oversees all sales functions, training of sales representatives, and a staff of seven sales representatives. **Career Steps:** District Sales Manager, GS Roofing Products (1989–Present); Sales Representative/Estimator, Greenville Lumber Company (1980–1984); Sales Representative, Bird & Son, Inc. (1975–1980). **Associations & Accomplishments:** Florida Roofing and Sheet Metal Association; National Association of Homebuilders. **Education:** Millsaps College (1975); Northeast Mississippi Junior College, Associate's degree in Business (1973). **Personal:** Married to Nancy in 1982. Three children: Corey, James, and Carly. Mr. Keith enjoys golf, jogging, and reading.

Jose (Pepe) Capeles

President
Sunoco Caribbean
P.O. Box 487
Yabucoa, Puerto Rico 00767–0487
(809) 893–2320
Fax: (809) 893–2550

2992

Business Information: Sunoco Caribbean, a subsidiary of Sun Oil Company based in Pennsylvania, is a manufacturer and marketer of lubricants. Other activities include manufacturing, blending and packaging. International in scope, Sunoco Caribbean concentrates on the Caribbean and Central American markets. As President, Mr. Capeles provides leadership, overall direction, and administration of all Company activities to accomplish operational and financial goals. **Career Steps:** President, Sunoco Caribbean (1993–Present); Sun Oil Company, P.A.: General Manager, Blending Plant (1991–1993), Process Development Manager, Lubes R&D (1989–1991), Refinery Operations Manager (1984–1989). **Associations & Accomplishments:** President of Energy Committee of the Manufacturers Association; Independent Lubricants Manufacturers Association; Licensed Engineers and Member of College of Engineers and Surveyors, Puerto Rico; A.I.C.H.E. **Education:** Tuck–Dartmouth, Business (1989); University of Puerto Rico, B.S.C.H.E. (1974). **Personal:** Married to Eva in 1976. Three children: Jose E., Maria A., and Gabriel E. Mr. Capeles enjoys golf, gardening and guitar.

Mr. F. Norman Christopher

Managing Director of Business Development Division
Lubrizol Corporation
29400 Lakeland Boulevard
Wickliffe, OH 44092
(216) 943–4200
Fax: (216) 944–6847

2992

Business Information: Lubrizol Corporation is a leading full–service supplier of performance chemicals to diverse markets worldwide. These specialty chemical products are created through the application of advanced chemical, mechanical and biological technologies to enhance the performance, quality and value of the products in which they are used. Founded in 1928, in Cleveland, Ohio, the Company now operates manufacturing and blending facilities (30 wholly–owned subsidiaries and 17 manufacturing plants), laboratories and offices staffed by more than 4,500 employees around the world. Lubrizol is a recognized leader in specialty additive systems for lubricating oils used in gasoline and diesel engines, for automatic transmission fluids, gear oils, marine and tractor lubricants. The Company also supplies specialty products for industrial fluids, fuel additives and process chemicals. In addition, they develop performance chemicals for specialized markets. The Company places much emphasis on safeguarding the environment, fuel economy, extended durability and determining both the primary and secondary effects accruing from the use of lubricants and fuels. Lubrizol works with their customers to achieve their product performance goals in the most effective, timely and cost–efficient manner. Their committment is to provide top quality products and services to meet both consumer and environmental demands. Lubrizol Corporation reports annual revenue of $1,599 MM. As Managing Director of Business Development Division, Mr. Christopher is responsible for developing new specialty chemical businesses and providing support services to his division. **Career Steps:** Managing Director of Business Development Division, Lubrizol Corporation (1994–Present); Senior Vice President, Lubrizol Performance Products Co. (1993–1994); Senior Vice President, Lubrizol Business Development Co. (1991–1992); Director of Planning and Development, Lubrizol Business Development Co. (1989–1990); Venture Manager, Consultant for Olin Corporation (1974–1985). **Associations & Accomplishments:** President–Elect, Commercial Development Association; President, Continue Life, Inc.; Licensing Executive Society; Published in business journals. **Education:** University of North Carolina, A.B. (1965); University of Connecticut, M.B.A. (1978); Harvard Business School, Program for Management Development (1989) **Personal:** Married to Anita in 1968. Two children: Paige and David. Mr. Christopher enjoys outdoor sports, including tennis, fishing, golf, community service and foreign missions.

Thad R. Hogan II

Director of International Sales of Quaker State Products
Quaker State Corporation
225 E. John Carpenter Freeway
Irving, TX 75062
(214) 868–0463
Fax: (214) 868–0678

2992

Business Information: Quaker State Corporation is one of the leading manufacturers and marketers of automotive oils and lubricants. As Director of International Sales of Quaker State Products, Mr. Hogan directs all sales of Quaker State branded products outside of North America. He locates distributor licensees and end users, while supporting them with technical support and marketing assistance to obtain more international business, especially in Canada and Mexico. **Career Steps:** Quaker State Corporation: Director of International Sales of Quaker State Products (1996–Present), International Marketing Manager (1990–1995), Sales Representative – Southern (1987–1990); Account Sales Manager, Industrial Lubricants Corporation (1990). **Associations & Accomplishments:** Overseas Automotive Council. **Education:** Texas A&M University, B.B.A. in Management (1987). **Personal:** Married to Susan L. in 1991. Two children: Michelle and Thad III. Mr. Hogan enjoys golf, tennis, fishing, and water and snow skiing.

Imtiyaz Patel

Managing Director
ISA Industries, Inc.
5 Jane Lane
Barrington, IL 60010
(547) 516–1583
Fax: (847) 516–2730

2992

Business Information: ISA Industries, Inc. is an international contract manufacturer and marketer of automotive lubricants and car care products. As Managing Director, Mr. Patel oversees daily operations, buying and selling functions, and attends various trade shows throughout the year. **Career Steps:** Managing Director, ISA Industries, Inc. (1993–Present); President, Leader Automotive, Inc. (1996–Present); Marketing Manager, Old World Industries, Inc. (1980–1983). **Associations & Accomplishments:** Who's Who in Executives and Professionals; Various other automotive associations. **Education:** University of Illinois, B.S. in Marketing (1986). **Personal:** Married to Salma Ahmed in 1986. Two children: Shahir Ahmed and Irshaad Ahmed. Mr. Patel enjoys travel and meeting new people.

Robert K. Zuccarello

Manager of Laboratory Services
Dryden Oil Company
9300 Pulaski Highway
Baltimore, MD 21220–2418
(410) 682–9468
Fax: (410) 682–9415

2992

Business Information: Dryden Oil Company is the heavy duty lubricants division of Castrol North America specializing in the blending, distributing and marketing of lubricating oils. Prior to its acquisition by Castrol North America, it was the largest independent manufacturer of heavy duty lubricants serving the industry for 100 years. His career began in 1957 when Mr. Zuccarello joined Dryden Oil Company as Manager of Laboratory Sciences in 1989. He is responsible for the testing for the corporate laboratories, including both new and used lubricating oils. Mr. Zuccarello has authored several papers and been recognized as a recipient of the "Best Paper of the Year" for his work in thermal analysis. **Career Steps:** Manager of Laboratory Services, Dryden Oil Company (1989–Present); Consultant, Chem–Sultants (1987–1989); Manager, Analytical Lab, Cities Service (1980–1987); Chemist and Technician (1967–1980); Microscopist, National Lead Company (1964–1967); Chemist, Textile Research Institute (1962–1967); Technician, FMC (1957–1962). **Associations & Accomplishments:** ASTM; Society of Automotive Engineers; Society of Accredited Marine Surveyors; President, Board of Education; Softball Umpire, American Softball Association. **Education:** Oklahoma University; Drexel University; Mercer County Community College. **Personal:** One child: Robert, Jr. Mr. Zuccarello enjoys golf and computers.

Steven R. Johnson

Lead Engineer II
Texaco, Inc., Alternate Energy Department
654 Otono Drive
Boulder City, NV 89005
(702) 651–1213
Fax: (702) 644–1474

2999

Business Information: Texaco, Inc. is a major producer and worldwide distributor of petroleum products and technology.

The Alternate Energy Department includes gas turbine powered simple and combined cycle cogeneration plants which supply electricity to utilities and process heat to other production plants. Mr. Johnson is the plant engineer responsible for operations, engineering and project improvements for two 85 MW facilities. **Career Steps:** Lead Engineer II, Texaco, Inc., Alternate Energy Department (1992–Present); Project Engineer, Texaco Cool Water Project (1989–1992); Chemical Engineer, Cool Water Coal Gasification Project (1986–1989); Plant Engineer, Southern California Edison, Solar One and the Cool Water Generating Station (1984–1986). **Associations & Accomplishments:** Member of Board, Western Turbine Users, Inc.; Certified Cogeneration Professional, Association of Energy Engineers; Professional Development Recognition, American Institute of Chemical Engineers; IGTI Author; American Society of Mechanical Engineers; Assistant District Commissioner, Boy Scouts of America; Author of several articles in industry periodicals. **Education:** University of Redlands, M.A. in Management (1988); Brigham Young University, B.S. in Chemical Engineering (1978). **Personal:** Married to Kim in 1979. Two children: Joshua and Kaleb. Mr. Johnson enjoys skiing, biking, hiking, spelunking, reading, travel, boating, radio and music.

3000 Rubber and Miscellaneous Plastics Products

3011 Tires and inner tubes
3021 Rubber and plastics footwear
3052 Rubber and plastics hose and belting
3053 Gaskets, packing and sealing devices
3061 Mechanical rubber goods
3069 Fabricated rubber products, NEC
3081 Unsupported plastics film and sheet
3082 Unsupported plastics profile shapes
3083 Laminated plastics plate and sheet
3084 Plastics pipe
3085 Plastics bottles
3086 Plastics foam products
3087 Custom compound purchased resins
3088 Plastics plumbing fixtures
3089 Plastics products, NEC

Dennis S. Chrobak

President
American Tire Corporation
446 W. Lake Ave.
Ravenna, OH 44266–3649
(216) 296–8778
Fax: (216) 296–9787

3011

Business Information: American Tire Corporation is a designer and manufacturer of 'trouble–free' tire/wheel assemblies. Established in 1995, the Ohio–based company focused primarily on bicycle tires and licensed a wheel manufacturer to produce dynamic steerable springs which have been patented. Since inception, corporate assets have increased to $10 million the first year, $22 million the second, with aspirations of doubling revenue by next year. As President, Mr. Chrobak provides the overall vision and strategy for the Corporation, ensuring quality product output, customer satsifaction and effective strategies to keep the company a viable presence in the current market. **Career Steps:** President, American Tire Corporation (1995–Present); Vice President, Alanco Enviromental Resources (1994); Chief Engineer, Strategic Technology & Business Planning, Goodyear (1993–94). **Associations & Accomplishments:** Society of Automotive Engineers; Boy Scouts of America. **Education:** Case Western Reserve University, M.B.A. (1989); Case Institute of Technologies, B.S. in Chemical Engineering (1961). **Personal:** Married to Bonnie Jean in 1962. Three children: Catherine, Philip, and James. Mr. Chrobak enjoys technology creation.

Anders T. Doll

Quality Assurance Manager
Hisan, Inc.
1849 Industrial Dr.
Findlay, OH 45840
(419) 425–7431
Fax: (419) 425–2602

3052

Business Information: Hisan, Inc. is a supplier of automotive fluid–handling tubing from three locations in Ohio. Established in 1987, Hisan, Inc. reports annual revenue of $60 million and currently employs 480 people. With twelve years experience in the quality assurance field, Mr. Doll joined Hisan, Inc. in 1989. Serving as Quality Assurance Manager, he is responsible for the management of quality assurance activities and oversight of fifteen employees at three plants, as well as serving as an ISO 9000 Management Representative. **Career Steps:** Quality Assurance Manager, Hisan, Inc. (1989–Present); Quality Assurance Manager, Jacobs Industries (1983–1988); Wheat Inspector, Star of the West Milling (1979–1983). **Associations & Accomplishments:** American Society for Quality Control; Society of Automotive Engineers. **Education:** Central Michigan University, B.S.B.A. (1983). **Personal:** Married to Jill in 1984. One child: Wesley. Mr. Doll enjoys sports and hunting.

Judith L. Bland

Corporate Director of Benefits Administration & Training
Goshen Rubber Company, Inc.
1525 South Tenth Street
Goshen, IN 46527
(219) 533–1111
Fax: (219) 533–5332

3053

Business Information: International in scope, Goshen Rubber Company, Inc. specializes in the manufacture and sale of mechanical rubber and plastic components (primarily seals), for the automotive industry. Products manufactured include elastomer, urethane and silicone. Established in 1916, Goshen Rubber Company reports annual revenue of $150 million and currently employs 2,000 people. As Corporate Director of Benefits Administration & Training, Mrs. Bland is responsible for the coordination and establishment of corporate–wide training programs. Concurrent with her position as Corporate Director, she serves as Team Leader of Manufacturing Reengineering. **Career Steps:** Goshen Rubber Company, Inc.: Corporate Director of Benefits Administration & Training (1994–Present), Team Leader of Manufacturing Reengineering (1995–Present); Director of Welfare Plans, Holy Cross Shared Services (1990–1994). **Associations & Accomplishments:** Listed in Who's Who in American High Schools, Who's Who in Professional Women; Michigan Association of Institutional Researchers (MAIR); Career Women's Guild. **Education:** Andrews University, M.B.A. (1990), B.B.A. in Managed Information Services (MIS), A.S. in Business Administration, A.T. in Information Science; Organizational Dynamics, Inc., Certified Facilitator of TQM. **Personal:** Married to R. Kirk Bland, Plant Manager of Mixing at Goshen Rubber Company, Inc., in 1995. Mrs. Bland enjoys golf, international cuisine, languages, nonverbal communications, puns, watercolor & oil painting, and learning anything new.

Mr. James O. Elledge

President
Elledge Gasketing and Supply Company
2579 Ferris Road
Columbus, OH 43224
(614) 471–3958
Fax: (614) 471–0131

3053

Business Information: Elledge Gasketing and Supply Company manufactures gaskets and other die–cut items to specifications. Established in 1964, the company currently employs 10 professionals. As President, Mr. Elledge is responsible for all aspects of operations including, sales, marketing and equipment purchasing. **Career Steps:** President, Elledge Gasketing and Supply Company (1964–Present); Sales, Southland Printing Company (1963–1966); Sales, Stoneman Press (1961–1962); Sales, Scioto Printing Co. (1957–1961). **Associations & Accomplishments:** Goodale Lodge #372 F. & A.M.; Worshipful Master (three terms); York Rite Bodies and Shrine; Head Chapter Advisor (12 years), Chairman Of State (two terms) Demolay; Demolay Chapter Advisor; Advisory Council; Sunday School Teacher (five years); President, Jr. High School and High School P.T.A.; Secretary of Civitan (three years); On Guard Council of N.F.I.B.; Guardian. **Education:** Ohio State University, B.A. (1950). **Personal:** Mr. Elledge enjoys writing, sports and travel.

Judith N. Lavey

Pension Administrator
GenCorp, Vehicle Sealing Division
P O Box 1002
Welland, Ontario L3B 5R9
(905) 735–5631 Ext. 218
Fax: (905) 735–5564

3053

Business Information: GenCorp is a publicly–traded United States company that has its roots with the General Tire and Rubber Company. When General Tire and Rubber sold its tire business in 1986, GenCorp, with three distinct divisions, was formed. One division produces polymer–based consumer products. The Aerospace Division produces solid and liquid rocket propulsion systems. The Vehicle Sealing Division is a leading producer of extruded rubber sealing and molded rubber parts for domestic and European passenger cars and light trucks. As Pension Administrator, Ms. Lavey educates, administer, updates all pension policy and procedures for the Canadian plant of GenCorp and reports to the 920 employees on all significant information in regards to pensions. **Career Steps:** Pension Administrator, United Way of South Nicaragua, Coordinator for Gencorp (1992–Present); Supervisor of Personnel/Benefits Administrator, pension Clerk, Personal Clerk, Norton Advanced Ceramics (1962–1992). **Associations & Accomplishments:** Human Resource Professional Association; United Way for Niagara South. **Education:** Humber College, PPAC (Pension Plan Administration Certificate) (1995); Niagara College, Management Labor Relations Certificate; Certified Human Resource Professional (1990). **Personal:** Three children: Barbara Atkinson (Son–in–Law David), David (entering Queen's University, Kingston, Ontario), and Christine (O.A.C.'s, St. Michael's High School, Niagara Falls). Grandchildren, Dustin and Emily. Ms. Lavey enjoys golf, walking, travel, reading for pleasure and business, and trips with her Grandchildren.

Keith R. Miller

Unit President
Garlock, Inc.
1666 Division Street
Palmyra, NY 14522
(315) 597–4811
Fax: (315) 597–3180

3053

Business Information: Garlock, Inc., established in 1887, is a manufacturer of industrial packaging, gasketing, oil seals, expansion joints, custom molded parts, and metallic gaskets for the automotive industry. Working out of eleven international offices, the Company employs over 1,500 people. As Unit President, Mr. Miller supervises administration of manufacturing, sales, purchasing, shipping, and engineering of several domestic and international locations. He handles all aspects of Company operations, including finance, human resources, and international activities. Mr. Miller joined the Company in 1980 as a Product Line Coordinator. **Career Steps:** Garlock Mechanical Packing, Inc.: President (1994–Present), Vice President of Sales & Marketing (1993–1994), Manager of Nuclear Services (1992–1993), Regional Manager – Southwest (1990–1992). **Associations & Accomplishments:** Fluid Sealing Association. **Education:** Union College, B.S. (1980). **Personal:** Married to Elizabeth in 1980. Two children: Emma and William. Mr. Miller enjoys coaching youth soccer and gardening.

Robert D. Myers

Vice President – Automotive Group
Sika Industry Division USA
22211 Telegraph Road
Southfield, MI 48034
(810) 354–6555
Fax: (810) 354–6559

3053

Business Information: Sika Industry Division USA is a manufacturer of elastomeric acoustical, sealing, and adhesive materials for the OEM automotive market. International in scope, Sika Industry Division has more than 50 locations throughout the world. Joining Sika Industry Division USA as Director of Product Development in 1988, Mr. Myers was appointed as Vice President in 1995. He is responsible for sales, marketing, strategic plannings, and international relations with the OEM level people. **Career Steps:** Sika Industry Division USA: Vice President (1995–Present), Director of Product Development (1988–1995); Manager of Elastomerics, Essex Speciality Producers (1986–1989). **Associations & Accomplishments:** Society of Plastic Engineers; Vice President, Providence Foundation. **Education:** Longview College; Southwestern Junior College, A.A. in Business Administration. **Personal:** Married to Anita in 1982. Two children: John and Christy.

Charles E. Phelps, CPA

Co–Owner
Phelps Industrial Products
6300 Washington Boulevard
Baltimore, MD 21227–5347
(410) 796–2222
Fax: (410) 796–1277

3053

Business Information: Phelps Industrial Products is a manufacturer of industrial sealing products, including gaskets, rubber products, mechanical seals, and mechanical packing. As Co–Owner, Mr. Phelps is responsible for many aspects of Company operations, including administrative activities, accounting, and data processing. **Career Steps:** Co–Owner, Phelps Industrial Products (1991–Present). **Associations & Accomplishments:** American Institute of Certified Public

Accountants; Maryland Society of Accountants. **Education:** Florida Atlantic University, B.B.A. (1974); Certified Public Accountant (1993). **Personal:** Married to Peggy L. in 1973. Two children: Gregory B. and Timothy A.

Terry T. Threlfall
Director of Technology
Freudenberg–NOK
Route 104
Bristol, NH 03222
(603) 744–1706
Fax: (603) 744–1706

3053

Business Information: Freudenberg–NOK is an international producer of elastomeric sealing devices for the OEM automotive industry. The Bristol, New Hampshire location produces precision elastomeric oil and grease seals primarily for the automotive market. As Director of Technology, Mr. Threlfall is responsible for the New Hampshire facility, the Company's largest facility. He is responsible for research and development, material development, CAD/CAM engineering, test labs, tool design, and tool and mold manufacturing. **Career Steps:** Director of Technology, Freudenberg–NOK (1989–Present); Engineering Manager, Albert Trostel Packings Company (1987–1989); Engineering Manager, Acushnet Corporation (1981–1987); Tool and Process Engineering Supervisor, Aeroquip Corp. (1978–1981). **Associations & Accomplishments:** Society of Automotive Engineers. **Education:** New Hampshire College, B.S.; New Hampshire Technical College, A.A.S. **Personal:** Married to Donna in 1971. Two children: Jessica and Terry Jr. Mr. Threlfall enjoys hiking, hunting, and camping.

Daniel C. Frickey
Senior Product Manager
Busak & Shamban
2531 Bremer Road
Ft. Wayne, IN 46803
(219) 422–1005
Fax: (219) 422–8420

3061

Business Information: Busak & Shamban specializes in the manufacture of hydraulic and pneumatic seals out of PTFE and plastic for the aerospace, automotive, and construction industries throughout the world. Established in 1952, the Company employs 325 people and has an estimated annual revenue of $30 million. As Senior Product Manager, Mr. Frickey is responsible for all aspects of the product line including advertising, pricing, and sales and engineering. **Career Steps:** Busak & Shamban: Senior Product Manager (1996–Present), Product Manager (1992–1996), Sales Manager (1988–1992). **Associations & Accomplishments:** American Management Association; Society of Automotive Engineers. **Education:** Washburn University, B.A. in Education (1976). **Personal:** Married to Elaine in 1981. Three children: Amanda, Scott, and David. Mr. Frickey enjoys golf, fishing, and coaching.

Krista W. Arthur
National Manager, Sales Administration
Oliver Rubber Company
P.O. Box 1827
Athens, GA 30607–1827
(706) 354–0810
Fax: (706) 354–4152

3069

Business Information: Oliver Rubber Company provides rubber products and retread–related products to the retreading industry. Ms. Arthur has held various positions within the Company, first as a Telemarketing Representative in 1990, Central Billing Administration Manager in 1993, and promoted to National Manager of Sales Administration in 1995. She currently oversees the Service Department, National Account Billing Department, and all administrative sales functions including sales force support. **Career Steps:** Oliver Rubber Company: National Manager, Sales Administration (1995–Present), Central Billing Administration Manager (1993–1995), Telemarketing Representative (1990–1993); Assistant Account Representative/Coop, G.E. Lighting Division (1989–1990). **Education:** University of Georgia, B.B.A. (1989). **Personal:** Married to David S. in 1991. Two children: William Cole and Mason Scott. Ms. Arthur enjoys spending time with her family.

Mr. Guillermo Cardona Valdez
Plant Manager
Poliuretanos Summa Woodbridge
Avenue Asociacion Nacional de Industrial #3
Cuautitlan, Izc. Edo., Mexico 54730
011–5258722409
Fax: 011–5258722123

3069

Business Information: Poliuretanos Summa Woodbridge, a subsidiary of Goodrich Corporation, is a manufacturer and international distributor of foam utilized in the manufacture of automotive seating. As Plant Manager, Mr. Cardona Valdez oversees finance, operations, quality control, materials, engineering, and production. **Career Steps:** Plant Manager, Poliuretanos Summa Woodbridge (1991–Present); Molding & Tool Shop Manager, Gillette de Mexico (1986–1991); Manufacture Manager, Coramex (1984–1986); Product Engineer, Lanzagorta Cop. (1981–1982). **Associations & Accomplishments:** Casa Blanca Club, Sport Tennis and Squash. **Education:** Engineer Mechanic, Master; Master in Implementatis of Culture in Total Quality. **Personal:** Married to Yolanda Villagomez Vega. One child: Guillermo Cardona Villagomez. Mr. Cardona Valdez enjoys soccer, tennis, and squash.

Thomas L. Carrell
Vice President of Information Services
Pioneer Balloon Company
5000 East 29th Street North
Wichita, KS 67220
(316) 685–2266
Fax: (316) 688–8702

3069

Business Information: Pioneer Balloon Company, a privately–owned company, is the world's leading manufacturer of latex and metallic balloons. International in scope, Pioneer Balloon Company has locations throughout the U.S., Canada, Thailand, United Kingdom, Mexico, and Australia. With eighteen years expertise in information technology, Mr. Carrell joined Pioneer Balloon Company as Data Processing Manager in 1983. Currently serving as Vice President of Information Services, he is responsible for all aspects of operations of the Finance and Information Services divisions, including finances, accounting, and strategic planning. **Career Steps:** Pioneer Balloon Company: Vice President of Information Services (1993–Present), Data Processing Manager (1983–1993); Programmer/Analyst, ASI Computer Systems, Inc. (1979–1983). **Associations & Accomplishments:** Data Processing Management Association; American Production Inventory Control Society; American Management Association. **Education:** Luther College, B.A. in English (1974); University of Northern Iowa, B.A. **Personal:** Married to Elizabeth in 1981. Four children: Andrea, Hunter, Parker, and Samuel. Mr. Carrell enjoys gardening, basketball, golf, surfing the Internet, softball and coaching.

Billy McGittigan
Market/Product Manager
Ansell Perry
1875 Harsh Avenue, SE
Massillon, OH 44646–7123
(330) 833–2811
Fax: (330) 833–5991

3069

Business Information: Ansell Perry is a manufacturer of sterile surgical and non–sterile examination gloves. As Market/Product Manager, Mr. McGittigan is directly responsible for North American marketing and product development for the Company. Additionally, he supervises the introduction of new and the maintenance of existing products. **Career Steps:** Ansell Perry: Market/Product Manager (1995–Present), Account Manager (1993–1995); Sales Representative, William C. Brown (1990–1993); District Executive, Boy Scouts of America (1987–1990). **Associations & Accomplishments:** Boy Scouts of America; Rotary Club; March of Dimes. **Education:** Nicholls State University, B.S. (1985). **Personal:** One child: Lauren. Mr. McGittigan enjoys flying, golf, jogging, and reading.

Robbi G. Mooney
Chief Operations Officer
Mid South Roller Company
200 Porter Industrial Road
Clarksville, AR 72830
(501) 754–6993
Fax: (501) 754–3417

3069

Business Information: Mid South Roller Company is a national manufacturer and servicer of industrial rubber rollers.

Established in 1980, Mid South Roller Company currently employs 44 people. With seventeen years experience in the manufacturing industry, Mrs. Mooney joined Mid South Roller Company in 1982. Currently serving as Chief Operations Officer, Mrs. Mooney is responsible for the oversight and control of all functions of the Company, including supervision of the department heads of sales, administration and production departments. **Career Steps:** Chief Operations Officer, Mid South Roller Company (1982–Present); Executive Secretary, Jacuzzi Bros., Inc. (1978–1981). **Associations & Accomplishments:** American Business Women's Association; Rotary Club; Chamber of Commerce; Advisory Counsel, Arkansas Valley Vocational Technical Institute; Rubber Roller Group. **Education:** Arkansas Technical University (1990); University of Arkansas – Little Rock; Arkansas Valley Vocational Technical School. **Personal:** Married to Timothy in 1991. Two children: Daymond and Ginger. Mrs. Mooney enjoys camping and reading.

Mrs. Zelda A. Parson
Controller
Dayco Products, Inc.
2300 South Highway 265
Springdale, AR 72764
(501) 750–1190
Fax: (501) 756–2126

3069

Business Information: Dayco Products, Inc. is the world's leading manufacturer and distributor of automotive and industrial rubber products. Products include belting, hoses, tires, tubing, etc. The Springdale plant is an assembly operation of front engine accessories for use in automotive manufacturing applications. As Controller, Mrs. Parson is responsible for the administration and direction of all financial activities at the Springdale plant. Established in 1985, the Springdale Plant employs approximately 125 people. **Career Steps:** Controller, Dayco Products, Inc. (1990–Present); City of Fayettville (1985–90): Budget Analyst, Accounting Supervisor, Special Projects Officer. **Associations & Accomplishments:** American Institute of Certified Public Accountants; Arkansas Society of Certified Public Accountants; Northwest Arkansas Chapter of Certified Public Accountants; Institute of Internal Auditors. **Education:** University of Arkansas, B.S. in Business Administration (1985), Major Accounting/Data Processing; Licensed Certified Public Accountant (1985). **Personal:** Married to Mark D. in 1982. One child: Tyler Wayne. Mrs. Parson enjoys golf and volleyball.

Mr. Koichi Tsukamoto
Executive Vice President
Zeon Chemicals Incorporated
4100 Bells Lane
Louisville, KY 40211
(502) 775–7724
Fax: (502) 775–7714

3069

Business Information: Zeon Chemicals Incorporated is a synthetic rubber producer primarily to the automotive industry. Offices: Texas, Mississippi, and Kentucky. Established in 1989, Zeon Chemicals Incorporated presently employs 400 people and has an estimated annual revenue in excess of $135 million. In his current capacity, Mr. Tsukamoto is responsible for all financial activities. **Career Steps:** Executive Vice President, Zeon Chemicals Incorporated (1994–Present); Vice President, Zeon Chemicals U.S.A., Inc. (1992–1994); President, Zeon Chemicals Texas, Inc. (1989–1992). **Education:** Keio University – Japan, Accounting (1962). **Personal:** Married to Yoko Tsukamoto in 1966. Three children: Toshiko, Tomoko, and Daisuke. Mr. Tsukamoto enjoys golf and traveling in his leisure time.

Edward A. Bernheim
President
Exxene Corporation
5939 Holly Road
Corpus Christi, TX 78414
(512) 991–8391
Fax: (512) 991–9057

3081

Business Information: Exxene Corporation is a manufacturer and retailer of the application of optical coatings to plastic or glass. Established in 1974, Exxene's Corpus Christi plant reports annual revenue of $5 million and currently employs 55 people. As President, Mr. Bernheim is responsible for all aspects of operations. **Career Steps:** President, Exxene Corporation (1976–Present); Technical Director, Hydrosol (1972–1976); R & D Group Leader, Alberto Culver (1969–1972). **Associations & Accomplishments:** Society of Mechanical Engineers; Society of the Plastic Industry; Society of Plastics Engineers; Society of Automotive Engineers.

Education: University of Missouri, M.S. in Chemistry (1969); Illinois Institute of Technology, B.S. in Chemistry (1967). **Personal:** Married to Shelley L. Bernheim.

William A. Burke

Executive Director
International Window Film Association
41815 North 12th Street
Phoenix, AZ 85027–7365
(602) 465–5730
Fax: (602) 465–5575

3081

Business Information: The International Window Film Association (IWFA) is an international trade association serving the window film industry. Since its inception five years ago, its members now number over 1,200 in 37 countries and include all window film manufacturers, 80% of the distributors and 25% of the professional installers within this industry. As Executive Director, Mr. Burke provides the overall vision and strategy of, ensuring quality product output, customer satisfaction and the effective strategies to keep the company a viable presence in the international market. **Career Steps:** Executive Director, International Window Film Association (1993–Present); Executive Director, International Sp. Reflector Association; Committee Manager, Association of Metalizers, Coater, and Laminators. **Associations & Accomplishments:** Scottsdale City's Man of the Year; Electric League of Arizona Man of the Year; Warner B. Lambert Award (1973) by TEAM; Executive Committee TEC, Edison Electric Institute. **Education:** Attended: University of Zaragoza; University of Maryland, A.S.W. **Personal:** Married to Audrey Ann in 1962. Two children: William H. and Patrick A. Mr. Burke enjoys spending time with family.

Elliott E. Fowler Jr.

Plant Manager
ITW Hi Cone
1140 West Bryn Mawr
Itasca, IL 60143–1509
(708) 773–9300
Fax: (708) 773–3015

3081

Business Information: ITW manufacturers plastic packaging products, with product lines to include extrusion and punch press operations. A Certified Plastics Engineer, Mr. Fowler joined ITW Hi Cone in 1991. Serving as Plant Manager, he is responsible for the operation and management of the Itasca, Illinois facility. **Career Steps:** Plant Manager, ITW Hi Cone (1991–Present); Facility Engineer, Galt Packaging (1990–1991); Maintenance Manager, ITW Hi Performance Plastics (1989–1990); ADCS E8, United States Navy (1963–1989). **Associations & Accomplishments:** Fleet Reserve Association; Citizens Flag Alliance; AARP; American Society of Quality Control; Society of Plastics Engineers. **Education:** Attended: Newberry College (1962). **Personal:** Married to Marina in 1985. Two children: Mike and Amy. Mr. Fowler enjoys aviation and classic automobiles.

LeRoy W. Gillmer

Vice President and General Manager
Continental Vinyl Window Company
11705 Lennon Road
Lennon, MI 48449
(810) 621–4660
Fax: (810) 621–3989

3081

Business Information: Continental Vinyl Window Company is a manufacturer and retail marketer of vinyl windows. Established in 1981, Continental Vinyl Window Company, with locations in Nashville, TN and Lennon, MI, currently employs 100 people. As Vice President and General Manager, Mr. Gillmer is responsible for the oversight of daily operations. **Career Steps:** Continental Vinyl Window Company: Vice President & General Manager (1990–Present), Plant Manager (1987–1990), Purchasing Agent (1983–1987). **Education:** General Education – Self Taught. **Personal:** Two children: Wayne and Tara. Mr. Gillmer enjoys collecting sports cards, cookie jars, stamps, and antique bottles.

Frank D. Graziano

Senior Vice President of Technology
Material Sciences Corporation
2300 East Pratt Boulevard
Elk Grove Village, IL 60007
(847) 806–2165
Fax: (847) 439–0737

3081

Business Information: Material Sciences Corporation is an international technology–based manufacturer of continuously processed specialty–coated materials and services. The Corporation's three primary areas of concentration are: Specialty Films – used in windows to protect from UV rays; Electrigalvanized Steel – used for cars, appliances, and buildings; and Pure Silver Coil Coating – used for lamps and lights to save energy. One recent project was the retrograde of the Empire State Building, with future plans including introducing a new paint which is applied at high speeds (600 feet per minute), and a clear coating for UV ray protection. As Senior Vice President of Technology, Dr. Graziano serves as the Chief Technical Officer responsible for bringing new technology and developing technologies into the Corporation throughout the world. His duties include public speaking at seminars and symposiums worldwide to share ideas and new products, as well as conducting presentations to the Company to implement new programs. **Career Steps:** Senior Vice President of Technology, Material Sciences Corporation (1972–Present); Vice President of Technical Direction, Midland Division, The Dexter Corporation (1963–1972); Supervisor, National Steel Corporation (1960–1963). **Associations & Accomplishments:** National Coil Coaters Association; American Chemical Society; Federation of societies for Paint Technology; American Institute of Chemists; Society of Automotive Engineers; Society of Plastic Engineers; Society of Manufacturing Engineers; Society of Sigma Xi; American Men in Science; Who's Who Worldwide. **Education:** University of Buffalo: Ph.D. in Chemistry (1960), M.A. in Chemistry (1956); Iona College, New Rochelle, New York, B.S. in Chemistry (1954). **Personal:** Married to Florence in 1954. Six children: Francis G., John P., Paul J., Thomas M., Jean M., and Robert M. Dr. Graziano enjoys golf, fishing, and entertaining his grandchildren.

Michael A. Nahmias

Manufacturing Technical Manager
Mobil Films Division
1150 Pittsford – Victor Road
Pittsford, NY 14534
(716) 248–1172
Fax: (716) 248–1465

3081

Business Information: Mobil Films Division is a designer and producer of plastic food packaging films in North America and Europe from seven plants. Customers include clientele responsible for Frito Lay, Musketeer, and Dorito brand products. A Chemical Engineering Master, Inventor, and a Patent Holder, Mr. Nahmias joined Mobil Films Division in 1983. Appointed as Manufacturing Technical Manager in 1993, he is responsible for solving world–wide technical problems in manufacturing. Career milestones include manufacturing a bag for Frito Lay – Ruffles to hold oxygen in and nitrogen out; initiating the idea of the Musketeer plastic wrapper in 1982; and create a new bag for Doritos to lengthen shelf life to 15 days in 1991–1992. **Career Steps:** Mobil Films Division: Manufacturing Technical Manager (1993–Present), Technical Account Manager (1990–1993), Special Projects Manager (1986–1989), Product Development Manager (1983–1986). **Associations & Accomplishments:** Goldratt Institute – Jonah; Author, "Films and Films Manufacturing" – Encyclopedia of Polymer Science and Engineering; 14 U.S. and 27 Foreign Patents in the area of packaging films. **Education:** Princeton University, B.S.E. with honors (1968); University of Rochester: M.S. with honors (1970), M.B.A. with honors (1971). **Personal:** Married to Pamela in 1982. Two children: Lindsay and Brent. Mr. Nahmias enjoys J24 sailboat racing (competed in 1995 worlds).

Mr. Keith L. Casson

Vice President, Research & Development
Sheldahl, Inc.
1150 Sheldahl Road
Northfield, MN 55057
(507) 663–8307
Fax: (507) 663–8545

3083

Business Information: Sheldahl, Inc. are developers and manufacturers of flexible composite laminates and tapes, and flexible interconnect (electrical circuit) systems. Established in 1955, Sheldahl, Inc. presently employs 900 people, and has an estimated annual revenue in excess of $90 million. In his current capacity, Mr. Casson coordinates and directs Corporate research and development programs and activities. **Career Steps:** Vice President, Research & Development, Sheldahl, Inc. (1992–Present); Director of Interconnect Research & Development, Sheldahl, Inc. (1990–1992); Director of Automotive Marketing, Sheldahl, Inc. (1987–1990). **Associations & Accomplishments:** (SAE) Society of Automotive Engineers; (SME) Society of Manufacturing Engineers; ISHM; (IEPS) International Electronic Packaging Society; (IPC) Institute of Printed Circuits; The Who's Who Registry; Minnesota Chamber of Commerce. **Education:** Iowa State University, B.S. Degree in Industrial Engineering (1963); University of Wisconsin, Graduate of Business Schooling; St. Thomas University, St. Paul, MN, M.I.N.I. M.B.A. program; Wharton School – University of Pennsylvania, Marketing seminar programs. **Personal:** Married to Karen in 1960. Two children: Kristi Nystuen and Kevin Casson. Mr. Casson enjoys skiing, outdoor activities, reading, and writing in his leisure time.

Douglas B. Johnson, P.E., Esq.

Product Development Manager
Brunswick Corporation
4600 Birch Hollow Drive
Lincoln, NE 68516–5107
(402) 464–8211
Fax: (402) 464–2247

3084

Business Information: Brunswick Corporation is an international manufacturer and marketer of advanced composite tubulars and pressure vessels for aerospace, defense, and industrial/petroleum applications. Brunswick Corporation serves clientele nationally and internationally from two locations: Lincoln, Nebraska and Camden, Arkansas. A Registered Professional Engineer and an Attorney–at–Law admitted to practice in Nebraska state and federal courts since 1980, Mr. Johnson has twenty–one years experience in business development and project management. He joined Brunswick Corporation as Program Manager in 1987 and was appointed as Product Development Manager in 1992. Reporting to the General Manager, he is responsible for the development of new product lines, including design, development, testing, qualifications, and production. **Career Steps:** Brunswick Corporation: Product Development Manager (1992–Present), Program Manager (1987–1992); Enron Corporation: Business Development Manager (1985–1986), Senior Engineer (1983–1985), Senior Project Engineer (1980–1983); Exxon Chemical Company: Cost and Contracts Engineer (1978–1980), Project Engineer (1975–1978); Project Engineer, E.I. Du Pont de Nemours and Company (1974–1975). **Associations & Accomplishments:** American Bar Association; American Society of Heating, Refrigeration and Air Conditioning Engineers; American Society of Mechanical Engineers; American Trial Lawyers Association; National Association of Corrosion Engineers; Nebraska State Bar Association; Society of Advanced Materials and Processes Engineering; American Electrical Engineers; Lincoln Bar Association; Triangle Fraternity. **Education:** Seton Hall University Law School, J.D. (1980); University of Nebraska, B.S. in Mechanical Engineering (1974). **Personal:** Married to Pamela J. in 1975. Five children: Richard A., Lauren S., Diana B., Scott N., and Catherine J. Mr. Johnson enjoys spending time with his children.

Ron Pershing

Road Sales Manager
Crumpler Plastic Pipe
P.O. Box 2068
Roseboro, NC 28382–2068
(910) 525–4046
Fax: (910) 525–5801

3084

Business Information: Crumpler Plastic Pipe is a manufacturer of corrugated plastic pipe, distributing throughout the southeastern United States. With twenty–six years of experience in the plastics industry, Mr. Pershing joined Crumpler Plastic Pipe as Road Sales Manager in 1992. He is responsible for hiring and training road sales personnel, as well as overseeing marketing, pricing structures, and assisting on manufacturing ideas. **Career Steps:** Road Sales Manager, Crumpler Plastic Pipe (1992–Present); Division President, Vinyler Corporation (1980–1990); Regional Sales Manager, Hancor Inc. (1970–1980). **Associations & Accomplishments:** Mason, York Rite; Scottish Rite; Past President, Shaine Club; Past Worthy Patton, Eastern Star; Elks Club; Rotary Club. **Education:** Paul Smith's College (1957). **Personal:** Married to Joyce in 1958. Two children: Laurie and Donna. Mr. Pershing enjoys golf, tennis, and public speaking.

Barry A. Peterson

Geothermal Sales Manager
Phillip Driscopipe
2929 North Central Expressway #300
Richardson, TX 75080
(214) 783–2614
Fax: (214) 783–2639

3084

Business Information: Phillip Driscopipe manufactures and supplies high density polyetholene pipe for sewer, water, heating, natural gas, and heat pump uses. National in scope, the Company has five locations throughout the U.S. and intends to expand into the overseas market within the next three to five years. As Geothermal Sales Manager, Mr. Peterson oversees management of territory sales representatives, and is directly responsible for five regions and managers. Additional duties include establishing new wholesale distributors, promoting new technologies, and expanding into new territories. **Career Steps:** Geothermal Sales Manager, Phillip Driscopipe (1995–Present); Owner, Geo Energy, Inc. (1993–1995); Project Manager, Contract Engineering Corporation (1987–1993). **Associations & Accomplishments:** International Ground Source Heat Pump Association; Geothermal Heat Pump Consortium; California Energy Commission; Geothermal Heat Pump Collaborative. **Education:** Western Kentucky University, Bachelor of Science (1986). **Personal:** Mr. Peterson enjoys travel, reading, home improvement projects, and gardening.

Richard J. Caldwell

Superintendent Project Engineer
Bayer Corporation
P.O. Box 500 State Route #2 North
New Martinsville, WV 26155
(304) 455–4400
Fax: (304) 455–2911

3086

Business Information: Bayer Corporation is an establishment primarily engaged in the manufacturing of chemicals, specifically isosyanates (i.e. foam insulation, clearcoat on cars, computer housings, plastic on rollerblades, materials in Nerf Balls, etc.). Headquartered in Germany, the Company has 54 locations throughout the U.S., and also owns Miles Laboratories. Established in 1955, the West Virginia division employs 1,000 people, and has an estimated annual revenue of $60,000,000. As Superintendent Project Engineer, Mr. Caldwell oversees draftsmen, project, and contract engineers, being directly responsible for five. He is also responsible for maintaining half of the plant's operations, and was instrumental in saving the Company $700,000 by fixing a malfunctioning valve for $6,000. **Career Steps:** Bayer Corporation: Superintendent Project Engineer (1995–Present), Division Engineering Superintendent (1993–1995), Maintenance Superintendent (1989–1993); Engineering Services Manger, G.E. Plastics (1987–1989). **Associations & Accomplishments:** Jaycees; National Rifle Association. **Education:** West Virginia University, B.S.Ch.E. (1979); Potomac State College, A.A. in Pre–Pharmacy. **Personal:** One child: Jim. Mr. Caldwell enjoys hunting, fishing, camping, and travel.

E. Ragland Coxe

Marketing Projects Manager
Sonoco Products Company
1 North Second Street, Ms W31
Hartsville, SC 29550–3300
(803) 383–3516
Fax: (803) 339–6015
EMAIL: See Below

3086

Business Information: Sonoco Products Company is an international consumer packaging company, with headquarters in Hartsville, SC. Established in 1897 with 15,000 employees, the Company's estimated average sales are over $3 billion. Serving in various managerial capacities for Sonoco Products since 1985, Mr. Coxe was appointed to his current position in 1995. As Marketing and Sales Manager, Mr. Coxe is responsible for all aspects of international business development and marketing, primarily covering Latin American sectors. Internet users can reach him via: Rags.Coxe@Sonoco.com. **Career Steps:** Sonoco Products Company: Marketing Projects Manager (1995–Present), Sales Operations Associate (1990–1992), Customer Service Manager (1985–1988). **Associations & Accomplishments:** Director, South Carolina Waterford Association; Vestry, St. Bartholomew Episcopal Church; Hartsville Rotary Club. **Education:** Wake Forest University, M.B.A. (1990). **Personal:** Married to Suiter Whitehead in 1986. Two children: Betty Suiter and Ragland Jr. Mr. Coxe enjoys athletics, hunting, and fishing.

James R. Eaton

Vice President of Sales and Marketing
Bemis Company, Inc.
8000 Centerview Parkway, Suite 101
Cordova, TN 38018–4010
(901) 759–3300
Fax: (901) 759–3350

3086

Business Information: Bemis is a principal manufacturer of flexible packaging and specialty coated and graphics products. More than 70 percent of the Company's sales are packaging related. Flexible packaging products include coated and laminated films and polyethylene packaging; packaging machinery; multiwall paper bags and consumer–size paper packaging. The Company's specialty coated and graphics products include pressure–sensitive materials, label applicating equipment and rotogravure cylinders. The primary market for the Company's products is the food industry which accounts for approximately 70 percent of sales. Other markets include chemical, agribusiness, pharmaceutical, medical, printing and graphic arts, and a variety of other industrial end uses. The Company holds a strong or dominant position, in many markets it serves and seeks out special market segments where the Company's technological or other capabilities give it a competitive advantage. A marketing executive with Bemis since 1982, James Eaton was appointed to his current position in 1900. As Vice President, he provides the overall executive administration for all sales and marketing activities for the Paper and Bag Division. **Career Steps:** Bemis Company, Inc.: Vice President of Sales and Marketing (1995–Present), Vice President of Sales (1988–1995), National Account Sales Manager (1984–1988), National Account Executive (1982–1984). **Associations & Accomplishments:** Long–Time Member, American Management Association; Institute of Packaging Professionals (IOPP) – formerly SPHE – Society of Packaging and Handling Engineers; Former President, Philadelphia Chapter; Outstanding Sales Achievement Award (1981 & 1984); Member, The 110 Club (1977–1981). **Education:** Pennsylvania State University, B.B.A. (1981); Niagara County Community College, Associates Degree in Accounting; American Management's four week management course. **Personal:** Married to Connie Eaton in 1972. Two children: Derek and Karen, who both attend Rhodes College in Memphis, TN. Mr. Eaton enjoys golf, skiing, theater, and family activities.

Edward P. Murphy, Jr.

Chief Financial Officer
Universal Protective Packaging, Inc.
61 Texaco Road
Mechanicsburg, PA 17055
(717) 766–1578
Fax: (717) 766–6049

3086

Business Information: Universal Protective Packaging, Inc. is a privately–held, plastic packaging manufacturer of ESD plastic clamshells. They are substituting box and bag foam with clamshells. Established in 1993, Universal Protective Packaging, Inc. has customers in Canada, Europe and in the Far East. Annual revenue of $8 million is reported and there are currently 60 corporate–wide employees. As Chief Financial Officer, Mr. Murphy is responsible for all aspects of financial matters, with duties including: bank relations, all controller functions within operations, and cost and purchasing of products. **Career Steps:** Chief Financial Officer, Universal Protective Packaging, Inc. (1993–Present); Assistant Division Controller, Ingersoll Rand Company (1978–1993). **Associations & Accomplishments:** Institute of Management Accountants; Knights of Columbus; American Legion; Coaches Little League baseball. **Education:** King's College, B.S. (1978). **Personal:** Married to Deborah C.. Three children: Edward, Patrick and Ryan. Mr. Murphy enjoys baseball and basketball.

Gary T. Storie

Credit Director
Carlisle Plastics
1314 North 3rd Street, Suite 300
Phoenix, AZ 85004–1751
(602) 407–2133
Fax: (602) 407–2128

3087

Business Information: Carlisle Plastics is a manufacturer of pre–formed plastic products. Established in early in the 1980's, the Company produces garment hangers, plastic film, bottles, trash bags, and shrink wrap for international distribution. In September 1996, the Company is in for some major changes, plans are for TYCO International to purchase Carlisle Plastics. As Credit Director, Mr. Storie is responsible for all credit collection function control for Carlisle Plastics. His staff handle credit research, establish new credit accounts, monitor current accounts, and anticipate and evaluate problem accounts. Mr. Storie handles all administrative duties, develops a business plan, and does long term strategic planning for his department. **Career Steps:** Credit Director, Carlisle Plastics (1992–Present); Credit Manager, International Resistor Company (1986–1991); Credit Manager, TRW (1978–1986). **Education:** East Tennessee State, B.S. (1973). **Personal:** Married to Donna in 1979. Mr. Storie enjoys outdoor activities and travel.

Daryl L. Westermeyer

Operations Manager
Contracted Operations
Township Road 295 US Route 50
Little Hocking, OH 45742–0452
(614) 423–6193
Fax: (614) 989–5350

3087

Business Information: Contracted Operations is a manufacturer of plastic compounding products, provided to companies on a contractual basis. Joining the Company as Plant Engineer in 1994, Mr. Westermeyer was appointed as Operations Manager in 1995. He is responsible for the supervision and planning of the day–to–day and long–term operations of the production facility, as well as overseeing all administrative operations for associates and a support staff of 50. **Career Steps:** Contracted Operations: Operations Manager (1995–Present), Plant Engineer (1994–1995); Hi–Vac Corporation: Regional Sales Manager (1993–1994), Chief Engineer (1991–1993). **Associations & Accomplishments:** Volunteer Fireman. **Education:** University of Missouri – Rolla, B.S. in Engineering Management (1986). **Personal:** Married to Kerry in 1995. Mr. Westermeyer enjoys auto racing and golf.

Sergio A.F. Alves

President
Vulcan Material Plastic S.A.
Estrada do Colegio No. 380
Rio de Janeiro, Brazil 21235–280
55–21–3622010
Fax: 55–21–3712828

3089

Business Information: Vulcan Material Plastic S.A. is a manufacturer of thermal plastics and a series of different products such as clear films (both rigid and flexible), auto door panels, and dash panels. The Company also makes adhesive paper for Rubbermaid and credit cards for Visa and Mastercard. As President, Mr. Alves is responsible for all aspects of Company operations, including administration, finance, public relations, and strategic planning. **Career Steps:** President, Vulcan Material Plastic S.A. (1992–Present); General Manager, Petroleo Ipiranga (1983–1992); Corporate Planning Manager, Exxon (1968–1982). **Associations & Accomplishments:** Vice President, Brazilian Plastics Association (ABRAPLA); Treasurer, Acao Comunitaria; Director, State of Rio De Janeiro Industry Federation (FIRJAN). **Education:** Universidade Federal do Rio De Janeiro, Economy (1967). **Personal:** Married to Elizabeth in 1970. Two children: Andre B. and Flavio B. Mr. Alves enjoys tennis, jogging, and music.

Terese M. Banas

Controller
Optrex America Inc.
44160 Plymouth Oaks Boulevard
Plymouth, MI 48170–2584
(313) 416–8500
Fax: (313) 416–8520

3089

Business Information: Optrex America Inc. is a manufacturer and distributor of plastic assembly units with LCD components. Established in 1981, Optrex American, Inc. reports annual revenue of $130 million and currently employs 55 people. As Controller, Ms. Banas is responsible for the areas of Human Resources, Inventory Management, Finances, Accounting, and MIS. **Career Steps:** Controller, Optrex America Inc. (1989–Present); Supervisory of Financial Reporting, CBS/Fox Video (1985–1989). **Associations & Accomplishments:** Weight Watcher's leader. **Education:** Walsh College, M.S. in Management (1996); Aquinas College, B.S. in Business Administration. **Personal:** Married to Michael Banas in 1982. One child: Steven Banas. Ms. Banas enjoys antiques, reading, and race walking.

Michel M. Bitritto, Ph.D.

Director of Recycling Services
Hoechst Technical Polymers
90 Morris Avenue
Summit, NJ 07901
(908) 598–4391
Fax: (908) 598–4165

3089

Business Information: Managing recycle services for industrial plastics companies and minor consumer recyclers, Hoechst Technical Polymers engineers, manufactures and distributes plastics within the Summit, New Jersey area. As Director of Recycling Services, Dr. Michel Bitritto oversees all recycling services concerning plastics to industrial companies, as well as non–industrial consumers. **Career Steps:** Director of Recycling Services, Hoechst Technical Polymers

(1991–Present); Marketing Development Manager, Hoechst Celanese (1987–1991); Resources Manager, Celanese Corporation (1982–1987). **Associations & Accomplishments:** American Chemical Society, Polymer Division; Twin Management Forum; Municipal Alliance for Prevention of Substance Abuse. **Education:** University of Connecticut, Ph.D. (1976); University of Maryland, Post–Doctorate Studies. **Personal:** Married to Sunil Garg in 1982. One child: Neena Marie.

Richard E. Bonnet
President and Chief Executive Officer
Plastic Recycling Service
1001 Depot Street
Parkersburg, WV 26101–5207
(304) 485–8062
Fax: (304) 485–8062
EMAIL: See Below

3089

Business Information: Plastic Recycling Service is a national post–consumer plastic recycling and processing company, specializing in servicing the greenhouse industry. Established in 1990, the Company also performs custom processing for plastics manufacturing companies. As President and Chief Executive Officer, Mr. Bonnet oversees daily operations, supervises personnel, and provides corporate leadership. Internet users can reach him via: PRSDICK@AOL.COM **Career Steps:** President and Chief Executive Officer, Plastic Recycling Service (1990–Present); Vice President GNHS Operations, Dudley's Florist (1977–1990); Marine Science Technician – E6, United States Coast Guard (1969–1973). **Associations & Accomplishments:** Ohio Florist Association; Industrial Development Committee, Mid Ohio Valley Chamber of Commerce. **Education:** University of New Hampshire, B.S. (1975). **Personal:** Married to Mary in 1970. Two children: David M. and Candace G. Mr. Bonnet enjoys rowing, bicycling and cooking.

John A. Cipolla
Founder
Countertops of Topeka I
840 North East Highway 24
Topeka, KS 66608
(913) 357–0005
Fax: (913) 357–1762

3089

Business Information: Countertops of Topeka I, established in 1993, specializes in the fabrication, installation, and sale of all types of countertops to individuals and retailers. As Founder, Mr. Cipolla is responsible for all aspects of Company operations, including handling all negotiations and contracts. **Career Steps:** Founder, Countertops of Topeka I (1993–Present). **Associations & Accomplishments:** National Federation of Independent Businesses; Board of Directors, Chamber of Commerce; Better Business Bureau. **Personal:** Mr. Cipolla enjoys karate, hunting, fishing, and snow and water skiing.

Antonio Fernando Cornelio
President
Cipla Ind. de Mats de Cons. SA
Avenue Getulio Vargas, 1.619
Joinville, SC, Brazil 89202–003
55–47–4416006
Fax: 55–47–4332258
EMAIL: See Below

3089

Business Information: Cipla Ind. de Mats de Cons. SA, one of the 40 companies belonging to the HB Corporation, is one of five plastics companies in Brazil. The Cipla Company transforms plastic into usable products (i.e., wine tanks, gas tanks, pipes, etc.). All Brazilian cars have at least 14 kilos of plastic made by Cipla, 55% of the plastic in construction market is made by Cipla, and 5% of the total Brazilian plastic market is Cipla. As President, Mr. Cornelio is responsible for all aspects of Company operations, including administration, sales and marketing, legal, and strategic planning. **Career Steps:** President, Cipla Ind. de Mats de Cons. SA (1994–Present); Chief Executive Officer, GEO Company SA (1992–1995); Director, Ensan Construction Company (1987–1992); Director, Group Columbia SA (1984–1987). **Associations & Accomplishments:** American Society of Public Administration; American Management Association. **Education:** University of Southern California – School of Business Administration: Ph.D. (1977), M.P.A. (1975); Getulia Vargas Foundation, M.B.A.; Attended, Stanford University; Fountainbleau, Business Training Program. **Personal:** Married to Aide Maria in 1981. Five children: Claudio Marcius, Monica Patricia, Fernando Jefferson, Aline, and Fernanda. Mr. Cornelio enjoys sailing, chess, tennis, and stamp collecting.

Todd D. Eby
Vice President of Finance
Bonar Inc.
2380 McDowell Road
Burlington, Ontario L7R 4A1
(905) 637–5611
Fax: (905) 637–9954

3089

Business Information: Bonar Inc. is a manufacturer of industrial packaging and rigid plastics. The Company has 14 sites in the U.S. and Canada. As Vice President of Finance, Mr. Eby is responsible for managing all aspects of corporate insurance, taxation, banking and treasury functions, and oversees all field accounting offices. Established in 1896, Bonar Inc. employs 1,300 people with annual sales of $290 million. **Career Steps:** Vice President of Finance, Bonar Inc., (1989–Present). **Associations & Accomplishments:** Financial Executive Institute; Society of Management Accountants; Toronto Board of Trade. **Personal:** Married. Four children.

Frank K. Facey
Director of Sales and Marketing
Norden Packaging
2781 Blume Drive
Los Alamitos, CA 90720–4702
(908) 534–1222
Fax: (908) 534–9555

3089

Business Information: Norden Packaging, a Swedish–owned packaging and plastics company, is the world's largest manufacturer of packaging equipment and servicing. As Director of Sales and Marketing, Mr. Facey is responsible for the direction of all sales and marketing activities, including strategic design targeted toward moving the Company forward. **Career Steps:** Director of Sales and Marketing, Norden Packaging (1991–Present); American National Can Company: Operations and Sales Manager (1991), Regional Sales Manager (1984–1991). **Associations & Accomplishments:** California Packaging Club; YMCA Black Achievers in Industry Award (1982); Lifetime member of Kappa Alpha Psi Fraternity. **Education:** Hartwick College, B.A. (1972); Universidad Ibero Americana – Mexico City. **Personal:** Mr. Facey enjoys tennis and music (Jazz).

Sean Gillespie
Manager of Associate Relations
Rubbermaid Commercial Products, Inc.
3124 Valley Avenue
Winchester, VA 22601–2636
(540) 542–8448
Fax: (540) 542–8582

3089

Business Information: Rubbermaid Commercial Products, Inc. is an international manufacturer and distributor of commercial plastic products to consumers. As Manager of Associate Relations, Mr. Gillespie is responsible for the management of salary and associate relations staff. Mr. Gillespie enjoys being involved with the Company and helped to form a peer review system in order to make the Company's associates feel more involved with their surroundings. **Career Steps:** Manager of Associate Relations, Rubbermaid Commercial Products, Inc. (1988–Present); Technical Executive and Search Consultant, R. Merriman Associates (1986–1988); Manager of Technical Services, TSI, Inc. **Associations & Accomplishments:** Society for Human Resource Management; Employment Management Association; American Society of Production and Inventory Control; Winchester Manufacturing Human Resources Association. **Education:** Indiana University of Pennsylvania, M.A. in Labor Relations (1983); St. Vincent College, B.A. **Personal:** Married to Rita in 1984. Three children: Taylor, Kalyn, and Brennan. Mr. Gillespie enjoys physical fitness, music (guitar), and sports (basketball, running, and light weightlifting).

William R. (Bill) Goodberlet
Account Manager
G.I. Plastek
25 Chapelwood Drive
York, PA 17402
(717) 840–4236
Fax: (717) 840–4934
EMail: See Below

3089

Business Information: Mr. Goodberlet is a professional in the plastics industry with manufacturing experience of injection–molded products beginning in 1978. Bill currently works with GI Plastek, who specializes in the design and custom molding of thermoplastic and RIM thermostats resins. As Account Manager, Mr. Goodberlet is responsible for the development and management of key accounts in the Mid–Atlantic district. Internet users can reach him via: 102257,1431@compuserve.com. **Career Steps:** Account Manager, G.I. Plastek (1994–Present); General Industries: Technical Service Manager (1992–1994), Project Engineer (1989–1992); Product Engineer, Plastic Components, Inc. (1986–1989). **Associations & Accomplishments:** Senior Member, Society of Manufacturing Engineers; Society of Plastics Engineers; Minister, Antioch Churches and Ministries; The Gideons International. **Education:** Concordia College, A.A. (1975); Seminars and college level courses in: Computers, CAD, Plastic Design, Assembly of Plastics, Quality Assurance, SPC, Project Management, and Quoting and Estimating. **Personal:** Married to Susan in 1977. Two children: Rachael and Elisabeth. Mr. Goodberlet enjoys golf, reading, public speaking, and playing the guitar.

Charles A. Gorman III
President & Owner
Florida Plastics Machinery
2200 Winter Springs Boulevard, Suite 106–301
Oviedo, FL 32765–9346
(407) 365–4088
Fax: (407) 365–4658

3089

Business Information: Florida Plastics Machinery is a manufacturers representative organization for the retail/wholesale sale of plastics processing equipment. As President & Owner, Mr. Gorman is responsible for all facets of Company operation. He handles the marketing of new and existing products, financial concerns, establishing budgets, general accounting practices, and public relations. Mr. Gorman also plans for future expansion and hopes to double the $3 million in sales in the next five years. **Career Steps:** President & Owner, Florida Plastics Machinery (1994–Present); Sales Engineer, Florida Plastics Machinery, Inc. (1988–1994). **Associations & Accomplishments:** Society of Plastics Engineers. **Education:** W. Connecticut State University, B.B.A. Degree in Marketing (1988). **Personal:** Married to Stacey in 1993. One child: Patrick. Mr. Gorman enjoys basketball, golf, and whitewater rafting.

Sharon K. Haught
Associate Counsel
Rubbermaid, Inc.
1147 Akron Road
Wooster, OH 44691
(330) 264–6464
Fax: (330) 287–2340

3089

Business Information: Rubbermaid, Inc. is a multi–national manufacturer of consumer and commercial plastic products from more than 30 locations worldwide. A practicing attorney in Ohio state courts since 1984, Mrs. Haught joined Rubbermaid, Inc. as Associate Counsel in the Corporate Law Department in 1985. She specializes in environmental law, contract review and drafting, and advertising law. **Career Steps:** Associate Counsel, Rubbermaid, Inc. (1985–Present); Associate Attorney, Bank One–Dayton OH (1983–1985). **Associations & Accomplishments:** American Bar Association; Ohio Bar Association; Wayne County Bar Association; Phi Alpha Delta Law Fraternity International. **Education:** University of Dayton School of Law, J.D. (1984); Ball State University, B.S. **Personal:** Married to Jeffrey P. in 1991. Two children: Don Roger and Stephanie Marie. Mrs. Haught enjoys international travel, photography and crafts.

Gary Hollingshead
General Manager
Carrera Industries
1141 West Grant Road
Tucson, AZ 85705–5312
(520) 622–8111
Fax: (520) 622–8444

3089

Business Information: Carrera Industries manufactures custom injection molding plastics. As General Manager, Mr. Hollingshead is responsible for diversified administrative activities, personnel supervision, and strategic planning. **Career Steps:** General Manager, Carrera Industries (1994–Present); Tech Medical: Operations Manager (1992–1994), Technical Services Manager – Engineering (1991–1992); Plant Manager, Spears Manufacturing (1990–1991). **Associations & Accomplishments:** Society of Plastics Engineers; Society of Manufacturing Engineers. **Education:** Des Moines Area Community College, A.A. in Manufacturing (1970). **Personal:** Married to Suzanne in 1963. Two children: Melisa and Kristen. Mr. Hollingshead enjoys flying, golf, and travel. He is also a lapidary.

Mr. Joseph C. Hurosky, II

President
Tri–Tech Plastics, L.P.
8756 Freeway Drive
Macedonia, OH 44056
(216) 468–0606
Fax: (216) 468–2145

3089

Business Information: Tri–Tech Plastics, L.P. processes custom injection molding for automotive, railroad and consumer industries. Established since 1993, Tri–Tech Plastics, L.P. presently employs 100 people and has an estimated annual revenue in excess of $10 million. In his current capacity, Mr. Hurosky is responsible for all aspects of Company operations, as well as finance and training. **Career Steps:** President, Tri–Tech Plastics, L.P. (1986–Present); Vice President and General Manager, Preston Plastics, Inc. (1981–1986); Plastics Operations, Division Manager, Par Industries, Inc. (1987–1989); Vice President and General Manager, H & H Engineering Molded Products, Inc. (1980–1993). **Associations & Accomplishments:** Society of Plastics Engineers; Ferris State University Plastics Engineering Technology Advisory Board; Technical Training Advisory Board, University of Akron. **Education:** Ferris State University, Plastics Engineering Technology (1973); Attended, Baldwin Wallace to finish his B.S. Degree in Business. **Personal:** Married to Nancy in 1977. Four children: Norman Joseph, John William, Dawn Elizabeth, and Matthew Corey. Mr. Hurosky enjoys golf, basketball, and yardwork in his leisure time.

Richard E. Husby

Vice President of Marketing
Duraco Products
1109 East Lake Street
Streamwood, IL 60107–4332
(708) 837–6615
Fax: (708) 837–7139

3089

Business Information: Duraco Products is an international manufacturing company whose headquarters is located in Streamwood, Illinois. The Company is the largest manufacturer of plastic decorative planterware for retail sales and used by interior landscape designers. As Vice President of Marketing, Mr. Husby directs the sales, marketing, merchandising, and advertising for Duraco Products. He is a member of The Board of Directors and as such is instrumental in planning the strategy of the company. **Career Steps:** Vice President of Marketing, Duraco Products (1983–Present); Marketing Manager, Phillips Products (1976–1983); National Sales Manager, Phillips Films (1973–1976). **Associations & Accomplishments:** Active in church, civic, and music organizations throughout Oklahoma and Illinois; Citizen of the Year, Carol Stream (1971); City Council, Carol Stream. **Education:** University of Minnesota, B.S. in Engineering (1957); University of Southern California, Advanced Management. **Personal:** Married to Patricia in 1955. Three children: Richard, Donald, and Dianne. Mr. Husby enjoys snow and water skiing, golf, vocal and instrumental music.

Patricia K. Kingsley

Accounts Receivable/Assistant Controller
Davidson Plastics Corporation
18726 East Valley Highway
Kent, WA 98032
(206) 251–8140
Fax: (206) 251–8303

3089

Business Information: Davidson Plastics Corporation is a plastic extrusion manufacturing company, manufacturing devices for fencing, highway products, and calculators, as well as plastic piping, molding, and treadmills. Ms. Kingsley manages the Accounts Receivable and is responsible for calculating commissions, A/R control and collection, and preparing internal reports and administers the General Ledger. Additionally, she acts as the Assistant to the Controller and handles state revenue returns for two states. **Career Steps:** Accounts Receivable/Assistant Controller, Davidson Plastics Corporation (1994–Present); Accounting Manager Davidson Plastics Company (1984–1994); Accountant, Production Plastics, Inc. (1979–1984). **Education:** Central Missouri State University (1967–1969); Highline Community College; Bellevue Community College. **Personal:** One child: Jessica C. P. Maldonado. Ms. Kingsley enjoys computers, gardening, animals, reading, and theatre.

Clark P. Lee, Ph.D.

Process Development Biochemist
Chronopol, Inc.
4545 McIntyre Street
Golden, CO 80403
(303) 271–7431
Fax: (303) 271–7461
EMail: See Below

3089

Business Information: Chronopol, Inc. is a research and development company specializing in degradable plastics. As Process Development Biochemist, Dr. Lee is responsible for, or directly involved in, the purchasing, construction, method development, and operation of laboratories involved in industrial microbiology. A recognized authority on water quality biosystems, he also lectures frequently and serves as an adjunct faculty research member for the College of Continuing Education and Department of Biochemistry at the University of Hawaii. Internet users can reach him via: CLLEE@GTCINC.COM. **Career Steps:** Process Development Biochemist, Chronopol, Inc. (1993–Present); Research Associate, University of Hawaii (1981–1989); I.H. Chemist, Occidental Oil Shale (1980). **Associations & Accomplishments:** American Chemical Society; American Society of Metals; S.I.M.; A.H.A. **Education:** University of Hawaii, Ph.D. (1989); Colorado School of Mines, N.I.O.S.H. Trainee (1979); Colorado State University, B.S. in Chemistry (1974–1978). **Personal:** Dr. Lee enjoys zymergy, mule and donkey training, riding, and driving.

Upendra S. Mehta

Corporate Quality Manager
Plaxicon Company
10660 Acacia Street
Rancho Cucamonga, CA 91730–5409
(909) 944–6868
Fax: (909) 944–8983

3089

Business Information: Plaxicon Company specializes in the manufacture of plastic containers (PET). Established in 1981, the Company employs over 250 people, has an estimated annual revenue of $50 million, and has locations in California, Alabama, and Ohio. As Corporate Quality Manager, Mr. Mehta directs the quality improvement program, establishes, implements, and maintains the quality system (based on ISO 9001), and oversees SPC program, GMP program, as well as the product development process. **Career Steps:** Corporate Quality Manager, Plaxicon Company (Present); Quality Assurance Manager, Santa Fe Plastic/Kerr Group (1991–1995); Quality Assurance Manager, Anchor Swan (1988–1991); Quality Control Manager, Andercraft Inc. (1987–1988); Industrial Engineer, Jyoti Engineering, Baroda India (1984–1986). **Associations & Accomplishments:** American Society of Quality Controls; Society of Plastic Engineers; Toastmasters Club. **Education:** California State Polytechnic University, M.B.A. (In Progress); M.S. University: M.S. in Industrial Engineering, B.S. in Textile Engineering; C.S.C., India, Certificate in Computer Science. **Personal:** Married to Parul U. in 1985. Two children: Juhi and Yash. Mr. Mehta enjoys travel, camping, photography, Indian music, cricket, and basketball.

Kurt D. Meyers

President
Windows of the World Manufacturing Inc.
1189 Rt. 46 East
Little Falls, NJ 07424–1830
(201) 890–0222
Fax: (201) 890–7491

3089

Business Information: Windows of the World Manufacturing Inc. specializes in the manufacturing of vinyl replacement windows, distributing their product through retail store operations, as well as wholesale direct from the manufacturer. Established in 1982, Windows of the World Manufacturing, Inc. currently employs 20 people and has an estimated annual revenue of $2.5 million. Future plans include franchising throughout the United States. In addition to the Little Falls location, manufacturing facilities are also located in Virginia as follows: 1500 Chestnut Street; Portsmouth, VA 23704; Bus. Phone: (800) 233–0665 and FAX: (804) 399–8526. As Owner and President, Mr. Meyers is responsible for all aspects of operations. Mr. Meyers began in automobile sales in 1976. Almost immediately he became one of N.J. top salesman. Three years later he was in charge of the entire sales force for one of the largest dealers in the country responsible for over 10 stores. **Career Steps:** Owner and President, Windows of the World Manufacturing Inc. (1982–Present). **Associations & Accomplishments:** Better Business Bureau of New Jersey Business and Industry Association; Chamber of Commerce; National Federation of Independent Business Remodelers and Contractors Association; National Association of the Remodeling Industry; Construction Trade Association; Northeast Window and Door Association; As an accomplished model for many years he was on the cover of the Archies album, Life Magazine, The New York Times and many other publications. He has also been in many TV commercials and fashion shows at such places as The Waldorf Astoria and The Hotel Piere. As an accomplished drummer he has recorded and toured the country playing with such bands as The Rolling Stones. **Education:** Ramapo College, B.A. (1973). **Personal:** Married to Jayne in 1977. One child: Ashley. Mr. Meyers enjoys reading, computers, sports and music.

Michael J. Molenda

Senior Marketing Manager
Hoechst Celanese, Advanced Materials Group
801 Brickell Avenue, 9th Floor
Miami, FL 33131
(305) 374–8226
Fax: (305) 372–0189

3089

Business Information: Hoechst Celanese, Advanced Materials Group specializes in the manufacture of plastic resins used in automotive, industrial, electrical and packaging industries. Established in 1940, Hoechst Celanese currently employs 40,000 people worldwide. As Senior Marketing Manager, Mr. Molenda is responsible for all Latin American sales and marketing operations and strategies. **Career Steps:** Hoechst Celanese, Advanced Materials Group: Senior Marketing Manager (1991–Present), Sales Executive (1980–1991); Engineer, Motorola (1979–1980); Technical Marketing Specialist, Monsanto (1976–1978). **Associations & Accomplishments:** SER (Latin training for service and technical careers); Education Chairperson and Former President, Society of Plastics Engineers; International Business Executive Advisory Board, Florida Atlantic University; American Bar Association. **Education:** University of Miami, J.D. (1984); Michigan Technological University, B.S. in Mechanical Engineering (1976). **Personal:** Mr. Molenda enjoys automobiles, thoroughbred horses, and travel.

Mr. Jorge Ramirez–Serrano

Controller
Precision Plastics Products
P.O. Box 2289
Toa Baja, Puerto Rico 00951–2289
(809) 794–1422
Fax: (809) 794–1530

3089

Business Information: Precision Plastics Products is an international manufacturer and producer of plastics and plastic closures. Established in 1971, Precision Plastics Products reports annual revenue of $3 million and currently employs 28 people. As Controller, Mr. Ramirez–Serrano is responsible for all aspects of financial and accounting matters. **Career Steps:** Precision Plastics Products: Controller (1983–Present), Administrative Manager (1978–1983), Accountant (1972–1978). **Associations & Accomplishments:** President of local Rotary Club; Rotary International; Lions International; Puerto Rico Manufacturing Association; Society of Plastic Engineer Caribbean Section. **Education:** International American University, Masters (1988), B.B.A. (1972). **Personal:** Married to Camelia Medina in 1972. Three children: Jorge, Ingrid, and Agustin. Mr. Ramirez–Serrano enjoys participating in community service.

John Joseph Rego

Vice President of Marketing and Development
The Hanson Group Limited
410 Beacon Street
Avon Lake, OH 44012
(216) 933–3539
Fax: (216) 933–9930
EMAIL: See Below

3089

Business Information: The Hanson Group Limited is a privately–held company specializing in the manufacture of injection–molded plastic products, mold building, and assembly systems. International in scope, the Company also has divisions that produce automotive, houseware, and school supply products, as well as satellite dishes. Established in 1960, the Company employs 250 people, and has an estimated annual revenue of $23–25 million. As Vice President of Marketing and Development, Mr. Rego is responsible for product design and development, project management, and implementation. A member of the Company for fourteen years, he also oversees all Company marketing functions. Internet users can reach him via: JJregohgl1@aol.com. **Career Steps:** The Hanson Group Limited: Vice President of Marketing and Development (1994–Present), Vice President Sales and Marketing (1987–1994), National Accountants Manager (1983–1987); Sales Manager, Universal Plastics (1981–1983). **Associations & Accomplishments:** Students in Free Enterprise (SIFE); National Tooling and Machining Association (NTMA); American Mold Builders Association (AMBA); Core Knowledge Foundation. **Education:** Miami University, Ohio, B.Phil. in Interdisciplinary Studies (1981). **Personal:** Married to Diane K. in 1982. Two children: Lindsay Diane and Robyn Antonette. Mr. Rego enjoys golf, cigars, reading, and spending time with family and friends.

Mark A. Roberts
Vice President
Alpha Enterprises, Inc.
6370 Wise Avenue, North West
Canton, OH 44720
(330) 490–2000
Fax: Please mail or call

3089

Business Information: Alpha Enterprises, Inc. is the primary manufacturer of plastic packaging and security products for media products (i.e., Video, CD, CD Rom, Audio Book, and photo industrial packaging for high grade tape). One of the largest manufacturers of these products, Alpha Enterprises, Inc. is headquartered in North Canton, Ohio with four other facilities throughout the United States. As Vice President for the Packaging and Security Divisions, Mr. Roberts is responsible for sales leadership strategic planning and implementation, marketing, new product development, recruiting, training and product forecasting. He supervises a team of six sales people. **Career Steps:** Alpha Enterprises, Inc: Vice President (1994–Present), Division Manager (1987–1994); Unit Manager, Frito–Lay (1982–1987). **Associations & Accomplishments:** American Marketing Association; ITA; VSDA; NARM. **Education:** Kent State: E.M.B.A. (1995), Bachelor in Business Administration. **Personal:** Married. Mr. Roberts enjoys martial arts and swimming.

Gerald L. Robertson, Ph.D.
Director of Research and Development
Shakespeare Electronics and Fiberglass
19845 U.S. Highway 76
Newberry, SC 29108
(803) 276–5504
Fax: (803) 276–8940

3089

Business Information: Shakespeare Electronics and Fiberglass is a manufacturer of fiberglass–reinforced plastic products — best–known for their radio antennas and fishing poles. Established in 1897, Shakespeare reports annual revenue of $45 million and employs 400 people. With eleven years expertise in materials process research and development, Dr. Robertson directs all facets of research and product development. **Career Steps:** Director of Research and Development, Shakespeare Electronics and Fiberglass (1995–Present); Senior Research Scientist, Amoco Performance Products (1988–1994); Supervisor of Composite Material Development, Thiokol Corporation (1984–1988). **Associations & Accomplishments:** American Chemical Society; Society for the Advancement of Materials and Process Engineering (SAMPE); Society of Plastics Engineers; Volunteer, Charis Housing Project in Atlanta (helping to build houses for the working poor). **Education:** Colorado State University, Ph.D. (1983); New Mexico State University, B.S. (1973). **Personal:** Married to Jackie in 1985. One child: Trever. Dr. Robertson enjoys golf, model building, and gardening.

Michael R. Rochester
Human Resources Manager
Patriot Manufacturing Inc.
South Egg Harbor Road
Hammonton, NJ 08037
(609) 567–0090
Fax: (609) 567–4177
EMAIL: See Below

3089

Business Information: Patriot Manufacturing Inc. is a manufacturer and distributor of vinyl windows for construction and remodeling industries. Established in 1975, the Company distributes products primarily in the Northeast and Mid–Atlantic states. With thirty years expertise in human resources management, Michael Rochester joined Patriot Manufacturing, Inc. as Human Resources Manager in 1995. He is responsible for managing all personnel matters, including hiring, firing, personnel issues, training, legal compliances, recruitment, benefits, health insurance, and health and safety issues. Internet users can reach him via: MRocheste@AOL.com. **Career Steps:** Human Resources Manager, Patriot Manufacturing Inc. (1995–Present); Director of Human Resources, Glenco Star (1991–1994); Vice President, Health/ Norton Associates (1984–1991); Director of Human Resources, Lesney Production Ltd. (1981–1984). **Associations & Accomplishments:** Youth Aid Panels; Society of Human Resource Management. **Education:** Cornell University, M.S. (1963); Rensselaer Le Faivre, Polytechnic

Institute, B.S. (1961). **Personal:** Married to Carole LeFaivre in 1994. Three children: Benjamin, Marne, and Andrew. Mr. Rochester enjoys reading, golf, tennis, and travel.

Yuri Efraim Rodosli

Director/President
Ameropa Industrias Plasticas Ltda
Avenida Marginal Direita Do Rio Tiete 810
Sao Paulo, Brazil Sp 05118–1
55–011–8317300
Fax: 55–011–2611177

3089

Business Information: Ameropa Industrias Plasticas Ltda develops and manufactures profiles, tubes, and rods of technical precision. As Director/President, Mr. Rodosli is responsible for all aspects of Company operations, including administration, finance, public relations, and strategic planning. **Career Steps:** Ameropa Industrias Plasticas Ltda: Director/President (1995–Present), Vice President (1994); Assistant Managing Director, Hellerman do Brasil (1990–1994). **Associations & Accomplishments:** 2nd Tenent Officer of Brazilian Army – Reserve; Brazilian Association of Plastics Industry; Brazilian Institute of Plastics; Estate of Sao Paulo Industry Federation. **Education:** Getulio Vargas Fundation, M.B.A. (1996), M.B.A. (1996); Faculdades Metropolitanas Unidas, Graduate in Business Administration (1992). **Personal:** Mr. Rodosli enjoys tennis, horses, sailing, and reading.

Ronald S. Rosenthal
Director of Operations
Absolute Coatings
38 Portman Road
New Rochelle, NY 10801
(914) 636–0700
Fax: Please mail or call

3089

Business Information: Absolute Coatings, a family–owned business, is an international manufacturer and formulator of clear coatings and finishes, such as polyurethane, stain, wood cleaner, and sealants. As Director of Operations, Mr. Rosenthal is responsible for the direction of all operational activities for warehouse shipping and receiving, as well as ordering all materials with the exception of chemicals. **Career Steps:** Director of Operations, Absolute Coatings (1981–Present); Customer Service Supervisor, J.C. Penney Company (1986–Present); Wholesale, Grolice Interstate (1980–1981). **Associations & Accomplishments:** Harrison Volunteer Ambulance Corporation; Amateur Photographer. **Education:** White Plains High School, Diploma. **Personal:** Mr. Rosenthal enjoys photography.

Christopher D. Roy
Vice President of Operations
Mid America Plastics, Inc.
P.O. Box 128
Gardner, KS 66030–0128
(913) 856–6550
Fax: (913) 856–6763

3089

Business Information: Mid America Plastics, Inc. is a privately–owned company specializing in the manufacture of injection–molded plastics. Established in 1990, the Company employs 180 people, and has an estimated annual revenue of $18 million. A second facility, located in Maryville, Tennessee, has a projected start–up date of October 1. The Tennessee plant will initially employ 50 personnel. As Vice President of Operations, Mr. Roy has complete responsibility. His duties include administration, finance, sales, public relations, marketing, and strategic planning. **Career Steps:** Mid America Plastics, Inc: Vice President of Operations (1990–Present), General Manger, Sales Manger, Materials Manager. **Associations & Accomplishments:** American Production and Inventory Control Society; Society of Plastics Engineers. **Education:** Southwest Missouri State, B.S. in Finance (1988), graduated first in class in School of Business. **Personal:** Married to Lisa A. in 1989. Mr. Roy enjoys physical fitness, golf, and travel.

W.M. Schermerhorn
Managing Director
AC Technology Europe
Slotzichweg 15
7533 CB Emschede, The Netherlands
31–53–403–6331
Fax: 31–53–483–6332
SCHERMERHORN@CMOLD.NL

3089

Business Information: AC Technology Europe, is the European headquarters for the American company, AC Technology. AC Technology, Europe, which specializes in plastic product and mold simulation/optimizational, is dedicated to software development in the plastic industry. Established in 1986, the Company is located in The Netherlands. As Managing Director, Mr. Schermerhorn is responsible for 39 employees in 17 countries, as well as maintaining the emphasis in the European market on the Company's C–mold product. Internet users can reach him via: SCHERMERHORN@CMOLD.NL **Career Steps:** Managing Director, AC Technology Europe (1993–Present); CAE Development Manager, Intergraph Europe (1988–1993); CAE Manager, AKZO_ Mobel (1982–1988). **Associations & Accomplishments:** Dutch Professional Association; Kiwi. **Education:** University, iR (M.Sc.) (1977). **Personal:** Married to Linda Marie Meijers in 1991. Two children: Victoria and Elizabeth. Mr. Schermerhorn enjoys historic car racing and work.

Roger Smallwood
Plant Manager
D.A., Inc.
101 Quality Court
Charlestown, IN 47111
(812) 256–3351
Fax: (812) 256–3352

3089

Business Information: D.A., Inc. specializes in the manufacture of injection molding (i.e., clips, clamps, covers for wires) for the automotive industry. As Plant Manager, Mr. Smallwood is responsible for all aspects of Company operations, including quality control, human resources, customer service, and customer relations. **Career Steps:** D.A., Inc.: Plant Manager (1994–Present), Administrative Manager (1993–1994), Quality Manager (1992–1993). **Associations & Accomplishments:** Southern Indiana Chamber of Commerce; Charlestown Chamber of Commerce; American Society of Quality Control. **Education:** Indiana University – Southeast. **Personal:** Married to Teresa in 1988. Two children: Dillon and Taylor. Mr. Smallwood enjoys fishing and golf.

Gerald A. Smith Jr.
Vice President – Sales and Marketing
ABTCO
3250 W. Big Beaver Road, Suite 200
Troy, MI 48084–2902
(810) 649–7775
Fax: (810) 649–0458

3089

Business Information: ABTCO is a manufacturer of building products. Joining ABTCO at its conception in 1992 as General Sales Manager – West, Mr. Smith was appointed as Vice President of Sales and Marketing in 1995. He is responsible for all aspects of sales and marketing in the Hardboard Plastics Division. **Career Steps:** ABTCO: Vice President – Sales and Marketing (1995–Present); National Sales Manager (1994–1995); General Sales Manager–West (1992–1994). **Education:** University of Kansas, B.G.S. – Bachelor of General Studies (1983); Duke University, Advanced Management Program; University of Michigan, Strategic Marketing Planning. **Personal:** Married to Deborah K. in 1977. Three children: Jeremy, Dustin and Nicholas. Mr. Smith enjoys golf and skiing during his leisure time.

Sheryl D. Solakian, CPIM
Vice President
Solakian Plastics
2657 North Argyle Avenue
Fresno, CA 93727–1304
(209) 294–7071
Fax: (209) 294–7159

3089

Business Information: Solakian Plastics specializes in the manufacture of custom plastic injection molding, and mold making. Established in 1975, Solakian Plastics currently employs 34 people. As Vice President, Controller and Co–Owner, Ms. Solakian is responsible for all aspects of operations, particularly focusing with financial administration and oversight of all accounting operations. **Career Steps:** Solakian Plastics: Vice President, Controller and Co–Owner (1993–Present), Cost Accountant (1980–1993); Typesetter, Dumont Printing (1975–1977); Master Tape Librarian, United Artists Records (1969–1974). **Associations & Accomplishments:** APICS: Local Chapter Treasurer; Former Secretary, Private Elementary School Board of Education; Fresno Lyric Opera Theater and Guild; Fresno Chamber of Commerce; National Association of Female Executives; Junior High School Student Mentor; Software Training Consultant. **Education:** Fresno City College, currently working towards her B.S. and M.B.A. in Finance and CIRM Certification. **Personal:** Married to Harry M. in 1973. Two children: Nicholas Michael and Thomas Peter. Ms. Solakian enjoys singing, reading, camping, cooking, baking, computers, playing the piano and the flute, crafts and making stained glass projects.

Michael S. Sullivan
Director of Manufacturing
Del Met
921 West Main Street, 3rd Floor
Hendersonville, TN 37075–2855
(615) 264–6667
Fax: (615) 264–6698
E MAIL: See Below

3089

Business Information: Del Met is a manufacturer and distributor of injection molded plastic parts for the automotive industry. Services include painting and assembly for wheel trim, center caps, and interior trim. Company sales are primarily to U.S. locations with a small percentage to international markets. As Director of Manufacturing, Mr. Sullivan has oversight of all manufacturing operations for three facilities. He is responsible for meeting established sales deadlines, quality standards, and plant safety standards. Internet users may contact him via: Miksulli@aol.com. **Career Steps:** Director of Manufacturing, Del Met (1992–Present); Director Marketing and Technical services, Prime Colorants, Inc. (1985–1992); Assistant to President, Tennessee Fan Company (1980–1985). **Associations & Accomplishments:** Society of Plastics Engineers. **Education:** Brescia College, B.S. (1975). **Personal:** Married to Rebecca in 1981. Two children: Matthew and Ashley. Mr. Sullivan enjoys golf, bowling, and surfing the net.

Vernal G. Vincent
Vice President of Sales and Management
New Plastics Corporation
3232 Cobb Parkway, Suite 250
Atlanta, GA 30339–3896
(404) 842–1081
Fax: (404) 842–1074

3089

Business Information: New Plastics Corporation specializes in the manufacture of custom and stock blow–molded plastic articles, as well as turning pure recycled plastic into plastic lumber. Established in 1968, New Plastics Corporation is a family–owned business and distributes its products throughout the United States and Canada. Currently, the Company employs over 200 people and has an estimated annual revenue of $18 million. As Vice President of Sales and Management, Mr. Vincent is responsible for all aspects of country–wide sales, as well as Company management. **Career Steps:** New Plastics Corporation: Vice President of Sales and Management (1992–Present), Sales Manager (1984–1992), Purchasing Agent (1979–1983). **Associations & Accomplishments:** Plastic Lumber Trade Association; Luxemburg Chamber of Commerce; Published in local newspapers. **Education:** NWTI, A.S. in Business (1979). **Personal:** Married to Jennifer Gregorich in 1990. Mr. Vincent enjoys sports, cars, golf, fishing, and travel.

Richard C. Whicker
Vice President
GTM Plastics
P. O. Box 462105, 114 North 3rd Street
Garland, TX 75046–2105
(214) 494–3551
Fax: (214) 272–8447

3089

Business Information: GTM Plastics specializes in the manufacture of thermoplastic injection molding, tooling and design. Established in 1964, GTM Plastics currently employs 55 people and has an estimated annual revenue of $5 million. As Vice President, Mr. Whicker is responsible for all aspects of sales, plant operations and general administration. **Career Steps:** Vice President, GTM Plastics (1972–Present). **Associations & Accomplishments:** Society of Plastic Engineers; American Business Clubs; Board of Directors, Local Baseball Team; Published in trade magazines such as "DuPont Design" and "Injection Molding Magazine." **Education:** University of North Texas (1977); Accounting and Information Systems Certification. **Personal:** Married to Valerie in 1974.

Two children: Eric and Emily. Mr. Whicker enjoys trap shooting, golf, and coaching youth sports.

William Wicks
President
R.W. Displays, Inc.
51 North Gates Avenue
Buffalo, NY 14218–1029
(716) 824–0772
Fax: (716) 824–5950

3089

Business Information: R.W. Displays, Inc. is a manufacturer of food display units, racks, and other associated products for the supermarket industry. National in scope, R.W. Displays, Inc. operates from two locations (New York and Pennsylvania). As President, Mr. Wicks is responsible for all aspects of operations, including the oversight of sales, production, and design. **Career Steps:** President, R.W. Displays, Inc. (1987–Present); Refrigeration Mechanic, Cold Spot (1984–1987); Refrigeration Mechanic, Wheels and Floors (1979–1984); Refrigeration Mechanic, State Refrigeration (1975–1979). **Personal:** Married to Carol in 1981. Two children: William J. and Joshua L. Mr. Wicks enjoys snowmobiling and boating.

3100 Leather and Leather Products

3111	Leather tanning and finishing
3131	Footwear cut stock
3142	House slippers
3143	Men's footwear, except athletic
3144	Women's footwear, except athletic
3149	Footwear, except rubber, NEC
3151	Leather gloves and mittens
3161	Luggage
3171	Women's handbags and purses
3172	Personal leather goods, NEC
3199	Leather goods, NEC

Ms. Carole Cary
Vice President, Human Resource Development
Woolworth Corporation, Speciality and Athletic Footwear Divisions
233 Broadway
New York, NY 10279–0001
(212) 720–4215
Fax: (212) 720–4028

3149

Business Information: Woolworth Corporation, Specialty Footwear/Athletic Footwear & Apparel Divisions, specializes in the manufacture, distribution and sale of famous footwear products for retailers such as Foot Locker, Lady Foot Locker, Kinney, Kids Foot Locker, Colorado, Footquarters and Champs Sports Stores throughout the United States. Established in 1889, Woolworth Corporation currently employs over 119,000 people worldwide. As Vice President and Director of Human Resource Development, Ms. Cary is responsible for training associates in technical management development and EEO matters in stores throughout the United States, Mexico and Canada. **Career Steps:** Vice President, Human Resource Development, Woolworth Corporation, Speciality Footwear/Athletic Footwear & Apparel Divisions (1993–Present); Player Programs Coordinator, National Football League (1991–1993); Passaic County Police Reporter, Bergen Record (1988–1991); Feature Story Reporter, Philadelphia Inquirer (1986–1988). **Associations & Accomplishments:** NAACP; NUL; American Management Association; American Society of Training and Development. **Education:** Columbia University, M.S. (1990); University of Virginia, B.A. (1985).

Gerardo Hernandez

Quality Manager
COACH International
URB Villa Barinquen, Calle Emilo Catro
Larer, Puerto Rico 00669
(809) 897–5120
Fax: (809) 897–5357

3172

Business Information: COACH International is an international manufacturer and distributor of fine leather products. Product lines include purses, boots, belts, wallets, etc. Head-

quartered in New York, COACH distributes products worldwide from two locations in the U.S. (New Jersey & Florida) and one in Puerto Rico. A Certified Quality Engineer with eight years of experience in quality assurance, Mr. Hernandez joined COACH International's Puerto Rico office as Quality Manager in 1995. He is responsible for the management of all quality assurance functions, including the implementation of special projects, quality planning, client relations, product development, inspection receipts, quality at the source, and HPLUS. **Career Steps:** Quality Manager, COACH International (1995–Present); Quality Engineer, Baxter Healthcare (1992–1995); Design Engineer, Raytheon Missile System (1988–1992). **Associations & Accomplishments:** American Society for Quality Control **Education:** University of Puerto Rico, B.S.in Electrical Engineering; Attending, University of Massachusetts, M.S. in Engineering Management; Certified Quality Engineer. **Personal:** Married to Marisal Velazquez in 1989. Three children: Wesley Xavier, Gerryel and Xiomarie. Mr. Hernandez enjoys playing basketball and reading.

James Saccacio
Executive Vice President
Elite Leather Company
28542 Cedar Ridge Road
Trabuco Cannon, CA 92679
(909) 468–0555
Fax: (714) 589–2250

3199

Business Information: Elite Leather Company is a manufacturer of mid– to mid–high contemporary leather furniture. Established in 1959, Elite Leather Company currently employs 100 people. Joining the Company as Vice President of Finance and Administration, Mr. Saccacio was appointed as Executive Vice President in 1993. He serves as the chief operating officer for the Company, providing the overall vision and strategies for the ensurance of quality product output, customer satisfaction, and the overall development to keep the company a viable presence in the international market. **Career Steps:** Elite Leather Company: Executive Vice President (1993–Present), Vice President of Finance and Administration (1986–1993); Assistant Vice President, Bank of America NT and SA (1982–1986). **Associations & Accomplishments:** University of California – Irvine Alumni Association; SMU Alumni Association; Young Entreprenuers Association; Sigma Alpha Epsilon; Young Furniture Manufacturers Association. **Education:** University of California – Irvine, M.B.A. (1993); SMU, B.B.A. (1982). **Personal:** Married to Enza in 1990. Mr. Saccacio enjoys weight training, golf, and travel.

3200 Stone, Clay, and Glass Products

3211	Flat glass
3221	Glass containers
3229	Pressed and blown glass, NEC
3231	Products of purchased glass
3241	Cement, hydraulic
3251	Brick and structural clay tile
3253	Ceramic wall and floor tile
3255	Clay refractories
3259	Structural clay products, NEC
3261	Vitreous plumbing fixtures
3262	Vitreous china table and kitchenware
3263	Semivitreous table and kitchenware
3264	Porcelain electrical supplies
3269	Pottery products, NEC
3271	Concrete block and brick
3272	Concrete products, NEC
3273	Ready–mixed concrete
3274	Lime
3275	Gypsum products
3281	Cut stone and stone products
3291	Abrasive products
3292	Asbestos products
3295	Minerals, ground or treated
3296	Mineral wool
3297	Nonclay refractories
3299	Nonmetallic mineral products, NEC

Jeffrey M. Klein
General Manager
Milgard Manufacturing, Inc.
1802 Shelton Drive
Hollister, CA 95023
(408) 636–0114
Fax: (408) 636–0274

3211

Business Information: Milgard Manufacturing, Inc. is a manufacturer of windows, doors, and skylights in vinyl, wood, fiberglass, and aluminum, and distributes the products to dealer networks internationally. As General Manager, Mr. Klein is responsible for operations management, the sales force, manufacturing groups, production, scheduling, and product quality. **Career Steps:** General Manager, Milgard Manufacturing, Inc. (1991–Present); Tour Marketing, Bullet Golf, Inc. (1989–1991); Human Resource Specialist, Union Federal Savings Bank (1987–1989). **Associations & Accomplishments:** National Association of Home Builders; Private Industry Council; Rotary International. **Education:** Stanford University: B.A. in Economics (1986), M.A. in Organizational Development (1987). **Personal:** Married to Elizabeth in 1987. Two children: Dionna and Elijah. Mr. Klein enjoys golf, running, fishing, and weightlifting.

John F. McConnell
Manufacturing Engineer
PPG Industries, Inc.
Glass Technology Center, P.O. Box 11210
Pittsburgh, PA 15238–0472
(412) 820–8117
Fax: (412) 820–8111

3211

Business Information: PPG Industries, Inc., ranked #1 in the industry nationwide, manufactures glass, fiberglas, chemicals, and coatings. Established in 1883, the Company currently employs 32,000 people and has annual sales of $7 billion. As Manufacturing Engineer, Mr. McConnell oversees the production and engineering of the Flat Glass Department. **Career Steps:** PPG Industries, Inc: Manufacturing Engineer, Flat Glass (1989–Present), Manager, Mechanical Engineering (1984–1989), Chief Furnace Engineer (1974–1984). **Associations & Accomplishments:** The American Ceramic Society; The American Society of Mechanical Engineers. **Education:** Bucknell University, B.S. in Mechanical Engineering (1956). **Personal:** Married to Lillie in 1956. Five children: Rebecca, Janet, John Jr., Carol, and Karen. Mr. McConnell enjoys camping and music.

Amy L. Brown
Plant Controller
Ball–Foster Glass Container Co., L.L.C.
1200 North Logan Street
Lincoln, IL 62656–1707
(217) 735–1511
Fax: (217) 735–1184

3221

Business Information: Ball–Foster Glass Container Co., L.L.C. is a manufacturer and distributor of glass containers nationally and internationally. Joining Ball–Foster Glass Container Co., L.L.C. in 1988, Mrs. Brown was appointed as Plant Controller in 1991. She is responsible for all operational and financial reporting for the Lincoln, Illinois plant, in addition to overseeing a support staff who conducts the day–to–day accounting procedures. **Career Steps:** Ball–Foster Glass Container Co., L.L.C.: Plant Controller (1991–Present), Cost and Inventory Analyst (1990–1991), Staff Accountant (1988–1990), Staff Accountant, Life of Indiana Insurance Company (1987–1988). **Associations & Accomplishments:** National Association of Female Executives. **Education:** Ball State University, B.A. in Accounting (1988). **Personal:** Married to Brian in 1990. Three children: Derek, Nicholas, and Amelia. Mrs. Brown enjoys travel.

Mr. Matthew C. Hollingsworth
General Manager and Training Specialist
Corning Consumer Products Company, Inc.
354 Shadowtown Road, Suite 150
Blountville, TN 37617
(615) 323–0546
Fax: (615) 323–0594

3221

Business Information: Corning Consumer Products Company, Inc. specializes in the manufacturing and retail sale of housewares, including Corningware, Pyrex, Corelle, Visions and many more. Mr. Hollingsworth serves as General Manager and Training Specialist (new managers) for the Factory Outlet Division. **Career Steps:** General Manager and Training Specialist, Corning Consumer Products Company, Inc. (1991–Present); General Manager, Colonial Heights Hardware Company (1986–1991); Accounts Manager, Commonwealth Insurance Company (1985–1986). **Associations & Accomplishments:** Member, Kiwanis Club; Volunteer with the Red Cross. **Education:** Ft. Wayne Business College, Bachelors Degree; American Institute of Consumer Credit – many other forms of training through seminars. **Personal:** Married to Debbie Hollingsworth in 1988. One child: Kaytlin B. Hollingsworth.

Scott G. Proudfoot
Director of Corporate Transportation and Distribution
Corning, Inc.
Houghton Park A–2
Corning, NY 14830
(607) 974–8756
Fax: Please mail or call

3221

Business Information: Corning, Inc. is a manufacturer and distributor of specialty glass and ceramic products (Corningware and Visionware), and is also a health service provider. As Director of Corporate Transportation and Distribution, Mr. Proudfoot is responsible for procuring domestic and international transportation and distribution services for the corporation. Established in 1856, Corning, Inc. employs 30,000 people with annual sales of $4.5 Billion. **Career Steps:** Director of Corporate Transportation and Distribution, Corning, Inc. (1992–Present); Manager of International Transportation, Corning, Inc. (1985–1992); Plant Manager, Corning, Inc. (1982–1985); Distribution Center Manager, Corning, Inc. (1979–1982). **Associations & Accomplishments:** Board of Directors, National Industrial Trans–League; Council of Logistics Management; Certified Member, American Society of Transportation and Logistics; Industry Sector Advisory Committee; U.S. Trade Representative, Department of Commerce; Southern Tier World Commerce Association, New York State; First Presbyterian Church; Little League programs. **Education:** University of Maryland, B.S. (1966); Brookings Institute, Management Program. **Personal:** Married to Janet K. Proudfoot in 1966. Two children: Stephen M. Proudfoot and Scott R. Proudfoot. Mr. Proudfoot enjoys golf and painting.

Mr. Stuart K. Sammis
Manager of Corporate Records
Corning, Inc.
HP–AB–02–Z
Corning, NY 14831
(607) 974–8120
Fax: (607) 974–8612

3221

Business Information: Corning, Inc. is a consumer products manufacturer of Corningware and Pyrex cookware, telecommunications and environmental products, and also provides laboratory testing services. As Manager of Corporate Records, Mr. Sammis is responsible for records management and imaging technology applications. He develops policies, litigation support, information security procedures, and records management procedures. Established in 1851, Corning, Inc. employs over 40,000 and reports annual revenue of more than $4 billion. **Career Steps:** Manager of Corporate Records, Corning, Inc. (1985–Present). **Associations & Accomplishments:** Association of Records Managers and Administrators; Institute of Certified Records Managers; Association of Information and Image Managers. **Education:** New York University, M.A. (1981); Fairleigh Dickinson University, B.A.

Shira Shapiro
Manager, General Accounting
Corning Costar
1443 Beacon Street
Brookline, MA 02146
(617) 868–6200
Fax: Please mail or call

3221

Business Information: Corning Costar, a Fortune 500 Company, is a manufacturer of glass products for cooking, and scientific testing equipment from beakers to flasks. As Manager of General Accounting, Ms. Shapiro handles all customer service, customer relations, advertising, marketing, employee relations, employee benefits, and budgetary concerns. **Career Steps:** Manager General Accounting, Corning Costar (1996–Present); Assistant Controller, Lightbridge, Inc. (1988–1996); Cost Accountant, Harris Corporation (1982–1985). **Associations & Accomplishments:** American Management Association; Boston Jewish Food Bank. **Education:** Boston University, M.S.M. (1986); University of Cincinnati, B.B.A. (1981). **Personal:** Ms. Shapiro enjoys music and dance.

Joao Batista de Araujo
Marketing and Sales Director
ABC Cristais Microelectonica, S.A.
Av Brasil 20.201
Rio de Janeiro, Brazil 21515–000
55–021–3756363
Fax: 55–021–3726950

3229

Business Information: ABC Cristais Microelectonica, S.A., established in 1974, is a privately–owned manufacturer of crystal units for the computer, audio, video, VCR, video game, and telecommunications industries worldwide. ABC Cristais Microelectronica has three manufacturing plants: cultured quartz (as grown bars), blanks, and final crystal unit. Established in 1974, the Company employs 250 people. As Marketing and Sales Director, Mr. Batista de Araujo is responsible for the development of new, and updates to existing marketing techniques to increase sales of Company products. He is responsible for administrative duties for his staff including personnel and budgetary concerns, and strategic planning. **Career Steps:** ABC Cristais Microelectonica, S.A.: Marketing and Sales Director (1996–Present), Marketing Director (1986–1996); ABC Xtal: Industrial Director (1983–1986), General Planning and Quality Manager (1979–1982). **Education:** PDG–EX, M.B.A. (1990); Rio de Janeiro University, Master Manufacturer Administration; Catholic University, Economy Graduate. **Personal:** Married to Ana Aurora in 1980. Two children: Cinthia and Marcella. Mr. Batista de Araujo enjoys tennis, swimming, and soccer.

Jose L. Feliciano–Castro
Accountant II
Essilor Industries
Sabanetas Industrial Park
Mercedita, Puerto Rico 00715
(787) 848–4130
Fax: (787) 848–4690

3229

Business Information: Essilor Industries, established in 1986 and employing over 300 people, specializes in manufacturing lenses. As Accountant II, Mr. Feliciano–Castro supervises the general accounting area. He is responsible for payroll, budgeting, taxes, and supervision of a three–person staff. **Career Steps:** Accountant II, Essilor Industries (1989–Present). **Associations & Accomplishments:** Associate Member, Institute of Management Accountants. **Education:** Catholic University of Puerto Rico, M.B.A. (1996); University of Puerto Rico, Ponce, B.B.A. (1989). **Personal:** Mr. Feliciano–Castro enjoys being an amateur singer, playing the organ, and reading computer books.

Carla Y. Kuntz
Group Human Resources Manager
Lancaster Colony
4460 Lake Forest Drive, Suite 200
Cincinnati, OH 45242
(513) 563–1113
Fax: (513) 563–9639

3229

Business Information: Lancaster Colony, the parent company of Candle–Lite Division, is a manufacturer of candles and glassware. Products include drinking glasses, candy dishes, and light fixtures. Joining Lancaster Colony in 1977, Ms. Kuntz was appointed as Group Human Resources Manager of the Candle–Lite Division in 1992. She is responsible for all administrative functions for personnel in the Candle–Lite Division, including hiring, firing, and counseling. **Career Steps:** Lancaster Colony – Candle–Lite Division: Group Human Resource Manager (1992–Present), Personnel Manager (1990–1992), Office Manager (1982–1990). **Associations & Accomplishments:** SHRM; GCHRA. **Education:** Xavier University. **Personal:** Two children: James and Brian. Ms. Kuntz enjoys reading and bicycling.

Nivia I. Ayala
Environmental Manager
San Juan Cement Company
P.O. Box 366698
San Juan, Puerto Rico 00936
(787) 721–5878
Fax: (787) 883–5747

3241

Business Information: San Juan Cement Company, Inc. is cement manufacturer, maintains contracts with both corporate and residential interests. As Environmental Manager, Ms. Ayala is responsible for the establishing procedures and monitoring to ensure daily compliance with all environmental regulations, including the handling, treatment, storage and disposal of all waste, toxic and hazardous material. She also supervises the Community Regulations Program. **Career Steps:**

Environmental Manager, San Juan Cement Company (1993–Present); Engineer, Puerto Rico Environmental Quality Brd. (1992–1993). **Associations & Accomplishments:** Air & Waste Management Association; National Registry of Environmental Professionals. **Education:** University of Puerto Rico, B.S.M.E. (1991). **Personal:** Ms. Ayala enjoys hiking and ECO tourism.

Clinton R. Wilkins

Technical Services Manager
Phoenix Cement Company
P.O. Box 43740
Phoenix, AZ 85080
(602) 264–0511
Fax: (602) 581–1836

3241

Business Information: Phoenix Cement Company, a subsidiary of Portland Cement Manufacturing Company, specializes in the manufacturing of cement and related products, and services concrete industries in the Northern half of the state. Established in 1959, the Company employs 120 people. As Technical Services Manager, Mr. Wilkins provides assistance to customers, and oversees quality assurance for the Company. Additional duties include management of the concrete lab and testing facility, compiling data, spreadsheets, and analyzing information, and problem solving. **Career Steps:** Phoenix Cement Company: Technical Services Manager (1995–Present), Technical Manager (1992–1995), Technical Service Engineer (1984–1995). **Associations & Accomplishments:** Phoenix Valley Church of Christ; Coordinate Children's Ministry; Coordinate Pre–Teen Ministry. **Education:** Arizona State University, Bachelor of Science (1983). **Personal:** Married to Kristine in 1984. Two children: Melissa and Jordon. Mr. Wilkins enjoys church related activities, basketball and other sports.

Benjamin F. Williams

Environmental and Safety Manager
Lone Star Industries, Inc.
P.O. Box 68
Pryor, OK 74362–0068
(918) 825–1937
Fax: (918) 825–3353

3241

Business Information: Lone Star Industries, Inc. is a nationwide manufacturer and distributor of Portland cement products. National in scope, Lone Star Industries, Inc. has five locations in Texas, Indiana, Illinois, Mississippi, and Oklahoma. As Environmental and Safety Manager, Mr. Williams is responsible for the management of all environmental policies and compliance and safety regulations, in addition to serving as the Personnel Manager. **Career Steps:** Environmental and Safety Manager, Lone Star Industries, Inc. (1993–Present); Plant Manager, InterPlastic Corporation (1986–1993); Technical Manager, Owens Corning Fiberglass Corporation (1977–1986). **Associations & Accomplishments:** Board of Directors, United Way of Mayes County; First United Methodist Church; Treasurer, Pryor Athletic Booster Club; JCI Senator; Oklahoma Safety Council; Region II Representative, Oklahoma School–to–Work Program; Coach, Summer League Girl's Softball. **Education:** Clemson University, B.S.Ch.E. (1968). **Personal:** Married to Charlene in 1974. Two children: "McK"and "C.C.". Mr. Williams enjoys spending time with his family and supporting his children's activities, such as coaching the summer league softball team.

Terry J. Hampton

Controller
Acme Brick Company
P.O. Box 425
Ft. Worth, TX 76101–0425
(817) 390–2463
Fax: (817) 390–2480
EMAIL: See Below

3251

Business Information: Acme Brick Company, the largest U.S.–owned company in the U.S., is a brick manufacturer. A Certified Public Accountant with over fifteen years of account management expertise, Mr. Hampton joined Acme Brick Company as Controller in 1990. He is responsible for all corporate financial aspects. Mr. Hampton can also be reached through the Internet as follows: HAMPSTER@DFWNET.COM **Career Steps:** Controller, Acme Brick Company (1990–Present); CPA Manager, Lockhart, Altaras & Thompson (1982–1990). **Associations & Accomplishments:** President, Fort Worth Chapter of Financial Executives Institute; Ducks Unlimited; Jaycees; Ridglea Country Club. **Education:** Tarleton State University, B.B.A. (1980); Certification: Certified Public Accountant. **Personal:** Mr. Hampton enjoys golf and gaming.

Charles G. Marvin

Executive Vice President
The Refractories Institute
650 Smithfield Street, Suite 1160
Pittsburgh, PA 15222–3907
(412) 281–6787
Fax: (412) 281–6881

3255

Business Information: The Refractories Institute is a national trade association for the refractories industry (clay and non–clay). Established in 1951, the association currently consists of 98 corporate members. As Executive Vice President, Mr. Marvin is responsible for coordinating and managing all nine committees, legislative and regulatory affairs, as well as environmental, safety, and health issues. **Career Steps:** Executive Vice President, The Refractories Institute (1980–Present); Professor of Military Science, University of Missouri at Rolla (1976–1980); Facilities Engineer, Nurnberg, Germany (1973–1975); Director of Facilities Engineering, Fort Eustis, VA (1970–1973); Engineer Construction Advisor, USARV, Viet Nam (1969); Facilities Engineer Operations Officer, U.S. Military Academy, West Point (1963–1966); Ceramic Engineer, General Refractories Company (1958–1960). **Associations & Accomplishments:** Fellow, American Ceramic Society; Iron and Steel Society; Air and Waste Management Association; The Retired Officers Association; Legion of Merit Medal and Bronze Star Medal. **Education:** University of Missouri at Rolla, M.S. in Engineering Management (1969); Alfred College, B.S. in Ceramic Engineering (1958); U.S. Army Command and General Staff College (1976). **Personal:** Married to Sandra B. in 1971. Mr. Marvin enjoys raising and showing Samoyeds.

Michael E. Tomlinson

Vice President – Sales
Lenox Brands
100 Lenox Drive
Trenton, NJ 08648–2309
(609) 844–1493
Fax: Please mail or call

3262

Business Information: Lenox Brands, a subsidiary of Brown–Forman, is a distributor of fine china, crystal and metal tabletop products (i.e. stainless steel flatware, sterling silver flatware, holloware), collectibles, and luggage and leather goods. Its brands include Lenox, Gorham, and Dansk tabletop products and Hartmann luggage. As Vice President of Sales, Mr. Tomlinson oversees all global corporate sales and marketing operations. **Career Steps:** Vice President of Sales, Lenox Brands (1994–Present); PepsiCo: Vice President of Business Re–engineering (1991–1994), Area Vice President – Florida (1990–1991). **Education:** Memphis University, B.B.A. (1973). **Personal:** Mr. Tomlinson enjoys sailing, running and golf during his leisure time.

Mark W. Mays

Manager of Corporate Planning
Southdown, Inc.
1200 Smith Street, Suite 2400
Houston, TX 77002
(713) 653–6855
Fax: (713) 653–6950
EMAIL: See Below

3271

Business Information: Southdown, Inc. specializes in the manufacture of cement and concrete. National in scope, the Company is headquartered in Texas, and has 100 locations throughout the U.S. Established in 1930, the Company employs 2,500 people and has estimated annual revenue of $600 million. As Manager of Corporate Planning, Mr. Mays handles profitability, strategic planning, budgeting, profit and loss analysis, review, and forecasting. Internet users can reach him via: Captnmark@aol.com. **Career Steps:** Southdown, Inc: Manager of Corporate Planning (1991–Present), Director of Taxation (1985–1991); Director of Taxes, Continental Group (1983–1985). **Associations & Accomplishments:** Arbor Software Users Group; Licensed Captain. **Education:** University of Connecticut, M.B.A. (1982); Duke University/University of Connecticut, B.S. in Accounting. **Personal:** Two children: Kaitlin and Conner. Mr. Mays enjoys being a licensed Captain, sailing, fishing, and model trains.

Riyad A. Abboud

General Manager
Ameron Gulf Company Ltd.
Box 1313 Al Ain
Abu Dhabi, United Arab Emirates
(971) 3–826555
Fax: (971) 3–826842

3272

Business Information: Ameron Gulf Company Ltd. is a manufacturer and supplier of reinforced concrete gravity and pressure pipe (storm drain & sewage) to the Arabian Peninsula and Persian Gulf Region. As General Manager, Mr. Abboud directs all activities related to the manufacture and installation of products, as well as coordinating with consultants and contractors. **Career Steps:** General Manager, Ameron Gulf Company Ltd. (1987–Present); Engineering Manager, Ameron Saudi Arabia Ltd. (1979–1986); Engineer, Canron Ltd. – Canada (1986–1987). **Associations & Accomplishments:** American Society of Civil Engineers; American Concrete Institute; American Society for Testing & Materials; American Society for Quality Control; Professional Engineers of Ontario–Canada; Lebanese Order of Engineers. **Education:** Louisiana State University, B.S. in Civil Engineering (1971). **Personal:** Married to Nabiha in 1974. Two children: Rana and Rima Lee. Mr. Abboud enjoys tennis, squash, skiing, golf, and reading, in addition to being a scholar of the Bible.

Ken Hawley

Regional Manager
Ready Mixed Concrete
P.O. Box 1067
Dunn, NC 28334
(910) 892–5116
Fax: (910) 892–4621

3272

Business Information: Ready Mixed Concrete is a concrete producer specializing in the distribution of concrete for construction, small home projects, etc. Established in 1935, the Company is regional in scope with ten locations throughout the area. As Regional Manager, Mr. Hawley is responsible for all area plants, 120 employees, and four division managers. He handles all administrative and operational duties, and strategic planning. **Career Steps:** Regional Manager, Ready Mixed Concrete (1994–Present); General Manager, V.J. Rose and Son (1983–1992); Plant Manager, Paul Beasley Concrete (1974–1983). **Associations & Accomplishments:** Portland Cement Association; American Concrete Institute; Carolina Concrete Association. **Personal:** Married to Vickie P. in 1974. Two children: Sarah and Melissa. Mr. Hawley enjoys golf and church.

Jon E. Loewer

Distribution Manager
W.R. Grace & Company – Conn.
6606 Marshall Boulevard
Lithonia, GA 30058–8959
(770) 484–1508 Ext.22
Fax: (770) 482–5670

3272

Business Information: W.R. Grace & Company specializes in the manufacturing and distribution of concrete chemical admixtures. International in scope, the Company has over 160 offices and 80 manufacturing and distribution facilities throughout the world, including Europe, South America, and the Far East. The Company was established in 1854 as a shipping, trading, and manufacturing group based primarily in Latin America. The specialty chemical division was formed in the 1950's and today is the largest manufacturer and supplier of specialty chemicals in the world employing over 50,000 people in 46 different countries with gross sales of over $7 billion. As Distribution Manager, Mr. Loewer oversees operation of the private delivery fleet, has P/L responsibility for a $1.7 million budget, and is responsible for customer relations within the delivery department. Additional duties include coordination with the Human Resources Manager, keeping abreast of changing Department of Transportation regulations, and management of the Company's fleet of drivers to maintain an efficient, safe, and legal delivery system. Mr. Loewer also manages the coordination of seven manufacturing facilities, including production planning, regarding delivery to approximately 1,500 customer locations in eight states. Mr. Loewer has been instrumental in the design, development programming, and implementation of a computerized database automated dispatch system, Mr. Loewer will be completing his CPFM "Certified Private Fleet Manager" school and test in January 1997, and will be officially certified in his field. **Career Steps:** Distribution Manager, W.R. Grace & Company (1995–Present); Traffic Logistics Manager, Louis Dreyfus Energy (1992–1995); Operations Manager, US Trans Service, Inc. (1990–1992). **Associations & Accomplishments:** Board of Directors, Atlanta Traffic Association; Certified National Safety Council DDC Professional Truck Driver Safety

Course Instructor; DOT Hazardous Material Certified. **Personal:** Married to Teresa in 1992. Three children: Adam, Jamie, and Megan. Mr. Loewer enjoys boating and skiing.

Eric J. Martin
Plant Manager
Mack Industry of Pennsylvania, Inc.
2207 Sodom Hutchings Road, NE
Vienna, OH 44473
(330) 638-7680
Fax: (330) 638-1277

3272

Business Information: Mack Industry of Pennsylvania, Inc. is a privately-owned company that manufactures precast concrete. The Company provides their products to contractors, home owners, general contractors, and the Departments of Transportation of Pennsylvania, Ohio, and Michigan for septic tanks, cemetaries, etc. through direct distribution. As Plant Manager, Mr. Martin is responsible for diversified administrative activities, including ordering, inventory control, personnel, training, and consistent production. **Career Steps:** Plant Manager, Mack Industry of Pennsylvania, Inc. (1993-Present); Job Placement Specialist, Trumbull County Board of Education (1992-1993); Chapter I Reading Instructor, Badger Local School District (1992). **Associations & Accomplishments:** Optimist Club of Bazzetta Township; ABC; Coach for wrestling and football. **Education:** Hiram College (1989). **Personal:** Married to Karen M. in 1991. One child: Kevin Kingsley. Mr. Martin enjoys all sports, reading, and woodworking.

Cristobal Soler
General Manager
Master Builders Technologies
Parque Industrial Aeropuerto Los Coigues 701 Quilicura
Santiago, Chile
562-739-0162
Fax: 562-739-0163

3272

Business Information: Master Builders Technologies, a division of Sandoz (an international pharmaceutical company), is a manufacturer of concrete additives, repair products, and protective chemicals. As General Manager, Mr. Soler is responsible for supervising 15 employees, Company sales and production. **Career Steps:** General Manager, Master Builders Technologies (1992-Present); Regional Manager S.E. Asia, MAC International (1982-1988); Division Manager, MBT Ausmalia (1988-1991). **Education:** University of North Carolina – Charlotte, B.S. Degree in Engineering (1982). **Personal:** Married to Paulina in 1986. Three children: Cristobal, Javiera, and Sebastian. Mr. Soler enjoys tennis and skiing.

John H. Barry
· · · ◄██ ◎ ██► · · ·

Vice President of Human Resources
Rinker Materials Corporation
1501 Belvedere Road
West Palm Beach, FL 33406
(407) 820-8310
Fax: (407) 820-8509

3273

Business Information: Rinker Materials Corporation is one of the leading U.S. producers of ready-mix concrete, crushed stone, concrete blocks, and other construction products. Established in 1926, Rinker Materials Corporation reports annual revenue in excess of $600 million and currently employs 3,000 people corporate-wide. As Vice President of Human Resources, Mr. Barry is responsible for the direction of all personnel matters, as well as engineering, environmental, quality, purchasing and administrative matters. **Career Steps:** Vice President of Human Resources, Rinker Materials Corporation (1992-Present); Vice President of Human Resources, ATC Telecommunications (1990-1991); Division Manager, AT&T Corporation (1964-1990). **Associations & Accomplishments:** Eastern Region Human Resources Council, American Management Association; American Compensation Association; Human Resources Planning Society. **Education:** Columbia University, M.B.A. (1964); Brown University, B.A. (1963). **Personal:** Married to Patricia in 1963. Two children: Anne G. and John H. Mr. Barry enjoys golf, jogging, and snorkeling.

Raymond L. Rhees
· · · ◄██ ◎ ██► · · ·

Chief Operating Officer of the Central Region
Oldcastle Precast/DBA AMCOR Precast
8392 Riverview Parkway
Littleton, CO 80125-9790
(303) 791-1100
Fax: (303) 791-1120

3273

Business Information: AMCOR Precast, a wholly-owned subsidiary of Oldcastle Precast, is a national producer of a variety of concrete construction materials. Established in 1932, AMCOR Precast employs 250 people. As Chief Operating Officer of the Central Region, Mr. Rhees is in charge of seven companies throughout fourteen states. **Career Steps:** AMCOR Precast: Chief Operating Officer of the Central Region (1992-Present), General Manager (1984-1992), Division Manager (1979-1984), Distribution Manager (1968-1979). **Associations & Accomplishments:** Pleasant View City Councilperson; President, Mountain States Concrete Pipe Association; Chamber of Commerce; National Precast Association; American Concrete Pipe Association; Little League Coach for football and basketball; Rocky Mountain Corrugate Steel Association; Publisher of several industry articles. **Education:** University of Phoenix; Weber State College, A.S. **Personal:** Married to Vickie J. Rhees. Four children: Alison, Brian, Jason, and Tiffani. Mr. Rhees enjoys spending time with his family, golf, hunting, fishing, and his work.

Eddie Scott
· · · ◄██ ◎ ██► · · ·

Owner and Chief Executive Officer
J. Graves Insulation Company
801 West 62nd Street
Shreveport, LA 71148
(318) 861-3526
Fax: (318) 865-2167

3292

Business Information: J. Graves Insulation Company is an industrial and commercial insulation asbestos abatement company. Established in 1983, J.W. Graves reports annual revenue of $8 million and currently employs 60 people. A twenty-year veteran of J.W. Graves, Mr. Scott joined the Company in 1975. He currently serves as Owner and Chief Executive Officer, responsible for all aspects of Company operations. In addition, he oversees all administrative operations for associates and a support staff of 60. **Career Steps:** Owner and Chief Executive Officer, J. Graves Insulation Company (1975-Present). **Associations & Accomplishments:** Board of Advisors, Louisiana State University; Occupational Safety of Health. **Education:** University of Texas, Construction Engineering (1984). **Personal:** Married to Karen Patrice in 1978. Four children: Jason, Daniel, Kristen, and Britney. Mr. Scott enjoys hunting and fishing.

Thomas E. Van Dame
· · · ◄██ ◎ ██► · · ·

Manager of Engineering
Motion Control Industries, Inc.
1441 Holland Street
Logansport, IN 46947
(219) 753-6391
Fax: (219) 722-5531

3292

Business Information: Motion Control Industries, Inc., a subsidiary of Carlyle, is a manufacturer of friction material parts (i.e., mold compounds, machine, bond) for non-automotive industrial applications. Established in 1967, Motion Control Industries, Inc. reports annual revenue of $18 million and currently employs 145 people. As Manager of Engineering, Mr. Van Dame is responsible for industrial, plant, project, and tooling manufacturing engineering operations, and all maintenance of facilities. **Career Steps:** Manager of Engineering, Motion Control Industries, Inc. (1993-Present); Senior Manufacturing Engineer, Rubbermaid, Inc. (1989-1993); Senior Product Engineer, Greg Engineering (1986-1989). **Associations & Accomplishments:** Society of Manufacturing Engineers; Society of Plastic Engineers; Society of Die Casting Engineers. **Education:** Lake Michigan College, Associate in Business Management (1982); Purdue University, B.S. in Material Engineering Technology; Law Technology Institute, A.S. in Industrial Engineering. **Personal:** Married to Linda in 1987. Two children: Jennifer and Jason. Mr. Van Dame enjoys golf, guitar, and computers.

Mr. Gregory A. Menke
Manager for Market Development in Europe – AURA Superinsulator
Owens–Corning Fiberglas, Inc.
413 Blue Smoke Trail
Peachtree City, GA 30269
(614) 321-7413
Fax: (404) 631-0845

3296

Business Information: Owens–Corning Fiberglas, Inc. is a major worldwide manufacturer of mineral wool and mineral wool insulation products made of such siliceous materials as rock, slag, and glass, or combinations thereof. The Corporation is the largest producer and distributor of glass insulation (fiberglass insulation) and glass compound materials. The Corporation is also in the process of developing a new customer base for AURA, a revolutionary superinsulator. As Manager for Market Development in Europe – AURA Superinsulator, Mr. Menke is responsible for creating the market demand for AURA, new customer relations and applications. Established in 1939, Owens–Corning Fiberglas, Inc. employs 17,000 people with annual sales of $3.4 billion. **Career Steps:** Manager for Market Development in Europe – AURA Superinsulator, Owens–Corning Fiberglas, Inc. (1993-Present); New Business Development Manager, Owens Corning (1993); Instructor EWD, USAF (1987-1989). **Associations & Accomplishments:** Selected among several candidates to be one of four people presently representing the Georgia Rotary 6900 in a global business exchange to Finland for four weeks (March, 1994); Interviewed for European magazine. **Education:** University of Michigan, M.B.A. (1991); Purdue University, Engineering Degree. **Personal:** Married to Victoria Menke in 1985. Four children: Jessica Katherine, Ross and Garrett. Mr. Menke enjoys golf, reading, and gardening.

Singh Manocha, Ph.D.
Manager of Analytical Services
PPG Industries, Inc. – Glass Technology Center
Guys Run Road – P.O. Box 11472
Pittsburgh, PA 15238-0472
(412) 820-8091
Fax: (412) 820-8161

3299

Business Information: PPG Industries, Inc. is a manufacturer and global distributor of chemicals operating through three distinct divisions: Coating & Resins, Glass, and Chemicals. PPG's Glass Technology Center, located at the Pittsburgh conglomerate headquarters, serves as the research and development arm providing all technology development and testing, focusing on fiberglass and coatings developments. As Manager of Analytical Services, Dr. Manocha is responsible for 57 people and the efforts of the analytical services. **Career Steps:** Manager of Analytical Services, PPG Industries, Inc. – Glass Technology Center (1985-Present); Senior Engineer, Analytical, Westinghouse (1979-1985); Senior Chemist, Analytical, Bayer (1977-1978). **Associations & Accomplishments:** Pittsburgh Conference of Analytical Chemistry and Applied Spectroscopy; ASTM; Analytical Laboratory Managers Association; Spectroscopy Society of Pittsburgh; Society for Analytical Chemistry of Pittsburgh. **Education:** Carnegie Mellon University, Ph.D. (1974); University of Delhi, India, M.Sc. in Chemistry (1968); University of Delhi, India, B.Sc. (Honors) in Chemistry (1966). **Personal:** Married to Connie in 1977. Two children: Eric and Sonia. Dr. Manocha enjoys spending time with his children.

Mary A. McDonnell
· · · ◄██ ◎ ██► · · ·

Director of Sales and Marketing
Tempo Technology Corporation
500 Apgar Drive
Somerset, NJ 08873-1155
(908) 563-4833 Ext. 519
Fax: (908) 563-4977

3299

Business Information: Tempo Technology Corporation is a manufacturer of synthetic diamonds for industrial applications (i.e., construction tools, saw blades, drill bits for the oil and gas industries, cutting tools). Established in 1987, Tempo Technology Corporation currently employs 80 people. Joining Tempo Technology Corporation in 1993 as Product Manager, Ms. McDonnell was appointed as Director of Sales and Marketing in 1995. She is responsible for the direction of all aspects of sales and marketing for the Corporation. **Career Steps:** Tempo Technology Corporation: Director of Sales and Marketing (1995-Present), Product Manager (1993-1995); Regional Sales Manager, General Electric Corporation (1991-1993). **Associations & Accomplishments:** Society of Petroleum Engineers (SPE); Polycrystalline Products Association (PPA); Concrete Sawing and Drilling Association

(CSDA); National Association of Female Executives (NAFE). **Education:** Columbia University, M.B.A. in Marketing and Finance (1985); Rutgers University, B.A. in Chemistry (1981). **Personal:** Ms. McDonnell enjoys running, skiing, and reading.

3300 Primary Metal Industries

3312 Blast furnaces and steel mills
3313 Electrometallurgical products
3315 Steel wire and related products
3316 Cold finishing of steel shapes
3317 Steel pipe and tubes
3321 Gray and ductile iron foundries
3322 Malleable iron foundries
3324 Steel investment foundries
3325 Steel foundries, NEC
3331 Primary copper
3334 Primary aluminum
3339 Primary nonferrous metals, NEC
3341 Secondary nonferrous metals
3351 Copper rolling and drawing
3353 Aluminum sheet, plate, and foil
3354 Aluminum extruded products
3355 Aluminum rolling and drawing, NEC
3356 Nonferrous rolling and drawing, NEC
3357 Nonferrous wiredrawing and insulating
3363 Aluminum die–castings
3364 Nonferrous die–casting exc. aluminum
3365 Aluminum foundries
3366 Copper foundries
3369 Nonferrous foundries, NEC
3398 Metal heat treating
3399 Primary metal products, NEC

Juan Aguirre
Manager of Human Resources
Acme Steel Company
10730 S. Burley Avenue
Chicago, IL 60617–6501
(312) 933–5020
Fax: (313) 933–5163

3312

Business Information: Acme Steel Company custom produces steel in small order lots, in special chemistries and widths, with exact product quality and steel processing service matched by few mills make Acme Steel unique. Its integrated steelmaking process coupled with the new continuous thin slab casting/hot strip mill technology will put Acme Steel in the commodity market by expanding market penetration. The Company specializes in the production of sheet, strip, and semi–finished steel in low, mid, and high carbon; alloy; high–strength, low alloy, and special grades. Its principal markets are agricultural, automotive components, industrial equipment, industrial fasteners, pipe and tube, process/converter, and tool manufacturing industries. As Manager of Human Resources, Mr. Aguirre provides guidance and professional expertise by providing a framework for Union and Management to increase the quality, profitability and competitiveness of the Company and its products. Additionally, he assures safety, medical, plant protection, and salaried administration programs are functioning according to Management goals and policies, and serves as spokesman at contract negotiations. **Career Steps:** Manager of Human Resources, Acme Steel Company – Chicago Plant (1990–Present); U.S.X. Steel: Staff Supervisor of Labor Relations (1986–1990), Administrator – Employment Practices (1979–1986), Supervisor of Employment (1974–1986). **Associations & Accomplishments:** Calumet Industrial Relations Group; Calumet Personnel Association, South Chicago YMCA Board of Directors and Campaign Chairman. **Education:** Indiana University, B.S. in Business (1974). **Personal:** Married to 'Pat in 1978. Two children: Michelle and Justin. Mr. Aguirre enjoys running and golf.

James A. Gough
Vice President of Operations
Robinson Steel
4303 Kennedy Avenue
East Chicago, IN 46312
(219) 398–4600
Fax: (219) 398–2977

3312

Business Information: Robinson Steel is a producer and distributor of cold reduced sheet and plate. As Vice President of Operations, Mr. Gough is responsible for overall supervision of all facilities, to include production and expenses. **Career Steps:** Robinson Steel: Vice President of Operations (1995–Present), Plant Manager (1991–1995), Plant Superintendent (1989–1991). **Personal:** Married to Brenda in 1994.

Two children: Christopher and Keith. Mr. Gough enjoys computers, outdoor activities and spending time with his family.

Edna E. Hernandez
Controller
Alonso & Carus Iron Works, Inc.
P O Box 566
Catano, Puerto Rico 00963–0566
(787) 788–1065
Fax: (707) 700–0350

3312

Business Information: Alonso & Carus Iron Works, Inc., established in 1961 and employing 100 people, manufactures and installs steel products such as tanks, pressure vessels, and structural steel. The Company has operations in Puerto Rico and the Virgin Islands. As Controller, Mrs. Hernandez is responsible for all aspects of financial activities, including cash management, inventory, accounts payable, and associated administrative matters. **Career Steps:** Controller, Alonso & Carus Iron Works, Inc. (1993–Present); Controller, Berlitz School of Languages (1989–1991); Cost Account Manager, Lederle Parenterals, Inc. (1975–1987). **Associations & Accomplishments:** First Baptist Church of Puerto Rico. **Education:** University of Puerto Rico: B.B.A (1974) and Graduate Business School. **Personal:** Married to Rafael A. Lopez in 1978. Four children: Eduardo, Edna Melissa, Adriana, and Jorge Gabriel Lopez. Mrs. Hernandez enjoys movies, her children, and being active in her church.

Terry L. Japhet
Plant Manager
Trico Manufacturing Corporation
5353 Franklin Street
Denver, CO 80216–6213
(303) 297–8727
Fax: (303) 297–8727

3312

Business Information: Trico Manufacturing Corporation is a steel fabrication job shop, producing all areas of alloy production. Exporting internationally to Ecuador and Pakistan, Trico's primary focus is as a government and defense contractor. It is currently working under a U.S. Dept. of Defense contract in the dismantling of the U.S. Army's chemical warfare bases — to be completed by year 2010 (destroying over 2 million lbs of Agent Orange). Originally serving in managerial roles for Trico since 1990, Terry Japhet rejoined the Company in 1993. As Plant Manager, he oversees all fabrication process operations and personnel at the Denver, Colorado facility. **Career Steps:** Plant Manager, Trico Manufacturing Corporation (1993–Present), (1991–1993); Plant Manager, Barshield (1991–1993); Plant Manager, Custom Metal Manufacturing (1985–1990). **Associations & Accomplishments:** International Jet Sport Boating Association: 6th Place at World Finals, Region 4 Champion, World Finalist. **Education:** Lamar Community College, Welding. **Personal:** Married to Gina in 1986. Mr. Japhet enjoys jet ski racing, water skiing, snow skiing, and hunting.

John J. Price Jr.
Plant Accountant
MacSteel–Arkansas
P.O. Box 1592
Ft. Smith, AR 72902–1592
(501) 648–5515
Fax: (501) 648–5592

3312

Business Information: MacSteel–Arkansas, a Division of Quanex, manufactures hot roll bar steel. A self–employed Public Accountant since 1973, Mr. Price joined MacSteel in 1985 as Plant Accountant. He is presently responsible for financial oversight, staff supervision, and cost analysis functions. **Career Steps:** Plant Accountant, MacSteel–Arkansas (1985–Present); Self Employed Public Accountant (1973–Present); Senior Accountant, Rheem Manufacturing Company, Inc. (1975–1985); Staff Corporate Tax Auditor, Derderian, Kann, Seyferth & Salucci, C.P.A.'s (1970–1975). **Associations & Accomplishments:** Institute of Management Accountants; American Accounting Association; National Society of Public Accountants; Arkansas State Chamber of Commerce; Manufacturers Tax Committee. **Education:** University of The Ozarks, B.S. in Management, B.S. in Accounting (1982); Walsh College of Accountancy – Detroit, Michigan (1982); Schoolcraft Community College – Livonia, Michigan, Associate Degree in Business (1969). **Personal:** Married to Nina M. in 1977. Three children: J.J., Stewart, and Lance. Mr. Price enjoys golf, bowling, and jazz music.

Christopher Wagner
President
The Bradbury Company of Puerto Rico, Inc.
P O Box 1495
Bayamon, Puerto Rico 00960
(787) 787–1125
Fax: (787) 785–3283

3312

Business Information: Bradbury Company of Puerto Rico, Inc. is a customized sheet metal fabricating company for the pharmaceutical, hotel, restaurant, and hospital industries. Established in 1982, the Company currently employs 30 people and expects to post sales/revenues in excess of $2 million in 1996. As President, Mr. Wagner oversees all operational aspects including sales and technical staff, sub–contractors/associates, strategic planning and customer relations. Other responsibilities include personnel director and advisor, financial control, inventory control, purchasing, and safety officer. **Career Steps:** President, Bradbury Company of Puerto Rico, Inc. (1987–Present); Site Foreman (Bridge Builder), Rhoades Construction Company (1980–1987); SP4 Platoon Leader, US Military Police (1977–1980). **Associations & Accomplishments:** Rotary Club; Puerto Rico Manufacturers Association; Puerto Rico Homebuilders Association. **Education:** Military Police Academy; Kansas State Police Academy. **Personal:** One child: Stephanie. Mr. Wagner enjoys golf, running, wind surfing, snorkeling, hiking, travel, and reading.

Timothy T. Wells
Manufacturing Manager
Metal Enterprises, Inc.
P.O. Box 6767
Greenville, SC 29606–6767
(864) 234–4864 (864) 234–4888
Fax: Please mail or call

3315

Business Information: Metal Enterprises, Inc. is a general steel manufacturer and steel service center. As Manufacturing Manager, Mr. Wells is responsible for the management of materials and production. Mr. Wells is also the owner of Scuba Ocean Sports and conducts private scuba diving lessons and trips. **Career Steps:** Manufacturing Manager, Metal Enterprises, Inc. (1983–Present); Engineered Products, Inc.: Contracts Manager (1980–1983), Project Manager (1978–1980); Project Manager, Metal Products, Inc. (1976–1978). **Associations & Accomplishments:** Toastmasters; Society of Manufacturing Engineers; Professional Association of Dive Instructors; South Carolina Archaeology and Anthropology Association. **Education:** USCS, B.S. (1981); Greenville Technical College, A.S. in Mechanical Engineering; A.S. in Met., Technology (1976); A.S. in Civil Technology (1977). **Personal:** Married to Susan in 1983. Mr. Wells enjoys scuba diving and golf.

Mr. Edward J. Kruk
Controller
Samuel Strapping Systems, Division Samuel Manu–Tech Inc.
2370 Dixie Road
Mississauga, Ontario L4Y 1Z4
(905) 279–9580
Fax: (905) 279–8016

3315

Business Information: Samuel Strapping Systems, Division Samuel Manu–Tech Inc. manufactures and distributes steel strapping products. They also distribute plastic strapping and shrink wrap. Forty percent of their business is in the United States, the other sixty percent is in Canada. As Controller, Mr. Kruk is responsible for all financial matters except income taxes. He oversees a staff of 15, provides monthly financial statements and performs various financial analyses. Established in 1985, Samuel Strapping Systems, Division Samuel Manu–Tech Inc. employs 185 people with annual sales of $70 million. **Career Steps:** Controller, Samuel Strapping Systems, Division Samuel Manu–Tech Inc. (1994–Present); Corporate Accountant, Samuel Manu–Tech Inc. (1989–1994); Income Tax Auditor, Province of Ontario (1987–1989); Reinsurance Accounting Manager, CIGNA Canada (1982–1986). **Associations & Accomplishments:** Member, Canadian Institute of Chartered Accountants. **Education:** Chartered Accountant (1980); University of Toronto, M.B.A (1978); University of Toronto, B.A.Sc. in Industrial Engineering (1975). **Personal:** Married to Christine in 1991. Two children: Christopher and Carmen. Mr. Kruk enjoys travel, reading, foreign affairs, stamp collecting, art collecting, running and hockey.

April M. Osborne, CPA
Controller of Corporate Accounting
Alcatel Canada Wire
140 Allstate Parkway
Markham, Ontario L3K 0Z7
(416) 424–5321
Fax: (416) 424–5333

3315

Business Information: Alcatel Canada Wire manufactures and distributes wire and cable worldwide. Products produced include magnet wire, power cable, transformer wire, and equipment cable. The Company currently employs approximately 1,500 people. As Controller of Corporate Accounting, Ms. Osborne oversees all financial aspects of the Company. **Career Steps:** Controller of Corporate Accounting, Alcatel Canada Wire (1993–Present); Audit Manager, Arthur Andersen (1988–1993). **Associations & Accomplishments:** Institute of Management Accountants; American Institute of Certified Public Accountants. **Education:** California State Polytechnic University, B.A. (1988); Certified Public Accountant (1992) **Personal:** Married to Evan Kimmel in 1996. Ms. Osborne enjoys golf, travel, and cooking.

Al Valzone
Director of Human Resources
Amercord, Inc.
P.O. Box 458
Lumber City, GA 31549
(912) 363–6207
Fax: (912) 363–4991

3315

Business Information: Amercord, Inc. is a national manufacturer of steel wire for the radial tire industry, distributing products to such companies as Bridgestone, Dunlap, and Goodyear. Established in 1972, the company presently employs 700 people. As Director of Human Resources, Mr. Valzone is responsible for personnel, employee relations, training & development, and organizational development. **Career Steps:** Director of Human Resources, Amercord, Inc. (1995–Present); Manager of Human Resources, Tel Plus Communications (1986–1995); Manager of Training and Development, Mitel, Inc. (1981–1986); Training Supervisor, International Minerals and Chemicals Corporation (1976–1981). **Associations & Accomplishments:** Society of Human Resource Management; Rotary International; Ducks Unlimited; Developed and implemented HRIS systems for Tel Plus Communications and other companies in the Southeast; Published corporate operations, training, and safety manuals; Created "Slurry" cartoons for internal publications. **Education:** Nova University, M.S. in Human Resource Management (1980); University of Miami, B.Ed. (1972). **Personal:** Married to Lorraine in 1959.

Abdulaziz M. Al Ariefy

Managing Director
Al Jazera Factory For Steel Products Limited
P.O. Box Number 1943
Jeddah, Saudi Arabia 21441
966–2–6362288
Fax: 966–2–6367823

3317

Business Information: Al Jazera Factory For Steel Products Limited is the Industrial Division of a family–owned business which manufactures steel pipes and tubes. The Company's other divisions are in the areas of real estate, travel agencies, and construction. Joining Al Jazera Factory For Steel Products Limited (founded by his father) as Managing Director of the Industrial Division in 1990, Mr. Al Ariefy provides the overall administrative and operational direction for the Saudi Arabia plant. **Career Steps:** Managing Director, Al Jazera Factory For Steel Products Limited (1990–Present); Administrative Supervisor, King Khaled National Guard Hospital (1987–1990). **Associations & Accomplishments:** American Tube Association; FMA; TPFA; Metal Bulletin **Education:** California State University: M.B.A. (1986), B.A. in Management. **Personal:** Married to Albanderi in 1979. Five children: Farrah, Mohammed, Sarah, Bushra and Abdullah. Mr. Al Ariefy enjoys swimming, hunting, and reading.

Gary W. Miller Jr.

General Manager
Frichtl Steel and Welding
P.O. Box 325
Newton, IL 62448–0325
(618) 783–8323
Fax: (618) 783–3118

3317

Business Information: Frichtl Steel and Welding was established in 1976 and posted revenues in excess of $7 million dollars in 1995. The Company has two locations in Newton, Illinois and currently employs 45 people. Frichtl Steel manufactures rolled and welded steel pipe for the construction industry. As General Manager, Mr. Miller is responsible for the overall profitability of the business and the safety of all employees. He is involved in developing marketing strategies for new and existing products, recruitment of management staff, compliance with OSHA and other safety rules and regulations, training of employees and accounts payable and receivable. Mr. Miller assists with long range planning for expansion and the development of new markets for existing products. **Career Steps:** General Manager, Frichtl Steel and Welding (1994–Present); General Manager, Mechanics Laundry (1993–1994); Department Manager, Menards (1992–1993). **Associations & Accomplishments:** American Management Association; National Utility Contractors Association; Lions Club; The Rotary. **Education:** University of Missouri/Rolla, Economics (1992). **Personal:** Mr. Miller enjoys golf, skiing, and basketball.

Bill C. Teague
Transportation Director
Charlotte Pipe & Foundry
2109 Randolph Road
Charlotte, NC 28207–1521
(704) 348–6454
Fax: (800) 233–6231

3317

Business Information: Charlotte Pipe & Foundry, established in 1901, is a manufacturer of plastic and cast iron pipes and fittings. The Company distributes to wholesalers, some retailers, and plumbing suppliers. As Transportation Director, Mr. Teague is responsible for all carrier selection, contracts, and rate negotiations. **Career Steps:** Transportation Director, Charlotte Pipe & Foundry (1991–Present); Distribution Service Manager, National Gypsum (1978–1991); Lighting Supervisor, GTE Sylvania (1973–1978) **Associations & Accomplishments:** North Carolina Traffic League **Education:** University of North Carolina, B.S. in Business Administration (1973) **Personal:** Married to Nancy in 1974. Mr. Teague enjoys golf and basketball.

Thomas R. Brockman
Information Systems Manager/Assistant Controller
Grede Foundries, Inc.
711 West Alexander Avenue
Greenwood, SC 29646–2303
(864) 388–2271
Fax: (864) 388–2317
EMail: See Below

3321

Business Information: Grede Foundries, Inc. is a manufacturer of quality steel, gray and ductile iron castings. As Information Systems Manager/Assistant Controller, Mr. Brockman is responsible for computer management, telecommunications, audio/visual equipment, training, accounting, budgeting, network administration, and department purchasing. Internet users can reach him via: grede@ais.ais–gwd.com. Being self–motivated and having the support of peers and family has been Mr. Brockman's inspiration to succeed. The company's Guiding Principles: Profit benefits everyone, Individualism and Recognition of Merit, Security in Performance, Community Responsibility, and Be Fair, Be Firm, and Smile have helped him in attaining current and establishing future goals. **Career Steps:** Grede Foundries, Inc.: Information Systems Manager/Assistant Controller (1994–Present), Systems Analyst (1988–1994); Computer Programmer/LAN Administrator, Whitehead Specialties (1986–1988). **Associations & Accomplishments:** Optimist Club; Just Say No: Chairman, Board of Directors. **Education:** University of Wisconsin – Madison (1984–1986); Creighton University (1982–1984). **Personal:** Married to Sue in 1989. Two children: Erick and Elizabeth. Mr. Brockman enjoys outdoors, sports, computers, and spending time with his family.

Marc A. Schmucker
Health, Safety, and Labor Relations Director
New River Castings
1701 1st Street
Radford, VA 24141–1221
(540) 731–9197
Fax: (540) 731–9057

3321

Business Information: New River Castings is a special manufacturer of ductile foundry. As Health, Safety, and Labor Director, Mr. Schmucker is responsible for diversified administrative activities. **Career Steps:** Safety Director, New River Castings (1994–Present); Melt Supervisor, Ward Manufacturing (1991–1994); Shift Superintendent, Vulcan Mold and Iron (1979–1991). **Education:** University of Pittsburgh, B.S. cum laude (1991). **Personal:** Married to Brenda S. in 1978. Two children: Eric and Jeffrey. Mr. Schmucker enjoys golf and baseball.

Randall J. Elser
Plant Manager
Steel Technologies, Inc.
1001 Konica Drive
Elkton, MD 21921–6347
(800) 305–6104
Fax: (410) 392–5745

3325

Business Information: Steel Technologies, Inc. is a sheet and strip steel processor. One of the top companies in the country in this industry and listed on NASDAQ, 60% of Steel Technologies' material is used in automobile applications. National in scope, with headquarters located in Louisville, Kentucky, it also has three facilities in Indiana, Michigan and Maryland. Joining Steel Technologies, Inc. as a slitter operator in 1984, Randall Elser has consistently moved up the corporate structure to attain his recent promotion as Plant Manager of the Elkton, Maryland facility. He is responsible for managing everyday operations involving manufacturing, management, personnel, training, technical services, and quality. **Career Steps:** Plant Manager, Steel Technologies, Inc. (1984–Present); Account Representative, Investors Diversified Services (1980–1984); Police Officer, Trumbull County – Ohio (1970–1980). **Associations & Accomplishments:** Lion's Club; Active in fund raising for Easter Seals; Fabricators and Manufacturers Association; Team McGlynns – Newark, DE. **Personal:** Married to Diane in 1969. One child: Randy Jr. Mr. Elser enjoys bowling, golf, fishing, and piloting private aircraft.

Mark D. Holcomb
Site Safety Director
Schueck Steel Company
2125 Ashfork Avenue
Kingman, AZ 86401–4651
(520) 718–1800
Fax: (520) 718–1804

3325

Business Information: Schueck Steel Company specializes in new construction of steel mills, steel erection, and installation of mill equipment. With seventeen years of providing Safety and EMT services in the oilfield and industrial construction industries (wastewater treatment plants, pulp and paper mills, power plants, fuel processing units, steel mills) Mr. Holcomb joined Schueck in 1995 as Site Safety Director. He is presently responsible for site safety and health for more than 100 employees in steel erection, millwrights, and general construction. **Career Steps:** Site Safety Director, Schueck Steel Company (1995–Present); Site Safety and Medic, Industrial Safety and Health (Jan.1995–Feb.1995); Corp Safety Director, JM&M Construction (Jun.1994–Nov.1994); Safety Inspector II, Raytheon Engineers and Constructors (1993–1994); Safety Inspector, H.B. Zachry Company (1992–1993); Owner, Independent Safety Consultants (1992); Paramedic, Calcasieu Medical Transportation and Ambulance (Jun.1992–Sept.1992); Safety Inspector/Paramedic, Med Tech International (1991–1992); Paramedic, Holston Ambulance Service, Inc. (1984–1991); XCalcasien County Sheriff's Office (1982–1994); Firefighter/Operator, Moss Bluff Fire Department (1979–1984). **Associations & Accomplishments:** National Fire Protection Association; American Society of Safety Engineers; Boy Scouts of America; National Registry of Emergency Medical Technicians; North American Hunting Club; Gold Prospectors Association of America; Bass Anglers Sportsman Society. **Education:** Columbia Southern University, B.S. in Safety and Health (1996); South West Louisiana Technical Institute, EMT/Paramedic; Numerous courses on Life Saving, Emergency, and Safety–Related Subjects. **Personal:** Married to Tina in 1991. Four children: Kalene, Marlene, Travis, and Antoinette. Mr. Holcomb enjoys diving, hunting, camping, fishing, prospecting, scouting, coins, and stamps.

Nick J. Morganti
Business Technology Partner
Carpenter Technology Corporation
P.O. Box 14662
Reading, PA 19612–4662
(610) 208–2718
Fax: (610) 208–3105

3325

Business Information: Carpenter Technology, originally a producer of specialty metals, now focuses primarily on the manufacture and international distribution of specialty ceramic materials and steel products for the automotive, aerospace, oil, and electronic industries. International in scope, the Company has branches in Brussels, Taiwan, Canada, Mexico, the U.S., and the United Kingdom. Established in 1889, the Company employs 4,212 people and has an estimated annual revenue of $757 million. As Business Technology Partner, Mr. Morganti serves as account representative from information services to end user areas. He is responsible for providing computer–related services for finance, human resources, legal functions, and engineering products business units. **Career Steps:** Carpenter Technology: Business Technology Partner (1995–Present), Manager of Information Services (1995), Divisional Financial Controller (1994–1995). **Associations & Accomplishments:** Board of Directors, Pennsylvania Southeast Conference; United Church of Jesus Christ. **Education:** Lehigh University, M.B.A. (1982); Albright College, B.S. in Accounting (1978); Certified Management Accountant (1982). **Personal:** Married to Roseann in 1978. Two children: Christina and Laura. Mr. Morganti enjoys competing in middle and long distance running events.

Stephen E. Oyler

Sales Manager
Geneva Steel
P.O. Box 2500 MS63
Provo, UT 84603–2500
(801) 227–9753
Fax: (801) 227–9059

3325

Business Information: Geneva Steel is an integrated steel producer, manufacturing steel from raw materials. Products manufactured include carbon steel plates, carbon steel coils, sheets, and pipes for the oil and gas industries. Joining Geneva Steel in 1987, Mr. Oyler was appointed as Sales Manager in 1993. She is responsible for overseeing pipe production and distribution nationally, as well as handling export sales for all products. **Career Steps:** Geneva Steel: Sales Manager (1993–Present), Marketing Manager (1992–1993), Marketing Analyst (1990–1992), Metallurgist (1987–1990). **Associations & Accomplishments:** Southern Gas Association; National Association of Steel Pipe Distributors; National Association of Pipe Coaters of America; Varsity Scout Leader, Boy Scouts of America. **Education:** University of Utah, M.B.A. (1992); Brigham Young University, B.S. in Business (1976); USAF Defense Language Institute, Vietnamese Language (1973). **Personal:** Married to Lauralyn in 1973. Six children: Kimlan, Rachel, Jennie, Timothy, Matthew, and Christopher. Mr. Oyler enjoys sports and gardening.

Howard J. Price
Vice President of Specialty Products
Fisher Brothers Steel Corporation
502 Nordhoff Place, P.O. Box 592
Englewood, NJ 07631–4808
(201) 567–2400
Fax: (201) 567–9530
(800) 631–1543

3325

Business Information: Fisher Brothers Steel Corporation is a full–line steel service center engaged in the buying, selling, storing, cutting, and processing of steel for consumers. He has conducted over 100 Quality Assurance Audits. As Vice President of Specialty Products, Mr. Price is responsible for diversified administrative activities, including sales and purchasing, and quality assurance. **Career Steps:** Vice President of Specialty Products, Fisher Brothers Steel Corporation (1983–Present); Director of Quality Assurance and Engineering, Pressure Vessel Nuclear Steel (1978–1983); Inside Sales/Work Order Manager, Fisher Brothers Steel (1976–1978). **Associations & Accomplishments:** Steel Service Center – New York Chapter; A.S.T.M.; American Society of Manufacturing Engineers; American Society for Quality Control; Published paper "A Material Suppliers Quality Assurance System for Auditing Nuclear Vendors". **Education:** Newark College Engineering, Division of Technology, Certificate of Mechanical Design. **Personal:** One child: Andrew. Mr. Price enjoys golf, tennis, flyfishing, rollerblading, and travel.

Silvio Roberto Badenes De Gouvea

Finance Director
Billiton Metals, S.A.
Praia De Botafogo, 228 4th Floor
Rio De Janeiro, Brazil 22359–900
55–21–553–1980
Fax: 55–21–553–0692
EMAIL: See Below

3334

Business Information: Billiton Metals, S.A. is a manufacturer of primary aluminum. The Company sells to traders (70% exported, 30% sold domestically), and to companies. As Finance Director, Dr. De Gouvea is responsible for all financial aspects of the Company, including controllership, systems, and treasury. Internet users can reach him via: silvio@bmsarj.attmail.com. **Career Steps:** Finance Director, Billiton Metals, S.A. (1981–Present); Financial Advisor, Billiton International Metals, The Netherlands (1984–1987); Associate Professor, Instituto Militar De Engenharia, Brazil (1974–1978). **Associations & Accomplishments:** Institute for Operation Research and Management Sciences. **Education:** University of California – Berkeley: Ph.D (1974), M.Sc. (1972); Instituto Militar De Engenharia – Rio, Brazil, B.S. (1969). **Personal:** Married to Lucia in 1970. Two children: Andre and Paulo. Dr. De Gouvea enjoys cheese–making and jogging.

James L. Helms
Quality Assurance Auditor
Alcoa Aluminum Company
74 North U.S. Highway 421
Delphi, IN 46923–9395
Fax: Please mail or call

3334

Business Information: Alcoa Aluminum Company is a primary manufacturer of extrude aluminum for industries such as Boeing and McDonnell Douglas. As Quality Assurance Auditor, Mr. Helms assures that the metal meets all specifications, and is also responsible for checking corrosion levels on aluminum. **Career Steps:** Quality Assurance Auditor, Alcoa Aluminum Company (1995–Present); Purchasing Administrator, General Seating of America (1990–1995); President, Jim Helms Lawn Care (1984–Present); Materials Manager, Random House Publishing (1986–1989); Farm Manager, Carol Floral Farms (1972–1985). **Associations & Accomplishments:** Masonic Lodge; Ancient Accepted Scottish Rite; Order of Eastern Star; American Legion; Retired IHSAA Basketball Official; Inventing. **Education:** Porter Business, Associates (1965); Purdue University. **Personal:** Married to Orvilla M. in 1968. Two children: Kristina and Cheryl. Mr. Helms enjoys gardening and automotive repairs.

George A. Hill
President
American Aluminum Enterprises
1315 Neptune Drive
Boynton Beach, FL 33426–8407
(407) 732–8106
Fax: (407) 732–9989

3334

Business Information: American Aluminum Enterprises is a commercial sales, manufacture, and installation contractor of customized hurricane shutters and aluminum railings primarily serving the South Florida region. Acquire Leasing, Inc., also owned and operated by the Hill Family, is a four year old company that leases vehicles and equipment, both commercially and privately. As President, Mr. Hill is responsible for all aspects of both family enterprises. **Career Steps:** President, American Aluminum Enterprises (1994–Present); President, Acquire Leasing, Inc. (1992–Present); President, American Aluminum and Insulation (1985–1994); President, Southern Insulation (1978–1985). **Associations & Accomplishments:** Paralyzed Veterans. **Personal:** Married to Barbara in 1972. Nine children: George, Richard, April, Christine, Marla, Keith, Moira, Tara, and Tami. Mr. Hill enjoys reading and teaching the Bible.

Cornell O. Ward
Director of Human Resources Can Division
Reynolds Metals Company
7900 Reycan Road
Richmond, VA 23237
(804) 743–5101
Fax: (804) 743–5436

3334

Business Information: Reynolds Metals Company — Can Division, a wholly–owned subsidiary of aluminum manufacturing conglomerate Reynolds Aluminum, specializes in the production and distribution of aluminum cans utilized by consumer products industries. A human resources and labor relations management executive for various Reynolds Metals divisions since 1972, Cornell Ward was transferred to the Richmond, Virginia headquarters in 1993. As Director of Human Resources, Mr. Ward is responsible for all human resource activities for the North American Can Division. **Career Steps:** Reynolds Metals Company: Director of Human Resources – North American Can Division (1993–Present), Manager of Industrial Relations – McCook Mill Products Division (1984–1993), Supervisor of Labor Relations – McCook Mill Products Division (1980–1984), Assistant Personnel Manager – Listerhill Reduction Division (1978–1980); Personnel and Labor Relations Specialist, Alloys Mill Products Division (1972–1978). **Associations & Accomplishments:** Alpha Phi Alpha Fraternity; Board of Directors, LaGrange Hospital Foundation; Board of Directors, Illinois Benedictine College Management Institute; Village of Bolingbrook Planning Board of Appeals and Planning Commission. **Education:** University of Alabama at Huntsville, M.S. in Administrative Science (1977); Alabama State University, B.S. in Education (1971). **Personal:** Married to Linda F. in 1971. Two children: Gillian Brooke and Cornell O'Bryant, Jr. Mr. Ward enjoys reading, electronic music recording, music publishing, songwriting, music production, golf, history, and art.

Jean Maccinile
Area Sales Manager
Clark Metals, Inc.
14605 South Main Street
Gardena, CA 90248
(310) 532–8000
Fax: (818) 765–6738

3336

Business Information: Clark Metals, Inc. specializes in the distribution of aluminum sheet, plate and extruded shapes; brass, bronze, copper, shapes and sheet. Stainless steel sheet No. 10 finish (mirror non–directional polish) and alucobond. As Area Sales Manager, Ms. Maccinile is responsible for training, marketing, operations, administration, and strategic planning. Additional duties include management of sales quotas and territories. **Career Steps:** Area Sales Manager, Clark Metals, Inc. (1995–Present); Sales Manager, Specialty Extr. (1993–1995); Sales Engineer, Ametek/Ketema (1974–1993). **Associations & Accomplishments:** Past President, Association of Women in Metal; Vice President, City of Hope; Volunteer, St. Joseph Medical Center, Burbank. **Education:** University of A.L.A. **Personal:** Married to Paul in 1969. Ms. Maccinile enjoys golf, walking, skiing, and bicycling.

Thomas F. Kern
Technical Manager
Elkem Metals Company
P.O. Box 613
Alloy, WV 25002–0613
(304) 779–3209
Fax: (304) 779–3297

3339

Business Information: Elkem Metals Company is a major alloy manufacturer, specializing in the production of ferro alloys and silicon metals. As Technical Manager, Thomas Kern oversees all North American silicon production development, technical resource support staff and overall divisional strategies. **Career Steps:** Technical Manager, Elkem Metals Company (1991–Present); Production Engineer, Union Carbide (1975–1981). **Associations & Accomplishments:** Iron and Steel Society; Representative, Electric Furnace Conference Organizations Committee. **Education:** Michigan Technical University, Metallurgic Engineering (1975). **Personal:** Married to Mary A. Beetham in 1975. Two children: Bill and Katie. Mr. Kern enjoys golf, tennis, and skiing.

A. Stephen Marini
Director – Human Resources – North America
Engelhard–Clal
700 Blair Road
Carteret, NJ 07008–1221
(908) 205–5973
Fax: (908) 634–7696

3339

Business Information: Engelhard–Clal is a fabricator of precious metals. As Director of Human Resources, Mr. Marini is responsible for employee relations, labor, hiring, business relations, and organizational development. **Career Steps:** Engelhard Corporation: Director of Human Resources (1994–Present), Corporate Manager (1991–1994), Director Industrial Relations – Specialty Metals (1988–1991). **Associations & Accomplishments:** American Management Association; American Society for Training and Development; New Jersey Vietnam Veterans; New Jersey Planning Group; Virginia Vietnam Veterans. **Education:** Rutgers University B.S. (1970).

Robert J. Milligan

Process/Project Engineer
Advanced Silicon Materials, Inc.
3322 Road N, N.E.
Moses Lake, WA 98837
(509) 766–9136
Fax: (509) 766–9123
EMAIL: See Below

3339

Business Information: Advanced Silicon Materials, Inc. specializes in the manufacture of polycrystalline silicon and silane gas. Established in 1990, the Company employs 350 people and has an estimated annual revenue of $75 million. As Process/Project Engineer, Mr. Milligan oversees research and development and is currently involved in finding a new process for the production of granular polysilicon from silane. Internet users can reach him via: Milligan@asimi.com. **Career Steps:** Process/Project Engineer, Advanced Silicon Materials, Inc. (1990–Present); Process/Project Engineer, Union Carbide Chemicals and Plastics Company (1988–1990); Graduate Assistant, University of Idaho (1986–1988). **Associations & Accomplishments:** Tau Beta Pi, Engineering Honor Society; Phi Kappa Phi National Honor Society; American Institute of Chemical Engineers. **Education:** University of Idaho: M.S. Ch.E. (1988), B.S. Ch.E. (1986). **Personal:** Married to Norma L. in 1989. Three children: Abinadi V.J., Aaron H. and Ammon L.. Mr. Milligan enjoys gardening, fishing, and reading.

Frederick A. Schweizer

Director of Metallurgy and Quality Insurance
Special Metals Corporation
4317 Middle Settlement Road
New Hartford, NY 13413–5317
(315) 798–2942
Fax: (315) 798–2016
EMAIL: See Below

3339

Business Information: Special Metals Corporation is a special metals manufacturing corporation, providing vacuum melting of high temperature nickel–based alloys utilized in gas turbine applications. Products marketed include reforge bar and billets. International in scope, Special Metals Corporation has locations in New York (New Hartford, Dunkirk), Princeton, Kentucky and Ann Arbor, Michigan. Serving in various managerial capacities at Special Metals Corporation since 1990, Frederick Schweizer was appointed Director Metallurgy and Quality Assurance in 1993. He is responsible for directing the technical end of the business, including overseeing the Process Metallurgy, Product Metallurgy, and Quality Assurance departments. Internet users can also reach him via: FAS9150@AOL.COM **Career Steps:** Special Metals Corporation: Director Metallurgy and Quality Assurance (1993–Present), Forged Products Manager (1992), Rolled Products Manager (1990–1991). **Associations & Accomplishments:** Board Member, Mohawk Valley Community College Foundation Board; Professional Association of Diving Instructors; American Society of Metals; Holder of four patents dealing with alloys; Published in Frontiers of High Temperature Metallurgy and has given a number of paper presentations. **Education:** Renssalaer Polytechnic Institute, M.S. (1982); University of Missouri at Rolla, B.S. **Personal:** Married to Elizabeth Ann in 1995. Four children: Lawrence, Steven, Kerri, and Kenneth. Mr. Schweizer enjoys scuba diving, underwater photography, and cycling.

Leon M. Ryan

General Manager
Southern Aluminum Manufacturing Inc.
P.O. Box 884
Magnolia, AR 71753–0884
(501) 234–8660
Fax: (501) 234–2823

3354

Business Information: Southern Aluminum Manufacturing Inc. is a manufacturer of aluminum tables and fixtures. As General Manager, Mr. Ryan is responsible for 50 people and oversees product design, design engineering and production, costing, trouble shooting, training, and employee relations. **Career Steps:** General Manager, Southern Aluminum Manufacturing Inc. (1992–Present); Virco Manufacturing Corporation: Manager of Engineering (1982–1992), Product Engineer (1970–1992). **Associations & Accomplishments:** EMTA; Chairperson, Red Cross Disaster; Commander, Faukner County Rescue Squad; CPuerto Rico Instructor. **Education:** ASTC (1965); University of Arkansas, Management. **Personal:** Married to April in 1992. Five children: Ben, Todd, Tammy, Matt, and Joe. Mr. Ryan enjoys race car driving at I–30 raceway, hunting, and fishing.

Souheil Ibrahim Hatoum

Managing Partner
Marconi Inter–Design Co. L.L.C.
P.O. Box 50007
Dubai, United Arab Emirates
9714–222–741
Fax: 9714–238–005

3355

Business Information: Marconi Inter–Design Co. L.L.C. is a steel, aluminum fabrications manufacturer, primarily for the production of roll–formed aluminum false ceiling strips and related formed and pressed steel sheetings and suspension carriers. International in scope, the Company primarily markets throughout the Middle East and United Arab Emirate countries. Marconi Inter–Design Co. L.L.C. is an exclusive agent for European decorative ceilings and partitions manufacturers. As Managing Partner, Mr. Hatoum provides vision and strategy for the company, ensuring quality product output, customer satisfaction, and the effective techniques needed to keep the company a viable presence in the international market. **Career Steps:** Managing Partner, Marconi Inter–Design Co. L.L.C. (1986–Present); Marketing Manager, Al Omran Decovinyl – United Arab Emirates (1984–1986); Assistant Commercial Manager, Al Gezairi Shipping – Lebanon (1981–1983). **Associations & Accomplishments:** YMCA. **Education:** Lebanese American University, B.S. (1982). **Personal:** Married to Lina Rostom in 1992. One child: Bilal. Mr. Hatoum enjoys reading, travel, and camping.

J.R. Johnsen

Optical Fiber Plant Manager
Alcatel Telecommunications
2512 Penny Road
Claremont, NC 28610
(704) 459–8467
Fax: (704) 459–1031
EMAIL: See Below

3357

Business Information: Alcatel Telecommunications is a manufacturer of optical fiber for the telecommunication industry. As Optical Fiber Plant Manager, Mr. Johnsen is responsible for production, engineering, and support functions of the optical fiber manufacturing facility. He is in charge of personnel concerns, budget compliance, and maintaining OSHA, EPA, and general safety standards. Internet users can reach him via: ric_johnsen@ccm.useable.alcatel.com. **Career Steps:** Alcatel Telecommunications: Optical Fiber Plant Manager (1995–Present), Technology Manager, Fiber Optic Cable (1994–1995), Customer Support Engineering Manager (1991–1994); Signal Corps Officer, U.S. Army (1979–1990). **Associations & Accomplishments:** United States Swimming National Certified Official. **Education:** Naval Postgraduate School, M.S. in Electrical Engineering (1986); United States Military Academy, B.S. (1979). **Personal:** Mr. Johnsen enjoys skiing, scuba diving, running and cycling.

Thomas D. Klein

Director of Operations
Custom Cabling Northwest
P.O. Box 440, 4403 Russell Road, Building 2B, Suite 116
Mukilteo, WA 98275–0440
(206) 745–3432
Fax: (206) 352–2253

3357

Business Information: Custom Cabling Northwest is a national company engaged in the installation of copper and fiber optic cable systems for the communications industry. Primarily covering the pacific northwest area, they perform work on a contract basis. As Director of Operations, Mr. Klein is responsible for all aspects of Company operations, as well as contract negotiations. **Career Steps:** Director of Operations, Custom Cabling Northwest (1993–Present); SSGT., Washington Air National Guard (1992–Present); Manager, Ivar's (1990–1992). **Personal:** Two children: Ian and Nichole. Mr. Klein enjoys spending time with his children and martial arts.

Philippe E. Lamy

General Counsel
Alcatel Cable
30 rue des Chasses
Clichy, France 92111
33–147566741
Fax: 33–147566654

3357

Business Information: Alcatel Cable is a manufacturer of telecommunication cables (copper and fiber optics), power cables (high, medium and low voltage), including submarine cables and insulated wire cables. Alcatel Cable consists of 257 subsidiaries, reporting annual revenue of 8 billion FF and currently employs 28,000 people company–wide. A practicing attorney in international law since 1975, Mr. Lamy joined Alcatel Cable in 1991. Serving as Group General Counsel, he provides legal consultation and representation in patent and corporate law, as well as serving as Secretary of the General Assembly. **Career Steps:** General Counsel, Alcatel Cable (1991–Present); Senior International Counsel, Air Liquide (1984–1991); Legal Counsel, Framatome (1979–1984); Legal Counsel, Bechtel Corporation (1975–1979). **Associations & Accomplishments:** International Bar Association; Cercle Montesquieu; Association Des Res Ponsables Juridiques D'Entreprise; Commander, Reserve Officer French Navy. **Education:** Insead, Advanced Management Program – Pontaine Bleau (1986); Dess Propriete Industrielle, Patent Law (1981); University of Paris, Business Administration (1975); Maitrise De Droit Prive (Private Law) – Paris (1969). **Personal:** Married to Decazes Francoise in 1974. Four children: Edouard, Christophe, Guillaume, and Amaury. Mr. Lamy enjoys hiking, swimming, and gardening.

Richard D. Snowden

Vice President of Sales
Cable Systems International
505 North 51st Avenue
Phoenix, AZ 85043–2701
(602) 233–5146
Fax: (602) 233–5634

3357

Business Information: Cable Systems International (CSI) is a manufacturer of cable used in the communications industry. Products include copper toll and exchange cable, service distribution wire, and electronic wire and cable. Purchased from AT&T in 1995 (formerly the AT&T Phoenix Works – which was established in 1968), CSI reports annual revenue of $400 million and currently employs 1,800 people. With an extensive background in telecommunications, Mr. Snowden joined CSI in 1995. Serving as Vice President of Sales, he is responsible for sales for the entire western area of the U.S. **Career Steps:** Sales Vice President, Cable Systems International (1995–Present); AT&T: Sales Vice President (1994–1995), Sales Manager (1989–1994). **Education:** University of LeVerne, MBA (1986), Bachelors in Business Management. **Personal:** Married to Kathryn in 1967. Two children: Kimberly and Donald. Mr. Snowden enjoys golf, gardening, and reading.

Paul G. Suchoski, Ph.D.

Vice President of Sales and Marketing
UTP (Uniphase Telecommunications Products)
1289 Blue Hills Avenue
Bloomfield, CT 06002–1302
(860) 769–3012
Fax: (860) 769–3001

3357

Business Information: UTP (Uniphase Telecommunications Products) is a manufacturer of fiber optic components and subsystems for telecommunications and CATV. International in scope, UTP operates from locations in Connecticut and Philadelphia. As Vice President of Sales and Marketing, Dr. Suchoski is responsible for all sales and marketing activities, as well as product definition and business development. **Career Steps:** U.T.P./Uniphase Telecommunications Products: Vice President of Sales and Marketing (1995–Present), Business Development Manager (1995); Operations Manager, UT Phonics (1992–1994); United Technologies Research Center: Group Leader (1989–1991), Research Scientist (1986–1988). **Associations & Accomplishments:** Institute of Electrical and Electronic Engineers; Society of Cable TV Engineers; Recipient, George Mead Award, given by UTC for outstanding contributions to technology; Publisher of more than 25 articles in the telecommunications field. **Education:** University of Florida: Ph.D. (1986), M.E. (1985), B.S.E.E. (1982). **Personal:** Married to Sharon in 1981. Three children: Matthew, Ashley and Christopher. Dr. Suchoski enjoys outdoor activities, hiking, jogging and tennis.

Natalie A. Veres

Facilities Manager
Alcatel Telecommunications
P.O. Box 400
Claremont, NC 28610–0400
(704) 459–8670
Fax: (704) 459–1031
EMAIL: See Below

3357

Business Information: Alcatel Telecommunications is the 3rd largest manufacturer of optical fiber and optical fiber cables for voice and data communications in the United States, serving such clients as Nynex, AT&T, MCI, and the Time Warner Corporation. Ms. Veres joined Alcatel in 1991 after an honorable discharge from the United States Army where she served as Tactical Operations Officer in the Signal Corps. Promoted to Facilities Manager in 1995, she is presently responsible for supervision of industrial utilities and support of manufacturing processes, managing site–wide contracts, cost reduction, and environmental concerns. Internet users may reach her via: natalie_veres@ccm.uscable.alcatel.com **Career Steps:** Alcatel Telecommunications: Facilities Manager (1995–Present), Team Developer and Operations Coordinator (1992–1995), Training and Documentation (1991–1992); Tactical Operations Officer, U.S. Army Signal Corps. (1988–1991). **Education:** Ohio University, B.S. in Telecommunications (1988). **Personal:** Ms. Veres enjoys outdoor activities, hiking, bicycling, camping, and skating.

Mr. Fred J. Murphy

Executive Vice President, Chief Operating Officer
Fisher Gauge Limited
194 Sophia Street
Peterborough, Ontario K9J 6Y9
(705) 748–9522
Fax: (705) 748–4015

3364

Business Information: Fisher Gauge Limited, established in 1942, is a manufacturer of small zinc die castings and special purpose die casting machinery. Eighty percent of company products are exported to the U.S., with the remainder shipped to European markets. The Company has three plants in Canada, one in New York, U.S.A, and one in Wales, Great Britain. As Executive Vice President and Chief Operating Officer, Mr. Murphy oversees all corporate manufacturing and marketing operations. **Career Steps:** Fisher Gauge Limited : Executive Vice President & Chief Operating Officer (1992–Present), Vice President of Finance and Administration (1986–1992); Vice President of Operations, Westclox Canada Ltd. (1980–1986). **Associations & Accomplishments:** Peterborough Chamber of Commerce; Certified Management Accountants; Human Resources Management Association; Kawartha Manufacturers; Greater Peterborough Economic Council; Junior Achievement of Canada; Kawartha Skills Development Committee; United Way Executive. **Education:** University of Toronto, C.M.A. (1980) **Personal:** Married to Carol in 1967. Two children: Scott and Jill. Mr. Murphy enjoys sports, reading, and community involvement in his leisure time.

Otto A. Knaisch

President and Chief Executive Officer
Aluminerie Alouette, Inc.
400, chemin de la Pointe–Noire, P.O. Box 1650
Sept–Iles, Quebec G4R 5C7
(418) 964–7102
Fax: (418) 964–7277

3365

Business Information: Aluminerie Alouette, Inc. is a multi–national consortium aluminum smelter concern. Members of the consortium are: AUSTRIA METALL AG – a major producer of non–ferrous metal in Austria; KOBE STEEL & MARUBENI CORPORATION – respectively one of the biggest iron ore and steel producers and involved in world–wide marketing of value–added products; LA SOCIETE GENERALE DE FINANCEMENT – a Quebec government–owned corporation promoting and developing various industrial activities in the Province of Quebec; HOOGOVENS – a Netherlands–based corporation and one of the largest steel producers in Europe and a leader among the aluminum producers; VAW – a German–based company and a leader in aluminum activities from bauxite mining to flexible packaging materials. VAW provides to Aluminerie Alouette Inc. technical assistance in areas such as design, construction, training, start–up and operation of the aluminum smelter. Aluminerie Alouette, Inc. has its head office in Sept–Iles, Quebec where all of its activities are performed. The corporation's involvement in the community is one of Alumineri Alouette, Inc.'s main achievements. The aluminum smelter is producing 215,000 tpy and is operating three main production areas: the carbon plant to provide anodes for the electrolytic process, the potroome for the transformation of the raw material (aluminum oxide) into liquid aluminum and the casthouse where liquid metal is cast into ingots. In addition, administrative and support services such as finances and procurement, human resources, technical services including laboratory are provided on site. Mr. Otto Knaisch is the President and Chief Executive Officer of the aluminum consortium and Chairman of the Board of Aluminerie Alouette Inc. His main role is in the planning and implementation of innovative technology and overall strategic growth. A world–renowned expert in the field of smelter technology (he holds the patent for the electrolysis smelter process), Mr. Knaisch was invited in 1993 by the Chinese government to evaluate their aluminum smelter technology. He was also appointed as Mediator for the Alusaf Hillside Smelter Project in South Africa. His modern hands–on approach management style has contributed significantly to one of Aluminerie Alouette Inc.'s major achievement whereby the smelter has evolved from its start–up in mid–1992 to a steady–state mode of operation with 600 employees without a labour union which is considered rather unusual in such an industrial environment. **Career Steps:** President and Chief Executive Officer, Aluminerie Alouette, Inc. (1993–Present); Plant Manager, VAW Aluminum Ltd., Germany (1991–1993); Vice President, Swiss Eternit Group (1989–1990); Assistant Vice President, Swiss Aluminum Ltd. (1967–1988). **Associations & Accomplishments:** Patent holder, Numerous published articles in magazines and newspapers; Lecturer at seminars and meetings; Member, German Institute of Mining & Metallurgical Engineers. **Education:** Technical University, Stuttgart, Germany, Electrical Engineering (1965).

Arne L. Watland

Vice President of Marketing and Sales
Progress Casting Group
2600 Niagara Lane North
Plymouth, MN 55447
(612) 470–6661
Fax: (612) 557–0320

3365

Business Information: Progress Casting Group is an aluminum foundry. Established in 1935, Progress Casting Group presently employs 300 people. Mr. Watland currently serves as Vice President of Marketing and Sales. **Career Steps:** Vice President of Marketing and Sales, Progress Casting Group (1993–Present); Director of Sales, Rosemount, Inc. (1988–1994); Vice President of Marketing, PPT, Inc. (1983–1988); Sales Manager, Modicon, Inc. (1978–1983). **Associations & Accomplishments:** Board of Directors, Wayzata Community Church; Board of Directors, M3F Foundation; Who;'s Who in Technology; Speaks at high schools and colleges; Wrote numerous articles. **Education:** Oakland University, M.B.A. (1979); Purdue University, B.S. in Aeronautical Engineering. **Personal:** Married to Janice in 1993. Four children: Jordan, Alexis, Katie, and Kellie. Mr. Watland enjoys flying, coins, and golf in his leisure time.

Jorge W. De Queiroz

President
Eluma S/A Ind. E. Com.
R. Dr. Julio Pignatari, 109
Santo Andre, Brazil 09220–901
55–11–446–5228
Fax: 55–11–446–4034

3366

Business Information: Eluma S/A Ind. E. Com. is a brass milling company and manufacturer of copper and copper products. The products are distributed to the auto industry, home appliance industry, civil construction concerns, engineers, refrigeration and air conditioning manufacturers, and wholesalers. The Company is international in scope and exports products to Asia, South American, Europe, and the United States. As President, Mr. De Queiroz has oversight of the daily operations. He is responsible for public relations, recruiting of upper management, marketing strategies, development of new sales markets, and cash management. Mr. De Queiroz assumed leadership in 1994 and brought the Company from bankruptcy to posting over 200 million dollars in revenue in 1995. **Career Steps:** President, Eluma S/A Ind. E. Com. (1994–Present); Corporate Financial Director, Iochpe Maxion S.A. –(1992–1994); Financial Director, Citro Pectina S.A. (1991–1992); Tax Department Manager, Exxon Corporation (1987–1990). **Associations & Accomplishments:** President, Brazilian Copper Institute. **Education:** marquette University, Engineering Degree (1974); Massachusetts Institute of Technology, Post Graduate Finance. **Personal:** Married to Ana Paula in 1995. Three children: Gabriel, Eduardo, and Victor. Mr. De Queiroz enjoys playing golf, tennis, and sailing.

H. Wade German

Converting Mill Manager
Wolverine Tube, Inc.
2100 Market Street
Decatur, IL 35601
(205) 353–1310
Fax: (205) 355–3818

3369

Business Information: Established in 1916, Wolverine Tube, Inc. is the leading international manufacturer of non–ferrous tubing, specializing in copper and alloy production. As Converting Mill Manager, Mr. German is responsible for receiving, melting and extrusion of raw materials. **Career Steps:** Converting Mill Manager, Wolverine Tube, Inc. (1986–Present); Smelter Superintendent, Cities Service Oil (1969–1986). **Associations & Accomplishments:** T.M.S. **Education:** University of Alabama – Huntsville, B.S. in Human Resources (1988). **Personal:** Married to Connie in 1968. Mr. German enjoys running and fly fishing.

Barrie W. Guibord

Executive Vice President
Plattco Corporation
7 White Street
Plattsburgh, NY 12901–3417
(518) 563–4640
Fax: (518) 563–4892

3369

Business Information: Plattco Corporation is a wholly–owned family corporation established in 1897, currently employing over 100 people. While the Corporation began as a foundry and machine shop servicing the mining industry, today Plattco manufactures valves with expertise in ferrous alloy castings and has an in–house research and development department. As Executive Vice President, Mr. Guibord concentrates on the development of international markets for products produced by Plattco. He works closely with Company engineers on the development of new and existing products and with the marketing department on marketing/sales of these products. Other duties Mr. Guibord has include customer relations, employee relations, and employee motivation. **Career Steps:** Plattco Corporation: Executive Vice President (1985–Present), Vice President (1980–1985), Plant Manager (1976–1980). **Associations & Accomplishments:** World Furture Society; Chamber of Commerce; Advisory Council, State University of New York; Advisory Board of Clinton Community College; Business Person of the Year, 1991; American Management Association. **Education:** State University of New York at Plattsburgh, C.A.S. (1977); 60 hours of Post Graduate study in Social Sciences; Permanent Teacher Certification K–12 (1975); Fordham University, B.A. in English. **Personal:** One child: Bari Ayn. Mr. Guibord enjoys piano, classical music, global culture and world government, reading, writing, skiing, skating, swimming, jogging, and travel.

Sheri L. Lytle

Director of Human Resources
FPM, L.P.
1501 Lively Boulevard
Elk Grove Village, IL 60007–5029
(847) 228–2525
Fax: (847) 228–9887

3398

Business Information: FPM, L.P. is a heat–treating company specializing in the heating of metals to a variety of hardness levels. Products are used for different types of commercial and construction applications. As Human Resources Director, Ms. Lytle is responsible for all human resource operations, including employee benefits. **Career Steps:** Director of Human Resources, FPM Heat Treating (1994–Present); Director of Human Resources, Accra Pac Group, Inc. (1989–1994); Human Resources Manager, Electro Transfer Systems (1988–1989). **Associations & Accomplishments:** Society for Human Resources Management; Elk Grove Rotary Club; Northwestern Human Resources Council; American Management Association. **Education:** Indiana Wesleyan University, M.S.A. (1994); Indiana University, Bachelor of Management, Administration, Personnel, and Industrial Relations. **Personal:** Married to Stephen. Two children: Rachel, Joel and Ashley. Ms. Lytle enjoys camping, boating, bicycling, traveling and reading.

Wayne H. Samuelson

Division Manager
Lindberg Heat Treating Company
6111 Cochran Road
Solon, OH 44139
(216) 248–4000
Fax: (216) 248–9515

3398

Business Information: Lindberg Heat Treating Company is a wholly–owned, commercial heat treating and metallurgical service which changes mechanical components' properties by heat treating. Based in Canada, Lindberg Heat Treating Company currently employs 26 people. As Division Manager, Mr. Samuelson, a Metallurgist by trade, is responsible for the management of all operations of the Solon Division. **Career Steps:** Division Manager, Lindberg Heat Treating Company (1995–Present); President, Shore Metal Treating, Inc. (1968–1995). **Associations & Accomplishments:** Heat Treat Network; ASM International; Published in trade journals and lectures on technical subjects. **Education:** Case Institute of Technology, B.S. in Metallurgy (1970). **Personal:** Married to Rosemary in 1988. Three children: Carina, Renee, and Rachel. Mr. Samuelson enjoys golf, woodworking, and metallurgical consulting.

Scott H. Anderson

Computer Systems Development and Support Manager
BHP Steel Building Products
2141 Milwaukee Way
Tacoma, WA 98421–2705
(206) 922–4982
Fax: (206) 535–0722

3399

Business Information: BHP Steel Building Products specializes in the process manufacture of colored steel panels; purchasing steel stock in coil form, then running it through dye processes for final production. As Computer Systems Development and Support Manager, Mr. Anderson is responsible for software and hardware integration, troubleshooting, and equipment upgrades. **Career Steps:** Computer Systems Development and Support Manager, BHP Steel Building Products (1991–Present); Assistant Lab Manager, Weyerhaeuser (1987–1991). **Associations & Accomplishments:** Aircraft Owners and Pilots Associaton; Digital Equipment Corporation Users Society; C.V.N.A. **Education:** Pacific Lutheran University, M.B.A. (1996); University of Puget Sound: B.S. Physics, B.S. in Computer Science. **Personal:** Married to Natalie in 1989. Two children: Mitchell and Dane. Mr. Anderson enjoys flying, golf, and basketball.

Ron E. Horne

Controller
Intech Enterprises, Inc.
P.O. Box 630, 477 South 28th Street
Washougal, WA 98671
(360) 835–8785
Fax: (360) 835–5144

3399

Business Information: Intech Enterprises, Inc. is a manufacturer of package handling equipment. Estsablished in 1989, Intech Enterprises, Inc. reports annual revenue of $2 million and currently employs 19 people. As Controller, Mr. Horne is responsible for business management and financial controls. **Career Steps:** Controller, Intech Enterprises, Inc. (1992–Present); Controller, Blind Enterprises, Inc. (1991–1992); Accounting Manager, Goodwill Industries (1966–1990). **Associations & Accomplishments:** Lions International. **Education:** International Accounts, B.S. (1972); Major in Accounting and Finance; Well versed in computer application. **Personal:** Married to Sandy in 1967. One child: Bernice. Mr. Horne enjoys flying.

William T. Nachtrab, Ph.D.

Vice President of Technology
Nuclear Metals, Inc.
2229 Main Street
Concord, MA 01742
(508) 369–5410
Fax: (508) 369–0918

3399

Business Information: Nuclear Metals, Inc. specializes in the production and development of specialty metals utilized in aerospace, electronic and energy applications. Products are predominantly beryllium, titanium, uranium and other nonferrous and ferrous alloys utilized in castings, extrusions powders, and semi- finished forms. Company management projects a continuous growth based on new product introductions the next three to five years. As Vice President of Technology, Dr. Nachtrab directs all technical activities, as well as managing the research and development staff of five professionals and three technicians. Established in 1972, Nuclear Metals, Inc. employs 130 people and reports annual revenue in excess of $27 million. **Career Steps:** Vice President of Technology, Nuclear Metals, Inc. (1993–Present); Manager of Research and Development, Nuclear Metals, Inc. (1988–1993); Senior Member Technical Staff, Thomson Consumer Electronics (1985–1988). **Associations & Accomplishments:** ASM International; The Minerals, Metals and Materials Society; American Powder Metallurgy Institute; Materials Research Society . **Education:** Lehigh University, Ph.D. in Metallurgical Engineering (1982); Illinois Institute of Technology, M.S. in Metallurgical Engineering (1980); Lehigh University, B.S. in Metallurgy and Materials Science.

Roland J. Theriault

General Manager
Fers et Metaux Recycles, Ltd.
1975 J.M. Langlois
La Prairie, Quebec J5R 5Z8
(514) 444–4424
Fax: (514) 444–4499
EMail: See Below

3399

Business Information: Fers et Metaux Recycles, Ltd., established in 1974, specializes in purchasing, processing, and selling ferrous and non–ferrous metals for recycling. As General Manager, Mr. Theriault manages all Company functions, including reporting to a Steering Committee representing both parent companies. Internet users can reach him via: 73353.1404@compuserve.com. **Career Steps:** General Manager, Fers et Metaux Recycles, Ltd. (1991–Present); Heckett Canada (Div. HARSCO): General Manager (1991–1985), Plant Supervisor (1982–1985); Plant Manager, Sidbec – Feruni, Inc. (1976–1981). **Associations & Accomplishments:** Canadian Association of Recycling Industries; Institute of Scrap Recycling Industries. **Education:** University of Ottawa (1961); Concordia University, Business Administration. **Personal:** Married to Patricia M. Peel in 1969. Four children: Katherine, Steven, Christine, and David. Mr. Theriault enjoys church activities, flying, skiing, gardening, and handicrafts.

Mrs. Carol M. Winters, CPA

Controller
Micro Precision
1206 Ann Street, P.O. Box 488
Delavan, WI 53115
(414) 728–5262
Fax: (414) 728–6829

3399

Business Information: Micro Precision specializes in the manufacture of machine parts (i.e., screws) as well as metal stampings. Established in 1986, the Company currently employs 110 people and has an estimated annual revenue of $8 million. As Controller, Mrs. Winters is responsible for all financial activities including budgeting and taxes. She also oversees the office and human resource department. **Career Steps:** Controller, Micro Precision (1993–Present); General Accounting Supervisor, Sta–Rite Industries, Inc. (1986–1993); Cash Management Analyst, Inryco, Inc., a subsidiary of Inland Steel (1984–1986). **Associations & Accomplishments:** Wisconsin Institute of Certified Public Accountants; Member in good standing, Institute of Management Accountants; Former Member, Financial Committee at Brookfield Presbyterian Church, Brookfield, WI. Current Member of Personnel Committee, First Presbyterian Church, Waukesha, WI. **Education:** University of Wisconsin, Milwaukee, B.B.A. (1983); CPA exam in Wisconsin (passed – 1987). **Personal:** Married to Gregory in 1989. Two children: Bryan G. and Andrew J. Winters. Mrs. Winters enjoys golf, camping, volleyball, card games, aerobics, and teaching Sunday School.

3400 Fabricated Metal Products

3411 Metal cans
3412 Metal barrels, drums, and pails
3421 Cutlery
3423 Hand and edge tools, NEC
3425 Saw blades and handsaws
3429 Hardware, NEC
3431 Metal sanitary ware
3432 Plumbing fixtures fittings and trim
3433 Heating equipment, except electric
3441 Fabricated structural metal
3442 Metal doors, sash and trim
3443 Fabricated plate work (boiler shops)
3444 Sheet metal work
3446 Architectural metal work
3448 Prefabricated metal buildings
3449 Miscellaneous metal work
3451 Screw machine products
3452 Bolts, nuts, rivets, and washers
3462 Iron and steel forgings
3463 Nonferrous forgings
3465 Automotive stampings
3466 Crowns and closures
3469 Metal stampings, NEC
3471 Plating and polishing
3479 Metal coating and allied services
3482 Small arms ammunition
3483 Ammunition, exc. for small arms, NEC
3484 Small arms
3489 Ordnance and accessories, NEC
3491 Industrial valves
3492 Fluid power valves and hose fittings
3493 Steel springs, except wire
3494 Valves and pipe fittings, NEC
3495 Wire springs
3496 Misc. fabricated wire products
3497 Metal foil and leaf
3498 Fabricated pipe and fittings
3499 Fabricated metal products, NEC

Linda L. Bobo

Senior Environmental Engineer
Ball Corporation
P.O. Box 2407
Muncie, IN 47037–0407
(317) 747–6580
Fax: (317) 747–6553
EMAIL: See Below

3411

Business Information: Ball Corporation, international in scope, is a Fortune 500 company specializing in the manufacture of metal containers for food and beverages, aerospace and glass containers, and pet plastics. The Company was established in 1880 and employs approximately 7,000 people. Estimated annual revenue for Ball Corp. is $2.6 billion. As Senior Environmental Engineer, Ms. Bobo is responsible for all environmental categories (air, water, and waste) and manages all environmental audit programs and environmental management system assessment programs. Internet users can reach her via: LBOBO@BALL.COM. **Career Steps:** Senior Environmental Engineer, Ball Corporation (1990–Present); Indiana Department of Environmental Management: Environmental Scientist Group Leader (1986–1990), Environmental Manager (1986–1990). **Associations & Accomplishments:** Institute of Hazardous Materials Managers (CHMM #2515); Air & Work Management Association; California Registered Environmental Assesor; Author of six reports for the U.S. Geological Survey. **Education:** Indiana University: M.P.A. in Management (1986), Chemistry and Math (1971); Butler University, Legal Studies (1984). **Personal:** Ms. Bobo enjoys training and showing her German Shepard dogs and skiing.

Eng. Lambert Dempster–Edwards, P.E.

Engineering Manager
Reynolds Metal Company
P.O. Box 2937
Guayama, Puerto Rico 00785
(787) 864–1414
Fax: (787) 864–6232

3411

Business Information: Reynolds Metal Company is a beer and beverage aluminum can manufacturing plant. As Engineering Manager, Mr. Dempster–Edwards manages the Engineering, Maintenance, and Environmental Department of the Company. He maintains all schedules, ensures operations are in accordance with the budget, and all environmental reports are submitted in a timely manner. **Career Steps:** Reynolds Metal Company: Engineering Maintenance and Environmental Manager (1994–Present), Quality Assurance Manager (1992–1994); Plant Superintendent, Bristol Myers Squibb Company (1988–1990). **Associations & Accomplishments:** National Society of Professional Engineers; American Institute of Plant Engineers; American Institute of Mechanical Engineers; Society of Manufacturing Engineers. **Education:** Frankly University – PA, B.S. in Mechanical Engineering (1990); Manufacturing Engineering Institute, Certificate of Manufacturing Engineering (1987); Catholic University, B.A. in Engineering (1984). **Personal:** Married to Maria E. Rosario in 1987. Three children: Sharon, Don, and Allan. Mr. Dempster–Edwards enjoys reading technology magazines, music, and playing the guitar.

Mark A. Klug

Plant Manager
Brockway Standard, Inc.
11440 Pacific Avenue
Fontana, CA 92337
(909) 685–1007
Fax: (909) 685–6856

3411

Business Information: Brockway Standard, Inc., one of nine manufacturing plants, is a national manufacturer of metal containers for the paint industry. Products include pint, quart, and gallon size paint and utility cans, which are distributed directly to the paint manufacturers. Mr. Klug is responsible for the overall management and maintenance of the Fontana, California plant, including the oversight of personnel, budgeting, etc. **Career Steps:** Plant Manager, Brockway Standard, Inc. (1990–Present); Armstrong Containers: Assistant Plant Manager (1988–1990), Plant Superintendent (1986–1988), Production Supervisor (1976–1986); Miller Brewing Company (1975–1976); Continental Can Company (1970–1975).

Associations & Accomplishments: Southern California Paint and Coatings Association. **Personal:** Married to Jan F. in 1989. One child: Rebecca Jean. Mr. Klug enjoys golf, fishing, and computers.

Peter J. Brunn

Vice President and Director of Marketing
Hoover Material Handling Group
2001 Westside Parkway, Suite 155
Alpharetta, GA 30201
(770) 664–4047 Ext. 108
Fax: (770) 664–2850

3412

Business Information: Hoover Material Handling Group, international in scope, is a manufacturer of shipping containers for liquids. The containers are manufactured to UN specifications and are made of a variety of materials, including stainless steel, carbon, steel, plastic, or plastic metal. As Vice President and Director of Marketing, Mr. Brunn is responsible for diversified administrative activities, including sales and marketing, and oversees all management. **Career Steps:** Hoover Material Handling Group: Vice President and Director of Marketing (1996–Present), Southeast Region Sales Manager (1994), Product Manager (1990–1994). **Associations & Accomplishments:** Institute Packaging Professionals; American Association of Textile Chemists and Colorists; National Account Marketing Association; Chemical Club of Charlotte. **Education:** Arizona State University, B.A. in Business Administration (1970). **Personal:** Two children: Michael P. and Kevin M. Mr. Brunn enjoys golf, tennis, and furniture making.

Terry G. Leseberg

Engineering Manager
American Tool Companies, Inc.
415 Industrial Row
Beatrice, NE 68310
(402) 223–7460
Fax: (402) 223–7491

3423

Business Information: American Tool Companies, Inc. manufactures hand tools and power tool accessories for professional do–it–yourself end users. Products include ViseGrip Locking–Pliers, Prosnip, Tin Snips, QuickGrip Bar Clamps, Chesco Hex Keys, Jack Saw Hand Saws, and a variety of taps, dies, drill bits, and router bits. Established in 1984, the Company employees 2,000 people in seven locations worldwide. As Engineering Manager, Mr. Leseberg oversees engineering, tool and die, quality, and federal EPA standards. **Career Steps:** American Tool Companies, Inc.: Engineering Manager (1993–Present), Design Engineer (1986–1993), Tool Maker (1981–1986). **Associations & Accomplishments:** Society of Manufacturing Engineers (SME) since 1989. Granted a design patent on the ViseGrip large capacity locking plier. Pat. No. 5,351,585. **Education:** Southeast Community College, Associate (1981). **Personal:** Mr. Leseberg enjoys hunting, archery, and English cars.

Jerry D. Coleman Jr.

Vice President
Porta–Nails, Inc.
315 North 17th Street
Wilmington, NC 28401
(910) 762–6334 (800) 634–9281
Fax: (910) 763–8650
EMail: See Below

3429

Business Information: Porta–Nails, Inc. specializes in the manufacture of specialty tools and fasteners, including Porta–Nailer, Buffer Mate, Router Mate, Wood Hog, Cutting Tools, Wing Template, Ring Master, and Dowel Mate. As Vice President of Sales and Marketing, Mr. Coleman is responsible for all aspects of Company operations, including sales, marketing, and finances. Internet users can reach him via: PORTA–NAILS@AOL.COM. **Career Steps:** Vice President of Sales and Marketing, Porta–Nails, Inc. (1993–Present); Senior Marketing Representative, Carolina Powerland Light (1982–1993). **Associations & Accomplishments:** Cape Fear Area United Way: Campaign Chairman, Former Board of Directors. **Education:** East Carolina University, B.S.B.A. (1982). **Personal:** Married to Susan B. in 1990. One child: Jerry D. III. Mr. Coleman enjoys golf and travel.

Harold R. McGough

Product Engineer
Imperial Products, Inc.
P.O. Box 726
Williamsburg, IN 47393–0726
(317) 966–0322
Fax: (317) 966–2403

3429

Business Information: Imperial Products, Inc. is a leading manufacturer of door and window hardware (i.e., thresholds, astragals) for the residential home market. As Product Engineer, Mr. McGough has 20 years of experience in the transportation industry and 6 years in the home building industry. Appointed to his current position in 1989, he is responsible for all the duties of an engineering department, including product research, design, and layout. He drafts detail, assembly, and shop instruction drawings, and produces shop instruction and CAD drawing manuals. Mr. McGough concurrently operates a CAD service business out of his home. **Career Steps:** Product Engineer, Imperial Products, Inc. (1989–Present); Senior Design Engineer, Wayne Corporation (1969–1989); Draftsman, Cooper–Bessemer Company (1966–1969); Sheet Metal Template Maker, Flexible Coach Company (1959–1966). **Associations & Accomplishments:** Williamsburg Church of the Nazarene. **Education:** Bliss Business College (1959–1960); Olivet Nazarene College (1960–1961); International Cooresponding Schools (1964–1986); Earlham College, Executive Training Program (1976–1977); Wright State University; Ivy College (1988). **Personal:** Married to Naoma Mae in 1961. Two children: Wanda Jean and Harold Raymond Jr. Mr. McGough enjoys fishing and his computer.

Duane B. Nixon

Project Manager – Corporate
Best Lock Corporation
6161 East 75th Street
Indianapolis, IN 46250
(317) 849–2225
Fax: (317) 845–7651

3429

Business Information: Best Lock Corporation specializes in the manufacture, wholesale/retail market and distribution of commercial grade locking systems. Product lines include: door hardware, key systems for universities, as well as commercial buildings. A management engineer with Best Lock since 1989, Duane Nixon was appointed to his current position in 1996. As Project Manager, he directs operations and coordinates teams involved in all major corporate projects. **Career Steps:** Best Lock Corporation: Project Manager (Since Jan. 1996), Operations Manager (1995–1996), Manufacturing Engineer Manager (1989–1995). **Associations & Accomplishments:** Society of Manufacturing Engineers; Four U.S. Patents. **Education:** Letourneau University, B.S. in Engineering (1982); Butler University, M.B.A. in progress; Certified Manufacturing Engineer. **Personal:** Married to Susan L. in 1987. One child: Isaac B. Mr. Nixon enjoys golf, church activities, and photography.

Roger L. Pollack

New Products Manager
Hartmann Luggage
P.O. Box 550
Lebanon, TN 37088
(615) 444–5000
Fax: (615) 443–4619

3429

Business Information: Hartmann Luggage specializes in the manufacture, marketing, and sale of luggage worldwide. As New Products Manager, Mr. Pollack manages the cross–functional introduction team tasked with bringing new products to market meetings. He also handles cost, schedule, and quality objectives. **Career Steps:** New Products Manager, Hartmann Luggage (1995–Present); Senior Manufacturing Engineer, Daisy Manufacturing Company (1989–1995); Senior Industrial Engineer, Lockheed Missile & Space Company (1984–1989); Materials Manager, Weed Instruments Company (1982). **Associations & Accomplishments:** Society of Manufacturing Engineers; Professional Engineer, Arkansas. **Education:** Texas A&M University, M.B.A. (1982); University of Arkansas, B.S. in Industrial Engineering. **Personal:** Married to Kristin in 1988. Three children: Andrew, Katharine, and Alexander. Mr. Pollack enjoys playing the guitar, jogging, and walking.

Sherman J. Smith

Director of Customer Service
Cooper Automotive
901 Roosevelt Parkway
Chesterfield, MO 63017
(314) 530–8350
Fax: (800) 882–2713

3429

Business Information: Cooper Automotive specializes in the manufacture of parts for the automotive after–market. A subsidiary of Cooper Industries, the Company provides head lights, lighting components, wiper blades, spark plugs, etc. to retailers and distributors worldwide. Headquartered in Houston, Texas, the Company has thirty–seven locations serving clients both nationally and internationally. As Director of Customer Service, Mr. Smith is responsible for processing customer orders, pricing of all merchandise, and direct supervision of twenty–one people. **Career Steps:** Director of Customer Service, Cooper Automotive (1992–Present); Director of Sales Administration, Champion Spark Plug (1989–1992); Manager, Customer Service and Domestic/Export, Cooper Tool (1969–1991). **Associations & Accomplishments:** 50 Men and Women; Rotary Club. **Education:** Clemson Business Management. **Personal:** Four children: Wendall, Brian, Sherman Jr., and Duane. Mr. Smith enjoys gourmet cooking, and golf.

Martin G. Wells

Managing Director – South American Operations
Delphi Energy & Engine Management Systems
Av. Indianopolis, 3096 Bloco B 5o And.
Sao Paulo–SP, Brazil 04062–003
55–11–5582–041
Fax: 55–11–189–6216

3429

Business Information: Delphi Energy & Engine – S. Am. specializes in the manufacture, OEM, and aftermarket sale of high–tech auto parts. A division of General Motors, one the U.S.'s "Big 3" automakers, the Company was established in 1990, employs in S. Am. 450 people, and has an estimated annual revenue of $200 million. As Managing Director, Mr. Wells is responsible for all aspects of Company operations in South America. He oversees new business development, and assists in ensuring the growth and expansion of the Company. **Career Steps:** Managing Director, Delphi Energy & Engin S. AM. (1995–Present); Govern./Industrial/Public Relations Director, General Motors of Argentina (1993–1995); Administration/Finance Director, Delco Remy of Brazil (1990–1993). **Personal:** Mr. Wells is a professional Chemical and Industrial Engineer with stron background in Industrial Relations, Negotiations and Finance Administration. Married to Alicia in 1971. Two children: Alan and Marvin. Mr. Wells enjoys being an artist (oil on canvas).

Russ Yeager

Director of Human Resources
Simpson Industries, Inc.
917 Anderson Road
Litchfield, MI 49252
(517) 542–5555
Fax: (517) 542–4200

3429

Business Information: Simpson Industries, Inc. specializes in the manufacture of automotive parts for companies within the automotive industry. As Director of Human Resources, Mr. Yeager is responsible for all human resource functions, including workers compensation issues, safety, benefits, and training. **Career Steps:** Director of Human Resources, Simpson Industries, Inc. (1994–Present); Human Resource Manager, ADALET–PLM – Division of Scott Fetzer (1987–1994). **Associations & Accomplishments:** Society of Human Resource Management. **Education:** Gannon University, B.A. (1982). **Personal:** Married to Karen in 1981. Mr. Yeager enjoys coaching childrens' hockey and spending time with family.

Sonja C. Johnston

Director of Human Resources
Faucet Queens, Inc.
650 Forest Edge Drive
Vernon Hills, IL 60061–4115
(847) 821–0777
Fax: (847) 821–0277

3431

Business Information: Faucet Queens, Inc. specializes in manufacturing, packaging, and distributing houseware, hardware, and plumbing items to drug and food stores. International in scope, the Company has seven national and five international export locations. As Director of Human Resources, Ms. Johnston is responsible for employee benefits, employee relations issues, training and public relations. Additionally, she oversees all hiring, new employee orientation, and daily administration and operations, including landscaping, housekeeping, and general grounds and building maintenance. **Career Steps:** Director of Human Resources, Faucet Queens, Inc. (1983–Present); General Office, Drexel Ice Cream Company (1980–1983). **Associations & Accomplishments:** Society for Human Resources Management; Total Quality Matrix Group; Northern Illinois Business Association. **Personal:** Two children: Patrick and Nicholas. Ms. Johnston enjoys spending free time with her children and going to the movies.

Mr. Kenneth F. Kames

Vice President of New Business Development
The Gillette Company
Prudential Tower Building
Boston, MA 02199
(617) 421–7728
Fax: (617) 421–8318

3431

Business Information: The Gillette Company is a global manufacturer of blades and razors, toiletries, writing instruments, small appliances, and oral care products. Mr. Kames is responsible for acquisitions, divestitures, joint ventures, and license agreements worldwide. Established in 1901, The Gillette Company employs over 30,000 people and reports revenue in excess of $5 billion. Company operations are conducted in over 200 countries worldwide. **Career Steps:** Vice President of New Business Development, The Gillette Company (1968–Present); Director Special Financial Projects, The Gillette Company (1981–1988); Assistant Director Financial Projects, The Gillette Company (1974–1981); General Manager–Japan, The Gillette Company (1970–1973); Manager – Branch Administration, Honeywell (1957–1968). **Associations & Accomplishments:** Vice President and Director of Boston Chapter, Association for Corporate Growth; National Committee on Government Liaison, Financial Executives Institute; Board of Directors, Digital Learning Systems, Inc.; Treasurer and Board Member, Broadview Condominium Association. **Education:** Suffolk University, B.S. (1961); Suffolk University Graduate School of Business (1969–1970); Bentley College, A.A. in Accounting.

Bryan L. Benson

Director, Engineering Services
York International
631 South Richland Avenue
York, PA 17403
(717) 771–7598
Fax: (717) 771–7838
E MAIL: See Below

3433

Business Information: York International is a manufacturer of heating, ventilation, air conditioning, and refrigeration products. Established in 1874, the Company currently has over 19,000 employees and expects to post sales in excess of $3 billion in 1996. York International supplies air conditioning units for large corporations (i.e. World Trade Centers, Navy Department, nuclear submarines). The Company was an official sponsor of the 1996 US Olympic Games and is also sponsoring the 1998 Winter Olympics in Nogana, the 2000 Olympics in Sydney, and the 2002 Winter Olympics in Salt Lake City. As Director of Engineering Services, Mr. Benson is responsible for large capital projects and manufacturing/engineering computer integration worldwide. He develops and implements all new projects and follows them through to completion. Internet users may contact him via: bbenson405@aol.com. **Career Steps:** York International: Director, Engineering Services (1996–Present), Division Manager (1992–1996), Manager, CAM (1988–1992), Senior Systems Analyst (1986–1988); Cincinnati Milacron Systems Integrator (1983–1986). **Associations & Accomplishments:** Society of Manufacturing Engineering; Board Member, Strand/Capital Performing Arts Center; Certified Manufacturing Technologist; Outstanding Young Men of America (1989). **Education:** Cedarville College, B.S. (1983). **Personal:** Married to Bethany in 1984. Mr. Benson enjoys golf, tennis, and racquetball.

Richard H. Rice

Operations Manager
Thermalex, Inc.
2758 Gunter Park Drive
Montgomery, AL 36109–1016
(334) 272–8270
Fax: (334) 244–0308

3433

Business Information: Thermalex, Inc. is a metal fabrication industry, supplying extruded/fabricated aluminum micro and micro–micro tubing utilized in the manufacturing applications of environmentally–safe heat exchangers. Joining Thermalex in 1992 upon completion of his military duty, Rick Rice was recently promoted as Operations Manager. He provides the overall operational management for plant production, ensuring a safe work environment and maintaining the Company's high–level quality product output. **Career Steps:** Thermalex, Inc.: Operations Manager (1995–Present), Manufacturing Manager (1992–1995); Director of Flight Training and Quality Control, Aeroscout Branch (1989–1992). **Associations & Accomplishments:** Ambassador, Montgomery Chamber of Commerce; Technical Services Committee Member, Aluminum Extruders Council; American Management Association. **Education:** Embry–Riddle Aeronautical University: B.S. (1990), M.B.A. **Personal:** Married to Kimberly in 1981. Two children: Kylie and Nathan. Mr. Rice enjoys golf, hiking, learning and teaching.

Thomas M. Bradley Sr.

Corporate Secretary and Chief Executive Officer
Bradley Window Corporation
699 East Tropicana Avenue
Las Vegas, NV 89119–6608
(702) 739–7466
Fax: (702) 739–1554

3442

Business Information: Bradley Window Corporation is a regional manufacturer and distributor of aluminum products (i.e., aluminum windows, aluminum doors, etc.), serving the home building industry (95%) throughout Western United States. Joining Bradley Window Corporation as Corporate Secretary and Chief Executive Officer in 1978, Mr. Bradley is responsible for all management and sales functions, including the day–to–day operations. Concurrent with his position at Bradley Window Corporation, he serves as a consultant with the Corporation's affiliate, Bradley Architectural Systems, Ltd, an international architectural design and consulting firm. **Career Steps:** Corporate Secretary and Chief Executive Officer, Bradley Window Corporation (1978–Present); President and Chief Executive Officer, Bradley Architectural Systems, Ltd. (Present). **Associations & Accomplishments:** Nevada Development Authority; Southern Nevada Home Builders; U.S. Chamber of Commerce; Score International Racing Association. **Education:** University of Alabama (1965–1968). **Personal:** Married to Theresa Ann in 1993. Two children: Tom Jr. and Kathryn Lee. Mr. Bradley enjoys professional race car driving, soda, and APBA.

Steve W. Spears

Vice President
Crawford Door Company
400 North Van Buren
Amarillo, TX 79107–5150
(806) 374–8591
Fax: (806) 374–8594

3442

Business Information: Crawford Door Company is a full–line supplier, distribution sales and installation servicer of overhead coiling and sectional doors, traffic and dock equipment utilized in commercial, residential, industrial and governmental applications. Joining the company in 1983 as a service manager, Mr. Spears was appointed to his current position in 1992. As Vice President he oversees all sectors of project development, including estimating and sales. **Career Steps:** Crawford Door Company: Vice President (1992–Present), Sales (1989–1992), Service Manager (1983–1989). **Associations & Accomplishments:** Vice President, Associated Sub Contractors; Amarillo Contractors Association; Associated General Contractor Association. **Education:** Amarillo College, Business (1994). **Personal:** Married to Janice in 1986. One child: Derek. Mr Spears enjoys golf, softball, and spending time with family.

Kay E. Zimmerman

Human Resource Manager
Sugarcreek Industries, Inc.
P.O. Box 460
Sugarcreek, OH 44681–0460
(338) 852–2417
Fax: Please mail or call

3442

Business Information: Established in 1940, Sugarcreek Industries, Inc. is a manufacturer of aluminum storm doors and storm windows; aluminum, vinyl, and aluminum/vinyl replacement windows; and new construction windows. As Human Resource Manager, Ms. Zimmerman is responsible for recruiting, hiring, payroll, administering all benefits, safety, policies, procedures, and personnel functions. In addition, she is responsible for employee training and counselling. **Career Steps:** Human Resource Manager, Sugarcreek Industries, Inc. (1995–Present); Human Resources Manager, Sugarcreek Window and Door Corporation (1986–1995); Personnel Manager and Employee Relations Manager, ARCO/Alsco (1981–1986); Manager Employee Services, Alsco/Anaconda (1974–1981); Alsco: Assistant Personnel Manager (1964–1974), Order Department Supervisor (1959–1964), Senior Order Clerk (1958–1959), Order Clerk (1957–1958), Factory Employee and Order Clerk (1956–1957). **Associations & Accomplishments:** Tuscarawas County Personnel Association; Tuscarawas Valley Safety Council; United Way Planning Committee; Buckeye Joint Vocational School Advisory Committee; Retirement Planning; Red Cross (Gray Lady); Visit nursing homes and work with elderly people; Various Church activities. **Education:** Associates in Administrative Management (1958), Countinuing Studies: Effective Speaking (1966), Human Relations (1967), Safety Training (1976); Anaconda: Human Relations I, Simulated Bargaining (1977), Pre–Retirement Planning (1981); Ohio State Council, Safety Training (OSHA) (1983). **Personal:** Married to Gene in 1951. Four children: Jennifer (Deceased), Terry, Gregory and Jay. Ms. Zimmerman enjoys hiking, biking, dancing, crafts with grandchildren, sports (baseball, track, field, basketball) and working with elderly people.

N. J. Henry Holroyd, Ph.D.

Senior Vice President of Research and Development
Luxfer U.S.A. Limited
1995 Third Street
Riverside, CA 92507
(909) 341–2245
Fax: (909) 351–0790

3443

Business Information: Luxfer U.S.A., Limited is an international manufacturer of high pressure aluminum alloy gas cylinders. Products include: beverage CO2 cylinders, fire extinguishers, scuba tanks and cylinders for medical oxygen, breathing apparatus and industrial gases. Established in the United Kingdom in 1958, the U.S. plant was established in 1971 and currently employs 446 people. As Senior Vice President of Research and Development, Dr. Holroyd is responsible for all aspects of global research and development. This position, initially based in the United Kingdom, moved to the U.S. with a global responsibility and focus on product development and manufacturing process monitoring. Prior to July 1995, Dr. Holyrod was Senior Consulting Scientist with Alcan International Limited in Banbury, UK; and for the last two years he has been on full–time secondment to Luxfer Gas Cylinders as Director of Materials Science. Projects include the development of getting natural gas to vehicles via cylinders. Concurrent with his position, he also serves as Adjunct Professor in the Department of Materials Science and Engineering at Case Western Reserve University, and Visiting Professor at the University of Central England. **Career Steps:** Senior Vice President of Research and Development, Luxfer U.S.A., Limited (1995–Present); Director of Materials Science, Luxfer Gas Cylinders (1993–Present); Senior Consulting Scientist, Alcan International, Ltd, Banbury, United Kingdom (1981–1995); Adjunct Professor in the Department of Materials Science and Engineering, Case Western Reserve University (1993–Present); Visiting Professor at University of Central England, Birmingham, United Kingdom (1994–Present). **Associations & Accomplishments:** Professional Member of Institution of Materials (MIM); Corporate Member of Institute of Corrosion (M.I.Corr); Chartered Engineer (C.Eng.), Member of TMS; Director, Institute of Corrosion Science & Technology (1987–1990); Research Board Member, TWI (The Welding Institute) (1992–1995); United Kingdom Representative on European Corrosion Federation (1992–1995); Director of Natural Gas Vehicles Association Limited (1993–Present); Published over 70 papers in technical journals; Former semi–professional cricketer; Golf handicap of 14; RESEARCH INTERESTS: Environment–Sensitive Fracture (SCC/CF), Fracture Mechanics, Process Monitoring and Physical Metallurgy of non–ferrous alloys. **Education:** University of Newcastle Upon Tyne, England, Ph.D. in Engineering (1977), B.Sc. (1972), Chartered Engineer (C.Eng.). **Personal:** Married to Mary in 1978. Dr. Holroyd enjoys playing the saxophone, jazz, collecting fine wine, golf, and specializing in DIY avoidance.

Carl E. Stevens

Vice President of Sales & Marketing
Trinity Industries, Inc.
3910 Washington Avenue
Houston, TX 77007
(713) 861–8181
Fax: (713) 861–7356

3443

Business Information: Trinity Industries, Inc. is a metal forming fabrication industry, specializing in the formation of metal plates into container ends utilized in process and pressure vessel manufacturing applications — i.e., chemical and oil industries. Established more than 50 years ago, Trinity Industries, Inc. currently employs 240 people. As Vice President of Sales & Marketing, Mr. Stevens directs all sales efforts to achieve the highest possible sales and return on sales. **Ca-**

reer Steps: Vice President of Sales & Marketing, Trinity Industries, Inc. (1993–Present); Director of Sales, Explosive Fabricators, Inc. (1990–1993); Lukens Steel Company: New Products Manager (1983–1990), Quality Control Manager (1975–1978). **Education:** Temple University, M.B.A. in Marketing (1983); University of Cincinnati, B.S. in Metallurgical Engineering. **Personal:** Married to Hetty in 1983. Two children: Kimberly and David. Mr. Stevens enjoys golf and tennis.

Ronald S. Szilagyi

Health, Safety, and Environmental Officer
B–Braun Biotech, Inc. USA
999 Postal Road
Allentown, PA 18103
(610) 266–6262 (800) 258–9000
Fax: (610) 266–9319

3443

Business Information: B–Braun Biotech, Inc. USA is the world's leading manufacturer of bio–fermentation equipment used by pharmacies for production and conducting research. International in scope, B–Braun Biotech, Inc. has locations in Canada, Germany, and the U.S. As Health, Safety, and Environmental Officer, Mr. Szilagyi is responsible for the enforcement of health, safety, and environmental laws, conducting negotiations for the Company, and has direct supervision over a staff of twenty. He also serves as the Electropolishing Foreman. Concurrently, he is the owner of a local bar. **Career Steps:** Health, Safety, and Environmental Officer, B–Braun Biotech, Inc. USA (1991–Present); President /Owner, R.T.J. Associates (1995–Present); Head Welder, Martin Sprocket and Gear (1989–1991). **Personal:** Mr. Szilagyi enjoys hunting and fishing.

Raymond E. Zbacnik

Process Engineer
Babcock & Wilcox
20 South Van Buren Avenue, #57
Barberton, OH 44203–0351
(330) 860–6551
Fax: (330) 860–2045
EMAIL: See Below

3443

Business Information: Babcock & Wilcox is a designer and manufacturer of boilers and environmental equipment for environmental and utility industries of the world. With over seventeen years of experience in the chemical, petroleum, and utility industries with increasing responsibility, including supervision of senior level process engineers, Mr. Zbacnik joined Babcock & Wilcox as Process Engineer in the Utility and Environmental Power Division in 1990. He is responsible for the process design and development of flue gas desulfurization (FGD) plants for the utility industry. Career highlights include the preparation of proposals for wet and dry FGD plants; carrying out contract work on FGD plants for Public Service of Indiana, Taiwan Power Company, KEPCO (Korea), and National Power – Pembroke (Wales); helping to establish and manage the division library; and performing additive and forced oxidation testing at Michigan South Central Power Agency. Internet users can reach him via: ZBACNIKR@PGG.McDERMOTT.COM. **Career Steps:** Process Engineer, Babcock & Wilcox (1990–Present); Process Engineer, Norton Company (1988–1990); Foster wheeler Energy Corporation: Process Supervisor (1981–1984), Senior Process Engineer (1979–1981), Process Engineer (1974–1979). **Associations & Accomplishments:** American Institute of Chemical Engineers; American Chemical Society; Institution of Chemical Engineers – British; World Apostolate of Fatima – Blue Army; Elected to Marquis' Who's Who in Science and Engineering (1996–1997). **Education:** Manhattan College, M.E. in Chemical Engineering (1977); Purdue University, B.S. in Chemical Engineering (1973); Attended: Indiana University, Purdue University at Fort Wayne, Fairleigh Dickinson University, Stevens Institute of Technology. **Personal:** Mr. Zbacnik enjoys spending time with his family, hiking, reading, and writing.

Dennis F. Gareau

Director of Quality Assurance
Gunver Manufacturing Company
255 Sheldon Road
Manchester, CT 06040
(860) 649–2888
Fax: (860) 649–8128

3444

Business Information: Gunver Manufacturing Company is a manufacturer of sheet metal components for the aerospace industry. As Director of Quality Assurance, Mr. Gareau directs and manages the Company's quality system to meet and comply with a multi–aerospace customer base, including international certification to ISO 9000–02. His background in Quality Control is vast and varied, beginning in 1962 in the Engine Assembly and Test Division of United Technologies. His career with United Technologies continued through 1988, with positions in Field Quality Control, Manager of Quality Assurance of the Automotive Division, and Quality Engineering Supervisor of the United Technologies Space Program. **Career Steps:** Director of Quality Assurance, Gunver Manufacturing Company (1993–Present); Director of Quality Assurance, J.T. Slocomb Company (1989–1993); Corporate Contract Auditor, Fansteel Corporation (1987–1988); United Technologies (1962–1988). **Associations & Accomplishments:** American Society for Quality Control; New England Quality Council; Knights of Columbus; Received Pratt and Whitney's highest Award for Management Effectiveness (1982). **Education:** Springfield College, Management; East Coast Aero Tech, A.S.; Springfield Tech. College, A.S.; Malcolm Baldridge School For Auditors. **Personal:** Married to Ann M. in 1963. Two children: Michael D. and Christopher J. Mr. Gareau enjoys golf, skiing, and softball.

Cheryl S. Grisar

Director of Marketing
Garmat USA
1401 West Stanford Avenue
Englewood, CO 80110–5579
(303) 781–6802
Fax: (303) 781–2683
EMAIL: See Below

3444

Business Information: Garmat USA is a manufacturer of automotive spray/bake booths. An international company, Garmat USA focuses on providing downdraft spray booths, preparation areas, sanding stations, and paint mix rooms to the automotive industry. Comprised of nineteen distribution offices in the U.S. and one manufacturing division, the Company handles international sales on an individual basis, with domestic orders being processed through distributors. As Director of Marketing, Ms. Grisar oversees all advertising and sales. Additional responsibilities include handling promotions, organizing two trade shows a year, managing production schedules, and attending seminars. Internet users can reach her via: cgrisar@aol.com. **Career Steps:** Director of Marketing, Garmat USA (1991–Present). **Associations & Accomplishments:** Golden Key National Honor Society. **Education:** Colorado State University, M.S. in Marketing (1990); SUNY, Buffalo, B.S. in Business Administration. **Personal:** Married to Nicholas DiPirro in 1995. Ms. Grisar enjoys skiing, hunting (archery), and canoeing.

Brent A. Holcomb

General Manager
Pendleton Technologies, Inc.
PO Box 60
Pendleton, IN 46064–0060
(317) 778–8048
Fax: (317) 778–7730
EMAIL: See Below

3444

Business Information: Pendleton Technologies, Inc. specializes in custom sheet metal fabrication, matched to customer specifications, as well as provides full custom design work. Joining Pendleton in 1989 as a project manager, Mr. Holcomb was appointed as General Manager in 1995. He is responsible for the overall operations, directly overseeing the areas of programming and engineering. He can also be reached through the Internet via: brent@indy.net **Career Steps:** Pendleton Technologies, Inc.: General Manager (1995–Present), Projects Manager (1989–1995); Laser/Service Technologist, Vaser Inc. (1986–1989). **Education:** Vincennes University, A.S. (1984). **Personal:** Married to Mary in 1984. Two children: Brian and Megan. Mr. Holcomb enjoys golf, computers, farming and family activities.

Paul P. Ilchuk

Controller
Walsh Sheet Metal Works
380 North Avenue
Abington, MA 02351
(617) 451–3658
Fax: (617) 871–8596

3444

Business Information: Walsh Sheet Metal Works is a fabricator of HVAC and sheet metal. Joining Walsh Sheet Metal Works as Controller in 1991, Mr. Ilchuk maintains all financial records and computer equipment. **Career Steps:** Controller, Walsh Sheet Metal Works (1991–Present); MIS Manager, Computer Processing Institute (CPI) (1985–1991); Operations Manager, Compugraphic (1983–1985); Operations Specialist, Honeywell (1967–1983). **Associations & Accomplishments:** William Sewall Gardner Masonic Lodge; Scottish Rite Valley of Lowell Chapter: 32nd Degree. **Education:** Bryant and Stratton, A.A. (1967). **Personal:** Two children: Philip and Peter. Mr. Ilchuk enjoys basketball and playing saxophone in the Big Band 'After Hours'.

Edward F. Rafalski Jr.

Engineer
Ductmate Industries, Inc.
R.R. 136
East Monongahela, PA 15063
(412) 258–0500
Fax: (412) 258–5494
EMAIL: See Below

3444

Business Information: Ductmate Industries, Inc. is a manufacturer of roll formed and stamped support products for the sheet metal industry. National in scope, the Company has a second location in Stockton, California. As Engineer, Mr. Rafalski oversees projects ranging from new product development, production line development, product improvement, literature for products, and customer inquiries. He also provides support to the accounting and technical departments, and conducts research. Internet users can reach him via: ductmate@usaor.net. **Career Steps:** Engineer, Ductmate Industries, Inc. (1992–Present); Graduate Research Assistant, University of Pittsburgh (1991–1992). **Associations & Accomplishments:** Pi Tau Sigma; Phi Eta Sigma; Society of Automotive Engineers (SAE). **Education:** University of Pittsburgh: M.S.M.E. (1993), B.S.M.E. (1991). **Personal:** Mr. Rafalski enjoys golf and motorcycling.

Ron Lecomte

General Manager
Klemp Corporation
Klemp Road
Dayton, TX 77535
(409) 258–5521
Fax: Please mail or call

3446

Business Information: Klemp Corporation Southern Division has revenue in excess of $12 million and employs over 100 people. Established in 1969, the Company is an international manufacturer and supplier of metal bar grating for oil companies, warehouses, construction companies, etc. As General Manager, Mr. Lecomte coordinates the day–to–day operations of the Southern Division (two locations). He is responsible for human resource and budgetary concerns, public relations, and strategic planning for his division. **Career Steps:** General Manager, Klemp Corporation (1995–Present); General Manager, W. Pat Crow Forgings (1994–1995); Operations Manager, Rockford Forge Company (1992–1994). **Associations & Accomplishments:** Liberty County Chamber of Commerce; Lions Club; Association of Building Contractors. **Education:** Upper Iowa University, B.A. (1983). **Personal:** Married to Mary in 1990. Two children: Chris LeComte and Shelli Guerra. Mr. Lecomte enjoys sports, racquetball, and reading.

Tony Elsinger

Director of Sales
McKey Perforating Company
3033 South 166th Street
New Berlin, WI 53151–3555
(414) 786–2700
Fax: Please mail or call

3449

Business Information: McKey Perforating Company, established in 1954, is a small, family–owned business, providing design assisted products to OEM's; serving 35 different markets in approximately 450 specific end uses. Marketed product divisions include: construction equipment, agricultural equipment, automotive equipment, laundry equipment, and car and consumer stereo products. As Director of Sales, Mr. Elsinger supervises the sales force and handles internal sales activities and training. In addition, he is responsible for price setting, major client accounts, marketing, pricing, balances, and account based accounting. **Career Steps:** McKey Perforating Company: Director of Sales (1993–Present); National Sales Manager (1992–1993); Manager of New Business Development (1992); Regional Sales Manager (1992). **Education:** University of Wisconsin at Milwaukee, B.S. in Business (1975). **Personal:** Married to Julie Ann in 1985. Mr. Elsinger enjoys hiking, fishing, books, and travel.

Henry E. Hildebrand

President and Chief Executive Officer
Ideal Metals Group
268 Orenda Road
Brampton, Ontario L6T 4A9
(905) 456–3970
Fax: (905) 456–8691

3449

Business Information: Ideal Metals Group, traded on the Canadian Stock Exchange, is a distributor of metals nationwide. Established in 1953, Ideal Metals Group reports annual revenue of $150 million and currently employs 300 people. With twenty years experience in the paper and packaging industry,

Mr. Hildebrand joined the Company in 1992. Serving as President and Chief Executive Officer, he is responsible for all aspects of operations, including administration, marketing, and strategic planning. **Career Steps:** President and Chief Executive Officer, Ideal Metals Group (1992–Present); Vice President, Abitibi Price Inc. (1990–1992); President, Barber–Ellis (1988–1990); President, Price Daxion (1984–1988). **Associations & Accomplishments:** Director, Mississauga Opera Company; Director, National Association of Aluminum Distributors. **Personal:** Married to Grace in 1967. Two children: Jason and Julie. Mr. Hildebrand enjoys sports and travel during his leisure time.

Jeffrey L. Daniels
Midwest Regional Service Center Manager
ITW Buildex
320 Industrial Drive, Unit C
West Chicago, IL 60185
(708) 231–0071
Fax: (708) 231–0145

3452

Business Information: ITW Buildex is a manufacturer of fasteners, tools, and roofing products for the construction products industry. As Midwest Regional Services Center Manager, Mr. Daniels is responsible for inventory, storage, packaging, and distribution. Additionally, he handles all customer services for the Company, i.e., questions, comments and complaints. **Career Steps:** Midwest Regional Services Center Manager, ITW Buildex (1995–Present); Distribution Manager, Venture Stores (1993–1995); Midwest Consolidation Center Manager, Baxter Health Care Corporation (1991–1993). **Associations & Accomplishments:** Alpha Phi Alpha Fraternity; American Legion; Veteran Officer, United States Air Force. **Education:** Central Michigan University, M.B.A. (1989); Howard University, Bachelor of Business Administration. **Personal:** Married to Eugenia C. in 1986. Mr. Daniels enjoys running, racquetball, and golf.

Rick Fine
Product Manager
USM Corporation
400 Research Drive
Wilmington, MA 01887
(508) 657–4700 Ext. 232
Fax: (508) 658–7459

3452

Business Information: USM Corporation is a national manufacturer and importer of industrial fasteners used in paint brushes, lighting fixtures, tackless carpet strip, furniture, and many other products. The Corporation deals mainly in machine quality nails and import screws, bolts and washers. As Product Manager, Mr. Fine handles the selling and marketing of manufactured products. He also assists in the development of sales procedures and policies and the designing of new marketing strategies. **Career Steps:** Product Manager, USM Corporation (1993–1996); National Sales Manager, Cambridge–Lee Industries (1987–1990); National Sales Manager, Sentnel Specialty Products (1983–1987); National Sales Manager, Frelen Corporation (1981–1983). **Associations & Accomplishments:** Wire International Association; American Marketing Association; Specialty Tool & Fastener Association; American Brush Manufacturers Association; Beta Gamma Sigma Scholarship Society. **Education:** University of Michigan, MBA (1969); Babson College, BSBA (1967) **Personal:** Married to Harriet in 1969. Three children: Scott, Robyn, and Jeffrey. Mr. Fine enjoys reading.

John A. Herr
Director of Quality Assurance
Applied Bolting Technology Products, Inc.
P.O. Box 255, 101 Main St.
Ludlow, VT 05149
(802) 228–7390
Fax: (802) 228–7204
EMAIL: See Below

3452

Business Information: Applied Bolting Technology Products, Inc. is the second largest domestic manufacturer of direct tension indicating washers used in bridges and high steel buildings. International in scope, the Company sells to companies in Thailand, Korea, Canada, and Colombia. As Director of Quality Assurance, Mr. Herr is responsible for product design and all aspects of product and service quality. He establishes all systems, procedures, production, and training programs for the Company. Internet users can reach him via: abtpdti@souer.net. **Career Steps:** Director of Quality Assurance, Applied Bolting Technology Products, Inc. (1994–Present); Project Coordinator – Engineering, C.R. Bard – USCI Division (1988–1994); Production Supervisor, Continental Cable Company (1985–1988); Track Foreman, Boston and Maine R.R. (1976–1985). **Associations & Accomplishments:** CMI Certification, American Society of Quality Con-

trol; Society of Manufacturing Engineers. **Education:** Franklin Pierce College, B.A. magna cum laude (1973). **Personal:** One child: Aurora. Mr. Herr enjoys landscaping, carpentry, and weightlifting.

Mr. Joseph J. Maida
Vice President
Empire Silver Company
120 Hathaway Drive
Stratford, CT 06497–7361
(203) 378–1881
Fax: (203) 378–8763

3471

Business Information: Empire Silver Company is a manufacturing job shop specializing in silver electroplating. Established in 1946, Empire Silver Company reports annual revenue of $1 million and currently employs seven people. As Vice President, Mr. Maida is responsible for the oversight of all daily operations. **Career Steps:** Mr. Maida has been with the Empire Silver Company 25 years. He was promoted to Shop Foreman in 1978, General Manager in 1985, and Vice President in 1990. **Associations & Accomplishments:** American Electroplates and Surface Finishers Society; Awards & Recognition Association; Milford Riders Motorcycle Club; Main Street Riders Motorcycle Club; Harley Owners Group. **Education:** Fannie A. Smith Preparatory School, Stratford High School, Diploma (1974). **Personal:** Married to Gail in 1976. Two children: Joseph and Andrew. Mr. Maida is an avid motorcycle enthusiast, who enjoys collecting them as well as riding. His Harley Davidsons have won numerous awards and he still enjoys riding in supercross and motorcross competitions.

Thomas L. Marino
General Manager
Light Metals Coloring Company, Inc.
270 Spring Street
Southington, CT 06489–1517
(203) 621–0145 Ext: 226
Fax: (203) 621–6312

3471

Business Information: Light Metals Coloring Company, Inc. specializes in aluminum metal refinishing and anodizing. Established in 1945, Light Metals Coloring Company, Inc. currently employs 100 specialists and has an estimated annual revenue of $6 million. As General Manager, Mr. Marino is responsible for all aspects of operations for the Company. **Career Steps:** General Manager, Light Metals Coloring Company, Inc. (1994–Present); Director of Product Finishing, The Napier Company (1986–1994); Vice President, Technical Director, American Chemical Works Company (1980–1985); Laboratory Manager/Chemist, Sigmund Cohn Corporation (1975–1980). **Associations & Accomplishments:** Connecticut Business and Industry Association; Connecticut Metal Finishers Association; United States Representative in Europe, Manufacturers, Jewelers, and Silversmiths Association; American Electro–Platers and Surface Finishers Association. **Education:** University of New Haven, M.B.A. (1994); Regents College, SUNY – Albany, B.A. **Personal:** Married to Theresa in 1982. Two children: Thomas Edward and Catherine Elizabeth. Mr. Marino enjoys electronics, boating, and music.

Saud Algosaibi
Managing Director
Arabian Pipecoating Company Limited
106 Al Khobar
Al Khobar, Saudi Arabia 31952
966–3–8642666
Fax: 966–3–8940901

3479

Business Information: Arabian Pipecoating Company Limited, a family–owned enterprise, is an international manufacturer of coatings used for pipes and the Algosaibi Group (cans, can–end making, bottling, chemical manufacturing, insurance, banking), which has 28 different investments. As Managing Director, Mr. Algosaibi is responsible for the management of the Arabian Pipe Coating Group, as well as serving as Group Vice President of Ahmad Hamad Algosaibi & Brothers. Prior to these positions, he was involved in the financial and strategic planning of the Company businesses. **Career Steps:** Managing Director, Arabian Pipecoating Company Limited (Present); Ahmad Hamad Algosaibi & Bros.: Vice President and Director (1991–Present), Assistant Vice President (1989–1991), Investment Manager (1988–1989). **Associations & Accomplishments:** Industrial Committee, Kingdom of Saudi Arabia; Industrial Committee, Chamber of Commerce; Industrial Committee, Industry Eastern Province. **Education:** Saint Edward University – Austin, TX, B.A. in Finance (1988). **Personal:** Married to Abeer Alzaid in 1986.

Four children: Suha, Ghaliah, Farah, and Noura. Mr. Algosaibi enjoys reading.

Robert H. Comstock

Director of Operations – The Americas
Dexter Packaging Products
90 Carson Road
Birmingham, AL 35215
(205) 854–5454 Ext: 200
Fax: (205) 520–0206

3479

Business Information: Dexter Packaging Products is a leading producer of protective specialty coatings, utilized for cans and flexible packaging materials. International in scope, the Company distributes throughout North America, South America, Latin America, Europe, South Africa, the Middle East, Japan, Singapore, China and Australia. A Chemical Manufacturing Engineer working with some of the leading consumer products conglomerates for the past thirty years, Robert Comstock was recruited to his current position with Dexter Packaging in November of 1993. As Director of Operations, he oversees manufacturing and production operations for plant facilities in all the Americas. **Career Steps:** Director of Operations – The Americas, Dexter Packaging Products (1993–Present); Director of Manufacturing – Mexico, PPG Industries (1989–1993); Section Manager – Technical Support Operations, Procter & Gamble (1966–1989). **Associations & Accomplishments:** American Institute of Chemical Engineers; Engineer Council of Birmingham; Association of Professional Inventory Control Specialists; Business Council of Alabama; Coach, Birmingham Youth Hockey League; Coach, Gardendale First Baptist Church Roller Hockey League. **Education:** University of Tennessee, Graduate work (1988); Lehigh University, B.S. in Chemical Engineering **Personal:** Married to N. Edith in 1979. Four children: Craig, Patricia, Douglas and Michael Earle. Mr. Comstock enjoys hockey, boating, music and playing the guitar during his leisure time.

Ivan M. Faigen
President/Treasurer
Stainless Steel Coatings, Inc.
Box 1145, 835 Sterling Road
South Lancaster, MA 01561
(508) 365–1703
Fax: (508) 365–1704

3479

Business Information: Stainless Steel Coatings, Inc. is an establishment engaged in the manufacture and distribution of specialty anti–corrosive coatings for the Food and Drug Administration, maritime, and various other industries both nationally and internationally. Established in 1974, the Company employs twelve people and has estimated annual revenue of $3 million. As President/Treasurer, Mr. Faigen oversees all aspects of the Company. Concurrent with his present position, he is Vice President of D&M/Chu Technology, Inc., as well as President of Divecomm, Inc. (an underwater communications company), and President of Dispensing Technologies International Corporation (developer of a two–part computerized dispensing machine). **Career Steps:** President/Treasurer, Stainless Steel Coatings, Inc. (1974–Present); Vice President, D&M/Chu Technology, Inc. (1992–Present); President/Treasurer, Chu Associates, Inc. (1955–1992); President, Divecomm, Inc. (1991–Present); President, Dispensing Technologies International Corporation (Present). **Associations & Accomplishments:** Senior Life Member, Institute of Electronics and Electrical Engineers; Board of Governors, Academy of Applied Science. **Education:** Northeastern University, M.S.E.E. (1953); Carnegie Institute of Technology, B.S.E.E. (1948). **Personal:** Married to Soma M. in 1949. Three children: Martha, Ronn, and Michael. Mr. Faigen enjoys scuba, snorkeling, gardening, music, and reading.

Henry Stewart
Quality Control Manager
Advanced Industrial Coating
581 Dado Street
San Jose, CA 95131–1207
(408) 383–9480
Fax: (408) 383–0854
EMAIL: See Below

3479

Business Information: Advanced Industrial Coatings, specialists in Fluoropolymer Coatings, is a national manufacturer of powder coating, fluoropolymer coating, and nylon applications. As Quality Control Manager, Mr. Stewart is responsible for the direction of quality control, scheduling, pro–active programs, and various operations management functions, in addition to overseeing a staff of more than 30. Internet users can reach him via: HSTEW95812@AOL.COM. **Career Steps:** Quality Control Manager, Advanced Industrial Coating, Inc. (1995–Present); General Manager, A & I Chemicals

(1992–1995); Environmental Compliance Director, Tri–City Circuits (1991–1992); Waste Treatment/Process Engineer, Data Circuit Systems (1990–1991). **Education:** DeAnza College (1995); Georgia College, University of California Extension. **Personal:** Married to Alexandra in 1995. Mr. Stewart enjoys golf, reading, and continuing his education.

Gary L. Zent
Strategic Materials Manager
Stoody Deloro Stellite
P.O. Box 807
Goshen, IN 46527
(219) 533–5127
Fax: (219) 534–3417

3479

Business Information: Stoody Deloro Stellite is an international producer of alloy coating powder, castings, PM parts, welding rod and wire. Mr. Zent has served in various positions with SDS since 1985, most recently promoted to Strategic Materials Manager in 1995. He is presently responsible for purchasing raw materials (e.g., elemental metals) such as cobalt, nickel, and chrome for three North American plants. **Career Steps:** Stoody Deloro Stellite: Strategic Materials Manager (1995–Present), Material Manager (1985–1995); Planner, Wear Technologies – Cabot Corporation (1978–1985). **Associations & Accomplishments:** American Production and Inventory Control Society. **Education:** Ball State University, B.S. (1977). **Personal:** Married to Monica in 1987. Two children: Joe and Melissa. Mr. Zent enjoys golf.

Alton G. Drury
Chairman of the Board
Talon Manufacturing Co.
Martinsburg, WV
(612) 427–1934
Fax: (612) 427–1934

3482

Business Information: Talon Manufacturing Co. is an ammunition demilitarization company, whose function is to take apart, recycle, and load small caliber (pistol and rifle) ammunition. The Company has six locations, including a new corporate office recently opened in Martinsburg, West Virginia. A former president of the Company, Mr. Drury was appointed as Chairman of the Board in 1994. Serving as an executive consultant to the Company's new president, he provides advice in management and technical areas, as well as helping in the setting up of operations. **Career Steps:** Talon Manufacturing Co.: Chairman of the Board (1994–Present), President (1992–1993); President, Shamrock Services (1989–1992); Technical Director, Federal Cartridge Co. (1975–1989). **Associations & Accomplishments:** Anoke–Hennepin District II Board of Education; American Defense Preparedness Association. **Education:** Montana State University, B.S. in Chemical Engineering (1960); Lincoln Institute, Degree in Industrial Management. **Personal:** Married to Mary in 1955. Three children: Claude, Mark, and Kathleen. Mr. Drury enjoys trap shooting, and riding motorcycles.

Richard C. McEntee
Director of Marketing
Marion Power Shovel Company
617 West Center Street
Marion, OH 43302–3509
(614) 383–5211
Fax: (614) 382–6773

3483

Business Information: Marion Power Shovel Company, established in 1884, designs, manufactures, and sells large capital goods (mining shovels, walking draglines, etc.) to the surface mining industry. With approximately 525 employees, the Company boasts annual income in excess of $118 million. As Director of Marketing, Mr. McEntee directs the Division's activities in Russia, India, and Japan, as well as directs the global marketing activities for new equipment. **Career Steps:** Marion Power Shovel Company: Director of Marketing (1994–Present), Manager of Joint Ventures (1986–1990); President, SDC Corporation (1988–1994). **Associations & Accomplishments:** AIME; Junior Achievement; Dublin Coffman High School Booster Group. **Education:** Murray State University, B.S. (1969). **Personal:** Married to Patricia in 1968. Two children: Randy and Kristin. Mr. McEntee enjoys golf, soccer, high school basketball and soccer booster.

Michelle Von Robinson
Manager – Personnel Accounting Benefits and Banking
Lockheed Martin Specialty Components, Inc.
P.O. Box 2908
Largo, FL 34649
(813) 541–8210
Fax: (813) 545–6022

3483

Business Information: Lockheed Martin Specialty Components, Inc. — a subsidiary of international aerospace technology conglomerate Lockheed Martin Corporation — currently under assignment as a Department of Energy contractor, is now in the process of transitioning into private sector business for the production of low volume, high technology environmental testing and precision machining projects. Serving in various accounting and financial management capacities for Lockheed Martin subsidiaries since 1989, Michelle Von Robinson was appointed Manager of Personnel Accounting Benefits and Banking for LMSC's Largo, Florida plant in 1995. In this capacity, she is responsible for management, design and implementation of all policies, procedures and systems for payroll, employee benefits and Company banking requirements. **Career Steps:** Lockheed Martin Specialty Components, Inc.: Manager of Personnel Accounting Benefits and Banking (1995–Present), Advanced Benefit Analyst (1992–1994); Tax Specialist, Lockheed Martin Electronics and Missiles (1989–1992). **Associations & Accomplishments:** International Foundation of Employee Benefits (1993–1996); International Society of Certified Employee Benefit Specialists (1995–1996); Suncoast Human Resources Management Association (1996). **Education:** Auburn University, B.S. in Business (1989); Certified Public Accountant; Certified Employee Benefit Specialist (1996). **Personal:** Ms. Robinson enjoys theater, aerobics and snow skiing.

Michael J. Smith
President and Chief Executive Officer
Investment Arms
1876 Horsecreek Road
Cheyenne, WY 82009–9342
(307) 635–2241
Fax: (307) 638–4043

3484

Business Information: Investment Arms is an international marketer, developer, and distributor of premiere–grade commemorative and limited edition firearms. As Chief Executive Officer, Mr. Smith is responsible for all aspects of operations, including administration, contract negotiations, training and employee management. **Career Steps:** Chief Executive Officer, Investment Arms (1993–Present); Patrolman, Cheyenne Police Department (1991–1994); General Manager, Cheyenne Trading Post (1988–1991). **Education:** Ricks College, A.A.; Attended: Regis University (1993). **Personal:** Married to Deana R. in 1986. Five children: Michael, Brittney, Jakeb, Kaleb, and Ciara. Mr. Smith enjoys hunting, fishing, writing, speaking on self–motivation and visioneering.

Arie P. Bregman
General Manager
Neles–Jamesbury, Inc.
1 Polito Drive
Shrewsbury, MA 01545
(508) 799–6190
Fax: (508) 799–6497

3491

Business Information: Neles–Jamesbury, Inc. specializes in the design, manufacture, sales, and service of valves for industrial applications. As General Manager, Mr. Bregman oversees service and repair for all North American service centers. He is also responsible for administrative duties, client services, and public relations. **Career Steps:** Neles–Jamesbury, Inc.: General Manager (1996–Present), Marketing Manager/ Pulp and Paper (1995–1996), Plant Manager (1990–1995), Chief Engineer (1982–1990). **Associations & Accomplishments:** Instrument Society of America; American Society of Mechanical Engineers. **Education:** Worcester Polytechnic Institute M.S.M.E. (1996); Lowell Technological Institute, B.S.M.E. (1975)' Repola Business School, Pori, Finland, Business Management (1994). **Personal:** Married to Ona in 1975. Two children: Eric and Ashley. Mr. Bregman enjoys golf, downhill skiing, and tennis.

Sean Natarjan
International Director
Universal Valve Company, Inc.
478 Schiller Street
Elizabeth, NJ 07206–2113
(908) 351–0606
Fax: (913) 268–5284
EMAIL: See Below

3491

Business Information: Universal Valve Company, Inc. manufactures valves and fittings for service stations and the oil and petroleum industries around the world. As International Director, Mr. Natarjan is responsible for all international business sales, marketing, and operations. Internet users may reach him via: seann36@aol.com **Career Steps:** International Director, Universal Valve Company, Inc. (1995–Present); Marley Pump Company: Director, Asia–Pacific (1993–1995), Managing Director – Marley Pump Company Asia P/L (1990–1993), Marketing Manager (1986–1990). **Associations & Accomplishments:** International Chamber of Commerce; Vietnam Chamber of Commerce. **Education:** Rockhurst College, M.B.A. (1985); University of Calcutta, India, B.S. in Economics. **Personal:** Married to Diana in 1982. Two children: Joy and Kelly. Mr. Natarjan enjoys cars, reading, and travel.

Kevin R. Peterson
Marketing Manager
Salina Vortex Corporation
3024 Arnold Avenue
Salina, KS 67401–8105
(913) 825–7177
Fax: (913) 825–7194
EMail: See Below

3491

Business Information: Salina Vortex Corporation is a manufacturer of slide gates and diverter valves for the handling of dry bulk materials (plastics, minerals, chemicals, grain, fibers, foodstuffs) for many Fortune 500 companies. As Marketing Manager, Mr. Peterson is responsible for all aspects of marketing for the Company, including marketing strategy, layout and design, photography, statistics, press releases, writing and publications, and product sales. Internet users can reach him via: krpeterson@salnet.org. **Career Steps:** Marketing Manager, Salina Vortex Corporation (1995–Present); Grain Strategies Consultant, Wright–Lorenz Grain Company (1987–1995); Vice President of Marketing, Producer Marketing, Inc. (1983–1987); Industrial Sales Manager, Waters True Value, Inc. (1981–1983). **Associations & Accomplishments:** American Marketing Association; Saline County Marketing Association; IFPA Photographers Association; Awarded Silver Beaver, National Boy Scouts of America; Published author; Who's Who in American Colleges & Universities; Who's Who Among Rising Young Americans; Who's Who Among Photographers. **Education:** Bethany College, B.A. in Business/Economics (1973). **Personal:** Married to Lynn in 1972. Two children: Kip and Kendra. Mr. Peterson enjoys photography, softball, volleyball, and golf.

Bert O. Smith
Director of Valve Automation Division
Caltrol, Inc.
2011 East Financial Way
Glendora, CA 91741–0809
(818) 852–3519
Fax: (818) 963–9629

3491

Business Information: Caltrol, Inc. is a manufacturer and distributor of valves and services. Products include control, relief, and on/off valves. Caltrol, Inc. runs a subsidiary company called Basin Valve Company. Established in 1947, Caltrol, Inc. currently employs 127 people. A management executive with Caltrol since 1987, Mr. Smith was appointed to his current position in November 1995. As Director, he oversees all operational aspects for Caltrol's Valve Automation Division. **Career Steps:** Caltrol, Inc.: Director of Valve Automation Division (1995–Present), Sales Director (1993–1995), Branch Manager (1987–1993). **Associations & Accomplishments:** Instrument Society of America; Southern California Metal Association. **Education:** California State University – Los Angeles (1971). **Personal:** Married to Tebbe Smith in 1976. Three children: Todd, Shelley, and Jamie. Mr. Smith enjoys golf, skiing, and weight lifting.

Andrew C. Long
Production Manager
Vemco Corporation
305 South Acacia Street
San Dimas, CA 91773–2925
(909) 599–6745 Ext: 206
Fax: (909) 599–1440

3492

Business Information: Vemco Corporation, Go, Inc. Division, is an international manufacturer of pressure regulators for the distribution of gases and liquids utilized in the Semi–conductor and Petro–chemical markets. Other product venues include the manufacture of drafting equipment and artificial windows. As Production Manager, Mr. Long is responsible for the oversight of manufacturing components and shipments of the finished product. **Career Steps:** Vemco Corporation: Production Manager (1994–Present), Industrial Engineer (1992–1994); Communications Technician, NTCC Long Beach (U.S. Navy) (1989–1992); U.S. Navy (1982–1988). **Associations & Accomplishments:** U.S. Naval Reserve: Petty Officer First Class Radioman (5 years active duty and 9 years reserve duty); Member, Veterans of Foreign Wars (VFW). **Personal:** Married to Jasmine in 1986. Three children: Glenn, Anna Marie, and Leah Michelle. Mr. Long enjoys sports, travel, and camping.

Terry A. Peterson

Director
Sargent Control and Aerospace
5675 West Burlingame Road
Tucson, AZ 85743–9453
(520) 744–1000
Fax: (520) 744–9390

3492

Business Information: Sargent Control and Aerospace manufactures hydraulic control valves and servo control valves. Mr. Peterson has served in various supervisory positions with Sargent Controls, most recently promoted to Director of Operations and Engineering in 1995. He is presently responsible for overseeing all designs, construction, and production, contractor interface, and various administrative functions. **Career Steps:** Sargent Control and Aerospace: Director (1995–Present), Production Manager (Jan.1995–Oct.1995), Quality Assurance Manager (1994–1995), Manufacturing Engineering Manager (1992–1994). **Associations & Accomplishments:** Society for Manufacturing Engineers; American Society for Quality Control; American Welding Society. **Personal:** Married to Cyndie in 1994. Four children: Dustin, Ryan, Brandon, and Angel. Mr. Peterson enjoys golf and softball.

Andre E. Papillon

Group Leader of Advanced Product Engineering
Associated Spring
10 Main Street
Bristol, CT 06010–6527
(860) 583–1331
Fax: (860) 589–3934

3493

Business Information: Associated Spring, part of the Barnes Group, is a a publicly–owned company specializing in the manufacture and design of precision springs, metal forms, and subassemblies for automotive, telecommunications, industrial, and medical markets. International in scope, Associated Spring spans Brazil, Mexico, Europe, and Canada. As Group Leader of Advanced Product Engineering, Mr. Papillon is responsible for the direction of the corporate product engineering group, consisting of M.S. and Ph.D. engineers who define the systems, tools, and training necessary to drive divisional product engineering into a future driven by technology. He also conducts internal presentations and seminars for training and the Board of Directors. Internet users can reach him via: andre@asbg.com **Career Steps:** Group Leader/Senior Product Design Engineer, Associated Spring, Bristol, CT (1992–Present); Applications Development Engineer, ICI Polyurethanes, Sterling Heights, MI (1990–1992); Project Engineer, ICI Rubicon, Geismar, LA (1989–1990). **Associations & Accomplishments:** Society of Manufacturing Engineers; Tau Beta Pi; Phi Beta Kappa; Society for Biomaterials; Hartford Chorale, Hartford, CT; Volunteer: Special Olympics; United Way; Various political campaigns. **Education:** Dartmouth College, M.S. in Biomedical Engineering (1990); University of California, Irvine, B.S. in Mechanical Engineering (1986). **Personal:** Mr. Papillon enjoys tennis, baseball card collecting, drawing, bicycling, travel, and U.S. History.

Mr. Glenn D. Mason

Branch Manager
McJunkin Corporation
2221 Westgate Drive
Rock Springs, WY 82901
(307) 382–7101
Fax: (307) 362–2427

3494

Business Information: McJunkin Corporation, a third generation family–owned company, is one of the world's leading supplier of pipes, valves and fittings, as well as electrical supplies. Currently, McJunkin Corporation is comprised of more than 80 branches and sales offices located in principal industrial centers, with more than 1,400 employees. The principal marketing divisions are Tubular Products, Stainless and Corrosion–resistant Products, Valves and Fittings, and Oil and Gas Suppliers. McJunkin also supplies a wide range of fabricating, manufacturing and engineering services in job shops located in Charleston and Nitro, West Virginia. In addition to these services, McJunkin also offers a variety of electrical products at eleven branches in Kentucky, Illinois, West Virginia, Ohio and Pennsylvania. In 1992, McJunkin's Electrical Division contracted with Goro to be the French company's sole distributor in the United States for a new line of belt fasteners. Principal industries served include: chemical, petrochemical, power generation and utilities, paper, refining, mining, metals, oil and gas production and distribution, engineering and construction. The Corporation has three subsidiaries: McJunkin Controls, Inc. (specializing in valve automation and other valve services, including quarter turn repair), McJunkin Appalachian Oil Field Supply Company (serving the oil and gas industries in West Virginia, Pennsylvania, Virginia, Kentucky, Ohio, Tennessee and Michigan); and McJunkin–Republic Supply Corporation (serving the Western United States). With corporate headquarters in Charleston, West Virginia, McJunkin Corporation reports annual revenue of $3 million company–wide and currently employs five people in the Rock Springs, Wyoming offices. As Branch Manager of McJunkin–Republic Supply Company (subsidiary of McJunkin), Mr. Mason is responsible for the oversight of all operations of branch locations and reporting conditions to the home office. **Career Steps:** Branch Manager, McJunkin Corporation (1985–Present); Sales Manager, Windustrial Company (1974–1985); Office Manager, Mid–Mountain Supply (1972–1974). **Associations & Accomplishments:** Sterling Who's Who; White Mountain Lion's Club; Council #2441 Knights of Columbus; BPOE #624 Elks Club; PVF Roundtable. **Education:** University of Wyoming (1968); FDIC Banking School; Various trade and training seminar schools. **Personal:** Married to Jeanne in 1961. Two children: Richard and James. Mr. Mason enjoys golf and any sporting game.

Sohel Anwar Ahmed Sareshwala

Materials, Purchasing & Quality Manager
Lokring Corporation
396 Hatch Drive
Foster City, CA 94404–1106
(415) 578–9999
Fax: (415) 578–0216

3494

Business Information: Lokring Corporation is a designer, manufacturer, and distributor of proprietary and patented tube and pipe fittings. A Mechanical and Industrial Engineer with over ten years experience in design, manufacturing and quality engineering, Mr. Sareshwala joined Lokring in 1988. Appointed as Materials and Purchasing Manager in 1994, he is responsible for the management of quality and engineering prototype, in addition to the management of materials, production and purchasing. **Career Steps:** Lokring Corporation: Materials, Purchasing & Quality Manager (1994–1996), Materials and Production Manager (1993–1994), Engineering Project Manager (1988–1992). **Associations & Accomplishments:** Three United States patents for designing Lokring Fittings; Senior Member, Society of Manufacturing Engineers; Senior Member, Institute of Industrial Engineers; APICS; Life Member, Tau Beta Pi. **Education:** San Jose State University, M.S. in Industrial and Systems Engineering (1988); Gujarat University (India), B.S. in Mechanical Engineering (1985). **Personal:** Married to Asfiya in 1989. Two children: Sidra and Zoya. Mr. Sareshwala enjoys cricket and table tennis.

James S. Campbell

Sales Manager
Maryland Specialty Wire, Inc.
100 Cockeysville Road
Cockeysville Hunt Valley, MD 21030
(410) 785–2500
Fax: Please mail or call

3496

Business Information: A subsidiary of Handy & Harmen, Maryland Specialty Wire, Inc. is a manufacturer of stainless steel and nickel based alloy wire. Established in 1945, Maryland Specialty Wire currently employs 200 people in the New Jersey, New York, Baltimore and England plants. The Company reports assets of over $44 million. As Sales Manager, Mr. Campbell is responsible for all aspects of customer service. The Company was ISO 9000 certified in less than 13 months, the result of Mr. Campbell's hard work and committment. **Career Steps:** Maryland Specialty Wire, Inc.: Sales Manager (1995–Present), Salesman (1994–1995), Project Coordinator (1993–1994), Management Trainee (1990–1993). **Associations & Accomplishments:** Roanoke College Alumni Association. **Education:** Roanoke College, B.B.A. (1989); Johns Hopkins University, graduate courses. **Personal:** Mr. Campbell enjoys swimming and spending time with his family.

Stephen E. Hall

Vice President/General Manager
Alcatel Wire & Cable
25 Ramble Wood Road
Toronto, Ontario M3C 3J4
(416) 467–4073
Fax: (416) 467–4065

3496

Business Information: Alcatel Wire & Cable is a manufacturer of wire and cable for Canada, the United States, and off-shore countries. As Vice President/General Manager, Mr. Hall is responsible for all aspects of Company operations, including production, human resources, accounting, and sales. He oversees all American operations. **Career Steps:** Alcatel Wire & Cable: Vice President/General Manager (1994–Present), Operations Manager (1992–1994), Planning Manager (1989–1992), Director, Information Technology (1989). **Education:** York University, M.B.A. (1986); McMaster University, Bachelor of Engineering (1975). **Personal:** Mr. Hall enjoys golf.

John R. Scott

Director of Operations
CORELLA ELECTRIC Wire & Cable, Inc.
4910 West Roosevelt
Phoenix, AZ 85043
(602) 272–9932
Fax: (602) 272–1376
EMAIL: Oraibi@MSN.com

3496

Business Information: CORELLA ELECTRIC Wire & Cable, Inc., ISO 9002 Certified, is a manufacturer of telecommunication wire for such companies as AT&T, Packard Bell, Bell South, and other telephone companies nationwide. As Plant Manager/Director of Operations, Mr. Scott is responsible for the management of all Company operations, including profit & loss concerns, personnel, plant operations, purchasing, and transportation. Concurrently, he serves as an Instructor of Management and Business courses at Rio Salado Community College and at a satellite campus of Park College in Kansas City, Missouri. **Career Steps:** Director of Operations, CORELLA ELECTRIC Wire & Cable, Inc. (1993–Present); Instructor, Rio Salado Community College (Present); Instructor, Park College Satellite Campus (Present); U.S. Air Force: Military Officer (1979–1993), Military NCO (1972–1979). **Associations & Accomplishments:** The Wire Association – International; Air Force Association; The Retired Officer Association; ORSA/TIMS, now Informs. **Education:** University of Oklahoma, Master's Degree. **Personal:** Married to Teresa in 1985. Three children: Adrienne, Patrick, and Laura. Mr. Scott enjoys golf and teaching.

Thomas Anthony Diemer

Senior Design Engineer
Parker Hannifin
124 Columbia Street
Clyde, NY 14433–1049
(315) 923–2311 Ext. 313
Fax: (315) 423–9306

3498

Business Information: Parker Hannifin is a manufacturer of stainless steel instrumentation tubing fittings, specializing in the manufacture of fuel nozzles for jet aircraft in the aerospace industry. As Senior Design Engineer, Mr. Diemer is responsible for the management of the CF6 Engine Family Nozzle line. **Career Steps:** Team Leader and Senior Design Engineer, Parker Hannifin (1992–Present); Senior Design Engineer, Sundstrand Corporation (1985–1992); Mechanical Engineer, Government, Naval Weapons Support Center (1983–1985). **Associations & Accomplishments:** Society of Automotive Engineers. **Education:** University of Wisconsin – Platteville, B.S. in Mechanical Engineering, minor in Math (1983). **Personal:** Married to Mary Ellen in 1990. Three children: Ryan, Becky and Sean. Mr. Diemer enjoys refinishing old furniture and reading science fiction.

Dean Sarah Walter–Lafferty

Personal Computer Coordinator
Penn Machine Works
100 Bethel Road
Aston, PA 19014
(610) 497–3300 Ext. 591
Fax: (610) 497–3325

3498

Business Information: Pennsylvania Machine Works, Inc. is a manufacturer of small high pressure forged pipe fitting in a variety of alloys. The company conducts business in the USA, Mexico, South America, Canada, and the Middle East. As Personal Computer Coordinator, Ms. Walter–Lafferty is responsible for PC related hardware, software, and peripheral devices, repair, installations, upgrades, troubleshooting, solution planning, research and development, purchasing, and AS/400 client access connectivity. **Career Steps:** Personal Computer Coordinator, Penn Machine Works (1992–Present); Founder DP Program/Lead Instructor, CHI Institute (1990–1992); Director of Education, Tracey Warner (1990). **Associations & Accomplishments:** Officer, Order of Eastern Star; Board of Advisors, Widener University; Student Alumni Liaison for Widener University; Christ Church Episcopal; Our Lady of Perpetual Help; Delta Phi Epsilon Alumni; Delaware Valley Users Group. **Education:** Widener University: B.S. (1984), M.Ed. (1988). **Personal:** Married to Ronald C. Jr. in 1991. One child: Jaimie Lillian. Ms. Walter–Lafferty enjoys gardening, cooking, collecting clothes for the homeless, exercise, friends, and attending water babies with her daughter.

Dixie D. Wilcox
Vice President
Bend It, Inc.
P.O. Box 752024
Houston, TX 77275–2024
(713) 991–0745
Fax: (713) 991–0827

3498

Business Information: Bend It, Inc. is a custom pipe–bending and coiling concern located in Houston, Texas with a staff of 15. As Vice President, Ms. Wilcox is responsible for the scheduling of all jobs and making sure the job is done correctly and finished in a timely manner. Other responsibilities include invoicing, management of personnel, customer relations, and shop supervision. **Career Steps:** Vice President, Bend It, Inc. (1992–Present); Supervisor, U.S. Government (1990–1992). **Associations & Accomplishments:** Kiwanis Club of Pearland; PL Citizens Police Academy Alumni Association. **Personal:** Married to Jim in 1986. Three children: Bridget, Jamie, and Kurtis. Ms. Wilcox enjoys her grandchildren and bowling.

Sandy Coffman
Operations Manager
Berlin Packaging
907 NW Platte Valley Drive
Riverside, MO 64150
(816) 587–5333
Fax: (816) 587–6269

3499

Business Information: Berlin Packaging is the largest distributor of steel, plastic and glass containers in the United States with 15 locations nationwide. As Operations Manager, Ms. Coffman is responsible for asset management, customer service and warehouse supervision, budget oversight, and daily operations. **Career Steps:** Operations Manager, Berlin Packaging (1991–Present); Operations Manager, Packaging West (1981–1991); Customer Service, Avery Label Systems (1975–1978). **Associations & Accomplishments:** Humane Society; American Society for the Prevention of Cruelty to Animals (ASPCA); National Honor Society. **Education:** East High School, Diploma (1968). **Personal:** Ms. Coffman enjoys movies, dancing, cat shows, and traveling.

Michael J. Lubas
Manager of Production Technology
Carpenter Technology Corporation – Steel Division
P.O. Box 14662
Reading, PA 19612–4662
(612) 208–2057
Fax: (610) 208–2462

3499

Business Information: Carpenter Technology Corporation – Steel Division is an integrated producer and distributor of specialty metal–alloyed products and materials (i.e., stainless, hi–temperature alloys, ceramics). Serving in various managerial capacities for CTC's Steel Division since 1986, Michael Lubas was appointed Manager of Production Technology in 1994. In this capacity, he is responsible for identifying technology which could be useful to the Company in the production of specialty metals, as well as managing teams to implement new technology. **Career Steps:** Carpenter Technology Corporation – Steel Division: Manager of Production Technology (1994–Present), Manager of Wire & Bar Finishing (1991–1994), Manager of Bar Finishing (1986–1991). **Associations & Accomplishments:** American Iron and Steel Engineers; Chairman and Vice Chairman, Exeter Township Planning Commission; Coach Exeter TWP Athletics for Girls (softball, basketball). **Education:** LaSalle University – Philadelphia, Pennsylvania, B.S. in Industrial Management (1969); Attended various professional and collegiate non–degree courses. **Personal:** Married to Martha S. in 1982. Two children: John M. and Susanna L. Mr. Lubas enjoys fishing, hunting, trap–shooting, skiing, and woodworking.

Thomas J. Manenti
Senior Vice President
Mitek Industries, Inc.
14515 North Outer Forty
Chesterfield, MO 63017
(314) 434–1200
Fax: (314) 434–5343

3499

Business Information: Mitek Industries, Inc. is one of the world's leading manufacturers of building components; with primary focus on the manufacture of galvanized steel connector plates utilized in roof truss production and flooring systems. The Company also provides software, engineering services and product support equipment. International in scope, Mitek has eight (8) facilities in the U.S. and ten (10) in various overseas locations. Established in 1956, Mitek reports annual revenue of $110 million and currently employs 450 people. With nine years in the building manufacturing sector, Mr. Manenti was appointed Senior Vice President for Mitek in 1991. As such, he is responsible for the oversight and overall administration for sales and marketing activities, as well as the supervision of all sales representatives. **Career Steps:** Mitek Industries, Inc.: Senior Vice President (1994–Present), Division Vice President (1991–1994); Gang–Nail Systems, Inc.: President (1988–1990), Vice President of Sales (1986–1988). **Associations & Accomplishments:** Promise Keepers International; Fellowship of Christian Athletes; Delta Kappa Epsilon Fraternity; Advisory Council, Rockwood School District Curriculum; Society for American Baseball Research; Published in Industrial Trade Magazines on marketing and sales of connector plates for the industry. **Education:** Nova University, B.S. (1985); Attended: Wharton School, Strategic Management; Rutgers University, Accounting. **Personal:** Married to Kathy in 1979. Two children: Joseph and Elena. Mr. Manenti enjoys baseball memorabilia, drums, golf, and church drama team.

John H. Naybor

President
Digitel Network Services, Inc.
1335 Old Norcross Road
Lawrenceville, GA 30245
(770) 682–4600
Fax: (770) 682–4500
EMAIL: See Below

3499

Business Information: Digitel Network Services, Inc. is a developer of hybrid fiber coax telecommunication systems for use in the Information Super Highway. Joining Digitel Network Services, Inc. as President in 1994, Mr. Naybor is responsible for developing new business and overseeing the day–to–day performance of existing projects. Internet users can reach him via: Digitel@Mindspring.com. **Career Steps:** President, Digitel Network Services, Inc. (1994–Present); Vice President of Marketing, CADD Services Group, Inc. (1993–1994); Vice President of Marketing, C.I.S., Inc. (1990–1993); Director of Sales, A.D.S., Inc. (1984–1990). **Associations & Accomplishments:** Society of Cable Television Engineers. **Education:** University of Hartford. **Personal:** Two children: John Jr. and Jaclyn.

Gregory J. Olsen
Manager of Special Projects
CBI Services, Inc.
St. George Road and RR 50 North
Bourbonnais, IL 60914
(815) 933–2200
Fax: (815) 933–0863

3499

Business Information: CBI Services, Inc. specializes in design fabrication and erection of metal plate products; providing designs to meet its clientele's specific needs. Working with the manufacturing department, Greg Olsen is the coordinator of non–standard contracts and specifications with engineering, purchasing and construction of specially designed products. **Career Steps:** CBI Services, Inc.: Manager of Special Projects (1992–Present), Production Superintendent (1982–1992); Manufacturing Expert, CBI/GBC Joint Venture – Australia (1981–1982). **Associations & Accomplishments:** Registered Professional Engineer – Illinois. **Education:** Illinois Institute of Technology, B.S.M.E. (1969). **Personal:** Married to Kathleen in 1995. Two children: Elizabeth and Timothy. Mr. Olsen enjoys baseball, golf, and bowling.

James G. Petri
Engineering Manager
Pacific Coast Technologies
434 Old Station Rd.
Wenatchee, WA 98801
(509) 664–8000
Fax: (509) 663–5039

3499

Business Information: Pacific Coast Technologies is a designer and manufacturer of hermetic, aluminum compatible connectors. Additionally, the Company manufactures and assembles aluminum and metal–matrix hermetic packaging. As Engineering Manager, Mr. Petri manages the engineering department and provides technical support to the engineering staff. **Career Steps:** Engineering Manager, Pacific Coast Technologies (1994–Present); Design Engineer, Texas Instruments – Defense Systems (1989–1994). **Associations & Accomplishments:** North Central Washington Society of Professional Engineers; Tau Beta Pi; Pi Tau Sigma; Texas Tech University Century Club. **Education:** University of Texas – Austin, M.S.in Mechanical Engineering (1989); Texas Tech University, B.S. in Mechanical Engineering (1987). **Personal:** Mr. Petri enjoys snow skiing, hiking, cycling, and fly–fishing.

Kevin M. Roche
Controller
Haven Manufacturing
370 Sterling Industrial Park
Brunswick, GA 31525
(912) 265–7536
Fax: (912) 264–9001

3499

Business Information: Haven Manufacturing, established in 1956, is a manufacturer of tube cutting machinery. Located in Brunswick, Georgia, the Company provides tube cutting machinery to the automotive and other industries. As Controller, Mr. Roche oversees all aspects of accounting, financial reporting, taxes, payroll, 401K administration, cost accounting, and human resource management. **Career Steps:** Controller, Haven Manufacturing (1995–Present); Auditor, Price Waterhouse (1994–1995); Accountant, Pioneer Group (1992–1994). **Education:** Boston University, B.S.B.A. (1992). **Personal:** Married to Michelle in 1996. Mr. Roche enjoys outdoor activities, reading, water sports, tennis, and golf.

Samuel J. Thomas
Vice President of International Sales
Polyken Pipeline Coating
15 Hampshire St.
Mansfield, MA 02048–1139
(508) 261–6222
Fax: (508) 261–6271

3499

Business Information: Polyken Pipeline Coating specializes in the manufacture of anti–corrosion pipeline coatings utilized by the oil, gas and water industries worldwide. Polyken is a subsidiary of Kendall, an international medical products conglomerate. Serving in various managerial capacities for Polyken since 1979, Samuel Thomas was appointed as Vice President of International Sales in 1994. In this capacity, he is responsible for new business development, expanding sales efforts worldwide, and ensuring profitability of the company. **Career Steps:** Polyken Pipeline Coating: Vice President of International Sales (1994–Present), Vice President of Marketing (1989–1994), Director of Marketing (1986–1989), Manager of Research and Development (1979–1982). **Associations & Accomplishments:** National Association of Corrosion Engineers; American Waterworks Association; USA – Russian/CIS Trade and Economic Council; International Pipeline and Offshore Contractors Association; Boy Scouts of America – Eagle Scout. **Education:** University of Massachusetts, M.S. in Plastics (1974); Norwich University, B.S. in Chemistry (1967). **Personal:** Married to Susan Stemporzewski in 1990. Mr. Thomas enjoys sailing, skiing, and golf.

Mr. Danny R. White
Marketing and Sales Manager
Lanxide Electronic Components L.P.
1300 Marrows Roads
Newark, DE 19714
(302) 456–6203
Fax: (302) 456–6223

3499

Business Information: Lanxide Electronic Components L.P. is a manufacturer of metal matrix composite products for thermal management and structural electronic applications. Established in 1990, Lanxide Electronic Components L.P. reports annual revenue in excess of $3 million and currently employs 30 people. As Marketing and Sales Manager, Mr.

White is responsible for the oversight and management of sales and marketing matters, as well as traveling and teaching sales methods on behalf of the Company. **Career Steps:** Marketing and Sales Manager, Lanxide Electronic Components L.P. (1990–Present); Lanxide Corporation: Market Development Specialist (1988–1990), Member of Technical Staff (1985–1988). **Associations & Accomplishments:** International Society of Hybrid Microelectronics; International Electronic Packaging Society; Phi Kappa Phi Honor Fraternity; Masonic Lodge. **Education:** Purdue University, Ph.D. (1985), M.S. (1980), B.S. (1978). **Personal:** Married to Carol Lewis–White in 1992. Mr. White enjoys restoring antique cars, beekeeping and computers.

Phyllis K. Yollin
Purchasing Manager
Palmer International, Inc.
P.O. Box 8
Worcester, PA 19490–0008
(610) 584–3245
Fax: (610) 584–4870

3499

Business Information: Palmer International, Inc. is a chemical manufacturer for the automotive industry (friction particles). The Company is privately held with 3 locations and 90 employees. As Purchasing Manager, Ms. Yollin is responsible for all aspects of Company purchasing. She is directly responsible for three people. **Career Steps:** Purchasing Manager, Palmer International, Inc. (1994–Present); Purchasing Manager, Glenco Star Refrigeration (1992–1994); Purchasing Assistant, C.W. Thomas, Inc. (1989–1992); Purchasing Assistant, Jomac, Inc. (1980–1989). **Associations & Accomplishments:** Philadelphia Chapter – Alzheimer Association. **Education:** Attended: Pennsylvania State University. **Personal:** Four children: Cathy, Michelle, Patti, and Diane. Ms. Yollin enjoys singing, sewing, and gardening.

3500 Industrial Machinery and Equipment

Alfredo R. Collado

President
IMPSA do Brasil
Rua Florida 1821 Brooklin Novo
Sao Paulo SP, Brazil 04565–001
55–11–5505–425
Fax: 55–11–5505–176

3511

Business Information: IMPSA do Brazil – is an international designer and manufacturer of capital goods. As President, Mr. Collado is responsible for all day–to–day operations of the Brazilian IMPSA location, including administration, finances, sales, public relations, accounting, taxes, marketing, and strategic planning. **Career Steps:** IMPSA: President IMPSA do Brazil (1995–Present), Marketing Manager (1993–1995), Commercial Developer (1992–1993), Chief of Engineering Department (1987–1992), Design Engineer (1982–1987). **Associations & Accomplishments:** Brazilian Chamber of Commerce; Argentina Chamber of Commerce; Engineers Association of Argentina. **Education:** Universidad Nac S. Juan, Civil Engineering (1982). **Personal:** Married to Monica in 1983. Two children: Alejandra and Federico. Mr. Collado enjoys surfing, sports, and walking.

Jon Lantz
Operations Manager
Zond Maintenance Corporation
13000 Jameson Road
Tehachapi, CA 93561
(805) 823–6835
Fax: (805) 823–6752

3511

Business Information: Zond Maintenance Corporation, a wholly–owned subsidiary of wind–generated electric conglomerate Zond Systems, Inc., specializes in the manufacture, market and service of wind turbine generators. Regional in scope, Zond's customer base is primarily focused to U.S. utility industries, however recent expansion now includes International. Serving as Manager of the Wind Facilities Operations since September of 1982, Jon Lantz provides the management and oversight for operations and maintenance of over 2,400 wind turbine generators. This also includes the direction for support functions areas including: warehouse, inventory, anemometry, motor pool, training, parts rebuild shop and special projects. Mr. Lantz also serves as the Projects Trend Analysis Specialist insuring the Turbines and Support functions operate at the highest reliability level possible. **Career Steps:** Operations Manager – Wind Facilities Operations, Zond Maintenance Corporation (1982–Present); Pan American, Inc. – Lantz Converters (1960–1982), Grandson of orginator and Son of Inventor. **Associations & Accomplishments:** Windsmith, American Wind Energy Association; Tehachapi Heritage League. **Education:** Bakersfield Community College. **Personal:** Married to Helen M. in 1983. Two children: Cameron Scoutt and Levi Hawk. Mr. Lantz enjoys art, ranching, and is a do–it–yourselfer. His goal is to be self–reliant on his ranch, selling his art work, crafts, restoring antiques, and making electricty form the wind and the Lantz Converter.

James R. Nelson

Chairman of the Board of Directors
Allison Advanced Development Company
1469 Forest View West
Prescott, AZ 86301
(317) 230–3105
Fax: (317) 230–3110

3511

Business Information: Allison Advanced Development Company (AADC) is a manufacturer and developer of jet engine (turbine) technology for the U.S. Department of Defense, as well as U.S. and international aerospace companies. The Company was formed as an affiliate of Allison Engine Company and Rolls–Royce, Inc., after the acquisition of Allison Engine Company by Rolls–Royce was approved by the U.S. DOD in February 1995. Key classified and controlled unclassified technology programs executed by Allison Engine Company for the DOD were transferred to the new AADC to satisfy DOD technology transfer requirements as a condition of approval for Rolls–Royce ownership. Invited out of retirement to become a Director and Proxy Holder of AADC in April 1995, Mr. Nelson was elected Chairman of the Board of Directors in the same year. With more than thirty years of experience in aerospace engineering and systems acquisition management, both with the U.S. Air Force and at General Electric Aircraft Engines, he uses this experience to help set the long range goals of AADC to assure total business growth while

satisfying unique DOD security requirements. He also serves as the Chairman of the Defense Security Committee for AADC. **Career Steps:** Allison Advanced Development Company: Chairman of the Board of Directors, Proxy Holder, Director, and Chairman of the Defense Security Committee (1995–Present); General Electric Aircraft Engines: Manager of the Engine Quality Assurance & Total Quality Management (TQM) (1989–1994), Manager of Evandale Quality Ops (1984–1989); U.S. Air Force (Systems Command): Colonel/USAF and Director of ASD/YZ Systems Program Office (SPO) (1981–1984), Colonel/USAF and Commander of AF Wright Aeronautical LABS (1977–1981), Colonel, Commander AF Aero Propulsion LAB (1975–1977), Colonel, Director, Aeromech.Systems, AF Systems Command (1974–1975), 12 Years, USAF Combat Crew Duty, Various Aircrafts including service in Korea (1953–1954), and Vietnam (1969–1970), 244 Combat Mission. **Associations & Accomplishments:** Associate Fellow, AIAA; Air Force Association (AFA); The Retired Officers Association (TROA); Aircraft Owners & Pilots Association (AOPA); Tau Beta Pi; 55th SRW (SAC) and 98th Bomb Wing (SAC) Associations; General Electric Member, Aerospace Industries Association; Quality Assurance Committee (1987–1993); Published several articles in professional journals and magazines; Holder of numerous USAF decorations and awards, including the Distinguished Service Medal, Legion of Merit w/OLC, Distinguished Flying Cross, and the Air Medal with 7 OLCs, and the Air Force Association 1984 National Award for Major Program Management. **Education:** U.S. Air Force Institute of Technology – WPAFB, Ohio: Distinguished graduate of both M.S. and B.S. programs at USAFIT, M.S. in Aerospace Engineering (1965), B.S. in Aeromechanical Engineering (1964); Yankton College, South Dakota, B.A. in Mathematics & Physical Education, magna cum laude (1951); Attended while in USAF: Squadron Officers School, Air Command & Staff College, Air War College, Defense Systems Management College. **Personal:** Married to Ruth in 1954. Four children: Nancy, David, Jeffrey, and Kathy, and five grandchildren. Mr. Nelson enjoys piloting and owning private aircraft, dry fly fishing (trout), and golf.

Ajit K. Rakhit, Ph.D.
Consulting Design Engineer
Solar Turbines, Inc.
2200 Pacific Highway
San Diego, CA 92186
(619) 544–5204
Fax: (619) 544–2682

3511

Business Information: Solar Turbines, Inc. is a manufacturer of gas turbomachinery, such as gas turbines and compressors. Established in 1932, Solar Turbines currently employs 2,200 people company–wide. With thirty years expertise in the engineering industry, Dr. Rakhit joined the Corporation in 1990 as a Consulting Design Engineer. He is responsible for the design and development of mechanical power transmission equipment used in gas turbomachinery. **Career Steps:** Consulting Design Engineer, Solar Turbines, Inc. (1990–Present); Senior Engineer Specialist, AlliedSignal Aerospace (1987–1990); Advanced Development Engineer, Reliance Electric Co. (1976–1987). **Associations & Accomplishments:** Member, American Society of Mechanical Engineers; Member, Standards Development Committees (Epicyclic Gear Drives and Aerospace Gearing) of American Gear Manufacturers Association; Chairperson, 1993 North American Bengali Conference in Los Angeles – an annual cultural gathering of Bangalees of North America. **Education:** Concordia University – Montreal, Canada, Ph.D. (1974); University of Birmingham – England, M.S. in Engineering; University of Calcutta – India, B.S. in Engineering. **Personal:** Married to Ratna in 1967. Two children: Roma and Dr. Amit Rakhit, M.D. Dr. Rakhit enjoys organizing and staging social drama activities and playing bridge.

Ronald L. Stutesman
General Manager
Stewart and Stevenson
3300 Unicorn Road
Bakersfield, CA 93308
(805) 399–8992
Fax: (805) 399–9764

3511

Business Information: Stewart and Stevenson specializes in the installation, start–up, and warranty of GE LM2500, LM5000, and LM6000 gas turbine cogeneration power plants (i.e., universities, hospitals, institutes, etc). After start–up, the Company supplies parts and service support as necessary. As General Manager, Mr. Stutesman is responsible for the activities of the entire western region, including parts and service. **Career Steps:** Stewart and Stevenson: General Manager (1989–Present); Branch Manager (1983–1986); Assistant General Manager (1979–1983). **Associations & Accomplishments:** Rotary International. **Education:** American Graduate School of International Management, M.A. (1974); University of Colorado, B.A. in 1973. **Personal:** Married to Nancy A. in 1970. Two children: Todd and Michael. Mr. Stutesman enjoys golf, snow and water skiing, and reading.

Mrs. Shelley J. Tarrant
Human Resources Director
Foras
63665 19th Avenue
North Palm Springs, CA 92258
(619) 329-1437 Ext.120
Fax: (619) 251-6573

3511

Business Information: Foras, originally founded in Denmark, owns and services over 1,000 wind turbines that provide electricity for the North Palm Springs community. Established in the U.S. in 1992, the Company employs 66 people. As Human Resources Director, Mrs. Tarrant oversees all phases of personnel management. She is responsible for recruitment and employee reviews, benefits including insurance plans, and development and implementation of policies. Additional duties include ensuring compliance with all state and federal labor laws, and quality control. **Career Steps:** Human Resources Director, Foras (1994–Present). **Education:** College of the Desert (1990); Vocational for Computer Accounting (1990). **Personal:** Married to Thomas in 1987. Six children: Justin, Jordan, Candess, Cody, Cierra, and Summer. Mrs. Tarrant enjoys swimming, and spending lots of time with her family.

J.J. (Jack) Vranich

Materials Manager
Voith Hydro
E. Berlin Road
York, PA 17402-0712
(717) 792-7853
Fax: (717) 792-7250

3511

Business Information: Voith Hydro, formerly Allis Chalmers, is a full-service manufacturer and distributor of hydro turbine equipment and control systems, marketing worldwide to power generation industries. Voith Hydro is one of six plants owned worldwide by Voith Group. As Materials Manager, Mr. Vranich is responsible for purchasing, receiving, warehousing, material & inventory control, and short and long term production planning for the North American plant. He is also responsible for coordinating procurement activities for Voith Group worldwide. **Career Steps:** Voith Hydro: Materials Manager (1989–Present), Manager of Production and Inventory Control (1983–1989); Project Manager, Allis Chalmers (1979–1983); Assistant Plant Manager, Alpha Cement Company (1975–1979). **Associations & Accomplishments:** APICS Certified; Purchasing Management Association; Manufacturers Association: Active Member of Legislation Committee. **Education:** Duquesne University, B.A. in Economics (1968); Pennsylvania State University, Strategic Purchasing; University of Pennsylvania – Wharton College: Executive Management and Strategic Re-Engineering.

Martin K. Barrett
Plant Manager
G S Electric
1301 Industrial Street
Hudson, WI 54016
(715) 386-6233
Fax: (715) 386-4124

3519

Business Information: G S Electric is a manufacturer of fractional horsepower motors, including permanent magnet and universal DC motors. National in scope, with limited international presence, G S Electric has manufacturing and distribution facilities in Pennsylvania (2) and Hudson, Wisconsin. Joining G S Electric as Plant Manager in 1992, Mr. Barrett is responsible for all aspects of management and direction of the business, as well as P & L of the Hudson facility. **Career Steps:** Plant Manager, G.S. Electric (1992–Present); Manufacturing Consultant, Pollack & Skan Inc. (1991–1992); Plant Manager, Molon Motor & Coil Corporation (1982–1991). **Associations & Accomplishments:** American Management Association; American Legion Post 703; Chamber of Commerce; Industrial Council. **Education:** CCU, B.S. (1995); CLC, A.A.S. in Industrial Management (1982). **Personal:** Married to Rita E. in 1979. Two children: Victoria and Kristen. Mr. Barrett enjoys fly-fishing.

Dave J. Kramer
OEM Sales Manager
Mercury Marine
W 6250 West Pioneer Road, P.O. Box 1939
Fond du Lac, WI 54937
(414) 929-5000
Fax: (414) 929-5437

3519

Business Information: Mercury Marine is a world leader in the manufacture of marine engines and marine engine accessories. Global in scope, Mercury has marine engine manufacturing facilities in Fond du Lac, Wisconsin; Stillwater, Oklahoma; and Belgium. The Fond du Lac facility specializes in the manufacture of Mercury, Mariner, and Force Outboard Motors. A seventeen year veteran, Mr. Kramer was appointed OEM Sales Manager at the Wisconsin location in 1993. He is responsible for OEM sales management of outboard motors to and through 70 U.S. Boat Manufacturers. **Career Steps:** Mercury Marine: Outboard OEM Sales Manager (1993–Present), Marketing (1991–1993), MerCruiser Sales Manager (1989–1990), Dealer Sales (1978–1988); Retail Management (1975–1977); Manufacturer's Representative (1972–1974). **Associations & Accomplishments:** FACES; Ducks Unlimited; Toastmasters; American Marketing Association; Published interviews; Co-produced award winning training video; Developed new protection plan program called Q-GUARD. **Personal:** Mr. Kramer enjoys attending his daughters soccer and basketball games, Green Bay Packer games, fishing, hunting, and outdoors.

David G. Kusek
Division Controller
Mercury Marine
P.O. Box 1939
Fond Du Lac, WI 54936-1939
(414) 929-5309
Fax: (414) 929-5395

3519

Business Information: Mercury Marine, a division of Brunswick Corporation, is a world leader in the manufacture of marine engines and marine engine accessories. Global in scope, Mercury has marine engine manufacturing facilities in Fond du Lac, Wisconsin; Stillwater, Oklahoma; and Belgium. The Fond du Lac facility specializes in the manufacture of Mercury, Mariner, and Force Outboard Motors. Mr. Kusek has served in various supervisory positions with the company, most recently promoted to Division Controller in 1994. His present responsibilities include all accounting, payroll, and budgeting functions. **Career Steps:** Mercury Marine: Division Controller (1994–Present), Director Financial Planning (1989–1993); Finance Director – Europe Sub, Marine Power Europe–Europe (1985–1989). **Associations & Accomplishments:** Board of Directors, YMCA – Fond Du Lac. **Education:** University of Wisconsin – Oshkosh, M.B.A. (1978); University of Notre Dame, B.B.A. in Finance (1974). **Personal:** Married to Connie in 1978. two children: Elizabeth and Mary Rose.

Andrea M. McCubbin, CPIM
MIS Director
Diesel Technology Company
2300 Burlingame Company
Wyoming, MI 49509-1700
(616) 246-2606
Fax: (616) 246-2620

3519

Business Information: Diesel Technology Company is the international manufacturer and distributor of the diesel engine fuel injectors used by the trucking industry and is a joint venture between Robert Bosh Ltd and Penske. The Company was established in 1989 and currently has 1,200 employees. As MIS Director, Ms. McCubbin is responsible for the management of all computer operations, telecommunications and business and engineering applications. The Company is consolidating locations which will require reworking all the networks and installing the upgraded applications systems into the new building. **Career Steps:** MIS Director, Diesel Technology Company (1994–Present); Grant Thornton: Manager (1994), Senior Consultant (1993–1994); Master Scheduler/MMIS Coordinator, Aero–Motive (1992–1993). **Associations & Accomplishments:** President, CA–PRMS Midwest User Group; Humane Society of US; Alpha Kappa Psi; Alumni Association of University of Iowa; Former Member and Officer of NMA, DPMA, and AAUW; United Way Gold Award (1983). **Education:** University of Iowa, B.B.A. (1982). **Personal:** Married to Jeffrey in 1986. Two children: Jason Charles and Andrew James. Ms. McCubbin enjoys flower gardening, crafts, working with family pets, and doing family activities.

Diego Dorronsoro Tenorio
General Manager
Maquinarias S. A.
Apartado Aereo 8103
Cali, Colombia
(572) 664-4241
Fax: (572) 665-5510

3523

Business Information: Maquinarias S. A. is a family–owned business originally founded as an automotive parts distributorship. Reorganized in 1982, the Company now specializes in import, sale and repair of agricultural machinery and farm–related equipment. Employing 52 people, Maquinarias S.A. has an estimated annual revenue of $5 million. As General Manager, Mr. Dorronsoro oversees all administrative and operational functions regarding the Company. He is also responsible for Company growth and researches and imports new products from all over the world. **Career Steps:** General Manager, Maquinarias S. A. (1982–Present); Sales Manager, Magrin S.A. (19745–1982); Manager, Jaime Dorronsoro Y Cia. S. en C. (1972–1975). **Associations & Accomplishments:** Chamber of Commerce. **Education:** Mississippi State University, B.S. (1970); Centro Internacional de Agricultura Tropical, Crop Production Specialist–Ciat (1970–1972). **Personal:** Married to Lamia in 1974. Two children: Diego and Daniel. Mr. Dorronsoro Tenorio enjoys horseback riding.

Mark Huenemann
Director of Training (Sales & Marketing)
Case Corporation
700 State Street
Racine, WI 53404
(414) 636-7581
Fax: (414) 636-6834

3523

Business Information: Case Corporation, currently the second largest company in the industry, manufactures and markets agricultural and construction equipment. The Corporation has over 1600 independently–owned businesses in North America. Established in 1842, Case Inc. presently has 17,000 employees. As Director of Training for Sales and Marketing, Mr. Huenemann oversees a staff of 55 people who manage performance analysis, and develops and delivers training programs. **Career Steps:** Case Corporation: Director of Training, Sales, and Marketing (1995–Present); Regional Sales Manager (1989), Sales Operations Manager (1987), Manager, Dealer Development (1985). **Associations & Accomplishments:** American Management Association; Beta Gamma Sigma. **Education:** University of Wisconsin–Milwaukee, M.B.A. (1982); University of South Dakota, M.A., B.S.E. **Personal:** Married to Renee in 1967. Three children: Timothy, Matthew, and Christine. Mr. Huenemann enjoys photography and travel.

Donald E. McGrath

President and Chief Executive Officer
Tyler Industries
P.O. Box 249
Benson, MN 56215
(320) 843-3333
Fax: (320) 843-2467

3523

Business Information: Tyler Industries is primarily engaged in the international manufacturing and marketing of equipment to blend and apply commercial fertilizers and pesticides. Established in 1958, the Company employs 265 people. As President and Chief Executive Officer, Mr. McGrath oversees the day–to–day operations of the Company and is responsible for strategic planning, administration, finance, marketing and public relations. Internet users can reach him via: www.Teautyler.com. **Career Steps:** President and Chief Executive Officer, Tyler Industries (1973–Present); Vice President and General Manager, Cornelius Company (1964–1973); Department Manager, Procter & Gamble (1958–1964). **Associations & Accomplishments:** Boy Scouts of America; Dove Township Planning Board. **Education:** University of Minnesota: M.B.A. (1986), Bachelor of Geological Engineering (1958). **Personal:** Married to June in 1956. Four children: Gustaf, Eric, Gretchen and Duncan. Mr. McGrath enjoys skiing, sailing, golf, and tennis.

Mr. Ed Moloney
President and Chief Executive Officer
Feed–Rite, Ltd.
17 Speers Road
Winnipeg, Manitoba R2J 1M1
(204) 233-8418
Fax: (204) 235-1260

3523

Business Information: Feed–Rite, Ltd. is a manufacturer and distributor (international) of stockfeed, pet food, livestock equipment, and animal health and pig breeding products. As President and Chief Executive Officer, Mr. Moloney is responsible for all aspects of company operations. Established in 1939, Feed–Rite, Ltd. employs 420 people with annual sales of $175 Million. **Career Steps:** President and Chief Executive Officer, Feed–Rite, Ltd., (1994–Present); General Manager of Finance, Ridley Corporation, Ltd. (1990–1994); Financial Controller, Goodman Fielder, Ltd. (1983–1990). **Associations & Accomplishments:** Fellow, Institute of Chartered Secretaries and Administrators (FCIS); Fellow, National Institute of Accountants (FNIA); Fellow, Corporate Institute of Management (FCIM). **Personal:** Married to Catherine in 1975.

Donald E. Rieser

Director
Case Corporation
287 Herrick Road
Riverside, IL 60546–2046
(708) 887–2177
Fax: (708) 887–2146

3523

Business Information: Case Corporation manufactures agricultural and construction equipment, maintaining facilities in the United States, Canada, Great Britain, France, and Germany. Mr. Rieser has served in various supervisory positions with Case, most recently promoted to Director in 1994. He is presently responsible for the design and development of small and medium agricultural tractors and current product design maintenance. **Career Steps:** Case Corporation: Director (1994–Present), Chief Engineer (1992–1994), Director–Construction Equipment Liaison (1990–1992). **Associations & Accomplishments:** Society of Automation Engineers; Sigma Iota Epsilon Business Fraternity. **Education:** Illinois Institute of Technology: M.B.A. (1984), B.S.M.A.E. (Mechanical Aerospace Engineering) (1970). **Personal:** Married to Marilyn in 1971. Mr. Rieser is a commercial pilot, and enjoys scuba diving and golf.

Jim L. Jenkins

Corporate Training Director
Poulan/Weed Eater
5020 Flournoy Lucas Road
Shreveport, LA 71149
(318) 683–3932
Fax: (318) 683–3567

3524

Business Information: Poulan/Weed Eater, a subsidiary of Electrolux and a division of WCI Outdoor Products, Inc., is a national manufacturer and distributor of lawn and garden equipment. Products include weed eaters, chain saws, edgers, lawnmowers, blowers, and tillers which are distributed through major retail companies, such as Lowes, Sears, Wal–Mart, Home Depot, and K–Mart. Headquartered in Shreveport, Louisiana, Poulan/Weed Eater Corporation also has eight manufacturing plants located throughout the nation. As Corporate Training Director, Mr. Jenkins is responsible for the development of management and training programs within the company, including conducting on–site training at the plants and in the corporate location. Career highlights which include being responsible for the initiation of the manager's training programs for the Corporation. **Career Steps:** Corporate Training Director, Poulan Weed Eater (1994–Present); Director of Manpower Development and Recruiting, Murray Ohio Manufacturing Company (1977–1994); Group Director of Personnel, Texfi Industries, Inc. (1972–1977); Personnel Director, Burlington Industries (1967–1972). **Associations & Accomplishments:** Former President, Lawrenceburg Rotary Club; Former President, Middle Tennessee Executive Committee – Boy Scouts of America; Advisor, Columbia State Community College; Advisor, Middle Tennessee State University; Advisor, University of North Alabama; Governor's Committee, Tennessee Hire the Handicapped; Former President, Lawrence County Leadership; Community Chairman, American Red Cross; Published article in American Society of Training Directors; Conducts lectures and teaching at colleges. **Education:** Pembroke University, B.A. (1963). **Personal:** Married to Mary Lynn in 1969. One child: Meredith. Mr. Jenkins enjoys reading, fishing, and hunting.

Lynwood Keller

Area Supervisor
Homelite
PO Box 40
Greer, SC 29652–0040
(803) 877–6401
Fax: (803) 879–1612

3524

Business Information: Homelite, a division of Deere & Co., is one of the nation's leading consumer lawn and garden equipment manufacturers. Best–known for its chain saw product line, Homelite also manufactures blowers, pumps, string trimmers, and other related lawn and home maintenance products. Established in 1934, Homelite distributes its products globally. A member of the Homelite management team since 1973, Mr. Keller now serves as Area Supervisor. He has full supervisory capacity in the oversight for six manufacturing divisions at the Greer, South Carolina facility. **Career Steps:** Homelite: Area Supervisor (1991–Present); Plant Superintendent (1987–1991); Supervisor (1973–1987). **Associations & Accomplishments:** Gideon; Master Mason; Sunday School Teacher and Trustee of his church. **Education:** Clemson University; Greenville Technical College, Management Science **Personal:** Married to Martha in 1981. Three children: Scott, Steven and Derrick. Mr. Keller enjoys fishing, golf, teaching Sunday School and serving as Director of Sunday School programs at his church.

Ed Waddles

Corporate Environmental Manager
MTD Products
979 S. Conwell Avenue
Willard, OH 44890–9301
(419) 935–6611
Fax: Please mail or call

3524

Business Information: MTD Products is the world's largest power equipment manufacturer, specializing in lawn and garden care products such as lawn mowers, tillers, and snow blowers. As Corporate Environmental Manager, Mr. Waddles ensures compliance with environmental regulations, prepares the Divisions for upcoming requirements, and is responsible for various administrative activities. **Career Steps:** Corporate Environmental Manager, MTD Products (1986–Present). **Associations & Accomplishments:** Chair, ASTM; Society of Manufacturing Engineers; Council President, Village of Plymouth, Ohio. **Education:** Environmental Management Degree (In Progress). **Personal:** Married. Three children.

Steven L. Clark

General Manager
Denardi Equipment
22099 Knabe Road
Corona, CA 91719
(909) 277–2477
Fax: (909) 277–0349

3531

Business Information: Denardi Equipment is a heavy equipment dealer representing Volvo Construction Equipment, Hitachi Construction Equipment, Esco Buckets & Teeth, Tesmac Trenchers, and other product lines for distribution to California and Southern Nevada. With thirty–one years of managerial experience, Mr. Clark joined Denardi in 1992. He personally coordinated the establishment of the Nevada location and now serves as General Manager of both the Corona Branch, which covers the Los Angeles market, and the Las Vegas Branch, which covers Southern Nevada. His responsibilities include staffing decisions, business development, and various administrative duties. **Career Steps:** General Manager, Denardi Equipment (1992–Present); General Manager – International Sales, Esco Corporation, Portland Oregon (1965–1992); Football Player, Green Bay Packers (July 1965–Sept.1965); Baseball Player, Boston Red Sox (Jan.1965–July 1965). **Associations & Accomplishments:** Association of Equipment Dealers; American Mining Congress; Engineering Contractors Association; Southern California Contractors Association. **Education:** Oregon State University, B.S. in Business Administration with Technical Minor in Construction (1965). **Personal:** Married to Joan in 1985. Two children: Chris and Brady. Mr. Clark enjoys golf, fishing, and hunting.

Nasirali A. Emadi

Senior Manufacturing and Systems Engineer
Caterpillar, Inc.
P.O. Box 787
York, PA 17402
(717) 751–5470
Fax: (717) 751–5217

3531

Business Information: Caterpillar, Inc. is the world's largest manufacturer of earthmoving and construction equipment and is a global leader in the manufacture of diesel and natural gas engines. As Senior Manufacturing and Systems Engineer, Ms. Emadi performs various functions within the business resources department including implementing business plans, and performance, financial, cost, and commodity analysis. She is also responsible for project management and serves as the Company liaison for suppliers. **Career Steps:** Caterpillar, Inc: Senior Manufacturing and Systems Engineer (1995–Present), Senior Manufacturing Engineer (1988–1995). **Associations & Accomplishments:** Council Member of ISGH; President of Homeowners Association; Consultant, Junior Achievement of South Central Pennsylvania. **Education:** Drexel University, B.S. in Mechanical Engineering (1988). **Personal:** Married to Maleka N. in 1988. Two children: Junaid and Safdar. Ms. Emadi enjoys golf, target shooting, having a small business background, and learning to fly.

Ron W. Leadmon

Director of Customer Service
Hahn Systems Incorporated
2401 Production Dr.
Indianapolis, IN 46241
(317) 243–3796
Fax: (317) 243–5919

3531

Business Information: Hahn Systems Incorporated is an international distributor of construction supplies, such as pneumatic power tools, electric power tools, staplers, nails, corrugated fasteners, adhesives, and compressors. Hahn Systems Incorporated services the U.S. (Indiana, Ohio, Kentucky, Illinois, Michigan) and Canada. As Director of Customer Service, Mr. Leadmon is responsible for all aspects of the Customer Service operation and administration, as well as overseeing retail operations, warehousing, distribution and processing of orders. **Career Steps:** Director of Customer Service, Hahn Systems Incorporated (1994–Present); Senco Products, Inc.: Manager of Customer Service (1989–1994), Manager of Product Information (1984–1989), Manager of Sales Services (1980–1984), Manager of Production Planning & Inventory Control (1976–1980), Customer Service Department (1971–1976) **Associations & Accomplishments:** Telemarketers of Cincinnati, Ohio; Tri–State Tele Communications, Cincinnati, Ohio; **Education:** University of Cincinnati (1985); Crosby Quality College: Certificate, QWG Trainer/Instructor Certified; Management by Objective & Results Certificate; Advancement through Projects (ATP) Certificate; N.A. F.T.A. Seminars/Training; Carlson Advertising (Cincinnati, Ohio) Certificate. **Personal:** Married to Virginia (Ginny) in 1972. Two children: Lorena (Lori) and Krystal. Mr. Leadmon enjoys playing golf, family events and nature tours.

Phillip W. Wise

Vice President and Operations Manager
Hamm Compactors, Inc.
25403 Oakhurst
Spring, TX 77386
(713) 987–0778
Fax: (713) 987–0778

3531

Business Information: Hamm Compactors, Inc. is a manufacturer, sales distributor, and marketer of heavy construction machinery to distributors worldwide. The machinery is used for building roads, foundations, etc. International in scope, Hamm Compactors has four manufacturing facilities located in France, Germany, Mexico, and the U.S. Joining Hamm Compactors as Vice President of RACO Division and Operations Manager in 1990, Mr. Wise is responsible for the oversight and management of the RACO Division, one of two divisions, manufacturing slabizing asphalt. **Career Steps:** Vice President and Operations Manager, Hamm Compactors, Inc. (1990–Present); National Sales Manager, Bomag USA, Inc. (1975–1990); Vice President of Sales and Marketing, Tide Equipment Company, Inc. (1972–1975); Regional Sales Manager, American Poclain Inc. (1968–1972). **Associations & Accomplishments:** Asphalt Recycling and Reclamation Association; American Society of Certified Engineering Technicians; National Association of County Engineers; American Public Works Association; Associated Equipment Distributors; Associated General Contractors. **Education:** Northwest Florida University (1957). **Personal:** Married to Altona O. in 1959. Three children: Christopher, Kevin, and Patrick. Mr. Wise enjoys golf, fishing, and ranching.

Mr. Steven Y. Chi

President of the Mining Group
Morrison Knudsen Corporation
7550 Ih–10 West, Suite 1400, P.O. Box 400090
San Antonio, TX 78229–1990
(210) 244–4618
Fax: (210) 244–4610

3532

Business Information: Morrison Knudsen Corporation specializes in mining & IPP development and engineering construction (bridges and dams). The Company primarily serves large U.S. corporations and has business ventures in Peru and Indonesia. Established in 1912, Morrison Knudsen Corporation presently employs 12,000 people and has an estimated annual revenue in excess of $2.7 billion. In his current capacity, Mr. Chi is responsible for all aspects of Company operations to include marketing and management. He also negotiates new contracts and new business ventures. Concurrently, he serves as Chairman and CEO of the East Asia Group and President of MK Peru, S.A. **Career Steps:** Morrison

Knudsen Corporation: President of the Mining Group (1996–Present), Chairman and CEO of the East Asia Group (1986–Present), President of MK Peru, S.A. (1993–Present); Vice President, Sunedco (1982– 1985). **Associations & Accomplishments:** Board, MK Gold; Vice Chairman, U.S. Mongolian Business Council; Member, AIME; Member, American Management Association. **Education:** University of Idaho, M.S. Degree (1963); Stanford University; Taipei Institute of Technology. **Personal:** Married for 23 years to Ling K. Chi. Three children: Jane, Stephanie and Kathy. Mr. Chi enjoys tennis and reading in his leisure time.

Steven L. Crabtree

President and Chief Executive Officer
DRC International, Inc.
3415 South 116th Street, Suite 125
Seattle, WA 98168–1978
(206) 246–7810
Fax: (206) 246–8711
EMAIL: See Below

3532

Business Information: DRC International, Inc. is a manufacturer and distributor of heavy equipment and parts for mining industries (silver, gold, platinum). Established in 1994, DRC International has manufacturing facilities in Germany, Italy, and the U.S., serving clientele in Far East Russia, Vietnam, and Mongolia. Founding DRC International as President and Chief Executive Officer in 1994, Mr. Crabtree oversees all administrative operations for associates and a support staff of 21, in addition to the oversight of all financial operations, investments, and expansion of the Company. He currently has two partners assisting in operations, one of whom is bilingual. Mr. Crabtree can also be reached through the Internet as follows: 102217.236@compuserve.com **Career Steps:** President and Chief Executive Officer, DRC International, Inc. (1994–Present); Vice President, BESCO International (1994–1995); Bearing Engineering and Supply: Branch Manager (1992–1994), Sales Manager (1989–1992). **Associations & Accomplishments:** Alaska Miners Association; Mongolian Commerce; Independent Distributors Association; Associated Equipment Distributors. Published in Voice of America in Russia and local newspapers. **Personal:** Married to Tracey Rene in 1984. One child: Danail Reed. Mr. Crabtree enjoys golf and snow skiing.

Bernard C. Curty
Credit Manager
I R Montabert
203 Rue De Grenoble
St. Priest, France 69800
(33) 72229780
Fax: (33) 72229793

3532

Business Information: I R Montabert is a multi–faceted international firm involved in construction, mining, and factories. The Corporation makes machines, machine accessories and does construction on public works projects. As Credit Manager, Mr. Curty is responsible for international financing, credit line control, and establishment of credit contacts. He directly supervises 14 employees in his department. **Career Steps:** Credit Manager, I R Montabert (1993–Present); Credit Manager, Ingersoll–Rand International, Ltd. (1984–1993); Credit Manager, Polysar International, Ltd. (1974–1984). **Associations & Accomplishments:** Finance Credit and International Business; Import–Export Club; Federation Europeene Credit Manager Association. **Education:** Fribourg University, M.B.A. (1964); Graduate School London: International Credit and Finance **Personal:** Married to Dechelette Carole in 1981. Three children: Philipe, David, and Gary. Mr. Curty enjoys classical music, riding, sailing, and golf.

Dalph S. McNeil
President
Brookville Mining Equipment Corporation
20 Pickering Street
Brookville, PA 15825–1224
(814) 849–7321
Fax: (814) 226–4499

3532

Business Information: Brookville Mining Equipment Company specializes in the manufacture of diesel and battery–operated mining locomotives, personnel carriers, rubber–tired tractors and all–terrain vehicles, and industrial locomotives. According to a survey published by the National Mining Association, Brookville Mining Equipment produces 70 to 80% of the domestic market of mining diesel locomotives for the past three years. A growing export business, the Company now has 30 overseas representatives, shipping to over 80 countries worldwide. Following an extensive academic career in post–secondary business administration education, Mr. McNeil joined Brookville's Locomotive Division in 1977. Appointed in 1989 as President of Brookville Mining Equipment Corp., he provides the vision and strategies for the overall corporate development, quality production output, P&L, and international relations. He was instrumental in the company's breakthrough developments of two new products: 8–wheeled locomotive utilized in industrial and cement operations facilities, and battery–powered equipment. **Career Steps:** President, Brookville Mining Equipment Company (1989–Present); Vice President, Brookville Locomotive Divison (1977–1989); Assistant Dean of Admissions, University of Pennsylvania – Edinboro (1969–1977). **Associations & Accomplishments:** Vice President, Clarion County YMCA Board; Jefferson County Development Council; Pinebrook Industrial Park Director; S&T Bank Board Member. **Education:** University of Pittsburgh, courses toward Doctorate (1977); Cannon University, M.B.A.; University of Pennsylvania – Edinboro, B.S. in Economics. **Personal:** Married to Nancy in 1978. Three children: Brent, Joel, and Shaina. Mr. McNeil enjoys golf, hunting, snow skiing, being out on the water, and bicycling with his children.

Margaux Palmiere

Vice President
American Parts & Equipment Corporation
27 Progress Street
Edison, NJ 08820
(908) 755–2700
Fax: (908) 755–1524

3532

Business Information: American Parts & Equipment Corporation is an international manufacturer and distributor of mining equipment. Products include trucks, shovels, and conveyors used exclusively for the energy mining industry (i.e., coal, oil, gas). Gobal in scope, products are marketed throughout North, South and Latin America, Russia, Asia and Northern Europe. Future plans include expanding into the diamond and ore mine industries. One of two founding partners, Vice President Margaux Palmiere is responsible for all sales and engineering projects. She also directs all administrative and strategical planning operations, **Career Steps:** Vice President, American Parts & Equipment Corporation (1991–Present); Vice President, AEC America (1989–1991); Purchasing Manager, Pamic International (1985–1989). **Education:** Herriot Watt University – Edinburgh, Scotland, B.A. (1983). **Personal:** Married to Paul in 1991. Three children: Richard, Christopher, and Nicole. Ms. Palmiere enjoys horses and the Opera.

Ron Schnoor

Vice President of Operations
HAM Marine, Inc.
P.O. Box 43
Pascagoula, MS 39568–0043
(601) 769–0275
Fax: (601) 769–1826

3533

Business Information: HAM Marine, Inc. specializes in the modification, conversion and repair of mobile offshore oil rigs, primarily in the Gulf of Mexico. Established in 1982, HAM Marine currently employs 300 people and has estimated annual revenue of $50 million. As Vice President of Operations, Mr. Schnoor is responsible for the overall management of marine operations, sales and marketing. **Career Steps:** Vice President of Operations, HAM Marine, Inc. (1984–Present); Civil Discipline Engineer, Brown & Root (1975–1984). **Associations & Accomplishments:** Propeller Club; Pascagoula Dugout Club. **Education:** Campbell College, B.S. (1974); University of Houston, M.S. in Civil Engineering. **Personal:** Married to Debbi D'Amato in 1975. Two children: Ryan and Zachary. Mr. Schnoor enjoys golf, boating and family activities.

Terry D. Holmes
Plant Manager
Schindler Elevator Corporation
821 Industrial Drive
Clinton, NC 28328–9749
(910) 590–5599
Fax: (910) 590–5595

3534

Business Information: The U.S. division of Schindler Elevator Corporation — the leading elevator company in Europe — specializes in the manufacture of escalator stairways. As Plant Manager, Mr. Holmes is responsible for the management and supervision of all plant activities. **Career Steps:** Plant Manager, Schindler Elevator Corporation (1990–Present); Westinghouse Electric Corporation: Manager of Manufacturing and Industrial Engineering (1986–1990), Manufacture of Manufacturing Engineering (1980–1985). **Associations & Accomplishments:** Former Chairman, Society of Manufacturing Engineering – Triangle Chapter, Raleigh–Durham, N.C.; Advisory Staff, Clinton City Schools Technology System Wide Committee; Advisor, Clinton City Schools Technology Preparation Program. **Education:** Central Michigan University, M.A. in Business (1981); North Carolina State University, B.S. in Mechanical Engineering. **Personal:** Married to Deborah in 1980. Two children: Doug and Blake. Mr. Holmes enjoys golf, piloting his private aircraft, and reading.

Robert H. Gardiner

President
Fenner (C.B.), Inc.
459 Georgetown Road, P.O. Box 459
Lawrence, PA 15055–0459
(412) 745–7100
Fax: (412) 745–2863

3535

Business Information: Fenner (C.B.), Inc. is an international manufacturer of conveyor belting, primarily used for the mining industry world–wide, focusing on the mineral extraction market. Fenner, a multi–national company, is a subsidiary of J.H. Fenner Limited in the United Kingdom with manufacturing facilities world–wide. As President, Mr. Gardiner has total business responsibility for all Fenner (C.B.), Inc. interests in the U.S., Canada, and South America. He focuses on improving the profile of the Company in the market place. Career milestones include tripling sales in the U.S. market during the first year he was with Fenner. **Career Steps:** President, Fenner (C.B.), Inc. (1992–Present); The Gates Rubber Company – UK: Industrial Sales and Marketing Director (1990–1992), Operations Manager (1986–1990); Engineering Manager, Uniroyal Ltd. – UK (1982–1986). **Associations & Accomplishments:** Society of American Institute of Mining, Metallurgical, and Petroleum Engineers; UK Institute of Mechanical Engineers and Chartered Engineer; Rubber Manufacturers Association; Published numerous articles in Europe dealing with quality assurance and ISO9000, as well as conducting seminars on the same topic. **Education:** Paisley University – Scotland, B.Sc. in Mechanical Engineering (1970). **Personal:** Married to Catherine in 1994. Five children: Audrey, Emma, Rebecca, Dawn, and Justin. Mr. Gardiner enjoys computer technology, golf, and skiing.

DeWitt H. Pendergrass
Director of Organizational Development
Best Diversified Products, Inc.
107 Flint Street, P.O. Box 4017
Jonesboro, AR 72401–4017
(501) 935–0970
Fax: (501) 935–3661

3535

Business Information: Best Diversified Products, a subsidiary of NorthStar, Inc., manufactures expandable conveyor systems with locations in Europe and various sister companies in the United States. As Director of Organizational Development, Mr. Pendergrass is responsible for professional development, recruitment, training, general human relations functions, plant safety, and compliance with environmental regulations. **Career Steps:** Best Diversified Products, Inc: Director of Organizational Development (1995–Present), Risk Manager (1994–1995); Safety Supervisor, Campbell Soup Company (1989–1994). **Associations & Accomplishments:** World Safety Organization; American Society of Safety Engineers; Society for Human Resource Management; American Management Association; Advisory Committee, Northeast Arkansas Occupational Health and Safety Administration. **Education:** University of Arkansas, B.S.B.A. (1988). **Personal:** Married to Brenda in 1974. Two children: Michael and Jennifer. Mr. Pendergrass enjoys woodworking and remodeling.

Qing Liang
Engineer Manager
American Lifts
601 W. McKee Street
Greensburg, IN 47240
(812) 663–4085
Fax: (812) 663–6017

3536

Business Information: Established in 1946, American Lifts is a manufacturer of material handling equipment, including hydraulic lifts, tilters, turntables, and conveyors. As Engineer Manager, Mr. Liang is responsible for operational activities, including finance, budget, and customer service. **Career Steps:** Engineer Manager, American Lifts (1989–Present); Mechanical Engineer, Coal Mining Machinery Research Institute of Shanghai, China (1983–85). **Associations & Accomplishments:** American Society of Mechanical Engineering (ASME), Golden Key National Honor Society and Outstanding College Students of America in 1989. **Education:** University of Louisville, M.S. (1989) **Personal:** Married to Yau Lu Liang. One child: Maria J. Mr. Liang enjoys basketball, fishing and stamp collecting.

Mr. Bjorn Tollefsrud
Chairman and Chief Executive Officer
Canadian Overhead Handling, Inc.
801 Cure Boivin
Boisbriand, Quebec J7G 2J2
(514) 430–6500
Fax: (514) 430–6611

3536

Business Information: Canadian Overhead Handling, Inc. engineers and manufactures manual and robotic electric overhead traveling cranes and associated equipment. As Chairman/Chief Executive Officer and Founder, Mr. Tollefsrud is responsible for the administration, financial matters and engineering for the company. Established in 1969, Canadian Overhead Handling, Inc. employs 75 people with annual sales of $15 million. **Career Steps:** Chairman/Chief Executive Officer and Founder, Canadian Overhead Handling, Inc. (1969–Present); General Manager, Munck Canada, Inc. (1965–1969); Electrical Engineer, CERN, Geneva, Switzerland (1960–1964); Electrical Engineer, Brown, Boveri & Cie, Baden, Switzerland (1957–1960); Electrical Engineer, Oerlikon Engineering Co., Zurich, Switzerland (1954–1957). **Associations & Accomplishments:** Norwegian Engineers Association; Corporation of Engineers of Quebec; Corporation of Engineers of Ontario. **Education:** E.T.H., Zurich, Diploma in Engineering (1955). **Personal:** Married to Randi. Four children: Lisbet, Sine, John and Bjorn. Mr. Tollefsrud enjoys cross–country skiing, bicycling, jogging and salmon fishing.

William "Bill" Nelson
Plant Manager
Western Rock Bit Company, Ltd
1026 Western Drive
Crossfield, Alberta, Canada T0M 0S0
(403) 946–5678
Fax: (403) 946–4358

3537

Business Information: Western Rock Bit Company, Ltd is an establishment primarily engaged in the manufacture of pressure vessels and truck/transport equipment (i.e. propane, flatbed, and refrigerated trucks). As Plant Manager, Mr. Nelson is responsible for all office staff, and supervises eight managers that assist in oversight of all aspects of the Plant, including, engineering, purchasing, and receiving. **Career Steps:** Western Rock Bit Company Limited: Plant Manager (1990–Present), Plant Superintendent (1975–1990), Fitter/Welder (1965–1975). **Associations & Accomplishments:** Alberta Pressure Vessel Manufacturer's Association (APVMA); Alliance of Manufacturers and Exporters, Canada. **Personal:** Two children: Audra and Greg. Mr. Nelson enjoys golf and camping.

Alan C. Lyons
Manager of MWS Engineering
Kennametal, Inc.
5171 Glennwood Avenue, P.O. Box 30700
Raleigh, NC 27622
(919) 829–5323
Fax: (919) 829–5340

3541

Business Information: Kennametal, Inc. specializes in the manufacture and distribution of steel and carbide metal–working products, cutting tools and tool holders. The number one Company of its kind in the U.S., the Company is headquartered in Latrobe, Pennsylvania. Established in 1938, Kennametal, Inc. employs 7,000 people worldwide, and has an estimated annual revenue of $1 billion. As Manager of MWS Engineering, Mr. Lyons manages a group of ten engineers and designers focused on development of rotating tools. He is responsible for design and development of machining center systems and holds a number of patents. **Career Steps:** Manager of MWS Engineering, Kennametal, Inc. (1981–Present); Design Engineer, Parkway Consultant Engineering, UK (1978–1981); Design Engineer, Dominion Glass, Inc., Canada (1978–1979); Design Engineer, Rolls Royce Aeroengines, UK (1970–1978). **Associations & Accomplishments:** Senior Member, Society of Manufacturing Engineers; Senior Member, Machining Technology Association of Society of Manufacturing Engineers; Speaker, International Manufacturing Technology Show. **Education:** Rolls Royce Institute, B.S. in Production Engineering (1977). **Personal:** Married to Annette in 1975. Two children: Lee and Emma. Mr. Lyons enjoys go–cart racing and classic cars.

Rick Alley
National Parts Manager
Mazak Corporation
8025 Production Drive
Florence, KY 41042
(606) 342–1790
Fax: (606) 342–1833

3542

Business Information: Mazak Corporation, the largest manufacturer of machine tools in the world, is a Japan–based Corporation with subsidiaries located around the world. The Florence, Kentucky branch is the largest division, with a higher production rate than any other, and boasts a 96% same–day–shipment rate. As National Parts Manager, Mr. Alley is responsible for sales, replacements, new product training, training of sales representatives, and managing the Spare Parts National Distribution Center. **Career Steps:** National Parts Manager, Mazak Corporation (1989–Present); Parts Manager, Lodge & Shipley (1974–1989). **Education:** University of Cincinnati, Bachelors (1980). **Personal:** Married to Debora in 1995. Mr. Alley enjoys watching Notre Dame teams play.

David J. Fiebelkorn
President and Chief Executive Officer
Komo Machine
11 Industrial Boulevard
Sauk Rapids, MN 56379
(320) 252–0580 (320) 252–0480
Fax: (320) 656–2472

3542

Business Information: Komo Machine is a custom design automation manufacturer, specializing in the production of machine tools. Product lines include CNC vertical wood routers and vertical mill machines. As President and CEO, David Fiebelkorn provides the overall vision and strategies, ensuring quality product output, customer satisfaction, and the continued development of the Company as a whole. **Career Steps:** President and CEO, Komo Machine (1995–Present); General Manager, A.J. Manufacturing (1993–1995); Frigidaire Company, Freezer Division: Director of Operations, Director of Materials, Manager of Quality Control (1981–1993); Teacher, District 748 (1975–1981). **Associations & Accomplishments:** APICS; Minnesota Pheasants Forever; American Society of Quality Control; Ducks Unlimited; Minnesota Waterfowl Association; National Association of Purchasing Management; Board Member, Sartell School; Former President–Elect, Sartell Education Association; St. Cloud Parents' Coalition; Property and Finance Committee, Atonement Lutheran Church; Religious Instructor at Celebration Lutheran Church. **Education:** St. Cloud State University, B.S. magna cum laude (1975); CPM Certification. **Personal:** Three children: Erin, Kathryn and Jill. Mr. Fiebelkorn enjoys hunting, horses, conservation farming, and teaching religion.

Hank Snow
Manufacturing Engineer
PHB Machining Division
8150 West Ridge Road
Fairview, PA 16415–1805
(814) 474–1552
Fax: (814) 474–1132
EMAIL: See Below

3542

Business Information: PHB Machining Division is a manufacturing company comprised of four divisions: die cast, machining, molding, and tool and die. The Machining Division specialized in complex machining operations on CNC Lathes, vertical and horizontal Machining Centers, and specialized equipment on a variety of materials. The Company prides itself on working directly with the customer, ensuring satisfaction in the item produced. As Manufacturing Engineer, Mr. Snow oversees all aspects of new product development, current process review, cellular manufacturing, and non–conforming material review. Internet users can reach him via: whyme94@aol.com. **Career Steps:** Manufacturing Engineer, PHB Machining Division (1994–Present); Vice President of Operations, Sonil, Inc. (1990–1994); Industrial Engineer/Production Supervisor, Weasler Engineering (1986–1990); Industrial Engineer/Production Supervisor, Mich. Special Products (1983–1986). **Associations & Accomplishments:** North America Fishing Club; Lake Erie Mustang Owners Club; American Cruisers; SCCA Member of the Year (1992). **Education:** Edinboro University, A.M.E.T. (1996); Illinois Institute of Technology. **Personal:** One child: Scott. Mr. Snow enjoys hunting, fishing, car clubs and shows.

Jeffrey L. Foreman
Vice President of Operations
Galgon Industries, Inc.
37399 Centralmont Place
Fremont, CA 94536–6549
(510) 792–8211
Fax: Please mail or call
EMAIL: See Below

3544

Business Information: Galgon Industries, Inc. is a designer and manufacturer of custom tools & dies, providing turnkey assembly and custom sheet metal fabrication. Established in 1966, Galgon Industries, Inc. currently employs 180 people. A Certified Public Accountant, bringing with him over ten years of industrial operations and accounting administration expertise, Mr. Foreman oversees all administrative operations, with focus in financial reporting, P&L and accounting sectors. He can be reached through the Internet via: jeff_foreman@aol.com **Career Steps:** Vice President of Operations, Galgon Industries, Inc. (1994–Present); Controller, UFCW, Local 588 (1991–1994); Vice President of Operations, Great-West Technology Limited (1986–1991). **Associations & Accomplishments:** American Institute of Certified Public Accountants (AICPA); California Society of CPA's. **Education:** California State University, M.B.A. (1990), B.S. in Business Administration and Accounting. **Personal:** Married to Rosemary in 1978. Two children: Jennifer and Brett. Mr. Foreman enjoys travel and children's school activities.

Theodore J. Leczo

• • •⬤ ━ • • •

President
Berry Metal Company
2408 Evans City Road
Harmony, PA 16037–7724
(412) 452–8040 Ext. 611
Fax: (412) 452–4115

3544

Business Information: Berry Metal Company, one of the leading suppliers for the steel industry, manufactures water cooled lances for injection of oxygen and carbon into steelmaking vessels. As President, Mr. Leczo provides the overall vision and strategy for the Company, ensuring quality product output, customer satisfaction and the effective techniques to keep the Company a viable presence in the international market. **Career Steps:** Berry Metal Company: President (1991–Present), Staff Engineer (1973–1990); Supervisor, Bethlehem Steel Corporation (1970–1973). **Associations & Accomplishments:** Member, Steelmaking Division Executive Board, American Institute of Mechanical Engineers (AIMES) – Iron and Steel Society; Member of Associate Members Committee, AISI; SMA; AISE. **Education:** Ohio State University, B.S. in Metal Engineering (1966). **Personal:** Married to Marilyn in 1985. Three children: Jeffrey, Jason, and Nicole. Mr. Leczo enjoys golf.

Geoff L. Lowery
Operations Manager
Tech Mold Manufacturing
504 South Madison Drive
Tempe, AZ 85281–7214
(602) 968–8324
Fax: (602) 921–0755

3544

Business Information: Tech Mold Manufacturing is a manufacturer of end production from injection molded plastics. Joining Tech Mold Manufacturing as Processing Engineer in 1990, Mr. Lowery was appointed as Operations Manager in 1993. He is responsible for directing all operations of the Company, in addition to overseeing all administrative operations for associates and a support staff of 25. **Career Steps:** Tech Mold Manufacturing: Operations Manager (1994–Present), Process Engineer (1989–1994); Production Manager, Pixley Richards (1986–1989); President and Owner, U.P.T. (1980–1986). **Associations & Accomplishments:** Society of Plastics Engineers. **Education:** Bowling Green University, B.A. in Education (major) and Mechanical Engineering (minor) (1970). **Personal:** Married to Lois in 1970. Two children: Aaron and Shannon. Mr. Lowery enjoys working, hunting, and riding dirt bikes.

Robert W. Miller
Plant Manager
Diamond Products International, Inc.
15955 West Hardy Street, Suite 300
Houston, TX 77060–3158
(713) 847–4181
Fax: (713) 999–1125

3545

Business Information: Diamond Products International (DPI), Inc. is a manufacturer of drill bits for use in the oil field industry. As Plant Manager, Mr. Miller is responsible for the management and oversight of all plant operations. He also organized the Company's in–house training program, and now conducts the employee training seminars. **Career Steps:** Plant Manager, Diamond Products International, Inc. (1994–Present); Plant Superintendent, Baroid Corporation (1991–1994); Manufacturing Supervisor, Strata–Bit Corporation (1985–1991). **Associations & Accomplishments:** Society of Mechanical Engineers; Church of Christ; East Montgomery County Sports Association. **Education:** Attended numerous Continuing Education credit courses and seminars. **Personal:** Married to Vickie in 1976. Two children: Jennifer and Travis. Mr. Miller enjoys gardening and coaching baseball.

Eric Pfeiffer
Market Development Manager
Simonds Industries, Inc.
135 Intervale Road
Fitchburg, MA 01420–6519
(508) 343–3731
Fax: (508) 343–3571
EMail: See Below

3545

Business Information: Simonds Industries, Inc., established in 1832, is the second largest cutting tool manufacturer in the industry. As Market Development Manager, Mr. Pfeiffer examines new markets, new market approaches, and new products, and learns how to utilize new techniques in the field. Internet users can reach him via: pfeiffer@simondsind.com. **Career Steps:** Market Development Manager, Simonds Industries, Inc. (1994–Present); Neill Tools, Inc.: Vice President of Marketing (1990–1994), Marketing Manager (1987–1990); Production Control Manager, Capewell Manufacturing Company (1982–1987). **Associations & Accomplishments:** IDA/ASMMA Young Executives Forum. **Education:** Dartmouth College, Bachelor's degree (1980). **Personal:** Married to Eileen in 1982. Four children: Erin, William, Robert, and John. Mr. Pfeiffer enjoys music, sports, and rock climbing.

Eric L. Burton
Regional Manager
Duo–Fast Corporation
11100 North East 34th Circle
Vancouver, WA 98682
(360) 254–2976
Fax: (360) 260–7843
EMAIL: See Below

3546

Business Information: Duo–Fast Corporation is a manufacturer of pneumatic tools and fasteners. As Regional Manager, Mr. Burton oversees sales, service and distribution on the west coast. Internet users can reach him at: erburton@aol.com. **Career Steps:** Regional Manager, Duo–East Corporation (1992–Present); Purchasing Manager, Crossroads Industries (1986–1991); Security Supervisor, Contemporary Services (1985–1986). **Education:** Arizona State University (1984). **Personal:** Married to Kelly in 1992. Mr. Burton enjoys sports and outdoor activities.

Michael J. Ward
President
American Point and Grind
5119 Mallard Drive
Bensalem, PA 19020
(215) 639–7799
Fax: (215) 639–7298

3546

Business Information: American Point and Grind is a manufacturers' representative with emphasis on industrial cutting tools and hand tools. Mr. Ward established AP&G in 1988, overseeing sales and marketing, payables, various administrative functions, and contract solicitation. Concurrently, he serves as an Instructor at Dale Carnegie & Associates. **Career Steps:** President, American Point and Grind (1988–Present); Instructor, Dale Carnegie & Associates (1988–Present); District Manager, Precision Twist Drive (1978–1987). **Associations & Accomplishments:** Dale Carnegie Sales Course Instructor (Avocational). **Education:** Central Michigan University, B.S. (1978). **Personal:** Married to Janet in 1980. Three children: James, Lindsay, and Katelyn. Mr. Ward enjoys golf, boating, and coaching Little League Baseball.

Alfredo Dannenberg
• • • —— ◉ —— • • •

President
Acos Dannenberg, Ltda.
Av Afonso De Sampaio E. Sousa 299
Sao Paulo, Brazil 08270–000
55–11–2056776
Fax: 55–11–9445926

3547

Business Information: Acos Dannenberg, Ltda. is the only rolling steel mill specializing in the production of net shapes, in the Southern Hemisphere. The Company produces steel from which manufacturers produce sections for manifolds, truck wheel side rings, automotive hinges, thresher bars, bulb flats for shipyards, patrol blades, pole shoes for electric motors, and a wide range of products for many other industries. As President, Mr. Dannenberg coordinates, supervises, and authorizes all the operational activities of the Company. **Career Steps:** President, Acos Dannenberg, Ltda. (1954–Present). **Associations & Accomplishments:** Americas Society, Inc.; National Geographic Society; Nacional Club; Sao Paulo Golf Club. **Education:** Educated in Germany and Switzerland. **Personal:** Mr. Dannenberg enjoys playing saxaphone, electric organ, and piano, classical and jazz music, golf, and reading Shakespeare.

Edward L. Blackmon
Vice President of Management Information Systems
The ESAB Group, Inc.
411 South Ebenezer Road
Florence, SC 29501–0545
(803) 664–4271
Fax: Please mail or call

3548

Business Information: The ESAB Group, Inc. is a worldwide manufacturer of welding and cutting products at seven principal locations in North America. Established in the early 1900s, The ESAB Group, Inc. currently employs over 2,000 people in North America. With 28 years in the manufacturing industry, Mr. Blackmon joined The ESAB Group in 1989. Currently serving as Vice President of Management Information Systems, he oversees all informations systems organization in North America. **Career Steps:** Vice President of Management Information Systems, The ESAB Group, Inc. (1989–Present); Vice President of Management Information Systems, LTEC (1985–1989); Various Management Positions, Union Carbide Corp. (1967–1985). **Associations & Accomplishments:** DPMA; APICS. **Education:** University of South Carolina; APICS–CFPIM. **Personal:** Mr. Blackmon enjoys golf, reading, computing, fitness, travel, and music.

Norman M. Sted Jr.
Regional Manager
Lincoln Electric
5717 North West 158th Street
Hialeah, FL 33014
(305) 556–0142
Fax: (305) 822–9129

3548

Business Information: Lincoln Electric is one of the largest manufacturers and distributors of ARC welding products in the world. Products manufactured at the 16 plants are shipped to consumers worldwide. The Company, with estimated sales in excess of 1 billion dollars, was established in 1895 and currently employs over 6,000 people. As Regional Manager, Mr. Sted has oversight of the Latin America Region. He supervises a staff of nine people and is responsible for all personnel concerns, human resource concerns, and training of his staff. Mr. Sted reviews new contracts, handles distribution of products to his region, oversees all current accounts, and develops new accounts for the Company. **Career Steps:** Lincoln Electric: Regional Manager (1991–Present), Country Manager (1981–1991), Technical Representative (1978–1981). **Associations & Accomplishments:** American Welding Society; American Management Society. **Education:** Adrian College, B.S. (1978); Metallurgy, Engineering, Professional Sales Course. **Personal:** Married to Kathy in 1984. Two children: Norm M. III and Brittany. Mr. Sted enjoys golf.

Zigmund Tytko Jr.
Plant Manager
Lincoln Electric Company
22801 St. Clair Avenue
Euclid, OH 44117–2524
(216) 383–2710
Fax: (216) 383–2889

3548

Business Information: Lincoln Electric Company is a manufacturing company primarily focused on the production of arc welding machines and related supplies for heavy construction (i.e. automotive, industrial equipment, and bridge constructing industries). International in scope, the Company is growing through acquisition, and has offices in the U.S., France, Canada, Australia, and Norway. Established in 1895, the Company employs 3,000 people and has an estimated annual revenue of $1 billion. As Plant Manager, Mr. Tytko oversees all aspects of manufacturing and production, and is directly responsible for 1,000 people, and 13 supervisors who report directly to him. **Career Steps:** Lincoln Electric Company: Plant Manager (1992–Present), Assistant Superintendent (1989–1992), General Foreman (1980–1989), Shift Foreman (1978–1980). **Education:** Cleveland State University, B.B.A. (1973). **Personal:** Married to Lorraine in 1977. Two children: Gina and Jill. Mr. Tytko enjoys hunting and fishing.

George Partyka
Director of Transfer System Division
Ann Arbor Machine Company
3388 Landings Drive
Ann Arbor, MI 48103
(313) 475–0505 Ext: 221
Fax: (313) 475–4336

3549

Business Information: Ann Arbor Machine Company is an industrial machinery fabrication plant, specializing in the manufacture of metal removal equipment. A design engineer with over 15 years expertise in machine tool design, George Partyka serves as Director of Ann Arbor's Transfer System Division. His primary responsibilities involve the process and conceptual design of machine products, as well as the overall operational direction of the Division. **Career Steps:** Director of Transfer System Division, Ann Arbor Machine Company (1993–Present); Project Engineer, Standard Tool & Manufacturing Company (1985–1993); Design Engineer, Edson Tool Company (1982–1985). **Associations & Accomplishments:** Society of Manufacturing Engineers; Coast Guard Auxiliary. **Education:** Silesian Polytechnic, M.S. (1974). **Personal:** Married to Mary in 1974. Two children: Alexandra and Anna. Mr. Partyka enjoys sailing, photography, and snow–skiing.

Joseph H. Hollander
Executive Vice President
Automated Components International/Pennsylvania Sewing Research Corporation
1321 East Drinker Street
Scranton, PA 18512–2612
(717) 344–4000
Fax: (717) 343–0618
EMAIL: See Below

3552

Business Information: Automated Components International/Pennsylvania Sewing Research Corporation is an establishment engaged in the manufacture of machinery used in the sewn products industry. As Executive Vice President and Owner, Mr. Hollander oversees all aspects of Company operations. Internet users can reach him via: jhh18@epix.net. **Career Steps:** Executive Vice President, Automated Components International/Pennsylvania Sewing Research Corporation (1988–Present); President, Jaycee Manufacturing, Inc. (1978–1988). **Associations & Accomplishments:** Executive Board, American Apparel Manufacturers Association; Associate Member, Congress; First Vice President, Temple Israel Scranton; Executive Board, Jewish Community Center of Scranton; Board of Directors, St. Francis of Assisi Soup Kitchen; Board of Directors, Scranton Primary Health Care Center; Board of Directors, Association for Retarded Citizens; Recognized for Service to his Industry form AAMA (1996). **Education:** New York University, B.S. in Business Administration (1979). **Personal:** Married to Ruth K. in 1983. Three children: Neil, Allison, and Max.

Sheryl S. Packard, CPA
Controller
Accent Color Science
800 Connecticut Boulevard
East Hartford, CT 06108
(860) 610–4109
Fax: (860) 610–4001

3552

Business Information: Accent Color Science specializes in the development and production of a line of printing systems for use in combination with high speed, black and white laser printers. As Controller, Ms. Packard manages the accounting department, treasury, risk management, and systems implementation. **Career Steps:** Controller, Accent Color Science (1996–Present); The Stanley Works: Team Leader/Systems Configuration and Implementation (1995–1996), Senior Internal Auditor (1993–1995); Public Accountant, Price Waterhouse LLP (1990–1993). **Associations & Accomplishments:** American Institute of Certified Public Accountants; Connecticut Society of Certified Public Accountants. **Education:** University of California – Los Angeles, B.A. (1990). **Personal:** Ms. Packard enjoys golf, piano, skiing, hiking, and singing.

Mary Louise Bovenzi
Human Resource Director
Double E Company, Inc.
319 Manley Street
West Bridgewater, MA 02379–1034
(508) 588–8099
Fax: (508) 580–2915

3554

Business Information: Double E Company, Inc. specializes in the design and manufacture of core chucks, shafts, and other web tension devices for the paper, film and foil industries. Established in 1975, Double E Company currently employs 100 people. As Human Resource Director, Mrs. Bovenzi is responsible for all aspects of human resource activities, including recruiting, retention, salary administration, benefits management, employee relations and safety. **Career Steps:** Human Resource Director, Double E. Company, Inc. (1995–Present); Human Resource Director, Evanswood Center (1992–1995); Human Resource Director, Falmouth National Bank (1990–1992). **Associations & Accomplishments:** New Member Committee, North East Human Resource Association. **Education:** Emmanuel College, W.M.S. Program; Clark University, B.A. in English and Education. **Personal:** Mrs. Bovenzi enjoys health and fitness.

W. G. Cook
Technical Manager
Valmet
27 Allen Street
Hudson Falls, NY 12839–1901
(518) 747–1504
Fax: (518) 747–1321

3554

Business Information: The Non–Wovens Machinery Group of Valmet is a developer, seller, designer, manufacturer, and start–up specialist for papermaking machines. Products include paper for tea bags, filters, and currency. As Technical Manager, Mr. Cook is responsible for leading research and development activities, technical engineering, and guiding project managers. **Career Steps:** Valmet: Technical Manager (1995–Present), Chief Engineer – Sandy Hill (1990–1995); Sandy Hill: Chief Design Engineer (1988–1990), Chief Development Engineer (1978–1988). **Associations & Accomplishments:** Chairman, TAPPI Engineering Division; Past Chairman TAPPI Fluid Mechanic Committee; International Association of Scientific Papermaking. **Education:** Adirondack Community College; Hudson Valley Community College, A.A.S. (1964). **Personal:** Married to Susan in 1968. Two children: Christopher M., and Craig W. Mr. Cook enjoys building and racing mountain bikes.

Allen D. Moore
Applications Engineer
AES Engineered Systems
436 Quaker Road
Queensbury, NY 12804
(518) 793–8801
Fax: (518) 793–9392

3554

Business Information: AES Engineered Systems is an original equipment manufacturer, specializing in the fabrication of paper machine and related papermill production auxillary equipment. An expert in applications design with over 10 years expertise, Mr. Moore joined AES in 1989 as an Applications Engineer. In this capacity, he provides sales consulting, application design and engineered installations of systems utilized in the performance of paper shard quality. **Career Steps:** Applications Engineer, AES Engineered Systems (1989–Present); Albany International: Applications Specialist (1986–1989), Applications Designer (1985–1986). **Associations & Accomplishments:** Technical Association of Pulp and Paper Industry, National and Eastern District. **Education:** Buffalo State College, BET (1984), AAS in Mechanical Engineering. **Personal:** Married to Lisa in 1988. Mr. Moore enjoys racquetball, snow mobiling, hiking, travel, and corvettes.

Chris A. Sparks
Systems Support Specialist
Lexmark, Inc.
740 New Circle Road, NW, Building 42
Lexington, KY 40511
(606) 232–1207
Fax: (606) 232–2873
EMAIL: See Below

3555

Business Information: Lexmark, Inc. is a manufacturer of printers and printer accessories for various wholesalers and retailers. As Systems Support Specialist, Mr. Sparks supports and develops new technology and is responsible for product development, maintenance, computer functions, and Information Systems. **Career Steps:** Systems Support Specialist, Lexmark, Inc. (1994–Present); Hospital Corpsman, U.S. Navy (1987–1992). **Associations & Accomplishments:** American Statistical Association. **Education:** National University, B.S. in Mathematics (1992); Attending: Eastern Kentucky University Graduate School. **Personal:** Married to Denise in 1988. Mr. Sparks enjoys weightlifting and firearm competitions.

Bill E. Davis
Executive Vice President
Sasib Bakery North America, Inc.
P.O. Box 869034
Plano, TX 75086–9034
(214) 422–5808
Fax: (214) 424–5041

3556

Business Information: Sasib Bakery North America, Inc. is an international designer and manufacturer of large wholesale bread and bun bakery equipment. The Company is composed of five bakeries and three package companies (buns, breads, products), in addition to the manufacturing division. International in scope, Sasib spans North America, Holland, Denmark, Italy and England. Established in 1948, Sasib Bakery North America, Inc. reports annual revenue in excess of $32 million and currently employs 150 people. As Executive Vice President, Mr. Davis is responsible for all aspects of sales and marketing, including marketing his own equipment for the Company all over the world and assisting other companies with technical support world–wide. **Career Steps:** Executive Vice President, Sasib Bakery North America, Inc. (1982–Present); Vice President of Sales and Marketing, Stewart Systems (1982–1986); Vice President and Engineer, Mrs. Baird's Bakery (1980–1982). **Education:** University of Texas, B.S. in Mechanical Engineering (1959); Tyler Junior College, A.A.; SMU, graduate work in Engineering Administration. **Personal:** Married to Nelda R. in 1959. Three children: Scott J., Andrew B., and Todd H. Mr. Davis enjoys sports, reading, and teaching.

Laura Freeman
Controller
Ala Cart Inc.
4400 K. Stuart Andrew Boulevard
Charlotte, NC 28217
(704) 527–7779
Fax: (704) 527–7702

3556

Business Information: Ala Cart Inc. manufactures and sells food service equipment (dish ware and food carts) to healthcare facilities. Distributing to the United States and Canada, the Company was established in 1989 and has estimated annual sales of $11 million. As Controller, Ms. Freeman is responsible for all financial aspects of the Company, including all financial reporting, budgeting, and cash management. **Career Steps:** Controller, Ala Cart Inc. (1994–Present); Math Tutor, College of Charleston (1990–Present); Accountant, Medical University of South Carolina (1991–1994). **Associations & Accomplishments:** Who's Who Among American College Students; Phi Kappa Pi; Omicron Delta Kappa; National Business Honor Society; National Latin Honor Society; Former Charleston Symphony Orchestra Singers Guild Member; Church Choir. **Education:** College of Charleston, B.S. in Accounting. **Personal:** Married to Melvin in 1994. Ms. Freeman enjoys singing, piano, cooking, and cross–stitch.

Timothy G. Kemper, P.E.
Director of Engineering
French Oil Mill Machinery Company
P.O. Box 920
Piqua, OH 45356–0920
(513) 773–3420 Ext. 430
Fax: (513) 773–3424

3556

Business Information: French Oil Mill Machinery Company designs custom plants and equipment for extraction of vegetable oil from seeds and nuts. Mr. Kemper joined the Company as Project Manager in 1986 after attaining his Mechanical Engineering Degree from the University of Cincinnati. Promoted to Assistant Product Manager in 1987, and to Product Manager in 1989, he moved into his present position as Director of Engineering in 1993. His responsibilities now include management of product development, engineering, and purchasing functions for the Oilseed Division. **Career Steps:** French Oil Mill Machinery Company: Director of Engineering (1993–Present), Product Manager (1989–1992), Assistant Product Manager (1987–1988); Project Engineer (1986). **Associations & Accomplishments:** National Society of Professional Engineers; Thomas Newcomen Society; American Oil Chemists Society; Ohio Society of Professional Engineers; Tau Beta Pi National Engineering Honor Society. **Education:** University of Cincinnati, B.S. in Mechanical Engineering (1986). **Personal:** Married to Joyce in 1986. Two children: Molly and Morgan. Mr. Kemper enjoys basketball, genealogy, gardening, and computers.

Michael B. Wilcox
Sales and Marketing Director
Elopak, Inc.
30000 South Hill Road
New Hudson, MI 48165
(810) 486–4600
Fax: (810) 486–5292

3556

Business Information: Elopak, Inc. is a manufacturer of packaging machinery and material used to fill cartons for the liquid food industry (i.e., Minute Maid, Dean Foods Tropicana). They also produce the actual cartons (forms and fills packaging). Holding various managerial roles with Elopak since 1985, Mr. Wilcox was appointed to his current executive role in 1994. He is responsible for directing all aspects of the sales and marketing functions of the Company's products, as well as supervision of sales support staff. **Career Steps:** Elopak, Inc.: Sales and Marketing Director (1994–Present), National Account Manager (1992–1994), Marketing Manager (1989–1992), Product Manager (1985–1988). **Associations**

& Accomplishments: Dairy and Food Industry Supplier Association; Institute of Packaging Professionals; City of Wixom, Michigan: Economic Development Committee, Strategic Planning Task Force. **Education:** University of Detroit, M.B.A. (1991); Michigan State University, B.S. in Packaging (1978). **Personal:** Married to Lucile in 1977. Two children: Corinne and Brendan. Mr. Wilcox enjoys managing a Little League baseball team, golf, and cross–country skiing.

Jeet Bhatia

Executive Vice President
Harper International Corp.
100 W. Drullard Avenue
Lancaster, NY 14086–1649
(716) 684–7400
Fax: (716) 684–7405

3559

Business Information: Harper International Corp. is a designer and manufacturer of industrial furnaces and kilns. Established in 1924, Harper International reports annual revenue of $20 million and currently employs 90 people. As Executive Vice President, Mr. Bhatia serves as Chief Operating Officer, responsible for all Corporate administrative operations and financial aspects. **Career Steps:** Harper International Corp.: Executive Vice President and Chief Operating Officer (1995–Present), Vice President (1994–1995); Vice President, Bocedyne Corp. (1989–1994). **Associations & Accomplishments:** American Institute of Chemical Engineers; American Chemical Society. **Education:** Rutgers University: M.B.A. (1978), B.S. in Chemical Engineering. **Personal:** Two children: Remy and Neta. Mr. Bhatia enjoys reading, writing, travel, art, and films.

Alexander Esparra

Manufacturing Engineering
Bryant Electric
P.O. Box 2008
Aibonito, Puerto Rico 00705–2008
(809) 735–8011
Fax: (787) 735–9223

3559

Business Information: Bryant Electric is a manufacturer of electrical components. The company has three central warehouses and approximately 300 sales locations world wide. As Manufacturing Engineering, Mr. Esparra is responsible for the maintenance of machinery and the physical plant at his location. He is in charge of the computers, general administration, and manufacturing standards of the Aibonito operation. **Career Steps:** Bryant Electric: Manufacturing Engineering (1993–Present), Engineer (1992–1996); Sparatec: Puerto Rico, President (1982–1989), New Jersey – President (1970–1982). **Associations & Accomplishments:** President, Board of Trustees, Ramapo State College; Committee of Planning, City of Paterson. **Education:** Newark School of Engineering (1955–1960). **Personal:** Married to Nerida in 1968. Four children: Michelle, Jacquie, Jorge, and Luis. Mr. Esparra enjoys private piloting.

Karl–Heinz Giebmanns

Owner and President
International Tool Machinery of Florida
5 Industry Drive
Palm Coast, FL 32137–5104
(904) 446–0500
Fax: (904) 445–5700

3559

Business Information: International Tool Machinery of Florida is one of the leading international manufacturers of precision computer–controlled grinding machines. Established in 1981, International Tool Machinery of Florida reports annual revenue of $5 million and currently employs 30 people. Immigrating to the U.S. from Germany in 1978, Mr. Giebmanns has vast international expertise in mechanical engineering design. Founding International Tool Machinery in 1981, as President he provides the overall direction and vision for the Company's continued growth, quality product output, and development. **Career Steps:** Owner and President, International Tool Machinery of Florida (1981–Present); Chief Engineer and Plant Manager, Hertlein – USA (1978–1980); Technical Manager, Belau S.A. – Mexico (1975–1978); Design Manager, Junker – Germany (1969–1975). **Associations & Accomplishments:** Published in newspapers in Florida and Connecticut. **Education:** Mr. Giebmanns completed his education in Mechanical Engineering in Germany in 1968. **Personal:** Married to Karola in 1969. Two children: Susanne and Thomas. Mr. Giebmanns enjoys sailing.

Roger M. Hoy, Ph.D.

New Product Development Manager
Hennessy Industries, Inc.
1601 Hennessy Drive
La Vergne, TN 37086
(615) 641–7533
Fax: (615) 641–7556

3559

Business Information: Hennessy Industries, Inc. is a manufacturer of products for the wheel service industry, including tire changers and wheel balancers. As New Product Development Manager, Dr. Hoy handles new product development and various other administrative activities. **Career Steps:** New Product Development Manager, Hennessy Industries, Inc. (1995–Present); Jacobs Vehicle Equipment Company: Product Development Manager (1990–1995), Senior Engineer (1989). **Associations & Accomplishments:** SAE; ASAE. **Education:** North Carolina State University: Ph.D. (1990), M.S. (1986); University of Georgia, B.S. (1984). **Personal:** Married to Diane A. in 1989. Dr. Hoy enjoys being with his family.

Yoichiro (Sunny) Ishikawa

Senior Vice President of Research and Development
Union Special Corporation
1 Union Special Plaza
Huntley, IL 60142–7007
(708) 669–4299
Fax: (708) 669–5765

3559

Business Information: Established in 1881, Union Special Corporation is an international manufacturer of industrial sewing equipment. Mr. Ishikawa has been employed with Union Special Corporation for over 15 years, starting out as a Product Line Manager. He was promoted to Sr. Vice President of Development in 1989. In this capacity Mr. Ishikawa manages the research and development activities of the company, including German and Japanese Subsidiaries. **Career Steps:** Union Special Corporation: Senior Vice President of Research and Development (1989–Present), Product Line Manager (1979–1984); Manager of Corporate Design Engineering, William Wrigley, Jr. Company (1984–1989). **Associations & Accomplishments:** American Society of Mechanical Engineers; Charter Member, MAPI Council on Engineering and Technology; Advisory Committee, McHenry County College on Council on Technology. **Education:** Illinois Institute of Technology, B.S. MAE (1973). **Personal:** Two children: Miki Thomas and Sumi Ann. Mr. Ishikawa enjoys golf, skiing, and is a private pilot with instrument rating.

Mr. Quinton "Coles" Marsh

Vice President
JCV, Inc.
7492 Old Alexandria Ferry Road
Clinton, MD 20735
(301) 868–2221
Fax: (301) 856–2688

3559

Business Information: JCV, Inc. is a regional leader in petroleum marketing equipment distribution. Headquartered in Clinton, MD, JCV, Inc. has additional branches in Salisbury, MD, and Roanoke, VA. In his current capacity, Mr. Marsh is responsible for all marketing and sales management. Established in 1967, JCV, Inc. presently employs 26 people, and has an estimated annual revenue in excess of $13 million. **Career Steps:** Vice President, JCV, Inc. (1979–Present); Sales Representative, Pump & Tank Company (1972 – 1979); Restaurant Manager, Commander Hotels, Inc. (1968–1972). **Associations & Accomplishments:** Former President, Current Membership Chairman, American Society of Petroleum Operations Engineers (ASPOE); Board of Directors, Group 10 Chairman, Petroleum Equipment Institute (PEI). **Education:** Chouau College; Palm Beach University, B.S. (1971). **Personal:** Married to Renee in 1971. Two children: Angela and Quinn. Mr. Marsh enjoys golf, sailing, tennis, and racquetball in his leisure time.

Jerry R. O'Donniley

Quality Assurance Manager
Noell, Inc.
2411 Dulles Corner Park, Suite 410
Herndon, VA 22071–3430
(703) 793–2247
Fax: (703) 793–4974

3559

Business Information: Noell, Inc. is a manufacturer of power plant equipment. International in scope, Noell has four manufacturing plants throughout the U.S. and distributes through over 200 global locations. As Quality Assurance Manager, Mr. O'Donniley is responsible for quality assurance for all U.S. divisions, in addition to designing and implementing quality projects and management teams. **Career Steps:** Noell, Inc.: Quality Assurance Manager (1996–Present), Site Construction Manager (1995–1996); Technical Services Manager, Dynasteel, Inc. (1988–1992); Technical Services Supervisor, Bechtel Power Corporation (1983–1986). **Associations & Accomplishments:** American Society for Quality Control; Civil Air Patrol – Auxiliary of the U.S. Air Force; American Legion. **Education:** State Technical Institute, A.E.T. with high honors (1978). **Personal:** Married to Carole in 1985. One child: Monica. Mr. O'Donniley enjoys piloting private aircraft and restoring automobiles and aircraft.

Mr. Masashi Osada

Treasurer/Controller of Mexico Operations
TKS Industrial Company
26100 American Drive, Suite 400
Southfield, MI 48034
(810) 355–0722
Fax: (810) 355–0360

3559

Business Information: TKS Industrial Company is an engineering and construction firm for automobile paint finishing systems. Customers include GM, Ford, Honda and Toyota. Corporate headquarters are located in Japan, with subsidiaries in Mexico, U.S., Canada and throughout the world. As Treasurer, Mr. Osada is the company officer responsible for receipt, custody, investment and disbursement of funds for the North American operations. As Controller of Mexico Operations, Mr. Osada is responsible for treasury functions, as well as overseeing accounting functions. Established in 1981, TKS Industrial Company employs 120 people with annual sales of $60 million. **Career Steps:** Treasurer – North American Operations (1992–Present), Controller of Mexico Operations (1990–Present), TKS Industrial Company. **Education:** Keio University, B.A in Economics (1983); University of Toronto, Graduate Studies (1987). **Personal:** Married to Takako in 1991. One child: Junpei. Mr. Osada enjoys travel and is bilingual in Japanese and English.

Michael E. Sharpless

Hewlett–Packard Strategic Alliance Manager
Texas Instruments, Inc.
1920 Main Street, Suite 900
Irvine, CA 92714–7228
(714) 660–8135
Fax: (714) 553–0857
EMAIL: mycl@msg.ti.com

3559

Business Information: Texas Instruments, Inc. is a one of the world's largest suppliers of the semiconductor products which are the core of today's electronic equipment. The Company consists of five business groups: Semiconductors, Defense Electronics, Software, Personal Productivity Products, and Materials and Controls. In the Semiconductor group, TI remains the acknowledged leader in the rapidly growing digital signal processor market. At the Irvine, California office, Mr. Sharpless serves as the HP Strategic Alliance Manager in the Semiconductor group, where he manages the technology alliance and joint venture efforts between Hewlett–Packard and Texas Instruments. Joining Texas Instruments in 1989, Mr. Sharpless was appointed as Hewlett Packard Strategic Alliance Manager in 1993. Although employed by Texas Instruments, he is responsible for developing and facilitating technology arrangements that will benefit both corporations. TI revenues in 1995 were $13.1 billion, up 27 percent from 1994. **Career Steps:** Texas Instruments, Inc.: Hewlett–Packard Strategic Alliance Manager (1993–Present), Western U.S. Design Center Manager (1992–1994), Southwest ASIC Design Center Manager (1989–1992); Western U.S. ASIC Design Center Manager, Arrow Electronics (1986–1989); Gate Array Development Engineer VLSI Technology, Inc. (1984–1986); ASIC Design Engineer, American Microsystems, Inc. (1981–1984). **Associations & Accomplishments:** American Management Association; Chair, TI – Irvine United Way; Published in technical conferences, IEEE, and electronic periodicals. **Education:** University of Santa Clara, M.S. in Engineering Management (1985); California State University – Sacramento, B.S. in Electrical Engineering

(1981); Certificate in Strategic Management, American Management Association (1995). **Personal:** Married to Wendy Housman, J.D. in 1991. One child: Katherine Anne. Mr. Sharpless enjoys spending time with his family, travel, wine appreciation, art, music, and reading.

James Simmons

President
Mico Equipment and Supply Corporation
RR Box 9B
New Berlin, NY 13411
(607) 847–6815
Fax: (607) 847–8323

3559

Business Information: Mico Equipment and Supply Corporation designs, manufactures, sells, and installs processing and cleaning systems for food, dairy, beverage, and pharmaceutical production facilities. Established in 1989, the Company currently employ 20 people and expects to post sales in excess of $5 million in 1996. As President, Mr. Simmons manages all aspects of company operations, concentrating on sales, marketing, and staff training and development. **Career Steps:** President, Mico Equipment and Supply Corporation (1989–Present); Sales and Design, W.A. Tompkins Company (1985–1988); Sales, United Dairy Machinery Corporation (1982–1985); Sales and Sales Manager, Plan a Home of Sidney (1980–1982). **Associations & Accomplishments:** Rotary International; Northeast Ice Cream Association; Food Industry Suppliers Association; New York Sanitations; New York State Dairy Boosters; District 3 Congressman for American Motorcycle Association. **Education:** St. Lawrence University. **Personal:** Married to Jacalyn in 1993. Five children: Lisa, Corrina, Shannon, Larissa, and Jason. Mr. Simmons enjoys motorcycles and off road activities.

AMF REECE
Better Ideas, Better Made

John Suddarth

President and Chief Executive Officer
AMF Reece Inc.
P.O. Box 15778
Richmond, VA 23227
(804) 559–5000
Fax: (804) 559–5210

3559

Business Information: AMF Reece Inc. is the only American–based manufacturer of specialized industrial sewing machines. AMF Reece invents, manufactures, and markets innovative products which enhance quality, increase productivity, and simplify operations in its customer's factories. AMF Reece invented each machine it sells. International in scope, AMF Reece has offices and distributors worldwide and factories in the U.S. UK, and Czech Republic. As President and CEO reporting to the Board of Directors, John Suddarth sets the strategic direction for the Company. In the intensely competitive sewing industry, constant product innovation,continuous improvement in quality, and practical cost reduction are key. John Suddarth leads an enthusiastic and responsive team which supplies, serves and supports AMF Reece products and customers worldwide. **Career Steps:** President and Chief Executive Officer, AMF Reece Inc. (1994–Present); Manager Lane Products, AMF Bowling Inc. (1990–1994); System Integration Engineer, General Electric Company (1987–1988); U.S. Army Officer, U.S. Army (1981–1987). **Associations & Accomplishments:** Sewn Products Equipment Suppliers Association; Hanover Association of Businesses; Boy Scouts of America; Fluent in German. **Education:** Stanford University, M.B.A. (1990); U.S. Military Academy, B.S. (1981). **Personal:** Married to Sigrid in 1985. Mr. Suddarth enjoys running, rollerblading, hiking, reading, and gardening.

Keizo Yamada

General Manager
Kubota Corporation
2372 A Qume Drive
San Jose, CA 95131
(408) 474–0200
Fax: (408) 474–0207

3559

Business Information: Kubota Corporation, established in 1889, is an international machinery manufacturer with five divisions worldwide: consolidated machinery; water conveyance; environmental; materials; and building and housing materials. With an estimated revenue of $12.5 billion, the Company presently employs over 16,000 people. As General Manager, Mr. Yamada operates out of the Silicon Valley office in the Department of Business Planning and Development. His responsibilities include tracking corporate investments and the development of new business opportunities. **Career Steps:** General Manager, Kubota Corporation (1989–Present); General Manager, Taiyo Consultants Company, Ltd. (1981–1989). **Education:** San Jose State University, B.A. (1971); International Development Center of Japan, M.B.A. Equivalent (1981). **Personal:** Married to Nitaya in 1983. Two children: Keiko and Takashi. Mr. Yamada enjoys travel.

Richard E. Hines

Manager – MIS CAD/CAM
Carver Pump Co.
2415 Park Avenue
Muscatine, IA 52761–5636
(319) 263–3410
Fax: (319) 263–4565
EMAIL: See Below

3561

Business Information: Carver Pump Co., established in 1937 and an ISO–9001 certified manufacturer, specializes in the manufacture, development and design of centrifugal pumps. Products are distributed to commercial and military entities throughout the U.S. A certified engineering technician with special expertise in CAD/CAM applications, Richard Hines has served as Carver Pump's Information Systems Manager since 1994. His duties involve the supervision of systems support staff, as well as the implementation and maintenance of all computer systems (i.e., MRP, CAD/CAM, Payroll, PC–based software applications). A community and civic minded individual, Richard is active in numerous sports and educational enhancement projects, as well as serves as an EMT with the Muscatine Ambulance Service. Internet users can also reach Richard via: CARVERPUMP@MUSCA-NET.COM **Career Steps:** IS Manager, Carver Pump Co. (1984–Present); EMT, Muscatine Ambulance (1980–Present); Design Technician, Stanley Consultants (1974–1982). **Associations & Accomplishments:** National Institute for Certification of Engineering Technicians; President & Board of Directors (2 terms), Applicon CAD/CAM User Group; Active Volunteer: United Way of Muscatine; Childrens Miracle Network. **Education:** Morrison Institute of Technology, A.S. (1973); Board of Medical Examiners – EMT (1985); Continuing Education – Computer Sciences. **Personal:** Married to Beverly in 1974. Three children: Richard, Perry and Amber. Mr. Hines enjoys family, schools & community activites, and computers.

Andrew M. Ondish

Regional Sales Manager
Hazleton Pumps, Inc.
225 North Cedar Street
Hazleton, PA 18201
(717) 455–7711
Fax: (717) 459–2852
EMAIL: See Below

3561

Business Information: Hazleton Pumps, Inc. specializes in the manufacture of centrifugal pumps, (i.e. horizontal, vertical, and submersible), for mining, steel manufacturing, and water/solid filtration. Established in 1917, the Company employs 250 people, and has an estimated annual revenue of $26 million. As Regional Sales Manager, Mr. Ondish oversees sales, marketing, public relations, and strategic planning. He is responsible for direct supervision of three manufacturers sales agencies, increasing product knowledge through training, personnel management, and support. Internet users can reach him via: atoz@prolog.net. **Career Steps:** Regional Sales Manager, Hazleton Pumps, Inc. (1995–Present); Product Engineer, Sundstrand Fluid Handling (1989–1995); Lease Analyst Supervisor, Source One, Inc. (1985–1989). **Associations & Accomplishments:** U.S. Army Reserve, Captain with twelve years commissioned service. **Education:** Colorado School of Mines, B.Sc. (1984); U.S. Army Quartermaster Officer Basic Course; U.S. Army Officer Advance Course. **Personal:** Married to Zelda K. in 1987. Three children: Andrew D., Hannah R., and Christopher A.. Mr. Ondish enjoys golf, rugby, fishing, and camping.

Mark C. Schaub

Engineering Manager
BW/IP International
1132 North 7th Street
San Jose, CA 95112–4427
(408) 298–0123
Fax: (408) 297–7461

3561

Business Information: BW/IP International is a manufacturer of customized pump equipment for the petroleum and power industries, such as centrifugal pumps. Projects have included manufacturing pumps for the Alaskan Pipeline. Established in 1872, BW/IP International reports annual revenue of $450 million and currently employs 2,000 company–wide. A veteran of the Company for twenty–one years, Mr. Schaub was appointed as Engineering Manager of the San Jose Operations in 1988. He is responsible for the management of all engineering activities, including being personally involved in made–to–order systems by taking customer requirements and turning them into pumps. **Career Steps:** BW/IP International: Engineering Manager – San Jose Operations (1988–Present), Technical Services Manager – Los Angeles (1987–1988), Engineering Manager – Los Angeles (1981–1986). **Associations & Accomplishments:** American Society of Mechanical Engineers (ASME). **Education:** Michigan State University, B.S. in Mechanical Engineering (1974); University of California – Los Angeles, Executive Management Program. **Personal:** Mr. Schaub enjoys running and bicycling.

John C. Bandrowski

Chief Engineer of Applications and Linear Technology
Thomson Industries, Inc.
2 Channel Drive
Port Washington, NY 11050
(516) 883–8000
Fax: (516) 883–9039

3562

Business Information: Thomson Industries, Inc. manufactures linear anti–friction bearings and accessories for the automotive, packaging, and medical industries. Mr. Bandrowski joined Thomson upon the conferral of his Engineering Degree in 1968. Promoted to Chief Engineer of Applications and Linear Technology in 1987, he presently manages the Applications Engineering Department, providing services, training, and technical recommendations to clients and distributors. **Career Steps:** Thomson Industries, Inc.: Chief Engineer of Applications and Linear Technology (1987–Present), Applications Engineer (1980–1987), Sales Engineer (1969–1980). **Associations & Accomplishments:** Vice–Chairman, Bearing Technology Committee of American Bearing Manufacturing Association; Chairman, Linear Bearing Subcommittee of International Standards Organization; Chairman, Linear Bearing Subcommittee of ABMA; American National Standards Institute; AMT. **Education:** Rensselaer Polytechnic Institute, B.S. in Materials Engineering (1968). **Personal:** Married to Christine in 1995. Mr. Bandrowski enjoys gardening, golf, reading, music, and watching sports.

Richard A. Gedig

Division Controller
Rexnord Corporation
7601 Rockville Road
Indianapolis, IN 46206
(317) 273–5618
Fax: (317) 273–5760

3562

Business Information: Rexnord Corporation, a subsidiary of BTR, p.l.c. – based in London, England, is a manufacturer of Rex and Link–Belt Power Transmission products (industrial bearings). International in scope, Rexnord Corporation has fourteen locations throughout the U.S. (12), Germany (1), and Italy (1). A management executive with Rexnord since 1984, Richard Gedig was promoted to his current position as Division Controller in 1994. In this capacity, he is responsible for all accounting and payroll functions for two plant operations – one in Indiana and one in Tennessee. **Career Steps:** Rexnord Corporation: Division Controller (1994–Present), Manager of Finance & Accounting (1990–1994), Manager of Financial Planning (1985–1990), Accounting Manager (1984–1985). **Associations & Accomplishments:** Elder, Community Church of Greenwood. **Education:** University of Indianapolis, M.B.A. (1982); Indiana University, B.S. in Accounting. **Personal:** Married to Karen in 1978. Two children: Callie and Cole. Mr. Gedig enjoys spending time with his family, water sports activities, watching sports, and golf.

James Stuart Goddard

Plant Manager
Rotek, Inc.
8060 Production Drive
Florence, KY 41042
(606) 342–8430
Fax: (606) 342–8460
E–MAIL: See Below

3562

Business Information: Rotek, Inc., established in 1966, is part of an international group with three locations in the United States. The Corporation is a manufacturer of large diameter (60 inches) precision bearings and slewing rings used in a variety of satellite and commercial industries. As Plant Manager, Mr. Goddard has oversight of the Kentucky plant. His responsibilities include personnel, production, and general day–to–day operations of the facility. Internet users can reach him via: jgoddard@fuse.net. **Career Steps:** Rotek, Inc.: Plant Manager (1995–Present), Manufacturing Engineer Manager (1993–1995), Chief Inspector (1991–1993). **Associations & Accomplishments:** Integrated Quality System Beta Test Co–op; Non–destructive Testing Certificates. **Education:** Lorain Community College (1975); Level III NDT Test Qualification in magnetic particle and liquid penetrant inspection. **Personal:** Married to Joanne in 1975. Three children: Suzanne, Jarret, and Jim. Mr. Goddard enjoys golf and spending time with his family.

James O. Ferguson
Leader of Engineering Services
Ingersoll–Rand
Highway 45 South
Mayfield, KY 42066
(502) 251–1278
Fax: (502) 247–9851
EMAIL: See Below

3563

Business Information: Ingersoll–Rand, CENTAC Division, is a manufacturer of centrifugal air compressors for the automotive, textile, petroleum, and skiing industries. International in scope, this Division has offices in Kentucky and Italy. As Leader of Engineering Services, Mr. Ferguson manages the Technical Media Center, coordinates engineering changes, and reviews engineering quality costs. He is also an ISO 9001 auditor and coordinates all engineering correspondence with the Italy facility. Internet users can reach him via: JIMO_FERGUSON@INGERAND.ATTMAIL.COM. **Career Steps:** Ingersoll–Rand: Leader of Engineering Services (1995–Present); Engineering Coordinator (1984–1995), Spare Parts Consultant (1982–1984). **Education:** Murray State University, Bachelors (1996); University of Kentucky, Via Paducah Community College, Associate of Arts. **Personal:** Married to Roxanne Carol in 1976. One child: Jessica. Mr. Ferguson enjoys golf and restoring his 1971 Corvette.

Gilbert V. Laurin
Industrial Division Manager
Atlas Copco Compressors Canada
30 Rue Montrose
Dollard Des Ormeaux, Quebec H9B 3J9
(514) 421–4121
Fax: (514) 421–2092

3563

Business Information: The Atlas Copco Group is an international industrial company with its head office in Stockholm, Sweden. The Company has subsidiaries in more than 60 countries and independent distributors in a further 80. Atlas Copco Canada, Inc. was founded in 1949 as Canadian Copco Ltd., a sales company located in Port Arthur (now Thunder Bay), Ontario. It was opened mainly to service accounts related to Canada's mining industry. Products include: industrial compressors, oil–free compressors, portable compressors, air dryers, after coolers, energy recovery systems, control systems, filters, and specially built gas and process compressors, expansion turbines, and cryogenic pumps. As Industrial Division Manager, Mr. Laurin oversees all marketing, engineering, and advertising, and is responsible for management of profit/loss ratios. **Career Steps:** Industrial Division Manager, Atlas Copco Compressors (1969–Present). **Education:** Concordia University, Marketing; Montreal Institute of Technology. **Personal:** Married to Anne Marie Gitto in 1980. Mr. Laurin enjoys photography and mountain biking.

Richard A. Steben, CPA
General Accounting Manager
Ingersoll–Rand Company – Centrifugal Compressor Division
Highway 45 South
Mayfield, KY 42066
(502) 247–8640
Fax: (502) 247–9851

3563

Business Information: Ingersoll–Rand Company – Centrifugal Compressor Division is a manufacturer of centrifugal air compressors for the automotive, textile, and skiing industries. International in scope, the Centrifugal Compressor Division is a multi–site manufacturing division with locations in Kentucky, Italy, and India. As General Accounting Manager and a Certified Public Accountant, Mr. Steben manages worldwide forecasting and budgeting for the Centrifugal Compressor Division. **Career Steps:** Ingersoll–Rand Company: General Accounting Manager – Centrifugal Compressor Division (1992–Present), Cost Accountant – Portable Compressor Division (1991–1992), Internal Auditor – Corporate Headquarters (1990–1991). **Associations & Accomplishments:** Certified Public Accountant – North Carolina (1992). **Education:** Bentley College, B.S. in Accounting (1988). **Personal:** Mr. Steben enjoys recreation, sports, and outdoor activities.

L. Gail Susik
Marketing Director
Compressor Systems, Inc.
3809 S. Farm to Market Road 1788
Midland, TX 79703
(915) 563–1170
Fax: (915) 561–9732

3563

Business Information: Compressor Systems, Inc. is an international manufacturer of natural gas compressors. Celebrating its 25th anniversary, the Corporation is a strong part of this relatively young industry — technology has only made it cost effective to retrieve natural gas for the last 25 to 30 years. As Marketing Director, Ms. Susik is responsible for marketing and public relations. **Career Steps:** Marketing Director, Compressor Systems, Inc. (1996–Present); Marketing Director, Permian Telco Federal Credit Union (1992–1995); Community Coordinator, Midland ARC (1991–1994); Owner, Total Image Marketing (1989–1991). **Associations & Accomplishments:** Midland Chamber of Commerce; Leadership Midland (1995); Board Member, Centers for Children & Families; Midland College Continuing Education; Instructor, Building Better Board Fund Raising & Marketing; Outstanding Young Women of America (1985). **Education:** Southwest Texas State University, B.S. (1981). **Personal:** Married to Robert in 1985. Three children: Tiffany, Ashley, and Marybeth. Ms. Susik enjoys golf, volunteering, and her church youth group.

Mr. Brian W. Combs
Executive Vice President – Finance and Control
Acme Engineering and Manufacturing
1820 N York, Box 978
Muskogee, OK 74402
(918) 684–0540
Fax: (918) 682–0134

3564

Business Information: Acme Engineering and Manufacturing specializes in the design, manufacture, and distribution of fans, blowers and ventilation equipment. Serving both commercial and industrial clients with sales representatives, the Company sells both nationally and internationally. In business for 50 years, Acme Engineering and Manufacturing currently employs 530 persons and has an estimated annual revenue of $50 million. As Executive Vice President of Finance, Mr. Combs is responsible for accounting, data processing, and communications systems and administration for the Company. **Career Steps:** Executive Vice President–Finance & Control, Acme Engineering & Manufacturing (1993–Present); Controller, Baldor Electric Company (1985–1993); Systems Coordinator, General Dynamics (1984–1985); Financial Analyst/Cost Accountant, North American Philips (Magnavox) (1981–1984). **Associations & Accomplishments:** American Institute of Certified Public Accountants; National Association of Accountants; National Credit Managers Association; Ft. Smith Chamber of Commerce. **Education:** East Tennessee State University, B.A. in Accounting (1981). **Personal:** Two children: Austin and Myriah. Mr. Combs enjoys enjoys water skiing, racquetball, and motorcycling.

Michael J. Feuser
Project Engineering Manager
American Fan Company Woods USA Division
2933 Symmes Road
Fairfield, OH 45014–2001
(513) 874–2400
Fax: (513) 870–5577
EMAIL: See Below

3564

Business Information: A manufacturer of large tunnel emergency ventilation equipment, American Fan Company Woods USA Division specializes in the manufacture of small to ten feet diameter fans. As designer of fan components, overseeing project testing and engineering, Michael Feuser serves as Project Engineering Manager, responsible for a quarter of the company sales. Other duties involve receiving new inquiries, budgetary pricing, preparation of submittals, drawings, and manufacturing operations. Internet users can reach him via: FEUSER.1. **Career Steps:** Project Engineering Manager, American Fan Company Woods USA Division (1992–Present); Engineer, Industrial Air (1990–1991). **Associations & Accomplishments:** ASLRAE – local sports. **Education:** University of Cincinnati, B.S. (1990). **Personal:** One child: Michael C. Mr. Feuser enjoys soccer and fitness activities.

Jeffrey R. Hoffer
Operations Manager
Airguard Industries
2501 Ampere Drive
Jeffersontown, KY 40299–3863
(502) 267–0355
Fax: (502) 267–0466

3564

Business Information: Airguard Industries is a manufacturer of high efficiency filtration products, including ASHME, HEPA, and dust collector filters. As Operations Manager, Mr. Hoffer is responsible for all aspects of operations, including customer service and delivery. **Career Steps:** Operations Manager, Airguard Industries (1994–Present); Operations Manager, Hefco (1992–1994); Manufacturing Manager, Clank Filter (1989–1992). **Associations & Accomplishments:** American Production and Inventory Control Society; Jeffersontown, KY Chamber of Commerce. **Education:** Franklin & Marshall University; APICS Certification (1991). **Personal:** Married to Jody L. in 1990. Three children: Jennifer, Donovan, and Jonah. Mr. Hoffer enjoys collecting Grateful Dead memorabilia, hiking, and sports.

Dennis Wierzbicki
Manager, Global Programs
Donaldson Company Inc.
P.O. Box 1299
Minneapolis, MN 55440–1299
(612) 887–3542
Fax: (612) 887–3843

3564

Business Information: Donaldson Company Inc. is one of the world's leading manufacturers of air and fluid filtration systems for all industrial applications. International in scope, Donaldson Company, Inc. has 20 manufacturing plants worldwide. As Manager of Global Programs, Dennis Wierzbicki is responsible for the management and coordination of overseas manufacturing, foreign business partners, and manufacturing associations. He also serves in the Gas Turbine Division, overseeing the manufacture of air filtration systems for gas turbines utilized in electrical power generation, mechanical pumping stations, etc. **Career Steps:** Manager, Global Programs, Donaldson Company Inc. (1993–Present); Director, Technical Services, Alexus Group (1992–1993); International Sales Manager, Alliant Tech Systems (1990–1992). **Associations & Accomplishments:** Minnesota World Trade Center; International Gas Turbines Institute; Young Astronauts Club. **Education:** University of St. Thomas; Tulane University, B.S. in Engineering (1979). **Personal:** Mr. Wierzbicki enjoys the outdoors.

Jeffrey L. Bigger

Vice President, Operations
Douglas Machine, L.L.C.
3404 Iowa Street
Alexandria, MN 56308–3345
(612) 763–6587
Fax: (612) 763–3624

3565

Business Information: Established in 1966, Douglas Machine, L.L.C. is a packaging machinery manufacturer. As Vice President of Operations, Mr. Bigger is responsible for overseeing manufacturing, materials, field service, and industrial engineering activities. **Career Steps:** Vice President of Operations, Douglas Machine, L.L.C. (1995–Present); Manufacturing Practice Leader, Arthur Anderson, L.L.C. (1992–1995); Staff Consultant, Anderson Consulting (1990–1992); Industrial Engineer, IBM (1988–1990). **Associations & Accomplishments:** American Production and Inventory Control Society; North Dakota State University Advisory Board – Industrial Engineering; Trustee, University of Minnesota State 4–H Foundation; Local Steering Committee, Habitat for Humanity. **Education:** North Dakota State University, B.S. (1990); University of Minnesota Executive Program (1996). **Personal:** Married to Julie in 1992. Two children: Jacob and Amanda. Mr. Bigger enjoys golf, basketball, carpentry, and reading.

William S. Hickok
Director of Logistics Planning
Riverwood International Inc.
3350 Cumberland Circle NW, Suite 1400
Atlanta, GA 30339–3357
(770) 644–3278
Fax: (770) 644–2920

3565

Business Information: Riverwood International Inc. is a manufacturer of high speed packaging machines and the fiber cartons that run through the machines. The main headquarters is located in Atlanta and is a privately–owned company. Established in 1979, Riverwood International Inc., employs 8,000 people with annual sales of $1.5 billion. As Director of Logistics Planning, Mr. Hickok is responsible for basic logistic functions, negotiations, and determines warehouse space. **Career Steps:** Director of Logistics Planning, Riverwood International Inc. (19–Present); Director of Global Logistics, Riverwood International Inc. (1994–1996); Director of Business Development, Roadway Logistics (192–1994); Vice President of Sales and Customer Service, American President Distribution (1988–1991). **Associations & Accomplishments:** Council of Logistics Management; American Forestry & Paper Association. **Education:** Southern Illinois University, B.S. (1975). **Personal:** Married to Elizabeth in 1975. Mr. Hickok enjoys power boating, tennis, running, and skiing.

Derald R. Bogs
General Manager
Control Techniques–Emerson
95 North Brandon Drive
Glendale Heights, IL 60139–2024
(708) 893–5249
Fax: (708) 893–4156

3566

Business Information: Control Techniques–Emerson is an AC/DC drive manufacturer. Headquartered in St. Louis, Missouri, the Company conducts business worldwide. As General Manager, Mr. Bogs manages all aspects of the business. His responsibilities include sales, marketing, engineering production, human resources, and direct supervision of twenty–five people. **Career Steps:** General Manager, Control Techniques–Emerson (1994–Present); Project Manager, LTV Steel Corporation (1987–1994); Operations Manager, Menusoft, Division of Allied Products (1985–1987); Electrical Engineer, Republic Steel (1981–1985). **Associations & Accomplishments:** American Iron and Steel Engineers; International Wire Association. **Education:** Keller, M.B.A. (1988); Purdue University, B.S.E.E. **Personal:** Married to Kathleen in 1992. Two children: Jonathan and Brittany. Mr. Bogs enjoys tennis, skiing, and wine making.

Tony J. Celli
Director/Procurement/Spare Parts & Customer Service
ITAM Techint Italimpianti
100 Corporate Center Dirve
Coraopolis, PA 15108
(412) 269–6500
Fax: (412) 262–3064

3567

Business Information: ITAM Techint Italimpianti, established in 1987, is an engineering firm involved in the design and manufacturing of reheating furnaces and process line equipment for the steel industry. The Company currently has 91 employees. As Director/Procurement/Spare Parts & Customer Service, Mr. Celli is responsible for the following groups purchasing, expediting, spare parts and customer service. He was responsible for developing his Department Quality Assurance Manual, Standard Operating Procedures, and Internal Operating Procedures, to meet ISO 9001 Standards. **Career Steps:** Director/Procurement/Spare Parts & Customer Service, ITAM Techint Italimpianti (1990–Present); Purchasing Manager, Davy Mckee Corporation (1983–1990); Senior Buyer/Expediting Manager Aetna–Standard Engineering Co. (1980–1983). **Associations & Accomplishments:** American Management Association; Former Chairperson/President Lawrence County Vocational Technical School (1990–1995); Ellwood City Area Outstanding Citizen (1995); National Association of Purchasing Managers; American Society for Quality Control; Former Member, Ellwood City Area School District Board of Education (1971–1995); President, Ellwiid City Area School District Board of Education (1974–1975, 1981–1982, 1986–1987, 1990–1995); Ellwood City Area Chamber of Commerce; Third Degree, Knights of Columbus; Pittsburgh Chapter Italy–America Chamber of Commerce; Director, Midwestern Free Enterprise Partnership; Former President, St. Agatha Parish Council (1987–1990); Purchasing Manager, Association of Pittsburgh; Ellwood City Area Outstanding Young Person Distinguish Service Award (1971). **Education:** Youngstown State University, B.A. (1971); Valley Forge Military Academy (1964). **Personal:** Married to Mary Ann in 1979. One child: Claire Elizabeth. Mr. Celli enjoys working on his antique sports car.

Brian John Walsh
International Sales Manager
Industrial Engineering and Equipment Company
425 Hanley Industrial Court
St. Louis, MO 63144–1511
(314) 644–4300
Fax: (314) 644–5332

3567

Business Information: Established in 1929, Industrial Engineering and Equipment Company is a manufacturer of industrial and commercial heating equipment. As International Sales Manager, Brian Walsh is responsible for the overall management of international sales and marketing support staff and operations. A practicing attorney since 1988, he also serves as in–house legal counsel, providing all aspects of legal support on behalf of IEEC. **Career Steps:** International Sales Manager, Industrial Engineering and Equipment Company (1992–Present); Vice President and Associate Counsel, International Registries, Inc. (1990–1992); Associate Attorney, Burt Maner & Miller (1988–1989). **Associations & Accomplishments:** American Bar Association. **Education:** George Washington University, J.D. (1988); Colgate University, B.A. (1985). **Personal:** Married to Rebecca Epstein in 1991.

Thomas R. Barth
• • • ━━━◉━━━ • • •
General Manager
Deutsche Babcock Energie UND Umwelttechnik AG
P.O. Box 46698
Abu Dhabi, United Arab Emirates 971 2 331
971–2–328–134
Fax: 971–2–331–765

3569

Business Information: Deutsche Babcock Energie UND Umwelttechnik AG is a major global manufacturer of boilers and pressure vessels, as well as a power plant construction and maintenance company. Established in 1973, Deutsche Babcock currently employs 410 people. As General Manager, Mr. Barth is responsible for all aspects of daily operations, including customer relations, supply contacts, large project management, and inter–company relationships. With his commercial background, Mr. Barth has been instrumental in the success of the company. **Career Steps:** Deutsche Babcock Energie UND Umwelttechnik AG: General Manager (1994–Present), Commercial Manager (1990–1994); Deputy General Manager, Nico International, Abu Dhabi (1988–1990). **Associations & Accomplishments:** Power Plant Maintenance Association. **Education:** Ecolle Des Roches Ch, M.B.A. (1974). **Personal:** Married to Franziska in 1995. Mr. Barth enjoys skiing, scuba diving, fishing and music.

Steven P. Kreamer
Manager, Manufacturing Technology Development
Cooper Turbocompressor, Division of Cooper Cameron Corporation
3101 Broadway
Buffalo, NY 14227–1034
(716) 891–3846
Fax: (716) 891–3859

3569

Business Information: Cooper Turbocompressor is a manufacturer of large multi–stage centrifugal compressors for process/air separation and plant air supply. As Manager, Manufacturing Technology Development, Mr. Kreamer manages Advanced Manufacturing Engineering, Tool Design, and Tool Room personnel. He is also responsible for coordinating the Capital investment for the Division. **Career Steps:** Cooper Turbocompressor: Manager, Manufacturing Technology Development (1995–Present), Manager, Manufacturing Engineering (1994–1995), Supervisor, Computer Aided Manufacturing Engineering (1987–1994), Senior Tool Design Engineer (1984–1987); Curtis Screw, Tooling Coordinator (1983–1984); Ness Automatic Machine, Tool Design Engineer (1977–1983). **Associations & Accomplishments:** Society of Manufacturing Engineers (1977–Present); Assistant Scoutmaster/Treasurer, Boy Scouts of America. **Education:** Canisius College, M.B.A. (1987); Buffalo State College, B.T. in Mechanical Engineering (1977). **Personal:** Married to Dawn in 1978. Two children: Joseph and Stephanie. Mr. Kreamer enjoys skiing, gardening, and cars.

Alex Lisachenko
Partner and Vice President of Operations
Somerwill Engineering, Inc.
1761 Highland Road
Twinsburg, OH 44087
(216) 425–3971
Fax: (216) 425–2162

3569

Business Information: Somerwill Engineering, Inc. provides the remanufacture of machines, including control and drive retrofits, software development, and scraping, as well as providing parts and service assistance, either at their site or client–based sites nationwide. Co–Founding Somerwill Engineering, Inc. as Partner and Vice President of Operations in 1992, Mr. Lisachenko is responsible for the direction of all marketing, manufacturing, and mechanical engineering functions, as well as providing consulting services. He owes his success to his very hardworking parents, his wife and children. **Career Steps:** Partner and Vice President of Operations, Somerwill Engineering, Inc. (1992–Present); Senior Sales Engineer, Giddings & Lewis/Warner & Swasey (1964–1992). **Associations & Accomplishments:** Veterans of Foreign Wars; American Legion; Vietnam Veteran; Recipient of Army Commendation Medal, Good Conduct Medal and numerous others. **Education:** Cuyahoga Community College, A.S. (1972); Warner & Swasey Company, 4 year Apprenticeship Program. **Personal:** Married to Cheryl in 1969. Four children: Laura, Mark, Gregory, and Jason. Mr. Lisachenko enjoys fishing, gardening, and spending time with his family.

Tom Patnaik
Product Manager
Ketema Process Equipment
9484 Mission Park
Santee, CA 92071
(508) 668–0400 (800) 553–8362
Fax: (508) 668–6855 (800) 953–8362

3569

Business Information: Ketema Process Equipment is a manufacturer of centrifuges and filters for pharmaceutical and chemical industries. As Product Manager, Mr. Patnaik manages the marketing and sales of various solid/liquid separational devices worldwide. **Career Steps:** Ketema Process Equipment: Product Manager (1995–Present), Applications Engineer (1994–1995); Applications Engineer, Flowseal/Mark Controls (1992–1994). **Associations & Accomplishments:** American Institute of Chemical Engineers; American Filtration and Separation Society; International Society of Pharmaceutical Engineers. **Education:** Texas A&M University – College Station: M.B.A. (1990), M.S. in Mechanical Engineering, B.S. in Mechanical Engineering. **Personal:** Married to Sunita in 1990. Two children: Suman and Amy. Mr. Patnaik enjoys tennis, badminton, table tennis, weight training, and physical fitness.

Mr. Ronald D. Potter
President
Creative Robotic Applications
1780 Corporate Drive
Norcross, GA 30093–2929
(770) 717–5227
Fax: (770) 717–5166

3569

Business Information: Creative Robotic Applications specializes in the manufacture, development and implementation of robotics and factory automation systems. Established in 1988, Creative Robotic Applications currently employs 25 people and has an estimated annual revenue of $6 million. As President and Founder, Mr. Potter is responsible for all aspects of operations, including sales, marketing and project engineering. **Career Steps:** President, Creative Robotic Applications (1988–Present); Vice President and General Manager, Advanced Manufacturing Systems (1985–1988); Vice President, Robot Systems, Inc. (1978–1984); Vice President, Auto–Place, Inc. (1969–1978). **Associations & Accomplishments:** Robotics International of SME; 1995 Joseph F. Engelberger Award, and will accept it in Singapore. **Education:** Michigan State University, B.S. in Mechanical Engineering. **Personal:** One child: Angela. Mr. Potter enjoys softball, wine and travel.

Kenneth N. Rapp
Vice President
Zymark Corporation
208 East Street
Upton, MA 01568–1212
(508) 435–9500
Fax: (508) 435–3439
EMAIL: See Below

3569

Business Information: Zymark Corporation is an establishment engaged in developing automation with robotics for pharmaceutical research and quality control laboratories. As Vice President, Mr. Rapp is responsible for running the world-wide business unit for dosage form analysis automation. This includes areas such as development, production, sales, and marketing. Internet users can reach him via: Ken.rapp@zy-mark.com. **Career Steps:** Zymark Corporation: Vice President (1995–Present), North American Business Manager (1993–1995), Eastern Sales Manager (1991–1993), Engineering & Marketing (1984–1987). **Associations & Accomplishments:** American Society of Mechanical Engineers; American Chemical Society; New Jersey Robotics Group; Alpha Epsilon Pi Fraternity. **Education:** Northeastern University, B.S.M.E. (1984). **Personal:** Married to Karen in 1988. Two children: Jonathan and Erik. Mr. Rapp enjoys music (including writing and recording guitar music), weightlifting, exercise, family, and outdoor activities.

William H. Reeve
Director of Systems/Software
Cybo Robots, Inc.
2701 Fortune Circle East
Indianapolis, IN 46241
(317) 484–2926
Fax: (317) 241–2727
EMAIL: See Below

3569

Business Information: Cybo Robots, Inc. is a full service provider of turnkey robotic automation solutions and services. The Company focuses on providing a wide range of services to medium– to large–sized companies with difficult or complex automation problems. As Director of Systems/Software, Mr. Reeve is responsible for all aspects of Company manufacture and software development for robotic systems. Mr. Reeve has 24 years experience in the Air Force and in computer engineering and his knowledge is vital to the success of the Company. Internet users can reach him via: wreeve@iquest.net. **Career Steps:** General Manager, Cybo Robots, Inc. (1994–Present); U.S. Air Force: Commander, 552nd Computer Group (1992–1994), Commander, 84th Radar Evaluation Squadron (1989–1992); Director, NATO, 4th Allied Tactical Air Force (1986–1989). **Associations & Accomplishments:** Tau Beta Pi Engineering Society. **Education:** Air Force Institute of Technology, M.S. in Computer Engineering (1978); Utah State University, B.S. in Computer Science. **Personal:** Married to Carol in 1968. Six children: Debora, Robert, Jared, Julie, Matthew, and Tyler. Mr. Reeve enjoys skiing.

Reinaldo Romero
Vice President
West India Machinery & Supply
P.O. Box 364308
San Juan, Puerto Rico 00936–4308
(809) 721–7640
Fax: (809) 721–6192

3569

Business Information: West India Machinery & Supply is a factory representative providing sales and services of construction, industrial and agricultural equipment throughout Puerto Rico. Equipment offered includes loaders, bulldozers, excavators, cranes, gensets, forklift trucks, quarries, and asphalt equipment. Established in 1924, West India Machinery & Supply reports annual revenue in excess of $8 million and currently employs 49 people. Joining the Company in 1958 as an administrative assistant, Mr. Romero worked his way up the corporate ladder to his current position as Vice President. He is responsible for all aspects of sales, finances and general supervision of operations and employees. He also serves as a member of the Board of Directors and Secretary of three subsidiaries: West India Machinery, West India Manufacturing and Service Company, and Garlam Enterprises Corporation. **Career Steps:** Administrative Assistant to Vice President, West India Machinery & Supply (1958–Present); Parts Department Supervisor, General Equipment Corporation (1956–1958); Non–Commissioned Officer, U.S. Army Artillery Batallion (1953–1955). **Associations & Accomplishments:** Chamber of Commerce; Puerto Rico Manufacturers Association; Asphalt Producers Association; Puerto Rico Ready Mix Association; Municipality of Bayamon Economic Development Corporation; Lions International: Club President, District 51–C Deputy Governor, Multiple District 51 Secretary General (1987) and Convention Chairman (1982); Puerto Rico Electrical Contractors Association; Aggregates Producers Association; Aggregates and Materials Wholesalers Association; Consultant Board Member, Catholic Social Services; Red Cross; American Legion. **Education:** University of Puerto Rico, B.B.A. (1960); Puerto Rico Commercial Institute; Attended numerous business and technical seminars in Puerto Rico and U.S.A. mainland. **Personal:** Married to Carmen Romero in 1946. One child: Milagros Romero. Mr. Romero enjoys music (singing and dancing), dominoes, volleyball, and civic activities in which he can help needy people.

Charles L. Wooddell Jr.
General Manager
Alfa Laval Inc.
955 Mearns Road
Warminster, PA 18974–2811
(215) 443–4002
Fax: (215) 443–4112

3569

Business Information: Alfa Laval Inc. is the world's leading manufacturer of centrifugal separators used in food, chemical, marine, power, and environmental applications for the chemical, food, pharmaceutical, and beverage industries. Established in 1883, Alfa Lava, Inc. currently employs 12,000 world–wide. With twenty–six years expertise in mechanical engineering, Mr. Wooddell joined Alfa Laval Inc. as General Manager of Industrial Separation in 1994. He is responsible for overall management and operational activities, as well supplying separators to the various industries. **Career Steps:** General Manager, Alfa Laval Inc. (1994–Present); Director of Marketing, Leeds & Northrup (1993–1994); Honeywell: Marketing Manager (1990–1993), Product Manager (1988–1990). **Associations & Accomplishments:** West Virginia Association of Professional Engineers; American Society of Mechanical Engineers. **Education:** Virginia Tech, B.S.M.E. (1969). **Personal:** Married to Laquita M. Wooddell in 1980. One child: C. Russell. Mr. Wooddell enjoys travel, golf and walking.

Mr. Farhat Ali
Vice President of Compatible Systems Operations
Amdahl Corporation
1250 E. Arques Avenue, MS 134
Sunnyvale, CA 94088
(408) 746–6014
Fax: (408) 746–6676

3571

Business Information: Amdahl Corporation is a leading manufacturer and developer of mainframe systems, including computers, software products and information storage products. International in scope, Amdahl has offices in every major country in the world, with a major manufacturing facility located in Ireland. As Vice President of Compatible Systems Operations, Mr. Ali is responsible for operations management for worldwide manufacturing, procurement and quality control. He is the administrator in charge of all administrative and personnel at the Sunnyvale, California operations headquarters. Established in 1970, Amdahl Corporation employs in excess of 6,000 corporate–wide people with annual sales of $1.7 billion. **Career Steps:** Vice President of Compatible Systems Operations, Amdahl Corporation (1994–Present); Vice President of Manufacturing, Amdahl Corporation (1993–1994); Director of Product Operations, Amdahl Corporation (1990–1992). **Associations & Accomplishments:** Industry Advisory Board, Minority Engineering Program, Santa Clara University **Education:** Harvard University Business School, M.B.A. (1979); Princeton University, B.S.E.E. in Computer Science **Personal:** Married to Memuna Ali in 1979. One child: Yasmin Ali. Mr. Ali enjoys golf, tennis and travel.

Connie L. Brock
Manager of VIP Customer Support
Texas Instruments
5701 Airport Road, MS 3268
Temple, TX 76503–6102
(817) 774–6912
Fax: (817) 774–6660
EMAIL: See Below

3571

Business Information: Texas Instruments, Inc. is a major international design, manufacturer and marketer of high–tech products, including computers and peripherals, semiconductors, defense electronics, software and other diverse components and materials. Texas Instruments currently has a working relationship with Hewlett Packard to introduce new products, as well as involvement on a worldwide basis with numerous joint ventures. Serving in various quality control management capacities with TI since 1989, Connie Brock was appointed to her current position in November of 1994. As Manager of VIP Customer Support, Ms. Brock is responsible for the management of customer support and service for both printers and notebook customers of Texas Instruments. She also manages the group technical support staff for printer and office solutions, as well as the Call Center for desk to desk support and other customer service functions. Beginning her career seventeen years ago in the quality control field, she found that customer service and customer satisfaction worked hand–in–hand, thereby developing an interest in the Customer Service field. Internet users can reach her via: Connie.Brock@dcepl.ltg.TI.com **Career Steps:** Texas Instruments: Manager of VIP Customer Support (1994–Present), Notebook Customer Service (1993–1994), Supplier Development Manager (1992–1994), Procurement Quality Manager (1989–1992). **Associations & Accomplishments:** Loaned Executive to United Way Campaign (1994); American Quarter Horse Association; Help Desk Institute. **Education:** University of Mary Hardin–Baylor, M.B.A. (1992). **Personal:** Ms. Brock enjoys breeding thoroughbred horses.

Karel H. Broekhuis
Segment Manager for Latin America
IBM Brazil, Limited
Rua Tutoia 1157–19 Andar
Sao Paulo, Brazil 04007–900
55–11–886–5499
Fax: 55–11–886–5295
E MAIL: See Below

3571

Business Information: IBM Brazil, Limited, a division of IBM, researches, develops, manufactures and markets computer and office products and services globally over a wide range of markets. The Research Division creates technology and makes contributions to the development of key evolving IBM strategies. As Segment Manager for Latin America, Mr. Broekhuis develops decision support solutions for the Latin American markets. Other responsibilities include definition of marketing and product strategies and development. Internet users can reach him via: Karel47@ibm.net. **Career Steps:** IBM Brazil, Limited: Segment Manager for Latin America (1996–Present), Information Asset Management Consultant (1993–1995); IBM Nederland N.V.: Special Product Manager Banking (1991–1993), Manager Marketing System (1987–1990). **Associations & Accomplishments:** Member of the American Management Association. **Education:** Erasmus University (1990); Technical University, Eindhoven B.Sc. **Personal:** Married to Beny Makiyama Lopes in 1993. One daughter: Mayra Priscilla. Mr. Broekhuis enjoys music, film, reading, travel, and spending time with his family.

Andrea V. Cotter
Senior Direct Marketing Strategist
IBM North America
9 Hillside Drive
Ballston Lake, NY 12019–9364
(518) 877–0484
Fax: (518) 877–0485
E MAIL: See Below

3571

Business Information: IBM Corporation researches, develops, manufactures and markets computer and office products and services throughout a wide range of worldwide markets. As Senior Direct Marketing Strategist, Ms. Cotter works with IBM Product Managers and Segment Leaders to develop and execute integrated marketing strategies. She oversees database marketing projects which include inbound and outbound telephone calls, direct mail, direct response advertising and electronic messaging. Internet users can reach her via: avc@vnet.ibm.com. **Career Steps:** IBM North America: Senior Direct Marketing Strategist (1996–Present), Campaign Strategist (1992–1995), Marketing Representative (1990–1992). **Associations & Accomplishments:** Executive Board Member, Junior Achievement of the Capital District; Board Member, Schenectady Swim Club; Professional Women's Network; Shenendahowa Central School District Partnership Team; Board Member, American Marketing Association. **Education:** SUNY at Albany, M.L.S. Cum Laude (1986); SUNY at Oswego, B.A. Cum Laude (1974). **Personal:** Married to James in 1974. One child: Christina. Ms. Cotter enjoys walking, swimming, playing the piano, gourmet cooking, and gardening.

Duane C. Crockett
Design Engineer
Cabletron Systems
570 South Clearwater West
Post Falls, ID 83854
(208) 773–1711
Fax: (208) 773–4001
EMAIL: See Below

3571

Business Information: Cabletron Systems, which manufactures and markets network hardware and network management software, serves the United States, Ireland, Singapore, Great Britain, Europe, Australia, and Brazil. As Design Engineer, Mr. Crockett designs local and wide area networks and provides technical support to both the customer base and inside sales force. Internet users can reach him via: duane_crockett_at_techsupp@ccmailpc.ctron.com **Career Steps:** Design Engineer, Cabletron Systems (1992–Present); Company CDR Captain, United States Army (1981–1992). **Associations & Accomplishments:** Washington National Guard Association; Usher at local church (1993–1994); U.S. Biathalon Association – Competes on Washington State Team, winner of Bronze Metal in Patrol Race; U.S. Army Bronze Star in Operation Desert Storm. **Education:** National University, M.B.A. (1992); Eastern Washington University, B.A. (1981); Community College of the Air Force, A.S. in Electronics; North Idaho College, A.A. (1973). **Personal:** Married to Candice in 1974. Three children: Ryan Duane Crockett, Heidi Dawn Crockett, and Bradley Clayton. Mr. Crockett en-

International Who's Who of Professionals™
Classified by Standard Industrial Code

3571   3571

joys mountain biking and cross country skiing, and is the author of the book, Ride Canfield Mountain.

Ken A. Faircloth

Vice President of Sales and Marketing
Xylog, Inc.
1750 Courtwood Crescent, Suite 101
Ottawa, Ontario K2C 2B5
(613) 723–2123
Fax: (613) 723–9825

3571

Business Information: Xylog, Inc. is a manufacturer, distributor, and reseller of microcomputers throughout Canada from three offices. With thirteen years experience in the computer sales, Mr. Faircloth joined Xylog, Inc. as Vice President of Sales and Marketing in 1993. He is responsible for the oversight of all sales and marketing for the company, in addition to supervising four internal sales people and eight independent agents. **Career Steps:** Vice President of Sales and Marketing, Xylog, Inc. (1993–Present); Government Sales Manager, Commodore Business Machines (1986–1993); Sales Representative, CompuMart (1983–1986). **Education:** University of Western Ontario, B.A. (1992); St. Lawrence College, England, A Levels. **Personal:** Married to Ana Weber in 1990. Mr. Faircloth enjoys music, golf, and tennis.

Mr. Donald L. Hough

Consultant
IBM Corporation
1605 LBJ Freeway
Dallas, TX 75234
(214) 280–4265
Fax: (214) 280–2241

3571

Business Information: IBM Corporation designs, manufactures and markets high–tech products globally, including information systems products and services, computers, semiconductors, networking hardware and software, computer hardware and software as well as outsourcing services and consulting. As Consultant, Mr. Hough consults in management topics in information technology specializing in process acceleration. Established in 1924, IBM Corporation employs 200,000 people with annual sales of $64 billion. **Career Steps:** Consultant, IBM Corporation (1989–Present); Consultant, Multiple Technologies Corporation (1988–1989); Consultant, Computer Task Group (1986–1988); Consultant, Amoco Oil Co., Tulsa, (1984–1986); Programmer, First National Bank, Tulsa, (1977–1984). **Associations & Accomplishments:** Data Administration Management Association; Association for Computing Machinery; authored "Rapid Delivery: an evolutionary approach for application development," IBM Systems Journal (1993). **Education:** Northeastern Oklahoma State University; Tulsa Junior College. **Personal:** Married to Monica Hough in 1975. Two children: Justin Todd Hough and Megan Blair Hough. Mr. Hough enjoys music and gardening.

Albert A. Irato

President and Chief Executive Officer
Hypercom
2851 W. Kathleen Road
Phoenix, AZ 85023–4053
(602) 866–5399
Fax: (602) 504–6455

3571

Business Information: Hypercom is the fastest growing POS device and POS network company in the U.S. The Company engineers and markets a spectrum of Integrated Network Devices which are sold in over 40 countries. Joining Hypercom as President and Chief Executive Officer in 1992, Mr. Irato is responsible for all aspects of operations, and providing the overall vision and strategies to keep the Company at the leading edge of the financial telecommunications marketplace. **Career Steps:** President and Chief Executive Officer, Hypercom (1992–Present); Senior Vice President, American Express (1986–1992); President and Chief Executive Officer, Financial Cards Systems, Inc. (1983–1984) **Associations & Accomplishments:** Board Member, Electronic Funds Transfer Association; American Management Association; Board Member, Continental Circuits Inc. **Education:** Spring Hill College, B.B.S. (1960); University of Virginia – Darden Graduate School, Advanced Management Program **Personal:** Married to Sarah in 1995. One child: Capucine.

Daniel (Dan) A. Lugar

General Manager
Opal Technologies, Inc.
9687 Gerwig Lane
Columbia, MD 21046
(410) 290–7700
Fax: (410) 290–9447
EMAIL: DLUGAR@MSN.COM

3571

Business Information: Opal Technologies, Inc., owned by private investors, is a manufacturer and reseller of personal computers and computer components. Distributing worldwide, Opal's primary market is Richmond to Philadelphia. Joining Opal in early 1995, Mr. Lugar is the sole reporter to the investors and is responsible for all aspects of company operations, including strategic and financial planning, marketing, purchasing, sales and manufacturing. World Wide Web users can reach him via: Http://www.industry.net/opal.technologies. **Career Steps:** General Manager, Opal Technologies, Inc. (1995–Present); President, Pree–Vue, Inc. (1991–995); Intel Corporation: International Sales Manager (1987–1991), Intel Marketing Specialist (1983–1986); Owner, Fair Haven Mobil & Gilmore Home Center (1976–1983). **Associations & Accomplishments:** Howard County, MD Chamber of Commerce; 1988 Intel "Winners Circle" award, top 5% of worldwide Intel sales. **Education:** American Graduate School of International Management, Masters in International Management (AZ – 1983); Westminster College, BA (PA – 1971). **Personal:** Mr. Lugar enjoys Flying, Skiing, Gourmet Cooking, Camping & Horses. Two children; Kara & Dana.

Monica Luketich, Ed.D.

Instructional Designer for Human Resource Development
Texas Instruments, Inc.
P.O. Box 3928
Dallas, TX 75265
(214) 917–1908
Fax: (214) 917–7519

3571

Business Information: Texas Instruments, Inc. is a manufacturer of defense systems, semiconductors, and electronic systems. As Instructional Designer for Human Resource Development, Dr. Luketich is responsible for administrative duties, constructing performance plans, training, and developing programs. **Career Steps:** Texas Instruments, Inc.: Instructional Designer for Human Resource Development (1985–Present), Coordinator of Training Antenna Department (1985–1988) **Associations & Accomplishments:** International Society for Performance Improvement; World Tang Soo Do Association. **Education:** West Virginia University, Ed.D. (1993), M.A., B.S. Degree in Secondary Education. **Personal:** Dr. Luketich enjoys karate, sewing, gardening, lace making, wine making, needle work, and reading.

Mr. James N. Marshall

Director of Operations – Americas International Group
Tandem Computers, Inc.
200 Galleria Parkway
Atlanta, GA 30068
(404) 618–1490
Fax: Please mail or call

3571

Business Information: Tandem Computers, Inc. is a manufacturing distributor of on–line processing systems for large enterprises. Established in 1974, the Company reports revenue of $2 billion and currently employs 8,500 people. As Director of Operations – Americas International Group (a subsidiary of Tandem Computers, Inc.), Mr. Marshall is responsible for all aspects of operations, including marketing, marketing sales, planning and opening of new markets. **Career Steps:** Director of Operations – Americas International Group, Tandem Computers, Inc. (1994–Present); Area Manager, Tandem Computers, Inc. (1991–1994); District Manager, Tandem Computers, Inc. (1986–1991); Branch Manager, Burroughs Corporation (1982–1986). **Education:** University of South Florida, B.A., B.S. (1975). **Personal:** Married to Carla. One child: Leanne. Mr. Marshall enjoys diving, photography and racquetball.

Luc Moyen

Director
Seagate Technology
920 Disc Drive
Scotts Valley, CA 95066–4544
(408) 439–3678
Fax: (408) 438–3047
EMAIL: See Below

3571

Business Information: Seagate Technology is one of the nation's leading manufacturers of data storage technology, with products including: disc drives, tape backups, data management software, and peripheral components. With over ten years expertise in computer integration and systems testing, Mr. Moyen serves as Director for Seagate's reliability design assurance and testing, encompassing all California products lines (disc drives). Mr. Moyen can also be reached through the Internet at: LUC_MOYEN@NOTES.SEAGATE.COM **Career Steps:** Director, Seagate Technology (1995–Present); IBM Corporation: Senior Manager Integration (1992–1995), Manager Product Test (1982–1992). **Associations & Accomplishments:** Tau Beth Pi; Eta Kappa Nu; University of Illinois President's Club; Fluent in: Portuguese, Luxembourguish, and Spanish (Fair). **Education:** University of Illinois Urbana–Champaign, M.S.E.E. (1982); Universidade Catolica de Minas Gerais, Brazil, B.S.E.E. **Personal:** Born and raised in Brazil. Parents are from Luxembourg. Married to Jennifer in 1981. Two children: Nicole and Vanessa. Mr. Moyen enjoys woodworking, drawing, soccer, travel, and tennis.

Michael S. Nichols

Senior Manager of ACD Systems Management
Dell Computers
2300 Greenlawn Boulevard, Building #3
Round Rock, TX 78664–7090
(512) 728–8261
Fax: (512) 728–0601
EMAIL: See Below

3571

Business Information: Dell Computers is a developer, manufacturer, seller, marketer, and servicer of all types of computers (i.e., laptops, notebooks, workstations, servers), as well as a reseller of computer software. Joining Dell Computers as Senior Manager of ACD Systems Management, Mr. Nichols is responsible for the management of a team of telecommunications analysts, applications developers, and project leaders for the highly sophisticated telecom platform. He also oversees client relations, forecasting, and marketing. Internet users can reach him via: MIKE_NICHOLS@ DELL.COM **Career Steps:** Senior Manager of ACD Systems Management, Dell Computers (Present); Manager of Base Operations, Banctec Service Corporation (1986–1993); AT&T Supervisor, SWB & AT&T (1982–1986). **Associations & Accomplishments:** Founding Member, Call Center Network Group – Dallas; Multiple AIDS Charitable Organizations. **Education:** Texas Tech University; New Mexico Junior College. **Personal:** Mr. Nichols enjoys travel, film and water sports.

Mr. Yosh Sato

Vice President of Manufacturing
Proxim, Inc.
295 North Bernardo Avenue
Mountain View, CA 94043
(415) 960–1630
Fax: (415) 964–5181

3571

Business Information: Proxim, Inc. is a manufacturer of wireless LAN adapter products. As Vice President of Manufacturing, Mr. Sato is responsible for manufacturing activities, manufacturing engineering, materials, and quality control. Established in 1984, Proxim, Inc. employs 75 people with annual sales of $11.2 million. **Career Steps:** Vice President of Manufacturing, Proxim, Inc. (1993–Present); Director of Operations, Maxoptix Corporation (1989–1992); Program Manager, MIPS Computer Systems (1988–1989). **Associations & Accomplishments:** American Production and Inventory Control Society; American Society for Quality Control. **Education:** San Jose State University, B.A. (1968). **Personal:** Married to Dorothy in 1972. Two children: Cristine and Georgine.

Jay D. Seifried

Director Information Services, Texas
AST Computer
1001 Northeast Loop 820
Ft. Worth, TX 76131–1417
(817) 230–5570
Fax: (817) 230–5565
EMAIL: See Below

3571

Business Information: AST Computer is a world–wide manufacturer, marketer, and supporter of a multibillion dollar personal computer business. With corporate offices located in Irvine, California, AST Computer has numerous sales offices throughout the U.S. International offices are located throughout Europe and Asia, and manufacturing facilities are in Texas, Ireland, Hong Kong, Taiwan, and the People's Republic of China making AST Computer one of the top ten manufacturers of personal computers in the world. As Director of Information Services for Texas, Mr. Seifried is responsible for the management of systems support, development, and I.T. for the Texas operation, which includes a one million per year PC assemble plant, 10,000 calls per day support center, and other distribution and engineering facilities, with a total of 2,000 employees. Internet uses can reach him via: Jay.Seifried@AST.COM. **Ca-**

reer Steps: AST Computer: Director, Information Services–Texas (1993–Present); GRiD Systems Corporation: Director (1991–1993), Manager Marketing Operations (1989–1991); Radio Shack Business Products: District Sales Manager (1986–1989). **Education:** Chase College of Law (1980); Thomas More College, B.S. (1977). **Personal:** Married to Janet in 1980. Three children: Craig, Jill, and Blaire. Mr. Seifried enjoys music, community theater, sports, and spending time with his family.

Michael H. Uhm
Vice President of Sales and Marketing
Daytek Electronics Corporation
105–3830 Jacombs Road
Richmond, British Columbia V6V 1Y6
(604) 270–3003
Fax: (604) 270–3022

3571

Business Information: Daytek Electronics Corporation, a subsidiary of Dawoo of Korea and the #1 company in Canada for monitors, is a manufacturer and distributor of computer monitoring equipment and computer notebooks for North America from two locations in Canada and one in the U.S. (Dallas, Texas). As Vice President of Sales and Marketing, Mr. Uhm is responsible for all aspects of sales and marketing functions, including conducting business with mass merchandisers, federal government and resellers. **Career Steps:** Vice President of Sales and Marketing, Daytek Electronics Corporation (1993–Present); Vice President of Marketing, STD Computers (1992–1993); Vice President, DARIUS (1991–1992). **Associations & Accomplishments:** Beach Grove Country Club for Golf (1 Handicap); Korean Business Group; Rotary Club. **Education:** University of British Columbia, B.S. in Economics (1986). **Personal:** Mr. Uhm enjoys golf, travel, music, and opera.

Ellen Beth Van Buskirk
Director of Communications
IBM Research Division
P O Box 218, Route 134
Yorktown Heights, NY 10598
(914) 945–3981
Fax: (914) 945–2131
E MAIL: See Below

3571

Business Information: IBM Corporation researches, develops, manufactures and markets computer and office products and services worldwide throughout a wide range of markets. The Research Division creates technology and makes contributions to the evolution of key IBM strategies. As Director of Communications, Ms. Van Buskirk is responsible for all marketing aspects of the Research Division of IBM. These functions include public relations, advertising, customer relations, and executive relations. Ms. Van Buskirk works closely with other members of management in the development and implementation of marketing techniques for new and existing IBM products. Internet users can reach her via: EBVB@Watson.IBM.com. **Career Steps:** Director of Communications, IBM Research Division (1994–Present); Director of Marketing Services, SEGA (1991–1994); Marketing Services Manager, Resort at Squaw Creek (1989–1991); Partner, Van Buskirk Morris Webster Smith (1987–1989). **Associations & Accomplishments:** Founding Member, Women in Interactive Entertainment; Girls, Inc. **Education:** University of Southern California, B.A. (1982). **Personal:** Married to Robert Knapp in 1994. Ms. Van Buskirk enjoys baseball, video games, and detective novels.

Benjamin Willis, Ph.D.
Director of Human Resources
Apple Computer, Inc.
One Infinite Loop, MS301–1 HR
Cupertino, CA 95014
(408) 974–4513
Fax: (408) 974–7892

3571

Business Information: Apple Computer Inc. designs, manufactures and markets high–tech products globally, including information systems products and services, computers, networking hardware and software, computer hardware and software, as well as outsourcing services and consulting. Dr. Willis has worked for Apple since 1986 and has over 1,100 clients. As Director of Human Resources, he is responsible for planning, design, system software technology, and human resource strategies. **Career Steps:** Director of Human Resources, Apple Computer Inc. (1986–Present); Senior Management Consultant, PGE (1984–1986). **Education:** Stanford University, Ph.D. (1987); Harvard University: M.Ed., B.A.; Teachers College Columbia University. **Personal:** Two children: Daria and Kyle. Dr. Willis enjoys travel, music, jogging, and raising daughters.

Mr. James R. Booth
Vice President, Corporate Materials and Purchasing
Quantum Corporation
500 McCarthy Boulevard, Mail Stop 12124
Milpitas, CA 95035
(408) 894–4451
Fax: (408) 894–3222

3572

Business Information: Quantum Corporation is one of the largest manufacturers of hard disk drives and mass storage devices worldwide. As Vice President of Corporate Materials and Purchasing, Mr. Booth is responsible for the management and direction of all facets of materials including commodity and sourcing strategies, supplier relationships, material cost, worldwide procurement, incoming material quality and measurement correlation. He also manages materials and commodity engineering departments, including component quality and reliability, supplier process capability and component maturity programs; corporate shipping and receiving, freight and traffic management. Prior to joining Quantum Corporation in 1988, Mr. Booth spent 17 years in various senior management positions in materials and operations organizations. Established in 1980, Quantum Corporation employs 7,000 people with annual sales of $4 Billion. **Career Steps:** Vice President, Corporate Materials and Purchasing, Quantum Corporation (1993–Present); Director of Materials, Quantum Corporation (1991–1993); Manager of Strategic Supplier Development, Quantum Corporation (1988–1991); Director of Materials, Anicon, Inc.; Manager of Procurement and Production Control, Memorex; Manager for 10 years, Zeta Laboratories. **Associations & Accomplishments:** National Association of Purchasing Managers; Authored numerous articles and executive viewpoints for several purchasing trade publications, including "Electronics Purchasing and Electronic Buyer's News."

Michael J. Fioravanti
Director of Channel Sales
Pinnacle Micro
19 Technology
Irvine, CA 92718
(714) 789–3002 (800) 553–7070
Fax: (714) 789–3033
EMail: See Below

3572

Business Information: Pinnacle Micro, established in 1987, specializes in the manufacture of optical storage devices for the computer industry. With 180 employees, Pinnacle Micro estimates annual revenue in excess of $81 million. As Director of Channel Sales, Mr. Fioravanti manages the sales efforts of 40% of the total Company revenue, dealing primarily with wholesale distribution. Internet users can reach him via: http://www.pinnaclemicro.com. **Career Steps:** Director of Channel Sales, Pinnacle Micro (1995–Present); District Sales Manager, Sony Electronics (1992–1995); Senior Sales Representative, NEC Technologies (1985–1991); Sales Associate, Personal Computer Products, Inc. (1984–1985). **Education:** National University, Certificate (1983). **Personal:** Married to Laurie in 1989. Two children: Alyssa and Nicole. Mr. Fioravanti enjoys softball.

Jack Hardy
Director of Special Systems
Encore Computer Corporation
6901 West Sunrise Boulevard, Mail Stop 401
Ft. Lauderdale, FL 33313–4406
(954) 587–2900
Fax: (954) 797–2494
EMAIL: See Below

3572

Business Information: Encore Computer Corporation is a developer, manufacturer, and integrater of mainframe–compatible I/O and Open Systems Mainframes. Joining Encore as Director of Special Systems in 1990, Mr. Hardy is responsible for the development, integration, and testing of I/O controllers and devices. He also designs customer specific computer systems and provides customer service. Internet users can reach him via: jhardy@encore.com. **Career Steps:** Director of Special Systems, Encore Computer Corporation (1990–Present), Gould Inc.: Senior Section Manager of Development (1987–1990), Section Manager of Development (1984–1987). **Associations & Accomplishments:** United Way; Active in church activities. **Education:** Nova University. **Personal:** Married to Susie J. in 1979. Two children: Christina and Jaclyn. Mr. Hardy enjoys golf.

Mr. Thomas W. McDorman
Executive Director of Engineering
Seagate Thailand
Bangkok, Thailand
(662) 531–0321
Fax: Please mail or call

3572

Business Information: Seagate Thailand, a Fortune 200 company, specializes in the design and manufacture of disk drives for computers (hard disk drives). Established since 1981, Seagate Thailand presently employs 60,000 people and has an estimated annual revenue in excess of $4 billion. In his current capacity, Mr. McDorman is responsible for process engineering for California–based products. **Career Steps:** Executive Director of Engineering, Seagate Thailand (1995–Present); Executive Director of Quality & Reliability, Seagate Technology, Inc. (1993–1995); Manager, Mechanical Development, Insite Peripherals (1990–1992); Executive Director, Manufacturing Engineering, Seagate (1985–1990); Other Drive Companies worked for: CMI; IMI; ISS; Aerospace: Martin Marietta. **Associations & Accomplishments:** Mr. McDorman attributes his personal success to his ability to lead both technical and non–technical people through difficult challenges, while building strong team relationships. **Education:** Pepperdine University, M.B.A. Degree; Cal Poly, San Luis Obispo, B.S.M.E. **Personal:** Married. Three children. Mr. McDorman enjoys jet skiing and computers in his leisure time.

Mary H. Hinthorne
North American Inside Sales Manager
Intel Corporation
2111 NE 25th Avenue, #JF3325
Hillsboro, OR 97124–5961
(503) 264–1169
Fax: Please mail or call
EMail: See below

3575

Business Information: Intel Corporation is an international manufacturer of computer systems, including motherboards, microprocessors, microcontrollers and memory chips. Field sales offices are located in every region of the world, with ten campuses having several manufacturing plants each. With thirteen years of experience in sales, Ms. Hinthorne joined Intel Corporation as North American Inside Sales Manager in 1994. She is responsible for the management of all inside sales activities, including system analyst sales and sales management, in addition to a staff of 40 outbound senior sales representatives for the North American Region. Internet users can reach her via: mary_hinthorne@ccm.jf.intel.com **Career Steps:** North American Inside Sales Manager, Intel Corporation (1994–Present); Internal & NA Director of Sales, Quantum Corporation (1991–1993); Director NA/Internet Sales, Basic Four Corporation (1988–1991). **Education:** Old Dominion University (1962–1965); Honeywell Programming, Certification A.A. **Personal:** Married to Richard V. in 1985. Two children: Arthur Travis and Erin Alexandra (Duffey). Ms. Hinthorne enjoys snowskiing, swimming, and gardening.

Jeffrey A. Lambert, C.P.M., A.P.P.
Purchasing Manager
NEC Technologies
1414 Massachusetts Avenue
Boxboro, MA 01719
(508) 393–1151
Fax: (508) 393–1040
EMAIL: See Below

3575

Business Information: NEC Technologies is a leading manufacturer of computers, computer peripherals, and other technology products for the North American market. The Company also develops and markets a wide range of optical storage products, fully–configured computers with secure Internet services for a dedicated Internet connection and various technology products for the automotive market, including airbag sensoring systems and flat–panel display monitors. NEC Technologies, Inc. is a subsidiary of NEC Corporation. As a Purchasing Manager, Mr. Lambert oversees Contract Manufacturing of electronic Sub–Assemblies and other related SBU activities. He is responsible for the cost–effectiveness and quality of these products. Internet users can reach him via: Jlambert@nectech.com. **Career Steps:** Purchasing Manager, NEC Technologies (1987–Present); Purchasing Supervisor, Raster Technologies (1984–1987); Senior Buyer, Aritech Corporation (1983–1984). **Associations & Accomplishments:** NAPM; Former President, Central Massachusetts Director of National Affairs; Board of Corporators, Lowell Boys Club; Merrimack Valley United Fund Volunteer of the Year (1987). **Education:** New Hampshire College, M.B.A.; Boston University, B.S.B.A. **Personal:** Married to Linda in 1979. Two children: Ryan and Kylee. Mr. Lambert enjoys sports, reading, travel, and family time.

Jeffery J. Peterson

Marketing Manager
Amdahl Corporation
M/S 380, 1250 East Arques Avenue
Sunnyvale, CA 94086–5401
(408) 992–2489
Fax: Please mail or call
3575

Business Information: Established in 1970, Amdahl Corporation is a primary manufacturer and re–seller of server and main frame computer systems and software. International in scope, the Company is headquartered in Sunnyvale, California, and has twenty–six other locations worldwide. As Marketing Manager, Mr. Peterson is directly responsible for a staff of four. He also oversees research, consulting, and vender interfacing, and handles product management. **Career Steps:** Marketing Manager, Amdahl Corporation (1995–Present); Manager, Systems Services, Bell Atlantic Corporation (1993–1995); Manager, Database Systems, Witco Chemical Corporation (1991–1993). **Associations & Accomplishments:** Sierra Club; Institute of Electronics and Electrical Engineers. **Education:** Rensselaef Poly Technical Institute, B.S. (1973). **Personal:** Mr. Peterson enjoys Pre–Columbian American art, bicycling, and hiking.

Dennis R. Robinson

Senior Project Manager
Compuware Corporation
31440 Northwestern Highway
Farmington Hills, MI 48334–2564
(810) 737–7300
Fax: (810) 737–7339
3575

Business Information: Compuware Corporation is a leading computer software manufacturer. As Senior Project Manager, Mr. Robinson supervises six software development groups, including 51 managers and technical leaders. He is responsible for product development, strategic planning and analysis, client requirements and application technology. **Career Steps:** Senior Project Manager, Compuware Corporation (1994–Present); Product Author, Technologic Software (1992–1994); Director of Development, Legent Corporation (1991–1992); Director of Development, Sterling Software (1983–1991). **Education:** C.L.C. – L.A., Computer Technology (1981); CDI, Computer Technology (1974); ELAC Biology (1972). **Personal:** Married to Jackee in 1972. Mr. Robinson enjoys golf and landscaping.

Mr. Michael Albrecht Jr.

General Manager for Utilities Industry
IBM
One IBM Plaza, 5th Floor
Chicago, IL 60611
(312) 245–5600
Fax: (312) 245–4414
3577

Business Information: IBM is the world's leading manufacturer and producer of data processing equipment, software and services in the information handling field. Products include data processing systems and software, telecommunications systems, office systems and workstations. In his current capacity, Mr. Albrecht manages all developmental marketing strategy operations, business transformation services and systems integration coordination for the Utilities Industry Division (marketing to electric, gas, water and waste management industries) in North America. He also oversees all functions for IBM's Consultancy and Solutions Groups. Established in 1994, IBM Utility Industry Division employs 120 people. **Career Steps:** General Manager for Utilities Industry, IBM (1994–Present); Vice President of Consulting, IBM Consulting Group (1991–1994); Managing Principal, Nolan Norton & Co. (1985–1991); Consultant, (1981–1985). **Associations & Accomplishments:** Data Processing Management Association; Former Member, Illinois Jaycees; former member of Phi Gamma Mu. **Education:** Michigan State University, M.B.A. (1978); Illinois State University, B.S. in Mathematics (19 63).

Mr. Jeffrey S. Bain

Staff Engineer
Lockheed Martin
9500 Godwin Drive, 110/016
Manassas, VA 22110–4157
(703) 367–3243
Fax: (703) 367–3149
3577

Business Information: Lockheed Martin organizations. Established in 1969 and once a division of IBM, Lockheed Martin currently employs over 2,000 people. As Staff Engineer, Mr. Bain is an on–site facilities engineer responsible for site clean rooms, HVAC maintenance, chilled water, and all controls. **Career Steps:** Staff Engineer, Lockheed Martin (1994–Present); Senior Associate Engineer, IBM (1985–1994). **Associations & Accomplishments:** American Society of Heating, Refrigeration, and Air Conditioning Engineers. **Education:** Virginia Technical Institute, B.S. in Mechanical Engineering (1985). **Personal:** Married to Margaret in 1995. Mr. Bain enjoys snow skiing, weightlifting, tennis, horseback riding and biking.

Beth A. Barber

Environmental Engineer
Nordson Corporation
555 Jackson Street
Amherst, OH 44001–2408
(216) 985–4074
Fax: (216) 985–1743
3577

Business Information: Nordson Corporation is a manufacturer of applications equipment. Established in 1966, Nordson Corporation reports annual revenue of $500 million and currently employs 2,300 people corporate–wide. As Environmental Engineer, Mrs. Barber is responsible for corporate environmental engineering, compliance, management and environmental issues. **Career Steps:** Environmental Engineer, Nordson Corporation (1992–Present); Process Engineer, Packaging Corporation of America (1991–1992); Process Engineer, Weyerhaeuser Paper Company (1989–1991). **Associations & Accomplishments:** Lorain County Solid Waste Policy Committee; American Institute of Chemical Engineering; STLE; Technical Association of the Pulp & Paper Industry (TAPPI). **Education:** State University of New York at Buffalo, B.S. in Chemical Engineering (1987). **Personal:** Married to Joseph Lacinak, Jr. in 1993. One child: Tara M. Lacinak. Mrs. Barber enjoys music (piano, viola & violin) and sports.

George J. Bliss

Sales Director
Western Digital
1701 Golf Road Tower#3, Room 803
Rolling Meadows, IL 60008
(847) 290–9888
Fax: (847) 290–9996
3577

Business Information: Western Digital specializes in high technology sales, specifically RAID Systems, WANs, removable disks, and hard drives for distributors and retailers. The first Fortune 500 company in the world to receive ISO certification, the Company plans to move into the retail section of the market. As Sales Director, Mr. Bliss oversees sales personnel in several locations. He is responsible for assigning distribution (channeling) to specific sales personnel in accordance with territorial requirements. **Career Steps:** Sales Director, Western Digital (1992–Present); Sales Manager, Seagate Technology (1983–1991); Representative, First Rep Intel (1974–1983). **Associations & Accomplishments:** Juvenile Diabetes Foundation; Child Abuse Prevention Services (CAPS); March of Dimes, Chicago Chapter; Michael Jordan Foundation; Lettuce Entertain You Charity Staff; Chicago Bulls Charities; Chicago White Sox Charities. **Education:** Northern Illinois University, B.S.E. (1971); University of Illinois, M.B.A. Program. **Personal:** Married. Two children: James and George. Mr. Bliss enjoys speech writing and T.V. production.

Joanne M. Bohigian

Worldwide Business Development Manager
Lotus Development Corporation
1 Bush Street Suite 600
San Francisco, CA 94104–4412
(415) 955–8627
Fax: (415) 421–0621
EMAIL: See Below
3577

Business Information: Lotus Development Corporation, a subsidiary of IBM, is an establishment primarily engaged in the supply and distribution of computer software. Established in 1982, the Lotus Development Corporation currently employs 5,000 people. As Business Development Manager, Ms. Bohigian is responsible for business development worldwide for the designated Lotus Global Accounts organization. She negotiates contracts with worldwide customers and is involved in contract reviews from development through completion. Ms. Bohigian developed strategies for pricing and contracts, delivery and procurement, third party participation, services and support, and customer communication. Internet users may contact Ms. Bohigian at joanne_bohigian@crd.lotus.com. **Career Steps:** Lotus Development Corporation: Worldwide Business Development Manager (1993–Present), Senior Corporate Business Development Manager and cc:Mail Business Development Manager (1992–1993), cc:Mail Sales Coordinator/Transition Project Manager (1991–1992); Assistant to Vice President of Finance, Aviation Methods, Inc. (1989–1990). **Associations & Accomplishments:** American Marketing Association; National Notary Association; Commonwealth Club. Lotus Global Accounts awards for Outstanding Individual Contributor – 1994 and 1995; Lotus Worldwide Sales award for Outstanding Individual Excellence – 1995. **Education:** Golden Gate University, E.M.B.A. (1992); University of San Francisco, Bachelor of Science in Business Administration (1988). **Personal:** Ms. Bohigian enjoys music, cooking, biking, and travel.

Wilma Bolsonni

President
Bolsonni Tecnologia Multimidia
Brig. Luiz Antonio, 2367 18 Andar Cj. 1813
Sao Paulo SP, Brazil 01311–000
0115511–287–34
Fax: 0115511–287–70
Email: See Below
3577

Business Information: Bolsonni Tecnologia Multimidia is a production and distribution service of multimedia titles on CD–ROM, training software home pages for the internet, electronic catalogs, and educational children's programming. As President, Ms. Bolsonni is responsible for all daily operations, customer relation, employee supervision, administrative duties, and manages the export and distribution of software. **Career Steps:** President, Bolsonni Tecnologia Multimidia (1994–Present); Director, Data Trade (1990–1994); Manager, Jaavco Poyry Engenharia (1984–1990). **Associations & Accomplishments:** Sociedade Dos Usuarios De Informatica E Telecomunicagoes. **Education:** University of MacKenzie, Administration (1983). **Personal:** Three children: Eliza B. Castilla, Daniel B. Castilla, and Renata B. Castilla. Ms. Bolsonni enjoys tennis, volleyball, and oil painting on canvas.

Debra S. Brackeen

Senior Manager of Strategic Partner Programs
Apple Computer, Inc.
1 Infinite Loop MS305–3A
Cupertino, CA 95014–2083
(408) 974–6875
Fax: (408) 974–2326
EMAIL: See Below
3577

Business Information: Apple Computer Inc. designs, manufacturers and markets high–tech products globally, including information systems products and services, computers, networking hardware and software, as well as outsourcing services and consulting. Apple Computer, Inc. currently employs 14,000 corporate–wide. As Senior Manager of Strategic Partner Programs, Ms. Brackeen is responsible for technology licensing, support, and services for strategic partners and developers. Career milestones include being a part of the Power McIntosh Development efforts. She can also be reached through the Internet via: Brackeen@newton.apple.com **Career Steps:** Senior Manager of Strategic Partner Programs, Apple Computer Inc. (1987–Present) **Associations & Accomplishments:** Co–Authored "Diversity at Apple." **Education:** Stanford University, B.A. (1986)

Rebecca J. Butler

Senior Direct Marketing Strategist
IBM
400 Locust Street
Des Moines, IA 50309
(515) 283–4346
Fax: (515) 283–4333
EMAIL: See Below
3577

Business Information: IBM develops and delivers technology solutions to customers by providing hardware, software, and services to meet business requirements. A Certified Professional Direct Marketer, Ms. Butler joined Big Blue in 1985 and has served in various marketing positions. She was promoted to Senior Direct Marketing Strategist in 1994. Her present responsibilities include development of direct marketing strategy and marketing communications for IBM software in North America. Internet users can reach her via: 103726.3057@compuserve.com **Career Steps:** IBM: Senior Direct Marketing Strategist (1994–Present), Advisory Campaign Strategist (1993–1994), Advisory Marketing Representative (1991–1993), Various Positions (1985–1993). **Associations & Accomplishments:** Optimist International: Former Governor of Iowa District (1993–1994) and serves on various international committees; Noon Optimist Club of Western Des Moines; Drake University: Alumna, Chair for Student Life National Advisory Board. **Education:** Drake University: B.S. in Business Administration (1985), Undergraduate Majors in Marketing and Human Resource Management; University of Missouri, Certified Professional Direct Marketer (1995). **Personal:** Ms. Butler enjoys travel, music, piano, singing, volleyball, and tennis.

Donald P. Bynum
President
Itac Systems
3113 Benton Street
Garland, TX 75042–7411
(214) 494–3073
Fax: (214) 494–4159
EMAIL: See Below

3577

Business Information: Itac Systems is an inventor and manufacturer of user interface technology for computers. Itac is best known for its trademarked "Trackball" — the newest technology development designed to replace the traditional "mouse". The Trackball is self–cleaning and eliminates the pain caused in the hand and wrist by operating the commonly–used mouse. As President, Mr. Bynum is responsible for the oversight of all aspects of operations, including administration, finances, public relations, and strategic planning. Internet users can reach him via: bynum@moustrak.com **Career Steps:** President, Itac Systems (1993–Present); Director of Business Development, MCC (1990–1991); Vice President of Worldwide Marketing, Data Point Corporation (1987–1990). **Associations & Accomplishments:** Quoted in a number of trade journals regarding the Trackball. **Education:** University of Texas, B.A. in Mathematics (1967). **Personal:** Married to Peggy in 1967. Two children: Russell and Brad. Mr. Bynum enjoys sailing, flying, and skiing.

Mr. Joseph R. Cannizzaro
Vice President of Worldwide Marketing
Digital Equipment Corporation
2 Results Way (MRO2–4/D16)
Marlboro, MA 01752
(508) 467–6874
Fax: (508) 467–1110

3577

Business Information: Digital Equipment Corporation, the third largest computer company in the world, provides a full line of computer hardware, software and services. With corporate headquarters in Maynard, Massachusetts, Digital currently employs 62,000 people worldwide. Established 35 years ago, Digital reports annual revenue of $14 billion. Joseph Cannizzaro, a 19–year veteran of Digital's engineering and manufacturing organizations, provides the focal point for all marketing activities worldwide for the Components and Peripherals Business Unit. Mr. Cannizzaro's role encompasses the strategy and operational direction of the business unit's marketing organization and programs in the U.S., Europe and Asia/Pacific, including advertising, direct marketing, trade shows, external events, public relations, analyst relations, customer relations, sales tools, product literature and training. He also serves as the senior marketing liaison to marketing functions internal and external to Digital. He works collaboratively with the business segments in the Components and Peripherals Business Unit to achieve established business goals. **Career Steps:** Vice President of Worldwide Marketing–Components & Peripherals Business Unit, Digital Equipment Corporation (1992–Present); Group Engineering Manager/LES/VIPS, Digital Equipment Corporation; Group Enginering Manager/LES/LESSE, Digital Equipment Corporation (1987–1990); Staff Engineer, IBM Corporation (1964–1975). **Associations & Accomplishments:** Published in trade journals; Wrote two chapters in Printed Circuit Handbook (McGraw Hill); **Education:** Long Island University, graduate; Lesley College, M.S. in Management (1989); INSEAD Executive Program, attended a 7–week International/Advanced Management Program, Fontainebleau, France. **Personal:** Married to Dolores in 1964. Two children: Joseph and Christopher. Mr. Cannizzaro enjoys boating, cars and skiing.

Carl P. Chesal
Market Development Manager
Sun Microsystems, Inc.
350 Albert Street
Ottawa, Ontario K1R 1A4
(613) 787–4265
Fax: (613) 237–9828
EMAIL: See Below

3577

Business Information: Sun Microsystems, Inc. is a national manufacturer and marketer of computer hardware and software. Established in 1982, Sun Microsystems Inc. reports annual revenue of $6 billion and currently employs 14,500 people corporate–wide. As Market Development Manager of the Sun Micro Computers Division, Mr. Chesal is responsible for the marketing development of national government contracts and electronic commerce in Eastern Canada and Ottawa. He can also be reached through the Internet via: carl.chesal@canada.sun.com **Career Steps:** Sun Microsystems, Inc.: Market Development Manager – Computers Division (1991–Present), National Technical (SE) Manager (1988–1991); SE Manager, Hewlett–Packard – Canada (1984–1988). **Associations & Accomplishments:** Canada Information Processing Society; Ontario Provincial Police/

Community Police Officer Volunteer; Junior Achievements Fund Raiser. **Education:** York University, Executive MBA in Marketing (1987); Saint Mary's University, B.Sc. in Math (1976). **Personal:** Married to Janet in 1974. Two children: Ian and Sharon. Mr. Chesal enjoys music, gardening, and photography.

Raymond Y. V. Chik, Ph.D.
Design Engineer
Quantum Corporation
135 Michael Cowpland Drive, Suite 300
Kanata, Ontario K2M 2E9
(613) 836–3134 Ext. 381
Fax: (613) 836–0796
E/M: chik@mosaid.com

3577

Business Information: Quantum Corporation designs and manufactures storage products for today's digital world. Widely recognized as the industry's quality leader, Quantum sells a broad range of storage products of OEM and distribution customers worldwide. As a Design Engineer in the mixed–signal design team of the Technology and Engineering group, Dr. Chik is responsible for designing high speed analog integrated circuits for state–of–the–art hard disk drive read–channel chips. Concurrent with his duties as Design Engineer at Quantum, he is the Vice President of Power Thinkings, a computer system consulting frim. **Career Steps:** Design Engineer, Quantum Corporation (1996–Present); Integrated Circuit Design Engineer, MOSAID Technologies, Inc. (1995–1996); Vice President, Power Thinkings (1994–Present). **Associations & Accomplishments:** Member of Institute of Electrical and Electronics Engineers; Author/Co–Author of several publications in international technical journals. **Education:** University of Toronto: Ph.D. in Electrical and Computer Engineering (1996), M.A.Sc. (1991) and B.A.Sc. (1988) in Electrical Engineering.

Gautam Chitnis
Managing Director – Asia/Pacific Operations
Trippe Manufacturing
500 North Orleans
Chicago, IL 60610
(508) 229–2247
Fax: (312) 329–1363
E–mail: see below

3577

Business Information: International in scope, Trippe Manufacturing specializes in the manufacture and distribution of power protection products for the computer industry. Established in 1922, Trippe Manufacturing currently employs 400 people and has an estimated annual revenue of $200 million. As Managing Director and Founder of the Asia–Pacific Division, Mr. Chitnis is responsible for all aspects of management, sales, marketing and distribution operations in the Asia–Pacific region. He can also be reached through the Internet via: GCHITNIS@mcimail.com **Career Steps:** Managing Director–Asia/Pacific, Trippe Manufacturing (1993–Present); Regional Director, Nippon – Falcon Electric (1991–1993); South Asia Manager, American Power Conversion (1990–1991). **Associations & Accomplishments:** Asian Information Technology Association; World Wildlife Foundation; Active Member, National Geographic Society; Numerous publications; Guest Lecturer, International Strategic Planning and Management at the Indian Institute of Management, the Asian Institute of Management, and the University of Rhode Island. **Education:** University of Rhode Island, M.B.A. (1991); University of Madras – India, B.S. in Engineering (1988). **Personal:** Mr. Chitnis enjoys nature activities.

Alan D. Clark, Ph.D., FIEE
Vice President of Advanced Communication Products
Hayes Microcomputer Products, Inc.
5835 Peachtree Corners East
Norcross, GA 30092–3404
(404) 840–9200
Fax: (404) 840–6830
EMAIL: See Below

3577

Business Information: Hayes Microcomputer Products, Inc. is a data communication product manufacturer, best known for its Smart Modem modems. Established in 1978, Hayes Microcomputer Products, Inc. reports annual revenue of $300 million and currently employs 800 people. As Vice President of Advanced Communications Products, Dr. Clark is responsible for development and management of new business opportunities and products. Career milestones include the development of the V42 big data compression standard and major technical contributions to the modem industry. Internet users can also reach Alan via: aclark@hayes.com **Career Steps:** Vice President of Advanced Communications Products, Hayes Microcomputer Products, Inc. (1994–Present); Vice President, Product Planning, Hayes (1993–1994); Director of Research, Dowty/Cray Communications (1991–1993); Technical Director, Dowty Information Systems (1989–1990). **Associations & Accomplishments:** Fellow, Institute of Electrical Engineers (IEE); Member, Institute of Electrical and Electronic Engineers (IEEE); Chartered Engineer. **Education:** Leicester Polytechnic, Ph.D. (1986), B.Sc. in Electronic Engineering. **Personal:** Married to Glenis in 1973. Two children: Elizabeth and Adam. Dr. Clark enjoys table tennis, reading, music, and walking.

Gregory T. Cortese
• • • —————◉————— • • •
Corporate Vice President of Law and Business Affairs
PAR Technology Corporation
8383 Seneca Turnpike
New Hartford, NY 13413
(315) 738–0600 Ext. 249
Fax: (315) 738–0411

3577

Business Information: PAR Technology Corporation specializes in the manufacture of computer and medical systems, including industrial data software and medical devices. Major clientele includes the healthcare industry, government agencies and fast food chain operations. Established in 1968, PAR Technology Corporation currently employs 1,100 people and has an estimated annual revenue of $100 million. As Corporate Vice President of Law and Business Affairs, Mr. Cortese is responsible for all legal functions for the parent company. Concurrently, Mr. Cortese holds the positions of Secretary and acting Chief Executive Officer of the PAR Medical Division. **Career Steps:** Corporate Vice President of Law and Business Affairs, Secretary, and Acting CEO of the PAR Medical Division, PAR Technology Corporation (1979–Present); Assistant Staff Judge Advocate, United States Air Force Reserves Ballistic Missile Office (1977–1979). **Associations & Accomplishments:** American Bar Association; American Corporate Counsels Association; American Society of Corporate Secretaries; Air Force Association; Massachusetts Bar Association; Computer Law Association; AYSO Soccer Coach. **Education:** Boston College of Law, J.D. (1974); Rensselaer Polytechnic Institute, B.S. in Engineering Science (1971). **Personal:** Married to Ruth (Susan). Two children: Shawn and Alyssa. Mr. Cortese enjoys reading, tennis and weightlifting.

Antonio Sergio Covas Pereira
• • • —————◉————— • • •
Assistant Treasurer
IBM Brazil
Avenue Pasteur, 138/146–MB–07
Rio De Janeiro, Brazil 22296–900
(021) 546–5384
Fax: (021) 546–5467

3577

Business Information: IBM Brazil specializes in information processing and business solutions. Mr. Covas Pereira has held various positions within IBM Brazil, serving as Country Administrative Manager from 1985 to 1987, Pension Fund Executive from 1988 to 1990, Treasury Operations Manager from 1991 to 1992, and moving into his present position as Assistant Treasurer in 1992. His current responsibilities include oversight of the Treasury Department and all financial activities. Concurrently, he serves as Chief Financial Officer of IBM Brazil Leasing Company, supervising product leasing, daily operations, and related financial activities. **Career Steps:** IBM Brazil Leasing Company, Chief Financial Officer (1992–Present); IBM Brazil: Assistant Treasurer (1992–Present), Treasury Operations Manager (1991–1992), Pension Fund Executive (1988–1990), Country Administration Manager (1985–1987). **Associations & Accomplishments:** IBEF (Financial Executives Association); Jockey's Country Club. **Education:** PUC – Rio: Engineering (1969), M.S.C., in Industrial Engineering, concentration in Finance (1971). **Personal:** Married to Marilia in 1974. Two children: Carlos Alexandre and Ana Carolina. Mr. Covas Pereira enjoys sports, volleyball, tennis, and snorkeling.

Mr. Christophe P. Daligault
Senior Marketing Manager
Microsoft Europe
One Microsoft Way
Redmond, WA 98052–8300
33–146–351077
Fax: 33–146–351111

3577

Business Information: Microsoft Corporation is the world's leading software development corporation. Starting during the 70's, Microsoft pioneered the standard computer languages for the Apple II and other early personal computers, then moved on to the development of the operating system, MS–DOS, for IBM's landmark PC. Envisioning the market expansion of the PC industry, Microsoft joined forces with the microprocessor giant, Intel Corporation, along with other entrepreneurs and thus created the PC clone industry which now dominates the market. Microsoft's introduction of the Windows program is what has brought the company into one of the world's profit leading enterprises, exceeding that of corporations with revenues ten times as large. Established in 1975, Microsoft currently employs 75,000 people world–wide. As Senior Marketing Manager, Mr. Daligault is responsible for all aspects of marketing and strategic planning for European operations. **Career Steps:** Senior Marketing Manager, Microsoft Europe (1993–Present); Group Product Manager, Microsoft France (1990–1993); Sales Director, CRAS France (1986–1990); Account Manager, BDDP Advertising France (1986–1989). **Education:** EDMEC, M.B.A. (1982); Graduate Business School, France. **Personal:** Married to Sandrine. One child: Louis.

Sam Danon

Founder and Managing Director
Tel–Call TV
73 Monza Place, Cayalami Park
Michaud, South Africa
27–114661803
Fax: 27–114661911

3577

Business Information: Tel–Call TV is an international distributor of television and radio signals for MATV and CATV in South Africa, Zambia, and Zaire. With thirty–eight years of experience in the radio and television industry, Mr. Danon founded Tel–Call TV in 1978 and serves as its Managing Director. He is responsible for the management and direction of the Company, as well as policy making and sourcing of new businesses. **Career Steps:** Founder and Managing Director, Tel–Call TV (1978–Present). **Associations & Accomplishments:** SCTE (1993); SBCA (1996); Johannesburg Chamber of Commerce; Midand Chamber of Commerce; Born in Bulgaria and educated in Israel; Nominated for Business Man of the Year (1996) **Education:** Television Engineering, (1958). **Personal:** Married to Nelida in 1971. Two children: Orly and Doron. Mr. Danon enjoys bowling.

Theresa G. DiStefano
HW Engineer Program Coordinator
COMPAQ Computer Corporation
MS 090404, 20555 SH 249
Houston, TX 77070
(713) 514–6224
Fax: (713) 518–7445
EMAIL: See Below

3577

Business Information: COMPAQ Computer Corporation, a Fortune 500 company, is a manufacturer of computers and peripheral equipment. Established in 1982, COMPAQ Computer Corporation reports annual revenue of $1 billion and currently employs 8,000 people. As HW Engineer Program Coordinator, Ms. DiStefano coordinates all aspects of program management support (i.e., schedules, forecast, technical data) for high end server products. Internet users can also reach Theresa via: TheresaD @ Compaq.com **Career Steps:** COMPAQ Computer Corporation: HW Engineer Program Coordinator (1993–Present), Operations Program Coordinator (1992–1993), Research and Development Program Coordinator (1990–1991). **Associations & Accomplishments:** Member, Tomball High School Drill Team Booster Club; PTO at Decker Prairie Elementary School. **Education:** Tomball College; Sam Houston University; Completed high school as

a mid–term graduate (1981). **Personal:** Two children: Michelle Butterworth and Natalie DiStefano. Ms. DiStefano enjoys horseback riding.

Jo–Ann F. Driscoll
Training Director
Powersoft Corporation
561 Virginia Road
Concord, MA 01742–2727
(508) 287–1595
Fax: Please mail or call

3577

Business Information: Powersoft Corporation designs and develops software applications. As Training Director, Ms. Driscoll develops training materials and coordinates training sessions for three user conferences attended by more than 4,000 users. **Career Steps:** Training Director, Powersoft Corporation (1991–Present); Education Consultant, Cullinet Software (1983–1991); Senior Instructor, GTE Sylvania (1976–1980). **Associations & Accomplishments:** Association of Data Processing Trainers; National Society for Performance and Instruction; Town of Carlisle Personnel Committee. **Education:** University of Massachusetts – Boston, M.Ed. (1996); Babson College, M.B.A. (1985); Bates College, B.A. (1968). **Personal:** Married to David in 1968. Ms. Driscoll enjoys hiking and cross–country skiing.

Mark Durst, C.A.

President
Patriot Computer Inc.
25 Minthorn Court
Thornhill, Ontario L3T 7N5
(416) 969–8123
Fax: (416) 969–8121

3577

Business Information: Patriot Computer Inc., the only name–brand manufacturer of computers in Canada, is an international manufacturer of personal computers. Comprised of a Vice President of Marketing (his brother), and Vice President of Technology (Rob Cherenko), the Corporation distributes directly to other corporations and government entities, as well as distributing through Canadian retailers and exporting to the U.S. and other countries. The Company is currently fulfilling a contract to manufacture 500,000 18" satellite receivers for a private corporation. These receivers provide 500 channels vice the normal 40 channel dishes. As President, Mr. Durst is responsible for the daily operations, including managing sales and marketing functions. He also oversees a support staff of 75 people at the Thornhill, Ontario location, as well as more than 275 people in three other locations. **Career Steps:** President, Patriot Computer Inc. (1991–Present); Vice President of Sales and Marketing, Primax Computer (1989–1991); Vice President of Sales and Marketing, Business World; Vice President of Sales and Marketing, Computer Solutions International (1986–1987). **Associations & Accomplishments:** Young President's Organizations; Young Entrepreneurs Organization; Participates in Patriot Computer, Inc.'s hockey team, The Patriots; Named in the Top 40 of the under–40 year old executives in Canada; the Firm was named one of the Top 50 best–managed companies in Canada by the Financial Post. **Education:** Chartered Accountant (1987); University of Waterloo, Bachelors of Mathematics (1986). **Personal:** Married with three children. Mr. Durst enjoys hockey.

Gustavo A. Eichelmann

Region Manager – Latin America
EMC Corporation
Textitlan no. 66 apt. 18
Mexico City, Mexico 14420
(525) 655–0760
Fax: (508) 497–6920

3577

Business Information: EMC Corporation is the world leader in enterprise–wide information storage and retrieval technology. Joining EMC as Region Manager for Latin America in 1995, Mr. Eichelmann is responsible for all aspects of the business in Latin America, including distribution, sales, marketing, and new business development. **Career Steps:** Region Manager – Latin America, EMC Corporation (1995–Present); Digital Equipment Corporation – Mexico: Director of Marketing and Business Development (1993–1995), General Manager – Northern Region (1991–1993), Sales Manager – Indirect Channels (1990–1991), Marketing Manager (1989–1990); Channel Development Manager, Hewlett–Packard – Mexico (1989). **Education:** INSEAD, International Management Education Program (1993); Universidad Anahuac, B.S. (1986). **Personal:** Married to Brigitte Goirand in 1986. Mr. Ei-

chelmann enjoys movies, theater, reading, and outdoor activities.

Mr. Stephen Elia
Director of Product Development
Leading Edge Products Inc.
117 Flanders Road
Westborough, MA 01581
Fax: Please mail or call

3577

Business Information: Leading Edge Products Inc., one of the top 100 in volume sales and brand name recognition, specializes in the manufacture of IBM clone personal computers. Established in 1980, Leading Edge Products, Inc. was the first company to clone the IBM PC. The Company currently employs 300 people and has an estimated annual revenue of $150 million. As Director of Product Development, Mr. Elia is responsible for all aspects of product definition, marketing, engineering and testing, as well as the supervision of a staff of 20. **Career Steps:** Director of Product Development, Leading Edge Products Inc. (1981–Present); Sales Executive, Royal Business Forms (1980–1981). **Associations & Accomplishments:** Voting Member of the VESA Committee; Taunton Massachusetts School Computing Advisory Board; Member, Boston Computer Society; American Association of Individual Investors. **Education:** Southeastern Massachusetts University, B.S. in Business Administration. **Personal:** Married to Janet Ann in 1983. Two children: Matthew Thomas and Victoria Colleen. Mr. Elia enjoys fishing, golf, chess and reading.

Daniel T. Feeney
Director of Peripherals
Mitac U.S.A.
3797 Spinnaker Court
Fremont, CA 94538–6537
(510) 440–3631
Fax: (510) 252–6991
EMAIL: See Below

3577

Business Information: Mitac U.S.A., a division of Synnex and a subsidiary of Mitac International, manufactures computers and computer equipment. As Director of Peripherals, Mr. Feeney manages the peripherals product line and is the Program Manager for OEM manufacturing. Internet users can reach him via: DanF @ Synnex.com **Career Steps:** Director of Peripherals, Mitac U.S.A. (1995–Present); Director, IPC Singapore (1994–1995); Director, Wearnes Brothers Limited, Singapore (1990–1994); Director, ACI (1987–1990). **Education:** Drexel University, B.S. in Physics (1972). **Personal:** Married to Nancy in 1986. One child: Shelby. Mr. Feeney enjoys sport car restoration and antique car racing.

Mr. Roy J. Finney III
Software Engineer
Compaq Computer Corporation
20555 S.H. 249
Houston, TX 77070
(713) 370–0670
Fax: (713) 378–0750

3577

Business Information: Compaq Computer Corporation, a Fortune 100 company, is one of the world's leading manufacturers of personal computers, software and related peripheral systems. In his capacity as a Software Engineer, Mr. Finney is responsible for the development and support of software applications for Compaq manufacturing sites. Established in 1982, Compaq Computer Corporation employs over 11,000 people worldwide and has annual revenue in excess of $14.8 billion. **Career Steps:** Software Engineer, Compaq Computer Corporation (1991–Present). **Associations & Accomplishments:** Association of Former Students, Texas A&M University; Eagle Scout, Boy Scouts of America; Member, First United Methodist Church; National Rifle Association. **Education:** Texas A&M University, B.S. (1990); Houston Baptist University, M.B.A. (1996).

Jean Guy Fournier
Communications Manager
IBM Canada Limited
23 Airport Boulevard
Bromont, Quebec J0E 1L0
(514) 534–6389
Fax: (514) 534–6059
EMAIL: See Below

3577

Business Information: IBM Canada Limited designs, manufactures and markets high–tech products globally. This includes information systems products and services, computers, semiconductors, networking hardware and software, and computer hardware and software. Services include outsourcing, multivendor support, and consulting. As Communications Manager, Mr. Fournier is responsible for all communication programs, donations, and overseeing daily operations. Internet users can reach him via: BRMVM1 (JAFOURNI). **Career Steps:** IBM Canada Limited: Public Relations Manager (1986–Present), Human Resources Manager (1984–1986), Manufacturing Manager (1980–1984); Supervisor, Royal Bank of Canada (1975–1977). **Associations & Accomplishments:** Canadian Society of Public Relations; Quebec Society of Public Relations; International Society for Communication Professionals. **Education:** Montreal University: M.B.A. (1986), B.Sc. in Industrial Relations. **Personal:** Mr. Fournier enjoys golf, skiing, rollerblading, rollerskating, and reading.

David E. Fulford
Process Engineer
Digital Audio Disc Corporation
1800 North Fruitridge Avenue
Terre Haute, IN 47804–1780
(812) 462–8326
Fax: (812) 462–8760

3577

Business Information: Digital Audio Disc Corporation manufactures CD, CD–ROM, LD, and DVD discs. Mr. Fulford joined DADC in 1992 and now serves as the Process Engineer overseeing the Printing Department. His responsibilities include quality control, productivity improvement, and project development. **Career Steps:** Digital Audio Disc Corporation: Process Engineer (1994–Present), Engineering Assistant (1992–1994); CIM Lab Assistant, Indiana State University (1991–1992). **Education:** Indiana State University, B.S./CIM (1993). **Personal:** Mr. Fulford enjoys sports, saltwater aquariums, basketball, and playing guitar.

Bruce C. Gayliard
Principal Software Engineer
Digital Equipment Corporation
200 Route 9 North
Manalapan, NJ 07726–9455
(908) 577–6198
Fax: (908) 577–6003
E MAIL: See Below

3577

Business Information: Digital Equipment Corporation specializes in the manufacture, distribution and service of computer systems worldwide. As Principal Software Engineer, Mr. Gayliard oversees the design and development of computer software and user support applications for clients. Internet users may contact him via: bg@unx.dec.com. **Career Steps:** Principal Software Engineer, Digital Equipment Corporation (1996–Present); Consulting Engineer, Concurrent Computer Corporation (1977–1996). **Associations & Accomplishments:** Institute of Electrical and Electronics Engineers; Institute of Electrical and Electronics Engineers Computer Society; Association for Computing Machinery. **Education:** Monmouth College, M.S.S.E. (1990), B.S.E.E. (1978). **Personal:** Married to Deborah A. in 1980. Three children: Justin, Nicholas, and Gillian. Mr. Gayliard enjoys model rocketry, scouts, and electronics.

Mark A. Gill
Director of Marketing Research and Development
Graphic Enterprise of Ohio
P.O. Box 3080
North Canton, OH 44720–8080
(800) 321–9874 Ext. 536
Fax: (216) 494–5481
EMAIL: See Below

3577

Business Information: Graphic Enterprise of Ohio, established in 1970, specializes in the development, manufacture, market and maintenance of high resolution, large format laser printers and related software. International in scope, Graphic Enterprise has eight locations throughout the world. Joining Graphic Enterprise as Manufacturing Division Manager in 1992, Mr. Gill was appointed as Director of Marketing, Research and Development in 1994. He is responsible for the oversight of all research and development facets of the laser printer line, as well as directing international sales and marketing. Internet users can reach him via: GEIOHIO.COM. **Career Steps:** Graphic Enterprise of Ohio: Director of Marketing Research and Development (1994–Present), Manufacturing Division Manager (1992–1994); Electrical and Instrumentation Supervisor, James River Corporation (1990–1992); First Lieutenant, US Army (1986–1990). **Associations & Accomplishments:** American Marketing Association; Association for Manufacturing Excellence; American Management Association; Institute of Electronics and Electrical Engineers; Knights of Columbus, Parish Council. **Education:** University of Dayton, B.S.E.E. (1986); Baily INFI 90 and Network 90 DCS Qualified. **Personal:** Married to Kathy in 1986. Mr. Gill enjoys golf, skiing, basketball, and woodworking.

Bernard F. Girbal

Managing Director, Southern Europe
CHIPCOM Europe
3Con Avenue de l'Arlanhique, 2 A Courtaboeuf
Les Ulis, France 91976
331–69–86–68–0
Fax: 331–69–86–68–8
E–mail: see below

3577

Business Information: E Com, the Leadership in Global Data Networking, has 16 years of data networking experience. Established in 1979 E Com Corporation reports annual revenue for the fiscal year 1995 (ending May of 1995) of $1.3 billion and currently employees 3,000 people in 40 countries. As Managing Director, Southern Europe, Mr. Girbal is responsible for all aspects of operations management. Mr. Girbal can also be reached through the internet as follows: BGirbal @ Email. E Com. **Career Steps:** General Manager, Western Europe, CHIPCOM Europe (1991–Present); General Manager of Sales, Marketing and Finance, Reseaux de Communication d'Entreprises (R.C.E.) (1988–1991); Hewlett–Packard: International Major Account Sales Manager (1984–1988), Customer Support Director (1980–1984). **Associations & Accomplishments:** Recipient of the "Excellence Award" in Clarinet at the Paris Classical Music Conservatory (1979); Director of the Hewlett–Packard Alumni Club, which is the association of former Hewlett–Packard employees. **Education:** Paris University of Technology, Engineering Degree (1979); Institut d'Administration d'Entreprises of Paris (I.A.E.), Business Administration Degree (1981). **Personal:** Married to Aline in 1985. Three children: Clementine, Marie, and Clara. Mr. Girbal enjoys classical music and golf.

Derek J. Groniger
Vice President of Sales & Marketing
DDI Business Systems
3800 W. 80th Street, Suite 1050
Minneapolis, MN 55431
(612) 831–4777
Fax: (612) 831–3672

3577

Business Information: DDI Business Systems is a value–added remarketer of manufacturing computer software, specifically ERP/MRPII. The Company produces turnkey products for software only.. As Vice President of Sales & Marketing, Mr. Groniger is responsible for sales and marketing management. He handles all customer relations, marketing products update, and clients. **Career Steps:** Vice President of Sales & Marketing, DDI Business Systems (1995–Present); Sales, American Software (1992–1995); Sales, Symex Computer Systems (1992). **Associations & Accomplishments:** American Production and Inventory Control Society. **Education:** University of Wisconsin – Madison, B.S. in Agriculture (1988). **Personal:** Married to Claudine in 1990.

Matthew J. Guardiola
Systems Applications Engineer
Silicon Graphics
2060 East Algonquin Road
Schaumburg, IL 60173
(847) 925–2905
Fax: (847) 925–2930
EMAIL: See below

3577

Business Information: Silicon Graphics is an international manufacturer of premium computer work stations (graphics work stations). Silicon Graphics is the world's first consistent real–time elections–display and simulation company (electronic display of the election outcomes, reported on the news). As Systems Applications Engineer, Mr. Guardiola is responsible for the technical consulting for sales, marketing, and engineering. Internet users can reach him via: Mattg@sgi.com **Career Steps:** Systems Applications Engineer, Silicon Graphics (1989–Present); Systems Engineer, Hewlett Packard (1987–1989). **Associations & Accomplishments:** De-Paul University Computer Science Club; Illinois Java Users Group; Chairman, Silicon Graphics Chicago Users Group. **Education:** De Paul University, Masters in Computer Science (1996); DeVry Institute of Technology, B.S. in Electrical Engineering (1989). **Personal:** Married to Susan Stelter in 1995.

Vivek Gupta
Manager of Capacity Planning
Intel Corporation
5000 W. Chandler Blvd.
Chandler, AZ 85226
(602) 554–2195
Fax: Please mail or call

3577

Business Information: Intel Corporation is an international manufacturer of computer systems, including motherboards, microprocessors, microcontrollers and memory chips. Field sales offices are located in every region of the world, with ten campuses having several manufacturing plants each. Serving in various managerial capacities for Intel since 1984, Vivek Gupta was appointed to his current position in 1996. As Manager of Capacity Planning, he oversees strategic planning activities, ensuring manufacturing capabilities and capacities are able to meet product demands for business units. **Career Steps:** Intel Corporation: Manager of Capacity Planning (1996–Present), Manager of North America Logistics (1993–1995), Manager of Manufacturing Engineering (1984–1993). **Associations & Accomplishments:** India Association: President (1994, 1995), Vice President (1993); Council of Logistics Management; Tau Beta Pi; Phi Kappa Phi; Writes articles on community issues and edits a newsletter with a circulation of 1,000; Actively involved in community activities. **Education:** Southern Illinois University, M.S. in Thermal Engineering (1983); Indian Institute of Technology, B.Tech in Mechanical Engineering (1977). **Personal:** Married to Mamta in 1980. Two children: Charu and Sasha. Mr. Gupta enjoys community work, tennis, pingpong, music, sightseeing, and writing.

Joe (Youssef) N. Haddad

General Manager
Computer Age Products SARL (CAP)
Sinel Fil
Beirut, Lebanon 55522
971–4–836181
Fax: 971–4–836809
EMAIL: See Below

3577

Business Information: Computer Age Products SARL (CAP) is involved in the development and integration of computer business solution, assembly of PC's, and the distribution of IT products. Established in 1986, the Company's main office is in Lebanon, with branches in San Diego, Cypress, and Dubai. As General Manager, Mr. Haddad is responsible for diversified administrative and operational activities. In addition, he serves as marketing manager and purchasing manager. Internet users can reach him via: comage@dm.net.lb. **Career Steps:** General Manager, Computer Age Product SARL (CAP) (1986–Present); Marketing and Sales Manager, E.O.S. Computer Solution (1982–1986). **Education:** Lebanese University, B.S. (1981). **Personal:** Married to Feyrouz Hanna in 1990. Two children: Angela and Nehme. Mr. Haddad enjoys chess and problem solving.

Thomas S. Harvey
Country Planning Coordinator, IBM Latin America
IBM
Rockwood Road, Route 9
North Tarrytown, NY 10591
(914) 332–2494
Fax: Please mail or call

3577

Business Information: IBM (International Business Machines) is a major manufacturer and distributor of information technology hardware and services to customers worldwide. As Country Planning Coordinator, IBM Latin America, Mr. Harvey is responsible for analysis and recommendation of financial plans to five subsidiaries in Latin America. Established in 1917, IBM employs 5,000 people with annual sales of $3 billion. **Career Steps:** Country Planning Coordinator (1994–Present), Manager of Accounting (1993–1994), Advisory Analyst in Finance (1992–1993), Financial Analyst (1990–1992), IBM Latin America, IBM. **Associations & Accomplishments:** Aristotle 2000, a mentoring program affiliated with Big Brothers. **Education:** New York University Stern School of Business, M.B.A. (1989); Wesleyan University, B.A. (1985); The Polytechnic School, Pasadena, CA (1981); Fluent in Spanish. **Personal:** Mr. Harvey enjoys basketball, making videos, playing golf, skiing and creative writing.

Mr. Jean–Francois L. Heitz

Assistant Treasurer
Microsoft Corporation
One Microsoft Way
Redmond, WA 98052–6399
(206) 936–9588
Fax: (206) 641–0798

3577

Business Information: Microsoft Corporation is the world's leading software development corporation. Starting during the 70's, Microsoft pioneered the standard computer languages for the Apple II and other early personal computers, then moved on to the development of the operating system, MS–DOS, for IBM's landmark PC. Envisioning the market expansion of the PC industry, Microsoft joined forces with the microprocessor giant, Intel Corporation, along with other entrepreneurs and thus created the PC clone industry which now dominates the market. Microsoft's introduction of the Windows program is what has brought the company into one of the world's profit leading enterprises, exceeding that of corporations with revenues ten times as large. Jean–Francois Heitz has been an executive member of the Microsoft organization since 1989, where he was Manager of Operations for Microsoft France. He transferred to the Corporate Headquarters in Redmond, Washington upon his appointment as Assistant Treasurer in 1994. In this capacity, Mr. Heitz is responsible for the administrative oversight for all corporate mergers and acquistions, risk management, and major customer financial relations. A native of France, he graduated from the prestigious institute Ecole des Mines de Paris, attaining a Diplome D'Engenieur, summa cum laude and first in his class of 1969. It is his unique ability to adapt to different environments and cultures which led him to the Microsoft Corporate "family." Established in 1975, Microsoft Corporation employs 15,000 world–wide people with annual sales of $4.65 billion in annual sales and market capitalization of $38.5 billion. **Career Steps:** Assistant Treasurer, Microsoft Corporation (1994–Present); General Manager of Business Operations, Microsoft France (1991–1994); Deputy General Manager, Finance and Accounting, Microsoft France (1989–1991); Vice President of Finance and Legal President, Matra Systems/Matra Technology (1987–1989). **Associations & Accomplishments:** President, Alumni Association of Ecole des Mines de Paris; Director, Centre National de Recherche Financiere. **Education:** Ecole des Mines de Paris, France, Diplome D'Engenieur, summa cum laude (1969); Stanford University, M.S.; Harvard University, C.F.M.P. **Personal:** Married to Catherine Coiffard in 1982. Three children: Fabien, Nathalie and Aurelia. Mr. Heitz enjoys jogging, mountain skiing, computers, and music (accomplished pianist).

Stephen E. Houlihan

Worldwide Accounting Manager
The Open Group, Inc.
11 Cambridge Center
Cambridge, MA 02142–1405
(617) 621–7262
Fax: (617) 621–8781
EMAIL: See Below

3577

Business Information: The Open Group, Inc. is a worldwide consortium of collaborative R&D/Branding of Unix based open systems computer software. The Company was created by large companies for the design of Unix software and to set standards for new technology. As Worldwide Accounting Manager, Mr. Houlihan is responsible for managing the accounting function through annual audit, financial reporting, and the administration of the corporate accounting group's financial network. At various times he has had additional the responsibility of hiring, training, and directing staff within the corporate, international and government accounting functions; providing timely consolidated financial reporting to the president and staff; daily financial support for a multi–functional customer service group and research group; developing and maintaining costing, budget, and financial models for multi–year private and government R&D contracts; computer hardware and software support for the financial group; internal user support for the financial group; and supported the budgeting process. Mr. Houlihan feels that one of the key factors to success is having a great support team at home; his wife Patricia. Internet users can reach him via: seh@OSF.org. **Career Steps:** Worldwide Accounting Manager, The Open Group, Inc. (1993–Present); Senior Accountant, Open Software Foundation (1990–1993); Senior Accountant/Network Administrator, Phoenix Technologies, Ltd. (1989–1990); Financial Applications Analyst, Cullinet Software, Inc. (1986–1989); Assistant Controller, Lansbrook Development Corporation (1984–1986); Assistant to the Controller, Leejay, Inc., dba Bed & Bath (1982–1984); Staff Accountant, Apparel Retail Corporation dba Dimensions (1980–1982). **Associations & Accomplishments:** Institute of Management and Administration; International Alliance of Theatrical Stage Employees. **Education:** St. Michael's College, B.A. in Business Administration (1980); Wescon. Novell Training at CNE Level, (1993); Northwestern University, COBOL programming language (1988); Cullinet Software Inc., User Applications and Culprit (1986). **Personal:** Married to Patricia L. Trundley in 1988. Mr. Houlihan enjoys sports, landscaping and home restoration.

David F. Hunter

Manager of IBM Pacific Development Center
IBM Canada Limited
P.O. Box 10132
Vancouver, British Columbia
(604) 664–6602
Fax: (604) 980–3321
EMAIL: See Below

3577

Business Information: IBM Canada Limited designs, manufactures and markets high–tech products globally. This includes information systems products and services, computers, semiconductors, networking hardware and software, and computer hardware and software. Services include outsourcing, multivendor support, and consulting. As Manager of IBM Pacific Development Center, Mr. Hunter is responsible for the attraction of development missions to the lab, building industry solutions for the global market place, and recruiting employees. Internet users can reach him via: Dhunter@vnet.IBM.com. **Career Steps:** IBM Canada Limited: Manager of IBM Pacific Development Center (1996–Present), National Sales Manager (1991–1995), Western Sales Manager (1987–1990), Development Manager–Expo '86 (1985–1986), Systems Engineer (1971–1984). **Associations & Accomplishments:** British Columbia Technology Information Association; Executive Director, Johnstone Straight Killer Whale Interpretive Centre. **Education:** University of Victoria, B.Sc. (1966). **Personal:** Married to Nancy in 1967. Two children: Paula and Philip. Mr. Hunter enjoys tennis, ocean kayaking, and hiking.

Yusuf Hussain

Project Manager
Cressoft, Inc.
10 Inverness Drive, East, Suite 220
Englewood, CO 80112–5612
(303) 754–6156
Fax: (303) 799–3345
EMail: See Below

3577

Business Information: Cressoft, Inc. is a computer software developer for state–of–the–art telecommunications and entertainment companies. Mr. Hussain has managed the Time Warner Communications Project since 1994, supervising American and foreign design teams in design process. Internet users can also reach him via: YUSUF.HUSSAIN@TWCABLE.COM. **Career Steps:** Project Manager, Time Warner Communications (1994–Present); Area Manager, Cressoft, Inc. (1992–1994); Assistant Technology Advisor, Government of Pakistan (1990–1992). **Associations & Accomplishments:** Pakistan Adventure Foundation; Pakistan Futuristics Foundation and Institute; Published several articles on the future of technology in Pakistan; Instrumental in formulating the National Technology Policy of Pakistan. **Education:** University of Texas – Austin, M.S. (1988); Rice University, B.S. (1985); Cornell University (1981–1982); American University of London, M.A. (1991). **Personal:** Married to Shandana in 1995. Mr. Hussain enjoys squash, cricket, and hot air ballooning.

D. K. Jackson

Director of Corporate Development
Sun Microsystems, Inc.
1643 Garnet Street
Broomfield, CO 80020–6607
(303) 796–7100
Fax: Please mail or call

3577

Business Information: Sun Microsystems, Inc. is one of the world's leading computer network systems design manufacturers, providing development and marketing of design automation software and services to accelerate and advance the process of designing electronic systems. In addition, the Company is a manufacturer of desktop scanners and computer work stations. As Director of Corporate Development, Mr. Jackson is responsible for mergers, corporate partnering activities, acquisitions and joint developments. **Career Steps:** Director of Corporate Development, Sun Microsystems, Inc. (1994–Present); Programming Manager, Storage Technology (1992–1994); Vice President of Business Development, Telwatch T.V. (1989–1994). **Education:** Columbia College, B.A. (1991). **Personal:** Married to Jean in 1976. Three children: Jennifer, Daniel, and Jaclyn. Mr. Jackson enjoys golf and fishing.

Joy James

Director – West Coast Development
ERS Imaging Supplies
4378 Sepulveda Boulevard, Suite 402
Sherman Oaks, CA 91403–3930
(818) 981–2840
Fax: (919) 386–0712
EMAIL: See Below

3577

Business Information: ERS Imaging Supplies is a value–added reseller within the computer peripheral industry, primarily focusing on the distribution of commodity goods with pro–environmental implications. As Director of West Coast Development, Joy James implements all business development and expansion throughout the West Coast U.S. Additionally, she is responsible for public relations and oversees 15 employees within the division. Internet users can reach her via: JOYOUS111@AOL.COM **Career Steps:** Director of West Coast Development, ERS Imaging Supplies (1995–Present); Business Manager, Data Products (Hitachi KoKi) (1993–1995); Consultant, Brother International (1993); Various Consulting Assignments (1990–1993). **Associations & Accomplishments:** Founder, Project Scholar (non–profit organization providing low–income student loans); Agoura Big Sister Program; Fellowship, Small Business Institute (1992). **Education:** Cal State University – Northridge, B.S. with Honors (1992); University of California – Los Angeles, Anderson School of Business, working towards M.B.A. **Personal:** Married to Mark in 1992. Ms. James enjoys outdoor activities and giving public speeches to young women about setting career goals.

Rebecca Jepson

Vice President of Sales & Marketing
Network Translation, Inc.
2464 Embarcadero Way
Palo Alto, CA 94303–3328
(415) 842–2111
Fax: (415) 843–1111

3577

Business Information: Network Translation, Inc. is a manufacturer and international marketer of computer equipment for corporate security and internet connectivity. Products include a firewall product based on IP address translation and network address translation. Established in 1994, Network Translation, Inc. has two locations in California and Georgia, reporting annual revenue of $4 million. With 17 years expertise in the industry, Ms. Jepsen joined Network Translation, Inc. as Vice President Sales & Marketing in 1995. She is responsible for running sales, public relations, product marketing, and trade shows, as well as managing direct and indirect channels of sales and marketing. **Career Steps:** Vice President Sales & Marketing, Network Translation, Inc. (1995–Present); Account Executive, AUSPEX System (1993–1995); Account Executive, SUM Microsystems (1988–1993). **Associations & Accomplishments:** Official with the Special Olympics. **Education:** University of Maryland, Liberal Arts; Defensive Language Institute, Monterey, California, Russian and Spanish Linguist; Attended many technical and sales training classes. **Personal:** Married in 1995. Ms. Jepson enjoys teaching aerobics, playing soccer, scuba diving, running, lifting weights, cycling, travel, and landscaping.

Carl R. Johnson

Senior Principal Programmer /Analyst
NCR Corporation
3644 Cairnbrook Drive
Columbia, SC 29210–4817
(803) 939–7483
Fax: (803) 939–6100
EMAIL: See Below

3577

Business Information: NCR Corporation is an international computer manufacturing company. A former division of AT&T, the Corporation has manufacturing locations in Rancho Bernardo, California, Columbia, South Carolina, Dublin, Ireland, and Augsburg, Germany, and develops computing solutions for a number of retail and financial institutions, as well as branches of the Federal Government. As Senior Principal Programmer/Analyst, Mr. Johnson offers technical support and consultation to software developers. His long–term goal is to help establish the Corporation as one of the major contenders in the mainframe market. Internet users can reach him via: carl.johnson@columbiasc.ncr.com. **Career Steps:** NCR Corporation: Senior Programmer/Analyst (1989–Present), Customer Services Engineer (1986–1989). **Associations & Accomplishments:** Team Captain, Valley National Eight – Ball Association; President, Hawkeye Pool League – Burlington, IA; Annual March of Dimes Walkathon Participant and Contributor; University of Iowa Alumni Association; Vietnam Veteran, U.S. Navy (1968–1972); Involved in recoveries of

Appollos 8, 11, and 12. **Education:** University of Iowa, B.S. (1986). **Personal:** Married to Rosemary in 1974. One child: Dawn. Mr. Johnson enjoys billiards, gardening, and computing.

John Paul (J.P.) Jones
Director of Sales and Marketing
Datametrics Corporation
21135 Erwin Street
Woodland Hills, CA 91367
(818) 598–6281
Fax: (818) 598–6300
EMAIL: See Below

3577

Business Information: Datametrics Corporation is a manufacturer of specialized computers for national military defense, and high speed digital color printers which are capable of yielding up to 20,000 pages per minute. As Director of Sales and Marketing, Mr. Jones directs all marketing and sales functions, including industrial presentations and trade shows. Internet users can reach him via: CYMAX@AOL.COM. **Career Steps:** Director of Sales and Marketing, Datametrics Corporation (1994–Present); Product Marketing Manager, Dataproducts Corporation (1984–1994). **Associations & Accomplishments:** Toastmasters International. **Education:** Pepperdine University, M.B.A. (1988); California State University, B.S. in Computer Science (1984). **Personal:** Married to Tracy Henare in 1996. Four children: Sarah, Meghan, Alexis, and Cassandra.

Henry Boon Kelly
System Architect
Doug Carson & Associates
1515 East Pine Street
Cushing, OK 74023–9161
(918) 225–0346
Fax: Please mail or call
EMAIL: See Below

3577

Business Information: Doug Carson & Associates is a compact disk and digital versatile disk manufacturer. As System Architect, Mr. Kelly designs and assists implementation of all products that are sold by the Company. Internet users can reach him via: BKELLY1053@AOL.com. **Career Steps:** Doug Carson & Associates: System Architect (1995–Present), Senior Software Engineer (1988–1995); Software Engineer, TMS (1985–1988). **Education:** Oklahoma State University: Master of Electrical Engineering (1985), B.S. in Electrical Engineering. **Personal:** Married to Lisa in 1991. One child: Christy. Mr. Kelly enjoys photography and amateur radio.

Jay A. Kerutis
Vice President of Sales & Marketing
New Media Corporation
1 Technology Drive Building A
Irvine, CA 92718–2339
(714) 453–0100
Fax: (714) 453–0114
E/M: See Below

3577

Business Information: Established in 1990, New Media Corporation is a manufacturer and worldwide retailer of PCMCIA cards for notebook computers. With an estimated annual sales of $40 million, New Media employs 47 people. As Vice President of Sales & Marketing, Mr. Kerutis is responsible for overseeing all marketing, advertising, programming, and sales for the Company. Internet users can reach him via: JKerutis@newmediacorp.com. **Career Steps:** Vice President of Sales & Marketing, New Media Corporation (1995–Present); Director of Sales, Merisel, Inc. (1993–1995); Director of Marketing, Silo, Inc. (1990–1993); Vice President & Merchandise Manager, Emporium Department Stores (1989–1990). **Education:** University of Kansas, B.A. (1983). **Personal:** Mr. Kerutis enjoys golf and various other outdoor activities.

James H. Kueffner
Lead Engineer
Applied Communications, Inc.
330 South 108 Avenue
Omaha, NE 68154
(402) 390–7923
Fax: Please mail or call
EMAIL: See Below

3577

Business Information: Applied Communications, Inc. is a manufacturer and vendor of software applications for electronic funds transfer products. Established in 1977, ACI's operations span worldwide, with over 1,200 employees. In addition to leading a support staff of 11, Mr. Kueffner, as Lead Engineer, is responsible for the design and implementation of fault–tolerant software for electronic funds transfer applications, in addition to overseeing a support staff of 11. He may be reached through the Internet via: Jim_Kueffner@MSN.com **Career Steps:** Applied Communications, Inc.: Lead Engineer (1991–Present), Senior Engineer (1987–1991), Engineer (1985–1987). **Associations & Accomplishments:** ACM; Midlands Triathlon Club; Volunteer for the Nebraska AIDS Project. **Education:** Iowa State University, B.S. (1982). **Personal:** Mr. Kueffner enjoys triathalons.

Choon Lian Liew

Senior Manager
Matsushita Electric Industrial Co., Ltd., Display Monitor Division
6–4–1 Tsujidomotomachi
Fujisawa, Kanagawa, Japan 251
81–466–351307
Fax: 81–466–366142

3577

Business Information: Matsushita Electric Industrial Co., Ltd. is a manufacturer of high–end computer display monitors and next–generation display devices, including electronic components, video and audio equipment, home appliances, communication industrial equipment, kitchen–related products, entertainment products, DVD, GPS, car navigation systems, STBs, semiconductors, motors, and batteries. Headquartered in Osaka, Matsushita Electric is the largest home electronics manufacturer in the world. As Senior Manager, Mr. Liew is responsible for planning and worldwide operations, including corporate strategies, procurement, marketing, logistics, and technological analysis. **Career Steps:** Senior Manager, Matsushita Electric (1994–Present); Vice President of Worldwide Operations, Fuji–Keizai USA, Inc. (1990–1994); Manager of Business Development, B.S.W. (M) Sdn Bhd (1984–1985). **Associations & Accomplishments:** U.S. National Dean's List (1982–1983); Who's Who Among Students in American Universities and Colleges; Alpha Chi National Honor Society; Malaysian Tae Kwon Do Black Belt Board; Most Outstanding Employee Award (1991); Published several highly successful market reports; Researched and written many single–client reports; Top Leadership Award, Outward Bound School Leadership Course; Various college level achievements. **Education:** Monmouth College, M.Sc. (1988); University of Dubuque, B.Sc. in Computer Science, Business Administration, and General Science – Magna Cum Laude (1981–1984); Royal Military College, Full Certificate and Military Certificates (1976–1980). **Personal:** Married to Sugama Yuko in 1989. One child: Midori. Mr. Liew enjoys movies and all kinds of sports.

Mr. Charles I.R. Loarridge
Vice President of Operations and Logistics
Zenith Data Systems
211 Hilltop Road
St. Joseph, MI 49085
(616) 982–5023
Fax: (616) 982–5005

3577

Business Information: Zenith Data Systems designs and manufactures personal computers. The company has worldwide distribution to businesses in the United States, Europe, Latin America, China, the Pacific Rim and Russia. As Vice President of Operations and Logistics, Mr. Loarridge is responsible for worldwide operations and logistics, including the supply line chain, manufacture and distribution of products. Established in 1889, Zenith Data Systems employs 2,000 people. **Career Steps:** Vice President of Operations and Logistics, Zenith Data Systems (1994–Present); Vice President of Portable Systems, Zenith Data Systems (1993–1994); AVP Operations, NCR Corporation Clemson (1992–1993); General Manager, NCR Corporation Clemson (1989–1991). **Associations & Accomplishments:** Member, The Institute of Electrical Engineers (United Kingdom); Fellow, Institute of Management; Member (United Kingdom). **Education:** Dundee, Scotland, D.M.S. (1982); Dundee, BSC in Electrical Engineering (1969), Certified Chartered Engineer. **Personal:** Married to Carol in 1975. Two children: Graeme and Euan. qMr. Loarridge enjoys history, modelmaking, railways and tennis.

Mr. Denis R. Lueders
General Manager
Gateway 2000
610 Gateway Drive
North Sioux City, SD 57049
(605) 232–2000
Fax: Please mail or call

3577

Business Information: Gateway 2000 is an OEM (Original Equipment Manufacturer) of IBM PC clones. Satellite offices are located in Souix Falls, SD, and Kansas City, MO. The Company is publicly traded on the NASDAQ exchange. As General Manager, Mr. Lueders is responsible for managing all aspects of operations at the Sioux Falls satellite facility. Established in 1985, Gateway 2000 employs 800 people. **Career Steps:** General Manager, Gateway 2000, (1994–Present); Technical Support Manager, Gateway 2000 (1992–1994); Customer Service Manager, Gateway 2000 (1991–1992). **Associations & Accomplishments:** Sioux City Better Business Bureau; Sioux Falls Chamber of Commerce. **Education:** Wayne State College, B.S. (1984). **Personal:** Married to Janeen A. in 1985. Two children: Grant and BreAnn. Mr. Lueders enjoys sports, camping, and computing.

Ruth Lutes
Engineering Program Management
Hewlett Packard
3404 E. Harmony Road, MS 66
Ft. Collins, CO 80525
(970) 229–3305
Fax: (970) 229–4545
E MAIL: See Below

3577

Business Information: Hewlett Packard designs, manufactures, and services electronic products and systems for measurement computing and communications. Established in 1939, the Company currently employs over 90,000 people worldwide. As Engineering Program Management, Ms. Lutes assists in the building of cross–function teams to deliver product lines on time. She handles general administrative duties for the Company. Internet users may contact her via: lutes@fc.hp.com. **Career Steps:** Engineering Program Management, Hewlett Packard (1992–Present). **Associations & Accomplishments:** People to People International Sponsor. **Education:** University of Colorado, B.A. in Chemistry (1975); University of Texas, Post Graduate in Chemistry; Colorado State University, Post Graduate in Computer Science. **Personal:** Married to Frank in 1975. Ms. Lutes enjoys international travel.

Kris L. McHam
Operations Director
Elsner Technologies Company
5020 Mark IV Parkway
Ft. Worth, TX 76106–2219
(817) 626–4110
Fax: (817) 626–5330

3577

Business Information: Elsner Technologies Company is a marketer, servicer, and supporter of original manufactured goods of sharing and extension devices utilized in computer peripheral applications. Established in 1994, Elsner Technologies reports annual revenue of $1.5 million. As Operations Director, Ms. McHam is responsible for the areas of marketing, sales, and public relations; as well as directing technical support activities. **Career Steps:** Operations Director, Elsner Technologies Company (1994–Present); Systems Engineer, Zadall Systems Group (1992–1994); Technical Support and Training, Bluff Creek Systems (1990–1992); Marketing Secretary, National Pride Systems (1988–1990). **Associations & Accomplishments:** League of Women Voters; Sierra Club. **Education:** East Texas State University. **Personal:** Two children: Madison and Makenzi. Ms. McHam enjoys golf, tennis, and writing.

Wayne Meng
President
Sanbor Corporation
6330 Hedgewood Drive
Allentown, PA 18106–9268
(610) 366–7899
Fax: (610) 366–7885

3577

Business Information: Sanbor Corporation specializes in the manufacture of computer cable and telecom cable assemblies. The Company presently operates two manufacturing plants in Pennsylvania and two in China. Established in 1990, Sanbor Corporation currently employs 550 people and has an estimated annual revenue of $10 million. As President, Mr. Meng provides the overall direction and vision of the company's continued growth, quality delivery to customers and strategic developments, as well as the supervision of all manufacturing, research and development, finance and marketing functions. Mr. Meng hopes to expand the business and take it public within the next few years. **Career Steps:** President, Sanbor Corporation (1990–Present). **Associations & Accomplishments:** Society of Cable Telecommunication Engineers. **Personal:** Mr. Meng enjoys tennis.

Gaita Marie Mompoint

Senior Financial Analyst
Hewlett–Packard
19447 Pruneridge Avenue   Bldg 49B/AGO
Cupertino, CA 95014
(408) 343–7783
Fax: (408) 343–7766

3577

Business Information: Hewlett–Packard Company, established in 1939, manufactures computer equipment and systems, peripheral products and other software. They also provide computer services. As Senior Financial Analyst, Mrs. Mompoint is responsible for the oversight of the World–Wide Business Processing Centers including supporting the Sales organization. Her major role is to minimize financial risk for Hewlett Packard, while optimizing their growth. She is also responsible for developing the advocacy program with these centers. Her future aspirations within Hewlett Packard are in the area of International Business Development in the marketing organization. She is presently in pursuit of a position in this area. Mrs. Mompoint is also fluent in French and is a native of Port–au–Prince, Haiti. **Career Steps:** Hewlett–Packard: Senior Financial Analyst (1993–Present), Collections Analyst (1988–1993); Finance Manager, American Electronics Association (1985–1987); Loan Consultant, Downey Savings Bank (1983–1985). **Associations & Accomplishments:** Professional Business Womens Association; Black MBA Association; Delta Sigma Theta Sorority; Sonoma County Wine Finders. **Education:** San Jose State University, M.A. in Economics; University of California, Berkeley, M.B.A. Program; Loyola University, B.S.; University of California, Santa Cruz, Ph.D. (In Progress). **Personal:** Married to Raynald in 1983 who is now Director of Engineering at Baynet Works, Santa Clara, CA. Three children: Ashley, Alyssa, and Anthony. Mrs. Mompoint enjoys aerobics, piano, and wine collecting with the Sonoma County Wine Finders Club.

Neil W. Morris

Director of Human Resources
United States Robotics/Megahertz
605 N 5600 W
Salt Lake City, UT 84116–3738
(801) 320–7306
Fax: (801) 320–6012
EMAIL: See Below

3577

Business Information: U.S. Robotics/Megahertz manufactures modems and communications access devices for personal computers, workstations, and mobile computers. As Director of Human Resources, Mr. Morris is responsible for personnel recruitment, hiring and training, payroll functions, dispute management, and various administrative activities. Internet users can reach him via: NMorris@MHz.com **Career Steps:** Director of Human Resources, U.S. Robotics/Megahertz Corporation (1994–Present); Manager of Human Resources, Megahertz Corporation (1992–1994); Administrative Manager of Distribution, NuSkin International (1990–1992). **Associations & Accomplishments:** Society of Human Resource Management; ICBA (local ACA chapter). **Education:** University of Phoenix, M.A.O.M. (1990); Brigham Young University, B.A.; University of Helsinki; Utah State University. **Personal:** Married to Kyra in 1988. Four children: Clinton, Kyler, Taylor, and Mitchell. Mr. Morris enjoys white water rafting, skiing, and camping.

Charles Morrison

President
Informedia Interactive
700–702 W. Main St.
Louisville, KY 40202
(502) 893–9966
Fax: (502) 583–9973
EMail: See Below

3577

Business Information: Informedia Interactive is a multi–media software development company designing systems for marketing and sales in the real estate industry. Established in 1983, Informedia now employs 8 people and grosses $1.5 million a year in sales. As President, Mr. Morrison is responsible for overseeing all business operations and marketing functions. Internet users can reach him via: MORRISON@INFORMEDIA.COM **Career Steps:** President, Informedia Interactive (1995–Present); President, The Morrison Group (1994–Present); Director, Principal Financial Group (1990–1994); Divisional Vice President, National Association of Realtors (1985–1990). **Associations & Accomplishments:** Rotary Club; Chamber of Commerce; Theatre Guild; Omicron Delta Kappa; Who's Who in America; Omega Tau Rho; AD Club; A.S.T.D. **Education:** Northern Illinois University, M.B.A. (1971); Bradley University, B.A.; Northwestern University, working toward a Ph.D.; California Poly; Fullerton; Alabama. **Personal:** Married to Judin in 1996. Five children: Kelleen, Patrick, Matthew, Craig, and Lauren. Mr. Morrison enjoys tennis, golf, skiing, woodworking, and boating.

Mr. Naren Nath

Lead Product Manager
Microsoft Corporation
One Microsoft Way, Building 9
Redmond, WA 98052
(206) 936–7365
Fax: (206) 936–7329

3577

Business Information: Microsoft Corporation is the world's leading software development corporation. Starting during the 70's (1979) with computer languages for early personal computers, Microsoft made its mark with the development of the MS–DOS Operating System for the IBM PC. Envisioning the market expansion of the PC industry, Microsoft joined forces with the microprocessor giant, Intel Corporation, along with other entrepreneurs and thus created the PC clone industry which now dominates the market. Microsoft's flagship Windows product now forms the foundation for an overwhelming majority of personal computers sold today. As Lead Product Manager, Mr. Nath has helped chart Microsoft's expansion into visionary new consumer markets, and now directs interactive content and applications activities in interactive television for Microsoft. Microsoft Corporation presently employs 15,000 people and has an estimated annual revenue in excess of $5 billion. **Career Steps:** Lead Product Manager, Microsoft Corporation (1992–Present); Project Leader, Unisys Corporation (1987–1990). **Associations & Accomplishments:** 1979 National Talent Scholar Award, India; Fellowship of the University of California at Santa Barbara. **Education:** Stanford University, M.B.A. (1992); University of California, Santa Barbara, CA, M.S. in Computer Science; Indian Institute of Technology, B.Tech., with honors, in Computer Science. **Personal:** Mr. Nath enjoys cross–training, volleyball and international travel.

Thomas Neubert

Vice President and General Manager
ELSA, Inc.
2150 Trade Zone Boulevard, Suite 101
San Jose, CA 95131
(408) 935–0350 Ext. 103
Fax: (408) 935–0370
EMAIL: See Below

3577

Business Information: ELSA, Inc. is a manufacturer of graphics accelerators for PC's, ISDN products, modems, video conferencing and MPEG play–back technology. As Vice President and General Manager, Mr. Neubert is responsible for oversight of daily operations, sales support, marketing and public relations functions, and maintaining communications with corporate headquarters in Germany. Internet users can reach him via: ThomasN@ELSA.com **Career Steps:** Vice President and General Manager, ELSA, Inc. (1994–Present); Director of Marketing, Orchid Technology (1991–1994); Marketing Manager, Access Computers – Germany (1989–1991). **Associations & Accomplishments:** International Interactive Communication Society; ELSA, Inc. has received nine awards through "Byte" and "News Media Magazine." **Education:** University of Pavervarn – Germany, Degree in Computer Engineering and Communications; San Francisco State University: Introduction to the Interactive Multimedia, Production Multimedia; Stanford University, Management Executive Program for Growing Companies. **Personal:** Mr. Neubert enjoys skiing, mountain biking, playing drums, and hiking.

Ron Niederer

Director of Customer Service
Informative Graphics
706 East Bell Road, Suite 207
Phoenix, AZ 85022–6642
(602) 971–6061
Fax: (602) 971–1714
EMAIL: See Below

3577

Business Information: Informative Graphics is a developer of consumer and industrial software equipment. As Director of Customer Service/Quality Assurance/MIS, Mr. Niederer is responsible for the direction of all customer services, quality assurance, and managed information system activities, including ensuring products are of the highest standards and he works as a liaison between customers and the Company. Internet users can reach him via: ronn@netzone.com **Career Steps:** Director of Customer Service/Quality Assurance/MIS, Informative Graphics Corporation (1993–Present); Senior Product Specialist, CalComp Digitizer Division, (1989–1993). **Education:** DeVry Institute, B.S. in Electronics Engineering Technology **Personal:** Mr. Niederer enjoys motorcross and mountain biking.

Bob O'Connor

Manager
Letraset, Nielsen & Bainbridge
40 Eisenhower Drive
Paramus, NJ 07652–1404
(201) 845–6100
Fax: (201) 845–0803
EMAIL: See Below

3577

Business Information: Letraset, Nielsen & Bainbridge, a division of Esselte Pendaflex Corporation based in Sweden, is the U.S. operations company for two divisions of manufacturing: graphic design software development and arts, which are distributed to stores; and framing and mattboard products for retail stores. International in scope, Letraset, Nielsen & Bainbridge has 20 subsidiaries worldwide. With twenty–eight years of experience in the computer industry, Mr. O'Connor joined Letraset, Nielsen & Bainbridge as Manager in 1990. He is responsible for the management of software and product development for both MacIntosh and PC/Windows products. Internet users can also reach him via: boconnor@esselte.com **Career Steps:** Manager, Letraset, Nielsen & Bainbridge (1990–Present); Typographic Development Manager, Photo Lettering, Inc. (1978–1990); Senior Design Manager, Linotype – Hell, (1973–1978); Systems Development Manager, Dymo Industries (1968–1973). **Associations & Accomplishments:** Type Directors Club; American Management Association; Apple Computer Developer; Microsoft Developer; Hewlett Packard Developer; Kodak Photo Exchange. **Education:** New York University, Certificate (1988); Bergen Technical College (1990); Monclair, Certificate (1993) **Personal:** Mr. O'Connor enjoys collecting coins and carpentry.

Mr. Robert G. O'Malley

Senior Vice President Services
MicroAge, Inc.
2400 South MicroAge Way
Tempe, AZ 85282
(602) 366–2990
Fax: (602) 366–2444
3577

Business Information: MicroAge, a Fortune 500 Company, is a leading provider of information systems technology to corporations worldwide, and to institutions and governmental agencies throughout the U.S. Mr. O'Malley currently serves as Senior Vice President, MicroAge Services. MicroAge Services provides marketing, information, and product–based services to MicroAge business units, associates, franchise owners, suppliers and enterprise clients. MicroAge Services is operated as a P&L center. In addition, Mr. O'Malley directs the information technology research and development activities of MicroAge, Inc. **Career Steps:** MicroAge Inc.: Senior Vice President, Services (1996–Present), President, MicroAge Data Services (1995–1996); General Manager of PC Desktop Systems, IBM (1994–1995); Vice President of Marketing and Brand Management – Americas, IBM PC Company (1994); Managing Director for Asia Pacific PC Operations, IBM (1992–1994); Vice President of Sales for the National Distribution Division, IBM (1990–1991); Director of Finance and Planning for U.S. Marketing, IBM (1988–1989). **Associations & Accomplishments:** Global Advisory Council, American Graduate School of International Management (Thunderbird), Phoenix, AZ. **Education:** Arizona State University, M.B.A. (1973); University of Minnesota, B.S. in Aeronautical Engineering (1967). **Personal:** Married to Barbara in 1968. Two children: David and Brian. Mr. O'Malley enjoys reading (business structures and leadership), golf, jogging and coaching youth baseball.

Robert J. Ott

Project Manager
Domino Control Print Division
67 Sand Park Road
Cedar Grove, NJ 07009
(201) 857–0901
Fax: (201) 857–0607
3577

Business Information: Domino Control Print Division develops and manufactures industrial ink jet printers for production date codes. The multi–million dollar company was established in 1982 and has approximately 200 employees. As Project Manager, Mr. Ott handles public relations duties for the company, developing sales strategies, and marketing of products. **Career Steps:** Project Manager, Domino Control Print Division (1991–Present); Director of Technology, Loveshaw Corporation (1987–1991); Director of Operation Inks, Domino–Amtet (1982–1987). **Education:** University of Rochester, B.S. in Science (1972). **Personal:** Married to Susan in 1979. Two children: Dennis and Dan. Mr. Ott enjoys making stained glass, candles, and playing golf.

Craig W. Pampeyan

Senior Industry Consultant – Professional Services Organization
Hewlett Packard
19111 Pruneridge Avenue
Cupertino, CA 95014–0765
(408) 447–6283
Fax: (408) 447–0218
E–Mail: pampeyan@hp.com
3577

Business Information: Hewlett Packard designs, manufactures and services electronic products and systems for measurement, computation and communications world–wide. The Professional Services Organization serves as Hewlett Packard's consulting practice. A management consultant and manufacturing executive with various affiliates of Hewlett Packard since 1981, Mr. Pampeyan was appointed as Senior Industry Consultant to the Professional Services Organization in 1995. Serving as Consultant for manufacturing companies in North and South America, he works with senior executives of Fortune 100 companies on busniess planning, manufacturing processes, product development, and information technology consulting. **Career Steps:** Hewlett Packard: Senior Industry Consultant – Professional Services Organization (1995–Present), Manufacturing Manager – Interactive Television Group (1992–1995), Manufacturing Consultant – Personal Computer Group (1990–1992). **Associations & Accomplishments:** IEEE; Association of Manufacturing Excellence; California Polytechnic State University Industrial Advisory Council; Awarded College of Engineering Medallion Award for Outstanding Alumnus 1995, California Polytechnic State University. **Education:** Santa Clara University, M.B.A. (1988); Stanford University, M.S. in Electrical Engineering (1984); California Polytechnic State University, B.S. in Electrical Engineering (1981). **Personal:** Married to Julie in 1995. Mr. Pampeyan enjoys photography, home remodeling, motorcycling, and travel.

R. James Parsons

Vice President of Marketing
New Tek
1200 South West Executive Drive
Topeka, KS 66615–3850
(913) 228–8000
Fax: (913) 228–8001
EMAIL: See Below
3577

Business Information: New Tek develops and sells desktop hardware and software for video and 3D digital computing. The Company is well known for Lightware, which accounts for 75% to 80% of all computer generated images on television. As Vice President of Marketing, Mr. Parsons is responsible for new business development, marketing, public relations, trade shows, negotiations with strategic partners, and strategic accounts. Internet users can reach him via: Jim@Newtek.com. **Career Steps:** Newtek: Vice President of Marketing (1996–Present), Director of Product Management (1995–1996), Manager, CD–Rom Development (1994–1995); Market Analyst, Wordperfect (1993–1994). **Associations & Accomplishments:** Advisory Board, American Marketing Association; Chairman, Consumer Electronics Show. **Education:** Brigham Young University, B.S. in Marketing (1992). **Personal:** Married to Cynthia in 1988. Three children: McKell, Jamie, and Cherstin. Mr. Parsons enjoys spending time with his family, church activities, working with the deaf, Boy Scouts, snow and water skiing, reading, and coaching and playing soccer.

Pamela R. Partch

Marketing Director
Futuresoft Inc.
3592 Darrow Road
Stow, OH 44224–4039
(330) 688–1716
Fax: (330) 688–3688
3577

Business Information: Futuresoft Inc. is an international software development company specializing in the electronic transmission of transactions of value (e.g., ATM and POS devices) for the financial industry. As Marketing Director, Ms. Partch is responsible for defining markets and distribution channels, marketing communication, development costs, production, sales, and strategic planning. Additionally, she oversees public relations, trade shows, and product requirements. **Career Steps:** Marketing Director, Futuresoft Inc. (1993–Present); Marketing Manager, Interbold (1991–1993); Diebold: Marketing Manager (1990–1991), Proposal Manager (1989–1990). **Associations & Accomplishments:** Woodridge Booster Club; Chamber of Commerce. **Education:** Iowa State University, Masters Degree (1978); Kent State University, Ph.D. in progress. **Personal:** Two children: Meghan and Brittany. Ms. Partch enjoys reading and home renovation.

Stacey M. Patulski

Vice President
Amptech, Inc.
62 West Freeman Road
Free Soil, MI 49411
(616) 464–5497
Fax: (616) 464–5320
3577

Business Information: Amptech, Inc., a family–owned business, is a manufacturer of electronic sub–assemblies for auto security systems. Providing services mostly in the state of Michigan, the Company has also expanded to the East Coast. Established in 1980, Amptech, Inc. employs 65 persons and has an estimated annual revenue of $4.2 million. Holding several positions within the Company since the age of thirteen, Mr. Patulski currently serves as Vice President. In this capacity, he is responsible for the management of the Personnel, Inventory Control, and Shipping departments. **Career Steps:** Vice President, Amptech, Inc. (Present). **Associations & Accomplishments:** Board of Directors, Alumni Association, West Shore Community College; Chairperson, Michigan Job Service Employers' Council; Mason County Human Resource Association. **Education:** Ferris State University, B.S. in Health Systems Management (1992); West Shore Community College, A.A.S. in Marketing/Management. **Personal:** Mr. Patulski enjoys snowboarding, officiating at basketball games, and collecting sports cards during this leisure time.

Duy H. Phan

Corporate Human Resources Manager
United States Robotics
6201 Oakton Street
Morton Grove, IL 60053
(847) 470–2155
Fax: (847) 965–4292
EMAIL: See Below
3577

Business Information: U.S. Robotics is an international manufacturer of modems, LAN/WAN products, and communications access devices for personal computers, workstations, and mobile computers. Mr. Phan has served in various capacities with U.S Robotics, most recently promoted to Corporate Human Resources Manager in 1996. His present responsibilities include oversight of the human resources integration process, employee placement for new divisions, and various administrative activities. Internet users may reach him via: dphan@usr.com **Career Steps:** U.S. Robotics: Corporate Human Resources Manager (1996–Present), Divisional Human Resources Manager (1994–1996); Benefits/Compensation/Human Resources Manager (1985–1994). **Associations & Accomplishments:** Society of Human Resource Management; A.C.A. **Education:** Northeastern University, B.S. (1982). **Personal:** Mr. Phan enjoys real estate investment and private business ownership.

Pote Pruettiangkura, Ph.D.

Director – Process/Equipment Engineering
Submicron Technology
PO Box 451118
Garland, TX 75045–1118
(662) 948–5470
Fax: (214) 530–6572
3577

Business Information: Submicron Technology is a manufacturer of computer chips and integrated circuits at two locations in Texas and one location in Bangkok. Established in 1994, Submicron Technology currently employs 1,000 people. As Director of Process/Equipment Engineering, Dr. Pruettiangkura is responsible for introducing and developing new technology for present and future generations of devices, as well as supervising a staff of 200 employees. **Career Steps:** Director – Process/Equipment Engineering, Submicron Technology (1995–Present); Advisory Board Member, Implanted Technology, Inc. (1995); Manager – Worldwide Product & Process Support and Development, Texas Instruments, Inc. (1989–1995). **Associations & Accomplishments:** American Chemical Society; Institute of Electrical and Electronic Engineers; Alpha Chi Sigma; Thailand Reversed Brain Drain Association. **Education:** University of North Texas: Ph.D. (1978), M.S. in Chemistry; Northwestern Oklahoma State University: B.S. in Mathematics and Chemistry. **Personal:** Married to Shirley in 1971. One child: Scott. Dr. Pruettiangkura enjoys reading and investing.

David J. Rauch

Vice President of Wafer Fabrics Operations
Read–Rite Corporation
345 Los Coches Street
Milpitas, CA 95035–5428
(408) 956–2215
Fax: (408) 956–3170
3577

Business Information: Read–Rite Corporation is an international manufacturer of Read–Rite head components for disk drives. Headquartered in Milpitas, California, the Corporation has a sales office in Colorado, a small office in San Diego, plants in Thailand, Malaysia and the Philippines, and a joint venture with Japan. Beginning his career as an Engineer with the Corporation at its inception in November 1983, Mr. Rauch currently serves as Vice President of Wafer Fabrics Operations. He is responsible for the management of operations for wafer fabric chips and semi–conductors at the corporate location in Milpatas. Career milestone include changing his college major from Physics to Electrical Engineering at the beginning of the computer age. **Career Steps:** Read–Rite Corporation: Vice President of Wafer Fabrics Operations (1995–Present), Director of Wafer Fab (1995), Program Manager (1992–1995). **Associations & Accomplishments:** Published in "Read–Rite Recorder," an internal publication. **Education:** University of Minnesota, B.S.E.E. (1980). **Personal:** Married to Lucy in 1990. Three children: Amie, Jacob, and Carly. Mr. Rauch enjoys skiing and camping.

Tod W. Replogle
Vice President
Business Computer Technologies
2412 East Washington Street
Bloomington, IL 61704–4497
(309) 662–2275
Fax: (309) 663–0506

3577

Business Information: Business Computer Technologies, evolved from a major CPA firm, provides the design, implementation and market of industry–specific value added software. Targeting manufacturing industries, BCT markets in the greater St. Louis metro area, as well as throughout the State of Illinois. A telecommunications management executive and systems network expert, Tod Replogle joined Business Computer Technology in March of 1995. As Vice President of Business Development, he is responsible for the administration and oversight for the areas of marketing, sales, advertising and Human Resources. **Career Steps:** Vice President, Business Computer Technologies (1995–Present); General Manager, Great Lakes Telecomunications (Jan. 1995–Mar. 1995); Territory Manager, Consolidated Communications (1990–1994). **Associations & Accomplishments:** Professional Network Association; Leadership Communication, McLean County; Peoria Chamber Golf Committee; St. Joseph Hospital Committee. **Education:** Illinois State University. **Personal:** Married to Sherri in 1986. Two children: Cori and Steven. Mr. Replogle enjoys golf, and coaching softball.

Mr. Ricardo H. Rodriguez
Professional Services & Business Administration Manager
Hewlett–Packard, Latin America Region
5200 Blue Lagoon Drive, Suite 950
Miami, FL 33126
(305) 267–4285
Fax: (305) 267–4651

3577

Business Information: Hewlett–Packard, Latin America Region is a computer systems manufacturer and reseller. As Professional Services & Business Administration Manager, Mr. Rodriguez is responsible for managing the delivery of technological consulting services as well as the adminstrative services for the computer systems operations for Latin America, excluding Brazil and Mexico. **Career Steps:** Hewlett–Packard: Professional Services & Business Administration Manager (1993–Present), Support Business Administration Manager (1992–1993), Financial Reporting Manager (1989–1991), Various Positions (1982–1991). **Education:** ITAM–Mexico, M.B.A. (1991); UBA–Argentina, C.P.A. (1985). **Personal:** Married to Elisa D'Ambrosio in 1985.

Salvador Romo–Fragoso
MCA Distribution Operating Manager
Hewlett–Packard
5200 Blue Lagoon Drive, Suite 950
Miami, FL 33126
(305) 265–6009
Fax: (305) 267–4298

3577

Business Information: Hewlett–Packard designs, manufactures, and services electronic products and systems for measurement computing and communications. As MCA Distribution Operating Manager, Mr. Romo–Fragoso handles all South America distribution for Hewlett Packard Personal Computer Products, but Mexico and Brazil. Responsible for business, inventory control, and logistics among this design. **Career Steps:** Hewlett–Packard: MCA Distribution Manager (1995–Present); Peripheral Distribution Manager (1992–1995); Distribution Service Manager (1990–1992); Several Engineering and Management at Hewlett–Packard (1983–1990). **Education:** Instituto Tecnologico y De Estudios/Superiores De Monterrey (ITESM) M.B.A. (1991); Mechanical Engineer (1983) Major in Control, Graduated with Honors. **Personal:** Married to Hilda in 1987. Mr. Romo–Fragoso enjoys mountain biking and violin music.

Albert John Sartor Jr.
National Sales Manager
Power Play Products, Inc.
1678 East 31st Street
Brooklyn, NY 11234–4211
(718) 382–0222
Fax: (718) 382–7339
EMAIL: See Below

3577

Business Information: Power Play Products, Inc. manufactures and distributes computer equipment (e.g., surge protectors, outlet strips, and safety devices) to major chain retailers such as Bill's Dollar Stores, Ames, and West Building Sup-

plies. As National Sales Manager, Mr. Sartor is responsible for overseeing all sales representatives and distributors throughout the country, managing some of the larger accounts personally. The Company grossed $3.5 million dollars in sales for 1995, and projects $6 million dollars for 1996. **Career Steps:** National Sales Manager, Power Play Products, Inc. (1995–Present); City Sales Manager, Yellow Freight Systems (1981–1995); Vice President of Operations, Garafolo Imports (1979–1981); Operations Manager, Tru–Con Container (1977–1979). **Associations & Accomplishments:** President and Founder (1992), Delta Nu Alpha Transportation Fraternity – Nassau Community College; Knights of Columbus, 3rd Degree Member. **Education:** Nassau Community College (1996); Sorbelsohn School, Certified Paralegal; H&R Block School, Certified Preparer. **Personal:** Married to Deborah in 1994. One child: Bryan. Mr. Sartor enjoys golf, school, and fishing.

Fumiaki Sato
••• ◖◉◗ •••

President
Texas ISA Inc.
14825 Saint Mary's Lane
Houston, TX 77079–2904
(713) 493–9925
Fax: (713) 493–2724

3577

Business Information: A subsidiary of the Japan–based ISA Co., Ltd., Texas ISA Inc. specializes in the manufacture, import and export of computer peripherals and computer products, as well as oil field products. Established in 1991, Texas ISA reports estimated annual revenue of $2 million. As Founder, Shareholder, and President, Mr. Sato is responsible for all aspects of operations, including business consulting. **Career Steps:** President, Texas ISA Inc. (1991–Present); Director, ISA Company, Ltd. (1991–1995); General Manager, Daiichi Jitsuqyo America, Inc. (1984–1991); Sales Manager, Daiichi Jitsuqyo Company, Ltd. (1976–1984). **Associations & Accomplishments:** Society of Petroleum Engineers; Geothermal Resource Council. **Education:** Waseda University, B.S. in Engineering (1976). **Personal:** Married to Sakiko in 1982. Two children: Natsumi and Louis. Mr. Sato enjoys golf, tennis and travel.

Ms. Nancy R. Simon
Patent Counsel
Apple Computer Inc.
One Infinite Loop, MS: 38 – PAT
Cupertino, CA 95014
(408) 974–9598
Fax: (408) 974–5436

3577

Business Information: Apple Computer Inc. designs, manufactures and markets high–tech products globally, including information systems products and services, computers, networking hardware and software, computer hardware and software, as well as outsourcing services and consulting. As Patent Counsel, Ms. Simon advises groups within the Company on intellectual property matters, primarily concentrating in the area of patent law. Apple Computer, Inc. presently employs over 10,000 people. **Career Steps:** Patent Counsel, Apple Computer Inc. (1993–Present); Associate Attorney, Felsman, Bradley, Gunter & Dillon (1991–1993); Engineer, Texas Instruments, Inc. (1986–1988). **Associations & Accomplishments:** MENSA; Phi Delta Phi Legal Fraternity; Sigma Iota Epsilon Management Fraternity; Zeta Tau Alpha; Who's Who Worldwide; Who's Who of American Law; Who's Who Among Law Students; Who's Who of Worldwide Business Leaders; State Bar of California; State Bar of Texas; Co–Authored: "Attorney's Fees and Intellectual Cases." **Education:** Southern Methodist University, J.D. (1991); University of Dallas, M.B.A. (1988); Iowa State University, B.S. in Electrical Engineering (1985). **Personal:** Ms. Simon enjoys sports, reading, and all aspects of education.

Gary D. Smith
National Service Director
Linotype – Hell Company
425 Oser Avenue
Hauppauge, NY 11788–3640
(516) 434–2798
Fax: (516) 434–3034

3577

Business Information: Linotype – Hell Company is an Electronic Pre–Press Company, specializing in scanning, Desktop Publishing, and computer toplate manufacturing. The Company's North America main office is in Hauppauge, NY. The worldwide home office is in Kiel, Germany. Joining Linotype – Hell Company in 1984, Mr. Smith serves as National Service Director, directing all field service activities for the service operation, which includes the responsibility of ISO people located throughout the U.S., who perform field service functions.

Career Steps: Linotype – Hell Company: National Service Director (1995–Present), Director East Area Service (1994–1995), Regional Manager (1993–1994), District Manager (1984–1993). **Associations & Accomplishments:** American Field Service Managers Association. **Education:** DeVry Institute of Technology, (1976). **Personal:** Married to Debby in 1982. One child: Jamie. Mr. Smith enjoys golf, tennis, basketball, and church.

Ramon Solano Jimenez
Distribution Systems Coordinator
IBM de Mexico S.A.
Av. Casa de la Moneda No. 333, Col. Lomas de Sotelo
Mexico City, Mexico 11200
(525) 327–5747 (525) 563–3155
Fax: (525) 271–1579
Email: See Below

3577

Business Information: IBM de Mexico S.A. designs, manufactures and markets high–tech products globally, including information systems products and services, computers, semiconductors, networking hardware and software, computer hardware and software. As Distribution Systems Coordinator, Mr. Solano Jimenez is responsible for the design, development, installation and operation of all the distribution systems, including domestic and international traffic systems. Career milestones include introducing automatic identification technology in the distribution systems, implementation of international distribution systems, and when serving as a business analyst, the development of distribution operation strategies that enhance performance of domestic traffic operations with important cost reductions. Internet users can also reach Ramon via: RAMON@VNET.IBM.COM **Career Steps:** IBM de Mexico, S.A.: Distribution Systems Coordinator (1995–Present), Distribution Operations Coordinator (1993–1994), Systems Analyst (1991–1992). **Associations & Accomplishments:** Active member, Club Fotografico de Mexico (photographer's group); Participated in photographic exhibitions in Mexico and other countries. **Education:** Universidad Nacional – Mexico, Engineering Master Degree – Operations Research, thesis in combinatorial optimization (expected in 1996); Universidad Panamericana, Industrial Engineering Degree. **Personal:** Married to Ernestina Guevara de Solano in 1993. Mr. Solano Jimenez enjoys photography, guitar, music, and mountain biking.

Xavier Soule, D.P.L.G.
••• ◖◉◗ •••

President Director General
ABVENT
3 Rue Decres
Paris, France 75014
33–1–43950505
Fax: Please mail or call
E–mail: see below

3577

Business Information: ABVENT specializes in the research, development and publishing of imaging and design computer software. Established in 1985, ABVENT currently employs 45 people and has an estimated annual revenue of $8.5 million. A major European computer architecture firm with offices in Switzerland, Italy and France; ABVENT is concentrating its strategy focus in the expansion of U.S. market presence. As President Director General, Mr. Soule is responsible for all aspects of operations, primarily in the areas of marketing, sales, new business development and strategic planning. He can also be reached through the worldwide Internet as follows: APPLELINK.ABVENT. **Career Steps:** President Director General, ABVENT (1985–Present); Architect, ABS (1980–1985); Architect, LSB (1975–1980). **Associations & Accomplishments:** Organist, Notre Dame Bon Conseil Church; Expert Judiciaire, Tribunal Paris; Published numerous times in European technical journals. **Education:** ENS-BA – UP7, Architect.DPLG (1975); Dea Histoire De L'Art Contemporain/Maitre En Sciences Et Techniques Restauration et Conservation/maitre es Lettres/Dess Archeometrie; Cnam: Geme Civil er Mathematiques. **Personal:** Married to Claire Andrieu in 1975. Two children: Augustin and Mathilde. Mr. Soule enjoys architecture and playing the organ.

Mr. Kurt P. Steubing
Manager of Business Evaluation, Research Division
IBM
P.O. Box 218, Route 134
Yorktown Heights, NY 10598
(914) 945–1270
Fax: (914) 227–7748

3577

Business Information: IBM Corporation researches, develops, manufactures and markets computer and office products and services worldwide in a wide range of markets. The Research Division creates technology, and makes contributions to the development of key evolving IBM strategies. As Manager of Business Evaluation, Research Division, Mr. Steubing manages a department of commercial and government pricers who prepare financial analysis and evaluate business cases. The Reasearch Division employs a staff of approximately 2,500. **Career Steps:** Manager of Business Evaluation (1994–Present), Financial Program Administrator (1993–1994), IBM Research Division; Manager, Financial Planning, IBM International Distribution Center (1991–1993). **Associations & Accomplishments:** Commercialization Achievement Award, IBM Research Division Award (1994); Finance Reeingineering, IBM Research Division Award (1994); Income Planning, IBM Research Division Award (1994); IBM Research Income Planning and Measurements (1993); IPODC Financial Plan (1991); Advanced Function Printing Software Pricing Award (1990); AFP Entry Pricing Promotion Award (1989); Financial Advisor, Campfire Girls; Volunteer, United Way. **Education:** Siena College, B.B.A. in Accounting (1983); Pace University, IBM Management School sponsored: Finance, International Accounting, Multinational Corporations, Leadership Development, and Business Communications. **Personal:** Married to Elizabeth in 1983. Two children: Megan and Kyle. Mr. Steubing enjoys skiing, volleyball, computers, fathering.

Sam E. Stimson

Senior Supplier Quality Engineer
Dell Computer
7000 Meadow Run
Austin, TX 78745
(512) 728–5289
Fax: (512) 728–3653
EMAIL: See Below

3577

Business Information: Dell Computer is a developer, manufacturer, seller, marketer, and servicer of all types of computers (i.e., laptops, notebooks, workstations, servers), as well as a seller of computer software. The Company has three divisions on a world–wide level: Notebook Computer Division, Desk Top Division, and Servers; as well as three manufacturing facilities (marketing and sales are also conducted): The U.S., Europe, and the Far East. Joining Dell Computer as Senior Supplier Quality Engineer in 1991, Mr. Stimson is responsible for the engineering quality of portable products in the Notebook Division on a world–wide level. He also works as the liaison between the Division (design and manufacturing) and the markets in the Far East and Europe. Internet users can reach him via: Sam.Stimson@ccmail.us.dell.com **Career Steps:** Senior Supplier Quality Engineer, Dell Computer (1991–Present); Quality Assurance Director, Carroll Touch (1989–1991); Quality Manager, Dresser Industries (1986–1989); Manufacturing Engineer Manager, Semcor (1984–1986). **Associations & Accomplishments:** American Society for Quality Control; Society of Manufacturing Engineers; Presented numerous papers at conferences; Ham Radio Operator. **Education:** St. Edwards University, M.B.A. (1982); Southwest Texas State University, B.A.A.S. (1977). **Personal:** Married to Jeannette in 1967. One child: Ian. Mr. Stimson enjoys golf and amateur radio.

Austin Sui

Chief Financial Officer
Acom, Inc.
46600 Landing Parkway
Fremont, CA 94538–6420
(510) 252–0500
Fax: (510) 252–0600
EMAIL: See Below

3577

Business Information: Acom, Inc. is a manufacturer and distributor of notebook computers and accessories, and is involved in development technology in the multimedia field. The Company was ranked tenth best by the research center that publishes "Computer Shoppers." As Chief Financial Officer, Mr. Sui is responsible for diversified financial operations of the Company. Internet users can reach him via: MigiUSA@Earthlink.com **Career Steps:** Chief Financial Officer, Acom, Inc. (1987–Present); Vice President, Northwater Engineering, Inc. (1995); Chief Financial Officer, MIG, Inc. (1993). **Education:** California State University at San Francisco, M.B.A. (1990); National Taiwan University, B.A. in Chemical Engineering. **Personal:** Married to Grace in 1987. Two children: Haidee and Mendi. Mr. Sui enjoys golf.

Olgierd O. Swida

OEM Manager/Latin America
Microsoft Corporation
899 West Cypress Creek Road
Ft. Lauderdale, FL 33309
(954) 489–4827
Fax: (954) 491–1616
E MAIL: See Below

3577

Business Information: Microsoft Corporation is the world's leading software development corporation. Starting during the '70s, Microsoft pioneered the standard computer languages for the Apple II and other early personal computers, then moved on to the development of the operating system, MS–DOS, for IBM's landmark PC. Envisioning the market expansion of the PC industry, Microsoft joined forces with the microprocessor giant, Intel Corporation, along with other entrepreneurs and thus created the PC clone industry which now dominates the market. Microsoft's introduction of the Windows program is what has turned the Company into one of the world's profit leading enterprises, exceeding that of corporations with revenues ten times as large. As OEM Manager/Latin America, Mr. Swida Internet users may reach him via: olgswid@microsoft.com. **Career Steps:** Microsoft Corporation: OEM Manager/Latin America (1996–Present), Marketing Manager/Latin America (1994–1996), Licensing Manager (1993–1994), Account Manager Eastern Europe (1989–1992). **Associations & Accomplishments:** With a flair for languages, Mr. Swida is fluent in English, Spanish, German, Russian and Polish and has a working knowledge of several others. **Education:** Universitat zu Koln, Diplom–Kaufmann (MBA) (1989). **Personal:** Married to Mariona Raventos in 1986. Two children: Oscar and Olaf. Mr. Swida enjoys skiing, flying, computers, languages, travel, and the internet.

Sonia Syngal

Technical Program Manager
Sun Microsystems Computer Company
2550 Garcia Avenue
Mountain View, CA 94043–1109
(408) 276–1396
Fax: (408) 945–9178
EMAIL: See Below

3577

Business Information: Sun Microsystems Computer Company manufactures software, hardware, servers, and microprocessors for business. Established in 1982, Sun presently employs 15,000 people. As Technical Program Manager for External Manufacturing, Ms. Syngal coordinates technical design and development with contracted manufacturing corporations. Internet users can reach her via: Sonia.Syngal@EBAY.SUN.COM **Career Steps:** Technical Program Manager, Sun Microsystems Computer Company (1995–Present); Ford Electronics: Process Engineer (1992–1994), Equipment Engineer (1991–1992), Process Development Engineer (1989–1991). **Associations & Accomplishments:** Stanford Engineering Club for Automation and Manufacturing; Women in Technology International; Gold Prize – Lincoln Arc Weldens Foundation; National Design Award (1995). **Education:** Stanford University, M.S. in Manufacturing Systems Engineering (1995); GMI Engineering & Management Institute, B.S.M.E. (1993). **Personal:** Ms. Syngal enjoys travel, foreign languages, reading, and tennis.

William M. Tatham

President/Chief Executive Officer
Janna Systems, Inc.
3080 Yonge Street, Suite 6060
Toronto, Ontario M4N 3N1
(416) 483–7711
Fax: (416) 483–3220
EMail: See Below

3577

Business Information: Janna Systems, Inc. is a management consultancy, specializing in the development of financial and document management software serving the finance, insurance and professional services industries. A former senior systems analyst with IBM, as well as a management consultant with one of the world's foremost financial consulting firms, Bill Tatham founded Janna Systems in 1990. Under his leadership, the Company has grown from a sole consultancy to its present 40 technological team staff, with revenue in excess of $8 million. **Career Steps:** President and Chief Executive Officer, Janna Systems, Inc. (1990–Present); Management Consultant, Anderson Consulting (1981–1990); Systems Engineer, IBM Canada, Ltd. (1978–1980). **Associations & Accomplishments:** Progressive Conservative Party. **Education:** University of Waterloo, B.A.Sc. (1983). **Personal:** Married to Janna in 1983. Three children: Michael, Janine and Colin. Mr. Tatham enjoys skiing, golf, electronics, and gardening.

William P. Taylor

Sales Administrator
Global Information Systems Technology, Inc.
100 Trade Center Drive, Suite 301
Champaign, IL 61820–7237
(217) 352–1165
Fax: (217) 352–9307
EMail: See Below

3577

Business Information: Global Information Systems Technology, Inc. is a manufacturer of computer software and a developer of custom computer–based training. International in scope, GIST, Inc.'s corporate office is located in Champaign, Illinois with two other national locations in Dayton, Ohio and San Antonio, Texas and international offices located in England, Germany, and Canada. As Sales Administrator, Mr. Taylor is responsible for the administration and direction of all computer and associated equipment sales, in addition to directing hands–on sales and presentations, and overseeing a sales staff of six. Internet users can reach him via: btaylor@gist.com **Career Steps:** Sales Administrator, Global Information Systems Technology, Inc. (1992–Present); United States Air Force: Technical Writer (1987–1992), Instructor (1980–1987). **Associations & Accomplishments:** Lions Club; Moose; Boy Scouts of America. **Education:** Eastern Illinois University, M.S. (1987); Southern Illinois University – Carbondale, B.S. in Electronic Systems; Community College of the Air Force, A.S. in Instructor Technology, Electronic Systems, and General Electronics. **Personal:** Married to Deborah Lynn in 1973. Two children: Katherine and Stephen. Mr. Taylor enjoys camping, backpacking, and woodworking.

Mr. Carsten Thomsen

Vice President of Engineering
National Instruments
6504 Bridge Point Parkway
Austin, TX 78730
(512) 795–6935
Fax: (512) 794–5641

3577

Business Information: National Instruments is a full–service electronics and software manufacturer specializing in the development of virtual instrumentation software and hardware. The Company is international in scope and distributes to over 21 countries. As Vice President of Engineering, Mr. Thomsen manages all new product development of computer hardware and software. Established in 1976, National Instruments employs 950 people with annual sales of $125 million. **Career Steps:** Vice President of Engineering, National Instruments (1994–Present); Division Manager, CMS, Bruel & Kjaer, Denmark (1993–1994); Division Manager, TMS, Bruel & Kjaer, Denmark (1983–1993). **Associations & Accomplishments:** Member, Institute of Electronics and Electrical Engineers. **Education:** Andrews University, B.A. (1971). **Personal:** Married to Kristen in 1973. Two children: Kristina and Maj. Mr. Thomsen enjoys travel and nature.

J. Patrick Timms

Vice President
Insilco Technologies Group
2411 North Oak Street, Suite 105
Myrtle Beach, SC 29577–3164
(803) 946–6200
Fax: (803) 846–9459

3577

Business Information: Insilco Technologies Group consists of four business units that manufacture components for the data, computer, and telecommunication markets. The four business units include: Insilco Technologies Group; S. Scott – wire and cable production; Signal Transformers – transformer manufacturing; and Stuart Stamping – metal stamping and die cut production. Joining Insilco Technologies Group as Vice President in 1995, Mr. Timms is responsible for the identification and promotion of synergy between the four business units, as well as the reduction of redundancy and development of opportunities for the group. **Career Steps:** Vice President, Insilco Technologies Group (1995–Present); Escol Industries: Vice President of Operations (1993–1995), General Manager (1990–1993). **Associations & Accomplishments:** Advisory Board Member, National Institute of Justice – Department of Justice; Founding Member, Wiring Harness Manufacturers Association; BICSI – A telecommunications association. **Education:** University of South Carolina, B.A. (1980); Duke University Fuqua School of Business, General Management Program. **Personal:** Married to Pamela in 1973. One child: Sarah Elizabeth. Mr. Timms enjoys fishing, golf, and sports.

Mr. Robert L. Trivett, Esq.
Director of Contracts Department – Communications Division
Tandem Computers, Inc.
200 Galleria Parkway, Suite 1300
Atlanta, GA 30339
(404) 951–0199
Fax: (404) 951–8255

3577

Business Information: Tandem Computers, Inc. is an innovative technology manufacturer and international distributor of specialized computer equipment, specifically a fault–tolerant processor utilized primarily by banking industry clientele, as well as law enforcement agencies and telecommunications firms. In his capacity as the Director of Contracts Department for the Communications Division, Mr. Trivett is responsible for the management and administration for sales contracts functions. Duties include customer sales, contracts negotiations, software development contracts and service contracts. Established in 1974, Tandem Computers, Inc. employs over 8,600 technical support and administrative staff personnel, and reports annual revenue in excess of $2 billion. **Career Steps:** Director of Contracts Department – Communications Division, Tandem Computers Inc. (1991–Present); Contracts/Leasing Manager, UNISYS Corporation (1981–1991); Executive Officer and Hearing Officer, State of California Womens Board of Terms and Parole (1971–1977). **Associations & Accomplishments:** Georgia Bar Association; American Bar Association; American Corporate Counsel Associatio n. **Education:** Woodrow Wilson Law School, J.D. (1987); University of Southern California, M.P.A. (1975); California State University, B.A. (1971).

Paul D. Trompeter
Software Designer
Tandem Computers, Inc.
2842 Cabrillo Avenue
Santa Clara, CA 95051–2323
(408) 285–9614
Fax: (408) 285–9594

3577

Business Information: Tandem Computers, Inc. is an innovative technology manufacturer and international distributor of specialized computer equipment, specifically a fault–tolerant processor utilized primarily by telecommunications firms clientele, as well as law enforcement agencies and banking/finance industries. Joining the Company in 1986 as Software Designer, Mr. Trompeter designs and maintains software courses for the research and development audience, as well as traveling and instructing global workforces in India, China, Europe, and Japan. He also serves as Curriculum Manager for research and development of education. **Career Steps:** Software Designer, Tandem Computers, Inc. (1986–Present); Senior Software Consultant, Motorola (1980–1985); Assistant Section Manager, Litton (1977–1980). **Associations & Accomplishments:** American Society for Quality Control; Institute of Electronics and Electrical Engineers; ACM. **Education:** Pepperdine University, M.S.T.M. (1996); San Jose State University, B.A. in Math (1977). **Personal:** Married to Lily Weckerly in 1983.

Mr. Daniel E. Udell
Director of Software Marketing Communications
IBM Corporation
Route 100
Somers, NY 10589
(914) 766–1699
Fax: (914) 766–9136

3577

Business Information: IBM Corporation, established in 1914, designs, manufactures and markets high–tech products globally, including information systems products and services, computers, semiconductors, networking hardware and software, computer hardware and software as well as outsourcing services, multivendor support services and consulting. Mr. Udell currently serves as the Director of Software Marketing Communications responsible for developing worldwide communications strategies and programs to promote IBM software. **Career Steps:** Director of Software Marketing Communications, IBM (1994–Present); Director of Communications – IBM Workforce Solutions – IBM's Human Resources spinoff (1992–1994); Director of Communications, IBM, U.S. (1990–1992) – responsible for all internal and external communications programs for IBM M&D units. **Associations & Accomplishments:** New York Academy of Sciences; International Center of Photography; Society of Human Relations Professionals; (PRSA) Public Relations Society of America; Along with his wife, Mr. Udell currently runs an internationally recognized art gallery, The Sound Shore Gallery. **Education:** Rensselaer Polytechnic Institute, B.S. in Physics (1957). **Personal:** Married to Mary Elizabeth in 1989. Four children: Seanne Elise Jersey, Moira Ann Oliver, Brian Udell and Kevin Udell. Mr. Udell enjoys photography.

Adrian F. Warner
Operations Director
Dewar Information Systems Corporation
3050 Finley Road, Woodland Courts
Downers Grove, IL 60515
(708) 241–3500
Fax: (708) 241–3587
E–mail: see below

3577

Business Information: Dewar Information Systems Corporation specializes in the development of pre–press publication software. Established in 1975, Dewar Information Systems Corporation currently employs 21 people. As Operations Director, Mr. Warner is responsible for all aspects of business management, profit and loss. He can also be reached through the Internet as follows: AWARNER@DEWAR.MHS.COM-PUSERV.COM **Career Steps:** Operations Director, Dewar Information Systems Corporation (1995–Present); Engineering Manager, Mortara Instrument Inc. (1993–1995); Technical Director and General Manager, Cambridge Medical Equipment (1985–1991). **Associations & Accomplishments:** Institute of Electrical Engineers; Institute of Electrical and Electronics Engineers Inc.; Chartered Engineer; FEANII accredited European Engineer. **Education:** CCAT, B.S. in Electronic Engineering (1985); CCAT, HND Electrical Engineering (1982). **Personal:** Married to Andrea in 1995. Mr. Warner enjoys building PC's, reading, movies and going to the coffee shop.

Ayao Yamazaki
Chairman of the Board
Megatek Corporation
16868 Via Del Campo Court
San Diego, CA 92127–1714
(619) 675–4000
Fax: (619) 675–4343

3577

Business Information: Megatek Corporation specializes in the development, manufacture, sales, and support of computer graphics accelerator hardware and software, mainly for CAD/CAM. Major clientele includes the automobile industry in Japan, the U.S. and Europe. Established in 1972, Megatek currently employs 150 people and has an estimated annual revenue of $30 million. As Chairman of the Board, Mr. Yamazaki is responsible for all aspects of operations. **Career Steps:** Chairman of the Board, Megatek Corporation (1992–Present); Managing Director, Nihon Unisys Ltd. (1993–Present); General Manager of Corporation Planning, Nihon Unisys Ltd (1990–1992). **Education:** Jiyu–Gukuen, Tokyo, B.S. equivalent (1961). **Personal:** Married to Yumiko in 1965. Two children: Makoto and Takako. Mr. Yamazaki enjoys golf, skiing, and listening to classical music.

Nancy Kim Yun
Director of Strategic Management
Rockwell
3770 Miraloma Avenue
Seal Beach, CA 92803
(714) 762–1739
Fax: (714) 762–0130
Email: See Below

3577

Business Information: Rockwell is a manufacturer of high–tech products from ICBM guidance computers and automotive vision sensors to aerospace satellites and modems. As Director of Strategic Management, Ms. Yun is responsible for strategic planning, supervising market research, and administrative duties. Internet users can reach her via: nkyun@anet.rockwell.com. **Career Steps:** Director of Strategic Management, Rockwell (1996–Present); Senior Associate, Booz–Allen K. Hamilton (1993–1996); Director of Strategic Focus, Burlington Air Express (1991–1992). **Associations & Accomplishments:** Beta Gamma Sigma **Education:** UCLA, M.B.A. (1988); UC Irvine, B.S. Degree in Computer Science, B.A. Degree in Psychology. **Personal:** Married to Keith in 1987. Two children: Lauren and Jessica.

Ptech Inc.

Oussama Ziade
Chief Executive Officer & Chairman
Ptech Inc.
160 Federal Street, 13th Floor
Boston, MA 02110
(617) 577–7100
Fax: (617) 577–7400
EMAIL: ziade@ptechinc.com

3577

Business Information: Ptech Inc. is an international manufacturer of business software products. The Ptech product, FrameWork, provides an integrated set of object–oriented methods and tools that enables companies to create an interactive blueprint of the information, activities, and processes driving their businesses. Founding the Company in 1994, Mr. Ziade serves as Chief Executive Officer, Chief Architect, & Chairman. He is responsible for all aspects of operations, including administration, finances, public relations, accounting, marketing, and strategic planning. **Career Steps:** Chief Executive Officer, Chief Architect, & Chairman, Ptech Inc. (1994–Present); Associative Design Technology (ADT); Chief Executive Officer (1993–1994), Vice President of Research and Development (1990–1993), Chief Architect (1989–1990). **Education:** Boston University, M.S. (1988); Harvard University, Post Graduate studies in High Energy Physics and Artificial Intelligence. (1987). **Personal:** Mr. Ziade enjoys building companies, swimming, writing, and building models.

Srdan Zirojevic
Applications Engineer
National Instruments
6504 Bridgeport Parkway
Austin, TX 78730
(512) 794–5374
Fax: (512) 794–5678
EMAIL: See Below

3577

Business Information: National Instruments is a virtual instrumentation, software and hardware company. As Applications Engineer, Mr. Zirojevic is responsible for technical support. His duties include, oversight of operations, strategic planning, product design and development. Internet users can reach him via: Srdan.Zirojevic@natinst.com. **Career Steps:** Applications Engineer, National Instruments (1996–Present). **Associations & Accomplishments:** Institute of Electronics and Electrical Engineers; Tau Beta Pi; ACM. **Education:** LaMar University, B.S.E.E. (1996). **Personal:** Mr. Zirojevic enjoys reading.

Mr. Robert W. Lovely
Vice President of Human Resources
Brandt, Inc.
705 South 12th Street
Watertown, WI 53094
(414) 261–1780
Fax: (414) 261–1783

3578

Business Information: Brandt, Inc. is a leading manufacturer of money processing equipment which is distributed worldwide to financial institutions, retailers, and gaming organizations. As Vice President of Human Resources, Mr. Lovely has full responsibility for domestic and international human relations functions. Established in 1890, Brandt, Inc. employs 540 people. **Career Steps:** Vice President of Human Resources, Brandt, Inc. (1992–Present); National Human Resources Manager, American Appraisal Associates (1988–1992); Assistant Director of Personnel, St. Mary's Medical Center (1986–1988); Human Resources Manager, Nicolet Instrument Corporation (1981–1986). **Associations & Accomplishments:** Society for Human Resource Management. **Education:** University of Wisconsin, M.B.A. (1990); Western Illinois University, B.A. in Political Science (1974).

Linda Susette Ballard
Account Executive
Xerox Business Services
10695 Frank Daniels Way
San Diego, CA 92131
(619) 495–3006
Fax: (619) 279–5669

3579

Business Information: Xerox Business Services is a division of the world's leading manufacturer and marketer of copiers, facsimile equipment, medical resonant image scanners, personal computers, and related chemical products. Established in 1956, Xerox Corporation reports annual revenue of $18 billion and currently employs 90,000 people corporate–wide. Xerox Business Services provides outsourcing document management services to clients. As Account Executive, Ms. Ballard is responsible for establishing budgets, overseeing financial concerns for individual accounts, scheduling equipment usage, and customer relations. **Career Steps:** Xerox Business Services: Account Executive (1978–Present), Sales Representative (1976–1978) **Associations & Accomplishments:** San Diego Host Lions Club. **Education:** National University, B.B.A. (1985); Miramar College, A.A. (1983). **Personal:** Married to Wallace in 1992. Two children: Laura Martin and David Ballard. Ms. Ballard enjoys being a certified doll artisan (porcelain antique reproductions).

James H. Cunningham
Managing Director
Stansa S.A.
Av. Conquistadores 1112
San Isdro, Lima, Peru 27
(511) 422–4790
Fax: (511) 440–9015

3579

Business Information: Stansa S.A. is an international distributor of office equipment. Operating from twelve sales and service locations in Lima and Peruvian cities, Stansa's product lines include digital copiers, digital duplicators, facsimile machines, printers, computers, office supplies and furniture. As Managing Director, Mr. Cunningham oversees all financial and administrative facets, as well as serving on the executive board in implementing strategic and development growth plans. **Career Steps:** Managing Director, Stansa S.A. (1983–Present). **Associations & Accomplishments:** Treasurer, American Association of Peru (1995, 1996). **Education:** St. Mark's School, Southborough, Massachusetts; Hobart College, B.A. in Economics (1983). **Personal:** Married to Caroline in 1995. Mr. Cunningham enjoys Colonial art, windsurfing, running, and waterskiing.

Arun Daga

Vice President/General Manager
Xerox Corporation
116 Wild Duck Road
Wilton, CT 06897–2831
(203) 968–3098
Fax: (203) 968–4556

3579

Business Information: Xerox Corporation is the world's leading manufacturer and marketer of copiers, facsimile equipment, medical resonant image scanners, personal computers, and related chemical products. Established in 1946, Xerox Corporation reports annual revenue of $17 billion and currently employs 80,000 corporate–wide. Mr. Daga heads the Xerox Multivendor Services, a business unit with worldwide operations, and Network Devices with $1 million in sales operating in the United States, France, Chile, and Canada. He is responsible for all aspects of Company operations for the unit, including administration, sales and marketing, and strategic planning. **Career Steps:** Xerox Corporation: Vice President/General Manager (1995–Present), Director of Xerox Community Office (1993–1995), General Manager of Xerox Services Division/President of Xerox Realty Corporation (1990–1993), Chief Financial Officer of Xerox Development and Manufacturing Group (1987–1990). **Associations & Accomplishments:** American Management Association. **Education:** University of Michigan – Ann Arbor: M.B.A. (1966), M.S.E. in Industrial Engineering, B.S.E. in Industrial Engineering. **Personal:** Married to Sharon in 1968. Two children: Renu and Sawjay. Mr. Daga enjoys travel and reading.

John L. Elter, Ph.D.
Vice President – Strategic Programs & Platforms
Xerox Office Document Products Division
200 Crosskeys, Building 815
Fairport, NY 14450
(716) 425–6000
Fax: (716) 425–6164

3579

Business Information: Xerox Corporation is the world's leading manufacturer and marketer of copiers, facsimile equipment, medical resonant image scanners, personal computers, and related chemical products. Established in 1954, Xerox currently employs 85,000 people and has an estimated annual revenue of $16 billion. A corporate and research executive with various divisions of Xerox since the conferral of his Doctorate in Engineering in 1969, Dr. John Elter currently serves as Vice President of Strategic Programs for the Office Document Products Division. Reporting directly to the President of this $8 billion Division, Dr. Elter is responsible for developing, manufacturing, and integrating Xerox strategic digital imaging products and services, including the development of strategic marking engines, image capture and processing modules, controllers and network, and client services. He is currently accountable for an $85 million budget and 500 staff. **Career Steps:** Xerox: Vice President of Strategic Programs and Platforms – Office Document Products Division (1993–Present), Vice President and General Manager of Departmental Printing – Office Document Systems Division (1992–1993), Chief Engineer of Product Strategy & Architecture – Mid Volume Development Department (1990–1992), Manager of Product Assurance – Xerox Quality Office Division (1989–1990), Technical Program Manager – 5090 Program Division (1983–1989), Manager of Technology Development – Fusing to Development Competency Centers (1969–1983). **Associations & Accomplishments:** Industrial Advisory Board and Industry Laboratory Tech Transfer Co–Chair, American Society of Mechanical Engineers; Industrial Research Institute; Optical Society of America; American Management Association; Pi Tau Sigma; Tau Beta Pi; American Men and Women of Science; Frequent lecturer and keynote speaker for University, Symposia and conference proceedings. **Education:** University of Rochester, Ph.D. in Mechanical & Aerospace Sciences (1969); New York University, M.S. in Mechanical Engineering (1965); Purdue University, B.S. in Mechanical Engineering (1963); Harvard Graduate School of Business, Creating Corporate Advantage Course (1995); University of California–Berkeley, Executive Briefing Program (1994), Executive Development Program (1990). **Personal:** Married to Margaret in 1965. One child: Sarah. Dr. Elter enjoys yoga, philosophy, sailing, fly–fishing, and whitewater rafting.

Anthony M. Federico
• • • ━━━◉━━━ • • •

Vice President of Technology & Document Production Services
Xerox Corporation
70 Linden Oaks Parkway
Rochester, NY 14625
(716) 383–7972 (716) 383–9723
Fax: Please mail or call

3579

Business Information: Xerox Corporation is the world's leading manufacturer and marketer of copiers, facsimile equipment, medical resonant image scanners, personal computers, and related chemical products. An electrical engineer with twenty–eight years experience, Mr. Federico was the Chief Engineer and key developer of the Xerox DocuTech System, a high quality printing machine combining modern computers and laser printers. He now serves as Vice President of Technology & Document Production Services, responsible for managing the outsourcing arm of Xerox, specifically the technical and business divisions. **Career Steps:** Vice President of Technology & Document Production Services, Xerox Corporation (1968–Present). **Associations & Accomplishments:** ACM; Institute of Electronics and Electrical Engineers. **Education:** Rochester Institute of Technology, B.S. in Electrical Engineering and Math. **Personal:** Mr. Federico enjoys windsurfing, sailing, travel, sports, golf, and computers.

Joseph Michael Giacalone
Regional Service Manager – LA/CARIB
Pitney Bowes – LA/CARIB Region
2424 North Federal Highway, Suite 360
Boca Raton, FL 33431
(407) 347–2040
Fax: (407) 347–2041

3579

Business Information: Pitney Bowes International specializes in the manufacture, retail sale, research and development, and design of office automation mailing equipment, postage meters and bases, inserting systems, barcode and sorting systems, folders, copiers, and fax machines. As Regional Service Manager – LA/CARIB., Mr. Giacalone oversees oversea dealer operations, service and customer related issues, repair procedures training, organizational recommendations, and parts stock. **Career Steps:** Pitney Bowes: Regional Service Manager, International Division (1993–Present), International Service Specialist, International Division (1988–1993), Regional Technical Specialist, Domestic Division (1985–1988). **Associations & Accomplishments:** North American Amateur Paintball Association. **Education:** Attended: Palm Beach Atlantic (1996), Michigan State University, Ohio State. **Personal:** Married to Tina Anne in 1991. Mr. Giacalone enjoys all sports, scuba diving, paintball, 4 wheeling, and motocrossing.

Gilbert J. Hatch
Vice President/General Manager
Xerox Corporation
200 Canal View Boulevard
Rochester, NY 14623
(716) 427–5999
Fax: (716) 427–3334

3579

Business Information: Xerox Corporation is the world's largest producer of document processing equipment. The Corporation has over 100,000 employees worldwide, including 15,000 at the New York Branch. As Vice President and General Manager of the Departmental Copier Business Unit, Mr. Hatch is in charge of the largest business unit within the Corporation. He is responsible for all personnel and the overall development of the unit. **Career Steps:** Xerox Corporation: Vice President/General Manager, Departmental Copier Division (1996–Present), Vice President/General Manager, Office Network Copying (1995–1996), Vice President/General Manager, Workgroup Copier (1992–1995). **Associations & Accomplishments:** Chairman of Xerox Office Document Products Group; United Way Leadership Campaign. **Education:** Rochester Institute of Technology: M.S. (1980), B.S. (1972). **Personal:** Married to Bernice in 1969. Three children: Amy, Karen and Adam. Mr. Hatch enjoys boating and skiing.

John J. Holland
Director of the Supply Chain
Xerox Corporation
P.O. Box 1600 Long Ridge Road
Stamford, CT 06904–1600
(203) 968–4210
Fax: (203) 968–4286
EMAIL: See Below

3579

Business Information: Xerox Corporation is the world's leading manufacturer and marketer of copiers, facsimile equipment, medical resonant image scanners, personal computers, and related chemical products. Established in 1946, Xerox Corporation reports annual revenue of $17 billion and currently employs 100,000 corporate–wide. A veteran of Xerox for twenty–five years, Mr. Holland joined the Corporation in 1959. Currently serving as Director of the Supply Chain, Mr. Holland is responsible for managing exports and logistics for the Latin American operations, as well as supervising 50 people directly and over 1,000 people indirectly, and managing world class systems. He can be reached through the Internet via: JackHolland@ea.xerox.com **Career Steps:** Xerox Corporation: Director of the Supply Chain (1992–Present), Director of Operations Control (1980–1992); Director of Asset Management, Rank Xerox, London (1975–1980). **Education:** Niagara University, B.S. (1959). **Personal:** Married to Suzanne in 1962. Four children: John III, Mary Sue, Patricia, and Annie. Mr. Holland enjoys golf.

Frederick B. Lanka
Assistant Facilities Manager
Ricoh Corporation
3001 Orchard Drive
San Jose, CA 95134
(408) 954–5352
Fax: (408) 944–3377

3579

Business Information: Ricoh Corporation specializes in office automation equipment manufacturing, (i.e. fax machines, laser printers, and copiers) sales and service. As Assistant Facilities Manager, Mr. Lanka is responsible for all aspects of the department. His duties include: oversight of building maintenance, including plumbing and electrical, partician configuration, outside vendors, tele–communications, and security. **Career Steps:** Assistant Facilities Manager, Ricoh Corporation (1981–Present); Adjunct Associate Professor, San Jose State Continuing Education (1996–Present). **Education:** De Anza College, A.A. (1972). **Personal:** Married to Milena in 1974. One child: Aimee. Mr. Lanka enjoys golf and reading.

Terry W. Mangalier
Director of Worldwide Services
Polaroid Corporation
201 Burlington Road
Bedford, MA 07130
(617) 386–5525
Fax: (617) 386–5611
EMAIL: See Below

3579

Business Information: Polaroid Corporation is a multi–billion dollar concern established in 1945 with over 9,000 employees. The Corporation designs, manufactures, and sells photographic and electronic imaging products worldwide. As Director of Worldwide Services, Mr. Mangalier is responsible for service and support of the Corporation's electronic imaging products worldwide market. Internet users can reach him via: Mongalt@Pol.Com. **Career Steps:** Polaroid Corporation: Director of Worldwide Services (1996–Present), Director of Services/Electronic Imaging (1994–1996), Director of Services, Identificational (1992–1994); Director of Service, Federal Systems Division, Wang Laboratories, Inc. (1974–1992). **Associations & Accomplishments:** Association of Field Service Managers International; Bedford Chamber of Commerce. **Education:** LaSalle University, B.S. in Business (1996); Louisiana State University, Executive Development Program; North Eastern University, Business Management Program. **Personal:** Married to Susan in 1979. Two children: Sara and Renee. Mr. Mangalier enjoys hiking, canoeing, and camping.

Terri R. Mason
Senior Systems Analyst
Xerox Engineering Systems
Rr 1 Box 28–ee
Farmersville, TX 75442–9767
(214) 389–5330
Fax: Please mail or call
EMAIL: See Below

3579

Business Information: Xerox Corporation is the world's leading manufacturer and marketer of copiers, facsimile equipment, medical resonant image scanners, personal computers, and related chemical products. Xerox Engineering Systems, a Division of Xerox, provides engineering document solutions to Fortune 500 Corporations. As Senior Systems Analyst, Ms. Mason provides pre– and post–sales support to sales personnel and clients, integrating engineering document solutions for clients. Internet users can reach her via: Terri_Mason@XN.XEROX.COM **Career Steps:** Senior Systems Analyst, Xerox Engineering Systems (1991–Present); Computer Specialist, Soil Conservation Service (1985–1991). **Education:** Kansas State University, B.S. (1980). **Personal:** One child: Jordan.

Janice K. O'Rourke

Director of Marketing
Xerox Corporation
8777 Purdue Road
Indianapolis, IN 46268–3104
(317) 875–6574
Fax: (317) 875–1544

3579

Business Information: Xerox Corporation is the world's leading manufacturer and marketer of copiers, facsimile equipment, document management software and hardware. Holding various management roles with Xerox since 1990, Janice O'Rourke was appointed as Director of Marketing in 1995. In this capacity, she is responsible for marketing assessment, development, and implementation of marketing programs. **Career Steps:** Xerox Corporation: Director of Marketing (1995–Present); International Marketing – Europe, South America, Canada (1993–1995); Manager, Xerox Alternate Channels (1990–1993); District Sales Manager, Burroughs Corporation (1980–1982). **Associations & Accomplishments:** Network of Women in Business; Indianapolis, Indiana Chamber of Commerce; Board of Directors, The Women's Alliance, Rochester, NY; Homeless Mission, Rochester, NY, food support committee; Children's Guardian Home, recreation committee. **Education:** University of Dayton, B.S. in Education (1974); St. John Fisher University, MBA courses (1985). **Personal:** Married to Kevin in 1974. Four children: Mickey, Daniel, Christine, and Tommy. Ms. O'Rourke enjoys travel, tennis, doing church volunteer work, and spending time with her family.

Paul E. Rossi
Research and Development Manager
Canon Virginia, Inc.
12000 Canon Boulevard
Newport News, VA 23606
(804) 881–6228
Fax: (804) 881–9507

3579

Business Information: Canon Virginia, Inc. is a manufacturer of office equipment, including copiers, printers, and peripheral supplies. As Research and Development Manager, Mr. Rossi is responsible for diversified administrative activities, including handling projects in parallel with materials. **Career Steps:** Canon Virginia, Inc: Research and Development Manager (1994–Present), Senior Manager (1987–1994); Senior Manager, Kodak (1986–1987). **Associations & Accomplishments:** American Chemical Society; Alpha Chi Sigma; Society of Plastic Engineers; Imaging Society and Technicians. **Education:** RIT, B.S. (1979); Polytechnic Institute of New York; University of New Haven; College of William and

Mary. **Personal:** Married to Beth in 1985. One child: Paul Baylor. Mr. Rossi enjoys photography.

Michael T. Stragmaglio

Senior Vice President of The Imaging Products Group
Ricoh Corporation
5 Dedrick Place
Caldwell, NJ 07006
(201) 882–2092
Fax: (201) 882–2097

3579

Business Information: Ricoh Corporation, the sales and distribution arm of Ricoh Japan, is a global manufacturer and distributor of copiers, facsimile equipment, multi–functional products, color systems, etc. International in scope, Ricoh Corporation has twelve manufacturing sites worldwide, with annual revenue of $12 billion worldwide and $1 billion nationally. The New Jersey office also serves as the distribution arm for corporate handling. As Senior Vice President of The Imaging Products Group, Mr. Stragmaglio is responsible for sales, marketing, and P & L for wholesale and retail distribution in North and South America. **Career Steps:** Senior Vice President of The Imaging Products Group, Ricoh Corporation (1994–Present); Minolta Corporation: Vice President of Graphics Group (1992–1994), Vice President and Business Director (1983–1992), Vice President of Sales (1987–1988). **Associations & Accomplishments:** Business Technology Association; UNICO; AIIM **Education:** University of Illinois, Business (1972). **Personal:** Married to Maureen in 1978. Two children: Michael Jr. and Jenna Marie. Mr. Stragmaglio enjoys golf, tennis, and auto racing.

Gloria Wadsworth
Account Executive
Pitney Bowes
6300 Wilshire Boulevard, 8th Floor
Los Angeles, CA 90040
(800) 322–8000 Ext. 1323
Fax: (213) 737–7315

3579

Business Information: Pitney Bowes is a worldwide manufacturer and distributor of business equipment. Established in 1920, the Company employs over 200,000 people and posted revenues in excess of $8 billion dollars in 1995. As Account Executive, Ms. Wadsworth oversees over 400 individual accounts. She is responsible for marketing new and existing products to clients and providing excellent customer service. Ms. Wadsworth works with clients on the installation of equipment and the training of employees in its use. She provides executive presentations and acts as mentor to junior sales representatives. **Career Steps:** Account Executive, Pitney Bowes (1996–Present); Speaker and Trainer, Self–Employed (1992–Present); Administration Manager, IBM Corporation (1983–1988). **Associations & Accomplishments:** National Association for Female Executives; Professional Speakers Association; St. Brigid's Lector Ministry; Professional Industrial Relations Association; Volunteer, LPGA Junior Golf Program. **Education:** University of South Carolina, B.S. (1982); Currently attending the University of Phoenix. **Personal:** One child: Gregory Timothy. Ms. Wadsworth enjoys classical dance, exercising, and studying philosophy.

Ed Young
Vice President of Sales and Customer Service
Sheridan Systems
10661 Falls Creek Lane
Dayton, OH 45458
(513) 278–2651
Fax: (513) 274–5719

3579

Business Information: Sheridan Systems designs and manufactures bindery machinery and systems for the production and distribution of books, magazines, catalogs, directories and newspapers. Established in 1835, Sheridan Systems currently employs 850 professionals and has an estimated annual revenue of $175 million. As Vice President of Sales and Customer Service, Mr. Young is responsible for all sales, marketing and customer service activities for the North American region. **Career Steps:** Vice President of Sales and Customer Service, Sheridan Systems (1994–Present); Vice President of Sales, AM Graphics (1984–1994); Sales Representative, National Account Manager, East and West Regional Manager, Harris Graphics Corp. (1979–1984). **Associations & Accomplishments:** Board of Directors, Web Offset Association Supplier Advisory Board; Printing Industries of America; Research & Engineering Council. **Education:** Indiana University of Pennsylvania, B.S. (1979). **Personal:** Married to Shelley A. in 1976. Two children: Erin E. and Matthew J. Young. Mr. Young enjoys golf, tennis, travel, and coaching baseball, softball, and soccer.

Dirk A. Laceur

President
IPSO USA, Inc.
7455 New Ridge Road, Suite A
Hanover, MD 21076
(410) 850–0909
Fax: (410) 850–5959

3582

Business Information: IPSO USA, Inc., daughter company of Belgian manufacturing company IPSO International, is an importer and distributor of commercial laundry equipment throughout the U.S., i.e., washers and dryers, to include coin–operated units for laundromats. As President, Mr. Laceur is responsible for all aspects of operations, including management, marketing, and planning. **Career Steps:** President, IPSO USA, Inc. (1994–Present); International Sales Manager, IPSO International, Belgium (1993–1994); National Sales Manager, PCZ, Belgium (1989–1993); Regional Sales Manager, Publi Ariane, Belgium (1986–1989). **Education:** University of Louvain, Psychology (1968). **Personal:** Mr. Laceur enjoys baseball, reading, and collecting stamps.

Juan B. Alvarez Jr.

Vice President
JB Alvarez Specialty Inc.
P.O. Box 29587, 65 Infanteria Station
Rio Piedras, Puerto Rico 00929
(809) 765–5361
Fax: (809) 250–6472

3585

Business Information: JB Alvarez Specialty Inc. specializes in the sale, service and maintenance of air conditioning units, serving corporate, commercial and private customers throughout Puerto Rico and the Caribbean Islands. Established in 1981, JB Alvarez Specialty Inc. currently employs 14 people. As Vice President, Mr. Alvarez is responsible for sales, accounting, and the supervision of technical support. **Career Steps:** Vice President, JB Alvarez Specialty Inc. (1987–Present). **Associations & Accomplishments:** Puerto Rico National Guard. **Education:** Ramirez College, Associate (1995); Escuela Tecnica De Electricidad, A/C Technician. **Personal:** Two children: Danaira Joan and Juan Dabid. Mr. Alvarez enjoys diving and vacationing on the beach.

James Fink
Controller
PRO Kontrol
1989 Rue Michelin
Laval, Quebec H7L 5B7
(514) 973–7765
Fax: (051) 473–6186
E MAIL: See Below

3585

Business Information: PRO Kontrol is a wholesaler of HVAC (heating, ventilation, and air conditioning) controls and other temperature control devices. Established in 1991, the Company currently has two locations in Quebec and hopes to expand internationally by the year 2000. As Controller, Mr. Fink is responsible for all aspects of financial operations, including accounting, financial reports, payroll, taxes, management, and budgets. Internet users may contact him via: JIM7497@aol.com. **Career Steps:** Controller, PRO Kontrol (1994–Present); Budget Analyst, Comp U Card (1989–1994). **Education:** University of Quebec, Bach. Admin. (1989). **Personal:** Mr. Fink enjoys hockey, tennis, reading, and movies.

Jeanette Flowers Cornett
Corporate Controller
Williamson Thermo King Dealership, Inc.
P.O. Box 3565
Wilson, NC 27895–3565
(919) 291–5045
Fax: Please mail or call

3585

Business Information: Williamson Thermo King Dealership, Inc. markets, sells, and services transport refrigeration vehicles (i.e. cooling trailers, ship containers, railroad cars, buses, ice cream trucks, etc.) and their parts. Celebrating their 25th anniversary, the Corporation currently has four locations and has estimated annual sales of $25 million. Williamson Thermo King was recently ranked as the ninth largest dealership in the nation. As Corporate Controller, Mrs. Flowers Cornett oversees all financial reporting and activities for the locations in North Carolina, South Carolina and Georgia. Her duties include responsibility for the accounting department, bank negotiations, auditing, and human resources concerns. **Career Steps:** Williamson Thermo King Dealership, Inc: Corporate Controller (1988–Present), Accounting Manager (1984–1988), Clerical/Accounting (1977–1984). **Associations & Accomplishments:** Local professional women's association; Dealer Advisory Council. **Education:** Wilson County Technical College, Accounting (1978). **Personal:** Married to Roger D. Cornett. Three children: Dale, Michele, and Michael. Three grandchildren. Mrs. Flowers Cornett enjoys antique cars, street rods, walking, and the mountains.

Michael W. Gebert

Controller
Carrier North America
P.O. Box 4808
Syracuse, NY 13221
(315) 432–7323
Fax: (315) 433–4057
EMail: See Below

3585

Business Information: A division of United Technologies, Carrier Corporation (North American Operations) is a leading manufacturer of residential and commercial heating and air conditioning products, gas furnaces, and heat pumps. Mr. Gebert joined Carrier Corporation in 1989, serving in various subsidary divisions until his promotion in 1995 to Corporate Controller for North American Operations. He is currently responsible for all transaction processing, financial, and accounting functions. Internet users can also reach him via: MIKE.GEBERT@CARRIER.WLTK.COM. **Career Steps:** Carrier: North America Operations, Controller (1995–Present), Assistant Controller (1994–1995); Asia–Pacific Operations, Controller (1991–1994); Manager of Financial Controls (1989–1991). **Associations & Accomplishments:** I.C.M.A. **Education:** Michigan State University, B.A. (1981). **Personal:** Mr. Gebert enjoys private piloting and small sailboats.

John Ostap Goshulak

General Manager
Hydrotherm Canada Corporation
5211 Creekbank Road
Mississauga, Ontario L4W 1R3
(905) 625–2991
Fax: (905) 625–6610

3585

Business Information: Hydrotherm Canada Corporation is a division of Mestek Canada Inc., a manufacturer of heating and air conditioning products, specializing in hot water heating for both residential and commercial marketplaces. International in scope, Hydrotherm Canada Corporation is the Canadian headquarters of Mestek Inc., with locations and activities spanning the globe. Joining Hydrotherm Canada Corporation as General Manager in 1992, Mr. Goshulak is responsible for all Canadian operations. Primary duties involve the coordination of sales, marketing, production and engineering for all of Canada. **Career Steps:** General Manager, Hydrotherm Canada Corporation (1992–Present); National Sales Manager, Danfoss Manufacturing – Canada (1989–1992); Automation System Engineer, Honeywell Canada, Ltd. (1987–1989); Technical Sales Engineer, Hydrotherm Canada Inc. (1984–1987). **Associations & Accomplishments:** Professional Engineers of Ontario (PEO); Association of Heating, Refrigeration & Air Conditioning Engineering (ASHRAE); Chairman, Hydronics Marketing Group of Canada (HMG); Education Chairm, Canadian Hydronics Council (CHC–CIPH); Reed Institute of Canada Hydronics Training Instructor. **Education:** University of Toronto, Bachelor of Applied Science, Mechanical Engineering (1984). **Personal:** Married to Debra in 1986. Three children: Peter, Emily, and Larissa.

Ricardo Guidini

Controller
Auto Kool Manufacturing Co., Inc.
Avenue Munoz Rivera 759
Rio Piedras, Puerto Rico 00925
(809) 765–8575
Fax: (809) 764–7760

3585

Business Information: Auto Kool Manufacturing Company, Inc. is a manufacturer of air conditioning units for automobiles and mini–split air conditioning units for homes. Established in 1992, Auto Kool Manufacturing has two locations in Rio Piedras, reporting annual revenue of $1.5 million and employing 50 people. As Controller, Mr. Guidini is responsible for all aspects of financial activities, including inventory, accounts payable, and associated administrative matters. **Career Steps:** Controller, Auto Kool Manufacturing Company, Inc. (1993–Present); Administrative Director, Caribe Hilton & Casino (1990–1993); Income Auditor, San Juan Hotel & Casino (1985–1990). **Associations & Accomplishments:** Voluntary consultant for non–profit organizations on the financial area providing service to victims of domestic violence; Teenage Group Activities Leader. **Education:** Attended: University of Phoenix, Monroe Community College – Rochester; Inter-american University, B.A. in Economics and Political Sciences. **Personal:** Mr. Guidini enjoys playing soccer.

John E. Hudson

Managing Director
Thermo King Corporation
314 West 90th Street
Minneapolis, MN 55420–3630
(423) 215–7624
Fax: (423) 242–4204

3585

Business Information: Thermo King Corporation is a manufacturer of mobile temperature control equipment, such as refrigeration for buses, recreational vehicles, etc. International in scope, Thermal King has fourteen factories in seven different countries. Joining Thermo King as Vice President of Finance in 1982, Mr. Hudson was appointed as Managing Director in 1992. He is responsible for managing and directing the activities of the Czech Republic office, as well as purchasing, strategic planning, and overall manufacturing operations. **Career Steps:** Thermo King Corporation: Managing Director (1992–Present), Vice President of Finance (1982–1992); Controller, Westinghouse Division (1979–1982). **Education:** Syracuse University, M.B.A. (1972); Harvard University, A.P.M. (1988). **Personal:** Married to Jane R. in 1967. Two children: James and Jennifer. Mr. Hudson enjoys golf and jogging.

Mr. James S. Kiriakos

Vice President of Sales Administration
Lennox Industries, Inc.
2100 Lake Park Boulevard
Richardson, TX 75080
(214) 497–5110
Fax: (214) 497–5427

3585

Business Information: Lennox Industries, Inc. specializes in the manufacture and distribution of heating and air conditioning equipment for residental dwellings and small commercial businesses. Established in 1895, Lennox Industries, Inc. currently employs 2,500 people and has an estimated annual revenue of $800 million. As Vice President of Sales Administration, Mr. Kiriakos is responsible for the direction of all distribution, customer service, and technical support areas for North America. **Career Steps:** Vice President of Sales Administration, Lennox Industries, Inc. (1991–Present); Corporate Controller, Lennox Industries Ltd., Canada (1990–1991); Division Controller, Eastern Division, Lennox Industries, Columbus, OH (1986–1990); Division Controller, Southeast Division, Lennox Industries, Atlanta, GA (1982–1986). **Associations & Accomplishments:** American Manufacturers Association; NAA; ICSA; American Society of Heating, Refrigeration, and Air Conditioning Engineers; Greek Orthodox Church. **Education:** University of Iowa, B.A. in Accounting (1973). **Personal:** Married to Diane in 1976. Two children: Georgia and Samuel. Mr. Kiriakos enjoys reading, golf and swimming.

Lin Tao Lu

Engineering Manager
RHEEM Manufacturing Company
P.O. Box 17010
Ft. Smith, AR 72917–7010
(501) 648–4116
Fax: (501) 648–4962

3585

Business Information: RHEEM Manufacturing Company is an international manufacturer of air conditioning units, warm air gas furnaces, and water heaters. RHEEM is ranked #2 in the North American Continent for the above three product lines. As Engineering Manager, Mr. Lu is responsible for the management of all engineering of commercial equipment, as well as the design, research, and development of products. **Career Steps:** RHEEM Manufacturing Company: Engineering Manager (1995–Present), Senior Project Engineer (1989–1995); Senior Research Associate, Illinois Institute of Technology (1987–1989). **Associations & Accomplishments:** American Society of Mechanical Engineers; American Society of Heating, Refrigeration and Air Conditioning Engineers; The Combustion Institute; Air Conditioning and Refrigeration Institute; Author of six publications and a number of technical reports; Holds five U.S. Patents. **Education:** National Polytechnic Institute of Grenoble – France: Doctorate (1986), M.S.M.E.; Dalian Marine College – China, B.S.M.E. **Personal:** Married to Lily Wang in 1990. Mr. Lu enjoys reading, tennis, Chinese chess and other games.

Mario Marrero

Controller
Port Distributors Inc.
P.O. Box 4437
Hollywood, FL 33083–4437
(305) 963–3800
Fax: (305) 963–3811

3585

Business Information: Port Distributors Inc. is a wholesale distributor of central air conditioning equipment. Established in 1977, Port Distributors currently employs 27 people and has an estimated annual revenue of $7 million. As Controller, Mr. Marrero is responsible for all aspects of financial operations. **Career Steps:** Port Distributors Inc.: Controller (1991–Present), Systems Analysist (1990–1991). **Associations & Accomplishments:** Key National Honor Society; Fort Lauderdale Chamber of Commerce; AIDS Walk Miami, Sponsor and Representative. **Education:** University of Miami, B.S. in Business (1990); Presently working on Master's degree. **Personal:** Mr. Marrero enjoys tennis, computers, reading and lifting weights.

Boris M. Meyerson, Ph.D.

MIS Director
Engelhard/ICC
441 North 5th Street, Suite 102
Philadelphia, PA 19123–4008
(215) 625–0700
Fax: (215) 625–8910
EMAIL: See Below

3585

Business Information: Engelhard/ICC specializes in the manufacture of commercial desiccant–based air conditioners. Primarily distributing to OEM's and other industries throughout the U.S., the Company also has partnership holdings with Japan and Korea. A native of Russia where he served in academic and administrative technology roles, Dr. Meyerson emigrated to the U.S. in 1994, and thereupon was appointed to his current position with Englehard/ICC. As MIS Director, he is responsible for the management of all computer operations, which involves order fulfillment, financial and manufacturing systems, as well as network support and users training. He can also be reached through the Internet via: 75702.1003@compuserve.com **Career Steps:** MIS Director, Engelhard/ICC (1994–Present); Associate Professor, Ufa Aviation University, Russia (1984–1994); Deputy Chief, Rep. Center for New International Tech., Russia (1991–1993). **Associations & Accomplishments:** NASPA. **Education:** Drake Training Tech., CNA (1994); Russian Academy of Sciences, Ph.D. in Engineering (1990); Ufa Aviation University, M.S. in Engineering (1984). **Personal:** Married to Anna in 1983. One child: Michael. Dr. Meyerson enjoys reading and his cats.

Mr. Gary R. Mirsky

Vice President of Sales
Hamon Cooling Towers, Division of Hamon Corporation
245 Highway 22 West
Bridgewater, NJ 08807
(908) 725–3337
Fax: (908) 725–3421

3585

Business Information: Hamon Cooling Towers, a Division of Hamon Corporation, is an international designer, manufacturer, and supplier of industrial cooling towers and related products and systems. Distributing primarily to power stations, the company is the major supplier world–wide of water cooling towers for the electricity generating industry. They also provide natural and mechanical draft cooling towers used in the petroleum chemical and pulp/paper industries. Established in 1906, Hamon Corporation, having their corporate office located in Brussels, Belgium, has offices located in: British Isles, France, Germany, Italy, Spain, South Africa, Australia, South Korea, South America, Thailand, and the U.S. (five continents). Hamon Cooling Towers' New Jersey office currently employs 35 persons and reports an annual estimated revenue of $30 million. In his current capacity, Mr. Mirsky is responsible for all U.S. sales operations and administration. **Career Steps:** Vice President of Sales, Hamon Corporation (1993–Present); Vice President/Division Manager, Hamon Cooling Towers (1992–1993); Vice President of Operations, Hamon Cooling Towers (1985–1992); Product Manager, Research Cottrell (1978–1985). **Associations & Accomplishments:** Chairman–Engineering Standards and Maintenance Committee, Cooling Tower Institute; ASHRAE; NJSPE; Numerous articles published in industry and engineering journals and periodicals. **Education:** Northeastern University, M.S./EM (1973); New Jersey Institute of Technology, B.S. in Mechanical Engineering. **Personal:** Married to Sandra in 1983. Three children: Michael, Debbie, and John. Mr. Mirsky enjoys fishing, tennis, and golf in his leisure time.

Gregory A. Osterman
Vice President of International Operations
Tyler Refrigeration Corporation
17288 Pencross Drive
Granger, IN 46530–9772
(616) 684–9737
Fax: (616) 684–9739

3585

Business Information: Tyler Refrigeration Corporation is a manufacturer of commercial refrigeration for supermarkets worldwide. As Vice President of International Operations, Mr. Osterman is responsible for all international operations, including strategic planning, manufacturing, and sales. **Career Steps:** Tyler Refrigeration Corporation: Vice President of International Operations (1986–Present), Marketing Manager – Europe (1982–1985), Export Sales Manager (1978–1982). **Education:** Attended Indiana University. **Personal:** Married to Sharon L in 1969. Two children: Zoanne G. and Zara L. Mr. Osterman enjoys golf, reading, and computing.

Jason Powell
Engineering Manager
IMI Cornelius, Inc.
1 Cornelius Place
Anoka, MN 55303
(612) 422–3035
Fax: (612) 422–3232
EMAIL: See Below

3585

Business Information: Cornelius, Inc. specializes in the manufacture of refrigerated beverage dispensing equipment. Established in the 1930's, the Company employs 500 people, and has an estimated annual revenue of $180 million. As Engineering Manager, Mr. Powell oversees reliability engineering, research and development, testing services, and regulatory affairs. Internet users can reach him via: jasonp@skypoint.com. **Career Steps:** IMI Cornelius, Inc: Engineering Manager (1993–Present), Policy and Procedures Specialist (1990–1993); Supplier Quality Engineering, ADC Telecommunications (1988–1990). **Education:** University of Minnesota, B.S. (1987). **Personal:** Mr. Powell enjoys woodworking, photography, skiing, and fishing.

Gerald Robinson
Health, Safety, Environment Manager
Lennox Industries (Canada), Ltd.
400 Norris Glen Road
Etobicoke, Ontario M9C 1H5
(416) 621–9321 Ext. 208
Fax: (416) 621–6303

3585

Business Information: Lennox Industries (Canada), Ltd. is one of the top six manufacturers of furnace, air conditioning, and ventilation. International in scope, the Company's corporate, international, and global headquarters are located in Dallas, Texas. As Health, Safety, Environment Manager, Mr. Robinson provides updates on regulations, disseminates them, and ensures they are implemented. He is also responsible for transport of hazardous materials and training employees for certification in ozone depletion prevention. **Career Steps:** Health, Safety, Environment Manager, Lennox Industries (Canada), Ltd. (1990–Present); Class "A" Miner, Rio Algom, Ltd. (1980–1990). **Associations & Accomplishments:** Ontario Association of Certified Engineering Technicians and Technologists; Canadian Environmental Auditing Association; International Accident Prevention Association; Canadian Manufacturing Association; Speaker, Institute of Canada; Recipient: Institute of Canada Excellence for Environmental Award, Nine P4 and Large Industry of the Year Awards. **Education:** Georgian College (1994); Communications Systems Technician, Canadian Armed Forces. **Personal:** Mr. Robinson enjoys fishing and hunting.

Mr. Mark A. Sawyer
Vice President
McNutt Service Group, Inc.
111 Sugar Loaf Road
Hendersonville, NC 28792
(704) 693–0933
Fax: (704) 696–9906

3585

Business Information: McNutt Service Group, Inc. specializes in heating, air conditioning, electric, and plumbing service and installation. Established since 1979, McNutt Service Group, Inc. presently employs 80 people. In his current capacity, Mr. Sawyer manages commercial accounts, general administration, training, and sales. **Career Steps:** Vice President, McNutt Service Group, Inc. (1983–Present); Owner, Evergreen Care Company (1979–1983); Owner, Focus Photo Products (1977–1979). **Associations & Accomplishments:** Past President, Toastmaster International – Asheville Chapter; Public speaker; Aircraft Owners and Pilots Association; Associated General Contractors. **Education:** Memphis State University (1975); Towson State University. **Personal:** Married to Debra in 1989. Two children and two step children: Jaime, Joey, Geoffrey, and Joey. Mr. Sawyer enjoys flying and horseback riding in his leisure time.

Christopher James Shimek
Plant Manager
Heat – N – Glo
800 W. Jefferson Street
Lake City, MN 55041–1370
(612) 437–1549
Fax: (612) 437–5121

3585

Business Information: Heat – N – Glo is a manufacturer of gas appliances. Joining Heat – N – Glo as Plant Manager in 1988, Mr. Shimek oversees all related manufacturing activities, in addition to all administrative operations for associates and a support staff. **Career Steps:** Heat – N – Glo: Plant Manager (1992–Present); Materials Manager (1990–1992); Purchasing/Buyer (1988–1990) **Associations & Accomplishments:** Lake City Chamber of Commerce; APICS – Twin Cities Chapter **Education:** St. Cloud State University, M.B.A. in Operations Management (1992); Winona State University, B.S. in Business Administration. **Personal:** Married to Kristin in 1994. Mr. Shimek enjoys hunting, fishing, volleyball and racquetball.

Elisa L. Simmonds
Controller
ICE (US), Inc.
140 Airport Lane
Bolivar, TN 38008
(901) 658–7000
Fax: (901) 658–3090

3585

Business Information: ICE (US), Inc. is a manufacturer of industrial commercial heaters with manufacturing and distribution facilities located in Canada and Tennessee. Established in 1993, ICE (US), Inc. reports annual revenue of $3.4 million and currently employs 44 people. A Canadian citizen with seven years of expertise as a controller, Miss Simmonds joined ICE, Inc. in 1986. She currently serves as Controller in the U.S. office responsible for all operational and financial matters, including accounting, computer systems, and health plan administration. **Career Steps:** Controller, ICE (US), Inc. (1993–Present); Controller, ICE Manufacturing, Ltd (Canada) (1990–1993); Controller, CDWEST, Ltd/ICES/TCL Canada (1988–1990). **Associations & Accomplishments:** Member, Certified Management Accountants – Canada. **Education:** University of Manitoba, two years of a B.A. (1989); Garden City Collegiate, Grade 12; Certificates in Seminar Programs. **Personal:** Miss Simmonds enjoys walking, reading, and meeting new people.

Dave P. Smith
Director of Human Resources
Elkhart Products
P.O. Box 740
Geneva, IN 46740–0740
(219) 368–7246
Fax: (219) 368–7889

3585

Business Information: Elkhart Products specializes in the manufacture of automotive air conditioning and refrigeration industry tubular components. Established in 1969, the Company employs 220 people and has estimated annual revenue of $24 million. As Director of Human Resources, Mr. Smith handles all aspects of personnel management. He is responsible for training, safety, benefits, wages, compensation, and employee benefits. **Career Steps:** Director of Human Resources, Elkhart Products (1996–Present); Goodyear Tire and Rubber: Manager, Industrial Engineer, and Training (1994–1996), Human Resources Manager)1989–1994, Coordinator, Industrial Engineer and Training (1987–1989). **Associations & Accomplishments:** Charter President of Optimist Club; Rotary; Past President for Parks and Recreation Board; Business Education Committee. **Education:** University of Akron, Business Administration (1977). **Personal:** Married to Lori in 1976. Three children: Natalie, Tim, and Dan. Mr. Smith enjoys golf and travel.

Roger Traboulay
Director/General Manager – Air Conditioner Mfg.
Peake Industries Limited
177 Western Main Road, Cocorite, PO Box 1221
Port of Spain, Trinidad
(809) 622–7325
Fax: (809) 662–4580
EMail: See Below

3585

Business Information: Peake Industries Limited is an air conditioning manufacturing facility. A member of the Thomas Peake and Company Group of Companies, and located in the twin–island Republic of Trinidad and Tobago in the West Indies, Peake Industries currently offers 18 product lines representing a range of over 200 different air conditioner models from 1–40 tons. Exports represent approximately 80% of its total business. With the capacity to produce 75,000 tons of air conditioning equipment per year utilizing the latest in manufacturing technology, Peake Industries has been able to live up to its vision of Quality and Flexibility. Serving in managerial capacities for Peake since 1989, Roger Traboulay was appointed Director and General Manager in 1995. He is responsible for the day–to–day operations of the Air Conditioning Manufacturing facility, ensuring quality product output and overall strategies. Mr. Traboulay is also a member of the Board of Directors at Peake Industries, and serves on the Export Advisory Board of TIDCO. Internet users can reach him via: roger@peake.trinidad.net **Career Steps:** Peake Industries Limited: Director/General Manager of Air Conditioner Manufacturing (1995–Present), General Manager (1993–1995), Plant Manager (1989–1992). **Associations & Accomplishments:** American Society of Heating, Refrigeration, and Air Conditioning Engineers; Vice President, Squash Association. **Education:** University of the West Indies: E.M.B.A. (1996), B.Sc. in Electrical Engineering (1988). **Personal:** Mr. Traboulay enjoys cycling, squash, and water sports.

Claus D. Wissler
Manager of Operations
BEHR Climate Systems, Inc.
5020 Augusta Drive
Ft. Worth, TX 76106
(817) 624–7273
Fax: (817) 624–3328

3585

Business Information: BEHR Climate Systems, Inc. is an international manufacturer of air conditioning and heater modules for all major automotive and truck industries. Established in 1969, BEHR Climate Systems, Inc. reports annual revenue of $55 million and currently employs 220 people. A Certified Manufacturing Engineer, Mr. Wissler joined BEHR Germany in 1991 as Assistant to the President of Production. Currently serving as Manager of Operations at BEHR Climate Systems, he is responsible for production, production support (industrial engineering, manufacturing engineering, maintenance, tooling) and logistics (purchasing, planning, warehousing). **Career Steps:** Manager of Operations, BEHR Climate Systems, Inc. (1993–Present); Assistant to the President of Production, BEHR Germany (1991–1993). **Associations & Accomplishments:** Society of Industrial Engineers; Society of Manufacturing Engineers; American Management Association. **Education:** Technical University – Stuttgart, Dipl–Ing (equivalent to M.S. in Engineering) (1991); Technical High School – Stuttgart, Pre–Engineering Diploma, Major: Math and Physics. **Personal:** Mr. Wissler enjoys photography, music, American "muscle" cars, and football.

Caio De Almeida Cunha
Finance Director
Ingersoll–Dresser Pumps do Brasil Ind. Com. Ltda.
Av. Suburbana, 5.451 Todos os Santos
Rio De Janeiro, Brazil 20771–001
55–21–269–8812
Fax: 55–21–592–6933

3586

Business Information: Ingersoll–Dresser Pumps holds approximately 30% of the Brazilian pump industry. As Finance Director, Mr. De Almeida Cunha is responsible for all financial aspects of the Company, including accounting and taxes. His audit experience is fundamented in large multinational companies. **Career Steps:** Finance Director, Ingersoll–Dresser Pumps (1994–Present); Director of Auditing, Price Waterhouse (1991–1993). **Associations & Accomplishments:** Vice President of Fiscalization, Accounting Boards; President, Rio de Janeiro Branch of the National Association of Accountants (ANEFAC). **Education:** Catholic University, B.A. (1981); Accounting Degree (1983). **Personal:** Married to Ana Luiza in 1985. Two children: Gabriel and Henrique. Mr. De Almeida Cunha enjoys spending time with his kids and biking.

Kent D. Reid

Director of Engineering Research & Development
Marley Pump Company
9650 Alden Road
Lenexa, KS 66215–1127
(913) 541–2985 (913)498–5538
Fax: (913) 498–5537
EMAIL: See Below

3586

Business Information: Marley Pump Company is a researcher and developer of environmental monitoring systems for underground storage tanks and pipelines and sites. Activities also include conducting ground surveys to monitor for leakage, creating new devices, such as submersible pumps for petroleum, and promoting awareness in Third World countries. As Director of Electronic Engineering Research & Development, Mr. Reid is responsible for the direction of all research and development, including new product development and working on water systems for Third World countries. Internet users may reach him via: reid@gvi.net **Career Steps:** Director of Engineering Research & Development, Marley Pump Company (1991–Present); Engineering Manager, Level Tech (1990–1991); Senior Design Engineer, Cambell Scientific (1987–1990). **Education:** Utah State University, B.S. Enviromental Engineering (1987) **Personal:** Married to Robena in 1984. Three children: Vanessa, Tyson and Kassidy. Mr. Reid enjoys single engine piloting, skiing, boating and water sports.

Vern M. Dawson

Executive Vice President
Hungerford & Terry, Inc.
226 Atlantic Avenue
Clayton, NJ 08312–1335
(609) 881–3200
Fax: (609) 881–6859

3589

Business Information: Hungerford & Terry, Inc. specializes in the manufacture of water treatment equipment. Established in 1909, Hungerford & Terry, Inc. currently employs 58 people and has an estimated annual revenue of $10 million. Joining the Company in 1972 as a purchasing manager, Mr. Dawson has been promoted through the corporate ladder to his current position as Executive Vice President. He is responsible for directing the areas of affirmative action, sales, production and salary administration. **Career Steps:** Hungerford & Terry, Inc.: Executive Vice President (1989–Present), Vice President, Secretary and Treasurer (1986–1989), Purchasing and Production Manager (1972–1986). **Associations & Accomplishments:** ELC of Gloucester County. **Education:** Rowan College, B.A. (1972); Graduate studies taken at Rowan College, (formerly Glassboro State College). **Personal:** Widower of Susan L. (married: 1964, deceased: 1995). Two children: Karen S. and Kathy A. Mr. Dawson enjoys volleyball.

Josef Meringer

Vice President of Marketing/Executive Chief
RATIONAL Cooking Systems, Inc.
Governor's Square Office Center, Suite 245
Hoffman Estates, IL 60195–2400
(847) 884–9950
Fax: (847) 884–9949

3589

Business Information: RATIONAL Cooking Systems, Inc., is a joint venture between RATIONAL Grosskuechentechnik GmbH in Landsberg, Germany, and The Middleby Corporation in Elgin, Illinois. An international company, RATIONAL Grosskuechentechnik is the inventor (1977) and world's leading manufacturer of the "Original RATIONAL Combi–Steamer", which is equipped with two cooking energies. Moist heat, dry heat, steam and hot air. These two cooking media can be used either individually, in sequence, or combined. The RATIONAL Combi–Steamer offers the possibility to operate almost all cooking methods of the traditional and modern cuisine in only one unit. Mr. Merringer is the number one expert in Combi–Steamer Technology and has nineteen years' specialized experience in different target groups throughout the world. A certified chef, certified by the industry, he has over fourteen years of technical experience in vacuum cooking and processing, and was instrumental in developing "RATIONAL Educational Culinary Curriculum", a comprehensive course for vocational and professional schools, culinary academies, institutes, and universities such as Johnson & Wales University. He has been invited to be a guest speaker at several international institutes and universities. Mr. Meringer also developed and teaches the RATIONAL Certified Chef Program. Executive Chefs nationwide participate in a three day seminar. The program is taught on a master chef level with precise technical transfer of knowledge, which results in the most unique modern cooking in the world. After successful completion of the course, these chefs support RATIONAL's customers as RATIONAL Certified Chefs. Years ago, Mr. Meringer established a special training program for the representatives, sales persons and service technicians of RATIONAL Combi–Steamers. A native of Tyrol, Austria, Chef Meringer has hosted such world dignitaries as former U.S. Presidents Nixon and Ford, and conductor Leonard Bernstein. Positively characterized by world–renowned business consultant Tom Peters, in his book "Liberation Management" as the Customer's Lawyer, Chef Meringer also plays a part in his video "World Class Quality". An active member of several culinary groups, Chef Meringer gives seminars on Modern Cooking technology, spices, vacuum cooking and kitchen marketing and management. **Career Steps:** RATIONAL Cooking Systems: Vice President of Marketing, Product Manager, Sales Manager, Director of Technical Applications and Sales Promotion, Freelance Representative (1977–Present); Hotel Bristol: Executive Chef, Kitchen Director. **Associations & Accomplishments:** American Culinary Federation; Chef of Cuisine Association; ACF–Chicago Chapter; WACS; VKD–Germany; FCSI; NAFEM Education Committee; Les Toques Blanches International; Euro–Toques; Supervisor for Three Culinary Olympics in Frankfurt, Germany; American Culinary Award (1995); Gold Medal fom the American Tasting Institute (1996). **Education:** Apprenticeship in Tyrol and Salzburg, Austria, at the Oesterreichischer Hof; Several gold medals, Chef de Partie. **Personal:** Married to Renate. One child: Melanie. Mr. Meringer enjoys tennis, bicycling, mountain hiking and climbing, skiing, photography, and fine food; his business travels around the world have enabled him to fulfill his interest in various cultures and histories.

H. Robert Michels

President
H. Robert Michels Inc.
540 Officenter Place, Suite 285
Gahanna, OH 43230–5317
(614) 471–1700
Fax: (614) 471–7773

3589

Business Information: Starting his sales career in 1975 at the age of eighteen working for a RainSoft dealer, Robert Michels earned enough money to buy out the dealer only one year later. By 1977 he had even opened a second dealership. In 1979, at the age of 22, the parent company – RainSoft (an international water treatment equipment company), offered him a position as a sales trainer to teach others what he was doing so well. He accepted their offer and sold both dealerships. From there, he was promoted in 1982 to District Manager, responsible for all sales in the states of Indiana and Ohio. Promoted to Regional Manager in 1989, Mr. Michels formed his own RainSoft distributorship, H. Robert Michels, Inc. His district included, and continues to operate in, the states of Indiana, Ohio, Michigan, Tennessee, Kentucky, Central Illinois, Western Pennsylvania, and Western New York. Under his management as District Manager and now Regional Manager, he has been responsible for quadrupling business. Wanting to insure his Company would continue if he retired (he had no relatives), the Founder of RainSoft formed Aquion Corporation in 1990. Aquion bought out all assets of RainSoft, including all trademarks and patents, concluding the process in 1995. Appointed as one of seven Board of Directors in 1994 (consisting of successful RainSoft dealers), he serves as General Partner and Major Stockholder of Aquion Corporation. In 1995, Aquion reported over $30 million in wholesale business around the world. **Associations & Accomplishments:** International Arabian Horse Association; American Horse Show Association; Water Quality Association; Arthritis Foundation; Chamber of Commerce; Better Business Bureau; Donate to numerous charities. **Personal:** Married to Elizabeth M. in 1982. Mr. Michels enjoys boating, fishing, sports, and Arabian horses.

Jesse Rodriguez

Partner and Vice President of Sales & Marketing
Ideal Horizons, Inc.
1 Ideal Way
Poultney, VT 05764–1042
(802) 287–4488
Fax: (802) 287–4486

3589

Business Information: Ideal Horizons, Inc. is an international manufacturer and marketer of ultraviolet water treatment systems used to eliminate harmful bacteria in water with chemical–free applications. A well–known specialist with commercial/industrial applications, Mr. Rodriguez has a degree in administration and over fifteen years experience in the ultraviolet field. As Co–Owner, Partner, and Vice President of Sales and Marketing, he is uniquely qualified to serve the high purity and other technically–advanced aspects of the commercial/industrial water treatment industry. **Career Steps:** Co–Owner, Partner, and Vice President of Sales and Marketing, Ideal Horizons, Inc. (1983–Present). **Associations & Accomplishments:** World Water Quality Assembly Committee on Industrial Education; Water Quality Association: Educational Services Committee: Who's Who Environmental Registry for Water Treatment Design; Purification & Disinfection Committee; Publications and Presentations on: Liquid Purificaton by Ultraviolet Radiation and Its Many Applicaitons; The Utilization of Ultraviolet Radiation for the Co–Generation Industry; Ultraviolet Water Equipment Design and Application; Applying Quality Assurance Concepts to Ensure the Performance of Pharmaceutical High Purity Water Treatment Systems. **Education:** El Camino College, A.A. in Business Administration (1976). **Personal:** Mr. Rodriguez enjoys fishing, boating, sports, and snow skiing.

David E. Sheldon, MBA

Operations Director
Miracle Marketing Mfg. Corp.
3350 S. 275 East St.
Salt Lake City, UT 84115–4520
(801) 487–0417
Fax: (801) 487–0494

3589

Business Information: Miracle Marketing Mfg. Corp. is a manufacturer and marketer of backpack vacuums for commercial use. As Operations Director, Mr. Sheldon is responsible for the coordination of operations with the other functions of the Company, including purchasing, correspondence between companies and manufacturers, monitoring and controlling customer relations, MIS, etc. **Career Steps:** Operations Director, Miracle Marketing Mfg. Corp. (1993–Present); Controller, Chrislow's Department Store (1982–1992); Store Manager, Jones Paint and Glass (1976–1982). **Education:** San Jose State University: M.B.A. (1990), B.S. in Business (1987). **Personal:** Married to Colleen in 1976. Six children: Stephanie, Melanie, Kimberly, Valerie, Jonathan, and Kellie. Mr. Sheldon enjoys camping with his family, geneology, and history.

Mr. Ronald S. Spice

Vice President of Sales
Carl O. Goettsch Company
4300 Carew Tower
Cincinnati, OH 45202
(513) 421–4200
Fax: (513) 421–4494

3589

Business Information: Carl O. Goettsch Company is an export management company of capital machinery for the corrugated box industry. In his capacity as Vice President for Sales, Mr. Spice is responsible for all sales and marketing in Latin America. Established in 1950, Carl O. Goettsch Company employs a full–time staff of 20 and reports annual revenues in excess of $25 million. **Career Steps:** Vice President of Sales, Carl O. Goettsch Company (1984–Present); Territorial Manager, Continental Group (1983–1984); Sales Representative, Union Camp (1979–1983). **Associations & Accomplishments:** Technical Association of Paper and Pulp Industry (TAPPI); Association of Independent Corrugated Converters (AICC); World Trade Association; Cincinnati Chamber of Commerce. **Education:** Indiana University, M.A. (1978); Indiana University, M.A. in Latin American Studies (1975); Indiana University, B.A. with Honors (1973).

Anthony A. Corriero

Senior Engineer
Bosch
P O Box 2488
Sumter, SC 29151
(803) 481–6506
Fax: (803) 481–6072
E MAIL: See Below

3593

Business Information: Bosch is an international manufacturer of OEM products, foundation brakes, and actuation products. Established in 1906, the Company estimates annual revenue of $600 million and presently employs over 900 people at this location. As Senior Engineer, Mr. Corriero, oversees product launch and tracks production, sales, and service from twenty four months prior to production through the first six months the item is on the market. Other responsibilities include staff supervision and strategic planning for the future. Internet users can reach him via: Corriet@summp001.allied.com. **Career Steps:** Senior Engineer, Bosch (1993–Present); Continuous Improvements Manager, ABB (1990–1993); Senior Engineer, Eaton (1985–1989). **Associations & Accomplishments:** Former Board Member, Red Cross of Columbia, South Carolina. **Education:** Rochester Institute of Technology, B.T. in Manufacturing Engineering (1987). **Personal:** Mr. Corriero enjoys refurbishing his half century old home and collecting cars, furniture, and glassware.

Richard A. Brock

Manufacturing Manager – Worldwide
Wolverine (Massachusetts) Corporation
51 E. Main St.
Merrimac, MA 01860
(508) 346–4541
Fax: (508) 346–4213

3599

Business Information: Wolverine (Massachusetts) Corporation is a manufacturer of pollution control equipment and ovens for the cereal industry (Kelloggs, General Mills, etc.), as well as converting industrial dryers. International in scope, Wolverine owns Proctor & Schwartz in North Carolina, an assembly manufacturing facility in the United Kingdom, as well as a subcontracting company. With nineteen years experience in the manufacturing industry, Mr. Brock joined Wolverine in 1988. Serving as Manufacturing Manager – Worldwide, he oversees overall global manufacturing operations, as well as diagnosing and solving problems, maintaining quality, designing work with the Engineering Department, and traveling extensively on behalf of the Company, both internationally and in the states south of Massachusetts. **Career Steps:** Manufacturing Manager – Worldwide, Wolverine (Massachusetts) Corporation (1988–Present); Plant Manager, SWM Ease, Inc. (1987–1988); Buyer, Causeway Ent. Inc.(1976–1980). **Education:** Northern Essex Community College (1990). **Personal:** Married to Sharon in 1978. Two children: Ross Alan and Nichole Elizabeth. Mr. Brock enjoys high performance automobiles.

Sharon M. Cardone, CPA

Chief Financial Officer
Versa–Matic Pump Company
6017 Enterprise Drive
Export, PA 15632
(412) 327–7867
Fax: (412) 327–4300

3599

Business Information: Versa–Matic Pump Company specializes in the manufacture of air–operated double diaphragm pumps utilized in food and chemical industries process applications. An ISO 9001 Certified manufacturer, Versa–Matic markets through world–wide distributors. As Chief Financial Officer, Ms. Cardone is responsible for the overall financial operation of the Company, including strategical and long range planning. **Career Steps:** Versa–Matic Pump Company: Chief Financial Officer (1996–Present), Manager of Finance (1994–1995); Senior Auditor, KPMG (1989–1991). **Associations & Accomplishments:** American Institute of Certified Public Accountants; Pennsylvania Institute of Certified Public Accountants; American Management Association; Society for Human Resource Management; American Production and Inventory Control Society. **Education:** Duquesne University: M.B.A. (1993), B.S.B.A. (1988). **Personal:** Ms. Cardone enjoys being a part–time gymnastics instructor.

Shao Li Chu

Vice President of Asia Pacific Operations
Systems Chemistry Inc.
3901 Burton Drive
Santa Clara, CA 95054
(408) 496–1177 Ext. 114
Fax: (408) 496–1188

3599

Business Information: Systems Chemistry Inc. specializes in the production and manufacturing of specialty chemical industry applications systems, such as automatic bulk chemical distribution, chemical mixing, and chemical generation systems. Established in 1985, Systems Chemistry Inc. reports annual revenue of $45 million. As Vice President of Asia Pacific Operations, Mr. Chu is responsible for sales and marketing of chemical mixing equipment (fully–automated, semi–automated, manual, dry tool equipment for all company equipment) in Asia countries and Asia project operations. **Career Steps:** Systems Chemistry, Inc.: Vice President of Asia Pacific Operations (1993–Present), Vice President of Engineering (1990–1993). **Education:** University of Southern California, M.S. (1983); National Chiao–Tung University, Taiwan, B.S.

Personal: Married to Yen–Yu Cheng in 1983. Two children: Mignon and Michel Chu. Mr. Chu enjoys electronics.

Michael G. Fokken

Executive Vice President
Aaladin Industries
RR 1 Box 2B
Elk Point, SD 57025–9702
(605) 356–3325
Fax: (605) 356–2330

3599

Business Information: Aaladin Industries is a manufacturer of pressure washers, steam cleaners, and environmentally safe parts washers. Established in 1981, the Company employs 89 people, and has an estimated annual revenue of $11 million. As Executive Vice President, Mr. Fokken oversees marketing, sales, and production. He also manages the cleaning systems division of the Company. **Career Steps:** Executive Vice President, Aaladin Industries (1985–Present); Aftermarket Sales Manager, CMI Road King Division (1971–1985); Plant Manager, Revolco, Inc. (1969–1971). **Associations & Accomplishments:** Past Chairman of the South Dakota Industry and Commerce Association; Past Chairman, Southern Union County Development Corporation/Union County Development Corporation; Past Chairman, Community Health Clinic; Past Chairman, Elk Point Commercial Club; Past Mayor, City of Elk Point; Board Member, Clay Union Health Foundation; Author of various newspaper articles. **Education:** Morningside College. **Personal:** Married to Monnie in 1969. Three children: Tricia, Scott, and Andrea. Mr. Fokken enjoys sprint cars, hunting, and golf.

Joel Lynn Godwin

President
Process Design and Fab, Inc.
Highway 74 East, P.O. Box 210
Peachland, NC 28133
(803) 537–7645
Fax: (704) 272–8915

3599

Business Information: Process Design and Fab, Inc., established in 1982, designs and fabricates machinery for the textile industry. As President, Mr. Godwin oversees daily operations, performs design work for new inventions in the textile industry, ensures OSHA standards, and is responsible for varied administrative activities. He is also the President of Process Mechanical Piping & Erection, a mechanical contractor servicing all Fortune 500 companies in the textile industry, and Vice President & Secretary of Anson Machine, a manufacturer of valve parts. **Career Steps:** President, Process Design and Fab, Inc. (1994–Present); President, Process Mechanical Piping (1982–Present); Vice President and Secretary, Anson Machine (1989–Present). **Associations & Accomplishments:** Anson County Development Corporation; Elder, Local Church; Sunday School Teacher; Work with Senior Citizens in Community. **Personal:** Married to Jane B. in 1966. One child: Joel Lynn Jr. Mr. Godwin enjoys fishing and cooking.

Diane Hardekopf

National Sales Manager
Matthiesen Equipment Company
566 North W.W. White Road
San Antonio, TX 78219
(210) 333–1510
Fax: (210) 333–1563

3599

Business Information: Matthiesen Equipment Company specializes in the manufacture of ice handling and processing equipment, including baggers, conveyors, crushers, bins and bag closers. Established in 1945, Mattiesen currently employs 20 people. As National Sales Manager, Ms. Hardekopf is responsible for the general management and administration of the company, as well as marketing strategies such as designing advertisements, brochures and cards. **Career Steps:** National Sales Manager, Matthiesen Equipment Company (1988–Present); Inside Sales Manager, ISSI (1987–1988);

Sales Representative, Starrett Corporation (1982–1987). **Associations & Accomplishments:** Membership Chairperson, Southwestern Ice Association; Mid Atlantic Ice Association; Packaged Ice Association; Southern Ice Exchange; Missouri Valley Ice Association; Western Ice Association; New England Ice Association; Great Lakes Ice Association. **Education:** SWMV, B.S. (1972); Trade Seminars and Continuing Education courses. **Personal:** Ms. Hardekopf enjoys painting, writing, reading, and illustrating.

Marko Koorneef

General Manager/Vice President
TECHNOPLAST International, Inc.
2807 S. 5th Court
Milwaukee, WI 53207
(414) 483–9266
Fax: (414) 483–4810

3599

Business Information: Technoplast International, Inc. is a sales and service office for an Austrian based tool and machine manufacuturer of extruders, calibration tables, pullers and auxiliary equipment for the production of PVC. profiles and complete PVC. windows systems. As General Manager, Mr. Koorneef is responsible for the direction, operation and profitability of the corporation, as well as for the Sales and Marketing. **Career Steps:** General Manager/Vice President, TECHNOPLAST, International, Inc. (1996–); Plant Manager, Bielomatik (1995–1996); General Sales and Marketing Manager, Kiefel Systems Inc. (1990–1995). **Education:** HTS Arnhem (Holland), Masters (1989). **Personal:** Married to Kimberley in 1992. Mr. Koorneef enjoys horseback riding and skiing.

Thomas M. Kurata, P.E.

Manager of International Business Development
Oil Systems Inc.
545 Estudillo Avenue
San Leandro, CA 94577–4640
(510) 297–5846
Fax: (510) 357–8136

3599

Business Information: Oil Systems, Inc. specializes in the development and marketing of the Plant Information (PI) System Software utilized by the refining, chemical, power, pulp and paper, and the food and beverage industries. The System is marketed internationally through trade shows and by word of mouth. Established in 1981, Oil Systems Inc. currently employs 50 people and has an estimated annual revenue of $16 million. As Manager of International Business Development, Mr. Kurata is responsible for identifying and developing sales strategies in Latin America and Asia, as well as following through on the utilization of new systems, from start–up to post–installation services. **Career Steps:** Manager of International Business Development, Oil Systems Inc. (1990–Present); Simulation Services Inc.: Director of Japan Operations (1989–1990), Senior Process Engineer (1988–1989); Systems Engineer, Department of Energy (1983–1986). **Associations & Accomplishments:** Registered Professional Engineer (1994); American Institute of Chemical Engineers; American Chemical Society; Society of Petroleum Engineers; Society of Mining Engineers; Instrument Society of America; Technical Association of Pulp and Paper Industry. **Education:** University of New Mexico, B.S. in Chemical Engineering (1983); University of Kansas, B.A. in Spanish and East Asian Studies (1975); University of California – Berkeley, Certificate in Information Systems. **Personal:** Married to Sachi in 1991. One child: Ken. Mr. Kurata enjoys tennis, fishing, and game hunting.

Mr. Conrado Mangapit Jr.

Marketing Manager, Power Apparatus Group, Industrial Division
Toshiba International Corporation
13131 West Little York Road
Houston, TX 77041–5807
(713) 466–0277
Fax: (713) 466–8773

3599

Business Information: Toshiba International Corporation is a major manufacturer and supplier of a wide variety of motor controlling and power equipment for the North American market. As Marketing Manager, Power Apparatus Group, Industrial Division, Mr. Mangapit is responsible for the Division's North American marketing and product development. The Division has three manufacturing facilities located in Houston, Texas for electric motors, inverter and UPS Systems, and motor control/switchgear products for major customers such as Weyerhauser, Georgia Pacific and Union Carbide. As of January 1, 1995 he was charged with the additional responsibilty as Manager of the Packaging Group. The Packaging Group handles projects involving two or more core products within the industrial division. Established in 1973, Toshiba International Corporation employs over 800 in the Industrial Division. **Career Steps:** Marketing Manager, Power Apparatus Group, Industrial Division, Toshiba International Corporation (1980–Present); Manufacturing Engineer (Electrical), Continental Can Company (1979–1980); Commissioned Officer, U.S. Navy (1969–1979). **Associations & Accomplishments:** Institute of Electrical and Electronics Engineers; Naval Officer's Association; Member, Naval Officer Retention Study conducted by the Chief of Naval Operations, whose recommendations were incorporated into official policies on Affirmative Action, Equal Employment Opportunity, and related Human Resources Regulations. **Education:** University of Southern California, B.S. in Electrical Engineering (1969).

Patrick N. McDonnell

President and Chief Executive Officer
Spectrum Diagnostix
20 New England Business Center
Andover, MA 01810–1022
(508) 686–8801
Fax: (508) 686–8809

3599

Business Information: Spectrum Diagnostix, a wholly-owned subsidiary of Physical Sciences, Inc., specializes in the development and manufacture of process control and emissions instrumentation, primarily lasers and advance electro–optical techniques. Major clientele include petro–chemical companies, refineries, chemical plants, and industrial power and raw material refineries. Established in 1992, Spectrum Diagnostix currently employs 20 people and has an estimated annual revenue of $2 million. As President and Chief Executive Officer, Patrick McDonnell oversees all manufacturing operations and overall Company strategy, reporting directly to the parent company's Board of Directors. A widely–acknowledged small business technology expert, he also provides independent consulting services for small business owners and those wishing to venture in technology–based business. **Career Steps:** President and Chief Executive Officer, Spectrum Diagnostix (1994–Present); Vice President and General Manager, Spire Corporation (1992–1994); Division Manager, TRW Space and Technology (1981–1992). **Associations & Accomplishments:** American Management Association; New England Business Council; Technology Coalition Chair, White House Conference on Small Business; Advisory Board, National Science Foundation; Academy of Technology Innovators; National Coalition of Small Businesses; Published six articles in trade conference publications. **Education:** San Diego State University, B.A. (1979); University of Southern California, Advanced Management School. **Personal:** Married. Mr. McDonnell enjoys golf and technology commercialization.

Gregory T. Novak
Director – Acquisition Support
General Signal
High Ridge Park Box 10010
Stamford, CT 06904
(203) 329–4347
Fax: (203) 329–4250
EMAIL: See Below

3599

Business Information: General Signal is a leading equipment manufacturer for the process control, electrical and industrial technology industries. Established in 1904, General Signal reports annual revenue of $2 billion and currently employs 12,669 people company–wide. As Director of Acquisition Support, Mr. Novak is responsible for establishing a superior process of conducting acquisitions to promote the growth of the Company. Mr. Novak can also be reached through the Internet: GREG.NOVAK@HQ.GENSIG.COM **Career Steps:** Director, General Signal (1995–Present); FMC: Operations Manager (1993–1995), Corporate Consultant (1991–1993); Production Operations Manager, GE Aircraft Engine Factory of the Future (1989–1991). **Associations & Accomplishments:** Mentor, International MBA Development Program; United Way; Young Leadership Club. **Education:** Purdue University – Krannert, M.B.A. (1990); University of Pittsburgh, B.S. in Mechanical Engineering. **Personal:** Married to Cynthia Novak in 1985. Mr. Novak enjoys running, hiking, snow skiing, and golf.

Gerard W. Osborne
Vice President of Energy Marketing
Babcock Materials Handling, Inc.
2365 Pleasantdale Road
Atlanta, GA 30340
(770) 448–6655
Fax: (770) 440 0763

3599

Business Information: Babcock Materials Handling, Inc., a division of Babcock International, is an international manufacturer and distributor of bulk material handling systems and equipment for the electric utility, industrial cogeneration, and pulp & paper industries. Established in 1975, the U.S. operations of Babcock Materials Handling reports annual revenue of $60 million and currently employs 60 people. As Vice President of Energy Marketing, Mr. Osborne is responsible for directing business development and sales & marketing activities related to the power and energy markets in North and South America. **Career Steps:** Vice President of Energy Marketing, Babcock Materials Handling, Inc. (1995–Present); Director of Business Development, Tampella Power Corporation (1989–1995); Director of Marketing, Detroit Integrated Systems (1987–1989); Numerous management and professional positions in Engineering, Sales and Marketing, Manufacturing and International Business (1966–1987). **Associations & Accomplishments:** Rotary International; American Society of Mechanical Engineers; Sales and Marketing Executives Association; Delta Mu Delta National Business Honor Society. **Education:** Ashland University, M.B.A. (1987); Stevens Institute of Technology, B.S. in Engineering (1966). **Personal:** Married to Carolyn in 1978. Three children: David, Brian, and Kevin. Mr. Osborne enjoys church choir, sailing, guitar, trap shooting, and wine making.

Rockne Porter

Managing Director
Tuthill Asia, Ltd.
Room 909–910 Kornhill Metro Tower #1 Kornhill Road
Quarry Bay, Hong Kong
852–2513–7113
Fax: 852–2513–7793

3599

Business Information: Tuthill Asia Ltd. is the Asia subsidiary of Tuthill Corporation. Worldwide, Tuthill has over 20 manufacturing facilities for industrial products. Mr. Porter is responsible for managing Asia, including 85 distributors. **Career Steps:** Managing Director, Tuthill Asia, Ltd. (1990–Present); Marketing Director of Industrial Products, Alcatel Trade International (1987–1989); Marketing Director of Industrial Products, ITT Asia Pacific (1980–1986). **Associations & Accomplishments:** Reserve Officers Association; American Society of Training Directors; Armed Forces Communications Society; American–Japan Society; American Chamber of Commerce – Japan; Published in various journal articles. **Education:** Peabody College, M.A.; Middle Tennessee State University, B.S. **Personal:** Married to Judy in 1974. Mr. Porter enjoys writing on comparative studies of Asian industrial training practices.

Amy J. Reichert
Controller
Berco of America, Inc.
W229 N1420 Westwood Drive
Waukesha, WI 53186
(414) 524–2222
Fax: (414) 524–2230

3599

Business Information: Berco of America, Inc. is a subsidiary of the Italy–based Berco, Inc. National in scope, the Corporation is responsible for U.S. distribution of heavy equipment parts. Established in 1995, the American division employs 19 people, and has an estimated annual revenue of $36 million. As Controller, Ms. Reichart is responsible for all financial and administrative functions, including oversight of daily transactions, budgetary concerns, monthly and quarterly financial reports, and accounts payable and receivable. **Career Steps:** Controller, Berco of America, Inc. (1995–Present); Accounting Manager, Raphael Limited (1988–1994); Payroll Supervisor, N.R.M.I. (1985–1988); Accounts Payable, Pizza Hut District Office (1983–1985). **Associations & Accomplishments:** MRA. **Education:** University of Wisconsin, Stevens Point, B.A. (1983). **Personal:** Married to Paul in 1991. Two children: Jessica and Mitchell. Ms. Reichert enjoys bowling and volleyball.

Charlie W. Sawyer
Vice President
TorqMaster Systems, Inc.
8430 NE Killingsworth
Portland, OR 97220
(503) 254–9292
Fax: (503) 254–5718

3599

Business Information: TorqMaster Systems, Inc. specializes in the manufacture of complex hydraulic systems, particularly large variable speed drives. Established in 1995, TorqMaster reports annual sales of $4 – $5 million. As Vice President, Mr. Sawyer is responsible for all aspects of operations management, including manufacturing, engineering, and OEM sales. **Career Steps:** Vice President, TorqMaster Systems, Inc. (1995–Present); Branch Manager, Fluid–Air Components (1987–1995); Engineering Manager, Vancouver Extrusion Company, ALCOA (1983–1987); Division Mechanical Engineer, ALCOA Aluminum (1981–1983). **Associations & Accomplishments:** American Society of Mechanical Engineering; Oregon, Washington and Arkansas Registered Professional Engineer; National Fluid Power Society; Registered Professional Fluid Power Specialist. **Education:** University of Oregon, M.B.A. (1995); Oregon State University, B.S. in Mechanical Engineering. **Personal:** Married to Debby Kay in 1980. Two children: Jason Charles and Jeffery Lewis. Mr. Sawyer enjoys fishing, baseball and horses.

Diane M. Schleicher

Vice President
Arroyo Process Equipment
1351 State Road 60 West
Mulberry, FL 33860–8571
(941) 425–1145
Fax: (941) 425–2936

3599

Business Information: Arroyo Process Equipment is a job shop fabrication facility, providing industrial equipment repair for equipment utilized in the phosphate, pulp and paper and chemical industries. As Vice President, Mrs. Schleicher has executive responsibility for all financial controls, administrative functions, banking and insurance relations. **Career Steps:** Vice President, Arroyo Process Equipment (1990–Present); Assistant Manager, Lilie Rubin (1988–1990). **Associations & Accomplishments:** St. Petersburg Yacht Club. **Education:** International School of Merchandising and Design, A.A. (1988); Dale Carnegie Management Seminar. **Personal:** Married to Kurt in 1993. Two children: Madison and Ariel Schleicher. Mrs. Schleicher enjoys billards, boating, travel, and spending time with her family.

3600 Electronic and Other Electric Equipment

3612 Transformers, except electronic
3613 Switchgear and switchboard apparatus
3621 Motors and generators
3624 Carbon and graphite products
3625 Relays and industrial controls
3629 Electrical industrial apparatus, NEC
3631 Household cooking equipment
3632 Household refrigerators and freezers
3633 Household laundry equipment
3634 Electric housewares and fans
3635 Household vacuum cleaners
3639 Household appliances, NEC
3641 Electric lamps
3643 Current–carrying wiring devices
3644 Noncurrent–carrying wiring devices
3645 Residential lighting fixtures
3646 Commercial lighting fixtures
3647 Vehicular lighting equipment
3648 Lighting equipment, NEC
3651 Household audio and video equipment
3642 Prerecorded records and tapes
3661 Telephone and telegraph apparatus
3663 Radio and TV communications equipment
3669 Communications equipment, NEC
3671 Electron tubes
3672 Printed circuit boards
3674 Semiconductors and related devices
3675 Electronic capacitors

3676 Electronic resistors
3677 Electronic coils and transformers
3678 Electronic conNECtors
3679 Electronic components, NEC
3691 Storage batteries
3692 Primary batteries, dry and wet
3694 Engine electrical equipment
3695 Magnetic and optical recording media
3699 Electrical equipment and supplies, NEC

Sakher Al Shara

Director/President
Ts Shara Tecn De Sist Ltda
R. Do Curtume, 274
Sao Paulo, Brazil 05065–001
55–11–861–0011
Fax: 55–11–861–0011
EMAIL: See Below

3612

Business Information: Ts Shara Tecn De Sist Ltda manufactures low potential energy components such as voltage regulators, and UPs. As Director/President, Mr. Al Shara oversees the financial and administrative duties of the Company. Internet users can reach him via: tsshara@tecepe.com.br. **Career Steps:** Director/President, Ts Shara Tecn De Sist Ltda (1990–Present); Engineering Supervisor, Military House United (1987–1989); Software Engineer, Digital (1989–1990). **Education:** University of Sao Paulo, M.B.A. (1994/96); University of Paris, Electronics Master Degree; University of Damascus, Electronics. **Personal:** Married to Tania Chofi in 1990. One child: Rodolfo. Mr. Al Shara enjoys being a pilot.

Edward R. Leininger

Vice President and General Manager
GSE Inc.
23640 Research Drive
Farmington Hills, MI 48335
(810) 476–7875
Fax: (810) 476–7249

3612

Business Information: GSE Inc. specializes in the production and distribution of diversified industrial electrical components, consisting of three divisions: Measurement Control Devices; Electric Weighing and Scale Devices; and Electric Hand Tools. Joining GSE in 1972 as an Applications Engineer, Mr. Leininger has consistently moved up the corporate ladder, attaining the position as Vice President and General Manager of the Measurements and Controls Division in 1993. This Division manufactures electric transducers and torque measurement devices utilized in diversified automotive and transportation industrial applications. Mr. Leininger has full executive responsibility for all profit & loss encompassing two manufacturing facilities in Detroit, 13 U.S. sales locations and 11 global satellite sales operations. His duties involve the oversight of all sales, service, marketing and engineering sectors. **Career Steps:** GSE Inc.: Vice President and General Manager (1993–Present), International Sales Manager (1990–1993), National Sales Manager (1987–1990), Applications Engineer (1972–1987); Engineer, NACO Electric (1969–1971); Engineer, General Electric (1968–1969). **Associations & Accomplishments:** Society of Manufacturing Engineers; American Society of Quality Control; JCI Senate; Former Mayor Protem and Councilman, City of Novi; Boy Scouts of America; Parks & Recreation Commissioner; County Solid Waste Delegate; Novi Yacht Club; Rotary International. **Education:** Michigan State University; Syracuse University; RETS Eng. School. **Personal:** Married to Mary Jane in 1968. Three children: Jeffrey, Christopher, and Elizabeth. Mr. Leininger enjoys golf, volleyball, boating, travel, dancing, and softball.

John C. Gardner, P.E.

Director of Operations
Curlee Manufacturing Company
13639 Aldine Westfield
Houston, TX 77039–3007
(713) 449–6271
Fax: (713) 449–4760

3613

Business Information: Curlee Manufacturing Company is an international manufacturer of electrical switchgear for use in hazardous (classified) locations. With eighteen years of experience in the manufacturing industry and a Professional Engineer licensed in the State of Texas, Mr. Gardner joined Curlee Manufacturing Company as Manager of Engineering in 1990. Appointed as Director of Operations in 1995, he is responsible for the overall day–to–day operations, with duties including accounting, sales, human resources, administra-

tion, in addition to managing shipping operations and overseeing all support staff. **Career Steps:** Curlee Manufacturing Company: Director of Operations (1995–Present), Manager of Engineering (1990–1995); Thermon Manufacturing: Project Manager (1989–1990), Product Development Manager (1978–1989). **Associations & Accomplishments:** Professional Engineer in State of Texas; Institute of Electrical and Electronics Engineers; Instrument Society of America. **Education:** Texas A&I University, B.S.E.E. (1994). **Personal:** Married to Karen McPhail in 1980. Mr. Gardner enjoys music and travel.

Robert P. McAlpine

Senior Vice President of Sales & Marketing
Pesa Switching Systems, Inc.
35 Pinelawn Road, Suite 99E
Melville, NY 11747–3111
(516) 845–5020
Fax: (516) 845–5023

3613

Business Information: Pesa Switching Systems, Inc. is a privately owned video, audio, and data equipment wholesaler and manufacturer, specializing in switching equipment. Acquired from the 3M Company in 1990, Pesa Switching is international in scope and employs 66 people. As Senior Vice President of Sales & Marketing, Mr. McAlpine is responsible for all marketing decisions for the Company, overseeing growth and strategic planning, as well as marketing, and sales. A member of the Company for six years, he is responsible for eight direct sales managers, forty two dealers, and two rep firms. **Career Steps:** Pesa Switching Systems, Inc: Senior Vice President of Sales & Marketing (1992–Present), National Sales Manager (1990–1992); Eastern Regional Sales, 3M Company (1988–1990). **Associations & Accomplishments:** Society of Motion Picture & Television Engineers (SMPTE); Society of Broadcast Engineers (SBE). **Education:** Polytechnic University, B.S.E.E. (1988); Suffolk Community College: A.A. in Engineering, A.A. in Liberal Arts. **Personal:** Married to Patricia Helgesen in 1982. Four children: Jessica, Robert, Michael, and Meghan. Mr. McAlpine enjoys scuba, sailing, and being a Little League Coach.

John R. McCallum, C.P.M.

Senior Buyer
Siemens Energy
7000 Siemens Road
Wendell, NC 27591
(919) 365–2234
Fax: (919) 365–2255

3613

Business Information: Siemens Energy is primarily engaged in the manufacture of switchgears, specifically for the power industry. Established in 1978, the Company employs 750 people, and has an estimated annual revenue of $150 million. As Senior Buyer, Mr. McCallum is responsible for the Manual Requirements Purchasing System (MRPS), and oversees the purchase of raw materials such as copper, steel, and electrical components, and ensuring the cost effectiveness of all materials purchased. **Career Steps:** Senior Buyer, Siemens Energy (1996–Present); Senior Buyer, American Sterilizer (1990–1996); Purchasing Manager, Rexnard/Thomas Coupling (1987–1990). **Associations & Accomplishments:** American Purchasing Society. **Education:** New Castle Business, Associates (1971). **Personal:** Married to Julia A. in 1972. Three children: Nicholas J., Elissa A., and Matthew W.. Mr. McCallum enjoys golf, coin collecting, and gardening.

Otto DeMuth

Director of Sales and Marketing
Dumore Corporation
1030 Veterans Street
Mauston, WI 53948–9314
(608) 847–6420
Fax: (800) 338–6673

3621

Business Information: Dumore Corporation specializes in the production of industrial electrical motors and hand tools, distributing directly to OEM's, as well as the international wholesale market through distributors. Established in 1910, the Mauston, Wisconsin headquarters employs a staff of 204, and reports overall corporate earnings in excess of $18 million. Joining Dumore in 1992 as a regional sales manager for the Motor Division, he was appointed Director of Sales and Marketing in 1994. He has full executive oversight for all engineering development, sales and marketing strategies, and staff supervision for both corporate divisions (hand tools, motors). **Career Steps:** Dumore Corporation: Director of Sales and Marketing (1994–Present), Regional Sales Manager (1992–1994); Vice President of Sales, Lesson Fleet (1989–1992); President, Motronics Corporation (1987–1989). **Associations & Accomplishments:** Small Motor Manufacturing Association; Chamber of Commerce. **Education:** Herkimer Community College, A.A. (1974). **Per-**

sonal: Mr. DeMuth enjoys golf, bowling, and spending time with his family.

Julia A. Fraser

Vice President of Market Strategy
Berclain Group Inc.
P.O. Box 292
Cummaquid, MA 02637–0292
(508) 362–3480
Fax: (508) 362–4162

3621

Business Information: Berclain Group Inc. is a manufacturer of synchronized mechanisms for the manufacturing industry. Services include detailed manufacturing schedulings of all resources. Headquartered in Quebec City, Canada, Berclain Group Inc. was established in 1986. Joining the Berclain Group Inc. in 1995, Ms. Fraser has the unique opportunity to work in her home in the capacity of Company Vice President of Marketing Strategy and Spokesperson. She spends most of her time conducting business on the Internet, through the use of three computers, and the telephone. Her responsibility is to ensure that the Company and the products serve the manufacturing community well. **Career Steps:** Vice President of Market Strategy, Berclain Group Inc. (1995–Present); Senior Industry Analyst, Advanced Manufacturing Research (1991–1995); Editor of CIM Strategies, Cutler Information Corp. (1985–1991); Senior Editor of Digital Design, Morgan-Grampian (1983–1985). **Associations & Accomplishments:** American Production and Inventory Control Society; Society of Manufacturing Engineers; Computer and Automated Systems Association. **Education:** Lawrence University, B.A. (1980). **Personal:** Married to Robert G. in 1990. Ms. Fraser enjoys needlepoint, tennis, jogging, exercising, scuba diving, and bird watching.

Ms. Nancy C. Mohn

Director of Commercial Analysis
ABB Global Boiler Business Area
2000 Day Hill Road
Windsor, CT 06095
(860) 285–5748
Fax: (860) 285–4900

3621

Business Information: ABB's Boiler Business Area ia a division of Swiss–based global industrial equipment conglomerate, Asea Brown Boveri. The Windsor, CT, facility is the headquarters for engineering and fabrication of electric power plant equipment for utilities, independent power producers, and industrial companies worldwide. As Director of Commercial Analysis, Ms. Mohn is responsible for the management of marketing functions for the boiler business. ABB employs over 200,000 people worldwide. Annual revenue is reported in excess of $30 billion, with over $10 billion in revenues from the power generation segment. **Career Steps:** ABB Boiler Business: Director of Commercial Analysis, (1995–Present), Director of Sales Analysis (1990–1995); Combustion Engineering (now ABB): Director of Strategic Planning (1985–1990), Marketing Manager (1983–1985), Supervisor of Chemical Systems (1979–1983), Product Development Engineer (1975–1979). **Associations & Accomplishments:** Leonhard Center Advisory Board, Penn State University; Advisory Board, Hartford College for Women; Women's Executive Committee, Hartford Chamber of Commerce. **Education:** University of Connecticut, M.B.A. (1982); University of Wisconsin, M.S. in Civil and Environmental Engineering; Penn State University, B.S. in Civil Engineering **Personal:** Married to Robert Keen in 1976. Ms. Mohn enjoys sailing, cross country skiing, and working with volunteer organizations including Habitat for Humanity.

Bill Shepherd

President
FASCO Industries, Ozark Division
1600 West Jackson Street
Ozark, MO 65721–9156
(417) 485–2311
Fax: (417) 485–6512

3621

Business Information: FASCO Industries, Ozark Division is a manufacturer of electrical motors for original equipment manufacturers (i.e., heating, air conditioners, pumps, etc). The Company produces 22–25 thousand motors a day. As President, Mr. Shepherd is responsible for all aspects of Company operations, including administration, finance, sales and marketing, and strategic planning. **Career Steps:** President, FASCO Industries, Ozark Division (1994–Present); Magnetek: Vice President/Managing Director, Budapest, Hungary (1992–194), Vice President/Director, GmbH, Germany (1989–1991), Vice President/General Manager, IHP Business Unit, St. Louis (1983–1989). **Associations & Accomplishments:** Chamber of Commerce; Small Motor Manufacturing

Association; The Presidents Club (1995). **Education:** University of Missouri, M.B.A. (1970). **Personal:** Married to Carole in 1988. Two children: Mellissa and Sarah. Mr. Shepherd enjoys sailing, golf, and skiing.

Mr. Robert L. Silvernell

Advanced Manufacturing Engineer
General Electric
1600 Industrial Parkway
Mebane, NC 27258
(919) 563–7346
Fax: Please mail or call

3621

Business Information: General Electric is the world's leading producer and distributor of industrial and consumer electrical and electronic products. General Electric's Mebane, North Carolina facility specializes in the production of electric motor and control assemblies utilized in electric vehicle applications (e.g., forklifts, golf carts, electric passenger vehicles). As Advanced Manufacturing Engineer, Mr. Silvernell is the senior engineer responsible for the design and implementation of new products and technological advances. **Career Steps:** Advanced Manufacturing Engineer, General Electric (1993–Present); Manager of Consolidation, General Electric, Caribe and Puerto Rico (1983–1993); Manufacturing Engineer, General Electric, Shreveport, LA (1979–1983). **Associations & Accomplishments:** Elfun Society; Society of Plastics Engineers; Adult Supervisor, Junior Achievement. **Personal:** Married to Carol in 1961. Two children: Debra Lynn and Dale Kevin; four grandchildren. Mr. Silvernell enjoys the restoring and collection of classic cars, and is also an avid bass fisherman.

Robert R. White Jr.

Industry Marketing Manager
Kollmorgen Motion Technologies Group
201 Rock Road
Radford, VA 24141
(540) 633–4129
Fax: (540) 731–0847

3621

Business Information: Kollmorgen Motion Technologies Group is a manufacturer of motion control products, including servo motors & drives, spindle motors & drives, specialty motors, steppers, and linear motors. Headquartered in Massachusetts, Kollmorgen Motion Technologies Group conducts business internationally. With fifteen years experience in marketing, Mr. White joined Kollmorgen Motion Technologies Group in 1981 and was appointed as Industry Marketing Manager in 1993. He is responsible for conducting research to direct the Company as to what products and services are needed in the industry, as well as overseeing the industry marketing activity. **Career Steps:** Kollmorgen Motion Technologies Group: Industry Marketing Manager (1991–Present), Western Region Manager (1988–1991), Advanced Systems Manager (1984–1988), Applications Engineer (1981–1984). **Associations & Accomplishments:** Volunteer Photographer, Marching Virginians; Kappa Kappa Psi – Honorary Band Fraternity. **Education:** Virginia Tech, B.S. in Electrical Engineering (1981). **Personal:** Married to Bonnie Maccubbin in 1982. Two children: Taylor and Mac. Mr. White enjoys photography, music, volleyball, hiking and camping.

Michelle H. Wooldridge

Director of Human Resources
Carbone of America
P.O. Box M – RT 15 460 W
Farmville, VA 23901–0276
(804) 395–8258
Fax: (804) 395–8206

3624

Business Information: Carbone of America is an electrical manufacturer of carbon brushes for electric motors in cars and trucks. Established in 1896, the Company employs 400 people and has an estimated annual revenue of $35 million. As Director of Human Resources, Ms. Wooldridge is responsible for recruiting and staffing, wage and salary administration, and affirmative action. She also oversees safety, security, public relations, corporate donations, training, employee counseling and assistance program administration, employee services and benefits administration, manpower planning, timekeeping, and payroll organization. **Career Steps:** Director of Human Resources, Carbone of America (1989–Present); Region Personnel Manager, Pizza Hut of America, Inc. (1985–1988); Heublin, Inc: Corporate Manager, Staffing (1982), Corporate Manager, Human Resources (1982–1983), Corporate Director, Human Resources (1983–1985); Phillip Morris, U.S.A.: Production Supervisor/Management Trainee (1977–1978), Manpower Supervisor (1977–1978), Non–Exempt Recruiter (1978), Supervisor, Hourly Department (1978), Senior Recruiter (1978–1979), Employee Relations Generalist (1979–1982). **Associations & Accomplishments:** Board of Directors, Fuqua School; Business Partnership Team Chair, Prince Edward County, VA Schools; Co–Chair, Employment Advisory Council; Co–Chair, Region Literacy Council; Adjunct Professor, Southside Virginia Community College; Board of Directors, Urban League of Greater Hartford and Atlanta; American Society for Personnel Administration; Employment Management Association; Who's Who in American Business; Outstanding Young Women in America Award; Youth Motivation Service Award; Black Achievers Award. **Education:** Yale University, B.A. in Sociology and African American Studies (1976). **Personal:** Married to Farley in 1990. Four children: Ashley, Justin, Lorna, and Farley II. Ms. Wooldridge enjoys spending time with family and participating in their sports and activities.

Frank Collette III

Network and Computer Operations Manager
Siemens Energy and Automation
444 Highway 19 South
Richland, MS 39218
(601) 936–9146
Fax: (601) 932–9961
EMAIL: See Below

3625

Business Information: Siemens Energy and Automation is a manufacturer of breakers and regulators for utilities. As Network and Computer Operations Manager, Mr. Collette is responsible for the administration, public relations, and strategic planning for network and computer operations. Concurrently, he owns his own computer business called, MICRO4000, Inc., in which he sells computers and associated software. Internet users can reach him via: frank@tec/ink.net **Career Steps:** Network and Computer Operations Manager, Siemens Energy and Automation (1989–Present); Data Processing Manager, Southern Crop Inc. Agency (1983–1988); Warehouse Clerk, Shell Oil Company (1982–1983). **Education:** Attended: Milsaps College, Mississippi State, Hinds Junior College and Phillips College. **Personal:** Married to Tereese in 1980. Three children: Frank IV, Christopher and Daniel. Mr. Collette enjoys fishing and skiing.

Leif P. Nygaard

Financial Manager
Johnson Controls
1701 West Civic Drive A7
Milwaukee, WI 53209–4433
(414) 228–3626
Fax: (414) 228–3675

3625

Business Information: Established in 1885, Johnson Controls is an international manufacturing corporation with four divisions: Batteries (car batteries), Plastics (bottles), Automotive (car seats), and Controls (automation controls). Mr. Nygaard has served in various senior administrative positions with the Company since 1990. Promoted to Financial Manager in early 1994, he is currently responsible for financial analysis, general controller activities, oversight of sales operations, and installation and service of commercial building heating and temperature control devices. **Career Steps:** Johnson Controls: Financial Manager (1994–Present), Senior Financial Analyst (1993); Senior Financial Auditor (1990–1993). **Associations & Accomplishments:** American Institute of Certified Public Accountants; Wisconsin Institute of Certified Public Accountants. **Education:** University of Wisconsin – Milwaukee, M.S. in Finance (1988); Marquette University, B.S. in Accounting. **Personal:** Married to Tracie in 1988. Two children: Britt and Nathaniel. Mr. Nygaard enjoys golf, camping and church activities.

Dan G. Reshel

Director of District Sales
Allen Bradles Company
1201 South 2nd Street
Milwaukee, WI 53204
(414) 382–3534
Fax: (414) 382–3970

3625

Business Information: Allen Bradles Company manufactures automation controls and software, providing systems solutions for the automotive industry by enabling them to program machinery for repetitive tasks. International in scope, the Company plans on expanding their overseas market, becoming second in Europe, and third or fourth in Asia. As Director of District Sales, Mr. Reshel handles all human resource duties. He is responsible for writing all authorizations for the Company, as well as overseeing annual evaluations, employee performance, and trade procedures. **Career Steps:** Allen Bradles Company: Director of District Sales (1994–Present); Sales Engineer (1985–1994). **Associations & Accomplishments:** National Association of Electrical Distributors; NAW. **Education:** University of Wisconsin, Mechanical Engineering (1983). **Personal:** Married to Lynn Vice in 1983. Two children: Max and Leann. Mr. Reshel enjoys reading, history, coaching soccer, and swimming.

Dominick L. Chiumento

Plant Manager
Ecolaire Corporation
1550 Lehigh Drive
Easton, PA 18042
(610) 260–1064
Fax: (610) 250–1071

3629

Business Information: Ecolaire Corporation is a manufacturer of surface condensers, dampers and related heat transfer products for the utility industry. International in scope, Ecolaire Corporation operates a plant in Pennsylvania, and has affiliated engineering groups in Europe. As Plant Manager, Mr. Chiumento is responsible for the management of all plant activities, including manufacturing, plant engineering, and conducting capability evaluations in selected plants worldwide. He is currently involved in a feasibility study to open a plant in China. **Career Steps:** Plant Manager, Ecolaire Corporation (1993–Present); President/Owner, Chiumento Development, Inc. (1991–1993); Foster Wheeler Energy Corporation: Plant Superintendent (1987–1991); Manager Plate &Tubular Products (1985–1987). **Education:** S.U.N.Y., Alfred; Florida State; Canal Zone College. **Personal:** Two children: Dominick Jr. and Julie Ann. Mr. Chiumento enjoys golf and boating.

Stephen G. Szychowski, Ph.D

Human Resources Manager
Cooper Power Systems/Transformer Products
1900 North Street
Waukesha, WI 53188–3844
(414) 524–4389
Fax: (414) 524–4344

3629

Business Information: Cooper Power Systems is a manufacturer of equipment for electrical transmission and distribution systems. As Human Resources Manager, Dr. Szychowski directs and coordinates activities related to planning, development, and implementation of policies, programs, and practices in support of ER for six plants. **Career Steps:** Human Resources Manager, Cooper Power Systems/Transformer Products (1995–Present); Manager of Employee Relations, Cooper Hand Tools – Sumter, SC (1992–1995); Manager of Labor Relations, Cooper Energy Services – Springfield, OH (1988–1992); Manager of Personnel, Doehler–Jarvis – Toledo, OH/Greeneville, TN (1973–1988). **Associations & Accomplishments:** Society of Human Resource Managers; American Society of Safety Engineers; Board Member, National Association for the Advancement of Colored People – Freedom Fund. **Education:** Central University, Ph.D (1993); University of Toledo: Ed.S. (1989), M.Ed. (1980), B.S. (1976). **Personal:** Dr. Szychowski enjoys being a football official for college and high school games.

Avi Valik

Trade Division Manager
Herouth LTD
31 Hamerkava Street
Holon, Israel 58851
9723–557–1190
Fax: 9723–556–9269

3629

Business Information: Herouth LTD provides electromechanical services for the commercial and industrial industries in Israel. Established in 1917, the Company employs 830 people and has estimated annual revenue of $100 million. As Trade Division Manager, Mr. Valik oversees the day–to–day management of the division. His duties include human resources, finance, and administration. **Career Steps:** Trade Division Manager, Herouth LTD (Present). **Education:** Reknati, B.S., Tel Aviv, M.B.A. (1976). **Personal:** Married in 1972. Two children: Gilad and Michal. Mr. Valik enjoys spending time with his family.

Felipe E. Wallace

Unit Manager
Chamberlain Group, Inc.
Carretera Luis Donaldo Colosio Kilometer 4–1/2
Nogales, Sonora, Mexico 84000
(520) 761–5458
Fax: (520) 761–5404

3634

Business Information: Chamberlain Group, Inc. is a manufacturer of automatic garage door openers. As Unit Manager of the Motor Area, Mr. Wallace is responsible for staff supervision, departmental direction, and varied administrative activities. **Career Steps:** Unit Manager, Chamberlain Group, Inc. (1989–Present); Operations Unit Manager, General Motors of Mexico (1980–1989); Quality Control Manager, Electro Partes de Matamoros (Zenith) (1976–1980); General Manager, Bolgar Enterprises de Mexico (1972–1980); Teacher, Universidad Autonoma Del Noroeste; Over 30 years experience in manufacturing. **Associations & Accomplishments:** President, Desarrollo Empresarial Mexicano (Junior Achievement) – Saltillo, Mexico; Service Director, Club Rotario Internacional – Saltillo, Mexico; Who's Who in Mexico (1987); APICS member since 1992, Actual President: Ambos Nogales Chapter. **Education:** Universidad Autonoma de Mexico, Physics (1964); I.T.T. – Germany. **Personal:** Married to Elvira. Three children: Ivan, Veronica, and Patricia. Mr. Wallace enjoys Born in Mexico City in 1940. Mr Wallace is bilingual Spanish/English.

Robert L. Ottobre

Product Manager
Leybold Vacuum Products
5700 Mellon Rd.
Export, PA 15632
(412) 325–6516
Fax: (412) 723–1217
EMAIL: See Below

3635

Business Information: Leybold Vacuum Products is a manufacturer of vacuum and vacuum–related equipment for a variety of different industries. In addition, Leybold manufactures dry compression pumps for the semiconductor industry. In his capacity, Mr. Ottobre is a worldwide product manager for Leybold's Dryvac (dry compression pump), which is used primarily in the manufacturing and processing of semiconductor wafers. Internet users can reach him via: 102730,3635@compuserve.com **Career Steps:** Leybold Vacuum Products: Product Manager – Pittsburgh (1994–Present), Sales Engineer – Los Angeles (1990–1994), Field Supervisor – Pittsburgh (1989–1990). **Associations & Accomplishments:** Institute of Electronics and Electrical Engineers; American Vacuum Society; East Hills Pitt Club; University of Pittsburgh Alumni Club. **Education:** University of Pittsburgh: B.S. in Electrical Engineering, Currently enrolled at the Katz Graduate School to obtain his Executive M.B.A. to be completed in 1997. **Personal:** Mr. Ottobre enjoys working out, golf and is an enthusiastic sports fan.

J. Husseini

Vice President
The Singer Company
4500 Singer Road
Murfreesboro, TN 37129–2913
(615) 893–6493
Fax: (203) 254–2755

3639

Business Information: Established in 1851, The Singer Company is one of the leading manufacturers, distributers and marketers of household and commercial electronic components, internationally famous for their industrial and household sewing machines and vacuum cleaners. As Vice President, Mr. Husseini is responsible for all aspects of manufacturing and distribution of Singer industrial products in North America. **Career Steps:** The Singer Company: Vice President (1986–Present), Director (1983–1986); Managing Director, Singer– Mid East Africa (1959–1983). **Education:** U.B.H. – Los Angeles, CA, M.B.A. (1986); Columbia University, International Program for Business Executives (1979). **Personal:** Married to Lamia in 1962. Two children: Mounier and Maher. Mr. Husseini enjoys tennis, golf, gardening and swimming.

Lee Propst

Regional Service Manager
Maytag
1611 Downing Drive
Lebanon, OR 97355
(503) 258–3833
Fax: (503) 258–5413

3639

Business Information: Maytag Corporation is an international manufacturer of home appliances, and is best known for their washers and dryers. Established in the 1890's, the Company reports an annual revenue of $5 billion and currently employs 23,000 people worldwide. As Regional Service Manager, Mr. Propst is responsible for the supervision of service operations in the Western United States and Canada, including 18 states and 4 provinces. He is also responsible for 10 district manager's reports. **Career Steps:** Maytag Corporation: Regional Service Manager (1988–Present), District Service Manager (1980–1988); Owner and President, Capital Refrigeration and Appliance, Inc. (1968–1980). **Associations & Accomplishments:** Refrigeration Service Engineers Society; Optimist Club; Scouting Leader, Boy Scouts of America. **Education:** San Jose State University, A.A. (1967); Continuing Education Courses, various schools and locations. **Personal:** Married to Mary in 1958. Five children: Deanna, Denise, Lisa, Amy and Andrew. Mr. Propst enjoys hunting, fishing, golf, softball and Scouting.

Sergio Varela

Vice President of Sales
Anaheim Manufacturing Co.
P.O. Box 4146
Anaheim, CA 92803–4146
(714) 524–7770
Fax: (714) 996–7073

3639

Business Information: Anaheim Manufacturing Co. is a manufacturer of garbage disposals. A fourteen–year veteran of the Company, Mr. Varela joined Anaheim Manufacturing Company in 1981. As Vice President of Sales and Part–Owner, he directs all sales and marketing operations, including the supervision of regional sales management staff, and overall strategies planning. **Career Steps:** Vice President of Sales, Anaheim Manufacturing Co. (1981–Present). **Associations & Accomplishments:** Building Industry Association; National Association of Plumbing – Heating – Cooling Contractors; National Council of Home Builders; National Apartment Association. **Personal:** Married to Anna in 1974. Two children: Andrea and Sergio, Jr. Mr. Varela enjoys golf, travel, and trying new French food restaurants.

Kent F. Wolfe

Quality Assurance Manager
Maytag–Jackson
2500 Doctor F.E. Wright Road
Jackson, IN 38305
(901) 424–3500
Fax: Please mail or call

3639

Business Information: Maytag–Jackson is a division of the Maytag Corporation an international manufacturer of home appliances, and is best known for their washers and dryers. Established in the 1992, the Jackson division employs 600 people, and has an estimated annual revenue of $250 million. As Quality Assurance Manager, Mr. Wolfe coordinates the functions of two teams that are involved in ensuring quality (one engineering team, and one receiving inspection team). He is also responsible for representing issues involving quality assurance, and is involved in plant direction, strategy, and training coordination. **Career Steps:** Maytag: Quality Assurance Manager, Jackson (1992–Present), Project Engineer (1990–1992), Quality Engineer (1988–1990), Reliability Engineer (1986–1988). **Associations & Accomplishments:** Workforce 2000; American Society for Quality Control. **Education:** Drake University, M.B.A. (1990); Kansas State, B.S. in Mechanical Engineering. **Personal:** Married to J. Diane in 1988. Three children: Ashley, Anna, and Grant. Mr. Wolfe enjoys golf, tennis, and basketball.

Katherine L. Johnson

Training Director
Lamps Plus
20250 Plummer Street
Chatsworth, CA 91311–5449
(818) 886–5267 Ext. 230
Fax: (818) 886–1011

3641

Business Information: Lamps Plus is a privately–owned national company based in Chatsworth, California. Established in 1976 by Mr. Dennis Swanson, the Company has thirty seven retail stores in five western states. Lamps Plus established and owns Pacific Coast Lighting Manufacturing and Centennial Contract Division. Lamps Plus is the World's Largest Lighting Manufacturer. Training Director, Katherine Johnson is responsible for the Training Department, which includes training sales staff, store office staff, computer register, and manager development. She develops and writes all training manuals and training material, plus she is editor of the Company newsletter. **Career Steps:** Training Director, Lamps Plus (1993–Present); Franchise Consultant, Supercuts (1986–1990); District Sales Manager, Avon (1981–1996). **Associations & Accomplishments:** Exchange Club; Toastmasters; Chamber of Commerce; Community College Instructor, and Is Published. **Education:** University of Michigan, Psychology (1982); Washtenaw Community College, Communications (1978). **Personal:** Married to Edmund in 1992. Three children: Stephen, Ben, and Michael. Ms. Johnson enjoys writing, travel, sailing, painting, and horseback riding.

Brian K. Kenyon

Purchasing Manager
Philips Lighting Company
P O Box 6800
Somerset, NJ 08875–6800
(908) 563–3038
Fax: (908) 788–6018

3641

Business Information: Philips Lighting Company is the number one manufacturer of lighting products in the world, and second in the U.S. International in scope, the Company is headquartered in Holland, and has twenty–nine divisions located throughout the world. Established in 1891, Philips Lighting Company employs 30,000 people, and has an estimated annual revenue of $750 million. As Purchasing Manager, Mr. Kenyon is responsible for purchasing non–bom and other raw materials. He also oversees coordination of ten manufacturing locations in the U.S., and is directly responsible for ten purchasing managers. **Career Steps:** Philips Lighting Company: Purchasing Manager (1988–Present), Purchasing Agent (1987–1988); Purchasing Agent, Rexham Corporation (1982–1987); Buyer, American Cyanamid Company (1978–1982). **Associations & Accomplishments:** National Association of Purchasing Management. **Education:** Upses College, B.A. Business Administration (1977); C.P.M., Purchasing Management Association. **Personal:** Married to Barbara in 1981. Nine children: Sunni, Ian, Joshua, Heather, Jessica, Rachel, Jeremiah, Samuel, and Jennifer. Mr. Kenyon enjoys water skiing, snow skiing, Aikido, horseback riding, astronomy, and his two horses received through the Standard Breed Foundation.

Debra Capua

Manager of Employee Communications
Philips Electronics North America
100 E. 42nd Street
New York, NY 10017–5613
(212) 850–5376
Fax: (212) 850–7350

3643

Business Information: Philips Electronics North America is a major international design manufacturer and marketer of high–tech products, including semiconductors, diversified components, consumer electronics and software. Philips consists of 25 divisions in several locations. Joining Philips as Manager of Employee Communications in 1995, Ms. Capua is responsible for employee communications for 30,000 employees in North America, including Company newsletters and benefits communications. Concurrent with her position at Philips, she serves as an Adjunct Instructor at St. John's University, teaching communications, speech, and English undergraduate courses. **Career Steps:** Manager of Employee Communications, Philips Electronics North America (1995–Present); Adjunct Instructor, St. John's University (1987–Present); Manager of Employee Communications, Home Insurance (1994–1995); Communications and Public Relations Manager, D'Arcy Masius Benton & Bowles (1992–1994); Editor, Tambrands (1988–1991). **Associations & Accomplishments:** International Association of Business Communications **Education:** St. John's University Graduate School of Arts & Sciences, M.A. (1983); St. Vincent's College of St. John's University, B.S. (1980). **Personal:** Married to Alan Danulevith in 1980.

William S. Ford

President and Chief Executive Officer
Ford Wire & Cable Corporation
P.O. Box 1299
Roseland, FL 32957–1299
(407) 388–3660
Fax: (407) 388–3698

3643

Business Information: Ford Wire & Cable Corporation is a national manufacturer and distributor of electrical wire. Products are distributed through agents and OEM's to electrical wholesalers and air conditioning, heating, and irrigation companies. Established in 1986, Ford Wire & Cable Corporation reports annual revenue of $6 million and currently employs 35 people. With thirty–one years in the manufacturing industry, Mr. Ford founded the Company in 1986. Serving as President and Chief Executive Officer, he is responsible for all aspects of operations, including administration, finances, sales, public relations, accounting, marketing, and strategic planning. **Career Steps:** President and Chief Executive Officer, Ford Wire & Cable Corporation (1986–Present); President and Chief Executive Officer, State Wire & Cable Corporation (1974–1985); President, AA Equipment, Inc. (1964–1974). **Associations & Accomplishments:** Florida Aero Club. **Education:** Holyoke Junior College, A.A. (1951). **Personal:** Married to Charlotte in 1951. Four children: Deborah, Laurie, Dale, and Stephan. Mr. Ford enjoys flying and rebuilding antique and classic aircraft.

Anthony M. Oh
Vice President of Marketing and Sales
Phelps Dodge High Performance Conductors
1570 Campton Road, P.O. Box 508
Inman, SC 29349–0508
(864) 472–0405
Fax: (864) 472–3381

3643

Business Information: Phelps Dodge High Performance Conductors (PDHPC) is a manufacturing establishment specializing in the production of conductors for aerospace, electronics, computers, medical, and automotive markets. A global leader in the wire cable industry, the Company was established in 1902 (formerly known as Hudson International Conductors). PDHPC employs over 1,000 associates and has an estimated annual revenue of $160 million. As Vice President of Marketing and Sales, Mr. Oh is responsible for the strategic positioning of the Company in the global marketplace through joint ventures, acquisitions, marketing initiatives, and development of new products. He also leads the revenue team in major negotiations, marketing roll–outs, and advertising campaigns including print and video materials. **Career Steps:** Phelps Dodge High Performance Conductors : Vice President of Marketing and Sales (1995–Present); Manager, Strategic Planning and Business Development (1993–1995); Manager, Corporate Quality Control (1991–1993). **Associations & Accomplishments:** Planning Forum; American Society for Quality Control (ASQC); Chair–PD Quality Council and Global Business Council; Big Brother/Big Sister, OCA; Chamber of Commerce. **Education:** Columbia University, B.S. in Engineering (1986). **Personal:** Married to Jodi L. Wu in 1993. Mr. Oh enjoys bicycling, volleyball, reading, and tennis.

Samuel Joseph Morrone II
Plant Manager
Philips Lighting
3861 South 9th Street
Salina, KS 67401
(913) 826–3509
Fax: (913) 826–3577

3645

Business Information: Philips Lighting is an international manufacturer and distributor of lighting products to lighting and department stores throughout the world. Comprised of sixteen plants, Philips Lighting products include fluorescent lamps. As Plant Manager, Mr. Morrone is responsible for the management of the Kansas plant, in addition to overseeing 600 employees. **Career Steps:** Philips Lighting: Plant Manager (1993–Present), Plant Manager – Paris, Texas (1990–1993), Project Manager – Fairmont, West Virginia (1988–1990), Factory Manager – Fairmont, West Virginia (1982–1990). **Associations & Accomplishments:** BPOE (Elks); Knights of Columbus; Director (Board), Saline County Chamber of Commerce. **Education:** West Virginia University, B.S. (1978). **Personal:** Married to Mary Anne in 1984. Four children: Sammy, Matthew, Kristyn, and Caitlyn. Mr. Morrone enjoys golf, music, and coaching children.

Alan E. Sueskind
Director of the Design Department
Quoizel, Inc.
325 Kennedy Drive
Hauppauge, NY 11788–4006
(516) 273–2700
Fax: (516) 231–7102

3645

Business Information: Quoizel, Inc. designs and manufactures residential and commercial lamps, lighting fixtures, mirrors, and retail displays. Headquartered in Hauppauge, the Company is currently transitioning to a new location in South Carolina. As Director of the Design Department, Mr. Sueskind is responsible for new line development, catalog information and photographic management, product development data system design, network management, instructional/technical illustration and literature, and UL/CSA Certification. Other responsibilities include copy writing, presentation graphics, print media management, satisfying overseas product requirements, and training with regards to graphics, data handling, and systems management. **Career Steps:** Quoizel, Inc.: Director of the Design Department (1995–Present), Director of Graphic Design (1990–1995); New Product Development Manager, A & G Industry (1977–1981). **Education:** Hofstra University, B.A. (1973). **Personal:** Married to Christine in 1993. Mr. Sueskind enjoys mountain biking, scuba diving, flying, Bridge, crossword puzzles, sculpting, and jazz.

Susan B. Ruud

Vice President/Co–Founder
Ruud Lighting, Inc.
9201 Washington Avenue
Racine, WI 53406–3750
(414) 886–1900
Fax: (414) 884–3395

3646

Business Information: Ruud Lighting, Inc. manufactures, assembles, and distributes lighting products to contractors primarily for industrial use. The Corporation, established in 1982, currently has 500 employees. As Vice President, Ms. Ruud oversees all human resource functions of the Corporation. Her responsibilities include recruiting, training, evaluating, counseling employees, and all payroll functions. As a Co–Founder of the Corporation, Ms. Ruud is the Corporate Secretary and a member of the Board of Directors. **Career Steps:** Vice President/Co–Founder, Ruud Lighting, Inc. (1982–Present); Teacher, Wisconsin Schools (1969–1970); Cost Accounting, Modini Manufacturing (1965). **Associations & Accomplishments:** Trustee, Carthage College, Outstanding Alumni Award winner; Vice President of the Board, Taylor Home; Board Member, Racine Area Geriatric Assessment Center; Junior League of Racine; AMA; APA. **Education:** Carthage College, B.A. Elementary Education (1969). **Personal:** Married to Alan in 1967. Two children: Christopher Alan and Cyndi Ann. Ms. Ruud enjoys reading, travel, and golf.

Edward P. Sepulveda
Senior Technical Support Analyst – High Intensity Division
Cooper Lighting
5035 Highway 61 South
Vicksburg, MS 39180
(601) 634–9620
Fax: (301) 634–9792

3646

Business Information: Cooper Lighting is an international manufacturer of commercial lighting fixtures. The High Intensity Division is one of three divisions within Cooper Companies — a Fortune 100 corporation headquartered in Houston, Texas. Cooper Companies operates one plant in Canada and two in Mexico, providing products and services for projects such as lighting Yankee Stadium, businesses, and high–end residential homes. As Senior Technical Support Analyst, Mr. Sepulveda is responsible for all communications equipment, computer equipment, and PCs, including setups, wiring, phones in Vicksburg, as well as the Mexican facility. In addition, he is responsible for all purchases of all related supplies. **Career Steps:** Cooper Lighting High Intensity Division: Senior Technical Support Analyst (1991–Present), Supervisor Computer Operations (1981–1991); Supervisor Delta Processing, Westinghouse (1975–1981). **Associations & Accomplishments:** Board Member, Mississippi Future Business Leaders of America – PBL Foundation through Vicksburg Junior College. **Education:** West Virginia Wesleyan College, B.M.E.; Attended Hinds Community College. **Personal:** Married to Barbara in 1960. Two children: Dawn and S. David. Mr. Sepulveda enjoys wood working, personal computers and David Winter collectible ceramics.

Judy Beach
Training Manager
Osram Sylvania
100 Endicott Street
Danvers, MA 01923
(508) 750–2534
Fax: (508) 750–2240
EMAIL: See Below

3648

Business Information: Osram Sylvania, formed in 1993 by the merger of Sylvania (established in the U.S. in 1924) and Osram (established in 1919 in Osram, Germany), is one of the world's leading manufacturers of lighting equipment. Osram Sylvania is located in 23 manufacturing sites in the United States and numerous others around the world. As Training Manager, Ms. Beach is responsible for designing and implementing employee training and education. Internet users can reach her via: BEACH@SLD.SYLVANIA.COM. **Career Steps:** Osram Sylvania: Training Manager (1995–Present), Senior Industrial Engineer (1986–1995); Senior Industrial Engineer, General Motors (1983–1986). **Associations & Accomplishments:** American Society of Training and Development; American Business Womens Association. **Education:** Golden Gate University, M.B.A. (1989); General Motors Institute, Bachelor in Industrial Engineering. **Personal:** Married to Wallace L. Jr. in 1995. Ms. Beach enjoys water sports and skiing.

Larry L. Murray
Vice President/Director of Operations
Economic Lighting
12580 Stowe Drive
Poway, CA 92064–6804
(619) 679–4100
Fax: (619) 679–4112

3648

Business Information: Economic Lighting is a manufacturer and distributor of light equipment for retailers and wholesalers. As Vice President/Director of Operations, Mr. Murray is responsible for all aspects of Company operations, including personnel and production. **Career Steps:** Vice President/Director of Operations, Economic Lighting (1991–Present); CEO, T.L.C. Electric, Inc. (1988–1991); Electrical Supervisor, H.G. Fenton (1985–1988); Electrical Supervisor, Calmat of Arizona (1981–1985) **Personal:** Married to Carol A. Kenney–Murray in 1987. Three children: Trenton Robert, Sean Jamison, and Ian Michael. Mr. Murray enjoys the outdoors.

N. Eric Petersen
Director of Marketing
IDD Aerospace Corporation
18225 Northeast 76th Street
Redmond, WA 98052–5021
(206) 885–4353
Fax: (206) 883–0387
EMAIL: See Below

3648

Business Information: IDD Aerospace Corporation is a manufacturer of avionics and lighting products, keyboards, and light plates utilized in flight decks. As Director of Marketing, Mr. Petersen is responsible for the sales and marketing functions of the Company. Internet users can reach him via: ericp@iddmail.attmail.com. **Career Steps:** Director of Marketing, IDD Aerospace Corporation (1991–Present); Regional Engineering Manager, Grimes Aerospace (1986–1991); Regional Sales Manager, Mark Controls Corporation (1980–1986). **Associations & Accomplishments:** Society of Automotive Engineers; American Marketing Association; American Electronic Association. **Education:** University of Washington, B.S.M.E. (1968). **Personal:** Married to Rebecca A. in 1984. Mr. Petersen enjoys sailing, flying, and golf.

Chris Carabini
Director of Operations
Berel Industries, Inc. (d.b.a. Craig Consumer Electronics)
13845 Artesia Boulevard
Cerritos, CA 90703–9000
(310) 926–9944
Fax: (310) 926–9269

3651

Business Information: Craig Consumer Electronics, a wholly–owned entity of Berel Industries, Inc., manufactures, markets and distributes consumer electronics throughout the U.S, as well as internationally in Hong Kong and China. As Director of Operations, Mr. Carabini is responsible for logistics, daily operations and product distribution for all sales locations. **Career Steps:** Director of Operations, Berel Industries, Inc. (d.b.a. Craig Consumer Electronics) (1995–Present); Telemarketing Manager, FHP Healthcare (1993–1995); Ski Patrolman, Vail Associates (1985–1990); Director, Monex International (1978–1982). **Associations & Accomplishments:** Finance Committee for Harry Browne; Special Skiman Patrol (1984–1990). **Education:** Northern University, M.S. (1980); Loyola Marymount, B.B.A. **Personal:** Married to Michelle in 1994. Two children: Anthony and Louanne.

Antonio Covarrubias Jr.
Director of Electronic Manufacturing
MTX
4545 East Baseline Road
Phoenix, AZ 85044–5306
(602) 438–4545
Fax: (602) 438–8734

3651

Business Information: Established in 1970, MTX is an international manufacturer of home and car audio products (e.g., stereo speakers, car audio amplifiers, and DJ mixers). As Director of Electronic Manufacturing, Mr. Covarrubias is responsible for staff supervision, product quality, and varied administrative activities. **Career Steps:** Director of Electronic Manufacturing, MTX (1992–Present); Plant Manager, Milo Technology (1991–1992); Manufacturing Manager, JSR Electronics (1990–1991); Senior Engineering Specialist, Marconi Institute. **Education:** University of Phoenix, currently working toward Bachelor's Degree in Business; DeVry Institute of

Technology. **Personal:** Two children: Michael and Jennifer. Mr. Covarrubias enjoys boating and skiing.

Paul J. Klingberg
Director of Digital Media Productions
CurtCo Media Group
29160 Heathercliff Road
Malibu, CA 90265–4125
(310) 589–3100
Fax: (310) 589–3111
EMAIL: See Below

3651

Business Information: CurtCo Media Group is a company that creates audio, video, multimedia and Internet productions with a home entertainment theme. Paul Klingberg is director of all audio, video and multimedia productions. He is currently working on a production project, developing and producing a series of demonstration videos to be used as a marketing tool for the home theater systems listed in CurtCo's partner magazine publishing company, the CurtCo/Freedom Group. A widely acknowledged expert in sound engineering, he was the audio engineer for gold selling records by recording artists Earth, Wind, and Fire, Cher, and Cheap Trick. Paul was also nominated for a Grammy in the Recording Engineer classification, and was awarded the prestigious 3M visionary award in 1994. **Career Steps:** Director of Digital Media Production, CurtCo Media Group (1993–Present); Producer–Audio Engineer, PJK Productions (1986–1993); Chief Audio Engineer, Pierce Arrow Studios (1978–1986). **Associations & Accomplishments:** National Association of Broadcasters; Audio Engineering Society; National Academy of Recording Arts and Sciences; Musician and Composer. **Education:** Trinity College, B.A.; U.C.L.A., Instructor of Audio Engineering. **Personal:** Married to Kathryn Conn in 1994. Mr. Klingberg enjoys classical music, cooking and being a private pilot.

Edward N. Mims
Sales Director
Cerwin Vega
549 Nobletree Court
Agoura, CA 91301
(805) 584–9332
Fax: (805) 583–0865

3651

Business Information: Cerwin Vega is a manufacturer of high quality speaker systems for home theater (consumer market), aftermarket mobile audio, professional application, and sound reinforcement. International in scope, the Company is headquartered in California with offices in Denmark and Canada. As Sales Director, Mr. Mims is responsible for all sales and marketing worldwide, and dealing directly with distributors and sales representatives. **Career Steps:** Cerwin Vega: Sales Director (1995–Present), National Sales Manager of U.S. (1993–1995); Bose Corporation: Director of Sales North America (1991–1993), Director of Special Marketing (1989–1991). **Education:** University of Texas – Austin, B.A. (1970). **Personal:** One child: Matthew. Mr. Mims enjoys golf, stamp collecting, sightseeing, and sports.

Dan M. Murphy
Regional Vice President
Sony Electronics, Inc.
8400 Esters Boulevard, Suite 500
Irving, TX 75063–2231
(214) 915–3124
Fax: Please mail or call

3651

Business Information: Sony Electronics, Inc. designs, manufactures and markets high–tech products. They are the world's largest consumer electronics and professional hardware and software product manufacturers. Mr. Murphy has advanced steadily within Sony's corporate structure, serving in several managerial positions before being promoted to Regional Vice President in 1995. He is currently responsible for all merchandising and distribution of consumer products within the Southwestern United States. **Career Steps:** Sony Electronics, Inc.: Regional Vice President, (1995–Present); Director of SIS/Nonretail Market (1992–1995); Director of SIS/Market CD–Rom (1990–1992); Director of Product Planning (1988–1990). **Associations & Accomplishments:** North Dallas Soccer Association; Make A Wish Foundation; various publications. **Education:** Attended, C.W. Post (1977–1979); Harvard Business School; P.D.I.; A.M.A. **Personal:** Mr. Murphy enjoys soccer and is a Division One Semi–Pro player.

John J. Pogorelec
Director of Operations
LG Electronics USA, Inc.
1000 Sylvan Avenue
Englewood, NJ 07632–3302
(201) 816–2044
Fax: (201) 816–2178

3651

Business Information: LG Electronics USA, Inc., a U.S. subsidiary of LG Electronics – based in Seoul, Korea, is a national and international manufacturer and distributor of consumer electronics, such as televisions, VCRs, stereos, CD players, etc. With U.S. corporate offices located in Englewood, New Jersey, products are marketed under the brand name, Gold-Star throughout numerous sales offices across the Nation. As Director of Operations, Mr. Pogorelec is responsible for the management of all functions related to importing, warehousing, transportation, and Quick Response (EDI). He also serves as a member of the Business Process Re–Engineering Team. **Career Steps:** Director of Operations, LG Electronics USA, Inc. (1993–Present); Sharp Electronics: Manager of Distribution and Administration (1990–1993), Operations Manager (1988–1990), Assistant Marketing Manager (1985–1987). **Associations & Accomplishments:** V.I.C.S./E.D.I. **Education:** William Paterson College: B.A. in Business Administration (1980), 36 credits toward M.B.A. in Business Management; Attended numerous logistics and EDI seminars. **Personal:** Married to Susan in 1983. Two children: Joseph and Janice. Mr. Pogorelec enjoys skiing, baseball, basketball, and ice hockey.

Madeline Di Nonno
Executive Director of Marketing, Sell–Through
MCA Universal Home Video, Inc.
70 Universal Plaza, Suite 435
Universal City, CA 91608
(818) 777–3267
Fax: (818) 866–1482
EMAIL: MCA.COM

3652

Business Information: MCA Universal Home Video, Inc. is a manufacturer and marketer of pre–recorded programming for home entertainment. As Executive Director of Marketing, Ms. Di Nonno is responsible for supervising marketing and promotional activities for theatrical, television, and children's programming released on video for the "sell–through" market. Career milestones include: development and execution of a multi–million dollar marketing campaign for the video release of Jurassic Park; established a year–round business for "sale" product, which has positioned the company with a broad-based catalog; providing greater selling/purchase opportunities for trade and consumer audiences; increased average sales volume with "new to video" launches including: Babe, Apollo 13, and Casper. Classic collections include: Ma and Pa Kettle, Abbott & Costello, and Universal Classic Monsters. **Career Steps:** MCA Universal Home Video: Executive Director of Marketing, (1994–Present), Director of Marketing, Sell–Through (1991–1994); Account Supervisor, Associated Marketing Group (1989–1991); Manager of Business Development, Alley Marketing (1987–1989); Regional Promotion Planner, Lancome Cosmetics (1984–1987); Publicity Assistant, ABC/Capital Cities, Inc. (1982–1984). **Associations & Accomplishments:** Co–Chair – Entertainment Council, Promotion Marketing Association of America; Women in Film; Hollywood Women's Political Committee; Independent Feature Project/West. **Education:** Boston University, B.A. in English; Post–graduate Studies: The New School; New York University; The School of Visual Arts; University of California at Los Angeles. **Personal:** Ms. Di Nonno enjoys painting and photography.

Conrad Tracy M. Enriquez

•••◄▬▬◉▬▬►•••

Vice President and CFO
ASR Recording Services
840 East Walnut Street
Carson, CA 90746
(310) 327–3180
Fax: (310) 461–0111

3652

Business Information: ASR Recording Services is a manufacturer of CD's, custom packages for CD's, floppy disks, audio and video. Conducting business on an international basis from locations in the San Fernando Valley and Carson, California, ASR distributes its products to studios and other retail audio/video entities. In charge of accounting, finance and overall administrative operations, Conrad Enriquez serves as President and Chief Financial Officer. **Career Steps:** Vice President and CFO, ASR Recording Services

(1990–Present); Chief Financial Officer, El Mar Plastics, Inc. (1990–Present); Controller, Fanamation, Inc. (1988–1990); Accounting Manager, Los Palos Hospital (1985–1988). **Education:** University of Phoenix, taking M.B.A. (1995–Present); University of Philippines, B.S.B.A. in Accounting (1985); Licensed CPA, Philippines. **Personal:** Mr. Enriquez enjoys fishing and hunting.

Leslie P. Haas
Director of Operations
Sony Pictures Entertainment, Inc.
10202 Washington Boulevard
Culver City, CA 90232
(310) 280–8489
Fax: (310) 280–1518

3652

Business Information: Sony Pictures Entertainment, Inc., the parent company of Columbia, Tri–Star, and Merv Griffin Enterprises, is a motion picture and television production company. As Director of Operations, Ms. Haas is managing the start–up operation of the new Digital Versatile Disk facility. Additionally, she handles business administration, operations, budgets, and various other related functions. **Career Steps:** Director of Operations, Sony Pictures Entertainment, Inc. (1994–Present); Program Manager, Schaeffer Magnetics (1992–1994); Project Manager, Rockwell International (1986–1992). **Associations & Accomplishments:** Starlight Foundation Volunteer. **Education:** Pepperdine University, M.B.A. (1990); Texas A&M, B.S. (1985). **Personal:** Married to Christopher in 1986. Ms. Haas enjoys tennis.

Franz Pusch
Creative Director
3D Sound, Inc.
1048 Irvine Avenue, Suite 321
Newport Beach, CA 92660
(714) 644–6475
Fax: (714) 644–0453
EMAIL: See Below

3652

Business Information: 3D Sound, Inc. designs and develops 3–Dimensional sound for compact disks, movie soundtracks, computers, sampling keyboards, and amusement park rides. Franz Pusch began his career in classical music in Vienna, Austria, traveling to the United States to direct the movie soundtrack for "Dune." After serving as Audio Engineer and Sound Programmer for various organizations, including four years as Chief Audio Engineer for Warner Bros., he established 3D Sound in 1994. Mr. Pusch presently focuses his attention on sound programming and engineering, software research, virtual reality and sound concepts. Internet users can reach him via: Fpusch@aol.com **Career Steps:** Creative Director, 3D Sound, Inc. (1994–Present); Chief Audio Engineer, Warner Bros. (1990–1994); Audio Engineer, Various (1981–1990). **Associations & Accomplishments:** National Academy of Recording Arts and Sciences. **Education:** Institute of Communication Electronics – Vienna, Austria, B.A. (1980); Academy of Music, Vienna. **Personal:** Mr. Pusch enjoys music composition, attending cultural events and classical concerts, and playing the guitar, keyboard, and Chaplin stick.

Eugene B. Alston
Business Manager
Lucent Technologies Services Company
4022 Stirrup Creek Drive, Suite 308
Durham, NC 27703
Fax: Please mail or call

3661

Business Information: Lucent Technologies Services Company, a newly formed branch of the corporate AT&T, is the manufacturing arm of the old AT&T, manufacturing switching equipment in all its factories worldwide. As Business Manager, Mr. Alston is responsible for the management of all construction primarily in the U.S., but in some foreign areas as well. In addition, he oversees all federal projects and a staff of 500. **Career Steps:** Business Manager, Lucent Technologies Services Company (1992–Present); AT&T Services Company (1989–1992); General Market Manager, Micro Computer Systems (1987–1989); Division Construction Manager, GTE South (1984–1987). **Associations & Accomplishments:** City Council of Creedmor; U.S. Army (1953–1955); Lions Club; Butner Lions Club; Republican Methodist; Recipient, Service Award, Governor James Holshouser (1973) **Education:** Wake Forest University. **Personal:** Married to Linda Sue in 1991. Three children: Ruby Lynn, Micheal Claude, and Carl Branch. Mr. Alston enjoys writing, competitive shooting, hunting (quail), reading, and spending time with his grandchild.

Michael R. Black
Vice President/Sales & Managed Services
Ameritech
2 Westbrook Corporate Center Suite 900
Westchester, IL 60154
(708) 409–5340
Fax: (708) 409–9420

3661

Business Information: Ameritech is a multi–billion dollar telecommunications corporation headquartered in Chicago. The Corporation sells and services the products it distributes. Ameritech also offers an equipment management service for the provision of information movement between consumers. As Vice President/Sales & Managed Services, Mr. Black is in charge of the sales teams primarily headquartered in Illinois, Michigan, Wisconsin, Indiana, and Ohio which service the entire country. His division provides managed voice, data, and video services for clients. Mr. Black handles the day–to–day operations of his department which include customer service, personnel concerns, and budgets. **Career Steps:** Ameritech: Vice President/Sales & Managed Services (1996–Present); Vice President Strategic Accounts (1994–1996); Assistant Vice President Sales, US West (1989–1993). **Associations & Accomplishments:** Board of Directors, Sandstone Corporation; Colorado Health Systems Agency. Education: Kensington University, MBA; Colorado State University, BS in Psychology; Columbia University Graduate School of Business, Executive Management Program. **Personal:** Married to Patty in 1987. Three children: Amy, Doug, and Shanna. Mr. Black is an audiophile who also enjoys skiing and Harley–Davidson motorcycles."

Mohammad A. Chaudry, Ph.D.

Chief Financial Officer – Public Relations Division
AT&T Corporation
58 Manor Drive
Basking Ridge, NJ 07920–2217
(908) 204–2133
Fax: (908) 204–2135
EMAIL: See Below

3661

Business Information: AT&T Corporation is a diversified telecommunications company providing global voice, data and video conferencing services and related products. They are well known for their long distance, local and business telephone services. Established in 1890, AT&T reports annual revenue of $75 billion and currently employs 304,000 people corporate–wide. A twenty year veteran with AT&T, Dr. Chaudry joined the Company in 1975. Currently serving as Chief Financial Officer of the Public Relations Division, he is responsible for all division financial activities, including budgeting and cost analysis. **Career Steps:** AT&T Corporation: Chief Financial Officer – Public Relations Division (1991–Present); Business Planning Manager (1984–1991); Productivity Analyst (1975–1984). **Associations & Accomplishments:** American Economic Association; Elected Member, Bernard Township Board of Education (1990–1995) and Vice President (1992–1994); Trustee–Treasurer, Pakistan American Foundation; Author of numerous articles and handbooks. **Education:** Tufts University: Ph.D. (1971), M.A. in Economics (1969); London School of Economics, B.Sc. with honors in Economics. **Personal:** Married to Victoria in 1969. Three children: Amin Reza, Yasmeena Farah and Alia Pia. Dr. Chaudry enjoys reading, and is an active elected political official in local, county, state and national political offices and programs.

Erwin W. Cook Jr.
Senior Operations Support Manager
Lucent Technologies
225 Schilling Executive Plaza 3, Seventh Floor
Cockeysville Hunt Valley, MD 21031–1102
(410) 584–6173
Fax: (410) 584–6394
EMAIL: See Below

3661

Business Information: Lucent Technologies, a newly formed branch of the corporate AT&T, is the manufacturing arm of the old AT&T, manufacturing switching equipment in all its factories worldwide. As Senior Operations Support Manager, Erwin Cook travels internationally, forming methods and procedures in expediting overseas orders, as well as training how to properly receive and account for equipment. Mr. Cook wrote and is responsible for the International Export Packing and Marketing Specifications used Globally by AT&T (Lucent Technologies) and several International Freight Forwarders located throughout the United States, Mexico, Asia and Europe. Internet users can reach him via: !ecookjr **Career Steps:** Senior Operations Support Manager, Lucent Technologies (1989–Present); Staff Manager, AT&T International (1982–1987); Section Chief, Western Electric International (1980–1982); International Project Coordinator, Western Electric Company (1980–1976); Customer Service Repre-

sentative (1965–1976). **Associations & Accomplishments:** National Association of Foreign Trade Zones; Veterans of Foreign Wars; American Legion; Special Forces Association; Baltimore and Harford Counties Volunteer Fireman's Associations; Assistant Chief of the Norrisville Volunteer Fire Company; Awarded the Theodore N. Vail Bronze and Silver Medals for courage and the saving of human lives. Mr. Cook is the only AT&T employee to ever receive two of the awards since the Vail Medal Award was established in 1920. Mr. Cook was also presented The Maryland Medal of Valor by the Governor of the State. **Education:** Towson State University, A.A. (1976); University of Maryland, Fire Engineering; JFK Warfare Center (1982). **Personal:** Married to Kathleen in 1964. Mr. Cook enjoys hunting, fishing, reading, and travel.

*"They make the product...
we make the difference."*

Richard E. McKay
Chief Executive Officer and President
1 Nation Technology Corporation
8016 State Road 54
New Port Richey, FL 34653
(813) 372-3132
Fax: (813) 372-2825

3661

Business Information: 1 Nation Technology Corporation is an independent remanufacturer, wholesaler, and distributor of telecommunications equipment for companies such as Northern Telecom and AT&T. Working on a national level, the Company plans to expand internationally. With six years experience in the telecommunications industry, Mr. McKay established 1 Nation Technology Corporation as Chief Executive Officer and President in 1995. He is responsible for all aspects of operations, including management of managers, marketing, advertising, research, training, and negotiations. In addition, he oversees all administrative operations for associates and a support staff of 15. **Career Steps:** Chief Executive Officer and President, 1 Nation Technology Corporation (1995–Present); Senior Vice President, A1 Teletronics (1991–1995); Sales Manager, Genesis Communications (1990–1991); Auditor, Federal Express (1988–1990). **Associations & Accomplishments:** North American Telecommunication Dealers; Northern Telecom Chapter – Tampa, ISLUA; Advisor, CCI; Board of Directors, 1 Nation Technology. **Education:** Memphis Institute Technology, A.A. (1988); University West Florida. **Personal:** Married to Renee W. in 1988. Two children: Skylar R. and Madison Rhea. Mr. McKay enjoys sports and computers.

Abdol Saleh, Ph.D.
Member of Technical Staff
Lucent Technologies
101 Crawfords Corner Road, Room 3J–338
Holmdel, NJ 07733
(908) 949–1915
Fax: Please mail or call

3661

Business Information: Lucent Technologies is an international manufacturer of telecommunication equipment, ranging from chips to telephone systems. Major customers include AT&T and Bell. As a Member of the Technical Staff Team in the Advanced Technologies Area, Dr. Saleh is responsible for providing consulting services in the different product lines within Lucent. His specialty includes product development and realization. Internet users can reach him via: savs@attquest.att.com. **Career Steps:** Member of the Technical Staff Team, Lucent Technologies (1996–Present); Member of the Technical Staff, AT&T (1988–1996). **Associations & Accomplishments:** IRAN. **Education:** Lehigh University, Ph.D. (1988), M.Sc. in Industrial Engineering, B.Sc. in Chemical Engineering, B.Sc. in Business and Economics. **Personal:** Dr. Saleh enjoys mountain climbing, movies, attending art exhibits, tennis, bicycling, reading, poetry, and travel.

Mr. James A. Sykes
Director, Technology Planning
AMP Incorporated
P.O. Box 3608, MS 140–009
Harrisburg, PA 17105–3608
(717) 986–3859
Fax: (717) 986–3334

3661

Business Information: AMP develops, manufactures and distributes electrical, electronic, optical and opto electronic and wireless interconnection systems and services. Established in 1940, AMP Incorporated currently employs 43,000 and has an estimated annual revenue of $5.5 million. As Director of Technology Planning, Mr. Sykes is responsible for general management, strategic and tactical planning, analysis, technology, business integration, and R&D efficiency and effectiveness. **Career Steps:** Director of Technology Planning, AMP Incorporated (1994–Present); General Manager of Technical Planning and Resource Services, Air Products and Chemicals (1974–1994); Technical Manager, Shell Development Company (1968–1974); Process Development Engineer, W.R. Grace Company (1964–1968). **Associations & Accomplishments:** American Institute of Chemical Engineers; American Chemical Society; World Futures Society; Strategic Management Society; Institute of Electrical and Electronics Engineers; Torch Club; Registered Professional Engineer; President (2 years), Board Member (6 years) Girl's Club of Allentown; Mr. Sykes is President of a Pennsylvania corporation. **Education:** University of Maryland, Ph.D. (1968). **Personal:** Married to Sharon Frances (O'Brien) in 1960. Two children: Brian Frances and David Aubrey. Mr. Sykes enjoys business management, architecture, travel and reading.

Richard Waldor

Roll–Out Manager
AT&T Global Information Systems
1290 Avenue of the Americas
New York, NY 10104
(212) 484–5505
Fax: (212) 484–5729
E–mail: see below

3661

Business Information: AT&T Global Information Systems, a division of AT&T, the world's largest communications company, is a computer–based equipment manufacturer, distributor and wholesaler. The Company is also engaged in training. Major clientele includes the financial, commercial and communications industries. Established in 1878, AT&T currently employs 32,000 people worldwide and has an estimated annual revenue of $32 billion. As Roll–Out Manager, Mr. Waldor is responsible for all aspects of supervision for the deployment, installation and maintenance of computer hardware and software. **Career Steps:** Roll–Out Manager, AT&T Global Information Systems (1990–Present); Vice President of Engineering, Infergen (1988–1990). **Associations & Accomplishments:** Project Management Institute; Trustee, Horizon Health Center. **Education:** George Washington University: M.B.A. in progress, Certified in Project Management; University of Rochester, B.S. in Statistics (1981). **Personal:** Married to Vivian Kerstein in 1995. One child: Simone Schiffmacher.

Chris J. Wolff
Technology Director
AT&T
1975 Lakeside Parkway #350
Tucker, GA 30084–5860
(770) 908–6760
Fax: (770) 908–3665

3661

Business Information: AT&T is an international telecommunications conglomerate providing global voice, data, and video teleconferencing services worldwide. As Technology Director, Mr. Wolff is responsible for designing and developing communication systems for BSM Data Sales, and distributing the hardware and software to branch offices. Once the hardware and software are distributed, the department becomes the support group for the branch offices and assists in the disbursement of information and updates on product changes. **Career Steps:** Technology Director, AT&T (1995–Present); Territory Manager, AT&T GIS (1994–1995); Financial Planning Manager, NCR Corporation (1986–1994). **Associations & Accomplishments:** Young Republicans. **Education:** University of Dayton, B.S. in Finance (1988); AT&T School of Business, Mini M.B.A. in Global Finance (1996) **Personal:** Mr. Wolff enjoys running, being a physical fitness enthusiast, and travel.

Mr. William Schupp
Vice President, North American Personnel
Matsushita Electric Corporation of America
One Panasonic Way
Secaucus, NJ 07094
(201) 392–4590
Fax: (201) 392–4180

3662

Business Information: Matsushita Electric Corporation of America is a subsidiary of one of the world's largest manufacturers and distributors of consumer and industrial products. Products include televisions, radios, video cassette recorders, stereo systems, and other electronics under the trade names of Panasonic and Quasar. The Parent Company is headquartered in Osaka, Japan. In his capacity as Vice President, North American Personnel, Mr. Schupp is responsible for direct staff training, labor relations, employee relations, benefits, compensation, and general personnel management functions. Established in 1959, Matsushita Electric Corporation of America employs over 5,000 people. **Career Steps:** Vice President, North American Personnel, Matsushita Electric Corporation of America (1992–Present); General Manager, Personnel, Quasar Division of Matsushita Electric Corporation of America (1984–1992); Director, Personnel and Industrial Relations, UNR–Leavitt Division, Leavitt Industries (1981–1984); Corporate Personnel Manager, Borg–Warner Corporation (1977–1981). **Associations & Accomplishments:** Society of Human Resource Management; Electronic Industries Association Human Resource Council. **Education:** University of Chicago, M.B.A. (1970); Loyola University, B.A.

Frank A. Adams, Ph.D.

Director of Strategic Programs
Motorola
1301 E. Algonquin Road
Schaumburg, IL 60196
(847) 576–6926
Fax: (847) 576–1961

3663

Business Information: Motorola is one of the leading global manufacturers and distributors of consumer and industrial electronic communications equipment, with product lines including radio/telephone communications, components, semiconductors, computer systems and peripherals, and home appliances. Established in 1928, the Corporation employs over 140,000 people worldwide. As Director of Strategic Programs, Dr. Adams is responsible for strategic change management and general strategic planning programs for the Corporation. He works closely with other members of management designing and implementing future change processes and systems. **Career Steps:** Motorola: Director of Strategic Programs (1994–Present), Director of Human Resources, World Wide Radio Products (1991–1994), Director of Human Resources, World Wide Mobile Products (1989–1991); Independent Management Consultant (1991–Present). **Associations & Accomplishments:** American Management Association; International Guild of Professional Consultants; Software Engineering People Management Network; Human Resources Strategic Planning Society. **Education:** Walden University, Ph.D. (1994); Liberty University, M.A. in Counseling; Arizona State University, M.B.A. Equivalent; Western New Mexico University, B. A. in Sociology, Psychology, and Business. **Personal:** Married to Vernell. Three children: Chris, Scott, and Jaime. Dr. Adams enjoys golf, reading, and sports.

Syed Saadat Ahmed
Facilities Project Engineer
Motorola
4000 Commercial Avenue
Northbrook, IL 60062
(847) 205–3466
Fax: (847) 205–2860
EMail: See Below

3663

Business Information: Motorola is headquarters for an automotive and industrial electronics division, offering sensor and power control technology, GPS navigation production, electrical vehicles, powertrain and chasis manufacturing, and overall electronics. As Facilities Project Engineer, Mr. Ahmed handles space and facilities planning, forecasting, designing, budgeting for buildings, and renovating building space for Motorola. Internet users can reach him via: g12118@email.mot.com. **Career Steps:** Motorola: Facilities Project Engineer (1994–Present), Facilities Coordinator/Engineer (1990–1994); Design Architect, Alan L. Foss & Associates (1990). **Associations & Accomplishments:** International Facility Management Association: Chairman, Public Relations Committee, Northern Illinois Chapter; American Institute of Architects; Illinois Society of Architects; Moto-

rola AWP Committee; Vice President of Pakistan Students Association, University of Oklahoma. **Education:** University of Oklahoma, B.S. in Architecture (1988); University of Karachi – Pakistan, B.S. in Chemistry; Lake Michigan College, A.S. in Engineering; Jamia Millia Institute of Technology, Diploma in Civil/Building/Technology/Drafting. **Personal:** Married to Salma in 1987. One child: Asad. Mr. Ahmed enjoys high–impact aerobics, biking, fishing, rollerblading, jogging, flying, sightseeing, and travel.

Mr. Anis R. Ally
Manufacturing Engineer Manager
California Amplifier
460 Calle San Pablo
Camarillo, CA 93012–8563
(805) 987–9000
Fax: (805) 388–2627

3663

Business Information: California Amplifier (CA) is a design manufacturer of microwave amplifiers utilized in satellite and wireless cable TV applications. Global in scope, with headquarters located in Camarillo, California, CA operates distribution offices throughout the U.S. as well as Brazil, France and Malaysia. An industrial engineering executive with over ten years expertise, Anis Ally serves as California Amplifier's Manufacturing Engineer Manager. His primary responsibility is to provide direction and supervision to all manufacturing and industrial engineer associates; ensuring optimal production, implementing automation and technology innovations as well as full profit & loss accountability. **Career Steps:** Manufacturing Engineer Manager, California Amplifier (1992–Present); Industrial Engineer (Contract), AlliedSignal Aerospace Division (1988–1992); Industrial Engineer, Oklahoma League for the Blind (1987–1988). **Associations & Accomplishments:** Institute of Industrial Engineers; Society of Manufacturing Engineers; Surface Mount Technology Association. **Education:** University of Oklahoma, M.S. in Industrial Engineering (1993); University of Pittsburgh, M.S. in Petroleum Engineering; B.S. in Mechanical Engineering, University of Energy and Technology, Karani, Pakistan; Presently enrolled in MBA program at California Lutheran University. **Personal:** Married to Shahla Nargis in 1991. Two children: Sarah and Abbas. Mr. Ally enjoys tennis, racquetball and spending time with his family.

Robert W. Andrews

President
ICG Wireless Services, Inc.
9351 Grant Street, Suite 600
Denver, CO 80229–4358
(303) 705–6900
Fax: (303) 705–6990
EMAIL: See Below

3663

Business Information: ICG Wireless Services, Inc., a wholly–owned subsidiary of international telecommunications conglomerate IntelCom Group, Inc. (ICG), specializes in the integration of satellite communications for voice, video, data and enhanced services. Joining the corporate parent company ICG in July of 1993 as Director of Finance, Mr. Andrews was transferred to the Wireless division to serve as Vice President of Finance, appointed President in November of 1995. Prior to joining ICG, Mr. Andrews started and owned Genesee Software, Inc., a developer of enhanced connectivity and communication software. For the preceding five years, he served as a Regional Sales Manager for Dynamic Information Systems, Corp. in Boulder, Colorado. In this role he was responsible for opening, developing and managing the two largest sales offices in that company. He was also employed by MidCon Corp., a wholly–owned $5 billion subsidiary of Occidental Petroleum. While there, Mr. Andrews was responsible for business planning and forecasting for their world–wide operations. He can also be reached through the Internet via: bandrews@icgws.com **Career Steps:** ICG Wireless Services, Inc.: President (1995–Present), Vice President – Finance (1994–1995); Director of Finance, IntelCom, Inc. (1993–1994); President, Genesee Software, Inc. (1991–1993); Regional Sales Manager, Dynamic Information Systems – Boulder, CO (1986–1991); Associate, Smith Barney – Chicago, IL; Business Planning Director, MidCon Corp. **Education:** University of Denver: M.B.A. (1982), B.S.B.A. in Finance (1976); Post–graduate work: Northwestern University Kellogg School of Management and Johns Hopkins University **Personal:** Married to Paula in 1984. Mr. Andrews enjoys snowboarding, jet ski racing and motorcycles.

W. Charles Austin
National Sales Manager
Sonic Communications, Inc.
4 Colonial Center, P.O. Box 287
New Ipswich, NH 03071–0287
(800) 688–1944
Fax: (603) 525–4745
EMail: See Below

3663

Business Information: Sonic Communications, Inc. specializes in the manufacture and marketing of audio and video accessories for law enforcement agencies and commercial applications. As National Sales Manager, Mr. Austin is responsible for diversified administrative activities, including researching new markets. Internet users can reach him via: Charles.Austin@pobox.com. **Career Steps:** National Sales Manager, Sonic Communications, Inc. (1995–Present); Adjunct Professor: Embry–Riddle Aeronautical University, Daniel Webster's Aviation College, New Hampshire Technical College (Present); Marketing Manager, Prudential Insurance (1994–1995); Commander, Lt. Colonel, United States Air Force (1971–1994). **Associations & Accomplishments:** Kiwanis; Civil Air Patrol; Aircraft Owners and Pilots Association; Founder/President, Vermont Aviation Educational Advisory Council; Frequent lecturer and publisher. **Education:** University of South Florida, B.S. in Economics and Finance; Webster's University, M.S. in Management; Certificate in Airline Transport Pilot; Lufthansa German Airlines Training School, Graduate; FAA Certified Flight and Advanced Ground Instructor. **Personal:** Married to Gigi in 1972. One child: Thalia. Mr. Austin enjoys flying, public speaking, and teaching.

Marjorie Baxter–Errickson
Manager of NPD Methods
Motorola
5005 E. McDowell Road, B–114 Mail Stop
Phoenix, AZ 85008–4229
(602) 244–4007
Fax: (602) 244–5408

3663

Business Information: Motorola is one of the leading global manufacturers and distributors of consumer and industrial electronic communications equipment, with product lines including radio/telephone communications, components, semiconductors, computer systems and peripherals, and home appliances. Joining Motorola in 1981 as an equipment engineer, Ms. Baxter–Errickson was appointed to her current position in 1992. As Manager of NPD Methods, she oversees the development of new product methodologies, focusing on research and TQM for cycle time reduction strategies. **Career Steps:** Motorola: Manager of NPD Methods (1992–Present); Staff Engineer (1990–1992); Equipment Engineer (1981–1990). **Associations & Accomplishments:** Sponsor and Instructor, Junior Achievement; Leadership, Local United Way Campaign; Consultant, Arizona State University. **Education:** Arizona State University, B.S. in Mechanical Engineering Technology (1982); Motorola University, management training. **Personal:** Married to Thomas K. in 1994. Two children: son, Adam Baxter; and step–daughter, Rachel Errickson. Mrs. Baxter–Errickson enjoys travel, gardening, piano, and supporting her children in sports activities.

Paul M. Harrison
President and Chief Executive Officer
Rock N Good Times
10225 East Coopers Hawk Drive
Sun Lakes, AZ 85248–7605
Fax: (602) 802–0713

3663

Business Information: Rock N Good Times is a manufacturer of disguised satellite TV RO systems and home theater. The satellites can be disguised as rocks or trees to cause others to believe that the owner really does not have a satellite. As Chief Executive Officer, Mr. Harrison is responsible for all aspects of Company operations, including conducting training, sales, and logistics. **Career Steps:** Chief Executive Officer, Rock N Good Times (Present); Defense Contract Management Quality Assurance, United States Government (Present); United States Air Force: Squadron Executive Officer (Present), Program Manager (1991–1994). **Associations & Accomplishments:** Air Force Association; Reserve Officers Association. **Education:** Air Command and Staff, M.P.A. (1994); California State University – Hayward, B.A. in Political Science (1980). **Personal:** Married to Vicky in 1978. Mr. Harrison enjoys international travel.

Wayne Carter McLachlan
Manufacturing Engineering Manager
Tektronix, Grass Valley Products
P.O. Box 1114
Grass Valley, CA 95945–1114
(916) 478–3462
Fax: Please mail or call
EMAIL: See Below

3663

Business Information: Tektronix, Grass Valley Products manufactures television equipment, including transport, routing, switchers, and digital effects. Established in 1960, the company maintains locations in the United States, Japan, and Great Britain. An Electronic Engineer with 20 years experience, Mr. McLachlan has served in various Engineering positions at Tektronix since 1976. Promoted to Manufacturing Engineering Manager in 1994, he is currently responsible for Engineering and Advanced Testing, staff supervision, and various administrative functions. Internet users can reach him via: Wayne.McLachlan@TEK.COM **Career Steps:** Tektronix, Grass Valley Products: Manufacturing Engineering Manager (1994–Present), Staff Engineer (1986–1994); Instructor, Yuba College (Present). **Associations & Accomplishments:** Manager SMPTE; Co–Author "Applied Electronic Instrumentation & Measurement." **Education:** National University, B.S.M.E.T. (1990); California Polytechnic, San Luis Obispo, B.S.E.E. (1975). **Personal:** Married to Donna in 1971. Three children: Jason, Carrie and Emily. Mr. McLachlan enjoys skiing and teaching broadcast video.

Lawrence F. McManus Jr.

Manager of Business & Strategic Development
Ericsson
Mountain View Road, Room #4400
Lynchburg, VA 24502
(804) 528–7359
Fax: (804) 522–3061

3663

Business Information: Ericsson is a major manufacturer and marketer of two–way radios and radio networks with locations in 110 countries worldwide. Mr. McManus joined Ericsson in 1994, managing business development in Canada and the United States. Promoted to Manager of Business & Strategic Development in 1995, he is presently responsible for the development and operation of all North American projects and oversight of all major telecommunications systems in North America. **Career Steps:** Ericsson: Manager of Business & Strategic Development (1995–Present), Business Development – Canada/Western United States (1994–1995); Vice President of Marketing & Sales, First DeFence (1993–1994). **Associations & Accomplishments:** APCO; ACA; NASTD; FCCA; Habitat for Humanity. **Education:** University of South Carolina, M.B.A. (1990); Copenhagen School of Business and Economics – Copenhagen, Denmark, A.P.I.M. Degree (1989). **Personal:** Married to Hannah Pinckney in 1990. Two children: Elizabeth and Thomas. Mr. McManus enjoys bicycling, home repair projects, restoring old cars, reading, and travel.

Charles E. Trimble

President and Chief Executive Officer
New Eagle Communications
139 First Street Terrace
New Strawn, KS 66839
(316) 364–5102
Fax: (316) 364–5380

3663

Business Information: New Eagle Communications is a manufacturer of electronic headsets and communication systems for police, military, auto racing, and other sports. As President/CEO, Mr. Trimble is responsible for all aspects of company operations, including sales, developing new products, and managing the Engineering Department. **Career Steps:** President/CEO, New Eagle Communications (1989–Present); Vice President of Operations, Republic Telecom (1985–1989); Vice President of Engineering, Ohio Teleport Corporation (1982–1985); Vice President of International Operations, United Telecom Companies (1969–1982). **Associations & Accomplishments:** Chaplain, Masonic Lodge; Rotary Club; President, Coffey County Chamber of Commerce; President, Coffey County Strategic Planning and Advisory Council; New Strawn Zoning Board; Burlington High School Youth and Business Council; Volunteer work for numerous committees. **Education:** Central Tech, A.S. in Electrical Engineering (1961). **Personal:** Married to Joyce in 1957. Two children: Jay and Edward. Mr. Trimble enjoys flying his private airplane.

Dennis G. Acton

Director – Partners & Distribution
Northern Telecom (Nortel)
221 Lakeside Blvd.
Richardson, TX 75082–4399
(214) 684–1673
Fax: (214) 684–3789
EMAIL: See Below

3669

Business Information: Northern Telecom Inc., one of the world's leading telecommunications marketers, specializes in the design, manufacture and service for a diverse range of products including telephone, data communications and semi–conductor production. Established in 1895, Northern Telecom Inc. currently employs 60,000 professionals and has an estimated annual revenue of $9 billion. A member of the Corporate family of Nortel since 1985, as Director of Partners & Distribution, Mr. Acton manages all external partnerships deemed strategic to meeting business objectives. He can also be reached through the Internet via: den.acton0244563@nt.com **Career Steps:** Nortel (Northern Telecom): Director – Partners & Distribution (1993–Present); Director of Operations (1991–1993); Director of International Sales & Marketing (1985–1991). **Associations & Accomplishments:** Associate Member, Professional Engineering Society – Province of Ontario **Education:** Queen's University, B.Sc. with honours in Engineering Physics (1963). **Personal:** Married to Heide–Marie in 1984. Three children: Molly J., Kirstie L. and William D. Mr. Acton enjoys skiing, swimming and hiking.

Raymond Aldridge

General Manager
ORR Protection Systems
13015 Middletown Industrial Boulevard
Louisville, KY 40223–4762
(502) 244–4500
Fax: (502) 244–4548

3669

Business Information: ORR Protection Systems provides engineering, installation and servicing of fire detection and fire suppression systems from five regional offices (one office in each state – Ohio, Missouri, Indiana, Georgia, and Kentucky). As General Manager, Mr. Aldridge is responsible for leadership of the Company, as well as establishing the mission, the promoting of a positive corporate culture. Mr. Aldridge can also be reached through the Internet: aldridge@iglou.com **Career Steps:** General Manager, ORR Protection Systems (Present); General Manager, Environmental Compliance Systems Corporation (1993–); Director of Project Management, Columbia Scientific Environmental (1992–1993); Director of Project Management, KVB, Inc. (1989–1992). **Associations & Accomplishments:** Air and Waste Management Association; Kentucky Environmental Marketing Association; Fire Suppression Systems Association. **Education:** Pepperdine University, M.B.A. (1989); University of Redlands, B.B.A. **Personal:** Married to Annette in 1984. Two children: Andrew and Luke. Mr. Aldridge enjoys his family and playing tennis (USTA Tournament Tennis).

Mikael Aronowitsch

Managing Director
Comex Electronics AB
Tumstockzvajen 11B
Taby, Sweden 18766
(468) 630–8230
Fax: (468) 630–1271

3669

Business Information: Comex Electronics AB is a manufacturer of anti–eavesdropping computer systems and data communications products for the defense force in Sweden. The Company is the market leader in this technology and has been a supplier to the Swedish Defense Force since 1986. The Company was founded primarily to protect the Company's brand name, Comex, which is the name of secure computers and peripherals manufactured by associated companies. All development, manufacturing, and marketing of the Comex product range is now carried out in–house. Comex also has patent rights worldwide on "Atac," a device that prevents emission signals from the defense force to reach civilians. As Managing Director, Mr. Aronowitsch is responsible for all aspects of Company operations including administration, finance, sales and marketing, and public relations. **Career Steps:** Managing Director, Comex Electronics AB (1987–Present); Managing Director, Commerivest Systems AB (1989–1994); Managing Director, MDS Sverblem Ab (1985–1986). **Associations & Accomplishments:** Sallskapet in Stockholm; Board Member, Comex Electronics AB. **Education:** Handelghogskolan i Sateborg: M.B.A. (1972), M.Sc. (1978).

Personal: Married to Ulrika Claesson in 1983. Two children: Louisa and Katarina. Mr. Aronowitsch enjoys sailing and golf.

Vivian Ayuso

Human Resources Director
Motorola Radio Products Americas Group
8000 West Sunrise Boulevard
Plantation, FL 33322
(954) 723–6349
Fax: (954) 723–4490
EMAIL: See Below

3669

Business Information: Motorola is one of the leading global manufacturers and distributors of consumer and industrial electronic communications equipment, with product lines including radio/telephone communications, components, semiconductors, computer systems and peripherals, and home appliances. The Radio Products America's Group (RPAG) is headquartered in Plantation, Florida. The Facility specializes in the research, development, and manufacture of two–way radio communication systems. In addition, RPAG includes distribution organizations for North America and Latin America, and a second manufacturing facility in Mt. Pleasant, Iowa. As Human Resources Director, Ms. Ayuso is responsible for a staff of 24 employees, including functions involving staffing, compensations, EEO/AA, employee relations, organizational development, work and family, wellness, health services, community relations, educational relations, change programs, and HRIS for a work force of 2,500 in South Florida, 750 in Mt. Pleasant, and 150 in Illinois. Internet users can reach her via: CCSCO5@email.mot.com. **Career Steps:** Human Resources Director, Motorola – Radio Products Americas Group (1994–Present); Diversity Director, Motorola – Land Mobile Products Sector (1992–1994); Human Resources Manager, Motorola – Radius Division (1991–1992), H.R. Operations Manager, Motorola C&E (1989–1991). **Associations & Accomplishments:** National Hispanic Corporate Council; Human Resources Roundtable of Florida; Internal Awards and Recognitions. **Education:** University of Louisville, B.S.C. (1978); Loyola University, Towards Master's in Industrial Relations. **Personal:** Married to Ramon Sanchez in 1982. Two children: Cristina and Monica. Ms. Ayuso enjoys plants, fitness/health, and spending time with her family.

Ahmed Y. Banafa

Chairman
Primevision Technologies
5000 Hopyard Road Suite 170
Pleasanton, CA 94588
(510) 469–0300
Fax: (510) 469–0347
EMAIL: See Below

3669

Business Information: Primevision Technologies is an establishment primarily providing video conferencing services. Established in 1995, the Company provides hardware/software for desktop video conferencing using special telephone lines at very low prices. Employing 15 people, the Company estimates annual revenue to be in excess of $4,000,000. As Chairman, Mr. Banafa is responsible for client recruitment, product installation and development, and system analysis. Internet users can reach him via: banafa@primevision.com. **Career Steps:** Chairman, Primevision Technologies (1995–Present); Ph.D. Researcher, Lehigh University (1990–1995); Engineer, B.T.C., Saudi Arabia (1987–1989). **Associations & Accomplishments:** The Institute of Electrical and Electronics Engineers (IEEE); P.C. Magazine Reader's Advisory Panel; Reviewer for IEEE Potentials Magazine. **Education:** Lehigh University, Master's Degree in Electrical Engineering (1993); K.A.A.U., Saudi Arabia, B.S.; L.C.C.C., Management Certificate. **Personal:** Married to Anessia in 1987. Four children: Bassem, Halla, Abdul, and Malik. Mr. Banafa enjoys surfing the Internet, reading, sailing, and flying.

ALCATEL

ESPACE

Augustin E. Coello–Vera, Ph.D.

Head of Technology
Alcatel Espace
26 Av J–F Champollion BP1187
Toulouse Cedex, France 31037
33–61195493
Fax: 33–61444990
EMAIL: See Below

3669

Business Information: Alcatel Espace is a manufacturer of satellites, satellite payloads, and satellite systems. Established in 1972, Alcatel Espace reports annual revenue of $350 million and currently employs 1,300 people. With expertise in Microelectronics in FLSI Systems, Dr. Coello–Vera joined Alcatel Espace in 1990 as Head of Technology. He is responsible for all aspects of technological operations, including strategic planning, implementation, and research and development of new products. He can also be reached through the Internet via: FRDK8X88@IBMMAIL.COM **Career Steps:** Head of Technology, Alcatel Espace (1990–Present); Director of Microelectronics, Alcatel SESA – Madrid (1987–1990); Manager of Wafer Fab, Thomson – CSF (1982–1987). **Associations & Accomplishments:** Member, Institute of Electrical and Electronic Engineers; JSHM. **Education:** UCSB, Ph.D. (1978), M.A., M.S. **Personal:** Married to Sylvie in 1979. Three children: Barbara, Christopher, and Aymeric. Dr. Coello–Vera enjoys mountain hiking and skiing.

Cynthia J. Comparin

Vice President and General Manager
Northern Telecom (Nortel)
2221 Lakeside Boulevard, MS C0327
Richardson, TX 75082
(214) 684–7500
Fax: (214) 684–3241

3669

Business Information: Northern Telecom, one of the world's leading telecommunications marketers, specializes in the design, manufacture and service for a diverse range of products to include telephone, data communications and semiconductors. Established in 1895, Northern Telecom reports annual revenue of $10 billion and currently employs 60,000 company–wide. As Vice President and General Manager of Network Transformation Services, Ms. Comparin provides consulting, project management, and sourcing services to Fortune 500 companies. **Career Steps:** Vice President and General Manager, Northern Telecom (1995–Present); Corporate Vice President of Business Development, Teknekron Infoswitch Corp. (1994); Strategic Unit Director for International Business, EDS (1984–1994). **Associations & Accomplishments:** Greater Dallas Chamber of Commerce; Women in Finance. **Education:** University of Texas at Austin, B.B.A. in Finance (1980); Financial Management Executive Course, Wharton; Executive Corporate Financial Management, Harvard; Integration of Marketing and Financial Strategic Plans, Wharton; M.B.A. Program, Somerset University, Ilminster, Somerset, England. **Personal:** Ms. Comparin enjoys golf, tennis, and travel.

Monica L. Creamer

Payroll Accountant
Interdigital Communications Corporation
781 3rd. Avenue
King of Prussia, PA 19406–1409
(610) 878–7800
Fax: (610) 992–9432

3669

Business Information: As Payroll Accountant, Ms. Creamer processes the semi–monthly payroll for approximately 195 employees, reconciles all payroll general ledger accounts, updating of equity roll forward and patents schedule, project labor, employee business expenses, and must be up–to–date on all state and federal payroll rules and regulations. **Career Steps:** Interdigital Communications Corporation: Payroll Accountant (1995–Present), Accounts Payable Clerk (1994–1995); Various Positions, Robert Half Account Temps (Jun.1994–Aug.1994). **Associations & Accomplishments:** American Society of Women Accountants; Pennsylvania Institute of Certified Public Accountants; Kappa Sigma Omega. **Education:** Cabrini College: B.S., B.A. (1994). **Personal:** Ms. Creamer enjoys tennis, swimming, softball, and reading.

Jan Dehesh

Director, Corporate Telecommunications
Qualcomm, Inc.
6455 Lusk Blvd.
San Diego, CA 92121
(619) 658–3003
Fax: (619) 658–3700

3669

Business Information: Qualcom, Inc., a leader in digital wireless communications technologies, manufactures, markets, licenses, and operates advanced communications systems and products based on digital wireless technology. A publicly held corporation based in San Diego since 1985, Qualcom, Inc. operates 10 locations nationally and 4 internationally, employing a total of 4500 people. As Director, Corporate Telecommunications, Ms. Dehesh is responsible for the corporate telecommunications department of the Corporation and handles all of the communications needs for 4,500 employees. Concurrently, Ms. Dehesh operates a consulting business called f.y.i. Communication Solutions. Ms. Dehesh may also be reached through E–Mail: JDehesh@qualcomm.com. **Career Steps:** Director, Corporate Telecommunications, Qualcomm, Inc. (1987–Present); Support Services, Linkabit Corporation. **Associations & Accomplishments:** San Diego Definity Users Group, founding member; International Definity Users Group, Inc.: Board of Directors, Western Region Director; San Diego Women Who Mean Business Award – Telecommunications Division (1994); Outstanding Young Women of America (1987). **Education:** University of California–San Diego, BA in Communications (in progress); Miramar Community College, honors. **Personal:** Married to Houtan in 1983. Two children: Gary James and Gabriel Ann. Ms. Dehesh enjoys being active in the community with Mira Mesa High School and the Children's Museum of San Diego.

Oscar J. Fontalvo

Market Manager
Ascom Timplex
8925 South West 148th Street
Miami, FL 33176
(305) 238–8505
Fax: (305) 238–8403
EMAIL: See Below

3669

Business Information: Ascom Timplex, located in Miami, is a manufacturer of communication and telecommunication equipment. The Company was established in 1969 and has approximately 5,000 employees. As Market Manager, Mr. Fontalvo handles the marketing of services and products in Latin America. He is also a senior systems engineer and assists in the development and design of telecommunication equipment. **Career Steps:** Ascom Timplex: Market Manager (1995–Present); Regional Service Director (1994–1995), Senior Systems Engineer (1993–1994). **Associations & Accomplishments:** Mr. Fontalvo has been published in local magazines. **Education:** New York City College, B.E. (1987). **Personal:** Married to Audrey in 1988. Two children: Andrew and Adrian. Mr. Fontalvo enjoys sports, playing soccer, racquetball, computers, and on–line services.

Devra D. Fuller

Marketing Communications Manager
Decibel Products
8635 Stemmons Freeway
Dallas, TX 75247
(214) 819–4281
Fax: (214) 631–4706

3669

Business Information: One of seven divisions of Allen Telecom Group, Decibel Products is a manufacturer of antennas and filtering products for telecommunication network systems. International in scope, Decibel markets to distributors, dealers, and OEM's in the cellular and personal communication services industries. As Marketing Manager, Devra Fuller's primary duty is promoting new products, with other duties as follow: overseeing advertising sectors, organizing and marketing trade shows, as well as writing and designing literature and pamphlets. She also provides support to Company public relations, promoting new products, and special events. **Career Steps:** Marketing Communications Manager, Decibel Products (1995–Present); Sales & Marketing Support Manager, Del Norte Tech. (1984–1993). **Associations & Accomplishments:** American Marketing Association. **Education:** University of Texas – Arlington: B.B.A. (1993), A.A. in Business (1990). **Personal:** Ms. Fuller enjoys travel, mystery novels, and animals.

Peter G. Kastner

Assistant Vice President of Finance & Acquisitions
Northern Telecom
3 Robert Speck Parkway
Mississauga, Ontario L4Z 3C8
(905) 566–3101
Fax: (905) 566–3403

3669

Business Information: Northern Telecom Inc., one of the world's leading telecommunications marketers, specializes in the design, manufacture and service for a diverse range of products including telephone, data communications and semiconductor production. Established in 1895, Northern Telecom, Inc. currently employs 60,000 people globally, and reports estimated annual revenue in excess of $9 billion. A tax accountant with over twenty years of corporate expertise, Peter Kastner joined Nortel's Canadian offices in 1981. Currently serving as Assistant Vice President of Finance & Acquisitions, he oversees all customer relations financial transactions and reporting. **Career Steps:** Northern Telecom: Assistant Vice President of Finance & Acquisitions (1996–Present), Assistant Vice President of Finance (1994–1996), Assistant Vice President of Canadian Taxes (1981–1994); Senior Manager, Revenue Canada – Taxation (1971–1981). **Associations & Accomplishments:** Certified General Accountants Association; Tax Executive Institute; Advisory Committee, Revenue Canada; Director, Ex Trade; Frequent Speaker & Writer on Tax Policy Issues. **Education:** University of Toronto; Wharton School of Business. **Personal:** Married to Rina in 1995. Three children: Sara, Amy, and Sarah. Mr. Kastner enjoys skiing, golf, and softball.

David E. McKeon

Director
Ameritech
2000 West Ameritech Center Drive 4E50
Hoffman Estates, IL 60196
(847) 248–4183
Fax: Please mail or call

3669

Business Information: Ameritech provides telecommunications products and services, including computer software, cellular accessories, and communications solutions to a five state region. With 1,700 employees in the region, the small business services has locations in Illinois, Wisconsin, Michigan, and Ohio. As Director, Mr. McKeon is responsible for all human resource functions related to the small business unit of the Company and is directly responsible for nine people. **Career Steps:** Director, Ameritech (1994–Present); Mobil: Manager, Human Resources (1992–1994), Manager, Employee Relations (1990–1992). **Education:** Michigan State University, M.L.I.R. (1986); Michigan State University, B.S. in Psychology (1983). **Personal:** Married. Mr. McKeon enjoys spending time with his family, travel, and 5k/10k races.

William Neighbors

President and Chief Operating Officer
Digital Theater Systems, L.P.
31352 Via Colinas, #101
Westlake Village, CA 91362
(818) 706–3525
Fax: (818) 706–1868

3669

Business Information: Digital Theater Systems (DTS), L.P. specializes in digital sound systems for movie theaters and digital sound recording equipment for film production (worldwide supplier). DTS is an international company with offices in Westlake Village, California and Brussels, Belgium. Established in 1993, DTS presently employs 26 people and has an estimated annual revenue in excess of $10 million. As President and Chief Operating Officer, Mr. Neighbors is responsible for all P & L, manufacturing functions, marketing functions, and strategic growth. **Career Steps:** Digital Theater Systems, L.P.: President and Chief Operating Officer (1994–Present), Executive Vice President and General Manager (1993–1994); Manager of Quality Improvement, PTI Technologies (1991–1993); Director of Operations, RTS Systems, Inc. (1988–1991); Manager of Finance and Planning PTI Technologies (1986–1988). **Associations & Accomplishments:** Board of Managers, YMCA; Certified ISO9000 Lead Assessor; 1st Employee of DTS Systems, The Leading Supplier of Digital Playback Systems for Movies in the World. **Education:** California State University at Northridge, B.S. in Finance (1982). **Personal:** Mr. Neighbors enjoys water skiing, mountain biking, guitar playing, music, and travel in his leisure time.

David G. Petersen

Product Manager
Fire Control Instruments
269 Grove Street
Newton, MA 02166–2239
(617) 965–2010
Fax: (617) 965–0659

3669

Business Information: Fire Control Instruments, a privately–owned company, is a manufacturer of commercial and industrial fire alarm control equipment. Fire Control Instruments has five regional sales offices (4 in the U.S. and 1 in England), selling worldwide through distribution. Joining Fire Control Instruments in 1978, Mr. Petersen was appointed as Product Manager in 1993. He is responsible for three of four product lines, as well as a number of new projects in research and development. He is also in charge of the upkeep of existing products and updating technology, as well as writing specifications for new products. **Career Steps:** Fire Control Instruments: Product Manager (1993–Present), various manufacturing positions (1978–1993). **Associations & Accomplishments:** National Fire Protection Association; National Rifle Association; American Mototcyclists Association. **Education:** St. Francis College (1975–1977). **Personal:** One child: Christian Gregory. Mr. Petersen enjoys hunting and motorcycles.

Kenneth R. Selig

Director/Advanced Marketing
Harris Corporation
809 Calle Plano
Camarillo, CA 93012–8516
(805) 389–2274
Fax: (805) 389–2301
E MAIL: See Below

3669

Business Information: Harris Corporation is a leading manufacturer and supplier of diversified electronics and telecommunications equipment. Harris Corporation, with worldwide sales of more than $3.3 billion, is focused on four major businesses: electronics systems, communications, semiconductors, and Lanier Worldwide office equipment. The Dracon Division of Harris Corporation is a major supplier of 85% of telecommunications test equipment. As Director/Advanced Marketing, Mr. Selig is responsible for developing new, major product lines and cooperative alliances to solve customer problems. Internet users may contact him via: KSELIG@HARRIS.COM. **Career Steps:** Harris Corporation: Director/Supertech (1994–Present), Director of Marketing (1990–1994); Director LMS–3192, Rockwell International (1987–1990); Program Manager, XEL Communications (1981–1987). **Education:** University of Northern Colorado, M.B.A. (1976); Ohio State University, B.S. **Personal:** Married to Lynne in 1976. Two children: Christy and Scott. Mr. Selig enjoys golf, tournament bass fishing, and wine making.

Colette C. Sun

Director/Environmental Affairs & Safety, Radio Products Group
Motorola
8000 West Sunrise Boulevard, Room 1153
Ft. Lauderdale, FL 33322
(954) 723–5605
Fax: (954) 723–5900
EMAIL: See Below

3669

Business Information: Motorola is one of the world's leading providers of wireless communications, semiconductors and advanced electronic systems, components and services. Environmental leadership is one of Motorola's key beliefs: constant respect for people and uncompromising integrity. As Director/Environmental Affairs & Safety, Radio Products Group, Ms. Sun directs the environmental health and safety (EHS) activities to ensure compliance of Corporate Policy. Ms. Sun also serves on the Corporation's Executive EHS Council, and is actively participating in establishing EHS vision, objectives and strategies, as well as setting policies and EHS directives to steer the Company into the 21st century towards its "best–in–class" vision. Internet users can reach her via: ECS005@email.mot.com. **Career Steps:** Director/Environmental Affairs & Safety, Radio Products Group, Motorola (1981–Present); Senior Engineer, Westinghouse Research & Development Center (1969–1981); Research Associate, Mellon Institute (1965–1969). **Associations & Accomplishments:** American Chemical Society; South Florida Manufacturing Association; Environmental Health Safety Committee; Chinese Cultural Association of Coral Springs, Florida; Coral Springs Philharmonic Society. **Education:** Kansas State University, M.S. in Chemistry (1965); Benedictine College, B.S. in Physical Chemistry (1963). **Personal:** Married to Shan C. in 1965. Two children: Charlotte Sun Bratka, and Wen Sun. Ms. Sun enjoys music, piano, singing, tennis, swimming, and sewing.

Michael R. Wallace

Regional Manager
DSC
5251 DTC Parkway, Suite 950
Englewood, CO 80111–3304
(303) 721–6514
Fax: (303) 721–6679

3669

Business Information: DSC Communications Corp. is a leading designer, developer, manufacturer and marketer of digital switching, transmission, access and private network system products for the worldwide telecommunications market place. As Regional Manager, Installation and Customer Services, Mr. Wallace has direct responsibility for site supervisors, planning and managing multiple projects. He is responsible for monitoring job cost, quality, safety, and customer satisfaction. Mr. Wallace interacts daily with DSC management and management from other telecommunications companies to provide timely installation, while keeping customer satisfaction as the primary objective. **Career Steps:** Regional Manager, DSC (1992–Present); Project Supervisor, Aerotek Telecommunication Services (1992); Project Supervisor Installation, Northern Telcom, Inc. (1985–1992); Installer, Wilco–Centel, Inc. (1980–1985); Installer, Blake Telecommunications (1976–1980). **Associations & Accomplishments:** Awards: DSC Directors Award for Continuous Excellence (1996), DSC Committed to Excellence Award (1994), DSC Night Out Award (1993); NTI Installation Top Service Sales System Revenue (1989–1992); Northern Star Award (1991); NTI Southwest Region Customer Commitment Award (1990); NTI Zero Defects Team Award, Quality Assurance (1988–1992). **Education:** Attended, Texas A & M Extension Service, Telecommunications Training Division; Northern Telcom Department of Installation Manpower Development, Various self–improvement, safety, and leadership classes; Dun & Bradstreet, Management courses; Microsoft Excel 5.0 and Project 3.0; The Pace Group Business Communication Skills; DSC Training, Various quality assurance and management training seminars. **Personal:** Married to Donna. Five children: Monica, Misty, Michelle, Bradley, and Marissa. Mr. Wallace enjoys fishing, hunting, and spending time with family.

Rudi Willems

Marketing Director Americas
Motorola
20 Cabot Boulevard
Mansfield, MA 02048–1153
(508) 261–4000
Fax: Please mail or call
EMAIL: See Below

3669

Business Information: Motorola Corporation is the leading telecommunications and datacommunications corporation in the world. As Marketing Director Americas, Mr. Willems oversees all aspects of marketing in the Information Systems Division. His duties include management of a staff of twenty–three, administrative functions, and strategic planning. He can be reached through EMail: VE0002@email.mot.com. **Career Steps:** Motorola: Marketing Director Americas (1995–Present), Marketing Director Europe (1989–1995), General Manager, Belgium. **Education:** Kath Universiteit, Belgium: M.B.A. (1983). Masters Degree in Engineering (1981). **Personal:** Married to Helga in 1981. Two children: Tine and Ilse. Mr. Willems enjoys scuba diving, rafting, tennis, and bicycling.

David L. Williams

Manager of Support Systems
Siemens Rolm Communications
4900 Old Ironside Drive
Santa Clara, CA 95054–1811
(408) 492–4138
Fax: (408) 492–3152

3669

Business Information: Siemens Rolm Communications, headquartered in Germany, is a manufacturer and servicer of private PBX telephone systems. Previously, Rolm began as an independent company started by four college students ("ROLM" stands for the initials of each student). After IBM took over Rolm Company, Siemens bought the Company in 1991. Siemens, considered the "AT&T" of Germany, repairs phone connection problems that other companies can't, with third and fourth level support, as well as serving clientele worldwide and providing New Software codes. It's goal is to grow from a $5 million company to a $2 billion company within the next three years. As Manager of Support Systems, Mr. Williams is responsible for the management of all support systems functions, in addition to oversight of a staff of 15, including development and field trial engineers and product support and product testing personnel. **Career Steps:** Siemens Rolm Communications: Manager of Support Systems (1994–Present), Product Support Engineer (1992–1994), Manager of Rolm Europe Division (1970–1992). **Education:** Oakland University, B.A. (1974); Attended several Manager Training Classes and several technical classes to learn and stay current with new technologies; Attended several Dr. Deming seminars and is a member of his Quality Group. **Personal:** Four children: Shannon, Marion, Melissa and Robert.

Danny Windham

Director of Marketing
ADTRAN
901 Explorer Boulevard
Huntsville, AL 35806–2807
(205) 971–8756
Fax: (205) 971–8699
E–mail: see below

3669

Business Information: Established in 1986 and incorporated in 1994, ADTRAN (Advanced Transmission) is a manufacturer of digital communications products (i.e., transceivers), utilized by telephone companies and their customers. ADTRAN operates 40 distribution points and 100 retail outlets. In two years the Company expanded its revenues 243% from $72 million to $175 million due to its products and marketing strategies. An Electrical Engineer with a graduate degree in Management, Mr. Windham combines his technical expertise with managerial talents to guide the strategic planning of the Company. As the Director, he is reponsible for all marketing activities. Mr. Windham attributes his success to a quick mind, good communication skills, his knowledge of telecommunications technology, early involvement in high growth industries, and the fact that he hand picks the members of his team. He can also be reached through the Internet via: DWINDHAM@ADTRAN.com **Career Steps:** Director of Marketing, ADTRAN (1990–Present); Founder and Vice President of Engineering, Processing Telecom Tech (1986–1990); Engineering Manager, Universal Data Systems (1982–1986). **Associations & Accomplishments:** Division Chairman of the Networking Division, North American Telecom Association; Volunteer, CASA — providing home repair and improvement to the aged and infirm; Eta Kappa Nu; Phi Kappa Phi; Care of the Aging; Optimists Club. **Education:** Florida Technical College, M.B.A. (1994); Mississippi State University, B.S. in Electrical Engineering (1981). **Personal:** Married to Jill in 1983. Two children: Amanda and April. Mr. Windham enjoys snow skiing.

David E. Woodcock

Facility Director
Nokia Mobile Phones
5650 Alliance Gateway Freeway
Ft. Worth, TX 76178–3736
(817) 491–7909
Fax: (817) 490–7517

3669

Business Information: Nokia Mobile Phones specializes in the manufacture of cellular phone products (national and international). The Company is the second largest builder of cellular phones in the United States providing global telecommunications. As Facility Director, Mr. Woodcock is responsible for security, engineering, maintenance, food service, fitness center, and administration. In addition, he oversees the Dallas Fort Worth area and leasing and real estate area. **Career Steps:** Facility Director, Nokia Mobile Phones (1994–Present); Martin Marrietta: Facilities Manager (1992–1994), Facilities Chief Engineer (1988–1992), Facilities Engineer (1981–1988). **Associations & Accomplishments:** International Facilities Management Association; American Society of Industrial Security. **Education:** Florida Institute of Technology, M.B.A. (1988); Georgia Institute of Technology, B.S.I.E. **Personal:** Married to Sharon in 1986. Three children: Daniel, Chris, and Mike. Mr. Woodcock enjoys weightlifting, jogging, boys' sports, and church.

Mahdi Q. Al Shammari

Chairman and Managing Director
Electrical Boards Manufacturing Company
P.O. Box 25428
Safat, Kuwait 13115
(965) 476–1304
Fax: (965) 476–3016

3672

Business Information: Electrical Board Manufacturing Company (EBOMAC) is a manufacturer and distributor of low to medium range boards up to 33,000 KV. The Company, established in 1978, does only custom work, taking orders and design by specification locally and internationally. The Company exports mainly to Egypt, Bahrain, Qatar, Oman, Sudan, Ghana, and Yemen. EBOMAC designed and erected the telecommunications tower in Kuwait, the fourth largest and tallest in the world. As Chairman and Managing Director, Mr. Al Shammari, whose background is in industrial planning and engineering, is responsible for all aspects of Company operations.

He was appointed Chairman when the company he was working for bought EBOMAC. **Career Steps:** Chairman and Managing Director, Electrical Board Manufacturing Company (1985–Present); Head of Projects FV, IIC (1983–1985); Site Engineer, Kuwait Municipality (1981–1983). **Associations & Accomplishments:** American Urban Planning Association; Kuwaiti Alumni. **Education:** Canady University, M.B.S. (1994); Greely University – Colorado, M.B.S. in Industrial and Planning (1981). **Personal:** Married to Nawal Bu Qaiss in 1981. Seven children: Khalid, Firas, Moh'd, Anfal, Wasayef, Amina, and Mishari. Mr. Al Shammari enjoys swimming, camping, volleyball, and travel.

Joseph G. Andersen
· · · ◉ · · ·

Chief Financial Officer/Vice President
Comptronix Corporation
3 Maryland Farms, Suite 140
Brentwood, TN 37027–5005
(205) 582–1865 Ext. 1865
Fax: (615) 377–3993

3672

Business Information: Comptronix Corporation is a design and manufacturing company of products mainly containing printed circuit boards, such as PC boards, telephone switches, and printers. As Chief Financial Officer/Vice President, Mr. Andersen is responsible for all aspects of Company operations, including finances, inventory, MIS, receivables, and strategic planning. **Career Steps:** Chief Financial Officer/ Vice President, Comptronix Corporation (1993–Present); Cost Accounting Manager, Augat Wiring Systems (1991–1993); Augat International: European Financial Controller (1987–1990), Internal Audit Manager (1987–1990). **Associations & Accomplishments:** American Institute of Certified Public Accountants. **Education:** University of Notre Dame, B.B.A. (1978). **Personal:** Married to Nancy in 1980. Two children: Kelly and Kevin.

Bruce E. Baumann

Vice President of Strategic Market Channels & Packaging
ABB Power T&D Company, Inc.
1021 Main Campus Drive
Raleigh, NC 27606–5202
(919) 856–3803
Fax: (919) 856–3810
EMail: bruce.e.bumann@us

3672

Business Information: ABB Power T&D Company, Inc. specializes in the design, manufacture, and development of electrical transformers, capacitors, circuit breakers, switches, meters, and automated distribution and energy management systems. The primary market for ABB is in North and South America. As Vice President of Strategic Market, Mr. Baumann is responsible for distributors, key market channels, packaging and field sales management. He has been working for ABB for 26 years. Internet users can reach him via: bruce.e.baumann@ustra.mail.abb.com. **Career Steps:** ABB Power T&D Company, Inc.: Vice President of Strategic Marketing (1994–Present), Vice President of Domestic Sales (1992–1994), BA Marketing Manager – Meters (1991–1992). **Associations & Accomplishments:** Various neighborhood associations; Member of community country club; Association of Edison Illumination Companies. **Education:** Purdue University, B.S.E.E. (1970). **Personal:** Married to Becky in 1970. Two children: Brian and Anne. Mr. Baumann enjoys golf, gardening, and various projects.

Bryant Bogren

Executive Vice President
DeGussa Electronics
222 West Lockeford Street, Suite 8
Lodi, CA 95240–2054
(209) 333–0303
Fax: (209) 333–0233

3672

Business Information: DeGussa Electronics specializes in the production and distribution of diversified products which include: printed circuit boards, metals, chemicals and pharmaceuticals. Global in scope, DeGussa's headquarters are located in Germany and Singapore, with U.S. offices in New Jersey and a manufacturing plant in Alabama. As Executive Vice President, Mr. Bogren is responsible for all aspects of Company operations, including sales, management, and strategic planning. **Career Steps:** Executive Vice President, DeGussa Electronics (1994–Present); National Sales Manager, Citation Circuits (1991–1994); Director of Marketing and Sales, Lika Corporation (1988–1991); Industrial Sales Manager, Ingram Paper Company (1982–1988). **Associations & Accomplishments:** Boy Scouts of America; Exchange Club. **Education:** Brigham Young University, B.S. (1967). **Personal:** Married to Judy in 1969. Four children: Ryan, Kris-

ta, Dane, and Cade. Mr. Bogren enjoys golf, water skiing, snow skiing, and racquetball.

Joseph H. Castle

Manufacturing Manager
Triangle Circuits of Pittsburgh
931 3rd Street
Oakmont, PA 15139–1939
(412) 828–5322
Fax: (412) 828–5803

3672

Business Information: Triangle Circuits of Pittsburgh is a national manufacturer of printed circuit boards, specializing in multi–layered circuits. With thirty–one years of experience in circuitry, Joseph Castle has served Triangle Circuits in managerial roles at various subsidiaries since 1989. Appointed as Manufacturing Manager for the Pittsburgh division in 1992, he provides the overall management of all manufacturing, facilities, environmental processes, and equipment purchases, in addition to directly and indirectly supervising a staff of 94. **Career Steps:** Manufacturing Manager, Triangle Circuits of Pittsburgh (1992–Present); Manufacturing Manager, Triangle Circuit of Danbury (1989–1992); Facility Engineer, Design Circuits (1980–1989); General Manager, Diventco Inc. (1965–1979). **Associations & Accomplishments:** Interconnection Technology Research Institute; Recipient, Special Recognition Award. **Personal:** Married to Barbara J. in 1995. Mr. Castle enjoys video production, coin collection and collecting Barbie dolls.

Samuel L. Fouquet

Senior Sales Account Manager
S3, Inc.
2770 San Tomas Expressway
Santa Clara, CA 95051
(408) 748–3022
Fax: (408) 980–7791
EMAIL: See Below

3672

Business Information: S3, Inc., established in 1989, is an international manufacturer of graphics accelerator integrated circuits for PC's, serving such companies as Compac, Dell, and IBM. While very successful ($500 million annual sales), the Company hopes to redirect their efforts more toward the multimedia market rather than the Internet. As Senior Sales Account Manager, Mr. Fouquet is responsible for the development and maintenance of existing accounts for both the West Coast and Central Region. He also provides support to the sales force and maintains customer satisfaction through support and quick resolution of any customer concerns. Internet users can reach him via: SAM@S3.COM **Career Steps:** Senior Sales Account Manager, S3, Inc. (1992–Present); Tactical Marketing Engineer, Chips & Technologies (1989–1992); System Analyst, Synetics (1987–1989). **Associations & Accomplishments:** Aircraft Owners & Pilots Association; Peninsula Bible Church; Boyton Neighborhood Group; International Networking Association. **Education:** Massachusetts Institute of Technology, S.B. (1987); Harvard Business School; Alicante University, Spain. **Personal:** Married to Mary Ann in 1994. Mr. Fouquet enjoys flying, outdoor activities, the beach, and mountain biking.

Greg J. Gross

Assistant Treasurer
Reptron Electronics
14401 McCormick Drive
Tampa, FL 33626–3021
(813) 854–2351
Fax: (813) 855–1697

3672

Business Information: Reptron Electronics is a distributor of electronic components and a contract manufacturer of circuit boards and related electronic equipment. As Assistant Treasurer, Mr. Gross is responsible for cash management, SEC reporting, capital expenditure management, budgeting, and projects. **Career Steps:** Assistant Treasurer, Reptron Electronics (1996–Present); Grant Thornton, LLP: Audit Manager (1994–1996), Audit Supervisor (1993–1994). **Associations & Accomplishments:** American Institute of Certified Public Accountants. **Education:** University of South Florida, B.A. (1988). **Personal:** Married to Debbie in 1996. One child: Kaley. Mr. Gross enjoys classic cars.

Wilfredo Leon

Purchasing Agent
AMP Circuits
200 Fairforest Way
Greenville, SC 29607–4609
Fax: (864) 675–7641
E MAIL: See Below

3672

Business Information: AMP Circuits is a manufacturer of printed circuit boards. The Company has three manufacturing facilities located in Long Island, New York, Delaware, Maryland, and Greenville, South Carolina. The Company deals with sophisticated printed circuit boards and is the largest supplier of connectors in the world. Established in 1996, AMP Circuits employs 500 people and estimates annual sales in excess of $60 million. As Purchasing Agent, Mr. Leon is responsible for purchasing products and services, vendor selection, and management for the operation. Internet users may reach him via: leon@amp.com. **Career Steps:** Purchasing Agent, AMP Circuits (1992–Present); Digital Equipment Corporation: Material Manager (1989–1992), Production Control Manager (1985–1989), Product and Inventory Control Manager (1980–1985). **Associations & Accomplishments:** Purchasing Management Association; American Production and Inventory Control Society; Founder, Carolinas Minority supplier Development Council; Founder, South Carolina Hispanic Coalition; Exchange Club of Mauldin; Rotary Club of Mauldin; Greenville Literacy Association. **Education:** University of Puerto Rico, B.S. (1971). **Personal:** Married to Daisy in 1987. Three children: Wilgia, Wil, and Litza. Mr. Leon enjoys gardening, professional sports, dancing, hiking, and being a Porsche enthusiast.

Amy Plant

Senior Program Manager
Taxan USA Corporation
2880 San Tomas Expressway, Suite 101
Santa Clara, CA 95051
(408) 748–0200
Fax: (408) 748–9190
EMAIL: See Below

3672

Business Information: Taxan USA Corporation is a turnkey manufacturing subsidiary of Kaga Electronics of Japan. Specializing in electronic sub–assemblies, the Company manages materials and manufactures and tests the completed products as per the customers' specifications. Established in 1981, Taxan USA Corporation employs 25 people and has estimated annual revenue of $40 million. As Senior Program Manager, Ms. Plant is responsible for all projects and operation of the Turnkey Division. Additional duties include customer service and coordination, as well as strategic planning. Internet users can reach her via: aplant@taxan.com. **Career Steps:** Taxan USA Corporation: Senior Program Manager (1994–Present), Program Manager (1991–1994), Administration Manager (1986–1991). **Education:** University of Dallas, B.A. (1984). **Personal:** Married to Leonard in 1996. Ms. Plant enjoys jet skiing, camping, and travel.

Timothy Lynn Solomon

Assistant Plant Controller
Philips Consumer Electronics – Greeneville
465 Bruce Collins Lane
Greeneville, TN 37743–7439
(423) 636–5382
Fax: (423) 636–5217

3672

Business Information: Philips Consumer Electronics – Greeneville is an electronics manufacturing company, specializing in televisions, printed circuit boards, computer monitors, and computer projections (LCD). Joining Philips Consumer Electronics as Accountant in 1981, Mr. Solomon was appointed as Assistant Plant Controller in 1994. He is responsible for inventory reconciliations, budgeting, and purchase orders. Concurrent with his position at Philips, he operates his family–owned cattle ranch, Houston Valley Ranch, consisting of 100 head of cattle. **Career Steps:** Philips Consumer Electronics – Greeneville: Assistant Plant Controller (1994–Present); Accounting Supervisor (1991–1994); Accountant (1983–1991). **Associations & Accomplishments:** Solomon Lutheran Church: Council Member, Chairman of Music and Worship Committee; Philips Managers Club; Philips Activities Club. **Education:** East Tennessee State University: M.B.A. (1992), B.B.A. in Accounting; Walters State Community College, A.S. in Business. **Personal:** Mr. Solomon enjoys owning and managing his beef ranch — Houston Valley Ranch. He also enjoys hiking, listening to and playing music, and photography.

Robert E. Burkhardt
Regional Sales Manager
Integrated Solutions, Inc.
3190 Coronado Drive, Suite A
Santa Clara, CA 95054
(408) 970–0997
Fax: (408) 986–1891
EMail: See Below

3674

Business Information: Integrated Solutions, Inc., a division of IBM/Integrated, is a manufacturer of semiconductor equipment. As Regional Sale Manager, Mr. Burkhardt is responsible for diversified administrative activities, including strategic planning and sales force development. Internet users can reach him via: Burkhardt@mail.insol.com. **Career Steps:** Regional Sale Manager, Integrated Solutions, Inc. (1993–Present); District Service Manager, GCA, a unit of General Signal (1982–1993). **Associations & Accomplishments:** International Society for Hybrid Microelectronics; American Management Association; Red Cross. **Education:** California Coast University, B.A. in Electronic Technology (1990). **Personal:** Married to Robin in 1987. Two children: Courtney Danielle and Taylor Joseph. Mr. Burkhardt enjoys woodworking, tennis, and photography.

Joseph A. Cestari
Vice President of Advanced Technology
Tylan General
3019 Alvin Devane Boulevard, Suite 230
Austin, TX 78741–7412
(512) 385–8996
Fax: (512) 385–7941
EMAIL: See Below

3674

Business Information: Tylan General is a designer, manufacturer and distributor of components, subsystems, and control systems utilized in semiconductor manufacturing equipment. Tylan's product line includes mass flow controllers, capacitance diaphragm gauges, and gas delivery systems. Global in scope, the Company markets to OEM and device manufacturers from locations in the U.S. (7), England, France, Germany, Japan, Korea, Singapore, and Taiwan. A management executive with Tylan General since 1990, Joseph Cestari was appointed to his current position in November of 1995. As Vice President of Advanced Technology, he is responsible for overall corporate technological development and strategies. Internet users can reach him via: CESTARI@AOL.COM **Career Steps:** Tylan General: Vice President of Advanced Technology (1995–Present), Director of Operations (1994–1995), General Manager (1990–1994); Technical Staff, Advanced Micro Devices (1986–1990). **Associations & Accomplishments:** Institute of Electronics and Electrical Engineers, SEMI; Austin Chamber of Commerce; Baylor Alumni State Board of Directors. **Education:** Baylor University, B.S. in Computer Engineering (1984); Masters in Management of Technology in process. **Personal:** Married to Beth in 1985. Two children: Nicholas and Zachary. Mr. Cestari enjoys family time, weightlifting, travel, and being "Daddy".

Mr. John Edward Chambers
President
Thermo–Kinetics Industries
P.O. Box 6747
Greenville, SC 29606–6747
(803) 277–8080
Fax: Please mail or call

3674

Business Information: As President of Thermo–Kinetics Industries, Mr. Chambers is responsible for all aspects of the company's daily operations.

Charles D. Clark
Planning Manager
Advance Micro Devices
5204 East Ben White Boulevard, MS 612
Austin, TX 78741–7306
(512) 602–4198
Fax: (512) 602–7430
EMAIL: See Below

3674

Business Information: Advance Micro Devices, established in 1969, is one of the leading semiconductor manufacturers in the U.S., distributing its products on the global market, with distribution offices in Germany and Japan. Serving in manufacturing management roles for some of the world's leading semiconductor industries spanning the period 1978 to the present, Charles Clark joined Advance Micro Devices in 1989. As Planning Manager, he provides the overall direction and implementation for production strategies, with duties including modeling simulation and fabrications layouts, wafer fabrication logistics, tracking delivery, customer relations, clean room control and maintenance. Internet users can reach him via: Charles.Clark@AMD.com. **Career Steps:** Planning Manager, Advance Micro Devices (1989–Present); Operations Manager, National Semiconductor, Inc. (1988–1989); Manufacturing Manager, Texas Instruments, Inc. (1978–1988). **Associations & Accomplishments:** American Production Inventory Control Society. **Education:** University of Oklahoma, B.S. (1978); Southeastern Oklahoma State University, M.B.A. (1984). **Personal:** Married to Vicki in 1974. Three children: Kaci, Kendra, and Kara. Mr. Clark enjoys golf and basketball.

Gerald M. Cox
Director, New Business Development
Fusion Semiconductor Systems
19841 Helmond Way
Gaithersburg, MD 20879
(301) 738–0022 ext. 5578
Fax: Please mail or call

3674

Business Information: Fusion Semiconductor Systems is the leading global supplier of asher and photostabilizer manufacturing equipment for use in the largest semiconductor fabrication sites worldwide. Located in Rockville, Maryland, the Corporation employs over 600 people. As Director of New Business Development, Mr. Cox is responsible for corporate mergers and acquisitions, alliances, and strategic planning for future expansion. As Director of Engineering, he managed 91 professionals in R&D, electrical, software, mechanical, design services, test engineering and three program managers in design of new products. **Career Steps:** Fusion Systems, Director, New Business Development (1996–Present) and Director, Engineering (1992–1996), Rockville, MD; Texas Instruments, Branch/Program Manager, Dallas, TX (1972–1992); Rockwell–Collins, Design Engineer (1966–1972) Dallas, TX. **Education:** Texas A & M University, B.S. in Electrical Engineering (1966). **Personal:** Married to Barbara in 1973. Two children: Cynthia and Catherine. Mr. Cox enjoys darkroom photography and travel.

Gary E. Dashney
Manager of Characterization
Motorola
5005 East McDowell Road
Phoenix, AZ 85008
(602) 244–3471
Fax: (602) 244–5218
Email: See Below

3674

Business Information: Established in the late 1950's, Motorola is one of five manufacturers of power semiconductors. The Power Semiconductor Product Sector is one of four Divisions in the plant, and the plant is one of five in the Phoenix area. As Manager of Characterization, Mr. Dashney is responsible for handling fiscal matters, directing daily operations, public relations, and supervising strategic planning. Additionally, he manages a group of 12 in the laboratory performing characterization by electrical and thermo abilities of products. Internet users can reach him via: rsfr40@email.sps.mot.com. **Career Steps:** Motorola: Manager of Characterization (1992–Present), Product Eng–Tmos (1986–92); Product ENg–Bipolar (1981–86). **Associations & Accomplishments:** Institute of Electrical & Electronics Engineers. **Education:** DeVry Institute, B.S.E.E.T. (1981). **Personal:** Married to Deborah in 1989. Three children: Crystal, Rochelle, and Brian. Mr. Dashney enjoys reading and computers.

Ronald L. DeHays
Regional Manager
Spectra Physics Laserplane
5475 Kellenburger Road
Dayton, OH 45424–1013
(513) 233–8921
Fax: (513) 667–8249

3674

Business Information: Spectra Physics Laserplane manufactures and markets lasers for construction and agriculture. Mr. DeHays joined Spectra as Branch Manager in 1985, moving into his present position as Regional Manager in 1992. He is presently responsible for overseeing all sales operations, sales training of independent dealers, and distribution management in Latin America. **Career Steps:** Spectra Physics Laserplane: Regional Manager (1992–Present), Branch Manager–3 (1985–1992); Manager, Miller Printing (1982–1984). **Education:** Wright State University, B.S. (1978); University of Phoenix, Currently Enrolled in Online Masters of International Marketing Program. **Personal:** Married to Margie in 1986. Four children: Christopher, Lauren, Matthew, and Thomas. Mr. DeHays enjoys skiing and reading.

Andre F. Hawit
President and Owner
Innovative Data Solutions
1035 East Hillsdale Boulevard
Foster City, CA 94404
(415) 349–0500
Fax: (415) 349–0101

3674

Business Information: Innovative Data Solutions is a data software company, specializing in specifically designed software (i.e., wafer mapping) for the the semi–conductor industry. As President and Owner, Mr. Hawit provides the overall vision and stategy for the company, ensuring quality product output, customer satisfaction and the effective techniques needed to keep the company a viable presence in the national market. **Career Steps:** President and Owner, Innovative Data Solutions (1991–Present); Engineering Manager, Analog Devices (1984–1991); Design Engineer, Micro Test (1983–1984). **Associations & Accomplishments:** Institute of Electrical and Electronics Engineers. **Education:** National University, M.B.A. (1988); San Francisco State University, B.S. (1983). **Personal:** Married to Rana in 1984. Mr. Hawit enjoys sports, chess, music and skiing.

John T. Hoback
Electronics Venture Manager
Amoco Chemical Corporation
150 West Warrenville Road, Building 500 C–1, P.O. Box 3011
Naperville, IL 60566
(708) 420–5454
Fax: (708) 420–3634
EMAIL: See Below

3674

Business Information: Amoco Chemical Corporation is a manufacturer of electronic materials provided for the semiconductor, assembly, and interconnect markets. As Electronics Venture Manager, Mr. Hoback handles the marketing and sales of current products, research and development of new products, and planning for division expansion. Internet users can reach him via: Jthoback@Amoco.com. **Career Steps:** Electronics Venture Manager, Amoco Corporation (1985–1988); Vice President/Sales & Marketing, EKS (1985–1988z); EMCA–Subs Rohm & Haas: Director of Marketing (1984–1985), Manager, New Business Development (1980–1984). **Associations & Accomplishments:** I.P.C.; T.M.R.C.; I.S.H.M.; S.E.M.I./SEMATECH; S.E.M.I. **Education:** University of Maryland, M.S. (1966); Gettysburg College, B.A. (1962). **Personal:** Married to Judy Zilker in 1964. Two children: Amy N. and Peter F. Mr. Hoback enjoys golf.

Patricia Ann Holzworth
Manager of Worldwide Compensation
Advanced Micro Devices
1 AMD Place, Mail Stop 7
Sunnyvale, CA 94088–3905
(408) 749–4604
Fax: (408) 749–3229
EMail: See Below

3674

Business Information: Advanced Micro Devices (AMD) is a manufacturer of integrated circuits, focusing on the personal and networked computing and communications market. This global, high–technology, state–of–the–art manufacturer of semiconductor devices has operations in the United States, throughout Asia, and in Eastern Germany and Sales Offices in more than 15 countries. As Manager of Worldwide Compensation, Mrs. Holzworth has corporate responsibility for base, executive, and sales compensation as well as expatriate administration. Internet users can reach her via: PATTI.HOLZWORTH@AMD.COM. **Career Steps:** AMD: Manager of Worldwide Compensation (1995–Present), Manager of Corporate/Domestic Compensation (1994–1995), Senior Compensation Analyst (1987–1994). **Associations & Accomplishments:** American Compensation Association; Peninsula Compensation Association; Western International Personnel Association; Radford Association – A&A Steering Committee. **Education:** Santa Clara University, B.S. (1983). **Personal:** Married to Ray in 1991. Three children: Ray Jr., Madison, and Meaghan. Mrs. Holzworth enjoys playing with her children, piano, and golf.

Michael C. Ingster
Vice President of Sales
Crosspoint Solutions, Inc.
694 Tasman Drive
Milpitas, CA 95035–7460
(408) 324–0200
Fax: Please mail or call

3674

Business Information: Crosspoint Solutions, Inc. is an international manufacturer of semiconductors established in 1990 and currently employing 50 people. The Company offers an alternative solution to medium to low end ASIC designers. As Vice President of Sales, Mr. Ingster has oversight of the sales department and handles all administrative duties. Other responsibilities include marketing new and existing products, budgetary concerns, strategic planning for the future, and general overview of day–to–day operations. **Career Steps:** Vice President of Sales, Crosspoint Solutions, Inc. (1995–Present); Director of Sales, LSI Logic Corporation (1984–1995). **Education:** Harvard University, B.S.E.E. (1982).

Jonathan P. Jansky

Plant Manager
MEMC Electronics
501 Pearl Drive
St. Peters, MO 63376–1071
(314) 279–5425
Fax: Please mail or call

3674

Business Information: MEMC Electronics is the second largest manufacturer of silicon wafers for the electronic materials industry. Mr. Jansky has served in various supervisory positions with MEMC since 1983, most recently promoted to Plant Manager in 1992. He is presently responsible for daily operations of the manufacturing facility and overseeing safety and environmental regulation compliance. **Career Steps:** MEMC Electronics: Plant Manager (1992–Present), Manufacturing Operations Manager (1989–1992), Manufacturing Manager (1985–1989), MTCE Manager (1983–1985). **Associations & Accomplishments:** Judge, Missouri Excellence Foundation State Award for Quality. **Education:** University of Missouri at Rolla, B.S.M.E. (1973); Advanced Training in Statistics. **Personal:** Married to Barbara in 1974. Mr. Jansky enjoys golf, fishing, camping, hiking, and reading.

John E. Jarvise
Quality Leader
Apex Microtechnology Corporation
5980 North Shannon Road
Tucson, AZ 85741–5230
(520) 690–8623
Fax: (520) 888–3329

3674

Business Information: Apex Microtechnology Corporation opened for operation in 1980 and currently employs 120 people. The Corporation expects to post sales in excess of $12 million dollars in 1996. Apex Microtechnology manufactures and distributes hybrid microcircuits for the electronics industry. As Quality Leader, Mr. Jarvise is head of the Quality Department and is responsible for the direction of quality control, scheduling, pro–active programs, and various operational management functions. He leads the corporate quality program for the Steering Committee and is also the safety compliance officer. **Career Steps:** Quality Leader, Apex Microtechnology Corporation (1987–Present); Vice President, Brentwood Investment Company, Inc. (1980–1987); Assistant Manager, Stephen & Company, Inc. (1978–1980). **Associations & Accomplishments:** American Society for Quality Control; Advanced Technology Advisory Committee, Pima Community College. **Education:** University of Phoenix, B.S.B.A. in Business Administration Management (1995). **Personal:** Mr. Jarvise enjoys breeding and exhibiting championship great danes.

Robert M. Lamendola

Vice President of Information Technology
General Instrument – Power Semiconductor Division
10 Melville Park Road
Melville, NY 11720
(516) 847–3035
Fax: (516) 847–3006

3674

Business Information: General Instrument – Power Semiconductor Division is a worldwide manufacturer of power rectifier and transient voltage supressor devices. A data systems management executive with General Instrument since 1992 and employee since 1986, Mr. Lamendola was appointed to his current position in May 1995. As Vice President of Information Technology, he is responsible for planning and directing all information technology–related activities for the organization. **Career Steps:** General Instrument – Power Semiconductor Division: Vice President of Information Technology (1995–Present), Director of MIS (1993–1995), Manager of Systems Development (1992–1993), Project Leader (1989–1992), Programmer/Analyst (1986–1989). **Education:** Bloomsburg University, B.S. in Computer and Information Science (1985). **Personal:** Married to Paula in 1986. One child: Courtney. Mr. Lamendola enjoys golf, skiing, and sports.

Jeffrey A. Levine
Founder and President
Galt, Inc.
6325 9 Falls of the Neuse
Raleigh, NC 27615–6325
(919) 847–7387
Fax: (919) 847–7636

3674

Business Information: Galt, Inc. is a vertically–integrated manufacturer, distributor and wholesaler of electrical equipment and components, including consumer electronics (car stereo equipment), printed circuit boards, and CATV equipment for the broadcasting industry. National in scope, Galt, Inc. has locations in North Carolina, Virginia, New Mexico, New York, California, and Arizona. Founding Galt, Inc. in 1990, Mr. Levine serves as President, responsible for all aspects of operations, including administration, advertising, product research and development, corporate purchasing and marketing, and strategic planning. He also works with engineers and handles public relations. **Career Steps:** Founder and President, Galt, Inc. (1990–Present). **Education:** Thunderbird/AGSIM, M.I.M. (1992); SUNY– Stonybrook, B.A. in Economics. **Personal:** Married to Valerie in 1990. One child: Michael. Mr. Levine enjoys coaching Little League baseball and basketball.

Gene R. Miller
President
Astec Semiconductor
255 Sinclaire Frontage Road
Milpitas, CA 95035–5415
(408) 263–8300
Fax: (408) 263–8340

3674

Business Information: Astec Semiconductor specializes in the design and manufacture of semiconductors. A subsidiary of the largest power supply company in the world, Astec distributes semiconductors internationally to China, Manila, Malaysia, and other countries. As President, Mr. Miller is responsible for all aspects of Company operations, including administration, finance, marketing, and strategic planning. **Career Steps:** President, Astec Semiconductor (1992–Present); President, Semicon (1990–1992); Division Manager, Digital Equipment Corporation (1980–1992). **Associations & Accomplishments:** I.T.T.T.; A.P.E.X. **Education:** Harvard University, M.B.A. (1990); San Jose State University, B.A. **Personal:** Married to JoAnn in 1961. Four children: Cindy, Robert, James, and Karen. Mr. Miller enjoys motorcycle riding and spending time at his ranch with his family. He is very involved with the Mentor program, a community program to help disadvantaged kids in the San Jose Valley area.

Mr. Akinori Mukasa
Executive Vice President
Intelmatec Corporation
41353 Albrae Street
Fremont, CA 94538
(510) 249–4802
Fax: (510) 659–1210

3674

Business Information: Intelmatec Corporation designs and manufactures flexible automation machines for semiconductor and disc media industries. They distribute to electronic, computer and chemical companies in the U.S., Asia and Japan. Established in 1982, Intelmatec Corporation employs 25 persons in their Fremont office and reports having estimated revenue in excess of $5 million. Mr. Mukasa is responsible for all aspects of financial functions and administration for the Corporation. **Career Steps:** Executive Vice President, Intelmatec Corporation (1991–Present); Managing Director, REP-IC Corporation (1976–1991); Director, DAIWA Trading Co., LTD (1953– 1975). **Education:** Aoyama Gakuin University, Tokyo, Japan, B.C.S. in Commercial Science (1953). **Personal:** Married to Miyoko in 1962. Two grown daughters: Junko and Noriko. Mr. Mukasa enjoys playing golf in his leisure time.

Donald E. Myers
Plant Manager
Intel Corporation
1350 Elwood Drive
Los Gatos, CA 95030
(408) 765–9518
Fax: (408) 765–9518

3674

Business Information: Intel Corporation is manufacturer and developer of semiconductors and other microprocessor products. Established in 1971, the Corporation revolutionized the computer industry with the development of the microprocessor computer chip. As Plant Manager, Mr. Myers handles the daily operations of the Los Gatos, California location. He is involved in the technical development of new products and works with others on redefining existing manufactured products. Internet users can reach him via: DMYERS@Access-com.com. **Career Steps:** Intel Corporation: Plant Manager (1991–Present), Engineering Manager (1987–1991), Operations Manager (1981–1987). **Education:** Santa Clara University, B.S.E.E. (1976). **Personal:** Married to Diane. Five children: Jacob Ryan, Amber, Jessica, Rochelle, and Angela. Mr. Myers enjoys writing, sky diving, white water rafting, and scuba diving.

Faramarz Nateghian, Ph.D.
Software/Applications Consultant
Asyst Technologies, Inc.
48761 Kato Road
Fremont, CA 94538
(510) 661–5063
Fax: (510) 661–5101
EMail: See Below

3674

Business Information: Asyst Technologies, Inc. is a leading provider of automated work–in–process (WIP) material systems for the semiconductor industry. The Company provides integrated systems based on three technology areas: minienvironment and interfaces to protect material from contamination; material tracking and validation to prevent misprocessing; and automated storage and transportation linked with factory–wide logistics control software to optimize manufacturing productivity. As Software/Applications Consultant, Dr. Nateghian conducts a comprehensive study of customer requirements. Based on a clear understanding of the customer's requirements, he creates a technical presentation explaining Asyst's solution, and continues his technical assistance during the sale, furnishing support throughout the negotiation of the contract. After submission of a formal customer request, Dr. Nateghian plans out the technical side of the project, ensures the software engineers understand what is needed, and maintains personal contact with the customer so as to remain abreast of any minute–to–minute changes to the requirements. Dr. Nateghian's responsibilities continue throughout the completion of the project, and on to the customer's product satisfaction. As Senior Staff Software Engineer, Dr. Nateghian heads a task force responsible for stabilizing a group of existing Asyst products, to include the MSC 6650, MSC 6610, and Smart–Tag. Additionally, he is responsible for the design and implementation of several software subsystems, including subsystems for the SMART Traveler System (STS). Internet users can reach him via: fnateghian@asyst.com. **Career Steps:** Software/Applications Consultant, Asyst Technologies, Inc. (1993–Present); Professor, Golden Gate University (1988–Present); Software Engineering Manager, U.S. Windpower, Inc. (1988–1993); Senior Software Engineer, Texas Instruments (1983–1987); Software Engineer, Dictaphone (1982–1983); Analyst, Stanford Research Institute (1981–1982). **Associations & Accomplish-**

ments: Center for Iranian Research and Analysis (CIRA); National Institute of Business Management; Decision Sciences Institute; Union Institute Alumni Association; Following is a partial list of Dr. Nateghian's published articles: "Iran's Industrial Challenges and Their Conceivable Solutions" (Forthcoming in 1997), "Civil Society in the Islamic Republic?" (CIRA Bulletin, Forthcoming Fall, 1996), "Industrial Challenges Facing Iran in the Third Millenium" (CIRA, March 1996), "Does Iran Need Technology Policy or State Ownership of Industry?" (AmirKabir University of Technology, Tehran, Iran, December 1995), and "Obstacles to Industrial Development In Iran" (CIRA, April 1994). **Education:** The Union Institute, Management Science, Ph.D. (1992); California State University at Hayward, M.B.A. (1988), B.S. in Computer Science (1981). **Personal:** One child: Mercedes. Dr. Nateghian enjoys chess, reading, writing, and running.

Demetris E. Paraskevopoulos, Ph.D.
Director of Strategic Planning and Market Development
National Semiconductor Corporation
2900 Semiconductor Drive
Santa Clara, CA 95052
(408) 721–5150
Fax: Please mail or

3674

Business Information: National Semiconductor Corporation (NSC) is a leading manufacturer and international distributor of semiconductors. In his current capacity, Dr. Paraskevopoulos oversees corporate strategic marketing developments and is responsible for the selection process of new business ventures and innovative products. In his prior position at National he was responsible for marketing and sales of PC–enhancement board level products in both OEM and retail channels. He has a very strong background in general management, marketing, sales, engineering, and product development, as well as experience in strategic planning, technology investment analysis, technology assessment and forecasting, intercorporate negotiations in the U.S. and Europe. He has extensive involvement with PC enhancement add–in products, PC networking, microelectronics and ASIC's, direct marketing technologies, advanced electronics and solid state sciences, and has acted as a change agent to drive organizational change at NSC and Xerox. In his previous position with National, Dr. Paraskevopoulos directed the worldwide marketing and sales activities for the Company's board level products. National Semiconductor Corporation, with over 12 manufacturing plant facilities located worldwide, employs 23,000 men and women. Annual revenue for fiscal year 1994 is reported in excess of $2.4 billion. **Career Steps:** Director of Strategic Planning and Market Development, National Semiconductor Corporation (1993–Present); Director Retail Channel of Operations, National Semiconductor (1991–1993); Vice President of Marketing and Sales, National Semiconductor (1989–1991); Vice President of Marketing, National Semiconductor (1989–1990); Manager, ASIC Device Operations, Xerox Corporation (1987–1989); Manager, Customer Services & Marketing, Xerox (1986–1987); Manager, Regional Design Centers, Xerox (1984–1986); Applications Manager, Xerox (1983–1984); Manager, Electrical Technology (1981–1982); Manager, Advanced Marking Technology Integration, Xerox (1980); Manager, Document Processor Concepts, Xerox (1979); Technical Specialist, Xerox (1978); Post–Doctoral Research Staff, Massachusetts Institute of Technology (1976–1977). **Associations & Accomplishments:** American Physical Society; Institute of Electrical and Electronic Engineers; Over thirty (30) publications in professional journals (IEEE, APS) and Xerox or NSC internal technical reports in the areas of science, microelectronics, technology economics and management. Over twenty (20) professional society speeches. Four (4) patents issued. Many studies in ASIC economics were often quoted by Dataquest, ICE, and McGraw–Hill. **Education:** Massachusetts Institute of Technology, National Magnet Lab, Post Doctoral studies in superconductivity, instrumentation and solid state devices (1976–1977); Boston University, Ph.D. in Physics (1976); University of Rochester, M.B.A. in Financial Economics (1982); ; Boston University, M.A. in Physics (1973); Brown University, Sc.M. in Electrical Engineering (1971); University of Athens, Greece, Diploma of Sciences, Physics (1969); Numerous corporate training courses in Management, Marketing, and Engineering Subjects.

Frank Pfefferkorn
Vice President – Manufacturing and Engineering
Matsushita Semiconductor Corporation of America
1111 39th Avenue, SE
Puyallup, WA 98374
(206) 841–6002
Fax: (206) 841–6516

3674

Business Information: Matsushita Semiconductor Corporation of America (MASCA) is an affiliated company of Matsushita Electric Industrial Co., Ltd., of Japan, acknowledged to be a leading diversified international manufacturer and marketer of consumer and industrial electronics carrying the trade names Panasonic, Technics, and Quasar. MASCA is a global leader in the manufacture of semiconductors and is the only semiconductor plant for Matsushita in the U.S. One of more than 150 plants in 38 countries, Matsushita's Puyallup factory employs over 400 workers and reports revenue in excess of $130 million. Bringing with him a vast knowledge in the field of semiconductor industry design and operations management, Frank Pfefferkorn was appointed as Vice President for the Puyallup plant in 1992. He is responsbile for spearheading all manufacturing and engineering operations, which also include the organization of all in–house computer technology systems and the day–to–day maintenance of the plant and its effective operations. **Career Steps:** Matsushita Semiconductor Corporation of America: Vice President – Manufacturing and Engineering (1992–Present), Fab Operations Manager (1991–1992); National Semiconductor: Operations Manager (1988–1991), Engineering Manager (1977–1988); Photo Engineer, Mostek Corporation (1974–1977). **Associations & Accomplishments:** Director, Eastern Pierce County Chamber of Commerce; Director, Pierce County Economic Development Board; Shared Leadership Support Committee, Puyallup School District; Fabless Semiconductor Associaton; American Electronic Association; ISO 9000. **Education:** University of Phoenix, B.S.B.A. (1987); Idaho State University, A.A. in Electronics. **Personal:** Married to Patsy in 1974. Two children: Nathan and Joshua. Mr. Pfefferkorn enjoys skiing, boating and reading.

Lance P. Riley
Advanced Technology Director
Unicircuit
14 Inverness Drive East, Bldg. E, Suite 128
Englewood, CO 80112
(303) 799–1533
Fax: (303) 790–8034
E MAIL: See Below

3674

Business Information: Unicircuit, a designer, manufacturer, and tester of complex interconnect technologies, was established in 1979. The Company employs 50 people and projects sales/revenues in excess of $6 million in 1996. Unicircuit does design analysis and product development for companies like Lockheed Martin, Motorola, Rockwell and Texas Instruments. The Company manufactures P.C.B.'s and conducts research on new and emerging technologies in the electronics field. As Advanced Technology Director, Mr. Riley assists in the development of new and emerging technologies, products packaging, and equipment acquisitions for the electronics industry. Other responsibilities include acting as technical liaison to employees, employee training, and technical presentations. Concurrently, Mr. Riley is coordinating research in advanced packaging with several higher learning institutions (i.e. University of North Carolina, Georgia Tech, and Princeton) and NASA. Internet users may reach Mr. Riley via: Lance@Unicircuit.com. **Career Steps:** Unicircuit: Advanced Technologies Director (1996–Present), Sales Engineer (1988–1990); Technical Sales, Alternate Circuit (1990–1996). **Associations & Accomplishments:** Surface Mount Technology Association (SMTA); International Society of Hybrid Manufactures (ISHM); International Electronic Packaging Society (IEPS). **Personal:** Married to Natalie in 1984. One child. Mr. Riley enjoys mountain biking, sports, teaching Bible study, and playing the drums in a band.

Mark A. Santorelli
Director of Engineering
M.E.C. Technology, Inc.
1889 Route 9 Unit 49
Toms River, NJ 08755–1271
(908) 505–0308
Fax: (908) 505–2151
E. MAIL: See Below

3674

Business Information: M.E.C. Technology, Inc., established in 1987, is a privately–owned manufacturer of semiconductor parts and supplier of engineering services. The Company redesigns existing parts, tailoring them to specific requirements for clients. As Director of Engineering, Mr. Santorelli has oversight of the entire engineering staff, including field services. His responsibilities include project scheduling, compiling project budgets, and monitoring project progress. Internet users can reach him via: HOBIEBRAT1@WORLDNET.ATT.NET. **Career Steps:** Director of Engineering, M.E.C. Technology, Inc. (1995–Present); Mechanical Designer, Bell Labs (1988–1995); Customer Service Manager, North American Reiss (1983–1987); Engineering Services, Tecknit (1980–1983). **Education:** Kean College, B.A. (1987). **Personal:** Mr. Santorelli enjoys racing Hobie Cats, bicycling, tennis, and kite flying.

R. Kevin Sellers
Finance Manager, Cable Products Division
Intel Corporation
6505 W. Chandler Boulevard, CH – 11 – 93
Chandler, AZ 85226–3324
(602) 554–3296
Fax: (602) 554–4880
E MAIL: See Below

3674

Business Information: Intel Corporation, established in 1894, is the world's leading marketer of semiconductors. Intel's Personal Conference Division designs, manufactures, and markets video and data conferencing software and hardware components. As Finance Manager, Mr. Sellers manages all financial services at the Chandler, Arizona location including accounts payable, accounts receivable, price analysis, cost targeting, and cash management. **Career Steps:** Intel Corporation: Finance Manager (1994–Present), Senior Finance Analyst (1992–1994), Financial Analyst (1991–1992). **Associations & Accomplishments:** Boy Scouts of America **Education:** Brigham Young University: M.B.A. (1991), Bachelors Degree (1989). **Personal:** Married to Rochelle in 1987. Three children: Collin, McKenzie, and Jackson. Mr. Sellers enjoys golf, Korean cooking, Korean language studies, and tennis.

J. Wayne Stewart
Executive Vice President of Operations
FSI International, Inc.
322 Lake Hazeltine Drive
Chaska, MN 55318–1034
(612) 448–8002
Fax: (612) 448–1300

3674

Business Information: FSI International, Inc. is a manufacturer of semiconductor processing equipment used in processing silicon wafers in the worldwide semiconductor industry. International in scope, FSI has five manufacturing plants, including four domestic and one in the United Kingdom. With more than twenty–three years of experience in the manufacturing industry, Mr. Stewart joined FSI as Vice President of Operations in 1994. Appointed as Executive Vice President of Operations in 1995, he is responsible for the management of worldwide manufacturing, including materials, quality, facilities, and information systems. Concurrently, he is a member of the Board of Directors for FSI Metron Europe. **Career Steps:** FSI International, Inc.: Executive Vice President of Operations (1995–Present), Vice President of Operations (1994–1995); Texas Instruments: Manager of Custom Manufacturing Services–Dallas (1992–1994), Worldwide Manufacturing Systems Manager (1990–1992), Operations Manager of Missile Systems Business (1983–1990). **Associations & Accomplishments:** Board of Directors and Volunteer, United Way of Metropolitan–Dallas; Texas Governor's Long Range Task Force on Education. **Education:** University of Texas–Austin, Bach. degree in Engineering Management (1972). **Personal:** Married to Dorothy in 1973. Two children: Brad and Christie. Mr. Stewart enjoys hunting, fishing, and golf.

Sherif Sweha
Design Manager
Intel Corporation
1900 Prairie City Road, Fm 3 99
Folsom, CA 95630–9501
(916) 356–2233
Fax: (916) 356–6795
E–Mail: See Below

3674

Business Information: Intel Corporation is an international manufacturer of computer systems, including motherboards, microprocessors, microcontrollers and flash memory. Field sales offices are located in every region of the world, with ten campuses having several manufacturing plants each. Serving in various managerial capacities for Intel since 1984, Vivek Gupta was appointed to his current position in 1996. As Manager of Capacity Planning, he oversees strategic planning activities, ensuring manufacturing capabilities and capacities are able to meet product demands for business units. **Career Steps:** Intel Corporation: Manager of Capacity Planning (1996–Present), Manager of North America Logistics (1993–1995), Manager of Manufacturing Engineering (1984–1993). **Associations & Accomplishments:** India Association: President (1994, 1995), Vice President (1993); Council of Logistics Management; Tau Beta Pi; Phi Kappa Phi; Writes articles on community issues and edits a newsletter with a circulation of 1,000; Actively involved in community activities. **Education:** Southern Illinois University, M.S. in Thermal Engineering (1983); Indian Institute of Technology, B.Tech in Mechanical Engineering (1977). **Personal:** Married to Mamta in 1980. Two children: Charu and Sasha. Mr. Sweha enjoys community work, tennis, pingpong, music, sightseeing, and writing.

Helena Maria Ting, Ed.D.
Senior Manager
Temic Semiconductor
1473 Parkwood Drive
San Mateo, CA 94403
(408) 567–8905
Fax: (408) 567–8970
E MAIL: See Below

3674

Business Information: Temic Semiconductor, established in 1966, is a division of Mercedes Benz–Diemler Benz. The Company manufactures hi–tech computer chips for Mercedes Benz automobiles. The chips are part of the electronic computer controls for speedometer, air bag and temperature control. As Senior Manager, Ms. Ting is responsible for human resources development and worldwide organizational development. Other responsibilities include executive planning and development, employee recruitment, employee assessment, and all in–house education programs. Concurrently, Ms. Ting serves as a Trustee at the Pacific School of Psychology and is a Professor at the University of San Francisco. Internet users can reach her via: Helena.Ting@temic.com. **Career Steps:** Senior Manager, Temic Semiconductor (1996–Present); Professor, University of San Francisco (1995–Present); Trustee, Pacific School of Psychology (1990–Present). **Associations & Accomplishments:** Museum Society; Friends of Filolt; American Society of Society of Training and Development; Bay Area Network of Organization Development. **Education:** University of San Francisco: Ed.D. (1991), Master's Degree; San Francisco State University, B.A. **Personal:** Married to Dr. Alan Ting in 1990. Ms. Ting enjoys travel, music, and reading.

Charles W. Weisel Jr
Senior Engineer
Kemet Electronics Corporation
P.O. Box 5928
Greenville, SC 29606
(864) 963–6439
Fax: (864) 963–6456
E MAIL: See Below

3675

Business Information: Kemet Electronics Corporation is a manufacturer and distributor of ceramic and tantalum electronic capacitors. Currently, the Company operates seven manufacturing plants in Mexico, five manufacturing plants in the United States and has distribution centers worldwide. The Company was a division of Union Carbide and split off in 1988. Kemet Electronics currently has over 6,000 employees worldwide and expects to post sales in excess of $400 million in 1996. As a Senior Engineer, Mr. Weisel is an electrical engineer for the Company and is responsible for the development of software for automatic test equipment used in the production testing of electronic capacitors. He is responsible for programming of machine control computers and provides support and maintenance of systems in the United States and Mexico. Internet users may contact him via: charlieweisel@kemet.com. **Career Steps:** Senior Engineer, Kemet Electronics Corporation (1986–Present); Systems Engineer, NCR Corporation (1980–1986); Manager, Milertronics (1978–1980); Electrical Engineer, J. E. Sirrine Company (1975–1978). **Associations & Accomplishments:** Project Management Institute. **Education:** Georgia Institute of Technology, B.E.E. (1974). **Personal:** Married to Sabyl Jones in 1982. Two children: Catherine and Blake. Mr. Weisel enjoys designing and building homes and being a leader of the Boy's Royal Rangers, a Christian Scouts Program.

Steven M. Hegyi
General Manager
ABB Power T & D
200 Newton Bridge Road
Athens, GA 30613
(706) 548–3121
Fax: (706) 549–2371

3677

Business Information: ABB Power T & D is an international designer, manufacturer, and marketer of distribution transformers to the utility industry. Established in 1958, ABB Power T & D reports annual revenue of $125 million and currently employs 650 people. With eighteen years experience in electrical engineering, Mr. Hegyi joined the Company in 1992 as Manager of the Productivity Center, with a promotion to Vice President of Quality Programs in 1993. Appointed as General Manager in 1994, he is responsible for the general management of the business, selling electrical transformers to both domestic and international markets. He also provides leadership and vision to increase profitability by changing design, manufacturing and information system technologies and improve operating efficiencies through the implementation of cellular manufacturing and total quality concepts. Under his leadership, Mr. Hegyi has been responsible for a sixty percent profitability improvement, twenty–five percent reduction in total labor and compensation costs, twenty–four percent quality improvement, fifty percent safety improvement, forty percent inventory reduction, and thirty percent floor space reduction. Other areas of management include public relations, marketing, and strategic planning. **Career Steps:** ABB Power T & D: General Manager – Athens, GA (1994–Present), Vice President Quality Programs – Raleigh, NC (1993–1994), Manager of Productivity Center – ABB Transmission Technology Institute, Raleigh, NC (1992–1993); Manager of Manufacturing, Engineering, and Quality, J.I. Case Company (1988–1992); General Electric Company: Quality Resources Consultant – Bridgeport, CT (1979–1988, 1986–1988), Manager of Advanced Quality Engineering – Milwaukee, WI (1983–1986), Senior Design Engineer – Hickory, NC (1981–1983), Development Engineer – Hickory, NC (1979–1981); Senior Project Engineer, Sperry Flight Systems (1977–1979). **Associations & Accomplishments:** Institute of Electrical and Electronic Engineers; American Society for Quality Control; Board of Directors (1996), Georgia Industry Association; Athens Technical Advisory Board; Productivity Center Advisory Board; Scout Master (1978–1986). **Education:** Arizona State University, M.S. in Electrical Engineering (1977); Colorado College, B.A. in Physics (1971); GE Manufacturing Management Courses (1979–1988); Certification: Certified Quality Engineer, by American Society for Quality Control (1990). **Personal:** Married to Katherine in 1971. Two children: Sarah and Laura. Mr. Hegyi enjoys restoring English manufactured antique motorcycles, gardening, and basketball.

Mr. Udo W. Werner
Controller
Framatome Connectors Daut and Reitz
Austr, 26
Neurnberg, Germany D–90411
49–(0911)52720
Fax: 49–(0911)52306

3678

Business Information: Framatome Connectors Daut and Reitz specializes in the worldwide manufacture of automotive electrical connectors. Established in 1957, Framatome Connectors currently employs 550 people. As Controller and Chief Financial Officer, Mr. Werner is responsible for all global corporate financial operations. **Career Steps:** Controller and Chief Financial Officer, Framatome Connectors Daut and Reitz (1993–Present); Controller and Chief Financial Officer, S F Steering Gear/Lensforden (1989–1993); Chief Financial Officer and Executive Vice President of Finance and Administration, Porsche Aviation Products (1985–1989). **Associations & Accomplishments:** VWI, Germany. **Education:** University of Fridericiana, Ph.D. in Economy Manufacturing and Planning (1986). **Personal:** Married to Ursula in 1988. Three children: Jessica, Nicole and Natascha. Mr. Werner enjoys scuba diving, sailsurfing and skiing.

Ronald E. Baker
Manager of Manufacturing
Philips Technologies
813 S. Grandstaff Drive
Auburn, IN 46706
(219) 925–8867
Fax: (219) 925–8710

3679

Business Information: Philips Technologies — a subsidiary of Philips NA Electronics Company, a "Tier 1" supplier to automotive OEM's — is a manufacturer of electronic systems and electromechanical sensors. Products include distributor–less ignition systems. Headquartered in Cheshire, Connecticut and established in 1977, Philips Technologies has three locations, reporting annual revenue of $55 million, and currently employs 400 people. As Manager of Manufacturing, Mr. Baker directs the daily efforts of manufacturing engineering, process support engineering, and maintenance; as well as participating in strategic planning. **Career Steps:** Manager of Manufacturing, Philips Technologies (1992–Present); Manager of Operations, Magnetek, Inc. (1988–1992); Plant Manager, Allen Bradley (1983–1988); Industrial Engineer, Delco Electronics (1980–1983). **Associations & Accomplishments:** Surface Mounted Technology Association; Provides leadership training to teens through a church–sponsored Youth Ministry. **Education:** Purdue University, B.S. (1979). **Personal:** Married to Judy in 1975. One child: Nick. Mr. Baker enjoys hunting, fishing and woodworking during his leisure time.

Robert J. Ball
Material Planning Manager
Micron Electronics, Inc.
900 East Karcher Road
Nampa, ID 83687
(208) 893–3825
Fax: (208) 893–8979
EMail: See Below

3679

Business Information: Micron Electronics, Inc. (MEI) manufactures electronic products for a wide range of computing and digital applications. The Company develops, markets, manufactures and supports systems for consumer, business and government use for Desktop, Servers, and Notebook products. MEI also provides contract manufacturing services to OEM's and maintains a component recovery operation. The Company conducts business domestically and internationally with over 1.5 billion in sales. As Material Planning Manager, Mr. Ball is responsible for components forecasting, master scheduling, MRP regens, inventory management, and production scheduling of the PC operations. Internet users can reach him via: RBALL@Micron.Com **Career Steps:** Material Planning Manager, Micron Electronics, Inc. (1995–Present); Master Scheduler, Megahertz Corp./US Robotics (1993–1994); Material Planner, Hewlett Packard (1989–1993). **Associations & Accomplishments:** Treasure Valley Chapter, American Production and Inventory Control Society (APICS). **Education:** Boise State University, M.B.A. (1991); Albertson's College of Idaho, B.B.A. in Financial/Administration and Management (1988); Utah Technical College – Provo/Orem, A.S. (1986). **Personal:** Married to Linda M. in 1985. Six children: Corey, Cambra, Caitlin, Jaron, Evan, and Kammon. Mr. Ball enjoys spending time with his family, camping, fishing, and baseball. He also enjoys international import/export opportunities and entrepreneurial opportunities.

Maureen A. Callahan–Saia, CPA
Controller
Genlyte Controls
2413 South Shiloh Road
Garland, TX 75041
(214) 840–3803
Fax: (214) 271–4077

3679

Business Information: Genlyte Controls, a division of Genlyte Group, is a manufacturer of electronic lighting controls. Established in 1985, Genlyte Controls reports annual revenue of $16 million and currently employs 90 people. A Certified Public Accountant in New Jersey, Mrs. Callahan–Saia joined the parent company, Genlyte Group in 1992. Transferring to their subsidiary, Genlyte Controls, in 1994, she was appointed as Controller, responsible for all financial reports and analysis, human resource management, and MIS management. **Career Steps:** Controller, Genlyte Controls (1994–Present); Manager of Financial Reporting, Genlyte Group (1992–1994); Supervisor of Accounting, CIT Group (1991–1992). **Associations & Accomplishments:** American Institute of Certified Public Accountants; New Jersey Society of Certified Public Accountants. **Education:** Montclair State College, B.S.

(1987). **Personal:** Married to Steve in 1994. Mrs. Callahan–Saia enjoys horses, reading, travel, and walking.

Sandy Cate
Human Resources Manager
Avnet, Inc.
620 West Industry Drive
Oxford, NC 27565
(919) 690–2001
Fax: (919) 690–1307

3679

Business Information: Avnet, Inc. is one of the nation's leading electronic and computer components manufacturer's distributor. Serving as the "middle man" for computer and semiconductor industries, Avnet processes all orders, inspects, packages, assembles and ships all products for its industry clientele. As Human Resources Manager, Sandy Cate is responsible for all aspects of employee relations, including personnel policies, recognition programs, safety, wellness training, job bidding, attendance, and vending services for the employee fund. **Career Steps:** Avnet, Inc.: Human Resources Manager (1994–Present), Senior Human Resources Representative (1992–1994); Human Resources Assistant, USCO Distribution Services, Inc. (1988–1992). **Associations & Accomplishments:** Society for Human Resource Management; Granville County Chamber of Commerce; Capital Associated Industries, Inc.; Active Member, White Memorial Presbyterian Church. **Education:** University of North Carolina – Chapel Hill, B.A. (1988); Certified Zenger–Miller Instructor. **Personal:** Ms. Cate enjoys snow skiing, camping, boating, reading, photography, travel and piano.

Mr. Eugene R. Chapdelaine
Owner
ERC Enterprises
27 Sandstone Drive
Bedford, NH 03110
(603) 425–5035
Fax: (603) 622–4073

3679

Business Information: ERC Enterprises develops interactive wholesale distribution networks. Established in 1990, ERC Enterprises is now active in four countries, and has achieved 100% growth rate. The parent company has been in business for 35 years and reported $6.5 billion in sales for Fiscal 1996. **Career Steps:** Owner, ERC Enterprises (1990–Present); Chief Engineer, Discom/TDK USA (1989–1996); Senior Video Engineer, Computervision (1981–1989); Engineer, Andersen Labs (1976–1989). **Associations & Accomplishments:** Institute of Electrical and Electronic Engineers (IEEE); Society for Information Display (SID); Boy Scout Leader; Previous Director of New England Escadrille; Experimental Aircraft Association (EAA). **Education:** University of Hartford, B.S. (1979); S.I. Ward Technical College, A.S. **Personal:** Married to Suzanne in 1983. Two children: Neil and Luke. Mr. Chapdelaine enjoys business developing, aircraft restoration and piloting.

Lance Criscuolo
Product Manager
Cybex
9910 Royal Lane #408
Dallas, TX 75231
(214) 578–1911
Fax: (214) 578–8676
EMAIL: See Below

3679

Business Information: Cybex specializes in the manufacture of integrated high precision robotics equipment for the semiconductor industry. Established in 1991, the Company has a sister company in Malaysia. The Company estimates annual revenue in excess of $7 million. As Product Manager, Mr. Criscuolo is responsible for sales and marketing efforts worldwide. Internet users can reach him via: lcriscuolo@cybextech.co. **Career Steps:** Product Manager, Cybex (1996–Present); Marlow Industries: Product Manager (1993–1996), Design Engineer (1991–1993); Design Engineer, E–Systems (1989–1991). **Associations & Accomplishments:** World Wild Life Fund (WWF); Humane Society of the United States (HUS). **Education:** Texas Tech University, B.S.M.E. (1989). **Personal:** Mr. Criscuolo enjoys golf, any outdoor sport, and animals.

Jack A. Enright
Manager
Hazeltine Corporation
450 East Pulaski Road
Greenlawn, NY 11740–1609
(516) 262–8331
Fax: (516) 262–8290
EMAIL: See Below

3679

Business Information: Hazeltine Corporation specializes in the manufacture of defence electronics including: Display systems, C3I, Commercial Antennas, Cellular Base Stations and Interrogation Equipment. A manufacturing engineer with over twenty years experience, Jack Enright serves as Manager of Manufacturing Engineering and Performance Measurement for Hazeltine's Greenlawn, New York manufacturing facility. **Career Steps:** Manager, Hazeltine Corporation (1986–Present); Senior Industrial Engineer, Fairchild Republic Corporation (1980–1986); Manufacturing Manager, Universal Fasteners (1976–1980). **Associations & Accomplishments:** National Management Association: Sustained Member, Former Vice President, Former Treasurer; American Management Association; American Production Inventory Control Society; Association for Quality and Participation; MTM Association; Chairman, Inclusion Special Education PTA Committee. **Education:** State University of New York: B.A. in Business Management (1987), currently in senior year completing a B.T. in Industrial Technology. **Personal:** Married to Patricia in 1981. One child: Jennifer. Mr. Enright enjoys teaching design engineering to 9–10th graders at Elwood School District.

Francisco A. Fiorotto

President
Brascabos
Presidente Kennedy 284
Rio Claro, SP, Brazil 13501–270
55–19–5249133
Fax: 55–19–5349377

3679

Business Information: Brascabos specializes in the production of electrical harness and power cords for appliance, automotive, telephone, and computer industries. The Company controls 90% of the market share in Brazil, and is contracted with companies such as Whirlpool in the United States. As President, Mr. Fiorotto is responsible for all aspects of Company operations, including administration, finance, sales and marketing, and strategic planning. **Career Steps:** President, Brascabos (1992–Present); Industrial Director, Brastemp S.A. (1988–1992); Marini E. Daminelli S.A. a division of Westinghouse Electric Corporation: General Manager (1983–1987), Engineering Manager (1979–1982). **Associations & Accomplishments:** Councelor, Federacao das Industrias do Estado de Sao Paulo. **Education:** Escola Federal Engenharea de Itajuba, Electrical Engineer (1972). **Personal:** Married to Maria Isabel G. in 1973. Three children: Katharine, Guilherite, and Gustavo Adolfo. Mr. Fiorotto enjoys horse endurance.

Martin D. Forbes
Director of International Sales and Marketing
Toshiba America MRI, Inc.
280 Utah Avenue
South San Francisco, CA 94080–6801
(415) 872–2722
Fax: (415) 742–6080

3679

Business Information: Toshiba America MRI, Inc. is a manufacturer of medical imaging systems, including magnetic resonance imaging. Established in 1989 with approximately 250 employees, the Company's estimated annual sales are over $75 million. As Director of International Sales and Marketing, Mr. Forbes is responsible for diversified operations, including sales, marketing, public relations, and strategic planning. **Career Steps:** Toshiba America MRI, Inc.: Director of International Sales and Marketing (1990–Present), Manager of International Service (1989–1990); Manager of Installations, Diasonics (1987–1989). **Education:** University of San Francisco, B.S. (1985); University of Bristol – England, B.S. (1980). **Personal:** Married to Shahnaz in 1989. One child: Cyrus Alexander. Mr. Forbes enjoys sailing and travel.

Keith I. Gray
Engineering Manager
Joslyn Hi Voltage Corporation
4000 East 116th Street
Cleveland, OH 44105–4310
(216) 271–6600
Fax: (216) 341–3615
EMail: See Below

3679

Business Information: Joslyn Hi Voltage Corporation is a manufacturer of medium voltage reactive control switches and control systems. As Engineering Manager, Mr. Gray is responsible for all engineering functions, including development, drafting, product development, strategic planning, and personnel responsibilities. Internet users can reach him via: k.i.gray@ieee.org. **Career Steps:** Engineering Manager, Joslyn Hi Voltage Corporation (1994–Present); Product Engineering Manager, Locke Insulator Company (1991–1994); Development Engineering Manager, Siemens (1988–1991); Manager of Circuit Breaker Division, Golden Gate Switch Board (1982–1988). **Associations & Accomplishments:** Institute of Electrical and Electronics Engineers. **Education:** Staffordshire College of Technology, HNC in Electrical Engineering (1963). **Personal:** Married to Rosemary in 1963. Three children: Claire, Nicola, and Sarah. Mr. Gray enjoys bicycling.

Ann M. Hill
LPN/OHN
Thomas & Betts Corporation
8735 Hamilton Road
Southaven, MS 38671–3103
(601) 342–1545
Fax: (301) 342–0246

3679

Business Information: Thomas & Betts Corporation is a manufacturer of electrical components (i.e., grounding rods, etc.) for residential properties. The Company has 37 plants internationally. As LPN/OHN, Ms. Hill takes care of injuries, physicals, Worker's Compensation, safety talks, and other parts of safety (safety team, inspection, etc.). **Career Steps:** LPN/OHN, Thomas & Betts Corporation (1994–Present); LPN/OHN – Safety Director, Landau Uniform, Inc. (1990–1994); LPN – Doctor's Assistant, Dr. Phil Lieberman (1982–1989). **Associations & Accomplishments:** American Society of Safety Engineers; American Industrial Hygiene; Mid–South Workman Compensation Association. **Education:** NWJC, LPN (1980); Sea Isle Vo Tech. **Personal:** Married to Jessie W. in 1965. Two children: Roger W. and Melissa A. Ms. Hill enjoys church activities, singing, and playing with her grandchildren.

Michael J. Hooper
Government Marketing Manager
Matsushita Electric
2430 Don Reid Drive
Ottawa, Ontario K1H 8P5
(613) 247–1501
Fax: (613) 247–1502
EMAIL: hooper@igs.net

3679

Business Information: Panasonic, a division of Matsushita Electric, was established March 17th, 1918 and currently employs 254,059. The Company manufactures electronic components for the broadcast and television industries. As Government Marketing Manager, Mr. Hooper is the manager for federal government accounts for industrial and broadcast systems. He is involved in developing marketing strategies for new and existing products. **Career Steps:** Government Marketing Manager, Matsushita Electric (1979–Present); Sales Representative, Turnelle Associates (1974–1979); Technician, Statistics Canada (1973–1974). **Associations & Accomplishments:** Society of Motion Picture and Television Engineers. **Education:** Algonquin College. **Personal:** Married to Karen in 1977. Two children: Shawn and Kevin. Mr. Hooper enjoys camping and skiing.

Walter J. Jenkins
Principal Analyst
Digital Equipment Corporation
301 S. Rockrimmon Boulevard
Colorado Springs, CO 80919
(719) 548–3142
Fax: (719) 548–2020
Email: See Below

3679

Business Information: Digital Equipment Corporation is an electronic manufacturing company. The Corporation produces the electronic components, assembles them, installs them, and then tests the products in which the components are installed. As Principal Analyst, Mr. Jenkins is responsible for analyzing materials, including researching what they are capable of doing and that the components allow products to function properly. Internet users can reach him via: Jenkins@ImTDev.ENET.DEC.COM. **Career Steps:** Principal Analyst, Digital Equipment Corporation (1977–Present). **Education:** Phoenix Community College, A.A. (1984). **Personal:** Married to Karen in 1987. Two children: Candice and Michael. Mr. Jenkins enjoys drag racing.

ADALET-PLM
A SCOTT FETZER COMPANY

Jeremias A. Martins
Vice President of Engineering
ADALET – PLM
4801 West 150th Street
Cleveland, OH 44135
(216) 267–5590 Ext. 237
Fax: (216) 267–6710

3679

Business Information: ADALET – PLM is one of the top six companies in the nation manufacturing small closure outside weatherproof switches, OEM sales, explosion proof industrial equipment, and off shore drilling rigs. As Vice President of Engineering, Mr. Martins is responsible for supervising 10 employees, managing new product development, and directing existing product maintenance. **Career Steps:** Vice President of Engineering, Adalet – PLM (1995–Present); Manager of Engineering, O–Z GEDNEY (1977–1995); Project Engineering, Scouill Manufacturing Company (1973–1977). **Associations & Accomplishments:** National Electrical Manufacturers Association; NFPA; Underwriter Laboratory Industrial Advisory Group for UL5O; Professional Engineer. **Education:** University of New Haven, B.S.M.E. (1983). **Personal:** Married to Debra A. in 1976. Two children: Kristen and Melissa. Mr. Martins enjoys sports, particularly golf and outdoor sports.

Jorge L. Montalvo
Process Engineer
Thomas & Betts Caribe, Inc.
224 F. Marbella
Aquadilla, Puerto Rico 00603
(809) 855–3046
Fax: (809) 855–2688

3679

Business Information: Thomas & Betts Caribe, Inc. is a major electronics components manufacturer and international distributor. Global in scope, the Company has operations in Europe, the Far East, the U.S. and Puerto Rico. The Puerto Rican operations specialize in the production of electrical terminals. A professional engineer with over ten years expertise in process manufacturing, design and mechanical engineering, Mr. Montalvo joined Thomas & Betts' Puerto Rican facility in March of 1991. As a Process Engineer, he implements process flow improvement concepts, testing and equipment improvement design and development. Additionally, he serves on the Safety Committee and Suggestions Programs, as well as an Element Director of the Loss Control Program. **Career Steps:** Process Engineer, Thomas & Betts Caribe, Inc. (1991–Present); Project Engineer, Avon Corporation (1986–1990); Junior Design Engineer, Naval Ocean Research and Development Activity (1985–1986). **Associations & Accomplishments:** American Society of Mechanical Engineers; Society of Manufacturing Engineers. **Education:** University of Puerto Rico – Mayaguez Campus, B.S.M.E. (1985); University of Phoenix – Guaynabo, Puerto Rico Campus, Towards M.B.A. in Marketing. **Personal:** Married to Annette Justiniano De Montalvo in 1992. One child: Jorge L. Montalvo Justiniano. Mr. Montalvo enjoys reading, model building, inventing and meditation.

Bruce R. Morrisseau
Business Unit Manager
Fenwal Electronics
450 Fortune Boulevard
Milford, MA 01757–1722
(508) 478–6000
Fax: (508) 473–6035

3679

Business Information: Fenwal Electronics is the world's leading manufacturer of thermistors (temperature sensors) for a broad range of appliance, automotive, industrial, medical, telecommunications, and military/aerospace applications. International in scope, Fenwal Electronics has three plants located in the U.S. (headquartered in Massachusetts), United Kingdom, and the Caribbean. Joining Fenwal in 1985, Mr. Morrisseau was appointed as Business Unit Manager in 1994.

He is responsible for managing one half of plant operations, including manufacturing, production, quality control, engineering, design engineering, equipment development, automation, and plant engineering for multiple product lines, consisting of 60% of annual sales. **Career Steps:** Fenwal Electronics: Business Unit Manager (1994–Present), Manufacturing Engineering Manager (1992–1994), Facilities/Safety Manager (1990–1992). **Associations & Accomplishments:** Benevolent and Protective Order of Elks. **Education:** Syracuse University, B.S. in Electrical Engineering (1985). **Personal:** Married to Tammy in 1993. Mr. Morrisseau enjoys oil painting, gourmet cooking, and general contracting.

Edenislao Negron Hernandez
Senior Products Engineer
Caribe General Electric
P.O. Box 1575
Anasco, Puerto Rico 00610
(787) 826–2590
Fax: (787) 826–5065

3679

Business Information: Caribe General Electric is the world's leading producer/distributor of consumer electrical and electronic products. Established in 1971, the Company specializes in the manufacture of protective relays, control switches, and electronic meters to an international market. Located in Anasco, Puerto Rico, the Company has eleven locations throughout the island. As Senior Products Engineer, Mr. Negron provides engineering support on all special orders, trouble–shoots problems and complaints from all over the world, and supervises a small support staff of engineers. **Career Steps:** Senior Products Engineer, Caribe General Electric (1996–Present); Product Owner, Caribe General Electric Relays, Inc. (1995–1996); Process Control Engineer, Caribe General Electric Products, Inc. (1990–1995). **Education:** University of Puerto Rico, B.S.E.E. (1983). **Personal:** Two children: Kristel and Stephanie. Mr. Negron Hernandez enjoys target shooting, reading, and travel.

Linda S. Perry

Vice President – Human Resources
General Instrument Corporation/PSD
10 Melville Park Road
Melville, NY 11747–9023
(516) 847–3030
Fax: (516) 847–3060

3679

Business Information: General Instrument Corporation/PSD specializes in the manufacture of electronic components. Established in 1932, PSD currently employs 3,285 people. Starting as Manager of Human Resources for General Instrument in 1984, Linda Perry now serves as Vice President over global human resource operations, with duties involving employee benefits, training, recruitment, strategies and objectives. **Career Steps:** General Instrument Corporation/PSD: Vice President – Human Resources (1995–Present), Director, Human Resources (1988–1995), Manager, Human Resources (1984–1988). **Associations & Accomplishments:** Society for Human Resource Management; International Institute of Human Resources; National Association of Female Executives; Long Island Association Economic Development Committee. **Education:** SUNY Empire State College, B.S. (1995). **Personal:** Ms. Perry enjoys reading, sailing and walking.

Lisa Ng Podsadecki
Accounting Manager
Taxan USA Corporation
2880 San Tomas Expressway, Suite 101
Santa Clara, CA 95051
(408) 748–0200 Ext. 223
Fax: (408) 748–9190
E MAIL: See Below

3679

Business Information: Taxan USA Corporation is a wholly–owned subsidiary of Kaga Electronics Co., Ltd. (Japan). Established in 1981, Taxan U.S.A. provides electronic parts procurement adn PCB assembly services to companies in Silicon Valley and from spring of 1994, the Company started the importing, exporting and sale of semicincustors and conmoputer peripheral equipment. As the primary financial professional and manager in the Company, Mrs. Podsadecki oversees and is fully responsible for all financial, budgetary, treasury, costing, and accounting functions to maintain the statutory accounts and to produce timely and effective management reporting. Other duties include indentification of cost problems and operation system inporvement. Internet users may contact her via: lpodsadzcki@taxan.usa.com. **Career Steps:** Accounting Manager, Taxan USA Corporation (1995–Present);

Commercial and Financial Controller, SGB Far East Ltd., Hong Kong (1993–1994); Financial Controller, Acer Consultants Pte Ltd., Singapore (1990–1993); Senior Accountant (auditor), Deloitte & Touche, Hong Kong (1986–1989). **Associations & Accomplishments:** The Chartered Association of Certified Accountants (Hong Kong and British); Institute of Certified Public Accountants of Singapore. Mrs. Podsadecki was born in Chinca PRC and studied for secondary and tertiary education in Hong Kong, and she has been working in three major international cities including Hong Kong, Singapore and Santa Clara, hence, she is fluent in both English and Chinese (Mandarin, Cantonese and Fukinese). **Education:** Hong Kong Baptist College, Honors Diploma (1986). **Personal:** Married to Ted in 1994. Mrs. Podsadecki enjoys arranging flowers.

Benjamin Sandzer–Bell

President
Thomson–CSF, Inc.
99 Canal Center Plaza, Suite 450
Alexandria, VA 22314–1588
(703) 838–5640
Fax: (703) 838–1688

3679

Business Information: Thomson–CSF, Inc. is a subsidiary of Thomson–CSF, a multi–national company headquartered in Europe, which specializes in business development and marketing of defense electronics. Serving various technical and global executive positions within the Thomson–CSF conglomerate since 1987, Benjamin Sandzer–Bell was appointed President of Thomson–CSF, Inc. in 1995. His primary focus involves government and international relations, contractual liaison and overall corporate strategy. **Career Steps:** President, Thomson–CSF, Inc. (1994–Present); President, Thomson–CSF Japan (1992–1994); Program Operations Manager, Wilcox Electric (1990–1992); Technical Transfer/Purchasing, Thomson–CSF MSE Program (1987–1990). **Associations & Accomplishments:** AUSA; Armed Forces Communications & Electronics Association (AFCEA); Navy League of the U.S.; American Defense Preparedness Association (ADPA); Fluent in Japanese. **Education:** Johns Hopkins University, M.A. in International Relations (1989); University of California – Los Angeles, B.A. in Political Science (1982). **Personal:** Married to Karen Sandzer–Bell.

Joel Yocom

President
Litchfield Precision Components
1 Precision Dr.
Litchfield, MN 55355–2610
(612) 693–2891
Fax: (612) 693–4444

3679

Business Information: Litchfield Precision Components specializes in the manufacture of flexible printed circuits and electronic components. A technical leader in the industry, Litchfield Precision Components is well–known for their complexity and development of new products. Established in 1975, the Company currently employs 200 people and has an estimated annual revenue of $12 million. As President, Mr. Yocom is responsible for all aspects of operations, as well as the overall vision and growth of the Company, quality delivery of products to customers and all strategic planning. **Career Steps:** President, Litchfield Precision Components (1993–Present). **Associations & Accomplishments:** Institute for Interconnecting and Packaging Electronic Circuitry; Presidental Award, IPEC (1992); Southeast Champion for Case Marketing, University of Tennessee; Published in Printed Circuit Fabrication Journal; Active public speaker. **Education:** University of Tennessee, M.B.A. in Marketing and Finance (1994). **Personal:** Married to Marcia Cole–Yocom in 1993. Mr. Yocom enjoys golf.

Ho Y. Yu, Ph.D.
President and Chief Executive Officer
Mobius Green Energy, Inc.
3333 Bowers Avenue, Suite 236
Santa Clara, CA 95054
(408) 654–1981
Fax: (408) 253–7336

3691

Business Information: Mobius Green Energy, Inc. is an international manufacturer and distributor of rechargeable NIMH batteries. Established in 1993, the Company has an estimated annual revenue of $15 million and currently employs 300 people. They also have two manufacturing sites in China. As President and Chief Executive Officer, Dr. Yu is a founding partner and is responsible for all aspects of operations. **Career**

Steps: President and Chief Executive Officer, Mobius Green Energy, Inc. (1994–Present); Vice President, VLSI Technology, Inc. (1988–1994); Manager of Process Development, Motorola (1986–1988); Executive Vice President, Quesel, Inc. (1985–1986). **Associations & Accomplishments:** Institute of Electrical and Electronical Engineering; Electrochemical Society; Board of Trustee, International Technologist University, Santa Clara, CA. **Education:** University of Notre Dame, Ph.D. (1968); Chiao Tung University, Taiwan, M.S. in Electrical Engineering (1965); Cheng Kung University, Taiwan, B.S. in Electrical Engineering (1962). **Personal:** Married to Chi–Yuan Yu in 1973. Two children: Henry Yu and Katie Yu.

Carol L. Kirk

President and Founder
Advanced Energy Sources
1031 South Santa Fe Avenue
Compton, CA 90221–4334
(310) 763–5544
Fax: (310) 763–5545

3692

Business Information: Advanced Energy Sources, d.b.a. Keystone Batteries, is a manufacturer of lead acid and gel batteries selling to distributors in the US and worldwide. The GEL Batteries are used for standby Power–Medical Equipment, phone equipment, computer equipment, also for storage power for solar energy. They power electric wheelchairs, toys and all forms of cars, trucks, motorhomes and boats. Our liquid line of batteries are used to start engines in heavy equipment, utility trucks, trucking lines, busses, etc. Established in 1992, Advanced Energy Sources report annual revenue of $3 million and currently employs 30 people. As President and Founder, Ms. Kirk is responsible for the supervising of all phases of operations, including manufacturing, office management, employee training, safety, EPA regulations, and sales. **Career Steps:** President and Founder, Advanced Energy Sources (1992–Present); Fundraising, Childhelp USA – Orange County (1982–1992); Real Estate Sales, Miller Real Estate (1975–1980). **Associations & Accomplishments:** Member of Childhelp USA – an organization to fight child abuse (a volunteer for 10 years). **Education:** Valley Junior College, A.A. (1982); Orange Coast College. **Personal:** Two children: Judy Ann and Jeffrey Lee Miller. Ms. Kirk enjoys spending time with her family, playing golf and snow skiing in the winter months.

Kirstin Litz Henry

Senior Programmer/Analyst
KOMAG
275 South Hillview Drive
Milpitas, CA 95035–5417
(408) 957–4463
Fax: (408) 946–9653
E MAIL: See Below

3695

Business Information: KOMAG is the world's largest supplier of thin film media for computer hard disk drives. International in scope, the Company is headquartered in Milpitas, California with additional offices in Malaysia. The product manufactured by KOMAG is considered to be the data storage industries' most advanced disk products. As Senior Programmer Analyst, Ms. Litz Henry oversees information systems manufacturing and is responsible for assisting in the automation of the production line. Internet users can reach her via: KirstinL@komag2.komag.com. **Career Steps:** Senior Programmer Analyst, KOMAG (1995–Present); Programmer/Analyst, Xilinx (1995); Programmer/Analyst, IDT (Integrated Device Tech.) (1989–1995); Teacher, Yvipa High School (1987). **Associations & Accomplishments:** National Association for Female Executives; Make–A–Wish Foundation. **Education:** University of Redlands–Johnston College, B.A. (1987); Yucaipa High School. **Personal:** Married to Michael in 1995. Ms. Litz Henry enjoys basketball, fishing, boating, and reading.

Adel Risaat Adib

Owner and General Manager
Alfa Electronics
5 Misr Development Buildings, Airport Road Heliopolis
Cairo, Egypt 11511
(202) 267–2816
Fax: (202) 266–0184

3699

Business Information: Alfa Electronics is a consultation, design, manufacturer, assembler, and servicer of electronic equipment and devices. Products include energy savers for hotel rooms, currency exchange boards, educational electronics, telephone timers, and custom–made equipment for third parties. Alfa Electronics is also an agent in Egypt for gasoline dispensers, ink jet printers, sound systems, hotel equipment, and access control systems for all commercial and industrial development. Founding Alfa Electronics in 1987 and serving as its Owner and General Manager, Mr. Adib is responsible for all aspects of operations, including strategic planning, management, and policymaking. He also writes for a technical magazine in Egypt, providing a monthly column where he presents opinions and ideas. **Career Steps:** Owner and General Manager, Alfa Electronics (1987–Present); Schlumberger: Middle East Markerting Manager (1983–1987), Operations Manager – Iraq (1979–1983), Location Manager – Egypt (1975–1979). **Associations & Accomplishments:** Board Member, New Civic Forum; Chamber of Electronic Industry, Egyptian Industry Federation; General Committee, Tech Industries Development. **Education:** Cairo University – Faculty of Engineering, B.Sc. (1972). **Personal:** Married to Nahed Nassif in 1975. Three children: Mary, Fadi, and Shady. Mr. Adib enjoys public work, writing, music, and art.

Sharon M. Andrews

Director of Finance
Buchanan Construction Products
101 Bilby Road
Hackettstown, NJ 07840–1715
(908) 813–3604
Fax: (908) 850–3726
EMAIL: See Below

3699

Business Information: Buchanan Construction Products, a subsidiary of Ideal Industries, is a manufacturer and distributor of electrical products, distributing through OEM marketing, direct sales, representative sales, and retail sales (Home Depot). Ms. Andrews joined Buchanan in 1994 as Accounting Manager, moving into her present position as Director of Finance the following year. Her responsibilities include all financial requirements, staff management, financial action program administration, accounting functions, and long range planning. Internet users can reach her via: SAndrews@wirenut.com **Career Steps:** Buchanan Construction Products: Director of Finance (1995–Present) Accounting Manager (1994–1995); Senior Financial Analyst, Integrated Network Corporation (1990–1994); Senior Accountant, Adidas U.S.A., Inc. (1988–1990). **Education:** Lehigh University, M.B.A. (1992); Muhlenberg College, B.A. in Accounting. **Personal:** Ms. Andrews enjoys golf.

David J. Besser

Director of Operations
PMI Food Equipment Group
701 S. Ridge Avenue
Troy, OH 45374–0001
(513) 332–2709
Fax: (513) 332–2959

3699

Business Information: PMI Food Equipment Group, a subsidiary of Illinois based Premark International, is comprised of three divisions, consumer products, building products, and food equipment, with the Troy Ohio plant specializing in the manufacture and marketing of commercial restaurant products. Established in 1986, the Company employs 10,000 people and has estimated annual revenue of $1.2 billion. As Director of Operations, Mr. Besser oversees all aspects of manufacturing operations for the food preparation equipment division. He is responsible for customer service and quality control, and has ten direct reports. **Career Steps:** Director of Operations, PMI Food Equipment Group (1985–Present); Manager of Systems Engineer, Litton (1985–1988); Manufacturing Engineer Manager, John Deere (1975–1985). **Associations & Accomplishments:** Outdoor Writers Association of America; Board of Directors, Southeastern Outdoor Press Association. Mr. Dorsey is an award–winning author and photographer of six books on outdoor and nature subjects. **Education:** Iowa State University, B.S.I.E. (1972); University of Cincinnati, Executive Program. **Personal:** Married to Christine in 1982. Two children: Chelsea and Alison. Mr. Besser enjoys tennis and golf.

Robert Blanchard

President
Plano Microwave Inc.
1601 Capital Avenue, Suite 101
Plano, TX 75074–8195
(214) 578–8155
Fax: Please mail or call

3699

Business Information: Plano Microwave, Inc. is a developer and manufacturer of ELINT and ESM systems and subsystems for the U.S. government and friendly foreign governments. PMI also provides support for the systems and subsystems it develops in the form of training, support equipment, field engineers, depot support, and technical data. Founding the Company three years ago, Mr. Blanchard serves as President and Chief Executive Officer and is responsible for all aspects of Corporate operations. **Career Steps:** President and Chief Executive Officer, Plano Microwave, Inc. (1992–Present); Business Area Director, UTL Corporation (1984–1992); Subcontracts Management, Lockheed (1980–1984). **Personal:** Mr. Blanchard enjoys outdoor sports and is involved in youth athletics coaching football.

Thomas A. Brown, Ph.D.

Human Resources Development Manager
Crown International, Inc.
1718 W. Mishawaka Rd.
Elkhart, IN 46515
(219) 294–8377
Fax: (219) 294–8083

3699

Business Information: Crown International, Inc. is a manufacturer and distributor of sound amplification equipment, microphones, radio broadcast, and electrical power equipment worldwide. As Human Resources Development Manager, Dr. Brown coordinates internal and external training, and administers employee education loan programs and grants administration. **Career Steps:** Human Resources Development Manager, Crown International, Inc. (1990–Present); Training Facilitator, General Motors – Fort Wayne (1986–1987); Associate Professor, Indiana Wesleyan University (1972–1983). **Associations & Accomplishments:** National Speakers Association; Indiana Speakers Association; Toastmasters International, Crowning Achievers Club; Elkhart County (Indiana) Business Development Task Force; Workforce Development Services/Northern Indiana, One Stop Information Center Advisory Board. **Education:** Ball State University, Ph.D. (1974); California State University – Northridge, MA (1967); Fuller Theological Seminary – Pasadena, California, M.Div. (1958); Taylor University, B.A. (1954). **Personal:** Married to Mary Martha in 1952. Three children: Bonnie Lynn, Marilee Anne, and Daniel Harry Brown. Dr. Brown enjoys photography, writing, and collecting stamps.

Joseph Y. Chen

Engineering Director
Cirrus Logic
3100 West Warren Avenue
Fremont, CA 94538–6423
(510) 226–2101
Fax: Please mail or call
EMAIL: See Below

3699

Business Information: Cirrus Logic, established in 1984, is an international manufacturer of multimedia video control logic, mass storage, and telecommunications and modem control logic. The Company boasts three locations and over 3,000 employees worldwide, and estimates sales in excess of $1.2 billion this year. As Engineering Director, Mr. Chen supervises the international distribution of software components for mass storage, oversees software development, and performs various administrative duties. Internet users can reach him via: CHEN@CIRRUS.COM **Career Steps:** Engineering Director, Cirrus Logic (1996–Present); Firmware Manager, Xebec (1986–1996). **Associations & Accomplishments:** Institute of Electronics and Electrical Engineers; X3T10; X3T13. **Education:** East Texas State, M.S.B.S. (1984). **Personal:** Married to Gracie in 1981. Two children: Winnie and David. Mr. Chen enjoys photography, travel, and movies.

Russell Childs

Associate Vice President
NEC Electronics, Inc.
7501 Foothills Boulevard
Roseville, CA 95661–9022
(916) 786–3900 Ext. 4830
Fax: (916) 786–7991

3699

Business Information: NEC Electronics, Inc. is a merchant manufacturer of digital MOS integrated circuits. Joining NEC Electronics in 1983, Mr. Childs was appointed as Associate Vice President in 1992. He is responsible for human relations, MIS, site administration, public relations, and customer relations (from time to time). **Career Steps:** NEC Electronics, Inc.: Associate Vice President (1992–Present), Associate Vice President of Operations (1992), Director of Operations (1990–1992), Department Manager (1983–1990). **Education:** Portsmouth Polytechnic – England, B.Sc. in Applied Physics (1969) **Personal:** Four children: Russell, Louise, Craig, and Lyndsey. Mr. Childs enjoys snow skiing and golf.

Ms. Patricia Ray Cobb
Director of Operations
EPE Technologies/Square D Company
1660 Scenic Avenue
Costa Mesa, CA 92626–1410
(714) 513–7345
Fax: (714) 434–1982

3699

Business Information: EPE Technologies, a subsidiary of Square D Company, is a designer, manufacturer, and servicer of uninterruptible power supplies and power protection equipment. Established in 1973, EPE Technologies reports annual revenue of $80 million and currently employs 360 people. As Director of Operations, Ms. Cobb is responsible for all aspects of Company operations. Assets include extensive engineering, product and process knowledge, as well as comprehensive quality methodology and systems background. She possesses effective verbal/written communication, interpersonal and analytical skills. She has also demonstrated the ability to develop and successfully execute tactical plans and elicit enthusiasm from subordinates. **Career Steps:** EPE Technologies, Inc.: Director of Operations (1994–Present), Director of Engineering (1993–1994); Square D Company, Columbia, SC: Total Quality Manager (1990–1993); Square D Company, Raleigh, NC: Manager of Plant, Engineering and Environmental Control (1989–1990), Manager of Fabrication and Environmental Control (1987–1989), Quality Assurance and Engineering Lab Supervisor (1985–1987), Plant Metallurgist (1980–1985). **Associations & Accomplishments:** AWARDS: Tribute to Women and Industry Award (1992); South Carolina Manufacturer of the Year (1991–1992); Industry Week Magazine Best Plant Finalist (1993); National Management Association Outstanding Manager Award (1989); Board of Trustees, El Toro Baptist Church, Lake Forest, California (1995); Chamber of Commerce Quality Committee, Columbia, South Carolina (1990); Chamber of Commerce Environmental Committee, Raleigh, North Carolina (1988); American Society for Quality Control (ASQC) (1980–Present); American Society of Metals (ASM) (1980–Present); 4th Grade teacher in Sunday School; Published in Global Environment Management Initiatives article titled: "Total Quality Management Certification Process" (1991); National Speaker for various organizations on Total Quality Management (1989–Present). **Education:** North Carolina State University, B.S. in MAT (1980), M.S. in Metallurgy, 15 hours (1980); Center for Creative Leadership (1992); Total Quality Management and Technical (1992); Customer Focus (1992); Total Quality Methodology (1992); Kellogg Management School (1991); Certified Trainer (1990); Master Trainer (1990); Vision College Faculty Training (1987). **Personal:** Married to Russell Liles Cobb (Manager of Environmental Programs for Rust Environmental, Inc.) in 1980. One child: Timothy Liles Cobb (plays football for the Saddleback Bears and is in the Gifted and Talented Education Program). Ms. Cobb enjoys watching her son play football, sports, swimming, reading, travel, music, and church activities.

Pietro Comerro
Managing Director
Comtest Italia SRL, a subsidiary of Thermo Voltek, a Thermo Electron company
Via Emilo Brusa 20
Torino, Italy 10149
39–11–455–1388
Fax: 39–11–455–1522

3699

Business Information: Comtest Italia SRL specializes in research and development, training, systems engineering, and distribution of electomagnetic compatibility products. As Managing Director, Mr. Comerro is responsible for the day–to–day activities of the Company, including management, operations, strategic growth and ensuring the profitability and growth of the Company. **Career Steps:** Managing Director, Contest Italia SRL (1994–Present); Sales Director, TESEO Spa (1990–1993); Research & Development Manager, ITACA Srl (1987–1990); Engineer, Alenia Spa (1986). **Associations & Accomplishments:** Institute of Electrical and Electronics Engineers; "Comunita L'Acco Glienza" for International Adoption. **Education:** Politecnico di Torino, Ingegnere (1986). **Personal:** Married to Silvia Vannelli in 1994.

Brian Marquis Davis
Sales Manager
General Electric
1465 Henry Brannan, Suite H
El Paso, TX 79936–6806
(915) 860–5720
Fax: (915) 860–5799
EMAIL: See Below

3699

Business Information: General Electric is the world's leading producer and distributor of industrial and consumer electrical and electronic products. General Electric's El Paso, Texas facility (established 1983) specializes in the production of industrial and consumer component capacitors. A Professional Engineer with extensive expertise in technology and design engineering, Brian Davis serves as International Sales Manager. He is responsible for all marketing and sales strategies for the Texas and Mexico sectors. Internet users can also reach him via: DAVIS.BRIAN@MLINK.MOTORS.GE.COM **Career Steps:** Sales Manager, General Electric (1994–Present); Engineering Manager, AGM Electronics (1990–1994). **Associations & Accomplishments:** Regent, Theta Tau – National Professional Engineering Fraternity (1990); Tau Beta Pi – Engineering Honorary; Toastmasters. **Education:** University of Arizona: M.S. (1993), B.S. **Personal:** Married to Alicia in 1994. Mr. Davis enjoys outdoor adventure sports.

Robert S. Eden, CPM
Corporate General Purchasing Manager
Eaton Corporation
1111 Superior Avenue, East
Cleveland, OH 44114
(216) 523–4390
Fax: (216) 479–7390

3699

Business Information: Eaton Corporation is a leading global manufacturer of highly engineered products which serve vehicle, industrial, construction, commercial, aerospace and marine markets. Principle products include truck transmissions and axles, engine components, hydraulic products, electrical power distribution and control equipment, ion implanters and a wide variety of controls. Headquartered in Cleveland, Ohio the company has 57,000 employees and 150 manufacturing sites in 22 countries. As Corporate General Purchasing Manager, Mr. Eden is responsible for negotiating corporate agreements with major companies to be used by all worldwide locations. He is also responsible for managing the contracting of major construction projects, training and development, along with directing numerous commodity strategic supplier sourcing programs. **Career Steps:** From 1973 to present, Mr. Eden has held numerous progressive management positions at several company locations to his present position as Corporate General Purchasing Manager. **Associations & Accomplishments:** Earned the Certified Purchasing Manager (CPM) designation awarded by the National Association of Purchasing Management, Inc.; Elks; VFW; Ohio State Highway Patrol Auxiliary; American Arbitration Association; Decorated U.S. Army combat infantry Vietnam veteran. **Education:** Case Western Reserve University, M.B.A. (1985); Northwood University, B.B.A. (1970). **Personal:** Married to Linda in 1970. Two children. Mr. Eden enjoys boating, golf, snow and water skiing.

Dayle B. Ellis
Vice President and General Manager
Peerless Manufacturing Company
2819 Walnut Hill Lane
Dallas, TX 75229–5711
(214) 353–5525
Fax: (214) 351–0194

3699

Business Information: Peerless Manufacturing Company is an international manufacturer of technically engineered environmental equipment (e.g., air pollution control for oxides of nitrogen, carbon monoxide, and HC). Established in 1933, the Company is headquartered in Dallas, Texas, and has three satellite locations in Singapore, the Netherlands, and Great Britain. As Vice President and General Manager, Mr. Ellis oversees all new business development, engineering functions, and reporting. **Career Steps:** Vice President and General Manager, Peerless Manufacturing Company (1991–Present); West Coast Manager, Norton Chemical Process (1990–1991); Owner, Airquest Environmental Company (1985–1990); Area Manager, Orbit Valve Company (1976–1985). **Associations & Accomplishments:** Air and Waste Management Association; American Boiler Manufacturers Association, Government Affairs Committee. **Education:** University of Houston, B.S. in Business Administration (1979); Ohio State University – Columbus, OH. **Personal:** Married to Sharon L. in 1977. Two children: Jenna and Mat-

thew. Mr. Ellis enjoys golf, skiing, travel, and spending time with his children.

Gary Conway Fields
President/Chief Engineer
Merge Technologies Group
211 Gateway Road, West
Napa, CA 94558–6279
(707) 252–6686
Fax: (707) 252–6686

3699

Business Information: Mr. Fields began his Company in 1992 with five other investors. In 1993, he bought stock in the Company and became a major stockholder. Merge Technologies Group is a Company that builds high–technology testing equipment (i.e., emulators, central office switches, etc). Mr. Fields has, unfortunately, passed on, but his Company is still strong in business, yielding $3 million in revenue annually. Mr. Fields was a very generous man who loved to spend time working on computers and investing. He made many donations to St. Helena Hospital and served as a member of their Presidents Club. **Career Steps:** President/Chief Engineer, Merge Technologies Group (1992–Present); President, Conway Engineering, Inc. (1977–1991); Vice President of Engineering, Lermah Telecom, Inc. (1975–1977). **Associations & Accomplishments:** Senior Member, National Association of Radio and Telecommunications Engineers; Presidents Club, St. Helena Hospital; Been published in technical articles and papers; Owner of 13 patents. **Education:** California Polytechnic University, B.A. (1959). **Personal:** Four children: Mark, Walter, Marie, and Nancy. Mr. Fields enjoyed ham radio, yachting, photography, and computers.

David P. Futkos
General Manager
Ericson Manufacturing Company
4215 Hamann Parkway
Willoughby, OH 44094
(216) 951–8000 Ext. 238
Fax: (216) 951–1867
H: (216) 942–6403

3699

Business Information: Ericson Manufacturing Company provides the fabrication of electric and electronic safety devices for human protection. These devices are manufactured for electrical, industrial, and safety distribution markets. As General Manager, Mr. Futkos is responsible for all corporate operations, manufacturing, and engineering research and development. **Career Steps:** General Manager, Ericson Manufacturing Company (1994–Present); Manufacturing Engineer and Manager, Tridelta Industries (1990–1994); Manufacturing Engineering Manager, Robertshaw Controls (1988–1990); Senior Manufacturing Engineer, Therm–O–Disc (Emerson) (1986–1988); Process Engineer, Packard Electric (General Motors). **Associations & Accomplishments:** Surface Mount Technology Association; Electronic Association; American Society of Quality Control; American Production Inventory Control Society; American Society of Mechanical Engineers; Ohio Society of Professional Engineers; National Society of Professional Engineers. **Education:** Youngstown University, B.S.M.E. (1986). **Personal:** Married to Dawn Marie in 1994. One child: Amanda Marie. Mr. Futkos enjoys woodworking, antiques, and electronic benchwork.

Anthony P. Gabriel
Vice President of Engineering
General Cable Corporation
4 Tesseneer Drive P.O. Box 61
Highland Heights, KY 41076–8497
(606) 572–8756
Fax: (606) 572–8497

3699

Business Information: General Cable Corporation is a billion dollar corporation based in Highland Heights, Kentucky. A division of Wassall PLC in the United Kingdom, the Corporation manufactures electrical and electronic data, wires, and cables nationally and worldwide. As Vice President of Engineering, Mr. Gabriel leads and directs the engineering efforts and initiatives for the Corporation, as well as orchestrates and directs new product initiatives for the Corporation. Additionally, he is responsible for all activities of General Cables' Technology Center. **Career Steps:** Vice President of Engineering, General Cable Corporation (1994–Present); Director of Electronic Engineering, Carol Cable Company (1987–1994); Director of Engineering, Alpha Wire Corporation (1978–1987). **Associa-**

tions & Accomplishments: Canadian Standards Association; National Electrical Manufacturers Association; Electronic Industries Association. **Education:** Farleigh Dickinson University, M.B.A.–S.E.T. (1983); State University of New York, Richmond Campus, B.S. in Engineering Sciences (1972); Staten Island Community College, Associate in Electrical Technology (1965). **Personal:** Married to Andrea L. in 1985. Three children: Kurt D., Christian D., and Erik D. Mr. Gabriel enjoys computers, conservation, fishing, and shooting sports.

Donald R. Garland
Regional Manager
Intermec
101 West Renner Road, Suite 400
Richardson, TX 75082–2002
(214) 231–8700
Fax: (214) 690–0957

3699

Business Information: Intermec, a division of Western Atlas, is a $2.4 billion company that manufacturers and sells bar code data collection systems. With 200 offices globally, products are marketed to end users in the manufacturing, distribution, and transportation industries. Joining Intermec as Regional Manager in 1989, Mr. Garland is responsible for the oversight of all sales and operations in the Western U.S.(consisting of 18 states), in addition to overseeing all administrative operations for a staff of 135. **Career Steps:** Regional Manager, Intermec (1989–Present); Vice President of Sales, U.S. Data (1981–1989). **Associations & Accomplishments:** Southern Methodist University Alumni Association. **Education:** Southern Methodist University, M.B.A. (1995). **Personal:** Married to Teresa in 1994. Two children: Donald Ray, II and Jesse Dean. Mr. Garland enjoys golf, racquetball, scuba diving, and snow skiing.

Robert P. Gray
Vice President of National Accounts
Woods Industries
11505 East Lakeshore Drive
Carmel, IN 46033–4424
(800) 428–6168 (317) 848–6984
Fax: (317) 846–0451

3699

Business Information: Established in 1935, Woods Industries is a major manufacturer of electrical products for home and office environments, currently employing 1,000 people. As Vice President of National Accounts, Mr. Gray performs sales and marketing functions with key accounts in the home improvement area. **Career Steps:** Woods Industries: Vice President of National Accounts (1995–Present), National Sales Manager (1994–1995), National Accounts Manager (1990–1994), Regional Manager (1986–1990); National Accounts Manager, Cooper Industries (1981–1986); Zone Manager, Ford Motor Company (1977–1981); Territory Manager, Coca–Cola, U.S.A. (1973–1976). **Associations & Accomplishments:** American Management Association; American Marketing Association; M.B.A. Executive Association; Young Executives Council, American Hardware Manufacturers Association; Member Board of Directors, Woodland Springs Neighborhood Association; National Tennis Academy Member. **Education:** Illinois State University: M.B.A. (1977), B.A. (1973); National Management Group, Inc., Training sessions completed in Time Management; Motivational Management Leadership Training; Technical Selling Skills. **Personal:** Married to Vicki in 1974. Three children: Jennifer, Lindsay, and Ali. Mr. Gray enjoys family activities, tennis, golf, reading, and travel.

Honey Jenkins
President
McLaughlin Electronics
17100 Gillette Avenue
Irvine, CA 92714–5603
(714) 442–9085
Fax: (714) 442–9087

3699

Business Information: McLaughlin Electronics is a manufacturer of electronic components, materials and process equipment, specializing in medical and automotive electronic devices. As President, Ms. Jenkins is responsible for all aspects of Company operations, including administration, finance, public relations, marketing, and strategic planning. **Career Steps:** President, Mc Laughlin Electronics (1993–Present); Director of Computer Learning, St. Angela's School (1985–1993); Engineer, Bechtel Corporation (1967–1975). **Associations & Accomplishments:** American Association of University Women; National Association of Female Executives. **Education:** University of California at Riverside, B.A. in Mathematics (1967). **Personal:** Married to Curtis in 1969. Two children: Gregory and Michelle. Ms. Jenkins enjoys travel.

Paul T. Klein, P.E.
Factory Engineering Manager
Philips Components
1033 Kings Highway
Saugerties, NY 12477
(914) 246–2811
Fax: (914) 246–9296

3699

Business Information: Philips Components, a division of Philips Electronics North American Corporation with N.V. Philips of the Netherlands as the parent company, is an international manufacturer of soft ferrites, an electronic ceramic used in electronic circuitry. The Company is ISO 9001 certified, which represents the highest rating of performance standards awarded. As Factory Engineering Manager, Mr. Klein is a Professional Engineer responsible for the management of efficiency and costing analysis, as well as the procedures of new products, estimates, through–put issues, and strategic planning. **Career Steps:** Philips Components: Factory Engineering Manager (1995–Present), Quality Supervisor (1993–1995), Manufacturing Manager (1986–1993), Senior Engineer/Line Supervisor (1984–1986); Manufacturing/Process Engineer/Line Supervisor, American AMCI (1982–1984). **Associations & Accomplishments:** Greene County Planning Board; Deputy Mayor/Trustee Village of Coxsackie, NY (1991–1995); American Society For Quality Control; Published an article on incinerator waste for the C.A.B.P. – a community–based organization. **Education:** Alfred University, B.S. in Glass Service (1979). **Personal:** Married to Theresa M. Everingham in 1978. Three children: Erika, Stefan, and Jacqueline. Mr. Klein enjoys spending time with his family and camping.

Robert E. Lee
Purchasing Manager
Toshiba International Corporation – Industrial Division
13131 West Little York Road
Houston, TX 77041
(713) 896–5300
Fax: (713) 896–5213

3699

Business Information: Toshiba Corporation, established in Japan in 1875, is a world leader in high technology, and manufactures numerous products in the areas of heavy electrical apparatus, information/communications systems, electronic devices, and consumer products. As Purchasing Manager, Mr. Lee is responsible for the management of industrial, corporate, and motor plant purchasing, in addition to managing a support staff of nine. Internet users can reach him via: HCKR71A@prodigy.com. **Career Steps:** Purchasing Manager, Toshiba International (1996–Present); Materials Manager, Drexel Oil Field Services (1992–1996); Materials Manager, Compaq Computer (1989–1992); Sales & Service Branch Manager, Wang Laboratories (1980–1989). **Associations & Accomplishments:** American Production Inventory Control Society; Harvard Club of Houston. **Education:** University of Maine, B.A. (1978). **Personal:** Married to Judith in 1979. Two children: Adam and Sarah. Mr. Lee enjoys soccer, golf, and swimming.

Michael W. Lejsner
Sales Director
Tampoprint International Company
1400 26th Street
Vero Beach, FL 32960–0317
(407) 778–8896
Fax: (407) 778–8289

3699

Business Information: Tampoprint International Company is a U.S. manufacturer, distributor, and servicer of Tampoprint silicone pad printing equipment and accessories to major OEM companies. Clientele include Wilson, Spalding, Oster, Johnson & Johnson, Square D, Santa Cruz, Motorola, Ford, Chrysler, and GM. The printing equipment is used to put the "on/off" on wipers and headlight switches and lock buttons; window "up/down" buttons and speedometers; numbers on cellular phones; and printing on golf balls, TV's, VCR's, the remote controls, etc. Their parent company is located in Germany, G.M.B.H. International, with three offices worldwide. With six years of experience in sales, Mr. Lejsner joined Tampoprint International Company as Sales Director in 1994. He directs all strategic planning for the entire U.S., including the general management of the facility, ensuring compliance of company procedures, and overseeing sales and product flow in and out of the Company. **Career Steps:** Sales Director, Tampoprint International Company (1994–Present); Sales Associate, Florida Imprint Systems (1993–1994); Trans Tech America: Sales Engineer (1991–1993), Service Technician (1990–1991). **Associations & Accomplishments:** National Rifle Association; HOG; PADI; Society of Professional Engineers; SPI. **Personal:** Married to Christie. One child: Sara. Mr. Lejsner enjoys sail boating, diving (certified), motorboating, skiing, tennis and outdoor activities.

Xiangming Li, Ph.D.
Vice President
AEM, Inc.
6827 Nancy Ridge Drive
San Diego, CA 92126
(619) 587–8285
Fax: (619) 455–5528

3699

Business Information: AEM, Inc. is a manufacturer of electronic components, materials and process equipment (i.e., chip inductors and micro–fuse). The company currently has two patents: One in the U.S. (1987) and one in China (1988). As Vice President, Dr. Li is responsible for all aspects of Company operations, primarily focusing in the areas of new business strategies and product development. Established in 1986, AEM, Inc. employs 50 people with annual sales of $10 million. **Career Steps:** Vice President, AEM, Inc. (1995–Present); Assistant Professor, Hong Kong University of Science and Technology (1993–1995); Lecturer, Hong Kong Polytechnic University (1989–1993). **Associations & Accomplishments:** American Institute of Chemical Engineers; Many articles published in various journals. **Education:** University of Michigan, Ph.D. (1985); South China University of Technology, M.Eng.; South China University of Technology, B.Sc. **Personal:** Married to Panmin Li in 1978. Two children: Hoi and Roger Li. Dr. Li enjoys table tennis and swimming.

K. Louis Lukanovich
President
MVSI and MVS
4830 Cousens Street
Montreal, Quebec H4S 1X7
(514) 333–0140
Fax: (514) 333–8636
EMAIL: See Below

3699

Business Information: MVSI and MVS designs laser vision systems for monitoring and control of welding machines and robots, inspection of computer chips and lead frames. As President, Mr. Lukanovich is responsible for all aspects of Company operations, including administration, finance, marketing, and strategic planning. Internet users can reach him via: Lukres@ietc.ca. **Career Steps:** President, MVSI and MVS (1994–Present); President, Lukres (1990–1994); Vice President of Mill Wide Systems, Measurex, Inc (1985–1989); President/Chief Executive Officer, MDDC Systems, Ltd (1973–1985). **Associations & Accomplishments:** Awarded Order of Canada for Leadership in High Technology and Sports (1977); Queen Elizabeth Jubilee Medal; Edison Welding Institute; Former Member, Canadian Pulp and Paper Association; Chairman, Computer Systems Committee; Canadian Olympic Teams: Competitor (1960), Coach in Canoeing (1972,1976); World Class Masters Competitor in Canoeing and Skiing. **Education:** Concordia University, B.Sc. (1961); Ryerson Institute of Technology (1957); Bell Systems Labs, Operations Research (1960). **Personal:** Married to Jean in 1958. Two children: Karen and Julianne. Mr. Lukanovich enjoys canoeing and skiing.

Robert L. Lupica
Director of Operations
Productos Electronicos Industriales, A Division of Northrop Grumman, Inc.
112 Munoz Rivera P.O. Box 2802
Santa Isabel, Puerto Rico 00757
(809) 845–3590 Ext.2301
Fax: (809) 845–3690

3699

Business Information: Productos Electronicos Industriales, A Division of Northrop Grumman, Inc., established in 1978, specializes in producing government electronics such as radar equipment and assemblies. By being separated into 5 categories, complex cabling (air frame/radar site), printed wire Boards (computer processing boards), radio frequency technology (microwaves), bench top assemblies, and systems integration, the Company can concentrate on developing electronics for commercial application for such companies as Chrysler and Bluebird. As Director, Mr. Lupica is responsible for sales, investment, marketing, engineering, and the manufacture and development of new products. The self–proclaimed "band leader" of the organization, he loves to see everything work, create and recreate. In addition to his success at Productos Electronicos Industriales, Mr. Lupica is also the founder of the Palmas Academy, a non–profit bilingual school he started with his wife in a rural part of Puerto Rico. Established in 1992 with donated materials and parents' assistance, the school currently has an enrollment of approximately 200 students in grades Pre–K thru 8. **Career Steps:** General Manager, Productos Electronicos Industriales (1991–Present); Sistemas Electronicos Industriales: Plant Manager (1989–1991), Operations Manager. **Associations & Accomplishments:** Chairman of the Board of Directors of the Palmas Academy. **Education:** Allegheny College, B.S. (1983); University of Michigan, Manufacturing Executive Program; The Wharton School, Executive Development Program. **Personal:** Married to Barbara in 1984. Two children: Matthew and Nicholas. Mr. Lupica enjoys golf and tennis.

Alan Madsen

Chairman
Alphamation, Inc.
180 North 2400 West, Suite 300
Salt Lake City, UT 84116–2949
(801) 942–6100
Fax: (801) 322–0172

3699

Business Information: Alphamation, Inc., established in 1992, specializes in the simulation of sight, sound, and motion for the flight and entertainment industries globally. Its main function is to create simulations, at a low cost, for flight simulators and the entertainment industries. Current projects involve a prototype Beta Unit for the flight industry. Founding the Company in 1992, Mr. Madsen serves as Chairman and Chief Executive Officer responsible for all aspects of operations, including strategic planning and seeking out future markets for the Company to work in. **Career Steps:** Chairman and Chief Executive Officer, Alphamation, Inc. (1992–Present); President, A.L.M. Corporation (1972–1992); President, The Homestead, a Corporation (1972–1978). **Associations & Accomplishments:** Past President, Utah–Nevada Hotel Association; Past President, Wasateh County Chamber of Commerce; Past Director, Mountainland Travel Council. **Education:** University of Utah; Brigham Young University. **Personal:** Married to Rebecca in 1973. Seven children: Geoffrey, Michael, Gregory, Robert, Scott, Stephen, and David.

Mr. David D. Malthouse

Executive Vice President
Technidyne Corporation
100 Quality Avenue
New Albany, IN 47150
(812) 948–2884
Fax: (812) 945–6847

3699

Business Information: Technidyne Corporation is a manufacturer of electro–optical instruments, used to measure the appearance of materials, such as paper products. As Executive Vice President, Mr. Malthouse is the General Manager, overseeing daily operations, administration, sales, and production. Mr. Malthouse attributes his success to a broad background in science and mathematics. Established in 1974, Technidyne Corporation employs a full–time staff of 55 people. **Career Steps:** Executive Vice President, Technidyne Corporation (1984–Present); Regional Sales Manager, Applied Color Systems (1977–1984); Sales Manager, Diano Corporation (1973–1977); Sales Manager, Martin Sweets Company (1970–1973). **Associations & Accomplishments:** Technical Association of the Pulp and Paper Industry; Technical Association of Textile Chemists and Colorists; International Association of Scientific Paper Makers. **Education:** South Dakota School of Mines and Technology, B.S. in General Engineering (1959).

Paul Mandelik

Director of Quality
Hazeltine Corporation
Pulaski Road
Greenlawn, NY 11740
(516) 262–8330
Fax: (516) 262–8340
EMAIL: See Below

3699

Business Information: Hazeltine Corporation is a designer and international manufacturer of defense and commercial electronics. The Corporations also provides surveillance–related equipment and telecommunications antenna displays to the military services. As Director of Quality, Mr. Mandelik is responsible for product quality and customer satisfaction, as well as administration, public relations, marketing, and strategic planning. He also oversees the design and manufacturing departments, 800 employees, and assures outgoing product needs are met. He may be reached through the Internet via: Mandelik@Hazeltine.com **Career Steps:** Director of Quality, Hazeltine Corporation (1987–Present); Manager of Quality Assurance, Parker–Gulc (1981–1987). **Associations & Accomplishments:** Senior Member, American Society for Quality Control; Association for Quality and Participation (AQP); Past President, Citizens Opposed to Pollution (COP). **Education:** Adelphi University, B.S. in Management (1984). **Personal:** Married to Barbara in 1966. Three children: Sheryl Dagostino, Russell, and Ilissa. Mr. Mandelik enjoys running, golf, and the environment.

Andrey V. Mishin, Ph.D

Vice President of Research and Development
Schonberg Research Corporation
3300 Keller Street, Building 101
Santa Clara, CA 95054–2612
(408) 980–9729
Fax: (408) 980–8605
EMAIL: See Below

3699

Business Information: Schonberg Research Corporation is a designer, builder, tester, and marketer of electron beam devices, particle accelerators, and related products for various applications, as well as portable microwave accelerators for scientific labs worldwide. As Vice President of Research and Development, Dr. Mishin is responsible for the development and marketing of linear accelerators, as well as the management of the Research and Development Group. Concurrently, Dr. Mishin is the Chief Executive Officer of Traspace International Corporation, a company responsible for introducing new products (technology marketing) in Russia and other eastern European countries. Internet users can reach him via: AVMSRC@aol.com. **Career Steps:** Vice President of Research and Development, Schonberg Research Corporation (1993–Present); Chief Executive Officer, Traspace International (1995–Present); Senior Researcher, MEPLI (1985–1993). **Associations & Accomplishments:** IEEE, Associate Member; Board of Supervisors, Santa Clara – Moscow (Russia), Sister City Commission. **Education:** Moscow Engineering Physics Institute, Ph.D., (1992). **Personal:** Married to Galina in 1983. One child: Olga. Mr. Mishin enjoys painting, woodcarving, volleyball, and music.

Mr. Bud J. Mullanix

Vice President – U.S. Sales and Marketing
DeGussa Electronics
420 West Pine #9
Lodi, CA 95240
(209) 333–8302
Fax: (209) 333–0233

3699

Business Information: DeGussa Electronics specializes in the production and distribution of diversified products which include: printed circuit boards, metals, chemicals and pharmaceuticals. Global in scope, DeGussa's headquarter offices are located in Germany and Singapore, with U.S. offices in New Jersey and a manufacturing plant in Alabama. As the Vice President of U.S. Sales and Marketing, Mr. Mullanix is responsible for all sales operations within the United States, including the supervision of Production Control and profit and loss. Established in 1894, DeGussa Electronics employs 20 people through the Lodi, California office, and reports corporate revenue in excess of $100 million. **Career Steps:** Vice President – U.S. Sales and Marketing, DeGussa Electronics (1992–Present); Director of Sales, Citation Circuits (1991–1992); Senior Sales Representative, Morton International (1989– 1991); Manufacturing Manager, Hewlett Packard (1978–1989). **Associations & Accomplishments:** President, Lodi Exchange Club; Chairperson, United Way. **Education:** Stanton University, B.S. in Business Administration (1985).

John A. Norris

Vice President of Marketing
Mosler Inc.
8509 Berk Boulevard
Hamilton, OH 45015–2213
(513) 870–1006
Fax: (513) 870–1012

3699

Business Information: Mosler Inc. is a leading supplier of electronic security including advanced Windows–based Access Control Systems, Proprietary Alarm Monitoring record, and money safes, drive–in banking systems, high speed currency processing equipment, and the latest in portals, turnstiles and metal detection. The Company offers round the clock service from its strategically located branch offices across the country. As Vice President of Marketing, Mr. Norris is responsible for product line revenue and profitability. **Career Steps:** Mosler Inc.: Vice President of Marketing (1995–Present), General Manager of New York and New Jersey regions (1991–1995), Director of Marketing (1989–1991), NE Area Sales Manager (1985–1989). **Associations & Accomplishments:** American Society for Industrial Security. **Education:** Farleigh–Dickinson University, M.B.A. (1985); State College of New Jersey, B.A. (1974). **Personal:** Married to Beverly J. in 1978. Two children: Sean and Colin. Mr. Norris enjoys local and school volunteer work, coaching, and golf.

M. Todd Popson

North American Sales Manager
Technidyne Corporation
100 Quality Avenue
New Albany, IN 47150–2272
(812) 948–2884
Fax: (812) 945–6847

3699

Business Information: Technidyne Corporation is an international manufacturer, seller, and servicer of optical testing equipment for the pulp, paper, and allied industries. Their equipment tests glass color, brightness., opacity, fluorescence, and gloss. As North American Sales Manager, Mr. Popson is responsible for all sales and promotions in North America, in addition to conducting seminars and demonstrations of optical properties of paper, advertising, and producing products and literature. **Career Steps:** Technidyne Corporation: North American Sales Manager (1995–Present), Applications Engineer, (1994–1995), Assistant Quality Manager (1992–1994), Engineer (1992). **Associations & Accomplishments:** Technical Association of the Pulp and Paper Industry (TAPPI); Optical Properties Committee of Tappi; Co–Author of "Measurement and Control of the Optical Properties of Paper" (2nd Edition); Metro United Way. **Education:** Indiana University, M.B.A. (1994); Purdue University, B.S. in Electrical Engineering (1991). **Personal:** Married to Claudia Marie in 1992. One child: Brenden Michael. Mr. Popson enjoys baseball, tennis, basketball, golf, fishing and hiking.

Benjamin D. Ray

Product Development Manager
ALPHA Metals
600 State Route 440
Jersey City, NJ 07304–1059
(201) 324–3616
Fax: (201) 434–6548

3699

Business Information: ALPHA Metals is a manufacturer of flux and coating materials used in the electronic circuit assemblies. The Company is divided into several distribution divisions and has 19 manufacturing plants worldwide. As Product Development Manager, Mr. Ray works in the Chemical Division of ALPHA Metals and designs and develops chemicals used in the manufacture of Cathode Ray Tubes (CRT). He is involved in the marketing of new and existing products, and is responsible for the training of staff and clients on new products. **Career Steps:** ALPHA Metals: Product Division Manager (1992–Present), Applications Technology Manager (1988–1992); Technical Director, KENCO Industries/ALPHA Metals (1983–1988). **Associations & Accomplishments:** American Chemical Society; Corporate Representative, Interconnecting Circuitry and Packaging. **Education:** Western Illinois University, B.S. (1981). **Personal:** Married to Deborah in 1991. Two children: Christopher and Matthew. Mr. Ray enjoys computer programming and radio control modeling.

Kathy L. Riehle

Manager of Sales Planning and Administration
Itron, Inc.
2818 North Sullivan Road
Spokane, WA 99216–1834
(509) 891–3557
Fax: (509) 891–3313
EMAIL: See Below

3699

Business Information: Itron, Inc. specializes in the manufacture and service of automated meter reading systems. As Manager of Sales Planning and Administration, Ms. Riehle manages the sales revenue, planning, and handles hardware forecasting. Internet users can reach her via: Kathy.Riehle@Itron.com. **Career Steps:** Itron, Inc.: Manager of Sales Planning and Administration (1988–Present), Senior Customer Business Analyst (1986–1988); Business Analyst, Data Processing Systems (1981–1986); Accounting Manager, Ogden Foods Inc. (1980–1981). **Education:** Trend College, Accounting (1979); Pursuing degrees in Marketing and

Finance through part–time student further education. **Personal:** Two children: Jeff and Brian. Ms. Riehle enjoys camping, biking, and outdoor sports & activities.

Michael A. Ross
Manufacturing Manager
National Instruments
6504 Bridge Point Parkway
Austin, TX 78730–5017
(512) 433–8608
Fax: (512) 433–8087
EMail: See Below

3699

Business Information: National Instruments is full–service electronics and software manufacturer specializing in the development of virtual instrumentation software and hardware, including test & measurement equipment and industrial automation. International in scope, National Instruments distributes to over 21 countries. As Manufacturing Manager, Mr. Ross is responsible for the direction and management of the manufacturing plant, including production operations, shipping & distribution, purchasing, product control, and testing associated ideas. Internet users can be reach via: Mike.Ross@NATINST.COM **Career Steps:** Manufacturing Manager, National Instruments (1994–Present); Worldwide Engineering Managing, IBM (1984–1994). **Associations & Accomplishments:** Texas Professional Engineers; University of Texas Executive MBA Association; American Society of Quality Controls; Phi Beta Gamma. **Education:** University of Texas – Austin: M.B.A. (1993), M.S.M.E. (1980); Pennsylvania State University, B.S.I.E. (1973). **Personal:** Married to Christina in 1972. Three children: Courtney, Amanda, and Trevor.

Russ Shade

Vice President – Industrial Systems
General Electric Company
1501 Roanoke Boulevard
Salem, VA 24153
(540) 387–7982
Fax: (540) 387–7981

3699

Business Information: General Electric Company is a diversified conglomerate, with manufacturing, financial services, and broadcasting subsidiaries, as well as being the world's leading producer and distributor of industrial and consumer electrical and electronic products. The Salem, Virginia subsidiary, General Electric Motors & Industrial Systems, manufactures industrial controls and process automation for a variety of industries (i.e., power generation, steel, paper, materials handling, etc.). Joining GE in 1973, Mr. Shade was appointed as Vice President and General Manager of GE Industrial Systems in 1995. He is responsible for the overall corporate management and operational activities of industrial systems, including drives and turbine controls. Additional duties include providing cross–functional leadership and strategical planning; and the responsibility for global ventures of industrial systems, serving as liaison for business relations with China, Singapore, Japan, Mexico, Canada, and in the near future, Europe. Career milestones include obtaining early technical success with several corporate patents on turbomachinery, and two–phase flow boiling and condensation that are currently in operation. **Career Steps:** General Electric Company: Vice President (1994–Present), General Manager – Navy & Steam Turbine Biz (1993–1994), Plant Manager – Steam Turbine Biz (1990–1993), Power Generation Biz Engineering Manager (1979–1990), Development Engineer (1973–1978). **Associations & Accomplishments:** Board of Directors, Virginia Manufacturer's Association; Former Board of Directors, North Central Massachusetts Chamber of Commerce; American Society of Naval Engineers. **Education:** Massachusetts Institute of Technology, M.S. in Mechanical Engineering (1973); Purdue University, B.S. in Mechanical Engineering (1972). **Personal:** Married to Debbie since 1971. Two children: Russell and Sarah. Mr. Shade enjoys hiking, mountain climbing, golf, and skiing.

Michael E. Tschopp

Controller and Finance Manager
Radiation Dynamics Inc.
74 Mount Vernon Avenue, B 15
Patchogue, NY 11772–1329
(516) 254–6800
Fax: (516) 254–6810

3699

Business Information: Established in 1959, Radiation Dynamics Inc. is a manufacturer of electron beam accelerators. As Controller and Finance Manager, Mr. Tschopp is responsible for forecasting, budgeting, financial statements, and supervising payroll and accounting departments. **Career Steps:** Controller and Finance Manager, Radiation Dynamics Inc. (1983–Present); Air Traffic Controller, FAA (1977–1981); USAF Air Controller, United States Air Force (1969–1976). **Associations & Accomplishments:** Long Island Business Association; American Management Association; Professional Air Traffic Controllers Organization. **Education:** Long Island University, B.S. in Accounting (1989). **Personal:** Mr. Tschopp enjoys golf, bowling, and American Jiu–Jitsu.

Tony H. Wu
Senior Design Engineer
Cirrus Logic
1851 Flickinger Avenue
San Jose, CA 95131
(510) 623–8300 Ext.5054
Fax: (510) 252–6070
EMAIL: See Below

3699

Business Information: Cirrus Logic is an international manufacturer of multimedia video control logic, mass storage, and telecommunications and modem control logic. As Senior Design Engineer, Mr. Wu is responsible for supervising the logic design of PC peripheral chips. Internet users can reach him via: TONYWU@CORP.CIRRUS.COM **Career Steps:** Senior Design Engineer, Cirrus Logic (Present). **Associations & Accomplishments:** Institute of Electronics and Electrical Engineers. **Education:** University of Southern California: Ph.D., (1995), M.S., (1992); National Taiwan University, B.S. (1989).

Troy Wurth

Marketing Manager
Tridon, Inc.
8100 Tridon Drive
Smyrna, TN 37167
(615) 459–5800
Fax: (615) 355–1142

3699

Business Information: Tridon, Inc. is a manufacturer and marketer of automotive electronics, wiper system components, and hose clamps for automotive and industrial markets. As Marketing Manager, Mr. Wurth is responsible for advertising, public relations, promotional and special customer programs, involving multiple product lines and brands for U.S. markets. He is also responsible for market research, point–of–sale (POS), packaging, and trade shows. **Career Steps:** Marketing Manager, Tridon, Inc. (1992–Present); Account Executive, Burroughs & Associates, Inc. (1990–1992); Assistant Buyer, Castner Knott, Inc. (1990). **Associations & Accomplishments:** Automotive Communications Council (ACC): Officer (Recording Secretary), Former Member of the Board of Governors, and Chairman of the Trade Show Committee; Automotive Cooling System Institute (ACSI); Murray State University Advertising Department Alumni Committee. **Education:** Murray State University, B.A. (1990). **Personal:** Married to Lisa in 1990. Mr. Wurth enjoys mountain bike riding, and attending Classic auto shows.

3700 Transportation Equipment

3711 Motor vehicles and car bodies
3713 Truck and bus bodies
3714 Motor vehicle parts and accessories
3715 Truck trailers
3716 Motor homes
3721 Aircraft
3724 Aircraft engines and engine parts
3728 Aircraft parts and equipment, NEC

3731 Ship building and repairing
3732 Boat building and repairing
3743 Railroad equipment
3751 Motorcycles, bicycles, and parts
3761 Guided missiles and space vehicles
3764 Space propulsion units and parts
3769 Space vehicle equipment, NEC
3792 Travel trailers and campers
3795 Tanks and tank components
3799 Transportation equipment, NEC

Gary L. Dolan
President
World Trans, Inc.
1401 S. Spencer
Newton, KS 67114
(316) 283–9500
Fax: (316) 283–0566

3710

Business Information: World Trans, Inc. is a manufacturer of customized mid–sized buses; utilized as transit and shuttle vehicles designed for passenger capacity of 10–29 persons — including the handicapped wheelchair accessible community. The products are marketed to universities, airports, churches, auto rental agencies, parking shuttle operators, limousine and taxi operators and transit authorities. An automotive sales and manufacturing executive with over 25 years experience in heavy truck and specialty vehicles manufacturing, Mr. Dolan formed World Trans, Inc. in early 1995 as a subsidiary of Collins Industries, Inc. As President and General Manager, he provides the overall vision and corporate strategies, focusing on quality development, quality assurance, and customer relations. **Career Steps:** President, World Trans, Inc. (1995–Present); Director of Sales, Champion Motor Coach (1991–1994); Regional Vice President, Winnebago Industries (1989–1990); National Accounts Manager, Volvo White Truck Corporation (1982–1989); Various roles, International Harvester (1967–1982). **Associations & Accomplishments:** CTA; Mid–Size Bus Manufacturers Association **Education:** Western New Mexico University, B.A. (1967). **Personal:** Married to Sharon in 1965. Two children: Tawna and Shane.

G. Wesley Blankenship, Ph.D., P.E.
Engineering Manager
General Motors Corporation – Romulus Engineering Center
37350 Ecorse Road
Romulus, MI 48174–1396
(313) 595–5630
Fax: (313) 595–5794

3711

Business Information: Dr. Blankenship is an engineering manager in the Advanced Engineering Group of General Motors Powertrain Division which manufactures engines and transmissions for automobiles and trucks. Dr. Blankenship manages the operations and technical policies of a research and development laboratory working on current and future automotive powertrain products. **Career Steps:** General Motors Corporation: Laboratory Manager (1994–Present), Senior Scientist (1990–1994), Project Engineer (1988–1990); Research Associate, Ohio State University (1986–1988). **Associations & Accomplishments:** American Society of Mechanical Engineers; Society of Automotive Engineers; Institute of Noise Control Engineers; Author of over 30 technical articles and reports in the areas of gear noise and vibration, rotating machinery dynamics, and powertrain engineering. **Education:** Ohio State University: Ph.D. (1992), M.S., B.S. summa cum laude with distinction in Mechanical Engineering; Licensed Professional Engineer, State of Michigan. **Personal:** Dr. Blankenship is married (Kateri) with one child and enjoys piano, gardening, backpacking, and mountain climbing.

Mercedes P. Breton
Finance Comptroller
Opel Italia
Piazzale Dell' Industria, 40
Roma, Italy 00144
39–6–54653358
Fax: 39–6–59–16947

3711

Business Information: Opel Italia, part of General Motors, is a manufacturer of Opel cars in Europe. As Finance Comptroller, Ms. Breton is responsible for pricing, sales incentives, business planning development, finance reporting, and inventory control. **Career Steps:** Finance Comptroller, Opel Italia (1993–Present); Competitive Analyst/Sales Manager, General Motors Europe (1992–1993); Financial Analyst, Opel Espana (1982–1992). **Associations & Accomplishments:** Spanish Institute of Audit and Balance Control. **Education:** Strat X, Marketing (1995); University of Zaragoza, Degree in Economy; Spanish Institute of Audit, Master of Balance Control. **Personal:** Ms. Breton enjoys painting (using photography), skiing, computers, cinema and animals.

Jeffrey A. Brown

Vice President of Marketing
Tridon, Inc.
8100 Tridon Drive
Smyrna, TN 37167
(615) 355–1121
Fax: (615) 355–1421

3711

Business Information: Tridon, Inc. is an international manufacturer of parts and systems for new automobiles and retail parts dealers such as WalMart and AutoZone. The Corporation has manufacturing locations in the United States and Europe. As Vice President of Marketing, Mr. Brown is in charge of marketing products throughout the United States and Canada. He is also involved in creating marketing strategies for new products. Mr. Brown deals with the daily operations of his department, to include recruitment of upper management, personnel concerns, department budgets, and planning for new product lines. **Career Steps:** Vice President of Marketing, Tridon, Inc. (1995–Present); Senior Marketing Manager, Pillsbury Company (1993–1995); Product Manager, Gerber Products Company (1991–1993); Product Manager, Frito–Lay, Inc. (1988–1991). **Associations & Accomplishments:** Mr. Brown has been published in various trade magazines. **Education:** Themdesbird, Master International Management; Kent State University, BBA. **Personal:** Married to Pam in 1986. Two children: Clayton and Aubree. Mr. Brown enjoys outdoor activities, boating, backpacking, and coaching soccer.

George P. Cabanting

Manager of Customer Commitment
Porsche Cars of North America
P.O. Box 30911
Reno, NV 89520–3911
(702) 348–3155
Fax: (702) 348–3777

3711

Business Information: Porsche Cars of North America is a specialty automotive products manufacturer and distributor. As Manager of Customer Commitment, Mr. Cabanting oversees warranty, policy procedure, and owner relations functions with customers, as well as manages corporate customer databases. Considered a pioneer in his field, Mr. Cabanting designed, developed and tested all warranty systems as well as being the liaison to MIS for all service systems–related projects. **Career Steps:** Porsche Cars of North America: Manager of Customer Commitment (1994–Present), Manager, Warranty and Service Systems (1984–Present); Warranty Expense Analyst, Volvo Cars North America (1982–1984); Volkswagen of America: Field Compliance Engineer (1980–1982), Senior Technical Analyst (1973–1981), Senior Warranty Claims Specialist (1973–1976). **Associations & Accomplishments:** Society of Automotive Engineers; Who's Who of Asian Americans; Who's Who of Young American Professionals; Who's Who of US Executives; Licensed: ASE Automotive Refrigerant and Recycling, ASE Master Technician, Volvo Master Technician, Volkswagen, Porsche & Audi Registered Technician; Authored numerous warranty and service manuals; Frequent technical lecturer. **Education:** Bergen Community College, Associates in Business (1976); Bronx Community College, Associates in Electrical Technology (1973). **Personal:** Married to Patricia in 1971. Two children: Ryan and Stephen. Mr. Cabanting enjoys hiking, boating on Lake Tahoe, and Porsche restoration.

John Dolfato

Attorney
General Motors of Canada
Box 660
St. Therese, Quebec J7E 4K6
(514) 433–4360
Fax: (514) 433–4370

3711

Business Information: General Motors of Canada, is the Canadian division of General Motors Corporation, one of the top three in the American automobile industry, and a manufacturer of cars and trucks. As Attorney, Mr. Dolfato oversees all legal and related issues involving the Company. He is responsible for all commercial litigation, as well as cases involving retail sales and services. Additional duties include reviewing advertising for Quebec, ensuring legal purchasing, and providing advice to the Detroit, Michigan headquarters on litigations, and lawsuits in which they are directly involved. **Career Steps:** Attorney, General Motors of Canada (1988–Present); Attorney, General Trust (1986–1988); Attorney, Baker Nudleman Lamontagne (1983–1986). **Associations & Accomplishments:** Canadian Bar Association; Quebec Bar Association; Quebec Alliance of Manufacturers and Exporters; Quebec Federation for Venetian Associations. **Education:** McGill University: Bachelor of Arts With Honors, B.C.L., L.L.B. (1982); Vanier College, D.E.C. **Personal:** Married to Silvia Baccalaro in 1989. One child: Andrew. Mr. Dolfato enjoys skiing, cycling, reading, and travel.

Shay Fani

Quality Engineer
Saturn Corporation
Body System MD–N12, 100 Saturn Parkway
Spring Hill, TN 37174
(615) 486–6069
Fax: (615) 486–7299
EMAIL: See Below

3711

Business Information: Saturn Corporation is an international automobile manufacturer. Working in numerous engineering and administrative capacities for Saturn since 1988, Shay Fani was appointed to her current position in 1991. As Quality Engineer, she directs all quality control and related design staff, as well as oversees materials procurement at all plant facilities. Internet users can reach her via: Saturn.SFANI11@GMEDS.COM. **Career Steps:** Saturn Corporation: Quality Engineer (1991–Present), Operations Engineer (1989–1991), Safety and Environmental Specialist (1988–1989). **Associations & Accomplishments:** Member, American Society of Quality Control. **Education:** Tennessee State University, M.S. in Engineering Science (1991); Tennessee Technical University, B.S. in Chemical Engineering (1979). **Personal:** One child: Neggi. Ms. Fani enjoys aerobics, music, tennis, movies, and books.

Charles M. Hill

Data Base Administrator
Ford Motor Company
6201 Wood Pond Road
West Bloomfield, MI 48323–2264
(313) 322–1998
Fax: (313) 337–6932

3711

Business Information: Ford Motor Company, one of the world's leading automotive manufacturers, is an international designer and manufacturer of automobiles and trucks with five vehicle centers: two truck centers, three auto centers. As Data Base Administrator, Mr. Hill is responsible for the implementation and maintenance of DB2 and IMS data base systems for several applications, problem resolution of all DB2 and IMS jobstreams, training personnel, DASD monitoring/tuning, and ISPF panel and CLIST enhancement coordination to support the changing database environment. He is also responsible for utilizing change manager to implement DB2 changes/migrations, use interactive SPUFI, software evaluation, and special projects that include implementing ESA software data compression. **Career Steps:** Data Base Administrator, Ford Motor Company (1993–Present); Data Base Administrator/Consultant, Syntel, Inc. (1990–1993); Data Base Analyst, Grand Trunk Western Railroad (1989–1990); Consultant, Network Info Systems (1989). **Associations & Accomplishments:** Junior Achievement. **Education:** Lawrence Technical University, B.S. in Business Administration (1994); Oakland Community College, Associate's degree in Business. **Personal:** Married to Susan in 1984. Mr. Hill enjoys playing golf, travel, hiking, and walking.

Andrew K. Jacobson

Director of Design – Commercial Trucks Division
Ford Motor Company
VC #5 DTC, Ste. 4200 42G42 16630 South Field Rd.
Allen Park, MI 48101
(313) 322–1213
Fax: (313) 390–0798
EMAIL: See Below

3711

Business Information: Ford Motor Company, one of the world's leading automotive manufacturers, is an international designer and manufacturer of automobiles and trucks with five vehicle centers: two truck centers, three auto centers. A thirty–year veteran with Ford Motor Company, Mr. Jacobson currently serves as Director of the Design Studio for Commercial Trucks, responsible for the direction of all design activities for vehicles weighing over 8,500 gross vehicle weight, ranging from the F–Series transits in Europe to Class 8 trucks. Career milestones include designing the new F150 series trucks, the Explorer and the Splash. **Career Steps:** Ford Motor Company: Director of Design – Commercial Trucks Division (1995–Present), Executive Director of Truck Design (1989–1994), Director of Design – Ford of Europe (1981–1989). **Associations & Accomplishments:** Conrducts approximately five large presentations and six smaller speaking engagements annually. **Education:** Art Center College of Design, B.A. (1965). **Personal:** Married to Margaret C. in 1965. Three children: Danielle Ann, Dane Andrew and Darrin August. Two grandchildren. Mr. Jacobson enjoys motorcycle riding, racing, and collecting.

Dale R. Johnson

Executive Director, Production Control and Logistics
General Motors Corporation
1 Pontiac Plaza
Pontiac, MI 48340
(810) 857–1193
Fax: (810) 857–4248

3711

Business Information: General Motors Corporation, one of the top three in the American automobile industry, is a manufacturer of cars and trucks. General Motors has a global work force in excess of 170,000 people and reports annual revenue of $25 billion. As Executive Director, Production Control and Logistics, Mr. Johnson works in the Automotive Components sector of GM. His group supplies components to all major vehicle OEM's. Mr. Johnson coordinates production control and logistics activities for the group. He attributes his success to being a flexible person, able to be a generalist or detail oriented as needed. **Career Steps:** Executive Director, Production Control and Logistics, General Motors Corporation (1992–Present); Director, Quality and Materials Management, Delco Remy Division, GM (1989–1992); Director, Quality and Materials Management, New Department Hyatt Division, GM (1988–1989); Advisor, Materials Management, New United Motor Manufacturing Inc. (1985–1988); Manager, Reliability and Quality Assurance, Packard Electric Division, GM (1983–1985). **Education:** Carnegie Mellon University, M.S.I.A. (1968); Carnegie Mellon University, B.S. in Chemical Engineering. **Personal:** Three children: Christie, Richard and Carrie. Mr. Johnson enjoys competitive and recreational running, golf and skiing.

Ms. Mary V. Miko

Manager, Pre–Production Build
General Motors Corporation
39785 Mt. Elliott
Clinton Township, MI 48038
(810) 947–0770
Fax: (810) 947–2786

3711

Business Information: General Motors Corporation is an automotive manufacturing company (over 20 assembly factories in North America). As Manager, Ms. Miko is responsible for processing and assembly in advance vehicle development. **Career Steps:** General Motors Inc.: Manager, Pre–Production Build (1995–Present), General Manager, Industrial Engineering (1992–1995); Group Manager, General Motors (1989–1991); Superintendent – Quality, General Motors (1984–1989). **Associations & Accomplishments:** National Association of Female Executives; Board of Directors – Research Federal Credit Union; Board of Directors, Michigan State University, AMP Alumni Association. **Education:** Michigan State University, Executive M.B.A. (1992); Oglethorpe University, Bachelor of Arts (1989). **Personal:** Ms. Miko enjoys golf, bowling, boating, and travel.

David C. Reek

Senior Manufacturing Engineer
Saturn Corporation – GMC
3139 Harlo Apt.G
Madison Heights, MI 48071–1984
(810) 528–4059
Fax: (810) 528–5262

3711

Business Information: Saturn Corporation, a wholly–owned subsidiary of General Motors Corporation, is an automotive manufacturing, engineering, and development company. As Senior Manufacturing Engineer, Mr. Reek supervises advanced product quality activities in the development stages of manufacturing. **Career Steps:** Senior Manufacturing Engineer, Saturn Corporation – GMC (1991–Present); Senior Applications Engineer, Delco Electronics – GMC (1990–1991); Senior Quality Engineer, Delco Electronics (1984–1990). **Associations & Accomplishments:** Certified Quality Engineer, ASQC. **Education:** Michigan Technical University, B.S.E.E. (1979). **Personal:** Four children: Jamie Lynn, Elizabeth Ann, Katrina Joy, and Laura Lee. Mr. Reek enjoys sports, woodworking, and cabinet making.

Frank W. Vaughn Jr.
Craft Manager – New Mack Avenue Viper Assembly Plant
Chrysler Corporation
12000 Chrysler Drive, CIMS 451–00–00
Detroit, MI 48288–1919
(313) 956–7514
Fax: (313) 956–7498

3711

Business Information: Chrysler Corporation produces and makes cars and trucks for customers in 75 countries. In North America, the Company markets vehicles through three divisions: Chrysler/Plymouth, Dodge/Dodge Truck, and Jeep/Eagle. Chrysler is ranked the 11th U.S. company in sales on the Fortune 500 list. Established over seventy years ago, Chrysler Corporation presently employs over 110,000 people and has an estimated annual revenue in excess of $36 million corporate–wide. Mr. Vaughn is the Craft Manager for the production of the Dodge Viper RT/10 (V–10, 400–horsepower roadster) and is responsible for the direct management of plant trim, final, and assessment operations. The Dodge Viper started as a concept car in 1989, and the praise was so high it drew raves from publications ranging from U.S. News and World Report to Popular Science. As a result, Team Viper brought it to market in 1992. **Career Steps:** Chrysler Corporation: Craft Manager – New Mack Avenue Viper Assembly Plant (1992–Present), Supervisor – Warren Truck Assembly Plant (1989–1992), Manufacturing Staff Trainee (1988–1989); Mr. Vaughn has also held several management and training positions in Product and Quality Engineering, Assembly and Stamping quality, Assembly Operations (Body & Paint, Trim, Chassis and Final), Labor Relations, Pilot Operations, and Production Control. **Associations & Accomplishments:** He is a member of: University of Detroit–Mercy Alumni; University of Detroit–Mercy Department of Intercollegiate Athletics/Fencing Team; American Management Association; Engineering Society of Detroit; Economic Club of Detroit; Detroit Institute of Arts; Chrysler Corporation Management Club; Chrysler Manufacturing Stamping and Assembly Management Club; Boys and Girls Clubs of Southwestern Michigan. He is also a Guardian Member of the Boy Scouts of America–Detroit Council. **Education:** University of Detroit, B.A. (1986); University of Detroit–Mercy, Graduate Studies; Has attended several business and management seminars, quality and productivity seminars. **Personal:** Mr. Vaughn enjoys the restoration of classic cars, professional auto racing, current events, and art.

Robert Grussing IV
Vice President
Mack Trucks Inc.
2100 Mack Boulevard
Allentown, PA 18105–5000
(610) 709–3660
Fax: (610) 709–2291
EMAIL: See Below

3713

Business Information: Mack Trucks Inc. is an international manufacturer of heavy duty motor trucks. International in scope, the Company has seven global manufacturing plants (4–U.S., 1–Canada, 1–Australia, 1–Venezuela). Established in 1900, Mack Trucks Inc. reports annual revenue in excess of $2 billion and currently employs 5,600 people corporate–wide. Joining Mack Trucks in 1992 as commercial controller, Mr. Grussing was appointed Vice President in 1995. He is responsible for the direction of the Highway Customer Focus division, which consists of marketing, product management, and all in–line customer services. He can also be reached through the Internet via: BPQXA@prodigy.com **Career Steps:** Mack Trucks Inc.: Vice President, Highway Customer Focus (1995–Present), Commercial Controller (1992–1995); GE Plastics Sales, General Electric Co.: Manager of Finance (1989–1992), Manager of Financial Planning and Analysis (1986–1989). **Associations & Accomplishments:** Truck Maintenance Council; American Trucking Association National Accounting and Finance Council; Phi Beta Kappa. **Education:** University of Vermont, B.A. in Economics (1980). **Personal:** Married to Theresa in 1986. Three children: Katherine, Timothy, and Rachael. Mr. Grussing enjoys golf, skiing, and has been a long suffering fan of the Boston Red Sox.

Paul M. Lenker
Plant Manager
North American Transit
7300 North Fm 2818 400
Bryan, TX 77807–1000
(409) 778–7816
Fax: (409) 778–2948

3713

Business Information: North American Transit Inc., is a Texas–based manufacturer of public transit buses. Specializing in diesel or natural gas powered public transportation, North American's primary production is the Model UDTV30 — a state–of–the–art, 30 foot, 25 passenger capacity transit vehicle. The UDTV, an all–American components vehicle, is designed from the ground up for low cost maintenance. A transportation manufacturing executive for over ten years, Mr. Lenker joined North American Transit in 1994. As Plant Manager, he oversees all plant operations, primarily focusing on quality product assurance, maintenance and customer service relations, and overall logistics. **Career Steps:** Plant Manager, North American Transit (1994–Present); Director of Manufacturing Operations, Dorsey Trailers (1993–1994); Plant Manager and Director of Quality Assurance, Transportation Manufacturing Corporation (1987–1993). **Associations & Accomplishments:** American Society for Quality Control; Toastmasters International; American Management Association; American Society for Training and Development. **Education:** Century University, B.A. (1992). **Personal:** Married to Donna L. in 1966. Two children: Matthew and Marc. Mr. Lenker enjoys sports officiating, golf, gardening, and lectures.

David A. Miller
Director of Product Safety
Clark Material Handling Company
749 W. Short Street
Lexington, KY 40508–1200
(606) 288–1479
Fax: (606) 288–1482
EMail: See Below

3713

Business Information: Clark Material Handling Company is a manufacturer of fork lift trucks, with over 753,000 trucks sold to date. As Director of Product Safety, Mr. Miller handles product safety and is considered an expert witness for liability defense. He utilizes data from accidents to make safer products. Internet users can reach him via: DMILLER726@AOL.COM. **Career Steps:** Clark Material Handling Company: Director of Product Safety (1993–Present), Director of Current Engineering (1989–1993), Director of Engineering – Electric Trucks (1987–1989). **Associations & Accomplishments:** Society of Automotive Engineers; American Society of Mechanical Engineers; American Society of Safety Engineers. **Education:** North East Essex Technical College, Higher National Diploma (1963). **Personal:** Married to Bonnie in 1966. Two children: Mark Allan and Michelle Anne. Mr. Miller enjoys golf.

Marco A. Najera Sixto
Human Resources Director
Kenworth Mexicana
4492 Camino De La Plaza
San Ysidro, CA 92173
52–656–28019
Fax: 52–656–28110

3713

Business Information: Kenworth Mexicana specializes in the manufacture and distribution of trucks and heavy trucks. The Company distributes domestically and exports to Asia, Australia, the United Kingdom, the United States, South America, and Africa. As Human Resources Director, Mr. Najera is responsible for all employee relations, including hiring, training, benefits, and staff motivation. **Career Steps:** Human Resources Director, Kenworth Mexicana (1994–Present); HR Consultant and Trainer (1990–1994); Human Resources Manager, Fisher Price de Baja California (1992–1994); Industrial Relations Manager, Mattel Toys – Mexico (1985–1990); Personnel Manager, Tijuana International Airport (1977–1985). **Associations & Accomplishments:** Tijuana Industrial Relations Association; Executives in Industrial Relations Association (Mexicali); Society for Human Resources Management; Conducted personnel turnover research in the Maquiladora Industry of Tijuana (1988–1992); Author of seven training programs and two training movie scripts. **Education:** Instituto Tecnologico de Tijuana, B.A. in Human Resources (1983); San Diego State University, TQM Certificate; Centro de Ensenanza Tecnica y Superior (Mexicali), M.B.A. in progress. **Personal:** Married to Lorena V. in 1984. Three children: Lorena Berenice, Karla Judith, and Marco Antonio. Mr. Najera Sixto enjoys reading and writing.

Jeffrey Sanders
Controller
Motor Coach International, Inc.
1850 North Central Avenue, Suite 910
Phoenix, AZ 85004–4527
(602) 207–6966
Fax: (602) 207–6603

3713

Business Information: Motor Coach International, Inc. is a manufacturer of intercity motor coaches, and is a distributor of coach and transit bus replacement parts. As Controller, Mr. Sanders is responsible for accounting and controls tax, corporate development, and investor relations. **Career Steps:** Motor Coach International, Inc.: Controller (1995–Present), Director – Financial Reporting (1993–1994); Senior Manager – Audit, Deloitte & Touche (1985–1993). **Associations & Accomplishments:** Manufacturers Alliance Financial Council III. **Education:** Arizona State University, B.A. (1984). **Personal:** Married to Kim in 1985. Two children: Matthew and Mitchell. Mr. Sanders enjoys family.

Grady Alexander
Purchasing/Production Coordinator
Automotive Motors Thomasville
113 Sunrise Center Drive
Thomasville, NC 27360–4928
(910) 474–2800
Fax: (910) 472–8862

3714

Business Information: Automotive Motors Thomasville, a subsidiary of Nissan (Toyota), manufactures power window motors for Chrysler. As Purchasing/Production Coordinator, Mr. Alexander is responsible for all financial scheduling and budgeting, production, control inventory, and shipping procedures. **Career Steps:** Purchasing/Production Coordinator, Automotive Motors Thomasville (1994–Present); Materials Manager/Plant Manager, Columbia Panel (Apr.1993–Dec.1993); Engineer, Alma Desk Company (1991–1993); Production Control Manager, High Point Furniture (1989–1991). **Education:** North Carolina State, B.S. (1973). **Personal:** Married to Terrianne W. in 1970. One child: Christopher. Mr. Alexander enjoys the internet, sci–fi, softball, model building, reading, and collecting coins, Disney items, & comic books.

Alan E. Anderson
Field Service Manager
Horton Vehicle Components, Inc.
P.O. Box 9455
Minneapolis, MN 55440–9455
(612) 627–5742
Fax: (612) 953–4635

3714

Business Information: Horton Vehicle Components, Inc. is a manufacturer of semi truck parts and is a vendor of hard parts, such as pneumatic clutches and brakes for transportation industry, as well as industrial applications. Mr. Anderson brings many years of experience with him to his position as Field Service Manager in which he is responsible for the sales and service to the largest trucking fleets in the United States, Canada, and Mexico. In addition, Mr. Anderson supervises all technical information which in turn keeps the Company's extensive training program current. **Career Steps:** Horton Vehicle Components, Inc.: Field Service Manager (1992–Present), Fleet Account Manager (1989–1992); Regional Sales Manager, Rudkin Wiley Corporation (1984–1989). **Associations & Accomplishments:** American Trucking Association, Maintenance Council; Equipment Managers Maintenance Council; Society of Automotive Engineers; National Hot Rod Association; Published in "Truck Parts and Service" (May 1994). **Education:** Northeast Missouri State University. **Personal:** Mr. Anderson enjoys motor sports, and drag racing – car owner and spectator.

Dennis L. Anderson
Vice President of Human Resources
Sears Manufacturing Company
1718 South Concord Street
Davenport, IA 52802–2901
(319) 383–2800
Fax: (319) 383–2810

3714

Business Information: Sears Manufacturing Company is a privately–held manufacturer of vehicular seating. Mr. Anderson joined Sears Manufacturing in 1989 as Director of Human Resources, moving into his present position as Vice President of Human Resources in 1994. He is responsible for all aspects of personnel management including benefits administration, OSHA, EPA, DOT, and labor relations. **Career Steps:** Sears Manufacturing Company: Vice President of Human Resources (1994–Present), Director of Human Resources (1989–1994); Manager, Labor Relations, J.I. Case (1985–1989). **Associations & Accomplishments:** Society for Human Resource Management; Job Service Employers Council; Quad Cities Industrial Relations Society; Private Industry Council; Chamber of Commerce; Quality Achievement Award, State of Iowa; J.T.P.A. **Education:** Western Illinois University, M.B.A. (1980); Northeast Missouri State University, B.S. (1973). **Personal:** Two children: Eric and Erin. Mr. Anderson enjoys running, biking, and gardening.

Nancy Andrews
Regional Director of Global Sourcing
Federal Mogul Corporation
P.O. Box 1966
Detroit, MI 48235–0906
(810) 354–8863
Fax: (810) 354–7939

3714

Business Information: Federal Mogul Corporation is a manufacturer and distributor of automotive parts (e.g., seals, engine parts, fuel parts) with 30 manufacturing plants worldwide distributing to Europe, Africa, Puerto Rico, Latin America, Russia, Australia, and the United States through wholesalers and resellers such as Pep Boys and NAPA. Ms. Andrews joined FMC as an Inventory Control Analyst in 1976, and has held various supervisory positions, including Product Team Manager and Materials Manager. Promoted to Regional Director of Global Sourcing in 1995, she is directly responsible for all operations in the African Region, including oversight of supplies, finances, and sourcing management. **Career Steps:** Federal Mogul Corporation: Regional Director of Global Sourcing (1995–Present), Materials Manager (1994–1995), Product Team Manager (1991–1994). **Associations & Accomplishments:** American Production & Inventory Control; Council of Logistics Management. **Education:** Lawrence Institute of Technology, B.B.A. (1983). **Personal:** Ms. Andrews enjoys reading and physical fitness.

Craig A. Ayres
Senior Project Engineer
NU–TECH and Engineering, Inc.
449 McCormick Drive
Lapeer, MI 48446
(810) 667–3240 (810) 667–4038
Fax: (810) 667–3029
CAYRES@TIR.COM

3714

Business Information: NU–TECH and Engineering Inc. specializes in automotive development in instrument panels (cluster containing speed, fuel, temperature, gauges, and driver information). As Senior Project Engineer, Mr. Ayres is responsible for diversified engineering and administrative activities, including managing developing projects and customer relations. Internet users can reach him via: CAYRES@TIR.COM. **Career Steps:** Senior Project Engineer, NU–TECH and Engineering Inc. (1993–Present); Project Engineer, Trialon Corporation (Contract at Delco Electronics Corporation – Cluster Engineer) (1991–1993); Project Engineer, Balance Engineering (Software Control for Manufacture Automation) (1990–1991). **Associations & Accomplishments:** Promise Keepers. **Education:** Michigan Technological University, B.S.E.E. (1990); Many supervising and managing courses. **Personal:** Married to Kathleen in 1990. Three children: Kaitlyn, Nicholas, and Matthew. Mr. Ayres enjoys home repair, computers, and most sports, including fishing.

Clark W. Babb
Production Manager
Jamestown Industries, Inc.
671 Bellbrook Avenue
Xenia, OH 45385
(513) 372–6939
Fax: (513) 372–8814

3714

Business Information: Jamestown Industries, Inc. is an integrated supplier for Delphi Chassis and provides synchronous manufacturing and shipment of Liteflex fiberglass leaf spring for General Motors Corporation. As Production Manager, Mr. Babb is responsible for the purchase of all raw materials, production scheduling, management of the research and development laboratory, manpower studies, plant layout, inventory control, and shipping and receiving functions. Concurrently, he is Co–Owner of Graphic Attitude Silk Screen Printing. **Career Steps:** Production Manager, Jamestown Industries, Inc. (Present); Co–Owner, Graphic Attitude Silk Screen Printing (1995–Present); Warehouse Manager, Jamestown Plastic Molders, Inc. (1979–1980); Security Specialist, U.S. Air Force (1975–1979). **Associations & Accomplishments:** Red Cross: Founding Member – Laramie County Executive Red Cross Committee, Selected as Chairman at F.E. Warren Air Force Base – Wyoming (oversees all training on base), CPuerto Rico Instructor, Advanced First Aid, Instructor Trainer. **Education:** Attended, Sinclair Community College; Los Angeles Community College, Certified Emergency Medical Technician. **Personal:** Two children: Clark II and John. Mr. Babb enjoys bicycling, canoeing, golf, and bowling.

Mr. Anil Bansal
Director of Product Engineering
Dana Corporation
P.O. Box 2229
Ft. Wayne, IN 46801
(219) 481–3106
Fax: (219) 481–3115

3714

Business Information: Dana Corporation is the third largest independent vehicular components and system manufacturer, serving all major original equipment manufacturers around the world. Established in 1905, Dana Corporation employs over 36,000 people in North America and has an estimated annual revenue of $7.0 billion. A Staff Engineer with Spicer Heavy Axle and Brake Division (SHABD) of Dana Corporation since 1985. In his current position Anil Bansal is responsible for the global direction of product engineering, research and development, and manufacturing planning for the SHABD. **Career Steps:** Dana Corporation: Director of Product Engineering, Manufacturing and Planning (1988–Present), Director of Product and Manufacturing Engineering (1985–1988); Chief Engineer Axle, Hayes Dana (1981–1985). **Associations & Accomplishments:** Society of Automotive Engineers; Society of Manufacturing Engineers; Association of Profession Engineers, Ontario, Canada; Computer and Automated Systems; Received Canadian National Productivity Award (1983); Keynote Speaker – National Engineer's Week – Ft. Wayne (1990); Keynote Speaker – Automotive Component Manufacturing Association, India (1990); Presented and Published Productivity Enhancement Paper – World Productivity Congress, Sweden (1993). **Education:** Bowling Green University, M.B.A. (1989); McMaster University, M. in Engineering (1977); I.I.T., New Delhi, India: M. in Technology (1975), B.S. in Mechanical Engineering, with Honors (1973). **Personal:** Married to Dr. Rosemary Leitch in 1983. Two children: Alexandra Lindsey and Neil Elliott. Mr. Bansal enjoys golf and the theatre.

Johan J. Beeckmans, Ph.D.
Director of Training and Development
ITT Automotive Inc.
3000 University Drive
Auburn Hills, MI 48326–2356
(810) 340–4277
Fax: Please mail or call

3714

Business Information: ITT Automotive Inc. specializes in the manufacturing of brakes, systems, electrical systems, structural systems, and fluid handling systems for the automotive industry. Currently, ITT Automotive employs 36,000 people and has an estimated annual revenue of $5.2 billion. As Director of Training and Development, Dr. Beeckmans is responsible for all aspects of executive development, executive assessment, and succession planning. **Career Steps:** Director of Training and Development, ITT Automotive Inc. (1994–Present); Manager of Management Development, ITT World Directories, Brussels (1989–1994); Manager of Human Resource Development, Ladbroke PLC, Brussels (1987–1989); Manager of Management Development, Bell Telephone Manufacturing Company (1983–1987). **Associations & Accomplishments:** American Society of Training and Development; Speaks French, Dutch, German, Portugese, Spanish, Italian, and English. **Education:** University, Ph.D. in Industrial Sociology; Postgraduate studies in Micro-Economics. **Personal:** Married to Christel in 1980. Two children: Peter and Inge. Dr. Beeckmans enjoys tennis, fitness, mountaineering and outdoor activities.

Sheldon C. Begley
Facilities Manager
Nishikawa Standard Company
P.O. Box 308
Topeka, IN 46571–0308
(219) 593–2156
Fax: (219) 593–2397

3714

Business Information: Nishikawa Standard Company, a joint venture between the Standard Products Company of the U.S. and Nishikawa Rubber Company of Japan, is an international manufacturer and distributor of dynamic sealing systems utilized in automotive industrial manufacturing production. Serving in managerial capacities for Nishikawa Standard since 1991, Sheldon Begley was appointed as Facilities Manager in 1993. Working from the main production facility in Topeka, Indiana, he oversees all facility–related functions corporate–wide, including the smooth maintenance of plant

operations for all three plant locations. **Career Steps:** Nishikawa Standard: Facilities Manager (1993 – Present), Manufacturing Manager (1991–1993); Production Manager, Starcraft Marine (1974–1989). **Associations & Accomplishments:** Topeka Town Council (1988–1992), President (1990–1991). **Personal:** Married to Pamela in 1975. Three children: Andrew, Brandon and Joshua. Mr. Begley enjoys family activities.

Michael T. Bigger
Maintenance and Tooling Manager
Winsert
2645 Industrial Parkway, P.O. Box 198
Marinette, WI 54143–0198
(715) 735–8127
Fax: (715) 732–2824

3714

Business Information: Winsert manufactures valve seat inserts for the automotive industry (machine/foundry). Joining Winsert in 1978 as a Maintenance Mechanic and Machinist, Mr. Bigger was named Foreman in 1981 and promoted to Maintenance and Tooling Manager in 1984. He is presently responsible for managing all mechanical maintenance, fabrication tooling, engineering and developing processing equipment within the plant. **Career Steps:** Winsert: Maintenance and Tooling Manager (1984–Present), Maintenance Foreman (1981–1984), Maintenance Mechanic/Machinist (1978–1981). **Associations & Accomplishments:** Local Technical Institute Advisory Board; Environmental HAZMAT Cleanup; OSHA. **Education:** North Wisconsin Technical College, Machine Tool Design (1978). **Personal:** Mr. Bigger enjoys woodworking, weightlifting, biking, and home building.

Steven M. Blomgren
Vice President of Original Equipment Sales
Tenneco Automotive – Monroe Auto Equipment Division
1 International Drive
Monroe, MI 48161–9345
(313) 243–8312
Fax: (313) 243–8031

3714

Business Information: Monroe Auto Equipment – a Division of Tenneco Automotive, is the largest manufacturer of ride control equipment (shock absorbers and struts) for the automobile industry. With ten manufacturing plants worldwide, Monroe Auto Equipment distributes to OEM's and after–market industry. Joining Monroe Auto Equipment in 1982, Mr. Blomgren was appointed as Vice President of Original Equipment Sales in 1995. He is responsible for administration and strategic planning for the original equipment manufacturer's business globally, including the management of O.E. sales for North America and the coordination of global sales. **Career Steps:** Tenneco Automotive – Monroe Auto Equipment Division: Vice President of Original Equipment Sales, (1995–Present), Director of Advanced Engineering (1993–1995), Director O.E. Sales (1990–1993), Chief Engineer, O.E. (1982–1990). **Associations & Accomplishments:** Society of Automotive Engineers; American Defense Preparedness Association; Professional Engineer – State of Michigan. **Education:** University of Illinois, B.S.M.E. (1966); Alexander Hamilton Institute, Certificate; Northern Illinois University. **Personal:** Married to Sheril in 1966. Two children: Scott and Stuart. Mr. Blomgren enjoys bowling, swimming, and golf.

James D. Bolton, P.E.
Validation Manager
Valeo Thermal Systems
2709 Bond Street
Rochester Hills, MI 48309
(810) 853–4560
Fax: (810) 853–5115

3714

Business Information: Valeo Thermal Systems, a French–based manufacturer, specializes in the design and manufacture of automotive HVAC and engine cooling components. As Validation Manager, Mr. Bolton coordinates all validation activities, including thermal and reliability laboratory research support, prototype and advanced quality design support. **Career Steps:** Validation Manager, Valeo Thermal Systems (1994–Present); Project Manager, Delphi Harrison Thermal Division (1971–1994). **Associations & Accomplishments:** Society of Automotive Engineers; American Society of Mechanical Engineers; National Society of Professional Engineers. **Education:** Purdue University M.S.M.E. (1976), B.S.M.E. (1975); Insead, CEDEP; GMI, Engineering. **Personal:** Married to Mary in 1976. Two children: Andrew Toby and Sarah Marie.

Steven M. Bonsall

Applications Engineer
Bowles Fluidics Corporation
6625 Dobbin Road
Columbia, MD 21045
(410) 381–0400
Fax: (410) 381–2718
3714

Business Information: Bowles Fluidics Corporation supplies fluidic devices (e.g., washer nozzles, defroster ducts, HVAC vents) to the automotive industries. An Applications Engineer with BFC since earning his degree in Mechanical Engineering in 1991, Mr. Bonsall is presently responsible for project management, product design, and customer contact. **Career Steps:** Applications Engineer, Bowles Fluidics Corporation (1991–Present). **Associations & Accomplishments:** Society of Automotive Engineers. **Education:** University of Maryland, Baltimore County, B.S.M.E. (1991). **Personal:** Mr. Bonsall enjoys drag racing.

Jon W. Bossoli

Engineering Manager
Philips Automotive Electronics
150 Knotter Drive
Cheshire, CT 06410–1136
(203) 271–6141
Fax: (203) 271–6035
3714

Business Information: Philips Electronics North America is a major international design manufacturer and marketer of high–tech products, including semiconductors, diversified components, consumer electronics and software. Philips consists of 25 divisions in several locations. The Automotive Electronics Division manufactures OEM shaft position and shaft speed sensors, distributing to the "Big 3" automotive manufacturers. An electronics and medical products specialty engineer with over twenty–five years expertise, Jon Bossoli has served in various divisions of Philips since 1975. Asked to rejoin Philips in 1988 to head its Engineering Unit at the new Automotive Electronics Division in Cheshire, Connecticut, Mr. Bossoli oversees all areas of product design and technology development, providing hands–on engineering design development as well. Mr. Bossoli is credited as the pioneer developer of Philips' sensor technology products. **Career Steps:** Engineering Manager, Philips Automotive Electronics (1988–Present); Engineering Manager, Sensor Engineering (1981–1988); Senior Engineer, Siemens Medical Manufacturing (1978–1981); Product Engineer, Philips Medical Manufacturing (1975–1978). **Associations & Accomplishments:** Society of Automotive Engineers. **Education:** University of Connecticut, B.S. (1969). **Personal:** Mr. Bossoli enjoys playing the guitar and sailing.

Robert L. Brock

Executive Vice President
Profiles Incorporated
277 Palmer Road
Ware, MA 01802–0659
(413) 967–3171
Fax: (413) 967–6847
3714

Business Information: Profiles Incorporated, a thirty year old company, produces automobile piston rings, cam wires, commutator wire for electric motors (for drills and vacuum cleaners), and other related products. The Company also specializes in cold rolling and drawing of precision wire shapes. As Executive Vice President, Mr. Brock is responsible for all aspects of Company operations, including all day–to–day operations. **Career Steps:** Executive Vice President, Profiles Incorporated (1993–Present); International Sales Manager, Snow Machines, Inc. (1991–1993); Vice President, CTEC, Inc. (1989–1991); Sales Manager, LMC, Inc. (1984–1989). **Education:** Dartmouth College, B.A. (1969). **Personal:** Married to Susan in 1969. Two children: Kimberly and Rebecca. Mr. Brock enjoys skiing, sailing, golf, scuba diving, canoeing, and water skiing.

Mr. Italo Caroli

President
DBM Reflex Enterprises, Inc.
1620 Boulevard Dagenais Ouest
Laval (Montreal), Quebec H7L 5C7
(514) 622–3100
Fax: (514) 622–3017
3714

Business Information: DBM Reflex Enterprises, Inc.specializes in the engineering, prototyping, product development and fabrication tooling of automotive lighting equipment. An international concern, more than half of their products are distributed outside of Canada. Purchasing DBM in 1981, Mr. Caroli is responsible for the administration and oversight of all operational aspects, focusing primarily on research and development and marketing strategies. Established in 1971, DBM Reflex Enterprises, Inc. employs 120 people with annual sales of $10 million. **Career Steps:** President, DBM Reflex Enterprises, Inc., (1975–Present); Vice President, DBM Industries Limited (1972–1975); Engineering Manager, DBM Industries Limited (1968–1972). **Associations & Accomplishments:** Corporation of Professional Engineers of Quebec; American Association for the Advancement of Science; Society of Plastic Engineers; American Society for Metals; Chamber of Commerce of Quebec; Chamber of Commerce of Laval; Patron: The Museum of Modern Art; Montreal Symphony Orchestra; Fundraiser, Centraid. **Education:** Polytechnic of Turin, Italy, Master in Mechanical Engineering (1967). **Personal:** Married to Michelle in 1971. One child: Francesca. Mr. Caroli enjoys astronomy, astrophysics, and horseback riding.

Bruce G. Christenson

Manager of Product Development
Eagle Picher Automotive Hillsdale Tool Division
263 Industrial Drive
Hillsdale, MI 49242–1078
(517) 439–0737
Fax: (517) 437–0323
3714

Business Information: Hillsdale Tool Division, established in 1940, designs, manufactures and distributes automotive parts (i.e., engine, transmission, driveline components). Serving in various management and engineering capacities for HTD since 1986, Bruce Christenson was appointed as Manager of Product Development in 1993. In this capacity, he is responsible for testing components, prototype, and supervision for a staff of 40. **Career Steps:** Hillsdale Tool Division: Manager of Product Development (1993–Present), Sales Engineer (1988–1993), Manufacturing Engineer (1986–1988); Territory Manager, Airoyal Company (1986). **Associations & Accomplishments:** Board of Directors, Hillsdale County Habitat for Humanity; Board of Directors, Kimball YMCA Nature Center. **Education:** Purdue University, B.S.M.T. (1983); University of Michigan, currently working towards an M.B.A. degree. **Personal:** Married to LeAnna in 1990. One child: Ryan.

Kyle P. Chura

Manager of Corporate Relations
ASC Incorporated
1 Sunroof Center Drive
Southgate, MI 48195
(313) 246–0559
Fax: (313) 246–0029
3714

Business Information: ASC Incorporated is the industry leader in the production of convertible cars, sunroofs, vehicle interior trim, and specialty vehicles. Established in 1965, the Company employs 2,200 people, and has an estimated annual revenue of $450 million. As Manager of Corporate Relations, Mr. Chura oversees all aspects of his department. He is responsible for writing speeches, press releases and collateral material, and handles all direct advertising, in addition to acting as the Company's spokesman. **Career Steps:** ASC Incorporated: Manager of Corporate Relations (1990–Present), Senior Marketing Coordinator (1988–1990), Account Representative (1988). **Associations & Accomplishments:** Adcraft Club of Detroit; International Motor Press Association; Motor Press Guild; International Motorsports Association Professional Racing License Holder; Sports Car Club of America Professional Racing License Holder. **Education:** Northwood University, B.B.A. (1987). **Personal:** Mr. Chura enjoys golf, running, and weightlifting.

John P. Corrunker

Product Quality Assurance Manager
AlliedSignal
780 Arcata Boulevard
Clarksville, TN 37040
(615) 553–6545
Fax: (615) 553–6577
3714

Business Information: AlliedSignal is an advanced technology and manufacturing company serving customers worldwide with aerospace and automotive products, chemicals, fibers, plastics and advanced materials. International in scope, AlliedSignal has three principal divisions: Aerospace, Automotive, and Engineered Materials. A Fortune 500 Company, AlliedSignal reports annual revenue in excess of $12.8 billion. As Product Quality Assurance Manager for AlliedSignal's Automotive Braking System Division, Mr. Corrunker is responsible for all aspects of internal and external quality assurance functions, primarily through warranty and reliability analysis. Established in 1986, AlliedSignal's Braking Division specializes in the manufacture of automotive and medium–sized truck anti–lock braking systems. There are currently over 370 people employed at the Clarksville, Tennessee manufacturing facility, generating over $40 million in revenue. **Career Steps:** Product Quality Assurance Manager, AlliedSignal (1993–Present); Quality Director, Stanadyne (1992–1993); Vice President of Quality, Borg Warner (1988–1992); Quality Manager, Ford Motor Company (1962–1988). **Associations & Accomplishments:** American Society of Quality Control; Society of Materials Engineers; Rotary International; NHRA; Soap Box Derby; Henry Ford Technological Award. **Education:** Kennedy Western University, B.S. in Quality Reliability (1995); Ferris; Lawrence; University of Michigan, Dearborn. **Personal:** Married to Carrol in 1964. Two children: Scott and Ian. Mr. Corrunker enjoys boating and golf.

Steven Crabtree

Sales and Product Manager
United States Gear Corporation
9420 South Stony Island Avenue
Chicago, IL 60617–3645
(312) 375–4900
Fax: (312) 375–4557
3714

Business Information: United States Gear Corporation, a privately–held company, was established in 1963 to provide high quality ring and pinion and differential components for industrial, truck, and automotive markets. The Corporation offers an expanding line of light duty truck and automotive ring and pinion gear sets, differential internal kits, installation kits, and TORQ–LINE limited slip differentials, made with pride in the USA. Special areas of expertise include ring gear and pinion cutting capacities, operating one of 200 Gleason gear machines used for cutting hypoid, spiral bevel, formate, and helix form tooth form, as well as differential side gears, side pinion gears, and differential cross shafts. Their heat treat operation – under the name Heat Treat Corporation of America – is a certified and approved heat treater and the sole source of heat treatment for U.S. Gear products. As Sales and Product Manager of the Light Duty Division, Mr. Crabtree is responsible for the management of the "TORQ–LINE FOR LIGHT DUTY TRUCKS" Program, overseeing all manufacturing activities for the products. **Career Steps:** Automotive After Market Sales (1978–93); Sales and Product Manager, United States Gear Corporation, Light Duty Division (1993–Present). **Associations & Accomplishments:** Peak Performance Network; Quota Buster Club. **Personal:** Married to Ann Marie in 1984. One child: Steven Herbert. Mr. Crabtree enjoys golf and is a drag racing enthusiast.

Jack R. Dawson

Vice President of Engineering
Preferred Technical Group
2044 Austin
Rochester Hills, MI 48309
(810) 299–7367
Fax: (810) 299–3979
3714

Business Information: Preferred Technical Group, a Division of Echlin, is a designer and manufacturer of power steering, hydrauliic brakes and air conditioning hoses. Products are distributed nationally and internationally at five locations in the U.S. Acquired by Echlin in 1992, Preferred Technical Group reports annual revenue of $300 million and currently employs 2,200 people. As Vice President of Engineering, Mr. Dawson oversees all product design and development internationally. **Career Steps:** Vice President of Engineering, Preferred Technical Group (1993–Present); Vice President of Engineering, S & H Fabricating & Engineering (1990–1993); Director of Engineering, Calsonic (1988–1990); Consultant, National Summit Group (1984–1987). **Associations & Accomplishments:** Society of Automotive Engineers. **Education:** General Motors Institute, B.S. in Mechanical Engineering (1970). **Personal:** Married to Kathleen M. in 1969. Mr. Dawson enjoys skiing, tennis, sports, reading, attending seminars, and country dancing.

Vicki R. Dobberteen

Director of Human Resources
Tokai Rika U.S.A., Inc.
100 Hill Brady Road
Battle Creek, MI 49015
(616) 966–0100
Fax: (616) 966–0818
3714

Business Information: Tokai Rika U.S.A., Inc. is an automotive switch manufacturer. Established in 1987, Tokai Rika U.S.A., Inc. employs 750 people and boasts annual revenue in excess of $180 million. As Director of Human Resources, Ms. Dobberteen is responsible for hiring, training, safety, payroll, benefits, Associate Relations and Associate activities. **Career Steps:** Tokai Rika U.S.A., Inc: Director of Human Resources (1994–Present), Manager, Human Resources (1993–1994), Assistant Manager, Human Resources (1991–1993). **Associations & Accomplishments:** Society for Human Resource Management (SHRM); American Management Association (AMA). **Education:** Olivet Nazarene College, B.A. (1973). **Personal:** Married to Kurt J. in 1988. One child: Wendy C. Geselle.

Thomas Dunk
General Manager
Spiral Industries
1572 North Old US 23
Howell, MI 48843
(810) 632–6300
Fax: (810) 632–9270

3714

Business Information: Spiral Industries is a manufacturer and international distributor of coupled hose assemblies utilized medium- to heavy–duty truck assembly manufacturers. Primarily distributing to OEM automotive industries in the U.S., Spriral also has marketing operations in Australia and Mexico. As General Manager, Thomas Dunk is responsible for the supervision and overall day–to–day operations in the areas of engineering, A2LA third–party accredited lab, the tool room and production manufacturing. In addition, he is an engineering designer, holding patents for injection molding applications, as well as continues to implement prototype designs for future development. **Career Steps:** Spiral Industries: General Manager (1994–Present), General Manager (1985–1990); General Manager, Cobra Enterprises (1991–1994); Former Owner: Putitan Machine Company, Puritan Automatic Screw Machine Company, Dun–Mor Products. **Personal:** Two children: Thomas W. and Tracy F. Mr. Dunk enjoys photography, golf and travel.

Donald L. Ecton Jr.
Manager of Production Engineering
Topy Corporation
P.O. Box 1010
Frankfort, KY 40602–1010
(502) 695–6163
Fax: (502) 875–5424

3714

Business Information: The Topy Corporation specializes in the manufacture of steel and aluminum wheels for passenger vehicles and light trucks. Established in 1985, the Topy Corporation currently employs 525 people. As Manager of Production Engineering, Mr. Ecton is responsible for all aspects of product engineering. **Career Steps:** Topy Corporation: Manager of Production Engineering (1992–Present), Assistant Manager of Engineering (1989–1992), Staff Engineer (1986–1989); Project Engineer, Lectrodryer Division of Ajax (1981–1986). **Associations & Accomplishments:** American Welding Society, Lexington Chapter Charter Member; Society of Manufacturing Engineers; American Society of Mechanical Engineers. **Education:** University of Kentucky, B.S. in Mechanical Engineering (1981). **Personal:** Married to Lelia M. in 1986. Mr. Ecton enjoys softball, golf and farm work.

Brian D. Evanson
Production Control Manager
Nasco Sec Wheels
9801 Almeria Street
Fontana, CA 90023
(213) 269–0283
Fax: (213) 265–2017

3714

Business Information: Nasco Sec Wheels manufactures and distributes aftermarket aluminum wheels for both street and racing wheel applications. As Production Control Manager, Brian Evanson schedules production for all departments, including new product development, blueprints and external products testing. In addition, he supervises all information systems operations, ensuring the smooth flow of computer network and data technology applications. **Career Steps:** Production Control Manager, Nasco Sec Wheels (1992–Present); CNC Programmer, Dynamark Ltd. (1990–1992); CNC Specialist, General Dynamics – Pomona (1988–1990); Apprentice, Harrington Mold (1985–1988). **Associations & Accomplishments:** Vocational Industrial Clubs of America; International Youth Skill Olympics – Birmingham, England (placed 5th). **Personal:** Married to Lisa in 1991. Three children: Jessica, Erik, and Samantha. Mr. Evanson enjoys camping and dirtbike riding.

Bryan C. Fossen
Business Team Manager
TRW Safety Systems
4051 North Higley Road, Building 23
Mesa, AZ 85315–1210
(602) 396–1906
Fax: (602) 396–1309

3714

Business Information: Utilizing thirty–three manual and automatic assembly processes for the production of nine products, TRW Safety Systems is the leading manufacturer of inflater/sub–assembly, driver–side airbags. Controlling a department budget of $12.5 million and a team of over 500 people, Bryan Fossen is the Business Team Leader responsible for the manufacture of the nine products and utilization of the assembly processes, producing 6.9 million inflators. **Career Steps:** Business Team Manager, TRW Safety Systems (1988–Present); Operation Officer, Major, US Army – Arizona National Guard (1980–Present); Headquarter Company Commander, 1–285th Aviation Battalion Attack – Helicopter Company (1990–1992); Production Manager, Great Western Silicon (1980–1988). **Associations & Accomplishments:** Arizona Army National Guard; US Association of Officers; National Guard Officer Association of Arizona. **Education:** 6224th Army Reserve School, Command and General Staff College in progress; Southwest University, B.S. in Aviation Administration; US Army Officer Rotary Course; Mesa College, A.A.S. in Management. **Personal:** Married to Teresa in 1992. Four children: Jacob, Jenna, Rebecca and Brooke. Mr. Fossen enjoys flying, running, racquetball, and military history.

Lary W. Graves
Bargaining Chairman
General Motors Corporation
13489 Riker Road
Chelsea, MI 48118
(313) 481–6428
Fax: Please mail or call

3714

Business Information: General Motors is one the U.S.'s "Big Three" automakers. Mr. Graves is the elected Bargaining Chairman for the 6,000 United Auto Workers (UAW) Union members working in six General Motors automatic transmission manufacturing plants. Mr. Graves handles grievance procedures, plant appointments, liaison between the International UAW and the local chapters, employee health and safety issues, and is involved with the Employee Health Program committee. Established in 1960, General Motors Corporation employs 6,000 people with annual sales of $1 billion. **Career Steps:** Bargaining Chairman, General Motors (1993–Present); Pipe Fitter, General Motors (1979–1993); Professional Baseball Player, Detroit Tigers. **Associations & Accomplishments:** Washtenaw County Work Consortium; Make a Wish Foundation. **Education:** Eastern Michigan University, B.S. (1990); Washtenaw Community College, A.A. **Personal:** Married to Jessica in 1978. Two children: Jessica and Cole.

Everett Greenli
Senior Industrial Engineer
Special Devices
11350 E. Sahuaro Drive, Apt. 211
Scottsdale, AZ 85259
Fax: (602) 451–4167
E MAIL: See Below

3714

Business Information: Special Devices, headquartered in California, primarily manufactures airbag igniters for the automobile industry. The Company is also expanding into the aerospace industry. As Senior Industrial Engineer, Mr. Greenli is involved in process realignment, methodology and implementation, and systems integrations. Other areas of involvement include cost collection systems, cost and finance, and design. Internet users can reach him via: egreenli@net-zone.com. **Career Steps:** Senior Industrial Engineer, Special Devices (1996–Present); Industrial Engineer/Financial Analyst, McDonnell Douglas (1989–1992); Industrial Engineer, Arizona Public Service (1986–1988); Contract Performance Measurement Specialist, HQ ARRCOM (1981–1984). **Associations & Accomplishments:** Institute of Industrial Engineers, Committees, Vice President, President; Performance Management Association, Committees, Vice President; National Contract Management Association, Committees; Society of Cost Estimating and Analysis; Arizona Professional Employment Network, Committees. **Education:** Florida Institute of Technology, M.S. Professional Management (1981); Montana State College, B.S. Industrial Engineering/Arts. **Personal:** Mr. Greenli enjoys golf, skiing, racquetball, tennis, hiking, and fishing.

David Harris
Group Vice President of Marketing & Communications
Crane Cams
530 Fentress Boulevard
Daytona Beach, FL 32114–1210
(904) 252–1151
Fax: (904) 947–5107

3714

Business Information: Crane Technologies is the parent company of Crane Cams, Crane Automotive Parts, and Cam Shaft Machine Corporation. Crane Cams is an automobile parts manufacturer. Crane Technologies holds contracts such as NHRA, IHRA, Ford, and Chrysler Corporation. As Group Vice President of Marketing & Communications, Mr. Harris is responsible for all aspects of Company operations, including marketing and sales, communications, MIS, and strategic planning. **Career Steps:** Group Vice President of Marketing & Communications, Crane Cams (1993–Present); Business Unit Executive, IBM (1978–1993); Planning Manager, Martin Marietta (1976–1978). **Associations & Accomplishments:** Director, Crane Technologies Group, Inc.; Director, Crane Cams Europe, Ltd.; Director, Crane Cams N.V. **Education:** Harvard, Executive M.B.A. (1985); Rollins College, M.B.A.; University of Central Florida, B.S. in Computer Science & Math. **Personal:** Married to Kaye in 1970. Two children: Cory and Jennifer. Mr. Harris enjoys golf, tennis, and jogging.

Robert A. Harrison
Manager of Sales and Marketing
Specialty Stampings, Inc.
Adel Division, 12500 East Nine Mile Road
Warren, MI 48089
(810) 758–6620
Fax: (810) 758–6043

3714

Business Information: Specialty Stampings, Inc. is a manufacturer of stamped and fabricated assemblies (i.e., air bag doors, instrument panel metals, decorative trim, hub caps). With estimated annual sales of $20 million, Special Stampings currently employs 150 people. As Manager of Sales and Marketing in the Adel Division, Mr. Harrison is responsible for diversified activities, including customer interface, and some international sales and marketing for the Company. **Career Steps:** Manager of Sales and Marketing, Specialty Stampings, Inc. (1988–Present); Senior Account Executive, Mascotech Ind. Comp. **Education:** Det. Institute of Technology, Bachelor of Industrial Engineering (1951). **Personal:** Married to Edith in 1989. Four children: David, Elizabeth, Sheila, and Steven. Mr. Harrison enjoys golf, sailing, and skiing.

John David Hurley
Engineering Manager
Manchester Plastics, Inc.
300 Elm Street
Homer, MI 49245–1337
(517) 568–6134
Fax: (517) 568–4662

3714

Business Information: Manchester Plastics, Inc., a division of Collins & Aikman, is an international automotive trim (i.e., urethane foam products) manufacturer. Established in 1968, the Company currently has five branches in the United States and three in Canada. As Engineering Manager, Mr. Hurley is responsible for a variety of administrative activities and the direct supervision of eleven engineers. With 25 years experience in the urethane industry, he joined Manchester in 1993 after holding several administrative positions in related industries. **Career Steps:** Engineering Manager, Manchester Plastics, Inc. (1993–Present); General Manager, RIM, Inc. (1991–1993); President, Urea–Tech, Inc. (1989–1991); Program Manager, Excel Industries (1985–1989). **Education:** Napoleon High School (1965). **Personal:** Married to Patricia in 1978. Two children: Nekiya and Jon. Mr. Hurley enjoys raising horses, hunting, fishing, and flint knapping.

Thomas E. Johnson
Vice President of Engineering
Horton Vehicle Components, Inc.
1170 15th Avenue, South East
Minneapolis, MN 55414
(612) 378–6454
Fax: (612) 627–5722

3714

Business Information: Horton Vehicle Components, Inc. is a manufacturer of fan clutches and brakes used in the diesel industry. The Corporation established this division in 1951 and currently employs over 400 people. Horton offers products through direct sale to customers and through a chain of distributors. As Vice President of Engineering, Mr. Johnson is involved in the research and development of new and existing products. Along with other members of the management staff, he develops proposals for prospective clients. **Career Steps:** Vice President of Engineering, Horton Vehicle Components, Inc. (1994–Present); Manager/Diesel Engine Design, General Electric (1981–1994); Senior Engineer, Bendix Corporation (1979–1981); Materials Development Engineer, Chrysler Corporation (1978–1979). **Associations & Accomplishments:** M.S.P.E. – Professional Engineer. **Education:** University of Minnesota, B.S. in Metallurgical Engineering (1974). **Personal:** Married to Donna in 1980. Two children: Derek II and Alison. Mr. Johnson enjoys his children.

Mr. Richard L. Keller

Vice President of Sales and Marketing
Lear Corp. – Ford Division
17425 Federal Drive
Allen Park, MI 48101
(313) 982–7301
Fax: (313) 982–7400

3714

Business Information: A Fortune 500 company, Lear Corp. is the world's largest independent supplier of automotive interior systems with sales of about $6.0 billion. In his current capacity, Mr. Keller is responsible for all aspects of sales and marketing for the Ford Division of Lear, which represents sales of about $2.5 billion, as well as the supervision of a 40–member sales staff. **Career Steps:** Automotive Industries Sales, Inc.: Vice President of Sales and Marketing (1994–1995), Director of Ford Sales (1987–1994); Sales Manager, Allen Industries (1978–1987). **Associations & Accomplishments:** Sales and Marketing Executives of Detroit. **Education:** Wayne State University, Masters of Business Administration (1973); University of Michigan, Bachelors in Business Administration (1969). **Personal:** Married to Christine in 1973. Two children: Thomas and Jaime. Mr. Keller enjoys tennis and golf.

Duncan A. MacMaster

Director of Canadian Operations
Arrow Automotive Industries
3883 Nashua Drive, Unit 8
Mississauga, Ontario L4V 1R3
(905) 677–7010
Fax: (905) 677–0474

3714

Business Information: Arrow Automotive Industries is a remanufacturer of automotive parts, taking used automotive parts that are traded in for new ones and remanufacturing them into new parts. At the present time, there are two regional locations in Canada, with future plans to expand nationwide. Joining the Company as Director of Canadian Operations in 1994, Mr. MacMaster is responsible for all aspects of operations at the Canadian offices, including sales, credits, warehousing, accounts payable, and accounts receivable. In addition, he oversees all administrative operations for associates and a support staff of ten. **Career Steps:** Director of Canadian Operations, Arrow Automotive Industries (1994–Present); Manager, Barlain Tire; Owner and Operator, BCBC Transport. **Associations & Accomplishments:** Board of Directors, The Mississauga Reps Hockey Association. **Education:** Humber College, Business Administration (1989). **Personal:** Married to Suzanne in 1990.

Paul A. Mallorey

Vice President of Technology Group
The Becker Group
6100 19 Mile Road
Sterling Heights, MI 48314–2102
(810) 726–3107
Fax: (810) 726–4598

3714

Business Information: The Becker Group is a tier one supplier of Automotive Interior Trim. Processes utilized by Becker include Injection molding, LD SRIM, Foam molding, Wood processing, and painting. The Becker Group presently supplies products to General Motors, Chrysler, and Ford Motors. International in scope, The Becker Group has 14 plants and spans the U.S. (Nashville, Tennessee and Southeastern Michigan) and Mexico. The Becker Group reports annual revenue of $600 million. As Vice President of Technology Group, Mr. Mallorey is responsible for all aspects of technology and oversight of research and development. **Career Steps:** Vice President of Technology Group, The Becker Group (1995–Present); Vice President and General Manager, Chivas Urethane, Inc. (1994–1995); Vice President of Engineering, Chivas Urethane, Ltd. (1990–1994). **Associations & Accomplishments:** Society of Automotive Engineers (SAE); Holder of two patents on low–density polyurethane techniques. Education: Lawrence Institute of Technology (LIT), B.S. in Mechanical Engineering (1984); United Air Force Academy (transferred to LIT). **Personal:** Mr. Mallorey enjoys golf."

Robert J. McCabe

Chief Financial Officer and Group Director of Finance
General Motors Corporation– Powertrain Group
895 Joslyn Avenue
Pontiac, MI 48340–2920
(810) 857–0532
Fax: (810) 857–0564

3714

Business Information: General Motors Corporation– Powertrain Group specializes in the design, manufacture and sales of engines, transmissions, iron and aluminum castings. A financial executive with GM since 1970, Mr. McCabe was appointed to his current position in 1992. As Chief Financial Officer and Group Director of Finance, Mr. McCabe oversees all aspects of financial operations for the Group. The Powertrain Group is GM's largest group in North America. **Career Steps:** Chief Financial Officer and Group Director of Finance, General Motors Corporation– Powertrain Group (1992–Present); Finance Director, GM – Packard Electric Division (1989–1992); Executive Director, Packard International (1989–1992); Chairman and Chief Executive Officer, Terex Equipment Ltd. (1987–1989). **Associations & Accomplishments:** City of Cortland, Ohio: Chairman, Charter Review Committee (1988–1989), Planning and Zoning Commission (1989–1992); Assistant Coach, NCAA Championship Cornell Ice Hockey Teams (1967 & 1970). **Education:** Cornell University: M.B.A. (1970), B.S. (1967). **Personal:** Married to Susan L. Lynch in 1989. Five children: Christa, Kasey, Kami, John, and Katie. Mr. McCabe enjoys scuba diving, sky diving, ice skating, and skiing.

Robert B. McNamee

Vice President of Sales
GO/DAN Industries
481 Covered Bridge Road
Cherry Hill, NJ 08034–3108
(800) 755–2160
Fax: (203) 865–3723

3714

Business Information: GO/DAN Industries is a national manufacturer of automotive radiators and heaters for the aftermarket. As Vice President of Sales, Mr. McNamee is responsible for all sales activities nationally and internationally, as well as serving as a member of the Executive Staff and overseeing strategic planning. **Career Steps:** Vice President of Sales, GO/DAN Industries (1990–Present); Daniel Radiator Corporation: Vice President of Sales and Marketing (1987–1990), General Sales Manager (1987) **Associations & Accomplishments:** President and Founder, Cherry Hill Pop Warner Football League. **Education:** Attended: University of Bridgeport and various AMA Programs. **Personal:** Married to Joyce in 1957. Five children: Brian, Mary–Beth, Sue–Ellen, Scott, and Mark. Mr. McNamee enjoys reading.

Jose Melgar

Executive President
Metalcon
P.O. Box 028537
Miami, FL 33102–8537
58–41–33–2993
Fax: Please mail or call

3714

Business Information: Metalcon is the leading manufacturer of automotive parts in Venezuela, exporting products to countries in three continents (i.e., Japan, Mid–East, Africa, Liberia, North & South America). Serving in managerial roles for Metalcon since 1991, Jose Melgar was appointed Executive President in 1993. He provides the oversight and administration for manufacturing operations and financial areas. **Career Steps:** Metalcon: Executive President (1993–Present), Finance Director (1991–1993), Treasury Manager (1983–1988); General Manager, WIX Venezuela (1988–1991). **Associations & Accomplishments:** Association of Automotive Parts Manufacturers; President, The Rotary Club Valencia (1996); Camara de Industriales – Carabobo. **Education:** University of Honduras: CPA (1973), B.A. in Business Administration; Dana University – Toledo, Certified Supervisor. **Personal:** Married to Maria in 1971. Two children: Jose Ismael and Erwin. Mr. Melgar enjoys golf, and amateur journalism (essays).

Garrett E. Mikita

Director of Manufacturing
United Technologies Automotive
1641 Porter Street
Detroit, MI 48216–1935
(313) 237–3658
Fax: (313) 962–4389

3714

Business Information: United Technologies Automotive is a full service supplier of automobile interiors, instrument panels, consoles, door panels, and trim for the automotive and trucking industries. The Company has five main divisions: Wiring Systems, Input Controls, Motors, European, and Interiors. As Director of Manufacturing at the Interiors Division, Mr. Mikita is responsible for providing leadership to eight manufacturing plants across the Midwest. His primary objective is to institute fundamental changes through World Class Manufacturing, reorganizing and performing a seven–step process. He will assure that his facilities reach their profit potential and improve product quality and the atmosphere within the Company. **Career Steps:** Director of Manufacturing, United Technologies Automotive (1995–Present); Pratt & Whitney Aircraft: Operations Manager (1995–1996), Business Unit Manager (1993–1995), Unit Leader – Advanced Coatings (1991–1993). **Associations & Accomplishments:** Certified in Production and Inventory Management by American Production and Inventory Control Society; Protagonist, Harvard Business School Case Study N9–696—67. **Education:** University of New Haven, M.B.A. (1992); Central Connecticut State University, B.S. in Engineering. **Personal:** Married to Deborah Lynnette in 1987. Mr. Mikita enjoys golf and travel.

Randall C. Miller

Senior Project Engineer
Atwood Automotive
1400 Eddy Avenue, Department 21
Rockford, IL 61103–3171
(815) 636–3279
Fax: (815) 877–4136

3714

Business Information: Atwood Automotive is a leading designer and builder of automotive parts for major automotive OEM's. Established in 1952, Atwood Automotive reports annual revenue of $225 million and currently employs 1,100 people. As Senior Project Engineer, Mr. Miller is responsible for the oversight of the implementation, testing, and research & development of parking brakes through production. Concurrent with his position at Atwood Automotive, he owns and operates full time, a custom golf club fabrication and repair shop. Career milestones include designing parts and equipment for companies to get patents (his name is listed on those patents as the designer). **Career Steps:** Senior Project Engineer, Atwood Automotive (1988–Present); Senior Designer, Amerock (1986–1988); Design Engineer, Evans Rule (1982–1986); Design Engineer, Orscheln (1976–1982). **Associations & Accomplishments:** Member, SAE; Member, Professional Clubmakers Society; Member, Golf Clubmakers Association. **Education:** North East Missouri State University, I.E. (1973). **Personal:** Married to Flora E. Miller in 1987. Two children: Andy and Teresa. Mr. Miller enjoys golf.

Paul A. Mlasko

Human Resources Manager
CMI Southfield, Inc.
26290 West Eight Mile Road
Southfield, MI 48034–3650
(810) 357–5180
Fax: (810) 357–2008

3714

Business Information: CMI Southfield, Inc. is a major supplier of automotive components for machining, engine and chassis components for the "Big 3" automotive industries (Chrysler, GM, Ford). Product lines include front wheel knuckles, cylinder heads and manifolds. With over twenty years expertise in human relations and personnel management, Paul Mlasko joined CMI–Southfield in 1992. As Human Resources Manager he oversees all personnel functions, with primary duties including benefits administration and implementation, employee relations, recruiting, safety, and all governmental regulations compliance. **Career Steps:** Human Resources Manager, CMI Southfield, Inc. (1992–Present); Human Resources Manager, American Plastic Toys, Inc. (1987–1992); Personnel Manager, Holloway Sand & Gravel Company, Inc. (1972–1987). **Associations & Accomplishments:** Society of Human Resource Managers; Michigan Manufacturers Association; American Management Association. **Education:** San Jose State University, B.A. in Business Administration (1972). **Personal:** One child: Maureen. Mr. Mlasko enjoys antiques, fishing, and golf.

David H. Mosier

····━━◆◉◆━━····

Chief Financial Officer
Rostra Precision Controls, Inc.
2519 Dena Drive
Laurinburg, NC 28352–4000
(910) 276–4853
Fax: (910) 276–1354
EMAIL: See Below

3714

Business Information: Rostra Precision Controls, Inc. is the number one domestic leader in the manufacture and distribution of automotive products to the automotive aftermarket and OE. Specializing in solenoids, transmission modulators, and cruise controls, the Company is international in scope and provides products to the Malaysian, Australian, and European markets. Established in 1991, the Company employs 217 people, and has an estimated annual revenue of $35 million. As Chief Financial Officer, Mr. Mosier is responsible for all financial analysis and reporting. Internet users can reach him via: Davidmos@Rostra.com. **Career Steps:** Chief Financial Officer, Rostra Precision Controls, Inc. (1995–Present); Senior Accountant, Deloitte & Touche (1991–1995). **Associations & Accomplishments:** North Carolina Association of Certified Public Accountants. **Education:** North Carolina State University, Bachelors in Accounting (1991). **Personal:** Mr. Mosier enjoys golf and antique car restoration (Mustangs and T–Birds).

Sean Z. Nobari
Vice President of Quality Systems
Horizon Technologies Group
20600 Eureka Road, Suite 200
Taylor, MI 48180
(313) 282–7322
Fax: (313) 285–3465
E MAIL: See Below

3714

Business Information: Horizon Technologies Group, established in 1943, provides machining and cold forming products to the automotive supplies market. As Vice President of Quality Systems, Mr. Nobari develops and implements corporate–wide Quality Systems and ensures compliance with national and international Quality System Standards. He is also responsible for the day–to–day quality operations of the Company and for maintaining customer satisfaction with Company products. Internet users can reach him via: 103063.2365@compuServe.com. **Career Steps:** Vice President of Quality Systems, Horizon Technologies Group (1994–Present); International Quality Assurance Manager, Bundy N.A. (1989–1994); Adjunct Professor, St. Clair community College (1990–Present). **Associations & Accomplishments:** American Society for Quality Control; Society of Manufacturing Engineers; American Statistical Association; RAB Certified Quality System Auditor (QS–A). **Education:** Wayne State University: M.S. in Operations Research (1988), B.S. in Planning and Computer Applications (1979). **Personal:** Married to Tonya Adli–Nobari in 1979. Three children: Matt, R. J., and Victoria. Mr. Nobari enjoys sports, scientific reading, and teaching.

Michael R. Peters
Plant Manager
Walker Manufacturing Company
704 Highway 25 South
Aberdeen, MS 39730
(601) 369–8161 Ext: 210
Fax: (601) 369–4352

3714

Business Information: Walker Manufacturing Co., Div. of Tenneco Automotive, is the world leader in automotive exhaust systems for both Original Equipment (OE) and After Market (AM) applications. Walker has thirteen North American lcoations, with three of those focused on After Market and the others on Original Equipment, including Ford, GM, Chrysler, and FOS. Joining Walker Manufacturing Company in 1987, Mr. Peters was appointed Plant Manager in January 1996. He manages all functional areas, including Production Quality, Materials, Finance, Human Resources, and Engineering for the Aberdeen and Prairie, Mississippi and Haleyville, Alabama locations. **Career Steps:** Walker Manufacturing Company: Plant Manager (1996–Present), Plant Operations Manager (1995–1996), Quality Manager (1991–1995), Senior Accountant (1987–1991). **Associations & Accomplishments:** Institute of Management Accountants; American Society for Quality Control; Board Member, Several Local and Civic Organizations; Exchange Club. **Education:** University of Mississippi, B.P.A. (1992). **Personal:** Married to Cheryl Ingersoll in 1992. Two children: Michael

"Ty" Tyler and Cori Marie. Mr. Peters enjoys golf, reading, outdoor activities, and spending time with his family.

John D. Phillips
Engineering Manager
DELPHI–E
2401 Columbus Avenue
Anderson, IN 46018
(317) 646–7176
Fax: (317) 646–7305
EMAIL: See Below

3714

Business Information: Formerly known as Delco–Remy and AC Delco, DELPHI–E is a manufacturer of automotive components. Products include ignition systems for all types of internal combustion engines, primarily used for automotive applications. With corporate headquarters in Flint, Michigan, DELPHI–E has more than 40 locations nationwide from which products are distributed to customers nationally and internationally. As Engineering Manager, Mr. Phillips is responsible for the oversight of all engineering departments to include production engineering, manufacturing engineering, process and tool engineering, and new product development engineering. He may also be reached through the Internet via: jdp@indy.net **Career Steps:** Engineering Manager, DELPHI–E (1989–Present); New Product Development, AC Delco Systems (1989–1992); Research Coordinator, Delco Remy (1986–1989). **Associations & Accomplishments:** Tau Beta Pi; Muncie Area Amateur Radio Club. **Education:** Stanford University, M.S. in Electrical Engineering (1985); General Motors Institute, B.S. in Electrical Engineering (1979); Attended Ball State University (1982–1984). **Personal:** Married to Kristin in 1979. Three children: Benjamin, Donald Scott, and Daniel. Mr. Phillips enjoys being active in amateur radio (NV9A), utilizing amateur, non–geosynchronous communications satellites.

Michael B. Potts
Manager of Strategic Planning
Eaton Corporation
191 East North Avenue
Carol Stream, IL 60188–2019
(708) 260–3176
Fax: (708) 260–3208

3714

Business Information: Eaton Corporation is one of the world's leading manufacturers of automotive and truck components, electrical components, industrial and commercial controls, and accessories. Established in the 1900's, Eaton Corporation reports annual revenue of $7 billion and currently employs 50,000 people corporate–wide. As Manager of Strategic Planning, Mr. Potts is responsible for all aspects of strategic planning operations, including joint ventures, mergers, and strategic alliances. **Career Steps:** Manager of Strategic Planning, Eaton Corporation (1993–Present); Plant Manager, U.S. Postal Service (1992–1993). **Associations & Accomplishments:** Association of Home Appliance Manufacturers. **Education:** Case Western Reserve University, M.B.A. (1993); Bradley University, B.S.in Industrial Engineering. **Personal:** Married to Pamela in 1987. Two children: Brooks and Tyler. Mr. Potts enjoys golf, reading, and chess.

James Rasmus
Executive Director
Tenneco
1010 Milam Street, Suite 1FP
Houston, TX 77002
(713) 757–6316
Fax: Please mail or call

3714

Business Information: Tenneco is a producer of automotive parts, packaging, gas pipeline, and shipbuilding with offices located throughout the world. As Executive Project Director, Human Resources/Payroll, Mr. Rasmus is responsible for the HR/payroll Shared Services initiative for Tenneco. In the next year, Mr. Rasmus plans to complete the development and implementation of a centralized payroll system. He sees each role he has filled as being a success for the organization and fulfilling a career milestone for himself. **Career Steps:** Executive Director, Tenneco (1995–Present); Case Corporation: Director Quality (1994–1995), Director of Marketing Support – International (1992–1994); Director of Human Resources – International Business Group (1990–1992). **Education:** University of Illinois: M.A. (1975), B.A. (1974). **Personal:** Married to Jo Goss Rasmus in 1984. One child: Kendall Marie. Mr. Rasmus enjoys jogging and tennis.

Carlos E. Richa
Director of Arms & Aftermarket Business Units
Trico Products Corporation – Plant 5
1995 Billy Mitchell Boulevard
Brownsville, TX 78521–5625
(210) 544–0342 Ext. 2310
Fax: (210) 544–0409

3714

Business Information: Trico Products Corporation – Plant 5 is the worldwide distributor, designer, and manufacturer of windshield wiper systems for original equipment manufactures and replacement markets with plants in Australia, Mexico, Great Britain, and the United States. As Director of Arms & Aftermarket Business Units, Dr. Richa is responsible for operations of the Brownsville, Texas plant and for 1,000 employees. He oversees recruitment of management staff, personnel concerns, financial accountability, marketing of new and existing products, and developing and training of sales personnel. Mr. Richa works with his managers on the establishment of workable budgets and monitors production costs to avoid deficit spending. **Career Steps:** Trico Products Corporation – Plant S: Director of Arms & Aftermarket Business Units (1995–Present), Director of Engineering (1992–1995); Quality Network Representative, Delphi Chassis–General Motors Corporation (1988–1992). **Associations & Accomplishments:** A.S.Q.C. **Education:** Wright State, M.S. Degree in Math (1991); Texas A&M University, Doctor of Engineering, Ind. Eng. (1988), Master of Engineering, Ind. Eng. (1985); The University of Texas–Austin, B.S. Degree in Electrical Engineering (1980). **Personal:** Married to Lucila in 1985. Two children: Carlos Eduardo and Javier Andres. Dr. Richa enjoys reading, sailing, and travel.

Debra Ryder
Director of Finance
G.T. Development Corporation
14601 Interurban Avenue South
Burien, WA 98168
(206) 244–1305
Fax: (206) 244–2842

3714

Business Information: G.T. Development Corporation is a manufacturing and assembling company of heavy duty, Class A truck components on an international level. As Director of Finance, Ms. Ryder is responsible for accounting, supervising employees, managing human resources, overseeing information services and handling administrative duties. She is also the Senior Manager in charge of working with banks and all legal departments. **Career Steps:** Director of Finance, G.T. Development Corporation (1994–Present); Controller, TIE Communications; Controller, Preservative Paint; Account Manager, Milgard Manufacturing. **Associations & Accomplishments:** WSCPA; IMA; APICS. **Education:** University of Montana, B.S. (1986).

Bruce J. Ryman
Director of Marketing
Praxair Surface Technologies
1500 Polco Street
Indianapolis, IN 46224
(317) 240–2447
Fax: (317) 240–2447
EMAIL: See Below

3714

Business Information: Praxair Surface Technologies is an international company specializing in thermal spray, metallic and ceramic coatings, and specialty powders for OEM and after–market applications. Concurrently, the Company provides aircraft component repair for turbine engines, as well as other specialty codine services. Praxair Surface Technologies has a development team at their R&D Center located in Indianapolis to develop and test patents. As Director of Marketing, Mr. Ryman is responsible for global marketing concepts, awareness, business development and coordination. A professional in the field of transportation equipment, he has served as Vice President and General Manager of TRW Heavy Duty Parts Division for over 17 years. Mr. Ryman can also be reached through the Internet via: 75361,2473@compuserve.com **Career Steps:** Director of Marketing, Praxair Surface Technologies (1994–Present); Director of Marketing, GTE Valenite Corporation (1991–1994); Vice President and General Manager, TRW Heavy Duty Parts Division (1972–1989); Vice President of Operations, MacKay and Company (1989–1991). **Associations & Accomplishments:** American Management Association; American Society of Mechanical Engineers. **Education:** Baldwin Wallace College: M.B.A. (1984), B.A. in Marketing (1982). **Personal:** Married to Lynda in 1972. Three children: Jeff, Jason, and Heather. Mr. Ryman enjoys barbershop singing and playing guitar.

Miss Kimberly L. Sheffey

Manager of International Sales
Neapco Inc.
Queen & Bailey Streets
Pottstown, PA 19464
(610) 323–6000
Fax: (610) 326–3857

3714

Business Information: Neapco Inc. is a manufacturer of automotive aftermarket parts (replacement parts for general repair). With an international distributorship, the company markets to major automotive warehouses and are then distributed to repair shops and retail automotive concerns. As Manager of International Sales, Miss Sheffey oversees all aspects of operations for the company's international division. She is also responsible for the coordination and administration of trade advertising and trade shows. Established in 1921, Neapco Inc. employs over 600 people. **Career Steps:** Manager of International Sales, Neapco Inc. (1992–Present); Marketing Representative of Export, Neapco, Inc. (1984–1992). **Associations & Accomplishments:** Member and Board of Directors, Overseas Automotive Council **Education:** Lebanon Valley College, B.S./B.A. (1984); Unversidad de Granada–Espana, B.A. (1982). **Personal:** Miss Sheffey enjoys playing the piano and also plays racquetball for relaxation.

Paul Slade

Plant Manager
Takata Restraint Systems Inc.
650 Chesterfield Highway
Cheraw, SC 29520
(803) 537–8247
Fax: (803) 537–8465

3714

Business Information: Takata Restraint Systems Inc. – Airbag Division is an international manufacturer of airbag restraint systems for the automobile industry. With seventeen years experience in plastics engineering, Mr. Slade joined Takata in 1991. Serving as Plant Manager, he is responsible for all aspects of plant operations in the Injection Molding/Painting Department. Established in 1988, Takata Restraint Systems Inc. employs 600 people. **Career Steps:** Plant Manager, Takata Restraint Systems Inc. (1991–Present); Product Manager, TRW (1987–1991); Product Engineer Manager, TRW Europe (1978–1987). **Associations & Accomplishments:** Society of Plastic Engineers. **Education:** Bachelors Degree (1970). **Personal:** Married to Amada in 1971. Two children: Chloe and Tanya. Mr. Slade enjoys gardening.

Don Smith

President/Owner
National Reconditioning, Inc.
1 Recon Drive
Houston, MS 38851
(601) 456–2371
Fax: (601) 456–9754
EMAIL: See Below

3714

Business Information: National Reconditioning, Inc. is a national re–manufacturer and distributor of diesel engine components (i.e., engine heads, rods, cam followers, accelerator drives, rocker boxes) to 80 dealers located in 17 states. Products are delivered and picked up via a fleet of Corporate trucks. Having founded National Reconditioning in 1987, Mr. Smith currently serves as President and Owner. He is responsible for the oversight of every facet of the Company, including strategic planning, product line decisions, targeting future state locations and clientele, and providing leadership. Internet users can also reach him via: Recond@1x.netcom.com **Career Steps:** President /Owner, National Reconditioning Inc. (1987–Present); Manager, Ford Motor Company (1972–1986). **Associations & Accomplishments:** Jaycees; Kiwanis. **Education:** Memphis State University, Mechanical Engineering (1975). **Personal:** Married to Lynda in 1979. Three children: Donnie, Joshua, and Daniel. Mr. Smith enjoys rebuilding old cars and water skiing.

Bob W. Smyser

Sales Manager
Wright Way, Inc.
605 HWY, 201 North
Mountain Home, AR 72653
(501) 425–8868
Fax: (501) 425–3688

3714

Business Information: Wright Way, Inc. is a manufacturer and wholesale distributor of exhaust and tail pipes for automobiles. Headquartered in Mountain Home, Arkansas, Wright Way, Inc. markets and distributes its own products, as well as markets products of other manufacturers to installers in seven states. In addition to warehouses across the country, future plans include going international. Serving in managerial roles for Wright Way since 1991, Bob Smyser was appointed corporate Sales Manager in 1994. In this capacity, he is responsible for the direction of all sales and marketing, including overseeing services, sales & marketing personnel, budgeting, and forecasting. **Career Steps:** Wright Way, Inc.: Sales Manager (1994–Present), Branch Manager – Dallas (1993–1994), Route Sales Manager (1991–1993). **Associations & Accomplishments:** State Director, Sedgwick Jaycees (1982). **Personal:** Married to Rebecca E. in 1995. Five children: Kristie, Gloria, Jason, Bobby–Joe and Misty. Mr. Smyser enjoys golf, fishing, basketball, song writing, and bowling.

Chris C. Stickney

Vice President
Explorer ProComp
2758 Via Orange Way
Spring Valley, CA 91978
(619) 670–5222
Fax: (619) 670–5690
EMAIL: See Below

3714

Business Information: Explorer ProComp is a manufacturer of shocks, suspension, lighting, and accessories for light trucks and offroad vehicles. As Vice President, Mr. Stickney is responsible for all aspects of Company operations, including sales, marketing, and advertising. Internet users can reach him via: ProComp2@Aol.Com. **Career Steps:** Explorer ProComp: Vice President (1995–Present), Vice President/General Manager (1992–1995), Vice President/Sales and Marketing (1991–1992). **Associations & Accomplishments:** SEMA; Christadelphians. **Education:** Pepperdine University (1990). **Personal:** Married to Kathleen in 1989. Mr. Stickney enjoys water sports, all athletic sports, and offroading.

Scott L. Striggow

Synchronous Manufacturing Business Unit Manager
Glacier Vandervell, Inc.
1215 Greenwood Street
Bellefontaine, OH 43311–1628
(513) 592–5010
Fax: (513) 593–8874

3714

Business Information: Glacier Vandervell, Inc., a subsidiary of TNN–Autos in the United Kingdom, is an international manufacturer of fluid film products, such as, half shell engine bearings and strippings, for the automotive industry. With corporate headquarters and sales offices located in Troy, Michigan, Glacier Vandervell, Inc. has four manufacturing facilities in Ohio. As Synchronous Manufacturing Business Unit Manager, Mr. Striggow is responsible for all aspects of forced manufacturing activities, including profit and loss of the Business Unit and oversight of a staff of 144 hourly wage earners and 11 salaried. **Career Steps:** Glacier Vandervell, Inc.: Synchronous Manufacturing Business Unit Manager (1995–Present), Engineering Manager (1994–1995); Product Engineering Manager, Gabriel Ride Control (1992–1994). **Associations & Accomplishments:** Society of Automobile Engineers (1986–Present). **Education:** Western Michigan University, B.S. (1983). **Personal:** Married to Rachel in 1981. Three children: Amanda, Nancy, and Scotty. Mr. Striggow enjoys racquetball, hunting, and fishing.

Mr. Suguru Suzuki

President
Nippondenso Mexico, S.A. de C.V.
Parque Industrial Monterrey
Apodaca, N.L., Mexico 66600
52–8–386–3821
Fax: 52–8–386–3818

3714

Business Information: Nippondenso Mexico, S.A. de C.V. is an international manufacturer and developer of vehicle instrument clusters (speedometers, gauges) and system products. Established in 1994, Nippondenso Mexico, S.A. de C.V. expects to employ over 500 and have an annual revenue of $100 million by the year 1999. Mr. Suzuki is responsible for all Nippondenso Mexico operations. **Career Steps:** President, Nippondenso Mexico, S.A. de C.V. (1994–Present); Nippondenso Tennessee Inc.: Executive Vice President (1991–1994), Vice President (Sept. 1989–1991); Nippondenso Co., Ltd.: Assistant General Manager (1986–1989), Manager of Production Engineering (1978–1986), Production Engineer (1965–1978). **Associations & Accomplishments:** Past Chairman, Blount County Japanese School; Honorary Citizen, City of Maryville, Tennessee. **Education:** KEIO University, Japan, B.S. (1965). **Personal:** Married since 1972 to Ritsuko. Three children: one son, Osanori and two daughters, Chikako and Akiko. Mr. Suzuki enjoys playing golf during his leisure time.

Virginia C. Vanark

Corporation Metallurgist of R&D Engineering
Excel Industries, Inc.
1120 North Main Street
Elkhart, IN 46514
(219) 264–2131
Fax: (219) 264–4621

3714

Business Information: Excel Industries, Inc. is a leading designer, manufacturer, and supplier of window and door systems to the combined ground transportation vehicle markets in North America. As Corporate Metallurgist of Research and Development Engineering, Ms. Vanark is responsible for conducting materials research for new product development, as well as serving as Metallurgy Consultant to manufacturing plants. **Career Steps:** Corporate Metallurgist of Research & Development Engineering, Excel Industries, Inc. (1994–Present); Metallurgist, Wix Division–Dana Corporation (1992–1994); Engineering Specialist–Materials, Electronics & Space Corporation (1989–1992). **Associations & Accomplishments:** ASM International; Society of Plastics Engineers; Alpha Gamma Delta. **Education:** University of Wisconsin–Milwaukee, B.S. (1986); Milwaukee Area Technical College, A.S. (1980). **Personal:** Ms. Vanark enjoys reading, needlepoint, and cake decorating.

Steven Weimar

Vice President, Sales and Marketing
Trim Master, Inc.
2310 Locust Court
Ontario, CA 91761–7613
(800) 548–7113
Fax: (909) 923–9500

3714

Business Information: TrimMaster, Inc., a subsidiary of the Philadelphia–based Berwind Group, is a manufacturer of real wood, carbon fiber, and graphic automotive interior trim, exterior stainless steel rocker panel moldings, and interior door sills. With corporate headquarters in Ontario, California, TrimMaster, Inc. is a global supplier to most major automotive companies, including Toyota, General Motors, Chrysler, Ford, Nissan, Mazda, Hyundai, Subaru, Suzuki, Rover and Renault. As Vice President of Sales and Marketing, Mr. Weimar is responsible for global sales and marketing functions, technical writing, budgetary planning, future vision, and product research and development. He is personally responsible for Trim Master's growth from $1.6 million in sale (1992) to over $30 million projected in 1996. **Career Steps:** Vice President of Sales & Marketing, Trim Master, Inc. (1992–Present); President, Weimar Marketing Group, Inc. (1989–1992); Vice President of Sales & Marketing, Kustom Fit Manufacturing, Inc. (1987–1988); President, Performance Marketing, Inc. (1985–1986); Vice President & General Manager, The Pattrax Corporation (1982–1985); Vice President of Sales & Marketing, Levan Specialty Co., Inc. (1974–1982); Partner, Watson Marketing (1971–1974). **Associations & Accomplishments:** Specialty Equipment Market Association (SEMA); Professional Restylers Organization (PRO); Chairman, SEMA Manufacturers Committee (1980–1981); SEMA Board of Directors (1982); Man–of–the–Year – Auto Merchandising News (1980); Guest Speaker at numerous conferences and association events. **Education:** Santa Monica City College, A.A.; Attended California State University – Long Beach (1973) and have attended numerous advanced training seminars/classes over the years. **Personal:** Married to Tammy in 1992. Seven children: Michelle, Melissa, Natalie, Jordan, Savannah, Matthew, and Madison. Mr. Weimar enjoys water and snow skiing, jogging, golf, and basketball.

Larry A. Wright

Executive Vice President
Multimatic, Inc.
85 Valleywood Drive
Markham, Ontario L3R 5E5
(905) 470–9149
Fax: (905) 470–6292
EMAIL: See Below

3714

Business Information: Multimatic, Inc. is a tier 1 supplier of automotive body hardware and suspension components and systems for the big three U.S. automotive industries, as well as Japanese manufacturers. Focusing primarily on door systems, the Company also offers advanced engineering services. . As Executive Vice President, Mr Wright oversees short and long term strategic planning. He is responsible for all legalities and managing the Company's growth into global markets. Internet users can reach him via: lwright@multi-line.com. **Career Steps:** Executive Vice President, Multimatic, Inc. (1993–Present); Borden and Elliot: Partner (1974–1993), Member of Executive Committee (1980–1992). **Associations & Accomplishments:** Board of Directors, The Wellesley Central Hospital; Alliance Management Committee, Healthcare Alliance of Women' s College and Wellesley

Central Hospitals. **Education:** University of Western Ontario, LL.B. (1996); University of Western Ontario, B.A. (1963). **Personal:** Married to Anne in 1966. Three children: David, Christopher, and Graham. Mr Wright enjoys golf, opera, live theater, and showing Bernese Mountain dogs.

Kevin J. Borkowski

Plant Superintendent
Heil Trailer International
3249 Hemp Land Road, P O Box 4807
Lancaster, PA 17604
(717) 397–7771 Ext. 262
Fax: (717) 394–5908

3715

Business Information: Heil Trailer International, a division of Dover Enterprises, is a manufacturer of bulk tank trailers for transporting liquid and dry bulk items. As Plant Superintendent, Mr. Borkowski is in charge of the Lancaster manufacturing plant. He ensures the smooth running of the manufacturing process. He is responsible for plant rearrangements and relocations. **Career Steps:** Heil Trailer International: Plant Superintendent (1995–Present) and Production Supervisor (1992–1995). **Associations & Accomplishments:** American Society for Quality Control. **Education:** California University of Pennsylvania, B.S. in Industrial Technology (1992). **Personal:** Married to Gina in 1992. One child: Dylan. Mr. Borkowski enjoys fly fishing and being an amateur baseball player.

Marsha Gail Chapman

Senior Graphics Specialist
Douglas Aircraft Company
3855 Lakewood Boulevard
Long Beach, CA 90846
(310) 593–1597
Fax: Please mail or call

3721

Business Information: Douglas Aircraft Company is the commercial division of McDonnell Douglas Corporation, providing commercial transportation aircraft in four different models (MD80, MD90, MD95, and MD11). The Company has 154 customers and operators worldwide for the MD80, MD90, and MD95, and 91 customers and operators worldwide for the MD11 and DC10. As Senior Graphics Specialist, Ms. Chapman conceives, designs, lays out, and coordinates illustrations and creative artwork for publications (handbooks, brochures, posters, and magazines), translating facts and features of subject material into graphic terms that best convey meaning. These publications are then distributed to the sales force and employees for better understanding of the airlines. **Career Steps:** McDonnell Douglas Corporation: Senior Graphics Specialist (1996–Present), Senior Writer (1985–1996), Writer (1980–1985). **Associations & Accomplishments:** President, National Council of Negro Women – Long Beach Section; Former President/Chairman of the Board, McDonnell Douglas Long Beach Management Club – Member of the Year (1992); Board Member, National Association for the Advancement of Colored People; Board Member, Long Beach American Lung Association; Douglas Aircraft Company Volunteer of the Year (1991). **Education:** West Coast University, B.S., A.S. (1991); Long Beach City College, A.A.; California State – Long Beach, Communications Certificate. **Personal:** Three children: Charmain, Charlene, and Cheryl. Ms. Chapman enjoys teaching Sunday School, ushering, reading, and volunteer work.

Karol L. Eller

Director of Strategic Sourcing
Lockheed Martin Skunk Works
1011 Lockheed Way
Palmdale, CA 93599
(805) 572–4386
Fax: (805) 572–2343

3721

Business Information: Lockheed Martin Skunk Works is a highly–classified, advanced technology aerospace company servicing both military and commercial customers. It is most recognized recently for the design and manufacture of jets and F–117A carriers flown during Operation Desert Storm. An aerospace procurement professional with various divisions of Lockheed Martin since 1966, Karol Eller was appointed to his current position in 1994. As Director of Strategic Sourcing, he oversees all programs and operations support staff involved in advanced programs requirements, particularly working closely in conjunction with participating aerospace industries (i.e., the supplier community). Concurrent with his duties with Lockheed Martin, Mr. Eller is also the founder and senior consultant of KLE Enterprises — a consulting and holding company. **Career Steps:** Director of Strategic Sourcing, Lockheed Martin Skunk Works (1994–Present); Director of Sourcing, Lockheed Transportation Systems (1992–1993); Manager of Subcontract Finance and Chief Negotiator – Advanced Tactical Fighter Program, Lockheed California Company (1989–1992). **Associations & Accomplishments:** American Management Association; Institute of Internal Auditing; Institute of Cost Analysis; Society of Cost Estimating and Analysis; Treasurer, County Supervisor – Ventura, California. **Education:** University of California – Los Angeles (1980); CERTIFICATIONS: Internal Auditor (1976), Cost Analyst (1983), Cost Estimator (1991); Lockheed Management Institute, USC (1982). **Personal:** Married to Jane in 1985. Two children: Paige and Todd. Mr. Eller enjoys camping, golf, and trapshooting.

John A. Fergione

Engineering Manager
Lockheed Martin
44207 20th Street West
Lancaster, CA 93534–4060
(805) 942–4565
Fax: (805) 945–0507

3721

Business Information: Lockheed Martin is a major manufacturer of military and commercial aircraft (i.e., F–16, F–117, Saturn rocket missles). The Corporation currently employs over 170,000 people. As Engineering Manager, Mr. Fergione serves as an experimental test pilot for all F–16 models, as well as manages all facilities and engineering development for the F–16 design program. Concurrent with his duties at Lockheed, he is also the Founder and President of J&A Enterprises — an industrial employment placement and recruitment services firm. **Career Steps:** Engineering Manager, Lockheed Martin (1988–Present); President, J&A Enterprises (1994–Present); Experimental Test Pilot, General Dynamics (1981–Present). **Associations & Accomplishments:** Director, Antelope Valley Board of Trade; Former President and Sustaining Member of Board of Directors, The Society of Experimental Test Pilots; Lancaster, Palmdale, and Quartz Hill Chambers of Commerce; President, The Izaak Walton League of America – Antelope Valley Chapter; Lockheed Management Association; Institute of Certified Professional Managers. **Education:** Southern Methodist University, M.S. (1987); University of West Florida, M.S. in Aeronautical Systems (1972); Villanova University, B.S. in Electrical Engineering (1971). **Personal:** Married to Anita in 1986. One child: John III. Mr. Fergione enjoys fishing, hunting, and computer software programming and design.

Robert (Bob) W. Fischer

Chief Engineer
Lockheed Martin Skunk Works
1011 Lockheed Way
Palmdale, CA 93530–3099
(805) 572–3052
Fax: (805) 572–2795

3721

Business Information: Lockheed Martin Skunk Works is a highly–classified, advanced technology aerospace company servicing both military and commercial customers. It is most–recently recognized for the design and manufacture of jets and F–117A carriers flown during Operation Desert Storm. As Chief Engineer, Mr. Fischer is responsible for development, engineering services, and successful task operations. **Career Steps:** Lockheed Martin Skunk Works: Chief Engineer (1990–Present), Manager, Aircraft Design (1986–1990), Manager, Derivative Design (1982–1986); Group Engineer (1978–1982); Design Specialist (1974–1978); Design Engineer – Electrical (1955–1974). **Education:** California State University – Los Angeles, B.M.E. (1960). **Personal:** Married to Janis in 1953. Three children: Michael, Todd and Corey. Mr. Fischer enjoys woodworking, umpiring and coaching.

James M. Hackworth Jr.

Staff Engineer
Lockheed Martin
320 Clinch Avenue
Clinton, TN 37716–4232
(423) 574–4244
Fax: (423) 574–4142
E MAIL: See Below

3721

Business Information: Within Lockheed Martin is a division that supports research activities pertaining to energy resource development.. The Company also handles the research for other companies and the D.O.D. on fossil fueling and energy conservation. As Staff Engineer, Mr. Hackworth is responsible for waste certification, regulations, marketing, and proposals and programs. He supervises class crews, shares information with employees, and provides guidance. His division provides services for other divisions such as equipment maintenance and construction rework for facilities. Internet users may contact him via: pe.ornl.gov. **Career Steps:** Staff Engineer, Lockheed Martin (Martin Marietta) (1989–Present); Martin Marietta: Field Engineering Support (1979–1989), Design Draftsman (1974–1979); Commissioner, Anderson County (1978–1990). **Associations & Accomplishments:** Habitat for Humanity; National Organization on Disability; Board of Directors, Anderson County Rescue Squad; Vice President, Anderson County Fair Association; Benevolent and Protection Order of Elks; Anderson County Democrat Party; Claxton Optimist Club; Honorary Member, Anderson County Women's Democrat Club; Anderson County Tourism Association; Chairman, Anderson County Civil Service Board; Chairman, Anderson County's Tennessee 200 Bicentennial Volunteer Day; Board of Directors, Anderson County Chamber of Commerce; Oak Ridge Chamber of Commerce. **Education:** Tusculum College: M.A.A.O.M., Master's Degree in Applied Organizational Management (1996), B.S. in Applied Organizational Management (1994); Roane state, Associates in Supervision and Management (1994); Harvard School of Public Health–Management and Disposal of Radioactive Waste (1996). **Personal:** Married. Two children: Matthew and Michael. Mr. Hackworth enjoys fishing, politics, golf, and youth sports.

Robert Held

Director of Structural Integrity
Cessna Aircraft
6107 Maple Street
Wichita, KS 67209–2130
(316) 941–6747
Fax: Please mail or call

3721

Business Information: Cessna Aircraft is an international manufacturer of small aircraft. Serving Cessna in various engineering supervisory capacities since 1966, Robert Held was appointed as Director of Structural Integrity in 1991. In this capacity, he is responsible for directing the activities of the Department, including the development and certification of airframes. **Career Steps:** Cessna Aircraft: Engineering Director of Structural Integrity (1991–Present), Manager of Structural Integrity (1980–1991); Supervisor of Structural Integrity (1966–1980). **Associations & Accomplishments:** Inter–Faith Ministries. **Education:** University of Arizona, B.S.M.E. (1958); Wichita State University, Engineering. **Personal:** Five children: Calvin, Audrey, Matthew, Emily and Brian. Mr. Held enjoys being an Emu Rancher.

Glen Hodges

Director of Technical Services
Weber Aircraft, Inc.
1300 E. Valencia Drive
Fullerton, CA 92831
(714) 449–3180
Fax: (714) 449–3045

3721

Business Information: Weber Aircraft, Inc. is a manufacturer of military and commercial aircraft interiors which includes crew seats, ejection seats, galleys, galley inserts, lavatories, toilets, and the 737 airstairs. As Director of Technical Services, Mr. Hodges manages quality assurance, inspection, technical data, materials and process engineering, proto, engineering test labs, and facilities maintenance. Mr. Hodges also oversees a staff of 45. **Career Steps:** Weber Aircraft, Inc.: Director of Technical Services (1993–Present), Director of Quality Assurance (1988–1993), Manager of Quality Assurance (1986–1988) in addition to 20 plus years in manufacturing. **Associations & Accomplishments:** American Society of Quality Control; American Society of Material; 1981 U.S. Shooting Team. **Education:** University of Oregon; Oregon State University; Mount Hood Community College; Pacific Lutheran; Clackamas Community College. **Personal:** Mr. Hodges enjoys four wheeling, shooting, hunting, and camping.

Eric P. Jones

Senior Buyer
Evergreen Helicopters, Inc.
3850 Three Mile Lane
Mcminnville, OR 97128–9402
(503) 434–4025
Fax: (503) 434–4212

3721

Business Information: Evergreen Helicopters, Inc., established in 1959, is the leader in rotary wing operations throughout more than 20 states and 138 countries. As Senior Buyer, Mr. Jones is responsible for all aspects of purchasing operations for the Company. **Career Steps:** Senior Buyer, Evergreen Helicopters, Inc. (1988–Present). **Education:** Linfield College, B.S. in Psychology, with a minor in Management

(1996). **Personal:** Mr. Jones enjoys flying, waterskiing, hunting, and fishing.

James S. Luby

Quality Department Manager
McDonnell Douglas Helicopter Systems
5000 East McDowell
Mesa, AZ 85215
(602) 891–2058
Fax: (602) 801 4508

3721

Business Information: McDonnell Douglas Helicopter Systems, a wholly–owned subsidiary of McDonnell Douglas Corporation, is a worldwide leading manufacturer of civil and military helicopters, military fighter aircraft, and ordnance. As Department Manager, Mr. Luby oversees a team of over 100 employees responsible for product quality. **Career Steps:** McDonnell Douglas Helicopter Systems: Department Manager (1995–Present), Quality Manager (1993–1995), Quality Engineer (1990–1993). **Associations & Accomplishments:** University of Phoenix Alumni Association; Graduated Top Graduate, 1995 (3.95 G.P.A. out of a 4.0). **Education:** University of Phoenix: Master of Business Administration (1995), Bachelor of Science in Business Administration (1992). **Personal:** Married to Mary in 1982. Two children: Michael and Anthony. Mr. Luby enjoys being a private pilot and flying radio controlled aircraft.

Karen M. Nagle

Human Resource Director
Aerospace Dynamic
25540 Rye Canyon Road
Valencia, CA 91355–1109
(805) 257–3535
Fax: (805) 257–2143

3721

Business Information: Aerospace Dynamic is a manufacturer of aircraft parts. As Human Resource Director, Ms. Nagle is responsible for handling all insurances, billing, grievances, legal claims, and payroll for 210 employees. **Career Steps:** Human Resource Director, Aerospace Dynamic (1995–Present); Human Resource Assistant, Aerospace Dynamics Int. (1992–1995); Customer Service/A.R. Rep., Santa Clarita Disposal (1991–1992). **Education:** Currently attending California State University Northridge; College of the Camyon, A.S. in Business Administration. **Personal:** Ms. Nagle enjoys motorcycle riding, travel, and riding her sea doo watercraft.

Mary H. Nickerson

Facility Layout Engineer
Boeing Defense and Space Group
145 Kirks Mill Road
Nottingham, PA 19362–9033
(610) 591–2522
Fax: Please mail or call

3721

Business Information: Boeing Defense and Space Group, a wholly–owned entity of The Boeing Company — an international commercial and defense airplane manufacturer primarily engaged in research and development of aircraft — specializes in the development and support of defense aircraft and space exploration craft. The Facilities Department provides support for the V22 Osprey Aircraft by designing space requirements and determining the support equipment required. The Boeing Company employs over 90,000 people worldwide and has annual revenue in excess of $12 billion. As Facility Engineer, Ms. Nickerson is responsible for providing the required layout designs for assembly areas, including flight test. This includes off–site locations at Bell Helicopter, Textron, NAWC Patuxent River Naval Base, Halifax Ice Testing, Nova Scotia & High Altitude Testing Requirements at Hot Springs, VA. Concurrent with her position at Boeing, Ms. Nickerson is also an Adjunct Faculty member at Wilmington College in the College of Business Administration teaching Management Courses. **Career Steps:** Facility Engineer, Boeing Defense and Space Group (1985–Present); Adjunct Faculty, Wilmington College (1991–Present); Marketing Editor, Hewlett Packard (1979–1984). **Associations & Accomplishments:** Society of Industrial Engineers; 4H Leader, Gunn Tree 4H; American Helicopter Society. **Education:** Wilmington College, M.B.A., M.S.M., dual degree (1991); Delware Technical College, B.S. in Industrial Engineering; Neumann College, B.S. in Business Administration. **Personal:** Two children: Moriah A. and Sam J. Ms. Nickerson enjoys running marathons, hiking and horseback riding.

Charles R. Prochaska

Engineering Manager
Boeing Company
3676 S. Shorewood Avenue
Greenbank, WA 98253
(306) 294–7390
Fax: (360) 222–3071
EMAIL: See Below

3721

Business Information: Boeing Company is one of the world's leading aircraft manufacturers, producing commercial jet transports, helicopters, military aircraft and space flight systems. Established in 1916, Boeing presently employs over 90,000 people worldwide and has an annual revenue in excess of $12 billion. A Boeing senior engineer serving with various subsidiary divisions since 1965, Charles Prochaska was recently assigned to the Insulation Payload Systems division. As Engineering Manager, he is responsible for the design of new insulation blanket technology for all new 777 and 737 generation aircraft models. Internet users can also reach him via: WHIDSTAR@WHIDBEY.COM. **Career Steps:** BOEING COMPANY: Engineering Manager, Insulation – New Process Payload Systems (1995–Present); Engineering Manager, 777 Division Cargo Systems (1991–1995); Principal Engineer, 777 Division (1990–1991); Principal Engineer, Sea Lance, Aerospace & Electronics Division (1987–1990); Senior Specialist Engineer, Marine Systems (1983–1985); Senior Specialist Engineer, 767 Division (1979–1982); Senior Specialist Engineer, AWACS (E–3); Specialist Engineer, BCAC/BMS/BAC (1965–1979). **Associations & Accomplishments:** Seattle Professional Engineering Association. **Education:** University of Michigan, B.S. in Aerospace Engineering (1965). **Personal:** Married to Judith in 1975. Five children: Roland Anthony, Meikle John and Peter Henry Prochaska; and Diane Elayne and Greg Andrew Petet.

Joseph C. Ramsey

Aeronautical Engineer (Retired)
General Dynamics/Convair
2011 Garfield Road
San Diego, CA 92110–1230
(619) 275–1111
Fax: Please mail or call

3721

Business Information: Mr. Joseph C. Ramsey, an Aeronautical Engineer for 37 years, retired in 1986. During his successful career, Mr. Ramsey was an Engineer for the Convair Division of General Dynamics. As such, he conducted wind tunnel testing and made aerodynamic studies on numerous aircraft from vertical takeoff airplanes to cruise missiles. He was a member of the American Institute of Aeronautics and Astronautics. Currently he is enjoying his time at home by adding to his computer knowledge, and writing a family genealogy. He also contributes his time to area Methodist church community programs and to affordable housing programs. **Career Steps:** Aeronautical Engineering Specialist, General Dynamics/Convair (1950–1987). **Associations & Accomplishments:** Past Chairman and current Secretary of Board of Directors, San Diego Interfaith Housing Foundation; Treasurer of Board of Directors, Ecumenical Council of San Diego County; Published a paper and contributed to USAF Data Compendium on powered aerodynamic lift. **Education:** Purdue University, B.S. in Aeronautical Engineering (1950). **Personal:** Married to Lois Ella Jones in 1954. Three children: Charles Perry Ramsey, Cheryl Mae Eubanks, and Richard Herbert Ramsey. Seven grandchildren. Mr. Ramsey enjoys genealogy.

Loy E. Rovenstine

Director of Quality Assurance
Lockheed Martin Electronic Defense Systems
Ridge Hill, MS #63
Yonkers, NY 10710–5598
(914) 964–2675
Fax: (614) 964–2777
EMAIL: See Below

3721

Business Information: Lockheed Martin Electronic Defense Systems is a manufacturer of electronic warfare, radar warning receivers, and radar jamming equipment intended for civil and military applications. As Director of Quality Assurance, Mr. Rovenstine is responsible for all deliverable hardware and software. He performs quality inspections on products and processes prior to delivery to clients. Mr. Rovenstine handles customer service concerns, day–to–day processes and product improvement and works to comply with the total mission of his division. Internet users can reach him via: lrovenstine@eds.lmco.com. **Career Steps:** Director of Quality Assurance, Lockheed Martin (1988–Present); Vice President of Tactical Missiles, Textron Aerostructures (1982–1988); Manager of Quality Assurance, Fairchild Republic (1977–1982); Program Manager, Martin Marietta – Denver (1957–1977); U.S. Marine Corps (1953–1962). **Associations & Accomplishments:** Aerospace Industries Association; American Society of Quality Control; Past President, American Association of Owners and Breeders of Peruvian Paso Horses. **Education:** Vanderbilt University, M.B.A. (1987); Columbia College, Management; University of Utah, Math and Physics. **Personal:** Married to Joan in 1982. Four children: Lori, Andrea, Barrie, and Dean. Mr. Rovenstine enjoys woodworking, fishing, reading, and horses.

Frances E. Sharples, Ph.D.

Head of Environmental Analysis Section
Lockheed Martin Energy Research Corporation
Building 1505, MS 6036, P.O. Box 2008
Oak Ridge, TN 37831
(423) 576–0524
Fax: (423) 576–8543
EMAIL: See Below

3721

Business Information: Lockheed Martin Energy Research Corporation is a division of Lockheed Martin, a major manufacturer of military and commercial aircraft (i.e., F–16, F–117, Saturn rocket missiles). As Head of Environmental Analysis Section, Dr. Sharples is line manager of approximately 75 staff in 3 research groups devoted to environmental impact assessment, environmental information analysis and management, and improving U.S. Department of Energy compliance with environmental laws and regulations. She is also directly responsible for five different departmental sections: environmental impact assessment, ecological risk assessment, global change data management, water resource management, and regulatory commissions. Internet users can reach her via: sef@ornl.gov. **Career Steps:** Lockheed Martin Energy Research Corporation: Head of Environmental Analysis Section (1992–Present), Group Leader, Environmental Compliance Group (1987–1992), Research Staff Member, Hazardous Waste Remedial Actions Program (1985–1987); Legislative Assistant for Energy and Natural Resources, Office of Senator Albert Gore, Jr. United States Congress (1984–1985); ORNL: Research Associate, Program Planning and Analysis Office (1982–1984), Research Associate, Environmental Impacts Program (1978–1982). **Associations & Accomplishments:** American Association for the Advancement of Science's Committee on Science, Engineering, and Public Policy; Consultant to the Center for Public Issues in Biotechnology; U.S. EPA Environmental Biology Peer Review Panel; Consultant to the United Nations Industrial Development Organization, World Health Organization, Environment Programme Working Group; Special Legislative Assistant to U.S. Senator Albert Gore, Jr.; Organizer and Transcript Editor, Hearing on Antibiotic Resistance; Recombinant DNA Advisory Committee, National Institute of Health; Special Research Consultant for U.S. Environmental Protection Agency; Fellow, American Association for the Advancement of Science (1992); Award of Excellence, U.S. Department of Energy' Congressional Science and Engineering Fellowship, American Association for the Advancement of Science; American Institute for Biological Sciences; Association for Women in Science; Ecological Society of America; National Association of Environmental Professionals; Sigma Xi. **Education:** University of California, Davis: Ph.D. (1978), M.A. (1974); Barnard College, A.B. (1972).

Janis K. Snook

Project Manager
The Boeing Company
1328 144th Street, South East
Mill Creek, WA 98012
(206) 865–4324
Fax: Please mail or call

3721

Business Information: The Boeing Company is one of the world's leading aircraft manufacturers, producing commercial jet transports, helicopters, military aircraft and space flight systems. Established in 1916, Boeing presently employs over 30,000 people worldwide and has an annual revenue in excess of $25 billion. As Project Manager, Ms. Snook is responsible for the production and release of 300 Catia software with applications in Blockpoint releases and all Boeing software. **Career Steps:** The Boeing Company: Project Manager (1995–Present), Systems Analyst (1990–1995), Train Administrator (1987–1990). **Education:** Attending City University. **Personal:** Married to Gerald in 1992. One child: Jennifer Ashley Collins. Ms. Snook enjoys theater, music, travel, and gardening.

Lisa E. Wilson
Contracts Manager
Lockheed Martin Energy Systems, Inc.
P.O. Box 628, M.S. 7606
Piketon, OH 45661
(614) 897–3605
Fax: (614) 897–2040

3721

Business Information: Established in 1993, Lockheed Martin Energy Systems, Inc., The Portsmouth Plant, is an environmental restoration and waste management facility. A division of Lockheed Martin, a major manufacturer of military and commercial aircraft and related aerospace, electronics, and radar devices, the Portsmouth site employs approximately 270 people. As Contracts Manager, Ms. Wilson is responsible for oversight of contract management, and memorandums of understanding. **Career Steps:** Lockheed Martin Energy Systems, Inc: Contracts Manager (1995–Present), Award Fee Coordinator/Assistant Division Manager (1992–1995), Procedures Management Section Head (1990–1992); EEO Program Manager, City of Chillicothe, Ohio (1990); Case Manager, Ross Correctional Institute (1988–1990); Technical Writer/Assistant Quality Control Supervisor, Rockwell International (1982–1988); Various Positions, Goodyear Atomic Corporation (1977–1982). **Associations & Accomplishments:** National Association Advancement of Colored People (NAACP); Alpha Kappa Mu Honor Society. **Education:** The Ohio State University, M.L.H.R. (Masters in Labor and Human Resources) graduation expected in December of 1996; Ohio University, B.A. (1976). **Personal:** Married to Lloyd A. in 1994. One child: Bryan D. Morris. Ms. Wilson enjoys bowling, creative writing, reading, and walking.

David A. Castetter
Manufacturing Bill of Material Leader
GE Aircraft Engines
1 Neumann Way, B23
Cincinnati, OH 45215
513 243–1637 w 513 683–3583 h
Fax: (513) 243–6025

3724

Business Information: GE Aircraft Engines, a General Electric Company Business is a manufacturer of jet aircraft engines for the military, commercial airline, marine vessels, and power generation industries. As Manufacturing Bill of Material Leader, Mr. Castetter is responsible for product configuration and integrated manufacturing planning and scheduling for all GE Aircraft engines and manufacturing sites. **Career Steps:** Manufacturing Bill of Material Leader, GE Aircraft Engines (1984–Present); Supervisor – Manufacturing Consulting, Ernst & Whinney (1980–1983); Manufacturing Systems Engineer, IBM (1976–1979). **Associations & Accomplishments:** ICCP; Masonic Lodge; Registrar and Coach in Community Youth Soccer Association. **Education:** Wright State University, Master's Degree (1976); Andrews University, B.A. **Personal:** Married to Robin J. in 1982. Three children: Jeremy, Blake, and Jonathan. Mr. Castetter enjoys song writing.

Patrick Quinn O'Connor
Director
AlliedSignal Engines
111 South 34th Street
Phoenix, AZ 85034
(602) 231–7600
Fax: (602) 231–7519

3724

Business Information: A subsidiary of Allied Signal, Inc. – an advanced manufacturing company serving customers worldwide with aerospace, automotive and engineered materials – AlliedSignal Engines specializes in commercial and military applications of small gas turbine engines. Serving in various subsidiary divisions of AlliedSignal since 1984, Mr. O'Connor joined the Company in 1993. As Enterprise Business Director, he is responsible for project management, operations and client interface for the Commercial Auxilary Power Enterprise. **Career Steps:** AlliedSignal Engines: Enterprise Business Director (1993–Present), Director of Airline Programs; Manager of Marketing, AlliedSignal Landing Systems. **Associations & Accomplishments:** Republican National Committee; United States Golf Association; Executive Council of Boys and Girls Clubs. **Education:** American Graduate School of International Management – Thunderbird, EMIM (In Progress); University of Arizona, Bachelor in Mechanical Engineering (1984).

HOWMET CORPORATION   PECHINEY GROUP

C. M. Protko
Director of Human Resources
Howmet Corporation – Dover Casting
9 Roy Street
Dover, NJ 07801–4308
(201) 328–2129
Fax: (201) 328–2137
EMAIL: See Below

3724

Business Information: Howmet Corporation – Dover Casting is an aerospace engineering and manufacturing Company. The Company makes aircraft blades and related products. As Director of Human Resources, Mr. Protko is responsible for all aspects of human resources for the Company, including recruiting, advising councils, and labor and employee relations. Internet users can reach him via: S.Protko@Howmetcorp. **Career Steps:** Director of Human Resources, Howmet Corporation – Dover Casting (1993–Present); Manager of LR/HR, Arnold Engineering Company (1989–1993); Director of Human Resources, Fluor Daniel, Inc. (1987–1989). **Associations & Accomplishments:** Society of Professional Human Resource Managers. **Education:** Idaho State University, M.B.A. (1977); Kentucky Wesleyan College: B.A. in Sociology (1972), B.A. in Education (1973). **Personal:** Married in 1973. Two children: Brooke and Matthew. Mr. Protko enjoys all athletics and sports.

Ramasar Singh
Director of Quality
Northwest Airlines
208 Crescent Oak
Peachtree City, GA 30269
(404) 530–3212
Fax: (404) 530–3898

3724

Business Information: Northwest Airlines is a major national and international carrier with over 45,000 employees worldwide. The Airline also has a manufacturing division where they rebuild and/or remanufacture jet engines. As Director of Quality, Mr. Singh has general management of the 400 employees of the Jet Engine Division. He handles personnel concerns, budgets, quality control concerns, and OSHA and other safety compliance regulations. Mr. Singh is involved in strategic planning for future expansion. **Career Steps:** Director of Quality, Northwest Airlines (1990–Present). **Education:** University of Saint Thomas, M.B.A. (1983); St. Cloud State University, B.S. in Industrial Engineering (1978). **Personal:** Married to Karrie in 1976. Two children: David and Matthew. Mr. Singh enjoys reading and golf.

Jeffrey D. Wood
General Manager
Interturbine Corporation
2800 Avenue E. East
Arlington, TX 76011
(817) 640–0895
Fax: (817) 649–7325

3724

Business Information: Interturbine Group of Companies is a Dutch–owned manufacturer and remanufacturer (overhaul) of specially large commercial engine components. International in scope, Interturbine has eleven companies in five countries. Interturbine Dallas Casings employs 75 people in Arlington, Texas (FAA Repair Station #ISO 9002). Approximately 60% of its sales are derived from overseas. As General Manager, Mr. Wood is fully responsible for all aspects of this Company. **Career Steps:** Interturbine Corporation: General Manager (1994–Present), Corporate Business Development: Netherlands (1992–1993), Singapore (1993–1994); Associate, Donaldson, Lufkin, & Jenrette (1991); Corporate Auditor, General Electric (1987–1990). **Associations & Accomplishments:** Managed philanthropic construction projects in Underdeveloped Regions of Columbia, Peru, and Philippines through the DePauw University Missions Programs (1984–1987). **Education:** Harvard Business School, M.B.A. in Operations Management (1992); DePauw University, B.A. (1987); G E Financial Management Program (1989). **Personal:** Married to Sapiah Anwar Wood in 1994. One child: Kelsey Diana. Mr. Wood enjoys travel and fitness.

John Richard Yates
Vice President of New Industrial Business
Rolls–Royce Canada, Ltee
9500 Cote De Liesse Road
Lachine, Quebec H8T 1A2
(514) 631–3541 Ext. 2375
Fax: (514) 636–0326

3724

Business Information: Rolls–Royce Canada Limitee is a manufacturer of large Aero derivative Industrial Gas Turbines for worldwide sales to the gas, oil, and power generation industries. As Vice President and General Manager of New Industrial Business, Mr. Yates is responsible for the complete manufacturing process, profits, and ensuring that the business grows in accordance with Company targets. Teaming with Product Support and Marketing departments, he ensures new business sales are maximized. **Career Steps:** Rolls–Royce Canada, Ltee: Vice President of New Industrial Business (1996–Present), Vice President of Engineering Services (1994–1996), Vice President of Engineering and Quality (1987–1994). **Associations & Accomplishments:** Executive – Airworthiness Committee, Aerospace Industries Association of Canada; President, Canadian Aeronautics and Space Institute. **Education:** Southampton University, H.N.C. (1959). **Personal:** Married to Lieve Cupers in 1983. Three children: Anick, Robert, and Helen. Mr. Yates enjoys yachting, athletics, photography, and gardening.

Dr. Nancy Crews
Senior Manager Marketing/Long Range Planning
Lockheed Martin Specialty Components, Inc.
P.O. Box 2908
Largo, FL 34649–2908
(813) 541–8376
Fax: (813) 541–8822

3728

Business Information: Lockheed Martin Specialty Components, Inc. is a manufacturer of electronic control systems intended for industrial and other applications. The Company is currently converting from a defense–related business to a commercial business centering on high–tech products and services. As Senior Manager Marketing/Long Range Planning, Dr. Crews is responsible for managing the marketing, sales, and customer support functions involved in the commercialization process, in addition to overseeing a staff of 10. **Career Steps:** Senior Manager Marketing/Long Range Planning, Lockheed Martin Specialty Components, Inc. (1994–Present); Adjunct Faculty, College of Business and Management, National Louis University (1993–Present); Marketing Director/Reprographics, Eastman Kodak Company (1990–1993). **Associations & Accomplishments:** American Chemical Society; Phi Kappa Phi Honor Society; American Association of University Women. **Education:** Virginia Polytechnic Institute and State University, Ph.D (1975); University of Florida, B.S. (1970); North Florida Junior College, A.A. (1968). **Personal:** Married to Larry in 1970. Two children: Michael and Christopher. Dr. Crews enjoys reading and bicycling.

John P. Doran
Manager of Product Assurance and Compliance
Lockheed Martin Control Systems
600 Main Street
Johnson City, NY 13790
(607) 770–2840
Fax: (607) 770–2914

3728

Business Information: Lockheed Martin Control Systems is a manufacturer of electronic control systems intended for civil and military aircraft, automotive, locomotive, industrial, and other applications. Joining Lockheed Martin Control Systems as Manager of Product Assurance and Compliance in 1994, Mr. Doran's primary focus is in assuring total customer satisfaction. He serves as the Quality Manager for several areas, including the test engineering design and support unit, electronic products, and software quality assurance. In addition, he also conducts auditing and systems integration to ensure readiness and quality for the customer. **Career Steps:** Manager of Product Assurance and Compliance, Lockheed Martin

Control Systems (1994–Present); Manager of Shop Operations, Martin Marietta Control Systems (1989–1994); Manager of Printed Circuit Assembly, General Electric (1988–1989). **Associations & Accomplishments:** Team Coach, Odyssey of the Mind, ISO 9001 Registration. **Education:** State University of New York, M.B.A. (1987); University of Lowell, B.S. in Civil Engineering (1980). **Personal:** Married to Tami in 1983. Three children: Michael, Katherine, and Megan. Mr. Doran enjoys skiing, camping, and family activities.

Fabio G. Grossi

Marketing Analysis
AVIALL, Inc.
2075 Diplomat Drive
Dallas, TX 75234–8999
(214) 406–2377
Fax: (817) 545–2525
EMAIL: See Below

3728

Business Information: AVIALL, Inc. specializes in aircraft parts distribution. As Marketing Analyst, Mr. Grossi is responsible for diversified administrative activities, including sales and marketing, and marketing analysis. Internet users can reach him via: 70410.3451@COMPUSERVE.COM. **Career Steps:** Marketing Analysis, AVIALL, Inc. (1995–Present); President, Venture Focus, Inc. (1994–1995); Project Manager, Vought Aircraft Company (1988–1994); Senior Analyst, Douglas Aircraft Company (1987–1988). **Associations & Accomplishments:** Experimental Aircraft Association; The Lighter Than Air Society; The Airship Association. **Education:** Embry–Riddle Aero University, M.B.A. (1983); Cornell University, B.S. (1981). **Personal:** Mr. Grossi is an FAA–certificated private pilot and enjoys aviation activities.

Wilbur Hinkston

Director of Manufacturing
Lord Corporation
2000 West Grandview Blvd., P.O. Box 10038
Erie, PA 16514–0038
(814) 868–5424
Fax: (814) 866–1916

3728

Business Information: Lord Corporation, a privately–held corporation, owns diversified aerospace manufacturing divisions. Headquartered in Cary, NC, division entities include as follows: Chemical Products — manufacture of rubber and metal adhesives; and Mechanical Products — manufacture of industrial components (i.e., vibration control, aerospace engine mounts, rotor blades). Serving in managerial roles for the Mechanical Products division of Lord Corporation since 1991, Wilbur Hinkston was promoted to Director of Manufacturing in 1993. Based at the Erie, PA plant, he provides the overall direction and oversight of the Mechanical Products Division's four plant facilities (2–PA; 1–KY; 1–OH), with primary focus on procurement and process engineering production. **Career Steps:** Lord Corporation: Director of Manufacturing (1993–Present), Business Manager (1991–1992); Division Vice President, Bausch and Lomb, Inc. (1986–1988). **Associations & Accomplishments:** Senior Member, Society of Manufacturing Engineers; Business Advisor, InRoads Program; American Helicopter Society. **Education:** Rochester Institute of Technology, M.B.A. (1981); St. John Fisher College, B.S. in Finance. **Personal:** Married to Kathy in 1977. Two children: Laura and Lisa. Mr. Hinkston enjoys coaching children's sports and drag racing.

Mike W. Lennon

Director
Northrop Grumman
600 Hicks Road Room H6110
Rolling Meadows, IL 60008–1015
(708) 259–9600
Fax: (708) 870–5727

3728

Business Information: Northrop Grumman is a manufacturer of advanced electronic composites for the aerospace and commercial aircraft industry. Established in 1994 as a result of the merger between Northrop Corporation and Grumman Aerospace Corporation, Northrop Grumman currently employs 40,000 people company–wide with 2,500 people in the Rolling Meadows plant. Mr. Lennon has been the Senior Project Director for a number of Northrop Grumman developments over the past 8 years, including the B–52 Bomber, the B–2 Bomber, and most recently, the Air Force F–15 Fighter Jet. **Career Steps:** Norhrop Grumman: Director F–15 Project (1990–Present), Director B–2 Project (1990), Director B–52 Project (1987–1990); United States Air Force Reserve; Admissions Liaison Officer, United States Air Force Academy. **Associations & Accomplishments:** Association of Old Crows; Air Force Association; Society of Logistics Engineers; Board of Directors, Society for the Preservation of Human Dignity. **Education:** University of Wyoming, M.B.A. (1976); University of Tennessee, B.S. (1972). **Personal:** Married to Judy in 1974. One child: Ryan.

Mr. P. Del MacFall

Facility Engineer
Northrop Grumman
90 Highway 22 West
Milledgeville, GA 31061
(912) 454–4415
Fax: (912) 451–0289

3728

Business Information: Northrop Grumman is a manufacturer of advanced composites for the aerospace and commercial aircraft industry. Established in 1994 when Northrop Corporation and Grumman Aerospace Corporation merged, Northrup Grumman currently employs 40,000 people company–wide and 500 people at the Milledgeville, Georgia location. As Facility Engineer, Mr. MacFall is responsible for design and specifications of manufacturing systems and machinery, as well as performing energy engineering functions. **Career Steps:** Facility Engineer, Northrop Grumman (1986–Present); President, Republic Machinery Corporation (1980–1986); President and Founder, Teleros Energy Group, Inc. (1987–1989); Instructor, Georgia College (1989–1995). **Associations & Accomplishments:** Association of Energy Engineers (AEE); Institute of Electrical and Electronic Engineers (IEEE). **Education:** Milwaukee School of Engineering, B.S. in Electrical Engineering (1962). He self–taught himself five computer languages and teaches at a college level, part–time and on a substitute basis. **Personal:** Married to Florence in 1963. Three children: Martha Earwood, Steve MacFall, Marie Rosenthal and four grandchildren.

Martin R. O'Conner

Director of Material Administration and Requirements
Northrop Grumman
1015 Wisconsin Ave.
Oak Park, IL 60304–1817
(708) 259–9600
Fax: (708) 870–5747

3728

Business Information: Northrop Grumman is a manufacturer of advanced composites for the aerospace and commercial aircraft industry. Established in 1994 when Northrop Corporation and Grumman Aerospace Corporation merged, Northrup Grumman currently employs 40,000 people company–wide. As Director of Material Administration and Requirements, Mr. O'Conner manages the process for procurement, and defines material requirements. **Career Steps:** Northrop Grumman: Director of Material Administration and Requirements (1995–Present), Material Specialist (1990–1995), Director of Financial Reporting and Accounting (1984–1990). **Associations & Accomplishments:** American Institute of Certified Public Accountants; Illinois Certified Public Accountants Society; Institute of Internal Auditors. **Education:** University of Illinois, B.A. (1972); State of Illinois, Certified Public Accountants. **Personal:** Married to Maureen P. in 1972. Five children: Brigid, Maureen Ann, Nora, Alana, and Brendan. Mr. O'Conner enjoys gardening.

Donald J. Paladino

Controller – Landing Gear Division
BF Goodrich
8000 Marble Avenue
Cleveland, OH 44141–2874
(216) 429–4049
Fax: (216) 429–4800

3728

Business Information: Established in 1894, BF Goodrich is one of the world's leading rubber and chemical products manufacturers, best–known for the manufacture of tires. Global in scope, the Company operates two main divisions: Aerospace, and Specialty Chemicals. Serving as Controller for BF Goodrich's Aerospace Landing Gear Division, Mr. Paladino oversees all financial and MIS activities, including general accounting, cost accounting, cost control, forecasting, strategic planning, and new system implementation. He also represents the division in board matters involving capital financing, budgeting, internal audit, regulatory compliance, and strategic planning. **Career Steps:** Controller, BF Goodrich Landing Gear Division (1991–Present); Director of Corporate Finance, Recon/Optical, Inc. (1985–1991); Manager of Financial Planning, Martin Marietta (1983–1985). **Associations & Accomplishments:** American Institute of Certified Public Accountants; Who's Who Worldwide; Who's Who Executive Club. **Education:** Pace University, B.B.A. (1976). **Personal:** Married to Ruth in 1975. Two children: Melissa and Justin. Mr. Paladino enjoys racquetball, golf, and skiing.

Albert L. Pease

Project Controls Manager
Tamsco
62 North Central Drive
O'Fallon, MO 63366
(314) 272–7447
Fax: (314) 272–7683

3728

Business Information: Tamsco (Technical Management Services Corporation) develops and delivers intermediate test program sets (software, hardware, and data) for intermediate level support of military aircraft. Established in 1991, the Company estimates revenue in excess of $5 million and presently employs 27 people. As Project Controls Manager, Mr. Pease is responsible for all cost and scheduling control functions, proposal preparations, and labor recording. Other duties include development and implementation of project budgets and monitoring compliance with accepted budgets. **Career Steps:** Project Controls Manager, Tamsco (1995–Present); Contract Consultant, McDonnell Douglas Technical Services (1992–1995); Contracts Administrator, McDonnell Douglas Missile Systems (1986–1992); Finance Administrator, McDonnell Douglas Information Systems (1974–1986). **Associations & Accomplishments:** Assistant Scout Master, Boy Scouts of America; President, Parents Organization Youth Tour Choir; Captain, United States Navy Reserve, Retired. **Education:** United States International University, M.B.A. (1974); Ohio University, B.S. Economics. **Personal:** Married to Roberta in 1975. One child: Derek. Mr. Pease enjoys golf and gardening.

Mr. James R. Peterson

Market Development Associate
Furon Company
4412 Corporate Center Drive
Los Alamitos, CA 90720
(714) 220–6557
Fax: Please mail or call

3728

Business Information: Furon Company manufactures and develops polymer based materials and products (Teflon, aircraft interiors) for the aerospace, medical and petrochemical industries. The Company has five divisions (retro–chemical, electrical, medical, transportation and industrial) and seventeen locations (fifteen in the U.S., one in England, one in Belgium). Furon is traded on the New York Stock Exchange. Mr. Peterson works in the retro–chemical segment. As Market Development Associate, he leads the Company's marketing resources towards growing markets and customers by developing new products and strategic alliances. An important career milestone for Mr. Peterson was establishing the value model: a program that quantifies the value of a product or service as opposed to its price. Established in 1960, Furon Company employs 2,500 people with annual sales of $320 million. **Career Steps:** Furon Company: Market Development Associate (1994–Present); Business Manager (1992–1994); Sales Manager (1990–1992). **Associations & Accomplishments:** Society of Manufacturing Engineers; Quoted in "Modern Plastics" and an aircraft newsletter; Speaker at professional seminars. **Education:** Pepperdine University, M.B.A. (1995); Western Washington University, B.S. in Industrial Technology. **Personal:** Married to Molly E. Peterson in 1985. Two children: Kyle J. Peterson and Kathleen E. Peterson. Mr. Peterson enjoys triathlon, scouting, surfing, bicycling and family time.

Rick Seeker

Marketing Manager
Atec
12600 Executive Drive
Stafford, TX 77477
(713) 240–1919
Fax: (713) 240–2682
EMAIL: See Below

3728

Business Information: Established in 1956, Atec is a designer and manufacturer of jet engine test stands and equipment for aerospace and energy service companies. As Marketing Manager, Mr. Seeker is responsible for marketing plans, advertisements, contract administration department, estimating department, business development, and customer calls. Internet users may reach him via: Flex@atec.com.www.atec.com **Career Steps:** Marketing Manager, Atec (1995–Present); Executive Account Representative, Halliburton Logging (1990–1995); Dresser Atlas: Executive Account Representative (1986–1990), Sales Manager (1979–1986), Sales (1975–1979). **Education:** Texas A&M University, B.B.A. in Marketing (1975). **Personal:** Married to Lisa in 1986. Two children: Kelly and Madison. Mr. Seeker enjoys ranching, golf, and hunting.

E. Denise Walker, P.H.R.
Benefits Administrator
B/E Aerospace, Inc.
1455 Fairchild Road
Winston–Salem, NC 27105
(910) 767–2000
Fax: (910) 744–6909

3728

Business Information: B/E Aerospace, Inc., formerly Burns, is a manufacturer of airline seats. The Company began operations in the 1940's and currently employs 600 people. As Benefits Administrator, Ms. Walker is responsible for the administration, coordination, evaluation, and implementation of benefits for the Winston–Salem facility. **Career Steps:** Benefits Administrator, B/E Aerospace, Inc. (1993–Present); Industrial Relations Administrator, The Stroh Brewery Company (1990–1993); Blood Services Consultant, American Red Cross (1987–1990). **Associations & Accomplishments:** Winston–Salem Society of Human Resource Professionals; Mineral Springs Volunteer Fire Department; Winston–Salem Junior Chamber of Commerce; Centenary United Methodist Church Chancel Choir. **Education:** Salem College, B.A., Professional in Human Resources and Emergency Medical Technician (1981). **Personal:** Ms. Walker enjoys sports, reading, and crafts.

Darren L. Washausen
Director
Fairchild Fasteners U.S.
3000 Lomita Boulevard
Torrance, CA 90505–5103
(310) 784–4382
Fax: (310) 784–2680

3728

Business Information: Fairchild Fasteners U.S. is an international supplier of aerospace and industrial fasteners for commercial and military aircraft. Established in 1955, Fairchild has four operations in California, one in France, two in Germany and one sales office in England. As Director of total product engineering of the South Bay facility, Darren Washausen has responsibility over design engineering, manufacturing engineering, waste treatment, metallurgical engineering, research and development, and customer sales aspects. **Career Steps:** Director, Fairchild Fasteners U.S. (1994–Present); Aircraft Braking Systems: Director Testing and Engineering Services (1994), Manager Testing and Engineering Services (1990–1994). **Associations & Accomplishments:** The Metallurgical Society; American Society for Metals; Heat Treat Association. **Education:** Kent State University, M.B.A. (1988); University of Missouri, B.S. in Metallurgical Engineering. **Personal:** Married to Stacia in 1984. One child: Britt. Mr. Washausen enjoys biking, volleyball, bowling, guitar, and golf.

Paul D. Hunt
Vice President
Peterson Builders, Inc.
41 North 3rd Avenue
Sturgeon Bay, WI 54235–0650
(414) 743–5574 ext 410
Fax: (414) 743–3987
Email: See Below

3731

Business Information: Peterson Builders, Inc. is an international shipbuilder offering procurement and logistic services to foreign and domestic governmental agencies and commercial industries. They currently provide materials to 82 countries. Established in 1946, Peterson Builders, Inc. reports annual revenue of $50 million and currently employs 300 people. As Vice President, Mr. Hunt is responsible for the oversight of all procurement, logistics and material processing, as well as contracting, subcontracting and marketing efforts for the Corporation. He can be reached through the Internet via: 75444.1657@ compuserve.com **Career Steps:** Vice President, Peterson Builders, Inc. (1989–Present); Department Manager, CACI, Inc. (1981–1989); Logistic Specialist, Lockheed Shipbuilding Company (1980–1981). **Associations & Accomplishments:** Society of Logistics Engineers; American Society of Naval Engineers; American Defense Preparedness Association; Retired U.S. Navy veteran of 20 years. **Education:** University of Kansas, M.S. (1969); Concord College, Athens, WV, B.S. **Personal:** Married to Bobbie in 1957. Mr. Hunt enjoys photography.

Bruce R. Majka
President and Chief Operating Officer
Cheoy Lee Shipyards North America
801 Seabreeze Boulevard, Bahiamer Yachting Center Tower Office
Ft. Lauderdale, FL 33316
(305) 527–0999
Fax: (305) 527–4947

3731

Business Information: Cheoy Lee Shipyards North America, the U.S. subsidiary of Cheoy Lee Shipyards, Ltd. – a Hong Kong–based company, is a designer, purchaser, and marketer of large pleasure yachts. With eighteen years experience in the shipyard industry, Mr. Majka set up and organized Cheoy Lee Shipyards North America office in 1994. Serving as President and Chief Operating Officer, he is responsible for all aspects of operations, including coordinating sales efforts with brokerage firms, advertising, and setting up boat shows. **Career Steps:** President and Chief Operating Officer, Cheoy Lee Shipyards North America (1994–Present); Director of New Construction, Rex Yacht Sales (1988–1994); President and Chief Operating Officer, Harbour Towne Marina (1981–1984); President, Yachts, Ltd. (1974–1981). **Associations & Accomplishments:** Southern Yacht Brokers Association; Marina Industries Association; National Marine Manufacturing Association; Active in Big Brothers/Sisters and Women Industries organizations. **Education:** University of Miami (1971); University of Connecticut Electrical Engineering (1968); U.S. Navy Nuclear Submarine Service, Nuclear Engineering. **Personal:** Married to Terry in 1972. Mr. Majka enjoys yachting, scuba diving, fishing, and computers.

Eugene M. McAvoy
Reactor Services, Training Supervisor
Newport News Shipbuilding
432 Mowbray Arch #1
Norfolk, VA 23507–2220
(804) 380–3529
Fax: (804) 624–1840
EMAIL: See Below

3731

Business Information: Newport News Shipbuilding is the largest ship builder in the United States. Established in 1886, the Company provides nuclear carriers and submarines for the Navy, and also specializes in commercial ship repair. As Reactor Services Training Supervisor, Mr. McAvoy is responsible for providing training in reactor service, leadership, and business conduct. Internet users can reach him via: emcavoy@concentric.net **Career Steps:** Reactor Services Training Supervisor, Newport News Shipbuilding (1994–Present); Literary Reviewer, The Virginian Pilot (1995–Present); Owner and Freelance Writer, EMM Enterprises (1989–Present). **Associations & Accomplishments:** Phi Kappa Phi–National Academic Honors Society. **Education:** University of the State of New York, B.A. (1994); Currently pursuing MFA at Old Dominion University. **Personal:** Mr. McAvoy enjoys writing and is currently writing a book entitled, The Final Approach.

George M. Simmerman Jr.
Assistant General Counsel
Ingalls Shipbuilding, Inc.
P.O. Box 149
Pascagoula, MS 39568–0149
(601) 935–3662
Fax: (601) 935–4864

3731

Business Information: Ingalls Shipbuilding, Inc., a wholly-owned entity of Litton Industries, Inc., specializes in the construction, overhaul and repair of Naval surface combatant and commercial ships. Established in 1938, Ingalls Shipbuilding Inc. currently employs 13,400 people. Employed by Litton Industries, Inc. as Assistant General Counsel to Ingalls, Mr. Simmerman represents the Company in the areas of Employment and Labor Law, Government and Commercial Contracts, Worker's Compensation and Litigation. **Career Steps:** Ingalls Shipbuilding, Inc.: Assistant General Counsel (1995–Present), Staff Attorney (1991–1995); Associate Attorney, Ott & Purdy, Ltd. (1990–1991). **Associations & Accomplishments:** American Bar Association; Alabama Bar Association; Mississippi Bar Association; Jackson County Bar Association; Board of Directors, Mississippi Bar's Young Lawyers Section; Labor and Employment and Public Law Section, American Bar Association; Former Staff, Mississippi Law Journal; Former Staff, Journal of Space Law; American Inns of Court; Law School Senate; Honor Board; National Dean's List; Outstanding Young Man in America (1983); Former President, Law School Student Body; Former President, Political Science Club; College Judicial Board; Fraternity Officer; Political Science Honor Society. **Education:** University of Mississippi School of Law, J.D. (1983); Spring Hill College, B.S. in Political Science (1980). **Personal:** Married to Valerie in 1984. Three children: Meredith, Sydney and Laithan. Mr.

Simmerman enjoys tennis, running, fishing and family activities.

Robert K. Snelling
Director of Sales and Marketing
Springfield Marine Company
P.O. Box 588, 1093 Cynthia St.
Nixa, MO 65714
(417) 725–2667
Fax: (417) 725–2667

3732

Business Information: Springfield Marine Company specializes in the manufacture of seats and pedestal hardware for the marine industry; originally established in 1953 as an aluminum sandcast foundry. A sister company in the same city works with expandable polystyrene for the automotive industry. As Director of Sales and Marketing, Mr. Snelling is responsible for all internal and external sales staff, international trade shows, advertising, customer relations and budgeting. **Career Steps:** Director of Sales and Marketing (1994–Present), Aftermarket Coordinator (1988–1994) Springfield Marine Company; Division Manager (1986–1988), Assistant Manager (1984–1986) Sunshine Automated Carwashes Inc. **Associations & Accomplishments:** Humane Society; Greater Ozarks Marine Dealers Association. **Education:** Southwest Missouri State University, Marketing and Sales degree, in progress. **Personal:** Married. Mr. Snelling enjoys playing golf, softball, and other spectator sports. Also enjoys tinkering with his two collector cars.

⚓ SUNBIRD

Blaine E. Timmer
President
Sunbird Boat Company
2348 Shop Road
Columbia, SC 29201–5164
(803) 799–1125
Fax: (803) 343–3662

3732

Business Information: Sunbird Boat Company, owned by Outboard Marine Company, is a manufacturer of pleasure boats. The Company offers complete packages of Sunbird boats, including EZ loader trailers and Evinrude and Johnson Motors. As President, Mr. Timmer is responsible for all aspects of Company operations, including administration, public relations, and marketing. **Career Steps:** President, Sunbird Boat Company (1994–Present); Vice President of Operations, Four Winns Boats (1986–1991); President, Century Boats (1985–1986); Vice President, Sales and Marketing, S–Z Yachts (1983–1985). **Associations & Accomplishments:** President, Chamber of Commerce – Cadillac, Michigan; Rotary Club, Cadillac, Michigan and Columbia, S.C.; LCDA. **Education:** U.S. Naval Academy, B.S. (1960). **Personal:** Married to Nancy in 1961. Three children: Stephen, Andrew and Christopher. Mr. Timmer enjoys golf and boating.

Cynthia Carothers
Manager of Customer Service Parts
Adtranz
1501 Lebanon Church Road
Pittsburgh, PA 15236–1491
(607) 737–3056
Fax: (412) 655–6900

3743

Business Information: Adtranz, a spinoff joint venture of ABB Traction, Inc., is an international manufacturer of passenger rail transportation vehicles, including locomotives, Amtrak, and others. As Manager of Customer Service Parts, Ms. Carothers manages all aspects of operations for the aftermarket business. **Career Steps:** Manager of Customer Service Parts, Adtranz (1995–Present); ABB Traction, Inc.: Manager of Customer Service Parts, (1992–1995), Project Manager (1991–1992), Contract Administration (1989–1991). **Associations & Accomplishments:** Society of Women Engineers. **Education:** Rider University, M.B.A. (1982); Lafayette College, B.S. in Civl Engineering. **Personal:** Married to Stuart in 1986.

Grover (E.J.) E. Johnson
Director of Coating and Linings
American Railcar Industries
100 Clark Street
St. Charles, MO 63301–2075
(314) 940–6035
Fax: (314) 940–6044

3743

Business Information: American Railcar Industries specializes in the manufacture and repair of railcars. A subsidiary of

ACF industries, the Company is international in scope, with branches throughout North America. Established in 1994, the Company employs 100 people. As Director of Coating and Linings, Mr. Johnson oversees all personnel involved in the repair, painting, and lining of new and existing railcars. **Career Steps:** Director of Coating and Linings, American Railcar Industries (1994–Present); Manager of Coatings, ACF Industries (1983–1994); Marketing and Technical Service, Carboline Company (1980–1983). **Associations & Accomplishments:** National Association of Corrosion Engineers (NACE); Steel Structural Painting Council (SSPC). **Education:** Southern Illinois University, Edwardsville (SIUE), Chemistry (1980). **Personal:** Married to Christine in 1975. Three children: Andrea, Sara and Samantha. Mr. Johnson enjoys flying (IFR pilot), fishing, family time and computers.

John Neugent

President
Sachs Bicycle Components
4980 E. Landon Drive
Anaheim, CA 92807
(714) 701–0254
Fax: (714) 701–0255

3751

Business Information: Sachs Bicycle Components is the US division of a bicycle components manufacturing company based in Germany and France. As President, Mr. Neugent oversees all aspects of Company operations, including staff supervision, administration, correspondence with the parent company, finance, and sales and marketing. **Career Steps:** President, Sachs Bicycle Components (1989–Present); Vice President of Marketing, Service Cycle (1986–1989); Vice President of Purchasing, Bike Rack (1985). **Associations & Accomplishments:** Board Member, Bicycle Wholesale Distributors Association. **Education:** University of Connecticut. **Personal:** Married to Linda in 1982. One child: Kathryn. Mr. Neugent enjoys golf and cycling.

Mark Allen Parrish

Operations Manager
Harley–Davidson, Inc.
18 Cross Falls Circle
Sparks, MD 21152
(717) 852–6840
Fax: (717) 852–6857

3751

Business Information: Harley–Davidson, Inc. is an international manufacturer of motorcycles and associated leisure/recreational products. While the Company's origins are in Milwaukee, Wisconsin. Harley–Davidson motorcycle assembly operations are located in York, Pennsylvania. The Company's primary chrome and zinc electro–plating operations are also located at the York facility. As Operations Manager, Mr. Parrish is currently responsible for all plating activities to include: plated part quality and delivery in support of daily production, planning and executing all continuous improvement initiatives, implementing technological innovations, and training all area personnel in electro–plating skills. Career milestones include extensive cross–functional exposure to manufacturing, marketing, finance, and strategic planning. **Career Steps:** Harley–Davidson, Inc.: Operations Manager (1996–Present), Production Supervisor (1995–1996); U.S. Army Assistant Operations Officer, 2–227 Aviation Battalion, Hanau, Germany (1991–1993); AH–64 Apache Attack Helicopter Platoon Leader, 2–227 Aviation Battalion, Ft. Hood Texas & Hanau, Germany (1989–1991). **Associations & Accomplishments:** New York Academy of Sciences; Honor Society of Sigma Xi (MIT Chapter); Honor Society of Phi Kappa Phi (West Point Chapter); FAA Certified, Rotary–Winged, Multi–Engine, Commercial Instrument Aviator and Fixed–Winged Student Pilot; MIT Copyrighted entitled "The Impact of Indirect Distribution Strategies on Supply Chain Operations"; Military awards include the Bronze Star and the Air Medal with Valor device for heroism during combat operations. **Education:** Massachusetts Institute of Technology, M.S.M., M.S.M.E. (1995); United States Military Academy, B.S. in Operations Research (1987). **Personal:** Married to Allison Gaines Hull in 1987. Two children: Elizabeth Gaines and Emily Rose Parrish. Mr. Parrish enjoys flying and motorcycle riding.

D. Scott Shelton

Credit Manager
MARWI USA
1 Union Drive
Olney, IL 62450
(618) 392–2000
Fax: (618) 395–1404

3751

Business Information: MARWI USA is a manufacturer and distributor of bicycle pedals, spokes, nipples, hubs, and lighting systems. As Credit Manager, Mr. Shelton is responsible for global credit and collections of 2,500 active accounts. Other duties include developing and writing credit policy, market forecasting and computer enhancements. **Career Steps:** Credit Manager, MARWI USA (1993–Present); Branch Manager, Citizens Budget Company (1991–1992); ITT Consumer Financial Corporation: Assistant Vice President/Regional Manager (1989–1991), Branch Manager (1984–1989). **Associations & Accomplishments:** National Association of Credit Management; National Bicycle Credit Association; Appointed Member, Vincennes, Indiana Redevelopment Commission; President, Vincennes Youth Soccer association; Board Member Vincennes Tennis Club; Board Member, St. John's United Church of Christ. **Education:** Kellogg Community College. **Personal:** Married to Juli in 1980. Two children: Stephanie and Kevin. Mr. Shelton enjoys cycling, tennis, snow skiing, and childrens activities.

Burl D. Dunlap

Chief of Program Contracts
Lockheed Martin Corporation
2514 Willena Drive Southeast
Huntsville, AL 35803–2474
(205) 544–0911
Fax: (205) 544–9156

3761

Business Information: Lockheed Martin Corporation is an Aerospace/Defense contractor for the government providing products such as space shuttle fuel tanks, military aircraft, missiles, etc. As Chief of Program Contracts, Mr. Dunlap is responsible for maintaining and monitoring contract changes, government property, and contract negotiations. **Career Steps:** Lockheed Martin Corporation: Chief of Program Contracts (1985–Present), Senior Contract Specialist (1978–1983); Technical Illustrator, Northrop Corporation (1968–1970). **Associations & Accomplishments:** National Contract Management Association; ALA Junior & Community College Basketball Conference; ALA High School Athletic Association; Southside Baptist Church; March of Dimes; Walk America. **Education:** New Orleans Theological Seminary; Athens College; University of Alabama, Huntsville. **Personal:** Married to Becky in 1962. Two children: Angie, Tina, and two grandchildren. Mr. Dunlap enjoys golf, softball, travel, camping, woodworking, and church work.

Tena M. Marangi

Director of Contracts
Atlantic Aerospace Electronics Corporation
6404 Ivy Lane, Suite 300
Greenbelt, MD 20770–1408
(301) 982–5270
Fax: (301) 982–5297
EMAIL: See Below

3761

Business Information: Atlantic Aerospace Electronics Corp., an employee–owned company, specializes in government defense contracts and is expanding to include commercial interests with electronic commercial and Blazer acceleration boards. Established in 1985, the Company employs 100 people, and has an estimated annual revenue of $18 million. As Director of Contracts, Ms. Marangi negotiates contracts and sub–contracts with the government, manages staff and program analysts, and ensures legality and accuracy of all commitments. Internet users can reach her via: marangi@dc.aaec.com. **Career Steps:** Director of Contracts, Atlantic Aerospace Electronics, Corp. (1986–Present); Director of Operations, Carter Marketing Group (1985–1986); Assistant to Senior Vice President of Marketing, MCI Telecom (1982–1985). **Associations & Accomplishments:** National Contract Management Association. Ms. Marangi has been published in a book on Quaker Parrots called "The Quaker Handbook" and three times in Feathered Friends Newsletter **Education:** National Louis University, Bachelors in Management and Behavioral Science (1990); Northern Virginia Community College, A.S. in Biology (1983). **Personal:** Ms. Marangi has been a runner for twenty years, plays tennis, has a Quaker Parrot who speaks over 200 words, and is writing her first novel.

Maria A. Sellers

Systems Engineer
Rockwell International
20615 47th Avenue
Bayside, NY 11361
(516) 574–2924
Fax: (516) 574–9010
EMAIL: See Below

3761

Business Information: Rockwell International is a privately–owned, multi–faceted, and diversified high technology company. The Company is involved in many different areas, including auto, space, defense, etc. Ms. Sellers works for the Autonetics and Missile Systems Division. She has dual functions, as a field engineer supporting and maintaining Rockwell built navigation equipment at a test lab facility. She currently has been assigned to the Navigation Subsystem of the Future project. As a Systems Administrator for the lab, she is currently programming in C & ValX and VxWorks, upgrading existing software codes and adding additional codes as necessary. Ms. Sellers is located in Great Neck, NY with Lockheed Martin (a company that contracts its services from Rockwell International) and works in conjunction with the software engineers at Rockwell's main plant in Anaheim, CA. Internet users can reach her via: masellers@anet.rockwell.com or maria–af–am.msn.com. **Career Steps:** Member of the Technical Staff/Systems Engineer, Rockwell International (1981–Present). **Education:** New York Institute of Technology, Master of Computer Science (1996); Ohio Institute of Technology: Associate's degree in Electronic Engineer, Bachelor's degree in Electronic Engineering Technology. **Personal:** Ms. Sellers enjoys networking, bowling, tennis, bike riding, and running.

Harold G. Watson

President and General Manager
Universal Propulsion Company, Inc.
25401 North Central Avenue
Phoenix, AZ 85027–7837
(601) 869–8067
Fax: (802) 869–8176

3764

Business Information: Universal Propulsion Company, Inc. specializes in the manufacture of ballistic devices and components required on escape systems (ejection seats) for military aircraft, space shuttle, and un–manned vehicle systems. Established 27 years ago, the Company presently employs 250 people, and has an estimated annual revenue of $32 million. As President and General Manager, Mr. Watson is responsible for management, as well as overseeing all aspects of Company operations. **Career Steps:** Universal Propulsion Company, Inc.: President and General Manager (1978–Present), Vice President and Director of Engineering (1968–1978); Director of Engineering, Space Ordnance Systems, Inc. **Associations & Accomplishments:** Life Member, Past President, SAFE Association; Member, American Defense Preparedness Association; Member, International Pyrotechnic Society; Member, AUVS Association; Member, AIAA Association; Member, AF Association. **Education:** University of Arizona, Tucson, AZ, B.S. in Engineering (1953). **Personal:** Married to Kathy in 1991. Three children: one son, Harold G. Watson Jr., and two daughters, Linda Valdivia and Patty Vanderlann.

Mr. Darryl F. Johnson

Director
Hughes Aircraft Company
19420 Eddingtor
Carson, CA 90746
(310) 616–0540
Fax: Please mail or call

3769

Business Information: Hughes Aircraft Company is a leading member of the aerospace industry. As Director, Group Administration/Services, Electro–Optical & Data Systems Group, Mr. Johnson is in charge of facilities management which includes facilities operations, support operations, security, proposals, communication media and central material. **Career Steps:** Director, Hughes Aircraft Company (1991–Present); Laboratory Manager, Hughes Aircraft (1990–1991); Material Manager, Hughes Aircraft (1988–1990); Procurement Manager, Hughes Aircraft (1984–1988); Material Program Administrator, Hughes Aircraft (1979–1984); Lieutenant Colonel, United States Army Reserves (1979–Present); Captain, United States Army, Active Duty: Executive Officer, DENTAC (1973–1978); Company Commander, 2nd Med. BN (1972–1973); Medical Advisor to Group Commander, 7th Special Forces Group (1971–1972). **Associations & Accomplishments:** President, Hughes Document Production Services; Past President, Hughes Black Professional Forum; Company Team Member, United Way, Western Region; Board Member/Chairman Fundraising Committee, African American Unity Center; Vice President, Board of Directors, Girl Scouts, Long Beach CA; UCLA Mentor, Tri–Mentor Program; Guest Alumni Speaker, UCLA Graduating Seniors (1990); Participant, Youth Motivation Task Force; Participant, Junior Achievement; Member, Fulfillment Fund for Los Angeles area; Board Member, Southern California Professional Basketball/Football Association (high school and college official); Member, Alpha Phi Alpha; Board Member, Black Military Officers Association; Awards: Army Commendation Medal with two OLC; Army Achievement Medal; National Defense Medal; Armed Forces Expeditionary Medal; Expert Field Medical Badge; Parachutist Badge; Four Year Army ROTC scholarship to UCLA; Distinguished Military Graduate, UCLA; Military Excellence Award, Kiwanis Club; Outstanding Young Men of America, US Jaycees (1977, 1985); Who's Who in the West (1987,1988). **Education:** UCLA, Executive Management Certificate (1992); Golden Gate University, Masters Degree in Public Administration (1975); UCLA, B.A. in Pscholo-gy (1970). **Personal:** Mr. Johnson enjoys golf, sports (basketball and football) and karate.

Wendy C. Carlo
Plant Accountant
Rockwell International
1801 West Stone Avenue
Fairfield, IA 52556–2148
(515) 469–2217
Fax: (515) 469–2275

3799

Business Information: Established in 1961, Rockwell International is a leader in aerospace, defense, automotive, avionics, and semi–conductor industry design and manufacture. With 43 plants, the Automotive Division specializes in the manufacture of drivelines and components for heavy and medium trucks. As Plant Accountant, Ms. Carlo is responsible for bookkeeping, tracking property for three locations, and inter-company transactions. **Career Steps:** Rockwell International: Plant Accountant (1996–Present), Accounting Clerk (1994–1996); Administrative Assistant, The Planners Professional Service (1992–1993). **Associations & Accomplishments:** Mission Trip to Mexico to build a church. **Education:** Buena Vista University, Bachelor's degree (1996); American Institute of Business. **Personal:** One child: Donny. Ms. Carlo enjoys auto racing, outdoors, and motorcycles.

Kenneth Harriman
Plant Manager
Midwest Industries, Inc.
Highway 59 & 175
Ida Grove, IA 51445
(712) 364–3365
Fax: (712) 364–4274

3799

Business Information: Midwest Industries, Inc. manufactures Shore Land'r Boat Trailers and Shore Station Dock and Hoist. As Plant Manager, Mr. Harriman is responsible for all manufacturing, maintenance, research and development, and tooling aspects of design. **Career Steps:** Plant Manager, Midwest Industries, Inc. (1989–Present); Plant Manager, Byron Originals (1980–1989). **Associations & Accomplishments:** American Welding Society; Petroleum Marketing Association of America; APEX. **Personal:** Mr. Harriman enjoys boating, hunting, fishing, snowmobiling, and skiing.

Albert A. Mardikian
Owner and Chief Design Engineer
Mardikian Design
15662 Commerce Lane
Huntington Beach, CA 92649
(714) 895–7139
Fax: (714) 895–7139

3799

Business Information: Mardikian Design, a family–owned enterprise, specializes in the manufacture and design of water craft (jet skis, pleasure boats) and sports cars. Mr. Mardikian is responsible for all aspects of Company operations. He holds over 22 patents for exotic automobile and watercraft designs and prototypes. Established in 1984, Mardikian Design currently employs 95 persons. **Career Steps:** Owner and Chief Design Engineer, Mardikian Design (1984–Present); President and Engineer, Laser Jet Performance (Since 1994); President and Engineer, Hydro Ski (Since 1990). **Associations & Accomplishments:** IJSBA Racing; APBA Racing. **Education:** Northrup University, B.S. (1971). **Personal:** Married to Nellie in 1975. One child: Chris. During his leisure time, Mr. Mardikian enjoys auto and jet ski racing.

Sharon D. Montgomery

Manager, Material Production Control
Delco Electronics Corporation
P.O. Box 9005
Kokomo, IN 46904–9005
(317) 451–4102
Fax: (317) 451–4215
EMAIL: See Below

3799

Business Information: Delco Electronics, a division of General Motors, is an establishment primarily engaged in the manufacture of automotive electronics (i.e., car stereos, and computer, airbag and A/C systems). Established in 1936, the Company employs 31,500 people, and has an estimated annual revenue of $5.4 billion. As Manager, Material Production Control, Mrs. Montgomery manages the material flow process globally (includes all materials systems, processes, policies, and procedures). She is also responsible for oversight of the logistics department, and supervision of 63 people. Internet users can reach her via: sdmontgo@mail.delcoelect.com. **Career Steps:** Delco Electronics: Manager, Material Production Control (1995–Present), Superintendent, Central Material Control (1989–1995); Manager, Production Control, Delco Remy, Division General Motors Corporation (1980–1989). **Associations & Accomplishments:** American Red Cross: Chairman of the Board of Directors, Chairman Finance Development Committee State Service Council, Board of Directors Ft. Wayne Blood Center; Board of Directors, Family and Children Services; Hopewell Center and Madiwon County Crippled Childrens Society; Alpha Kappa Alpha Sorority; American Management Association; National Association of Female Executives. **Education:** Ball State University, B.S. (1968); University of Illinois Executive Development Program (1990). **Personal:** Married to Herbert in 1970. Three children: Kelli, Herbert, and Stacee. Mrs. Montgomery enjoys public speaking, reading, and church activities.

Ronald G. Newton
Senior Vice President of Sales & Marketing
Hennessy Industries, Inc.
P.O. Box 3002, 1601 J.P. Hennessy Blvd.
La Vergne, TN 37086–1982
(615) 641–7533 Ext. 7272
Fax: (615) 647–6069

3799

Business Information: Established in 1955, Hennessy Industries, Inc. is a worldwide manufacturer of automotive service equipment, employing 400 people and grossing $115 million annually. Mr. Newton joined Hennessy in 1990 with 14 years of sales and marketing experience. In his current capacity as Senior Vice President of Sales & Marketing, he is responsible for diversified administrative activities and providing Company leadership toward growth. **Career Steps:** Hennessy Industries: Senior Vice President of Sales & Marketing (1993–Present), Vice President of Sales (1990–1993); Maremont: Vice President of Marketing (1984–1990), Vice President of Sales (1982–1984). **Associations & Accomplishments:** Automotive Sales Council. **Education:** Auburn University, B.S. (1969). **Personal:** Married to Wanda in 1969. Three children: Melissa, Marsha, and Allen. Mr. Newton enjoys golf, racing, and music.

Phil B. Santamaria
Graphic Design Specialist
Lockheed Martin
3428 Hickerson Drive
San Jose, CA 95127–4314
(408) 742–4394
Fax: Please mail or call

3799

Business Information: Lockheed Martin is a United States Defense contractor. As Graphic Design Specialist, Mr. Santamaria develops and generates complex classified and diversified graphics and illustrations, creative typesetting, and a newsletter. He also trains others and deals in developing materials. **Career Steps:** Graphic Design Specialist, Lockheed Martin (1977–Present); Building Designer, Southland Corporation (1974–77); Industrial Engineer, Di Giorgio Leisure Products (1972–1974). **Associations & Accomplishments:** Lions Clubs International, District 4–6C, California; Knights of Columbus. **Education:** University of Santo Tomas, Philippines, B.A. **Personal:** Married to Magdalena A. in 1974. Mr. Santamaria enjoys photography, listening to classical music, gardening and helping those in need.

Jeffery A. White, C.P.M.
Manager of Procurement Compliance
United Defense GSD
15 Windham Boulevard
Aiken, SC 28901
(803) 643–2503
Fax: (803) 643–2504
EMAIL: See Below

3799

Business Information: United Defense GSD is a manufacturer of military vehicles. As Manager of Procurement Compliance, Mr. White oversees all aspects of the purchasing department with U.S. government regulations and laws. Internet users can reach him via: jeffery_white@fmc.com. **Career Steps:** Manager of Procurement Compliance, United Defense GSD (1996–Present); United Defense L.P. (1995–1996), Compliance Training Leader (1994–1995). **Associations & Accomplishments:** National Association of Purchasing Management; National Contract and Management Association; Past Chairman, William Goodridge Minority Business Center; Awarded, Pennsylvania Entrepreneur of the Year; Adjunct Professor, Penn State University and Midland Technical College; Published numerous articles. **Education:** South Carolina State University, B.S. (1983). **Personal:** Married to Sylvia A. Toussaint in 1987. Three children: Jeffery A. II, Tiffany Alicia, and Salina Joy. Mr. White enjoys computer programming, mentoring teens, and golf.

3800 Instruments and Related Products

3812 Search and navigation equipment
3821 Laboratory apparatus and furniture
3822 Environmental controls
3823 Process control instruments
3824 Fluid meters and counting devices
3825 Instruments to measure electricity
3826 Analytical instruments
3827 Optical instruments and lenses
3829 Measuring and controlling devices, NEC
3841 Surgical and medical instruments
3842 Surgical appliances and supplies
3843 Dental equipment and supplies
3844 X–ray apparatus and tubes
3845 Electromedical equipment
3851 Ophthalmic goods
3861 Photographic equipment and supplies
3873 Watches, clocks, watchcases and parts

T. W. Foss
Director of Manufacturing
AEL Industries Inc./Cross Systems
1355 Bluegrass Lakes Parkway
Alpharetta, GA 30201–7700
(770) 475–3633
Fax: (770) 476–0176

3812

Business Information: AEL Industries Inc./Cross Systems is a manufacturer of radar environment simulators and night vision heads up display systems. As Director of Manufacturing, Tom Foss is responsible for the oversight and administration of the Departments of Purchasing, Inventory Control, Production Engineering, Production Control, Assembly and Testing. **Career Steps:** Director of Manufacturing, AEL Industries Inc./Cross Systems (1988–Present); Department Manager, Electromagnetic Sciences (1986–1988); Advanced Technology Manager, Rockwell International/ MSD (1983–1986); Plant Manager, Rockwell International/ CGAD (1979–1982). **Associations & Accomplishments:** Tau Beta Pi. **Education:** Iowa State University, Masters (1976); University of Iowa, B.S. in Industrial Engineering (1969). **Personal:** Married to Sarah L. in 1968. Four children: Elisabeth, Victoria, Nicholas, and Adam. Mr. Foss enjoys reading and coaching youth sports.

P. Douglas Groseclose
Director of Employee Development and Human Resource Management
Lockheed Martin Electronics and Missiles
5600 Sand Lake Road, MP–229
Orlando, FL 32819–8907
(407) 356–3226
Fax: (407) 356–0919

3812

Business Information: Lockheed Martin Electronics and Missiles, a division of Lockheed Corporation – a major manufacturer of military and commercial aircraft — is an aerospace research and manufacturer of defense–related systems (i.e. missiles). Established in 1957, Lockheed Martin Electrics and Missiles reports annual revenue of $1 billion and currently employs 4,800 company–wide. As Director of Employee Development and Human Resource Management, Douglas Groseclose is responsible for personnel matters, including management of staffing, outplacement, training, OD, policies and procedures, and providing Human Resources services to the $500 million Fire Control Systems business unit. Concurrent with his position at Lockheed Martin, he serves as Executive Vice President of MindForms, Inc. **Career Steps:** Director of Employee Development and Human Resource Management, Lockheed Martin Electronics and Missiles (1991–Present); Executive Vice President, MindForms, Inc. (Present); Martin Marietta: Manager of Training and Organization Development (1989–1991), Manager of Organizational Development (1981–1989); Private Consultant (1980–1981). **Associations & Accomplishments:** Association for the Management of Organizational Design; American Society for Training and Development; Organizational Development Institute; Advisory Board, Valencia Community College; American Society for Quality Control. **Education:** North Carolina Wesleyan College, B.A. (1967). **Personal:** Married to Debbra in 1982. Two children: Scott and Deeanna.

Benny C.W. Lau

Vice President of Product Planning
ATI Technologies, Inc.
33 Commerce Valley Drive, East
Thornhill, Ontario L3T 7N6
(9058) 825–262
Fax: (905) 882–9339
EMAIL: See Below

3812

Business Information: ATI Technologies, Inc. designs and manufactures computer graphics accelerators, multimedia, and other computer related products for distribution to retailers and OEM's. International in scope, the Company has six locations throughout Germany, Canada, and the United States. Established in 1985, the Company employs 700 people, and has an estimated annual revenue of $500 million. As Vice President of Product Planning, Mr. Lau coordinates between engineers and strategic customers. He is also responsible for all administrative and operational aspects of his department. Internet users can reach him via: Benny@Unix.atitech. **Career Steps:** Vice President of Product Planning, ATI Technologies, Inc. (1985–Present); Design Engineer, Litton Industries (1984–1985); Design Engineer, Semi–Tech (1982–1984). **Associations & Accomplishments:** Association of Professional Engineers of Ontario. **Education:** University of Ontario: M.A.Sc. (1981), B.A. Sc. (1979). **Personal:** Married to Ruby in 1982.

Maritza Zayas

Operations Manager
PEI Division of Northrop Grumman Electronicos, Inc.
fMunoz Rivera 112 Route One
Santa Isabel, Puerto Rico 00757
(809) 845–3590
Fax: (809) 845–3690

3812

Business Information: PEI Division of Northrop Grumman Electronicos, Inc., established in 1978, is a manufacturer of high quality, high reliability electronic devices using sophisticated technology. As Operations Manager, Mrs. Zayas is responsible for product manufacturing and shipping, customer relations, directing production stages, and coordinating engineering and production groups. With 47 employees, the Corporation estimates annual sales in excess of $45 million. **Career Steps:** PEI Division of Northrop Grumman Electronicos, Inc.: Operations Manager (1996–Present), Material Senior Supervisor (1992–1995), Senior Test Engineer (1987–1991). **Education:** University of Puerto Rico, B.S.E.E. (1987). **Personal:** Married to Jose A. Santiago in 1989. Two children: Angie L. and Jose A. Mrs. Zayas enjoys being an active participant in church–related activities.

Timothy J. King
Purchasing Director
Ika Works
2635 North Chase Parkway
Wilmington, NC 28405
(910) 452–7059
Fax: (910) 452–7693

3821

Business Information: With locations in Germany, the U.S. and Malaysia, Ika Works is an international manufacturer of laboratory and processing equipment. Providing and researching for companies such as Procter and Gamble, Gillette, Kraft Foods, Estee Lauder and schools and institutions, the Company produces processing and lab equipment which includes high sheer mixers, magnetic stirrers and shakers. As Purchasing Director, Tim King is responsible for administering all procurement of goods and services, inventory control, vendor relations and traffic coordination. **Career Steps:** Purchasing Director, Ika Works (1994–Present); Area Supervisor, Worsley Companies (1990–1994). **Associations & Accomplishments:** Outstanding College Students of America (1988); National Association of MBA Executives (1994). **Education:** University of North Carolina – Wilmington, M.B.A. (1994); Florida State University: B.S. in Management, B.S. in Marketing. **Personal:** Married to Kimberly in 1995. Mr. King enjoys sports (i.e. golf and basketball) and gardening.

Vladimir E. Ostoich, Ph.D.
Vice President of Engineering
Abaxis, Inc.
1320 Chesapeake Terrace
Sunnyvale, CA 94089–1100
(408) 745–6840
Fax: (408) 734–2874

3821

Business Information: Abaxis, Inc. develops, manufactures, and markets portable blood analysis systems for medical doctors and veterinarians. Established in 1989, Abaxis, Inc. employs 75 people with annual sales of $10 million. As Vice President of Engineering, Dr. Ostoich, who is also one of the Founders of the Company, handles all research and development of new products. Depending on the size of the project, Dr. Ostoich's staff varies. **Career Steps:** Vice President of Engineering, Abaxis, Inc. (1989–Present); Vice President of Engineering, Proxim (1986–1989); Director of Engineering, Biotreck (1984–1986). **Education:** Technical University of Denmark: Ph.D. (1977), M.Sc. in Electrical Engineering (1975); Universidad Santa Maria, B.S. in Electrical Engineering (1968). **Personal:** Married to Liliana in 1969. Two children: Tonka and Ivan. Dr. Ostoich enjoys sailing.

Rebecca Liner Sheriff
Corporate Controller
Chase Instruments Corporation
6760 Jimmy Carter Boulevard, Suite 125
Norcross, GA 30071–1256
(770) 729–7413
Fax: (770) 729–7429

3821

Business Information: Chase Instruments Corporation manufactures laboratory glassware for the medical and veterinary fields. A Certified Public Accountant, Ms. Sheriff joined Chase as Corporate Controller in 1990. She is responsible for the oversight of all financial aspects of operations, including accounting, billing, cash receipts, receivables, management of financial packages, and various administrative duties. Concurrently, Ms. Sheriff is a published poet, recognized by the International Society of Poets. **Career Steps:** Corporate Controller/CPA, Chase Instruments Corporation (1990–Present); Accounting Manager/CPA, Academy Life Insurance (1988–1990); Accounting Manager/Tax/CPA, Blue Cross/Blue Shield of Georgia (1974–1988). **Associations & Accomplishments:** American Institute of Certified Public Accountants; Georgia Society of Certified Public Accountants; International Society of Poets; Belvedere Civic Club; Who's Who of Professional Women; Who's Who in Georgia. **Education:** Georgia State University, B.B.A. (1981); Certified Public Accountant; Certified Professional Secretary. **Personal:** Ms. Sheriff enjoys collectibles and writing poetry.

Phillip R. Smith

President/General Manager
Caron Product Services, Inc.
P.O. Box 715
Marietta, OH 45750
(614) 373–6809
Fax: (614) 374–3760

3821

Business Information: Caron Product Services, Inc. is a manufacturer of laboratory equipment such as constant temperature chambers, environmental chillers, various OEM products, and other related products. The Company distributes their products on an international scale. As President/General Manager, Mr. Smith is responsible for all aspects of Company operations, including administration, sales and marketing, finance, and strategic planning. **Career Steps:** President/General Manager, Caron Product Services, Inc. (1995–Present); Director of Technical Operations, Cincinnati Sub–Zero (1983–1995). **Associations & Accomplishments:** Institute of Electronics and Electrical Engineers; I.S.A. **Education:** University of Cincinnati, M.B.A. (1992); Western Kentucky University, B.S.E.E.T. **Personal:** Married to Tracie in 1984. Two children: Alexander and Matthew. Mr. Smith enjoys gardening, golf, and water skiing.

Sajaad A. Chaudry
Vice President of Engineering and Technical Services
Facility Robotics, Inc.
875 Old Roswell Road, Suite C–400
Roswell, GA 30076
(404) 640–0071
Fax: (404) 640–7224

3822

Business Information: Facility Robotics, Inc. is a system integrator for state of art in building automation systems including heating, cooling, and communication systems. Established in 1986, Facility Robotics, Inc. reports annual revenue of $4 million and currently employs 20 people. As Vice President of Engineering and Technical Services, Mr. Chaudry is responsible for engineering, development of software, and the provision of technical assistance to the rest of the Company. **Career Steps:** Vice President of Engineering and Technical Services, Facility Robotics, Inc. (1995–Present); Director of Technical Services, Teletrol Systems, Inc. (1988–1995); Project Engineer, NYPRO, Inc. (1987–1988). **Associations & Accomplishments:** Tau Beta Pi, National Engineering Honor Society; Pi Tau Sigma, Mechanical Engineering Honor Society; The Association of Energy Engineers; Published in ASHRAE Journal. **Education:** University of Lowell, Massachusetts, B.S. in Mechanical Engineering (1985), One year of M.S. in Mechanical Engineering; St. Lawrence College, Cornwall, Ontario, Canada, Mechanical Engineering Technology Degree. **Personal:** Married to Nishat Sajaad Chaudry in 1993. One child: Mariam Sajaad Chaudry. Mr. Chaudry enjoys flying model helicopters, travel, and sightseeing.

Jerry Kidd

Vice President
Hurckman Mechanical
P O Box 10977
Green Bay, WI 54307–0977
(414) 499–8771
Fax: (414) 499–6769

3822

Business Information: Hurckman Mechanical, headquartered in Wisconsin, is a multi–million dollar conglomerate which sells and installs monitoring systems for buildings throughout the United States. The systems monitor, via computers, the lighting, heating, and air conditioning systems in both large and small buildings. As Vice President, Mr. Kidd is responsible for all Company training programs. He works with clients and management on the development of improved customer service techniques and technical service. **Career Steps:** Vice President, Hurckman Mechanical (1968–Present). **Personal:** Married to Malinda in 1982. Four children: Geri, Jodi, Bret, and Jamie. Mr. Kidd enjoys breeding cockatiels and working with the Wisconsin Wildlife Sanctuary.

Martin J. Plebon

President/General Manager
Spirax Sarco Canada LTD
383 Applewood Crescent
Concord, Ontario L4K 4J3
(905) 660–5510
Fax: (514) 620–2703

3822

Business Information: Spirax Sarco Canada LTD specializes in the manufacturer of commercial and industrial steam ancillary equipment (i.e. controls, humidifiers, screens, valves, and pumps). International in scope, the Company services thirty–six countries, with subsidiaries in the U.S., Canada, and England. A family–owned business, Spirax Sarco Canada LTD was established in 1908. As President/General Manager, Mr. Plebon is responsible for identifying market need, overseeing the financial status of the Company, handling profit/loss ratios, and keeping current on the market share. **Career Steps:** Spirax Sarco Canada LTD: President/General Manager (1996–Present), Regional Manager (1990–1996), Provincial Manager (1988–1989), Sales Representative (1986–1988). **Associations & Accomplishments:** Alliance Quebec, West Island Chapter; Canadian Professional Sales Association. **Education:** Ryerson Polytechnic, C.E.T. in Chemical Engineering Technology (1984). **Personal:** Married to Caroline Samne in 1995. Mr. Plebon enjoys skiing, golf, and computers.

Garry E. Gladfelter Sr.

Account Engineer, MSS
Landis and Gyr, Inc.
19501 NE 10th Avenue, Suite H
Miami, FL 33179
(305) 652–5111
Fax: (305) 651–1506

3823

Business Information: Landis and Gyr, Inc., formerly Powers Regulator Company, is a national manufacturer, installer, designer, and servicer of automatic temperature controls, card accesses, and fire/security and mechanical systems. The Company is comprised of more than 60 main branches and numerous sub–branches domestically, targeting commercial markets, such as hospitals, laboratories, prisons, residential, and businesses. As Account Engineer, MSS, Mr. Gladfelter is responsible for the operation of one–half the division which handles the Florida State area for Bell South. With 111 buildings under his direction, he ensures that all contracting is complete and done correctly, as well as supervising 20 mechanics who service and install the systems. **Career Steps:** Account Engineer, MSS, Landis and Gyr, Inc. (1990–Present); Senior Project Manager, Barton Associates, Inc. (1973–1990); HVAC Designer, Glassglow and Associates, Inc. (1968–1973). **Associations & Accomplishments:** American Society of Heating, Refrigerating and Air Conditioning Engineers, Inc.; International Maintenance Institute; Speaker for ASHRAE. **Education:** Attended, York College of Pennsylvania (1983). **Personal:** Married to Helen in 1969. One child: Garrison Jr. Mr. Gladfelter enjoys golf and going to the beach.

Lee W. Hoevel

Vice President and Chief Technical Officer
AT&T Global Information Solutions
1700 South Patterson
Dayton, OH 45479–0001
(513) 445–5555
Fax: (513) 445–1728

3823

Business Information: AT&T Global Information Solutions is a global communications networks company specializing in voice, video and data communications (information movement and management). As Vice President of Architecture, Technology and Design (AT&D) and Chief Technical Officer of the Computer Systems Group, Mr. Hoevel is responsible for the overall technical health of the Company. He champions the achievements of the technical community, nurtures productivity and promotes innovation throughout the Company. Dr. Hoevel's department deals directly with technology management—the planning, acquisition and full exploitation of core competencies and new enabling technologies. Mr. Hoevel focuses on developing the technical community, hosting several technical conferences each year to ensure the Computer Systems Group remains current in key areas. He can be reached through the internet via: Lee.Hoevel@DaytonOH.ATT-GIS.COM **Career Steps:** AT&T Global Information Solutions: Vice President and Chief Technical Officer (1993–Present), Vice President of Technology and Development (1991–1992); NCR Corporation: Chief Architect (1988–1991), Director of Advanced Architecture (1985–1988); Senior Manager of Architecture, IBM (1983–1985); Consultant, Palyn Associates (1972–1978); Research Assistant, Stanford University (1972–1978); Johns Hopkins University Applied Physics Laboratory (1967–1972). **Associations & Accomplishments:** Sigma Xi; Institute of Electrical and Electronic Engineers; Association for Computing Machinery; AT&T Board Member, Micro–Computer Corporation (4 years); Various publications in trade journals; Numerous patents. **Education:** Johns Hopkins University, Ph.D. in Electrical Engineering (1978); Rice University, B.A. in Economics (1968), B.A. in Mathematics (1967). **Personal:** Married to Betty in 1972. Two children: Anne and Barbara. Mr. Hoevel enjoys chess, bridge, woodworking, and historical restorations.

Bruce Jorgensen

President
X–Rite, Inc.
3100 44th Street, SW
Grandville, MI 49418–2567
(616) 534–7663
Fax: (616) 534–8342

3823

Business Information: X–Rite, Inc. is a producer of quality control instruments measuring color, optical, and photo density for the paint, plastics, textile, graphic art, photo, medical & packaging markets. International in scope, X–Rite, Inc. has three overseas locations (Manchester, United Kingdom; Cologne, Germany; Hong Kong). Established in 1958, X–Rite, Inc. reports annual revenue of $75 million and currently employs 500 people. With 27 years expertise in the chemical engineering industry, Mr. Jorgensen joined X–Rite in 1994. Serving as President and Chief Operating Officer, he is responsible for all aspects of operations, providing the overall strategic direction and vision for the Company's continued growth development, quality product output and international market presence. **Career Steps:** President and Chief Operations Officer, X–Rite, Inc. (1994–Present); Various Managerial Positions, Exxon Chemical Company (1966–1994). **Associations & Accomplishments:** American Management Association; Board Member, Metropolitan Foundation; Board Member, West Michigan Horticultural Society; West Michigan World Affairs Council; World Trade Association. **Education:** Michigan State University: M.B.A. in Marketing (1966), B.S. in Chemical Engineering (1965). **Personal:** Married to Linda in 1968. Two children: Lisa Marie and Erik. Mr. Jorgensen enjoys boating, jogging, and tennis in his leisure time.

Salvatore Monteforte

Chairman and Chief Executive Officer
SIMENT, Inc.
76 Merkley Square
Scarborough, Ontario M1G 2Y7
(416) 289–4448
Fax: (416) 289–2669
EMAIL: See Below

3823

Business Information: SIMENT, Inc., established in 1973, is engaged in the research, development, manufacturing and marketing of scientific instruments. Recent developments have been in the design of bioreactor instrumentation. With a thirty–one year experience in engineering design and manufacturing, Dr. Monteforte joined SIMENT in 1983. Serving as Chairman and Chief Executive Officer, he is responsible for all aspects of operations, including planning and supervising the design and implementation of all engineering and investment projects. He also plans, organizes, and directs the activities of NEAITON, Inc., serving as Chairman and Chief Executive Officer. NEAITON, Inc. is a consulting firm providing engineering services to manufacturing companies, including project management and assistance for financing, in Canada, the U.S., Mexico, and Italy. Dr. Monteforte can be reached through the Internet via: 102011.3226@compuserve.com **Career Steps:** Chairman and Chief Executive Officer, SIMENT, Inc. (1983–Present); Chairman and Chief Executive Officer, NEAITON, Inc. (1973–Present); Investment Project Consultant, Central American Research Institute for Industry (ICAITI), Guatemala, and Industrial Development Bank of El Salvador (1958–1969). **Associations & Accomplishments:** Association of Professional Engineers of Ontario (PEO); The New York Academy of Sciences; University Professor, Universities of Turin, El Salvador, and Landivar. **Education:** Polytechnic of Turin, Doctorate in Engineering (1951); Attending: University of Toronto. **Personal:** Married to Maria L. Bazzarello in 1952. Six children: Lucia, Rodolfo, Guglielmo, Anna Isabella, Enrico, and Roberto. Dr. Monteforte enjoys history and mathematics.

Dan Rigato

Treasurer
MRM Air Products
22777 Heslip Drive
Novi, MI 48375
(810) 348–6900
Fax: (810) 348–2150

3823

Business Information: MRM Air Products is a distributor of application–based pneumatic control devices such as air cylinders, air management systems, and vacuum systems. The majority of the products are produced for the automotive industry. As Treasurer, Mr. Rigato is responsible for all aspects of cash management, securities administration, credit, collections, and remittance processing for the Company. Other responsibilities include bank relations, budgetary concerns, and providing funding for the purchase of capital assets and acquisitions. Concurrently, Mr. Rigato is a part–time instructor at the Detroit College of Business. **Career Steps:** Treasurer, MRM Air Products (1994–Present); Ameritech: Product Development (1992–1994), Product Management (1985–1992). **Education:** Wayne State University: M.B.A. (1986), B.S./B.A. in Operations Management (1980). **Personal:** Married to Mary in 1981. Two children: Erin and Caitlin. Mr. Rigato enjoys rock climbing, backpacking, fishing, hunting, and gardening.

Willfried Schramm, Ph.D.

Vice President of Research and Development
Saliva Diagnostic Systems, Inc.
11719 North East 95th Street
Vancouver, WA 98682
(360) 696–4800
Fax: (360) 254–7942
EMail: See Below

3823

Business Information: Saliva Diagnostic Systems, Inc. is a biotechnology company which develops diagnostic tests that can be used in non–laboratory conditions. The Company has offices in Singapore and London, and distributor locations in Europe, Africa, and South America. As Vice President of Research and Development, Dr. Schramm is responsible for directing efforts in developing diagnostic testing. He heads a group of fifteen that focuses on infectious diseases and manufacturing procedures. Dr. Schramm may be reached through the Internet via: Schramm@Pacifier.com **Career Steps:** Vice President of Research and Development, Saliva Diagnostic Systems, Inc. (1993–Present); Vice President of Research and Development, Bio Quant, Inc. (1985–1993); Research Scientist, University of Michigan – Ann Arbor (1984–1990). **Associations & Accomplishments:** American Association for the Advancement of Sciences; American Association of Clinical Chemists; American Chemical Society; New York Academy of Sciences; Society for the Study of Reproduction; Contributes frequently to publications on organic chemistry, physiology, and analytical biochemistry. **Education:** University of Hamburg, Germany, Ph.D. (1977); University of Rostock, Germany. **Personal:** Married to Gudrun in 1968. Two children: Frauke and Antje. Dr. Schramm enjoys the outdoors, hiking, bicycling, horseback riding, and swimming.

Mr. Willem B. Tijmann

President
E & T Instrumentation
P.O. Box 80033 (101A Pond Street)
Stoneham, MA 02180–0901
(617) 438–3889
Fax: (617) 438–9414

3823

Business Information: E & T Instrumentation provides instrumentation and consultation for large projects worldwide. Established in 1987, E & T Instrumentation currently employs 4–8 people. As President, Mr. Tijmann is responsible for geotechnical & structural instrumentation and soil & rock mechanics applications. His clientele includes large companies, their governments and universities in the promotion of instrumentation for support of technical and international trade in the construction industry, and estimating the cost of large overseas and domestic projects as a member of the design team. Additionally, he organizes, plans and participates in engineering seminars in the U.S. and overseas with emphasis of the Pacific Rim countries (i.e., Hong Kong, Philippines, Thailand, R.O.C., Malaysia, Singapore, Indonesia, Europe, Central and South America). Mr. Tijmann travels extensively throughout the U.S. and overseas on behalf of the company's projects and has gathered a wide range of experience in design and practical applications, monitoring of instruments and interpretations of results covering deep and shallow foundations, excavations, structural earthfill embankments, earthfill and concrete dams, lined and unlined tunnels (NATM) and underground structures in soil and rock for conventional and nuclear projects. Concurrent with his duties at E & T Instrumentation, he serves as President and Senior Consultant for the consulting firm W.B.T.C. **Career Steps:** President, E & T Instrumentation (1992–Present); President, W.B.T.C. (Consultants) (1987–Present); Vice President of the International Division, Slope Indicator Company (1976–1987); Project Manager, Dames & Moore (1964–1976). **Associations & Accomplishments:** American Society of Civil Engineers (Honorary Member) since 1956 (ASCE); International Society for Soil Mechanics & Foundation Engineers (ISSMFE); Affiliate Member Association of Engineering Geologists (ASEG); Senior Member, American Society of Testing & Materials (ASTM); National Association of Underwater Instructors (NAUI) Certified Diver; Inventor of USA Patents 5038622 – Strain Gauge Assembly for Measuring, 3344869 – Earth Coring Device, 3146838 – Patented Soil Sampling Device and other Canadian and International Patents Pending; Proficient in eight languages; Numerous articles and publications. **Education:** University of California at Berkley, Rock Mechanics Courses (1954); Polytechnical H.T.S. Amsterdam, The Netherlands, M.S. and B.S. in Civil Engineering (1955). **Personal:** Married to Mirna Aeschlimann, M.D. in 1991. One child: Sonja Maria Strand Tijmann. Mr. Tijmann enjoys scuba diving, sailing, tennis and hiking.

Mr. Charles S. Walker

Vice President, Corporate Account Director
Measurex Corporation
19947 Garnett Court
Saratoga, CA 95070
(408) 741–0731
Fax: (408) 741–5701

3823

Business Information: Measurex Corporation manufactures, markets and services process control and information systems designed to enhance the product quality and manufacturing efficiencies of industrial manufacturing operations. In his current capacity, Mr. Walker is responsible for Corporate Account activities in selected accounts in the Paper Industry, including Corporate and Division Executives and Managers, Engineering, R&D, and Information Technology. Established in 1968, Measurex Corporation presently employs 2,300 people and has an estimated annual revenue in excess of $250 million. **Career Steps:** Vice President, Corporate Accounts Director (1990–Present). Various management positions, including Vice President, Division Manager, within Measurex Systems, Inc. (1973–1990). Various positions, including Division Manager, within AccuRay Corporation, now ABB Automation (1958– 1972). U.S. Naval Officer (1953–1957). **Associations & Accomplishments:** Technical Association of the Pulp and Paper Industry; Paper Industry Management Association; Instrument Society of America; Naval Academy Alumni Association; Naval Academy Athletic Association; Assigned three patents on Process Control: Zone Average Cascade Control, Zone Average Cross Direction Control, Economic Optimization Control; Pioneered corporate account programs in the industrial manufacturing market segment during the early 1960's under the tutelage of Mr. Howard Begg, the Father of Institutional Selling; Continually refining such programs to date. **Education:** U.S. Naval Academy, B.S. (1953). **Personal:** Married to Dana Walker in 1954. Three children: Pam, Charles Jr., and Kelly.

Tasos Zografos

Director of Operations
Lockheed Martin IMS
188 The Embarcadero, Suite 450
San Francisco, CA 94104
(415) 512–9493
Fax: (415) 512–0844

3823

Business Information: Lockheed Martin IMS is a division of Lockheed Martin, a manufacturer of electronic control systems intended for civil and military aircraft, automotive, locomotive, industrial, and other applications. The IMS Division works with Federal, State, and local governments on developing new technology in the field of transportation. This division explores new business operations (i.e. automation of tolls, trucks, weigh stations, international border crossings) to save time and eliminate existing traffic problems. The IMS Division was established in 1985 and currently employs over 2,000 people. As Director of Operations, Mr. Zografos is responsible for all operations including planning, implementation, operational support for all networking activities, and sales support. Concurrently, Mr. Zografos is a California real estate broker and investor. **Career Steps:** Lockheed Martin IMS: Director of Operations (1993–Present), Program Manager (1993–1995); Lockheed Missiles and Space: Director (1991–1993), Project Manager (1989–1991). **Associations & Accomplishments:** Public Relations Director, Greek American Political Association; Volunteer work for/with the homeless; Mr. Zagrafos is a guest speaker on the plight of underprivileged high school students. **Education:** University of Southern California, M.S. (1986); San Jose State University, B.S. in Aerospace. **Personal:** One child: Sam. Mr. Zografos enjoys playing basketball and soccer.

Fouad Gabr Ahmed Khodier

General Manager
Juma Al Majid Establishment for Electro Mechanical Works
P.O. Box 60204
Dubai, United Arab Emirates
(04) 851034
Fax: (04) 857890

3824

Business Information: Juma Al Majid Establishment for Electro Mechanical Works provides electro–mechanical engineering and contracting services for central air conditioning, electrical, plumbing, and elevators throughout the United Arab Emirate. Established in 1976, Juma Al Majid Establishment employs 1,300 people. Joining the Company in 1982 as Design Manager, Mr. Khodier was appointed to his current role in 1991. As General Manager, he is responsible for the direction and management of engineering matters, as well as the contracting business. **Career Steps:** Juma Al Majid Establishment for Electro Mechanical Works: General Manager (1991–Present), Contracting Manager (1986–1991), Design Manager (1982–1986). **Associations & Accomplishments:** American Society of Heating, Refrigeration and Air Conditioning Engineer; United Arab Emirates Engineering Associations. **Education:** Faculty of Engineering, B.Sc. (1976). **Personal:** Married to M. Sabri in 1977. Four children: Yasmin, Ahmed, Noora, and Akram. Mr. Khodier enjoys sports and reading.

Gerald F. Obermeyer, P.E.

Senior Engineer
Joseph Pollak Corporation
11801 Miriam Drive
El Paso, TX 79936
(915) 592–5700
Fax: (915) 592–4196

3824

Business Information: Joseph Pollak Corporation is a manufacturer and distributor of electro–mechanical instrumentation for cars, trucks, buses and others, such as ATVs and snowmobiles to OEMs. As Senior Engineer with the Transportation Electronics Division, Mr. Obermeyer is responsible for implementation and integration of new products into production, as well as scheduling, designing and developing new products. Concurrent with his position as Senior Engineer, he serves as the Staff Assistant to the Vice President. **Career Steps:** Senior Engineer – Transportation Electronics Division, Joseph Pollak Corporation (1992–Present); Engineer, General Instruments (1951–1992); Engineer, Westinghouse (1949–1951). **Associations & Accomplishments:** Knights of Columbus; American Legion; Texas Society of Professional Engineers; National Society of Professional Engineers. **Education:** University of Maine, BSME (1949); University of Connecticut; Holy Cross College; University of Massachusetts; American International College. **Personal:** Married to Mary Eileen in 1945. Three children: William, Stephen, and Paul. Mr. Obermeyer enjoys tennis and woodworking.

Ricardo Ampudia

President
AMTEK Group
Blvd. M. de Cervantes Saavedra # 394–37, Col. Irrigacion
Mexico City, Mexico 11500
(525) 580–4223
Fax: (525) 395–5974

3825

Business Information: AMTEK Group is formed by three companies: AMTEK, ECOBIOL Labs., and CPU. The Group specializes in quality and saving energy products, ecological and biodegradable products, engineering, and commercialization. As President, Mr. Ampudia oversees all aspects of the Company. He is responsible for day–to–day operations, business strategy, administration, and strategic planning. **Career Steps:** President, AMTEK Group (1982–Present); General Manager, SEPAC (1972). **Associations & Accomplishments:** President, Friendship Canada–Mexico Association; Institute of Electrical and Electronics Engineers. **Education:** Purdue University, M.S.M. (1992); McGill University, M.Eng. (1982); Anahuac University, Mexico, B.Eng. (1977); G.E. Control, Charlottesville. **Personal:** Married to Ena in 1978. Two children: Erika and Alexis. Mr. Ampudia enjoys music and playing the piano and guitar.

Thomas J. Pritchett

Principal Scientist
Beckman
2500 North Harbor Boulevard
Fullerton, CA 92634–3100
(714) 773–8022
Fax: (714) 773–8883
EMAIL: See Below

3825

Business Information: Beckman is a manufacturer and tester of scientific instruments and equipment. As Principal Scientist, Dr. Pritchett is responsible for strategic marketing, equipment development, analytical methods, and various administrative duties including technical consulting and data sheets. With the Company for three years, Dr. Pritchett also oversees all literature regarding the Company, and holds seminars discussing bio–pharmaceutical control. Internet users can reach him via: TJpritchett@ccgate.dp.beckman.com. **Career Steps:** Principal Scientist, Beckman (1993–Present); Manager, AD&QC, Cytel (1991–1993); Scientist II, Genetles Institute (1990–1991); Senior Scientist, Baxter Health Care (1989–1990). **Associations & Accomplishments:** Parenteral Drug Association; American Association of Pharmaceutical Scientists; Judge, Orange County Science; Published in Generic Engineering News, (January 1996). **Education:** University of California, Los Angeles, Ph.D. (1987); California State University, Chico, B.A. **Personal:** Married to Laureen Little in 1992. One child: Catherine Lynn. Dr. Pritchett enjoys rock climbing, hiking, camping, and helping his wife with a market campaign she conducts.

Georgia Hastings Sievwright

General Counsel – Secretary & Director of Corporate Relations
Hewlett Packard (Canada), Ltd.
5150 Spectrum Way
Mississauga, Ontario L4W 5G1
(903) 206–3297
Fax: (905) 206–4122
EMAIL: See Below

3825

Business Information: Hewlett–Packard (Canada), Ltd. designs, manufactures and services electronic products and systems for measurement, computation and communications worldwide. As General Counsel – Secretary & Director of Corporate Relations, Ms. Sievwright is responsible for general counsel and strategic management of law and corporate relations. Internet users can reach her via: GEORGIA_Sievwright@HPCanada–OM1.OM.HP.Com. **Career Steps:** General Counsel – Secretary & Director of Corporate Relations, Hewlett–Packard (Canada), Ltd. (1988–Present); IBM Canada, Ltd (1985–1988). **Associations & Accomplishments:** Law Society of Upper Canada; Canadian Bar Association; Canadian Corporate Counsel Association; Toronto Computer Lawyers Group; International Computer Law Association; Canadian Society of Corporate Secretaries; Legislative Committee, CMA; Board of Governors, The Bishop Strachan School, Information Technology Association of Canada. **Education:** Osgoode Hall Law School, LL.B. (1983); York University, B.A. with Honors (1980). **Personal:** Married to Johnnie–Mike Irving in 1992. One child: Campbell Graham Hastings. Ms. Sievwright enjoys skiing, golf, water sports, and cycling.

Paul R. Hemmes, Ph.D.

Vice President of Research & Strategic Planning
Environmental Test Systems
53438 Valley Springs Court
Granger, IN 46530
(219) 262–2060
Fax: (219) 262–2495
EMAIL: see below

3826

Business Information: Environmental Test Systems is a national manufacturer and distributor of environmental test kits, biosensors, and medical diagnostics; particularly focusing on water quality testing products, such as chlorine tests for swimming pools and salt and concrete analysis testing in Japan. Established in 1985, Environmental Test Systems reports annual revenue of $11 million and currently employs 80 people. With extensive expertise in biochemical research and academic studies, prior to entering the manufacturing industry, Dr. Hemmes joined Environmental Test Systems as Vice President of Operations in 1992. Currently serving as Vice President of Research & Strategic Planning, he is responsible for overall research and development of testing products. Career milestones include taking a sabbatical to the USSR for six months, in which he established an on–going relationship with Russian scientists. He can also be reached through the Internet at: 71172,2277@compuserve.com **Career Steps:** Environmental Test Systems: Vice President of Research & Strategic Planning (1994–Present), Vice President of Operations (1992–1993); Vice President of Manufacturing, Angenics Inc. (1988–1989); Director of Process Development, Miles Laboratories; Professor of Physical Chemistry, Rutgers University (11 years). **Associations & Accomplishments:** Former Vice President, Jaycees – Oldbridge, New Jersey; American Chemical Society (ACS); Microchemical Society; Associate Editor, Microchemical Journal; American Math Society; Exchange Visitor to USSR (1978 & 1981); Published in several publications, such as Journal of Physical Chemistry and Journal of Inorganic Chemistry; Holder of eight patents; Guest lecturer on matters dealing with the manufacturing of latex–based diagnostic products. **Education:** Polytechnic Institute of Brooklyn, Ph.D. (1976); Clarkson College, B.S. (1966). **Personal:** Two children: Paul C. and Jeffrey M. Hemmes. Dr. Hemmes enjoys travel and reading.

Mr. Dudley M. Boden

Instrument Systems Division
Minolta Corporation
101 Williams Drive
Ramsey, NJ 07446
(201) 818–3183
Fax: (201) 825–4374

3827

Business Information: Minolta Corporation, Instrument Systems Division is a wholly–owned entity of one of the world's leading photo–optical products manufacturers. The Division specializes in the manufacture and international distribution of industrial quality control and color measurement equipment, particularly spectrophotometers and color analyzers. As General Manager, Mr. Boden is responsible for the oversight of all Instrument Division operations corporate–wide in the Americas (North, South and Central). The Instrument Systems Division of Minolta Corporation was established in 1981 and employs 60 people at the Ramsey, New Jersey headquarters and throughout the United States. **Career Steps:** General Manager, Minolta Corporation, Instrument Systems Division (1994–Present); National Sales & Marketing Manager, Minolta Corporation (1991–1994); Technical Manager, Macbeth Division of Kollmorgen Corporation (1988–1991); Product Marketing Manager, Crosfield Electronics (1985–1988). **Associations & Accomplishments:** Society of Imaging Science and Technology; American Association of Textile Chemists and Colorists; Automated Imaging Association; Inter Society Color Council; Treasurer and Council Member, King of Kings Lutheran Church. **Education:** Long Island University, working towards MBA; Rochester Insitute of Technology, B.S. with honors in Photographic Science and Instrumentation (1978). **Personal:** Married to Karen in 1981. One child: Laura. Mr. Boden enjoys golf, canoeing and tennis.

Thomas A. Cellucci, Ph.D.

Senior Director
Newport Corporation
1791 Deere Avenue
Irvine, CA 92714
(714) 253–1688
Fax: (714) 253–1650
EMAIL: See Below

3827

Business Information: Newport Corporation is a manufacturer of laser/electro–optic equipment. Products include motion control, vibration control, optics, photonics, components and instruments. Established in 1969, Newport Corporation currently employs 400 people. A highly–motivated and proven performer, Dr. Cellucci has a broad base of experience in selling and marketing both high–end capital equipment and commodity–like products under both rapid growth and declining market conditions. Joining Newport Corporation in 1989 as Manager of the Eastern Regional Office, he has climbed the corporate ladder serving as Director of Worldwide Market Development in the Vibration Control Division to his present position as Senior Director and Member of the Executive Staff. Dr. Cellucci is directly responsible for the profit and loss of the Vibration Control Division which he developed and is currently implementing plans for Newport's entrance into semiconductor equipment market niches through major strategic alliances and new product development. He also works directly with CEO/Chairman of the Board on long–range strategic issues for the entire firm. His most recent accomplishment involves the growth of the Vibration Control business into industrial niche markets. He also led the integration of products from two major acquisitions, Micro–Controle and Klinger Scientific, into one consolidated worldwide offering. The Scientific and Laboratory business that Dr. Cellucci ran prior to his current role saw operating income grow by over 6 points in a two year period, making it the most profitable business at Newport today. His participation as a member of the Company's Quality Council also contributed to ISO–9002 certification for the Firm. **Career Steps:** Newport Corporation: Senior Director (1993–Present), Director (1991–1993), Director of Worldwide Market Development (1991–1993), Manager (1989–1990); Senior Sales Engineer, Coherent, Inc. (1987–1989); Associate Research Chemist, Shell Development Company (1984–1989); Professor of Physics and Laser/Electro–Optic Technology, Camden County College (1988–1990); Instructor in Department of Chemistry, University of Pennsylvania (1983–1984). **Associations & Accomplishments:** Board of Directors (1993), Laser Energetics, Inc.; Advisory Board (1989–1992), Princeton University's Advanced Photonics and Opto–electronics Materials Center; American National Standards Institute Board, (Chartered to write Standard Z136.5 for The Safe Use of Lasers in Educational Institutions) (1991–Present); American Chemical Society; American Institute of Chemists; American Physical Society; Optical Society of America; Laser Institute of America; President (1984), Phi Lambda Upsilon; American Management Association; Notary Public of New Jersey; Big Brothers/Big Sisters Program; Marquis' Who's Who in Science and Engirering (1993). **Education:** University of Pennsylvania, Ph.D. (1984); Rutgers University, M.B.A. (1991); Fordham University, B.S. (1980); University of Pennsylvania's Wharton School of Business, Executive Education Program (1994). **Personal:** Married to Marsha D. in 1987. One child: Bradford T. Dr. Cellucci enjoys anitque refinishing, cycling, and restoring scientific antiques.

Robert D. Claflin

President
Labsphere Inc.
P.O. Box 70
North Sutton, NH 03260–0070
(603) 927–4266
Fax: (603) 927–4694

3827

Business Information: Labsphere, Inc. is an international manufacturer of electro–optical products (instruments that measure light) for the aerospace, photographic, paint, lighting, and medical industries. Established in 1979, Labsphere, Inc. reports annual revenue of $10 million and currently employs 100 people. As President, Mr. Claflin is responsible for all aspects of operations. **Career Steps:** President, Labsphere Inc. (1989–Present); President, CCA Information Systems (1986–1989); President, Arcus Corporation (1984–1986); Vice President, Reeves Communications (1977–1982). **Associations & Accomplishments:** Served two years in the U.S. Navy as a Lieutenant, serving in Viet Nam, near Da Nang and Vung Tau. **Education:** Columbia University, M.B.A. (1972); Harvard University, B.S. (1968). **Personal:** Married to Kyri Watson Claflin in 1982. Two children: Thomas and Henry.

Patrick J. Novak

Engineering Manager
Meson Design and Development
4 Valley Street
Binghamton, NY 13905–2417
(607) 722–3776
Fax: (607) 722–3945

3827

Business Information: Meson Design and Development designs and manufactures fiber optic test equipment and monitoring systems. As Engineering Manager, Mr. Novak is responsible for the organization and control of existing product offerings, as well as all new product design and development. In addition, he assists in marketing. **Career Steps:** Engineering Manager, Meson Design and Development (1994–Present); Design Engineer, Control Concepts/Liebert (1990–1993); Design Engineer, C.E. Systems Inc. (1989–1990); Design Engineer, Unique Power Inc. (1983–1989). **Education:** Missouri Institute of Technology, B.S.E.E.T. (1979). **Personal:** Married to Maria in 1980. Two children: Jarad and Brandon. Mr. Novak enjoys personal computers, music, art, lacrosse, and fishing.

Dan Turner

Director of Sales
ITT Night Vision
7635 Plantation Road
Roanoke, VA 24019–3222
(540) 362–8000
Fax: (540) 362–4574

3827

Business Information: ITT Night Vision is a manufacturer of commercial night vision devices for the U.S. military, NATO Armies, law enforcement, outdoor sporting equipment (hunting, etc.) and marine (water) consumers. With eleven years experience in marketing, Mr. Turner joined ITT as a Marketing Manager in 1990. Appointed Director of Sales in 1993, he is responsible for all commercial sales activities, as well as supervising the managers of Marine Sales, Outdoor Consumer Sales, Law Enforcement Sales and all International Sales activities. **Career Steps:** ITT Night Vision: Director of Sales (1993–Present), Marketing Manager (1990–1993); Marketing Manager, Honeywell (1985–1990); Major, U.S. Army Infantry/Special Forces (1960–1985). **Associations & Accomplishments:** National Sheriffs Association; Special Forces Decade Association; National Marine Manufacturer's Association; 173d Airborne Association; Coach, Dixie Youth Softball – Fast–pitch. **Education:** William Carey College, B.S. in Business Administration (1973). **Personal:** Married to the former Barbara Gilbert of Hattiesburg, MS in 1974. Two rchildren: Niki and Katy. Mr. Turner enjoys flying, coaching youth softball, and outdoor yardwork.

Peter Galanis

Director of Quality Assurance
Dynisco Instruments
4 Commercial Street
Sharon, MA 02067–1653
(617) 784–8400
Fax: (617) 784–2902

3829

Business Information: Dynisco Instruments is a manufacturer and exporter of pressure transducers and sensors worldwide. Dynisco Instruments has two plants, one in the U.S. (Massachusetts) and one in Germany, in addition to sales offices around the world. As Director of Quality Assurance, Mr. Galanis led the effort to ISO9032 Certification of the Quality Management System, and is responsible for managing the quality, safety, and environmental compliance systems. **Career Steps:** Dynisco Instruments: Director of Quality Assurance (1992–Present), Purchasing Manager (1990–1992); Purchasing Manager, Temptronic Corporation (1983–1990); Purchasing Manager, Compo Industries (1981–1983). **Associations & Accomplishments:** National Association of Purchasing Managers; American Society of Quality Control; Certified Purchasing Manager. **Education:** Northeastern University, M.B.A. (1986). **Personal:** Married to Mary Ellen in 1979. Three children: Jonathan, Rebecca, and Jennifer. Mr. Galanis enjoys sports, reading, learning, and coaching his children's basketball team.

LUXTRON

Robert J. Goodman

President and Chief Executive Officer
Luxtron Corporation
2775 Northwestern Parkway
Santa Clara, CA 95051–0947
(408) 727–1600
Fax: (408) 727–1664

3829

Business Information: Luxtron Corporation, an ISO 9001 certified company and one of 17 companies owned by the British company Fairey Group, provides the development, manufacture and support of instrumentation utilized in fiber optic temperature sensing, semiconductor process monitoring, and other process measurement applications. Clientele include semiconductor, medical and microwave industries. Based in California, Luxtron also has regional offices in Chicago, Illinois, Texas, and Phoenix, Arizona. Joining Luxtron Corporation as President and Chief Executive Officer in 1995, Mr. Goodman is responsible for all aspects of operations, including administration, accounting, public relations, and strategic planning. **Career Steps:** President and Chief Executive Officer, Luxtron Corporation (1995–Present); Wyse Technology: General Manager, Amdek (1992–1995), Director of Channel Marketing (1987–1992); Texas Instruments: Account Manager (1985–1987), Marketing Manager (1983–1985), Manufacturing Manager (1980–1983). **Associations & Accomplishments:** Semiconductor Equipment and Materials International; American Management Association. **Education:** St. Edward's University, M.B.A. (1984); United States Military Academy – West Point, NY, B.S. in Engineering (1975). **Personal:** Married to Natalie in 1992. One child: Julie. Mr. Goodman enjoys sailing, art, and travel.

Richard L. Guild

Founder and President
SKC South, Inc.
P.O. Box 2016
Appomattox, VA 24522
(804) 352–7149
Fax: (804) 352–5754
EMAIL: See Below

3829

Business Information: SKC South, Inc., a subsidiary of SKC, Inc., is an international manufacturer and distributor of environmental air sampling instruments with 40 locations worldwide. Working with his father (founder of SKC, Inc.) throughout his high school and college education, upon graduation from college, Richard Guild founded the subsidiary SKC South, Inc. Serving as President and Chief Executive Officer he is responsible for all aspects of operations, including administration, finances, sales, public relations, marketing, and strategic planning. He also serves as President of the parent company. Internet users can reach him via: Rich-Guild@aol.com **Career Steps:** Founder, Owner, President, and Chief Executive Officer, SKC South, Inc. (Present); President, SKC, Inc. (Present). **Associations & Accomplishments:** American Industrial Hygiene Association: Carolina, Tennessee Valley and Central Virginia Sections; Editor, Virginia Canal and Navigators Society. **Education:** University of Pittsbugh. **Personal:** Married to Lynah C. in 1991. Two children: Andrew K. and Susan R. Mr. Guild enjoys being editor of non–profit publications and is a pioneer of Living History/Local Historical Society.

W.A. (Tony) Harmon

President
Polar Electro Inc.
2501 West Burbank Boulevard, Ste. 301
Burbank, CA 91505
(818) 563–2865
Fax: (818) 563–2867

3829

Business Information: Polar Electro Inc. is a manufacturer and marketer of heart rate monitors for use in exercise, training, and cardiac rehabilitation. The monitor is a two–piece system which is worn on a belt around the chest. The Company sells to independent contractors such as bike shops and sporting goods stores. The monitor is also available to all members of the Olympic team. As President, Mr. Harmon is responsible for the day–to–day operations of the Company, including administration, finance, public relations, and strategic planning. **Career Steps:** President, Polar Electro Inc. (1994–Present); President, Federated Foodservice, Inc. (1993–1994); Vice President of Sales, Sugar Foods Corporation (1989–1992). **Associations & Accomplishments:** Chairman, Fitness Products Council. **Education:** Pepperdine University, M.B.A. (1993); University of Tennessee, B.S. Degree in Industrial Management (1974). **Personal:** Married to Curti in 1974. Two children: Lanny and Brent. Mr. Harmon enjoys golf, running, and cycling.

Gary J. Johanning

General Manager
Geodetic Services, Inc.
1511 South Riverview Drive
Melbourne, FL 32901
(407) 724–6831
Fax: (407) 724–9253

3829

Business Information: Geodetic Services, Inc., established in 1977, is a manufacturer of industrial measuring instruments for tasks requiring a high degree of accuracy. The Company's products are used in airplanes, ships, aerospace technology, and the automotive industry. With estimated annual revenue of $2 million, the Company presently employs 15 people. As General Manager, Mr. Johanning oversees the day–to–day operations of the Company. He is responsible for developing and implementing sales and marketing techniques for new and existing products. Other responsibilities include oversight of personnel, technical support and customer service. Mr. Johanning is also responsible for production process supervision. **Career Steps:** Geodetic Services, Inc: General Manager (1993–Present), Engineer (1990–1993); Program Analyst, DBA Systems, Inc. (1986–1990). **Associations & Accomplishments:** American Society of Civil Engineers; American Society of Photogammetry and Remote Sensing; Chi Epsilon Civil Engineering Honor Society; Tau Beta Pi, All Engineering Honor Society. **Education:** University of Wisconsin, Madison, B.S.C.E.E. (1986). **Personal:** Married to Deborah C. in 1988. Mr. Johanning enjoys singing, golf, gardening, and animals.

Douglas C. Kapsa

Vice President of Sales and Marketing
Fastest, Inc.
2315 Hampden Avenue
St. Paul, MN 55114
(612) 645–6266
Fax: (612) 645–7390

3829

Business Information: Fastest Inc. is a dedicated manufacturer of productivity and quality improvement tools for pressure and vacuum testing. Customers of Fastest produce a wide range of products, from micro–medical components to heavy duty hydraulic equipment. Users of the Company's products have ensured the quality and performance of the products they make. Products used daily, from air conditioners to automobiles. As Vice President of Sales and Marketing, Mr. Kapsa oversees the sales and marketing operations of the Company, including administration, finances, and strategic planning. He also oversees research on new products and engineering development plans for new products. He works closely with the engineering personnel in the design, manufacture, patent, and market introduction of the product. **Career Steps:** Vice President of Sales and Marketing, Fastest, Inc. (1990–Present); National Sales Manager, Cherne Industries (1987–1990); Sales Manager, Vincent Brass and Aluminum (1982–1987). **Education:** Northwestern University, M.B.A. (1972); Loyola University, B.B.A. (1969). **Personal:** Mr. Kapsa enjoys rebuilding old, foreign cars.

Boris A. Krivopal

Director of Chemical Engineering
Tek–Scan, Inc.
307 West 1st Street
Boston, MA 02127
(617) 464–4500 Ext. 250
Fax: (617) 464–4266

3829

Business Information: Tek–Scan, Inc. develops and manufactures pressure sensor systems. The technology is used in diverse fields such as dental occlusion analysis, in–shoe foot pressure and gait analysis, orthopedic, surgical and other cromedical and athletic areas, aerospace, automotive and other industrial areas. As Director of Chemical Engineering, Dr. Krivopal heads a research team in all areas of development and formulation of pressure sensitive conductive dialectric inks and adhesives. His duties include administrative oversight of his team, planning for future projects, budget concerns, quality assurance of research data, and the reporting of team–finding to management. **Career Steps:** Director of Chemical Engineering, Tek–Scan, Inc. (1991–Present); Research and Development Engineer, Tra–con, Inc. (1988–1991). **Associations & Accomplishments:** American Chemical Society; The New York Academy of Sciences; American Association for the Advancement of Science; Published in approx. 80 Technical Publications (articles, reports, books and patents). **Education:** Institute of Material Science, Ph.D. (1970); M.S. in Mechanical and Material Engineering (1966); Center for Professional Advancement: Adhesives for Coatings, Industrial Ink Technology, Inherently Conductive Polymers, Electrically Conductive Composites, Applied Surface and Collard Chemistry. **Personal:** Married to Irene in 1969. Two children: Yakov and Mark. Dr. Krivopal enjoys music, tennis, and chess.

Thomas L. Mann

Information Resource Management (IRM) Supervisor
JAYCOR
1401 Spring Hill Road, #300
McLean, VA 22102–3008
(703) 397–9336
Fax: (703) 397–9300
EMail: See Below

3829

Business Information: JAYCOR is a technical services company, specializing in Business Process Re–engineering (BPR), Database design and development, research, and programming specialized applications. As Information Resource Management Supervisor for the Nuclear Test Personnel Review (NTPR) project, Mr. Mann is responsible for the NTPuerto Rico Local Area Network (LAN), all programming of database access programs, data administraiton, database administration, and data entry activities. The NTPuerto Rico program provides information on and to all military veterans who were exposed to nuclear radiation during the atmospheric nuclear tests from 1945 to 1963 and the occupation forces of Hiroshima and Nagasaki. Internet users can reach him via: mannt@va,jaycor.com or tlmann@nmaa.org **Career Steps:** Information Resource Management Supervisor, JAYCOR (1994–Present); Senior Analyst, General Research Corporation (1988–1993); Senior Programmer/Analyst, UNISYS (1986–1987); Senior Programmer/Analyst, SAIC (1984–1986); Physicist/Senior Programmer, US Army Ballistic Research Lab (1979–1984); Doctrine Specialist/Programmer, U.S. Army Ordnance & Chemical Center & School (1977–1979); U.S. Army Officer (1962–1976). **Associations & Accomplishments:** National Multimedia Association of America; Mid–Atlantic Oracle Users Group; Aircraft Owners & Pilots Association; National Rifle Association; North American Hunting Club. **Education:** Bowling Green State University, B.S. (1962); University of Delaware, advanced studies in Math and Computer Science; Johns Hopkins, advanced studies in Computer Science. **Personal:** Married to Carolyn in 1986. Three children: Robert, Kenneth, and Jeffrey. Mr. Mann enjoys flying, travel, and hunting.

Claribel Rodriguez Gonzalez, C.P.A.

Senior Financial Analyst
Hewlett Packard
P.O. Box 4048
Aguadilla, Puerto Rico 00605–4048
(787) 882–6285
Fax: (787) 882–6693

3829

Business Information: Hewlett Packard, the second largest computer company in the world, designs, manufactures and services electronic products and systems for measurement, computation and communications. Hewlett Packard specializes in five areas: Medical Services, Analytical, Computers, Personal Equipment, and Services Support. As Senior Financial Analyst, Mrs. Rodriguez Gonzalez oversees all business portfolios and financial aspects. She is also responsible for target and research marketing, auditing for ISO 9000, new products, and customer service. **Career Steps:** Hewlett Packard: Senior Financial Analyst (1990–Present), Accountant (1989–1990). **Associations & Accomplishments:** State Society of Certified Public Accountants of Puerto Rico. **Education:** University of Puerto Rico: M.B.A. (1989), B.S.B.A. (1986); Certified Public Accountant (1993). **Personal:** Married to William Guerra in 1993. Mrs. Rodriguez Gonzalez enjoys stamp collecting (worldwide), beach, watersports, reading, music, and handicrafts.

Carolyn Ray Strong

Director of Worldwide Customer Communications
Tektronix, Inc.
P.O. Box 500
Beaverton, OR 97077
(503) 627–3070
Fax: (503) 627–5593
EMAIL: See Below

3829

Business Information: Tektronix, Inc. is a portfolio of measurement, color printing, video, and networking businesses dedicated to applying technology excellence to customer challenges. Headquartered in Wilsonville, Oregon, Tektronix has presence in 23 countries outside of the United States. A management executive with Tektronix since 1973, Carolyn Strong was appointed to her current position in May of 1995. As Director of Worldwide Customer Communications involved with the Test and Measurement segment of the Company, she is primarily responsible for global marketing communications. Other duties involve assisting in corporate pre–sale communications, advertising, public relations, and trade show coordination. Carolyn also coordinates all customer documentation, providing manuals for the over 1,500 product lines offered, as well as coordinates all global programs, Internet site updates, catalogs, and customer magazines. Internet users can reach her via: carolyn.ray.strong@tek.com. **Career Steps:** Tektronix, Inc.: Director of Worldwide Customer Communications (1995–Present), Customer Documentation Manager (1986–1995), Computer Training Manager (1985–1986); Technical Publications Manager (1979–1985); Assistant Adjunct Professor, University of Oregon. **Associations & Accomplishments:** Chairman of the Board, 1st Technology Federal Credit Union; Senior Member, Society for Technical Communications; Association of Computer Machinery; SIGDOC. **Education:** University of Oregon, M.S. (1992); Whitworth College, B.A. **Personal:** Ms. Strong enjoys collecting Coca–Cola memorabilia, and the study and support of autism.

Ralph D. Taylor

Director of Engineering
DIT–MCO International
5612 Brighton Terrace
Kansas City, MO 64130
(816) 444–1111
Fax: Please mail or call
EMAIL: See Below

3829

Business Information: DIT–MCO International is an international manufacturer of automatic test equipment (i.e., wire analyzers). As Director of Engineering, Ralph Taylor is responsible for the direction of the research and development engineering operations, and reporting to the Company's President. Internet users can reach him via: rtaylor@ditmco.com. **Career Steps:** Director of Engineering, DIT–MCO International (1974–Present); Senior Engineer, Allied Signal (1968–1974). **Associations & Accomplishments:** Institute of Electronics and Electrical Engineers; Beta Gamma Sigma; Kappa Kappa Psi. **Education:** University of Missouri at Kansas City, M.B.A.; University of Missouri at Columbia, M.S.E.E. (1972); University of Missouri at Rolla, B.S.E.E. (1968). **Personal:** Married to Cynthia C. in 1991. Four children: Jennifer Lee, Nathan Ralph, Rachel Ann, and Scott Mathew. Mr. Taylor enjoys genealogy and coins.

Fernando G. Valenzuela

Financial Administrator
Hewlett–Packard
5200 Blue Lagoon Drive, Suite 950
Miami, FL 33126–2089
(305) 267–4246
Fax: (305) 267–4635

3829

Business Information: Hewlett–Packard, the second largest company in the world, designs, manufactures and services electronic products and systems for measurement, computation and communications. Hewlett–Packard specializes in five areas: Medical Services, Analytical, Computers, Personal Equipment, and Services Support. Joining Hewlett–Packard in 1990, Mr. Valenzuela was appointed as Financial Administrator in 1993. He is responsible for all financial and administration management, as well as maintenance for services and development of procedures for the Latin America. **Career Steps:** Hewlett–Packard: Financial Administrator (1993–Present), Process Manager (1992–1993), Information Technology Manager (1990–1992); Professional Soccer Player in Mexico. **Education:** University of Miami, M.B.A. (1995); Universidad Iberoamericana, B.S. in Computer Science; Colegio de Graduados en Alta Direccion, M.B.A. in Management. **Personal:** Married to Marina in 1991. One child: Santiago.

Mr. Peter R. Escobal
President
Aquatronics/Filtronics
1620 Beacon Place
Oxnard, CA 93033
(805) 486-2614
Fax: (805) 486-2491

3840

Business Information: Aquatronics/Filtronics is a design manufacturer of pharmaceutical and medical related products utilized in the pet industry and aquaculture (e.g., magnetic drive pumps, ultraviolet sterilizers). Established in 1969, Aquatronics/Filtronics employs 40 persons. As President for the Company, Mr. Escobal is responsible for all aspects of operations to include product design and marketing. **Career Steps:** President, Aquatronics/Filtronics (1987–Present); Technical Staff, Aerospace Corporation (1985–1987); Senior Engineer, Jet Propulsion Labs (1975–1985); Assistant Department Manager, TRW Systems Group (1968–1975). **Associations & Accomplishments:** Author, Methods of Orbit Determination (1965), and Methods of Astrodynamics (1969), John Wiley Publishers; Winner, Chance Vought Memorial Prize for Airplane Design, New York University (1960). **Education:** University of California–Los Angeles, M.S. (1960); New York University, B.A.E. and B.A. **Personal:** Married since 1967 to Gayle. Two children: Don and Ramon Escobal. Mr. Escobal enjoys writing and music.

Koichi Abe, Ph.D.
Vice President of Technology
JDS–FITEL, Inc.
570 W. Hunt Club Road
Nepean, Ontario K2G 5W8
(613) 727-1304
Fax: (613) 727-8284
EMAIL: See Below

3841

Business Information: JDS–FITEL, Inc. is a Canadian-based, high–technology company that specializes in the manufacture and distribution of a broad range of fiber optic components, instruments, and installation products for the communications industry. Regional in scope, the Company has four locations throughout Canada. Established in 1984, JDS–FITEL, Inc. employs 700 people and has estimated annual revenue of $80 million. As Vice President of Technology, Mr. Abe oversees management of research and development projects, and intellectual properties. Additional duties include strategic planning and direct supervision of a fifty person staff. Internet users can reach him via: koichi_abe@jdsfitel.com. **Career Steps:** Vice President of Technology, JDS–FITEL, Inc. (1992–Present); Senior Researcher, National Optics Institute (1988–1992); Consultant, Nokia Cables (1987); Director of Technology, Northern Telecom (1982–1987). **Associations & Accomplishments:** Optical Society of America; Author of fifty published papers. **Education:** University of Tokyo, Japan, Ph.d. (1971). **Personal:** Married to Shelly R. Richards in 1992. Dr. Abe enjoys outdoors, skiing (cross country and downhill), and biking.

Nelson Allan, Ph.D.
Director of Engineering
KMC Systems, Inc.
220 Daniel Webster Highway
Merrimack, NH 03054-4809
(603) 886-7558
Fax: (603) 594-7010
EMAIL: See Below

3841

Business Information: KMC Systems, a division of Kollsman, Inc. since January of 1996, manufactures and designs medical devices for distribution throughout the world. After twenty–five years as a Software Engineer for General Electric, Dr. Allan joined Kollsman in 1987 as an Avionics System Scientist. In 1996, he was named Director of Engineering for KMC Systems and is presently responsible for all engineering activities. Internet users can reach Dr. Allan via: nallan@Kollsman.com **Career Steps:** Director of Engineering, KMC Sys-

tems, Inc. (1996–Present); Scientist Avionics Systems, Kollsman (1987–1990); General Electric: Manager, Software Engineering (1980–1987), Manager, Advanced Engineering (1978–1980). **Associations & Accomplishments:** Knights of Columbus; Kiwanis; Sigma Pi Sigma. **Education:** Polytechnic Institute of Brooklyn, Ph.D., in Systems (1972); University of Maine, B.S. in Engineering Physics (1961). **Personal:** Married to Patricia in 1960. Five children: John, Joseph, Jackie, Jennifer, and Jessica. Dr. Allan is a commercial pilot instructor and loves to fly.

Vivek Bhargava
International Market Manager
Baxter Healthcare Corporation
1500 Waukegan Road Boulevard K
McGaw Park, IL 60085-6728
(847) 578-2379
Fax: (847) 689-2715

3841

Business Information: Baxter Health Care is a wholly–owned subsidiary of Baxter International, one of the world's leading medical products manufacturers and distributors. Based in Deerfield, Illinois, the parent company has two product groups — Medical Specialties (products for blood processing, dialysis systems, cardiovascular devices), and Medical/Laboratory Products and Distribution (anesthetics, surgery supplies and products, intravenous systems, sales and distribution services). Baxter International markets over 200,000 products in 100 countries, with over 30,000 items being manufactured through Health Care's Surgical Group alone. Serving in marketing management positions for Baxter since 1993, Vivek Bhargava was appointed as International Market Manager in June of 1994. In this capacity, he directs all international sales and marketing strategies for the operating room products unit corporate–wide. **Career Steps:** Baxter Healthcare Corporation: International Marketing Manager (1994–Present), Associate Product Manager (1993–1994); Consultant, International Business Center (1992–1993). **Associations & Accomplishments:** American Marketing Association; Round Table. **Education:** Michigan State, M.S. in International Business (1993); Virginia Tech, M.B.A.; Panjah Engineering College, B.S. in Industrial Engineering. **Personal:** Married to Renu Anne in 1993. Mr. Bhargava enjoys travel, hiking and cultural interaction.

Dean A.J. Coates

Treasurer/Controller
BOC Canada, Ltd.
5975 Falbourne Street, Unit 2
Mississauga, Ontario L5R 3W6
(905) 501-2533
Fax: (905) 501-1717

3841

Business Information: BOC Canada, Ltd. is a manufacturer and distributor of industrial and medical gases and equipment. The Company distributes equipment (anaesthesia machines, dialysis units, respirators, etc.) throughout Canada for residences and small and medium–sized companies. As Treasurer/Controller, Mr. Coates is responsible for financial and management accounting and reporting, tax, treasury, internal and external auditing of retail areas and production facilities, and all aspects of treasury. **Career Steps:** BOC Canada, Ltd.: Treasurer/Controller (1989–Present), Corporate Accountant (1987–1989); Senior Auditor, KPMG (1987). **Associations & Accomplishments:** Canadian Institute of Chartered Accountants; Ontario Institute of Chartered Accountants. **Education:** Wifrid Laurier University, B.A. in Economics (1983). **Personal:** Married to Hilary in 1984. Mr. Coates enjoys most sports.

Danna C. Cochran
National Sales Manager
Therapy Concepts, Inc.
1245 South Cleveland Massillon Road, Suite 220
Akron, OH 44321
(216) 666-9109
Fax: (216) 666-8654
EMAIL: See Below

3841

Business Information: Therapy Concepts, Inc. is a medical manufacturer of support services and orthotics, specializing in equipment for the long term health care markets (i.e., nursing homes, home care agencies). The Corporation has two divisions: Distribution – to dealers that sell to customers, and Retail – marketing directly to home care agencies and nursing homes. Hired as the first Sales Representative by Therapy Concepts, Inc. in January 1991, Ms. Cochran was appointed National Sales Manager in 1995. She is responsible for the overall operations of the Retail Division, including technology, operations, personnel, sales, and customer service, in addition to overseeing 56 employees nationally. Internet users can

reach her via: danna2@IX.netcom.com **Career Steps:** Therapy Concepts, Inc.: National Sales Manager (1995–Present), Sales Representative (1991–1995); Marketing Manager, Circle Health (1990–1991); Sales, The Mediscus Group (1989–1990). **Associations & Accomplishments:** National Association of Female Executives; United States Tennis Association; Wound Ostomy and Continence Nurses Society. **Education:** Akron University, B.S.B.A. in Marketing (1994); Univ. of Akron. **Personal:** Ms. Cochran enjoys tennis, skiing, and photography.

John B. Collins
Vice President of Technology
Xylum Corporation
670 White Plains Road
Scarsdale, NY 10583
(914) 725-0606
Fax: (914) 725-1158
E MAIL: See Below

3841

Business Information: Xylum Corporation, established in 1988, is a manufacturer of medical instruments and blood analyzers. The Company presently employs 34 people. As Vice President of Technology, Mr. Collins oversees the research, engineering, and development of new, as well as the redevelopment of existing, products. Internet users can reach him via: WeeThree@aol.com. **Career Steps:** Vice President of Technology, Xylum Corporation (1995–Present); Vice President of Research and Development, Kollmorgan, Inc. (1992–1995); Engineering Manager, Perkin–Elmor (1983–1992); Senior Systems Analyst, American Cyanamid (1977–1983). **Associations & Accomplishments:** Association of Comp. Machinery; Institute of Electronics and Electrical Engineers; American Chemical Society. **Education:** New York University, M.S. C.S. (1983); Princeton University, Ph.D. Chemistry; Holy Cross, B.A. Chemistry. **Personal:** Married to Sylva in 1980. Three children: Susan, John Jr., and Michael. Mr. Collins enjoys boating and photography.

John E. Connors
Director of Corporate Human Resources
Becton Dickinson and Company
1 Becton Drive
Franklin Lakes, NJ 07417
(201) 847-6715
Fax: (201) 587-0089
EMAIL: See Below

3841

Business Information: Becton Dickinson and Company is a $3 billion, publicly–traded firm providing medical diagnosis technology and medical devices such as microbiological diagnostic reagents, microbial collection products, and microbiological mini–environment products. As Director of Corporate Human Resources, Mr. Connors directs all phases of personnel management. He encompasses organizational effectiveness, human resource flow, and compensation of benefits. His duties include personnel recruitment and evaluation, benefits, payroll and compensations, and ensuring compliance with all labor laws. Internet users can reach him via: Jecnj@aol.com. **Career Steps:** Director of Corporate Human Resources, Becton Dickinson and Company (1991–Present); T.J. Lipton, Inc: Manager, Corporate Human Resources (1989–1991), Manager, Human Resources (1981–1989). **Associations & Accomplishments:** Corporate Leadership Council; Society of Human Resource Management. **Education:** Avila College, M.B.A. (1988); University of Kansas, B.S. **Personal:** Mr. Connors enjoys sports, and volunteer work/activities.

J. Francisco Cuesta Z.

General Manager
Farquemic
Casilla: 17–11–06477 CCI
Quito, Ecuador
(593) 246-0034
Fax: (593) 246-0034

3841

Business Information: Farquemic is a representative of three German companies which manufacture, export, and market medical supplies (surgical instruments). Products are imported to Ecuador and sold by Farquemic to hospitals (75%) and private practices (25%). As General Manager and First Partner, Mr. Cuesta Z. is responsible for all aspects of operations, including day–to–day activities, administration, finances, sales, public relations, accounting, marketing, and strategic planning. Ninety percent of the business is owned by himself, his wife, and children, with the remaining ten percent owned by his brother–in–law. **Career Steps:** General Manager and First Partner, Farquemic (1981–Present); B. Braun Melsungen – Ecuador: Regional Manager (1975–1981), Marketing Director (1981–1986); Regional Sales Representative,

Upjohn Laboratories (1972–1975). **Associations & Accomplishments:** Executive Association of Guayaquil; Alemana Chamber of Commerce; Espanola Chamber of Commerce; Municipal Tennis Club – Quito. **Education:** Universidad Central de Venezuela, Business Administration (1972); Centro Internacional de Formacion Empresarial Barcelona – Espana (1978); I.N.C.A.E. San Jose – Costa Rica (1981); Attended different courses and seminaries dictated in Germany, Spain, Brazil, and Ecuador. **Personal:** Married to Maritza Bustamante in 1993. Three children: Juan Martin, Nicolas Alejandro, and Maria Jose Cuesta. Mr. Cuesta Z. enjoys tennis, traveling, and chess.

Thomas A. Cycyota
Vice President of Marketing
New Dimensions in Medicine
3040 East River Road
Dayton, OH 45439
(513) 294–1767 Ext: 465
Fax: (513) 294–8363

3841

Business Information: New Dimensions in Medicine is a manufacturer of disposable medical devices. Joining New Dimensions in Medicine as Director of Marketing in 1991, Mr. Cycyota was then appointed as Group Director of Marketing in 1992. Currently serving as Vice President of Marketing (since 1994), he reports to the President of Marketing regarding the marketing activities of the Company. **Career Steps:** New Dimensions in Medicine: Vice President of Marketing (1994–Present), Group Director of Marketing (1992–1994), Director of Marketing (1991–1992); Product Manager, Kendall Healthcare Products (1989–1991). **Education:** Loyola University – Chicago, M.B.A. (1988); University of Illinois – Urbana, B.S. in Biology (1980). **Personal:** Married to Cyndy in 1985. Mr. Cycyota enjoys reading, exercising, and children's activities.

Dr. Eido Digati
Chief Executive Officer
Schiapparelli Biosystems, Inc.
368 Passaic Avenue
Fairfield, NJ 07004
(201) 882–8630
Fax: Please mail or call

3841

Business Information: Schiapparelli Biosystems, Inc. is a medical diagnostics company. Established in 1988, Schiapparelli Biosystems, Inc. presently employs 178 people. As Chief Executive Officer, Dr. Digati is responsible for all aspects of Company operations, as well as financial matters. **Career Steps:** Schiapparelli Biosystems, Inc.: Chief Executive Officer (1991–Present), President (1987–1991); President, Business Technology Advisors, Inc. (BTA) (1979–1987); Vice President, CTIP – Engineering Company (1973–1978); Assistant to the President, ESSO Italiana (1965–1972). **Associations & Accomplishments:** (GEI) Gruppo Esponenti Italiani. **Education:** University of Rome – Italy, Ph.D. in Economics (1965); Harvard Business School, Executive Program (1969); Northwestern University, International Business Program (1970).

Prof. dr. Margaret Furay Fay
Global Medical Affairs Director
Regent Hospital Products, Ltd.
80 International Drive
Greenville, SC 29615
(864) 234–9516
Fax: (864) 234–9518
EMail: See Below

3841

Business Information: Regent Hospital Products, Ltd. is the world's largest manufacturer of condoms and surgical gloves. A division of London International plc., Regent is a medical device company. With over 30 years of Clinical Experience, Dr. Fay has served as Director of Surgery, PACU, department of anesthesia, surgical intensive care, burn units, and cardiac catheterization laboratories. Dr. Fay founded a medical marketing, research, and communications firm in 1980. Presently, she serves as the Global Director of Medical Affairs for Regent Hospital Products, Ltd. She is responsible for medical research and the overall direction of medical affairs. Dr. Fay is Research Professor of Surgery at the University of Virginia School of Medicine, Department of Plastic Surgery, Charlottesville. She is considered an international expert in the field of latex allergy and outcomes research. Internet users can reach her via: drmFay@ix.netcom.com. **Career Steps:** Global Medical Affairs Director, Regent Medical Corporation (1990–Present); Chief Executive Officer, AMCI Corporation (1989–1990); Chief Executive Officer/President, Five Points Communications Corporation (1981–1988); Director OR, SICU, PACU, and Anesthesia, Hennepin City Medical Center (1980–1981). **Associations & Accomplishments:** American Association of University Women; International Society of Contact Dermatology; International Surgical Society; Society

for Hospital Epidemiology in America; American Association for the Advancement of Science; Creighton University Alumnae Association; American Society for Medical Staff Affairs; Nurse Consultants Association; Association of Operating groom Nurses; American Women business Owners Association; National Science Foundation; European Panel of Infection Control in Dentistry; Who's Who in American Nursing; Who's Who in U.S. Executives; Who's Who Personalities of America; Who's Who in American Women; Who's Who in Professional and Executive Women; Outstanding Young Women of America; Numerous publications. **Education:** University of Minnesota, Doctor of Philosophy (1990); Columbia Pacific University: Master in Psychology, magna cum laude (1980), Bachelor of Arts in Business Administration (1978); Creighton University – St. Catherine's Hospital, Nursing Diploma (1960).

Gerald K. Flakas
Manager of Engineering
Fischer Imaging
2301 Windsor Court
Addison, IL 60101
(630) 627–0900
Fax: (630) 628–3120

3841

Business Information: Fischer Imaging designs, manufactures, and distributes medical x–ray equipment to hospitals and other facilities. Supporting clients worldwide, the Company has two locations in Denver, Colorado and Addison, Illinois. Established in 1920, the Company employs 450 people, and has estimated annual revenue of $80 million. As Manager of Engineering, Mr. Flakas oversees all phases of the engineering department. He supervises sixteen engineers and a support staff. Mr. Flakas also designs x–ray equipment for the Company. With estimated annual sales of $80 million, Fischer Imaging currently employs 450 people. **Career Steps:** Fischer Imaging: Manager of Engineering (1996–Present), Senior Engineer (1991–1996); General Electric Company: Senior Engineer (1985–1990), Project Engineer (1978–1985). **Associations & Accomplishments:** Institute of Electronic and Electrical Engineers. **Education:** University of Wisconsin: M.S.E.E. (1968), B.S.E.E. (1966). **Personal:** Married to Esther in 1967. Two children: Polly and Alexander. Mr. Flakas enjoys curling, golf, and antiques.

A. Michael Foster

Worldwide Demand and Inventory Manager
ETHICON ENDO–SURGERY, Inc. a Johnson & Johnson Company
577 Belle Meade Farm Drive
Loveland, OH 45140
(513) 786–7305
Fax: (513) 483–8755

3841

Business Information: ETHICON ENDO–SURGERY, Inc., a Johnson and Johnson company, is a manufacturer and worldwide distributor of Endoscopic and Mechanical surgical products. In his current position, Mr. Foster is responsible for Worldwide materials management, with emphasis on Inventory Management, Demand and Production Planning. **Career Steps:** ETHICON ENDO–SURGERY Inc. a Johnson and Johnson company, Worldwide Demand and Inventory Manager (1994–Present); Digital Equipment Corporation (Storage Division): Corporate Distribution, Customer Service and Materials Manager (1990–1994), Plant Distribution Manager (1988–1990). **Associations & Accomplishments:** Certified Production and Inventory Manager (CPIM) from APICS; Board Member, YMCA (1993); Board Certified Production and Inventory Manager (CPIM) fir APICS; Board Member, YMCA (1993); Board Member, Christ Emanuel Christian Academy, United Way (1983); Recognized by Federal Express for an enhanced International Just–in–Time Logistics Model; Recognized by Boeing aircraft for Inventory Process Velocity and High Performance Work Team Models; Exceeded benchmarked materials management categories in all industries. **Education:** Florida Institute of Technology, M.S. (1980); Western Illinois University, B.S. (1975). **Personal:** Married to Cathy in 1977. Three children: Shannon Rae, Kasi Marie, and Mychal Ryan. Mr. Foster enjoys reading, fishing, tennis, jogging, and spending time with his family.

Lloyd W. Gaedke
Director of Quality and Documentation Systems
Becton Dickinson
2350 Qume Drive
San Jose, CA 95131–1812
(408) 954–4150
Fax: (408) 577–1409

3841

Business Information: Becton Dickinson is a manufacturer of medical devices and supplies for hospitals, physicians, clinics, and the home health care industry. As Director of Quality and Documentation Systems, Mr. Gaedke is responsible for the quality systems effort. He is responsible for maintaining continuous ISO 9000 registration and is the management representative with BSI. He oversees the system, making sure it meets Company regulations and the standards set by FDA and ISO. **Career Steps:** Becton Dickinson: Director of Quality and Documentation Systems (1995–Present), Director of Regulatory Affairs and Quality Management (1994–1995), Director of Regulatory Affairs and Quality Assurance (1993–1994), Manager of Quality Assurance (1989–1993). **Associations & Accomplishments:** Regulatory Affairs Professional Society; American Society for Quality Control. **Education:** University of North Texas, B.A. (1973). **Personal:** Married to Joan in 1968. One child: Tobin. Mr. Gaedke enjoys bicycling and nature photography.

Fernando J. Gonzalez Rodriguez
Production Supervisor/Manufacturing Engineer
St. Jude Medical
P.O. Box 998
Caguas, Puerto Rico 00726–0998
(787) 746–1111
Fax: (787) 746–5272

3841

Business Information: St. Jude Medical is a manufacturer of mechanical heart valves. The Company distributes to hospitals throughout Puerto Rico. As Production Supervisor, Mr. Gonzalez Rodriguez is responsible for production facilitation and manufacturing engineering. He also coordinates quality systems and training. **Career Steps:** St. Jude Medical: Production Supervisor (1994–Present), Planner/Buyer (1992–1994); Planner/Buyer, Baxter Pharmasul (1990–1992). **Associations & Accomplishments:** American Production and Inventory Control Society. **Education:** University of Puerto Rico – Mayaguez Campus, B.S.I.E. (1987); Currently attending Universidad Del Turabo for Masters Degree in Materials Management. **Personal:** Married to Carlota Asencio in 1992. One child: Carla Giselle. Mr. Gonzalez Rodriguez enjoys plastic model building, computers, and music.

Kathy Hohenberger
Regional Director of Sales
Hill–Rom Company
12303 Delta Drive
Taylor, MI 48180
(313) 946–2055
Fax: (313) 945–2015

3841

Business Information: Hill–Rom Company is a medical capital equipment manufacturer and sales organization. Headquartered in Indiana, the Company is international in scope, with several locations in the U.S. and overseas. As Regional Director of Sales, Ms. Hohenberger oversees customer relations, marketing, and strategic planning. She is also responsible for new employee training, personnel management and performance reviews, profitability of the region, and directly supervises a staff of sixteen. Additionally, She serves as Company mentor for the succession planning for management. **Career Steps:** Regional Director of Sales, Hill–Rom Company (1994–Present); Support Systems International: Regional Manager (1993–1994), Sales Representative (1987–1993). **Associations & Accomplishments:** National Association of Female Executives; Active in International Exchange Program for foreign students. **Education:** Northern Michigan University, B.S.N. (1984). **Personal:** Married to Ronald in 1987. Two children: John and Megan. Ms. Hohenberger enjoys tennis, aerobic exercise, and reading.

Douglas P. Keys
Director of Global Logistics Management
Baxter, Cardiovascular
17221 Red Hill Avenue
Irvine, CA 92714
(714) 250–2462
Fax: (714) 756–4020

3841

Business Information: Baxter, Cardiovascular provides third stage cardiovascular medical devices (i.e. catheters, heart valves and rings, pressure monitoring and blood oxygenation instruments) to the healthcare industry. Baxter is comprised of four groups, Cardiovascular, Renal, Biotech, and I.V. Systems, the Company is international in scope, with branches worldwide. Established in 1931, the Company employs 60,000 people corporate-wide, with the Irvine division reporting an estimated annual revenue of $800 million. As Director of Global Logistics Management, Mr. Keys oversees U.S. and international customer service, distribution and planning. He is also responsible for materials management, and is currently involved in a project involving a divestiture of Baxter's U.S. hospital distribution business into a seperate corporation, allegiance. **Career Steps:** Baxter: Director of Global Logistics Management, Cardiovascular Group (1995–Present), Director of Logistics, Biotech Group, Europe (1992–1995), Project Manager, Fenwal Division (1990–1992), Materials Planning Manager, Fenwal Division (1988–1990). **Associations & Accomplishments:** Council of Logistics Management. **Education:** Webster University, M.B.A. (1991); Penn State University, B.S. in Logistics (1984); APICS Certification, CPIM. **Personal:** Married to Linda in 1988. Mr. Keys enjoys cycling and being a wine enthusiast, a hobby he picked up while living in Belgium.

Richard C. Kindberg
Director of Marketing, Sales Development & International Sales
Richard Allan Medical
8850 M 89
Richland, MI 49083
(616) 629–5811 Ext. 230
Fax: (616) 629–9654

3841

Business Information: Richard Allan Medical manufactures, sells, and markets surgical instruments for both minimally invasive and traditional open procedures. As Director of Marketing, Sales Development & International Sales, Mr. Kindberg is responsible for all marketing–related activities, project development, clinician interface, and oversight of sales personnel training and development. **Career Steps:** Director of Marketing, Sales Development & International Sales, Richard Allan Medical (1995–Present); Director of New Product Development, Focal, Inc. (1994–1995); Director of Marketing and Professional Education, Ethicon Endo–Surgery – Johnson & Johnson (1983–1994). **Education:** Bowling Green State University, B.S.B.A. in Marketing, Selling, and Sales Management (1979). **Personal:** Married to Michele P. in 1994. Three children: Elizabeth, Ashley, and Brittany. Mr. Kindberg enjoys golf, reading, cooking, jogging, travel, and rollerblading.

Bernd J. Larsen
Director
Maersk Medical (USA)
26133 U.S. Highway 19 North, Suite 202
Clearwater, FL 34623–2019
(813) 791–8303
Fax: (813) 791–6266

3841

Business Information: Headquartered in Denmark, Maersk Medical is the world's largest manufacturer of such medical products as PVC catheters and urology bags, and is a major manufacturer of other devices as foley catheters, scalpels and blades, and calcium alginate wound dressings. As Director of the United States liaison office in Clearwater, Florida, Mr. Larsen supervises all North American corporate activities, including product distribution, client interface, and budget management. **Career Steps:** Pharma–Plast/Maersk Medical: Director (USA) (1985–Present), Director (Germany) (1980–1986); Regional Export Manager, Modulex (Denmark) (1978–1980). **Associations & Accomplishments:** Healthcare Manufacturers' Marketing Council. **Education:** Arizona Graduate School of International Management, Master's in International Management (1977); Arizona State University, B.A. in Political Science (1976). **Personal:** Married to Marianne in 1973. Five children: Eva, Karina, Brita, Eric, and Aaron.

Peter Lawes, Ph.D.
Vice President of Quality Assurance, Technical and Regulatory Aff
Pfizer Hospital Products, Ltd.
Ash House, Fairfield Ave.
Staines, England TW18 4AN
44–1784444612
Fax: 44–1784444500

3841

Business Information: Pfizer Hospital Products, Ltd., a division of Howmedica International, Inc., is an international manufacturer, distributor, and marketer of orthopaedic implants and associated surgical instruments, in addition to conducting research and designing products. As Vice President of Quality Assurance, Technical and Regulatory Affairs, Dr. Lawes is responsible for design and development management of products, as well as serving as a decision maker, ensuring compliance of quality assurance, regulatory affairs, and

clinical trials management. He also conducts "hands on" product design and testing. **Career Steps:** Vice President of Assurance, Technical and Regulatory Affairs, Howmedica International, a division of Pfizer Hospital Products Group Ltd (1989–Present); Howmedica International, Inc.: Vice President of Quality, Regulatory Affairs & Technical (1987–1989), Director of Product Development (1985–1987), Director of Quality Assurance & Regulatory Affairs – Ireland Division (1981–1984). **Associations & Accomplishments:** Vice Chair, Bath (University) Institute of Medical Engineering (UK); President and Chair, International Association of Medical Prosthesis Manufacturers; Institution of Mechanical Engineers (UK): Sustaining Member, Committee Member – Engineering in Medicine Committee; European Orthopaedic Research Society; Biological Engineering Society (UK). **Education:** University of Strathclyde, Ph.D. in Bio–Engineering (1982); Loughborough University of Technology, M.Tech. in Engineering Design – United Kingdom (1973); University of Leicester, B.Sc. in Special Physics – United Kingdom (1969); Irish Management Institute – Dublin, Ireland, I.M.I. Diploma in Management (1983). **Personal:** Married to Hilary in 1970. Five children: Kate, Frances, Jo Anne, Daniel and Fionnuala. Dr. Lawes enjoys playing the guitar, piano, music, chess, and spending time with his family.

Charles H. Lawyer
Director of Technical & Professional Affairs
Howmedica
359 Veterans Blvd.
Rutherford, NJ 07070
(201) 507–7796
Fax: (201) 507–7254

3841

Business Information: Howmedica specializes in the design and manufacture of orthopaedic implants. The Company also distributes the implants to hospitals throughout the United States. As Director of Technical & Professional Affairs, Mr. Lawyer coordinates and implements compliance with European regulations, and implements labeling upgrades. **Career Steps:** Howmedica: Director of Technical & Professional Affairs (1993–Present), Director of Quality Assurance (1987–1993), Assistant Director of Quality Assurance (1982–1987). **Associations & Accomplishments:** American Society of Technical Manager; American Society of Mechanical Engineers; RAPS; Orthopaedic Surgical Manufacturers Association; Director, Meadowlands YMCA; US Delegate to ISO. **Education:** New Jersey Institute of Technology, M.S.M.E. (1976). **Personal:** Married to Dolores in 1962. Three children: Jeffrey, Catherine, and Susan. Mr. Lawyer enjoys golf, gardening, and bicycling.

Joseph Librizzi, Ph.D.

President
Misonix, Inc.
1938 New Highway
Farmingdale, NY 11735
(516) 694–9555
Fax: (516) 694–9412

3841

Business Information: Misonix, Inc. is a developer and manufacturer of ultrasonic research and medical devices and environmental safety equipment. As President, Dr. Librizzi is responsible for all management and operations of the Company. **Career Steps:** President, Misonix, Inc. (1972–Present); Research Engineer, Grumman Aerospace (1970–1972); Research Associate, Polytechnic Institute of Brooklyn (1965–1970). **Associations & Accomplishments:** Semiconductor Safety Association. **Education:** Polytechnic Institute of Brooklyn: Ph.D. (1970), M.S. in Aerospace, B.Ae.E. **Personal:** Married to Bonnie in 1993. Four children: Stephen, Teresa, Gina, and Anthony. Dr. Librizzi enjoys auto racing and golf.

James J. Lotze

Vice President of Engineering
ETHICON, Inc.
Route 22
Somerville, NJ 08876
(908) 218–2959
Fax: (908) 218–3518

3841

Business Information: ETHICON, Inc., a Division of Johnson & Johnson, is a manufacturer of medical instruments used in surgical procedures. Products include sutures, needles and other surgical devices for medical use. International in scope, ETHICON, Inc. has fourteen locations nationally (Illinois, New Jersey, Georgia, Texas, Puerto Rico) and internationally (India, Mexico, Italy, Japan, China, Brazil, Scotland, France, Ger-

many). Established in 1945, ETHICON currently employs approximately 5,000 people domestically. A twenty–three year veteran of the Company, Mr. Lotze joined ETHICON, Inc. in 1973. Appointed as Vice President of Engineering in 1990, he is responsible for all engineering: electrical and mechanical engineering, computer systems e.g. CAD/CIM for manufacturing development, and design and development of all major equipment. He also oversees the sterilization operations, engineering technical services, and international engineering groups. For the past five years, he has made ETHICON an example of what technology can do for Johnson & Johnson, becoming a high tech state–of–the–art company. **Career Steps:** ETHICON, Inc., a Division of Johnson & Johnson: Vice President of Engineering (1990–Present), Director of Engineering (1989–1990), Director of Affiliate and International Engineering (1987–1988), Director of International Engineering (1982–1987). **Associations & Accomplishments:** Member of the Raritan Valley Community College Foundation; Member of the Somerset County Vocational and Technical School Foundation; Member of the Advisory Board for Somerset County Vocational and Technical Schools; Montgomery Township Planning Board. **Education:** Long Island University, M.B.A. (1972); University of Dayton, B.S.I.E. (1967). **Personal:** Married to Mary in 1970. Two children: Michael and Christine. Mr. Lotze enjoys tennis, snow skiing, and scuba diving.

B. Gail Macik, M.D.
Medical Director
Cardiovascular Diagnostics, NC
7200 Bluffside Court
Raleigh, NC 27615
(919) 954–9871
Fax: (919) 954–9932

3841

Business Information: Cardiovascular Diagnostics, NC is a research and development company for medical devices. Established in 1985, the Company currently employs fifty people. A practicing physician since 1983, Dr. Macik joined Cardiovascular Diagnostics in 1995. Serving as Medical Director, Dr. Macik is responsible for developing and performing clinical trials of medical devices. **Career Steps:** Medical Director, Cardiovascular Diagnostics, NC (1995–Present); Assistant Professor of Medicine and Pathology, Duke University Medical Center (1989–1995). **Education:** University of Texas Health Science Center, M.D. (1983). **Personal:** Dr. Macik enjoys outdoor activities.

Gerald A. Mayer
Employment Manager
Siemens Medical Systems, Inc.
186 Wood Avenue South
Edison, NJ 08830
(908) 321–4520
Fax: Please mail or call

3841

Business Information: Siemens Medical Systems, Inc. is the world's leading supplier of medical electronics for the hospital/medical market. Headquartered in Edison, New Jersey, Siemens Medical maintains 19 district offices and 13 subdivision offices. There are over 400 Siemens offices throughout the United States. As Employment Manager, Mr. Mayer manages employment and recruiting activities nationwide, administering all Company policies and procedures. His responsibilities include employee counseling, training and orientation, and development of internal and external education. **Career Steps:** Employment Manager, Siemens Medical Systems, Inc. (1987–Present); Independent Consultant, Digital Equipment Corporation (1984–1987); Manager, Recruiting and Employment, Mobil Oil Corporation (1974–1984). **Associations & Accomplishments:** Employer Advisory Group; Presbyterian Church Session; National Wildlife Federation. **Education:** Missouri Valley College, B.S. (1964). **Personal:** Married to Eileen in 1968. Three children: Laurie, Kim, and Keith. Mr. Mayer enjoys gardening, home remodeling, travel, and reading.

James E. McGee
Director of Sales & Marketing
Command Medical Products, Inc.
15 Signal Avenue
Ormond Beach, FL 32174–2984
(904) 672–8116
Fax: (904) 677–7781

3841

Business Information: Command Medical Products, Inc. is an FDA–registered contract manufacturer of disposable medical devices. As Director of Sales & Marketing, Mr. McGee is responsible for all aspects of sales and marketing. **Career Steps:** Director of Sales & Marketing, Command Medical Products, Inc. (1993–Present); Area Sales Manager, Medisense, Inc. (1988–1993); Regional Sales Manager, Baxter (1982–1988). **Education:** University of Central Florida, B.S. (1979). **Personal:** Married to Debbie in 1983. Three children: Matthew, Patrick, and Christopher. Mr. McGee enjoys spending time with family, attending his children's sports activities, church, CCD, and is an avid Orlando Magic fan.

Mark R. Miklos

Chief Financial Officer
Health Factors, Inc.
6925 112th Circle, Suite 102
Largo, FL 34643–5200
(813) 547–4441
Fax: (813) 541–9880

3841

Business Information: Health Factors, Inc. is a specialized mail order respiratory pharmacy, providing products from five locations nationally. As Chief Financial Officer, Mr. Miklos is responsible for all financial functions of the Corporation, including accounting and banking. He also directs the activities of managed care, marketing, sales, collection, budgeting, computers, etc. **Career Steps:** Chief Finance Officer, Health Factors, Inc. (1996–Present); Administrator, Pediatric Otolaryncology (1992–1996); Controller, Oxygen Services, Inc. (1989–1992). **Associations & Accomplishments:** Professional Association of Health Care Office Managers; South Pinellar Medical Executive Association; Chamber of Commerce; IDF, Pediatric Society; Church. **Education:** Troy State University, B.A. (1989); St. Peter's Junior College, A.A. **Personal:** Married to Paula in 1990. One child: Mark Jr. Mr. Miklos enjoys fishing, scuba diving, baseball, football, and other sports.

John N. Morgan

Vice President of Sales and Operations
MEDIQ–PRN
1 Mediq Plaza
Pennsauken, NJ 08110
(609) 662–3200
Fax: (609) 268–9731
E MAIL: See Below

3841

Business Information: MEDIQ–PRN is a distributor of critical care medical equipment. The Company was established in 1974 and currently employs over 700 people. As Vice President of Sales and Operations, Mr. Morgan manages the sales and operations of the Eastern Division, which encompasses 52 branch offices. He is involved in the development of sales techniques for new and existing products. Mr. Morgan works with other members of management in the development of short– and long– term plans for his division and for the Company as a whole. Internet users can reach him via: medprn@aol.com. **Career Steps:** Vice President of Sales and Operations, MEDIQ–PRN (1988–Present); Regional Sales Trainer, Pharmacia (1984–1988). **Associations & Accomplishments:** American College of Healthcare Executives; University of Connecticut Alumni Association; Los Angeles Chamber of Commerce. **Education:** University of Connecticut, B.S. (1981). **Personal:** Married to Venetia in 1992. Three children: Jamee, Ellen, and John. Mr. Morgan enjoys golf and other outdoor sports.

Wayne Morrow

International Business Manager
Chattanooga Group Limited
P.O. Box 572
Concord, NH 03302–0572
(603) 224–6867
Fax: (603) 224–6252

3841

Business Information: Chattanooga Group Limited is an international manufacturer of healthcare devices and physiotherapy equipment, providing rehabilitation equipment for homes, hospitals, sports clinics, and gyms. Established in 1949, Chattanooga Group Limited reports annual revenue of $65 million and currently employs 400 people. Joining Chattanooga Group Limited in 1995, Mr. Morrow serves as International Business Manager. He is responsible for all aspects of international administration, including directing and distributing new products and overseeing new districts interfacing in the United Kingdom offices. **Career Steps:** International Business Manager, Chattanooga Group Limited (1993–Present); President and Chief Executive Officer, Ergomed, Inc. (1991–1995); Director of Marketing, Abbott Labs (1990–1991); Vice President, Chase Walton/SF Medical (1988–1990). **Associations & Accomplishments:** Published in American Chemical Society paper; Patents (polymers). **Education:** Union College, M.S. studies (1982), B.S. (1979); Graduate studies in Chemistry and Economics. **Personal:** Married to Patti in 1976. Four children: Christine, Dan, Nickolas, and Jill. Mr. Morrow enjoys outdoor sports, skiing, basketball, and hiking.

Darlene G. Osborn

Regional Health Network Manager
Bayer Corporation
32 Encore Court
Newport Beach, CA 92663–2364
(800) 581–2432 3806
Fax: (714) 645–3519
E MAIL: See Below

3841

Business Information: Bayer Corporation, established in 1867, is a manufacturer of X–ray film, film processors, and laser cameras. The Company also sells Picture Archiving and Communication Systems (PACS). With estimated revenue in excess of $7.2 billion, the Company presently employs over 22,000 people. As Regional Health Network Manager, Ms. Osborn is responsible for monitoring the Kaiser HMO in Southern California. She handles customer service and does all of the Corporation's insurance billing. **Career Steps:** Regional Health Network Manager, Bayer Corporation (1993–Present); MRI Product Specialist, Picker International (1992–1993); Nuclear Medicine Specialist, General Electric Medical Systems (1990–1992); Sales Representative, General Electric Plastics (1986–1990). **Associations & Accomplishments:** Young Professionals Against Cancer; American marketing Association. **Education:** Pepperdine University, M.B.A. (1992); SUNY–Oswego, B.S. Business Administration (1983). **Personal:** Married to John in 1995. Ms. Osborn enjoys spending time with her husband, biking, hiking, camping, and other outdoor activities.

Barrett Edward Rabinow, Ph.D.

Director, Strategic Technical Development
Baxter Healthcare Corporation
Baxter Technology Park
Round Lake, IL 60073
(847) 270–5802
Fax: (847) 270–5690

3841

Business Information: Baxter International, of which Baxter Healthcare is the principal domestic operating subsidiary, is the leading manufacturer and marketer of health–care products and services worldwide. The Company concentrates R & D efforts in biotechnology, cardiovascular medicine, renal therapy and related medical fields. Dr. Rabinow joined Baxter in 1977 as a Research Scientist and has served in various supervisory positions. Affiliated with the I.V. Systems Division, he is responsible for identifying, evaluating, and creating new business opportunities; manufacturing troubleshooting; and acting as a trade group/regulatory liaison. **Career Steps:** Baxter Healthcare Corporation: Director, Strategic Technical Development (1991–Present), Director, Chemistry Research and Development (1983–1991), Manager, Analytical (1978–1982); Director of Chemistry, Norwegian–American Hospital (1976–1977); NIH Post–Doctoral Fellow in Clinical Chemistry, Michael Reese Hospital (1975–1976). **Associations & Accomplishments:** HIMA; PDA; AAMI; Numerous Company awards for problem solving and business creation; industry position papers, as well as publications in pharmaceutics, materials science, analytical and clinical chemistry, and packaging. **Education:** University of Chicago: Ph.D. (1974), M.S. (1969); Cornell University, A.B. (1968). **Personal:** Three children: Daniel, Jonathan, and Jessica.

Ramon Ricart

Director of Quality Systems
National Medical Care
6620 South 33rd
McAllen, TX 78503
(210) 682–1571
Fax: (210) 682–2442

3841

Business Information: National Medical Care is an international bloodlines manufacturer for dialysis treatment equipment. Established in 1974, National Medical Care currently employ 600 people. With thirteen years of experience in quality assurance, Mr. Ricart joined the Company in 1993 after the plant was closed for ten months by the FDA. Serving as Director of Quality Systems and using his expertise in quality assurance, he was able to have the Company up and running in three months. He is currently responsible for the direction of all quality systems throughout Texas, Mexico, and Latin America. **Career Steps:** Director of Quality Systems, National Medical Care (1993–Present); Director of Quality Assurance, Bristol–Myers–Squibb (1987–1993); Laboratories Manager, Alcon Labs (1982–1987). **Associations & Accomplishments:** American Society for Quality Control; Chemist's College Puerto Rico. **Education:** University of Puerto Rico, Computers (1984); Interamerican University: B.S. in Chemistry (1974), B.S. in Math (1974). **Personal:** Mr. Ricart enjoys bike riding and dancing.

Carlos L. Rodriguez

Senior Quality Engineer
CPI Del Caribe
Road 698, Lot 12
Dorado, Puerto Rico 00646
(787) 796–8217
Fax: (787) 796–4848

3841

Business Information: A subsidiary of Guidant, CPI Del Caribe is an establishment primarily engaged in the manufacture of medical devices, specifically lead cables for pacemakers and defibrillators. Established in 1990, the Company employs 270 people. As Senior Quality Engineer, Mr. Rodriguez provides support and counseling to all manufacturing areas. He is also responsible for supervision of QCRI, receiving, shipping, crib, and quality control quarantine. He has performed manufacturing processes and sterilization validations. He has conducted cost reduction initiative resulting in annual savings of $500,000. **Career Steps:** Guidant/CPI Del Caribe: Senior Quality Engineer (1994–Present), Quality Engineer (1990–1994); Staff Manufacturing Engineer, Baxter Edwards (1986–1990). **Associations & Accomplishments:** Children International; United Funds; American Society for Quality Control; IIE; Excellence Award Guidant Corp. **Education:** University of Puerto Rico: M.S.I.E. (1991), B.S.I.E. (1985); Certified Quality Engineer (1992); Certified Quality Auditor (1994); P.E. License (1989). **Personal:** Married to Rosa Sanchez in 1994. Mr. Rodriguez enjoys basketball, tennis, cycling, movies, video games, and reading.

Dan Rogers

Branch Operations Manager
Butler Company
1302 Avenue R
Grand Prairie, TX 75050–1603
(214) 602–0866
Fax: (214) 602–1349

3841

Business Information: The Butler Company specializes in the distribution, sales and service of veterinary products to veterinary clinics and veterinary professionals. Established in 1988, the Butler Company currently employs 30 people and has an estimated annual revenue of $20 million. As Branch Operations Manager, Mr. Rogers is responsible for all aspects of operations, including purchasing, transporting and personnel management. ' **Career Steps:** Branch Operations Manager, Butler Company (1988–Present). **Education:** University of Evansville, Indiana (1977). **Personal:** Married to Sharon Lee in 1983. Two children: Nikki Lee and Chad Douglas Muffler. Mr. Rogers enjoys gardening and woodworking.

Rose Marie C. Salah

Educational Services Manager
Behring Diagnostics, Inc.
151 University Avenue
Westwood, MA 02090
(617) 320–3011
Fax: (617) 251–2023

3841

Business Information: Behring Diagnostics, Inc. specializes in the manufacture, research and development of pharmaceutical and medical diagnostic instrumentation equipment. Products are utilized in the analyzation of infectious diseases, thyroid scans, fertility, cardiac and tumor markers. Joining Behring Diagnostics, Inc. in 1989 as a Senior Systems Engineer, Ms. Salah was appointed to her current role in 1992. As Educational Services Manager she provides the overall coordination and supervision for customer training programs. Implementing the program with only one part–time classroom and one program, the division has now expanded to providing five different programs, including new hire orientation and international training. **Career Steps:** Behring Diagnostics, Inc.: Education Services Manager (1992–Present), Senior Systems Engineer (1989–1992); Product Evaluation Manager, Nova Biomedical (1986–1989). **Associations & Accomplishments:** Junior League of Boston; American Association of Clinical Chemists; Ace of Clubs – Boston; American Society of Clinical Pathologists. **Education:** Northeastern University, M.S. (1978). **Personal:** Ms. Salah enjoys ice skating, skiing, dancing, and travel.

Rolf Schild

Board Chairperson
Huntleigh Technology plc
310–312 Dallow Road
Luton, United Kingdom LU1 1TD
44(0)1582 4131
Fax: 44(0)1582 4025

3841

Business Information: Huntleigh Technology plc is the holding company for international device manufacturers. Entities include: Huntleigh Technology — specialists in the manufacture of medical devices; and, Tedea Huntleigh — an industrial distributor for weights and measurement product lines. The designer of many quality design products for Huntleigh, Rolf Schild now serves as Executive Chairman of the Board. He continues on a consultory basis for hands–on design projects, as well as overseeing the direction of the company. **Career Steps:** Huntleigh Technology plc: Chairman of the Board (1983–Present), Joint Chief Executive (1975–1982); Chair and Joint Managing Director, S.E. Laboratories Ltd (1963–1972). **Associations & Accomplishments:** Fellow, Institute of Electrical Engineers. **Education:** Polytechnic, C. Eng., (1957). **Personal:** Married to Daphne in 1959. Three children: Julian, David, and Annabel. Mr. Schild enjoys reading and listening to music.

Peter Schreiber II

•••◄━━◉●━━►•••

International Division Director
North American Drager
3135 Quarry Road
Telford, PA 18969
(215) 721–5404
Fax: (215) 721–9561

3841

Business Information: North American Drager is a manufacturer of high quality medical devices, such as anesthesia systems, patient monitors, and data management products. Products are distributed throughout 42 countries, excluding Europe. Established in 1968, North American Drager currently employs 500 people. As Director of the International Division, Mr. Schreiber directs a corporate division that is responsible for establishing, maintaining and expanding business through a network of international distributors. **Career Steps:** North American Drager: Director of the International Division (1992–Present), International Sales Manager (1990–1992); Manager of Sales, Merchants Press (1983–1990). **Associations & Accomplishments:** Born and raised in Germany; he has lectured at symposia and conference proceedings around the world, such as: China, Egypt, Turkey, Europe, South Africa, and South America. **Education:** Boston University, B.A. (1981). **Personal:** Married to Diane in 1988. Three children: Alexander, Nikolas, and Lisa. Mr. Schreiber enjoys spending time with his family, soccer, and studying History of Strategies in Political and Military Interactions.

Peter Serpentino
Director, Materials Science
Becton Dickinson Vacutainer Systems
1 Becton Drive
Franklin Lakes, NJ 07417–1815
(201) 847–4750
Fax: (201) 847–4851

3841

Business Information: Becton Dickinson and Company manufactures and sells a broad range of medical supplies, devices and diagnostic systems for use by health care professionals, medical research institutions and the general public. With 19 years experience in the research and development industry and a Clinical Chemist, Dr. Serpentino joined Becton Dickinson as Director of Materials Science in 1995. He is responsible for the direction of all materials science research and development activities, and overseeing the activities of 25 other scientists. **Career Steps:** Director, Becton Dickinson Vacutainer Systems (1995–Present); Kimberly Clark Corporation: Senior Research and Development Manager – Nonwovers (1984), Senior Research and Development Manager – Absosency (1984–1995). **Associations & Accomplishments:** American Association of Clinical Chemist's. **Education:** University of Rochester: Ph.D. (1977), M.S. in Chemistry; St. John's University, B.S. in Chemistry. **Personal:** Married to Margaret (Peggy) in 1973. Two children: Tracy and Megan. Mr. Serpentino enjoys technology management and tennis.

Rosa Servera Lugo
Training Coordinator
McGaw of Puerto Rico, Inc.
P.O. Box 729
Sabana Grande, Puerto Rico 00637–0729
(787) 873–4600
Fax: (787) 873–3027

3841

Business Information: McGaw of Puerto Rico, Inc. manufacturers and internationally distributes medical devices in Puerto Rico, Europe, the United States, and Australia. A subsidiary of IVAX Corporation, a producer of pharmaceuticals, the Company has three locations, one each in California, Puerto Rico, and Texas. As Training Coordinator, Ms. Servera Lugo is responsible for various projects in the Company, for designing

and implementing all training curriculum, policies, and procedures, and supervising management training and recruitment. **Career Steps:** McGaw of Puerto Rico, Inc: Training Coordinator (1994–Present), Manufacturing Supervisor (1988–1994), Documentation Coordinator (1975–1988). **Associations & Accomplishments:** Scoutmaster, Boy Scout Troop #122; Boy Scouts of America, Order of the Arrow; John XX; Chairman, Boy Scouts of America Roundtable, Puerto Rico Chapter. **Education:** Inter American University, Post Graduate (1992); Colegio Agricultura y Artes Mecanicas B.B.A. in Arts. **Personal:** Married to Juan E. Mendez Sanchez in 1979. Five children: Mikito, Doynet, Nany, Juancito, and Juan Carlos. Ms. Servera Lugo enjoys camping, reading, and helping in the community.

Aatish Shah
Manager of Accounting & Analysis
Baxter Healthcare Corporation – Novacor Division
7799 Pardee Lane
Oakland, CA 94621
(510) 568–8338 Ext. 2418
Fax: (510) 633–0467

3841

Business Information: Baxter Healthcare Corporation is a Fortune 500 company which manufactures and distributes life saving medical products. Over half of its $5 billion revenue is generated from Europe, Japan, and emerging markets, such as Latin America, China, and India. Its major product line represents life saving medical technology products. Novacor, a startup company located in Northern California, is currently developing and marketing an Artificial Heart Device. The product is commercially approved for sale in Europe and is under clinical study in U.S. The Company employs 180 people and has an estimated annual revenue of $15 million. As Manager of Accounting and Analysis, Mr. Shah is responsible for management reporting, forecasting, and budgeting. **Career Steps:** Baxter Healthcare Corporation: Manager of Accounting & Analysis – Novacor Division (1995–Present), Senior Operations Analyst – Interventional Cardiology Division – participated in the divestiture of $40 million division (1994–1995); Co–Owner, Kapali Foods, Inc. – established financial and marketing systems for a newly incorporated ethnic wholesale distributor (1994); Assistant Accounting Manager, Kerr Group, Inc. (1987–1994). **Associations & Accomplishments:** Fluent in Indian languages, namely Gujrati and Hindi; President, Tri–Valley Indian Association. **Education:** University of Arizona, M.B.A. (1986); University of Baroda, India: M.A. in Accounting (1982), B.A. in Accounting (1979). **Personal:** Married to Archana in 1985. Two children: Shuchee and Saarth. Mr. Shah enjoys music and travel.

Osmo Suovaniemi, MD, Ph.D.

•••◄━━◉━━►•••

Chairman of the Board
Biohit Oy
Verkkosaarenkatu 4
Helsinki, Finland 00580
358–0–773–2900
Fax: Please mail or call

3841

Business Information: Biohit Oy is an international manufacturer and retailer of electronic and manually–operated pipettes for the medical and research fields. The Company has been awarded over 70 patents within Finland, and several hundred worldwide, in the fields of laboratory diagnostics, optics, and mechanics. As Founder and Chairman of the Board, Mr. Suovaniemi oversees the daily operation of Biohit Oy. He was granted the Club of Business Journalists Award for the economic feat of the year in 1984 – managing an exceptionally innovative Company, export–oriented and focused on high technology. Dr. Suovaniemi has produced over 100 inventions, with two over–shadowing the others. The vertical photometer analyzer, e.g., Multiskan, FP–9 and FP–900 and the single– and multi–channel, adjustable Finnpipettes have, since the 1970s, served as examples for numerous companies worldwide and created highly valuable opportunities for the rapid development of the EIA–test kits, which was especially good news for the blood banks. Later on the entire HIV–diagnostic field which, in its early years was based on the use of EIA–test kits, benefited from Multiskans and Finnpipettes. Currently the concept of the vertical photometer with complementary products and the adjustable Finnpipettes have generated multi–billion dollar global businesses. Both the Finnpipette and the vertical photometer may justifiably be called the industrial standards of the future, which is the highest and most valuable goal for an inventor. The Multiskan and other analyzers based on the vertical photometry invention, the Finnpipette, the consumables used with these products, and HIV– and other EIA–test kits form the basis of the equipment delivered to the blood banking center to be constructed in China. **Career Steps:** Chairman of the Board, Biohit Oy (1987–Present); Chairman and CEO, Labsystems Oy and Eflab Oy (1974–1986). **Associations & Accomplishments:**

Former member of the board, Vice Chairman, and Chairman, General Industry Group (General Industry Federation); Member of the board, Confederation of Finnish Industry (Confederation of Finnish Industry and Employers). Dr. Suovaniemi has been published in numerous trade journals, and has been frequently quoted in the Finnish newspapers. **Education:** University of Helsinki, Ph.D. (1994) and M.D. (1972). **Personal:** Married to Oili in 1964. Three children: Vesa, Joel, and Ville. Mr. Suovaniemi enjoys sailing and piano.

Edward V. Tancredi
Plant Manager
National Medical Care
1816 Underwood Boulevard
Delran, NJ 08075–1233
(609) 764–1222
Fax: (609) 764–1160

3841

Business Information: National Medical Care specializes in the manufacture and development of kidney dialysis medical devices utilized in hemodialysis treatments. A management executive with National Medical, employed since 1975, Ed Tancredi was appointed as Plant Manager in May of 1992. In this role, he is responsible for the implementation and development of policies and procedures, developing job scope and budgets, overall day–to–day operations, as well as interfaces with the departments of Human Resources, Planning, Traffic, Distribution, Engineering, Accounting, Maintenance, and R&D Quality Control. **Career Steps:** National Medical Care: Plant Manager (1992–Present), Production Manager (1990–1992), Plant Lead Operator, NMC – Union Representative (1978–1989); Union Representative, Oil, Chemical, Atomic Workers Local 8–398. **Associations & Accomplishments:** American Management Association; National Association of the Self–Employed; Towing and Recovery Association of America; National Rifle Association. **Education:** Burlington County College, A.S. Psychology; ISO 9000; GMP's; TCM. **Personal:** Married to Donna in 1971. Two children: Edward and Mary Ann. Mr. Tancredi enjoys hunting, fishing, drag racing, and auctions.

Peter A. Thompson, M.D.
Vice President of Research and Development
Becton Dickinson Immunocytometry Systems
2350 Qume Drive
San Jose, CA 95131–1812
(408) 954–2287
Fax: (408) 954–2506
EMAIL: See Below

3841

Business Information: Becton Dickinson Immunocytometry Systems is a $3 billion, publicly–traded firm, providing medical diagnosis technology and medical devices. A practicing physician since 1984 and a Board–Certified Medical Oncologist, Dr. Thompson joined Becton Dickinson as Associate Medical Director in 1991. He was then promoted to Medical Director in 1992 and to his present position as Vice President of Research and Development in 1994. He oversees all the research and development of the Immunocytometry Systems Division, a bio–technology division of the Company, producing high–tech instrumentation systems for bio–technical research. Dr. Thompson can also be reached through the Internet as follows: pthompson@bdis.com **Career Steps:** Becton Dickinson Immunocytometry Systems: Vice President of Research and Development (1994–Present), Medical Director (1992–1994), Associate Medical Director (1991–1992); Staff – Division of Cancer Treatment, National Cancer Institute (1987–1991). **Associations & Accomplishments:** Board of Trustees, San Francisco State University; Published numerous articles and book chapter in the field of Oncology. **Education:** Brown University: M.D. (1984), B.A. (1980).

John Timte
Director of Engineering
Roxane Laboratories
1809 Wilson Road
Columbus, OH 43228–9579
(614) 276–4000 Ext. 2477
Fax: (614) 276–0095

3841

Business Information: Roxane Laboratories, a subsidiary of the Germany–based international corporation Boehornger Ingelheim, is a manufacturer of generic pharmaceuticals. As Director of Engineering, Mr. Timte manages all engineering and maintenance functions, as well as project management operations. **Career Steps:** Director of Engineering, Roxane Laboratories (1994–Present); The Scotts Company: Director of Engineering (1990–1994), Manager of Plant Engineering and Maintenance (1987–1990). **Associations & Accomplishments:** International Society of Pharmaceutical Engineers; Registered Professional Engineer – State of Ohio. **Education:** Michigan State University, B.S. in Mechanical Engineering (1975). **Personal:** Married to Linda A. in 1975. Two children: Emily and Laura. Mr. Timte enjoys flying, music, and Corvettes.

Dale A. Wahlstrom
Director of Operations
Medtronic
7000 Central Avenue, #6
Fridley, MN 55432–3568
(612) 574–3323
Fax: (612) 574–4284
EMail: See Below

3841

Business Information: Medtronic specializes in the manufacture and distribution of implantable medical devices. As Director of Operations, Mr. Wahlstrom is responsible for design, engineering, production, purchasing, planning, and other various activities. Internet users can reach him via: dale.Wahlstrom@Medtronic.com. **Career Steps:** Medtronic: Director of Operations (1990–Present), Director of Engineering – The Netherlands (1988–1990), Director of Implantable Battery and Polymer Operations (1982–1988); Manager of Engineering, Litton Microwave (1978–1982). **Associations & Accomplishments:** University of St. Thomas – St. Paul, MN: President of Alumni Association, Industrial Advisory Board; Society of Manufacturing Engineers; American Management Association; Board of Directors, Anoka County Quality Association; Member, PDMA. **Education:** University of St. Thomas – St. Paul, MN, Master's of Science in Manufacturing Systems (1995); St. Cloud State University, B.S. in Engineering Technology (1978). **Personal:** Married to Diane in 1972. Two children: Jessica and Lindsey. Mr. Wahlstrom enjoys hiking, travel, and cross country skiing.

Gerard P. Walsh
Corporate Director
C.R. Bard, Inc.
730 Central Avenue
Murray Hill, NJ 07974
(908) 277–8394
Fax: (908) 756–5982
EMail: See Below

3841

Business Information: C.R. Bard, Inc. is a manufacturer of medical and surgical products for the health care industry. As Corporate Director, Mr. Walsh handles executive management by directing global functions in training, computer networks, applications, and research technology solutions. Internet users can reach him via: 76656.3203@Compuserve.com. **Career Steps:** Corporate Director, C.R. Bard, Inc. (1981–Present); Production Manager, ADM Corporation (1974–1980); Engineer, NCR Corporation (1971–1974). **Associations & Accomplishments:** Technology Forum; DPMA; PC Group; Who's Who in the Computer Industry (1991); Executive Managers Group; American Consultants League; Volunteer fire department associate; President, Local Neighborhood Association; President of company credit union; Disabled American Veterans. **Education:** New York University, M.B.A. (APC) (1981); Wagner College, M.B.A. (1978); Kean College, B.S. (1976). **Personal:** Married to Kathleen in 1976. Two children: Casey and Katelyn. Mr. Walsh enjoys sports cars, mountain biking, fishing, and family life.

Dale G. Bramlet
President, Chief Executive Officer, and Founder
Orthopedic Designs, Inc.
3542 Morris St.
St. Petersburg, FL 33713
(813) 526–9100
Fax: (813) 822–4340

3842

Business Information: Orthopedic Designs, Inc., established in 1995, is a designer and manufacturer of orthopedic implants. As President, Chief Executive Officer, and Founder, Mr. Bramlet is responsible for all aspects of operations, including management, strategic planning, direction of the Company, supervision of employees, and overall planning. He currently has five patents pending. Concurrently, he is the Founder and an investing partner of the Florida Orthopedic Associates, a surgical practice, as well as a Vice President of a real estate company. **Career Steps:** President, Chief Executive Officer, and Founder, Orthopedic Designs, Inc. (1995–Present). **Personal:** Mr. Bramlet enjoys scuba diving.

James P. Bremer
Vice President of Credit
Starkey Laboratories, Inc.
6700 Washington Avenue South
Eden Prairie, MN 55344
(612) 828–9174
Fax: Please mail or call

3842

Business Information: Starkey Laboratories, Inc., a privately-owned company, specializes in the manufacture of hearing instruments. With over 26 locations, the Company supplies their products to distributors internationally. As Vice President of Credit, Mr. Bremer handles the administrative services. He oversees a support staff of 51 employees, customer administration, billing, discounts, credit cards, and financial management services. **Career Steps:** Starkey Laboratories, Inc.: Vice President of Credit (1989–Present), Corporate Credit Manager (1981–1989), Purchasing/Credit Manager (1975–1980); Accountant, Qualtone, Inc. (1968–1975). **Associations & Accomplishments:** Lions Club of Eden Prairie; Equipment Leasing Association; National Association of Credit Management; 1996 Trustee of the Starkey Laboratories 401k plan. **Education:** University of Minnesota, B.A. (1971). **Personal:** Married to Bebe R. in 1995. Four children: Elizabeth, Katherine, Rebecca, and James Jr. Mr. Bremer enjoys golf and tennis.

Ricardo Burgos

Quality Director
Zimmer Caribe, Inc.
Valle Alto, 14th Street, J–13
Ponce, Puerto Rico 00731
(809) 259–5959
Fax: (809) 259–5960

3842

Business Information: Zimmer Caribe, Inc., a division of Bristol–Myers Squibb, is a manufacturer of orthopaedic implants. Established in 1992, Zimmer Caribe, Inc. reports annual revenue of $60 million and currently employs 190 people. As Quality Director, Mr. Burgos is responsible for all aspects of quality assurance, ensuring the distribution and supply of quality products, as well as regulatory compliance for safety and effective product distribution. **Career Steps:** Quality Director, Zimmer Caribe, Inc. (1991–Present); Productos Electronicos, Division of Westinghouse: Manager of Quality and Reliability Assurance (1987–1991), Engineer of Quality Assurance (1980–1987). **Associations & Accomplishments:** Lions International Club; American Society of Quality Control. **Education:** University of Catolica de Puerto Rico, M.B.A. (1990); Recinto Universitario de Puerto Rico – Mayaguez Campus, B.S. in Mechanical Engineering; Recinto Universitario de Puerto Rico – Ponce Campus, A.S.; Recognized by the American Society of Quality Control as: "ASQC Certified Quality Engineer" and "ASQC Certified Quality Auditor." **Personal:** Married to Maria de Lourdes Colon in 1985. Three children: Ricardo, Lenis Anel, and Melanie. Mr. Burgos enjoys softball and basketball.

Bart H. Burrow
Vice President of Engineering
King Systems Corporation
15011 Herriman Boulevard, P O Box 1138
Noblesville, IN 46061
(317) 776–6823
Fax: (317) 776–4164

3842

Business Information: King Systems Corporation is a manufacturer and distributor of disposable anesthesia circuits. As Vice President of Engineering, Mr. Burrow oversees the design of equipment, parts, and systems used in the manufacturing of the disposable circuits. He is currently involved in the research and development of a profile design on extruded tubing in anesthesia circuitry. **Career Steps:** Vice President of Engineering, King Systems Corporation (1994–Present); Vice President Sales/Project Director, Burco Corporation (1977–1994). **Associations & Accomplishments:** Society of Plastic Engineers; Society of Manufacturing Engineers. **Personal:** Married to Lee Anne in 1991. Three children: Nicholas, Alexander, and Lucas. Mr. Burrow enjoys camping, snow skiing, and racing.

James B. Carnation

Executive Vice President of Operations
Neuromed, Inc.
5000 A Oakes Road
Ft. Lauderdale, FL 33314
(305) 584–3600
Fax: (305) 581–9580

3842

Business Information: Quest/Neuromed, Inc. is an international manufacturer of medical devices, such as implantable spine stimulators. Established in 1982, Neuromed, Inc. reports annual revenue of $30 million and currently employs 200 people. With more than ten years expertise in aerospace electronics, Mr. Carnation joined Neuromed, Inc. in 1993 as Executive Vice President of Operations. He is responsible for all operations, including manufacturing, testing, quality assurance, purchasing, materials, scheduling, shipping, and receiving. One of the highlights of his career was training the first seven astronauts to repair electrical devices in space if it was needed. **Career Steps:** Executive Vice President of Operations, Neuromed, Inc. (1993–Present); Director of Manufacturing, Unipower (1992–1993); Director of Manufacturing, Litton Data Systems (1988–1992); President, Tri–Tech Electronics (1985–1988); NASA (Prior to 1985). **Associations & Accomplishments:** Senior Member, IIE; Knights of Columbus; APICS. **Education:** Ramapo College of New Jersey, B.S. (1976). **Personal:** Married to Frances in 1957. One child: Melanie. Mr. Carnation enjoys golf and computers.

Bill G. Copeland
Clinical Director
NovaCare – Sabolich Prosthetics of Florida
5411 Beaumont Center Boulevard #785
Tampa, FL 33634
(813) 249–0449
Fax: (813) 249–0524

3842

Business Information: NovaCare – Sabolich Prosthetics of Florida, a subsidiary of NovaCare, is a national manufacturer of prosthetic devices, as well as providing fittings of devices. NovaCare, Inc. is a rehabilitative services company providing physical, occupational, and speech therapy to nursing homes (Contract Services Division). The Company has outpatient clinics providing orthopedic and support services nationally (Outpatient Services Division), and 130 orthotic and prosthetic laboratories which specialize in the manufacture of artificial limbs (Manufacturing Division). Novacare, Inc. currently has the number one market share in the U.S. for all three divisions. As Clinical Director, Mr. Copeland manages all facility operations, focusing in the areas of quality control, patient relations, professional client services representation, and marketing. He also interacts with corporate offices, serves as a physical therapist, and fits patients with prosthetic devices. An above–the–knee amputee himself, he is able to relate to new amputees, visiting them in the hospital, and providing them with counseling. **Career Steps:** Clinical Director, NovaCare – Sabolich Prosthetics of Florida (1985–Present); Computer Operations Manager (1981–1985); Trackman Maintenance of Way, Sante Fe Railroad (1973–1980). **Associations & Accomplishments:** Florida Association of Prosthetics. **Education:** Attended: Central State University (1982). **Personal:** Married to Elizabeth Ann in 1992. Four children: Gwendolyn, Amber, Steffany, and Alexander. Mr. Copeland enjoys tennis, golf, martial arts, and playing the guitar.

Mark A. Croasmun
Operations Manager
Oilind Safety
4901 Cripple Creek Drive
Houston, TX 77017–5937
(713) 947–8990
Fax: (713) 947–8990

3842

Business Information: Oilind Safety is a manufacturer of breathing air, breathing air respirators, gas monitoring instruments, and fall protection equipment. As Operations Manager, Mr. Croasmun is responsible for the renting of equipment, purchasing equipment, and personnel employment. **Career Steps:** Operations Manager, Oilind Safety (1996–Present); Shop Manager, Total Safety (1988–1996). **Education:** Lafayette Vo-Tec (1994); Emergency Medical Technician. **Personal:** Married to Judy.

Andrew Dingman
Safety Director
Wadleigh Energy
37362 Brownvillage Road
Slidell, LA 70459–0188
(504) 847–0688
Fax: (504) 649–1554

3842

Business Information: Wadleigh Energy Group is comprised of several companies involved in construction, fabrication, equipment and crew rentals, and safety equipment re–furbishment. As Safety Director, Mr. Dingman does employee safety training for the Energy Group. He is responsible for making sure Company safety and OSHA regulations are up–to–date and being met. Mr. Dingman investigates Company accidents to determine if safety regulations were followed or if they were inadequate. **Career Steps:** Director, Wadleigh Energy (1992–Present); Safety Director, Mallard Bay Drilling (1992–1994); Barge Master, Global Marine Drilling (1988–1992). **Associations & Accomplishments:** American Society of Safety Engineers. **Education:** University of Alaska, B.S. in Business (1968); Ellis Hospital, Paramedic (1971). **Personal:** Married to Pauline in 1977. One child: Shauna Mary. Mr. Dingman enjoys golf and spending time with family.

James (Jimmy) E. Dixon
MIS Director
Med Covers
1103 Transport Drive
Raleigh, NC 27603
(919) 772–4250 EXT. 133
Fax: (919) 772–3917
E MAIL: See Below

3842

Business Information: Med Covers is a design and manufacturing facility engaged in the production of soft–sided cases for the medical, data capture, and electronic industries. As MIS Director, Mr. Dixon is responsible for the Management Information Systems Department and the LAN network. He handles all administrative, marketing, public relations, strategic planning, and implementation for the Department. Mr. Dixon works closely with other management staff on the development and implementation of an annual budget. Internet users may reach Mr. Dixon via: jedixon@mercury.interpath.com. **Career Steps:** MIS Director, Med Covers (1993–Present); Owner, Technical Support Services (1993); Systems Engineer, Accounting Computer Services (1991–1993); Senior Systems Engineer, Tandy Corporation (1989–1991). **Associations & Accomplishments:** AIDS Service Agency of Wake County; Girl Scout Council of Coastal Carolinas; Institute of Electrical and Electronic Engineers; NaSPA; Board of Directors, Wake County Community Services. **Education:** North Carolina State University, B.S. in Computer Science (1984); Tarrant County Junior College, Point of Sale Specialist Training, Artisoft Certified Instructor, Notary Public Instructor, KEE Systems Learning Laboratory Instructor, RealWorld Authorized Consultant. **Personal:** Mr. Dixon enjoys mainstream level square dancing, computers and ham radio (KF4KHU).

Danita Evans
National Sales Manager
Micro Tech
106 Pine Street, P.O. Box 838
Monticello, MN 55362–0838
(800) 745–4327
Fax: (612) 295–8898

3842

Business Information: Micro Tech is a manufacturer and marketer of custom hearing instruments (hearing aids) internationally. Specializing in small cosmetic instruments, Micro Tech is part of the leading edge of technology and cosmetic industries producing a difficult product to manufacture. Products are sold to audiologists (ear, nose, throat) in both hospitals and private settings in the U.S. and Canada. Initially becoming involved with Micro Tech as an investor, Ms. Evans watched her life savings investment go to zero. Deciding that she could turn the company around, she came into the Company as National Sales Manager and Primary Shareholder in 1990. Through her leadership, management, and motivation of all inside sales staff, Micro Tech has had a 30% growth rate during the last three years, with plans to go public in the near future. **Career Steps:** National Sales Manager, Micro Tech (1990–Present); Xerox Corporation: Senior Account Executive (1988–1989), Supply Account Manager (1986–1987). **Associations & Accomplishments:** Donatsu President; Chamber of Commerce; PTA; SCC School Consultant; Toastmasters; Dale Carnegie; Sioux Falls College Alumni Association; National Republican Committee. **Education:** Sioux Falls College, B.S. in Biology and Psychology (1981). **Personal:** Married to Gordon Bye in 1987. Three children:

Brittany, Westin, and Danae. Ms. Evans enjoys rock climbing, hiking, reading, working with gifted children, sales training, and public speaking.

Shirley Fang
Engineer
Sigtron Technologies, Inc.
11537 Berryknoll Circle
Draper, UT 84020
(801) 5715048
Fax: (801) 571–8317

3842

Business Information: Crystal Instruments is a Hi–Tech research and development company, specializing in PCMCIA, video products, and etc. Their current products include PCMCIA digital signal analyzer, portable PCMCIA–based DSP box, film viewing box (consumer product), and etc. As Engineer, Ms. Fang is responsible for the design and creation of computer chips and the development of algorithms. **Career Steps:** Engineer, Sigtron Technologies (1995–Present); Engineer (design digital hearing aid), Sonix Technologies (1995–Present); Engineer (design wireless phone system), Phonex (1994–1995); Research Assistant, University of Utah (1990–1994). **Education:** University of Utah, Ph.D. (1996); Zhejiang University, China, M.S. and B.S. in Engineering. **Personal:** Ms. Fang enjoys reading stories with her children, watching television, and music.

Kellye Frederick
Human Resources and Payroll Manager
Hartzell Manufacturing Inc.
2600 North I–35
Denton, TX 76207
(817) 387–3535
Fax: (817) 383–2087
EMAIL: See Below

3842

Business Information: Hartzell Manufacturing Inc. is a manufacturer of plastic injection molding and secondary operations used in the medical industry. Customers include Motorola and Fisher. Hartzell Manufacturing, Inc. operates five regional facilities in Florida, Wisconsin, Minnesota, and Texas. As Human Resources and Payroll Manager, Mrs. Frederick is responsible for all aspects of personnel operations, including payroll, human resources, benefits, and Worker's Compensation. She also serves as Safety Manager, overseeing all safety activities. Internet users can reach her via: Kellye@Hartzell.com. **Career Steps:** Human Resources and Payroll Manager, Hartzell Manufacturing Inc. (1994–Present); Shipping and Order Entry, EMC–Hartzell (1993–1994); Administrative Assistant, Action Carpets (1992–1993). **Associations & Accomplishments:** Denton Human Resources Association. **Education:** North Central Texas College; Brookhaven Community College, UNT. **Personal:** Married to Tim in 1991. Mrs. Frederick enjoys reading, crossword puzzles, boating, swimming, and fitness.

Louisa M. Hayashi
Director of Marketing
A.J. Reynolds Company, Inc.
3435 West Lomita Boulevard
Torrance, CA 90505–5010
(310) 784–3800
Fax: (310) 784–3833
EMAIL: See Below

3842

Business Information: A.J. Reynolds Company, Inc. is a distributor of cleanroom products including gloves, garments, face masks, swabs, and wipers serving the pharmaceutical, bio–tech, and disk drive industries. As Director of Marketing, Ms. Hayashi manages and supervises the Customer Service Department, designs and coordinates trade magazine advertisements and is an ISO 9000 coordinator. She is involved in the development and creative direction of the Company catalog. Internet users can reach her via: Lhajr@aol.com. **Career Steps:** Director of Marketing, A.J. Reynolds Company, Inc. (1991–Present); Marketing Specialist, Coventry Manufacturing (1988–1991). **Education:** California State, Bachelor of Science in Business Administration (1989); Polytechnic University, Pomona. **Personal:** Married to Craig A. in 1991. Ms. Hayashi enjoys volleyball, aerobics, and reading.

Ralf Marbach, Ph.D.
Project Manager
Biocontrol Technology
300 Indian Springs Road
Indiana, PA 15701
(412) 349–1811
Fax: (412) 349–8610

3842

Business Information: Biocontrol Technology, Inc. is a manufacturer of biomedical devices and environmental products. Established in 1972, the Company developed and manufactured cardiac pacemakers, heart valves, and related accessories. The Company is currently developing and producing noninvasive blood glucose sensors for use by persons with diabetes. As Project Manager and lead engineer, Dr. Marbach provides leadership and technical support for engineers involved in an advanced sensing concept which employs proven technology and is aimed at providing state–of–the–art accuracy and precision at the reduced cost and improved ruggedness of a consumer–type product. **Career Steps:** Biocontrol Technology: Section Manager (1994–Present), Systems Engineer (1993–1994); Research Associate, Institute for Spectrochemistry and Applied Spectroscopy, Dortmund, Germany (1989–1993). **Associations & Accomplishments:** Member of the Society for Applied Spectroscopy. Twelve peer–reviewed papers in the field of glucose sensing and infrared spectroscopy including first–published successful analysis of glucose in human blood samples using mid–IR spectroscopy, first–published successful analysis of glucose in blood samples using near–IR spectroscopy, and first–published noninvasive determination of glucose in–vivo. Several conference proceedings, patents, and patent applications. **Education:** University of Dortmund – Dortmund, Germany, Ph.D. in Electrical Engineering (1993). **Personal:** Married to Birgit in 1993. One child: Richard. Dr. Marbach enjoys turkey hunting and measuring Glucose non–invasively.

Mr. William H. Patterson
••• ◉ •••

Vice President and Chief Operations Officer
Monarch Products, Inc.
4555 North Jackson Street, P O Box 1899
Jacksonville, TX 75766
(903) 586–0914
Fax: (903) 586–0866

3842

Business Information: Monarch Products, Inc. is a manufacturer of medical devices, created specifically to produce sterilization system containers, and distributed solely through Johnson & Johnson. Established in 1984, Monarch Products, Inc. reports annual revenue of $8 million and currently employs 50 people. As Co–Founder, Vice President, and Chief Operations Officer, Mr. Patterson is responsible for all aspects of the business. **Career Steps:** Co–Founder, Vice President, and Chief Operations Officer, Monarch Products, Inc. (1984–Present); President and Chief Executive Officer, Texas Processed Plastics (1981–1984); Executive Vice President, Tally–Ho Plastics (1971–1981); Plant Engineer, Shell Oil Company (1969–1972). **Associations & Accomplishments:** American Society of Mechanical Engineers; Society of Plastic Engineers; Texas Society of Professional Engineers; National Society of Professional Engineers; American Management Association; Marquis Who's Who; Alpha Phi Omega Service Fraternity; Who's Who Worldwide; Who's Who Among Colleges and Universities. **Education:** Lamar University, B.S. in Mechanical Engineering (1969). **Personal:** Married to Katherine in 1969. Three children: Lee, David, and Margaret. Mr. Patterson enjoys coin collecting and water skiing.

Robert K. Rasmussen
General Manager
Zero Gravity Medical, Inc.
459 Universal Circle
Sandy, UT 84070
(801) 566–7800
Fax: (801) 566–1700

3842

Business Information: Zero Gravity Medical, Inc. specializes in medical manufacturing, specifically advanced composite injection molded wheel–chairs, and pressure relief wheelchair cushions. A division of Ottobock, a German–based company, Zero Gravity Medical, Inc. distributes products internationally and has plans to expand with a new product line. As General Manager, Mr. Rasmussen is responsible for all administrative and marketing duties, in addition to coordinating research and development, and oversight of new products. **Career Steps:** Zero Gravity Medical, Inc: General Manager (1995–Present), Director, Marketing Sales (1994–1995), National Sales Manager (1994); International Account Manager, Honeywell (1988–1993). **Associations &**

Accomplishments: Previous President, ASHRAE. **Education:** University of Utah, B.S. in Civil Engineering (1984). **Personal:** Married to Kathleen in 1979. Five children: Jeff, Marc, Chris, Kim, and Emily. Mr. Rasmussen enjoys family activities, the outdoors, fly fishing, and mountain biking.

Jorge Ros

General and Plant Manager
Johnson & Johnson Professional
P.O. Box 2015
Las Piedras, Puerto Rico 00771
(809) 733–2424
Fax: (809) 733–9888

3842

Business Information: Johnson & Johnson Professional is an entity of the global consumer/professional/pharmaceutical healthcare products conglomerate – Johnson & Johnson. This division manufactures and markets Johnson & Johnson orthopaedic products (i.e., castings for bones, splints, bracing materials, braces) to managed care organizations and health care providers. Established in 1980, Johnson & Johnson Professional reports annual revenue of $50 million and currently employs 90 people. As General and Plant Manager, Mr. Ros is responsible for all aspects of management and plant operations, including administration, sales, accounting, strategic planning, and the supervision of five managers. **Career Steps:** Johnson & Johnson Professional: General and Plant Manager (1994–Present), Operations Manager (1991–1994); Johnson & Johnson Consumer Products: Materials Management (1989–1991), Engineer (1986–1989). **Associations & Accomplishments:** American Production and Inventory Control Society, Inc. (APICS); Chamber of Commerce, Puerto Rico; Puerto Rico Manufacturers Association (PRMA). **Education:** Worcester Polytechnic Institute, B.S. in Electrical Engineering (1985). **Personal:** Married to Wanda E. Torregrosa in 1985. Two children: Nicole M. and Jorge J. Mr. Ros enjoys volleyball, basketball, and computers.

Douglas C. Thomson

President
Depuy Canada, Ltd.
6695 Millcreek Drive, Unit 3
Mississauga, Ontario L5N 5R8
(905) 542–6077
Fax: (905) 567–4615

3842

Business Information: Depuy Canada, Ltd. is a national and international manufacturer and marketer of orthopaedic implants. As President and General Manager of Canadian Operations, Mr. Thomson is responsible for all the Company's Canadian operations, concentrating on sales, marketing, and staff training and development. **Career Steps:** President, Depuy Canada, Ltd. (1994–Present); President, Zimmer of Canada (1993–1994); Director of International Marketing, Zimmer, Inc. (1990–1992); Vice President of Orthopaedic Division, Zimmer of Canada (1987–1990). **Associations & Accomplishments:** Canadian College of Health Service Executives; Brampton Flying Club; Medical Devices Canada. **Education:** University of Guelph, B.Sc. Honors (1978). **Personal:** Married to Debra in 1977. Two children: Julie and Kelly. Mr. Thomson enjoys being a private pilot and camping.

Thom Goracy

Manager
Smith Holden, Inc.
325 Murphy Road
Hartford, CT 06134–2105
(203) 522–1134
Fax: (203) 246–4285

3843

Business Information: Smith Holden, Inc. is a family–owned company providing dental supplies and equipment to businesses in New England and Eastern New York. Established in 1850, Smith Holden, Inc. currently employs more than 20 people. As Manager, Mr. Goracy is responsible for all aspects of management, as well as serving on the Strategic Planning Committee. Concurrent with his position, he serves as Management Consultant in his own private consulting practice. **Career Steps:** Manager, Smith Holden, Inc. (1992–Present); President, Goracy Management Associates, Inc. (1982–1992); President, SRC Systems, Inc. (1989–1990); Partner, Dental Environments (1982–1986). **Associations & Accomplishments:** Committee Member, American Dental Trade Association; Institute of Business Appraisers; Published in magazines and industry journals. **Education:** Our Lady of the Lake University, M.B.A. (1992); Walden University, Doctoral Program. **Personal:** Married to Patricia G. in 1980. Five children: Tom, Missey, Sheila, Alex, and TJ. Mr. Goracy enjoys golf and running.

Steve A. Hunter

Vice President and Co–Owner
Barth Dental Lab
8820 East 33rd
Indianapolis, IN 46226–6501
(317) 897–8434
Fax: (317) 898–9658

3843

Business Information: Barth Dental Lab is a manufacturer of dental appliances, including crowns, bridges, partials, dentures, and cosmetics. Established in 1958 with 45 people, the Company's estimated annual sales are over $2.5 million. As Vice President and Co–Owner, Mr. Hunter is responsible for all aspects of Company operations, including administrative activities and research. **Career Steps:** Vice President and Co–Owner, Barth Dental Lab (1981–Present); Manager, Barth Lab Shelbyville (1979–1981). **Associations & Accomplishments:** United Methodist Church. **Education:** Elkhart Institute of Technology (1975). **Personal:** Married to Kim in 1992. Four children: Ryan, Dustin, Alex, and Allison. Mr. Hunter enjoys golf and cooking.

Mr. Michael A. Williamson

International Manager
3M Healthcare – Dental Division
3M Center, Building 275 – 2SE–03
St. Paul, MN 55133–3275
(612) 733–6660
Fax: (612) 733–2481

3843

Business Information: 3M Healthcare – Dental Division, a wholly–owned subsidiary of 3M Healthcare, specializes in manufacture and international distribution of dental equipment. With headquarter operations located in St. Paul, MN and a satellite office in Austin, TX, 3M Healthcare has over 54 subsidiary concerns around the world. In his capacity as International Manager, Mr. Williamson is responsible for all international operations for the Dental Division, as well as serve as liaison with all international subsidiaries, ensuring product compliance and proper distribution and marketing strategies. 3M Healthcare – Dental Division employs over 400 people and has annual corporate revenue in excess of $160 million. **Career Steps:** International Manager, 3M Healthcare – Dental Division (1993–Present); Marketing Operations Director, 3M (1989–1993); Business Manager – Europe, 3M (1984–1989). **Associations & Accomplishments:** American Dental Trade Association; Chairman, World Trade Commission; International Dental Manufacturers; Lions Club International. **Education:** Wilfrid Laurier University, B.Sc. (1971); McMaster University, B.A. in Business Administratio n.

NEY
DENTAL INTERNATIONAL

Henry G. Wolfe Jr., CDT

President and Chief Executive Officer
Ney Dental International Inc.
1280 Blue Hills Avenue, Ney Industrial Park
Bloomfield, CT 06002
(860) 242–2281
Fax: (860) 769–6047

3843

Business Information: Ney Dental International Inc. (NDI) is a manufacturer and international distributor of dental precious metals and dental laboratory equipment and supplies. As President and Chief Executive Officer, Mr. Wolfe provides the overall executive administration and vision, ensuring quality product output, customer relations, strategies and technological developments to keep the Company a viable presence in the international market. NDI's manufacturing facility is ISO 9001 certified and CE awarded. **Career Steps:** Ney Dental International Inc.: President and Chief Executive Officer (1995–Present), President (1994–1995); Vice President, The J.M. Ney Company (1988–1994). **Associations & Accomplishments:** National Association of Dental Laboratories; Grove Port Lodge #24, F&AM; American Dental Trade Association; Hartford Lodge #19 BPOE; Lu Lu Temple – A.A.O.N.M.S.; Hartford Club; Scottish Rite Valley of Columbus; American Legion Post 84. **Education:** Baldwin–Wallace College, B.A. (1968). **Personal:** Married to Betty L. in 1968. Two children: Jennifer and Joshua. Mr. Wolfe enjoys golf, hunting and bridge during his leisure time.

John R. Lubben

Manager of Strategic Accounts
General Electric Company – GE Medical Systems
20 Waterview Boulevard
Parsippany, NJ 07054
(201) 402–3938
Fax: (201) 402–3912

3844

Business Information: General Electric Company – GE Medical Systems a wholly–owned division of global electronics technology conglomerate, General Electric, specializes in the manufacture, service and international distribution of diagnostic imaging equipment for the health care industry. Products include Magnetic Resonance Imaging (MRI) and Computerized Axial Tomography (CAT) Scanners. They also market transportable diagnostic cassette imagers, particularly utilized in military field operations. As Manager of Strategic Accounts, Mr. Lubben's primary role is in the coordination and administration of GE Medical Systems Academic Centers located in conjunction with New York University and Columbia University. He also is responsible for the training of all sales force teams for the Southeast Asia entities. Established in 1920, General Electric Company – GE Medical Systems has annual sales of $3.7 billion. **Career Steps:** Manager of Strategic Accounts, General Electric Company – GE Medical Systems (1991–Present); District Sales Manager, Motorola, Inc. – Communications and Electronics Division (1984–1991). **Associations & Accomplishments:** American Management Association **Education:** Monmouth College, M.B.A. (1991); Monmouth College, B.S. in Marketing and Management **Personal:** Married to Janice in 1985. One child: Donald.

Robert S. Pryor

Senior Vice President, Americas
Sterling Diagnostic Imaging
P.O. Box 6101
Newark, DE 19714–6101
(302) 451–0575
Fax: (302) 451–0588

3844

Business Information: Sterling Diagnostic Imaging — a former division of E. I. du Pont de Nemours and Company — is an international developer, manufacturer, marketer, and distributor of diagnostic imaging products, including x–ray film, consumables and associated equipment, to radiology and x–ray practices worldwide. As Senior Vice President, Americas, Mr. Pryor is responsible for the direction of all marketing, sales and equipment services, as well as all administration and support operations for the Americas. **Career Steps:** Senior Vice President, Americas, Sterling Diagnostic Imaging (1996–Present); Director of North American Sales and Equipment Service/Support Operations, E. I. du Pont de Nemours and Company, Medical Products (1994–1995); E. I. du Pont de Nemours and Company, Medical Products; Glasgow Plant Manager (1993–1994); Newtown Plant Manager (1991–1993); variety of positions in marketing, sales and business management (1973–1990). **Associations & Accomplishments:** Member of Executive Council, Sterling Diagnostic Imaging; former Board member ASRT Education Foundation; Outstanding Graduate, Chemical Officer Basic Training; Recipient of the Meritorious Service Award during active duty assignment, U.S. Army. **Education:** North Georgia Military College, B.S. in Physical Chemistry (1971); Wharton School of Business, Executive Management Series; Columbia, Executive Management Series. **Personal:** Married to Pamela P. in 1981. Three children: Bobby, Blake, and Catherine. Mr. Pryor enjoys golf, boating, and activities associated with driving business cultural change through business process reengineering and high performance work systems.

Richard Tarrance

President
Custom Medical Concepts
P.O. Box 537
Vinemont, AL 35179–0537
(205) 739–9400
Fax: (205) 739–3812
EMAIL: See Below

3844

Business Information: Custom Medical Concepts develops teleradiology and x–ray communication systems to transfer information through the Internet with clarity to remote pathologists and orthopedic surgeons. Mr. Tarrance founded CMC in 1994, developing and marketing his unique product to medical institutions and private practices. As President and Chief Executive Officer, he is responsible for all administrative activities, marketing, and personnel decisions. Concurrently, he serves as President of Advanced Digital Computers. Internet users can reach him via: RICK@CNETI.COM **Career Steps:** President, Custom Medical Concepts (1994–Present); President, Advanced Digital Computers (1986–Present). **Educa-**

tion: Gadsden State College, B.A. (1972). **Personal:** Married to Ramona in 1981. Three children: Britney, Blake and Chace. Mr. Tarrance enjoys the Internet, tennis, and spending time with his children.

Felix Adorno
Production Manager
Millipore Cidra, Inc.
P.O. Box 11977
Cidra, Puerto Rico 00739–1977
(809) 273–8495
Fax: (809) 747–6553

3845

Business Information: Millipore Cidra, Inc. is a manufacturer of Medical Devices and Membranes for filtration and Diagnostic applications. Recent developments have been in the design of new membranes for diagnostic applications. Established in 1978, Millipore Cidra, Inc. currently employs 250 people. With twenty years expertise in Chemical and Biopharmaceutical manufacturing, Mr. Adorno joined Millipore Cidra, Inc. in 1988. Serving as Production Manager, he directs manufacturing areas within the plant, such as production activities and research and development of new products. Career milestones include working in the creation of new membranes for diagnostic applications for Millipore and improving the efficiency of steel furnaces electrodes while employed by Union Carbide. **Career Steps:** Production Manager, Millipore Cidra, Inc. (1990–Present); Senior Engineer, Waters (1988–1990); Assistant Head of Quality Control, Union Carbide (1981–1988). **Associations & Accomplishments:** American Society for Quality Control; Rosicruzian Order. **Education:** University of Turabo, M.B.A. (1991); University of Puerto Rico, B.S. in Chemical Engineering (1975). **Personal:** Married to Carmen Davila in 1980. Three children: Felix Jr., Rebbeca, and Adriana. Mr. Adorno enjoys airplanes, model aviation, and music.

Dorothea Hemphill Astl, M.D.
Vice President of Regulatory Medical Affairs
Electropharmacology
2301 N.W. 33rd Court, Suite 102
Pompano Beach, FL 33069
(800) 678–8020 Ext: 233
Fax: (305) 975–4021

3845

Business Information: Electropharmacology is a national manufacturer of medical devices and short wave diothermy for physicians, nursing homes, and hospitals, as well as research development in new technology for medical devices. A practicing physician for the past eleven years, Dr. Astl joined the Company in 1994. Serving as Vice President of Regulatory Medical Affairs, she is responsible for the oversight and management of projects, data entry, documentation, human resources, quality assurance, and quality control. She also regulates sales representatives to insure that products are within regulations and are recovered when not in use. **Career Steps:** Vice President of Regulatory Medical Affairs, Electropharmacology (1994–Present); Clinical Laboratory Director, Medical Associates (1990–1994); Scientist I, Bio–Dynamics (1983–1984); Director of Clinical Laboratory Services, Emergency Centre (1982–1983). **Associations & Accomplishments:** American Association for the Advancement of Science; Regulatory Affairs Professional Society (RAPS); International Society of Clinical Laboratory Technologists (ISCLT); Florida Technician License; Radiological Health Services; Author of articles published on pharmaceuticals and pharmaceutical research; Nominee to Who's Who in American Women; International Who's Who of Professionals; Harry Gold Pharmacology Award Co–Author; Fluent in Spanish; Conducted numerous clinical research studies in the areas of: Drug Interactions, Mechanism of Action of Drugs, New Drugs Bioavailability, Pharmacodynamics, Drug Efficacy, Clinical Trials; Author of numerous journal articles and abstracts. **Education:** Center of University Studies, School of Medicine, M.D. (1988); Nova University, B.S.; Northwest Institute of Medical Laboratory and X–ray Techniques, A.S.; Internship: Regional Military Hospital, El Cipres, B.C. (1988–1989); Fellowship and Clinical Research: Florida College of Medical and Dental Assistants (1979–1981), John E. Stambaugh, Jr., M.D., Ph.D. (1976–1978), Thomas Jefferson University – Department of Pharmacology (1973–1978). **Personal:** Married to John Daniel in 1973. Dr. Astl enjoys mystery and mystery movies.

Boudewijn L.P.M. Bollen

Vice President and Managing Director for European Division
Nellcor Puritan Bennett
Hambauenwetering 1
S–Hertogenbosch, The Netherlands 5231 DD
(31) 736485200
Fax: (31) 73420199

3845

Business Information: Nellcor Puritan Bennett is a designer, manufacturer, and marketer of specialty medical monitoring equipment and medical monitoring sensors (i.e., oxygen, ventilation, home care division, analysis equipment, therapeutic equipment). International in scope, Nellcor Puritan Bennett manufactures and distributes products all over the world. With more than twenty–one years experience in management, Mr. Bollen joined Nellcor Puritan Bennett as Vice President and Managing Director for the European Division in 1986. He is responsible for the direction and management of operations in Europe. **Career Steps:** Vice President and Managing Director for European Division, Nellcor Puritan Bennett (1986–Present); Vice President of Marketing and Sales, AHS/Baxter (1981–1986); General Sales Manager, Dico Bv (1978–1981); General Manager, Hilton Hotels (1975–1978). **Education:** Hotel Business School, M.B.A. (1968). **Personal:** Married to Ilona in 1974. Two children: Nathalie and Sander. Mr. Bollen enjoys golf, field hockey, tennis, sailing, and skiing.

David M. Cordier
Manufacturing Engineering Manager
Precision Interconnect
16640 SW 72nd Avenue
Tigard, OR 97224–7756
(503) 603–4748
Fax: (503) 620–7131
EMail: See Below

3845

Business Information: Precision Interconnect provides cables and cable assemblies for medical, diagnostic, ultrasound, and surgical equipment. International in scope, the Company is a division of AMP. As Manufacturing Engineering Manager, Mr. Cordier manages the manufacturing and process engineers in the cable plant. Internet users can reach him via: dave.cordier@precisionint.com. **Career Steps:** Precision Interconnect: Manufacturing Engineering Manager (1996–Present), Process Engineering Manager (1995–1996), Fine Wire Cable Team Coordinator (1995), Product Development Engineer (1987–1995). **Education:** Portland State University: M.B.A. (1994), B.S. in Electrical Engineering. **Personal:** Married to Julie in 1988. Two children: Nicole and Alex. Mr. Cordier enjoys tennis, Estes model rockets, playing the guitar, and singing.

Nina Davis, C.P.I.M.
Chief Operating Officer/Chief Financial Officer
New Star Lasers, Inc.
11802 Kemper Road
Auburn, CA 95603–9500
(916) 823–1434
Fax: (916) 823–1446
EMail: See Below

3845

Business Information: New Star Lasers, Inc. develops and distributes all medical lasers to hospitals and physicians, and provides the renting of lasers to laboratories. As Chief Operating Officer/Chief Financial Officer, Ms. Davis is responsible for the management of operations and finance. He handles materials, production, accounting, and product engineering. Internet users can reach her via: NynaD@aol.com. **Career Steps:** Chief Operating Officer/Chief Financial Officer, New Star Lasers, Inc. (1994–Present); Materials Manager, Sunrise Technologies, Inc. (1990–1994); Applications Engineer, Margaux Controls (1983–1986); Journeyman Welder, FMC Corporation (1975–1978). **Associations & Accomplishments:** American Production and Inventory Control Society; National Association of Female Executives. **Education:** California State University – Fresno, B.A. (1983); De Anza Community College, A.A. (1980). **Personal:** Married to James in 1986. One child: Sarah. Ms. Davis enjoys playing piano.

Sherri Marie Donaldson
Director of Operations/Marketing
International Magnetic Images
2424 North Federal Highway, Suite 410
Boca Raton, FL 33431
(561) 362–0917
Fax: (407) 347–5341

3845

Business Information: International Magnetic Images is an international medical diagnostic imaging company. The Company provides magnetic equipment such as MRI (Magnetic Resonance Image) machines to hospitals throughout the world. As Director of Operations/Marketing, Ms. Donaldson handles all marketing and operation aspects of the Company. She is responsible for customer relations, public relations, and strategic planning. **Career Steps:** Director of Operations/Marketing, International Magnetic Images (1993–Present); Johnson City: Medical Rehabilitation, Chief Executive Officer (1988–1992), Cardio–Diagnostics, Chief Operating Officer (1990–1992). **Associations & Accomplishments:** Beta Sigma Phi International. **Education:** Century University, B.S. (1994); Johnson County Community College, R.N. **Personal:** Married to John in 1988. Ms. Donaldson enjoys reading.

James L. Higgins
Owner
Home Health Care Plus
316 Neosho Street
Burlington, KS 66839
(316) 364–8055
Fax: (316) 364–8001
EMAIL: See Below

3845

Business Information: Home Health Care Plus, established in 1986, is a supplier of durable medical equipment and hospital supplies. As Owner and President, Mr. Higgins oversees all financial aspects of the Company, does strategic planning for the future, markets Company products to new clients, and introduces new products to established clients. Future plans for the Company include expansion into other markets and the establishment of new and larger stores. **Career Steps:** Owner, Home Health Care Plus (1986–Present); Command Senior Chief, MIOWU (1989–Present); Director of Emergency Medical Services, Coffey County E.M.S. (1991–Present); Foreman Ironworker, Daniels International (1980–1984). **Associations & Accomplishments:** Kansas Association of E.M.S. Administrators; United States Naval Reserve; Coffey County Chamber of Commerce; Rotary International. **Education:** Midwest Medical Academy of Pre–Hospital Sciences; Paramedic (1990). **Personal:** Married to Valorie in 1976. Three children: Joshua, Austin, and Blake. Mr. Higgins enjoys golf.

Steven E. Kaska
Director
Acoustic Imaging Technologies Corporation
10027 South 51st Street
Phoenix, AZ 85044–5204
(800) 541–8174
Fax: (602) 496–6679

3845

Business Information: Acoustic Imaging Technologies Corporation, a division of Daimler Benz Aerospace, is an international manufacturer of medical ultrasound instrumentation, utilized for radiology obstetrics and gynecology diagnostics. Future plans include entering new international markets by developing advanced cost effective high resolution ultrasound. Established in 1983, Acoustic Imaging Technologies Corporation currently employs 270 people. Joining Acoustic Imaging in 1993 as general manager, Steven Kaska was appointed Director in 1994. He has full executive administration over all global strategic marketing, as well as supervision of all staff at the Phoenix division. **Career Steps:** Acoustic Imaging Technologies Corporation: Director (1994–Present), General Manager (1993–1994); Vice President of Marketing, Diasonics Ultrasound (1991–1992); Director of Cardiology, Advanced Technology Labs, Inc. (1988–1991). **Associations & Accomplishments:** ATUM; Medical Marketing Association. **Education:** Wilkes College, B.S. in Commerce and Finance. **Personal:** Married to Rosalind Ann in 1983. One child: Steven Christopher. Mr. Kaska enjoys American history, writing, fly fishing, and travel.

Terry Paladini
Partner, Vice President, and Treasurer
Auragenics, Inc.
277 Broadway Mezzanine
New York, NY 10007
(212) 233–1925
Fax: (212) 233–1965

3845

Business Information: Auragenics, Inc. is a world–wide, exclusive distributor and marketing company of new technology in the medical and dental field, including the CUPID–Cardiac Ultra–Phase Information Diagnostic (a supplement to the EKG machine). Auragenics, Inc. currently employs 20 people. An economist with an extensive background in international banking/financing and consulting, Ms. Paladini serves on the Board of Directors of Auragenics, Inc. as the Executive Vice President and Treasurer. She is also responsible for all international matters, including administration and finances. Concurrently, she is the President and Partner of Federal Plaza International, an international consulting firm specialized in mergers and acquisitions, joint ventures, trade/finance and international banking. She is also the Corporate Director of Mhega Trade, Inc., an exporter of a Pig Iron from Brazil, with duties including the negotiation of discounts on Letters of Credit and pre–production financing. Career milestones include the restructuring and implementation of Zepter International USA, Inc. (a European multi–national company brought to the U.S. by Federal Plaza International) in the U.S., where she served as Vice President and Corporate Director during its restructuring phase (Jul. 1993 – Aug. 1995). **Career Steps:** Partner, Vice President, and Treasurer, Auragenics, Inc. (1995–Present); Vice President and Director, Zepter International USA, Inc. (1993–1995); President and Partner, Federal Plaza International (1990–Present); International Consultant, Self–Employed (1988–1990). **Associations & Accomplishments:** National Association of Executive Women (NAFE); East Side Chamber of Commerce, NY; American Association of University Women (AAUW); The Brazilian American Chamber of Commerce; The Brazil U.N. 95 Committee, Inc.; Lyons of Brazil; The James Beard Foundation. **Education:** PUC, Economics (1964); International Banking Institute, International Banking. **Personal:** Two children: Miriam and Jonathan. Ms. Paladini enjoys opera and tennis.

Barry G. Phillips

Vice President of Corporate Development and Government Relations

Racal Health and Safety, Inc.

7305 Executive Way
Frederick, MD 21704–8354
(301) 695–8200
Fax: (301) 695–4413

3845

Business Information: Racal Health and Safety, Inc. is a division of a British–owned company established in 1976. The Company manufacturers health and safety equipment for respiratory protection. As Vice President of Corporate Development and Government Relations, Mr. Phillips oversees and develops corporate synergistic opportunities, international sales, government relations and regulating activities, business partnerships, and corporate expansion. He is involved in the development of long–term strategic planning for expansion into other markets and locations. **Career Steps:** Racal Health and Safety, Inc.: Vice President of Corporate Development and Government Relations (1996–Present), Vice President of Marketing (1995–1996); Industrial Marketing Manager, Scott Aviation (1991–1995); Industrial Sales Manager, Ciehl Company (1987–1991). **Associations & Accomplishments:** Industrial Safety Equipment Association; Standards Committee – American National Standards Institute; American Industrial Hygiene Association; National Fire Protection Association; ISO Technical Advisory Group; International Society for Respiratory Protection; Safety Equipment Distributors Association; Environmental Assessment Association; "Who's Who in Sales and Marketing" (1989); "Who's Who in Environmental Registry" (1992). **Education:** California Coast University, M.B.A. (1996); Government Institutes; Marshall University; University of Wisconsin Business School; Milwaukee School of Engineering. **Personal:** Married to Suzette in 1988. Mr. Phillips enjoys scuba diving and outdoor activities.

Vincent Pluvinage, Ph.D.

President of International Operations

Resound Corporation

49 Spencer Lane
Atherton, CA 94027
(415) 780–7820
Fax: (415) 321–9568

3845

Business Information: Resound Corporation is a medical electronics manufacturer (sound processing chip for hearing aids – AT&T spin–off). In his current capacity, Dr. Pluvinage is responsible for all aspects of general management for international operations. Established in 1984, Resound Corporation presently employs 320 people and has an estimated annual revenue in excess of $60 million. **Career Steps:** President of International Operations, Resound Corporation (1991–Present); Vice President of Research and Development, Resound Corporation (1987–1991); MTS, AT&T – Bell Labs (1985–1987). **Associations & Accomplishments:** Little Flowers in New York – children's organization; Written for scientific journals, books, and trade magazines. **Education:** University of Michigan, Ph.D. (1984); UCL – Belgium, Master of Engineering.

R. Edwin Powell

President/Chief Executive Officer

Caire, Inc.

3505 County Road, 42 West
Burnsville, MN 55306
(612) 882–5007
Fax: (612) 882–5172

3845

Business Information: Caire, Inc. is a Minnesota–based manufacturer of medical devices which globally markets and distributes home respiratory products. As President/Chief Executive Officer, Mr. Powell is responsible for all aspects of Company operations, including management, employee supervision, strategic planning, and product development. **Career Steps:** President/Chief Executive Officer, Caire, Inc. (1993–Present); Vice President of Sales and Marketing, MVE, Inc. (1985–1993); Sales and Marketing Manager, Joy Manufacturing (1974–1984); Officer, United States Air Force (1969–1974). **Associations & Accomplishments:** Health Industry Manufacturers Association – Chair of the Home Care Committee; Board Member, Health Industry Distributors Association Educational Foundation; Board, Medical Alley; NAMES; Board Member, the Navigators. **Education:** University of Colorado, M.B.A. (1978); U.S. Air Force Academy, Baccalaureate Degree (1969); Texas A&M University, post–graduate studies. **Personal:** Married to Wendy in 1969. Six children: Elizabeth, Ralph Edwin III, Jonathan Edwin, Eleanor, David Edwin, and Emily. Mr. Powell enjoys golf, skiing, fly fishing, reading, and sailing.

Lee Schamus

Scientist & Engineer

Hughes Aircraft

2000 El Segundo Boulevard
El Segundo, CA 90245
(310) 616–6210
Fax: (310) 616–0394
EMail: See Below

3845

Business Information: Hughes Aircraft is a leading member of the aerospace industry. The Company provides electro–optical systems for military and commercial applications. As Scientist & Engineer, Mr. Schamus is responsible for software development, mostly for real–time systems. Internet users can reach him via: lschamus@ix.netcom.com. **Career Steps:** Hughes Aircraft: Scientist & Engineer, (1990–Present), Senior Systems Engineer (1982–1989); Principle Software Engineer, Honeywell Training & Control Systems Division (1989–1990). **Associations & Accomplishments:** Secretary–Treasurer, American Institute of Aeronautics & Astronautics – San Fernando Valley Section; Airplane Owners & Pilots Association; Scripp's Institute; Discovery Team, UC Regents. **Education:** University of Rhode Island; Southern Illinois University, M.S. Degree in Physics (1980); Washington University – St. Louis: B.S.E.E. (1977), B.S. in Physics (1977). **Personal:** Mr. Schamus enjoys flying, horseback riding, music, and computers.

Lorna Vega

Area Manager

Dade International

SJ 59 Valle San Juan Encantada
Trujillo Alto, Puerto Rico 00977–1307
(787) 755–2790
Fax: (787) 283–3211

3845

Business Information: Dade International specializes in the sales and service of diagnostic instrumentation for chemistry departments at hospitals and laboratories (both private and government). The Company owned 51% of Dupont Medical Products, but as of May 1995, Dade bought out Dupont in Puerto Rico. As Area Manager, Ms. Vega administers the sales office for Puerto Rico and the Caribbean, supervising market development. She visits hospitals to assess their equipment needs, presents products to the Med–techs, produces a proposal, and installs products with the service representatives. **Career Steps:** Dupont Medical Products: Area Manager (1993–Present), Technical/Sales Representative (1989–1993), Technical Representative (1988–1989). **Associations & Accomplishments:** Association of Medical Technologists in Puerto Rico; First Woman President, Club Exchange of Puerto Rico. **Education:** University of Puerto Rico – Medical Center Campus, Post Bachelor – Medical Technology (1984). **Personal:** Ms. Vega enjoys reading books, music, travel, meeting new people, gardening, and bowling.

Pearline Brown

Senior Scientist

Vistakon

5985 Richard Street
Jacksonville, FL 32216
(904) 443–3346
Fax: (904) 443–3342

3851

Business Information: A subsidiary of Johnson & Johnson, a global professional and pharmaceutical healthcare products conglomerate, Vistakon is a manufacturer of medical devices, specifically contact lenses (i.e. Acuview and Sureview). These medical devices must pass strict clinical trials regarding safety and efficiency. Employing approximately 1,800 people, the Company has an estimated annual sales of $500 million in 1996. As Senior Scientist, Ms. Brown is responsible for quality assurance related issues, internal and external auditing, and supplier certification (Lead ISO9000 Auditor). She is also responsible for test method development and transfer of products from Research and Development to production. She serves as a company wide quality trainer, and assists with facility set up. **Career Steps:** Senior Scientist, Vistakon (1995–Present); Quality Assurance Manager, NAmSA (1993–1995); Supervisor Quality Assurance and Regulatory Affairs Difco Scientific (1992–1993). **Associations & Accomplishments:** American Society of Microbiology (ASM); American Chemical Society; Alpha Kappa Alpha Sorority, Inc.; American Society of Quality Control. **Education:** Alabama State University, Master's in Biology (1988). **Personal:** Ms. Brown enjoys tennis and other exercise–related activities, reading westerns, and travel.

Alan R. Sartain

Vice President of Marketing and Customer Support

Polymer Technology

100 Research Drive
Wilmington, MA 01887–4406
(508) 694–1178
Fax: (508) 658–6111
EMAIL: See Below

3851

Business Information: Polymer Technology, an affiliate of Bausch & Lomb, is the leading manufacturer of rigid contact lenses, lens materials and solutions — marketed under the Boston brand name. Polymer Technology has one main location, with numerous general sales offices worldwide. Joining Polymer Technology in 1991, Mr. Sartain was appointed as Vice President of Marketing and Customer Support in 1994. He is responsible for all aspects of product marketing and customer support activities, including marketing and sales information, customer service, consumer affairs, and market research. Internet users can reach him via: alan_sartain@polymer.com **Career Steps:** Polymer Technology: Vice President of Marketing and Customer Support (1994–Present), Director of Marketing (1991–1994), Marketing Manager – Personal Products Division (1987–1991). **Education:** Montana State University, B.S. in Business (1983). **Personal:** Married to Melissa in 1983. Two children: Christopher and Matthew. Mr. Sartain enjoys snow skiing, hiking, golf, and jogging.

Jane C. Viscolosi

Distribution Account Manager

UVEX

27 Beth Avenue
Warren, RI 02885
(401) 245–0094
Fax: (401) 245–1322

3851

Business Information: A subsidiary of The Bacou Group based in Germany, UVEX specializes in the manufacture of safety products, primarily concentrating on eye protectors for factory workers and sports protection. The leading manufacturer of protective eyewear, UVEX has been in operation for over 20 years. Currently the Company employs 300 people. As Distribution Account Manager, Mrs. Viscolosi is responsible for all aspects of distribution and end user sales in New England, Eastern New York and Northern New Jersey. Concurrent to her position with UVEX, Mrs. Viscolosi is also an aerobics instructor and has been the Director of the New England Health and Racquet Club since 1985. **Career Steps:** UVEX: Distribution Account Manager (1992–Present), Manager of Customer Service (1989–1992), Technical Sales Representative and Marketing Service Manager (1987–1989). **Associations & Accomplishments:** National Safety Council; Rhode Island Safety Association; American Fitness Association **Education:** University of Rhode Island, B.S. in Business Administration (1983). **Personal:** Married to Lawrence L. Jr. in 1987. Mrs. Viscolosi enjoys aerobics.

Richard O. Austin

Vice President/General Manager of High End System Printing
Xerox Corporation
101 Continental Avenue
El Segundo, CA 90245
(310) 333–2059
Fax: (310) 333–6416
3861

Business Information: Xerox Corporation is the world's leading manufacturer and marketer of copiers, facsimile equipment, medical resonant image scanners, personal computers, and related chemical products. As Vice President/ General Manager of High End System Printing, Mr. Austin is responsible for development, delivery, marketing, and sales of high end cut sheet printers. **Career Steps:** Xerox Corporation: Vice President/General Manager of High End System Printing (1992–Present), Chief Engineer Software (1989–1992), Vice President of Client Services (1985–1989). **Associations & Accomplishments:** Board of Directors, Engineering Executive Institution Xerox Corporation. **Education:** Westcoast University, A.A., B.S. (1972). **Personal:** Married to Elma E. in 1963. One child: Heather M. Mr. Austin enjoys golf.

Paul Forte

Controller
Colex
P O Box 1487
Paramus, NJ 07653
(201) 265–5670
Fax: Please mail or call
3861

Business Information: Colex is a major manufacturer of photographic equipment and supplies used for developing everything from pictures to billboards. Established in 1971 and with estimated annual revenue of $13 million, the Company presently employs 86 people. As Controller, Mr. Forte oversees all financial reporting and activities. Duties also include responsibility for accounts receivable and payable, filing of sales tax information, commission program, treasury and investments, and Company and employee insurance. **Career Steps:** Controller, Colex (1993–Present); Corporate Controller, Diacolor–Pope, Inc. (1989–1990); Chief Financial Officer, W. R. Grace & Company (1969–1989). **Education:** Pace University, M.B.A. (1978); City University of New York, M.A. in Economics (1974). **Personal:** Three children: Francesca, Matthew, and Sandra.

David E. Getzik, CPA

Vice President of Finance
International Communication Materials, Inc. (ICMI)
P.O. Box 716, Route 119 South
Connellsville, PA 15425–0716
(412) 628–1014
Fax: (412) 628–1214
3861

Business Information: International Communication Materials, Inc. (ICMI), a wholly–owned subsidiary of NuKote, Inc., is one of the leading manufacturers of toner and developers for copiers, laser printers and fax machines in the world. Established in 1978 and acquired by NuKote in 1992, ICMI currently employs 200 people. As Vice President of Finance, Mr. Getzik is responsible for all aspects of financial operations reporting to the Senior Vice President. **Career Steps:** Vice President of Finance, International Communication Materials, Inc. (ICMI) (1994–Present); Joy Technologies, Inc.: Manager of Financial Reporting (1984–1994), Controller–Division (1980–1984); Senior Accountant, Price Waterhouse & Co. (1976–1980). **Associations & Accomplishments:** American Institute of Certified Public Accountants; Pennsylvania Institute of Certified Public Accountants. **Education:** Waynesburg College, B.S. in Business Administration (1976). **Personal:** Married to Debi in 1977. Three children: Kristopher, Timothy, and Stefan.

Ray A. Linn

Cardiology Manager
Eastman Kodak Company
Four Consourse Parkway, Suite 300
Atlanta, GA 30328
(770) 668–0500
Fax: (770) 926–3043
3861

Business Information: Eastman Kodak Company – the official imaging sponsor of the Olympic Games and the "World Leader in Images" – was established in 1880 and employs more than 100,000 people around the globe (54,000 of them in the U.S.). With major manufacturing plants in the U.S., Canada, Mexico, Brazil, England, France, Germany and Australia, Eastman Kodak markets a broad range of imaging products in more than 150 countries. In 1994, the Company's sales totaled $18 billion – about half of that came from outside the U.S., while exports from the U.S. totaled more than $2 billion last year. The Company invested about $850 million in research and development and more than $1 billion in plants and equipment. Kodak products include photographic films, papers and chemicals for amateur and professional use, motion picture films, copier–duplicators, electronic imaging products, including scanners, sensors, and printers, microfilm, image management systems, and diagnostic imaging film and equipment. As Cardiology Manager, Mr. Linn is responsible for the Cardiology Business, comprised of the Southeast Region of the United States of the Health Imaging division of Kodak. **Career Steps:** Eastman Kodak Company: Cardiology Manager (1992–Present), Account Manager – Boston, MA (1990–1992), Technical Sale Representative – Dayton, OH (1984–1986), Technical Sales Representative – Columbus, OH (1986–1990), Film Manufacturing (1972–1984). **Associations & Accomplishments:** American Legion; Veteran of Foreign Wars. **Education:** U.S. Army Still Photographers School (1968); Eastman Kodak Company Schools, Black and White Photography, Color Photography, Marketing Training. **Personal:** Married to Barbara in 1971.

Scott J. McCormac

Vice President of Finance
Houston Fearless 76 Inc.
203 West Artesia Boulevard
Compton, CA 90220–5517
(310) 645–0755
Fax: (310) 608–1181
3861

Business Information: Houston Fearless 76 Inc. specializes in the manufacture of film equipment, processors, cameras, and duplicators. The Company is also an integrator of electronic image equipment and software. Established in 1976, Houston Fearless 76 Inc. currently employs 125 people. As Vice President of Finance, Mr. McCormac is responsible for all aspects of financing, including banking, as well as the Accounting and MIS Departments. Mr. McCormac was with the Company from 1974 to 1979, and returned in 1982 as the Controller. **Career Steps:** Vice President of Finance, Houston Fearless 76 Inc. (1982–Present); Assistant Controller, Eldon Industries, Electric Power Division (1979–1982). **Associations & Accomplishments:** Active in his local Church. **Education:** University of Southern California: M.B.A. (1975), B.S. (1974); Attended the Witter School of Law.

John G. Ochs

Manager of Engineering Excellence
Xerox Corporation
800 Phillips Road
Webster, NY 14580
(716) 422–0388
Fax: (716) 265–5384
EMAIL: See Below
3861

Business Information: Xerox Corporation is the world's leading manufacturer and marketer of copiers, facsimile equipment, and related chemical products. Established in 1946, Xerox Corporation reports annual revenue of $17 billion and currently employs 80,000 corporate–wide. As Engineering Excellence Manager for the Print Engine Development Unit, Mr. Ochs is responsible for development and delivery of training materials to upgrade skills in the Design Engineering community. Mr. Ochs is also the corporate Subject Matter Expert for Quality Function Deployment. Internet users can also reach him via: John_Ochs@wb.xerox.com. **Career Steps:** Xerox Corporation: Engineering Excellence Manager (1993–Present); Quality Engineering Manager – New Programs (1987–1993), Quality Engineering Specialist (1982–1986); Senior Quality Engineer (1974–1981). **Associations & Accomplishments:** American Society for Quality Control; Xerox Management Association; Speaker, Automation Forum (1994); Speaker, Sensor Expo (1995); Vice President, Penfield Volunteer Emergency Ambulance (1985). **Education:** Rochester Institute of Technology, M.S. (1975); Lowell Technological Institute, B.S. (1969); National Registry of Emergency Medical Technicians; Certified EMT (1978); New York State Certified Advanced EMT–R (1983). **Personal:** Married to Janet in 1975. Three children: Joanna, Matthew, and Suzanne. Mr. Ochs enjoys reading, collecting baseball cards, and ballroom dancing.

Glen H. Pearson

Division Director – MREO Polymer Processing Division
Kodak Corporation
B2 Kodak Park
Rochester, NY 14652–4713
(716) 722–9138
Fax: (716) 722–7072
3861

Business Information: Kodak Corporation – the official imaging sponsor of the Olympic Games and the "World Leader in Images" – was established in 1880 and employs more than 100,000 people around the globe (54,000 of them in the U.S.). With major manufacturing plants in the U.S., Canada, Mexico, Brazil, England, France, Germany and Australia, Kodak markets a broad range of imaging products in more than 150 countries. In 1994, the Company's sales totaled $18 billion – about half of that came from outside the U.S., while exports from the U.S. totaled more than $2 billion last year. The Company invested approximately $850 million in research and development, and more than $1 billion in plant and equipment. Kodak products include: photographic films, papers and chemicals for amateur and professional use; motion picture films; copier–duplicators; electronic imaging products, including scanners, sensors, and printers; microfilm; image management systems; and diagnostic imaging film and equipment. Serving in various research and administrative roles for Kodak divisions since 1985, Glen Pearson was appointed to his current position in 1992. As Director of the MREO Polymer Processing Division, Mr. Pearson serves as the research manager, responsible for research and development in the area of polymer processing (injection moldings, extrusion, film manufacturing, extrusion coatings) and resin coatings. **Career Steps:** Kodak Corporation: Division Director – MREO Polymer Processing Division (1992–Present), Unit Director – Physical Perrformance (1989–1992), Laboratory Head – Electronic Interconnects (1987–1989), Laboratory Head – Polymer Physical Chemicals (1985–1987). **Associations & Accomplishments:** Society of Rheology; American Chemical Society. **Education:** University of Massachusetts, Ph.D. in Chemical Engineering (1976); Virginia Polytechnic Institute, B.S. in Chemical Engineering (1971). **Personal:** Married to Karen in 1971. Mr. Pearson enjoys golf, squash, and music.

Douglas Pileri

Director of Strategic Planning
Eastman Kodak Company
P.O Box 92988
Rochester, NY 14692
(44)–181–424–3
Fax: (44)–181–424–4
EMAIL: See Below
3861

Business Information: Eastman Kodak Company, established in 1880, employs more than 96,000 people around the globe, 54,000 of them in the U.S. With major manufacturing plants in the U.S., Canada, Mexico, Brazil, England, France, Germany and Australia, the Company markets a broad range of imaging products in more than 150 countries. Almost two thirds of the Company's sales come from outside the U.S. Kodak products include: photographic films, papers and chemicals for amateur and professional use; motion picture films; copier–duplicators; electronic imaging products including scanners, sensors, and printers; microfilm; image management systems; and diagnostic imaging film and equipment. As Director of Strategic Planning, Mr. Pileri oversees business development and product commercialization for Kodak's digital and applied imaging division. Mr. Pileri is a leading spokesperson on imaging futures. Internet users can reach him via: dcpileri@aol.com. **Career Steps:** Eastman Kodak Company: Director of Strategic Planning (1992–Present), Assistant to President, Paris, France (1992), Manager, S/W Platform Center, Rochester, NY (1990). **Associations & Accomplishments:** American Management Association International; The Conference Board, Board of Directors – Rochester Hemophilia Center. **Education:** University of Rochester, Executive M.B.A. (1990); Rochester Institute of Technology, B.S. in Computer Engineering. **Personal:** Married with two daughters. Mr. Pileri enjoys music, tennis, digital imaging, computers, and other cultures.

Jeffrey L. Smolinski

Vice President of Operations
X–Rite, Inc.
3100 44th Street SW
Grandville, MI 49418
(616) 534–7663
Fax: (616) 534–1295
3861

Business Information: X–Rite, Inc. is a national manufacturer and international marketer of color photometric instruments (i.e., photography equipment, printing presses, photocopiers) and instruments that remove silver from X–rays. The Company also owns Labsphere, a manufacturing company that produces a device measuring light for General Electric products. As Vice President of Operations, Mr. Smolinski is responsible for all aspects of operations for the Grandville manufacturing plant. **Career Steps:** Vice President of Operations, X–Rite, Inc. (1994–Present); La–Z–Boy Chair Company: Director of Operations (1991–1994), Director of Advanced Technologies (1988–1991); Advanced Systems Engineer, IBM (1987–1988). **Associations & Accomplishments:** American Society of Mechanical Engineers; Society of Mechanical Engineers; Voted Outstanding Alumni (1995); Member, Executive Network; Co–authored article for ASME; Co–authored, Tool & Dye Makers Handbook; Frequent speaker. **Education:** Michigan Technological University, B.S. in Mechanical Engineering (1983). **Personal:** Married to Barbara in 1983. Three children: Jennifer, Megan, and Kylo. Mr. Smolinski enjoys spending time with his family, boating, fishing, and camping.

Mary L. Trupo
Director of Area Communications
Eastman Kodak Company
4 Concourse Parkway, NE
Atlanta, GA 30328–5397
(770) 392–2935
Fax: (770) 392–2851

3861

Business Information: Eastman Kodak Company – the official imaging sponsor of the Olympic Games and the "World Leader in Images" – was established in 1880 and employs more than 100,000 people around the globe (54,000 of them in the U.S.). With major manufacturing plants in the U.S., Canada, Mexico, Brazil, England, France, Germany and Australia, Eastman Kodak markets a broad range of imaging products in more than 150 countries. In 1994, the Company's sales totaled $18 billion – about half of that came from outside the U.S., while exports from the U.S. totaled more than $2 billion last year. The Company invested about $850 million in research and development and more than $1 billion in plant and equipment. Kodak products include: photographic films, papers and chemicals for amateur and professional use; motion picture films; copier–duplicators; electronic imaging products, including scanners, sensors, and printers; microfilm; image management systems; and diagnostic imaging film and equipment. Joining Eastman Kodak as Sales Representative in 1984, Ms. Trupo was appointed to her present position as Director of Area Communications in 1991. She is responsible for all communications and public relations for the Southeastern states and Washington, D.C. Her duties include increasing the overall awareness of Kodak to internal associates and external constituents. **Career Steps:** Eastman Kodak Company: Director of Area Communications (1991–Present); Regional Property Manager (1989–1991); Sales Manager (1988–1989); Sales Representative (1984–1988). **Associations & Accomplishments:** Junior League of Atlanta; Spelman College Corporate Partners Council; Leadership Atlanta Inc.; Foundation Board, Camp Best Friends; Advisory Board, Children's Museum of Atlanta; Advisory Board, Atlanta Educational Partnerships (Atlanta Chamber of Commerce). **Education:** Old Dominion University, B.S. (1982). **Personal:** Ms. Trupo enjoys reading, swimming and motorcycle riding.

Gregory T. Walker
Worldwide Category Manager of Cartridge Film Products
Eastman Kodak Company
343 State Street Mc 0104
Rochester, NY 14650–0001
(716) 724–0702
Fax: Please mail or call

3861

Business Information: Eastman Kodak Company, established in 1880, employs more than 100,000 people around the globe, 54,000 of them in the U.S. With major manufacturing plants in the U.S., Canada, Mexico, Brazil, England, France, Germany and Australia, it markets a broad range of imaging products in more than 150 countries. In 1994, the Company's sales totaled $13.6 billion. About half of the Company's sales came from outside the U.S., while exports from the U.S. totaled more than $2 billion last year. The Company invested about $850 million in research and development and more than $1 billion in plant and equipment. Kodak products include: photographic films, papers and chemicals for amateur and professional use; motion picture films; copier–duplicators; electronic imaging products including scanners, sensors, and printers; microfilm; image management systems; and diagnostic imaging film and equipment. As Manager, Mr. Walker is responsible for worldwide category management and cartridge film products. **Career Steps:** Manager/Marketing, Eastman Kodak Company (1992–Present); Manager/Communications, Eastman Kodak Company (1988–91); Group Advertising Director/Vice President, Uniworks Group, Inc. (1986–88). **Associations & Accomplishments:** Greater Rochester Area Five Cross/Five Shield; Rochester Council; Alpha Phi Alpha Fraternity. **Education:** Miami University, B.A. (1976). **Personal:** Married to Sharon E. B. in 1977. Two children: Gaelyn and Erryn.

SECTOR
SPORT WATCHES

Alberto Carlo Milani
Executive Vice President
Artime U.S.A. Corporation
505 Park Avenue
New York, NY 10022–1106
(212) 826–0700
Fax: (212) 826–1018
EMAIL: See Below

3873

Business Information: Artime U.S.A. Corporation, a subsidiary of Artime S.P.A., is an international manufacturer and marketer of watches, such as Sector Sports Watches, Sector No Limits, Cadet, Philip Watch, and Lucien Rochat. Artime S.P.A. is the Italian Company of the Swiss group Artima–Philip Watch, based in Neuchatel, Switzerland. Italian headquarters are located in Milan, Rome, Naples, and Padua. Products are distributed worldwide through Artima S.A. of Neuchatel and is sold in 54 countries by authorized distributors. As Executive Vice President, Mr. Milani is responsible for the direction of the day–to–day operations of U.S. and Canadian markets, in addition to serving as liaison with the Italian parent corporation. Internet users can reach him via: SECTOR.NYC@AOL.COM. **Career Steps:** Executive Vice President, Artime U.S.A. Corporation (1993–Present); National Sales Manager, Artime S.P.A. – Naples, Italy (1992–1993); General Manager, Artime S.P.A. – Milan, Italy (1991–1992). **Associations & Accomplishments:** Jewelry Industry Council. **Education:** Herisau University – Switzerland, M.B.A. (1988). **Personal:** Mr. Milani enjoys marathons, snowmobiling, and mountaineering.

Michael A. Pucci
Director of Sales
Artime U.S.A. Corporation
505 Park Ave,
New York, NY 10022–1106
(708) 778–8052
Fax: (708) 778–8057

3873

Business Information: Artime U.S.A. Corporation, the U.S. arm of Naples, Italy–based Artime, SPA, is a manufacturer and marketer of fine sports watches — marketing under the brand name "Sector". As Director of Sales, Mr. Pucci oversees all sales aspects and personnel, covering the Western Hemisphere, Carribean and South Pacific regions. **Career Steps:** Director of Sales, Artime U.S.A. Corporation (1992–Present); Regional Manager, Raymond Weil Watch (1990–1992); National Account Manager, SMH Watch/Tissot (1985–1990); Vice President of Sales, Hallmark Jewelery Company (1979–1985). **Education:** University of Illinois (1979). **Personal:** Married to Sharon in 1982. Four children: Anthony, Nicholas, Bianca, and Gianna. Mr. Pucci enjoys computer science, golf, and language.

3900 Miscellaneous Manufacturing Industries

3911 Jewelry, precious metal
3914 Silverware and plated ware
3915 Jewelers' materials and lapidary work
3931 Musical instruments
3942 Dolls and stuffed toys
3944 Games, toys, and children's vehicles
3949 Sporting and athletic goods, NEC
3951 Pens and mechanical pencils
3952 Lead pencils and art goods
3953 Marking devices
3955 Carbon paper and inked ribbons
3961 Costume jewelry
3965 Fasteners, buttons, needles and pins
3991 Brooms and brushes
3993 Signs and advertising specialties
3995 Burial caskets

3996 Hard surface floor coverings, NEC
3999 Manufacturing industries, NEC

Craig J. Bailey
President/CEO
Landstrom's Original Black Hills Gold Creations
405 Canal Street
Rapid City, SD 57701–3100
(605) 343–0157
Fax: (605) 343–0535
EMAIL: bailey@Landstroms

3911

Business Information: Landstrom's Original Black Hills Gold Creations is one of the largest and oldest privately–held jewelry design, manufacturing, and distribution companies in the country. The Company produces tri–colored gold jewelry from materials found in the Black Hills of the Dakotas. By United States Law, Black Hills Gold products must be manufactured in the region. As President/CEO, Mr. Bailey controls the daily operation of the Corporation and its subsidiaries. He is involved in marketing strategies, cash management, product quality, human resource management, sales policies, and expansion planning. Mr. Bailey is also the owner of BMA, a management consulting company providing ISO 9000 consulting. **Career Steps:** President/CEO, Landstrom's Original Black Hills Gold Creations (1994–Present); President/Owner, BMA (1994–Present); Operations Manager, Graco, Inc. (1981–1994). **Associations & Accomplishments:** Rotary International; American Society for Quality Control; American Production and Inventory Control Society. **Education:** University of St. Thomas, MBA (1989); University of Minnesota, BA (1984). **Personal:** Mr. Bailey enjoys golf, traveling, and being a student.

Marie Colaianni
Controller
Tracey, Ltd.
2407 Boyd Avenue
Gallup, NM 87301
(505) 863–3635
Fax: Please mail or call

3911

Business Information: Tracey, Ltd. is a designer of contemporary Indian jewelry in silver, gold, and platinum. As Controller, Ms. Colaianni is responsible for all aspects of Company finances, including financial statements, taxes, and accounting. **Career Steps:** Controller, Tracey, Ltd. (1993–Present); Manager/Owner, JCOLAI, Inc. dba Class Act (1993–1996). **Associations & Accomplishments:** Soroptimist International. **Education:** University of New Mexico, B.A. (1988). **Personal:** Ms. Colaianni enjoys playing the piano.

Julieanne D. Wade, CPA

Controller/Vice President – Finance and Administration
Cathedral Art Metal Company, Inc.
250 Esten Avenue
Pawtucket, RI 02860–4827
(401) 726–2100
Fax: (401) 726–1790

3911

Business Information: Cathedral Art Metal Company, Inc. is a domestic and international manufacturer of import/export inspirational giftware and jewelry. A certified public accountant with over ten years expertise, Julieanne Wade serves as Cathedral's Controller/Treasurer. She is responsible for diversified financial and administrative activities, primarily overseeing all finance, accounting, and human resources divisions. **Career Steps:** Controller/Vice President – Finance and Administration, Cathedral Art Metal Company, Inc. (1994–Present); Manager, Kahn, Litwin and Company, Ltd. (1991–1994); Senior Accountant, Sansiveri, Ryan, Sullivan and Company, (1987–1990). **Associations & Accomplishments:** Rhode Island Society of Certified Public Accountants; American Institute of Certified Public Accountants. **Education:** Bryant College: B.S. in Business Administration (1987), M.S.T. in progress; Certified Public Accountant, Rhode Island. **Personal:** One child: Brandon C. Wade.

Vinod M. Zaveri

Vice President
Cinco Star, Inc.
22 West 48th Street, Suite 1005
New York, NY 10036–1803
(212) 921–1536
Fax: (212) 921–1628

3911

Business Information: Cinco Star, Inc., a family–owned and operated business since 1990, is a manufacturer of fine gold jewelry. International in scope, the Company distributes through sales people, telemarketing, trade shows, and magazines. As Vice President, Mr. Zaveri is responsible for all aspects of Company operations, including administration, sales and marketing, finances, and strategic planning. **Career Steps:** Vice President, Cinco Star, Inc. (1990–Present). **Associations & Accomplishments:** Jewelers Board of Trade; Manufacturers Jewelers and Silversmiths of America. **Education:** SPCE, B.E. (1979); IGI Diploma. **Personal:** Married to Usha in 1982. One child: Krishny. Mr. Zaveri enjoys reading.

Magalis Cruz

Manager of Safety, Environmental, and Human Relations
Wallace International de P.R., Inc.
P.O. Box 1177
San German, Puerto Rico 00683–1177
(787) 892–2065
Fax: (787) 892–5550

3914

Business Information: Wallace International de P.R., Inc. is a manufacturer of sterling silver tableware, featuring names like Towle, Wallace, Tuttle Sterling, International Silver, etc. As Manager of the Safety, Environmental, and Human Resources departments, Ms. Cruz is responsible for maintaining an accident–free workplace by means of employee education, audits, and coordination with management. She also serves as Chief of Security. **Career Steps:** Manager of Safety, Environmental, and Human Resources Departments and Chief of Security, Wallace International de P.R., Inc. (1991–Present); Operations Manager, E.P.A. Wood Specialties, Inc. (1990–1992); Safety and Personnel Manager, Henlo Industries, Inc. (1988–1990). **Associations & Accomplishments:** Professionals Association for Accident Prevention; National Association of Female Executives; Crozados de America, (Former Association). **Education:** Interamerican University, B.B.A. (1994); Numerous seminars and conferences: Enviromental, Health, and Safety Field and Human Resources Field. Graduate from OSHA Institute–Chicago, Train the Trainer. **Personal:** Ms. Cruz enjoys reading, sight seeing, travel and get–together activities.

Kenneth H. Ballantyne

President
Latin Percussion Inc.
1670 Belmont Avenue
Garfield, NJ 07026–2344
(201) 478–6903
Fax: (201) 478–7975

3931

Business Information: Latin Percussion Inc., a privately–owned family business, is the world's leading distributor and manufacturer of hand–percussion musical instruments. Joining Latin Percussion as President and Chief Executive Officer in 1995, Mr. Ballantyne is responsible for all aspects of daily operations, including overseeing all manufacturing functions. In addition, he oversees all administrative operations for associates and a support staff of 90. **Career Steps:** President, Latin Percussion Inc. (1995–Present); President (North America), Dendrite International (1993–1995); Block Drug Company: Vice President and General Manager (1983–1992), Vice President of Marketing (1981–1983). **Education:** Syracuse School of Business, M.B.A. (1969); St. Lawrence University, B.A. (1967). **Personal:** Married to Suzanne in 1969. Mr. Ballantyne enjoys the cultivation of hybrid tea roses, model ship building (Fighting Sail vessels), and collecting computer war games.

Mr. C. Terence Lewis

Vice President and General Manager
Yamaha Corporation of America, Keyboard Division
6600 Orangethorpe
Buena Park, CA 90620
(714) 522–9471
Fax: (714) 522–9301

3931

Business Information: Yamaha Corporation of America, Keyboard Division, the United States' number one musical instrument company, specializes in the manufacturing, marketing and distribution of keyboard musical instruments. Products include acoustic pianos, the Clavinova Digital Piano, the Disklavier reproducing piano and Silent Pianos. Yamaha was established in 1887, with total U.S. revenues of $710 million and currently employs 970 people. As Vice President and General Manager, Mr. Lewis is responsible for the administration and oversight of all U.S. operations for the Keyboard Division. **Career Steps:** Vice President and General Manager of Keyboard Division, Yamaha Corporation of America (1991–Present); General Manager of Keyboard Division, Yamaha Corporation of America, (1989–1991); General Manager of Piano Division, Yamaha Corporation of America (1986–1989). **Associations & Accomplishments:** First Vice President, National Piano Foundation (1988–1990); Chairman, Public Relations Committee, Piano Manufacturers Association International (1987–1989); Major involvement with: Smithsonian Institute; Make–A–Wish Foundation; National Endowment for the Arts; and numerous musical–related organizations. **Education:** Pepperdine University, M.B. in Administration (1994); University of Minnesota; Columbia University. **Personal:** Married to Margaret in 1983. Two children: Preston and Richard. Mr. Lewis enjoys music, lecturing, traveling, photography, skiing and wilderness trekking.

Jacqueline Randler–Buxo

Account Manager
Gibson Guitar Company
1422 Amberwood Circle
Murfreesboro, TN 37129
(615) 871–4500
Fax: Please mail or call

3931

Business Information: Gibson Guitar Company is one of the world's leading manufacturers of musical instruments. Product lines include guitars, accessories, banjos, and audio and acoustical amplifiers. As Account Manager, Jacqueline Randler–Buxo is responsible for the development and coordination of all marketing strategies for Latin America, Eastern Europe and Africa. Her prior expertise as an international customer relations management executive with major technological industries in Puerto Rico is definitely the key element in her successful sales strategies. **Career Steps:** Account Manager, Gibson Guitar Company (1996–Present); International Parts Specialist, General Electric Technological Services (1988–1993); International Customer Service Representative, Grand Island Biological Company (1986–1988). **Associations & Accomplishments:** Middle Tennessee State University MBA Association; Omicron Delta Epsilon (International Economics Honor Society). **Education:** Middle Tennessee State University, M.B.A. (1995); New York State University at Buffalo, B.A. (1986). **Personal:** Married to Arturo M. in 1994. Mrs. Randler–Buxo enjoys reading, travel, arts & crafts, the Internet, and art & history museums.

Mr. Eugene B. Reglein

Owner and Chairman of the Board
J.J. Babbitt Company Inc.
2201 Industrial Parkway
Elkhart, IN 46516
(219) 293–6514
Fax: (219) 293–9465

3931

Business Information: J.J. Babbitt Company Inc., established in 1939, is a manufacturer and international distributor of mouthpieces and caps for Clarinets and Saxophones. As Owner and Chairman of the Board, Mr. Reglein is responsible for overseeing management of all Company operations and directing strategic planning execution. In July of 1994, Mr. Reglein's son, William R. Reglein, was named the Company's President. **Career Steps:** Owner and Chairman of the Board, J.J. Babbitt Company Inc. (1994–Present); President, J.J. Babbitt Company Inc. (1939–Present). **Associations & Accomplishments:** Member, Former Board Member and Secretary Treasurer, National Association of Musical Instrument Manufacturers; Scottish Rite of South Bend; Active in Elks Lodge and Lions Club; Beautification Committee, Elkhart Chamber of Commerce; Lay Leader and Endowment Committee, First United Methodist Church of Elkhart.

Mark R. Blackford

Manager of Sales
Little Tikes Commercial Play Systems (OMNI), Inc.
14724 Proctor Avenue
City of Industry, CA 91746
(818) 333–8830
Fax: (818) 961–0111

3944

Business Information: Little Tikes Commercial Play Systems (OMNI), Inc. is a manufacturer and distributor of soft–contained play systems. Currently acquiring OMNI, the Corporation assembles and installs playgrounds for fast food restaurants, large family fun centers, small toys for individual marketing, etc. International in scope, Little Tikes Commercial Play Systems currently distributes products within the U.S., Australia, South Korea, Germany, and Austria. Joining Little Tikes as Manager of Sales in 1993, Mr. Blackford is responsible for the management of all aspects of the Sales Department, including inside sales for Asia and Pacific locations, sales support, marketing, and installation departments, as well as the development of policy and procedures for operations and providing leadership for team projects. **Career Steps:** Manager of Sales, Little Tikes Commercial Play Systems (OMNI), Inc. (1993–Present); Operations Manager, Modern Faucet (1985–1993); Vice President of Operations, Amartec, Inc. (1983–1985). **Associations & Accomplishments:** American Bar Association; California Bar Association. **Education:** Western State University, J.D. (1989); California State University–Fullerton, B.A. in Business Finance. **Personal:** Married to Jane in 1985. Two children: Jonathan and Nicholas. Mr. Blackford enjoys family, sports, and coaching son's soccer team.

Gary P. Brennan

Director of Manufacturing Operations
Hasbro Games Group
443 Shaker Road
East Longmeadow, MA 01028
(413) 525–6411
Fax: (413) 525–1823

3944

Business Information: Hasbro Games Group is the world's leading manufacturing company of toys, games, and puzzles. The Company has acquired Tonka Brothers and Calico, the manufacturers of cabbage patch dolls. As Director of Manufacturing Operations, Mr. Brennan is responsible for handling daily operations and strategic planning. **Career Steps:** Director of Manufacturing Operations, Hasbro Games Group (1985–Present); Plant Manager, Playskool (1982–1985); General Supervisor, MB Electronics (1979–1982). **Associations & Accomplishments:** Society of Plastics Engineers; Society of Mechanical Engineers; American Society of Quality Control. **Education:** Lehigh University, B.A. (1979). **Personal:** Married to Patricia in 1988. Two children: John and Michael. Mr. Brennan enjoys tennis, basketball, and fishing.

Kevin P. England

Director of Environmental Affairs
Hasbro, Inc.
1027 Newport Avenue
Pawtucket, RI 02861
(401) 727–5621
Fax: (401) 727–5883

3944

Business Information: Hasbro, Inc., established in 1920, is a leading manufacturer and distributor of toys and board games to retailers. As Director of Environmental Affairs, Mr. England is responsible for environmental compliance, remediation, auditing, and international affairs, as well as all funding and real estate activities. **Career Steps:** Director of Environmental Affairs, Hasbro, Inc. (1989–Present); Environmental Engineer, A.T. Cross (1989); Corporate Environmental Engineer, Textron, Inc. (1986–1989); Corporate Environmental Engineer, Augat, Inc. (1983–1986). **Associations & Accomplishments:** Chairman, Board of Directors, Recycling for Rhode Island Education; Waste Water Operators Association. **Education:** Bryant College, M.B.A. (1983); Providence College, B.A. (1979).

Lynn E. Hvalsoe

General Counsel
Nintendo of America Inc.
4820 150th Avenue, NE
Redmond, WA 98052–5111
(206) 882–2040
Fax: (206) 882–3585

3944

Business Information: Nintendo of America Inc. is an international manufacturer and distributor of consumer electronics, including video game hardware, software and accessories. As the world leader in video games, Nintendo's sales exceeded $4 billion worldwide in 1995. A practicing attorney in Washington state courts since 1981, Ms. Hvalsoe joined Nintendo of America as General Counsel in 1988. She is actively involved in the business affairs of the company and is responsible for the supervision and direction of Nintendo's legal affairs worldwide, including the oversight of all litigation, intellectual property protection, licensing, distribution, contracts, governmental relations on legal matters and international antipiracy programs. **Career Steps:** General Counsel, Nintendo of America Inc. (1988–Present); Partner, Karr Tuttle Campbell (1986–1988); Associate, Sax & MacIver (1981–86). **Associations & Accomplishments:** Frequent speaker on intellectual property licensing and protection at meetings and seminars. **Education:** University of Washington, J.D. (1980) **Personal:** Married to Clinton G. Chapin in 1978. Two children: Adam and Mark.

Jerroid N. Marks

President/Owner
MediaRave
320 Wisconsin Avenue, Suite 319
Oak Park, IL 60302–3459
(708) 524–9416
Fax: Please mail or call

3944

Business Information: MediaRave is a manufacturer of leading–edge interactive entertainment (Virgin and Aclaim), including video games for home systems, arcades, and the Internet. Established in 1995 with four employees, MediaRave has an estimated annual sales of over $5 million. As President/Owner, Mr. Marks, who began his career at the age of 23, is responsible for all aspects of company operations, to include overseeing development of new products. **Career Steps:** President/Owner, MediaRave (1995–Present); Senior Technical Consultant, Chicago Stock Exchange (1994–1996); Desktop Specialist, Kemper Securities (1992–1994). **Education:** Jones Metropolitan, HS Diploma (1991). **Personal:** Mr. Marks enjoys travel to the Orient, outdoor activities, parasailing, and whitewater rafting.

Linda Muren
Director of Customer Service
Century Products
9600 Valley View Road
Macedonia, OH 44056–2059
(216) 468–4391
Fax: (216) 650–6519

3944

Business Information: Century Products specializes in the manufacturing and distribution of juvenile furniture and accessories (i.e. infant carseats, strollers, highchairs, etc.). International in scope, the Company is headquartered in Macedonia, with manufacturing plants in Canton, Ohio, and Mexico as well as a central customer service center in Twinsburg, and subsidiaries in Oklahoma and Arkansas. Established in 1949, Century Products, with their Mexican subsidiary, employs 1,400 people, and has an estimated annual revenue of $160 million. As Director of Customer Service, Ms. Muren oversees all aspects of customer service for retailers. She is also responsible for administration, operations, public relations, marketing, strategic planning, and manages production and planning. Additional duties include direct supervision of eight customer service representatives, and handling of materials and shipping. **Career Steps:** Director of Customer Service, Century Products (1995–Present); Reliance Electric: Customer Service Manager, Distributor Products (1993–1995), Customer Service Manager, Drive Systems (1992–1993). **Associations & Accomplishments:** American Production and Inventory Control Society (APICS); Ohio Society of Certified Public Accountants. **Education:** Case Western, Masters (1994); Baldwin Wallace, Undergraduate. **Personal:** Married to Phillip in 1994. One child: Erika. Ms. Muren enjoys travel, team sports, and swimming.

Martin Tucker
President
Topsales, Inc., d.b.a. Topco Sales
11960 Borden Avenue
San Fernando, CA 91341–9010
(818) 365–9263
Fax: (818) 361–1295

3944

Business Information: Topsales, Inc., d.b.a. Topco Sales is a manufacturer and distributor of gifts, toys, and novelties. Main products include electronic light/water decorative gifts, novelty gifts, radio–controlled cars, Bugs Bunny toys, and cosmetic/bath products. Established in 1973, Topsales, Inc. presently employs over 260 people, has offices in Taiwan, Hong Kong,

and Los Angeles, and has an estimated annual revenue in excess of $14 million. As President, Mr. Tucker oversees all aspects of Company operations. **Career Steps:** President, Topsales, Inc., d.b.a. Topco Sales (1973–Present); Research Scientist, McDonald Douglass Aircraft (1961–1973); University of California – Los Angeles and Long Beach Community College: Adjunct Faculty (1965–1968), Faculty (1966–1967); Scientist, Hughes Aircraft; Scientist, Douglass Aircraft; Instructor, Metals Engineering Institute (1969–1971). **Associations & Accomplishments:** Director, Sheba's Society; Director, American Society for Technion (1990–Present); Member, American Welding Society for Metals (1959–Present); Member, Elks (1979–Present); Regional Professional Engineer, CA (1967); Fellowship Award, Hughes Aircraft (1962–1963); Fellowship Award, American Welding Society (1960); Professional Achievement Award, Douglas Aircraft (1967); Honorary Member, Veterans of Foreign Wars of the United States; Mr. Tucker is the author of two books: "Secret Joys" and "Crystal Energy"; Received U.S. Patent on May 31, 1994, entitled: "Inflatable Figure from Flexible Plastic Sheet Material." **Education:** University of California – Los Angeles, M.S. (1965); Washington University, B.S. (1961). **Personal:** Two children: Scott and Tracy. Three grandchildren: David, Megan, and Ethan Irving. Mr. Tucker enjoys tennis, volleyball, and basketball in his leisure time.

M. Joseph Brough
Vice President of Information Systems and Operations
Icon Health & Fitness
1500 South 1000 West
Logan, UT 84321
(801) 750–7789
Fax: (801) 750–7755

3949

Business Information: Icon Health & Fitness is a manufacturer and distributor of home exercise equipment to end buyers and all major retail stores. As Vice President of Information Systems and Operations, Mr. Brough manages all information technology, communications network, production loading in various plants, and order processing and shipping. **Career Steps:** Vice President of Information Systems and Operations, Icon Health & Fitness (1990–Present); Senior Consultant, Price Waterhouse (1989); Senior Consultant, Andersen Consulting (1987–1989). **Associations & Accomplishments:** Safari Club International. **Education:** University of Utah: M.B.A. (1987), B.A. in Finance. **Personal:** Married to Emily in 1985. Mr. Brough enjoys outdoor activities.

Robert J. Corliss

President/Chief Executive Officer
Infinity Sports, Inc.
28 Ridge Road
Lebanon, NJ 08833
(908) 832–6229
Fax: (908) 832–6040

3949

Business Information: Infinity Sports, Inc. is a manufacturer and retailer of sporting goods. International in scope, the Company manufactures under the "Bike" brandname. As President/Chief Executive Officer, Mr. Corliss is responsible for all aspects of Company operations, including management, marketing, and strategic planning for new opportunities, mergers, and acquisitions. **Career Steps:** President/Chief Executive Officer, Infinity Sports, Inc. (1993–Present); President/CEO, Herman's Sporting Goods, Inc. (1990–1993); President/Principal, Senn–DeLaney International (1985–1990); Director of Sales, Best Products Company, Inc. (1974–1985). **Associations & Accomplishments:** National Retail Federation: Board of Directors, Executive Committee; Board of Directors, National Retail Institute. **Education:** University of Maryland, B.A. (1976). **Personal:** Married to Melanie L. in 1974. Two children: Shelby and Bobby. Mr. Corliss enjoys sports and travel.

Peter J. Gilbert

Senior Design and Research Engineer
Titleist
2839 Laker Avenue East
Carlsbad, CA 92008
(619) 930–2114
Fax: (619) 930–2125

3949

Business Information: Titleist, established in 1940, is a designer, manufacturer, and distributor of a full line of golf products including socks, hats, golf clubs, and golf balls. The Company currently has 3500 employees and expects to post sales/revenues of over $500 million in 1996. As Senior Design

and Research Engineer, Mr. Gilbert oversees the design of the golf clubs produced by Titleist. His team consists of computer designers and skilled tool makers who design and develop prototype masters and mockups of golf clubs. **Career Steps:** Senior Design and Research Engineer, Titleist (1990–Present); Senior Naval Architect and Marine Engineer, John Gilman and Associates (1986–1990); Packaging Engineer, Hamilton Standard (1986). **Associations & Accomplishments:** American Society of Mechanical Engineers; Society of Manufacturing Engineers; American Society of Physics. Mr. Gilbert currently has received 2 patents and has 5 pending. **Education:** University of Massachusetts, B.S. (1986). **Personal:** One child: Evan. Mr. Gilbert enjoys golf, tennis, biking, exercising, reading, and travel.

Norman S. Leighty
Vice President and General Manager – International Business Unit
Zebco Corporation
6101 East Apache Street
Tulsa, OK 74115
(918) 831–6860
Fax: (918) 836–2616

3949

Business Information: Zebco Corporation is one of the world's leading manufacturing distributors of fishing tackle and electric fishing motors. Established in 1949, Zebco Corporation currently employs 750 people corporate–wide. An executive with Zebco since 1987, Mr. Leighty was appointed to his present role in November 1994. Currently serving as Vice President and General Manager for the International Business Unit, he is responsible for all sales and marketing of all products sold outside the U.S. He also manages numerous General Managers in foreign countries and 47 distributors, and is responsible for establishing processes and brokerage delivery. Career milestones include building the International Business Unit from zero to over 20% of Zebco Corporation operations. **Career Steps:** Zebco Corporation: Vice President and General Manager – International Business Unit (1994–Present), Vice President and General Manager – Browning Business Unit (1993–1994), Vice President of Marketing (1987–1993). **Associations & Accomplishments:** Board of Directors, Tulsa World Trade Association; Conducted numerous seminars; Published newspaper column in Boulder Daily Camera on fishing and hunting. **Education:** Indiana University: M.S. (1969), B.S. (1968). **Personal:** Married to Sharon in 1995. Three children: Jane, Ted and John. Mr. Leighty enjoys fishing, auto racing and playing the guitar during his leisure time.

Jack A. Martinez
President and Owner
Black Flys Eyewear
1560–B Superior
Costa Mesa, CA 92627
(714) 646–3389
Fax: (714) 646–0372

3949

Business Information: Black Flys Eyewear specializes in the manufacture of quality athletic protective eyewear (i.e., goggles and glasses) and snow boards. Established in 1990, Black Flys Eyewear currently employs 20 people and has an estimated annual revenue of $25 million. As President and Owner, Mr. Martinez provides the overall direction and vision of the Company's continued growth, quality delivery of products to customers, and all strategic developments, as well as all aspects of daily operations. **Career Steps:** President and Owner, Black Flys Eyewear (1990–Present); Owner, Lava Magazine. **Associations & Accomplishments:** Ski Industry Association. **Education:** Two years post–secondary education in Architecture. **Personal:** Mr. Martinez enjoys surfing, snowboarding, and skateboarding.

Matthew T. Morrett
Promotional Director
Hunters Specialties
6000 Huntington Court Northeast
Cedar Rapids, IA 52402–1268
(319) 395–0321
Fax: (319) 395–0326

3949

Business Information: International in scope, Hunters Specialties is a manufacturer of sporting goods and hunting accessories. Established in 1977, Hunters Specialities currently employs 200 people. As Promotional Director, Mr. Morrett is responsible for organizing and conducting national promotions, as well as directing his 50–person promotional staff. **Career Steps:** Promotional Director, Hunters Specialties. **Associations & Accomplishments:** National Rifle Association; National Wild Turkey Federation. **Personal:** Mr. Morrett enjoys hunting, fishing, and the outdoors.

Susan D. Daniels
Director, Corporate Gifts/Special Market Division
Montblanc, Inc.
75 North Street
Blooms Bury, NJ 08804
(908) 479–1600 EXT. 415
Fax: (214) 596–9289

3951

Business Information: Montblanc, Inc. is the world's leading manufacturer and wholesaler of writing instruments, desk and leather accessories, hand–crafted paper, and many other luxury items. As Director, Ms. Daniels is responsible for sales, marketing and advertising for the North American subsidiary of Montblanc, Inc., Corporate Gifts/Special Markets Division. **Career Steps:** Montblanc, Inc.: Sales Director (1995–Present), National Account Director (1993–1995); Field Sales Manager/Regional Sales Manager, Yves Saint Laurent Parfums/Cosmair, Inc. (1986–1991). **Associations & Accomplishments:** Incentive Manufactures Rep Association; General Management Award, (1995–1996); Budget Performance Award (1995–1996); National Account Management Award (1995–1996); Member: Incentive Manufacturers Rep. Association. **Education:** University of Texas – Dallas (1978); University of Texas – Arlington, Business Administration (1976–1978). **Personal:** Married to David in 1990. Two children: Katherine and Michael. Ms. Daniels enjoys family, exercise, entertaining, golf, and reading.

Paul C. Fisher

President
Fisher Space Pen Company
711 Yucca Street
Boulder City, NV 89005
(702) 293–3011
Fax: (702) 293–6616

3951

Business Information: Fisher Space Pen Company is an international manufacturer and distributor of the pressurized Space Pen used for U.S. and Russian space programs. Products are also distributed for retail sale in the better department and specialty stores. A pioneer in the ball point pen industry, Paul Fisher is the inventor and patent–holder of the erasable ball pen and the pressurized Space Pen (used on all manned space flights – American and Russian). After several years of designing tools and automatic machines, he founded Fisher Space Pen Company in 1948. As President, he is responsible for all aspects of operations, including administration, finances, public relations, marketing, strategic planning, and inventions. Career highlights include the recent creation of the "2010" pen, which is guaranteed to write until the year 2010. In addition, he is the author of four books on the importance of accuracy and fairness and how to apply the scientific technique (which has been used successfully in the physical sciences to the social sciences), and is the designer and builder of the first efficient automatic machine used to make tips for ballpoint pens. **Career Steps:** President, Fisher Space Pen Company (1948–Present); Assistant to the President, Aetna Ball Bearing Manufacturing Company (1993–1995); Fisher–Armour Manufacturing Co.: President, Consulting Engineer, Tool & Machine Designer, and General Manager (1946–1950); General Manager, Cedar Rapids Bakery (1936–1938). **Associations & Accomplishments:** Rotary Club – Boulder City, Nevada; Chamber of Commerce – Boulder City, Nevada; Writing Instrument Manufacturers Association; Recipient, Governor's Distinguished Nevada Business Award (1989); Advisor for the Government of Chile on how to cope with serious economic problems in inflation (1983); Recommended to serve on President Reagan's Team of Economic Advisors by Nevada Senator Paul Laxalt (1981); Selected by the Small Businesss Administration as Small Business Person of the Year for the State of Nevada (1980); Candidate for President of the United States in the New Hampshire Primary (1960); Author of four books: Common Sense Today (1952), Road to Freedom (1960), TAX REFORM – America at the Brink (1968), and THE PLAN – To Restore The Constitution and Help Us All Get Out Of Debt (1988). **Education:** Kansas State University, B.S. (1939); Attended: Coe College (1934) and Kansas Wesleyan University (1931–1934). **Personal:** Six children: Terry Fisher Hough, Pomm Fisher Olsen, Marteen Fisher Moore, and Cary, Morgan, and Scott Fisher. Mr. Fisher enjoys philosophy, economics, social science, writing, and business.

Mary T. Anton
Materials Director
M Grumbacher, Inc.
30 Englehard Drive
Cranbury, NJ 08512–3721
(609) 655–8282 Ext. 593
Fax: Please mail or call

3952

Business Information: M Grumbacher, Inc., a part of Koh–I–Noor, is a business dedicated to the manufacturing of artist and hobby craft paint and paper. Headquartered in Bloomsbury, New Jersey, the Company currently employs 100 people. As Materials Director, Ms. Anton handles the purchasing, planning, shipping, receiving, and warehouse functions of the Company. She is also responsible for key interfacing with the Marketing Department. **Career Steps:** Materials Director, M Grumbacher, Inc. (1991–Present); Manager of Logistics, Cosmair, Inc.; Manager of Master Schedules, Ortho Pharmaceutical – J&J Company. **Associations & Accomplishments:** APICS; Troup Leader, U.S. Girl Scouts. **Education:** William Paterson College, B.A. (1974). **Personal:** Married to Kenneth in 1981. Two children: Jenny and Ryan. Ms. Anton enjoys bowling, arts, and crafts.

Kenny Walker
Chief Executive Officer
Walker Stamp and Seal Company
121 Northwest 6th Street
Oklahoma City, OK 73102–6014
(405) 235–5319
Fax: (405) 235–1698

3953

Business Information: Walker Stamp and Seal Company is a family–owned manufacturer of marking devices, signage, and promotional specialties. The Company was established in 1951 and has approximately 17 employees. As Chief Executive Officer, Mr. Walker has oversight of all functions of the Company. He handles financial matters, personnel concerns, marketing of products and services, sales, public relations, and general day–to–day operations of the Company. By the year 2001, when Walker Stamp and Seal Company celebrates its 50th anniversary, Mr. Walker plans to have doubled the size of the Company and their revenue. **Career Steps:** Chief Executive Officer, Walker Stamp and Seal Company (Present). **Associations & Accomplishments:** Board of Education, Oklahoma City Public Schools; President, Downtown Lions Club of Oklahoma City; Board Member, Downtown NOW; Board Member, Carpenter Square Theatre, Inc.; Class 15 Leadership Oklahoma City; Board Member, Lake Hefner Boat Owners Association; Co–Chair, 1995 Opening Night Event. **Education:** Attended, University of Central Oklahoma (1972). **Personal:** Married to Kathy in 1992. One child: Natallie. Mr. Walker enjoys sailing, travel, and community service.

Theresa Morabito
Director Production Planning
ITW Medalist, Inc.
2700 York Road
Elk Grove Village, IL 60007
(847) 766–9000
Fax: Please mail or call

3965

Business Information: ITW Medalist, Inc. is a manufacturer of fasteners for automotive, distributor, and OEM businesses. The parent company, Illinois Tool Works, is located in 34 countries worldwide. Headquartered in Elk Grove Village, ITW Medalist has two manufacturing facilities and five branch offices around the United States. As Director of Production Planning and Control, Ms. Morabito is responsible for production planning and control at both manufacturing facilities. She is accountable for delivery schedule performance, inventory management, and department of 14 employees. As Director of Production Planning and Control, Ms. Morabito handles all production planning for the two Elk Grove facilities. She is responsible for the budget, schedule performance, and direct reports for her support staff. **Career Steps:** Director, ITW Medalist, Inc. (1995–Present); United Technologies Corporation: Operations Program Manager (1993–1994), Project Engineer (1986–1992). **Associations & Accomplishments:** Institute of Industrial Engineers; American Production and Inventory Control Society. **Education:** Western Connecticut University, M.B.A. (1992); Rochester Institute of Technology, B.S. in Industrial Engineering (1986); American Production and Inventory Control Society: C.P.I.M., C.I.R.M. (1996).

Melvin C. Seitz Jr.
Director of Corporate Relations
Service Supply Company, Inc.
603 E. Washington Street
Indianapolis, IN 46204
(317) 638–2424
Fax: (317) 638–6120

3965

Business Information: Service Supply Company, Inc. is a distributor of industrial fasteners and deals with original equipment manufacturing companies. A family–owned business established in 1948, the Company boasts 40 locations nationwide. As Director of Corporate Relations, Mr. Seitz is in charge of public relations and human resource management. He handles all personnel concerns including recruiting of management personnel and hiring. Concurrently, Mr. Seitz serves as President of the Seitz–Owing Foundation which assists not–for–profit groups in regions where the Service Supply Company offices are located. **Career Steps:** Service Supply Company, Inc., Director of Corporate Relations (1995–Present), President, Treasurer – Has been with the company for 40 years. **Associations & Accomplishments:** National Fastener Distributors Association; Nation Association of Wholesaler–Distributors; Metropolitan Development Commission, City of Indianapolis; President, Cole Commercial Arts District; Vice President, Cole Motor Car Club of America. **Education:** Butler University **Personal:** Married to Bette. Four Children. Mr. Seitz enjoys antique automobiles and Cole Motor Car Club of America.

Michael W. Ward
Divisional Operations Manager
YKK USA, Inc.
1306 Cobb Industrial Drive
Marietta, GA 30066–6607
(770) 427–5521
Fax: (770) 429–9324

3965

Business Information: YKK USA, Inc. is a division of YKK Corporation of America, a Japanese–owned holding company based in Tokyo. The Marietta, Georgia operation is a manufacturer of zippers and related closure product groups (i.e. hook and loop, plastic buckles, webbing, and Levi jeans buttons). As Divisional Operations Manager, Mr. Ward is directly responsible for five branches in the Southeast region and a staff of 15. The Southeast region includes the Caribbean, Puerto Rico, North Carolina, South Carolina, Tennessee, Alabama, Florida, Virginia, and Kentucky. One of Mr. Ward's functions is to establish excellent customer service with new and existing clients in the region. Other responsibilities are developing a viable budget, budgetary compliance, and planning for the expansion of his office. **Career Steps:** YKK USA, Inc.: Divisional Operations Manager, (1986–Present) and various positions within the Company (1976–1986). **Education:** Capital University, B.A. (1977); Marietta Cobb Vocational–Technical, Data Processing Technology. **Personal:** Married to Carrie in 1976. Two children: Robert and Monica. Mr. Ward enjoys fishing, going to flea markets, and writing, publishing, and recording music.

Jerry M. Robbins
General Manager
M&E Manufacturing Company
266 Union Avenue
Laconia, NH 03246–3139
(603) 528–1217
Fax: (603) 528–6306

3991

Business Information: M&E Manufacturing Company specializes in the manufacture and distribution of professional dental and consumer cosmetic brushes. As General Manager, Mr. Robbins oversees all areas for the cosmetics sector of the Company, including sales, marketing and overall production controls. **Career Steps:** General Manager, M&E Manufacturing Company (1991–Present); Anchor Advanced Products: Department Manager (1983–1991), Supervisor (1980–1983). **Associations & Accomplishments:** Write Your Congressman. **Education:** Attended: Walter State. **Personal:** Married to Trudy in 1992. Two children: Jessica and Joshua. Mr. Robbins enjoys golf and reading.

William J. Bell
Vice President of Sales and Marketing
Spindle Company
3710 Park Place
Montrose, CA 91020
(818) 957–0900
Fax: (818) 957–0035

3993

Business Information: Spindle Company is a manufacturer and designer of display signs and sign components. In 18 years the Company has expanded from a custom sign maker into a full–stock catalog operation, currently holding 60 percent of the national market. Established in 1975, Spindle Company currently employs 65 people and has an estimated annual revenue of $5 million. As Vice President of Sales and Marketing, Mr. Bell is responsible for the supervision of all inside and outside sales personnel, as well as the direction of all marketing activities. **Career Steps:** Vice President of Sales and Marketing, Spindle Company (1982–Present); Director of Operations, J C Penney Company (1968–1982); Store Manager, W.T. Granet Company (1963–1968). **Education:** Ohio State University, B.S. (1963). **Personal:** Married to Barbara J. in 1982. Two children: Tamara and Renee. Mr. Bell enjoys downhill skiing, studying Western History, and restoring classic and antique automobiles.

Robert L. Boggs Jr.

Corporate Quality Manager
Fred B. Johnston Company
P.O. Box 1359
Hillsborough, NC 27278
(919) 732–2126
Fax: (919) 732–5540

3993

Business Information: Fred B. Johnston Company is a manufacturer of high quality nameplates, faceplates, decorative overlays, and point of purchase displays. As Quality Assurance Manager, Mr. Boggs is responsible for the ongoing quality improvement efforts and ISO registration efforts. **Career Steps:** Corporate Quality Manager, Fred B. Johnston Company (1995–Present); Nameplate Division of W.H. Brady: Quality Assurance Manager (1994–1995), Manufacturing Systems Manager (1993–1994), Customer Service Manager (1992). **Associations & Accomplishments:** American Society for Quality Control: Certified Quality Engineer, Certified Quality Auditor; U.S.A. Volleyball: National Referee, Jr. National Scorekeeper, Treasurer of Carolina Region (1987–1992); North Carolina Volleyball Officials Board; Treasurer Atlantic Coast Conference Volleyball Official; National Society Sons of the American Revolution; National Society Children of the American Revolution; Senior National Chairman, Tomb of the Soldier of the American Revolution (1982–1984); National Convention Committee (1982–1996); National Second Vice President (1975); Youth Soccer Coach, Guilford College YMCA; Delta Upsilon Fraternity; Benevolent and Protective Order of the Elks; First Presbyterian Church. **Education:** Guilford College – Certificate of Accomplishment in Accounting; University of North Carolina – Chapel Hill, B.S.B.A. (1979). **Personal:** Married to Lisa in 1987. Three children: Trey, Ashley, and Kristin. Mr. Boggs enjoys family, volleyball, swimming, and coaching soccer.

Eugene C. Gillespie

President
Indoor Media Group, Inc.
3102 Maple Aveste 260
Dallas, TX 75201–1259
(214) 871–2277
Fax: (214) 871–2277

3993

Business Information: Established in 1992, Indoor Media Group, Inc. is a unique developer of media advertising sales products, currently marketing a floor–mounted image unit which allows brand image advertising at the point of sale. As President, Mr. Gillespie provides the overall direction and vision for the Company's continued growth, the quality delivery of products to customers, and business strategic planning. He entered a company and built it up in an industry that was very competitive, took a concept with no commercial value and turned it into an international success; personally reponsible for the promotion of the product. Starting his career as a sales representative, he has continuously worked his way up through various career steps with diverse commodities manufacturing companies such as: National Accounting Manager, Canadian National Sales Manager, Vice President of National Accounts, and Vice President. **Career Steps:** President, Indoor Media Group, Inc. (1992–Present); Vice President of National Accounts, United Distillers, Schenley Affiliated Brands (1990–1992); Canadian National Sales Manager of Food Service Division, Ernest and Julio Gallo Winery of Canada (1988–1990); National Access Manager of East Region, Ernest and Julio Gallo Winery, U.S.A. (1982–1988); Sales Representative, Procter & Gamble Company (1980–1982). **Education:** University of Missouri at Columbia, B.A. in Communication (1980). **Personal:** Mr. Gillespie enjoys sports, cultural activities, International Affairs, travel and the Arts.

W. Anthony Colson

Director of National Accounts
Batesville Casket Company
One Batesville Boulevard
Batesville, IN 47006
(812) 934–8004
Fax: (812) 934–8618

3995

Business Information: Batesville Casket Company is one of the world's leading manufacturers of burial caskets and cremation products. Batesville Casket Company is a subsidiary of Hillen Brand, (IN) — a publicly–traded Fortune 500 Company based in Batesville. With several years of marketing and training experience, as well as experience in intense strategic planning, Mr. Colson joined Batesville Casket Company in 1988. Currently serving as Director of National Accounts since 1992, he directly works with two large corporations that own and operate many funeral homes and cemetaries. He also does acquisitions for corporate travel. **Career Steps:** Batesville Casket Company: Director of National Accounts (1992–Present), Manager of Business Planning (1990–1992), Manager of Sales Training (1988–1990). **Associations & Accomplishments:** Indianapolis Athletic Club; American Society of Training and Development. **Education:** Indiana University, B.S. (1985). **Personal:** Three children: Lora, Sarah, and Erin. Mr. Colson enjoys boating, outdoor activities, and cars.

M. Ned Rogers

Senior Product Engineer
Batesville Casket Company
1 Batesville Boulevard, M/S E–30
Batesville, IN 47006
(812) 934–8474
Fax: (812) 934–7926

3995

Business Information: Batesville Casket Company is a funeral service and manufacturer of burial and cremation caskets and urns. As Senior Product Engineer, Mr. Rogers is responsible for product management of premium products and development, and creating new products. **Career Steps:** Senior Product Engineer, Batesville Casket Company (1990–Present); Advanced Manufacturing Engineer, PMI Food Equipment Group (1989–1990); Manager of Robotic Applications, Hobart Brothers Company (1984–1989). **Associations & Accomplishments:** American Welding Society; Society of Manufacturing Engineers; ASM International; Publication: Co–Author of One Chapter in the American Welding Society Technical Handbook (1996). **Education:** GMI Engineering & Management Institute, M.S. Degree in Manufacturing Management (1994); Le Tourne Au University, B.S. Degree in Welding Engineering (1984). **Personal:** Married to Mary in 1982. One child: Katherine. Mr. Rogers enjoys competitive volleyball and cycling, and spending time with his daughter.

Gregg Taylor

Director of Strategic Markets
Hillenbrand Industries
1 Batesville Boulevard
Batesville, IN 47006
(800) 622–8373
Fax: (812) 934–8618

3995

Business Information: Hillenbrand Industries is a manufacturer and seller of burial products, including caskets and cremation urns. Established in 1884, with over 3,000 employees, the Company has estimated annual sales of over $550 million. As Director of Strategic Markets, Mr. Taylor manages the sales and marketing efforts nationally to Hispanic, Asian, and African–American customer bases. **Career Steps:** Hillenbrand Industries: Director of Strategic Markets (1994–Present), Territory Manager (1991–1994); Owner, Spectrum Group (1986–1991). **Associations & Accomplishments:** NAACP; Boys and Girls Club; Phi Beta Sigma Fraternity, Inc.; Central Antelope Jaycees; Antelope Valley Republican Assembly; President, 3G Corp. **Education:** University of Oklahoma, B.S. (1983). **Personal:** Married to Laura in 1988. Four children: Brandon, Blaine, Bryce and Blake.

Sergio Velasquez

Country Manager
Stonhard Co. Inc.
Los Juarez 26
Col. San Jose Insurgentes, Mexico D.F 03900
(525) 563–9900
Fax: (525) 598–4614

3996

Business Information: Stonhard Co. Inc., a division of RPM, is the world's leading supplier and installer of high performance industrial seamless floors, coatings and linings; serving food processing, pharmaceutical, automotive, parts manufacturing, and beverage industries. International in scope, Stonhard Co. Inc. has locations in the U.S., Europe, Latin America, and Asia and reports annual sales of $150 million. As Country Manager, Mr. Velasquez is responsible for the management of the corporate business unit with a staff of 25 and annual sales of $5 million. He handles all aspects of profits and losses, including annual budgets and plans, directing activities of sales, marketing, operations and accounting departments, as well as developing and implementing short and long–term strategies for operations in Mexico. Additionally, he interacts daily with banks, lawyers and governmental agencies on issues, such as credit lines, employee benefits, and compliance with foreign investment regulations. **Career Steps:** Stonhard Co. Inc.: Country Manager – Mexico (1995–Present), Sales Manager – Latin America (1993–1995), Field Sales Manager – Northern Mexico (1992–1993), Project Engineer – Latin America (1991–1992); Sales Engineer – Colombia, Invisa S.A. (1989–1991). **Associations & Accomplishments:** Fluent in Spanish, English, and Portuguese. **Education:** Universidad EAFIT, Medellin, Colombia, B.S. in Civil Engineering. **Personal:** Mr. Velasquez enjoys soccer, sports, and spending time with his family.

Mr. Daniel Ackerman

President
Clestra CleanRoom, Inc.
7000 Performance Drive
North Syracuse, NY 13212–3448
(315) 452–5200
Fax: (315) 452–5252

3999

Business Information: Clestra CleanRoom, Inc. is a mechanical contractor specializing in the design and construction of clean rooms for high–technology, semi–conductor, and pharmaceutical manufacturing industries. The Company distributes internationally throughout the United States, Canada, South America, Mexico, Europe, and Asia. Mr. Ackerman is responsible for the direction and management of all corporate operational functions in America. Established in 1983, Clestra Cleanroom, Inc. currently employs 85 persons and reports estimated annual revenue in excess of $20 million. **Career Steps:** President, Clestra CleanRoom, Inc. (1989–Present); Division Manager, Clestra Cleanroom Europe (1985–89); Product Manager, Clestra Hauserman Europe (1981–1985); Development Engineer, Clestra Hauserman Europe (1978–1980). **Associations & Accomplishments:** International Society of Pharmaceutical Engineering; American Management Association; Fluent in French and German. **Education:** Ecole Nationale Superieure Des Arts et Industries, B.S. in Mechanical Engineering (1978); Institut Francais De Gestion – Paris, France, M.B.A. in Marketing (1984). **Personal:** Married to Kathy in 1980. Two children: Gael and Yann. Mr. Ackerman enjoys boating and motorcycling.

Harold A. Allen, Ph.D.

Owner and Chief Executive Officer
Quality Manufacturing Services
6000 Welch Avenue, Suite 15
El Paso, TX 79905–1840
(915) 779–1115
Fax: (915) 779–1335

3999

Business Information: Quality Manufacturing Services is a contract manufacturer located in Mexico. With corporate headquarters in El Paso, Texas, Quality Manufacturing Services manufactures electronic, mechanical, and medical products for U.S. companies. Establishing Quality Manufacturing Services in 1993, Dr. Allen serves as Owner and Chief Executive Officer. He is responsible for managing Company operations and finances, in addition to overseeing all administrative operations for associates and a support staff of 450. **Career Steps:** Owner and Chief Executive Officer, Quality Manufacturing Services (1993–Present); Chief Executive Officer and President, Texas Optoelectronics, Inc. (1981–1993); Vice President, Honeywell – Optometric Division (1977–1981). **Associations & Accomplishments:** American Electronics Association; Advisory Council, University of Texas at Dallas; Rotary – El Paso; Published technical articles and is owner to several patents; Frequent speaker at conferences. **Education:** Purdue University, Ph.D. in Physical Chemistry (1966);

Whitman College, B.A. **Personal:** Three children: Michael, Timothy, and Robert. Dr. Allen enjoys tennis and skiing.

Amy Arrow, Ph.D.

Executive Vice President
Oligos Etc.
15 Equestrian Ridge Road
Newtown, CT 06470–1869
(800) 888–2358
Fax: (800) 869–0813
EMAIL: See Below

3999

Business Information: Oligos Etc. is a manufacturer of synthetic DNA. As Executive Vice President, Dr. Arrow is responsible for all aspects of Company operations, including administration, research, and strategic planning. Internet users can reach her via: OEIOT2@AOL.COM. **Career Steps:** Executive Vice President, Oligos Etc. (1989–Present); Vice President, Co–Founder, and Co–Owner, Biotix, Inc. (1987–1989); Director of Research and Development, International Biotechnologies, Inc. (1986–1987); Fellowship, Department of Hematology, Yale Medical Center – New Haven, CT (1985–1986); Fellowship, Strong Memorial Hospital Cancer Center – Rochester, NY (1984–1985); Fellowship, Strong Memorial Hospital Department of Pediatrics and Infectious Disease – Rochester, NY (1983–1984). **Associations & Accomplishments:** New York Academy of Sciences; American Association of Pharmaceutical Scientist; American Society for Microbiology; American Chemical Society; American Association of the Advancement of Science; National Association of Female Executives; Sigma Xi Research Society; Who's Who in the World; Who's Who in American Women; Who's Who in Science and Engineering; Who's Who in Young Professionals; Who's Who in Emerging Leaders; Frequent publisher of various medical articles. **Education:** Ph.D. in Eukaryotic/Prokaryotic Drug Resistance (1986); Albany Medical College, Ph.D. in Antibiotic Resistance and Transport (1983); Colgate University, B.S. in Chemistry and Fine Arts. **Personal:** Married to Ed Yasko in 1986. Three children: Melissa, Jessica, and Cassandra.

Jonathan W. Ayers

Vice President, Strategic Planning
United Technologies Corporation
1 Financial Plaza
Hartford, CT 06101
(860) 728–7686
Fax: (860) 728–6355
E MAIL: See Below

3999

Business Information: United Technologies Corporation provides a broad range of high technology products and support services to the building systems, automotive, and aerospace industries. The Corporation has six operating units: Otis Elevator, Carrier Air Conditioning, Pratt & Whitney, UT Automotive, Sikorsky Aircraft and Hamilton Standard. Established in 1953, the Corporation currently employs over 180,000 people and expects sales/revenues in excess of $23 billion in 1996. As Vice President for Strategic Planning, reporting directly to the Chief Executive Officer, Mr. Ayers is responsible for acquisitions and mergers, corporate development, and strategic planning for all divisions within United Technologies Corporation. Internet users can contact him via: Ayersjw@cac.corphq.utc.com. **Career Steps:** Vice President for Strategic Planning, United Technologies Corporation (1995–Present); Principal, Corporate Finance, Morgan Stanley and Company (1986–1995); Manager, Bain and Company (1982–1985); Systems Engineer, IBM Corporation (1978–1981). **Associations & Accomplishments:** Board Member, Dow–United Technologies Composite Products, Inc.; Board Member, Greater Hartford Arts Council; Mason's Island Yacht Club. **Education:** Harvard Business school, M.B.A. Graduated with High Distinction (Baker Scholar) (1983); Yale University, B.A. in Molecular Biophysics and Biochemistry (1978). **Personal:** Married to Helaine. Three children: Kimberly, Lauren, and Margaret. Mr. Ayers enjoys sailing, skiing, art, and music.

Doris D. Bergamo

Vice President of Accounting
Devon Precision Industries
Munson Road
Wolcott, CT 06716
(203) 879–1437
Fax: (203) 879–5556

3999

Business Information: Devon Precision Industries is a manufacturer of over 200 items, including Swiss screws machine products. Joining Devon Precision Industries as Payroll Clerk in 1990, Mrs. Bergamo was appointed as Vice President of Accounting in 1993. She is responsible for all accounting functions, including the supervision of support staff, bank reconciliations, taxes, and financial matters. Concurrent with her position at Devon, she serves as Secretary/Treasurer of Alden Corporation, a manufacturer of broken bolt extractors, drill–outs, and new micro broken bolt extractors (which are only manufactured by Alden in sizes #5, #8, #10, and 1/4 inch). **Career Steps:** Devon Precision Industries: Vice President of Accounting (1993–Present), Assistant Controller (1993), Payroll Clerk (1990–1993); Secretary/Treasurer, Alden Corporation (Present). **Associations & Accomplishments:** Notary Public; Participated in Miss Wolcott Scholarship Pageant – Miss America Preliminary (1988–1991). **Education:** University of Hartford, B.S. in Accounting (1987). **Personal:** Married to Peter in 1988. Three children: Peter, Stephanie, and Valerie.

Carl E. Byrne

President
Imaginary Voyage, Inc.
8211 Evergreen Drive
Parkville, MD 21234–5508
(410) 668–0031
Fax: (410) 668–0031
EMAIL: See Below

3999

Business Information: Imaginary Voyage, Inc. designs and manufactures high tech display elements and special effects for the retail display industry, "creating fantasy through design." Mr. Byrne established Imaginary Voyage in 1986. As President, he is the central guiding force for the Company, leading the design process and coordinating project development from inception to completion. Internet users can reach him via: carlbrn@aol.com **Career Steps:** President, Imaginary Voyage, Inc. (1986–Present); Technical Specialist, Xerox Corporation (1976–1986). **Personal:** Married to Darlene in 1972. Two children: Laura and Kara. Mr. Byrne enjoys spending time with family.

Margaret C. Cegelski

Chief Financial Officer
Accessories Marketing Inc.
231 Beckett Place, Unit A
Grover Beach, CA 93433–1917
(805) 489–0490
Fax: (805) 489–1920

3999

Business Information: Accessories Marketing Inc. specializes in the manufacture of Slime, a flat tire prevention product, and private labels and decals for children's helmets. Established in 1993, Accessories Marketing Inc. currently employs 17 people and has an estimated annual revenue of $2 million. As Chief Financial Officer, Ms. Cegelski is responsible for all aspects of financial operations, as well as the coordination of all advertising efforts. **Career Steps:** Chief Financial Officer, Accessories Marketing Inc. (1992–Present); Controller, Access Marketing (1983–1992); Administrative Assistant, Cassette Productions (1982–1983). **Associations & Accomplishments:** President, Parent–Teacher Association. **Education:** Cuesta College (1981); F.I.D.M., Degree in Interior Design. **Personal:** Married to Steve in 1983. Three children: Danielle, Johannes and Alexander. Ms. Cegelski enjoys hiking, mountain biking, and designing, building and remodeling homes.

Mr. Michael E. Connors

Vice President of Sales and Marketing
Boston Retail Products
400 Riverside Avenue
Medford, MA 02155
(617) 395–7417
Fax: (617) 395–0155

3999

Business Information: Boston Retail Products is a manufacturer of merchandising equipment and impact protection products. Established in 1937, Boston Retail Products reports annual revenue of $25 million and currently employs 170 people. As Vice President of Sales and Marketing, Mr. Connors is responsible for coordinating sales, marketing and new product development. **Career Steps:** Vice President of Sales and Marketing, Boston Retail Products (1995–Present); Director of Marketing Paper Products Division, Avery Dennison (1993–1995). **Education:** Nichols College, M.B.A. (1992); University of Massachusetts – Amherst, B.S. in Marketing (1978). **Personal:** Married to Joan M. in 1979. Two children: McKenzie and Molly. Mr. Connors enjoys hunting, fishing, basketball, and gardening.

Susan Croft

Western Zone Sales Manager
E. I. DuPont de Nemours and Company
175 North Harbor Drive, Apt. 2604
Chicago, IL 60601–7345
(800) 472–1791
Fax: (708) 310–3233

3999

Business Information: E.I. DuPont de Nemours and Company, the ninth largest company in the world, is a research and technology–based global chemical and energy company offering high–performance products based on chemicals, polymers, fibers and petroleum. Committed to better things for better living, DuPont serves worldwide markets in the aerospace, apparel, automotive, agriculture, construction, packaging, refining and transportation industries. Established in 1968, the Medical Products Business Unit reports annual revenue in excess of $1 billion. Holding several positions during the last seventeen years with Medical Products, Ms. Croft was appointed as Western Zone Sales Manager in 1994. Serving as the sales manager for DuPont Diagnostics, she is responsible for 50% of U.S. revenue and 38% of worldwide revenue. She also manages and directs all sales managers and sales representatives, consisting of 66 people, including six district managers. **Career Steps:** E. I. DuPont de Nemours and Company: Western Zone Sales Manager–Chicago, IL (1994–Present), Western Sales Manager – Los Angeles, CA (1989–1994), Business Manager–Toronto, Canada (1985–1989), Market Development Manager–Wilmington, DE (1984–1985), National Sales and Marketing Manager–Toronto, Canada (1982–1984), Sales Development Manager–Wilmington, DE (1980–1982), Technical Representative – Indianapolis, IN (1978–1980); Laboratory Manager, Sandusky Memorial Hospital (1974–1978); Medical Technologist, Johns Hopkins Hospital (1970–1974). **Associations & Accomplishments:** Clinical Laboratory Managers Association; American Society of Clinical Pathologists. **Education:** Claremont College, M.A. in Management (1995); Jacksonville University, B.S. in Biology (1970); Certification: Board Certified Medical Technologist by The American Society of Clinical Pathologists MT (ASCP) #76666. **Personal:** Ms. Croft enjoys sports and exercising.

Lisa Dorr

Director of Controls Engineering
Vanguard Automation, Inc.
10900 North Stallard Place
Tucson, AZ 85737–9527
(520) 297–2621
Fax: (520) 544–0535
EMAIL: See Below

3999

Business Information: Vanguard Automation, Inc. is a national manufacturer of custom automation systems utilized in the manufacturing industry. National in scope, Vanguard Automation spans Arizona, California, and Minnesota. Established in 1984, Vanguard Automation reports annual revenue of $20 million and currently employs 175 people. As Director of Controls Engineering, Ms. Dorr is responsible for technical and functional management of 25–30 control engineers, quoting and concepting new designs, and developing engineering standards. She can also be reached through the Internet via: HOST!TUCSON!LISAD@vai.attmail.com **Career Steps:** Vanguard Automation, Inc.: Director of Controls Engineering (1994–Present), Manager/Engineer (1993–1994); Engineer/Scientific Analysis, General Dynamics (1990–1992); Research Assistant/Ultrasonic Hyperthermia, Arizona Cancer Center (1988–1990). **Associations & Accomplishments:** National Institute of Electronics and Electrical Engineers; Center for Software Excellence. **Education:** University of Arizona: M.S. in Electrical Engineering (1990), B.S. in Agriculture (1982). **Personal:** Married to Mark A. Taylor in 1995. Ms. Dorr enjoys scuba diving, horseback riding, and camping.

Mr. Gary E. Dove

Program Manager
Hopeman Brothers, Inc.
P.O. Box 820
Waynesboro, VA 22980
(540) 949–9201
Fax: (540) 949–9206

3999

Business Information: Hopeman Brothers, Inc. is a Marine joiner sub–contractor and is a turn–key supplier of ship interiors and accomodations. As Program Manager, Mr. Dove is accountable for schedule, product, budget, etc. for a particular program of the ship. **Career Steps:** Hopeman Brothers, Inc.: Program Manager (1989–Present), R & D Manager (1989), CAD/CAM System Manager (1986–1988). **Personal:** Married to Robin in 1979. Two children: Bridget and Gregory.

Christian Drapeau

Director of Research and Development
Cell Tech
1300 Main Street
Klamath Falls, OR 97601–5914
(541) 885–7585
Fax: (541) 885–7788

3999

Business Information: International in scope, Cell Tech is a developer and marketer of blue–green algae and related products through Network Marketing. Joining the Company as an independent speaker in 1994, Mr. Drapeau was responsible for giving weekend seminars and workshops for the Company's independent distributors. In 1995, he was appointed as Director of Research and Development, responsible for all aspects of research and development activities, in addition to conducting weekend seminars in North America. He works closely with 300,000 independenet distributors (as of April 1st, 1996) to provide them with scientific information and is involved in cutting edge scientific research in areas of nutrition and human physiology. He participates in designing harvest facilities to preserve all the nutritional values of the algae. He is also involved in the scientific aspect of public relations. Career milestones include developing and teaching a new approach to accelerated learning to teachers and students of various disciplines – this technique of accelerated learning was briefly described in Sheila Ostrander and Lynn Schroeder's book, "Superlearning 2000," describing how through the practical application of these techniques, Mr. Drapeau became the North American Champion (Black Belt) in Tae Kwon Do. He later created a manual on the self–use of accelerated learning techniques, entitled "J'apprends a apprendre" (I learn to learn) that will be published in April 1996. During his course of independent study, which was heavily influenced by his monastic experience, he explored the profound impact that forgiveness and spirituality can have on health, which he promotes to more than 300,000 Company distributors. He also studied herbal medicine and the use of essential oils, nutrition, fasting, and yoga. After his extensive private research, he wrote another book, entitled "Natural Healing," which will be published in 1997. He is also the author of another book, a piece of fiction meant for the average reader, giving them an introduction to French philosophers of the 18th and 19th centuries, Plato, Pythagorus and the teaching of the great religions. **Career Steps:** Director of Research and Development, Cell Tech (1995–Present); Trainer and Writer, Christian Drapeau, Inc. (1993–Present). **Associations & Accomplishments:** Association for Global Learning; AQETA – Quebec Association for Learning Disabilities; APMDQ – Quebec Association of Alternative Medicine Practitioners; Earth Save; ACLO – Association of Knights of the Golden Lotus – spiritual brotherhood; Lived in a monastery in the South of France after receiving Masters Degree; Co–Hosted a health and science radio show which aired weekly in Montreal (1993–1994); Wrote and hosted a three–hour special on Radio–Canada, on the life of Mahatma Gandhi and the practical implementation of non–violence as a powerful political strategy for social reform in North America. **Education:** McGill University: M.S. in Neurology and Neurosurgery (1991), B.S. **Personal:** Mr. Drapeau enjoys reading, writing, horseback riding, and wild river canoeing.

Carmen E. Emery

Executive Manager – Customer Relations
Brother International
200 Cottontail Lane
Somerset, NJ 08875
(908) 356–0880 Ext: 3716
Fax: (908) 563–4226

3999

Business Information: Brother International is an international manufacturer of home office equipment. Established in 1954, Brother International reports annual revenue of $1 billion. As Executive Manager – Customer Relations, Ms. Emery directs all customer relations (policies and procedures) for all product groups and conducts all professional training. **Career Steps:** Brother International: Executive Manager – Customer Relations (Aug. 1995–Present), Manager – FAX Diagnostic Center (1994–1995); Manager – Sales Administration and Marketing Support, TEMCO HealthCare; Manager of Customer Service, Regina Corporation. **Associations & Accomplishments:** National Association of Female Executives. **Personal:** One child: George.

Mr. Juan A. Fernandez

Director
TeleBrands Corporation
81 Two Bridges Road
Fairfield, NJ 07004–1039
(201) 244–0300
Fax: (201) 244–0233
EMAIL: See Below

3999

Business Information: TeleBrands Corporation is a national and international manufacturer, wholesaler and retailer of "As Seen On TV" products. Clientele include K–Mart, Wal–Mart, and Sam's Wholesale Club. Sixty to eighty percent of the products are imported. International in scope, TeleBrands has locations in the U.S., Hong Kong, London, India, and Spain. Joining TeleBrands Corporation as Director in 1993, Mr. Fernandez is responsible for the direction of the Manufacturing, Procurement and Quality Control divisions. Internet users can reach him via: (201)206–0577@MCIMAIL.COM **Career Steps:** Director, TeleBrands Corporation (1993–Present); Electronic Engineer, Gemini Industries (1990–1993); Consulting Engineer, Lewis S. Goodfriend & Associates (1987–1989). **Associations & Accomplishments:** American Society for Quality Control; National Association of Purchasing Management. **Education:** Stevens Institute of Technology, B.S. in Electrical Engineering (1986). **Personal:** Mr. Fernandez enjoys skiing, music, travel, and scuba diving.

Daniel J. Frantz

Director of Public Affairs
Jet Blast Products Corporation
6800 Fort Smallwood Road
Baltimore, MD 21226–1710
(410) 636–0816
Fax: Please mail or call
HOME:(410)547–0249

3999

Business Information: Jet Blast Products Corporation manufactures and distributes a DIY line for the consumer. As Director of Public Affairs, Mr. Frantz coordinates all press releases, interviews, radio and print advertising, and maintains the media database. Responsible for all pre & post trade show publicity. **Career Steps:** Director of Public Affairs, Jet Blast Products Corporation (1995–Present); Public Affairs Coordinator, Pennsylvania Resources Council (1990–1994); Director of Sales/Promotions Coordinator, Pulsation's Entertainment Complex (1986–1990). **Associations & Accomplishments:** Maryland Chamber of Commerce; Lambda Iota Tau International Literature Honor Society. **Education:** Cabrini College, B.A. in English /Communication (with Literature and Theater concentration) (1995).

Paul J. Gerstenberger

Chief Executive Officer
Child Safe International, L.L.C.
3065 Center Green Drive, Suite 220
Boulder, CO 80301
(303) 444–7474
Fax: (303) 444–4438

3999

Business Information: Child Safe International, LLC is an international manufacturer of child safety products. The Company's main product is a stuffed animal backpack with an electronic device to prevent child abduction, called "Safe Pack." Returning to the business world after retiring several years ago, Mr. Gerstenberger established Child Safe International in 1995. As an inventor and Chief Executive Officer, he is responsible for all aspects of operations, in addition to overseeing all administrative operations for associates and a support staff of 12. He previously served as Chief Executive Officer of P.J.G. International in which he was the inventor of various products from toys to medical equipment. His career milestone is the invention of "Safe Pack." Additionally, Mr. Gerstenberger established a company in October of 1995 — 3C273 — and serves as Chief Executive Officer. **Career Steps:** Chief Executive Officer, Child Safe International, LLC (1995–Present); Chief Executive Officer, P.J.G. International, Inc. (1988–1995). **Associations & Accomplishments:** Okinawan Shurite Karate Association. **Education:** University of Colorado. **Personal:** Married to Tana in 1985. Four children: Joseph, Aliene, Mandi and Erin. Mr. Gerstenberger enjoys skiing and sports cars.

Paul E. Glassman

Manager of Planning and Materials
Magnetek–Ohio Transformer
2001 US Highway 301
Palmetto, FL 34221–6513
(941) 729–5606
Fax: (941) 722–2549

3999

Business Information: Magnetek–Ohio Transformer, established in 1988, remanufactures oil–filled transformers. Boasting $13 million in annual sales and employing 100+ people, the Company hopes to dramatically increase sales and market recognition in the near future. As Manager of Planning and Materials, Mr. Glassman is responsible for diversified administrative activities, including purchasing, human resources, and accounting. **Career Steps:** Manager of Planning and Materials, Magnetek–Ohio Transformer (1993–Present); Waukesha Electric: Engineering and Marketing Planner (1990–1993), Materials Planner (1987–1990), Shop Floor Planner (1982–1987). **Associations & Accomplishments:** APICS Certified (CPIM); Board of Governors–School Board for Manatee Area Technical College; SAC–Chairman–Manatee Area Technical College. **Education:** Cardinal Stritch College, B.S. in Business Administration (1990). **Personal:** Married to Dawn in 1985. Two children: Robert and Madeline. Mr. Glassman enjoys golf, raising children, reading and community service.

Patricia S. Grigg

Human Resources Manager
MCL, Inc.
501 South Woodcreek Road
Bolingbrook, IL 60440
(708) 759–9500
Fax: (708) 759–0902

3999

Business Information: MCL, Inc. is a manufacturer of high power amplifiers for the satellite communications industry. Established in 1961, MCL, Inc. reports annual revenue of $30 million and currently employs 132 people. As Human Resources Manager, Ms. Grigg oversees all personnel matters, including recruiting, salary administration, benefits, safety, employee counseling, training, etc. **Career Steps:** Human Resources Manager, MCL, Inc. (1990–Present); Human Resources Administrator, Interlake (1986–1990); Administrative Coordinator, JCAH (1982–1986). **Associations & Accomplishments:** Society for Human Resources Management (SHRM); Society for Human Resources Professionals (SHRP); Management Association of Illinois (MAI); American Compensation Association (ACA). **Education:** De Paul University, B.A. in Business Administration (1993). **Personal:** Married to William in 1992. One child: Amanda. Ms. Grigg enjoys spending time with her family, bike riding, travel, reading, and volleyball.

William W. Heminghous

Director of Quality and Technology
Thomson Bay Company
1645 Marquette Street
Bay City, MI 48706–4179
(517) 776–5111
Fax: (517) 686–7920

3999

Business Information: Thomson Bay Company, located in Bay City, Michigan, is a manufacturer of linear motion systems, ballscrews, and linear slides. The corporation was established in 1987 and has approximately 125 employees. As Director of Quality and Technology, Mr. Heminghous is in charge of product quality assurance and makes sure manufactured items meet industry safety standards. He is also responsible for the development and implementation of new technological changes in the field of linear motion systems. Mr. Heminghous was instrumental in instituting a quality assurance program at Thomson Bay and is constantly monitoring and changing the company standards. **Career Steps:** Director of Quality and Technology, Thomson Bay Company (1991–Present); Director of Quality, Thomson Saginaw Ballscrews Company (1988–1991); Manager Science Labs, Sverdenp Tech/NASA (1986–1988); Manager Quality Services, Teledyne continental Motors (1983–1986). **Associations & Accomplishments:** American Society for Metals; Society of Automotive Engineers; American Society for Quality Control; Who's Who in the Midwest, 1995; Young American Men and Women of Science, 1994. **Education:** Eastern Michigan University, Attending for MS; University of Illinois, BS. **Personal:** Married to Brenda in 1970. Three children: Lydia, John, and William, Jr. Mr. Heminghous enjoys fishing, hunting, walking, and using the computer.

Mark Allen Henslee
Manufacturing Engineering Manager
Globe Motors Division – Labinal Components and Systems
3887 Napier Field Road
Dothan, AL 36303
(334) 983–3542
Fax: Please mail or call

3999

Business Information: Globe Motors Division – Labinal Components and Systems is a manufacturer of custom and semi–custom micromotor devices used in aerospace, medical, computer, and automotive markets. Established in 1943, Globe Motors Division reports annual revenue in excess of $60 million and currently employs 500 people. Experienced in engineering and product management, Mr. Henslee joined Globe Motors Division as Manufacturing Engineering Manager in 1993. He is responsible for managing the Manufacturing Engineering Department in the Dothan, Alabama plant and re-establishing the manufacturing engineering function in the Reynosa, Mexico plant. He also implemented a derivative product release procedure shortening the process from eight weeks to two weeks, formalized the cost reduction program, introduced cellular manufacturing techniques successfully, and started up over fifteen million dollars of new business. **Career Steps:** Manufacturing Engineering Manager, Globe Motors Division – Labinal Components and Systems (1993–Present); Prestolite Electric Inc. (1988–1993): Program Manager – Heavy Duty Motor Products; Unit Operations Manager – Starter Motor Products; General Foreman – Machining Operations; Foreman – Casting Machining; Supervisor – Production Engineering; Production Engineer; Borg-Warner Automotive Control Systems: Manufacturing Engineer (1986–1988), Tooling Design Engineer (summer 1985). **Associations & Accomplishments:** American Society of Engineering Management; American Management Association; Society of Management Engineers; Institute of Industrial Engineers; Society of Automotive Engineers. **Education:** University of Missouri – Rolla, B.S. in Engineering Management (1985). **Personal:** Married to Dana in 1989. One child: Aaron Neal Henslee. Mr. Henslee enjoys sailing and rebuilding old cars.

Larry P. Holleran
Vice President
FMC Corporation
1315 Greenwood Avenue
Wilmette, IL 60091
(312) 861–5882
Fax: (312) 561–5913

3999

Business Information: FMC Corporation, a Fortune 500 company, is a diversified international manufacturer of chemicals, defense equipment and food machinery. A twenty–three year veteran of FMC, Mr. Holleran has served as Vice President since 1985, reporting directly to the President and overseeing all administrative operations for the Company. **Career Steps:** FMC Corporation: Vice President (1985–Present), Director of Human Resources (1977–1985), Group on Human Resources (1972–1977). **Associations & Accomplishments:** Former Director and President, Human Resource Management of Chicago; Distinguished Colleague Award (1995); Board of Directors, Plaza Club; Chairman Executive Com, University of Illinois Center for Human Resource Management. **Education:** University of Chicago, M.B.A. (1972); University of Pittsburgh, B.S. (1956). **Personal:** Married to Kathleen in 1957. Four children: Mark, Martin, Lynn, and Scott.

Ernest A. Hopcus
Senior Manufacturing Engineer
3M Austin Center
6801 River Place Boulevard, Building 141–4S–03
Austin, TX 78726–9000
(512) 984–5206
Fax: (512) 984–5109

3999

Business Information: 3M is a diversified manufacturer of products ranging from tapes (Scotch) to Post–it Notes (R) to medical and dental devices. Established in 1905, 3M currently employs 85,000 people worldwide and has an estimated annual revenue of $15 billion. As Senior Manufacturing Engineer, Mr. Hopcus is responsible for the scale–up of new products, the introduction of new technologies, leading cost reduction efforts, and troubleshooting in the molded rubber area used for medium voltage splicing cables. **Career Steps:** Senior Manufacturing Engineer, 3M Austin Center (1986–Present); Chemist, Michelin Americas R & D Corporation (1978–1985); Chief Chemist and Quality Control Manager, Lawrence Hose Company (1976–1978). **Associations & Accomplishments:** Rubber Division, American Chemical Society; Phi Kappa Phi; local charitable work; volunteer with live theatre group. **Education:** Canisius College, B.S. (1968). **Personal:** Married to Frances in 1968. Three children: Joelle,

Christopher and Kevin. Mr. Hopcus enjoys cooking, reading, camping and volunteering.

Hubert Jacobs van Merlen
Senior Vice President and Chief Financial Officer
Commercial Intertech
1775 Logan Avenue
Youngstown, OH 44505–2622
(330) 740–8555
Fax: (330) 744–1142

3999

Business Information: Commercial Intertech is an international manufacturer of hydraulic components, filtration equipment, metal products and pre–engineered buildings. Traded on the New York Stock Exchange, Commercial Intertech operates 20 factories worldwide, with 45% of their business coming form the international market. Bringing with him eight years of experience as the European Finance Director at Commercial Intertech's Luxembourg office, Mr. Jacobs van Merlen was appointed Senior Vice President and Chief Financial Officer 1995. In his current capacity, he is responsible for all financial activities, in addition to assisting in strategic acquisitions. **Career Steps:** Commercial Intertech: Chief Financial Officer (1995–Present), European Finance Director (1987–1995). **Education:** Catholic University of Louvain, License (1975). **Personal:** Married. Two children: Celine and Andrew. Mr. Jacobs van Merlen enjoys sailing, tennis, skiing, and golf.

Francisco A. Jeannot
President and Comptroller
Boringuen Rivets Inc.
R Street, Building #4, El Comandante Industrial Park
Carolina, Puerto Rico 00983
(809) 750–6140
Fax: (809) 750–0640

3999

Business Information: Boringuen Rivets Inc. specializes in the manufacture of tubular rivets. Established in 1991, Boringuen Rivets Inc. currently employs 18 people. As President and Comptroller, Mr. Jeannot is responsible for all aspects of operations and all financial functions. Concurrent to his position with Boringuen Rivets Inc., Mr. Jeannot is also the Executive Vice President of K–Love Fashions, Inc., a manufacturer of fine jewelry. **Career Steps:** President and Comptroller, Boringuen Rivets Inc. (1991–Present); Executive Vice President and Comptroller, K–Love Fashions, Inc. (1983–Present); Comptroller, Gar Creations, Inc. (1977–1983); Senior Auditor, Orlando Vargas–Colon, C.P.A. (1973–1977). **Associations & Accomplishments:** Saint Mark Evangelical Lutheran Church. **Education:** University of Puerto Rico, Accounting Degree (1972). **Personal:** Married to Irma Sanchez in 1957. Four children: Irma, Lourdes, Yvonne and Francisco. Mr. Jeannot enjoys basketball, fishing and music.

Mrs. Kathleen I. Jennings
Corporate Secretary
N & K Enterprises Inc.
1495 N.E. 129th Street
North Miami, FL 33161
(305) 893–9559
Fax: (305) 893–8536

3999

Business Information: N & K Enterprises Inc. is a national manufacturer and distributor of janitorial supplies. In addition, the Company also provides contracted janitorial services to industries and business companies. Established in 1986, N & K Enterprises Inc. employs over 80 persons and reports estimated annual revenue in excess of $2 million. As Corporate Secretary, Ms. Jennings is responsible for the administration of all office functions which include office staff supervision, accounting, financial reports. **Career Steps:** Corporate Secretary, N & K Enterprises Inc. (1990–Present); Financial Counselor, 1st National Bank (1981–1990); Personnel Officer, Government of Jamaica (1962–1978). **Personal:** Married to Neville Jennings in 1978. Two children: Neale B. and Nathalee Jennings. Mrs. Jennings enjoys clothing design and coordination and reading during her leisure time.

Allen R. Jensen
Executive Vice President and Chief Legal Counsel
E. Khashoggi Industries
800 Miramonte Drive
Santa Barbara, CA 93109
(805) 897–2299
Fax: (805) 899–3517

3999

Business Information: E. Khashoggi Industries is a research and development company, specializing in concrete– and starch–based materials, as well as other items that can be made out of paper or plastic. Additional products include biodegradable materials used in the fast food industry packaging, etc. International in scope, E. Khashoggi Industries span the U.S. (California, Utah, Washington, DC) and numerous foreign countries. Established in 1985, E. Khashoggi Industries currently employs 50 people. A practicing attorney in Utah and California state courts, Mr. Jensen joined E. Khashoggi Industries in 1994. Serving as Executive Vice President and Chief Legal Counsel, he provides legal consultation and representation in the areas of patent, trademark, copyright, and corporate law. **Career Steps:** Executive Vice President and Chief Legal Counsel, E. Khashoggi Industries (1994–Present); Officer, Director and Founding Shareholder, Workman, Nydegger & Jensen (1987–Present); Adjunct Professor, Brigham Young University (1985–1994); Technical Advisor & Law Clerk, U.S. Court of Customs & Patent (1977–1979); Associate and Shareholder, Fox, Edwards & Gardiner (1979–1984). **Associations & Accomplishments:** National Inventors Hall of Fame (1987–1990); National Council of Intellectual Property Law Association (1977–1991); Patent, Trademark, and Copyright Section (1980–Present), Utah State Bar; Patent, Trademark, and Copyright Section (1988–1990), American Bar Association; American Intellectual Property Law Association (1981–Present). **Education:** George Washington University, J.D. (1977); Brigham Young University, B.S. in Chemistry (1974). **Personal:** Married to Carlyn P. in 1975. Three children: Ashley, Kirstin, and Christopher. Mr. Jensen enjoys family activities and is also an accomplished classical pipe organist.

A. W. Johnny
Vice President
Yesmin International
1419 30th Road, Suite 2
Long Island City, NY 11102
(718) 726–1749
Fax: (718) 726–1749

3999

Business Information: Yesmin International imports and exports aviation and textile machinery, chemicals, food, and garments. As Vice President, Mr. Johnny conducts international market research and is responsible for international commodity investments. Concurrently, he serves as President and Chief Executive Officer of Daiwan's World. **Career Steps:** Vice President, Yesmin International (1991–Present); President and Chief Executive Officer, Daiwan's World (Present); Executive Director, Alpha Enterprises (1992); Chairman, Atlantis U.S.A. International (1982). **Associations & Accomplishments:** Vice Chairman, Bangladesh–American Republican Party; Executive Member, Bangladesh–American Friendship Association; Treasurer, Queen's County Republican Party; Executive Member, The New York Immigration Coalition. **Education:** City College, Electrical Engineer (1986); International Correspondence School, P.A., Civil Engineering Technology. **Personal:** Married to Yesmin Wahab in 1988. One child: Daiwan Wahab. Mr. Johnny enjoys travel, fishing, boating, and helping the community.

Susan G. Kirby
Assistant Treasurer
Tektronix, Inc.
P.O. Box 1000, MS 63–844
Wilsonville, OR 97070
(503) 685–4110
Fax: (503) 685–4108

3999

Business Information: Tektronix, Inc. is a portfolio of measurement, color printing, and video and networking businesses dedicated to applying technology excellence to customer challenges. Tektronix, Inc. is headquartered in Wilsonville, Oregon and has operations in 23 countries outside of the United States. Founded in 1946, the company reports an annual revenue of $1.5 billion. As Assistant Treasurer, Mrs. Kirby is responsible for the areas of Credit, Collection, Accounts Receivable and Foreign Exchange Risk Management Divisions. **Career Steps:** Tektronix, Inc.: Assistant Treasurer (1994–Present), Sales Controller (1991–1994), Leasing General Manager (1988–1991). **Associations & Accomplishments:** Past coach for basketball and soccer. **Education:** East Oregon State, B.S. (1972). **Personal:** Married. Four children. Mrs. Kirby enjoys running and reading.

Isidora K. Lagos
Director of Marketing
Candle Corporation of America (CCA)
627 Bay Shore Drive
Oshkosh, WI 54901–5216
(414) 232–3381
Fax: (414) 231–3487

3999

Business Information: Candle Corporation of America (CCA) is a manufacturer and marketer of candles, accessories, and related home fragrance products. CCA has approximately 2,000 employees and an estimated annual sales of $350 million. As Director of Marketing, Ms. Lagos manages three Brand Managers as well as the entire Marketing Department, works closely with the Vice President of Sales and Marketing, as well as with the sales personnel. In addition, she supervises the financial management of the brands, and manages product development. She is responsible for the marketing direction of the Class brands and channel of trade: Colonial Candle of Cape Cod, Carolina Designs, and Mrs. Baker's. **Career Steps:** Director of Marketing, Candle Corporation of America (CCA) (1995–Present); Hallmark Cards: National Account Manager (1992–1995), Regional Operations Manager (1991–1992), Marketing Strategist/Product Manager (1984–1989). **Associations & Accomplishments:** National Association of Female Executives; Phi Beta Kappa; Published articles in Discount Store News and the Journal of International Business. **Education:** Indiana University: M.B.A. (1984), B.A. (1992); Lajos–Kossuth University – Budapest, Fulbright Scholar (1983). **Personal:** Ms. Lagos enjoys being an aerobics instructor, travel, stamp collecting, and her Black Lab, Max.

Frank J. Lazowski

Director of Manufacturing
Cummins Allison Corporation
891 Feehanville Drive
Mount Prospect, IL 60056–6002
(847) 299–9550
Fax: (847) 299–9130
EMAIL: See Below

3999

Business Information: Cummins Allison Corporation is a manufacturer of specialized office equipment. Marketed product lines include: coin and currency handling equipment, paper shredders, and other specialty office products. International in scope, Cummins Allison has manufacturing facilities in the U.S. (Illinois) and United Kingdom. As Director of Manufacturing, Mr. Lazowski is responsible for all manufacturing functions, including plant management, quality control, purchasing, production, distribution, and management information systems. He is also responsible for the supervision of 380 production and support staff. Internet users can reach him via: FJLIIID@INTERNETMCI.COM **Career Steps:** Director of Manufacturing, Cummins Allison Corporation (1993–Present); Senior Consultant, Deloitte & Touche (1989–1992). **Associations & Accomplishments:** Society of Manufacturing Engineers; Institute of Industrial Engineers; APICS; Published two articles in Managing Automation Magazine. **Education:** Lake Forest Graduate School, M.B.A. (1995); Millikin University, B.S. in Industrial Engineering (1987). **Personal:** Married to Denise in 1993. Mr. Lazowski enjoys boating, skiing, tennis, and golf.

James A. Life
President – Contract Division
Rockline Industries
1583 East Mountain Road
Springdale, AR 72764
(501) 756–9251
Fax: (501) 756–9075

3999

Business Information: Rockline Industries specializes in the manufacture and distribution of private label moist toweletts and baby wipes under contract conversions from major manufacturing corporations. Established in 1979, Rockline Industries currently employs 400 people. As President – Contract Division, Mr. Life is responsible for all aspects of contract operations. A paper products management executive and engineer for over 20 years, Mr. Life was the Founder and President of Midwest Converting, and continued to serve in the same capacity when Rockline acquired the company in 1989. **Career Steps:** President – Contract Division, Rockline Industries (1989–Present); President and Founder, Midwest Converting (1979–1989); Plant Manager, Scott Paper Company (1975–1979). **Associations & Accomplishments:** Focus Business Leader, Sam's Wholesale Conference; Trade

speaker. **Education:** Louisiana State University, B.S. in Mechanical Engineering (1962). **Personal:** Married to Judy in 1978. Five children: Keith, Jeff, Lynn, Deann Hunt and Leslie Kester. Mr. Life enjoys backpacking, barbershop singing, old automobiles, and photography.

Mr. Larry J. Maier
Manager of Graphic Design/Art Director
Bally Gaming International, Inc.
6601 South Bermuda Road
Las Vegas, NV 89119–3605
(702) 896–7721
Fax: (702) 896–7770

3999

Business Information: Bally Gaming International, Inc., with corporate headquarters in Chicago, Illinois, is an international manufacturer of gaming devices (slot machines). Established in 1932, Bally Gaming reports annual revenue of $130 million and currently employs 350 people. As Manager of Graphic Design/Art Director, Mr. Maier is responsible for the overall art design of the games. **Career Steps:** Manager of Graphic Design/Art Director, Bally Gaming, Inc. (1989–Present); Designer/Illustrator, Masterpiece Studio – Chicago (1987–1989); Owner and Freelance Illustrator (1981–1987). **Associations & Accomplishments:** Recipient of awards for art design on Bally's gaming devices. **Education:** Memphis State University, B.F.A. (1981). **Personal:** Married to Elaine in 1989. Two children: Joseph and Alex. Mr. Maier enjoys golf and all sports.

Thomas L. Mann
Director of Manufacturing
Thermoscan, Inc.
10421 Pacific Center Court
San Diego, CA 92121
(619) 550–2124
Fax: Please mail or call

3999

Business Information: Thermoscan, Inc. designs, manufactures, and markets tympanic thermometers for the international professional and consumer market. As Director of Manufacturing, Mr. Mann is responsible for all Manufacturing, Purchasing, and Materials functions worldwide. This includes subcontract manufacturing in China, Malaysia, and the United States. Additionally, this includes in–house manufacturing in San Diego. **Career Steps:** Thermoscan, Inc.: Director of Manufacturing (1992–Present), Director of Materials (1993), Materials Manager (1994). **Education:** San Diego State University, B.S. in Management, emphasis on Production and Operations Management (1984) **Personal:** Married to Elizabeth in 1990. Two children: Thomas and Joseph. Mr. Mann enjoys backpacking and travel.

Philip K. Marshall
Manager of Quality Assurance
Chelsea Building Products
565 Cedar Way
Pittsburgh, PA 15139
(412) 826–8077
Fax: (412) 826–0113

3999

Business Information: Chelsea Building Products is a manufacturer of PVC window and door extrusions. Established in 1975, Chelsea Building Products currently employs 400 people. As Manager of Quality Assurance, Mr. Marshall is responsible for the management of all quality assurance activities, including the production of 100,000 pounds of products daily, policy procedures, oversight of twelve auditors and group leaders, 250–300 windows daily, product verification design, warehouse organization, customer service, and supplier programs. He also serves as a TQM trainer. **Career Steps:** Manager of Quality Assurance, Chelsea Building Products (1985–Present); Supervisor, Vyn–All Window Company (1980–1985); Educator and Coach, St. Agnes School (1983–1984). **Associations & Accomplishments:** American Society of Quality Control; Society of Plastic Engineers. **Education:** Edinboro State University, B.S. (1980). **Personal:** Married to Susan in 1982. Three children: Kelli–Lynn, Lauren, and Courtney. Mr. Marshall enjoys sports.

Scott G. Martin
Project Manager
International Game Technology
P.O. Box 10580
Reno, NV 89510
(702) 448–1984
Fax: (702) 448–2003
EMAIL: See Below

3999

Business Information: International Game Technology is the world's leading designer and manufacturer of slot machines, video gaming equipment, and proprietary software for computerized wide–area game monitoring systems. Currently serving as Project Manager for International Game Technology in Reno, Nevada, Scott G. Martin has thirteen years of experience in the Engineering and Manufacturing fields. He oversees the development, implementation, and improvement of processes, procedures, and techniques in Quality Assurance. Trained as an Engineer, Mr. Martin has held progressively demanding managerial responsibilities, in Quality, Manufacturing Engineering, Materials, Production, and Technical Support. He has worked for multinationals at both the branch and parent–level in Canada and the United States including Motorcoach Industries, Standard Aero Limited, Unisys Defense Systems, and International Game Technology. Scott is a past Vice–President of the Winnipeg chapter of APICS, served as liaison for the Manitoba chapter of the Canadian Manufacturers Association and served on the Red River College curriculum advisory council for Industrial Electronics. He was also a member of Total Quality Manitoba and the Winnipeg Chamber of Commerce. Scott Martin serves as Director of Programs for the APICS Northern Sierra Chapter in Reno Nevada. He also speaks and teaches on a number of Operations, Management, and Quality subjects and is an APICS Train the Trainer. Scott has written articles for "Integration 2000" and "The APICS Link." His latest article is entitled "Identifying effective paths to increased profitability." Internet users can also reach him via: grzly@aol.com. **Career Steps:** International Game Technology: Project Manager (1994–Present), Quality/Operations Manager, IGT – Canada (1992–1994); Engineering Specialist, Unisys Defense Systems (1990–1992); Quality Assurance Inspector, Standard Aero, Ltd. (1988–1990). **Associations & Accomplishments:** APICS: Director of Programs – Northern Sierra Chapter, Former Vice President – Winnipeg Chapter, Liaison to Canadian Manufacturers Association; Former Member, Red River College Curriculum Advisory Council; Former President, Unisys Employees Association; KJBA National Association: School Head, Board Member. **Education:** Canadian Forces Fleet School – Esquimalt, Marine Engineer (Top Student Award); Canadian Forces Fleet School – Halifax, Marine Engineer (Top Student Award); Canadian Forces School of Aerospace, Ordinance, and Engineering, Aero Engine Technician. **Personal:** Married to Camille in 1987. Three children: Ryan, Jesse, and Alycia.

Rafael Marxuach Del Toro
Director/House Counsel
Lausell Enterprises
P.O. Box 362413
San Juan, Puerto Rico 00936–2413
(809) 798–7610
Fax: (809) 740–3415

3999

Business Information: Lausell Enterprises, established in 1947, is an industrial manufacturing organization. A practicing attorney since 1963, Mr. Marxuach Del Toro joined Lausell Enterprises as Director and House Counsel in 1970. **Career Steps:** Director/House Counsel, Lausell Enterprises (1970–Present); Principal, R. Marxuach Del Toro (1970–Present); President, Invermar, Inc. (1994–Present); Principal, R. Marxuach Brokerage Firm (1993–Present); Lawyer, R. Paniagua Diez (1968–1970); Lawyer, Department of Justice – Commonwealth of Puerto Rico (1964–1968). **Associations & Accomplishments:** Counsel for Special Events, Puerto Rico Cultural Institute (1995); Involved in charitable and other associations to help persons with handicaps; Director, Felisa Rincon de Gautier Foundation (1996); Member, Puerto Rico Conservation Trust (1996); American Bar Association; Puerto Rico Bar Association; Inter American Bar Association; Economic Advisory Committee of the Senate of Puerto Rico; Museum of Modern Art – New York Association; Caparra Country Club; Rio Mar Golf and Country Club; Ateneo de Puerto Rico; Manufactures Association of Puerto Rico; General Contractors Association; Home Builders Association; Chamber of Commerce. **Education:** Tulane Law

School, L.L.B. Doctor in Law (1963); University of Puerto Rico, B.B.A. in Finance (1960); Real Estate Courses (1993); Various Seminars, Courses, and Lectures in Investments, Real Estate, Business, Finance, and Law (1970–Present). **Personal:** Married to Matil in 1961. Five children: Rafael A., Michelle, Miguel A., Ginette, and Matlisha. Mr. Marxuach Del Toro enjoys boating, walking, reading, art, and travel.

David L. Massey
Chief Financial Officer
Ving Card, Inc.
9333 Forest Lane
Dallas, TX 75243–4205
(214) 907–2273
Fax: (214) 907–2771

3999

Business Information: Ving Card, Inc. is a manufacturer of hotel security card access locking devices. The Company is also the inventor of recodeable locking technology. Ving Card, Inc. deals mainly with hospitals, colleges, universities, government contracts, apartments, and hotels. As Chief Financial Officer, Mr. Massey is responsible for overseeing all financial operations, administrative duties, and personnel. **Career Steps:** Ving Card, Inc.: Chief Financial Officer (1996–Present), Controller (1994–1996); Administrative and Finance Manager, Vetrotex Certainteed Corporation (1980–1993). **Education:** Midwestern State University: M.B.A. (1989), B.B.A. (1983). **Personal:** Married to Jill Stevenson in 1996. Two children: David Ryan and Christopher Kyle. Mr. Massey enjoys golf, disc golf, snow skiing, tennis, and playing piano and drums.

Kathleen M. Massey
Assistant General Counsel
A. O. Smith Corporation
11270 West Park Place
Milwaukee, WI 53223–0973
(414) 359–4109
Fax: (414) 359–4143

3999

Business Information: A. O. Smith Corporation is a diversified manufacturer. Major product lines include: automotive structural components; fractional horsepower and hermetic electric motors; residential and commercial water heaters; fiberglass piping systems; protective industrial coatings; livestock feed storage systems; and water, wastewater, and dry storage tanks. A practicing attorney since 1981, Ms. Massey joined A. O. Smith Corporation as Senior Counsel in 1972. Appointed as Assistant General Counsel in 1993, her practice area includes product liability litigation, specializing in mass torts (repetitive litigation involving a number of people). **Career Steps:** A. O. Smith Corporation; Assistant General Counsel (1993–Present), Senior Counsel (1992–1993); Shareholder, Habush, Habush & Davis, S.C. (1987–1990). **Associations & Accomplishments:** American Bar Association; Wisconsin Bar Association; Minnesota Bar Association; Language Proficiency – French. **Education:** University of Wisconsin School of Law, J.D. (1981); Kalamazoo College, B.A., cum laude (1978); L'Universite de Claremont–Ferrand, France, Matriculated Student (1976–1977). **Personal:** Married to Steven J. in 1990. Ms. Massey enjoys travel.

Kevin McCoy
CEO
The Corporate Image
2203 Airport Way, Suite #8055
Seattle, WA 98134–2027
(206) 382–7771
Fax: (206) 382–7775
E–MAIL: SEE BELOW

3999

Business Information: The Corporate Image is a designer, developer, manufacturer, and distributor of superb P.O.P. materials, ad specialty innovators, and corporate identity merchandise. As CEO, Mr. McCoy is responsible for all aspects of company operations, including administration, finance, sales, public relations, accounting, legal, taxes, marketing, and strategic planning. **Career Steps:** CEO, The Corporate Image (1990–Present); CRP Inn, CEO (1986–1990); President, J. Lampert Promotion (1972–86). **Associations & Accomplishments:** TEC, POPAI and ASI. **Education:** SUA, BA (1965). **Personal:** Married to Sandra in 1990. Four children: Christopher, Regan, William and Bradley. Mr. McCoy enjoys golf, painting, antiques, autos and motorcycles.

Linda S. McGinnis
Vice President
Appalachian Regional Manufacturing
1101 Lakeside Drive
Jackson, KY 41339–9678
(606) 666–2433
Fax: (606) 666–4750

3999

Business Information: Appalachian Regional Manufacturing specializes in high–tech component fabrication and assembly production, providing sub–assembly, final assembly, testing, packaging, distribution, and sublimation. Current contracts are with IBM for the assembly and fabrication of keyboards, as well as Mas–Hamilton Engineering Group providing lock assembly. Joining Appalachian Regional Manufacturing as Operations Manager in 1994, Ms. McGinnis currently serves as Vice President. She is responsible for all aspects of administrative and management activities, including accounts payable, new operations quotes, day–to–day business management, long–term business direction, and financial planning. **Career Steps:** Vice President, Appalachian Regional Manufacturing (1994–Present); Drop–Out Prevention Coordinator, Martin County Board of Education – Inez, Kentucky (1992–1994); Associate Professor of History, Marshall University – Huntington, West Virginia (1991–1992). **Associations & Accomplishments:** Phi Alpha Theta (historical society); Elementary and junior high school basketball coach; Former K.H.S.A.A. official; City of Jackson Chamber of Commerce. **Education:** Marshall University, M.A. (1989); Eastern Kentucky University, B.S. (1975). **Personal:** Two children: David Michael and Mark Douglas. Ms. McGinnis enjoys exercise, reading, coaching, and watching her youngest son play basketball.

Robert H. Menchhofer
Vice President
Northwest Awards
5744 West 79th Street
Indianapolis, IN 46278
(317) 876–8838
Fax: (317) 876–1308

3999

Business Information: Northwest Awards specializes in the manufacture of awards and trophies, performs engraving services, and produces promotional and personalized products. As Vice President and Chief Administrative Officer, Mr. Menchhofer is responsible for all aspects of sales, operations and finance. **Career Steps:** Vice President, Northwest Awards (1995–Present); National Sales Manager, Champ Products, Inc. (1994–1995); Stewart Warner South Wind Corporation: Sales Manager (1988–1994), Field Sales Representative (1980–1988); Coordinator of the Service Center, Link Belt Division, FMC Corporation (1974–1980); Systems Analyst, Packard Electric Division, GMC (1972–1974). **Associations & Accomplishments:** President, Brownsburg Jaycees (1978–1979); State Chairman, Indiana Jaycees (1979–1984); Member, 500 Fesitval Associations; Member, Society of Automotive Engineers; Appaloosa Horse Club; Treasurer (1987), President (1988–1989), Central Indiana Appaloosa Horse Club; U.S. Jaycees Senate; Phi Gamma Delta. **Education:** GM Institute, Flint, MI (1966–1968); Purdue University, B.S. in Industrial Management (1972). **Personal:** Married to Donna Lee in 1969. Two children: Christopher and Angela. Mr. Menchhofer enjoys restoring automobiles and woodworking.

Mr. Richard A. Merluzzi
Business Director, Specialty Products
FMC Corporation
1735 Market Street
Philadelphia, PA 19103
(215) 299–6714
Fax: (215) 299–5819

3999

Business Information: FMC Corporation is one of the world's leading producers of chemicals and machinery for industry, government and agriculture. Company sales were $4 billion including international sales of more than 100 countries accounting for 49% of annual revenue. As Business Director of Specialty Products, Mr. Merluzzi oversees all business aspects of the world–wide Specialty Products business of the Peroxygen Chemicals Division. His responsibilities include strategy development and implementation and profit and loss management. The Specialty Products business is global in scope with a portfolio of products used primarily as polymerization catalysts, chemical synthesis intermediaries and sanitizer/biocides. The business has revenues of $40 million, operates manufacturing facilities in Buffalo, NY, Santa Clara, Mexico and Fuji City, Japan and currently employs 160 people. **Career Steps:** FMC Corporation: Business Director, Specialty Products (July 1992–Present), Division Controller (April 1990–July 1992), Marketing Manager (November 1988–April 1990). **Associations & Accomplishments:**

World Affairs Council of Philadelphia; Pennsylvania State University Alumni Association; Junior Achievement; Tau Beta Pi – National Engineering Honor Society; Chi Epsilon – National Civil Engineering Honor Society. **Education:** Drexel University, M.B.A. (1983); Pennsylvania State University, B.S. in Civil Engineering; Executive Education Courses at Harvard University, Columbia University and University of Virginia Darden School. **Personal:** Married to Kathryn in 1986. Three children: Richard III, Alexander and Andrew. Mr. Merluzzi enjoys golf and biking.

Barry Miller
Vice President of Taxation
American Trading and Production Corporation
P.O. Box 238
Baltimore, MD 21203–0208
(410) 347–7131
Fax: (410) 347–7050

3999

Business Information: American Trading and Production Corporation is a manufacturer and distributor of office products, a real estate development and Management Company, and is involved in oil and gas exploration and development. As Vice President of Taxation, Mr. Miller is responsible for diversified administrative activities, including all corporate tax functions. **Career Steps:** American Trading and Production Corporation: Vice President of Taxation (1995–Present), Assistant Treasurer and Director of Taxation (1987–1995), Tax Manager (1984–1987). **Associations & Accomplishments:** Tax Executives Institute; National Society of Tax Professionals; Assistant Scoutmaster, Boy Scouts of America; Maryland Chamber of Commerce Tax Committee. **Education:** University of Baltimore, B.S. in Accounting (1974). **Personal:** Married to Tracy L. in 1980. Four children: Tara, Jason, Megan, and Erica. Mr. Miller enjoys stamp and coin collecting, golf, hiking, and travel.

Martin Miller
National Sales Manager
Channel Kor Systems, Inc.
3337 South Old Hwy 37
Bloomington, IN 47402–2297
1–800–CHAN–KOR
Fax: (812) 336–8047

3999

Business Information: Channel Kor Systems, Inc. is a manufacturer of trade show exhibits and CAD designs for approximately 150 vendors. As National Sales Manager, Mr. Miller is responsible for all U.S. and international sales, dealer sales, development and sales personnel management. In addition, he is responsible for coordinating the National Dealer Network in the United States and Canada; design, marketing and advertising programs; newsletters; and internal growth strategies. **Career Steps:** National Sales Manager, Channel Kor Systems, Inc. (1992–Present); Condit Exhibits: Showroom/Systems Manager (1990–1992), Account Executive (1988–1990). **Associations & Accomplishments:** World Wildlife Fund; International Exhibitors Association. **Education:** Indiana University School of Business, B.A. (1988). **Personal:** Married to Candace Marie in 1989. One child: Kiernan Mae. Mr. Miller enjoys alpine skiing, fishing, hunting, golf, acoustic guitar, and most importantly, spending time with his family.

Martin T. Miller
Vice President of Sales
Melitta North America, Inc.
17757 U.S. Highway 19 North, Suite 600
Clearwater, FL 34624
(813) 524–4829
Fax: (813) 535–5798

3999

Business Information: Melitta North America, Inc., a German–based corporation, is a leading manufacturer and distributor of coffee and coffee preparation products for distribution throughout North America. With extensive background in food industries sales, Mr. Miller joined Melitta in 1992. As Vice President of Sales, he oversees all sales and marketing operations and related sales representatives support covering the U.S., Canada and Latin America. **Career Steps:** Vice President of Sales, Melitta North America, Inc. (1992–Present); Vlasic Food Inc.: Director of Sales Planning (1989–1992), Regional Sales Manager (1988–1989); Zone Manager, No Nonsense Fashions (1986–1988). **Associations & Accomplishments:** Board of Trustees, National Food Brokers Association. **Education:** Western Michigan

University, B.S. (1980). **Personal:** Married to Linda in 1980. Three children: Matthew, Michael and Robert.

Robert H. Mitchell

Technical Supervisor
3M Corporation
915 Highway 22 South
Hutchinson, MN 55350–2900
(320) 234–1864
Fax: (320) 234–1629
EMAIL: See Below

3999

Business Information: 3M Corporation is a diversified international manufacturer of chemicals, plastic products, abrasives, and various taping systems (marketed under the Scotch brandname), as well as reflective sheeting for traffic control systems, and medical/dental products. Established in 1905, 3M currently employs 85,000 people worldwide and has an estimated annual revenue of $15 billion. Serving with 3M in various consulting and supervisory positions since 1981, Mr. Mitchell was promoted to Technical Supervisor in 1992 and is currently the production General Supervisor for Surface Mount Supplies project within the Industrial Tape and Specialties Division, supervising 39 hourly and 8 technical personnel. Internet users can also reach him via: BOB3M@HUTCH-TEL.NET. **Career Steps:** 3M Corporation: Technical Supervisor (1992–Present), Statistical Consultant (1988–1992), Quality and Process Engineer (1981–1988). **Associations & Accomplishments:** American Society For Quality Control: Officer, Statistics Division, Chemical and Process Industries Division, Quality Management Division; Quality Management Consultant, Hutchinson, MN of McLeod County. **Education:** University of Minnesota at Morris, B.S. (1980). **Personal:** Married to Lori in 1982. Two children: Jacob and Kyle. Mr. Mitchell enjoys reading, Internet, camping, and tennis.

Hicks B. Morgan, Esq.

Secretary, Treasurer and General Counsel
Morgan Buildings, Spas, Pools & RV's
2800 McCree Road
Garland, TX 75046
(214) 840–1200
Fax: (214) 278–9121

3999

Business Information: Morgan Buildings, Spas, Pools & RV's is a retailer of above ground swimming pools and recreational vehicles, and is a manufacturer and retailer of portable and modular buildings and portable hot tubs. Mr. Morgan currently serves as Secretary, Treasurer and General Counsel for the Company. Established in 1960, Morgan Buildings, Spas, Pools & RV's employs 1,000 people with annual sales of $90 million. **Career Steps:** Secretary, Treasurer and General Counsel, Morgan Buildings, Spas, Pools & RV's (1977–Present). **Associations & Accomplishments:** American Bar Association; Texas Bar Association; Dallas Council on World Affairs; Self–Insurance Institute of America; Treasury Management Association; American Management Association; Active in church. **Education:** Georgetown University, J.D. (1977); Dartmouth College, A.B. in History and Economics (1970). **Personal:** Married to Vicki in 1971. Five children: Hope, Michelle, Heather, Nathan and Andrew. Mr. Morgan enjoys travel, fishing, and skiing.

Richard F. Nestler

President and Chief Executive Officer
R. F. Nestler & Associates, Inc.
4 West Manilla Avenue
Pittsburgh, PA 15220–3310
(412) 921–7001
Fax: (412) 921–7279

3999

Business Information: R. F. Nestler & Associates, Inc. is the manufacturer and marketer of a cigarette dispenser called the "ADmatic" (TM), a merchandise machine used in supermarkets and convenience stores. Rented to retailers, the units prevent children from purchasing and/or stealing cigarettes, saving the retailer $10,000 a month. It also offers advertising space and dispenses samples and coupons for promotions. This unique invention uses presently–wasted air space instead of valuable floor space; delivers products down an acrylic chute to each check–out counter; removes item from inventory and charges it to the cashier's register; and places it on the reorder guide automatically (sensors verify the cashier received the product). The unit also automatically lowers to floor level for restocking. The unit can also can dispense cassettes, film, batteries, and other easily pocketed items, as well as tracking inventory. A seasoned inventor and entrepreneur, Mr. Nestler established R. F. Nestler & Associates, Inc. in 1980. Mr. Nestler serves as its President and Chief Executive Officer, responsible for all aspects of operations, including administration, finances, sales, public relations, accounting, marketing, strategic planning, and inventions. He is the inventor of the ADmatic (TM), which was first installed in stores in 1988 and is now in stores located in Pittsburgh, Pennsylvania and throughout Kentucky. He is also the inventor of the plastic bags used in place of paper bags, perforated bags used to hold vegetables, and dispensing units used in supermarkets. **Career Steps:** President and Chief Executive Officer, R. F. Nestler & Associates, Inc. (1980–Present); President, Nestler May Corporation (1966–1980); Store Manager, Kroger Company. **Associations & Accomplishments:** President, Greentree Athletic Association (10 years); Cub Master, Greentree Troop 202 (8 years); Rotary International (5 years); Honorable Order of Kentucky Colonels (5 years); Lecturer at numerous universities. **Education:** Louisiana State University (1957); Attended: Allegheny Tech; West Pennsylvania Tech; Dale Carnegie; Pitt University, Corness Extension. **Personal:** Married to Marjorie Anne in 1957. Four children: Cheryl, Lori, David, and Rick. Mr. Nestler enjoys inventing, writing poetry, golf, baseball, football, bowling, hunting, fishing, gardening, and cooking.

Richard A. Newmark, Ph.D.

Corporate Scientist
3M
Building 201–BS–07
St. Paul, MN 55144
(612) 733–7679
Fax: (612) 733–0648

3999

Business Information: 3M is a diversified manufacturer of plastic, video, and audio tape and sandpaper; marketing under the brandname Scotch, as well as reflective sheeting for traffic signs. Established in 1905, 3M currently employs 85,000 people worldwide and has an estimated annual revenue of $15 billion. As Corporate Scientist, Dr. Newmark is an Analytical Chemist and Supervisor of the Nuclear Magnetic Resonance Facility. One of only thirty corporate scientists within 3M, Dr. Newmark is the Senior Scientist serving as mentor to other corporate members. **Career Steps:** 3M: Corporate Scientist (1992–Present), Staff Scientist (1981–1992), Senior Research Specialist (1977–1981). **Associations & Accomplishments:** American Chemical Society; Society of Applied Spectroscopy; District I Community Council, St. Paul; Bicycle Advisory Board; Sigma Xi; Phi Betta Kappa. **Education:** University of California – Berkeley, Ph.D. (1964); Harvard College, A.B. (1961). **Personal:** Married to Joan Friedman in 1965. Two children: Merel and David. Dr. Newmark enjoys bicycling and travel.

Gary Michael Niceswanger

Manager – Financial Reporting
Dexter Corporation
1 East Water Street
Waukegan, IL 60085–5635
(847) 625–4406
Fax: (847) 623–4297

3999

Business Information: Established in 1767, Dexter Corporation is a specialty materials manufacturer, employing 4,800 people and grossing $1.1 billion annually. The Packaging Products Division produces coatings for rigid containers and closures for packaging food and beverages. As Manager of Financial Reporting for the Packing Products Division, Mr. Niceswanger's responsibilities include the preparation, consolidation, and analysis of divisional financial statements for all locations. He has served with Dexter in various capacities since 1990. **Career Steps:** Manager of Financial Reporting, Dexter Corporation (1994–Present); Controller/Accounting Manager, Dexter – Aerospace Materials Division (1990–1994); Senior Accountant, Deloitte & Touche (1986–1990). **Associations & Accomplishments:** Institute of Management Accountants, Illinois Northeast Chapter; American Institute of Certified Public Accountants; Iowa Society of Certified Public Accountants. **Education:** University of Northern Iowa, B.A. (1986). **Personal:** Mr. Niceswanger enjoys tennis, reading, and jogging.

Wanda I. Nieves

President
Escaparates, Inc.
Calle Pereiera Leal #629 Urb Valencia
San Juan, Puerto Rico 00923
(787) 767–0094
Fax: (809) 767–0094

3999

Business Information: Escaparates, Inc. is a designer and manufacturer of exhibits and displays used in the commercial industry, such as light boxes and display furniture for Cosmair Caribe and Sony of Puerto Rico stores. As President, Ms. Nieves is responsible for all aspects of operations, including administration, finances, quotes for design projects, and overseeing project designs. **Career Steps:** President, Escaparates, Inc. (1987–Present); Story Board Designer, University of Puerto Rico – Cayey (1994–1996); Creative Consultant, WIN Promotions (1983–1986); Theater Scenery Designer, Centro de Bellas Artes de Puerto Rico (1980–1985). **Associations & Accomplishments:** Exhibit Designer and Producer Association; Puerto Rico Manufacturers Association; Villa Marina Yacht Club; San Juan Art League; Listed in Who's Who in Hispanic American. **Education:** Fine Arts School of the Institute of Culture of Puerto Rico, B.A. (1983). **Personal:** Ms. Nieves enjoys painting, filming, and boating.

Eduardo Pallette

President
Buena Veritas Arg. SA
E. Dela Carreras 486
San Isidro, Argentina 1642
54–1–315–1738
Fax: 54–1–315–1738

3999

Business Information: Buena Veritas Arg. SA is a quality control and technical assesment company. The Company is also involved in the ship registry industry. As President, Mr. Pallette is responsible for all aspects of Company operations in the South America region. **Career Steps:** President, Buena Veritas Arg. SA (1980–Present); Vice President, National Railways (1978–1980). **Associations & Accomplishments:** Argentina Association of Engineers. **Education:** Catholic University, M.B.A. (1969); University of Buenos Aries, B.S. in Engineering. **Personal:** Married to Maria Gavina in 1970. Three children: Eduardo, Tomas, and Paula. Mr. Pallette enjoys sports, skiing, and golf.

Jason M. Pashko

International Market Research Director
American Saw
301 Chestnut Street, P.O. Box 504
East Longmeadow, MA 01028–0504
(413) 525–3961
Fax: (413) 525–9621

3999

Business Information: American Saw specializes in the manufacture of band saw blades. Established in 1915, American Saw currently employs 900 people. As International Market Research Director, Mr. Pashko is responsible for all aspects of marketing in Germany and Austria, working from the Hannover, Germany international headquarters. Germany Office location: American Saw, Freiding Strasse #12; Hannover, Germany 30559; 011–(49) 511525314. **Career Steps:** International Market Research Director, American Saw (1970–Present). **Associations & Accomplishments:** Phi Beta Kappa; University of Osuabrueck, Fulbright Alumni Association. **Education:** University of Osuabrueck, Fulbright Fellowship, Germany (1993–1994); College of the Holy Cross, A.B. (1993). **Personal:** Mr. Pashko enjoys running, swimming, biking and hiking.

Maricelis Penzort

Controller
Pall P.R., Inc.
P.O. Box 729
Fajardo, Puerto Rico 00738–0729
(809) 863–1124
Fax: (809) 863–7214

3999

Business Information: Pall P.R., Inc. specializes in the manufacture of industrial filter elements utilized by Fortune 500 companies. Established in 1974, the Company currently employs 210 people and has an estimated annual revenue of over $50 million. As Controller, Ms. Penzort is responsible for all aspects of financial operations, customer service, and the Accounting Controls. Concurrent to her position with Pall P.R, Inc., Ms. Penzort also owns her own Partyland franchise store, and hopes to open three more in the next two years. She attributes her success to a positive attitude and the ability to continue working toward her goals. **Career Steps:** Controller, Pall P.R., Inc. (1976–Present); Staff Accountant, Rudolph & Rudolph, CPA's. **Associations & Accomplishments:** Institute of Management Acountants. **Education:** New Hampshire College, M.B.A. (1984). **Personal:** Married to Ismael Ramos in 1977. Two children: Ismael Ramos, Jr. and Anjanette Marcano. Ms. Penzort enjoys sports, movies, dancing, plays, festivals and travel.

Hans Peter
President
Phoenix Label Company
P.O. Box 695
Olathe, KS 66051
(913) 780–5200
Fax: Please mail or call

3999

Business Information: Phoenix Label Company is a manufacturer of labels. As President, Mr. Peter is responsible for all aspects of operations. He supervises general management, oversees budgeting, monitors financial matters, handles employee situations, approves all sales and contracts, and develops strategic plans for the future of the Company. **Career Steps:** President, Phoenix Label Company (1987–Present). **Personal:** Mr. Peter enjoys boating, collecting old cars, and church activities.

COIN MECHANISMS INC.

Rhoda D. Pierz
Executive Vice President
Coin Mechanisms, Inc.
400 Regency Drive
Glendale Heights, IL 60139–2284
(708) 924–7070
Fax: (708) 924–7088

3999

Business Information: Coin Mechanisms, Inc. is a family–founded, owned, and operated business which has been in existence for over 25 years. Manufacturing coin handling and verifying devices primarily for the gaming and amusement industries, their coin comparitor has set industry standards in the casino market place. International in scope, Coin Mechanisms' products can be found all over the world, to include England, Denmark and Australia. Products include cash boxes for video machines and handles for slot machines. After 12 years absence, Ms. Pierz rejoined Coin Mechanics in 1987 as a payroll manager, and was appointed as Executive Vice President in 1991. Among her responsibilities are finance, human resources, payroll and employee benefits. **Career Steps:** Coin Mechanics, Inc.: Executive Vice President (1991–Present), Payroll Manager (1987–1991); Special Education Teaching Assistant, Hayward Community Schools in Wisconsin (1983–1987); Veterinary Assistant in Hayward WI (1979–1983). **Associations & Accomplishments:** Re-established Girl Scouting Program in Hayward, WI; Hugger, Special Olympics; Volunteer, Dreamflight. **Education:** College of Dupage; University of Wisconsin at Superior. **Personal:** Married to Michael Parratore. Two children: Jason Poreda and Brandi Blaesing. Two Grandchildren: Jennifer and Michael Blaesing. Ms. Pierz enjoys Harley–Davidson motorcycle riding, travel, and raising domestic & farm animals.

Phillip A. Pittman

President & Chief Executive Officer
Diverse Environmental Products Inc.
910 Reuter Drive
West Sacramento, CA 95605
(916) 371–7013
Fax: (916) 489–7804

3999

Business Information: Diverse Environmental Products Inc. (DEP), specializes in recycling post consumer waste tires. The Company, using an ambient grind method of size reduction, granulates waste tires into custom sized Crumb Rubber which the Company then markets as a feedstock to other value added consumer product line producers. The Company has developed a process to chemically mix Crum Rubber with plastic to make rubberized plastic products such as waste baskets, refuse containers, toys, tools, alternative lumber and playground safety surfaces. Established in 1989, Diverse Environmental Products exports goods to Canada, Saudi Arabia, U.K., and many other countries in Europe. As President and Founder, Mr. Pittman is considered as one of the top five tire recycling authorities in America, and is responsible for all aspects of operations. **Career Steps:** President and Founder, Diverse Environmental Products Inc. (1989–Present); Owner, Dixie Lee Construction Co., Inc. and Dixie Lee Development Corporation (1975–1989). **Personal:** Married with four daughters, Mr. Pittman is considered an Environmentalist who enjoys taking his grandsons fishing.

Joel A. Remillard
Engineering Manager/Project Coordinator
SPM/Portland
1600 NE 25th Avenue
Hillsboro, OR 97124
(503) 693–3425
Fax: (503) 640–0964
EMail: See Below

3999

Business Information: SPM/Portland is a manufacturing company specializing in injection molding, medical testing equipment, and tool and dye work for the medical and consumer electronics industries. As Engineering Manager, Mr. Remillard oversees the Tooling Engineers, Project Engineers, Bills of Materials, CAD Support, and Quoting. While managing Engineering, he acts as Program Manager for strategic customers such as Intel, Abbott Laboratories, and INFOCUS Systems. Additionally, Mr. Remillard has prepared multilevel value added processes for key customers, multilevel mechanical assemblies, shielding, and decorative applications. Internet users can reach him via: Joel@spm–pdx.com. **Career Steps:** Engineering Manager/Project Coordinator, SPM/Portland (1992–Present); Tooling Coordinator, Quality Plastics (1989–1992); Toolmaker, Plastics Development, Inc. (1979–1989). **Associations & Accomplishments:** Society of Manufacturing Engineers. **Education:** Oregon Institute of Technology, currently pursuing a B.S. in Industrial Engineering; Five year Tool and Dye Apprenticeship. **Personal:** Mr. Remillard enjoys water skiing, snow skiing, and bicycling.

Thomas Rendina
President
Anchor Pad International
4050 Chandler Way
Santa Ana, CA 92704
(714) 427–1290
Fax: (714) 427–1292
EMAIL: See Below

3999

Business Information: Anchor Pad International is a manufacturer of computer and office products security systems. Owned by Ivie Industries, Anchor Pad manufactures and sells a device that locks computers down to their workstations. As President, Mr. Rendina is responsible for all aspects of Company operations, including administrative management, and international sales and marketing. Internet users can reach him via: Anchor@anchor.com. **Career Steps:** President, Anchor Pad International (1995–Present); Chief Operating Officer, Ivie Industries (1995–Present); Director of Operations, Birtcher Medical Systems (1990–1995); General Manager, LEA Dynatech (1986–1990). **Associations & Accomplishments:** World Trade Association; American Society of Industrial Security. **Education:** California Poly – Pomona, M.B.A. (1989); San Diego State University, B.S. in Business Finance. **Personal:** Married to Terri in 1982. Four children: Juliet, Thomas II, Hilary, and Raymond. Mr. Rendina enjoys golf.

Robert L. Rickards
Manager Technical Training
AlliedSignal Inc.
P.O. Box 29003
Phoenix, AZ 85038–9003
(602) 365–2678
Fax: (602) 365–2832

3999

Business Information: AlliedSignal Inc. is an advanced technology and manufacturing company serving customers worldwide with aerospace and automotive products, chemicals, fibers, plastics and advanced materials. International in scope, AlliedSignal has three principal divisions as follows: Aerospace, Automotive and Engineered Materials. A Fortune 500 company, AlliedSignal, Inc. reports annual revenue in excess of $12.8 billion. As Manager of Technical Training, Robert Rickards is responsible for all in–house technical training and associated support staff at AlliedSignal's Phoenix, Arizona Marketing, Sales, and Service Depts. **Career Steps:** Manager Technical Training, AlliedSignal Inc. (1988–Present); Training Supervisor, Intel Corporation (1982–1986); Training Supervisor, ITT Corporation (1981–1982); United States Air Force (1960–1981). **Personal:** Married to Kuniko in 1962. One child: Deborah. Mr. Rickards enjoys golf.

Pedro L. Rodriguez

President
Caribbean Engineering & Safety Controls, Inc. (CESCI)
P.O. Box 191253, Hato Rey Station
San Juan, Puerto Rico 00919–1253
(787) 792–9840
Fax: (787) 783–5975

3999

Business Information: Caribbean Engineering & Safety Controls, Inc. (CESCI), a family–owned business, is a company dedicated to improving worksite safety for construction, road, and auto mechanic workers. CESCI provides the latest non–personal safety products in the market, as well as offers the most complete line of products geared toward the prevention & control of hazardous substance spills. Products include: Clayton brake & clutch washers, Backsaver truck drum dollies, HEPA filter vacuums & sanders, spill prevention & control products, Ready Road Repair cold asphalt, Artic insulated water coolers, plastic safety construction fencing, traffic control products, flexible traffic delineators, reflective plastic drums, traffic–marking equipment, aerosol & pail traffic paint, commercial & residential solar–powered lights, and Nelson firestop products. The Company is divided into three sections: 1) Traffic Control and Construction Safety Products; 2) Brakewasher Equipment for garages; and 3) Spill Control and Prevention Products. Bringing with him twenty–five years of experience in hazardous materials while serving with the military, Mr. Rodriguez established Caribbean Engineering & Safety Controls, Inc. in 1991 to improve health and safety at the workplace. Serving as its Owner and President, he is responsible for all aspects of operations, including administration, finances, sales, public relations, marketing, and strategic planning. Career highlights includes the planning, organization, and development of maintenance plans for the Puerto Rico Army National Guard, which ensured the efficiency of maintenance operations at all levels; prepared policies and Standard Operating Procedures (SOPs) and ensured implementation of them to assure quality control and uniformity in managerial and jobs performance. **Career Steps:** President, Caribbean Engineering & Safety Controls, Inc. (CESCI) (1991–Present); Puerto Rico Army National Guard: Maintenance Manager (1990–1993), Maintenance Assistance Team Supervisor (1988–1990), Electronics Section Supervisor (1983–1988). **Associations & Accomplishments:** United Retailers Association – Puerto Rico; Association of Professionals for Accidents Prevention; Fluent in English & Spanish (written & spoken); Army National Guard (ARNG) Construction Criteria Review Committee; Coordinating Committee for "Gran Regata Colon–92, Fifth Centenary" for the Commonwealth of Puerto Rico; Chairperson of the Transportation Committee, National Science Teachers Association (NSTA) Area Convention – assigned to work with the Puerto Rico Department of Education; Transportation Committee, First Puerto Rico International Science and Engineering Fair. **Education:** Metropolitan University – Cupey, PR, B.S. in Business Administration – In Progress; Puerto Rico Tourism Department – Barranquitas Hotel – Barranquitas, PR, Training in Hotel Management & Administration (1972); San Juan Technological Institute – San Juan, PR, Training in Computer Programming (1970); Training: Fifteen courses, trainings, and seminars offered by the Office of Personnel Management (OPM) geared toward the enhancement of managerial, supervisory and administrative skills and knowledge and twenty-four courses intended to increase the maintenance knowledge in a variety of Army–owned equipment; Fort Gordon, Georgia: Attended and graduated from the Warrant Officers Advanced Course and from the Communications Electronics Material Management Course (CEMMOC); Numerous supervisory, administrative, and technical education courses and Army correspondence courses. **Personal:** Married to Ivonne Quinones in 1989. Mr. Rodriguez enjoys reading, model and antique cars, and archaeology documentals.

George W. Schroeder
QS9000 Coordinator
Grand Rapids Controls
P.O. Box 360
Rockford, MI 49341–0360
(616) 866–9551
Fax: (616) 866–5065

3999

Business Information: Established in 1968, Grand Rapids Controls is a manufacturer of mechanical control cables which distributes worldwide. The Company currently employs 400 people. As QS9000 Coordinator, Mr. Schroeder is responsible for plant operations, teaching and developing the business, and assuring compliance to QS9000. **Career Steps:** QS9000 Coordinator, Grand Rapids Controls (1992–Present); Director Quality, Teledyne – Continental Motors (1987–1992); Director Quality, Cast Metal Industries (1980–1987). **Associations & Accomplishments:** American Association of Quality Control; Society of Automotive Engineers; Society of Manufacturing Engineers; S.D.C.E.; A.F.S. **Education:** Illinois Central College (1975). **Personal:** Mr. Schroeder enjoys hunting, fishing, and shooting.

Charlette Sears
General Manager
Tenneco Packaging
2024 Norris Road
Bakersfield, CA 93308
(805) 392–4020
Fax: (805) 392–4093

3999

Business Information: Tenneco Packaging is one of four divisions with Tenneco Corp. and manufactures a comprehensive line of packaging products to include container board, paper board, corrugated products, folding cartons and molder fiber, aluminum and plastic packaging products. As General Manager, Ms. Sears manages the activities of 300 associates in the production of high quality plastic products for a low cost. **Career Steps:** Plant Manager, Tenneco Packaging (1994–Present); Mobil Chemical: Unit Manager for Cinch Sak (1993–1994), General Supervisor (1989–1993). **Associations & Accomplishments:** Board of Directors, Kern County United Way. **Education:** Attended: University of Mary Hardin Baylor; University of Kansas, B.G.S. in Personnel Administration. **Personal:** Married to Victor Joe in 1977. Ms. Sears enjoys reading business and self–improvement books and playing the piano.

Christine L. Seering
President
Prenatal Cradle, Inc.
P.O. Box 443
Hamburg, MI 48139
(810) 231–2983
Fax: (810) 231–2941

3999

Business Information: Prenatal Cradle, Inc. is a national manufacturer and marketer of patented maternity garments, which include the Prenatal Cradle (a support garment for the tummy), Criss–Cross Cradle (patent pending), and V2 Supporter (patent pending) trademarks. Physician recommended, the products are distributed throughout retail outlets and catalogs from two locations in Michigan (Clare and Hamburg). Establishing Prenatal Cradle, Inc. after the invention of a maternity product used to support pregnant women's stomachs in 1987, Mrs. Seering proceeded, as Co–Inventor, to patent the product and went into partnership with her sister–in–law (who the product was invented for). Serving as President, she is responsible for many aspects of operations, including business administration, public relations, strategic planning, shipping, quality control, catalog sales, and new product development. **Career Steps:** President, Prenatal Cradle, Inc. (1987–Present); Registered Nurse, University of Michigan Hospitals; Registered Nurse, Family Home Care; Registered Nurse, St. Joseph Mercy Hospital. **Associations & Accomplishments:** NFIB; Boy Scout Troop Committee Member; Shepherding Committee; Treasurer, New Church START; Recipient as co–inventor for new patent granted on V2 Supporter; Active, Discipleship Committee Chairperson for the church with which she is a member; Member, Small Ladies Ensemble Singing Group; ICEA. **Education:** Eastern Michigan University; Lansing Community College, A.A. **Personal:** Mrs. Seering enjoys swimming, sailing, bicycling, singing, and family activities.

Stan D. Seitz

Senior Vice President
PSC Inc.
675 Basket Road
Webster, NY 14580
(716) 265–1600
Fax: (716) 265–6431

3999

Business Information: PSC Inc. specializes in the manufacture of bar code laser scanning devices. Established in 1969, PSC Inc. currently employs 500 people and has an estimated annual revenue of $85 million. As Senior Vice President, Mr. Seitz is responsible for all aspects of operations. **Career Steps:** Senior Vice President, PSC Inc. (1993–Present); Senior Director of Operations, Compusa (1992–1993); President, P C Brand, Inc. (1989–1992); Vice President of Manufacturing, Dell Computer Corporation (1986–1989). **Associations & Accomplishments:** Phi Beta Kappa Honor Society; Phi Kappa Phi Honor Society; Knights of Columbus; Interviewed for articles, recently in Modern Material Handling.

Education: University of Chicago, M.B.A. (1981); University of Arizona, B.S. with high distinction (1972). **Personal:** Married to Nancy M. in 1976. Four children: Kimberly, Kirk, Kristina and Kara. Mr. Seitz enjoys running, camping, and his children's activities.

David Settle
Director of Transportation
Lasco Bathware
888 West Broadway
Three Rivers, MI 49093–1900
(616) 279–7461
Fax: (616) 278–8220

3999

Business Information: Lasco Bathware — a division of England–based Tomkins Industries, Inc. — is a major manufacturer of fiberglass and acrylic bathtubs, showers, and whirlpools. In the U.S., Tomkins Industries, Inc. owns companies such as: Murray of Ohio, Red Wing Foods, Smith & Wesson, Gates Rubber, Philips Products, Dexter Axle, etc. With headquarters located in England, Tomkins Industries, Inc. has more than 120 locations worldwide (100 are in the U.S.). Joining Lasco Bathware in 1982, Mr. Settle was appointed as Director of Transportation in 1994. He is responsible for the entire scope of fleet and distribution of both inbound and outbound products, including operations, sales, public relations, and strategic planning. **Career Steps:** Lasco Bathware: Director of Transportation (1994–Present), National Fleet and Distribution Manager (1991–1994), Regional Fleet and Distribution Manager (1982–1991). **Associations & Accomplishments:** American Trucking Association; Private Fleet Management Institute; National Private Truck Council; Nominated for Fleet Executive of the Year and Fleet Safety Professional of the Year; Youngest recipient in England to recieve his CDL, known as HGL. **Education:** Turton County (1966); Bolton Technical College, Transportation; Certified Private Fleet Manager (1994). **Personal:** Married to Carole in 1973. Mr. Settle enjoys outdoor sports, fitness training, and reading.

Jack P. Shields
Assistant Plant Manager
First Brands Corporation
101 Old Mill Road
Cartersville, GA 30120–4128
(770) 382–2330
Fax: (770) 387–9883
EMAIL: See Below

3999

Business Information: First Brands Corporation, a Fortune 200 company, is a leading manufacturer and distributor of consumer products. These products include: "Glad" plastic bags and wrap, "STP" car care products, "Johnny Cat," "Everclean," and "Scoop Away" cat litters, and "Simoniz" car waxes. Joining First Brands in 1980 as an engineer, Mr. Shields was appointed to his current position in 1994. As Assistant Plant Manager he provides the overall technical leadership for the Cartersville plant, ensuring its efficient operation. He can also be reached through the Internet via: SHIELDSJP@AOL.COM **Career Steps:** First Brands Corporation: Assistant Plant Manager (1994–Present); Manager of Technology (1992–1994); Production Department Manager (1988–1992); Department Head – Maintenance (1986–1988); Assistant Department Head – Engineering (1984–1986); Maintenance Supervisor (1983–1984); Production Supervisor (1981–1983); Project Engineer (1980–1981). **Associations & Accomplishments:** Christmas in April; Governor's School for Science and Technology; Little League Baseball Coach. **Education:** New Jersey Institute of Technology, B.S. in Mechanical Engineering (1980). **Personal:** Married to Cindy in 1982. Three children: Meghan, Danny and Taylor. Mr. Shields enjoys reading and golf.

Lucia Smigel

President
Robell Research, Inc.
635 Madison Avenue
New York, NY 10022
(212) 755–6577
Fax: (212) 755–3263

3999

Business Information: Ms. Smigel is the acknowledged conceiver of the $12 whitening toothpaste category. She also invented the patented delivery system for the acclaimed "Supersmile" Whitening Mouthwash and the patented design for the "Supersmile" 45 Degree Toothbrush. Ms. Smigel was responsible for licensing Robell's patented line of products to a multi–

national oral care company which generated over $90 million in sales during the second year of its introduction. Prior to starting Robell Research in 1989, Ms. Smigel was President of Smigel Research, and prior to that she managed the offices of the world's first dental aesthetic practice and set the standard for fee structures in the industry. **Career Steps:** President, Robell Research, Inc. (1989–Present); President, Smigel Research (1983–1988); Office Manager, Irwin Smigel, D.D.S., P.C. (1970–1982). **Education:** New York University, Washington Square College, NYC, B.S. (1956). **Personal:** Married to the renowned aesthetic dentist, Dr. Irwin Smigel.

Jack Stella
Manager of Safety System Product Programs
Adapto, Inc.
122 South Litchfield Road
Goodyear, AZ 85338
(602) 925–6711
Fax: (602) 932–0939

3999

Business Information: Adapto, Inc. is a manufacturer of precision–machined components, focusing on safety system products. Product line includes air bags for the automotive industry. Adapto has three manufacturing plants: two in Arizona and one in Southbend, Indiana. As Manager of Safety System Product Programs, Mr. Stella is responsible for the management of all programs related to safety system products, including serving as customer liaison and being instrumental in the design of a total automation robotic system, as well as implementation and integration systems. **Career Steps:** Manager of Safety System Product Programs, Adapto, Inc. (1994–Present); General Manager, SkyBlazer, Inc. (1993–1994); Senior Support Engineer, TRW Vehicle Safety Systems (1989–1993); President, Precision Wire Cut, Inc. (1984–1989). **Education:** Spring Garden College, Tool Engineer; Dobbins Vocational School, Mechanical Engineering and Machining Shop Technology, Journeyman Tool & Die Marker. **Personal:** Married to Colleen Nesbitt in 1982. Two children: Judith and John III. Mr. Stella enjoys golf, hiking, and travel.

Kevin R. Tillery
Production Manager
Calculex, Inc.
P.O. Box 339
Las Cruces, NM 88004–0339
(505) 525–0131
Fax: (505) 524–4744

3999

Business Information: Calculex, Inc. manufactures and designs high–end multiplexers and demultiplexers for recording systems, mainly Armor I and Armor II projects. Established in 1989, the company now has a second location in California. As Production Manager, Mr. Tillery serves as the Program Manager for contracts and Engineer Manager for new R&D. He supervises the engineering and programming teams, overseeing 25 employees in troubleshooting and meeting project deadlines. **Career Steps:** Production Manager, Calculex, Inc. (1995–Present); Program Manager, Physical Science Laboratory (1989–1993). **Education:** New Mexico State University, M.S. (1989). **Personal:** Married to Lisa in 1994. Four children: Jeremy, Joshua, Zachary, and Karen. Mr. Tillery enjoys mountain biking.

Steven R. Treon
East Regional Sales Manager
Interkal/GDS Seating, Inc.
5981 East Cork Street
Kalamazoo, MI 49003
(610) 746–9785
Fax: (616) 746–3408

3999

Business Information: Interkal/GDS Seating, Inc. is a design and manufacturing firm supplying stadium and arena seating to the educational and commercial market. Established in 1974, Interkal/GDS Seating, Inc. employs 175 people with estimated annual sales in excess of $35 million. As East Regional Sales Manager, Mr. Treon is responsible for all sales and marketing in Kalamazoo, MI and Fountain Inn, SC. **Career Steps:** East Regional Sales Manager, Interkal/GDS Seating, Inc. (1995–Present); Major Project Sales, Dant Clayton Corporation (1992–1995); Director of Sales and Technical Services, Contour Seats, Inc. (1986–1992). **Associations & Accomplishments:** International Facilities Manager Association; I.A.A.M. **Education:** Lincoln Technical Institute, Associate's Degree in Architecture (1983). **Personal:** Married to Debra in 1984. Three children: Brittany, Trisha, and Dillon. Mr. Treon enjoys family activities, sports, and travel.

Dennis D. Tuel Sr.
Chief Executive Officer
Shoremaster Inc.
P.O. Box 358
Fergus Falls, MN 56538–0358
(218) 739–4641
Fax: (218) 739–4008

3999

Business Information: Shoremaster Inc. is a manufacturer of waterfront equipment (i.e., marinas, boat lifts, docks). Established in 1973, Shoremaster Inc. currently employs 100 people and has an estimated annual revenue of $10 million. As Chief Executive Officer, Mr. Tuel is responsible for all aspects of operations. **Career Steps:** Founder and Chief Executive Officer, Shoremaster Inc. (1973–Present). **Associations & Accomplishments:** Board of Directors, Tri–State Manufacturers Association; Secretary, Minnesota Buffalo Association; Political Campaign Chairman; Ducks Unlimited. **Education:** St. Cloud State University, B.A. in Chemistry and Biology. **Personal:** Married to Marsha in 1960. Five children: Lisa, Lori, Melissa, Dennis Jr. and Tricia. Mr. Tuel enjoys managing his buffalo ranch (Buffalo Pass Ranch Inc.).

Thomas J. Walz
President
Carbide Processors
2733 South Ash Street
Tacoma, WA 98409–7850
(206) 272–1708
Fax: (206) 383–5802

3999

Business Information: Carbide Processors specializes in the manufacture of cutting tool parts, as well as cutting tool and new materials research and implementation. In 1989, Carbide Processors was named one of the top 500 fastest growing companies by "Inc." magazine. Established in 1981, Carbide Processors currently employs 25 people. As President, Mr. Walz is responsible for all aspects of operations, including research, safety, sales and marketing. **Career Steps:** President, Carbide Processors (1981–Present). **Associations & Accomplishments:** Chamber of Commerce; Volunteer Economic Development Board; City Club; President, Friends of China Lake; Elks; National Tech Transfer Center; Focus Group; Mensa; International Society for Philosophical Enquiry; Guest Speaker and Instructor, Pierce College and Tacoma Community College; Various professional and charitable associations. **Education:** Creighton University, B.A. (1974).

William W. West IV

Director of Operations
Lawson Mardon Label
P.O. Box 0, 1403 Fourth Avenue
New Hyde Park, NY 11040–5544
(516) 355–2522
Fax: (516) 775–8723

3999

Business Information: Lawson Mardon Label is a manufacturer of flexible packaging for beverages and paper labels for food and beverages. Owned by a Swiss Company, Lawson Mardon Label is one of five North American divisions. As Director of Operations, Mr. West is responsible for all aspects of Company operations of the New York and Maryland facilities. **Career Steps:** Director of Operations, Lawson Mardon Label (1992–Present); Plant Manager, Astro Valcour, Inc.; Regional Sales Manager, Cab Tek, Inc.; Plant Superintendent, James River, Inc. **Associations & Accomplishments:** American Management Association; American Society for Quality Control; Flexible Trade Association; Sterling Who's Who. **Education:** DePaul University – Paris, France, M.B.A. (1963). **Personal:** Married to Helen in 1965. Mr. West enjoys chess, golf and, poetry.

Kwang Yang, M.D., C.C.F.P.
Chairman
Worldwide Ginseng Corporation
10751 King George Highway
Surrey, British Columbia V3T 2X6
(604) 581–2611 (604) 588–5988
Fax: (604) 581–5069 (604) 590–4569

3999

Business Information: Worldwide Ginseng Corporation is an emerging company well–suited to a new market environment, taking a revolutionary approach to ongoing cultivation by introducing the first–ever development of commercial scale hydroponically–grown ginseng. Two programs are carried through agreements with Agriculture and Agri–Food Canada, and the University of British Columbia at Vancouver. As Chairman, Dr. Yang is responsible for all aspects of Company operations. Concurrently, Dr. Yang is a physician with his own private practice. **Career Steps:** Chairman, Worldwide Ginseng Corporation (1994–Present); Doctor, Dr. Kwang Yang (1971–Present). **Associations & Accomplishments:** Canadian Medical Association; College of Family Physicians of Canada; Surrey Medical Society; British Columbia General Practitioner's Society; Surrey Delta Chinese Community Society; British Columbia Medical Association; National Taiwan University Medical School Alumni; Former Principal and Director, Universal Institute; Certifications: Canada, China, England, Hong Kong, Canadian Family Physician, Acupuncture – State of California, Advanced Cardiac Life Support, Advanced Trauma Life Support; Publication: "Urinary Tract Infection in Children," Canadian Family Physician Journal (1971). **Education:** National Taiwan University Medical School, M.D. (1969); Dalhousie University Medical School: Rotating Internship Program (1969–1970), Family Medicine Residency Program (1970–1971). **Personal:** Married to Catherine in 1974. Four children: Florian, Lawrence, Alexander, and Felix. Dr. Yang enjoys gardening, hiking, swimming, chess, tennis, and biking.

Renaud Zigmann
Executive Chairman
Xsalto
Les Francons
Lans en Vercors, France 38250
(33) 76954153
Fax: Please mail or call

3999

Business Information: Xsalto, established in 1995, is a national developer and marketer of products in the areas of artificial intelligence and scientific computing. As Executive Chairman, Mr. Zigmann is responsible for all aspects of operations, including the design and development of products, including new business development and serving as expert in the fields of artificial intelligence and scientific computing. **Career Steps:** Executive Chairman, Xsalto (1995–Present); Technical Manager of Research and Development, ITMI, France (1993–1995); Research Engineer, idem (1988–1992). **Associations & Accomplishments:** Association Francaise d'intellegence Artificielle; Association de independants en informatique; Member, Institute of Electronics and Electrical Engineers. **Education:** University of Grenoble, D.E.A. (Doctorat d'etudes Approfondics) (1987). **Personal:** Mr. Zigmann enjoys mountain sports, literature, computer science, and philosophy.

4000 – 4999
TRANSPORTATION
AND
PUBLIC UTILITIES

4000 Railroad Transportation

Curtis S. McGhee II
Account Executive
CSX Transportation
200 Galleria Parkway, Suite 430
Atlanta, GA 30339–3129
(770) 859–1909
Fax: Please mail or call

4011

Business Information: CSX Transportation is one of the oldest and largest railroad transportation units in the Nation. Originally established in 1827, with the merger of Seaboard Coast Line Railroad and the Chesapeake and Ohio Railroad companies it now employs approximately 29,000 people and has an estimated revenue of $4.7 billion. As Account Executive, Mr. McGhee is responsible for developing and providing logistics solutions to Fortune 100 corporations. **Career Steps:** CSX Transportation: Account Executive (1990–Present), Growth Team Leader (1996–Present), Management Trainee (1990). **Associations & Accomplishments:** Big Brothers/Big Sisters of Cobb County; Virginia Polytechnic Institute and State University Alumni Association. **Education:** Georgia State University, M.B.A. in Finance (1995); Virginia Polytechnic Institute and State University, B.S. in Management. **Personal:** Married to Angela in 1995. Mr. McGhee enjoys sports, spending time with his wife, and taking his "little brother" to sporting events.

Patrick J. Mead
General Manager, Eastern Business Group
Amtrak
360 W. 31st Street
New York, NY 10001
(212) 630–7220
Fax: (212) 630–6326

4011

Business Information: Amtrak is national passenger railroad company specializing in rail transportation throughout the U.S. Established in 1971, the Company employs 23,000 people corporate wide (700 in New York) with estimated annual revenue of $74 million. As General Manager, Eastern Business Group, Mr. Mead directs all operational aspects of the Company. He oversees trains from the east coast to the midwest, and handles all marketing, transportation, on–board services, ticket offices, etc. **Career Steps:** Amtrak: General Manager, Eastern Business Group (1995–Present), Transportation Superintendent (1993–1995), District Superintendent, New England (1988–1993), Superintendent for Operations, Washington, DC Headquarters (1986–1988). **Associations & Accomplishments:** American Association of Railroad Superintendents. **Education:** University of Virginia, Executive Development (1985). **Personal:** Married to Barbara in 1984. Three children: Jamie, Jennifer, and Jessica. Mr. Mead enjoys golf, decoy carving, and gardening.

K. S. Pahk
President
Hyundai Intermodal, Inc.
897 West 190th Street, Suite #7
Gardena, CA 90248
(310) 217–8260
Fax: (310) 527–8261

4011

Business Information: Hyundai Intermodal, Inc. is a domestic transportation company specializing in stack train operations across the United States. As President, Mr. Pahk oversees the operation of the Corporation. He is responsible for financial planning, marketing of services, human resource utilization, and planning for the continued growth of the Corporation. **Education:** Choong–Ang, Korea, B.A. **Personal:** Married to Wanda. Two children: Eugene and Edwin. Mr. Pahk enjoys golf.

Michael J. Tallarico
Project Manager
Conrail
1810 Round Street
Bethlehem, PA 18018–4560
(610) 861–5657
Fax: (610) 861–5753
EMAIL: See Below

4011

Business Information: Conrail provides freight rail transportation throughout the northern region of the U.S., including nine offices located in the northeast with headquarters in Philadelphia, Pennsylvania. As Project Manager, Mr. Tallarico is responsible for major construction in the field from the office in Bethlehem, supervising installation of rail signals and new technologies. Internet users can reach him via: Mtalla@aol.com. **Career Steps:** Conrail: Project Manager (1996–Present), Senior Project Engineer (1994–1996), Engineer Service Test (1990–1994), Project Engineer (1984–1990). **Associations & Accomplishments:** Association of American Railroads. **Education:** Ryder Technical Institute, Associate in Technology (1974). **Personal:** Married to Patricia in 1976. Two children: Patrick and Jennifer. Mr. Tallarico enjoys music, computers, and books.

Alison Conway–Smith

Vice President and Chief Engineer
Amtrak
30th Street Station, Fourth Floor
Philadelphia, PA 19104
(215) 349–1131
Fax: (215) 349–2628

4012

Business Information: Amtrak is a national passenger railroad, as well as freight forwarding. As Vice President and Chief Engineer, Ms. Conway–Smith is responsible for design, construction, and maintenance of all Amtrak owned infrastructures. **Career Steps:** Vice President and Chief Engineer, Amtrak (1994–Present); New Jersey Transit: Deputy General Manager (1993–1994), Superintendent of M&E Line (1990–1993), Engineer Special Projects (1985–1990). **Associations & Accomplishments:** American Railway Engineering Association; Metropolitan Railroad Club. **Education:** University of Connecticut, B.S.C.E. (1979). **Personal:** Married to William Peter in 1989. Two children: Molly and Peter. Ms. Conway–Smith enjoys painting.

4100 Local and Interurban Passenger Transit

4111 Local and suburban transit
4119 Local passenger transportation, NEC
4121 Taxicabs
4131 Intercity and rural bus transportation
4141 Local bus charter service
4142 Bus charter service, except local
4151 School buses
4173 Bus terminal and service facilities

Robert S. Ator

General Manager
ATC/Vancom Paratransit Services
4660 West Tropicana
Las Vegas, NV 89103–5212
(702) 222–0113
Fax: (702) 222–0698 (702) 256–7807
EMAIL: See Below

4111

Business Information: ATC/Vancom Paratransit Services, a division of ATC/Vancom of Nevada Limited Partnership, Inc., is a mass transit management company, providing management services, including city bus and paratransit systems. An expert in public transit management spanning a period of twenty years, Robert Ator has served at ATC/Vancom's Las Vegas, Nevada, CAT Paratransit division since 1994. Working under contract with the Regional Transportation Commission of Clark County, he oversees all day–to–day operations and support staff connected with the production of public transit vehicles. Internet users can also reach Robert via: rator@anv.net **Career Steps:** General Manager, ATC/Vancom (1994–Present); Assistant Transportation Supervisor, ATE Management & Services Company (1979–1983); Safety and Training Director, American Transit Corporation (ATC) (1976–1979). **Associations & Accomplishments:** Clark County Business Development Advisory Council; Former Member of Board of Directors, Florida Transit Association; Former Member of Board of Directors, Boys' Club; Former Member, Technical Coordinating Committee of Metropolitan Planning Organization. **Education:** University of Texas – Austin. **Personal:** Married to Fannie Mae in 1969. Three children: Scarlett, Robert Jr., and Mary. Mr. Ator enjoys computers, photography, and travel.

Dennis M. Cristofaro

Maintenance Manager
Chicago Transit Authority
2600 West Pershing Road
Chicago, IL 60632–1629
(312) 847–3114
Fax: (312) 927–0389
E Mail: See Below

4111

Business Information: Chicago Transit Authority is the municipal agency responsible for administering public transportation services within the Chicago metropolis. With twenty–four years of experience in the transportation industry, Mr. Cristofaro joined Chicago Transit Authority originally in 1966. After spending five years in other companies in the transportation industry (i.e., Ruan Truck Leasing, Leaseway of Illinois), he re–joined the Company as Maintenance Manager in 1983. He is responsible for all maintenance operations for a fleet of 239 buses. Internet users can reach him via: Transitman@msn.com or Dennis.cristofaro@afol.com **Career Steps:** Maintenance Manager, Chicago Transit Authority (1983–Present) (1966–1978); Maintenance Superintendent, Ruan Truck Leasing (1980–83); Maintenance Manager, Leaseway of Illinois (1978–1980). **Associations & Accomplishments:** Village Trustee, Village of Orlando Hills (198–93); Planning Commissioner, Village of Orlando Hills (1985–1989); Automotive Engine Rebuilders (1991–93); Instructor, Diesel Technology – Triton College (1982–1983, 1984–1985). **Education:** Daley College. **Personal:** Married to Barbara in 1967. Four children: Brian, Denise, Rosemary, and Jennifer. Mr. Cristofaro enjoys travel, dining out, and remodeling homes.

Earl J. Fairfax III

Transit Director
Maple Heights Transit
5501 Dunham Road
Maple Heights, OH 44137–3645
(216) 587–9685
Fax: (216) 662–2880

4111

Business Information: Maple Heights Transit is a public transit system for the City of Maple Heights. Established in 1935, Maple Heights Transit currently employs 45 people. As Transit Director, Mr. Fairfax is responsible for general management. **Career Steps:** Transit Director, Maple Heights Transit (1992–Present); Greater Cleveland RTA: Superintendent of Transportation (1988–1992), District Superintendent (1985–1988). **Associations & Accomplishments:** Cleveland Jaycees; Conference of Minority Transportation Officials. **Education:** Baldwin Wallace College (1992); Certificate in Human Resources Management; Certificate in Communications; Northeastern University; Cuyahoga Community College. **Personal:** Mr. Fairfax enjoys tennis, chess, fishing, and camping.

Rosemary A. Kalagher

Transportation Director
Montachusett Regional Transit Authority
R1427 Water Street
Fitchburg, MA 01420–7243
(508) 345–7711 Ext. 243
Fax: (508) 343–2719

4111

Business Information: Montachusett Regional Transit Authority is the agency responsible for providing public bus and van service for the elderly and disabled in the county and surrounding regions. As Transportation Director, Ms. Kalagher manages contracts and bidding for special education and Early Intervention programs. **Career Steps:** Transportation Director, Montachusett Regional Transit Authority (1988–Present); Vocational Counselor/Math Instructor, Career Education Training Center (1986–1988); Adolescent Specialist, Lipton Mental Health (1982–1985). **Associations & Accomplishments:** Published in "The Fitchburg Sentinel & Enterprise" and "The Worchester Telegram & Gazette." **Education:** Assumption College, B.A. (1977). **Personal:** Ms. Kalagher enjoys travel, photography, fishing, and reading.

Narendra Prasad, P.E.

General Superintendent
MTA New York City Transit
847 5th Avenue
Brooklyn, NY 11232
(212) 690–9618
Fax: (212) 690–9541

4111

Business Information: MTA New York City Transit is a public agency for public transportation in New York City. The Department of Subways operates 6,000 subway cars; and the Department of Buses operates 3,800 buses. The Company currently employs approximately 40,000 people system–wide. There are 22 depots under the Department of Buses where bus maintenance activities are performed. From these depots, bus service to the public is also available. Mr. Prasad is responsible for all aspects of facilities/plant & equipment maintenance of 10 depots through 6 superintendents, 15 maintenance supervisors and 150 hourly employees. **Career Steps:** General Superintendent, MTA New York City Transit (1994–Present); Superintendent, MTA New York City Transit (1986–1994); Resident Engineer, MTA New York City Transit (1982–1986); Sub Division Engineer, BSEB, India (1976–1982). **Associations & Accomplishments:** Institute of Electrical & Electronics Engineers; Association of Energy Engineers; International Facilities Management Association. **Education:** Long Island University, M.B.A.; India Institute of Technology, B.S. in Electrical Engineering (1970); State University of New York, Professional Engineer. **Personal:** Married to Madhuri Prasad in 1973. One child: Ayush Prasad.

Mrs. Deborah J. Ward

Director of Finance
Hillsborough Area Regional Transit Authority
4305 East 21st Avenue
Tampa, FL 33605–2300
(813) 623–5835
Fax: (813) 664–1119

4111

Business Information: Hillsborough Area Regional Transit Authority is a public mass transportation serving the Hillsborough area with bus service. Established in 1980, the Transit Authority currently employs in excess of 400 people, operates 170 buses and has an estimated annual revenue of $30 million. As Director of Finance, Mrs. Ward manages all aspects of finance, budget, procurement, payroll and accounting. **Career Steps:** Hillsborough Area Regional Transit Authority: Director of Finance (1990–Present), Accounting Manager (1981–1990); Bookkeeper, Marlin Steel (1979–1981); Cost Accountant, Great Southwest Corporation (1977–1979). **Associations & Accomplishments:** Institute of Management Accountants; National Association of Female Executives; Governmental Financial Officers Association. **Education:** University of Southern Florida, M.B.A. (1993); Carson–Newman College, B.S. in Accounting (1977). **Personal:** Married to Richard in 1974. Mrs. Ward enjoys golf, needlecrafts and teaching Sunday School.

Ms. Mary Sue Big Crow

Program Director
OST Ambulance Service
P.O. Box 346, Old PHS Hospital
Pine Ridge, SD 57770–0346
(605) 867–5999
Fax: (605) 867–5285

4119

Business Information: OST Ambulance Service is a Tribal (Oglala Sioux) program funded by the 93638 Fund under the directorship of PHS Hospital. OST provides a full–range of emergency medical services (EMS) treatment and transportation of the sick or injured. A practicing EMT since 1977 and an EMT Instructor since 1988, Ms. Big Crow joined OST Ambulance Service as Program Director in 1994. She is responsible for coordinating all aspects of the EMS Program, including compliance of policies and procedures, billing, overseeing a staff of 43 (29—EMTs, 10—First Responders, 4–Field Supervisors), serving as an ambulance attendant, and coordinating and training EMTs in Basic First Aid and CPuerto Rico classes. **Career Steps:** Program Director, OST Ambulance Service (1994–Present); Pine Ridge Reservation Ambulance Service: Assistant Director (1981–1993), Secretary and Billing Clerk (1976–1981). **Associations & Accomplishments:** South Dakota EMT Association; 2nd Vice President, Aberdeen Area Native American EMS Association; Tribal Emergency Response Commission (for hazardous materials and disaster preparedness). **Education:** Oglala Lakota College, B.A. in Business Administration in progress; Certified Emergency Medical Technician (1977); EMT Instructor, Black Hills Training Center (1988). **Personal:** Married to Raymond in 1976. Four children: Travis, George, Kara, and Krysti. Ms. Big Crow enjoys sewing, beadwork, and music.

Beverly G. Courtney
Chief Operating Officer
AAA Ambulance Service
207 South 28th Avenue
Hattiesburg, MS 39401
(601) 264-0175
Fax: (601) 264-3981

4119

Business Information: AAA Ambulance Service provides emergency and non–emergency transportation of the sick and injured. As Chief Operating Officer, Miss Courtney is responsible for the daily activities of the business and the operations division. Additionally, she provides support and direction to the administrative and support staff of 120. **Career Steps:** AAA Ambulance Service: Chief Operating Officer (1995–Present), Director of Operations (1990–1995); SAA: EMT–Basic (1986–1987), EMT–Paramedic (1987–Present). **Associations & Accomplishments:** Vice President, Mississippians for Emergency Medical Services; Active Member, American Ambulance Association. **Education:** Attended: PRCC; Currently working towards a Degree in Business Administration with an emphasis in Health Care. **Personal:** Two children: William and Jennifer. Miss Courtney enjoys reading, jet skiing, and softball.

Norberto D. Curitomai
President
Spanish Transportation Service Corporation
995 Main Avenue
Clifton, NJ 07011
(901) 470-0633
Fax: Please mail or call

4119

Business Information: Spanish Transportation Service Corporation is a provider of public passenger transportation (buses) — with a fleet consisting of 28 mini–buses capable of holding 13–20 passenger groups. STS currently provides service from New Jersey to New York, with future plans to expand to Washington, D.C., as well as the establishment of an export business, exporting farm machinery to South America. Established in 1993, Spanish Transportation Service Corporation currently employs 12 people. As President, Mr. Curitomai is responsible for all aspects of operations. **Career Steps:** President, Spanish Transportation Service Corporation (1993–Present); New Jersey Van Supervisor, New Jersey Van Corporation (1993); Driver, Broadway Taxi (1992–1993); Driver, Rohen Transportation (1990–1992). **Associations & Accomplishments:** American Bus Association; Peruvian Parade, Inc. **Education:** World Trade Institute, Export; E.P.A.E., Peru, Business Administration. **Personal:** Married to Elizabeth Matias in 1985. Four children: Carmen, Masali, Ansel, and Roberth. Mr. Curitomai enjoys reading books.

Scot C. Graham
Captain
Mutual Aid Ambulance Service
P.O. Box 350
Greensburg, PA 15601-0350
(412) 837-6134
Fax: (412) 834-2810

4119

Business Information: Mutual Aid Ambulance Service provides emergency medical transport services throughout the major Westmoreland County, PA sector. Services provided include CPuerto Rico education, ambulatory transit services to area medical facilities, disaster relief and response. Its motto is "Service.....so others may live". An emergency staff support member with Mutual Aid Ambulance since August 1985, Scot Graham has served as Captain of the Greensburg, PA team since March of 1992. He oversees all special operations services, which includes Disaster Planning & Management, serving as Speciality Response Team Leader, Public Relations, and supervision of the Communication Center. A certified EMS–Paramedic Instructor, he also conducts frequent classes on CPR, Basic Life Support and other specialized public educational programs. One such program he developed and implemented is "Andy the Ambulance" — a fictional character which he uses to educate Preschool through 2nd Grade children on emergency and disaster response services. **Career Steps:** Mutual Aid Ambulance Service: Captain (1992–Present), Manager (1991–1992), Crew Chief/Shift Supervisor (1985–1991). **Associations & Accomplishments:** Federal Emergency Management Agency: Urban Search and Rescue Team, Electronic Search Division; Assistant Chief, Marquerite Volunteer Fire Department; Pennsylvania Department of Health: EMT/Paramedic Advisory Board, Mass Casualty Incident Committee; Award: Citation for Pennsylvania Senate, House of Representatives, Governors Highway Safety Award, National American Legion Community and Youth Services, Corporate Livesaving Unit Citation. **Education:** University of Pittsburgh; Numerous licenses and certifications from National Fire Academy, Pennsylvania Department of Health, Environmental Protection Agency; Pennsylvania

State Fire Academy; Federal Emergency Management Agency; Pennsylvania Separtmentof Environmental Resources; American Heart Association; National Academy of Trauma; Center for Emergency Medicine; National Academy of EMD. **Personal:** Married to Elizabeth M. in 1991. Mr. Graham enjoys golf and collecting EMS and Fire Department patches from the world over.

Michael D. Griffus

Regional Vice President
Laidlaw Transit, Inc.
1340 Treat Boulevard, Suite 210
Walnut Creek, CA 94596
(510) 939-1299
Fax: (510) 685-3513

4119

Business Information: Laidlaw Transit, Inc., a wholly–owned subsidiary (and largest division) of Laidlaw, Inc., provides public transportation services on a contract basis to corporate, municipal, governmental, educational and healthcare/emergency medicine (ambulance) sectors. The parent company, Laidlaw, Inc. is a $3.5 billion multi–divisional transportation conglomerate traded on the NYSE. Headquartered in Toronto, Canada, it has three distinct industry divisions: Laidlaw Waste, Laidlaw Environmental and Laidlaw Transit, Inc. With sixteen years experience in the transportation industry, Mr. Griffus joined Laidlaw Transit, Inc. as Regional Vice President in 1991. Covering the areas encompassing Northern California, Washington, Oregon, Alaska, Eastern Colorado and Utah, he is responsible for the supervision of over 4,500 staff, P&L accountability, customer relations and administrative support for the Transit Division. **Career Steps:** Regional Vice President, Laidlaw Transit, Inc. (1991–Present); Area Manager, Leaseway Transportation (1980–1991). **Associations & Accomplishments:** Associate Member, Regional Productivity Committee. **Education:** University of Washington, B.A. in Business (1980). **Personal:** Married to Melissa in 1980. Two children: Daniel and Sarah. Mr. Griffus enjoys coaching, golf, and hiking.

Grant Helferich
Director
Butler County Emergency Medical Services
701 North Haverhill
Eldorado, KS 67042
(316) 321-9260
Fax: (316) 321-9264

4119

Business Information: Butler County Emergency Medical Services is a paramedical ambulance service organization, providing emergency medical services on–site and enroute to hospitals from accident sites. With fifteen years expertise in the medical field, Mr. Helferich joined Butler County Emergency Medical Services in 1990. Currently serving as Director, he is responsible for the overall administration and management of paid employees and volunteers, as well as budgeting. **Career Steps:** Butler County Emergency Medical Services: Director (1990–Present), Operational Supervisor (1980–1988); Cardiovascular Specialist, HCA – Wesley Medical Center (1988–1990). **Associations & Accomplishments:** Member, Leadership Butler; Kansas Certified Mobile Intensive Care Technician; National Certified Paramedic; National Association of Emergency Medical Services; International Association of Fire Chiefs; National Association of EMS Physicians; Kansas Certified Training Officer; National Society of EMS Administrators; American Ambulance Association. **Education:** Wichita State University; Hutchinson Community College; Butler County Community College; Southwestern University – Paramedical. **Personal:** Married to Hope K. in 1984. Four children: Peter, Tim, Ben and Hannah. Mr. Helferich enjoys golf and fishing.

Carolyn E. Kleck
General Manager
A–1 Handicapped Transportation
2541 East Jackson Street
Phoenix, AZ 85034
(602) 275-3224
Fax: (602) 275-4623

4119

Business Information: A–1 Handicapped Transportation provides wheelchair and stretcher van transportation for people with special needs. Established in 1989, the Company employs 12 people and has an estimated annual revenue of $500 thousand. As General Manager, Ms. Kleck is responsible for negotiating contracts, all accounting, personnel management, and the monitoring and dispatch of all equipment. **Career Steps:** General Manager, A–1 Handicapped Transportation (1995–Present); Office Manager, Phoenix Sheraton

(1990–1992); Office Manager, AZ Office Equipment (1986–1989); Operations Manager, 1st Interstate Bank of Arizona (1977–1986). **Associations & Accomplishments:** Glendale Chamber of Commerce; Womens International Bowling Association. **Education:** Glendale Community; Rio Salado Community College. **Personal:** Married to Richard Scott in 1985. Three children: Kandis M. Councilor, Dawn C. and Lawrence W. Potts. Ms. Kleck enjoys drawing, pastels, bowling, reading, camping, and fishing.

Mrs. Claire H. Klein
President
Action Transit Enterprises, Inc.
330 Popper Street
Pittsburgh, PA 15223-2295
(412) 781-7906
Fax: (412) 781-8230

4119

Business Information: Action Transit Enterprises, Inc. is a local transport company providing school buses, coaches, vans and triaxle trucks to the public in the Pittsburgh community. Established in 1976, Action Transit Enterprises, Inc. currently employs 200 people and has an estimated annual revenue of $7 million. As President, Mrs. Klein is the Director of Human Resources, responsible for operations and administration. **Career Steps:** President, Action Transit Enterprises, Inc. (1976–Present); Office Manager, Edward A. Schultz, Esq. (1943–1949). **Associations & Accomplishments:** Member, Pittsburgh Bus Association; Board of IVC; Former President, Pittsburgh Chapter of Hadassah, American Zionist Federation; Pittsburgh Conference of Jewish Women; Jewish National Fund; Vice President, B'nai Israel Congregation. **Education:** Chatham College, B.A. (1943). **Personal:** Married to Seyour in 1949. Two children: Alan H. and Evan A. Mrs. Klein enjoys stamp collecting, knitting and gardening.

George T. Kosue Jr.
Director of Administration
American MedTrans
33315 33rd Place Southwest
Federal Way, WA 98023
(206) 649-6910
Fax: (206) 549-9490

4119

Business Information: American MedTrans, a subsidiary of the Laidlaw Engineering Company (a hazardous waste disposal and passenger transportation company), is an ambulance service provider, providing emergency transportation to clientele in a six–county area in the state of Washington. With corporate headquarters located in San Diego, California, American MedTrans is located in the Mountain Region Branch (one of six regions in the U.S.), serving the Northwestern U.S. sector. The regional office is located in Las Vegas, Nevada. Operating a fleet of 4,000 ambulances nationwide, MedTrans is the largest company of its kind in the U.S. Serving for the past twenty–five years in executive positions, Mr. Kosue joined American MedTrans in 1992 as Director of Operations. Appointed as Director of Administration in 1993, he oversees the day–to–day administrative functions to include budgeting, manpower utilization, statistical analysis, and business office functions. **Career Steps:** Director of Administration, American MedTrans (1995–Present); American MedTech: Director of Administration (1993–1995), Director of Operations (1992–1993); Director of Operations, Shepard Ambulance (1970–1992). **Associations & Accomplishments:** Executive Board, Washington Ambulance Association; King County Fire Chiefs Association; Association of Public Safety and Communications Officers; Washington State Trauma Care Council – North Region. **Education:** Central Washington University, B.S. (1985). **Personal:** Married to Julie L. in 1972. One child: Connie L. Mr. Kosue enjoys computers, photography, and reading.

Paul H. Wain
Director
Pinkerton Services, Inc.
1014 California Avenue
Pittsburgh, PA 15202
(412) 766-5600
Fax: (412) 766-4951

4119

Business Information: Pinkerton Services, Inc. provides emergency and non–emergency ambulance services to Pittsburgh and surrounding areas. Established in 1946, the Company employs 35 people. As Director, Mr. Wain provides oversight of administrative and operational duties. He is also responsible for staff, billing, and handling of emergency calls. **Career Steps:** Pinkerton Services, Inc: Director (Present), Director of Operations, Manager. **Associations & Accomplishments:** Scoutmaster/Council, Boy Scouts of America; Memorial Park Church Youth Leader; Assistant Chief, Peebles District Volunteer Fire Company.

Ted Wilson
Regional Vice President
Laidlaw Transit Limited
30 Heritage Road
Markham, Ontario L3P 1M4
(905) 294–5104
Fax: (905) 294–6377

4151

Business Information: A subsidiary of Laidlaw, Inc., a multi–divisional company providing various services, i.e., environmental, hazardous waste and waste management (fourth largest), and health care transportation (under the name Med Trans with 2,200 ambulances). Additionally, Laidlaw Transit Limited is the largest provider of home–to–school transportation in North America. The Company, utilizing a fleet of 35,000 buses, contracts with various schools to provide safe and cost effective student transportation. Established in 1967, the Company employs 50,000 people and has an estimated annual revenue of $1.2 billion. As Regional Vice President, Mr. Wilson is responsible for both financial and operational performance of those divisions in central Ontario, managing a fleet of 1,500 school buses and coordinating with 23 school boards throughout the Province. **Career Steps:** Laidlaw Transit Limited: Regional Vice President (1990–Present), Division Manager, Ottawa (1988–1989), Division Manager, Kingston (1980–1985). **Associations & Accomplishments:** Delegate to 1995 Governor General's Canadian Study Conference; Fund Raising Committee for Metro Toronto Association for Community Living; Past Director, Ontario School Bus Operators Association; United Empire Loyalists Association. **Education:** University of Waterloo, B.A. with Honors (1976). **Personal:** Married to Christine in 1992. Four children: Bianca, Tristan, Tracey, and Ruth. Mr. Wilson enjoys camping and golf.

James R. Saffley
Partner & Executive Vice President
JetCorp
18152 Edison Avenue
Chesterfield, MO 63005–3708
(314) 530–7000
Fax: (314) 530–7001

4173

Business Information: JetCorp is a maintenance company for private jets of Fortune 500 and Fortune 100 companies. Maintenance accounts for 70% of the Company's business, the rest is in fueling, hangar storage, and charter. As Partner & Executive Vice President, Mr. Saffley is responsible for aircraft sales, accessories, avionics, maintenance, ramp service, charter, and the interior shop. **Career Steps:** Partner & Executive Vice President, JetCorp (1992–Present); Senior Vice President of Technical Support, Aviation Material and Technical Support (1991–1992); Senior Vice President of Technical Services (1982–1991), Vice President of Technical Services (1975–1982), Manager & General Manager (1974–1975). **Associations & Accomplishments:** Professional Aviation Maintenance Association, Inc.: Board of Directors, Former President, Former Central Region Director; National Aviation Maintenance Technician of the Year Award, Industry/FAA Award (1982); The Airwork Kudos Knight Award (1982). **Education:** NATA Management Institute, Aviation Management (1979); Harry Woehr & Associates, Business Management (1976); Beech Aircraft Corporation, Beech King – Air 100 Factory School (1970); Sabreliner Familiarization Course; Airframe and Systems, Aero Commander Factory School (1963); O'Fallon Technical School, Jet and Reciprocal Powerplant Courses (1962). **Personal:** Married to Barbara. They have three children Sandra, Donna, and Suzane. Mr. Saffley enjoys golf and fishing.

4200 Trucking and Warehousing

4212 Local trucking, without storage
4213 Trucking, except local
4214 Local trucking with storage
4215 Courier services, except by air
4221 Farm product warehousing and storage
4222 Refrigerated warehousing and storage
4225 General warehousing and storage
4226 Special warehousing and storage, NEC
4231 Trucking terminal facilities

Robert Hall
General Manager and Assistant Secretary
Cowan Systems, Inc. and Subsidiaries
100 Lums Road
North East, MD 21901–2410
(410) 287–5077
Fax: (410) 287–5812

4212

Business Information: Robert Hall, with over 20 years expertise in the trucking industry, is the General Manager and Assistant Board Secretary to Cowan Systems, Inc. and its subsidiary companies, which consist as follows: Cowan Systems, Inc. — provider of long–haul truck transportation; and PDS, Inc. (dba Peninsula Distribution Services) — providing contract truck and intermodal trailer transportation services. Established in 1989, the parent company reports annual revenue of $6 million. **Career Steps:** General Manager and Assistant Secretary, Cowan Systems, Inc. and Subsidiaries (1989–Present); Lease and Sales Branch Management, Rollins Leasing (1981–1989); Manager, Brody Truck Rental (1981); Lease and Sales Management, Tri–State Vehicle Leasing (1978–1981). **Associations & Accomplishments:** Cecil County Chamber of Commerce; Maryland Motor Trucking Association; American Trucking Association, National Committee. **Education:** University of Baltimore, B.S. (1972); Central Michigan University, M.S. in progress. **Personal:** Married to Elizabeth in 1976. Two children: Jerry and Jason. Mr. Hall enjoys sailing, and train collecting.

Mr. Paul L. Ingram
President
Ingram Trucking Inc.
1601 Beaver Dam Road, P.O. Box 249
Morgantown, KY 42261
(502) 526–3727
Fax: (502) 526–5739

4212

Business Information: Ingram Trucking Inc. is a (intermodal) truckload carrier. National in scope, Ingram primarily covers the Central and Southwestern United States. Their major contract is with Sumitomo, a major manufacturer of automotive wiring harnesses. As President, Mr. Ingram oversees all operational aspects of the Company, focusing on client relationships and contracts with major clients. Established in 1981, Ingram Trucking Inc. employs a staff of 48. **Career Steps:** President, Ingram Trucking Inc. (1981–Present).

Alice F. Peacock
Safety Director
Cartwright Van Lines Incorporated
11901 Cartwright Lane
Grandview, MO 64030–1151
(816) 763–2700
Fax: (816) 763–7863

4212

Business Information: Cartwright Van Lines Incorporated is a family–owned international freight line headquartered in Grandview, Missouri. Established in 1934, the corporation handles the hauling of household goods and some general freight to local, national, and international destinations. As Safety Director, Ms. Peacock is responsible for driver qualifications, driver logs, accident reports, equipment, inspections, and licensing as well as consulting with the fleet manager to hire drivers. She is required to be current on all rules and regulations regarding the hauling of merchandise across state and international borders. **Career Steps:** Cartwright Van Lines Incorporated: Safety Director (1983–Present), Safety Supervisor (1978–1983), Safety Clerk (1970–1978). **Education:** Attended, Concordia Teachers College. **Personal:** Married to James in 1965. Two children: James and Tamera. Ms. Peacock enjoys music and hand sewing.

Gregory M. Bartus
Regional Manager
Trailer Bridge, Inc.
8700 Joliet Road
McCook, IL 60525
(708) 447–5505
Fax: (708) 447–5767

4213

Business Information: Trailer Bridge, Inc. is an intermodal truck load/ocean carrier company, providing service between the U.S. and Puerto Rico via company–owned tractors and vessels. National in scope, Trailer Bridge spans three locations: Florida, Illinois, and Puerto Rico. Joining Trailer Bridge, Inc. as Regional Manager in 1992, Greg Bartus is responsible for the management of all trucking operations in the Northern Region. Duties include coordinating all pickup and deliveries for the Northern Region, ensuring that certain customers are

taken care of, and costs are kept at a minimum. **Career Steps:** Regional Manager, Trailer Bridge, Inc. (1992–Present); Operations Manager, Allen Freight Lines (1990–1992); Manager of Truck Operations, Cargo, Inc. (1988–1990); Supervisor of Truck Operations, Al–Ways Air Freight (1982–1988). **Education:** Pennsylvania State University, B.S. in Business Logistics (1980). **Personal:** Married to Carol L. in 1985. Three children: Allison Greer, Molly Lauren, and Gemma Rose.

Gottlieb W. Baumann
President
Iowa Western Transport, Inc.
2328 East 24th Street
Polk, IA 50317
(515) 266–1844
Fax: (515) 266–1844

4213

Business Information: Iowa Western Transport, Inc. is a regional, interstate transportation company providing general freight hauling for businesses within the domestic United States. As President, Mr. Baumann supervises the everyday operations of the Company, including finances, personnel, equipment, and strategic planning. He also performs dispatching duties. ensuring that the proper type and size of vehicle is sent to the jobsite. **Career Steps:** President, Iowa Western Transport, Inc. (1996–Present); President, Sarah Marie Transportation (1988–1995); President, J&D Trucking (1980–1995). **Personal:** Married to Dorothy in 1977. Mr. Baumann enjoys fishing.

Judy J. Burkhardsmeier
Controller
Carlile Enterprises, Inc.
1813 East 1st Avenue
Anchorage, AK 99501
(907) 276–7797
Fax: (907) 278–7301

4213

Business Information: Carlile Enterprises, Inc. is an Alaskan–owned intra/interstate freight carrier with three branches in Alaska and one in Federal Way, Washington. As Controller, Ms. Burkhardsmeier is responsible for all financial statements, supervises twenty people in general ledger, payroll, accounts receivable, accounts payable, and collections functions, and reports directly to the President. **Career Steps:** Controller, Carlile Enterprises, Inc. (1995–Present); Staff Accountant, Providence Hospital (1993–1995); Assistant Controller, Chugach Fisheries, Inc. (1991–1992). **Associations & Accomplishments:** Church Outreach Program; Women's Aglow. **Education:** Minot State University, B.S. in Accounting (1983). **Personal:** Married to Ronald in 1987. Three children: Paul, Amy, and Sean Case. Ms. Burkhardsmeier enjoys reading, camping, fishing, and spending time outdoors.

Mr. Larry J. Chapman
President
Chapman Trucking Co., Inc.
P.O. Box 4210
Casper, WY 82604–0210
(307) 472–7000
Fax: (307) 472–3835

4213

Business Information: Chapman Trucking Co., Inc. is a small trucking firm specializing in the heavy haul of machinery and equipment for companies and oil fields. Established in 1979, Chapman Trucking Co., Inc. reports annual revenue of $1 million and currently employs 14 people. As President, Mr. Chapman is responsible for all aspects of operations. **Career Steps:** President, Chapman Trucking Co., Inc. (1979–Present). **Associations & Accomplishments:** President, Wyoming Trucking Association. **Education:** University of Wyoming. **Personal:** Married to Carol in 1969.

Marion S. Hall

Vice President
Caldwell Freight Lines, Inc.
P.O. Box 620
Lenoir, NC 28645–0620
(704) 728–9231
Fax: (704) 728–0445

4213

Business Information: Caldwell Freight Lines, Inc. is a common carrier specializing in the delivery of new furniture from dealers and retailers in the Northeast, Southwest, and Midwest. The Corporation is headquartered in North Carolina and has two other locations nationwide. As Vice President, Mr. Hall is currently responsible for all financial aspects of the

Corrporation. Other duties include the administration of employee benefits and data processing. Mr. Hall is currently making the transition from day–to–day administration of the Corporation to long range planning and will soon be assisting with mergers and acquisitions. **Career Steps:** Caldwell Freight Lines, Inc: Vice President (1992–Present), Secretary/Treasurer (1989–1992), Controller (1986–1989). **Associations & Accomplishments:** American Institute of Certified Public Accountants; American Management Association; International Management Association; North Carolina Association of Certified Public Accountants. **Education:** University of North Carolina/Chapel Hill, B.S. in Business (1982). **Personal:** Married to Stephanie C. in 1982'. Mr. Hall enjoys gardening and woodworking.

Gary B. Hill

Training Director
Milan Express Company
1091 Kefauver Drive
Milan, TN 38358–3412
(901) 686–7428
Fax: (901) 686–8829

4213

Business Information: Milan Express Company is a trucking company providing services for LTL commodities as well as truck loading facilities. Established in 1969, the Company currently employs 900 people. As Training Director, Mr. Hill is responsible for the oversight of the Milan management systems, training programs, and internal and external communications. Mr. Hill is personally responsible for implementing the Milan University program for terminal managers, a post–graduate one–week program. Mr. Hill was a high school Psychology and American History Teacher prior to joining Mistletoe Express in 1981. **Career Steps:** Training Director, Milan Express Company (1992–Present); Manager of Loss Prevention, Smalley Transportation (1989–1992); Terminal Manager, Estes Express Company (1986–1989); District Manager, Mistletoe Express (1981–1986); Operations Manager, SATOL Trucking Co., Saudi Arabia (1979–1981); High School Teacher. **Associations & Accomplishments:** Applicant, West Tennessee Speakers Association; Numerous public speaking appearances. **Education:** University of Memphis, B.A. in Psychology and B.S. in Secondary Education (1993). **Personal:** Mr. Hill enjoys tennis, quail hunting, public speaking, and conducting self improvement training seminars.

Terance Littlefield
Information Systems Administrator
Hartt Transportation Systems, Inc.
262 Bomarc Road
Bangor, ME 04401–2624
(207) 947–1106
Fax: (207) 941–0839

4213

Business Information: Hartt Transportation Systems, Inc. is an interstate trucking company. Mr. Littlefield joined Hartt as Informations System Administrator in March of 1991. In five short years he has put a PC on every desk and networked every department, bringing explosive growth to the small transportation company with the competitive edge of computer technology. Concurrently, Mr. Hartt has administered the computer systems for Northern Log Homes, Inc. since 1995. **Career Steps:** Information Systems Administrator, Hartt Transportation Systems, Inc. (1991–Present); Computer Systems Administrator, Northern Log Homes, Inc. (1995–Present). **Personal:** Three children: Jeffrey, Melissa and Stephanie. Mr. Littlefield enjoys spending time with his family, which includes his fiance Gail and her daughter Megan.

M. Jane Michaelsen
Corporate Collections Manager
Arrow Transportation Company
10145 North Portland Road
Portland, OR 97283
(503) 240–4363
Fax: (503) 240–4303

4213

Business Information: Arrow Transportation Company is a trucking firm which transports liquid bulk. As Corporate Collections Manager, Ms. Michaelsen is responsible for diversified administrative activities, including finance, public relations, accounting, strategic planning, customer service, and traffic management. **Career Steps:** Arrow Transportation Company: Corporate Collections Manager (1995–Present), Corporate Traffic Manager (1993–Present), Rate Analyst (1981–1993). **Education:** ONABEN Small Business (1996);

PCC, Basic rules and tariffs. **Personal:** Three children: Raymond K. Ditzler, Elizabeth J. Rabon, and Samantha J. Burnside. Ms. Michaelsen enjoys woodworking, haircutting, quilt making, and sewing.

Robert G. Olterman
General Manager and Director
Yellow Integrated Logistics, Inc.
10990 Roe Avenue
Shawnee Mission, KS 66211
(913) 344–5030
Fax: Please mail or call

4213

Business Information: Yellow Integrated Logistics, Inc., an affiliate of Yellow Freight, provides all aspects of freight transportation and storage facilities. Established in 1938, the Corporation reports annual revenue of $2.8 billion and currently employs 25,000 corporate–wide. Joining the Corporation as General Manager and Director in 1992, Mr. Olterman is responsible for all aspects of operations and management of the Shawnee Mission, Kansas location. **Career Steps:** General Manager and Director, Yellow Integrated Logistics, Inc. (1992–Present); Regional Vice President, Routing Technology Software, Inc. (1986–1992); Senior Vice President of Sales and Marketing, Interstate Motor Freight System (1982–1986). **Associations & Accomplishments:** Council of Logistics Management; American Society of Transportation and Logistics; Association of Transportation Law; American Marketing Association. **Education:** University of Tennessee, B.S.B.A. (1965); Attended: LaSalle Law School, Columbia University. **Personal:** Married to Arlene in 1963. Four children: Stephanie, Fran, Richelle, and Rob. Mr. Olterman enjoys golf and boating.

Daniel H. Popky
Vice President of Finance
Allied Holdings, Inc.
160 Clairemont Avenue, Suite 570
Decatur, GA 30030–2529
(404) 370–4277
Fax: (404) 370–4342

4213

Business Information: Allied Holdings, Inc. is a transportation company, specializing in automotive distribution (shipping cars from the manufacturers to the dealers). The largest car carrier for Ford companies, Allied Holdings, Inc. also transports for General Motors and Chrysler companies, serving customers from eight national locations. With ten years of experience in accounting, Mr. Poppy joined Allied Holdings, Inc. as Vice President and Controller in 1994. Appointed as Vice President of Finance in 1995, he is responsible for the direction of all administrative operations for the entire company, from finance to the registration of vehicles. **Career Steps:** Allied Holdings, Inc.: Vice President of Finance (1995–Present), Vice President and Controller (1994–1995); Audit Manager, Arthur Anderson LLP (1986–1994). **Associations & Accomplishments:** American Society of Certified Public Accountants; Georgia Society of Certified Public Accountants; National Accounting and Financial Council of American Trucking Association; Georgia Chamber of Commerce. **Education:** Lehigh University, B.S. in Accounting (1986). **Personal:** Married to Kim in 1993. Mr. Popky enjoys golf, jogging, and water skiing.

Roberto Quintanilla Buendia

Chief Executive Officer
Tranportes Quintanilla S.A. de C.V.
305 Windsor Road
Laredo, TX 78041
(210) 717–4550
Fax: Please mail or call

4213

Business Information: Tranportes Quintanilla S.A. de C.V. is an intermodal freight transportation company, serving Puerto Rico and the Caribbean. Founding the company in 1979, as Chief Executive Officer, Mr. Quintanilla Buendia provides the overall vision and strategy for the company's continued development and growth, primarily focusing on international relations. **Career Steps:** Chief Executive Officer, Tranportes Quintanilla S.A. de C.V. (1979–Present). **Associations & Accomplishments:** President, Central de Carga de Nuevo Laredo; Advicer to Mexican Banks: Bancresser and Somex (Nuevo Laredo Branch); Speaker of Mexican Transporters; Young Presidents' Organization; Owns race car team, has raced in Indy 500 (since 1988). **Education:** Texas A&I, Degree in Marketing (1970). **Personal:** Married to Guadalupe in

1969. Four children: Michelle Patricia, Roberto, Rolando, and Rodrigo. Mr. Quintanilla Buendia enjoys motor sports, and golf.

Stanley McKenney Stricklen
Director of Operations
APL Automotive Logistics
17197 North Laurel Park Drive, Suite 200
Livonia, MI 48152
(313) 953–8210
Fax: (313) 953–5528

4213

Business Information: APL Automotive Logistics is an international transportation company, providing intermodal and truck transportation and logistics services for the global automotive industry (i.e., Toyota, Chrysler, General Motors, Ford). Freight is first shipped from China and from Asia to the U.S. West Coast, then by major railroad to the trucking industry. Joining APL Automotive Logistics as Division Manager In 1991, Stan Stricklen was appointed as Director of Operations in 1995. He is responsible for the direction of operational flow and distribution of products, in addition to information transfers and ensuring contracts are in good standing with major railroads. **Career Steps:** APL Automotive Logistics: Director of Operations (1995–Present), Manager of Operations (1993–1995), Division Manager (1990–1993); Operations Manager, Builders Transport (1989–1990); Driver–Manager, Stoops Express (1988–1989). **Associations & Accomplishments:** C.L.M.; Detroit Traffic Club; Mississippi Army National Guard. **Education:** University of Alabama, B.A. (1978). **Personal:** Married to Jan in 1978. Three children: Lauren, Melinda, and Rachel. Mr. Stricklen enjoys deer hunting and fishing.

William J. Walters
Vice President
Audubon International
739 South White Horse Pike, Suite 7
Audubon, NJ 08106
(609) 346–0933
Fax: (609) 546–7050

4213

Business Information: Audubon International provides transportation of material (printed matter, chemicals, plastics, metal) via van and flatbed trucks throughout the United States and Canada. As Vice President, Mr. Walters is responsible for overseeing sales, daily operations, and customer service functions. **Career Steps:** Vice President, Audubon International (1992–Present). **Associations & Accomplishments:** Industrial Soap and Recycling Industry; American Cancer Society – March of Dimes; American Metal Association. **Education:** Drexel University, Marketing (1990). **Personal:** Mr. Walters enjoys volleyball, softball, weight lifting, and golf.

Duane Westbrook
Application System Manager
J. B. Hunt Transport, Inc.
615 J. B. Hunt Corporate Drive
Lowell, AR 72745
(501) 820–8431
Fax: (501) 820–8395
EMAIL: See Below

4213

Business Information: J.B. Hunt Transport, Inc. is the holding company for freight transportation entities, providing comprehensive transportation and logistics services. Divisions include: DryVan, Flatbed, Special Commodities, Logistics, and Dedicated Contract Services – dedicating equipment, people, and systems to customer accounts. Transport and Shipping; Flatbed – the nation's largest; Commodities; Logistics – specializes in the transportation needs of Company; and Contract Services – delivering special equipment to customers. As Application System Manager, Mr. Westbrook is responsible for the management of software development for the J.B. Hunt's Logistics Division. Internet users may also reach him via: WestBr@mail.JBHUNT.com **Career Steps:** J.B. Hunt Transport, Inc.: Application Systems Manager (1994–Present), Senior Systems Analyst (1992–1994), Systems Analyst (1991–1992). **Associations & Accomplishments:** Council of Logistics Management (CLM); United States Tennis Association (USTA); Published in "Computer World" – the Campus edition for seniors going into the field (1993). **Education:** School of the Ozarks, B.S. in Computer Science (1988); North West Arkansas Community College, A.S./C.S. **Personal:** Married to Kathleen in 1986. One child: Austin. Mr. Westbrook enjoys tennis, audio/visual/computers, and sports cars.

Robert D. Clouse

President
Transportation Management, Inc.
9822 SE 50th
Milwaukie, OR 97222
(503) 653–7194
Fax: (503) 659–6539
EMAIL: See Below

4214

Business Information: Transportation Management, Inc., established in 1987, is a transportation consulting company, providing third party logistic freight brokering for domestic trucking companies. Founding the Company in 1987, Mr. Clouse is responsible for all aspects of operations, in addition to providing consulting services to the Company's clientele. Mr. Clouse provides expertise in pool distribution in all fifty states, claim settlement and most forms of motor carrier freight service. Internet users can reach Robert via: BCPDX@AOL.COM **Career Steps:** President, Transportation Management, Inc. (1987–Present). **Associations & Accomplishments:** American Trucking Association. **Education:** Portland Community College (1989). **Personal:** Married to Linda in 1975. Three children: Elliot, Emily, and Christopher. Mr. Clouse enjoys golf, fishing, and camping.

John J. Mascia

World Wide Corporate Security Manager
United Parcel Service
55 Glenlake Parkway North East
Atlanta, GA 30328
(404) 828–7250
Fax: (404) 828–6361

4215

Business Information: United Parcel Service (UPS) specializes in domestic and international package and document distribution. As World Wide Corporate Security Manager, Mr. Mascia is responsible for the security of all equipment planes, vehicles, facilities, as well as corporate assets. **Career Steps:** United Parcel Services: World Wide Corporate Security Manager (1992–Present); Domestic Corporate Director of Security (1987–1992); Regional Manager of Security, Northeast Region (1978–1987); District Delivery Information Services Manager and Security Manager, in New York (1972); Operations Center Manager (1970); Operations Supervisor (1969); Package Delivery Driver, New York (1966). **Education:** Attended United Parcel Service Internal Schools nationwide specializing in security and package delivery operations. **Personal:** Married to Margaret in 1981. Three children: Mike, Joe, and Lisa. Mr. Mascia enjoys equestrian activities, art, and travel.

William L. Peters Jr.

Chief Financial Officer
Washington Express Services
8541 Piney Branch Road
Silver Spring, MD 20901–3920
(301) 650–5350
Fax: (301) 608–0150

4215

Business Information: Washington Express Services, the leading courier company in the Washington, D.C. area, is an expedited freight courier, providing on–demand delivery services. As Chief Financial Officer, Mr. Peters is responsible for the financial stability of the Company, handling financial statements, tax issues, and evaluating new software. He is also involved in corporate restructuring, overseeing marketing and company operations, as well as serving as the Director of Human Resources. **Career Steps:** Chief Financial Officer, Washington Express Services (1995–Present); Branch Administrator, Cushman & Wakefield, Inc. (1993–1995); Consultant for Managed Health Care, Sandoz Pharmaceuticals (1992–1993); Financial Manager, Tetley Inc. (1990–1992); Warner Lambert (1989–1990). **Associations & Accomplishments:** Sterling Youth Soccer Association; Seneca Cause Home Owners Association. **Education:** Fairleigh Dickinson University, B.S. in Finance/Economics (1989); County College of Morris, A.A. in Liberal Arts; Strayer College, MBA in Business Administration (currently attending). **Personal:** Married to Suzanne in 1983. Three children: Christine, Katelyn, and Michael. Mr. Peters enjoys coaching youth soccer.

Mustafa El–Mubasher, Ph.D.

Owner and Executive Officer
Karam Savannah Products, Inc.
2750 East Mission Boulevard
Ontario, CA 91761–2901
(909) 947–5256
Fax: (909) 947–5775

4219

Business Information: Karam Savannah Products Inc., established in 1982 as a multi–national company specialized in livestock, meats, crops, and other agricultural products and equipment. With his extraordinary experience and educational background, Dr. El–Mubasher is doing a wide variety of jobs and he is moving goods and services across the globe. Concurrent with his active executive duties at Karam Savannah, he is a Corporate Officer at Laloo International Inc.; specializing in the manufacture and distribution of plumbing and hardware supplies and taking charge of its General Management. **Career Steps:** Owner and Executive Officer, Karam Savannah Products Inc. (1982–Present); Chairman, Danish Agro–Industrial Corporation, Denmark (1988–Present); Advisor, The World Bank of the United Nations (1976–1988). **Associations & Accomplishments:** The 1818 Society, Washington, D.C.; The Club of Tropical Veterinary Medicine, Scotland; American Institution of Professional Bookkeepers; American Management Association. **Education:** Century University – LA: Ph.D (1982), B.A.; Royal School of Veterinary Medicine – Edinburgh, D.T.V.M. (1978); Cairo University, B.V.S.C. (1968). **Personal:** Married to Claire in 1972. One child: Karam. Dr. El–Mubasher enjoys reading, music, sports, tennis, and education.

Joseph DelGreco

General Manager
Interstate Warehousing, Inc.
110 Distribution Drive
Hamilton, OH 45014
(513) 874–6500
Fax: (513) 874–6775

4222

Business Information: Interstate Warehousing, Inc. is a third–party cold storage and frozen foods distribution transport company. A food products and warehouse management executive with over ten years expertise, Mr. Del Greco serves as General Manager. In this capacity he oversees all aspects of the company, including customer service, profit and loss and sales. **Career Steps:** General Manager, Interstate Warehousing, Inc. (1994–Present); Regional District Manager, Specialty Brands; Executive Director, Universal Suppliers; Warehouse Manager, Nestle Foods. **Associations & Accomplishments:** Institute Internal Auditors. **Education:** Babson College, B.S. (1987). **Personal:** Married to Barbara in 1995. Mr. DelGreco enjoys the Boston RedSox, golf, and reading.

Richard A. Newton Jr.

Regional Operations Manager
D & A Refrigeration
1629 Alexander Avenue
Tacoma, WA 98421–4118
(206) 272–5808
Fax: (206) 272–5838

4222

Business Information: D & A Refrigeration serves as the North American service arm for Sydney, Australia–based RCC — a refrigeration equipment manufacturer. Operating from facilities in Tacoma and Seattle, Washington, D&A provides all warranty and general maintenance service, as well as provides distribution management for North American markets. As Regional Operations Manager, Mr. Newton is responsible for all operations and maintenance for North America, Japan and Russia. **Career Steps:** Regional Operations Manager, D & A Refrigeration (1993–Present); Broker, Dean Witter Reynolds (1990–1991); Broker and Manager, Blindor Robinson and Company (1988–1990). **Associations & Accomplishments:** Refrigerated Service Engineers Society; Phi Sigma Kappa Fraternity. **Education:** Montana State (1986). **Personal:** Mr. Newton enjoys snow & water skiing and rock climbing.

Bob Tremblay

General Manager
Associated Freezers of Canada
3691 Weston Road
Toronto, Ontario M9L 1W4
(416) 741–7820
Fax: (416) 741–4718

4222

Business Information: Associated Freezers of Canada is a public refrigerated warehouse. Marketing to six provinces in Canada, the Company currently has three 200,000 square foot freezers and coolers in Ontario. The Company is also hoping to market their freezers on an international scope in the near future. As General Manager, Mr. Tremblay is responsible for all Ontario operations and sales. **Career Steps:** General Manager, Associated Freezers of Canada (1993–Present); Logistics Manager, Maple Leaf Foods (1990–1993); Robin Hood Multifoods: General Manager (1986–1990), Distribution Manager (1983–1986). **Associations & Accomplishments:** CALM; CAWDS; Logistics Institute. **Education:** Concordia, Bachelor of Commerce (1962). **Personal:** Married to Katherine in 1964. Two children: Sharon and Sheryl. Mr. Tremblay enjoys bowling and golf.

Kurt Borne

Vice President of Operations
PSS Warehousing and Transportation, Inc.
7 Nicholas Ct.
Dayton, NJ 08810–1559
(908) 274–1333
Fax: (908) 274–1358

4225

Business Information: PSS Warehousing and Transportation, Inc. was established in 1983 as a small warehousing company. Through the addition of a small trucking fleet in 1987, the Company has expanded to five locations and the ability to warehouse anything except hazardous waste. Regional in scope, the Company has distribution authority in 48 states. As Vice President of Operations, Mr. Borne oversees all aspects of his department and is responsible for personnel management, scheduling, strategic planning, contact negotiations, and logistics. Concurrent to his present position, Mr. Borne is Co–Owner of a small vending business, Bulldog Enterprises. **Career Steps:** Vice President of Operations, PSS Warehousing and Transportation, Inc. (1991–Present). **Associations & Accomplishments:** Warehousing Educational Research Center (WERC); Council on Logistics Management (CLM). **Education:** Long Island University, Bachelors (1990). **Personal:** Mr. Borne enjoys reading and going to the gym.

Kerry K. Kelling

Vice President of Operations
Waterloo Warehousing & Services
324 Duryea Street
Waterloo, IA 50701–5317
(319) 236–0467
Fax: (319) 236–0314

4225

Business Information: Waterloo Warehousing & Services is a public warehouse, specializing in providing bulk warehousing. Established in 1982, Waterloo Warehousing & Services currently employs 75 people. With thirty–nine years experience in management, Mr. Kelling joined Waterloo Warehousing & Services in 1993. Serving as Vice President of Operations, he is responsible for the administrative, operational, finance, public relation, and strategic planning matters of the Operations Department. **Career Steps:** Vice President, Operations, Waterloo Warehousing & Services (1993–Present); Business Unit Manager, John Deere (1956–1993). **Personal:** Mr. Kelling enjoys sports.

Richard H. Matthews

Vice President Marketing and Safety
Kellar Bonded Warehouse
6340 Best Friend Road
Norcross, GA 30071
(770) 448–6526
Fax: (770) 449–6988

4225

Business Information: Kellar Bonded Warehouse is a 370,000 square foot general merchandise public warehouse. As Vice President, Mr. Matthews is responsible for handling all new business development, customer relations, managing follow–ups, compliance, and safety, including hazardous materials, training, and inspections. **Career Steps:** Vice President, Kellar Bonded Warehouse (1993–Present); Director of

Training, MTI Education Services (1991–1993); Corporate Logistics Manager, Oxford Chemicals (1968–1991). **Associations & Accomplishments:** Delta Nu Alpha Transportation Fraternity; National Transportation Claims Prevention Council; National Association of Purchasing Management; Board of Directors, Georgia Freight Bureau March (1991); Gideon International; Christian Motorcyclists Association; Quest Outreach 1996 Olympics; ACOG Security Team 1996 Olympics; Life Member, American Motorcyclists Association; AMA Road Rep. of the Year (1979), (1980), (1981); AMA Top Road Promoters (1984), (1985), (1986); Top Fundraiser for Muscular Distrophy (1985), (1986); Awarded Top Recognition, Scottish Rite Hospital for 1981 Fundraiser. **Education:** Massey College, Associates in Accounting & Business Administration cum laude (1964); Transportation Safety Institute (1992); Graduate Intermodal Transportation Hazardous Materials; Dun & Bradstreet Telemarketing (1996). **Personal:** Married to Brenda in 1975. Two children: Dana Lynn Matthews Roden and Candace Kay Wright. Mr. Matthews enjoys being a 220 average bowler and avid motorcyclist.

Timothy B. Burnam

Vice President of Construction
Storage Trust Realty
2407 Rangeline
Columbia, MO 65201
(314) 499–4799
Fax: (314) 442–5554

4226

Business Information: Storage Trust Realty is a real estate investment company listed on the New York Stock Exchange. Currently the company operates 125 self–storage facilities in 16 states. A family–owned and operated business, Storage Trust Realty has grown at an enormous rate, buying out half of its competitors in 1994. In operation since 1974, Storage Trust Realty currently employs 325 people and has an estimated annual revenue of $100 million. As Vice President of Construction, Mr. Burnam is responsible for all construction and renovations fo 125 self–storage facilities in 16 states, as well as the budget. **Career Steps:** Vice President of Construction, Storage Trust Realty (1994–Present); President, Burnam Construction (1987–1994); President, E–Z Rent – All and Supply Company (1977–1987). **Education:** University of Missouri. **Personal:** Married to Mary Ruth in 1986. Two children: Megan and Sadie. Mr. Burnam enjoys woodworking, travel and spending time with his family.

Gary Johnson

Vice President
Automotive Northern Warehouse, Inc.
2400 19th Street, South West
Mason City, IA 50401
(575) 422–5002
Fax: (515) 423–7372

4226

Business Information: Automotive Northern Warehouse, Inc. is an automotive aftermarket distributor. The Company is a cooperative of 88 shareholders and 200 stores. Established in 1956, Automotive Northern Warehouse employs 120 people with annual sales of $60 million. As Vice President, Mr. Johnson oversees every aspect of the warehouse operations. **Career Steps:** Vice President, Automotive Northern Warehouse, Inc. (1994–Present); Warehouse Manager, Batteries, Inc. (1988–1989); Warehouse Manager, Varta Batteries (195–1988). **Associations & Accomplishments:** Employers Association; National Rifle Association; Automotive Warehouse Distributors Association; North American Hunting Retriever Association; Chamber of Commerce; Independent Automotive Parts of America. **Personal:** Married to Sharon in 1978. Mr. Johnson enjoys hunting.

John M. Kane

President
E.I. Kane, Inc.
6810 Deerpath Road
Baltimore, MD 21227
(410) 799–3200
Fax: (410) 799–3208

4226

Business Information: E.I. Kane, Inc. is a holding company which operates five subsidiary companies. These companies provide such services as commercial moving and storage, hauling, limousine services, installation of furniture for manufacturing companies, and temporary labor services. As President, Mr. Kane is responsible for all aspects of Company operations, including strategic planning, marketing, and assuring the growth and success of the Company. **Career Steps:** E.I. Kane, Inc.: President (1993–Present), Executive Vice President (1989–1993); Office Movers, Inc.: Vice President at Large (1985–1989), Branch Manager (1983–1985). **Associations & Accomplishments:** Knights of Malta; American Trucking Association; Maryland Motor Trucking Association; Washington D.C. Board of Trade. **Education:** Mount St. Mary's, B.S. (1983); Wharton Executive Management Program. **Personal:** Married to Mary in 1986. Three children: Jack, Grace, and Elizabeth. Mr. Kane enjoys golf and tennis.

Mitchell A. Zulinick

General Manager – Interior Operation
Arrow Transportation Systems, Inc.
1320–B McGill Road
Kamloops, British Columbia
(604) 374–3831
Fax: (604) 374–0250
EMAIL: See Below

4226

Business Information: Arrow Transportation Systems, Inc. is an international trucking company, providing transportation, materials handling, terminal reloading and consulting services from 18 locations throughout Canada and Alaska. Joining Arrow Transportation Systems, Inc. in 1989, Mr. Zulinick was appointed as General Manager of Interior Operations in 1993. He is responsible for all aspects of interior operations of the Kamloops, British Columbia location, including marketing, business development, contract negotiations, budgeting, financial analysis, corporate quality control, human resources, training systems, and contract negotiation with teamsters. Internet users can reach him via: zulinick@netshop.net. **Career Steps:** Arrow Transportation Systems, Inc.: General Manager – Interior Operations (1993–Present), Director of Marketing (1992–1993), Manager Organizational Development & Strategic Planning (1989–1992). **Associations & Accomplishments:** American Marketing Association; Mining and Metalurgical Association; British Columbia Forestry Alliance; British Columbia Quality Council; British Columbia Trucking Association. **Education:** University of British Columbia, B.Commerce (1988). **Personal:** Mr. Zulinick enjoys golf, ice hockey, tennis, and guitar.

Kenneth (Ken) W. Barrios

Executive Vice President
National Auto Truckstops
3100 West End Avenue Suite 300
Nashville, TN 37203
(615) 783–2630
Fax: (615) 385–2365

4231

Business Information: National Auto Truckstops was formed to purchase the truckstop assets of Unical 76 (97 truck stops, with licensing rights, in 38 states). The Company franchises most of their truck stops but operate 15 sites of their own. As Executive Vice President, Mr. Barrios is responsible for daily operations, franchising programs, advertising, training, handling fuel supply, public relations, and engineering. **Career Steps:** National Auto Truckstops: Executive Vice President (1995–Present), Vice President (1993–1995); AIG Trading Corporation, Vice President (1991–1993). **Associations & Accomplishments:** Commodity Trading Advisor; Helping Hands; Springfield Illinois Symphony. **Education:** University of North Carolina, M.B.A. (1975). **Personal:** Married to Carla in 1971. Two children: Megan and Matt. Mr. Barrios enjoys golf, reading, and gardening.

4300 U.S. Postal Service

4311 U. S. Postal Service

Pablo Alvarez Jr.

Postmaster
United States Postal Service
160 Calle 14 De Julio
Luquillo, Puerto Rico 00773
(787) 889–3170
Fax: (787) 889–1449

4311

Business Information: U.S. Postal Service is the mail processing, transportation and delivery system serving citizens and residents of the United States and commonwealths associated with the U.S. Established in 1790, the United States Postal Service currently employs 700,000 people nation–wide. As Postmaster, Mr. Alvarez is responsible for directing all mail in Puerto Rico. Additional duties include providing delivery of mail service in compliance with customer requests, including Express Mail, as well as the oversight of budget compliance, marketing, Human Resources, and transportation. **Career Steps:** U.S. Postal Service: Post Master (1991–Present), Manager Address Information (1990–1991), Superintendent Postal Operations (1987–1990), Supervisor Station and Branches (1983–1987). **Associations & Accomplishments:** President, National Association of Postmasters of the United States – Puerto Rico and Virgin Islands. **Education:** University of Puerto Rico, B.A. in Labor Relations (1986). **Personal:** Two children: Cristina M. and Ricardo J.

Melvin Francis

Manager of Distribution Operations
United States Postal Service
4600 Aldine Bender Road
North Houston, TX 77315
(713) 985–4275
Fax: (713) 985–4196

4311

Business Information: United States Postal Service uses highly automated and mechanized operations for distribution activities and processing mail, in order to be able to deliver mail throughout the United States. As Manager of Distribution Operations, Mr. Francis works in the North Houston Postal Office and is responsible for mail processing activities on the tour from 2:30 p.m. until 11:30 p.m. daily. **Career Steps:** United States Postal Service: Manager of Distribution Operations, (1993–Present), Tour Superintendent (1990–1993), General Supervisor (1986–1990). **Associations & Accomplishments:** Branch Resident, National Association of Postal Supervisors; Certified Teacher, State of Texas; Co–Chairman Deacon Board, New Pleasant Grove Missionary Baptists Church; Joint Steering Committee, Quality of Work Life, U.S. Postal Service. **Education:** Texas Southern University, B.A. (1971); Houston Community College, A.A. (1973). **Personal:** Married to Betty in 1969. Two children: Tonya and Melodie. Mr. Francis enjoys public speaking, cooking, and attending social events.

William J. Henderson

Chief Operating Officer and Executive Vice President
United States Postal Service
475 Lenfant Plaza Southwest
Washington, DC 20260
(202) 268–4842
Fax: (202) 268–4243

4311

Business Information: United States Postal Service is the mail processing, transportation and delivery system serving citizens and residents of the United States. The U.S. Postal Service is considered to have begun July 26, 1775, when the Second Continental Congress convened in Philadelphia and appointed Benjamin Frankin to serve as the first Postmaster General. Except for Indian Affairs, the U.S. Postal Service is the second oldest government agency. A 23–year veteran of the U.S. Postal Service, Mr. Henderson was appointed as Chief Operating Officer and Executive Vice President in 1994. He is responsible for the U.S. Postal Service operations efforts which include the direction of all mail processing, distribution and delivery operations, and engineering, transportation, facilities construction and purchasing functions on a national level. The immediate supervisor of eight Vice Presidents at Postal Service Headquarters and all ten Vice Presidents of Area Operations, he also is responsible for the oversight of the administrative operations of 715,000 postal employees nation–wide. **Career Steps:** United States Postal Service: Chief Operating Officer and Executive Vice President (1994–Present), Chief Marketing Officer and Senior Vice President (1993–1994), Vice President of Employee Relations (1992–1993). **Associations & Accomplishments:** National Literacy Council; Planning Committee, UNC Bicentennial; Harley Davidson Club; Universal Postal Union. **Education:** University of North Carolina, B.S. (1972).

John Malave

Postmaster and District Manager
United States Postal Service
585 Avenue, F.D.Roosevelt
San Juan, Puerto Rico 00936–9312
(809) 767–2159
Fax: (809) 250–8065

4311

Business Information: U.S. Postal Service is the mail processing, transportation and delivery system serving citizens and residents of the United States and commonwealths associated with the U.S. Established in 1790, the United States Postal Service currently employs 700,000 people nation–wide. As Postmaster and District Manager, Mr. Malave is responsible for directing the Caribbean District Postal Service, composed of Puerto Rico, Saint Thomas, St. John, and St. Croix. Additional duties include providing delivery of mail service in compliance with customer requests, including Express Mail, as well as the oversight of budget compliance, marketing, Human Resources, transportation, and four labor unions. **Career Steps:** U.S. Postal Service: Postmaster and District

Manager (1995–Present), Plant Manager (1993–1995), Director of City Operations (1991–1993). **Associations & Accomplishments:** National League of Postmasters; National Association of Postal Supervisors; National Association of U.S. Postal Supervisors; National League of Postmasters – U.S. **Education:** University of Puerto Rico, B.B.A. (1978); Colorado Management Academy, Potomac, Maryland, Center for Creative Leadership. **Personal:** Married to Josabeth Del Valle in 1969. One child: Gamaliel Malave.

Soraya Noland, Ph.D., CPE
Ergonomist – Engineering
United States Postal Service
P.O. Box 341
Merrifield, VA 22116–0341
(703) 280–7250
Fax: Please mail or call

4311

Business Information: United States Postal Service is the U.S. quasi–government agency charged with the processing and distribution of mail throughout the U.S. and internationally. The engineering distribution center is centrally–located near one of the largest processing centers in the U.S. – the U.S.Postal Service headquarters in Washington, D.C. As Ergonomist in the Engineering & Development Center, Dr. Noland is responsible for the design, test, and evaluation of equipment to insure that the design accomodates the postal workforce without jeopardizing the health of employees. **Career Steps:** Ergonomist, United States Postal Service (1995–Present); Postdoctoral/Assistant Professor, Iowa State University (1979–1982); President and Founder, Farabi Regional University (1976–1979). **Associations & Accomplishments:** Board of Certification, Professional Ergonomists; Transportation Research Board, National Research Council; Who's Who of American Women; 1982 and 1983 Marquis Publication; Who's Who in Midwest; Special Commendation: Appointed and inaugurated by the Queen of Iran, Dr. Noland established Farabi Regional University in Iran; Publisher of over 30 published articles with two more to be published on Macro and Microergonomics. **Education:** State University of New York–Buffalo, Ph.D. (1976); Iowa State University, Post-doctoral studies (1982). **Personal:** Dr. Noland enjoys classical music, hiking, and doing research on Albert Einstein.

Marvin Price
Manager of Customer Service
United States Postal Service
4001 SW 25th Street
Hollywood, FL 33023–4405
(954) 987–4912
Fax: (954) 962–4549

4311

Business Information: Established in 1790, the United States Postal Service is the mail processing, transportation and delivery system serving citizens and residents of the United States. As Manager of Customer Service, Mr. Price is responsible for the daily work activities of 95 employees and 3 supervisors in mail delivery to 22,158 customers in the 33022 zip code area of Florida. **Career Steps:** Manager of Customer Service, United States Postal Service (1991–Present); OIC/Postmaster, Opa Locka Post Office (1991). **Associations & Accomplishments:** Blacks in Government; NAACP; A+ (Afro–American Postal League); Veterans of Foreign Wars; President, Carver Ranches HomeOwners Association; Code Enforcement Board of Broward County. **Personal:** Married to Betty R. in 1971. Two children: Letitia Wynette and Brian Demon. Mr. Price enjoys fishing, golf, and community activities.

Ana L. Torres
Supervisor
United States Postal Service
585 FD Roosevelt Avenue
San Juan, Puerto Rico 00936
(787) 767–3047
Fax: Please mail or call

4311

Business Information: U.S. Postal Service is the mail processing, transportation and delivery system serving citizens and residents of the United States and commonwealths and territories associated with the United States. Established in 1790, the United States Postal Service currently employs 700,000 people nation–wide. As Supervisor, Ms. Torres is in charge of employees detailed to handle the manual jobs associated with processing mail. She organizes training programs for her staff, develops division budgets, monitors staff production and handles the daily operational duties associated with her position. **Career Steps:** Supervisor, U.S. Postal Service (1981– Present); Bio Equipment Technician, Bellview Hospital (1981–1983); Laboratory Technician, Long Island Hospital (1979–1981). **Associations & Accomplishments:** Summit Hills Crafts Association. **Education:** New

York Technical College, A.A.S. (1979). **Personal:** Ms. Torres enjoys gardening, volunteer work, and recreational activities.

4400 Water Transportation

4412 Deep sea foreign trans. of freight
4424 Deep sea domestic trans. of freight
4432 Freight trans. on the Great Lakes
4449 Water transportation of freight, NEC
4481 Deep sea passenger trans, ex. ferry
4482 Ferries
4489 Water passenger transportation, NEC
4491 Marine cargo handling
4492 Towing and tugboat service
4493 Marinas
4499 Water transportation services, NEC

Guillermo Berriochoa

President
Grupo Transportes Inter–Mex S.A. de C.V.
Av. Industriales No. 26 Zona Industrial
Cuautitlan, Izcalli, Mexico 54730
(525) 872–2945
Fax: (525) 872–2945
EMail: See Below

4412

Business Information: Grupo Transportes Inter–Mex S.A. de C.V. is a group made up of 18 companies in Mexico and Brownsville, TX. The Company's main business is a trucking company servicing Mexico, the United States, and Canada. The Group, which transports such cargo as petroleum, hazardous materials, and waste, began in 1965 as a family trucking business. In 1974, the business was split up, and is now four different major trucking companies (Transportes Nacionales Mexicanos, S.A. de C.V.; Transportes a Granel de Mexico, S.A. de C.V.; Transportes Nortimex, S.A. de C.V.; Ameri–Liquid Transport, Inc.). All equipment is owned by the Company and all services are door–to–door. Various other companies under the Group are Inmobiliaria Solomex, S.A. de C.V., which is the company controlling all investments in real estate (land and buildings); Administraciones Norquim, S.A. de C.V., the company which sells administrative services; Administraciones Inter–Mex, S.A. de C.V. which promotes new business through all of North America; Industria de Remolques Mexicanos, S.A. de C.V., the manufacturer of the trailers and transportation vehicles, with DOT–ASME U & R Stamps; Beico, the distributor of computers, phones, fax machines, and other office equipment; and ESEMEX, S.A. de C.V., the emergency response company in Mexico. Grupo Transportes Inter–Mex, S.A. de C.V. has represented Mexico in the North American Free Trade Agreement (NAFTA). As President, Mr. Berriochoa handles all operations of the Group. He owns over 95% of Grupo Transportes Inter–Mex and serves as Chairman of the Board as well. Internet users can reach him via: kbg@mail.Internet.com.mx. **Career Steps:** President, Grupo Transportes Inter–Mex S.A. de C.V. (1975–Present). **Associations & Accomplishments:** National Tank Truck Carriers; American Trucking Association; Camara Nacional del Autotransporte de Carga; Canadian Trucking Association; North American Transportation Alliance; Camara Nacional de la Industria de la Transformacion; Western Highway Institute; Commercial Vehicle Safety Alliance. **Personal:** Four children: Guillermo, Miguel, Kimberly, and Victoria. Mr. Berriochoa enjoys travel and going to the beach.

Steven R. Borseti
Regional Sales Manager
AEI
440 McClellan Highway
East Boston, MA 02128
(617) 569–6300
Fax: (617) 569–1085

4412

Business Information: AEI is an international transportation and logistics company. AEI provides international transport services by air, sea, and ground as well as customs brokerage and warehouse distribution. With over 300 facilities internationally, the Company is the oldest freight forwarder in the United States. As Regional Sales Manager, Mr. Borseti develops sales and marketing strategies for 11 districts, hires and develops all salespeople, and helps customers expand their services with AEI. **Career Steps:** AEI: Regional Sales Manager (1994–Present), District Sales Manager – Boston (1993–1994), Account Executive – Boston (1990–1993).

Associations & Accomplishments: Council of Logistics Management; Foreign Commerce Club – Boston. **Education:** College of the Holy Cross, B.A. in Political Science (1987); Fordham University (1983). **Personal:** Married to Linda in 1989. One child: Sam. Mr. Borseti enjoys golf, basketball, movies, and music.

Luz Burgos
Controller
Perez & Cia de Puerto Rico, Inc.
P.O. Box 2209
San Juan, Puerto Rico 00902–2209
(787) 721–6010
Fax: Please mail or call

4412

Business Information: Perez & Cia de Puerto Rico, Inc. is Steamship Agent, Stevedores and Terminal Operator. The Company also operates the only drydock in Puerto Rico. As Controller, Ms. Burgos is in charge of the Administration and Finance Departments for the Ship Repair Division. **Career Steps:** Controller, Perez & Cia de Puerto Rico, Inc. (1994–Present); Controller, Economic Development Administration (1988–1994); Auditor, Puerto Rico Comptroller Office (1971–1988). **Education:** Interamerican University: B.A. (1974), 12 Grades in Master. **Personal:** Ms. Burgos enjoys reading, theater, and travel.

C. Eric Britten
Sales Manager
Sea–Land Service, Inc.
2550 Denali Street, Suite 1604
Anchorage, AK 99503–2737
(907) 263–5611
Fax: (907) 274–0430
E–mail: see below

4424

Business Information: A division of the CSX Corporation, Sea–Land Service, Inc. is the largest United States–flagged container shipping company providing worldwide water transportation of container goods. Established in 1956, Sea–Land Service, Inc. currently employs over 8000 people worldwide and 250 in Alaska. As Sales Manager, Mr. Britten is responsible for all aspects of sales and marketing of transportation services for the Alaska area. **Career Steps:** Sales Manager, Sea–Land Service, Inc. (1990–Present); Sodexho Alaska: Operations Manager (1987–1990), Facility Manager (1985–1987). **Associations & Accomplishments:** Anchorage Chamber of Commerce, Municipal Committee; Municipality of Anchorage, Budget Advisory Commission; Anchorage Municipal Task Force on Consolidation; Volunteer, Alaska Rapid Reading Service for the Blind. **Education:** University of Connecticut, B.S. in Urban Economics (1972). **Personal:** Two children: Edward Van Duyn Verbeck and Sherryll V. Duplechein. Mr. Britten enjoys all outdoor activities, including camping, and being a freelance writer.

Christopher J. Connor
Vice President of Sales and Marketing
Wallenius Lines North America, Inc.
188 Broadway
Woodcliff Lake, NJ 07675
(201) 307–1300
Fax: (201) 307–9740

4424

Business Information: Wallenius Lines North America, Inc. specializes in the ocean transportation of automobiles, mobile industrial equipment and recreational vehicles. In operation since 1934, Wallenius Lines North America, Inc. currently employs 108 people and has an estimated annual revenue of over $100 million. As Vice President of Sales and Marketing, Mr. Connor is responsible for all aspects of sales and the generation of revenue. **Career Steps:** Vice President of Sales and Marketing, Wallenius Lines North America, Inc. (1994–Present); Crowley American Transport: Area Manager of Corporate Sales (1991–1994), Director of Marketing and Sales in Europe (1987–1990); Manager of USA Sales, United States Lines – Hong Kong (1985–1986). **Education:** Villanova University, B.A. in Finance (1980). **Personal:** Married to Tracy in 1986. Three children: Christopher, Sean, and Griffin. Mr. Connor enjoys golf and running.

William R. Barbour
Manager of Rail Disbursements
American President Lines
6060 Primacy Parkway, Suite 300
Memphis, TN 38119
(901) 684–7975
Fax: (901) 684–7750
EMAIL: See Below

4449

Business Information: American President Lines is an international steamship corporation with 5,000 employees worldwide. The Company owns a stack train network in North America, plus twenty steamship vessels. As Manager of Rail Disbursements, Mr. Barbour manages $250 million in accounts payable per year to 30 to 40 major transportation providers. Additionally, he is responsible for a support staff of auditors for rail builders. Internet users can reach him via: bill.Barbour@ccgate.Apl.com. **Career Steps:** American President Lines: Manager of Rail Disbursement (1994–Present), Supervisor of Invoicing (1991–1994), Customer Service Representative (1989–1991). **Associations & Accomplishments:** Memphis Traffic Club; Honorary Memphis City Councilman (1992). **Education:** University of Memphis, B.B.A. in Finance (1987). **Personal:** Married to Wendy in 1988. Mr. Barbour enjoys golf and hunting.

Robert Goolsby
Senior Operations Manager
Dixie Carriers Inc.
2102 Broadway
Houston, TX 77012–3806
(713) 649-3232
Fax: (713) 649-7928
EMAIL: See Below

4449

Business Information: Dixie Carriers, Inc. — a wholly-owned entity of international transportation conglomerate Kerby Corporation — is involved in the maritime transportation of chemicals, working with such major industries as Shell Oil. As Senior Operations Manager, Mr. Goolsby is responsible for the day–to–day activities of the Canal Group, consisting of 33 inland towboats and 82 inland barges, wherein seven managers report directly to him. Internet users can reach him via: Robert.Goolsby@KMTC.com. **Career Steps:** Senior Operations Manager, Dixie Canal Group (1989–Present); Personnel Manager, Alamo Inland Marine (1986–1989); Personnel Manager, Rio Marine (1981–1986). **Associations & Accomplishments:** Houston Propeller Club; Texas Waterway Operators, Navigation Committee; American Waterways Operations, Navigation Committee; Gulf Intercoastal Canal Association, Navigation Committee; Galveston Bay Foundation. **Personal:** Married to Diann in 1976. Three children: Bryce, Hillary, and Tyler. Mr. Goolsby enjoys fishing and Corvette restoration.

Hector V. Mella Jr.
Executive Vice President
Gencia Maritima Y Comercial
I.D. #10082E. 7303 North West 56th Street
Miami, FL 33166
(809) 537-2570
Fax: (809) 537-2752
EMAIL: See Below

4449

Business Information: Founded in 1981 by Ramon Mella, Gencia Maritima Y Comercial is a family–owned business with international scope. The third largest company in the Dominican Republic, where it is headquartered, the Company specializes in shipping, including cruise travel, stevedoring, and cargo. As Executive Vice President, Mr. Mella is responsible for the day–to–day operations of the Company, including administration, operations, finance, marketing, and strategic planning. Additionally, he oversees a small support staff, and handles all public relations. Concurrent to his position with Gencia Maritima Y Comercial, Mr. Mella also owns Unitrade South America, the largest power protections company in the United States which specializes in uninterrupted power suppliers. Internet users can reach him via: V.Mella@Codetel.net.do. **Career Steps:** Executive Vice President, Gencia Maritima Y Comercial (1981–Present); Private Entrepreneur. **Associations & Accomplishments:** Rotary International; Councilman of the City of Santo Domingo, Dominican Republic. **Education:** Maritime College, B.S. (1981). **Personal:** Married to Mildred in 1983. Four children: Valerie Michelle, Marielle Marie, Gabrielle, and Marielou. Mr. Mella enjoys fishing, yachting, and hunting.

Nair Pinto De Oliveira Vitielli

Manager
Transworld Mudancas International
Av. Rio Branco 26/10
Rio De Janeiro, Brazil Rj20090–00
(021) 263-8112
Fax: (021) 253-6492

4449

Business Information: Transworld Mudancas International is an international transportation and trading company. TMI is a shipper of large cargo, including corn, sugar, and soybean, as well as conducting household moves, operating internationally from three locations in Brazil. As Manager, Ms. Vitielli is responsible for the management of all commercial sales and operations of sea, air, and sea–air shipments besides inland

and surface logistics. **Career Steps:** Manager, Transworld Mudancas International (1996–Present); Director of the International Department, Ultramar Forwarding Co. (1990–1993); Manager, Export/Import, Group TAI (1986–1990); Administration Manager, Metropolitan Transportation (1985–1986). **Associations & Accomplishments:** International and National Trade Associations. **Education:** University of Sao Paulo, Dr. in Language (1972); Continuing Education courses: International Transportation, International Trading (Sales and Purchase), Logistic and Business Administration. **Personal:** Married to Paulo Sergio S. Vitielli in 1978. Two children: Paula and Mario. Ms. Vitielli enjoys swimming, walking, reading, computer courses and writing.

Craig Newnan
Owner/Chief Executive Officer
Hone Heke Corporation, d.b.a. Expeditions
P O Box 10
Lahaina, HI 96767
(808) 661-3756
Fax: (808) 661-0544

4482

Business Information: Hone Heke Corporation, d.b.a. Expeditions specializes in inter–island passenger transportation via ferry between Lahaina, Maui, and Manele Harbor, Lanai. "The Casual Best" (Translation of Hone Heke), is comprised of three ferries that offer ten trips a day. Incorporated in 1976, with current operations established in 1989, the Company employs eleven people, and has an estimated annual revenue of $2 million. As Chief Executive Officer, Mr. Newnan oversees and manages all aspects of the Company. His duties include administration, scheduling, personnel management, marketing, strategic planning, and customer relations. **Career Steps:** Chief Executive Officer, Hone Heke Corporation – DBA Expeditions (1982–Present); Construction Manager, Pacific Construction Company, Ltd. (1979–1980); Construction Manager, Swinerton & Walberg Company (1971–1976). **Associations & Accomplishments:** Rotary Club of Lahaina; Paul Harris Fellow; Sullivan Fellow; Board of Directors, Lahaina Rotary Foundation; Sponsor, Community Fire Arms Education; Sponsor, Lanai Youth Programs and Inter Island Athletics. **Education:** University of California at Berkeley: M.B.A. (1971), B.S. Business Administration (1970), B.S. Civil Engineering (1970); Additional Graduate work at Stanford University. **Personal:** Mr. Newnan enjoys scuba diving for research and IPSC Combat Pistol Competition.

Richard S. Hickey Jr.
District Sales Manager
Celebrity Cruises
5201 Blue Lagoon Drive
Miami, FL 33126
(800) 437-6111
Fax: (954) 346-5189

4489

Business Information: Celebrity Cruises located in Coral Springs, Florida, provides luxury cruises to Bermuda, Alaska, and the Caribbean, aboard a fleet of 5 ships. Established in 1989, they are a growing company, with plans to add 2 more ships. With 8 years experience in sales, Mr. Hickey is responsible for promoting the cruise line through advertising and sales coordination with the 300 agents in his territory. In his official position as District Sales Manager, he is additionally responsible for servicing client and corporate accounts, and overseeing all advertising campaigns. **Career Steps:** District Sales Manager, Celebrity Cruises (1996–Present); District Sales Manager, Norwegian Cruise Line (1988–1996); Mortgage Broker, Home Financing Center (1987–1988). **Education:** Western State College of Colorado, B.A. (1986). **Personal:** One child: Richard S. III. Mr. Hickey enjoys martial arts.

Ms. Catherine A. Young
Director of Internal Audits
Royal Caribbean Cruises Limited
1050 Caribbean Way
Miami, FL 33132–2028
(305) 539-6640
Fax: (305) 539-6654

4489

Business Information: Royal Caribbean Cruises Limited is an international cruise line, with 14 ships, offering 4 to 14–day cruises in Asia, Europe, Caribbean, Alaska, Mexico, and Bermuda. Future plans include offering cruises to the Far East and adding five new ships in 1997. Established in 1970, Royal Caribbean Cruises Limited reports annual revenue of $1.1 billion and currently employs employs 1,800 people at the Miami office. As Director of Internal Audits, Ms. Young is responsible for performing operational and EDP audits of the Company, both land–based and shipboard. **Career Steps:** Director of Internal Audits, Royal Caribbean Cruises Limited (1993–Present); Director of Internal Audits, Capital Bank (1989–1993); Audit Manager, Price Waterhouse (1982–1989). **Associations & Accomplishments:** Board Member, Leukemia Society of South Florida; Founding Board Member, Young Professional Group of Leukemia Society; Junior League of Miami. **Education:** University of Miami, B.B.A. (1982). **Personal:** Married to Mike Buhai in 1993. Ms. Young enjoys racing sailboats and gourmet cooking.

Francisco A. Padilla
General Manager
South Puerto Rico Towing and Boat Services
P.O. Box 427
Guayanilla, Puerto Rico 00656–0427
(787) 844-6415
Fax: (787) 844-6838

4492

Business Information: South Puerto Rico Towing and Boat Services is a marine transportation company specializing in the towing of ships/boats from harbor to harbor in Puerto Rico. The towing service mainly handles petroleum ships that are no longer in service. As General Manager, Mr. Padilla handles the day–to–day operations and administration of the towing service and sees that everything runs smoothly and efficiently. He is responsible for the docked, undocked, and dead ship transportation boat services at Guayanilla, Tallaboa, Guanica, and Ponce harbors. **Career Steps:** South Puerto Rico Towing and Boat Services: General Manager (1991–Present); President (1974–1990), Staff Member (1966–1974). **Associations & Accomplishments:** Navieros De Puerto Rico; Puerto Rico Manufacturers Association; Camara De Comercio De Ponce. **Education:** University of Puerto Rico, M.A. (1990); University of Bridgeport, M.S. (1989). **Personal:** Married to Norma in 1987. One child: Gustavo. Mr. Padilla enjoys walking outdoors.

C. Eugene Baker
General Manager – Operations Caribbean
NAVIERAS NPR, Inc.
GPO Box 71306
San Juan, Puerto Rico 00936
(809) 793-3000
Fax: (809) 793-6055

4499

Business Information: NAVIERAS NPR, Inc., formerly owned by the government, is a privately–owned steamship container shipping line and terminal operator, providing shipping services throughout the world on a contractual basis. Joining NAVIERAS NPR, Inc. as General Manager of Caribbean Operations in 1995, Mr. Baker is responsible for the overall operations of the Caribbean operations, including the management of terminal and related operations in San Juan and Caribbean Islands feeder services. **Career Steps:** General Manager – Operations Caribbean, NAVIERAS NPR, Inc. (1995–Present); Port Manager, Puerto Rico Marine Management, Inc. (1993–1995); Port Manager, Ryan–Walsh, Inc. (1983–1989); Assistant Vice President, Ellen & Company, Inc. (1979–1983). **Associations & Accomplishments:** Propeller Club; Maritime Association Port of Charleston; Former President, South Carolina Stevedores Association; South Atlantic Employers Negotiating Committee; Trustee Joint Welfare–Pension Fund. **Education:** University of South Carolina, B.S. in Business Management (1975). **Personal:** Married to Debra in 1972. Two children: Juli and Gene. Mr. Baker enjoys hunting and golf..

Orlando Bravo
President
Orlando Bravo Steamship
P.O. Box 3186
Mayaguez, Puerto Rico 00681–3186
(809) 833-0988
Fax: (809) 834-3588

4499

Business Information: Orlando Bravo Steamship is a shipping agency with offices in Mayaguez and San Juan, Puerto

Rico. Established in 1945, Orlando Bravo Steamship currently employs 12 people. As President, Mr. Bravo is responsible for all aspects of operations, including administration, finances, sales, public relations, accounting, marketing, and strategic planning. Concurrent with his position at Orlando Bravo Steamship, he serves as President of Bravo Shipping Agency. Upon completion of his studies in 1970, he went to work for his father, the founder of both companies, becoming President and Chief Executive Officer of both companies in 1972. **Associations & Accomplishments:** Treasurer, Puerto Rico Shipping Association; Propellers Club of USA; Bankers Club of San Juan, Puerto Rico; Chaine de Rotisseurs; Chamber of Commerce; Interviewed in "International Maritime Magazine" in London. **Education:** University of Puerto Rico, B.A. (1970). **Personal:** Married to Artemis Bravo in 1969. Two children: Orlando III and Alejandro Bravo – both attending universities in the U.S. (Brown University – Rhode Island and Stanford University). Mr. Bravo enjoys tennis, golf and thoroughbred racing.

MARITIME BUREAU, INC.

MARINE SURVEYORS & CONSULTANTS

Captain D. Brian Dufour
Executive Vice President
Maritime Bureau, Inc.
122 West Bay Street
Savannah, GA 31401–1109
(912) 236–6366
Fax: (912) 236–1704

4499

Business Information: Maritime Bureau, Inc. is a marine management consultancy, serving major maritime shipping industries and insurers with services which include damage assays, shipping evaluations and maritime TQM studies. Bringing with him an extensive background in maritime industry management, spanning a twenty year time frame, Capt. Dufour serves as Executive Vice President. In this capacity, he has full executive charge for all administrative operations, as well as provides consulting services to major clients in regards to compliance and regulatory affairs. **Career Steps:** Executive Vice President, Maritime Bureau, Inc. (1993–Present); Owner and Consultant, Captain Brian Dufour, Inc. (1986–1993); Captain, Stena Lines – AB Sweden (1974–1986). **Associations & Accomplishments:** Society of Consulting Marine Engineers and Ship Surveyors; Navy League; Propeller Club; Chairman of Sub–Committee for Planning and Prevention; The Savannah Area Contingency Plan Committee. **Education:** Warsash College, B.S. in Marine Science (1977). **Personal:** Married to Patricia S. in 1984. Three children: Jessica, Daniel, and Leon. Captain Dufour enjoys carpentry, gardening, and golf.

Paul Hagstrom
Managing Director
Transoceanic Cable Ship Co., Coastal Cable Ship Co.
340 Mount Kemble Avenue, Room S113
Morristown, NJ 07960–6656
(201) 326–5500
Fax: (201) 927–8506

4499

Business Information: Transoceanic Cable Ship Co.and the Coastal Cable Ship Co., wholly–owned subsidiaries of AT&T, are installers and maintainers of fiber optic communication cable in all oceans of the world. The Companies own and operate five U.S. and Marshall Islands flag ships. As Managing Director, Mr. Hagstrom is responsible for all Company activities, including ship operations and engineering, business functions, sales, etc. Career milestones include serving as the Master of the Icebreaker Polar Star and the Naval Engineering Program Director for the U.S. Coast Guard. **Career Steps:** Managing Director, Transoceanic Cable Ship Co. (1995–Present); Naval Engineering Program Director, United States Coast Guard (1993–1995); Master Icebreaker Polar Star, United States Coast Guard (1991–1993); Various Assignments, United States Coast Guard (1966–1995). **Associations & Accomplishments:** American Society of Naval Engineers, Chairman of Flagship Section, Washington, DC (1994–1995), and a member since 1968; U.S. Naval Institute. **Education:** Massachusetts Institute of Technology, Ocean Engineer (1975), Masters in Mechanical Engineering (1975); United States Coast Guard Academy, B.S. (1970).

Personal: Two children: Christine and Jeffrey. Mr. Hagstrom enjoys golf and sailing.

Khalid Mohamed Mattar

Managing Director
Awal Contracting & Trading Company
P.O. Box 741
Manama, Bahrain
(x) 725100
Fax: (x) 728659

4499

Business Information: Awal Contracting & Trading Company owns and operates a fleet of vessels servicing the offshore oil industry The Company also has a side business in real estate and serves as an affiliate of an air conditioning business. Established in 1961, Awal Contracting & Trading Company currently employs 100 people. A twenty–year veteran of AWALCO, Mr. Mattar was appointed as Managing Director in 1985. He is responsible for the overall running of the Company's day–to–day activities, future planning, and financial management. **Career Steps:** Awal Contracting & Trading Company (AWALCO) W.L.L.: Managing Director (1985–Present), Administration Manager (1975–1979); Managing Director, Awal Products Company W.L.L. (1979–1985). **Associations & Accomplishments:** Steering Committee, Gulf Regional Propeller Club. **Education:** Arabic University of Beirut, Business Administration & Economy (1975). **Personal:** Married to Dr. Amel K. Algosaibi in 1988. One child: daughter, Nouf. Mr. Mattar enjoys swimming, running, boating, and spending time with his family.

William M. McDaniel
Human Relations Manager
Wilhelmsen Lines U.S.A., Inc.
401 East Pratt Street
Baltimore, MD 21202–3117
(410) 659–7900
Fax: (410) 659–7995

4499

Business Information: Wilhelmsen Lines U.S.A., Inc., a subsidiary of Wilhelmsen Lines A.S. Oslo Norway, is a global maritime shipping line. Joining the Company as Human Relations Manager in 1994, Mr. McDaniel is responsible for all aspects of personnel administration and management functions. He also serves as Senior Manager, responsible for total quality management, communications, and employee training. **Career Steps:** Human Relations Manager, Wilhelmsen Lines U.S.A., Inc. (1994–Present); Quality Manager, Alaska Railroad Corporation (1992–1994); Joint Training Manager, ALCOM (1991–1992); Training Division Manager, USAISC (1990–1991). **Associations & Accomplishments:** American Society for Quality Control; Published in the "New Port Authority Magazine"; U.S. Army Retiree (20 years). **Education:** Purdue University, M.S. (1980); U.S. Military Academy at West Point, New York, B.S. (1972). **Personal:** Married to Paula in 1973. Four children: Ryan, Maura, Bridget, and Siobhan. Mr. McDaniel enjoys running, skiing, and camping.

Donald R. Salsbury
Vice President and General Manager
Mid–South Towing Company
P.O. Box 790, Foot of Scott Street
Metropolis, IL 62960–0790
(618) 524–3100
Fax: (618) 524–8680

4499

Business Information: Mid–South Towing Company, a subsidiary of Teco Transport & Trade, is a contract carrier of bulk commodities, by towboat and barge fleets on the Mississippi and Ohio River systems. As Vice President and General Manager, Mr. Salsbury is responsible for providing overall leadership and direction of Mid–South vessels and terminal operations. **Career Steps:** Vice President and General Manager, Mid–South Towing Company (1979–Present); Professional Engineer, Midland Enterprises Inc. (1973–1979); Marine Engineer, The Ohio River Company (1956–1973); Licensed United States Merchant Marine. **Associations & Accomplishments:** Board of Directors, Dinamo – Pittsburgh, PA; Board of Directors, Combank – Metropolis, IL; Board of Directors, Massac County Chamber of Commerce; The American Waterways Operators. **Education:** Delgato College – New Orleans, LA (1974); Licensed United States Merchant Marine. **Personal:** Married to Virginia in 1962. One child: Kimberly R. Eaton. Mr. Salsbury enjoys golf, hunting, and fishing.

Frank Schumann
Vice President
Unitek Technical Services, Inc.
P.O. Box 29177
Honolulu, HI 96820–1577
(808) 832–9008
Fax: (808) 832–9011

4499

Business Information: Unitek Technical Services, Inc., a division of Pacific Marine & Supply, specializes in ship repair of commercial vessels, as well as provides commercial painting, insulation, flooring, and ultra high pressure water–jetting systems. Established in 1988, Unitek is the only "Blow in Blanket" insulation licensed contractor in the industry. Bringing with him over fifteen years construction management expertise, Frank Schumann was appointed Vice President of Unitek in 1988. In this capacity, he serves as Project Manager with other duties to include: estimations, personnel recruitment, purchasing and subcontract negotiations. **Career Steps:** Project Manager, Unitek Technical Services, Inc. (1988–Present); General Manager, R. Slayen, Inc. (1983–1988); Field Foreman/Estimator, M&R Slayen, Inc. (1980–1982). **Associations & Accomplishments:** Blow in Blanket Contractors Association; Propellor Club of Honolulu; University of Maine Alumni Association. **Education:** University of Maine, B.S. (1977); NIOSH 582, Asbestos Abatement Supervisor. **Personal:** Married to Mary Ellen in 1987. One child: Ashley Rose. Mr. Schumann enjoys golf.

4500 Transportation By Air

4512 Air transportation, scheduled
4513 Air courier services
4522 Air transportation, nonscheduled
4581 Airports, flying fields and services

Elbert Earl Atlas
Director of Training
Burlington Air Express
16808 Armstrong Avenue
Irvine, CA 92713–0185
(714) 752–1212 Ext. 2143
Fax: (714) 955–9028
EMAIL: See Below

4512

Business Information: Burlington Air Express is an international business–to–business transportation service of heavy air freight. As Director of Training, Mr. Atlas is responsible for the organization, development, and training functions of the Company. Internet users can reach him via: BAXEARL@AOL.COM. **Career Steps:** Director of Training, Burlington Air Express (1991–Present); Second Vice President of Field Development and Communications, Transamerica Life Companies (1980–1991). **Associations & Accomplishments:** Organizational Development Network, Los Angeles, CA Chapter. **Education:** Pepperdine University, M.S.O.D. (In Progress); Ambassador College, B.A. **Personal:** Married to Patricia in 1963. Three children: Jeffrey, Judith, and Jonathan. Mr. Atlas enjoys sport fishing, wine making, reading, and racquetball.

Michael Blake
Manager
United Airlines
1200 East Algonquin Rd.
Elk Grove Village, IL 60006
(847) 700–7460
Fax: (847) 700–5033

4512

Business Information: United Airlines, established in 1929, is an international commercial airline specializing in passenger and freight transportation. As Manager, Mr. Blake is responsible for planning, developing, and administering the capital and operating plan for the Information Services Division, a $500 million division of UAL. **Career Steps:** United Airlines, Manager (1995–Present); Senior Staff Analyst of Strategic Planning (1994–1995); Associate, Price Waterhouse Personal Financial Services (1991–1993); Staff Analyst, Baxter (1989–1991). **Associations & Accomplishments:** AICPA; Illinois CPA; ICMA; Chairman, Business Advisory Committee; Local Education & Economic Development Council; Certified Management Accountant; Certified Public Accountant. **Education:** University of Chicago, M.B.A. (1994); University of Utah, B.S. in Accounting. **Personal:** Married to Natalie in 1989. Mr. Blake enjoys snowboarding, basketball, and fishing.

Jackie R. Elliott
District Sales Manager
Northwest Airlines
P.O. Box 30937
Memphis, TN 38130–0937
(901) 332–6646
Fax: (901) 332–2074
EMAIL: See Below

4512

Business Information: Northwest Airlines is a major national and international airline with over 45,000 employees worldwide. Joining Northwest Airlines in 1984, Ms. Elliott was appointed as District Sales Manager in 1995. She is responsible for the national and corporate sales activities of an eight–state regional area. She directs all staff accounts, joint sales, and corporate and national accounts, as well as setting up corporate and international contracts. Internet users can reach her via: CELLIOTT@MEM.NET **Career Steps:** Northwest Airlines: District Sales Manager (1995–Present), National and Corporate Sales Manager (1993–1995), Corporate Sales Manager (1992–1993). **Associations & Accomplishments:** President, Women in Travel – Memphis; Board of Directors, Better Business Bureau – Memphis; Vice President, Kansas City Chamber of Commerce, Aviation Committee; Former President, Women in Travel – Kansas City; Sales and Marketing Executives – Memphis; Adult Student Association – Memphis. **Education:** University of Memphis, attending and expected graduation is in 1996; Normandale Community College, A.A.S. in Marketing and Management, graduated with honors (1989). **Personal:** Married to Charles in 1986. One child: Ryan. Ms. Elliott enjoys golf and travel.

Mr. John R. Fowler
Vice President
Alaska Airlines
P.O. Box 68900
Seattle, WA 98168–0900
(206) 433–3200
Fax: (206) 433–3311

4512

Business Information: Alaska Airlines is a U.S. commercial airline primarily serving Alaska and the West Coast, with routes extending from Mexico to the Russian Far East. In his current capacity, Mr. Fowler is responsible for all aspects of technical operations for the Airline to include administration, planning, quality control, technical training, schedule coordination, aircraft routing, maintenance, and engineering. Established in 1932, Alaska Airlines presently employs 6,000 people and has an estimated annual revenue in excess of $1 billion. **Career Steps:** Vice President, Alaska Airlines (1991–Present); Vice President, Pan Am (1989– 1991); Managing Director, Pan Am (1988–1989); Director, Pan Am (1986–1988). **Associations & Accomplishments:** Senior Advisory Committee, Air Transport Association; Management Partners Pepperdine University; Adult Learning Center, Tacoma Community College; Alaska Raptor Rehabilitation Center. **Education:** Pepperdine University, M.B.A. (1995); Adelphi University, undergraduate. **Personal:** Married since 1981 to Diana. Five children: John R., Jeanne M., James E., William A., and Thomas J. Mr. Fowler enjoys golf, yachting, photography, scuba diving, and management study in his leisure time.

Robert R. Gurley
Director of International Marketing and Sales
Aeromexico Airlines
13405 Northwest Freeway, Suite 240
Houston, TX 77040
(713) 744–8415
Fax: (713) 939–7242

4512

Business Information: Aeromexico Airlines, based in Mexico, is an international commercial airline specializing in freight and passenger transportation throughout Mexico, Europe, and the U.S. As Director of International Marketing and Sales, Mr. Gurley is responsible for marketing programs, business development, and sales for the U.S. and Europe. **Career Steps:** Aeromexico Airlines: Director of International Marketing and Sales (1995–Present), Managing Director of Reservations (1991–1995); Continental Airlines: Regional Manager of Reservations (1988–1991), Director Onepass Service Center (1985–1988). **Associations & Accomplishments:** Southwest Communications Association; Go Texan Committee. **Education:** South West Texas State University, B.B.A. (1974). **Personal:** Married to Kathleen in 1983.

Richard K.C. Hee
Vice President of Marketing and Services
Island Air, Inc.
99 Kapalulu Place
Honolulu, HI 96819
(808) 836–7693
Fax: (808) 833–5498

4512

Business Information: Island Air, Inc., a sister company to Aloha Airlines, is a scheduled airline providing inter–island flights to clients. With twenty–two years of experience in management and marketing, Mr. Hee joined Island Air, Inc. as Vice President of Marketing and Services in 1990, after serving in a management capacity at Aloha Airlines. He is responsible for sales and marketing functions, as well as airport operations. **Career Steps:** Vice President of Marketing and Services, Island Air, Inc. (1990–Present); Aloha Airlines: Director of Sales in Hawaii and South Pacific (1989–1990), Regional Manager of Oahu (1988–1989); Manager of Visitor Sales (1987–1988). **Associations & Accomplishments:** Japanese Chamber of Commerce; Honolulu Chamber of Commerce; ASTA; Member, Kuakini Hospital Fund Raiser. **Education:** Chaminade College, B.S. in Management and Marketing (1973). **Personal:** Married to Sandy Hee in 1980. Two children: Daniel and Michelle. Mr. Hee enjoys spending time with his family, golf, basketball, and volleyball.

Kenneth A. Pettit

President Emeritus
Pettit & Pettit Consulting Engineers, Inc.
201 East Markham Street, Suite 400
Little Rock, AR 72201
(501) 374–3731
Fax: (501) 374–1802

4512

Business Information: Pettit & Pettit Consulting Engineers, Inc. specializes in heating, ventilation, air conditioning, plumbing, and electrical consulting. Mr. Pettit co–founded the Firm upon conferral of his Mechanical Engineering degree from the University of Texas, Austin, in 1949. He has since maintained the Firm's tradition of customer satisfaction as a Partner and then as Sole Proprietor from 1968 on into his retirement to President Emeritus in 1996. **Career Steps:** Pettit & Pettit Consulting Engineers, Inc: President (1980–Present), Sole Proprietor (1968–1980), Partner (1949–1968). **Associations & Accomplishments:** Rotary Club; American Society of Heating, Refrigeration, and Air Conditioning Engineers; National Society of Professional Engineers; American Society of Professional Engineers; Tau Beta Pi; American Association of Mechanical Engineers. **Education:** University of Texas – Austin, B.S. in Mechanical Engineering (1949). **Personal:** Married to Joan Carroll in 1956. Two children: Allen Marshall and Andrew Scott. Mr. Pettit enjoys auto repairs and golf.

Chester J. Piolunek Jr.
Director of Operations and Chief Pilot
Pennsylvania Aviation, Inc.
1501 Narcissa Road
Blue Bell, PA 19422
(215) 646–1800
Fax: (215) 628–3594

4512

Business Information: Pennsylvania Aviation, Inc. is a regional, fixed base operation, providing fuel to airplanes and a chartered airline. With ten years expertise in the aviation industry, Mr. Piolunek joined Pennsylvania Aviation, Inc. in 1992 as Director of Operations and Chief Pilot. He is responsible for all aspects of management in the Charter Department. **Career Steps:** Pennsylvania Aviation, Inc.: Director of Operations and Chief Pilot (1992–Present), Pilot (1985–1986); Pilot, Pan-American World Airways (1986–1991). **Associations & Accomplishments:** Aircraft Owners & Pilots Association (AOPA); NBAA; NATA; Published in local newspaper in regards to annual air shows given by the Company, showing Mr. Piolunek's antique airplanes. **Education:** Florida Institute of Technology, B.S. (1982); Northern Virginia Community College, A.A.S. (1979). **Personal:** Married to Julie Ann in 1988. Mr. Piolunek enjoys collecting model railroads and antique motorcycles & airplanes.

Robert T. Policastro
Manager of Aircraft Maintenance Operations
United Airlines
6016 Avion Drive
Los Angeles, CA 90045–5679
(310) 646–2120
Fax: (310) 646–3108

4512

Business Information: United Airlines is an international commercial airline specializing in freight and passenger transportation. Mr. Policastro began his career with United Airlines in 1978 as a Foreman Aircraft MTC and worked his way up to Manager of Aircraft Maintenance Operations in 1994. He is responsible for 400 mechanics and 100 administrative and management support staff, in addition to the daily maintenance of aircraft. **Career Steps:** United Airlines: Manager of Aircraft Maintenance Operations (1994–Present), Shuttle By United Designs Team (1994), Manager of Maintenance Operations (1989–1994), Foreman Aircraft MTC (1978–1989). **Associations & Accomplishments:** Council of Airline Maintenance Managers; Board of Advisors, College of Aeronautics; Corvette Club of Ventura; received the Diamond Award from the FAA (1994, 1995). **Education:** Rutgers University, B.S. (1979); Teterboro School of Aeronautics, Aircraft and Powerplant License. **Personal:** Married to Sandra in 1969. Two children: Matthew and Marc. Mr. Policastro enjoys golf.

Mr. David R. Retz
Tax Counsel
American Airlines, Inc.
P.O. Box 619616, MD5656
DFW Airport, TX 75261
(817) 967–3965
Fax: Please mail or call

4512

Business Information: American Airlines, Inc. is a major international commercial airline specializing in passenger and freight transportation. As Tax Counsel, Mr. Retz directs all aspects of excise taxation, sales and use taxation, petroleum and alcoholic beverage regulation, customs and international taxation. Established in 1934, American Airlines, Inc. employs 124,000 people with annual sales of $15 billion. **Career Steps:** Tax Counsel, American Airlines, Inc. (1991–Present); Senior Staff Specialist, United Airlines (1989–1991); Corporate Counsel, Marshall Field & Company (1986–1989). **Associations & Accomplishments:** American Bar Association; Illinois Bar Association; Chicago Bar Association; H.M. Customs and Excise Joint Industry Consultancy; IATA Fuel Trade Forum; Jet Fuel Inteligence; World Jet Fuel Report. **Education:** DePaul Law School, L.L.M. – Tax (1993); Illinois Institute of Technology Chicago Kent College of Law, J.D.; Cornell College, B.S. in Special Studies. **Personal:** Mr. Retz enjoys world travel and off beat musical and cultural events.

Sigmar Sigurdsson

Vice President of the Americas
Cargolux Airlines International
238 Lawrence Avenue
San Francisco, CA 94080–6817
(415) 225–0747
Fax: (415) 225–0988

4512

Business Information: Cargolux Airlines International is an air cargo airline for freight forwarders worldwide. Established in 1970, Cargolux Airlines reports annual revenue of $350 million worldwide and currently employs 50 people at the San Francisco, California location. With fifteen years experience in the air cargo industry, Mr. Sigurdsson has held various executive positions with Cargolux since 1980. Rejoining Cargolux in 1990 following his employment in an Iceland–based airline, he now serves as Vice President of the Americas; responsible for all Cargolux activities in the Americas, including administration, operations, finances, sales, and marketing. **Career Steps:** Cargolux Airlines International: Vice President of the Americas (1990–Present), Director of Asia/Pacific (1980–1985); Cargo Director, Icelandair – Iceland (1986–1990). **Education:** Business School of London; Business College in Iceland. **Personal:** Married to Edda in 1969. Two children: Hjalmar Gunnar and Anna Lisa. Mr. Sigurdsson enjoys camping, hiking, tennis, bicycling, and reading.

P. Juan Van Rensburg

Vice President – South America
South African Airways
Av. Santa Fe 794 3rd Floor
Buenos Aires, BA, Argentina 1059
(541) 311–8199
Fax: (541) 311–5825
Email: See Below

4512

Business Information: South African Airways is an airline comprised of 48 aircraft and 10,500 employees. The airline flies to Europe, London, Asia, the Middle East, India, Australia, South America, New York, and Miami. As Vice President – South America, Mr. Van Rensburg is responsible for managing Company operations and reports to the President – Americas. Internet users can reach him via: juansaaba@sicoar.com. **Career Steps:** Vice President, South African Airways (1993–Present); Assistant Vice President, SAA (1990–1993); Management Consultant, Transnet (1986–1990). **Associations & Accomplishments:** South African Medical & Dental Council. **Education:** Stellenboselt, Bachelor's in Communications Honors, Industrial Psychology Honors (1986). **Personal:** Married to Hannelie in 1989. Two children: Adeline and Armin Juan. Mr. Van Rensburg enjoys squash, windsurfing, golf, and travel.

Larry L. Vaughn
Director of Maintenance
Rasmark Jet Charter
6915 Boeing Drive
El Paso, TX 79925–1107
(915) 772–4616
Fax: (915) 779–5387
EMAIL: See Below

4512

Business Information: Rasmark Jet Charter is an on–demand jet aircraft line with charter flights to North and South America. As Director of Maintenance, Mr. Vaughn ensures the safety and airworthiness of the aircraft, as well as managing the day–to–day operations of the Company. Internet users can also reach him via: Falcon10@MSN. **Career Steps:** Director of Maintenance, Rasmark Jet Charter (1993–Present); Director of Maintenance, Junction Jet Center (1989–1993); Chief Inspector, Skybird Aviation (1984–1993). **Associations & Accomplishments:** Professional Aircraft Maintenance Association. **Education:** University of California – Los Angeles, B.E. (1971); Flight Safety International for Lear Jets, Falcon Jets, J.E.T. Auto Pilot, etc. **Personal:** One child: Jamie Lynn. Mr. Vaughn enjoys snow skiing.

Samuel Wilkinson
Assistant Financial Controller
BahamasAir Holdings Company Ltd.
P.O. Box SS–5472
Nassau, Bahamas
(809) 377–8451
Fax: (809) 377–7408

4512

Business Information: BahamasAir Holding Company Ltd. is an airline company that specializes in international and domestic flights to Florida, New York and the Family Islands of the Bahamas. A Certified Public Accountant, Mr. Wilkinson joined BahamasAir Holding Company as Assistant Financial Controller in 1995. He is responsible for all matters which directly or indirectly pertain to or affect company revenues, including Passenger Sales Revenue, Lifted Coupons, Interline Revenue, Cargo Revenue, and Credit Card Revenue. Also included are data input controls which pertain to revenue, revenue analysis and reporting, Bi–lateral and Multi–lateral Airline Agreements, external reporting to the Bahamas Government and all receivables which impact on revenues. **Career Steps:** Assistant Financial Controller, BahamasAir Holding Company Ltd. (1995–Present); Financial Controller, Happy Tours/Pleasure Tours, Ltd. (1992–1995); Financial Controller, National Workers Bank, Ltd. (1990–1992); Management Officer, Bank of Nova Scotia (1983–1990); Revenue Officer, Bahamas Customs (1979–1983); Accounts Clerk, CitiBank (1978–1979); Part–time Lecturer, St. John's University; Part–time Lecturer, Sojourner Douglas College; Part–time Lecturer, College of the Bahamas. **Associations & Accomplishments:** Beta Gamma Sigma – Academic Excellence; Certificate of Recognition for Academic Excellence; Golden Key National Honour Society – Academic Excellence. **Education:** University of Miami: M.B.A. in Finance and Management, B.B.A. in Management and Marketing; College of the Bahamas, A.A. in Accounting; Institute of Financial Accountants – London, Certified Accountant; Association of Cost & Executive Accountants – London; Fellow, Institute of Professional Financial Managers – London; Fellow, International Association of

Bookkeepers – London; Fellow in Business Administration, Faculty of Business Administrators – London. **Personal:** Married to Melanie S. in 1990. One child: Samuel James, Jr. Mr. Wilkinson enjoys reading, music, theatre, and lecturing.

Mr. Darryl L. Wilson
Manager of Health and Occupational Benefits
United Airlines
O'Hare International Airport, Chicago, IL
Chicago, IL 60666
(312) 601–4005
Fax: (312) 601–4141

4512

Business Information: United Airlines Inc. is an international commercial airline specializing in freight and passenger transportation. United Airlines Inc. currently employs 82,000 industry professionals. As Inflight Operations Manager, Mr. Wilson is responsible for 15 Inflight Supervisors who manage 2,500 Flight Attendants. **Career Steps:** United Airlines: Manager of Health and Occupational Benefits (1995–Present), Inflight Operations Manager (1991–1995); Attorney of Labor Relations, United Airlines Inc. (1986–1991); Grants Coordinator, Milwaukee County Executive's Office (1979–1983); Casualty Underwriter, Insurance Company of North America (1977–1979). **Associations & Accomplishments:** Member, Operating Board of Directors Ravinia Associates; Member and Treasurer, Board of Directors Jazz Institute of Chicago; Member, Who's Who Among Young Rising Americans (1991); Member, American Biographical Institute Board of Advisors; Member American Bar Association; Member, Chicago Bar Association; Member, Association of Trial Lawyers; Recipient, United Airlines Award of Merit (1990); Named, "Best and Brightest" in "Dollars and Sense Magazine" (1991). **Education:** University of Wisconsin Law School, J.D. (1986); West Virginia State College, B.S. in Education (1974). **Personal:** Married to Gail LaVette in 1986. One child: Jeffery. Mr. Wilson enjoys being a jazz collector.

Zahmari M. Hernandez

Translator/Administrative Assistant
United Parcel Service
150 Sector Central Cafcas Building
2nd Floor LMM Intl. Airport, C, Puerto Rico 00979
(809) 253–2877
Fax: Please mail or call

4513

Business Information: United Parcel Service (UPS) specializes in domestic and international small package and document distribution. Maintaining facilities in Puerto Rico since 1985, the Company presently employs 632 people in Puerto Rico and the Virgin Islands. As Translator and Administrative Assistant in the Business Development Department, Ms. Hernandez is responsible for translating and processing reports and documents. **Career Steps:** Translator/Administrative Assistant, United Parcel Service (1993–Present); Office Aid, Barry University Work Study Program (1988–1991); Office Aid, Economic Development Administration (1988–1992). **Associations & Accomplishments:** School of Arts and Sciences, Barry University: Outstanding Graduate, President's List, Dean's List; Who's Who Among Students in American Universities & Colleges; National Dean's List Alumni Association; Kappa Gamma Pi National Catholic College Graduate Honor Society; Delta Epsilon Sigma National Scholastic Honor Society; Lambda Iota Tau International Literature Honor Society; Alpha Mu Gamma Foreign Languages Honor Association. **Education:** Barry University – Miami, Florida, B.A., Magna Cum Laude (1991); Seminars Attended: Management Skills (1995), "Segundo Simposio sobre la Traduccion en Puerto Rico" (1994), "Primer Simposio sobre la Traduccion en Puerto Rico" (1992). **Personal:** Ms. Hernandez enjoys sports and listening to music.

Guy B. Kriske
District Industrial Engineering Manager
United Parcel Service
3312 Broadway Street, North East
Minneapolis, MN 55413
(612) 379–6676
Fax: (612) 376–6530
EMAIL: See below

4513

Business Information: United Parcel Service (UPS) specializes in domestic and international small package and document distribution. As District Industrial Engineering Manager, Mr. Kriske is responsible for managing the industrial engineering, technical support, and customer resources departments. Internet users can reach him via: TQGuy@Aol.Com. **Career Steps:** District Industrial Engineering Manager, United Parcel Service (1975–Present); Information Services Supervisor,

American Chain and Cable (1973–1975). **Associations & Accomplishments:** Institute of Industrial Engineering Council of Logistics; Transportation Committee, Minnesota Chamber of Commerce; Cub Scout Leader. **Education:** Northeastern Illinois University, B.S. in Computer Science (1978). **Personal:** Married to Tina in 1984. Four children: Brandon, Adam, Justin and Andrew. Mr. Kriske enjoys golf, white water rafting and scouts.

Roy E. Lancraft
Engineering Division Manager
Roadnet Technologies, United Parcel Service
2311 York Road
Timonium, MD 21093–2215
(410) 560–4014
Fax: (410) 560–4329
E–mail: see below

4513

Business Information: Roadnet Technologies, United Parcel Service specializes in domestic and international package and document distribution utilizing land, air and sea transportation and state–of–the–art logistical tracking methods. Established in 1907, UPS currently employs 300,000 people worldwide and has an estimated annual revenue of $20 billion. As an Engineering Division Manager, Mr. Lancraft is responsible for all aspects of technical development, including software and hardware systems such as the electronic clipboard, cellular communications, wireless dispatch systems, and shipping improvements. Mr. Lancraft can also be reached through the Internet as follows: REL@Roadnet.UPS.Com. **Career Steps:** Engineering Division Manager, Roadnet Technologies, United Parcel Service (1987–Present); Principal Member of the Technical Staff, Westinghouse/Unimation Robotics (1984–1987); Staff Scientist, Bolt Bertnick & Newman (1978–1984). **Associations & Accomplishments:** Institute of Electrical and Electronics Engineers; Tau Beta Pi and Eta Kappa Mu, Engineering Honor Societies; Troop Committee Member, Boy Scouts; Youth Sports Soccer Coach. **Education:** University of Connecticut: M.S. in Electrical Engineering (1979), B.S. in Electrical Engineering, magna cum laude (1976). **Personal:** Married to Sandra L. in 1977. Two children: Michael James and Erin Courtney. Mr. Lancraft enjoys sports, golf and tennis.

Mary A. Montgomery
Accounting Administrator
Emery Worldwide
303 Corporate Center Drive
Vandalia, OH 45377
(513) 454–3989
Fax: (513) 454–2979

4513

Business Information: Emery Worldwide is one of the leading parcel delivery services. Established in 1952, Emery specializes in air freight, ocean, and truck delivery. As Accounting Administrator, Ms. Montgomery maintains domestic and international fuel usage records for the Company's aircraft, ensuring the aircraft has enough fuel to reach its destination. **Career Steps:** Emery Worldwide: Accounting Administrator (1995–Present), Quality Assurance Specialist (1992–1995), International Specialist (1988–1992). **Associations & Accomplishments:** Job Enrichment Task Force; Active Supporter for Quality Education for Children. **Education:** International Broadcasting School (1982). **Personal:** One child: Matthew Cole. Ms. Montgomery enjoys boating and camping.

Thomas J. Papenthien
District Automotive Manager
United Parcel Service
795 South Springfield Road
Waukesha, WI 53186–1406
(414) 785–7221
Fax: (414) 524–9259
E Mail: See Below

4513

Business Information: United Parcel Service (UPS) specializes in domestic and international small package and document distribution. Starting as an auto mechanic with UPS in 1976, Thomas Papenthien steadily moved through the corporate structure to attain the position as District Automotive Manager in 1988. In this capacity, he directs all automotive services operations for the State of Wisconsin. Internet users can reach him via: trappy@execpc.com. **Career Steps:** United Parcel Service: District Automotive Manager (1988–Present), Auto Fleet Manager (1985–1988), Auto Fleet Supervisor (1984), Auto Mechanic (1976–1984). **Personal:** Married to Cathy in 1974. Three children: Steve, Kelly, and Doug. Mr. Papenthien enjoys electronics, computers, reading, exercise, and investigating stocks and bonds.

Rhea Roberson

Managing Director
Federal Express
P.O. Box 727–Comat 4231
Memphis, TN 38194
(901) 922–6857
Fax: (901) 922–3286

4513

Business Information: Federal Express is an international express package delivery service with corporate headquarters in Memphis, Tennessee. The corporation has approximately 26,000 employees. As Managing Director, Mr. Roberson directs the research, conceptual, mechanical and electrical design of sortation facilities around the world. He oversees the packages sorted through conveyors, computer systems, and container handling. Mr. Roberson directly supervises approximately 70 employees. **Career Steps:** Federal Express: Managing Director (1996–Present), Manager, FM Engineering (1991–1996), Project Engineer, Electrical Design (1989–1991), Project Engineer, MX Engineering (1987–1989). **Associations & Accomplishments:** National Society of Professional Engineers; Tennessee Society of Professional Engineers. **Education:** Christian Brothers University, Masters of Engineering Management (1996); Mississippi State University, B.S. in Electrical Engineering; Northwest Mississippi Junior College, A.S. **Personal:** Married to Regina in 1994. Mr. Roberson enjoys golf, boating, and reading.

Lisa L. Rossello
Executive Vice President
Tol Air Services, Inc.
P.O. Box 37670, LMM International Airport
San Juan, Puerto Rico 00937
(809) 791–5235
Fax: (809) 791–8385

4513

Business Information: Tol Air Services, Inc. is an airline cargo transportation company, concentrating in serving the commercial airline industry. Established in 1981, Tol Air Services, Inc. currently employs 56 people. As Executive Vice President, Ms. Rossello is responsible for general management and conducting seminars and lectures on behalf of the Company. **Career Steps:** Executive Vice President, Tol Air Services, Inc. (1988–Present); Sales, Exhibition Group (1978–1988). **Personal:** Married to Jorge Toledo in 1988. Two children: Georgina and Jorge Toledo. Ms. Rossello enjoys flying aircraft and spending time with her family.

Clifford L. Stockman
District Human Resources Manager – New York District
United Parcel Service
75 Smith Street
East Farmingdale, NY 11735–1022
(516) 755–7841
Fax: (516) 755–7828

4513

Business Information: United Parcel Service (UPS) specializes in domestic and international small package and document distribution. Established in 1907, UPS currently employs 3,200 people in the New York District. As District Human Resources Manager of the New York District, Mr. Stockman is responsible for all aspects of personnel matters, including hiring, training, labor relations, and benefits. **Career Steps:** United Parcel Service: District Human Resources Manager of the New York District (1994–Present), District Human Resources Manager of the South Carolina District (1991–1994), Operations Manager of the South New England District (1990–1991), Corporate Human Resources Employee Manager at the Corporate Office in Greenwich, Connecticut (1986–1990). **Associations & Accomplishments:** Society of Human Resource Managers (SHRM); Works closely with the Long Island United Way; Member, Long Island NAACP. **Education:** University of West Florida, B.A. (1978). **Personal:** Mr. Stockman enjoys travel, boating, water skiing, camping and hiking.

W. J. Stoner
National Account Sales Executive
Royal Transportation
5140 S. 3rd Street
Milwaukee, WI 53207
(414) 482–3397 (414) 679–9970
Fax: (414) 482–4474

4513

Business Information: Royal Transportation is a national and Canadian contract carrier and worldwide airfreight forwarder. Royal Transportation transports raw and finished goods by land, air and water for small and large corporations for international distribution by wholesalers and retailers (importing and exporting). As National Account Sales Executive, Ms. Stoner is responsible for all national accounts with major companies, including contracts, logistics management, and acquiring new accounts. Key responsibilities include defining market lanes and establishing goals; devising and implementing plans for account penetration; budget ing resources; and monitoring and evaluating results. Major accomplishments include increasing sales through account penetration. **Career Steps:** National Account Sales Executive, Royal Transportation (1992–Present); Vice President of Operations, Badger Lines, Inc. (1989–1992); Express Freight Lines, Inc.: Vice President of Operations and Human Resources (1985–1989), Vice President of Special Services Division (1973–1985). **Associations & Accomplishments:** Delta Nu Alpha Transportation Fraternity; Published article on freight business activities. **Education:** Concordia University, B.A. in Management and Communications, summa cum laude; Carthage College, Certified Paralegal; University of Wisconsin, A.A. in Transportation and Distribution. **Personal:** Ms. Stoner enjoys racquetball, target shooting, and travel.

Mangala Srirangam
Manager of Information Systems
Virgin Atlantic Cargo
1983 Marcus Avenue Suite 100
New Hyde Park, NY 11042–1016
(516) 775–2600
Fax: (516) 354–3760

4522

Business Information: Virgin Atlantic Cargo is the cargo division of Atlantic Airways. Making four runs a day, the Company is headquartered in London, England which three branches in the U.S. Established in 1984, the Company employs 300 people and has estimated annual revenue of $30 million. As Manager of Information Systems, Ms. Srirangam establishes maintains, and operates the time systems department. She supervises the staff, manages an AS 400 system that is uses as a platform for program development, and researches and approves new hardware. **Career Steps:** Manager of Information Systems, Virgin Atlantic Cargo (1992–Present); Financial Analyst, CGI Systems (19991–1992); Financial Analyst, Met Life (1989–1991). **Education:** West Virginia University, M.B.A. (1989); Madras University: M.A. in Political Science, Masters in Commerce. **Personal:** Married to Cimi Sivaneri in 1995. Ms. Srirangam enjoys boats, music, and gardening.

Ibis I. Valles
Vice President of Human Resources
Jet Aviation
980 Moonachie Avenue
Teterboro, NJ 07608
(201) 462–4053
Fax: (201) 462–4054

4522

Business Information: Jet Aviation is a multi–operational aviation business. The company supplies corporations with aircraft, flight crews, aircraft services, and maintenance. In addition, it is an FBO (Fuel–based Operations), providing fueling and maintenance for aircraft at national and international airports. Established in the 1967, Jet Aviation employs 500 people and has estimated annual revenue of $90 million. As Vice President of Human Resources, Mrs. Valles is responsible for all aspects of human resources to include, training and development, hiring and termination, and counseling. **Career Steps:** Vice President of Human Resources, Jet Aviation (1992–Present); Director of Human Resources, Honeywell Space Systems Division (1986–1972); Sperry Aerospace Division: Manager of Personnel (1981–1986); Human Resources Manager (1974–1981); Instructor of Adult Education, Phoenix Area Institutions (1969–1974). **Associations & Accomplishments:** Board of Directors, Cancer Association (1992); United Way; Instructor to 7th Grade Students, Junior Achievement; American Management Association; American Compensation Association; Society of Human Resource Management. **Education:** University of Nebraska, B.S. in Education (1969); ASU, Graduate courses taken; Harvard School of Business, Leadership classes. **Personal:** Married to Robert in 1976. One child: Max. Mrs. Valles enjoys skiing, reading, and playing the piano during her leisure time.

Kenneth L. Below

Chief Financial Officer and Assistant Director
Lambert St. Louis International Airport
P.O. Box 10212
St. Louis, MO 63145–0125
(314) 426–8026
Fax: (314) 426–5733

4581

Business Information: Lambert St. Louis International Airport is the 11th largest international airport in the United States. As Chief Financial Officer and Assistant Director, Mr. Below is responsible for all billing and invoice activities, oversight of accounting functions, MIS and facilities management. **Career Steps:** Chief Financial Officer and Assistant Director, Lambert St. Louis International Airport (1995–Present); Manager, Martin Marietta (1986–1995); Senior Engineer, McDonnell Douglas (1982–1986); Manager, Southwestern Bell (1980–1982). **Associations & Accomplishments:** American Association of Airport Executives; Airport Council International – North America; National Forum for Black Public Administrators. **Education:** Webster University: M.B.A. (1992), M.A.; Washington University, A.B. **Personal:** Mr. Below enjoys skiing, sports, travel, and reading.

Patrick S. Graham
Executive Director
Savannah Airport Commission
400 Airways Avenue
Savannah, GA 31408–8000
(912) 964–0514
Fax: (912) 964–0877

4581

Business Information: The Savannah Airport Commission (S.A.C.) controls all functions pertaining to the operation of the Savannah Airport and its support personnel. Joining S.A.C. as director of finance in 1981, Mr. Graham has served as its Executive Director since 1988. He has full administrative charge of all budgetary, human resources, federal regulatory compliance, and public relations. **Career Steps:** Savannah Airport Commission: Executive Director (1992–Present), Deputy Executive Director (1988–1992), Finance Director (1985–1988); Controller, Continental Forest Industries (1980–1985). **Associations & Accomplishments:** Rotary International; American Association of Airport Executives; Alee Shrine Temple. **Education:** Central Michigan University, M.A.A. (1985); Armstrong State College, B.B.A.; Certified Public Accountant (1985). **Personal:** Two children: Kathleen and Kristen. Mr. Graham enjoys golf, softball, boating, and fishing.

Garry R.J. King

Vice President of Marketing and Corporate Development
Edmonton International Airport
P.O. Box 9860
Edmonton, Alberta T5J 2T2
(403) 890–8084
Fax: (403) 890–8329
EMAIL: See Below

4581

Business Information: Edmonton International Airport is one of four private airports in Canada, providing world class international airport and air service. The Airport was privatized from transport in 1992. As Vice President of Marketing and Corporate Development, Mr. King heads business development in the areas of air service, land development, concessions, industrial parks, job creation, passenger service, aerospace development, corporate and general aviation, and tourism. Internet users can reach him via: GarryK@oanej.com. **Career Steps:** Vice President of Marketing and Corporate Development, Edmonton International Airport (1993–Present); Vice President of Marketing and Development, Trenton Industries (1990–1993); Brigadier General, Canadian Air Force (1959–1990). **Associations & Accomplishments:** Director, Greater Edmonton Visitors and Convention Association; Director, Alberta Aerospace Association; Airports Council International North America–Marketing Steering Group. **Education:** Royal Military College, Bachelor of Communications (1963). **Personal:** Mr. King enjoys sports, music, travel, and collecting fine wines.

Roy Lamb
Controller
UNC Accessory Services
86 Cleveland Avenue
Bay Shore, NY 11706
(516) 242–4330
Fax: Please mail or call

4581

Business Information: Established in 1966, UNC Accessory Services specializes in aviation overhaul and repair of accessory components with locations in New York, Texas, and Florida. As Corporate Controller for the accessory component area, Mr. Lamb oversees eighteen employees in conducting all financial and accounting functions. **Career Steps:** Controller, UNC Accessory Services (1993–Present); Naval Products: Controller (1992–1993), General Accounting Manager (1987–1992). **Associations & Accomplishments:** Institute of Management Accountants. **Education:** University of New Haven, M.B.A. (1990). **Personal:** Married to Kathleen in 1992. Two children: Michele and Melissa. Mr. Lamb enjoys golf and boating.

Michael A. Landry

Manager of International Flight Following
Universal Weather & Aviation, Inc.
8787 Tally Ho Road
Houston, TX 77061
(713) 944–1622
Fax: (713) 943–4625
E Mail: See Below

4581

Business Information: Universal Weather & Aviation, Inc. has a staff of 11 dedicated Flight Followers assigned to the task of keeping track of all aircraft locations, 24 hours a day, seven days a week. Universal Flight Following is considered the hub of communcations between the aircraft and the thousands of airfields and handlers around the world. As Manager of International Flight Followers, Mr. Landry is responsible for confidentially monitoring global tracking of general aviation aircrafts. He can be reached via the Internet at MLANDRY@UNIV–WER.COM. **Career Steps:** Manager, Universal Weather & Aviation, Inc. (1986–Present); Overhead Crane Operator, U.S. Steel (1984–1986), Air Traffic Controller, U.S. Navy (1979–1984). **Associations & Accomplishments:** President Elect, Hobby Airport Exchange Club; Statistician of Progressive State Convention; Secretary of Progressive State Convention; Post Adjutant, American Legion Post 628. **Education:** Conroe Norman Industrial College; Air Traffic Control School, N.A.S. – Memphis (Navy); Communication Center School – Fort Gordon, Georgia (Army). **Personal:** Two children: Candace Antonette and Andrew Michael Landry, Jr. Mr. Landry enjoys basketball, reading, bowling, and cooking.

Marjan J. Mazza
Airport Manager/Grant Administrator
Broward County Aviation
1400 Lee Wagener Boulevard
Ft. Lauderdale, FL 33315–3558
(954) 359–6176
Fax: (954) 359–1292

4581

Business Information: Broward County Aviation is a full–service airport operation. As Airport Manager/Grant Administrator, Ms. Mazza is responsible for diversified administrative activities, including acting as the federal and state liaison. **Career Steps:** Airport Manager/Grant Administrator, Broward County Aviation (1993–Present); Dade County Aviation: Administrative Officer (1992), Aviation Special Assistant (1989). **Associations & Accomplishments:** American Association of Airport Executives; Florida Airport Managers Association. **Education:** Embry Riddle Aeronautical University, M.B.A. (1992); Currently pursuing a Ph.D. in Public Administration at Florida Atlantic University. **Personal:** Married to Sunil Harman in 1995. Ms. Mazza enjoys reading and music.

Charlotte A. Pashley
Director of Purchasing – Airline Catering
Ogden Aviation Services
JFK Building 125
Jamaica, NY 11430
(718) 995–8584
Fax: (718) 995–8584

4581

Business Information: Ogden Aviation Services provides contractual services to the airline industry at John F. Kennedy International Airport. With seventeen years experience in the airline industry, Ms. Pashley joined Ogden Aviation Services as Director of Sales and Marketing in 1985. Appointed as Director of Purchasing – Airline Catering in 1995, she is responsible for directing, managing, and coordinating all aspects of purchasing activities for airline catering to include contracts, pricing, negotiations, and computer software design. **Career Steps:** Ogden Aviation Services: Director of Purchasing – Airline Catering (1995–Present); Director of Sales and Marketing (1985–1995); Director of Food and Beverage, Pacific Southwest Airlines (1979–1985). **Associations & Accomplishments:** Inflight Food Service Association; National Restaurant Association – Food Service Purchasing Managers Group. **Education:** Arizona State University, B.S. in Dietetics (1973); American Management Association, Bottom Line Course; Vendor Negotiations; Strategic Management of Suppliers. **Personal:** Married to Bruce R. in 1991. One child: Brooke. Ms. Pashley enjoys working out, reading, and arts.

Kathy J. Pettit
Director of Customers
Southwest Airlines Company
2702 Love Field Drive, P.O. Box 36611
Dallas, TX 75235–1611
(214) 904–4000
Fax: (214) 509–7995

4581

Business Information: Southwest Airlines Company, established in 1971, is a commercial business providing on demand charter airline services. As Director of Customers, Ms. Pettit is responsible for managing consumer affairs, providing executive legal correspondence, maintaining open communications, and designing interior configurations for 737–700 jets. **Career Steps:** Southwest Airlines Company: Director of Customers (1994–Present), Director of Communications (1993–Present), Manager of Corporate Communications (1990–1993); Manager of Inflight Services, Braniff International (1978–1981). **Associations & Accomplishments:** American Management Association; Recipient of Over 400 Commendations & Citations for Customer Service Excellence. **Personal:** One child: Johnny L. Meaney. Ms. Pettit enjoys attending her son's little league baseball games.

George L. Smith
President
SNH Aerospace Services L.L.C.
1966 1st Ave. Hanger 1
San Antonio, TX 78216
(210) 822–4318
Fax: (210) 822–3164

4581

Business Information: SNH Aerospace Services L.L.C. is a certified FAA repair station offering specialized services in aerospace welding to the regional airlines, commercial airlines, general and corporate aviation industry. As President and Co–Founder, Mr. Smith is responsible for the development of new business projects, as well as providing sales efforts to the current fleet. He recently oversaw the development of a Supplemented Type Certificate (STC) to convert the Fairchild's Merlin/Metro Series from Ni–Cad batteries to a sealed lead acid battery which reduced the operators cost of operation. **Career Steps:** President, SNH Aerospace Services L.L.C. (1996–Present); Director of Business Development, Fairchild Aircraft Services (1993–1996); Manager of Regional Airlines Technical Services/Sales, Midcoast–Little Rock (1985–1993); Manager of Customer Services, Gulfstream Aerospace – Commander Division (1981–1985). **Education:** University of Arkansas–Little Rock; Emry Riddle, Hawkeye Technology, A&P License. **Personal:** Married to Kathy A. in 1976. Two children: Sheri Lynn and Stacey Noel.

Marcela Zeman
Finance Director
BAA Indianapolis, L.L.C.
2500 South High School Road, Box 100
Indianapolis, IN 46241
(317) 487–5100
Fax: (317) 487–5034

4581

Business Information: BAA Indianapolis, LLC manages the Indianapolis International Airport and Reliever Airports for, and on behalf, of the Indianapolis Airport Authority. The BAA/IAA Management Contract is the first of its kind in the U.S. and is the first partial privatization of airports in the U.S. BAA Indianapolis LLC's ultimate parent company is BBA plc, a United Kingdom–based company that is the largest private airport operator in the world. As Finance Director, Ms. Zeman oversees all financial management operations and has key responsibilities in financial strategic planning for both the Airport and the BAA management company. **Career Steps:** Finance Director, BAA Indianapolis, LLC (1995–Present); BAA plc United Kingdom: Chief Internal Auditor (1994–1995), Internal Audit Supervisor (1992–1994); Audit Senior, Ernst & Young Australia (1989–1992). **Associations & Accomplishments:** Institute of Chartered Accountants (Australia); Institute of Internal Auditors (UK); American Association of Airport Executives. **Education:** University of South Australia, B.A. Accounting (1989).

4600 Pipelines, Except Natural Gas

4612 Crude petroleum pipelines
4613 Refined petroleum pipelines
4619 Pipelines, NEC

Jane A. Thomas
Human Resources Coordinator
Alyeska Pipeline
P.O. Box 300
Valdez, AK 99686
(907) 835–6523
Fax: Please mail or call

4612

Business Information: Alyeska Pipeline brings oil from the North slope of Alaska, via pipeline, to be shipped out internationally. The Company also supplies its own ships. As Human Resources Coordinator, Ms. Thomas is responsible for the Valdez Marine Terminal Business Unit, Ship Escort, and Response Vessel System Business Unit. She handles all human resource functions, including employee benefits, payroll, hiring, policies, and procedures. **Career Steps:** Alyeska Pipeline: Human Resources Coordinator (1995–Present), Human Resources Generalist (1994–1995), Human Resources Specialist (1992–1993), Human Resources Analyst (1991–1992). **Associations & Accomplishments:** Society of Human Resource Management. **Education:** Boston University, M.B. in Education (1991); Alaska Pacific University, B.A. **Personal:** Ms. Thomas enjoys reading, hiking, and plants.

4700 Transportation Services

4724 Travel agencies
4725 Tour operators
4729 Passenger transport arrangement, NEC
4731 Freight transportation arrangement
4741 Rental of railroad cars
4783 Packing and crating
4785 Inspection and fixed facilities
4789 Transportation services, NEC

C.J. Armstrong
Sales Consultant
Saigon Travel Services
27 Breezway Drive
Asheville, NC 28803
(704) 654–9920
Fax: (704) 654–9921

4724

Business Information: Saigon Travel Services is a consulting service, establishing contacts between United States and Vietnamese businesses and schools. The company arranges travel between the two countries for government personnel, businesses, and individuals, developing transportation plans, Visa acquisition, and appropriate foreign contacts. As Sales Consultant, Mr. Armstrong is responsible for customer travel arragements, business development, and serves as a foreign liason. Concurrently, he is furthering his education and hopes to aid in the development of Vietnam's business districts. **Career Steps:** Sales Consultant, Saigon Travel Services (1993–Present); Guest Lecturer in Organizational Development, Lotus Business College, Vietnam (1993–1994); Lt. Colonel, U.S. Army (1962–1992). **Associations & Accomplishments:** Member, U.S.–Vietnam Chamber of Commerce – Chicago, Illinois; Boy Scouts of America; Numerous Veterans Organizations; Voting Member, Board of the Military Coalition, Washington, D.C. **Education:** UNC–Asheville, Elementary and Secondary Teaching Certification (1996); Western Kentucky University, M.A. in Public Administration (1984); Florida State University, B.S. in Government (1973); Johns–Hopkins University, Graduate Level Business Courses (1994–1995). **Personal:** Mr. Armstrong enjoys travel, reading, and working with Boy Scouts.

Espinola Brunson
Director of Operations
Carlson Wagonlit Travel
1616 East Indian School Road, Suite 135
Phoenix, AZ 85016
(602) 230–2633
Fax: (602) 230–2668
EMAIL: See Below

4724

Business Information: Carlson Wagonlit Travel (CWT) provides travel management and services. As Director of Operations for all Arizona branches of CWT, Ms. Brunson is responsible for sales, customer service, and personnel management. Internet users can also reach her via: EBrunson@ctg.otc3.carlson.com **Career Steps:** Director of Operations, Carlson Wagonlit Travel (1974–Present). **Associations & Accomplishments:** American Business Women's Association; Touchstone Committees; Arizona Center for Law in the Public Interest; Advisory Board, Maricopa Community Colleges Travel Curriculum. **Education:** Arizona State University, B.A. (1971); Attending University of Phoenix, M.B.A in Progress. **Personal:** Married to Michael in 1971. Two children: Michael and Marcus. Ms. Brunson enjoys reading, cooking, and hiking.

Mark E. Herbert
Vice President
WorldTravel Meetings & Incentives
402 Broadway, Ste. 700
San Diego, CA 92101
(619) 702–9800
Fax: (619) 702–9802
EMAIL: See Below

4724

Business Information: WorldTravel Meetings & Incentive, an incentive and meeting services company located in San Diego, California, provides incentives/meetings for corporations and businesses. Established in 1988, the company strives to motivate clients' employees. As Vice President, Mr. Herbert handles all operational aspects of the company including Human Resources, MIS, financial and budgetary aspects, as well as employee oversight and travel arrangements. Internet users can also reach him via: MHERBERT@WTPSAN.Com. **Career Steps:** WorldTravel Meetings & Incentive: Vice President (1995–Present), Director of Operations/Purchasing (1993–1995); Manager–Travel Services, Tri Companies, Inc. (1989–1993). **Associations & Accomplishments:** San Diego Junior Chamber of Commerce. **Education:** Bentley College, B.S. in Management (1988). **Personal:** Mr. Herbert enjoys golf, skiing, and boating.

Becky Messmer
Human Resource Director
Ross & Babcock Travel
9075 North Meridian Street
Indianapolis, IN 46260
(317) 844–7616
Fax: (317) 848–9475

4724

Business Information: Ross & Babcock Travel is a full service agency providing travel and related services to clients. National in scope, the Company has branches in Indiana, New York, Ohio, and Florida. Established in 1949, the Company employs 140 people, and has an estimated annual revenue of $50 million. As Human Resource Director, Ms. Messmer is responsible for interviewing, administering benefits, payroll, policy development and implementation, and indirectly supervises the Human Resource trainees. **Career Steps:** Human Resource Director, Ross & Babcock Travel (1996–Present); Human Resource Manager, National Car Rental (1989–1995). **Associations & Accomplishments:** Society of Human Resource Managers; HRACI. **Education:** Indiana University. **Personal:** Married to Ron in 1979. Three children: Sarah, Elizabeth, and Andy. Ms. Messmer enjoys dancing, horseback riding, and antique hunting.

Osama M. Sabbah
Director General
Baz Tours & Cargo
P.O. Box 21271
Safat, Kuwait 13073
(965) 2452718 Ext. 111/116
Fax: (965) 2452919

4724

Business Information: Baz Tours & Cargo is the number one tour operator in the Persian Gulf, specializing in custom travel, tours, and vacation plans, holiday clubs, and cargo handling. As Director General, Mr. Sabbah is responsible for overseeing daily operations, taking a specific interest in travel to Austria. **Career Steps:** Director General, Baz Tours & Cargo (1990–Present); General Manager, Burgan International

Travel (1985–1990); Route Budget & Planning Supervisor, Kuwait Airways (1981–1985). **Associations & Accomplishments:** Kuwaiti Travel & Tourism Association. **Education:** Ain Shams University, Faculty of Commerce – Cairo, Bachelor's (1980); American University – Cairo, Computer Science Diploma (1980). **Personal:** Married to Mercia Khalil in 1988. Two children: Mariam Sabbah and Ameera Sabbah. Mr. Sabbah enjoys reading and playing football.

Amal E. Waked, Ph.D.
•••◖▬◉▬◗•••

General Manager
World Travel Service
P.O. Box 830
Manama, Bahrain, Saudi Arabia
973 224 679
Fax: 973 210 277

4724

Business Information: World Travel Service is a travel agency which provides all aspects of travel and cargo services, by air, land, and sea. The company is the General Sales Agent in Bahrain, for Cathay Pacific, Air Nevada, Ansett Australia, Ansett Newzealand, Canadian Airlines International, Delta Airlines, Finnair, Icelandair, Philippine Airlines and TAP Air Portugal; including Eurail, Britrail, international tour operators, and industry suppliers. Established in 1974, World Travel Service reports an annual revenue of $30 million and currently employs 89 people. As General Manager, Dr. Waked is responsible for planning, organizing, directing, motivating, controlling, and policy and decision making activities. **Career Steps:** General Manager, World Travel Service (1989–Present); Manager Cargo Operations, Abudhabi Airport Service (1977–1988); Manager Travel, Whittaker Corp. – Saudi Arabia (1974–1977); Managing Director and Co–Owner, Flying Carpet Corp. – Beirut (1971–1974). **Associations & Accomplishments:** President, Advisory Committee of Bahrain Travel and Tours Association (1990–Present); Board of Directors, Arab Exchange Company. **Education:** Pacific Southern University, Ph.D. (1988). **Personal:** Married to Maureen Callahan in 1984. Two children: Elias Robert and Janeva Lauren Waked. Dr. Waked enjoys fishing, and reading.

Kimberly Burshek
Vice President, Chief Financial Officer
Hawaiian Vacations, Inc.
1010 Northern Lights Boulevard
Anchorage, AK 99503–3715
(907) 261–2728
Fax: (907) 261–2744

4725

Business Information: Hawaiian Vacations, Inc. is a wholesale tour operation providing non–stop service from Anchorage, Alaska to Hawaii. Focusing primarily on travel packages which include airfare, auto and hotel accomodations, the Company offers services year round. As Vice President, Chief Financial Officer, Ms. Burshek oversees the accounting departments facilities and administration. He is responsible for preparing financial statements, budgets, and manages cash flow projections. **Career Steps:** Hawaiian Vacations, Inc: Vice President, Chief Financial Officer (1996–Present), Director of Finance (1995–1996), Controller (1994–1995); Certified Public Accountant, Stanley M. Carrothers Accounting Corporation (1989–1992). **Associations & Accomplishments:** American Institute of Certified Public Accountants; Chairman of Membership/Benefits Committee, Alaska Society of Certified Public Accountants. **Education:** California State University, Sacramento, B.S. in Accounting (1988). **Personal:** Married to Sean P. in 1994. Ms. Burshek enjoys aerobics, riding motorcycles with her husband, and cross country skiing.

Maria Angelica Mesas
Managing Director
All Patagonia
Juana Fadul 26, Ushuaia
Tierra del Fuego, Argentina 9410
(549) 013–3622
Fax: (549) 013–0707

4725

Business Information: All Patagonia specializes in tour operations, receiving people from all over the world, and utilizing Company–owned busses and guides, to provide them with customized torus of Argentina. The Company also operates a nautical shop which markets ship merchandise, and a boat repair facility. Esntablished in 1991, the Company employs twelve people. As Managing Director, Ms. Mesas oversees all aspects of the Company and is responsible for administration, operations, finance, marketing, sales, public relations, and customer service. **Career Steps:** Managing Director, All Patagonia (Present). **Associations & Accomplishments:** FAYT; CAT. **Personal:** Married in 1991. Ms. Mesas enjoys walking, tennis and golf.

Hal F. Ryder
President
Galaxy Tours
997 Old Eagle School Road, Suite 207
Wayne, PA 19087
(610) 964–8010
Fax: (610) 964–8220

4725

Business Information: Galaxy Tours is the world's leader in custom–designed group travel including incentive award programs. With more than 35 years experience, Galaxy is the original pioneer of custom–designed and personalized tours for veterans in 57 nations. All branches of the service have participated in tours, including divisions, battalions and companies from all over the globe. The tours allow visits to special places requested by the customer, provides trained and educated escorts, and can be accompanied by written materials. Welcome receptions at all levels of governments and ceremonial events are selected if possible and customers are given an itinerary that is helpful and flexible. Established in 1960, Galaxy Tours was the creator and pioneer of the military veterans tours and events in 1962 commemorating and honoring World Wars I, II, Korea, and Vietnam veterans. Currently the company employs 12 people and reports an estimated annual revenue of $8 million. As President and Chief Executive Officer, Mr. Ryder provides the overall direction and vision for the company's continued growth, quality delivery of services to customers, and all business strategic planning, as well as marketing, sales and daily operations. Mr. Ryder served in the United States Army and retired as Lt. Col. **Career Steps:** President, Galaxy Tours (1960–Present); Chicago & North Western Railway: Director of Research and Marketing (1956–1959), Manager of Freight Services (1954–1956); Legal Administrative Officer, Western Base Section, United States Army (1945–1946). **Associations & Accomplishments:** Retired Officers Association; Reserve Officers Association; Army and Navy Club, Washington, D.C.; Military History Association of the United States; American Legion; Veterans of Foreign Wars; American Society of Travel Agents; Numerous military veterans associations; United States and Foreign. **Education:** LaSalle University (1958); Attended the University of California, the University of Tulsa and the University of Indiana. **Personal:** Married to Margarget in 1953. Two children: Andrew and Susan. Mr. Ryder enjoys writing, tennis and bowling.

Paul A. Walsh
National Sales Manager
Gray Line of Alaska
300 Elliott Avenue West
Seattle, WA 98119
(206) 286–3910
Fax: (206) 281–0621
EMAIL: See Below

4725

Business Information: Gray Line of Alaska, a division of Holland American Lines, is the largest tour group in Alaska. The Company provides over 150 motor coaches, 12 deluxe rail cars and three day boats for clients/customers. As National Sales Manager, Mr. Walsh is responsible for accounts located in the United States, Canada and other international countries. He markets and sells existing tour packages and assists in the development, marketing, and selling of new packages. Internet users may contact him via: pwalsh.sea@aol.com. **Career Steps:** National Sales Manager, Gray Line of Alaska (1996–Present); Holland America Line: Sales Supervisor (1994–1996), Sales Trainer (1994), Sales Representative (1992–1994). **Associations & Accomplishments:** Toastmasters International; Alaska Visitors Association. Mr. Walsh has been published in numerous trade magazines and press releases. **Education:** Seattle University, B.A. (1988).

Mr. Steven F. Paul
President and Chief Executive Officer
Tran–Star Executive Transportation Services, Inc. – New York Office
P.O. Box 2574
North Babylon, NY 11703
(516) 243–3800
Fax: (516) 586–7543

4729

Business Information: Tran–Star Executive Transportation Services, Inc. is a corporate car service, providing transportation for executives to and from airports using vans, limos, town cars, and sedans. As President and Chief Executive Officer, Mr. Paul oversees management of all company operations, concentrating on strategic planning, corporate structure, and profit and loss. Mr. Paul designed, developed, and implemented the Direct Reservation System which enables customers such as travel agents to make car service reservations directly via computer terminals. Established in 1991, Tran–Star Executive Transportation Services, Inc. employs a staff of 60 and reports annual revenue of $2.3 million. **Career Steps:** President and Chief Executive Officer, Tran–Star Executive Transportation Services, Inc. (1991– Present); General Manager, Arrow Island Transportation, Inc. (1989–1991); General Manager, Delux Transportation Services, Inc. (1984–1989). **Associations & Accomplishments:** Long Island Association (Transportation Committee); Better Business Bureau; The American Legion; The National Safety Council; The Veterans of Foreign Wars. **Education:** Indian River College, A.S. (1973); Dale Carnegie Institute.

Carol Balmain–Lapoint

General Manager
Vecta Transportation Systems, Inc.
P.O. Box 38346
Sacramento, CA 95838–0346
(916) 921–6696
Fax: (916) 921–6243

4731

Business Information: Vecta Transportation Systems, Inc. is a common LTL freight carrier, covering the states of California, Nevada, and Arizona. Its fleet currently consists of 225 tractors and over 800 trailers operating from 15 terminal stations. Reporting directly to the President, as General Manager Carol Balmain–Lapoint provides the overall management for all key management personnel and sales representatives, as well as ensures customer service satisfaction and the smooth operation of corporate administrative activities. **Career Steps:** General Manager, Vecta Transportation Systems, Inc. (1991–Present); Sales Representative, Pella Company, Inc. (1989–1991); Business Management Consultant, Craig Makashima, DDS, Keith Judd, DDS (1988–1989). **Education:** Success Alliance Business Management Training (1987–1989). **Personal:** Three children: Gabriel, Zachary and Serenity. Ms. Balmain–Lapoint enjoys water skiing and boating.

Mark A. Barker

Vice President/General Manager
Key Customs Brokers
P.O. Box 63 Station Toronto A M F
Mississauga, Ontario L5P 1A2
(905) 672–0490
Fax: (905) 672–0494

4731

Business Information: Key Customs Brokers specializes in arranging customs clearance and freight forward services for corporations importing/exporting goods to and from Canada. Headquartered in Toronto, the Company has six other locations throughout Canada. As Vice President/General Manager, Mr. Barker oversees all functions, including accounting, import/export, and invoicing. He is directly responsible for twenty–three people, and troubleshoots any problems that arise. **Career Steps:** Vice President/General Manager, Key Customs Brokers (1989–Present); Manager, Affiliated Customs Brokers (1972–1989). **Associations & Accomplishments:** The Transportation Club of Toronto; Canadian Association of Customs Brokers; Transportations Clubs International; Mississauga Board of Trade. **Education:** Canadian Institute of Customs Brokers (1979). **Personal:** Married to Cathie in 1984. Two children: Ashley and Storm. Mr. Barker enjoys sports of all kinds, and coaching hockey and ringette.

Laura A. Cap

Vice President of Marketing
Allied Van Lines, Inc.
215 West Diehl Road
Naperville, IL 60563
(708) 717–3625
Fax: (708) 717–3023

4731

Business Information: Allied Van Lines, Inc. is a national transportation company specializing in the transport of high–value products and household goods relocation. Services are provided through 700 dealers throughout the U.S. Becoming the first female vice president in Allied Van Lines in 1994, Ms. Cap serves as Vice President of Marketing, responsible for the Quality Service Division mechanism, in addition to overseeing a staff of 34. Duties include overseeing customer service, public relations, advertising, and internal communications operations. **Career Steps:** Allied Van Lines, Inc.: Vice President of Marketing (1994–Present), Director of Marketing (1992–1994), Manager of Marketing Comm. (1988–1992), Manager of Corporate Comm. (1986–1988). **Associations & Accomplishments:** International Association of Business Communications; American Marketing Association; Mentiium 100 – an organization that consists of 100 high–profile executives in the Chicago area; Board of Directors, Dupage Council of Girl Scouts. **Education:** University of Wisconsin, B.A. (1982). **Personal:** Married to Larry in 1990. Two children: Ryan and Adam.

Luiz Fernando Fleury Da Rocha

Controller
Burlington Air Express Do Brasil
Candido Vale 319 Tatuape
Sao Paulo SP, Brazil 03068–010
55–11–941–7314 Ext 204
Fax: 55–11–942–7461
V/M (USA): (770) 997–8052

4731

Business Information: Burlington Air Express, a subsidiary of Pittston Company, is a full service freight company headquartered in California. The Company deals in international air and ocean freight brokerage, logistics and custom clearance. Participating in both importing and exporting, the Company does business with large corporations such as Xerox, IBM, and Ford. As Controller, Mr. Fleury Da Rocha is in charge of all financial matters for Brazil, Mexico, and Chile. He oversees contract negotiations, budgets, and tax reporting for the Latin American operation of Burlington Air Express. Mr. Fleury Da Rocha is also fluent in Portuguese, Spanish, and English. **Career Steps:** Controller, Burlington Air Express (1994–Present); Internal Auditor, The Pittston Company (1992–1994); Senior Auditor, KPMG – Peat Marwick (1988–1992). **Associations & Accomplishments:** Certified Fraud Examiners; National Rifle Association; American Chamber of Commerce, Sao Paulo, Brazil; Certified Trade Specialist. **Education:** Metropolitan University Sao Paulo, B.A. (1988); C.P.A. (1990); Cambridge University (UK): Bachelor Degree in Accounting (1990), Proficiency in English Degree (1982). **Personal:** Married to Patricia in 1996. Mr. Fleury Da Rocha enjoys photography, scale modelling, and hunting.

Michael P. Foley

Vice President
Karl Schroff & Associates
3750 West Centry Boulevard
Inglewood, CA 90303–1106
(310) 673–5900
Fax: (310) 673–6969
EMAIL: See Below

4731

Business Information: Karl Schroff & Associates is an international freight forwarder and U.S. Customs House Broker, dealing in export/import shipping to and from any world–wide port or airport. They also have exclusive partners under contract to serve as liaison between entities. International in scope, Karl Schroff & Associates spans 60 countries. Joining the Firm as Vice President in 1990, Mr. Foley serves as the assistant to the President, in addition to directing the Divisions of North American Corporate Sales & Operations and Overseas Agency Activity. Internet users can reach him via: MikeF15404@aol.com **Career Steps:** Vice President, Karl Schroff & Associates (1990–Present); Regional Manager, U.S. Group Consolidators (1986–1990); Account Executive, Air Express International (1981–1986). **Associations & Accomplishments:** Minnesota World Trade Association; International Trade Association of Chicago; National Customs Brokers and Freight Forwarders Association of Los Angeles; Los Angeles Air Cargo Forwarders Association; Westchester/LAX Chamber of Commerce. **Education:** United States Air Force Academy (1979); IATA/FIATA Professional Air Cargo Certification (1982). **Personal:** Married to Susan in 1979. One child: Jonathan. Mr. Foley enjoys camping, sailing, golfing, and is an outdoorsman.

Manuel Gonzale Tapia

Board of Directors
Transportes Tramaca Cargo Limitada
Uribe 936
Antofagasta, Chile
(565) 520–0220
Fax: (565) 522–6203

4731

Business Information: Transportes Tramaca Cargo Limitada provides transportation of cargo and individuals across Chile via Company–owned trucks and busses. Focusing primarily on the mining industry, the Company was established in 1940, employs 1,583 people, and has an estimated annual revenue of $70 million. As a Member, Board of Directors, Mr. Gonzale Tapia is part owner of the Company and, utilizing his experience as an engineer, advises on strategic planning and technical issues. **Career Steps:** Transportes Tramaca Cargo Limitada: Board of Directors (1995–Present), Manager (1993–1995). **Associations & Accomplishments:** SKAL Club. **Education:** University of Chile, Engineer (1972). **Personal:** Married in 1973. Three children: Jose, Macarend, and Francisco. Mr. Gonzale Tapia enjoys reading and music.

Judith L. Haggin

Vice President of Government Compliance
George S. Bush & Company, Inc.
600 NW Front Avenue
Portland, OR 97209–3771
(503) 228–6501
Fax: (503) 294–0432

4731

Business Information: George S. Bush & Company, Inc. is an international customs broker and freight forwarder which sets up importing systems in–house and processes international orders. Primary focus is on the importation of lumber and agricultural products, as well as textiles and food products. As Vice President of Government Compliance, Ms. Haggin is responsible for work quality and corporate compliance with U.S. Customs. She also oversees integration training, set–up of in–house importing systems for companies, processing all international orders, and introducing importing strategies. She also oversees the Import Manager and Management Team Head. Concurrently, she serves as Director of Customer Development, responsible for developing processes and systems within clients' structure. **Career Steps:** George S. Bush & Company, Inc.: Vice President of Government Compliance (1991–Present), Director of Customer Development (1991–Present), Import Manager (1984–1991); Air Import Supervisor, Circle International (1983–1984); Import Specialist, J.T. Steeb & Co. (1978–1983). **Associations & Accomplishments:** World Trade Center (PTLD) – Educator on Staff – courses include NAFTA, Processing International Orders, Duty Drawback, Importing Strategies; CRCBA (Columbia River Customs Brokers & Forwarders Association: President (1996–1998), Import Chair (1992–1996). **Education:** Attended Portland State University (1977). **Personal:** Married to Larry in 1985. Three children: Christa and Taber Oglesby and Camille Haggin. Ms. Haggin enjoys Girl Scout activities, travel, and conducting lectures and seminars on behalf of NAFTA.

James R. Hall

Brokerage Director
Southland Brokerage, Inc.
P.O. Box 653
Lawrenceburg, IN 38464–0653
(615) 762–6509
Fax: (615) 762–7217

4731

Business Information: Southland Brokerage, Inc. is a transportation logistics and brokerage services firm. Acting as a third–party intermediary, Southland's services include inventory auditing, delivery routing, accounts receivable and billing, storing, and trafficking, as well as providing drivers and trucks. As Brokerage Director, James Hall is responsible for the management of the entire company, including overseeing all company employees, evaluating and developing customer and carrier contracts, and controlling Quality Assurance functions. He also represents the Company at trade association shows, formulates and develops budgets, assists individuals with customer service problems or complaints. Additionally, he provides the overall implementation and strategies for future development and service expansions. **Career Steps:** Director of Brokerage Operations, Southland Brokerage, Inc. (1991–Present); Brokerage Director, ABC Brokerage (1986–1991); Dispatch Supervisor, ABC Express. **Associations & Accomplishments:** Regional Vice President, Delta Nu Alpha Transportation Fraternity; Transportation Intermediaries Association. **Education:** University of North Alabama, B.S.N. in progress. **Personal:** Married to Cyndi in 1978. Two children: Kristopher and Nicole. Mr. Hall enjoys spending time with his children, golf, horseback riding, music, reading, and fishing.

Phil Hasson

Distribution and Logistics Manager
3 Com Corporation
5400 Bayfront Plaza
Santa Clara, CA 95052
(408) 764–7042
Fax: (408) 764–7021
E MAIL: See Below

4731

Business Information: 3 Com Corporation, established in 1979, manufactures quality network adapters used to connect computers to networks. The Company also offers products for small business, small site and individual user environments, inter–networking platforms, digital modems and adapters. With estimated annual revenue of $2.5 billion, the Company presently employs over 4,500 people worldwide. As Distribution and Logistics Manager, Mr. Hasson oversees the sales and distribution of products to markets in the United States, South America, and APR. Internet users can reach him via:

Phil_Hasson@3mail.3com.com. **Career Steps:** 3 Com Corporation: Distribution and Logistics Manager (1990–Present), Inventory Control Manager (1989–1990), Financial Analyst (1988–1989), Inventory Analyst (1985–1988). **Associations & Accomplishments:** Council of Logistics Management. **Education:** RCC/CSB, FCC Certificate (1982). **Personal:** Married to Elizabeth in 1986. Three children: Quinton, Valerie, and Lindsay. Mr. Hasson enjoys golf, photography, and the outdoors.

Alain C.W. Lau

Managing Director
Vinpac Lines (Canada), Inc.
8321 Willard Street
Burnaby, British Columbia
(604) 525–8082
Fax: (604) 525–8093
E MAIL: See Below

4731

Business Information: Vinpac Lines (Canada), Inc. is an international freight forwarder, air, ocean and warehousing firm. The Company is a subsidiary of Vincent Intetrans (Holdings) Ltd., a public listed company in Hong Kong. As Managing Director, Mr. Lau oversees and coordinates North & Central South America offices as well as agents in the Far East and Europe. His responsibilities include problem solving, marketing, budgetary concerns and strategic planning for expansion into new markets. **Career Steps:** Managing Director, Vinpac Lines (Canada), Inc. (1990–Present); Sinotrans – Shuahai, Peoples Republic of China: General Manager (1987–1990), General Manager – Overseas Development (1985–1987); Marketing Manager, Fritz International, Hong Kong (1983–1985). **Associations & Accomplishments:** Vancouver Cathay Lions Club; Pacific Rim Cargo Association; British Institute of Management; Charter Institute of Transport; Charter Institute of Supervisory Management, FIATA. **Education:** Hong Kong Polytechnic, D.M.S. **Personal:** Married to Andy Luk in 1976. One child: Sheung Lau. Mr. Lau enjoys studying art and furniture design, basketball and golf.

Brian W. Loy

District Manager
SurfAir
9414 Aero Space Drive
St. Louis, MO 63134–3826
(314) 428–8822
Fax: (314) 428–6222

4731

Business Information: SurfAir, a division of Winship Group, Inc., is a multi–service transportation company providing air–freight forwarding services. Mr. Loy joined Surfair in 1990 as District Operations Manager in Kansas City, Missouri, moving into his present position as District Manager of all Sales and Operations for the St. Louis facility in 1993. **Career Steps:** SurfAir: District Manager, St. Louis (1993–Present), District Operations Manager, Kansas City (1990–1993); Operations Manager, All American Delivery (1984–1990). **Associations & Accomplishments:** MENSA. **Education:** William Jewell, Music (1986). **Personal:** Married to Debra in 1986. Two children: Kevan and Alecia. Mr. Loy enjoys church and family activities, and composing music via his personal computer.

The Jackson Kearney Group

David G. Mannella

Vice President
The Jackson Kearney Group
P.O. Box 53255
New Orleans, LA 70153–3255
(504) 943–1835
Fax: (504) 942–4239

4731

Business Information: The Jackson Kearney Group is a diversified logistics services company, providing stevedoring, terminal operations, warehousing (dry and refrigerated), freight forwarding, customs house brokerage, and transportation services. A logistics and commodities executive working with some of the world's leading consumer commodities conglomerates for more than fourteen years, David Mannella was appointed as Vice President in 1991. Serving on the Company's Executive Committee, his primary responsibilities include development and growth strategies, implementing and maintaining TQM, contract negotiations, and P&L responsibility of JKG operating subsidiaries. **Career Steps:** Vice President, The Jackson Kearney Group (1991–Present); Procter & Gamble Company: Manager – Traffic and Port Operations, for The Folger Company (subsidiary of P&G) New Orleans, LA (1987–1991), Distribution Analyst – The Folger Company, Cincinnati, OH (1985–1987), Various Managerial Roles, Procter & Gamble Distributing Co. (1982–1985). **Associations & Accomplishments:** Council of Logistics Management; American Warehouse Association; International Association of Refrigerated Warehouses; Clemson University P.E.O.P.L.E. Advisory Group; Equipment Maintenance Council. **Education:** Clemson University, B.S. in Industrial Management, cum laude (1982) Tiger Letterman Association for Football, Beta Gamma Sigma, Who's Who in American Universities and Colleges; University of Cincinnati, Post–graduate courses in Business Administration; Professional Enhancement Courses: Quality Improvement, Effective Negotiations, Statistical Methods for Quality, Covey's Seven Habits of Highly Effective People, Team Building. **Personal:** Married to Ann Lee Hall in 1988. Two children: Lauren and Christopher. Mr. Mannella enjoys athletic activities, golf, and collecting antiques during his leisure time.

Mr. James R. Munson

Vice President of Business Development
Xonex Relocation
1599 Rock Mountain Industrial Drive
Stone Mountain, GA 30083
(404) 373–3328
Fax: Please mail or call

4731

Business Information: Xonex Relocation, a $33 million dollar company, is a corporate relocation company with offices in New Jersey, New York, Delaware, Georgia, Florida, and Texas. Mr. Munson is responsible for domestic and international sales. **Career Steps:** Vice President of Sales, Wansley International Relocations (1985–Present); President, Ransler Moving & Storage (1983–1985). **Associations & Accomplishments:** French–American Chamber; British Olympic Associations; Alliance Francaise d'Atlanta, Inc.; Confr□ Du Tasteduvine. **Education:** Memphis State University, Bachelors Degree (1976). **Personal:** Married to Elizabeth in 1986. Two children: Meredith and Eric.

Wayne G. Paul

Region Director
J.B. Hunt Dedicated Contract Services
3500 Parkway Lane, Suite 460
Norcross, GA 30092–2832
(770) 263–6983
Fax: (770) 263–8591
EMAIL: See Below

4731

Business Information: J.B. Hunt is a truck load carrier, logistics, and full–service transportation company with branches in the United States and subsidiaries in Mexico and Canada. As Region Director, Mr. Paul is responsible for delivery and set–up, route design, scheduling, and implementing operations from beginning to end. In addition, he oversees Company branches in Mexico, Canada, and international operations. Internet users can also reach him via: wgp2001@aol.com **Career Steps:** J.B. Hunt Dedicated Contract Services: Region Director (1994–Present), Director of Operations – Mexico (1993–1995); Vice President of Sales and Marketing, North American Van Lines – H.V.P. (1992–1993); Area Manager, Ryder Dedicated Logistics (1986–1992). **Associations & Accomplishments:** American Management Association; Council of Logistics Management; National Defense Transportation Association; Outstanding Young Men of America Award; Sales Marketing Executive Club. **Education:** Attending, Northwestern University – Kellogg Graduate School of Management, Executive Masters Program, Degree Candidate (June 1997); University of Alabama, B.S. in Transportation (1980). **Personal:** Married to Verlinda Farrar in 1982. One child: Daniel H.. Mr. Paul enjoys golf, photography, basketball, and travel.

Bill D. Price

Vice President of Safety
Oklahoma Tank Lines
4312 South Georgia Place
Oklahoma City, OK 73129
(405) 677–6633
Fax: (405) 672–0301

4731

Business Information: Oklahoma Tank Lines is an interstate carrier of refined petroleum products. Established in 1966, the Company presently employs 250 people. As Vice President of Safety, Mr. Price screens all applicants for driver and owner/operator positions. He teaches defensive driving courses to employees, investigates accidents, and oversees the safety operations at five terminals. Mr. Price is responsible for implementing all rules and regulations established by OSHA, DOT, Workman's Compensation, and Company policies. Other responsibilities include development of driver training programs, coordination of quarterly safety meetings, and public relations. **Career Steps:** Vice President of Safety, Oklahoma Tank Lines (1982–Present); Oklahoma Highway Patrol: Lieutenant, Supervisor, Trooper (1960–1982); Apprentice Helper, Norman Plumbing & Heating (1956–1960); Professional Driver, Masters Mayflower Trucking (1955–1956). **Associations & Accomplishments:** Associated Motor Carriers of Oklahoma; Board of Directors, Oklahoma Safety Council; Kansas Safety Council; Texas Safety Council; NTTC Safety Council. Awards: NTTC Merit Award, 11–15 Million Mile Class (1993); NTTC Merit Award, 6–8 Million Mile Class (1992); Advisory Member of Central Oklahoma Vocational–Technical School (1991). **Education:** South Oklahoma City Junior College, Associates degree (1960). **Personal:** Married to Joyce in 1958. Three children: Jeff, Shelli, and Terri. Mr. Price enjoys spending his off time with his entire family and his grandchildren.

Ted P. Roberts, CPA

Controller
TS Expediting Services, Inc.
P.O. Box 307
Perrysburg, OH 43552
(419) 837–2401
Fax: (419) 837–5535

4731

Business Information: DBA Tri–State Expedited Services, Inc. handles urgent freight or same day (overnight) freight for the United States and Canada. The Company contracts 600 different independently owned operators for freight transportation. As Controller, Mr. Roberts is responsible for all financial and accounting functions, including cash management. **Career Steps:** Controller, TS Expediting Services, Inc. (1992–Present); Vice President of Finance, Advantage Electric, Inc. (1984–1991); Assistant Controller, Hickory Farms of Ohio (1982–1984); Senior Accountant, Alexander Grant & Company (1976–1982). **Associations & Accomplishments:** American Institute of Certified Public Accountants; Ohio Society of Certified Public Accountants. **Education:** University of Toledo, B.B.A. (1976); Bowling Green State University. **Personal:** Married to Shelly in 1988. Five children: Nicholas, Jacob, Marc, Shawn, and Katie. Mr. Roberts enjoys boating, fishing, and golf.

J. Kent Rountree

Vice President of Sales and Operations
Oklahoma Southern Transportation
P.O. Box 687
Tahlequah, OK 74465–0687
(918) 458–0653
Fax: (918) 458–0655

4731

Business Information: Oklahoma Southern Transportation is a national contract motor carrier and freight brokerage. Based in Tahlequah, Oklahoma, OST specializes in the distribution of dry freight throughout 48 states. As Vice President of Sales and Operations, Mr. Rountree is responsible for the direction of sales, marketing, customer service, dispatch, maintenance, safety, and recruiting. Concurrently, he serves as a Reservist in the U.S. Army. **Career Steps:** Vice President of Sales and Operations, Oklahoma Southern Transportation (1992–Present); United States Army: Reservist (1992–Present), Active Duty (1987–1992). **Associations & Accomplishments:** Association of the United States Army; National Federation of Independent Businessmen; The Retired Officer Association; National Riflemen Association; Tahlequah Airport Advisory Board; Tahlequah Industrial Development Committee; Northeastern State University Alumni Association; Cub Scout Leader. **Education:** Northeastern State University, B.S. Management (1987); Commercial Rotor Wing Pilot License. **Personal:** Married to Ellen S. in 1982. Two children: Jared K. and Breanna L. Mr. Rountree enjoys coaching youth soccer, running and fishing.

Bob W. Sneed

Vice President of Sales
Comdata Corporation
1421 Champion Drive, Suite 101
Brentwood, TN 37027
(800) 638–9364
Fax: (800) 749–8171
E MAIL: See Below

4731

Business Information: Comdata Corporation is a subsidiary of Cerdian Corporation, an information service company specializing in transaction processing for the transportation, trucking, and gaming industries. Established in 1970, Comdata Corporation employs 1,800 people, and has an estimated annual revenue of $300 million. As Vice President of Sales, Mr. Sneed is responsible for national account sales organization. He also oversees all administrative functions, and handles strategic planning and all over–the–road services. Internet users can reach him via: BobSneed@aol.com. **Career Steps:** Vice President of Sales, Comdata Corporation (1991–Present); Vice President of sales, Cummins Cash and Information Systems (1986–1991). **Associations & Accomplishments:** American Management Association; National Restaurant Management Association. **Education:** Abilene

Christian, B.B.A. (1981). **Personal:** Married to Lynnette in 1980. Three children: Robby, Charla, and Matt. Mr. Sneed enjoys boating, horseback riding, and soccer.

Tim Stueck
Controller
Ruan Transport Company
601 Locust Street, Suite 1333
Des Moines, IA 50309–3751
(515) 245–2739
Fax: (515) 245–2780

4731

Business Information: Ruan Transport Company is a freight transportation and logistics company. It deals with companies from small privately–owned companies to the Fortune 500. As Controller, Mr. Stueck provides financial analysis, daily management of all financial issues, process engineering, and is a member of the Company's Strategic Planning Team. **Career Steps:** Ruan Transport Company: Controller (1993–Present), Managing Auditor (1992–1993); Supervising Auditor, Union Pacific (1989–1992). **Associations & Accomplishments:** Institute of Management Accountants; Certified Public Accountant (CPA); Certified Management Account (CMA). **Education:** University of Iowa: M.A. in Accounting (1989), B.B.A. in Accounting and Finance. **Personal:** Married to Tamara in 1991. Mr. Stueck enjoys weightlifting and golf.

Hank F. Verschoote
Regional Vice President
ABF Freight System, Inc.
151 Reverchon
Pointe Claire, Quebec H9P 1K1
(514) 636–1490
Fax: (514) 636–4611

4731

Business Information: ABF Freight System, Inc. is the fourth largest commercial, less–than–truckload trucking company in the world. The Company, a division of AR Best Corporation headquartered in Fort Smith, Arkansas, operates throughout North America and has international operations in Europe, South America, and the Far East. Established in 1935, the Company presently employs over 12,000 people and estimates annual revenue in excess of $1.2 billion. As Regional Vice President, Mr. Verschoote is responsible for the development of national accounts in Canada. Other responsibilities include the administration of his staff and reporting on staff and regional progress to the Vice President of National Sales at Corporate Headquarters in Arkansas. **Career Steps:** ABF Freight System, Inc.: Regional Vice President (1996–Present), Senior Director of National Sales (1982–1996), Director of National Accounts (1973–1982). **Associations & Accomplishments:** Canadian Industrial Transportation League; Traffic Club of Montreal, Inc. **Education:** Loyola University, B.A (1958); Graham's Business College. **Personal:** Married to Carol in 1964. Two children: Carolyn and Mark. Mr. Verschoote enjoys king, art, and golf.

Allison Dean Wright
Executive Director
South Carolina Insurance News Service
1136 Washington Street, Suite 508
Columbia, SC 29201
(803) 252–3455
Fax: (803) 779–0189
EMAIL: See Below

4731

Business Information: South Carolina Insurance News Service provides insurance information to the media and consumers in South Carolina. Operated by a Board of Directors who are members of major insurance companies in the state, the Insurance News Service was established in 1977, employs two people, and has an estimated annual budget of $200 K. As Executive Director, Ms. Wright oversees media relations, tracks legislation, and appears on television shows and participates in radio talk shows. Additional duties include answering reporters' questions, preparation of video news reports, handling the South Carolina Arson Hotline, and works closely with the SC Department of Insurance. Internet users can reach her via: Scins@scsn.net. **Career Steps:** Executive Director, South Carolina Insurance News Service (1996–Present); Director, Charleston Metro Chamber of Commerce (1993–1995); Personnel Specialist/Recruiter, Interim Healthcare (1990–1993); Placement Counselor, Human Resources, Inc. (1988–1990). **Associations & Accomplishments:** Planning Board, Trident United Way; Board, Parents Empowered to Save Teens; The Citadel M.B.A. Association; Alpha Omicron Pi Alumnae; Founder of a campaign against running red lights in Charleston, South Carolina, that has sparked a national campaign in 54 cities. **Education:** The Citadel,

M.B.A. (1993); Middle Tennessee State University, B.B.A. (1986). **Personal:** Married to Patrick in 1988. Ms. Wright enjoys photography, horseback riding, flying and travel.

David H. Baggs
Assistant Vice President of Corporate Strategy
CSX Corporation
One James Center, Suite 1800
Richmond, VA 23219–4037
(804) 782–1508
Fax: (804) 782–1409

4789

Business Information: CSX Corporation is a Fortune 500 transportation company providing rail, intermodal, ocean shipping, barging, trucking, and contract logistics services worldwide. With an extensive background in financial management, Mr. Baggs joined CSX's rail subsidiary in 1985 as an Economic Analyst, and was named Manager of Economic Analysis the following year. After a two–year assignment as Assistant Director of Business Planning, he joined the parent Company as Director of Corporate Strategy. In this capacity, Mr. Baggs helped lead an effort to realign management's interests with those of its shareholders. This was accomplished by reorienting the planning process and incentive compensation programs to emphasize Economic Value Added, and by increasing senior management ownership through a leveraged stock program. Mr. Baggs was named Assistant Vice President of Corporate Strategy in August of 1994 and currently advises senior management on a broad spectrum of issues ranging from mergers and acquisitions to emerging market and technological opportunities. **Career Steps:** CSX Corporation: Assistant Vice President of Corporate Strategy (1994–Present), Director of Corporate Strategy (1990–1994), Assistant Director of Business Planning (1988–1990), Manager of Economic Analysis (1986–1988); Economic Analyst (1985–1986). **Education:** The College of William and Mary, M.B.A. (1985); University of Arizona, B.B.A. (1981). **Personal:** Married to Linda Escalera in 1985. Two children: Nathan Alexander and Joshua Christopher. Mr. Baggs enjoys tennis, golf, racquetball, backgammon, and art collecting.

Keith Burnett
Director of Invoicing and Collections
Yellow Freight System
10990 Roe Avenue
Overland Park, KS 66211–1213
(913) 344–3658
Fax: (913) 344–4711

4789

Business Information: Yellow Freight System, established in 1948 in Overland Park, Kansas, is a transportation motor carrier serving the U.S. nationwide, as well as international services within Europe, the Pacific Rim, Mexico, and Canada. Starting with the Company as a clerk in November 1982, Mr. Burnett currently serves as Director of Invoicing and Collections. He is responsible for the direction of all invoicing and collection activities. **Career Steps:** Yellow Freight System: Director of Invoicing and Collections (1995–Present), Manager of Imaging Technologies (1993–1995), Manager of Customer Satisfaction (1990–1993). **Associations & Accomplishments:** Association of Information and Image Management; National Accounting and Finance Council of American Trucking Association; Published in trade journals and interviewed for newsletters. **Education:** Rockhurst College, M.B.A. (1990); William Jewell College, B.A. in History (1979). **Personal:** Married to Kimberly in 1982. Three children: Ian, Kyle, and Crosby. Mr. Burnett enjoys gardening, camping, and history.

Jeff Clark

District Manager
Celadon Jacky Maeder
2801 Fortune Circle East Drive, Suite B
Indianapolis, IN 46241
(317) 247–8100
Fax: (317) 248–3054

4789

Business Information: Celadon Jacky Maeder is an international transportation and logistics company consisting of 25 terminals serving the U.S., Canada, and Mexico. Aggressive plans include expanding into South America and Africa. Established in 1991, Celadon Jacky Maeder Indianapolis reports annual revenue of $11 million and currently employs 13 people. As District Manager, Mr. Clark is responsible for the management of export & import operations and sales & development of more than 300 accounts throughout Indiana, Kentucky, and Southern Ohio. **Career Steps:** District Manager, Celadon Jacky Maeder (1991–Present); District Manager, In-

tertrans Corporation (1983–1991); Air Export Manager, Circle International (1977–1983). **Associations & Accomplishments:** World Trade Club of Indiana; World Trade Club of North Eastern Indiana; Indiana CLM; Published in Indianapolis Business Journal and Indiana Industrial Journal. **Education:** Indiana – Purdue University (1977); IATA; FIATA. **Personal:** Married to Bethany in 1984. Two children: Meghan and Matthew. Mr. Clark enjoys travel, swimming and outdoor activities.

Tom Culbertson
Vice President
Thomson Terminals LTD
55 City View Dr.
Rexdale, Ontario M9W 5A5
(416) 442–2314
Fax: (416) 442–2365

4789

Business Information: Thomson Terminals LTD, is a wholly–owned Canadian Group of companies. A major provider of distribution, warehousing, and logistics management in the Ontario, Quebec and Northeast United States. Employing over 200 people involved with operations based in Ontario. **Career Steps:** Manager, Ault Transportation Services (1990–Present); Operations Manager, Servall International (1988–1989). **Associations & Accomplishments:** Ontario Trucking Association; Toronto Trucking Association; Private Motor Truck Council of Canada. **Education:** Attended Humber College (1982) and York University, Finance Programs. **Personal:** Married to Ann in 1987. Two children: Tyler and T.J. Mr. Culbertson enjoys golf.

Michael F. Davidson
Director of Safety and Maintenance
Giroux Brothers Transportation
40 Ballard Street
Worcester, MA 01607
(800) 899–4523
Fax: (508) 753–8527

4789

Business Information: Giroux Brothers Transportation is a transportation Company comprised of two divisions, the first of which is the largest distributor of carpets in the Northeast, while the second deals in the delivery of dry bulk plastic. As Director of Safety and Maintenance, Mr. Davidson handles the safety programs for both companies, 50 drivers, and a total of 125 employees. He assures that all programs comply with Department of Transportation and OSHA regulations. Additionally, he is in charge of all maintenance and purchasing. **Career Steps:** Director of Safety and Maintenance, Giroux Brothers Transportation (1988–Present); Operations Manager, Overnite Transportation Company (1978–1988). **Associations & Accomplishments:** National Safety Council. **Education:** Attended, Assumption College (1978). **Personal:** Married to Teresa in 1990. One child: Brittney Paige. Mr. Davidson enjoys fishing, reading, and gardening.

David B. Edmonds

Vice President of Corporate Sales
Caliber System, Inc.
3560 West Market Street, PO Box 5459
Akron, OH 44334–0459
(330) 665–8847
Fax: (330) 665–8853

4789

Business Information: Caliber System, Inc. is a major holding company, owning and operating transportation and logistics strategic management companies. Entities include: RPS (Roadway Package System); Caliber Logistics; Roberts Express; and Viking Freight Systems. International in scope, Caliber System has presence in over 1,500 global offices. Serving in managerial roles for the RPS division since 1986, David Edmonds was promoted and transferred to serve as Caliber System's Vice President of Corporate Sales in 1994. He has full executive oversight for all corporate sales activity corporate–wide, as well as serves as an officer involved in all corporate strategies and development. **Career Steps:** Vice President of Corporate Sales, Caliber System, Inc. (1994–Present); RPS – A Caliber Company: Director of National Sales (1993–1994), Manager of National Sales (1990–1993), Retail Specialist (1986–1989). **Associations & Accomplishments:** Council of Logistics Management; American Management Association. **Education:** Kent State University, B.B.A. (1980). **Personal:** Married to Lynn in 1985. Mr. Edmonds enjoys golf, motorcycles, and American history.

Oswaldo Sartori Filho

Financial Director
Luxor Transport Ltda
R. Lauro Muller 116–S1.1703
Rio de Janeiro, Brazil 22290–160
5521–542–1850
Fax: 5521–571–9927
EMAIL: See Below

4789

Business Information: Luxor Transportes is one of the most important brazilian transport companies. As Financial Director, Mr. Filho is responsible for all financial aspects of operations including general finances, accounting, taxes, budgeting, costs, and strategic planning. Internet users can reach him via: sartori@montreal.com.br. **Career Steps:** Financial Director: Luxor Transport Ltda (1995–Present); Supergasbras (1995); Mesbla S/A (1994). **Associations & Accomplishments:** Instituto Brasileiro De Executivos Financeiros. **Education:** Coppead/UFRJ, POS Graduation (1989); IBMEC, Financial M.B.A. **Personal:** One child: Gabriela Jullanelly. Mr. Filho enjoys chess, music, and diving.

Stanley H. Hall

Managing Partner
American Service Association/Airport Parking Mgmt
360 Grand Avenue, Suite 302
Oakland, CA 94610
(510) 832–1057
Fax: (510) 632–7608

4789

Business Information: American Service Association/Airport Parking Management is a government support and transportation services, providing reports development for parking citations in the City, servicing buses and charters for airport services, as well as serving private companies and government agencies. Estabishing American Service Association/Airport Parking Management in 1991, Mr. Hall serves as its Owner and Managing Partner. He is responsible for all management and operations, including initiating reports for the City and making all arrangements for services. Concurrent with his private business, he serves as City Manager of the City of Hollister, responsible for the administration of day–to–day business affairs of the city, initiating policy considerations, and implementing policy directives. **Career Steps:** Managing Partner, American Service Association/Airport Parking Management (1991–Present); City Manager, City of East Palo Alto (1987–1991); Special Assistant and Director of Government Affairs, Port of Oakland (1980–1987). **Associations & Accomplishments:** International City Managers Association; American Society of Public Administrators; Kappa Alpha Psi Fraternity; 100 Black Men of the Bay Area; National Forum for Black Public Administration; California City Managers Foundation. **Education:** Golden Gate University, M.P.A. (1972); San Francisco State University, B.A. **Personal:** Mr. Hall enjoys golf, racketball, tennis, writing, and poetry.

Cynthia Levin

Director of Information and Processing Improvement
Burlington Northern Santa Fe
1700 E. Golf Rd., 3rd Floor
Schaumburg, IL 60173–5804
(847) 995–2051
Fax: (847) 995–2929
EMAIL: See Below

4789

Business Information: Burlington Northern Santa Fe is a national provider of intermodal transporation of freight. As Director of Information and Processing Improvement, Mrs. Levin is responsible for the process improvement and introduction of new technologies to intermodal employees and the Company's customers. She is also involved with the strategic focus for intermodal business groups, increasing productivity, and reducing costs. Internet users can also reach her via: CLEVIN3951@AOL.COM **Career Steps:** Director of Information and Processing Improvement, Burlington Northern Santa Fe (1994–Present); Altschuler, Melvoin and Glasser: Practice Director – Software Improvement Implementations (1993–1994), Practice Director – Distribution (1991–1992). **Associations & Accomplishments:** School Board Member, Congregation B'nai Tikvah; Volunteer work within local area; Published articles on marketing. **Education:** Loyola University, M.B.A. (1984). **Personal:** Married to Alan in 1978. Two children: Jessica and Alex. Mrs. Levin enjoys camping, reading, and skiing.

Mark Loranger

President
Takeout Taxi
5301 Beethoven St., Suite 135
Los Angeles, CA 90066–7061
(310) 301–7074
Fax: (310) 301–7014

4789

Business Information: Takeout Taxi is a multiple restaurant marketing and delivery service franchise. Providing a unique customer service, Takeout Taxi offers the pickup and delivery of restaurant food (the customer's choice) to the customer's home or place of business. Founding the Los Angeles franchise in 1992, Mr. Loranger serves as President, Chief Executive Officer, and Chairman of the Board. He is responsible for all aspects of operations, focusing on marketing and financial management. **Career Steps:** President, Takeout Taxi (1992–Present); IBM: Advisory Marketing Representative (1986–1992), Engineer (1983–1986) **Associations & Accomplishments:** Institute of Electrical and Electronics Engineers (IEEE); Volunteer, KCRW (National Public Radio's Santa Monica, CA affiliate) **Education:** George Washington University, M.B.A. (1991); University of California – Davis, Electrical Engineering **Personal:** Married to Katie Lichtig in 1986. Mr. Loranger enjoys sailing, running, computers and skiing.

Michael H. Mack

Director of Operations
UPS Worldwide Logistics
2 Concourse Parkway, Suite 850
Atlanta, GA 30328–5588
(404) 828–4768
Fax: (404) 828–4505

4789

Business Information: A subsidiary of United Parcel Service, UPS Worldwide Logistics is an international third–party warehousing and transportation company. Established in 1990, UPS Worldwide Logistics currently employs 375 people and has an estimated annual revenue of $500 million. As Director of Operations, Mr. Mack is responsible for all aspects of domestic operations and the implementation of new customers. **Career Steps:** UPS Worldwide Logistics: Director of Operations (1995–Present), Operations Manager (1994–1995), Senior Project Manager (1992–1993); Industrial Engineering Manager, United Parcel Service (1988–1991). **Associations & Accomplishments:** International Association of Industrial Engineers; Council of Logistics Management. **Education:** David Lipscomp University, B.A. in Sociology (1977); LaSalle University, J.D. (expected 1996). **Personal:** Married to Marilyn in 1973. Two children: Christy and Kimberly. Mr. Mack enjoys golf, self–improvement, his family, and being an energetic leader.

Len Peterson

President
Copy Carriers
19110 South Vermont Avenue
Gardena, CA 90248–4413
(310) 324–9922
Fax: (310) 324–3502

4789

Business Information: Copy Carriers is an electronics transportation carrier, specializing in the delivery of electronic copiers and high–level electronic products. Copy Carriers, Inc. covers the regional area of California, Arizona, and Nevada. Founding the Company in 1985 and serving as President since 1992, Mr. Peterson is responsible for all aspects of Company operations, in addition to the administrative operations for associates and a support staff of 32. **Career Steps:** Copy Carriers Inc.: President (1992–Present), Owner (1985–1992); General Manager, Truck Air Transfer (1984–1985); General Manager, Pams Delivery Inc. (1980–1984). **Personal:** Married to Renee in 1995. One child: Ransom Vanoy Felts. Mr. Peterson enjoys karate (4th degree black belt), golf, and water skiing.

Emilio Rodriguez Luciano

Comptroller
Island Wide Express
A St., Bldg 9, Location 5 Dr. Mario Julia Industrial Pk
San Juan, Puerto Rico 00920
(809) 273–0715
Fax: (809) 273–6684

4789

Business Information: Island Wide Express, a subsidiary of A. Sus Ordenes, Inc., is a provider of island wide package delivery and transportation services. Established 25 years ago, Island Wide Express reports annual revenue of $5 million and currently employs 150 people. As Comptroller, Mr. Rodriguez Luciano is responsible for all aspects of Company financial matters, including accounting and budgeting. He also serves as Manager of Information Systems, overseeing all computer operations. **Career Steps:** Comptroller, Island Wide Express (1987–Present); Senior Auditor, Rosaly, Perez, Villarini, C.P.A. (1982–1987); Assistant Treasury, Municipio de Ponce (1976–1982). **Associations & Accomplishments:** Asociacion Profesional de Contadores. **Education:** Universidad Catolica de Puerto Rico, B.B.A. in Management and Biology (1986). **Personal:** Married to Alma Rosa Lopez in 1977. Three children: Emilio, Eduardo, and Marycelis. Mr. Rodriguez Luciano enjoys computer teaching.

Scott Shearer

President
Total Transportation Consultants, Inc.
191 Woodport Rd., Suite 204D
Sparta, NJ 07871–1122
(201) 729–0699
Fax: (201) 729–8850

4789

Business Information: Total Transportation Consultants, Inc. (TTC) provides transportation logistics services for all types of companies. These services include pre–audit and freight payment, carrier negotiations and preparation of freight routing guides. TTC works on the basis of "shared savings" and charges its clients no fees or retainers. Mr. Shearer founded TCC in 1990. He is responsible for directing a 10 person sales force, as well as overseeing recruitment of new sales personnel and maintaining his own accounts. Concurrent with his position at TTC, he serves as Vice President of Sales for CRST Logistics, arranging for the movement of any type of freight via truck, air, or rail. **Career Steps:** President, Total Transportation Consultants, Inc. (1990–Present); Area Sales Manager, Roadway Express (1978–1988). **Associations & Accomplishments:** Transportation Intermediaries Association; Presidents Ring of Honor, Roadway Express (1987). **Education:** University of Pennsylvania, B.A. (1974). **Personal:** Married to Alicia in 1994. Three children: Jessica, Jaclynn, and Rebecca. Mr. Shearer enjoys travel, golf, tennis, and skiing.

Steven A. Stumpo

Price Manager – Northeast Region
CSX Intermodal
200 International Circle
Hunt Valley, MD 21030
(410) 584–0100
Fax: (800) 848–9301

4789

Business Information: CSX Intermodal is a national train and trucking company, providing door–to–door shipping services of low–priced, finished goods. CSX headquarters is scheduled to be relocated to Jacksonville, Florida in the very near future. Established in 1988, CSX Intermodal reports annual revenue of $1 billion and currently employs 2,000 people. As Price Manager – Northeast Region, Mr. Stumpo is responsible for constructing, negotiating and regulating rates for transportation from the origins of Maine to Portsmouth, Virginia. **Career Steps:** CSX Intermodal: Price Manager – Northeast Region (1994–Present); Pricing Supervisor (1993–1994), Pricing Coordinator (1992–1993), Operations Supervisor (1992). **Associations & Accomplishments:** CSXI Company Chairperson, United Way, Baltimore Campaign; Toastmasters – International; Baltimore Traffic Club; Philadelphia Traffic Club. **Education:** Pennsylvania State University, B.S. in Business (1990). **Personal:** Mr. Stumpo enjoys organizing parties and events, skiing, golf, water skiing, and mountain biking.

Timothy J. Watson

President and Chief Executive Officer
WTSN Enterprises, Inc.
39111 Center Ridge Road
North Ridgeville, OH 44039
(216) 327–5705
Fax: (216) 327–9404

4789

Business Information: WTSN Enterprises, Inc. is a family–owned company consisting of 4 divisions: Chapin Trucking Line, Inc., T&T Equipment, Inc., T&T Trucking, Inc., and T&T Properties, Inc., providing local–haul trucking, the lease of tractors, trailers, and warehouse facilities for businesses that distribute and assemble products. Established in 1936, WTSN Enterprises, Inc. currently employs 25 people. A third–generation President and Chief Executive Officer, Mr. Watson is responsible for the oversight of all activities, as well as strategic planning for the Company's future growth. **Career**

Steps: WTSN Enterprises, Inc.: President and Chief Executive Officer (1994–Present), Vice President, Operations, Dispatcher, Driver, Yard Help. **Associations & Accomplishments:** COSE – a small local business association; Lorain County Chamber of Commerce; Chairman, Businessman's Round Table Group of Lorain County (Junto); Akron Businessman's Round Table Group. **Education:** Baldwin Wallace College: B.A. (1971), Strategic Planning Course (1995), Managing Your Vision: The Perils of Leading a High–Growth Company (1995), How to Win in Sales (1995), Power Keys to Power Selling (1995), Financial Keys to Growth (1995), Success is a Team Effort (1995). **Personal:** Married to Jennifer in 1994. Two children: Timothy II and Jason. Mr. Watson enjoys auto dirt racing and reading.

4800 Communications

4812 Radiotelephone communications
4813 Telephone communications, exc. radio
4822 Telegraph and other communications
4832 Radio broadcasting stations
4833 Television broadcasting stations
4841 Cable and other pay TV services
4899 Communications services, NEC

Ethel M. Arguello

Chief Financial Officer/Chief Information Officer
AT&T of Puerto Rico, Inc./AT&T of the Virgin Islands
250 Munoz Rivera 10th Floor
Hato Rey, Puerto Rico 00902
(809) 729–2770
Fax: (809) 729–2744
EMAIL: earguello

4811

Business Information: AT&T of Puerto Rico, Inc. is a diversified telecommunications company providing global voice, data and video conferencing services and related products. They are well known for their long distance, residential and business communication services and equipment. As of August 1995, the company presently employs approximately 4,000 people throughout the CALA region. Including a couple of factories in Mexico and some joint ventures in other South American countries the total reaches over 10,000. Specific to Puerto Rico and Virgin Islands there are approximately 550 employees. An executive member of the AT&T Corporation, Ethel M. Arguello started with Pacific Telephone in 1970, where she held several supervisory jobs. Transferred to AT&T in 1982, she has had many positions in the various AT&T subsidiaries and Divisions in different States and countries. These changes have helped her increase her domestic and international experiences in the areas of communications, financials, systems and enhanced her management knowledge and skills. Current duties as Chief Financial Officer and Chief Information Officer of AT&T Puerto Rico and Virgin Islands involve ensuring integrity of financial results, compliance with GAAP and any other local financial, fiscal or legal requirements. The development and implementation of new systems platforms, the maintenance of financial and marketing applications, the network expansions and enhancements, the end user support and computer operations. The managing and oversight of 55 employees performing these functions. Other duties as an Executive Vice President includes the reviewing of corporate strategies for sound economic value. **Career Steps:** Chief Financial Officer and Chief Information Officer, AT&T of Puerto Rico and Virgin Islands (1995–Present); President/Founder, AT&T of Nicaragua, S.A. (1991–1995); Regional Controller, AT&T – American Region (1988–1991). **Education:** San Francisco City College, B.S. in Management (1980); University of Central Florida, courses taken toward M.B.A. in Finance & Accounting. **Personal:** Married to Juan in 1970. Three children: Carolina, Jonny and Jennifer. Ms. Arguello enjoys singing, tennis, movies, and swimming.

Marilyn Mcauslan

General Manager
Bell Operator Service Canada
100 Dundas Street, Floor 4A
London, Ontario N6A 4L6
(519) 663–6343
Fax: (519) 439–7814

4811

Business Information: Bell Operator Canada Service develops and operates logistics systems for Bell Canada telecommunications. As General Manager, Ms. Mcauslan is responsible for the operation, management, and administration for her region. **Career Steps:** General Manager, Bell Operator Canada Service (Present). **Personal:** Married to Ken. Three children: Sierra Dawn, Nevada Dawn, and Cheyenne Dawn. Ms. Mcauslan enjoys working and spending time with her family.

James W. Akerhielm

Regional Vice President/Southeast
Bell Atlantic Nynex Mobile
80 International Drive, Suite 500
Greenville, SC 29615–1811
(864) 987–2302
Fax: (864) 676–0042

4812

Business Information: Bell Atlantic Nynex Mobile is a wireless communications provider. In the Southeastern United States, Bell Atlantic Nynex Mobile provides wireless services in Virginia, North Carolina, South Carolina, and Georgia. As Regional Vice President/Southeast, Mr. Akerhielm is responsible for increasing the customer base and acquiring other properties to expand his geographic region. It is his responsibility to make sure that the services offered are of the highest quality for the most economical price. Mr. Akerhielm's duties include extensive public relations, marketing of existing services, and general oversight of the Greenville office. **Career Steps:** Regional Vice President/Southeast, Bell Atlantic Nynex Mobile (1995–Present); Bell Atlantic: Executive Director, Network Planning (1994–1995), Director–Network (1993–1994). **Associations & Accomplishments:** Greenville, South Carolina 300, for Greenville Chamber of Commerce; Mr. Akerhielm has been published in the Greenville, South Carolina newspapers and has also appeared on WSPA TV Channel 7, the local CBS affiliate. **Education:** University of Pennsylvania, Executive Masters of Science in Engineering (1994); Lafayette College, B.S. in Mechanical Engineering (1986). **Personal:** Married to Karen in 1991. Mr. Akerhielm enjoys jogging, "Over 30" basketball, the beach, and his wife.

Thomas J. Aprahamian

Controller
Metrocall, Inc.
6910 Richmond Highway
Alexandria, VA 22306
(703) 660–6677 Ext: 5110
Fax: (703) 768–3958

4812

Business Information: Metrocall, Inc., ranked the 8th largest in the U.S., is a paging service provider, providing service and products to 945,000 customers nationally from 36 sales offices. A Certified Public Accountant, Mr. Aprahamian joined Metrocall, Inc. as Controller in 1994. He is responsible for all aspects of financing and accounting for the Company. **Career Steps:** Controller, Metrocall, Inc. (1994–Present); Audit Senior, Arthur Andersen, LLP (1990–1994). **Associations & Accomplishments:** Certified Public Accountant; Treasurer, Pi Kappa Phi (1988–1989); Homeowner Association. **Education:** James Madison University, B.B.A. (1990). **Personal:** Married to Jennifer in 1990. One child: Tyler. Mr. Aprahamian enjoys softball and baseball.

Dennis Arroyo Audiffred

Assistant Manager
Celulares y Beepers Telefonica
Calle Cinco D–4 URB Buso
Humacao, Puerto Rico 00791
(787) 863–2599
Fax: (787) 860–0264

4812

Business Information: Celulares y Beepers Telefonica has provided all communication services to Puerto Rico since 1915. The Company is one of the largest and most technologically advanced communications companies in the world. As Assistant Manager, Mr. Arroyo Audiffred is in charge of two islands and all the marketing, sales, and purchasing for his wireless communications division. **Career Steps:** Assistant Manager, Celulares y Beepers Telefonica (1995–Present); Puerto Rico Telephone Company: Assistant Manager (1995), Supervisor, Customer Service (1988–1995), Supervisor (1981–1988); Departmento de Instruccion Publica, Teacher, Social Studies (1979–1981); Latin American Community Center, Wilmington, Deleware, Social worker (1978–1979); Delegate, Union Independiente de Empeados Telefonicos (1982–1987). **Associations & Accomplishments:** Club Artes; Instituto de Culture Puertorrigueno; Centro Cultural (1987–1990); Ana Roque Humaca. **Education:** Universidad Turabo, M.B.A. (1996). **Personal:** Married to Waleska Rivera in 1990. Three children: Desiree, Denisse, and Dennis Omar. Mr. Arroyo Audiffred enjoys fishing, gardening, and reading.

Oscar O. Bakir

President
SISTECO, Ltda.
P.O. Box 1455
Cochabamba, Bolivia
59–142–85500
Fax: 59–142–85100
EMail: See Below

4812

Business Information: SISTECO, Ltda. is a telecommunications company that specializes in the integration and resale of communication, data processing, and industrial control systems. The Company sells, installs, services the equipment, and trains people in its use. SISTECO does business with large companies, including banks, hospitals, airports, government offices, etc. The Company works in conjunction with Northern Telecom, and together they service both the public and private sectors with over 50 million telecommunication lines. Currently, SISTECO, in conjunction with Packard Bell, has three retail store in Bolivia and is working on a fourth. Headquartered in La Paz, the Company is the largest of its kind in Bolivia. As President, Mr. Bakir handles all Company operations, including finances, sales and marketing, public relations, and strategic planning. He has two partners in the business and additionally serves as Chairman of the Board. Internet users can reach him via: GER@DICYT.NRC.E-DU.BO. **Career Steps:** SISTECO, Ltda.: President (1991–Present), Vice President (1989–1991), Regional Manager of Cochabamba Branch (1983–1989). **Associations & Accomplishments:** Cochabamba Chamber of Commerce: Director, Vice President, President; Federation of Private Entrepreneurs of Cochabamba: Director, Vice President, President; Director of Educational Anti–Drug and Social Rehabilitation System (SEAMOS); Director, Development Corporation of Cochabamba. **Education:** Universidad Mayor de San Andres, Engineer (1979). **Personal:** Married to Veronica Rojas in 1978. Four children: Alejandro, Monica, Isabel, and Jimena. Mr. Bakir enjoys reading, music, and sports.

Eduardo Barreto

Vice President and General Manager
MTI
Avenue Nogal T–1 Lomas Verdes
Bayamon, Puerto Rico 00956
(809) 780–7450
Fax: (809) 780–7701
EMAIL: See Below

4812

Business Information: MTI provides cellular telecommunications service for the Puerto Rico Telephone Company, paging systems, automobile security systems, & electromechanic services, and the new division of marketing data information for pharmaceutical fields. Working in various sales and technical management roles for MTI since 1984, Eduardo Barreto was appointed to his current position in May of 1994. As Vice President and General Manager, he is responsible for operations, budgeting, and coordinating all marketing efforts. Internet users can reach him via: MTI@caribe.com. **Career Steps:** MTI: Vice President and General Manager (1994–Present), Sales Manager (1991–1994), Technician and Sales (1984–1991). **Associations & Accomplishments:** Puerto Rico Chamber of Commerce. **Education:** University Politecnica de Puerto Rico, Engineering degree in progress. **Personal:** Married to Vanessa Nadal in 1993. One child: Eduardo Antonio. Mr. Barreto enjoys boating and week–ends.

Jose Ignacio Bolivar

Chief Accountant
Cellular One
P.O. Box 192830
San Juan, Puerto Rico 00919–2830
(787) 397–5007
Fax: (787) 397–5121

4812

Business Information: Cellular One, offering cellular and paging systems to Puerto Rico and the Virgin Islands, is a telephone reseller and provider of monthly access and airtime service to the general public. Established in 1988, the Puerto Rico division employs 600 people. As Chief Accountant, Mr. Bolivar is in charge of all financial reporting, including SEC. He also oversees all purchasing systems and monitors the accounting cycle. **Career Steps:** Chief Accountant, Cellular One (1994–Present); Senior Auditor, Price Waterhouse (1987–1992). **Associations & Accomplishments:** American Institute of Certified Public Accountants; Colegio de Contadores Publicos Autorizados de Puerto Rico. **Education:** Bentley College: Associates in Management, Bachelors in Accounting (1987). **Personal:** Married to Georgina Vega in 1993. Mr. Bolivar enjoys going to the beach and spending time at home with his wife.

Wayne Bradley
General Manager
Palmer Wireless d.b.a. Cellular One
14680 South Taimiami Trail
Ft. Myers, FL 33912
(941) 433–2355
Fax: (941) 433–8130

4812

Business Information: Palmer Wireless d.b.a. Cellular One is a telephone reseller and provider of monthly access and airtime service to the general public. As General Manager, Mr. Bradley is responsible for retail/corporate sales, engineering, installation and service, credit/collections, office administration, site selection, and customer relations. **Career Steps:** General Manager, Palmer Wireless dba Cellular One (1995–Present); Vice President of Marketing, Pacific Telecom Cellular (1993–1995); General Manager of Texas, Nextel, Inc. (1990–1993); General Manager of South East Florida, McCaw Cellular, Inc. (1984–1990). **Associations & Accomplishments:** Sigma Chi; U.S. Marine Corps (1964–1966); U.S. Coast Guard (1966–1969); Chamber of Commerce, Lee County; Florida Board of County Communications award for outstanding assistance in the disaster response to Hurricane Opal, (October, 1995). **Education:** Texas Christian University, B.S. (1964). **Personal:** Married to Barbara in 1980. Mr. Bradley enjoys watching sports, running, swimming, and dog breeding.

Cheryl P. Carl
Vice President of Operations and Director
Cityscape Corporation
565 Taxter Road
Elmsford, NY 10523–2300
(914) 592–6677
Fax: (914) 592–6070

4812

Business Information: Cityscape Corporation As Vice President of Operations and Director, Ms. Carl **Career Steps:** Vice President of Operations and Director, Cityscape Corporation (1993–Present); Executive Vice President and Director, Astrum Funding Corporation (1983–1993); Vice President, Gramatan Home Investment (1978–1980). **Education:** Adelphi University, B.A. (1974). **Personal:** Ms. Carl enjoys spending time with her family.

Sheri L. Carl
Retail Sales Manager
360 Communications
5425 Jonestown Road, P.O. Box 6840
Harrisburg, PA 17112–0840
(717) 545–3300
Fax: (717) 540–1838

4812

Business Information: Formerly known as Sprint Cellular, 360 Communications provides cellular phone and pager sales and service. As Retail Sales Manager, Miss Carl manages all operations and staff in five retail cellular stores. **Career Steps:** 360 Communications: Retail Sales Manager (1994–Present), Sales Representative (1992–1994); Front Office Manager, Holiday Inn (1991–1992). **Associations & Accomplishments:** Lebanon Valley Chamber of Commerce. **Education:** WMS Valley High School, Diploma (1985). **Personal:** Miss Carl enjoys all sports.

Ronald R. Carney
Vice President of Advanced Products Department – CTO
AirNet Communications Corporation
100 Rialto Place, Suite 300
Melbourne, FL 32901–3074
(407) 676–6703
Fax: (407) 953–6607
EMAIL: See Below

4812

Business Information: AirNet Communications Corporation is a provider of wireless communication for infrastructures. Co–founding AirNet Communications Corporation in January, 1994, Mr. Carney serves as Vice President of Advanced Products Department and Chief Technical Officer. He is responsible for all aspects of advanced products, including administration, strategic planning, and the design and development of new product technology. Internet users can also reach him via: RCARNEY@AIRCOM.COM **Career Steps:** Co–founder and Vice President of Advanced Products Department, AirNet Communications Corporation (1994–Present); Research & Development Manager, Harris Corporation (1984–1994); Research Engineer, NASA Lewis Research Center (1983–1984). **Associations & Accomplishments:** Eta Kappu Nu; IEEE. **Education:** University of Akron, M.S. in Electrical Engineering (1984), B.S. in Electrical Engineering; Littleton Community College, Associates in Engineering Technology. **Personal:** Mr. Carney enjoys sailing.

John Coccimiglio
General Manager
Allegan Cellular
134 Water Street
Allegan, MI 49010
(616) 673–5171
Fax: (616) 673–8794

4812

Business Information: Allegan Cellular is a cellular phone carrier established in 1990 with one location in Allegan, Michigan. As General Manager, Mr. Coccimiglio, is responsible for the daily operation of the business, including quality control, and maintaining a high level of customer service. **Career Steps:** General Manager, Allegan Cellular (1990–Present); General Manager, Michiana Metronet (1987–1990). **Associations & Accomplishments:** Rotary. **Education:** Western Michigan University, Bachelor (1983). **Personal:** Married to Soraya in 1986. One child: Laurelle Muelenberg. Mr. Coccimiglio enjoys sports.

Beverley Cox
Vice President – Human Resources
Glenayre Technologies
5935 Carnegie Boulevard
Charlotte, NC 28209–4617
(704) 553–0038
Fax: (704) 643–0921

4812

Business Information: Glenayre Technologies, Inc. is a leading worldwide supplier of telecommunications equipment and related software used by service providers in the paging and other wireless personal communications markets. Established in 1962, the Company has offices around the world including: Beijing; China; Dubai; Prague; The Netherlands; Mexico City; and Sao Paulo, Brazil and employs over 1,800 people. Glenayre was recently recognized by "Financial World's" 'Growth 100' list as a top growth company with sales in excess of $300 million and is included in the NASDAQ 100. As Vice President of Human Resources, Ms. Cox has worldwide responsibility for setting the strategic direction in human resources, as well as managing and directing the functional areas including: recruitment and selection, training, career development, benefit and salary administration, employee relations and corporate administration. **Career Steps:** Vice President – Human Resources, Glenayre Technologies (1992–Present); Vice President of Human Resources, Cadmus Communications (1989–1992); Regional Director of Human Resources, Radisson Hotel Corporation (1984–1989); Personnel Manager, Iveys – Division of Batus (1979–1984). **Associations & Accomplishments:** Society of Human Resources Managers; Charlotte Area Personnel Association; Women Executives. **Education:** University of South Carolina, B.S. in Psychology (1979). **Personal:** Married to Charles M. Berger in 1987. Ms. Cox enjoys tennis, golf and photography.

Jan Dehesh
Director of Corporate Telecommunications
Qualcomm, Inc.
6455 Lusk Boulevard
San Diego, CA 92121
(619) 658–3003
Fax: (619) 658–3700
E MAIL: See Below

4812

Business Information: Qualcomm, Inc. sells, manufactures, and distributes satellite and cellular communications systems. A publicly–held, international Corporation based in San Diego, California, Qualcomm, Inc. boasts ten national and four international locations. As Director of Corporate Telecommunications, Ms. Dehesh oversees operations, public relations, sales, and marketing. **Career Steps:** Director of Corporate Telecommunications, Qualcomm, Inc. (1987–Present); Support Services, Linkibit Corporation. **Associations & Accomplishments:** San Diego Region Definity Users Group; Western Region Director, International Definity Users Group, Inc.; Children's Museum of San Diego; Recipient of San Diego Women Who Mean Business Award in the Telecommunications division (1994); Named an Outstanding Young Women of America (1987). **Education:** Miramar Community College. **Personal:** Married to Houtan in 1983. Two children: Gary James and Gabriel Ann. Ms. Dehesh enjoys community activities.

Debra A. Depping
Director – Customer Services
Western Wireless
2001 NW Lake Sammamish Road
Issaquah, WA 98027
(206) 313–5206
Fax: (206) 313–5206

4812

Business Information: Western Wireless is a national telecommunications company, providing personal communications services (e.g., cellular phone, paging) to Washington State residents. Established in 1992, the company presently employs approximately 1,000 people and seeks to expand their services and consumer base in the near future. As Director of Customer Services, Ms. Depping manages the Customer Service Center for centralized operations, supervising a staff of 50. She is additionally responsible for all credits and new accounts. **Career Steps:** Western Wireless: Director of Customer Services (1996–Present), Director (1992–1996), Manager (1991–1992); Director, McCaw Cellular (1986–1991). **Associations & Accomplishments:** National Circle Award of Excellence. **Education:** Washington State University, B.A. (1974). **Personal:** Two children: Dara A. and Danelle E. Ms. Depping enjoys bicycling, music, skiing, and running.

Jay Flakowitz
Project Analyst
AT&T Wireless Services
7 Seneca Court
New York, NY 10956–5713
Fax: (914) 634–3953

4812

Business Information: AT&T Wireless Services, formerly known as Cellular One, is a wireless communication provider. This division, of the world famous long–distance telecommunication provider AT&T, is responsible for providing cellular, wireless data, paging, messaging, and air–to–ground communication for service customers in the United States. As Project Analyst, Mr. Flakowitz oversees all project analyst and strategic planning. He conducts the production cost analysis for new and existing programs. **Career Steps:** Project Analyst, A T & T Wireless Services (1995–Present); Accountant, Giant Carpet (1994); Payroll Specialist, Paychex (1993–1994). **Associations & Accomplishments:** Institute of Management Accountants; American Management Association; NY-SACPA. **Education:** Attending, St. Thomas Aquinas, M.B.A. program ; Dominican College, B.S. in Business Administration; Rockland Community College, A.A.S. in Accounting. **Personal:** Mr. Flakowitz enjoys golf, reading, and outdoor activities.

Yvonne G. Gallimore
Manager
Americatel Corporation
4045 NW 97th Street
Miami, FL 33178
(305) 716–8700
Fax: (305) 994–7295

4812

Business Information: Americatel Corporation is an international telecommunications company specializing in services to Latin America and the Caribbean. Headquartered in Miami, the Company offers point–to–point service, satellite communications, and enhanced messaging systems. Americatel has 50 employees and estimates sales in 1996 to exceed $8 million. As Manager, Ms. Gallimore controls the functionality and operations of the billing system (i.e. set–up, taxation, invoicing). She is involved in development of new business pricing and viability and accounting policy maintenance. Ms. Gallimore works closely with the marketing department in the implementation and development of new marketing techniques. **Career Steps:** Manager, Americatel Corporation (1994–Present); Assistant Controller, Peoples Telephone Company (1987–1994); Accountant, Citibank (1986–1987); Assistant Auditor, KPMG (1980–1983). **Associations & Accomplishments:** Black Alumni, Florida International University; United Pentecostal Church; American Institute of Certified Public Accountants, Pending–Application in process. **Education:** Florida International University, Master's in Accounting (1995); University of the West Indies, B.Sc. in Accounting (With Honors) (1985); Certified Public Accountant examinations (1994). **Personal:** Married to Daniel in 1982. One child: Scott–Dane. Ms. Gallimore enjoys tennis, swimming, working with children, and church work.

Mitchell A. Gilley
Operations Manager
Cellular One
621 Boll Weevil Circle, Suite 31A
Enterprise, AL 36330–2768
(334) 393–2355
Fax: (334) 393–9898

4812

Business Information: Cellular One is a telephone reseller and provider of monthly access and airtime service to the general public, serving a six–county area in Alabama. As Operations Manager, Mr. Gilley is responsible for the management of all day–to–day operations, including inventory control, personnel, price structure, literature design, network design/management, marketing, writing of policy & procedures, training, supervision of all administrative departments, and fraud control. **Career Steps:** Operations Manager, Cellular One (1994–Present); Sales Associate, Alltel Mobile (1993–1994); Account Representative, AAMP of America (1992–1993); Business Owner, Action Auto (1988–1992). **Associations & Accomplishments:** New Home Baptist Church; Certified IASCA Judge; Certified Automotive Installation Technician. **Education:** Wallace College, Drafting (1993); Enterprise State Junior College, Business Administration; Cellular Fraud Control Training. **Personal:** Married to Jennifer Waddell in 1990. One child, Katelyn Arianna. Mr. Gilley enjoys water skiing, hunting, and fishing.

Barbara LaFleur
District Manager
Century Cellunet
3505 Summerhill Road, #4 Summer Place
Texarkana, TX 75503
(903) 793–3710
Fax: (903) 792–0283
EMAIL: See Below

4812

Business Information: Century Cellunet is a subsidiary of Century Telephone Enterprises, Inc., a Louisiana Company with more than 65 years of telecommunications experience. Today, Century is among the largest cellular service operators in the United States. Century Cellunet provides high quality cellular service to subscribers in six states. As District Manager, Ms. LaFleur oversees all aspects of market operations to maximize long–term profits. **Career Steps:** Century Cellunet: District Manager (1996–Present), Account Executive (1989–1996); Senior Account Representative, Executone (1981–1986). **Associations & Accomplishments:** The Commission Group; Texarkana Chamber of Commerce; Atlanta Chamber of Commerce; Hope, Arkansas Chamber of Commerce. **Education:** East Texas State University (1994). **Personal:** Married to Daryl in 1986. Two children: Tiffany Dawn Hamilton and Sammy Lynn Hamilton Jr. Ms. LaFleur enjoys reading and sewing.

Tim J. Link
Director of Carriers Relations
U.S. Communications, Inc.
6140–C Northbelt Pkwy.
Norcross, GA 30071
(770) 613–8206
Fax: (707) 840–0905

4812

Business Information: U.S. Communications is the only company that provides national centralized information services, automated activation processing and marketing support for major national retailers to wireless communications carriers. Tim Link coordinates all efforts between U.S. Communications and the wireless carriers including contract negotiations, renewals and financial support generation. Tim Link brings with him an extensive background in telecommunications and cellular product management, having worked for several major companies in the industry (AT&T, Sprint, Bell South). **Career Steps:** Director of Carrier Relations, U.S. Communications (1996–Present); General Manager, Palmer Wireless (1994–1996); General Manager/Product Manager, Bell South Cellular (1992–1994); Major Account Executive, Sprint (1991–1992) Account Executive, AT&T (1988–1991). **Associations & Accomplishments:** Trustee, Southwest Florida Chamber; Outstanding Young Alumni Circle of Achievement Award, Ball State University; Membership Chairman, Ft. Myers Property Owners Association; Advisory Board, Edgewood Renaissance Academy; International Management Council; Rotary International; Founder, Central Indiana Baseball League; Former President, Men's Adult Baseball League; Key Note Speaker, ReAct National Conference; Key Note Speaker, Anderson Business Club. **Education:** Ball State University, B.S. (1986). **Personal:** Married to Kim Kendrick in 1986.

Jim Mahoney
Director
Airtouch International–Poland
2999 Oak Road MS 750
Walnut Creek, CA 94596
(510) 210–3535 Ext. 7750
Fax: 4822–695–0484
EMAIL: See Below

4812

Business Information: Airtouch International is the largest global wireless service provider in the world. With branches in eleven countries, the Company offers cellular phones and paging services, and plans to expand through the addition of satellite and personal communication systems, and by implementing digitalized services. As Director, Mr. Mahoney is responsible for creation and project management of business start–up activities, currently in Poland. His duties include providing technological expertise, human resources, coordination, and project implementation. Internet users can reach him via: Jim.Mahoney@ccmail.airtouch.com. **Career Steps:** Airtouch International: Director–Poland (1996–Present), Director, Program Management, Headquarters (1994); Staff Manager, Quality, Pacific Bell (1992). **Education:** San Diego State College, B.S. **Personal:** Two children: Michael Paul and Nathaniel Ryan. Mr. Mahoney enjoys biking and sports.

Ms. Joan T. Mancuso
Managing Director of the Americas and Asia Regions
AT&T Tridom
840 Franklin Court
Marietta, GA 30067
(404) 514–3618
Fax: (404) 514–1737

4812

Business Information: AT&T Tridom, a wholly–owned division of AT&T, is primarily engaged in the operation, manufacturing and sale of VSAT products, utilized in satellite telecommunications. In her current capacity, Ms. Mancuso is responsible for managing the sales and marketing of export products to the Americas and Asia regions, as well as meet all regulatory policies and guidelines of each end–country. Established in 1988, AT&T Tridom employs over 300 people with annual sales of in excess of $100 million. **Career Steps:** Managing Director of the Americas and Asia Regions, AT&T Tridom (1990–Present); Vice President of Marketing, IDB International (1989–1990); Director of International Services, Contel ASC (1986–1989); Director of Sales, COMSAT, International Communications (1983–1986). **Education:** George Washington University, M.B.A. (1980); University of Maryland, B.S. (1971). **Personal:** Married to Joseph J. in 1977. Ms. Mancuso enjoys art work, museums, and golf. Ms. Mancuso has adapted to a wide range of cultures and is fluent in Mandarin (Chinese).

Mr. Michael A. Marino
Executive Vice President & Chief Operating Officer
NYNEX Mobile Communications Company
1095 Avenue of the Americas, Room 2654
New York, NY 10036
(212) 395–2272
Fax: (212) 730–0621

4812

Business Information: NYNEX Mobile Communications Company specializes in wireless telecommunications serving the New York and New England Regions. Anticipating rapid growth, the Company is merging with Bell Atlantic Mobile Systems. In his capacity as Executive Vice President & Chief Operating Officer, Mr. Marino is responsible for overseeing all operations, including marketing, technical, sales, customer service and support, external affairs, employee relations. Established in 1983, NYNEX Mobile Communications Company employs over 1600 people and reports annual revenues in excess of $600 million. **Career Steps:** Executive Vice President & Chief Operating Officer, NYNEX Mobile Communications Company (1992–Present); Vice President, Strategy & Planning, NYNEX Worldwide Services Group (1991–1992); Executive Vice President and Chief Operating Officer, NYNEX Business Centers (1988–1991); Vice President, Finance and Administration, NYNEX Business Information Systems Company (1987–1988). **Associations & Accomplishments:** Alumni Association, Tufts University; Alumni Association, Pace University, Lubin Graduate School of Business; American Management Women; March of Dimes; Juvenile Diabetes Foundation. **Education:** Pace University, Lubin Graduate School of Business, M.B.A. (1979); Tufts University, B.A. (1969).

Rick C. McClure
Automated Call Distribution and Operations Manager
Pagemart, Inc.
1604 North Davis
Arlington, TX 76012
(214) 706–3704
Fax: Please mail or call

4812

Business Information: Pagemart, Inc. is a national customer service center, providing paging services throughout the U.S. from four state–of–the–art, high–tech customer service centers. Handling 400,000 to 500,000 calls per month and serving 1.3 million subscribers, Pagemart is the fastest growing paging company in the nation, ranking the fifth largest in the U.S. As Automated Call Distribution and Operations Manager, Mr. McClure is responsible for call routing, scheduling, policy & procedures, and development of reporting technology. **Career Steps:** Automated Call Distribution and Operations Manager, Pagemart, Inc. (1995–Present); Director of Client Services, Regency Communications, Inc. (1994–1995); Administrative Coordinator, National Non Profit Corporation (1987–1994). **Associations & Accomplishments:** SLI Users; ISLUA; Professional Managers Association; Published in Telemarketing Magazine. **Education:** Texas Tech University, B.B.A. (1980) **Personal:** Mr. McClure enjoys consulting with small businesses and non–profit organizations in his spare time.

Daniel G. Murphy
Vice President/General Manager
Pagenet Wisconsin
400 South Executive Drive, Suite 202
Brookfield, WI 53005–0883
(414) 785–8050
Fax: (414) 785–0883

4812

Business Information: Pagenet Wisconsin is the world's largest wireless message service in the world. International in scope, the Company is expanding into such countries as South America, Brazil, and Europe. As Vice President/General Manager, Mr. Murphy oversees all aspects of the Company, and is responsible for sales, accounting and finance, marketing and strategic planning. **Career Steps:** Vice President/General Manager, Pagenet Wisconsin (1995–Present); Sales Manager, Chgo. Communications Service (1980–1992). **Associations & Accomplishments:** Recipient of the President's Award (1995+1996); #1 Sales Manager Award. **Education:** St. Norbert College. **Personal:** Married to Therese in 1991. Two children: Sara and Caitlin. Mr. Murphy enjoys golf, reading, and motorcycling.

Mr. Mark O. Nelson
Director of Customer Service
Cellular One
1120 South Loop 360, Building 1, Suite 100
Austin, TX 78746
(512) 750–7510
Fax: (512) 750–7702

4812

Business Information: Cellular One is a telephone reseller and provider of monthly access and airtime service to the general public, serving 240,000 customers in a 15 county/metro area in Texas and Louisiana. Mr. Nelson currently serves as Director of Customer Service for Cellular One. He has directed over 100 cellular service centers and established sources for service delivery for the Texas and Louisiana districts. Established in 1986, Cellular One (Texas) currently employs 250 people. **Career Steps:** Director of Customer Service, Cellular One (1989–Present); Sales Administration Manager, Woodtape, Inc. (1986–1989); Customer Service Manager, Mastermark, Inc. (1979–1986). **Associations & Accomplishments:** Member of the Board of Directors, (ICSA) International Customer Service Association (1994–1996); Speaker at: Call Center (1992), ICSA National Conference (1992 and 1993); Lrg. P.C. Conference (1995); Published in "Marketng Survey" and "Quality Service Update." **Education:** University of Washington, B.A. (1977). **Personal:** Mr. Nelson enjoys photography and public speaking.

Bert G. Offers
Director
Nortel
2350 Lakeside Boulevard
Richardson, TX 75082–4399
(214) 684–7923
Fax: (214) 685–8840
EMAIL: See Below

4812

Business Information: Nortel is a major telecommunications vendor specializing in public switching, wireless communications, broadband networks, and enterprise networks for companies such as Bell Companies, GTE, and various other long distance carriers. Established in 1896, the Company employs over 50,000 people, and operates worldwide. As Director, Mr. Offers oversees product management and marketing, and is responsible for the long distance marketplace in America. **Career Steps:** Nortel: Director (1995–Present), Senior Manager (1994–1995); Senior Manager/Germany (1992–1994). **Education:** University of Alberta, Engineering (1984). **Personal:** Married to Nancy in 1986. Two children: Nathan and Matthew. Mr. Offers enjoys children and water–sports.

Roberto I. Ortiz
Inventory Control Specialist
Cellular One – Puerto Rico
Metro Office Park, Building #6
Guaynabo, Puerto Rico 00969
(809) 397–5174
Fax: (809) 397–5101

4812

Business Information: Cellular One – Puerto Rico is a telephone reseller and provider of monthly access and airtime service to the general public. The Guaynabo office serves as headquarters for all Cellular One branch locations throughout Puerto Rico, as well as administers office locations in The Caribbean sectors at St. Thomas and St. Croix. As Inventory Control Specialist, Mr. Ortiz is responsible for evaluating various models of computer equipment and their vendors, as well as purchasing them according to the Company's needs and his evaluations. **Career Steps:** Inventory Control Specialist, Cellular One – Puerto Rico (1994–Present); Assistant Manager, El Canario Inn (1992–1994); Sales Order Entry Manager, Moore Industries International (1988–1990); Computer Programmer/Operator, Softkay, Inc. (1987–1988). **Associations & Accomplishments:** Society of American Magicians (1990–Present); Archivist, Puerto Rican Society of Illusionists (1990–Present). **Education:** World University – Puerto Rico, B.A. (1984). **Personal:** Married to Myriam D. Garcia in 1996. Mr. Ortiz enjoys performing Christian music and children's magic shows; as well as enjoys outdoor activities, particularly the beach, nature hiking, and photography.

John C. Parry Jr.

President
NYNEX Network Systems (Bermuda) Limited
The Emporium Building; 69 Front Street
Hamilton, Bermuda HM12
(809) 295–5756
Fax: (809) 295–5708

4812

Business Information: NYNEX Network Systems (Bermuda) Limited is the marketing agent for the FLAG (Fiber–optic Link Around the Globe) project. Covering a distance of more than 27,000 km, and operating at 50 Gbps on each of two fiber pairs, the FLAG cable is designed to achieve a bearer circuit capacity of 120,000 64 Kbps circuits end–to–end. The System is expected to be operational in 1997. International in scope, NYNEX has offices in London, Hong Kong, and Bermuda. Established in 1993, NYNEX Network Systems (Bermuda) Limited reports annual revenue of $200 million and currently employs 20 people. As President, Mr. Parry is responsible for all aspects of operations, including directing sales and marketing efforts of international sales force with offices in London, Brussels, Hong Kong and Dubai. **Career Steps:** President, NYNEX Network Systems (Bermuda) Limited (1993–Present); Managing Director of Quality, NYNEX (1992–1993); Division Manager of South Manhattan, New York Telephone (1990–1992); Director of Labor Relations, New York Telephone (1989–1990). **Associations & Accomplishments:** Captain, U.S. Naval Reserves (Retired). **Education:** Pace University, M.B.A. (1980); University of South Carolina, B.A. (1966); Tuck Executive Program – Dartmouth (1991). **Personal:** Married to Vicki Keller Parry in 1968. Two children: Liana and Alicia.

Mel Reed
District Sales Manager
Nextel Communications
8000 East Quincy Avenue
Denver, CO 80237
(303) 721–3675
Fax: Please mail or call

4812

Business Information: Nextel Communications, established in 1989, is the premier provider of wireless communications in North America. With locations in most major metropolitan areas in the United States, the Company employs over 4,500 people. As District Sales Manager, Mr. Reed oversees the daily operations of the Denver office and manages a sales force

that directly and indirectly sells Motorola made products to major companies and individuals. **Career Steps:** District Sales Manager, Nextel Communications (1993–Present); National Sales Manager, Allcom Communications; Sales Manager, Motorola Communications. **Associations & Accomplishments:** Mr. Reed has written articles for numerous trade publications; Attained "Master Trainer" level achieved with various companies. **Education:** Colorado Christian University (1996); Adams State College (1978). **Personal:** Married to Maureen in 1982. Five children: Aimee, Matthew, Micheal, Joseph, and Jacob. Mr. Reed enjoys fishing, restoring antique trucks, travel, and coaching sports, football, track, and basketball.

Mr. Jean–Guy Riverin
Director of Real Estate
Bell Mobility Cellular
200 Bouchard
Dorval, Quebec H9S 5X5
(514) 822–3098
Fax: (514) 893–3732
EMAIL: See below.

4812

Business Information: Bell Mobility Cellular is an international radio communications business providing every aspect of communications (cellular, paging, satellite, etc.). With B.C. Mobile as its holding company, Bell Mobility currently has 1.8 million customers internationally. As Director of Real Estate, Mr. Riverin is responsible for directing all real estate services, lease negotiations, and inter–company relations for 800 network sites in Quebec and Ontario. In addition, he is responsible for new acquisitions, leases, accounts payable, office space, point of sales, and warehousing. Internet users can reach him via: JGRiveri@Mobility.com. **Career Steps:** Bell Mobility – Cellular: Director of Real Estate (1996–Present), Director of Regulated Services (1990–1996); Director of Operations, Bell Mobility – Skytel (1987–1990). **Associations & Accomplishments:** Canadian Institute of Management (CIM); IFMA; BOMA; ARAS/SARA Board of Director. **Education:** University of Montreal, B.S. (1996); University of Quebec, Engineering. **Personal:** Married to Diane Bernard in 1980. Two children: Josee and Manon. Mr. Riverin enjoys being an amateur radio operator.

R. A. Robinson

General Manager
Horizon Cellular Group d.b.a. Cellular One
580 Northern Avenue
Hagerstown, MD 21742–2811
(301) 791–2355
Fax: (301) 331–5701
EMAIL: See Below

4812

Business Information: Administering fifteen FCC licensed markets nationally, Horizon Cellular Group d.b.a. Cellular One is a wireless telecommunications firm. The Hagerstown, MD office is responsible for four licensed markets and six retail locations. As General Manager, R.A. Robinson is accountable for all functions of the Hagerstown business, overseeing sales, accounting, collections, finance, operations and customer service. Internet users can reach him via: RRobin2492@AOL.COM. **Career Steps:** General Manager, Horizon Cellular Group d.b.a. Cellular One (1994–Present); United States Cellular: Area Manager (1992–1994), Market Manager (1990–1992). **Associations & Accomplishments:** USGA; CTIA. **Education:** California College of Arts (1976); Everett College, A.A. **Personal:** Married to Roxanne in 1984. Four children: Bronson, Bianca, Dawn and Nicole. Mr. Robinson enjoys golf, gourmet cooking and wine collecting.

Robert H. Sage

General Manager
360 Communications
349 Southport Circle, Suite 101
Virginia Beach, VA 23452–1161
(800) 473–2355 Ext: 3004
Fax: (804) 473–5762

4812

Business Information: 360 Communications, formerly known as Sprint Cellular Company, a division of Sprint Corporation (a diversified international telecommunications company with more than $12.6 billion in annual revenues and the United States' only nationwide all digital, fiber–optic network), is a provider of cellular phones and services to more than 1.2 million customers in nearly 100 cities in 14 states. With seventeen years experience in the communications industry, Mr.

Sage joined Sprint Cellular Company as General Manager in 1988. He is responsible for the direction of all aspects of operations for seven area locations. **Career Steps:** General Manager, 360 Communications (Sprint Cellular Company) (1988–Present); Sales Manager, Central Cellular (1985–1988); Account Executive, Metromedia Paging (1979–1985). **Associations & Accomplishments:** Board of Directors, Old Dominion Inter Collegiate Foundation; Junior Achievement: Board of Directors, Treasurer; Board of Directors, Pembroke Kiwanis Club; Norfolk Sports Club. **Education:** Clinch Valley College of University of Virginia, B.S. (1979). **Personal:** Married to Laura in 1982. Two children: Brandon Robert and Ryan Allen. Mr. Sage enjoys golf, attending local sporting events, and participating in civic activities.

Michael A. Sasarman
Senior Engineer
Nortel, Inc.
P.O. Box 3511 Station C
Ottawa, Ontario K1Y 4H7
(613) 763–9735
Fax: (613) 763–2626
EMAIL: MSAS@nortel.ca

4812

Business Information: Nortel, Inc. is an international telecommunications company. Canada's flagship high–tech company, Nortel is one of the major players in global telecommunication networks. The corporation employs 60,000 people in over 100 countries. As Senior Engineer, Mr. Sasarman is responsible for technical leadership and development of A.I.N. services for carrier networks, as well as strategic planning for the continued development of A.I.N. services. Mr. Sasarman has recently received an international assignment in Germany in technical sales. He will be in charge of a major account supplying switching technology to the German market. **Career Steps:** Senior Engineer, Nortel, Inc. (1994–Present); Design Engineer, Bell Northern Research (1992–1993); Senior Consultant, Artis (1990–1992). **Associations & Accomplishments:** Professional Engineers, Ontario; Board of Directors of the National Arts Centre Orchestra Association; IEEE; Mr. Sasarman has participated in many IEEE conferences. **Education:** University of Ottawa, M.A.Sc. (1996) and B.A.Sc.EE (1988). **Personal:** Mr. Sasarman enjoys sailing and tennis.

Robert J. Stokes
Director Marketing & Material
Motorola
CH 180 1300 North Alma School Road
Chandler, AZ 85224–2939
(602) 814–4464
Fax: (602) 814–4566
EMAIL: See Below

4812

Business Information: Motorola is one of the leading global manufacturers and distributors of consumer and industrial electronic communications equipment, with product lines including radio/telephone communications, components, semiconductors, computer systems and peripherals, and home appliances. As Director Marketing & Material, Mr. Stokes directs the marketing, production control, and customer service organization for the ASIC Division. Internet users can reach him via: RJStokes1@aol.com. **Career Steps:** Motorola: Director Marketing & Material (1994–Present), Product Manager (1991–1994), Product Engineer (1984–1991), Sales Executive (1982–1984). **Associations & Accomplishments:** Board of Directors, State of Alaska Emergency Medical Services; American Production and Inventory Control Society; Professional Bowhunters Society. **Education:** Self educated to equivalent of B.S.E.E.; Certified by Motorola's Engineering Review Board. **Personal:** Married to Laurie E. in 1977. Four children: Robert Jr., Dustin, Joseph, and Timothy. Mr. Stokes enjoys camping, hiking, bow hunting, and, shooting traditional archery tackle (longbows).

Peter M. Taddeo
Vice President of Marketing
Nextel Communications
301 East Ocean Boulevard, #2000
Long Beach, CA 90802–4828
(310) 624–5049
Fax: (310) 544–9394

4812

Business Information: Nextel Communications owns and operates integrated wireless telecommunications systems nationwide with a subsidiary, Nextel International. The Company maintains offices in China, Canada, and Mexico. As Vice President of Marketing, Mr. Taddeo is responsible for the development of tactical and strategic marketing initiatives. **Career Steps:** Vice President of Marketing, Nextel Communications (1994–Present); Executive Director of International Business Development, Bell Atlantic International (1993–1994); Director of Product Development, Bell Atlantic Mobile (1985–1993). **Associations & Accomplishments:**

American Marketing Association; Cellular Telephone Industry Association; Economic Development Council – Los Angeles, California; Porche Owners Club; Quoted in: "Fortune," "Business Week," and "RCR." **Education:** Pace University, M.B.A. (1979); Iona College, B.B.A. (1975). **Personal:** Married to Christine in 1984. One child: Amy. Mr. Taddeo enjoys skiing and motor sports (car racing).

William L. Tant Jr.
Switching Engineer
360 Communications
3651 Junction Boulevard
Raleigh, NC 27603
(919) 880–9967
Fax: (919) 446–1529

4812

Business Information: 360 Communications, formerly Sprint Cellular, provides cellular and wireless communications. Mr. Tant served as an RF System Performance Engineer at Sprint Cellular until his Transfer to Switching Engineer at the newly renamed 360 Communications in 1996. He is presently responsible for the maintenance of the cellular network – ensuring clear communications – for offices in Raleigh and Durham, North Carolina, covering an area from the Carolina Coast to Danville, Virginia. **Career Steps:** Switching Engineer, 360 Communications (1986–Present); RF System Performance, Sprint Cellular Company (1994–1995). **Education:** Wilson Community College, A.A.S. in Electronics (1973). **Personal:** Married to Ruth V. in 1981. Two children: Justin and Elizabeth. Mr. Tant enjoys spending time with his family.

Rod Douglas Taylor
General Manager
AT&T Wireless Services
210 Imi Kala Street, Ste. 204
Wailuku, HI 96793–1274
(808) 242–4999
Fax: (808) 244–0936

4812

Business Information: AT&T Wireless Services, formerly known as Cellular One, is a wireless communication service company, providing cellular, wireless data, messaging, and air–to–ground communication. Joining the Company as General Manager in 1993, Mr. Taylor is responsible for the overall management of AT&T wireless services in Hawaii. **Career Steps:** General Manager, AT&T Wireless Services (1995–Present); General Manager, Cellular One (1993–1995); General Manager, RAM Paging Hawaii (1988–1993). **Education:** University of Central Florida, Marketing (1984). **Personal:** Married to Linda in 1987. Two children: Rachael and Travis. Mr. Taylor enjoys surfing.

Paul L. Turner

Vice President of Customer Service
Pagemart Wireless, Inc.
6688 North Central Expressway, Suite 800
Dallas, TX 75206–3914
(214) 706–3750
Fax: (214) 373–7698

4812

Business Information: Pagemart Wireless, Inc. is the 5th largest wireless communications company in the United States, providing fax, voice–mail, and paging services to 1.4 million subscribers. Mr. Turner joined Pagemart in 1994 as the Vice President of Customer Service. He immediately developed the Customer Support Division with a staff of 700 employees at four locations. His present responsibilities include providing support for a wide spectrum of wireless services, personnel coordination, and executive leadership. **Career Steps:** Pagemart Wireless, Inc.: Vice President of Customer Service (1995–Present), Vice President – Nationwide (1994–1995); Senior Manager, MCI (1985–1994). **Associations & Accomplishments:** St. Luke Community Methodist Church; American Diabetes Association; America's Managers Association; Advisory Board, Brookhaven College; Officer of Society for Advancement of Managers (SAM). **Education:** Southern Methodist University, Mid–Management Executive Program (1995); University of New Orleans, Marketing (1980). **Personal:** One child: Kyle. Mr. Turner enjoys travel, reading, and basketball.

Jill J. Woods
Distributional Sales Manager
BellSouth Mobility
5600 Glenridge Drive, NE
Atlanta, GA 30342–1357
(404) 847–2429
Fax: (404) 705–0403

4812

Business Information: BellSouth Mobility provides diversified wireless telecommunications services & products (i.e., cellular phones, fax, paging, and digital technology). As Distributional Sales Manager, Ms. Woods is responsible for national retail accounts to provide cellular services to customers, including such companies as Radio Shack, AT&T, and Kroger. **Career Steps:** Distributional Sales Manager, BellSouth Mobility (1987–Present); Regional Merchandiser, T.J.Max & Company (1986–1987); Buyer – Mens Clothes, Pitiz Department Stores (1985–1986). **Associations & Accomplishments:** Junior League Cobb/Marietta. **Education:** University of Alabama, Bachelors (1985). **Personal:** Married to Doug in 1987. Two children: Turner Elizabeth and Caitlyn James. Ms. Woods enjoys oil painting, horseback riding, decorating, and reading.

Lillie M. Woods
Vice President for Fiscal Affairs
Tougaloo College
500 West County Line Road
Tougaloo, MS 39174
(601) 977–7718
Fax: (601) 977–7866

4812

Business Information: Tougaloo College, affiliated with the United Church of Christ, is a private, four–year, coed, liberal arts college. Majors with the largest enrollment include Economics, Biology, and Political Science. Preprofessional programs are in Law, Medicine, Veterinary Science, Dentistry, and Theology. Established in 1869, The College currently employs 185 faculty. Joining Tougaloo College in 1975, Ms. Woods was appointed as Vice President for Fiscal Affairs in 1990. She is responsible for the fiscal operations management of the Institution, including budget management, program planning, financial projections, student financial assistance, purchasing, personnel, institutional support services, administrative data processing, and plant/construction operations. **Career Steps:** Tougaloo College: Vice President for Fiscal Affairs (1990–Present), Business Manager (1986–1990), Associate Business Manager (1985–1986), Controller (1977–1986), Federal Grants Accountant (1976–1977), Junior Accountant (1975–1976); Accounting Clerk, W. E. Walker Stores (1974–1975); Sales Associate, J. C. Penny (1973–1974). **Associations & Accomplishments:** National Association of Colleges and Universities Business Officers (1995); Southern Association of Colleges and Universities Business Officers (1995); American Association of University Women (1995); Board Member (1995), Mississippi Chapter of American Heart Association; Planning Team Member (1994), UNCF Fiscal Affairs Workshop; National Association of Independent Colleges and Universities Task Force on Direct Lending (1993); Chaired Mississippi Black Women's Political Action Forum (1991); Treasurer (1990), Mississippi Chapter of Sigma Gamma Rho Sorority; Outstanding Young Women of America (1980); Who's Who Among Students in American Universities and Colleges; AWARDS: Distinguished Service Award by Tougaloo College (1992); Distinguished Service Award by Sigma Gama Rho Sorority, Inc. (1989); The Mississippi Association of Certified Public Accountants Scholarship Award (1974). **Education:** Jackson State University: M.P.A. (1980), B.S. in Accounting (1974); Harvard University, Certificate in Management Development Program (1987). **Personal:** One child: Paula Renee Woods. Ms. Woods enjoys arts & crafts and working with the youth. As an active member of Cherry Grove M.B. Church, she serves as Director of the Sunshine Band, Chairperson of the Church Quarterly newsletter, and publicity committee member.

Robert A. Yeager
Marketing Manager
Cellular One
RR 1 Box 3A
Winfield, PA 17889–9799
(717) 524–2351
Fax: (717) 522–5251
EMail: See Below

4812

Business Information: Cellular One is a telephone reseller and provider of monthly access and airtime service to the general public. As Marketing Manager, Mr. Yeager is responsible for daily operations in two markets, MSA/RSA, and ensuring profitability and excellence. Internet users can reach him via: RAYEAGER@POSTOFFICE.PTD.NET. **Career Steps:** Marketing Manager, Cellular One (1995–Present); General Man-

ager, Sunshine Cellular (1992–1995); Account Executive, Bell Atlantic (1991–1992); Advisory Market Representative, IBM (1977–1990). **Education:** Univerity of Phoenix, Business Management (1996); Lincoln Technical Institute, Associate of Applied Science in Electronics. **Personal:** Married to Karen in 1974. Five children: Elizabeth, Suzanne, Robert Jr., Rachael, and Leah. Mr. Yeager enjoys reading, motivation, training, and music. He has also played guitar and banjo in various blues bands.

Tom J. Zenisek
Senior Business Manager
Northern Telecom, Inc.
200 Athens Way
Nashville, TN 37228–1397
(615) 734–4481
Fax: (615) 734–5116
E/MAIL: See Below

4812

Business Information: Northern Telecom, Inc., one of the world's leading telecommunications marketers, specializes in the design, manufacture and service for a diverse range of products including, telephone, data communications, and semi–conductor production. Established in 1895, Northern Telecom Inc. currently employs 55,000 professionals and has an estimated annual revenue of $10.2 billion. With more than thirteen years of experience in the telecommunications industry, Mr. Zenisek joined Northern Telecom in 1982. Presently serving as Senior Business Manager for Business Alliances, his current work focus is in the development of the Company's products for computer telephony integration. Prior to assuming this position, he was Manager of Business Analysis and Research at Northern Telecom Limited. He spent four years in research and development for business communication products at Bell–Northern Research — Northern Telecom's research and development affiliate. Concurrent with his position at Northern Telecom, he is the President and Chairman of the Board of the Enterprise Computer Telephony Forum, Inc. (ECTF) – an industry organization formed to promote an open, competitive market for Computer Telephony Integration (CTI) technology. ECTF is an open, mutual benefit, volunteer membership, non–profit organization incorporated in the State of California. It is comprised of Computer Telephony Integration (CTI) end users, computer vendors, telecommunications vendors, hardware component vendors, software developers and systems integrators; all seeking to grow and enhance the CTI marketplace via the implementation of international standards. He is also a Member of the Board of Governors of the Multi Media Telecommunications Association. **Career Steps:** Senior Business Manager, Northern Telecom, Inc. (1982–Present); Professor of Management, University of Calgary and University of Saskatchewan; Manager of Business Analysis and Research, Northern Telecom Limited. **Associations & Accomplishments:** Enterprise Computer Telephony Forum, Inc. (ECTF): President, Chairman of the Board; Board of Governors, Multi Media Telecommunications Association; Numerous publications on management topics; United States Army Security Agency – Radio Telecommunications Intelligence Experience. **Education:** Ohio State University: Ph.D., MBA, B.A. **Personal:** Married to Margaret in 1988. Two children: Chris and Janet. Mr. Zenisek enjoys boating.

Paul A. Zukowski
President
U.S. Wireless Cable
1803 West Avenue
Austin, TX 78701
(512) 320–8522
Fax: (512) 892–3795
Email: See Below

4812

Business Information: As President of U.S Wireless Cable, Mr. Zukowski is responsible for organization, management, and control over all of the Company's wireless cable operations. He is also responsible for all Company–related business decisions, development, and fiscal strength. He has implemented strategies to improve the Company's position in its market, corporate procedures improving control over all of the the Company's operations, and he has redesigned the remote accounting and inventory control systems, resulting in much lower costs and expenditures at the individual satellite offices. Internet users can reach him via: 74452.3212@compuserve.com. **Career Steps:** President, U.S. Wireless Cable (1995–Present); Chief Corporate Engineer Operations, United States Wireless Cable, Inc. (1994–1995); Chief Systems Engineer, Computer Express (1993–1994); Programmer for UNIX and DOS Systems, Siemens Ag. Production Telecommunications Department (1989–1991). **Associations & Accomplishments:** Institute of Electronics and Electrical Engineering; WCA; The Setan Medical Fund. **Education:** Texas Tech University, B.Sc.E.E. (1992). **Personal:** Married to Jimmie in 1994. Mr. Zukowski enjoys computers and scuba diving.

Clifford Gayler Ackley

President and Owner
Industry Telephone Company
P.O. Box 40, Highway 159 West
Industry, TX 78944
(409) 357–4411
Fax: (409) 357–2323

4813

Business Information: Industry Telephone Company, a family–owned business, is an independent, rural telephone company that provides its own construction operations. Established in 1955, Industry Telephone Company currently employs 21 people. As President and Owner, Mr. Ackley is responsible for the oversight of daily operations of the business. **Career Steps:** Industry Telephone Company: President and Owner, Vice President and General Manager. **Associations & Accomplishments:** 100 Club of Austin County; 100 Club of Houston; Austin County Peace Officers Association; Masonic Lodge; Colorado Valley Shrine Club; Liberty Bell Award, Austin County Bar Association; Outstanding Community Leader Award; Outstanding Citizen Award. **Education:** Bellville High School (1958). **Personal:** Married to Mary Ackley in 1973. Four children: Mark and Larry Ackley, Robin Marek and Sheila Raeke. Mr. Ackley enjoys music, golf, and fishing.

Mary K. Artis

Marketing Manager
AT&T
227 West Merrow Street
Chicago, IL 60606
(312) 230–2291
Fax: (708) 554–6217

4813

Business Information: AT&T is a diversified telecommunications company providing global voice, data and video conferencing services and related products. They are well known for their long distance, local and business telephone services. Established in 1886, AT&T currently employs 180,000 people worldwide. As Marketing and Sales Manager, Mr. Artis is responsible for managing and coaching a team of special account executives. **Career Steps:** AT&T: Marketing Manager (1994–Present), Human Assets/Learning (1993–1994), Account Executive (1991–1993); Sales Representative, Shorr Paper Products (1987–1991). **Associations & Accomplishments:** National Association of Female Executives; Board of Directors, Aurora Hispanic Chamber of Commerce; Member, 2000 Notable American Women; Staff Member, Main Baptist Children's Church. **Education:** Aurora University: M.B.A. (1996), B.A. (1982); Howard University, M.A. (1984). **Personal:** Two children: Brittany and Adrianna. Ms. Artis enjoys reading, exercising, and travel.

Roger W. Bailey

Strategic Alliance Vice President
AT&T Solutions
15 Vreeland Road
Florham Park, NJ 07932
(201) 443–2230
Fax: (201) 443–2659
EMAIL: See Below

4813

Business Information: AT& T Solutions is an international networking outsourcing company. Established in 1995, they are a subsidiary of AT&T comprised of three divisions: Consulting, which is headquartered in Washington, D.C.; Systems Integration, also headquartered in Washington, D.C.; and Outsourcing, located in Florham Park, New Jersey. With sixteen locations worldwide, ten in the United States and six overseas, the Company hopes to expand their operation to include four to eight more locations within the next year. As Strategic Alliance Vice President, Mr. Bailey draws upon over twenty years of experience in the field. Responsible for negotiating strategic alliances as required for corporate ventures, he presents relevant information to analysts. Internet users can reach him via: rwbailey@attmail.com. **Career Steps:** AT& T Solutions: Strategic Alliance Vice President (1996–Present), Customer Engagement Vice President (1995–1996); Director, Government Affairs, Dell Computer Corporation (1993–1995); Consultant, Self–Employed (1992–1993); Perot Systems Corporation: General Counsel (1991–1992), Manager of Competitive Analyst (1990–1991); Electronic Data Systems: Group General Counsel (1985–1989), Associate General Counsel (1978–1985); U.S. Air Force (1969–1978). **Associations & Accomplishments:** Texas Bar Association; Virginia State Bar Association. **Education:** University of Puget Sound, J.D. (1977); California State University, M.B.A.; Stanford University, M.S. in Aero/Astro Engineering; U.S. Air Force Academy, B.S. in Astro Engineering/Mathematics. **Personal:** Married to Sally in 1973. Mr. Bailey enjoys scuba diving.

Thomas E. Barber

Senior Analyst and Project Manager
BellSouth Telecommunications
Attn: InfoTech 2835 Brandywine Road, Suite 300
Atlanta, GA 30342
(770) 452–4528
Fax: Please mail or call
EMAIL: See Below

4813

Business Information: BellSouth Telecommunications is an exclusively diversified telecommunications company providing voice, data and other advanced network products. BellSouth is the result of a merger between Southern Bell and South Central Bell with offices located in eight states (South Carolina, North Carolina, Georgia, Florida, Mississippi, Tennessee, Alabama and Kentucky). BellSouth currently employs 74,000 people throughout the Corporation. Mr. Barber joined Southern Bell in 1979 as a Programmer and Analyst, continuing with BellSouth after the merger in 1985 as a Manager and Lead Analyst. After serving in various consulting positions, he moved into his present position as Senior Analyst and Project Manager in 1996. He is now responsible for project scheduling and budgeting, systems development, technology advisement, and introduction of new software. Internet users can reach him via: Ed.Barber@bridge.bellsouth.com **Career Steps:** BellSouth Telecommunications: Senior Analyst and Project Manager (1996–Present), Object Technology Consultant (1994–1996), Information Technology Consultant (1990–1994), Manager and Lead Analyst (1985–1990), Programmer and Analyst (1979–1985). **Associations & Accomplishments:** Certified Data Professional by ICCP; Alpha Iotta National Honor Society for Decision Sciences. **Education:** Georgia State University, M.S. in Decision Science (1994); University of North Carolina – Greensboro, B.S. in Math; Attended: Georgia Institute of Technology. **Personal:** Married to Deborah in 1972. Two children: Jennifer and Lori. Mr. Barber enjoys computer programming and spending time with his daughters.

Thomas A. Bartlett

Regional Vice President
Bell Atlantic Mobile
8 Neshaminy Interplex, Suite 317
Trevose, PA 19053
(215) 638–6281
Fax: Please mail or call

4813

Business Information: Bell Atlantic Mobile is a cellular telephone provider of monthly access and airtime services to the general public. As Regional Vice President, Mr. Bartlett is responsible for all aspects of operations, including marketing, sales, human resources, and finance for the Pennsylvania (Philadelphia), Delaware and Southern New Jersey areas. Established in 1984, Bell Atlantic Mobile employs 350 people. **Career Steps:** Regional Vice President, Bell Atlantic Mobile (1992–Present); Chief Financial Officer, Bell Atlantic Business Systems (1989–1992); Financial Director, Sorbus Europe (1987–1989). **Associations & Accomplishments:** American Institute of CPA's; American Institute of Judicial Engineers; American Cancer Association; Listed in Philly's 1993 Top People to Watch; Featured in many articles, television programs, interviews and talk shows. **Education:** Rutgers University, M.B.A. (1981); Lehigh University, B.S. in Engineering. **Personal:** Married to Francesca in 1982. Two children: Matthew and Brittany. Mr. Bartlett enjoys coaching, tennis and golf.

Eric B. Blaustein, D.P.A.

Director
MCI Telecommunications, Inc.
7000 Weston Parkway
Cary, NC 27513–2119
(919) 677–5677
Fax: (919) 677–5625

4813

Business Information: MCI Telecommunications, Inc. is a diversified telecommunications company providing global voice, data and video services and related products. Principal business units include the Long Distance Division and the local telephone companies. Joining MCI as Senior Manager in 1988, Dr. Blaustein was appointed as Director in 1995. He is responsible for directing the activities of all network surveillance and performances, including national transmission surveillance, national switch operations, fiber security, and all performance modeling and measurements. **Career Steps:** MCI Telecommunications, Inc.: Director (1995–Present), Senior Manager (1988–1995); Assistant Professor, American University (1985–1988). **Associations & Accomplishments:** Published article on the planning for the implantation of new software; Interviewed for the Journal of Assistant Management and Journal of Quality Assurance Software Q&A. **Education:** George Washington University, D.P.A. (1984); University of Denver, M.P.A. (1976); Drexel University, M.S. in Information Sciences (1975). **Personal:** Two children: Erin Rebecca and Michael Brian. Dr. Blaustein enjoys camping, golf, exercise, and skiing.

Peggy M. Bloodworth

National Account Executive
Northern Telecom
Dept. 7208, 4001 East Chapel Hill Nelson Highway
Research Triangle Park, NC 27709
(919) 992–3132
Fax: Please mail or call
EMAIL: See Below

4813

Business Information: Northern Telecom is a telecommunications company, which sells services to businesses and individuals. As National Account Executive, Ms. Bloodworth is responsible for selling services to rural residential areas, marketing services, and all other accounts. Internet users can reach her via: peggy.bloodworth@nt.wm. **Career Steps:** Northern Telecom: National Account Executive (1996–Present), Director Marketing (1989–1995). **Associations & Accomplishments:** North Carolina Wine Growers Association. **Education:** Virginia Commonwealth University, B.S. (1977); Attended: Virginia Polytechnic Institute, Virginia State University. **Personal:** Married to P. Jeffrey in 1979.

John W. Brown, CPA

Purchasing Manager
Lufkin–Conroe Telephone Exchange
P.O. Box 1568
Conroe, TX 77305–1568
(409) 539–7250
Fax: (409) 788–1229
EMAIL: See Below

4813

Business Information: Lufkin–Conroe Telephone Exchange is an independent telephone utility company. Texas' fifth largest independent telecommunications provider, it currently serves over 85,000 customers from locations in Lufkin and Conroe. Serving Lufkin–Conroe in various supervisory roles since 1989, John Brown was appointed as Purchasing Manager in August of 1984. In this capacity, he has full administrative direction of all materials procurement and inventory for both locations. Additionally, he is responsible for the monitor and preparation of corporate capital and budgetary allocations. Internet users can reach him via: jbrown@tcac.com. **Career Steps:** Lufkin–Conroe Telephone Exchange: Purchasing Manager (1994–Present); Staff Manager – Budget (1991–1994); Supervisor – General Accounting (1989–1991). **Associations & Accomplishments:** American Institute of Certified Public Accountants; Texas Society of Certified Public Accountants – Houston Chapter; Leadership Montgomery County (1995–1996). **Education:** Stephen F. Austin State University: M.B.A. (1990), B.B.A. (1984); Certified Public Accountant in State of Texas (1987). **Personal:** Married to Mary Elizabeth in 1991. Mr. Brown enjoys the raising and training of AKC Golden Retrievers.

Phillip H. Brown

Director
Bell Atlantic
1490 Prospect Street
Trenton, NJ 08638
(609) 882–2606
Fax: (609) 393–1211

4813

Business Information: Bell Atlantic is a provider of communications, telecommunications, and information systems. As Director of Residence Collection Centers, Mr. Brown directs all activity of residence collection centers for four out of the seven states operating under Bell Atlantic's jurisdiction (New Jersey, Maryland, Virginia, Delaware). **Career Steps:** Bell Atlantic: Director of Residence Collection Centers (1993–Present), Director of Toll Services (1992–1993), Director of Industrial Healthcare (1991–1992), Director of Business Services Planning and Integration (1989–1991). **Education:** Wharton School – University of Pennsylvania, M.B.A. (1977); Brown University, B.A. (1975). **Personal:** Married to Robin in 1978. Two children: Khalid and Jahi. Mr. Brown enjoys casting "positive" shadows on African–American youth and coaching his son's basketball team.

Robert J. Bruno
Director of Corporate Marketing
GTE Corporation
P.O. Box 152092
Irving, TX 75015–2092
(214) 718–1815
Fax: (214) 718–3034

4813

Business Information: GTE Corporation is a world–leading telecommunications company providing voice, data, and video communications throughout the United States and various regions around the world. As Director of Corporate Marketing, Mr. Bruno is responsible for integrating the marketing capabilities of the companies that comprise GTE, in order to ensure increased effectiveness in the GTE marketplace. He also ensures the required capabilities are available in order to develop the highest quality marketing and sales professionals and processes. **Career Steps:** Director of Corporate Marketing, GTE Corporation (1983–Present); District Manager, AT&T (1973–1983); Sales Manager, Nynex (1965–1973); Manager, JC Penney (1963–1965). **Associations & Accomplishments:** American Marketing Association; He has been a guest speaker for the Conference Board, The Marketing Institute, and the Institute for International Research. His article, "The Evolution to Market–Driven Quality," was published in the Journal of Business Strategy (September/October 1992). **Education:** Indiana University; University of Buffalo; Niagara University, M.A.; Seton Hall University, B.A. **Personal:** Married to Connie in 1963. Three children: Eric, Nicholle, and Danielle. Mr. Bruno enjoys coin collecting, swimming, and golf.

Ashlie M. Bryant
Marketing Communications Manager
VOYSYS
48634 Milmont Drive
Fremont, CA 94538–7353
(510) 252–1100
Fax: (510) 252–1101
EMAIL: See Below

4813

Business Information: VOYSYS is a computer telephony solution provider, providing telecommunication and voice mail solutions as an OEM. Headquartered in Fremont, California, VOYSYS markets hardware and software products to distributors/dealers of various businesses with locations throughout the world. As Marketing Communications Manager, Mrs. Bryant is responsible for the management of the Marketing Communications Department, including public relations, advertising, direct mail, channel marketing, trade shows, promotions, and investor relations across three different business channels. Internet users can reach Ashlie via: abryant@voysys.com **Career Steps:** Marketing Communications Manager, VOYSYS (1993–Present); Atwork Corporation: International Business Development (1992–1993), Marketing Assistant (1991–1992). **Associations & Accomplishments:** American Marketing Association; Bilingual in English and French; Author of various articles for the San Francisco Chronicals, Press Briefing, and PC magazines. **Education:** University of California – Davis, B.A. (1990); La Sorbonne, L'Universite de Grenoble. **Personal:** Married to H. Ray in 1991. Mrs. Bryant enjoys reading, walking, and travel.

Frank Calabrese
Director of U.S. Sales
Voicecom Systems, Inc.
2 Corporate Drive, Suite 636
Shelton, CT 06484
(203) 926–0936
Fax: (203) 929–1437

4813

Business Information: Voicecom Systems, Inc. provides value–added communication services for mobile professional consultants, sales representatives, and people who usually do business on the road. They can access their voice mail, faxes, and e–mail with one number from anywhere in the nation. As Director of U.S. Sales, Mr. Calabrese manages the field sales organization nationwide. He is responsible for the supervision of 60 account executives and sales representatives. **Career Steps:** Voicecom Systems, Inc.: Director of U.S. Sales (1995–Present), Regional Sales Manager (1992–1995); Regional Sales Director, Wang Information Services (1985–1992); Branch Regional Manager, Western Union

Telegraph (1982–1985). **Associations & Accomplishments:** Little League. **Education:** Northeastern University, B.S. (1977). **Personal:** Married to Deborah in 1983. Four children: Frank, Kristyn, Kayla, and Anthony.

David Carlucci
Senior Buyer
Bell Atlantic
650 Park Avenue
East Orange, NJ 07017
(201) 414–7749
Fax: (201) 672–9602

4813

Business Information: Bell Atlantic is an exclusively diversified telecommunications company providing voice, data and other advanced network products. As Senior Buyer, Mr. Carlucci is responsible for preparing, negotiating, and writing agreements and contracts for specific lines of business within the company. **Career Steps:** Senior Buyer, Bell Atlantic (1993–Present); Staff Manager, Bell Communications Research (1989–1993); Staff Specialist, New Jersey Bell Telephone Company (1981–1989). **Associations & Accomplishments:** National Association of Purchasing Managers; The National Library of Poetry; Randolph Township Little League; Calvary Temple Assembly of God; Purchasing Management Association of New Jersey. **Education:** Thomas Edison College, B.A. (1990); County College of Morris County; Monmouth College of New Jersey. **Personal:** Married to Regina in 1964. Two children: David William and Brian Anthony. Mr. Carlucci enjoys writing, reading, sports, and physical fitness.

Mr. Charles F. Columbus
President
Shared Communications Services, Inc.
1095 25th Avenue, S.E.
Salem, OR 97301
(503) 399–7000
Fax: (503) 399–1459

4813

Business Information: Shared Communications Services, Inc. provides long distance and other communication services including voice mail, 800 numbers, and credit travel cards (call to home only). They are the largest regional communications company in the Northwest. In his current capacity, Mr. Columbus is responsible for all aspects of Company operations and establishes the mission and vision for continued growth. Established since 1986, Shared Communications Services, Inc. presently employs 36 people (7 offices), and has an estimated annual revenue of $24 million. **Career Steps:** Co–founder, President, Shared Communications Services, Inc. (1986–Present); Manager, U.S. West (1970–1986); Sales Manager, New Jersey Bell (1965–1970); Field Representative, New Jersey Bell (1960–1965). **Associations & Accomplishments:** America Carriers Telecommunications Association; National Carriers Buyers Association; Chamber of Commerce; Rotary Club; Active in community projects. **Education:** Rutgers, B.A. Degree in Marketing (1962). **Personal:** Married to Beverly for 14 years. Two children: Charles and Cynthia Jean. Mr. Columbus enjoys hunting, fishing, and golf in his leisure time.

Frank J. DeJoy
Director of Operations
Teleport Communications Group
275 Old New Brunswick Road
Piscataway, NJ 08854–3722
(908) 981–4402
Fax: Please mail or call

4813

Business Information: Teleport Communications Group is a national provider of local telecommunications services, including private line, voice, and ATM; serving major metropolitan areas. Customers include long distance telephone companies, corporations in geographic serving areas, and other networking companies. As Director of Operations, Mr. DeJoy is responsible for all operations in New Jersey including planning, implementation, operational support for all networking activities, and sales support. **Career Steps:** Director of Operations, Teleport Communications Group (1994–Present); Systems Engineering Manager, AT&T Bell Laboratories (1992–1994); Technical Consultant, AT&T Network Systems (1989–1992); Computer Engineer, IBM Corporation (1988). **Associations & Accomplishments:** Institute of Electrical and Electronics Engineers; Member, Board of Directors, Garden State Underground Plant Location Service. **Education:** Rutgers Graduate School of Management, M.B.A. (1993); Rutgers College of Engineering, B.S. in Electrical Engineering. **Personal:** Mr. DeJoy enjoys reading, exercising, and sports.

Manuel del Toro
Vice President – Marketing
Telefonica Larga Distancia
P.O. Box 70325
San Juan, Puerto Rico 00936–8325
(787) 749–5800
Fax: (787) 749–5858

4813

Business Information: Telefonica Larga Distancia is the leading long distance telephone company serving Puerto Rico. Services are provided in three areas: Residential – $30 million in revenue; Government – $5 million (80% of the Puerto Rican government is serviced by TLD); and in the Private Sector – $12 million, which includes small, medium, and large companies in Puerto Rico. TLD is the first telecommunications company to surpass AT&T in Puerto Rico, with 44% of the market share, leaving AT&T with 40%. Future plans include expanding long distance services into the U.S.; opening new markets in Puerto Rico; expanding into the Internet; and using the PCS (Personal Communications System). As Vice President of Marketing, Manuel del Toro is responsible for all sales and marketing activities, in addition to managing a staff of 90. **Career Steps:** Vice President – Marketing, Telefonica Larga Distancia (1992–Present); President/Owner, M&L Communications (1990–1992); Sales Manager, ITT Business Communications (1973–1989). **Associations & Accomplishments:** Sales and Marketing Executive Association; Puerto Rico Chamber of Commerce. **Education:** University of Puerto Rico, B.A. in Architectural Design (1972). **Personal:** Married to Lirsa Pabon in 1987. Two children: Carlos and Manuel Jesus. Mr. del Toro enjoys reading and religious activities.

Dana K. Devine
Executive Director
EXCEL Telecommunications
22 Fernwood Drive
Conway, AR 72032–3602
(501) 327–9235
Fax: (501) 327–8767

4813

Business Information: EXCEL Telecommunications, established in 1988, provides long–distance telephone service to customers at discounted rates. As Executive Director, Mr. Devine is responsible for recruiting and training new representatives as well as bringing renewed inspiration to the company's experienced personnel. **Career Steps:** Executive Director, EXCEL Telecommunications (1995–Present); Branch Manager, Norwest Mortgage (1990–1994); Senior Vice President Investment Banker, Brittenum & Associates (1980–1986). **Associations & Accomplishments:** Faulkner County Executive Association. **Education:** University of Arkansas, B.B.A. in Finance; Mississippi State University, B.A. **Personal:** Married to Jennifer in 1992. Three children: Danielle, Denton, and Taylor. Mr. Devine enjoys gardening with his wife, Jennifer and scuba diving with his family.

John Drake
Manager of Service Operations
Sprint–United Telephone
197 Route 94
Lafayette, NJ 07848
(201) 579–4474
Fax: (201) 579–4488

4813

Business Information: Sprint/United Telephone – New Jersey is a subsidiary of Sprint Corporation. Sprint is a diversified international telecommunications company with more than $12.6 billion in annual revenues and the United States' only nationwide all digital, fiber–optic network. It's divisions provide global long distance voice, data and video products and services, local telephone services to more than 6.5 million subscriber lines in 19 states, and cellular services to more than 1.2 million customers in nearly 100 cities in 14 states. Sprint/United Telephone – New Jersey is the second largest telephone company in New Jersey. Sprint provides service in five counties, serving approximately 171,000 access lines covering more than 1,128 square miles. Products and services are offered to major businesses, educational institutions and government institutions, serving areas within its franchised territory. As Manager of Service Operations, Mr. Drake oversees the field maintenance and installation of communications equipment in Northwest New Jersey. **Career Steps:** Sprint – United Telephone: Manager of Service Operations (1993–Present), Manager of the Service Center (1991–1993); President, Tri

State Dock & Door (1979–1982). **Associations & Accomplishments:** Director, Sussex County Chamber of Commerce; Director, United Way of Sussex County; Board of Commission, New Jersey Crimestoppers; Boy Scouts of America. **Education:** LaSalle University, B.S. (1989); University of Michigan, Management. **Personal:** Married to Ann in 1980. Mr. Drake enjoys golf, brewing his own beer and restoring Porsches.

Keith Dunford
Vice President
California Microwave
125 Kennedy Drive
Hauppauge, NY 11788–4072
(516) 272–5606
Fax: (516) 736–8772
EMAIL: See Below

4813

Business Information: California Microwave is a manufacturer of telecommunications and satellite communication products. The Company supplies voice, data, and television broadcast materials and services to such companies as AT&T, MCI, and British Telecommunications. Established in 1976, California Microwave currently employs 500 people and posted revenues of over $130 million dollars in 1995. As Vice President/Business Development, Mr. Dunford handles the marketing of new services and products to new and existing clients. He handles the daily administrative duties of the Business Development Division, to include recruiting staff, personnel concerns, scheduling, and developing a viable budget. Mr. Dunford reports to the Board of Directors on the development of new markets and products. Internet users can reach him via: 102667.2300@Compuserve.com. **Career Steps:** Vice President/Business Development, California Microwave (1993–Present); Vice President/Operations, Spar Aerospace/Comtel (1985–1992); Executive Vice President, Spatial Communications (1983–1985). **Associations & Accomplishments:** National Association of Fucak Instructors; Civil Air Patrol; Institute of Electronics and Electrical Engineers; American Management Association; Aircraft Owners and Pilots Association; American Society of Quality Control; Certified Flight Instructor. **Education:** London School of Economics, B.A. (1961); Manchester University, B.Sc. (1958). **Personal:** Married to Ena Louise in 1957. Three children: Jillian, Michael, and Angela. Mr. Dunford enjoys flying, and search and rescue.

David J. Easter
Vice President of Network Services
United States Signal Corp.
2855 Oak Industrial Drive, NE
Grand Rapids, MI 49506–1272
(616) 224–4253
Fax: (616) 224–5106
EMAIL: See Below

4813

Business Information: U.S. Signal Corp. is a telecommunications provider of long distance, local service, CAP, Internet, and PCS services. Its customer base includes such major companies as Ameritech Region, NYNEX, and Bell Atlantic. Joining U.S. Signal as Vice President of Network Services in 1987, Mr. Easter has the ultimate responsibility for network planning, operations, and costing for the Network Services. Internet users can reach him at the following address: bodhi1@ix.netcom.com **Career Steps:** Vice President of Network Services, U.S. Signal (1987–Present). **Education:** Calvin College, B.A. (1984).

BCI CORP.

James T. Evans, J.D.
Vice Chairman of the Board/General Counsel
Brittan Communications International Corporation
2103 Commonwealth Avenue
Houston, TX 77006–1805
(713) 523–7191
Fax: (713) 523–9130

4813

Business Information: Brittan Communications International Corporation is the largest long distance reseller in America. Headquartered in Houston, Texas, and active in 11 states, the Company plans to open offices in Mexico and Great Britain. Established in 1994, the Company is active in a great many philanthropic endeavors, donating 2% of its annual revenue to such charities as Adult Literacy, Child Advocacy, and the National Alliance on Literacy. As Vice Chairman of the Board/

General Counsel, Mr. Evans is responsible for all aspects of legal services: general business, real estate and governmental regulations. In addition to his responsibilities with Brittan Communications International Corporation, Mr. Evans also holds three other positions concurrently: He is the Host of his own radio talk show, "Houston Head–On", on radio station KNUZ, and has interviewed such well known personalities as Ross Perot; he is the Chairman of Commonwealth Publishing, Inc., a company he founded to publish books dealing with political topics, including one he authored, "Where Liberals Go to Die," and his newest release in progress "Melt Down 2000: The End of Public Education;" Mr. Evans has also been a practicing attorney since 1978, concentrating in all forms of Business Law, including Business Transactions and Negotiations. **Career Steps:** Vice Chairman of the Board/General Counsel, Brittan Communications International Corporation (1994–Present); Host, Houston Head–On, KNUZ Radio Station (1995–Present); Chairman, Commonwealth Publishing, Inc. (1994–Present); Attorney, James T. Evans, Attorney & Counselor (1978–Present). **Associations & Accomplishments:** American Bar Association; Texas Bar Association; American Judges Association; Admissions: U.S. Supreme Court, U.S. Tax Court, Court of Veterans Appeals, Supreme Court, State of Texas, Fifth Circuit Court of Appeals, U.S. District Courts, Southern and Northern Districts of Texas. **Education:** University of Houston: J.D. Cum Laude (1968), B.B.A. (1965). **Personal:** Married to Linda Arlene in 1983. Mr. Evans enjoys sky diving.

Gordon G. Eyre
General Manager
AT&T
4460 Rosewood Drive, Room 6210
Pleasanton, CA 94588–3050
(510) 224–4800
Fax: (510) 224–4560
EMAIL: See Below

4813

Business Information: AT&T is a diversified telecommunications company providing global voice, data and video conferencing services and related products. They are well known for their long distance, local and business telephone services. Joining AT&T in 1964, Gordon Eyre was appointed as General Manager in 1990. He oversees data provisioning for private line customers in the western half of the U.S. Internet users can reach him via: !Eyre **Career Steps:** AT&T: General Manager (1990–Present), District Manager – Engineering (1985–1990), District Manager – Operations (1981–1985), District Labor Relations Manager (1979–1981). **Associations & Accomplishments:** Who's Who in Colorado; Chairman, Parks and Recreation – Denver; Best Company, Junior Achievement – Salt Lake City; Bishop, The Church of Jesus Christ of Latter Day Saints; Member, Sunshine Singers; Partners in Education. **Education:** University of Utah (1964–1965); Radio Institute – Salt Lake City, A.A. **Personal:** Married to Margene Hunsaker in 1973. Eleven children: Ken, Darrell, Linda, Kathy, Diana, Jill, David, Ben, Anna, Emily and Sarah. Mr. Eyre enjoys bicycling and photography.

Larry Flegle, C.S.E.
National Accounts Manager
LDDS World Com
1 Ravina Drive, Suite 1310
Atlanta, GA 30346
(770) 512–3333 Ext. 327
Fax: (770) 512–3334
E MAIL: See Below

4813

Business Information: LDDS World Com is the fourth largest long distance telephone carrier in the United States. As National Accounts Manager, Mr. Flegle is responsible for selling and maintaining long distance telephone services to Fortune 500 and other large companies. Internet users can reach him via: lflegle@ix.netcom.com. **Career Steps:** National Accounts Director, LDDS World Com (1994–Present); National Account Manager, MCI Communications (1982–1994). **Associations & Accomplishments:** Past President, Sales and Marketing Executives of Atlanta; Academy of Management; Georgia Telecommunications Association; Fellow, Sales Marketing Executives International Academy of Achievement (1996). Several sales awards dated from (1982–1996) and has had articles printed in trade magazines and journals. **Education:** NOVA Southeastern University, Doctoral candidate; Pepperdine University, M.P.A.; University of South Florida, B.A. **Personal:** Married to Jan Flegle, R.N. in 1969. Mr. Flegle enjoys being an amateur radio operator (N4TMW).

Pete Fournier
Manager, Real Estate Technical Engineering
U S WEST
4022 East Edgemont
Phoenix, AZ 85008–1409
(602) 630–7564
Fax: (602) 235–3964

4813

Business Information: U S WEST, Inc. is a diversified telecommunications company providing global voice, data and video conferencing services and related products. Established in 1984, U S WEST currently employs 56,000 persons corporate–wide. As Manager, Real Estate Technical Engineering, Mr. Fournier provides technical support for all aspects concerning the real estate needs of 14 states. His principal duties include the design and construction, and budgeting and funding of office buildings. **Career Steps:** Manager, Real Estate Technical Engineering, U S WEST (1990–Present); Real Estate Project Manager, U S WEST/Mountain Bell (1978–1990); Construction Supervisor, Bechtel (1976–1978). **Associations & Accomplishments:** American Society of Heating, Refrigeration and Air Conditioning Engineers; Maricopa County Indoor Air Quality Council; Arizona Indoor Air Quality Council; Rancho Ventura Neighborhood Association; Mesa Restaurant Owners Association; Numerous memberships and involvement with German and German/American Associations. **Education:** Tri State College (1969); Various trade and professional training sessions. **Personal:** Married to Treva in 1972. Mr. Fournier enjoys folk and classical music, and travel.

Ed Fukunaga
Manager – Marketing Research
Sprint
7015 College Boulevard, Suite 200
Overland Park, KS 66211
(913) 323–7420
Fax: (913) 323–7410
EMAIL: See Below

4813

Business Information: Sprint is a world–wide provider of diversified telecommunications and information products and services. As Manager – Marketing Research, Mr. Fukunaga provides marketing research consultation, design, and implementation services to both Sprint and external marketing professionals. Internet users can reach him via: fukunaga@sky.net **Career Steps:** Manager – Marketing Research, Sprint (1994–Present); Marketing Research Specialist, Steelcase (1988–1994); Research Director, Customer Satisfaction Research Institute (1983–1988). **Associations & Accomplishments:** American Marketing Association. **Education:** University of Kansas: M.S. in Marketing (1983), Masters of Business Administration (1979). **Personal:** Married to Diane in 1977. Two children: Edwin and Elaine. Mr. Fukunaga enjoys classical music (vocal).

Mr. Joseph F. Gatt
Chairman and Chief Executive Officer
Telecel International Limited
36 Grove Street
New Canaan, CT 06840
(203) 966–4623
Fax: (203) 966–7477

4813

Business Information: Telecel International is an international telecommunications company providing telecommunications traffic to African countries. Established in 1985, Telecel International currently employs 250 individuals and has an estimated annual revenue of $60 million. As Chairman and Chief Executive Officer, Mr. Gatt is responsible for all aspects of operations focusing primarily with strategic and political planning. **Career Steps:** Chairman and Chief Executive Officer, Telecel International (1985–Present); President and Chief Executive Officer, Transtate (1980–1981); Director General and Chief Executive Officer, Air Zaire (1973–1977); Vice President, Pan Am (1964–1979). **Associations & Accomplishments:** Wings Club; A.O.P.A.; Published in industry magazines. **Education:** Hunter College, B.S. (1965). **Personal:** Married to Theodora L. in 1962. Two children: Sharon E. and Karen J. Mr. Gatt enjoys being a pilot and playing tennis.

Mrs. Margaret M. George
Director of Marketing Communications
U S WEST Communications
5090 North 40th Street
Phoenix, AZ 85018
(602) 351–6170
Fax: (602) 954–4270

4813

Business Information: U S WEST Communications furnishes telephone voice and data communications to residences and businesses in 14 western and midwestern states. Mrs. George is responsble for strategy development and tactics for advertising, brand image, customer information, product promotions, business relations and internal and external communications for the company's Small Business Group, which serves over 900,000 customers. She works closely with the Product Development, Product Management and Sales organizations to deliver finished programs. **Career Steps:** U S WEST Communications: Director of Marketing Communications (1994–Present); Director of Strategic Planning (1993–1994); Product Manager (1993). **Associations & Accomplishments:** Board of Directors, Phoenix Chamber of Commerce; Forest Ridge School Alumni Board; Instructor, Religious Education. **Education:** University of Washington, B A (1978). **Personal:** Married to Thomas in 1979. Two children: Johnathan and Emily. Mrs. George enjoys horseback riding and skiing.

Teri L. Granier
Area Coordinator
EXCEL Telecommunications Company
25123 Harper Drive
The Woodlands, TX 77380
(713) 364–0078
Fax: (713) 364–0037

4813

Business Information: EXCEL Telecommunications great long–distance services with competitive rates and tremendous discounts. EXCEL not only offers long distance services, it offers a perfect business opportunity. As Area Coordinator, Ms. Granier recruits and trains independent representatives for an exciting and profitable career. She holds seminars for large and small groups to give detailed information on the services EXCEL Telecommunications offers. **Career Steps:** Area Coordinator, EXCEL Telecommunications (1995–Present); Administrative Manager, Self Leveling Machines, Inc. (1994–Present); Regional Manager, Tidewater Temps, Inc. (1993–1994); Licensed Real Estate Sales Agent, Keller Williams Realty (1995–Present). **Associations & Accomplishments:** American Business Women's Association; Society for Human Resource Management; National Notary Association; National Association of Realtors; Texas Association of Realtors; Montgomery County Association of Realtors; Volunteer, Longview Museum and Art Center; Notary Public – Texas. **Education:** Killgore College, Real Estate License (1992); Art Instruction School: Basic Art Certificate and Fundamentals of Commercial Art Certificate. **Personal:** Married to Jo in 1990. Ms. Granier enjoys travel, cooking, poetry, and networking, among many other things.

Rafael E. Graulau
Management Information Systems Director
Telefonica Larga Distancia (TLD)
P.O. Box 70325
San Juan, Puerto Rico 00936–8325
(787) 273–5407
Fax: (787) 273–5421

4813

Business Information: Telefonica Larga Distancia (TLD) is a long distance carrier providing telecommunication services for customers in Puerto Rico. The service provides access to the internet, private lines, calling cards, and prepaid calling cards. As Management Information Systems Director, Mr. Graulau directs a staff comprised of librarians and programmers. He is in charge of developing and implementing programs and products to improve the quality of services offered to customers. **Career Steps:** Management Information Systems Director, Telefonica Larga Distancia (TLD) (1994–Present); Management Information Systems Manager, Bella International (1989–1992); Systems Analyst, Wang Laboratories (1988–1989); Officer, U.S. Air Force (1983–1988). **Education:** Ohio State University, B.S. in Industrial Engineering (1983). **Personal:** Married to Nydia L. Medina in 1989. One child: Rafael E. Graulau Medina. Mr. Graulau enjoys golf, baseball, and reading.

Gladys M. Haecker
Manager of Safety and Health
Southwestern Bell Corporation
1010 North Saint Mary's, Room 1014
San Antonio, TX 78215
(210) 222–5052
Fax: (210) 222–6136

4813

Business Information: Southwestern Bell Corporation is an exclusively diversified telecommunications company providing voice, data and other advanced network products. A thirty–one year veteran of Southwestern Bell Corporation, Mrs. Haecker has been in the safety field for the past seven-

teen years. Currently serving as the Manager of Safety and Health, she is responsible for the management of all safety, health, and environmental issues, as well as ensuring regulatory compliance, training, and program development. Following the guidelines set by federal and state government agencies, she works on a team of three traveling throughout South Texas and Houston, conducting "hands on" inspections and training. **Career Steps:** Southwestern Bell Corporation: Manager of Safety and Health (1979–Present), Manager of Network C/O (1976–1979), Various clerical position (1962–1976). **Associations & Accomplishments:** American Society of Safety Engineers; Greater South Texas Safety Council; Professional Women of Southwestern Bell; Secretary/Treasurer, Catholic Life Insurance Union (CLIU) Branch #4 **Education:** Certifications: Certified Safety Professional; Construction Health & Safety Technician; Occupational Health & Safety Technologist; Professional Source – Texas Worker's Compensation Commission. **Personal:** Married to Ralph in 1964. Three children: Julie, Suzanne, and Michael. Mrs. Haecker enjoys singing, snow skiing, playing the guitar, and spending time with her family.

Atikem Haile–Mariam
Manager
Corning Incorporated Telecommunications
35 West Market Street Mp–ro–02 Products Division
Corning, NY 14831
(607) 974–7541
Fax: (607) 974–7522
EMAIL: See Below

4813

Business Information: Corning Incorporated Telecommunications invented fiber optics and is chartered to manufacture and market this product. As Manager, Mr. Haile–Mariam is responsible for diversified administrative activities, including market development for premises data com applications. Internet users can reach him via: Hailemariam@Corning.com **Career Steps:** Corning Incorporated Telecommunications: Manager (1994–Present), Senior Sales Engineer (1993–1994), Market Specialist (1992–1993); Analyst, ICF–Kaiser (1988–1990). **Associations & Accomplishments:** B.I.C.S.I.; ATM Forum; American Marketing Association. **Education:** University of Virginia, M.B.A. (1992); Washington University – St. Louis, B.S. in Engineering (1986); Knox College, B.A.'s in Physics and History (1984).

Quinlan Halbeisen
Manager
Southwestern Bell Telephone Company
1832 SW Meadow Lane
Topeka, KS 66604–3567
(913) 272–6578
Fax: Please mail or call

4813

Business Information: Mr. Quinlan Halbeisen, a Manager of Southwestern Bell Telephone Company since 1967, retired in 1991. During his career with Southwestern Bell, Mr. Halbeisen was responsible for quality assurance and quality inspection of the installation of new telephone machines for the entire state of Kansas. Under his supervision, the City of Topeka was the second city in the United States to use a local/toll machine. It was his personal goal to see old systems converted to new, more productive systems smoothly, and that the transition not disrupt service. Mr. Halbeisen was awarded the NOVA award when he retired for his development of a computer program that could track the performance of drafting contractors. Though his title changed many times during his career at Southwestern Bell, Mr. Halbeisen's function remained the same: to supervise others in the updating, additions to existing machines, and/or the total replacement of electro–mechanical machines with electronic and, most recently, digital machines. **Career Steps:** Southwestern Bell Telephone Company: Manager (1972–Present), Engineer (1967–1972); Engineer, Alpha Engineering (1961–1967); Engineer, Western Electric Company (1955–1961). **Associations & Accomplishments:** Topeka Chapter, Kansas Engineering Society; National Society of Professional Engineers; Former Local President, 3 United Way agencies; Shawnee Council of Camp Fire; Community Resources Council; Topeka Catholic Services. **Education:** Illinois Institute of Technology, B.S. in Electrical Engineering (1965); Loras College, Iowa, Two–year undergraduate degree; Iowa State University, 7 quarters in Electrical Engineering College. **Personal:** Married to Ann in 1963. One child: Mary. Mr. Halbeisen enjoys computers.

Clyde C. Hamby
Engineering Director
Lucent Technologies, Inc.
6701 Roswell Road
Atlanta, GA 30328–2599
(770) 587–5913
Fax: (770) 643–7836

4813

Business Information: Lucent Technologies, Inc. was formed from the former manufacturing and research organizations of AT&T. As Engineering Director, Mr. Hamby directs operations of teams of professionals who are tasked with designing and configuring telecommunications networks for Lucent's Global Commercial Markets customers. **Career Steps:** Engineering Director, Lucent Technologies, Inc. (formerly AT&T Network Systems) (1966–1996). **Associations & Accomplishments:** U.S. Air Force Reserve, Texas, South Carolina, Korea, and Vietnam (1966–1972); Security Clearances, Cryptography Endorsements (1966–1972); Society of Military Engineers (1968); Institute of Electronics and Electrical Engineers; Riyadh Businessmen's Club (1980–1981); International Chamber of Commerce (1984–1987); Diversity Council Member (AT&T Network Systems) (1994); "Who's Who Worldwide" (1994); Member, Roswell First Baptist Church. **Education:** Georgia Institute of Technology, B.S. in Industrial Engineering (1966); Over 5,000 hours of postgraduate level classes, including advanced technology, management leadership, scientific course development, seminars and speaking engagements to professional societies in the U.S. and abroad; Federal Communication Commission, Licensed Amateur Radio Operator (1957); Journeyman, Apprentice in Electrical Contracting (1961); USAF ROTC Graduate, Georgia Tech (1966). **Personal:** Mr. Hamby enjoys golf, non–fiction reading, amateur radio, gardening, travel, and continuing education courses.

Katherine J. Harless
• • • ◄━━● ◉ ●━━► • • •

President
GTE Airfone
2809 Butterfield Road
Oak Brook, IL 60522–9000
(708) 575–1201
Fax: (708) 573–0270

4813

Business Information: GTE Airfone is the world's leading provider of airborne telecommunications systems, serving passengers on more than 1,800 commercial aircraft representing 21 U.S.–based and international carriers. Holding numerous executive positions throughout her twenty–three years with GTE, Ms. Harless was appointed President in July of 1996, after serving as President for GTE's Texas/New Mexico Region. She is responsible for all operations of the Company. Career highlights include piloting the process of reengineering for GTE Telephone Operations in 1991 and doubling positive results in different areas of responsibility. **Career Steps:** President, GTE Airfone (July 1996–Present); GTE Telephone Operations: Regional President (1994–July 1996), Vice President of IC Markets (1992–1994), Assistant Vice President of Consumer Sales (1990–1992); Assistant Vice President of Financial Support (1988–1990). **Associations & Accomplishments:** Leadership America; American Business Women's Association; Committee of 200; National Association of Accountants; National Executive Association; University of Texas – Austin, College of Business Administration – Foundation Advisory Council. **Education:** University of Texas, B.A. in Accounting (1972). **Personal:** Married to Skip in 1973. Three children: Skip Jr., Ely, and Bill. Ms. Harless enjoys gardening, golf, and education.

Michael J. Hascall
Field Engineer
PTI Communications
290 North Main Street
Kalispell, MT 59901–3946
(406) 758–1221
Fax: (406) 758–1234

4813

Business Information: PTI Communications furnishes telephone voice and data communications to residences and businesses in several western and northwestern states. Established in 1903, the Company services approximately 550,000 customers. As Field Engineer, Mr. Hascall works with communities to determine routes and receive permits for new phone lines to cross private property. He is responsible for insuring quality transmission to customers through existing lines and installing new cable when existing lines are full. **Career Steps:** PTI Communications: Field Engineer (1993–Present), Senior OSP Field Engineer (1979–1993), OSP Field Engineer (1976–1979). **Education:** Oregon Institute of Technology, Bachelor in Technology (1972). **Personal:** Married to Susan in 1988. Two children: Alicia and Bethany. Mr. Hascall enjoys reading, bowling, photography, music, and spending time with his family.

Bradley C. Hickman
Consultant and Plan Administrator
SBC Communications Inc.
175 East Houston, 4–F–9
San Antonio, TX 78205–2233
(210) 351–2639
Fax: (210) 351–2652
EMAIL: See Below

4813

Business Information: SBC Communications Inc. is one of seven Bell operating companies, a result of the recent structural reorganization of Southwest Bell Corporation. Headquartered in San Antonio, SBC is the largest cellular company internationally, and 34th in the U.S. Starting with one of Southwest Bell's subsidiaries in 1980, Brad Hickman was appointed to his current position with SBC in 1991. As Consultant and Plan Administrator, he is responsible for retirement benefits, 401(K) plans, vendor relationships, training, policies and procedures, regulatory compliance, and serving as liaison with business units. Internet users can reach him via: BHICKMA%MSITXHUB@SWGATE2.SBC.COM. **Career Steps:** Consultant and Plan Administrator, SBC Communications Inc. (1991–Present); Associate Director of Human Resources, SBC Adminsitrative Services, Inc. (1990–1991); Manager of Benefits, Southwestern Bell Telephone Company (1985–1989). **Associations & Accomplishments:** American Compensation Association; International Foundation of Employee Benefits. **Education:** St. Louis University, M.B.A. (1988); Southwest Missouri State University, B.S. in Mathematics. **Personal:** Married to Linda in 1981. Two children: Lauren and Amanda. Mr. Hickman enjoys spending time with his children, traveling, and listening to music.

Sandy E. Hickombottom
NY Global Business Planning & Results
Manager–Northeast Region
AT&T – Consumer & Small Business Division
P.O. Box 788
Morristown, NJ 07963
(212) 387–4000
Fax: (212) 387–6269

4813

Business Information: AT&T is a diversified telecommunications company providing global voice, data and video conferencing services and related products. They are well known for their long distance, local and business telephone services. With more than ten years of varied, broad–based business management experience, Miss Hickombottom joined AT&T in 1985. Appointed as Planning & Results Manager of the Northeast Regional Segment Organization – Consumer and Small Business Division in 1996, she is responsible for the market planning and business management of the New York Global consumer and small business territory. Career highlights include leading the Consumer Communications Service Accessible Communications SBU in the development of an effective customer–focused business plan and the design of Global Consumer Communications Services Distribution Segmentation customer service offers. **Career Steps:** AT&T: New York Global Planning & Results Manager of the Northeast Regional Segment Organization – Consumer & Small Business Division (1996–Present); Customer Service/Sales Operations Manager (1994–1996); Global Markets and Services, International Consumer Long Distance Marketing Manager (1993–1994); Accessible Communication Services, Product Manager (1991–1993); General Business Systems Marketing Manager, Distribution Strategy (1989–1991); Staff to Field Sales Rotation (1990–1991); Government Affairs, Marketing Services Cost Analyst, Access Matters, Rates & Tariffs (1988–1989); Business Markets Group, DMDR/Advertising Systems Analyst, Marketing Information Systems (1986–1988); Business Marketing Services Pricing Analyst, Marketing Plans Implementation (1985) **Associations & Accomplishments:** "I AM..."ACADEMY Board of Directors and Advisory Team; American Marketing Association; American Management Association; Toastmasters International Inc.; National Association of Female Executives; Subcommittee National Professional Development Conference, Alliance of Black Telecommunications Employees Inc.; AT&T's Minority Recruitment Advisory Board; Former President, Metropolitan Jackson State University Alumni Chapter; AWARDS & HONORS: AT&T Product Management/Operations Quarterly Director's Award (1996), AT&T Global Acclaim Award–Project Leadership–Innovative Customer Service Design/Development (1995), AT&T True Spirit Award— "Project Platinum" (1994), Outstanding Team Leader Award—Morristown Home Bible Fellowship (1994–1995), Excellence in Leadership & Growth Award–Faith Fellowship Home Bible Fellowship (1992), Honor and Recognition Award—CCS ACS SBU—(1992), Program Support Award—ALLIANCE of Black Telecommunications Employees (1991,1995), GBS Vice President of Marketing Quarterly Outstanding Project Recognition Award (1991), GBS Director of Marketing Excellence

Award (1991), AT&T Human Resources Outstanding Contribution Award (1991), GBS Senior Team Marketing & Product Management Solutions Celebration Award (1990), Marketing Service Organization Spotlight Award—Diversity Initiatives (1988), (3) Director of Marketing Outstanding Performance Recognitions within 8 months (1989–1990); Listed In: International Who's Who of Professional and Business Women; Two Thousand Notable American Women (1996); Outstanding Young Women of America (1985). **Education:** Fairleigh Dickinson University, M.B.A. in Marketing (1991); Jackson State University, B.S. in Marketing (1986); University of Michigan, Executive **Education:** Mid–management Development (1993); George Washington University, AT&T Project Management Professional Development Program (1995–1997), in pursuit of Master Certification in Professional Project Management; Faith Fellowship Ministries(FFM) World Outreach School of Ministry (1994); Faith Fellowship World Outreach Bible School Diploma, Biblical Studies (1992); AT&T "How to Run Your Business" Series (1992). **Personal:** Miss Hickombottom enjoys teaching, reading, cooking, "Debt–Free and Prosperous Living" consulting, and listening to Christian music.

John W. Howard
Director
Houston Cellular
1 West Loop Street, Suite 300
Houston, TX 77027–9009
(713) 553–2375
Fax: (713) 964–9139

4813

Business Information: Houston Cellular is a cellular telecommunications provider. A Certified Public Accountant, Mr. Howard joined Houston Cellular as Controller in 1991. Promoted to Director in 1995, he is presently responsible for the oversight of credit, collections, and customer activation activities. **Career Steps:** Houston Cellular: Director (1995–Present), Controller (1991–1995); Controller, National Convenience Stores, Inc. (1985–1990); Audit Manager, Price Waterhouse (1977–1985). **Associations & Accomplishments:** Texas Society of Certified Public Accountants; Financial Executives Institute; American Financial Association. **Education:** Texas Tech University: M.S. (1977), B.B.A. (1975). **Personal:** Married to Susan in 1989. Two children: Kelly and Kristen. Mr. Howard enjoys golf.

Eric I. Khounlo
Sales Planner
Lucent Technologies
9410 Pierce St.
Westminster, CO 80021
(303) 707–4017
Fax: (303) 707–4116
E MAIL: uswct!eikhounlo

4813

Business Information: Lucent Technologies, formerly AT&T Systems and Technology Business, is a $22 billion corporation that designs, builds, and delivers a wide range of public and private networks, communications systems, software,and microelectronic components. As Sales Planner, Mr. Khounlo prepares business cases to solve customer problems and identify sales potential, performs competitive, statistical, financial, and economic analyses to determine sales revenue. He also assists in developing and implementing budgets, sales, and marketing techniques. Other duties include performing financial, economic, and statistical analyses to assist in sales forecasting. Internet users may contact him via: leikhounlo. **Career Steps:** Sales Planner, Lucent Technologies (1996–Present); US West Communications: Geographic Market Analyst (1995–1996), GIS Specialist (1992–1995); Market Analyst (1990–1992). **Associations & Accomplishments:** Denver Association of Business Economists. **Education:** University of Denver, Master degree, Telecommunications (1996), Graduate Certificate in GIS; University of Iowa, B.A. in Economics; Des Moines Area Community College, Diploma in Printing. **Personal:** Married to Nina in 1990. One child: Ryan. Mr. Khounlo enjoys tennis, fishing, reading, and spectator sports.

Tim Kingsbury
Associate Director
Bell Canada Logistics
20 Norelco Drive
North York, Ontario
(416) 747–6720
Fax: (519) 763–6587

4813

Business Information: Bell Canada Logistics develops and operates logistics systems for Bell Canada telecommunications. Mr. Kingsbury has served in various supervisory positions with Bell Canada, most recently promoted to Associate Director in 1995. His present responsibilities include strategic planning and technical support for systems, business transformation, applications development on all platforms, and cor-

porate systems operations. **Career Steps:** Bell Canada Logistics: Associate Director (1995–Present), Senior Projects Manager (1991–1995), Systems Manager (1989–1991). **Associations & Accomplishments:** Digital Work Group; Perception Technology User Group; EIIC Data Users Group; PMAC; Trustee and Chair of Finance Committee, Board of Education. **Education:** Conestoga College, Materials Management (1982). **Personal:** Married to Julie in 1991. One child: Daniel Charles Amaziah. Mr. Kingsbury enjoys spending time with his family and working on his 100 acre farm.

Robert D. Lyons
Staff Manager
AT&T
295 North Maple Avenue, Room 2136 F3
Basking Ridge, NJ 07920–1002
(908) 221–2605
Fax: (908) 221–5059
EMAIL: See Below

4813

Business Information: AT&T is a diversified telecommunications company providing global voice, data and video conferencing services and related products. The Company is well known for its long distance, local and business telephone service, and information technologies. As Staff Manager, Mr. Lyons is the strategic database marketing manager responsible for implementing database information into marketing strategies. In addition, he is responsbile for in–market trials and customer relationship analysis. Internet users can reach him via: Rdlyons@mailATT.com. **Career Steps:** AT&T: Staff Manager (1995–Present), Business Analyst – I.S. Systems (1988–1995), Human Resource Management (1984–1988). **Associations & Accomplishments:** Alpha Sigma Lambda **Education:** Lehigh University, M.B.A. (1996); Caldwell College, B.S. in Business Administration. **Personal:** Married to Donna in 1985. Three children: Matthew, Daniel and Rebecca. Mr. Lyons enjoys outdoor activities, particularly hiking.

Manuela C. McCall

Executive Director
Pacific Bell
2410 Camino Ramon #0240
San Ramon, CA 94583–4203
(510) 806–5830
Fax: (510) 806–5949
EMAIL: See Below

4813

Business Information: Pacific Bell, a leading diversified telecommunications company in the U.S., provides leading edge technologies such as data, voice, video transport and application services to customers. Based in California and Nevada, the Company has national and international relationships with Fortune 500 companies. Established in the 1870's, Pacific Bell currently employs 40,000 employees and has an estimated annual revenue of $9 billion. As Executive Director, Ms. McCall is responsible for all aspects of marketing and product development associated with Pacific Bell's consumer broadband network. She can also be reached through the Internet via: MCMCCAL@PACBELL.COM **Career Steps:** Pacific Bell: Executive Director (1994–Present), Director of Wholesale Marketing (1992–1994), Strategic Pricing Manager (1989–1991); Staff Director of Corporate Strategy, Pacific Telesis (1991–1992). **Associations & Accomplishments:** Phi Kappa Phi Harvard Alumni Association. **Education:** California State University, M.B.A. in Finance (1989); Harvard Business School, P.M.D. (1992); Mississippi University for Women, B.S. in Mathematics (1977). **Personal:** Ms. McCall enjoys nature hiking, golf, and surfing the internet.

John D. McNaughton
Vice President of Marketing and Customer Solutions
Northern Telephone Limited
P. O. Box 1110, 850 Birch Street South
Timmins, Ontario P4N 7J4
(705) 360–2271
Fax: (705) 360–2302
EMAIL: See Below

4813

Business Information: Northern Telephone Limited, a subsidiary of Bell Canada Enterprises, provides local telephone services to North Eastern Ontario. Established in 1905, the Company employs 345 people and has estimated annual revenue of $47 million. As Vice President of Marketing and Customer Solutions, Mr. McNaughton oversees the Marketing, Planning, Sales and Customer Services aspects of the company's operations and also supervises a staff of sixty–five. Internet users can reach him via: Mcnaught@nt.net. **Career Steps:** Vice President, Marketing and Customer Solutions, Northern Telephone Ltd. (1995–Present); Managing Director –WorldPlus, AT&T Canada, Inc. (1994–1995); Vice President – Card Marketing, Diners Club/en Route (1993–1994).

Associations & Accomplishments: Board of Directors, Timmins Chamber of Commerce; Board of Directors, NorTel Mobility, Inc. **Education:** Concordia University, Business Administration (1983). **Personal:** Married to Patricia in 1989. Three children: Veronica, Tyler, and William. Mr. McNaughton enjoys cycling and skiing.

Mr. Richard S. McPherson

Director of Property Management Services
U S WEST Business Resources, Inc.
188 Inverness Drive, Suite 420
Englewood, CO 80112
(303) 397–8420
Fax: Please mail or call

4813

Business Information: U S WEST is a telecommunications and information services company. Business Resources, Inc., a division of U S WEST, provides property, materials and fleet management services. Established in 1984, U S West currently employs 55,000 people corporate–wide, with Business Resources, Inc. employing 3,000 people. As Director of Property Management Services, Mr. McPherson is responsible for the management of 11 million square feet of commerical properties in Arizona, New Mexico, Colorado, Nebraska and Wyoming. **Career Steps:** Director of Property Management Services, U S WEST Business Resources, Inc. (1993–Present); Area Manager of Strategic Planning, U S WEST (1991–1993); Area Manager of Materials Management, U S WEST (1985–1991); District Manager of National Product Scheduling, AT&T (1984–1985). **Associations & Accomplishments:** International Development Research Council – currently on Education Committee, Past Chairperson of the Rocky Mountain Chapter; Board of Directors & Treasurer, Balloon Federation of America; Past President of the Colorado Balloon Club; Published various articles: "Site Selections" workshop article, article in Balloon Federation Journal. **Education:** Arizona State University, B.A. in Business (1979). **Personal:** Mr. McPherson enjoys hot air ballooning, skiing, scuba diving, golf and traveling.

Louis E. Metcalf III

General Sales Manager
AT&T Network Systems
12450 Fair Laks Circle, Suite 302
Fairfax, VA 22033–3810
(703) 802–3859
Fax: (703) 802–3852
EMAIL: See Below

4813

Business Information: AT&T Network Systems is one of the world's largest manufacturers of network telecommunications equipment and suppliers of end–to–end solutions used by communications services providers and other network operators around the world. The "world's networking leader," AT&T is the largest long–distance carrier in the U.S. and the world's largest provider of wireless services. AT&T's Worldwide Intelligent Network carries more than 185 million voice, data, video and facsimile messages every business day and AT&T Bell Laboratories provides basic research, product, and service development. As a result of merging with McCaw Cellular Communications, Inc. in 1994, AT&T is the largest cellular services provider in the world. Joining AT&T Network Systems in 1987, Mr. Metcalf was appointed as General Sales Manager in 1993. He is responsible for the oversight of a team that provides telecommunication systems and devices for the U.S. Government Department of Defense, as well as overseeing contract negotiations and business development. Internet users can reach him via: attmail!lmetcalf. **Career Steps:** AT&T Network Systems: General Sales Manager (1993–Present), Program Director (1991–1993), Program Manager (1987–1991). **Associations & Accomplishments:** Armed Forces Communications & Electronics Association; Former Board Member, Manassas Area Soccer Association; Former Board Member, Greater Manassas Baseball League; Former Area Director, Boy Scouts of America. **Education:** George Mason University, B.S. in Business Administration (1978). **Personal:** Married to Marcia A. in 1972. Two children: Louis and Audrey. Mr. Metcalf enjoys being a baseball historian.

David E. Morton

Manager of National Support Assistance Center
GTE Telephone Operations
P.O. Box 152134
Irving, TX 75015–2134
(214) 724–3970
Fax: (214) 724–3782

4813

Business Information: GTE Telephone Operations is a world leading telecommunications technology conglomerate. Working in administrative and operations roles for various GTE subsidiaries since 1986, David Morton was promoted to his current position in May of 1994. As Manager of National Support Assistance Center, Mr. Morton is responsible for providing administrative support to the Support Assets Department, as well as national support to the building, construction, and fleet organizations. **Career Steps:** GTE Telephone Operations: Manager of National Support Assistance Center (1994–Present), Senior Staff Engineer (1990); State Coordinator – BF&E, GTE of Indiana (1986). **Associations & Accomplishments:** Boy Scouts of America; Building Operation Manager Association; National Association of Watch and Clock Collectors; National Corvette Restorers Society. **Education:** University of Wyoming, Associates Degree (1974); Wyoming Technical Institute, Technical Degree in Automotive Maintenance. **Personal:** Married to Cheryll in 1988. Four children: Mike, Malinda, Jaimee, and Allison. Mr. Morton enjoys automotive restoration, clock restoration, and fishing.

Ms. Tracie A. Muesing

Vice President of Transformation Systems
U S WEST Communications
Suite 5200, 1801 California Street
Denver, CO 80202
(303) 896–1241
Fax: (303) 896–0946

4813

Business Information: U S WEST Communications is a regional telecommunications provider, serving both residential and business customers covering a 14–state area in the Western U.S. As Vice President of Transformation Systems, Ms. Muesing provides strategic direction for reengineering of information systems operations, development and internal data communications. Established in 1876, U S WEST Communications employs 55,000 people with annual sales of $9 billion. **Career Steps:** Vice President of Transformation Systems, U S WEST Communications (1994–Present); Vice President of Information Application Development, US WEST Technologies (1992–1994); Vice President of Quality, US WEST, Inc. (1990–1992); Executive Director of Strategic Planning, US WEST, Inc. (1988–1990). **Associations & Accomplishments:** Colorado Womens Chamber of Commerce; Conference Board, Council of North American Information Management Executives. **Education:** Univesity of Phoenix, M.B.A. (1986); University of South Dakota, Computer Science (1970). **Personal:** Married to Travis in 1979.

Barbara Jean Nagle

Regional Director/Regional Training Director
EXCEL Telecommunications Company
1943 SW Import Drive
Port St. Lucie, FL 34953
(561) 461–7861
Fax: (561) 461–7986
Voice Mail: 1–800–969–080

4813

Business Information: EXCEL Telecommunications is an innovative long distance telecommunications company providing alternative voice, data services and related products to residential and commercial clientele. Services are marketed through a network of independent representatives sponsored by others already working for the Company. EXCEL is currently the third largest long distance carrier in the nation providing telecommunication services worldwide. As Regional Director/Regional Training Director, Ms. Nagle brings people into Multi–Level Marketing and trains them to become professional, successful EXCEL representatives. **Career Steps:** Regional Director/Regional Training Director, EXCEL Telecommunications (1995–Present); Computer Programmer, St. Lucie County School Board (1987–Present). **Associations & Accomplishments:** Executive Board Member, Classroom Teachers Association; Zone Chairperson, Crimewatch; Eucharistic Minister; Lector at Church; Volunteer, Lawnwood Regional Hospital; Helped organize SAFESPACE – home for battered women and children; Past President, Democratic Club, Port St. Lucie, Florida. **Education:** Indian River Community College; Webster College, A.A. (1985); Albion College. **Personal:** Married to Thomas in 1984. Four children: Vickie, Jeffrey, Kim, and Pam. Ms. Nagle enjoys being with her nine grandchildren, golf, walking, and listening to music.

Mr. Mark S. Neft

Senior Analyst
MCI
707 17th Street
Denver, CO 80202
(303) 291–6887
Fax: (303) 291–6365

4813

Business Information: MCI is a diversified telecommunications company providing global voice, data and video services and related products. Principal business units are the Long Distance Division and the local telephone companies. In his capacity as Senior Analyst, Mr. Neft is the senior technical leader on a variety of projects for the Corporation. The focus of the projects may be in the business or consumer market division. He is instrumental in the creation of innovative technological programs establishing advanced technological business networks and residential service improvements goals for the organization. Twenty–five years after its founding, MCI Communications Corporation has grown into a company with nearly $12 billion in annual revenue, over 36,000 employees worldwide and more than 65 offices in 60 countries and places. According to the International Institute of Communications, MCI was ranked as the world's sixth largest international carrier for 1992. **Career Steps:** Senior Analyst, MCI; Manager, Mauville; Manager, Unocal. **Education:** Syracuse University, B.S. in Computer Science (1988).

Mr. Michael Nessler

Director of Strategic Business Planning
AT&T – American Transtech Division
8000 Baymeadows Way, Room 5–2–010
Jacksonville, FL 32256–7520
(904) 636–2558
Fax: (904) 636–3579

4813

Business Information: AT&T is a diversified telecommunications company providing global voice, data and video conferencing services and related products. They are well known for their long distance, local and business telephone services. AT&T's American Transtech division provides customer outsourcing. Established in 1984, the Division currently employs 10,000 people. An AT&T engineering executive since 1992, Michael Nessler currently serves as Director of American Transtech's Strategic Business Planning Division, responsible for functional disciplines, short– and long–term strategies. **Career Steps:** AT&T: Director of Strategic Business Planning – American Transtech Division (May 1995–Present); Director of TQM/Re–engineering – American Transtech Division (1993–May 1995); Client–Server Development – Corporate Information Technology Services Division (1992–1993). **Associations & Accomplishments:** Association of Quality and Participation; American Society of Quality Control; Florida Steding Examiner. **Education:** University of Massachusetts, B.S. (1981); Indiana University, Executive Education Program (1993). **Personal:** Married to Anne in 1985. Mr. Nessler enjoys the beach, golf and spending time with his two children.

Cheraldine S. Oliver

Director of Education and Training
AT&T
55 Corporate Drive, Room 13C01
Bridgewater, NJ 08807–1265
(908) 658–6095
Fax: (908) 658–2723
EMAIL: See Below

4813

Business Information: AT&T is a diversified telecommunications company providing global voice, data and video conferencing services and related products. They are well known for their long distance, local and business telephone services. Established in 1886, AT&T currently employs 180,000 people worldwide. An expert in international communications training specializing in the areas of Curricula Design, Competency Models and Courseware Development in Latin America, Asia and Europe, Cheraldine Oliver joined AT&T as Director of Education and Training in 1980. She is responsible for providing solutions for the training of international and domestic sales and client business managers. Internet users can reach her via: icsoliver@aol.com **Career Steps:** Director of Education and Training, AT&T (1980–Present). **Associations & Accomplishments:** American Society for Training and Development; American Horse Show Association. **Personal:** Two children: Jennifer and Johnathan. Ms. Oliver enjoys competing and training in all aspects of equestrian competition.

James M. Olson

General Manager
AT&T
170 South Warner Road
Wayne, PA 19087–2121
(610) 341–5200
Fax: (610) 989–0870
EMAIL: See Below

4813

Business Information: AT&T is one of the world's largest providers of telecommunications equipment and services to customers in 120 countries. Joining AT&T in 1982, Mr. Olson was appointed as General Manager of the Business Communication Services of the Long Distance Division in 1994. He is responsible for the oversight of the entire department which provides long distance service to small businesses in the Pennsylvania and Southern New Jersey areas. Internet users can also reach him via: jolson@bem1.attmail.com **Career Steps:** AT&T: General Manager (1994–Present), Branch Manager – Virginia (1993–1994), International Sales Director (1991–1993), Senior Staff Manager (1989–1990). **Associations & Accomplishments:** Ranked tennis player; Member of 100+ corporate memberships. **Education:** University of Maryland, M.B.A. (1982); University of North Carolina, B.A. in Journalism (1978). **Personal:** Married to Suzanne in 1986. Mr. Olson enjoys tennis, basketball, and softball.

Frederic Papeians

Board of Directors
Metrotel
Calle 75 No 58–30
Barranquilla, Colombia
(575) 368–3311
Fax: (575) 368–9991

4813

Business Information: Metrotel specializes in local telecommunications, Internet, and information systems networks for area companies and individuals. Established in 1994, the Company employs 170 people and has estimated annual revenue of $48 million. As a member of the Board of Directors, Mr. Papeians designs and constructs networks and procures implementation systems. **Career Steps:** Board of Directors, Metrotel (1995–Present); Alcatel: Assistant General Manager (1994–1995), Sales Manager (1990–1992), Sales Coordinator (1989–1990). **Associations & Accomplishments:** Harvard Club of Belgium; Fulbright Alumni Association. **Education:** Harvard Business School, M.B.A. (1994); Ecole Polytechnique, Brussels, Belgium, Engineering (1987). **Personal:** Married to Manuela in 1990. Two children: Boris and Gabriel.

Wilson H. Parran

Vice President – Technology Services
Frontier Corporation
180 S. Clinton Avenue
Rochester, NY 14646
(716) 777–4534
Fax: (716) 325–7639
EMail: See Below

4813

Business Information: Frontier Corporation provides long distance and local telecommunication services, including phone service, paging, cellular, and audio and visual conferencing. As Vice President – Technology Services, Mr. Parran handles service technology, strategic planning, and development. Internet users can reach him via: WPARRAN@FRONTIERCORP.COM. **Career Steps:** Vice President – Technology Services, Frontier Corporation (1996–Present); Chief Information Officer & President, Frontier Information Technology (1995–1996); Vice President of Corporate Systems, Bell Atlantic (1993–1995). **Associations & Accomplishments:** Association of Computing Machinery; Institute of Electronics and Electrical Engineers; Society of Information Managers. **Education:** George Washington University, M.S. (1993); Columbia Union College, B.S.; Prince Georges College, A.A. **Personal:** Married to Deborah Ann in 1973. Two children: Damani K. and Khalil M. Mr. Parran enjoys travel and photography.

Jerome J. Pasierb

Quality Manager
MCI Telecommunications, Inc.
501 63rd Street
Downers Grove, IL 60516–2024
(708) 515–6721
Fax: (708) 719–5232

4813

Business Information: MCI Telecommunications, Inc. is a diversified telecommunications company providing global voice, data and video services and related products. Principal business units are the Long Distance Division and the local telephone companies. Joining MCI as Sales Support Manager in 1988, Mr. Pasierb was appointed as Quality Manager in 1992. He is responsible for management of the quality of products and services offered by MCI. **Career Steps:** MCI Telecommunications, Inc.: Quality Manager (1992–Present), Sales Support Manager (1988–1992); Officer, United States Army (1983–1988). **Associations & Accomplishments:** American Society of Quality Control; American Quality and Productivity; Leukemia Team in Training. **Education:** Keller Graduate School of Management, M.B.A. (1993); United States Military Academy – West Point, B.S. in Engineering (1983). **Personal:** Married to Cathy in 1988. One child: Christopher. Mr. Pasierb enjoys reading, running and cross county skiing.

Scott V. Payton

Vice President of Technology
Pegasus Information Systems
P.O. Box 35
Clear Creek, IN 47426–0035
(812) 334–0000
Fax: (812) 333–4185

4813

Business Information: Pegasus Information Systems is a long distance telephone service provider, providing services from three locations (2 in Indiana and 1 in Florida). Joining Pegasus Information Systems as Vice President of Technology in 1994, Mr. Payton is responsible for the development and implementation of information systems for the entire organization. He is also involved with the creativity and the "what" and the "how" of the implementation of the technologies, in addition to supervising a staff of six. **Career Steps:** Vice President of Technology, Pegasus Information Systems (1994–Present); I.S. Developer, Indiana University (1992–1994); G.I.S. Developer, American Market Metrics (1990–1992); Nuclear Missile Technician, United States Air Force (1987–1990). **Associations & Accomplishments:** Featured in several magazines in 1995 on the applications he wrote on the telephone industries. **Education:** Indiana University (1992); United States Air Force, Technical Certificate ICBM Master Technician. **Personal:** Mr. Payton enjoys music, songwriting, running, roller blading, and mountain biking.

Kim Phillips

Vice President, Service
Popp Telecom
620 Mendelssohn Avenue North
Golden Valley, MN 55427
(612) 797–7939
Fax: (612) 544–9798

4813

Business Information: Popp Telecom specializes in reselling the telecommunications networks of AT&T and MCI. As Vice President, Service, Ms. Phillips overseas customer service, operator services, and inside sales. **Career Steps:** Popp Telecom: Vice President Service (1993–Present), Regional Manager (1991–1993), Account Representative (1990–1991). **Associations & Accomplishments:** Executive Women International. **Education:** University of St. Thomas, M.B.A. (In Progress); St. Olaf College, B.A. in Chemistry and Math; University of Lancaster, England, B.A. in Chemistry and Math (1986). **Personal:** Ms. Phillips enjoys language, music, and history.

Frank J. Presuto

General Manager
AT&T
32 Avenue of the Americas, Room 2612
New York, NY 10013
(212) 387–6568
Fax: (212) 387–6569
E–mail: see below

4813

Business Information: AT&T is a diversified telecommunications company providing global voice, data, and video conferencing services and related products. They are well known for their long distance, local, and business telephone services. Established in 1886, AT&T currently employs 180,000 people worldwide. An employee of AT&T for 29 years, Mr. Presuto is now the General Manager responsible for the support of all eastern region network management center operations, from Boston to North Carolina. His unit is also responsible for the company infrastructure and network management. **Career Steps:** AT&T: General Manager/AMS (1992–Present), National Account Manager (1987–1992), Operations Manager (1982–1987). **Associations & Accomplishments:** Grand Lodge of the State of New York Composite Lodge #819; F & A Masons; St. Anthony Fathers Guild; Telephone Pioneers of America; New York City Mayors Task Force for Telecommunications Disaster Recovery; Wall Street Telecommunications Association; Published in Network World, Computer World, Project Management Journal, and others. **Education:** Nassau Community College, A.B. (1978). **Personal:** Married to Elizabeth Ann in 1975. Four children: Chris, Marisa, Frank, and Melissa. Mr. Presuto enjoys golf, scuba diving, and physical fitness activities.

James M. Pulfrey

Manager, Infrastructural Planning
U S WEST Communications
700 West Mineral Avenue, Room IAf 13.16
Littleton, CO 80120–4511
(303) 707–7601
Fax: (303) 707–9716
EMAIL: See Below

4813

Business Information: U S WEST Communications is a diversified telecommunications company providing global voice, data and video conferencing services and related products. As Manager, Infrastructural Planning, Mr. Pulfrey is responsible for overseeing development of all architectural standards relating to telecommunications infrastructures. Internet users can reach him via: jpulfre@USwest.com. **Career Steps:** U S WEST Communications: Manager, Architecture Planning (1993–Present), Manager, Infrastructure Planning (1990–1993), Manager Switch Planning (1983–1990). **Associations & Accomplishments:** Master Status, National Association of Radio and Telecommunications Engineers (NARTE). **Education:** New York University, B.E. in Civil Engineering (1971); St. Joseph's College, B.A. in Math/Physics (1971). **Personal:** Married to Lorraine in 1970. Three children: Jimmy, Michelle, and Lauren. Mr.. Pulfrey enjoys sports and being an ambassador for Promise Keepers.

Paul A. Quaiser

Director – Pacific/West Market
AT&T
26 W. Dry Creek Circle
Littleton, CO 80120–4475
(303) 707–4050
Fax: (303) 707–4125

4813

Business Information: AT&T Network Systems is one of the world's largest manufacturers of network telecommunications equipment and suppliers of end–to–end solutions used by communications services providers and other network operators around the world. The "world's networking leader," AT&T is the largest long–distance carrier in the U.S. and the world's largest provider of wireless services. AT&T's Worldwide Intelligent Network carries more than 185 million voice, data, video and facsimile messages every business day and AT&T Bell Laboratories provides basic research, product, and service development. As a result of merging with McCaw Cellular Communications, Inc. in 1994, AT&T is the largest cellular services provider in the world. Joining AT&T Network Systems in 1990, Mr. Quaiser was appointed as Director of the Pacific/West Market. He is responsible for determining market opportunities and direction, as well as developing market plans, allocating resources (R&D and people), and implementing plans and transition programs to account teams. **Career Steps:** AT&T Network Systems: Director – Pacific/West Market (1995–Present); Regional Sales Manager (1992–1995); Sales / Marketing Planning Consultant (1990–1992). **Associations & Accomplishments:** INROADS Intern Program; Denver Metro Big Brothers; Colorado Wildlife Association; National Audobon Society; Rocky Mountain Porsche Club; USA Volleyball Association; Telephone Pioneers. **Education:** Rutgers University, in process; University of Denver, M.B.A. in International Marketing & Business Administration (in process); Regis University, B.S. in Computer Science; AT&T Leadership Continuity Program; AT&T Executive Education Program **Personal:** Mr. Quaiser enjoys competitive volleyball, mountain biking, canine agility training, and wildlife preservation.

Sheryl L. Radetsky

Member Technical Staff
U S WEST Communications
931 14th Street, Room 810
Denver, CO 80202–2903
(303) 624–1767
Fax: (303) 624–0500
EMAIL: See Below

4813

Business Information: U S WEST Communications (formerly known as Mountain Bell) is a regional telecommunications provider, serving both residential and business customers covering a 14–state area in the western United States. A manager and service center consultant, with U S WEST since 1973, Sheryl Radetsky was appointed as a Technical Staff Manager in 1990. In this capacity, she is responsible for providing leadership, direction and support for information technology in the area of software tools. This includes tool evaluations, tool trials, project management, and providing software tool support on a regional level. Internet users can reach her via: SLRADET@USWEST.COM. **Career Steps:** U S WEST Communications: Project Manager (1990–Present), Service Center Consultant (1993–1994), Manager – Technical Staff (1989–Present), Supervisor (1986–1989), Computer Specialist (1977–1985), Computer Attendant (1975–1977). **Personal:** Married to Sam in 1981. Two children: Jaclyn and

Rachel. Ms. Radetsky enjoys running, aerobics, weights, and skiing.

Mr. Jacques H. Richard

Director of Asia Pacific Branch
AT&T
1535F, 32 Avenue of the Americas
New York, NY 10013
(212) 780–7800
Fax: (212) 780–7806

4813

Business Information: AT&T is a diversified telecommunications company providing global voice, data and video services and related products. They are well known for their long distance, local and business telephone services. As Director of the Asia Pacific Branch, Mr. Richard is responsible for the marketing and distribution of network services, as well as directing sales efforts of a 40 person organization. **Career Steps:** Director of Asia Pacific Branch, AT&T (1995–Present); General Manager of Sales, AT&T (1993–1995); Director of International Sales, Japan, AT&T (1990–1993); Manager of the Personnel Exchange Program, Japan, AT&T (1989–1990). **Associations & Accomplishments:** Japanese Communications Association of New York City; Fluent in Japanese. **Education:** University of Chicago, M.B.A. (1983); Brigham Young University, B.A. **Personal:** Married to Noriko in 1991. Mr. Richard enjoys golf, traveling, music and contemporary Japanese fiction.

Deb Ricketson

Quality Consultant
Southern Bell
13936 Ketch Cove Place
Jacksonville, FL 32224
(904) 350–3001
Fax: (904) 350–3005

4813

Business Information: Southern Bell is a telecommunications company specializing in telephone operations. As Quality Consultant, Ms. Ricketson is responsible for training, consulting, and facilitating teams and individuals through the quality process. **Career Steps:** Quality Consultant, Southern Bell (1991–Present). **Associations & Accomplishments:** Jacksonville Quality Exchange; Jacksonville Volunteer Association; Jacksonville Crises Intervention Center; Public Relations Student Society of America. **Education:** Currently attending University of North Florida; University of North Florida, B.A. (1990); Florida Community College, A.A. **Personal:** Married to A.J. in 1993. Two children: Justin and Chris. Ms. Ricketson enjoys working at the YMCA, sports, and travel.

Rick Rivera

General Manager
Valley Network Partnership
401 Spring Lane, Suite 300
Waynesboro, VA 22980
(540) 946–3525
Fax: (540) 946–3598
EMAIL: See Below

4813

Business Information: Valley Network Partnership, owned by four independent telephone companies, is a telecommunications firm, providing dedicated access at DS–1 and DS–3 levels to telecommunication carriers (i.e., AT&T) and other companies. As General Manager, Mr. Rivera is responsible for marketing and selling service, as well as P&L responsibilities, administration, operations, and customer service. His main priority is to negotiate high–dollar, high level contracts of more than $1 million. Internet users can also reach Rick via: rrivera@cfw.com **Career Steps:** General Manager, Valley Network Partnership (1994–Present); Marketing Director, KINI, L.C. (1992–1994); Assistant Vice President, National Bank for Cooperatives (1989–1991). **Associations & Accomplishments:** Former Board of Director, Contel Pioneers of Georgia; Former Associate Advisory Council Member, National Telephone Cooperative Association; Published in 1994–95 Registry of Business Leaders. **Education:** Georgia State University, B.B.A. in Management (1985); Northern Virginia Community College, A.A.S. in Management (1979). **Personal:** Married to Karla B. in 1987. Two children: Karmen Alyse and Meagan Elizabeth. Mr. Rivera enjoys golf.

Hayes N. Robertson

Vice President of National Accounts
Conference Call USA, Inc.
2913 Sequoia Drive
Edgewood, KY 41017
(800) 305–0989
Fax: (606) 344–9863

4813

Business Information: Conference Call USA, Inc. provides international tele–conferencing, audio conferencing, and call–back service to Fortune 100 companies and non–profit professionals. Established in 1986, the Company employs 100 people, and has an estimated annual revenue of $15 million. As Vice President of National Accounts, Mr. Robertson handles all administrative duties related to his department. He is responsible for providing a cost effective way for business to communicate on a national and international basis. Additional responsibilities include accounting, marketing, strategic planning, and public relations, ensuring customers remain satisfied with the level of service they receive. **Career Steps:** Vice President of National Accounts, Conference Call USA, Inc. (1989–Present); Assistant Vice President, Illinois Company INV. (1987–1989); District Sales Manager, CIT Group EF Division (1986–1987). **Associations & Accomplishments:** Cook County Republican Party; International Tele–Conferencing Association; National Association of Sales Professionals; Sales and Marketing Executives; Executive Club of Chicago; Telecommunications Resellers Association; American Management Association; Republican National Committee. **Education:** Texas Christian University, B.B.A. (1984). **Personal:** Married to Evelyn in 1993. Mr. Robertson enjoys trading on the commodities market and being a private pilot.

Teri M. Rogers

Network Environmental Coordinance and Compliance Manager
BellSouth
675 West Peachtree Street NE, 22J64
Atlanta, GA 30375
(404) 529–2504
Fax: Please mail or call

4813

Business Information: BellSouth Telecommunications, Inc. is an exclusively diversified telecommunications company providing voice, data and other advanced network products. BellSouth is the result of a merger between Southern Bell and South Central Bell. With offices located in nine states (South Carolina, North Carolina, Georgia, Florida, Mississippi, Tennessee, Alabama and Kentucky), BellSouth currently employs 74,000 people throughout the Corporation. Joining BellSouth as Supervising Engineer in 1991, Ms. Rogers was appointed as Network Environmental Coordinance and Compliance Manager in 1995. She is responsible for environmental coordination and compliance for the Network Department. **Career Steps:** BellSouth: Network Environmental Coordinance and Compliance Manager (1995–Present), Transport Engineer Manager (1994–1995), Supervising Engineer (1991–1994). **Associations & Accomplishments:** Lion's Club; Habitat for Humanity; Board of Directors, Georgia Tech Club for BellSouth Employees; Nature Conservancy. **Education:** Georgia Tech, B.S.I.M. (1977). **Personal:** Ms. Rogers enjoys scuba diving, snowskiing, and pottery.

Jeannie A. Salonya

Training and Development Consultant
U S WEST Communications
1365 West Gill Place
Denver, CO 80223–2303
(303) 763–1033
Fax: (303) 763–1006

4813

Business Information: U S WEST Communications is a regional telecommunications provider, serving both residential and business customers covering a 14–state area in the western United States. Starting with U S WEST in 1972 as an installer, Jeannie Salonya has steadily moved up the corporate structure, appointed to her current position as Training and Development Consultant in 1992. In this role, Ms. Salonya is primarily responsible for assessing training needs and developing team–building workshops. **Career Steps:** U S WEST Communications: Training and Development Consultant (1992–Present), Circuit Design Engineer (1982–1992), Residental Telephone Installer (1972–1982). **Associations & Accomplishments:** Chairperson, Electronic Advisory Committee; North Community Action Team; Big Sisters America; Volunteer Reading Program, Regis University. **Education:** Regis University: currently working toward B.A. in Psychology; Electronic Degree; Certificate in Management; B.A. in Business. **Personal:** One child: James Thomas Lloyd Jr. Ms. Salonya enjoys horses, water and snow skiing, and scuba diving.

Silveria Sanchez

Manager for Design, Methods and Analysis
GTE Corporation
700 Hidden Ridge, HQW03B37
Irving, TX 75038
(214) 718–4025
Fax: (214) 718–7469
EMAIL: See Below

4813

Business Information: GTE Telephone Operations is a world–leading telecommunications technology conglomerate. In her capacity, Ms. Sanchez oversees design, methods, and analysis. She manages all longitudinal and special studies relative to customer satisfaction – domestically and support GTE's international entitites. In addition, she is responsible for industry bench marking, consultation to the organization relative to customer perception, outside vendors, and data collection. Internet users can reach her via: Silveria.flores@Telops.gte.com **Career Steps:** GTE Corporation: Manager, Design, Methods and Analysis (1994–Present), National Account Manger (1989–1992), Account Management, Sales (1984–1989). **Associations & Accomplishments:** American Marketing Association; Dallas Hispanic Chamber of Commerce. **Education:** Dallas Baptist University, M.B.A. (1992); University of North Texas, B.A. of Applied Arts and Sciences. **Personal:** One child: Dominica. Ms. Sanchez enjoys racquetball, volleyball and attending sports events.

Mr. Richard L. Schaulin

Vice President of Human Resources
GTE Telephone Operations
600 Hidden Ridge, HQE04J10, P.O. Box 152092
Irving, TX 75015–2092
(214) 718–6306
Fax: (214) 718–1987

4813

Business Information: GTE Telephone Operations is a world leading telecommunications technology conglomerate. As Vice President of Human Resources, Mr. Schaulin is responsible for the overall administration and oversight for human resources policy staff support and guidance. Duties include: compensation and benefits, staffing, employee and labor relations, safety, education and training. Established in 1918, GTE Telephone Operations employs 70,000 people with annual sales of $15.7 billion. **Career Steps:** Vice President of Human Resources, GTE Telephone Operations (1988–Present); Vice President of Human Resources, GTE Service Corporation (1987–1988); Vice President of Human Resources, GTE California (1984–1987). **Associations & Accomplishments:** University of Southern California Advisory Board, Center for Effective Organizations; University of Illinois Center for Human Resource Management. **Education:** Southern Illinois University, B.A. (1964). **Personal:** Married to Mary Jane in 1963. Two children: Jeffrey and Jennifer. Mr. Schaulin enjoys golf.

Janice Lee Scites

Vice President of Business Customer Care
AT&T
11 North Stonehedge Drive
Basking Ridge, NJ 07920
(908) 234–8120
Fax: (908) 234–5370
EMAIL: jlscites@attmail.

4813

Business Information: A T & T is a diversified telecommunications company providing global voice, data and video conferencing services and related products. They are well known for their long distance, local and business telephone services. Established in 1886, AT&T currently employs 180,000 people worldwide. As Vice President of Business Customer Care, Ms. Scites works with customers on satisfying their needs for quality service. She is responsible for developing, implementing, and compliance to a billion dollar annual budget. Coordinating with other management staff, Ms. Scites designs and develops strategic plans for the Company. **Career Steps:** Vice President of Business Customer Care, A T & T (1995–Present); Connecticut Mutual: President of Customer Service Group (1993–1995), Senior Vice President of Individual Life Insurance Line (1992–1993). **Associations & Accomplishments:** American Bar Association; Hartford Bar Association; Connecticut Bar Association; New Jersey Bar Association; Society for Information Management, New Jersey; Winner of the Carnegie Mellon Business technology Innovation in 1993; Chartered Life Underwriter; Chartered Financial Consultant. **Education:** University of Connecticut Law School, J.D. (1977); Ohio University, B.A. (1971). **Personal:** Two children: Alexandria and Greta Colflesh. Ms. Scites enjoys reading and exercising.

Norma M. Scuri
Executive Director
Pacific Bell
2600 Camino Ramon, 1S051
San Ramon, CA 94583–5009
(510) 823–6555
Fax: (510) 355–9371
4813

Business Information: Established in 1906, Pacific Bell is a telecommunications company based in California and Nevada specializing in voice, video, and data. The Company is the largest in California and provides integrated network services. As Executive Director, Ms. Scuri is responsible for process management, technical support, and product introduction for network operations. **Career Steps:** Executive Director, Pacific Bell (1995–Present); General Manager, Network and Loop Technology (1991–1995). **Associations & Accomplishments:** Advisory Board, Department of Engineering – San Francisco State University. **Education:** St. Mary's College, B.A. (1988). **Personal:** Married to Andrew in 1975. Ms. Scuri enjoys golf, travel, knitting, reading, crochet, and the Internet.

Fakhruddin A. Siddiqui
Manager – Houston Office
AT&T
5 Greenway Plaza Estates
Houston, TX 77046
(713) 968–5326
Fax: (713) 968–5031
EMAIL:fsiddiqui
4813

Business Information: AT&T is a diversified telecommunications company providing global voice, data and video conferencing services and related products. They are well–known for their long distance, local and business telephone services. As Manager, Mr. Siddiqui is responsible for managing and operating the Houston Office and all field support laborers, in addition to supervising one of three core sales and marketing management teams. **Career Steps:** Manager – Houston Office, AT&T (1993–Present); Regional Manager, Data Digital Corporation (1982–1993); Exxon (1970–1981). **Associations & Accomplishments:** International Marketing Association of Professionals; American Association of Petroleum Engineers. **Education:** University of Pennsylvania: M.B.A. (1957), B.S. in Petroleum Engineering (1955); United Nations Institue of Advance Technological Studies – Geneva, Switzerland, Post Graduate Diploma; Institute of Commerce, School of Business – London, United Kingdom, Diploma. **Personal:** Married to Najma in 1959. Three children: Seem, Huma, and Noma. Mr. Siddiqui enjoys research writing, tennis, golf, and public speaking.

Lorraine M. Siegworth
General Manager of Human Resource Operations
Sprint
900 Springmill Street
Mansfield, OH 44906
(419) 755–8560
Fax: (419) 774–0145
4813

Business Information: Sprint is one of the top three long distance telecommunications companies in the U.S., currently employing 60,000 people. As General Manager of Human Resource Operations, Miss Siegworth is responsible for delivering Human Resource Services, with a staff of 17, to the employee base (i.e., labor, staffing, benefits, development) throughout the states of Indiana and Ohio. **Career Steps:** Sprint: General Manager of Human Resource Operations (1995–Present), Manager of Human Resource Re–engineering (1993–1995), Regional Manager of Business Office Operations (1992–1993). **Associations & Accomplishments:** North Central Technical College Business Advisory Board; Mansfield City Schools Business Advisory Council – Partners in Progress Program; American Society for Training and Development; Society for Human Resource Management. **Education:** Bowling Green State University, B.A. in Communications (1989); Currently pursuing a Masters Degree from The Ohio State University. **Personal:** Miss Siegworth enjoys motosports, travel, and reading.

William M. Staffeld
Director of Carrier Sales
Trescom International
200 East Broward Boulevard, 21st Floor
Ft. Lauderdale, FL 33301
(954) 763–4000
Fax: (954) 713–1522
4813

Business Information: Trescom International is a telecommunications company that provides international long distance for carriers such as Sprint, AT&T, etc. International in scope, the Company owns fiberoptic lines worldwide, coordinating and contracting foreign governments to provide voice and data communications, as well as Internet access. As Director of Carrier Sales, Mr. Staffeld oversees sales and negotiates long distance contracts for the southeastern United States and is directly responsible for representatives and managers located throughout the U.S. **Career Steps:** Trescom International: Director of Carrier Sales (1996–Present), Branch Manager, Commercial Markets (1995–1996); International Network Sales, AT&T (1993–1995). **Associations & Accomplishments:** South Florida Telcom Forum; American Cancer Society. **Education:** Florida State University, B.S. (1990); University of North Carolina, Greensboro. **Personal:** Mr. Staffeld enjoys all outdoor sports/activities and travel.

Karl A. Sweigart
Vice President of Corporate Human Resources
Sprint Corporation
10937 Oak Drive
Kansas City, KS 66109–3452
(913) 624–2438
Fax: (913) 624–2467
4813

Business Information: Sprint Corporation is a world–wide provider of diversified telecommunications and information products and services. They are best known for their long distance and business services. With twenty–five years experience in Human Resources, Mr. Sweigart joined Sprint Corporation in 1982. Appointed as Vice President of Corporate Human Resources in 1995, he is responsible for overseeing the day–to–day operations of corporate center human resources, including staffing, compensation, employee relations, etc. He also serves as the Chief Human Resources Strategic Planning Officer for all Corporate matters. Career milestone includes piloting the establishment of independent Human Resource departments in each business unit throughout the Corporation. In 1987, Sprint only had a Human Resources Department at the corporate level. **Career Steps:** Sprint Corporation: Vice President of Corporate Human Resources (1995–Present), Vice President of Human Resources Strategic Planning (1993–1995), Vice President of Benefits and Systems (1990–1993), Vice President of Human Resources (Network Division) (1987–1990). **Associations & Accomplishments:** American Management Association; Human Resource Planning Society; Lt. Governor, Kansas District, Optimist International; Former President, Piper Optimist Club. **Education:** American University, M.S. (1986). **Personal:** Married to Rhonda. Four children: Amy, Angela, Derek, and Blair. Mr. Sweigart enjoys working with youth.

Joseph D. Tesson
Director of Finance
Southwestern Bell
12851 Manchester Road Room 10 3–E
St. Louis, MO 63131
(314) 505–0005
Fax: (314) 505–0064
4813

Business Information: Southwestern Bell is an exclusively diversified telecommunications company providing voice, data and other advanced network products. As Director of Finance, Mr. Tesson is responsible for all financial functions in the St. Louis Market Area. He is involved in all strategic planning, financial functions, process improvement, budgeting and forecasting functions. **Career Steps:** Southwestern Bell: Director of Finance (1996–Present), Director – Billing (1993–1996), Director – Financial Planning (1992–1993), Director – Chief Accountant (1991–1992). **Associations & Accomplishments:** Certified Public Accountant; American Institute of Certified Public Accountants; Missouri Society of Certified Public Accountants; President, Alumni Board of Directors, Washington University. **Education:** Washington University, M.B.A. (1993); Southwest Missouri State University, B.S. in Accounting (1981). **Personal:** Mr. Tesson enjoys jogging and sports.

Karen S. Treat
Director
Pacific Bell
RM 3S250L, 2600 Camino Ramon
San Ramon, CA 94583
(510) 823–6505
Fax: (510) 866–3510
4813

Business Information: Pacific Bell is a San Francisco–based telecommunications company specializing in voice, video and data services. It provides long distance and local communications services and is building a new network for the information superhighway and wireless communications for California's customers. With six years expertise in the area of process re–engineering employing state–of–the–art software and statistical sampling techniques, Ms. Treat joined Pacific Bell as an Accounting Manager in 1986. Promoted to Director in 1992, she is responsible for the direction of product costing studies and several payroll and time reporting functions for technicians and sales employees. **Career Steps:** Pacific Bell: Director (1992–Present), Accounting Manager (1986–1992); Information Systems Manager, Pacific Telesis (1983–1986); Systems Developer, Pacific Telephone (1972–1983). **Associations & Accomplishments:** American Society Quality Control (ASQC); Published in Telephony Magazine (1993); Simply the Best Quality Award (1993). **Education:** Golden Gate University, M.B.A. in Marketing (1989); Loyola University of Los Angeles, B.B.A. (1973) **Personal:** Ms. Treat enjoys hiking, skiing, walking, traveling, cooking, and music.

Justo Varela, J.D.
Vice President of Corporate Planning
AT&T of Puerto Rico
P.O. Box 3746
San Juan, Puerto Rico 00902–3746
(809) 729–6205
Fax: (809) 729–2705
4813

Business Information: AT&T of Puerto Rico is a telecommunications company providing local and long distance communications, infrastructure equipment, consumer and business products, and systems integration services for individuals and businesses in the Puerto Rico area. Established in 1987, AT&T of Puerto Rico currently employs 400 people. As Vice President of Corporate Planning, Mr. Varela is responsible for the direction of the design and development of the AT&T of Puerto Rico long term strategy, regulatory issues, market requirements and company/competitor capabilities. Concurrent to his position with AT&T, Mr. Varela is also a part–time university instructor. **Career Steps:** Vice President of Corporate Planning, AT&T of Puerto Rico (1994–Present); Vice President of Corporate Planning, Puerto Rico Telephone Company (1986–1994); Engineer and various management positions, Puerto Rico Electric Power Authority (1960–1979). **Associations & Accomplishments:** Puerto Rico Engineers and Surveyors Association; Puerto Rico Bar Association; Federal Communications Bar Association. **Education:** University of Puerto Rico, J.D. (1973), B.S. in Electrical Engineering (1960). **Personal:** Married to Margarita in 1981. Five children: Sandra, Jafet, Wilka, Linette and Gabriel. Mr. Varela enjoys sports, chess, computers, and Church activities.

Lorna L. Waggoner
General Manager
One Star Long Distance
6200 Aurora Avenue, Suite 305E
Des Moines, IA 50233
(800) 950–7644
Fax: (515) 251–8798
4813

Business Information: One Star Long Distance is a reseller of long distance services, specializing in small– to medium–sized businesses. Established in 1982, One Star Long Distance reports annual revenue of $20 million and currently employs 300 people. As General Manager, Ms. Waggoner oversees total operation for three states (Nebraska, Iowa, and Illinois), including hiring, training, and motivating a staff of 40 people. **Career Steps:** General Manager, One Star Long Distance (1994–Present); State Director, LDDS Communications (1992–1994); Territory Manager, TMC Long Distance (1984–1992). **Associations & Accomplishments:** Member, National Association of Female Executives; Former President, Sales & Marketing Executives of the Midlands; Former President, Greater Resources for Omaha Women; Former Vice President, American Business Women's Association. **Education:** Sinclair College (1980); Miami Jacobs College. **Personal:** Married to Paul in 1982. Two children: Keith and Angela. Ms. Waggoner enjoys family activities, boating, and reading mysteries.

Helmy Hamed Wasief
General Manager
Beed Trading Company
P.O. Box 9173
Riyadh, Saudi Arabia 11413
966–1–4026239
Fax: 966–1–4034075
4813

Business Information: Beed Trading Company is a telecommunications company, providing the import, implementation and maintenance of private telecommunication, paging systems, and GSM terminals. Joining Beed Trading Company as General Manager in 1993, Mr. Wasief is responsible for all aspects of general management and Marketing. **Career Steps:** General Manager, Beed Trading Company (1993–Present); Marketing Manager, Switching, AT&T Saudi Arabia (1991);

Communications Division Manager, NESCO Saudi Arabia (1983–1989); Switching Expert, International Telecommunications Union (ITU) (1983). **Associations & Accomplishments:** Engineers Syndicate – Egypt; International Telecommunications Union – Geneva; shared the committees preparing specifications for Saudi telephone network expansion project TEP (1982–1983); A native of Egypt. **Education:** University of Alexandria, Egypt: Faculty of Engineering, B.Sc., Telecommunications Division (1968). **Personal:** Married to Fawkia EL Nahhas in 1974. Three children: Sons, Ahmed and Mohamed; and daughter, Marwah. Mr. Wasief enjoys chess, swimming and fishing.

Russell Todd Webster
Product Manager
A T U Telecommunications Company
600 Telephone Avenue
Anchorage, AK 99503
(907) 564–1525
Fax: (907) 257–4774
E MAIL: See Below

4813

Business Information: A T U Telecommunications Company is the largest municipally–owned telephone company in the United States and the 27th largest telephone in the country, serving 300,000 residents within a 100 square mile area of Anchorage, Alaska. As Product Manager, Mr. Webster administers the Voice Mail, Business Systems, and the Yellow Pages departments of the telephone company. He is involved in the development of new sales and marketing techniques for services offered. Internet users may contact him via: twebster@adr.com **Career Steps:** Product Manager, A T U Telecommunications Company (1996–Present); General Sales Manager, Anchorage Daily News (1994–1996). **Associations & Accomplishments:** Kiwanis Club of Anchorage; Listed in Who's Who in American High School Students (1981) **Education:** University of Alaska, M.P.A. (1995). **Personal:** Mr. Webster enjoys dog mushing, hunting, fishing, and repairing automobiles.

Warren H. Weiner
Vice President & General Manager
PCSI
9645 Scranton Road
San Diego, CA 92121–1761
(619) 535–9505
Fax: (619) 535–1785

4813

Business Information: PCSI, a wholly–owned subsidiary of Cirrus Logic, is an international manufacturer and distributor of wireless communications products. One of five owners, Mr. Weiner co–founded PCSI as Chief Financial Officer in 1987. He now serves as Vice President and General Manager in addition to his responsibilities as CFO, overseeing the design, manufacture, and marketing of wireless modems and communications modules (including two–way pagers and a cellular phone with an integrated pager, two–way messaging, and internet access). **Career Steps:** PCSI: Vice President & General Manager (1987–Present), Chief Financial Officer (1987–1994); Strategic Planner, IU International (1981–1983). **Associations & Accomplishments:** United Jewish Foundation; Bethel Synagogue. **Education:** Wharton School, University of Pennsylvania: M.B.A. (1979), B.S. (1978). **Personal:** Married to Nurith in 1982. One child: Sandy McBride. Mr. Weiner enjoys golf and bicycling.

Mr. Richard S. Wetmore
Director
Lucent Technologies
480 Red Hill Road, Room 2N–208
Middletown, NJ 07748
(908) 615–5900
Fax: (908) 615–5914

4813

Business Information: Lucent Technologies is a telecommunications systems and technology company. Mr. Wetmore's projects include operations systems software which improves the call completion performance of large public switched telephone networks, including network management systems which support network surveillance, analysis, and control during disasters, overloads, and other types of catastrophic failures. As Director, Mr. Wetmore manages a team of 400 people. Their technology is used by more than thirty telephone companies around the world. Mr. Wetmore is also a leading contributor to the International Telecommunication Union's Network Management Development Group. The ITU is a United Nations agency. Lucent Technologies provides telecommunications services and products worldwide. Internet users can reach him via: wetmore@lucent.com. **Career Steps:** Director of Network Performance Applications, Lucent Technologies' Laboratories (1991–Present); Network Management Department Head, AT&T Bell Laboratories

(1986–1991); Network Architecture Planning, AT&T Communications (1986–1986); Network Operations, AT&T Communications (1983–1985); Network Routing & Management, AT&T Bell Laboratories (1982–1983). **Associations & Accomplishments:** Institute of Electrical and Electronics Engineers; Tau Beta Pi Engineering Honor Society; Eta Kappa Nu Electrical Honor Society; Telephone Pioneers of America; Published articles in press and technical journals. **Education:** Cornell University, Master of Engineering (1978); Clarkson University, B.S. (1977); Licensed Commercial Sailplane Pilot.

Diana D. Wilson
Customer Advocate Manager
U S WEST Communications
200 S. 5th St., Room 1800
Minneapolis, MN 55402
(612) 663–5509
Fax: (612) 663–4347

4813

Business Information: U.S. West Communications is a diversified telecommunications company providing global voice, data and video conferencing services and related products. As Customer Advocate Manager, Ms. Wilson provides customers with project management services and data communications installations requirements. **Career Steps:** U.S. West Communications: Customer Advocate Manager (1996–Present), Corporate Project Manager (1994–1996), Sales Manager, Small Business (1993–1994), Sales Manager, Residential (1989–1992). **Associations & Accomplishments:** Board of Directors, St. Paul Rehabilitation; IMC; Project Management Institute (PMI)/ **Education:** Phoenix University, Certification in Technical Project Management (1995); Bellevue University: Master of Arts in Management, B.A. in Sociology (1994); Certified Project Management Professional (1995). **Personal:** Married to Milton S. in 1977. Three children: Sherri, Erick, and Ashley. Ms. Wilson enjoys singing, walking, and working with children.

Jim Wolak
Director
Ameritech
232 East Maple Road
Troy, MI 48083–2716
(810) 589–7676
Fax: (810) 589–7657
EMAIL: See Below

4813

Business Information: Ameritech, a telecommunications "Baby Bell" provides phone service to commercial interests in the mid–western United States. International in scope, with locations world–wide, the Company offers such state of the art communications as CPE cellular, and data and media services. Ameritech was established in 1984 with Divestiture, the mid–western branch, located in Troy, Michigan, is comprised of three divisions, Small Business, Custom Business Services, and Enhanced Business Services. As Director, Mr. Wolak oversees the service and repair needs of 49 direct reports, and handles the "I&M", with the non–regulated side of the Company. In the future, Mr. Wolak looks forward to integrating the Business Culture of the regulated and non–regulated entity, enabling Ameritech to offer a higher quality of customer service thru streamlined repair and billing. Internet users can reach him via: Jim.Wolak@Ameritech.com. **Career Steps:** Ameritech: Director (1995–Present), Manager, Distribution (1986–1995); President, Wolak Contracting Company, Inc. (1974–1986). **Associations & Accomplishments:** Volunteers to help the needy through various charities. **Education:** Elgin Community College: Bachelors in Psychology (In Progress), Associate in Climate Control Technology, Associate in Business.; **Personal:** Married to Vicki in 1982. Two children: Olivia, and Erin. Mr. Wolak enjoys carpentry, camping, flying, and inventing.

Sonny Works
Executive Director
EXCEL Telecommunications Company
18 Stevens Court
Villa Hills, KY 41017–1023
(606) 891–9122
Fax: Please mail or call

4813

Business Information: Excel Telecommunications Company is an innovative long–distance telecommunications company providing alternative voice, data services and related products to residential and commercial clientele (i.e., fundraising products). Services are marketed through a network of independent companies built by distributors. As Executive Director, Mr. Works provides all aspects of training to independent companies on a national level. **Career Steps:** Executive Director, Excel Telecommunications Company (1991–Present); Supervisor, Shaklee Company (1981–1989); Chemicals, Hilton Davis Company

(1971–1990). **Associations & Accomplishments:** Excel Team Soccer Coach (1995–Present); First Baptist Church: Treasurer, Deacon. **Education:** Cincinnati Baptist College (1978); Bill Gothard Youth Conflict Seminars. **Personal:** Married to Mary Elizabeth in 1975. One child: Benjamin Edward. Mr. Works enjoys golf, sports, and involvement with his son.

Willie F. Wright Jr.
Supervisor of Electrical Engineering
NISE East – Detachment Norfolk Code 526
Box 1376
Norfolk, VA 23501–1376
(804) 785–6422 Ext. 216
Fax: (804) 485–6467
EMAIL: See Below

4813

Business Information: NISE East – Detachment Norfolk Code 526 is a communications company, providing telephone installation and support services for U.S. Navy bases and Afloat commands. As Supervisor of Electrical Engineering, Mr. Wright is responsible for the management of the Telephone System Manager and Engineers who provide engineering and installation of switched systems. Internet users can also reach Mr. Wright via: WRIGHTW@gnome.nosc.mil **Career Steps:** Supervisor of Electrical Engineering, NISE East – Detachment Norfolk Code 526 (1993–Present); NAVE-LEXCEN – Portsmouth: Supervisor of Electrical Engineer (1987–1993), Program Manager (1980–1987); Nuclear Production Manager (Electrical Engineer), Norfolk Naval Shipyard – Portsmouth, VA (1974–1980). **Associations & Accomplishments:** AFCEA; Naval Reserve Officers Association; Naval Institute Society; U.S. Sailing Association; Norfolk Naval Sailing Association; Navy Sailing Association – Annapolis, MD; Who's Who World Wide. **Education:** Old Dominion University, B.S. in Engineering (1970). **Personal:** Two children: Deborah E. and Barbara E. Mr. Wright enjoys swimming, sailing, and cruising on the Chesapeake Bay.

Fred Y. S. Yoo
Executive Director
Bellcore
RRC 1M322, 444 Hoes Lane
Piscataway, NJ 08854
(908) 699–7200
Fax: (908) 336–3506
EMAIL: See Below

4813

Business Information: Bellcore is a leading provider of communications software and consulting services based on world–class research. Bellcore creates the business solutions that make information technology work for telecommunications carriers, businesses, and governments worldwide. As Executive Director – Network Services/Technology Services, Mr. Yoo is responsible for worldwide deployment and support for Bellcore Network Planning, Network Element Management, and Advanced Intelligent Network systems. Mr. Yoo began his career with Bell Laboratories in 1983, and joined Bellcore in 1984. Since joining Bellcore, Mr. Yoo project managed the development of large–scale telecommunications operations support systems for network provisioning and operations to support advanced telecommunications technology such as CCS, ISDN, FDLC, and multi–vendor switch generics. Internet users can reach him via: ysy1@cc.bellcore.com. **Career Steps:** Bellcore: Executive Director – Network Services and Technology (1993–Present), Executive Director – Technical Support to Chief Technical Officer (1990–1992), Executive Director – Integrated Software Project Management (1992–1993). **Associations & Accomplishments:** Software Support Professionals Association. **Education:** Columbia University, M.B.A. (1996); Brown University, M.S. in Computer Science (1984); Harvey Mudd College, B.S. in Math/CS. **Personal:** Married to Linda Lee in 1990. One child: Esther. Mr. Yoo enjoys golf, skiing, and travel.

Edward D. Young III

•••━━◖◉◗━━•••

Vice President of External Affairs
Bell Atlantic
1310 North Courthouse Road, 11th Floor
Arlington, VA 22201–2501
(703) 974–1200
Fax: (703) 974–8261

4813

Business Information: Bell Atlantic is an exclusively diversified telecommunications company providing voice, data and other advanced network products. As Vice President of External Affairs, Mr. Young serves as liaison between the FCC and the Company and ensures compliance with regulations. Concurrent with his position, he serves as Associate General Counsel providing legal advice. He was admitted to practice law in the District of Columbia courts and national courts in

1981. **Career Steps:** Vice President of External Affairs, Bell Atlantic – NSI (1993–Present); Vice President and General Counsel, New Jersey Bell (1991–1993); Assistant Vice President and General Attorney, Bell Atlantic Corporation (1988–1991); Senior Attorney, Bell Atlantic Corporation (1987–1988). **Associations & Accomplishments:** American Bar Association; National Bar Association; Washington Bar Association; Board of Directors, Bloomfield College; Board of Directors, United States Telephone Association (USTA); Board of Directors, United States Telecommunications Training Institute (USTTI). **Education:** Harvard Law School, J.D. (1980); Amherst College, B.A., cum laude. **Personal:** Married to the Rev. Gina Tillman–Young. Six children.

Ralph A. Young Jr., RPA, FMA
Group Property Manager
AT&T
2355 Dulles Corner Boulevard
Herndon, VA 22071
(703) 713–5100
Fax: (703) 713–5107
EMAIL: See Below

4813

Business Information: AT&T is a diversified telecommunications company providing global voice and data networking services and related products. AT&T is internationally recognized for its business and consumer long distance telephone services. Established in the early 1900's, AT&T currently employs 350,000 people worldwide. Holding various managerial roles with AT&T for the past 29 years, Ralph Young was appointed to his current position in 1994. As Group Property Manager, he is responsible for managing and maintaining 60 properties covering an area over two million square feet, as well as coordinates with the tenants to ensure the maintenance of the value of the buildings and achieve goals more efficiently. During his tenure with AT&T, he was the innovator in implementing a program to utilize microchip cards for security purposes as opposed to using guard personnel. Internet users can reach him via: ATTMAIL!rayoung. **Career Steps:** AT&T: Group Property Manager (1994–Present), Group Team Leader (1990–1994), Region Administrative Manager (1985–1989). **Associations & Accomplishments:** Society of Property Professionals; Optimist Club of Herndon, VA. **Education:** American College of Nutrition, M.S. (1994); East Carolina University. **Personal:** Married to Kathleen in 1967. Three children: Randy, Geoff, and Tony. Mr. Young enjoys coaching, gardening, and collecting baseball memorabilia.

Cheng Yong (Robert) Zhang, Ph.D.

Vice President
Asian American Network, Inc.
520 North Ethel Avenue
Alhambra, CA 91801–1817
(818) 452–2150
Fax: (818) 293–1846
EMail: See below

4813

Business Information: Asian American Network, Inc. is an international telecommunications company, providing business development, marketing, and consulting services in the Asia–Pacific/China Region. Sprint/AAA is a joint venture between Sprint and Asian American Association. As Vice President, Mr. Zhang serves as the major decision–maker and senior executive on all international–related business for telecommunication projects, especially in the Asia/China area. Internet users can reach him via: rzhang@aan.net. **Career Steps:** Vice President, Asian American Network, Inc. (1995–Present); Vice President, Sprint/AAA (1995–Present); Vice President, CDMA Communications, Inc. (1994–1995). **Associations & Accomplishments:** Institute of Electronics and Electrical Engineers; Senior Consultant, China Association for International Science & Technology Cooperation, China. **Education:** University of Southern California: Ph.D. in Electrical Engineering (1991), M.S. in Electrical Engineering; University of California – Los Angeles, Post Doctoral; Sichuan University – China, B.S. in Electrical Engineering. **Personal:** Married to Rong Zhou in 1987. Mr. Zhang enjoys photography and travel.

Jose D. Quinones
Special Channel Manager
AT&T of Puerto Rico, Inc.
250 Munoz Rivera Avenue, 10th Floor
Hato Rey, Puerto Rico 00918
(787) 729–6278
Fax: (787) 729–6260

4831

Business Information: AT&T is a diversified telecommunications company providing global voice, data and video conferencing services and related products. They are well known for their long distance, local and business telephone services. Established in 1886, AT&T currently employs 180,000 people worldwide. As General Manager, Mr. Quinones manages and implements special projects to generate revenues and increase market sales. **Career Steps:** AT&T: Special Channel Manager (1996–Present), General Manager Products and Services (1995–1996), Director Customer Service (1994), Sales Manager (1988–1994). **Associations & Accomplishments:** Industrial Association; Disabled Veterans Association. **Education:** New Hampshire University, B.B.A. (1985). **Personal:** Married to Yolanda in 1994. Two children: Jose Enrique and Dalyl. Mr. Quinones enjoys breeding birds, playing guitar, and bowling.

Lola M. Blais

Business Manager
Sconnix Broadcasting/WLNH/WBHG
P.O. Box 7326, Building One Village West
Gilford, NH 03246–7326
(603) 524–1323
Fax: (603) 528–5185

4832

Business Information: Sconnix Broadcasting is the largest and oldest radio broadcasting station in New England, providing the broadcasting for three radio stations for the Lakes Region. Stations include WLNH – Adult Contemporary; WBHG – Classic Rock; WAMJ–AM Talk Show, featuring such celebrities as Rush Limbaugh, Oliver North, and Dr. Joy Brown. As Business Manager, Ms. Blais is responsible for the management of all three radio stations, including accounting, payroll, insurance, purchase approval needs, etc. Concurrently, she is Owner and Operator of Blais Accounting Services, providing income tax services for individuals and small corporations, as well as payroll services. **Career Steps:** Business Manager, Sconnix Broadcasting/ WLNH/WBHG (1992–Present); Owner/Operator, Blais Accounting Services (1984–Present); Insurance Representative, State Farm Insurance (1990–1991). **Associations & Accomplishments:** DAR Recipient (1963); Laconia/Weirs Beach Chamber of Commerce; Participant in numerous fundraising–type programs, such as Santa Fund, an annual auction conducted to raise money for the needy. **Education:** Franklin Pierce, Masters in Business Management (1984); Real Estate License. **Personal:** Married to Wayne in 1994. Three children: Kristen Davenport, Dirk Zinn and David Relf. Ms. Blais enjoys golf and dancing.

Ruddy Bravo
Operations Manager
KDIF Radio
1465 Spruce Street, Suite A
Riverside, CA 92507
(909) 784–4210
Fax: (909) 784–4213

4832

Business Information: KDIF Radio is a local community Spanish language radio station. As Operations Manager, Mr. Bravo oversees all national and local sales, traffic, special events, and advertisements for the station. **Career Steps:** Operations Manager, KDIF Radio (1990–Present); Branch Manager, Electrolux Corporation (1982–1987); Chancellor Nicaraguan Consulate at Los Angeles, Nicaraguan Government (1976–1979). **Education:** San Bernardino Valley College, A.A. (1989); Private Autonome University – Managua Nicaragua, Private Accountant; Attended, Electrolux Management Training Center. **Personal:** Two children: Karla and Ruddy Joe. Mr. Bravo enjoys running and chess.

R. Charles Dusic III

Controller and Chief Financial Officer
West Virginia Radio Corporation
1251 Earl L Core Road
Morgantown, WV 26505
(304) 342–8131
Fax: (304) 344–4745

4832

Business Information: West Virginia Radio Corporation was founded in 1940 in Morgantown, West Virginia with WAJR–AM. In 1948, WAJR–FM was put on the air as the first FM station in West Virginia and one of the first commercial FM stations licensed in the United States. West Virginia Radio Corporation currently owns and operates eight radio stations and a state–wide news network. As Controller and Chief Financial Officer, Mr. Dusic oversees all financial matters for the three corporations, with primary duties involving financial reporting, annual fiscal analysis for distribution to stockholders, and overall budgetary matters. **Career Steps:** Controller and Chief Financial Officer, West Virginia Radio Corporation (1995–Present); Manager – Accounting and Auditing, Arnett & Foster, CPA's (1992–1995); Manager – Accounting, KPMG Peat Marwick (1988–1992). **Associations & Accomplishments:** West Virginia Society of Certified Public Accountants; American Institute of Certified Public Accountants; Broadcast Cable Financial Managers; United States Golf Association; West Virginia Golf Association; Previous Member of the GFOA Special Review Committee; Vice–Chair of the WVSCPA Cooperation with State and Local Government Committee; Board Member, Boyd Memorial Church of Christ; Member, Berry Hills Country Club, Charleston, WV. **Education:** Baylor University, B.B.A. in Accounting (1987). **Personal:** Married to Becky in 1992. Two children: Jake and Emily. Mr. Dusic enjoys golf.

Christopher E. Fleming

Director of Marketing
105.9 WHCN Liberty Broadcasting Group
1039 Asylum Avenue
Hartford, CT 06106
(203) 247–1060
Fax: (203) 247–1059

4832

Business Information: 105.9 WHCN Liberty Broadcasting Group is a radio broadcasting station consisting of nineteen privately–held stations. As Director of Marketing, Mr. Fleming is responsible for the overall marketing plan and execution. **Career Steps:** Director of Marketing, 105.9 WHCN Liberty Broadcasting Group (Present); Morning Show Host, WXPC Charlotte, NC; Assistant Program Director, WYBB Charleston, SC; Morning Show Host, WSUE Sault Ste Marie, MI. **Education:** Ithaca College, B.S.

Michael H. Ford
General Sales Manager
KWEN FM K. 95
7136 South Yale Avenue, Suite 500
Tulsa, OK 74136
(918) 493–8533
Fax: (918) 493–2889

4832

Business Information: Established in 1980, KWEN FM K. 95 is a radio broadcasting and advertising agency. As General Sales Manager, Mr. Ford is responsible for all sales of advertisements for two radio stations, KWEN and KJSR. **Career Steps:** General Sales Manager, KWEN FM K. 95 (1987–Present); Account Manager, WZZK (1985–1987); Local Sales Manager, KCYY–KKYX–KDIL (1987–1993); General Sales Manager, KWEN–KJSR (1994–Present). **Associations & Accomplishments:** American Marketing Association; Broadcast Executives of Tulsa (B.E.T.); San Antonio Radio Advertising & Broadcasting Executives (SARABE); Rocky Mountain Elk Foundation; Ducks Unlimited. **Education:** University of Alabama, B.S. in Marketing (1984). **Personal:** Married to Angela in 1985. Two children: Justin and Jacob. Mr. Ford enjoys hunting, tennis and racquetball.

Nancy B. Golden
Promotions Director
WBWN, B–104 FM
1303 Morrissey Drive
Bloomington, IL 61701–7033
(309) 663–1041
Fax: (309) 662–8598

4832

Business Information: WBWN, B–104 FM is a hot country music station serving central Illinois. As Promotions Director,

Ms. Golden plans and directs all aspects of special events and promotions for the station. **Career Steps:** Promotions Director, WBWN, B–104 FM (1995–Present); Retail Floral Manager, Owen Nursery & Florist (1992–1995); Retail Floral Manager, Imagine That! (1988–1992); Retail Floral Manager, Flower Town, Inc. (1994–1988); Floral Design Instructor (1978–1995). **Associations & Accomplishments:** Ambassador, McLean County Chamber of Commerce; Director of "Jam in June III" for the Children's Foundation; Board of Directors, Junior Achievement of Central Illinois; Board of Directors, Heart of Illinois Holiday Tree Festival. **Education:** Attended Illinois Central College. **Personal:** Married to Curtis A. in 1994. Two children: Michael and Rochelle. Ms. Golden enjoys country music (Tim McGraw's Number One Fan) and beginning to design the family's new log home.

Peter M. Johnson

Executive Producer and Creator
Classical Crossovers!
P.O. Box 333
Divide, CO 80814
(719) 687–8190
Fax: (719) 687–3077

4832

Business Information: "Classical Crossovers!", a unique weekly classical music appreciation hour heard on over 50 radio stations nationwide, is a production of PMJ Productions. Founder Peter Johnson is a former WGBH, Boston host and author of the thesis, "The Future of Classical Music on Radio in America." **Career Steps:** Executive Producer and Creator, PMJ Productions (1994–Present); Music Director, KZAZ–FM (1991–1992); Music Director, WDAV–FM (1988–1991); Producer and Host, WGBH–FM (1986–1988). **Associations & Accomplishments:** Licensed Colorado Realtor; Pikes Peak Hospice Volunteer; Association of Independents in Radio; Sierra Club. **Education:** Boston University: M.S. (1990), M.B.A. (1987); Williams College, B.A. (1975). **Personal:** Mr. Johnson enjoys landscape photography, Rockies and Utah backpacking, and readings on Catholicism.

James C. King

Director of Broadcasting
The X–Star Radio Network
3800 Victry Parkway, MS 7211
Cincinnati, OH 45207
(513) 731–9898 EXT: 108
Fax: (513) 745–1004

4832

Business Information: The X–Star Radio Network is one of the largest privately–owned public radio stations in the U.S. The Network owns a chain of seven radio stations located in four states (Michigan, Ohio, Kentucky, Indiana). A recent recipient of the George Foster Peabody Award (the highest award in broadcasting with 1 in 15,000 vying for the award), The X–Star Radio Network has a 1950's–style in broadcasting. Established in 1970, the Network has grown from a 10–watt station to the 26,000–watt station it is today. Beginning his career as an educator in Broadcasting and History, Dr. King serves as Director of Broadcasting at The X–Star Radio Network, responsible for the direction of all broadcasting activities, including fundraising, risk–taking, and radical thinking. In addition, he oversees the growth of the Company, new technology, and conducting updates on the Internet, as well as supervising a staff of 25. **Career Steps:** Director of Broadcasting, The X–Star Radio Network (1976–Present); Director of Broadcasting, Xavier University (1976–Present); Assistant Professor of Radio–TV, University of Cincinnati (1973–1976). **Associations & Accomplishments:** National Association of Broadcasters; Michigan Association of Broadcasters; N.A.R.A.S. **Education:** University of Michigan, Ph.D. (1973); Western Michigan University: M.A., B.A. **Personal:** Married to Kathleen C. in 1967. Three children: Ryan, Justin, and Nolan. Dr. King enjoys computers, video production, reading, and ancient history.

Lutchman Bob Mahabir

President/Owner
WHIZ Communications Network
6073 NW 167th Street, Suite C–7
Miami Lakes, FL 33015–4314
(305) 826–5414
Fax: (305) 826–4715

4832

Business Information: WHIZ Communications Network is the voice of Caribbean America in South Florida, managing radio broadcasting on WAVS 1170 AM and WVCG 1080 AM. Mr. Mahabir established WHIZ in 1990, serving as President, General Manager, and Program Host, providing music, talk shows, guest speakers, and information to the community. **Career Steps:** President/Owner, WHIZ Communications Network (1990–Present); Vice President, Capital Bank (1974–1978); Vice President, County Bank (1972–1974); Commercial Loan Officer, Virgin Islands National Bank (1970–1972). **Associations & Accomplishments:** Lions Club of St. Croix, Virgin Islands; Lions Club of Ives/Sky Lake, Miami; Miami–Dade Chamber of Commerce. **Education:** New York Tech at Nova University; American Institute of Banking; Naparima College, Trinidad. **Personal:** Married to Joy Yuklin in 1969. Two children: Analisa and David. Mr. Mahabir enjoys parties and family get–togethers.

Albert Rodriguez Sr.

President
KAZA Spanish Radio
P.O. Box 1290
San Jose, CA 95108–1290
(408) 984–1290
Fax: (408) 985–9322

4832

Business Information: KAZA Spanish Radio is the only existing traditional Spanish station in the South Bay locale serving the Hispanic community for nearly a quarter of a century. Its ADI spans over a largely Hispanic six–county region and has listeners in Santa Clara, San Mateo, Santa Cruz, Monterey, San Benito, and Alameda Counties. It is strategically located in the middle of an Hispanic community which ranks Number 1 in Hispanic Household Effective Buying Income in the nation, and provides marketing excellence with its skillful mix of radio promotion with other people–to–people direct contact strategies. As President, Mr. Rodriguez is responsible for operational decisions concerning the future of the station. He is currently retired and his family runs the business, however, he is still involved in the day–to–day operations of the company, and remains the majority shareholder. Concurrent with his duties as President of KAZA Spanish Radio, he is also the President of LUZ/AL Promotions. Albert's impressive career in entertainment began in 1963 when he established a small movie house in Maryville, California. Within three years, he had expanded his enterprise into seven theaters throughout California and Arizona. He also has distinguished himself as a leading promoter in the state and the Bay Area, bringing top–name entertainers and celebrities from Mexico to perform at various Hispanic cultural events. For his tireless devotion to public service, Albert and Radio KAZA have won numerous awards, including commendations from the U.S. Department of Commerce for voter registration radio programs, his assistance in the Mexico City earthquake, and his generous scholarship support and help with veterans' issues. **Career Steps:** President, KAZA Spanish Radio (1973–Present); President; LUZ/AL Promotions (1968–Present). **Associations & Accomplishments:** Board Member, Hispanic Chamber of Commerce of Santa Clara Valley; Past State Chair, American G.I. Forum; San Jose Police Crime Stoppers; United Way of Santa Clara County: Co–founder of Hipanic Charity Ball; International Lions Club; The American National Red Cross; Appreciation Awards for his coverage and attention to AIDS, Immigration, Health, Drugs, Politics, and Art; Contributes to Hispanic Scholarships; Exemplary Leadership Award – presented by the Hispanic Development Corp., KNTV Channel 11 and The Mercury News in honor of National Hispanic Month; Special Commendation: 1991 "Profiles of Success" – by Santa Clara County Board of Commissioners for extraordinary community leadership.. **Personal:** Married to Luz Maria Sidhu in 1960. Four children: Veronica R. Yanez, Sonia S., Albert Jr. and Juan Manuel. Seven grandchildren. Mr. Rodriguez enjoys golf, fishing, and providing entertainment to the public.

Karen E. Slade

Vice President and General Manager
KJLH–FM Radio
161 North La Brea Avenue
Inglewood, CA 90301
(310) 330–2200 Ext. 221
Fax: (310) 330–5565

4832

Business Information: KJLH–FM Radio, a subsidiary of Taxi Productions, Inc., is a "Class A" radio broadcasting station, servicing Compton and Los Angeles, California. The station offers urban adult contemporary music. With nineteen years of experience in broadcasting, Ms. Slade joined KJLH–FM Radio as Vice President and General Manager in 1989. She is responsible for all profits and losses at the station, in addition to overseeing all programming, sales, and administration. **Career Steps:** Vice President and General Manager, KJLH–FM Radio (1989–Present); Xerox Corporation: Regional Sales Manager (1988–1989), Dealer Sales Manager (1985–1988), Marketing Consultant (1985–1987). **Associations & Accomplishments:** Board of Directors, National Association of Black Owned Broadcasters; Ladders of Hope – a Los Angeles–based program and affiliate; Advisory Board, Mentoring Our Students Through Experience. **Education:** Pepperdine University, M.B.A. (1991); Kent State University, B.S. in Broadcasting (1977). **Personal:** Ms. Slade enjoys reading, step aerobics, and old movies.

Doug Whitman

Senior Vice President
Noalmark Broadcasting Corporation
P.O. Box 104
Fayetteville, AR 72702–0104
(501) 521–0104
Fax: (501) 443–3100

4832

Business Information: Noalmark Broadcasting Corporation owns and operates thirteen radio stations in Arkansas, Texas, and New Mexico. The Stations offer a wide variety of programs including news, talk, country, and rock and roll. Established in 1973, the Company presently employs 115 people. As Senior Vice President, Mr. Whitman is one of three partners in the Company. He is a member of the Board of Directors. Responsibilities include public relations, providing vision and general management of operations, and strategic planning for the future. **Career Steps:** Senior Vice President, Noalmark Broadcasting Corporation (1983–Present); Vice President, KITN Corporation (1973–1983). **Associations & Accomplishments:** Chairman, Long Range Planning Committee, Fayetteville School District; Officer/Director, Arkansas Broadcasting Association; High Council and Young Men's President, Church of Jesus Christ of Latter Day Saints; Board Member, First Financial Bank; District Chairman, Boy Scouts of America. **Education:** Brigham Young University, Associate's degree (1980). **Personal:** Married to Pamela in 1976. Two children: Jessica and Andrew. Mr. Whitman enjoys family activities, travel, boating, skiing, and being a baseball coach.

FOX SPORTS NET

Sheryl D. Adams

Vice President of Corporate Sponsorship
Liberty Sports, Inc./Fox Sports Network
1800 W. Loop South #1680
Houston, TX 77027
(713) 963–8500
Fax: (713) 963–0924

4833

Business Information: Fox Sports Net is the national cable network division of the global sports alliance recently formed between News Corp., the parent company of Fox Sports, and Liberty Media, the parent company of Liberty Sports. Fox Sports Net consists of fX, the general entertainment and sports network, the Liberty Sports' nationwide family of Prime Sports regional networks. As Vice President of Corporate Sponsorship Sales, Ms. Adams is responsible for the strategic development and solicitation of network partnership alliances with clients seeking to further broaden corporate branding and name. **Career Steps:** Vice President of Corporate Sponsorship Sales, Liberty Sports, Inc./Fox Sports Network (1983–Present); Events Tournament Director, Liddun & Associates (1979–1983). **Associations & Accomplishments:** Chairman, Regional Sports Networks Advisory Board, Cable Advertising Bureau; Women's Sports Foundation; Association of Women in Communications; Pi Beta Phi Sorority; Alabama Alumni Association. **Education:** University of Alabama, Bachelor of Arts in Communication (1979). **Personal:** Ms. Adams enjoys tennis, golf, snow and water skiing.

Susan W. Allen

Regional Vice President
MTV Networks
950 East Paces Ferry Road, Suite 2440
Atlanta, GA 30326
(404) 814–7810
Fax: Please mail or call

4833

Business Information: MTV Networks is a highly successful cable television broadcasting company featuring programs like Beavis & Butthead and Headbangers Ball, in addition to an eclectic variety of music. Appointed to Regional Vice President in 1993, Ms. Allen oversees and directs affiliate sales and marketing staff activities, which includes local advertising and service terms. **Career Steps:** Regional Vice President, MTV Networks (1993–Present); Marketing Manager, Rainbow Programming (1984–1986). **Associations & Accomplish-**

ments: Women in Cable; CTAM. **Education:** University of North Carolina, B.A. in Journalism (1982). **Personal:** Married to Gene in 1987. Two children: Hunter and Samuel.

Mr. Geoffrey S. Calnan

Senior Vice President of Advertising and Promotion

Fox Broadcasting Company

10201 West Pico Boulevard
Los Angeles, CA 70035
(310) 203–1587
Fax: (310) 788–9745

4833

Business Information: Fox, Inc. incorporates Fox Broadcasting Company, Fox Television Stations, Fox Children's Network, Twentieth Century Fox Film Corp., FoxVideo, Twentieth Century Television, and Fox Music Group. Fox Broadcasting Company (FBC) achieved record profits in fiscal 1993. These gains resulted from both the addition of three new nights of regularly scheduled prime time programming, and modest firming of advertising pricing. As in prior periods of expansion, FBC's ratings declined slightly as the new nights debuted with primary new programming against established line–ups at the other three networks. The average household rating dropped only 2% from the previous year to 7.3 (each rating point represents 1% of all households with television sets, or 931,000 homes). However, as compared to the previous year, FBC held its ground on its strong Wednesday through Sunday prime time schedule with a 6.3 rating in the key Adult 18– 34 demographic. The average prime time rating of the other three networks declined 5%, from 6.2% in 1992 to 5.9% in 1993. Two hit shows were launched in 1993 – Martin and Melrose Place – complementing Fox's stable of veteran shows. Fox has also established itself as a major force in children's programming. The Fox Children's Network, which programs 19 hours each week of children's programming, is the #1 source of children's programming six days a week. Fox Children's Network has consistently beaten its other network competitors on Saturday morning with the #1 lineup for the season. It also ranked #1 in weekday afternoon programming with shows, such as The X–Men and Batman: The Animated Series, continuing to lead in their time slots. As Senior Vice President of Advertising and Promotion, Mr. Calnan oversees over 60 employees and supervises the creation and production of all creative print and on–air advertising, as well as design ON–AIR look. **Career Steps:** Senior Vice President of Advertising and Promotion, Fox Broadcasting Company (1988–Present); Vice President of Special Projects, ABC–TV (1985–1988); Secretary, NBC–TV (1981–1984). **Associations & Accomplishments:** Alcoholics Anonymous (1978). **Education:** Palo Vercles High School (1968).

Stephen Carrol

Vice President of Network Distribution

Fox Broadcasting Company

1211 Avenue of America, Floor 2
New York, NY 10036
(212) 556–2461
Fax: (212) 556–8568

4833

Business Information: Fox Broadcasting Company is a national provider of network television. Offering a large selection in programming, the Company offers production and distribution of news, sports, and movies, along with weekly prime time shows. Established in 1987, FOX has estimated annual sales of $1 billion. As Vice President of Network Distribution, Mr. Carrol is charged with the task of ensuring the distribution of network programming, and working with affiliate relations to improve their signal reception and promotional responsibilities. He also strives to enhance and develop the distribution of FOX to new markets and personally handles all contract negotiations. **Career Steps:** Vice President of Network Distribution, Fox Broadcasting Company (1994–Present); Regional Manager of Affiliate Relations, CBS (1989–1994); Cameraman, ABC (1984–1986); Technical Director, WTTG – TV (1977–1984). **Associations & Accomplishments:** International Radio & Television Society; National Association of Television Program Executives. **Education:** Columbia University, M.B.A. (1988); Ithaca College, B.S. **Personal:** Mr. Carrol enjoys running, weightlifting, and hiking.

Yolanda E. Carter

Production Manager

Black Entertainment Television

1899 9th Street Northeast
Washington, DC
(202) 608–2803
Fax: (202) 526–0795

4833

Business Information: Black Entertainment Television (BET) is a cable television network, providing a premiere source of television entertainment for African Americans. African American–owned and operated, BET also owns two magazines and a jazz and radio network. BET has recently launched a Web–site in partnership with Microsoft. Joining Black Entertainment Television as Production Manager in 1993, Miss Carter is responsible for the oversight of day–to–day "hands on" technical operations. She has direct supervision of a support staff of 7, with the indirect oversight of 60. **Career Steps:** Production Manager, Black Entertainment Television (1993–Present); Sole Proprietor, The PC Solution (1992–1993); Administrative Manager, Interface Video Systems Inc. (1983–1993). **Associations & Accomplishments:** Board of Directors, Women in Film and Video; The Village Center for Youth Development and Achievement: Executive Director, Co–Chair – Mentoring/Internship Committee; Executive Producer, Union Temple Baptist Church Television Ministry. **Education:** Howard University, English Major. **Personal:** Miss Carter enjoys reading, jazz music, writing, photography and gospel singing.

Jerry C. Corns

Director of Facilities

Liberty Sports

100 E. Royal Lane, Suite 300
Irving, TX 75039–3101
(214) 868–1000
Fax: (214) 868–1787

4833

Business Information: Liberty Sports, the largest producer of broadcast sports nationwide, handles broadcasting for regional sports networks. As Director of Facilities, Mr. Corns manages the corporate Facility and assists at the eight other locations. He oversees new construction, phone systems, and general communications work. **Career Steps:** Director of Facilities, Liberty Sports (1994–Present); Broadcast Quality Control Manager, Sportscom (1988–1994); Owner, New Tech Development (1979–1988); Mechanical and Nuclear Field Engineer, General Electric (1977–1979). **Associations & Accomplishments:** Building Owners and Managers Association; International Facilities Managers Association. **Education:** Pierce Junior College, A.A. (1973); Installation and Service Engineering Course; (Mechanical and Nuclear) Field Service and Management Course. **Personal:** Married to Janet L. in 1977. Mr. Corns enjoys home and furniture refinishing and mechanical antiques.

John M. Florescu

Chief Executive Officer

David Paradine Television, Inc.

9000 Sunset Boulevard
Los Angeles, CA 90069
(310) 275–5644
Fax: (310) 275–5670

4833

Business Information: David Paradine Television, Inc. specializes in the production of public affairs, news, and entertainment programming for worldwide distribution. Mr. Florescu is Executive Producer of the longest–running PBS interview series "Talking with David Frost." Executive Producer " The Next President with David Frost" (1986–1988). **Career Steps:** Chief Executive Officer/Executive Producer, David Paradine Television, Inc. (1986–Present); Director, Communications Department, Democratic National Committee, D.C. (1985–1986); Executive Producer, Great Confrontations At The Oxford Union/P.B.S. (1982–1985); Vice President, Programming, American Program Bureau, Inc. (1981–1985). **Associations & Accomplishments:** Contributor to Editorial Pages of Washington Post, The Christian Science Monitor, Boston Globe, and San Francisco Chronicle; Oxford Cambridge Society of California; National Democratic Institute; U.S. Election Observer in Romania and Kenya; Guest lecturer – Stanford, Yale, and Harvard universities. **Education:** Boston College, B.A. in History, Magna Cum Laude (1976); Campion Hall – Oxford University, Matriculated, Fall (1974). **Personal:** Married to Gina in 1993. Mr. Florescu enjoys tennis and skiing.

Douglas W. Garlinger

Director of Engineering

LeSea Broadcasting WHMB–TV40

10511 Greenfield Avenue
Noblesville, IN 46060–4127
(317) 773–5050
Fax: (317) 776–4051
dgarlinger@prodigy.com

4833

Business Information: Established in 1968, LeSea Broadcasting is one of the nation's largest Christian broadcasting networks with outlets owned and operated in 7 states. As Director of Engineering, Mr. Garlinger is responsible for overseeing all technical aspects of nine television facilities, one FM station, a satellite uplink facility and two international shortwave stations. Mr. Garlinger is also active in LeSEA Global Feed the Hungry, a missionary program delivering food and supplies worldwide. Since 1988, Mr. Garlinger has made numerous visits to Africa and other crisis spots as part of a LeSEA Global logistical team and video documentary crew. He was present in Rwanda, Burundi and Goma, Zaire shortly after the Rwandan massacres. He has visited over 50 nations as a result of his work with LeSEA Global and LeSEA Broadcasting. Internet users can reach him via: dgarlinger@prodigy.com. **Career Steps:** Director of Engineering, LeSea Broadcasting WHMB–TV40 (1980–Present); Broadcast Engineer, WTHR–TV13 – Indpls, In (1972–1979); Broadcast Engineer, WIMA–TV35 – Lima, OH (1970–1972). **Associations & Accomplishments:** Society of Broadcast Engineers; Board of Directors, National Association of Shortwave Broadcasters; Trustee, Ennes Educational Foundation; SBE Educator of the Year (1994); U.S. Patent, Video Periodicity Indicator (1978); Co–Authored SBE TV Operations Certification Handbook; Cleveland Institute of Electronics, Outstanding Graduate of the Year (1996). **Education:** Cleveland Institute of Electronics, A.A.S.Electronics Engineering Technology (1994). **Personal:** Married to Cheryl in 1987. Three children: Angela, Kelly Garlinger, and Josh Boyle. Mr. Garlinger enjoys aviation and being an amateur radio operator, callsign WAGPQX.

Mr. Jim S. Gilmore, Jr.

Chairman and Chief Executive Officer

Gilmore Enterprises Corporation

162 East Michigan Avenue
Kalamazoo, MI 49007
(616) 381–6744
Fax: (616) 381–5326

4833

Business Information: Gilmore Enterprises Corporation is the parent company for diverse business concerns throughout Michigan. Business entities include: Continental Corporation of Michigan (Real Estate Operations), Continental Corporation of Michigan (Gilmore Rading Team), and Jim Gilmore Enterprises Industrial Farms, Richland, MI. Established in 1962, Gilmore Enterprises Corporation employs 100 people. In his current capacity as Chairman and Chief Executive Officer, Mr. Gilmore oversees all aspects of operations for Gilmore Enterprises Corporation and its subsidiaries. He also serves as Chairman and Chief Executive Officer of Gilmore Broadcasting Corporation which includes Gim Gilmore Productions and WEHT–TV (an ABC Affiliate), both of Evansville, Indiana. **Career Steps:** Chairman and Chief Executive Officer, Gilmore Enterprises Corporation (Present); Chairman and Chief Executive Officer, Gilmore Broadcasting Corporation (Present); Partner and Chairman, Cole–Gilmore Pontiac–Cadillac/Nissan; Board of Directors, Biggs/Gilmore Association; Board of Directors, Fabri–Kal Corporation; President and Director, Stadium Management Co., Inc. **Associations & Accomplishments:** National Broadcasters Club; National Communications Club; Classic Car Club of America; The Park Club; The Beacon Club; Kalamazoo Country Club; The Metropolitan Club; Mid–America Club; Cheeca Lodge; Capitol Hill Club; Dictionary of International Biography; Jim Gilmore Foundation; Former Member, Board of Directors, American Cancer Society; March of Dimes Life Member; Board of Directors, National Captioning Institute; Boys Clubs of America Associate Director; NAB Advisory Committee to Corporation for Public Broadcasting; Former Member, National Association of Manufacturers; Jewish National Fund "Tree of Life" Award; Honored at the White House Reception for Selected Broadcasters; Selected by Radio Free Europe to represent United States on group visit to RFE and NATO facilities in West Germany; United States Auto Club (ASAC) Life Member; Republican National Advisory Council; Republican Congressional Leadership Council; Former Mayor, City of Kalamazoo; Supervisor, Kalamazoo County; Honorary Doctor of Humane Letters, Nazareth College; Boy Scouts of America–Southwest Michigan Council, "Distinguished Citizen Award"; Michigan Young Man of the Year (1960); Michigan Motor Sports Hall of Fame Member. **Education:** Culver Military Academy; Kalamazoo College. **Personal:** Five children: Bethany Lass, Sydney McElduff, James S. Gilmore, III, Elizabeth Bystrycki and Ruth Langs.

Mr. Ira H. Goldstone

Vice President and Director of Engineering

Tribune Broadcasting Company

5800 Sunset Boulevard
Los Angeles, CA 90028
(213) 460–3987
Fax: (213) 460–5787

4833

Business Information: Tribune Broadcasting Company, a Fortune 500 Company, is a broadcast group focusing on major market independent television and radio stations. Established in 1945, Tribune currently employs 1,000 people in the Engineering Division. As Vice President and Director of Engineering, Mr. Goldstone is responsible for capital planning and purchasing, as well as long–term technological planning and research. **Career Steps:** Vice President and Director of Engineering, Tribune Broadcasting Company (1993–Present); Director of Engineering, KTLA–TV Inc., Los Angeles, California (1983–1993); Vice President of Corporate Engineering, Standard Communications (1981–1983); Director of Technical Services, WCVB–TV, Boston, Massachusetts (1972–1981). **Associations & Accomplishments:** Board of Overseers, Emerson College; Society of Motion Picture Television Engineers (SMPTE); Society of Broadcast Engineers (SBE); Society of Television Engineers (STE); Jewish Big Brother Association. **Education:** Emerson College, B.S. in Mass

Communications (1971). **Personal:** Mr. Goldstone enjoys computer technology, photography and skiing.

Carmen Irizarry Bult
Comptroller
WAPA TV/Pegasus Broadcasting of San Juan
P.O. Box 362050
San Juan, Puerto Rico 00936
(787) 273–1440
Fax: (787) 793–8060

4833

Business Information: WAPA TV/Pegasus Broadcasting of San Juan is a television station providing local broadcasting services to the San Juan area. As Comptroller, Ms. Irizarry Bult is responsible for supervising eight people, managing the accounting department, and establishing accounting procedures and policies, handling financial statements, budgets, purchasing, and payroll operations. **Career Steps:** Comptroller, WAPA TV/Pegasus Broadcasting of San Juan (1995–Present); Pegasus Broadcasting of San Juan: Accounting Manager (1989), Chief Accountant (1987). **Education:** Catholic University of Puerto Rico, B.B.A. (1977). **Personal:** Married to David in 1982. One child: Joe. Ms. Irizarry Bult enjoys fishing, painting, and writing.

Hector M. Martinez
• • • ━━━◉━━━ • • •

Senior Vice President
Teleonce
P.O. Box 10000
Santurce, Puerto Rico 00907
(809) 721–7294
Fax: (809) 722–3505
EMail: See Below

4833

Business Information: Teleonce, affiliated with an Ohio television station, is an independent station that telecasts 21 hours a day in Puerto Rico. As Senior Vice President, Mr. Martinez handles all sales and marketing, including sales budgets, presentations, audience forecasts, and analysis. Internet users can reach him via: HMarti3071@aol.com. **Career Steps:** Senior Vice President, Teleonce (1991–Present); WAPA–TV: Senior Vice President (1986–1991), Sales Manager (1984–1986). **Associations & Accomplishments:** Sales and Marketing Executives Association; Chamber of Commerce. **Education:** InterAmerican University, M.B.A. (1987); Villanova University, B.S.B.A. (1978). **Personal:** Married to Mari Valldejuli in 1984. Two children: Hector Luis and Jose Jaime. Mr. Martinez enjoys bowling, basketball, travel, and reading.

Jacyn A. Meyer
Regional Vice President
Z Music Television
3010 Lyndon B. Johnson Freeway, Suite 1050
Dallas, TX 75234–2709
(214) 620–8800
Fax: (214) 620–1115

4833

Business Information: Z Music Television, a subsidiary of Nashville, Tennessee–based Fortune 500 entertainment conglomerate — Gaylord Entertainment, provides a family–oriented music video programming service. As Regional Vice President, Jacyn Meyer is responsible for selling Z Music Television to entertainment distributors (i.e. cable, DBS, wireless, MMDS, and telephone companies) located in the areas west of the Great Lakes to Hawaii. **Career Steps:** Regional Vice President, Z Music Television (1993–Present); Regional Director, NBC (1991–1992); Director – Affiliate Relations, Nostalgia Television (1990–1991). **Associations & Accomplishments:** Women In Cable and Telecommunications (WICT); Cable Television Administrative & Marketing Association (CTAM); Phi Theta Kappa. **Education:** University of Texas at Dallas in progress; Collin County Community College; University of Minnesota. **Personal:** One child: Adam. Ms. Meyer enjoys golf, tennis, and reading.

Bruce F. Miller
Vice President
Public Broadcasting Service
1320 Braddock Place
Alexandria, VA 22314–1698
(703) 739–5000
Fax: (703) 739–3223
Email: See Below

4833

Business Information: Public Broadcasting Service is a television network providing advanced, educational, and cultural programming to all PBS members in compressed digital format. Strategic goals for the network include providing high definition TV service to all members beginning this year. As Vice President of Broadcast and Technical Services, Mr. Miller is responsible for delivering advanced television services to stations, handling operations, maintenance and satellite uplinking. Internet users can reach him via: bmiller@pbs.org. **Career Steps:** Public Broadcasting Service: Vice President (1994–Present), Director of I/C Transition Planning (1993–1994); General Manager, Advanced Television Test Center (1991–1993); Manager of Studio Field Operations, ABC Washington News Bureau (1982–1991). **Associations & Accomplishments:** Chairman, Society of Motion Picture & Television Engineers, Washington, D.C.; Former President, Vice President, & Treasurer, Washington Executive Broadcast Engineers; Elder, E.P. Church; NRF Community Association. **Education:** Fordham University, MBA (1971); Drexel University, BSEE. **Personal:** Married to Barbara in 1963. Two children: Deborah and David.

Alfonso Espinosa de los Monteros
• • • ━━━◉━━━ • • •

Vice President, News Department/National News Director
Ecuavisa National Television Network
Bosmediano y Carbo
Quito, Ecuador
593–244–6979
Fax: 593–244–5488

4833

Business Information: As of March 1996, Alfonso Espinosa de los Monteros holds the record for the longest career in a single news program for Latin America, serving as National News Anchor at Ecuavisa National Television Network – the largest television network in Brazil – since 1967. During his long career at Ecuavisa Channels 2 and 8, Mr. Monteros has anchored and moderated a variety of opinion programs, debates, and panel presentations, conducting many one–on–one interviews with national and international personalities. Results of various national surveys find him to be the journalist with the most credibility nationwide. Concurrent with his Anchor position at the station, he has also taken on the duties of Vice President of the News Department since 1995 and also serves as magazine correspondent for "Vistazo" and "Close–Up." **Career Steps:** Ecuavisa National Television Network: Vice President, News Department – Channels 2 and 8 (1995–Present), National News Anchor – Channels 2 and 8 (1967–Present), Regional Vice President, News Department – Channel 2 (1992–1994). **Associations & Accomplishments:** Vice President of A–E–R (Ecuadorian Radio–Broadcasting Association). **Education:** Honorary Journalism Degree from the Ministry of Education (1971). **Personal:** Married to Priscila Rendon in 1972. Two children: Paula and Juan Jose. Mr. Monteros enjoys music and plays classical guitar.

Phyllis A. Ned
Vice President and General Manager
Pulitzer Broadcasting Company d.b.a. KETV
2665 Douglas Street
Omaha, NE 68131
(402) 978–8971
Fax: (402) 978–8922

4833

Business Information: Pulitzer Broadcasting Company d.b.a. KETV, based in St. Louis, Missouri, is the owner of a television broadcasting station in Omaha, Nebraska. Affiliated with ABC, KETV broadcasts syndications in the morning and evening hours, with focus on local news. Established in 1957, Pulitzer Broadcasting Company reports annual revenue of $15.5 million and currently employs 110 people. Joining KETV in 1990, Mrs. Ned has held numerous management positions. Appointed as Vice President and General Manager in 1994, she is responsible for all day–to–day operations, in-

cluding management of the direction of the entire television station. **Career Steps:** Pulitzer Broadcasting Company d.b.a. KETV: Vice President and General Manager (1994–Present), General Sales Manager (1994), Local Sales Manager (1991–1993), National Sales Manager (1990–1991). **Associations & Accomplishments:** American Women in Radio and Television; Advisory Committee, Television Bureau of Advertising Sales; Omaha Ad Club; Board of Directors, Omaha Crimestoppers. **Education:** Recipient, Degree in Business and Accounting (1965). **Personal:** Married to David in 1968. Four children: Denise, Diana, Rebecca, and Addie. Mrs. Ned enjoys tennis and golf.

Peter C. Neefus
Lead Systems Analyst/Programmer
Christian Broadcasting Network
977 Centerville Turnpike
Virginia Beach, VA 23463
(757) 579–3264
Fax: (757) 579–6122
EMAIL: See Below

4833

Business Information: Christian Broadcasting Network is a non–profit organization specializing in broadcasting Christian and family–oriented programs including The 700 Club. Among its affiliates is Operation Blessing, a humanitarian aid organization. Established in 1960, the Company employs 1,000 people and has estimated annual revenue of $100 million. As Lead Systems Analyst/Programmer, Mr. Neefus manages the Business Systems Group and is responsible for designing, implementing and maintaining custom software. He also supports the accounting, human resources, and other departments, and directly supervises a staff of six. Internet users can reach him via: peter.neefus@cbn.org. **Career Steps:** Lead Systems Analyst/Programmer, Christian Broadcasting Network (1989–Present); Contracts Manager, American Systems Engineering Corporation (1988–1989); Manager of Administration, Information and Control Systems (1986–1988); Management Trainee, Ferguson Enterprises (1983–1986). **Associations & Accomplishments:** Kempsville Presbyterian Church. **Education:** University of North Carolina, Chapel Hill, M.B.A. (1983); Davidson College, B.S. in Chemistry (1981). **Personal:** Married to Marie in 1990. Two children: Suzanne and John. Mr. Neefus enjoys sports, jogging, and spending time with his family.

Sarah E. Noddings
Vice President of Legal Affairs
Warner Brothers Television
300 Television Plaza
Burbank, CA 91505
(818) 954–7159
Fax: (818) 954–7104

4833

Business Information: Warner Brothers Television (p.k.a. Lorimar Productions) — a subsidiary of telecommunications conglomerate Time Warner — is a major television production company. A practicing entertainment attorney admitted to California, Nevada and New Jersey courts since 1975/76, Sarah Noddings has served in legal capacities for Warner Brothers Television and Lorimar Productions, Inc. since 1983. Starting as an attorney with Lorimar Productions, Inc. prior to the Company's acquisition by Warner Communications in 1989, Ms. Noddings has served in the capacity of Vice President of Legal Affairs since her promotion in 1987. She also handles legal matters for Telepictures Productions and affiliated companies. **Career Steps:** Vice President of Legal Affairs, Warner Brothers Television (1989–Present); Lorimar Productions: Vice President – Legal Affairs (1987–1989), Attorney (1983–1987); Of Counsel to Taft Entertainment Company, Russell & Glickman (1981–1983); Attorney, International Creative Management (1978–1981); Attorney, O'Melveny & Myers (1976–1978); Law Clerk, Hon. Howard W. Babcock – Eighth Judicial District Court, Las Vegas, NV (1975–1976); School Social Worker, Carteret Board of Education – Carteret, New Jersey (1970–1975); Director – County Youth Program & Research Analyst, Sonoma County People for Economic Opportunity, Santa Rosa, CA (1968–1969). **Associations & Accomplishments:** National Awards Committee, Academy of Television Arts and Sciences; Los Angeles Copyright Society: Member Since 1979, Former Trustee; Women in Film; Honorary Membership in American Trial Lawyers Association; Officer, Arlington Elementary and Casimir Middle School PTA Boards; Listed in: Who's Who in American Law, Who's Who of American Women and Who's Who in California; Women Entertainment Lawyers; Los Angeles County Bar Association: Intellectual Property Section, Barrister's Executive Board (1978–1979); Co–chair – Barrister's Settlement Officer Program (1976–1978); VISTA Volunteer – Kings County Community Action Organization, Hanford, CA; AWARDS: Dedication of Home Garden Neighborhood Center; YMCA Outstanding Service to Youth Award; Certificate of Appreciation from President Lyndon B. Johnson; Featured Guest on syndicated television program "The Home Show." **Education:** Seton Hall University – School of Law, J.D. cum laude (1975); Stanford

University – School of Law; Rutgers University: Graduate School of Social Work, M.S.W. (1968); Douglass College/Rutgers University, B.A. (1965); University of California – Los Angeles. **Personal:** Two children: Christopher and Aaron. Ms. Noddings enjoys family activities, travel, outings, tennis, skiing, bicycling, swimming, and photography.

Jillian Robinson
Program Development and Production Manager
KAET–TV Channel 8
Box # 871405, Arizona State Univ.,KAET/CH8
Tempe, AZ 85287–1405
(602) 965–3506
Fax: (602) 965–1000

4833

Business Information: KAET–TV Channel 8 is the P.B.S. television broadcast affiliate in Phoenix (19th largest TV market). Established in 1961, KAET–TV currently employs 75 people. With over eight years expertise in broadcast production, Ms. Robinson serves as Program Development and Production Manager, joining KAET in 1993. She is responsible for developing new television productions, supervising from inception to completion (production and producers), and exploiting merchandising/ancillary rights for shows. **Career Steps:** Program Development and Production Manager, KAET–TV Channel 8 (1993–Present); President, Robclif Productions – London (1988–1994); Script Consultant, ITC Entertainment – London (1987–1988); Producer, Tim Miller Productions (1987). **Associations & Accomplishments:** Arizona Production Association; Media Panelist, Arizona Humanities Council. **Education:** Colorado College, B.A. cum laude (1987); Attended: University of California – Los Angeles (1986); Syracuse University – Florence, Italy (1986). **Personal:** Ms. Robinson enjoys tennis, international travel, hiking, reading, and horseback riding.

Joan E. Russell
Financial Director
3 Angels Broadcasting Network
P.O. Box 220
West Frankfort, IL 62896–0220
(618) 627–4651
Fax: (618) 627–4678

4833

Business Information: 3 Angels Broadcasting Network is a satellite television ministry network specializing in religious, educational, health, and family programs. As Financial Director, Ms. Russell is responsible for all accounting functions, including accounts receivable, accounts payable, and funding for special projects. **Career Steps:** Financial Director, 3 Angels Broadcasting Network (1993–Present); Controller, KDL Foods, Inc. (1986–1993); Accountant, Lanny Branner Co. (1984–1993); Self–Employed (1979–1984). **Education:** James Madison University, M.S. (1993); Southern College, B.S. in Accounting (1974). **Personal:** Married to Robert in 1988. Three children: Heather M. Dillon Turner, Heidi Dillon and Daniel I. Russell (stepson). Ms. Russell enjoys music, reading and health.

Gaitree Sahadeo
Owner/Producer
Viddyms
P.O. Box 1988 – Madison Square Station
New York, NY 10159
(212) 228–6000 Ext. 385
Fax: Please mail or call

4833

Business Information: Viddyms is a television production company with a focus on the Caribbean culture and Reggae music. As Owner/Producer, Ms. Sahadeo is responsible for the production, publishing, and hosting of the Company, as well as promoting her productions and singers. **Career Steps:** Owner/Producer, Viddyms (1987–Present); Circulation Manager, Rodman Publishing Corporation (1995); Fulfillment Manager/Group Sub Manager, Institutional Investor (1989); Circulation Assistant, Adweek Magazine (1988). **Associations & Accomplishments:** National Business Circulation Association. **Education:** Hunter College, B.A. (1989); Attended, New York University – School of Continuing Education. **Personal:** Ms. Sahadeo enjoys bicycle riding, racquetball, and walking.

Thomas Randall Scott
•••◄━━━◉◯━━━►•••

President
Liberty Broadcasting Network, Inc.
745 Custer Drive
Lynchburg, VA 24502
(804) 534–8100
Fax: (804) 534–8119

4833

Business Information: Liberty Broadcasting Network, Inc., a Dr. Jerry Falwell affiliate television broadcasting network, provides nationwide, private educational and religious programming. The Network also does programming for Liberty University, the largest evangelical university in the United States. As President, Mr. Scott oversees all operations, marketing, promotions, and senior management. In addition, he serves as a frequent guest lecturer and is an adjunct professor in Marketing at Liberty University. **Career Steps:** Liberty Broadcasting Network, Inc.: President (1987–Present), Vice President; Chief Operating Officer, Old Time Gospel Hour; President, Liberty Alliance. **Associations & Accomplishments:** Direct Marketing Association of Washington; American Marketing Association; National Association of Christian Counselors. **Education:** Liberty University, M.B.A. (1990). **Personal:** Married to Linda D. in 1973. Two children: Stephanie and Brandon.

Jocelyn E. Smith, M.B.A., C.P.A.
Director of Finance
WJCT, Inc.
100 Festival Park Avenue
Jacksonville, FL 32202
(904) 358–6321
Fax: (904) 358–6331

4833

Business Information: WJCT, Inc. is a non–profit public broadcasting television and radio station. As Director of Finance, Mrs. Smith oversees all financial aspects of the Station's operations, including the business office and audits. **Career Steps:** WJCT, Inc.: Director of Finance (1994–Present), Accounting Manager (1991–1994); Accountant, Boys & Girls Club of NE Florida (1990–1991). **Associations & Accomplishments:** American Institute of Certified Public Accountants; Florida Institute of Certified Public Accountants; Beta Gamma Sigma MBA Business Fraternity. **Education:** University of North Florida, M.B.A. (1991); Certified Public Accountant. **Personal:** Married to David Lee in 1994. One child: Michael (Ryan) Mulligan. Mrs. Smith enjoys movies, dining out, being with friends, and spending time with her son.

Peggy M. Soucy
Deputy Bureau Chief and Chief of Washington News Operations
CNN America, Inc.
820 First Street, NE
Washington, DC 20002
(202) 898–7900
Fax: (202) 898–7904

4833

Business Information: CNN, the world's first 24–hour all news network, provides in–depth live coverage and analysis of breaking news events. In addition to comprehensive news events, CNN offers a full range of programs covering the latest in Business, Politics, Weather, Sports, Entertainment, Health and Science news, as well as topical interviews. Joining CNN as assignment manager in 1983, Peggy Soucy was named Deputy Bureau Chief in 1986. She was appointed to her current position of Deputy Bureau Chief and Chief of Washington News Operations in January of 1996. In this capacity, she has direct operations responsiblity over the network's largest domestic bureau, supervising over 350 employees. Specific duties involve strategic planning, administration and the coordination of special news projects. Working with the bureau chief, she represents all four networks with the White House, Congress, Department of Defense and other government agencies when the network pool chair position falls to CNN. Her major asssignments have included pool coverage of U.S. President Clinton's overseas trips, with the most recent being President Clinton's Middle Eastern trip in October, 1994. Other assignments were the supervision of Department of Defense pool coverage during the crises in Haiti, Cuba and the Gulf War. **Career Steps:** CNN America, Inc.: Deputy Bureau Chief and Chief of Washington News Operations (1996–Present), Deputy Bureau Chief (1986–1995), Senior Assignment Editor (1984–1986), Assignment Manager – Washington Assignment Desk (1983–1985); Various Assignment Desk Positions, CBS News – Washington (1978–1983). **Associations & Accomplishments:** International Women's Media Foundation; Society for Professional Journalists; Radio-Television News Directors Association. **Education:** James Madison University, B.A. in Communications (1978). **Personal:** Married to Denis in 1979. Ms. Soucy enjoys reading, skiing, kayaking, and snorkeling.

Ronald M. Stravinsky
Director of Financial Operations
WVIA TV FM
70 Old Boston Road
Pittston, PA 18640
(717) 826–6144
Fax: (717) 655–1180

4833

Business Information: WVIA TV FM is a non–profit public broadcasting station specializing in television and radio programming educational documentaries. As Director of Financial Operations, Mr. Stravinsky is responsible for handling a $4.5 million budget, revenues, fund raising, and supervising five employees. **Career Steps:** Director of Financial Operations, WVIA TV FM (1982–Present); Finance Director, City of Scranton (1974–1982). **Education:** Bloomsburg University, B.S. (1974); University of Scranton. **Personal:** Married to Donna in 1975. One child: Jenifer. Mr. Stravinsky enjoys golf, running, and activities at the beach.

Lori D. Terwell
Director of Advertising and Promotions
WBBM–TV – CBS Chicago
630 North McClurg Court
Chicago, IL 60611
(312) 951–3554
Fax: (312) 951–3571

4833

Business Information: WBBM–TV – CBS Chicago, a CBS affiliate, is the third largest ADI television station in the country with an audience of over 7 million. As Director of Advertising and Promotions, Ms. Terwell serves as the Creative Director for the station, in charge of all advertising, promotions, creative marketing, and all external media relations. **Career Steps:** WBBM–TV – CBS Chicago: Director of Advertising and Promotions (1995–Present), Promotion Manager (1994–1995); Writer/Producer, CBS–TV Miami (1993–1994); Writer/Producer, NBC–TV, KFOR–TV – Oklahoma City, Oklahoma (1991–1993). **Associations & Accomplishments:** Board Member, Chicago Coalition for the Homeless; Chicago Broadcast Advertisers Club; Promax International: Member and Nominee of Promax International's Gold Medal; NATAS; Recipient of three Emmy's for promotional sports. **Education:** University of Oklahoma, Bachelors in Journalism (1986).

Roberto Vizcon
News Director
WSCV Channel 51 News
2340 West 8th Avenue
Hialeah, FL 33010–2019
(305) 889–7602
Fax: (305) 889–7699

4833

Business Information: WSCV Channel 51 News is a Spanish–speaking television station primarily geared to the Hispanic population in South Florida. With fifteen years experience in broadcasting, Mr. Vizcon joined WSCV Channel 51 News as News Director in 1992. He is responsible for the direction of all news broadcasts and managing a support staff of more than 45. **Career Steps:** WSCV Channel 51 News: News Director (1992–Present), Executive Producer; Producer of Hola America, Univision Network (1989–1992); Producer, WLTV–TV Univision; Producer, WTVJ–TV (1988–1989); Producer, WCMH–TV (1987–1988); Producer, WINK–TV (1986–1987); Producer and Assistant News Director, WSCV–TV (1985–1986); Producer, WLTV–TV (1982–1984); News Production Assistant, WUSA–TV (1981–1982); News Producer and Reporter, WQBA–AM/FM Radio (1980–1981). **Associations & Accomplishments:** Radio Television News Directors Association AeRho; Secretary, National Honorary Broadcasting Society; Society of Professional Journalists; SDX; National Association of Hispanic Journalist; Florida Association of Hispanic Journalists; UPI Award of Excellence, Florida News Division A, Best Newscast Category, TV: Outstanding Achievement (1987), Honorable Mention (1984), Series/Documentary Category, Radio, Outstanding Achievement (1981). **Education:** University of Florida, B.S. in Broadcasting (1979); Northwestern University, Toward M.S. in Broadcast Journalism; Paid Broadcasting Intership, WQBA Radio – Miami, Florida. **Personal:** Mr. Vizcon enjoys jogging, going to the gym, reading, movies, bike riding, and rollerblading.

Peter A. Wood
Director of Computer Services
Crossroads Christian Communications
1295 North Service Road P.O. Box 5100 Station LCD 1
Burlington, Ontario L7R 4M2
(905) 845–5101 Ext.3521
Fax: (905) 332–6655
EMAIL: See Below

4833

Business Information: Crossroads Christian Communications, Inc., a non–profit organization, has the largest Christian website in Canada. CCCI is also involved in Christian television production throughout Canada. Hired three years ago to help consolidate the three systems and to develop new software, Mr. Wood has gained the title of Director of Computer Services. He oversees the department responsible for all computer operations. Internet users can reach him via: pwood@myna.com. **Career Steps:** Director of Computer Services, Crossroads Christian Communications (1993–Present); Senior Technical Editor, Spar Aerospace, Ltd. (1991–1993); Technical Writer, Atlantis Aerospace, Ltd. (1990); Systems/Documentation Consultant (1984–1994). **Associations & Accomplishments:** Chancellor of Knights of Columbus Council 3296. **Education:** Memorial University – Newfoundland, B.A. (1985).

Neil L. Abramson
Program Manager – HFC Telephony
Time Warner Communications
160 Inverness Drive West
Englewood, CO 80112–5001
(303) 799–3310
Fax: (303) 799–5681
EMAIL: See Below

4841

Business Information: Time Warner Communications is a national alternate access telecommunications provider and competitive local exchange carrier. The Engineering Corporate Headquarters is located in Englewood, Colorado, with two other headquarters in Stanford, Connecticut and New York City, New York. As Program Manager of HFC Telephony, Mr. Abramson is responsible for the development and implementation of hybrid fiber/coax (HFC) telephone systems to provide residential telephone service. Internet users can reach him via: neil.abramson@twcable.com **Career Steps:** Program Manager – HFC Telephony, Time Warner Communications (1994–Present); Senior Reliability Engineer, NEC America Inc. (1985–1992); Project Manager, GTE Sprint Communications (1984–1985); Operations Support System Engineer, Southwestern Bell (1980–1984). **Associations & Accomplishments:** Society of Cable Telecommunications Engineers; American Management Association; Institute of Electrical and Electronics Engineers. **Education:** Southern Methodist University: M.S.E.M. (1988), B.S.E.M. (1980). **Personal:** Married to Teresa in 1987. Two children: Clifton Lee and Melissa Laurel. Mr. Abramson enjoys scale modeling and tennis.

Duane M. Anderson
Systems Engineer
Sioux Falls Cable
3507 South Duluth
Sioux Falls, SD 57105
(605) 339–9393
Fax: (605) 335–1987

4841

Business Information: Sioux Falls Cable is a cable television and data networks company. One of its recent major projects was a data link–up for the Sioux Falls School District. Starting as an installer with Sioux Falls Cable in 1978, Duane Anderson has steadily worked his way up the corporate structure, appointed to his current position in 1987. As Systems Engineer, he oversees and implements all system technology design, as well as maintains satellite receiving equipment, automated commercial insertion, data links, and oversees capital budget dispersals. **Career Steps:** Sioux Falls Cable: Systems Engineer (1987–Present), Chief Service Technician (1985–1987), Installer (1978–1985). **Associations & Accomplishments:** Former President, Sioux Falls East Kiwanis Club; Society of Cable Telecommunications Engineers, Inc.; Board Member, Crime Stoppers. **Education:** Western Iowa Tech, Elec. Tech (1975); FCC Licensed; Dale Carnegie Human Relations; Advanced Technician, National Cable Television Institute. **Personal:** Married to Jerri in 1990. Two children: Jason and Laura. Mr. Anderson enjoys Civil War reinacting.

Ms. Susan E. Binford

Executive Vice President
Turner Entertainment Group
1050 Techwood Drive
Atlanta, GA 30318
(404) 885–4290
Fax: (404) 885–4298

4841

Business Information: Turner Entertainment Group is a public relations and corporate communications company providing worldwide programming, production, and entertainment distribution. Established in 1970, Turner Entertainment Group currently employs 8,000 company–wide. As Executive Vice President, Ms. Binford is responsible for all public relations. **Career Steps:** Turner Entertainment Group: Executive Vice President (1995–Present), Senior Vice President of Public Relations (1993–1995); Senior Vice President of Media Relations, NBC (1989–1993). **Associations & Accomplishments:** Women in Film; Women in Cable; National Academy of Television Arts & Sciences (NATAS). **Personal:** Ms. Binford enjoys golf and skiing.

Michael D. Burke
Manager of PCS
Cox Communications
1400 Lake Hearn Drive Northeast
Atlanta, GA 30319
(800) 241–1084
Fax: (404) 843–5711

4841

Business Information: Cox Communication is an international company, providing communications through newspapers, radio stations, and television stations worldwide. Joining Cox Communication as Manager of PCS and Partner in a corporate position in 1993, Mr. Burke is responsible for interfacing with the Regional company, as well as negotiating contracts and recruiting. **Career Steps:** Manager of PCS, Cox Communications (1993–Present); GTE Mobilnet: Network Planner (1993), Transition Manager (1991–1992), Radio Engineer (1990). **Associations & Accomplishments:** Published article in Wireless Product News called "PCS Standards Will Determine Site Equipment." **Education:** University of Southern Florida, B.S.E.E. (1988); Charles County Community College, General Engineering Studies; G.W.U.; Registered E.I.T. in Virginia. **Personal:** Married to Denise in 1990. Two children: Nicole and Timothy. Mr. Burke enjoys golf, tennis, gardening, and coaching his kids' sports.

Terri J. Burkhart
Senior Account Executive
TCI of Kansas
2012 First
Dodge City, KS 67801
(316) 227–8425
Fax: (316) 227–7212

4841

Business Information: TCI Media Services is the largest media sales organization in the world. The Advertising Department was established five years ago in Dodge City and Garden City, Kansas where Terri sells, she also sells in the Pratt, Kansas area which TCI added in 1993. As Senior Account Executive, her responsibility is for cable television advertising and creative promotions in all three markets. She is involved in production and scripting in TV commercials and directly supervises employees, including a secretary. With offices in Dodge City, and Pratt, Kansas, she also promotes a local cable show called Summer Scene 96. **Career Steps:** Senior Account Executive, TCI Media Services (1992–Present); News Anchor/Production/Sales, KBSD T.V. (C.B.S.) (1990–1992); News and Weather Co–Anchor, KTVC T.V. (C.B.S.) (1981–1990). **Associations & Accomplishments:** National Association of Female Executives; Chairman of Discover Dodge; Graduated Auctioneer; Ventriloquist for over 20 years; Past Assistant Director, Mrs. U.S.A. Pageant; Miss America Preliminary Judge; Involved in Television and Radio Broadcasting since age 16; Recipient: Young Carriest Award (1986), Award of Excellence, Marketing and Promotion (1994); Member of a Country Western Gosple and Rock and Roll Group (early 1980s). **Education:** Dodge Community College, Associate of Arts (1977); Kansas City Missouri School of Auctioneering. **Personal:** Married to Kenny in 1996. Two children: Chelsea and Katie. Ms. Burkhart enjoys fishing, hunting, trap shooting, singing, pit crew detail for her husband who races sprint cars.

Mario Cairella

Financial Director
Time Warner–Warner Music Argentina
Castro Barros 848
Buenos Aires, Argentina
(541) 957–6075
Fax: (541) 957–6073

4841

Business Information: Time Warner–Warner Music Argentina is an international entertainment company, providing television, cable, music, and related services to area residents. As Financial Director, Mr. Cairella oversees accounting and administration, and is responsible for finance, legal affairs, budget, and forecast activities for imports, logistics, international trade, collections and credits, and reporting IT and treasury activities. Mr. Cairella is an expert in reengineering and restructuring divisions as well as in optimizing the different lines of business profitability. **Career Steps:** Financial Director, Time Warner–Warner Music Argentina (1991–Present); Audit Manager, Unisys (1989–1991); Audit Manager, Kodak (1987–1989). **Education:** Columbia University, Executive M.B.A. (1984). **Personal:** Public Accountant/Systems Analyst. **Personal:** Married to Gabriela Raponi in 1989. Two children: Lucas and Florencia. Mr. Cairella enjoys reading and tennis.

James R. Craig

Vice President
Craig Communications
1740 South Interstate 35, Suite 128
Carrollton, TX 75006
(214) 245–5022
Fax: (214) 245–4922
EMAIL: See Below

4841

Business Information: Craig Communications is a communications cabling company specializing in local area network design, building, and installation. The Company installs fiberoptics using autocad drawings and autocad revisions. As Vice President, Mr. Craig is responsible for all aspects of Company operations, including overseeing daily operations, providing customer quotations, designing networks, and consulting services. Concurrently, Mr. Craig owns and operates his own consulting firm, focusing on campus design and communications network proposals. Internet users can reach him via: JRCRAIG008@AOL.COM. **Career Steps:** Vice President, Craig Communications (1984–Present); National Field Service Manager, Nova Data Systems (1982–1984); Regional Manager, Northern Telecom (1979–1982); Director of Satellite Service, Western Union (1962–1979). **Associations & Accomplishments:** Building Industry Consulting Services International (BICSI); International Facility Management Association; American Subcontractors Association (ASA); Association of General Contractors (AGC). **Education:** Graceland College (1958); Registered Communications Distribution Designer (RCDD); LAN Specialist. **Personal:** Married to Laura in 1988. Mr. Craig enjoys golf.

Jeff D. Del Monte
Director of National Operations
Time Warner Communications
160 Inverness Drive West
Englewood, CO 80112
(303) 799–5688
Fax: (303) 754–6155
EMAIL: See Below

4841

Business Information: Time Warner Communications is a national alternate access telecommunications provider and competitive local exchange carrier. The Engineering Corporate Headquarters is located in Englewood, Colorado, with two other headquarters in Stamford, Connecticut and New York City, New York. As Director of National Operations, Mr. Del Monte directs the national operations surveillance and maintenance organization. He is responsible for developing and implementing programs, operations and software, as well as conducting research for new program development. Internet users can reach him via: Jeff.delmonte@twcable.com. **Career Steps:** Director of National Operations, Time Warner Communications (1994–Present); Intel Communications Group: Director of Quality Assurance (1995), Director, National Control Center (1994–1995); Manager of Network Operations, Bay Area Teleport (1991–1994). **Associations & Accomplishments:** National Association for Radio Technology Engineers. **Education:** University of Maryland. **Personal:** Married to Petra in 1981. Two children: Daniel and Dominic. Mr. Del Monte enjoys computers and music.

Angela M. Donohue
Marketing Manager
Primestar
365 North Science Park Road
State College, PA 16803
(814) 238–0308
Fax: Please mail or call

4841

Business Information: Primestar is a direct–to–home satellite service with corporate headquarters located in Engelwood, Colorado. Customers are served nationwide. As Marketing Manager, Ms. Donohue is responsible for supervising distribution and sales offices, managing the Northeast Region, administering demos, and directing the sales force. **Career Steps:** Marketing Manager, Primestar (1995–Present); State Marketing Manager, TCI of Virginia (1992–1995). **Associations & Accomplishments:** President, CTAM Virginia Chapter (1994); Women in Cable and Telecommunications. **Education:** College of William & Mary, M.B.A. (1992); University of Scranton, B.A. **Personal:** Married to Michael in 1992. Ms. Donohue enjoys golf, gardening, and bicycling.

CABLEVISION

Lawrence M. Drake II
Senior Vice President and General Manager, Midwest Region
Cablevision Systems Corporation
3300 Lakeside Avenue
Cleveland, OH 44114
(216) 575–8016
Fax: (216) 575–0212

4841

Business Information: Cablevision Systems Corporation, the fifth largest operator in the United States, is a multiple system operator with interests in cable television, cable programming, telephony and sports and entertainment properties. Through its Rainbow Programming Division, Cablevision operates American Movie Classics (AMC), SportsChannel, and Bravo. The Company's sports and entertainment properties include the Madison Square Garden, the NBA New York Knicks and the NHL New York Rangers. As Senior Vice President and General Manager for the Midwest Region, Mr. Drake is responsible for the management and delivery of telecommunication services for 410,000 customers in a three–state region (Ohio, Illinois, Michigan), including systems operating results, revenue, cash flow, cost control, programming and customer service efficiency. Prior to joining Cablevision Systems, Mr. Drake had many years in the retail and food service industry, holding positions with such giants as Kraft Foods, Coca–Cola and KFC–Pepsico. **Career Steps:** Senior Vice President and General Manager of Midwest Region, Cablevision Systems Corporation (1995–Present); KFC – Division of Pepsico, Inc.: Vice President of New Concepts and Business Development (1993–1995), Vice President and General Manager (1991–1993), Vice President of Administration (1990–1991). **Associations & Accomplishments:** Executive Leadership Council; Executive Fellows Alumni Association at Rockhurst College; Life Member, Alpha Phi Alpha Fraternity, Inc.; National Black MBA Association; Director, Marketing Associates International, Inc. **Education:** Rockhurst College, M.B.A. (1990); Georgia State University, B.A. in Sociology and Business (1977). **Personal:** Married to Sharon in 1994. Two children: Kia Nichol and Kory Lawrence. Mr. Drake enjoys music, athletics, and reading.

Steven M. Dyche
Technical Operations Manager
News–Press & Gazette Company
102 North Woodbine
St. Joseph, MO 64506–3448
(816) 279–1234
Fax: (816) 279–8773
EMAIL: See Below

4841

Business Information: News–Press & Gazette Company is a cable television multi–system operator, with 100,000 cable television subscribers and 9 cable television systems. News–Press owns several television stations, as well as regional and community newspapers throughout the states of Missouri, Arizona and California. As Technical Operations Manager, Mr. Dyche is responsible for the engineering of both the newspaper and television stations. He develops new technology, integrates the technologies, as well as trains staff for projects and new innovations. Mr. Dyche's experience started in the industry when he was still in college working for a small Cable company. In addition to his duties as Technical Operations Manager, he is also the General Manager for Macon Cablevision, News–Press & Gazette Company's satellite system. Internet users can reach him via: SDyche@AOL.COM. **Career Steps:** Technical Operations Manager, News–Press & Gazette Company (1994–Present); General Manager, Macon Cablevision (1994–Present); Plant Engineer, Bermuda Cablevision Ltd. (1992–1993); Plant Operations Manager, United Video (1986–1992). **Associations & Accomplishments:** Institute of Electronics and Electrical Engineers; SCTE. **Education:** College of the Ozarks, B.S. (1972); Tennessee State Technical School, A.S. in Electronics. **Personal:** Married to Mary in 1970. Mr. Dyche enjoys his family and career.

Casey C. Flynn
Director of Sales – Western Region
Lodgenet Entertainment
4100 Spring Valley Road, Suite 800
Dallas, TX 75255
(214) 851–4223
Fax: (214) 851–4228
EMAIL: See Below

4841

Business Information: Lodgenet Entertainment is a lodging entertainment provider of cable television, in–room movies, in–room games, interactive services, shopping. As Director of Sales, Mr. Flynn is responsible for field sales organization in the western United States and Canada. Internet users can reach him via: CASEY.FLYNN@LODGENET.COMM. **Career Steps:** Lodgenet Entertainment Company: Director of Sales (1992–Present), Regional Sales Manager (1989–1992); President, World Marketing Group (1986–1989). **Personal:** Married to Cheryl in 1990. Three children: Kelsie, Pam, and Jeff. Mr. Flynn enjoys spending time with his family, golf, fly fishing, and skiing.

Francisco Framil
General Manager
Cable Adnet of Puerto Rico, Inc.
P.O. Box 366741
San Juan, Puerto Rico 00936–6741
(809) 273–1022
Fax: (809) 273–6420

4841

Business Information: Cable Adnet of Puerto Rico, Inc. specializes in advertising sales for cable television. The Company, owned by Telecommunications, Inc., represents different systems, providing marketing, sales, and service for advertising inventory. As General Manager, Mr. Framil is responsible for all aspects of Company operations, including sales, marketing plans, administration, budgeting, hiring, and personnel. **Career Steps:** General Sales Manager, Cable Adnet of Puerto Rico, Inc. (1992–Present); Telemundo, Inc.: Sales Manager (1990–1991); Sales Supervisor (1977–1987); Account Executive, WADA–TV (1988–1989). **Associations & Accomplishments:** Board of Directors, Sales and Marketing Executives Association; Advertising Committee, Chamber of Commerce. **Education:** University of Puerto Rico, B.A. in Political Science (1976). **Personal:** Two children: Carlos and Francisco Juan. Mr. Framil enjoys movies, fiction writing, chess, the beach, and basketball.

Stephen J. Frantela
District Manager
Century Communications
51 6th Avenue West
Huntington, WV 25701–1715
(304) 522–2373
Fax: (304) 523–5493

4841

Business Information: Century Communications is a cable television company, providing cable service to 45,900 subscribers, with 800 miles of plant throughout 28 communities in the Huntington, West Virginia area. Established in 1969, Century Communications has three locations in the region and currently employs 90 people at the Huntington Branch. With 14 years expertise in the communications industry, Mr. Frantela joined Century Communications in 1992. Currently serving as District Manager, he is responsible for the overall administration, management and operations of the district, including finances, sales, public relations, marketing, and strategic planning. Noted accomplishments include securing a contract for Marshall University, providing cable service to 1,200 resident dormitories; rebuilding the Huntington System to a 750mz two–way fiber optic sonet ring system, including budget, design, construction schedule, head–end upgrade, satellite dish replacement, and converter upgrade – projections include telephony, video conferencing, and data transmission by 1996–1997; improving public and government relations; successful negotiations of franchise renewals in many of the communities served; regaining a positive employee relations in a union environment; repairing hostile government and public sentiment requiring an effective media campaign, including personal TV appearance, meetings with the editorial board of the local newspaper, and radio; surpassing customer performance standards set by the FCC; negotiating union agreement renewals with the CWA; and exploring alternative revenue sources, such as: pay–per–view, leased access, telephony, and data services. **Career Steps:** District Manager, Century Communications (1992–Present); Continental Cablevision: General Manager – Salem, New Hampshire (1990–1992), Sales & Marketing Manager – Lawrence, Massachusetts (1990), Regional Marketing Manager of Sales & Service – Portsmouth, New Hampshire (1987–1989); Director of Sales & Marketing, ML Media Cable TV (1986–1987); Sales & Marketing Manager, Group W Cable, Inc. (1985–1986); Sales Manager, Rogers Cablesystems (1981–1985); Sales Representative, The Upjohn Company (1978–1981). **Associations & Accomplishments:** Board of Directors: West Virginia Cable Television Association, United Way, Valley Health Company; Rotary Club; Board of Directors, Art Museum; Clean Up Green Up; Homeless Food Drive; Recipient, Governor's Award two years in a row while employed at Continental Cable; Member, Telecommunication Subcommittee formed by the West Virginia Public Service Commission (PSC) to assist in establishing parameters for telephone competition; Recipient, "Achievement Award" from the National Association for Minorities in Cable (1993); Recipient, Cable Television Administration and Marketing Society (CTAM) "National Award" for a newspaper insert designed to favorably heighten public opinion (1994). **Education:** University of Minnesota Medical School, Graduate studies in Medical Science (1975–1978); Carroll College, B.A. in Biology and Chemistry, cum laude, on a football scholarship (1971–1975); Completed a course for business leaders throughout the State and Tri–State area – "Leadership West Virginia and Tri–State Leadership." **Personal:** Married to Diane M. in 1986. Two children: Alexander S. and Andrew J.

Peter W. Gaillard
Vice President of Strategic Planning
Booknet
45 Rockefella Plaza, 20th Floor
New York, NY 10111
(212) 698–2470
Fax: (212) 698–2472

4841

Business Information: Booknet is a new cable television company which will premier in 1997. The new 24–hour cable channel with be highlighting authors, reviews, and book sales. Advertising will be available on the channel and it will be aired nationwide. As Vice President of Strategic Planning, Mr. Gaillard is involved in all the groundwork for the Company. His responsibilities include creating time lines, developing strategies, marketing, affiliate sales, and satellite connections. **Career Steps:** Vice President of Strategic Planning, Booknet (1995–Present); Executive Director for Affiliates, NET–TV (1993–1995); Advance Representative, The White House under President Bush (1992–1993). **Education:** Kenyon College, A.B. in Economics (1988). **Personal:** Mr. Gaillard enjoys golf and tennis.

Jennifer L. Gatti
Director of Accounting
Harron Communications Corporation
70 Lancaster Avenue
Frazer, PA 19355
(610) 993–1038
Fax: (610) 644–2790

4841

Business Information: Harron Communications Corporation is a communications company with a direct interest in cable, direct broadcast TV, cable advertising, and media. As Director of Accounting, Ms. Gatti manages the accounting department at the corporate level, overseeing five regional accounts and one corporate account. In addition, she oversees all profit and loss, and statements, in addition to the overseeing the efforts of 15 employees. **Career Steps:** Director of Accounting, Harron Communications Corporation (1995–Present); Senior Accountant, Deloitte & Touche LLP (1992–1995). **Education:** University of Delaware, B.S.A.C. (1992). **Personal:** Ms. Gatti enjoys golf, travel, and reading.

L. W. (Lenny) Hannigan
General Manager
CVI – Cablevision Industries
233 South Third Street
Clarksburg, WV 26301
(304) 623–3933
Fax: (304) 624–4805

4841

Business Information: CVI – Cablevision Industries, recently merging with Time Warner, is a national cable television service provider. Joining CVI as Acting Office Manager in 1992, Mr. Hannigan was appointed as General Manager in 1994. He is responsible for the financial performance of the system, as well as government relations, personnel relations, public relations, and ensuring compliance with all policies, procedures, and regulations. Part–time Teacher: AIB classes at Fairmont State College (1992–1993). **Career Steps:** CVI – Cablevision Industries: General Manager (1994–Present), Acting Office Manager (1992–1994); Credit Department Manager, Empire National Bank (1989–1992); Loan Officer, Empire National Bank,(1985–1989); Customer Service and Operations, Empire National Bank,(1982–1985); Independent Contractor,(1977–1982); State Inspector, West Virginia Department of Highways,(1976); Part–time Teacher, Salem Teikyo University Radio, TV and Cable Programming. **Associations & Accomplishments:** Board of Directors, Clarksburg Salvation Army; Board of Directors, West Virginia Cable Television Association; Board of Directors, Nutter Fort Community Center; Harrison County Chamber of Commerce: Chairman, Partnerships in Education and Ambassadors Council; Greater Clarksburg Associates; Director of Youth and Music, First Baptist Church of Nutter Fort; Assistant Leader, Boy Scouts of American – Clarksburg Baptist Church Troop; Who's Who of Outstanding Young Men. **Education:** Attending: Fairmont State College; West Virginia Undergraduate School of Banking, Graduate; American Institute of Banking; Graduate Assistant for Dale Carnegie; Alderson Broaddus College: Music Education; Dun & Bradstreet Business Education Services; Information Technology, Inc. Certificate in Data Processing; Franklin International Institute, Inc. Advanced Time Management: DOCMOM, Inc., Leadership Education and Development; Crowe Chizek & Company, Loan Review, Loan Documentations: National Business Institute, Commercial Loans, Mortgage Foreclosure. **Personal:** Married to Cheryle L. (Sherry) in 1985. Two children: Jody Michael and Sarah Jane. Mr. Hannigan enjoys teaching and church activities. He is also an accomplished jazz musician, and enjoys writing and performing contemporary Christian Music.

Richard A. Human

Director of Sales and Marketing
TimeWarner Communications
11252 Cornell Park Drive, Suite 410
Cincinnati, OH 45242
(513) 489–5805
Fax: (513) 489–0439

4841

Business Information: Time Warner Communications is the telecommunications subsidiary of Time Warner Inc., the world's largest media and entertainment company, and a recognized leader in publishing, music, video entertainment and cable television. Time Warner AXS of Greater Cincinnati is a division of Time Warner Communications that provides competitive local access services. As Director of Sales and Marketing, Mr. Human is responsible for the direction of all sales and marketing activities including sales, budget preparation, network planning, the development of plans for products and services, costing programs, and the creation of innovative ways to market products and services. He lives by the motto, "The refusal to fail and the tenacity to overcome." **Career Steps:** Director of Sales and Marketing, Time Warner Communications (1994–Present); Sales Manager, Norstan Communications (1991–1994); National Account Manager, LCI International (1991): National Account Executive, MCI Telecommunications (1988–1991); Major Account Executive (1986–1988). **Associations & Accomplishments:** Mason; Deerfield Township Rotary Club; Tri–State Telecommunications Association; Lakota Business Advisory Council. **Education:** Wilmington College, B.A. in Management (in progress). **Personal:** Married to Michele in 1982. Two children: Ricky and Lauren. Mr. Human enjoys golf and fishing with his children.

David R. Humphrey

Senior Vice President
International Family Entertainment
2877 Guardian Lane, P.O. Box 2050
Virginia Beach, VA 23450–2050
(757) 459–6110
Fax: (757) 459–6421

4841

Business Information: International Family Entertainment, owned by Tele–Communications, Inc., specializes in the production of family–oriented television programming. Owners and operators of "The Family Channel", and "MTM Entertainment" (owners of the "Bob Newhart" and "Mary Tyler Moore" shows), the Company produces and distributes T.V. programs aimed at family–style viewing with programs suitable to all family members. The Company also owns the Ice Capades and Carolina Opry. Established in 1977, the Company employs 840 people, and has an estimated annual revenue of $295 million. As Senior Vice President, Mr. Humphrey oversees investor relations, stockholder meetings and strategic planning (i.e. mergers, acquisitions, and related finance). Additional responsibilities include managing of SEC filings, negotiating loans and protecting interest rates, and serving as Company liaison with Wall Street analysts. **Career Steps:** International Family Entertainment: Senior Vice President (1993–Present), Vice President of Financial Relations (1992–1993); Tele–Communications, Inc: Assistant Vice President of Financial Reporting (1989–1992), Director of Financial Reporting (1981–1989). **Associations & Accomplishments:** American Institute of Certified Public Accountants (AICPA); Colorado Society of Certified Public Accountants (CSCPA); National Investor Relations Institute (NIRI); Quoted in "The Wall Street Journal" and "Multi–Channel News." **Education:** Colorado State University: B.S., B.A, (1977). **Personal:** Married to Karen in 1977. Two children: Robert and Heather. Mr. Humphrey enjoys golf and camping.

Sandra S. Mitchell

Regional Vice President
Home Box Office (HBO)
12750 Merit Drive
Dallas, TX 75251–1209
(214) 450–1033
Fax: (214) 387–5670

4841

Business Information: Home Box Office (HBO) is an international distributor of subscription cable television services providing HBO and Cinemax to cable operators throughout the country. The Dallas Regional Office — covering the States of Texas, Oklahoma, Louisiana, Arkansas and New Mexico — currently employs 1,000 people. As Regional Vice President, Ms. Mitchell is responsible for the management of the Dallas Regional Office, including ensuring the achievement of goals, dealing with subscribers, achieving maximum penetration in the area for new clients, financial deals, and negotiating with clients. **Career Steps:** Home Box Office (HBO): Regional Vice President (1994–Present), Director and Regional Manager. **Associations & Accomplishments:** CTAM – Texas Board Member; National Association of Minorities in Cable; Women in Cable. **Education:** University of Wisconsin, M.B.A. (1980); Southern University, B.S. in Accounting (1977). **Personal:** Married to William in 1987. Two children: Charles and Justin. Ms. Mitchell enjoys spending time with her sons, fitness, jogging and racquetball.

Adolphus M. Ohaya

Manager of Materials/Purchasing
TCI of Pennsylvania, Inc.
300 Corliss Street
Pittsburgh, PA 15220–4815
(412) 771–8700 Ext: 1224
Fax: (412) 331–7452

4841

Business Information: TCI of Pennsylvania, Inc. is the largest provider of Cable Television/ Telecommunications Services to homes in Western Pennsylvania. Established in 1968, TCI is the world's largest cable service provider which operates from four groups. As Manager of Materials and Purchasing for TCI of PA, Inc., Mr. Ohaya manages the assets in the system's warehouse, including all requests for purchase orders, as well as implements policies and procedures for asset management and control. **Career Steps:** Manager of Materials/Purchasing, TCI of Pennsylvania, Inc. (1995–Present); Tax Department Customer Service Manager, PayAmerica (1993–1995); Senior Payroll Tax Administrator, Ceridian Corporation (1986–1993). **Associations & Accomplishments:** Executive Director, African Relief Fund Inc. – a non–profit charitable organization (non–salaried and voluntary); Americian Planning Association; Fellow, Walter Kaitz Foundation (1995–1996); National Association of Minorities in Cable. **Education:** Morgan State University: Master of City and Regional Planning (1986), B.A. Geography, magna cum laude (1981). **Personal:** Married to Cynthia Ann in 1981. Two children: Lauren and Nicole. Mr. Ohaya enjoys soccer and volunteering for any activities to enhance the quality of life for less fortunate people.

Mary H. Oldak

Vice President of Business Operations and Finance
Home Box Office (HBO) – Direct to Home Satellite
1100 Avenue of the Americas
New York, NY 10036
(212) 512–1002
Fax: (212) 512–1794

4841

Business Information: Home Box Office (HBO), a division of TimeWarner, is a provider of pay television, as well as a creator of programs for its own multi–channel HBO and Cinemax channels. Joining HBO in 1981, Ms. Oldak was appointed as Vice President of Business Operations and Finance in 1994. She is responsible for overseeing the complex operational and financial challenges for distribution of HBO and Ciniemax to satellite dishes, including the various database systems, and telecommunications that support businesses as well as the customer service centers located in Chicago. **Career Steps:** Home Box Office (HBO): Vice President of Business Operations and Finance (1994–Present), Vice President and Assistant Controller (1990–1994), Director of Revenue Accounting (1986–1990). **Associations & Accomplishments:** American Management Association; Women In Cable & Telecommunciations; National Association For Female Executives. **Education:** St. John's University, B.S. and M.B.A. **Personal:** Two children: Lauren and Ryan Byrne. Ms. Oldak enjoys tennis, water–skiing, and reading.

John Pait

Operations Manager
TKR Cable of Greater Louisville
1800 Neville Drive
Louisville, KY 40216–3820
(502) 448–7336
Fax: (502) 447–2477

4841

Business Information: TKR Cable of Greater Louisville is a cable television company, providing paid television services to over 200,000 customers in the areas of Jefferson County, Louisville, and the Metro area. With thirteen years experience in the cable television industry, Mr. Pait joined TKR as Operations Manager in 1992. He is responsible for all customer operations, including telephones, customer service, billing, dispatch operations for after–repair calls, and meeting all Federal communications standards. He also oversees a staff of more than 75 full–time, 20–25 temporaries, and eight customer service supervisory employees. **Career Steps:** TKR Cable of Greater Louisville: Operations Manager (1992–Present), Installation Manager (1989–1992); Financial Planner, American Express Financial Services (1987–1989); General Manager, First Carolina Communications (1986–1987); General Manager, Greenville Cable TV, Inc. (1983–1986). **Associations & Accomplishments:** Association for Quality and Participation; Vice President, Little League. **Education:** Gardner Webb University, B.S. in Business Administration (1978). **Personal:** Married to Debbie in 1977. Two children: Matt and Ashley. Mr. Pait enjoys outdoor sports (i.e. golf, fishing, and hunting) and being an assistant coach for high school basketball team.

William A. Paquin, CPA

Chief Financial and Information Officer
ICS Communications, Inc.
520 West Arapaho Road
Richardson, TX 75080
(214) 669–6011
Fax: (214) 669–6016

4841

Business Information: ICS Communications, Inc. is a provider of shared tenant services, selling private cable television and security services to multi–dwelling properties. ICS is owned by MCI, NewsCorp. and two other investers, having a national presence in 28 cities. With ten years experience in communications and a Certified Public Accountant, Mr. Paquin joined ICS Communications in 1995. As Chief Financial and Information Officer, He provides the overall executive administration in the areas of financial and accounting, data informations and systems implementations. Career milestones include the formation of a venture that brought telecommunications to the troops in Desert Storm. **Career Steps:** Chief Financial and Information Officer, ICS Communications, Inc. (1995–Present); Vice President of Finance and Information Services, MCI International, Inc. (1986–1995); Vice President of Planning and Analysis, Paine Webber. **Associations & Accomplishments:** Financial Executives Institute; American Institute of Certified Public Accountants; New Jersey Society of Certified Public Accountants. **Education:** Fairleigh Dickenson University, B.S. (1971); Certified Public Accountant. **Personal:** Married to Carolee in 1985. Four children: Bill, Ryan, Elene and Terese Ann. Mr. Paquin enjoys golf.

Ricardo "Rick" A. Perez

Vice President of Programming
Turner Broadcasting
1050 Techwood Drive Northwest
Atlanta, GA 30318–5604
(404) 885–2438
Fax: (404) 885–2489
EMAIL: See Below

4841

Business Information: Turner Broadcasting is a public relations and corporate communications company providing worldwide programming, production, and entertainment distribution. As Vice President of Programming, Mr. Perez heads the programming schedule and acquisitions department for TNT in Latin America. Internet users can reach him via: RPEREZ@ATL.MINDSPRING.COM. **Career Steps:** Turner Broadcasting: Vice President of Broadcasting (1993–Present), Director of Broadcasting (1990–1993). **Education:** Texas Technical College: M.A. in Mass Communications (1988), B.A. in Telecommunications (1984). **Personal:** Married to Connie in 1984. Three children: Luke, Meredith, and Nicholas. Mr. Perez enjoys playing the guitar and running triathlons.

Roger M. Ponder
*Senior Executive Director – Division Operations
Development*
Time Warner Communications
*160 Inverness Drive West
Englewood, CO 80126
(303) 754–6189
Fax: (303) 799–3331*

4841

Business Information: Time Warner Communications is a facilities–based provider of telecommunications services, including private line, switched, and data. The Company is responsible for the development, implementation and integration of cable, entertainment, and telephony communication services with Time Warner divisions. As Senior Executive Director – Division Operations Development, Mr. Ponder is responsible for developing business plans, supervising staff and senior staff, operation results, and budgets. In addition, he is responsible for the overall management of Time Warner Communications' alternative access operations and telephony switching divisions, covering the Southwest U.S. sectors. **Career Steps:** Senior Executive Director – Division Operations Development, Time Warner Communications (1994–Present); Sprint/United Management Company: Director of Business Development and Product Management (1990–1994), Director of New Business Development (1989–1990); Manager, United Telephone Company of Florida (1972–1989). **Associations & Accomplishments:** American Management Association. **Education:** Rollin College, Florida: B.S. in Business Management (1983), B.S. in Economics (1981); University of Florida (1971). **Personal:** Married to Karen Diane in 1976. One child: Jason. Mr. Ponder enjoys water sports, snow skiing, fishing, diving, and tennis.

Timothy Ryerson
Vice President of Planning & Scheduling
Encore Media Corporation
*5445 Dtc Parkway, Suite 600
Englewood, CO 80111–3051
(303) 267–4000
Fax: (303) 796–8176*

4841

Business Information: Encore Media Corporation is a television production company for eight domestic and two international pay television channels. Established in 1991, Encore Media Corporation currently employs 200 people. As Vice President of Planning & Scheduling, Mr. Ryerson is responsible for the supervision of 25 people, planning, scheduling, interstitial scheduling, traffic, and quality control for all domestic channels. He also serves as Production Executive for original programming. **Career Steps:** Vice President of Planning & Scheduling, Encore Media Corporation (1993–Present); Director of Program Planning, Showtime Networks, Inc. (1989–1993); Vice President of Programming, Z Channel (1985–1989). **Associations & Accomplishments:** Board Member and Vice President, Colorado Film & Video Association; Member, Cable Positive; Director and Writer of "The Dear One" – an independent feature film. **Education:** University of Southern California, A.B. in Cinema (1974). **Personal:** Married to Naomi J. Ryerson in 1989. Three children: Michael Rae, Lia Victoria, and Jordana Martine. Mr. Ryerson enjoys alpine skiing.

Elizabeth Sanderson–Burke

President
Peoples Broad Band Communications
*710 Cherry Street
Seattle, WA 98040–5325
(206) 622–3042
Fax: (206) 623–5951
EMAIL: See Below*

4841

Business Information: Peoples Broad Band Communications, an entity of family–owned Wisconsin–based People's Communications, is a cable television provider, serving over 3,000 rural subscribers in the state of Washington. The parent company, People's Communications (est. 1901) prides itself on keeping abreast of all the latest telecommunications technology, with current expansion strategies leading into video data and Internet services. Continuing in the excellent reputation established by her great–grandfather who founded the company, Ms. Sanderson–Burke was appointed President of PBBC in 1992. A practicing attorney since 1981, she continues to practice law part–time, serving clients in the areas of real estate law and transactions, estate planning and communications law. Internet users can also reach her via: LizB@Peoples.net **Career Steps:** President, Peoples Broad Band Communications (1992–Present); Attorney, Sanderson & Ewalt, P.S. (1986–1995); Attorney, Security Properties (1984–1985); Environmental Consultant, Rescan Mining

Company (1983–1984). **Associations & Accomplishments:** National Cable Television Cooperative – Lenexa, Kansas: Sustaining Member, Immediate Past Chair; Director, Peoples Communications, Inc. **Education:** Pepperdine University, J.D. (1981); University of Washington, Mediation Certificate. **Personal:** Married to Michael in 1987. Two children: Ryan and Stuart.

Terry Tatum
National Sales Manager
Home Cable Concepts
*611 Yvonne Drive
Goodlettsville, TN 37072
(615) 860–6100
Fax: (615) 860–6214*

4841

Business Information: Home Cable Concepts is a provider of cable programming through DSS products to customers who do not normally have access to hardline cable. Established in 1990, the Company presently employs 800 people and estimates 1996 revenues to exceed $60 million. As National Sales Manager, Mr. Tatum is responsible for approximately 500 salespeople located in 25 different offices across the nation. He monitors the progress and production of his sales staff and evaluates and handles employment counseling. **Career Steps:** National Sales Manager, Home Cable Concepts (1991–Present); President, American Diamond Exchange (1986–1991); Managing Partner, Street Jewelry and Loan (1982–1986). **Associations & Accomplishments:** USGA; USTA; Championship coach of Dixie Youth Baseball; Listed in High School Who's Who. **Education:** Gemological Institute of American, C.D.A. (1984); VSCC, A.S. (1982). **Personal:** Married to Crystal in 1991. One child: Hamilton "Brock". Mr. Tatum enjoys softball, golf, tennis, and water sports.

Pamela S. van der Lee

Vice President – Ad Sales & Promotions Marketing
Nickelodeon
*1515 Broadway
New York, NY 10987
(212) 258–7758
Fax: (212) 258–7676*

4841

Business Information: Nickelodeon, established in 1979, is an international entertainment company owned and operated by Viacom. Divisions include domestic television, recreation, consumer products, Nickelodeon movies, and international networks located in the United Kingdom, Australia, and Germany. Products provided include Nickelodeon Magazine, home video and audio, toys, books, etc. Pam van der Lee, as Vice President, Advertising Sales & Promotions Marketing, oversees the promotional activity across all businesses of Nickelodeon and Nick at Nite. She is responsible for setting the strategy, as well as developing and executing promotions in support of priority brands, programs and new businesses. In addition, she is responsible for identifying strategic partners through which the network and its various businesses can increase awareness, exposure and sales. She and her staff act as an internal sales promotion group to create effective promotions on behalf of the network's advertisers and business partners. Joining Nickelodeon in February 1988, she has served in the roles of Promotion Coordinator, Marketing Manager and Director of Marketing and was steadily promoted to achieve her current executive role. During her tenure she has handled affiliate promotions and event marketing, oversaw Nickelodeon's mall tours, arena tours and special events including the grand opening of the widely popular Nickelodeon Studios at Universal Studios Florida. She was instrumental in forming Nickelodeon's first strategic marketing alliance with Pizza Hut, a multi–year promotional partnership which included a national tour, multiple store promotions and sponsorship of an exhibit at Nickelodeon Studios. She has also generated wide exposure yielding millions of dollars in media for the Nickelodeon and Nick at Nite brands, products and services. **Career Steps:** Nickelodeon: Vice President, Ad Sales and Promotions Marketing (1993–Present); Director of Marketing (1991–1993); Marketing Manager (1989–1991); Promotions Coordinator (Feb. 1988–Dec. 1988); Promotions Coordinator, Up With People (1985–1987). **Associations & Accomplishments:** Advertising Women of New York; Women in Cable, CTAM; Voted "Top 10" promotional executives y Promo Magazine. **Education:** Rollins College – Winter Park, FL, B.A. in English and Speech Communications (1985). **Personal:** Married to Henncus C. in 1989. One child: Graham Marius. Ms. van der Lee enjoys tennis, antiquing and biking during her leisure time.

Anil K. Agarwal, DDS, MS, PC
President, CEO, and Chairman
Cable Auditor of America, Inc.
*10624 South Cicero, Second Floor
Oaklawn, IL 60453
(708) 424–0882
Fax: (312) 582–9869*

4899

Business Information: Cable Auditor of America, Inc. is an auditing company, providing cable piracy services to cable service companies. Founding Cable Auditor of America, Inc. in 1995 and serving as its President, Dr. Agarwal is responsible for all aspects of operations, including administration and strategic planning. He also operates a private dental practice, specializing in prosthodontics and subspecializing in implantation. Since 1991, Dr. Agarwal has started five other companies, including A.G. Packaging & Shipping, H.P. Services, Inc., Eyecom Security Ltd., Voice of Success, Inc., FCC Licensing, and Telecommunications. **Career Steps:** Tenured Associate Professor at Northwestern University; Diplomate Status in International Organization in Implant; President & CEO, H.P. Services Inc.; President & CEO, A.G. Packing & Shipping; President & CEO, Cable Auditors of America, Inc.; President & CEO, Eyecon Security Ltd.; President & CEO, Anilk Agarwal, DDS, MS, PC (1982–Present). **Associations & Accomplishments:** International Congress of Implantology; Appointed by Governor of Illinois on two Committees; Community Man of The Year; Awarded by Mayor of City of Chicago. **Education:** Northwestern University: D.D.S. with specialty certification in Prosthodontics; M.S. (1982), B.S. **Personal:** Married to Shashi in 1975. Three children: Amal, Shelly, and Sheena. Dr. Agarwal enjoys tennis, exercise, reading, giving lectures, and scientology.

Rex Anderson
General Manager
The Furst Group, Inc.
*304 5th Street
North Platte, NE 69101
(308) 534–3400
Fax: (308) 532–0304*

4899

Business Information: The Furst Group, Inc., was named the fastest growing private company in America by "Inc 500" magazine for 1995. The Furst Group provides communications services including: inbound and outbound long distance, pagers, internet access and is continuing to expand their products and services. As General Manager, Mr. Anderson is responsible for developing and implementing strategic sales plans, as well as all administration, customer service and all other aspects of business at his location. **Career Steps:** General Manager, The Furst Group, Inc. (1994–Present); Owner, Earthsong Landscaping (1992–1994); General Manager, White Crane Trading Company (1991–1992); Project Manager/Computer Consultant, Ciber, Inc. (1986–1991). **Associations & Accomplishments:** Special Olympics: Mr. Anderson's accomplishments include many very successful endeavors starting with providing General Brown with the information necessary to gain Congressional approval for the B–1 bomber very early in his career. Mr. Anderson has designed and managed the implementation of large scale international payroll systems, inventory forecast systems, as well as standard accounting systems. He is an accomplished speaker who has been invited and spoken to many large groups on a variety of subjects, including personal development subjects, current event topics, and technical development seminars. Special Olympics: Board Member, Fundraiser, Coach; Treasurer, Association of Retarded Citizens; Festival of Trees: Board Member, Organizer; Business Computer Professional and Personal Workshop Organizer. **Education:** University of Nebraska (1976). **Personal:** Married to Susan M. in 1994. Three children: Eric, Adrienne, and Matthew. Mr. Anderson enjoys racquetball, tennis, softball, scuba diving, and snow and water skiing. Mr. Anderson would like to progress to CEO of an international company. His organizational, management, and leadership skills make him a prime candidate for that goal in the near future.

H. Charles Baker, Ph.D., P.E.
Owner and Consultant
Telecommunications Engineering, Inc.
*9611 Woodmen Circle
Dallas, TX 75238–1859
(214) 343–3229
Fax: (214) 343–3229
EMAIL: See Below*

4899

Business Information: Telecommunications Engineering, Inc. is an independent engineering consultancy. A Professor of telecommunications for thirty years and a Professional Engineer, Dr. Baker founded Telecommunications Engineering, Inc. in 1979. He is responsible for all aspects of operations, in addition to providing consulting in engineering issues. Concurrent with his consulting firm, he serves as an Adjunct Professor at Southern Methodist University. Internet users can reach him via: hbaker@seas.smu.edu **Career Steps:** Owner and Consultant, Telecommunications Engineering, Inc. (1979–Present); Adjunct Professor, SMU (1980–1996); Telecommunications Advisor, Exxon (1968–1980); Associate Professor, SMU (1962–1968). **Associations & Accomplishments:** International Communications Association; Institute of Electrical and Electronic Engineers; The Gideons International. **Education:** University of Texas – Austin, Ph.D. in Electromagnetic Antennas (1962); Southern Methodist University: M.S. in Electrical Engineering (1959), B.S. in Electrical Engineering (1956). **Personal:** Married to Barbara in 1967. Two children: Jennifer and Rachel. Dr. Baker enjoys camping, fishing, and boating.

Jacques A. Blanche
Senior Executive Assistant to the Executive Office
Alcatel CIT
10, rue Latecoere
Velizy Villacoublay, France 78141
331–30678517
Fax: 331–30679383

4899

Business Information: Alcatel CIT, one of the world's leading manufacturers of communications equipment, specializes in turnkey contracting for the telecommunications industry. Established more than 100 years ago, the Company reports annual revenue of $2.4 billion and currently employs 9,400 people company–wide. Alcatel CIT is part of the Alcatel Group reporting annual revenue of $22 billion and approximately 123,700 employees. A veteran with the Company for the past twenty four years, Mr. Blanche joined Alcatel CIT as Technical Director of Switching Operations, then Commercial Manager, before being in charge of U.S. Operations in 1982. Currently serving as Senior Executive Assistant to the Executive Office, he is involved in strategic planning, coordination of European Affairs and responsible for South African operations. **Career Steps:** ALCATEL CIT: Senior Executive Assistant to the Executive Office, (1987–Present), Director of Corporate Development (1983–1987), Director of U.S. Operations (1982–1983); Commercial Drive (1978–1982); Technical Director (1972–1977). **Associations & Accomplishments:** Vice President, AFNOR (French Standardization Body); Vice President, Institute for Audiovisual and Telecommunications in Europe (IDATE); European Telecommunications Suppliers Association (ECTEL); Member, Chairperson – Regulatory Affairs Specialist Group; Founder and 1st Chair, ONP CCP (European Regulatory Organization); Founder, Inter–Industries Group for the Information Society; Chairperson, Fulmen South Africa. **Education:** Ecole Polytechnique; Ecole Nationale Superieure des Telecommunications **Personal:** Married to Jacqueline in 1960. Two children: Valerie and Sophie. One grandson. Mr. Blanche enjoys the Arts, antics, wildlife, and history.

Robert S. Block
Co–Founder, Chairman, Chief Executive Officer
International Communication Technologies, Inc.
12555 West Jefferson, Suite 300
Los Angeles, CA 90066
(310) 301–7680
Fax: (310) 301–7680

4899

Business Information: International Communication Technologies (ICT), Inc. is a telecommunications company, with three areas of activity: operations, technical, and manufacturing. ICT has subsidiary and affiliate communication operations and manufacturing joint ventures in Poland, Czech Republic, Armenia, Russia, Bangladesh, Philippines, India, and China. As an experienced senior executive in the communications industry, Robert Block co–founded International Communication Technologies, Inc. in 1989. Serving as Board Chairman and Chief Executive Officer, he is responsible for the oversight of all operations, primarily focusing on administration, finances, accounting, and strategic planning. An electronics entrepreneur with a long and successful career in the communications industry in the U.S. and internationally, he is an inventor and holds numerous patents. These include: Parental control for TV (required by Telecommunications Act of 1996 to be included in all TV sets imported or made in U.S.

effective in 1998), Impulse Pay–Per–View, Conditional Access Systems for Direct Broadcast Satellite (DBS), Cable–TV, and Subscription TV, and Encryption and scrambling systems. He is a founder of: R.P. Telekom, licensed to provide telephone and other communication services to more than 20% of Poland's population, Cable Plus, Czech largest cable TV system with more than 450,000 subscribers. He serves as Shareholder and Corporate Director of KWHY–TV (Ch 22), a Los Angeles TV station (since March 1982), and a Shareholder and Corporate Director of Block & Associates (owner of the MMDS, 4 microwave TV stations, in Houston, Texas for more than seven years.) **Career Steps:** Co–Founder, Chairman, and CEO, International Communication Technologies, Inc. (1989–Present); Co–Founder, Chairman, and CEO, The ICT Group, Inc. (Present); Founder, R.P. Telekom, Warsaw, Poland (Present); Shareholder and Corporate Director, KWHY–TV (Ch 22) (1982–Present); Shareholder and Corporate Director, Block & Associates – Houston, Texas (1989–Present); Founder, Major Shareholder, President, and CEO, SelecTV – U.S. (1970–1980); Founder and Shareholder, SelecTV – United Kingdom (Present); Regional Director, North American Airlines, the largest coach airline in the U.S.; Co–Founder, Past President, and currently a Trustee, U.S. Sports Academy. **Associations & Accomplishments:** Inventor and Patent Holder, Impulse Pay–Per–View and Parental Control which have worldwide influence on the marketing of entertainment, sports, information, and education services. Earlier experiences include: Owner and operator of the 55th largest advertising agency in the world, Regional Manager for a large syndicated television programming company, and as an Educator – serving as an advisor to several Universities; Co–Author of "Guide to Finance" and numerous articles on communications, technology, and finance; Provided expert testimony and consultation to many governments and business organizations, including the U.S. Congress, FCC, Australian Broadcast Tribunal, BBC, Singapore Broadcasting, European Broadcast Union, TDF, Canal Plus, Argentine Cable, and many others; Mentioned in The Guiness Book of World Records for being the first family to take a vacation at the bottom of the sea. **Education:** University of Wisconsin, Degree in Education; United States Sports Academy, Honorary Doctorate in Philosophy. **Personal:** Mr. Block enjoys skiing, scuba, music and travel.

Constance Tegge Cameron
Director of Internal Communications
Ameritech Network Services
2000 West Ameritech Drive
Hoffman Estates, IL 60196–5000
(708) 248–2140
Fax: (708) 248–3756

4899

Business Information: Ameritech Corporation, a major international telecommunications company and information provider, provides a wide array of local phone, data and video services in Illinois, Indiana, Michigan, Ohio, and Wisconsin. Established in 1984, Ameritech has 14 business units and approximately 64,000 employees. Ameritech network services is the company's largest unit with approximately 40,000 employees. A management executive with Ameritech and its subsidiaries since 1987, Ms. Cameron now serves as Director – Internal Communications for Ameritech network services. She is responsible for the management of print, electronic communication and special projects. **Career Steps:** Director – Internal Communications, Ameritech Network Services (1993–Present); Director of Corporate Communications, Ameritech Services (1987–1993); Manager – Employee Communications, Ameritech Publishing (now Ameritech Advertising Services) (1987–1989). **Education:** University of Michigan: M.A. in Journalism (1973), B.A. in English (1969). **Personal:** One child: Alexander. Ms. Cameron enjoys reading about the Civil War and supporting women in the business environment through various special projects. She is the recipient of numerous awards, including the International Association of Business Communicators (IABC) Gold Quill; the Women in Communications Jacob Scher award and the Northwestern University Video Restor award.

James S. Cardwell
Chief Financial Officer and Board Director
Good Galaxy Entertainment
226 West 47th Street, Suite 900
New York, NY 10036
(212) 869–1118
Fax: (212) 997–0326

4899

Business Information: Good Galaxy (GGE) is a children's television production and distribution company in over 60 countries worldwide. Established in 1993, GGE currently has estimated annual revenues and production costs of $5–10 million (London, New York & Hong Kong). Mr. Cardwell is also an executive officer for Daglow Exploration, Inc., an Alaskan gold exploration and mining company with a multi–million ounce proven gold reserve (New York, Fairbanks and Sydney). As CFO for both companies, Mr. Cardwell is responsible for all fi-

nancial aspects, including co–productions, drilling programs, and equity offerings. A successful entrepreneur, Mr. Cardwell was a producer of the hit musical "Nunsense" in New York, with worldwide grosses nearly $100 million. Long–term plans include the development of Theatre America, a company that will produce and distribute a series of new plays on Broadway, television and film, and restore several historic theatres. **Career Steps:** Chief Financial Officer/Board Director, Good Galaxy Entertainment (1995–Present); CFO/President, Daglow Exploration, Inc. (1994–Present); President, Theatre America Enterprises (1991–Present); Cardwell Productions (1986–Present); Senior Tax Consultant (CPA), Arthur Andersen & Company (1981–1985). **Associations & Accomplishments:** Author, "Inside Broadway, the Missing Profits"; Board of Trustees/Lay Leader, John Street United Methodist Church (the oldest Methodist Church in America). **Education:** Illinois State University, B.S. in Accounting (1981). **Personal:** Mr. Cardwell enjoys computers, speaking, travel, antiques, music and art.

Patrick A. Cataldo Jr.
Vice President
Bellcore
331 Newman Springs Road, NVC 2Z359B
Red Bank, NJ 07701
(908) 758–5180
Fax: (908) 758–4308

4899

Business Information: Bellcore is a leading provider of communications software and consulting services based on world–class research. Bellcore creates the business solutions that make information technology work for telecommunications carriers, businesses, and governments worldwide. Mr. Cataldo is responsible for Bellcore's Learning Services unit, which delivers an extensive program of technical educational offerings to improve job performance of customers managing telecommunications syustems and services related to Bellcore and vendor products. Training is available in multiple delivery formats, including lecture/lab, multimedia options, and embedded performance support systems. Bellcore Learning Services employs 375 people, serving 387 companies in 93 countires. The organization has direct contact with 29,000 students per year, in addition to serving as an Internal resource for technical training of the company's 6,500 employees. Learning Services is ISO 9000 certified for quality procedures in design, development, delivery, and servicing of its products. **Career Steps:** Vice President–Learning Services, Bellcore (1995–Present); Chief Executive, Digital Equipment Ireland Ltd. (1992–1994); Digital Equipment Corporation: Corporate Vice President–Consulting and Education (1990–1992), Corporate Vice President–Education (1985–1990). **Associations & Accomplishments:** American Society of Training and Development: Past recipient of "International Trainer of the Year" Award, Former Treasurer, Former Board Member; Sales and Marketing Training: Former Board Member; Lesley College: Corporator; Clark University: President's Council; Stevens Institute: Master's in Technology Management Board. **Education:** Boston College, M.B.A.; Grand Valley State University, Honorary Ph.D.; St. Francis College, B.A. **Personal:** Married to Kathleen. Three children: Patrick, Peter, and Caitie. Mr. Cataldo enjoys golf and photography.

Katrina C. Cochran
Manager, Global Market Research
MTC – Telemanagement Corporation
1304 Southpoint Boulevard
Petaluma, CA 94954
(707) 776–1310
Fax: (707) 769–6190
EMAIL: See Below

4899

Business Information: MTC – Telemanagement Corporation is an international telecommunications management firm. As Marketing Manager, Ms. Cochran is responsible for global market research, focusing on market assessments in Europe, Asia, and South America. In addition, she is responsible for identifying critical issues, projecting the impact on the Company as a whole. Internet users can reach her via: kcochran@mtcworld.com **Career Steps:** Marketing Manager, MTC – Telemanagement Corporation (1996–Present); Director of Strategic Planning, Polish–American Printing Association (1991–1992). **Associations & Accomplishments:** World Affairs Council in San Francisco; Commonwealth Club in San Francisco; San Francisco Ballet Association. **Education:** Fletcher School of Law & Diplomacy, M.A.L.D. (1995); Harvard Law School, Program on Negotiation (1995); California Polytechnic State University, B.A. in Political Science (1988). **Personal:** Ms. Cochran enjoys dance (23 years of classical ballet and jazz).

Bruce L. Cook, Ph.D.
Executive Director
Illinois Municipal Institute
P. O. Box 451
Dundee, IL 60118
(312) 859–8090
Fax: (847) 428–8974

4899

Business Information: Illinois Municipal Institute (IMI), an innovative communications services concern, provides diverse programs to include: political surveys, media advertising through tabloids and data processing applications. As Executive Director, Dr. Cook is responsible for all aspects of operations. Concurrent with his duties at IMI, he also teaches courses on Business Communication at the Keller Graduate School of Management. **Career Steps:** Executive Director, Illinois Municipal Institute (1983–Present); Instructor, Keller Graduate School of Management; Instructor, Columbia College; Research Analyst, Marketing Department, Fox Valley Press – Copley Publications (1995–Present); Research Director, David C. Cook Foundation (1972–1983); Operations Officer, USAF – ADC (1967–1972). **Associations & Accomplishments:** Author of monograph, "Understanding Pictures in Papua, New Guinea (Elgin, IL: David C. Cook Foundation, 1981). **Education:** Temple University, Ph.D. (1978); San Diego State University, M.A.; Ohio Wesleyan University, B.A. **Personal:** Married to Eileen in 1973. Four children: Steven, Chris, Helen and Bruce. Mr. Cook enjoys reading and computer applications in his leisure time.

Wayne D'Ambrosio
Director of Government Sales
COMSAT Mobile Communications
6560 Rock Spring Drive
West Bethesda, MD 20817
(301) 214–3252
Fax: (301) 214–7205
EMAIL: See Below

4899

Business Information: COMSAT Mobile Communications provides telecom and satellite communication services. International in scope, the Company serves over 200 countries. As Director of Government Sales, Mr. D'Ambrosio sells satellite services to networks in the United States and several foreign governments. U.S. governmental consumers include the Department of Defense. Internet users can reach him via: Wayne.Dambrosio@comsat.com. **Career Steps:** Director of Government Sales, COMSAT Mobile Communications (1993–Present); Vice President/Partner, Capital Consulting Group (1986–1993); Principal, Marlar International (1984–1986); Senior Consultant, Booz Allen & Hamilton (1980–1984); United States Navy (1974–1980). **Associations & Accomplishments:** AFCEA; NTDA; RTCM; United States Naval Academy Alumni Association; Retired Naval Reserve Commander activated for Desert Shield/Desert Storm. **Education:** Webster College, M.B.A. (1980); United States Naval Academy, B.S. (1974). **Personal:** Married to Rita Poore in 1996. Mr. D'Ambrosio enjoys sailing and rugby.

Bruce Dines
Independent Telecommunications Executive
–Independent–
330 Cliff Falls Court
Colorado Springs, CO 80919
(719) 548–8192
Fax: Please mail or call
E–MAIL: bdines@usa.net

4899

Business Information: Mr. Dines has fifteen years of entrepreneurial experience in the cable television and wireless communications business. During the last five years (1991–1996), Mr. Dines served as Senior Operating Officer of a wireless cable television company, American Telecasting, Inc. Along with the founding members, he built the enterprise from its infancy to a $280 million company, the largest in its industry today. He was heavily involved in all aspects of business operations, including product development, marketing, budgeting, contract negotiation, business acquisitions, sales and customer support. He played a key role in bringing the Company public ($60 million) in 1993, and again in 1995, when the Company successfully raised $100 million in a high yield offering. Both offerings positioned the Company to dominate the industry, not only by successfully capitalizing internal growth, but also by providing the resources to make strategic and timely acquisitions and become the major consolidator of the industry. In early 1996, Mr. Dines left to seek new entrepreneurial ventures and currently serves as an independent telecommunications executive. In that capacity, he has worked with a PCS company ("Personal Communications Services" – the "next generation" technology for mobile and portable telephony) where he developed the business plan and financial model for the company to take to the capital markets. He is currently working with an Internet Access and software development company where he is designing the organizational infrastructure and administrative processes to support their ex-

plosive growth. **Career Steps:** Telecommunications Executive, Independent (1996–Present); Vice President of Operations, American Telecasting, Inc. (1991–1996); Director of Operations, Leonard Communications (1989–1991); Operations Analyst, Daniels Communications (1986–1989). **Associations & Accomplishments:** Chairman, Rotary "Artist of the West" Fundraiser (1996); Board Member, Junior Achievement of Colorado Springs; Former Chair of the Customer Service Subcommittee, Wireless Cable Association; Numerous publications throughout his career in "Cable Television Business" and other trade journals. **Education:** Louisiana State University, M.S. (1984); Stanford University, B.S. (1976); Extensive Post Graduate Business and Leadership Training. **Personal:** Mr. Dines enjoys fly–fishing, skiing, tennis, squash, and writing.

Dan H. Edel
Partner
Edel Enterprises
222 E. Eau Gallie Boulevard
Indian Harbour Beach, FL 32937–4874
(407) 777–9195
Fax: (407) 777–9294
EMail: See Below

4899

Business Information: Edel Enterprises has retail stores, representing Bell South Mobility, that sells and services cellular phones and pagers. Mr. Edel is responsible for all aspects of Company operations, including business development, marketing, strategic planning, and sales and marketing. Mr. Edel has accomplished reaching Regional Director in Excel Communications at a rapid pace, while simultaneously assisting other Excel Representatives in becoming independent successful business owners. Internet users can reach him via: edel@metrolink.net. **Career Steps:** Edel Enterprises: Owner (1991–Present); Sales (1990–1991); U.S. Army (1987–1990). **Associations & Accomplishments:** Chamber of Commerce; Better Business Bureau. **Personal:** Mr. Edel enjoys boating, diving, fishing, and golf.

D. Roderick Elford, B.P.E. (Hon), M.D. (CCFP)
Telemedicine Fellow
Telemedicine Centre, Faculty of Medicine
Memorial University of Newfoundland
St. John's, Newfoundla A1B 3V6
(709) 737–6654
Fax: (709) 737–7054
EMail: See Below

4899

Business Information: In 1995, Dr. Elford began the world's first two–year Clinical Fellowship in Telemedicine and a part–time Faculty position at Memorial University of Newfoundland. He is one of a few individuals formally trained in telemedicine research. His research focuses on designing, implementing and evaluating telemedicine systems with a special interest in underserved/isolated communities (e.g. far north, third world, offshore, space). He has worked as a telemedicine consultant for Hughes Aircraft of Canada and the Canadian Space Agency. His future plans include completing his Fellowship studies in Europe and the US, seeking a full–time academic appointment at a distinguished institution and working as a telemedicine consultant/educator. Internet users can reach him via: relford@morgan.ucs.mun.ca. **Career Steps:** Clinical Fellowship in Telemedicine, Telemedicine Centre, Memorial (1995–1996); Clinical Lecturer in Family Medicine, Memorial (1995–1996). **Associations & Accomplishments:** Graduated with First Class Honors, Faculty of Kinesiology (1989); Peter Lougheed Scholar, Faculty of Medicine (1993); Exemplary Family Medicine resident in Canada (1995); Presentations on telemedicine at the International Space University Summer Session (1994), the Mayo Clinic (1995), the World Congress in Telemedicine (1995). **Education:** Calgary, B.P.E. (1989); Toulouse, International Space University Diploma (1991); Alberta, M.D. (1993); Calgary, CCFP (1995). **Personal:** Dr. Elford enjoys travel, sports (wind surfing, mountain biking, snow boarding, hockey), and computers.

Nique Fajors
Vice President of Marketing
Digital Telemedia, Inc.
91 Fifth Avenue, Suite 401
New York, NY 10003–3039
(212) 255–0827
Fax: (212) 255–1339
EMAIL: See Below

4899

Business Information: Digital Telemedia, Inc. has been a local Internet access provider in New York City since 1993. As Vice President of Marketing, Mr. Fajors is responsible for marketing, sales, and strategic alliances. Internet users can reach

him via: nique@dti.net **Career Steps:** Vice President of Marketing, Digital Telemedia, Inc. (1995–Present); Brand Management, Proctor & Gamble (1993–1995); Executive Producer, "The Invisible Men" Educational Video (1992–1995). **Associations & Accomplishments:** Harvard Business School Alumni Association; Mentor to Boston Youth (since 1990); Published several articles in The New England Business Tribune, Urban Profiles Magazine, and Barutiwa Newspaper; Member of Who's Who Online. **Education:** Harvard Business School, M.B.A. (1993); Suffolk University – Sawyer School of Management, B.S.B.A. (1989).

Bari K. Faudree
Corporate Audit Manager
GTE Service Corporation
P.O. Box 407 19845 U.S. 31 North
Westfield, IN 46074
(317) 896–6563
Fax: (317) 896–3734

4899

Business Information: GTE Service Corporation is a world leading telecommunications technology conglomerate, providing voice, data, and video wireline and wireless communications throughout the United States and various regions around the world. Mr. Faudree has served in various managerial positions with GTE since 1982. Promoted to Corporate Audit Manager in 1989, he is now responsible for planning, directing, administering, organizing, and supervising various audit activities within GTE including Financial, Operational, and EDP in the United States. Additionally, he is responsible for training GTE audit staff and course development worldwide. **Career Steps:** Corporate Audit Manager, GTE Service Corporation (1989–Present); GTE Telephone Operations: Midwest Audit Manager (1987–1988), Accounting Manager (1982–1986). **Associations & Accomplishments:** Institute of Internal Auditors; Institute of Management Accountants; Manchester College Alumni Association; Orchard Park Presbyterian Church; Fishers Soccer Youth Organization; Fishers Basketball Youth Association. **Education:** Indiana University – Ft. Wayne, M.S.B.A. (1982); Manchester College, B.S. in Accounting and Economics (1977); Certified Management Accountant (1989). **Personal:** Married to Rachel Faudree in 1977. Four children: Rebecca, Melissa, Joshua, and Kristina. Mr. Faudree enjoys golf, tennis, basketball, fishing, and family vacations.

Robert (Dan) Daniel Frame
Engineering Manager
Telco Systems
45550 Northport Loop East
Fremont, CA 94538–6408
(510) 624–5592
Fax: (510) 490–9396
EMAIL: See Below

4899

Business Information: Telco Systems is a designer, manufacturer, and marketer of integrated service access multiplexers for telecommunications equipment users. Telco is ISO 9001 certified. As Engineering Manager, Mr. Frame is responsible for the departments of component reliability and regulatory engineering. Internet users can reach him via: danf@nad.telco.com **Career Steps:** Engineering Manager, Telco Systems (1990–Present); Component Engineering Supervisor, Racal Datacom (VADIC) (1983–1990); Product Engineering, ATANI (1981–1983). **Associations & Accomplishments:** IEEE; ASQC; Boy Scouts of America Committee Chairman (three sons involved in scouting); Served one year in the U.S. Army in the Vietnam Infantry and Air Mobile Division. **Education:** California Polytechnic University, B.S. in Electrical Engineering (1974); West Valley College, A.S. in Electrical Technology, A.A. in Drafting; University of San Francisco: recipient of additional certificates in Telecommunications; SJSU, Reliability Engineering. **Personal:** Married to Mary Alice in 1978. Four children: Derek, Brian, Steven, and Kevin. Mr. Frame enjoys fishing, hiking, boating, furniture making, and restoring automobiles.

Sanjeev Garg
Vice President
Esprit Telecom
2021 L Street Northwest, Suite 300
Washington, DC 20036–4909
(202) 467–1992
Fax: (202) 736–5065
EMAIL: See Below

4899

Business Information: Esprit Telecom is a telecommunications company with headquarters based in Europe. A Certified Novell Engineer, Mr. Garg, joined Esprit Telecom as Vice President of the Management Information Systems in 1994. He manages all aspects of Information Services for Esprit's group of companies. Mr. Garg can also be reached through the Internet via: SANJEEVG@ESPRITTELE.COM **Career Steps:** Vice President, Esprit Telecom (1994–Present); Regional Information Systems Manager, Frontier Telecommunication (1993–1994); Manager of Information Systems, Mid Atlantic Telecom (1992–1993); Program Analyst, The American University, Telecom (1990–1992). **Education:** The American University, M.S. (1992); Certified Novell Engineer; Undergraduate Degree: B.S. in Computer Engineering. **Personal:** Mr. Garg enjoys swimming, squash, tennis, and classical music.

Dale V. Geminder

Executive Director
AccessVision
67 W. Michigan Avenue, Suite 112
Battle Creek, MI 49017
(616) 968–3633
Fax: (616) 968–2924
4899

Business Information: AccessVision, established in 1987, is a community, industrial television facility. As Executive Director, reporting directly to the Board of Directors, Mr. Geminder is responsible for all AccessVision's community access center activities, including budgeting (developing, monitoring, and reviewing) and grants (preparing, submitting, and monitoring). He also is responsible for evaluating employees; advising the Board on relevant federal, state, and local legislation; and maintaining effective written and oral communication skills, including the ability to initiate, develop and maintain good relationships with a broad range of people. Concurrent with his executive role for AccessVision, Mr. Geminder is an adjunct instructor with Kellogg Community College, teaching broadcast programming and the basic fundamentals of television production. **Career Steps:** AccessVision: Executive Director (1992–Present), Operations Manager (1989–1992); Photojournalist, WWMT – TV (1986–1989). **Associations & Accomplishments:** Board of Directors, Calhoun County Unit–American Cancer Society (1992–1995); United Way of Greater Battle Creek: Member, Community Relations Central Committee (1991–Present); City of Battle Creek Planning Commission (Since 1993); Communications Technology Advisory Committtee, Kellogg Community College (Since 1991); Communications Advisory Committee, Operation G.R.A.D. (Since 1990); Task Force Committee, Food Bank of South Central Michigan; Battle Creek Recreation Department; Lakeview Little League. **Education:** Ferris State College, B.S. (1980), A.S. **Personal:** Married to Tammy in 1991. Two children: David M. and Steven D. Mr. Geminder enjoys golf, camping and coaching youth baseball and softball leagues.

Victor J. Giordani

Director of Operations and Engineering
Bell Atlantic Network Integration
4979B Mercantile road
Baltimore, MD 21236
(410) 933–1000 Ext. 224
Fax: (410) 933–1026
4899

Business Information: Bell Atlantic Network Integration, a division of Bell Atlantic, installs and maintains local and wide area integration networks including wire, fiber, and video. As Director of Operations and Engineering, Mr. Giordani provides sales support and post sale implementation activities for Maryland, Washington DC and Northern Virginia. Concurrently, Mr. Giordani is an Adjunct Professor of Telecommunications at Baltimore City Community College. **Career Steps:** Director of Operations and Engineering, Bell Atlantic Network Integration (1994–Present); Adjunct Professor, Baltimore City Community College; Manager of Premise Laboratories, Bell Atlantic of Maryland (1992–1994); Manager of Special Services, C & P Telephone of Maryland (1989–1992). **Associations & Accomplishments:** The Exchange Club of Towson, Maryland. **Education:** Loyola College, B.S. (1972). **Personal:** Married. Mr. Giordani enjoys golf, skiing, walking, and reading.

Ivan R. Gorgeon

Product Marketing Manager
INFONET Services Corporation
2100 E. Grand Avenue
El Segundo, CA 90245
(310) 335–2130
Fax: (310) 335–2876
4899

Business Information: INFONET Services Corporation is the leading provider of international data, fax, and voice communications solutions to Fortune 500 multi–nationals. The Company provides global, managed networks and desktop applications, such as messaging, for companies which outsource their communications needs. INFONET's network is accessible from 175+ countries, with local support in 57 countries. The Company is jointly owned by a number of the world's leading telecom operators. As a Product Marketing Manager, Mr. Gorgeon oversees INFONET's X.25, SNA, and remote access network services. His responsibilities include P&L, new product development, strategy, training, sales forecasts, and customer service. **Career Steps:** Product Marketing Manager, INFONET (1995–Present); Telematics International, U.S.A.: Product Marketing Manager (1991–1995); Communication Consultant, Telemedies International FRANCE (1988–1990). **Associations & Accomplishments:** Lifeguard, French Atlantic Ocean. **Education:** High Institute of Computer Technology, Paris France (1982); Bachelors in Math, Physics, and Language (1980). **Personal:** Married in 1985. Mr. Gorgeon enjoys painting, arts, antiques, windsurfing, biking, soccer, and travel.

Stephen K. Graham

Safety and Environmental Manager
DSC Communications Corporation
1000 Coit Road
Plano, TX 75075–5802
(214) 519–4025
Fax: (214) 867–3103
EMail: See Below
4899

Business Information: DSC Communications Corporation is an international telecommunications company, providing software/hardware research and development, as well as the manufacture of switch gears, access products, video on demand, cross connects, and printed circuit board assemblies. Clientele include MCI, Sprint, Bell, and Motorola. As Safety and Environmental Manager, Mr. Graham is responsible for all safety and environmental issues nationally and internationally for 5,000 employees as it pertains to Worker's Compensation, in addition to the oversight of industrial hygiene throughout the areas of Costa Rica, Puerto Rico, and Denmark. Internet users can reach him via: SGRAHAM@ccmail.DSCC.com. **Career Steps:** Safety and Environmental Manager, DSC Communications Corporation (1993–Present); Project Scientist, Law Engineering (1992–1993); Research Assistant, ARCO Oil & Gas Company (1983–1992). **Associations & Accomplishments:** Steering Committee, North Texas Safety Consortium; Executive Officer, Collin County Recycling; American Association of Safety Engineers; North Texas Association of Environmental Professional; Published technical publication in IEEE, entitled: "Process Design and Optimisation for Environmentally Conscious Printed Circuit Board Assembly" – turned in at the International Symposium on Electronics and the Environment. **Education:** University of Oklahoma, B.S. in Microbiology/Chemistry (1990). **Personal:** Married to Renee in 1983. Two children: twin boys, Scott and Kyle. Mr. Graham enjoys scuba diving, fishing, sailing, and sports.

Patricia K. Graves

President
Caption First, Inc.
3238 Rose Street
Franklin Park, IL 60131–2145
(847) 671–3376
Fax: (847) 671–6611
4899

Business Information: Caption First, Inc. is a captioning service offering real–time live captioning for the deaf and hearing impaired individuals. Using her extensive court reporting skills and modern technology, spoken words are translated into text instantaneously for viewing in business and personal settings. As President, Ms. Graves is responsible for administrative duties, receiving new clients, and captioning. She performs all captioning for the Company herself. With extensive courtroom experience, she is able to live–caption within 1/10th of a second. **Career Steps:** President, Caption First (1989–Present); Court Reporter, Wolfe, Rosenberg (1983–1989); Court Reporter, Subcontractor (1979–1983). **Associations & Accomplishments:** National Court Reporters Association; Association of Late–Deafened Adults. **Education:** Triton College, Associates (1978). **Personal:** Married to Roy K. in 1981. Two children: Matthew and Malia.

Paula S. Haley

Manager of Accounting
Kansas Direct Broadcast Satellite Limited Liability Company
1111 East 30th
Hays, KS 67601
(913) 625–3334
Fax: (913) 625–7432
4899

Business Information: Kansas Direct Broadcast Satellite LLC, established in 1993, serves two–thirds of the state of Kansas by providing CD quality sound and laser disk quality video through direct programming, the ultimate in new television technology. As Manager of Accounting, Ms. Haley is responsible for oversight of all aspects of accounting, including account management, preparation of financial statistics, and general accounting procedures and practices. **Career Steps:** Manager of Accounting, Kansas Direct Broadcast Satellite LLC (1994–Present); Accountant, State of Kansas (1986–1994); Accounting Clerk, R.P. Nixon Operations (1983–1986). **Associations & Accomplishments:** Soroptimists International of Hays; National Association of Female Executives. Ms. Haley is listed in Who's Who in American High School Students (1979). **Education:** Ft. Hays State University, B.S. (1985). **Personal:** Married to Jerry in 1984. One child: Kyle. Ms. Haley enjoys being an aerobics instructor.

M. Jahan Hassan

President and Co–Owner
Expose Communications, Inc.
P.O. Box 15126
North Hollywood, CA 91615–5126
(818) 786–9292
Fax: (818) 786–8760
EMAIL: See Below
4899

Business Information: Expose Communications, Inc., headquartered in Los Angeles, California, is a reseller of AT&T, Sprint, and MCI telecommunication products to the commercial and residential industries. They also publish the Internet internationally. International in scope, Expose Communications spans the U.S. (Los Angeles, California and New York) and Bangladesh. Co–founding Expose Communications in 1990, as President Mr. Hassan is responsible for all aspects of operations, including client relations (various telephone companies), finances, and marketing. In addition, he oversees all administrative operations for associates and a support staff of 120. **Career Steps:** President and Co–Owner, Expose Communications, Inc. (1990–Present); Manager, Thrifty Corporation (1988–1990); Professional Service Representative, Pfizer Lab (BD), Ltd. (1982–1988). **Associations & Accomplishments:** Narayanganj Bar Association; FITA; TIA; Bangladesh Chamber of Commerce. **Education:** Dhaka University: LL.B. (1982), B.Sc. **Personal:** Married to Shirin A. in 1984. One child: Mayoukh J. Mr. Hassan enjoys reading and travel.

Carolyn E. Hazard

Art Director
Newscope Technology/Legacy Creative Ventures, L.L.C.
1000 2nd Avenue #1601
Seattle, WA 98104
(206) 343–1032
Fax: (206) 343–1183
4899

Business Information: Newscope Technology and Legacy Creative Ventures, L.L.C. are national, multi–specialty communications companies, consisting of three phone services, providing telecommunications, audio–visual, and multi–media functions. Established in 1992, Newscope Technology currently employs approximately 200 people. Being involved from the very beginning when the company was barely more than an idea, Carolyn worked several multi–media campaigns to establish their service. In 1995, they have expanded from one city to twelve, and are still currently growing. Then in February of 1995, Legacy Creative Ventures was established and with that came more opportunity. Legacy Creative Ventures is a Metaphysical company consisting of two psychic lines, a national metaphysical magazine which she serves as Graphics Editor, and soon to be added: a metaphysical mail–order Catalog, two Web sites, Interactive CD–Rom programs, and a series of informative and instructional tapes on metaphysics. She is responsible for ad–campaigns, recruiting, media buying, and overseeing creative development and production planning. **Career Steps:** Art Director and Media Buyer, Newscope Technology (1992–Present); Art Director, Legacy Creative Ventures, L.L.C. (1995–Present); Freelance Artist (1989–Present). **Education:** Colorado Institute of Art, A.A. (1990).

Michael D. Hinds

Partner, Vice President, and Operations Manager
ESP Communications, Inc.
28170 SW Boberg Road
Wilsonville, OR 97070–9205
(503) 682–4195
Fax: (503) 682–2781
4899

Business Information: ESP Communications, Inc. is a low voltage contractor of data communications, fire, security, and telephone systems serving the Northwest U.S. from its location in Wilsonville, Oregon. Services include the installation and service maintenance of voice and data cable and associated equipment, including tele–systems, hubs, routers, etc. Major clients include IBM, Hewlett Packard, Siemans Rolm, and Symantec Corp. As Partner, Vice President, and Operations Manager, Mr. Hinds is responsible for assisting in the financial decisions and growth of the business, in addition to focusing on the establishment of quicker response times, quality assurance, and the supervision of technical staff. **Career Steps:** Partner, Vice President, and Operations Manager, ESP Communications, Inc. (1990–Present); Operations Manager, Allen/Falk Communications (1989–1990); Operations Manager, U.S. West (1984–1989). **Associations & Accomplishments:** Board of Directors, State Apprenticeship Training Program; American Builders and Contractors; Independent Electrical lContractors; Trustee, Silverston Elks Lodge 2210. **Education:** Technical, Journeyman (1989); Attended various communications–related training and management courses. **Personal:** Married to Carroll in 1979. Two children: Nicole and Nathan. Mr. Hinds enjoys hunting, fishing, mountain biking, camping, and most outdoor activity.

Maureen S. Justice
Assistant Vice President – Marketing and Associate Communications
NCR Corporation
1334 South Patterson Boulevard
Dayton, OH 45479–0001
(513) 445–7341
Fax: (513) 445–6942

4899

Business Information: NCR Corporation (formerly AT&T Global Information Solutions) is a major international company, providing communications and information solutions worldwide. Established in 1884, NCR currently employs 38,300 people worldwide and has an estimated annual revenue of $7 billion. Joining the NCR "family" upon conferral of her Masters in Business Adminintration in 1983, Ms. Justice was appointed Assistant Vice President, Marketing and Associate Communications in December, 1995. **Career Steps:** NCR Corporation: Director of Strategic and Operational Planning (1994–1995), Manager of Communications Industry Marketing (1994), Manager of Strategic Marketing (1993–1994). **Associations & Accomplishments:** National Association for Female Executives; Planning Forum. **Education:** Wright State University: M.B.A. (1983), B.S. in Management and Marketing.

Drew J. Kaplan

· · · ➤━━●━━◀ · · ·

Chief Executive Officer
Voice Telephone Company
880 Hampshire Road, Suite V
Westlake Village, CA 91361–2811
(805) 449–2080
Fax: (805) 449–2081
EMAIL: See Below

4899

Business Information: Voice Telephone Company, a family–owned business, is a resaler of prepaid calling cards through Inter Exchange Carrier (IXC) to Cash Express Grocery Stores. One of the first companies to develop and market prepaid cellular in the U.S., Voice also provides private label prepaid calling cards for other companies. Co–founding Voice Telephone Company in 1993, Mr. Kaplan co–owns the Company with his father. Serving as Chief Executive Officer, he is responsible for the oversight of all operations, including administration, finances, sales, public relations, accounting, marketing, and strategic planning. Mr. Kaplan was also the first to develop the Smart Survey Reward Program (or SSRP), an electronic survey tied into a phone card which rewards survey–takers with free long–distance service. Internet users may reach him via: Debitcard@aol.com **Career Steps:** Chief Executive Officer, Voice Telephone Company (1993–Present); Secretary, Kiripaka – New Zealand (1991–1993); Treasurer, Kaplan Enterprises (1985–1991); President, Audio Impressions (1985–1991). **Associations & Accomplishments:** Licensed Realtor, State of California; Mexican–American Grocers Association; Better Business Bureau; Dun & Bradstreet. **Personal:** Married to Gail in 1992. Mr. Kaplan enjoys fund raising activities, computers, and loves high end audio and video equipment.

QUINTILIAN —TRAINING—

Brian J. Kiell
Director
Quintilian Training, Ltd.
75 Harvesters Way, Weavering, Maidstone
Kent, Great Britain, United Kingdom ME14 5SH
44–1622–734567
Fax: 44–1622–738322

4899

Business Information: International in scope, Quintilian Training, Ltd. provides training in telecommunications and related areas such as managerial skills in the telecommunications industry. Established in 1995, Quintilian Training, Ltd. currently employs two people. As Director, Mr. Kiell is responsible for all aspects of operations, including training, direction, and acting as the Company secretary. **Career Steps:** Director, Quintilian Training, Ltd. (1995–Present); BT P/C: Product Marketing Manager (1993–1994), Senior Tutor for Customer Training (1991–1993), Communications Manager (1989–1991). **Associations & Accomplishments:** Published in UK–based professional magazines. **Education:** Stoke–on–Trent College; Erith College; St. George's College. **Personal:** Married to Wendy Marie in 1983. Two children: Nadine and Hayley. Mr. Kiell enjoys walking and travel.

Elaine R. Klein
Vice President of Employee and Community Relations
APAC TeleServices
425 Second Street SE, P.O. Box 3300
Cedar Rapids, IA 52406–3300
(319) 369–2948
Fax: (319) 399–2495

4899

Business Information: APAC TeleServices provides telemarketing services, and inbound and outbound outsourcing services for customer service and sales solutions. APAC is in the top five of the top 50 telemarketing companies in the United States. Established in 1973, APAC currently employs 5,000 people. As Vice President of Employee and Community Relations, Ms. Klein is responsible for all aspects of employee satisfaction, community relations, public relations and publications. **Career Steps:** Vice President of Employee and Community Relations, APAC TeleServices (1987–Present); Vice President, Telebusiness USA (1980–1987); Master Teacher, Skokie Illinois School District #68 (1964–1970). **Associations & Accomplishments:** American Telemarketing Association; Professional Management Association; Women's Network; Local Chamber of Commerce; Junior League; Madge Phillips Center (a women and children's homeless shelter); YWCA. **Education:** Northwestern University, M.A.; University of Michigan, B.A. **Personal:** Three children: Wendy, Jordan and Daniel. Ms. Klein enjoys antique collecting, and flower arranging.

Dean W. Kokko
Production Services Manager
NEXTLINK Interactive
707 Southwest Washington, 8th Floor
Portland, OR 97205–3536
(503) 727–6457
Fax: (503) 241–8156
EMAIL: See Below

4899

Business Information: NEXTLINK Interactive is an international provider of interactive voice technology. As Production Services Manager, Mr. Kokko is responsible for the day–to–day operations of equipment, and manages national and international services. Internet users can reach him via: DKOKKO@NEXTLINK.NET **Career Steps:** Production Services Manager, NEXTLINK Interactive (1995–Present); Director of Information Services, Food Services of America (1988–1995); Data Processing Manager, Automotive Products (1978–1988). **Associations & Accomplishments:** Past President, Sunrise Toastmasters; Past President, Cascade AS400 Users Group; Oregon Speakers Association. **Education:** Lewis & Clark College, Art and Psychology (1970). **Personal:** Married to Marj in 1976. Mr. Kokko enjoys automobile rallying, volleyball, and blues music.

Joseph J. Laschober
Vice President of Finance
Conference Call USA, Inc.
1349 South Wabash Avenue
Chicago, IL 60605–2504
(312) 987–1964
Fax: (312) 765–6773
EMAIL: See Below

4899

Business Information: Conference Call USA, Inc. specializes in telecommunications, including audio and video teleconferencing, enhanced platform services, and international long–distance services. As Vice President of Finance, Mr. Laschober is responsible for a wide variety of activities, as they relate to the operation of the Company. He oversees all aspects of financial operations, including presentation planning and tax consulting. Internet users can reach him via: jlasch@interserv.com. **Career Steps:** Vice President of Finance, Conference Call USA (1994–Present); Vice President of Finance, Dial Services, Ltd. (1994–Present); Accounting Manager, Sachnoff & Weaver, Ltd. (1991–1994). **Associations & Accomplishments:** University of Illinois Alumni Association. **Education:** University of Illinois, B.S. in Accountancy (1985); Certified Public Accountant, State of Illinois. **Personal:** Married to Catherine in 1989.

David A. Lucas
Vice President and Chief Operating Officer
Cleveland Telecommunications
5351 Naiman Parkway, Suites E & F
Solon, OH 44139–1014
(216) 498–9400
Fax: (216) 498–9408

4899

Business Information: Cleveland Telecommunications is a telecommunications conglomerate divided into three business units: Terrestrial, wireless and satellite communications equipment; Facilities operation and maintenance; and Research and Development. Established in 1982, Cleveland Telecommunications currently employs more than 150 people. As Vice President and Chief Operating Officer, Mr. Lucas is responsible for all aspects of operations, including administration and business development in each business unit. Additional responsibilities include sales, accounting, marketing and strategic planning. **Career Steps:** Vice President and Chief Operating Officer, Cleveland Telecommunications (1992–Present); Director of Operations, Star Services (1991–1992); Account Manager, Capital Analysts (1990–1991). **Associations & Accomplishments:** Member, National Contract Management Association; Amateur musician. **Education:** John Carroll University, B.S. in Business Administration (1990). **Personal:** Mr. Lucas enjoys hiking, hunting, remodeling his home, and music.

DIRECTV

Robert L. Meyers
Executive Vice President and Chief Financial Officer
DirecTV
2230 East Imperial Highway
El Segundo, CA 90245
(310) 535–5093
Fax: (310) 535–5222

4899

Business Information: DirecTV, a subsidaryof GM Hughes Electronics, is a direct broadcast television service. The service began in 1994 and currently has over 1.7 million subscribers. Subscribers pay a monthly programming fee for service and receive approximately 175 channels (i.e. pay for view events, sports, movies, music, special events, Best of cable, etc.). As Executive Vice President and Chief Executive Officer, Mr. Meyers is responsible for the financial aspects of operations, i.e., forecasting, accounting, strategic planning, budgetary requirements, and revenue enhancement. **Career Steps:** DirecTV, Executive Vice President and Chief Financial Officer (1996–Present); Director of Corporate Financial Planning and Investor Relations (1993–1996); Hughes Electronics, Controller Electro Optical Systems (1989–1993); Assistant Controller Electro Optical Systems (1987–1989).

Associations & Accomplishments: National Investor Relations Institute. **Education:** University of Southern California: M.B.A. (1972), B.S. Business Administration (1970). **Personal:** Married to Karen in 1972. One child: Rob, Jr. Mr. Meyers enjoys skiing, golf, and fishing.

Phyrell R. Mills

President and Chief Executive Officer

Conference Worldwide, Inc.

3340 Peachtree Road, Tower Place, Suite 2000
Atlanta, GA 30326–1026
(404) 812–8200
Fax: (404) 812–8201
EMAIL: See Below

4899

Business Information: Conference Worldwide, Inc. (CWI), a privately–held corporation, provides audio and video teleconferencing services worldwide. Using the MultiLink System 70's 100% direct digital fiber optic systems and network, CWI was the first and only teleconferencing service provider to install the system. This equipment enables CWI to guarantee that users will hear perfect voice communication with no distortion, interruptions, or broken connections. Its customers are assured that neither Acts of God nor primary long distance failures will ever interrupt service, due to CWI operating on the same priority power and telephone grid as the Metropolitan Fiber System's Network. With twenty–two years experience in senior management and sales in the telecommunication industry, Mrs. Mills founded Conference Worldwide, Inc. in 1994 and serves as its President and Chief Executive Officer. She is responsible for all aspects of operations, including administration, finances, public relations, strategical planning, and developing and executing strategies, programs and plans to capture Fortune 500 companies and other major clients in the telecommunications industry. Career milestones include being instrumental in capturing or servicing AT&T, United Telecommunications Corporation, Southeastern Communications Association, National Data Corporation, and RBOC's. Internet users can reach her via: PMILLS@CWW.com. **Career Steps:** President and Chief Executive Officer, Conference Worldwide, Inc. (1994–Present); National Sales Manager, MultiLink, Inc. (1987–1994); Executive Vice President of Sales and Marketing, AllNet Communications (1984–1987). **Associations & Accomplishments:** International Teleconferencing Association (ITCA); The Kentucky Society; General Motors Crest Club; Ford Marketing Institute; National Women's Association. **Education:** Addison State University, M.B.A. (1966); Attended: University of Kentucky, AT&T Telecommunications, General Motors Institute, Ford Marketing Institute.

Nina Moore

Director of Training and Development

Allen Telecom Group

30500 Bruce Industrial Parkway
Solon, OH 44139
(216) 349–8659
Fax: (216) 349–8738

4899

Business Information: Allen Telecom Group is a manufacturer of wireless communications equipment and systems specializing in cellular, land mobile, paging and personal communications applications. Established in 1953, Allen Telecom Group reports annual revenue of $200 million and currently employs more than 500 people. As Director of Training and Development, Ms. Moore is responsible for directing corporate–wide training programs for employees and customers (technical, sales, team building, management development) and design, develop and present many programs. **Career Steps:** Director of Training and Development, Allen Telecom Group (1993–Present); Manager of Training and Development, Allen Telecom Group (formerly Antenna Specialists Co.) (1991–1993); District Training Manager, Virginia Department of Transportation (1985–1991). **Associations & Accomplishments:** American Society for Training & Development (national and local); Society for Human Resources Managers; American Management Association; Training Director's Consortium. **Education:** Youngstown State University, B.S. in Education (1970); University of Akron, M.S. candidate in Technical Education (1996). **Personal:** Married to John in 1980. Two children: Becky and Jennifer. Ms. Moore enjoys walking, travel, reading, and golf.

Larry Dean Newell

Director of Communications

Marshall County 911

P.O. Box 955
Moundsville, WV 26041–2955
(304) 845–1920
Fax: (304) 843–1551

4899

Business Information: Marshall County 911 provides Enhanced 911 emergency services, through radio and telephone communications for police, fire, rescue, and EMS. With twenty–two years experience in communications, Mr. Newell joined the Marshall County 911 office as Director of Communications in 1993. He is responsible for directing the daily operations of all Marshall County 911 services and operations, in addition to overseeing the administrative operations for associates and a support staff of eleven. He is also responsible for the development of policies and future development of 911 programs. **Career Steps:** Director of Communications, Marshall County 911 (1993–Present); Sgt./Deputy Sheriff, Marshall County Sheriff's Office (1974–1993); Communications, West Virginia State Police (1973–1974). **Associations & Accomplishments:** Moundsville Baptist Church: Deacon, Youth Leader, Sunday School Class Teacher & Usher; Association of Public Safety Communication Officials; National Emergency Number Association; Fraternal Order of Police; West Virginia Enhanced 911 Council. **Education:** West Virginia Northern Community College, A.S. (1974). **Personal:** Married to Ronna in 1977. Two children: Rebekah and Jack. Mr. Newell enjoys church related activities and church youth group.

Carole A. O'Brien

Executive Director–Telecom Reform Business Development

Bellcore

445 South Street, Room 1C253B
Morristown, NJ 07960–6438
(201) 829–4641
Fax: (201) 829–1336
EMAIL: See Below

4899

Business Information: Bellcore is a leading provider of communications software and consulting services based on world–class research. Bellcore creates the business solutions that make information technology work for telecommunications carriers, businesses, and governments worldwide. As Executive Director–Telecom Reform Business Development, Mrs. O'Brien is responsible for providing leadership within marketing and sales account teams developing solutions supporting Telecom Reform (ie., number portability, network unbundling, wholesale/retail business processes, etc). Internet users can reach her via: caob@cc.bellcore.com. **Career Steps:** Bellcore: Executive Director–Telecom Reform Business Development (1995–Present), Managing Director/Canada (1991–1995); Account Executive–GTE (1989–1991); Account Executive–International (1985–1989). **Associations & Accomplishments:** Zonta Club of Morristown Area (Service); 200 Club of Morris County; Project Community Pride; Sales and Marketing Executives; Licensing Executives Society. **Education:** Syracuse Sales & Marketing, Certificate (1989); New Jersey Institute of Technology: B.S.I.E. (1976), M.S. in Management Science (1983). **Personal:** Married to Robert Skeele in 1989. Mrs. O'Brien enjoys boating, gardening, reading, and golf.

Daniel P. Owen

Engineering Director

Selectronics

P.O. Box 9, Route 100
Waitsfield, VT 05673–0009
(802) 496–8322
Fax: (802) 496–8209

4899

Business Information: Selectronics is the parent company of Waitsfield Telecom, Champlain Valley Telecom and Waitsfield Cable Television. These Companies provide telephone and CATV services to customers in Central Vermont. As Engineering Director, Mr. Owen is responsible for managing all engineering, construction, warehousing, purchasing activities, and supervision of employees. **Career Steps:** Engineering Director, Selectronics (1991–Present); Engineer, Contel (1977–1991); Radar Technician, U.S.A.F. (1973–1977). **Associations & Accomplishments:** Rotary Club; Chair, Telephone Association of New England RSAC Committee. **Education:** St. Michael's, M.S.A. (1996); Johnson State College, B.S. (1991); University of Alaska, A.S., Industrial Electronics (1982). **Personal:** Married to Vicky L. in 1973. One child: Nathaniel G. Mr. Owen enjoys golf and Antique British Motorcycles.

Guillermo E. Paiz

Administrative Director

Amtech

7441 N.W. 8th Street, Building M
Miami, FL 33126–2940
(305) 262–1661
Fax: (305) 267–7171
E/MAIL: See Below

4899

Business Information: Amtech is an international telecommunications company, providing cable television and DTH services throughout most of the 25+ countries in Latin America and the Caribbean. Amtech has its own offices in Brazil, Chile, Guatemala, and in the near future, Mexico. Established in 1984, Amtech reports annual revenue of $22 million and currently employs 30 people. As Administrative Director, Mr. Paiz is responsible for the management of all operations and administrative departments, including Logistics, Human Resources, Accounting, and MIS. He can also be reached through the Internet via: Willy@amtechnet.com **Career Steps:** Administrative Director, Amtech (1992–Present); Wang Caribbean and Latin America: Software Manager (1991–1992), Marketing Consultant (1988–1991). **Associations & Accomplishments:** American Amateur Racquetball Association. **Education:** Texas A&M University, M.S. in Economics (1987); Francisco Marroquin University, Systems Engineer (1982). **Personal:** Married to Belia in 1986. One child: Guillermo J. Mr. Paiz enjoys racquetball, computers, family, and sports.

Curtiss B. Peabody

President and Chief Informations Officer

Atlantic of Tampa

5912–D Breckenridge Pkwy
Tampa, FL 33610
(813) 744–2001
Fax: (813) 744–2006

4899

Business Information: Atlantic of Tampa, associated with AT&T, is a telecommunications company, providing telecommunication systems and services to businesses in Florida (Tampa), Michigan (Detroit), Illinois (Chicago), Pennsylvania, and New Jersey. Services include service maintenance, maintenance agreements and selling breakthrough products. The Company is 51%–owned by Atlantic of Tampa and 49%–owned by AT&T. Established in 1984, Atlantic of Tampa reports annual revenue of $40 million and currently employs 520 people. As President and Chief Informations Officer, Mr. Peabody is responsible for all aspects of operations, as well as information services. **Career Steps:** President and Chief Informations Officer, Atlantic of Tampa (1984–Present). **Education:** Hunter College, New York (1983–1984). **Personal:** Married to Debbie in 1986. Mr. Peabody enjoys golf, water sports, motorcycling, and tennis.

Barry E. Phetteplace

Senior Engineer and PCP Specialist

AT&T

7200 South Alton Way
Englewood, CO 80112–2201
(303) 457–9425
Fax: (303) 843–5051
EMAIL: See Below

4899

Business Information: AT&T is a global communications networks company specializing in voice, video and data communications (information movement and management). They are well known for their long distance, local and business telephone services. Appointed as Senior Engineer in 1995, Mr. Phetteplace is a Novell specialist. He heads the team of system administrators, serving data needs internally. Concurrent with his position at AT&T, Mr. Phetteplace founded his own company in 1992 — B&G Computer Sources. A diversified telecommunications company, B&G provides phone systems and other related products to clients. As President, Mr. Phetteplace oversees and directs all operations, including administration, payroll, training, public relations and expansion. He can be reached through the Internet via: !bphetteplace@ATT-MAIL.COM **Career Steps:** Senior Engineer and PCP Specialist, AT&T (1995–Present); Senior Engineer of Voice Mail,

AT&T BCS (1991–1995); Training Manager, AT&T GBCS (1989–1991). **Education:** Regis University, B.S. in CIS; Novell Certification. **Personal:** Married to Geneve in 1975. Three children: Brent, Brian, and Rebecca. Mr. Phetteplace enjoys fly fishing and collecting baseball cards.

Mr. Gino O. Picasso
President
GE Capital Spacenet Services, Inc.
1750 Old Meadow Road
McLean, VA 22102
(703) 848–1300
Fax: (703) 848–1036

4899

Business Information: GE Spacenet provides point–to–multipoint, satellite–based private and shared network products and services for data, voice, fax and digital video communications to customers in domestic and international markets. The service offerings include the Skystar Advantage(TM) communications network which features VSAT (very small aperture terminal) remotes, private hub and shared hub equipment and services, satellite services, as well as program management, field maintenance and network management and control. After acquiring GE Capital Spacenet Services, Inc. in 1994, the General Electric Organization appointed Mr. Picasso (after three years in his expertise with the Organization) to the President capacity where he is responsible for the expansion of the company's global service offerings, as well as the oversight of all operational functions of the Company. Established in 1981, GE Capital Spacenet Services, Inc. currently employs 200 people and is a wholly–owned subsidiary of GE Capital Services, a $20 billion financial services unit of General Electric Corporation. **Career Steps:** President, GE Capital Spacenet Services, Inc. (1994–Present); Vice President of Business Development and International Marketing, GE American Communications, Inc. (1993–1994); Vice President of Business Development, GE American Communications, Inc. (1992–1993); Associate, McKinsey & Company, Inc. (1985–1991). **Education:** University of Pennsylvania, Wharton School of Business, M.B.A. (1985); University of Maryland, M.S. in Computer Science (1981); Georgetown University, B.S. in Mathematics (1977). **Personal:** Married to Linda I. in 1981. Three children: John, Lauren and Michael. Mr. Picasso enjoys tennis and swimming.

Benjamin Piza de Rocafort
President
ViaCom C.R. International S.A.
P.O. Box 811
San Jose, Costa Rica 1000
11–506–2570607
Fax: 11–506–2232040
EMAIL: See Below

4899

Business Information: ViaCom C.R. International S.A. is a full service cellular communication company, with sales over a million dollars, which services five Latin American countries. The Company has a service division which handles the calling card and conference calls and an equipment division which handles the sales of phone systems. As President, Mr. Piza de Rocafort controls and coordinates all the offices in Central America and recommends investments to the Board of Directors. He is in charge of the day–to–day operations of the corporation and for long–range strategic planning which includes expanding service to all of Latin America. Internet users can be reach via: Elecom@sol.racsa.co.cr. **Career Steps:** President, ViaCom C.R. International S.A. (1992–Present); President, Exportaciones del Mundo S. A. (1987–Present); President, Costa Rica Celular S.A. (1985–Present). **Associations & Accomplishments:** Costa Rica Chamber of Commerce; Guatemala Chamber of Commerce; Chamber of Industries; Central America Cellular Association; National Association of Economic Fomentation; National Geographic Society; Founder, National Professional Group – Costa Rica, El Salvador, Honduras, and Guatemala. **Education:** University of Latinoamericana, M.B.A. (1992); Attended: Miami University, International Business, National University, Economic Politics; New York University, Business in English, Wireless Telecommunications Industry /Ericsson; VFR Pilot. **Personal:** Married to Lizzy Ungar in 1983. Two children: Viviana Piza Ungar and Fabiola Piza Ungar. Mr. Piza de Rocafort enjoys flying, surfing, skiing, and horseback riding.

Richard A. Rommel
Vice President of Operations
North Communications
13274 Fiji Way
Marina Del Rey, CA 90292
(310) 577–7700 Ext. 7326
Fax: (310) 574–2869
EMAIL: See Below

4899

Business Information: North Communications is an international multimedia company, specializing in the manufacture of software and multimedia networks. As Vice President of Operations, Mr. Rommel is responsible for all aspects of operations, including manufacturing, software engineering, management, strategic planning, and administration. Internet users can reach him via: RRommel@Infonorth.com. **Career Steps:** North Communications: Vice President of Operations (1995–Present), Director of Software Engineering (1995), Manager of Software Engineering (1994–1995); Operations Leader, Hughes Info Tech Company (1993–1994). **Associations & Accomplishments:** Institute of Electronics and Electrical Engineers; A.C. M. **Education:** Loyola Marymount: M.S.C.S. (1986), B.S. in Physics (1982). **Personal:** Married to Monica in 1987. Two children: Eric and Cassandra. Mr. Rommel enjoys reading, jogging, skating, and skiing.

Joseph M. Roscitt Jr.

President
Telcom Engineering Group Inc.
3525 South Ocean Boulevard, Apartment 208
Palm Beach, FL 33480–5792
(305) 646–0082
Fax: (407) 533–0539

4899

Business Information: Telcom Engineering Group Inc. specializes in the installation and testing of cellular telephones, equipment and digital data. International in scope, Telcom serves the U.S. in Georgia, South Carolina, North Carolina, and the countries of Brazil and Colombia. Established in 1989, Telcom Engineering currently employs 10 people and has an estimated annual revenue of $1.5 million. As President and Founder, Mr. Roscitt is responsible for the overall success of the company, the quality of the services provided, and all strategic planning. Mr. Roscitt started his company from scratch, and has a personal goal to expand his business and cover more geographic territory. **Career Steps:** President, Telcom Engineering Group Inc. (1989–Present); President, J.P.J. Consulting Group (1986–Present); Partner, P.F. Roscitt Electric (1981–1989). **Associations & Accomplishments:** Local #164 IBEW (1970–Present); Elks of Cliffside Park, N.J. (1983–1995). **Education:** Fairleigh Dickinson, Associates; Local #164, Estimating School. **Personal:** Married to Debra S. in 1973. Two children: Cassandra Fogarty and Joseph M. III. Mr. Roscitt enjoys boating, boat racing, and spending time with his family, including his two grandchildren.

Alex S. Ruiz–Casanova
Director of Strategy and Marketing
Pacific Bell
4376 Conejo Drive
Danville, CA 94506
(510) 901–8460
Fax: (510) 866–2969

4899

Business Information: Pacific Bell is a global telecommunications network, specializing in voice, video and data. They provide communication services and in the process of building a new network for the information superhighway. Established in 1984, Pacific Bell currently employs 52,000 people and has an annual revenue of $8.1 billion. As Director of Strategy and Marketing of the Ethnic Markets Group, Mr. Ruiz–Casanova is responsible for the design and implementation of Hispanic and Asian marketing programs for Pacific Bell. **Career Steps:** Director of Strategy and Marketing, Pacific Bell (1994–Present); Marketing Director, Domecq International (1993–1994); Regional Marketing Manager, EJ Gallo Winery (1991–1993); Market Development Manager, Colgate Palmolive Company (1984–1991). **Associations & Accomplishments:** Member of the Counciling Committee for Educational Projects, Hispanic Education and Media Group; Imagen Award Winner for "Each Mind is a World" Documentary; Mr. Ruiz–Casanova has been recognized on numerous occasions for his creative talent. His most recent accomplishments are the development of Pacific Bell calling card audio–visual execution and a P.S.A. to promote public phones featuring Rita Moreno. **Education:** Tulane University, M.A., International Studies (1982); St. Mi-

chael's College, B.A., Economics and Fine Arts (1980); Mr. Ruiz–Casanova completed the marketing management program at Columbia University Graduate School of Business (1995). **Personal:** Married to Anita Tonnessen in 1991. Three children: Lindsay, Sarah and Sofia. Mr. Ruiz–Casanova enjoys racquet sports, the outdoors, and the Arts.

Carmen M. Sabater
Corporate Controller
MasTec, Inc.
3351 NW 77 Ave
Miami, FL 33122
(305) 599–1800
Fax: (305) 406–1908

4899

Business Information: MasTec, Inc. is an international telecommunications services company, providing installation, service, and maintenance functions for communications infrastructure. MasTec consists of thirty–five field offices and four regional offices. Established in 1963, MasTec, Inc. reports annual revenue of $400 million and currently employs 5,000 people company–wide. As Corporate Controller, Mrs. Sabater is responsible for internal and external financial reporting and treasury responsibilities, human resources, and management information. **Career Steps:** Corporate Controller, MasTec, Inc. (1994–Present); Deloitte & Touche LLP: Senior Manager (1993–1994), Manager (1989–1993). **Associations & Accomplishments:** Hands in Action/Manos en Accion; University of Miami Alumni Association; University of Miami Hurricane Club. **Education:** University of Miami: M.B.A. (1986), B.B.A. (1985). **Personal:** Married to Carlos. Two children: Erika and Victoria. Mrs. Sabater enjoys reading and cycling.

Dana L. Schuh
Program Manager, Sales and Marketing
NCR Corporation
1529 Brown Street EMD/4
Dayton, OH 45479
(513) 445–2087
Fax: (513) 445–0375
EMAIL: See Below

4899

Business Information: NCR Corporation (formerly AT&T Global Information Solutions) is a major international company, providing communications and information solutions worldwide. Established in 1884, NCR currently employs 38,300 people worldwide and has an estimated annual revenue of $7 billion. As Program Manager, Sales and Marketing, Ms. Schuh manages global information technology programs from concept to deployment. She is responsible for oversight of technical infrastructure, support and hardware resources, and development of ongoing releases. Internet users can reach her via: dana.schuh@daytonoh.ncr.com. **Career Steps:** Program Manager, Sales and Marketing, NCR Corporation (1996–Present); AT&T Global Information Solutions: Program Manager, Manufacturing Engineering and Logistics (1995–1996), Senior Business Consultant, Logistics (1994–1995). **Associations & Accomplishments:** Professional Golfers Association; Conservation International. **Education:** University of Dayton, M.B.A. (1993); Bowling Green State University, B.S. (1981). **Personal:** Married to Jeffery in 1983. Ms. Schuh enjoys golf, cooking, and reading.

Mr. Anthony J. Sciacca
Director of Network Systems
networkMCI Conferencing
8750 West Bryn Mawr Avenue, Suite 900
Chicago, IL 60631
(312) 399–1735
Fax: (312) 399–1710

4899

Business Information: networkMCI Conferencing provides audio, video and data conferencing for the general business public in five major city locations in the U.S., Canada, United Kingdom and Hong Kong. Specialty products include investor–relations conference and telemanagement services. Established in 1969, networkMCI Conferencing reports annuals revenue of $150M (1996) and currently employs 700 people. As Director of Network Systems, Mr. Sciacca is responsible for all aspects of engineering consulting for the overseas offices, as well as staff and technology management, design direction, and implementing operations and maintenance of the Conference Network. **Career Steps:** Director of Network Systems, networkMCI Conferencing (1993–Present); Manager of World–Wide Network Services, Abbott Laboratories (1988–1993); Senior Communications Analyst, Abbott Laboratories (1984–1988); Senior Telecommunications Analyst, Digital Equipment Corporation (1981–1984); Administrative

Assistant for Data Processing, Combined Insurance (1970–1981); Lt. Colonel of U.S. Army Reserve, 84th Division (Training), Milwaukee, Wisconsin, U.S. Army (1968–1970). **Education:** Boston University, M.B.A. (1983); Boston University, B.A. (1968). **Personal:** Married to Joyce. Mr. Sciacca enjoys singing in church choir, golf and reading.

James B. Sellman
President
Advanced Digital Technologies, L.L.C.
2001 Marcus Avenue, Suite 205
New Hyde Park, NY 11042–1011
(516) 488–8171
Fax: (516) 488–8175

4899

Business Information: Advanced Digital Technologies, LLC is an international telecommunications design, and development firm of digital radio systems and equipment for the cellular industry. Advanced Digital Technologies receives most of their business from governmental agencies (75%) and commercial businesses (25%). Establishing Advanced Digital Technology, LLC in 1994, Mr. Sellman serves as President and Chief Executive Officer. He is responsible for all aspects of operations for the business, in addition to overseeing all administrative operations for a support staff of 21. **Career Steps:** President, Advanced Digital Technologies, LLC (1994–Present); Vice President of Operations, InterDigital Communications Corp. (1990–1993); Director of Systems Engineering, ARINC (1989–1990); Deputy Program Executive Officer, U.S. Government (Civil Service) (1966–1988). **Associations & Accomplishments:** AFCEA, Institute of Electrical and Electronics Engineers. **Education:** University of Colorado, M.S. (1987); Loretto Heights College – Denver, CO, B.A.; University of Notre Dame, B.S in Electrical Engineering **Personal:** Married to Joan in 1962. Three children: Darryl, Holly and Heidi. Mr. Sellman enjoys speed walking.

Stephen J. Seuntjens
International Controller
ADC Telecommunications
4900 West 78th Street
Minneapolis, MN 55435
(612) 946–3201
Fax: Please mail or call
EMAIL: See Below

4899

Business Information: ADC Telecommunications is a provider of telecommunications equipment and services worldwide. A Management Accountant, Mr. Seuntjens joined ADC as Financial Analyst in 1994. He was appointed as International Controller in 1995, responsible for all accounting and budgeting worldwide. Internet users can also reach him via: steve_seuntjens@adc.com **Career Steps:** ADC Telecommunications: International Controller (1995–Present), Financial Analyst – International (1994–1995); Financial Analyst – International, National Computer Systems (1991–94). **Associations & Accomplishments:** Institute of Management Accountants. **Education:** University of St. Thomas, M.I.M. (1994); Creighton University, B.S.B.A. (1988). **Personal:** Mr. Seuntjens enjoys biking, reading, and meeting new people.

Mr. Glenn D. Slovenko
Senior Vice President
Citzens Equality Plus Telecommunications
26A Barnes Park Road – North
Wallingford, CT 06492
(203) 284–1511
Fax: (203) 949–0097

4899

Business Information: Citizens Equality Plus Telecommunications sells state–of–the–art telecommunications cost reduction and productivity enhancement services through its nationwide franchise and license network. As Senior Vice President and division head, Mr. Slovenko manages all aspects of the rapidly expanding operation which include its association with the 5th largest independent phone company, Citizens Telecom the dominant division of Citizens Utilities (NYSE:CZN). Established in 1977, Citizens Equality Plus Telecommunications employs over 260 people directly and has independent representation approaching 1,000. Established in 1977, Citzens Equality Plus Telecommunications employs over 40 people. **Career Steps:** Senior Vice President, Citizens Equality Plus Telecommunications (1995–Present); Vice President, Franchise Development, Equality Plus Telecommunications (1995); Director, Franchise Development, Manhattan Bagel Company, Inc. (1993–1995); President, Feuntes Associados (1992–1993); Internal Consultant, Mi-

das International Corporation (1987–1992). **Associations & Accomplishments:** Active in several wildlife and wilderness protection efforts, eg. Delaware & Raritan Greenway, Inc.; University of California, Davis, Alumni Association; International Franchise Association; A.S.E. certified Technician and Member; Several educational planning boards; Mr. Slovenko has been featured in many articles, and edited, "The Combined Family" (Plenum 1993) book. **Education:** New York University, Human Resource & Training Development; University of California at Davis, B.S. (1986); Bel–Rae Institute of Animal Technology (Denver University Affiliate), A.S. (1982); Zenger–Miller Certified Instructor (1991). **Personal:** Married to Jin Victoria Slovenko in 1988. Mr. Slovenko enjoys bicycling, racquetball, photography, travel and reading.

Gordon H. Smith
Vice President of Sales
Communications Engineering Company
1000 27th Avenue Southwest
Cedar Rapids, IA 52404
(319) 364–0271
Fax: (319) 364–6970

4899

Business Information: Communications Engineering Company designs and installs video, data, voice, and wireless communications systems, specializing in LAN/WAN, fiberoptics, audio, security, and access control. They are also a Motorola service center. Mr. Smith has served in various supervisory positions with CEC since joining the Company as a Sales Representative in 1978. Promoted to Vice President of Sales in July, 1995, he is presently responsible for providing executive leadership, strategic direction, and coordinating product development. **Career Steps:** Communications Engineering Company: Vice President of Sales (1995–Present), Director of Data Systems (1990–1995), Sales Representative (1978–1990). **Associations & Accomplishments:** National Sound Contractors Association. **Education:** Hawkeye Institute of Technology, Electronic Service Technician (1976). **Personal:** Married to Sandra in 1980. Two children: Katie and Sara. Mr. Smith enjoys golf.

Robert A. Steinkrauss
President and Chief Executive Officer
Raptor Systems, Inc.
69 Hickory Drive
Waltham, MA 02154–1011
(617) 487–7700
Fax: (617) 487–5799
E–mail: see below

4899

Business Information: Raptor Systems, Inc. is a developer of Internet security software for the telecommunications industry. Raptor Systems, Inc. provides the software needed to secure individual Internet business ventures and protect them from outside intervention. The Company was established in 1992, and with the recent growth and popularity of the Internet and the World Wide Web systems, Raptor Systems has expanded from one to fifty employees in less than a year. The Company markets its product over the Internet, the WWW, Direct Mailings, trade shows and public relations firms. As the President and Chief Executive Officer, Mr. Steinkrauss provides the overall direction and vision for the company's continued growth, quality delivery to customers, and strategic development. Mr. Steinkrauss is also on the Board of Directors and attributes the success of his company to his vast experience in sales, engineering, marketing and international exposure. Mr. Steinkrauss can also be reached through the Internet as follows: BOBS@ Raptor.com **Career Steps:** President and Chief Executive Officer, Raptor Systems, Inc. (1992–Present); President and Chief Executive Officer, Racal Interlan (1993–1995); Senior Vice President and General Manager of Internetworking, Racal Datacom Group (1991–1993); Senior Vice President of Finance and Operations, Racal Milgo (1990–1991). **Associations & Accomplishments:** Massachusetts Software Council; Massachusetts High Tech Council. **Education:** Boston College, B.S. in Accounting (1973); Certified Public Accountant, State of Massachusetts. **Personal:** Married to Louise in 1981. Four children: Bobby, Billy, Krista and Courtney. Mr. Steinkrauss enjoys golf and boating.

Zulma N. Suarez
Controller
General Instrument (P.R.), Inc.
Box 11515
Barceloneta, Puerto Rico 00617
(809) 845–8509
Fax: (809) 846–8575

4899

Business Information: General Instrument (P.R.), Inc. is an international manufacturer and supplier of telecommunications equipment utilized in cable television and satellite distribution applications. GIC is a major supplier of cable settop

converters, cable transmission equipment, home satellite receivers, and satellite decryption modules. Established in 1983, General Instrument (P.R.), headquartered in Chicago, Illinois, reports annual revenue of $700 million and currently employs 1,200 people at their Puerto Rico plant. As Controller, Ms. Suarez is responsible for all aspects of financial matters for the Finance Department, including sales and accounting. **Career Steps:** Controller, General Instrument (P.R.), Inc. (1994–Present); Finance Manager, Allergan Medical Optics (1992–1994); Financial Planning and Analyst Manager, Digital Equipment (1987–1992); Financial Analyst, Westinghouse (1985–1987). **Associations & Accomplishments:** National Justice Commission, PCUSA (1991–1994); Institute Management Accountant – Mayaguez Chapter (1992–Present); Board of Directors, Gaucio Conference Center (1990–1993). **Education:** Interamerican University, M.A. in Industrial Management (1994); University of Puerto Rico, B.B.A. in Accounting (1982). **Personal:** Ms. Suarez enjoys spending time with her family and volunteering her time with young adults.

Shawnee D. Swarengin
Managing Director
Newscope Technology
1000 Second Avenue, Suite 1601
Seattle, WA 98104
(206) 292–9508
Fax: (206) 343–1183

4899

Business Information: Newscope Technology is a national, multi–specialty communications company, consisting of three psychic telephone lines and providing telecommunications, audio–visual, and multi–media functions. Established in 1992, Newscope Technology currently employs 100 people. Founding the Company in 1992, Ms. Swarengin serves as Managing Director, responsible for all aspects of operations and management, including strategic planning and the supervision of 260 support staff. **Career Steps:** Managing Director, Newscope Technology (1992–Present). **Personal:** One child: Nick. Ms. Swarengin enjoys dancing, travel, music and song writing.

Lesa V. Thomas
President
Texas Captioning Inc.
9708 South Padre Island Drive
Corpus Christi, TX 78418
(512) 939–8998
Fax: (512) 939–8207

4899

Business Information: Texas Captioning Inc. provides interpretation and closed caption communication services, as well as awareness training for persons deaf and hard–of–hearing by real time. Established in 1994, Texas Captioning Inc. currently employs 10 communication specialists serving Corpus Christi, Texas and surrounding areas. Ms. Thomas was inspired to establish Texas Captioning Inc. upon the birth of her daughter Katherine who was born profoundly deaf and is currently attending public school. As President, she serves as a State of Texas Level III Interpreter for the deaf and is responsible for all aspects of operations including captioning processes; managerial duties and staff supervision. **Career Steps:** President, Texas Captioning Inc. (1994–Present); Interpreter – Level III, Corpus Christi Area Council for the Deaf (Present); Lead Interpreter, Corpus Christi Independent School District (1990–1994). **Associations & Accomplishments:** Partners in Policymaking through Governor's Committee for Person with Disabilities; Mayor's Committee with Persons with Disabilities; Texas Society of Interpreters for the Deaf. **Education:** Texas A&M University – Corpus Christi, B.A. in Communications (1993). **Personal:** Married to George Falk, Jr. One child: Katherine Murch. Ms. Thomas enjoys skiing, scuba diving, and crafts.

Scott A. Tonarelli
District Manager
Cable and Wireless, Inc.
1275 K Street Northwest, Suite 200
Washington, DC 20005
(202) 371–1716
Fax: (202) 842–2293

4899

Business Information: Cable and Wireless, Inc. is a provider of business–oriented telecommunications through switch and private–line networks. Joining the Company as Switch Technician in 1986, Mr. Tonarelli was appointed as District Manager in 1994. He is responsible for the management of field operations in the Mid–Atlantic Region, including overseeing installations and materials on daily operations. In addition, he oversees the overall administrative operations for associates and a support staff of 35. **Career Steps:** Cable and Wireless, Inc.: District Manager (1994–Present), District Supervisor (1993–1994), Lead Technician (1988–1992), Switch Technician (1986–1988). **Associations & Accomplishments:** Advisory Board, Penn Technical Institute. **Education:** Penn

Technical Institute, A.S. in Technology (1986); Attending: Capitol College for an Engineering Degree in Telecommunications. **Personal:** Married to Katherine in 1988.

Pierre L. Touchette
President
Amerimage Communications
1001, Rue Lenoir, A–212
Montreal, Quebec H4C 2Z6
(514) 931–2111
Fax: (514) 931–1411
EMAIL: See Below

4899

Business Information: Amerimage Communications is a television production company specializing in music videos, alternative music (Jazz, world music, gospel, etc.) videos and concerts, documentaries, and educational productions. Products are also exported internationally. As President and Founder, Mr. Touchette serves as the Executive Producer responsible for all aspects of operations, including day–to–day management. He can be reached through the Internet via: pierre.touchette@sympatico.ca. **Career Steps:** President, Amerimage Communications (1994–Present); TVONTARIO: Program Director (1990–1994); Producer–Director (1982–1990). **Associations & Accomplishments:** Academy of Canadian Cinema & Television. **Education:** University of Ottawa, B.A. (1975). **Personal:** Married to Claire in 1993. Four children. Mr. Touchette enjoys reading and music.

Beverly Ventura

Vice President of Sales – West Region
Wiltel
1110 West Taft Avenue
Orange, CA 92665–4150
(714) 282–3585
Fax: (714) 282–3543

4899

Business Information: Wiltel provides national voice, data, and video communications service. As Vice President of Sales for the Western Region, Ms. Ventura is responsible for eighty–two people in nine states, overseeing all sales and marketing efforts. **Career Steps:** Wiltel: Vice President of Sales – West Region (1995–Present), Director of Sales, West Coast (1993–1995); Regional Sales Manager, Bell South (1991–1993). **Associations & Accomplishments:** Women in Business. **Education:** Chapman University, Master's In Psychology (In Progress); Redlands University, B.S. (1981). **Personal:** One child: Andrea. Ms. Ventura enjoys golf, skiing, reading, travel, and spending time with her family.

Sandra E. Walton
Director of Marketing
INTERNOC
603 Navarro Street, Suite 402
San Antonio, TX 78205
(210) 299–4662
Fax: (210) 229–1483
EMail: See Below

4899

Business Information: INTERNOC is an inter–networking and telecommunications integration firm focusing on the design, installation, and management of service providers within the industry. As Director of Marketing, Ms. Walton is responsible for everything related to managing sales programs, print, and media, as well as industry research and positioning. Internet users can reach her via: swalton@internoc.com. **Career Steps:** Director of Marketing, INTERNOC (1996–Present); President/Owner, White Owl Designs (1993–1995); Artist/Photographer, Aadland Advertising (1990–1991). **Associations & Accomplishments:** National Association of Female Executives; Contributor, Prepung Counseling Educational Fund; Works with the Mentally Ill and the Homeless; Volunteer, Aiding to those who have recently lost both parents. **Education:** Attended, University of Texas – San Antonio (1992). **Personal:** Ms. Walton enjoys oil painting, studying cognitive archeology, the history of philosophy, and psychology.

Bruce D. White
President
White Enterprises
545 Park Drive
St. Claire, MO 63077
(314) 343–9977
Fax: (314) 343–5684
EMAIL: See Below

4899

Business Information: Mr. White founded White Enterprises in 1973, designing and constructing communications networks for outside plant installations. He is presently under contract with the Sovran Leasing Corporation to provide interconnection design and construction management for St. Louis University. Internet users can reach him via: Bruce@mvs.st-claire.nb.us **Career Steps:** White Enterprises: President (1973–Present); Danella Companies: District Superintendent (1983–1990 and 1992). **Associations & Accomplishments:** Charter Member, Connect Missouri; United Way. **Education:** University of Illinois, B.S. (1972). **Personal:** Married to Jeanette in 1995. Mr. White enjoys golf and fishing.

William W. Whitehead
Manager of National Logistics Center
GTE Supply
6550 Jimmy Carter Boulevard
Norcross, GA 30071
(770) 441–6200
Fax: (770) 441–6226

4899

Business Information: GTE Supply is a world–leading telecommunications company providing voice, data, and video communications throughout the United States and various regions around the world. GTE Supply–Norcross handles the logistical services producing 25,000 to 30,000 lines of activity a month with 30M dollars of throughput a month. As Manager of National Logistics Center, Mr. Whitehead handles national distribution of cellular products for GTE affiliates, Module Network, and other companies. **Career Steps:** GTE Supply: Manager of National Logistics Center (1995–Present), Material Coordinator – Logistics Services (1995), Supervisor – Supply Operations (1994–1995). **Associations & Accomplishments:** Council of Logistics Management. **Education:** St. Andrew's Presbyterian College, B.A. (1989). **Personal:** Married to Shonna G. in 1993. Mr. Whitehead enjoys soccer and horticulture.

Mr. Wei Yuan
Vice President of China Business Development
International Wireless Communications, Inc.
400 South El Camino Real
San Mateo, CA 94402
(415) 548–0808
Fax: (415) 548–1842

4899

Business Information: International Wireless Communications, Inc., established in 1991, is a pioneer in provision of wireless communications networks to developing countries. Its business is the startup, operation and ownership of major wireless–based communications projects in countries around the world. The IWC vision is to bring the lowest cost, most modern wireless technologies to developing countries and thereby provide affordable communications services to the largest possible number of people. A true leader in wireless communications services in developing countries, IWC has invested in more than 20 wireless communications projects through operating companies in Mexico, Brazil, Indonesia, Malaysia, Philippines, India, Pakistan, New Zealand, Sri Lanka, the United States and China. As Vice President of China Business Development, Mr. Yuan is responsible for developing and structuring wireless communications ventures in the Chinese market. **Career Steps:** Vice President of China Business Development, International Wireless Communications, Inc. (1994–Present); Director, SR Telecom, Inc. (1993–1994); Sales Manager, SR Telecom, Inc. (1992–1993); Associate, NGL Consulting (1991); Industrial Policy Research Associate, China Ministry of Electronics Industry (1985–1988). **Education:** University of Western Ontario, M.B.A. (1991); Hangchou Institute of Electronics Industry, China, M.S. in Engineering; University of Science and Technology of China, B.S. in Electronics. **Personal:** Married to Shuang Xie. Two children: Michael Lihan Yuan and Patric Lifan Xie.

4900 Electric, Gas and Sanitary Services

4911 Electric services
4922 Natural gas transmission

4923 Gas transmission and distribution
4924 Natural gas distribution
4925 Gas production and/or distribution
4931 Electric and other services combined
4932 Gas and other services combined
4939 Combination utilities, NEC
4941 Water supply
4952 Sewerage systems
4953 Refuse systems
4959 Sanitary services, NEC
4961 Steam and air–conditioning supply
4971 Irrigation systems

David Lee Armstrong
Director of Finance and Accounting
Kaufmann County Electric
P.O. Box 941
Kaufmann, TX 75142–0941
(214) 932–2214
Fax: (214) 932–6466

4911

Business Information: Kaufmann County Electric is a non–profit electric cooperative serving 24,000 customers within four counties. Established in 1938, Kaufmann County Electric currently employs 86 people. As Director of Finance and Accounting, Mr. Armstrong is responsible for the management of the Investing, Finance, Accounting, and Information Systems departments. Other duties include tax reporting. **Career Steps:** Director of Finance and Accounting, Kaufmann County Electric (1986–Present). **Associations & Accomplishments:** Institute of Management Accountants; Friends of the Sterling C. Evans Library; Texas Electric Cooperatives Accounting Association: Treasurer (1992–1993); Texas Society of Certified Public Accountants; TAMU Association Former Students Century Club Member; National Association of Investors Corporation Member. **Education:** Texas A&M University, Agricultural Economics (1985). **Personal:** Mr. Armstrong enjoys investing, reading, travel, and making friends.

Ronald G. Barnes
Manager, Marketing and Member Services
Coast Electric Power Association
P.O. Box 2430, 302 Highway 90
Bay St. Lou, MS 39521–2430
(601) 467–6535
Fax: (601) 467–6069
EMAIL: See Below

4911

Business Information: Coast Electric Power Association is an electric distribution cooperation serving three counties in South Mississippi. The Association, affiliated with Statewide Rural Electric Power Association, supplies electricity to 53,000 customers. As Manager of Marketing and Member Services, Mr. Barnes is responsible for all marketing programs for the Company, and marketing the Good Cents program (encouraging customers to use heat pumps in their homes). Internet users can reach him via: RGB2000@GNN.COM. **Career Steps:** Manager of Marketing and Membership Services, Coast Electric Power Association (1995–Present); Field Director, Boy Scouts of America (1989–1995); Area Sales Manager, McRaes, Inc. (1986–1988). **Associations & Accomplishments:** Home Builders Association of Mississippi; Mississippi Economic Development Council; Harrison County Economic Development Council; Boy Scouts of America; United Way of South Mississippi; Co–Founder, Pine Beet Regional Youth Coalition. **Education:** University of Southern Mississippi, B.S. in Business Administration (1986). **Personal:** Married to Angela S. Barnes in 1986. Two children: Amy and Hayley. Mr. Barnes enjoys golf.

Kelly Bishop–Fulton
School Program Coordinator
Dayton Power & Light
1065 Woodman Drive
Dayton, OH 45432–1423
(513) 259–7251
Fax: (513) 259–7813

4911

Business Information: Dayton Power & Light sells electricity and natural gas to residential, commercial, industrial, and governmental customers within a 6,000 square mile area of West Central, Ohio. The Company provides service for 24 counties through 21 service centers. As School Program Coordinator, Ms. Bishop–Fulton manages and coordinates the Company's School Programs department in which our mission is to teach young people about the wise use of energy through more than ten free educational programs. **Career Steps:** School Program Coordinator, Dayton Power & Light (1993–Present); Presenter's Network Coordinator, American Red Cross (1996–Present); Communications Specialist, Airborne Express (1990–1993). **Associations & Accomplishments:**

Associate Board, American Red Cross; American Red Cross Emergency Translator; Board Member, Ohio Energy Project – National Energy Education Development; Alliance for Education – Excellence in Teaching Awards Committee; Dayton Boy's & Girl's Club; Former President, Sigma Delta Pi International Honor Society for Spanish; Team Member, Battle of the Businesses for Special Olympics. **Education:** Wilmington College of Ohio, Bachelor of Arts (1993). **Personal:** Married to Dale in 1996. Ms. Bishop–Fulton enjoys tutoring in English and Spanish on a volunteer basis for low income students, athletics, and being a member of DP&L's basketball and softball leagues.

Steve C. Blose
Supervisor of Purchasing and Contract Services
Atlantic Electric
6801 Black Horse Pike
Pleasantville, NJ 08234–4131
(609) 645–4488
Fax: (609) 645–0582

4911

Business Information: In operation for over 100 years, Atlantic Electric provides electric services in combination with other services such as energy conservation to the residents and businesses in Pleasantville and surrounding communities. In his current capacity, Mr. Blose is responsible for the supervision of all purchasing and contract services. **Career Steps:** Atlantic Electric: Supervisor of Purchasing and Contract Services (1993–Present), Supervisor of Fixed Asset Accounting (1991–1993), Senior Auditor and Supervisor of Internal Auditing (1983–1991). **Associations & Accomplishments:** Institute of Internal Auditors. **Education:** Monmouth College, M.B.A (1980); Catawba College, B.A. (1975); Certified Internal Auditor (1983). **Personal:** Married to Sharon M. in 1988. Five children: Kristi, Greg, Jamie, Katie, and Carly. Mr. Blose enjoys sports and the outdoors.

Shirley Briones
Treasurer
Central and South West Services Corporation
P.O. Box 21928
Tulsa, OK 74121–1928
(918) 594–2188
Fax: (918) 594–3831

4911

Business Information: Established in 1939, Central and South West Services Corporation manages four utility companies that provide electric power to residents and businesses in Tulsa and the surrounding area. Currently the company employs 14 people and has an estimated annual revenue of $3.6 billion. As Treasurer, Ms. Briones is responsible for all aspects of cash management, securities administration, credit, collections and remittance processing for all four utility companies that make up the corporation. **Career Steps:** Treasurer, Central and South West Services Corporation (1994–Present); Central Power and Light Company: Manager of Budgets and Accounting Systems (1991–1994), Supervisor of Financial Planning (1988–1991), Statistician and Analyst (1983–1988). **Associations & Accomplishments:** Institute of Management Accountants; Treasury Management Association. **Education:** Texas A & M – Corpus Christi: M.B.A. (1988), B.B.A. in Accounting (1980). **Personal:** Married to Joseph in 1987.

Denise Y. Campbell
Senior Environmental Project Engineer
Pepco
1900 Pennsylvania Avenue N.W. Room 710
Washington, DC 20068
(202) 331–6640
Fax: (202) 331–6197
Email: See Below

4911

Business Information: Pepco, established in 1896, is an electric utility company with six generating facilities. As Senior Environmental Project Engineer, Ms. Campbell is responsible for administrative duties, preparing and submitting annual reports for state agencies, compliance orders, auditing, following changes in federal laws, consulting, and providing guidance. Internet users can reach her via: DCampbell@HPI.PEPCO.com. **Career Steps:** Pepco: Senior Environmental Project Engineer (1994–Present), Environmental Project Engineer (1989–1994), PCB Coordinator (1987–1989), Environmental Engineer (1986–1987). **Education:** Michigan Technical University, B.S. Degree in Engineering (1980). **Personal:** Ms. Campbell enjoys scuba diving.

Kenneth P. Carter
Attorney
Entergy Services, Inc.
639 Loyola Avenue, Suite 2600
New Orleans, LA 70113–3125
(504) 576–2761
Fax: (504) 576–2106

4911

Business Information: Entergy Services, Inc. is an investor–owned, public electric utility company consisting of several utilities in four states. A practicing attorney in Louisiana state and federal courts since 1974, Mr. Carter joined Entergy Services in 1995. He is responsible for managing, supervising, and handling litigation cases, primarily on casualty issues for Entergy companies. **Career Steps:** Attorney, Entergy Services, Inc. (1995–Present); Partner, Monroe & Lemann, P.L.C. (1975–1995). **Associations & Accomplishments:** Louisiana State Bar Association; New Orleans Bar Association; Federal Bar Association. **Education:** Tulane University School of Law, J.D. (1974); Washington and Lee University, B.A. (1971). **Personal:** Married to Nancy Carter, M.D. in 1975. Two children: Erin E. and Meghan E. Mr. Carter enjoys golf.

Shirley F. Cox
Vice President of Human Resources
Jones Onslow Electric Membership Corporation
259 Western Blvd.
Jacksonville, NC 28546
(910) 353–0707
Fax: (910) 353–8000

4911

Business Information: Jones Onslow EMC is a member–owned cooperative electric utility distribution service, serving businesses and residents within the coastal North Carolina counties of Onslow, Lenoir, Pender, Jones, Duplin, and Craven. As Vice President of Human Resources, Ms. Cox is responsible for all personnel administrative activities, including hiring, payroll, benefits, wellness, affirmative action, employment policies, evaluations, and employment laws. **Career Steps:** Jones Onslow Electric Membership Corp.: Vice President of Human Resources (1992–Present), Human Resources Manager (1990–1992), Administrative Assistant (1988–1990). **Associations & Accomplishments:** National Society of Human Resource Professionals; Board of Directors, Onslow County Women's Center; Board of Directors, Peers Family Development; Soroptimist. **Education:** Mount Olive: currently working toward a B.S. in Business Management. **Personal:** Married to Kenneth in 1975. One child: Jessica Jean. Ms. Cox enjoys gardening, the beach, and reading.

James E. Curtin
Corporate Controller
Besicorp Group Inc.
1151 Flatbush Rd.
Kingston, NY 12401–7011
(914) 336–7700 Ext: 125
Fax: (914) 336–7172

4911

Business Information: Besicorp Group Inc. is a fabricator and distributor of solar and radiant heat transfer technology products, systems, and solar electric products and systems, as well as an owner and developer of independent power production projects through its partnership interests. Current holdings consist of six plants in the state of New York, with expansion underway or planned in various developing countries. As Corporate Controller, James Curtin oversees all financial and accounting areas, primarily focusing on treasury functions, financial reporting, and tax–related issues. **Career Steps:** Corporate Controller, Besicorp Group Inc. (1995–Present); Ebasco Services, Inc.: Financial Reporting Manager (1990–1995), Principal Financial Analyst (1984–1990), Senior Internal Auditor (1981–1984); Corporate Accounting Manager, Dun & Bradstreet International, Ltd. (1979–1981), Corporate Auditor, The Dun & Bradstreet Corporation (1975–1979). **Associations & Accomplishments:** American Institute of Certified Public Accountants; New York State Society of Certified Public Accountants. **Education:** Pace University, B.B.A. (1971). **Personal:** Married to Jeanette in 1982. Two children: Christopher and Sean. Mr. Curtin enjoys golf, reading, and all spectator sports.

James E. Daniels
Working Foreman
Jacksonville Electric Authority (JEA)
8703 Burkhall Street
Jacksonville, FL 32211–5096
(904) 632–6916
Fax: (904) 632–6955

4911

Business Information: Jacksonville Electric Authority (JEA) is a public utility providing electrical utility services to residents and businesses in Duval County, part of Clay County, and St. John County. With two major service centers (Westside Service Center and Southside Service Center), JEA provides services to the Westside, Northwest, and the Southside of Jacksonville. As Working Foreman, Mr. Daniels is responsible for supervising a crew of eight, which includes preparing needed equipment and material for electrical jobs throughout the city. He also manages all work that is contracted out from JEA. Concurrently, he serves as a Real Estate Broker for Prudential Network Realty and as Broker–Owner of Daniels & Associates Realty, Inc. **Career Steps:** Working Foreman, Jacksonville Electric Authority (JEA) (1982–Present); Real Estate Broker, Prudential Network Realty (1994–Present); Broker–Owner, Daniels & Associates Realty, Inc. (1996–Present). **Associations & Accomplishments:** Jacksonville Board of Realtors; Electric Authority Supervisor Association; Distinguished Friends; Who's Who Among Students in American Universities and Colleges. **Education:** Principles Practices II of Real Estate (Broker Course) (1995); Jones Business College, B.S. (1974). **Personal:** Two children: Robin and Kindra Woodham. Mr. Daniels enjoys football, basketball, tennis, and dancing.

William A. Dore
Marketing Coordinator
Virginia Power–Eastern Division Energy Efficiency
5301 Robin Hood Road, Suite 100
Norfolk, VA 23513
(757) 857–2082
Fax: (757) 857–2048

4911

Business Information: Virginia Power is an investor–owned utility company specializing in electricity, with district offices and substations serving customers throughout Virginia. North Carolina Power, a subsidiary of Virginia Power, serves customers in the Northeastern part of North Carolina. Established in 1894, the Company currently employs 10,000 people. As Marketing Coordinator, Mr. Dore develops, coordinates, and helps to implement marketing plans for residential energy efficiency programs. Other responsibilities include public relations and strategic planning for the future. Concurrently, Mr. Dore is a requested speaker and lecturer on a variety of topics related to marketing and performs independent marketing consulting. **Career Steps:** Marketing Coordinator, Virginia Power (1995–Present); Vice President of Research and Development, Rose and Krueth Realty Corporation (1991–1995); President and CEO, Source, Inc. (1985–1991). **Associations & Accomplishments:** Treasurer Elect, Old Dominion University Real Estate Advisory Board; Urban Land Institute; National Association of Homebuilders. Mr. Dore is the recipient of several military and marketing awards and is conducts lectures and speaking engagements in marketing techniques. **Education:** Western Kentucky University, M.P.A. (1977); Ohio University, B.S. (1970); CBN University; Catholic University. **Personal:** Married to Carol in 1979. Two children: David W. and Debra K. Mr. Dore enjoys public speaking and lecturing.

Mr. William L. Drennen
Manager
New Martinsville Municipal Electric Utility
191 Main Street
New Martinsville, WV 26155
(304) 455–9138
Fax: (304) 775–2732

4911

Business Information: New Martinsville Municipal Electric Utility is a municipal electric distributor for the New Martinsville, West Virginia locale. Established in 1929, New Martinsville Municipal Electric Utility currently employs seven people. As Manager, Mr. Drennen is responsible for all aspects of operations, including planning and design, administration, public relations, field supervision, accounting, personnel, and community leadership. **Career Steps:** Manager, New Martinsville Municipal Electric Utility (1981–Present); Owner and Manager, Drennen Excavating Company (1978–1980); Line Construction to Accountant, Southern California Edison Company (1958–1974). **Associations & Accomplishments:** Charter Member of Jaycees, Santa Paula, California; President of Parent Teachers Association; Member of Board of Directors, New Martinsville Regatta; Advisor, Boy Scouts of

America; Member, Friends of the College; Advisor to Main Street, USA; Advisory to Library; Member of The American Public Power Association. **Education:** Kennedy Western University; Ventura Junior College; New Martinsville Community College. **Personal:** Married to Eulalia R. in 1952. Three children: John H. and Matthew L. Drennen, and Shelly I. (Drennen) Brown. Mr. Drennen enjoys reading, Quarterhorse breeding, and carpentry.

Richard Alan Eckersley
Manager, Applied Technology and I & E Engineering
Houston Lighting and Power Company
12301 Kurland Drive
Houston, TX 77034–4811
(713) 945–8245
Fax: (713) 945–8176
E MAIL: See Below

4911

Business Information: Houston Lighting and Power Company is an investor–owned electric utility company. As Manager of Applied Technology and Industrial & Electrical Engineering, Mr. Eckersley is responsible for managing the identification and applications of new technology in existing and new power plants, as well as providing technical direction to I&C and Electrical Engineers assigned to the Fossil Plant Engineering Department. Previously managed the design engineering on all plant betterment projects, as well as a two unit, combustion turbine based congeneration project. Internet users may contact him via: rick–eckersley@hlp.com. **Career Steps:** Houston Lighting and Power Company: Manager, Applied Technology and I & E Engineering (1995–Present), Manager, Design Engineering (1992–1995), Supervising Project Engineer (1981–1992), Senior Electrical Engineer (1979–1981). **Associations & Accomplishments:** Institute of Electrical and Electronic Engineers; Authored article titled "Utility–led cogen meets tight specs on steam supply", Power Magazine, August, 1995. **Education:** University of Texas at Arlington, B.S.E.E. (1975). **Personal:** Married to Wanda in 1976. Two children: Richard and Erica. Mr. Eckersley enjoys computers, hunting, and golf.

Rick Ferguson, CCP

Manager of System Compensation and HRIS
Entergy Services, Inc.
639 Loyola Avenue, 14th Floor
New Orleans, LA 70113–3125
(504) 569–4000
Fax: (504) 576–4428

4911

Business Information: Entergy Services, Inc. is a national and international producer and distributor of electricity. Established prior to 1900, Entergy Services, Inc. reports annual revenue of $6 billion and currently employs 15,000 people. As Manager of System Compensation and HRIS, Mr. Ferguson is responsible for human resource management for non–regulated, national, and international departments. Career milestones include the introduction of Redesign of Compensation System, that resulted in a cost savings in excess of $30 million for Entergy Services, Inc. in 1994. **Career Steps:** Manager of System Compensation and HRIS, Entergy Services, Inc. (1992–Present); Head of Human Resources Operations, Society (1991–1992); Head of Compensation and Benefits, TRW Automotive (1989–1991). **Associations & Accomplishments:** American Compensation Association; Certified Compensation Professional; Conference Board Council on Compensation; Published article on Compensation in the 90's. **Education:** University of Dayton, M.B.A. (1981); Wright State University (1976). **Personal:** Married to Bea in 1975. Mr. Ferguson enjoys travel, golf, and tennis.

OGDEN *POWER*

Mr. Theodore L. Flood
Vice President
Ogden Power Development
3211 Jermantown Road
Fairfax, VA 22030
(703) 246–0662
Fax: (703) 246–0782

4911

Business Information: A Division of the Ogden Corporation, Ogden Power Development owns and operates electric production facilities throughout the world. Established in 1983, Ogden Power Development currently employs 2,400 people and has an estimated annual revenue of $700 million. The Ogden Corporation reports $2.4 billion in sales and employs 47,000 people corporate–wide. As Vice President, Mr. Flood is responsible for all aspects of business development, U.S. and Latin American marketing strategies, and project management. **Career Steps:** Vice President, Ogden Power Development (1989–Present); Director of Government Sales, Weitz Resource (1987–1989); Director of Government Relations, Time Energy Systems (1985–1987); Federal Energy Office, Federal Energy Administration and the United States Department of Energy, Office of the Secretary of Energy (1972–1985); U.S. Army (1968–1970); Vietnam Service (1969–1970). **Education:** East Tennessee State University, M.B.A. (1972). **Personal:** Married to Mary in 1968. One child: Scott. Mr. Flood enjoys hunting, fishing, camping and bicycling.

Victor M. Fontane
Head, Customer Service Division
Puerto Rico Electric Power Authority
P.O. Box 364267
San Juan, Puerto Rico 00936–4267
(787) 289–4134
Fax: (787) 289–4131
EMAIL: See Below

4911

Business Information: Puerto Rico Electric Power Authority provides electric and related services to 1.3 million customers, including the federal government, industries, and residences. Established in 1941, the Company employs 10,000 people and has an estimated annual revenue in excess of $1 billion, 560 million. Plans for the future include a power increase from 2.8 to 3.5 megawatts. As Head, Customer Service Division, Mr. Fontanet supervises customer relations. He is responsible for training 1600 customer service representatives and manages all wholesale and government billings and collections. Internet users can reach him via: Jhigh@coqui.net. **Career Steps:** Puerto Rico Electric Power Authority: Head, Customer Service Division (1993–Present), Assistant Head, Supply Division (1984–1993), District Manager (1980–1984). **Associations & Accomplishments:** Puerto Rico Treasury Management Association; Puerto Rico Electric Power Authority Management Association. **Education:** University of Puerto Rico, B.B.A. (1971). **Personal:** Married to Julie A. High Littleton in 1993. Four children: Yasmin, Brenda, Gaby, and Christian. Mr. Fontane enjoys reading and sports.

Mr. Brian E. Forshaw
Director, Power Supply
CT Municipal Electric Energy Cooperative
30 Stott Avenue
Norwich, CT 06360–1508
(860) 889–4088
Fax: (860) 889–8158
EMail: See Below

4911

Business Information: CT Municipal Electric Energy Cooperative is a joint action municipal electric system power supply agency, responsible for meeting bulk power needs of municipal electric utility systems in Norwich, Connecticut and surrounding communities. As Director of Power Supply, Mr. Forshaw is responsible for negotiating electric power supply and transmission contracts, identifying and implementing strategic planning options, regulating sales of power supplies, and representing municipals. He can also be reached through the Internet via: BForshaw@aol.com **Career Steps:** CT Municipal Electric Energy Cooperative: Director of Power Supply (1993–Present), Manager of Power Planning and Operations (1990–1993), Supervisor of Power Contracts (1983–1993). **Associations & Accomplishments:** New England Power Pool: Public Power Representative, Operations Committee, Review Committee, North East Regional Transmission Group Negotiations; Northeast Public Power Association: Regional Power Supply Committee Retail Wheeling; Town of Waterford: Representative Town Meeting Member, Sub Base Realignment Coalition. **Education:** Rensselaer Polytechnic Institute, M.S. in Operations Management (1991); Bates College, B.A. in Mathematics. **Personal:** Married to Angela in 1982. Three children: Brittany, Bethany and Robert. Mr. Forshaw enjoys sports, reading and family activities.

Mr. John W. Greenlee
General Manager
Gascosage Electric Cooperative
P.O. Drawer G
Dixon, MO 65459
(573) 759–7146
Fax: (573) 759–6020

4911

Business Information: Gascosage Electric Cooperative is a rural utility providing electrical services to the surrounding areas of Dixon, Missouri. Established in 1945, Gascosage Electric Cooperative currently employs 27 people. As Chief Executive Officer and General Manager, Mr. Greenlee is responsible for all aspects of operations, including administration, strategic planning, and the market & distribution of electricity. **Career Steps:** Chief Executive Officer and General Manager, Gascosage Electric Cooperative (1992–Present); Assistant General Manager for Administration, East River Electric Power Cooperative (1990–1991); Division Manager of Accounting, Eastern Iowa Light & Power Cooperative (1982–1990). **Associations & Accomplishments:** President, Dixon Lions Club (1994–1996); Vice President, Dixon Chamber of Commerce (1994, 1995, 1996); Dixon Senior Citizens Board of Directors (1994, 1995, 1996); Community Drug Abuse Advisory Committee; Dixon Economic Development Committee; Fort Leonard Wood Regional Commerce and Growth Association. **Education:** Kansas State Teachers College, Emporia, Kansas, B.S. in Business (1969). **Personal:** Married to Wilma Jean. Four children: Dawn, Diane, Shelly and Tom. Mr. Greenlee enjoys golf, fishing and hiking.

Ronald C. Hall
Plant Manager of Combustion Turbines
Tennessee Valley Authority
1101 Market Street, BR 2G
Chattanooga, TN 37402
(423) 751–7202
Fax: (423) 751–8599

4911

Business Information: Tennessee Valley Authority (TVA) is an electric utility providing electrical services to the Tennessee Valley region through the operation of 12 fossil and three nuclear plants. Tennessee Valley Authority also has 48 combustion turbines units located at four sites. As Plant Manager of Combustion Turbines, Mr. Hall is responsible for overseeing all operations, maintenance, and engineering support of TVA's combustion turbines. He is responsible for high availability factors and improving starting reliability from 23% in 1991 to 97.4% in 1995. **Career Steps:** Tennessee Valley Authority: Plant Manager of Combustion Turbines (1993–Present), Manager of Operations and Technical Support (1991–1993); Florida Power & Light: Departmental Quality Manager (1990–1991), Performance Engineer (1988–1990). **Associations & Accomplishments:** American Society of Mechanical Engineers; Published technical papers. **Education:** Auburn University, B.S. in Mechanical Engineering (1988). **Personal:** Married to Tonya in 1992. Mr. Hall enjoys water skiing and restoring antique automobiles.

Richard F. Heany

Division Manager, U.S.A. Operations

Energy Performance Services, Inc.
2003 Renaissance Boulevard
King of Prussia, PA 19406
(610) 278–6633
Fax: (610) 278–7255

4911

Business Information: International in scope, Energy Performance Services, Inc. implements energy cost reduction measures in commercial, industrial, and institutional facilities, and guarantees that the total cost of implementation will be paid by the savings in energy costs. Established in 1986, Energy Performance Services, Inc. currently employs 35 people. As Division Manager, U.S.A. Operations, Mr. Heany oversees all day–to–day operations, which includes sales and marketing, engineering and project development. **Career Steps:** Division Manager, U.S.A. Operations, Energy Performance Services, Inc. (1994–Present); Project Manager, Heatac Systems (1988–1994); Sales Engineer, Philadelphia Gas Works (1986–1988). **Associations & Accomplishments:** Senior Member, Association of Energy Engineers; Certified Energy Manager, Association of Energy Engineers; Member, International Ground Source Heat Pump Association. **Education:** LaSalle University, M.B.A. in Finance (1989); Drexel University, B.S. in Civil Engineering (1983). **Personal:** Married to Marjorie Ann in 1992. Three children: Marjorie Ann, Jennifer Marie and Deanna Elizabeth. Mr. Heany enjoys golf and personal investing.

Kathryn R. Hood

Manager of Financial Services

El Paso Electric Company
303 North Oregon
El Paso, TX 79901–1329
(915) 543–5842
Fax: (915) 521–4779

4911

Business Information: El Paso Electric Company is an electric utility, servicing over 250,000 customers from the southeast corner of New Mexico — including an Army base and an Air Force base, to as far North as Van Horn, Texas. Joining El Paso Electric Company in 1982, Ms. Hood was appointed as Manager of Forecasting and Budgeting in 1991. She is responsible for the oversight of budget functions, O & M, cash and capital, sales forecasting, bond issuance, training of personnel, as well as overseeing long term forecasts. In 1996 Ms. Hood was named Manager of Financial Services and in addition to her other duties, was assigned the responsibility of Investor Relations. **Career Steps:** El Paso Electric Company: Manager of Forecasting and Budgeting (1991–Present), Assistant Manager of Finance Planning (1989–1991), Supervisor of Subsidiary Accounts (1986–1989). **Associations & Accomplishments:** American Society of CPA's; Texas Society of CPA's; El Paso Chapter TSCPA; El Paso Electric Employees Political Action Committee; National Association for Female Executives. **Education:** New Mexico State University, B.A. (1982). **Personal:** Two children: Dustin and Russell. Ms. Hood enjoys golf and bowling.

John M. Hoskins

Vice President and Treasurer

Tennessee Valley Authority
400 W. Summitt Hill Drive — WT4E
Knoxville, TN 37902–1499
(423) 632–3366
Fax: (423) 632–6673

4911

Business Information: Tennessee Valley Authority (TVA) is the largest public utility in the United States. Established in 1933, TVA currently employs more than 16,000 people. Beginning his TVA career in 1978 as an auditor in TVA's Internal Audit Branch, John Hoskins was appointed as Vice President and Treasurer in October of 1994. His primary duties focus on the administration and oversight of all loan programs and risk management, and responsibility for developing plans for long–term debt management to provide capital funds for the power program at a minimal cost. This also includes the review of long–term financing proposals, and making applicable recommendations to TVA's Chief Financial Officer. Mr. Hoskins has worked on $30 billion in new debt financings since TVA's return to the public bond market in 1989. Of these financings, $23 billion were for advance refunding of existing debt, resulting in annual interest expense savings to TVA of over $300 million. Two of these bond sales have been recognized by "Institutional Investor" magazine as "Deals of the Year" which are the financial community's equivalent of Oscars. TVA was named as the most outstanding agency borrower worldwide for 1995 by "Euroweek" magazine. A Certi-

fied Public Accountant and a member of the American Institute of Certified Public Accountants, Mr. Hoskins recently was part of a five–person advisory team that interviewed candidates and recommended a new firm to represent Knox County government as its financial advisor. John has worked on a variety of special projects for TVA, some major ones including two papers on TVA for the Clinton Administration; electronic data transmission of a variety of financial and statistical information from TVA's 160 power distributors; and the establishment of a $200 million capital improvement projects loan fund for the TVA power distributors. **Career Steps:** Tennessee Valley Authority: Vice President and Treasurer (1994–Present); Program Manager (1992–1994); Financial Analyst (1987–1992); Supervisor of Revenue and Accounting (1985–1987). **Associations & Accomplishments:** American Institute of Certified Public Accountants. **Education:** University of Tennessee, M.B.A. concentration in Finance (1987); Tennessee Technological University, B.S. in Accounting (1977). **Personal:** Married to Karen in 1978. Two children: Justin and Aaron.

Jack M. Huether

Director of Marketing, HVACR

Emerson Electric Company
8100 W. Florissant Ave., Bldg. A.
St. Louis, MO 63136–1417
(314) 553–3162
Fax: (314) 553–1097

4911

Business Information: Emerson Electric Company is an international conglomerate, consisting of over 50 divisions involved in the manufacture and global distribution of consumer and industrial products. Serving in managerial roles for Emerson Electric's Specialty Motors Division since 1986, Jack Huether was appointed Director of HVAC Marketing in 1995. In this capacity, he is responsible for the direction of marketing activities in North America for fractional horsepower motors to major HVAC OEM's (i.e., Lennox, Whirlpool, ICP), in addition to overseeing profitability and sales activities. **Career Steps:** Emerson Electric Company: Director of Marketing (1994–Present), Marketing Manager (1990–1994), Sales Engineer (1986–1990). **Associations & Accomplishments:** Lay Director at his church; Board of Directors, SSPMA; Recipient, Salesman of the Year. **Education:** Southern Illinois University, M.B.A. (1992); University of Missouri – Columbia, B.A. (1977). **Personal:** Married to Teresa in 1979. Two children: Kathleen and Timothy. Mr. Huether enjoys all sports, reading, and coaching childrens sports teams.

Ray M. Hugo

Director of Customer Services

Virginia Power
13000 James Madison Highway
Orange, VA 22960
(540) 672–6102
Fax: (540) 672–6140

4911

Business Information: Virginia Power is an electric public utility serving most of Virginia and parts of North Carolina. As Director of Customer Services, Mr. Hugo manages engineers, meter readers, the business office, and storeroom. He is also responsible for all phases of customer services and ensures client satisfaction. **Career Steps:** Virginia Power: Director of Customer Services (1987–Present), Division Staff Administrator (1984–1987), Senior Personnel Representative (1982–1984), Service Representative (1979–1982). **Associations & Accomplishments:** Orange County Chamber of Commerce; Piedmont United Way; Boy Scouts of America; Governors Regional Economic Development Advisory Council, Region 7; Chamber's Award for Excellence (1994); Resolution of Appreciation, Orange County Board of Supervisors (1992). **Education:** University of Richmond, M.B.A. (1983); Brigham Young University, B.S. in Business Management (1978). **Personal:** Married to Diane Rose Beatty in 1978. Five children: Nathan, Janelle, Benjamin, Brandon, and Jessica. Mr. Hugo enjoys gardening, working with youth at his church, travel, and Golden Retrievers.

Mr. Konstantinos N. Kappatos

Vice President of Engineering and Operations

Old Dominion Electric Cooperatives
4201 Dominion Boulevard
Glen Allen, VA 23233
(804) 747–0592
Fax: (804) 747–3742

4911

Business Information: Old Dominion Electric Cooperatives is a generation and transmission electric utility selling wholesale electric power in the states of Virginia, Maryland, Delaware, and West Virginia. The Company has over 360,000 customers, and is currently growing at a rate of 4% per year. As Vice President of Engineering and Operations, Mr. Kappatos is responsible for engineering operations and construction, including contract negotiations, rate setting, load forecasts, and integrated resource planning. Arriving in the U.S. in 1969, Mr.

Kappatos attributes his success to luck, hard work, perseverance, and his ability to keep up with the pace of change in the industry. He has been involved in the electrical power generation industry for over 15 years. Old Dominion Electric Cooperatives employs 77 people and reports an annual income of $340 million. **Career Steps:** Vice President of Engineering and Operations, Old Dominion Electric Cooperatives (1984–Present); Principal Utility Consultant, Dalton Associates (1983–1984); Electrical Engineer, Rural Electrification Administration (1979–1983). **Associations & Accomplishments:** National Society of Professional Engineers; National Society of Energy; The Greek Orthodox Church. **Education:** George Washington University, M.S. (1977); Virginia Polytechnic Institute & State University, B.S. in Electrical Engineering; Registered Professional Engineer in Virginia and Delaware.

Milton B. Lee II

Chief Operating Officer

City of Austin Electric Utility Department
721 Barton Springs Road
Austin, TX 78704
(512) 322–6571
Fax: (512) 322–6037

4911

Business Information: City of Austin Electric Utility Department provides the generation, transmission and distribution of electricity for the City of Austin, Texas. Established in 1895, City of Austin Electric Utility Department reports annual revenue of $540 million and currently employs 1,100 people. As Chief Operating Officer, Mr. Lee is responsible for the executive management of the electric utility. **Career Steps:** Chief Operating Officer, City of Austin Electric Utility Department (1990–Present); Director of Planning and Fuels, Lower Colorado River Authority (1988–1989); Assistant Director of Engineering, Public Utility Commission (1976–1984). **Associations & Accomplishments:** Engineering Foundation Advisory Council – University of Texas at Austin; National Society of Black Engineers Region V Advisory Board; LBJ Science Academy Advisory Board; Texas Alliance of Minority Engineers; Leadership Austin Board; United Way. **Education:** University of Texas – Austin, B.S. in Mechanical Engineering (1971). **Personal:** Married to Sarah Lee in 1994. Three children: Quentinn, Chanda and Shannon. Mr. Lee enjoys travel.

Mr. Larry D. Leftner

Owner

Smokey's Electric
P.O. Box 748
Edgewater, FL 32141
(904) 428–6211
Fax: Please mail or call

4911

Business Information: Smokey's Electric provides electric services in combination with other services such as customer relations and energy conservation research to residents and businesses in Edgewater and surrounding areas. A family operated business since 1964, Smokey's Electric currently employs three people. As Owner, Mr. Leftner is responsible for all aspects of operations. **Career Steps:** Owner, Smokey's Electric (1979–Present). **Personal:** Mr. Leftner enjoys boating and four–wheeling.

Edward W. C. Leung

Manager of Environmental Health Safety – Nuclear Energy Division

General Electric Company
175 Curtner Avenue
San Jose, CA 95125–1014
(408) 925–1940
Fax: (408) 925–2421
EMAIL: See Below

4911

Business Information: General Electric Company is the world's leading producer and distributor of industrial and consumer electrical and electronic products. Established in 1953, General Electric's San Jose, California facility specializes in the production of nuclear energy, employing 3,000 people. As Manager of Environmental Health Safety – Nuclear Energy Division, Mr. Leung is responsible for all aspects of management of environmental, health and safety issues. She can also be reached through the Internet via: LeungE@SJCP02.NE.GE.COM **Career Steps:** General Electric Company: Manager of Environmental Health Safety – Nuclear Energy Division (1991–Present), Manager of Environmental Health Safety – Semiconductor Division (1984–1991), Manager of Environmental Health Safety – Aerospace Division (1979–1993). **Associations & Accomplishments:** Member, American Industrial Hygiene Association; Board of Directors, Peninsula Industrial and Business Association. **Education:** Hunter College – City University of New York, M.S. (1978); Pace University, B.S. (1977). **Personal:** Married to Cleo in 1979. Two children: Charles and William. Mr. Leung enjoys visiting environmentally sensitive areas of the world.

Mark S. Lynch

Project Director
Southern Electric International
900 Ashwood Parkway, Suite 500
Atlanta, GA 30338–4780
(770) 392–7659
Fax: (770) 673–7726

4911

Business Information: Southern Electric International, an unregulated subsidiary of The Southern Company, is an independent power producer of electricity, concentrating in acquisitions and privatization of utility companies. Established in 1980, Southern Electric International currently employs 365 people. As Project Director, Mr. Lynch is responsible for developing green field projects and heading up the team, including obtaining and negotiating all agreements, permits and financing to construct and operate an acquired asset. Current projects include a job in Indonesia. **Career Steps:** Project Director, Southern Electric International (1988–Present); Project Manager, Reynolds, Smith and Hills (1980–1988); Superintendent, L K Comstock (1978–1980). **Associations & Accomplishments:** Registered Professional Engineer State of Florida; Institute of Electronics and Electrical Engineers; Co-author "Reliability Centered Design: Power Plant Conceptual Design Optimization." **Education:** Villanova University, B.E.E. (1976). **Personal:** Married to Kim in 1981. Three children: Maura, Matthew, and Patrick.

Edwin J. Mantel

Director Information Projects – Nuclear
Commonwealth Edison
1400 Opus Place, Ste. 300
Downers Grove, IL 60515–1198
(708) 663–7583
Fax: (708) 663–2999

4911

Business Information: Commonwealth Edison is a member–owned electric utility, serving customers throughout the greater Downers Grove, Illinois area and surrounding county communities. Mr. Mantel has been with Commonwealth Edison since 1987, starting out as a district manager and working his way up. Currently as Director of Information Projects – Nuclear, Mr. Mantel oversees the installation of management across the division and ensures proper staffing. In addition, he has a series of project managers who report to him (7 direct & 60 nuclear plant background). **Career Steps:** Commonwealth Edison: Director Information Projects – Nuclear (1992–Present), Services Director – Dresden Nuclear Power Station (1989–1992), District Manager (1987–1989). **Associations & Accomplishments:** Project Management Institute; Strategic Planning Committee – Riverside, Illinois; Nuclear Records Management Association. **Education:** University of Chicago, M.B.A. (1974); Illinois Institute of Technology, B.S. in Math (1969). **Personal:** Married to Bernadette in 1971. Four children: Julie, Peter, Matt and Joey. Mr. Mantel enjoys collecting antique model trains and fishing.

David W. Miller, Ph.D.

Corporate Health Physicist
Illinois Power Company
760 Stevens Creek Boulevard
Forsyth, IL 62535
(217) 935–8881 Ext. 3880
Fax: (217) 935–4632
EMAIL: See Below

4911

Business Information: Illinois Power Company (IPC) is an international provider of public utility electrical generations and global informational data systems on nuclear power occupational doses. IPC also provides support operations to the Clinton Power Station. As Corporate Health Physicist, Dr. Miller is the North American Regional Coordinator for the NEA/IAEA ISOE Program. He may be reached through the Internet via: DWMPHD@AOL.COM **Career Steps:** Illinois Power Company: Corporate Health Physicist (1993–Present), Director of Plant Radiation Protection (1988–1992); Supervisor of Radiological and Environmental Services, Pennsylvania Power & Light Company (1980–1988). **Associations & Accomplishments:** Nuclear Energy Agency; OECD; ISOE–IAEA, Paris, France (President, ISOE Bureau 1995–1999); Health Physics Society: National Board Member (1996–2000); Adjunct Professor, College of Engineering, University of Illinois; Member, Governor's Radiation Advisory Council, Illinois; Elected Public Official, Village Trustee, Forsyth, Illinois. **Education:** Purdue University: Ph.D. (1976), M.S. (1973). **Personal:** Married to Kathleen J., M.D. in 1976. One child: Robert. Dr. Miller enjoys golf, tennis, and serving as Forsyth Village Trustee (elected official) and hospital board trustee.

Jerome Murray

Charlotte Area Planner of Electrical System Design
Duke Power Company
6325 Wilkinson Boulevard
Charlotte, NC 28214
(704) 382–5925
Fax: (704) 382–5601

4911

Business Information: Duke Power Company is an electrical power supplier for the midwest regions of North and South Carolina. As Charlotte Area Planner of Electrical System Design, Mr. Murray plans, designs, and implements major electrical distribution facilities for the western quadrant of the City of Charlotte (metropolitan area). Established in 1905, Duke Power Company currently employs 17,052 people and has annual assets in excess of $4.5 billion. **Career Steps:** Charlotte Area Planner of Electrical System Design, Duke Power Company (1993–Present); Power Quality Services Reliability Engineer, Duke Power Company (1990–1993); Electrical System Design Engineer, Duke Power Company (1987–1990). **Associations & Accomplishments:** Institute of Electrical and Electronic Engineers; Institute of Electronics and Electrical Engineers Computer Society; Delta Epsilon Sigma Honor Society; Registered North Carolina Notary Public. **Education:** Belmont Abbey College, B.A. in Business (1994); DPC's Leadership School, L.E.A.D.; DPC's Distribution Engineering School, A.D.S.; Beaufort County Community College, A.A.S. in Electrical Engineering Technology. Pfeiffer University, M.B.A. **Personal:** Married to Lynette N. in 1986. One child: Marcus Terran. Mr. Murray enjoys audio listening, biking, car maintenance, and computer programs.

A. Reed Newland

Principal Attorney of International Development
CMS Enterprises Company
330 Town Center Drive, Suite 1100, Fairlane Plaza South
Dearborn, MI 48126
(313) 436–9344
Fax: (313) 441–0282

4911

Business Information: CMS Enterprises Company, a subsidiary of CMS Energy, is a worldwide independent power production company, as well as a power plant development firm. CMS Enterprises is also actively involved in oil and gas exploration and production, and is in the pipeline business. Presently, the Company operates power plants in Argentina, the Philipines and ten other countries; employing over 8,000 people, with assets of $3.5 billion reported for FY 1995. Assigned to the non–utility segment of the Company, Mr. Newland is responsible for the management of all legal aspects of international development projects. **Career Steps:** CMS Enterprises Company: Principal Attorney of International Development (1994–Present), Principal Attorney of Latin America (1993–1994); General Counsel, Gundle Environmental Systems (1992–1993). **Associations & Accomplishments:** American Bar Associations; Member, Episcopal Church; Internal publications. **Education:** University of Houston Law Center, J.D. (1984); Stanford University, A.B. in History (1980). **Personal:** Mr. Newland enjoys soccer, tennis, golf, reading, and keeping physically fit.

J.Terry Rennie

Plant Manager
Modesto Energy Limited Partnership
P.O. Box 302, 4549 Ingram Creek Road
Westley, CA 95387
(209) 894–3161
Fax: (209) 894–3170

4911

Business Information: Modesto Energy Limited Partnership, a division of United American Energy Operation Corporation, supplies electricity to Pacific Gas & Electric through the use of waste tires. United Arab Emirates maintains thirteen facilities processing rice hulls, natural gas, waste coal, waste tires, and hydro–power to produce electricity. A Marine Engineer with sixteen years experience, Mr. Rennie joined MELP in 1993. As Plant Manager of the Westley, California location, he supervises all operations, maintenance, business, environmental, and personnel activities of the facility. **Career Steps:** Plant Manager, Modesto Energy Limited Partnership (1993–Present); Maintenance and Engineering Supervisor, Mission Operations & Maintenance (1991–1993); Plant Engineer, GWF Power Systems (1988–1991); Marine Engineer, United States Merchant Marines (1972–1988). **Associations & Accomplishments:** Marine Engineering Beneficial Association; Active in Fundraising for Education and Historical Preservations; Published in Power Magazine. **Education:** B.S. in Marine Engineering (1972); Licensed Marine Engineer. **Personal:** Married to Marcia J. in 1978. Two children: Jason and Sara. Mr. Rennie enjoys camping, fishing, and bicycle riding.

Richard D. Rinck

Market Development Coordinator
Atlantic Electric
6801 Black Horse Pike
Pleasantville, NJ 08232
(609) 645–4852
Fax: (609) 383–0582

4911

Business Information: Atlantic Electric specializes in electric power generation, serving 450,000 customers throughout the southern third region of New Jersey. Established in 1886, Atlantic Electric currently employs 1,400 people and has an estimated annual revenue of $1 billion. As Market Development Coordinator, Mr. Rinck provides leadership in developing new and existing markets and coordinates geothermal heating and cooling activities with regional and national organizations. **Career Steps:** Atlantic Electric: Market Development Coordinator (1995–Present), Coordinator of Marketing Planning (1994–1995), Senior Analyst of Marketing (1989–1994), Senior Analyst of Strategic Planning (1986–1989). **Associations & Accomplishments:** Chairman, Northeastern Utilities Group for Geothermal Energy Technology; Consortium for Energy Efficiency, Advisory Committee and Chairman Geothermal Heat Pump Committee, Vice Chairman Geothermal Heat Pump Consortium Technology Confidence Committee; Chairman, Geothermal Heat Pump Consortium National Awareness Committee; NJ Heat Pump Council–Professional Education Committee; National Youth Sports Coaches Association; Church council; Speaker, Rotary, Lions, Kiwanis and Republican Clubs. **Education:** Monmouth College, M.B.A. (1985); Stockton College, B.A. in Psychology. **Personal:** Married to Judith in 1977. Two children: Melinda and Jesse. Mr. Rinck enjoys water and snow skiing, basketball, volleyball, golf and youth sports coaching.

Eduardo A. Rodriguez

Senior Vice President and General Counsel
El Paso Electric Company
303 North Oregon Street
El Paso, TX 79901
(915) 543–2037
Fax: (915) 521–4704

4911

Business Information: El Paso Electric Company is an electric public utility company serving residents and businesses in the El Paso locale. Established in 1901, El Paso Electric Company, reports annual revenue of $500 million and currently employs 1,101 people. A practicing attorney in Texas since 1979, Mr. Rodriguez joined El Paso Electric Company as Staff Counsel in 1981 becoming the General Counsel and Secretary in 1989. Currently serving as Senior Vice President, General Counsel, and Chief Legal Officer, he is responsible for the oversight of the Secretary's Office and Corporate Communications, in addition to his legal practice. **Career Steps:** El Paso Electric Company: Senior Vice President and General Counsel (1993–Present), Vice President and General Counsel (1991–1993), General Counsel and Secretary (1989–1991). **Associations & Accomplishments:** American Bar Association; Texas Bar Association; New Mexico Bar Association; Instructor of Constitutional Law (1981–1983), El Paso Police Academy; Hispanic Bar Association. **Education:** St. Mary's University School of Law, J.D. (1979); Texas Tech University, B.A. in Political Science, with high Honors. **Personal:** Married to Maria Del Rosario in 1988. Three children: Jason Michael, Stacey, and Victoria. Mr. Rodriguez enjoys aerobic exercises, weight training, and reading political, historical novels and biographies.

Richard W. Roop

Plant Manager –Ratts Generating Facility
Hoosier Energy – Rural Electric Cooperative, Inc.
P.O. Box 126, Blackburn Road
Petersburg, IN 47567
(812) 354–8491
Fax: (812) 354–3777

4911

Business Information: Hoosier Energy – Rural Electric Cooperative, Inc., headquartered in Bloomington, Indiana, is an electrical generating and transmitting cooperative with three locations in Indiana (Bloomington, Marion, and Petersburg). Serving in various engineering and managerial roles for HEREC since 1986, Richard Roop has served as the Ratts Generating Facility Plant Manager since 1995. He is responsible for the overall day–to–operations of the Facilty, with duties to include planning, organizing, controlling, and project coordination associated with operations and the betterment of the 250 mega watt generation station. **Career Steps:** Hoosier Energy – Rural Electric Cooperative, Inc.: Plant Manager – Ratts Generating Facility (1995–Present), Instrument and Electrical Engineer (1986–1995); Senior Instrument Engineer, Southern Indiana Gas and Electric (1981–1986). **Associations & Accomplishments:** Instrument Society of America; Petersburg Chamber of Commerce; Board Member, Pike County United Way; Board Member, Pike County Growth Council; Advisory Board Member, Indiana State University, Department of Electronics and Computer Technology; Advisory Board Member, Ivy Tech State College, Technology Department. **Education:** Indiana State University, M.B.A. (1995); Murray State University, B.S.E.E.T. (1980). **Personal:** Married to Laura D. in 1980. Two children: Lauren and Brandon. Mr. Roop enjoys spending time with his family, golf, softball, and coaching his son's little league games.

Kenneth W. Seaton

Commercial Markets Manager
ComEd
1919 Swift Drive
Oak Brook, IL 60521–1502
(708) 684–3828
Fax: (708) 684–3819

4911

Business Information: ComEd is an investor–owned public utility. As Commercial Markets Manager, Mr. Seaton is responsible for sales to all commercial customers. **Career Steps:** ComEd: Commercial Markets Manager (1992–Present), Operations Manager (1990–1992), Area Manager (1987–1990). **Associations & Accomplishments:** Former President, Crystal Lakes Ambutol Advisor Board for Sherman Hospital; Former Vice President, Industrial Section of The Crystal Lake Chamber of Commerce; Former President, Church of the Cross Board of Trustees. **Education:** Northwestern University – Kellogg School of Management, M.B.A. (1972); University of Illinois, B.S.E.E. (1969). **Personal:** Married to Marilyn in 1973. Two children: Mark and Traci. Mr. Seaton enjoys golf, skiing, and home projects and repairs.

Stephen L. Smith

Superintendent
Lower Colorado River Authority
9309 Tea Rose Trail
Austin, TX 78748–5013
(512) 473–3310
Fax: (512) 473–4010

4911

Business Information: Lower Colorado River Authority is a wholesale electrical provider servicing the Austin, Texas region. As Superintendent, Mr. Smith supervises daily operations, handling employee reviews, scheduling of staff, budgetary concerns, compliance with OSHA safety regulations, and facilities maintenance. Mr. Smith also supervises the underground power plant construction. **Career Steps:** Superintendent, Lower Colorado River Authority (1992–Present); Operations Manager, Trammell Crow Company (1984–1992); Assistant Chief Engineer, Dobie Center Limited (1979–1984). Education: Lee College, Associate Degree. **Personal:** Married to Belinda in 1988. Six children: Corey, Zach, Lauren, Christy, Rochelle, and Kellyn. Mr. Smith enjoys sports and his kids."

David Stanley

Director of Finance and Accounting
Rappahannock Electric
P.O. Box 7388
Fredericksburg, VA 22404–7388
(540) 891–5888
Fax: (540) 891–0781

4911

Business Information: Rappahannock Electric is an electric cooperative, providing electrical services to over 70,000 residences and business throughout the North Central and Mountain regions of Virginia. A Certified Public Accountant, Mr. Stanley joined Rappahannock Electric as Financial Analyst in March 1995 and was appointed as Director of Finance and Accounting in September 1995. He is responsible for directing the activities of the accounting process, debt financing and investments, financial training, analysis and development of new business ventures. Concurrent with his position at Rappahannock Electric, he serves as a financial and leadership consultant to mid–size firms. **Career Steps:** Rappahannock Electric: Director of Finance and Accounting (Sept. 1995–Present), Financial Analyst (Mar. 95–Sept. 95); Accounting Supervisor, Commonwealth Gas (Mar. 1987–Mar. 1995). **Associations & Accomplishments:** Certified Public Accountant; Faculty Member, Averette College; Member, Institute of Management Accountants. **Education:** Averett College, M.B.A. (1984); Virginia Commonwealth University, B.S. in Accounting (1985). **Personal:** Married to Crystal in 1991. Mr. Stanley enjoys public speaking, financial training, and athletics.

Mr. James S. Thomson

Vice President and General Manager–Asia/Pacific
Mission Energy Company
18101 Von Karman Avenue, Suite 1700
Irvine, CA 92715
(714) 752–5588
Fax: (714) 752–6319

4911

Business Information: Mission Energy Company is one of the world's largest investors in privately–owned, foreign and domestic, independent power plants. Established in 1986, Mission Energy Company employs 700 people. In his current capacity, Mr. Thomson directs the development, legal, financial, and operations of the Company's Asia–Pacific business. Additionally, he is responsible for the field offices in Melbourne, Australia, Jakarta, Indonesia, and Singapore. **Career Steps:** Vice President and General Manager–Asia/Pacific, Mission Energy Company (1990– Present); Vice President–Operations, Energy Factors, Inc. (1983–1990); Manager, Financial Planning, San Diego Gas & Electric Company (1976–1983). **Associations & Accomplishments:** Registered Professional Engineer–California and Arizona. **Education:** University of Michigan; Iowa State University, M.S. Engineering Economics; Georgia Institute of Technology, B.S. Operations Research. **Personal:** Married to Jacklyn (Jackie) in 1971. Two children: Jonathan and Jessica. Mr. Thomson enjoys scuba diving, sailing, skiing, tennis, and golf during his leisure time.

Julio (Mutch) Usera

Manager of Marketing & Economic Development
Black Hills Power and Light Company
625 9th Street
Rapid City, SD 57701
(605) 348–1700
Fax: (605) 342–2464

4911

Business Information: Black Hills Power and Light Company (BHP&L) is an investor–owned, electric utility servicing residential and business customers in the Rapid City, South Dakota locale. Established in 1941, BHP&L currently employs 360 people. Mr. Usera joined BHP&L in 1992 as Manager of Marketing & Economic Development, responsible for the development, planning, and implementation of all marketing and economic development programs. **Career Steps:** Manager of Marketing & Economic Development, Black Hills Power and Light Company (1992–Present); Manager of Public Affairs, Black Hills Corporation (1980–1992). **Associations & Accomplishments:** Black Hills Homebuilders Association; Rapid City Toastmasters Club; Edison Electric Institute; Black Hills Advertising Federation; Board Member, YMCA; Board Member, Boy's Club; Board Member, Rapid City Area Economic Development; Advisory Board, South Dakota Commission of Civil Rights. **Education:** Attended: Black Hills State University, 2 years. **Personal:** Two children: Joshua and Matthew. Mr. Usera enjoys martial arts (instructor), outdoors, and skiing.

Michael Whiteside

Executive Vice President and General Manager
Coweta Fayette Electric Membership Corporation
PO Box 488
Newnan, GA 30264–0488
(770) 502–0226
Fax: (770) 251–9788

4911

Business Information: Coweta Fayette Electric Membership Corporation, one of the top 25 cooperative companies in the U.S., is an electric utility cooperative serving more than 42,000 customers in the Newnan, Georgia locale. Joining Coweta Fayette as Administrative Assistant in 1974, Mr. Whiteside was appointed as Executive Vice President and General Manager in 1983. He is responsible for all aspects of operations and management, in addition to overseeing all administrative operations for associates and a support staff of 125. **Career Steps:** Coweta Fayette Electric Membership Corporation: Executive Vice President and General Manager (1995–Present), Administrative Assistant (1974–1983); Engineer, Southern Engineering Company (1966–1974) **Associations & Accomplishments:** Former President, Newnan Coweta Chamber of Commerce; Secretary, Georgia Electric Membership Corporation; Rotary Club; Board Member for following: First Union Bank, Gresco–Oglethorpe Power, Fayette Chamber of Commerce **Education:** Middle Georgia College, A.S. in Electrical Engineering; Georgia State University; DeKalb College **Personal:** Married to Lynn in 1964. Five children: Tracy, Kevin, Scott, Nicole and Julie. Mr. Whiteside enjoys golf and photography.

Brian M. Wirz

Executive Vice President of Power Supply
Jacksonville Electric Authority (JEA)
21 West Church Street
Jacksonville, FL 32202–3155
(904) 632–7270
Fax: (904) 632–7366

4911

Business Information: Jacksonville Electric Authority (JEA) is a publicly–owned utility with five power plants (four in Florida and one in Georgia), serving customers in North East Florida. As Executive Vice President of Power Supply, Mr. Wirz is responsible for the direction of all power supply activities, including power supply planning, bulk power sales, purchase of fuel, as well as licensing, designing, constructing, operating and maintaining the utilities' coal, oil and gas fired facilities. **Career Steps:** Jacksonville Electric Authority (JEA): Executive Vice President of Power Supply, (1995–Present), Associate Managing Director (1983–1995), Director of Power Engineering (1978–1992), Division Manager of Power Engineering (1976–1978). **Associations & Accomplishments:** Member American Society of Mechanical Engineers; Elected to "Who's Who in Electrical Utility Industry" (1991); Member, Executive Board of the North Florida Council, Boy Scouts of America; Past Chairman American Public Power Association, Generating and Fuels Committee; Second Degree Black Belt Tae Kwon Do. **Education:** University of North Florida, M.B.A.,(1981); Georgia Institute of Technology, B.S. in Mechanical Engineering. **Personal:** Married to Carolyn. Four children: Jennifer, Kathleen, Jacob and Timothy. Mr. Wirz enjoys reading, music, martial arts, as well as antique and high–performance automobiles.

Sandra Fraley Abel

Senior Attorney
Kentucky West Virginia Gas Company, L.L.C.
630 North Lake Drive
Prestonsburg, KY 41653–1040
(606) 886–2311
Fax: (606) 889–9084

4922

Business Information: Kentucky West Virginia Gas Company, L.L.C. is a subsidiary of Equitable Resources, Inc., a full service energy marketing company with operations for the exploration, production, storage, transportation and distribution of natural gas. As Senior Attorney, Ms. Abel acts as agent and representative for the Company, dealing with natural gas and energy law, property law, and administrative law. She started out as a Staff Attorney with Equitable Resources Energy Company, an oil and gas production company, and transferred into the newly created position of Senior Attorney with Kentucky West Virginia Gas Company, a natural gas transmission company in 1996. **Career Steps:** Senior Attorney, Kentucky West Virginia Gas Company (1996–Present); Staff Attorney, Equitable Resources Energy Company (1991–1996). **Associations & Accomplishments:** American Bar Association; Virginia Bar Association; Kentucky Bar Association; American Association of Professional Landmen; Kentucky Oil and Gas Association; Virginia Oil and Gas Association. **Education:** University of Kentucky, J.D. (1991); Eastern Kentucky University, B.A.

Bernard M. Otis

Vice President of Transmissions
Iroquois Pipeline Operating Co.
One Corporate Drive, Suite 600
Shelton, CT 06484
(203) 925–7216
Fax: (203) 929–9501

4922

Business Information: Iroquois Pipeline Operating Company is a provider of natural gas transmissions spanning from Canada to New England and New York. Established in 1991, Iroquois Pipeline Operating Company reports annual revenue of $150 million and currently employs more than 80 people. As Vice President of Transmissions, Mr. Otis is responsible for system design, operations, transportation rate & tariff issues, marketing, and business development. **Career Steps:** Vice President of Transmissions, Iroquois Pipeline Operating Company (1991–Present); Director of Gas Supply, Gaz Metropolitain (1988–1991); Senior Manager of Transportation, TransCanada PipeLines (1986–1988). **Associations & Accomplishments:** New England Gas Association (NEGA); American Gas Association (AGA). **Education:** University of Ottawa, Basic Mechanical Engineering (1973). **Personal:** Married to Francine in 1973. Two children: Madeleine and Melanie. Mr. Otis enjoys golf, tennis, skiing, and bowling.

Jacqueline L. Rains
Employee Development Consultant
Southern California Gas Company
19848 Welby Way
Winnetka, CA 91306–4341
(213) 244–2848
Fax: (818) 702–9212
EMAIL: See Below

4922

Business Information: Southern California Gas Company is a natural gas utility providing energy services to residents of the Southern California area. Established in 1890, the Company employs 6,900 people, and has an estimated annual revenue of $13 billion. As Employee Development Consultant, Ms. Rains works with various internal clients to assess organizational needs for professional and work–place development, strategic planning, and design and implementation of employee benefits and programs. Internet users can reach her via: Swanmaker@aol.com. **Career Steps:** Southern California Gas Company: Employee Development Consultant (1995–Present), Energy Partnership Manager (1994–1995); Marketing Manager/Western Region, Energy Investment (1992–1994); Product Development Manger, Hly-oh Company, C/O Southern California Edison (190–1992). **Associations & Accomplishments:** American Society for Training and Development (ASTD); National Association of Female Executives; American Association of University Women; Pepperdine Alumni Association. **Education:** Pepperdine University, M.B.A. with Honors (1987); California State University, Northridge, B.A. Magna Cum Laude; Los Angeles Valley Jr. College, A.A. Cum Laude. **Personal:** Married to Jeffrey Alan Turk in 1991. One child: Grace Elizabeth Rains–Turk. Ms. Rains enjoys scuba diving, doll collecting, public speaking, and travel.

Debbie A. Ristig
Director of Environment
NorAm Gas Transmission
P.O. Box 21734
Shreveport, LA 71151–0001
(318) 429–2808
Fax: (318) 429–3927
EMAIL: See Below

4922

Business Information: NorAm Gas Transmission Company (all Locations) specializes in natural gas transmission. As Director of Environment, Health & Safety (all locations), Ms. Ristig supervises the environmental and safety programs, including permitting, regulatory review and compliance, reporting, and training. Internet users can reach her via: DRISTIG@PRYSM.NET. **Career Steps:** NorAm Gas Transmission: Director of Environment (1993–Present), Regional Construction Supervisor (1988–1993), Design Engineer (1982–1988). **Associations & Accomplishments:** Louisiana Engineering Society; National Society of Professional Engineers; American Society of Mechanical Engineers; American Society of Safety Engineers; Arkansas Environmental Federation; Louisiana Environmental Federation. **Education:** Louisiana Tech University M.B.A. (1987), B.S. in Mechanical Engineering (1982). **Personal:** Married to Kyle in 1990. Ms. Ristig enjoys dog obedience and agility, and water skiing.

David M. Webb
Gas Controller
Northern Plains
1400 Smith EB 4248
Houston, TX 77002
(713) 853–3906
Fax: (713) 646–3425
E/M: Dwebbeflash.net

4922

Business Information: Northern Plains, one of three divisions of Euron, is a natural gas pipeline built to transport Canadian gas to markets in the mid–west and other parts of the U.S. As Gas Controller, Mr. Webb supervises the Northern border and is responsible for overseeing transportation, delivery, and operation, ensuring timely processing of customer orders and stability of the pipeline. **Career Steps:** Enron/Northern Plains: Gas Control Coordinator (1995–Present), Transportation Specialist (1994–1995), Gas Controller (193–1994). **Associations & Accomplishments:** Black Employees Development Association (BEDA). **Education:** Electronics Institute, Associates Degree (1989). **Personal:** Married to Karen in 1985. One child: Courtney. Mr. Webb enjoys fishing and the Internet.

Patricia K. Jorczak
Information Technical Standards Architect
Indiana Gas Company
1630 North Meridan Street
Indianapolis, IN 46202–1402
(317) 321–0693
Fax: (317) 321–0499
EMAIL: See Below

4923

Business Information: Indiana Gas Company is a local gas distribution utility serving one third of central Indiana. As Information Technical Standards Architect, Ms. Jorczak is responsible for corporate communications and managing internet services, including Internet access, web pages, company intranet maintenance, and personnel training. Internet users can reach her via: PJORCZAK@INDIANA–GAS.COM **Career Steps:** Information Technical Standards Architect, Indiana Gas Company (1989–Present); Branch Manager, J.T.S. Computer Services (1988–1989); Technical Services Manager, Computer Task Group (1980–1988). **Associations & Accomplishments:** Network of Women in Business; Member of the Indianapolis Chamber of Commerce Connect Project. **Education:** Indiana State University: M.S. (1978), B.A.; Attended, Purdue University. **Personal:** Three children: Jennifer, Nicholas and Edwin. Ms. Jorczak enjoys reading and gardening.

Robert Weaver
Superintendent of Human Resources
UGI Utilities, Inc.
2121 City Line Road
Bethlehem, PA 18017
(610) 807–3148
Fax: (610) 807–3167

4923

Business Information: UGI Utilities, Inc. is a natural gas distribution company serving three counties in Texas. The Company provides service to consumers, industrial, and commercial users. As Superintendent of Human Resources, Mr. Weaver oversees all aspects of personnel management. He is responsible for benefits, policies, recruitment, and reviews, as well as payroll, safety, discipline, and labor/employee relations. **Career Steps:** Superintendent of Human Resources, Ugi Utilities, Inc. (1992–Present); Manager of Human Resources, Exide Corporation (1990–19*91); Assistant Plant Manager, Russell Stanley Corporation (1989–1990); Administrator of Employee Relations, Allied/Signal Aerospace (1987–1988). **Associations & Accomplishments:** Board of Governors, Allentown Lehigh County Chamber of Commerce; Chairman of Human Resources Committee, Allentown Lehigh County Chamber of Commerce; Chairperson, Employee's Advisory Council, Pennsylvania Department of Labor; Ambassador Board, Lehigh Carbon Community College; Numerous other community organizations; Teaches evening classes at the local community College. **Education:** Lincoln Technical Institute, A.S. (1985); University of Maryland, B.S. **Personal:** Married to Suzanne in 1986. One child: Jacob. Mr. Weaver enjoys golf, and spending time with his family.

Alex C.W. Cheng
General Manager
Yankee Gas Services Company
47 Eagle Street
Waterbury, CT 06708
(203) 596–3126
Fax: (203) 596–3130

4924

Business Information: Yankee Gas Services Company is the largest natural gas distribution company in Connecticut serving approximately 177,000 customers in 69 cities and towns throughout Connecticut. Joining Yankee Gas as an Engineer in 1982, Mr. Cheng has risen through the ranks of General Manager. In his current position, he oversees the Distribution, Engineering, Fleet Management, Material Procurement, Research and Development, and Technical Support. **Career Steps:** Yankee Gas Services Company: General Manager (1995–Present); Superintendent (1992–1995); Business Manager (1988–1992); Area Supervisor (1987–1988); Engineer (1982–1987). **Associations & Accomplishments:** Society of Gas Operators; Northeast Gas Distribution Council; New England Gas Association; American Gas Association; Chinese Culture Center; Chinese Language School; Volunteer: Special Olympics, American Diabetes Society. **Education:** University of New Haven: coursework towards M.B.A., B.S. in Mechanical Engineering (1982); American Management Association. **Personal:** Married to Ana in 1980. Three children: Philip, Christine and Derrick. Mr. Cheng enjoys golf.

Daniel Commella
Director
Southern Connecticut Gas
855 Main Street
Bridgeport, CT 06604–4915
(203) 795–7718
Fax: (203) 795–7716

4924

Business Information: Southern Connecticut Gas is a local natural gas distribution company, serving residential and business customers in the Bridgeport and New Haven, Connecticut locale. With thirteen years experience in the gas industry, Mr. Commella joined Southern Connecticut Gas in 1994. Serving as Director, he oversees the administrative operations of a support staff of ten, in addition to the direction of short– and long–term purchasing, strategic planning, regulatory affairs at the federal level, and large commercial and industrial sales functions. **Career Steps:** Director, Southern Connecticut Gas (1994–Present); Director of Gas Supply, Western Gas Resources (1992–1994); Director of Gas Purchasing, J. Makowski, Inc. (1984–1992); Vice President, Gazocean USA (1982–1984); Caltex Petroleum Corp.: Entry level leading to Manager of International Sales (1970–1982). **Associations & Accomplishments:** GISBI; NEGA; West Haven Chamber of Commerce, East Coast Natural Gas Cooperation. **Education:** New York University, B.S. (1970); Adelphi University, Post–Graduate Studies. **Personal:** Two children: Adam and Caitlin. Mr. Commella enjoys golf, skiing, and gardening.

Robert L. Cosentino
Southern Area Engineer
Pacific Gas Transmission
1440 Lake Road
Redmond, OR 97756–9617
(541) 548–9251
Fax: (541) 548–9225
EMAIL: See Below

4924

Business Information: Pacific Gas Transmission is the largest importer of Canadian natural gas, as well as an exporter to the United States. As Southern Area Engineer, Mr. Cosentino is responsible for contracting and engineering aspects of the Oregon Operations. Internet users can reach him via: RLCosen@Bendnet.com. **Career Steps:** Southern Area Engineer, Pacific Gas Transmission (1990–Present); Power Production Engineer, Pacific Gas & Electric (1985–1990). **Associations & Accomplishments:** National Association of Corrosion Engineers; American Society of Mechanical Engineers. **Education:** California Polytechnic University, B.S. (1985). **Personal:** Married to Valerie in 1987. One child: Gina. Mr. Cosentino enjoys collecting and restoring Mercedes Benz in his spare time.

Lloyd J. Duggan Jr.
Manager, Market Research & Planning
Yankee Gas Services Company
599 Research Parkway
Merriden, CT 06450–8326
(203) 639–4411
Fax: (203) 639–4426
EMAIL: See Below

4924

Business Information: Yankee Gas Services Company is the largest natural gas distribution company in Connecticut, serving approximately 177,000 customers in 69 cities and towns throughout Connecticut. Mr. Duggan began his career with Yankee Gas in an administrative position in March of 1993. Promoted to Manager of Market Research & Planning in 1995, he is currently responsible for market research advertising, promotions, and new product development. He also serves as Chief Media Spokesperson. Internet users can also reach him via: LLOYD55@AOL.COM. **Career Steps:** Yankee Gas Services Company: Manager, Market Research & Planning (1995–Present), Corporate Communications and Reg. Planning Administrator (1993–1995); Senior Consultant, Hampton Strategies, Inc. (1992–1993). **Associations & Accomplishments:** American Marketing Association; Market Research Association. **Education:** American University, M.B.A. (1983); Howard University, B.B.A. (1977). **Personal:** Married to Gem P. in 1980. Three children: Taneisha, Tatiana and Lloyd III. Mr. Duggan enjoys golf, body building, total health fitness, science–fiction, and collecting jazz music.

Neil A. Fortkamp
Executive Vice President and Chief Operating Officer
Gateway Energy Corporation
10842 Old Mill Road 5
Omaha, NE 68154
(402) 330–8268
Fax: (402) 330–7738

4924

Business Information: Gateway Energy Corporation, a public company, is a natural gas transmission and transportation company, providing direct pipelines, as well as joint ventures. Other business venues include oil/gas production, development of oil/gas leases for production, as well as operating a few systems involved in the delivery of gas to end users. Gateway Energy Corporation's main office is located in Omaha, Nebraska, with a subsidiary in Houston, Texas. Joining Gateway Energy Corporation as Executive Vice President and Chief Operating Officer in 1993, Mr. Fortkamp is responsible for supervising and managing Company operations, including joint ventures and supervision of accounting and reporting functions. **Career Steps:** Executive Vice President and Chief Operating Officer, Gateway Energy Corporation (1993–Present); President, Data Duplicating Corporation (1991–1993); Vice President, Regency Affiliates, Inc. (1988–1989); Vice President, KVI Associates, Inc. (1989–1990). **Associations & Accomplishments.** Board of Directors, Visiting Nurse Association of Midlands; Board of Directors, Data Duplication Corporation; Active in his church. **Education:** University of Nebraska–Lincoln, B.S. (1968). **Personal:** Married to Jo in 1975. Two children: Scott and Mark. Mr. Fortkamp enjoys golf, reading, and bowling.

Kimberley M. Futch
New Market Developer
West Florida Natural Gas
316 SW 33rd Avenue
Ocala, FL 34471–4519
(352) 622–0111
Fax: (352) 622–1612
EMAIL: See Below

4924

Business Information: West Florida Natural Gas is a natural gas distributor in Central Florida servicing customers from two regional locations (Ocala and Panama City). As New Market Developer, Ms. Futch is responsible for the development of new markets by using direct mail, TV and radio advertisements, commercial and industrial sales, and marketing functions (i.e., marketing plans, forecasting, etc.). Internet users can also reach her via: MKINVEST.COM@AOL. **Career Steps:** West Florida Natural Gas: New Market Developer (1994–Present), Residential Sales Agent (1993–1994), Credit/Customer Service Manager (1987–1993). **Associations & Accomplishments:** Board of Directors (1990–1995), Executive Board (1996–1999), Vice Chair Membership (1996–1997), Economic Development Council; Board of Regents, Leadership Ocala (1994–1996); Leadership Youth Board (1996–1999). **Education:** Nova University, B.A. (1993). **Personal:** Married to Michael Leshman in 1996. One child: Kyle K. Futch. Ms. Futch enjoys golf, cooking, and growing herbs.

Richard C. Lindley
Vice President of Natural Gas Marketing
FINA Oil and Chemical Company
P.O. Box 2159
Dallas, TX 75221
(214) 890–1844
Fax: (214) 750–2570

4924

Business Information: FINA Natural Gas Company, a subsidiary of FINA Oil and Chemical Company, is a marketer of natural gas purchased from gas producers located throughout the U.S. Established in 1989, FINA Oil and Chemical Company reports annual revenue of $486 million. With over 30 years expertise in petroleum and natural gas exploration and marketing, Richard Lindley joined FINA in 1988. Appointed to his current position in April 1995, as Vice President of Natural Gas Marketing, he is responsible for all aspects of marketing natural gas. **Career Steps:** President, FINA Natural Gas Co. (1992–Present); FINA Oil and Chemical Company: Vice President of Natural Gas Marketing (1995–Present), General Manager of Exploration and Production (1988–1992), President, Indian Wells Oil Company (1985–1987). **Associations & Accomplishments:** Member, Executive Board of Circle Ten Council of Boy Scouts of America; Member, Natural Gas Supply Association; Member, Gas Industry Standards Board. **Education:** Oklahoma State University, B.S. (1963). **Personal:** Married to Deborah A. in 1988. Two children: Christopher Webb and Nicholas Lindley. Mr. Lindley enjoys golf, bridge, exercise, and attending sporting events.

Craig A. Lynch
General Manager of Distribution Engineering
New Jersey Natural Gas (NJNG)
1078 Timesquare Boulevard
Lakewood, NJ 08701–5524
(908) 938–7885
Fax: Please mail or call

4924

Business Information: New Jersey Natural Gas Company (NJNG) is a natural gas utility distributor, providing service to customers residing in the Lakewood, New Jersey locale. As

General Manager of Distribution Engineering, Mr. Lynch directs all activities of the Distribution and Distribution Engineering departments. **Career Steps:** New Jersey Natural Gas Company (NJNG): General Manager – Distribution Engineering (1995–Present), Engineering Manager (1991–1995), Management Engineer (1990–1991). **Education:** West Virginia Univeristy, B.S. in Chemical Engineering (1984). **Personal:** Married to Donna Marie in 1984. Three children: Kristen, Rebecca and Devin. Mr. Lynch enjoys spending time with his family, snow skiing, and freshwater fishing during his leisure time.

Charles A. Phillips
Marketing Support Specialist
Michigan Consolidated Gas Company – MICHCON
500 Griswold
Detroit, MI 48226
(313) 256–6872
Fax: (313) 256–5825

4924

Business Information: Michigan Consolidated Gas Company – MICHCON is a natural gas utility business marketing natural gas products to new and existing companies throughout Michigan. As Marketing Support Specialist, Mr. Phillips is responsible for marketing and information systems, data bases, and distributing data to market consultants. Established in 1894, Michigan Consolidated Gas Company – MICHCON employs 3,040 people with annual sales of $432 million. **Career Steps:** Michigan Consolidated Gas Company – MICHCON: Marketing Support Specialist (1995–Present), Staff Accountant (1991–1995), Material Accountant (1988–1991). **Associations & Accomplishments:** Vice President, Institute of Management Accountant. **Education:** Currently attending Walsh College for an M.S. Degree in Finance; University of Detroit, B.S. Degree in Accounting (1990). **Personal:** Married to Marie in 1987. Two children: Jeff and Jason. Mr. Phillips enjoys PCs.

David G. Unruh
Senior Vice President, Law and Corporate Secretary
Western Energy, Inc.
Suite 3400, 666 Burrard Street
Vancouver, British Columbia
(604) 488–8015
Fax: (604) 488–8088

4924

Business Information: Westcoast Energy, Inc. began operations in 1949 and currently employs over 6,000 people. An energy–based corporation, Westcoast Energy is primarily in the natural gas industry. The Corporation gathers, processes, stores, and distributes natural gas. Westcoast Energy provides energy services, power generation and international ventures. As Senior Vice President, Law and Corporate Secretary, Mr. Unruh is responsible for all legal aspects of Westcoast Energy, Inc. As Corporate Secretary, Mr. Unruh is a member of the Corporate Leadership Team (CLT), the highest committee in the Company. **Career Steps:** Senior Vice President, Law and Corporate Secretary, (1993–Present); Lawyer and Partner, Aikins, MacAulay & Thorvaldson (1984–1993); Lawyer and Partner, Christie, DeGraves, MacKay (1975–1984); Lawyer and Associate, Pitblado & Hoskin (1971–1975). **Associations & Accomplishments:** Canadian Bar Association; Manitoba Bar Association; International Directors Association. **Education:** University of Manitoba: Bachelor of Laws (1970), Bachelor of Arts (1966); Certified General Accountant (Honourary) (1979). **Personal:** Married to Joanne. Two children: Christine and Paul. Mr. Unruh enjoys outdoor sports, skiing, golf, and reading.

Ramon R. Gonzalez–Simounet

Vice President
Empire Gas Company, Inc.
P.O. Box 363651
San Juan, Puerto Rico 00936–3651
(809) 751–5725
Fax: (809) 751–9904

4925

Business Information: Empire Gas Company, Inc. is a major manufacturer and distributor of liquified petroleum gas in Puerto Rico, with 48 billion gallons having been sold in the country since the Company's start in 1967. Empire Gas Company, Inc. currently employs 150 professionals. Joining Empire in 1984, as Vice President Ramon Gonzalez–Simounet is responsible for Company operations and strategic planning. His strategic plans for the future will focus on the development of business expansion utilizing his expertise as a lawyer, with concentration in banking law. **Career Steps:** Vice President,

Empire Gas Company, Inc. (1984–Present). **Associations & Accomplishments:** American Bar Assn.; Tennis Club Caribe Hilton Hotel; Asociacion Residentes Paseo Alto. **Education:** Boston Univ., Banking Law (1986); Attended: Interamericana School of Law; Loyola University – New Orleans. **Personal:** Married to Roxanne Mayol Lopez in 1985. Three children: Priscilla, Juan Ramon, and Mara. Mr. Gonzalez–Simounet enjoys music, art, history, travel, tennis, and spending time with family.

Stephen L. Moore III
Vice President
Jardine Petroleum
102 West 500 So. Street, Suite 402
Salt Lake City, UT 84101–2333
(801) 532–3211
Fax: (801) 532–2021

4925

Business Information: Jardine Petroleum is a wholesale distributor of refined petroleum products in Utah and four surrounding states. Established in 1942, Jardine Petroleum reports annual revenue of $65 million and currently employs 51 people. Serving as Vice President, Stephen Moore is responsible for marketing and treasury, in addition to working on the succession of the Company. He will become one of three owners within the next five years. Mr. Moore also serves on the Board of Directors. **Career Steps:** Vice President, Jardine Petroleum (1994–Present); Vice President, Triton Fuel Group (1990–1994); Senior Vice President, Cornerstone Bank (1986–1990). **Associations & Accomplishments:** Western Petroleum Marketers Association; Chairman of Finance Committee, Park City Community Church. **Education:** Southern Methodist University, B.B.A. (1981). **Personal:** Married to Julie in 1994. Three children: Brandon, Landon, and Teia. Mr. Moore enjoys snow skiing and photography.

Herbert L. Beacher
Engineer
Southern Nuclear Operating Company
P O Box 1295
Birmingham, AL 35201
(205) 992–5133
Fax: (205) 992–5465

4931

Business Information: Southern Nuclear Operating Company, established in 1989, operates nuclear power plants in Georgia and Alabama. As Engineer, Mr. Beacher functions as an auditor with the Safety Engineering Review Group within the Corporate office, conducting quality assurance auditing and project procedures for different departments' policies and procedures. **Career Steps:** Engineer, Southern Nuclear Operating Company (1992–Present); Engineer, Georgia Power Company (1982–1992); Engineer/Co–op Student, IBM (1978–1980). **Associations & Accomplishments:** Board of Directors, Big Brother/Big Sisters; Board of Trustees, Southside Christian Methodist Episcopal Church. **Education:** Tuskegee Institute, B.S. Electrical Engineering (1981). **Personal:** One child: Harrison Lyle. Mr. Beacher enjoys reading, keeping up on current events, football, softball, baseball, basketball, and golf.

Ellis P. Cadenhead
Assistant General Manager
Newnan Water & Light Commission
70 Sewell Road, P.O. Box 578
Newnan, GA 30264
(770) 253–5516
Fax: (770) 253–0292
EMail: See Below

4931

Business Information: Newnan Water & Light Commission is a utility company serving Coweta County, GA with water, sewer, electrical, and fiber optic utility services. The Commission works to improve economic development in Coweta County, which is Georgia's sixth fastest growing county and in the top 30 in the United States. As Assistant General Manager, Mr. Cadenhead coordinates the distribution system of all utilities along with the administrative functions, including engineering and design, and distribution automation. Internet users can reach him via: ellis@nwsl.west.ga.net. **Career Steps:** Newnan Water & Light Commission: Assistant General Manager (1992–Present), Assistant Manager – Administration (1990), Electrical Superintendent (1989–1990). **Associations & Accomplishments:** Mason; Shriner; Electric Cities of Georgia Board of Directors, Former Chairman Municipal Electric Authority of Georgia Telecommunications Committee. **Education:** LaGrange College; West Georgia College. **Personal:** Married to Carol S. in 1980. Four children: Roy, Ken, James, and Jason. Mr. Cadenhead enjoys woodworking.

Mr. Eddie Cuevas–Silvagnoli
Attorney
Puerto Rico Electric Power Authority
P.O. Box 50306
Toa Baja, Puerto Rico 00950–0306
(809) 289–4453
Fax: Please mail or call

4931

Business Information: Puerto Rico Electric Power Authority (PREPA), established in 1947, is a public utility, providing electrical service to residences and businesses residing in San Juan, Puerto Rico locale. A practicing attorney in Puerto Rico courts since 1985, Mr. Cuevas–Silvagnoli joined PREPA in 1987. Serving as Attorney, he provides legal representation on behalf of the Company, focusing on litigation of civil cases, torts, breech of contracts, and bids. **Career Steps:** Attorney, Puerto Rico Electric Power Authority (1987–Present); Attorney, Gonzalez, Bennazar & Colorado (1985–1987); Law Clerk, Fiddler, Gonzalez & Rodriguez (1984–1985). **Associations & Accomplishments:** Puerto Rico Bar Association. **Education:** University of Puerto Rico: J.D. (1985), B.S. in Mathematics. **Personal:** Married to Myriam Melindez in 1986. One child: Lauren. Mr. Cuevas–Silvagnoli enjoys writing and tennis.

Julio H. Morales
Marketing Consultant
Consumer's Power Company
4000 Clay Avenue SW
Grand Rapids, MI 49548
(616) 530–4249
Fax: (616) 530–4105

4931

Business Information: Consumer's Power Company is an electric and gas utility serving all of Michigan via sixty offices statewide. Established in 1889, the Company employs over 9,000 people and has estimated annual revenue of over $2 billion. As Marketing Consultant, Mr. Morales oversees and coordinates projects, and advises customers on energy management techniques for economic savings. **Career Steps:** Consumer's Power Company: Marketing Consultant (1995–Present), Systems Engineer (1987–1995). **Associations & Accomplishments:** Advisor, Junior Achievement Program; Southwest Society of Healthcare Engineers (SWSHE). **Education:** Aquinas College, M.B.M. (In Progress); Ferris State University, B.S.M.E.; Grand Rapids Community College, A.A.S. **Personal:** Married to Michelle in 1993. One child: Michael. Mr. Morales enjoys restoring exotic automobiles.

Francis Obi
President
Law Offices of Francis Obi
40 Union Avenue, Suite 102
Irvington, NJ 07111–3277
(201) 373–0065
Fax: (201) 373–0477

4931

Business Information: Law Offices of Francis Obi is a full–service, general practice law firm specializing in personal injury and medical malpractice. The private firm consists of three legal specialists. Admitted to practice in 1991, Mr. Obi began his legal career as a Law Clerk with the N.J. Attorney's Office. Establishing his individual law practice in 1993, he is responsible for all aspects of the firm. Mr. Obi can also be reached at his New York office at 42 North Main Street, 2nd Floor; Spring Valley, NY 10977. **Career Steps:** President, Law Offices of Francis Obi (1993–Present); Associate Attorney, B. Giscombe P.A. (1992–1993); Law Clerk, N.J. Attorney General's Office (1990); Auditor/Manager, Loews Corporation (1985–1989). **Associations & Accomplishments:** American Bar Association; American Trial Lawyers Association; National Bar Association; National Conference of Black Lawyers. **Education:** Cardozo Law School, Yeshiva University, J.D. (1991); Ramapo College of New Jersey, Mahwah, NJ, B.A.; Institute of World Affairs, Diploma in International Affairs. **Personal:** Married to Lawana King Obi in 1987. One child: Tokuubo. Mr. Obi enjoys soccer, boxing, and traveling internationally.

Isaac Ineh Obi
Project Manager of Engineering and Technical Services
Niagara Mohawk Power Corporation
300 Erie Boulevard
Syracuse, NY 13220
(315) 349–4294
Fax: (315) 349–7661
EMAIL: See Below

4931

Business Information: Niagara Mohawk Power Corporation is a public utility providing electric and nuclear power, and natural gas to Upstate and Central New York State. Mr. Obi joined NMPC as a Systems Analyst in 1990. Promoted to Project Manager of Engineering and Technical Services in 1996, he is now responsible for designing information management systems for the Engineering Department, including software code design, system support, and engineering supervision. Internet users can reach him via: IIOBI@MAILBOX.SYR.EDU **Career Steps:** Niagara Mohawk Power Corporation: Project Manager of Engineering and Technical Services (1996–Present), System Analyst (1990–1995); Project Control Manager, Fluor Daniel (1989–1990). **Associations & Accomplishments:** Coach, Young Boys Soccer Club. **Education:** Syracuse University, M.S. (1995); University of Houston, B.S. (1979). **Personal:** Married to Adelina in 1980. Two children: Joanne and Jaffat. Mr. Obi enjoys soccer, travel and reading.

Debbi P. Poppiti
Manager of Media Relations
Delmarva Power Company
800 Kings Street
Wilmington, DE 19899
(302) 429–3854
Fax: (302) 429–3141

4931

Business Information: Delmarva Power Company provides electricity to 450,000 customers in Delaware, Maryland, and Virginia, and natural gas to 100,000 in Northern Delaware. As Manager of Media Relations, Ms. Poppiti is responsible for internal and external communication, publication of the weekly newsletter, coordination of the monthly newscast, development of annual and quarterly reports, press inquiries and relations, and shareholder communications. **Career Steps:** Manager of Media Relations, Delmarva Power Company (1995–Present); Press Secretary, New Castle County Executive Office (1991–1995); Editor, Reporter, News Anchor, WILM Newsradio (CBS Affiliate) (1987–1991). **Associations & Accomplishments:** Board Member, Chair of Public Relations Committee, Family and Children of Delaware; Founder, Fund for Women at the Delaware Community Foundation; Public Relations Society of America; Board Member, Bill Frank Gridiron Dinner Scholarship Fund. **Education:** Syracuse University S.I. Newhouse School of Public Communications, B.S. Broadcast Journalism (1987). **Personal:** Married to Vincent in 1993. Ms. Poppiti enjoys theatre (musical comedy) and outdoor activities.

Mr. Kenneth C. Riead
Senior Certified Energy Manager
City of Independence, Missouri Power & Light Department
PO Box 1019
Independence, MO 64051
(816) 325–7495
Fax: (816) 325–7470

4931

Business Information: City of Independence, Missouri Power & Light Department is a municipal electric utility serving approximately 50,000 consumers in Independence and the surrounding vicinity. The City is presently upgrading the energy efficiency of City–owned buildings under an Energy Performance Contract. As Senior Certified Demand Side Manager, Mr. Riead is responsible for energy conservation programs and demand side management related services. He administers the rebate program, oversees energy work needed by the city and evaluates energy related services. Established in 1901, City of Independence, Missouri Power & Light Department employs over 250 people with annual sales of $56 million. **Career Steps:** City of Independence, Missouri Power & Light Department, Energy Applications Administrator (1990–1996), Senior Certified Energy Manager (1996–Present); President, Energy Independence/Ener–Home, Inc. (1981–1990); Consultant, Custom Controls/American Multi–Cin (1984–1986); Director, State of Colorado/Arapahoe Energy Extensive Service Energy Conservation Lab (1980–1981). **Associations & Accomplishments:** Certified Energy Manager, Association of Energy Engineers (AEE); Senior Certified Demand–Side Manager, AEE; Senior Member, AEE; Full Member, American Society of Heating, Refrigeration & Air Conditioning Engineers; Distinguished Service Award, City of Independence Energy & Environment Committee; Certified

Energy Conservation & Solar Energy Instructor, Missouri, Kansas & Colorado. Mr. Riead has also published articles in newspapers and magazines on energy related topics. **Education:** Red Rocks Community College, Solar Design Degree (1981); Central Missouri State University, B.S., Pub.R (1977). **Personal:** Married to Sharla H. Riead in 1979. Two children: Lorien H. and Kaycie P. Mr. Riead enjoys energy consulting and growing experimental energy crops at his energy demonstration home, the "Replete Residence" and research farm.

Eric L. Robey
Electric Sales Manager
South Carolina Electric and Gas Company
Mail Code I–24
Columbia, SC 29218
(803) 733–2854
Fax: (803) 376–2180

4931

Business Information: South Carolina Electric and Gas Company (SCE&G) provides electric and gas utilities to the region for commercial and private use. SCE&G has 480,000 electric customers (400,000 private and 80,000 commercial) and 240,000 gas customers. A Certified Internal Auditor, Eric Robey has held various marketing and account management positions with SCE&G since 1980. Since 1994 he has served as Electric Sales Manager of the Northern Division, responsible for new business development and business retention in the residential and commercial markets. Mr. Robey also oversees a staff of 17 professionals and 3 clerical, a $2 million operating budget and maintains relations with trade allies. **Career Steps:** South Carolina Electric and Gas Company: Electric Sales Manager – Northern Division (1994–Present), National Accounts Coordinator – Industrial Marketing (1993–1994), Senior Accont Representative – Commercial Marketing (1991–1993), Sales Representative – Commercial and Industrial Sales (1990–1991), Sales Representative – Residential Sales, Lexington District (1987–1990), Junior Auditor (1980–1987). **Associations & Accomplishments:** Member, Corporate Speaker's Bureau; American Society of Heating, Refrigeration, and Air Conditioning Engineers; Mechanical Contractors Association of South Carolina; Chairman, Stewardship Committee for the Peachtree Rock Preserve, South Carolina Nature Conservancy. **Education:** Florida Atlantic University, B.B.A. (1980); Certified, Internal Auditor (1984). **Personal:** Married to Reneé in 1981. Mr. Robey enjoys hiking, canoeing, and the outdoors.

Stephen Stone
Manager Voice/Data
Graybar Electric Company
11828 Lackland Road
St. Louis, MO 63146–4206
(314) 692–5880
Fax: (314) 569–3638
EMAIL: See Below

4931

Business Information: Graybar Electric Company is an international distributor of electrical and communication products. Established in 1870, with an estimated annual revenue in excess of $3 billion, Graybar currently employs 20 people. In his capacity, Mr. Stone is responsible for managing all voice, data, and WAN activities throughout the Company. **Career Steps:** Manager Voice/Data, Graybar Electric Company (1994–Present); Manager of Technical Services, MCI (1988–1994); International Manager, General Dynamics (1985–1987); Manager, AT&T (1973–1984). **Education:** Attended: Texas A&M, University of Houston, and Houston Community College. **Personal:** Married to Diane Lynn in 1986. Two children: Katlin and Matthew. Mr. Stone enjoys gardening and automobiles.

Thomas A. Wojtalik
Supervisor of Environmental Compliance
Tennessee Valley Authority
1101 Market Street, MR 5K
Chattanooga, TN 37402
(423) 751–3130
Fax: (423) 751–4760

4931

Business Information: Tennessee Valley Authority specializes in providing electrical service for sale to domestic, commercial, and industrial use, including power generation, transmission, and distribution. Established in 1933, and employing over 16,000, it provides service in seven states. As Supervisor of Environmental Compliance, Mr. Wojtalik oversees the operations impact of transmission lines, compliance on environmental programs, disposal of solid and hazardous waste materials, obtaining permits, negotiating terms and conditions for projects, annual reports to regulatory agencies, and construction and technical requirements at the Chattanooga facility. **Career Steps:** Tennessee Valley Authority: Supervisor of Environmental Compliance (1991–Present), Staff Environmental Engineer (1988–1991), Staff Environmental Siting Engineer (1979–1988). **Associations & Accomplishments:** Bioelectromagnetics Society; National Association Environmental Professionals. **Education:** University of Minnesota, (1968); Michigan State University: M.S., B.S. **Personal:** Married to Mary (Jackie) in 1970. Three children: Shari Lee Morgan, Candace, and Amanda. Mr. Wojtalik enjoys gardening, ornithology, hiking, and reading.

JoAnn M. Bauer

Vice President
Peco Energy
2301 Market Street
Philadelphia, PA 19103
(215) 841–6786
Fax: (215) 841–5306

4932

Business Information: Peco Energy is an investor–owned gas and electric utility company serving the East Coast. Established in 1850, the Company currently has 7,200 employees and estimated annual sales of $3.0 billion. As Vice President, Ms. Bauer handles all customer services, including meter reading, credit collections, field management, and client relations. **Career Steps:** Peco Energy: Vice President of Customer Service (1994–Present), Regional Manager (1992–1994), Manager of Nuclear Administration (1989–1992). **Associations & Accomplishments:** Leadership, Inc.; National Association of Female Executives. **Education:** University of Pennsylvania, presently working toward an M.S. in Dynamics of Organization (1997); LaSalle University: B.S. in Electronic Physics, A.A. in Computer Science. **Personal:** One child: Michele. Ms. Bauer enjoys sailing, skiing, and golf.

Lamont B. Cornwell

Director of Market Development
ARKLA
400 East Capital
Little Rock, AR 72201
(501) 377–4872
Fax: (501) 377–4762

4932

Business Information: ARKLA is a natural gas distribution company serving residents and businesses in Arkansas, Oklahoma, Texas and Louisiana. ARKLA delivers 130,000 BCF of natural gas a year. Established in the 1800's, ARKLA currently employs 1,200 people and has an estimated annual revenue of $125 million. As Director of Market Development, Mr. Cornwell is responsible for all aspects of marketing for industrial and commercial customers. With 15 people in his department, Mr. Cornwell and his staff contact prospective customers and advise them how to best utilize natural gas services, which can sometimes mean refering the customer to another energy source. **Career Steps:** ARKLA: Director of Market Development (1993–Present), Manager of Marketing, Arkansas Division (1985–1993), Air Conditioner Sales Coordinator, Arkansas Division (1979–1985), District Sales Manager (1969–1979). **Associations & Accomplishments:** Founder and First President, Arkansas Gas Association; Board of Directors, Salive County Boys Club; School Board Member, Benton Arkansas Public Schools; Various civic and Community support groups; Member, Director of Classes, and Teacher, First Baptist Church; Directed training seminars and marketing plans. **Education:** Ouachita Baptist University, B.S.E. (1969). **Personal:** Married to Billie in 1987. Four children: Monty, Brian, Meredith, and Mitchell. Mr. Cornwell enjoys hunting, fishing, golf, and all outdoor sports.

Richard N. Longenecker

General Manager of Sales and Service
Public Service Electric and Gas
80 Park Plaza, Suite T6
Newark, NJ 07102
(201) 319–3202 (201) 430–6078
Fax: Please mail or call

4932

Business Information: Public Service Electric and Gas (PSE&G) is the fourth–largest integrated electric and gas utility in the U.S. As General Manager of Sales and Business Service, Mr. Longenecker is responsible for revenue retention and growth for over 200,000 industrial and commercial customers. This includes field sales and service operations at four locations in New Jersey Department, including over 130 associates. His responsibilities also include management of Demand Side Management (DSM) auditing services. **Career Steps:** General Manager of Sales and Service, Public Service Electric and Gas (1994–Present); Various Sales and Marketing Positions, Cargill, Inc. (1988–1994). **Education:** University of Toledo, M.B.A. (1988). **Personal:** Married to Debbie in 1988. One child: Kayla. Mr. Longenecker enjoys jogging and reading.

Luis J. Rengel

President
Bahamas Oil Refining
Box 21048
Ft. Lauderdale, FL 33335–1048
(809) 352–9811
Fax: (809) 352–4029

4932

Business Information: Bahamas Oil Refining, a wholly–owned subsidiary of Venezuelan oil company PDVSA, is an oil and petroleum products storage and terminal operation, as well as a third–party rental storage facility. Established in 1970, Bahamas Oil Refining reports annual revenue of $12 million and currently employs 116 people. As President, Mr. Rengel is responsible for ensuring the safety and security of PDVSA's investment while moving the Company towards self–sufficiency and profitability. **Career Steps:** President, Bahamas Oil Refining (1993–Present); Lagoven S.A. (PDVSA) Venezuela: Materials & Procurement General Manager (1991–1993); Eastern Division General Manager (1988–1990), Maintenance Manager (1986–1988). **Associations & Accomplishments:** American Management Association; Venezuelan Engineers Association; Published two articles about the oil industry and economy; Frequent international speaker. **Education:** Pennsylvania State University, Administration and Management CS (1990); Oklahoma City University, Industrial Engineering; University of Missouri, Drilling Operation Seminar; Venezuelan Ministry of Defense, National Defense and Security. **Personal:** Married to Virginia in 1962. Three children: Luis J., Veronica and Mrs. Virginia Kefalas. Mr. Rengel enjoys reading, golf and travel.

Michael D. Rind, Esq.

Director of Employment
Baltimore Gas & Electric Company
P.O. Box 1475, Gas & Electric Building
Baltimore, MD 21203–1475
(410) 234–6153
Fax: (410) 234–5126

4932

Business Information: Baltimore Gas & Electric Company, one of the largest employers in the State of Maryland and a Fortune 50 company, is an energy producer and services corporation, specializing in electric and gas utility and energy services. BG&E services the regional area of Baltimore, Maryland, covering 2,300 square miles. As Director of Employment, Mr. Rind is responsible for the direction of all employment activities, including hiring, retaining, leading staff, planning functions, and all other areas of employment for the Company. Due to his law background, he also provides advice in legal matters. **Career Steps:** Baltimore Gas & Electric Company: Director of Employment (1994–Present), Director of Human Relations (1986–1993), Counsel (1982–1986). **Associations & Accomplishments:** American Gas Association Employment/AA/EEO Committee; Chesapeake Human Resources Association; Employment Management Association; President, Kiwanis Club of Mountain Road – Pasadena, MD. **Education:** Duke University – School of Law, J.D. (1969); University of Chicago, B.A. in Political Science (1966). **Personal:** Married to Bernice in 1985. Mr. Rind enjoys bridge.

Larry D. Rose

Telecom Project Manager
Consumers Power Company
1945 West Parnall Road, Ms: P14–204
Jackson, MI 49201–8658
(517) 788–8966
Fax: (517) 788–0426

4932

Business Information: Consumers Power Company is an investor–owned gas and electric utility. Established in 1886, Consumers Power Company contracts with a variety of major telecommunication vendors for company network services. Services include voice and data, wire and wireless networks. Mr. Rose joined Consumers Power Company in 1986 after his graduation from Michigan State University. Promoted to Telecommunications Project Manager in 1990, he is presently responsible for managing major telecommunications projects, leading teams of analysts and engineers, and performing a variety of administrative functions. **Career Steps:** Consumers Power Company: Telecom Project Manager (1990–Present), Project Engineer (1986–1990). **Associations & Accomplishments:** Served two year mission in Belgium and France (1979–1980); Phi Betta Kappa. **Education:** Michigan State University, B.S.E.E. (1986); Lansing Community College, A.S. magna cum laude. **Personal:** Married to Marlene in 1982. Four children: Krystal, Elisha, Jessica and Timothy.

Wendy Alys Stern

Senior Systems Analyst
National Utility Investors
Bedminster, NJ 07083–1975
(908) 289–5000 Ext. 5481
Fax: (908) 351–2890

4932

Business Information: A national utilities company, National Utility Investors (NUI) is a multi–state gas distribution, sales and service Corporation serving more than 360,000 customers along the eastern seaboard. NUI Corporation provides natural gas services to residents and businesses in New Jersey, Florida, North Carolina, Pennsylvania, Maryland, and New York. As Senior Systems Analyst, Ms. Stern is responsible for the management of project teams, the analysis of proposed systems or enhancements, and the work needed to implement systems. An expert in her field, Ms. Stern completed a prisoner tracking system for the Essex County Jail 14 years ago that is still in operation today. In may of 1996, she implemented a Leak Management System. **Career Steps:** Senior Systems Analyst, National Utility Investors (1982–Present); Senior Programmer Analyst, Essex County Department of Data Processing (1980–1982); Programmer Analyst, American Express Company (1978–1980); Programmer, New York City Department of Health and Hospitals (1976–1978). **Associations & Accomplishments:** National Association for Female Executives; Cub Scout Den and Patrol Leader; Who's Who of Colleges and Universities (1974). **Education:** New York Institute of Technology, B.S. in Computer Science (1974). **Personal:** Married to David Eugene in 1974. Two children: Renny and Gene. Ms. Stern enjoys being a soccer team mother.

Charles W. Anderson

Project Manager
Northern Indiana Public Service Company
5265 Hohman Avenue
Hammond, IN 46320–1722
(219) 647–4513
Fax: (219) 647–4600

4939

Business Information: Northern Indiana Public Service Company is a public utility provider, serving 700,000 customers in Indiana. Mr. Anderson joined NIPSCO in 1974. After serving in various customer service positions, he was promoted to Project Manager of Customer Information Systems in 1992 and is currently responsible for coordinating a staff of 30 employees in new information system implementation. **Career Steps:** Northern Indiana Public Service Company: Project Manager (1992–Present), Manager of Customer Service Center (1989–1991), Assistant to the Senior Vice President (1985–1989), Customer Services Management (1974–1985). **Associations & Accomplishments:** Indiana University Alumni Association; Customer Service Committee, AGA/EEI. **Education:** Indiana University: M.B.A. (1979), B.S. in Accounting (1974). **Personal:** Married to Debra A. in 1987. Two children: Paige R. and Wesley M. Mr. Anderson enjoys spending time with his family.

Mr. Ernest J. Boutte

Division General Manager – Stockton, California
Pacific Gas & Electric Company
4040 West Lane Avenue, P.O. Box 930
Stockton, CA 95201–0930
(209) 942–1455
Fax: Please mail or call

4939

Business Information: Pacific Gas & Electric Company, the nation's largest combined utility provides the generation, transmission, and distribution of electricity and gas to the major portion of Northern and Central California. The Company serves a customer base of 12 million. PG&E is one of California's largest employers with over 20,000 employees, and reports annual revenue of $10 billion. Ernest Boutte has held various engineering and management position's with the company since 1965. In his current capacity as Division Manager for the Stockton Division, he is responsible for all aspects of operations for those facilities, key management personnel and employees within a 4,000 square mile area in the San Joaquin Region of California. **Career Steps:** Pacific Gas & Electric Company: Division Manager, Stockton Division (1993–Present); Division Manager, Vaca Valley Division, Sacramento Valley Region (1991–1993); Executive Assistant to Region Vice President, San Joaquin Valley Region (1987–1991); Region Superintendent, Substation Operations (1983–1987); Division Superintendent of Generation, Hydro Generation (1981–1983), Supervisor of Electrical Maintenance (1978–1981), Hydro Electric; Electrical Test Engineer, General Construction (1975–1978); Various operations and Electrical Maintenance positions (1965–1975); U.S. Navy, Electronics Technician – Radar Specialty; Flight Air Controller (1962–1965). **Associations & Accomplishments:** Harvard University Alumni Association; Western Energy and Communications Association; Pacific Coast Gas Association; University of Idaho Alumni Association; American Heart Association; Boy Scouts of America Executive Board of Directors; San Joaquin Business Partnership Association; University of Pacific Advisory Board of Directors; San Joaquin Business Council; Various Chambers of Commerce and Employee Associations (Black, Hispanic, Filipino, Asian); National Rifle Association; Pacific Service Employee Association; United Way; Mayor's Waterfront Revitalization Committee; Chair–Division Community Involvement Project Committe; Business Incubator Economic Development Benefactor; American Management Association; Service Medal of Honor – Vietnam. **Education:** Hartnell College, Salinas, California, A.A. in Electrical/Electronics Engineering (1975); Federal Telecommunications Commission Electronics Engineering License (1977); Fresno State University, Engineering Industrial Technology (1978); University of San Francisco, B.S. in Business Management (1983); University of Idaho, Utility Executive Training Program (1988); Harvard University, Executive M.B.A. Program (1992). **Personal:** Married to Eleanor. Two children: Mark and Marlo.

Mr. Neil H. Butterklee

Staff Attorney
Consolidated Edison Company of New York, Inc.
4 Irving Place, Room 1815–S
New York, NY 10003
(212) 460–1089
Fax: (212) 677–5850

4939

Business Information: Consolidated Edison Company of New York, Inc. is an establishment engaged in the generation, transmission, and distribution of electricity, gas and steam. As Staff Attorney, Mr. Butterklee is responsible for certain legal aspects of the Corporation, including negotiating and drafting contracts, counseling Corporate clients and litigation. Established in 1850, Consolidated Edison Company of New York, Inc. employs 17,500 people. **Career Steps:** Consolidated Edison Company of New York, Inc.: Staff Attorney (1995–Present), Attorney (1993–1995); Senior Planning Analyst, Consolidated Edison Company of New York (1989–1993); Analyst, Consolidated Edison Company of New York (1983–1989). **Associations & Accomplishments:** Law Licensures; New York State; Connecticut; Washington, D.C.; Federal Court (Eastern and Southern Districts of New York); American Bar Association; New York State Bar Association; Connecticut Bar Association; Former Member of the Board of Directors, United States Fencing Association; Published in articles concerning home construction. **Education:** New York Law School, J.D. (1992); Adelphi University, M.B.A. Degree (1987); SUNY at Stony Brook, B.S. (1980), M.S. Degree (1982). **Personal:** Married to Arlene Butterklee in 1982. Mr. Butterklee enjoys golf, writing, and is a former nationally–ranked fencer.

Michael J. Cyrus

President
Natural Gas Clearinghouse, Canada
707 8th Avenue SW, Suite 800
Calgary, Alberta T2P 3V3
(403) 781–3375
Fax: (403) 781–3155

4939

Business Information: The Natural Gas Clearinghouse, Canada, is a multi–energy service corporation providing financial and physical services for natural gas, electricity, and NGL's crude industries. Established in 1985, Natural Gas Clearinghouse currently employs 1,100 people. As President, Mr. Cyrus is responsible for all commercial operations in Canada. **Career Steps:** President, Natural Gas Clearinghouse, Canada (1995–Present); Executive Vice President, Novagas Clearinghouse Ltd. (1995–Present); Vice President of Risk Management, Natural Gas Clearinghouse Corporation (1992–1995); Commodity Trader, Chicago Mercantile Exchange (1988–1992). **Education:** University of Arkansas: M.B.A. (1992), B.S.; University of Texas, Gas Technology Program Graduate. **Personal:** Married to Mariet Cyrus in 1984. Two children: Maura G. and Mary Audrey.

Lorie Farkas–Van Linden

Director of Public Information
Water, Gas & Light Commission
P.O. Box 1788
Albany, GA 31703
(912) 435–2020 Ext. 345
Fax: (912) 434–1813

4939

Business Information: The Water, Gas & Light Commission, established in 1912, is the largest public utility company in Georgia. A fifth generation native of Albany, Georgia, Lorie Farkas has served as The Water, Gas & Light Commission's Director of Public Information for the past eight years. While WGL has alway remained on the cutting edge of technology, previous to Ms. Farkas' arrival at WGL, there was only one program to assist customers with specific needs and no community involvement or educational programs in the community. She has established and created various programs to benefit WGL customers, as well as the community. Her WGL educational film "Working For You" won the highest ADDY Award in its category in 1988. She has since gone on to garner numerous ADDY, Community Service and Letter of Commendation awards from local, state and national governmental entities. She is a frequent lecturer to civic groups, clubs and schools concerning WGL and the related subjects of conservation, ecology and recycling. Lorie follows the credo — "Community Service Is The Rent We Pay For Living." **Career Steps:** Director of Public Information, Water, Gas & Light Commission (1988–Present); Public Relations for Southwest Georgia, Nations Bank (1974–1986). **Associations & Accomplishments:** Board of Directors, Chamber of Commerce; President, 'Fall on the Flint' Board; Heart Board; Ritz Cultural Board; Wowega Council on Aging; Co–Chair, Martin Luther King Day Dinner — hosted over 1,000; Co–Chair, COPS (Community Oriented Police) Leadership Council; Coordinator in partnership with Albany, GA Mayor Coleman of Annual Christmas Parade (reinstated after 31 years); Featured on nationally syndicated ABC News programs for her coordination in the send off of National Guard Troops during the Desert Storm event; National Public Relations Committee, American Public Power Administration; Chair, 2nd Annual Jo Marie Payton Celebrity Volley Ball Classic – Albany State College; Coalition for Racial Diversity; Leadership Albany Class; Chair, Leadership Alumni Board; Leadership Albany Foundation Board; SPECIAL AWARDS: ADDY Award for Albany/Dougherty Chamber of Commerce Video she co–produced (1992); National Community Service Award for K I D S program she created; Twice received Personal Letters of Recommendation from President Bush and from Oprah Winfrey; Who's Who in Energy Conservation for the Nation; Albany, Georgia's "Career Woman of the Month" (June 1993). **Education:** Univ. of Miami (1968). **Personal:** Married to William A. in 1991. Two children: Lane Alexander and Joshua Chandler. Ms. Farkas–Van Linden enjoys bead work, travel, gourmet cooking, providing free interior decorating to her friends, and creating one–of–a–kind angels (heavenly hosts)."

Mr. Richard T. Felago

Vice President
Wheelabrator Environmental Systems Inc.
Liberty Lane
Hampton, NH 03842
(603) 929–3000
Fax: (603) 929–3123

4939

Business Information: Wheelabrator Environmental Systems Inc. is an international developer, owner and operator of large scale trash–to–energy, power, water, and wastewater plants. Wheelabrator Technologies Inc. is traded on the New York Stock Exchange with $3.5 billion in assets, and employs over 3,000 people worldwide. As Vice President of the Hampton, New Hampshire facility, Richard Felago is responsible for licensing, contracting and front–end development which includes initiation, management, and permitting. His career milestones include the implementation of the Wheelabrator Falls Recycling and Energy Recovery Facility; and the Wheelabrator Gloucester Resource Recovery Facility, the nation's first regulated solid waste energy recovery utility. **Career Steps:** Wheelabrator Environmental Systems Inc.: Vice President (1993–Present), Vice President of Business Development (1990–1993), Regional Vice President (1988–1990); Associate Department Head, The Mitre Corporation (1981–1982). **Associations & Accomplishments:** Solid Waste Association of America; Independent Power Producers of India; IWSA; NSWMA; Toastmasters; Recipient of 1995 Power Plant Award presented by Power Magazine; Published in the 4th Annual Business Industry Environment Conference Exhibition and China Excursion in Wan Chai (1995) – "Waste to Energy Project Implementation – Lessons Learned"; Co–author of "The Resource Recovery Management Model" – a 500–page step–by–step guide for public officials; Annual guest lecturer at Tufts University; Speaker at Spring Garden College in Pennsylvania and various other colleges and conferences. **Education:** Polytechnic Institute of New York, M.S. in Civil Engineering (1977); University of Detroit, B.S. in Mechanical Engineering (1970); Licensed Professional Engineer in Pennsylvania, New York and Massachusetts. **Personal:** Married to Susan Stephens Felago in 1972. Four children: Christina, Thomas, Brigette and Anne Marie. Mr. Felago enjoys golf, swimming, running and reading.

John E. Ferren

Assistant General Manager
Greenville Utilities Commission
P.O. Box 8147
Greenville, NC 27835–8147
(919) 551–1502
Fax: (919) 551–1597

4939

Business Information: Greenville Utilities Commission provides public utilities, including water, sewer, electric and natural gas service to two thirds of Pitt County, North Carolina, servicing approximately 60,000 customers. Established in 1905, the Greenville Utilities Commission currently employs 350 people and has an estimated annual revenue of $120 million. As Assistant General Manager, Mr. Ferren is the Chief Operating Officer and Secretary to the Board of Commissioners. As such, he is responsible for all construction, customer service needs, support, daily operations and administration. **Career Steps:** Assistant General Manager, Greenville Utilities Commission (1981–Present); Marketing Representative, GRW Engineering, Inc. (1976–1980); Assistant Director of Planning, Barren River Area Development District (1968–1973). **Associations & Accomplishments:** First Vice President and Campaign Co–Chair, Pitt County United Way; American Management Association; Chair, Strategic Planning Committee, Pitt County Chamber of Commerce; Frequent public speaker. **Education:** Western Kentucky University, M.P.S. (1973); Georgia State University, B.A. in Sociology. **Personal:** Married to Arlene M. in 1985. Two children: Beth Ferren Britt and Jennifer Ferren Brodeur. Mr. Ferren enjoys music, boating, golf, painting, woodworking and playing the guitar.

Gregory W. Haddow

Manager of Marketing Programs and Planning
San Diego Gas and Electric Company
8306 Century Park Court, Cp4200D, 2nd Floor
San Diego, CA 92123–1593
(619) 654–1230
Fax: (619) 654–1117
EMAIL: See Below

4939

Business Information: Established in 1881, San Diego Gas and Electric Company is a gas, electricity, and energy efficiency company. A wholly–owned subsidiary of ENOVA, SDG&E serves over 1.2 million customers. Serving in various managerial roles for SDG&E since 1986, Gregory Haddow was appointed to his current position in 1992. As Manager of Marketing Programs and Planning, he is responsible for all marketing activities within San Diego Gas and Electric Company and ENOVA. Internet users can reach him via: haddow@imx.sdge.com **Career Steps:** San Diego Gas and Electric Company: Manager of Marketing Programs and Planning (1992–Present), Manager of Marketing Information and Planning (1986–1992); Supervisor of Market Research, Pacific Gas and Electric (1979–1986). **Associations & Accomplishments:** Board of Directors, AESP formerly ADSMP, (Award for Excellence) (1989–1992); ACEEE, Advisory Committee, Marketing Chair (1990–1991); Pacific Coast Gas Association, Chairman's Award; EPRI Marketing Tools and DSM Business Unit Council; American Marketing Association; Parish Council (1993–1995); Board of Directors, Scripps Ranch Little League. **Education:** San Francisco State University, M.A.; San Diego State University, B.A. Executive Challenge Program, **Personal:** Married to Cynthia in 1979. Two children: Mark and Sarah. Mr. Haddow enjoys running, surfing, guitar, and Little League Baseball.

Ann M. Hatch

Director of News and Information
Texas Women's University
P.O. Box 425619
Denton, TX 76204
(817) 898–3456
Fax: (817) 898–3463
EMail: See Below

4939

Business Information: Texas Women's University is a public, four–year, coed, liberal arts university. Established in 1901, the main campus is located in Denton. Currently there are 292 full–time and 92 part–time faculty instructing predominately women undergraduate students. Major course studies with the largest enrollment include Nursing, Business Administration and Interdisciplinary Studies. Special preprofessional programs are offered in Law, Medicine and Dentistry. As Director of News and Information, Mrs. Hatch is responsible for all news, media relations and related duties, as well as acting as the University's spokesperson. She can also be reached through the Internet as follows: S_HATCH@VENUS.TWU.EDU **Career Steps:** Texas Women's University: Director of

News and Information (1995–Present), Assistant Director of Media Relations (1988–1995); News Services Coordinator, Auburn University at Montgomery (1983–1988). **Associations & Accomplishments:** Council for Advancement and Support of Education; Texas Public Relations Association; American Cancer Society; Texas Special Olympics; Leadership Denton; Denton Rotary; City of Denton Community Development Advisory Committee; Denton Chamber of Commerce Economic Development Committee; Vision for Denton 2000 Communications Committee. **Education:** Auburn University: M.S. (1988), B.S. in Applied Communications. **Personal:** Married to Jim in 1974. One child: Robert. Mrs. Hatch enjoys reading, writing, and community service through publicity and promotions.

R. K. Moorthy

Director of Corporate Compensation and Benefits
Ontario Hydro
700 University Avenue H2 CO2
Toronto, Ontario
(416) 592–2501
Fax: (416) 593–3552

4939

Business Information: Ontario Hydro, created in 1906, is today among the largest electric utilities in North America, with a total revenue of about $9 billion and 23,000 employees. A skilled Human Resources executive with over 30 years experience working with large companies in the utility, banking, computer, and oil industries, Mr. Moorthy joined Ontario Hydro in 1986. Serving as Director of Corporate Compensation and Benefits in the Head Office, he is responsible for directing the development of objectives, strategies, policies and programs in Compensation and Benefits. His major strengths are in strategy development and implementation, and management of programs and services through a highly–motivated team. Career milestones include establishing the Division with challenging and pro–active mission and programs, as well as developing and implementing a comprehensive compensation strategy. The new initiatives include: pay for performance, pension changes, pay equity, suggestion plans, recognition programs, downsizing programs, negotiation support, joint problem solving, executive compensation/incentives, and competency pay. **Career Steps:** Director of Corporate Compensation and Benefits, Ontario Hydro (1986–Present); Bank of Montreal: Vice President of Compensation and Benefits (1983–1986), Senior Manager of Compensation and Benefits (1980–1983), Manager of Compensation and Benefits (1978–1980); I.B.M. World Trade Corporation – Southeast Asia Region: Manager of Personnel Programs (1976–1978), Compensation and Benefits Manager (1975–1976), Special Advisor (1974–1975), Plan Personnel Manager (1971–1974), Personnel Services Manager (1969–1971); Executive Personnel Assistant and Personnel Manager Caltex, Ltd. (1961–1969); Assistant Manager, Lee & Muirhead, Ltd. and Hind Musafir Agency (1956–1961). **Associations & Accomplishments:** Former Chair, Canadian Compensation Association; Former Director, American Compensation Association; Former Chair, Canadian Bankers' Pension Committee; Advisory Council, Conference Board of Canada; Association of Canadian Pension Management; American and Canadian Management Associations; Instructor, Canadian Compensation Association Education Program; Rated as a top practitioner in Compensation by Canadian HR Reporter (1989); First "Key Stone Award" with life membership in American Compensation Association (1995). **Education:** Bombay University, B.A. in Economics and Statistics, Post–Graduate Diploma in Industrial and Labour Laws; International Management School, IBM Blaricum, Netherlands. **Personal:** Married to Sugantha in 1968. Two children: Malini and Raja. Mr. Moorthy enjoys reading and tennis.

Ramy Nahas

Engineer
Consolidated Edison Company of New York, Inc.
225 East 82nd Street, Apt. 2A
New York, NY 10028
(212) 561–2785
Fax: (212) 561–2620

4939

Business Information: Consolidated Edison Company of New York, Inc. is a marketer of electricity, gas, and steam to five borroughs of New York City and Westchester. Consolidated Edison Company of New York currently employs 17,000 people company–wide. As Engineer, Mr. Nahas serves as system engineer at one of the Company's fossil power plants and is responsible for maintenance engineering and new capital installations. Mr. Nahas is also responsible for daily technical support and root cause failure analysis. **Career Steps:** Consolidated Edison Company of New York, Inc.: Engineer (1993–Present), Construction Inspector (1990–1992), Management Intern/Assistant Engineer (1987–1990). **Associations & Accomplishments:** Professional Engineer in New York State. **Education:** Columbia University – SEAS, M.S. (1987), B.S. in Mechanical Engineering (1986). **Personal:** Mr. Nahas enjoys running marathons and playing tennis.

Carlos H. Sierra

General Manager
Empresa's Publica's Municipales De Palmira
Calle 31 # 2486
Palmira Valle, Colombia
57–222756334
Fax: 57–222757025

4939

Business Information: Empresa's Publica's Municipales De Palmira is a pubic utility company which services public telephones, electrical service, gas service, and shopping centers. These services are both commercial and residential, only in Colombia. As General Manager, Mr. Sierra is responsible for all finances, sales & marketing, legal, and administration. **Career Steps:** General Manager, Empresa's Publica's Municipales De Palmira (1993–Present); Presidente, Colmundo Radio S.A. (1989–1993); Presidente, La Garantia S.A. Dishington S.A (1983–1989); Presidente, Copeq LTDA (1979–1983). **Associations & Accomplishments:** Miembro Junta Directiva, Asociacion Nacional De Medios De Comunicaciones; Presidente, Asociacion Nacional De Consultores De Gerencia. **Education:** Attended: Universidad De Medellin (1968), Uniandes, Mercadeo Internacional. **Personal:** Married to Rosario de Sierra in 1968. Five children: Carlos Alberto, Francisco, Alicia Tatiana, Juan David, and Santiago. Mr. Sierra enjoys preaching the word of God.

Jacqueline M. Sierra

Vice President
L. S. Quilting Inc.
J. Oliver Street, M Camunas Street
Hato Rey, Puerto Rico 00918
(809) 754–7065
Fax: (809) 759–7270

4939

Business Information: A family–owned and operated business, L. S. Quilting Inc. specializes in the manufacture of bedspreads, bedsheets, pillows and cushions. Established in 1987, L. S. Quilting currently employs 60 people. As Vice President and General Manager, Ms. Sierra is responsible for the overall day–to–day adminstratvie operations, working in partnershjp with her husband who serves as President. **Career Steps:** Vice President, L. S. Quilting Inc. (1992–Present); Project Manager, Flair Carpets (1990–1992). **Associations & Accomplishments:** Puerto Rico Industrials Association. **Education:** Muhlenberg College, Bachelor's Degree (1983). **Personal:** Married to Luis A. in 1992. One child: Brian Rios.

Keith Stamm

Vice President
Utilicorp United
10700 East 350 Highway
Kansas City, MO 64138
(816) 737–7981
Fax: (816) 737–7985
EMAIL: See Below

4939

Business Information: Utilicorp United is a multi–national holding company, owning and operating regulated and non–regulated utility properties. Serving in various managerial capacities for Utilicorp United since 1990, Keith Stamm was appointed Vice President of Energy Trading in 1995. His primary duty is for the direction and oversight of domestic regulated utilities power marketing operations. **Career Steps:** Utilicorp United: Vice President (1995–Present), Director of Planning (1993–1995), Director of Fuels (1990–1993). **Education:** Rockhurst College, M.B.A. in Finance (1986); University of Missouri, B.S. in Mechanical Engineering. **Personal:** Married to Peggy in 1982. Three children: David, Brian, and Rebecca.

Sergio Rodriguez Zubieta

Executive Director
Camuzzi Argentina
Av Davila 240 Piso 3
Buenos Aires, Argentina 1107
(541) 319–7983
Fax: (541) 319–7954

4939

Business Information: Camuzzi Argentina, a holding company of Gruppo Camuzzi from Italy, is controlling several public services utilities related to natural gas distribution, drinking water, and sewage treatment, plus electricity. Established in 1991 for the privatization of the argentinian state own gas company, Camuzzi serves well over a million customers in 45% of Argentina geography. The group is exploring new business opportunities in the rest of Latin American. Mr. Rodriguez Zubieta was responsible for the winning bid offer and today is Chairman and Vice–Chairman of the operating companies, definition of business strategies and leading the new business development teams. **Career Steps:** Executive Director, Camuzzi Argentina (1992–Present); Chief Executive Officer, Contarsul Service S.A. (1990–1992); Senior Surveyor, Det Norske Veritas (Oslo) (1986–1987). **Associations & Accomplishments:** Board Member, Argentinian Petroleum Institute; Board Member, CAMMESA; Argentine Society of Engineers; Member of TFII of International Gas Union. **Education:** University of Buenos Ares, Naval Architect & Marine Engineer (1983); Off Shore Technology, Trondheim (Norway); Quality Service & Surveyor, Oslo (Norway). **Personal:** Married to Mercedes Ramos Oromi in 1988. One child: Valentin. Mr. Zubieta enjoys mountain skiing, fishing, and horseback riding.

Ashraf (Art) M. Azmi

Principal Engineer
Metropolitan Water District
350 South Grand Avenue, Suite 12–103
Los Angeles, CA 90071–3406
(213) 217–7676
Fax: (213) 217–7650
EMAIL: See Below

4941

Business Information: Metropolitan Water District is the leading water utility company in the U.S., providing the conveyance, treatment, and delivery of water to Southern California (60%), including the building and designing of dams. Established in 1932, the Company employs 2,000 people, and has an annual revenue of $900 million. As Principal Engineer, Mr. Azmi is responsible for the management and direction of the Survey Engineering Group consisting of approximately 95 people. Duties include construction, cadastral, geodetic and right–of–way surveys, in addition to planning and developing GIS projects. Internet users can reach him via: aazmi@mwd.dst.ca.us **Career Steps:** Metropolitan Water District: Principal Engineer (1995–Present), Manager (1992–1995); Project Engineer, DGA Consultants (1988–1990). **Associations & Accomplishments:** American Society of Civil Engineers; IRWA. **Education:** SDSM & T, M.Sc. in Civil Engineering (1988); Ain Shams University – Cairo, Egypt, B.Sc. in Civil Engineering; Currently enrolled in a Doctorate Program at University of La Verne in Public Administration (estimated graduation 1996). **Personal:** Married to Kimberly in 1986. Mr. Azmi enjoys travel, reading, scuba diving, and soccer.

Dean Jason Chingman

Tribal Water Engineer Well Technician
Office of the Tribal Water Engineer
Shoshone & Arapahoe Tribes, P.O. Box 217
Ft. Washakie, WY 82514
(307) 332–3164
Fax: (307) 332–3230

4941

Business Information: Office of the Tribal Water Engineer is the water administration office for the Wind River Indian Reservation in Fremont County, Wyoming, serving the Shoshone and Northern Arapaho tribes. It functions under a multi–legal system of laws and procedures by the Water Resource Control Board, which administers water on the Reservation in accordance with the mandates of the Wind River Water Code. A Native American born and raised on the Wind River Indian Reservation, Mr. Chingman was hired as Tribal Water Engineer Well Technician by the Office of the Tribal Water Engineer in 1994 to complete court–mandated work. His duties include the inventory and identification of all groundwater on the Reservation, resulting in the creation and preparation of the required forms and procedures which the Office will use to administer the well database verification process. He is currently in the process of compiling a ground water department proposal for the Eastern Shoshone and Northern Arapaho Tribes. In addition, he serves as a Permits Technician. **Career Steps:** Tribal Water Engineer Well Technician, Office of the Tribal Water Engineer (1994–Present); Clerk, Department of Health &

Human Services (Jun. 1994–Aug. 1994); Bookkeeper, Shoshone Tribe Finance Department (Jun. 1993–Aug. 1993). **Associations & Accomplishments:** Founder and Former President, American Indian Science and Engineering Society – Fremont County Chapter; Wyoming Representative, Native American Church Organization for North American Indian College; American Indian Education Advisory Board Secretary, Central Wyoming College; Born and raised on the Wind River Indian Reservation. **Education:** Attended: Central Wyoming College.

Robert E. Elder
Deputy Assistant Director
City of Houston – Public Works and Engineering
7000 Ardmore
Houston, TX 77054
(713) 741–7690
Fax: (713) 748–2056

4941

Business Information: City of Houston administers Water Production division of the Department of Public Works and Engineering requirements to continuously produce a safe, potable water at desired flows and pressure to those persons and businesses residing within the boundaries of the city of Houston, Texas. As Deputy Assistant Director, Mr. Elder is responsible for managing and directing all field maintenance operations and labor staff for the City of Houston Water Production sectors. **Career Steps:** Deputy Assistant Director, City of Houston – Public Works and Engineering (1991–Present); Owner, Pt. Arthur Construction, Inc. (1987–1991); Regional Construction Manager, McDonald's Corporation (1983–1987). **Associations & Accomplishments:** American Public Works Association; American Water Works Association; Charter Member, Public Works Toastmasters; National Forum for Black Public Administrators; Alpha Phi Alpha Fraternity, Inc.: President, Epsilon Tau Lambda Chapter; Parliamentarian, Booker T. Washington Alumni Association – Class of 1953; Board Member/Former President, Palm Beach Civic Club, Inc.; Houston/Harris County Ecumenical Council, Inc. — a 501(c)(3) organization: Chair – Executive Committee/Vice Chairman, Vice President; President, The Cronies, Inc.; Society of American Military Engineers; Central Garden Baptist Church: Trustee – Deacons & Trustees Board, Treasurer – Usher Board **Education:** Tuskegee University, B.S. (1957); Attended: Air War College. **Personal:** Married to Albertina B. Harris in 1958. Two children: Kenneth E. and Derrick W. Mr. Elder enjoys basketball, coin collecting, and working with youth.

James E. Heath
Assistant Director
Detroit Water Department
6425 Huber Avenue
Detroit, MI 48211
(313) 237–7426
Fax: (313) 267–6284

4941

Business Information: Detroit Water Department provides water and sewer systems for the city of Detroit, Michigan. Regional in scope, the Department services 123 communities, and approximately four million customers. As Assistant Director, Mr. Heath oversees the operations group, as well as water and production for five plants. **Career Steps:** Detroit Water Department: Assistant Director (1995–Present), Superintendent, Maintenance and Repair Division (1982–1995), Assistant Superintendent, Maintenance and Repair (1980–1982). **Education:** Highland Park Community College. **Personal:** Married to Cleo G. in 1958. One child: James W.. Mr. Heath enjoys golf, bowling, and walking.

John H. Huston, Esq.
Vice President and Director
Western Water Company
4660 LaJolla Village Drive, Suite 680
San Diego, CA 92122
(303) 933–9423
Fax: (303) 933–9461

4941

Business Information: Western Water Company with headquarters in San Diego and offices in Denver, Reno, and Sacramento is concerned with water rights acquisition from farmers and ranchers. The Company is also involved in the investment in and resale of water rights. Western Water Company has an interest in Integrated Water Company where Mr. Huston serves as Chairman. As Vice President and Director, Mr. Huston administers the operation of the Colorado office. He is involved in facets of the day–to–day operations of his office. **Career Steps:** Vice President and Director, Western Water Company (1992–Present); Chairman, Integrated Water Company (1992–Present); General Partner, Procyon Group (1981–1992). **Associations & Accomplishments:** Geolog-

ic Society of America; American Bar Association; Board of Regents, California Lutheran University; Mr. Huston has had articles published in the Wall Street Journal and various Denver newspapers. **Education:** University of Colorado, J.D. (1976); Stanford University: M.S. in Geology (1973), B.S. in Geology (1973). **Personal:** Married to Candace in 1975. Two children: Matthew and Lauren. Mr. Huston enjoys scuba diving, power boating, four wheeling, and tennis.

Ian M. Knapp
Director of Marketing
Wheelabrator Water Technology, Inc.
55 Shuman Blvd.
Naperville, IL 60563
(708) 717–4567
Fax: (708) 717–2247

4941

Business Information: Wheelabrator Water Technology, Inc. specializes in industrial and municipal water and waste water treatment, systems, products, and services. As Director of Marketing, Mr. Knapp is responsible for global marketing, strategic planning, and acquisitions. **Career Steps:** Director of Marketing, Wheelabrator Water Technology, Inc. (1992–Present); President, Memtek Corporation (1984–1992); Director of Business Development, Progress Technologies Corporation (1989–1991); Vice President Operations, XYDEX Corporation (1984–1988) **Associations & Accomplishments:** Water Environment Federation; Water Quality Association **Education:** University of South Florida, B.A. (1973) **Personal:** Married to Cristina in 1975. Two children: Dylan and Connor. Mr. Knapp enjoys tennis, sailing, and boxing.

Marilyn Ware Lewis
Chairman of the Board
American Water Works Company, Inc.
1025 Laurel Oak Road, Box 1770
Voorhees, NJ 08043
(717) 687–9703
Fax: (717) 687–8561

4941

Business Information: American Water Works Company, Inc., the largest investor–owned utility in the United States, operates 23 water service companies in 21 states and serves more than 6 million people living in over 700 communities. As Chairman of the Board, Ms. Lewis oversees all Company operations. During her time as Chairman of the Board, the market capitalization has risen from $520 million to $1.6 billion. She also serves on the Board of Directors of the American Enterprise Institute. **Career Steps:** American Water Works Company, Inc.: Chairman of the Board (1988–Present), Vice Chairman (1984–1988), Chairman of the Compensation Committee (1984–1988), Chairman of the Executive Committee (1989–Present), Director (1982–Present); Member of Board of Directors, CIGNA Corporation (1993–Present); Member of Board of Directors, Penn Fuel Gas, Inc. (1982–Present). **Associations & Accomplishments:** American Enterprise Institute – a think tank which sponsors research and public policy development in the areas of defense, trade, economics, social issues, and politics; Board Member, Pennsylvania Chamber of Business and Industry; Eisenhower Exchange Fellowships; Pennsylvanians of Effective Government; PENJERDEL Council; Trustee and Executive Committee, University of Pennsylvania Health Systems; Board of Overseers, School of Medicine of the University of Pennsylvania Medical Center; President, Solanco Publishing Company; Business Leader of the Year by the PA House Republicans (1993); Director's Choice Award for the National Women's Economic Alliance Foundation (1992); Executive Women of New Jersey Award (1992). **Personal:** Three children: Amy, Mark, and Scott Strode.

Sun Liang, Ph.D.
Section Manager
MWD
700 Moreno Avenue
La Verne, CA 91750–3303
(909) 392–2914
Fax: (909) 392–5246
EMAIL: See Below

4941

Business Information: MWD is a water wholesaler specializing in supplying 1.3 to 1.6 billion gallons of water per day to La Verne area residents. Established in 1928, the Company employs 3,000 people and has estimated annual revenue of $844 million. As Section Manager, Dr. Liang serves as process engineer, responsible for treatment of all water, design and implementation of new treatment processes, and management of all related staff. Internet users can reach him via: sliang@mwd.dst.ca.usa. **Career Steps:** Section Manager,

MWD (1992–Present); Project Engineer, Parson Engineering Science, Inc. (1984); Research Associate, The University of Michigan (1980). **Associations & Accomplishments:** International Ozone Association; American Society of Civil Engineers; National Ground Water Association (NGWA); AWWA. **Education:** The University of Michigan, Ann Arbor, Ph.D. in Design Engineering (1984); University of California, Berkeley, Master of Science in Civil Engineering; National Taiwan University, Taipei, R.O.C. in Agricultural Engineering. **Personal:** Married to Ping in 1979. Three children: Sharon, Karen, and Terri. Dr. Liang enjoys basketball, fishing, and travel.

Richard Osborn, C.P.A., C.F.E.
Controller/Human Resource Director
Highline Water District
P.O. Box 3867
Kent, WA 98032–0367
(206) 824–0375
Fax: (206) 824–0806

4941

Business Information: Highline Water District is a local water utility company, providing water to homes in Kent, Des Moines, Federal Way, Seatac, Burien, Tukwila, and unincorporated King County. A Certified Public Accountant with twenty–one years experience, Mr. Osborn joined Highline Water District as Controller and Human Resource Director in 1995. He is responsible for all financing, human resources, client relations, and the oversight of his staff. **Career Steps:** Controller/Human Resource Director, Highline Water District (1995–Present); Assistant Audit Manager, Office of State Auditor, State of Washington (1979–1995); Assistant Audit Supervisor, Department of Labor and Industries (1975–1979). **Associations & Accomplishments:** Past President, Association of Government Accountants; Association of Certified Fraud Examiners; Association of Certified Public Accountants – Washington State. **Education:** University of Puget Sound, Master (1982). **Personal:** Married to Sandra in 1971. Two children: Kevin and Amanda. Mr. Osborn enjoys coaching softball, refereeing soccer, and attending his daughter's hockey games.

Terrace W. Stewart
Director
Dallas Water Utilities
1500 Marilla Street 4AN
Dallas, TX 75201
(214) 670–3144
Fax: (214) 670–3154

4941

Business Information: Dallas Water Utilities is the municipal management office for the municipal water and wastewater utility in Dallas. Joining Dallas Water Utilities as Deputy Director in 1992, Mr. Stewart was appointed as Director in 1995. He is responsible for the direction of all aspects of operations, including engineering, strategic planning, business functions, and media relations. **Career Steps:** Dallas Water Utilities: Director (1995–Present), Assistant Director (1993–1995), Deputy Director (1992–1993). **Associations & Accomplishments:** American Water Works Association; Water Environment Federation; Immediate Post Chair/Board Member, Arlington Night Shelter. **Education:** University of Texas – Arlington, B.S. (1982). **Personal:** Married to Kim in 1975. Three children: Kemesha, Kelton and Auriyelle. Mr. Stewart enjoys fishing and oil painting.

Jeffrey A. Arnold
President/General Manager
Envirosystems Supply, Inc.
11820 North West 37th Street
Coral Springs, FL 33065
(954) 796–3390
Fax: (954) 796–3405

4953

Business Information: Envirosystems Supply, Inc., a wholly–owned subsidiary of Aquacare Systems, Inc. designs, manufactures, installs, and supplies waste water treatment systems for industries and municipalities. As President/General Manager, Mr. Arnold oversees the operation of the Company. He is responsible for contract negotiations, invoicing, shipping, prioritizing, scheduling, and human resource concerns. Other responsibilities include development of new sales and marketing techniques for products and services. **Career Steps:** President/General Manager, Envirosystems Supply, Inc. (1995–Present); Regional Sales/Marketing Manager, Hi–Ran Systems, Inc. (1992–1995); Business Manager, Parkson Corporation (1983–1992). **Associations & Accomplishments:** American Water Works Association; Water Environment Federation. **Education:** Florida Atlantic University, Masters Candidate; Wartburg College, B.A. in Biological Sciences. **Personal:** Married to Jeanie. Mr. Arnold enjoys golf, gardening, and all sports.

Joseph C. Call
Division Vice President and Controller
Waste Management International
80 E. Chambers Street
Colorado Springs, CO 80907
(719) 442–2107
Fax: (719) 578–0425

4953

Business Information: Waste Management International specializes in the collection of solid waste, and the management of area landfills. Established in 1972, Waste Management International currently employs 180 people. As Division Vice President and Controller, Mr. Call is responsible for all aspects of the Accounting Department, including financial statements, analysis acquisitions, the development of information systems, and internal control. **Career Steps:** Division Vice President and Controller, Waste Management International (1989–Present); Staff Accountant, James & Company, CPA's (1986–1988); Internal Auditor, Davis County School District (1985–1986). **Associations & Accomplishments:** Webelos Scout Advisor; Explorer Scout Advisor; Various Church positions; Church Youth Group Advisor. **Education:** Weber State University, B.S. (1985). **Personal:** Married to Raquelle Waite in 1977. Two children: Amanda and McKenzey.

Yo–Yoon Cho, Ph.D.

Executive Consultant
International Technology
240B Cherry Street
Shrewsbury, MA 01545–4054
(508) 842–5643
Fax: (508) 842–5438
EMAIL: See Below

4953

Business Information: International Technology is a hazardous waste designing firm. Established in 1926, the Company reports annual revenue of $450 million and currently employs 2,800 people. With twenty–two years experience in environmental consulting, Dr. Cho joined International Technology as Executive Consultant in 1995. He is the corporate executive consultant for the Firm's clientele. Dr. Cho can also be reached through the Internet via: YYC@World.Std.com **Career Steps:** Executive Consultant, International Technology (1995–Present); Senior Consulting Engineer, S. Webster (1984–1995); Staff Consultant, E. D'Appolonia Consulting (1973–1984). **Associations & Accomplishments:** Elder, Presbytery of Boston; Presbyterian Churches of U.S.A. **Education:** University of South Carolina: Ph.D. (1975), M.S. (1970); Seoul National University – Korea, B.S. (1967). **Personal:** Married to Young H. in 1967. Four children: Esther, Michelle, Melissa, and Abraham. Dr. Cho enjoys ham radio, golf, and tennis.

James R. Hare
District Sales Manager
Browning–Ferris, Inc.
7790 Tessman Road, P.O. Box 201690
San Antonio, TX 78219
(210) 661–4104
Fax: (210) 661–0689

4953

Business Information: Browning–Ferris, Inc. is one of the world's leading publicly–held solid waste service companies, which primary focus is to collect, transport, treat, and dispose of commercial, residential, and municipal solid waste. The Corporation provides a variety of services, including recycling, resource recovery, municipal and commercial sweeping, medical waste services, portable restroom services, and landfill operations throughout the world. With corporate headquarters located in Houston, Texas, Browning–Ferris, Inc. serves North America from five regions within the Domestic U.S. and in Canada, and serves the Southern Region from nine divisional locations. Joining Browning–Ferris, Inc. as Landfill Sales Manager in 1989, Mr. Hare has held several management positions during the past eight years, including Business Development Manager and Landfill Market Development Manager of the Houston Office, and Landfill Sales Manager of the Austin Office. Appointed as District Landfill Sales Manager of the San Antonio Office in 1995, he is responsible for the oversight of all revenue management and sales activities for each district location, as well as overseeing market growth, technical/regulatory development, training, and administration. His duties also include providing technical support (directing and coaching) to the sales staff and directing the activities of six landfill operations. **Career Steps:** Browning–Ferris, Inc.: District Sales Manager – San Antonio (1995–Present), Business Development Manager – Houston (1994–1995), Landfill Market Development Manager – Houston (1989–1994), Landfill Sales Manager – Austin (1989); l Landfill Sales Consultant, Oklahoma City (1988). **Associations &**

Accomplishments: Task Force Committee to develop Solid Waste Regulations for New Mexico, San Antonio Manufacturers Association; API Development of Area–Specific Waste Management Plans for Exploration and Production Operations, Air and Waste Management Association. **Education:** Southwest Texas State University, B.S. (1976); University of Texas – Austin (1973–1974). **Personal:** Married to Patty in 1972. Three children: Michael, Matthew, and Elizabeth. Mr. Hare enjoys golf, softball, reading, movies, and attending his children's school/sporting events.

Victor Jarnegan
Plant Manager
Post Consumer Recycling Plant
101 Inteplast Boulevard
Lolita, TX 77971
(512) 874–3400
Fax: (512) 874–3405

4953

Business Information: Post Consumer Recycling Plant, a division of World–Pak Corporation, is a post consumer recycling plant, servicing the Lolita, Texas locale. World–Pak Corporation is a division of AMTOPP Corporation, which is a division of CPP Plant–AMTOPP Corporation. Established in 1995, Post Consumer Recycling Plant currently employs 46 people. Joining the parent company AMTOPP in 1991 as operations manager of the CPP Plant, Victor Jarnegan was appointed as Plant Manager for World Pak's recycling plant in 1995. He is responsible for all aspects of daily operations of the plant, as well as strategic planning and training of employees. **Career Steps:** Plant Manager, World–Pak Corporation d.b.a. Post Consumer Recycling Plant (1995–Present); Special Projects Manager, AMTOPP Corporation (1992–1995); Operations Manager, CPP Plant – AMTOPP Corporation (1991–1992). **Associations & Accomplishments:** Society of Plastic Engineers; Association for Quality and Participation; American Society for Quality Control; American Legion; Veterans of Foreign Wars; Kappa Alpha Psi Fraternity; American Management Association. **Education:** University of Texas – Austin, working on Ed.D.; American Technological University, Killeen, TX, M.S. in Human Resource Management/Business Management (1985); Webster College, St. Louis, MO, B.A. in Management Sciences (1975). **Personal:** Married to Phyllis Ann in 1972. One child: Joseph (JT) Jarnegan. Mr. Jarnegan enjoys golf, softball, basketball, and computer applications.

Michael W. Jasperson
District Controller
Laidlaw Environmental Service – LES
P.O. Box 22285
Salt Lake City, UT 84122–0285
(801) 252–2000
Fax: (801) 252–2075

4953

Business Information: Laidlaw Environmental Service (LES) is the largest hazardous waste firm in North America and the most modern in the world. LES handles all services for hazard waste disposal for North America consisting of three regions. Joining Laidlaw Environmental Service as District Controller for the Western Division in 1994, Mr. Jasperson is responsible for overseeing all aspects of financial activities for two regions and accounting activities for the third. Duties include forecasting annual budgets, receipts, accounts payable, CIP, capital management, and tracking. **Career Steps:** District Controller, Laidlaw Environmental Service – LES (1994–Present); USPCI: Regional Accounting Manager (1993–1994), Accounting Supervisor (1991–1993). **Associations & Accomplishments:** Institute Management Accountants; Volunteer Income Tax Assistance. **Education:** University of Houston, B.S. in Accounting (1987). **Personal:** Married to Jana in 1993. Mr. Jasperson enjoys golf, skiing, racquetball, basketball, and hiking.

Stephen L. Kesinger
Director, Procurement and M.I.S.
American Ref–Fuel
777 North Eldridge Parkway
Houston, TX 77079
(713) 584–4550
Fax: (713) 584–4583
Email: See Below

4953

Business Information: American Ref–Fuel is a waste conversion and energy production concern. Established in 1986 and currently employing 600 people, the Company posted revenues in excess of $300 million dollars in 1995. American Ref–Fuel is in the business of converting fuel waste products into alternate energy sources. As MIS Director, Mr. Kesinger is responsible for the day–to–day operations of the Company. He is involved in developing a workable budget, managing in-

formation technology expenditures, assessing and implementing technology needs and developing staff. As Director of Procurement, Mr. Kesinger is in charge of short and long–term purchases for American Ref–Fuel. He specializes in developing long term procurement strategies for goods and services, as well as developing supplier partnerships. Internet users can reach him via: KESINGER@IX.NETCOM.COM. **Career Steps:** Director, Procurement and M.I.S. – American Ref–Fuel (1993–Present); Shell Oil Company: Internal Consultant (1992–1993), Manager of Materials Procurement (1992). **Associations & Accomplishments:** National Association of Purchasing Managers; Certified Purchasing Manager. **Education:** Currently attending LaSalle University for a Doctorate; Eastern Illinois University, B.S. Degree in Business. **Personal:** Married to LeAnn in 1988. Three children: Courtney, Cameron, and Cassidy. Mr. Kesinger enjoys travel.

Denis Liggins
Division President and General Manager
Waste Management of Ohio–Akron
1339 Main Street
Cuyahoga Falls, OH 44221–4924
(330) 945–5151
Fax: (330) 923–3365

4953

Business Information: Waste Management of Ohio–Akron, a division of WMX Technologies Corporation, provides solid waste collection, hauling and disposal, recycling collection and processing, and environmental services. As Division President and General Manager, Mr. Liggins manages maintenance, sales, service, administration, transfer, processing, and recycling plant operations. **Career Steps:** Division President and General Manager, Waste Management of Ohio–Akron (1994–Present); President, Human Effectiveness Development Group/EI (1987–1993); Zone Employee Relations Manager, Chemlawn Services Corporation, (1984–1987); Director of Employment & Employee Relations, JCPenney Casualty Insurance Company (1976–1984). **Associations & Accomplishments:** Rotary; Human Resource Management; American Society of Training & Development; National Solid Waste Management Association. **Personal:** One child: Erin D. Mr. Liggins enjoys music and golf.

Mr. Glenn R. Madelmayer
Facility Manager
Ogden Martin Systems of Alexandria/Arlington
5301 Eisenhower Avenue
Alexandria, VA 22304
(703) 370–7722
Fax: (703) 461–3097

4953

Business Information: Ogden Martin Systems of Alexandria/Arlington specializes in resource recovery (waste to energy). Established in 1987, The Company currently employs 40 people. As Facility Manager, Mr. Madelmayer is responsible for daily operations, including maintenance, environmental compliance, safety and budget. **Career Steps:** Facility Manager, Ogden Martin Systems of Alexandria/Arlington (1993–Present); Chief Engineer, Ogden Martin Huntington (1990–1993); Project Manager, Ogden Decon Services (1989–1990). **Education:** Polytechnic Institute of New York, B.S. in Mechanical Engineering (1982). **Personal:** Married to Loretta in 1984. Three children: Robert, Sean, and Lauren. Mr. Madelmayer enjoys sports, woodworking, and classic auto restoration.

Monica Shannon
Branch Industrial Manager
Safety Kleen
5050 Salida Boulevard, P.O. Box 555
Salida, CA 95368
(209) 545–1011
Fax: (209) 545–3680

4953

Business Information: Safety Kleen is the largest international recycler of contaminated waste. As Branch Industrial Manager, Ms. Shannon is responsible for achieving Company objectives through direct sales to industrial manufacturers while maintaining compliance with numerous regulatory agencies. **Career Steps:** Branch Industrial Manager, Safety Kleen (1989–Present); Branch Manager, Breuners Furniture Rental (1985–1989). **Associations & Accomplishments:** National Association of Female Executives; National Parks/Conservation Association; Modesto Chamber of Commerce; Devlin Society. **Education:** Candidate for Bachelor of Science in Business Management (1999). **Personal:** Ms. Shannon enjoys gardening, reading, and water sports.

Glenn C. Sinclair
Division Vice President and Controller
Waste Management Inc.
3329 Street Road, Three Greenwood Square
Bensalem, PA 19020
(215) 736–2000
Fax: Please mail or call

4953

Business Information: Waste Management Inc., a subsidiary of WMX Technologies, provides environmental services such as hauling and landfills. The company has many locations worldwide. As Division Vice President and Controller, Mr. Sinclair manages the Financial Service Group for Waste Management's Mid–Atlantic Group. His responsibilities include administration, operations, finance and strategic planning. Established in 1971, Waste Management Inc. employs 65,000 people with annual sales of $10 billion. **Career Steps:** Division Vice President and Controller, Waste Management Inc. (1993–Present); Vice President, The Sinclair Corporation (1994–Present); Vice President and Controller, Italy, Waste Management Inc. **Education:** Lewis University, B.A. (1979). **Personal:** Mr. Sinclair enjoys travel.

John Sullivan
President
C.I.D. Refuse Service, Inc.
10860 Olean Road
Chaffee, NY 14030
(716) 496–5000 (716) 822–2100
Fax: (716) 496–5500

4953

Business Information: C.I.D. Refuse Service, Inc., a family–owned business, handles commercial, industrial, and domestic refuse hauling. Serving the western New York area, the Company is involved in transfer stations and recycling. As President, Mr. Sullivan plans, develops, establishes, and implements policies in accordance with Board directives. He is responsible for all aspects of Company operations, including overseeing five section chiefs, sales, recycling, shop maintenance, and hiring of staff. Additionally, he wrote all the computer software for the Company and built the network. **Career Steps:** C.I.D. Refuse Service, Inc: President (1993–Present), Systems Administrator (1992–1993). **Associations & Accomplishments:** Hamburg Chamber of Commerce; Waste Leadership Council; Environmental Industries Association. **Education:** State University of New York – Buffalo, B.A. in Psychology (1992). **Personal:** Married to Elizabeth in 1993. One child: Abigail. Mr. Sullivan enjoys golf and the Internet.

John S. Walker

Director of Marketing
John–Glenn Sanitation Service
930 West Long Avenue
Du Bois, PA 15801–1737
(814) 342–4166
Fax: (814) 371–2532
EMAIL: See Below

4953

Business Information: John–Glenn Sanitation Service identifies and disposes of waste according to administrative regulations and guidelines. As Director of Marketing, Mr. Walker is responsible for generating new revenue, developing proposals, market projects, and advertising literature, accounts receivable and payable, and public relations functions. Concurrently, he serves as President and Family Historian of the A.D. Johnson Family Association, a family geneaology research organization. He also writes a bi–weekly family research series ("Root, Branches, Twigs") for "The Progress" of Clearfield, Pennsylvania. Internet users may reach him via: RBT@PENN.COM **Career Steps:** Director of Marketing, John–Glenn Sanitation Service (1994–Present); Owner, Research–Resource (1994–Present); President and Family Historian, A.D. Johnson Family Association (Present); Marketing, B.F.I. (1991–1994). **Associations & Accomplishments:** Board of Directors, Camp Cadet; Board of Directors, Clearfield County Historical Society. **Education:** Juniata College, B.S. (1973); Pennsylvania State University – Altoona School of Commerce, Masters and Honorary Doctorate. **Personal:** Married to LeeAnne in 1977. One child: Gretchen. Mr. Walker enjoys gardening and working with youth.

Andrew Wilfork

Director of Solid Waste
Metro Dade Solid Waste Management
8675 NW 53rd Street, Suite 201
Miami, FL 33166–4566
(305) 594–1520
Fax: (305) 594–1591

4953

Business Information: Metro Dade Solid Waste Management, the largest curbside recycling program in the U.S., is a waste collection and disposal company with three landfills. Serving customers in the Miami metropolitan areas and the surrounding Dade County, the Company is responsible for collecting garbage for 250,000 homes and providing city–wide disposal for other companies. Joining Metro Dade Solid Waste Management in 1979, Mr. Wilfork was appointed as Director of Solid Waste in 1995. He is responsible for the direction of all solid waste collection activities in unincorporated Dade County. **Career Steps:** Metro Dade Solid Waste Management: Director of Solid Waste (1995–Present); Deputy Director of Operations (1989–1995); Superintendent (1980–1986); Waste Foreman 2 (1979–1980) **Associations & Accomplishments:** National Association for the Advancement of Colored People; Public Works Association; National Forum for Black Public Administrators; General Refuse Collection and Disposal Association **Education:** Florida International University, B.S. (1974) **Personal:** One child: Jermaine. Mr. Wilfork enjoys antique cars, biking, and helping with his church youth group.

Mr. Paul H. Wyche, Jr.

Vice President, Community Relations & Governmental Affairs
Safety–Kleen Corporation
1000 North Randall Road
Elgin, IL 60123–7857
(708) 468–2212
Fax: (708) 468–8536

4953

Business Information: Safety–Kleen Corporation is the world's largest recycler of contaminated fluids from automotive and industrial markets and the largest re–refiner of used motor oil with over 500,000 customers worldwide. Established since 1968, Safety–Kleen Corporation presently employs 6,500 people, and has an estimated annual revenue in excess of $800 million. In his current capacity, Mr. Wyche is responsible for directing the Company's public affairs, community relations and local, state, and federal government relations activities. **Career Steps:** Vice President, Community Relations & Governmental Affairs, Safety–Kleen Corporation (1991–Present); Public Affairs Manager, E.I. DuPont (1980–1991); Associate Public Affairs Director, U.S. EPA (1975–1980); Senior Legislative Assistant, U.S. House of Representatives (1970–1975). **Associations & Accomplishments:** Board of Directors, National Association of Chemical Recyclers; Society of Professional Journalists; State Governmental Affairs Council; Brandywine Professional Association; Environmental Equity Task Force, Chemical Manufacturers Association; Environmental Equity Task Force, National Association of Manufacturers. **Personal:** Married to Louise in 1970. Two children: Shaina Nicole and Kimberly Elise. Mr. Wyche enjoys tennis and reading in his leisure time.

Robert R. Bye

Vice President of Operations
Allstate Power Vac, Inc.
2515 Brunswick Avenue
Linden, NJ 07036
(908) 862–3800
Fax: (908) 862–8014

4959

Business Information: Allstate Power Vac, Inc. specializes in industrial cleaning and environmental remediation. The Company works with major refinery companies (i.e., Exxon) in hauling solid and hazardous waste. As Vice President of Operations, Mr. Bye handles all operations of the Company, including directing all efforts for new customers, major client interface, and new business development. **Career Steps:** Vice President of Operations, Allstate Geotech Corporation (1994–Present); Senior Production Manager, OHM Corporation (1991–1994); Projects Director, Chemical Waste Management (1988–1991). **Associations & Accomplishments:** American Society of Mechanical Engineers; American Soci-

ety of Corrosion Engineers. **Education:** New Jersey Institute of Technology, B.S.M.E. (1983); Camden Community College, A.S. in Engineer Science. **Personal:** Two children: Tessa and Meghan. Mr. Bye enjoys private piloting, and served in the U.S. Navy from 1992–1995, participating in the Cuban blockade.

John D. Dyson
Project Engineer
Infilco Degremont, Inc.
P.O. Box 71390
Richmond, VA 23255
(804) 756–7691
Fax: (804) 756–7788

4959

Business Information: Infilco Degremont, Inc. specializes in water and wastewater treatment, with their focus being primarily on municipal and industrial water and wastewater. The Company works on projects throughout the world. Established in 1894, the Company employs 170 people. As Project Engineer, Mr. Dyson handles many phases of projects such as chemical and process testing, field work, engineering and marketing. Additional duties include piloting, development, proposals and presentations. **Career Steps:** Infilco Degremont, Inc: Project Engineer (1993–Present), Pilot Engineer (1991–1993); Chemist, Henrico Company, VA (1988–1991). **Associations & Accomplishments:** American Water Works Association; Active Church Member. **Education:** Longwood College, B.S. in Chemistry (1988). **Personal:** Married to Jacquelin Raye in 1995. Mr. Dyson enjoys hunting, fishing, and softball.

Annette V. Murdaca
Vice President of Finance
California Waste Removal Systems, Inc.
P.O. Box 241001
Lodi, CA 95241
(209) 369–8274
Fax: (209) 369–6894

4959

Business Information: California Waste Removal Systems, Inc. provides waste hauling, material recycling facilities and composting operations to individuals and businesses in Lodi and surrounding communities. As Vice President of Finance, Mrs. Murdaca is responsible for all aspects of finance and administration, including the management of the Accounting Department and all governmental correspondence. **Career Steps:** California Waste Removal Systems, Inc.: Vice President of Finance (1993–Present), Vice President of Administration (1989–1993), Public Awareness Coordinator (1985–1989). **Associations & Accomplishments:** Soroptomist, Sister Cities Program, Lodi; Lodi Boys and Girls Club; Lodi Women's Club; Lodi Memorial Hospital Board of Directors; San Joaquin County Legal Secretary Association; Member California Refuse Removal Council; Member, Women in Waste; Member, National Solid Waste Management Public Relations Committee; President, Rivergate Homeowners Association. **Education:** Chico State University. **Personal:** Married to Jim in 1988. Two children: Alexis and Pietro. Mrs. Murdaca enjoys golf, reading, the beach and spending time with her children.

MBI
MARITIME BUREAU INC.

John Peck
President
MBI Maritime Bureau, Inc.
122 West Bay Street
Savannah, GA 31401
(912) 236–6366
Fax: (912) 236–1704

4959

Business Information: Maritime Bureau, Inc. (MBI), specializes in providing environmental remediation and related hazardous materials solutions to the maritime industry. MBI is uniquely qualified, staffed and equipped to immediately respond to and manage hazardous or oil spill incidents of any size, anywhere and anytime. Its Command Center, which features the latest in technological computer systems, provides crisis mapping for the entire country, including electronic navigation charts for plotting sea responses, spill trajectories and emergency plans for every U.S. port. Responding with speed and skill, MBI's Incident Commander takes charge of the response and engages the most qualifed response contractor available. Maritime Bureau's dedicated, highly–trained and experienced associates are located throughout the U.S. Close liaison with P&I interests, underwriters and legal representatives are maintained and fully coordinated throughout the response. With the extensive legislative regulations and international standards applying to the shipping industry, Maritme Bureau can provide the assistance needed by managing every aspect of the compliance process. MBI can provide certification assistance, policies and procedures development, compiling of procedural and operational manuals and compliance requirements audit. The Company can also assist in internal safety, pollution prevention, and quality control by conducting quality control audits, accident analyzation and investigation, and other organizational shortcomings. Services in this area include: OPA 90 – Vessel and Facility Plans; IMO – Marpol Regulation; Operations Manuals; ISM Compliance and Certification; ISO 9000 Code Quality Assurance. Finally, MBI offers a wide spectrum of marine survey services for all types of vessels. Services in this area include: Cargo Surveys; Draft Surveys; Port Captain or Supercargo; Hull and Machinery; Vessel Condition and Valuation; Pre–Load and Stowage; Yachts. Founding Maritime Bureau in 1969, John Peck provides the overall vision and strategies to keep the Company a viable presence in the international market. With more than 25 years as an independent surveyor, he is experienced in general cargoes and commodities spanning all types of steel products, cocoa, coffee, meat and frozen foods, fruit, fish, wood and paper. He also is skilled in loading and discharge surveys, cargo and hull damage, and yacht surveys. John has supervised hazardous material loading; is trained in handling oil pollution claims, and is a certified Incident Commander. Additionally, he also is experienced in ship fire and damage control. An acknowledged expert in condensation, Mr. Peck has published several papers and developed and patented Cargo Dry, a unique and inexpensive solution to overhead condensation problems. **Career Steps:** President, MBI Maritime Bureau, Inc. (Present); Marine Safety Inspector, The Republic of Vanuatu; Independent Surveyor. **Associations & Accomplishments:** Society of Naval Architects and Marine Engineers; American Boat and Yacht Council; National Fire Protection Association; Technical Institute of Pulp and Paper; Cocoa Merchants Association; Author of two papers on cocoa and a manual on its proper stowage. **Education:** University of Maryland; New York University; Transylvania College; Institute of Marine Design (Naval Architecture); Licensed Insurance Adjuster; Continuing courses through SNAME: vessel rolling, forensic engineering, stress, and operations.

Bruce O. Schmucker, P.E.

Director of Engineering and Environmental Affairs
Rumpke
10795 Hughes Road
Cincinnati, OH 45251–4523
(513) 851–0122
Fax: (513) 825–4839

4959

Business Information: With headquarters in Cincinnati, Rumpke is one of the largest privately–held solid waste collection firms in the United States. The Corporation handles the collection, disposal, and recycling of non–hazardous solid wastes. Rumpke operates a total of 13 solid waste disposal facilities located in Ohio, Kentucky, and Indiana. The Corporation was established in 1945 and currently has approximately 3,000 employees. As Director of Engineering and Environmental Affairs, Mr. Schmucker is responsible for the management of 35 engineers and environmental specialists to support waste collection, recycling and disposal facilities. Mr. Schmucker has been quoted in industry magazines and is currently working on a description of the largest refuse slide in the world. A paper on this subject will be published shortly and is tentatively being called "Rumpke's Refuse Slide". **Career Steps:** Director of Engineering and Environmental Affairs, Rumpke (1995–Present); Divisional Engineer & Regulatory Compliance Manager, Browning–Ferris Industries (1991–1995); Assistant Project Engineer, Wodward–Clyde Consultants (1987–1991). **Associations & Accomplishments:** American Society of Civil Engineers; International Solid Waste & Public Cleansing Association; G.S.I.; S.W.A.N.A. **Education:** University of Akron: M.S. in Geotechnical Engineering (1987), B.S. in Civil Engineering. **Personal:** Married to Margaret in 1991. One child: Zachary. Mr. Schmucker enjoys woodworking, weight lifting, golf and fishing.

Mr. Martin G. Terry
President
Beko Condensate Systems Corporation
4140 Tuller Road, Suite 108
Dublin, OH 43017–5013
(614) 798–5275
Fax: Please mail or call

4959

Business Information: Beko Condensate Systems Corporation is an international specialist company dealing with the removal and treatment of compressor condensate prior to discharge to drain (remove water from compressed air systems). With the manufacturer located in Germany, Beko Condensate Systems Corporation has offices in the U.S., England, France, Italy, Korea, and the Netherlands. The U.S. subsidiary was established in 1992, and currently employs five people. As President, Mr. Terry is responsible for all aspects of company–wide operations, including setting up distribution network and sales & marketing. **Career Steps:** President, Beko Condensate Systems Corporation (1988–Present); Export Manager, Belliss & Morcom – United Kingdom (1985–1988); Export Manager, CompAir – United Kingdom (1982–1984). **Education:** Surrey University – United Kingdom, B.Sc. (1969). **Personal:** Married to Maureen in 1970. Two children: Maria and Mark. Mr. Terry enjoys golf.

Steven N. Tranotti
Director – Technical Development
Advanced Environmental Recycling
2591 Mitchell Avenue
Allentown, PA 18103–6609
(610) 797–7608
Fax: (610) 797–7696
EMAIL: See Below

4959

Business Information: Advanced Environmental Recycling provides recycling and remediation of mercury and other heavy metals from hazardous waste. As Director of Technical Development, Mr. Tranotti is responsible for developing technology and processes for recycling heavy metals. In addition, he is responsible for research and development, training processes, design, and specifying and modifying research equipment. Internet users can reach him via: TRANOTTI@POSTOFFICE.PTD.NET. **Career Steps:** Director – Technical Development, Advanced Environmental Recycling (1990–Present); Advanced Environmental Technology Corporation: Manager Reactive Chemicals (1987–1990), Manager Safety and Training (1983–1987). **Associations & Accomplishments:** Volunteer Firefighter; Emergency Medical Team; CPuerto Rico Instructor; Soccer Coach. **Education:** Allentown College of St. Francis De Sales, B.S. in Chemistry (1980). **Personal:** Married to Katherine in 1983. Two children: Amanda and Daniel. Mr. Tranotti enjoys fishing and soccer.

Eric C. Watson
Executive Director
Plainfield Municipal Utilities Authority
7–9 Watchung Avenue, P.O. Box 5110
Plainfield, NJ 07061–5110
(908) 226–2518
Fax: (908) 226–2561

4959

Business Information: Plainfield Municipal Utilities Authority is responsible for city–wide sewer collection treatment and disposal, city–wide residential garbage collection and disposal, and city–wide resident recycling. As Executive Director, Mr. Watson is responsible for day–to–day operations and administrative management decisions. **Career Steps:** Executive Director, Plainfield Municipal Utilities Authority (1995–Present); City of Plainfield: Director of Public Works (1994–1996), Deputy City Administrator (1995). **Associations & Accomplishments:** Alpha Phi Alpha Fraternity; Prince Hall Masons, Stone Square Lodge #38. **Education:** Rutgers University, B.A. (1979). **Personal:** Married to Tanya

in 1985. Two children: Erica and Korey. Mr. Watson enjoys fishing and hunting.

5000 – 5199
WHOLESALE
TRADE

5000 Wholesale Trade – Durable Goods

5012 Automobiles and other motor vehicles
5013 Motor vehicle supplies and new parts
5014 Tires and tubes
5015 Motor vehicle parts, used
5021 Furniture
5023 Homefurnishings
5031 Lumber, plywood, and millwork
5032 Brick, stone and related materials
5033 Roofing, siding and insulation
5039 Construction materials, NEC
5043 Photographic equipment and supplies
5044 Office equipment
5045 Computers, peripherals and software
5046 Commercial equipment, NEC
5047 Medical and hospital equipment
5048 Ophthalmic goods
5049 Professional equipment, NEC
5051 Metals service centers and offices
5052 Coal and other minerals and ores
5063 Electrical apparatus and equipment
5064 Electrical appliances, TV and radios
5065 Electronic parts and equipment
5072 Hardware
5074 Plumbing and hydronic heating supplies
5075 Warm air heating and air–conditioning
5078 Refrigeration equipment and supplies
5082 Construction and mining machinery
5083 Farm and garden machinery
5084 Industrial machinery and equipment
5085 Industrial supplies
5087 Service establishment equipment
5088 Transportation equipment and supplies
5091 Sporting and recreational goods
5092 Toys and hobby goods and supplies
5093 Scrap and waste materials
5094 Jewelry and precious stones
5099 Durable goods, NEC

Don Burdick

Partner
Clubview Imports
2231 C Michigan Avenue
Arlington, TX 76013
(817) 795–3895
Fax: (817) 795–7365

5012

Business Information: Clubview Imports is a wholesale provider of luxury import motorcars to the trade or individuals. The Company specializes in the buying and selling of Mercedes, BMW, Porsche, Lexus, Jaguar, Infinity, and Ferrari automobiles, and Harley–Davidson motorcycles. One of three Partners in the Company, Mr. Burdick is responsible for many aspects of Company operations including administration, finance, sales and marketing, and strategic planning. **Career Steps:** Partner, Clubview Imports (1995–Present); Chairman, Clubview Holding, Inc. (1982–1993); President, Graybird Leasing, Inc. (1976–1982); Owner, South West Executive Air (1970–1976). **Associations & Accomplishments:** U.S. Senatorial Advisory Board. **Education:** University of Texas (1964–1967); Air Traffic Controller; Commercial Pilot; Multi–Engine Instrument; Aircraft Dispatcher. **Personal:** Two children: Jennifer and Charles Zachery. Mr. Burdick enjoys golf and boating.

Dimitri Gauguier
Owner
Ultimate Transex U.S.A., Inc.
9049 Byron Ave.
Surfside, FL 33154
(305) 868–7212
Fax: (305) 868–7212

5012

Business Information: Ultimate Transex U.S.A., Inc. is an export company based in Miami, Florida. Established in 1991, the Company exports cars all over Europe and South America, providing a broker between customers and suppliers. In addition, Ultimate Transex U.S.A., Inc. is an export division for clothing stores. As Owner, Mr. Gauguier is responsible for all aspects of Company operations, including finance, sales, and public relations. **Career Steps:** Owner, Ultimate Transex U.S.A., Inc. (1992–Present); V.D.V. International: General Manager (1988–1991), Sales Manager (1987–1988); Sales, Cars Trading Group (1984–1987). **Associations & Accomplishments:** Belgian Chamber of Commerce. **Education:** University of Brunel, Master's Degree in Marketing (1992); University of Charleroi – Belgium, Computers Studies. **Personal:** Married to Danielle in 1985. Two children: Elodie and Bradley. Mr. Gauguier enjoys spending time with his family.

Scott D. Lilja
Director of Training and Development
FinishMaster
4259 40th Street, SE
Kentwood, MI 49512–4100
(616) 949–7604
Fax: (616) 949–1264

5012

Business Information: FinishMaster is an automotive wholesale distribution center, currently operating from 61 sites throughout the U.S. As Director of Training and Development, Mr. Lilja provides all direction, coordination and instruction for corporate personnel training programs. **Career Steps:** Director of Training and Development, FinishMaster (1992–Present); Marketing Manager, 3M (1983–1992). **Associations & Accomplishments:** EIUS; American Sociological Association, National. **Education:** Macalester College, B.A. in History (1983). **Personal:** Mr. Lilja enjoys golf and tennis.

Mrs. Linda S. Olson
Secretary/Treasurer
Ray Dennison Chevrolet, Inc.
2320 North 8th Street
Pekin, IL 61554
(309) 347–3101
Fax: (309) 347–7258

5012

Business Information: Ray Dennison Chevrolet, Inc. is a new and used truck and automobile dealership, with a full-service parts, repair, and body shop facility. As Secretary/Treasurer, Mrs. Olson is responsible for overseeing management of all accounting and finance functions, tax preparation, financial statements, and administration of the 401K and employee pension programs. Established in 1974, Ray Dennison Chevrolet, Inc. employs 100 full–time employees. **Career Steps:** Secretary/Treasurer, Ray Dennison Chevrolet, Inc. (1992–Present); Assistant Office Manager, Ray Dennison Chevrolet, Inc. (1974–1992); Midwest Mazda (1972–1974); Office Manager, Peoria Motors Ford (1966–1971). **Associations & Accomplishments:** Worthy Matron of Central City Chapter (1972, 1983, 1987), Grand Officer for Illinois (1991), Grand Representative of Nebraska in Illinois (1995–1997), Order of the Eastern Star of Illinois; Fundraising for the American Cancer Society, scholarships, and The Eastern Star Home for the Aged. **Education:** Midstate Business College, A.A. (1966); Reynold's and Reynold's Training Programs.

Steven Shelton
Customer Relations Manager
GMAC
14062 Monroe Circle
Omaha, NE 68137–4046
(402) 399–5423
Fax: (402) 896–3587

5012

Business Information: GMAC is an international financial subsidiary of General Motors Corporation, accomodating GM dealers in retail, leasing, and wholesale functions. Serving in various supervisory capacities at GMAC subsidiaries since 1992, Steve Shelton has served as the Omaha, Nebraska's office Customer Relations Manager since March of 1995. He is responsible for all retail and lease accounts, as well as oversees all Credit Department staff and activities. **Career Steps:** General Motors Acceptance Corporation (GMAC): Customer Relations Manager (1995–Present), Acquisitions Credit Supervisor (1994–1995), Dealer Credits Supervisor (1992–1994). **Associations & Accomplishments:** Bellevue University Alumni Association; University of Nebraska, Lincoln Alumni Association; Beta Sigma Psi Fraternity Alumni; Aid Association for Lutherans; Former Treasurer, Saint Thomas Lutheran Church. **Education:** Bellevue University: M.B.A. (1996), Masters in Management, with Distinction; University of Nebraska – Lincoln, B.S.B.A. **Personal:** Married to Cynthia in 1980. Three children: Nicholas James, Brandon Mitchell and Alexander Michael. Mr. Shelton enjoys golf, tennis and youth athletic coach (baseball, football and soccer).

David G. Wobst
Manager of Technical Training
Mitsubishi Motor Sales America
6450 Katella Avenue
Cypress, CA 90630–5208
(714) 372–6143
Fax: (714) 934–7654

5012

Business Information: Mitsubishi Motor Sales America serves as the import arm for all North American Mitsubishi automobile dealerships. Joining Mitsubishi in 1986 as an instructional designer, David Wobst was appointed to his current executive position in 1991. As Manager of Technical Training he develops and oversees all in–house systems training seminars. **Career Steps:** Mitsubishi Motor Sales America: Manager of Technical Training (1991–Present); Supervisor of Instructional Designs (1989–1991); Instructional Designer (1986–1989). **Associations & Accomplishments:** American Society for Performance/Instruction; American Vocational Association; International Television Association; Master ASE Auto Technician; National Association of Industrial Technology; National Society for Performance and Instruction; North American Council of Automotive Teachers; Society of Automotive Engineers. **Education:** California State University–Long Beach (in progress); Denver Automotive and Diesel College, Automotive Technology (1979). **Personal:** Married to Judy in 1984. Two children: Brian and Kelly. Mr. Wobst enjoys antique auto restoration.

Ken Ball, C.P.E., C.E.M.
Plant Engineering Manager
ITT Automotive
400 Ridgefield Court
Asheville, NC 28806
(704) 665–5138
Fax: (704) 665–5547

5013

Business Information: ITT Automotive specializes in the manufacture of motor vehicle parts primarily focusing on Anti-lock Braking Systems for such auto manufacturers as BMW, Chrysler, and Ford. Established in 1989, the Company currently employs 1,100 people. As Facilities Engineer, Mr. Ball manages all operations for the departments of facility maintenance, machine installation and construction. **Career Steps:** ITT Automotive: Plant Engineering Manager (1996–Present), Facilities Engineer (1991–1996), Maintenance Engineer (1989–1991); Preventive Maintenance Engineer, General Electric (1984–1989). **Associations & Accomplishments:** (ASHRAE) American Society of Heating, Refrigeration, and Air Conditioning Engineers; Association of Energy Engineers. **Education:** East Tennessee State University, B.S. (1983); Certified Energy Manager; Certified Plant Engineer. **Personal:** Married to Peggy in 1971. One child: Rhonda. Mr. Ball enjoys photography.

David J. Brown
General Manager
Federal Mogul Chile Limitada
Argomeda 494 Esq. Carmen
Santiago, Chile
56–2–634–4818
Fax: 56–2–634–1076
EMail: See Below

5013

Business Information: Federal Mogul Chile Limitada is a distributor of auto parts (i.e., engine parts, brake parts, and accessories) for the wholesale and retail markets in Chile. As General Manager, Mr. Brown is responsible for all aspects of Company operations, including sales and distribution of the Chilean branch of Federal Mogul. Internet users can reach him via: DIGEBRO@IBM.NET. **Career Steps:** Federal Mogul Corporation Limitada: General Manager – Chile (1995–Present), Latin America Product Manager (1993–1995), Latin American Inventory Manager (1991–1992), Operations Manager – Venezuela (1985–1986), Controller – Venezuela (1982–1984). **Associations & Accomplishments:** Fellow, Chartered Accountants – England, Wales. **Education:** City of London Polytechnic, Chartered Accountant (1975). **Personal:** Married to Marianecm in 1979. Two children: Alejandro and Miguel Eduardo. Mr. Brown enjoys cars, keeping fit, tennis, cycling, and reading.

Ryan C. Cochran
Administrative Executive
Smith Auto Parts
216 South Bridge Street
Visalia, CA 93291
(209) 734–1396
Fax: (209) 627–6708

5013

Business Information: Smith Auto Parts provides in–house engine repair, and markets auto parts in both the retail and wholesale trade. As Administrative Executive, Mr. Cochran is responsible for personnel, cash flow, administration, and project management. **Career Steps:** Smith Auto Parts: Administrative Executive (1995–Present), Warehouse Manager (1986–1995). **Associations & Accomplishments:** Northern California Golf Association; Professional Golfers Association; United States Golf Association. **Education:** Fresno Pacific College, B.A. (1995); Kings River Community College; New Mexico State University. **Personal:** Mr. Cochran enjoys golf, tennis, basketball, working out, and travel.

Dean Ryan Davidson
North American Quality Manager
Alfmeier Corporation
120 Elcon Drive
Greenville, SC 29605–5180
(864) 299–6300
Fax: (864) 299–3020

5013

Business Information: Alfmeier Corporation is a manufacturer and distributor of fuel components for the automotive industry. As North American Quality Manager, Mr. Davidson plans, directs, and controls corporate quality initiatives. **Career Steps:** North American Quality Manager, Alfmeier Corporation (1995–Present); VDO Yazaki Corporation: Quality Manager (1989–1994), Director of Cost Reduction Activity (1990–1991); Mechanical Engineer, Dana Corporation (1985–1989). **Associations & Accomplishments:** American Society for Quality Control; Society of Automotive Engineers; Society of Manufacturing Engineers; Tau Beta Pi National Engineering Honor Society; Chairperson, BMW Supplier Quality Council. **Education:** West Virginia University, B.S. in Engineering (1985). **Personal:** Married to Sherri in 1989. Two children: Ryan and Courtney. Mr. Davidson enjoys golf and sports.

James A. Dawson
Controls Engineer
Nelson Metal Products Corporation
2950 Prairie Street Southwest
Grandville, MI 49418
(616) 538–5660
Fax: (616) 538–6959

5013

Business Information: Nelson Metal Products Corporation is an automotive engine component supplier. As Controls Engineer, Mr. Dawson is responsible for the design, specifications, and approvals of electrical, hydraulic, and pneumatic machine controls. In addition, he also acts as the Project Leader on all implementation. He may also be reached through the Internet via: jadegr@aol.com **Career Steps:** Controls Engineer, Nelson Metal Products Corporation (1989–Present). **Associations & Accomplishments:** Institute of Electronics and Electrical Engineers; ISA. **Education:** Grand Valley State University, B.S. in Engineering; Attended Michigan State University. **Personal:** Married to Brenda in 1986. One child: Christopher. Mr. Dawson enjoys golf, computers and reading.

Vincent Ranucci, C.P.A.
Chief Financial Officer
Alden Autoparts Warehouse
535 Grand Army Hwy. Rte. 6
Somerset, MA 02726–1204
(508) 673–4233
Fax: (508) 674–4468

5013

Business Information: Alden Autoparts Warehouse is a wholesale/retailer automotive parts distributor. A franchise of international automotive parts conglomerate Parts Plus, Alden Autoparts currently operates eight retail stores and five warehouses. A Certified Public Accountant, Mr. Ranucci serves as Chief Financial Officer overseeing all financial and accounting functions of the Company, including acting as liaison for attorneys and banking institutions. **Career Steps:** Chief Financial Officer, Alden Autoparts Warehouse (1994–Present); Chief Financial Officer, Fiore Industries (1991–1994); Senior Accountant, Piccerelli and Gilstein (1987–1991). **Associations & Accomplishments:** Rhode

Island Society of Certified Public Accountants; Association of Independent Certified Public Accountants. **Education:** Bryant College, B.S. in Business (1985). **Personal:** Married to Rosetta in 1993. Mr. Ranucci enjoys family activities, exercise, and home improvement projects.

Eloy Veiga

President
Zorrilla Commercial Corporation
Ave. Barbosa #1062
Rio Piedras, Puerto Rico 00925
(809) 783–9315
Fax: (809) 783–0940

5013

Business Information: Zorrilla Commercial Corporation, a family–owned business, is a distributor of General Motors automobiles and AC Delco parts in four stores located throughout Puerto Rico and the Caribbean. A fifth store will be opening in the near future. Established in 1963, Zorrilla Commercial Corporation reports annual revenue of $12 million and currently employs 52 people. As President, Mr. Veiga is responsible for all aspects of operations, overseeing purchasing, sales, inventory and accounting departments for all five stores. **Career Steps:** President, Zorrilla Commercial Corporation (1974–Present). **Associations & Accomplishments:** Centro Gallego de Puerto Rico; Trade Leaders Club; Overseas Automotive Council; Recipient, International Chamber of Commerce in Paris, France Award (1995). **Education:** Business School in la Coruna, Spain (1954). **Personal:** Married to Elena Veiga in 1959. Two children: Yvonne and Yvette. Mr. Veiga enjoys exercise, fishing, and boating.

Cristina Asteinza Roman

Vice President
A. Unique Used Parts
1051 East 52nd Street
Hialeah, FL 33013–1752
(305) 685–8105
Fax: (305) 685–8858

5015

Business Information: A. Unique Used Parts specializes in the wholesale and retail sale and export of used automobile and truck parts to body shops and dealers. International in scope, the Company has stores throughout Florida and the Caribbean. Established in 1990, the Florida office employs eight people, and has an estimated annual revenue of $3 million. As Vice President, Ms. Roman oversees all aspects of the Company. Her duties include administration, logistics, operations, finance, personnel management, marketing, and strategic planning. **Career Steps:** Vice President, A. Unique Used Parts (1988–Present). **Associations & Accomplishments:** Florida Automobile Dismantlers and Recyclers Association. **Education:** Florida International University, B.A. (1988); Miami Dade Community College, A.A. **Personal:** Married to Manny in 1989. Two children: Alexandra and Gabriel. Ms. Roman enjoys boating.

Guillermo R. Alvarez

Executive Vice President and Chief Operating Officer
Borg Warner International Corporation, Inc.
250 Iturregiel Plaza, Ave. 65th Infantry KM5 HM2
Rio Piedras, Puerto Rico 00984
(809) 752–4050
Fax: (809) 276–7270

5021

Business Information: Borg Warner International Corporation, Inc. is a national furniture and appliance chain consisting of 16 stores throughout Puerto Rico. Established in 1960, Borg Warner International Corporation, Inc. reports annual revenue of $38 million and currently employs 360 people. As Executive Vice President and Chief Operating Officer, Mr. Alvarez manages two companies (Sales Co. and Finance Co.), as well as overseeing the manufacturing operations. **Career Steps:** Executive Vice President and Chief Operating Officer, Borg Warner International Corporation, Inc. (1993–Present); Area Director of Stores, Toys 'R' Us Company (1988–1993); Consultant, Photo Rapid, Inc./Borrero Inc. (1983–1988); Vice President and General Merchandise Manager, Barker's Department Stores (1979–1983). **Associations & Accomplishments:** Director, Better Business Bureau; Puerto Rico Chamber of Commerce; Phi Sigma Alfa Fraternity. **Education:** Pennsylvania Military Academy, B.B.A. (1965). **Person-**

al: Married to Liduvina Pagan in 1966. Three children: Guillermo, Vilma, and Ana. Mr. Alvarez enjoys deep sea fishing.

Sue Henderson

Controller
Franklin Interiors
1 Station Square, Suite 500
Pittsburgh, PA 15219–1122
(412) 255–4064
Fax: (412) 255–4089

5021

Business Information: Franklin Interiors is a wholesale and retail jobber distributor of Steelcase office furniture – the only one of its kind in the Pittsburgh area. Product lines include workstations, desks, chairs, partitions, and file cabinets. Established in 1992, Franklin Interiors currently employs 52 people. As Controller, Ms. Henderson is responsible for all financial business, budgets and concerns, as well as manages the departments of Business, Facilities and Systems Management. **Career Steps:** Controller, Business Manager, Facilities Manager, and Systems Manager, Franklin Interiors (1993–Present); Business Manager, YMCA, Beaver County (1990–1992); Senior Cost Accountant, Schroeder Brothers (1985–1989). **Associations & Accomplishments:** Treasurer of Jubilee Habitat in 1994. **Education:** Geneva College, B.S. in Mathematics (1983), B.S.B.A. in Accounting (1987). **Personal:** Married to Charles in 1983. One child: Chad. Ms. Henderson enjoys crafts and swimming.

Nancy S. Kramer

Treasurer
Sparrows, Inc.
4115 Howard Avenue
Kensington, MD 20895
(301) 530–0175
Fax: (301) 530–0189
EMAIL: See Below

5021

Business Information: Sparrows, Inc. specializes in wholesale/retail sales and import of antique French furniture and accessories, directly from France. The Corporation provides delivery nationwide, and will export if necessary. Established in 1983, the Corporation employs five people, and has an estimated annual income of $1.2 million. As Treasurer, Ms. Kramer is responsible for purchasing, sales, and accounting. A Co–Owner of the Corporation, she and her partner personally select all products. Internet users can reach her via: Nskramer@aol.com. **Career Steps:** Treasurer, Sparrows, Inc. (1983–Present); Treasurer, Kramer & Scott, Inc. (1979–1985); Management Analyst, Social Security Administration (1972–1979). **Associations & Accomplishments:** Current Secretary, Editor of Newsletter, Member of the Board, Antique Dealers Association of Maryland (ADAM); Maryland Retailers Association (MRA); National Association of Dealers in Antiques (NADA). **Education:** Keane State College of New Jersey, M.A. (1973); Ballard College, B.A. (1967); University of Milwaukee (1967–1968). **Personal:** One child: Henning Fritz Kramer. Ms. Kramer enjoys reading and antiquing.

Donald A. LeBuhn

President
Evolution Furniture Company, Inc.
271 Ninth Street
San Francisco, CA 94103
(510) 540–1296
Fax: (510) 540–0389
EMail: See Below

5021

Business Information: Evolution Furniture Company, Inc. is a retail and wholesale furniture and home furnishings business. Two stores serve the Bay area. The Company manufactures its own line of furniture at a facility in Berkeley, California. As President, Mr. LeBuhn is responsible for all aspects of Company operations, including design, manufacturing, and purchasing. Internet users can reach him via: LEBUHN@AOL.COM. **Career Steps:** President, Evolution Furniture Company, Inc. (1993–Present); Owner/CFO, CD & HB, Inc. (1993–1994); Sales Associate/Broker, Cushinan & Wakefield, Inc. (1986–1992). **Education:** New York University, Master's degree (1992); Lehigh University, B.S. in Finance (1986). **Personal:** Mr. LeBuhn enjoys biking, skiing, scuba diving, and fishing.

Scott W. Messmore

President
Memphis Business Interiors
P.O. Box 18479
Memphis, TN 38181
(901) 360–8899
Fax: (901) 360–8370

5021

Business Information: Memphis Business Interiors is a provider of wholesale and retail office furniture to major companies. Prior to establishing Memphis Business Interiors in 1995, Mr. Messmore was employed by Steelcase – the world's leading office furniture supplier and manufacturer for sixteen years. During his tenure, he served as Vice President of Sales and Marketing in the Canadian operations, as well as Manager of Dealer Alliance, and Regional Manager of U.S. Operations. Currently serving as President and Owner of Memphis Business Interiors, he is responsible for all aspects of operations, including administration, finances, sales, marketing, and strategic planning. **Career Steps:** President, Memphis Business Interiors (1995–Present); Vice President of Sales and Marketing, Steelcase Canada Ltd. (1992–1995); Steelcase, Inc.: Manager of Dealer Alliance (1991–1992), Regional Manager (1987–1991). **Associations & Accomplishments:** International Facility Management Association; Rotary. **Education:** University of Florida, B.S.B.A. (1974); University of Alabama, graduate studies; Northwestern University, graduate studies. **Personal:** Married to Joan Messmore in 1979. Three children: Michael, Jeffrey, and Allison. Mr. Messmore enjoys spending time with his family, flyfishing, and golf.

Anthony M. Silva

Executive Vice President
Com–Care Inc.
3221 Northwest Tenth Terrace
Ft. Lauderdale, FL 33309
(305) 568–3400
Fax: (305) 568–3401

5021

Business Information: Com–Care Inc. specializes in the retail and wholesale market of office furniture and related products. Established in 1991, Com–Care Inc. currently employs 13 people and reports an estimated annual revenue of $3 million. As Executive Vice President, Mr. Silva is responsible for the identification and design of the marketplace to ensure growth and stability of the Company, as well as the management of daily operations. **Career Steps:** Executive Vice President, Com–Care Inc. (1992–Present); President, Professional Systems Install (1990–1992); Project Coordinator, Liss Transportation (1988–1990). **Associations & Accomplishments:** Broward Beacon Council; Fort Lauderdale Chamber of Commerce. **Education:** Northern Essex Community College, A.A. (1986). **Personal:** Mr. Silva enjoys softball, golf, and skiing.

Rebecca S. Burcham

Office Manager
McCann's Floorcovering, Inc.
P.O. Box 3667
Seattle, WA 98124–3667
(206) 442–9019
Fax: (206) 389–0925

5023

Business Information: McCann's Floorcovering, Inc. is a specialty contractor which installs carpet, ceramic, laminate, glasbord, and marlite floorcoverings. As Office Manager, Ms. Burcham is responsible for all clerical aspects of the business and management personnel, including hiring, and training. She also handles cash flow management, and collections. **Career Steps:** Office Manager, McCann's Floorcovering, Inc. (1993–Present); Owner, Business Specialties (1993–Present); Owner, N.W. Waters Salmon Smokery (1995–Present); Resident Manager, Parkwood Apartment (1993–Present). **Personal:** Married to Ken in 1991. Three children: Shawn, David, and Larry. Ms. Burcham enjoys hiking, kayaking, remodeling, boating, and whale watching.

Lorna R. Catullo

Director of Sales
Country Floors
15 E. 16th Street
New York, NY 1003–3104
(212) 627–8300
Fax: (212) 424–1604

5023

Business Information: Country Floors is a direct importer and distributor of high–end ceramic tile and stone. As Director of Sales, Ms. Catullo manages, promotes, and oversees all sales activities and customer service functions in New York, Greenwich (Connecticut), and Philadelphia showrooms. **Career Steps:** Director of Sales, Country Floors (1992–Present); Sales Manager, Carminart, Inc. (1978–1992). **Associations & Accomplishments:** Industry Foundation Member, American Society of Interior Designs; National Association of Female Executives. **Education:** New York School of Interior Design, Certification Program (1978); Ithaca College – Ithaca, New York, B.S. **Personal:** Two children: Cynthia Ross and Christopher Scott. Ms. Catullo enjoys flower gardening.

Jane Edwards
Vice President, Marketing
The Pampered Chef, Ltd.
350 South Rohlwing Road
Addison, IL 60101–3030
(708) 261–8570
Fax: (708) 261–8586

5023

Business Information: The Pampered Chef, Ltd. is a national direct seller of kitchen tools. Established in 1980, the Company has approximately 25,000 independent contractors in the United States, and a catalog consisting of kitchen tools and recipe books. As Vice President, Ms. Edwards oversees products, public relations, communications, and handles all marketing. **Career Steps:** Vice President, The Pampered Chef, Ltd. (1995–Present); Director of Marketing, Discovery Toys Inc. (1992–1995); Director of Public Relations, The Fashion Institute of Design and Merchandising (1984–1992). **Associations & Accomplishments:** Public Relations Society of America; International Association of Business Communicators; Women in Communicators Inc.; The Publicity Club of Chicago; Board of Directors, The San Francisco Clothing Bank. **Education:** American Conservatory Theatre, Theatre Arts (1976). **Personal:** One child: Angelique Edwards Green. Ms. Edwards is also a published writer.

Joe Nickels

Vice President of Sales
Camden Flooring
1300 Route 38
Cherry Hill, NJ 08002–2855
(609) 662–4830
Fax: (609) 625–1605

5023

Business Information: Camden Flooring is a distributor and manufacturing representative of wholesale floor coverings. Products include carpet, vinyl, tile, and wood flooring for residential and commercial sites located throughout the Northeast U.S. and overseas. Established in 1926, Camden Flooring currently employs 46 people. With nineteen years experience in sales and marketing, Mr. Nickels joined Camden Flooring in 1994. Serving as Vice President of Sales, Mr. Nickels is responsible for the oversight of day–to–day operations in the Sales Department, including coordinating sales, marketing, and product introduction for the Company. **Career Steps:** Vice President of Sales, Camden Flooring (1994–Present); President, The Nickels Sales Agency (1988–1994); Vice President Sales and Marketing, Benj. Berman, Inc. (1976–1988); Drill Sergeant, United States Army (1968–1970). **Associations & Accomplishments:** Elected Committeeman, Township of Hamilton; Director, Greater Mays Landing Chamber of Commerce; Coach, Hamilton Township Soccer Club; American Legion; Coach, Mays Landing Athletic Association; Hamilton TWP Historic Society. **Education:** La Salle University, B.A. (1967). **Personal:** Married to Janet in 1984. Six children: Joseph, Daniel, Jeffrey, Allison, Kevin, and Michael. Mr. Nickels enjoys scuba diving, triathlons, and golf.

Thomas L. Fife
Manager
LumberOne
9 Railroad Street
Brownsburg, IN 46112–1243
(317) 852–8996
Fax: (317) 852–8999

5031

Business Information: LumberOne is a wholesale, contractor only, lumber operation. This includes a full–scale wall panelization plant. The second generation family–owned company is responsible for 18% of new house construction within their 45–mile radius, covering the suburban/rural Indianapolis area. Mr. Fife joined LumberOne in 1987 as Assistant Receiver, serving in various supervisory and management capacities before moving into his present position as Manager in 1994. In addition to management of the operations and office, he has assumed the larger role of consulting and advising the President/Owner, and encouraging further interaction and communications with customers. Concurrently, he is active in the lumber and building materials community as a seated member of the Educational Committee of the Indiana Lumberman &

Building Supplies Association. He further advances the concept of motivation through employee empowerment and Humanizing the Workplace with regular seminars presented in the state of Indiana, as well as other states throughout the Midwest region. **Career Steps:** LumberOne: Manager (1994–Present), Operations Manager/Office Manager (1993–1994), Operations Manager (1991–1993), Yard Foreman (1990–1991), Head Receiver (1989–1990), Driver (1988–1989), Assistant Receiver (1987–1988); Owner, Fife Forestry Management (1985–1987); Co–Owner/President, Sisson Studios (1980–1985). **Associations & Accomplishments:** Indiana Lumberman & Building Supplies Association: Education Committee (1995, 1996), Customer Service Instructor (1994, 1995, 1996), State Convention Keynote Speaker (1993, 1994, 1995), Appreciation Award for Outstanding Training & Teaching on Customer Service; Lumber-One: Employee of the Year (1988), Employee of the Month (Numerous); Armed Forces: Bronze Star Medal for Meritorious Service, National Defense Service Medal, Good Conduct Medal, Vietnam Campaign Medal – Two Overseas Bars; American Legion; Top Secret Crypto Security Clearance, U.S. Army. **Education:** U.S. Army: Classes on Juris Prudence, Code of Conduct, CBR Training, Service Signal Communications and Radio Teletype Operator School; Continuing Studies in Accounting, Sales Motivation, Customer Service and various other retail related subjects; Currently participating in the "Management for Excellence" Seminar by NLBMDA. **Personal:** Married to Lynne Foster Fife (Artist) in 1994. Two children: Anthony Layton Fife and Kristen Nicole Grove. Mr. Fife enjoys auto racing and outdoor nature activities. Mr. and Mrs. Fife spend considerable time marketing Mrs. Fife's paintings.

Nicholas R. Kent
Executive Vice President and Chief Executive Officer
North American Wholesale Lumber
3601 Algonquin Road, Suite 400
Rolling Meadows, IL 60008
(847) 870–7470
Fax: (847) 870–0201
E–Mail: See Below

5031

Business Information: North American Wholesale Lumber is an international trade association serving the wholesale lumber industry. Services of the organization include education programs, newsletters, industry statistical information, an annual meeting, various regional meetings, and a Traders Market each fall. As Executive Vice President and Chief Executive Officer, Mr. Kent is responsible for overall day–to–day operations, including enhancing education, professionalism, and communication in pursuit of efficient distribution. Internet users can also reach him via: NAWLA@AOL.COM **Career Steps:** Executive Vice President/CEO, North American Wholesale Lumber (1988–Present); Executive Director, Northwestern Lumber Association (1984–1988); Building Division Director, Associated General Contractors of Minnesota (1978–1984); Assistant Director of Administrative Services, Associated General Contractors of America – Washington D.C. (1973–1978); Commissioned 2nd Lieutenant, U.S. Air Force (1973). **Associations & Accomplishments:** American Society of Association Executives; Chicago Society of Association Executives; American Lumber Standard Committee; Forest Products Advisory Committee, Chicago Mercantile Exchange. **Education:** West Virginia University, B.S. (1973). **Personal:** Married to Paula in 1987. Two children: Jillian and Samuel.

James C. Stuckey
Vice President and Co–Founder
Wholesale Wood Products
P.O. Box 1325
Dothan, AL 36302
(334) 793–6028
Fax: (334) 794–6607

5031

Business Information: Wholesale Wood Products is the owner of diversified lumber products industries throughout Alabama. Entities include: a wholesale wood products company; a manufacturing company for southern yellow pine boards; and a lumber retailing company. With twenty–four years experience in the lumber industry, Mr. Stuckey joined Wholesale Wood Products in 1979. Serving as Vice President and Co–Founder, he is responsible for the oversight of all administrative operations for associates and a support staff of 100, in addition to financial matters and long range planning. **Career Steps:** Vice President and Co–Founder, Wholesale Wood Products (1979–Present); Salesman, Hathcock Lumber Company, Inc. (1971–1979). **Associations & Accomplishments:** NAWLA; SFPA; SLMA; AFA; Wiregrass United Way; Former President, SEACT. **Education:** University of Alabama, B.S. (1970); Executive Management Institute, University of Virginia. **Personal:** Married to Sally in 1969. Three children: Curt, Andy, and Reeves.

Dorene M. Brown, C.C.C.E.
Controller
Tamar Building Products
3957 Walker Road
Windsor, Ontario N8W 3T4
(519) 969–7060
Fax: (519) 969–5023

5033

Business Information: Tamar Building Products is a retail and wholesale building materials supplier (e.g., roofing, gutters, aluminum and vinyl siding). As Controller, Ms. Brown serves as General Manager and Financial Officer, conducting and supervising all financial aspects of company operations. **Career Steps:** Controller, Tamar Building Products (1980–Present); Credit Manager, Meikar Roofing, Ltd. (1974–1980). **Associations & Accomplishments:** Windsor Builders Supply Association; International Credit Association; Credit Association of Canada; United Way. **Education:** St. Claire College, Jr. Accounting Certificate (1975). **Personal:** Three children: Scot, Terry, and Melissa.

Danielle Huff Humphrey
Director of Finance and Administration
Washington Energy Conservation System
5875 Barclay Drive
Alexandria, VA 22315–5701
(703) 924–5715
Fax: (703) 924–5756

5033

Business Information: Washington Energy Conservation System is a full–service home improvement contractor, providing the sale, finance, service and installation of home improvement products (e.g., roofing, siding, windows, doors). As Director of Finance and Administration, Ms. Humphrey is responsible for overseeing corporate taxes and finances. **Career Steps:** Director of Finance and Administration, Washington Energy Conservation System (1995–Present). **Education:** American University, M.B.A. (1994); Michigan State University, B.A. in Political Science. **Personal:** Ms. Humphrey enjoys scuba diving, rock climbing, and hiking.

Lynn K. Whyte
Vice President of Administration
Ted Lansing Corporation
8501 Sanford Drive
Richmond, VA 23228
(804) 266–8893
Fax: (804) 262–7554

5033

Business Information: Ted Lansing Corporation is a wholesale distribution of exterior building products and a manufacturer of certainteed windows. Established in 1955, the Company currently employs 350 people. As Vice President of Administration, Mr. Whyte is responsible for all aspects of the departments of Payroll, Credit, Human Resources, Compliance and Safety, as well as all Company vehicles. Mr. Whyte spent 23 years on active duty with the United States Air Force, during which time he was awarded the Meritorious Service Medal with Three Oak Leaf Clusters, the Joint Service Commendation Medal, and numerous other military awards. **Career Steps:** Vice President of Administration, Ted Lansing Corporation (1994–Present); Legal Advisor/Humanitarian Relief in Operation Provide Comfort, United States Air Force (1993); Director of Plans and Requirments – Air Force Information Services, HQ United States Air Force (1990–1994). **Associations & Accomplishments:** Rotary; Arizona Bar Association; The Retired Officers Association; The Air Force Association; Former Boy Scout Leader; Participated in numerous church and civic activities including fund raising, service projects, clean–up and restoration. **Education:** Arizona State University, J.D. (1978); University of Nebraska – Lincoln, M.A. in Management (1978); Brigham Young University, B.S. in Accounting (1970). **Personal:** Married to Sherry G. in 1972. Two children: Kimber Dawn Brouse and Leslie Michelle Whyte. Mr. Whyte enjoys collecting antiques, gardening, and international travel.

Mr. David R. Andalcio
President
Abbott Industrial Supply
3129 West 36th Street
Chicago, IL 60632–2303
(312) 247–6555
Fax: (312) 890–9638

5039

Business Information: Abbott Industrial Supply is a leading distributor of construction materials and various industrial supplies, as well as computer and office equipment. Current projects that Abbott is involved with include: Construction Division – Chicago construction projects, including the McCormick

Place Expansion, Loyola University, University of Illinois Molecular Biology Lab, Chicago's 911 System, and USPS General Mail Facility; Computer and Office Equipment Division – installation of a 2,000–computer turnkey operation for the Chicago Public School System, North Western and Illinois Central railroads, City of Chicago, and Re/Max Realty. In his capacity as President, Mr. Andalcio oversees the overall operations of the Company, including financial and marketing strategies. The first full year under his management (1993), Abbott Industrial Supply saw a 58% sales increase to more than $6 million. Mr. Andalcio purchased the firm in October of 1992 from Nelson Carlo. From 1988 until this purchase, he had served Mr. Carlo as general manager of a subsidiary computer services business which was then folded into Abbott. A firm supporter of equal employment opportunity, Mr. Andalcio has been active in the minority community for more than a decade. A leader and role model, he believes success comes to those who "are innovative, resourceful, extremely focused and achievement– oriented and who never quit until the job is done." Established in 1978, Abbott Industrial Supply employs a staff of 15 and reports annual sales in excess of $6 million. **Career Steps:** President, Abbott Industrial Supply (1992–Present); Director of Marketing, Abbott Products, Inc. (1991–1992); General Manager, Great Lakes Office (1988–1991); President, D & D Electronics (1982–1986). **Associations & Accomplishments:** Hispanic American Cont. Indust. Association; CRPC; LAMB; Chicago United Way; Published and interviewed in various trade and media publications (e.g., Minority Business Report, Work Force 2000). **Education:** The British Educational System.

Louis H. T. Dehmlow

Chairman of the Board
GLS Corporation
1750 North Kingsbury Street
Chicago, IL 60614–4813
(312) 664–3500
Fax: (312) 664–2349

5039

Business Information: A privately–owned family business, GLS Corporation is a wholesale distributor of basic materials utilized in the fabrication of reinforced plastic products and synthetic rubber. With over 2,000 customers in 19 states and Canada, GLS distributes fiberglass–based plastic for a variety of trademarked products, and owns a fleet of trucks and two barge terminals. Established in 1940, GLS currently employs 250 people and has an estimated annual revenue of $180 million. Mr. Dehmlow was the President of GLS for 41 years. As such, he guided the corporation to its prominence and is now the Chairman of the Board. As Chairman, Mr. Dehmlow oversees all company activities. His son serves as the Company President and Chief Executive Officer. **Career Steps:** GLS Corporation: Chairman of the Board (1993–Present), President (1952–1993). **Associations & Accomplishments:** Chairman of the Board, National Association of Wholesale Distributors (1987–1988); President, National Association of Chemical Distributors (1984–1985); President, National Associaton of Plastic Distributors (1975–1976); First President, Former President and Director, Illinois Wholesale Distributors Association (1975–1976); Battalion Commander, Northwestern Military And Naval Academy; Published in several books. **Education:** University of Michigan, B.S. in Engineering and Chemical Engineering (1950); Northwestern Military and Naval Academy (1945). **Personal:** Married to Carla in 1947. Three children: Nancy, Steven Louis and Christine Dehmlow Smith. Mr. Dehmlow enjoys photography, writing and sailing.

Edward J. Keels

President
Keels Building Materials Inc.
PO Box 3442
Gulfport, MS 39505
(601) 452–2500
Fax: (601) 452–3555

5039

Business Information: Keels Building Materials Inc. is a supplier of wholesale building materials to retail lumber yards in Louisiana, Mississippi, Alabama, and Florida. Products include lumber (pine) bought from lumber mills located in the Southern part of the U.S. Future plans include expanding into four states, to include web page, special projects, and satellite operations. Local plans include streamlining their accounting department within the next four months. Establishing Keels BMI in 1995, Mr. Keels serves as President, responsible for all aspects of operations, including outside sales and the training of sales personnel. **Career Steps:** President, Keels Building Materials Inc. (1995–Present) **Associations & Accomplishments:** Founder and President, The Krewe of Zeus, Inc. —

private mardi gras organization **Education:** University of Southern Mississippi, Major in Psychology/Minor in Business **Personal:** Married to Louise R. in 1975. Three children: Edward J. III, Kimberly A. and Melanie R.

Eugenio C. Marotta
President
Perma–Lite of Pennsylvania
1717 Penn Avenue, Suite 320
Pittsburgh, PA 15221–5004
(412) 242–8010
Fax: (412) 242–5784

5039

Business Information: Perma–Lite of Pennsylvania is a national retailer, specializing in the custom replacement of windows and doors for the homeowners industry. Perma–Lite has two locations in Pennsylvania (Pittsburgh and New Castle). Purchasing 30% of the Company in 1985, Mr. Marotta became 100% owner in 1994. Serving as President, he is responsible for all aspects of operations, including the oversight of sales and telemarketing. **Career Steps:** President, Perma–Lite of Pennsylvania (1979–Present); Executive Director, Berlitz School of Languages (1973–1979). **Associations & Accomplishments:** Rotary Club of Pittsburgh; Italian Sons and Daughters; Spanish Cultural Club; Former President, National Association for the Remolding Industry. **Education:** University of Buffalo, B.A. (1973). **Personal:** Married to Elva Marotta in 1974. Two children: Franco and Jessica. Mr. Marotta enjoys photography, tennis, and skiing.

Mr. Steven S. Serowik
Vice President
Star Sales & Distributing Corp.
29 Commerce Way
Woburn, MA 01888
(617) 933–8830
Fax: (617) 933–2145

5039

Business Information: Star Sales & Distributing Corp. is a national wholesale distributor of construction supplies and materials, including: drywall and concrete screws, related fasteners, hardware, hand tools, and power tools. Established in 1922, Star Sales has two office locations, one in Woburn, Massachusetts, the other in Pompano Beach, Florida. In addition, Star Sales has stocking warehouses in St. Louis, Missouri and Greensboro, North Carolina. The Company currently employs approximately 50 people and reports annual revenue of $15 million. As Vice President, Mr. Serowik is responsible for strategic planning, financial management and general administration. **Career Steps:** Vice President, Star Sales & Distributing Corp. (1994–Present); Consultant, KPMG Peat Marwick (1992–1994); President, WCV, Inc. (1988–1990). **Education:** University of New Hampshire, M.B.A. (1992); Boston University, B.S. in Business Administration/Finance. **Personal:** Married to Erika in 1994. Mr. Serowik enjoys golf, skiing, reading and travel.

Luai Abdul Aziz Al Abdul Razzaq

Managing Director
Ashraf & Company, Ltd.
3555
Safat, Kuwait 13036
(965) 531–2960
Fax: (965) 533–6376

5043

Business Information: Ashraf & Company, Ltd. is a marketing and distribution firm for photographic products and accessories used in publishing, imaging, printing, and art graphics businesses in Kuwait. Joining Ashraf & Co. as General Manager in 1991, Mr. Al Abdul Razzaq was appointed as Managing Director in 1993. He is responsible for the complete supervision of all marketing, financial and administrative activities for the Company. **Career Steps:** Ashraf & Company, Ltd.: Managing Director (1993–Present), General Manager (1991–1993); General Manager, Aabdulaziz & Partner Trdg. (1989–1991). **Education:** Kuwait University, Bachelors (1989). **Personal:** Married to Manal in 1991. One child: Faisal. Mr. Al Abdul Razzaq enjoys swimming and water sports.

John T. Hopkins
Vice President and Director of Operations
Da–Lite Screen Company
11500 Williamson Road
Cincinnati, OH 45241
(513) 489–3222
Fax: (513) 489–4247

5043

Business Information: Da–Lite Screen Company is the global leader in the manufacture and distribution of projection screens and presentation products. Established in 1909, Da-Lite Screen Company reports annual revenue of $60 million and currently employs 400 people. A management executive with Da–Lite since 1988, John Hopkins is Vice President and Director of Operations responsible for all international operations, as well as overall general management of the Rear Projection Products Division. **Career Steps:** Da–Lite Screen Company: Vice President and Director of Operations (1994–Present), Vice President of International (1991–1994); Vice President of Manufacturing (1988–1991); Materials Manager, York International (1979–1988). **Associations & Accomplishments:** Rotary International; Phi Gamma Delta. **Education:** Purdue University, B.S. (1979). **Personal:** Married to Kathy in 1983. Four children: David, Josh, Timothy, and Katie. Mr. Hopkins enjoys gardening and international travel.

Thomas C. Bersch Jr.
Vice President of Sales
Corporate Express
4320 North 124th Street
Milwaukee, WI 53222–1008
(414) 466–2200
Fax: (414) 466–2541

5044

Business Information: Corporate Express is the largest office supply company in the United States, with 43 distribution centers worldwide. As Vice President of Sales, Mr. Bersch, in charge of the Midwest Centers, is directly responsible for approximately 11 employees and indirectly supervises another 102. Mr. Bersch handles customer service, furniture contracts for the Midwest, departmental budgets, and personnel concerns. **Career Steps:** Corporate Express: Vice President of Sales (1995–Present) and Sales Manager (1989–1995); Sales Representative, Siekert & Baum (1980–1989). **Personal:** Married to Karen in 1983. One child: Tyler Joseph. Mr. Bersch enjoys computers and golf.

Karen L. Finley
Comptroller/Director
FISource, Inc.
514 Carmony Road Northeast
Albuquerque, NM 87107
(505) 345–7575
Fax: (505) 345–7935

5044

Business Information: FISource, Inc. is a marketer and servicer of banking equipment, such as ATM's, vaults, cameras, alarms, and pneumatic tube drive–up systems. Established in 1985, FISource, Inc. reports annual sales of $6 million and currently employs 80 people. As Comptroller/Director, Ms. Finley serves as Head of the Finance and Service departments, responsible for all aspects of financial matters. She also is a member of the Board of Directors. **Career Steps:** FISource, Inc.: Comptroller/Director (1995–Present), Accountant (1992–1994); Accountant, The Rehabilitation Center, Inc. (1988–1992). **Associations & Accomplishments:** National Association for Female Executives (NAFE); New Mexico Professional Accountants Association. **Education:** University of New Mexico, B.A. (1988). **Personal:** Ms. Finley enjoys computers, reading, and interior decorating.

Paula S. Holman
Director of Human Resources
BMC, Inc.
P.O. Box 35910
Albuquerque, NM 87176–5910
(505) 837–2000
Fax: (505) 837–2070

5044

Business Information: BMC, Inc. specializes in the sale and service of copiers, fax machines, computer equipment, and other office products in New Mexico and the El Paso area of Texas. As Director of Human Resources, Ms. Holman is responsible for the development and implementation of all policies and procedures, payroll, orientation, and training for more than 140 employees. **Career Steps:** Director of Human Resources, BMC, Inc. (1994–Present); Systems Manager, CRS, Inc. (1990–1994). **Associations & Accomplishments:** Human Resource Management Association; Board, Albuquerque Civic Light Opera Association. **Education:** University of Wyoming, B.S. in Business (1991). **Personal:** Ms. Holman enjoys the outdoors, horseback riding, swimming, and tennis.

John A. Love
Vice President of Human Resources
Boise Cascade Office Products Corporation
800 West Bryn Mawr Avenue
Itasca, IL 60143–1503
(708) 773–5036
Fax: (708) 773–7107

5044

Business Information: Boise Cascade Office Products Corporation is an international office products distribution company offering distribution to large and small corporations, businesses as well as mail order to small work and home offices. As Vice President of Human Resources, Mr. Love is responsible for all Human Resource functional activities for the Company. **Career Steps:** Boise Cascade Office Products Corporation: Vice President of Human Resources (1995–Present), Director of Human Resources (1990–1995), Manager of Human Resources (1978–1990), Manager of Training and Development (1976–1978). **Associations & Accomplishments:** The Society For Human Resource Management; Multiple Sclerosis Society; Saratoga Institute. **Education:** University of Missouri, B.S. in Business Administration (1972). **Personal:** Married to Denise in 1990. Two children: Matthew and Melissa. Mr. Love enjoys travel and sports.

Larry W. Miller
President
E. H. Clarke & Bro., Inc.
19 South Second
Memphis, TN 38103
(901) 523–8228
Fax: (901) 523–9696

5044

Business Information: E. H. Clarke & Bro., Inc., at the same location since 1902, is a provider of office supplies and products, including office furniture, printing, and computer supplies. E. H. Clarke & Bro., Inc. also provides more than 23,000 items by catalog. Joining E. H. Clarke & Bro., Inc. as President in 1995, Mr. Miller oversees the entire operation, including administration, finances, sales, public relations, client relations, marketing, and strategic planning. **Career Steps:** E. H. Clarke & Bro., Inc.: President (1995–Present), Vice President and General Manager (1994–1995), Vice President (1993–1994); Senior Sales Representative, United Stationers Supply Company (1992–1993); Stationers Distributing Company: Eastern Regional Sales Coordinator (1989–1992), National Sales Coordinator (1988–1989); McKesson Office Products: National Sales Manager (1987–1988), Sales Representative (1984–1987); Sales Representative, Champion Office Products (1980–1984); Sales Representative, E. H. Clarke & Bro., Inc. (1968–1980). **Associations & Accomplishments:** President's Club 3rd Year Award (1992), National Office Products Association; Business Products Industry Association; Volunteer Office Products Association; Southern Travelers Association; Mid–South Travelers Association. **Education:** University of Memphis, B.A. (1967). **Personal:** Married to Fran in 1967. Three children: Lori, Allison, and Justin. Mr. Miller enjoys church, reading, and family activities.

J. Barry Sawyer
Customer Support Director
CWC Office Products
6670–C Corners Industrial Court
Norcross, GA 30092
(770) 849–0878
Fax: (770) 849–0664

5044

Business Information: CWC Office Products, a division of United States Office Products, is a supplier of office products, furniture, snacks, coffee and coffee products. Established in 1929, the Company estimates revenue of $56 million in 1996 and presently employs 185 people. As Customer Support Director, Mr. Sawyer oversees all customer service applications and facilities management at the Company's distribution center. Other areas of responsibility include development of marketing techniques and total quality management programs. **Career Steps:** Customer Support Director, CWC Office Products (1995–Present); Director of Customer Support, OSOS (1993–1995); National Account Director, Express Office Products (1985–1993); Store Manager, DeKalb Office Supply (1983–1985). **Associations & Accomplishments:** Advisor, Asher School of Business; President of Professional Division, Phi Beta Lambda; Phi Beta Lambda Business Person of the Year 1995; Listed in Who's Who in American Junior Colleges 1984. Mr. Sawyer prepared articles for presentation at the OSOS Convention in 1992 including "Is "Total Quality" All We've Cracked It Up to Be?" **Education:** Georgia State University, B.B.A. (1991); DeKalb Community College,

Associates in Business (1984); Pace Institute, Facilitator Training Certificate–Strategic Thinking (1996). **Personal:** Married to Deborah in 1985. Two children: Doug and Everitt. Mr. Sawyer enjoys softball, golf, tennis, and community involvement.

Cesar Adil D O Souto

President/Marketing Director
GSA–S International, Ltda.
Rua Dona Margarida, 795
Porto Alegre RS, Brazil 90420611
55–51–3371788
Fax: 55–51–3436393
EMail: See Below

5044

Business Information: GSA–S International, Ltda. is an exclusive distributor of Unibind office material in the Brazilian territory. The Company specializes in import, distribution, and service for copy machines, binding machines in general, and computer technology. As President/Marketing Director, Mr. Souto is responsible for all aspects of Company operations, including administration, finances, taxes, sales and marketing, and strategic planning. Internet users can reach him via: GSAS@conex.com.br. **Career Steps:** President/Manager Director, GSA–S International, Ltda. (1990–Present); Partner, South American Business Law Group (1989–1992). **Associations & Accomplishments:** Institute of Business Studies; Liberal Institute; Rotary Club; Mr. Suoto is fluent in Portuguese, English and Spanish, and can understand French. **Education:** Law School, Specialization in Law and Marketing and Business Administration, in progress. **Personal:** Mr. Souto enjoys tennis, music, and playing the guitar.

Mrs. Lynn L. Winkler
Controller
Perry Corporation
P.O. Box 7199
Lafayette, OH 45854
(419) 228–1360
Fax: (419) 224–8128

5044

Business Information: Perry Corporation is a retail sales, service, rental, and leasing organization for business systems and office automation products, such as fax machines, micrographics, laser disks, copiers, etc. In her capacity as Controller, Mrs. Winkler is responsible for all accounting functions, including managing accounting office personnel. Established in 1957, Perry Corporation has 4 retail locations, and employs a full–time staff of 120. **Career Steps:** Controller, Perry Corporation (1993–Present); Controller, Swaney Olds–Nissan (1985–1990); Staff/General Ledger Accountant, Abrams Construction (1978–1985). **Associations & Accomplishments:** Ohio Society of Certified Public Accountants. **Education:** Lima Technical College, A.A. (1978); Certified Public Accountant (1993).

Shawn Ashley
Vice President
Great Lakes Computer Services, Inc.
7546 Gratiot Road
Saginaw, MI 48609
(517) 781–4741
Fax: (517) 781–9987

5045

Business Information: Great Lakes Computer Services, Inc. specializes in the wholesale and retail market of computer systems, as well as provides full maintenance and warranty services; network systems consultation, design and implementation; and customized systems installation. As Vice President, Mr. Ashley directs operations in the areas of accounting, network design, and maintenance services, as well as provides network analysis and design consultation to major clientele. **Career Steps:** Vice President, Great Lakes Computer Services, Inc. (1993–Present); Senior Technician, Modware Computers (1989–1993); Tactile Specialist, U.S. Army (1985–1989). **Associations & Accomplishments:** Member, Computer Industry Technology Industry. **Personal:** Married to Barbara in 1994. Two children: Justin and Alyssa. Mr. Ashley enjoys music and travel.

Amy J. Bochman
Operations Manager
Practice Outlook, Inc.
7500 North Dreamy Draw Drive #133
Phoenix, AZ 85020
(602) 861–9972
Fax: (602) 943–5866

5045

Business Information: Practice Outlook, Inc. specializes in the retail sales of computers and software for the dental industry. Established in 1982, Practice Outlook, Inc., currently employs 15 people and has an estimated annual revenue of $2 million. As Operations Manager, Ms. Bochman is responsible for the overall direction of the Company and its continued growth in the absence of the President. **Career Steps:** Operations Manager, Practice Outlook, Inc. (1990–Present); Director of Operations, Merchants Funding Group (1987–1990); Manager and Agent, Jim Long & Associates (1984–1987); Controller, Ag Financial Systems (1982–1984). **Associations & Accomplishments:** Volunteer, Phoenix Children's Hospital. **Education:** Nettleton Business College (1974). **Personal:** Married to Otto in 1974. Ms. Bochman enjoys reading, walking, volunteer work and spending time with her two dogs.

Bradley D. Burris
Service Manager
Ameridata
4241 Veterans Boulevard
Metairie, LA 70006
(504) 833–1076
Fax: Please mail or call

5045

Business Information: Ameridata, a publicly–owned corporation, is an international personal computer reseller and service provider. International in scope, Ameridata has 72 locations in the U.S. and 15 globally. As Service Manager, Mr. Burris is responsible for the revenue and profitability of people, as well as conducting cost analysis reports. In addition, he manages a technical staff of 75 people in Louisiana and Mississippi. **Career Steps:** Service Manager, Ameridata (1995–Present); Entre Computer Center: Service Manager (1994–1995), Lead Technician (1992–1994); Field Engineer, TRW (1991–1929). **Associations & Accomplishments:** American Federation of Musicians; New Orleans Computer Club. **Education:** Southeastern Louisiana University, Masters of Music (1975); University of New Orleans, Bachelors of Music Education (1974). **Personal:** Mr. Burris enjoys playing the guitar and singing in the New Orleans area.

Christopher D. D'Anna Sr.

Executive Vice President
Reliable Computer Parts
7401–R Fullerton Road
Springfield, VA 22153
(703) 569–5300
Fax: (703) 569–5301
EMail: See Below

5045

Business Information: Reliable Computer Parts is a wholesaler of IBM and Compaq computer parts to computer maintenance and repair companies. As Executive Vice President, Mr. D'Anna is responsible for all aspects of Company operations, including personnel, purchasing, planning, and long range forecasting. Concurrently, Mr. D'Anna is President and Co–Founder of a holding company called ABTEI; he is Director and Co–Founder of Affordable Business Technology – selling previously–owned computer equipment, cellular phones, and pagers; and is a Volunteer Track Coach at T.C. Williams High School in Alexandria, VA. Internet users can reach him via: danna1@rcp.com. **Career Steps:** Executive Vice President, Reliable Computer Parts (1993–Present); Director, Afforable Business Technology (1995–Present); President, ABTEL (1995–Present). **Associations & Accomplishments:** Montclair Country Club; Alumnus, Sigma Pi Fraternity, Beta Phi Chapter; Head Track and Field Coach, Peekskill High School (1986–1990). **Education:** Pace University, B.S. (1989). **Personal:** Married to Colleen in 1993. One child: Christopher Jr. Mr. D'Anna enjoys golf, NBA basketball, and spending time with his family, he is a season football ticket holder for N.Y. Jets and basketball season ticket holder for Washington Bullets.

Herman Delatte

Chief Operating Officer
Micrografx, Inc.
1303 East Arapaho Road
Richardson, TX 75081–2444
(214) 994–6636
Fax: 011–41–22–7840

5045

Business Information: Micrografx, Inc., established in 1982, is one of the leading software vendors in the international computer market. The company specializes in computer graphics and works closely with Microsoft. International in scope, Micrografx has subsidiaries throughout the U.S., United Kingdom, France, the Netherlands, Germany, Japan, Italy, Canada, and Australia. Joining Micrografx in 1991 as Vice President for European operations, Mr. Delatte was appointed Chief Operating Officer and Vice President–International in January of 1994. He provides the overall executive administration for all operations world–wide, primarily focusing in the areas of localization of products, marketing, sales, international finance and controls. **Career Steps:** Micrografx, Inc.: Chief Operating Officer (1994–Present); Senior Vice President, International (1994); Vice President of Europe (1991–1993); Ashton–Tate (now Borland): Managing Director, Europe West – Benelux/France/Spain/Italy (1988–1991); Managing Director, Ores; Account and Sales Management, Control Data (Service Bureau Co./SBC). **Education:** Lindelei, Belgium, Computer Science Graduate (1973). **Personal:** Married to Silvana in 1984. One child: Sarah. Mr. Delatte enjoys tennis, jogging, and skiing.

Ed Eftekhary

Manager
Byte & Floppy Computers
7636 Clairmont Mesa Boulevard
San Diego, CA 92111–1535
(619) 571–9013
Fax: (619) 571–3169

5045

Business Information: Byte & Floppy Computers is one of California's largest and most–respected computer sales corporation, with future plans to expand nationwide. Clientele include Fortune 500 and 100 companies. As Manager, Mr. Eftekhary oversees all operations of the San Diego location, including sales, services, marketing, advertising, and training. **Career Steps:** Manager, Byte & Floppy Computers (1989–Present); Manager, SG Computers (1988–1989); Manager, Compu–Save Systems (1986–1988). **Associations & Accomplishments:** Children's baseball coach. **Education:** Illinois Institute of Technology, B.A. (1986). **Personal:** Married to Shokooh in 1986. One child: a son, Nima. Mr. Eftekhary enjoys reading, fishing, hiking, volleyball, and attending seminars.

Erik H. Engdahl

Vice President of Engineering
Ontrak Systems, Incorporated
1753 South Main Street
Milpitas, CA 95053
(408) 262–5200
Fax: (408) 262–9109

5045

Business Information: Ontrak specializes in the manufacture of chemical mechanical polishing and cleaning equipment. As Ontrak's newest executive officer, Erik Engdahl was appointed as Vice President of Engineering in November of 1995. Prior to joining Ontrak, Erik was Vice President of New Products at Thermco Systems' Orange, California plant. Thermco is a major manufacturer of diffusion and thin film furnaces and chemical reactors. He was responsible for all aspects of new product development, including the management of software, electrical, and mechanical engineering directly related to process engineering. In the process of transfering machines to the Chemical Processing Department, Mr. Engdahl utilized his leadership skills to build a world class team in just months when it takes others in his field years. **Career Steps:** Vice President of Engineering, Ontrak Systems (1995–Present); Vice President of New Products, Thermco Systems (1993–1995); Process Engineering Manager, Watkins–Johnson (1990–1993); Member of the Technical Staff, Space Power Incorporated (1987–1990); Edison Engineer, General Electric (1984–1987). **Associations & Accomplishments:** American Nuclear Society; John Grand Memorial Scholar; Youth Soccer League. **Education:** University of California – Berkeley, M.S. in Mechanical Engineering (1987); Oregon State University, B.S. in Nuclear Engineering; Graduate of General Electric's Advanced Engineering Program. **Personal:** Married to Brenda in 1983. Two children: Andrew and Brian. Mr. Engdahl enjoys water skiing, soccer and volleyball.

Gloria Espinosa

Sales/Marketing Manager
MEMOREX TELEX P.R., INC.
G.P.O. Box 71318
San Juan, Puerto Rico 00936–8418
(787) 754–7936
Fax: (787) 751–4555

5045

Business Information: MEMOREX TELEX P.R., INC. provides computer supply sales and service to Latin American distributors. As Sales/Marketing Manager, Miss Espinosa has total responsibility for the sales and marketing operations of products distributed throughout Latin America. **Career Steps:** Sales/Marketing Manager, MEMOREX TELEX PUERTO RICO, INC. (1984–Present); Traffic Manager, Radio Americas (1981–1984). **Associations & Accomplishments:** National Association for Female Executives. **Education:** International Trade, Special Course (1996); Master of Arts in Administration/Supervision; Bachelor of Arts in Social Work. **Personal:** Miss Espinosa enjoys writing, tennis, and being an expert in middle ages literature (10th to 13th century).

Thomas P. Farrell

President
Alternative Computer Technology
7908 Cin–Day Road, Suite W
West Chester, OH 45069
(513) 755–1957
Fax: (513) 755–1958

5045

Business Information: Alternative Computer Technology specializes in the resale of anti–virus software and hardware for the computer industry. The products are directly marketed through the Internet, magazines and telemarketing. Alternative Computer Technology is also involved in anti–virus materials and methods research. Established in 1990, Alternative Computer Technology currently employs 12 people. As President, Mr. Farrell is responsible for all aspects of daily operations. **Career Steps:** President, Alternative Computer Technology (1990–Present); Pioneer: Regional Manager (1986–1990), District Manager (1984–1986). **Education:** University of Florida, M.B.A. (1982); University of Ohio, B.S. in Electrical Engineering (1979). **Personal:** Married to Kimberly in 1990. Two children: Chelsea and Brady. Mr. Farrell enjoys skiing, and coaching youth baseball and basketball leagues.

Gail M. Ferrelli

National Sales Manager
Agency Management Services Inc.
82 Hopmeadow Street
Simsbury, CT 06070
(203) 658–1900 Ext. 2134
Fax: (203) 651–7402
E–mail: see below

5045

Business Information: Agency Management Services Inc. specializes in the development of software for the insurance industry. Established in 1960, Agency Management Services Inc. currently employs 1,020 people and has an estimated annual revenue of $150 million. As Vice President of National Sales, Ms. Ferrelli is responsible for the retail marketplace revenue generated by the independent agents, and the supervision of 35 people. She can also be reached through the Internet as follows: Gailcat@AOL.com **Career Steps:** Agency Management Services Inc.: Vice President of National Sales (1989–Present), Regional Sales Manager (1986–1989), Account Manager (1981–1986). **Associations & Accomplishments:** Former Director, American Water Ski Association; Numerous public speaking and seminar appearances. **Education:** Columbus College, B.A. (1972). **Personal:** Ms. Ferrelli enjoys golf and water skiing.

Sue H. Flore

Director of Sales
Director of Sales
Resource One Computer Systems
278 North 5th Street
Columbus, OH 43215–2604
(614) 241–5800
Fax: (614) 241–5810

5045

Business Information: Resource One Computer Systems is a reseller of computer hardware and software solutions, providing products, installation, maintenance, and computer service for corporate customers. Major brands include IBM, Packard, etc. With headquarters in Columbus, Ohio, Resource One Computer Systems has two locations in Ohio (Cincinnati, Columbus) and two in California. Joining Resource One Computer Systems as Director of Sales in 1996, Mrs. Flore is responsible for the direction of all sales activities, including vender relations, distribution, assisting the Marketing Department, product promotions, oversight of technical staff, and watching out for emerging technology. **Career Steps:** Resource One Computer Systems: Director of Sales (1996–Present), Technical Acquisition Center Director (1994–1996); Regional Account Manager, Micro Age Computer Centers (1992–1994); Account Manager, Micro Resources (1990–1992). **Associations & Accomplishments:** Eastland Career Center Advisory Council; School To Work Program; Ohio University Organizational Communications Mentor Program. **Education:** Ohio University, B.S. in Communications (1979). **Personal:** Married to Richard in 1991. Mrs. Flore enjoys tennis, golf, soccer, volleyball and travel.

Graham P. Fossey

Director of Field Operations
The Bradshaw Group
715 North Glenville, Suite 450
Richardson, TX 75081
(214) 644–7558
Fax: (214) 644–2534

5045

Business Information: The Bradshaw Group is a marketer and servicer of laser printers. Established in 1989, The Bradshaw Group reports annual revenue of $8 million and currently employs 36 people. With twenty years in service business, Mr. Fossey joined The Bradshaw Group in 1992. Serving as Director of Field Operations, he is responsible for the management of national services and parts, as well as training and technical support. **Career Steps:** Director of Field Operations, The Bradshaw Group (1993–Present); National Training Manager, Automatic Data Processing (1986–1992); Technical Support Manager, McDonnell Douglas (1983–1986); Service Manager, T.A.S.K. Kuwait (1977–1983). **Associations & Accomplishments:** Association of Field Service Managers; International American Management Association; Board of Directors, Local Community Service Organization. **Education:** Royal Air Force – U.K., B.S.C. (1969). **Personal:** Mr. Fossey enjoys models and computers.

Walter N. Garvey

Vice President of Operations and Logistics
GBC Technologies, Inc.
100 GBC Court
Berlin, NJ 08009–2424
(215) 487–2873
Fax: (609) 216–1156

5045

Business Information: GBC Technologies, Inc. is a high–end computer distributor and networks products and technical support. As Vice President of Operations and Logistics, Mr. Garvey is responsible for many aspects of Company operations, including administration, customer service, facility, human resources, inventory control, logistics/distribution, return merchandise operation, security, traffic, and warehousing. In his current capacity, Mr. Garvey has decreased on–hand carrying return merchandise inventory from $2 million to $300 thousand, reduced SGA by .003% saving the Company $500 thousand in 6 months, and numerous other accomplishments that saved the Company excess time and money. **Career Steps:** Vice President of Operations and Logistics, GBC Technologies, Inc. (1994–Present); General Manager, Power Logistics/Kraft (1992–1994); Vice President of Operations and Service, Silo, Inc.; Director of Operations, A. Pomerantz Company. **Associations & Accomplishments:** American Society for Quality Control; American Production and Inventory Control Society; Council of Logistics Management; Association for Quality and Participation; Warehouse Educational Research Council; International Association of Refrigerated Warehouses. **Education:** Saint Francis (1966). **Personal:** Married to Andrea in 1979. Two children: Lauren and Deanna. Mr. Garvey enjoys singing, baseball, hockey, public speaking, and working and supporting the Boy's and Girl's Club of America.

Kent Gaskill
District Manager
Inacom Info Systems
8601 Dunwoody Place, Suite 538
Atlanta, GA 30350–2500
(770) 643–2472
Fax: (770) 993–6375

5045

Business Information: Inacom Info Systems is a marketer of personal computers and related services to corporate accounts. Established in 1982, Inacom Info Systems report annual revenue of $2.2 billion and currently employs 1,800 people. As District Manager, Mr. Gaskill is responsible for all aspects of operations, including sales, engineering, maintenance and training services. **Career Steps:** District Manager, Inacom Info Systems (1992–Present). **Education:** Indiana University, B.A. (1981). **Personal:** Mr. Gaskill enjoys weightlifting, reading, and tennis.

Mark Gerhard
Sales Manager
Ascent Solutions, Inc. PkZip Compression Software
9009 Springboro Pike
Miamisburg, OH 45342–4834
(513) 847–2374
Fax: (513) 847–2375
EMAIL: See Below

5045

Business Information: Ascent Solutions Pk Zip Compression Software is a supplier of computer software to businesses and the public. The Company was established in 1988 and currently employs over 40 people. As Sales Manager, Mr. Gerhard oversees the North American sales force, manages existing customer accounts, and develops new accounts. He is involved in developing new marketing and sales techniques and customer service programs, and educational programs for staff and clients. Internet users may contact him via: mark@asizip.com. **Career Steps:** Sales Manager, Ascent Solutions PkZip Compression Software (1995–Present); Regional Sales Manager, Medair (1992–1995); National Sales Manager, A.L. Williams (1987–1992); Network Sales, TMC (1984–1987). **Associations & Accomplishments:** American Data Processing Association; American Defense Preparedness Association. **Education:** Kettering College of Medical Arts, Science (1992); Sinclair College (1980–1984). **Personal:** Spouse: Linda. Six children: Andrea, Tiffany, Alex, Katie, Zach, and Ryan. Mr. Gerhard enjoys his family, skiing, boating, theater, travel, building, racing, and diving.

Jack H. Hammell
Vice President and Chief Financial Officer
Elite Computer Services Inc.
1248 Sussex Turnpike, Suite B–12
Randolph, NJ 07869–2908
(201) 895–5008
Fax: (201) 895–5262

5045

Business Information: Elite Computer Services Inc. specializes in the sale of used IBM parts for maintenance, marketing to computer remanufacturers throughout the U.S. and Canada. The Company follows through with requests — returns calls even though the parts may not be available — and provides the best parts at fair prices and excellent service. Established in 1988, Elite Computer Services Inc. currently employs 9 people and has an estimated annual revenue of $2 million. Establishing the company with his son–in–law, Mr. Hammell serves as Vice President and Chief Financial Officer, responsible for all aspects of financial operations, as well as equipment analysis, procurement and stock management. **Career Steps:** Vice President and Chief Financial Officer, Elite Computer Services Inc. (1988–Present); Controller, Contract Packaging Corporation (1983–1988); Vice President, Hollander & Company (1978–1983); Treasurer, The Highton Company (1970–1978). **Associations & Accomplishments:** Treasurer of Local Chapter, Holiday Rambler Recreational Vehicle Club; America Model Association; New Jersey Business and Industry Association; Family Motor Coach Association; Make–A–Wish Foundation. **Education:** Rutgers University (1956–1957). **Personal:** Married to Harriet R. in 1956. Three children: Katherine DiGiacomo, Thomas Hammell, and Carol Kagdis. Mr. Hammell enjoys camping, magic, and radio–controlled model planes and boats.

Miss Zanifer Hosein
President
PC Elite Software Services Inc.
300 North Queen Street, Suite 106
Etobicoke, Ontario M9C 5K4
(416) 626–6764
Fax: (416) 626–7016

5045

Business Information: PC Elite Software Services Inc. specializes in the provision of software design and development, computer applications and training to private individuals, small business concerns and corporate companies throughout Ontario. As President, Miss Hosein oversees all aspects of business operations, including administrative, accounting, business planning and software development. She has specialized in database application design and development. Throughout her career, Miss Hosein has gained respect and admiration for her business and interpersonal skills. Established in 1985, PC Elite Software Services Inc. employs 20 computer training, consulting and administrative support staff. Annual sales for fiscal year 1994 were reported in excess of $1 million. **Career Steps:** President, PC Elite Software Services Inc. (1986–Present); EDI Specialist, Canadian General Electric Corporation (1985–1986); Applications Specialist, CGE (1982–1985). **Associations & Accomplishments:** Treasurer and Director, Toronto Chapter of Local Area Network Dealers Association; Treasurer, Trinidad and Tobago – Canada Chamber of Commerce. **Education:** University of Waterloo, B.Math (1982).

George (Rick) Hutchinson
President
Banklink Inc.
349 5th Avenue, 5th Floor
New York, NY 10016–5009
(212) 696–3131
Fax: (212) 532–2886

5045

Business Information: Banklink Inc. specializes in the development and distribution of financial software, electronic commerce products, and service bureau support for use by financial institutions. Established in 1978, Banklink Inc. currently employs 70 people. As President, Mr. Hutchinson is responsible for all aspects of operations. **Career Steps:** President, Banklink Inc. (1994–Present); Vice President, Chemical Bank (1991–1994); Vice President, Bankers Trust (1985–1991); Associate, Morgan Guaranty Trust (1984–1985). **Associations & Accomplishments:** Treasury Management Association; University of California – Berkeley Alumni Association. **Education:** Columbia University, M.B.A. (1984); University of California – Berkeley: B.A. in Journalism (1980), B.A. in Economics (1979). **Personal:** Married to Carolyn G. in 1993. One child: Maya.

Ms. Kathryn J. Lamon
Vice President
Proactive, Inc.
Two Concourse Parkway, Suite 650
Atlanta, GA 30328–5371
(770) 804–5680
Fax: (770) 804–5687

5045

Business Information: Proactive, Inc. located in Atlanta, Georgia is a supplier of computer software for compliance monitoring. The software is PC–based and is targeted to banks and thrift institutions. As Vice President, Ms. Lamon handles the training, installation, and support groups for Proactive, Inc. She periodically reviews the software for regulatory changes and updates as needed. Ms. Lamon works with other management personnel to develop a workable Corporate budget and monitors Corporate expenditures. She is involved with personnel concerns, financial responsibilities, public relations, and expansion plans. **Career Steps:** Vice President, Proactive, Inc. (1993–Present); Senior Analyst, Unisys Corporation (1985–1993); Product Coordinator, Decatur Federal S & L (1981–1985). **Associations & Accomplishments:** Toastmasters; Childrens Ministries at Redan UMC. **Education:** Mercer University – Atlanta, B.S. (1986). **Personal:** Married to Franklin in 1981. Two children: Ryan and Morgan. Ms. Lamon enjoys reading, horseback riding, and spending time with the family.

Ronald A. (Ron) Layton
President and Chief Operating Officer
International Telecomp Associates, Inc.
12523 Browns Ferry Road, Lower Level Suite 1
Herndon, VA 22070–5711
(703) 421–1433 (800) 229–2476
Fax: (703) 421–1434
EMAIL: See Below

5045

Business Information: International Telecomp Associates, Inc. is a global, total–spectrum, one–stop shopping company with worldwide exports of telecommunications and computing equipment and services. Products include offerings from underwater–based and maritime surface systems to the array of terrestrial–based and satellite–based telecommunications and computing capabilities. Founding International Telecomp Associates, Inc. in 1995, Mr. Layton and his wife hold 80% of Company stock, with 100% voting rights within the Company (employees own the other 20% stock). As President and Chief Operating Officer, he provides the overall leadership and management direction for a staff of 27, as well as the vision and strategies to keep the Company a viable presence in the ever-changing global telecommunications market. He can also be reached through the Internet via: ron@layton.com **Career Steps:** President and Chief Operating Officer, International Telecomp Associates, Inc. (1995–Present); GTE Spacenet Corp.: Director of International Programs (1993–1995), Senior Program Manager II (1992–1993); Colonel (Retired), U.S. Air Force (1970–1992). **Associations & Accomplishments:** Served as White House Special Assistant to then – Vice President George Bush (June 1985–January 1989) and White House Senior Policy Analyst (January–June 1989); International Chamber of Commerce; Inductee, USAF Air Weapons Controller Hall of Fame (1988). **Education:** West Virginia University: M.S. in Land Economics (1970), B.S. in Agricultural and Biological Sciences (1967); Air War College, M.S. equivalent (1990). **Personal:** Married to Vonda Sue in 1966. Two children: Rhonda and Mark. Mr. Layton is an avid fisherman.

Mr. Jean Luc le Brigand
President and Directeur General
Assistance Informatique Systeme
24 Bis Rue Monteil
Nantes, France 44000
33–51729010
Fax: 33–51729011

5045

Business Information: Assistance Informatique Systems is a computer systems development and integration, and systems network service company. Established in 1985 by two friends, Jean Luc le Brigand and Bruno Waconge, the company is the result of two great minds who shared the same belief that microcomputers are a unique and universal work tool. The two decided to leave their positions with Aerospatiale and go into business for themselves. The result was immediate success as the Company was able to market their systems to some of the largest French corporations such as Elf Antar France, EDF GDF, Alstrom ARB, La Poste, France Telecom, Le Minisiere De L'Economie and their ex–employer, Aerospatiale. AIS has expanded to include 6 independent locations and currently employs 15 people. The Company reports an annual revenue of $7 million. As President and Directeur General, Mr. le Brigand provides the overall vision and operational strategies for the continued development and viability of the Company as a whole. **Career Steps:** President and General Director, Assistance Informatique Systems (1985–Present); Specialiste Mesures Physiques, Aerospatiale (1979–1985). **Associations & Accomplishments:** ASBR (volleyball), Vice President (1980–1985); Ardent Supporter of Foot–ball Club Nantes Atlantique (FCNA). **Education:** I.U.T St. Nazaire, D.U.T Mesure Physique (1978). **Personal:** Married to Catherine in 1978. One child: Jonathan. Mr. le Brigand enjoys boating, travel, volleyball, tennis and squash.

Amy S. Lin
Director of Corporate Accounting
CMD Technology, Inc.
1 Vanderbilt
Irvine, CA 92718–2011
(714) 470–3139
Fax: (714) 470–3119

5045

Business Information: CMD Technology, Inc. is a manufacturer and wholesaler of computer products, primarily consisting of adapters. CMD Technology operates two regional offices in Irvine and one sales office in Boston, consisting of three divisions: DEC, RAID, and PC Disk Controllers. As Director of Corporate Accounting, Ms. Lin is responsible for all financial and accounting functions, including cash management and projections, in addition to overseeing and managing a corporate accounting staff of 10. **Career Steps:** Director of Corporate Accounting, CMD Technology, Inc. (1990–Present); Senior Accountant, Stylus Furniture (1988–1990); Accountant, Portola Venutres (1986–1988). **Education:** Emporia State University – Kansas, M.B.A. (1983). **Personal:** Ms. Lin enjoys sports, picnics and barbeques.

ELITE INFORMATION SYSTEMS
A BROADWAY & SEYMOUR COMPANY

Monty Lunn
Vice President
Elite Information Systems, Inc.
10336 Wilshire Boulevard
Los Angeles, CA 90024–4730
(310) 398–4900
Fax: (310) 398–4966
EMAIL: See Below

5045

Business Information: Established in 1947, Elite Information Systems, Inc. specializes in providing computer software for major law firms and corporate law departments. As Vice President, Mr. Lunn is responsible for the oversight of corporate marketing, as well as channel strategies and revenue expansion initiatives. He can also be reached through the Internet via: mlunn@elite.com **Career Steps:** Vice President, Elite Information Systems, Inc. (1994–Present); Regional Manager, CMS Data Corporation (1990–1994); Regional Sales Manager, CSS, Inc. (1987–1990); Senior Account Manager, Wang Labs, Inc. (1983–1987). **Associations & Accomplishments:** American Marketing Association; Toastmasters International; Young Leadership Council: Founder, Board of Directors (1986–1988); Who's Who in American Schools (1974); Metropolitan Area Committee New Orleans (1990); Council for Fiscal Reform (1989); National Merit Scholar. **Education:** Attended: Southeastern Louisiana University and University of Southwestern Louisiana. **Personal:** Married to Kathleen in 1987. Two children: Margaret and Jane. Mr. Lunn enjoys rugby, tennis, golf, and skiing.

Jacquelyn R. Lyons
Vice President of Product Development
The Leverage Group
68 National Drive
Glastonbury, CT 06033
(800) 892–3334
Fax: (860) 633–6106

5045

Business Information: The Leverage Group is an insurance software vendor. With eighteen years experience in computer science, Ms. Lyons joined The Leverage Group as Vice President of Product Development in 1994. She is responsible for development of new software products and enhancement of existing ones. **Career Steps:** Vice President of Product Development, The Leverage Group (1994–Present); Director, Computer Sciences Corporation (1984–1994); Senior Programmer Analyst, Vantage Computer Systems (1983–1984); Applications Manager, Bank One (1981–1983). **Associations & Accomplishments:** Association of Proposal Management Professional. **Education:** University of Dayton, B.S. in Computer Science (1977). **Personal:** Married to Christopher in 1971. One child: Bradley.

Shirish Nadkarni
President
Horizon Computers, Inc.
5 Lincoln Highway
Edison, NJ 08820–3964
(908) 603–0004
Fax: (908) 603–0066
EMAIL: See below

5045

Business Information: Horizon Computers, Inc. specializes in the development of computer software, as well as providing computer consulting services. Established in 1989, Horizon Computers currently employs 60 people and has an estimated annual revenue of $3 million. As President, Mr. Nadkarni is responsible for all aspects of operations, including business planning, marketing, business expansion and strategic and financial planning. Originally from India, Mr. Nadkarni has expanded his business to include some partnerships in his home country. He can also be reached through the Internet via: srn@horizoncomp.com **Career Steps:** President, Horizon Computers, Inc. (1989–Present). **Associations & Accomplishments:** Association of Indian Computer Professionals. **Education:** New York University – Stern Business School, M.B.A. (1992); New Jersey Institute of Technology, M.S. in Computer and Information Sciences; Indian Institute of Technology – Bombay, B. Tech. in Chemical Engineering. **Personal:** Married to Nutan S. in 1988. One child: Neel. Mr. Nadkarni enjoys music, painting and spending time with his family.

Elias Obadia Benzadon
Sales and Marketing Director
Microsoft Venezuela
P.O. Box 25255
Miami, FL 33102–5255
58–14–217034
Fax: 58–2–2855971
EMAIL: See Below

5045

Business Information: A subsidiary of Microsoft Corporation, Microsoft Venezuela develops and sells computer software to distributors and wholesalers worldwide. The new strategic product of Microsoft is Internet Microsoft, selling internationally at this time. Responsible for the large accounts of Microsoft in Venezuela, Elias Obadia Benzadon is Director of Sales and Marketing, initiating business in Columbia, Peru, Ecuador and the Carribean. Internet users can reach him via: 73000.411@compuserve.com. **Career Steps:** Sales and Marketing Director, Microsoft Venezuela (1991–Present); General Manager, Deloit & Touch I.S. Division Venezuela (1989–1991); General Manager, Way Computer Systems (1986–1989); Computer Science Professor, Simon Bolivar University. **Associations & Accomplishments:** Who's Who in Finance & Industry (1995). **Education:** Harvard Business School, Executive Program (1994); Simon Bolivar University, Science Magister in Computer Engineering. **Personal:** Married to Flora Serruya in 1991. One child: Menahem. Mr. Obadia Benzadon enjoys reading, computers, and spending time with his family.

Mr. Rick Orford
President
Microrom Computers
17 Du Mans Road
Blainville, Quebec J7C 4X8
(514) 434–0557
Fax: (514) 434–0557

5045

Business Information: Microrom Computers is a computer center generating the majority of its business from brokering memory and hard drives. They also provide custom computer design and peripherals; and also serve international markets. Mr. Orford is an extremely gifted 17–year–old, and probably the youngest President of a company in Canada. President of Microrom Computers, and the owner of two other companies, he oversees management of all company operations, concentrating on purchasing and strategic planning. Established in 1991, Microrom Computers reports a projected end revenue in 1996 of $50 million. **Career Steps:** President, Microrom Computers (1991–Present). **Education:** ICS, A.A. in Computer Science (1992), and courses in Business Administration. **Personal:** Mr. Orford enjoys swimming, aquatic sports, and spending time with his family.

Mr. Kevin Panhkham
Managing Director
Krystal KPC
24 Place Carnot
Rosny Sous Bois, France 93110
33–48947462
Fax: 33–48947457

5045

Business Information: Krystal KPC is an importer and exporter of computers and hardware and a distributor of memory components to the U.S., Europe, Bulgaria and North Africa. Additionally, Krystal provides consulting services to financial institutions, such as La Carjse d'epansne, France. Krystal KPC currently employs eight people. As Founder and Managing Director, Mr. Panhkham is responsible for all aspects of operations, including administration, finances, strategic planning, purchasing and public relations. His career steps include serving as a Comissaire and Director of Finance. **Career Steps:** Managing Director, Krystal KPC (1994–Present). **Associations & Accomplishments:** L'association des Sheiens Commissaires de L'armee. **Education:** Attended L'ecole de Commerce. **Personal:** Mr. Panhkham enjoys reading.

Graham B. Paterson
Vice President of Sales and Marketing
Computer Corporation of America
500 Old Connecticut Path
Framingham, MA 01701
(508) 270–6666
Fax: Please mail or call

5045

Business Information: Computer Corporation of America, a completely employee–owned Company, specializes in supplying large scale databases (software) to Fortune 1000 companies. As Vice President of Sales and Marketing, Mr. Paterson is responsible for sales, marketing, and consulting. He is also involved in customer relations and satisfaction, as well as strategic planning. **Career Steps:** Vice President of Sales and Marketing, Computer Corporation of America (1985–Present); General Manager, Tesdata (1981–1985); Sales Manager, ICL (1967–1981). **Associations & Accomplishments:** Institute of Directors. **Education:** University of York – UK, B.A. (honors) in Mathematics and Economics (1967). **Personal:** Married to Kath in 1971. Two children: Claire and Mark. Mr. Paterson enjoys bridge, skiing, and is a board member of a charity organization.

Mr. Steve K. Peng
Vice President
PC Express, Inc.
820 South Garfield Avenue, Suite 201
Alhambra, CA 91801
(818) 293–1661
Fax: (818) 293–1665

5045

Business Information: PC Express, Inc. is a major international multi–lingual software developer, specializing in developing Windows environments in Chinese, Japanese, Korean, and other languages. Its main product, TwinBridge Multi–Lingual System for Windows is the market leader in the Asian language computing market. Global in scope, PC Express' headquarters are located in the United States, with branch offices in China and Taiwan, and many distributorships throughout the world, including Japan, Hong Kong, Singapore, Canada, Australia, etc. As Vice President, Mr. Peng is responsible for all internal information systems and executive management, as well as database systems and marketing strategies. Established in 1989, PC Express, Inc. employs 25 people in the Alhambra office and reports corporate revenues in excess of $2 million. **Career Steps:** Vice President, PC Express, Inc. (1992–Present); Vice President, TrendWave Int. Corporation (1990–1991); Division Manager, Richfield Data Services, Inc. (1989–1990); Manager, InterWorld Corporation (1989). **Associations & Accomplishments:** Member, Software Publishers Association; Member, Institute of Electrical and Electronic Engineers. **Education:** University of Southern California, M.S. (1989); University of California–Berkeley, B.S. (1988).

Giselle G. Pickard
Chief Executive Officer
SBS Corporation
2084 Valleydale Road
Birmingham, AL 35244
(205) 444–1800
Fax: (205) 444–1805

5045

Business Information: SBS Corporation specializes in the development and sale of computer software, including complementary hardware particularly utilized in community banking environments. Established in 1989, SBS currently employs 369 people. As Chief Executive Officer, Mrs. Pickard is responsible for all aspects of operations, including administration, purchasing, accounting and personnel. **Career Steps:** Chief Executive Officer, SBS Corporation (1994–Present); University of Alabama at Birmingham: Director (1993–1994), Program Manager (1989–1993); Internal Auditor, Eastern Health System, Inc. (1987–1989). **Associations & Accomplishments:** Board of Directors, Birmingham Venture Club (1993–1995); Female Executive, March of Dimes (1990–1993); Alabama Society of Certified Public Accountants; Our Lady of Sorrows Catholic Church: Parish Council Secretary, Co–Chair of Young Adult Choir, Performed with Choir before the Pope in Rome; Frequent speaker at public relations and small business conferences. **Education:** University of Alabama – Birmingham: M.B.A. (1991); B.S. in Accounting (1984). **Personal:** Married to William P. in 1991. Mrs. Pickard enjoys travel, gardening, singing, speaking and studying French.

Paul H. Pincus

Chief Financial Officer, Secretary and Treasurer
Smith Renaud, Inc.
19 West 21st Street, Suite 1101
New York, NY 10010
(212) 645–6542
Fax: (212) 691–2157
E–mail: see below

5045

Business Information: Smith Renaud, Inc. specializes in the technological advancement and design of Internet software utilizing the Java language. Established in 1995, Smith Renaud, Inc. currently employs 6 people. As Chief Financial Officer, Secretary and Treasurer, Mr. Pincus is responsible for all aspects of business and financial operations. He can also be reached through the Internet as follows: php@market-place.net **Career Steps:** Chief Financial Officer, Secretary and Treasurer, Smith Renaud, Inc. (1995–Present); Bilbao Project Associate, Solomon R. Guggenheim Museum (1995–Present); Senior Finance Analyst, Solomon R. Guggenheim Foundation (1990–1995); Assistant Vice President of Marketing, Black and White International (1989–1990). **Associations & Accomplishments:** Committee of Museum Administration and Finance, American Association of Museums; Vice President of the Board of Directors, Waverly Mews Corporation. **Education:** Columbia University, B.S. (1989). **Personal:** Mr. Pincus enjoys hiking in the wilderness, sailing and the Arts.

Laura L. Rodemann
Director of Customer Services
Magnetic Data Inc.
6754 Shady Oak Road
Eden Prairie, MN 55344
(612) 942–4525
Fax: (612) 941–3248

5045

Business Information: Magnetic Data Inc. is a computer peripheral repair and logistics company, including the repair of drives, boards, AS400, laptops, portables and printers. Established in 1982, Magnetic Data Inc. currently employs 175 people. As Director of Customer Services, Ms. Rodemann is responsible for all aspects of customer service, accounting, logistics, receiving, shipping and inventory. **Career Steps:** Director of Customer Services, Magnetic Data Inc. (Present); Sales Manager, Comdata; Sales Manager, Empak. **Associations & Accomplishments:** American Cancer Center; Some internal publications. **Education:** University of Minnesota, B.A. (1982). **Personal:** Ms. Rodemann enjoys boating, coaching T–ball and soccer, and being a Hockey Mom.

J. Scott Runner
Director of ASIC Cores
Synopsys – Logic Modeling, Inc.
1550 NW Gibbs Drive
Beaverton, OR 97006
(503) 690–6900
Fax: (503) 690–6906
E–mail: see below

5045

Business Information: Synopsys – Logic Modeling, Inc. specializes in CAE software and logic device modeling development, distribution and support. Established in 1985, Synopsys – Logic Modeling currently employs 1,600 people and has an estimated annual revenue of $270 million. As Director of ASIC Cores, Mr. Runner utilizes his skills in engineering management, technical market understanding, ASIC design, applications engineering and CAE. He is also the Project Manager of a start–up team whose focus is on the tools development and modeling for embedded systems. Mr. Runner can also be reached through the Internet as follows: srunner@synopsys.com **Career Steps:** Synopsys – Logic Modeling, Inc.: Director of ASIC Cores (1995–Present), Manager of Designware Research and Development (1992–1995); Fujitsu Microelectronics, Inc.: Manager of ASIC Design Centers (1991–1992), Manager of ASIC Applications Engineering (1989–1991), Engineer (1987–1989), Field Applications Engineer and Design Center Engineer (1984–1987); Hardware and Software Systems Developer, Georgia Institute of Technology (1981–1984). **Associations & Accomplishments:** Institute of Electronics and Electrical Engineers; Chairman, Test and Reliabilty, CICC; Co–Chairman, Core Processors, ASIC Seminar; Who's Who in the West; Who's Who in American High School Students; Published numerous articles. **Education:** Georgia Institute of Technology, B.S. in Applied Physics (1984). **Personal:** Married to Athena Ellen McGinn. One child: Aiden Scott McGinn Runner. Mr. Runner enjoys distance running and writing.

Enrique Sanchez
Personnel Manager
Future Tech International
7630 North West 25th Street
Miami, FL 33122–1705
(305) 392–7366 (305) 567–0057
Fax: (305) 715–7166

5045

Business Information: Future Tech International is a multi–million dollar distributor of computer hardware components, peripherals, and systems to Latin America. The Company was recently voted into the Inc. 500. As Personnel Manager, Mr. Sanchez is responsible for recruitment, compensation, benefits, and employee relations. **Career Steps:** Personnel Manager, Future Tech International (1992–Present); Compensation & Benefits Manager, Pan American Hospital (1989–1991); Personnel Manager, Sheffield Industries (1983–1985). **Associations & Accomplishments:** Past Member; Personnel Association of Greater Miami; University of Miami Civic Chorale; South Florida's Composer's Alliance; Florida Grand Opera; Florida Philharmonic. **Education:** St. Thomas University, M.S.M. (1983); Florida International University, B.B.A. in Management (1979). **Personal:** Mr. Sanchez enjoys being a composer, singing opera, and playing the piano and violin. Mr. Sanchez studied music composition with Salil Sachdev and voice with Virginia Alonso.

Yuda Saydun

Vice President & General Manager
Tech Data Corporation
8501 Northwest 17th Street
Miami, FL 33126–1000
(305) 718–3210
Fax: (305) 599–8488

5045

Business Information: Tech Data Corporation is an international wholesale distributor of computer hardware, software, networking, and telecommunication products. As Vice President & General Manager, Mr. Saydun is in charge of the Latin American operations of the corporation. He is in charge of new business growth and development for this area. Mr. Saydun oversees marketing of products and services, public relations, some financial aspects, and continual growth plans for Latin America. **Career Steps:** Vice President & General Manager, Tech Data Corporation (1993–Present); American Express: DVP, Cardmember Marketing (1992–1993), RVP, Consumer Financial Services (1990–1992), VP Marketing Sales & Strat Planning (1988–1990). **Education:** University of California – Los Angeles, M.B.A. (1982); Universite Libre de Bruxelles, B.S. in International Relations (1975). **Personal:** One child: Sarah Marie. Mr. Saydun enjoys sailing and photography.

Youssif H. Shanshiry
President
International Computer Services
208 Pleasant Street
Watertown, MA 02172–2321
(617) 923–1707
Fax: (617) 923–4720
EMAIL: See Below

5045

Business Information: International Computer Services specializes in the export and marketing of computer products to Europe and the Middle East. As President, Mr. Shanshiry is responsible for all aspects of Company operations, including marketing, purchasing, and shipment of all products that are sold. Internet users can reach him via: YhShanshiry@msn.com. **Career Steps:** President, International Computer Services (1985–Present); Senior Vice President of International Sales, Business Computing International (1982–1984); Principal Planner/Analyst, Massachusetts Department of Education (1981). **Education:** Boston University: M.A. in Math (1978), Ph.D. Candidate; Suffolk University, B.S. in Math; Post Graduate Work in Computer Science: Salem State University, Lowel State College. **Personal:** Married to Janet in 1973. Two children: Rabih Y. and Yasmine Y. Mr. Shanshiry enjoys chess, music, swimming, and surfing the Internet.

Mr. Josh Spranger

Vice President of Technical Services
Innovation Computers
1240 East Newport Center Drive
Deerfield Beach, FL 33442
(305) 345–3750
Fax: (305) 422–9608

5045

Business Information: Innovation Computers is a computer reseller, network integrator and consulting firm. Established in 1988, Innovation Computers reports annual sales of $60 million and currently employs 65 people. As Vice President of Technical Services, Mr. Spranger is responsible for the oversight of all aspects of the technical services department, including installations, networking, consultations, and supervision of 22 people. **Career Steps:** Vice President of Technical Services, Innovation Computers (1992–Present); Owner, Software City Service (1990–1992); Director of Networking, QBE Information Systems (1982–1990); Service Manager, A–1 Business Systems (1979–1982). **Education:** University of Nevada – Las Vegas, B.S. in Computer Science (1978); Novell ECNE, Compaq ASE. **Personal:** Mr. Spranger enjoys horseback riding, boating, and camping.

Mr. John C. Tsai
General Manager
U.S. Sertek, Inc.
926 Thompson Place
Sunnyvale, CA 94086
(408) 733–3174
Fax: (408) 733–2569

5045

Business Information: U.S. Sertek, Inc. specializes in the import and export of electronic and computer related products (manufacturing, design and retail worldwide). As General Manager, Mr. Tsai is responsible for all aspects of administrative operations for the Company. **Career Steps:** General Manager, U.S. Sertek, Inc. (1985–Present); General Manager, Hi–Sun International (1980–1985); Manager, Linmark International (1969–1980). **Associations & Accomplishments:** Vice President of Civic Chinese School in San Jose, CA. **Education:** Chinese University, Business Department, B.S. (1968). **Personal:** Married to Catherine P. Tsai in 1971. Two children: Jackson and Michael Tsai.

Mr. Terry Turner
Vice President of Global Sales Operations
Dun & Bradstreet Software
3445 Peachtree Road, N.E.
Atlanta, GA 30326–1276
(404) 239–4407
Fax: (404) 239–3107

5045

Business Information: Dun & Bradstreet Software, a division of the Dun & Bradstreet Corporation, is a worldwide distributor of host–based business applications software solutions (accounts payable, accounts receivable, etc.). Products are geared toward the Fortune 5000 companies. In his capacity as Vice President of Global Sales Operations, Mr. Turner is in charge of global sales and operations. Responsibilities include sales force training and development; product development; sales methodology and automation; policies and procedures; motivation. He also manages corporate accounts, partnerships, and alliances. Established in 1971, Dun & Bradstreet Software employs a staff of over 2400 and reports revenues in excess of $450 million. **Career Steps:** Vice President of Global Sales Operations, Dun & Bradstreet Software (1993–Present); National Sales Manager, Dun & Bradstreet Software (1989–1993); Regional Sales Manager, Qronos Technology (1988–1989); District Sales Manager, Xerox Computer Services (1985–1988). **Education:** Pepperdine University, B.S. in Management (1981).

S. Vasu

President
Koni Ameritech Services
5105 Peachtree Industrial Boulevard
Atlanta, GA 30341
(404) 458–0467
Fax: (404) 455–9634
E–mail: see below

5045

Business Information: Koni Ameritech Services specializes in the development of fixed–price custom software, and time–material consulting for software development maintenance. Established in 1993, Koni Ameritech Services currently employs 16 people and has an estimated annual revenue of $1.7 million. As President, Mr. Vasu is responsible for all aspects of operations, including new client relations. Concurrent to his position with Koni Ameritech Services, Mr. Vasu is involved in two additional companies: Apollo Health Systems, a software development company, and Sky Services, an import and export company. **Career Steps:** President, Koni Ameritech Services (1993–Present); Account Manager, Fourth Technologics (1990–1993). **Associations & Accomplishments:** Local Chamber of Commerce; Institute of Electrical and Electronics Engineers. **Education:** M.S. in Electronics (1994); Pursuing M.B.A., to be completed in 1996. **Personal:** Married to Vijana Vasudevan.

Bruce A. Wood

Assistant Controller
Dallastone Inc.
2 Cote Lane, Unit
Bedford, NH 03110–5842
(603) 647–8168
Fax: (603) 624–2466

5045

Business Information: Dallastone Inc. specializes in the development of computer software and hardware backup systems for major corporations including AT&T and Boeing. Established in 1984, Dallastone Inc. currently employs 14 people and has an estimated annual revenue of $3 million. As Assistant Controller, Mr. Wood is responsible for all aspects of accounts receivable and payable, payroll, financial statements, purchasing, and month–end and year–end reports. **Career Steps:** Assistant Controller, Dallastone Inc. (1992–Present); Assistant Controller, Atom Contracting (1991–1992); Cost Accountant, Harvey Construction Company (1980–1991). **Associations & Accomplishments:** Advisor, Catholic Youth Organization. **Education:** Hesser College, A.S. (1980); New Hampshire Vocational Technical College, A.S. in Heating, Air Conditioning and Refrigeration. **Personal:** Married to Diane in 1973. Two children: Jason and Tiffany. Mr. Wood enjoys water skiing, snow skiing and camping.

Arend Zweekhorst

President
SQL Systems Inc.
6442 City West Parkway, Suite 400
Eden Prairie, MN 55344–7718
(612) 943–7270
Fax: (612) 943–7312

5045

Business Information: SQL Systems Inc. is a software manufacturer and service company providing asset and maintenance management. A subsidiary of Global, SQL Systems Inc. was established in 1985. Currently the two Companies employ 235 people and have an estimated annual revenue of $36 million. As President, Mr. Zweekhorst is responsible for all aspects of operations for SQL Systems North America. **Career Steps:** President, SQL Systems Inc. (1993–Present); SQL Systems BV: Senior Business Consultant (1991–1993), Sales Manager (1989–1990); Branch Manager, Engineering, Tecona (1980–1989). **Education:** College in the Netherlands, B.S. in Chemistry (1971); Institute of Social Sciences – The Hague, General Management. **Personal:** Married to Claudia Hasper in 1980. Three children: Augusta, Salome and

Bojoura. Mr. Zweekhorst enjoys golf, tennis, and collecting stamps.

Mr. Greg Londot

Director of Administration
Audio Visual America
237 South 23rd Street
Phoenix, AZ 85034–2503
(602) 275–6060
Fax: (602) 275–6696
EMAIL: See below

5046

Business Information: International in scope, Audio Visual America is an audio visual production company providing a full line of audio visual rentals, from data production to full–stage concert systems. The Company supplies lighting and staging for industrial trade shows, and provides installation of the hard equipment such as the video projectors. Established in 1969, Audio Visual America currently employs 160 people and has an estimated annual revenue of $5.5 million. As Director of Administration, Mr. Londot is responsible for all aspects of budgets and projections, internal audits, employee recruiting and training, inventory control, and all warehouse operations including shipping, receiving, transportation and quality control. Mr. Londot can also be reached through the Internet as follows: GregLl219@aol.com. **Career Steps:** Director of Administration, Audio Visual America (1992–Present); Manager of Production, Paulson & Company (1990–1992); Audio Visual Manager, The Pointe Resorts, Inc. (1987–1990). **Associations & Accomplishments:** American Diabetes Association, Arizona Chapter; Member of various support groups for diabetes. **Education:** Brooks Institute, B.A. (1986); Southern California College, Psychology and Education. **Personal:** Married to Donna in 1979. Two children: Nicole LaSandra and Zachary Tyler. Mr. Londot enjoys photography, reading Science Fiction and Star Trek.

Jeff Anderson

Territory Manager
Allied Healthcare
5306 Carolwood Drive
Greensboro, NC 27407
(910) 632–0230
Fax: (910) 632–0230

5047

Business Information: Allied Healthcare markets medical gas equipment, disposables, and respiratory equipment to dealers who, in turn, sell to hospitals and other health care providers. As Territory Manager, Mr. Anderson is responsible for coordinating dealer sales activities, including training, motivating, and organizing business functions for five specialty dealers. **Career Steps:** Territory Manager, Allied Healthcare (Present); District Manager, National Revenue Corporation (1991–1992); Sales Representative, Baxter Healthcare Corporation (1983–1990); Custom Products Manager, American Hospital Supply (1981–1983). **Associations & Accomplishments:** Executive Group, Westover Church. **Education:** University of Iowa, B.B.A. (1979). **Personal:** Married to Piper in 1982. Two children: Seth and Drew. Mr. Anderson enjoys golf, water skiing, hiking, camping, and reading.

Gabriel A. Carrillo Garibay

Chief Executive Officer and Chairman of the Board
Bard Mexico S.A. de C.V.
Jaime Balmes #11, 702D
Col. Los Morales Polanco, Mexico 11500
(525) 576–4145
Fax: (525) 395–6086

5047

Business Information: Bard Mexico S.A. de C.V. is a distributor of medical equipment and hi–tech medical disposables to Mexican markets. Established in 1983, Bard Mexico reports annual revenue of $4 million and currently employs 26 people. Starting with Bard Mexico in 1983 as a Sales Manager, Mr. Carrillo Garibay has held numerous management roles through the years. Appointed as Chief Executive Officer and Chairman of the Board in 1991, he provides the overall direction and vision for the Company's continued growth, strategic development, quality assurance, and customer satisfaction. **Career Steps:** Bard Mexico S.A. de C.V.: Chief Executive Officer and Chairman of the Board (1991–Present), General Manager (1987–1991), Sales Manager (1983–1987). **Education:** University of Iberoamericana, Biomedical Engineer (1980). **Personal:** Married to Pilar Valls Torrens in 1983. Two children: Jimena del Pilar and Gabriel Andres. Mr. Carrillo Garibay enjoys spending time with his family, politics, literature, tennis, and bowling.

John P. Caruso

Manager of Distribution
Graham Field, Inc.
12055 Missouri Bottom Road
Hazelwood, MO 63042–2313
(314) 731–5272
Fax: (314) 731–5567

5047

Business Information: Graham Field, Inc., established in 1946, is a national medical supplies distributor, offering a complete line of surgical, clinical, emergency and sanitary health products. With over thirteen years expertise in the distribution industry, John Caruso joined Graham Field, Inc. as Manager of Distribution in 1994. He is responsible for the management of all Distribution Center operations, including inventory control and the supervision of support staff. **Career Steps:** Manager of Distribution, Graham Field, Inc. (1994–Present); Warehouse Supervisor, Smithkline Beecham (1989–1994); Warehouse Operations Manager, Macro Systems Inc. (1986–1989); Warehouse Supervisor, Mid America Dairymen, Inc. (1983–1986). **Associations & Accomplishments:** Marine Corps Reserve Officer Association; APICS; Material Handling & Management Society. **Education:** Rutledge College, A.A. (1985); Southwest Missouri State University, B.S. **Personal:** Married to Jacquetta R. in 1973. Two children: Danielle and Preston. Mr. Caruso enjoys golf and swimming.

Sia Kee Chow

Division Manager
Antah Sri Radin Sdn Bhd
Petaling Jaya No. 3 Jalan 19/1
Selangor, Malaysia 46300
(603) 757–3435
Fax: (603) 756–7390

5047

Business Information: Antah Sri Radin Sdn Bhd, established in 1962, is a healthcare trading company with medical and diagnostic divisions, providing their services and products worldwide. As Division Manager, Mr. Sia is responsible for the Diagnostics Division, including P&L, development of existing and new markets, human resources, and the day–to–day management of the Division. **Career Steps:** Division Manager, Antah Sri Radin Sdn Bhd (1990–Present); Medical Lab Technologist, General Hospital Kuala Lumpur (1984–1990). **Education:** Institute of Medical Research, Medical Laboratory Technologist (1984). **Personal:** Married to Lisa Chan Siok Peng in 1989. Two children: Sia Wai Suan and Sia Wai Jen. Mr. Sia enjoys badminton, swimming, and reading.

Maria I. Damiani

Vice President
Southern Medical Products, Inc.
P.O. Box 7648
Ponce, Puerto Rico 00732–7648
(809) 843–4030
Fax: (809) 284–0876

5047

Business Information: Established in 1984, Southern Medical Products, Inc. specializes in the sale and rental of durable medical equipment. As Vice President, Ms. Damiani is responsible for administration, finance, sales, accounting and strategic planning. Her husband, Nestor Laboy, is the President of the Company. Together they hope to expand the business into other locations. **Career Steps:** Vice President, Southern Medical Products, Inc. (1982–Present); Executive Secretary, Metro–Dade Human Resources (1980–1982); Executive Secretary, St. Luke's Home Care Program (1971–1979). **Associations & Accomplishments:** SEMA, Puerto Rico Chamber of Commerce; Puerto Rico Chamber of Commerce; Names. **Education:** Catholic University: M.A. (1982), B.S.S. **Personal:** Married to Nestor Laboy in 1976. Two children: Mari Elena and Edwin. Ms. Damiani enjoys crochet, lace–making, and plastic canvas.

John T. Eads

President
Eads & Associates, Inc.
115 E. Granada Blvd., Suite 10
Ormond Beach, FL 32176–6634
(800) 676–7322
Fax: (904) 676–7621

5047

Business Information: Eads & Associates, Inc. is an international independent distributor of hi–tech medical diagnostic imaging equipment. Establishing Eads & Associates as President in 1988, Mr. Eads is responsible for the oversight and direction of all sales in the State of Florida. He also oversees all administration, sales forces, application personnel (people who demonstrate and install equipment), marketing, large contract closings, and personnel training. **Career Steps:** President, Eads & Associates, Inc. (1988–Present); Sales Manager, O.E.C. Medical Systems (1985–1988); Distributor, O.E.C. Diagnosis (1977–1984) **Education:** Holy Cross College, B.S. (1955); Temple University, pursuing M.B.A. in Marketing (1958–1960); Penn State University, Retail & Wholesale Services course (1957) **Personal:** Married to Veronica in 1959. Four children: Jolta, James, Christina and Elizabeth. Mr. Eads enjoys music (classical, Opera), golf and exercise.

Mr. Sam H. Eulmi
• • • ◦➖◉➖◦ • • •

President
Advanced Scientific Enterprises, Inc.
5474 Complex Street, Suite 501
San Diego, CA 92123–1118
(619) 492–1424
Fax: (619) 576–0721

5047

Business Information: Advanced Scientific Enterprises, Inc. is a distributor of medical devices and pharmaceuticals. Founding Advanced Scientific Enterprises, Inc. in 1989, Mr. Eulmi serves as President, responsible for all aspects of operations, including administration, and strategic planning. Concurrent with this position, he serves as Director of OKUNIS Consulting Group – a project financing consulting firm, and as Director of DANNAH Holdings, Ltd. – an international business consulting firm. **Career Steps:** Founder and President, Advanced Scientific Enterprises, Inc. (1989–Present); Director, OKUNIS Consulting Group (1994–Present); Director, DANNAH Holdings, Ltd. (1994–Present). **Associations & Accomplishments:** World Trade Association; Institute of the Americas; AHEPA; Who is Who Worldwide; Oxford Club; Fluent in French and Arabic. **Education:** San Diego State University, B.S. in Electrical Engineering (1983); University of San Diego, International Business. **Personal:** Married to Petroula in 1983. Two children: Stephen and Patrick. Mr. Eulmi enjoys languages, soccer, travel, watching documentaries, and reading.

Guy E. Halgren
• • • ◦➖◉➖◦ • • •

Executive Director
Peri, Inc.
6757 Edgewater Commerce Parkway
Orlando, FL 32810–4278
(407) 297–9999
Fax: (407) 297–6818
EMAIL:Peri@NetPass

5047

Business Information: Peri, Inc. is a marketer of new and recycled dental equipment. Established in 1983, Peri, Inc. currently employs 28 people. As Executive Director, Mr. Halgren is responsible for the oversight of all outside sales, production and purchasing. **Career Steps:** Peri, Inc.: Executive Director (1993–Present), Production Manager (1992–1993), Sales Executive (1990–1992), Shipping Manager (1988–1990). **Education:** St. Leo College. **Personal:** Mr. Halgren enjoys travel and golf.

John Hollingshead
• • • ◦➖◉➖◦ • • •

Director
Advanced Medical Concepts
7049 Perkins Road
Baton Rouge, LA 70808–4320
(504) 767–1844
Fax: (504) 767–2944

5047

Business Information: Advanced Medical Concepts is a wholesale provider of a full range of home medical equipment and services, including oxygen and respiratory therapy devices, enteral therapy, home infusion and compound pharmacy supplies, and ostomy and wound care. Established in 1988, the Company currently employs 35 people and has an estimated annual revenue of $4 million. As Director, Mr. Hollingshead is responsible for all aspects of the Company, including finances and operations, emphasizing customer ser-

vice. **Career Steps:** Director, Advanced Medical Concepts (1994–Present); Business Office Manager, Advanced Medical and the General Living Center (1989–1994). **Associations & Accomplishments:** National Association of Medical Equipment Dealers; Health Industry Distributions Association; Louisiana's Medical Equipment Dealers; Individual Case Management Association; Friends for Life; United Way; March of Dimes; Mid City Redevelopment. **Education:** College of St. Francis, M.H.A. (1996); University of Southern Mississippi, B.S. (1986). **Personal:** Hollingshead enjoys hiking, weight training, travel, tennis, camping, and being in nature.

Laura E. Holt, R.N., B.S.
Sales Consultant
Hill–Rom Company
454 McCormick Street
Shreveport, LA 71104
Fax: Please mail or call

5047

Business Information: Hill–Rom Company, a subsidiary of Hillenbrand Industries, is an international manufacturer and marketer of health care products, specializing in specialty beds, hospital beds, overbed tables and other hospital equipment (beds that rotate, relieve pressure – low air loft, and irrigate patients). The Company is on the cutting edge, with 100% of local business and 90–96% of national business. Hillenbrand Industries, the parent company, is a major manufacturer of the "cadillac" of caskets (Batesville Co.) and hospital beds. With nineteen years experience in health care, Ms. Holt joined Hill–Rom Company in 1995. Serving as Sales Consultant, she travels throughout the state, marketing the Corporation's products. **Career Steps:** Sales Consultant, Hill–Rom Company (1995–Present); Senior Account Manager, Caremark/Coram – world's largest home infusion therapy provider (1993–1995); Nurse, Shreveport Medical Center (1986–1993); Nurse, St. Patricks Hospital (1976–1986). **Associations & Accomplishments:** Junior League of Shreveport; Shreveport Metro Ballet Guild. **Education:** McNeece, B.S. in Nursing; Centenary College, participating in the MBA program (expected: May 1996).

Lisa M. Lainer
Supervisor of Chemistry Controls
CIBA Corning Diagnostics – A Chiron Business
115 Norwood Park South
Norwood, MA 02062
(617) 551–7819
Fax: (508) 339–4475

5047

Business Information: CIBA Corning Diagnostics – A Chiron Business — is an international marketer of diagnostic instrumentation and testing equipment, such as immunoassay and blood gas analyzers. CIBA Corning Diagnostics recently became a division of Chiron Corporation, a leader in biotechnology. As Supervisor of Chemistry Controls, Ms. Lainer is responsible for the oversight of all sales of chemistry control materials used to verify calibration of analyzers and patient results. In addition, she is an inventor of a variety of items and the holder of three patents (with three more pending), which includes: a hairstyle display and selection system – giving the consumer an opportunity to see how different styles and colors will look on them; a candy/gum holder with a pen; and a photograph/greeting card holder and display system. Upon the diagnosis of Lyme Disease in her mother, husband, 4–year old daughter, and herself, Ms. Lainer spends numerous hours volunteering her time to raise money for Lyme Disease Research, as well as speaking before the Board of Health on the disease. She has also appeared on NBC's "Real Life" show regarding the subject. Internet users can reach Ms. Lainer via: Lisa.Lainer@ Cibadiag.com **Career Steps:** Supervisor of Chemistry Controls, CIBA Corning Diagnostics – A Chiron Company (1992–Present); Supervisor of Retail Sales, Merkert Enterprises Food Brokerage (1990–1992); Mortgage Consultants, Great Western Bank (1989–1990). **Associations & Accomplishments:** Volunteer, National Lyme Disease Foundation – raised $40K for International Conference at Copley Plaza Hotel – Boston, MA (1996). **Education:** Clark University, B.A. (1987); The City University – London, England, studied International Economics (1986). **Personal:** Married to Steven D. in 1990. Two children: Samantha Hillary and Tyler Raymond. Ms. Lainer enjoys inventing, writing, walking, photography, and travel.

Sandra I. Lopez
Logistics Manager
Johnson & Johnson
6303 Blue Lagoon Drive #450
Miami, FL 33126–6002
(305) 265–2607
Fax: (305) 261–1899
EMail: See Below

5047

Business Information: Johnson & Johnson is a global consumer, professional, and pharmaceutical healthcare products conglomerate, providing a complete healthcare products line (i.e., medical/surgical products, prescription pharmaceutical, over–the–counter pharmaceutical and diagnostics). Established in 1886, Johnson & Johnson currently employs 80,000 people worldwide. As Logistics Manager, Ms. Lopez is responsible for strategic management of the professional sector of Latin America. Internet users can reach her via: SLopez@corus.jnj.com. **Career Steps:** Logistics Manager, Johnson & Johnson (1994–Present); Export Trade Specialist, Jim Walter Corporation (1993–1994); International Services Senior Coordinator, Critikon – a division of Johnson & Johnson. **Associations & Accomplishments:** Council of Logistics Management; International Customer Service Association; American Production and Inventory Control Society; South Florida Round Table. **Education:** University of Tampa, M.B.A. (1994); University of South Florida, B.A. in Marketing. **Personal:** Ms. Lopez enjoys reading and biking.

Jennifer R. Marr
Director of International Marketing/General Manager – Export Div.
Henry Schein, Inc.
135 Duryea Road
Melville, NY 11747–3834
(516) 843–5961
Fax: (516) 843–5681
EMAIL: See Below

5047

Business Information: Henry Schein, Inc. is a worldwide distributor of health care supplies to the medical profession. Headquartered in Melville, New York, the Company maintains three distribution centers, two telemarketing centers, and eight offices in Europe. Ms. Marr joined Henry Schein in 1991 as Director of International Marketing, taking on the additional responsibilities of General Manager of the Export Division in 1995. In her present capacity, Ms. Marr oversees daily operations, marketing, strategic planning, and various administrative functions. Internet users can reach her via: JDMarr@aol.com **Career Steps:** Henry Schein, Inc: Director of International Marketing & General Manager – Export Division (1995–Present), Director of International Marketing (1991–1995); Director/Dental Division, Medchoice, Inc. (1988–1991); Marketing Field Specialist, Patterson Dental Company (1981–1988). **Associations & Accomplishments:** International Council, Direct Marketing Association; Export Committee, Dental Manufacturers of America. **Education:** Marquette University, B.S. (1985). **Personal:** Married to David in 1994. Ms. Marr enjoys skiing, golf, and piano.

Anthony J. Merlino
• • • ◦➖◉➖◦ • • •

Imaging Consultant
Bayer Corporation – AGFA Division
100 Challenger Road
Ridgefield Park, NJ 07660
(201) 641–9566
Fax: (201) 288–8566

5047

Business Information: Bayer Corporation – AGFA Division, a leader in PACS (Picture Archive Communications Systems), is an international marketer of medical imaging (radiology equipment) covering the international marketplace. Widely-known for Bayer Aspirin products, Bayer Corporation is a multi-national company, providing research, development, manufacturing, and marketing of animal health pharmaceuticals and biologicals. Products include health care products, agricultural products, polymers, and organic chemicals. A conglomerate with 170 companies under its umbrella, Bayer Corporation employs 50,000 people worldwide. Divisions include Graphics, Motion Pictures, Non–Destructive Testing Division, Photography, Pharmaceutical, Diagnostics and Medical. As the Imaging Consultant for the Medical Division, Mr. Merlino is responsible for a $5 million territory, including sales of computer server platforms and computer soft copy review stations for Medical Imaging. His accounts have always been in the Top 5 in revenue and was the first to install three out of five new products this year. **Career Steps:** Imaging Consultant, Bayer Corporation – AGFA Division (1989–Present); Account Manager, International Ultrasound (1987–1989).

Associations & Accomplishments: One of the first to receive the "AGFA President's Club" award. **Education:** Pace University, B.B.A. (1988). **Personal:** Married to Catherine in 1986. Three children: Michael, Brandon and Meghan. Mr. Merlino enjoys motocross and auto racing.

Jerrold B. Miller
Vice President
Life Systems
4 Mall Terrace
Savannah, GA 31406–3602
(912) 355–9494
Fax: (912) 354–5190

5047

Business Information: Life Systems is a distributor of medical equipment and disposables, specializing in "Vital Signs" equipment (i.e., blood pressure equipment, blood oxygen level devices). As Business Planning Vice President, Mr. Miller is responsible for operations, finances, purchasing, human resources, administration, and tax management. **Career Steps:** Vice President, Life Systems (1995–Present); Vice President of Finance, Burke, Fox & Company (1987–1992); Vice President Corporate Controller, Parker Pen Company (1981–1983). **Associations & Accomplishments:** American Institute of Certified Public Accountants; March of Dimes, Greenbriar Children's Center. **Education:** Case Western Reserve University: M.B.A. (1968), B.B.A. (1960) **Personal:** Married to Linda G. in 1961. Two children: Boyd and Barbra. Mr. Miller enjoys tennis, travel, stamps, and wines.

Douglas W. Mitchell
Director of Purchasing
Telectonics Pacing Systems
7400 South Tucson Way
Englewood, CO 80112–3938
(303) 799–2451 (303) 790–8000
Fax: Please mail or call

5047

Business Information: Telectonics Pacing Systems, a subsidiary of Pacific Dunlop, is a manufacturer of pace maker medical equipment. With sites in Sydney, Miami Lakes, and Colorado, the Company distributes internationally. As Director of Purchasing, Mr. Mitchell is responsible for worldwide purchasing, including the administration and direction of all worldwide purchasing sites, hiring, training and contract negotiations. **Career Steps:** Director of Purchasing, Telectonics Pacing Systems (1995–Present); Cobe Renal Care: Manufacturing Operations Manager (1994–1995), Manufacturing Support and Systems Manager (1992–1994); Purchasing Manager, Ampex Corporation (1984–1992). **Education:** California Coast University, B.A. (1996). **Personal:** Mr. Mitchell enjoys golf and photography.

Alicia D. Morris
Vice President and Clinical Director
Healthcare Equipment and Supplies
2404 North Orange Ave.
Orlando, FL 32804–5513
(407) 898–6004
Fax: (407) 896–4032

5047

Business Information: Healthcare Equipment and Supplies is a provider of full–service durable medical equipment for the Central Florida area, with a heavy focus on seating and mobility, respirators, respiratory therapy services, and maternal infant services. As Vice President and Clinical Director, Mrs. Morris is responsible for the direction of day–to–day clinical needs for clientele base, including the assurance and oversight of quality care and meeting patient needs, JCAHO monitoring and evaluations, as well as in–house staff training. **Career Steps:** Vice President and Clinical Director, Healthcare Equipment and Supplies (1989–Present); National Medical Equipment: Clinical Director (1987–1989), Clinical Supervisor (1982–1987); NICU Respiratory Supervisor, Sierra Medical Center (1974–1982). **Associations & Accomplishments:** American Association for Respiratory Care; Florida Society for Respiratory Care. **Education:** Miami Institute of Health Sciences (1982); Kent State University; University of Texas – El Paso. **Personal:** Married to Harold Q. in 1968. Two children: Lawrence C. and Michelle Louise. Mrs. Morris enjoys swimming, crafts, and traveling.

John A. Mycek
Vice–President of Sales and Marketing
General Lab Supply
438 Pompton Road
Wayne, NJ 07470–2105
(201) 956–9292
Fax: (201) 595–8445

5047

Business Information: General Lab Supply is a leading international distributor of medical products and supplies. As Vice–President of Sales and Marketing, Mr. Mycek is responsible for the northeast region of the Company, as well as oversees sales training. **Career Steps:** General Lab Supply: Vice–President of Sales and Marketing (1995–Present), Warehouse Manager. **Associations & Accomplishments:** Volunteer Fire Fighter; Special Police Officer volunteer. **Personal:** Married to Linda in 1986. Three children: Carol, John, and Chris. Mr. Mycek enjoys camping with his kids.

Gilbert Perez

Branch Manager
Medline Industries, Inc.
Royal Industrial Pk, Bldg B., Local #5, RD869, Bo Palmas
Catano, Puerto Rico 00962
(809) 788–1094
Fax: (807) 788–1346

5047

Business Information: Medline Industries, Inc. is a major international manufacturer and distributor of surgical and medical supplies. Products are marketed through multi–national sales representatives, as well as offering an extensive full–scope health care supplies and equipment catalog. Product lines range from tongue depressors to high technology video imaging equipment. As Branch Manager, Gilbert Perez oversees all distribution and logistics operations for Puerto Rico. **Career Steps:** Branch Manager – Puerto Rico, Medline Industries, Inc. (1991–Present); Administrator – Parts Center, Caribe G.E. (1987–1991); Operations Manager, Quality Distributors (1981–1987). **Associations & Accomplishments:** National Rifle Association; Church Youth Counselor. **Education:** University of Phoenix, M.B.A. (1995); Brooklyn College, B.B.A. **Personal:** Married to Ludy in 1972. Two children: Denise and Carlos.

Kerry Persson
President
Swedish Health Care AB
PO Box 4443
S–203 15 Malmo, Sweden 20315
46–40–611–8200
Fax: 46–40–127810

5047

Business Information: Swedish Health Care AB is a private company established in 1989, supported by the City of Malmo, the County Council of Malmohus and Lund University and their affiliated hospitals in Lund/Malmo. Swedish Health Care AB has also an agreement with Uppsala University Hospital. The purpose is to promote and export equipment, supplies, products and services in the field of health and dental care internationally. In the field of services Swedish Health Care AB offers comprehensive training and education programs, patient care and consultancy e.g. feasibility studies, health policy and strategy, management and operation of hospitals, etc. The main markets are Eastern Europe, Japan, the Middle East, Africa and South East Asia. After working for Swedish Health Care for several years, Mr. Persson purchased the Company in 1993. As President and Owner of the Company, he is responsible for all management decisions regarding Swedish Health Care. Other responsibilities include contract negotiations, development of budgets, development of marketing and sales programs for products and services offered, and public relations. **Career Steps:** President, Swedish Health Care (1989–Present); Director Liaison Office, Lund University (1978–1989); Vice Chancellor, Teachers College (1965–1978). **Associations & Accomplishments:** International Hospital Federation; Swedish Trade Council; Swedish Chamber of Commerce; Travellers Club; Sweden–China Association; Sweden–Japan Association; North Cape Club; National Geographic Society. **Education:** Uppsala University, B.S. (1962). **Personal:** Married to Maria Isabel in 1963. Three children: Vivianne, Victoria, and Robert. Mr. Persson enjoys Literature, outdoor life, and travel.

Timothy A. Pritts
President/Chief Executive Officer
Bauerfeind U.S.A., Inc.
2100 Barrett Park Drive, Suite 508
Kennesaw, GA 30144
(800) 423–3405
Fax: (770) 929–8477
EMAIL: See Below

5047

Business Information: Bauerfeind U.S.A., Inc. is a subsidiary of Germany–based Bauerfeind GMBH. Specializing in the sales of orthopedic supports and braces to the medical field (i.e. orthopedic surgeons, athletic trainers, physical therapists, medical retailers and podiatrists). Established in 1986, the Company has a location in every U.S. state and Canada. As President/Chief Executive Officer, Mr. Pritts oversees all aspects of the Company in both the U.S. and Canada. His duties include administration, operations, public relations and strategic planning, and sales and marketing development **Career Steps:** President/CEO, Bauerfiend U.S.A., Inc. (1995–Present); OSTEONICS Corporation: Account Manager, Osteomedics, Inc. (1992–1995), Technical Representative, RATECH Corporation (1990–1992). **Associations & Accomplishments:** Athletics and Team Captain for Lacrosse Team, Rutgers University; High School All American; Academic All American; Member of Promise Keepers. **Education:** Rutgers University, B.S. (1990). **Personal:** Married to Vivain V. in 1992. Mr. Pritts enjoys golf, sports and outdoor activities.

Paul Vazquez
Vice President of Sales & Service Department
Pelegrina Medical, Inc.
P.O. Box 910
Saint Just, Puerto Rico 00978–0910
(809) 761–0000 Ext. 222
Fax: (809) 761–0404

5047

Business Information: Pelegrina Medical, Inc. is a provider of medical equipment, hospital supplies and bio–medical services to the healthcare industry. Established in 1985, Pelegrina Medical, Inc. reports annual revenue of $5.5 million and currently employs 30 people. With over ten years expertise in medical technology sales, Mr. Vazquez serves as Vice President directing all areas of sales and marketing. **Career Steps:** Vice President of Sales & Service Department, Pelegrina Medical, Inc. (1987–Present); Representative, Tecnologia Cardiovascular, Inc. (1985); Sergeant, U.S. Army (1982–1985). **Associations & Accomplishments:** Asociates de Residentes El Plantio. **Education:** University of Central de Bayamonon, Marketing Degree in progress; Interamerican University, Hato Rey, Accounting (1978–1982). **Personal:** Married to Nanette Jimenez in 1983. Two children: Michelle Vazquez and Paul Alexander. Mr. Vazquez enjoys drag racing, golf, scuba diving, and boating.

Rodolfo Vega Dencker
General Manager/Partner
Cosin Limited
16 July Avenue #18 Fourth Floor, Casilla 5993
La Paz, Bolivia
(591) 235–5311
Fax: (591) 239–1021

5047

Business Information: Cosin Limited specializes in the import and distribution of medical and industrial equipment. Established in 1975, the Company employs 30 people and has estimated annual revenue of $4 million. As General Manager/Partner, Mr. Vega Dencker oversees all aspects of the Company, to include administration, operations, finance, sales, marketing, and strategic planning. **Career Steps:** Cosin Limited: General Manager/Partner (1990–Present), Manager, Medical Division (1985–1990). **Associations & Accomplishments:** Chamber of Commerce and Industry; Vice President, Bolivian–Chilean Chamber of Commerce; Bolivian–French Chamber of Commerce; Bolivian–German Chamber of Commerce. **Education:** ICAI, Madrid, Spain, Telecommunications (1974). **Personal:** Married to Veronica Estenssoro in 1976. Three children: Claudia, Valeria, and Diego. Mr. Vega Dencker enjoys raquetball and tennis.

Joyce B. Gainey
Assistant Controller
Capo, Inc.
2 Sunshine Boulevard
Ormond Beach, FL 32174–8754
(904) 673–4966
Fax: (904) 672–8720

5048

Business Information: Capo, Inc. is a wholesale distributor of sunglasses and non–prescription reading glasses. As Assistant Controller, Mrs. Gainey provides assistance to the Controller on accounts payable, payroll, self–funded benefits for the Company, and financial reports. Concurrently, she serves as Manager of Human Resources, Office Functions, and Benefits departments. **Career Steps:** Assistant Controller, Capo, Inc. (1990–Present). **Education:** Edinboro University of Pennsylvania, B.A. in Business and Economics (1981). **Personal:** Married to Bryan in 1984. Two children: Kate and John. Mrs. Gainey enjoys golf and all types of sports.

Richard J. Laskowski
Vice President and Director, Manufacturing
Optical Gaging Products, Inc.
850 Hudson Avenue
Rochester, NY 14621–4839
(716) 544–0450 Ext. 249
Fax: (716) 544–0131

5049

Business Information: Optical Gaging Products, Inc. is a global force in the precision measurement market. Product lines provide solutions for many applications in the automotive, aerospace, clinical, ceramic, electronics, plastics, biomedical, and metal working industries. As Vice President and Director, Manufacturing, Mr. Laskowski oversees manufacturing operations that include: purchasing, production, control, production machine shop, machine assembly, finishing operations, electronics, and optical manufacturing services. **Career Steps:** Vice President and Director, Manufacturing, Optical Gaging Products, Inc. (1988–Present); General Measurement Research: Vice President of Manufacturing (1984–1988), Manufacturing Manager (1978–1984), Electrical Engineer (1975–1978). **Associations & Accomplishments:** American Management Association; Institute of Electronics and Electrical Engineers; Institute of Industrial Engineers; A.P.I.C.S.; Badon Street Settlement. **Education:** Rochester Institute of Technology, B.E.T. (1975).

Linda Jeanne Maynes
• • • ━━◉━━ • • •

Controller
Checkpoint Systems, Inc.
101 Wolf Drive
Thorofare, NJ 08086
(609) 384–2454
Fax: (609) 848–2042

5049

Business Information: Checkpoint Systems, Inc. specializes in the retail sale of security equipment. Listed on the New York Stock Exchange, Checkpoint Systems, Inc. currently employs 2,300 people and has an estimated annual revenue of $128 million. Joining Checkpoint in 1989 as staff accountant, Mrs. Maynes was appointed Controller in 1994. She is responsible for all aspects of accounting functions, as well as taxes and global cash management for U.S. corporations. She is also involved in acquisition analysis of the competition and evaluations. **Career Steps:** Checkpoint Systems, Inc.: Controller (1994–Present), Assistant Controller (1992–1994), Senior Accountant (1992). **Associations & Accomplishments:** American Institute of Certified Public Accountants; New Jersey Society of Certified Public Accountants. **Education:** Drexel University, M.S. (1992); Rutgers University, B.S.; Certified Public Accountant. **Personal:** Married to John in 1991. Two children: Jacqueline and Andrew. Mrs. Maynes enjoys crafts and rollerblading.

Lydia Dragan
Personnel Manager
Denman & Davis
1 Broad Street
Clifton, NJ 07011
(201) 684–3900
Fax: (201) 684–8723

5051

Business Information: Denman & Davis is a steel service center specializing in the distribution of steel and related products via three facilities. As Personnel Manager, Ms. Dragan oversees all aspect of human resources. She is responsible for compliance, compensation, benefits, training, and reviews. **Career Steps:** Personnel Manager, Denman & Davis (1976–Present). **Associations & Accomplishments:** Society for Human Resource Management; International Airlines Travel Agent Network; Certified Sandals Specialist. **Education:** Upsala, Certificate in Human Resource Management (1989); Katherine Gibbs School, Associates in Liberal Arts. **Personal:** Married to Donald in 1983. One child: Brandon. Ms. Dragan enjoys travel.

Mr. Shuhao Zhang
Vice President
Ning Shing (USA) Inc.
12 Route 17 North
Paramus, NJ 07652
(201) 712–1516
Fax: (201) 712–1364

5051

Business Information: Ning Shing (USA) Inc. conducts international trading in base metals, precious metals, steel products, also exporting metals to China and importing garments from China. As Vice President, Mr. Zhang is in charge of the metal trading and export business operations. Established in 1990, Ning Shing (USA) Inc. employs a full–time staff of six and reports annual revenue of $30 million. **Career Steps:** Vice President, Ning Shing (USA) Inc. (1990–Present); General Manager, Minmetals, Inc. (1987– 1990); Director, Section Chief, Minmetals Zhejiang Branch (1984–1987). **Education:** China Foreign Economic Relationship and Trade Ministry Management Institute, B.S. (1984).

Gerald L. Gilbert
Regional Manager of Financial Services
Wesco Distribution, Inc.
2233 6th Avenue South
Seattle, WA 98134
(206) 292–4010
Fax: (206) 292–4043

5061

Business Information: Wesco Distribution, Inc. is a wholesale distributor of electronic materials and equipment. Established in 1926, and acquired by Clayton, Dubilier & Rice in 1994, the Company offers a full line of products to serve industrial construction, utility and government companies, and modular and mobile home companies throughout the U.S. and Canada. As Regional Manager of Financial Services, Mr. Gilbert oversees the Northwestern area which includes Washington, Oregon, Montana, Colorado, Utah, Nevada, Idaho, Alaska, Arizona, and twenty branches in Northern California. His duties include setting collection priorities, implementing and enforcing collection policies, approving orders, negotiating contracts, management of legal personnel, and testifying in court cases as the Custodian of Records. **Career Steps:** Wesco Distribution, Inc: Region Manager/Financial Services (1989–Present), District Credit Manager (1982–1984); Mortgage Loan Officer, Interwest Bank (1987); Branch Loan Manger, First Interstate Bank (1984–1987). **Associations & Accomplishments:** Board of Directors, NACM; Board of Directors, The High Liners, Inc.. **Education:** Western Washington University, B.A. (1979). **Personal:** Married to Laine E. Coates in 1974. Two children: Rachel Christie and David Charles. Mr. Gilbert enjoys camping, gardening, making model rockets, and time with his family.

Keith A. Lennartson
Director of Communications
Bang & Olufsen of America
1200 East Business Center Drive, Suite 100
Mount Prospect, IL 60056–6041
(847) 299–9380
Fax: (847) 699–1475
EMail: See Below

5061

Business Information: Bang & Olufsen of America is the U.S. distribution center for the Denmark–based, residential music, theater, and telephone products Company. As Director of Communications, Mr. Lennartson directs marketing efforts and manages public relations and training areas. **Career Steps:** Bang & Olufsen of America: Director of Communications (1995–Present), Training Manager (1991–1993); Regional Manager, Elliott Sales Company (1988–1991). **Associations & Accomplishments:** Scandinavian–American Cultural Society; Professional Audio Retail Association; I.D.S.A. **Education:** University of Minnesota – Duluth. **Personal:** Married to Dawn Marie in 1993. Two children: Erik and Karsten. Mr. Lennartson enjoys skiing, photography, music, and rollerblading.

Jeffrey L. Brasure
Co–Owner and Corporate Secretary
Green Mountain Systems & Service, Inc.
P.O. Box 683
Essex Junction, VT 05453
(802) 878–6351
Fax: Please mail or call

5063

Business Information: Green Mountain Systems & Service, Inc. provides service, sales, engineering, installation and consultations for electronic building systems to consumers, end users and jobbers. Products include fire alarms, security and closed circuit devices, intercoms, heating and ventilation, and access control. As Co–Owner, Mr. Brasure is responsible for budgeting, customer service, and strategic planning, and customer satistaction. He also oversees operations and administration, and manages the budget. Concurrent with his present position, Mr. Brasure is Co–Owner and Secretary of New England Electronic Supply. **Career Steps:** Co–Owner and Corporate Secretary, Green Mountain Systems and Services (1996–Present); Co–Owner/President, New England Electronic Supply (Present); General Manager, Notifier Northeast Corporation (1995–1996); Sales and Marketing, Landis & Gyr Powers (1991–1995); Simplex Time Recorder (1984–1991); Brasure Construction Company (1978–1983). **Associations & Accomplishments:** Boy Scouts of America; Essex United Soccer Club; National Fire Protection Association. **Education:** Johnson State College, B.S. (1972); Various Business Management and Electrical Engineering courses. **Personal:** Married to Lorraine in 1979. Two children: Daniel and Michael. Mr. Brasure enjoys sports, reading, numismatics, camping, and family.

Earl Daniel
• • • ━━◉━━ • • •

General Manager
Herman Goldner Company, Inc.
200 Cleveland Rd. #7
Bogart, GA 30622
(706) 353–1465 (800) 550–4653
Fax: (706) 353–1347

5063

Business Information: Herman Goldner Company, Inc. specializes in engineered control components and equipment distribution. As General Manager, Mr. Daniel is responsible for profit/loss for six sales offices and one production facility. **Career Steps:** General Manager, Herman Goldner Company, Inc. (1983–Present); District Manager, Limitorque Corporation (1975–1983); Production Control Manager, Honeywell Aerospace Division (1973–1975). **Associations & Accomplishments:** Masons; Shriners; Chamber of Commerce; TAPPI; Instrument Society of America; Certified Purchasing Manager, National Association of Purchasing Managers. **Education:** Lynchburg College, M.A. (1978); University of South Florida, B.A. (1973). **Personal:** Married to Lisa in 1992. Two children: Jessica and Casey. Mr. Daniel enjoys hiking, camping, and tennis.

Daniel J. Flynn
• • • ━━◉━━ • • •

Chief Financial Officer
Allied Wire & Cable
401 East 4th Street
Bridgeport, PA 19405
(610) 272–9700
Fax: (610) 272–5826

5063

Business Information: Allied Wire & Cable, a family–owned business established in 1987, is an international distributor of electrical products, primarily to wholesalers of OEMS. As Chief Financial Officer, Mr. Flynn is responsible for all financial aspects of the Company. He personally oversees an accounting staff of three persons, and supervises warehouse operations. **Career Steps:** Chief Financial Officer, Allied Wire & Cable (1989–Present); District Sales Manager, Metal Lubricants (1987–1989). **Associations & Accomplishments:** Wire Harness Manufacturers Association; Philadelphia Chamber of Commerce; Reading Chamber of Commerce. **Education:** Villanova University, B.S. in Business Administration (1987). **Personal:** Married to Ann in 1990. Two children: Courtney and Shane. Mr. Flynn enjoys golf, weightlifting, and playing with his children.

Rodolfo E. Gonzalez

Executive Vice President of International Sales
Bright Point
1573 N.W. 82nd Ave.
Miami, FL 33126
(305) 470–8500
Fax: (305) 640–9684

5063

Business Information: Bright Point is one of the largest distributors of cellular phone hardware and accessories in the United States, representing major brands, including Motorola and Nokia. In addition, the Company recently merged with Allied Communications. As Executive Vice President of International Sales, Mr. Gonzalez is responsible for all sales and marketing in the South Florida and Latin America region. **Career Steps:** Executive Vice President of International Sales, Bright Point (1994–Present); Latin American Director, Allied Communications (1994); Vice President, Southern Star Holding (1990–1994); President, Investment Source Corporation (1989–1990). **Associations & Accomplishments:** World Trade Center; Alacel. **Education:** University of Florida, A.A. (1994); Real Estate license; Mortgaged Broker License. **Personal:** One child: Elizabeth A. Mr. Gonzalez enjoys racquetball, golf, and sailing.

Robert Leidner

Vice President
Regency Lighting, Inc.
16665 Arminta Street
Van Nuys, CA 91406–1611
(800) 284–2024
Fax: (818) 901–0118

5063

Business Information: Regency Lighting, Inc. is one of the largest wholesale lighting distributors in the U.S. Specializing in selling to large end users such as hospitals, large corporations, retail stores, etc., the Company has four other locations in Los Angeles, San Francisco, Dallas, and Atlanta. As Vice President, Mr. Leidner oversees operation of all national offices. He was responsible for developing the systems for the Company, and is the catalyst for growth. His duties include implementing policies and procedures, strategic planning, and administration. Concurrently, he is Co–Owner with his wife of a real estate management company, Leidner Properties. **Career Steps:** Vice President, Regency Lighting, Inc. (1982–Present); President, Improving Tomorrow Today (1979–1982); Director of Operations, Continental Conservation Systems (1977–1979). **Associations & Accomplishments:** Environmental Protection Agency–Green Light (Ally); Association of Professional Energy Managers. **Personal:** Married to Sue in 1992. Mr. Leidner enjoys boating and golf.

Jeffrey F. Litzinger

Director
Ohio Geo–Thermal Services
483 Lexington Avenue
Mansfield, OH 44907–1501
(419) 756–5959 (800) 554–1577
Fax: (419) 756–6067

5063

Business Information: Ohio Geo–Thermal Services is a wholesale distributor of geo–thermal equipment and supplies. Products include geo–thermal heat pumps. Established in 1992, Ohio Geo–Thermal Services reports annual revenue of $1 million and currently employs five people. As Director, Mr. Litzinger is reponsible for creation and direction of budgeting activities, all executive decisions made for the Company, management of staff, setting sales goals and marketing. **Career Steps:** Director, Ohio Geo–Thermal Services (1992–Present); Sales Coordinator, Water Furnace of Ohio (1989–1992); Owner and President, Woodshop Corporation (1981–1989). **Associations & Accomplishments:** Home Builders Association of Greater Akron (HBA); International Ground Source Heat Pump Association (IGSHPA); National Heat Pump Consortium; National Ground Water Association. **Education:** Capital University, B.S. (1982); Numerous CEU's in business related courses. **Personal:** Married to Kelley Litzinger in 1991. Two children: Kaitlin and Cassandra. Mr. Litzinger enjoys golf.

Allan I. Nowenstein

Corporate Credit Manager
Bell Industries
1161 North Fairoaks Avenue
Sunnyvale, CA 94089–2102
(408) 734–8570 Ext. 111
Fax: (408) 734–8631

5063

Business Information: Bell Industries is a major distributor of electronic equipment. Established in 1952, Bell Industries currently employs 1,400 people and has an estimated annual revenue of $451 million. As Corporate Credit Manager, Mr. Nowenstein is responsible for the credit operations for 7 hub regions in the United States. With a staff of 15, Mr. Nowenstein provides financial analysis, credit reconciliations and collections. With over ten years of financial experience, Mr. Nowenstein has learned how to use credit as a tool to generate sales, an asset to any company whose livelihood is based on sales revenues. **Career Steps:** Corporate Credit Manager, Bell Industries (1986–Present); Corporate Credit Manager, Silconix (1985–1986); Corporate Credit Manager, EPYX Computer Software (1983–1985). **Associations & Accomplishments:** President, National Electronic Distribution Credit Association; Member, National Distriburtors Credit Executive Association; Former President, Electronic Distributors Credit League. **Education:** Pace University, B.B.A. (1971). **Personal:** Married to Terry in 1972. Two children: Allison and Lauren. Mr. Nowenstein enjoys astronomy, electronics and science fiction.

Steven Schwai

Electrical Controls Engineer
Best Electrical Supply Corporation
P O Box 341190
Milwaukee, WI 53234–1190
(414) 545–8800
Fax: (414) 545–8849

5063

Business Information: Best Electrical Supply Corporation, established in 1976, distributes electrical distribution and control equipment. As Electrical Controls Engineer, Mr. Schwai concentrates on layout design and acts as the technical and applications expert for the Company. Other responsibilities include management of his administrative and engineering support staffs and being the training coordinator. **Career Steps:** Electrical Controls Engineer, Best Electrical Supply Corporation (1994–Present); Electrical Controls Engineer, WSA Engineered Systems (1992–1994); Unit Engineer, Commonwealth Edison (1992). **Education:** university of Wisconsin, B.S.E.E. (1992). **Personal:** Mr. Schwai enjoys being a youth soccer coach.

Phaedon S. Stylianides

Managing Director
Stylianides Broadcast Equipment Ltd
P.O. Box 3509
Limassol, Cyprus CY–3303
357–5353619
Fax: 357–5355357
EMAIL: See Below

5063

Business Information: Stylianides Broadcast Equipment Ltd. is an importer and distributor of electronic equipment, such as broadcasting and professional television equipment. The Company is a registered distributor of Sony products, marketing to related broadcasting companies, such as production facilities, video, etc. from two offices in Cyprus (Nicosia and Limassol). Starting his career out as Sales Manager in his father's business, Styliandes Brothers, Ltd. (a seller of brandy and other spirits), Mr. Stylianides founded his own company in 1985. Based on a need in the market and his increased interest in broadcasting, he established Stylianides Broadcast Equipment Ltd. Serving as Managing Director, he is responsible for all aspects of operations, including administration, finances, sales, public relations, marketing, and strategic planning. Concurrent with this company, he is Founder and Owner of Stylianides Computer Services, Ltd., a software and hardware company. Internet users can reach him via: 73064,1304.compuserve.com **Career Steps:** Managing Director, Stylianides Broadcast Equipment Ltd. (1985–Present); Owner, Stylianides Computer Services, Ltd. (1993–Present); Sales Manager Stylianides Brothers, Ltd. (1975–1984). **Associations & Accomplishments:** Cyprus Radio and Television Association; Famagusta Rotary Club; Famagusta Nautical Club. **Education:** Athens University in Greece, Economics (1975). **Personal:** Married to Elli in 1978. Two children: Nicole and Stella. Mr. Stylianides enjoys computers.

Ms. Cheryl L. Thompson

Chairman of the Board, Chief Executive Officer, and Co–Owner
Warren Electric Company
P. O. Box 67/77001
Houston, TX 77003
(713) 236–2186
Fax: (713) 236–2188

5063

Business Information: Warren Electric Company is an international electrical equipment wholesaler. Electrical supplies distributed include: conduit and cable, motor controls, variable frequency drives, and programmable controllers. Customers include: Dow, Oxydental Chemical and Houston Lighting & Power. As Chairman of the Board, Chief Executive Officer, and Co–Owner, Ms. Thompson is responsible for overseeing management of all operations, and final review of all proposals, new customer and vendor candidates, and financial decisions. Established in 1919, Warren Electric Company employs over 300 people in 12 locations in 2 states and Puerto Rico and reports annual revenue in excess of $130 million. **Career Steps:** Chairman of the Board, Chief Executive Officer, and Co–Owner, Warren Electric Company (1992–Present); Vice President, Warren Electric Company (1990–1992); Treasurer, Warren Electric Company (1987–1990). **Associations & Accomplishments:** Director, National Association of Electrical Distributors (NAED); Director, Houston Electrical League; Director, Theatre Under the Stars; Director, Houston Livestock Show & Rodeo; Director, Rotary Club of Houston Foundation; Director, San Jacinto Girl Scouts; "Women on the Move" 1995, for the City of Houston; Outstanding Family Owned Business for State of Texas (1995). **Education:** Houston Community College.

Andrew Cohan

Vice President of Merchandising
Emerson Radio Corporation
P.O. Box 430
Parsippany, NJ 07054–0430
(201) 428–2008
Fax: (201) 428–2019

5064

Business Information: Emerson Radio Corporation is a major supplier to large mass merchandise retailers. Primary product category is consumer electronics, such as radios. Established in 1962, Emerson Radio Corporation currently employs 250 people. With nine years experience in merchandising, Mr. Cohan joined Emerson Radio Corporation as Vice President of Merchandising in 1993. He is responsible for developing and merchandising all product categories, as well as developing new business categories. He also directs the O.E.M. business and international business activities. **Career Steps:** Vice President of Merchandising, Emerson Radio Corporation (1993–Present); Senior Vice President, McCrory Store Corporation (1992–1993); Ames Department Stores: Vice President of Merchandise Administration (1990–1992), Vice President and General Merchandise Manager (1986–1990). **Education:** Tulane University – New Orleans, B.A. in Liberal Arts (1976). **Personal:** Married to Desiree L. in 1982. One child: Alissa Sean. Mr. Cohan enjoys tennis, music, and art.

Niranjan H. Gidwani

Director
Agiv Group
P.O. Box 16885
Jebel Ali, Dubai, United Arab Emirates
(971) 4–816767
Fax: (971) 4–816237

5064

Business Information: Agiv Group is an international distributor of consumer electronic goods and home appliances, such as videos, televisions, audios, CDs, refrigerators, vacuums, washing machines, etc. With offices located on all continents and selling in 38 countries, Agiv Group also distributes the Company's brand products, called Shivaki. As Director, Mr. Gidwani is responsible for the direction of worldwide marketing of the Company's brand products, in addition to serving as Unit Head for all Gulf and African business divisions. Mr. Gidwani was instrumental in spreading the brand name for the Company and developing new businesses. **Career Steps:** Agiv Group: Director (1995–Present), Group General Manager (1990–1995); Operations Manager, Modi GBC Ltd. (1986–1990); Resident Officer, Hong Kong Bank (1984–1986). **Associations & Accomplishments:** American Management Association; Rotary Club, Pune, India; Indian Management Association; Lecturer and writer on general management issues. **Education:** Pune University: M.B.A. (1982), Bachelor of Mechanical Engineering. **Personal:** Married to Anita in 1985. One child: Arjun. Mr. Gidwani enjoys music and reading.

Paul D. Gustafson
Information Systems and Training
Servall Company
253 E. Milwaukee Street
Detroit, MI 48202–3233
(313) 872–3658
Fax: (313) 872–5312

5064

Business Information: Servall Company specializes in the wholesale distribution of appliance parts. Based in Detroit, Michigan, the Company has seventeen other distributorships throughout Ohio and Michigan. Established in 1929, the Company employs 108 people, and has an estimated annual revenue of $15 million. As Information Systems and Training, Mr. Gustafson oversees all information systems (hardware and software), and handles all training and related functions. A member of the "top management team", he is also responsible for shipping, receiving, and standardizing. **Career Steps:** Information Systems and Training, Servall Company (1996–Present); Director of Information Services and Training, VAMAC (1994–1996); Second Lieutenant, North Dakota Army National Guard (1992–1994). **Education:** University of North Dakota, B.B.A. (1993). **Personal:** Mr. Gustafson enjoys scuba diving.

Rick Swiers
Director of Broadcast Systems
Sony Electronics, Inc. – Business and Professional Group
3 Paragon Drive
San Jose, CA 95134
(408) 955–5808
Fax: (408) 955–5555

5064

Business Information: Sony Electronics, Inc. – Business and Professional Group markets professional audio and video products for distribution to high–end professional users, such as television, commercial, and program producers. The Business and Professional Group of Sony Electronics, Inc. reports annual revenue of $1.3 billion and currently employs 1,400 people. As Director of Broadcast Systems, Mr. Swiers is responsible for the direction of major product development projects, including taking emerging technology and making it practical by conducting research and development at customer sites. **Career Steps:** Sony Electronics, Inc. – Business and Professional Group: Director of Broadcast Systems (1995–Present), Director of Market Development (1994–1995), Market Development Manager (1991–1994), Marketing Manager (1988–1991). **Associations & Accomplishments:** Society of Motion Picture and Television Engineers. **Education:** Fairleigh Dickinson University, M.B.A. (1994); University of Tennessee at Martin, B.S. (1976). **Personal:** Married to Amy in 1991. One child: Emily. Mr. Swiers enjoys golf, flying, and travel.

Ronald J. Wydra
Director of Inventory
Marcone Appliance Parts
2300 Clark Avenue
St. Louis, MO 63103
(314) 231–7225
Fax: (314) 231–7645

5064

Business Information: Marcone Appliance Parts is a factory–authorized distributor for all major manufacturers of domestic appliances (i.e., Whirlpool, Maytag, etc.). As Director of Inventory, Mr. Wydra manages the inventory for 34 locations nationwide consisting of over 100 suppliers. Additionally, he tries to maximize profit and availability. **Career Steps:** Marcone Appliance Parts: Director of Inventory (1995–Present), Florida Inventory Manager (1988–1995), Branch Manager (1979–1988). **Education:** Valencia Community College (1978); Various Management Courses. **Personal:** Married to Homeyra in 1988. One child: Eric. Mr. Wydra enjoys chess, golf, football, and fishing.

Mr. Jim Shujun Chang
Vice President of Marketing and Sales
C & C Solutions, Inc.
2140 Winston Park Drive, #2 & 3
Oakville, Ontario, Canada L6H 5V5
(905) 829–3477
Fax: (905) 829–1252

5065

Business Information: C & C Solutions, Inc. is a stocking distributor on cable television and telecommunication equipment, including microwave and fiberoptic products. As Vice President of Marketing and Sales, Mr. Chang oversees all aspects of sales and marketing for People's Republic of China operations. He supervises the operations of the China office, including sales, warehouse and service center operations located in the Beijing headquarters. An esteemed technology scientist, Mr. Chang designed the key electronic board for computer system launching satellite and missile, and has been honored with numerous scientific awards from China for his scientific and technological accomplishments. Established in 1990, C & C Solutions, Inc. employs 15 people with annual sales of $8 million. **Career Steps:** Vice President of Marketing and Owner, C & C Solutions, Inc. (1990–Present); Purchasing Manager, China Electronics I/E Corp. (1983–1989); Computer System Designer, North China Computer Research Institute (1978–1982). **Associations & Accomplishments:** Recipient, First Class Awards of China National Scientific & Technology Result, the paper "Phase Lock Application in Computers" won first class awards in China National Science and Technology workshop. **Education:** Fudan University, China B.S. in Computers (1977). **Personal:** Married to Kathy Huang in 1979. One child: Jimmy. Mr. Chang enjoys playing bridge, swimming and skating.

Craig Conrad
Vice President of Sales and Marketing
TTI Inc.
2441 Northeast Parkway
Ft. Worth, TX 76106–1816
(817) 740–9000
Fax: Please mail or call

5065

Business Information: TTI Inc. specializes in the worldwide distribution of electronics. Currently the company operates 29 distribution sites, including those in North America, Latin America, California and Europe. Established in 1971, TTI employs 800 people and has an estimated annual revenue of $370 million. As Vice President of Sales and Marketing, Mr. Conrad is second in command responsible for the operations of the Company. **Career Steps:** Vice President of Sales and Marketing, TTI Incorporated (1993–Present); Vice President of Sales and Marketing, Avnet (1990–1993); Vice President of Sales and Marketing, Schweber/Lex (1978–1990). **Associations & Accomplishments:** National Electronics Distribution Association; Board Member, Education Foundation; Advisor, University Marketing Council; Various trade publications. **Education:** Northern Illinois University, B.S. (1975). **Personal:** Married to Ann in 1975. Two children: Allison and Theresa. Mr. Conrad enjoys fishing, basketball, boating and golf.

Judith Anne Davis, B.A., H.R.M., C.H.R.P.

• • • ◎ • • •

Director Human Resources
Electro Sonic Inc.
319 Broadway Avenue
Toronto, Ontario M4P 1W2
(416) 494–1666
Fax: (416) 487–9785

5065

Business Information: Electro Sonic Inc. is a leading Canadian–owned distributor of electronic and electrical components. As the Corporate Director of Human Resources, Ms. Davis is the senior individual responsible for all Human Resource activities. Reporting directly to the President, she is a key member of the Senior Management team, ensuring that all areas related to Human Resources support and foster progressive Corporate initiatives through quality processes and programs. Some of her key responsibilities include Strategic Planning, Policy Formulation, Organizational Change to Meet Progressive Initiatives, Continuous Learning, Empowerment, among others. Ms. Davis ensures that Human Resources is set on a visionary path to support the Corporate mission and strives to develop the best people in the industry. Since every employee at Electro Sonic is a customer, her goal is to provide continuous customer satisfaction through continuous employee education, training and development. **Career Steps:** Director Human Resources, Electro Sonic Inc. (1991–Present); President, Davis & Associates (1990–1991); Senior Manager Development & Communications, ICG Utilities (1988–1990); Senior Manager Employee Relations, Northern and Central Gas Corp. (1984–1988). **Associations & Accomplishments:** Human Resources Association of Ontario; Society for Training and Development; Western Business School; National Action Committee on the Status of Women; Former Member, Canadian Gas Association; Former Member, Canadian/American Compensation Association; Former Member, Canadian Relocation Association; Nominated to the Board of Directors for a Community College in Ontario; Employee Campaign Coordinator, United Way; Canvasser Canadian Cancer Society; Committed to Continuous Learning, an initiative Ms. Davis introduced and implemented was featured in the Toronto Star, the Canadian Broadcasting Television Evening News and CBC radio; Introduced a hiring policy committed to work place diversity which was featured in Canadian Business Magazine. **Education:** Western University, London, Human Resource Management (1984); York University, Toronto, B.A. in Economics (1974); York University, Toronto, Economics Research Graduate Student, project results and recommendations published by the Canadian Federal Government (1975); Einstein Institute, Search Professional, New York City (1989); Certified Human Resource Professional (1988). **Personal:** Ms. Davis enjoys photography (National Prize Winner), reading, skiing, renovating, interior design, and volunteering.

J. Scott Hagerty
Division Manager
Wyle Electronics
170 W. Election Drive # 100
Draper, UT 84020
(800) 414–4144
Fax: (801) 823–8557

5065

Business Information: Wyle Electronics specializes in the distribution of electronics (semiconductors). Established in 1948, the Company has over $1.1 billion in corporate sales with over 35 divisions, along with newly acquired international companies. As Division Manager, Mr. Hagerty manages a large support staff, sets market strategies, develops supplier programs and relations, and covers the North America customer base. **Career Steps:** Wyle Electronics: Division Manager (1995–Present), Operations Manager (1992–1995); Regional Production Manager, Hamilton Avnet (1988–1989). **Associations & Accomplishments:** Lost Dutchman Mining Association; Habitat for Humanity. **Education:** Arizona State University (1978); Scottsdale Community College. **Personal:** Married to Pamela Estelle in 1984. Three children: Lucas Tyler, Shane Peter, and Siera Jo. Mr. Hagerty enjoys gold mining, sports, and outdoor activities.

Thomas F. Herrmann
Manager of Database Administration
Newark Electronics
4801 North Ravensworth Avenue
Chicago, IL 60640
(312) 907–5285
Fax: (847) 680–3410

5065

Business Information: Newark Electronics sells and distributes electronic parts. As Manager of Database Administration, Mr. Herrmann is responsible for the supervision and maintenance of all computer information systems. **Career Steps:** Manager of Database Administration, Newark Electronics (1993–Present); Senior Database Analyst, Waste Management (1989–1993); Project Leader, Applied Information Development (1986–1989); Database Administrator, Velsicol Chemical (1985–1986). **Associations & Accomplishments:** Aldermanic Candidate in Wisconsin (1972–1980); Vernon Hills Youth Baseball/Softball Association; DPMA – Sioux Falls and Chicago. **Education:** University of Wisconsin; Gateway Technical College. **Personal:** Married to Gail in 1975. Four children: Aaron Matthew, Joel Michael, Andrew Jacob, and Justin Thomas. Mr. Herrmann enjoys music and sports.

Karen A. Johnian
Human Resources Manager
Contact East, Inc.
335 Willow Street
North Andover, MA 01845–5921
(508) 682–9844
Fax: (508) 681–7875

5065

Business Information: Contact East, Inc. is an electronic distributor for other companies. Contact East, Inc. serves as middle man, sending catalogues to other companies and individuals. As Human Resources Manager, Ms. Johnian implements, monitors, and tracks programs. She establishes policies, researches benefits, training, employee relations, and all other human resource responsibilities. **Career Steps:** Human Resources Manager, Contact East, Inc. (1995–Present); Compensation Analyst, W.R. Grace & Company – Conn. (1993–1995); Human Resource Coordinator/Generalist, Medtronic Interventional (1989–1993); Conference Coordinator, Digital Consulting, Inc. (1986–1989). **Associations & Accomplishments:** North East Human Resources Association; American Compensation Association; Merrimack Valley Chamber of Commerce. **Education:** Bentley College, Certificate in Human Resource Management (1993); St. Anselm College, B.A. in Business and Economics (1985). **Personal:** Married to Steven in 1994. Ms. Johnian enjoys attending human resource conferences and seminars, home renovation, and landscaping.

Mark H. Lawrence

Manager, Wireless Business Unit
Harris Corporation
809 Calle Plano
Camarillo, CA 93012–8519
(805) 389–2495
Fax: (805) 389–2301
EMail: See Below

5065

Business Information: Harris Corporation is a leading manufacturer and supplier of diversified electronics and office automation equipment. Harris Corporation, with worldwide sales of more than $3.4 billion, is focused on four major businesses: electronics systems, communications, semiconductors, and Lanier Worldwide office equipment. Network Support System is the test equipment division of Harris Corporation and is the leading supplier of craft tools to the U.S. telecommunications industry. As Manager of the Wireless Business Unit, Mr. Lawrence is responsible for profit and loss, marketing and sales, identification and introduction of new products, and strategic alliances related to wireless test equipment. Internet users can reach him via: MLAWREN1@HARRIS.COM. **Career Steps:** Manager – Wireless Business Unit, Harris Corporation (1996–Present); Vice President TeleCompcepts, Inc. (1994–1996); Marketing Director, Teledesic Corporation (1991–1994). **Associations & Accomplishments:** Chartered Engineer; Institute of Electrical Engineers; Association of Masters of Business Administration; Beta Gamma Sigma Masters of Business Administration Honors Society. **Education:** University of Southern California, M.B.A. (1991); University of London, B.Sc. in Physics and Electronics. **Personal:** Mr. Lawrence enjoys traveling and sporting activities.

Daniel J. Moncino II

Director of Marketing
Schlumberger Industries – Metes Communication Systems
3155–B Northwoods Parkway
Norcross, GA 30071–1539
(770) 368–3505
Fax: (770) 263–8104
EMAIL: See Below

5065

Business Information: Schlumberger Industries – Meter Communication Systems, established in 1993, is an international company primarily engaged in the distribution of meter communication systems for water, gas, and electrical utility companies. International in scope, the Company has numerous locations worldwide, though mainly in North America and Europe, and exhibits in various international trade shows. As Director of Marketing, Mr. Moncino oversees all aspects of marketing for meter communication systems division and is responsible for marketing and product management. Internet users can reach him via: moncino@norcross.slb.com. **Career Steps:** Schlumberger Industries: Director of Marketing (1996–Present), Manager of Business Development (1995–1996); Key Account Manager for Proctor & Gamble with BASF AG (1992–1995). **Associations & Accomplishments:** Automatic Meter Reading Association (AMRA); American Water Works Association (AWWA). **Education:** University of Chicago: M.B.A. (1992), B.A. in Business Administration/Finance; B.A. in International Business/Minor in German Literature and Language. **Personal:** Married to Dorothee M. in 1990. Two children: Kai Christian and Maiya Patricia. Mr. Moncino enjoys woodworking, nature hiking with his family, and sailing.

David Mullen

National Sales Manager
Crane Connectors
4700 Smith Road
Cincinnati, OH 45212
(513) 631–4700
Fax: (513) 631–5700

5065

Business Information: Crane Connectors is an international retailer of electronic connectors. As National Sales Manager, Mr. Mullen plays a major role in programming sales development and the extensive research it takes to find new and innovative ways to market Crane Connectors' products. He is also responsible for overseeing all operations, sales, public relations, marketing, and strategic planning activities. **Career Steps:** Crane Connectors: National Sales Manager (1995–Present), Regional Sales Manager (1993–1994); Regional Sales Manager, Deutsch IPD (1989–1993). **Associations & Accomplishments:** People Working Cooperatively (PWC) – conducts home repairs for the poor and elderly; American Management Association (AMA). **Education:** Wilmington College, B.A. in Marketing (1993); Cincinnati Technical College: A.A.S. in Laser Optics and Industrial Lab Technology. **Personal:** Mr. Mullen enjoys Tae Kwan Do, basketball, and travel.

Dwain A. Rittenhouse

Chief Operating Officer
JCH Enterprises, Inc.
4533 Andrews Street
North Las Vegas, NV 89031–2727
(702) 643–5000
Fax: (702) 643–5001

5065

Business Information: JCH Enterprises, Inc. is a wholesaler of electrical and electronic products specializing in wire and cable items, electrical harnesses, and assembling data. The Corporation was established in 1987, employs approximately 100 people, and posted sales in excess of 22 million dollars last year. As Chief Operating Officer, Mr. Rittenhouse directs and coordinates the daily operations of the Corporation, working through department and branch managers. He has oversight of all financial, marketing, personnel, public relations concerns, and is planning for Corporation expansion within the next five years. Under the direction of Mr. Rittenhouse, JCH Enterprises, Inc. has shown a 22% increase in growth in the last year. **Career Steps:** Chief Operating Officer, JCH Enterprises, Inc. (1994–Present); Operations Manager, JCH Wire & Cable; (1993–1994); Quality Assurance Supervisor/Specialist, EG& G Energy Measurements (1979–1993). **Associations & Accomplishments:** American Society for Quality Control; Community College of Southern Nevada; Clark County School District Joint Skills Committee. **Education:** University of Nevada, Las Vegas, Certificate in Business Management (1982–1984); Clark County Community College; Spartan School of Aeronautics. **Personal:** Married to Cheryll in 1986. Two children: Renee, and Justin. Mr. Rittenhouse enjoys family.

CAI MUELLER

Chet Rojice Sr.

Division President
Connector Accessories, Inc.
3939B Mogadore Industrial Parkway
Mogadore, OH 44260–1224
(330) 628–5700
Fax: (330) 628–6727

5065

Business Information: Connector Accessories Inc. (CAI)/Mueller Electric, a division of Mueller Electric Company, is a subcontractor of wiring harness assemblies, molded cable, electronic and electro–mechanical products and assemblies for smaller and larger companies throughout the nation, with some affiliates overseas. As Division President, Mr. Rojice is responsible for all aspects of operations over CAI. **Career Steps:** Division President, Connector Accessories, Inc. (1991–Present); General Manager, Assemblics, Inc. (1988–1991); General Manager, Minor Assembly & Design, Inc. (1985–1988); President, Station, Inc. (1982–1985). **Personal:** Married to Cynthia A. in 1967. Three children: Chet Jr., Christopher, and Caryn. Mr. Rojice enjoys camping and boating.

Dennis J. Sein

Vice President of Sales
Infinity Sales
20 Corporate Park, Ste. 100
Irvine, CA 92714
(714) 833–0300
Fax: (714) 833–0303

5065

Business Information: Infinity Sales provides sales and marketing services to semiconductor manufacturers, as well as serves a manufacturing representative for Southern California semiconductor industries. Infinity Sales has branch offices in Los Angeles, Irvine and San Diego. As Vice President of Sales, Mr. Sein is responsible for all Corporate sales force, training, and P&L accountability of products and services. **Career Steps:** Vice President of Sales, Infinity Sales (1989–Present); District Sales Manager, VLSI Technology (1987–1989); Sales Engineer, Advanced Micro Devices (1984–1987). **Associations & Accomplishments:** Electronic Representatives Association; Tau Beta Pi – Engineering Honor Society. **Education:** Stony Brook University, B.S. in Electrical Engineering (1984). **Personal:** Mr. Sein enjoys running, bicycling, and boating.

Jim S. Zhang

Vice President of Marketing and Sales
C & C Broadband Solutions, Inc.
1250 N. Lakeview Ave. #Q & R
Anaheim, CA 92807
(714) 701–0250
Fax: (714) 701–0253

5065

Business Information: C & C Broadband Solutions, Inc. is a stocking distributor of cable television and telecommunication equipment, including microwave and fiberoptic products. As Vice President of Marketing and Sales, Mr. Zhang oversees all aspects of sales and marketing for People's Republic of China operations. He supervises the China office, including sales, warehouse and service center operations located in Beijing. An esteemed technology scientist, Mr. Zhang designed the key electronic board for China's first satellite and has been honored with numerous scientific awards from China for his scientific and technological accomplishments. Established in 1990, C & C Broadband Solutions, Inc. employs 15 people with annual sales of $10 million. **Career Steps:** Vice President of Marketing and Owner, C & C Broadband Solutions, Inc. (1990–Present); Purchasing Manager, China Electronics I/E Corp. (1983–1989); Computer System Designer, North China Computer Research Institute (1978–1982). **Associations & Accomplishments:** Recipient, First Class Awards of China National Scientific & Technology Result, the paper "Phase Lock Application in Computers" won first class awards in China National Science and Technology workshop. **Education:** Fudan University, China B.S. in Computers (1977). **Personal:** Married to Kathy Huang in 1979. One child: Jimmy. Mr. Zhang enjoys playing bridge, swimming and skating.

Brian D. Cole

Vice President of Finance
J.C. Enterprises
35 Pine Street
Manchester, NH 03103–6206
(603) 647–5511
Fax: (603) 647–1310
EMAIL: See Below

5072

Business Information: J.C. Enterprises is an importer and wholesale distributor of CTT & Calhawk tools from China to the New England area. As Vice President of Finance, Mr. Cole is responsible for all aspects of financial operations, including accounting, taxes, and coordinating shipments from the Manchester facility. Internet users can reach him via: BCole@Empire.net. **Career Steps:** Vice President of Finance, J.C. Enterprises (1995–Present); Manager, Store 123 (1991–1995). **Associations & Accomplishments:** Knights of Columbus; Former President, Economics and Finance Association. **Education:** New Hampshire College, B.S. in Finance (1995); Hesser College, A.S. in Accounting. **Personal:** Mr. Cole enjoys bowling, golf, and skeet shooting.

James R. Proctor

Vice President of Operations
Odell Hardware Company
P.O. Box 20688
Greensboro, NC 27420–0688
(910) 299–9121
Fax: (910) 852–0450

5072

Business Information: Odell Hardware Company is a national distributor of 43,000 different hardware products. As Vice President of Operations, Mr. Proctor is responsible for managing the Warehouse Transportation Department, to include truck lines, drivers, tractors, and trailers. He also coordinates truck routes with sales routes, and oversees the warehouse, distribution center, shipping, receipts, storage, orders, and loading. In addition, he is responsible for Management Information Technology. **Career Steps:** Vice President of Operations, Odell Hardware Company (1992–Present); Vice President and Co–Founder, Integrated Professional Services (1990–1992); President, J.R. Proctor & Associates (1985–1992). **Associations & Accomplishments:** Tread Users Group (Midrange Systems); Triangle Users Group (Midrange Systems); Former Member, DPMA – Greensboro, North Carolina Chapter; Co–Founder and Treasurer, Jamestown, North Carolina Youth League; Published in trade and industrial magazines and internally with IBM and hardware magazines. **Education:** University of North Carolina – Chapel Hill: B.S. in Mathematics and Nuclear Physics (1968); Vanderbilt University, Executive Management Program. **Personal:** Married to Shirley in 1977. Three children: Bryon, Wesley, and Ashley. Mr. Proctor enjoys golf, skiing, and fishing.

Mark Seitz
Director of Advertising
Service Supply Company, Inc.
P.O. Box 732
Indianapolis, IN 46206
(317) 638–2424
Fax: (317) 634–9087
EMAIL: See Below

5072

Business Information: Service Supply Company, Inc., a family–owned business, is a distributor of industrial fasteners. As Director of Advertising, Mr. Seitz is responsible for the direction of advertising and marketing, as well as coordinating new projects and systems (i.e., Internet access, catalog production). Internet users can reach him via: MCSSSC **Career Steps:** Director of Advertising, Service Supply Company, Inc. (1994–Present); Owner/Operator, Midwest Tape Company; Owner/Operator, Marvins of Bloomington (1986). **Associations & Accomplishments:** Republican Round Table; National Fastener Distributor Association; Childrens Evangelist Fellowship. **Education:** DePauw University, B.A. (1986). **Personal:** Married to Amy Dione in 1990. Two children: Lauren and Macallister. Mr. Seitz enjoys waterskiing, mountain biking, and snow skiing.

James W. Stedman Sr.
Facilities Manager and Corporate Safety Officer
Moore Handley, Inc.
P.O. Box 786
Helena, AL 35080
(205) 663–8267
Fax: (205) 663–8374

5072

Business Information: Moore Handley, Inc. is a wholesale distributor of hardware and building supplies for the construction industry. The Company distributes to international markets, as well as seventeen southeastern states. As Facilities Manager, Mr. Stedman is responsible for the physical property, justification of new equipment, and all maintenance. As Corporate Safety Officer, he is responsible for all on–site safety of the entire facility. **Career Steps:** Facilities Manager and Corporate Safety Officer, Moore Handley, Inc. (1995–Present); Industrial Relations Manager, Ward's Cabinetry (1993–1995); Manager of Manufacturing, Coyne Cylinder Company (1990–1993); Manager of Manufacturing, Electrical Equipment Company, Inc. (1986–1989). **Associations & Accomplishments:** Senior Member, Institute of Industrial Engineers; American Production and Inventory Control Society; Chairman, Blount County Tourism Committee; Executive Vice President of Sales and Marketing, Sun Coast Management Services. **Education:** Utica College, A.S. in Business (1973); Numerous Executive Development Courses; Dale Carnegie Leadership Training, Graduate. **Personal:** Married to Lynn W. in 1993. Four children: Katherine Brodock, James Jr., Kevin Scott, and William M. Cooper. Mr. Stedman enjoys mentoring, computing, and consulting small business owners.

Michael C. Walch
• • • ━━◉━━ • • •
Vice President
Overland, Inc. d.b.a. Smithy Company
P.O. Box 1517
Ann Arbor, MI 48106–1517
(313) 913–6700
Fax: (313) 913–6663
EMail: See Below

5072

Business Information: Overland, Inc. d.b.a. Smithy Company is an international trading and marketing company specializing in metalworking and woodworking tools and accessories. Established in 1990 with approximately 40 employees, the Company's estimated annual sales is over $10 million. As Vice President, Mr. Walch oversees operations in the areas legal, financial, accounting, and administrative matters. A practicing attorney admitted to practice before state and federal courts in Michigan, Oregon and Washington since 1984, prior to joining Overland, Mr. Walch served as an administrative law judge as well as in associate legal practice concentrating in business and international law matters. Internet users can reach him via: mjwalch@aol.com **Career Steps:** Vice President, Overland, Inc. d.b.a. Smithy Company (1995–Present); Administrative Law Judge, Lane Council of Governments (1992–1994); Attorney, Foster & Pepper (1990–1991). **Associations & Accomplishments:** Michigan Bar Association; Oregon Bar Association; Former Chairman, Washington County Land Use Advisory Commission; Vice President, Stanford Law Society of Oregon; Phi Kappa Phi; Beta Gamma Sigma; Phi Eta Sigma; Oregon Public Accountant; Boy Scouts of America. **Education:** Stanford University Law School, J.D. (1984); Brigham Young University, B.A. magna cum laude. **Personal:** Married to Rebecca in 1984. Four children: Shannon, Trevor, Bria and Nolan. Mr. Walch enjoys Dead Sea Scrolls research and whatever interests his children.

Edith I. Harden
Vice President
Johnstone Supply
3232 44th Avenue, North
St. Petersburg, FL 33714–3810
(813) 525–1175
Fax: (813) 526–8659

5075

Business Information: Johnstone Supply is a wholesale air conditioning, heating, refrigeration, and electrical parts outlet for residential and commercial consumers. As Co–Owner and Vice President, Ms. Harden is responsible for clerical, banking, sales, and customer satisfaction. **Career Steps:** Vice President, Johnstone Supply (1986–Present); Nurse Aid, Heritage Acres Nursing Home (1982–1984); Nurse Aid, Big Horn County Hospital (1976–1981); Co–Owner/Office/Sales, Ideal Refrigerator & Electrical (1968–1976). **Associations & Accomplishments:** Rebecca's (Noble Grand) Community Projects (beautification and helping the needy); Church related projects (1976–1979). **Education:** Miles City Community College (1976–1979). **Personal:** Married to Ivan in 1949. Three children: Nikolina Ann Harden Hansen, Douglas Scott, and Dustan Ray; and nine grandchildren and one great grandchild. Ms. Harden enjoys sewing, painting, and travel.

Michael L. McCluhan
MIS/Telecommunications Manager
Johnstone Supply
7245 SW Durham Road
Tigard, OR 97224–7562
(503) 624–1982
Fax: (503) 968–1144
EMail: See Below

5075

Business Information: Johnstone Supply is a wholesale distributor of heating, ventilation, air conditioning, and refrigerants. With corporate headquarters in Tigard, Oregon, Johnstone Supply has seven locations in the U.S. (4–Oregon, 1–California, 2–Washington). As MIS/Telecommunications Manager, Mr. McCluhan is responsible for 85 employees throughout all seven stores, in addition to providing application software support, PC/Network support, and telecommunications support. Internet users can reach him via: SPUD-MAX@AOL.COM. **Career Steps:** MIS/Telecommunications Manager, Johnstone Supply (1995–Present); MIS/Telecommunications Manager, Deschutes County 911 (1990–1995); MIS/Support Services Manager, Morgan Hill Police Department (1989–1990). **Associations & Accomplishments:** Community Theater of the Cascades; President, Tillicum Village HOA; Technical Division, International Association of Chiefs of Police. **Education:** Portland State University; Lewis & Clark College; University of Oregon; Maple Woods Community College. **Personal:** Married to Sally in 1982. Two children: Aaron and Alyson. Mr. McCluhan enjoys photography and fishing.

Luther Sipe
Director of Training
ScottPolar Refrigeration Training Center
3009 W. Fairmont Avenue
Phoenix, AZ 85017–4615
(602) 274–5341
Fax: (602) 274–5472

5078

Business Information: ScottPolar Refrigeration Corporation specializes in commercial refrigeration service and installation of units for supermarkets. Established in 1949, the Company employs 300 people and has estimated annual revenue of $4 million. As Director of Training, Mr. Sipe oversees all technical training and is responsible for all administrative and operational functions related to his department. **Career Steps:** Director of Training, ScottPolar Refrigeration Training Center (1994–Present); Start–up and Troubleshooter, ScottPolar Refrigeration Corporation (1981–1994); Service Technician, ScottPolar Refrigeration Corporation, (1969–1981); Service Technician, Marine–Air (1967–1969); Service Technician, Somerset Refrigeration (1960–1969). **Associations & Accomplishments:** United State Air Force Veteran; Certificate Member, R.S.E.S.; Developed a training video that won first place in a national competition (1988). **Education:** Numerous Factory Schools and Seminars. **Personal:** Married to Kay in 1959. Three children: Jennifer, Lori, and Gary. Mr. Sipe enjoys hunting and fishing.

Douglas B. Kline
Vice President of Finance and Chief Executive Officer
BPS Equipment Rental and Sales
9016 Phillips Highway
Jacksonville, FL 32256
(904) 262–6155
Fax: (904) 262–5962

5082

Business Information: BPS Equipment Rental and Sales is a renter, seller, and servicer of construction–related equipment from eleven branch locations in Southeastern Florida. Main products include aerial work platforms, scaffolding, and suspended platforms. BPS Equipment Rental and Sales is a subsidiary of BET PLC in England, that owns 62 companies worldwide. With twenty–four years experience in accounting and finance and a Certified Public Accountant in Florida, Mr. Kline joined BPS as Vice President of Finance and Chief Executive Officer in 1989. He is responsible for all financing, accounting, human resources, and administration functions, as well as assisting the President in the direction and management of the Company. He is also involved in the activities of international business and transaction functions. **Career Steps:** Vice President of Finance and Chief Executive Officer, BPS Equipment Rental and Sales (1989–Present); Vice President of Finance, Markka Healthcare, Inc. (1987–1989); Vice President of Finance, Concord Food Corporation (1984–1987); Director of Internal Audit, Aegis Corporation (1979–1984); Audit Manager, Price Waterhouse (1972–1979). **Associations & Accomplishments:** American Institute of Certified Public Accountants; Treasurer of Northern Florida Chapter, Financial Executives Institute; Board of Directors, Rebound Care Corporation. **Education:** Florida State University, M.B.A. (1972), B.S. in Accounting (1971); Certification: Certified Public Accountant. **Personal:** Married to Delores in 1970. Mr. Kline enjoys running, tennis, and exercising.

Lynn E. Stoller
Vice President
Stoller International
RR 3 Box 5
Pontiac, IL 61764
(815) 844–6197
Fax: (815) 842–3203

5083

Business Information: Stoller International, a family–owned business, is an agricultural equipment sales company serving customers from three stores in Illinois throughout the U.S. and international companies. Established by Mr. Stoller's father in 1935 and incorporated in 1963, Stoller International reports annual revenue of $7 million and currently employs 48 people. As Vice President, Mr. Stoller serves as the manager of all stores, setting up scheduling, handling payroll, and administrative functions, as well as conducting financial analysis, and sales. **Career Steps:** Vice President, Stoller International (1985–Present). **Associations & Accomplishments:** Sunday School Teacher, Apostolic Christian Church. **Education:** Illinois State University, B.S. (1980); Illinois Central College, A.S. **Personal:** Married to Elaine in 1980. Four children: Candice, Holly, Natalie, and Wendy. Mr. Stoller enjoys hunting and shooting.

Paul V. Bleeker
Vice President of Operations
Cummins West, Inc.
788 Sandoval Way
Hayward, CA 94544–7111
(510) 429–2425
Fax: (510) 429–2425

5084

Business Information: Cummins West, Inc. is a distributor for Cummins Engines, Onan Generators and other associated components, parts and services. Established in 1942, Cummins West, Inc. reports annual revenue of $50 million and currently employs 180 people. As Vice President of Operations, Mr. Bleeker is responsible for daily operations in eight locations, including manufacturing systems, expenses, inventories, and vehicles. **Career Steps:** Vice President of Operations, Cummins West, Inc. (1987–Present); General Manager, Denver Freightliner (1981–1987); Service Manager, Ruan Leasing Company (1976–1981); Owner, Trucking & Service Station (1972–1976). **Education:** Milford Community High School, Graduate (1969). **Personal:** Married to Marcia G. in 1983. Two children: Lauren and Mindi. Mr. Bleeker enjoys woodworking (design and building furniture and houses), motor sports, and relaxing around the pool.

Larry Comparone
Director of Information Technology
Material Handling Division of Western Atlas, Inc.
2100 Litton Lane
Hebron, KY 41048
(606) 334–2557
Fax: (606) 334–2333

5084

Business Information: Material Handling Division of Western Atlas, Inc. is a manufacturer of industrial material handling systems. The Company was established in 1903 and produces conveyors, sortation equipment, palletizers and automated storage and retrieval equipment. Products are sold to clients such as PepsiCo, Nabisco and Ford Motor Company. As Director of Technology, Mr. Comparone is responsible for all information resources. He handles employee training classes and seminars dealing with the information processes. Mr. Comparone is responsible for updating and maintaining all computer systems. **Career Steps:** Material Handling Division of Western Atlas, Inc.: Director of Technology (1995–Present), Manager Corporate Reporting (1993–1995); Manager Budgets, Litton–Unit Handling Systems (1991–1993); Associate Financial Analyst, Litton–Winchester Electronics (1989–1991). **Education:** University of New Hampshire, B.A. (1979). **Personal:** Married in 1990.

Daniel F. Crowley
General Sales Manager
Power Lift
14815 Firestone Blvd.
La Mirada, CA 90638
(310) 632–0900
Fax: (714) 228–0900

5084

Business Information: Power Lift is an authorized Caterpillar lift truck franchise dealer. Established in 1993, Power Lift reports annual sales of $50 million and currently employs 286 people. As General Sales Manager, Mr. Crowley is responsible for the oversight of all sales and marketing functions. **Career Steps:** General Sales Manager, Power Lift (1993–Present); District Manager, Yuasa Exide (1984–1993); Operations Manager, International Contract and Trading (1980–1984). **Associations & Accomplishments:** UCLA Varsity Sailing Coach (1985–1989); Member, Distribution Management Association – Los Angeles, California. **Education:** University of Minnesota, B.S. in Civil Engineering (1979). **Personal:** Married to Connie in 1991. Two children: Rebecca and Max. Mr. Crowley enjoys golf, sailboat racing, tennis, fishing, and sports.

Dean C. Hirt Jr.

Chief Financial Officer and Treasurer
Honnen Equipment Company
5055 East 72nd Avenue
Commerce City, CO 80022
(303) 287–7506
Fax: (303) 288–2215

5084

Business Information: Honnen Equipment Company, licensed John Deere Industrial Equipment distributor in Colorado and Grove World Wide Industrial Crane distributor in Colorado, Wyoming, Nebraska, providing sales, rentals, parts and service from three locations. Joining Honnen Equipment Company as Controller in 1986, promoted to Chief Financial Officer and Treasurer in 1990, Mr. Hirt is responsible for all financial, administrative, IS, and financing functions. Honnen Equipment Company has received the John Deere Mark of Excellence Award seven consecutive years. Mr. Hirt serves on Honnen Equipment Companies Executive Committee Board. Career milestones include design and implementation of technology and communication systems that allowed growth of 200% with overall reductions in overhead. **Career Steps:** Chief Financial Officer and Treasurer, Honnen Equipment Company (1986–Present); Controller, MSF Corporation (1981–1986); Staff Accountant, Rhode, Scripter & Associates, CPA (1979–1981). **Associations & Accomplishments:** Written and published two articles for John Deere publications, speaker on financing and leasing in the construction industry; Organizer and Officer, National Computer User Group; Involved in children's and hunger related charities. **Education:** University of Northern Colorado, B.S. in Business (1979). **Personal:** Married to Ilene in 1981. Three children: Dean III, Brian, and Lisa. Mr. Hirt enjoys skiing, reading, tennis, and golf.

Charles S. Moss
Manager of Research and Development
Alfa Laval Celleco
1000 Laval Boulevard
Lawrenceville, GA 30243–5912
(770) 963–2100
Fax: (770) 822–2964

5084

Business Information: Established in 1972, Alfa Laval Celleco is a pulp and paper process equipment supplier, currently employing 150 people. As Manager of Research and Development, Mr. Moss supervises the development of new equipment, fiber lines, and process systems. **Career Steps:** Manager of Research and Development, Alfa Laval Celleco (1989–Present); Process Engineer, CRS Sirrine Engineers (1988–1989); Pulp and Paper Analyst, Bird Machine Company (1968–88). **Associations & Accomplishments:** Technical Association of Pulp and Paper Industries; Alfa Outstanding Achievement Award; Employee of the Year. **Education:** Clemson University, Chemical Engineering (1963); Northeastern University, Mechanical Engineering, Franklin Institute of Technology, Chemistry (1965). **Personal:** Married to Eileen in 1972. Four children: Meridith, Melissa, Muretta and Merrick. Mr. Moss enjoys photography, music and Frankensteinian testing with process involvements.

Mark S. Rigato
Executive Vice President
Magna Machinery Company, Inc.
1101 Whitcomb
Madison Heights, MI 48071
(810) 616–0080
Fax: (810) 616–0320

5084

Business Information: Magna Machinery Company, Inc. is an authorized distributor and servicer of CNC metal cutting machinery, such as CNC lathes and mills. Established in 1984, Magna Machinery reports annual revenue of $40 million and currently employs 60 people. Involved in industrial sales and distribution his entire career, Mr. Rigato joined Magna Machinery Company, Inc. in 1989 as Sales Manager. Currently serving as Executive Vice President, he is responsible for all aspects of national sales and marketing, manufacturing relations, and sales training. **Career Steps:** Magna Machinery Company, Inc.: Executive Vice President (1993–Present), Sales Manager (1989–1993); National Sales Manager, Mac Valves, Inc. (1986–1988); Sales Engineer, MRM Air Products (1982–1986) **Associations & Accomplishments:** American Machine Tool Distributors Association; Society of Manufacturing Engineers. **Education:** Hillsdale College, B.A. (1981). **Personal:** Married to Victoria L. in 1984. Five children: Theresa, Vincent, Dominic, John, and Maria. Mr. Rigato enjoys guitar and golf during his leisure time.

Rick Star

Vice President and General Manager
Engman–Taylor Company, Inc.
W142 N9351 Fountain Boulevard
Menomonee Falls, WI 53051
(414) 255–9300
Fax: (414) 255–6512

5084

Business Information: Engman–Taylor Company, Inc. is an industrial distributor of machine tools and industrial supplies, purchasing items from an international supplier base for market distribution to manufacturing concerns in Wisconsin and Illinois. Subsidiaries of Engman–Taylor include: Rockford Cutting Tools & Abrasives, Jacobsen & Daw, and Innovative Machine Tool Sales. Future plans include continued controlled growth and major investments in office automation systems, the goal being to reduce customer response times. Established in 1945 and incorporated in 1956, Engman–Taylor Company, Inc. reports annual revenue of $38 million and currently employs 103 people. As Vice President and General Manager, Mr. Star is responsible for the supervision of sales, customer service, and operational functions. **Career Steps:** Engman–Taylor Company, Inc.: Vice President and General Manager (1995–Present), Director of Sales (1991–1995), Zone Sales Manager (1989–1991). **Associations & Accomplishments:** National Association of Industrial Technology (NAIT); Industrial Distribution Association (IDA); Quoted in articles in "Industrial Distribution" and "Buy Lines" magazines. **Education:** University of Wisconsin – Stout, Bachelor of Science, magna cum laude (1984). **Personal:** Married to Lori Anne in 1986. Mr. Star enjoys music and sports.

Jeff Williamson
District Operations Manager
Honeywell, Inc.
3895 Vantech Drive, Suite #5
Memphis, TN 38115
(901) 367–5045
Fax: (901) 367–5070

5084

Business Information: Honeywell, Inc. is active in three areas: Space and aviation, e.g. government contracts and airplane cockpits; Industrial automation; and Home and Building control products, including security and environmental solutions. Honeywell is a worldwide Corporation active in 120 countries. Besides the main U.S. office in Minneapolis, there are major branch offices in Hong Kong, Toronto, Brussels, and Miami (serving South America). As District Operations Manager, Mr. Williamson is responsible for human resource management, organizational change management, service scheduling, performance management, and a multi–million dollar profit/loss management program. Other responsibilities include scheduling of sales and delivery of products, customer relations, and negotiating contracts for vendors. **Career Steps:** Honeywell, Inc.: District Operations Manager (1993–Present), Senior Account Manager (1985–1993); Factory Sales, Dover Elevator Company. **Associations & Accomplishments:** Awards Received from Honeywell: Operations Manager of the Year (1995); Award in Excellence (1993); Award in Divisional Sales (1991); Two Outstanding Performance Awards. **Education:** Christian Brothers University, B.S.M.E. (1983). **Personal:** One child: Joshua. Mr. Williamson enjoys golf, boating, and fishing.

Donald G. Burns
Assistant Controller
Unisource Southeast Region
7785 Baymeadows Way, Suite 200
Jacksonville, FL 32256–7561
(904) 693–5801
Fax: (904) 731–4939

5085

Business Information: Unisource Southeast Region is a sales, marketing, and distribution company specializing in industrial/packaging products and printing paper. Established in 1921, the Company employs 1,369 people and has estimated annual revenue of $1.2 billion. As Assistant Controller, Mr. Burns is responsible for financial reporting and general accounting functions. He oversees the general accounting department and performs scheduled profitability and financial analysis and forecasting. **Career Steps:** Assistant Controller, Unisource Southeast Region (1984–Present); Staff Accountant, Winn–Dixie Stores (1977–1984). **Associations & Accomplishments:** Christian Professional Resource. **Education:** University of North Florida, B.B.A. (1983). **Personal:** Married to Megan in 1979. Three children: Lauren, Christine and John. Mr. Burns enjoys snow skiing, fishing, volleyball, and basketball.

Winthrop Doolittle
General Manager
Revchem Plastics
P.O. Box 8190
Redlands, CA 92375
(909) 877–8477
Fax: (909) 877–8475

5085

Business Information: Revchem Plastics is a distributor of raw materials, process equipment, and industrial supplies into the composite industry. As General Manager, Mr. Doolittle is responsible for sales, marketing, and long range strategic planning. **Career Steps:** General Manager, Revchem Plastics (1985–Present); Operations Manager, Xerxes Corporation (1981–1985); Financial Analyst, Mobil Chemical (1979–1980). **Education:** Babson College: M.B.A. (1979), B.S. in Finance (1978). **Personal:** Married to Jeanne in 1984. Two children: Damon and Spencer. Mr. Doolittle enjoys golf and snow boarding.

Drew A. Tucci
Director of Sales
Eastern Bearings, Inc.
7096 South Willow Street
Manchester, NH 03103–2334
(603) 668–3300
Fax: (603) 669–5714

5085

Business Information: Eastern Bearings, Inc. is a bearings and industrial power supplies distributor, serving retail and wholesale customers throughout Vermont, Massachusetts, Maine, Rhode Island and New Hampshire. As Director of Sales, Mr. Tucci is responsible for sales, marketing, sales forecasting, budgeting, opening new markets and new branches, and integrating supply and vendor relations. In addition, he serves as General Manager for the newly merged company, Eastern Lane Industries. **Career Steps:** Eastern Bearings, Inc.: Director of Sales (1995–Present), Sales Manager (1992–1995); General Manager, Eastern Lane Industries (1995–Present); District Manager, Emerson Electric Company (1989–1992). **Associations & Accomplishments:** Manchester Chamber of Commerce; Pennsylvania State University Alumni Association; American Marketing Association; Power Transmission Distributor Association. **Education:** New Hampshire College, M.B.A. (1995); Pennsylvania State University, B.S. in Marketing. **Personal:** Married to Lynn A. in 1989. Mr. Tucci enjoys golf, tennis, and collectables.

Walterio R. Castillo

Director for Latin American Marketing, Sales, and Education
Sebastion International
18256 Northwest 61st Place
Hialeah, FL 33015–5603
(305) 826–7257
Fax: (305) 826–1772

5087

Business Information: Sebastion International distributes beauty products to independent salons around the world from its headquarters in Los Angeles, California. As Director for Latin American Marketing, Sales, and Education, Mr. Castillo is responsible for varied administrative activities and strategic planning, regularly embarking on marketing and educational forays to Mexico and the Caribbean. **Career Steps:** Director for Latin American Marketing, Sales, and Education, Sebastion International (1987–Present); General Manager, G.D. Searle and Company (1981–1987); Director of Marketing, CIBA – Geigy 91975–1981); Marketing Manager, Bristol Myers Company International Division (1964–1975). **Education:** University National Pedro H. Uresses, Masters of Business Administration (1976). **Personal:** Married to Cristina in 1986. Five children: Monnika, Walterio Jr., Elio, Christian, and John.

Robert M. Fey

Director of Technical Operations
Toro Company
5825 Jasmine Street
Riverside, CA 92504
(909) 785–3503
Fax: (909) 783–3647

5087

Business Information: Toro Company specializes in the design and manufacture of irrigation control and sprinkler systems. As Director of Technical Operations, Mr. Fey is the process leader of new product development for sprinkler systems and electronics. **Career Steps:** Director of Technical Operations, Toro Company (1994–Present); Director of Technical Operations, Thermador Division, Masco (1992–1994); Vice President of Engineering, Kohler (1989–1992); Vice President of Engineering, Roper (1983–1989); Vice President of Engineering, Speed Queen Division, Rayethon Corporation (1981–1983); Manager of Design Engineering, General Electric Corporation (1962–1981). **Associations & Accomplishments:** Society of Plastics Engineers; Granted 11 patents. **Education:** St. Louis University, Master's in Meteorology; University of Louisville, B.S. in Mechanical Engineering (1959). **Personal:** Married to Patricia in 1982. Six children: Natasha, Jessica, Jane, Tammy, Nancy, and Susan. Mr. Fey enjoys antiques, classic automobiles, and sailing.

Juan Grau

President
Grau Mechanical Enterprises, Inc.
6653 Powers Avenue, Suite 239
Jacksonville, FL 32217
(904) 268–0505
Fax: Please mail or call

5087

Business Information: Grau Mechanical Enterprises, Inc. is an importer and wholesale distributor of Italian–designed dry cleaning and laundry equipment — the exclusive importers of MAXClean. Established in 1993, the Company has an estimated annual sales of over $1 million. As President, Mr. Grau is responsible for all aspects of Company operations, including finance, administration, public relations, marketing, and strategic planning. **Career Steps:** President, Grau Mechanical Enterprises, Inc. (1993–Present); Chief Executive Officer, Star Engineering Inc. (1986–1991). **Education:** Florida International University (1991), Sporane Falls Community College, Pre–Electrical Engineering. **Personal:** Married to Elena in 1980. Two children: Eric and Melissa. Mr. Grau enjoys Piloting.

William L. Henry

General Manager and Sales Manager
Engleside Products, Inc.
355 East Liberty Street
Lancaster, PA 17602
(717) 397–9497
Fax: (717) 397–9095

5087

Business Information: Engleside Products, Inc. is a provider of wholesale home care products and janitorial supplies to hardware stores and supermarkets throughout the Nation. Products include paper products and chemical cleaning supplies. Servicing the Pennsylvania and New Jersey area, Engleside Products, Inc. has two subsidiaries, Excel Cleaning Service and Engleside Home Products. With more than ten years of experience in sales, Mr. Henry joined Engleside Products, Inc. in 1991 and serves as its General Manager and Sales Manager with a 10% interest in the Company. He is responsible for the management of the Company, as well as all sales activities. **Career Steps:** General Manager and Sales Manager, Engleside Products, Inc. (1991–Present); Sales Manager, Excel Cleaning Services (1993–1994); Operational Manager, Clean Way Professional Cleaning (1988–1993); Sales Representative, Bortek, Inc. (1986–1988). **Associations & Accomplishments:** Lancaster County Foster parent Association; Foster Parent (20 Years); U.S. Golf Association; Sales Managers and Executives Association; Vietnam Veteran (1968–1969). **Education:** Attended: University of New Mexico (1965–1966), Milton Hershey School, U.S. Airforce Institute, Various courses and seminars for Sales and Sales Managers. **Personal:** Married to Kathryn in 1974. Six children: Melissa, Bobby, Willie, Patrick, Iseha and Ericka. Mr. Henry enjoys golf, coaching baseball and camping with family.

Stephen L. Kovacs

Director of Sales and Marketing
Harris Offshore Services
60 East 42nd Street, Suite 1150
New York, NY 10165
(212) 808–0098
Fax: (212) 808–0198

5087

Business Information: Harris Offshore Services is a primary exporter of foodservice, laundry, and capital equipment for hotels and institutions around the world. The Company has agents in fifteen countries worldwide at the present time. Plans for expansion include the opening of an office in California. Established in 1972, the Company employs 18 people, and has an estimated annual revenue of $5 million. As Director of Sales and Marketing, Mr. Kovacs develops sales, set up computer operations and systems, and develops new markets and new products for distribution worldwide. In addition, he is responsible for developing food product sales from breakfast cereals to India, baking products to Russia, diverse food to Brazil, and cocktail mix to California. Concurrently, Mr. Kovacs is engineering a joint venture with a corporation for distribution to London, Russia, and Eastern Block countries. **Career Steps:** Director of Sales and Marketing, Harris Offshore Services (1994–Present); Purchasing Manager, Quest International Industries, Inc. (1985–1994); Assistant Manager, Projects Purchasing, Inter–Continental Hotels – World Headquarters (1975–1985). **Education:** F.I.T., Division of State University of New York, A.A.S. (1964).

Stuart Stine

Manager of Business Systems
Lockheed Martin Manned Space Systems
604 Swallow Court
Slidell, LA 70461
(504) 257–2015
Fax: (504) 639–0675
EMail: See Below

5088

Business Information: Lockheed Martin Manned Space Systems – the Space Shuttle External Tank Program, is the manufacturer of the space flight hardware fuel tank for the shuttle. As Manager of Business Systems, Mr. Stine is responsible for the design and implementation of all business automated systems. He can also be reached through the Internet as follows: Stuart.Stine@MAF.NASA.Gov **Career Steps:** Manager of Business Systems, Lockheed Martin Manned Space Systems (1990–Present); Administrator of Financial Analysis, Lockheed Martin Headquarters (1988–1990); Administrator of Financial Planning, Lockheed Martin Manned Space Systems (1984–1988). **Associations & Accomplishments:** Board of Directors, Christ Episcopal Church Vestry. **Education:** Tulane University, Executive M.B.A. program(24 hours completed toward requirement of 48 hours); University of Texas, B.B.A. in Finance and Marketing (1979). **Personal:** Married to Susan Kay in 1982. Three children: Samuel, Trevor, and Zachary. Mr. Stine enjoys church, youth soccer, youth swimming, and Boy Scout activities.

James D. Vigneau

Senior Manager of Human Resources
Alpine Electronics
19145 Gramercy Place
Torrance, CA 90501
(310) 783–7043
Fax: (310) 212–0884

5088

Business Information: Alpine Electronics, a wholly–owned subsidiary of the Japanese–based telecommunications company, Alpine of Japan, serves as the marketing distribution arm for the sale of high end audio, security and navigation systems. Major clientele include Honda, BMW, Mercedes and other major automotive manufacturers. As Senior Manager of Human Resources, Mr. Vigneau is responsible for all human resource and administration functions in North and South America. **Career Steps:** Senior Manager of Human Resources, Alpine Electronics (1990–Present); Senior Human Resource Representive, Northrop Corporation (1982–1990); General Manager, JMS, Inc. (1975–1982). **Associations & Accomplishments:** Society of Human Resource Management; Professionals in Human Resources Association; Chairman, Human Resource Professionals of Torrance; Torrance Rotary. **Education:** University of San Francisco, B.S. (1986). **Personal:** Married to Roberta in 1986. Two children: Lisa and Jeff. One grandchild: Joshua. Mr. Vigneau enjoys sailing, scuba diving, and golf.

James D. Anderson

President/CEO
Road Runner Skate Walkers – a Division of USSAT Corporation
338 East Mariposa Street
Phoenix, AZ 85012–1606
(602) 277–7617
Fax: Please mail or call

5091

Business Information: Mr. Anderson has been in the process of developing this product for four years. The invention is a cover for the bottom of in–line skates to allow the user to walk with them. Road Runner Skate Walkers has had the prototype, the patent, and the trademark, and will soon begin manufacturing and distribution of the product. Currently, Mr. Anderson is working on promoting the Road Runner Skate Walkers. **Career Steps:** President/CEO, Road Runner Skate Walkers – a Division of USSAT Corporation (1992–Present); Contractor – NDT Technician, MQS Inspection, Inc. (1996); Garrett Fluid Systems, Garrett (1986); Arizona Q.C. Engineer, Arizona Public Service (1983). **Associations & Accomplishments:** American Society of Non–Destructive Testing. **Education:** Arizona State University, M.E. (1960). **Personal:** Three children: John, James, and Karen. Mr. Anderson enjoys golf and model building.

Jerry A. Guisinger

Chief Financial and Administration Officer
Sand Trap Golf, Inc.
1515 Fruitville Road
Sarasota, FL 34236–8507
(941) 955–1958
Fax: (941) 365–0923

5091

Business Information: Sand Trap Golf, Inc. is an international retailer and wholesaler of golf products serving individual and major companies, such as Calloway, Spaulding, Footjoy, and Titleist. Shipped from three locations in Sarasota County, Sand Trap Golf, Inc. markets products both nationally and internationally. As Chief Finance/Administration Officer, Mr. Guisinger is responsible for all finances, administrative activities, and computer systems. His duties include overseeing accounting, investments, banking, hiring and firing of employees, the purchase of hardware and software solutions, and coordination of computer support. In addition, he serves as a liaison between Sand Trap and the employee leasing company. **Career Steps:** Chief Finance/Administration Officer, Sand Trap Golf, Inc. (Present); Controller, MYCO Trailers, Inc.; Comptroller, Stancon Management; Comptroller, Just Like Home, Inc. **Associations & Accomplishments:** Former military member. **Personal:** Mr. Guisinger enjoys going to the beach, canoeing, volleyball, and computers.

Thomas R. Reed
Vice President of Finance & Administration
Bolle America, Inc.
3890 Elm Street
Denver, CO 80207
(303) 321-4300
Fax: (303) 321-6952

5091

Business Information: Bolle America, Inc. markets and distributes Bolle sunglasses in the United States, the Caribbean, and Mexico to high end retailers. As Vice President of Finance & Administration, Mr. Reed is responsible for all finance, accounting, human resources, and MIS for the Company. He is heavily involved in forecasting and budgeting. **Career Steps:** Vice President of Finance & Administration, Bolle America, Inc. (1994–Present); Senior Auditor, Ernst & Young (1990–1994). **Education:** University of Denver: M.B.A. (1990), B.S.B.A. (1984). **Personal:** Married to Lori in 1995. Two children: Conner and Erin. Mr. Reed enjoys golf and shooting.

Debra L. Westenberger
Marketing Manager
Perry Austen Bowling Products
2700 Westown Parkway, Suite 430
West Des Moines, IA 50266-1411
(515) 224-7780
Fax: (515) 223-6095

5091

Business Information: Perry Austen Bowling Products, a division of international sports congolomerate — Brunswick Corporation, is a major distributor of bowling products. As Marketing Manager, Mrs. Westenberger is responsible for the promotion and advertising programs, including allocation of a $600,000 budget. **Career Steps:** Marketing Manager, Perry Austen Bowling Products (1993–Present). **Associations & Accomplishments:** Board of Directors, American Marketing Association – Iowa Chapter; Des Moines Leadership Institute (1996); Des Moines Prairie Club. **Education:** Drake University: M.B.A. (1991), B.S. in Marketing. **Personal:** Mrs. Westenberger enjoys dogs, reading, playing piano, and exercising.

Maria A. Drew

Director of Human Resources
Disney Consumer Products Latin America Inc.
1 Alhambra Plaza
Coral Gables, FL 33134
(305) 567-3734
Fax: (305) 567-3795

5092

Business Information: Disney Consumer Products Latin America, Inc. is an international marketing and development firm for Disney merchandise (consumer products). As Director of Human Resources, Ms. Drew is responsible for the human resources function for the Latin American region of Disney Consumer Products. **Career Steps:** Disney Consumer Products Latin America, Inc.: Director of Human Resources (1995–Present), Manager of Human Resources (1994–1995), Disney Consumer Products (domestic): Manager of Employee Relations (1992–1994); The Walt Disney Company: Manager of Equal Opportunity Programs & Employee Records (1989–1992), Manager of Equal Opportunity Programs (1985–1989). **Associations & Accomplishments:** GSHRM; Former Chair & President of the Los Angeles Basin Equal Opportunity League; Former Board Member of the Los Angeles Urban League; Former Member of the Hispanic Academy of Media Arts & Sciences. **Education:** University of LaVerne, B.S./B.A. (1989). **Personal:** Married to Dana in 1983.

Stella Wong

Vice President
Boley Corporation
2022 Violet Street
Los Angeles, CA 90021-1729
(212) 688-8802
Fax: (213) 688-7484

5092

Business Information: Boley Corporation is primarily engaged in the import and wholesale distribution of toys and related products to major retailers in the U.S., Canada, and Mexico. A family–owned Company, Boley Corporation accounts for 80% of their shipping to domestic retailers. Established in

1981, the Company employs 18 people, and has an estimated annual revenue of $13 million. As Vice President, Mrs. Wong handles all internal management and control and is responsible for all financial planning. A Co–Owner with her husband, she is also responsible for financial forecasting for the Company and oversight of the Company's strategic focus. **Career Steps:** Vice President, Boley Corporation (1981–Present). **Associations & Accomplishments:** Member of "Sterling's Who's Who." **Education:** California State, Northridge, Master of Science (1985). **Personal:** Married to Ronald in 1985. Three children: Reuben, Spencer, and Renee. Mrs. Wong enjoys singing and reading journals.

Richard J. Commerford
Operations Manager
Central Metals Recycling
950 Marietta St. NW
Atlanta, GA 30318-5504
(404) 874-7564
Fax: Please mail or call

5093

Business Information: Central Metals Recycling is a facility that buys recyclable metals, processes them, and sells them back to various manufacturers. The Company currently serves a regional market. Established in 1915, Central Metals Recycling employs 130 people. As Operations Manager, Mr. Commerford manages all phases of production operations including hiring, training, budgeting, scheduling, and purchasing. **Career Steps:** Operations Manager, Central Metals Recycling (1995–Present); Special Products Plant Manager, Clarke American (1985–1995); Captain, U.S. Army (1981–1985). **Associations & Accomplishments:** Cobb County Chamber of Commerce, member; Cobb County Business School Advisory Board, past Advisory Board Member; Army Commendation Medal – Army Achievement Medal. **Education:** Kennesaw State College, MBA (1995); Virginia Military Institute, BA in Economics (1981). **Personal:** Mr. Commerford enjoys the outdoors, hiking, and camping. He also enjoys golf.

Mark W. Hope, QEP
Vice President, Northwest Region
Waste Recovery, Inc.
8501 N. Borthwick
Portland, OR 97217
(503) 283-2261 ext 13
Fax: (503) 283-2498

5093

Business Information: Waste Recovery, Inc. specializes in scrap tire collection, recycling, processing and marketing. The Company has developed a pioneering approach to using tires as fuel products for the pulp and paper, cement, and utility industries; processing approximately 17 million tires in 1995. Established in 1982, Waste Recovery, Inc. currently employs 240 people in six different regions across the U.S. and has an estimated annual revenue of $20 million. In his current capacity, Mark Hope directs all aspects of management for the Northwest Region and acts as a resource for management of corporate environmental affairs. **Career Steps:** Waste Recovery, Inc.: Vice President, Northwest Region (1990–Present), Marketing & Governmental Affairs Manager (1985–1989), Procurement/Transportation and Governmental Affairs Manager (1982–1984); Oregon DEQ: Superfund Program Manager (1981–1982), RCRA Program Manager (1979–1981), Project Officer–Surface Impoundment Assessment (1980–1981), Staff Specialist–Urban Wood Waste Disposal and Recovery Alternatives (1979–1982); Environmental Specialist, Douglas County Health Department (1977–1978). **Associations & Accomplishments:** Technical Association of the Pulp and Paper Industry; Air and Waste Management Association; Qualified Environmental Professional (QEP), Institute of Professional Environmental Practice; Published in: TAPPI Engineering (1993), Council of Industrial Boiler Owners (1995), Air Pollution Control Association Specialty Conference (1988), The Akron Rubber Group, Inc. (1987), National Council of the Paper Industry for Air & Steam Improvement Bulletin (1985), Co–authored and managed quintessential consultant reports on scrap tires for the states of Minnesota (1985) and Ohio (1986). **Education:** Oregon State University, B.S. in Public Health. **Personal:** Married to Valerie in 1981. Two children: Nicholas and Anthony. Mr. Hope enjoys skiing, hiking and rollerblading.

Donald D. Tripler
Vice President of Foreign Operations
P & R Metals, Inc.
2222 North Alameda Street
Compton, CA 90222
(213) 774-0595
Fax: (310) 537-1624

5093

Business Information: P & R Metals, Inc. is an international recycling company specializing in the recycle of scrap non-ferrous metals. Established in 1962, P & R Metals, Inc. cur-

rently employs more than 100 people. As Vice President of Foreign Operations, Mr. Tripler is responsible for coordination of the financial and managerial aspects of the Company's domestic and Mexican affiliates, as well as operations, accounting, and strategic planning. **Career Steps:** Vice President of Foreign Operations, P & R Metals, Inc. (1993–Present); Senior Accountant – CPA, Alder, Green, & Hasson (1990–1993). **Associations & Accomplishments:** California State Board of Accounting; California State Society of Certified Public Accountants; American Institute of Certified Public Accountants; Latin Business Association; Mexican American Alumni Association – Loyola Marymount University. **Education:** Loyola Marymount University, B.S. in Accounting (1990). **Personal:** Mr. Tripler enjoys running, tennis, and basketball.

David Crowe

Chief Executive Officer
Gold Unlimited, Inc.
1645 Otter Lake Loop
Hanson, KY 42413-9650
(502) 322-3347
Fax: Please mail or call

5094

Business Information: Gold Unlimited, Inc. markets wholesale jewelry through more than 100,000 independent distributors in the United States, Canada, and Hong Kong. With eight years experience in the jewelry industry and twenty–seven years experience in network marketing, Mr. Crowe founded Gold Unlimited in 1992. In his capacity as Chief Executive Officer, he is presently responsible for business development, marketing, and strategic planning. **Career Steps:** Chief Executive Officer, Gold Unlimited, Inc. (1992–Present); President & Chief Executive Officer, American Gold Eagle (1990–1992); Chief Executive Officer, Perfect Combination, Inc. (1989–1990). **Associations & Accomplishments:** Direct Sales Association, Washington, D.C.; Multi–Level Marketing Association. **Education:** Attended: Radiological Technical Institute; Multiple business seminars and courses. **Personal:** Married to Martha in 1969. Two children: Joley Crowe Larkin and Mindy Crowe Cutler. Mr. Crowe enjoys bicycling and fishing. Mr. Crowe is especially proud of being a Vietnam Veteran.

George Molayem

President
Hill Street Jewelers, U.S.A.
510 West 6th Street, Suite 728
Los Angeles, CA 90014
(213) 688-0108
Fax: (213) 688-0107

5094

Business Information: Hill Street Jewelers, U.S.A. is a manufacturer and wholesaler of fine diamond jewelry in the U.S. and the Caribbean. Hill Street Jewelers also publishes a 40–page, bi–monthly trade magazine that is circulated through jewelry stores throughout the U.S. Joining Hill Street Jewelers as President in 1986, Mr. Molayem is responsible for the day–to–day operations and future direction of the Company. He also serves as the Company's publisher, top salesman, buyer, and a servicer of large clientele. **Career Steps:** President, Hill Street Jewelers, U.S.A. (1986–Present); Co–Manager and Director, Nau H. Mico, VA. **Education:** University of Maryland, Management, Economics, and Finance (1984). **Personal:** Married to Sharon in 1989. One child: Michelle. Mr. Molayem enjoys all family activities.

Ferdinand Vazquez
Director of Security
Sandburg & Sikorski
37 West 26th Street
New York, NY 10010
(212) 843-7464 Ext. 10
Fax: (212) 779-1998

5094

Business Information: Sandburg & Sikorski is a wholesale jewelry manufacturing firm based in New York, engaged in the manufacture and sales of such to over 600 retailers. As Director of Security, Mr. Vazquez is responsible for the implementation of all security procedures and policies for the corporation, such as an identification access/card program, and the supervision over the installation of all the Corporation's alarms and closed circuit television systems. He additionally secures the delivery routes and transportation of merchandise; conducts investigations into reports of missing merchandise; requisitions and maintains security equipment; screens employees, visitors, and contractors upon entry into restricted areas; supervises key access control; and the implementation of the Company's proprietary security department. **Career Steps:** Director of Security, Sandburg & Sikorski (1994–Present); Security Officer, St. Lukes/Roosevelt Hospital (Smithers Rehabilitation Center) (1992–1994); Mount Sinai Medical Center: Security Supervisor (1989–1991), Security Coordinator (1987–1989); Assistant Building Fire Safety Director/Loss Prevention Officer, The Trump Organization (1986–1987); Assistant Director of Security, Frederick Goldman, Inc. (1985–1986); Supervisor/Investigator (Special Assignment), Dignon Security Services, Inc. (1981–1986). **Education:** John Jay College of Criminal Justice, B.S. (1978–1980); New York State Certified Armed Guard.

Edward B. Bradley
President
Shared Marketing, Inc.
18965 University Avenue Northeast
Cedar, MN 55011
(612) 434–1036
Fax: (612) 434–8260

5099

Business Information: Shared Marketing, Inc. is an international distributor of nutritional products worldwide, such as health & fitness, weight control, etc. As President, Mr. Bradley is responsible for all aspects of operations, including administration, finances, public relations, marketing, and strategic planning. **Career Steps:** President, Shared Market, Inc. (1995–Present); National Sales Manager, Omnetics Connector Corp. (1988–1995); National Application Engineer, ITT Cannon (1977–1988); Customer Service Manager, PIC Wire and Cable (1972–1977). **Associations & Accomplishments:** Sales and Marketing Executives of Minneapolis; Instructor, American Red Cross. **Education:** Marquette University, B.S.E.E. (1970). **Personal:** Married to Carol in 1960. Four children: Linda, Patricia, Marianne, and Sharon. Mr. Bradley enjoys sailing, skiing, and golf.

dooley enterprises, inc.
WINCHESTER®
DISTRIBUTOR
1198 N. Grove St. • Anaheim, CA 92806
714-630-6436   FAX 714-630-3910

Cynthia A. Dooley
Vice President
Dooley Enterprises, Inc.
1198 N. Grove Street
Anaheim, CA 92806
(714) 630–6436
Fax: (714) 630–3910

5099

Business Information: Dooley Enterprises, Inc. is one of the nation's leading distributors of law enforcement ammunition — focusing primarily in the supply of Winchester brand small arms ammunition. With major clientele located in California, Dooley Enterprises also has clientele in the states of Alaska, Hawaii, Oregon, Arizona and Nevada. Serving as Vice President for this family business, Mrs. Dooley oversees all information systems areas, with duties also including computer programming, sales, operations, as well as accounting and financial audits controls. She implemented the Company's entire computer systems network operations which also led to quadruple growth in five years. **Career Steps:** Vice President, Majority Stock Holder, Dooley Enterprises, Inc. (1989–Present); Teleservicing/ATM Servicing Representative, Bank of America (1979–1989). **Associations & Accomplishments:** NRA; Ham Radio Licensed Technician. **Education:** California State University – Fullerton, B.A. in Business (1983). **Personal:** Married to Patrick J. in 1980. Two children: Christopher and Jimmy. Mrs. Dooley enjoys computers, step aerobics, target and clay shooting, and reading mystery novels.

Michael Estus
Product Manager
Eurpac Service Company
3001 Skyway Circle North, Suite 160
Irving, TX 75038
(214) 257–1194 Ext. 213
Fax: (214) 570–7126
EMAIL: See Below

5099

Business Information: Eurpac Service Company is a military exchange sales and service organization, supporting military exchanges worldwide, providing products to stores and commissaries. As Product Manager, Mr. Estus is responsible for business machines, computer peripherals, and price sensitive products. In addition, he is responsible for budgeting, fore-

casting of products, and communicating between the buyer (exchanges) and the manufacturer to ensure the best price for the product. Internet users can reach him via: MESTUS@airmail.net. **Career Steps:** Eurpac Service Company: Product Manager (1995–Present), Technical Trainer (1994–1995); Demonstrator, Watt/Spohn Military Sales (1993–1994); Sales Specialist, Pamco Enterprises (1992–1993); Sales Associate, Spec–4 Marketing (1992–1993); Vendor Demonstrator, Specialized Marketing (1991–1993); Oriental Specialist, Sysco Food Services (1992); Manufacture Representative, Mercury Luggage (1991–1992); Consultative Broker, Marketing Plus Associates (1991–1992); Vendor, Lindale Marketing (1991–1992); Vendor Representative, William Carter Company (1991–1993); Network Marketer, Estus Marketing Consultants (1990–1993); Radio Repairman, US Army Reserve (1988–1989). **Associations & Accomplishments:** Mitchell Award, Civil Air Patrol (US Air Force); Who's Who in High School; San Antonio World Trade Association; Association of American Chinese Professionals; Director of Minority Affairs, Search Committee; First Place, Packard Bell Holidays Contest in the Continental US; Asian American Professional Association, Houston Chapter; University of Texas – San Antonio: President – Chinese Student Association, Board Member – Student Research Group, Appointed Delegate – John Shepherd Leadership Forum. **Education:** University of Texas–San Antonio, B.A. in Criminal Justice (1991); San Antonio College, A.A.; Certifications: Private Investigator, Security Officer – Texas Board of Private Investigators; Radiotelephone Operator Permit — FCC. **Personal:** Married to Diana R. in 1991. Mr. Estus enjoys golf, rebuilding computers, and is fluent in Mandarin Chinese.

Anita T. Gittelson

Senior Vice President and Partner
WESSCO International
1950 Sawtelle Boulevard, Suite 360
Los Angeles, CA 90025–7014
(310) 477–4272
Fax: (310) 477–7910

5099

Business Information: WESSCO International is an amenity designer, importer, and domestic licensee for custom name brand products for hotels, airlines, cruise lines, and duty free industries. As Senior Vice President and Partner, Ms. Gittelson is responsible for sales, public relations, strategic planning, trade show coordination, and budget goal planning. Additionally, she is a Partner in the Retail Division. **Career Steps:** Senior Vice President and Partner, WESSCO International (1986–Present); Vice President – Hotel Division, Michaud Associates (1984–1986); Director of Development, Los Angeles Civic Light Opera (1982–1984). **Associations & Accomplishments:** National Association of Executive Women in Hospitality; Marine, Hotel, Catering and Duty Free Association; International Flight Association (National & International); International Duty Free Association; Women's Alliance for Israel; Past President, Encino Community Center; Past President and Founder, Encino Theatre Group; Los Angeles Mayor's Award; Chair, Bi–Centennial Parade; Los Angeles City Council Award for Contributions to the Arts in the City of Los Angeles; Honorary Award from California State Parent Teacher Association for Coordinating Inter–Racial Programs. **Education:** California State University at Northridge, B.A. (1971); University of California at Los Angeles, Master's classes in Business Administration. **Personal:** Three children: Robert Bruce, Gerald Jay, and Beverly Sue Gittelson Manitsky. Ms. Gittelson enjoys musical theatre, master choral, reading, travel, and gourmet cooking, and her grandchildren: Alex Ian, Jesse Andrew, and baby Manitsky.

Thomas L. Lynott
Chairman
Ural America, Inc.
8146 304th Avenue SE
Preston, WA 98050
(206) 222–7738
Fax: (206) 222–7739

5099

Business Information: Ural America, Inc. is an international importer and exporter of Russian and Chinese goods. Established in 1991, Ural America, Inc. reports annual revenue of $13 million and currently employs eleven people. As Co–Founder and Chairman, Mr. Lynott oversees all aspects of operations, including finances, purchasing, and contracts. After the fall of Communism in Russia in the Fall of 1989, Mr. Lynott read an article in the San Jose Mercury in 1990, discovering that fifty percent of all potatoes grown in Russia never got to market because of rotting. Seeing a marketing opportunity, he obtained a Visa, traveled to Russia and came home with partners, investors, and a $10 million project. His project included obtaining a contract to purchase, dehydrate, and ship potatoes to the U.S. The dehydrating process (taking out 92% of the potato's water), enabled the potatoes to be shipped, handled and stored more economically and without fear of spoiling. After one and a half years of trips, he established an office

with an office manager and a translator. He has been involved in other areas, such as marketing Russian motorcycles throughout the U.S., a Chinese tire recycling plant, and a cycle plant that supports a city of 50,000 people and employs 10,000 people in Siberia – helping the people modernize equipment at the plant and a 1940's equipment building by sharing technology techniques on cycles from WWII. **Career Steps:** Chairman, Ural America, Inc. (1991–Present); President, Pace Capital Corporation (1989–1991); President, World Class Marine (1986–1989); President, Lynott Securities (1979–1986); President, Reinell Industries, Inc. (1965–1977). **Associations & Accomplishments:** World Trade Club; Russian American Foundation for Economic Cooperation; Article done on him in the "Seattle Times." **Education:** University of California – Los Angeles, B.A. (1964). **Personal:** Married to Bobbette in 1995. One child: Beau. Mr. Lynott enjoys skiing, boating, and golf.

Peter B. Neuberger
General Manager
Strategic Distribution
12136 West Bayaud Avenue, Suite 320
Lakewood, CO 80228
(303) 233–4722
Fax: (303) 234–1468

5099

Business Information: Strategic Distribution is the fifth fastest growing company, specializing in industrial distribution of MRO supplies for manufacturing companies. Strategic Distribution has sixty locations throughout North America. Joining Strategic Distribution as General Manager in 1995, Mr. Neuberger oversees all aspects of operations with the in-plant store division. **Career Steps:** General Manager, Strategic Distribution (1995–Present); Norton Company: Director of Industrial Marketing (1993–1994), Manager of Industrial Distribution (1991–1993). **Associations & Accomplishments:** Industrial Distribution Association; World Wildlife Fund for Endangered Species. **Education:** Harvard University, M.B.A. (1991); Amherst College, B.A. (1986). **Personal:** Mr. Neuberger enjoys show horses.

Mr. Arturo Pimienta
Preisident and Chief Executive Officer
Universal Network, Inc.
1007 Grogan's Mill Road, #200
The Woodlands, TX 77380
(713) 363–4000
Fax: (713) 367–2619

5099

Business Information: Universal Network, Inc. is a wholesale trader specializing in U.S. exports into Mexico and Latin America. The Company presently employs 86 people, has an estimated annual revenue of $17 million and has been established for six years. As President and Chief Executive Officer, Mr. Pimienta is responsible for all aspects of operations for the Company. **Career Steps:** Senior Vice President, Interamericas Investments, Inc.; Chief Financial Officer, PBP Mexico; Chief Financial Officer, Dicopsa Mexico. **Associations & Accomplishments:** Member, Knights of Columbus; Member, Houston Hispanic Chamber of Commerce. **Education:** Attended Universidad Anahuac Mexico, Industrial Engineering Degree (1988). **Personal:** Married to Maria in five years. Two children: Arturo Kenneth and Juan Pablo. Mr. Pimienta enjoys tennis and music.

Anthony S. Radziminski Jr.
Co–Owner and Vice President
Ostar International, Inc.
7720 Lima Road
Ft. Wayne, IN 46818
(219) 497–7454
Fax: (219) 497–0159

5099

Business Information: Ostar International, Inc. is an import/export firm, providing technical services related to defense conversions to Eastern European countries, such as Russia, Poland, and Lithuania. Future plans include expanding operations to the Middle East. With twenty–eight years experience in the technical industry, Mr. Radziminski co–founded the Firm in 1994. Serving as Co–Owner and Vice President, he directs all operations and management activities of the Corporation, as well as conversing with multi–national clientele in fluent Polish, Russian, and English. **Career Steps:** Co–Owner and Vice President, Ostar International, Inc. (1994–Present); Program Manager, Magnavox (1988–1992); Senior NCO, United States Air Force (1967–1988). **Associations & Accomplishments:** Polish Falcons; Association of Old Crows; VFW; American Legion; Freedom Through Vigilance Association; National Rifle Association; The Retired Enlisted Association; The Air Force Association. **Education:** Attended: University of Maryland (1988); Indiana University, Graduate Intensive Russian Program. **Personal:** Married to Michiko in 1970. Two children: Christine N. and Monica M. Mr. Radziminski enjoys reading and writing.

5100 Wholesale Trade – Nondurable Goods

5111 Printing and writing paper
5112 Stationery and office supplies
5113 Industrial and personal service paper
5122 Drugs, proprietaries and sundries
5131 Piece goods and notions
5136 Men's and boys' clothing
5137 Women's and children's clothing
5139 Footwear
5141 Groceries, general line
5142 Packaged frozen foods
5143 Dairy products, exc. dried or canned
5144 Poultry and poultry products
5145 Confectionery
5146 Fish and seafoods
5147 Meats and meat products
5148 Fresh fruits and vegetables
5149 Groceries and related products, NEC
5153 Grain and field beans
5154 Livestock
5159 Farm–product raw materials, NEC
5162 Plastics materials and basic shapes
5169 Chemicals and allied products, NEC
5171 Petroleum bulk stations and terminals
5172 Petroleum products, NEC
5181 Beer and ale
5182 Wine and distilled beverages
5191 Farm supplies
5192 Books, periodicals and newspapers
5193 Flowers and florists' supplies
5194 Tobacco and tobacco products
5198 Paints, varnishes, and supplies
5199 Nondurable goods, NEC

Carroll M. Deal

Plant Manager
Paper Stock Dealers, Inc.
3226 Mid Pines Road
Fayetteville, NC 28306–9337
(910) 423–8700
Fax: (910) 423–6777

5111

Business Information: Paper Stock Dealers, Inc. is a multi–national, wholly–owned subsidiary of Sonoco Products, consisting of 28 divisions of paper stock dealers and producing one third of the tonnage for Sonoco. Joining Paper Stock Dealers, Inc. as Plant Manager in 1995, Mr. Deal is involved in the day–to–day operations of the plant, including the oversight of purchasing, selling, trucking, safety, and maintenance activities. **Career Steps:** Plant Manager, Paper Stock Dealers, Inc. (1995–Present); Owner and Operator, Industrial Services, Inc. (1991–1995); Owner and Operator, C. M. Deal/ U.S. Mail Contractor (1989–1992); Sales and Marketing Director, Sandwood Tire Company, Inc. (1981–1989). **Associations & Accomplishments:** American Trucking Association; United States Mail Haulers Association. **Personal:** Married to Joan B. Holland in 1996. Mr. Deal enjoys boating and drag racing.

Sean A. Keefe

Regional Manager
Spicers Paper Inc.
19027 72nd Avenue South
Kent, WA 98032–1024
(206) 251–6500
Fax: (206) 251–1898

5111

Business Information: Spicers Paper Inc. is a wholesale distributor of printing and imaging papers. Established in Australia in 1896, the Company employs 45 people and posted revenues in excess of $28 million dollars in 1995. As Regional Manager, Mr. Keefe is in charge of the Washington State area. He is responsible the development of sales strategies, marketing new and existing products, establishing viable budgets for his region, monitoring the approved budgets, and general cash management for the Washington Region. Mr. Keefe oversees public relations, strategic planning, and personnel concerns for his office. **Career Steps:** Spicers Paper Inc.: Regional Manager (1994–Present), Northwest Administrative Manager (1993–1994), Sales Administrative Manager (1992–1993). **Associations & Accomplishments:** Pacific Printing and Imaging; National Paper Trade Association; Various Conventions and Trade Shows. **Personal:** Married to Sandra in 1978. Two children: Michael and Valerie. Mr. Keefe enjoys camping, fishing, music, and travel.

Carlos Salcedo

Sales Representative
Kirk Paper/ResourceNet International
30535 Huntwood Avenue
Hayward, CA 94544
(510) 489–5475
Fax: (510) 489–9415

5111

Business Information: Kirk Paper/ResourceNet International is an international distributor of paper, including paper, xerographic, industrial supplies, and retail packaging. As Sales Representative, Mr. Salcedo is responsible for increasing the Company's client base and sales volume in Northern California. His goal is to continually improve and be happy. **Career Steps:** Sales Representative, Kirk Paper Company/Resource Net International (1994–Present); Promotions Representative, Unisource Corporation (1989–1994); Freelance Writer, Self Employed (1990–Present). **Associations & Accomplishments:** American Institute of Graphic Arts; Printing Industries of Northern California; Larkin Street Youth Center; Big Brothers/Big Sisters. **Education:** San Francisco State University, B.A. in English (1991); U.S. Army Reserves, Medic. **Personal:** Mr. Salcedo enjoys reading, writing, weightlifting, volleyball, and sky diving. He lives with his two cats, Tigger and Princess Toonces.

Greggory A. Bruce

Director of Operations; Corporate Secretary
Envelopes of Nevada, Inc.
3111 South Valley View Boulevard, Suite C 101
Las Vegas, NV 89102
(702) 365–1440
Fax: (702) 365–1822

5112

Business Information: Envelopes of Nevada, Inc. is a complete wholesale printing company specializing in envelopes. Regional in scope, the Company is in the process of establishing a web site, and expanding service on a national level. Established in 1989, the Company employs 20 people, and has an estimated annual revenue of $2.5 million. As Director of Operations, Mr. Bruce is responsible for all aspects of the Company. He oversees all personnel, marketing, community relations, and proudly serves as liaison between the Company and the community. Additional duties include staff training, human resources, safety and payroll. Concurrent with his present position, Mr. Bruce is Owner of GB Productions, a Company which combines his poetry and photography. **Career Steps:** Director of Operations, Corporate Secretary, Envelopes of Nevada, Inc. (1994–Present); Store Manager, Lucky Stores, Inc. (1980–1994); Floor Manager, Ardan Catalog Showrooms (1978–1980). **Associations & Accomplishments:** Las Vegas Chamber of Commerce; U.S. Chamber of Commerce; American Management Association; Public Broadcasting System; KUNV Community/University Radio; Alzheimer's Association Advocate – Las Vegas Region; International Society of Poets. Published his poetry in three publications. Recipient of annual award from the Alzheimer's Association. **Education:** University of Nevada, Las Vegas. **Personal:** Mr. Bruce enjoys being a poet, photographer and owner of GB Productions.

Robert W. Croes

President/Chief Executive Officer
Antraco Aruba N.V.
P.O. Box 598 L.G. Smith Boulevard 126
Oranjestad, N. Antille Aruba
(297) 8–23434
Fax: (297) 8–33006
EMAIL: See Below

5112

Business Information: Antraco Aruba N.V., originally a wholesale distributor for 3M, became diversified in 1970 and 1974 and is now a major wholesaler of office furniture, stationary, and educational products. The sole IBM dealer in the country, Antraco Aruba N.V. also offers automation hardware, software, and services, providing clients with everything needed for offices or school systems. Importing for five stores throughout Aruba, the Company serves clients in the retail, commercial, and industrial markets. With 108 employees and an estimated annual revenue of $12 million, the Company plans to expand their bookstore from 300 to 680 square meters. As President/Chief Executive Officer, Mr. Croes oversees every aspect of the business, including responsibility for profit and loss ratios, and a staff of eight managers. **Career Steps:** President/Chief Executive Officer, Antraco Aruba N.V. (1964–Present); Manager, PAC Agencies (1966–1970); Aruba Chemical Industries: Sales/Production Coordinator (1965–1966); Sales/Production Clerk (1963–1965). **Associations & Accomplishments:** President, Aruba Trade and Industries Association; Past President, Aruba Lions Club; A&ASR Consistory Solomon's Wisdom; Past President, Aruba Chamber of Commerce; Eastern Star Aruba Chapter #2; Supervisory Council, Social Security Bank; 32 Degree Mason. **Education:** Institute for Social Sciences, B.S.; Caribbean Business School, M.B.A. in International Management (In Progress). **Personal:** Married to Enid R. Marugg in 1967. Two children: Robert W. and Marielsa R.. Mr. Croes enjoys reading and philosophy.

Steven C. Hamel

Chief Financial Officer and Director of Operations
Copytronics, Inc.
2461 Rolac Road
Jacksonville, FL 32207
(904) 731–5100
Fax: (904) 448–5897

5112

Business Information: Copytronics, Inc. is a marketer and dealer of office products, providing sales, services, and supplies for products sold. Established in 1972, Copytronics, Inc. reports annual revenue in excess of $22 million and currently employs 213 people. As Chief Financial Officer and Director of Operations, Mr. Hamel provides strategic planning related to financial, operational, distributional, and acquisition issues (sales & marketing). **Career Steps:** Chief Financial Officer and Director of Operations, Copytronics, Inc. (1992–Present); Financial Director, BET Plant Services (1990–1992); Manager, McHaze, Ezzell & Company, CPA's (1986–1990); Controller, Profit Key International, Inc. (1983–1986); Supervisor, Coopers & Lybrand (1978–1983); Staff Accountant, Kirkland & Company, CPAs (1976–1978). **Associations & Accomplishments:** American Institute of Certified Public Accounting; Florida Institute of Certified Public Accounting; American Management Association; CFO Roundtable, Copier Dealers Association. **Education:** Auburn University, B.S. in Business Administration (1976). **Personal:** Married to Judy in 1985. Two children: Zachary and Alexander. Mr. Hamel enjoys sports, reading, and woodworking.

Omar G. Kerbage, Ph.D.

Directeur General
Armor
18 34 Rue Chevreuil
Nantes, France 44100
(33) 40384000
Fax: (33) 40582991

5112

Business Information: Armor is a manufacturer and marketer of business office supplies, such as impact and non–impact products. Concentrating in thermotransfer technology, Armor distributes products throughout England and Benelux, Africa, with a factory located in Morocco. Established in 1922, Armor reports annual revenue of $510 million FF and currently employs 600 people. As Directeur General, Dr. Kerbage serves as President and is responsible for all aspects of operations, including research and development, manufacturing, and quality and environmental control. Originally from Lebanon, Dr. Kerbage is fluent in French, Arabic, English, and basic knowledge of Spanish. His educational background is in engineering chemistry and physics. **Career Steps:** President and Directeur General, Armor (1983–Present); Manager Division Assistant, Thomson CSF (1981–1983); Engineer, HEF (1980–1981). **Education:** Ecole Centrale, Ph.D. in Physics (1980); (ESCIL) in Lyon, France, Engineer in Quemestry (1977). **Personal:** Married to Marie Christine Lambert in 1977. Four children: Valerie, Sandrine, Julie, and Nicolas. Dr. Kerbage enjoys sea activities, gardening, reading, and spending time with his family.

Harold S. Malen

Director of Information Technology
BT Office Products International
700 West Chicago
Chicago, IL 60610
(312) 633–4603
Fax: (312) 633–4729
EMAIL: See Below

5112

Business Information: BT Office Products International is primarily engaged in the distribution of office products (i.e. stationary, writing utensils, etc.). International in scope, the Company has thirty locations worldwide, with branches in Europe, Asia, and the U.S. Established in 1941, the Company employs 5,000 people, and has an estimated annual revenue of $1.4 billion. As Director of Information Technology, Mr. Malen oversees all aspects of the MIS/DP department and is responsible for computer programming and network, telecommunications, and the help desk. Internet users can reach him via: hmalen@chicago.btopi.com. **Career Steps:** Director of Information Technology, BT Office Products International (1995–Present); Development Manager, Metromail Corporation (1993–1995); Development Manager, Boise Cascade Office Products (1988–1992). **Associations & Accomplishments:** Who's Who in the Midwest (1988); Outstanding Quality Achievement Award (1995). **Education:** Roosevelt University, M.B.A. (1976); De Paul University, B.Sc. (1965). **Personal:** Married to Julie in 1973. Two children: Robert and Greg. Mr. Malen enjoys coaching his son's baseball team, golf and basketball.

Edward J. Panconi

Director of Sales, Planning and Administration
Office Depot
2200 Old Germantown Road
Delray Beach, FL 33445
(800) 937–3600
Fax: (407) 266–1095

5112

Business Information: Office Depot is an international retail leader in office supplies comprised of both a commercial and a business service division. As Director of Sales, Planning and Administration, Mr. Panconi is responsible for handling sales, communications, policies, and customer relations. Additionally, he oversees account executives and managers, manages special events, prices products, and supervises employees. **Career Steps:** Director of Sales, Planning and Administration, Office Depot (1995–Present); Vice President, Eastman Office Products Division Office Depot (1994); Systems Marketing Manager, BT Redwood (1992). **Associations & Accomplishments:** Board Director, Sigma Pi Fraternity International. **Education:** Loyola Marymount University, B.A. (1984). **Personal:** Mr. Panconi enjoys scuba diving and cooking.

Clinton L. Davis

Head of Operations
Western ResourceNet International
6000 N. Cutter Circle
Portland, OR 79217–3935
(503) 978–1345
Fax: (503) 285–8143

5113

Business Information: Western ResourceNet International, a subsidiary of International Paper, distributes paper and paper products globally. The Company distributes fine paper, graphics supplies, and industrial paper products. As Head of Operations, Mr. Davis is responsible for the warehouse, logistics, and facilities. He is a member of a five-person team which decides the best practices and policies for over 200 divisions nation-wide. **Career Steps:** Head of Operations, Western ResourceNet International (1995–Present); President, J oh's Coffee Inc. (1992–1996); Head of Operations for the Pacific Northwest, Alum Rock Foodservice, a subsidiary of Beatrice Foods (1989–1993). **Associations & Accomplishments:** Formerly a United Way volunteer. **Personal:** Mr. Davis enjoys golf, boating, and fishing.

Kyle Frick

Vice President Marketing and Business Development
Pacific Periodical Services
9914 32nd Avenue, South
Tacoma, WA 98409
(206) 581–1940
Fax: (206) 584–5941

5113

Business Information: Pacific Periodical Services is a wholesale distributor of magazines, books, and other products that relate to information, education, and entertainment. As Vice President Marketing and Business Development, Mr. Frick oversees outside contracts with customers and suppliers to ensure the Company's ability to remain competitive. **Career Steps:** Vice President Marketing and Business Development, Pacific Periodical Services (1995–Present); Regional Circulation Manager, Petersen Publishing (1994–1995); Senior Territory Manager, Time Distribution Services (Time/Warner) (1991–1994); Territory Manager, Valley Wine (1990–1991). **Associations & Accomplishments:** Professional Ski Instructors of America; University of Oregon Alumni Association – Puget Sound Chapter. **Education:** University of Oregon, B.S. in Marketing (1989). **Personal:** Mr. Frick enjoys golf, water and snow skiing, camping, and reading.

Tracy Lee Kondracki

Vice President
Fleet Data Forms, Inc.
3275 West Hillsboro Boulevard, Suite 100
Deerfield Beach, FL 33442–9410
(954) 429–2750
Fax: (954) 429–2782

5113

Business Information: Fleet Data Forms, Inc., soon to be Fleet Graphics & Promotions, Inc., deals with the making of business forms, distribution for medical facilities, travel, and large volume commercial accounts. Established in 1988, Fleet Data Forms employs 9 people with annual sales of over $1 million. As Vice President, Ms. Kondracki is responsible for managing in–house personnel and all sales staff, problem solving, graphic design, and strategic planning. **Career Steps:** Fleet Data Forms, Inc.: Vice President (1995–Present); Director of Operations (1989–1994); Pre–press Department Manager, Printers Emergency Service (1984–1987). **Associations & Accomplishments:** DMIA; ASI. **Education:** University of Cincinnati; Cincinnati Technical College. **Personal:** Married to Richard in 1994. Ms. Kondracki enjoys art, animal rights, and environmental issues.

Gabriele Maussner–Schouten

Manager of Customer Information Systems
Avenor
2 Kenview Boulevard
Brampton, Ontario L6T 5E4
(905) 793–0707
Fax: (905) 793–0153

5113

Business Information: Avenor, Inc. specializes in the manufacturing and distribution of white paper in North America. Corporately headquartered in Montreal, the Company has two other Canadian branches that deal in pulp and yellow paper. Established in 1993, the Company employs 1,000 people, and has an estimated annual revenue of $450 million. As Manager of Customer Information Systems, Mrs. Maussner–Schouten is responsible for overall strategy and customer/employee satisfaction. Her duties include marketing, administration and planning. **Career Steps:** Avenor, Inc: Manager of Customer Information Systems (1996–Present), Manager of Customer Service (1995–1996); Manager of Marketing Services, Siemens Electric Limited (1993). **Associations & Accomplishments:** American Society for Quality Control (ASQC); Hong Kong–Canadian Business Association. **Education:** Dalhousie University, M.B.A. (1990); Beltrieoswirhin, Diploma; Techhochacshule, Nurnberg, Germany. **Personal:** Married to Joe Schouten in 1991. One child: Katrina. Mrs. Maussner–Schouten enjoys her daughter, skiing, and travel.

Georges Mirza

President
Automation International
12705 South Kirkwood Road, Suite 214
Stafford, TX 7477–3813
(713) 240–5777
Fax: (713) 240–5888

5113

Business Information: Located just south of Houston, Texas, Automation International specializes in distributing and representing industrial control and factory automation products. Established in 1988, the Company primarily concentrates in the Latin American market, providing consulting expertise on distribution, advertising, translation services, and technical assistance to enable companies to expand into international markets. Through their efforts in simplifying Latin American expansion, Automation International has helped enhance the market in Latin American countries for various suppliers. As President, Mr. Mirza oversees the daily operations of the Company and is responsible for all administrative and financial duties, as well as strategic planning, sales, and public relations. **Career Steps:** President, Automation International (1988–Present); International Marketing Manager, GE/GE Finance (1984–1988); Area Sales Manager, IDT (Jun.1983–Dec.1983); District Sales Manager, Texas Instruments (1978–1983). **Associations & Accomplishments:** Instrumentation Society of America (ISA). **Education:** Laval University, B.S.E.E. (1975). **Personal:** Married to Janis Parsley in 1994. Mr. Mirza enjoys rollerblading, biking, and computer games.

Joe Pyryt

Director of Facilities & Engineering
PaperDirect, Inc.
100 Plaza Drive, 2nd Floor
Secaucus, NJ 07094
(201) 271–9300 Ext. 2193
Fax: (201) 271–9623
EMAIL: See Below

5113

Business Information: PaperDirect, a subsidiary of DELUXE Corporation, is the world's leading supplier of specialty papers and desktop publishing–related products and services. As Director of Facilities & Engineering, Mr. Pyryt is responsible for all facility management functions and industrial engineering activities, including internal administrative services departments – Communications/Mail, Corporate Records, Purchasing, Reproduction, Housekeeping, Building Maintenance Services, Environmental Health and Safety, Industrial Engineering, Security – and financial coordination of all corporate–related invoices. Internet users can reach him via: jpyryt@aol.com **Career Steps:** Director of Facilities & Engineering, PaperDirect, Inc. (1994–Present); Director of Central Operations, Carretta Trucking, Inc. (1993–1994); Operations Manager/Industrial Engineer, United Parcel Service of America (1979–1992). **Associations & Accomplishments:** Material Handling Society of New Jersey, Inc.; Institute of Packaging Professionals; Institute of Industrial Engineers, Metro NJ. **Education:** Fairleigh Dickinson University, M.B.A. (1982); William Paterson College, B.A. (1977).

Michael N. Ruest

Human Resources Manager
ResourceNet International
613 Main Street
Wilmington, MA 01887
(508) 988–8505
Fax: (508) 988–7401

5113

Business Information: ResourceNet International is primarily engaged in the sales and distribution of fine paper and industrial supplies on a wholesale basis. As Human Resources Manager, Mr. Ruest is responsible for personnel management at five locations. He oversees employee recruitment and review, and serves as Company liaison between three labor unions. **Career Steps:** Human Resources Manager, ResourceNet International (1996–Present); Employee Relations Manager, S.D. Warren Company (1993–1996); Employee Relations/Employment Manager, Raytheon Company (1986–1993). **Associations & Accomplishments:** Society for Human Resource Management. **Education:** Fitchburg State College: M.S. (1987), B.S. (1979); University of Michigan, Labor Relations Seminar (1996). **Personal:** Married to Ann in 1988. Two children: Hannah and Michael Jr. Mr. Ruest enjoys spending time with his family, international contacts of his children in Romania and Vietnam, woodworking and volunteer work with numerous community groups.

Margaret M. Thoma

President
Image Packaging by Horwitz
145 Philo Road West
Horseheads, NY 14845
(607) 739–3667
Fax: (607) 739–3457

5113

Business Information: Image Packaging by Horwitz is a wholesale retail packaging firm. Horwitz provides paper products and janitorial goods to hospitals, schools, and restaurants. Image markets retail packaging (toys, boxes, bows) throughout the country. Established in 1992, Image Packaging by Horwitz has two locations and currently employs four people at Image Packaging and 35 people at Horwitz. As President of Image Packaging by Horwitz, Mrs. Thoma is responsible for all aspects of operations, including daily operations. Concurrent with her position, she serves as Secretary and Treasurer for Horwitz. **Career Steps:** President, Image Packaging by Horwitz (1992–Present); Horwitz Paper & Packaging Co., Inc.: Secretary and Treasurer (1992–Present), Sales Representative (1983–1992). **Associations & Accomplishments:** Elmira Rotary; Retail Paper Manufacturer's Association (RPMA); National Paper Trade Association (NPTA). **Education:** Lemoyne College, B.A. in English (1983), Minor in Industrial Relations, cum laude. **Personal:** Married to Clifford Thoma in 1991. Mrs. Thoma enjoys mountain bike riding and restoring old homes.

Delia L. Beckman

Controller
Team Up International Inc.
P.O. Box 98236
Las Vegas, NV 89193–8236
(702) 361–5552
Fax: (702) 361–3170

5122

Business Information: Team Up International is a multi–level marketing company that prides itself on advanced high–level vitality products. The Company distributes herbal products and food supplements throughout the United States, Canada, and Virgin Islands. As Controller, Mrs. Beckman is responsible for diversified activities, including all finances, accounting, and payroll. **Career Steps:** Team Up International: Controller (1995–Present), Assistant Accounting Manager (1994–1995); Office Manager, Dynamic Piping (1992–1994); Owner, Beckman Tax Service (1992–Present). **Associations & Accomplishments:** National Association of Female Executives; Nevada Executive Women. **Education:** Community College of Southern Nevada, B.A. in progress. **Personal:** Married to Steven F. in 1990. Five children: Christopher, Virginia, Victoria, Angela, and Sabrina. Mrs. Beckman enjoys bowling, sewing, gardening and reading.

Mirena M. Bird

Comptroller
Elizabeth Arden – Puerto Rico Export
Post Office Box 191146
San Juan, Puerto Rico 00919–1146
(809) 753–7300
Fax: (809) 753–7327

5122

Business Information: Elizabeth Arden – Puerto Rico Export is an international distributor of prestige cosmetics, toiletries, and perfumery products to the Caribbean and Latin American markets. Joining Elizabeth Arden – Puerto Rico Export as Financial Analyst in 1987, Ms. Bird was appointed as Comptroller in 1990. She is responsible for the management of all financial and administrative functions, including budgeting, accounting, strategic planning, and oversight of personnel. **Career Steps:** Elizabeth Arden – Puerto Rico Export: Comptroller (1990–Present), Financial Analyst (1987–1989); Financial Analyst, Pearl Vision Center – Puerto Rico (1986). **Associations & Accomplishments:** Alumni, International Association of Alumni Students in Economic Sciences. **Education:** University of Puerto Rico, B.B.A. (1982). **Personal:** Ms. Bird enjoys sports, walking, wind surfing, and socializing with friends.

Luis Gerardo Castillo

Broker Real Estate/Mortgage
Northern Trade Realty/Northern Trade Mortgage
13365 SW 119th Street
Miami, FL 33186
(305) 281–2061 (305) 265–1835
Fax: (305) 265–1832

5122

Business Information: Northern Trade Realty is a real estate corporation specializing in the Miami South West area and affiliated with Northern Trade Mortgage and Imperial Land Title Corporation. Northern Trade Realty has a wide reach, involved in residential, commercial, industrial, and other real estate areas. Northern Trade Mortgage is involved in FHA, Conventional, Hard Equity, and other special loan programs. As a Licensed Broker in Real Estate and Mortgage, Mr. Castillo specializes in giving Full Service to the industry by taking care of clients from beginning to end in the acquisition of real estate. Mr. Castillo has also served as Personnel Manager at Continental Farms, a fresh cut flower importer, since 1982. **Career Steps:** Real Estate/Mortgage Broker, Northern Trade Realty (1993–Present); Personnel Manager, Continental Farms (1983–Present); Salesperson, Century 21 Executive One Realty (1991–1993). **Associations & Accomplishments:** Founder, Kendall Lions Club (1994); Member and Former Vice President, Miami Lions Club (1990–Present); Miami Lighthouse Feast Chairman (1992–1994); American Cancer Society (1995–Present); Nicaragua – Second Treasurer Miami Chamber of Commerce (1994–Present). **Education:** Gold Coast Real Estate, Broker Licensed (1995); Century 21, Salesperson Licensed (1990); National Assessment Institute, Mortgage Broker Licensed (1993); Miami Dade Community College, Office Manager (1992); University of Costa Rica, Economy (1982). **Personal:** Born in Nicaragua, Chinandega, August 12, 1961. Parents: Jose E. and Norma R. Arrived U.S.A. Oct. 10, 1982. Married to Rina Santamaria in 1985. One child: Melissa. Mr. Castillo enjoys meeting people and helping the community.

Ron T. Frederic

President and Chief Executive Officer
New Image International, Inc.
115 N. Water Street
Georgetown, KY 40324
(502) 867–1895
Fax: (502) 867–0389

5122

Business Information: New Image International, Inc. is a wholesale distribution company, utilizing Network Marketing to distribute a dietary food supplement. Established in 1993, New Image International, Inc. reports annual sales of $22 million and currently employs 38 people. As President and Chief Executive Officer, Mr. Frederic is responsible for the oversight of all day–to–day operations of the entire Corporate structure. **Career Steps:** President and Chief Executive Officer, New Image International, Inc. (1993–Present); National Marketing Director, National Safety Associates (1992–1993); Pastor, Harvest Baptist Church – Louisville, KY (1988–1992); Pastor, Bayview Baptist Church – Washington, IL (1984–1988). **Associations & Accomplishments:** Active in mission work and support in Mexico **Education:** Southeastern Louisiana University, B.A. in Business Administration (1967). **Personal:** Married to Audy in 1965. Four children: Tim, Christi, Joel and George. Mr. Frederic enjoys fishing and flying (licensed pilot).

Timothy G. Hayes

Vice President of Sales
Bayer Consumer Care
36 Columbia Road
Morristown, NJ 07960
(201) 254–4756
Fax: (201) 254–4852

5122

Business Information: Bayer Consumer Care specializes in the sale of Bayer Aspirin, Alka–Seltzer, One–A–Day Vitamins, and Phillips Milk of Magnesia to the retail consumer market. As Vice President of Sales, Mr. Hayes is responsible for all sales activity, customer marketing, trade and customer association activity, working in the field with his sales organization, and internal corporate marketing and finance. **Career Steps:** Bayer Consumer Care: Vice President of Sales (1994–Present), Director of Field Sales (1993–1994), Director of Trade Marketing (1992–1993); Director of Trade Marketing, Quaker Oats (1990–1992). **Associations & Accomplishments:** National Association of Food Brokers; National Association of Chain Drug Stores. **Education:** Furman University, B.A. in Business Administration (1980) **Personal:** Married to Susan in 1980. Three children: Christopher, Bryan, and Thomas Kelly.

John Joos–Vandewalle, M.D.

Chief Executive Officer
Teva Marion Partners
9300 Ward Park Way
Kansas City, MO 64114
(816) 966–3054
Fax: (816) 966–3977

5122

Business Information: Teva Marion Partners, the result of a joint venture between Hoechst Marion Roussel and Teva Pharmaceuticals, specializes in pharmaceutical marketing; throughout domestic U.S. and Canada. Dr. Joos–Vandewalle has seen it grow from inception to the present fifty–member partnership. As Chief Executive Officer, he is responsible for aspects of operations including; administration, public relations, marketing and strategic planning. **Career Steps:** Chief Executive Officer, Teva Marion Partners (1995–Present); Marion Merrell Dow: Vice President of Global Business Planning (1993–1995), Vice President of International Business Management (1992–1993), Director of Global Commercial Development (1989–1992). **Associations & Accomplishments:** Member and Past President, Board of Directors, Epilepsy Foundation for the Heart of America; Member, Board of Directors, Missouri Quality Foundation; Member, Board of Directors, Rockhurst College Executive Alumni Association; Sponsor, Multiple Sclerosis Society; Frequent speaker regionally and nationally; Published articles on the commercial side of pharmaceuticals. **Education:** Rockhurst College, M.B.A. (1993); University of Witwatersrand, Johannesburg, South Africa, M.D. and B.Sc. (Honors). **Personal:** Married to Jane in 1980. Two children: Catherine and Claire.

Veronica A. Labatkin

Director of Special Projects
Neuman Distributors
175 Railroad Avenue
Ridgefield, NJ 07657–2312
(201) 941–2000 Ext. 8345
Fax: (201) 941–0929

5122

Business Information: Neuman Distributors specializes in the wholesale distribution of pharmaceutical products. Established in the 1950s, the Company employs 755 people and has estimated annual revenue of $1.2 billion. As Director of Special Projects, Ms. Labatkin oversees all finance–related functions, including mergers and acquisitions. She is also responsible for writing projections and analytical reports. **Career Steps:** Director of Special Projects, Neuman Distributors (1994–Present); Audit Manager, Weidenbaum, Ryder & Company (1989–1993); Business Analyst, Simon & Schuster (1988–1989); Senior Auditor, Arthur Anderson & Company (1985–1989). **Education:** Pace University, B.A. in Finance (1985). **Personal:** Married to Bruce in 1989. Two children: Ryan and Kelsey. Ms. Labatkin enjoys skiing, personal fitness, and time with her family.

Dr. Barbara T. McKinnon

Director of Business Development
Nova Factor
1620 Century Center Parkway
Memphis, TN 38132–2140
(901) 385–3606
Fax: (800) 827–8987

5122

Business Information: Nova Factor is a national distributor of specialty pharmaceuticals for patients with chronic diseases. The Company educates patients about the drugs and insurance claims. As Director of Business Development, Dr. McKinnon contacts manufacturers of biotech drugs and negotiates agreements for value–added distribution services. **Career Steps:** Director of Business Development, Nova Factor (1994–Present); Manager of Pharmacy Services, Pharma-Thera (1988–1994); Director of Nutrition Supply, Humana Hospital Huntsville (1985–1988); Director of Pharmacy, Humana Specialty Hospital (1981–1985). **Associations & Accomplishments:** Executive Committee, Section of Home Care Practitioners – American Society of Health Systems Pharmacists; United States Pharmacopeial Convention Home Care Advisory Panel; Chair, Tennessee Home Infusion Committee; National Advisory Group on TPN Standards and Guidelines. **Education:** University of Tennessee: Pharm.D. (1984), B.S. in Pharmacy (1981). **Personal:** Married to Derek in 1991. Three children: Jessica Thompson, Tyler, and Samuel. Dr. McKinnon enjoys cross–training.

Kelly Nott

Independent Marketing Associate
Omnitrition
8474 Sopwith Boulevard
Reno, NV 89506
(702) 677–1647
Fax: (702) 785–3602

5122

Business Information: Omnitrition is a nationwide distributor of nutritional supplements, vitamins, and skin, facial, and body care products. As Independent Marketing Associate, Ms. Nott is responsible for the distribution of products. Concurrent with her duties as Independent Marketing Associate, she is also a Hotel Manager for Fitzgeralds Hotel, wherein she manages all aspects of hotel operations. **Career Steps:** Independent Marketing Associate, Omnitrition (1989–Present); Fitzgeralds Hotel: Hotel Manager (1994–Present), Guest Service Supervisor (1987–1993); Casino Cleaning Manager, Harolds Club with Fitzgeralds (1993–1994). **Associations & Accomplishments:** Reno Area Hotel Management Association. **Education:** TMCC; San Diego State University; San Jose City College; University of Nevada at Reno, Gaming Management Program. **Personal:** Married to Dane G. in 1993. Two children: Jessica and Tyler. Ms. Nott enjoys Omnitrition IMA, yardwork, biking, camping, fishing, computers, and school functions with her children.

Richard E. Owens, Ph.D.

Independent Distributor
Interior Design Nutritionals (IDN)
164 Spring Street
Ozark, MO 65721–9528
Fax: Please mail or call

5122

Business Information: Interior Design Nutritionals (IDN), a division of Nuskin, is a distributor of dietary/mineral supplements and vitamins. A primary producer of FIBERNET, a natural fat burner made from the fiber of shell fish, the Company is international in scope. As an Independent Distributor, Dr.

Owens oversees the marketing and distribution of Company products, and is responsible for all related administrative and operational functions. In the course of his career, Dr. Owens is most proud of his development of a Poison Control System for the state of Arkansas and implementing the Brussels Trade Nomenclature (BTN) for Saudi Aramco, the world's largest oil producer. The BTN system tracks imported and exported material worldwide. He was also instrumental in training Saudi nationals in business–related computer software. **Career Steps:** Independent Distributor, Interior Design Nutritionals (IDN) (1995–Present); Geophysicist, Saudi Aramco (1979–1994); Senior Analyst, Digital Equipment Corporation (1977–1979); Systems Manager, University of Arkansas Medical Center (1973–1976). **Associations & Accomplishments:** The Doctorate Association of New York Educators, Inc. **Education:** Walden University, Ph.D. in Business Administration (1992); University of Oklahoma, M.S. in Engineering Management; University of Missouri, M.A. in Managerial Economics; South East Missouri State University, B.S. in Mathematics; Control Data Institute, Top Graduate in Computer Science. **Personal:** Married to Marsha in 1965. Six children: Tanya, Karen, Christine, Sarah, Richard, and Nicole. Dr. Owens enjoys swimming, softball, and youth activities.

Sondra Trust

Founder, President, and Chief Executive Officer
Diabetic Medserv, Inc.
633 NE 167th Street, Suite 501
Miami, FL 33162–2443
(305) 652–9332
Fax: (305) 652–0703

5122

Business Information: Diabetic Medserv, Inc. is a national mail–order company specializing in the distribution of medical and diabetic supplies to senior citizens across the United States. A graduate with honors from Florida International University, Ms. Trust founded Medserv in 1995, fulfilling a need for increased compliance with medical treatments for senior citizens across the country. **Career Steps:** Founder, President, Chief Executive Officer, and Chairperson of the Board of Directors, Diabetic Medserv Inc. (1995–Present); President and Chief Executive Officer, American Complex Care (1985–1994); Nursing Supervisor, Jackson Memorial Hospital (1971–1978). **Associations & Accomplishments:** AACN; ONS; INS; American Diabetes Association. **Education:** Florida International University, B.A., B.S.N., Summa Cum Laude (1977). **Personal:** Married to Michael Levine in 1994. Two children: Jessica Raphael and Lauryn Raphael. Ms. Trust is also an opera singer.

John R. Yost

President
Chemical Sources, Inc.
P.O. Box 5180
North Muskegon, MI 49445
(616) 744–0554
Fax: (616) 744–0727

5122

Business Information: Chemical Sources, Inc. is a chemical brokerage, consultancy and sourcing intermediate, locating hard to find intermediates for pharmaceutical companies. As President, Mr. Yost manages all aspects of company operations, concentrating on sales, marketing, and consulting. Established in 1993, Chemical Sources, Inc. employs 2 people. **Career Steps:** President, Chemical Sources, Inc., (1993–Present); Business Manager, Koch Chemical (1986–1993); President, Muskegon Chemical (1974–1985); Executive Vice President, Story Chemical (1972–1974). **Associations & Accomplishments:** Past Board of Directors, Synthetic Organic Chemical Manufacturers Association; American Chemicals Society; American Institute of Chemical Engineers. **Education:** University of Pennsylvania, M.S. in Chemical Engineering (1949); Ursinus College, B.A. **Personal:** Married to Dorcas in 1976. Two children: Stephen and John. Mr. Yost enjoys sports and bridge.

Michael B. Moore

Director of Operations
General Fiberglass Supply
1335 East Wisconsin Avenue
Pewaukee, WI 53072
(414) 691–3500
Fax: (414) 691–3073

5131

Business Information: General Fiberglass Supply, established in 1972, is a distributor of reinforced plastic and urethane raw materials and equipment to RV's, boats, and industrial manufacturers. General Fiberglass Supply is a regional Company with five locations, a staff of 68, and 22 subordinates. As Director of Operations, Mr. Moore is responsible for all the trucking and warehousing aspects, the equipment, and

customer service departments. He is also responsible for the Western region, which includes Minneapolis and Kansas City. Mr. Moore oversees a staff of 5 who reports directly to him. **Career Steps:** General Fiberglass Supply: Director of Operations (1996–Present), Customer Service Manager (1994–1995), Technical Sales Representative (1993–1994), Inside Sales Representative (1992). **Associations & Accomplishments:** National Honor Society; Listed in Who's Who in High School Honor Students. **Education:** University of Wisconsin, B.A. in Finance (1990). **Personal:** Married to Kristen in 1995. Mr. Moore enjoys martial arts, photography, body building, and sports.

Reuben Abraham

Vice President
Harbor Footwear Group, Ltd.
55 Harbor Park Drive
Port Washington, NY 11050
(516) 621–8400
Fax: (516) 621–4957

5139

Business Information: Harbor Footwear Group, Ltd., a privately held company, is Brazil's largest exporter of men's shoes. The Company specializes in branded and private–label men's footwear. The Company is headquartered in New York, with offices in Brazil, Italy, Spain, Taiwan, and many other national and foreign ports. As Vice President of Far East Operations, Mr. Abraham is responsible for many of the administrative duties of the Far East locations. He handles direct sourcing from Asia, product development, quality control, and other related activities. **Career Steps:** Executive Vice President & COO, TriStar International Footwear, Ltd. (1987–Present); Senior Vice President of Marketing & Sales, SanShoe Trading Corporation (1981–1987); National Sales Manager, Bata Shoe Company (1971–1981). **Education:** Bryant College, B.S. (1971). **Personal:** Married to Linda in 1973. Two children: Aaron and Silas. Mr. Abraham enjoys playing tennis and coaching youth baseball.

Joseph Esber

Vice President
Lexi Trading Company
3402 W. MacArthur Blvd., Suite J
Santa Ana, CA 92704
(714) 437–9926
Fax: (714) 437–9927

5139

Business Information: Lexi Trading Company specializes in the wholesale import and export of general merchandise (i.e. clothing, shoes, and accessories), from Venezuela to South America and the U.S. As Vice President, Mr. Esber is responsible for purchasing all Company inventory, administration, sales, marketing, and strategic planning for both the California and Venezuela locations. Additional duties include customer service, public relations and finance. **Career Steps:** Vice President, Lexi Trading Company (1995–Present); Owner, Calzado Nikita (1985). **Education:** International Business. **Personal:** Mr. Esber enjoys soccer and golf.

Peggy H. Geolat

Director of Risk Management
Brown Group, Inc.
8300 Maryland Avenue
Clayton, MO 63105
(314) 854–4128
Fax: (314) 854–4098

5139

Business Information: Brown Group, Inc. is a wholesaler and retailer of footwear products. As Director of Risk Management, Ms. Geolat provides property/casualty insurance risk management, as well as management of claims and insurance programs. **Career Steps:** Director of Risk Management, Brown Group, Inc. (1996–Present); Risk Manager, Centermark Properties (1989–1993); Account Executive, Daniel & Henry Co. (1987–1989). **Associations & Accomplishments:** St. Louis Chapter, Risk Managers Society (RIMS). **Education:** University of Missouri – St. Louis, M.B.A. (1992); Southern Illinois University, B.S. in Business. **Personal:** Ms. Geolat enjoys tennis and golf.

Rowena Lam

Regional General Manager
Inchcape JDH Ltd.
2 On Ping Street, Siu Lek Yuen – 14/F JDH Centre
New Territories, Hong Kong
852–26355883
Fax: 852–26374691

5139

Business Information: Inchcape JDH – TBL Division is an international distributor of Timberland products in the Greater China area, with major sales and marketing activities covered on a regional basis. Products include shoes, boots, apparel, and accessories. A publicly–held company in the United Kingdom, Inchcape JDH also markets and distributes print labels. Joining Inchcape JDH in 1992, Ms. Lam was appointed as Regional General Manager for the Timberland Distribution Division in Hong Kong, China and Taiwan. She is responsible for the management of local offices within each area, including profits and losses for Hong Kong and Taiwan and administrative functions. **Career Steps:** Inchcape JDH Ltd.: Regional General Manager – Timberland Division (1995–Present), General Manager – Timberland Division (1994–1995); Divisional Manager – Wiltona Division (1992–1994), Marketing Manager – Wiltona Division (1992). **Associations & Accomplishments:** Recipient, Excellence Marketing Award. **Education:** Chinese University of Hong Kong: Diploma (1992), Diploma in Business Administration (1991); College of Education, Teacher's Certification (1986).

Michael J. Freda

President/Chief Operating Officer
Buckley Thorne Messina
23 Strathmore Road
Natick, MA 01760–2442
(508) 653–6000
Fax: Please mail or call

5140

Business Information: Buckley Thorne Messina is a food brokerage company representing over 80 different food manufacturers such as Quaker Oats and Kellogg, and Fortune 500 food and consumer products companies. The Company boasts six locations, three in New York and three in Massachusetts. As President/Chief Operating Officer, Mr. Freda oversees all aspects of Company operations, including administration, finance, sales and marketing, and strategic planning. **Career Steps:** President/Chief Operating Officer, Buckley Thorne Messina (1995–Present); Market Dynamics: President/Chief Executive Officer (1993–1994), Executive Vice President/Chief Operating Officer (1992–1993); Vice President, Roberts & Associates (1988–1991). **Associations & Accomplishments:** Grocery Manufacturers Association; Knights of the Grist. **Education:** University of Southern Connecticut, B.A. (1975). **Personal:** Married to Shirley in 1979. Mr. Freda enjoys sports, running, weights, baseball card collecting, reading, and history.

Susan H. Cameron

Corporate Specialist, Traffic and Customs
Best Foods Canada, Inc.
1949 Gagnon Street
Lachine, Quebec H8T 3M5
(514) 422–8123
Fax: (514) 636–8928

5141

Business Information: Best Foods Canada, Inc. specializes in the international distribution of high standard name brand food items to retail stores and clients. Headquartered in Lachine, Quebec, the Company is regional in scope with branches throughout the province. As Corporate Specialist, Traffic and Customs, Ms. Cameron negotiates and monitors transportation of all shipments, ensures customs compliance, and manages all stock and transfers. **Career Steps:** Corporate Specialist, Traffic and Customs, Best Foods Canada, Inc. (19–Present) **Personal:** Ms. Cameron enjoys golf and swimming.

Ramon A. Carrasco

General Manager
Tipp Distributors
1477 Lomaland E–7
El Paso, TX 79935
(915) 594–1618
Fax: Please mail or call

5141

Business Information: Tipp Distributors specializes in commercializing Mexican products (i.e. soft drinks, juices, and canned foods), throughout the United States, primarily in Hispanic areas. Headquartered in El Paso, Texas, the Company has joint ventures in Mexico and distributes products in thirty states. Established in 1986, the Company employs 23 people, and has an estimated annual revenue of $30 million. As General Manager, Mr. Carrasco oversees all aspects of the Company. His duties include marketing, operations, relations with suppliers, sales, freight, finances and accounting, and direct supervision of four district managers through his main sales office in California. **Career Steps:** General Manager, Tipp Distributors (1994–Present); Market Development Manager, Argos Corporation (1991–1994); Operations Representative, The Coca–Cola Company (1989–1991). **Education:** ITESM, Industrial and Systems Engineering (1988). **Personal:** Married to Olga Cecilia in 1996. Mr. Carrasco enjoys football, soccer, watching movies, and reading novels.

June Collett

Vice President of Sales
Alliant Foodservice
5445 Spellmire Drive
Cincinnati, OH 45246–4842
(513) 870–3913
Fax: (513) 874–5188

5141

Business Information: Alliant Foodservice, formerly Kraft Foodservice, is a $4 billion business responsible for supplying food and paper products to commercial institutes such as restaurants, hospitals, nursing homes, schools, and country clubs. As Vice President of Sales, Ms. Collett oversees all sales and marketing, assisting sales representatives and managers in stimulating sales growth and, in turn, profits. **Career Steps:** Vice President of Sales, Alliant Foodservice (1983–Present); Kraft Foodservice: District Sales Manager (1989–1994), Major Account Manager (1986–1989); General Manager, Bonanza Steakhouse (1979–1983). **Associations & Accomplishments:** Ohio Restaurant Association. **Education:** Attended: Raymond Walters, Business Courses,U.C., Business Courses. **Personal:** Married to Bill in 1990. Two children: Ben and Ann. Ms. Collett enjoys travel and golf.

Olivia M. Leale

Co–Owner and Secretary–Treasurer
Inmark International Marketing, Inc.
5427 North East Penrith Road
Seattle, WA 98105–2842
(206) 527–2369
Fax: (206) 523–5994
EMAIL: See Below

5141

Business Information: Inmark International Marketing, Inc. imports and exports food for industrial use, specializing in pea pods, water chestnuts, baby corn, and bamboo — primarily importing from the Far East and Central America. As Co–Owner and Secretary–Treasurer, Ms. Leale is responsible for accounting, invoicing, corporate expansion, and various administrative activities. Internet users may reach her via: OLEALE@IX.NETCOM.COM **Career Steps:** Inmark International Marketing, Inc.: Co–Owner, Secretary, Treasurer (1980–Present); Driver Guide, Autoguide – London, England (1976–1980). **Associations & Accomplishments:** AFFI. **Education:** Vassar College, B.A. (1966); School of Paralegal Studies, Certificate. **Personal:** Married to Douglas in 1980. Five children: Katrina, Jennifer, Douglas, Leslie and Barbara. Ms. Leale enjoys building collectible doll houses, reading, skiing and boating.

George Martin

Sales Manager for Exports
Furman Foods Inc.
P.O. Box 500
Northumberland, PA 17857
(717) 473–3516
Fax: (717) 473–7367

5141

Business Information: Furman Foods Inc. is a food processor in the United States, dealing with the countries of Canada, Mexico, many of the Caribbean countries, as well as many countries in the Middle East. As Sales Manager for Exports, Mr. Martin is responsible for all export sales and obtaining any international contracts for the Company. Additionally, he handles all government sales and contracts, both federal and state. **Career Steps:** Furman Foods Inc.: Sales Manager for Exports (1995–Present), Label Manager (1987–1995), Warehouse Worker (1986–1987), Production Worker (1975–1986). **Associations & Accomplishments:** Upper Augusta Volunteer Fire Company. **Personal:** Married to Alisa in 1995. Four children: George, Lucas, Zachary, and Zane. Mr. Martin enjoys practicing martial arts, being a published poet, and is actively interested in photography and sculpture.

B. Gen Douglas A. Riach, AUS–Ret

Account Executive
Sales Max Inc.
1900 Garden Tract Road
Richmond, CA 94801
(510) 232–9255
Fax: (415) 697–7146

5141

Business Information: Sales Max Inc., is a Discount Grocery Wholesaler specializing in closeouts, in and out items for independent supermarkets, drug stores, and other retailers. As an Account Executive, Mr. Riach handles new business developments. Prior to entering the civilian workforce, he spent 39 years with the United States Armed Forces. He enlisted in the Army in 1941, completed Officer Candidate School at Fort Benning, Georgia in 1942, and was commissioned as an Infantry Second Lieutenant. As a member of the 116th Infantry Regiment, 29th ID he participated in the D–Day (June 6th) landing on Omaha Beach, as well as the Normandy, Ardennes, and Rhineland campaigns. Upon his return to the United States, he joined the Army Reserves, held positions in the USAR and the CA National Guard, and after many successful assignments, retired from military services in 1987. BG Riach has been inducted into the Infantry Hall of Fame at Fort Benning, Georgia. **Career Steps:** Account Executive, Sales Max Inc. (1996–Present); Territory Manager, Ibbotson, Berri, DeNola Brokerage, Inc. (1990–1996); Territory Sales Manager, Mel Williams Co. (1981–1982); Territory Sales Manager, Long, Shipley & Bauer Association (1982–1983); Account Executive, Thunderbird Market Inc. (1983–1984); Executive Vice President, Visual Marketing Plans (1984–1987); Territory Manager, General Foods Corporation (1948–1980). **Associations & Accomplishments:** Who's Who in the West; Who's Who in California; Former Chairman of National Defense Section, Commonwealth Club of California; United States Army Reserve Officer's Association; Association of Former Intelligence Officers (AFIO); Association of the United States Army; 32 Degree Scottish Ritte, Shrine (Islam Templar); Master Mason, Lodge 400; The Retired Officers Association; Eagle Scout with Silver Palm; Magnus Officialis, SMOTJ (Knights Templars); Knight Commander, OSJ (Knights Hospitallers); Knight Commander, Polonia Restituta (Polish State Order); Commanders Cross with Star, order of St. Stanislaus (CSSTS) and Commander of Commandery of San Francisco, Ca: Knight Order of the Compassionate Heart (International); Former President, Merchandising Executives Club of San Francisco; Legion of Merit; Purple Heart; Bronze Star V and Cluster; Combat Infantryman's Badge; Medal of Merit with Cluster; Commendation Medal; French and Belgium Croix d'Guerre; 12 other foreign decorations (French, Belguiqe, Polish, Yugoslavan). **Education:** University of California at Los Angeles, B.A. (1948); Fenn College, Postgraduate work in Sales Management and Marketing; Command and General Staff College; Industrial College of the Armed Forces; Armed Forces Staff College. **Personal:** Married to Eleanor in 1942. One child: Sandra. During his leisure time he enjoys studying Military Science.

Jaime Kay Schneider

Controller
Metro Eagle
10711 Northend Avenue
Ferndale, MI 48220–2130
(810) 547–5760
Fax: (810) 547–0950

5141

Business Information: Metro Eagle is a wholesaler of snackfoods and a distributor of a private label for Farmer Jack chain stores. With 36 routes, the Company distributes and sells throughout Michigan and Ohio. As Controller, Ms. Schneider is responsible for all accounting, financial statements, and taxes of the Company. **Career Steps:** Controller, Metro Eagle (1994–Present); Certified Public Accountant, Bank & Bozin, CPAs (1993–1994); Certified Public Accountant, John L. Barker, C.P.A. (1985–1993). **Associations & Accomplishments:** American Institute of Certified Public Accountants; Michigan Association of Certified Public Accountants; Our Savior Lutheran Church. **Education:** Oakland University, B.S. (1985); Certified Public Accountant. **Personal:** Married to Alan in 1989. One child: Amanda Elizabeth. Ms. Schneider enjoys sports and family.

Robert (Bob) S. Skinner

Manager
Save A Lot Limited
21 Bristol Valley Court
St. Peters, MO 63376–7913
(314) 428–2250
Fax: (314) 428–6728

5141

Business Information: Save A Lot Limited is a wholesale grocery supply company with service departments for complete grocery store installations. As Manager, Mr. Skinner is involved in designing store fixture layouts, purchasing all necessary refrigeration equipment, scanning systems and all display fixtures. **Career Steps:** Manager, Save A Lot Limited (1989–Present); International Sales Director, Tempmaster International (1988–1989); Manufacturer's Representative, Paul Erickson, Inc. (1984–1987); Store Engineer, Associated Wholesale Grocers (1979–1984). **Education:** Southwest Missouri State University – Springfield, MO, B.S. (1979). **Personal:** Married to Michelle in 1979. Four children: Chris, Zack, Mallory, and Ethan. Mr. Skinner enjoys sports, coaching little league, yard work, and remodeling.

Ed Slagle

Vice President/General Manager
Acosta Sales Company
490 Commerce Park Drive
Marietta, GA 30060–2710
(770) 419–4000
Fax: (770) 419–4020
EMAIL: See Below

5141

Business Information: Acosta Sales Company is the largest food brokerage company in the Southeastern U.S. Specializing in cost effective marketing of manufactured goods, the Company has a large market penetration and can distribute client goods in retail and wholesale environments. Regional in scope, the Company has twenty–three locations throughout the Southeast, with corporate offices centralized in Jacksonville, Florida. Established in 1983, the Company employs 140 people, and has an estimated annual revenue of $200 million. As Vice President/General Manager, Mr. Slagle oversees the Acosta division and is responsible for all of the administrative and operational functions it encompasses. His duties include oversight of 138 manufacturer accounts comprised of 2,200 different items and supervision of 20 wholesale, 112 retail, 16 administrative, and 10 marketing associates through department managers who provide direct reports. Established in 1983, the Georgia Office of Acosta employs 140 people and has an estimated annual revenue of $200 million. Internet users can reach him via: eslagle@acostasales.com. **Career Steps:** Acosta Sales Company Vice President/General Manager (1995–Present), Account Executive (1993–1995); Branch Manager, Citibank (1990–1993). **Associations & Accomplishments:** North Florida Food Association; Georgia Food Industry Association; Atlanta Food Brokers Association. **Education:** University of Central Florida, B.S.B.A. (1978). **Personal:** Married to Heidi in 1979. Three children: Brian, Elaina and Laura. Mr. Slagle enjoys running, golf, and one on one basketball with his son.

Mr. Frederic N. Kelel

President
K & K Distributing
15360 Dale
Detroit, MI 48223
(313) 537–2630
Fax: (313) 537–2664

5143

Business Information: K & K Distributing is a dairy and ice cream distributor to supermarkets, restaurants and convenience stores. Products include milk, juice, cream, sour cream, yogurt, cheese, and ice cream. As President, Mr. Kelel manages all aspects of the business, including sales and marketing, route setting, driver training, finance and accounting, and delivery scheduling. Established in 1989, K & K Distributing employs a staff of 14 and reports annual revenue of $14 million. **Career Steps:** President, K & K Distributing (1989–Present); President, K & K Brokers (1987–1989); Route Driver, Kelel Distributing (1980–1987). **Associations & Accomplishments:** Detroit Police Reserve Officer; Business United with Officers and Youths (BUOY); Michigan Association of Petroleum Dealers. **Education:** Police Academy, P.O.R. (1994).

Jeanette M. Parr
Director of Human Resources Administrator
Presto Food Products, Inc.
18275 Arenth Avenue
Rowland Heights, CA 91748
(818) 854–7604
Fax: (818) 854–0655

5143

Business Information: Presto Food Products, Inc. processes and distributes creamers, toppings, and desserts to retailers and food services. As Director of Human Resources Administrator, Ms. Parr is responsible for human resources, hiring, firing, training employees, public relations, risk management, security, and administrative services. **Career Steps:** Director of Human Resources Administrator, Presto Food Products, Inc. (1990–Present); Vice President/Director of Human Resources, First Federal Savings and Loan (1985–1990); Human Resource Manager, Creftcon Industries. **Associations & Accomplishments:** President, California Human Resource Council; Women of Achievement Award, San Gabriel Valley (1996); First Woman President, Hacienda Heights Kiwanis. **Education:** California Poly – Pomona: M.B.A. (1990), B.S. (1986). **Personal:** Married to Warren in 1969. One child: Tim. Ms. Parr enjoys being a part–time teacher at Cal Poly–Pomona.

Mark L. Heide
Controller
Sweetheart Bakery
5150 Midland Road
Billings, MT 59104
(406) 248–4800
Fax: (406) 248–1499

5145

Business Information: Sweetheart Bakery is a wholesale bakery service. The Company sells bread, buns, and rolls to food stores, including Associated Foods, Super Value, Albertsons, and Buttreys. With over 60 locations, the Company supplies baked goods to stores throughout Northern Wyoming and Montana. As Controller, Mr. Heide oversees all Company budgets, financial transactions, expenses, and financial reports. **Career Steps:** Controller, Sweetheart Bakery (1982–Present). **Education:** University of Montana, M.B.A. (1995); Eastern Montana College, General Business (1978). **Personal:** Married to Melody in 1975. Two children: Jason and Garrett. Mr. Heide enjoys fishing, hunting, and reading.

A. Randy Smith
Account Executive
IBC/Dolly Madison Bakery
312 6th Street, Northwest
Winter Haven, FL 33880–4635
(941) 293–5982
Fax: (941) 293–5982

5145

Business Information: Dolly Madison Bakery, one of the world's leading consumer bakery conglomerates, has been a wholly–owned subsidiary of Interstate Brands Corporation (IBC) since 1937. The company produces breads, cakes, snack cakes, pies, and doughnuts at 63 bakeries across the United States. Mr. Smith began as a route salesman in 1983 with Dolly Madison and was promoted to Area Sales Manager later that year. He was subsequently promoted to District Sales Manager in 1986, and Account Executive 1987. He is now responsible for Company sales, interfacing with new and existing customers, soliciting new accounts, and developing sales expansion plans. **Career Steps:** IBC/Dolly Madison Bakery (1983–Present); Sales Supervisor, Bost Bakery – South Carolina (1978–1983); Sales Manager, Kern's Bakery – Virginia (1975–1978). **Associations & Accomplishments:** Florida Food Industry; Automatic Merchandising Association of Florida; HeJaz Shrine Temple; Dunean Masonic Lodge; Winter Haven Moose Lodge. **Education:** Cecil's Business College, Business & Accounting (1968); American Management Association – Dale Carnegie. **Personal:** Married to Sandra B. in 1968. Two children: Chris and Amy. Mr. Smith enjoys golf, fishing, motor sports, and spending time with his grandson.

Kamal Ahmed, M.D.

President/Chief Executive Officer
PLACID–NK Corporation
199–18 Keno Avenue
Hollisood, NY 11423
(718) 238–5183
Fax: (718) 523–8439

5146

Business Information: PLACID–NK Corporation is a importer/exporter of frozen seafood. Established in 1993, the Company is located in Brooklyn, New York. As President/Chief Executive Officer, Dr. Ahmed oversees all administrative and operational duties of the Company, including new business development and contract negotiation. Concurrent to his duties at PLACID–NK, Dr. Ahmed holds two other positions. He is the President/Chief Executive Officer of Bangladesh Express, a world–wide financial service, as well as a practicing Physician of Obstetrics/Gynecology in private practice, with privileges at New York's Methodist Hospital. **Career Steps:** President/Chief Executive Officer, PLACID–NK Corporation (1993–Present); President/Chief Executive Officer, Bangladesh Express, Inc. (1995–Present); Attending Physician, Department of Obstetrics/Gynecology, New York Methodist Hospital (1987–Present). **Associations & Accomplishments:** American Medical Association; New York State Medical Society; Good Size. **Education:** Dacca Medical College, M.B.B.S. (1976); New York State University, M.D. **Personal:** Married to Begum N. Ahmed, D.D.S. One child: Khaled. Dr. Ahmed enjoys sports and soccer.

Nicolas Del Castillo

General Manager
C.I. Oceanos, S.A.
Carretera A. Mamonal #1–504
Cartegena, Colombia
(575) 668–5188
Fax: (575) 668–5266

5146

Business Information: C.I. Oceanos, S.A. is a primary exporter of cultivated shrimp. Comprised of a processing plant, 340 acre farm, hatchery, seven trawlers and three lobster boats, as well as an ice factory, the Company is an established leader in the Colombian market. Established in 1982, the Company employs 505 people, and has an estimated annual revenue of $16 million. As General Manager, Mr. Del Castillo oversees every aspect of the Company including administration, finance, operations, marketing, and strategic planning. **Career Steps:** General Manager, C.I. Oceanos, S.A. (1987–Present). **Associations & Accomplishments:** Past President of the Board of Directors of the Andi; President of the Board of Directors of Acuanal; Member of the Board of Directors of the Chamber of Commerce of Cartagena. **Education:** London School of Economics, M.Sc. (1983). **Personal:** Married to Maria Claudia Trucco.

Richard Hobson
President
Lakeview Marketing, Inc.
222 East Main Street
Albert Lea, MN 56007–2977
(507) 373–7075
Fax: (507) 373–6875

5147

Business Information: Lakeview Marketing, Inc. is a meat brokerage and distributor. Mr. Hobson, founder of the company in 1994, is responsible for diversified administrative activities, sales, marketing, and the supervision of brokers nationwide. **Career Steps:** President, Lakeview Marketing, Inc. (1994–Present); Partner and Marketing, Albert Lea Marketing (1990–1994); Sales Representative, Gold Country Marketing (1986–1990). **Associations & Accomplishments:** President–Elect, Kiwanis Club; Former President, Albert Lea Youth Soccer Association. **Education:** Iowa State University, Agricultural Business (1973). **Personal:** Married to Pamela S. in 1972. Two children: Nathan and Kevin. Mr. Hobson enjoys youth sports, refereeing soccer, boating, and golfing.

Salem Kallel
Sales Manager
Texas Meat Purveyors
4241 Director Drive
San Antonio, TX 78219
(210) 337–1011
Fax: (210) 333–9410

5147

Business Information: Texas Meat Purveyors is a meat supply and distribution company. As Sales Manager, Mr. Kallel is responsible for acquisitions, personnel coordination, and development of policies and procedures. He has received numerous awards from the American Culinary Federation, instructs culinary students, and has authored several training tapes and manuals for the Beef Council. **Career Steps:** Texas Meat Purveyors: Sales Manager (1988–Present), Sales Representative (1978–1988); Department Manager, Bealls (1976–1978). **Associations & Accomplishments:** Texas Chef's Association, Subchapter of American Culinary Federation. **Education:** St. Syr Police School, Criminology and Police Science (1972); Universite De Tunis, Economic Sciences (1970). **Personal:** Married to Brenda in 1976. Two children: Leila and Hedi. Mr. Kallel enjoys coaching soccer, boating, fishing, and spending time with his family.

Frank Ballesteros

President
Fresh Western Marketing Docks and Cooling, Inc.
P.O. Box 5909
Salinas, CA 93915
(408) 758–1390
Fax: (408) 758–4310

5148

Business Information: Fresh Western Marketing Docks and Cooling, Inc. is a produce distribution center for fresh produce (lettuce, tomatoes, etc.) located in Salinas, California. As President, Mr. Ballesteros is responsible for all aspects of operations, including managing the distribution and cooling of approximately 20 million SKU per year, as well as human resources and strategic planning. **Career Steps:** President, Fresh Western Marketing Docks and Cooling, Inc. (1993–Present); Distribution Manager, Fresh Western Marketing (1983–1993); Distribution Manager, Royal Packing Company (1978–1983). **Associations & Accomplishments:** RPDA. **Personal:** Married to Darlene in 1995. Two children: Frank Jr. and Michael. Mr. Ballesteros enjoys horseback riding and boating.

Randolph I. Fleming
Terminal Manager
Dole Fresh Fruit Company
P.O. Box 1689
Gulfport, MS 39502–1689
(601) 867–2932
Fax: (601) 867–2919

5148

Business Information: Dole Fresh Fruit Company specializes in the production and distribution of fresh fruits and vegetables sourced from Latin America, the Far East, Africa, and North America. As Terminal Manager, Mr. Fleming manages the port operations at the facility in Gulfport, MS. **Career Steps:** Dole Fresh Fruit Company: Terminal Manager (1995–Present), President and General Manager, Dole Dominicano (1990–1995), General Manager, Honduras (1983–1990), Controller, Honduras (1980–1983). **Associations & Accomplishments:** Vice President, Caribbean Association of American Chambers of Commerce in Latin America; President, American Chamber of Commerce, Dominican Republic; Dominican "Consejo Nacional de Hombres de Empresa; Dominican Agribusiness Council Board of Directors; President, American Chamber of Commerce, Honduras. **Education:** Harvard University, M.B.A. (1972); Yale University, B.A. in Economics (1966); Phillips Academy (1962). **Personal:** Married to Vivianna in 1970. Six children: David, Baird, Aurora, Rebeccah, Nancy, and Rafael. Mr. Fleming enjoys weightlifting, diving, and windsurfing.

Nicholas E. Gibbone
Vice President and Chief Financial Officer
Missa Bay Citrus Company
508 Center Square Road
Swedesboro, NJ 08085–1708
(609) 241–0900 Ext. 120
Fax: (609) 241–0020

5148

Business Information: Missa Bay Citrus Company, established in 1974, is a distributor of citrus products to various food retailers, primarily the WaWa chain of stores, which has 200 stores, 199 of which are located in New Jersey. Currently, Missa Bay Citrus Company employs 87 people and expects to post revenues/sales in excess of $50 million in 1996. As Vice President and Chief Financial Officer, Mr. Gibbone is responsible for all financial aspects of the Company. He handles all bank relations, business and health insurance, cash management, and protects the assets of the Missa Bay Citrus Company. **Career Steps:** Vice President and Chief Financial Officer, Missa Bay Citrus Company (1981–Present); Senior Managerial Accountant, Baldt One (1978–1981); Financial Analyst, SKF Industries, Inc. (1974–1978). **Associations & Accomplishments:** National Association of Accountants; Treasurer, Wallingford–Swarthmore Aquatic Club. **Education:** Temple University, M.B.A. (1971); Villanova University, B.S. in Business Administration (1968). **Personal:** Married to Deborah in 1972. Two children: Chad and Pamela. Mr. Gibbone enjoys reading, walking, and looking for business opportunities.

Shawn S. Harris
Owner and Director
Harris Import and Export
Mercuriusweg 12
Schiedam, The Netherlands 3113AR
(31) 102730573
Fax: (31) 104263034

5148

Business Information: Harris Import and Export is an international commodities trading company, concentrating on the importation of South and North American fruits and vegetables to all European countries. Established in 1990, Harris Import and Export reports annual revenue of $7 million. As Owner and Director, Ms. Harris is responsible for all aspects of operations, including sales, marketing, management, administration, public relations, and strategic planning. **Career Steps:** Owner and Director, Harris Import and Export (1990–Present). **Associations & Accomplishments:** Published in local produce magazines in The Netherlands. **Education:** University of Wisconsin – La Crosse, B.A. (1989).

Salustiano Alvarez

President
Mendez & Company, Inc.
P.O. Box 363348
San Juan, Puerto Rico 00936–3348
(809) 793–8888
Fax: (809) 783–4085

5149

Business Information: Mendez & Company, Inc. is a food and beverage importer and distributor, operating from three locations in Puerto Rico (Rio Piedras, Ponce, Mayaguez). A forty–year veteran of Mendez & Company, Mr. Alvarez started with the Company as Manager of the Retail Grocery Division in 1956 and was appointed as Vice President of the Company since 1979. Serving as President of the Company since 1993, he is responsible for all aspects of operations, including finances, sales, marketing, and strategic planning. **Career Steps:** Mendez & Company, Inc.: President (1993–Present), Vice President of Liquors Division (1979–1993), Manager of Retail Grocery Division (1956–1979). **Associations & Accomplishments:** American Cancer Society Puerto Rico Division; American Red Cross Puerto Rico Chapter; Caribbean Food Bank of Puerto Rico; Foundation for Pediatric Oncology Department; The Keepers of the Quaich; Corporate Membership, Wholsalers Chamber of Commerce; Confrerie Du Taste-vin Puerto Rico; Equestrian Order of the Holly Sepulcher of Jerusalem. **Education:** Wharton School of Commerce, Pennsylvania, B.A. (1954). **Personal:** Married to Irma Fiol in 1956. Three children: Salustiano Jr., Luis, and Irma M. Mr. Alvarez enjoys participating in the affairs of the community as a responsible citizen.

Charles Branham
Independent Distributor
NIKKEN, Inc.
3517 Roosevelt Avenue
Tacoma, WA 98404–4841
(206) 272–5092
Fax: (206) 572–4684

5149

Business Information: NIKKEN, Inc., a Japanese–based company, is an international marketer of health and nutritional products throughout 13 countries. As an Independent Distributor of NIKKEN products, Mr. Branham and his wife, Claudia, distribute products nationwide and develop new network marketing businesses. Through "success" reading, personal development, time management, and help from their upline, Mr. Branham has built a successful business which earns them in excess of $30,000 a month. **Career Steps:** Independent Dis-

tributor, NIKKEN, Inc. (1993–Present). **Associations & Accomplishments:** Pierce County Chamber of Commerce. **Personal:** Married to Claudia in 1973. Ten children: David, John, Colleen, Marcia, Debra, Terry, Patti, Edward, Walter, and Martin. Mr. Branham enjoys reading and photography.

Thomas M. Coward
Director of Product Specialists
CONCO Food Service
524 West 61st Street
Shreveport, LA 71106
(318) 869–3061
Fax: (318) 868–4541

5149

Business Information: CONCO Food Service, established in 1896, is a distributor of a full line of products including food and non–food items for restaurants, schools, healthcare facilities, etc. With estimated revenue of $250 million, the Company presently has over 400 employees. As Director of Product Specialists, Mr. Coward is responsible for the activities of four product specialists in purchasing and sales. His duties include the development and implementation of sales techniques for new and existing products offered to clients. **Career Steps:** CONCO Food Service, Shreveport, LA: Director of Product Specialists (1996–Present), Buyer/Merchandiser (1993–1996), Buyer/Merchandiser, Bell–Sysco (1991–1993); Buyer/Merchandiser, CONCO Food Service, Jackson, MS (1981–1991). **Education:** Mississippi College: M.B.A. (1983), B.S. B.A. (1980); Hinds Junior College, A.A. (1978). **Personal:** Married to Pamela in 1987. Two children: Adam and Joey Watson. Mr. Coward enjoys scuba diving, pool, fishing, and boating.

Peter J. Crupe
Accounting Manager
Bruno Scheidt, Inc.
1533 64th St.
Brooklyn, NY 11219–5709
(212) 741–8290 Ext: 293
Fax: (718) 259–1170 Ext: 57

5149

Business Information: Bruno Scheidt, Inc. imports gourmet and ethnic food from the Far East, Italy, France, and Spain, for distribution to food service industries throughout the United States. The Company has one private warehouse in New Jersey and numerous public warehouses across the United States. As Accounting Manager, Mr. Crupe is responsible for accounts payable, accounts receivable, cash management, managing investments, reviewing tax returns, and coordinating financial audits. **Career Steps:** Accounting Manager, Bruno Scheidt, Inc. (1993–Present); General Accountant, Phibro Energy (1991–1992); Staff Accountant, Philipp Brothers (1982–1991); Assistant Operations Manager, Standard Financial Corporation (1979–1982). **Associations & Accomplishments:** Mystery Writers of America; Baker Street Irregulars; Xaverian High School Alumni Association; Boston College Alumni Association. **Education:** St. John's University, M.B.A. (1979); Boston College, B.A. in Economics and Sociology (1976). **Personal:** Mr. Crupe enjoys music, sports, theater, and reading.

Sadiq Khalil Dawani
Managing Director
Al Jazira Cold Store Company
P.O. Box 26087
Manama, Bahrain
097–3701100
Fax: 097–3702122

5149

Business Information: Al Jazira Cold Store Company is an importer and wholesaler of dry foods, pet foods, cosmetics, and processed meats for supermarkets throughout Bahrain, to include four under their management. Goods are imported from countries worldwide, including the U.S., U.K., Australia, France, Switzerland, and Denmark. As Managing Director, Mr. Dawani oversees all operations for the Company, and markets new contracts from around the world. **Career Steps:** Al Jazira Cold Store Company: Managing Director, (1994–Present), General Manager (1990–1994); Proprietor, Sadiq Dawani Trading Company (1995); Director, K.H.M. Dawani & Sons (1962). **Associations & Accomplishments:** Former President, Rotary Club of Sulmaniya; Director, Bahrain Family Leisure Co. **Education:** Educated from UK in Business Management. **Personal:** Married to Patricia June in 1962. Three children: Samir, Shayesta, and Eskander. Mr. Dawani enjoys squash, bridge, fishing, boating, and swimming.

Jose Diaz Garza H.
Vice President
Pacific Star
Eugenio Cuzin 930
Parque Ind, Zapopan, Mexico 45150
011–5236567636
Fax: 011–5236569153

5149

Business Information: Pacific Star, an affiliate holding of Pillsbury Industries, is an international food and restaurant supply distributor, serving major retail supermarkets and restaurants throughout Mexico. As Vice President, Mr. Diaz Garza H. oversees all marketing strategies, responsible for customer development, new product lines and overall business growth. He was the instrumental person bringing in such major customers as Wendy's, Whataburger and Sanborn's, the largest Mexican food chain. **Career Steps:** Vice President, Pacific Star (1995–Present); President of Mexican and Latin American Simple Green Distributorship (1990–1995). **Education:** Universidad Autonoma, Business Administration (1985). **Personal:** Mr. Diaz Garza H. enjoys water and snow skiing, mountain biking, and jogging.

Derk C. Doijer
Chief Executive Officer
Makro Atacadista S/A
Rua Carlos Lisdegno Carlucci, 519
Sao Paulo, Brazil 05536–900
55–11–842–3566
Fax: 55–11–842–1010

5149

Business Information: Makro Atacadista S/A is Brazil's largest self–service cash and carry wholesaler and sells a wide variety of food and non–food consumer goods. The Company caters to selected customer groups, such as small businesses and institutional markets. As Chief Executive Officer, Mr. Doijer oversees the day–to–day operations of the Company, including employee administration, finances, sales and marketing, and strategic planning. **Career Steps:** Makro Atacadista S/A: President and C.E.O. – Sao Paulo (1995–Present), President and C.E.O. – Holland (1993–1995), Argentina (1989), Operations Director – Argentina (1987). **Education:** University of Rotterdam, Lawyer (1974); Post Academic, Fiscal Sciences (1981). **Personal:** Married to Alexandra Van Der Valk in 1981. Two children: Derk Jr. and Alexander. Mr. Doijer enjoys golf and sports.

Carl R. (Bob) Eklund
Plant Engineer
Interstate Brands Corporation
5003 South Spruce
Sand Springs, OK 74063–2060
(918) 835–7695
Fax: (918) 838–8951

5149

Business Information: Interstate Brands Corporation is a wholesale bakery for Wonder Bread. As Plant Engineer, Mr. Eklund is responsible for all building and machine maintenance, as well as overseeing the capital budget. **Career Steps:** Plant Engineer, Interstate Brands Corporation (1993–Present); Assistant Engineer, Continental Baking Company (1983–1993). **Associations & Accomplishments:** Vice President, American Institute of Plant Engineers – Tulsa, OK Chapter. **Education:** Southern Nazarene, Master's Degree (1992). **Personal:** Married to Vicki A. in 1988. Five children: Lisa, Kendra, Jimmy, Mickey, and Willie. Mr. Eklund enjoys boating, camping, and hunting.

Jay Flekier
Marketing/Sales Director
Vaughan Brothers Company
424 West Country Lane Terrace
Kansas City, MO 64114
(816) 563–4141
Fax: (816) 563–5842
EMail: See Below

5149

Business Information: Vaughan Brothers Company has been supplying gourmet coffee and shelled eggs to the world since 1871. As Marketing/Sales Director, Mr. Flekier is responsible for sales efforts either directly or through a network of food brokers. Internet users can reach him via: JFLEKIER@AOL.COM. **Career Steps:** Marketing/Sales Director, Vaughan Brothers Company (1991–Present); District Sales Manager, E.J. Brach Company (1986–1990); District Sales

Manager, Swift Eckrich Company (1980–1986). **Associations & Accomplishments:** American Management Association; Young Republicans Association. **Education:** University of Missouri, B.A. in Political Science (1980). **Personal:** Mr. Flekier enjoys reading, computer technology, and golf.

David Hayes

President and Chief Executive Officer
HAZ Sales, Inc.
P.O. Box 5060, 2595 Katherine Avenue
Ventura, CA 93005
(805) 654–8175
Fax: (805) 654–0208

5149

Business Information: HAZ Sales, Inc. is a restaurant supplies distributor, serving fast food and "to go" industries throughout Santa Barbara counties. Supplies include paper & foam products, janitorial items, canned goods, frozen foods, and refrigerated food products. Establishing HAZ Sales, Inc. following his Naval career in 1986, David Hayes serves as General Manager, Sales Manager, and Chief Executive Officer. He is responsible for all aspects of operations, including day–to–day activities, administration, finances, sales, public relations, marketing, and strategic planning. **Career Steps:** President and Chief Executive Officer, HAZ Sales, Inc. (1986–Present); Warehouse Manager, Cal Mar, Inc. (1986); First Class Petty Officer, United States Navy (1980–1986). **Associations & Accomplishments:** Church of the Living Christ–California. **Personal:** Married to Cynthia Lee in 1994. Two children: Brandie Lynn and Brandin Richard Franklin. Mr. Hayes enjoys playing golf with his family and friends.

Mitchell W. Isner

Controller
Shasta Spring Water
P.O. Box 492066
Redding, CA 96049–2066
(916) 221–2158
Fax: (916) 221–2963

5149

Business Information: Shasta Spring Water is a regional company that bottles water for distribution to other locations. As Controller, Mr. Isner is in charge of all financial concerns of the Company, to include cash management, accounts receivable, accounts payable, purchasing, payroll, investments, departmental audits, and establishing Company–wide budgets. Mr. Isner is involved in investment plans for future Company expansion. **Career Steps:** Controller, Shasta Spring Water (1995–Present); Controller, Canteca Foods, Inc. (1993–1995); Owner, Mitchell W. Isner Accounting (1985–1993); Control & Compliance, CFA Securities (1984–1986). **Associations & Accomplishments:** American Institute of CPA's; Inland Society of Tax Accountants; Board Member, Fire Protection District; Parks & Recreation Commissioner; Board Member, Youth Baseball Organization. **Education:** University of California – Berkeley, B.A. (1988); California State – Chico. **Personal:** Married to Rebecca in 1984. Two children: Megan and Jordan. Mr. Isner enjoys the outdoors, golf and camping with his family.

Edgar J. Johnson

Vice President of Sales
Heinz Pet Products
1 Riverfront Place
Newport, KY 41071–4548
(606) 655–5030
Fax: (606) 655–5015

5149

Business Information: Heinz Pet Products, a division of H.J. Heinz Company, is a national and international distributor of pet foods. Products include: 9–Lives, Kibbles & Bits, Gravy Train, and many others. Established in 1869, Heinz Pet Products reports annual sales of $1.2 billion. Joining the Company as a factory worker at age 18, Mr. Johnson worked his way up the corporate ladder to his present position of Vice President of Sales. He is responsible for all aspects of product sales and

also does public speaking on behalf of the Company. **Career Steps:** Heinz Pet Products: Vice President of Sales (1991–Present), General Manager of Marketing (1988–1991); Vice President of Marketing, David & Sons (1984–1988). **Education:** California Coast University, M.B.A. (1988), B.S. **Personal:** Married to Dee in 1972. Two children: Kristina and Derek. Mr. Johnson enjoys tennis and music.

Mr. James D. Kennedy

President (Retired – 1991)
Kennedy Enterprises, Inc., and AuNaturel Foods, Inc.
1723 Baldwin Drive
McLean, VA 22101
(703) 356–9667
Fax: Please mail or call

5149

Business Information: Kennedy Enterprises, Inc. was established in 1967 with five health food stores in Virginia and Maryland. It also distributed a catalogue of its products which were shipped to customers throughout the world. In 1969, a subsidiary, AuNaturel Foods, Inc., opened a factory near Buff Bay, Jamaica, developing and producing new tropical food products, largely from breadfruit and surplus bananas. A major problem in all banana producing countries is the large, wasted surplus of bananas inherent in their cultivation. The world–wide publicity given to the possibility of the Jamaican factory being able to turn these surpluses into marketable and durable foods generated queries from almost all banana producing countries. However, by 1973 AuNaturel Foods, Inc. was experiencing a number of unforeseen bureaucratic and start–up problems. Even though the number of new products produced by the factory had reached eight, with more in prospect, financial losses forced the operation to close. As President of both corporations, Mr. Kennedy was responsible for supervising their operations until his retirement in 1991. Currently, he is drawing on his fascinating background and personal experiences while a CIA Case Officer, researching and writing a book on the ongoing controversial period of Indonesian history from 1948–1967, including the U.S. involvement therein. Mr. Kennedy was the recipient of a personal Letter of Commendation from President Kennedy for his activities during the Cuban Missile Crisis. **Career Steps:** President, Kennedy Enterprises, Inc. and AuNaturel Foods, Inc. (Retired 1991); Case Officer and Indonesian Specialist, Central Intelligence Agency (1950–1967); Captain and Special Agent, U.S. Army Military Intelligence and the U.S. Army Counterintelligence Corps (1942–1946), participating in five European battle campaigns, from the Normandy landing to the Ardennes and finally meeting the Russians at the Elbe. **Associations & Accomplishments:** Phi Gamma Delta Fraternity, University of Idaho; Central Intelligence Retirees Association; Army Counterintelligence Corps Veterans; Past Commander, Veterans of Foreign Wars. **Education:** University of Amsterdam, Graduate Study under Dutch Government Fellowship (1948–1949); Fletcher School of Law and Diplomacy at Tufts University, M.A. (1948); University of Idaho, B.A. **Personal:** Married to Elinor Lintner Kennedy in 1951. One daughter: Mary B. Kennedy. One Granddaughter: Kirsten B. Larsen.

Roberto J. Luciano, CPA

Controller
Mendez & Company, Inc.
P.O. Box 363348
San Juan, Puerto Rico 00936
(809) 793–8888
Fax: (809) 783–4085

5149

Business Information: Mendez & Company, Inc. is a distributor of liquor and groceries. Established in 1912, Mendez & Company, Inc. currently employs 460 people. As Controller, Mr. Luciano is responsible for all aspects of financial operations, including accounting, financial reports, payroll, taxes, management, and projects. **Career Steps:** Controller, Mendez & Company, Inc. (1993–Present); KPMG Peat Marwick: Senior Manager (1989–1993), Manager (1987–1989). **Associations & Accomplishments:** American Institute of Certified Public Accountants; Former Member, Finance and Planning Committee, Puerto Rico Association of Certified Public Accountants; Former President, Institute of Internal Auditors (1987); Institute of Management Accountants. **Education:** University of Puerto Rico, B.B.A. (1980); Certified Public Accountant; Certified Internal Auditor. **Personal:** Married to Marisol Marchand in 1993. Mr. Luciano enjoys golf and wine tasting.

Ted Pilato

Founder, President and Chief Executive Officer
Dynamic Food Sales
15707 Rockfield Boulevard, Suite 105
Irvine, CA 92718–2830
(714) 457–1969
Fax: (714) 457–9101

5149

Business Information: Dynamic Food Sales is a food brokerage, providing sales and marketing functions to bakery product industries. Current client base extends throughout southern California and all of Arizona, with future development to expand throughout the domestic U.S. Establishing Dynamic Food Sales in 1995 and serving as its President and Chief Executive Officer, Mr. Pilato is responsible for all aspects of operations, including the aggressive search for companies to fill their niche market. Concurrently, he is starting a spin–off company — a temporary personnel agency formed to serve the bakery industry. **Career Steps:** President, Dynamic Food Sales (1995–Present); Vice President Sales, Atlas–Horn Food Service (1993–1995); Western Regional Sales Manager, International Multifoods (1988–1993); District Sales Manager, Bunge Foods (1983–1988). **Associations & Accomplishments:** Board of Directors, City of Hope Bakery Committee; California Retail Bakers Association; Retail Bakers of America; Given numerous presentations to industry associations and schools. **Education:** San Diego State University, B.A. in Marketing (1981). **Personal:** Married to Beth in 1996. Three children: Gino, Mario, and Nicholas. Mr. Pilato enjoys golf and travel.

R. Herschel Wyatt

Vice President of Retail Services
Laurel Grocery, Inc.
P.O. Box 4100
London, KY 40743–4100
(606) 878–6601 Ext. 251
Fax: (606) 864–5693
EMAIL: See Below

5149

Business Information: Laurel Grocery, Inc. is a wholesale distributor of food and supplies (i.e. cash registers, computers, etc.) to grocery and convenience stores in seven states. As Vice President of Retail Services, Mr. Wyatt is responsible for all aspects of his department, including administration, operations, marketing, strategic planning, customer service, and public relations. Internet users can reach him via: rhwyatt@skn.net. **Career Steps:** Vice President of Retail Services, Laurel Grocery, Inc. (1994–Present); Consulting Analyst, Southern California Edison Company (1983–1994); Consulting Analyst, Airsearch Manufacturing Company (1978–1983). **Associations & Accomplishments:** MENSA. **Education:** University of California, Los Angeles, B.S.B.A. (1963). **Personal:** Married to Chrystal Gaye in 1983. One child: Matthew Levi. Mr. Wyatt enjoys computer graphics animation.

⌐┴INTERLINK

Herman H. Yermilov

President and Chief Executive Officer
INTERLINK U.S.A., Inc.
11 Deer Park Drive
Monmouth Junction, NJ 08852
(908) 329–1400
Fax: (908) 329–6906
EMAIL: See Below

5149

Business Information: INTERLINK U.S.A., Inc. provides export and sales/distribution of American food products and computer equipment to Russia. In 1993, INTERLINK became the first official distributor of Hershey Foods in Russia. Started as a consulting Company, INTERLINK ventured into publishing, producing in 1989–92 one of the first independent business–magazines in Russia. Consulting and marketing experience allowed INTERLINK to develop its own sales/distribution group and since 1992 the company became a noticeable importer on the Russian market. In 1994 INTERLINK initiated, as a principal shareholder, foundation of Special Investment Bank– a fast growing Russian private commercial bank. Founding INTERLINK in 1988, as President and Chief Executive Officer, Herman Yermilov provides the overall vision and strategies for corporate growth and day–to–day operation. Internet users can reach him via: INTERLINK2@aol.com. **Career Steps:** President and Chief Executive Officer, Interlink U.S.A., Inc. (1988–Present), Senior Economist in the U.S.S.R. State Bank (1985–1987). **Education:** Moscow Financial Institute (Russian State Academy of Finance), M.B.A. (1985). **Personal:** Married to Irina V. in 1985. Two children: Anna and Catherine. Mr. Yermilov enjoys computers, books, and tennis.

Menachem Zenziper

Managing Director
Zenziper Grains and Feedstuffs Importers
10 Haaliya Street
Tel Aviv, Israel 66061
9723–681–4666
Fax: 9723–681–0604

5149

Business Information: Zenziper Grains and Feedstuffs Importers specializes in the importing of grains, feedingstuffs and protein sources for animal feeding consumption. Grains and products are imported from all around the world. The company is the largest private company of its kind in Israel and distributes only throughout that country. Established in 1926, the company employs thirteen people and has an estimated annual revenue of $100 million. As Managing Director, Mr. Zenziper oversees all phases of the Company and is responsible for financial management, administration, operations, marketing and sales, and public relations. Concurrent with his present position, Mr. Zenziper is one of the founders and main stockholder of Eshed Robotec (1982) Ptd., a high–tech Company based in Israel. **Career Steps:** Managing Director, Zenziper Grains and Feedstuffs Importers (1976–Present). **Associations & Accomplishments:** Chamber of Commerce **Education:** M.Sc. (1969). **Personal:** Married in 1969. Three children: Sharon, Eran and Yael. Mr. Zenziper enjoys off road driving, and horse raising and riding.

Jim D. Coleman

Quality Improvement Team Leader
AgAmerica FCB
P.O. Box TAF–C5
Spokane, WA 99220–4005
(509) 838–9576
Fax: (509) 838–9512

5159

Business Information: AgAmerica FCB is a wholesale agricultural lender, funding Farm Credit Associations who in turn lend to farmers, ranchers, and aquatic producers. As a Team Leader, Mr. Coleman assesses internal controls, facilitates control and risk self assessment workshops, and manages credit reviews. **Career Steps:** AgAmerica FCB: Quality Improvement Team Leader (1996–Present), Quality Control Director (1994–1996), Senior Credit Reviewer (1990–1994), Regional Quality Control Director (1986–1990), Branch Manager (1980–1986). **Associations & Accomplishments:** Institute of Internal Auditors – National and Local Chapters; Habitat for Humanity; Church Youth Fund Raising Committee; 1977 Outstanding Young Men of America. **Education:** Black Hills State University, B.S. in Business Economics (1974). **Personal:** Married to Sheila in 1980. Two children: Callie and Christie. Mr. Coleman enjoys home remodeling, camping, and all types of sporting events.

Mary A. Greer

Laboratory Technician
Mallinckrodt Veterinary, Inc.
1331 S. 1st Street
Terre Haute, IN 47802
(812) 232–0121
Fax: (812) 232–4698

5162

Business Information: Mallinckrodt Veterinary, Inc. manufactures and sells human and animal healthcare products and specialty chemicals. As Laboratory Technician, Ms. Greer is responsible for quality control and analysis of the products. Concurrently, she owns her own flower and gift shop, called Country Creations, which evolved from a hobby to a business. Inspired at an early age by her mother's and sister's love for flowers, she realized that she possessed the gift of creating with flowers. Her shop was recently recognized for Outstanding Service in the Florist Industry by the National Florist Association. In a recent newspaper article, she stated, "With faith, determination and ambition, these are the tools which helped her pave the way from a hobby to opening Country Creations." **Career Steps:** Laboratory Technician, Mallinckrodt Veterinary, Inc. (1978–Present); Laboratory Technician, Union Hospital (1970–1978); Laboratory Technician, Regional Hospital (1962–1969). **Associations & Accomplishments:** American Society of Clinical Pathologist; Board of Directors, YWCA; Wabash Valley Herb Society. **Education:** Indiana State University, Medical Technician (1961); Ivy Tech, Computers; Indianapolis Floral Art Design (1989); Indiana University Continuing Education. **Personal:** Married to Samuel T.. Four children: Cheryl, Richard, Steven, and Patricia. Ms. Greer enjoys floral art design.

Lawrence R. Nessler

Director of Sales and Marketing
Vita–Foam
2222 Surrett Dr.
High Point, NC 27263
(910) 431–1171
Fax: (910) 889–6633

5162

Business Information: Vita–Foam is one of the world's leading distributors of polyurethane foam. The Company's main consumers are the automotive manufacturing and the retail furniture industries. As Director of Sales and Marketing, Mr. Nessler focuses on the marketing of the product and managing the sales department. **Career Steps:** Director of Sales and Marketing, Vita–Foam (1994–Present); Marketing Manager, Comfort Clinic (1994); Vice President of Sales and Marketing, Highland Fabrics, Inc. (1990–1994); Vice President of Sales – Foam Division, Leggett & Peatt, Inc. (1981–1990). **Education:** Guilford Community College, Accounting (1991); Porter College, Business (1968). **Personal:** Married to Vicki L. in 1976. Three children: Kim, Kelly, and Jay. Mr. Nessler enjoys hunting.

Brian L. Cunningham

Operations Manager
Mittler Supply, Inc.
810 South Liberty Street
Muncie, IN 47302–2319
(317) 289–6341
Fax: (317) 284–8934

5169

Business Information: Mittler Supply, Inc. is a distributor of industrial and medical gases, safety equipment, and welding supplies to hospitals and other healthcare entities, as well as industrial manufacturers. Established in 1946, Mittler Supply, Inc. has 13 branches located in Illinois, Michigan, and Indiana, and currently employs 11 people. As Operations Manager, Mr. Cunningham is responsible for the management of the Muncie, Indiana store and fill plant, including the oversight and direction of day–to–day operations. **Career Steps:** Operations Manager, Mittler Supply, Inc. (1994–Present); Manager of Purchasing, Muncie Reclamation Supply (1988–1994); Vice President and Owner, L & B Castings, Inc. (1987–1988). **Associations & Accomplishments:** Ancient Accepted Scottish Rite, Valley of Indianapolis; Masonic Lodge F & AM #730, Daleville, Indiana. **Education:** Purdue University. **Personal:** Married to Diana L. Cunningham in 1987. Mr. Cunningham enjoys woodworking and golf.

Ole Jacob Kjendlie

Managing Director
Thors Kemiske Fabrikker
12 Haraldsvei
Skaarer, Norway 1473
47–67904100
Fax: 47–67909183

5169

Business Information: Established in 1920, Thors Kemiske Fabrikker is a manufacturer and distributor of chemicals, detergents, and coatings in Norway. As Managing Director, Mr. Kjendlie is responsible for varied administrative activities, including sales, marketing, production supervision, logistics, and strategic planning. **Career Steps:** Managing Director, Thors Kemiske Fabrikker (1993–Present); Regional Commercial Manager, Dove Chemical Nordic (1991–1993); Managing Director, Dove Chemical Denmark (1988–1991). **Associations & Accomplishments:** American Club of Norway; Dino Club of Managers in Swedish Owned Companies; Sports Clubs. **Education:** B.A. in Business Administration; External Courses in: Human Relations, Management Communications; Quality and Productivity Management Essentials; Gustav Kaser's Management Training. **Personal:** Married to Anne Bente in 1978. Four children: Joachim, Karl, Frederick, and Martin. Mr. Kjendlie enjoys skiing, jogging, squash, and fishing.

Martin P. LaBenz

Chief of Staff
McCann International L.L.C.
4155 Blackhawk Plaza Circle, Ste 150
Danville, CA 94506–4613
(510) 736–0244
Fax: (510) 736–6745
E/Mail: Marty@mccanni.co

5169

Business Information: McCann International L.L.C. is an international business development firm with offices in Blackhawk, California and Johannesburg, South Africa. An architect and pioneer of a new model of international business development, McCann International brings unique products and services together with complementary human and financial resources, often taking an equity position in the resulting business enterprises. As Chief of Staff, Mr. LaBenz is responsible for articulating business goals, organizing business development projects and moving them forward to successful realization. He is assisted by a staff of pre–eminent professionals in the fields of international commerce, finance, and advanced telecommunications. He makes his home in San Ramon, CA. Internet users can reach him via: marty@mccanni.com. **Career Steps:** Chief of Staff, McCann International L.L.C. (1996–Present); Manager of Technical Services & Regulatory Affairs, Spectrum Chemical Manufacturing Corporation (1990–1996); Product Development Chemist, Castle International Resources (1986–1990); Proprietor, High Country Installation (1980–1986); Project Engineer, FedServ Industries (1978–1980). **Associations & Accomplishments:** Small Package Labeling Committee, Society for Chemical Hazard Communication; Responsible Care Coordinator, Chemical Manufacturers Association; TSCA Committee, Synthetic Organic Chemical Manufacturers Association. Implementation of expert system for development of chemical hazard information; Radiation Safety Officer; Licensed CA Pharmacy Exemptee (1992–1996); Licensed Pilot. **Education:** University of Colorado – Boulder, B.S. (1973). **Personal:** One child: Audrey Lark. Mr. LaBenz enjoys mountaineering, flying, sailing, and wood and metal working. He is currently engaged in collaborative authorship of a series of technical monographs.

Darwin H. Simpson

Vice President – Southern Region
Van Waters and Rogers, Inc.
P.O. Box 2169
Spartanburg, SC 29304–2169
(864) 580–2100
Fax: (864) 580–2134

5169

Business Information: Van Waters and Rogers, Inc., a subsidiary of Univar, is one of the leading international industrial chemical distributors. Established in 1924 and listed on the New York Stock Exchange, the Company has locations throughout the United States, Canada, and Europe. Serving in executive roles for Van Waters & Rogers since 1982, Darwin Simpson was appointed as Southern Region Vice President in 1996. He provides the overall direction of operations and management staff for 40 distribution centers encompassing the Southern U.S. Aside from his executive career, Mr. Simpson is a Brigadier General serving in the U.S. Army National Guard. **Career Steps:** Van Waters and Rogers, Inc.: Vice President – Southern Region (1996–Present), Vice President of Logistics (1994–1996), Southern Region Vice President (1986–1994), Eastern Region Vice President (1982–1986). **Associations & Accomplishments:** Rotary Club; Trustee, Wofford College; Association of the U.S. Army. **Education:** Pepperdine University, M.B.A. (1982); U.S. Army War College (1992). **Personal:** Married to Bonnie in 1968. Two children: Melissa and Brad. Mr. Simpson enjoys golf and model airplane building.

Laith H. Al Shebel

Regional Sales Manager
SABIC Far East, Ltd.
Suite 1208, Two Pacific Place
Queensway, Hong Kong
85–22–5243889
Fax: 85–22–5224733

5172

Business Information: SABIC (Saudi Basic Ind. Corp.) Far East, Ltd. specializes in the marketing of industrial petrochemicals and plastic raw materials. The Company has many joint ventures with companies such as Exxon, Mobile, and Shell. As Regional Sales Manager, Mr. Al Shebel is responsible for planning and monitoring sales activity and sales support staff of the Far East Region, including China, Taiwan, Korea, the Philippines, Vietnam, and New Zealand. **Career Steps:** Regional Sales Manager, SABIC Far East, Ltd. (1994–Present); Area Sales Manager, SABIC Marketing, Ltd. (1990–1994); Assistant Manager (RBG Marketing), SAUDI American Bank (1989–1989). **Associations & Accomplishments:** Army

Volunteer during Gulf War (1991); 6–month training in UCC R&D Center (1993); 6–month training with Societee de Enterprise et de Etudes General (Paris) (1983). **Education:** University of Petroleum & Minerals, B.S. (1985); Management Centre Europe, seminars; Chartered Institute of Management. **Personal:** Married to Walaa A. AlMuammar in 1991. One child: Danya. Mr. Al Shebel enjoys fishing, desert camping, and computers.

Jeffrey W. Gibbs

Manager – Amoco Marketing Institute
Amoco Petroleum Products
200 East Randolph Drive, MC 0301
Chicago, IL 60601–6401
(312) 856–2849
Fax: (312) 616–0637
EMAIL: See Below

5172

Business Information: Amoco Corporation is a worldwide producer of crude oil and natural gas, as well as a marketer of refined petroleum products. Established in 1891, Amoco currently employs 38,000 people and has an estimated annual revenue of $28 billion. Amoco Marketing Institute, the training arm of Amoco Petroleum Products' Marketing Department, provides the design, development and implementation of various training programs to field and management staff. A management executive and consultant with Amoco Corporation since 1981, Jeffrey Gibbs has served as Director of the Marketing Institute since July of 1995. In this capacity, he is responsible for strategic direction, managing activites, budgetary oversight, and staff development. Internet users can reach him via: JGIBBSADM@AOL.COM **Career Steps:** Amoco Petroleum Products: Manager – Amoco Marketing Institute (1995–Present), Manager of Product Supply and Logistics (1993–1995), Field Sales Manager (1991–1993), District Support Services Manager (1990–1991). **Associations & Accomplishments:** American Society of Training Directors; Golden Retrievers Club of Illinois; Church Leader. **Education:** University of Illinois, B.S. in Finance (1980). **Personal:** Mr. Gibbs enjoys dog training and competition.

Margaret Ryan Kreeger, Esq.

Senior Attorney
ARCO
515 South Flower Street, Suite 4527
Los Angeles, CA 90071
(213) 486–1520
Fax: (213) 486–1544

5172

Business Information: ARCO, one of the leading providers of oil and gas products throughout the world, is a fully–integrated oil company that markets oil and natural gas liquids to various industries. A practicing attorney in California state courts since 1978, Mrs. Kreeger joined ARCO as Senior Attorney in 1988. She is responsible for providing legal representation and litigation for all in–house employment law matters. **Career Steps:** Senior Attorney, ARCO (1988–Present); Senior Attorney, SCE (1985–1988); Assistant to Chairman, EEOC (1984–1985). **Education:** University of San Francisco, J.D. (1978); University of California at Irvine, B.A. in Spanish/Political Science (1975) **Personal:** Married to Withold in 1989. One child: Patrick. Mrs. Kreeger enjoys reading, spending time with her family, and community service activities.

Stephen P. Tymikiw
Controller
Clarks Petroleum Service
115 Ferndale Road
Syracuse, NY 13219
(315) 697–2278
Fax: (315) 697–2308

5172

Business Information: Clarks Petroleum Service is a retail and wholesale distributor of petroleum and petroleum–based products. Established in 1926, Clarks Petroleum Service currently employs 35 people. As Controller, Mr. Tymikiw is responsible for all aspects of financial and daily operations. **Career Steps:** Clarks Petroleum Service: Controller (1995–Present), Director of Management Information Systems (1991–Present), Assistant Supervisor (1986–1995). **Associations & Accomplishments:** Voluntary Board Member and Treasurer, Ukrainian National Home; Supervisory Committee Member, Self–Reliance FCU. **Education:** Lemoyne College, B.S. in Accounting (1986). **Personal:** Married to Irene in 1993. Mr. Tymikiw enjoys sports, including volleyball and golf.

Howard Custer
Executive Vice President
St. Louis Beer Sales
4233 Union Boulevard
St. Louis, MO 63115
(314) 383–5574
Fax: (314) 383–0001

5181

Business Information: St. Louis Beer Sales is an establishment primarily engaged in wholesale distribution of beverages, specifically beer. Established in 1994, the Company employs 151 people, and has an estimated annual revenue of $49,000,000. As Executive Vice President, Mr. Custer oversees all operational aspects of the Company, including sales, finances, and delivery. **Career Steps:** Executive Vice President, St. Louis Beer Sales (1995–Present); Miller Brewing Company: General Manager (1984–1994), Production Manager (1979–1984). **Education:** Drake University, B.A. (1968). **Personal:** Married. Mr. Custer enjoys golf and woodworking.

Jimmie Dixon

President/General Manager
City Beverage Company, Inc.
P.O. Box 1036
Elizabeth City, NC 27906–1036
(919) 330–5539
Fax: (919) 330–4880

5181

Business Information: City Beverage Company, Inc. is regional wholesaler of beer, wine, and water since 1939. As President/General Manager, Mr. Dixon is responsible for all aspects of Company operations, including administration, marketing, and strategic planning. **Career Steps:** City Beverage Company, Inc.: President/General Manager (1990–Present), Vice President (1960–1990). **Associations & Accomplishments:** Chamber of Commerce; Industrial Development Commission; Board of Trustees, Albemarle Hospital; North Carolina Beer and Wine Association; Kiwanis Club; Board of Directors, Centura Bank; Board of Directors, Northeastern Regional Economic Development Commission. **Education:** Attended: Old Dominion College (1961). **Personal:** Married to Annette in 1959. Three children: Jeff, Mike and J.T. Mr. Dixon enjoys fishing, golf, and hunting.

David Stinson
General Manager
Ben E. Keith Beers
1805 Record Crossing
Dallas, TX 75235
(214) 634–1500
Fax: (214) 638–4918

5181

Business Information: Ben E. Keith Beers is a wholesale distributor for Anheuser–Busch beers. The Company has two locations in Texas (Dallas and Fort Worth). A seventeen–year veteran with Ben E. Keith Beers, Mr. Stinson was appointed as General Manager in 1991. He is responsible for the distribution, sales, and merchandising of products from the Dallas office. **Career Steps:** Ben E. Keith Beers: General Manager of Dallas Branch (1991–Present), Assistant General Manager of Fort Worth Division (1983–1991). **Associations & Accomplishments:** Alumni Board, Delta Sigma Phi – University of North Texas; Board Member, Dallas Arts District Friends. **Education:** University of North Texas, B.B.A. (1979). **Personal:** Married to Laura in 1980. One child: Rachel. Mr. Stinson enjoys reading and classic movies.

Sang M. Truong
Creative Director
Paulaner–North American
8100 South Akron Street, Suite 313
Englewood, CO 80112
(303) 792–3242
Fax: (303) 792–3430
EMAIL: info@paulaner.com

5181

Business Information: Paulaner North American, a wholly–owned subsidiary of Germany's Paulaner Group AG, is the exclusive U.S. importer and marketing agency for Paulaner and Hacker–Pschorr beers. PNA portfolio also includes beers from London and Belgium. The European holding company is The Schorghuber Group, with brewery ownership in Europe, Asia, and South America. In addition to beer, The Schorghuber Group is a conglomerate involved in Coca–Cola, wine, commercial aircraft leasing, commercial construction, real estate development, hotel, resort and hospitality industries. As Creative Director, Mr. Truong works with advertising and Puer-

to Rico agencies to develop campaign and advertising design. Mr. Truong is also involved in the marketing aspect of PNA such as planning, forecasting and researching market trends. **Career Steps:** Creative Director, Paulaner North American (1996–Present); Graphic Designer, PST, now MCI Direct (1994–1996); Manager, TMS (1990–1992). **Education:** Colorado Institute of Art (1994); University of Northern Colorado (1991). **Personal:** Married to Anh T. Vo in 1992. Two children: Alexandria and Erika. Mr. Truong enjoys wines, golf, travel, painting and learning.

Brent J. Vanderstelt
General Sales Manager
Vanderplow Distributing Company
2623 Jarman
Muskegon Heights, MI 49444
(616) 733–2076
Fax: (616) 739–9320

5181

Business Information: Vanderplow Distributing Company, serving the beverage industry since 1943, is a wholesaler of alcoholic beverages, including beer and wine from two locations in Michigan (Muskegon Heights and Cadillac). Brand names include Miller Beer, Gallo Wine, and Pabst Blue Ribbon Beer. Established in 1968, Vanderplow Distributing Company reports annual revenue of $5 million and currently employs 28 people. As General Sales Manager, Mr. Vanderstelt is responsible for all office administration and direction, as well as warehouse operations, sales, and delivery. Concurrent with his management position at Vanderplow, he is the owner of 31 rental units and a residential construction company – he provides all bid and project negotiations, while his wife acts as the general contractor and supervises the construction of homes. **Career Steps:** Vanderplow Distributing Company: General Sales Manager (1995–Present), Sales Manager (1994–1995), Key Account Manager (1988–1994). **Associations & Accomplishments:** Muskegon Area Rental Association (MARA); American Entrepreneur Association (AEA). **Education:** Muskegon Community College, Associate Degree (1995). **Personal:** Married to Kimberly in 1990. Mr. Vanderstelt enjoys running, weight lifting, and travel.

John Xenos
General Manager
Monarch Beverage
7910 Rockville Road
Indianapolis, IN 46214–9539
(317) 273–1310
Fax: (317) 273–1313

5181

Business Information: Monarch Beverage specializes in the wholesale distribution of beer and wine. The Company imports products internationally, and stocks some 650 beer labels including Miller, Coors, Heineken, Pabst, Stroh, Heileman, Sam Adams, Corona, and all major imports. The Company also carries domestic and imported wines such as Gallo, Glen Ellen, and Kendall Jackson. Established in 1947, Monarch Beverage employs 310 people, and has an estimated annual revenue of $90 million. As General Manager, Mr. Xenos oversees the day–to–day operations of the Company. His duties include administration, customer service, sales, public relations, accounting, strategic planning and warehouse management. **Career Steps:** General Manager, Monarch Beverage (1994–Present); Division Manager, E & J Gallo Winery (1992–1994); State Manager, Gallo (1988–92); Sales Manager, Atomic Distributing Company (1983–1985). **Associations & Accomplishments:** Past President, Lambda Chi Alpha Fraternity. **Education:** Marshall University, B.A. in Management (1979). **Personal:** Married to Kim Williamson in 1995. Mr. Xenos enjoys all sports, running and, fishing.

Rino Armeni
Marketing Director
Southern Wine and Spirits
4500 Wynn Road
Las Vegas, NV 89103
(702) 876–4500
Fax: (702) 255–1216

5182

Business Information: Southern Wine and Spirits, established in 1966, is the largest distributor of fine wine and liquors in the United States. The Company presently employs 185 people. As Marketing Director, Mr. Armeni oversees the operation of the marketing department. He is involved in developing and implementing marketing techniques to sell new and existing products to clients. Mr. Armeni develops, implements, and monitors departmental budgets. **Career Steps:** Marketing Director, Southern Wine and Spirits (1994–Present); Executive, Caesar's Palace (1989–1994); Executive, Walt Disney Resort (1988–1989); Executive, Marriott Hotels (1980–1988). **Associations & Accomplishments:** Vice President, Chain De Rotisseur; Association Colinair de France; Italy–America Chamber of Commerce. **Education:** College of Stressa, Diploma (1969); Certificate of Wine and

Spirits, London. **Personal:** Married to Marie–Claire in 1974. Two children: Paola and Laura. Mr. Armeni enjoys all major sports.

David J. Casey
Manager of Financial Analysis
Eber Brothers Wine & Liquor Corporation
3200 Monroe Avenue
Rochester, NY 14618–4608
(716) 586–7700
Fax: (716) 586–0521

5182

Business Information: Eber Brothers Wine & Liquor Company is a wholesale distributor of wine and liquor. Serving in various accounting roles for Eber Brothers since 1990, David Casey has steadily moved up the corporate structure, achieving his current status as Manager of Financial Analysis in December of 1995. His primary duties in this role involve the overall direction and supervision of financial and cost analysis functions and support staff. **Career Steps:** Eber Brothers Wine & Liquor Company: Manager of Financial Analysis (1995–Present), Accounting Manager (1994–1995), Accounting Supervisor (1992–1994), Staff Accountant (1990–1992). **Associations & Accomplishments:** Institute of Managerial Accountants. **Education:** St. John Fisher College, B.S. (1990). **Personal:** Married to Christine in 1992. David is an avid golfer during his leisure hours.

Mr. Paul E. Davis
President
Maison Jomere, Ltd.
420 Common Street, Suite 105
Lawrence, MA 01840
(508) 682–0885
Fax: (508) 682–1292

5182

Business Information: Maison Jomere, Ltd. is an international importer and distributor of fine French and Californian wines. A renowned wine taster and wine industry expert, Mr. Davis oversees all aspects of operations for the Company, focusing on marketing and distributor contract negotiations. Established in 1980, Maison Jomere, Ltd. employs 2 persons and has annual revenues of $5 million. **Career Steps:** President, Maison Jomere, Ltd. (1980–Present); President, Castel Wines International (1976–1980); Vice President, S.S. Pierce (1973–1976). **Associations & Accomplishments:** Compagnon du Beaujolais; Compagnon du Bordeaux; U.S. Chamber of Commerce; Coach, various youth sports programs in North Andover. **Education:** Northeastern University, B.S. (1966).

William David Pananos
National Sales Director of Spirits
Sazerac
809 Jefferson Hwy
Jefferson, LA 70121
(504) 841–3438
Fax: (504) 831–2383

5182

Business Information: Sazerac is an importer/exporter, distributor, and bottler of alcoholic and non–alcoholic beverages. International in scope, Sazerac has two plants, one in Louisiana (grain neutral spirits), and one in Kentucky (bourbon). As National Sales Director of Spirits, Mr. Pananos is responsible for visiting wholesalers, training, building relations with customers, and evaluating processes of the recruiting networking. He is also head of the support level for 11 regional sales managers. **Career Steps:** National Sales Director of Spirits, Sazerac (19–Present); Sales Manager, Magnolia Marketing (1988–1996); Sales Manager, Glazer Wholesalers (1985–1988); Sales Manager, Quality Beverage (1978–1985). **Education:** Tulane University, M.B.A. (1995); University of Massachusetts, B.S. in Business (1977). **Personal:** Married to Janet in 1986. Two children: Nicole and Anthony. Mr. Pananos enjoys golf and running.

Matt A. Serviere
Director of International Sales
Harris Moran Seed Company
1601 Red Bud
McAllen, TX 78504–4621
(210) 972–0915
Fax: (210) 971–8386

5191

Business Information: Harris Moran Seed Company develops, produces, and distributes hybrid vegetable seeds, specializing in hardy plants and those possessing natural insecticides. Mr. Servere has served in various managerial positions since joining Harris Moran in 1986. Promoted to Director of International Sales in 1994, he now provides support to the international sales team, interfaces with foreign distributors, develops long–term sales plans, and designs training materials. **Career Steps:** Harris Moran Seed Company: Director of International Sales (1994–Present), Regional Sales Manager (1986–1994); Manager of Vegetable Production, Griffin and Brand Company (1978–1986). **Associations & Accomplishments:** FIS. **Personal:** Married to Tricia in 1982. Three children: Joshua, Sharon and Amy. Mr. Serviere enjoys game hunting, skiing, and carpentry.

Judy R. Allen, CMP
Conventions and Meetings Manager
Ingram Book Company
1 Ingram Boulevard
La Vergne, TN 37086–3629
(615) 793–5000
Fax: (615) 793–3939

5192

Business Information: Established in 1964, Ingram Book Company is an international wholesale trade book distributor. As Conventions and Meetings Manager, Ms. Allen plans all trade shows, conferences, author signings, Publisher Blitz Days, and more than 100 events annually. **Career Steps:** Conventions and Meetings Manager, Ingram Book Company (1993–Present); Program Coordinator, Tennessee Healthcare Association (1992–1993); Sales Representative, Orkin Plantscaping (1991–1992); Catering Sales Manager, Opryland Hotel (1985–1991). **Associations & Accomplishments:** Meeting Professional International; International Exhibitors Association; Associate of the Month, December 1993. **Education:** University of Tennessee – Knoxville, B.S. (1985); Certified Meeting Professional. **Personal:** Married to W. Clark in 1991. One child: Jacob Henry. Ms. Allen enjoys sewing, reading, and church activities.

Deborah K. Felt
Vice President
Western Readers Service
100 Railroad Avenue
Danville, CA 94526
(510) 820–4441
Fax: (510) 820–4125

5192

Business Information: Western Readers Service is a magazine broker with 800 lines and 200 magazines. The Service will custom create a variety of publications into one order for clients. Headquartered in Danville, California, the Service has offices in six locations with 45 employees. As Vice President, Ms. Felt is primarily concerned with administrative duties and acts as a liaison between departments to improve, correct, and streamline all corporate aspects. She has oversight of customer service, telecollections, purchasing and marketing of new and existing services. **Career Steps:** Vice President, Western Readers Service (1994–Present); Assistant Vice President, Mid Atlantic Data Service (1974–1994). **Associations & Accomplishments:** National Association of Female Executives; Full Gospel Church. **Personal:** Two children: Jimmy and Dana. Ms. Felt enjoys golf, traveling with the family, and teaching her daughter to embroider.

Denise L. Bellavance
Director of Merchandising
Petals
300 Central Avenue
White Plains, NY 10606–1210
(914) 946–7373
Fax: (914) 946–7342

5193

Business Information: Petals is a mail–order catalog for the consumer market. The Catalog sells artificial flowers and decorative products. As Director of Merchandising, Ms. Bellavance is responsible for diversified administrative activities, including all aspects of merchandising. **Career Steps:** Director of Merchandising, Petals (1993–Present); Giftware Product Development, Bloomingdales (1990–1993); Seasonal Import Buyer, Thrifty Drug Store (1988–1990); Giftware Buyer, Fortunoff's (1986–1988). **Associations & Accomplishments:** Women in Production; U.S. Figure Skating Association. **Education:** International Fine Arts College, B.A. (1976); Rhode Island School of Design, Advertising. **Personal:** One child: Danielle. Ms. Bellavance enjoys ice skating, antique hunting, and country line dancing.

Daniel J. Brooks
Retail Nursery Manager
McGinnis Farms
5610 McGinnis Ferry Rd.
Alpharetta, GA 30202–3925
(770) 442–8881 EXT. 249
Fax: (770) 442–3214

5193

Business Information: McGinnis Farms is a wholesale and retail company specializing in nursery, irrigation and chemical products. Products are marketed to nurseries and individuals from eight stores in Georgia (4), Tennessee (2), and North Carolina (2). As Retail Nursery Manager, Mr. Brooks is responsible for the management of the Retail Division, including operations, accounting, sales, marketing, and administration. Concurrently, he serves as a silent partner in Brooks Garden Center, where his father is the active and managing partner. His future plans include founding his own business with his wife. **Career Steps:** Retail Nursery Manager, McGinnis Farms (1994–Present); Partner, Brooks Garden Center (1990–Present); Subagent, Hansard Insurance Company (1993–1994). **Associations & Accomplishments:** Ducks Unlimited; Trout Unlimited. **Education:** University of Georgia, B.A. in History (1993); Gainesville College, A.S. in General Studies. **Personal:** Married to Pamela in 1994. Mr. Brooks enjoys music, fishing, hunting, and skiing.

Joseph M. LoMonaco
Controller
Riverdale Farms, Inc.
9440 North West 12th Street
Miami, FL 33172–2804
(305) 592–5760
Fax: (305) 592–3371

5193

Business Information: Riverdale Farms, Inc. is an importer of fresh cut flowers from Central and South America. The Company sells to wholesale flowers buyers throughout the United States and Canada. As Controller, Mr. LoMonaco oversees all functions of the Accounting Department; including actions taken on delinquent accounts, accounts payable, and the preparation of financial statements for presentation to the Board of Directors. Additionally, he oversees the Computer Information Systems area, sets Company policies, develops procedures, and negotiates employee benefits. **Career Steps:** Riverdale Farms, Inc: Controller (1994–Present), Senior Accountant (1993–1994); Credit Manger, Four Farmers, Inc. (1992–1993). **Associations & Accomplishments:** W.F. & F.S.A. Young Executives. **Education:** Florida International University, M.B.A. (1993); Syracuse University – Utica College, B.S. in Accounting (1989). **Personal:** Mr. LoMonaco enjoys golf and weight training.

Joao V. P. Diniz
Regional Director
Brown & Williamson Tobacco Corporation
Calle D Lote 30, Amelia Distribution Center
Guaynabo, Puerto Rico 00968
(809) 782–9877
Fax: (809) 782–9866

5194

Business Information: Brown & Williamson Tobacco Corporation manufactures and exports cigarette products. Brown & Williamson is headquartered in Louisville, Kentucky. A Sales and Distribution expert with thirty years experience in the market sales and export industry, Mr. Diniz joined Brown & Williamson Tobacco Corporation as Regional Director in 1986. He is responsible for the management of the Puerto Rico operations, including traveling on behalf of the company primarily in Puerto Rico. **Career Steps:** Regional Director, Brown & Williamson Tobacco Corporation (1986–Present); National/Export Manager, BAT – Venezuela (1966–1986). **Associations & Accomplishments:** Chamber of Commerce. **Personal:** Married to Betty in 1974. Two children: Juan Carlos and Juan Eduardo.

Muhammad A. Aboaisha
Owner
Nowres Trading Establishment
P.O. Box 5480
Dammam 31422, Saudi Arabia
966–3–8340788
Fax: 966–3–8345652

5199

Business Information: Nowres Trading Establishment (NTE) is a diverse activities, overseeing the operations of decorative doors, fabricating aluminum arches, powder coating for metals, metal casting, building materials, computer services and accessories, authorized dealers and distributors in the Eastern province for IBM PC, ZyXEL Modem, Software.

NTE is also associated with Al–Habib communication Mobile GSM. With 30 years experience in banking, Mr. Aboaisha established Nowres Trading Estabishment in 1980, with the assistance of his son Haitham, the General Manager. **Career Steps:** Nowres Trading Establishment: Owner and President (1980–Present); Riyadh Bank: Regional Manager (1985–Present), Branch Manager (1969–1985), Member of Board of Directors and Representative of Saudi Banks to Union of Arab Banks (1985–1990). **Education:** Riyadh University, B.S. in Economics (1967), Participated in many conferences and seminars in different topics. **Personal:** Married with four children: Haitham, Nawar, Rayed, and Abdulla. Mr. Aboaisha enjoys reading, classical music and travel.

Alexandre Henrique Caiado
Director
Greenwich
Rua Comendador Araujo, 143 5 andar – Cj. 55 centro
Curitiba, Parana, Brazil 80420–900
55–41–322–0805
Fax: 55–41–322–0849
E MAIL: See Below

5199

Business Information: Greenwich provide a global source service to small industrial companies in South America. The Company also imports baby strollers from Asia and distributes them to stores throughout Brazil for resale. As Director, Mr. Caiado is one of two partners in the firm and is responsible for all administrative and financial concerns. He handles human resource management, personnel, cash management, public relations, and strategic planning for the Company. Internet users may reach him via: greenwich@sul.com.br. **Career Steps:** Director, Greenwich (1995–Present); Director of Administration, Caiado Empreedimentos a Participardes (1995–Present); Director of Finance, Factoring House (1994–1995); Assistant, Agropecuaria Arroio (1989–1994). **Associations & Accomplishments:** Representative of Business Management University in his town while a student (1990–1994); President of GEL (group of liberal studies) (1993); Coordinator of Young Businessmen's Counsel at Parana's Chamber of Commerce. **Education:** Facuidades Positivo, M.B.A. (1994); Post Graduation at Faculdade de Direito de Curitiba, Commercial Law. **Personal:** Mr. Caiado enjoys tennis, skiing, swimming, and aviation.

Carlos Della Vedova

President
American Intertrading S/A
Libertade 836 Oficina 37
Buenos Aires, Argentina 1012
(541) 823–8718
Fax: (541) 823–8718

5199

Business Information: American Intertrading S/A is an international trading company specializing in wearing apparel. The Company contracts international companies (i.e. Levi's in the United States and Dufour in Italy) to distribute their wares in South America. As President, Mr. Della Vedova oversees all operational aspects including sales, management, public relations, and strategic planning. **Career Steps:** President, American Intertrading S/A (1992–Present); Levi's de Argentina: Export Manager, (1990–1992), Production Manager (1987–1990), Engineering Manager (1985–1987). **Associations & Accomplishments:** Investel S/A. **Education:** Buenos Aires University, Engineer (1976). **Personal:** Married to Ana Maria in 1978. Three children: Ana Ines, Carlos, and Maria Victoria. Mr. Della Vedova enjoys reading, travel, and sailing.

Dennis R. McDonald
Director of Distributor Services
New Image International, Inc.
115 North Water Street
Georgetown, KY 40324
(502) 867–1895
Fax: (502) 863–5640
EMAIL: See Below

5199

Business Information: New Image International, Inc. is a network marketing company in the weight–loss and nutritional supplement field distributing through direct retailers via word–of–mouth advertising. As Director of Distributor Services, Mr. McDonald serves as the Executive in charge of phone–order entry, distributor and customer services, internal affairs, and processing departments. In addition, he co–chairs various national conferences and edits "New Image News" – the Company newsletter. Internet users may reach him via: NIINTL@aol.com **Career Steps:** Director of Distributor Services, New Image International, Inc. (1994–Present); Manager of Sales, CIFA Supply, Inc. (1994); President, D&D Marketing (1988–1993); Manager, Schmitt's Furniture (1986–1988).

Associations & Accomplishments: Chamber of Commerce; Junior Achievement Institute; IHFRA; Downtown Retail Merchants Association; Direct Selling Association; Former Member, Kiwanis; Former Member, FGBMFI; Former Member, American Management Association. **Education:** Certified Home Furnishings Representative. **Personal:** Married to Deborah in 1976. Three children: Joshua, Tina, and Caleb.

Rick J. Pritikin
Vice President
Thomas Nelson, Inc.
404 BNA Drive, Suite 600 Building 200
Nashville, TN 37217
(615) 889–9000
Fax: (615) 883–7851

5199

Business Information: Thomas Nelson, Inc. is the largest distributor of Bible publications and Christian music in the United States. The Corporation is a manufacturer and distributor of gifts under the C.R. Gibson, Markings, Pretty Paper, Graphomania and Makings Inspirations labels. As Vice President, Mr. Pritikin is in charge of 4 divisions including all of Unison Music Distribution and the exclusive world–wide contact for the Round Towel(R). He is responsible for concept development, marketing, distribution, and all ad campaigns. He oversees all aspects of the business unit. He handles all personnel concerns for employees reporting directly to him. Mr. Pritikin works closely with all members of management to establish a workable budget for the Corporation and then works with department and division heads to ensure budgetary guidelines are followed. **Career Steps:** Vice President, Thomas Nelson, Inc. (1991–Present); Vice President of Sales & Marketing, Good News Publishers (1985–1991); Vice President of Sales & Marketing, Bresler Drexel Ice Cream Company (1974–1985); President, Pritco Group (1984–Present). **Associations & Accomplishments:** American Management Association; American Marketing Association; Delta MuDelta ETA Chapter; DePaul University; Gospel Music Association; National Association of Recording Merchandisers; National Association of Chain Drug Stores; Former Vice President, Christian Management Association. **Education:** Seattle Pacific, M.B.A. (1996); DePaul University, B.Sc. Degree in Business; Merchandising Institute; Purdue University. **Personal:** Married to Kimberly in 1981. Three children: Diane, Lauren, and Bethany. Mr. Pritikin enjoys golf, reading, and working out.

Sue A. Rodman
Vice President
Deer Track Traders, Ltd.
P.O. Box 448
Loveland, CO 80539–0448
Fax: (970) 667–8464

5199

Business Information: Deer Track Traders, Ltd. specializes in the procurement and wholesale trade of Native American arts and crafts. Crafted by more than 300 tribes, the products are sold throughout the United States and in 12 countries internationally. As Vice President, Ms. Rodman is responsible for all aspects of Company operations, including management, procurement, and education. **Career Steps:** Vice President, Deer Track Traders, Ltd. (1975–Present); Co–Manager, Traveling Traders (1974–1975); Sales/Silversmith, Pine Silver Shop (1970–1972). **Associations & Accomplishments:** Indian Arts and Crafts Association; Western and Eastern Salesman's Association. **Education:** Colorado State University (1970–1973); Woodbury Business College (1969). **Personal:** Married to Alpine C. in 1970. One child: Connie L. Ms. Rodman enjoys reading, writing, playing the piano, recreation, research, and being an artist.

5200 – 5999
RETAIL TRADE

5200 Building Materials and Garden Supplies

5211 Lumber and other building materials
5231 Paint, glass and wallpaper stores
5251 Hardware stores

5261 Retail nurseries and garden stores
5271 Mobile home dealers

Douglas L. Bowen
Corporate Vice President
The Contractor Yard, Inc.
259 Access Road
Spartanburg, SC 29305
(803) 599–5967
Fax: (803) 599–0962

5211

Business Information: The Contractor Yard, Inc., the wholesale professional arm of Lowe's Companies, Inc., is a national supplier of building materials, selling only to professional building contractors. Joining Lowe's Companies in 1986 as a Store Manager, Mr. Bowen was appointed to his current position as Corporate Vice President on January 1995. He has corporate executive charge of all operations for 25 regional Contractor Yard locations. **Career Steps:** Lowe's Companie's Inc.: Corporate Vice President – The Contractor Yard, Inc. (1995–Present), District Manager (1991–1994), Store Manager (1986–1990). **Associations & Accomplishments:** Mason; Eagle Scout B.S.A.; Tae Kwondo – 1st Dan Blackbelt, martial arts. **Education:** University of North Carolina – Wilmington, NC. **Personal:** Married to Laure I. in 1984. Two children: Weston Douglas and Joseph Cole Bowen. Mr. Bowen enjoys golf, basketball, and softball.

Chong Gu
Accounting Manager
City Mill Company, Ltd.
660 N. Nimitz Highway, P.O. Box 1559
Honolulu, HI 96806–1559
(808) 529–5821
Fax: (808) 521–9769

5211

Business Information: City Mill Company, Ltd. is a locally–owned home improvement and building material retailer. Founded in 1899, the Company currently operates seven store locations throughout the Island of Oahu. A certified public accountant with over ten years financial management experience, Chong Gu has served as City Mill's Accounting Manager since 1995. His primary role is the oversight and administration of all accounting aspects and support staff, with additional duties to include overall corporate strategies and development as a member of the executive team. **Career Steps:** Accounting Manager, City Mill Company, Ltd. (1994–Present); Accounting Manager, Servco Pacific Inc. (1993–1994); Accounting Manager, Pacific International Company, Ltd. (1991–1993). **Associations & Accomplishments:** American Institute of Certified Public Accountants – Guam Chapter. **Education:** University of Hawaii: M.A. in Economics (1991), M.B.A. (1989); People's University of China, Bachelor of Business Administration (1983). **Personal:** Married to Yuanyuan in 1980. One child: Yang. Mr. Gu enjoys photography and gardening.

Billie J. Hall
District Credit Manager
Foxworth Galbraith
520 North Telshor Boulevard
Las Cruces, NM 88011–8223
(505) 522–0153
Fax: (505) 522–2461

5211

Business Information: Foxworth Galbraith is one of the largest retail lumber sales and contractors in the country. As District Credit Manager, Ms. Hall has oversight of credit operations for the eleven stores in her district. Her responsibilities include approval/disapproval of credit applications, evaluation of credit liens, composing/sending letters of intent, and representing the Company at court hearings and filings. **Career Steps:** District Credit Manager, Foxworth Galbraith (1988–Present); Bookkeeping/Credit, Casey Carpet Company (1988); Assistant to President, New Mexico Activities Association (1987). **Education:** Donal Ana Community College, Certified Nursing Assistant Certificate; New Mexico Real Estate Course (1991). **Personal:** Married to James in 1974. Two children: Marti Jene and Misti Lynn. Ms. Hall enjoys stock car racing, boating, and water skiing.

Arnold N. Lakey
Vice President of Credit Management
Lowe's Companies, Inc.
613 Cherry Street
North Wilkesboro, NC 28659
(910) 651–4324
Fax: (910) 651–2637

5211

Business Information: Lowe's Companies, Inc. is a home improvement center–building supply retail chain with 350 retail stores located throughout Texas, Oklahoma, Michigan, and Pennsylvania. Eighty percent of Lowe's customers are retail, with twenty percent from commercial businesses. Established in 1947, Lowe's reports annual revenue of $7.3 billion and currently employs more than 35,000 people corporate–wide, including 78 people in the North Wilkesboro Office Credit Department. A thirty–nine year veteran with Lowe's, Mr. Lakey joined the Company in 1956 and has held numerous positions within the Credit Department. Appointed as Vice President of Credit Management in 1976, he is responsible for the oversight of all credit operations for commercial and building business accounts totaling $1.2 billion per year, as well as the supervision of a staff of five people. **Career Steps:** Lowe's Companies, Inc.: Vice President of Credit Management (1976–Present), Corporate Credit Manager (1973–1976), Office and Credit Supervisor (1968–1973). **Associations & Accomplishments:** National Association of Credit Management; NACM – Loss Prevention; North Wilkesboro Rotary Club: Former President, Former Director, Special Treasurer; Board of Trustees, Wilkes Community College. **Education:** Kings Business College, A.A. (1956). **Personal:** Married to Rebecca C. in 1959. Five children: Scott, Kevin, Robyn, Chris, and Jon. Mr. Lakey enjoys civic work.

Alberteen Y. Lewis
Budget Director
Fulton County Board of Education
786 Cleveland Avenue Southwest
Atlanta, GA 30315–7239
(404) 763–6760
Fax: (404) 763–5510

5211

Business Information: Fulton County Board of Education is the county governmental office responsible for the administration of all public, elementary, and secondary education facilities within its county jurisdiction. The Board establishes partnerships between community businesses and individuals which promote collaborative and mutually beneficial results, in order to enhance student achievement through these partnerships, and provide learning opportunities for the community. As Budget Director, Ms. Lewis oversees the preparation of budgets, monitors utilization of budgets, generates funds for school programs and new school projects for the district, as well as monitors revenue for the department. Concurrent with her position as Budget Director, Ms. Lewis owns her own acounting and tax service, Account Abilities. **Career Steps:** Budget Director, Fulton County Board of Education (1994–Present); Owner, Account Abilities (Present); United States Army: Management Officer (1985–1986); Assistant Finance Officer (1981–1985). **Associations & Accomplishments:** Institute of Management Accountants; Georgia Association of School Business Officials; Major, United States Army Reserves; PAW Minister's Wives Association. **Education:** Clark Atlanta University, M.B.A. in Finance (1991); Alcorn State University, B.S. in Business Administration; U.S. Army: Command & Staff Services School, Finance Officers Advanced Course. **Personal:** Married to Jonathan. Three children: John, Lina, and Talal. Ms. Lewis enjoys tennis and park activities with her children.

Richard A. Ludeman
Manager
Cooper Building Materials
1451 Bella Vista Way
Bella Vista, AR 72714–7622
(501) 855–3053
Fax: (501) 855–4572

5211

Business Information: Cooper Building Materials, an ACE Home Center, is a national retailer and wholesaler of building materials and supplies for residential construction. With corporate headquarters in Arkansas, Cooper Building Materials also serves as a builder for the retirement community in Missouri, Tennessee, and South Carolina, in addition to manufacturing Peachtree Windows and Doors for other lumber yards in Kansas and Missouri. As Manager, Mr. Ludeman is responsible for the oversight of all aspects of operations of the Retail and Wholesale Divisions. In addition to supplying materials to other Cooper locations, he oversees a support staff of 70. **Career Steps:** Manager, Cooper Building Materials (1994–Present); Store Manager, Payless Cashways (1982–1994). **Associations & Accomplishments:** Northwest Arkansas Home Builders Association; Lions Club; Habitat for Humanity. **Education:** University of South Dakota, B.S. in Business Administration (1982). **Personal:** Married to Monya in 1983. Two children: Ricky and Rachel. Mr. Ludeman enjoys golf, hunting, boating, and sports card collecting.

Michael S. McDole
Vice President and General Manager
JT's Home and Builders Center
75 Tupelo Street
Bristol, RI 02809
(401) 254–0200
Fax: (401) 254–0320

5211

Business Information: JT's Home and Builders Center is a retail lumberyard. Currently, 80 percent of sales are to professional contractors. In operation since 1907, JT's Home and Builders Center currently employs 25 people. As Vice President and General Manager, Mr. McDole is responsible for all aspects of operations, including sales, profits, inventory, receivables and payables, and personnel. **Career Steps:** JT's Home and Builders Center: Vice President (1993–Present), Assistant General Manager (1990–1993), Corporate Buyer (1987–1990), Contractor Sales (1983–1987). **Associations & Accomplishments:** Board of Directors, Bristol County Builders Association; Rhode Island Lumber and Building Materials Dealers Association; Writes a monthly column for Pro–Sales magazine, a national trade journal. **Education:** Roger Williams University. **Personal:** Married to Carol. Four children: Lynne, Kristen, Douglas, and Karen. Mr. McDole enjoys golf.

Jorge Luis Perez
Vice President
Almacenes Arilope, Inc.
P.O. Box 4003
Aguadilla, Puerto Rico 00605–4003
(809) 891–0560
Fax: (809) 891–0560

5211

Business Information: Almacenes Arilope, Inc. is a family–owned, retail hardware and building materials store providing services to local consumers. Future plans include expanding their customer base by opening a Home and Garden Center to the facility. As Vice President, Mr. Perez is responsible for assisting the President (his father) in all aspects of operations and purchasing matters. **Career Steps:** Vice President, Almacenes Arilope, Inc. (1990–Present); Texas Instruments. **Associations & Accomplishments:** Lions Club; Phi Sigma Alpha. **Education:** Marquette University, Electrical Engineering Degree (1980); Abilene University of Dallas, M.B.A.

Luis Perez Jr.
President
Almacenes Arilope, Inc.
P.O. Box 4003
Aguadilla, Puerto Rico 00605–4003
(809) 891–0560 (809) 891–0750
Fax: (809) 891–0560

5211

Business Information: Almacenes Arilope, Inc. is a family–owned, retail hardware and building materials store providing services to local consumers. Future plans include expanding their customer base by opening a Home and Garden Center to the facility. Founded by his father 30 years ago, Mr. Perez began his climb up the company ladder as Treasurer in 1967. Presently serving as President, Mr. Perez is responsible for all aspects of operations, including purchasing products for distribution to customers. His son, Jorge assists him as Vice President. **Career Steps:** Almacenes Arilope, Inc.: President (1980–Present), Treasurer (1967–1980); Manager, M. Perez & Sons (1956–1967). **Associations & Accomplishments:** Rotary Club; Lions Club; Nu Sigma. **Education:** Professional Commerce School, Accounting Degree (1954). **Personal:** Married to Elba in 1956. Three children: Jorge Luis, Martha, and Lourdes. Mr. Perez enjoys reading, music, and dominoes.

John L. Thomas
Branch Manager
Roofers Mart of Oregon
1679 Sage Road, Suite B
Medford, OR 97501
(541) 773–4730
Fax: (541) 779–6711

5211

Business Information: Roofers Mart of Oregon specializes in the wholesale distribution of materials specific to the roofing industry (with the exception of commercial roofing contractors). Regional in scope, the Company also has locations in Portland and Medford, Oregon. Established in 1970, the Company employs five people and has an estimated annual revenue of $4.5 million. As Branch Manager, Mr. Thomas oversees sales, service and training, and is responsible for coordinating all business activities and seminars. Additional duties include administration, operations, purchasing, marketing, and strategic planning. **Career Steps:** Branch Manager, Roofers Mart of Oregon (1987–Present); Owner, Operator, Island Roofing, Inc. (1981–1987); Assistant Manager, Newberry's, A Division of McCrory (1977–1981). **Associations & Accomplishments:** American Guild of English Handbell Ringers (AGEHR); Assistant Varsity Head Coach, Girls Basketball at North Medford High School; Coordinator of Handbell Music, United Methodist Church, Medford, Oregon; Habitat for Humanity. **Education:** Southern Oregon State; Portland State. **Personal:** Married to Linda K. Thomas in 1992. Three children: Zachary, Chelsea, and Seth. Mr. Thomas enjoys basketball, softball, golf, music, fund raising for youth activities, and Habitat for Humanity.

Brian Craig Underwood
Sales Coordinator
ACME Brick Company
3020 West Front
Midland, TX 79701–7145
(915) 699–5017
Fax: (915) 699–1839

5211

Business Information: ACME Brick Company specializes in the retail and commercial sale of bricks and tiles. Headquartered in Fort Worth, the Company does business in Texas and its surrounding states. As Sales Coordinator, Mr. Underwood oversees the operations of the Midland, TX facility, including sales, scheduling, public relations, and customer service. **Career Steps:** Sales Coordinator, ACME Brick Company (1994–Present). **Education:** Texas Tech University, B.S. (1991). **Personal:** Married to Kristi in 1996. Mr. Underwood enjoys hunting and other outdoor activities.

James A. Whatley
Director of Construction
Home Depot
1101 Perimeter Drive, Suite 300
Schaumburg, IL 60173–5024
(847) 413–4965
Fax: (847) 413–4973

5211

Business Information: Home Depot is the largest retailer of do–it–yourself supplies in the United States and the fifth largest in the world. As Director of Construction, Store Planning, and Maintenance, Mr. Whatley oversees development, construction, and maintenance for all facilities in 13 Midwestern States. **Career Steps:** Director of Construction, Home Depot (1992–Present); Vice President, Williams Construction (1986–1987); Vice President, Halsted Development Company (1984–1986); Construction Manager, Weingarten Realty Inc. – Houston, Texas (1976–1984). **Associations & Accomplishments:** American Mensa Society; Published in "Michigan Society of Engineers." **Education:** Louisiana State University, M.B.A. in Finance and Real Estate (1986). **Personal:** Married to Marilyn Kaye in 1972. Two children: Tiffany Christine and Brian Patrick. Mr. Whatley enjoys hunting, stained glass work, and golf.

Daniel K. Wilder
Senior Vice President
Home Base
3345 Michelson Drive
Irvine, CA 92715–1606
(714) 442–5289
Fax: Please mail or call

5211

Business Information: Home Base is a warehouse–style home improvements retail store, similar to Lowes or Home Depot stores, that has 80 locations in 13 western states, excluding Montana. Future plans include continuing to develop stores on the West Coast and remodeling their stores to the new prototype: Pilot Special Order System – an efficient order and delivery system for customers that enable them to receive orders directly from vendors. Established in 1983, Home Base reports annual revenue of $1.4 billion and currently employs 9,800 company–wide. As Senior Vice President, Mr. Wilder is responsible for all aspects of inventory management and logistics, including ordering, stocking, and EDI activity. **Career Steps:** Home Base: Senior Vice President (1993–Present), Senior Vice President of Finance & Logistics (1991–1993), Vice President and Controller (1987–1991). **Associations & Accomplishments:** Certified CPA in Utah; Member, President's Council, Hardline Technical Conference; Frequent public speaker; Published numerous articles. **Education:** California State University – Fullerton, B.A. in Accounting (1977); Utah State University, C.P.A. **Personal:** Married to Janet G. Wilder in 1976. Two children: Adam and Alexa. Mr. Wilder enjoys golf and cars.

John Corbin

District Manager
Tractor Supply Company
3480 W. Andrew Johnson Hwy.
Morristown, TN 37814
(423) 586–1721
Fax: (423) 586–1721
EMAIL: See Below

5251

Business Information: Tractor Supply Company is a retail supplier of specialty farm products. Established in 1938, the company maintains more than 200 locations in 25 states. Mr. Corbin has served in various capacities with TSC, most recently named District Manager in 1991. He is presently responsible for 16 stores, supervising daily operations and performing a variety of administrative activities. In addition, he is responsible for developing and coordinating corporate expansion plans. **Career Steps:** Tractor Supply Company: District Manager (1991–Present), Area Manager (1991), Manager (1988–1991). **Associations & Accomplishments:** Chamber of Commerce. **Education:** NTSU; various training seminars. **Personal:** Two children: Jennifer and Lauren. Mr. Corbin enjoys golf and camping.

Juan Cruz Melendez

President
La Casa De Los Tornillos
P.O. Box 1059
Manati, Puerto Rico 00674
(787) 884–4201
Fax: (787) 884–4341

5251

Business Information: La Casa De Los Tornillos is a retail outlet specializing in hardware sales to the pharmaceutical industry. With eight locations throughout Puerto Rico, the Company plans to open new facilities in the Virgin Islands in the near future. Established in 1992, the Company employs six people, and has an estimated annual revenue of $680,000. As President, Mr. Cruz Melendez is responsible for all functions related to the Manati branch. His duties include administration, operations, public relations, accounting and budgetary concerns, marketing, and strategic planning. **Career Steps:** President, La Casa De Los Tornillos (1992–Present); Inventory Specialist, Muebles Nuevo Concepto (1988–1992); Junior Accountant, Roberto Cruz, C.P.A. (1986–1988). **Education:** Universidad Inter–Americana: Bachelor's Degree (1988), Associates Degree in Economy and Accounting. **Personal:** Married to Yamele Vicens in 1989. One child: Juan Alejandro Cruz Vicens. Mr. Cruz Melendez enjoys sports (especially basketball) and church activities.

Ritch Flogstad

Director of Operations
Northern Hydraulics, Inc.
5635 S. Park Drive, P.O. Box 1219
Savage, MN 55378
(612) 895–6857
Fax: (612) 894–1020

5251

Business Information: Northern Hydraulics is a national retailer of industrial and commercial tools at discount prices throughout 32 stores around the country. Joining Northern Hydraulics as an accountant in 1984, Ritch Flogstad was appointed to his current position in 1994. As Director of Operations, his primary duties involve the distribution and transportation of goods, supervision of two warehouses, all warehouse personnel and the fleet operations. **Career Steps:** Northern Hydraulics, Inc.: Director of Operations (1994–Present), Regional Branch Manager (1986–1994), Accountant (1984–1986). **Education:** Simpson College, B.A. (1983). **Personal:** Married to Monika in 1988. Mr. Flogstad enjoys reading, basketball, and family activities.

Mr. Ricardo M. Freund

Corporate Director
Freund S.A.
39 Calle Ote y Pasaje Freund #2
San Salvador, El Salvador
(503) 276–3333
Fax: (503) 276–3250

5251

Business Information: Freund S.A., a family–owned business, is a retail hardware store chain located in San Salvador, El Salvador run by brothers, Eduardo and Ricardo Freund. There are 14 "mini home depot" type stores located throughout El Salvador. Established in 1913, Freund S.A. currently employs 450 people. As Corporate Director, Mr. Freund is responsible for designing IT systems, procedures and controls, as well as screens, hires and trains employees. Concurrent with his position at Freund S.A., Ricardo serves as Director en Compania General de Seguros (for the last six months) and Director of Sherwin Williams Central America (for the last three years). **Career Steps:** Corporate Director, Freund S.A. (1993–Present); Managing Director, MTB – Marketing Systems (1991–1993); Captain and Technical Manager, Israel Air Force (1987–1991); Stress Engineer, Israel Aircraft Industries (1985–1987). **Associations & Accomplishments:** Director of Virgin Forest Foundation Monte Cristo, Fundacion Max Freund – providing scholarships; Fundacion Amigos de Ilopango – Environmental Protection of Lake Ilopango Basin; Propemi – providing non–profit loans and development of small business; Noar Shelanu – training of young leaders in isolated communities. **Education:** Cornell University: M.S. in Engineering (1984) and B.Sc. (1983). **Personal:** Married to Laura Daniela in 1988. Mr. Freund enjoys bicycling, windsurfing, water skiing and designing remote control speed boats.

Patrick John Joyce

Call Center Manager
Trend–Lines, Inc.
135 American Legion Highway
Revere, MA 02151–2405
(617) 853–0900
Fax: (617) 853–0226

5251

Business Information: Trend–Lines, Inc. is an international specialty retailer of wood working tools and accessories, as well as golf equipment and supplies. Distributing through direct sales catalogs (entitled: Wood Workers Warehouse) and retail stores, Trend–Lines currently operates over 123 retail franchises across the U.S. As Call Center Manager, Patrick Joyce manages all in–bound telemarketing, customer service, technical assistance, data entry, mail operations and in–house telecommunications areas. **Career Steps:** Call Center Manager, Trend–Lines, Inc. (1992–Present); Branch Manager, Community Newsdealers, Inc. (1971–1992); Materials Control Coordinator, Baird–Atomic, Inc. (1968–1971). **Associations & Accomplishments:** International Association of Approved Basketball Officials, Inc. (IAABO); Sponsor and Donor: HLA Registry Foundation, Inc. (Bone Marrow); American Red Cross. **Education:** Rivier College, M.B.A. (1996); Merrimack College, B.A. of Business; University of Lowell, A.A. in Business; Certified Referee, IAABO. **Personal:** Married to R. Allison in 1968. Two children: Colleen and Patrick M. Mr. Joyce enjoys officiating for youth basketball events, reading, and is an avid Boston Bruins fan.

Ernesto Perez

Manager
Northern Hydraulics, Inc.
10576 Southwest Eighth Street
Miami, FL 33174–2602
(305) 221–0515
Fax: (305) 221–0568

5251

Business Information: Northern Hydraulics, Inc. is a national retailer of industrial and commercial tools at discount prices throughout 32 stores around the country. With nineteen years experience in executive positions, Mr. Perez joined Northern Hydraulics, Inc. as Manager in 1992. He is responsible for directing all store operations, including receiving products, operating the computer systems, and overseeing of a support staff of 17. **Career Steps:** Manager, Northern Hydraulics, Inc. (1992–Present); Vice President of Operations, Grand Union – Virgin Islands (1989–1992); Store Director, Pantry Pride (1977–1989). **Associations & Accomplishments:** St. Thomas Chamber of Commerce. **Education:** Rutgers University, M.B.A. (1969). **Personal:** Three children: Vivian, Ernest, and Dannette. Mr. Perez enjoys theater, playing basketball, swimming, and working out in the gym.

Paul David Tanner

Midwest Project Manager
Home Depot
1101 Perimeter Drive, Suite 300
Schaumburg, IL 60173–5024
(847) 413–4968
Fax: (847) 413–4973
EMAIL: See Below

5251

Business Information: Home Depot is the nation's leading home improvement retailer with over 435 stores serving 42 states. As Midwest Project Manager, Mr. Tanner manages and directs all construction and planning activities for the states of Michigan and Ohio, and controls design standards for the Midwest Region. Internet users can reach him via: pdtanner@aol.com. **Career Steps:** Midwest Project Manager, Home Depot (1993–Present); Project Manager – Health Care Facility, The Haswell Company (1988–1993); Professional Soccer – Danmark, Lynburg, Danmark – Masgengale's (1984–1986); College Recruiter, Andrew College (1983–1984). **Associations & Accomplishments:** Kappa Sigma Fraternity; Jackson's Men; Civic Volunteer, United Way; Jacksonville, FL Riverside Preservation Association; Annual Volunteer, PGA Golf Charities; Association of General Contractors. **Education:** University of Florida, Master of Building Construction (1988); LaGrange College, B.B.A. in Marketing/Management; Andrew College, A.S. in Chemistry/Physics. **Personal:** Married to Tracey Hardy in 1988. Mr. Tanner enjoys coaching, playing, & refereeing soccer, fly fishing, big trophy hunting, and riding Harleys.

Colin D. White

National Marketing Director
Higher Ideals Inc.
1329G Moanalualani Way
Honolulu, HI 96819
(808) 599–8889
Fax: (808) 528–0620
EMail: See Below

5251

Business Information: Higher Ideals, Inc. mission is to develop people of "primary greatness." Higher Ideals assists each individual in this process by making available to them current scientific and educational information that helps them understand important basic truths as well as what kinds of products are needed for optimal health. Higher Ideals offers patented world class vitamins, minerals, antioxidants and other nutritional formulations as well as skin care, cleaners and much more at price levels the average person can afford. As the National Marketing Director, Mr. White coordinates the research findings of leading experts, sets pricing strategies, heads training efforts, and heads development of new services and products. Internet users can reach him via: Higher Ideals.com **Career Steps:** National Marketing Director, Higher Ideals Inc. (1995–Present); Sales Manager, 21st Century Lighting (1985–Present); Director of Research & Development, International Management Services (1985–Present); Western Regional Manager, 21st Century Enterprises (1980–1982). **Associations & Accomplishments:** Sustaining Member, Boy Scouts of America; Green Lights, Certified Surveyor Ally; T.R.U.T.H. Foundation. **Education:** Utah State University, Bachelor's degree (1979). **Personal:** Married to Renee Poulson in 1978. Two children: Benjamin and Cheryl. Mr. White enjoys writing and being a guest writer for Adventure and other magazines. Also, Mr. White is very involved in the activities of his church, and is a strong advocate of returning to the constitutional values and rights revered and established by the founding fathers of the United States – and establishing these freedoms and values worldwide.

David H. Losek

Assistant Treasurer
General Host Corporation
6501 East Nevada
Detroit, MI 48234–2833
(313) 564–2828
Fax: (313) 564–2084

5261

Business Information: General Host Corporation, the parent company of Frank's Nursery & Crafts, is a specialty retailer of lawn, garden, nursery, crafts, and Christmas merchandise. Mr. Losek joined Frank's in 1993 as a manager. Promoted within GHC to his present position as Assistant Treasurer in 1995, his responsibilities include long and short term cash forecasting, budgeting, and serving as liaison in maintaining investor and banking relations. **Career Steps:** Assistant Treasurer, General Host Corporation (1995–Present); Frank's Nursery & Crafts: Assistant Controller (1995), Manager, Sales, Audit, Cash, Accounting (1993–1995); Manager, Inventory & Accounting, Perry Drug Stores (1989–1993). **Associations & Accomplishments:** American Institute of Certified Public Accountants – Tax and Personal Financial Planning Sections; Michigan Association of Certified Public Accountants. **Education:** Wayne State University: M.B.A. (1995), B.S. (1986). **Personal:** Married to Angela in 1992. Mr. Losek enjoys reading, golf, and bicycling.

Carol A. DeHart
President
Dehart's Homes Inc.
226 St. James
Hollister, MO 65672
(417) 335–8615
Fax: (417) 335–6919

5271

Business Information: Dehart's Homes Inc. is a manufactured housing dealership, providing sales, maintenance, installation and mortgage financial assistance. As President, Ms. Dehart is responsible for all aspects of Company operations, including administration, finance, sales, public relations, legal, taxes, marketing, and strategic planning. In addition, she is responsible for the decoration of touring homes, sales and purchase of homes, and coordinating all subcontractors utilized in the moving and maintenance of homes. **Career Steps:** President, Dehart's Homes Inc. (1989–Present); General Manager, Days Inn – Scottsboro, Al (1988–1989); Assistant Manager, Holiday Inn – Scottsboro, Al (1974–1988). **Associations & Accomplishments:** (PAWS) Branson Humane Society. **Education:** University of Alabama. **Personal:** Carol is an avid golfer in her leisure hours.

5300 General Merchandise Stores

5311 Department stores
5331 Variety stores
5399 Misc. general merchandise stores

Bob Dufour
Director of Hearing Centers/Director of Professional Services
Wal–Mart Stores, Inc.
702 South West 8th Street, Department 8037
Bentonville, AR 72716
(501) 273–4071
Fax: Please mail or call

5311

Business Information: Wal–Mart Stores, Inc. is the #1 retailer of general merchandise (hard lines, home lines, and soft lines) in the USA, having 2,046 stores. Wal–Mart Stores Division 1 is made up of four parts. Division 1A (Northwest), Division 1B (Southwest), Division 1C (Southeast), and Division 1D (Northeast). As Director of Hearing Centers/Director of Professional Services, Mr. Dufour is involved in the overall operations for the Centers, and is responsible for personnel management, and budgeting. He also oversees professional services management for government affairs and handles all aspects of compliance with laws and regulations related to pharmacy, managed, and related health care issues. **Career Steps:** Wal–Mart: Director of Hearing Centers/Director of Professional Services (1995–Present), Regional Manager, Pharmacy (1988–1995), District Manager, Pharmacy (1985–1988), Pharmacy Manager (1983–1985). **Associations & Accomplishments:** American Pharmacy Association; National Association of Chain Drug Stores; Boy Scouts of America. **Education:** Northeast Louisiana University, B.S. (1978). **Personal:** Married to Carole in 1978. Four children: Patrick, Lance, Jacob, and Shelby. Mr. Dufour enjoys fishing, baseball, soccer, snorkeling, and sailing.

Rachel Florey Reichenbach
Store Manager
Dillard's Department Store
4610 Milhaven Road
Monroe, LA 71203
(318) 323–8000 Ext. 201
Fax: (318) 323–3106

5311

Business Information: Dillard's Department Store is a retail apparel, accessories, cosmetics and home furnishings chain operation. Established in 1938, Dillard's currently employs 200 people in the Monroe store. As Store Manager, Ms. Florey Reichenbach is responsible for all aspects of operations, including personnel and merchandising. **Career Steps:** Dillard's Department Store: Store Manager (1992–Present), Buyer (1989–1992), Area Sales Manager (1987–1989). **Associations & Accomplishments:** American Business Women's Association; Ouachita Heritage Chapter; Monroe Chamber of Commerce. **Education:** University of Texas – Tyler, B.B.A. (1987); Northern Louisiana University, M.B.A. in progress. **Personal:** Married to Bret in 1991. Ms. Florey Reichenbach enjoys reading.

Lt. Col. Mary Louise Hicks
Director – Morale, Welfare & Recreation
United States Marine Corps – Quantico
Building 2034, C37 1
Quantico, VA 22134
(703) 784–3006
Fax: (703) 784–2936

5311

Business Information: The Morale, Welfare & Recreation Division, in operation with the United States Marine Corps base in Quantico, VA, administers military exchanges retail and department stores, food and hospitality for the Officer's and Enlisted Clubs, and for all sports and recreation on base. Serving as Director of the Morale, Welfare and Recreation division, Lt. Col. Hicks directs three branches of retail, food and recreation, and four support branches consisting of finance, human resources, marketing and facilities. Her future plans are to retire in August, 1996. She has accepted the position of Director of Institutional Development for the Marine Military Academy in Harlingen, Texas. **Career Steps:** United States Marine Corps: Rank of Lt. Colonel; Director – Morale, Welfare & Recreation Division, Quantico, VA (1991–Present); Head of Retail – Camp LeJeune, NC (1988–1991), Exchange Officer – Henderson Hall Exchange, Arlington, VA (1985–1988). **Associations & Accomplishments:** Phi Upsilon Omicron; Board of Governors, Marine Corps Association; Parents Club; US Naval Academy, Marine Military Academy, and Culver Military Academy. **Education:** Texas Tech University, B.S. in Home Economics/Merchandising (1975); Navy Exchange Officers Course; Marine Corps Command & Staff College; Senior Naval Officer's Total Quality Leadership Course. **Personal:** Married to Lt. Col. Michael K. Hicks, U.S.M.C. in 1973. Three children: Michael Keith, Jr. (MIDN U.S. Naval Academy), Christopher Brian (Cadet, Marine Military Academy), and Kevin Thomas (Cadet, Culver Military Academy). In her leisure time, Ms. Hicks enjoys scuba diving, sailing, sports, and athletics.

Sherry L. Hollock
Operating Vice President
Federated Department Stores, Inc.
7 West Seventh Street
Cincinnati, OH 45202
(513) 579–7726
Fax: (513) 679–7969

5311

Business Information: Federated Department Stores, Inc. is one of the nation's leading department store retailers. Currently operating 359 department stores, Federated also operates more than 100 specialty and clearance stores in 35 states. Established in 1929, Federated Department Stores, Inc. reports annual revenue of $14 billion and currently employs 112,000 people company–wide. With twenty–two years experience in personnel recruitment and development, Mrs. Hollock joined Federated in 1995. Serving as Operating Vice President, she directs all personnel activities as Head of the Human Resources Department. She is responsible for training and development, career development, succession planning, and staffing. **Career Steps:** Operating Vice President, Federated Department Stores, Inc. (1995–Present); Divisional Vice President – Recruitment & Development, Lazarus Department Stores–Cincinnati, OH (1987–1995); Divisional Vice President – Recruitment & Development, John Wanamaker Department Stores–Philadelphia, PA (1983–1987). **Associations & Accomplishments:** American Society of Training and Development; Society for Human Resource Management; Human Resource Planning Society; Junior Achievement Board of Directors. **Education:** Penn State University, B.S. (1973) **Personal:** Married to Barry in 1973. Mrs. Hollock enjoys boating, golf, water sports, photography and gourmet cooking during her leisure time.

Terrance D. Holt

Director of Energy Services
Hills Department Stores
3010 Green Garden Road
Aliquippa, PA 15001
(412) 378–0511 Ext: 241
Fax: (412) 378–4250

5311

Business Information: Hills Department Stores is a discount department store specializing in the retail sale of general merchandise. Established in 1954, Hills Department Stores currently employs 18,000 people nationwide and has an estimated annual revenue of $1.8 billion. As Director of Energy Services, Mr. Holt is responsible for all aspects of electric, gas and water usage, as well as cost, budgeting and capital projects in excess of $20 million a year. **Career Steps:** Hills Department Stores: Director of Energy Services (1994–Present), Manager of Maintenance and Energy Management (1991–1994). **Associations & Accomplishments:** Green Lights Surveyor Ally; Association of Energy Engineers; Western Pennsylvania Association of Energy Engineers; Edison Electric Institute National Account Participant; Environmental Energy Managers Institute; Energy Users News, Certificate of Merit Recipient (1994); Epsilon Eta Award (Energy Efficient building design) from Illinois Power; I.M.R.A. Electric Rate Task Force; Member, Coalition for Energy Reform. **Education:** Edinboro University, B.S. (1977); Pennsylvania State University, Physical Plant Certification. **Personal:** Married to Ernestina in 1989. Three children: Eric, Sara and Marissa. Mr. Holt enjoys racquetball and golf.

Mr. David E. Jackson
Senior Vice President of Store Operations Division 1B
Wal–Mart Stores, Inc.
702 South West 8th Street
Bentonville, AR 72764
(501) 273–8142
Fax: Please mail or

5311

Business Information: Wal–Mart Stores, Inc. is the #1 retailer of general merchandise (hard lines, home lines, and soft lines) in the USA, having 2,046 stores. Wal–Mart Stores Division 1 is made up of four parts. Division 1A (Northwest), Division 1B (Southwest), Division 1C (Southeast), and Division 1D (Northeast). In his current capacity, Mr. Jackson is responsible for all aspects of store operation and personnel in 463 Wal-Mart stores in the Southwest United States, Division 1B. Wal-Mart presently employs 75,000 people and has annual sales of approximately $10 billion. **Career Steps:** Senior Vice President of Store Operations Division IB, Wal–Mart Stores, Inc. (1993–Present); Regional Vice President, Wal–Mart Stores, Inc. (1989–1993); District Manager, Wal–Mart Stores, Inc. (1987–1989); Store Manager, Wal–Mart Stores (1983–1989). **Associations & Accomplishments:** Member, Omega Psi Phi Fraternity, Inc.; Salutatorian, Lincoln High School (1967); BRAG Award (Black Retail Action Group) Winner 199 4. **Education:** Tuskegee University, B.S. Degree in Economics (1971); University of Alabama (1975–1976).

Roger C. Trivette
Director of Construction/Store Planning/Facilities
Ames Department Stores
2418 Main Street (Mail Station 0410)
Rocky Hill, CT 06067
(203) 257–5007
Fax: (203) 257–2181

5311

Business Information: Over 25 years of consistent success in the design of discount stores, grocery stores, restaurants, and shopping centers, Mr. Trivette earned the title of Director of Construction/Store Planning/Facilities in 1994. His responsibilities include the design and construction of new stores, remodeling, take–over stores, and corporate facilities. He is also responsible for store planning, fixturing, store signage, store and corporate utilities and energy management systems, maintenance of 308 department stores, 2 distribution centers, print shop, photo studio, fixture storage facilities, records retention, and the company employee sample store; and the departmental budgets, totaling in excess of $61.5 million annually. While in this position, Mr. Trivette has achieved many things including: the design and construction of a new 75,000 square foot prototype store; the redesign and renovation of 12 take–over stores totaling 765,000 square feet; and 35 major store remodels totaling 1,500,000 square feet. **Career Steps:** Director of Construction/Store Planning/Facilities, Ames Department Stores (1994–Present); Vice President of Design and Construction, Rose's Discount Stores, Inc.

(1983–1994); Director of Design and Construction, Lowes Food Stores and World Food Systems, Inc. (1979–1983); Construction Manager and Designer/Developer, Self–Employed (1970–1979); Senior Designer, R.J. Reynolds Industries, Inc. (1958–1970). **Associations & Accomplishments:** Steering Committee, International Mass Retailers Association. **Personal:** Married to to the former Linda Eller in 1958. Two children: Todd and Heather. Mr. Trivette enjoys photography and auto racing.

Ms. Frances V. Valdez

Regulatory/Environmental Group Attorney
J.C. Penney Company, Inc.
P.O. Box 10001
Dallas, TX 75024–3698
(214) 431–1243
Fax: (214) 431–1134

5311

Business Information: J.C. Penney Company, Inc. is a major national retail department store chain having over 1,200 stores across the U.S. and also serves an international market through their catalog division. Plans call for the opening of the Company's first international stores in 1995 to be located in South America and Mexico. As Regulatory/Environmental Group Attorney, Ms. Valdez represents the corporation in all regulatory environmentally –related matters (licensed departments product safety, OSHA and ADA), as well as serve as Counsel involved in loss prevention matters for the Northeast regional stores. The J.C. Penney Company, Inc was established in 1902. **Career Steps:** Regulatory/Environmental Group Attorney, J.C. Penney Company, Inc. (1992–Present); Director, Shareholder and Attorney, Baker, Glast & Mills, P.C. (1985–1992); Law Clerk, Honorable John C. Ford, U.S. Bankruptcy Judge, Northern District of Texas (1984–1985). **Associations & Accomplishments:** Marquis Who's Who In American Law (1995, 1996, 1997); Miescuelita, Board of Directors; Environmental Section, International Section and Corporate Counsel Section, Dallas Bar Association; Hispanic Chamber of Commerce; Environmental Section and Corporate Counsel, American Bar Association; Yale Club of Dallas; Elihu Society; Mexican American/Hispanic Business Women's Association. **Education:** University of Texas School of Law, J.D. (1980); Yale University, B.A.; University of Texas–Dallas, International Management Program. **Personal:** Married to Joe A. Gonzales in 1981. Two children: Ana Lisa and Martin Esteban. Ms. Valdez enjoys sewing, crafts, rock climbing and basketball.

Audrey R. Walker

Human Resources Manager
Sears Roebuck & Company
3333 Beverly Road, Ms B2357B
Hoffman Estates, IL 60179–0001
(847) 286–8168
Fax: (847) 286–1777

5311

Business Information: Sears Roebuck & Company is a major national retail department store chain with stores across the U.S. As Human Resources Manager, Ms. Walker is responsible for diversified activities, including recruiting, administration, human resources, and information systems. **Career Steps:** Human Resources Manager, Sears Roebuck & Company (1985–Present); Administrator, New York City Board of Education (1975–1979). **Associations & Accomplishments:** Advisory Board, Salvation Army; Delta Sigma Theta; Board, DuPage County Girl Scouts; Board, Family Focus; Links, Inc. **Education:** Pace University, M.S. (1979); Hunter College in New York City, B.S. **Personal:** Married to Lee H. in 1968. Four children: Danette Judkins, Janine White, Lee II, and Darryl. Ms. Walker enjoys tailoring and needlepoint.

Annie M. Wilson

Deputy Exchange Officer
Navy Exchange – Norfolk Naval Base
1560 Mall Drive
Norfolk, VA 23511–3800
(804) 440–2201
Fax: (804) 440–2131

5311

Business Information: Navy Exchange provides a full selection of retail services including malls and marts, barber, video, liquor, etc. to active duty members of the U.S. Navy, their families, retirees and reservists. The Navy Exchange System has 42 locations and four branches throughout the U.S. With thirty years of experience in the Navy Exchange System, Ms. Wilson was promoted in the Norfolk, Virginia Exchange to Deputy Exchange Officer in 1993. She is responsible for the overall management of both the retail organization and customer services departments, with control of budget, sales, and administration. **Career Steps:** Navy Exchange – Norfolk: Deputy Exchange Officer (1993–Present), Retail Operations Manager (1989–1991); District Manager, NEX Service Center – Norfolk (1991–1993). **Associations & Accomplishments:** St. Mark AME Church: Executive Management Board, Finance Committee, Steward & Choir Member; Youth Group, Virginia Beach Jail Ministry; Commonwealth of Virginia, Senate Joint Resolution No. 24 – Salute from the General Assembly for Excellent and Exemplary Service to Virginia (1992); Department of the Navy: Meritorious Civilian Award (1991), Letter of Commendation (1989), Naval Base Norfolk Public Service Excellence Award (1991); Letter of Commendation, Secretary of the Navy (1986); Navy Exchange: Worldwide Association of the Year (1990, 1991), Woman of the Year (1985, 1987), Letter of Appreciation – received 14 (1987–1995), Customer Support Award (1991); Superior Accomplishment Recognition Award – received 3 (1985, 1988, 1989). **Education:** Executive Leadership Institute, Certificate (1995); Tidewater Community College, Leadership Training (1985), Human Relations (1977). **Personal:** Married to William in 1966. One child: Kowana. Ms. Wilson enjoys reading, walking, biking, singing in the choirs, witnessing about the Lord Jesus Christ, working with employees to help them achive goals and watching people.

Jose Raul De La Mora

Comptroller
Almacenes Pitusa, Inc.
P.O. Box 839
Hato Rey, Puerto Rico 00919
(809) 282–0202 Ext. 4500
Fax: (809) 282–0340

5331

Business Information: Almacenes Pitusa, Inc. is a chain of discount stores, 10 supermarkets, 5 autocenter stores, 19 furniture stores, 35 department stores, 19 lumber & hardware stores, and 26 one dollar stores. As Comptroller, Mr. De La Mora is responsible for the general supervision of all aspects of the Company, including finance, accounting, management, taxes, and other activities. Mr. De La Mora reports directly to the Chief Executive Officer of the Company. **Career Steps:** Comptroller, Almacenes Pitusa, Inc. (1976–Present). **Associations & Accomplishments:** President, Coderi of Puerto Rico; Scholarships Committee President of Coderi (a school for handicapped children and young adults). **Education:** University of Puerto Rico, B.A. in Accounting and Finance (1971). **Personal:** Married to Jorgelina in 1965. Two children: Ana Lourdes and Jose Raul Jr. Mr. De La Mora enjoys working with handicapped children, reading, and music.

Lisa Geyer

District Manager
Circle K
1052 West SR 436, Suite 1070
Altamonte Springs, FL 32714
(407) 786–5111
Fax: (407) 786–5115

5331

Business Information: International in scope, Circle K Stores, Inc. is a convenience store chain owning 2,500 stores in 22 states, and 2,500 stores in 18 countries. Circle K is the largest independent retailer of gasoline within the United States. As District Manager, Ms. Geyer is responsible for the operations and profitability of 22 stores. In 1996 Ms. Geyer won District Manager as well as three awards for the state of Florida which included highest sales increase, highest profitability and best expense control. **Career Steps:** District Manager, Circle K (1985–Present). **Education:** University of Pittsburgh (1985); working on M.B.A. **Personal:** Married to Mark in 1989. Three children: Chase Taylor, Alexis Briel, and Preston Quade.

Juanita M. Hester

Store Director
Super K–Mart Center
510 4th Street Plaza Southwest
Hickory, NC 28602–2868
(704) 345–6505
Fax: Please mail or call

5331

Business Information: Super K–Mart Center is a retailer for several worldwide merchandise concerns. As a part of the KMart Corporation nationwide chain of stores, Super KMart is one of the largest retail concerns in the United States. As Store Director, Ms. Hester is responsible for improvement in the quality of store services, and improving the relationship between employer and employees in her regional store. She has oversight of financial matters, purchasing, legal services, marketing, and strategic planning for the Hickory, North Carolina facility. **Career Steps:** Super K–Mart Center: Store Director (1995–Present), Store Manager (1991–1995), Assistant Manager (1982–1991). **Associations & Accomplishments:** Family and Community Education Development – Hickory. **Education:** Virginia Union University, B.A. in Business Administration (1982). **Personal:** Ms. Hester enjoys being a mentor for young ladies, reading, and retreating to the mountains for relaxation.

Gregory Wilson

Director of Human Resources
HOT Topic
3410 Pomona Boulevard
Pomona, CA 91768–3236
(909) 869–6373
Fax: (909) 869–6374

5331

Business Information: HOT Topic, headquartered in Pomona, is a specialty retail store, providing entertainment merchandise. Products include Gothic–alternative music, apparel (t–shirts), posters, pins, etc. Growing at a rate of 30 stores annually, HOT Topic has locations throughout the U.S. As Director of Human Resources, Mr. Wilson is responsible for the direction of all human resource activities, including the oversight of benefits for 700 individuals. He also directly oversees the Benefits/Support Field District Managers, and the Distribution Center, including all staffing, training programs, and quality operations of managers. **Career Steps:** Director of Human Resources, HOT Topic (1994–Present); Regional Human Resources Manager, Millers Outpost (1990–1994); Manager of Corporate Employment, Wherehouse Entertainment (1987–1990). **Associations & Accomplishments:** Professional Industrial Relations Association; Society for Human Resource Management; Board Member and Advisor, Alford Unified School District. **Education:** Minot State University, B.A. (1986); Palomar College, A.A.; SRI Certification/Interviewing Zenger Miller Training Certification. **Personal:** Mr. Wilson enjoys sports, music (Jazz and the Blues), travel, and writing.

Barry N. Adam

Director of System Development
Disney Store, Inc.
101 North Brand Boulevard, Suite 1000
Glendale, CA 91203–2619
(818) 543–3475
Fax: (818) 545–9224

5399

Business Information: Disney Store, Inc. is a specialty retail store for Disney–specific merchandise distributed to 900 franchises worldwide. As Director of System Development, Mr. Adam is responsible for all operations, marketing, and strategic planning. **Career Steps:** Disney Store, Inc.: Director of System Development (1993–Present), Manager of Merchandising and Distribution (1991–1993); Advanced Cybornetics: Project Manager (1988–1991), Senior Analyst (1984–1988). **Education:** East Stroudsburg University, B.S. in Computer Science (1983). **Personal:** Married to Kathy in 1991. One child: Karli. Mr. Adam enjoys skiing and soccer.

Michael W. Scheerer

Vice President of Assets Protection
Consolidated Stores Corporation
300 Phillipi Road
Columbus, OH 43228–1310
(614) 278–6590
Fax: (614) 278–6498

5399

Business Information: Consolidated Stores Corporation is a retail close–out chain operation with over 820 stores in 39 states. Established in 1983, Consolidated Stores Corporation currently employs 20,000 people nationwide and has an estimated annual revenue of $1.5 billion. As Vice President of Assets Protection, Mr. Scheerer is responsible for all aspects of property protection and safety, including the management of 50 guards and the in–store monitoring system for all 820 stores across the country. **Career Steps:** Consolidated Stores Corporation: Vice President of Assets Protection (1995–Present), Director of Assets Protection (1993–1995); Police Officer, City of Columbus, Ohio (1968–1986). **Associations & Accomplishments:** American Society of Industrial Security; Disabled American Veterans; Fraternal Order of Police. **Education:** Columbus State. **Personal:** Married to Carole in 1975. Two children: Tina and Mike, and two grandsons, Anthony and Nicholas. Mr. Scheerer enjoys golf.

Christine A. Walsh

Vice President of Merchandising
Holiday Companies
4567 West 80th Street
Bloomington, MN 55437
(612) 830–8021
Fax: (612) 832–8551

5399

Business Information: Holiday Companies is major retailer of general merchandise for gas, convenience, and grocery stores. The Company is also a food wholeseller and petroleum marketer, serving all Northern States from Washington to Michigan. As Vice President of Merchandising for 500 stores, Ms. Walsh is responsible for all advertising marketing, merchandising, and warehousing. She oversees a staff of 12 directly and coordinates activities for 300 employees. **Career Steps:** Holiday Companies: Vice President of Merchandising (1995–Present), Manager of Store Planning (1993–1995); Senior Tenant Coordinator, Melvin Simon & Associates (1990–1993); Senior Project Manager, Curt Johnson Properties (1986–1990). **Associations & Accomplishments:** Delegate to State Political Convention. **Education:** University of Minnesota: Bachelor of Science (1991), currently enrolled in Masters Program for Housing and Planning.

5400 Food Stores

5411 Grocery stores
5421 Meat and fish markets
5431 Fruit and vegetable markets
5441 Candy, nut and confectionery stores
5451 Dairy products stores
5461 Retail bakeries
5499 Miscellaneous food stores

Emily E. Adair

Environmental Director
Ericksons Diversified Corporation
509 2nd Street
Hudson, WI 54016
(715) 381–2350
Fax: (715) 386–1013

5411

Business Information: Ericksons Diversified Corporation is an owner and operator of 18 grocery stores in Wisconsin and Minnesota, along with a real estate business and a franchise of various retail stores. As Environmental Director, Ms. Adair is solely responsible for planning and implementing environmental management programs for the entire Company. **Career Steps:** Environmental Director, Ericksons Diversified Corporation (1994–Present); Environmental Intern, Larry's Market (1994). **Associations & Accomplishments:** Speaker at regional conferences on the topic of environmental management in the grocery industry. The Company has received three environmental awards Ms. Adair joined, including the prestigious Minnesota Governor's Award for Excellence in Pollution Prevention (1996). **Education:** Pacific Lutheran University, B.B.A. (1994). **Personal:** Ms. Adair enjoys skiing, camping, hiking, environmental voluntary programs, tennis, and travel.

Debbie Beall

Benefits Supervisor
Brookshire Grocery Company
P.O. Box 1411
Tyler, TX 75710–1411
(903) 534–3122
Fax: (903) 534–2200

5411

Business Information: Brookshire Grocery Company is a full–service, family–owned retail grocery business. Headquartered in Tyler, Texas, Brookshire Grocery operates over 120 retail stores throughout Louisiana, Texas, and Arkansas. Additionally, it operates 18 Super One convenience stores. As Benefits Supervisor, Ms. Beall is responsible for coordinating and supervising all functions of the Health Benefits Department, including overseeing customer service for employees and memberships and balancing all insurance reports. She also conducts five orientations per month in all three states for new partners (approximately 50–100 partners monthly), as well as processing disabilities, leave of absences, and part–time benefits for employees. **Career Steps:** Brookshire Grocery Company: Benefits Supervisor (1995–Present), Benefits Coordinator (1989–1995), Personnel Secretary (1984–1989). **Associations & Accomplishments:** Associate Member, Insurance Women of Tyler; Bronze Member, Disabled Veterans of America; Former Children's Church Director, Sunday School Teacher. **Education:** Tyler Junior College; Tyler Business School; Tyler Commercial College; Certified Executive Secretary. **Personal:** Married to John in 1989. Ms. Beall enjoys swimming, shopping for antiques, decorating her home, and reading.

Richard D. Beazer

President and Chief Executive Officer
Sav–U–Foods, Inc.
10670 Acacia Street
Rancho Cucamonga, CA 91730–5409
(909) 483–3700
Fax: (909) 483–3705

5411

Business Information: Sav–U–Foods, Inc. is a regional retail grocery chain. Established in 1992, there are currently 45 store locations throughout the southern California area. With forty years expertise in the retail/wholesale business, Mr. Beazer joined Sav–U–Foods as President, Chief Executive Officer, and Part–Owner in 1992. He is responsible for the overall corporate strategy and vision, including administration, finances, sales, public relations, accounting, marketing, and development. **Career Steps:** President and Chief Executive Officer, Sav–U–Foods, Inc. (1992–Present); Vice President of Corporate Marketing, Core–Mark International (1989–1992); Vice President of Corporate Merchandising, Melane Company, Inc. (1985–1989); Owner and Operator, Beazer's Super Value (1982–1985). **Education:** University of Michigan (1978). **Personal:** Married to Gail in 1961. Six children: Robert, Becky, Brian, Brenda, Blake, and Brent. Mr. Beazer enjoys swimming, running, and woodworking.

Kam K. Choi

Vice President of Administration
T&T Supermarket, Inc.
13331 Vulcan Way, Suite 14
Richmond, British Columbia V6V 1K4
(604) 276–9889
Fax: (604) 276–1627

5411

Business Information: T&T Supermarket, Inc. is a supermarket chain located throughout British Columbia. As Vice President of Administration, Mr. Choi is responsible for finance and accounting, administration, and new store development. He deals with all new ideas and projects, and handles outside consultants, architects, and project managers. **Career Steps:** Vice President of Administration, T&T Supermarket, Inc. (1993–Present); Chief Accountant, Nam Tai Electronics, Inc. (1992–1993); Director of Finance, Rembrandt Holdings, Ltd. (1989–1992); Chief Financial Officer, U–Save Foods, Ltd. (1985–1989). **Associations & Accomplishments:** Certified Member, Society of Management Accountants of British Columbia. **Education:** University of Calgary, B.Comm. (1979). **Personal:** Mr. Choi enjoys tennis, reading, and travel.

Joseph J. Cowhey

Director of Sales and Marketing
Delaware Supermarkets, Inc.
P.O. Box 3224
Wilmington, DE 19804–0224
(302) 999–1801
Fax: (302) 999–1227

5411

Business Information: Delaware Supermarkets, Inc., acquired by Bernard Kenny in January 1995, is a small successful supermarket and food business with two locations in Wilmington, Delaware. As Director of Sales and Marketing, Mr. Cowhey is responsible for all aspects of public relations, advertising, print advertising, newspapers, and television, in addition to serving as liaison between the Company and vendors. **Career Steps:** Director of Sales and Marketing, Delaware Supermarkets, Inc. (1995–Present); Sales Manager, The Boerner Company (1989–1995); Account Manager, Dietz & Watson (1983–1989). **Associations & Accomplishments:** Eastern Frozen Food Association; Eastern Dairy Deli Association; Tri–State Dairy Deli Organization; Philadelphia Food Trade Organization; Food Marketing Institute. **Education:** Allentown College, B.A. (1981). **Personal:** Married to Dawn in 1987. Mr. Cowhey enjoys relaxing with his wife.

Oral W. Edwards

Chairman & Owner
GES, Inc. d.b.a. Food Giant Supermarkets
3004 Forrest Lake Road
Forrest City, AR 72335
(501) 295–2484
Fax: (501) 295–3551

5411

Business Information: GES, Inc. is a corporation that owns and operates Food Giant Supermarkets and specializes in the development of shopping centers. As Chairman & Owner, Mr. Edwards is responsible for supervising daily operations of all the Food Giant Supermarkets, personally visiting all the stores, motivating personnel, handling fiscal matters, marketing, public relations, and strategic planning. **Career Steps:** Chairman & Owner, GES, Inc. (1965–Present). **Associations & Accomplishments:** Chairman, Forrest City Steering Committee; Board, Cities in School; Forrest City Industrial Development Committee; Finance Committee First Baptist Church; 1987 Arkansas Retail Grocer of the Year; Former President & Charter Board Member, Arkansas Retail Grocers and Merchants Association; Former Commissioner, Mississippi River Parkway Commission; Board of Directors, City Chamber of Commerce; Board of Directors, Arkansas State Chamber of Commerce. **Personal:** Married to Christine in 1952. Two children: Susan Marie DeRossitt and Stephen W. Mr. Edwards enjoys gardening and antiques.

Mr. Russell K. Kates

Chief Financial Officer, Secretary and Treasurer
Steele's Markets, Inc.
200 West Foothills Parkway
Ft. Collins, CO 80525
(303) 226–0654
Fax: (303) 225–9266

5411

Business Information: Steele's Markets, Inc. is a chain of four supermarkets serving the Fort Collins area. As Chief Financial Officer, Secretary and Treasurer, Mr. Kates is responsible for overseeing finance, accounting and treasury functions for the company, as well as the Bakery, Deli and Meat operations, and new store development projects. Established in 1940, Steele's Markets, Inc. employs 450 people with annual sales of $45 million. **Career Steps:** Chief Financial Officer, Secretary and Treasurer, Steele's Markets, Inc. (1984–Present); Owner, Jewelry Emporiums (1970–1990). **Associations & Accomplishments:** Director, Retail Bakers of America; Chairman, Retail Advisory Board, Colorado Lottery; Director, Bethpage Mission; Retail Advisory Board, Nash Finch Company; Member, Food Marketing Institute; International Deli & Dairy Association; National Grocers of America; American Association of Meat Processors. **Education:** Colorado State University, B.B.A. (1970); University of Southern California, Food Industry Management Seminars. **Personal:** Married to Carol Ann in 1973. Three children: Jennifer, Brian and Alisa. Mr. Kates enjoys automobile restoration, playing golf and traveling in his leisure time.

Kerry M. Larson

District Manager and Frozen Food and Dairy Director
Ericksons Diversified Corporation
509 2nd Street
Hudson, WI 54016
(715) 386–9315 Ext: 2394
Fax: (715) 386–5924

5411

Business Information: Ericksons Diversified Corporation, a family–owned business, is the owner of sixteen independent retail food store chains (Oconto Foods, Ericksons, Festival Foods, etc) located throughout Western Wisconsin and Minnesota. The first store chain was established in Clayton, Wisconsin in the 1930's by Steve Erickson and Doug Driskel, concentrating on specific markets for growth and strategic planning. Joining Ericksons as District Manager and Frozen Food and Dairy Director in 1990, Mr. Larson is responsible for the oversight of the entire district operations, including all merchandising, purchasing, pricing, and operations for the frozen and dairy section. **Career Steps:** District Manager and Frozen Food and Dairy Director, Ericksons Diversified Corporation (1990–Present); Market Operations Director, Festival Foods – P.A. (1988–1990); Store Operations Training Specialist, Cub Foods (1981–1988). **Education:** UM – Morris, Vocal Studies. **Personal:** Married to Linda. Two children: Jake and Ruby. Mr. Larson enjoys karate, weightlifting, softball, and singing.

John E. Mautner
President and CEO
The Nutty Bavarian
37 Skyline Drive Suite 2106
Lake Mary, FL 32746
(800) 382–4788
Fax: (407) 444–6335

5441

Business Information: The Nutty Bavarian, established in 1990, is a producer of cinnamon roasted almonds. The Company sells their roasted almonds in nut carts in theme parks, arenas, stadiums, and shopping centers. As President and CEO, Mr. Mautner is responsible for all aspects of company operations. Mr. Mautner was the original creator of the coating on the almonds. **Career Steps:** President and CEO, The Nutty Bavarian (1990–Present); Senior Financial Analyst, International Paper (1986–89). **Associations & Accomplishments:** National Association of Concessionars; International Association Amusement Parks and Attraction; Mobile Merchants Association. **Education:** Southern Illinois, B.A. Finance (1986). **Personal:** Married in 1986. Mr. Mautner enjoys sports and sailing.

Linda S. Arnold
President
TCBY Treats
19 Prospect Road
Strasburg, PA 17579
(717) 397–4411
Fax: (717) 394–2404

5451

Business Information: TCBY Treats is a frozen yogurt (soft serve and hand dipped), ice cream, shaved ice, salads, and sandwich restaurant. The Restaurant also offers its customers a cake and pie freezer, filled with professionally decorated cakes and pies, a bakery (bagels and fat–free muffins), TCBY cookies, and gourmet coffee. As President of TCBY, Ms. Arnold is responsible for the overall management of operation and accounting. She is also President of MLM Group, Inc. which is a check cashing and Western Union service. **Career Steps:** President, MLM Yogurt Corporation d.b.a. TCBY Treats (1991–Present); President, MLM Group, Inc. d.b.a. Cash–a–Check (1991–Present); Vice President, Olde Towne Realty, Inc. (1988–1991); Realtor–Associate, Olde Towne Realty, Inc. (1989–1991); Business Broker, Business Marketing Works, Inc. (1988–1991); Area Coordinator, Excel Communications, Inc. (1995–Present). **Associations & Accomplishments:** Lancaster Chamber of Commerce; Pennsylvania Dutch Convention and Visitors Bureau; NFIB. **Education:** Goldey Beacom, Associate of Arts (1971). **Personal:** Four children: Holly, David, Matthew, and Andrew. Ms. Arnold enjoys gardening and cooking.

Annette R. Wilmot–Gluck
Executive Manager
Cuba Cheese Shoppe
53 Genesee Street
Cuba, NY 14727–1133
(716) 968–3949
Fax: (716) 968–1746

5451

Business Information: Cuba Cheese Shoppe is a retail and wholesale cheese and gourmet gift shoppe. The Shoppe also handles mail orders, fund raising order programs, and has a limited truck delivery area in western New York and northern Pennsylvania. As Executive Manager, Mrs. Wilmot–Gluck has oversight of a variety of departments. These departments include accounting, mail order, fund raising, personnel, finance, and marketing and advertising. Mrs. Wilmot–Gluck attributes her success to her creativity and drive for success and accuracy. **Career Steps:** Cuba Cheese Shoppe, Executive Manager (1992–Present), Mail Order Director (1990–1992). **Associations & Accomplishments:** S.P.C.A. Volunteer; Y.M.C.A.; PCDI Fitness and Nutrition Certification. **Education:** Cazenovia College, A.A.S. (1987); Currently enrolled at Empire State College. **Personal:** Married to Chris in 1995. Mrs. Wilmot–Gluck enjoys fitness, animals, and travel.

Jorge Tostado Jr.
Human Resource Director
Grace Baking
548 Cleveland Avenue
Berkeley, CA 94710–1007
(510) 559–4573
Fax: Please mail or call

5461

Business Information: Grace Baking, a regional bakery, was established in 1987 and currently employs 200 people. Grace Bakery offers bread, pastries, danish, and wedding cakes to clients in the Northern portion of California. With retail stores attached to each bakery, the company expects sales of over $9 million dollars this year. As Human Resource Director, Mr. Tostado is responsible for all human resource functions of the Company. He handles staff recruitment, staff training and development, employee relations, employee compensation, payroll, and legalities relating to personnel management. Mr. Tostado assists in the establishment of the budget for his department and monitors expenses to comply with budgetary guidelines. **Career Steps:** Human Resource Director, Grace Baking (1994–Present); Human Resources Administrator, Memick Products, Inc. (1991–1994); Human Resource Supervisor, Page Packaging (1987–1991). **Education:** Attending, San Francisco State University. **Personal:** Mr. Tostado enjoys softball.

Collin Barr
Vice President of Store Development
Caribou Coffee
5432 Brookview Avenue
Minneapolis, MN 55424–1601
(612) 359–2707
Fax: (612) 359–2930

5499

Business Information: Caribou Coffee is a national gourmet coffee retailer, which develops and builds their own establishments. Presently in seven market areas with 54 stores, the market area includes Minneapolis, Detroit, Columbus, Chicago, Atlanta, Raleigh, and Charlotte. Joining Caribou Coffee as Vice President of Store Development in 1994, Mr. Barr is responsible for directing and managing a team of professionals in the acquisition and development of property and the overall building of stores (approximately 50–60 a year). **Career Steps:** Vice President of Store Development, Caribou Coffee (1994–Present); Principal, Tobin Advisors (1992–1994), Principal, Trammell Crow Company (1986–1991). **Associations & Accomplishments:** National Association of Industrial and Office Parks; International Council of Shopping Centers Association; Hospitality House Boys–Girls Club Board. **Education:** University of Minnesota, M.B.A. (1991); Bethel College – St. Paul, MN, B.A. (1984). **Personal:** Married to Brenda in 1985. Three children: Collin Jr., Connor, and Austin. Mr. Barr enjoys spending time with his children, backpacking, fly fishing, coaching, reading, and managing personal investments.

Robert W. Blaylock
Human Resource Manager
Circle K Stores, Inc.
658 Commerce Dr., Suite C
Roseville, CA 95678–6422
(916) 786–8440
Fax: (916) 786–8521

5499

Business Information: International in scope, Circle K Stores, Inc. is a convenience store chain owning 2,500 stores in 22 states, and 2,500 stores in 18 countries. Circle K is the largest independent retailer of gasoline within the United States. As Human Resource Manager, Mr. Blaylock is responsible for all employment issues, training, recruiting, and legal matters (EEOC– wage and contract disputes). In addition, he oversees 800 employees and is responsible for 77 stores in Northern and Central California. **Career Steps:** Circle K Stores, Inc.: Human Resource Manager (1993–Present), District Manager (1992–1993); Restaurant General Manager, Taco Bell (1989–1991). **Associations & Accomplishments:** Optimist International; Boy Scouts of America; National Thespian Society; Society of Human Resource Managers. **Education:** University of Phoenix, currently attending. **Personal:** Married to Linda J. Newland in 1975. Five children: Jennifer, Aaron, Adam, Deborah, and Michael. Mr. Blaylock enjoys dramatic arts and music.

Cindy V. Davinsizer
Section Manager
Sheetz, Inc. Office
5700 6th Avenue
Altoona, PA 16602
(814) 941–5167
Fax: (814) 941–5535

5499

Business Information: Sheetz, Inc. Office is a chain of convenience stores located primarily in Pennsylvania. Established in 1969, the Company estimates revenue of $700 million in 1996 and presently employs over 4,000 people. As Section Manager, Ms. Davinsizer is part of the General Accounting Department and is responsible for account reconciliations, new store licensing, lottery, and money order and credit card areas. **Career Steps:** Section Manager, Sheetz, Inc. Office (1995–Present); In Charge Accountant, Edwards Leap & Sauer, CPA's (1989–1995); Staff Accountant, Young Oakes Brown & Company, CPA's (1987–1989). **Education:** Pennsylvania State University, B.A. in Accounting (1985). **Personal:** Married to Kristopher in 1990. One child: Kyle Zachary. Ms. Davinsizer enjoys auto racing and gardening.

Angela Eaton
General Manager
Health Food Centers
400 East Indian River Road
Norfolk, VA 23523–1756
(804) 545–7357
Fax: (804) 545–0609

5499

Business Information: Health Food Centers is a privately–owned company, owning and operating six retail health and nutrional needs stores throughout the Norfolk and Virginia Beach, Virginia area. Joining the company in 1982 as a bookkeeper, Angela Eaton was promoted to General Manager in 1985. She is responsible for sales, marketing, P&L and all accounting administration for the company as a whole. **Career Steps:** General Manager, Health Food Centers (1982–Present); Accounting Clerk, Portsmouth Psychiatric Hospital (1979–1982); Clerk, A&P (1976–1979). **Associations & Accomplishments:** National Nutritional Foods Association. **Education:** Tidewater Community/Old Dominion University, Partial degree/courses as needed. Still pursuing educational seminars on a regular basis; Weight and Fat Management Certified (1996); Registered Model, John Robert Powers Modeling and Finishing School (1976). **Personal:** Married to Glenn in 1979. One child: Derek. Angela enjoys French Impressionist art, Monet, Renoir, and others. Also, flower gardens and watching birds in their natural habitats. She loves cooking and leading a healthy lifestyle, using natural vitamins and herbs and working out regularly. She is also very interested in the ageing process and preventative health care.

Kathryn D. Seipp–Hennis
Controller
Culligan Southwest
1034 Austin Street
San Antonio, TX 78208–1153
(210) 226–5344
Fax: (210) 226–1731

5499

Business Information: Culligan Southwest provides sales and rentals of water softeners, drinking water systems, and bottled water to residental and commerical customers in South Central Texas. Established in 1939, Culligan Southwest has five locations in the South Texas area and currently employs 100 people. A Certified Public Accountant since 1985, Mrs. Seipp–Hennis joined the Company as Controller in 1990. She is responsible for preparing financial statements, payroll reports, sales tax reports, and all related accounting functions. **Career Steps:** Controller, Culligan Southwest (1990–Present); Tax Accountant, Boehm & Boehm, CPA's (1988–1990); Self Employed, Kathryn D. Seipp, CPA (1988). **Associations & Accomplishments:** Texas Society of Certified Public Accountants; American Woman's Society of Certified Public Accountants; San Antonio Society of Women Certified Public Accountants; San Antonio Chapter of Certified Public Accountants; Beta Gamma Sigma; St. Mark Evangelist Choir. **Education:** University of Texas – San Antonio, B.B.A. (1982); Certification: Certified Public Accountant (1985). **Personal:** Married to Steve L. Hennis in 1994. Mrs. Seipp–Hennis enjoys bowling, gardening, and cooking.

Jerry L. Snearly

Vice President, Financial Operations Officer
Circle K Stores, Inc.
3003 North Central Avenue, Suite 1600
Phoenix, AZ 85012
(602) 530–5357
Fax: (602) 860–0329

5499

Business Information: Circle K Stores, Inc. is an international convenience store chain owning 2,250 stores in 18 states, and 2,400 stores in 18 countries. Circle K is also the largest independent retailer of gasoline within the United States. As Vice President and Financial Operations Officer, Mr. Snearly is responsible for the operational accounting and financing functions at the Corporate level, in addition to directing the quality of earning and development. He also travels on behalf of the Corporation, striving to improve store operations by showing them how to better utilize check cashing systems, electronic services, ATM's, and cutting costs. **Career Steps:** Circle K Stores, Inc.: Vice President and Financial & Operations Officer (1995–Present), Vice President of Finance (1993–1995); General Manager Check Collection, Southland (1991–1993). **Associations & Accomplishments:** Board of Directors, SSP; Serves on the Overview Committee for K–Cal in Las Vegas, Nevada (combined Circle K and Unocal). **Education:** New Hampshire College, B.S. in Accounting, Marketing, and Finance (1977). **Personal:** Married to Karen in 1974. Two children: Tara and Justin. Mr. Snearly enjoys music (plays the guitar) and golf.

Ernesto Archilla Jr.
Controller
Garage Isla Verde
RR 1, Box 29
Carolina, Puerto Rico 00979
(787) 791–1313
Fax: (787) 791–4206
EMAIL: See Below

5511

Business Information: Garage Isla Verde is a dealership representing Mercedes Benz, which sells new and used Mercedes; parts and service. As Controller, Mr. Archilla is responsible for all aspects of financial operations of the Company, including supervising procedures (financial statements, reports, and analysis), training of new employees, full responsibility of financial and accounting records, maintenance of accounting records, preparation of a profit forecast, and other related activities. Accounting is under A.L.P. computer system and duties are a matter of analysis of cost and revenues accounts, margins of profits, etc. Internet users can also reach him via: Garage Isla Verde Inc. **Career Steps:** Controller, Garage Isla Verde (1972–Present); Controller, Aviation Associates, Inc. (1966–1971); Chief Clerk, Auditor, Coodgean Western Hemisphere Corporation (1948–1965); Chief Accounting Clerk, Camp Torlinguero Exchange (1944–1947); Assistant Municipal Auditor, Municipal Government Voya Boga (1940–1943). **Education:** Instituto Casanova, B.B.A. (1937); La Salle Extension University, U.S.N. in Public Accounting and Certified Public Accounting Coaching. **Personal:** Three children: Orlando, Ernie, and Enery. Mr. Archilla enjoys reading, politics, and accounting.

5500 Automotive Dealers and Service Stations

5511 new and used car dealers
5521 Used car dealers
5531 Auto and home supply stores
5541 Gasoline service stations
5551 Boat dealers
5561 Recreational vehicle dealers
5571 Motorcycle dealers
5599 Automotive dealers, NEC

Susan E. Artaz

Comptroller
Glenwood Springs Ford Dealership
P.O. Box 668
Glenwood Springs, CO 81602–0668
(970) 945–2317
Fax: (970) 945–0469

5511

Business Information: Glenwood Springs Ford is an authorized Ford, Lincoln, Mercury automobile dealership, providing a full range of new and used car and truck sales and leases, maintenance service and parts supplies to Glenwood Springs, Colorado, and surrounding counties residents. As Comptroller, Mrs. Artaz is responsible for overall financial control of the Company, including financial reporting and operations, accounts receivable, credit approval, financial monitoring and analysis, payroll, and extended service contracts. **Career Steps:** Comptroller, Glenwood Springs Ford Dealership (1991–Present); Senior Accountant, Deloitte & Touche (1989–1991). **Associations & Accomplishments:** Colorado Society of Certified Public Accountants; American Society of Certified Public Accountants; Former Colorado State President of Distributive Education Clubs of America. **Education:**

University of Denver, B.S. in Accounting (1989). **Personal:** Married to Grady in 1989. Two children: Dusty Renae and Garrett Lee. Mrs. Artaz enjoys waterskiing, boating, and snowmobiling.

Dane R. Basl
Operations Manager
Vinco Management Services
12450 Fair Lakes Circle, Suite 380
Fairfax, VA 22033–3810
(703) 922–7900
Fax: (703) 802–3480

5511

Business Information: Vinco Management Services, owned and operated by Vince Sheehy and Company, is the corporate office for all Sheehy automotive dealerships. VMS has locations in Virginia (4) and Maryland (2), in addition to ten franchises, marketing Ford, Mitsubishi, Pontiac, Nissan, and Hyundai vehicles. As Operations Manager, Mr. Basl is responsible for operations of all dealerships owned and operated by Vince Sheehy and Company. His primary functions involve customer satisfaction, coordination with key dealership management staff for policies and procedures compliance; as well as the hiring and training of personnel. He has just completed his first book, "The Prevailing Car Salesman" and is currently seeking a publisher. **Career Steps:** Operations Manager, Vinco Management Services (1993–Present); Director of Recruiting and Training, Fitzgerald Automotive Group (1992–1993); Director of Training, Automotive Development Center (1991–1992); Director of Recruiting and Training, Koons Automotive Group (1987–1990). **Education:** Harford Community College (1970). **Personal:** Mr. Basl enjoys writing, golf, biking, tennis, snow skiing, and weightlifting.

Mark Borjon
Owner
Paso Robles GMC Truck, Inc.
P.O. Box 1108
Paso Robles, CA 93447–1108
(805) 238–4515
Fax: (805) 238–2829

5511

Business Information: Paso Robles GMC Truck Inc. is a retailer of automobiles from four locations in Paso Robles, specializing in GMC trucks, Lance campers, Sundowner trailers, and CM trailers. As Owner, Mr. Borjon is responsible for the day-to-day operations, including administration, finances, public relations, marketing, and strategic planning. **Career Steps:** Owner, Paso Robles GMC Truck Inc. (1994–Present); Managing Partner, Wallace Corporation (1991–1994); Manager, Rancho Grande Motors (1986–1991). **Associations & Accomplishments:** Elks; High School Rodeo. Published in "Trucking Magazine." **Personal:** Married to Shelia in 1976. Two children: Jennifer and Stephanie. Mr. Borjon enjoys horses and Mid State Fair.

Mr. Guy H. Burrous
Vice President/Treasurer
Classic Automotive Group
2301 North I–35
Round Rock, TX 78664
(512) 244–9000
Fax: (512) 244–6977

5511

Business Information: Classic Automotive Group is an authorized sales and service dealership for GMC, Pontiac, Oldsmobile, Honda and Toyota automobiles, serving the populace of Round Rock, Texas and surrounding areas. As Vice President/Treasurer, Mr. Burrous is responsible for the administration and oversight of all financial and administrative functions for the dealership, as well as strategic planning and public relations. Established in 1985, Classic Automotive Group employs over 290 sales, service and administrative personnel and reports estimated annual sales in excess of $140 million. **Career Steps:** Treasurer, Classic Automotive Group (1991–Present); Controller, Bluebonnet Motors (1991); Assistant Controller, Rountree Automotive Group (1987–1990); Controller, Dixie Trucks (1983–1987). **Associations & Accomplishments:** Round Rock Sertoma. **Education:** Midwestern State University, B.B.A. (1964).

James M. Carson

Co–Owner
Carson Chrysler
2695 East Main Street
Plainfield, IN 46168–2703
(317) 839–6554
Fax: (317) 839–9601

5511

Business Information: Carson Chrysler is a new auto and truck dealer, involved in sales and service of a full line of Chrysler, Plymouth, Dodge, and Jeep/Eagle trucks and automobiles. As Co–Owner, Mr. Carson is responsible for all aspects of Company operations, including administration, finance, sales and marketing, and strategic planning. Mr. Carson began working with his father in 1970, and in 1983 at the age of 25, he became the youngest Chrysler dealer in the United States. **Career Steps:** Co–Owner, Carson Chrysler (1983–Present); Part Service/Sales Fleet, Carson Ford Sales, Inc. (1970–1983). **Associations & Accomplishments:** Assistant Chief, Liberty District 3 Fire District; Cataract Yacht Club; NFPA; Masonic Lodge; Shelby Auto Club; Disabled American Veterans, Commanders Club; Hendricks County Postal Advisory Council; Plainfield and Indianapolis Chamber of Commerce; IVFA–NAVET Eagles. **Education:** Vincennes University and Indiana University, Master's degree in Business (1980); Ford Motor Company Marketing Institute; Chrysler Motors Corporation; Chrysler Corporation Institute; State of Indiana Fire Fighter Standards and Education; Skip Barber Racing School. **Personal:** Married to Kathy in 1989. Two children: Kyley and Katie. Mr. Carson enjoys parasailing, waterskiing, boating, camping, and car shows.

Carter L. Doolittle

Manager/Share Holder
Gary Miller Dodge Mazda
4827 Village Circle West
North East, PA 16428–6613
(814) 868–5551
Fax: (814) 866–3689

5511

Business Information: Gary Miller Dodge Mazda is an authorized Dodge/Mazda automobile dealership and authorized Detroit Discount Dealer. Specializing in providing a full range of new and used car and truck sales, maintenance service and parts supplies to Western New York, Ohio, Pennsylvania and surrounding areas. Comprised of a fourteen acre lot, the Dealership sells over 4,000 automobiles a year. As Manager/Share Holder, Mr. Doolittle oversees all aspects of the dealership including sales and marketing, administration, and customer service. **Career Steps:** Manager/Share Holder, Gary Miller Dodge Mazda (1981–Present). **Associations & Accomplishments:** AOPA, Pilot Association; Silver Award of Sales Professionals; Make a Wish Foundation; American Cancer Society Relay for Life Alot. **Personal:** Mr. Doolittle enjoys being a pilot (private, instrument and multi–engine and high performance), tennis, boating, travel, exercise, waterskiing, snow skiing, working out, and collecting Corvettes.

Charles M. Hill
Data Base Administrator
Ford Motor Company
6201 Wood Pond Road
West Bloomfield, MI 48323–2264
(313) 322–1998
Fax: (313) 337–6932

5511

Business Information: Ford Motor Company, one of the world's leading automotive manufacturers, is an international designer and manufacturer of automobiles and trucks with five vehicle centers: two truck and three auto centers. As Data Base Administrator, Mr. Hill is responsible for the implementation of DB2 and IMS data base systems. Additionally, he trains personnel, enhances data base, utilizes change, and performs software evaluation. **Career Steps:** Data Base Administrator, Ford Motor Company (1993–Present); Data Base Administrator/Consultant, Syntel, Inc. (1990–1993); Data Base Analyst, Grand Trunk Western Railroad (1989–1990); Consultant, Network Info Systems (1989). **Associations & Accomplishments:** Junior Achievement. **Education:** Lawrence Technical University, B.S. in Business Administration (1994); Oakland Community College, Associate's degree in Business. **Personal:** Married to Susan in 1984. Mr. Hill enjoys coin and first day cover collecting.

John T. Lunciano
General Manager
Dick Poe Motors, Inc.
6501 Montana Avenue
El Paso, TX 79925
(915) 778–9331
Fax: (915) 778–9136
Email: See Below

5511

Business Information: Dick Poe Motors, Inc., established in 1928, is an automobile dealership offering Dodge, Chrysler, Toyota, Honda, and Pontiac cars and trucks. The dealership currently employs 280 people, and boasts annual sales in excess of $100 million. As General Manager, Mr. Lunciano is responsible for daily business functions, sales, and customer relations. Internet users can reach him via: PHAQUA. Established in 1928, Dick Poe Motors, Inc. employs 212 people with annual sales of $100 million. **Career Steps:** General Manager, Dick Poe Motors, Inc. (1996–Present); General Manager, Mesa Ford (1995–1996); Sales Manager, Dick Poe Honda Pontiac (1992–1996); Owner, Courtesy Auto Sales (1989–1992). **Education:** Baylor University (1982); Ford Manager Training, Pacific Institute. **Personal:** Married to Kathleen in 1993. Mr. Lunciano enjoys boating, motorcycling, and street rods.

A. F. MacPhee
President
MacPhee Pontiac Buick GMC, Ltd.
636 Portland Street
Dartmouth, Nova ScotiaB2W 2M3
(902) 434–4100
Fax: (902) 435–2270

5511

Business Information: MacPhee Pontiac Buick GMC, Ltd. is an authorized General Motors automobile dealership, providing a full range of new and used car and truck sales, GMAC–Smart Lease programs, in–house leasing programs, maintenance services, and parts supplies to Dartmouth, Nova Scotia and surrounding area residents. As President, Mr. MacPhee oversees the day–to–day operations of the dealership. He works closely with local financial institutions in the development of lending programs for automobile purchases/leases. Other responsibilities include public relations, development of marketing and sales techniques, and strategic planning for the future. **Career Steps:** President, MacPhee Pontiac Buick GMC, Ltd. (1983–Present); Manager, Peterson Pontiac (1977–1983); Sales Representative, Forbes Chevrolet and Oldsmobile. **Associations & Accomplishments:** National Automobile Dealers Association; Director, Nova Scotia Automobile Dealers Association; Canadian Automobile Dealers Association (Maclean's Magazine Dealer of Excellence Award – 1995). **Education:** General Motors Institute, Dealer Management (1980); Xavier Junior College. **Personal:** Married to Mary in 1969. Three children: Shannon, Andrew, and David.

Tom Mahrer
General Sales Manager
Greiner Motor Company, Inc.
P.O. Box 2460
Casper, WY 82602
(307) 266–1680
Fax: (307) 265–2260

5511

Business Information: Greiner Motor Company, Inc. specializes in the sale and service of new Ford cars and trucks. As General Sales Manager, Mr. Mahrer coordinates all sales, promotions, and advertisements. He is responsible for training all sales and clerical personnel, assists with administrative duties, and manages over $7 million in inventory. **Career Steps:** General Sales Manager, Greiner Motor Company, Inc. (1982–Present); District Manager, GH Texas Reamer Company (1979–1982); Field Sales, Dresser Security (1977–1978). **Associations & Accomplishments:** Casper Petroleum Club; Casper Boat Club; Elks Lodge; Moose Lodge. **Education:** National College of Business. **Personal:** Married to Sandra L. in 1977. One child: Jessica. Mr. Mahrer enjoys fishing, hunting, and sporting events.

Wynette P. Rhodes
Treasurer
Cook Chevrolet Inc.
610 Troy Highway
Elba, AL 36323–1519
(334) 897–2297
Fax: (334) 897–2387

5511

Business Information: Cook Chevrolet Inc. is an authorized Chevrolet automobile dealership, providing a full range of new and used car and truck sales, maintenance service and parts supplies to Elba, Alabama, and surrounding counties residents. As Treasurer, Mrs. Rhodes serves as business manager and secretary, maintaining the Company's books and preparing financial statements. She also performs customer service, inventory, and troubleshooting functions. **Career Steps:** Treasurer, Cook Chevrolet Inc. (1969–Present); Elba General Hospital, (1966–1969). **Education:** MacArthur Trade School, Business degree (1966). **Personal:** Married to David in 1956. Three children: Dianne, Lydia and Jeffery. Mrs. Rhodes enjoys reading, piano and crafts.

Michael B. Ron

President
Delek Motors Limited
23 Timna Street
Holon, Israel 58813
9723–557–7101
Fax: 9723–556–5840

5511

Business Information: Delek Motors Limited specializes in the import, distribution and retail sales of Mazda vehicles. Owned by Delek Investments and Properties, the Company imports vehicles from Japan and distributes them throughout Israel. As President, Mr. Ron oversees all aspect of the Company. He is responsible for administration, operations, finance, sales, public relations and strategic planning. **Career Steps:** President, Delek Motors Limited (1991–Present); Consul in Los Angeles, California (1982–1987). **Associations & Accomplishments:** Introduced a new Mazda car in Israel. **Education:** Technician Israel Management: M.Sc. (1962), B.Sc., both in Electrical Engineering. **Personal:** Married to Bilha. Two children: Oded and Daphna. Mr. Ron enjoys tennis.

Mr. Joel E. Rosenwasser
Comptroller
PAL Auto Group
791 South Road
Poughkeepsie, NY 12601
(914) 298–1193
Fax: (914) 298–0628

5511

Business Information: PAL Auto Group is an authorized sales and service dealership for Chevrolet, GEO and Buick automobiles, serving Rockland and Dutchess Counties of New York, with two locations — one in Poughkeepsie and one in West Haverstraw, NY. As Comptroller, Mr. Rosenwasser is responsible for the administration of all general management and financial operations for the company and its subsidiary concerns. Established in 1976, PAL Auto Group employs 80 professional sales and administrative staff. **Career Steps:** Comptroller, PAL Auto Group (1992–Present); Comptroller, Erickson Olds/Toyota of Rockland (1989–1992); Comptroller, Curry Chevrolet Sales and Service (1986–1989); Comptroller, Harbor Isle Chevrolet (1983–1986). **Associations & Accomplishments:** Masonic Lodge; Chevrolet Council of Business Managers. **Education:** Baruch College, B.A. in Business Administration (1976).

Gloria J. Santori
Personnel Director
Saturn Corporation
100 Saturn Parkway – J10
Spring Hill, TN 37174
(615) 486–5758
Fax: (615) 486–6061

5511

Business Information: Saturn Corporation, a wholly–owned subsidiary of General Motors Corporation, is an automotive manufacturing, engineering, and development company. As Personnel Director, Ms. Santori is responsible for all personnel, safety, and training in the Powertrain plant. **Career Steps:** Saturn Corporation: Personnel Director (1996–Present), EEO Advisor (1994–1996), General Supervisor Products (1993–1994), Team Leader Material Flow (1991–1993). **Associations & Accomplishments:** Salvation Army; Volunteer, March of Dimes; Minority Purchasing Council. **Education:** University of Michigan, B.A. (1986). **Personal:** Two children: Delishia Jones and Leshunda Turner. Ms. Santori enjoys reading, travel, and socializing.

Jeffrey D. Sproul
Fixed Operations Director
Dave Yakim Ford
910 W. Murdock Avenue
Oshkosh, WI 54901
(414) 231–1610
Fax: (414) 231–3598

5511

Business Information: Dave Yakim Ford is an authorized Ford automobile dealership serving the greater Oshkosh, Wisconsin and surrounding 200–mile radius populace. Established in 1955, Dave Yakim Ford reports annual revenue of $6 million and currently employs 55 people. As Fixed Operations Director, Mr. Sproul is responsible for the oversight of service, parts, and body shop operations. Career milestones include bringing Dave Yakim Ford from last in the ratings in "CSI's" December 1993 listing to the #2 Ford dealership in Wisconsin — accomplished by going to a Group/Team System. **Career Steps:** Fixed Operations Director, Dave Yakim Ford (1993–Present); Service Manager, Carousel Motors (1991–1993); Service Manager, Sexton Ford (1984–1991). **Associations & Accomplishments:** Recipient, "Medallion Award" (1992, 1993, 1994 & 1995), Ford Motor Company; ASC Charter Forum Group; Ford Quality Committment Award (1992, 1993). **Education:** Black Hawk College, A.S. in Electronics Technology (1983) **Personal:** Married to Rita in 1992. Two children: Wesley and Dalton. Mr. Sproul enjoys fishing, hunting and softball.

Gerry Wood
Owner/President
Wood Group of Companies
7337 Macleod Trail South West
Calgary, Alberta T2H 0L8
(403) 253–2211
Fax: (403) 640–0130

5511

Business Information: Wood Group of Companies specializes in the retail sale of cars and trucks. Regional in scope, the Company has four locations: Woodridge Lincoln Mercury, Woodridge Lincoln Mercury of Okotoks, Advantage Ford and Crowfoot Village Honda. Established in 1983, the Group employs 250 people, and produces annual revenue over $140 million. Woodridge has consistently been the largest Lincoln Mercury dealership in Canada since its inception. They pioneered retail leasing in Western Canada dna now rank around the best in all of Canada. Advantage Ford is the latest acquisition to the group and is housed in an outstanding dealership facility in south Calgary. As Owner/President, Mr. Wood coordinates all strategic planning, marketing, and public relations. **Career Steps:** Owner/President, Wood Group of Companies (1983–Present); President, Gerry Wood Chevrolet/Olds (1979–1983); Sales Manager, Maclin Ford Sales, Limited (1969–1979). **Associations & Accomplishments:** Canadian Down Syndrome Society; World President's Organization; Calgary Burns Club; United Way. **Education:** Stow College, Glasgow, Scotland, Marketing (1966). **Personal:** Married to Elaine in 1975. Three children: Rory, Megan, and Cailean. Mr. Wood enjoys golf and looks forward to his free time at his residence in the Foothills of Alberta, south of Calgary and also his hideaway in Northern Montana.

Thomas Andrade
Controller
Everett's Auto Parts
553 Thatcher Street
Brockton, MA 02402
(508) 583–7478
Fax: (508) 583–7937
EMAIL: See Below

5531

Business Information: Everett's Auto Parts is a large automotive recycling operation specializing in used auto parts and scrap. Everett's primarily services the northeast, with an increasing presence in the international exporting industry. As Controller, Mr. Andrade is responsible for accounting, investments, reporting, strategic alliances, and taxes. Internet users can reach him via: tcandrade@aol.com **Career Steps:** Controller, Everett's Auto Parts (1996–Present); Blue Cross Blue Shield of Massachusetts: Director, Financial Systems (1995–1996), Manager, FSBSU (1994–1995). **Associations & Accomplishments:** Appalachian Mountain Club; Professional Association of Diving Instructors (PADI) Open Water Diver. **Education:** Bentley College, Bachelor (1992). **Personal:** Mr. Andrade enjoys winter mountaineering, skiing, hiking, camping, kayaking, and other outdoor activities.

Silvio Di Fiore

Director of Loss Prevention and Inventory Control
Strauss Discount Auto
9 A Brick Plant Road
South River, NJ 08882–1097
(908) 390–9000 Ext: 5260
Fax: (908) 390–9079

5531

Business Information: Strauss Discount Auto is a retailer of auto parts and accessories, as well as a servicer and repairer of automobiles. National in scope, Strauss Discount Auto has 125 stores located strategically throughout the Northeast, including New York, New Jersey, Pennsylvania, Connecticut, Massachusetts, and Delaware. Joining Strauss Discount Auto as Director of Loss Prevention and Inventory Control in 1994, Mr. Di Fiore is responsible for the direction of loss prevention and inventory control, including all facets of physical security, administration, investigation, auditing, training, and the development of policies and procedures. **Career Steps:** Director of Loss Prevention and Inventory Control, Strauss Discount Auto (1994–Present); Director of Loss Prevention, Bergdorf Goodman (1991–1994); Regional Loss Prevention Manager, SAKS Fifth Avenue (1985–1991). **Associations & Accomplishments:** American Society for Industrial Security; International Association of Credit Card Investigators; National Association of Chiefs of Police (1988); Retail Loss Prevention Association; National Criminal Justice Association. **Education:** Rutgers University, B.S. in Criminal Justice (1983); Institute of Paralegal Studies, Certified Paralegal. **Personal:** Married to Nancy in 1986. Two children: Danielle and Brian. Mr. Di Fiore enjoys sports (i.e. baseball, football, soccer).

Adrian Hidalgo H.

General Manager
Super Servicio, S.A.
P O Box 992–1000
San Jose, Costa Rica
(506) 222–5544
Fax: (506) 257–6873

5531

Business Information: Super Servicio, S.A. is a Firestone distribution center. The Company imports tires from Korea, Germany, and the United States. As General Manager, Mr. Hidalgo H. is responsible for all aspects of Company operations, including management, operations, strategic planning, and sales and marketing. **Career Steps:** General Manager, Super Servicio, S.A. (1984–Present); Vice President, Codesa (1982–1984); Manager, C.R. Stock Exchange (1978–1982). **Associations & Accomplishments:** President, Asociacion de Interclubes. **Education:** INCAE, M.B.A. (1970). **Personal:** Married to Bertha in 1977. Three children: Adrian, Maria Gabriela, and Roberto. Mr. Hidalgo H. enjoys running, tennis, boating, and fishing.

Conley P. Kyle

Vice President of Store Operations
HI/LO Auto Supply
2575 W. Bellfort
Houston, TX 77054–5025
(713) 663–9220
Fax: (713) 663–9276

5531

Business Information: HI/LO Auto Supply is a retailer and wholesaler of automobile parts to retail and commercial markets, such as garages and service stations. National in scope, HI/LO Auto Supply has 194 stores throughout Texas, Louisiana, and California. As Vice President of Store Operations, Mr. Kyle is responsible for the oversight of all 194 store operations and store employees, as well as sales operations and customer services. In addition, he directly supervises fourteen regional managers and two division managers. **Career Steps:** Vice President of Store Operations, HI/LO Auto Supply (1991–Present); Vice President of Operations, Advance Auto Parts (1973–1991). **Associations & Accomplishments:** Masonic Order, Star of West Lodge #114; Bay Area Baptist Church; Chamber of Commerce; Recipient of HI/LO's highest award "The HI/LO Circle of Excellence Achievement Award." **Education:** Wytheville Community College, A.A.S. (1970). **Personal:** Married to Helen in 1975. Two children: Rico and Michelle. Mr. Kyle enjoys golf, traveling, and gardening.

Mike J. Miller

Training Director
Tire Kingdom
2001 North Congress Avenue
Rivera Beach, FL 33404–5101
(407) 842–4290 Ext: 284
Fax: (407) 842–6314

5531

Business Information: Tire Kingdom is an independent retailer, providing tires, tire–related services, and mechanical repairs, including wheel alignments, and repairs to the braking, driveline, and steering systems. With 146 locations throughout Florida, Tire Kingdom just opened three locations and a warehouse in Charlotte, North Carolina, with two more opening in that area in the near future. Mr. Miller has worked as a mechanic since 1975, he started with Tire Kingdom in 1982. Seeing the need for a mechanic's training program, he pursued the idea until it was adopted by the company in 1986. Appointed as Training Director in 1992, Mr. Miller is responsible for the preparation of the training classes and classroom segment of retail computer operations and automotive mechanical theory. Customer satisfaction claims that are mechanical in nature are also on his duty list. **Career Steps:** Tire Kingdom: Training Director (1992–Present), Retail Computer Operations training (1990–1992), Mechanical Trainer (1986–1990), Automotive Mechanic (1982–1986); 7 years automotive mechanic experience; 4 years hotel/motel experience. **Associations & Accomplishments:** ASE Certified Master Automotive Technician (1985–Present); Certified in Dade and Broward Counties for Automotive Repair; Technical Advisor for Broward County Better Business Bureau; Vocational Industrial Clubs of America; Automotive Advisory Committee, North Technical Education Center, PBC; Automotive Training Managers' Council; ASE Refrigerant Certification; TRW Automotive Tech Team. **Personal:** Married to Deborah in 1992. Two children: son, Jeff and daughter, Jaime. Mr. Miller and his bride enjoy golf, biking, and flying (Private Pilot SEL).

Ismael Velazquez Jr.

Chief Executive Officer and Chief Operating Officer
Velazquez Auto & Body Parts
P.O. Box 900
Isabela, Puerto Rico 00662–0900
(787) 830–3013
Fax: (787) 830–7889

5531

Business Information: Velazquez Auto & Body Parts is a retailer and wholesaler of imported automotive parts throughout Puerto Rico. The Company is considered to be the largest retailer of Mitsubishi and Hyundai automotive products outside the metropolitan area of San Juan. As Chief Executive Officer, Chief Operating Officer, and a 25% Shareholder, Mr. Velazquez is responsible for all operations and relationships with suppliers, customers, and financial institutions, in addition to supervising all sales and purchasing. Concurrently, he is a 25% Shareholder in Hyundai de Isabela. **Career Steps:** Chief Executive Officer and Chief Operating Officer, Velazquez Auto & Body Parts (1983–Present). **Associations & Accomplishments:** American Institute of Certified Public Accountants; Puerto Rico State Society of Certified Public Accountants; Recognized as the Top Parts Dealer of Mitsubishi products in Puerto Rico (1991). **Education:** Inter–American University, B.B.A. (1993). **Personal:** Married to Maria in 1986. Two children: Ismarie and Ismael III. Mr. Velazquez enjoys scuba diving, reading, and conducting history research and accounting conferences.

Nouri A. Kashmeeri, Ph.D.

President
Anwar Management, Inc.
185 Rosedale Road
Yonkers, NY 1071–2526
(914) 337–5525
Fax: (914) 337–5868
E–MAIL: See Below

5541

Business Information: Established in 1994, Anwar Management, Inc. is an import and export company specializing in the retail sale of gasoline (ie., Shell stations). As President, Mr. Kashmeeri is responsible for all aspects of company operations, including decision–making, strategic planning, and international business. Concurrently, Mr. Kashmeeri is President of Micro Times, an import and export computer and software center. Internet users can reach him via: KASHMEERI@MSN.COM **Career Steps:** President, Anwar Management, Inc. (1994–Present); President, Micro Times, Inc. (1996–Present); Chairman, Anwar Trading International (1975). **Education:** University of Michigan, Ph.D. (1969) and University of Michigan, M.S. in Civil Engineering. **Personal:** Married to Faiza Al–Fassi in 1960. Three children: Abeer, Khalid and Badr.

Fred Pace

General Manager
Adventure Marine and Outdoor
1201 B Miracle Strip Parkway, South East #B
Ft. Walton Beach, FL 32548
(904) 244–1099
Fax: (904) 243–8677

5551

Business Information: Adventure Marine and Outdoor, established in 1980, is a marine dealership engaged in the sales and service of new and used boats and outdoor recreational supplies. Employing 83 people, the Company estimates annual sales in excess of $32 million. As General Manager, Mr. Pace is responsible for all aspects of daily store operations and personnel management. **Career Steps:** General Manager, Adventure Marine and Outdoor (1989–Present); General Manager, Duplessis Cadillac (1985–1989); General Manager, Clinton Cadillac (1983–1985). **Education:** University of Massachusetts, B.A. (1974). **Personal:** Mr. Pace enjoys boating, tennis, and running.

Wayne E. Hartmann

Owner and General Manager
Wheels Inc.
3471 South University Drive
Fargo, ND 58104–6225
(701) 235–6459
Fax: (701) 235–6450

5561

Business Information: Wheels Inc. sells and services recreational vehicles, including snowmobiles, motorcycles, personal watercraft, and ATV's. The Company has gone from $250,000 in sales in 1978 to $4.3 million in 1995. Establishing the Company in 1977 and serving as its Owner and General Manager, Mr. Hartmann oversees all daily operations, including personnel decisions, marketing, and bookkeeping functions, as well as the efforts of thirteen employees. **Career Steps:** Owner and General Manager, Wheels Inc. (1977–Present); Service Manager, F.M. Auto Mart (1974–1977). **Associations & Accomplishments:** AOPA Pilots Association; Snowmobile North Dakota. **Education:** Attended, Alexandria Vocational Technical (1972–1974). **Personal:** Married to Tracy in 1995. Three children: Ryan, Alicia and Kelsey. Mr. Hartmann enjoys flying, snowmobiling and travel.

Kurt Dimick

Owner
Tri–City Cycle
2028 East Jeffers Frontage Road
Loveland, CO 80538–8913
(970) 667–8697
Fax: (970) 667–1998

5571

Business Information: Tri–City Cycle is Colorado's largest used motorcycle dealer, specializing in all top line vehicle models, including Harley Davidson, as well as ATV's, watercraft, and snowmobiles. A top ranked motorcycle racer for ten years, Mr. Dimick established the dealership in 1991, concentrating on customer service and personal attention to detail. He is responsible for hiring and training sales representatives and a network of wholesale buyers, as well as public relations, marketing, and administrative functions. **Career Steps:** Owner and Operator, Tri–City Cycle (1991–Present); Owner and Operator, The Bike Buyer (1990–1991); Owner and Operator, Yamaha Motor Sports (1984–1990); Sales Manager, Laforte Yamaha (1979–1984). **Associations & Accomplishments:** American Motorcycle Association; Motorcycle Roadracing Association: Top Ranked Motorcycle Racer for ten years with three consecutive #1 Plates; Sports Riders Association of Colorado: 15 years of Pro Status. **Personal:** Two children: Dalton and Colter. Mr. Dimick enjoys dirt bike riding, snowmobiling, and boating.

Edward Hidalgo Jr.

Director, International Operations
International Aviation
1500 Perimeter Road, Building S
West Palm Beach, FL 33406
(561) 478–8700
Fax: (561) 747–7810 (561) 233–8549

5599

Business Information: International Aviation is a fixed–base operation that services, maintains, and sells general aviation and corporate aircraft. With four locations, the Company is directly involved with Corporate aviation, providing hangar storage, FAA approved maintenance service, aircraft fuel, as well as hotel and car reservations, and aircraft catering. As Director, International Operations, Mr. Hidalgo promotes the Company's services in Mexico, Central and South America, and the Caribbean. He is responsible for overseeing all services and maintaining customer satisfaction. **Career Steps:** Director, International Operations, International Aviation (1993–Present); Director, International Operations, Signature Flight Support (1982–1993); Director, International Operations, Hangar One, Inc. (1976–1982). **Education:** University of Virginia, B.A. (1971); Embry Riddle Aeronautical University, Flight Technology. **Personal:** Married to Nanette in 1981. Three children: Edoardo, Tila, and Nina. Mr. Hidalgo enjoys reading, physical fitness, automobiles, boating and sports.

5600 Apparel and Accessory Stores

5611 Men's and boys' clothing stores
5621 Women's clothing stores
5632 Women's accessory and specialty stores
5641 Children's and infants' wear stores
5651 Family clothing stores
5661 Shoe stores
5699 Misc. apparel and accessory stores

Skai S. Wallace
Director of Operations and Merchandising
IZOD Big & Tall
350 5th Avenue, Suite 2505
New York, NY 10118–2599
(212) 564–3742
Fax: (212) 736–2349

5611

Business Information: IZOD Big & Tall, a division of Block Industries, is a privately–owned corporation with offices in New York City and Wilmington, North Carolina. Specializing in men's big and tall sportswear, the IZOD Division was established in 1994 and has an estimated annual revenue of $7.2 million. As Director of Operations and Merchandising, Mrs. Wallace handles all aspects of developing and sourcing the entire line. She negotiates prices, inspections, and special key account programs. She travels extensively to all national trade shows, as well as to stores. Additional duties include planning and organizing samples, implementing merchandising plans, and assisting customers. **Career Steps:** Director of Operations and Merchandising, IZOD Big & Tall (1994–Present); Director of Merchandising, Gordon and Ferguson (1992–1994); Director of Merchandising, U2 Wear Me Out. **Associations & Accomplishments:** United A.B.A.T.E. of N.J.; H.O.G. **Education:** F.I.T., New York, NY, A.A.S. (1983). **Personal:** Married to Alan in 1995. One daughter: Zenija. Mrs. Wallace enjoys being with her family, travel, golf, and motorcycling.

Karen A. Brown
Vice President of Operations
Haddad Apparel
100 West 33rd Street, Room 1001
New York, NY 10001–2914
(212) 630–5444
Fax: (212) 630–5420

5641

Business Information: Haddad Apparel is a family–owned business that designs, imports and sells licensed children's clothing, with 14 locations worldwide. The Company was established in 1942 and currently has over 200 employees. As Vice President of Operations, Ms. Brown oversees all aspects of the Company operations. Her duties include coordinating, structuring, and organizing foreign offices, the New York office and the New Jersey warehouse in order to streamline and expedite the production process. Ms. Brown acts as an advisor to the Company owners on the future of the Company. **Career Steps:** Haddad Apparel: Vice President of Operations (1995–Present), Import Coordinator (1993–1995); Import Coordinator, May Merchandising Company (1992–1993); Buyer, Thalhimers (1991–1992). **Education:** University of North Carolina at Chapel Hill, B.S. in Industrial Relations (1985). **Personal:** Ms. Brown enjoys photography, knitting and designing sweaters, skiing, and travel.

Eric K. Goldstein
Director of Product Development
The Gap, Inc.
620 Avenue of the Americas
New York, NY 10011
(212) 886–7026
Fax: (212) 886–7086

5651

Business Information: The Gap, Inc., well known for "The Gap Jeans," is one of the nation's leading specialty retailers offering a diverse array of high quality women's, men's and children's casual clothing. As Director of Product Development, Mr. Goldstein is responsible for the direction of all research and development of new fabrics and finishing technology to be used throughout the world. **Career Steps:** Director of Product Development, The Gap, Inc. (1994–Present); Director of Product Development, Polo/Ralph Lauren Corporation 91991–1994); Director of Quality, Nationwide Formalwear (1989–1991). **Associations & Accomplishments:** Senior Member, American Association for Texile Chemists and Colorists; Active Alumni Member, Philadelphia College of Textiles and Science. **Education:** Philadelphia College of Textiles, B.S. in Textile Technology (1988); British School of Leather Technology; Clemson University. **Personal:** Married to Theresa in 1991. One child: Jacob. Mr. Goldstein enjoys travel, sports, and car restoration.

Kathy Snowden

Division Vice President
Eddie Bauer, Inc.
15010 NE 36th Street
Redmond, WA 98052
(206) 882–6333
Fax: (206) 556–7668

5651

Business Information: Eddie Bauer, Inc. is a privately–held retail and mail order business. Products include menswear, womenswear, outdoor functional gear, home furnishings, and casual and dress sportswear. International in scope, Eddie Bauer, Inc. has four hundred stores located throughout the U.S. and Canada, with joint ventures in Japan and Germany. With a Catalog Division and an Outlet Division, the Corporation focuses in three areas: home, a.k.a. Eddie Bauer, and sportswear. As one of 25 Corporate Vice Presidents, Ms. Snowden serves as Division Vice President for the Retail Stores Division, responsible for leading field organizations, located throughout the West Coast and Canada, to successfully run their own businesses. Ms. Snowden traveled to Osaka, Japan to stock and open the Eddie Bauer Store in the first outlet mall in Japan. **Career Steps:** Eddie Bauer, Inc.: Division Vice President (1995–Present), Regional Manager (1993–1995), Senior District Manager (1988–1993). **Associations & Accomplishments:** Board of Director Member, Bellevue Community College; NRMA – National Retail Association. **Education:** St. Olaf College, B.A. – majored in English and Political Science, minored in Music and Religion (1982). **Personal:** Married to Mark in 1985. One child: James John (Jamie). Ms. Snowden enjoys music theater, golf, rollerblading, and playing the flute and piccolo.

Joseph M. Dela Cruz
Director of Information Systems
Sneaker Stadium
2035 State Route 27, Suite 1100
Edison, NJ 08817–3351
(908) 248–9090 Ext. 2525
Fax: (201) 696–4771

5661

Business Information: Sneaker Stadium, with 18 locations, is a retail athletic superstore, providing athletic footwear and apparel. The Store, with over 20,000 square feet, stocks over 40,000 pairs of shoes. Currently, Sneaker Stadium is the 30th largest sporting goods Company in the nation. As Director of Information Systems, Mr. Dela Cruz develops and forecasts Company system needs for current and future growth. He is responsible for development, design, and implementation of client server systems, telecommunications, and satellite equipment. **Career Steps:** Director of Information Systems, Sneaker Stadium (1994–Present); Manager of Information Systems, Osh Kosh B'Gosh (1992–1994); Supervisor of System Operations, Ilio, Inc. (1989–1992). **Associations & Accomplishments:** Professional Association of Diving Instructors. **Education:** Rutgers University, B.S. in Computer Science (1990); New York University; Cittone Institute. **Personal:** Married to Patricia in 1994. Mr. Dela Cruz enjoys tennis, golf, reading, cycling, travel, and scuba diving.

Douglas P. Haensel
Chief Financial Officer
Butler Group, Inc.
400 Technology Court
Smyrna, GA 30082
(770) 801–1200 Ext. 205
Fax: (770) 801–0075

5661

Business Information: Butler Group, Inc., A subsidiary of General Electric Capital Corporation, is a chain of over 200 retail women's shoe stores nationwide. The Butler Group, founded in 1926 and employing over 1,200 people, estimates annual revenue in excess of $85 million. As Chief Financial Officer, Mr. Haensel is responsible for the day–to–day operations of the Company. Other responsibilities include overseeing any joint ventures to expand the Company, MIS, financial concerns, and strategic planning. **Career Steps:** Chief Financial Officer, Butler Group, Inc. (1994–Present); General Electric Capital Corporation: Vice President–Restructuring (1992–1994), Senior Account Executive (1990–1992). **Associations & Accomplishments:** Corporate Turnaround Association; Atlanta Chamber of Commerce; Retail Roundtable. **Education:** University of Wisconsin, B.B.A. (1985); General Electric Financial Management Program (1985–1987). **Personal:** Married to Paige in 1993. One child: Maxwell. Mr. Haensel enjoys working with charitable organizations and spending time with his family.

David Liberman
Director of Information Services
Just for Feet, Inc.
153 Cahaba Valley Parkway
Pelham, AL 35124–1144
(205) 403–8000
Fax: (205) 403–8200
EMAIL: See Below

5661

Business Information: Just for Feet, Inc. is a full–service retail athletic footwear chain, complete with in–store basketball courts, laser shows, restaurants, and 4,000 styles of footwear. Established in 1977, the Company presently employs 3,000 people and reports annual revenue of approximately $150 million. As Director of Information Services, Mr. Liberman is responsible for all corporate technological acquisitions, including computer systems, communications hardware and software, and audio/video equipment. Internet users can reach him via: DAVID@FEET.COM **Career Steps:** Director, Just For Feet, Inc. (1995–Present; 1990–1992); Producer – Computing, America Online, Inc (1992–1995). **Education:** University of Montevallo (1983). **Personal:** Married to Christine in 1988. One child: Corwin. Mr. Liberman enjoys auto racing and aviation. Additionally, he volunteers his time for celebrity benefits and does consulting and public speaking on telecommunications.

Lisa M. Danning
Quality Assurance Engineer
Transpec Fasteners, Inc.
1500 North Park Drive, Suite 150
Ft. Worth, TX 76102
(817) 877–1072
Fax: (817) 338–9645

5672

Business Information: Transpec Fasteners, Inc. is a distributor of military hardware and specifications, NAS ordinance and specials to customer drawings. The Company conducts in–house hardness testing of products. Established in 1988, Transpec currently employs 40 people. As Quality Assurance Engineer, Ms. Danning manages the day–to–day activities of the Quality Assurance Department. She is responsible for the quality of all manuals, product reporting, audits, technical inspections, and customer service. Other responsibilities include implementation of the ISO9002 standards and training of new inspectors on the Company standards. **Career Steps:** Transpec Fasteners, Inc.: Quality Assurance Engineer (1996–Present), Quality Assurance Manager (1992–1996), Inspector (1988–1992). **Associations & Accomplishments:** ASM International. **Education:** ISO Internal Auditor Course, (1994); Principles of Internal Audition of ISO 9002, ANSI/ASQC Q9002–1994 and Quality Systems in Accordance with ANSI/ASQC Q 10011–1–1994 (1994); James Madison High School (1983). **Personal:** Two children: Kyle A. and Travis J. Danning. Ms. Danning enjoys camping, horseback riding, and dog training.

David L. Petroski
General Manager
UNITOG
899 Market Street
Bloomsburg, PA 17815
(717) 784–4310
Fax: (717) 784–4312

5699

Business Information: UNITOG is a leading supplier of high quality uniform rental services to a variety of industries and sells custom–designed uniforms primarily to national companies in connection with their corporate image programs. Unitog manufactures a substantial amount of the uniforms that the Company rents or sells. As General Manager, Mr. Petroski is responsible for total sales, expenses, profit, and operations of the Bloomsburg facility. **Career Steps:** General Manager, UNITOG (1994–Present); General Manager, R.U.S. Division of OMNI Services (1986–1994); Terminal Manager, Roadway Express, Inc. (1976–1986). **Associations & Accomplishments:** Lions Club of Lewisburg; Bloomsburg, PA Chamber of Commerce; Pennsylvania Association of Industrial Laundries; Who's Who Worldwide (1993–1994); Who's Who in U.S. Executives (1989); Manager of the Year (1993); Salesman of the Year (1983); TQA and QAT Facilitator. **Education:** King's College, B.S. (1976). **Personal:** Married to Karen in 1980. Two children: Jennifer and Diana. Mr. Petroski enjoys golf, boating, gardening, woodworking and softball.

5700 Furniture and Homefurnishings Stores

5712 Furniture stores
5713 Floor covering stores
5714 Drapery and upholstery stores
5719 Misc. homefurnishings stores
5722 Household appliance stores
5731 Radio, TV and electronic stores
5734 Computer and software stores
5735 Record and prerecorded tape stores
5736 Musical instrument stores

Jodie M. Bargamin
Store Manager
Heilig Meyers Furniture
9225 North 76th Street
Milwaukee, WI 53223–1058
(414) 354–2066
Fax: (414) 354–2874

5712

Business Information: Heilig Meyers Furniture opened its first store in 1913 in Goldsboro, North Carolina. The national furniture retailer has since expanded to 718 locations, doubling in size the last three years. Ms. Bargamin was promoted in 1995 from Credit Manager in Memphis, Tennessee, to Store Manager for 76th Street facility, and City Manager for all three locations in the Milwaukee, Wisconsin, area. Her responsibilities include personnel decisions, financial oversight, and various administrative activities. **Career Steps:** Heilig Meyers Furniture: Store Manager (1994–Present), Credit Manager (1994–1995). **Education:** East Carolina University: M.B.A. (1993), B.S. in Business Management (1988). **Personal:** Married to Paul in 1995.

George C. Burnett Jr.

President
Burnett's Treasures
7310 Miramar Road, Suite 100
San Diego, CA 92126–4222
(619) 586–1900
Fax: (619) 506–6255
EMAIL: See Below

5712

Business Information: Burnett's Treasures, a retail furniture store and San Diego landmark, was established in 1915 by the Burnett Family, passing from father to son most recently in 1983. As President, Mr. Burnett oversees daily operations and performs various administrative activities. Concurrently, he serves as President of Designer Delivery, a furniture delivery service contracting with furniture companies in the San Diego–Los Angeles metro area. Internet users can reach him via: GBURN@IX.NETCOM.COM **Career Steps:** President, Burnett's Treasures (1983–Present); President, Designer Delivery (1984–Present). **Associations & Accomplishments:** Home Furnishings Association of San Diego. **Education:** At-

tended, California Western University. **Personal:** Married to Marie in 1976. Two children: George III and Richard. Mr. Burnett enjoys track bicycle racing.

Evelyn Kennedy Hudson
President
Office Images, Inc.
P.O. Box 6724
High Point, NC 27262–6724
(910) 841–6665
Fax: (910) 841–7402

5712

Business Information: Office Images, Inc. specializes in office furniture sales, space planning, bids and interior design specifications for offices, motels, medical facilities, and restaurants. As President, Ms. Hudson is responsible for all aspects of Company operations, including sales and interior designing. **Career Steps:** President, Office Images, Inc. (1994–Present); President/General Manager, Evelyn Hudson Interiors (1972–1994); Assistant Buyer/Interior Designer, Boyles Furniture Sales (1967–1972); President & General Manager, Hudson House, Inc. (1963–1967). **Associations & Accomplishments:** International Interior Design Association; Fellow, International Furnishings Design Asssociation; Allied Member, American Institute of Architects; International Toastmasters; Leader of Stephens Ministry. **Education:** New York School of Design, Interior Design (1967); Ashmore Business School; Randolph Community College. **Personal:** Widow to C.C. Hudson in 1936. Two children: James D. and Kenneth Allen. Ms. Hudson enjoys travel and reading.

Teri L. Olson
Owner/President/Chief Executive Officer
Diversified Office Furniture
2863 Bondesson
Omaha, NE 68112
(402) 451–8167
Fax: (402) 451–2316

5712

Business Information: Diversified Office Furniture Services is a retail and service establishment. Providing sale of new and recycled office furniture, design and layout, installation, re–configuration, maintenance/cleaning, and service of all types of office furniture including such specialty items as rolling file systems & ergonomic/modular systems etc. to companies and businesses in the midwest. Incorporated in 1991, the Company also specializes in the refurbishing of all used modular furniture, and plans on expanding through added locations. As Chief Executive Officer, Mrs. Olson oversees all aspects of the business, including design, sales, marketing, and supervision of the management staff. She also oversees all phases of customer service and personally reviews client accounts. **Career Steps:** Chief Executive Officer, Diversified Office Furniture (1990–Present); General Manager, Pete's Office Furniture, Inc. (1982–1990). **Associations & Accomplishments:** Greater Omaha Chamber of Commerce; North Omaha Commercial Club. **Education:** University of Nebraska at Omaha. **Personal:** Married to Michael J. in 1992. Two children: Micaela Cecilia Korin and Ryan Joshua Elias.

Jack Rayher
Director of Marketing
Dial–A–Mattress
31–10 48th Avenue
Long Island City, NY 11101
(718) 472–1200
Fax: (718) 472–1310

5712

Business Information: Dial–A–Mattress, the world's largest direct marketer of mattresses, is a privately–owned bedding retailer. Established originally as a store, Dial–A–Mattress moved into phone sales (1–800) and is headquartered in Long Island City, New York, offering their services through franchises, primarily along the East Coast. Joining Dial–A–Mattress as Director of Marketing in 1995, Mr. Rayher is responsible for all advertising, including public relations, promotions, market research, and management of the image of the Company. **Career Steps:** Director of Marketing, Dial–A–Mattress (1995–Present); Director of Marketing, 1–800–FLOWERS (1993–1995); Vice President and Director of Database Marketing, Citicorp PCS Information Services (1990–1993); Vice President and Account Supervisor, NW Ayer & Partners (1982–1990). **Education:** Bernard Baruch, M.B.A. (1978); St. Francis College, B.A. **Personal:** Married to Erica in 1974. Mr. Rayher enjoys photography, foreign travel, and scuba diving.

SUMMEY CABINETS INC.

Michael K. Summey
President
Summey Cabinets, Inc.
325 South Buncombe Road
Greer, SC 29650
(864) 877–9729
Fax: (864) 879–0788

5712

Business Information: Summey Cabinets, Inc. was established in 1968 by Mr. Summey's father. The Company currently has ten employees and expects annual sales to exceed $1 million. The Company builds cabinets for residential and commercial clients. As President, Mr. Summey oversees all aspects of the business. He is responsible for general administrative duties, sales and marketing of services and products, public relations, and planning for Company expansion. Mr. Summey works with clients on the design and cost estimates of products and on establishing good customer relations. Concurrently, Mr. Summey is Secretary/Treasurer of The Greer Group, a general contractor doing commercial and residential construction in and around Greer, South Carolina. **Career Steps:** President, Summey Cabinets, Inc. (1990–Present). **Associations & Accomplishments:** Greer High School Boosters Club; Greer Human Resources; Greenville County School District, Building and Grounds Committee. **Education:** Attended, Montreat–Anderson; Attended, University of South Carolina; Attended, Greenville Technical College. **Personal:** Married to Kathleen in 1979. Two children: Ryan and Brandon. Mr. Summey enjoys golf, fishing, snow skiing and computers.

Michael R. Wetzel
Sales Management/Account Executive
Workstyles, Inc.
1021 Euclid Avenue
Cleveland, OH 44115
(216) 781–9911
Fax: (216) 781–0926

5712

Business Information: Workstyles, Inc. is a contract furniture sales company, specializing in office furniture and interior design. As Sales Management/Account Executive, Mr. Wetzel is responsible for diversified administrative activities, including sales, marketing, and financing. **Career Steps:** Sales Management/Account Executive, Workstyles, Inc. (1993–Present); Regional Manager, Center Core, Inc. (1992–1993); Sales Manager, D & L Office Furniture (1989–1992); Account Executive, Weber, Hilmer & Johnson (1978–1989). **Associations & Accomplishments:** Notary Public; Elks Club. **Education:** Elmhurst College, B.S. (1990) **Personal:** Married to Kristin in 1986. Three children: Alexandra, Katelyn, and Francesca. Mr. Wetzel enjoys reading, golf, motorcycle riding, and travel.

Gene Wolf
President
A. L. Myers, Inc.
173 North Highland Avenue
Ossining, NY 10562
(914) 941–1408
Fax: (914) 941–5160

5712

Business Information: A. L. Myers, Inc., a major independent store in the Metro, New York area, is a retail furniture store, providing furniture and carpeting for home and office design. Established in 1891, A. L. Myers, Inc. currently employs 21 people. Joining the Company as Treasurer and Secretary in 1947, Mr. Wolf was appointed as President in 1994. He is responsible for the oversight of all aspects of operations, specifically including financial and planning involvement. Concurrent with his executive position with A. L. Myers, Inc., he serves as Chief Executive Officer and Treasurer with various affiliated real estate companies. **Career Steps:** A. L. Myers, Inc.: President (1994–Present), Treasurer and Secretary (1970–1994); Chief Executive Officer and Treasurer, Various Affiliated Real Estate Companies (1963–Present). **Associations & Accomplishments:** Member and Former President, Ossining Rotary Club; Former President, Ossining Chamber of Commerce; Former Member, Board of Trustees for Phelps Memorial Hospital Association and Center (6 years); Co-chaired committees in community and represented Ossining and Ossining Chamber of Commerce at meetings with senators and representatives in Washington, D.C. and Albany, New York. **Education:** New York University, B.S. in Financial Management (1951). **Personal:** Married to Lillian in 1979. Three children: Col. Robert L. Wolf (USMC–RET), Karol Ann Gerdts, and Randy Sue D'Iorio. Mr. Wolf enjoys golf, stamp collecting, architecture, and appraising antiques and furniture.

David S. Numark
President and Chief Executive Officer
Concorde Flooring Systems, Inc.
444 Park Avenue South
New York, NY 10016
(212) 685–1300
Fax: (212) 685–1485

5713

Business Information: Concorde Flooring Systems, Inc. is a national full–service floor covering dealership. As President and Chief Executive Officer, Mr. Numark is responsible for overseeing all aspects of business operations and development. Founded in 1993, Concorde Floording Systems, Inc. employs a full–time staff of nine. **Career Steps:** President and Chief Executive Officer, Concorde Flooring Systems, Inc. (1993–Present); Vice President, Corporate Carpet Systems (1990–1993); Assistant Vice President, Lasher Carpet Company (1989–1990); Regional Manager, Lotus Carpet Company (1987–1989). **Associations & Accomplishments:** International Facility Management Association (IFMA); International Association of Corporate Real Estate Executives (NACORE); Institute of Business Designers (IBD); United Jewish Appeal (UJA); Chamber of Commerce, Regional Business Partnership, Newark, New Jersey. **Education:** University of Delaware, B.A. (1982). **Personal:** Married to Gail in 1984. Two children: Jeffrey and Matthew.

Timothy J. Scanlon
Controller
Hiller Stores, Inc.
P O Box 6307
Rochester, MD 55903
(507) 288–1766
Fax: (507) 288–0362

5713

Business Information: Hiller Stores, Inc. is the largest floor covering retailer in southeastern Minnesota. Established in 1958, the Company employs 35 people, and has an estimated annual revenue of $10 million. As Controller, Mr. Scanlon oversees all monetary aspects of the Company, including purchasing, work process orders, accounting, taxes, and long–term contracts. **Career Steps:** Controller, Hiller Stores, Inc. (1994–Present); Audit and Accounting Manager, Coffman, Nehring, Christoperson & Ferguson (1987–1994). **Associations & Accomplishments:** American Institute of Certified Public Accountants; MNCPA; Treasurer, Possibilities of Southern Minnesota, Inc.; Local coordinator and instructor for CPA Review Course. **Education:** Winona State University, B.S. (1997). **Personal:** Married to Karen in 1989. One child: Robert. Mr. Scanlon enjoys biking and golf.

John D. Sloan
Director of Operations
Blakley Corporation, d.b.a. Blakley's
8060 East 88th Street
Indianapolis, IN 46256
(317) 576–8358
Fax: (317) 841–5651

5713

Business Information: Blakley Corporation, d.b.a. Blakley's, is a retailer and installer of floor coverings, such as carpet, vinyl, wood, and ceramic. Blakley's has two locations, with corporate headquarters in Indianapolis, Indiana. Joining the Corporation as Floor Covering Installer in 1976, Mr. Sloan was appointed as Director of Operations in 1986. He is responsible for the direction of all aspects of operations, including monitoring and supervising inventory control of two warehouse facilities; monitoring and supervising quality and quantity of the cutting of carpet; overseeing the scheduling and billing office operations; scheduling the daily routing of three field superintendents; and supervising approximately 60 sub–contracting crews daily. He also creates new research and develops new ideas, on a daily basis, that will improve the quality of this industry. Responsible for creating and supervising an installation training program to develop a well–rounded, quality instal-

lation professional, he also assists sales personnel in estimating labor speeds and costs for upcoming jobs. **Career Steps:** Blakley Corporation: Director of Operations (1986–Present), Floor Covering Installer (1976–1986). **Associations & Accomplishments:** Floor Covering Installation Contractors Association; Floor Covering Institute of Technical Services; Union Journeyman Floor Coverer. **Education:** Floor Covering Institute Technic, Cerificate (1995); Certification: Armstrong Service Flooring School; Ivy Tech, A.S. in Construction Engineering. **Personal:** Married to Kathy in 1989. Two children: Samantha and Zachary. Mr. Sloan enjoys golf.

Steven Johnson
Owner and President
Johnson's Parts & Service, Inc.
4901 1st Avenue North
Birmingham, AL 35222
(205) 591–3503
Fax: (205) 591–1039

5719

Business Information: Johnson Parts & Service, Inc. is a provider of parts and services for commercial cooking equipment and refrigeration. Serving under contract with manufacturers, Johnson Parts & Service, Inc. provides parts and services to owners (i.e. restaurants, schools, hotels, caterers, etc.) of commercial cooking equipment (i.e. ovens, fryers, stoves, coolers, freezers, HVAC, etc.). Founding Johnson Parts & Service, Inc. in 1981 when he was seventeen years old, Mr. Johnson serves as Owner and President. He is responsible for ensuring customer satisfaction within the service and parts departments. He also works on picking up new lines with manufacturers. **Career Steps:** Owner, Johnson Parts & Service, Inc. (1981–Present). **Associations & Accomplishments:** Commercial Food Equipment Service Association (CFESA); Master Gas Fitters; Master Plumber. **Personal:** Married to Tammy in 1988. Two children: Derek and Jonathan. Mr. Johnson enjoys scuba diving, fishing, boating, and golf.

James G. Quinn

Treasurer
IKEA
496 West Germantown Pike
Plymouth Meeting, PA 19462
(610) 834–0180 Ext. 5230
Fax: Please mail or call

5719

Business Information: Established in 1985, IKEA is the largest home furnishings retailer in the world. Based in Sweden and headquartered in Pennsylvania, the Company maintains 14 outlets in the United States. As Treasurer, Mr. Quinn is responsible for financial management, bank relations, and short and long term investments. **Career Steps:** IKEA: Treasurer (1993–Present), Financial Reporting Manager (1989–1993); Controller, Waste Management (1987–1989). **Associations & Accomplishments:** Treasury Management Association. **Education:** Villanova University, M.B.A. (1993); Drexel University, M.S. in Accounting. **Personal:** Married to Danielle in 1990. One child: Kevin.

Donald Ray Stewart

Comptroller
Big Sandy Furniture, Inc.
8375 Gallia Pike
Franklin Furnace, OH 45629
(614) 574–2113 Ext. 228
Fax: (614) 574–1078

5719

Business Information: Big Sandy Furniture, Inc. is one of the top 100 retailers of furniture and appliances in the United States. The Company owns seven main stores and three affiliates. As Comptroller, Mr. Stewart is responsible for all finances, controlling expenses, and overseeing all information systems. **Career Steps:** Comptroller, Big Sandy Furniture, Inc. (1990–Present); Manager, Family–Owned Grocery Store (1977–1990). Education: University of Kentucky, B.B.A. (1977)."

Stuart Teller
President
Madco
120 Royall St.
Canton, MA 02021–1028
(617) 828–8310
Fax: (617) 828–1533

5719

Business Information: Madco is a sales and manufacture representative organization in the gift and home furnishings industry. Gift products are distributed throughout New England and New York, as well as distributing books to the Carolinas (primarily college book store gifts). As President, Mr. Teller is responsible for all aspects of operations, including administration, finances, strategic planning, in addition to directing a staff of 43 sales representatives, two sales managers, and eight support staff. **Career Steps:** Madco, Inc.: President (1995–Present), General Manager (1983–1995); Buyer, Kings/Barkers (1978–1983). **Associations & Accomplishments:** Club 35; National Association of 35 of the largest gift/home furnishings representatives in the country; Regional Coordinator, Gift for Life. **Education:** Western Connecticut University. **Personal:** Married to Luanne in 1977. Two children: Joshua and Jacqueline. Mr. Teller enjoys golf.

Kent A. McCaughey
Vice–President
Joe McCaughey's Appliance
9340 West 87th Terrace
Shawnee Mission, KS 66212–3703
(913) 381–5656
Fax: (066) 212–3703

5722

Business Information: Joe McCaughey's Appliance is a retail and wholesale distributor of appliances established in 1943 by the McCaughey Family and passed down from father to son in 1958. As Vice–President, Mr. McCaughey is responsible for all administrative activities, sales, advertising, promotions, logistics, marketing, and business management. **Career Steps:** Vice–President, Joe McCaughey's Appliance (1981–Present). **Associations & Accomplishments:** Young Entrepreneurs of America; Board of Directors, Lions Club International; President, Breakfast at Eight Business Club; Kansas City Chamber of Commerce. **Education:** Kansas City–Kansas Community College (1982) **Personal:** Married to Teressa in 1982. Two children: Brooke and Nicole. Mr. McCaughey enjoys sports.

Robert E. White
MIS Director
Royce, Inc.
6565 Coffman Road
Indianapolis, IN 46268
(317) 290–3580
Fax: (317) 290–3585
EMAIL: See Below

5722

Business Information: Royce, Inc. specializes in rent–to–own electronics, appliances, and furniture; Buy here, pay here car lots; and financial loan offices. As MIS Director, Mr. White is responsible for the supervision of all computer operations Corporation–wide. Internet users can reach him via: 102671,3373@Compuserve.com. **Career Steps:** MIS Director, Royce, Inc. (1994–Present); Computer Supervisor, Best Buy, Inc. (1993–1994); Service Administrator, CCS Computers, Inc. (1992–1993); System Administrator, Student Care Services, Inc. (1989–1992) **Education:** Ivy Tech, Netware (1995); ITT Technical Institute, Associate's Degree in Electronics (1979); Certified Novell Administrator (1995) **Personal:** Married to Judith in 1995. Six children: Nathaniel, Cora, Bobby, James, Lana and Brandon. Mr. White enjoys programming in Clarion.

Ms. Sameer Aboabdo
President
Anaba USA Incorporated
1900 West Artesia Boulevard
Compton, CA 90220–5310
(310) 223–0400
Fax: Please mail or call

5731

Business Information: Anaba USA Incorporated is engaged in the retail sale of household audio, video, and mobile electronic equipment. Products include televisions, radios, video cassette recorders, cellular telephones, in addition to many other items. Starting as a small company, Anaba USA has grown more than 37% since it was established. Company goals for the future include striving to remain constant in their level of growth and expansion. As President, Mr. Aboabdo owns 34% of Anaba USA and has been with the Company and serving in his present position for five years. Duties and responsibilities include overseeing all general administration, supervising daily activities, approving buyers' selections, and presiding over employee training and sales transactions. Concurrently, Mr. Aboabdo serves as Chief Financial Officer, authorizing all financial transactions and supervising all accounting functions. He attributes his success to being straight forward with suppliers, as well as with customers. Mr. Aboabdo also maintains a close relationship with customers. **Career Steps:** President, Anaba USA Incorporated (19–Present) **Associations & Accomplishments:** Published in Car Electronics Magazine **Personal:** Mr. Aboabdo enjoys raquetball and volleyball.

Robert C. Caras
President/Chief Executive Officer
Multi–Systems
1804 Clovermeadow Drive
Vienna, VA 22182
(703) 255–3030
Fax: (703) 255–6060
EMAIL: See Below

5731

Business Information: Multi–Systems designs and installs custom residential media systems. Multi–Systems was established in 1989 and services the Northern Virginia area. As President/Chief Executive Officer, Mr. Caras manages the overall operation of Multi–Systems, to include marketing, selling, financial administration, personnel management, and strategic planning. The long term plans are for Multi–Systems to expand into related fields. Internet users can reach him via: Multi@nicom.com. **Career Steps:** President/Chief Executive Officer, Multi–Systems (1989–Present); President, S.H. Berman, Inc. (1976–1989). **Associations & Accomplishments:** Custom Electronics Design and Installation Association; Kentucky Colonel, for service to a non–profit organization. **Education:** The Citadel, Business Administration (1975). **Personal:** Married to Marie in 1980. Two children: Chris and Allison. Mr. Caras enjoys golf.

Terry Casey
General Manager
Best Buy
1949 East Camelback Road
Phoenix, AZ 85016–4140
(602) 266–3400 Ext: 2020
Fax: (602) 266–9433

5731

Business Information: Best Buy is a major retail electronics chain. Recruited from Circuit City, Terry Casey joined Best Buy as General Manager of the Phoenix branch in 1993. He provides the overall day–to–day supervision for operations and personnel. **Career Steps:** General Manager, Best Buy (1993–Present); Circuit City: Operations Manager (1990–1993), Distribution Manager (1987–1990). **Education:** North Virginia Community College (1974); Dale Carnegie; Steven Covey. **Personal:** Married to Shirley in 1980. Mr. Casey enjoys boating and fishing.

Francis Chen

Managing Director
Industrial Tobishi, S.A.
Ave Petit Thouars 4467
Miraflores, Lima 18, Peru
51–1–440–6877
Fax: 51–1–435–6642
EMAIL: See Below

5731

Business Information: Industrial Tobishi, S.A. specializes in the purchasing and re–selling of home appliances including television and audio–video items. With locations in Lima and southern Peru, the Company plans to expand sales to the international market. As Managing Director, Mr. Chen supervises and controls purchasing, sales, and public relations, and is responsible for procuring high quality products for re–sale. Internet users can reach him via: fschen@amauta.rep.net.pe. **Career Steps:** Managing Director, Industrial Tobishi, S.A. (1994–Present); Managing Director, Neon S.A. (1988–1990); Managing Director, Nisan S.R.L. (1987–1988). **Associations & Accomplishments:** Sociedad Nacional de Industras, Peru; Asociacion Country Club "La Planicie". **Education:** University of Miami, B.B.A. (1993). **Personal:** Married to Sophia in 1994. Mr. Chen enjoys golf and baseball.

Mr. Leonard H. Roberts
President
Radio Shack
1800 One Tandy Center
Ft. Worth, TX 76102
(817) 390–3231
Fax: (817) 390–2647

5731

Business Information: Radio Shack is a retailer of consumer electronics with more than 7,000 stores located throughout the U.S., South America, Canada, Russia, Australia, and Mexico. Products range from computers, televisions, telephones, stereos, to auto and home alarm systems, specialty radio equipment (short wave and scanning), and electronic components. As President, Mr. Roberts oversees operations for all Radio Shack stores worldwide. Established in 1921, Radio Shack employs 25,000 people with annual sales of $3 billion. **Career Steps:** President, Radio Shack (1993–Present); Chairman and CEO, Shoney's Inc. (1990–1993); President and CEO, Arby's Inc. (1985–1990); Managing Director, Ralston Purina Co. Inc. (1974–1985). **Associations & Accomplishments:** United Way of Metropolitan Tarrant County; National Crime Prevention Council; Big Brothers/Big Sisters of America; Clark Atlanta University; Belmont University; Students in Free Enterprise, Inc. **Education:** DePaul University of Law, J.D. (1974); University of Illinois, B.S. (1971). **Personal:** Married to Laurie in 1967. Three children: Dawn, Dina and Melissa.

Mr. John Adams, Ph.D.
Vice President/Technical Director – Network Integration Software
Digital Equipment Corporation
550 King Street
Littleton, MA 01460
(508) 486–7990
Fax: (508) 486–7417

5734

Business Information: Digital Equipment Corporation, the third largest computer company in the world and the leader in mainframe networked systems technology, provides a full line of computer hardware, software and services. With corporate headquarters in Maynard, Massachusetts, Digital currently employs 62,000 people worldwide. Established 35 years ago, Digital reports annual revenue of $14 billion. In his current capacity as Vice President and Technical Director of Network Integration Software, Dr. Adams oversees all aspects of operations for technical strategy and execution of integration software. An executive staff member and systems engineer with Digital Equipment since 1986, he was one of the integral designers in the creation of EtherNet — today's standard for local area networks (LAN). **Career Steps:** Digital Equipment Corporation: Vice President/Technical Director of Network Integration Software (1995–Present), Vice President of Network Operating Systems (1994–1995), Vice President of Open Network Software (1991–1993), Group Manager of Local Area Networks (1986–1990). **Associations & Accomplishments:** Sigma Xi; Chairman, Lincoln Massachusetts Recreation Committee; Published in Digital Publications. **Education:** Massachusetts Institute of Technology, Ph.D. (1972); Tufts University, M.S., B.S.; Harvard University, A.B. **Personal:** Married to Patricia in 1967. Two children: Sam and Darcy. Dr. Adams enjoys cycling, skiing and golf.

Trisha L. Christeson–Bach
Marketing Director
Gateway 2000, Inc.
810 Fulton Street
Rapid City, SD 57701
(605) 342–0935
Fax: (605) 342–7842
EMail: See Below

5734

Business Information: Gateway 2000, Inc. is a computer re-seller and A+ service center. Additionally, the Company has implemented a complete training facility to educate consumers on the various ways the computers can be utilized. As Marketing Director, Ms. Christeson–Bach handles all marketing, public relations, and promotions. She is also Director of Education, responsible for training and teaching courses about the network. Internet users can reach her via: regal@regalcomputer.com. **Career Steps:** Marketing Director, Gateway 2000, Inc. (1995–Present); Marketing Support Director, Grain Systems, Inc. (1993–1995); Retail Marketing Director, Comp USA, Inc. (1991–1993). **Associations & Accomplishments:** Women's Networking Group; Chamber of Commerce; Women Against Violence; Big Brother & Big Sisters; Volunteer, Storybook Island for Rotary Club. **Education:** University of South Dakota; University of Colorado – Boulder, worked toward Master's degree in Marketing and Public Relations; Morningside College, Bachelor's degree (1990). **Per-**

sonal: Married to Jeffrey M. in 19974. Ms. Christeson–Bach enjoys golf, travel, crafting, outdoor activities, and desktop publishing.

Michael A. Gauvin
Vice President, Sales
Breault Research Organization
6400 East Grant Road, Suite 350
Tucson, AZ 85715–3862
(520) 721–0500
Fax: (520) 721–9630

5734

Business Information: Breault Research Organization provides design, implementation, consultation and sales of optical and illumination software and hardware. Joining Breault in 1983 as manager of computer operations, Mr. Gauvin was appointed Vice President of Sales in 1993. He has full executive charge for all sales strategies and related sales support personnel Company–wide. **Career Steps:** Breault Research Organization: Vice President, Sales (1993–Present), National Sales Manager (1992–1993), Senior Systems Analyst (1986–1992), Computer Operations Manager (1983–1986). **Associations & Accomplishments:** Illumination Engineering Society. **Education:** University of Arizona, B.S. (1982). **Personal:** Married to Janet in 1982. Two children: Danielle and Jeffrey. Mr. Gauvin enjoys golf, soccer, and computers.

Rene W. Melchers

President/Owner
Micro Market, Inc.
7712 Kent Boulevard
Brockville, Ontario
(613) 342–2307
Fax: (613) 342–2321
E MAIL: See Below

5734

Business Information: Micro Market, Inc., established in 1987, is a regional computer retailer. The Corporation offers personal training to customers and service on its product. Micro Market, Inc. currently employs 16 people. As President/Owner, Mr. Melchers manages all aspects of company operations, concentrating on sales, marketing, and staff training and development. Other responsibilities include consulting for clients and directing on–site training for larger clients. Internet users may contact him via: rene@recorder.ca. **Career Steps:** President/Owner, Micro Market, Inc. (1987–Present); Computer Trainer, St. Lawrence College (1986–1987); Computer Trainer, MTS (1985–1986); Systems Support, J.R. Business Equipment, Ltd. (1982–1985). **Associations & Accomplishments:** Rotary International; Ontario Society Training and Development; Local Training Adjustment Board. **Education:** St. Lawrence College: Computer Program (1982), Historical Restoration Technician (1980). **Personal:** Married to Patti Broad–Merchers in 1982. Three children: Charles, Andrew, and Phillip. Mr. Melchers enjoys tennis, squash, camping, and coaching junior baseball.

Miguel E. Planas Velez

President and Owner
Acoss, Inc.
P.O. Box 6299
Ponce, Puerto Rico 00733–6299
(787) 848–3777
Fax: (787) 848–3799

5734

Business Information: Acoss, Inc. is a retailer and servicer of computers and associated equipment from showrooms and offices in Puerto Rico, providing consulting services, networks, assembly, and maintenance contracts. The fastest growing computer company in South Puerto Rico, Acoss, Inc. conducts international business, primarily in the U.S. and with Fortune 500 companies located in Puerto Rico, as well as the local government, and manufacturing companies. Future plans include expanding into more international businesses, especially in Central America. As President and Owner, Mr. Planas Velez is responsible for all aspects of operations, including administration, management, finances, public relations, marketing, and strategic planning. **Career Steps:** President and Owner, Acoss, Inc. (1994–Present); Manager, Centizo Caroiolugza del Sur (1992–1994); Accounting Officer, Perez Hermanos, Inc. (1991–1992). **Associations & Accomplishments:** National Mail Order Dealer's Association; U.S. Chamber of Commerce; Ponce and South Puerto Rico Chamber of Commerce. **Education:** LaGuardia Community College, A.A.S. (1980). **Personal:** Married to Naomi in 1993.

Two children: Miguel and Yamil. Mr. Planas Velez enjoys water sports and travel.

Charles Sharp
President
Digital Image Technology
3 Thomas Rice Drive
Westborough, MA 01581
(508) 836–4521
Fax: (508) 366–1775
EMAIL: See Below

5734

Business Information: Digital Image Technology is a marketer of high–end computer imaging systems and peripheral equipment. International in scope, Digital Image Technology conducts business in China, Italy, Germany, Argentina, and the United States. As President, Mr. Sharp is responsible for all aspects of operations, including Corporate management and sales, in addition to conducting public speaking at trade shows. Internet users can reach him via: CLSHARP100@AOL.COM. **Career Steps:** President, Digital Image Technology (1992–Present); President, Digital Graphics; Vice President, Sentinel Imaging; Director of OEM, Iris Graphics. **Associations & Accomplishments:** National Computer Graphics Association. **Education:** Boston University, M.B.A. (1985); Cornell University: Master's Degree in Engineering (1977), B.S. in Operations Research (1976). **Personal:** Married to Debra in 1977. Two children: Jessica and Gregory. Mr. Sharp enjoys reading and restoring antiques and classic sports cars.

S. K. Stephens, C.E.O.
Chief Executive Officer
Computer Applications Etc.
5630 Crowder Blvd
New Orleans, LA 70127
(504) 245–9913
Fax: (504) 245–9913

5734

Business Information: Computer Applications Etc. specializes in computer software and hardware sales and service. As Chief Executive Officer, Mrs. Stephens manages sales, oversees contracts, and provides training. Responsible for all phases of daily operations, she also handles all administrative duties, and manages human resource functions. **Career Steps:** Chief Executive Officer, Computer Applications Etc. (1995–Present); Director, NASA Regional Training Site (1995–Present); Member of Technical Staff, Bell Communications Research (1984–1993); Assistant Professor, Southern University at N.O. (1993–1995). **Associations & Accomplishments:** Who's Who Among American Teachers; National Technical Association; American Management Association; Who's Who in the Computer Industry; Pi Mu Epsilon; Alpha Kappa Alpha Sorority, Inc.; Society of Distinguished High School Students; Alpha Chi Scholarship Fraternity; Southern University President's Award. **Education:** Tulane University, M.H.A. (1996); Purdue University, Masters of Science in Computer Science; Southern University, Baton Rouge, Bachelor of Science in Compute Science, Cum Laude. **Personal:** Mrs. Stephens enjoys quilting, sewing, tennis, hiking, bowling, cross–stitch, and singing.

Steve Weaver
Director, Systems Development
Comp U.S.A.
14951 North Dallas Parkway
Dallas, TX 75240
(214) 982–4483
Fax: (214) 982–4869

5734

Business Information: Comp U.S.A. is an establishment primarily engaged in the retail and corporate sale of personal computers and related products. Headquartered in Dallas, Texas, the Company is national in scope, with 105 stores throughout the U.S. Established in 1985, the Company employs 10,000 people and has an estimated annual revenue of $4 billion. As Director, Systems Development, Mr. Weaver focuses on the infrastructure of the Company, providing tactical and strategic planning, enabling the Company to grow at a fast and innovative pace. **Career Steps:** Director Systems Development, Comp U.S.A. (1994–Present); Systems Manager, Chief Auto Parts (1992–1994); Distribution Systems Manager, Blockbuster Entertainment (1988–1992); Senior Consultant, Arthur Anderson & Company (1980–1985). **Associations & Accomplishments:** Texas A&M Corps Leadership Outreach; Past Member, Boy Scouts of America. **Education:** Texas A&M: M.B.A. (1980), B.S. in Industrial Distribution (1974). **Personal:** Married to Diana in 1990. Two children: Austin and Ben. Mr. Weaver enjoys hunting and reading.

Patrick M. Zapatka
District Manager
Electronics Boutique
3225 Southwest 325th Street
Federal Way, WA 98023
(206) 815–1850
Fax: (206) 815–0716
EMAIL: See Below

5734

Business Information: Electronics Boutique is a privately–owned company with over 500 stores worldwide. With Corporate Offices in Westchester, PA, the Company specializes in the retail sale of computer software, peripherals, accessories, and video game software, hardware, and accessories. As District Manager, Mr. Zapatka oversees the operations of stores in Washington, Oregon, and Western Canada. He is responsible for product knowledge, training, sales, and completions. Internet users can also reach him via: PZapatka@MSN.Com. **Career Steps:** District Manager, Electronics Boutique (1991–Present); Owner, Official Process Service (1987–1993); District Manager, Blockbuster Video (1987–1991). **Education:** University of Texas – El Paso, B.B.A. (1996). **Personal:** Married to Judy Beth in 1987. One child: Jaryd. Mr. Zapatka enjoys computers, reading, racquetball, boating, comic books, and action figures.

Marco Navarra
Head of Top 40 Music Promotions
Road Runner Records
536 Broadway
New York, NY 10012
(212) 274–7540
Fax: (212) 219–0301
EMail: See Below

5735

Business Information: Road Runner Records is a large, independently owned, international record company. The Company produces a large variety of music, including Heavy Metal, Top 40, Alternative, and R&B. As Head of Top 40 Music Promotions, Mr. Navarra promotes artists around the country by talking to DJs. Additionally, he is responsible for field promotions with the artists. Internet users can reach him via: NAVARRA@MAIL.ROADRUN.COM. **Career Steps:** Head of Top 40 Music Promotions, Road Runner Records (1995–Present); Director, Jive Records (1993–1995); Director, Next Plateau (1992–1993); Director, Atlantic Records (1990–1992). **Associations & Accomplishments:** NARAS. **Education:** U.S.F. **Personal:** Married to Lya in 1985.

5800 Eating and Drinking Places

5812 Eating places
5813 Drinking places

Rocky Aiyash
President and Chief Executive Officer
Pazzo Cucina Italiana
8725 West Higgins Road, Suite 850
Chicago, IL 60631
(708) 531–1112
Fax: (312) 714–0110

5812

Business Information: Kerry E., Inc. dba Pazzo Cucina Italiana is an upscale Italian restaurant. As President and Chief Executive Officer, Mr. Aiyash is responsible for the development of the Company, menu organization, marketing, design and decor, and all financial aspects of the Company. **Career Steps:** President and Chief Executive Officer, Pazzo Cucina Italiana (1993–Present); President and Chief Executive Officer, Arby's UK (1990–1993); Regional Director of Operations, Show Biz (1985–1990). **Associations & Accomplishments:** National Rifle Association; International Restaurant Association; National Pilots Association. **Education:** London Business School, M.B.A. (1993); Southern Illinois University, B.A. **Personal:** Married to Kerry in 1982. Three children: Matthew, Brittany, and Zachary. Mr. Aiyash enjoys hockey, basketball, and boating.

Mr. Robert C. Arbizzani
President
The Little Owl, Inc.
101 West State
Geneva, IL 60134
(708) 232–7994
Fax: Please mail or call

5812

Business Information: The Little Owl, Inc. is a unique restaurant and tavern, now celebrating its 75th anniversary. It is located in an historic 1850 building with the original tin ceilings. Daily specials and a diverse variety of American food are served. As President, Chief Executive Officer, General Manager, and Owner, Mr. Arbizzani oversees all aspects of the business including administration, operations, finance, sales, marketing and strategic planning. Established in 1920, The Little Owl, Inc. employs 20 people with annual sales of $750,000. **Career Steps:** President, The Little Owl, Inc. (1987–Present); Vice President, The Little Owl, Inc. (1972–1987); Sales, Proctor & Gamble (1968–1971). **Associations & Accomplishments:** Member, National Restaurant Association; Member, Illinois Restaurant Association; Member, Geneva Restaurant Association; Member, Geneva Zoning Board of Appeals. **Education:** Doane College, B.A. (1968). **Personal:** Married to Barbara in 1971. Two children: John and Chris. Mr. Arbizzani enjoys fishing, boating and golf.

Paula D. Ashley
Media Director
Long John Silvers Inc.
101 Jerrico Drive
Lexington, KY 40509–1809
(606) 263–6637
Fax: (606) 263–6716

5812

Business Information: Long John Silvers Inc. is one of the nation's leading fastfood seafood restaurant chains. Established in 1969, with Corporate headquarters located in Lexington, Kentucky, the Corporation reports annual revenue in excess of $900 million. An advertising executive with over ten years expertise, Ms. Ashley serves as Director of Media Services. In this capacity she is responsible for the overall Corporate administration of advertising functions, which includes the planning and execution of a $40 million budget and the supervision of Media Services support staff. **Career Steps:** Director of Media Services, Long John Silvers Inc. (1991–Present); Regional Marketing Director, Jerrico Inc. (1989–1991); Media Supervisor, Abbott Advertising (1987–1989). **Associations & Accomplishments:** Phi Kappa Phi; Board Member, Lexington Children's Theatre; Leader, Girl Scouts of America. **Education:** Eastern Kentucky University, B.A. in Public Relations (1981). **Personal:** One child: Erica Nicole. Ms. Ashley enjoys tennis, piano, travel and working with Children's Theatre productions.

Mr. David K. Bang
President
SunAM Corporation
4100 West Pico Boulevard
Los Angeles, CA 90019
(213) 734–6800
Fax: (213) 734–6155

5812

Business Information: SunAM Corporation is the management operations for a seafood restaurant/fish market chain – Pico Seafood (three locations throughout Los Angeles, CA). Established in 1988, the SunAM Corporation presently employs 28 people and has an estimated annual revenue in excess of $2 million. As President/Founder, Mr. Bang oversees all aspects of daily Corporate operations. **Career Steps:** President, SunAM Corporation (1988–Present); Vice President, Pacific Sons, Inc. (1986–1988); Purchasing Manager, Grocey Warehouse (1982–1986). **Associations & Accomplishments:** Chair, Community Redevelopment Agency; Member, Community Policing Agency – Wilshire Division; Chair, YMCA; Featured in the Los Angeles Times; Acknowledged by City Hall for helping the homeless. **Education:** Cal–State at Los Angeles (1982); Mt. San Antonio College, A.A. **Personal:** Married to Ranah Yoon in 1986. Two children: Rosemary and Heidi. Mr. Bang enjoys hiking and photography.

Rod Barham
Chief Financial Officer
Hot Dog On A Stick, Inc.
777 South Pacific Coast Highway
Solana Beach, CA 92075
(619) 755–3049
Fax: (619) 674–4666
EMAIL: rjbarham@aol.com

5812

Business Information: Hot Dogs On A Stick, Inc. was established in 1946 and has 100 locations in shopping malls throughout the United States, with approximately 1,000 employees. The Corporation is a fast food chain selling hot dogs. As Chief Financial Officer, Mr. Barham handles all financial aspects of the Corporation. He is responsible for accounts payable, accounts receivable, financial planning, budgets, and cash management. Mr. Barham is a member of the Board of Directors in charge of international franchising. **Career Steps:** Chief Financial Officer/Director, Hot Dog On A Stick, Inc. (1991–Present); Lieutenant Colonel, US Army (1987–1995); Controller, CompuCable (1985–1987). **Associations & Accomplishments:** National Eagle Scout Association; National Guard Association of California; Delta Chi Fraternity. **Education:** National University, MBA; University of Georgia, BBA and AA. **Personal:** Married to Jeannie in 1979. Two children: Sean and Eileen. Mr. Barham enjoys miniature wargames, the Boy Scouts, and the Army National Guard.

John Enix Batts
Director of MIS
Turf Catering Company
P.O. Box 4244, 4201 Versailles
Lexington, KY 40544–4244
(606) 253–0541
Fax: (606) 281–6452
EMAIL: See Below

5812

Business Information: Turf Catering Company is the catering firm which services the Keeneland Race Course in Lexington, Kentucky and the Oaklawn Jockey Club in Hot Springs, Arkansas. The Company has approximately 500 seasonal employees and caters to around 20,000 race fans daily. As Director of Management Information Services, Mr. Batts handles all computer related services. He is also responsible for financial decisions, accounts receivable, approval of computer purchasing requests, and all technical projects for the Company. Mr. Batts is involved in the planning of computer projects to be accepted by Turf Catering Company. Internet users can reach him via: JohnBatts@aol.com. **Career Steps:** Tuft Catering Company: Director, Management Information Services, (1995–Present); Accounts Receivable Clerk (1992–1995); Kentucky Revenue Cabinet: Programmer/Analyst Senior (1994–1995), Programmer/Analyst (1993–1994). **Associations & Accomplishments:** Board Member, Woodford County Chapter, American Red Cross; General Board Member and Deacon, Midway Christian Church; Past Co–President, Association of Computer Machinery, Transylvania University. **Education:** Transylvania University, B.A. (1992). **Personal:** Married to Cynthia in 1994. Mr. Batts enjoys origami, community theater, and studying Ancient Egypt.

Margie Beckerman
Co–Owner
Tony Bonos Restaurant & Bar
2024 Mid Rivers Mall Drive
St. Peters, MO 63376
(314) 397–8001
Fax: (314) 278–8238

5812

Business Information: Tony Bonos Restaurant is a family–owned restaurant and bar, focusing on Italian food, but including seafood and Mexican food. The business is run by Ms. Beckerman, her brother (who started the restaurant), and partner, Doug LeClair. With two locations in Missouri (St. Peters and Bridgeton), Tony Bonos Restaurant serves as host for parties and banquets, providing space for 50 people. Established in 1992, Tony Bonos Restaurant reports annual revenue of $1.2 million and currently employs 130 people. As Owner, Ms. Beckerman is responsible for all aspects of operations, including serving as general manager and bookkeeper. Additional responsibilities include, accounts payable, accounts receivable, employee payroll, computer programming, advisor, and food & liquor costs. **Career Steps:** Owner, Tony Bonos Restaurant (1992–Present); Customer Service Agent, Trans–World Express (1988–1992); General Manager, Payroll Manager, and Bookkeeper, Calico's Restaurants (1973–1990); Tour Guide for St. Louis, Destination St. Louis (1990–1991). **Associations & Accomplishments:** St. Peters Chamber of Commerce. **Education:** Mercy High School (1963); St. Louis University; TWA Travel Academy. **Personal:** Two children: Denny and Scott. Ms. Beckerman enjoys cooking, travel, movies, walking, and gardening.

Rosemarie Broussard, R.D.
Human Resources Director
Whitsons Corporation
379 Oakwood Road
Huntington Station, NY 11746
(516) 424–2700 Ext.206
Fax: (516) 424–2745

5812

Business Information: Whitsons Corporation is one of the top twenty–five growing companies on Long Island. A family–owned business, the Company specializes in food service

contract management, and services over sixty businesses and industries including, schools, colleges, restaurants, and health care facilities. The Company also caters special programs and seasonal events and employs 525 people. As Human Resources Director, Ms. Broussard is responsible for all aspects of personnel management including recruitment, training, employee reviews and benefits, and establishing policies and procedures. She also oversees adherence to union rules and handles disciplinary policies and procedures. A registered dietician, Ms. Broussard has been in the food service industry for twenty years. **Career Steps:** Human Resources Director, Whitsons Corporation (1996–Present); Aramark: Human Resources Manager (1994–1996), Director of Nutrition Services (1985–1994), Assistant Director (1976–1985). **Associations & Accomplishments:** American Dietetic Association; Society for Human Resource Management; LI Center for Business Professionals; Phi Epsilon Omicron. **Education:** Queens College, B.A. (1975). **Personal:** Two children: Rhys and Douglas. Ms. Broussard enjoys running, exercising, and spending time with her kids.

Charles R. Bruce
••• ◄══◉══► •••
Vice President of International Marketing
Wendy's International, Inc.
4288 West Dublin Granville Road
Dublin, OH 43017–1442
(614) 764–3067
Fax: (614) 764–3026
EMAIL: See Below

5812

Business Information: Wendy's International, Inc., the world's third largest hamburger restaurant chain, is the franchise headquarters for the Wendy's quick service food chain, started by Dave Thomas in 1969. With twenty years of experience in marketing, Mr. Bruce joined Wendy's International, Inc. as Vice President of International Marketing in 1994. His primary focus is to build Wendy's into a global brand through international marketing efforts. With his extensive international background, fluency in Spanish, and cross–cultural experiences, he is very comfortable working with people from different countries and cultures which has made him successful in his endeavors. Internet users may reach him via: 73041.11@compuserve.com **Career Steps:** Vice President of International Marketing, Wendy's International, Inc. (1994–Present); Vice President of Marketing, International Pizza Hut Franchise Holders Association, Inc. (1986–1994); International Marketing Manager, The Coleman Co., Inc. (1978–1986). **Education:** Kansas State University, B.A. (1973); Universidad Ibero–Americana – Mexico City, Summer Program; Wichita State University, M.B.A. Program. **Personal:** Married to Kay F. in 1979. One child: Kristen M. Mr. Bruce enjoys international travel (70+ countries), reading, watching football, and sailing.

Vanessa A. Cancel
Senior Operations Manager
Interfood Corporation
1492 Ave. Ponce de Leon Centro Europa
Guaynabo, Puerto Rico 00966
(809) 722–3195 (809) 725–8667
Fax: (809) 721–7314

5812

Business Information: Interfood Corporation, a subsidiary of Interlink Group, is the owner and operator of two casual theme restaurants in the Guaynabo, Puerto Rico area. As Senior Operations Manager, Ms. Cancel is the manager of managers, responsible for the daily oversight of operations, including management, hiring, training, hourly training, promotions, ordering, purchasing, marketing, and store openings. **Career Steps:** Interfood Corporation: Senior Operations Manager (1995–Present), General Manager (1994–1995), Assistant Manager (1992–1993); Director of Membership Services, Puerto Rico Hotel & Tourism Association (1991–1992). **Associations & Accomplishments:** Puerto Rico Hotel & Tourism Association; Certified Trainer; Pizzeria Uno Corporation; Recipient of leadership awards, such as "Best New Store of the Year." **Education:** Marquette University, B.S., with Minor in Sociology (1991). **Personal:** Ms. Cancel enjoys wine tasting, creative cuisine, kayaking, and travel.

Ms. Peggy T. Cherng
Vice Chairman
Panda Management Company
899 El Centro Street
South Pasadena, CA 91030
(818) 799–9898
Fax: (818) 403–8600

5812

Business Information: Panda Management Company manages a chain of Chinese fast food and fine dining restaurants. The Company has 160 restaurants located in 20 states. The

full–service fine dining restaurants feature 100 selections cooked–to–order, and the fast food restaurants offer 16 selections in a cafeteria style setting. As Vice Chairman, Ms. Cherng administers the strategic planning and departmental goalsetting process, and develops and implements the tactical plan in support of Company strategy. Established in 1973, Panda Management Company employs over 2,700 people and reports annual revenue in excess of $100 million. **Career Steps:** Vice Chairman, Panda Management Company (1993–Present); Various Positions, Panda Management Company (1982–1993); Project Manager, Actron/3M (1979–1982); Engineer, McDonnell Douglas (1977–1979). **Associations & Accomplishments:** Member, The Executive Committee; Member, American Compensation Association; School Board Member, Westridge School of Girls. **Education:** University of Missouri, Ph.D. in Electrical Engineering (1974); University of Missouri, M.S. in Computer Science (1971); Oregon State University, B.S. Applied Mathematics (1970).

Mr. Timothy J. Corbett
Director of Hardware Development
Hospitality Systems, Inc.
6401 Congress Avenue, Suite 175
Boca Raton, FL 33487
(407) 241–9998
Fax: (407) 241–2312

5812

Business Information: Hospitality Systems, Inc. is a point–of–sale systems company for restaurants and hotels, providing them with Windows–based POS systems nationwide. Established in 1992, the Company currently employs more than 30 people. As Director of Hardware Development, Mr. Corbett is responsible for the overall administration and oversight of new projects, entailing the testing and evaluation of new hardware platforms and subsystems; as well as oversees manufacturing operations. He is currently researching a new "touch screen" technology and is busy keeping the Corporation current and up–to–date on computer technology. **Career Steps:** Director of Hardware Development, Hospitality Systems, Inc. (1992–Present); Computer Technician, Carnival Cruise Lines (1989–1992). **Associations & Accomplishments:** Novell Certified Network Engineer (CNE); Licensed private pilot. **Education:** Devry Institute, A.S. in Electronic Engineering (1979). **Personal:** Married to Kathy Corbett in 1982. One child: Stacey Lynn Corbett. Mr. Corbett enjoys designing and building small computer interfaces and piloting aircraft.

Gloria J. Daniels
Senior Buyer
Krystal Company
1 Union Square
Chattanooga, TN 37402
(423) 757–1541
Fax: Please mail or call

5812

Business Information: Krystal Company is a fast–food operation with over 350 units in the Southeast. As Senior Buyer, Ms. Daniels is responsible for the administration of distribution programs, is a commodity buyer for paper goods and dry grocery items, prices over 250 line items monthly, and tends to the administrative lease car program. **Career Steps:** Senior Buyer, Krystal Company (1972–Present); Assistant to Credit Manager, Brock Candy Company (1968–72). **Education:** Chattanooga State. **Personal:** Married to William in 1990. One child: Gina. Two granddaughters: Jessica and Danielle. Ms. Daniels enjoys physical fitness and being active in Grace Episcopal Church.

Kathy J. Dreiling
Co–Owner and President
Picnic Basket Catering Company
1701 A. South Eight Street
Colorado Springs, CO 80906
(719) 635–0200
Fax: (719) 635–4653

5812

Business Information: Picnic Basket Catering Company, a subsidiary of Soup To Nuts, Inc., is an off–site corporate and social catering company, providing everything from box lunches to elegant dinners. The Company's highlights include catering a dinner for President Clinton and his staff at the local Air Force Academy. Services include catering food, flowers, rentals, and theme–oriented dinners. Co–Founding Picnic Basket Catering Company with her partner, Michelle R. Talarico in 1989, Ms. Dreiling serves as its President and Co–Owner, responsible for the direction of all administration, finances, and marketing. Concurrent with her position at the Company, she serves as Co–Founder and Co–Owner of the parent company, Soup To Nuts, Inc. and a subsidiary, A Trattoria, an Italian Southern California–style deli. **Career Steps:** Co–Owner and President, Picnic Basket Catering Company (1989–Present); Media Buyer, Graham Advertising (1988–1989).

Associations & Accomplishments: Colorado Springs, Small Business Persons (1995); Chamber of Commerce. **Education:** Ft. Hays State University, B.A. in Communications (1980). **Personal:** Ms. Dreiling enjoys the outdoors and music.

Cyndi P. Duncan
District Manager
Rusty's Pizza Parlors, Inc.
6673 Ming Avenue
Bakersfield, CA 93309–3491
(805) 835–5595
Fax: Please mail or call

5812

Business Information: Rusty's Pizza Parlors, Inc. is a pizza restaurant chain, consisting of seven restaurants located in California. Established in 1969, Rusty's Pizza Parlors, Inc. currently employs more than 120 people company–wide. With eleven years expertise in the restaurant industry, Ms. Duncan joined Rusty's Pizza Parlors, Inc. in 1987. She currently serves as District Manager, responsible for all aspects of operations within her district, including ensuring customer and employee satisfaction. **Career Steps:** District Manager, Rusty's Pizza Parlors, Inc. (1987–Present); Chef, Joh–Bert's Restaurant (1986–1987); Restaurant Manager, Bakers Square Restaurants (1984–1986). **Associations & Accomplishments:** N.A.F.E.; Harley Owners Group; Musician. **Education:** California Lutheran University, Bachelor's Degree (1984). **Personal:** Ms. Duncan enjoys riding motorcycles and playing the drums.

Stephanie L. Ennis
Human Resource Manager
American Restaurant Group
450 Newport Center Drive, Fl 6
Newport Beach, CA 92660–7610
(714) 721–8069 Ext 296
Fax: (714) 589–8490

5812

Business Information: American Restaurant Group is the parent holding company for a chain of restaurants such as Spoons, National Sports Grill, and spectrum Foods, Inc. Established in 1987 and headquartered in Redding, CA, the Company has over 3,500 employees nationwide. As Human Resource Manager, Ms. Ennis is responsible for all aspects of human resource activities, including recruiting, retention, salary administration, benefits management, employee relations, and safety. Other responsibilities include training and development, risk management, and employee law compliance. **Career Steps:** Human Resource Manager, American Restaurant Group (1995–Present); Human Resource Manager, Family Restaurants, Inc. (1994–1995); Human Resources Generalist, Restaurant Enterprises Group (1992–1995); Marketing Associate, John W. Henry Futures (1989–1991). **Associations & Accomplishments:** American Society of Training and Development; Newport Beach Sister City Association; Newport Harbor Jaycees; Volunteer naturalist for Upper Newport Bay Ecological Reserve. **Education:** University of Houston, B.B.A. (1984); Society of Human resources, Certified Human Resources Professional; National Futures Association, Series three license. **Personal:** Married to Billie in 1989. Ms. Ennis enjoys being a volunteer naturalist, crafts, travel, and reading.

Jerald A. Finch
Director of Food Services
Aramark
P.O. Box 4175
Durant, OK 74701
(405) 924–0121
Fax: (405) 924–7313

5812

Business Information: Aramark provides food, maintenance, grounds, and housekeeping services to university and college campuses across the United States. Mr. Finch has served in various capacities with Aramark, most recently promoted to Director of Food Services at Southeastern Oklahoma State University. He is responsible for supervising all campus services and personnel management. **Career Steps:** Aramark: Director of Food Services – Southeastern Oklahoma State University (1992–Present), Catering Director – San Antonio (1990–1992), Food Services Director – Sacramento (1986–1990), Operations Manager – San Antonio (1984–1986). **Associations & Accomplishments:** Southeastern Oklahoma State University Alumni Association; Oklahoma State University Alumni Association; Delta Upsilon Fraternity. **Education:** Southeastern Oklahoma State University, M.A.S. (1995); Oregon State, B.S. **Personal:** Married to Susan E. in 1983. Two children: Jacob and Hannah. Mr. Finch enjoys family, church, and anything outdoors.

Mr. David I. Goldfarb
Vice President
Maramont Corporation
5600 First Avenue, Building C
Brooklyn, NY 11220
(718) 439–3900
Fax: (718) 492–2985

5812

Business Information: Maramont Corporation is a national food commissary operation, providing packaged meals to schools, hospitals, penitentiary facilities, airlines, and industrial companies. In his current capacity, Mr. Goldfarb is responsible for management of purchasing operations for the Company. He also serves as Corporate General Counsel. Established in 1980, Maramont Corporation currently employs over 800 persons and reports estimated annual revenue in excess of $100 million. **Career Steps:** Vice President, Maramont Corporation (1983–Present); Attorney, Pomerantz, Levy (1981–1983). **Associations & Accomplishments:** American Bar Association; New York State Bar Association; American School Food Service Association; New York School Food Service Association. **Education:** Cardobo School of Law, J.D. (1980). **Personal:** Married to Joyce in 1981. They have seven children.

Frank Gruber
Assistant Vice President
Wood Company
6081 Hamilton Boulevard
Allentown, PA 18106–9687
(610) 706–3824
Fax: Please mail or call

5812

Business Information: Wood Company is a food and beverage hospitality distribution industry, servicing throughout 11 states in the northeastern U.S. Wood Company is divided in four sections: Housecare, Hospitality, Business Dining, Education. As Assistant Vice President, Frank Gruber oversees all operations for the divisions of Housecare and Hospitality, providing the overall management and supervision of 50 accounts, as well as the direction of key divisional management personnel. **Career Steps:** Assistant Vice President, Wood Company (1995–Present); Director, Bally's Parkplace Casino (1989–1995). **Associations & Accomplishments:** National Association of Catering Executives **Personal:** Married to Mai in 1993. One child: Christopher. Mr. Gruber enjoys outdoor activities, yardwork, and time with his son.

James T. Harrington

•••➤━●━◄•••

Vice President of Marketing
King's Country Shoppes, Inc.
1180 Long Run Road, Suite A
McKeesport, PA 15131–2033
(412) 751–0700
Fax: (412) 751–9008

5812

Business Information: King's Country Shoppes, Inc., well-known for its patented cinnamon ice cream, is a chain of twenty–nine family dining restaurants located throughout Western Pennsylvania. The Restaurant provides home-cooked meals at a low cost, serving over one million customers monthly. Mr. Harrington joined King's Country Shoppes, Inc. in 1969. Currently serving as Vice President of Marketing, he is responsible for all marketing activities, including advertising, promotions, restaurant openings, public relations, the Corporate Donations Program, and Corporate functions. **Career Steps:** King's Country Shoppes, Inc.: Vice President of Marketing (1995–Present), Director of Purchasing (1988–1995), District Manager (1984–1988), General Manager (1970–1984). **Associations & Accomplishments:** Marketing Executive Group NRA; West Pennsylvania Restaurant Association; Officer on Leukemia Society Board; Neighborhood Marketing Institute; National Restaurant Association. **Personal:** Married to JoAnn in 1975. One child: Valerie.

Jeffrey S. Harrison
Partner
Mason Harrison Jarrard, Ent.
1728 Lansdale Drive
Lewisville, TX 75028–2163
(214) 724–1916
Fax: (214) 724–0890
EMAIL: See Below

5812

Business Information: Mason Harrison Jarrard, Ent. is a franchisee of Sonic Drive–In fast–food restaurants whose theme takes it's customers back to the fifties when hamburgers and shakes were served to customers by car hops. Established in 1975, the national Company has an estimated annual revenue of over $100 million. As Owner of 7 drive–in restaurants and Partner of 15, Mr. Harrison oversees all development of the franchises in Dallas–Fort Worth, TX and Phoenix, AZ. **Career Steps:** Partner, Mason Harrison Jarrard, Ent. (1984–Present). **Associations & Accomplishments:** National Association of Sonic Franchises. **Education:** Attended: Oklahoma State University. **Personal:** Married to Maria C. Valle in 1994. Mr. Harrison enjoys snow skiing, reading, fishing, and spending time with his wife.

Angel Herrera
Vice President and Managing Director
PRI–PR/USVI (PepsiCo P.R., Inc.)
P.O. Box 11858
San Juan, Puerto Rico 00922–1858
(809) 277–7711
Fax: (809) 277–7780

5812

Business Information: PRI–PR/USVI (PepsiCo P.R., Inc.) provides customer services through a chain of 150 restaurants (i.e., Kentucky Fried Chicken, Taco Bell, and Pizza Hut) located throughout Puerto Rico (130) and the U.S. Virgin Islands (20). Established in 1969, PRI–PR/USVI reports annual revenue of $150 million and currently employs 5,000 company–wide. As Vice President and Managing Director, Mr. Herrera is responsible for the management and oversight of all three chains, including 150 restaurants. **Career Steps:** Vice President and Managing Director, PRI–PR/USVI (PepsiCo P.R., Inc.) (1995–Present); Kentucky Fried Chicken, PR/USVI: General Manager (1994–1995), Director of Operations (1994), Director of Marketing (1991–1994). **Associations & Accomplishments:** Sales and Marketing Executives (SME). **Education:** Bachelor in Science (Marketing and Finance); Boston College, School of Management; Interamerican University School of Law. **Personal:** Married to Lisa Casanova. Two children: Gabriel and Angel Enrique. Mr. Herrera enjoys golf and jogging.

Joseph J. Hollencamp
Senior Vice President
Summit Family Restaurants
440 Lawndale Drive
Salt Lake City, UT 84115
(801) 463–5641
Fax: (801) 463–5536

5812

Business Information: Summit Family Restaurants is a franchise management operations of Hometown Buffet restaurants. Established in 1991, the Corporation currently owns and manages 16 establishments within eight states and employs 1,300 people corporate–wide. With twenty–two years of expertise in the restaurant industry, Mr. Hollencamp joined Summit Family Restaurants in 1991. Serving as Senior Vice President, he directs operations of the Hometown Buffet Division, including purchasing, designing, real estate training, managing, construction, and operations. **Career Steps:** Senior Vice President, Summit Family Restaurants (1991–Present); Vice President of Operations, Southland Buffets, Inc. (1987–1990); District Manager, Showbiz Pizza Place (1981–1987); Management, Country Kitchen (1973–1981). **Associations & Accomplishments:** Interviewed for "Restaurant News" and local newspapers. **Education:** Attended: Showbiz College, OCB College, HTB College. **Personal:** Mr. Hollencamp enjoys hunting and carpentry.

Mrs. Beth Ann Horner, CPA
Owner
H & G Restaurant, Inc. & Beth A. Horner, CPA
8534 North Bend Road
Easton, MD 21601
(410) 820–5758
Fax: (410) 820–5758

5812

Business Information: H & G Restaurant, Inc. is a family–style restaurant serving homestyle cooking, and seating 125 people. The Restaurant has been featured many times on local television channel 13 WJZ. Beth A. Horner, CPA is a tax service and consulting firm. As Owner of H & G Restaurant, Inc., Mrs. Horner manages the restaurant, and handles all accounting and finance functions. Beth A. Horner, CPA is a sole–proprietorship with 85 clients – individuals, partnerships, and corporations. Established in 1947, H & G Restaurant, Inc. was purchased by Mrs. Horner and her husband in 1989, employs 44 people, and reports annual revenue of $1.5 million. Beth A. Horner, CPA was established in 1986. **Career Steps:** Owner, H & G Restaurant, Inc. (1989–Present); Owner, Beth A. Horner, CPA (1986–Present); Senior Accountant, Ellin & Tucker, Chartered (1985–1989). **Associations & Accomplishments:** American Institute of Certified Public Accountants;

Maryland Association of Certified Public Accountants (MACPA). **Education:** Mount Saint Mary's College, B.S. Accounting (1985).

Anne D. Huemme

Chief Financial Officer
Longhorn Steaks
8215 Roswell Road, Building 200
Atlanta, GA 30350
(770) 551–5445
Fax: (770) 551–6686

5812

Business Information: Longhorn Steaks is a chain of casual dining restaurants located throughout Georgia, Alabama, Tennessee, Florida, Kentucky, Ohio, North Carolina, and South Carolina. The Company, established in 1981, owns 71 locations with 6 more franchised, and employs approximately 3,000 people. The Company has annual sales in excess of $140 million. As Chief Financial Officer, Ms. Huemme manages all financial aspects for the Company, to include accounting, budgeting, payroll, and taxes. **Career Steps:** Chief Finance Officer, Longhorn Steaks (1995–Present); Pizza Hut: Director, Asset Development – Southern Division (1994–1995), Finance Director – Georgia Market (1991–1994); Vice President, Strategic Planning, Prudential Bache (1986–1990). **Education:** Fuqua School of Business, M.B.A. (1984); Duke University, B.A. (1983). **Personal:** Two children: Kyle and Grace. Ms. Huemme enjoys children, swimming, golf, jogging, and tennis.

Jeff Hunter

Director of Marketing
Captain D's Seafood
P.O. Box 1260
Nashville, TN 37202–1260
(615) 231–2324
Fax: (615) 231–2792

5812

Business Information: Captain D's Seafood is a national chain of dining establishments specializing in a variety of fried and broiled seafood. Established in 1969, the Company employs 25,000 people and has estimated annual revenue of $500 million. As Director of Marketing, Mr. Hunter is responsible for promoting expansion of the Company through marketing and advertising. His duties include overseeing promotions, public relations and marketing. **Career Steps:** Director of Marketing, Captain D's Seafood (1994–Present); Burgundy Group Advertising: Director of Operations (1991–1993), Management Supervisor (1990–1991); Production Manager, Bontin Advertising (1988–1990). **Associations & Accomplishments:** American Advertising Federation; IABC; National Restaurant Marketer's Association; Tennessee Performing Arts; Second Harvest Food Bank; Nashville Community Resource Center. **Education:** University of South America, B.S. in Marketing (1987). **Personal:** Married to Margo Boyd in 1992. Mr. Hunter enjoys golf, reading, and travel.

Jean M. Jenkins, CPP

Payroll Manager
Chi Chi's Mexican Restaurant
10200 Linn Station Road
Louisville, KY 40223–3841
(502) 426–3900
Fax: (502) 339–4373

5812

Business Information: Chi Chi's Mexican Restaurant specializes in serving fine foods and spirits in an ethnic atmosphere. Established in the early 1980's, Chi Chi's currently employs 31,000 people. As Payroll Manager, Ms. Jenkins is responsible for the supervision of staff and payroll for 311 restaurants country–wide. **Career Steps:** Chi Chi's Mexican Restaurant: Payroll Manager (1992–Present), Payroll Tax Analyst (1990–1992); Payroll Supervision, Grisanti's (1986–1990). **Associations & Accomplishments:** American Payroll Association. **Education:** Sullivan Junior College of Business, A.A. (1983). **Personal:** Married to David in 1986. Three children: Drew, Jamie and Wesley. Ms. Jenkins enjoys aerobics and Karate.

Rhonda K. Johannesen

Director of Food Service Operations
Allen & O'Hara, Inc.
3385 Airways Boulevard
Memphis, TN 38116–3841
(901) 345–7620 Ext. 328
Fax: (901) 946–2914

5812

Business Information: Allen & O'Hara, Inc. is a real estate, construction, and management services corporation for commercial properties and non–profit institutions. The Company owns and operates college residence halls and hotels, including food service facilities. As Director of Food Service Operations, Ms. Johannesen is responsible for managing operations in 13 states with 1000–plus employees and annual revenues exceeding $28 million. Established in 1952, Allen & O'Hara, Inc. employs 2,000 people with annual sales of $49.5 million. **Career Steps:** Allen & O'Hara, Inc.: Director of Food Service Operations (1996–Present), Corporate Marketing Director (1995–1996), Assistant Director of Food Service (1990–1995). **Associations & Accomplishments:** President of Memphis Chapter, National Board Member of Roundtable for Women in Food Service; Society for Technician Communication; National Restaurant Association; Certified Food Service Management Professionals. **Education:** University of Wisconsin–Stout, B.S. (1981). **Personal:** Married to Kevin Hagopian in 1986. Ms. Johannesen enjoys writing.

Scott R. Jones

Vice President of Research Development and Quality Control
El Pollo Loco Restaurants, Inc.
3355 Michelson, Suite 350
Irvine, CA 92715
(714) 251–5477
Fax: (714) 251–5180

5812

Business Information: El Pollo Loco Restaurants, Inc., a subsidiary of Flagstar, is a chicken and Mexican fast food chain offering dining–in, take–out and drive–thru services. International in scope, El Pollo Loco has 250 locations in the Western U.S., Mexico, Philippines, and Singapore. Established in 1980, El Pollo Loco reports annual revenue of $200 million and currently employs 1,500 people corporate–wide. With over 25 years experience in the restaurant management and development industry, Mr. Jones joined El Pollo Loco Restaurants, Inc. in 1993. Currently serving as Vice President of Research Development and Quality Control and as a senior management team member, he is responsible for research and development of products and equipment prototype technology, overseeing quality control and contributing to the design and implementation of marketing strategies. **Career Steps:** Vice President of Research Development and Quality Control, El Pollo Loco Restaurants, Inc. (1993–Present); Vice President of Research & Development and Quality Control, Carl's Jr. Restaurant, Inc. (1989–1993); Vice President of Operations, Marie Callander Restaurant, Inc. (1967–1989). **Associations & Accomplishments:** International Food Technologist (IFT); California Restaurant Association (CRA); Boy Scouts of America (BSA); Pediatric Cancer Research Foundation – Children's Hospital. **Education:** Long Beach City College, A.A. (1967). **Personal:** Married to Cindy in 1976. Four children: Jason, Jared, Jeanette, and Jake. Mr. Jones enjoys hunting, camping, and backpacking.

Yosoji Kanada

Production Manager
International In–Flight Catering Company, Ltd.
310 Rodgers Boulevard
Honolulu, HI 96819–1833
(808) 836–2431
Fax: (808) 836–5815

5812

Business Information: International In–Flight Catering Company, Ltd. provides in–flight catering services, serving major airline clientele such as Japan Airlines, Korea Airlines, and Northwest Airlines. An executive chef specializing in Japanese cuisine with over twenty years expertise, Mr. Kanada was appointed as Production Manager in 1982. In this capacity, he oversees all kitchen operations, with duties including the assembly of tray sets, as well as the preparation of Japanese menu entrees. **Career Steps:** Production Manager, International In–Flight Catering Company, Ltd. (1982–Present); Chef Instructor, Kyoto Culinary Art College – Japan (1979–1982); Cook for Japanese Food, Restaurant "Shoubu–En" – Japan (1975–1979). **Associations & Accomplishments:** Honolulu Chapter, ACF. **Education:** Doshisha University, Economics (1975); Chef's Certificate of Japan. **Personal:** Married to Keiko in 1990. Mr. Kanada enjoys social dancing, skiing, and classic guitar.

Thomas A. Kershaw

President
Hampshire House
84 Beacon Street
Boston, MA 02108–3496
(617) 227–9600
Fax: (617) 723–1898

5812

Business Information: Hampshire House is a restaurant and pub operation on Beacon Hill in Boston, situated in a turn–of–the–century mansion. The Hampshire House Restaurant, now known as the Library Grill, is celebrating fifty years of continuous operations. Boston Magazine has characterized the restaurant as one of the "most romantic" dining rooms in the city. The basement is the locale for the Bull & Finch Pub, a neighborhood bar. It was built in England and imported in 1969 to create a cozy, casual atmosphere for local residents. In 1982, the producers of the TV show "Cheers" used the interior of the Bull & Finch Pub as the inspiration for the set of their series. The exterior of the building was filmed for the lead–in to the show and for use at commercial breaks. In the final three years, episode portions were filmed on location at the Hampshire House. As a result of the popularity of the TV show, the Pub has become one of the most sought after tourist attractions in Boston. The Pub has been cited as the best in its category by Playboy Magazine, Cosmopolitan Magazine, and Nation's Restaurant News. Due to their popularity among Boston tourists, Bull & Finch Enterprises was created in 1985 to develop, manufacture, and sell a complete line of "Cheers" products. The 1992 edition of the Top 500 Restaurant Operations, by Restaurant Hospitality Magazine, listed the Hampshire House and Bull & Finch Pub in the Top 100. As President and Owner, Mr. Kershaw is responsible for all aspects of operations including serving as host for the restaurant and pub. **Career Steps:** President, Hampshire House Corporation (1969–Present); President, Bull & Finch Enterprises (1985–Present); President, Executive Townhouse Corporation (1969–1981); Market Development Manager, Bolt, Beramek & Newman (1966–1969); Owner, Primus Association (1965–1966); Production Manager, Data Packaging Corporation (1964–1965); Staff E.I., duPont de Nemours (1962–1964). **Associations & Accomplishments:** Chairman of the Board of Directors, Greater Boston Convention and Visitors Bureau (1986–Present); Founder and Co–Chairman, Massachusetts Visitor Industry Council (MVIC Inc.) (1993–Present); Chairman, New England USA (1994–Present); Founder and Chairman of the Board, Massachusetts Tourism Coalition (1987–1991); Board of Directors, National Restaurant Association (1986–Present); Board of Directors, Massachusetts Restaurant Association (1981–1993); President, Massachusetts Restaurant Association (1992–1993); Advisory Board, United States Travel and Tourism Administration (1990–Present); Governor's Council on Economic Growth and Technology (1992–Present); Light–A–Life Chairman, Christmas on the Common (1982–Present); Board of Directors, Friends of the Public Garden and Common (1983–Present); Founder and Chairman, The Salem Heritage Trail Committee (1984–1986); President, Beacon Hill Business Association (1981–1984); Chairman, Beacon Hill Business Association (1992–Present); Chairman, March of Dimes – Gourmet Gala (1986–1987); Advisory Committee, Suffolk University School of Management; Visiting Lecturer to the New Enterprises Course, Cornell University; Member of Corporation and Visiting Committees, Massachusetts General Hospital; Bunker HIll Community College Foundation; Board of Directors, Greater Boston Council of Boy Scouts (1988–Present); Local Council Representative, National Council, Boy Scouts of America (1991–Present); Member of the Corporation, Culinary Institute of America (1989–Present); Past Member of the Board of Directors, Beacon Hill Civic Association; Board of Directors of Executives Club, Greater Boston Chamber of Commerce (1991–1993); Republican National Committee: Team 100 (1989–1992), Republican Eagles (1986–Present), Republican Senatorial Trust (1989–1990), GOPAC, Executive Committee (1988–Present), Republican National Convention (Attended – 1992, Delegate – 1988, Alternate Delegate – 1984); George Bush for President/Victory '88 (1988); Bush–Quayle '92; Member of State Committee, Massachusetts Republican Party (1988–Present); Finance Chairman, State Committee, Massachusetts Republican Party (1991–1992); President, Boston Republican City Committee (1992–Present); Chairman, Ward Five Republican Committee (1982–Present); Restauranteur of the Year Award (1984); Venture Magazine Arthur Young Entrepreneur fo the Year Award (1987); Man of the Year, Boston City Republican Committee (1989); Outstanding Volunteer for Region Four–Massachusetts Republican State Committee (1989); Employer of the Year – Project Triangle (1989); Bunker Hill Community College Distinguished Service Award (1990); Massachusetts Tourism Leadership Award (1990); Massachusetts Tourism "Unity" Award (1990); Finalist, Entrepreneur of the Year 1991; Best Maintained Properties, City of Boston (1991); Salut Au Restaurateur, Florida State University (1984); Special Recognition by Raymond L. Flynn for efforts on the Light–A–Life, Christmas on the Common Committee (1986, 1987 and 1988); Commendation by Governor Michael S. Dukakis (June 1986); Proclamation from Raymond L. Flynn of Boston making "Thomas Kershaw" Day in recognition of business, community and charitable contributions to the city; National Head Injury Foundation; March of Dimes Distinguished Service Award for activities associated with organization activities; Who's Who in the World (1990–1992); Who's Who in Finance and Industry (1979–1992); Who's Who in the East (1981–1992). **Education:** Harvard University Business School, M.S. in Business Administration (1962); Swarthmore College, B.S. in Mechanical Engineering.

Charles R. Lawrence Jr.

General Manager
Volume Services, Inc.
2 Galleria Parkway, N.W.
Atlanta, GA 30339–5938
(770) 989–5024
Fax: (770) 989–5071
EMAIL: See Below

5812

Business Information: Volume Services, Inc. provides catering, concessions, and off–site catering to convention centers, and N.F.L. and N.B.L. sports centers, including the Cobb Galleria Centre in Atlanta, Georgia. National in scope, the Company has 90 locations throughout the U.S. Established in 1977, the Company employs 300 people, and has an estimated annual revenue of $7 million. As General Manager, Mr. Lawrence oversees two accounts in the Cobb Galleria Centre, which is rated the second busiest sports arena in the U.S., and one in the Palmetto Expo Centre in South Carolina. He is also responsible for twenty–five managers, and all concession activities. Internet users can reach him via: cobbgall@atlanta.com. **Career Steps:** General Manager, Volume Services, Inc. (1993–Present); Corporate Sales Manager, World Congress Centre/MGR Foods (191–1993); Hospitality Sales Manager, Atlanta Hilton & Towers (1989–1991). **Associations & Accomplishments:** National Association of Catering Executives; Meeting Professionals International. **Education:** Johnson & Wales: A.S. in Culinary Arts (1987), B.S. in Food Services (1989). **Personal:** Married to Sherrie in 1994. Mr. Lawrence enjoys golf, tennis, cooking, gardening, and reading.

Richard J. Layson
Manager of Operations
The Velvet Elvis
1906 McKinney
Dallas, TX 75201
(214) 969–5568
Fax: (214) 969–1888

5812

Business Information: The Velvet Elvis is a bar and restaurant chain with locations in Houston, Dallas, and proposed locations in Denver and New Orleans. The business is privately owned and was founded in 1990. As Manager of Operations, Mr. Layson is responsible for the operations of all locations. He handles the financial commitments, public relations, strategic planning, and marketing strategies. **Career Steps:** Manager of Operations, The Velvet Elvis (1994–Present); General Manager, Iggys Restaurant /Royal Jelly (1993–1994); Platters Restaurant (1991–1993). **Associations & Accomplishments:** Texas Restaurant Association; YMCA; American Softball Association; Uptown Merchant Association; University of St. Thomas Volunteer. **Education:** Attended, Peru State University, Peru Nebraska (1987–1990). **Personal:** Mr. Layson enjoys sports, chess, and working with kids at local YMCA.

Arne A. Lebrato, CPA, MBA
Regional Controller
McDonald's Corporation
1 Crossroads Drive
Bedminster, NJ 07921–2614
(908) 306–7965
Fax: (908) 306–7977

5812

Business Information: McDonald's Corporation is the corporate headquarters and a global franchiser of McDonald's Restaurants, a fast–food franchise specializing mainly in serving sandwiches, salads, breakfast and beverages. McDonald's has more than 17,000 restaurants in 85 countries and is a leader in the global food service industry. The Company had systemwide sales of $26 billion and net income of $1.2 billion in 1994. As Regional Controller, Mr. Lebrato is responsible for the management of the regional budget and $400+ million in systemwide sales for the Northern New Jersey, Pennsylvania and Southern New York areas, as well as M&A analysis on restaurants and capital expenditure analysis. **Career Steps:** Regional Controller, McDonald's Corporation (1993–Pres-

ent); Accounting Manager, Marine Transport Lines (1992–1993); Supervisor of International Accounting, Moody's, Inc. (1990–1991); Supervising Senior Accountant, KPMG Peat Marwick, Luxembourg and Grand Cayman (1986–1990). **Associations & Accomplishments:** American Institute of Certified Public Accountants; Illinois and Montana Society of Certified Public Accountants. **Education:** New York University – Stern School of Business, M.B.A. in Finance, Taxation, and International Business (1995); Bentley College: B.S. in Accounting, A.S. in Management. **Personal:** Married to Amy in 1988. Three children: Alexander, Nicholas, and Gregory. Mr. Lebrato enjoys golf, hiking, and travel.

Paul Liebman III

Director of Marketing, Sales, and Promotions
Phoenix Live
455 North Third Street, Suite 301
Phoenix, AZ 85004–3939
(602) 252–2502
Fax: (602) 252–0091

5812

Business Information: Phoenix Live is a multi–venue entertainment facility encompassing 40,000 sq. ft. of rental space, including three night clubs and a restaurant. Established in 1990, Phoenix Live is one of ten properties currently owned by parent company, Harborage I Ltd. employing 250 professionals with an estimated annual revenue of $5 million. As Director of Marketing, Sales, and Promotions, Mr. Liebman is responsible for all public relations and advertising activities including electronic print and media. **Career Steps:** Director of Marketing, Sales, and Promotions, Phoenix Live (1995–Present); General Manager, Health Fighters Bar & Grill (1994–1995); General Manager, Pierce Street Annex (1991–1994); General Manager, Catch A Rising Star (1990); General Manager, Jokers Comedy Clubs (1987–1989); General Manager, T–Bar (1980–1986). **Associations & Accomplishments:** Rotary International; Professional Comedians Association; Muscular Dystrophy Association. **Education:** Attended: Southern Methodist University, Pursuing International Business Degree; Southwest Texas State University; North Texas State University; Texas Military Institute. **Personal:** Mr. Liebman enjoys aikido, sailing, gourmet cooking, biking, motorcycles, flying, swimming, and skiing.

David G. Lloyd
Chief Financial Officer
Taco Cabana
8918 Tesoro Drive, Suite 200
San Antonio, TX 78217
(210) 804–0990
Fax: (210) 804–2135
EMAIL: See Below

5812

Business Information: Taco Cabana is a national chain of Tex–Mex patio cafe restaurants. A public company as of 1992, it is traded on the NASDAQ. Comprised of 104 Company–owned restaurants and twenty franchises, the Company has restaurants in Texas, Colorado, Georgia, New Mexico, Indiana, and Oregon. Established in 1978, Taco Cabana employs 3,300 people and has an estimated annual revenue of $140 million. As Chief of Financial Operations, Mr. Lloyd is responsible for all accounting, finance, MIS, purchasing, and loss prevention functions. Additional duties include preparation of financial analysis and reports, and direct supervision of a staff of forty. Internet users can reach him via: dlloyd@tacocabana.com. **Career Steps:** Chief of Financial Operations, Taco Cabana (1994–Present); Senior Audit Manager, Deloitte & Touche (1985–1994). **Associations & Accomplishments:** American Institute of Certified Public Accountants; Board of Directors, Texas Society of Certified Public Accountants; San Antonians Against Lawsuit Arise. **Education:** Trinity University, B.S. (1985). **Personal:** Married to Janine in 1987. Two children: Cassie and Emily. Mr. Lloyd enjoys running, tennis, basketball, and skiing.

Rocky Lucia
General Manager
Old Time Tavern
Dover Mall, Suite 2
Toms River, NJ 08753
(908) 349–8778
Fax: (908) 244–8127

5812

Business Information: Old Time Tavern, managed by Sunshine Enterprises, Inc., is a full–service restaurant chain providing full banquet facilities, as well as extensive bar services. As General Manager, Mr. Lucia is responsible for all aspects of

the operation, including employee supervision, training and recruitment of senior–level management, hosting, and P&L responsibility. **Career Steps:** General Manager, Old Time Tavern (wholly–owned subsidiary of Sunshine Enterprises, Inc.) (1994–Present); General Manager, Chef's International, Inc. (1980–1994). **Associations & Accomplishments:** NJRA; Chamber of Commerce. **Education:** Attended: DeVry Technical Institute. **Personal:** Married to Stacey Ann in 1991. One child: Kayla Rose. Mr. Lucia enjoys golf and drums.

Nicholas A. Lupoli Jr.
Vice President
Double N. Inc.
29 North Broadway
Salem, NH 03079
(603) 894–7396
Fax: (603) 894–7054

5812

Business Information: Double N. Inc. is a franchise management corporation, overseeing administrative operations for six Sal's Just Pizza fast food locations in New England. Mr. Lupoli and his brother founded the franchises in 1990. He is presently responsible for supervising all product inventory and employee relations. **Career Steps:** Vice President, Double N. Inc. (1990–Present); Forktruck Driver, Mighty Fine Wood Products (1989–1990); Sports Events, Northwestern University (1989); Painter, Self–Employed (1987–1988). **Education:** Northeastern University, M.E.T. (1988–1990). **Personal:** Mr. Lupoli enjoys working on cars and trucks.

Ronald S. Marino

Vice President of Development
Golden Corral Corporation
5151 Glenwood Avenue
Raleigh, NC 27612
(919) 781–9310
Fax: (919) 881–4654

5812

Business Information: Golden Corral Corporation is one of the leading family restaurant chains globally. The Corporation has 442 international locations and is growing rapidly. Established in 1973, it employs approximately 16,500 people and has an estimated annual sales of over $622 million. As Vice President of Development, Mr. Marino oversees all corporate development and strategies, involving the areas of real estate, legal matters and market research. **Career Steps:** Vice President of Development, Golden Corral Corporation (1979–Present); Vice President of Operations, Sambo's Restaurant, Inc. (1968–1978). **Associations & Accomplishments:** Nacor; International Restaurant Franchise; California Real Estate Association; National Restaurant Association; National Food Service Professionals. **Education:** University of California at San Francisco, Hotel and Restaurant (1968); University of California at Santa Barbara, Real Estate. **Personal:** Married to Susan in 1969. Two children: Anna and Stephen. Mr. Marino enjoys skiing, fishing, and hiking.

Bill Mathis
Vice President of Sales
Glazier Foods Company
1520 Oliver Street
Houston, TX 77007–6035
(713) 869–6411 Ext. 402
Fax: (713) 869–7852

5812

Business Information: Glazier Foods Company is a distributor of a full–line of food services, including health care, contract feeders, national chains, individual restaurants, and retail markets. A regional company covering a 300–mile radius in Texas from one location, Glazier Foods Company is a family–owned company, celebrating sixty years of operations in 1996. Mr. Mathis joined the business as Vice President of Sales in 1991. He is responsible for the direction of all divisions of sales and marketing, including the development and implementation of new procedures throughout the different departments within the Company. He also is responsible for directing the training of personnel and overseeing a staff of 60. **Career Steps:** Vice President of Sales, Glazier Foods Company (1991–Present); General Sales Manager, White Swan (1988–1991); General Manager, M&M Sales, Inc. (1984–1988). **Associations & Accomplishments:** Metropolitan Baptist Church; Sigma Chi. **Education:** Texas A&I, B.B.A. in Management (1982). **Personal:** Married to Laura in 1991. One child: Collin. Mr. Mathis enjoys racquetball and jogging.

Nick Mautone
General Manager
Gramercy Tavern
42 East 20th Street
New York, NY 10003
(212) 477–0777
Fax: (212) 477–1160

5812

Business Information: Gramercy Tavern is a high volume, high quality, fine dining establishment offering private dining rooms and a tavern. Established in 1994, the Company employs 120 people and has an estimated annual rovonuo of $10 million. As General Manager, Mr. Mautone has full responsibility over all Company functions. His duties include administration, operations, finance, staff management and strategic planning. **Career Steps:** General Manager, Gramercy Tavern (1996–Present); General Manger, Hudson River Club (1993–1996); General Manager, Gotham Bar and Grill (1990–1993); Owner, American Pie Restaurant (1982–1990). **Associations & Accomplishments:** National Restaurant Association; New York Restaurant Association; James Beard House. **Education:** Fordham University, B.S. in Business (1982). **Personal:** Married to Laurie Hampen in 1989. One child: Alexander Mautone. Mr. Mautone enjoys skiing, racquetball, and sports.

Mrs. Debra A. Maymi
Market Manager
PepsiCo/Taco Bell
11622 Knobcrest
Houston, TX 77070
(713) 320–7576
Fax: (713) 320–8417

5812

Business Information: Taco Bell Corporation, a subsidiary of PepsiCo, is the largest quick–service Mexican–style restaurant chain in the world, with approximately 4,500 locations in 50 states and a growing international market. At this time, over 100 restaurants are operating in Canada, Guam, the United Kingdom, Japan, Cayman Islands, Dominican Republic, St. Maarten, Honduras, Chile, Egypt, Oman, Poland, Russia, Costa Rica, Guatemala, the Bahamas, Puerto Rico, Saudi Arabia, Aruba, Qatar, and the American Virgin Islands. Approximately 30 percent of the units are owned and operated by independent franchises. Ms. Maymi currently serves as the Market Manager for the Corporation. Originated by Glen Bell, Taco Bell became a reality on March 21, 1962. The first Taco Bell restaurant was built in Downey, CA. The first franchise was sold in 1964. Taco Bell went public in 1969 and was acquired by PepsiCo in 1978. Today, Taco Bell employs over 120,000 people in company–operated and franchised units, and corporate offices across the United States. **Career Steps:** Market Manager, PepsiCo/Taco Bell (1992–Present); User Services Manager, Compaq (1989–1992); Systems Support Manager, Wang (1985–1989). **Associations & Accomplishments:** Zonta – international women's civic organization. **Education:** Our Lady of the Lake, M.B.A. (1991); Our Lady of the Lake, B.B.A. **Personal:** Married to Rafael in 1985. Three children: Rudy, Alexandra and Kara. Mrs. Maymi enjoys collecting Mexican folk art.

Steve Miguel

Executive Director of Worldwide Development
Hard Rock Cafe
5401 Kirkman Road
Orlando, FL 32819–7940
(407) 351–6000
Fax: (407) 351–0269

5812

Business Information: The Hard Rock Cafe is an international themed Rock and Roll memorabilia restaurant and merchandise outlet. Established in 1971, the Hard Rock Cafe currently employs 4,500 people worldwide. As Executive Director of Worldwide Development, Mr. Miguel is responsible for the site approval and design development, as well as construction and facilities fit out. **Career Steps:** Executive Director of Worldwide Development, Hard Rock Cafe (1993–Present); General Manager of Resort Development, Walt Disney World (1981–1993). **Associations & Accomplishments:** State of Florida General Contractors. **Education:** Valencia Community College, A.S. in Construction Technolgy (1984); University of Rhode Island, B.S. in Business Administration. **Personal:** Married to Tina in 1988. One child: Zachary Antone. Mr. Miguel enjoys boating, fishing, and skiing.

Bijan B. Modaressi
President
Chelsea's
1055 Thomas Jefferson Street, NW
Washington, DC 20007
(202) 298–8222
Fax: (301) 293–7092

5812

Business Information: Chelsea's Dinner Theatre is home to The Capitol Steps, a musical and political satire group. Chelsea's offers late evening live entertainment and bands, with a different cuisine each night. As President, Mr. Modaressi oversees the day–to–day operations of Chelsea's. He is responsible for recruiting entertainment, promoting productions, and assuring customer satisfaction with services and products offered. Other responsibilities include financial concerns, weekly cost analysis, cash management, and long–term expansion planning. **Career Steps:** President, Chelsea's (1981–Present); Energy Conservation Manager, Montgomery County Government (1978–1981); Manager of Design and Casting, Bechtel Power Corporation (1977–1978); Managing Director, Arvandan Shipyard Aluminum (1975–1977). **Associations & Accomplishments:** Sigma Tau Fraternity; American Society of Mechanical Engineers; Nominee for 1996 Nightlife and Entertainment Operator of the Restaurant Association of Metropolitan Washington. Chelsea's was listed as the # 1 Hot Spot in Washington, DC by the Washington Times. **Education:** George Washington University: M.S. M.E. (1977), B.S. M.E. (1970). **Personal:** Married to Mehri in 1978. One child: Mark. Mr. Modaressi enjoys travel, water sports, and theatre.

Laurie G. Moore
Corporate Employment Manager
Brinker International
6820 LBJ Freeway
Dallas, TX 75240
(214) 770–9366
Fax: (214) 770–9529

5812

Business Information: Brinker International is a full–service international restaurant company, owning and operating five restaurant chains in 45 states and 11 countries (Chili's, Macaroni Grill, On the Border, Cozy Mel's, Maggionos Little Italy, Corner Bakery). Joining Brinker International upon college graduation in 1986, Ms. Moore was appointed as Corporate Employment Manager in 1990. She is responsible for all recruitment and placement of personnel in the Corporate office, including all level staff positions and officers. **Career Steps:** Corporate Employment Manager, Brinker International (1986–Present). **Associations & Accomplishments:** Society of Human Resource Management; Women in Foodservice Forum; Dallas Human Resource Society; Volunteer, Junior League of Dallas. **Education:** Stephen F. Austin State University, B.A. in Communications (1986). **Personal:** Married to Robert in 1990. One child: Hailey. Ms. Moore enjoys sports, music, classic movies, and wine tasting.

Sonny Moore
Vice President of Commissary Operations
Donelson Foods
2960 Armory Drive
Nashville, TN 37204–3701
(615) 254–1563 Ext. 160
Fax: (615) 254–1569

5812

Business Information: Donelson Foods is a Division of O'-Charley's, Inc., a 67 unit casual dining restaurant chain in the southeastern United States. Mr. Moore serves as Vice President of Commissary Operations, responsible for purchasing, distribution, and manufacturing of food and other products for the O'Charley's restaurants. Donelson Foods is also a manufacturer of proprietary food products under O'Charley's and other labels, including meat, bread, and salad dressings. Mr. Moore provides the overall management and direction for O'Charley's Commissary Operations. **Career Steps:** Vice President of Commissary Operations, Donelson Foods (1986–Present); Production Supervisor, Shoney's Inc. (1982–1986); Manager, Cracker Barrel (1978–1979); Manager, McDonald's Franchise (1973–1978). **Associations & Accomplishments:** Board of Directors, Donelson Christian Academy (Nashville, TN). **Education:** Tennessee Technical University (1972); Hamburger University, Advanced Operations (1974). **Personal:** Married to Sherry in 1973. Two children: Travis and Ginny. Mr. Moore enjoys fishing and softball.

Robert N. Mulford Jr.
General Manager
Royal Exchange Pub/Flying Club
740 S. Salisbury Boulevard
Salisbury, MD 21801–5846
(410) 749–1263
Fax: (410) 749–1318

5812

Business Information: Royal Exchange Pub is a 50 table, full service restaurant that has been voted the area's Best American Restaurant. The Royal Exchange Pub has been in business for over 20 years, has become a Landmark in Salisbury and sets the standard for "Eastern Shore Dining." The restaurant is certified by AAA Motor Club and the National Restaurant Association, and has been recognized twice by Restaurant Hospitality for the "500 Achievement Award." There is also a banquet facility which can accommodate 75 people. Directly connected to the restaurant is the Flying Club, a dance club that holds 350 people, and is complete with high a high tech DJ booth, sound system and lights, an elevated dance floor and a stage facility for live entertainment. As General Manager, Mr. Mulford oversees the operations of both facilities. He is responsible for 100 employees, and handles all hiring, evaluating and terminating of employees, purchasing, budgeting, marketing, scheduling, as well as menu design, community involvement, and promotional activities. **Career Steps:** General Manager, Royal Exchange Pub/Flying Club (1995–Present); Nurse Recruiter, Maxim Health Care (1993–1994); Manager, Webster's 1801 Bar/Restaurant/Banquet Facility (1990–1992); Manager, Bowers Automotive (1986–1990). **Associations & Accomplishments:** Vice President, Rotoract Club, Salisbury, MD; Maryland Restaurant Association. **Education:** Salisbury State University, B.A. (1992); University of Maryland Eastern Shore, Hotel/Restaurant Management. **Personal:** Mr. Mulford enjoys golf, sailing, racquetball, mountain biking and travel.

Jeffrey S. Nicholas
Vice President of Procurement
Alliant Foodservice
5445 Spellmire Drive
Cincinnati, OH 45246–4842
(513) 874–3663
Fax: (513) 874–2948

5812

Business Information: Alliant Foodservice specializes in distributing packaged foods to hospitals, schools, and nursing homes in the Cincinnati, Ohio area. As Vice President of Procurement, Mr. Nicholas is responsible for all aspects of marketing, including all buying of projects, strategic planning, and product distribution to clients. **Career Steps:** Alliant Foodservice: Vice President of Procurement (1993–Present), Senior Buyer (1992–1993); Merchandiser, Clark Food Service (1989–1992). **Education:** University of South Mississippi, B.S. (1983). **Personal:** Mr. Nicholas enjoys golf and exercise.

Thomas Pane
Owner and Operator
Grapevine Restaurant
2545 Niagara Falls Boulevard
Amherst, NY 14228–3527
(716) 691–7799
Fax: (716) 691–6282
EMAIL: See Below

5812

Business Information: Grapevine Restaurant is a family–type restaurant serving foods, such as grilled chicken, salad, spaghetti, etc. surrounded by four saltwater fish tanks. Services also include catering for weddings and business functions. With nineteen years of experience in the restaurant business, Mr. Pane founded Grapevine Restaurant in 1983 and serves as its Owner and Operator. He is responsible for all aspects of operations, including administration, finances, sales, public relations, accounting, and strategic planning. Internet users can reach him via: Vettman@msn.com **Career Steps:** Founder, Owner, and Operator, Grapevine Restaurant (1983–Present); Panes Restaurant, General Manager (1977–1983). **Associations & Accomplishments:** Chamber of Commerce. **Personal:** Married to Liza in 1984. Three children: Krystina, Peter and Amanda.

Eric M. Paul
Senior Vice President
Ruby Tuesday
4721 Morrison Drive
Mobile, AL 36609–3350
(334) 344–3000
Fax: (334) 344–9513

5812

Business Information: Ruby Tuesday, a subsidiary of Morrison Restaurants Inc., is a casual dining restaurant chain with a relaxed family atmosphere. Established in 1972, Ruby Tuesday currently employs 19,016 employees. A member of Morrison Restaurants Inc. for over 16 years, Mr. Paul currently serves as Senior Vice President of Operations for Mozzarella's Cafe, where he is responsible for all aspects of operations for the concepts. **Career Steps:** Senior Vice President, Ruby Tuesday (1990–Present); Morrison Restaurants Inc.: Senior Vice President of Human Resources (1995), Vice President of Operations (1983–1994). **Education:** Emory University, B.A. in Psychology and Education (1975). **Personal:** Married to Alice. Two boys: Brian and Alan. Mr. Paul enjoys coaching soccer and playing paintball.

George Pease
Vice President of Sales
NATCO
1 Wamsutta Street
New Bedford, MA 02740–7335
(508) 997–7473
Fax: (508) 995–8543

5812

Business Information: NATCO is a foodservice distributor offering over 6,000 items to restaurants, bakeries, and institutions. The Company serves the New England area of Massachusetts, Rhode Island, and Southern New Hampshire. Established in 1907, NATCO currently employs 100 people and last year posted revenues of over 30 million dollars. As Vice President of Sales, Mr. Pease has oversight of the Company profitability through sales. He assists in developing marketing strategies for new and existing products, training sales personnel, and reviewing vendor products and services. Mr. Pease also involved in establishing working budgets and monitors expenditures to plan for the following year's budget. **Career Steps:** Vice President of Sales, NATCO (1991–Present); Sales, JP Foodservice–Monarch (1990–1991); Area Manager, Morris Alper (1989–1990); General Sales Manager, Rykoff Sexton (1979–1989). **Associations & Accomplishments:** United Way–Junior Achievement; Wamsutta Club; New England Wholesale Foodservice Distributors Association; Massachusetts Retail Bakers Association. **Education:** Northeastern University, Marketing Degree (1985); Eastern Connecitcut State University, BA. **Personal:** Married to Wendy in 1977. Two children: Geoff and Rand. Mr. Pease enjoys squash, soccer, community service, and coaching.

Dennis Peer
Director of Operations
Weinbaum Operations – d.b.a. McDonald's Restaurants
1106 Kings Highway
Rolla, MO 65401
(314) 341–2700
Fax: (314) 341–3203

5812

Business Information: Weinbaum Operations – d.b.a. McDonald's Restaurants manages eight McDonald's franchises in the Missouri area. As Director of Operations, Mr. Peer is responsible for managing the administrative office out of which fall of all eight restaurants are controlled, overseeing business expansion, supervising employees, and customer satisfaction. **Career Steps:** McDonald's Restaurants: Director of Operations, Weinbaum Operations (1994–Present), Director of Operations, McGraw Inc. (1993–1994), Director of Operations, Wyatt & Hillmeyer Operations (1963–1993). **Associations & Accomplishments:** McDonald's Charities, Fund raising, and McDonald House; Published Quotable Quotes in Reader's Digest and National Enquirer, Current Quote in Reader's Digest is "One Measure of Leadership is the Caliber of the People Who Choose to Follow You." **Education:** St. Louis University (1965). **Personal:** Four children: Kristin, Matthew, Laura, and Tricia. Mr. Peer enjoys sports and music.

Greg S. Pesky
Vice President
Sawtooth Enterprises d.b.a. The Buckin' Bagel
P.O. Box 2759
Ketchum, ID 83340–2759
(208) 726–0112
Fax: (208) 726–0113

5812

Business Information: Sawtooth Enterprises d.b.a. The Buckin' Bagel is a chain of New York–style bagel stores located throughout Idaho. As Vice President, Mr. Pesky heads all marketing and communications activities, oversees personnel management, interfaces with the President on operations issues, and is responsible for the maintenance of vendor relations. **Career Steps:** Executive Vice President, Sawtooth Enterprises d.b.a. The Buckin' Bagel (1995–Present); Managing Editor, Sporting Goods Business (1993–1995). **Associations & Accomplishments:** Quoted in The New

York Times and Wall Street Journal. **Education:** Lafayette College, B.A. (1990). **Personal:** Mr. Pesky enjoys running (New York Marathon), golf, and skiing.

Daniel D. Posner
President
Peppercorn Restaurant and Lounge
1813 Paul Bunyan Drive
Bemidji, MN 56601
(218) 759–2794
Fax: (218) 759–1093

5812

Business Information: The Peppercorn Restaurant and Lounge is an eating and drinking establishment providing fine dining in a relaxing atmosephore, as well as a full–service bar and lounge. Established in 1985, the Peppercorn Restaurant currently employs 30 people. As President and Co–Owner, Mr. Posner provides the overall direction and vision for the restaurant's continued business, quality delivery of foods and services to customers and all daily operations. **Career Steps:** President, Peppercorn Restaurant and Lounge (1991–Present); Manager, Pizza Hut (1988–1991). **Associations & Accomplishments:** NFIB; Foundation Member, Bemidji State University; Chamber of Commerce; National Deer Hunter Association. **Education:** Bemidji State University, B.S. in Business Management (1988). **Personal:** Married to Mechelle Posner in 1992. Mr. Posner enjoys hunting and fishing.

Christina M. Quesada
Owner
CQ's Place
301A South Avenue East
Westfield, NJ 07090
(201) 644–1312
Fax: (201) 644–8413
EMAIL: See Below

5812

Business Information: CQ's Place is an American/Tex–Mex Western restaurant located in Westfield, New Jersey. Christina Quesada opened CQ's in 1988 as the culmination of a lifetime dream and her most memorable accomplishment. As Owner and Operator she oversees all aspects of operations, financial management, and staffing administration. Concurrently, she has served as Tax Manager at AT&T since 1987. Internet users may reach her via: attmail!cquesada **Career Steps:** Owner, CQ's Place (1988–Present); AT&T: Tax Manager (1987–Present), Assistant Staff Manager (1984–1987); Tax Accountant, Manhattan Industries (1990–1984). **Associations & Accomplishments:** Northern New Jersey Miami University Alumni Club. **Education:** Fairleigh Dickenson University, M.B.A. (1984); Miami University (Ohio), B.S. in Accounting. **Personal:** Married to Rosendo (Chuck) in 1987. One child: Chantel Lee.

Bill Reigle
Director of Human Resources
Skyline Chilli Inc.
4180 Thunderbird Lane
Fairfield, OH 45014–2235
(513) 874–1188
Fax: (513) 874–3591

5812

Business Information: Skyline Chilli Inc., estatblished in 1949, is a chain of 85 fast food resturants that specialize in fast service and good food. Skyline Chili has approximately 600 employees. As Director of Human Resources, Mr. Reigle is responsible for all facets of Human Resource Management for the corporation. These responsibilities include hiring, service awards, pensions plans, and safety for the employees. Mr. Reigle's plans for the future include advancing to Vice President of Human Resources in order to become a strategic partner in the planning and upgrading of the staff and helping them to develop themselves. **Career Steps:** Director of Human Resources, Skyline Chilli Inc. (1993–Present); Director of Personnel, The Ohio River Company (1983–1993); Teacher, Cincinnati Public Schools (1978–1982). **Associations & Accomplishments:** Council Hotel and Restaurant Trainers; Society Human Resource Management; Greater Cincinnati Human Resource Association; Active in fund raising activities for various Boy Scout Troops; Mr. Reigle contributes articles to local and regional newspapers. **Education:** University of Cincinnati, B.S. in Education (1977). **Personal:** Married to Jennifer in 1989. One child: Benjamin. Mr. Reigle enjoys sports, politics, and history.

Mr. Timothy P. Reith
President
Tacoma, Inc.
209 East Main Street
Martinsville, VA 24112
(703)666–9417
Fax: (703)666–9427

5812

Business Information: Tacoma, Inc. owns and operates 15 Taco Bell franchises in the Southwest Virginia region. The Company has more than doubled in size and plans to increase it's market share by adding 5 more stores during the next year. As President and Part Owner, Mr. Reith is responsible for all financial aspects, marketing, current and future development, and overseeing the administration and operation of all 15 stores. Mr. Reith has recently developed the rights to the Golden Corral franchise for Southwest Virginia and plans to operate under the name ++++Good Good, Inc.++++ as president of the new company . Tacoma, Inc. established in 1988 employs over 300 management and service personnel and reports estimated annual income of over $12 million. **Career Steps:** President, Tacoma, Inc. (1992–Present); Franchise Director, Pepsi Cola Corporation (1986–1992); Regional Director, Marriott Corporation (1976–1986). **Associations & Accomplishments:** Member, Board of Trustees, Blue Ridge Chapter–National MS Society .

Kathy Ruiz
Corporate Executive Chef
Landrys Seafood Restaurants
1400 Post Oak Boulevard, Suite 1010
Houston, TX 77056
(713) 850–1010
Fax: (713) 963–8194

5812

Business Information: Landrys Seafood Restaurants is a chain of seafood restaurants (51 total). As Corporate Executive Chef, Ms. Ruiz is responsible for the menu development of all locations. Additionally, she hires chefs, and visits all store locations for problem solving and public relations. **Career Steps:** Corporate Executive Chef, Landrys Seafood Restaurants; Chef/Owner, Kathy's Restaurant; Consultant, Many – Houston; Consultant, Yucatan – Cancun. **Associations & Accomplishments:** Roundtable for Women in Food Service; International Association of Women Chefs and Restauranteurs. **Education:** Manhattanville College, B.S. (1979). **Personal:** Ms. Ruiz enjoys scuba diving, tennis, running, and reading.

Mr. Avtar S. Saini
President
Avatar & G Inc.
11780 S.W. 88 Street
Miami, FL 33186
(305) 274–1300
Fax: (305) 271–2666

5812

Business Information: Avatar & G Inc., established in 1991, owns and operates an ethnic East Indian restaurant franchise called Punjab Palace. Specializing in authentic East Indian cuisine, the restaurant serves lunch and dinner menus, as well as provides full catering and banquet facilities. As President, Mr. Saini is responsible for all aspects of operations, as well as being owner and manager of the business. **Career Steps:** President, Avatar & G Inc. (1991–Present); Cashier and Waiter, Sangeet of India (1989–1995); Waiter, New Punjab Indian Restaurant (1988–1989). **Associations & Accomplishments:** Published in Miami Herald. **Education:** India, Graduate (1973). **Personal:** Married to Gurmeet K. Saini in 1978. Two children: Damandeep and Sartaj Saini. Mr. Saini enjoys cooking and his family.

Norberto Sanchez
• • • ◄━━━ ◉ ━━► • • •

Chairman and Chief Executive Officer
Norsan Food Group
5060 North Royal Atlanta Drive, Suite 30
Tucker, GA 30084
(770) 414–5026 Ext: 15
Fax: (770) 414–5839

5812

Business Information: Norsan Food Group is the holding company for food and meat distribution companies and casual and fast food restaurants. They include Frontera Mex–Mex Grill, Inc.; Norsan Restaurant, Inc.; Norsan Restaurant of Kentucky, Inc.; Mexi–Tacos, d.b.a. Don Taco – is a fast food establishment; Valsan Meat, d.b.a. Prime Meats – is a USDA meat distribution plant; Norsan Foods, Inc. – is a food distribution company to restaurants; and Norsan Management – a provider of management services to all companies. Presently, the Company owns and operates a total of seven restaurants throughout Georgia and Kentucky. Establishing Norsan Food Group in 1987, Mr. Sanchez serves as its Owner, Chairman, and Chief Executive Officer. He is responsible for the management and oversight of all aspects of operations, including strategic planning. **Career Steps:** Chairman and Chief Executive Officer, Norsan Food Group (1987–Present); Manager of Engineering, Trinity Industries (1984–1986). **Associations & Accomplishments:** Atlanta Hispanic Chamber of Commerce; National Restaurant Association; Georgia Hospitality and Travel Association; Mexican Community Association. **Education:** Georgia Tech: MSME, MSIE (1981). Monterrey Institute of Technology BSME, BSEE. **Personal:** Married to Iracema in 1982. Three children: Pamela, Natalia, and Stephanie. Mr. Sanchez enjoys golf and reading.

Mr. John R. Scheible

Director of Operations
K & K Fast Foods, d.b.a. Checkers Hamburgers
2065 University Boulevard
Adelphi, MD 20783
(301) 439–1892
Fax: (703) 330–5133

5812

Business Information: K&K Fast Foods, Inc., d.b.a. Checkers Hamburgers is a fast food, double drive–through concept originating out of Florida. K&K Fast Foods, Inc. operates four Checkers franchises in Maryland. Established in 1992, K&K Fast Foods, Inc. reports annual revenue of $5.9 million and currently employs 320 people. As Director of Operations, Mr. Scheible is responsible for all aspects of company operations. **Career Steps:** Director of Operations, K&K Fast Foods, Inc., d.b.a. Checkers Hamburgers (1992–Present); Director of Operations, Champion Sports Bars (1990–1992); Director of Operations, Mr. Day's Sports Bars/Rally in Ally (1988–1990). **Associations & Accomplishments:** National Rifle Association (NRA); World Karting Association (WKA); Tech Racing (Driver); Bertel Roos Racing Series, 9th Place; National Restaurant Association (NRA), Washington Chapter; Bull Run Civic Association; Awards: Million Dollar Sales (1994), Franchisee of the Year (1994), #1 Sales Increase in Company Up 18% (1994). **Education:** Johnson St. College, B.S. (1981); Numerous schools and seminars: Roos Racing School; Tech Racing; Marriot T.Q.M. Seminars; Management by the Numbers Seminar; Behavior Seminar; Time Management Seminars; Dollars & Sense Seminar. **Personal:** One child: Jessica Noel Scheible. Mr. Scheible enjoys racing cars, motorcycles, and boats.

Kathleen Simas

Director of Corporate Publications
Hot Dog on A Stick, Inc.
777 South Pacific Coast Highway, Suite 114
Solana Beach, CA 92075
(619) 755–3049
Fax: (619) 755–5809

5812

Business Information: Hot Dog on A Stick, Inc. is an employee–owned fast food company which operates more than 98 restaurants across the United States. As the Company's Director of Corporate Publications, Ms. Simas is responsible for the writing, design, layout, and editing of the monthly corporate newsletters and operational notices. These writings facilitated Hot Dog on a Stick's selection for the 1993 ESOP Association Award for Printed Communications Excellence. Ms. Simas also writes, coordinates, and produces training and operational manuals and various other brochures regarding the Company. Ms. Simas has developed the printed materials and manuals necessary for the Company's international franchises. **Career Steps:** Director of Corporate Publications, Hot Dog on a Stick, Inc. (Present). **Education:** San Diego State University, M.P.H. (1990); University of California – San Diego, B.A. in Animal Physiology/Minor in Anthropology (1987).

Steve Stanley

Corporate Director of Kitchen Operations
Chuys Comida Deluxe
1623 Toomey Road
Austin, TX 78704
(512) 473–2783
Fax: (512) 473–8684

5812

Business Information: Chuys Comida Deluxe is a full–service, independent restaurant chain consisting of 10 units with four different concepts. As Corporate Director of Kitchen Operations, Mr. Stanley is responsible for the development and implementation of all recipes and kitchen procedures, as well as all centralized purchasing, development of new training

programs, and all restaurant openings. **Career Steps:** Corporate Director of Kitchen Operations, Chuys Comida Deluxe (1991–Present); Corporate Food and Beverages Manager, Guild Hotel Management (1988–1991); Co–Owner/Chef, Royce's Private Supper Club (1983–1988); Traveling Corporate Chef, Realm Hotel Management (1979–1983). **Associations & Accomplishments:** American Culinary Federation; Texas State Chef's Association. **Education:** University of Utah (1986); American Hotel Management Association. **Personal:** Married to Patricia in 1982. Two children: Mickell and Joshua. Mr. Stanley enjoys skiing, rock climbing, backpacking, racquetball, and reading.

Brian S. Stengl

Seafood Procurement Manager
Dardin Restaurant
7101 Lake Eleanor Drive
Orlando, FL 32809
(407) 245–4735
Fax: (407) 245–5093

5812

Business Information: Dardin Restaurant is a national chain of restaurants including Olive Garden, Red Lobster, and Bahama Breeze franchises (1,200 in all). Established in 1968, the Company employs 110,000 people and has estimated annual revenue of $3.2 billion. As Seafood Procurement Manager, Mr. Stengl is responsible for purchasing seafood for all restaurants in the chain. He buys direct from producers in thirty countries around the world, and is responsible for a support staff of ten. **Career Steps:** Seafood Procurement Manager, Dardin Restaurant (1991–Present); General Mills Restaurants: Quality Assurance Manager (1979–1981), Seafood Buyer (1981–1984); Senior Seafood Sales Manager (1984–1991). **Associations & Accomplishments:** NFI. Education: Westchester University, Bachelor of Science (1977). **Personal:** Married to Christina in 1979. Two children: Kyle and Sarah. Mr. Stengl enjoys fishing, boating, and shooting."

Lisa Lorraine Strippoli

Marketing Director
Delilah's Den/Cabaret
100 Spring Garden Street
Philadelphia, PA 19123
(215) 625–2800
Fax: (215) 625–2816
EMail: See Below

5812

Business Information: Delilah's Den/Cabinet is a full service bar and restaurant, as well as an upscale gentlemen's club featuring live entertainment (over 200 International showgirls since 1989). Primary customers are corporate businessmen, but the Club is also open to the general public. Memberships are available along with V.I.P. Services. As Marketing Director, Ms. Strippoli handles all marketing, advertising, public relations, and maintenance of customer database for the Restaurant. She is also responsible for the promotion of conventions, sporting events, VIP parties, booking special appearances, and establishing mailing lists. Internet users can reach her via: delilahs.com. **Career Steps:** Marketing Director, Delilah's Den/Cabinet (1993–Present); Promotions, Penn Distributors (1992–Present); Legal Secretary, Carl A. Price, Esq. (1991–1992); Legal Secretary, Foster C. Ergood, Esq. (1989–1991). **Associations & Accomplishments:** Chamber of Commerce; Pennsylvania Convention Center; International Restaurant Association; FBLA (1986–1987); National Honor Society (1984–1987). **Education:** Camden County Community College, working toward a Bachelor's degree. **Personal:** Ms. Strippoli enjoys fine wines & foods, quiet beaches, music, and mountain biking.

James T. Strobino

Director of Operations
Hard Rock Cafe International
131 Clarendon Street
Boston, MA 02116–5131
(617) 353–1400
Fax: (617) 424–7165

5812

Business Information: Hard Rock Cafe International is an international themed Rock and Roll memorabilia restaurant chain and merchandise outlet. Established in 1971, the Hard Rock Cafe currently employs 4,500 people worldwide. Joining Hard Rock Cafe as General Manager of the New York office in 1989, Mr. Strobino was appointed as Director of Operations of Hard Rock Cafe International in the Boston office in 1994. He oversees all U.S. operations for the Company, including overall responsibility for the units in the U.S. east of the Mississippi (Boston – 10, District of Columbia, New York, Atlanta, San Antonio, Dallas, Nashville, Orlando and Miami). **Career Steps:** Hard Rock Cafe International: Director of Operations

(1994–Present), Regional Director U.S. (1990–1994); General Manager, Hard Rock Cafe–New York (1989–1990); General Manager, TGI Fridays Inc. (1986–1988). **Associations & Accomplishments:** National Restaurant Association; Massachusetts Restaurant Association; American Management Association. **Education:** Trenton State College, B.S. (1983) **Personal:** Married to Colleen in 1991. Mr. Strobino enjoys rollerblading, baseball, music, running, and working with charitable organizations during his leisure time.

James H. Von Bergen

Franchise Area Director
Wendy's International, Inc.
6406 Willow Pond Drive
Fredericksburg, VA 22407–8407
(540) 785–9428
Fax: (540) 785–9428
EMAIL: See Below

5812

Business Information: Wendy's International, Inc. is the franchise headquarters for the Wendy's quick service food chain, started by Dave Thomas in 1970. As Franchise Area Director, Mr. Von Bergen is responsible for the oversight of the largest franchisee for Wendy's International, Inc. and 112 restaurants throughout six states. He also consults to the franchisees procedure compliance, business development, and organizational development, as well as locating sites, handling all aspects of new franchisees from site location to serving customers, as well as providing consultation on the business aspects. Internet users can reach him via: JIMVBERGEN@AOL.COM. **Career Steps:** Franchise Area Director, Wendy's International, Inc. (trademark) (1995–Present); Market Manager, KFC – USA, Inc. (PepsiCo) (1991–1995); Management Development Participant, Johnson and Wales University (1986–1991). **Associations & Accomplishments:** World Tae Kwon Do Federation; Jaycees; Action International Martial Arts Association. **Education:** Johnson Wales University: M.B.A. in International Business(1991), B.S. in Hospitality Management, A.S. in Hotel/Restaurant Management; Schiller International University – Strausburg, France, Hotel/Restaurant Certificate; College Preparatory at Sea Pines Abroad – Salzburg, Austria. **Personal:** Married to Julietta in 1994. Mr. Von Bergen enjoys martial arts, firearms, and computers.

Douglas K. Walker

Controller
Sieta Bar & Grill, Inc.
6553 Superior Avenue
Sarasota, FL 34231–5835
(941) 927–8807
Fax: (941) 924–2818

5812

Business Information: Sieta Bar & Grill, Inc. is a management company that oversees the daily operation of three company–owned restaurants. Based in Florida, the "bar & grill" style restaurants have two locations in Sarasota, and one in Maderra Beach. As Controller, Mr. Walker is responsible for financial record keeping, budgeting, projections, and insurance. Additional responsibilities include advising the Assistant Vice President in all operational matters, as well as overseeing all Human Resources and Administration matters, and making reports to the owners. **Career Steps:** Controller, Sieta Bar & Grill, Inc. (1994–Present); General Manager, Fat Tuesday (1992–1994); Financial Administrator, Retail Technologies Corporation (1989–1992); Assistant Vice President, First Union National Bank (1986–1989). **Education:** University of Notre Dame, B.B.A. in Finance (1984).

Cory A. Washburn

Director of Operations
East of Chicago Pizza Company
318 West Walton Street
Willard, OH 44890
(419) 935–3033
Fax: (419) 935–EAST

5812

Business Information: East of Chicago Pizza Company is a corporation that franchises retail pizza stores throughout Ohio and Indiana. As Director of Operations, Mr. Washburn is responsible for quality control inspections, product testing, research and development, franchise technical support, and creating operational standards. **Career Steps:** Director of Operations, East of Chicago Pizza Company (1992–Present). **Associations & Accomplishments:** Charter Member, Willard, Ohio Jaycees. **Education:** Heidelberg College. **Personal:** Two children: Trey Alan and Cassandra Inez. Mr. Washburn enjoys water sports, reading, and music.

Paul Wenner
Founder and Chief Executive Officer
Wholesome and Hearty Foods, Inc.
975 SE Sandy Boulevard, Suite 201
Portland, OR 97214
(503) 238–0109
Fax: (503) 232–6485

5812

Business Information: Established in 1985, Wholesome and Hearty Foods, Inc. specializes in the development of meatless, low–fat healthy food products. The Company provides healthy food alternatives to restaurants and fast food establishments. Wholesome and Hearty Foods' signature item is the Gardenburger (R), listed on 28,000 menus nationwide. As Founder and Chief Executive Officer, Mr. Wenner is responsible for all aspects of operations; he was also the inventor of the Gardenburger (R), receiving its patent in 1985. Mr. Wenner has been a Vegetarian for over thirty years after being in poor health as a child. Healthy foods are a part of his life, and he is very passionate about his company. **Career Steps:** Founder and Chief Executive Officer, Wholesome & Hearty Foods, Inc. (1985–Present). **Associations & Accomplishments:** Social Venture Network; Business for Social Responsibility; Published in Fortune and Time magazines. **Personal:** Mr. Wenner enjoys frisby golf, disc golf and walking.

Robert Yiannas
Vice President of Operations
Miami Subs Corporation
2928 Barrymore Court
Orlando, FL 32835
(305) 973–0000
Fax: (407) 299–7024

5812

Business Information: Miami Subs Corporation is a 196–unit restaurant chain located in thirteen states. Headquartered in Ft. Lauderdale, Florida, the Company specializes in quick service segment dining. As Vice President of Operations, Mr. Yiannas oversees 50% of the Company and franchise operations. He is responsible for all day–to–day activities. **Career Steps:** Vice President of Operations, Miami Subs Corporation (1995–Present); COO, M.G. III, Inc. (1990–1995); Director of Operations, Pavgar Restaurants, Inc. (1981–1990). **Associations & Accomplishments:** University of Central Florida Alumni Association. **Education:** University of Central Florida, B.S.B.A. (1987). **Personal:** Married to his wife in 1989. Mr. Yiannas enjoys sports and his church.

Bill Young

Proprietor
Big Fish/C.A. Muer Corporation
1548 Porter Street
Detroit, MI 48216–1936
(313) 336–6350
Fax: (313) 336–5711

5812

Business Information: Big Fish/C.A. Muer Corporation is a fine dining seafood restaurant chain with nineteen restaurants located throughout Florida, Ohio, Pennsylvania, District of Columbia, and Michigan. Holding various executive roles with C.A. Muer Corp. since 1987, Bill Young was appointed as Proprietor of the Big Fish restaurant chain in 1995. He is responsible for all aspects of operations, including administration, marketing, and strategic planning. **Career Steps:** Proprietor and Restauranteur, Big Fish/C.A. Muer Corporation (1995–Present); Charley's Crab/C.A. Muer Corporation: Proprietor (1992–1995), Executive Director (1987–1992). **Associations & Accomplishments:** Theta Xi Fraternity; St. Clare de Montefalco Men's Club; National Restaurant Association; Taster's Guild; Grand Action Committee. **Education:** University of Michigan (1982). **Personal:** Mr. Young enjoys hockey, fishing, golf, skiing, and cooking.

Daniel J. Zakour
General Manager and Director of Operations
Applegate Restaurant, Inc., d.b.a. Burger King
1881 Crater Lake Highway
Medford, OR 97504
(503) 773–3669
Fax: Please mail or call

5812

Business Information: Applegate Restaurant, Inc., d.b.a. Burger King is the management office for nine Burger King fast food restaurant franchises in the Southern Oregon region. Established in 1977, Applegate Restaurant, Inc. reports annual revenue of $12 million and currently employs 325 people corporate–wide. With 22 years expertise in the fast food industry, Mr. Zakour joined Applegate Restaurant, Inc. in 1992. Currently serving as General Manager and Director of Operations, he is responsible for all management and operations, including sales projections, opening new restaurants, overseeing daily operations of all restaurants, advertising and hiring. **Career Steps:** Applegate Restaurant, Inc., d.b.a. Burger King; General Manager and Director of Operations (1992–Present), General Manager (1982–1987); General Manager, Wendy's (1987–1992). **Associations & Accomplishments:** Youth for Christ; Operator of the Year (Wendy's International) (1991). **Education:** Oregon Institute of Technology; Hamburger University – McDonald's; Franchisee Training – Wendy's; Operator Training – Burger King. **Personal:** Married to Teresa L. in 1985. Two children: Briana D. and Nickolas S. Mr. Zakour enjoys spending time with his family, church activities, and all sports.

Mr. William J. Zierke
Senior Vice President
Paragon Steakhouse Restaurants, Inc.
10200 Willow Creek Road
San Diego, CA 92131
(619) 635–3828
Fax: (619) 689–2289

5812

Business Information: Paragon Steakhouse Restaurants, Inc. is a full–service fine dining restaurant chain. At present, there are 94 restaurants in ten states (Indiana, Virginia, North Carolina, California, Michigan, Arizona, Nevada, Illinois, Ohio and Wisconsin). Established in 1968, Paragon Steakhouse Restaurants, Inc. currently employs over 7,000 people, and reports annual revenue of $200 million. As Senior Vice President, Mr. Zierke heads the operational side of the Company and sets operational standards. Mr. Zierke is also responsible for financial and growth strategies. **Career Steps:** Senior Vice President, Paragon Steakhouse Restaurants, Inc. (1968–Present). **Education:** Bradley University, B.S. (1971). **Personal:** Married to Sherill in 1975, Mr. Zierke has three children. Mr. Zierke enjoys golf and his children's activities.

Walter S. Zuromski, C.E.C., C.C.E.
Director of Culinary Research and Development
Daka Restaurants
42 Westwood Rd.
Lincoln, RI 02865
(401) 722–2727
Fax: (401) 722–2777

5812

Business Information: Daka Restaurants is a food service management organization, specializing in service to businesses, institutions, colleges, hospitals, and schools. An Executive Chef with over twenty years of expertise, Walter Zuromski serves as Daka's Director of Culinary Research and Development. His primary duties involve new product development and strategies, as well as project management facilitation. Concurrent to his duties with Daka, he continues to consult industry and serves as adjunct faculty in the College of Culinary Arts at Johnson and Wales University. **Career Steps:** Director of Culinary Research and Development, Daka Restaurants (1995–Present); Executive Chef, Mill Falls Restau-

rant (1989–1994); Executive Chef, The Charles Hotel (1983–1988); Additionally Chef Zuromski's consulting assignments have taken him all over the World with Culinary Core Consulting (1989–Present). **Associations & Accomplishments:** Has competed successfully in Regional, National, and International Food Shows/Competitions, capturing many gold medals; American Culinary Federation – Certified Executive Chef & Certified Culinary Educator; Member of the New England Culinary Olympic Team in 1988, Frankfurt, Germany, World Champions; American Institute of Wine and Food; The James Beard Federation, Chosen as one of New England's Great Regional Chefs; Chefs in America, 1991 Boston, Chef of the Year; One of the Founder, Society for American Cuisine. **Education:** Johnson and Wales University, B.S. in Food Service Management (1976); Culinary Institute of America, AOS Occupational Studies, Culinary Arts. **Personal:** Married to Phoebe A. in 1978. Three children: Nicole, Jonathan, and PhoebeAna. Mr. Zuromski enjoys biking, skiing, and wine.

5900 Miscellaneous Retail

5912 Drug stores and proprietary stores
5921 Liquor stores
5932 Used merchandise stores
5941 Sporting goods and bicycle shops
5942 Book stores
5943 Stationery stores
5944 Jewelry stores
5945 Hobby, toy and game shops
5946 Camera and photographic supply stores
5947 Gift, novelty and souvenir shops
5948 Luggage and leather goods stores
5949 Sewing, needlework and piece goods
5961 Catalog and mail–order houses
5962 Merchandising machine operators
5963 Direct selling establishments
5983 Fuel oil dealers
5984 Liquefied petroleum gas dealers
5989 Fuel dealers, NEC
5992 Florists
5993 Tobacco stores and stands
5994 News dealers and newsstands
5995 Optical goods stores
5999 Miscellaneous retail stores, NEC

Mr. David W. Alexander
Facilities Manager
Longs Drug Stores
141 North Civic Drive
Walnut Creek, CA 94596
(510) 210–6999
Fax: (510) 210–6882

5912

Business Information: Longs Drug Stores specializes in the retail sale of prescription and over–the–counter drugs. Established in 1938, the Longs Drug Store chain currently employs 15,000 people in 325 stores in five states and has an estimated annual revenue of $2.6 billion. As Facilities Manager, Mr. Alexander is responsible for the overall management and engineering of all store facilities. **Career Steps:** Facilities Manager, Longs Drug Stores (1987–Present); Energy Coordinator, Mervyns (1984–1987); Manager of Energy Systems Engineering, International Energy Systems Corporation (1983–1984). **Associations & Accomplishments:** Association of Energy Engineers; Association of Professional Energy Managers; American Society of Heating, Refrigeration and Air Conditioning Engineers; Youth Softball Coach; Youth Soccer Referee; Hillside Covenant Church; National Ski Patrol. **Education:** California Polytechnic State University, San Luis Obispo, B.S. in Mechanical Engineering (1983). **Personal:** Married to Jeriann in 1985. Two children: Lara and Katie. Mr. Alexander enjoys skiing.

Daniel W. Barnes, D.Ph.
Director of Pharmacy
Maury Regional Hospital Pharmacy
1224 Trotwood Avenue
Columbia, TN 38401
(615) 380–4056
Fax: (615) 540–4145

5912

Business Information: Maury Regional Hospital Pharmacy is affiliated with a 275–bed acute and subacute medical facility in Columbia, Tennessee. As Director of Pharmacy, Mr. Barnes runs the daily operations. He works closely with the medical staff and hospital administration to maintain quality pharmaceutical service. Mr. Barnes supervises pharmacy staff, inventory, recruitment of qualified help, and assists in long–

range pharmacy expansion plans. **Career Steps:** Director of Pharmacy, Maury Regional Hospital Pharmacy (1992–Present); Administrator, Skilled Infusion Management (1992); Director, Pharmacy & Materials, South Community Hospital (1977–1992). **Associations & Accomplishments:** Tennessee State Hospital Pharmacists; American Society of Hospital Pharmacists; National Rifle Association; Tennessee Pharmacists Association; Central Christian Church: Secretary of Church Board and Church Deacon. **Education:** University of Oklahoma, MPH (1989); South West Oklahoma State University, BS Pharmacy (1976). **Personal:** Married to Mary Ruth in 1987. One child: Gina Elizabeth. Mr. Barnes enjoys collecting guns.

Herb Bobo

Senior Director, Healthcare Services
Big B Inc.
Box 10168
Birmingham, AL 35202–0168
(205) 424–3421
Fax: (205) 424–8087

5912

Business Information: Big B Inc. is a major retail pharmaceutical chain. Headquartered in Birmingham, Alabama, Big B encompasses a five–state area serving customers in 380 store locations. Services provided include pharmacy benefits management, durable medical goods, in–house long–term care pharmaceutical facilities, mail–order pharmacy provisions. A registered Pharmacist with over ten years expertise, Mr. Bobo serves as Senior Director responsible for the administration of all Managed Care Pharmacy Programs, focusing his duties in the areas of product development, contract negotiations, marketing and client relations. **Career Steps:** Big B Inc.: Senior Director, Healthcare Services (1995–Present), Senior Director, Managed Care (1992–1995); Facility Manager, Express Pharmacy Service (1987–1992); Pharmacist, Walker Regional Medical Center (1986–1987). **Associations & Accomplishments:** Academy of Managed Care Pharmacy; American Pharmaceutical Association; Alabama Pharmacy Association; Jefferson County Pharmacy Association; National Association of Chain Drug Stores; Tennessee & Alabama Retail Associations; Georgia Association of Chain Drug Stores; Director, Oxmoor Rotary Club; Alexis de Tocqueville Society (United Way); Literacy Volunteer; Outstanding Young Men of America. **Education:** Birmingham Southern College, M.A. (1992); Pharmacy Auburn University, B.S. **Personal:** Mr. Bobo enjoys golf and boating.

Marshall Clouser

Owner and Pharmacist
Clouser Drugs, Inc.
109 South Madison Street
Madisonville, TX 77864–1902
(409) 348–2184
Fax: (409) 348–5985

5912

Business Information: Clouser Drugs, Inc. is a retail pharmacy, providing pharmaceutical preparations, gifts, and sundries. Clouser Drugs has two stores in the Madisonville area. Establishing Clouser Drugs, Inc. in 1968, Mr. Clouser is responsible for all aspects of operations, in addition to dispersing pharmaceutical preparations and overseeing all administrative operations for associates and a support staff of 6. **Career Steps:** Owner and Pharmacist, Clouser Drugs, Inc. (1968–Present). **Associations & Accomplishments:** Texas Pharmaceutical Association; National Association of Retail Druggists; Chamber of Commerce; First United Methodist Church: Choir, Committees, Sunday School Teacher. **Education:** University of Houston, B.S. in Pharmacy (1966); Tyler Junior College; Stephen F. Austin University. **Personal:** Married to Sunny in 1967. Two children: Katherine Amanda and Edward Marshall Jr. Mr. Clouser enjoys golf, backpacking, fishing, and amateur radio.

Mr. Walter E. Dykes

President
Habana Hospital Pharmacy, Inc.
4710 North Habana Avenue
Tampa, FL 33614
(813) 872–7771
Fax: (813) 872–8295

5912

Business Information: Habana Hospital Pharmacy, Inc. is a full–service, retail and home infusion pharmacy specializing in mail order, prescriptions, home therapy and health care. The Pharmacy has 24–hour health care services. As President, Mr. Dykes is responsible for all aspects of operations for the business including: store management, dispensal of prescriptions, intravenous preparations, patient charting and counseling. He also serves as a medical resource for area physicians. Established in 1970, Habana Hospital Pharmacy, Inc. em-

ploys 8 people with annual sales of $1.6 million. **Career Steps:** President, Habana Hospital Pharmacy, Inc. (1970–Present); Manager/Pharmacist, Touchton Drug Store (1968–1970); Manager/Pharmacist, DeSoto Drug Store (1961–1968). **Associations & Accomplishments:** Deans National Advisory Committee, School of Pharmacy at the University of Florida; Past President of the Academy 100, School of Pharmacy at the University of Florida; Past President, Visiting Nurses Association; Past Member, State Omsbudsman Committee; Member, Hillsborough County Pharmacy Association; Member, Florida Pharmacy Association; Member, Southwest Florida Hospital Pharmacist; Member, National Association of Retail Druggists. **Education:** University of Florida, B.S. in Pharmacy (1961); Emory University, B.A. (1957). **Personal:** Married to Ann P.Dykes. Two children: Walter Edmund Dykes II and Stephanie D. Brooks. Mr. Dykes enjoys golf, tennis, photography and antiques.

Mark Eastham

Vice President
Value Rx
4500 Alexander Boulevard Northeast
Albuquerque, NM 87107
(505) 761–6157
Fax: (505) 761–6126

5912

Business Information: Value Rx is a provider of pharmacy management services to HMO's, employer groups, unions, self–insured groups, and hospitals. Established in 1987, Value Rx is the third largest in its field. As Vice President, Mr. Eastham is responsible for negotiating contracts with pharmaceutical companies. In addition, he monitors contract compliance and is a liasion between the company and drug wholesalers. **Career Steps:** Vice President, Value Rx (1995–Present); Vice President of Purchasing, Diagnostek (1994–1995); Director of Pharmacy, Cigna (1992–1994). **Associations & Accomplishments:** ASHP; NMPHA; PRN. **Education:** University of New Mexico, B.S. in Pharmacy (1986). **Personal:** Married to Michelle in 1992. Three children: Mark, Miranda, and Melanie. Mr. Eastham enjoys public speaking.

Wanda Gonzalez

Pharmacist
Farmacia Borinquen
Calle Barbosa #40
Isabela, Puerto Rico 00662–2912
(809) 872–3660
Fax: Please mail or call

5912

Business Information: Farmacia Borinquen is a full–service retail pharmacy. Joining Farmacia Borinquen as Pharmacist in 1990, Ms. Gonzalez is responsible for all aspects of operations, including sales, public relations and dispersement of pharmaceutical preparations. **Career Steps:** Pharmacist, Farmacia Borinquen (1990–Present); Pharmacist, Fondo del Seguro de Puerto Rico (1988–1990); Pharmacist, Farmacia de Diego (1987–1988). **Associations & Accomplishments:** Colegio de Farmaceuticos de Puerto Rico; Asoc. de Comercio Detallistas Unidos. **Education:** Universidad de Puerto Rico, B.A. (1978). **Personal:** Married to Mariano Perez in 1988. One child: Nicole Perez. Ms. Gonzalez enjoys reading, dancing, manual arts (i.e. lace making & sewing), and sports.

John T. Haun

Owner and Chief Pharmacist
King Pharmacy, Inc.
P.O. Box 490
Welch, WV 24801–0490
(304) 436–3624
Fax: Please mail or call

5912

Business Information: King Pharmacy, Inc. is a full–service retail pharmacy, offering pharmaceutical preparations, religious books, Christian soundtracks, cosmetics, sundries, and a convenience grocery section. With eighteen years expertise in pharmacology, Mr. Haun purchased King Pharmacy as Owner and Chief Pharmacist in 1980. He shares responsibility for all aspects of operations with his wife (who was his inspiration to become a pharmacist), including management of store activities and oversight of all administrative operations for associates and a support staff of 5. His other duties include dispersing pharmaceutical preparations. **Career Steps:** Owner and Chief Pharmacist, King Pharmacy, Inc. (1980–Present); Pharmacist in Charge, Rite and Pharmacy (1978–1980); College Student, West Virginia University and Bluefield State College (1971–1977); Radar Technician/Staff Sergeant, United States Air Force (1966–1971). **Associations & Accomplishments:** Vice President, Adkin District Neighborhood Watch; Sportsman's Club; Triangle Gun Club; Life Member, National Rifle Association; American Pharmaceutical Association; Southern Appalachian Pharmaceutical Association; American Legion. **Education:** West Virginia School of Pharmacy, B.S. (1977). **Personal:** Married to Doris

Ann in 1972. Four children: Crystal Dawn, Tabitha Leigh, LeeAnn Amber, and John T. II. Mr. Haun enjoys horse back riding and target shooting.

Mary Jasinski–Caldwell

Vice President/General Manager
City Pharmacy of Elkton, Inc.
723 North Bridge Street
Elkton, MD 21921–5309
(410) 398–4383 Ext.13
Fax: (410) 398–6903

5912

Business Information: City Pharmacy of Elkton, Inc. is one of the Top 250 independent retail drugstores in the U.S., providing pharmaceuticals, over–the–counter medicines, and home health care equipment. Successfully surviving seemingly insurmountable competition from surrounding drugstore chains, they continue to compete. Starting out performing janitorial services (cleaning bathrooms and dusting shelves) with the City Pharmacy of Elkton, Inc. in 1975, Ms. Jasinski–Caldwell was later promoted to Registry Clerk in the Billing Department, and was subsequently appointed as Pharmacy Technician. Currently serving as Vice President and General Manager, she is responsible for payroll, personnel, computer updates & integration, corporate policy, and decision–making. After the birth of her child in 1992, she became very active in Pro–Life, and as a result started a group called, PARTICIPATE for Life. Her goal is to educate the public with facts and figures about abortion and Pro–Life issues, enabling her to affect many people's lives. She continues to be involved on a very personal level, providing a philanthropic outlook to outreach groups. **Career Steps:** Vice President/General Manager, City Pharmacy of Elkton, Inc. (1975–Present). **Associations & Accomplishments:** American Management Association; National Association of Female Executives; National Federation of Independent Business; Board of Orthotic Certification; Goldey Beacom College Alumni Association; Board of Directors, Maryland Right to Life; Board of Directors, Mission America; Creator and Founder, Particip.a.t.e. for Life!; International Platform Association; National Republican Committee; National Right to Life; American Life League; Pro–Life Maryland; Alpha Chi Honor Society; Knights of Columbus; Bishop Beetler Council; Pro–Life Editorialist. **Education:** Goldey Beacom College, B.S. in Management (1983). **Personal:** Married to William A. in 1990. Two children: Helaina Marie, and Anna Leigh. Ms. Jasinski–Caldwell enjoys pro–life education, and being a pro–life columnist.

Joyce M. Lloyd

Vice President of Sales & Marketing
Wellpoint Pharmacy Management
27001 Agoura Road, Suite 325
Agoura, CA 91301–5334
(818) 878–2648
Fax: (818) 880–2219

5912

Business Information: Wellpoint Pharmacy Management is a nationwide organization specializing in the sale of prescription drugs to other Blue plans. The Company also has a program which updates doctors and pharmacists on new drugs, and any changes in those that have been available. As Vice President of Sales & Marketing, Ms. Lloyd is responsible for sales and marketing of pharmaceuticals. **Career Steps:** Vice President of Sales & Marketing, Wellpoint Pharmacy Management (1992–Present); Regional Director, Warner Lambert–Parke Davis (1989–1992); National Account Manager, Lederle Laboratories (1982–1989). **Associations & Accomplishments:** Academy of Managed Care Pharmacy; Group Health Association of America; National Managed Health Care Congress; Medical Marketing Association. **Education:** Fairleigh Dickinson University, B.S. Degree in Marketing (1984); Phi Omega Epsilon Honor Society; Delta Mu Delta Business Honor Society. **Personal:** Married to Rick in 1988. One child: Thomas. Ms. Lloyd enjoys golf.

Mr. George John Manos, R.Ph.

President
Village Apothecary, Inc.
346 Bleecker Street
New York, NY 10014
(212) 807–7566
Fax: Please mail or

5912

Business Information: Village Apothecary, Inc. is a full–service retail pharmacy. As President, Mr. Manos is responsible for overall corporate management. As a Registered Pharmacist, he also provides all pharmaceutical needs for the company. Mr. Manos also serves as a consultant to major pharmaceutical industries including: Uni Med, Ross Laboratories and Schering Laboratories. Established in 1983, Village Apothecary, Inc. employs 22 people and has $5 million in annual revenues. **Career Steps:** Village Apothecary, Inc.: President (1996–Present), Vice President (1993–1996); Vice President, Standard Importing Company (1980–1983); Assistant Vice President, Krinos Foods Inc. (1978–1980). **Associations & Accomplishments:** Empire State Pharmaceutical Society (PSSNY); Knights of Malta Order of St. George; Masonic Lodge, Franklin Lodge #213; National Association of Retail Druggist (NARD); National Rifle Association (NRA); Who's Who in America; Interviewed by television and other media publications. **Education:** Fairleigh Dickenson University, M.B.A.; Long Island University, B.S. in Pharmacy (1989); Wofford College, B.A.

Gary J. Misiaszek

Supply Chain Management/Logistical Analyst
Consumer Value Stores (CVS)
1 CVS Drive
Woonsocket, RI 02895–6146
(401) 765–1500
Fax: (401) 769–7748

5912

Business Information: Consumer Value Stores (CVS) is an establishment engaged in the retail sale of health and beauty aids and pharmaceuticals. Established in 1963, CVS employs 35,000 people and estimates annual revenue to be in excess of $5 billion. Mr. Misiaszek has been nominated to several task force committees affecting the distribution of merchandise from the various distribution centers. Acting as liaison between the Warehousing and MSI departments, he has been involved in the design and implementation of warehouse information systems. As Supply Chain Management/Logistics Analyst, Mr. Misiaszek is currently involved in a three year effort to re–engineer warehouse processes and implement an integrated warehouse management system into its three distribution centers. **Career Steps:** Consumer Value Stores (CVS): Supply Chain Management/Logistics Analyst (1994–Present), Warehouse Systems Manager (1986–1994), Warehouse Systems Engineer (1983–1986). **Education:** Bryant College, B.A. in Business Administration (In Progress). **Personal:** Married to Mary in 1980. Two children: Jason and Melissa. Mr. Misiaszek enjoys playing classical guitar and learning sign language.

Ronald L. Montgomery

Owner and Chief Pharmacist
F & M Drug, Co.
209 North Douglas Avenue
Ellsworth, KS 67439–3215
(913) 472–3131
Fax: Please mail or call

5912

Business Information: F & M Drug, Co. is a retail pharmacy, providing pharmaceutical preparations by prescription and sundries. Joining F & M Drug, Co. upon graduation from college in 1957 as a pharmacist, Ronald Montgomery has consistently worked his way up the "company ladder". Appointed as co–owner in 1966, he became Owner, President, and Chief Pharmacist in 1980. He is responsible for all aspects of operations, including dispersing pharmaceuticals and overseeing all administrative operations for associates and a support staff of 14. **Career Steps:** F & M Drug, Co.: Owner, President, and Chief Pharmacist (1980–Present), Co–Owner and Pharmacist (1966–1980); Pharmacist (1958–1966); Hospital Pharmacy Consultant (27 years). **Associations & Accomplishments:** Kansas Pharmaceutical Association; National Catholic Pharmaceutical Guild; NARD, Ellsworth Chamber of Commerce; Past President, Volunteer–Fire Department (23 years); Knights of Columbus; Fine Arts Club; Church choir and Lay Minister of Communion; National Guard (1958–1964). **Education:** Kansas University, B.S. (1957). **Personal:** Married to Marlene Mattas in 1964. Two children: Kristin M. Montgomery Bethea and James Andrew Montgomery. Mr. Montgomery enjoys following sports activities, music and musical events, gardening, and working with his hands.

Ike Neal

Owner and Chief Pharmacist
Neal Drug
P.O. Box 609
Cross Plains, TX 46443–0609
(817) 725–6424
Fax: Please mail or call

5912

Business Information: Neal Drug is a retail professional pharmacy, providing pharmaceutical preparations, gift items, and health and beauty aids. An independent druggist and founder of Neal Drug in 1954, Mr. Neal is the owner and Chief Pharmacist. He is responsible for all aspects of operations, in addition to overseeing all administrative operations for a support staff of two pharmacists and dispersing pharmaceutical preparations. He also is the owner of an orchard (peaches, apples, apricots, pecans) and vegetable garden. **Career Steps:** Owner and Chief Pharmacist, Neal Drug (1954–Present); Pharmacist, Frank's Rexal Drug (1951–1954). **Associations & Accomplishments:** American Phamaceutical Association; Texas Pharmaceutical Association; NARD; American Society Consultant Pharmacists; American Society Hospital Pharmacists; Big Country Pharmaceutical Association; Cross Plains Masonic Lodge #627; He and his wife were on the cover of "Drug Topics" magazine, saluting the independent drug operators (independent superstars) in 1992. **Education:** University of Texas, B.S. in Pharmacy (1950); Tennessee Technical University. **Personal:** Three children: Terri Jan Neal Bradford, Sherri Ann Neal Riney, and James Richard Neal, and eight grandchildren (4 boys and 4 girls).

Michael A. Ng, D.Pharm.

Owner and Pharmacist
Ng's Westside Pharmacy
5401 California Avenue SW
Seattle, WA 98136–1512
(206) 937–5722
Fax: (206) 935–0118

5912

Business Information: Ng's Westside Pharmacy is a community pharmacy, providing pharmaceutical preparations, gifts, and sundries. A practicing pharmacist since 1974, Mr. Ng founded Ng's Westside Pharmacy as Owner and Pharmacist in 1977. He is responsible for all aspects of operations, in addition to dispersing pharmaceuticals and overseeing all administrative operations for associates and a support staff of 10. **Career Steps:** Owner and Pharmacist, Ng's Westside Pharmacy (1977–Present); Staff Pharmacist, Long's Drugs (1974–1977) **Associations & Accomplishments:** NARD; APHA; NFIB; Washington State Pharmacists Association **Education:** University of the Pacific: D.Pharm. (1974), B.Pharm. (1973); NARD Management Institute (1993) **Personal:** Married to Arlene J. Mark, a pharmacist, in 1976. Three children: Marissa, Bethany and Joshua. Dr. Ng enjoys golf, skiing and tennis in his leisure time.

Bryan Noar

Vice President of Marketing
Soaring Eagle Ventures Inc.
9820 Willow Creek Road, Suite 490
San Diego, CA 92131
(800) 359–3245 (619) 271–0501
Fax: (619) 271–8375

5912

Business Information: Soaring Eagle Ventures Inc. formulates and markets nutritional supplements and health and personal care products. As Vice President of Marketing, Mr. Noar designs marketing materials and training tools for independent distributors, conducts seminars, and oversees daily operations. Additionally, he is responsible for public relations functions and development of new markets. **Career Steps:** Vice President of Marketing, Soaring Eagle Ventures Inc. (1995–Present); Vice President of Marketing, Vaxa International, Inc. (1992–1995); Nuskin Independent Distributor (1988–1992); Certified Public Accountant, West, Turnquist and Schmitt, CPA's (1986–1988); CPA, Alder, Green and Hasson, CPAs (1983–1986). **Associations & Accomplishments:** Multi–Level Marketing International Association; American Institute of Certified Public Accountants. **Education:** University of California – Los Angeles (Graduate Classes), C.P.A. (1983); University of Cape Town, B.A. in Commerce. **Personal:** Mr. Noar enjoys working out, fishing rand spiritual studies. Additionally, he is an avid supporter of several wildlife charities.

Lcda. Zaida Perez

President
Farmacia Modelo
MJ Cabrero #54, P.O. Box 1677
San Sebastian, Puerto Rico 00685–1677
(809) 896–1154
Fax: (809) 896–1154

5912

Business Information: Farmacia Modelo is a community pharmacy serving the San Sebastian, Puerto Rico locale. A practicing pharmacist and chemist since 1957, Ms. Perez established Farmacia Modelo in 1965. Serving as President of the Corporation, she provides pharmaceutical services and preparations to her customers. She also speaks publicly regarding pharmaceuticals and serves as President of the Volunteers for the American Red Cross. **Career Steps:** President, Farmacia Modelo (1965–Present). **Associations & Accomplishments:** Colegio de Farmaceuticos de Puerto Rico; Majority Leader, Municipal Council of San Sebastian, Puerto Rico; First Vice Governor, District Fourteen Altrusa International of Puerto Rico, Inc.; Red Cross Volunteer; Secretary, Volleyball Association; Governor–Elect for her district, scheduled to take office in 1999; Recipient, Pharmacist of the Year Award (1959). **Education:** University of Puerto Rico, B.S. in Pharmacy and Chemistry (1957). **Personal:** Four children: Manuel, Jose, Lilia, and Laura. Ms. Perez enjoys sports, reading, and volleyball.

Dr. James E. Stone

Director
Syncor International Corporation
330 Research Court
Norcross, GA 3092–2920
(800) 678–6799 Ext.2174
Fax: (770) 416–1299

5912

Business Information: Syncor International Corporation is a distributor of nuclear pharmaceuticals to hospitals and clinics (compounds and dispenses patient specific unit dose radio–pharmaceutical prescriptions). As Manager, Dr. Stone is responsible for process engineering, operations, customer process, networking, and information technology. **Career Steps:** Syncor International Corporation: Director (1994–Present), Project Director, Business Process Reengineer (1994–Present), Executive Director Operations (1991–1994), Director of Operations. **Associations & Accomplishments:** APHA; Society of Nuclear Medicine; Alabama Society of Nuclear Medicine; Florida Society of Nuclear Medicine. **Education:** Mercer University, Pharm D. (1980); Sanford University, B.S. in Pharmacy. **Personal:** Married to Ellen in 1973. Two children: Brian and Michelle. Dr. Stone enjoys tennis and water sports.

Mr. Timothy J. Tommaney

Media Manager
Thrift Drug, Inc.
615 Alpha Drive
Pittsburgh, PA 15328–2819
(412) 967–8064
Fax: (412) 967–8009
EMAIL: See Below

5912

Business Information: Thrift Drug, Inc. — a subsidiary of J.C. Penney, Inc. — is a national retail drug chain located throughout sixteen states and consisting of over 600 stores. Joining Thrift Drug, Inc. in 1984, Mr. Tommaney was appointed as Media Manager in 1993. He is responsible for collections, advertising, budgets, vendor invoicing, expenses, placing print media, and conducting market and Internet research. Internet users can reach him via: TTOMMAN@USAOR.net.com **Career Steps:** Thrift Drug, Inc.: Media Manager (1993–Present), Advertising Income Administration (1984–1988); Automation Analysts (1984–1988); Waste Water Treatment Manager, James Austin Company (1981–1982). **Associations & Accomplishments:** Pittsburgh Advertising Club; International Society of Poets; Literacy Council Volunteer. **Education:** Westmoreland County Community College, A.B.A. (1995); Indiana University of PA; Butler County Community College. **Personal:** Married to Maribeth in 1996. Two children: Todd and Katie. Mr. Tommaney enjoys basketball, golf, baseball, poetry and running.

Gisele Velazquez–Montero

Secretary and Chief Pharmacist
Farmacia La Variante
P.O. Box 1387
Anasco, Puerto Rico 00610–1387
(809) 826–6529
Fax: (809) 826–6549

5912

Business Information: Farmacia La Variante is a full–service, community pharmacy, providing pharmaceutical preparations, gifts, and sundries. With eleven years experience in the pharmaceutical industry, Ms. Velazquez–Montero joined Farmacia La Variante as Secretary of the Corporation and Chief Pharmacist in 1990. She is responsible for sales, public relations, and strategic planning, in addition to dispersing pharmaceutical preparations. **Career Steps:** Secretary and Chief Pharmacist, Farmacia La Variante (1990–Present); Staff Pharmacist, Farmacia Nelia (1988–1990); Staff Pharmacist, Farmacia Luna (1986–1988); Graduated Pharmacist, Farmacia Serrano (1985–1986). **Associations & Accomplishments:** APHA; Valu–Rite Program; Farmacias Aliadas; Colegio De Farmaceuticos de Puerto Rico. **Education:** University of Puerto Rico Medical Science Campus, B.S. (1985). **Personal:** Married to Juan D. Estevez in 1989. Two children: Eduardo E. Estevez and Natalia A. Estevez. Ms. Velazquez–Montero enjoys going to the beach and spending time with her family.

International Who's Who of Professionals™

5912   **Classified by Standard Industrial Code**   5942

Harry E. (Skip) Zamminer III
Chairman and Chief Executive Officer
Zambar Drug Inc., d.b.a. Drug Emporium Inc.
1655 N. Gallatin Road
Madison, TN 37115
(615) 860–0145
Fax: (615) 860–3106

5912

Business Information: Zambar Drug Inc., d.b.a. Drug Emporium. is a super drug store that is category–dominant and value–driven and continues to build good relationships between the consumer and pharmacist from a strong prescription base. A District Manager in store operations with Walgreens for 28 years, Mr. Zamminer joined Zambar Drug Inc. as Chairman and Chief Executive Officer in 1994. Purchasing a defunct Phar–Mor store in May 1995, he is responsible for all aspects of operations, including administration, human resources, store expansion, and overlooking store and pharmacy operations. **Career Steps:** Chairman and Chief Executive Officer, Zambar Drug Inc. (1994–Present); District Manager, Walgreen Drug (1965–1994) **Associations & Accomplishments:** Franchise Advisory Board, Drug Emporium **Education:** St. Louis College of Pharmacy; St. Louis University; Forest Park Junior College **Personal:** Married to Jean V. in 1972. Two children: Jon and Katherine. Mr. Zamminer enjoys tennis, model trains and walking.

Terry R. Zartman
Pharmacist/Manager
Weis Markets, Inc.
860 Carlisle Street
Hanover, PA 17331
(717) 632–7781
Fax: Please mail or call

5912

Business Information: Weis Markets, Inc. is a supermarket chain with 100 locations in and around Pennsylvania. Presently 70 of the 100 locations have pharmacies on the premises. The Company is in the process of developing all locations into one–stop shopping markets. As Pharmacist/Manager, Mr. Zartman is presently responsible for the total operations of the pharmacy department including staff recruitment, training, scheduling, and evaluating. Other responsibilities include conducting stock inventories and maintaining inventory levels to provide quality service to customers. **Career Steps:** Pharmacist/Manager, Weis Markets, Inc. (1986–Present); Pharmacist/Manager, Thrift Drug Company (1973–1986); Pharmacist/Manager, Coover's Pharmacy, Inc. (1971–1973). **Associations & Accomplishments:** Philadelphia College of Pharmacy and Science Alumni Association; Pi Lambda Phi Fraternity; Rho Chi Honorary Pharmacy Fraternity; Chairman, Spring Grove Borough Planning Commission. **Education:** Philadelphia College of Pharmacy and Science, B.Sc. Pharmacy (1971). **Personal:** Married to Sandra in 1971. One child: Melanie Ann. Mr. Zartman enjoys racquetball, coin collecting, and speaking with young people about drug abuse and his choice of career.

Heidi Bintz Friedman
Vice President, Co–Founder, and Co–Owner
Double Diamond of Vail, Inc., d.b.a. Kenny's Double Diamond Ski Shop, Inc.
P.O. Box 1110
Vail, CO 81658–1110
(970) 476–2704
Fax: (970) 476–7129

5941

Business Information: Kenny's Double Diamond Ski Shop, Inc., located at the base of Vail Mountain, is an exclusive, full–service ski shop, providing technical and service–oriented services, as well as offering the consumer the best equipment and clothing available. As Vice President, Co–Founder, and Co–Owner, Ms. Friedman is responsible for the general operations and direction of the office, including purchasing, producing advertising activities, product promotions, and sales. Concurrently, she serves as a ski instructor and Founder of the Double Diamond Clinic for Women Only. **Career Steps:** Vice President, Double Diamond of Vail, Inc. (1990–Present); Owner – Travel Service, Vacation Coordination (1986–1990); Ski Instructor, Vail Associates (1985–1987); Stock and Commodity Broker, Merill Lynch (1982–1985). **Associations & Accomplishments:** Vail Valley Tourism and Convention Bureau; American Morgan Horse Association; Professional Ski Instructors of America (20 year member); Chamber of Commerce; Lion's Head Merchant Association; Michigan State University Alumni; Named Michigan Apple Queen. **Education:** Michigan State University, B.S. (1981). **Personal:** Married to Kenneth in 1987. Two children: Elle and Sophe. Ms. Bintz Friedman enjoys spending time with her family, riding

and showing horses, skiing, hiking, swimming, and instructing her daughters in the art of skiing.

Gordon M. Boivin
Director of Training – Dive Division
Sport Chalet, Inc.
920 Foothill Boulevard
La Canada Flint, CA 91011–3338
(818) 790–2717 Ext. 244
Fax: (818) 790–0087

5941

Business Information: Sport Chalet, Inc. is a retail multi–recreational specialty store for outdoor activities. Divisions include Biking, Mountain Climbing, Scuba Diving, etc. Their Diving Division is the largest nationally. Sport Chalet, Inc. has 19 locations throughout Southern California. Starting his diving career in the commercial and construction industry, Mr. Boivin joined Sport Chalet, Inc. following his retirement from the Canadian Coast Guard in 1992, where he served as the developer and Chief Instructor for the Rescue Swimmer and Rescue Specialist Schools. For Sport Chalet, Inc. he serves as the Director of Training in the Dive Division, responsible for all aspects of operations, including pools, compressors, diving clubs, diving charters, scuba instructors. The majority of the scuba business is created from corporate executives and business people who visit Southern California on trips and want to take a dive or a scuba course. **Career Steps:** Director of Training – Dive Division, Sport Chalet, Inc. (1992–Present); Chief Instructor and Rescue Specialist, Canadian Coast Guard (1982–1992). **Associations & Accomplishments:** National Association of Underwater Instructors (NAUI); Co–Author of three textbooks and author of published articles on scuba diving. **Personal:** Married to Tammy in 1990. One child: Konner. Mr. Boivin enjoys Aikido and Iaido.

Lloyd J. Hart

President
Mad River Rocket Company
P.O. Box 548
Waitesfield, VT 05673
(802) 496–2455
Fax: Please mail or call
EMAIL: See Below

5941

Business Information: Mad River Rocket Company, international in scope, is a manufacturer of toys and sporting goods, including kneeboards for snow which were patented in 1987. Operating from one location, Mad River Rocket Company also has a stunt group, which travels around the country, performing stunts with kneeboards, such as a 360 degrees flip on a table and other available equipment. As President, Mr. Hart is responsible for all aspects of Company operations, including marketing, sales, and management. Internet users can reach him via: Rocket@Madriver.com. **Career Steps:** President, Mad River Rocket Company (1990–Present); Vice President, Aldis Hart Company (1984–1990); Self–Employed, Contract Chef (1980–1982). **Associations & Accomplishments:** Hanwood Hockey Association; Cambridge Hockey Association; Skatium Hockey Association; Brookline Hockey Association; Hockey and Baseball Coach. **Education:** Chef's Apprenticeship, Master Potter. **Personal:** Married to Namiko Z. in 1990. Three children: Alex Malony, and Julie and Glenn Ortiz. Mr. Hart enjoys hockey.

Debra S. Saunders
Vice President and Board Secretary
Golfmart
4200 Wyoming, NE
Albuquerque, NM 87111
(505) 296–5866
Fax: (505) 299–8723

5941

Business Information: Golfmart is a specialty retail store marketing golf products, such as golf equipment, clothing, and accessories. Golfmart is the largest golf retail store in New Mexico, consisting of 12,000 square feet of retail store space. An indoor golf instructional facility is also provided, offering golf lessons and clinics. Established in 1987, Golfmart reports annual revenue of $2.5 million and currently employs 15 people. As Vice President and Board Secretary, Ms. Saunders is responsible for all day–to–day operations, including all financial functions, advertising preparation (placement of TV and printed advertising), Internet catalogue preparation and servicing, and supervision of operations related to personnel. She also serves as a buyer of fashions and accessories. **Career Steps:** Vice President and Board Secretary, Golfmart (1990–Present); Vice President/Controller, Charter Bank for Savings (1987–1990); CPA, Krencik & Associates, CPA's (1986–1987); CPA, Deloitte – Touche (1982–1986). **Associa-

tions & Accomplishments:** American Institute of Certified Public Accountants; New Mexico Society of Certified Public Accountants. **Education:** New Mexico State University, B.A. in Accountancy (1982). **Personal:** Married to David in 1983. Two children: Steven and Sam. An avid golfer, Debra also enjoys reading and keeping fit (aerobics, health wellness fitness).

Sherrie L. Fox
Partner
The Olde Fox Book Shoppe
225 South Main Street
Mt. Vernon, OH 43050
(614) 393–1840
Fax: (614) 393–1849

5942

Business Information: The Olde Fox Book Shoppe is a retail book store, offering best–seller and Top 10 reading material and other publications. Ms. Fox and her husband recently established the store, intending to provide quality service and products to their clientele. Her responsibilities include oversight of daily operations, accounting, marketing, and administrative activities. Concurrently, she serves as Team Leader for Coopers and Lybrand, L.L.P., which is one of the "Big 6" accounting firms in the U.S., and a consulting firm for computer system development for government and private sector accounting systems. **Career Steps:** Partner, The Olde Fox Book Shoppe (1996–Present); Team Leader, Coopers & Lybrand, L.L.P. (1994–Present); Senior Financial Specialist, Defense Logistic Agency (1981–1994). **Associations & Accomplishments:** Treasurer, Critical Incident Stress Debriefing; Mt. Vernon Equine 4–H Advisor. **Education:** Attending, Ohio University; Columbus Technical Institute. **Personal:** Married to William C. in 1988. Four children: Misti D., Charles C., Dayna C., and Jennifer A.. Ms. Fox enjoys golf, horseback riding, and reading.

Blake Kovrig
Vice President
PC Mania/Bookware
6111 Boulevard East 2nd Floor
West New York, NJ 07093
(201) 854–7750
Fax: (201) 854–7747
EMAIL: See Below

5942

Business Information: PC Mania is an international distributor of computer books, specializing in discounted computer publications. Headquartered in Toronto, Canada, the Company distributes through wholesale direct sales marketing, trade shows, as well as retail store operations. Currently there are 36 U.S. and 300 Canadian retail stores in operation. As Vice President, Mr. Kovrig provides the overall executive administration for all operational strategies of the retail stores in the entire North American region. Prior to joining PC Mania, Blake was a successful interior design consultant. His motto for life is: "Confidence Breeds Success....Ego Breeds Stupidity". Internet users can reach him via: bkovrig@aol.com **Career Steps:** Vice President, PC Mania (1993–Present); Owner, Alek Blake Interiors (1992–1993); Home Consultant, Schreiter's Furniture (1990–1992). **Associations & Accomplishments:** K.M.H.A. Hockey Triple A: 2 Time All Star Ontario Champions, Former Assistant Captain, Former Captain. **Education:** Ontario Academy of Arts, Interior Design Certification (1989). **Personal:** Mr. Kovrig enjoys guitar, hockey, and poetry.

Mr. Gary S. McBrayer
Director of Store Administration
Barnes & Noble, Inc.
120 Fifth Avenue
New York, NY 10011
(212) 633–3302
Fax: (212) 645–6929

5942

Business Information: Barnes & Noble, Inc. is a national retail bookstore enterprise. As the largest book retailer in the U.S., Barnes & Noble, Inc. has over 300 store locations across the country. In his current capacity, Mr. McBrayer is responsible for the direction of all corporate store operations and also provides support for the superstore divisional field needs. Established in 1873, Barnes & Noble, Inc. employs over 6,000 persons corporate–wide and reports annual revenue in excess of $1.2 billion. **Career Steps:** Director of Store Administration, Barnes & Noble, Inc. (1992–Present); Director of Stores, Bookstop, Inc. (1983–1992); Director of Operations, Century Bookstores Inc. (1975–1981). **Associations & Accomplishments:** American Management Association; American Booksellers Association. **Education:** University of Texas–Austin, M.B.A. (1983); Baylor University, B. A.

Barbara I. Stuark
General Manager/ Director of Human Resources
Barbara's Bookstore
3130 North Broadway Street
Chicago, IL 60657
(312) 477-0412
Fax: (312) 281-9484
EMAIL: See Below

5942

Business Information: Barbara's Bookstore, with six stores in the city, is the largest independent bookstore chain in Chicago. The two divisions, Barbara's Bookstore and Barbara's Bestsellers, offer a wide variety of titles for Chicago residents. Established in 1963, the chain currently employs 100 people and plans to continue expanding in the Chicago area. As General Manager, Ms. Stuark is responsible for the daily operations of the bookstore chain. She oversees budgets, financial concerns, purchasing, sales training, marketing, and advertising. As Human Resource Manager, Ms. Stuark is in charge of personnel concerns, staffing of the six stores, employee evaluations, employee counseling, and employee benefits. **Career Steps:** General Manager/ Director of Human Resources, Barbara's Bookstore (1995–Present); Director of Guest Services Purchasing, Brookfield Zoo (1992–1995); Director of Retail Operations, Field Museum of National History (1983–1992). **Associations & Accomplishments:** American Management Association; American Booksellers Association; American Association of University Women; American Compensation Association; American Society for Quality Control; Museum Store Association; National Association of Female Executives. **Education:** Keller Graduate School of Management: M.H.R.M. (1996), M.B.A. (1995); Northwestern University, B.S. **Personal:** Ms. Stuark enjoys gardening, reading, and school.

Harrell Barrington
Vice President
Carlyle & Company
3984 Union Ridge Road
Burlington, NC 27217
(910) 227-3543
Fax: (910) 227-3543
Home: (910) 226-2688

5944

Business Information: Carlyle & Company, a three-generation, family-owned business, is a retail jewelry store. Originally established in North Carolina, as "Jewel Box Stores Corporation" before changing to its present name, Carlyle & Co., it now consists of 82 stores and three divisions (Jewel Box – Carlyle – Caldwell/Lavake). A forty-year veteran with Carlyle & Company, Mr. Barrington began his career as a salesman in 1955 in Greenville, North Carolina. Over the span of his career, he has held numerous positions, including Manager, Supervisor, Regional Manager, and District Manager. Appointed as Vice President in 1996, he is responsible for all aspects of operations for the Eastern North Carolina, consisting of ten stores. He also supervises all stores and associates in his district, as well as overseeing sales performances, manager and associate training, future manager development, and meeting with the Carlyle & Co. Home Office in order to improve stores and customer services. In October of 1995, he was inducted into the Company's Hall of Fame, an honor given to employees who have significantly contributed to the Company's growth, profit, and success. Mr. Barrington is quoted as saying, "I am very fortunate to have had the opportunity to learn from and work with some of the best people in this business, Bill Thunberg, Dick Backer, Milton Greenspon, and Ann Cranford, to name a few. I have always taken pride in having some of the best managers/associates in the Company working with me." **Career Steps:** Carlyle & Co. (since 1955): Vice President, District Manager; Regional Manager; Supervisor; Manager; Salesman. **Associations & Accomplishments:** Boy Scouts of America; Optimism Club; Lions Club; Jaycees; Inducted into the Carlyle & Co. Hall of Fame (1995). **Education:** Gemological Institute of America; People Management Courses. **Personal:** Married to Janice. Two children: Kenny and Allison Barrington; daughter-in-law, Patricia and grandson, Roger. Mr. Barrington enjoys fishing and horses.

Bonni G. Davis

Vice President, Secretary, and General Counsel
Finlay Fine Jewelry Corporation
521 5th Avenue, 3rd Floor
New York, NY 10175–0399
(212) 808-2080
Fax: (212) 557-3848

5944

Business Information: Finlay Fine Jewelry Corporation, a wholly-owned subsidiary of Finlay Enterprises, Inc., is the largest operator of licensed fine jewelry departments located in department stores in the U.S. and France. As of April 29, 1995, the Company operated 794 domestic fine jewelry departments in 30 host store groups, located in 43 states and the District of Columbia and 101 licensed departments in France. The Company's licensors include store groups owned by The May Department Stores Company, Federated Department Stores, Inc., Carson Pirie Scott & Co., and Broadway Stores, Inc., as well as numerous independent store groups, such as Liberty House, Maison Blanche, Belk Stores and Gottschalk's. Included in France are department stores owned by Galeries Lafayette. Admitted to the bar in 1986 and licensed in New York and New Jersey, Ms. Davis serves as General Counsel in the Legal Department. She is responsible for all legal matters concentrating in employment law, government business law, and procurement of the Company's insurance policies. Concurrent with her position, she serves as Vice President and Secretary of Finlay Fine Jewelry Corporation and Secretary and Corporate Counsel for Finlay Enterprises, Inc. **Career Steps:** Vice President, Secretary, and General Counsel, Finlay Fine Jewelry Corporation (1988–Present); Secretary and Corporate Counsel, Finlay Enterprises, Inc. (1988–Present); Secretary and General Counsel, Tru–Run Corporation (1988–1989); Secretary and General Counsel, Adrien Arpel, Inc. (1988–1990); S&L Acquisition Company: Secretary and General Counsel (1988), Secretary and Senior Corporate Counsel (1987–1988), Assistant Secretary and Associate General Counsel (1986–1987); Seligman & Latz, Inc.: Assistant Secretary and Law Clerk (1983–1986), Legal Assistant (1983–1986); Legal Assistant, Greene, Althoff & Bonaguidi (1980–1981); Legal Assistant, Weiss, Rosenthal & Schwartzman (1980). **Associations & Accomplishments:** American Bar Association (1986); New Jersey Bar Association (1987); New York City Bar Association; New York State Bar Association (1986), Member of Executive Committee to the Corporate Counsel Section of the New York State Bar; Listed in Who's Who in American Law. **Education:** Touro Law School, J.D. (1985); Trinity College, B.A. (1979). **Personal:** Ms. Davis enjoys competitive tennis.

Sandra L. Davis
Operations Manager
Weavers Gems and Minerals, Inc.
4251 Chestnut St.
Emmaus, PA 18049–1019
(610) 967-3156
Fax: Please mail or call

5944

Business Information: Weavers Gems and Minerals, Inc., d.b.a. GEMSTONE Jewelry, is a retail jewelry chain with more than 100 stores located throughout the United States. As Operations Manager, Ms. Davis oversees eight regional/district managers in ten states. She is responsible for recruiting, hiring, training, and supervising personnel and management staff. Other duties entail travel throughout the operational area to evaluate merchandise mix, competition, and location, as well as to provide directives to increase sales. **Career Steps:** Operations Manager, Weavers Gems and Minerals, Inc. (1993–Present); Training Supervisor, Payless Shoe Source (1989–93). **Associations & Accomplishments:** National Association of Female Executives. **Education:** Central Pennsylvania Business School, Associates in Retail Management; Continuing Education Courses at Lehigh County Community College. **Personal:** Ms. Davis enjoys NASCAR racing, billiards, shopping, volleyball, crafts, and playing with her godson.

Jamie Onate
Director of Global Expansion and Legal Compliance
Jewelway International, Inc.
5151E Broadway Boulevard, Suite 500
Tucson, AZ 85711–3712
(520) 747-9900
Fax: (520) 747-4813

5944

Business Information: Jewelway International, Inc. is an international retailer of fine jewelry via independent representatives throughout the United States, Canada, Australia and the United Kingdom. As Director of Global Expansion and Legal Compliance, Ms. Onate is responsible for the direction of all expansion and legal matters globally, including research of new markets, approving marketing materials, revision of all sales manuals, forms (Spanish, French, English), policies and procedures, and ensuring compliance with guidelines. **Career Steps:** Director of Global Expansion and Legal Compliance, Jewelway International, Inc. (1994–Present). **Education:** University of Arizona, B.S. in Business (1994).

Tina Perez, C.P.A.
President/Chief Financial Officer
Pacula & Gough Jewelry Company, Inc.
6378 West Jefferson Boulevard
Ft. Wayne, IN 46804–3075
(219) 459-6925
Fax: (219) 459-1326

5944

Business Information: Pacula & Gough Jewelry Company, Inc., established in 1986, is a retail jewelry concern with stores in Indiana and Michigan. The stores offer a variety of jewelry styles for all ages and currently employ approximately 60 people. As President/Chief Financial Officer, Ms. Perez has oversight of the stores in the chain. She monitors daily operations and corporate financial concerns. Ms. Perez reports to the Board of Directors regarding the status of the corporation and assists in planning future regional expansion. **Career Steps:** Pacula & Gough Jewelry Company, Inc.: President/ Chief Financial Officer (1996–Present), Controller (1994–1996); Division Controller, North American Van Lines (1991–1994); Division Controller, Northill Corporation (1989–190). **Associations & Accomplishments:** Indiana Certified Public Accountants Society; American Institute of Certified Public Accountants. **Education:** Manchester College, B.A. (1984). **Personal:** Married to Mark in 1988. Three children: Elena, Marina, and Hannah. Ms. Perez enjoys gardening.

Michele L. Williams
Vice President of Credit
Sterling, Inc.
375 Ghent Road
Akron, OH 44333–4601
(330) 668-5760
Fax: (330) 668-5971

5944

Business Information: Sterling, Inc. is a jewelery retailer located throughout the United States. As Vice President of Credit, Ms. Williams oversees the credit functions relating to credit extension, customer service, credit insurance, and credit projects. **Career Steps:** Sterling Inc.: Vice President of Credit (1995–Present), Assistant Vice President of Credit (1993–1995), Director of Credit (1991–1993), Manager of Methods/Procedures (1990–1991). **Personal:** Married to Mario P. Weiss in 1996. Ms. Williams enjoys free time, sports, and writing poetry.

Rawson V. Ingalls Jr.
Vice President
Strang–Hatcher Corp.
PO Box 6206
Richmond, VA 23230–0206
(804) 353-6466
Fax: Please mail or call

5945

Business Information: Strang–Hatcher Corporation, d.b.a. Ben Franklin Crafts, is a retailer of crafts, art supplies and custom framing. They currently have three stores in operation in Richmond, Virginia, with six to seven more planned in the future. With a background in banking, wholesale distribution, and financial planning, Mr. Ingalls joined Strang–Hatcher Corporation as Vice President and General Manager in 1992. He is responsible for all aspects of administration, financial and corporate planning, and human resources. Career milestones include taking the sales of a wholesale distribution company (White Leap Wholesale) in 1978, from $7 million to $48 million in seven years and being appointed as President and Chief Executive Officer. He also set State sales records in his first year with Lincoln Life Insurance Corp. **Career Steps:** Vice President, Strang–Hatcher Corp. (1992–Present); Agent, Lincoln Life Insurance Corp (1990–1992); President, White Leap Wholesale, Inc. (1978–1986) **Associations & Accomplishments:** Jaycees; Chamber of Commerce. **Education:** Virginia Commonwealth University, courses toward M.B.A. (1978); Lynchburg College, B.S. **Personal:** Married to Deborah in 1977. One child: Tyler. Mr. Ingalls enjoys fishing during his leisure time.

Mark R. Johnson, CPA
Assistant Controller
Kay–Bee Toy Stores
100 West Street
Pittsfield, MA 01201
(413) 499-0086 Ext: 379
Fax: Please mail or call

5945

Business Information: Kay–Bee Toy Stores is one of the nation's leading retail toy chain operations. Established in 1959, Kay–Bee reports annual revenue in excess of $1.1 billion. As Assistant Controller, Mr. Johnson is responsible for all external and internal reporting, budgeting, payroll and cash management. **Career Steps:** Assistant Controller, Kay–Bee Toy Stores (1994–Present); Associate, Kevin Jeffers & Company (1993–1994); Senior Manager – Accounting, Victoria's Secret Stores (1991–1993); Senior Manager, KPMG Peat Marwick (1979–1991). **Associations & Accomplishments:** Ohio Society of Certified Public Accountants. **Education:** Indiana University, M.B.A. (1979); Valparaiso University, B.S.B.A. (1977). **Personal:** Married to Debra in 1979. Two children: Ross and Kyle.

Ed R. McClane

Vice President of Marketing
Hobby Town, U.S.A.
6301 South 58th Street
Lincoln, NE 68516
(402) 434–5075
Fax: (402) 434–5055

5945

Business Information: Hobby Town, U.S.A., with 116 stores in 35 states, is the only national franchisor in the hobby industry. As Vice President of Marketing, Mr. McClane is responsible for franchise sales and marketing of products for all 116 stores in the chain. He assists in the development of budgets for his department and monitors expenditures to avoid deficit spending. Concurrently, Mr. McClane is a nationally–known motivational speaker on recruitment, member development, leadership, and organizational structure. **Career Steps:** Vice President of Marketing, Hobby Town, U.S.A. (1995–Present); Vice President of Sales, American Software and Hardware Distributors (1995); National Sales Manager, Hobbico (1986–1994); Branch Sales Manager, United Model Distributors (1983–1986). **Associations & Accomplishments:** International President, Sigma Pi Fraternity. **Education:** Eastern Illinois University, B.A. (1981). **Personal:** Mr. McClane enjoys public speaking, cooking, and walking.

Raymond H. Goodden

President
R. Goodden Corp. d.b.a. Renegade Music Company
P.O. Box 17011
St. Petersburg, FL 33733–7011
(800) 959–3786
Fax: (800) 434–2879

5961

Business Information: R. Goodden Corp., d.b.a. Renegade Music Company, is a direct mail advertising company specializing in catalog sales of musical instruments and equipment, to include guitars, banjos, amplifiers, guitar strings, etc., to musicians and the music industry. While extremely successful in the retail market, the Company hopes to expand into the school market. As President, Mr. Goodden is responsible for all aspects of Company operations, including catalog layout and purchasing from major manufacturers nationwide. **Career Steps:** President, R. Goodden Corp. d.b.a. Renegade Music Company (1994–Present); General Manager, Findeison Ent. dba Suncoast Music Dist. (1984–1994). **Personal:** Married to Amy B. in 1989. Two children: Kaitlin and Jesse. Mr. Goodden enjoys baseball, golf, and card collecting.

Joan T. Myers
Director of Customer Relations
Miles Kimball Company
41 West 8th Avenue
Oshkosh, WI 54901
(414) 231–6975 Ext.3216
Fax: (414) 231–6942

5961

Business Information: Miles Kimball Company specializes in catalog sales and direct mail. Comprised of two catalogs (one offering consumers gift items to fit their lifestyles and the other providing photography accessories.), the Company is international in scope with sales throughout the U.S. and Canada. As Director of Customer Relations, Ms. Myers oversees the day–to–day operations of the Company, assists in strategic planning for the future, and manages the telephone sales and customer service departments. **Career Steps:** Director of Customer Relations, Miles Kimball Company (1996–Present); Director of Call Centers, Service Merchandise (1995); Manager of Operations, Telephone Sales and Customer Services, Gander Mountain, Inc. (1991–1995); Supervisor, Customer Relations, Quill Corporation (1986–1991). **Associations & Accomplishments:** International Customer Service Association; Society of Consumer Affairs Professional in Business (SOCAP). **Personal:** Two children: Tracey Heather and Meghan Noelle. Ms. Myers enjoys interior decorating,

gardening, cycling, going to the races, her four dogs, and jogging.

Nancy C. Ottman
Personnel Manager
J.C. Penney Catalog
5555 Scarborough Boulevard
Columbus, OH 43232–4730
(614) 863–7004
Fax: (614) 863–7031

5961

Business Information: J.C. Penney Catalog is a division of J.C. Penney Corporation, responsible for the fulfillment of catalog retail sales nationwide. Employed by J.C. Penney since 1968, Ms. Ottman was appointed as Personnel Manager of the J.C. Penney Catalog Division in 1988. She serves as the Northeast Regional Personnel Manager, responsible for the oversight of hiring, firing, benefits, and personnel relations for exempt and non–exempt personnel. **Career Steps:** J.C. Penney Catalog: Regional Personnel Manager of the J.C. Penney Catalog Division (1988–Present), Manager of Client Services (1986–1987), Personnel Management (1968–1986). **Associations & Accomplishments:** Personnel Association of Columbus, Ohio (PACO). **Education:** Attended: Capital University. **Personal:** Ms. Ottman enjoys church music, cross–stitch, and the study of butterflies.

Leonard E. Smith
Director of Personnel
Brylane
P.O. Box 7226
Indianapolis, IN 46207–7226
(317) 266–3242
Fax: (317) 266–3393

5961

Business Information: Brylane specializes in the catalog sales of men and women's clothing under the names, Lane Bryant, Roamans, Lerner, and King Size. The Company handles the entire sale, from taking the phone/mail–in orders to shipping the ordered merchandise to the customers. As Director of Personnel, Mr. Smith is responsible for compensation, benefits, compliance, and employee relations. **Career Steps:** Director of Personnel, Brylane (1966–Present). **Associations & Accomplishments:** Indiana State Chamber of Commerce; Indiana Personnel Association; Human Resources Association of Central Indiana. **Education:** Northeast Technical College and School of Art – Colchester, U.K. **Personal:** Married to Michele in 1965. One child: Leonard, Jr. Mr. Smith enjoys barbershop quartet singing.

Jimmy Stevens
Vice President
Catalog Resources, Inc.
97 Commerce Way
Dover, DE 19904
(302) 741–8636
Fax: (302) 678–5439

5961

Business Information: Catalog Resources, Inc. is a catalog fulfillment and telemarketing service. A turnkey operation, the Company provides an 800# for various catalogs, and processes, packs, and ships customer orders from their two Delaware–located distribution centers. Established in 1988, the Company employs 50 people. As Vice President, Mr. Stevens oversees all aspects of the Company's two call centers. He is responsible for management of a large customer service and major clerical department. A lifetime member of the National Association for the Advancement of Colored People (NAACP), Mr. Stevens is also a member of the Urban League, Association of Work Life Professionals, and a recipient of the Penny Partnership Award. **Career Steps:** Vice President, Catalog Resources, Inc. (1995–Present); Manager, Client Services, J. C. Penney (1975–1995). **Associations & Accomplishments:** Franklin University Alumnae; Lifetime Member, National Association for the Advancement of Colored People (NAACP); Urban League; Association of Work Life Professionals. **Education:** Franklin University, B.A. (1972). **Personal:** Mr. Stevens enjoys reading and sports.

Gregory B. Benedict
President & Chief Executive Officer
Fisher Automatic Service
P.O. Box 447, County Road D & 1250
Bryan, OH 43506
(419) 636–2887
Fax: (419) 636–9220
EMail: See Below

5962

Business Information: Fisher Automatic Service is a family–owned, full–line food and refreshment vending and coffee services business. Serving a 50–mile radius in Indiana, Ohio, and Michigan, the Company operates in lunch rooms in both industrial and commercial locations, operating ten routes and one main commissary. As President & Chief Executive Officer, Mr. Benedict is responsible for all aspects of the day–to–day operations, including administrative, personnel, and focusing on legal and financial matters. Internet users can reach him via: fasico@bright.net **Career Steps:** Fisher Automatic Service: President & CEO, (1994–Present), Executive Vice President (1987–1994); Attorney, Erwin & Davidson (1984–1987); General Manager, Johns Automatic Vending (1979–1982); Route & Maintenance, Fisher Automatic Service (1972–1978). **Associations & Accomplishments:** Treasurer, Bryan Rotary Club; President, William County Bar Association; American Bar Association; New Mexico Bar Association; Bryan Area Foundation; Deacon, First Presbyterian Church; Council Board Member, Boy Scouts of America. **Education:** University of New Mexico, J.D. (1984); University of Colorado, B.S. in Finance (1977). **Personal:** Married to Rita in 1978. Mr. Benedict enjoys American history, constitutional/legal history, skiing, fishing, golf, shooting, and computers.

Robert E. Polentz
Senior Vice President & Chief Financial Officer
PIA Merchandising Services, Inc.
P.O. Box 19777
Irvine, CA 92713–9777
(714) 476–2200
Fax: (714) 476–8403

5962

Business Information: PIA Merchandising Services, Inc. is an international merchandising company providing in–store merchandising services for packaged goods manufacturers, grocery stores, and drug store chains. As Senior Vice President & Chief Financial Officer, Mr. Polentz is responsible for all aspects of financial operations, as well as overseeing investor relations, accounting, business planning, income taxes, and treasury. **Career Steps:** Senior Vice President & Chief Financial Officer, PIA Merchandising Services, Inc. (1993–Present); Senior Vice President & Chief Financial Officer, Mobile Technology, Inc. (1991–1993); Vice President of Finance, Hyundai Motor America (1985–1991). **Associations & Accomplishments:** Vice Chairman of the Board, Orange County March of Dimes; Treasurer, Golden West College Foundation. **Education:** University of Southern California, M.B.A. (1972); University of California – Los Angeles, B.S. (1968). **Personal:** Married to Susan in 1969. Three children: Kea, Dustin, and Tyler. Mr. Polentz enjoys snow skiing, fishing, and running.

Warren E. Barbieri
Vice President of Procurement
Alliant Foodservice
389 South Coley Road
Tupelo, MS 38801–7026
(601) 680–8134
Fax: (601) 841–9295

5963

Business Information: Alliant Foodservice is a distributor of over 5,000 foodservice products. Responsible for managing the buying staff and marketing the activities of the company, Warren Barbieri has served as the Vice President of Procurement since 1986. **Career Steps:** Vice President of Procurement, Alliant Foodservice (1986–Present); Buyer and Merchandiser, Kraft Foodservice, Inc. (1985–1986); Sales Representative, Institutional Food Distributors (1984–1985). **Associations & Accomplishments:** Outstanding Young Men of America (1985); Founder, Oleput Festival. **Education:** Delta State University, B.B.A. in Marketing (1983). **Personal:** Married to Michelle in 1993. One child: Noah Vincent. Mr. Barbieri enjoys antique car collecting, art, reading, spending time with his family, and golf.

BKB Direct Marketing Research Inc.

Katherine Chan

Vice President, Research and Analysis
BKB Direct Marketing Research Inc.
2255 Sheppard Avenue East, E400
Willowdale, Ontario M2J 4Y1
(416) 492–2006
Fax: (416) 756–9290
EMAIL: See Below

5963

Business Information: BKB Direct Marketing Research Inc. specializes in marketing research for the direct marketing industry. Founded in 1989, it was the first company in Canada to provide all the research services required by the direct marketing industry – consumer contact research, statistical analysis and database management and consulting, under one roof. BKB has established itself as an expert in direct mail and telemarketing. Recent examples of success include a number of new product development studies, image tracking, customer loyalty and retention strategies, lifetime value assessment, predictive modeling, market segmentation, revenue forecasting, attitude probing and political environment scanning. BKB's current clientele represent major retailers, insurance companies, cataloguers, banks, and petroleum companies in Canada, the United States, Mexico, and Europe. Joining BKB as Director, Research and Analysis in 1990, Ms. Chan was appointed as Vice President in 1995. She is responsible for client acquisition and client contact at the strategic level, translating research plans into marketing action. She also conducts training seminars and speaks at conferences to promote customer knowledge in marketing through research. Internet users may reach her via: katchan@ibm.net.com **Career Steps:** BKB Direct Marketing Research Inc.: Vice President of Research & Analysis (1995–Present), Director of Research & Analysis (1990–1995); Partner of Customer Information, Royal Trust (1988–1990). **Associations & Accomplishments:** Canadian Direct Marketing Association; Sustaining Member and Research Council Member, Direct Marketing Association; Professional Marketing Research Society; American Marketing Association – Toronto Chapter. **Education:** Andrews University, B.B.A. (1988). **Personal:** Ms. Chan enjoys skydiving and snowboarding in her leisure time.

Me. Linda Delorme

Corporate Counsel
Avon Canada, Inc.
5500 Trans–Canada Rte.
Pointe Claire, Quebec H9R 1B6
(514) 630–5443
Fax: (514) 630–8374

5963

Business Information: Avon Canada, Inc., is a division of Avon Products, Inc. the world's leading direct selling cosmetics company. National and international operations provide people throughout the world with the beauty, value and fine quality of Avon products. The most modern developmental and manufacturing techniques are utilized to provide sales representatives with products as up–to–the minute as today. All new product formulas are developed by their global research and development laboratories in Suffern, New York. The design of their packages is the result of a skilled artistic and creative group. Established in 1886, Avon Products, Inc. currently employs 32,000 people worldwide. As Corporate Counsel, Ms. Delorme oversees all legal functions of the Company's Canadian division. Her responsibilities include legal oversight of direct sales, trade marks, employment issues, and litigation. **Career Steps:** Avon Canada, Inc: Corporate Counsel (1995–Present), Legal Counsel (1992–1993); Attorney/Corporate Finance, McMaster Meighen –Lawyers (1991–1992). **Associations & Accomplishments:** Quebec Bar Association; Canadian Bar Association; Canadian Corporate Counsel Association. **Education:** University of Sherbrooke, LL.B. (1990); McGill University, B.A. in Political Science. **Personal:** Married to Antoine Chawky in 1994. Me. Delorme enjoys horseback riding and exercise.

Judy Gunderson

Director
Mary Kay Cosmetics
940 Southeast 4th Court
Deerfield Beach, FL 33441–5910
(305) 427–4697
Fax: Please mail or call

5963

Business Information: Mary Kay Cosmetics is one of the nation's leading direct–marketing cosmetics industries. Mary Kay markets their products through consultants providing at–home make over workshops to provide facials, skin care instruction and sales to the public. As Director, Ms. Gunderson is responsible for recruiting consultants, marketing products and conducting training seminars for consultants. **Career Steps:** Director, Mary Kay Cosmetics (1991–Present); Vice President, American Golf Unlimited Inc. (1995–Present); President and Owner, American Golf of Florida, Inc. DBA Golf and Tennis World (1971–1989); Secretary/Treasurer, Pennisular Properties, Inc. (1969–1971). **Personal:** Married to Jerry in 1971. Three children: Jamie, Jeff, and Marc. Ms. Gunderson enjoys photography and walking the beach.

Manuel N. Sousa

Director of Human Resources
Pepsi–Cola Company
1 Pepsi Way
Somers, NY 10589–2201
(914) 742–4520
Fax: Please mail or call

5963

Business Information: Pepsi–Cola Company is one of the world's leading producers and marketing distributors of soft drink beverages and consumer food products. As Director of Human Resources, Mr. Sousa is responsible for the development and execution of human resource management strategies for the Operations Group of the Company. **Career Steps:** Director of Human Resources, Pepsi–Cola Company (1996–Present); Avon Products, Inc.: Area Director of Human Resources & Administration – Asia–Pacific (1995–1996), Director of Human Resources Planning (1993–1995); Program Manager/Director of University Employment, MARS, Incorporated (1990–1993); Organization Development and Human Resources Manager, (MARS) EFFEM Foods–Canada (1986–1990). **Associations & Accomplishments:** International Association for Corporate Professional Resources (IACPR); Human Resource Professional Association of Ontario; Human Resource Planning Society; Lecturer and presenter at colleges. **Education:** McMaster University, B.S. in Sociology (1982); University of Toronto, Business Studies. **Personal:** Married to Katherine A.T. in 1984. Two children: Jonathan and Laura. Mr. Sousa enjoys squash, tennis, piano, reading, and investing.

Edgardo B. Viera

Vice President
JP Industrial Sales Company
717 Hernandez Street
Miramar, Puerto Rico 00907
(787) 722–0607
Fax: (809) 722–0657

5963

Business Information: JP Industrial Sales Company is a manufacturers representative for industrial and municipal machinery. The Company was established in 1971, currently employs 8 people and posted revenues in excess of $4 million dollars in 1995. As Vice President, Mr. Viera is involved in increasing machinery sales. **Career Steps:** JP Industrial Sales Company: Vice President (1992–Present), Sales Engineer (1979–1992). **Associations & Accomplishments:** Water Environment Foundation. **Education:** University of Puerto Rico, B.S. in Mechanical Engineering (1947).

Pawan K. Agarwal, Ph.D.

Engineering Associate
Exxon Chemical Company
5200 Bayway Drive
Baytown, TX 77522–5200
(713) 425–1372
Fax: (713) 425–2395

5983

Business Information: Exxon Chemical Company is one of the nation's leading producers of crude oil and natural gas, and the nation's industry leader in combined oil and gas reserves. High–quality gasoline and other automotive and convenience products are marketed through a chain of about 10,000 Exxon–Branded motor fuel outlets operated by dealers and distributors, as well as more than 400 such outlets operated by Exxon employees. An Engineering Associate at Exxon Chemical since 1977, Dr. Agarwal oversees all polymer and chemical research and development procedures at the rBaytown, Texas, facility. **Career Steps:** Engineering Associate, Exxon Chemical Company (1977–Present). **Associations & Accomplishments:** American Chemical Society; Society of Rheology. **Education:** University of Pittsburgh, Ph.D. (1975); Washington University – St. Louis, M.S. **Personal:** Married to Alka in 1975. Two children: Neal and Suneal. Dr. Agarwal enjoys reading, golf, and tennis.

Valerie Finneran

National Customer Service & Quality Improvement Manager
Suburban Propane
240 Route 10 West
Whippany, NJ 07981–2105
(201) 503–9964
Fax: (201) 515–5976

5984

Business Information: Suburban Propane is a national supplier of propane gas, serving nearly 1 million customers through 365 sales and service centers. The Company provides fuel service appliances, forklifts, and motor fuel to customers. Established in 1928, Suburban Propane has 3,500 employees and expects to post sales in excess of $700 million in 1996. As National Customer Service & Quality Improvement Manager, Ms. Finneran handles a nationwide call center. She is responsible for customer satisfaction studies and measurement, customer opinion surveys, and compiles quality satisfaction indices. Ms. Finneran makes recommendations to management for motivational programs, operational policies, and training programs. She is also responsible for measurement for performance management. **Career Steps:** National Customer Service & Quality Improvement Manager, Suburban Propane (1990–Present); Director of Customer Service, IMTECH Technologies (1987–1990); Customer Service Manager, Pandick Technologies (1984–1987). **Associations & Accomplishments:** International Customer Service Association; International Society for Performance Improvement; Active speaker at several international customer service associations. **Education:** Pace University, B.B.A. in Marketing (1983). **Personal:** Married to Andrew. Two children. Ms. Finneran enjoys sailing, skiing, running, and competing in 5K runs.

Charlotte R. Windham Hogenson

President
Hogenson Propane
Rt. 7, Box 139AA
Sherman, TX 75090
(903) 786–4456
Fax: (903) 532–6132

5984

Business Information: Hogenson Propane, established in 1994, is a family–owned business and one of the leading marketers of commercial and retail LP–gas in the area. As President, Ms. Hogenson is responsible for all aspects of operations, including the direction of sales and marketing, finances, public relations, and strategic planning. **Career Steps:** Hogenson Propane: President (1994–Present), Marketing Director (1995–Present); Office Manager, Hogenson Paving & Materials (1991–1995); Sales Director, Sheraton Hotels (1989–1991). **Associations & Accomplishments:** Business & Professional Women; Sponsor: Campfire, Inc. **Education:** Grayson Community College. **Personal:** Married to Casey in 1984. Two children: Caley and Colby. Ms. Hogenson enjoys music and travel during her leisure time.

Bruce Tripp

Manager
Star Gas Service
6428 Sullivan Trail
Wind Gap, PA 18091
(610) 863–9016
Fax: (610) 863–5855

5984

Business Information: Star Gas Service is a limited partnership propane company operating in 12 states with over 60 locations. Originally established in 1947 under the name Main Gas, Star Gas Service acquired Main Gas in 1987. The Wind Gap, PA branch, with twelve employees, currently reports annual sales of $2 million. As Manager of the Wind Gap branch, Bruce Tripp is responsible for the day–to–day operations of the business, including delivery services, bottom–line performance, and budgetary oversight. **Career Steps:** Manager, Star Gas Service (1991–Present); Manager, Main Gas (1983–1991). **Associations & Accomplishments:** Rotary International; Board of Managers, Better Business Bureau – Lehigh Valley; N.F.P.A.; N.P.G.A.; Association of String Instrument Artisans. **Education:** William Carey College; University of Southern Maine; Westchester Community College; Northampton Community College. **Personal:** Married to Susan in 1981. Two children: Travis Matthew and Douglas James. Mr. Tripp enjoys building electric guitars, music, computers and travel.

Donald E. Jackson

Manager
Big River Oil Company, Inc.
8538 County Road 418
Hannibal, MO 63401
(573) 221–0226
Fax: (573) 248–1132

5989

Business Information: Big River Oil Company, Inc. is a petroleum distributor with two subsidiaries – D.B. Gray Oil Company and Fowler Oil – and twelve convenience stores. As Manager, Mr. Jackson manages all sales personnel, the purchase and sale of heavy oils, and is responsible for supervision of special projects (e.g., rental property, convenience stores, etc.). **Career Steps:** Manager, Big River Oil Company, Inc. (1994–Present); Manager, Heilig Meyers Corporation Company (1991–1994); Sales Manager, Western Distributing Company (1989–1991). **Associations & Accomplishments:** Missouri Petroleum Marketers Association; Missouri Association of Convenience Stores. **Education:** Central Missouri State University, Bachelor's in Electronics (1987). **Personal:** One child: Amber Nicole. Mr. Jackson enjoys golf, trout fishing, and cars. He is presently restoring a '73 Mustang convertible.

Juan Carlos Sosa–Azpurua

International Marketing Analyst
Citgo Petroleum Corporation
P.O.Box 3758
Tulsa, OK 74102
(918) 497–5751
Fax: (918) 495–5022
EMAIL: See Below

5989

Business Information: Citgo Petroleum Corporation, a wholly–owned subsidiary of Venezuela Corporation and the third largest petroleum refining and marketing/distribution company in the United States, specializes in the production of gasoline, kerosene, distillate fuel oils, residual fuel oils, and lubricants. International in scope, the Company presently employs 6,000 people. As International Marketing Analyst, Mr. Sosa–Azpurua negotiates with international distributors, prepares economic analysis reports, and provides strategic direction. Internet users may reach him via: JSOSA@TUL4.CITGO.COM **Career Steps:** International Marketing Analyst, Citgo Petroleum Corp. (1994–Present); Attorney at Law, Nevet & Mesquita Law Firm (1992–1993); Law Clerk, Baker & MacKenzie Law Firm (1989–1991). **Associations & Accomplishments:** Caracas Bar Association – Caracas, Venezuela; Pro Bono Legal Service, Girl Scouts of America; Board Member, Tulsa Museum of Art; Newspaper Columnist; Class Agent, Harvard Law School. **Education:** Harvard Law School, L.L.M. (1994); J.D. Universidad Catolica Andres Bello, B.S in Sciences Los Arcos. **Personal:** Married to Ines Rohl–Sosa in 1993. One child: Alejandro Sosa–Rohl. Mr. Sosa–Azpurua enjoys running (Boston Marathon), reading, chess, and music.

Bill T. Merana

Managing Acquisition Developer
Supervision Optical Company
208 Lake Parson Green, Suite 1014
Brandon, FL 33511
(813) 662–5589
Fax: (813) 662–5589

5995

Business Information: Supervision Optical Company is an emerging forty–store optical chain located throughout Florida, formed from mergers and acquisitions. The Company has three operating divisions, those being Value Vision, Eye Deals Lab, and 20/20 Optical. Through this configuration, it is organizing private eyecare practitioners, while structuring a network and creating a mechanism by which professionals can competitively practice. Supervision's aim is to take this eyecare enterprise to a public stock offering. As Managing Acquisition Developer, Mr. Merana is responsible for the management of all acquisitions and development activities for the Company. Career milestones include developing and establishing programs and projects to promote savings and improve business, such as: authored VOG–ing As A Performance Tool; Innovated the Expression, Perfecting Profitable Practices; Designed Education and Training Curricula; Agile–Sizing Operations; Developing Financial Controls; Negotiating Unique Vendor Contracts; Setup JIT; Originated, Customer is Boss; Received Customer Care Awards, as well as many others; He is also a Licensed Optician. **Career Steps:** Managing Acquisition Developer, Supervision Optical Company (Present); Associate Manager, LensCrafters; General Manager of Optical Services, California Institute of Eye Surgery; State Educator, State of Virginia Opticianry Program; Managing Lead Optician, Pearl Express; Business Manager/Optician, Sears Opticals; Manager, Vision Works; Trainee, Family Business. **Associations & Accomplishments:** American Board of Opticianry; National Contact Lens Association. **Education:** California Coast University: M.B.A., P.H.D. Candidate; Penn State University, B.S.; Licensed Optician in North Carolina, Virginia, and Florida (in progress). **Personal:** Married to Mary Ward. Mr. Merana enjoys reading, health, Bible Study and family.

David J. Babulski

Master Technical Instructor
Lanier Worldwide, Inc.
5025–C North Atlanta Drive
Tucker, GA 30084
(770) 493–2732
Fax: (770) 493–2743
EMAIL: See Below

5999

Business Information: Lanier Worldwide, Inc. is an international distributor and servicer of business equipment throughout locations in Europe, Asia, North and South America. With headquarters in Atlanta, Georgia, Lanier Worldwide is a subsidiary of Harris Corporation, a Fortune 500 company located in Melbourne, Florida. In the ten year period 1976–1986, Mr Babulski served in various training capacities with the 3M Company in St. Paul Minnesota. Upon transferring to Lanier Worldwide in1986, he was appointed Master Technical Instructor where he is responsible for training technical employees on the functions needed to service, repair and install the Company's equipment. He also develops tutorials for technical programs, as well as screening tests. Internet users can also reach him via: DBABULSK@LANIER.COM **Career Steps:** Master Technical Instructor, Lanier Worldwide, Inc. (1986–Present); 3M Company: Master Instruction Developer (1982–1986), Instructional Developer (1976–1982). **Associations & Accomplishments:** Phi Delta Kappa (Honor Education Fraternity); National Association of Rocketry (NAR); National Science Teachers Association (NSTA); Volunteer Science Enrichment (Middle/High School); Author of 25 articles. **Education:** University of St. Thomas, M.A. in Education (1983); California State University, Northridge, B.A. in Earth Science (1973); Glendale College, A.A. (1969); Currently enrolled with California Coast University, Ed.D. Program – graduation in 1997. **Personal:** Married to Karen in 1969. Three children: Tamara, Katrina, and Timothy. Mr. Babulski enjoys model aviation and rocketry, astronomy, fine art, and operating ham radios.

Mario O. Campos

Vice President
MRC and Sons
P.O. Box 360689
San Juan, Puerto Rico 00936–0689
(809) 749–9398
Fax: (809) 749–9313

5999

Business Information: MRC and Sons, a family–owned business, is an international manufacturer's representative firm, providing marketing services for Puerto Rican manufacturers in all export and global trade ventures. Joining the family business upon graduation in 1991, Mr. Campos serves as Vice President responsible for all aspects of general management, as well as the oversight of all sales, marketing, and public relations functions. **Career Steps:** Vice President, MRC and Sons (1975–Present). **Associations & Accomplishments:** American Chamber of Commerce; Puerto Rico Chamber of Commerce. **Education:** Fordham University, B.A. (1991). **Personal:** Married to Martha Wiltz in 1992. One child: Mario A. Mr. Campos enjoys fishing, scuba diving, squash, and spending time with family.

John Diwishek

Director of Research and Development
Fingerhut
1250 Industrial Park Boulevard
Eveleth, MN 55734
(218) 744–1001
Fax: (218) 744–3552

5999

Business Information: Fingerhut is a nationally known catalog company which sells a wide variety of items. As Director of Research and Development, Mr. Diwishek runs the telemarketing center calling internal/existing customers with product offers. He is responsible for all training, research and development, and authoring publications for one of the tele–centers. **Career Steps:** Fingerhut: Director of Research and Development (1993–Present), Supervisor (1992–1993); Substitute Teacher, Hermantown/Duluth School District (1992–1993). **Education:** University of Minnesota – Duluth, B.A.A. (1992); Mesabi Community College, A.A. **Personal:** Mr. Diwishek enjoys martial arts, all sports, and music (guitar).

Linda Kaye Fourshee

District Manager
Corning Revere Factory Outlet Stores
763 Kentucky Highway 514
Princeton, KY 42445
(502) 365–2304
Fax: (502) 365–2118

5999

Business Information: Corning, Inc. is a global leader in the manufacture, research, development, and marketing of glass, optical fiber, health services, telecommunications, environmental, and consumer products. Corning and its subsidiaries are well–known for their ceramic tableware (Corelle) and bakeware (Corningware). Located in North and South America, Europe and Asia, Corning reports annual revenue of $4.8 billion and currently employs 39,000 people. Ms. Fourshee was named District Manager for the twelve Corning Revere Factory Outlet Stores in Kentucky, Ohio, and Tennessee in September of 1990. She is responsible for staff hiring and training, auditing, customer service functions, and various administrative duties. **Career Steps:** Corning Revere Factory Outlet Stores: District Manager (1990–Present), Manager (1988–1990); Buyer and Bookkeeper, Trigg Supply (1980–1988); Sales and Bookkeeper, Fourshee Building Supply (1973–1979). **Associations & Accomplishments:** Member, Former First Vice President and President, Women's Club of Cadiz; Member and Former Secretary, Cadiz Gateway Garden Club; Trigg County Homemakers: State Vice President, Extension District Board of Directors, Former County Vice President and President, Former Pennyville Area Vice President and President. **Education:** Attended, University of Kentucky. **Personal:** Ms. Fourshee enjoys gardening and needlepoint.

Mr. Robert S. Heath

Senior Vice President of Sales
Beauti Control Cosmetics, Inc.
2121 Midway Road
Carrollton, TX 75006
(972) 458–0601
Fax: (972) 776–4004

5999

Business Information: Beauti Control Cosmetics, Inc., headquartered in Carrollton, Texas, is an international direct sales company of cosmetics and skin care products. As Senior Vice President of Sales, Mr. Heath manages the entire internal and external sales force. Established in 1981, Beauti Control Cosmetics, Inc. currently employs 300 internal and 52,000 external sales representatives and has annual revenue in excess of $170 million. **Career Steps:** Vice President of Sales and Leadership Development, Beauti Control Cosmetics, Inc. (1992–Present); Managing Director of Leadership Development, Beauti Control Cosmetics, Inc. (1991–1992); District Director, Beauti Control Cosmetics, Inc. (1989–1991). **Associations & Accomplishments:** Active politically with support to local and national campaigns. **Education:** Mars Hill University, B.S. (1987); Attended Southern Methodist University. **Personal:** Married. One child: Taylor Elaine. Mr. Heath enjoys water skiing and scuba diving.

William (Jay) Jones Jr.

Software Quality Assurance Manager
Lanier Worldwide
4667 North Royal Atlanta Drive
Tucker, GA 30084–3802
(770) 493–2142
Fax: (770) 493–2491
EMAIL: wjjones@lanier.co

5999

Business Information: Lanier Worldwide is an international distributor and servicer of business equipment with locations in Europe, Asia, North and South America. With headquarters in Atlanta, Georgia, Lanier Worldwide is a subsidiary of the Harris Corporation, a Fortune 500 company located in Melbourne, Florida. As Software Quality Assurance Manager, Mr. Jones is responsible for leading the Corporation by being the Customer's Advocate and the Company's Conscience. Internet users can reach him via: wjjones@lanier.com. **Career Steps:** Software Quality Assurance Manager, Lanier Worldwide (1996–Present); Quality Systems Engineer, TSW International (1995); Owner, Business Physicians (1995); IBM: Corporate Consultant (1991), Software Product Developer (1989), Software Assurance Product Manager (1987), Hardware Quality Assurance, Product Manager (1980), Manufacturing Technician (1977). **Associations & Accomplishments:** American Management Association; IEEE Computer Society; Certified ISO 9000 Lead Assessor; Kepner Tregoe Problem Solving and Decision Making; SQL Database Administration; Lotus Notes Administration/Developer; OS/2 Lan Administration; C++, PLI, APL, REXX, XEDIT, KEDIT, SQL, QME, 1C1, AS, CMS, SAS, Script GML, Book Master, Book Manager; American Society for Quality Control; Alpha Kappa Mu Honor Society; Outstanding College Students of America; Outstanding Young Men of America; Authorized to teach the SEI Process Program's Personal Software Process Control. **Education:** North Carolina Central University, B.S. in Computer Science (1990); Durham Technical Institute, A.A.S. in Electronics Engineering Technology (1973). **Personal:** Married to Darah M. in 1976. Four children: Jennifer, Sarah, Jonathan, and Samuel. Mr. Jones enjoys spending time with his family.

Donna R. Latta
Director of Systems and Planning
The Longaberger Company
95 N Chestnut Street
Dresden, OH 43821
(614) 754–6537
Fax: (614) 754–6541

5999

Business Information: The Longaberger Company is a family–owned business known for the manufacture of hand–woven baskets. The baskets are sold at home parties nationwide. As Director of Retail Systems and Planning, Ms. Latta is currently working on the planning and development team for a retail/entertainment center the Company plans to open in the year 2000. **Career Steps:** Director of Systems and Planning, The Longaberger Company (1994–Present); Control Buyer, Victoria's Secret Stores (1990–1994); Manager of Planning and Distribution, Lazarus Department Stores (1986–1990); Merchandise Coordinator, The Limited Stores, Inc. (1980–1986). **Associations & Accomplishments:** Columbus Zoo; National Geographic Society; Parent Teacher Association. **Education:** Ohio University, B.A. (1973). **Personal:** One child: Tiffany Nicole. Ms. Latta enjoys show dogs and Little League sports.

Kathy M. LaVanier

Vice President of Merchandising
Wicks 'n' Sticks
P.O. Box 4586
Houston, TX 77210–4586
(713) 874–3677
Fax: (713) 874–3655
EMAIL: See Below

5999

Business Information: Wicks 'n' Sticks is one of the world's leading retailers of candles and home fragrance products. Established in 1968, Wicks 'n' Sticks has grown to 205 stores, 202 franchises, and 3 corporate stores. As Vice President of Merchandising, Mrs. LaVanier is responsible for product selection, vendor approval, assortment planning, corporate buying, and two large private trade shows each year. Internet users can reach her via: CANDLEKATH@AOL.COM **Career Steps:** Vice President of Merchandising, Wicks 'n' Sticks (1995–Present); Walt Disney Attractions: Senior Buyer (1993–1995), Character Buyer (1991–1993), Control Buyer for Souvenirs and Stationary (1990–1991); Summit Corporation: Giftware Buyer (1988–1991), District Manager (1986–1988); District Manager, Brookstone Company (1983–1986); Centre Point Mall: Store Manager (1980–1983), Mall Manager (1981–1983), Department Manager (1972–1979), Clerk (1968–1972). **Associations & Accomplishments:** Mentor, Orlando/Orange County Compact (1990–1995); Speaker, Teach–In 2000 (1992, 1993); The Heart of Florida United Way, Division Chairman, Special Task Force (1990–1995); The Greater Orlando Chamber of Commerce; Kissimee/Osceola Chamber of Commerce; Channel 24 Public Television, Operator, Annual Fund Raiser Auction; Beta House, Fund Raiser. **Education:** Willmar Community College, A.A. (1980). **Personal:** Married to William in 1975. Mrs. LaVanier enjoys gardening, painting, and reading.

Melvin B. Locklear Sr.
Director
Truth Haven, UBO
P O Box 39657
Baltimore, MD 21212
(410) 391–6886
Fax: (410) 391–6887
E MAIL: See Below

5999

Business Information: Truth Haven, UBO (Un–incorporated Business Organization) is dedicated to spreading the true good news of the Holy Bible, the Gospel, and more mundane news for the good health and well being of Christians and those seeking the truth. Communication is conducted by E–Mail, FAX, telephone, one–on–one, and through prearranged forums and meetings. As Director, Mr. Locklear maintains communications with the public primarily via Internet Home Page on the World Wide Web and by posting worthy comments from other seekers of the truth on the Internet Page. In addition, Mr. Locklear provides spiritual guidance counseling for those who seek it and provides Bible study lessons. Internet users may contact him via: melbatsan@sprynet.com. **Ca-**

reer Steps: Director, Truth Haven, UBO (1995–Present); Associate Professor, Lincoln University (1992–1993); Active Marketing and Systems Engineering, IBM (1965–1991). **Associations & Accomplishments:** Master Mason, Prince Hall Freemasons Jerusalem Piligrim; Certified International Financier; Jaycees; ToastMaster; Junior Achievement; **Education:** National University, M.B.A.; IBM Advanced Business Institute; Morgan State University, B.S. in Mathematics. Various Bible Study Courses. **Personal:** Four children: Lori, Melvin, Lelsie, and Myron. Mr. Locklear enjoys boating, fishing, painting, hiking, camping and Bible study.

Debra A. May
Director of Publications
Petland, Inc.
195 North Hickory Street
Chillicothe, OH 45601–2610
(614) 775–2464
Fax: (614) 775–2575

5999

Business Information: Petland, Inc. is a retail pet store franchise chain in the United States, Canada, Japan, and France. Established in 1967, the Corporation currently has over 150 franchise stores worldwide. As Director of Publications, Ms. May produces employee newsletters, press releases, educational materials, and a multi–color magazine on pets. **Career Steps:** Director of Publications, Petland, Inc. (1987–Present); Reporter/Photographer, Chillicothe Gazette/Gannett (1983–1987); Reporter/Photographer, The Daily Telegram/ Thompson Newspapers (1979–1983). **Education:** Adrian College, B.A. in English/Journalism (1980). **Personal:** Ms. May enjoys kite flying, rollerblading, and tennis.

Richard S. Siska
Senior Vice President Sales National/International Sales
Ben Franklin Stores
36 Pheasant Run
Lake Zurich, IL 60047–9785
(708) 462–6390
Fax: Please mail or call

5999

Business Information: Ben Franklin Stores is a franchisor and national wholesaler of craft and variety merchandise. Established in 1885, Ben Franklin Stores reports annual revenue of $400 million and currently employs 1,200 people. As Senior Vice President of National and International Sales, Mr. Siska is responsible for all national sales and public trade. **Career Steps:** Senior Vice President on National and International Sales, Ben Franklin Stores (1993–Present); Vice President of Sales and National Accounts, Wilton Industries (1987–1993); Vice President of Sales, R.A. Briggs Company (1972–1986). **Associations & Accomplishments:** Independent Mass Retailing Association (IMRA); American Creative Craft Industries (ACCI); Hobby Industries Association (HIA). **Education:** Christian Brothers University, B.S. in Business Administration (1969). **Personal:** Married to Christine in 1969. Two children: Cara and Kylene. Mr. Siska enjoys tennis, bicycling, and reading.

Rosamaria Sostilio
Corporate Loss Prevention Director
Saks Fifth Avenue
12 East 49th Street
New York, NY 10022
(212) 940–4403
Fax: (212) 940–4411

5999

Business Information: Saks Fifth Avenue is a major international chain of retail stores, providing high quality merchandise. Established in 1929, Saks Fifth Avenue reports annual revenue of $1.6 billion and currently employss 13,000 people company–wide. With fourteen years experience in loss prevention management, Ms. Sostilio joined Saks Fifth Avenue in 1989. Serving as Corporate Loss Prevention Director, she directs, and is accountable for, all aspects of asset protection and retail–loss prevention. **Career Steps:** Corporate Loss Prevention Director, Saks Fifth Avenue (1989–Present); Loss Prevention Management, Bloomingdales (1981–1989). **Associations & Accomplishments:** Make–a–Wish Foundation; American Society International Security; National Retail Federation; Retail Loss Prevention Association; Association of Women's Economic Development. **Education:** Boston University, B.A. in Psychology (1985). **Personal:** Ms. Sostilio enjoys golf, tennis, travel and reading during her spare time.

Charles R. Tilden
Vice President of Corporate Affairs
Alco Standard Corporation
825 Duportail Road
Wayne, PA 19087–5525
(610) 993–3608
Fax: (610) 644–1574
EMAIL: CTilden027

5999

Business Information: Alco Standard Corporation is an international holding company for office supply and equipment entities, distributing to customers throughout the U.S., United Kingdom, Canada, and Mexico. The Company's holdings are as follows: Alco Office Products – a marketer, distributor, and servicer of office copiers; and Unisource – a distributor of fine paper and supply systems, such as packaging supplies, tapes, shrink wrap, and sanitary maintenance supplies. Established in 1965, Alco Standard Corporation reports annual revenue of $10 billion and currently employs 32,000 people. As Vice President of Corporate Affairs, Mr. Tilden is responsible for the management of corporate communications and investor relations. **Career Steps:** Vice President of Corporate Affairs, Alco Standard Corporation (1994–Present); GENCORP: Vice President of Communications (1988–1994), Director of Communcations (1985–1988); Professor, Depauw University (1983–1985). **Associations & Accomplishments:** Arthur Page Society – Professional Communications Society; Vice President, Forum; Puerto Rico Seminar; St. Peter's Episcopal Church. **Education:** University of Chicago, M.B.A. (1982); DePauw University, B.A. (1975). **Personal:** Married to Beth in 1977. Three children: Matthew, Emily, and Michael. Mr. Tilden enjoys golf, tennis, cycling, and reading.

Ferdinand Vevante

Executive Vice President
Aquacade Swimming Pool Service
200 Levittown Pkwy
Hicksville, NY 11801–6131
(516) 433–5230
Fax: (516) 433–5230

5999

Business Information: Aquacade Swimming Pool Service is a pool and spa service company, supplying and building above ground and underground pools and spas. The Company also supplies and builds indoor pools primarily for residential use. As Executive Vice President, Mr. Vevante is responsible for all aspects of company operations, including administration, finance, sales, public relations, accounting, legal, taxes, marketing, and strategic planning. **Career Steps:** Executive Vice President, Aquacade Swimming Pool Service (1965–Present); Self Employed/President, Service Stations, Used Car Sales, Car/Truck Rental (1954–1964); Auto Mechanic/Supervisor, Nassau County Department of Public Works (1964–1990). **Associations & Accomplishments:** Elks Club; Sons of Italy; Little League; Various Political Parties. **Education:** Post College, B.S. in Business (1977); Various training and courses in automotive related subjects. **Personal:** Married to Theresa in 1949. Five children: Michael, Kevin, Brian, Ferdinand, and Barry. Mr. Vevante enjoys fishing, golf, and roller skating.

Manuel J. Yturbe, C.P.A.
Director
Dos Lunas, S.A., C.V.
9051–C Siempre Viva Road, Suite 40–450
San Diego, CA 92173
(52)114–31969
Fax: (52)114–31969

5999

Business Information: Dos Lunas, S.A., C.V. is a 1200 square–foot, Southwestern–style clothing, jewelry and art gallery located in Cabo San Lucas, specializing in the sale of one–of–a–kind items such as leather bags and paintings done by local artists or imported from exotic locations such as India, Guatemala, Indonesia, the United States and Mexico. As Director, Mr. Yturbe is responsible for all aspects of operations, including purchasing, personnel and advertising. Mr. Yturbe considers himself a promoter, arranging for balloon rides, doing radio talk shows, and other promotional strategies. **Career Steps:** Director, Dos Lunas, S.A., C.V. (1990–Present); Public Relations Manager, Cabo Real (1985–1994); Sales Director, Autos Mexico – Chrysler Dealership (1978–1984); Executive Accountant, Banco Internacional (1972–1978). **Associations & Accomplishments:** Amigos Delos Ninos, Cabo San Lucas, Mexico. **Education:** University of Anahuac, C.P.A. (1976); Salisbury School of Connecticut. **Personal:**

Mr. Yturbe enjoys golf, scuba diving, music, photography and skiing.

6000 – 6999

FINANCE,

INSURANCE

and

REAL ESTATE

6000 Depository Institutions

6011 Federal reserve banks
6019 Central reserve depository, NEC
6021 National commercial banks
6022 State commercial banks
6029 Commercial banks, NEC
6035 Federal savings institutions
6036 Savings institutions, except federal
6061 Federal credit unions
6062 State credit unions
6081 Foreign bank and branches and agencies
6082 Foreign trade and international banks
6091 Nondeposit trust facilities
6099 Functions related to deposit banking

Julia K. Holman
Economic Analyst
Federal Reserve Bank of Atlanta
104 Marietta Street, NW
Atlanta, GA 30303–2713
(404) 614–7986
Fax: (404) 521–8956
EMAIL: See Below

6011

Business Information: Federal Reserve Bank of Atlanta is a regional reserve and rediscount institution for their member banks. As Economic Analyst of the Latin America Research Department, Ms. Holman provides country–risk assessment for various Latin American countries, including monitoring economic and banking developments in Latin America. Internet users can reach her via: jholman@frbatlanta.org. **Career Steps:** Economic Analyst, Federal Reserve Bank of Atlanta (1995–Present); Institutional Sales and Trading Assistant, Kidder, Peabody, and Co., Inc. (1992–1993); Sales Assistant, Corporate Services Department, Montgomery Securities (1991–1992). **Associations & Accomplishments:** Atlanta Council on International Relations; Toastmasters International; Organization of Women in International Trade. **Education:** Johns Hopkins – School of Advanced International Studies, M.A. in International Relations (1995); Vanderbilt University, B.S. in European History (1991); Universite de Paris IV, La Sorbonne, Certificat de francais commercial et economique (1990). **Personal:** Ms. Holman enjoys hiking, biking, and swimming. She is fluent in French, Italian, Spanish, and Portuguese.

Dr. Frank Yutian Lei
Senior Operation Support Analyst
Federal Reserve Bank of New York
33 Liberty Street, Room 917
New York, NY 10045
(212) 720–2838
Fax: (212) 720–1379

6011

Business Information: Federal Reserve Bank of New York is the central bank of the United States acting as a government banker and supervisor of commercial banks. Established in 1914, the Agency currently employs 2,500 people. As Senior Operation Support Analyst, Dr. Lei is responsible for computer system and network administration with research and market analysis groups. **Career Steps:** Senior Operation Support Analyst, Federal Reserve Bank of New York (1995–Present); McWilliams Forge Company, Inc.: CAD/CAM Consultant (1995–Present), CAD/CAM Systems Specialist (1991–1995); Research Assistant, New Jersey Institute of Technology (1990–1991). **Associations & Accomplishments:** Numerous Publications including: "On the Natural Vibration of Thick Plates on Elastic Foundations," Journal of Vibration & Shock,

VI (1987), "Simplified Method for Elasto–Plastic Analysis of Structures under Variable Cyclic Loading," International Journal Pres. & Pipe, V49 (1992), "A Constitutive Model and Elastoplastic Analysis of Structures under Cycle Loading," ACTA Mechanica Solida Sinica, V4 N I (1991). **Education:** Tsinghua University, China, Ph.D. (1989); Zhongshan University, B.S. (1983). **Personal:** Dr. Lei enjoys swimming, tennis and music.

Eldon L. Richardson II
Senior Vice President of Lending/Mortgage Banking Division
Coast Federal Bank
P.O. Box 9115, CST Center
Van Nuys, CA 91409–9115
(818) 366–8732
Fax: (818) 831–8819
EMAIL: See Below

6011

Business Information: Coast Federal Bank is an 8 billion dollar federal financial institution, specializing in real estate lending. As Senior Vice President of the real estate lending/Mortgage Banking Division, Mr. Richardson directly manages all sales and operations of the 200 employee Division. His career milestones include development of a 500 acre Cedar Hills township in 1975, the creation of the inflation responsive mortgage (IRM) in 1980. The mortgage is now referred to as the price level adjusted mortgage (PLAM). The PLAM enabled mortgage interest rates to be at 8% during a period of history when rates were at 15%. Most recently he has centralized and IMAGED all loan processing along with automated loan origination through POS/EDI. Internet users can reach him via: BUBBADICK.AOL.COM **Career Steps:** Senior Vice President of Lending/Mortgage Banking Division, Coast Federal Bank (Present); Managing Director, R.E. Lending, Home Fed Bank; Executive Vice President/Chief Lending Officer, Gibralter Savings; Executive Vice President/CEO, McNeil–Mehew Group. **Associations & Accomplishments:** National Association of Mortgage Underwriters; National Association of Review Appraisers; Mortgage Bankers Association; Past State Vice President, National Association of Home Builders. **Education:** El Camino College (1972). **Personal:** Married to Christine in 1969. One child: Benjamin. Mr. Richardson enjoys golf and flyfishing.

Mr. David I. Robbins
Senior Consumer Affairs Specialist
Federal Reserve Bank of San Francisco
P.O. Box 7702
San Francisco, CA 94120
(415) 974–2967
Fax: (415) 393–1921

6011

Business Information: The Federal Reserve Bank of San Francisco promulgates and enforces Federal consumer banking for chartered banks that are members of the Federal Reserve. As Senior Consumer Affairs Specialist, Mr. Robbins counsels consumers regarding the law governing the Federal Reserve and investigates complaints involving consumer law including illegal discrimination. Established in 1914, Federal Reserve Bank of San Francisco employs 2,000 people. **Career Steps:** Senior Consumer Affairs Specialist, Federal Reserve Bank of San Francisco (1978–Present); Administrative Assistant, Veterans Administration (1975–1977). **Associations & Accomplishments:** California Bar Association; American Bar Association. **Education:** San Francisco Law School, LL.M. (1987); California Costa Junior College, A.A. (1968); California University at Hayward, B.A. (1973); California University at Hayward, M.A. (1977). **Personal:** Mr. Robbins enjoys creative writing and cardboard/paper sculpture.

Sherrill L. Shaffer, Ph.D.
Assistant Vice President
Federal Reserve Bank of Philadelphia
10 Independence Mall
Philadelphia, PA 19106
(215) 574–6416
Fax: (215) 574–2507

6011

Business Information: Federal Reserve Bank of Philadelphia is a regional reserve and rediscount institution for their member banks. Established in 1913, the Federal Reserve Bank of Philadelphia currently employs 1,100 people. As Assistant Vice President, Dr. Shaffer is the Discount Officer and head of Banking Studies. **Career Steps:** Assistant Vice President, Federal Reserve Bank of Philadelphia (1988–Present); Chief and Senior Economist, Federal Reserve Bank of New York (1980–1988); Economics Consulting Assistant, Rosse and Olszewski (1978–1980); Instructor, Teaching Assistant, Research Assistant, Stanford University (1976–1980).

Associations & Accomplishments: American Economics Association; Financial Management Association; Industrial Organization Society; North American Economics and Finance Association; American Mathematical Society; Mathematical Association of America; New York Academy of Sciences; Observing Chairman (1993), Publicity Chairman (1994–Present), Delaware Valley Amateur Astronomers (1993); Secretary and Board of Directors, New York Arts Group (1982–1983); Who's Who in the World (1995–1996); Who's Who in the East (1988–1996); Who's Who in Finance and Industry (1990–1995); Who's Who in U.S. Commercial and Savings Banks (1991); Who's Who Among Young American Professionals (1992–1993); Who's Who in Science and Engineering (1992–1993); Violinist with various orchestras: (university, civic and professional) including Concort Master, New York (1981–1983), Symphony for United Nations (1981–1983), New York Festival Orchestra (1981), Pacific Philharmonic (1978–1979). **Education:** Stanford University, Ph.D. in Economics (1978); Rice University, B.A. in Economics (1974). **Personal:** Married to Margaret in 1987. One child: David. Dr. Shaffer enjoys astronomy and playing the violin.

Mary R. Shiflet
Vice President/Senior Loan Officer
Home Federal Bank
1602 East Cumberland Avenue
Middlesboro, KY 40965–3228
(606) 248–1095
Fax: (606) 242–1010

6011

Business Information: Home Federal Bank is a full–service financial institution. As Vice President/Senior Loan Officer, Ms. Shiflet oversees the Lending Function of the Bank, and makes home and consumer loans. **Career Steps:** Vice President/Senior Loan Officer, Home Federal Bank, F.S.B. (1979–Present); Cashier, Daniel Boone Clinic (1974–1979). **Associations & Accomplishments:** President, Lions Club of Middlesboro. **Education:** Louisiana State University – Graduate School of Banking of the South, Banking (1995). **Personal:** Three children: Ronda, April, and Alicia. Ms. Shiflet enjoys church activities.

Steven C. Adams
City Executive
Huntington National Bank
PO Box 229, 61 S. Main Street
London, OH 43140–0229
(614) 852–1234
Fax: (614) 852–4298

6021

Business Information: Huntington National Bank is a full service commercial bank. National in scope, Huntington has branch offices in Ohio, Kentucky, Indiana, Michigan, Florida, West Virginia and Pennsylvania. Joining Huntington National Bank in 1987 as a Commercial Lender, Steven Adams was appointed to his current role in 1994. As City Executive he has full executive administration over all bank operations at the London, Ohio branch, as well as a branch office in West Jefferson, Ohio. **Career Steps:** Huntington National Bank: City Executive (1994–Present), Commercial Lender Vice President (1990–1994), Commercial Lender Assistant Vice President (1987–1990); Branch Manager, Farm Credit Services (1981–1987). **Associations & Accomplishments:** Kiwanis of London, Ohio; London First United Methodist Church; London City Council; London City Schools Business Advisory Committee. **Education:** Rio Grande College, B.A. in Public Administration (1979); Franklin University; Certificate from Ohio School of Banking **Personal:** Married to Paula J. in 1979. Three children: Samuel, Stephanie and Matthew. Mr. Adams enjoys competing in equestrian events, as well as riding for pleasure.

Matthew W. Barrett, O.C.

Chairman & Chief Executive Officer
Bank of Montreal
100 King St. W.
Toronto, Ontario M5X 1A1
(416) 867–4693
Fax: (416) 867–7061

6021

Business Information: Bank of Montreal is a leading international world banking institution providing lending and banking services. As Chairman & Chief Executive Officer, Mr. Barrett is responsible for overseeing all daily operations. At the age of 18 he joined the bank, and was elected Chairman of the Board at age 45. At the time he was among the youngest bank heads. In 1974, when appointed Manager, he played a central role in the development of the Bank's on–line, real–time banking system, one of the world's first. A key turning point in his career came in November, 1978 when appointed Vice President of the British Columbia Division, the largest of the Bank's nine divisions. Concurrently, he is the Director of The Molson Companies Limited, The Seagrams Company Limited, and Nesbitt Burns, Inc. **Career Steps:** Bank of Montreal: Chairman, Board of Directors (1990–Present), Chief Executive Officer (1989), President and Chief Operating Officer (1987–1989), Board of Directors (1987), Executive Vice President/Group Executive (1985), Deputy Group Executive, Treasury Group (1984), Deputy General Manager, International Banking (1981), Senior Vice President, Eastern/Northern Ontario (1980), Vice President, British Columbia Division (1978), Increasingly responsible positions in Support Services (1968–1978), Teller (1967), Trainee Clerk, London (1962). **Associations & Accomplishments:** Chairman, Capital Campaign for the University of Waterloo; Co–Chair, Royal Victoria Hospital Campaign; Trustee and Member of the Finance Committee of the Toronto Hospital; Member of the Policy Committee and Director of the Business Council on National Issues; Council for Canadian Unity; Conference Board of Canada; Montreal Board of Trade Heritage Foundation; Member, Board of Governors, Junior Achievement of Canada; Various Community Organizations; Outstanding CEO of the Year (1995); American Academy of Achievements "Golden Plate Award" (1993); Sales and Marketing Executive of the Year Award "Ursaki Award" (1994). **Education:** University of New Brunswick, D.Litt.; St. Mary's University, LLD; Bishop's University, D.C.L.; York University, LL.D.; University LL.D.; University of Waterloo, LL.D.

Greg Bashore
Manager, Human Resources Strategic Planning and Analysis
Signet Bank
701 East Franklin Street 6th Floor
Richmond, VA 23219
(804) 771–7808
Fax: (804) 771–7882

6021

Business Information: Signet Bank is a 12 billion dollar financial services institution which provides its customers with an array of financial services products. As Manager of Human Resources Planning and Analysis, Mr. Bashore is responsible for managing the analytical resources within the Human Resources Division focused on the following types of work: measuring value of products and services, identifying, recommending and implementing process improvement opportunities, new product development, financial measurement and Human Resources Strategic Planning. Initial accomplishments include: redesigning the recruitment department, redesigning the customer services delivery system, building a measurement MIS system, implementing APC costing and building a strategic planning process. **Career Steps:** Regional Manager, Norwest Mortgage, Inc. (1993–Present); Branch Manager, Comnet Mortgage Company (1988–1990); Branch Manager, Northeastern Mortgage Company (1986–1988); Loan Originator, RIHT Mortgage Corporation (1981–1986). **Associations & Accomplishments:** HRPS; SHRM; Strategic Leadership Societies; ECU Alumni. **Education:** Virginia Commonwealth University, M.B.A.; East Carolina University, B.A. in Economics. **Personal:** Married.

David J. Bennett, C.P.A.
Vice President of Comptroller's Department
Suffolk County National Bank
206 Griffing Ave.
Riverhead, NY 11901–3009
(516) 727–5270
Fax: Please mail or call

6021

Business Information: Established in 1890, Suffolk County National Bank is a full–service, commercial, community bank specializing in indirect automobile lending, with total assets of $800 million. A Certified Public Accountant, Mr. Bennett serves as the bank's Vice President of the Comptroller's department, responsible for all financial reporting functions of the bank. **Career Steps:** Vice President of Comptroller's Department, Suffolk County National Bank (1994–Present); Supervising Senior Accountant, KPMG Peat Marwick L.L.P. (1990–1994); Auditor, Long Island Savings Bank (1989–1990). **Associations & Accomplishments:** American Institute of Certified Public Accountants. **Education:** State University of New York – Old Westbury, Bachelors (1988). **Personal:** Mr. Bennett enjoys golf and hockey.

Ms. Sally A. Brady
Vice President
Citibank, N.A.
1 Court Square
Long Island City, NY 11120
(718) 248–7836
Fax: (718) 248–4678

6021

Business Information: Citibank, N.A. is a financial services organization providing banking services to consumers and corporate customers worldwide. Established in 1812, Citibank, N.A. presently has offices in more than 90 countries and employs over 80,000 people. As Vice President, Ms. Brady is responsible for marketing to a number of small business segments in the New York/Connecticut are a. **Career Steps:** Vice President and Director of Small Business Global Marketing, Citibank (1991–Present); Program Manager of Consumer Marketing, Citibank (1989–1991); Director of Human Resources Policy Development, Citibank (1985–1989). **Education:** St. John's University, B.A. (1966).

Mark O. Carter
Vice President of PC Consulting Services
NationsBank
3 Commercial Place, Floor 1
Norfolk, VA 23510–2108
(804) 446–3647
Fax: (804) 624–2829

6021

Business Information: NationsBank is a full–service financial institution (the 3rd largest in the country) operating in nine states and offering a complete array of consumer, commercial and corporate banking services. As Vice President of PC Consulting Services, Mr. Carter is responsible for all microcomputer applications throughout the Company. **Career Steps:** NationsBank: Vice President of PC Consulting Services (1993–Present), Project Manager (1989–1993); Manager EDP, Cox Communications (1986–1989). **Education:** Old Dominion University, B.S.B.A. (1986). **Personal:** Married to Janet in 1988. One child: Brandon Mark. Mr. Carter enjoys water skiing, weightlifting, and golf.

Dawn J. Cochran
Assistant Vice President – Operations
North Cascades National Bank
P O Box 1648
Chelan, WA 98816
(509) 682–4502
Fax: (509) 682–7333

6021

Business Information: North Cascades National Bank is a full–service bank established in 1986. The bank offers a wide range of services including checking, savings, loans, investments, safety deposit boxes, travelers checks, and trust accounts. With four locations throughout the state, the bank presently employs 60 people. As Assistant Vice President – Operations, Ms. Cochran oversees the activities of all tellers at all four branches, assists with new account processing, and training within the bank. Other responsibilities include investments, reconciliation of FED line, and numerous other activities associated with balancing daily operations. **Career Steps:** Assistant Vice President/Operations, North Cascades National Bank (1986–Present); Secretary/Loan Clerk/New Accounts Clerk, Whatcom State Bank (1981–1986); Loan Processor/New Accounts, Oregon Bank (1978–1981). **Education:** Chelan High School (1976). **Personal:** Four children: Andrew and Casey Newton, Kramer Cannon, and Hannah Cochran. Ms. Cochran enjoys being with her children and participating and watching their sporting activities.

Frederick E. Curry III
Assistant Vice President
Chase Manhattan Bank
95 Wall Street, 10th Floor
New York, NY 10005
(212) 493–4388
Fax: (212) 493–4049

6021

Business Information: Chase Manhattan Bank is the largest banking institution in the United States which provides financial services to private individuals, governments, and corporations world–wide. As Manager of the bank's Tax Reporting and IRS Compliance area, Mr. Curry oversees 1099 tax reporting, non–resident alien certification and solicitation, IRS B & C notice response processing, individual tax ID certifications, tax withholdings, interest calculations, adjustments, and telephone customer service. **Career Steps:** Chase Manhattan Bank: Assistant Vice President, Operations Manager (1995–Present), Assistant Treasurer, Training and Commu-

nications Manager (1993–1995), Customer Service Manager (1987–1993), Senior Operations Associate (1982–1987); Corporal, United States Marine Corps, 8th Combat Engineer Support Battalion, Camp Lejeune, North Carolina (1980–1982) **Associations & Accomplishments:** President, Former Vice President and Assistant Treasurer, New York Association of Urban Bankers; Consultant, Junior Achievement of New York, Inc.; Career Advisor, Medgar Evers College; Instructor, American Institute of Banking. **Education:** Fordham University, M.B.A. (May 97); Adelphi University, B.S. (1993); American Institute of Banking, Graduate (1989). **Personal:** Married to Beverly in 1985. Mr. Curry enjoys movies, chess, and Tae Kwon Do.

Ralph E. Day Jr.
Vice President, Trust Officer
First National Bank and Trust Company
P.O. Box 69
Ardmore, OK 73402–0069
(405) 223–1111
Fax: (405) 221–1139

6021

Business Information: First National Bank and Trust Company is an independent bank, primarily involved in trust banking management and estate planning. As Vice President and Trust Officer, Mr. Day oversees the entire trust department, including managing any non–standard customer relations matters. **Career Steps:** Vice President and Trust Officer, First National Bank and Trust Company (1991–Present); Vice President and Trust Officer, Bank IV of Olathe, Kansas (1989–1991); Senior Trust Officer, Commerce Bank of Kansas City, MO (1985–1989); Vice President and Trust Officer, First National Bank of Vinita, OK (1983–1985). **Associations & Accomplishments:** Missouri Bar Association; National Association for Community Leadership; Treasurer, Arbuckle Area Council; Boy Scouts of America; Communities–In–Schools; Rotary Club of Ardmore, OK; American Legion; Oklahoma Bankers Association. **Education:** University of Missouri at Kansas City, J.D. (1976). **Personal:** Married to Victoria A. in 1971. Three children: Bryan, Kevin, and Jennifer. Mr. Day enjoys golf and speaking about the banking industry to high school students.

Richard C. Ducharme, CPA

Treasurer and Chief Financial Officer
Central Bank
399 Highland Avenue
Somerville, MA 02144–2516
(617) 629–4229
Fax: (617) 629–4295

6021

Business Information: Central Bank is a full service bank established in 1915. The Bank currently employs 90 people and boasts assets of $320 million. Central Bank's services include checking, savings, trust accounts, and commercial and individual loans. As Treasurer and Chief Financial Officer, Mr. Ducharme manages an $80 million dollar bond portfolio for the Bank. He is involved in the accounting and financial operations of Central Bank. **Career Steps:** Treasurer and Chief Financial Officer, Central Bank (1994–Present); Senior Financial Advisor, Federal Deposit Insurance Corporation (1991–1994); Chief Financial Officer, Numerica Financial Corporation. **Associations & Accomplishments:** Financial Executive Institute; Chairman, New Hampshire Multiple Sclerosis; American Institute of Certified Public Accountants; Massachusetts Society of Certified Public Accountants; Chairman, New Hampshire Board of Accountancy. **Education:** Suffolk University Graduate School of Management, Completing Masters of Science in Finance; Northeastern University Graduate School of Business, M.B.A. (1972); New Hampshire College, B.S. in Accounting, cum laude (1968). **Personal:** Married to Pauline in 1967. One child: Laura. Mr. Ducharme enjoys swimming and cross country skiing.

Stephanie G. Duncan
Assistant Vice President
NationsBank
295 Greystone Boulevard
Columbia, SC 29210
(803) 765–8370
Fax: (803) 765–8293

6021

Business Information: NationsBank is a full–service financial institution (the 3rd largest in the country) operating in nine states and offering a complete array of consumer, commercial and corporate banking services. As Assistant Vice President, Ms. Duncan is responsible for the design, implementation, and follow through of an incentive program for the Teller population for the entire state of North Carolina. **Career Steps:** NationsBank: Assistant Vice President (1994–Present), Teller Certification Manager (1994–Present), Teller Trainer (1990–1994). **Associations & Accomplishments:** Urban Bankers Association. **Education:** Limestone College, B.S. (1995); Columbia Junior College, Associate's degree in Business. **Personal:** Married to Benjamin I., II in 1986. One child: Benjamin I., III. Ms. Duncan enjoys tennis, reading, travel, and church and family activities.

Susan P. Emerson
Vice President/Account Executive
Glendale Federal Bank
700 North Brand Boulevard, Suite 440
Glendale, CA 91203–1238
(800) 669–5100
Fax: (818) 409–5272

6021

Business Information: Glendale Federal Bank, established in 1934, is one of the largest savings institutions in the United States. Glendale Federal is evolving into a full service banking institution, serving the consumer and business banking needs of California. As Vice President/Account Executive, Ms. Emerson is involved in marketing consumer, business banking, and specialized financial products and services to individuals, corporations, and non–profit organizations. She also monitors client accounts and advises on changes in the financial market. **Career Steps:** Glendale Federal Bank: Vice President/Account Executive (1987–Present), Marketing Sales Coordinator (1983–1987), and Public Relations Assistant (1981–1983). **Associations & Accomplishments:** American Heart Association, Los Angeles County; Board Member, Agape International University; Christian Management Association; Oak Creek Presbyterian Church; Executive Board of Directors, Executive Board of Directors, Cystic Fibrosis Foundation of Southern California/Southern Nevada; Board of Directors, The Mustard Seed, Inc. **Education:** Taylor University, BA (1966). **Personal:** Married to Tom in 1982. Two children: Traci and Tom Jr. Ms. Emerson enjoys music, reading, shopping, and volunteer work.

Laurence S. Grafstein
Managing Director
CS First Boston
55 East 52nd Street
New York, NY 10055
(212) 909–2531
Fax: (212) 593–9079

6021

Business Information: CS First Boston is a global investment bank providing world–class financial services. As Managing Director, Mr. Grafstein serves as head of the Telecom practice, coordinating global investment through telecommunications. He has appeared on CNBC Evening and has been published in "The Wall Street Journal." **Career Steps:** Managing Director, CS First Boston (1995–Present); Managing Director, Wasserstein Perella & Company (1990–1995). **Associations & Accomplishments:** Wall Street Executive Committee, United Jewish Appeal; Board Member, Arts Connection – New York; Guggenheim Education Advisory Council; Co–Founder, Employment Channel; Published in Wall Street Journal; Appearances on CNBC Evening Television. **Education:** University of Toronto Law, LL.B (1988); Oxford University, M.Phil (1984); Harvard University, B.A. (1982). **Personal:** Married to Rebecca in 1989. Two children: Daniel and Edward. Mr. Grafstein enjoys sports and spending time with his kids.

Bert K. Harris
Executive Vice President/Chief Operating Officer
Pioneer National Bank
331 North Central Avenue
Duluth, MN 55807
(218) 624–3676
Fax: (218) 624–9066

6021

Business Information: Pioneer National Bank is a full–service commercial banking institution, providing lending, credit card, and mortgage services. Established in 1912, Pioneer National Bank operates three branches in the region. As Executive Vice President/Chief Operating Officer, Mr. Harris is responsible for all administrative activities of the Duluth branch, including business development, supervision of daily operations, oversight of SBH loans, and strategic planning. **Career Steps:** Executive Vice President/Chief Operating Officer, Pioneer National Bank (1995–Present); Managing Agent, Resolution Trust Corporation (1990–1995); Special Assets Officer, Northwest Bank Wyoming (1987–1989); President, Security Bank of Glevrock (1984–1986). **Associations & Accomplishments:** Duluth Chamber of Commerce; Economic Development Committee; Rotary Club of Duluth #25; Recipient of three Achievement Awards from Resolution Trust Corporation. **Education:** Colorado State University, B.S. (1960).

Personal: Married to Jo in 1976. Five children: Juli, Martha, Chad, Oliver, and Michael. Mr. Harris enjoys skiing, tennis, carpentry, old car restoration, and reading.

Elizabeth Hembree
Vice President and Cashier
First National Bank
P.O. Box 809
Pawhuska, OK 74056–0809
(918) 287–3612
Fax: (918) 287–2099

6021

Business Information: First National Bank, a family–owned bank, provides all aspects of commercial banking. Established in 1906, FNB currently employs 14 people. As Vice President and Cashier, Ms. Hembree is responsible for all aspects of financial operations, including regulatory reporting, hiring and firing. **Career Steps:** Vice President and Cashier, First National Bank (1989–Present). **Associations & Accomplishments:** Little League Football; ESA & PEO Salvation Army; Sunday school teacher; Women's Group. **Education:** Bartlesville Wesleyan College, B.S.; RSC Claremore, OK, A.A. **Personal:** Married to Greg in 1978. Two children: Tyler and Morgan. Ms. Hembree enjoys spending time with her family and travel.

Craig D. Henry
Vice President
First Union
6329 Teaneck Place
Charlotte, NC 28215–4016
(704) 590–2760
Fax: (704) 567–1830

6021

Business Information: First Union is a full–service commercial bank established in 1888 and headquartered in Charlotte, North Carolina. The Bank services offered include checking, savings, individual and commercial loans, investment counseling, trust accounts, and credit cards. First Union has approximately 2,000 branches throughout the southeast and approximately 44,000 employees. As Vice President, Mr. Henry is responsible for the consumer portion of the banking services offered by First Union (i.e. credit cards, ATM, and banking by computer). He is involved with the development and implementation of new marketing techniques for services offered. Some of the techniques used are telemarketing, direct mailings, and the internet. **Career Steps:** Vice President, First Union (1994–Present); Vice President, First Chicago (1990–1994). **Associations & Accomplishments:** Mr. Henry has been published in "Planning Review" **Education:** Ohio University: M.B.A. (1986) and B.A. **Personal:** Married to Lana in 1983. Mr. Henry enjoys research, reading, NASCAR, hunting, fishing, hiking, and being a Civil War buff.

Jason J. Hogg
Credit Sector Compliance Officer
MBNA America
555 Papermill Road 3rd Floor
Newark, DE 19711
(302) 458–0305
Fax: (302) 651–9783

6021

Business Information: MBNA America, an international banking and credit institution, is the second largest issuing bank of credit cards in the United States. As Credit Sector Compliance Officer, Mr. Hogg is responsible for handling compliance, auditing, electronic data processing, guiding relations with federal regulatory bodies, controlling policies and procedures, interacting with the Office Comptroller of Currency involved with auditing, and operating a large sector of the company. **Career Steps:** MBNA America: Credit Sector Compliance Officer (1996–Present), AVP Specialized Lending (1995–1996), Senior Officer Sports Marketing (1993–1995), Officer Co–Branding (1992–1993). **Associations & Accomplishments:** United Way; Institute for International Sport; World Athlete Games; Irish Peace Institute – Ireland. **Education:** Colby College, B.A. (1992). **Personal:** Married to Alexandra in 1994. Mr. Hogg enjoys water and snow skiing, hunting, and piano composition.

Lisa A. Hudy
Vice President of Communications
Franklin Bank
24725 West 12 Mile Road, Suite 210
Southfield, MI 48034
(810) 358–6495
Fax: (810) 358–4239
EMail: See Below

6021

Business Information: Franklin Bank is a full–service, community bank with four branches and $500 million in assets. Franklin Bank serves southeast metro Detroit and is active in three counties. As Vice President of Communications, Ms. Hudy manages the Investor Relations and Public Relations Departments. She also handles the telephone banking center and supervises sales administration functions. Internet users can reach her via: lah@FranklinBank.com. **Career Steps:** Franklin Bank: Vice President of Communications (1991–Present), Human Resource Assistant (1990–1991), Customer Information Processor (1987–1990). **Associations & Accomplishments:** National Association of Investor Relations: National and Local Chapters. **Education:** University of Michigan, B.A. (1987). **Personal:** Married to Alex in 1992. Ms. Hudy enjoys genealogy and church activities.

Carol Y. Kellum
Vice President
SouthTrust Bank
1000 Quintard Avenue
Anniston, AL 36201–5788
(205) 238–1000
Fax: (205) 231–4310

6021

Business Information: SouthTrust Bank is a full–service commercial banking institution. With twenty–three years experience in the banking industry, Ms. Kellum joined SouthTrust Bank's Anniston branch in 1982. Serving as Vice President, she is in charge of operations, compliance, special assets, and community reinvestment of the Anniston market. **Career Steps:** Vice President, SouthTrust Bank (1982–Present); Executive Secretary, Central Bank (1972–1982). **Education:** Jacksonville State University (1972); Numerous AIB courses attained: Basic, Standard, and Advanced diplomas. **Personal:** Married to Steve in 1971. Two children: Heather and Tony. Ms. Kellum enjoys needlework, reading, and playing the piano.

Gayle S. Kern
Senior Vice President
AmSouth Bank
P O Box 11007
Birmingham, AL 35288–0001
(205) 560–5613
Fax: (205) 560–5615

6021

Business Information: Bank is a full service commercial banking association with 250 branches in Alabama, Florida, Georgia, and Tennessee. This is a regional bank with over $17 billion in assets. As Senior Vice President, Ms. Kern is responsible for all call centers, inbound customer service, and sales calls for consumers and small businesses. Ms. Kern is responsible for a team of 150 employees and oversees the general activities of the department. **Career Steps:** Senior Vice President, AmSouth Bank (1995–Present); Vice President–Call Center Manager, Bank One (1990–1995); Vice President Retail and Operations and Vice President Retail Systems Ameritrust Bank (1986–1990). **Education:** Cleveland State University, B.A. (1980); University of Virginia, Consumer Bankers Associate. **Personal:** Married to Bill in 1984. Five children: Jeanette, Joyce, Terri, Sharon, and William. Ms. Kern enjoys golf, reading, walking, and Church activities.

Rhonda M. Land
Vice President and Operations Officer
First National Bank
403 North Jackson Street, P.O. Box 278
Salem, MO 65560–0278
(573) 729–6617
Fax: (573) 729–7393

6021

Business Information: First National Bank is a 90–year old, full–service community bank with assets of $80 million. With eighteen years of experience in data processing, Ms. Land joined First National Bank in 1978. Appointed as Vice President and Operations Officer in 1989, she is responsible for the direction of all operations and data processing at the Salem, Ohio branch. **Career Steps:** First National Bank: Vice President and Operations Officer (1989–Present), Vice President and Data Processing Officer (1984–1989); Data Processing Officer (1978–1984). **Associations & Accomplishments:** Board Member, Agape Home of Deny County. **Education:** Southwest Baptist University, B.S. in Business Management in progress. **Personal:** Ms. Land enjoys sports, music, and church related activities.

Mary E. Lane

Vice President of Marketing & Strategy
Chase Manhattan Bank
4 Chase Metrotech Center, 8th Floor
Brooklyn, NY 11245
(718) 242–2707
Fax: (718) 242–3819
EMAIL: Mlane1996@aol.com

6021

Business Information: Chase Manhattan Bank is a full–service banking institution offering checking, savings, lending, trust accounts, and investment counseling. As the largest bank in the United States, Chase Manhattan offers a wide variety of services nationally and globally. As Vice President of Marketing & Strategy, Ms. Lane assists with developing marketing strategies for the International Banking Division. She coordinates with product management, international customer relations, development of training programs, and international customer service. **Career Steps:** Chase Manhattan Bank: Vice President of Marketing & Strategy (1995–Present), Vice President Product Management (1994–1995); Vice President Relationship Management (1993–1994). **Associations & Accomplishments:** Advisory Committee, Finance, Credit and International Business; Product Management Committee, United States Council on International Banking. **Education:** Columbia University, MIA (1986); Middlebury College, BA Cum Laude (1982). **Personal:** Married to Paul Cristello in 1993. Ms. Lane enjoys modern dance and travel.

Harold R. Longley

Chief Operating Officer
Surety Bank and Trust Company Limited, Inc.
P.O. Box Ss 5857
Nassau, Bahamas
(809) 363–4380
Fax: (809) 363–4344

6021

Business Information: Surety Bank and Trust Company Limited, Inc. is a full service banking facility focused on providing banking and other trust services to high networth individuals and companies in a secure, privileged and discreet manner. Established in 1995, the Bank is newly incorporated, and has a class "A" rating. As Chief Operating Officer, Mr. Longley oversees all day–to–day activities. He is responsible for client recruitment, administration, operations, public relations, strategic planning, and enhancing customer service. **Career Steps:** Chief Operating Officer, Surety Bank an Trust Company Limited, Inc. (1995–Present); Royal Bank of Canada: Manager, Lending Services, Commercial Unit; General Manager, International Limited; Manager, Nassau Main Branch. **Associations & Accomplishments:** Director, Nassau Flight Services Limited; Director, Workers Bank Limited; Chairman, Crippled Children's Committee; Director, Bahamas Chamber of Commerce; Board, Salvation Army; President, Bridge Club. **Education:** University of Miami, M.B.A. (1978); St. John's University, Minnesota; St. Augustine's College, Nassau. **Personal:** Married to Calliope in 1959. Six children: Nicole Hillard, Rosemarie Symonette, Lisa Fields, Adrian, Lambert and Nicholas Longley. Mr. Longley enjoys racquet sports, bridge, and whist.

Priya L. Mackhrandilall
Chief Financial Officer
Marathon National Bank of New York
28–22–Steinway Street
Astoria, NY 11103
(800) 721–9516
Fax: (718) 721–0270

6021

Business Information: Marathon National Bank of New York is a full service commercial bank providing financial and related services to clients. Established in 1989, the Bank employs twenty people. As Chief Financial Officer, Ms. Mackhrandilall oversees all financial aspects of the Bank and is responsible for accounting, budget, payroll, management of assets, and serving as cashier. **Career Steps:** Marathon Na-

tional Bank of New York: Chief Financial Officer (1995–Present), Vice President, Controller (1994–1995), Assistant Vice President, Accounting Manager (1993–1994), Operations Manager (1991–1993). **Associations & Accomplishments:** Who's Who Among Students in American Universities and Colleges; Alpha Chi National Honor Society, D.C. Chapter. **Education:** Strayer College, B.S. (1990). **Personal:** Ms. Mackhrandilall enjoys travel, outdoor sports, hiking, yoga, and meditation.

Sandra Marrone
Vice President and Manager of Systems and Products International
Society National Bank
127 Public Square
Cleveland, OH 44114
(216) 689–5236
Fax: (216) 689–3683

6021

Business Information: Society National Bank, based in Cleveland Ohio, is a full–service financial and lending institition. International in scope and established in 1889, Society National Bank currently employs 3,000 people. As Vice President and Manager of Systems and Products International, Ms. Marrone is responsible for all aspects of international banking. **Career Steps:** Vice President and Manager of Systems and Products International, Society National Bank (19–Present). **Associations & Accomplishments:** Cleveland World Trade Association; Cleveland Growth Association; United States Council for International Banking. **Education:** Cleveland State University, M.B.A. (1984). **Personal:** Married to Jay in 1980.

Amaury Diaz Martinez

Deputy Comptroller
Government Development Bank for Puerto Rico
P.O. Box 42001
San Juan, Puerto Rico 00940–2001
(787) 722–4860
Fax: (787) 728–2265

6021

Business Information: Government Development Bank for Puerto Rico provides financing to public corporations, agencies, and municipalities. The Bank also serves as fiscal agent and financial advisor to the Commonwealth of Puerto Rico. As Deputy Comptroller, Mr. Diaz is responsible for all financial aspects of the Bank. **Career Steps:** Deputy Comptroller, Government Development Bank for Puerto Rico (1995–Present); General Auditor, Economic Development Bank for Puerto Rico (1994–1995); Audit Manager, Price Waterhouse (1987–1994). **Associations & Accomplishments:** Puerto Rico Society of Certified Public Accountants; American Institute of Certified Public Accountants; Institute of Internal Auditors; Institute of Certified Management Accountants; American Management Association. **Education:** Columbia University, New York, New York, M.B.A. (1986); Brandeis University, Waltham, Massachusetts, B.A. in Mathematics and Economics (1984). **Personal:** Mr. Diaz enjoys reading and collecting souvenirs from Olympic Games.

Oscar Marulanda Gomez

Director
Banco de la Republica
Cra. 7a, No. 14–78, Piso 6
Bogota, Colombia
(571) 286–7204
Fax: (571) 281–9734

6021

Business Information: Banco de la Republica is the central banking system of Colombia, providing full financial services. As Director, Mr. Marulanda Gomez is responsible for monetary, exchange rates, and credit management of the Republic of Colombia, with specific mandate to preserve the currency's purchasing power and the adequate functioning of the country's payment systems. **Career Steps:** Director, Banco de la Republica (1993–Present); Board of Directors, Interamerican Development Bank (1991–1993); Senior Advisor to the Minister, Ministry of the Treasury and Public Credit (1984–1991); Partner, Director, and Researcher, Oficina de Investigaciones Socioeconomicas y Legales (1971–1984); Head of the Macroeconomic Policy Division for Full Employment, Departamento Nacional de Planeacion (1969–1971). **Education:** Georgetown University, Candidate for the Master's Degree in Economics (1967–1968); George Washington University (1966–1967); Universidad de Los Andes (1966–1967); Uni-

versidad Javeriana, Civil Engineer (1960–1965); Various personal courses. **Personal:** Two children: Adriana and Valeria. Mr. Marulanda Gomez enjoys tennis, golf, and music.

Daniel E. McDill
Senior Vice President
First Bank
1675 Lakeland Drive, Suite 303
Jackson, MS 39216–4844
(601) 982–1237
Fax: (601) 982–0411

6021

Business Information: First Bank is a financial institution specializing in commercial lending to small businesses. As Senior Vice President, Mr. McDill is responsible for all aspects of Branch operations, including lending. Mr. McDill is also an Adjunct Professor, teaching adult continuing education courses through Hinds Community College. **Career Steps:** Senior Vice President, First Bank (1994–Present); Vice President, First National Bank of Vicksburg (1991–1994); Assistant Vice President, Deposit Guaranty National Bank (1981–1991). **Associations & Accomplishments:** President, Rankin County Chamber of Commerce; Director, Mississippi Future Farmers of America Foundation; Director, Brandon Youth Association; Trustee, Leadership Rankin and Service Award Recipient for Cystic Fibrosis Foundation of Mississippi; Outstanding Young Men of America (1989). **Education:** Mississippi College, B.S.B.A. (1981); University of Oklahoma, Graduate School of Commercial Lending (1991); University of Colorado, Graduate School of Banking (1993). **Personal:** Married to Vickie in 1978. Two children: Brad and Emily. Mr. McDill enjoys hunting and golf.

Trudie A. McGovern
Vice President – Corporate Management Reporting
Wachovia Bank of Georgia, N.A.
P.O. Box 4148
Atlanta, GA 30302–4148
(404) 332–5552
Fax: (404) 332–5742

6021

Business Information: Wachovia Bank of Georgia, N.A. is a full–service financial institution, specializing in commercial banking with branches throughout Georgia, North Carolina, and South Carolina. A managerial associate with Wachovia Bank of Georgia since 1987, Ms. McGovern was appointed as Vice President of Corporate Management Reporting in 1991. In this capacity, she is responsible for management reporting for the corporate line of business, as well as budget functions. **Career Steps:** Wachovia Bank of Georgia, N.A.: Vice President (1991–Present), Assistant Vice President of Management Reporting Retail (1989–1991), Accounting Officer of Management Reporting Corporate (1987–1989). **Associations & Accomplishments:** Junior League of Atlanta; Marymount Alumni Association; CPA – Licensed in Georgia; Olympic Volunteer; BellSouth Atlanta Golf Classic: Co–Chairman of the Juniors Committee. **Education:** Georgia State University, Post–graduate studies (1987); Marymount College, B.A. in Political Science. **Personal:** Two children: Sarah M. and Robert F. Ms. McGovern enjoys tennis, running, golf, and swimming.

W.C. Jack Miller
Vice President
CoreStates Financial
P.O. Box 1102
Reading, PA 19603
(610) 655–3735
Fax: (610) 655–2943

6021

Business Information: CoreStates Financial, formerly Meridian Bancorp, Inc., is a financial holding company with over $45 billion dollars in assets. Regional in scope, the Company has branches in New Jersey, Pennsylvania, and Delaware. As Vice President of Advantage Phone Center, Mr. Miller oversees two twenty–four hour phone centers that handle all inbound service and sales calls (i.e. loan applications, checking and savings account services, and customer relations). Additional duties include management of a staff of 260 and implementing self–directed work teams to develop the phone centers. **Career Steps:** CoreStates/Meridian: Vice President, Advantage Phone Center (1988–Present), Vice President, CoreStates Financial (1993–Present); Meridian Bancorp, Inc.: Product Marketing Manager, Marketing Officer (1987–1989), Sales Development (1985–1987), Community Banking (1983–1985), Commercial Loan Examiner (1982–1983). **Associations & Accomplishments:** Board Member, Mid–Atlantic Chapter, American Telemarketing Association; Philadelphia Direct Marketing Association; Founding Member, Telephone Marketing Council; Board Member and President, Albright College Alumni Association; Exhibit Chair, Scenic River Days Festival for Reading; Board Member, Early Cloud and Company User Group; Reading's Centre Park Historic District; Speaker at various ATA and

PDMA seminars and Albright College Career Programs. **Education:** Albright College A.B. (1982); Graduate School of Retail Bank Management, C.B.A. (1988–1990).

Shashank Mishra
Vice President
ABN AMRO Bank
135 South La Salle Street, Suite 200
Chicago, IL 60603–4105
(312) 904–7326
Fax: (312) 904–2084
EMAIL:smishra@pc.abn.com

6021

Business Information: ABN AMRO Bank is a national financial institution, specializing in banking. Joining ABN AMRO Bank as Vice President in 1993, Mr. Mishra serves as Chief Financial Officer, responsible for all mortgage aspects, securities, all financing matters, as well as non–mortgage areas and selling to investors. **Career Steps:** Vice President, ABN AMRO Bank (1993–Present); Vice President, Bank of America (1992–1993); Assistant Vice President, Security Pacific Bank (1990–1992). **Associations & Accomplishments:** Mortgage Bankers Association; Holder of Masters' (Ocean–going Ship Captain's Certificate) from Australia; Chicago Coalition for the Homeless; Author and publisher of article in Mortgage Banking; Edited and published internal newsletter for Security Banking. **Education:** Cornell University, M.B.A. (1990). **Personal:** Married to Neerja in 1984. Two children: Samir and Nishant. Mr. Mishra enjoys spending time with his family.

Carol J. Parry
Managing Director
Chemical Bank
270 Park Avenue
New York, NY 10017
(212) 270–5284
Fax: (212) 270–7544

6021

Business Information: Chemical Bank is a full–service global financial institution providing a full spectrum of services to include loans, investments, checking and savings, and mortgage financing. As a result of the impending merger between Chemical Banking Corporation and Manufacturers Hanover Bank. With over 30 years of management experience in the financial services industry, the public sector, and as a management consultant, Carol Parry joined Chemical Bank in 1978. Appointed as the Managing Director in charge of the Community Development Group in 1992, she is responsible for all lending for low– and moderate–income multi–family housing; commercial revitalization projects; Small Business Administration–guaranteed loans; loans to community–based, not–for–profit organizations; all corporate contributions and community outreach activities; the Bank's Minority and Women Vendor Program, as well as Fair Lending and Community Reinvestment Act compliance. She also chairs the Chemical Bank Community Development Corporation. Prior to the merger of Chemical Banking Corporation and Manufacturers Hanover Corporation in 1991, Ms. Parry was the Director of Manufacturers Hanover's Business Banking Group. She was responsible for the Bank's tri–state area relationships with small and mid–size businesses with annual sales of $3 million to $50 million. At Chemical Bank, from 1978 to 1989, she was one of the architects of that bank's successful middle–market and small business strategy and became one of Chemical's first women senior vice presidents in 1981. In addition to her tenure at Chemical Bank, Ms. Parry has been a management consultant at McKinsey & Co., headed her own consulting business, and was a partner at Personnel Corporation of America. In addition, she served as Administrator for the City of New York Special Services for Children agency with the responsibility of all child welfare services. **Career Steps:** Managing Director, Chemical Bank (1992–Present); Director of Business Banking Group, Manufacturers Hanover Trust (1990–1992); President, C. J. Parry Associates (1989–1990); Director of Private Banking, Chemical Bank (1987–1989). **Associations & Accomplishments:** Board of Directors, Health Insurance Plan of New York; Board of Directors, New York Landmarks Conservancy; Board of Directors, New York City Housing Partnership; Chair, CRA Committee, New York Clearing House. **Education:** Harvard Business School, AMP Certificate (1984); University of Connecticut, M.S.W. (1969); Tufts University, B.A. (1964). **Personal:** Married to John R. Fox in 1990.

Ralph D. Pina
Facilities Manager
Dedham Institute for Saving
55 Elm Street
Dedham, MA 02026–5996
(617) 329–6700
Fax: (617) 326–9893

6021

Business Information: Dedham Institute for Saving is a full service community bank established in 1831. The Bank offers a full line of services including savings, checking and loans. As Facilities Manager, Mr. Pina oversees all areas regarding real estate, facility design and construction, as well as the maintenance, security, communications, capital equipment, and the purchasing and maintenance of equipment for all bank branches. **Career Steps:** Facilities Manager, Dedham Institute for Saving (1991–Present); President, Norwood Door and Window (1986–1991); President/ Builder, C & R Associates (1981–1986). **Associations & Accomplishments:** International Facility Managers Association (IFMA); Licensed Construction Supervisor, Commonwealth of Massachusetts; Certified Facility Manager, North Eastern University. **Education:** North Eastern University, C.F.M. (1994); Peterson School of Steam Engineering (1984). **Personal:** Four children: Lisa, Mari–Kate, Jessica, and Rachel. Mr. Pina enjoys golf, weight training, exercise, and spectator sports.

Ronald L. Ploude
Vice President
United National Bank
1399 South West 1st Avenue
Miami, FL 33130
(305) 358–4334
Fax: (305) 381–6320
EMAIL: See Below

6021

Business Information: United National Bank is a local full–service banking institution specializing in lending to the legal profession. As Vice President, Mr. Ploude is in charge of the credit department which provides background checks and approvals to customers. He manages the day–to–day operation of his eight person staff, compiles annual department budgets, and does strategic planning for the anticipated rapid growth of the department. **Career Steps:** Vice President, United National Bank (1993–Present); Loan Officer, Community Bank of Homestead (1991–1993); Credit Review Manager, Southeast Bank (1990–1993); Lending Manager, Suntrust Bank (1985–1990). **Associations & Accomplishments:** Director, Miami Chapter, Robert Morris Associates; Director, Dade/Monroe Division of March of Dimes. **Education:** University of Connecticut, B.S. in Accounting (1974). **Personal:** Married to Faith in 1974. Two children: Laura and Veronica. Mr. Ploude enjoys sailing, period furniture woodworking, and hunting.

Richard M. Postiglione
Vice President of Auditing
IBJ Schroder Bank & Trust Company
1 State Street, 7th Floor
New York, NY 10004
(212) 858–2759
Fax: (212) 858–2114

6021

Business Information: IBJ Schroder Bank & Trust Company is a commercial bank and trust organization with a broad base of products and services. As Vice President of Auditing, Mr. Postiglione develops and manages the Annual audit programs for both financial and EDP staffs. He also provides control counseling to senior management. **Career Steps:** Vice President of Auditing, IBJ Schroder Bank & Trust Company (1984–Present); Senior Auditor, European American Bank (1983); Auditor, Marine Midland Bank (1980–1983). **Associations & Accomplishments:** Bank Administration Institute; Delta Mu Delta, National Honor Society of Business Administration; Cannon Financial Institute, Certified Trust Auditor; Catholic High School Athletic Association, High School Basketball Coach. **Education:** University of Wisconsin, Management (1987); Wagner College, B.S. in Business Administration/Economics. **Personal:** Married to Monica in 1990. Two children: Julia and Jenna. Mr. Postiglione enjoys quality family time and activities. He is also active in both High School and College athletics.

Silvio Luiz B. Prado
Director
Banco Rendiments S.A.
Alameda Corena 75 Apt. 151
Sao Paulo, Brazil 01424–000
55–11–816–0789
Fax: 55–11–212–9701

6021

Business Information: Banco Rendiments S.A. is a full service banking facility specializing in international trade, finance and correspondent banking. As Director, Mr. Prado oversees all aspects of the Company including administration, operations, finance, public relations, marketing and strategic planning. **Career Steps:** Director, Banco Rendiments S.A. (1992–Present); Resident Vice President, Citibank, NA (1986–1989); Joint Director, Banca ABC Roma S/A (1989–1991); Director, Banlatin S/A (1991–1994). **Education:** Economist (1977); Marketing International; International Finance. **Personal:** Married to Maria Tereza N.B. in 1985. Two children: Thiago Nocera B. and Thalita Nocera B.. Mr. Prado enjoys basketball and music.

Bonnie A. Rasmussen–Dougherty
Relationship Manager for Commercial Lenders
Fleet Bank
300 Broadhollow Road
Melville, NY 11747–4832
(516) 547–7838
Fax: (516) 547–7701

6021

Business Information: Fleet Bank, a subsidiary of Fleet Financial Group, is a diversified banking and financial services bank. Headquartered in Long Island, New York, Fleet Bank has locations throughout the North East from Maine to New Jersey. Joining Fleet Bank in 1991, Ms. Rasmussen–Dougherty was appointed as Assistant Vice President of Fleet Bank of the Long Island headquarters and Relationship Manager for Commercial Lenders in 1994. She is responsible for a forty million dollar portfolio of commercial loans. **Career Steps:** Fleet Bank: Relationship Manager for Commercial Lenders (1994–Present), Portfolio Manager and Credit Officer (1991–1994); Credit Analyst, Chemical Bank (1990–1991). **Associations & Accomplishments:** Interviewed for the Long Island Business News. **Education:** Adelphi University, B.A. (1990); Chemical Bank Credit Training Program. **Personal:** Married to Patrick Dougherty in 1995. Ms. Rasmussen–Dougherty enjoys sharp shooting, golf, and Ju Jitsu (black belt).

Frances Wamer Reeves
Personnel Officer
First National Bank
950 John C. Calhoun Drive
Orangeburg, SC 29115
(803) 531–0559
Fax: (803) 531–0524

6021

Business Information: First National Bank is a full–service financial institution serving South Carolina's southern counties. Ms. Reeves has served in various secretarial and administrative positions since joining First National in 1982. In 1987 she received her Bachelor's Degree in Business Administration from the Limestone College Management Program, a continuing education program for experienced professionals. Promoted to Personnel Officer in 1995, she is presently responsible for daily operations of the Human Resources Department, recruiting and hiring, and various administrative functions. **Career Steps:** First National Bank: Personnel Officer (1995–Present), Administrative Assistant (1987–1995), Secretary (1982–1987); Secretary, Georgia Pacific (1981–1982). **Associations & Accomplishments:** Ebenezer United Methodist Church; Moultrie Chapter DAR; Edicto Clemmon Club. **Education:** Limestone College, B.S. (1987); American Institute of Banking, General Diploma. **Personal:** Married to Thomas B. Jr. in 1974. Ms. Reeves enjoys cross–stitching.

Jacqueline Schneider
Vice President
Bank of America
185 Berry Street, 3rd Floor #5891
San Francisco, CA 94107
(415) 624–1300
Fax: (415) 624–1490

6021

Business Information: Bank of America is an international financial institution specializing in commercial banking. Bank of America is the largest retail bank in the U.S., as well as rated the second largest commercial bank. Established in 1904, Bank of America employs over 50,000 people worldwide and 90 people in the San Francisco branch. With thirteen years experience in the banking industry, Ms. Schneider joined Bank of America in 1988. Serving as Vice President, she is the Senior Finance Officer responsible for Capital Markets accounting and planning, reporting, and analysis. **Career Steps:** Vice President, Bank of America (1988–Present); Regulatory Reporting, Security Pacific Corporation (1987–1992); Auditor, Peat, Marwick (1983–1987). **Associations & Accomplishments:** California Society of Certified Public Accountants; League of Women Voters of California. **Education:** California State University – Fresno, B.S. (1983). **Personal:** One child: Derrick. Ms. Schneider enjoys ballroom dancing, skiing, and cycling.

Ernest L. Sullivan

Vice President of Human Resources
Banc One Corporation
800 Brooksedge Boulevard
Columbus, OH 43271
(614) 248–8816
Fax: (614) 882–1068

6021

Business Information: Banc One Corporation is the 10th largest bank in the United States, with over 50,000 employees in 13 states. Considered to be one of the top ten for profitability, making over $1 billion in net income, Banc One Corporation is a full–service financial institution. As Vice President of Human Resources, Mr. Sullivan's two primary areas of responsibility are staff and employee relations. He manages the recruitment and selection of all employees for Ohio, Kentucky, and West Virginia, the Corporation's largest region with over 21,000 employees. **Career Steps:** Banc One Corporation: Vice President of Human Resources, (1991–Present), Assistant Vice President of Human Resources (1988–1991); Manager of Staffing and Employee Relations, Rockwell International (1981–1988). **Associations & Accomplishments:** Personnel Association of Columbus; Society for Human Resources Management; President, Board for Jobs for Columbus Graduates; Board Member, St. Stephens Community House; Business Advisory Council, Central State University. **Education:** Capital University, B.A. in Business (1981). **Personal:** Mr. Sullivan enjoys swimming, Japanese culture, and tennis.

Quy Tran

Portfolio Manager
Peoples Bank
850 Main Street
Bridgeport, CT 06604
(203) 338–4137
Fax: (203) 338–6983

6021

Business Information: People's Bank is a financial institution specializing in savings and small business loans. Currently operating 80 branches, the Bank is the tenth largest bank in the United States and 50th in the world. As Portfolio Manager, Mr. Tran is responsible for approving and managing small business loans for the Bank. With almost ten years in the banking business, he enjoys helping Asian customers to become independent and assists in teaching them to speak English. **Career Steps:** Portfolio Manager, Peoples Bank (1990–Present); Credit Manager, First Federal Bank (1988–1990); Credit Manager, Bay Bank (1986–1988). **Associations & Accomplishments:** President, Asian Community Services, Inc.; President, Vietnamese Mutual Assistance Association; Connecticut Coalition of Mutual Assistance Association, Inc. **Education:** University of New Haven, M.B.A. (1981); Saigon University: B.A. in American English Literature (1970), B.A. in Education (1968). **Personal:** Married to My – Hanh Thi Tran in 1972. Two children: Cuong Doan Tran; Thanh – Lan Thi Tran. Mr. Tran enjoys table tennis, harmonica, and guitar.

Kenneth D. Walter, C.P.A./P.F.S., C.F.P.

Director of Auditing/Financial Planning Officer
Pamrapo Savings Bank
591 Avenue C
Bayonne, NJ 07002–3813
(201) 339–4600
Fax: (201) 823–2044
EMAIL: See Below

6021

Business Information: Pamrapo Savings Bank is a full–service financial institution specializing in banking and financial

planning. The Bank offers residential/commercial mortgages, consumer loans, personal and business checking, savings, and certificate accounts. The Bank also offers financial planning services such as estate planning, investment planning, retirement planning and individual tax return services. With 8 branches in the New Jersey area, the bank is considering expansion into other states in the near future. As Director of Auditing, Mr. Walter reviews all audits performed by his staff. He is responsible for writing and submitting audit reports to the Board of Directors along with submitting an audit plan for Board approval every year. As Financial Planning Officer, Mr. Walter supervises investment planning, estates, mortgages, and tax returns for customers. Internet users can reach him via: Ppxm36b@Prodigy.com. **Career Steps:** Director of Accounting, Pamrapo Savings Bank (1988–Present); Auditor, Stephen P. Radies & Company (1985–1987). **Associations & Accomplishments:** Institute of Internal Auditors; Metro New York Society of Institute of Certified Financial Planners; Treasurer of Bayonne Catholic Youth Organization; American Institute of Certified Public Accountants; New Jersey Society of Certified Public Accountants; Institute of Certified Financial Planners; F.M.S.; A.A.I.I.; Adjunct Professor at F.D.U., Madison, New Jersey. **Education:** Montclair State University, B.S. (1985); Certified Public Accountant, Certified Financial Planner, Series 7 and 63; Life and Health Authorities. **Personal:** Married to Trinidad in 1990. Two children: Kenneth II, and Joseph. Mr. Walter enjoys golf, billiards, and cooking.

James R. Weiss

Special Assets Manager
First Bank, N.A.
701 Lee Street
Des Plaines, IL 60016
(847) 390–5628
Fax: (847) 390–5700

6021

Business Information: First Bank, N.A., based in Minneapolis, Minnesota, is a national commercial banking institution serving customers through subsidiaries located throughout North America. First Bank has eleven branches, four of which are physical locations. With ten years of experience in the banking industry, Mr. Weiss joined First Bank, N.A. as Branch Manager in 1986. Serving throughout the years as Retail Manager and Business Development Manager, he was appointed as Special Assets Manager in 1994. He is responsible for managing special assets for trust customers located in the states of Illinois and Wisconsin, in addition to managing and overseeing business development activities for the department. **Career Steps:** First Bank, N.A.: Special Assets Manager (1994–Present); Business Development Manager (1992–1994), Retail Manager (1990–1992), Branch Manager (1986–1990). **Associations & Accomplishments:** Des Plaines Club; Former Treasurer, Downers Cerove Noon Lions; Former President, Downers Cerove Jaycees; Ambassador–Downers Cerove COC; Downers Cerove Total Community Development Project. **Education:** Benedictine University, M.B.A. in Finance (1996); Arizona State University, B.S. in Economics. **Personal:** Mr. Weiss enjoys the outdoors, fishing, and golf.

Ning Weng

President and Chief Executive Officer
Asian American National Bank
6100 Corporate Drive
Houston, TX 77036
(713) 771–2828
Fax: (713) 771–3689

6021

Business Information: Asian American National Bank is a full–service commercial bank, headquartered in Houston, Texas. By providing its expertise and connections throughout Asia, AANB serves not only Asian customers but also international business communities at large. As President and Chief Executive Officer, Mr. Weng is responsible for the overall management and operations. **Career Steps:** President/CEO, Asian American National Bank (1992–Present); Chairman of the Board/President/CEO, Texas First National Bank (1991–1992); Senior Vice President/Senior Corporate Officer, Pacific Southwest Bank, Texas (1989–1990); Senior Vice President/Chief Lending Officer, Liberty Bank, Hawaii (1985–1989); Vice President/Regional Manager, The Chase Manhattan Bank (1981–1984). **Education:** Rutgers University, M.B.A. (1976); New Jersey Institute of Technology, M.S. (1975). **Personal:** Married to Long in 1970. Two children: Elizabeth and Alexander. Mr. Weng enjoys reading, sports, chess, and travel.

Ted J. Williams

President and Chief Executive Officer
Boatmens National Bank
P.O. Box 351
Lebanon, MO 65536–0351
(417) 532–3184
Fax: (417) 588–1011

6021

Business Information: Boatmen's National Bank, a wholly–owned entity of Boatmen's Bancshares, is a full–service commercial bank. The Lebanon, Missouri office currently operates from two locations, and reports assets of $74 million in loans and over $80 million in deposits. The parent company (Boatmen's Bancshares), is the oldest banking institution west of the Mississippi (will be 150 years old 1997). Operating in nine states throughout the Midwest, it reports assets of over $41 billion. A banking executive with over ten years expertise, Ted Williams joined Boatmen's Bank in 1987, serving as Senior Vice President at the Cape Girardeau branch. Appointed as President and Chief Executive Officer for the Lebanon offices in December of 1993, he provides the overall executive administration for all day–to–day operations for both branch locations. He has the distinction of being Boatmen's Bancshares (holding company) youngest CEO ever appointed. Mr. Williams also personally manages over $10 million in portfolios. **Career Steps:** Boatmen's National Bank: President and Chief Executive Officer – Lebanon, Missouri offices (1993–Present); Senior Vice President – Cape Girardeau office (1987–1993); Lender, Farm Credit Services of Southeast Missouri (1985–1987). **Associations & Accomplishments:** Rotary International; Downtown Business Committee, Lebanon Chamber of Commerce; Membership Committee Chairperson, Lebanon Area Foundation; St. Francis Catholic Church Parish Council; Industrial Development Authority, City of Lebanon; Lebanon Planned Progress Committee. **Education:** Arkansas State University, B.S. (1985); Iowa Agri Banker's School, A.A. (1990). **Personal:** Married to Lori in 1994. Three children: Zachary, Taylor and Megan. Mr. Williams enjoys duck hunting, raising registered beef cattle, and spending time with his family.

Jayne Wirt

Assistant Vice President
First National Bank
501 East 20th Street
Farmington, NM 87401
(505) 326–9006
Fax: (505) 326–9007

6021

Business Information: First National Bank, a independently–owned bank, provides all aspects of commercial banking. As Assistant Vice President, Ms. Wirt is responsible for all aspects of the Branch operations, including finance, public relations, marketing, and strategic planning. **Career Steps:** First National Bank: Assistant Vice President (1993–Present), Branch Supervisor 20th (1990–1993), Head Teller, Main Office (1989–1990), Operation Supervisor, Aztec (1987–1989). **Associations & Accomplishments:** Financial Women International; American Institute of Banking; San Juan College – Business Advisory Committee. **Education:** San Juan College, currently attending; New Mexico School of Banking (1989). **Personal:** Married to Gerry A. in 1994. Two children: Annette L. Blivens and John E. Billingsley Jr. Ms. Wirt enjoys camping, four–wheeling, and spending time with her grandchildren.

Randy L. Withrow

Vice President – Mortgage Servicing Manager
First American National Bank
First American Center
Nashville, TN 37237–4503
(615) 748–1587
Fax: (615) 748–1598

6021

Business Information: First American National Bank is a national financial institution concentrating on banking. With sixteen years expertise in the banking industry, Mr. Withrow joined First American National Bank in 1988 and was appointed as Vice President and Mortgage Servicing Manager in 1995. He is responsible for all aspects of mortgage services, including conversion of mortgage portfolios because of mergers and acquisitions. **Career Steps:** First American National Bank: Vice President – Mortgage Servicing Manager (1995–Present); Vice President – Consumer Credit Administration (Jan. 1995–Jun. 1995); Vice President – MIS Business Systems (1992–1995); Vice President – User–Coordination Consumer (1988–1992). **Education:** Morehead State University; Ashland Community College, A.A. in Accounting (1980); BAI – Certified EDP Auditor and Trust Auditor. **Personal:** Married to Margaret (Maggie) in 1986. Mr. Withrow enjoys writing, photography, golf, and swimming.

John G. Acker

Group Vice President
Banque Paribas
2029 Century Park East, Suite 3900
Los Angeles, CA 90067
(310) 551–7316
Fax: (310) 556–8759

6022

Business Information: Banque Paribas is the 20th largest bank in the world. With a total of $240 billion in assets, Banque Paribas is a full–service, wholesale merchant bank. As Group Vice President, Mr. Acker co–heads the United States media–entertainment finance division. He has a staff of twelve and travels extensively working on customer calls. **Career Steps:** Group Vice President, Banque Paribas (1989–Present); Banking Officer, First Interstate, Ltd. (1987–1989); Sales Manager, Cable TV Industries (1983–1987). **Associations & Accomplishments:** Beta Alpha Psi; Sigma Iota Epsilon; Omicron Delta Epsilon; Beta Gamma Sigma. **Education:** University of Southern California, M.B.A. (1987); University of Colorado – Boulder, B.S. **Personal:** Married to Lisa in 1992. One child: Grant. Mr. Acker enjoys travel, golf, and skiing.

Iari de Andrade

Executive President
BIAPE International Bank Limited
Apartado 51–558
Caracas, Venezuela 1050–A
(582) 781–7622
Fax: (582) 781–1546

6022

Business Information: BIAPE International Bank Limited is an inter–American savings and loan. As Executive President, Mr. de Andrade has been with the Bank for almost 20 years, serving in several different positions. He currently handles all day–to–day operations for the Bank, including financial and administrative matters. **Career Steps:** BIAPE International Bank Limited: Executive Vice President (1986–Present), Vice President (1982–1986), Finance Manager (1976–1982). **Associations & Accomplishments:** American Management Association; Instituto Venezolano de Ejectivos de Finazas; Los Palos Grandes; Honorary Citizen of Texas; Director of World Savings Bank Institute Brussels. **Education:** University of Rio de Janeiro, Economic Engineering (1972–1974); University of Paris, Ecomometrics (1967–1968); University of Guanabara–Bazil, School of Economy, Administration and Finance, Economist (1963–1967). **Personal:** Mr. de Andrade enjoys snow skiing.

Steven L. Decatur

President
First Bank – St. Cloud
1010 West St. Germain
St. Cloud, MN 56301
(320) 654–2316
Fax: (320) 656–2320

6022

Business Information: First Bank – St. Cloud is a full–service commercial lending institution and holding company located in Northern and Western Central Minnesota. The Bank deals in investments, trusts, and personal banking. As President, Mr. Decatur manages all business banking functions and commercial lending for First Bank. He also ensures the overall economic development and public relations for the Bank. **Career Steps:** First Bank System: President (1993–Present); Vice President/Manager of FBS Lending (1990–1993), Vice President/Manager of High Tech Division (1985–1990). **Associations & Accomplishments:** Junior Achievement – Duluth, MN; United Way – Duluth Area; Marshall School. **Education:** Indiana University, M.B.A. (1977); Carleton College, B.A. (1975). **Personal:** Married to Mary in 1977. Three children: Krista, Anna, and Jacob. Mr. Decatur enjoys antique tractor restoring, tennis, hunting, and fishing.

Dave DeVos

Senior Vice President
Farmers & Merchants Bank
P.O. Box 848
Huron, SD 57350–8840
(605) 352–9403
Fax: (605) 352–6982

6022

Business Information: Farmers & Merchants Bank is a full service banking facility with over $150 million in assets, and a loan–to–deposit ratio of 70%. Considered one of the 100 most safe banks in the nation, Farmers & Merchants Bank has five branches throughout South Dakota. As Senior Vice President, Mr. DeVos oversees all agricultural lending, supervises the remote branch office, and is a member of the Bank's senior management team. **Career Steps:** Senior Vice President, Farmers & Merchants Bank (1986–Present); Vice President Management Supervision, Farm Credit Services (1985–1986); Assistant Vice President/Credit Management, Farm Credit Banks of Omaha (1982–1985). **Associations & Accomplishments:** South Dakota Bankers Association; Upper Midwest Agricultural Credit Council; Faculty Member, Midwest Banking Institute; Past President/Board Member, Huron Chamber of Commerce; Past Board Member, United Way; Huron Development Corporation; Sigma Alpha Epsilon Fraternity; Past State Board Member, South Dakota Agriculture in the Classroom Program. **Education:** South Dakota State University, B.S. in Agricultural Education (1975); American Bankers Association Commercial Lenders School (1990). **Personal:** Married to Doreen Vien in 1975. One child: Derek. Mr. DeVos enjoys fishing, hunting, basketball, softball, hobby farming, and participating in an investment club.

Mark A. Eppler

Chief Financial Officer
Pacific State Bank
6 South El Dorado
Stockton, CA 95202
(209) 943–7400
Fax: (209) 463–4054

6022

Business Information: Pacific State Bank is a full–service financial banking and lending organization. Established in 1987, Pacific State currently has three branch locations in the greater Stockton, California area, and reports assets in excess of $50 million. Joining Pacific State Bank's main branch as a commercial loan officer in 1993, Mark Eppler was appointed to his current position in 1995. As Chief Financial Officer, he is resonsible for all financial aspects of the company, as well as overseeing accounting, investments, and operational procedures. **Career Steps:** Pacific State Bank: Chief Financial Officer (1995–Present); Controller (1994–1995); Commercial Loan Officer (1993–1994); Bank Examiner, FDIC (1991–1993). **Associations & Accomplishments:** Rotary International; Golden Key Honor Society. **Education:** California State University at Sacramento, B.S. in Finance (1990). **Personal:** Married to Diane in 1987. One child: Tyler. Mr. Eppler enjoys water skiing, snow skiing, jogging, and biking.

Mr. Jonathan R. Fox

Chief Executive Officer and Chairman of the Board
Fowler State Bank
201 Main Street
Fowler, CO 81039
(719) 263–4276
Fax: (719) 263–4277

6022

Business Information: Fowler State Bank is a full–service financial banking and lending organization. Established in 1899, Fowler State Bank currently employs 11 people. As Chief Executive Officer and Chairman of the Board, Mr. Fox oversees all aspects of operations. **Career Steps:** Fowler State Bank: Chief Executive Officer and Chairman of the Board (1991–Present), Vice President (1985–1991), Assistant Vice President (1983–1984), Assistant Cashier (1980–1982), and Member of the Board of Directors since 1980. **Associations & Accomplishments:** Vice President and Board Member, Fowler Country Club and Cottonwood Links Golf Course; Advisory Council, Fowler High School Vocational Business Department; Member, Sons of the American Revolution; Member, Colorado Bankers Association and Independent Bankers Association; Former Board Member and Treasurer, Arkansas Valley Regional Medical Center (1986–1994); Treasurer, Missouri Day Association; University of Colorado Distinguished Service Award. **Education:** University of Colorado, B.S. (1980). **Personal:** Married to Shari L. in 1988. Two children: Sean and Ashleigh. Mr. Fox enjoys fishing, horseback riding, biking and skiing.

Julia S. Gouw

Senior Vice President and Chief Financial Officer
East West Bank
415 Huntington Drive
San Marino, CA 91108
(818) 799–5178
Fax: (818) 799–8410
EMAIL: See Below

6022

Business Information: East West Bank is a $1.3 billion commercial banking institution, serving customers in over 20 branches throughout California. As Senior Vice President and Chief Financial Officer, Ms. Gouw is responsible for all aspects of finances, including accounting, management information systems, asset/liability, and purchasing. Concurrently, she serves as Chairperson of Internal Asset Review and Management Information System Committees and Member of the Asset/Liability, Senior Management, and Compliance Committees. Internet users may reach her via: jgouw@aol.com **Career Steps:** East West Bank: Senior Vice President and Chief Financial Officer (1994–Present), Senior Vice President and Controller (1991–1994), Vice–President and Controller (1989–1991); Senior Audit Manager, KPMG Peat Marwick (1983–1989); Staff Accountant, Texaco, Inc. (1981–1983). **Associations & Accomplishments:** Financial Managers Society: National Member, Former President – Los Angeles Chapter; Certified Public Accountant; California Society of Certified Public Accountants; Marquis Who's Who of American Women (1987–1988). **Education:** University of Illinois – Urbana Champaign, B.S. in Accounting with Highest Honor (1981). **Personal:** Married to Ken in 1981. Ms. Gouw enjoys reading, travel, and personal finance and investing.

Mark J. Guillot

Internal Auditor
Bank One Louisiana
451 Florida Street
Baton Rouge, LA 70801
(504) 332–7338
Fax: (504) 332–7512

6022

Business Information: Bank One Louisiana is a full service commercial banking institution. Services offered include checking, savings, investment banking, trust accounts, and commercial and individual loans. Established in the late 1800's, Bank One currently employs over 50,000 people and has assets of over $97 billion. Mr. Guillot is senior internal auditor and is responsible for planning, coordinating and supervising various audits of company operations and products. His expertise is in the areas of trust auditing and regulatory compliance. **Career Steps:** Assistant Vice President–Auditing, Bank One Louisiana (1991–Present); Internal Auditor and Compliance Officer, Alerion Bank (1987–1991). **Associations & Accomplishments:** Treasurer, Baton Rouge Chapter, Institute of Internal Auditors; Treasurer, Cedarcrest Southmoor Parent Teacher Organization; Examination Committee, Bank Administration Institute–Certified Bank Compliance Officer Exam; Knights of Columbus; National Association of Trust Audit and Compliance Professionals. **Education:** University of New Orleans, M.B.A. (1994); Northwestern State University, B.A.; Certification Designations: Certified Internal Auditor; Certified Bank Auditor; Certified Bank Compliance Officer. **Personal:** Married to Angela in 1982. Two children: Paul and Matthew. Mr. Guillot enjoys relaxing with his family, movies, music, and 5K runs.

Edward M. Jamison

Vice Chairman, President and Chief Executive Officer
Community Bank of Nevada
1400 South Rainbow Blvd.
Las Vegas, NV 89102
(702) 878–0700
Fax: (702) 878–1060

6022

Business Information: Community Bank of Nevada is a full–service state chartered bank, member of the Federal Deposit Insurance Corporation and the Federal Reserve System. With twenty–one years of experience in the banking industry, Mr. Jamison founded Community Bank of Nevada in 1994 and serves as Vice Chairman, President and Chief Executive Officer. He founded Nevada Community Bank, located in Las Vegas, Nevada, in early 1989 and served as the Vice Chairman of the Board, President, and Chief Executive Officer until the bank was sold to a large multi–bank holding company in late 1993. He is responsible for all aspects of operations, in addition to overseeing all administrative operations for the bank and its officers and employees. **Career Steps:** Vice Chairman, President and Chief Executive Officer, Community Bank of Nevada (1994–Present); Executive Vice President, First Security Bank of Nevada, a wholly owned subsidiary of First Security Corporation (1994); Vice Chairman, President and Chief Executive Officer, Nevada Community Bank

(1989–1994); Senior Vice President, First Security Financial (1984–1989); Chairman of the Board, President, Executive Vice President, Commerce Financial (1976–1983). **Associations & Accomplishments:** Rotary Club; Director – Nevada Banks Association; Nevada Representative, American Bankers Community Bankers Council; Director, LLVA Foundation; Past President, ILGC of Utah; Director, Utah Consumer Bankers Association. **Education:** Weber State College, B.S. (1972) **Personal:** Mr. Jamison is married to Janalee and they have four children. Mr. Jamison enjoys golf, tennis and church activities.

Kelly D. Johnson

Vice President, Regional Retail Sales Manager
First of America Bank – Illinois, N.A.
1551 Sandy Hollow Road
Rockford, IL 61109
(815) 395–3664
Fax: (815) 391–5012

6022

Business Information: First of America Bank – Illinois, N.A. is an affiliate bank of First of America Bank Corporation, headquartered in Kalamazoo, Michigan. One of the largest bank holding companies in the Midwest, FOA serves more than 32 million households and businesses in Illinois, Michigan, Indiana, and Florida through a network of over 600 offices. Mr. Johnson presently serves as the Regional Retail Sales Manager for the Northern Illinois Region, consisting of 70 building locations, representing over $42 billion in assets. **Career Steps:** First of America Bank: Vice President, Regional Retail Sales Manager – Illinois, N.A. (1995–Present), Retail Sales Manager – Michigan (1993–1994), Branch Manager III – Michigan (1989–1993). **Associations & Accomplishments:** Former President, Southwest Michigan Chapter American Institute of Banking. **Education:** Evangel College, B.B.A. in Management (1985). **Personal:** Married to Velvet in 1985. Two children: Cole and Jordan. Mr. Johnson enjoys bowhunting, billiards, golf, and fishing.

Mark H. LaRoe

Senior Vice President
Comercia Bank – Texas
PO Box 650282 Mail Code 6607
Dallas, TX 75265
(214) 965–8981
Fax: (214) 965–8980

6022

Business Information: Comercia Bank–Texas is a wholly–owned subsidiary of Comerica Incorporated. With 55 locations throughout Texas, Comercia Bank–Texas is a full–service financial services provider. As Senior Vice President, Mr. LaRoe manages the Healthcare Banking Department for the Texas Region. **Career Steps:** Senior Vice President, Comercia Bank – Texas (1992–Present); Various positions at Comerica Bank – Texas and its predecessor bank purchased by Comerica Bank in 1988. **Associations & Accomplishments:** Board Member, Mental Health Association of Greater Dallas; Executive Committee, Presbyterian Healthcare Forum; Board Member, Hope Cottage; Assistant Treasurer, The Episcopal Diocese of Dallas; Leadership Dallas (1995–1996 class); Officer Brother, The Most Venerable Society of the Order of St. John of Jerusalem; Downtown Dallas Rotary Club. **Education:** Texas Tech University, B.B.A. (1980). **Personal:** Married to Dianne in 1982. Three children: Hamilton, Annie, and Trotter. Mr. LaRoe enjoys jogging, fishing, and outdoor activities.

Bruce A. Lieurance

Vice President and Financial Officer
The Sabina Bank
135 North Howard Street
Sabina, OH 45169–1152
(513) 584–2491
Fax: (513) 584–2494

6022

Business Information: The Sabina Bank, known as "the friendly bank on the corner," is a private, state–chartered financial institution, specializing in banking. With twelve years of experience in banking, Mr. Lieurance joined The Sabina Bank in 1984. Appointed as Vice President in 1991 and Financial Officer in 1995, he is responsible for the completion of regulatory reports, all types of lending activities, and investment portfolio maintenance. **Career Steps:** Vice President and Financial Officer, The Sabina Bank (1984–Present). **Education:** Wilmington College, B.S. (1984); Southern State Community College, A.S. in Business (1982). **Personal:** Mr. Lieurance enjoys golf and classic cars.

Jae M. Maxfield

President and Chief Executive Officer
Sparta State Bank
109 East Division
Sparta, MI 49345–0186
(616) 887–7366
Fax: (616) 887–7990

6022

Business Information: Sparta State Bank is a commercial financial institution, specializing in banking and insurance. Established in 1898, Sparta State Bank currently employs 65 people. With twenty–three years expertise in the banking industry, Mr. Maxfield joined Sparta State Bank in 1994. Serving as President and Chief Executive Officer, he oversees the administrative operations for associates and a support staff of 65, in addition to all aspects of bank finances. Concurrent with his executive position at Sparta State Bank, he serves as President and Chief Executive Officer of First Community BankCorp, a holding company. **Career Steps:** President and Chief Executive Officer, Sparta State Bank (1994–Present); President and Chief Executive Officer, Maxfield Associates (1993–1994); President and Chief Executive Office, First America Bank – Monroe (1990–1993); Senior Vice President, Erie State Bank (1975–1990). **Associations & Accomplishments:** President, Chamber of Commerce; Community Foundation. **Education:** University of Utah, M.B.A. (1968); Idaho State University, B.A. **Personal:** Married to Janice in 1982. Mr. Maxfield enjoys backpacking and cycling.

James W. Mays

Vice President and Manager of Cost Management
First Tennessee Bank
165 Madison Avenue
Memphis, TN 31803
(901) 523–5606
Fax: (901) 523–4945

6022

Business Information: First Tennessee Bank is one of the largest bank holding companies in the United States. The Bank offers a wide range of services for their customers from simple savings and checking accounts to complex trust and investment services. As Vice President and Manager of Cost Management, Mr. Mays develops and implements strategic profitability and risk management analysis systems for First Tennessee Bank. These systems incorporate the concepts of total quality management, activity–based cost management, benchmarking and process re–design used in indentifying operating performance standards and goals. Mr. Mays consults with Bank Management in the evaluation of products and processes in order to provide more cost effective work production. **Career Steps:** First Tennessee Bank: Vice President and Manager of Cost Management (1988–Present), Vice President and Manager of Planning and Financial Analysis (1986–1988), Vice President, Manager of Budgeting and Financial Analysis (1984–1986); Director of Finance and Administration, PDW Computer Systems (1982–1984); Budget Director, Humana, Inc. (1976–1981). **Associations & Accomplishments:** Guest lecturer, University of Memphis and Christian Brothers University MBA programs; Institute of Management Accountants; Memphis Partners, Inc.; Memphis Concert Ballet. **Education:** University of Louisville, MBA (1971) and BS Commerce (1970); Southwestern Graduate School of Banking; Southern Methodist University; Crosby Quality College. **Personal:** Married to Glenna in 1965. One child: Jennifer. Mr. Mays enjoys travel, golf, and horsemanship.

James Meyer

Vice President
Bank of Illinois – Leasing Division
101 Broadway Mall, Unit 3
Normal, IL 61761
(309) 862–3392
Fax: (309) 862–2773

6022

Business Information: Bank of Illinois – Leasing Division (B.O.I. Leasing) specializes in long–term business equipment leasing. The Bank Leasing Division designed and developed a specialized lease marketing program that has been endorsed by various equipment manufacturers across the nation as an additional sales tool for the manufacturer's marketing and distributor organizations. This lease marketing program promotes equipment leasing as a customer value added service through the leasing concept of "Equipment Purchasing Acquisition Choice" for the manufacturer's business customers. As Vice President, Mr. Meyer oversees the operations of the Leasing Division of the Bank. **Career Steps:** Vice President, Bank of Illinois – Leasing Division (1994–Present); Territorial Manager, Country Leasing (1993–1994); President, The Aaron Leasing Companies, Inc. (1980–1992). **Associations & Accomplishments:** Knights of Columbus; Developed and designed a dealer lease sales operation training manual and a lease marketing/training video tape. Also conducts lease training sales seminars for manufacturer's national sales personnel and equipment distributors. **Education:** Quincy University, B.S. in Business Management (1972); Various Equipment Leasing Seminars. **Personal:** Married to Gretchen in 1972. Mr. Meyer enjoys travel and camping.

1st FIRST TENNESSEE
Here for you.

Sarah L. Meyerrose

Regional President
First Tennessee Bank
235 East Center Street
Kingsport, TN 37660–4303
(423) 378–7001
Fax: (423) 378–7070

6022

Business Information: First Tennessee Bank National Association with $12 Billion in assets, provides retail, commercial, and mortgage banking services to metropolitan areas of Tennessee, including Kingsport. A full service commercial bank, First Tennessee is a subsidiary of First Tennessee National Corporation, whose nationwide business lines include mortgage banking, broker, agency and capital markets services, a credit card operation, and check cashing services. Named one of 10 best corporations in the United States for mothers to work by "Working Mother" Magazine, First Tennessee, established in 1864, looks forward to growing even stronger in the communities it serves and continuing to maintain its high level of customer service. In her various roles with the company, Mrs. Meyerrose has helped to incorporate several new programs into the infrastructure, including assistance with daycare and eldercare issues and an "800" number for employee families to call should they need help with personal issues. Additionally, Mrs. Meyerrose was instrumental in implementing various family–friendly programs, including "Flexplace", whereby some employees, with the aid of company furnished computers and modems, are allowed to work from home. **Career Steps:** Regional President, First Tennessee Bank (1995–Present); First Tennessee National Corporation: Senior Financial Officer (1988–1992), Vice President/Treasurer (1984–1988), Vice President/Assistant Treasurer (1982–1984); Executive Vice President (1992–1995). **Associations & Accomplishments:** Chair: Elect of Kingsport Tomorrow; Board Member of: Kingsport Area Chamber of Commerce, Girls, Inc., YMCA, United Way, Salvation Army, Kingsport Symphony Orchestra, Rotary International. **Education:** Owen School of Management of Vanderbilt University, Exec. M.B.A. (1987); Vanderbilt University, B.A. in Business/Economics, Magna Cum Laude (1978). **Personal:** Married to Michael J. in 1978. One child: Anna Michaela. Mrs. Meyerrose enjoys music, especially church, organ and piano, and being a gourmet cook.

Debra J. Noah

Second Vice President
Chase Manhattan of Oregon
5285 Southwest Meadows Road, Suite 199
Lake Oswego, OR 97035
(503) 684–0504
Fax: (503) 639–2256

6022

Business Information: Chase Manhattan of Oregon is a full–service financial institution specializing in banking as well as corporate pensions. As Second Vice President, Ms. Noah is responsible for marketing, underwriting, and Jumbo mortgages. In addition, she is a loan officer and certified credit officer. **Career Steps:** Second Vice President, Chase Manhattan of Oregon (1992–Present); Vice President, Bank of America/Security Pacific Bank (1988–1992); Senior Banking Officer, First Interstate Bank (1977–1988). **Associations & Accomplishments:** City Council President, City of Gresham (1995–Present); Treasurer of Board of Trustees, Waverly Children's Home (1991–Present); Past Matron and Past State Committee Member, Order of Eastern Star; Mother Advisor and Past State Officer, International Order of Rainbow for Girls; Elected Officer, Order of Amaranth; Business Banking Officer of the Year, Security Pacific (1988); Pacesetter of the Year, First Interstate (1987); Winner of District 7 International Speech Contest, Toastmasters International; Awards: CTM, ATM, ATM–Bronze, ATM–Silver, and Club Mentor. **Education:** Western Agricultural Credit School, Diploma with honors (1991); American Institute of Banking, General Banking Diploma; Northwest Intermediate Commercial Lending School, graduate (1989); Chase Professional Development Series, Completed (1994). **Personal:** Married to Lee in 1978. Two children: Jeanette and Meredith. Ms. Noah enjoys sewing, playing the organ, and chaperoning and volunteering at her children's school.

William H. Novosad
Vice President/Senior Lender
Tracy State Bank
P.O. Box 1069 250 3rd Street
Tracy, MN 56175–0069
(507) 629–4780
Fax: (507) 629–4765

6022

Business Information: Tracy State Bank is a commercial lending bank located in Tracy, Minnesota. The bank offers commercial lending services to consumers, agricultural concerns, and real estate firms. As Vice President/Senior Lender, Mr. Novosad has oversight of all bank operations and general administration functions. He also assists customers with step-by-step plans to increase their financial worth. **Career Steps:** Vice President/Senior Lender, Tracy State Bank (1994–Present); Farm Credit Services: Senior Loan Reviewer, St. Paul (1989–1994), Director of Special Credit, Southern Minnesota (1986–1988), Branch Manager, Loan Officer (1978–1985). **Associations & Accomplishments:** National Institute of Credit; Upper Midwest Agricultural Credit Council; Lions International; Boy Scout Advisor; Minnesota Deer Hunters Association; Viet Nam Veterans Association; Veterans of Foreign Wars; American Legion; Volunteer to Russia with Agricultural Cooperative Development International; N.C.F.C. **Education:** Mankato State University, B.S. in Finance (1978). **Personal:** Married to Miriam in 1973. Three children: Billy, Lucas, and Alexander. Mr. Novosad enjoys fishing, hunting, and auto racing.

Caroline Savage
Vice President
Riggs National Bank of D.C.
808 17th Street Northwest
Washington, DC 20006–3910
(202) 835–6708
Fax: (202) 835–6816

6022

Business Information: Riggs National Bank of D.C. – Washington, D.C.'s oldest, is a full-service commercial bank consisting of 60 branches located throughout D.C., Virginia and Maryland. In the banking industry for over twelve years, Caroline Savage has served in various executive roles for Riggs National since 1992. Working in the Trust Department, she serves as Vice President and Trust Officer, administering all personal trust accounts and related support staff. **Career Steps:** Riggs National Bank of D.C.: Vice President and Trust Officer (1992–1993), Cluster Manager – Personal Trust (1993–1995), Manager – Personal Trust Administrator (1995–Present). **Associations & Accomplishments:** Volunteer, Sibley Memorial Hospital – Washington, D.C. **Education:** Mary Baldwin College, B.A., (1982); National Trust School; National Graduate Trust School.

Jessica Ellen Schmeesing
Regional Human Resource Representative
AgriBank, FCB
375 Jackson Street
St. Paul, MN 55101
(612) 282–8336
Fax: (612) 282–8353

6022

Business Information: AgriBank, FCB provides agricultural lending and finance-related services to the 7th Farm Credit District, and an additional 30 farm credit service organizations nationwide. As Regional Human Resource Representative, Ms. Schmeesing provides human resource consulting to Farm Credit Service Associations in ten locations throughout a seven state region. She works with employment teams to help establish human resource departments in their subsidiaries. **Career Steps:** Regional Human Resource Representative, AgriBank, FCB (1993–Present); Assistant to Executive Director, American Cancer Society (1992–1993); Human Resource Representative, ARCO (1990–1992); Human Resource Representative, 3M Corporation (1990). **Associations & Accomplishments:** International Human Resource liaison with Russian, Polish, and Bulgarian Bankers; TCPA; Lakewood Community Leadership Academy. **Education:** University of Minnesota, M.A.I.R. (1990); Hamline University, B.A. (1988). **Personal:** Ms. Schmeesing enjoys volleyball, wally ball, basketball, and athletic activities with her family.

John Wagaman
Vice President
Ozark Bank
P.O. Box 220, 106–112 N. 2nd Avenue
Ozark, MO 65721
(417) 581–2321
Fax: (417) 581–2235

6022

Business Information: Ozark Bank is a high quality, full-service community bank, serving the Ozark area via three branches. As Vice President, Mr. Wagaman oversees Credit Administration and Loan Review. He manages loan quality from credit and documentation. **Career Steps:** Vice President, Ozark Bank (1988–Present); Credit Review Officer, Mercantile Bank Corporation (1984–1988); Assistant Vice President, Lewis & Clark Mercantile Bank (1979–1984). **Associations & Accomplishments:** Jaycees; First Baptist Church of Ozark. **Education:** Columbia College, B.A. in Business Administration (1979); RMA, Omega Commercial Loans; AIB School; National Compliance School; National Reg. 2 School. **Personal:** Married to Kathy A. in 1984. Three children: Lauren A., Thomas E., and Timothy D. Mr. Wagaman enjoys golf and walking.

James (Jim) A. Wills
Chief Operating Officer
Cowlitz Bank
P.O. Box 1518
Longview, WA 98632–7912
(360) 423–9800
Fax: (360) 423–1921

6022

Business Information: Cowlitz Bank is a state chartered, full service financial and lending organization. As Chief Operating Officer, Mr. Wills is responsible for all aspects of operations, including administration, finance, public relations, and strategic planning. In addition, he is part owner and holds a seat on the Senior Management Team. **Career Steps:** Chief Operating Officer, Cowlitz Bank (1988–Present); Assistant Vice President, Klickitat Bank (1982–1988); Assistant Vice President, Rainier Bank (1966–1982). **Associations & Accomplishments:** Washington Bankers Association; Chairman of the Board, Cowlitz County Economic Development Council; Rotary Club; President, Lions Club; Chamber of Commerce; Hospice Board Member. **Education:** Spokane Community, Associates (1970); Carroll College at Helena, MT; Northwest Ag. School at Pullman, WA; Commercial Credit School Rainier Bank; American Institute of Banking. **Personal:** Married to Sharon in 1972. Five children: James Jr., Kerry, Jennifer, Paul, and Carl. Mr. Wills enjoys RV traveling and golf.

Jack D. Wilson
Vice President of Compliance
Rancho Vista National Bank
1385 East Vista Way
Vista, CA 92084–4041
(619) 631–2512
Fax: (619) 631–2567

6022

Business Information: Rancho Vista National Bank is a full-service commercial bank providing savings, checking, and related financial services to clients. Established in 1982, and employing fifty people, the Bank has assets of approximately $98 million. As Vice President of Compliance, Mr. Wilson is also responsible for security, CRA, safety, and facilities management. Additional duties include administration, operations, and staff management related to his department. **Career Steps:** Vice President of Compliance, Rancho Vista National Bank (1989–Present); Vice President and Chief Financial Officer, Western Family Bank (1982–1988); Vice President and Cashier, Bank of Marina Del Rey (1981–1982); Medical Administrator, Valencia Mesa Medical Group (1978–1981). **Associations & Accomplishments:** Certified Internal Auditor, Institute of Internal Auditors; Certified Regulatory Compliance Manager, Institute of Certified Bankers (ABA); Youth Soccer Coach and Referee; Fullerton Soccer Club; Past Treasurer, Civitan, Carlsbad Chapter. **Education:** California State – Fullerton, B.A. (1969); National Graduate Compliance School. **Personal:** Two children: Gregg and Julie. Mr. Wilson enjoys golf.

Hwa Jin Yoon
Compliance Officer
California Cho Hung Bank
3000 West Olympic Boulevard
Los Angeles, CA 90006–2516
(213) 380–8300
Fax: (213) 386–7208
EMAIL: See Below

6022

Business Information: California Cho Hung Bank is a commercial bank which is state–chartered, FDIC insured, and is a FRB non–member. A practicing attorney in New York since 1993, Ms. Yoon joined California Cho Hung Bank as Compliance Officer in 1993. She is responsible for all of the Bank's regulatory matters, including legal issues and regulatory accounting, and serving as the Corporate Secretary. Future plans include serving as a director and senior executive officer. **Career Steps:** Compliance Officer, California Cho Hung Bank (1993–Present); Law Clerk, Hong & Chang (1992–1993); Paralegal and Assistant Manager, Korean Air (1980–1988). **Associations & Accomplishments:** New York Bar; New York State Bar Association; Amateur Golfers Association Tour of Southern California. **Education:** New York University School of Law, Master of Comparative Jurisprudence (1992); Korea Air and Correspondence University, LL.B.; Hankuk University of Foreign Studies, B.A. **Personal:** Ms. Yoon enjoys computers, golf, tennis, and swimming.

Mr. Michael G. Tomeczko
Vice President and Director of Senior Citizens Program
Pullman Bank of Commerce and Industry
6100 North Northwest Highway
Chicago, IL 60631
(312) 594–2227
Fax: (312) 775–3444

6028

Business Information: Pullman Bank of Commerce and Industry is a private chartered full service commercial banking institution. As Vice President and Director of Senior Citizens Program, Mr. Tomeczko provides the direction and administration for the senior programs of the bank. With a senior membership of over 3,500 persons, Pullman offers free checking and special activities for their members. Mr. Tomeczko is the coordinator for all special tours offered. Concurrent with his duties at Pullman, he has a private practice law firm, specializing in Senior law and litigation representation. Mr. Tomeczko is an ardent advocate for the senior citizen population citywide, acting on their behalf in many community and neighborhood councils and committees. He has been working with senior citizens for the past 25 years. On behalf of his tireless efforts for the senior community of the Northwest area of the City of Chicago and nearby suburbs, he was honored at a testimonial dinner given by the Norwood Park Chamber of Commerce. During the ceremony, he was presented numerous awards and accolades from city, state, governmental dignitaries (including Citation from President Clinton) and fellow peers. On this day, he also received proclamation by the Chicago City Council declaring September 22, 1994 as Michael G. Tomeczko Day. **Career Steps:** Vice President and Director of Senior Citizens Program, Pullman Bank of Commerce and Industry (1987–Present); Service Area Director, City of Chicago Department on Aging/Disability (1973–1987). **Associations & Accomplishments:** The Chicago Society; Knights of Columbus – 4th Degree; Advocates Society; American Bar Association; Chicago Bar Association; Royal Order of the Moose; Polish National Alliance; Polish Businessmen's Club; Treasurer, Norwood Park Chamber of Commerce; Member–Board of Directors, Retired Senior Volunteer Program, City of Chicago/Department on Aging–Northwest Service Area Advisory Council. **Education:** Chicago Kent College of Law, J.D. (1975); St. Ambrose University, B.A. (1971). **Personal:** Married to Patricia in 1965. Two children: Kathryn and Michael.

George Aristizabal
District Manager
World Savings & Loan
17350 State Highway 249, Suite 120
Houston, TX 77064
(713) 955–7593
Fax: (713) 955–0258

6029

Business Information: World Savings & Loan is a financial institution specializing in home mortgage loans and savings. Established in 1964, World Savings & Loan is a subsidiary of Golden West. As District Manager, Mr. Aristizabal is responsible for all loan origination aspects, including management, training, and support of ten loan officers. He also maintains and services wholesale accounts through mortgage brokers, who offer their unique loan products. **Career Steps:** World Savings & Loan: District Manager (1995–Present), Wholesale Representative (1994–1995), Retail Representative

(1993–1994). **Associations & Accomplishments:** Affiliate Member, Houston Association of Realtors. **Education:** San Jacinto College, A.A. in Aviation Management (1992). **Personal:** Married to Susan in 1992. One child: Lauren. Mr. Aristizabal enjoys scuba diving, ranching, hunting, golf and flying in his leisure time.

Mr. Howard I. Atkins
Executive Vice President and Chief Financial Officer
Midlantic Corporation
499 Thornall Street
Edison, NJ 08818
(908) 321–8125
Fax: (908) 321–8518

6029

Business Information: Midlantic Corporation is a full service financial services company and commercial bank. In his current capacity, Mr. Atkins is responsible for all of the Company's financial functions including asset–liability management, public relations, financial controls, tax management, corporate strategic planning, mergers and acquisitions, investor relations, insurance, and audit. Prior to joining Midlantic, he worked for seventeen years with Chase Manhattan Bank in a wide–range of domestic and international financial positions. He most recently served as Treasurer with responsibility for worldwide funding and balance sheet management, investment strategy, interest rate risk management, and debt and capital planning. He has served in London, Europe, Africa and the Middle East, with functions to include foreign exchange, securities trading, capital markets and precious metals businesses. Midlantic Corporation serves New Jersey and Pennsylvania with over 325 consumer and commercial branch locations. **Career Steps:** Executive Vice President and Chief Financial Officer, Midlantic Corporation (1991–Present); Treasurer, Chase Manhattan Corporation (1990–1991); Various Executive Positions, Chase Manhattan Corporation (1977–1990). **Associations & Accomplishments:** Financial Executives Institute, Association of North American Corporate Treasurers. **Education:** Ohio State University, M.S. (1973); City College of New York, B.S. in Mathematics.

Shariq Azhar

General Manager
MashreqBank PSC
255 5th Avenue
New York, NY 10016–6516
(212) 545–8200
Fax: (212) 545–0918

6029

Business Information: MashreqBank is a full–service commercial bank. As General Manager, Mr. Azhar oversees all areas of operations for the bank. **Career Steps:** General Manager, MashreqBank PSC (1992–Present); Vice President, Chase Manhattan Bank N.A. (1988–1992); Senior Research Analyst, Federal Reserve Bank of New York (1987–1988). **Associations & Accomplishments:** Bankers Association of Foreign Trade; Association of Forfeiters in America; U.S. Council on International Banking. **Education:** New York University, MBA (1987); University of Salford – United Kingdom, B.Sc. with Honours (1978). **Personal:** Married to Anjum in 1982. Two children: Herad and Mehreen. Mr. Azhar enjoys squash and soaring.

Marcel R. Badeau

Senior Vice President and Chief Financial Officer
Cambridge Trust Company
1336 Massachusetts Avenue
Cambridge, MA 02138
(617) 441–1516
Fax: (617) 441–1569
EMAIL: See Below

6029

Business Information: Cambridge Trust Company is a full–service commercial bank. Regional in scope with headquarters located in Cambridge, Massachusetts, CTC currently operates from seven branch locations throughout the greater Boston and Cambridge areas. Corporate assets are in excess of $500 million. As Senior Vice President and Chief Financial Officer, Mr. Badeau is responsible for all operations and financial aspects of the company. Internet users can reach him via: MBadeau@cambtrust.com. **Career Steps:** Senior Vice President and Chief Financial Officer, Cambridge Trust Company (1995–Present); Senior Manager, Arthur Andersen & Company (1986–1995). **Associations & Accomplishments:** American Institute of Certified Public Accountants; Massa-

chusetts Society of Certified Public Accountants; American Management Society; The Treasurers' Club of Boston; Trustee, Consumer Credit Counseling Services of Massachusetts, Inc,; Trustee and Treasurer, Danforth Museum of Art. **Education:** Bentley College, B.S. in Accounting (1986). **Personal:** Married to Margo. Two children: Jason and Crystal.

Edna L. Barbosa
Human Resources Manager
Hamilton Bank, N.A.
3750 Northwest 87th Avenue
Miami, FL 33178–2421
(305) 717–5553
Fax: (305) 717–5560

6029

Business Information: Established in 1983, Hamilton Bank, N.A. is an international trade and financing institution with 400 locations. As Human Resources Manager, Ms. Barbosa oversees personnel acquisition, record keeping, employee benefits, counseling, and training. **Career Steps:** Human Resources Manager, Hamilton Bank, N.A. (1995–Present); Quality Service Representative – Latin America, Eastern Airlines (1986–1988); Supervisor – Flight Attendents, Eastern Airlines – San Juan Base (1981–1986); Personal Appearance Supervision, Eastern Airlines – San Juan Base (1979–1981). **Associations & Accomplishments:** Vice President, Parents Association at Carrollton Catholic School for Girls (1994–1996); Social Justice Committee. **Education:** Barry University, B.S. (1993); University of Puerto Rico, Liberal Arts. **Personal:** Two children: Alexandra Maria and Joseph Suarez–Sarmiento. Ms. Barbosa enjoys walking, jazzercise, and rollerblading.

Parvez K. Bashir
Computer Consultant
The World Bank
1909 K Street, R–5091
Washington, DC 20433
(202) 473–6248
Fax: (202) 676–1370

6029

Business Information: The World Bank is a financial institution providing loans to third world countries for projects and developments. As Computer Consultant, Mr. Bashir provides consulting to OBP (research and development wing of the Bank) to provide state–of–the–art Operating Systems, Database and Communications services to World Bank Divisions. **Career Steps:** Computer Consultant, The World Bank (1993–Present); Senior System Analyst, Data Transformation Corporation (1992–1993); Senior Technical Specialist, KOH Systems, Inc. (1990–1991); Consultant, Support/Group (1989–1990). **Education:** University of Hawaii, M.S. in Electrical Engineering (1989); Indian Institute of Technology, New Delhi, M.Tech. in Control Engineering. **Personal:** One child: Ahmed Fadil Parvez. Mr. Bashir enjoys spending time with his family, travel, whitewater rafting, playing pool and table tennis.

Mrs. Ariel F. Chun
Chief Executive Officer
University of Hawaii Federal Credit Union
P.O. Box 22070
Honolulu, HI 96823–2070
(808) 956–8578
Fax: (808) 956–5199

6029

Business Information: University of Hawaii Federal Credit Union is a not–for–profit, member–owned full financial service organization for faculty, staff, student and alumni association members of the university. Established in 1955, University of Hawaii Federal Credit Union employs 42 persons. Currently #8 of 116 credit unions in Hawaii, UHFCU has 14,500 members and over $135 million in assets. Mrs. Chun is responsible for all aspects of operations for the Firm. **Career Steps:** Chief Executive Officer, University of Hawaii Federal Credit Union (1986– Present); Branch Administration, First Federal Savings & Loan Association of Hawaii (1966–1986). **Associations & Accomplishments:** Payment Systems for Credit Unions, Inc. Board of Directors; Mid–Pacific Institute Alumni Association (private educational facility); YMCA Board of Directors; National Association of Federal Credit Unions; Credit Union Executives Society; Altar Guild, Queen Emma Chapel (Episcopal); Volunteer/Fund Raiser: United Cerebral Palsy, United Way; Alzheimer's Association, Inc.; State of Hawaii Clearing House for Missing Children; Hawaii Food Bank. **Education:** Arizona State University, B.A. Executive Development (1986); Recipient of Bergengren Award, prestigious award for having completed all 24 executive study modules sponsored by the Credit Union National Association (CUNA); also the Filene and Raiffeisen Awards. **Personal:** Married

since 1962 to Larry. Two children: Terilyn and Randall. Mrs. Chun enjoys golf, craft–making, gardening, and gourmet Chinese cooking in her leisure time.

Marlene M. Cooper
Vice President, Manager, and Senior Personal Banking Officer
Capitol Bank and Trust
4801 West Fullerton Avenue
Chicago, IL 60639–2503
(312) 804–6048
Fax: (312) 622–1968

6029

Business Information: Capitol Bank and Trust specializes in commercial banking services. As Vice President, Mrs. Cooper is responsible for diversified administrative activities, including managing the retail banking area, and maintaining and upgrading computer and telephone equipment. **Career Steps:** Capitol Bank and Trust: Vice President (1994–Present), Senior Personal Banker, Personal Banking Supervisor, Personal Banking Manager/Officer, Personal Banking Vice President. **Education:** Newport University, B.A. in Business Administration. **Personal:** Married to Edward in 1991. One child: Dane Matthew. Mrs. Cooper enjoys swimming with her son, sports, and gardening.

Bonnie J. Davis
Vice President
Valley National Bank of Cortez
350 West Montezuma Avenue
Cortez, CO 81321
(970) 565–4411
Fax: (970) 565–4434

6029

Business Information: Valley National Bank of Cortez is a full–service financial institution specializing in commercial banking. As Vice President, Ms. Davis is responsible for the lending of commercial real estate mortgages and consumer lending. **Career Steps:** Vice President, Valley National Bank of Cortez (1989–Present); Lender, First National Bank of Montrose (1977–1987); Lender, Citizens Bank of Cortez (1971–1977). **Associations & Accomplishments:** Former President, Earned Dwight Bonham Award (1993); Kiwanis of Mesa Verde–Cortez–Charter; BOD: Chairman for Special Projects, "Prize of Cortez" cleanup campaign, Board of Directors; Four Corners Child Advocacy Center: Board Member, Volunteer; Red Cross Volunteer (20 years). **Education:** Numerous banking courses through Robert Morris Associates and American Banking Association. **Personal:** Two children: Robert Charles Davis and Kathleen J. Carricato. Ms. Davis enjoys golf and spending time with her grandchild.

William C. Davis
Vice President of Investment Trusts
Palm Beach National Bank & Trust Co.
11760 U.S. Highway 1, Suite 100
North Palm Beach, FL 33408
(407) 882–1776
Fax: (407) 627–2355

6029

Business Information: Palm Beach National Bank & Trust Co. is a full–service, boutique bank and trust operations, serving the population of the island of Palm Beach. With four branches in Florida, Palm Beach National Bank & Trust Co. reports assets of $150 million and $300 million in trusts. As Vice President of Investment Trusts, Mr. Davis is responsible for the management of the private funds ($40 million) of one hundred trust clients. After funds are placed in trusts, he re–invests it into real estate spanning from Miami area to Vero Beach. **Career Steps:** Vice President of Investment Trusts, Palm Beach National Bank & Trust Co. (1994–Present); Director of Operations, Bobo, Spicer, et al, P.A. (1989–1994); Senior Vice President of Lending, Ambassador Savings & Loan (1985–1989). **Associations & Accomplishments:** Chairman, Lou Groza National Collegiate Football Award; Vice President, Palm Beach County Sports Commission; President, The Forum Club of the Palm Beaches; President, Palm Beach County Seminole Boosters; President, Kiwanis Club of Palm Beach Gardens; Chairman, American Cancer Society; Chairman, State Special Olympics; Responsible for raising $700,000 to build Blum Stadium – where kids can go for sporting events and different activities. **Education:** Florida State University, B.A. (1968); Graduate School of Savings and Loan, Management and Finance; Indiana University Graduate School of Business (1980). **Personal:** Married to Barbara in 1974. Mr. Davis enjoys community service activities and helping young people.

Antonio de los Rios
Vice President
Citibank, N.A. – Citigold
666 Fifth Avenue, Fifth Floor
New York, NY 10103
(212) 830–4887
Fax: (212) 582–0441

6029

Business Information: Citibank, N.A. is a financial services organization providing banking services to consumers and corporate customers worldwide. Established in 1812, Citibank, N.A. presently has offices in more than 90 countries and employs over 89,000 people. The Citibank, N.A. – Citigold division of the company is a large–account (minimum balance of $100,000), customer–managed banking and investing organization available anywhere in the United States there is a Citibank Office. As Vice President, Mr. de los Rios is the Director of the organization that provides and maintains the systems utilized by Account Executives and other customers, and the systems that interface with the bank— including PC's, telephones, and teleconferencing equipment. Mr. de los Rios was instrumental in making the Citibank Citigold program available throughout the country and was recognized for the direct systemic conversion of the program in eight short months. **Career Steps:** Vice President, Citibank, N.A. – Citigold (1993–Present). **Personal:** Mr. de los Rios enjoys sailing.

Eric F. J. Di Benedetto
Managing Director
Banexi Corporation
3000 Sand Hill Road, Building 2, Suite 205
Menlo Park, CA 94025
(415) 854–3010
Fax: (415) 854–3015

6029

Business Information: Banexi Corporation, with parent company operations headquartered in France, is a financial institution specializing in managing venture capital funds and investment banking for U.S.–based companies. Established in 1969, Banexi Corporation reports annual assets of $200 million and currently employs 200 people. As Managing Director, Mr. Di Benedetto is responsible for all aspects of venture capital funds. **Career Steps:** Managing Director, Banexi Corporation (1991–Present); Vice President, Pargesa/Lambert Brussels (1989–1991); Associate, Bankers Trust (1988–1989). **Associations & Accomplishments:** American Horse Shows Association; United States Combined Training Association; United States Equestrian Team; World Affairs Council; Commonwealth Club of California; ESSEC Alumni Association. **Education:** ESSEC – France: M.B.A. (1989), B.A. in Mathematics and Physics. **Personal:** Mr. Di Benedetto enjoys competing in equestrian activities.

Ruth E. Fisk
Vice President of Marketing and Public Relations
First Bank of Highland Park
1835 First Street
Highland Park, IL 60035–3101
(708) 432–7800
Fax: (708) 433–2150

6029

Business Information: First Bank of Highland Park is a full–service banking and lending institution. Currently the bank employs 60 people. In her current capacity as Vice President, Ms. Fisk is responsible for all aspects of Marketing and Public Relations. **Career Steps:** Vice President of Marketing and Public Relations, First Bank of Highland Park (Present). **Associations & Accomplishments:** Great Dane Club and Rescue Effort; United States Holocaust Memorial Museum. **Education:** Duke University, M.B.A. (1987); Vassar College, B.A. in Economics.

Mr. Jeffrey R. Hall
Senior Vice President
First Tennessee National Corporation
300 Court Street, IMZ 8472
Memphis, TN 38103
(901) 523–5256
Fax: (901) 523–5243

6029

Business Information: First Tennessee National Corporation is one of the nation's 50 largest bank holding companies with assets of $12.1 billion. It's principal subsidiary, First Tennessee Bank National Association is the largest Tennessee-based bank holding company. Emphasizing convenient quality service, First Tennessee Bank N.A. offers general banking products through 236 locations which serve 3 states, including the five major metropolitan areas across Tennessee. As Senior Vice President, Mr. Hall is responsible for the lending activities of the Bank's Dealership Financing Center which has an estimated $200 million in assets. He leads the lending group in meeting the commercial and sales financing needs of big ticket consumer goods retailers, including automobile, boat and manufactured housing dealers. **Career Steps:** Senior Vice President, First Tennessee National Corporation (1993–Present); Senior Consultant, Coopers & Lybrand (1992–1993); Region Manager, Transamerica Commercial Finance (1990–1992); Area Sales Manager, Chrysler First Commercial Corp. (1981–1990). **Associations & Accomplishments:** Memphis Consumer Credit Association; Robert Morris Associates; Metropolitan Financial Group. **Education:** University of Dayton, B.S./B.A. (1981). **Personal:** Married to Susan in 1991. Two children: Bradley and Mitchell. Mr. Hall enjoys golf.

Norlan L. Hinke
President and Chief Executive Officer
First Central State Bank
914 6th Avenue
DeWitt, IA 52742
(319) 659–3141
Fax: (319) 659–3144

6029

Business Information: First Central State Bank is a full–service financial institution. Established in 1967, First Central State Bank currently employs 30 people. As President and Chief Executive Officer, Mr. Hinke is responsible for all aspects of management and operations. **Career Steps:** President and Chief Executive Officer, First Central State Bank (1981–Present); Vice President, Jackson State Bank, Maquoketa (1975–1981); Owner and Partner, D & H Construction (1973–1975); Office Assistant, Creditthrift of America (1972–1973). **Associations & Accomplishments:** Executive Officer, DeWitt Economic Development Committee (1982–Present); Trustee and Treasurer, DeWitt Community Hospital (1984–Present); Trustee and Administrative Council, DeWitt United Methodist Church (1993–Present); Board Member, Iowa Bankers Association (1994–Present); Outstanding Young Men of America (1982); DeWitt Community Citizen of the Year (1985–1986). **Education:** St. Ambrose University, M.B.A. (1988); University of Wisconsin Graduate School of Banking; University of Dubuque, B.S. in Business Administration (1982). **Personal:** Married to Cindy in 1972. Two children: Molly and Troy. Mr. Hinke enjoys various sports and outdoor activities, church and family activities.

Kitt K. Ho

Finance Officer
Marathon National Bank
11444 Olympic Boulevard
Los Angeles, CA 90064–1549
(310) 996–9883
Fax: (310) 996–9892
EMail: See Below

6029

Business Information: Marathon National Bank is a full–service commercial banking institution. Established in 1983, Marathon National Bank reports assets of $10 million and currently employs 40 people. As Finance Officer, Mr. Ho serves as system administrator of controller functions. He can also be reached through the Internet as follows: 75662.1571@compuserve.com **Career Steps:** Finance Officer, Marathon National Bank (1990–Present); Assistant Controller, California State University, Northridge Foundation (1989–1990); Senior Accountant, Imperial Premium Finance (1987–1989). **Associations & Accomplishments:** California Public Accountant; Novell System Administrator; American Bankers Association. **Education:** Central Michigan University, M.S. (1984). **Personal:** Married to Linda in 1986. One child: Tiffany. Mr. Ho enjoys reading, computers, and gardening.

Brian Hodges
Vice President
The Mechanics Bank
3170 Hilltop Mall Road
Richmond, CA 94806–1921
(510) 262–7224
Fax: (510) 262–7203
EMAIL:BHodges716@AOL.com

6029

Business Information: The Mechanics Bank is a financial institution specializing in full–service commercial banking, serving customers from 16 branches located throughout the California Bay area. Established in 1905, The Mechanics Bank reports annual assets of $950 million and currently employs 460 people. With 13 years expertise in the banking industry, Mr. Hodges joined The Mechanics Bank in 1982 as a bank teller, working his way up the corporate ladder to his current position. Now serving as Vice President and Head of Branch Operations, he is responsible for oversight of all branches in the Bay Area. **Career Steps:** The Mechanics Bank (Since 1982): Vice President, Branch Manager, Bank Teller. **Education:** St. Mary's College, B.A. in Business Management (1989); Pacific Coast Banking School, Graduate Certificate.

Clark L. C. Huang
Vice President
Signet Banking Corporation
4224 Cox Road, Suite 102
Glen Allen, VA 23060
(804) 967–2149
Fax: (804) 967–2123

6029

Business Information: Signet Banking Corporation is a medium–sized commercial banking and lending institution located in the Southeastern United States and reporting more the $12 billion in assets. Unique in nature, Signet Banking Corporation utilizes a philosophy that is geared to academia. Currently the bank employs more than 5,000 people corporate–wide. As Vice President, Mr. Huang is responsible for all aspects of administration, including finances, projects, strategic analysis, planning, all budget operations, and all "backroom" operations of the bank. **Career Steps:** Vice President, Signet Banking Corporation (1995–Present); Financial Analyst, Bank of Boston (1994–1995); Assistant Vice President, and Senior Project and Financial Analyst, First Interstate Bank (1992–1994). **Associations & Accomplishments:** Tutor, Richmond Literacy Council (READ Center); Los Angeles Junior Achievement. **Education:** University of California – Los Angeles, B.S. (1993); Harvard Extension School. **Personal:** Mr. Huang enjoys volleyball, photography, and travel. To date, he has been in 22 of the 50 states to visit family and friends.

Roseanne L. Jenkins
Vice President
SunTrust Bank, Central Florida, N.A.
200 South Orange Avenue
Orlando, FL 32802
(407) 237–5247
Fax: (407) 237–6904

6029

Business Information: SunTrust Bank, Central Florida, N.A., established in 1932, is a financial institution specializing in banking. With 20 years expertise in the banking industry, Ms. Jenkins joined SunBank N.A. in 1975 and is presently responsible for the management of the Corporate Customer Service Department. **Career Steps:** Vice President, SunTrust, Central Florida, N.A. (1995–Present); SunBank, N.A.: Product Manager (1994–1995), Assistant Manager of Corporate Customer Service (1992–1994), Operations (1975–1994). **Education:** Attended Oklahoma State University. **Personal:** Ms. Jenkins enjoys cooking, reading, crafts, and art & antique collecting.

Mr. Robert K. Kendrick
Second Vice President
Chase Manhattan Bank
3CMC Metrotech Center
Brooklyn, NY 11245
(718) 242–7390
Fax: (718) 242–2329

6029

Business Information: Chase Manhattan Bank is a full–service financial institution specializing in banking as well as corporate pensions. In his current capacity, Mr. Kendrick is responsible for project planning and analysis. Chase Manhattan

Bank presently employs three people. He is currently working on a project that will transform the company to a totally electronic and paper–free environment, internationally. **Career Steps:** Second Vice President, Chase Manhattan Bank (1993–Present); Service Manager, Chase Manhattan Bank (1992–1993); Accounting Manager, Chase Manhattan Bank (1990–1992). **Associations & Accomplishments:** Industry Standardization for Investment Translation Committee (ISITC); Previous School School board member. **Education:** PACE, B.A. Degree in Accounting (1979).

Thomas J. Kitrick Jr.
Vice President of Strategic Planning and Interactive Marketing
First Union National Bank, B.A.
1525 WT Harris Blvd.
Charlotte, NC 28269
(704) 590–2751
Fax: Please mail or call
E–mail: see below

6029

Business Information: First Union National Bank, B.A. is a full–service financial and lending organization. As Vice President of Strategic Planning and Interactive Marketing, Mr. Kitrick is responsible for strategic direction concerning the corporations Internet Marketing program relative to homebanking, EDI, EFT, Imaging and Customer Service. He has led and designed numerous marketing strategies for FUNB, coining the terms Cyberbanking(sm), Community Commerce(sm) and First Access Network(sm) to position FUNB's strategy within the industry; which also involved the management of graphics design, HTML programmers and project managers in the overall implementation. Mr. Kitrick can also be reached through the Internet as follows: TOMK@mail.mci.net **Career Steps:** Vice President of Strategic Planning and Interactive Marketing, First Union National Bank, B.A. (Present); Assistant Vice President of Corporate Communications, Bear Stearns and Company; Manager of Presentation Services, Goldman Sachs & Company; Specialist Clerk, New York Stock Exchange, Einhorn and Company. **Associations & Accomplishments:** Frequent speaker and presenter at Internet conferences; Interviewed and published in American Banker, Interactive Age, and The Charlotte Observer; Currently working on a book that relates to Individuation and Actualization of Humanist Psychology with the growing culture of the Internet. Education: Walden University, Ph.D. candidate (1996); Fairleigh Dickinson University, M.B.A.; New York University, B.A. in Organizational Communications.

Lucille T. Kolish
Vice President
Bay Bank
53 McDonald Drive
Chicopee, MA 01020–4943
(413) 731–4503
Fax: Please mail or call

6029

Business Information: Bay Bank is a full–service commercial bank with over 200 branch offices primarily serving retail concerns in the New England area. Bay Bank currently employs 4,000 people company–wide. As Vice President, Mrs. Kolish is responsible for marketing corporate banking products, including cash management, demand deposit accounts to Microlink, and loans. **Career Steps:** Vice President, Bay Bank (1970–Present). **Associations & Accomplishments:** Trustee, Elms College Chicopee, Massachusetts; Director and Past President, Chicopee Chamber of Commerce; Director, Galaxy Community Council; Chairman, Chicopee Development Corporation; Recipient of the Women of the Year Award; First Woman President of Chamber of Commerce; American Institute of Banking; United Way. **Education:** Bachelor of Arts. **Personal:** Married to Edward in 1954. Three children: Elaine and Theresa, who are both attorneys, and Anthony. Mrs. Kolish enjoys golf, interior decorating, and reading.

June D. Lehr
Vice President
Dauphin Deposit Bank and Trust Company
3607 Derry Street
Harrisburg, PA 17111
(717) 255–2205
Fax: (717) 237–6156

6029

Business Information: Dauphin Deposit Corporation, headquarted in Harrisburg, PA, is the parent company of Dauphin Deposit Bank & Trust Company. The Bank has 2500 employees and operates in over 100 branch offices in Pennsylvania. With forty–three years expertise in the banking industry,

Mrs. Lehr was appointed Vice President in 1992. She serves as Manager of Customer Management Information and Data Entry departments, with overall responsibility of maintaining the on–line customer and account relationships throughout the Bank for all departments. **Career Steps:** Vice President, Dauphin Deposit Bank and Trust Company (1992–Present); Assistant Vice President, Southern Pennsylvania Bank (1982–1992); Transit Supervisor, Monroe Security Bank of Stroudsburg (1952–1954). **Associations & Accomplishments:** President of the Local Chapter, Women of the ELCA; Celebration Chairman of the Church, Shrewsbury Lutheran Retirement Home; Works with the York Police Juvenile Department for the "Say No To Drugs" program; St. Paul Zeigler's Lutheran Church: Sunday school teacher, former Sunday school superintendent, choir member for the past 32 years. **Education:** Pennsylvania American Institute of Banking; Pennsylvania State – York Campus, Banking Courses. **Personal:** Married to Harold E. in 1951. Two children: Terence L. Lehr and Cheryl A. Breneman. Mrs. Lehr enjoys reading, singing, and collecting angels.

Paul T. Lilienthal

Vice President
Riverside Bank
800 LaSalle Avenue
Minneapolis, MN 55402
(612) 338–8600
Fax: (612) 338–8218

6029

Business Information: Riverside Bank is a financial institution, specializing in commercial banking primarily in small business lending with seven branches in the Minneapolis metropolitan area. Joining Riverside Bank as Vice President of Commercial Lending in 1993, Mr. Lilienthal is responsible for managing a portfolio of $11 million, as well as supervising a staff of six. He also serves as Chair of the Appraisal Committee and Member of the Senior Loan Committee. **Career Steps:** Vice President, Riverside Bank (1993–Present); Bank Examiner, Federal Deposit Insurance Corporation (1989–1993). **Associations & Accomplishments:** Big Brother/Big Sisters; Northeast Business Association in Minneapolis; The Collaborative; Minnesota Software Association; Teaches Classes for Junior Achievement. **Education:** St. Cloud State University, M.S. (1989); St. Thomas University.

Victoria Lopez–Negrete K.

Head of Marketing and Service Quality
Citibank, N.A. Chile
Providencia 2653– 3 Piso
Santiago, Chile
(562) 338–3312
Fax: (562) 338–3078

6029

Business Information: Citibank is a global financial services organization, with nearly a century of international experience, which offers a full range of banking services in over 40 countries. In Chile, Citibank–Global Consumer Bank has 23 branches, and as Marketing and Service Quality Head, Ms. Lopez–Negrete supports the core business objectives as well as branding and positioning. She also oversees all aspects of service quality, research and public relations. **Career Steps:** Marketing and Service Quality Head, Citibank, N.A. (1995–Present); Business Development and Payment Devices/Electronic Banking Director, Multibanco Mercantil Probursa (recently Banco Bilbao Viscaya–Mexico) (1993–1995); Mastercard–Mexico Office, General Manager (1992–1993); Membership Travel Services/Marketing Director, American Express–Mexico (1990–1992). **Education:** Anahuac University, Mexico City, Bachelor in Sciences of Social Communication, Specializing in Marketing, Business Administration, Advertising, and Journalism (1972). **Personal:** One child: Francisco Auera LN. Ms. Lopez–Negrete K. enjoys music, opera, film, history, and hiking.

Richard Lynn
Director of Planning and Budgeting
World Bank
1818 H. Street, NW, Room E9081
Washington, DC 20433
(202) 473–0114
Fax: (202) 522–3378

6029

Business Information: World Bank, a development finance affiliate of the United Nations, is an international financial institution dedicated to world economic development. Owned by countries of the United Nations, World Bank provides loans, at no interest, for economic development of primarily poor and underdeveloped countries. The Bank's revenue is received through the sale of bonds to world capital markets and contributions from Parliaments and the U.S. Congress. As Director of Planning and Budgeting, Mr. Lynn establishes the priority and direction of the Bank, and is responsible for preparing multi–year plans and administrative (operating) budgets, in addition to reviewing results against plans and budgets. **Career Steps:** World Bank: Director of Planning and Budgeting (1990–Present), Director of Administration (1986–1990), Director of Organization Planning (1983–1986); Assistant Executive Director for Management, U.S. Federal Trade Commission (1974–1975); McKinsey & Co., Management Consultants (1966–1974). **Associations & Accomplishments:** Board of Advisors, Advanced Management Institute; Judge, Arthur Flemming Awards (for outstanding U.S. government employees under 40); Religious Society of Friends. **Education:** University of Chicago, M.A. (1957); Hanover College, B.A.; University of Indiana (courses). **Personal:** Married to Christine in 1959. Four children: Eric, Catherine, Peter, and Evangeline.

Joseph B. Madamba Jr.

Vice President
Shawmut Bank
777 Main Street, MSN 980
Hartford, CT 06115
(203) 986–1647
Fax: (203) 986–4734

6029

Business Information: Shawmut Bank is a financial institution providing financial services and commerical banking. Shawmut Bank is currently in the process of merging with Fleet Bank to become the largest bank in New England. Established in 1792, Shawmut Bank reports annual assets of $35 billion and currently employs 10,000 people company–wide. As Vice President – Derivatives/Hedge Products, Mr. Madamba is responsible for managing the hedge products portfolio used in asset/liability management, trading interest rate derivatives for Bank hedging, as well as customer business, derivatives pricing, valuation and risk monitoring. **Career Steps:** Vice President – Derivatives/Hedge Products, Shawmut Bank (1995–Present); Consultant (1993–1995); Financial Analyst, AIG Trading Corporation (American International Group) (1992–1993); Commodity Analyst, Gruppo Ferruzzi, Ferruzzi Trading USA (1990–1992); Grain Trader, ConAgra, Inc. (1987–1989). **Associations & Accomplishments:** Recipient, Joaquin J. Gonzalez and Gamma Sigma Delta Gold Medal for Academic Excellence; Most Outstanding Student, University of the Philippines College of Agriculture (1984); Chancellor's List; Dean's List; Chancellor's Saber for Leadership (1983); Armed Forces Cadet Leadership Medal (1983); U.P. Honor Star Medal (1983–1984); Marksmanship Medal (1982–1984). **Education:** Purdue University – Krannert Graduate School of Management, M.S. in Industrial Administration, graduated top of the class (1986); University of the Philippines, UPLB, Philippines, B.S. in Agriculture, magna cum laude (1984). **Personal:** Mr. Madamba enjoys trading stocks, futures & options, global financial markets, travel, tennis, soccer, volleyball, softball, and rifle shooting.

Allan A. Miller
President and Chief Executive Officer
Bank of Verona
P.O. Box 930126, 108 North Main Street
Verona, WI 53593
(608) 845–6486
Fax: (608) 845–6728

6029

Business Information: Bank of Verona is an independent community bank, operating with $70 million in assets. Chartered in 1903 and opened in 1904, Bank of Verona is a full–service, progressive, pro–active bank. As President and Chief Executive Officer, Allan Miller started at the entry level position at Verona, and is now running the operations of the bank. His primary responsibilities include marketing, personnel management, and administration. **Career Steps:** Bank of Verona:

President and Chief Executive Officer (1994–Present); Executive Vice President (1991–1994); Controller (1977–1991). **Associations & Accomplishments:** Community Banks of Wisconsin; Independent Bankers Association of America; Wisconsin Bankers Association; WIMNUG; Verona Area Chamber of Commerce; Verona Optimists Club. **Education:** University of Wisconsin – Madison Graduate School of Banking, Community Bank Management (1983); Madison Area Technical College, Associates in Business Administration/ Accounting (1977).

Estrella Miranda

Senior Vice President of the Human Resources Department
Banco Santander
P.O. Box 362589
San Juan, Puerto Rico 00936–2589
(809) 759–7070
Fax: (809) 765–9622

6029

Business Information: The leading bank in Spain and the fourth largest in the world, Banco Santander is a full–service banking and commercial lending institution. Banco Santander recently aquired First Fidelity and First National Bank, and now employs over 1,700 people worldwide. The bank reports assets of over $35 billion. As Senior Vice President of the Human Resources Department, Ms. Miranda is responsible for all aspects of work force development and training for the Caribbean area, as well as mergers, outsourcing with EDS and the design of the compensation program. **Career Steps:** Banco Santander: Senior Vice President of the Human Resources Department (1993–Present), Senior Vice President (1988–1993); Human Resources, First National Bank of Boston (1986–1988); Labor Relations Manager, Caribe General Electric (1983–1986). **Associations & Accomplishments:** Society of Human Resources; Puerto Rico Bankers Association; Muscular Dystrophy Association; Puerto Rico Wheel Chair Tennis Association. **Education:** Interamerican University (1979); Advanced Management Schools; attended several American universities; Compensation and Labor Legislation. **Personal:** One child: Michelle Rodgiguez Miranda. Ms. Miranda enjoys tennis, bowling and windsurfing.

Judith F. Morin

Assistant Vice President
Bristol County Savings Bank
35 Broadway
Taunton, MA 02780–3120
(508) 828–5446
Fax: (508) 822–2070

6029

Business Information: Bristol County Savings Bank is a full–service financial institution, specializing in commercial banking. Established in 1847, the Bank currently operates out of six offices. Having started at Bristol County Savings Bank as a teller in 1973, Ms. Morin has worked her way up to the position she has today. As Assistant Vice President, Ms. Morin oversees and administrates five branch offices, and calls on area businesses to discuss current or potential bank relationships. **Career Steps:** Assistant Vice President, Bristol County Savings Bank (1973–Present). **Associations & Accomplishments:** Taunton Area Chamber of Commerce Mentor Program; United Way: Breakthrough Committee Chairman, Industrial Solicitor; Solicitor, YMCA; Kiwanis: Second Vice President, Assistant Treasurer; Auditor, Pilgrim Congregational Church; Sachem District Annawon Council; Director, Boy Scouts of America. **Education:** Bristol Community College, Associate's degree (1991); Bridgewater State College, Bachelor's Degree in Business (In Progress). **Personal:** Married to Raymond A. in 1986. Ms. Morin enjoys swimming, walking, and biking.

Jean B. Poindexter

Assistant Vice President
Macon Savings Bank
50 West Main Street
Franklin, NC 28734–3006
(704) 524–7000
Fax: (704) 524–8803
EMAIL: See Below

6029

Business Information: Macon Savings Bank, organized in 1922, is a full–service, financial institution with five locations in Western North Carolina. As Assistant Vice President, Ms. Poindexter is responsible for accounting functions, payroll, auditing, and coordinating employee's insurance. Ms. Poindexter has worked her way up to her current position from teller. She can also be reached through the World Wide Web: http://www.maconbank.com/maconbank. **Career Steps:** Macon Savings Bank: Assistant Vice President (1996–Present), Assistant Secretary (1987–1996), Teller/Insurance Clerk/Accounting (1974–1987). **Associations & Accomplishments:** Vice President, Ladies Auxiliary; Vacation Bible School – Kids Crusade Director; Franklin Church of God: Teacher, Assistant Song Leader; Member of Singing Group "His Servants." **Education:** Southwestern Community College, A.A.S. in Accounting (1992). **Personal:** Married to M. Carroll in 1986. Two children: Christopher M. Cheek and Justin C. Poindexter. Ms. Poindexter enjoys singing, church work, and working with people. Mrs. Poindexter is the daughter of Lawrence & Evelyn Brendle. She has 2 sisters; one of them is her identical twin..

Guilherme Rocha Rabello

Credit Director
Banco Rural South America
Rua Rio De Janeiro 927–14.0 And.
Belo Harizonte, Brazil 30160–9
55–31–2395301
Fax: 55–31–2227438
EMAIL: See Below

6029

Business Information: Banco Rural South America is a commercial financial institution with forty–four branches in Brazil, Uruguay, the Bahamas, and a broker in Miami, Florida. As Credit Director, Mr. Rabello oversees a staff of 100 in the management of credit approvals and contracts. He is also a member of the committee responsible for all final financial decisions. Internet users can reach Mr. Rabello via: guiller@br.homeshopping.com.br **Career Steps:** Credit Director, Banco Rural South America (1989–Present); Director, Exata Investments (1994–1995); Director, Tratex Investments E. Participacoes (1984–1989). **Education:** University of Michigan, Master of Science (1983); Universidad Catolica de Minas Gerais, Electronics Engineering; Universidad Federal de Minas Gerais, Civil Engineering. **Personal:** Married to Beatriz in 1981. Two children: Julia Fontes and Marina Fontes. Mr. Rabello enjoys squash, soccer, music, and sports.

Mary Jane Schank

Vice President of Retail Banking
Home Federal Bank
100 South 3rd Street
Hamilton, OH 45011–2816
(513) 867–7727
Fax: Please mail or call

6029

Business Information: Home Federal Bank, part of the First Financial Bank Corporation, is managed as an independent community bank providing all aspects of financial services. The Bank has six branches in Ohio and two newly acquired branches in Indiana. As Vice President of Retail Banking, Ms. Schank is responsible for all branch offices, marketing of those offices, product development, data processing, customer service, and security. **Career Steps:** Vice President of Retail Banking, Home Federal Bank (1993–Present); Charter Oak Savings Bank: Vice President of Retail Banking (1991–1993), Regional Manager (1988–1991). **Associations & Accomplishments:** Anderson Township Chamber of Commerce; Hamilton Chamber of Commerce; Volunteer work with an orphanage "Beech Acre." **Personal:** Married to Martin H. in 1972. Two children: Jennifer and Brian. Ms. Schank enjoys running.

Carol A. Siegel

Vice President of Technoloy Risk Management
The Chase Manhattan Bank
160 East 38th Street
New York, NY 10016
(212) 270–8445
Fax: Please mail or call

6029

Business Information: The Chase Manhattan Bank is a global financial institution specializing in commercial banking. As Vice President of Information Risk Management, Ms. Siegel is responsible for the direction and supervision for The Chase Manhattan Bank Division's Information Security, with duties involving performing data security administration for North America, Capital Markets, Treasury, Asia, Europe, Latin Americas and Emerging Marketing, management of a staff of 15 people and ensuring Global Bank compliance with corporate Information Protection Policies and Procedures. Additional duties include managing implementation of public Internet connectivity for The Chase Manhattan Bank, creating bankwide policies for administration, monitoring, and change control, including technical security specifications for firewalls, web servers, anonymous ftp servers and routers, as well as developing and implementing information security policies, standards, procedures, and guidelines for UNIX (Sun Solaris and SunOS, IBM RS/6000), AS/400, DEC VAX/VMS, Novell and PC platforms. Concurrent with her position at The Chase Manhattan Bank, she is writing a book on security and technical implementation for Internet sites (expected to sell 50,000 copies). **Career Steps:** Vice President of Technology Risk Management, The Chase Manhattan Bank (1994–Present); Manager of Information Technology Audit and Security Services, Coopers & Lybrand (1991–1994); Data Security Officer of Information Services Group, Participants Trust Company (1990–1991); Systems Officer in Corporate Division, CitiBank N.A. (1986–1990); Senior Programmer of Computer Resources Division, KPMG Peat Marwick (1984–1986); Partner and Manager of U.S. Operations, Francesco Donati, Inc. (1977–1982); Programmer, Information Systems Department, International Playtex, Inc. (1976–1977); Research Assistant of European Operations, Titan Industrial Corporation (1971–1976). **Associations & Accomplishments:** Israel Tennis Center; YMCA; United Jewish Appeal; First woman to graduate Computer Engineering from the computer curriculum from Boston University; PUBLICATIONS: Co–author, Internet Security for Business: "How To Do Business Safely on the Net," John Wiley & Sons, Inc. (1996); "Windows NT: Operating System Security Features," Security Series, Auerbach Publishers (1995); "Sun Microsystems Solaris Operating System Audit Considerations," EDP Auditing, Auerbach Publishers (1995); Co–author, Microsoft Windows NT 3.5 – Guidelines for Security, Audit and Control, Microsoft Press (1994); "Crisis in Information Technology," Digital Enterprise (1993); Basic Electronic Mail, IBM International Technical Support Centers (1992); "Electronic Commerce for Financial Institutions: A Risk Management Perspective". Data Security Management, Auerback Publishers, (1996), Audit Management, Auerbach Publishers (1996); PROFESSIONAL ORGANIZATIONS: Founder of the Security User Group (SUG); Board of Directors, New York Metro Region, Information Systems Security Association (ISSA); Member, Information Systems Audit and Control Associations (ISACA); International Who's Who 1995: FOREIGN LANGUAGE SKILLS: Fluent in Italian and French, and conversational Spanish. **Education:** CISA (Certified Information System Auditor) (1992); New York University, M.B.A. in Computer Applications (1984); Boston University, B.S. in Systems Analysis Engineering (1971).

Peggy Sue Sims

Corporate Payroll Manager
Union Planters Corporation
7130 Goodlett Farms Parkway
Cordova, TN 38018
(901) 383–6652
Fax: (901) 383–2830

6029

Business Information: Operating as a financial banking company, Union Planters Corporation has approximately forty separate entities in seven different states. After years of perseverance and dedication to Union Planters and her chosen profession, Peggy Sue Sims was appointed as Corporate Payroll Manager, in charge of processing payroll for over 6,000 employees. **Career Steps:** Corporate Payroll Manager, Union Planters Corporation (1989–Present); Payroll Supervisor, Deposit Guaranty National Bank (1980–1989). **Associations & Accomplishments:** American Payroll Association. **Education:** Hinds Junior College. **Personal:** Married to Joe J. in 1963. Three children: Sherry, Aimee and Joe II. Ms. Sims enjoys crafts, stamp collecting, travel and relaxing whenever possible.

Hector Soto, P.E.

Vice President Banking Operations
First Bank Puerto Rico
P.O. Box 9146
Santurce, Puerto Rico 00908–0146
(787) 729–8197
Fax: (787) 729–8330

6029

Business Information: First Bank Puerto Rico is a full–service financial institution specializing in commercial and residential banking. First Bank Puerto Rico has 35 branches: 33 in Puerto Rico, and 2 in the Virgin Islands. As Vice President Banking Operations, Mr. Soto is responsible for processing policy, procedures, new products, and managing products. Additionally, he maintains quality and service. **Career Steps:** Vice President Banking Operations, First Bank Puerto Rico (1991–Present); Assistant Vice President, First Federal (1989–1991); Manager, Citibank N.A. (1987–1989). **Associations & Accomplishments:** Alpha Pi Mu, Industrial Engineers Honor Society; Tau Beta Pi, International Engineers Honor Society; President and Director, American Institute of Industrial Engineers, Puerto Rico Chapter #188. **Education:** University of Puerto Rico–Mayaguez, B.S.I.E. (1984); Politecnic University of Puerto Rico, M.S.I.E. **Personal:** Mr. Soto enjoys tennis, fishing, and cycling.

Pauline M. Staner

Retired Vice President/Director
Charter Bank
815 Highway 146 South
La Porte, TX 77571–4837
(713) 422–2695
Fax: (713) 470–8536

6029

Business Information: During WWII, Ms. Staner worked in the Accounting Department at San Jacinto Shipyard located on the Houston Ship Canal. After the Company closed, she went on to the Houston Shipyard. There, she worked in the Cost Accounting Department. When, in 1945, the government no longer had need of the shipyards and decided to close them, Ms. Staner went to work for a local community bank, First National Bank of La Porte. Since the bank was small (only four employees), she wore many hats although her primary functions were as Assistant Cashier and Secretary. Through the years, the bank had changed its name and size, and with its growth Pauline was promoted several times (Lending Officer, Vice President, and finally Director). At the end of 1994, Ms. Staner decided to retire and looks forward to traveling. **Career Steps:** La Porte State Bank, now Charter Bank: Director (1990–Present), Lending & Vice President (1960–1994); Assistant Cashier & Secretary, First National Bank of La Porte (1945–1960). **Associations & Accomplishments:** Former President, La Porte Bay Area Heritage Society; Treasurer, La Porte Civic Club; La Porte Bayshore Chamber of Commerce; National Association of Bank Women; Former President, American Cancer Society, La Porte; Church of Christ – Baytown, TX. **Education:** San Jacinto College (1988); Lee College (1945–1947); Texas Vocational College (1941). **Personal:** Widow to William C. in 1993. One child: Deborah Kay Staner Fortune. Ms. Staner enjoys reading, farming, ranching, and travel.

James H. Stark

Chief Financial Officer
Community Capital Corporation and Greenwood Bank & Trust
109 Montague Avenue, P.O. Box 218
Greenwood, SC 29649
(803) 941–8206
Fax: (803) 941–8260

6029

Business Information: Community Capital Corporation and Greenwood Bank & Trust is a full–service lending and banking institution. Established in 1989, Community Capital Corporation and Greenwood Bank & Trust currently employs 42 people. As Chief Financial Officer, Mr. Stark oversees all operations of a two–bank holding company, including accounting, data processing, EDP and all financial operations. **Career Steps:** Chief Financial Officer, Community Capital Corporation and Greenwood Bank & Trust (1988–Present); Chief Financial Officer, Cumberland Valley National Bank (1982–1988); Vice President and Cashier, American National Bank (1968–1982); Treasurer, Water, Sewer, and Sanitation Committee (1967–1968). **Associations & Accomplishments:** Former President, Board, and Committee Chairman, Kiwanis Club; IBAA – South Carolina. **Education:** Western Kentucky University, B.S. (1957); ITI and UNISYS Computer Schools. **Personal:** Married to Jean in 1957. Two children: Stephen and Stuart. Mr. Stark enjoys golf.

Bruce A. Strand

Vice President
Key Bank of Washington
95 2nd Street South, P.O. Box 310
Friday Harbor, WA 98250–0310
(360) 378–2111
Fax: (360) 378–2599
EMAIL: See Below

6029

Business Information: Key Bank of Washington, owned by KeyCorp, is a corporate commercial bank, providing local banking accounts, investment, trust, and customized financial services. Headquartered in Cleveland, Ohio, Key Bank is the 10th largest bank holding company in the U.S., with 1,400 offices in 26 states. With nineteen years of experience in the banking industry, Mr. Strand joined Key Bank of Washington as Vice President in 1994. He serves as Branch Sales Manager and Area Manager for three San Juan County branches, responsible for administration, sales staff management, as well as serving as a customer liaison and corporate problem solver. Internet users can reach him via: bastrand@pacificrim.com. **Career Steps:** Vice President, Key Bank of Washington (1994–Present); Key Bank of Alaska: Manager – Credit Services (1992–1994), Southwest Region Manager (1988–1993); Branch Manager, National Bank of Alaska (1988); First Interstate Bank of Alaska (1982–1987); First National Bank of Anchorage (1977–1982). **Associations & Accomplishments:** Treasurer and Board Member, San Juan Island Chamber of Commerce; Founder, Treasurer and Board Member, United Way of San Juan County; Founder and Board Member, San Juan Island Community Foundation; Founder and Rotarian of the Year, Palmer Rotary Club in Alaska Paul Harris Fellow. **Education:** University of Washington: M.B.A. (1977), B.A. (1975); Pacific Coast Banking School (1985). **Personal:** Four children: Jamie, Melissa, Kylie and Andrew. Mr. Strand enjoys personal computers, photography and reading.

Ronald L. Thompson Jr., CPA

Vice President of Finance
Hancock County Savings Bank
351 Carolina Avenue
Chester, WV 26034
(304) 387–1620
Fax: (304) 387–1643

6029

Business Information: Hancock County Savings Bank is a community mutual savings bank, providing mortgage lending and savings services to individuals and businesses in seven counties from three branches. Established in 1899, Hancock County Savings Bank reports $185 million in assets and currently employs 70 people. As Vice President of Finance, Mr. Thompson is responsible for all aspects of financial matters, including accounting, finances, and investments. **Career Steps:** Vice President of Finance, Hancock County Savings Bank (1993–Present); Field Manager, Office of Thrift Supervision (1988–1993); Account Executive, Cunningham Schmentz (1987–1988). **Associations & Accomplishments:** American Institute of Certified Public Accountants (AICPA); American Cancer Society; March of Dimes. **Education:** West Virginia University, B.S. (1980); Stonier Graduate School of Banking (1987), **Personal:** Married to Tina in 1992. Two children: Stacy and William. Mr. Thompson enjoys sports.

Edward Torchia

Vice President
National City Bank of Pennsylvania
100 North 13th Street
Franklin, PA 16323
(814) 437–4054
Fax: (814) 437–3205

6029

Business Information: National City Bank of Pennsylvania is a full–service financial institution. As Vice President, Mr. Torchia is responsible for all aspects of operations, including administration and strategic planning. He is involved in pioneering the idea of "call center" in which all banking can be done by telephone. He is also involved in hiring handicapped or disabled people for the "call center." **Career Steps:** Vice President, National City Bank of Pennsylvania (1996–Present); Vice President – Collection Manager, Integra Financial Corporation (1991–1996); Assistant Vice President – Collections Manager, Gallatin National Bank (1989–1991); Banking Officer, Mellon Bank National (1979–1989). **Education:** University of Wisconsin, Retail Banking Management (1994). **Personal:** Married to Mary Ellen in 1989. One child: Matthew. Mr. Torchia enjoys biking and fishing.

Craig C. Wilcox

Senior Vice President
Grand Rapids State Bank
523 NW 1st Avenue
Grand Rapids, MN 55744
(218) 326–9414
Fax: Please mail or call

6029

Business Information: Grand Rapids State Bank is a full–service banking and lending institution. In operation for over 80 years, the Bank currently employs 60 people. As Senior Vice President, Mr. Wilcox is responsible for all aspects of Human Resources. He is also a loan officer and the Chief Operating Officer of the bank. An expert in the field of banking, he has been published in Money Magazine and North West Financial Review. **Career Steps:** Grand Rapids State Bank: Senior Vice President (1993–Present), Comptroller (1990–1993), Vice President (1980–1990). **Associations & Accomplishments:** Director, Grand Rapids Chamber of Commerce; Director, HASCA County Camp Fire; Volunteer, United Way of 1000 Lake; Former President Pastoral Council, St. Joseph's Catholic Church; Safari Club International; Ruffed Glouse Society. **Education:** St. John's University, B.S. (1972). **Personal:** Married to Lynn in 1981. Three children: Cameron, Ashley, and Stephanie. Mr. Wilcox enjoys hunting safaries in Africa, fishing, dogs, sports, and coaching sports.

Jeffrey W. Wolfers

Vice President
Marine Midland Bank
One Marine Midland Center
Buffalo, NY 14203
(716) 841–5237
Fax: (716) 841–7192
E–mail: see below

6029

Business Information: Marine Midland Bank is a full–service commercial financial and lending organization. Established in 1850, the Marine Midland Bank currently employs 8,500 people and reports assets of over $1 billion. As Vice President, Mr. Wolfers is responsible for the management of large–scale information technology projects. Mr. Wolfers can also be reached through the Internet as follows: CWOLFERS@AOL.COM **Career Steps:** Vice President, Marine Midland Bank (1992–Present). **Associations & Accomplishments:** Paradise Community Association; Friends of Olmstead. **Education:** Canisius College, B.A. (1979). **Personal:** Married to Joanna in 1979. Two children: Carrie Anne and Elizabeth Marie. Mr. Wolfers enjoys hiking, golf, history and travel.

Angela Wong

Assistant Vice President of Auditing
First Interstate Bancsystem
401 North 31st Street
Billings, MT 59101–1200
(406) 255–5877
Fax: Please mail or call

6029

Business Information: First Interstate Bancsystem is a full–service commercial banking institution. Regional in scope, FIB has over 19 branch locations throughout Montana. As Assistant Vice President of Auditing, Ms. Wong is responsible for audit review of internal control structures within all the branches, and supervision of staff to ensure audits are correct, conducting trusts and special audits herself. **Career Steps:** First Interstate Bancsystem: Assistant Vice President of Auditing (1994–Present), Audit Officer (1991–1993); Manager, Chinese Garden Restaurant (1985–1987). **Associations & Accomplishments:** Director, Family YMCA, Billings, Montana; Treasurer, Montana Association of Female Executives; Former President, Montana State University; Billings Toastmaster Club; Committee Member, The American Society of Women Accountants; Billings Society of CPA's; Montana Society of CPA's. **Education:** Montana State University – Billings, Accounting (1989); Certified Public Accountant Designation. **Personal:** Married to Chun Chin Wong in 1979. Two children: Jason and Jamie Wong. Ms. Wong enjoys hiking, backpacking, cross–country skiing, golf, and reading.

Pamela A. Wood

Vice President & Manager
Seafirst Bank
800 Fifth Avenue FAB–8
Seattle, WA 98104
(206) 358–3841
Fax: (206) 358–6325

6029

Business Information: Established in 1870, Seafirst Bank is the leading bank in the Pacific Northwest and the second largest division of the Bank of America network. Ms. Wood joined Seafirst in 1969 and advanced through branch operations positions to Loan Processing Supervisor in 1980 and has held various supervisory positions since, including Branch Customer Service Manager and Call Center Manager, moving into her present position as Vice President and Department Manager in 1994. A Human Resource Professional, Ms. Wood is responsible for oversight of daily operations, research functions, and various administrative activities. **Career Steps:** Seafirst Bank: Vice President & Manager (1994–Present), Call Center Manager: Services (1988–1994), Branch Customer Service Manager (1983–1988), Loan Processing Supervisor (1980–1983). **Associations & Accomplishments:** Seafirst Volunteers: Participation in various volunteer activities throughout the year (e.g., Christmas in April and School Supply Drive). **Education:** Attended, Everett Community College (1980). **Personal:** Two children: Jennifer and Victoria. One grandchild: Madison Rose. Ms. Wood enjoys fine lace crochet, reading, and travel.

E. J. Woodard Jr.

Chairman of the Board, President, and Chief Executive Officer
Commonwealth Bankshares, Inc. / Bank of the Commonwealth
403 Boush Street
Norfolk, VA 23510–1200
(804) 446–6904
Fax: (804) 446–6929
EMAIL: See Below
6029

Business Information: Commonwealth Bankshares, Inc. / Bank of the Commonwealth is a financial institution specializing in commercial banking. Established in 1970, Commonwealth Bankshares, Inc. reports annual assets of $92 million and currently employs 55 people. As Chairman of the Board, President, and Chief Executive Officer, Mr. Woodard is responsible for the administration of the bank, providing leadership, direction, and guidance of the Bank activity to insure the short and long term profitability. He can also be reached through the Internet via: EWoodard@infi.net **Career Steps:** Commonwealth Bankshares, Inc. / Bank of the Commonwealth: Chairman of the Board, President, and Chief Executive Officer (1973–Present), Senior Loan Officer (1972–1973); Assistant Vice President and Branch Manager, First Virginia Bank of Tidewater (1967–1972); Vice President – Lending, American Finance System (1964–1967); Military, Virginia National Guard (Army) (1964–1971). **Associations & Accomplishments:** American Institute of Banking – Tidewater Chapter: Member (Since 1967), Advisory Board Member (Since 1973); American Bankers Association; Virginia Bankers Association: Advisor, Banking Advisor Program, State Legislative Committee (1980–85, 1995–Present), Member of Task Force Committee, Congressional Team Captain for Congressman Owen Pickett, District II Representative BANKPAC Committee; Virginia Association of Community Banks; National Conference of Christians and Jews Dinner Committee; Talbot Park Baptist Church: Chair of Finance Committee, Budget Planning Committee, Church Council, Director of Median Adult Division, Teacher of Median Adult I Class, Member Median Adult 1 Calvary Class, Chair of Endowment Committee; Volunteer, Norfolk Emergency Shelter Team (N.E.S.T. Sheltering Ministry); Urban Business Development Corp.: President, Director, Chair of Loan Review Committee, Executive Committee; President and Director, Boush Bank Building Corp.; Trustee: Under Virginia Land Trust Agreement and Under North Carolina Trust Agreement; United Way of South Hampton Keel Club; Navy League of the United States; Phi Beta Gamma; Greater Norfolk Corporation: Director, Transportation Committee, Downtown Revitalization Committee, Business Retention Committee; Rotary Club of Norfolk: Hunger Committee, Holiday Luncheon Committee, Vocational Service and Career Information Committee, Tiel Rotary Exchange Committee; Economics Club of Hampton Roads; NOTABLE ACHIEVEMENT: Youngest individual ever elected to position of bank President for State of Virginia; Listed in: Who's Who in Virginia; Personalities of the South; Directory of International Biography; Who's Who in Finance and Industry; Personalities of America; Who's Who in the World; Who's Who in the South and Southwest; Personalities of America; Men of Achievement; Directory of Distinguished Americans; Who's Who in America; West's Who's Who in the U.S. Banking Industry; Official Registry of the Who's Who of American Business Leaders; Who's Who Registry of Business Leaders; Who's Who in Religion; Who's Who Registry of Global Business Leaders; Sterling's Who's Who; International Who's Who; SPECIAL AWARDS: Award for patriotic service through U.S. Savings Bond Program, presented by Secretary of Treasury–W. Michael Blumenthal; Outstanding Service Award – Downtown Norfolk Development Corporation; Meritorius Service Award – American Heart Association Virginia Affiliate, Inc.; Distinguished Service and Leadership for fifteen years service – American Heart Association **Education:** Frederick College, Concentration in Science (1961–1964); Old Dominion University, Business Administration (1967–1972); American Institute of Banking (1967–1972); Institute of Certified Bankers; Received designation of 'Certified Lender – Business Banking' **Personal:** A native of the Tidewater community, he is married to the former Sharon Ann Williamson of Norfolk, Virginia. They have one son, Troy Brandon.

Thomas R. Yenne

Senior Vice President and Managing Director
Guaranty Federal Bank
8333 Douglas
Dallas, TX 75225
(214) 360–2828
Fax: (214) 360–1660
6029

Business Information: Guaranty Federal Bank is a financial institution specializing in commercial, mortgage, and consumer banking. With sixteen years expertise in the banking industry, Mr. Yenne joined Guaranty Federal Bank in 1992. Currently serving as Senior Vice President and Managing Director, Mr. Yenne is responsible for the management of the Mortgage and Consumer Finance Group, including Mortgage Warehouse, Mortgage Investment and Consumer Lending. **Career Steps:** Senior Vice President and Managing Director, Guaranty Federal Bank (1992–Present); Senior Vice President and Manager, Bank One, Texas (1979–1992). **Associations & Accomplishments:** Member, Board of Directors, West Dallas Neighborhood Development Corporation; Member, Advisory Board, Chance Center of Dallas; Member, Board of Directors, Southern Methodist University Mustang Club; Volunteer Fund Drive, Southern Methodist University; Member, Mortgage Bankers Association of America; Member, Texas Mortgage Bankers Association. **Education:** Southern Methodist University: B.A. (1974), Two years Graduate study in Sociology. **Personal:** Married to Debra F. in 1974. Two children: Jordan and Andrew Yenne. Mr. Yenne enjoys golf, sports, and community involvement.

Robert Yuzwa

Director, Human Resources
Business Development Bank of Canada
5 Place Ville Marie, Bureau 500
Montreal, Quebec
(514) 283–4007
Fax: (514) 283–1668
6029

Business Information: Business Development Bank is an establishment primarily engaged in lending, venture capital, consulting, training, and business counseling. National in scope, the Bank has 80 locations throughout all provinces and two territories of Canada. As Director, Human Resources, Mr. Yuzwa directs development of human resource strategy, policy, and programs, including initial implementation, training, and communication. Additionally, he must link human resource management needs to the business needs and implement new requirements or changes to the satisfaction of all stakeholders. **Career Steps:** Business Development Bank: Director, Human Resources (1994–Present), Director, Compensation and Benefits (1991–1993); Manager, Compensation Planning and Development, Canadian National Railways (1984–1990). **Associations & Accomplishments:** Conference Board, Compensation Research Centre; Canadian Compensation Association; Regular Conference Speaker. **Education:** University of Saskatchewan, Bachelor of Commerce (1972); Canadian Compensation Association, CCP. **Personal:** Married to Gina. Mr. Yuzwa enjoys gardening, reading, and spending time with his four children and one grandchild.

Maureen A. Zvanut Gardiner

Vice President, Consumer Marketing
Mercantile Bank
12443 Olive Boulevard, 52–2
St. Louis, MO 63141
(314) 579–3698
Fax: (314) 579–3649
6029

Business Information: Mercantile Bank is a financial institution providing specialized financial services including the marketing of credit card products to consumers and focusing on customer satisfaction. Established in 1855, Mercantile Bank reports assets in excess of $16 billion and currently employs 4,000 people company–wide. As Vice President of Consumer Marketing, Ms. Zvanut Gardiner is responsible for developing, implementing, and managing partner credit card programs, such as Southwestern Bell Visa Co–Brand Program. **Career Steps:** Vice President, Consumer Marketing, Mercantile Bank (1993–Present); Vice President, Product Acceptance & Research (PAR) (1991–1993); Marketing Research Manager, Marine Bank (1988–1991); Senior Analyst of Advertising Research, Ralston Purina Company (1986–1988). **Associations & Accomplishments:** DMMA; Outstanding Young Women of America (1991); American Banking Association (ABA); Visa Association; Mastercard Association; University of Missouri – St. Louis Alumni Association; Southern Illinois University – Edwardsville Alumni Association; Active in church and school activities. **Education:** Southern Illinois University – Edwardsville, M.B.A.; University of Missouri – St. Louis, B.A. in English and French. **Personal:** Married to Gareth S. Gardiner. Two children: one daughter, Frankie, and one stepson, James. Ms. Zvanut Gardiner enjoys dancing, reading, and aerobics.

S. Kathryn Allen

Vice President & Chief Compliance Officer
Chevy Chase Bank
8401 Connecticut Avenue
Chevy Chase, MD 20815–5803
(301) 986–7383
Fax: (301) 986–7210
6035

Business Information: Chevy Chase Bank, the largest Federal Savings Bank in the District of Columbia area, is a financial institution, specializing in savings, mortgages, and banking services. As Vice President and Chief Compliance Officer, Ms. Allen is responsible for insuring the compliance of federal and state regulatory issues for the Bank and its subsidiaries. **Career Steps:** Vice President and Chief Compliance Officer, Chevy Chase Bank (1994–Present); Assistant General Counsel, US Environmental Protection Agency (1991–1994); General Counsel, Fleet Bank – New Hampshire (1986–1989); Associate, Warner and Stackpole (1984–1986). **Associations & Accomplishments:** Resource Sharing Network; African American Business Association; U.S. Pan Asian American Chamber of Commerce; The Washington Board of Trade; National Association of Female Executives; National Bar Association; Recipient, "Women of Courage" award from the National Federation of Black Women Business Owners. **Education:** Boston College Law School: Law Degree (1984); Smith College: double major in Biochemistry and African–American Literature; Boston University Law School: additional graduate work in Banking Law. **Personal:** Married to Robert Butler in 1995. Two children: Nathan Goshtigian and Gladstone A.E. Butler.

T. Bradford Canfield

Chief Financial Officer
Boeing Employees Credit Union
P O Box 97050
Seattle, WA 98124–9750
(206) 439–5973
Fax: (206) 439–5816
E MAIL: See Below
6035

Business Information: Boeing Employees Credit Union is a full–service credit union offering financial services to the employees of Boeing. The Facility is the fourth largest in the United States serving over 200,000 members with $2.2 billion in assets. Services offered include savings, checking, loans, on–line banking, and electronic delivery means. Established in 1935, the Credit Union presently has two locations in Washington state and employs over 500 people. As Chief Financial Officer, Mr. Canfield has oversight of all financial strategy for the group and is involved in the development of strategic planning for the future. Internet users can reach him via: bcanfield@becu.org. **Career Steps:** Chief Financial Officer, Boeing Employees Credit Union (1987–Present); Audit Manager, Touche Ross & Company (1980–1987). **Associations & Accomplishments:** Board of Directors, Woodland Park Zoological Society; Director, Center for Wildlife Conservation; Officer, King County Credit Union League; Executive Officer, Credit Union CFO Council. **Education:** Gonzaga University, B.B.A. (1980); Stanford University Executive Development. **Personal:** Married to Lesley in 1986. One child: Jessica. Mr. Canfield enjoys fly fishing, boating, golf, and woodworking.

Vickie L. Gill

Senior Vice President/Chief Appraiser
Hawthorne Savings FSB
2381 Rosecrans Avenue, Floor 2
El Segundo, CA 90245–4917
(310) 725–5775
Fax: (310) 725–5036
6035

Business Information: Hawthorne Savings FSB is a full–service, financial institution. As Senior Vice President/Chief Appraiser, Ms. Gill works in the Real Estate/Appraisal Division of the Bank. She is mainly responsible for real estate appraisal work for environmental problems and EPA permit regulations. **Career Steps:** Senior Vice President/Chief Appraiser, Hawthorne Savings FSB (1994–Present); Assistant Chief Appraiser, Guardian Bank (1992–1994); Review Lending Manager, R.T.C. (1990–1992); Residential Manager, Union Bank (1983–1989). **Associations & Accomplishments:** Designated Member, SRA Appraisal Institute; Designated Member, Environment Assessment Association; Instructor, Real Estate Appraisal at University of California – Los Angeles. **Education:** University of Oklahoma, B.A. (1966). **Personal:** Married to James in 1976. Ms. Gill enjoys reading and teaching.

Michelle E. Green

Vice President and Director of Accounting Operations
Bank United of Texas, FSB
3200 Southwest Freeway, Phoenix Tower 1400
Houston, TX 77027
(713) 543–6846
Fax: (713) 543–6351
6035

Business Information: Bank United of Texas, FSB is a $14 billion (total assets) federally–chartered savings bank, operating a fully–integrated national housing finance business. With banking divisions only in Texas, Bank United of Texas operates a mortgage division in 34 states. Spending the first five years of her career in public accounting, Ms. Green joined Bank United of Texas as Vice President and Director of Accounting Operations in 1991. She is responsible for corporate accounts payable, payroll, general ledger, and fixed assets. She also serves as a liaison with every area within the bank, including overseeing a support staff of 34. **Career Steps:** Vice President and Director of Accounting Operations, Bank United of Texas, FSB (1991–Present); Vice President and Account Acq. Manager, United Savings Association of the Southwest (1989–1991); Senior Vice President of Finance, Allen Park Federal Savings & Loan (1986–1988). **Associations & Accomplishments:** American Institute of Certified Public Accountants; Texas Society of Certified Public Accountants; National Association of Black Accountants; Association of Certified Fraud Examiners; University of Houston: Downtown Educational Talent Search Middle School Mentor Program; High School Athletics Parent Booster; Parent Teacher Organization: Treasurer, Volunteer; Who's Who in High School; Who's Who in College. **Education:** Florida A&M University, B.S. in Accounting (1976). **Personal:** Married to Roy L. Cook in 1978. Three children: Paula R., Christopher M. B., and Matheu B.

Allison W. Hall
Vice President/Internal Auditor
St. Clair Federal Savings Bank
1927 1st Avenue N.
Birmingham, AL 35094
(205) 583–3202
Fax: (205) 338–2228

6035

Business Information: St. Clair Federal Savings Bank is a full service financial institution providing banking and related services to clients. A subsidiary of Alabama National Bank Corporation, a multi–bank holding company with seven locations throughout Alabama, the Bank has $80 million in assets. As Vice President/Internal Auditor, Ms. Hall acts as liaison between external auditors and management, reviewing loans, reporting directly to the board, and overseeing internal audits, and financial reporting to stock holders and regulatory agencies. **Career Steps:** Vice President/Internal Auditor, St. Clair Federal Savings Bank (1993–Present); Staff Accountant, Dudley, Hopton, Jones, Sims and Freeman (1987–1993). **Associations & Accomplishments:** Past Director/Secretary/Vice President, ASWA **Education:** Birmingham Southern College, B.S. in Accounting (1987). **Personal:** Married to Kerry M. in 1984. Two children: Taylor and Joshua. Ms. Hall enjoys painting and floral arranging.

Lawrence M. Levine
President
Coutts & Co (USA) Inc.
65 East 55th Street
New York, NY 10022
(212) 303–2911
Fax: (212) 303–2916

6035

Business Information: Coutts & Co (USA) Inc., a member of the National Westminster Bank Group, is an international private banking facility. As President of the Service Management Company, Mr. Levine is responsible for all aspects of operations, service delivery, and technology that support the international private banking branches of both Coutts & Co AG and Coutts & Co (USA) International in the United States. **Career Steps:** President, Coutts & Co (USA) Inc. (1995–Present); Senior Vice President, Coutts & Co AG, New York Branch (1994–Present); Citibank, N.A.: Vice President and Service Quality Director – Citibank Private Bank (1988–1994), World Corporation Group (1986–1988), Vice President and City Administrative Officer – Citibank International Cleveland (1985–1986), Vice President – Citibank International Chicago (1982–1985), Assistant Vice President and Manager (1976–1981). **Associations & Accomplishments:** Chicago Civic Federation (1985). **Education:** Syracuse University – School of Management, M.B.A. in Finance (1974); Syracuse University, B.A. in Economics (1973). **Personal:** Married to Denise in 1979. Three children: Eric, Jason, and Gregory. Mr. Levine enjoys community affairs and coaching soccer, basketball, and little league baseball.

Rafael Ruiz
Director of Administration and Operations/Controller
Government Development Bank for Puerto Rico
P.O. Box 42001
San Juan, Puerto Rico 00940
(787) 722–8360
Fax: (787) 723–7388

6035

Business Information: Government Development Bank for Puerto Rico is a full–service, financial institution specializing in financing the private sector. As Director of Administration and Operations/Controller, Mr. Ruiz supervises the Management Information Systems operations and services, accounts payable, and is directly responsible for three employees. **Career**

Steps: Government Development Bank for Puerto Rico: Director of Administration and Operations/Controller (1995–Present), General Auditor (1993–1995); Business Assurance Manager, Coopers & Lybrand (1982–1993). **Associations & Accomplishments:** American Institute of Certified Public Accountants; Puerto Rico Society of Certified Public Accountants; The Institute of Internal Auditors. **Education:** University of Puerto Rico, B.B.A. (1982). **Personal:** Married to Anamaria Rosado in 1988. Two children: Anamaria and Rafael. Mr. Ruiz enjoys softball, baseball, basketball, and tennis.

Roland A. Turmol Jr.
Vice President
First Home Savings Bank, F.S.B.
P.O. Box 189
Pennsville, NJ 08070–0189
(609) 678–4415
Fax: (609) 678–8304

6035

Business Information: First Home Savings Bank, F.S.B. is a full–service, federal savings bank, specializing in residential mortgages, consumer loans, and student savings programs. With seventeen years experience in the banking industry, Mr. Turmol joined First Home Savings Bank as Controller in 1991. He serves as the Senior Administration Officer responsible for overseeing all administrative operations of the branch network. **Career Steps:** Vice President, First Home Savings Bank, F.S.B. (1991–Present); Vice President, First National Bank of New Jersey (1979–1991). **Associations & Accomplishments:** Big Brothers / Big Sisters of Salem County; Washington Club **Education:** Gloucester County College, A.A.S. (1978). **Personal:** Mr. Turmol enjoys arts and crafts, bowling and travel during his leisure time.

Brenda M. Wilkins
Controller
Passumpsic Savings Bank
124 Railroad Street
St. Johnsbury, VT 05819–1606
(802) 748–3196
Fax: (802) 748–6793

6035

Business Information: Passumpsic Savings Bank, established in 1853, is a full–service, community financial institution specializing in banking and savings. With eighteen years experience in accounting, Ms. Wilkins joined Passumpsic Savings Bank in 1990. Serving as Controller, she is responsible for all aspects of financial functions, including balance sheets, income statements, financial analysis, call reports, federal and state reporting, and assisting internal and external auditors. **Career Steps:** Controller, Passumpsic Savings Bank (1990–Present); Internal Auditor, Dartmouth Bank (1988–1990); Financial Analyst, Fairbanks Weighing Division (1981–1988); Staff Accountant, Barry A. McCormick (1979–1981). **Associations & Accomplishments:** Business & Professional Women's Club; American Heart Association. **Education:** Lyndon State College, B.S. in Business (1995); Champlain College, A.S. in Accounting (1977). **Personal:** Ms. Wilkins enjoys aerobics, nautilus conditioning, tennis and skiing.

Carolyn Williams–Goldman
Senior Vice President and Director of Human Resources
Bay View Federal Bank
2121 S. El Camino Real
San Mateo, CA 94403
(415) 312–7286
Fax: (415) 358–0128

6035

Business Information: Bay View Federal Bank was established in 1911 and has 26 offices in the Bay area. The Bank handles all types of banking, including loans, savings, checking, and other financial services. As Senior Vice President and Director of Human Resources, Ms. Williams–Goldman oversees all daily functions for the Human Resource Group (hiring, recruiting, benefits, compensation, payroll, etc.) and Corporate Services Group, which handles purchasing, maintenance of facilities, and the mail room. Additionally, she serves on the Bank's Senior Management Committee which formulates and implements the Bank's strategic objectives. **Career Steps:** Bay View Federal Bank: Senior Vice President and Director of Human Resources (1995–Present), Assistant Vice President and Associate Counsel (1991–1994); Vice President and Counsel, First Nationwide Bank (1991–1994); Associate, Winthrop, Stimson, Putnam & Roberts (1987–1990). **Associations & Accomplishments:** State Bar of California; State Bar of New York; San Mateo Bar Association; American Bar Association; Volunteer legal services for Legal Aid Society for San Mateo. **Education:** University of California – Boalt Hall School of Law, J.D. (1987); University of California – Berkeley, B.A. (1983). **Personal:** Married to Keith in 1986.

One child: Tyler. Ms. Williams–Goldman enjoys reading fiction, travel, and entertaining friends at her home.

Michael P. Donnelly
Vice President
Savings Bank of Finger Lake
470 Exchange Street
Geneva, NY 14456
(315) 789–3838
Fax: (315) 789–0651

6036

Business Information: Savings Bank of Finger Lake is a full–service community bank, offering all types of loans (consumer, commercial, and residential). As Vice President, Mr. Donnelly oversees residential and consumer lending services as well as strategic planning for the overall bank, product development, pricing, and management of an origination sales force. **Career Steps:** Vice President, Savings Bank of Finger Lake (1995–Present); Vice President of Direct Marketing, Sibley Mortgage Corporation (1990–1995); Operating Mer. President, Imaging Systems, Inc. (1983–1990). **Associations & Accomplishments:** Local MBA; Kiwanis; Chamber of Commerce; Rotary; Engaged Encounters. **Personal:** Married to Christine M. in 1982. Four children: Sean, Michael, Joseph, and Kevin. Mr. Donnelly enjoys golf, fishing, coaching kids activities, and being a Cub Scout leader.

James C. Neely III
Marketing Manager
Trumball Savings and Loan Company
P.O. Box 711
Warren, OH 44482–0711
(216) 373–8670
Fax: (216) 373–8629

6036

Business Information: Trumball Savings and Loan Company is a stock company, providing traditional savings and loans programs. With the corporate office located in Warren, Ohio and seven other offices in Ohio, Trumball Savings and Loan Company operates somewhat like a commercial bank, but without trusts. As Marketing Manager, Mr. Neely is responsible for managing all advertising activities, market research, and sales for the Company. His marketing research includes seeking weaknesses in market/customer information files and targeting solutions. Most of the research is conducted internally, focusing on direct marketing and advertising. **Career Steps:** Marketing Manager, Trumball Savings and Loan Company (1994–Present); Marketing Director, First National Bank of Pennsylvania (1992–1994); District Agent, Prudential (1991–1992); Vice President of Marketing, Central Trust Company of Northwestern Ohio. **Education:** Ohio University, Bachelors (1974); School of Bank Marketing, Boulder, CO; Ohio School of Banking. **Personal:** Married to Patricia in 1991. Three children: James IV, Kyle, and Coral. Mr. Neely enjoys home restoration, gardening, woodworking, and canoeing.

Karen S. White
Chief Financial Officer/Controller
Central Valley Bank
116 West Main Street
Ottumwa, IA 52501–2540
(515) 682–8355
Fax: (515) 682–8947

6036

Business Information: Central Valley Bank is a savings and loan association chartered in 1994. The Bank purchased three failing institutions and started out with their deposits. It has grown 27% in the first year with a loan volume of ten times what the Bank started out with. As Chief Financial Officer/Controller, Ms. White is responsible for all financial aspects of the Bank, including payroll, accounting, and other related functions. **Career Steps:** Chief Financial Officer/Controller, Central Valley Bank (1994–Present); Accountant, Tennyson Enterprises (1993–1994); Certified Public Accountant, Anderson Larkin & Company (1991–1993). **Associations & Accomplishments:** Iowa Society of Certified Public Accountants; American Institute of Certified Public Accountants; Quota; Parent Teacher Association; Chamber of Commerce;

SHIRM; Financial Managers. **Education:** Buena Vista College, B.A. (1988); Certified Public Accountant (1989). **Personal:** Married to Stephen L. in 1980. Two children: Melissa and Adam.

Dana C. Bice

Vice President of Marketing and Human Resources
Omega Federal Credit Union
206 Siebert Road
Pittsburgh, PA 15237
(412) 369–3030
Fax: (412) 369–3828

6061

Business Information: Omega Federal Credit Union, boasting four branch offices, is a full–service financial institution providing services to local corporations within a 30 mile radius. As Vice President of Marketing and Human Resources, Ms. Bice is responsible for supervising all marketing activities and overseeing all branches' administrative functions. **Career Steps:** Vice President of Marketing & Human Resources, Omega Federal Credit Union (1993–Present); Personnel Administrator, Rombro Health Services (1988–1990); Store Manager, Hit or Miss (1986–1988). **Associations & Accomplishments:** Board of Directors, Northern Allegheny County Chamber of Commerce. **Education:** LaRoche College, Masters; Pennsylvania State University, B.S. (1985). **Personal:** Married to Thomas G. in 1986. Two children: Taylor Tatyana and John Thomas. Ms. Bice enjoys raising her children, both of whom were adopted from Russia.

Kerry L. Caines

Credit Union Manager
State Farm Insurance Federal Credit Union
31303 Agoura Road
Westlake Village, CA 91363–0001
(818) 707–5350
Fax: (818) 707–5372

6061

Business Information: State Farm Insurance Federal Credit Union, formally established in 1975, is a financial institute providing benefits to State Farm Insurance associates, including employees and their dependents. Employed by State Farm Insurance for the past 21 years, Mr. Caines was appointed Credit Union Manager in 1993. He is responsible for the operation of a $44 million credit union, including investments, delinquent accounts, finances, and public relations. **Career Steps:** Credit Union Manager, State Farm Insurance Federal Credit Union (1993–Present); State Farm Insurance: Data Processing Supervisor (1988–1993), Computer Technician (1974–1988). **Education:** University of LaVerne, B.S. in Progress (1997); Attended: Moorpark College; Illinois State University. **Personal:** Married to Diane in 1981. Mr. Caines enjoys hunting, fishing, and continuing education.

Sandra Cirel DeLaus

Director of Information and Technology
The Summit Federal Credit Union
100 Marina Drive
Rochester, NY 14626
(716) 453–7066
Fax: (716) 453–7006
E–MAIL: See Below

6061

Business Information: The Summit Federal Credit Union is a federally–chartered credit union serving the financial needs of its community. The Credit Union offers high interest yields on savings, certificates, IRAs, and checking accounts and low rates on loans and mortgages. As Director of Information and Technology, Ms. Cirel DeLaus is accountable for three supervisors and 23 employees and is responsible for all administrative–related duties. She is responsible for the customer service telephone center, ATM entries from 12 machines, account adjustments, and items processing from Federal Reserve Banks. Internet users can reach her via: DeLaus@summitfcu.org. **Career Steps:** Summit Federal Credit Union: Director of Information Technology (1995–Present), Data Processing Manager (1990–1995), Data Processing Supervisor (1988–1990). **Associations & Accomplishments:** Ms. Cirel DeLaus has been published in the Credit Union magazine. **Education:** Rochester Institute of Technology: Masters of Science in Software Development & Management (1996), B.S. in Applied Computing. **Personal:** Married to Daniel in 1987. Three children: Mara, Kendra, and Daniel. Ms. Cirel DeLaus enjoys spending time with her family.

Michael B. Cornell

Manager, Training and Development/Shoppe Service Center
Marriott Federal Credit Union
1 Marriott Drive
Washington, DC 20058–0001
(301) 380–4092
Fax: (301) 380–5148
EMAIL: See Below

6061

Business Information: Marriott Federal Credit Union, recipient of Credit Union of the Year Award (1995), is a non–profit financial institution providing financial products and services to employees of Marriott International and Host Marriott. Established in 1953, Marriott Federal Credit Union reports annual assets of $80 million and currently employs 75 people. As Control Manager, Mr. Cornell is responsible for the management of training and development, space planning coordination, and facility support. In recognition of his outstanding service and dedication, he was awarded Marriott's 1995 "Employee of the Year." Concurrent to his position at Marriott Federal Credit Union, he serves in partnership with his wife as Co–owner and Business Manager of Calligraphers Ink — custom hand and computerized calligraphy. His wife is Owner and operates the business. He can also be reached through the Internet via: michael.cornell@marriott.com **Career Steps:** Marriott Federal Credit Union: Control Manager (1994–Present), Special Projects Manager (1991–1994), System Administrator (1990–1991), Lending & Delinquency Control (1988–1990); Co–owner and Business Manager, Calligrapher's Ink (1993–Present). **Associations & Accomplishments:** Innovative Thinkers Network; International Credit Association; Maryland Credit Union League; Franklin Quest FFT; World Wildlife Federation; Board of Directors, Oseh Shalom (Men's Club); Friends of the National Zoo; Published in local newspaper, Washington Post and in newsletters. **Education:** Loyola College, M.B.A. (1992); University of Maryland, B.A. (1980). **Personal:** Married to Bonnie in 1984. Two children: Zachary and Alana. Mr. Cornell enjoys coaching youth sports and playing racquetball.

Deborah D'Angelo

Marketing Project Coordinator
Affinity Federal Credit Union
P.O. Box 750
Bedminster, NJ 07921–0750
(908) 719–3912
Fax: (908) 719–3885

6061

Business Information: Affinity Federal Credit Union is a credit union owned by the members of AT&T, Global Information Systems, and Lucent Technologies. The Union offers a variety of financial services to members. As Marketing Project Coordinator, Ms. D'Angelo manages daily administration of existing marketing programs, and assists with marketing research, design, and layout of marketing materials. **Career Steps:** Marketing Project Coordinator, Affinity Federal Credit Union (1995–Present); Administrative Assistant, Premier Financial, Inc. (1994–1995); Video/Audio Studio Lab Manager, Rider University (1992–1994). **Associations & Accomplishments:** National Center for Missing and Exploited Children; Assistant at Soup Kitchen in New Brunswick; Assisted with the Jerry Kids Telethon. **Education:** Rider University, B.A. (1994). **Personal:** Ms. D'Angelo enjoys golf, skiing, and administering a club to help children learn how and why to save money.

K. Verline Forsberg, C.C.U.E.

President
Wyo Central Federal Credit Union
190 South David
Casper, WY 82601
(307) 234–5401
Fax: (307) 234–1523
EMAIL: See Below

6061

Business Information: Wyo Central Federal Credit Union is a full service financial institution servicing over 45 employee and organizational groups. Lending services include first and second mortgages, all types of consumer loans, credit and debit cards. Deposit services include share savings, checking, IRA's, and CD's. As President, Ms. Forsberg is responsible for all aspects of the credit union's operations including: serving as CFO reporting directly to the Board of Directors, future planning, policy implementation and administration, data processing, personnel administration, and compliance oversight. Internet users can reach her via: kvf@coffey.com. **Career Steps:** President, Wyo Central Federal Credit Union (1992–Present); Conoco Federal Credit Union: President (1980–1992), Assistant Treasurer (1978–1980) **Associations & Accomplishments:** Soroptomists: member, Past Matron of Fort Casper Chapter #4, E.O.S.; Member of various academic honor societies. **Education:** University of Wisconsin Graduate School of Business – Madison, Credit Union Management Diploma (1989); C.C.U.E. Certification (1991). **Personal:** Two children: Larry and Laura. Ms. Forsberg enjoys skiing, mountain biking, sewing, reading, and computing.

Valorie Grant

Marketing Director
Miami Postal Service Credit Union
P.O. Box 520622
Miami, FL 33152
(305) 592–7733
Fax: (305) 477–2736

6061

Business Information: Miami Postal Service Credit Union is a full service financial institution, providing its members with all their financial needs. Established in 1928, the Credit Union employs 37 staff, and continuously endeavors to live up to the Credit Union motto "People Helping People." As Marketing Director, Ms. Grant oversees all marketing related topics including staff training programs. During her tenure at the MPSCU, Mrs. Grant has been instrumental in the implementation of various new programs, including a weekly staff training program, an extensive mortgage program, and a montly staff newsletter. A recipient of the prestigious Certified Credit Union Executive Designation (CCUE), Ms. Grant is one of only 1,395 in the country to be so honored. The CCUE designation is the hallmark of professional credit union achievement. **Career Steps:** Marketing Director, Miami Postal Service Credit Union (1994–Present); Marketing Analyst, FPL Federal Credit Union (1988–1994); Mortgage Manager, Mercy Credit Union (1985–1988). **Associations & Accomplishments:** Secretary of the North Dade Chapter of the Florida Credit Union League; President for two years of the Coral Keys Chapter. **Education:** CUNA Marketing Management School, Certified Credit Union Executive; STAR Program, Realtor, SRN (England), also an Equestrian Trainer. **Personal:** Two children: Julia Christina and Jane Louise. Ms. Grant enjoys writing, reading, scuba diving, travel, and horseback riding,.

Brenda G. Grocott

Chief Executive Officer
Cleveland Center Federal Credit Union
326 East Lorain Street
Oberlin, OH 44074–1216
(216) 774–4818
Fax: (216) 647–4952

6061

Business Information: Cleveland Center Federal Credit Union is a full–service financial and lending organization. As Chief Executive Officer, Ms. Grocott is responsible for overseeing daily operations, various administrative functions, and serves as Treasurer of the Board of Directors. Additionally, she supervises personnel in financial bookkeeping, marketing, and advertising capacities. **Career Steps:** Chief Executive Officer, Cleveland Center Federal Credit Union (1980–Present). **Associations & Accomplishments:** President, Town & Country Ladies' Organization/Club; LaGrange Lions; Wellington Kiwanis; Oberlin Chamber of Commerce. **Education:** Lorain County Community College; Pennsylvania State University – Financial Management School. **Personal:** Two children: Robert L. and Krista N. Ms. Grocott enjoys baking, gardening, and crafts.

David J. Hamilton

President
Oteen V.A. Federal Credit Union
1100 Tunnel Road
Asheville, NC 28805
(704) 298–8521
Fax: (704) 298–8532

6061

Business Information: Oteen V.A. Federal Credit Union is a small, personal financial services institution, specializing in banking and financing. Established in 1936, Oteen V.A. Federal Credit Union reports annual revenue of $1 million and currently employs 8 people. As President, Mr. Hamilton is responsible for the day–to–day operations of the institution. **Career Steps:** President, Oteen V.A. Federal Credit Union (1993–Present); President, DECA Credit Union (1991–1993); Supervisory Examiner, Comptroller – Florida (1985–1990). **Associations & Accomplishments:** Veterans of Foreign War (VFW); American Legion; Speaker on Lending Philosophy and Risk Based Lending. **Education:** University of Tampa, M.B.A. (1982); California Coast University, currently in Ph.D. Program. **Personal:** Married to Donna in 1967. Two children: Thomas and Scott. Mr. Hamilton enjoys golf, bowling, and computers.

Claire Ippoliti
Mortgage Manager
Philadelphia Federal Credit Union
216 West Washington Square
Philadelphia, PA 19106
(215) 625–8743
Fax: (215) 625–0916

6061

Business Information: Philadelphia Federal Credit Union is a full service banking institution located in Philadelphia, Pennsylvania. The Credit Union offers mortgage and lending services to its members as well as savings and investment services. As Mortgage Manager, Ms. Ippoliti supervises a staff of six employees in the Mortgage Department, and is responsible for mortgage investments in excess of $80 million annually. Ms. Ippoliti enjoys the day–to–day challenges associated with her position and is continually developing new marketing strategies to introduce products and services to her new and existing clients. **Career Steps:** Philadelphia Federal Credit Union: Mortgage Manager (1995–Present), Student Loan Manager (1994–1995), Loan Officer (1992–Present). **Education:** Temple University, B.A. in Liberal Arts (1989).

Kenneth Jensen
Vice President of Finance
Pinellas County Employees Federal Credit Union
P.O. Box 2300
Largo, FL 34649–2300
(813) 586–4422
Fax: (813) 585–2274

6061

Business Information: Pinellas County Employees Federal Credit Union is a federal credit union serving county employees and other municipalities. Functioning as a full–service, financial institution with 7,600 members, Pinellas County Employees Federal Credit Union offers savings and checking accounts, credit cards, ATM's, audio response, CD's, IRA's, loans, and mortgages. Established in 1956, the Credit Union currently employs 21 people. With twelve years experience in credit unions, Mr. Jensen joined Pinellas County Employees Federal Credit Union in 1989. Serving as Vice President of Finance, he is responsible for overseeing the accounting area and in charge of complete financial operations and EDP, as well as the supervision of three staff members and serving as a backup to the President in his absence. **Career Steps:** Vice President of Finance, Pinellas County Employees Federal Credit Union (1989–Present); Pinellas County Teachers Credit Union: Finance Manager (1988–1989), Staff Accountant (1983–1988). **Associations & Accomplishments:** Secretary (1995), Pinellas Chapter–Florida Credit Union League; Seminole Kiwanis Club (1992–1994); Credit Union Executives Society (1994–1995); Secretary (1995), Coastal Oaks Homeowners Association. **Education:** University of South Florida, B.A. in Business (1982); St. Petersburg Junior College, A.A. in Business Administration (1980). **Personal:** Married to Janet in 1986. Two children: Susan Ames and Christopher Ames. Mr. Jensen enjoys sports, card collecting, and travel.

James Jordan
Chief Financial Officer
Dow Louisiana Federal Credit Union
P.O. Box 150
Plaquemine, LA 70765–0150
(504) 353–6310
Fax: (504) 353–6387

6061

Business Information: Dow Louisiana Federal Credit Union is a full–service financial institution, providing share and loan services to members. Membership to DLFCU is open to all Dow Louisiana employees and their family members – current membership totals more than 7,000. Services provided include ATM, 24–hour MARS System, and sharebranching. DLFCU belongs to the Member Shared Service Center Network with branches that service members of DLFCU. A Certified Public Accountant, Mr. Jordan joined DLFCU as Chief Financial Officer in 1993. He is responsible for all aspects of financial functions for the credit union, including administration, finances, sales, taxes, marketing, strategic planning, budgeting, accounting, asset/liability management, and case management. **Career Steps:** Chief Financial Officer, Dow Louisiana Federal Credit Union (1993–Present); Claims Specialist, Resolution Trust Corporation (1991–1993); Accountant, Charter Bank, FSB (1986–1991). **Associations & Accomplishments:** American Institute of Certified Public Accountants; Louisiana State Society of Certified Public Accountants. **Education:** University of Mississippi, Business Management (1986); Louisiana State University, CPA Prep

Program. **Personal:** Married to Karen in 1990. Mr. Jordan enjoys painting and playing the guitar.

Mr. Eugene P. Kelly
Operations Manager
U.S. Central Credit Union
7300 College Boulevard, Suite 600
Overland Park, KS 66210
(913) 661–3017
Fax: (913) 661–3826

6061

Business Information: U.S. Central Credit Union provides liquidity for the Corporate Credit Union Network by safely investing surplus funds of the nation's 12,000 credit unions. Forty Corporate Credit Unions make up the Corporate Credit Union Network. Established in 1974, U.S. Central currently employs 170 people. As Operations Manager, Mr. Kelly is responsible for managing the Securities Settlement and Safekeeping departments and the Asset/Liability trading desk operations. Concurrent with his position, he conducts internal lecturing and training. **Career Steps:** Operations Manager, U.S. Central Credit Union (1992–Present); Assistant Vice President, Donaldson, Lufkin, Jenrette (1987–1992); Operations Manager, Paine Webber (1982–1986). **Associations & Accomplishments:** Recipient, "People Helping People Award" (1994); Volunteer in local community. **Education:** Jersey City State College, B.A. (1979); Rutgers University; New York Institute of Finance; NASD Series 7,63, and 27 registered.

Joan M. Meagher
Vice President of Operations
Webster First Federal Credit Union
1 North Main Street
Webster, MA 01570–2229
(508) 943–1433
Fax: (508) 949–6621

6061

Business Information: Webster First Federal Credit Union is a federally–chartered credit union with assets of more than $216 million, serving the financial needs of its local community. It offers high interest yields on savings, certificates, IRAs, and checking accounts and low rates on loans and mortgages. ATMs are located in five out of nine branches. With twenty–eight years experience in the banking industry, Ms. Meagher joined Webster First Credit Union as a teller in 1967. Serving in several executive positions, she was appointed as Vice President of Operations in 1989. She is responsible for the day–to–day operations of the nine branches to assure high quality, efficient service to all customers, along with developing and implementing policies and procedures to attain short and long term goals and strategies of management. **Career Steps:** Webster First Federal Credit Union: Vice President of Operations (1989–Present), Assistant Vice President of Operations (1988–1989), Branch Manager (1987–1988), Loan Officer (1983–1987), Teller Supervisor (1969–1983), Teller (1967–1969). **Education:** Nichols College, Bachelor of Science in Business Administration (1993); Babson College, Financial Studies, Executive Education (1995). **Personal:** Married to Robert J. in 1958. Three children: Cheryl, Robert Jr., and Scott, and two grandchildren, Matthew and Danielle. Ms. Meagher enjoys camping, traveling, and reading in her leisure time.

Sherry Preston–Huguenin
Marketing Director
Forest Products Federal Credit Union
P.O. Box 1179
Klamath Falls, OR 97601–0281
(541) 884–1376 Ext. 209
Fax: (541) 885–8081

6061

Business Information: Forest Products Federal Credit Union is a full service financial institution offering financial services to over 100 chartered members. In addition to checking, savings, and related services, the Facility also offers two $1,000 scholarships. Established in 1936, the Company employs 60 people and has $84 million in assets. As Marketing Director, Ms. Preston–Huguenin oversees all advertising promotions, fund raisers, new charter members, and trade show events. She is also responsible for promoting staff team work and handling all advertising through television, radio, and newspapers. **Career Steps:** Marketing Director, Forest Products Federal Credit Union (1991–Present); Sales Representative, Amidon's Office Equipment (Three Years); Sales Representative, NEC America, Inc. (Five Years). **Associations & Accomplishments:** Klamath County Chamber of Commerce Ambassador; 1996 Graduate of Leadership Kla-

math; Financial Women International. **Education:** DeAnza Community College, Computer Programming. **Personal:** Married to Eric in 1994. Ms. Preston–Huguenin enjoys the adventurous spirit she inherited from her father and enjoys travel, pets, and family.

J. C. Sherman
Information Technology Executive
Navy Federal Credit Union
P.O. Box 3001
Merrifield, VA 22119
(703) 255–8368
Fax: (703) 255–7795

6061

Business Information: Navy Federal Credit Union, the world's largest credit union, is a financial institution with over $8 billion in assets and 1.4 million members, specializing in banking. Services include checking, savings, loans, financial advising, investment services, etc. Members are primarily members of the U.S. Navy, U.S. Marines, and government employees, who may initially establish an account during deployment status. At that time, the member obtains multi–benefits, both internationally and nationally, on most U.S. Naval bases located throughout the world. Established in 1934, Navy Federal Credit Union currently employs 3,200 people company–wide. As Information Technology Executive, Mr. Sherman is responsible for prime negotiation of hardware and software acquisitions. **Career Steps:** Information Technology Executive, Navy Federal Credit Union (1992–Present); Division Director, U.S. Air Force Communications Group (1991–1992); Branch Chief, U.S. Air Force Communications Squadron (1988–1991). **Associations & Accomplishments:** Semper Paratus Lodge, No. 49 (Masonic Lodge) of Washington, D.C.; Alexandria Scottish Rites of Alexandria, Virginia; American Legion Post, No. 10 of Manassas, Virginia. **Education:** Catholic University of America, M.A. (1990); East Texas State University, B.A. (1979); Defense Systems Management College; DoD Computer Institute; Air Force Communications School. **Personal:** Married to Lucy M. Sherman in 1977. Four children: Alex B., Baron N., Anna K., and J. Chancellor. Mr. Sherman enjoys chess, reading, golf, tennis, and softball.

Sharon A. Updike
President/Chief Executive Officer
San Diego Postal Credit Union
P.O. Box 81625
San Diego, CA 92138–1625
(619) 224–3521 Ext.101
Fax: (619) 224–5620
EMAIL: See Below

6061

Business Information: San Diego Postal Credit Union provides banking and related services to postal employees in the San Diego County area. A member–owned, full service, financial lending organization, the Facility was established in 1928 and has branches in Midway, Carmel Mountain, Chula Vista and El Cajon, California. As President/CEO, Ms. Updike oversees all four branches in the San Diego area. She provides direction and information to the board of directors and directly supervises three employees. Joining San Diego Postal Credit Union in 1994, Ms. Updike was responsible for converting the data processing from on–line to in–house. She has also implemented several new programs to enhance member service including deposit–taking ATMs at Postal facilities, audio response, in–house ATMs and Visa programs all while doubling the ROA and increasing the loan–to–share ratio from 32% to 56%. With background experience comprising twenty–one years in management, thirteen of which were in credit union management, Ms. Updike managed two credit unions in Orange County, California between 1977 and 1982. Additionally, she served as Training Director for May Company and as Personnel Director for TRE Security and Service Communications. A guest speaker and program leader at various California Credit Union League functions including the Financial Management Series, Ms. Updike has also conducted seminars in financial management including the Hawaii CUES Council in Honolulu. A graduate of Western CUNA Management School, she also holds a degree in business administration with an emphasis on organizational behavior from California State University, Fullerton and was listed in the 1992–1993 issue of Who's Who Worldwide. Internet users can reach her via: s–Updike@msn.com. **Career Steps:** President/Chief Executive Officer, San Diego Postal Credit Union (1994–Present); Senior Vice President, Orange County Teachers Union (1986–1993); Manager, Consulting Service, California Credit Union League (1982–1986). **Associations & Accomplishments:** President, Credit Union Chief Executives Association; Board Member, Credit Union Executives Society of Southern California. **Education:** California State, Fullerton, B.A.; Graduate of Western CUNA Management School. **Personal:** Ms. Updike enjoys outdoor activities, golf, skiing, gardening and spending time with her 20 month old child.

Carlos Enrique Vega–Perez, Esq.

General Counsel
Cooperativa A/C Arecibo (COOPACA)
P. O. Box 1056
Arecibo, Puerto Rico 00613
(787) 880–3225
Fax: (787) 878–6672

6061

Business Information: Cooperativa A/C Arecibo (COOPACA) provides financial services to its members. A practicing attorney since 1986, Mr. Vega–Perez joined Cooperative A/C Arecibo in 1992. There, he serves as General Counsel and Legal Department Director and is responsible for all litigation, and legal consulting and counseling. **Career Steps:** General Counsel, Cooperativa Credit Union (1992–Present); Staff Attorney, Puerto Rico Legal Services Corporation (1988–1991); Part–time professor at Pontificia Universidad Catolica de Puerto Rico, Aceribo campus since 1985. **Associations & Accomplishments:** Puerto Rico Bar Association; American Bar Association; Bankruptcy Bar Association of Puerto Rico; American Civil Liberties Union; Citizens in Defense of the Environment; Admitted to practice law before the Federal District Court for Puerto Rico, and the FIrst Circuit Court of Appeals and the Supreme Court of the U.S.A.; Citizens in Defense of the Environment; Phi Alpha Delta Law Fraternity International. **Education:** InterAmerican University – Law School: J.D. (1986), B.A. (1983); Studying toward a Master;s degree in Law and Economics. **Personal:** Mr. Vega–Perez enjoys collecting, reading, and water sports.

Christopher White

General Manager
RTN Federal Credit Union
600 Main Street
Waltham, MA 02154–5551
(617) 736–9805
Fax: (617) 736–9934

6061

Business Information: RTN Federal Credit Union is a full–service financial institution serving industrial employee groups. As General Manager, Mr. White oversees the entire operation of the Credit Union, including union negotiations, loan processing, and personnel issues, with emphasis on Voice and Data Communications. **Career Steps:** RTN Federal Credit Union: General Manager (1993–Present), Operations Manager (1986–1992). **Education:** Nichols College, B.S.B.A. (1982). **Personal:** Married to Regina L. in 1984. Three children: Christian, Rebecca, and Daniel. Mr. White enjoys playing and watching hockey.

Craig A. Wilson

Vice President
Atlantic Financial Federal Credit Union
EP 4, LL1, 11350 McCormick Road
Hunt Valley, MD 21031–1003
(410) 584–8076
Fax: (410) 771–1055
E–mail: see below

6061

Business Information: Atlantic Financial Federal Credit Union is a member–owned full–service lending and financial institution. Established in 1950, the Credit Union currently employs 6 people and reports assets of over $4 million. As Vice President, Mr. Wilson is responible for the management of the Accounting Department, Management Information Systems, human resources, ALM, investments, and is the acting Pension Administrator. Mr. Wilson has been in the finance and accounting business for over 10 years. Internet users can also reach Craig via: CWILSON32B@AOL.COM **Career Steps:** Vice President, Atlantic Financial Federal Credit Union (1991–Present); McElroy Metal, Inc.: Manager of Corporation Accounting Services (1989–1990), Division Controller (1985–1989). **Associations & Accomplishments:** American Management Association; West Virginia Society of Certified Public Accountants. **Education:** West Virginia University, B.S. in Business Administration (1979). **Personal:** One child: Dustin Joseph. Mr. Wilson enjoys golf, photography, baseball, computers and on–line services, and spending time with his family.

David W. Boone

Vice President
First Pioneer Farm Credit
9 County Road 618
Lebanon, NJ 08833
(908) 782–5215
Fax: (908) 782–5229

6062

Business Information: First Pioneer Farm Credit is a provider of credit and other financial services (i.e., tax preparation, recordkeeping, business consulting, appraisals) to farmers. With twenty–six years of experience in the banking industry, Mr. Boone joined First Pioneer Farm Credit as Vice President in 1994. He is responsible for the management of the Credit Office, as well as administration and finances. He also serves as a member of the Credit Committee. **Career Steps:** Vice President, First Pioneer Farm Credit (1994–Present); Vice President of Credit, North Central Jersey Farm Credit (1993–1994); Assistant Vice President and Branch Manager, North Central New York Farm Credit (1978–1993); Agriculture Loan Officer, National Bank Of N.N.Y. (1970–1978). **Associations & Accomplishments:** Former Member: Kiwanis International, former President, Northern New York Chapter AQP, Former President, Jefferson Community College Foundation; Special Olympics Volunteer. **Education:** Farm Credits NYPAR Management Development Seminar. **Personal:** Married to Jean in 1971. Two children: Kerry and Stephanie. Mr. Boone enjoys reading, golf and travel.

Debbie Guthery

Marketing Director
Lycomm Multimedia
1107 18th Avenue South
Nashville, TN 37212
(615) 532–6873
Fax: (615) 532–6870

6062

Business Information: Lycomm Multimedia is a full service credit union for state government employees. Lycomm Multimedia offers checking, savings, loans, and investment accounts for members. Established in 1971, the Credit Union currently has 23 employees. As Marketing Director, Ms. Guthery develops and implements new marketing techniques for services offered by Lycomm Multimedia. Other duties include educating employees on new services offered and how to promote existing services. Ms. Guthery monitors and tracks the growth of the Credit Union as changes occur in the marketplace. **Career Steps:** Marketing Director, Lycomm Multimedia (1994–Present); Assistant Manager, MECU (1992–1994); Business Manager, Davis Daniel Enterprises (1990–1992). **Associations & Accomplishments:** Director of Promotions, Celebrate the Child, Inc.; VIP Panelist, Easter Seals Presidents Council. **Education:** Attending: Volunteer State Community College; American Institute of Banking, Finance; Vannoy, Talent Agency. **Personal:** One child: Tyler J. Andrykowski. Ms. Guthery enjoys being a freelance writer.

Mark A. Kloeckner

Vice President of Finance
Saguaro Credit Union
P.O. Box 40875
Tucson, AZ 85717
(520) 624–8333
Fax: (520) 792–6169

6062

Business Information: Saguaro Credit Union is a banking credit union, providing a complete range of financial services to its members from three locations in Tucson, Arizona. A Certified Management Accountant, Mr. Kloeckner joined Saguaro Credit Union as Vice President of Finance in 1994. He is responsible for all Accounting Department activities, including financing, accounting, budgeting, asset/liability management, purchasing, Visa, student loans, and electronic transfers. **Career Steps:** Vice President of Finance, Saguaro Credit Union (1994–Present); Principal Examiner, National Credit Union Administration (1987–1994). **Associations & Accomplishments:** Institute of Management Accountants. **Education:** Mankato State University: M.B.A (1987), B.S. in Accounting (1985); Certified Management Accountant. **Personal:** Married to Deborah in 1990. Five children: Deborah, Belinda, Robert, Felicia and Domanic. Mr. Kloeckner enjoys home remodeling, sports, swimming, and backyard mechanics.

William L. Lambacher Jr.

Comptroller
Falls Catholic Credit Union
2237 State Road
Cuyahoga Falls, OH 44223
(330) 929–7341
Fax: (330) 929–9342

6062

Business Information: Falls Catholic Credit Union is a full service banking facility offering savings, checking, Certificates of Deposit, Individual Retirement Accounts and related services to clients. Regional in scope, the Credit Union was established in 1957, and employees ten people. As Comptroller, Mr. Lambacher is an electronic banking specialist (ACH, ATM), and oversees of all financial activity relating to the Company. He is responsible for balancing general ledger accounts and preparing financial statements, maintaining records in a neat and orderly fashion, distribution of dividends and handling of all certificates of deposit and individual retirement accounts, performing daily backups of all computer files, establishing and writing procedures pertaining to share drafts and other deposit activity, and ensuring timely reporting of pertinent information to the Internal Revenue Service. Additionally, Mr. Lambcher was one of the first recipients in the country to receive the prestigious "Designation of Accredited ACH Professional" award in 1993. **Career Steps:** Falls Catholic Credit Union: Comptroller (1988–Present), Bookkeeper (1986–1987), Teller (1985). **Associations & Accomplishments:** University of Akron Alumni Band; St. Vincent's Catholic Church Traditional Choir; Mid–America Automated Payment Operations Committee Member; Awarded Designation of Accredited ACH Professional (1993). **Education:** University of Akron: B.S. in Accounting (1989), B.S. in Business Administration/Finance (1985), Associate of Applied Business and Data Processing (1983). **Personal:** Married to Mary Anne Felker in 1996. Mr. Lambacher enjoys skiing, bicycling, photography and music.

Candido Lebron Santiago, MCR

Chairman of the Board of Directors
Cooperativa De Ahorro Y Credito Mauna Coop.
P.O. Box 127
Maunabo, Puerto Rico 00707–0127
(787) 861–2240
Fax: Please mail or call

6062

Business Information: Cooperativa De Ahorro Y Credito Mauna Coop. is a cooperative credit union. As Chairman, Mr. Lebron Santiago directs all meetings, makes all policy–related decisions, oversees loan approvals and expansion, and is responsible for all administrative activities. During his presidency, Company increased its assets from 27 million dollars to 84 million dollars. The Coop. also grew from one office to six branches, one shopping center, and one drugstore. Concurrently, he serves as Regional Director for the V.R. Program of the Family Department. **Career Steps:** Chairman, Cooperativa De Ahorro Y Credito Mauna Coop. (1986–Present); Regional Director for V.R. Program, Family Department (1988–Present); Rehabilitation Counselor, V.R. Program (1978–1988). **Associations & Accomplishments:** Puerto Rican Rehabilitation Counselor's Association; Liceo Puertriqueno de Procedimientos Parlamentarios; Futuros, Inc (Partnership of Private Industry & V.R. Program). **Education:** University of Puerto Rico, Master's in Rehabilitation Counseling (1973); Hartford University, Six Year Program in Counseling; Numerous Training Seminars in Management of Finance and Management of V.R. Services. **Personal:** Mr. Lebron Santiago enjoys reading and travel.

Randall J. Mims

President and Chief Executive Officer
Florida State University Credit Union
1530 Metropolitan Boulevard
Tallahassee, FL 32308
(904) 385–9999
Fax: (904) 385–8925

6062

Business Information: Florida State University Credit Union is a federal credit union, serving all banking and financial needs for its members, consisting of employees of Florida State University and their immediate family. A Certified Credit Union Executive with over twelve years expertise in credit union management, Mr. Mims joined Florida State University Credit Union in 1993. Serving as President and Chief Executive Officer, he oversees total operations of member financial affairs, as well as financial affairs of the institution. **Career Steps:** President and Chief Executive Officer, Florida State University Credit Union (1993–Present); Executive Vice President, The Credit Union of Palm Beach County (1989–1993); Vice President of Finance and Administration, Oak Ridge Federal Credit Union (1988–1989); Internal Auditor, ORNL Federal al Credit Union (1983–1988). **Associations & Accomplishments:** Secretary, Board of Directors, Florida Credit Union League; Director, Florida Credit Union Service Group; Director, NFECU Service Corporation; Director, Tallahassee Shared Services, Inc.; Committee Member, Florida Credit Union League Governmental Affairs; Member, Pi Kappa Phi National Fraternity; Published in Credit Union Time and other financial management journals. **Education:** Nova Southeastern University, M.B.A. (1993); Palm Beach Atlantic College, B.S. in Human Resource Management; Certified Credit Union Executive, a professional designation awarded in 1992. **Personal:** Mr. Mims enjoys tennis, racquetball, swimming and mountain biking.

Marc Mucroski
CEO/Manager
RMI Company Employees Credit Union
804 Warren Avenue
Niles, OH 44446–1139
(330) 652–3887
Fax: (330) 652–2681

6062

Business Information: RMI Company Employees Credit Union is a full–service, financial and lending institution. As CEO/Manager, Mr. Mucroski is responsible for all aspects of the Bank operations. **Career Steps:** CEO/Manager, RMI Company Employees Credit Union (1988–Present). **Associations & Accomplishments:** Past President, Hermitage Volunteer Fire Department; Hermitage Masonic Lodge #810; Board Member, City of Farrell Economic Development Loan Committee; President, Farrell Volunteer Fire Department; Church Volunteer. **Education:** Theil College: B.A. in Accounting (1986), A.A. in Computer Science. **Personal:** Married to Vicki in 1994.

Donna M. Russo
Vice President of Human Resources
Digital Employees Credit Union
141 Parker Street
Maynard, MA 01752–0130
(508) 461–6700 Ext.6752
Fax: (508) 461–6988

6062

Business Information: Digital Employees Credit Union is a full service financial institution providing banking and related services to clients. With assets of approximately $400 million, the Facility is the third largest credit union in the nation, with fifteen branches throughout the U.S. and a P.C. branch. Established in 1980, the Credit Union employs 195 people. As Vice President of Human Resources, Ms. Russo is responsible for employee relations, benefits administration, recruitment, and training. **Career Steps:** Digital Employees Credit Union: Vice President of Human Resources (1996–Present), Director of Human Resources (1995–1996), Human Resources Manager (1993–1995). **Associations & Accomplishments:** Society for Human Resource Management (SHRM); Northeast Human Resource Association (NHRA); National Association of Female Executives (NAFE). **Education:** Emmanual College, B.S. in Management (In Progress); Bentley College, Human Resource Management (1989). **Personal:** Married to Bill in 1970. Two children: Pamela and Paul. Ms. Russo enjoys jazz and tap dancing.

Roger G. Abbott
Data Architect
Bank of Montreal
101 King Street West, FCP 17th Floor
Toronto, Ontario M5X 1A1
(416) 956–2244
Fax: (416) 867–7157
EMail: See Below

6081

Business Information: Bank of Montreal is a full–service financial institution specializing in treasury trading systems development and management. The Treasury division has four major locations, London, Chicago, Toronto, and Singapore. As Data Architect, Mr. Abbott is responsible for the international data base components group. Internet users can reach him via: rabbott@bmo.com. **Career Steps:** Data Architect, Bank of Montreal (1995–Present); Vice President of Software Engineering, TX Base Systems, Inc. (1990–1994); Circle Associate, LinkAge, Inc. (1987–1990). **Associations & Accomplishments:** Toronto Island Resident; Royal Canadian Yacht Club. **Education:** Pennsylvania State University, B.S. in Chemical Engineering (1979). **Personal:** Married to Charlotte de Heinrich. Two children: Ryan and Alison. Mr. Abbott enjoys soccer, sailing, and woodworking.

Meloma F. Afuola
President
Development Bank of American Samoa
P.O. Box 9
Pago Pago, American S 96799
(684) 633–4031
Fax: (684) 633–1163

6081

Business Information: Development Bank of American Samoa is a banking institution, providing financial services to customers in American Samoa. As President and Board of Director, Mrs. Afuola is responsible for all aspects of operations, in addition to overseeing the administrative operations for associates and a support staff of 137. Prior to her present position, she served as Deputy Treasurer of the American Samoa Government. **Career Steps:** President, Development Bank of American Samoa (1995–Present); Deputy Treasurer, American Samoa Government (1993–1995); American Samoa Government: Director of Administrative Services (1985–1992), Acting Budget Director (1992–1993). **Associations & Accomplishments:** Director, Women's Village Organization in American Samoa; Board of Directors, The American Samoa Development Bank (1995–1997); President, Women's Church Organization in Village; Council member, Humanity Council in American Samoa. **Education:** Long Beach State University, B.S. (1983). **Personal:** Married to Hon. Kalasa Afuola, High Court of American Samoa in 1983. Twelve children, including step–children.

Michel Avramov, Ph.D.
Deputy Manager
Banque Saradar France
49 Avenue George V
Paris, France 75008
331–4443–4443
Fax: 331–4723–9920
EMAIL: See Below

6081

Business Information: Banque Saradar France is a financial institution, specializing in banking and investments such as checking, savings, commodities, etc. Joining Banque Saradar France as Systems Analyst in 1988, Dr. Avramov is Deputy Manager since 1990, responsible for all aspects of technical operations, including development and control of the Bank's computer systems. Internet users can also reach Dr. Avramov via: 100764.1775@compuserve.com **Career Steps:** Banque Saradar France: Deputy Manager (1990–Present), Systems Analyst (1988–1990); Professeur Informatique, Centre D'Etudes Pratiques en Informatique (1987–1988); Deputy Manager, University Center For Qualification (1985–1987); Research Associate to the Computer Department, Technical University of Sofia (1980–1987). **Associations & Accomplishments:** Association For Humanitarian Aid; Many papers and books on Computers and Computing. **Education:** Technical University of Sofia: Ph.D. in Computer Science (1978); M.Sc. in Applied Mathematics (1976); Electronics Engineer (1974). **Personal:** Married to Regina in 1977. One child: Lucien. Dr. Avramov enjoys photography, movies, tennis, music, skiing, and sports cars.

F. Dieter Beintrexler
Chief Representative – New York Representative Office
Raiffeisen Zentralbank Oesterreich AG
609 Fifth Avenue, 10th Floor
New York, NY 10017
(212) 593–7593
Fax: (212) 593–9870

6081

Business Information: Raiffeisen Zentralbank Oesterreich (RZB–Austria) is the representative office for a major foreign bank located in Austria and throughout Eastern Europe that is very active in the syndicated loan market. Established in 1980, the Office currently employs 6 people. With over 16 years expertise in the international banking market, Mr. Beintrexler joined RZB–Austria in 1990. Appointed to his current position in 1991, he serves as representative on behalf of all RZB–Austria interests in the U.S. **Career Steps:** Chief Representative, Raiffeisen Zentralbank Oesterreich AG (1989–Present); Oesterreichische Landerbank: Vice President and Manager of Foreign Department (1988–1989), Vice President and Manager of Syndications (1987–1988); Vice

President and Manager of Middle East and Africa, First City National Bank of Houston (1985–1987). **Associations & Accomplishments:** Director, United States – Austrian Chamber of Commerce in New York; Phi Beta Kappa; Omicron Delta Epsilon; Pi Sigma Alpha. **Education:** University of Delaware: M.A. in Economics (1979), B.A. in International Relations and Economics. **Personal:** Married to Jean Ellen in 1968. Three children: Inge, Heide, and Erika. Mr. Beintrexler enjoys scuba diving, skiing, biking, hiking, and reading.

Roberto L. Cabrera
Internal Auditor
Banco Popular de Puerto Rico
P O Box 362708
San Juan, Puerto Rico 00936–2708
(787) 723–0077
Fax: (787) 725–5440

6081

Business Information: Banco Popular de Puerto Rico is a full service banking facility. One of the largest and most prestigious banks in Puerto Rico, it was established in 1893. With numerous locations throughout Puerto Rico, New York and St. Thomas (U.S. Virgin Islands), the Bank offers consumer and commercial services and employs around 6,000 people. As Internal Auditor, Mr. Cabrera coordinates and performs financial, compliance, and operational audits for the bank and its subsidiaries. Mr. Cabrera provides technical support for branch management on financial questions and handles administrative duties for his staff. **Career Steps:** Internal Auditor, Banco Popular de Puerto Rico (1994–Present); Payroll Accounts Payable Office, Servi–Medical, Inc. (1992–1994). **Associations & Accomplishments:** Colegio de Contadores Publicos Autorizados de Puerto Rico (State Certified Public Accountants Association); American Institute of Certified Public Accountants; Institute of Management Accountants; University of Puerto Rico, Ex Alumni Association. **Education:** University of Puerto Rico, B.B.A. (1993); Certified Public Accountant (1994). **Personal:** Mr. Cabrera enjoys scuba diving.

Jorge Crespo–Velasco
President
Caja de Ahorro y Prestamo Los Andes S.A.
Casilla No. 369
La Paz, Bolivia
(5912) 358497
Fax: (5912) 356022

6081

Business Information: Caja de Ahorro y Prestamo "Los Andes" S.A. is a full–service financial institution providing services to small and micro enterprises. As President, Mr. Crespo–Velasco is responsible for all aspects of Company operations. **Career Steps:** President, Caja de Ahorro dy Prestamo "Los Andes" S.A. (1994–Present); Executive President, Siresa (Present); Executive President, EMCOS S.A. (1994–1995); Ambassador to the U.S., Government of Bolivia (1989–1993); Executive President, Industrias Albus, S.R.L. (1988–1989); Undersecretary of State, Ministry of Foreign Relations (1984–1985); Minister of Industry, Commerce, and Tourism, Government of Bolivia (1982–1983); Local Consultant, United Nations Development Program (1980–1981). **Associations & Accomplishments:** Consultative Council of the Ministry of Foreign Relations; Board Member, Commercial and Industrial Companies; Board Member, Quipus Cultural Foundation; President, Los Andes Savings and Loan Association; President, Protisa Trout Farm on Lake Titicaca; Secretary of Board of Directors, American Chamber of Commerce – Bolivia; Board of Directors, Seamos Drug Prevention Foundation. **Education:** London School of Economics, Certificate of Completion in International Relations (1982); Catholic University of Louvain – Belgium, Certificate of Completion in Political Science (1977); ISVE – Naples, Italy, Certificate of Completion in Economic Development (1965); University of Maryland, B.S. in Business and Public Administration (1961). **Personal:** Married to Adela in 1966. Three children: Flavia, Ximena, and Maria. Mr. Crespo–Velasco enjoys tennis and hiking.

Alberto Y. Cruz, CPA
Vice President and General Director
Banco Finadem, S.A.
P.O. Box 25273, Ce–338
Miami, FL 33102–5273
(809) 532–3000
Fax: (809) 535–7070
EMAIL: See Below

6081

Business Information: Banco Finadem, S.A., formerly doing business as a financial loan institution, is now authorized as a multi–service commercial bank serving the Dominican Republic — with established credit lines in seven international banking institutions. As Vice President and General Director, Mr. Cruz oversees all operations from the Miami, Florida headquarters, as well as establishing credit lines with other banks internationally. Internet users can reach him via: a.cruz@codetel.net.do. **Career Steps:** Vice President and General Director, Banco Finadem, S.A. (1994–Present); Corporate Finance Inter., McKee & Company (1994); Finance Manager, Bonanza Dominicana (1989–1993). **Associations & Accomplishments:** Institute of Certified Public Accountants of Dominican Republic; Finance Manager Association. **Education:** AGSIM (Thunderbird), Master in International Management (1994); UNPHU, B.S. in Accounting; PUCA-MAIMA, graduate studies in stock market; Certified Public Accountant. **Personal:** Married to Vivian Ravelo in 1996. Mr. Cruz enjoys stamp collecting, reading and spending time with his family.

Misako Ishimura
Assistant Vice President
The Sanwa Bank Limited
55 East 52nd Street
New York, NY 10055–0002
(212) 339–6300
Fax: (212) 754–1853
EMAIL: See Below

6081

Business Information: The Sanwa Bank Limited, head office in Osaka and headquarters in Tokyo, is the leading commercial bank in the world. Ms. Ishimura joinied The Sanwa Bank Limited in 1986. She is responsible for the control and management of expenses, such as the processing of expense reports. Internet users can reach her via: SANWAIRD@PAN-IX.COM. **Career Steps:** Assistant Vice President, The Sanwa Bank Limited (1991–Present); Executive Secretary, Mitsui OSK Limited (1985). **Associations & Accomplishments:** Sachiyo Ito Dance Company; Theodore Gordon Flyfishers. **Education:** Wakayagi, Natori for Japanese Traditional Dance; Kwansei Gakuin University, B.A. of Art. **Personal:** Ms. Ishimura enjoys flyfishing during her leisure time.

Kuldeep Kishore
Head of Strategic Planning
Michigan National Corporation
27777 Inkster Road (10–00)
Farmington Hills, MI 48333–9065
(810) 473–5281
Fax: (810) 473–3086

6081

Business Information: Michigan National Corporation, a wholly–owned subsidiary of National Australia Bank, Ltd., is a financial services provider. As Head of Strategic Planning, Mr. Kishore is responsible for strategic planning, practice transfers, mergers, and aquisitions. **Career Steps:** Director of Strategic Planning, Michigan National Corporation (1995–Present); National Australia Bank: Group Manager (1993–1995), Controller (1990–1993); Senior Consultant, Price Waterhouse Urwick (1989–1990). **Associations & Accomplishments:** Royal Automobile Club of Victoria; British Institute of Management. **Education:** Vanderbilt University, M.B.A. (1977); University of Delhi, M.A., B.Sc. Honors. **Personal:** Married to Mrs. Usha Kishore in 1976. Two children: Vishaal and Monica. Mr. Kishore enjoys photography.

Jonathan B. Lipschitz
Vice President
Chemical Bank
52 Broadway, 8th Floor
New York, NY 10004
(212) 701–6829
Fax: (212) 701–4829

6081

Business Information: Chemical Bank is a full–service global financial institution providing a full spectrum of services to include loans, investments, checking and savings, and mortgage financing. As Vice President, Mr. Lipschitz is responsible for all aspects of operations concerning the corporate tax compliance area, including the supervision of employees. Other duties include consolidated tax returns, tax savings and the management of overall tax liability. **Career Steps:** Vice President, Chemical Bank (1983–Present); Corporate Tax Manager, Spicer & Oppenheim CPA's (1981–1983); Senior Tax Accountant, Buchbinder, Stein, Tunick & Platkin CPA's (1977–1981). **Associations & Accomplishments:** American Institute of Certified Public Accountants; New Jersey State Society of Certified Public Accountants; New York State Society of Certified Public Accountants; Certified and licensed as a CPA in New York and New Jersey. **Education:** Ithaca College, B.S. in Accounting (1977); Certified CPA in

New York and New Jersey. **Personal:** Married to Debra K. Katcher in 1983. One child: Bryan. Mr. Lipschitz is an avid tennis player, enjoys all areas of sports and is also a bird enthusiast.

Gilberto Lopez
Work Out Loan Officer
Banco Santander
P O Box 193522
San Juan, Puerto Rico 00919–3522
(787) 759–7070 EXT: 212
Fax: (787) 754–4338

6081

Business Information: Banco Santander, headquartered in Spain, is a full service commercial bank offering checking, savings, personal and commercial loans, investment programs, and trust accounts. Banco Santander P.R. has total assets on deposit of $4,507 million and deposits over $3,290 million. As Work Out Loan Officer, Mr. Lopez collects past due accounts handling approximately 300 accounts worth over $24 million. He is currently assisted by two credit officers. **Career Steps:** Work Out Loan Officer, Assistant Vice–President, Banco Santander, Puerto Rico (1992–Present); Financial Analyst Assistant Treasurer, The Chase Manhattan Bank, N.A. (1989–92). **Associations & Accomplishments:** Certified Public Accountant (1993); Treasurer (1994) and Vice–President (1996) Home Owners Association; Secretary (1996) Banco Santander Bowling League. **Education:** University of Puerto Rico, B.S.B.A. Three (3) majors, Accounting, Finance & Marketing; GPA; 3.73: Interamerican University of P.R., MBA Finance; In Process, Current GPA: 4.00 **Personal:** Mr. Lopez enjoys bowling, basketball, tennis, and collecting music and movies.

John D. Lung Jr.
Marketing Manager
Coutts & Co. (Cayman) Limited
P.O. Box 1584
Grand Cayman, Cayman Island
(345) 945–4777
Fax: (345) 945–4799

6081

Business Information: Coutts & Co. (Cayman) Limited is one of the leading international private banking institutions, with offices in the world's top 20 financial centres. Coutts is regarded as the leading offshore private bank, serving high net worth individuals and Global Fortune 1000 companies by providing sophisticated investment management, trust administration, company management, mutual fund administration, and banking services. As Marketing Manager, Mr. Lung is responsible for developing a regional marketing strategy, new business development, and client service. He travels extensively on behalf of the Bank. **Career Steps:** Coutts & Co. (Cayman) Limited: Marketing Manager (1993–Present), Coutts & Co. Trust Holdings, Representative (Miami) (1992–1993). Coutts & Co. (Uruguay) S.A., Deputy Marketing Manager (1989–1991); Hong Kong and Shanghai Banking Corporation, (Madrid), Analyst (1987). **Associations & Accomplishments:** (Society of Trust and Estate Planners (STEP); Cayman Islands Bankers Association. **Education:** I.E.S.E. (Spain–Universidad de Navarra/Harvard), Bilingual M.B.A. (1988); University of Texas, Austin Bachelor's Degree in Art (1986). **Personal:** Married to Maria del Mar Batlle in 1989. Two children: John Nicholas Alexander and Carolina Alexandra Lung. Mr. Lung enjoys spending time with his family, scuba diving, rowing, sailing, cycling, skiing, golf, and reading.

Terrence A. Lyons
••• ◀▬▬ ◉ ▬▬▶ •••

President
B.C. Pacific Capital Corporation
1055 W. Georgia St., Suite 1632
Vancouver, British Columbia V6E 3R5
(604) 669–3141
Fax: (604) 687–3419

6081

Business Information: B.C. Pacific Capital Corporation is a merchant bank and investment company specializing in providing financial services and security investments to the mining, oil and gas industries. Established in 1988, the Company employs three people, and has estimated annual revenue of $20 million. As President, Mr. Lyons oversees all aspects of the Company. A Co–Founder, he is responsible for assisting clients with financial investments, administration, operations, finance, sales, public relations and strategic planning. **Career Steps:** President, B.C. Pacific Capital Corporation (1988–Present); Versatile Corporation: Executive Vice President (1986–1988), Vice President, Marine (1983–1986).

Associations & Accomplishments: Heart and Stroke Foundation; Governor of Trust, Special Olympics. **Education:** University of Western Ontario, M.B.A. (1974); University of British Columbia, B.A.Sc. in Civil Engineering (1972). **Personal:** Married to Julie Paul in 1990. One child: Whitney Samantha. Mr. Lyons enjoys charities, skiing, and golf.

Dominic J. Mercuri
Vice President of Target Marketing
Canada Trust
161 Bay Stroot, 33rd Floor
Toronto, Ontario
(416) 361–8006
Fax: (416) 361–8134

6081

Business Information: Canada Trust offers financial services to customers through 410 branch offices throughout Canada. Services offered include checking, savings, mutual funds, estate planning, insurance, and financial advice. As Vice President of Target Marketing, Mr. Mercuri is responsible for direct marketing of services, product advertising for various business lines, telemarketing, branch advertising, and media advertising. **Career Steps:** Vice President of Target Marketing, Canada Trust (1992–Present); General Manager, CIBC (1990–1992); Direct Marketing Manager, Royal Trust (1989–1990). **Associations & Accomplishments:** Canadian Direct Marketing Association. **Education:** McMaster University, B.A. (1980). **Personal:** Married to Carol in 1982. Two children: Jennifer and Frank. Mr. Mercuri enjoys golf and sports.

J. Nelson Avilla
Senior Economist
International Development Bank
3003 Van Ness Street, N.W., Apt. South 811
Washington, DC 20008–4701
(202) 623–1848 Ext.1848
Fax: (202) 623–2152

6081

Business Information: International Development Bank is the largest bank in Latin America, providing all aspects of banking and financial services to clients. Established in 1962, the Bank is headquartered in Washington, D.C., and has branches in Japan, Europe, and France, as well as several field offices worldwide. As Senior Economist, Mr. Nelson Avilla brings over forty years of experience to his position. He is responsible for overseeing and advising companies on financial matters, and forecasting revenues and profits for large corporations. **Career Steps:** Senior Economist, International Development Bank (1992–Present); Programs Coordinator, United Nations/U.N.D.P. (1988–1992); Professor, Central American Economics–Postgraduate (1986–1987). **Associations & Accomplishments:** President, Staff Association, International Development Bank (1992–1996); Former President, Honduran Association of Economists; Former President, Honduran Association of Certified Public Accountants; Former Dean, Honduran University. **Education:** Universite de Paris I, Doctorate (1985); Universite D'Aix, Marseille II, Master of Science (1981); INCAE, Nicaragua, Postgrade in Administration (1975); Honduran University; C.P.A., Economist (1977). **Personal:** Married to Belen Maria in 1975. Two children: Ana Luisa and Tania Libertad. Dr. Nelson Avilla enjoys reading, music, writing novels, and painting.

Andre Jafferian Neto
••• ◀▬▬ ◉ ▬▬▶ •••

Finance Director
Banco Sofisa, South America
R. Libero Badro, 509
Sao Paulo, Brazil 01009–000
(011) 605.0131
Fax: (011) 606.6867

6081

Business Information: Banco Sofisa, South America, is a financial group with a commercial bank, broker–dealer, leasing company, and an off–shore bank. As Finance Director, Mr. Neto is responsible for the oversight of all financial and accounting activities. **Career Steps:** Finance Director, Banco Sofisa, South America (1993–Present); Director, Banco Credito Sao Paulo (1989–1993); Director, Zogbi D.T.V.M. (1986–1989); Manager, Patente C.C.V.M. (1984–1986). **Education:** Universidade Sao Paulo, Engineering (1984). **Personal:** Married to Marcia in 1986. Two children: Fernando and Renata. Mr. Neto enjoys jogging.

Jose Felix Padilla Mejia

General Manager
Interbank S.A.
P O Box 3107
Managua, Nicaragua
505–2–785–95
Fax: 505–7–835–37

6081

Business Information: Interbank S.A. is a commercial private bank located in Nicaragua. The Bank offers services in checking, savings, loans, and investments in eight locations throughout Nicaragua. As General Manager, Mr. Padilla Mejia is accountable for the activities of all eight branches of the Bank. He handles public relations, strategic planning, and coordinates and controls all operations of the Bank. **Career Steps:** General Manager, Interbank S.A. (1994–Present); Vice General Manager, Banco Nicaraguense, S.A. (1984–1994); Attached Vice President, Banco Central De Nicaragua (1982–1984). **Associations & Accomplishments:** Asociacion Nicaraguense de Profesionales de la Administracion; Camara de Comercio de Nicaragua; American Nicaraguan Chamber of Commerce; Asociaion de Bancos Privados de Nicaragua–ASOBANP. **Education:** INCAE, M.S.C B.A. (1990); Unan Nicaragua: Master Degree in Business Economy, Bachelor in Business Administration (1974) **Personal:** Married to Patricia Leiva in 1974. Four children: Linda, Jose, Ilce, and Ruben. Mr. Padilla Mejia enjoys reading/writing about economic issues, swimming, chess, and jogging.

Luis E. Perez, CPA

Vice President and Controller
Roig Commercial Bank
P.O. Box 457
Humacao, Puerto Rico 00792–0457
(809) 850–6314
Fax: (809) 850–6377

6081

Business Information: Roig Commercial Bank is a full–service financial institution with 25 branch locations throughout Eastern Puerto Rico . As Vice President and Controller, Mr. Perez is responsible for all financial transactions regarding the lending institution. **Career Steps:** Vice President and Controller, Roig Commercial Bank (1983–Present); Senior Auditor, Ernst & Young (1980–1983). **Associations & Accomplishments:** Colegio de Contadores Publicos Autorizados de Puerto Rico. **Education:** University of Puerto Rico, B.B.A. (1980); Certifications: Certified Public Accountant, CBA. **Personal:** Married to Ivette Ramirez. Two children: Emmanuel and Elizabeth. Mr. Perez enjoys church activities and basketball.

Oneida Perez Acosta, J.D.

Attorney
Banco Popular de Puerto Rico
P.O. Box 36–6818
San Juan, Puerto Rico 00936
(787) 753–7849
Fax: (787) 751–7827

6081

Business Information: Banco Popular de Puerto Rico is a full service banking facility. One of the largest and most prestigious banks, it was established in 1893, and is native to the island. With numerous locations throughout Puerto Rico, New York and St. Thomas (U.S. Virgin Islands), the Bank offers consumer and commercial services. among others, and employs around 6,000 people. As Attorney, Mrs. Perez Acosta concentrates in bankruptcy, both consumer and corporate, and is responsible for assisting and advising the bank accordingly. **Career Steps:** Attorney, Banco Popular de Puerto Rico (1992–Present); Attorney, Chapter 13 Trustee, Puerto Rico (1990–1992). **Associations & Accomplishments:** Puerto Rico Bankruptcy Bar Association; American Bar Association; Colegio de Abogados de Puerto Rico. **Education:** University of Puerto Rico Law School, J.D. Cum Laude (1990); University of Puerto Rico, B.A. in Arts and Political Sciences, Magna Cum Laude. **Personal:** Married to Ray Jones Quinones in 1985. Two children: Ray Jones Jr. and Diego Alejandro. Mrs. Perez Acosta enjoys reading, calligraphy, movies, and bike riding.

Marcello Augusto Pinto

Manager
Lloyds Bank PLC
Av. Brig. Faria Lima 2020 15 Andar
Sao Paulo, Brazil 01481–900
(11) 818–8478
Fax: (11) 818–8373

6081

Business Information: Lloyds Bank PLC is an international wholesale bank offering security and expertise in local and international vices, encompassing trade finance, corporate finance, corporate and private banking custody, and investment products. Based in London, Lloyds Bank has locations worldwide, including eleven branches in Brazil. As Manager, Mr. Pinto is responsible for the management of all marketing activities, including interbank relations, products and services, marketing planning, institutional marketing, press communications, advertising, and database marketing. **Career Steps:** Lloyds Bank PLC: Manager (1995–Present), Senior Analyst (1993–1995), Trainee (1992–1993). **Associations & Accomplishments:** Associacao Brasileira de Anunciantes – ABA (Brazilian Advertisers Association); Associacao Brasileira das Emprasas of Marketing Direto – ABEMO (Brazilian Direct Marketing Companies Association); Clube dos Executivos de Marketing (Marketing Executives Club). **Education:** MacKenzie University, B.A. in Business Administration (1991). **Personal:** Mr. Pinto enjoys reading, diving, and cooking.

Yolanda Rosich

Assistant Vice President and Private Banker
Banco Popular de Puerto Rico
Munoz Rivera Avenue, No. 209 Banco Popular Center 4th Floor
Hato Rey, Puerto Rico 00918
(787) 281–5168
Fax: (787) 751–9118

6081

Business Information: Banco Popular de Puerto Rico is a full service banking facility. One of the largest and most prestigious banks, it was established in 1893, and is native to the island. With numerous locations throughout Puerto Rico, the Bank offers consumer and commercial loans, and employs 6,000 people. As Assistant Vice President and Private Banker, Ms. Rosich assists high networth clients with financial planning and investments. **Career Steps:** Assistant Vice President and Private Banker, Banco Popular de Puerto Rico (1995–Present); Assistant Under Secretary of the Administrative Appeals Division, Puerto Rico Department of the Treasury (1993–1995); Tax Manager, Price Waterhouse (1986–1993); Accountant, Vega Palau & Co. (1983–1986). **Associations & Accomplishments:** American Institute of Certified Public Accountants; Puerto Rico Society of Certified Public Accountants; Certified Financial Planner Licensee. **Education:** University of Puerto Rico, Bachelor (1986); Certified Public Accountant, Certified Financial Planner, License Series 7; Broker of bank and investment products. **Personal:** Married to Edgar Torrellas in 1989. Ms. Rosich enjoys volleyball and beach sports.

Daniel Strumphler

Group Vice President
ABN AMRO Bank
500 Park Avenue
New York, NY 10022–1606
(212) 446–4153
Fax: (212) 754–6114

6081

Business Information: ABN AMRO Bank, a U.S. subsidiary of a foreign–based financial institution, specializes in international banking, with emphasis on Western European and Asian countries. With regional headquarters located in Chicago, Illinois, ABN AMRO's locations encompass 64 countries in all. As Group Vice President, Mr. Strumphler is responsible for managing the group serving international companies conducting business in the U.S. **Career Steps:** ABN AMRO Bank: Group Vice President (1994–Present), Vice President (1990–1993); Senior Analyst, ING (1990–1991); Director, T–D Bank (1987–1989). **Associations & Accomplishments:** Dutch Citizen (Native Language); Conversant in German and French. **Education:** Delft University, M.B.A. (1981); Leiden University, J.D.

Miguel Garcia Suarez

Legal Counsel
First Financial Bank
P O Box 10832
San Juan, Puerto Rico 00922–0832
(787) 756–1881
Fax: (787) 756–1815

6081

Business Information: First Financial Bank is a mortgage bank holding company for several banks in Puerto Rico. The Bank also has offices in New York and Florida. First Financial Bank began operations in 1971 and currently has 300 employees. As Legal Counsel, Mr. Suarez concentrates on cases dealing with labor, taxes, and corporate and banking law. He is responsible for recruitment, training, scheduling, evaluating, and counseling of his staff members. **Career Steps:** Legal Counsel, First Financial Bank (1971–Present); Legal Counsel, Fomento Corporation (1968–1971). **Associations & Accomplishments:** Mortgage Bankers Association; Puerto Rico Bank; Federal Bank; Phi Eta Mu Fraternity. **Education:** University of Puerto Rico, L.L.B. (1968). **Personal:** Married to Clara in 1981. Six children: Richard, Maria Teresa, Javier, Rocio, Coral, and Mishel. Mr. Suarez enjoys surfing the internet and playing dominoes.

Hiroko Tatebe

Senior Vice President and Treasurer
Dai–Ichi Kangyo Bank of California
555 West Fifth Street
Los Angeles, CA 90013–3033
(213) 612–2810
Fax: (213) 612–2875

6081

Business Information: Dai–Ichi Kangyo Bank of California — a wholly–owned subsidiary of Japanese–based banking conglomerate Dai–Ichi Ltd. — is a full–service commercial bank, operating from three branches in Los Angeles, Torres, and San Jose. Serving in various executive roles for Dai–Ichi since 1986, Hiroko Tatebe was appointed as Senior Vice President and Treasurer in 1991. Working from the Los Angeles main branch, she provides the overall supervision for California support centers, with duties including operations, investments, human resources, administration, accounting, and EDP. In addition, she is in charge of the divisions of Planning, Credit and Loans. **Career Steps:** Dai–Ichi Kangyo Bank of California: Senior Vice President and Treasurer (1991–Present), Vice President and Treasurer (1990–1991), Vice President and Senior Operations Officer (1986–1990). **Associations & Accomplishments:** Women in Business; Financial Women International. **Education:** Whittier College, B.A. (1973); Bank Administrative Insitute – Graduate School of Banking (1983); Certified Financial Planner (1988). **Personal:** Ms. Tatebe enjoys the theater, music, and travel.

Angeles Torres Sanchez

Assistant Trust Officer
Oriental Bank and Trust
P.O. Box 191429
San Juan, Puerto Rico 00919–1429
(787) 766–1986
Fax: (787) 274–1165

6081

Business Information: Oriental Bank and Trust is a commercial service bank providing financial and related services to clients. Formerly a savings bank, the Facility has a subsidiary brokerage house "Oriental Financial Services Corporation", as well as sixteen locations throughout the island. Established in 1964, the Bank employs 310 people, and has assets of approximately $877 million. As Assistant Trust Officer, Mrs. Torres Sanchez assists the Senior Vice President of the trust department, supervises other employees, and manages all services, retirement, and financial planning. **Career Steps:** Assistant Trust Officer, Oriental Bank and Trust (1990–Present); Associate Lawyer, Lasa, Escalera & Reichard (1988–1990); Tax Accountant Senior, Ernst & Young (1986–1988). **Associations & Accomplishments:** Collegio de Abogados de Puerto Rico; Fund Raiser for Catholic Schools Scholarship Program; Fund Raiser for several Civic Entities. **Education:** University of Puerto Rico Law School, J.D. (1986); University of Puerto Rico, B.B.A. in Accounting; School of Mortgage Banking of the M.B.A., Washington D.C. **Personal:** Married to Henry Vitier in 1979. Three children: Nicole, Lauren, and Gregorie. Mrs. Torres Sanchez enjoys reading, recycling, and counseling.

David Cortina

Managing Director
Canadian Imperial Bank of Commerce
425 Lexington Avenue
New York, NY 10017–3903
(212) 856–3851
Fax: (212) 856–3892

6082

Business Information: The second largest bank in Canada and in the top ten of U.S. banks, Canadian Imperial Bank of Commerce is an international, full–service banking and lending organization. In operation since 1850, Canadian Imperial currently employs 1,200 people in the U.S. offices, and offers banking services in London, Canada, and the Far East, as well as Los Angeles, Houston, Atlanta and Boston. As Managing Director, Mr. Cortina is responsible for the supervision of auditing efforts in the United States, and global derivatives for brokers and dealers. In addition to his banking responsibilities, he has participated in financial management networks, lectures and internal presentations. The Canadian Imperial Bank of Commerce has featured Mr. Cortina numerous times in their internal publications as a result of his exceptional work. **Career Steps:** Managing Director, Canadian Imperial Bank of Commerce (1994–Present); Vice President of Auditing, Swiss Bank Corporation (1988–1994); Assistant Controller, Bowery Saving Bank (1987–1988). **Associations & Accomplishments:** New York State Society of Certified Public Accountants; American Institute of Certified Public Accountants; Education Committee Chairman, Association of International Bank Auditors. **Education:** Adelphi University, M.B.A. (1991); St. Bonaventure University, B.B.A. in Accounting (1977). **Personal:** Married to Debra Ann in 1978. Three children: Eric, Melissa and Michael. Mr. Cortina enjoys coaching Little League and soccer.

Armida Garaygordobil

Vice President
Bankers Trust Company
300 South Grand Avenue 41st Floor
Los Angeles, CA 90071
(213) 620–8353
Fax: (213) 620–8381

6082

Business Information: Bankers Trust Company is the 8th largest commercial banking and financial service institution in the United States with 82 offices worldwide and $104 billion in assets. As Vice President, Ms. Garaygordobil serves as the international private banker for the West Coast division, particularly focusing on all Mexican accounts management. **Career Steps:** Vice President, Bankers Trust Company (1992–Present); Vice President, First International Bank (1988–1992). **Associations & Accomplishments:** U.S. Mexico Chamber of Commerce; Marymount Alumni Association. **Education:** University of Arizona (1969) **Personal:** Ms. Garaygordobil enjoys needle point, courses, university computer.

Salomon Kalmanovitz, Ph.D.

Co–Governor
Banco de la Republica
Cra. 7 No. 14–78 Piso 6
Bogota, Colombia
(57) 13347380
Fax: (57) 12819734

6082

Business Information: Banco De La Republica is Colombia's Central Bank. It controls money, interest rates and foreign exchange policy. Appointed as Co–Governor of Banco de la Republica in 1993, Dr. Kalmanovitz is one of five full–time members of the Board, making decisions on macro–economic analysis and policy, monetary policy, and administration. The members of the Board are all nominated by the President of Colombia for a term of four years. **Career Steps:** Co–Governor, Banco de la Republica (1993–Present); Universidad Nacional: Dean of Economics (1991–1993), Professor (1975–1991). **Education:** New School: M.A. (1969), Ph.D. candidate (1970); University of New Hampshire, B.A. **Personal:** Two children: Manuel and Pablo. Dr. Kalmanovitz enjoys reading, computers, and studying history.

Georgia Kimble

Vice President
Bank of America
1000 West Temple Street, Department 5195
Los Angeles, CA 90012–1514
(213) 240–6036
Fax: (213) 240–6030

6082

Business Information: Bank of America is an international financial institution specializing in commercial banking. Bank of America is the largest retail bank in the U.S., as well as rated the second largest commercial bank. Joining Bank of America in 1990, Ms. Kimble was appointed as Vice President in 1993. She serves as the Customer Service Manager for lockbox remittance processing, serving about 900 customers and overseeing 1400 lockboxes. Her department is paper–based (processing checks), with future plans to expand into automation. She is responsible for a team of 8 people and 6 support offices, as well as managing the processing, corrections, taking telephone calls, and working with the sales force. **Career Steps:** Bank of America: Vice President (1993–Present), Manager Customer Service (1992–1993), Manager of Operations (1990–1992). **Associations & Accomplishments:** Urban League of Los Angeles; Recipient of awards for high quality performance and for working at the local men and women's shelter. **Education:** El Camino College, A.A. (1968); University of California – Los Angeles; Los Angeles City College. **Personal:** Married to Lonnie in 1965. Ms. Kimble enjoys working with women, children and men shelters, and creative NAS (Neighbors Always Sharing).

Hector P. Lanfranco

Foreign Debt Trader
Banco Medefin U.N.B.
25 De Mayo 489 2nd Piso
Buenos Aires, Argentina 1339
54–1–318–1300
Fax: 54–1–318–1328

6082

Business Information: Banco Medefin U.N.B., a wholly–owned Argentinian commercial banking institution, provides international banking and financial trading in Argentina and other Latin American countries. Established in 1975, Banco Medefin U.N.B. currently employs 260 people. With ten years experience in accounting and banking matters, Mr. Lanfranco joined Banco Medefin in 1989. Serving as Foreign Debt Trader, he is responsible for processing debt papers of Latin American countries, keeping up–to–date on current events, and following investments on a day–to–day basis. **Career Steps:** Foreign Debt Trader, Banco Medefin U.N.B. (1989–Present); Account Executive, Corresponsal de Bear Stearns (1985–1989). **Associations & Accomplishments:** Jockey Club de Argentina. **Education:** Cardenal Newman College, B.A. (1980). **Personal:** Married to Francis Obesio in 1993. Mr. Lanfranco enjoys golf, tennis, collecting stamps, coaching and playing rugby, and water skiing.

Manuel R. Manotas

Executive Vice President, General Manager
Banco Ganadero
1150 S. Miami Ave.
Miami, FL 33130–4111
(305) 374–3955
Fax: (305) 374–8187

6082

Business Information: Banco Ganadero is the largest international bank in Colombia, currently comprised of 185 branches in Colombia and one in Miami, Florida. A management executive with Banco Ganadero serving at various subsidiary locations since 1984, Manuel Manotas was transferred to the Miami, Florida branch in April of 1995. As General Manager and Executive Vice President, Mr. Manotas is responsible for the management and direction of all banking activities, concentrating on promoting trade finance between Colombia and the U.S. **Career Steps:** Banco Ganadero: General Manager, Miami (1995–Present), Senior Vice President International, Colombia (1988–1995), General Manager, Panama (1984–1988). **Associations & Accomplishments:** Colombian Banking Association, Miami Chapter. **Education:** Universidad Santo Tomas de Aquino, Law and Political Sciences (1975), Universidad "Colegio Mayor de Nuestra Senora del Rosario", B.A. in Private Law. **Personal:** Married to Magdalena. Mr. Manotas enjoys fishing, bicycling, scuba diving, and spending time with his family.

Jeremy Mitchell

Personnel Manager
Bank of New York
48 Deer Park Avenue
Babylon, NY 11702–2802
(516) 321–1978
Fax: (516) 669–3424

6082

Business Information: The Bank of New York, rated as #1 in cost efficiency, is a full–service international commercial banking establishment. Bank of New York has 389 branches in the regional area of Suffolk County, with other branches worldwide. Joining the Bank of New York as Personnel Manager in 1990, Mr. Mitchell directs the operations of the Management Training Program, as well as heading up the Personnel Department for 49 of the 389 branches in the New York area. **Career Steps:** Personnel Manager, Bank of New York (1990–Present); HM Forces – British Army (1978–1990). **Associations & Accomplishments:** The Life Guards Association; Combermere Barracks, Windsor, England. **Education:** Army Education Center Airbright, B.A. in History (1983); The City and Guilds of London, Certificate in Communication Skills and Management. **Personal:** Married to Susan in 1990. Mr. Mitchell enjoys tennis and sailing.

Kenneth C. Ng

Vice President and Branch Manager
Nanyang Commercial Bank, Ltd.
50 California Street, 31st Floor
San Francisco, CA 94111
(415) 398–8866
Fax: (415) 398–0871

6082

Business Information: Nanyang Commercial Bank, Ltd. is an international commercial bank with only one branch in the U.S. With corporate offices located in Hong Kong, Nanyang Commercial Bank, Ltd. specializes in the provision of commercial banking functions to corporate customers. As Vice President and Branch Manager, Mr. Ng is responsible for all aspects of operations for the San Francisco branch, including international import and export trading, trade finance, and supervision of a staff of 20. **Career Steps:** Nanyang Commercial Bank, Ltd.: Vice President and Branch Manager (1987–Present), Assistant Vice President and Head of Credit Department (1984–1987). **Education:** San Francisco State University, Finance (1995). **Personal:** Married to May M. in 1989. Two children: Yvonne and Melinda. Mr. Ng enjoys travel, jogging, and photography.

Mr. Mark A. Norton

President and Chief Executive Officer
International Merchant Finance, Ltd.
435 Sixth Avenue
Pittsburgh, PA 15219
(412) 288–8590
Fax: (412) 288–8589

6082

Business Information: International Merchant Finance, Ltd. (IMFIN) is a limited partnership specializing in analyzing, structuring, documenting, and arranging debt and equity financing for trade and project transactions worldwide. The Company also advises corporations and banks on international finance matters including mitigation of risks, privatization and joint venture financing. The general partner of IMFIN is International Merchant Finance Company, a Pennsylvania corporation (100% owned by Mr. Norton). As President and Chief Executive Officer, Mr. Norton is responsible for overseeing all aspects of company operations, profitability and efficiency. Mr. Norton founded IMFIN in 1993, following a 25–year career in international banking in both money center and regional commercial banks in the U.S. and Europe. He has successfully structured, negotiated, documented and implemented numerous multimillion dollar export and international project transactions as well as public and private offerings in capital markets totaling in excess of $5 billion (U.S.). He and his family emigrated from Poland to the U.S. in 1982 (when Martial Law was declared), and became naturalized citizens in 1990. **Career Steps:** President and Chief Executive Officer, International Merchant Finance, Ltd. (1993–Present); Senior Vice President and Manager, ABN AMRO Bank, N.V. (1990–1993); Senior Vice President and Manager, Security Pacific Trade Finance, Inc. (1987–1990); Vice President and Assistant Manager, PNC/Pittsburgh National Bank (1983–1987); Director, Bank Handlowy w Warszawie S.A. and Financial Attache of Poland to the United States (1979–1982); various management positions at Bank Handlowy w Warszawie S.A. (1970–1979). **Associations & Accomplishments:** Board of Directors, Pittsburgh Council for International Visitors (1990–1993). **Education:** Main School of Economics, Warsaw, Poland, M.Sc. in Economics (1970); Colgate Darden Graduate School of Business Administration at the University of Virginia.

Michael A. Reynal

Vice President
Union Bank of Switzerland
299 Park Avenue
New York, NY 10171-0002
(212) 821-6158
Fax: (212) 821-3778

6082

Business Information: The Union Bank of Switzerland is an international investment banking institution. Established in 1947, the Union Bank of Switzerland currently employs 2,000 people and reports assets of over $40 billion. As Vice President, Mr. Reynal is responsible for the origination and execution of international privatization and financing issues, as well as Corporate mergers. In the banking business for over ten years, Mr. Reynal is a world expert on economic relations and has been published in the English Oxford Library. **Career Steps:** Vice President, Union Bank of Switzerland (Present); Head of the Latin American Desk, Barclays de Zoete Wedd; Representative, Condor Securities; Associate, Chase Manhattan Bank. **Associations & Accomplishments:** Mr. Reynal is fluent in English, Spanish, French, Portuguese and Italian. **Education:** Yale University, B.A. (1983); Oxford University, Economic Relations; M.Litt Thesis Degree. **Personal:** Married to Michaela. Two children: Michael and Sophia. Mr. Reynal enjoys tennis, polo, Latin American art and wildlife.

Nelson Rodriguez–Lopez

General Counsel and Executive Vice President
Banco Bilbao Vizcaya – Puerto Rico
461 Sagrado Corazon
San Juan, Puerto Rico 00915
(809) 277-3793
Fax: (809) 277-3891

6082

Business Information: Banco Bilbao Vizcaya – Puerto Rico, the largest bank in Spain and one of the largest in the world, is an international financial institution, specializing in banking, commercial, trading, and securities. Banco Bilbao Vizcaya currently has 6,000 branches located throughout the world, reporting $110 billion in assets and employing 68,000 people corporate–wide. A practicing attorney in Puerto Rico courts since 1976, Mr. Rodriguez–Lopez joined the Corporation in 1991. Serving as General Counsel and Executive Vice President, he provides legal counseling in international commercial finance, regulatory, compliance, securities, legislation, and Corporate matters. **Career Steps:** General Counsel and Executive Vice President, Banco Bilbao Vizcaya – Puerto Rico (1991–Present); General Counsel and Vice President, Caguas – Central Federal Savings Bank (1984–1991); Chief Legal Counsel, Governor of Puerto Rico – Honorable Carlos Romero Barcelo (1981–1984); Chief Legal Counsel, President of the Senate – Honorable Luis A. Ferre (1977–1981). **Associations & Accomplishments:** Puerto Rico Bar Association; Federal Bar Association; Academia Interamericana; Supreme Court of the USA; Supreme Court of Puerto Rico; General Secretary, National Republican Party of Puerto Rico; Counseling Board, NAFTA; Board of Examiners (1983, 1984), Supreme Court of Puerto Rico; Counsel, Luis A. Ferre Foundation and Ponce Art Museum. **Education:** University of Puerto Rico: J.D. (1976), B.A. (1972); Oxford University – England, B.A. (1973); University of Sorbonne – Sorbonne, Paris, Summer International Program (1970). **Personal:** One child: Jaime A. Alcover Rodriguez. Mr. Rodriguez–Lopez enjoys painting, writing, music, and travel.

James L. Kermes

President and Chief Executive Officer
Glenmede Trust Company
1650 Market Street, Suite 1200
Philadelphia, PA 19103-7301
(215) 419-6036
Fax: (215) 419-6196

6091

Business Information: Glenmede Trust Company specializes in investment management and tax planning for high net worth individuals and institutions. Their main objective is to assist clients in the preservation and/or enhancement of their wealth by investments and minimizing unnecessary taxes. Glenmede Trust Company also has a complete division of 120 people that only administer grants for the Pugh Charitable Foundation, a $3.7 billion trust fund established by the founders of Sun Oil. Joining Glenmede Trust Company as President and Chief Executive Officer in 1995, Mr. Kermes is responsible for all aspects of operations. **Career Steps:** President and Chief Executive Officer, Glenmede Trust Company (1995–Present); Chief Investment Officer, The Northern

Trust Company (1991–1995); President and Chief Investment Officer, C&S Investment Advisors (1985–1991); Chief Investment Officer, SunBank (1980–1985). **Associations & Accomplishments:** Investment Performance Presentation Standards; Implementation Committee, Association for Investment Management and Research; Board Member, YMCA; Board Chairman, Metro Atlanta Recovery Residences; President Council, Arts and Sciences for Central Florida; Trinity Preparatory School: Board Member, Finance Committee Chairman. **Education:** Hamilton College, B.A. in History (1962). **Personal:** Married to Patricia in 1965. Two children: Kevin and Suzanne "Suki". Mr. Kermes enjoys restoration of old homes, gardening, and golf.

Sandra L. Sherman

Trust Operations Consultant
Union Bank of California
530 B Street, Suite 204
San Diego, CA 92101
(619) 230-3095
Fax: Please mail or call

6091

Business Information: Union Bank of California is an international establishment equipped to meet the needs of the banking and trust world. With a diverse background in Trust Operation Services, Ms. Sherman, a knowledgeable, progressive, analytical consultant, joined the Bank in March 1996. She exhibits expertise as a Systems Specialist, and has innovative ideas for implementing efficiencies, along with improving the quality of the outgoing services. While staying abreast of constant growth and change in the banking industry, she has placed herself in a select group of professionals. **Career Steps:** Trust Operations Consultant, Union Bank of California (1996–Present); North American Trust Company: Vice President of Operations (1990–1996), Operations Supervisor (1988–1990), Special Project Clerk (1987–1988). **Associations & Accomplishments:** American Bankers Association; Cuong Nhu Oriental Martial Arts Association; San Diego League. **Education:** Pepperdine University, B.S. (1986); CTOS – Canon Trust School. **Personal:** Ms. Sherman enjoys martial arts, water skiing, sailing, and teaching self–defense classes.

Robert L. Young

Vice President and Chief Internal Auditor
United National Bank & Trust Company
153 Lincoln Way East
Massillon, OH 44646
(216) 830-7250
Fax: (216) 830-7257

6091

Business Information: United National Bank & Trust Company is a governmental regulated, government or governmentally commercial bank specializing in commercial, mortgage and consumer lending. Established in 1854, United National reports assets of over $650 million. As Vice President and Chief Internal Auditor, Mr. Young is responsible for all audit functions, including the supervision of the audit staff to completion of regulatory and compliance requirements. He reports to the Audit Committee and the Board of Directors. Under his direction, the entire Auditing Department/Function were completely automated. **Career Steps:** Vice President and Chief Internal Auditor, United National Bank & Trust Company (1991–Present); Assistant General Auditor, P.N.C. Bank (1989–1991); Regional Audit Supervisor, Central Bancorporation (1986–1989); Branch Auditor, First National Bank of Ohio (1978–1986); Security Specialist, United States Air Force (1971–1975). **Associations & Accomplishments:** Cleveland, Akron, and Canton Chapters, Institute of Internal Auditors; Boy Scouts of America; Former Committee Chairman, Cub Scout Troop 3118. **Education:** University of Akron, B.S. in Business Administration and Accounting (1979); University of Wisconsin – Madison, Bank Administration Diploma; Ohio University, Ohio School of Banking, successfully completed courses in Bank Management, Personnel Administration, Funds Management, Profitability Analysis, Organizational Performance, Investment Policies, Bank Lending and Bank Law; The School for Bank Administration, Audit Training. **Personal:** Married to Carol in 1972. Two children: Brian and Zachary. Mr. Young enjoys golf, professional photography, and computer sciences and applications.

Keith F. Browning

Senior Risk Analyst
Travelers Express
1550 Utica Avenue, South
Minneapolis, MN 55416
(612) 591-3391
Fax: (612) 591-3399
EMail: See Below

6099

Business Information: Travelers Express is the world's largest processor of money orders and financial services, such as utility bill payments, home banking, and payment systems. As Senior Risk Analyst, Mr. Browning analyzes financial risk to Travelers Express and makes recommendations to reduce risk among customers. Internet users can reach him via: 102503,104@compuserve.com. **Career Steps:** Travelers Express: Senior Risk Analysts (1993–Present), Human Resource Representative (1994–1996); Credit Analyst, Oscar Mayer Foods Corporation (1990–1993). **Associations & Accomplishments:** United Way Chairperson: Fund raising, Charity; National W Club Alumni Association. **Education:** University of Wisconsin – Madison, B.A. in Economics (1987). **Personal:** Married to Elizabeth in 1989. Two children: Tatyana and Taylor. Mr. Browning enjoys competitive sports and investing.

Mr. J. Paul Leger

President and Chief Executive Officer
United States Foreign Exchange
71 Dewey Avenue
Warwick, RI 02886-2431
(401) 732-7000 Ext: 5550
Fax: (401) 732-7019
EMAIL: See Below

6099

Business Information: United States Foreign Exchange (USFX) is an international currency risk underwriter. Joining USFX as President and Chief Executive Officer in 1993, Mr. Leger is responsible for all aspects of administrative and operational procedures, in addition to overseeing an associate and administrative support staff of 50. He can also be reached through the Internet via: USFX@ICHANGE.COM **Career Steps:** President and Chief Executive Officer, United States Foreign Exchange (1993–Present); President, IRD (1981–1993); President, Commander Board Signs (1976–1981). **Associations & Accomplishments:** International Society of Financiers; Nautical Research Guild; U.S.S. Constitution Modelers Guild; Mystic Seaport Museum; American Management Association; International Society of Financiers; Who's Who of Executives. **Education:** SMU – Canada: MBA in Finance (1976), B.Comm. in Investments (1974), C.I.F. (1993). **Personal:** Married to Louise in 1974. Mr. Leger renjoys hiking, skiing, yachting, wood working, and building models.

6100 Nondepository Institutions

Pedro Alicea

Human Resources Director
Cooperative A/C Arecibo
P.O. Box 1056
Arecibo, Puerto Rico 00612
(809) 878-2095
Fax: (809) 880-1609

6111

Business Information: Cooperative A.C. Arecibo is a member–owned consumer banking institution serving members from eight branches throughout Puerto Rico — operating like U.S. credit unions. As Human Resources Director, Mr. Alicea directs all personnel policies and procedures, recruitment, benefits and training. **Career Steps:** Human Resources Director, Cooperative A.C. Arecibo (1994–Present); Human Relations, Me Salve, Inc. (1991–1994). **Associations & Accomplishments:** Quality Life Council, Chamber of Commerce of Puerto Rico; Founder, Puerto Rico Young Association; Vice President, National Employee Council of Puerto Rico Job Service. **Education:** Metropolitan University, M.B.A. (1995); University of Puerto Rico – Bayamon, Bachelor's Degree. **Personal:** Married to Edna R. Pagan in 1993. Mr. Alicea enjoys tennis, golf, and basketball.

James W. Hunter
Policy Analyst
Freddie Mac (Federal Home Loan Mortgage Corporation)
8200 Jones Branch Drive, MS# 275
McLean, VA 22102
(703) 903–2213
Fax: (703) 903–2338

6111

Business Information: Freddie Mac, a government enterprise in the secondary mortgage market, is a publicly traded security that represents participation in a pool of mortgages guaranteed by the Federal Home Loan Mortgage Corporation. As a Policy Analyst, Mr. Hunter establishes and monitors official credit policies. Established in 1970, Freddie Mac (Federal Home Loan Mortgage Corporation) employs 3,500 people. **Career Steps:** Policy Analyst, Freddie Mac (Federal Home Loan Mortgage Corporation), (1991–Present); Senior Credit Analyst, Continental Federal Savings Bank (1989–1991); Credit Analyst, S&T Bank (1986–1988). **Associations & Accomplishments:** American Bar Association; Pennsylvania Bar Association. **Education:** Georgetown University School of Law, LL.M. (1995); George Mason University School of Law, J.D. (1992); University of Miami, M.B.A. (1986); College of William & Mary, A.B. (1985). **Personal:** Married to Denise A. Hunter in 1994.

William G. Knight
President/Chief Executive Officer
Credit Union Central of Canada
300 The East Mall
Toronto, Ontario M9B 6B7
(416) 232–1262
Fax: (613) 730–1475

6111

Business Information: Credit Union Central of Canada is a national credit union that requires only a fee to become a member. As President/Chief Executive Officer, Mr. Knight is responsible for all aspects of Company operations, including administration, financial, and strategic planning. **Career Steps:** Credit Union Central of Canada: President/Chief Executive Officer (1995–Present), Vice President – Government Affairs Unit (1989–1995); Federal Secretary, New Democratic Party of Canada (1987–1988); Principal Secretary, New Democratic Federal Leader, the Hon. Ed Broadbent (1982–1987); Principal Secretary, Premier of Saskatchewan, the Hon. Allan Blakeney (1979–1982). **Associations & Accomplishments:** Commissioner, Royal Commission on Electoral Reform and Party Finance; Member of Board of Directors, Ontario International Trade Corporation; Member of Board of Directors, Credential Securities, Inc.; Member of Board of Directors, Douglas Coldwell Foundation; Member of Advisory Board, Centre for the Study of Business–Government–NGO Relations, Carleton University; Member of Executive Committee, Association of Former Parliamentarians; Member of Parliament (1971–1974). **Education:** University of Saskatchewan: Bachelor of Arts (1968), Bachelor of Education (with distinction) (1970). **Personal:** Married to Tessa Hebb in 1989. Five children: Andrea, Donald, Matthew, Ben, and Nick.

Nancy B. Parker
Vice President and Director of Information Services
Federal Home Loan Bank – Dallas Branch
5605 North MacArthur Boulevard, Suite 900
Irving, TX 75038–2617
(214) 714–8606
Fax: (214) 714–8783

6111

Business Information: Federal Home Loan Bank – Dallas Branch is part of the 12 Federal Reserve Bank Districts. The Dallas branch covers a five state, Southwestern–Midwest region and provides banks, insurance companies, mortgage companies, and other lending organizations the financing available for consumer home loans. As Vice President and Director of Information Technology, Ms. Parker is in charge of all data processing communication needs of the Dallas branch of the Federal Home Loan Bank. She is involved in the design and implementation of new communication and data systems. Ms. Parker works with other managers to determine exactly what data processing services are needed and assists with the development of training programs for staff members on new and existing systems. **Career Steps:** Vice President and Director of Information Technology, Federal Home Loan Bank – Dallas Branch (1993–1996); Senior Technical Specialist,

Champion International (1983–1987); Senior Analyst, Harris Computers (1983–1983); Programmer/Analyst, Cryovac Division of W. R. Grace (1978–1980). **Education:** Furman University, B.S. (1975). **Personal:** Married to John in 1991. One child: Michael. Ms. Parker enjoys gardening and reading.

Scott M. Callaway
Vice President and Manager
Barnett Bank
11800 Research Parkway
Orlando, FL 32833
(407) 650–5472
Fax: (407) 381–4020

6141

Business Information: Established in 1898, Barnett Bank is a financial services organization providing banking services, including personal loans, credit cards, investment packages and mortgages to consumers and corporate customers worldwide. At present, there are 629 branch locations in Florida. As Vice President and Manager, Mr. Callaway is responsible for all aspects of business development, the annual budget, marketing, and sales, as well as motivation and employee coaching. **Career Steps:** Vice President and Manager, Barnett Bank (1985–Present). **Associations & Accomplishments:** Kiwanis International; Board Member, Florida Hospital Foundation; Junior Achievement; American Institute of Banking. **Education:** Roy E. Crammer Graduate School – Rollins College, M.B.A (1992); University of Florida, Finance and Insurance. **Personal:** Married to Mary in 1986. Two children: Adam and Mitchell. Mr. Callaway enjoys riding his Harley Davidson motorcycle, golf, basketball, and camping.

Maxine Carr
President
Educational Loan Restructuring Service (ELRS)
3300 S. Gessner Road, Suite 259
Houston, TX 77063–5740
(713) 952–4623
Fax: (713) 952–7999

6141

Business Information: Educational Loan Restructuring Service (ELRS) is a company that assists consumers and organizations, in the areas of resolving defaulted student loan debt and student loans debt management. The Company does this through education, and instruction, and has worked with over 200 borrowers with defaulted student loans. ELRS has also consulted with large companies such as, Management Adjustment Bureau Collection Agency and Consumer Credit Counseling Service, and has successfully handled the restructuring of over $2 million in defaulted student loans. As President, Ms. Carr specializes in resolving consumers' defaulted student loan problems, and handling all aspects of Company operations. **Career Steps:** President, Educational Loan Restructuring Service (ELRS) (1994–Present); Chairperson – Political Involvement Committee, Coalition of 100 Black Women (1995); Collection Manager/Director of Training, Metropolitan Resource Corporation (1994); Collection Manager, Surpas Resource Corporation (1993). **Associations & Accomplishments:** Former Chairperson of Political Involvement Committee, National Coalition of 100 Black Women. **Education:** Educational Enrichment Center (1988); Center for Advanced Legal Studies; Houston School of Business, Paralegal Studies. **Personal:** Three children: John P., Ryan P., and Courtney M. Carr.

William Compton
Branch Director
Associates
2432 W. Main Street
Norristown, PA 19403–3049
(610) 539–6400
Fax: (610) 539–8537

6141

Business Information: Associates, owned by Ford, is an international full–service financial company with 1,200 offices located throughout the U.S., Puerto Rico, England, and Japan. As Branch Director, Mr. Compton manages a $13 million branch budget, wherein he controls expenses, losses, and profitability. He is additionally responsible for delinquencies, branch employees, and the general business of the Norristown branch. **Career Steps:** Associates: Branch Director (1995–Present), Branch Manager (1993–1995); Branch Manager, ITT (1987–1993). **Associations & Accomplishments:** Chamber of Commerce; Better Business Bureau. **Education:** Wilkes University, Bachelor's degree (1987); Lackawanna Junior College, Associate's degree in Accounting and Business Administration. **Personal:** Married to Trish in 1992. One child: Kaitlyn. Mr. Compton enjoys golf, boating, and skiing.

Tedd Craven
Director of Corporate Consulting
PHH Corporation
3 Rocklan Road
West Harrison, NY 10604
(203) 796–1299
Fax: (203) 796–3518
EMAIL: See Below

6141

Business Information: PHH Corporation is a services company with three major sectors: PHH Relocation Management Services, which assists clients with real estate and relocation needs, PHH Mortgage Services, which specializes in home financing, and PHH Vehicle Management Services, which provides clients with fleet leasing. Established in 1946, the Company has locations throughout the U.S., Canada, Germany, and the United Kingdom. As Director of Corporate Consulting, Mr. Craven is responsible for business process re–engineering facilitation coupled with technology identification and implementation. Concurrent to his position with PHH Corporation, Mr. Craven is also the owner of Topcatt Studios, a full service recording studio. Internet users can reach him via: Masc622@Gnn.com. **Career Steps:** Director of Corporate Consulting, PHH Corporation (1984–Present); Director of Data Processing, Medical Scientific International (1979–1984); Director of Information Services, Hospital Bureau Incorporated (1982–1984); Owner, Topcatt Studios (Present). **Associations & Accomplishments:** Board of Directors, PHH Atrium Insurance; House Captain, Past Five Years, Americares Homefront; Volunteer, West Chester Association for Retarded Children. **Education:** West Chester College, Civil Engineering (1969); United State Air Force, Electronics Major. **Personal:** Married to Melanie in 1977. Two children: Emily and Jesse. Mr. Craven enjoys playing in a number of orchestras and owning his own recording studio.

Michael J. Cunningham
Vice President of Operations
American Express Company
200 Vesey Street
New York, NY 10285–3490
(212) 640–3364
Fax: (212) 619–7080

6141

Business Information: American Express, established in 1960, specializes in worldwide financial and travel related services. The Company consists of three divisions: IDS, American Express and Travel Related Services. American Express currently employs 50,000 people worldwide and has an estimated annual revenue of $1 billion. As Vice President of Operations, Mr. Cunningham is responsible for all aspects of billing, payment processing, budget operations, as well as re–engineering and strategic design implementation. **Career Steps:** American Express Company: Vice President of Operations (1992–Present), Vice President of Finance (1984–1992); Finance Manager, Chemical Bank (1982–1984); Auditor, CIT Financial Corporation (1979–1982). **Associations & Accomplishments:** Association for Retarded Citizens; "Challenger" Little League; Special Olympics; National Down Syndrome Organization. **Education:** Pace University: M.B.A. (1984), B.S.; Certified Public Accountant, New York State (1981).

John C. DeSantis
Vice President
Fleet Credit Card Services
225 Rainbow Mall
Niagara Falls, NY 14303
(716) 286–2516
Fax: (716) 286–2594

6141

Business Information: Fleet Credit Card Services, a wholly–owned entity of Fleet Financial Group, provides the management and administration of credit card applications for the parent company. A managerial executive with Fleet Services subsidiaries since 1987, John DeSantis was appointed to his current position in March of 1995. As Vice President and Site Manager of the Niagra Falls credit card processing headquarters, he is responsible for the oversight of the departments of Accounting and Settlement, Security and Fraud, Card Holder Services, Merchant Services, and Systems Support. **Career Steps:** Vice President and Site Manager, Fleet Credit Card Services (1995–Present); Vice President and Senior Operations Group Manager, Fleet Services Corporation – Retail Loans (1989–1995); Assistant Vice President, Fleet/Norstar Services – Syracuse (1987–1989). **Associations & Accomplishments:** Past Chairman, United Way Campaign; Past Chairman, Finance Committee for James St. United Methodist Church. **Education:** SUNY–Oswego (1975); Onondaga Community College; American Institute of Banking. **Person-

al: Married to Judith Ann in 1982. Three children: Stephanie, Tiffany, and Elizabeth. Mr. DeSantis enjoys golf, football, and spending quality time with his family.

Ronald A. Donatelli
Vice President and Regional Manager
BTM Capital Corporation
Six PPG Place, Suite 820
Pittsburgh, PA 15222–5406
(412) 391–5200
Fax: (412) 391–3001

6141

Business Information: BTM Capital Corporation is a wholly-owned subsidiary of Bank of Tokyo – Mitsubishi, Ltd. As Vice President and Regional Manager, Mr. Donatelli provides administrative and marketing direction to the Pittsburgh Loan Production Office, overseeing personnel and developing future expansion plans. The Pittsburgh office specializes in asset based lending. **Career Steps:** Vice President and Regional Manager, BTM Capital Corporation (1995–Present); Vice–President, National Canada Finance Corporation (1984–1995). **Associations & Accomplishments:** Board Member, Commercial Finance Association – Pittsburgh Chapter. **Education:** LaRoche College, B.S. in Business (1981). **Personal:** Married to Mary Lynn in 1982. One child: Erik. Mr. Donatelli enjoys sports and golf.

(Gladys) Anahir Fuster
Credit Review Process Officer
Banco Popular de Puerto Rico
Home Mortgage Plaza 12th Floor 268 Ponce de Leon Avenue
Hato Rey, Puerto Rico 00918
(787) 765–9800
Fax: (787) 754–8845

6141

Business Information: Banco Popular de Puerto Rico is a full–service international bank offering checking, savings, commercial loans, personal loans, trust services, and investment services to residents of Puerto Rico, the Virgin Islands and portions of the United States. The Bank currently has 180 branches worldwide. As Credit Review Process Officer, Ms. Fuster conducts financial analysis of loans, analyzes risk involvement, approves and disburses funds, and calculates the percentages to be applied to applicants. **Career Steps:** Credit Review Process Officer, Banco Popular de Puerto Rico (1995–Present); Senior Auditor, Price Waterhouse (1992–1995). **Associations & Accomplishments:** Puerto Rico State Society of Certified Public Accountants; American Institute of Certified Public Accountants. **Education:** University of Puerto Rico, Bachelor degree (1992) and starting second year of law school; Certified Public Accountant (1994).

Richard F. Gaccione
Managing Director of Marketing
Citibank
430 Orienta Avenue
Mamaroneck, NY 10543
(718) 248–5446
Fax: Please mail or call

6141

Business Information: Citibank provides national credit card services for Citibank Mastercard and Visa cards. As Managing Director of Marketing, Mr. Gaccione directs all marketing aspects of Visa/Mastercard operations for Citibank in the U.S., as well as overseeing 25 million accounts, advertising functions, and card member relationships. **Career Steps:** Managing Director of Marketing, Citibank (1994–Present); President and Chief Executive Officer, Hieleman Brewery (1994); President–Consumer Products Division, Bristol Myers Squibb (1991–1993); President – Bayer Aspirin Co., Kodak (1988–1991); President, Lysol Products (Kodak) (1985–1988). **Associations & Accomplishments:** Board Member, YPO – Metro New York; Columbus Citizens Foundation; Board Member – Marketing Advisory, VISA. **Education:** Wharton Graduate, M.B.A. (1970); Brooklyn College, B.S. in Mathematics and Economics. **Personal:** Married to Rosanne in 1970. Two children: Victoria and Douglas. Mr. Gaccione enjoys skiing, tennis, and fundraising for Brooklyn College.

Donald J. Gleason

Executive Vice President
SmartCash, Inc.
2929 East Camelback Road, Suite 222
Phoenix, AZ 85016
(602) 954–7760
Fax: (302) 791–7644

6141

Business Information: SmartCash, Inc. is a financial services firm, providing stored value systems. Its mission is to develop and promote the use of SmartCard in the financial industry in the U.S. SmartCash, Inc. provides a liaison with the top 20 financial institutions, including Visa and Mastercard. Co-founding SmartCash, Inc. in 1995, Mr. Gleason serves as Executive Vice President. He serves as the Director of Market Development, providing market development consisting of sales, marketing, client relations, product development, and government relations. **Career Steps:** Executive Vice President, SmartCash, Inc. (1995–Present); Electronic Payment Services, Inc.: President of Smart Card Enterprises (1993–1995), President of Money Access Service (1991–1993); Senior Vice President, CoreStates Financial Corporation (1988–1991). **Associations & Accomplishments:** Electronic Funds Transfer Association; Visa Stored Value Working Group; Pi Kappa Alpha Alumni Association. **Education:** Villanova University, B.A. (1970). **Personal:** Married to Janice in 1989. Three children: Marc, Cary, and Steven. Mr. Gleason enjoys boating, golf, and jogging.

William D. Hooper
Vice President
Citicorp/Citibank
1 Court Square 12th Floor
Long Island City, NY 11120–0001
(718) 248–7901
Fax: (718) 248–7997
EMAIL: See Below

6141

Business Information: Urrutia Valles, Inc., the third largest insurance company in Puerto Rico, is an insurance broker for all lines of insurance, focusing on commerical and personal insurance in the San Juan area. Established in 1980, Urrutia Valles, Inc. reports premium revenue of $2.5 million and currently employs 25 people. As Vice President, Mr. Hooper is one of 450 such Officers for Citibank worldwide. Assigned to Citishare Corporation, as Marketing Director he oversees all marketing and customer relations for the subsidiary. Citishare is one of the world's foremost global ATM/POS electronic funds transfer networks. **Career Steps:** Vice President, Citicorp/Citibank (1979–Present); Instructor, Electronic Imaging, The New School/Parsons School of Design (1991–1993); Senior Profitability Analyst, American Airlines (1978); Senior Consultant, Arthur Andersen and Company (1975–1978); Research Assistant, Columbia University (1971–1973). **Associations & Accomplishments:** Electronic Funds Transfer Association; Electronic Banking and Economics Society; International Platform Association; Associate Member, Professional Photographers of America; Photo Marketing Association; Affiliate Member, American Society of Media Photographers; Theta Tau National Professional Engineering Fraternity; Former Vice President, Alumni Council St. Paul's School; St. Luke's Church; Who's Who of Emerging Leaders in America; Who's Who in the East; Dictionary of International Biography; International Book on Honor; 5,000 Personalities of the World; Community Leaders of America; Personalities of America; International Who's Who of Intellectuals; Men and Women of Distinction; International Leaders in Achievement; Men of Achievement; The International Directory of Distinguished Leadership; ABI Medal of Honor Commemorating Distinguished Lifelong Achievements; Two Thousand Notable American Men; International Cultural Diploma of Honor; Most Admired Men and Women of the Year; The 20th Century Award for Achievement; International Who's Who of Contemporary Achievement. **Education:** Columbia University: M.B.A. (1974), M.S. in Engineering (1973), B.S. in Engineering (1971), Dean's List (1970); Northwestern University, IBM Systems Science Institute; New York Institute of Photography, Certificate in Professional Photography (1990); Arthur Andersen Consultant's Training School. **Personal:** Married to Cathleen Collins in 1982. One child: W. Craig. Mr. Hooper enjoys sailing, cycling, photography, and classical & new age music.

Mitchell C. Kahn
President/Chief Executive Officer
First Merchants Acceptance Corporation
570 Lake Cook Road, Suite 126
Deerfield, IL 60015–4910
(847) 948–9300
Fax: (847) 948–9303

6141

Business Information: First Merchants Acceptance Corporation is a specialty consumer finance company that provides credit services to automobile dealers nationwide, enabling them to assist clients in the purchase of previously owned automobiles. As President/Chief Executive Officer, Mr. Kahn oversees the daily operation of the Company and as the Company's Principal Executive Officer is charged with the responsibility for the direction and supervision of all of the Company's business and operations. **Career Steps:** President/Chief Executive Officer, First Merchants Acceptance (1991–Present); President and Chief Executive Officer, First Credit (1989–1991); Senior Vice President, Mercury Finance (1983–1989); General Counsel, General Finance (1979–1983). **Associations & Accomplishments:** Illinois Financial Services Association; American Financial Services Association; Consumer Bankers Association; Entrepreneur of the Year, Illinois/Northwest Indiana Region (1995). **Education:** Illinois Institute of Technology, J.D. (1978); Kent College of Law; University of Illinois, B.A. (1975). **Personal:** Married to Susan in 1974. Two children: Andy and Tyler. Mr. Kahn enjoys tennis and golf.

Rajeev Kapur
Senior Project Manager
American Express
6225 North 24th Parkway, 2nd Floor
Phoenix, AZ 85016
(602) 553–6136
Fax: (602) 553–6139

6141

Business Information: American Express specializes in worldwide financial and travel related services. The Company consists of three divisions: American Express Financial Advisors, IDS, and American Express Bank and Travel Related Services. Mr. Kapur currently serves as Senior Project Manager for one out of eight worldwide initiatives to reengineer TRS. He is responsible for the formulation of the project mission, objectives and scope together with the tactical execution of all development and implementation strategies. He is currently involved with a project that integrates the total customer relationship by linking a combination of card products, services and benefits, across the American Express Credit card franchise. Established in 1958, American Express currently employs 50,000 people. **Career Steps:** Senior Project Manager, American Express (1991–Present); Airline Program Manager, AlliedSignal Aerospace Company (1990–1991); Sales and Marketing Manager, AlliedSignal Aerospace Company (1989–1991). **Associations & Accomplishments:** Authored article in Industrial Engineering (Dec. 1984). **Education:** University of Houston, M.B.A. (1983); Bangalore University, India, B.S. in Mechanical Engineering (1981). **Personal:** Married to Sadhana in 1983. Two children: Nikita and Sheena. Mr. Kapur enjoys racquet sports (tennis and squash), theater, and whitewater rafting.

Bozena Lesniowski
Executive Manager, Chief Executive Officer
United Poles, F.C.U.
412 New Brunswick Avenue
Perth Amboy, NJ 08861
(908) 442–5648
Fax: (908) 442–1443

6141

Business Information: United Poles, F.C.U. is a financial institution dedicated to serving the Polish community of the New Jersey area. A local credit union, the Bank is full–service and handles transactions, savings and checking accounts, rand loans. As Executive Manager and Chief Executive Officer, Ms. Lesniowski manages all personnel and interacts with loan officers. She is responsible for Bank advertising and marketing and for overall Bank administration. **Career Steps:** Executive Manager, Chief Executive Officer, United Poles, F.C.U. (1985–Present); Assistant Professor, E.P.A. Center Katowice (1972–1976); Assistant Professor, Jagiellonian University (1971–1972). **Associations & Accomplishments:** Z.P.A. United Poles in America; Polish Scouting Organization of America. **Education:** Economy Academy of Katowicki Poland, Ph.D. in Disseration (1975); Jagiellonian University, M.A. in Sociology. **Personal:** Married to Lester in 1968. One child: Lukasz. Ms. Lesniowski enjoys reading and theater.

Carlos H. Miyares Jr.

Vice President
Associates Financial
250 East Carpenter Freeway #3D
Irving, TX 75062
(214) 541–4958
Fax: Please mail or call

6141

Business Information: Associates Financial provides loans to consumers to finance real estate and or retail endeavors. A public Company as of May, 1996, Associates Financial focuses primarily on Hispanic clientele, and is national in scope, with twenty–one locations among Florida, Illinois, California and New York. As Vice President, Mr. Miyares oversees all aspects of branch expansion and improvement. Responsible for expanding the Company from five to eleven branches, and increasing revenue by $11 million, Mr. Miyares also handles various administrative and operational duties. **Career Steps:** Associates Financial: Vice President (1995–Present), Group Vice President (1994–1995). **Education:** University of South Florida, A.A. (1983). **Personal:** Married to Lora in 1986. Four children: Carlos IV, Sterling, Dillon and Berton. Mr. Miyares enjoys jogging, weightlifting, and racquetball.

Gil Moro

Vice President of Marketing
American Express D.O. Brasil
Av. Maria Coelho Aguiar 215 Bloco F 8th Floor
Sao Paulo, Brazil 05804–900
5511–3741–7171
Fax: 5511–3741–8281

6141

Business Information: American Express D.O. Brasil specializes in worldwide financial and travel–related services. The Company consists of three divisions: American Express Financial Advisors, IDS, American Express Bank and Travel Related Services. As Vice President of Marketing for Latin America, Mr. Moro is responsible for approximately 100 staff members and handles client retention, marketing, database, and related activities. **Career Steps:** Vice President of Marketing, American Express D.O. Brasil (1996–Present); Director of Marketing, American Express (1989). **Associations & Accomplishments:** Alumni Association of Engineers; Marketing Executives Association. **Education:** University of California – Los Angeles, M.B.A. (1985); University of Sao Paulo – Brazil, Civil Engineering (1981). **Personal:** Married to Simone Cenovicz. One child: Mariana Cenovicz. Mr. Moro enjoys fishing.

Pilar Rodriguez

Director of Human Resources
American Express Co.
14901 NW 79th Court
Hialeah, FL 33016
(305) 820–7581
Fax: (305) 820–7509

6141

Business Information: American Express Co. specializes in worldwide financial and travel related services. The Company consists of three divisions: American Express Financial Advisors, IDS, American Express Bank and Travel Related Services. As Director of Human Resources, Ms. Rodriguez's key responsibilities encompass assessing, developing, and implementing short– and long–term Human Resource strategies, and creating and integrating models and tools for assessing training and development needs. She is responsible for creating and staffing an internal and external executive database, identifying creative sourcing strategies to build high quality, diverse candidate pipelines, adhering to Human Resources compliance requirements. As part of employee benefit administration, she ensures business compliance with governmental regulations pertaining to Human Resources and the employee/labor laws for the Latin America region. **Career Steps:** American Express Co.: Director of Human Resources (1995–Present), Manager Human Resources Training and Development (1994–1995), Senior Management Development Consultant (1993–1994), International Consultant/Team Developer (1992–1993), Accounts Relations Manager (1991–1992), New Accounts Senior Analyst/Anti–Attrition Analyst (1988–1991). **Associations & Accomplishments:** Society of Human Resources Management; American Society for Training and Development; American Compensation Association; American Society for Quality Control; Institute of International Human Resources. PC experience: Excel, Word for Windows, Powerpoint, Horizon, and HRIS. Verbal and written fluency in English, Spanish, French and Portuguese (in progress). Ms. Rodriguez has written numerous articles for in–house publications for American Express. **Education:** NOVA University, M.B.A. (1992); Instituto Tecnologico de Santo Domingo, B.S. in Economics (1983). **Personal:** Ms. Rodriguez enjoys tennis, landscaping and travel.

Mr. David Douglas Stone

Vice President of Worldwide Technologies Strategies
American Express TRS Co., Inc.
American Express Tower, World Financial Center, 40th Floor
New York, NY 10285
(212) 640–4697
Fax: Please mail or

6141

Business Information: American Express Co., Inc. specializes in worldwide financial and travel related services. The Company consists of three divisions: IDS, American Express Bank, and Travel Related Services. Mr. Stone is employed in the Travel Related Services Division. As Vice President of Worldwide Technologies Strategies, he is responsible for planning and executing technologies strategies to enable re-engineering and new product development. Established in 1850, American Express Co., Inc. employs over 65,000 people worldwide. **Career Steps:** Vice President of Worldwide Technologies Strategies, American Express TRS Co., Inc. (1994– Present); Vice President of Global Reengineering, American Express International (Asia/Pacific) (1993–1994); Vice President of Marketing and Sales, American Express International (Hong Kong) (1991–1993); Vice President of Marketing and Sales, American Express International (East Asia) (1990–1991). **Associations & Accomplishments:** Department of State Fellowship, U.S. Embassy, Bonn, Germany (1979). **Education:** The Fletcher School of Law, M.A. in International Relations (1992); Tufts University, B.A. in Political Science and German Studies (1980).

Lynn Zeck

Regional Senior Marketing Manager
American Express
12201 Merit Dr., Ste. 850
Dallas, TX 75251–2264
(505) 820–2693
Fax: (505) 820–2697

6141

Business Information: American Express specializes in worldwide financial and travel related services. The Company consists of three divisions: American Express Financial Advisors, IDS; American Express Bank and Travel Related Services. As Regional Senior Marketing Manager, Mrs. Zeck is responsible for all marketing and strategic planning, as well as working with merchants and sales organizations to develop market campaigns for card members. In addition, she is responsible for promoting tourism to a designated market. **Career Steps:** American Express: Regional Senior Marketing Manager (1992–Present), Account Executive (1983–1992), Territory Manager (1979–1983). **Associations & Accomplishments:** Santa Fe Restaurant Association; Santa Fe Opera; Southwestern Association of Indian Artists. **Education:** Georgia Southern College, Master of Education (1972).

Randal B. Gunn

Director of Collection Operations
National Credit Service
444 North Frederick Avenue, Suite 401
Gaithersburg, MD 20877–2432
(301) 670–6545
Fax: (304) 670–9731

6153

Business Information: National Credit Service provides the management of delinquent receivables for national and regional corporations and government agencies. As Director of Collection Operations, Mr. Gunn holds the senior management position responsible for joint management of operational departments. He establishes and implements corporate policy, procedures, and he directly manages delinquent receivables exceeding $180 million annually. **Career Steps:** Director of Collection Operations, National Credit Service (1988–Present); Field Representative, Mid State HOmes (1986–1988); Branch Manager, Jim Walter Homes (1983–1986). **Associations & Accomplishments:** Vice President, Seaboard Collectors Association; American Collectors Association; Scottish Heritage USA, Inc.; The Clan Gunn Society of North America. **Education:** Virginia Tech, B.S. (1981). **Personal:** Married to Paula M. Gregg in 1996. Mr. Gunn enjoys gardening, cooking, and reading.

Dane A. James

Group Vice President for Business Development
NOVUS Services, Inc.
2500 Lake Cook Road
Riverwoods, IL 60015–3851
(847) 405–3413
Fax: (847) 405–4520

6153

Business Information: NOVUS Services, Inc., a division of Dean Witter, Discover & Co., Inc., is a merchant account acquisition/management concern for credit cards. As Group Vice President for Business Development, Mr. James oversees the activities of seven managers at the Vice President level and their support staff. He is responsible for account management of over 900 top merchant clients as determined by sales volume with emphasis on the supermarket and warehouse club industries. Mr. James works with his staff in the development and implementation of marketing strategies, sales strategies, and budgets. **Career Steps:** Group Vice President for Business Development, NOVUS Services, Inc. (1995–Present); Discover Card Services, Inc.: Vice President–Supermarket Industry (1993–1995), National Manager–Franchise Development (1991–1993) **Education:** Indiana University, B.S. in Business (1983); University of Michigan, Executive Management Program. **Personal:** Married to Loraine in 1995. Mr. James enjoys running, skiing, and golf.

Ann Kathryn Rush

Project Manager
World Financial Network National Bank
4590 E. Broad Street
Columbus, OH 43213
(614) 755–3510
Fax: (614) 755–3456
EMail: See Below

6153

Business Information: World Financial Network National Bank provides proprietary and retail credit card services. As Project Manager, Ms. Rush designs, builds, and maintains mainframe and PC–based marketing systems for retail credit card portfolios. She also aids in the growth of the Company by acquisition of new accounts, setting up acquisition programs, and consulting with clients. Internet users can reach her via: arush@msgway.limited.net. **Career Steps:** World Financial Network National Bank: Project Manager (1992–Present), Senior Programmer Analyst (1989–1992), Programmer Analyst (1987–1989); Programmer Analyst, Bank One Support Services (1985–1987). **Education:** Ohio University, B.B.A. (1984). **Personal:** Married to Phillip in 1988. Ms. Rush has two daughters, and enjoys sewing, needlework, and cooking.

Renee R. Mang

Director
Sallie Mae
777 North Twin Creek Dive
Killeen, TX 76543
(817) 554–4882
Fax: (817) 554–4722

6155

Business Information: Sallie Mae is a Fortune 500 company specializing in originating loans for external lenders who, in turn, provide student loans and financial aid to college and university students. National in scope, the Company has branches throughout the United States and is the largest lending service in the Country. As Director, Ms. Mang oversees loan originations, lender, and college/university relations. Additional responsibilities include management of 200 employees, product development, and financial issues and budgeting. **Career Steps:** Director, Sallie Mae (1990–Present); Assistant Vice President, Marine Midland Bank (1988–1990); Manager, Goldome Bank (1986–1988). **Associations & Accomplishments:** Humane Society; Disabled Children; Associations for the Homeless; Associations for AIDS Patients. **Personal:** Married to Michael in 1978. One child: Michael. Ms. Mang enjoys theater.

William H. Holloway II

Director of Human Resources
Delta Card Services
16211 Park 10 Place
Houston, TX 77084
(713) 579–4471
Fax: (713) 579–4499

6159

Business Information: Delta Card Services provides Visa, Mastercard and American Express financial outsourcing for over 400 financial institutions nationwide. A branch of Delta Card Services is located in Jamaica providing data entry and credit card application processing for individuals and businesses located outside of the United States. Established in 1982, Delta Card Services currently employs 1,200 people and has an estimated annual revenue of $10 million. As Director of Human Resources, Mr. Holloway is responsible for all aspects of personnel, accounting and data processing. **Career Steps:** Director of Human Resources, Delta Card Services (1991–Present); Director of Human Resources, ECO Resourcers (1989–1991); Principal, Information Management (1985–1989); Marketing Representative, IBM (1975–1980). **Associations & Accomplishments:** Vice President, Human Resource Systems Professionals; Houston Personnel Association; Chairman, Every Member Canvass, Christ Church Cathedral; Parade Committee, Houston Livestock Show and Rodeo; Houston Chamber of Commerce, Chairman's and President's Awards; Board Member, Fort Bend Independent School District, Education Committee; Published in Human Resource Systems Professionals Magazine. **Education:** University of Houston, M.B.A. (1975); University of Texas, B.A. with honors; Wharton School of Finance, Certified Employee Benefit Specialist. **Personal:** Married to Lynn in 1977. Mr. Holloway enjoys jogging, tennis and scuba diving.

Charles W. Idol
Director of Process Engineering Design and Support
Citicorp/Citibank
14700 Citicorp Drive
Hagerstown, MD 21742–2201
(301) 790–4273
Fax: (301) 714–5814
EMAIL: See Below

6159

Business Information: CitiCorp/CitiBank is a financial services industry organization providing banking services to consumers and corporations worldwide. As Director of IST, Mr. Idol is responsible for the oversight of various operational functions of requirements, systems design, testing, and support. He has been responsible for the continued integration of emerging technology, such as Bankcards, Intranets and computer–based training. Mr. Idol has overseas experience supporting startup operations in Spain, Greece, Germany, and Brussels. In addition, he has owned and operated two successful private business ventures. **Career Steps:** CitiCorp/CitiBank (1985–Present): Director of IST, Director of Customer Service Phone Center, Multimedia CBT, Global Documentation, Advanced Workstation Development, Requirements Planning and Analysis. Other businesses: Sear Roebuck, American Express (Manager of Operations). **Associations & Accomplishments:** Mr. Idol has held positions on various organizational boards, such as The American Cancer Society. **Education:** St. Anselms College (1978); Various certificates and awards for continued education: AT&T Voice Data Communications, Capability and Maturity Model, Project Management, etc. **Personal:** Married to Lisa for 15 years. Mr. Idol enjoys enjoys being a musician and Maryland State soccer referee.

Allan L. Ludwigson
Senior Credit Officer
AgriBank, FCB
375 Jackson Street
St. Paul, MN 55101
(612) 282–8389
Fax: (612) 282–8462

6159

Business Information: Agribank, FCB, part of the Farm Credit System, established in 1916, and covering an 11–state area, is a wholesale lender to farm credit associations and other financial institutions. As Senior Credit Officer, Mr. Ludwigson specializes in the areas of the cattle, sugar beet, and potato industries and keeps current on the status of these industries. He is responsible for loan approval of loans which exceed farm credit associations' delegated authority. Each of these loans generally exceeds $3 million dollars. **Career Steps:** Agribank, FCB: Senior Credit Officer (1995–Present), Director of Association Credit Audit (1994–1995); Director of Loan Review (1992–1994). **Associations & Accomplishments:** Robert Morris Associates; Active in St. Patrick's Catholic Parish. **Education:** University of Wisconsin, B.S. in Agricultural Education. **Personal:** Married. Mr. Ludwigson enjoys golf, reading, and singing in the church choir.

Mrs. O. Machelle Morris
General Counsel
American Lenders Service Co.
312 E. Second Street
Odessa, TX 79761
(915) 332–0361
Fax: (915) 332–1065

6159

Business Information: American Lenders Service Co. is an international franchisor of collateral recovery businesses. As General Counsel, Mrs. Morris is responsible for all legal functions for the Company. Established in 1979, American Lenders Service Co. employs a staff of 45. **Career Steps:** General Counsel, American Lenders Service Co. (1979–Present). **Associations & Accomplishments:** Junior Women's Association of Midland, TX; Phi Alpha Delta Law Fraternity; Texas State Bar Association; American Bar Association. **Education:** Texas Tech University Law School, J.D. (1992); University of Texas at Austin, B.B.A. in Management (1989).

Mr. James G. Petcoff
Senior Financial Analyst
Finova Capital Corporation
95 North Route 17 South
Paramus, NJ 07652
(201) 712–3366
Fax: Please mail or call

6159

Business Information: Finova Capital Corporation is an international financial services company serving commercial and corporate clients. Headquartered in Phoenix, Arizona, Greyhound's service criteria include the lease and/or loan provision for commercial equipment, franchise support, aircraft lease, vendor services. As Senior Financial Analyst, Mr. Petcoff is responsible for portfolio valuation, financial pricing, modeling, cost of funds analysis, present value theory and internal rate of return. **Career Steps:** Senior Financial Analyst, Greyhound Financial Corporation (1993–Present); Staff Accountant and Financial Analyst, G.S. Imaging Services (1991–1993); Senior Cost Accountant, Simon & Schuster Inc. (1988–1990). **Associations & Accomplishments:** CompuServe Online Service; Rockland Astronomy Club; Computer Instructor. **Education:** St. Bonaventure University, B.B.A. (1988). **Personal:** Mr. Petcoff enjoys computers, softball, weightlifting and motorcycling.

Edward J. Shada
Vice President/Director of Public Finance
Advanta Financial Corporation
TransAm Plaza Dr., Suite 200
Oak Brook Terrace, IL 60181
(800) 423–8314
Fax: (801) 264–2953

6159

Business Information: Advanta Financial Corporation, a division of Fuji Banking in Japan, is a multi–billion dollar asset–based financing company for states and municipalities. As Vice President/Director of Public Finance, Mr. Shada is responsible for the public finance department of the Utah office. His department handles corporate programs valued in excess of $100 million dollars. **Career Steps:** Vice President/Director of Public Finance, Advanta Financial Corporation (1996–Present); Vice President, Clayton Brown Capital Corporation; Vice President, Westpac Banking Corporation; Vice President, The LINC Group, Inc. **Associations & Accomplishments:** Equipment Leasing Association; Association for Governmental Leasing and Finance; Government Finance Officers Association. **Education:** Creighton University, B.S. in Mathematics (1979). **Personal:** Married to Paula S. in 1982. One child: Alex. Mr. Shada enjoys skiing, fishing, hunting, motorcycle riding, and scuba diving.

Paul Snider

Senior Vice–President
Auto Marketing Network
2101 Corporate Boulevard, NW, Suite 316
Boca Raton, FL 33431
(407) 997–2440
Fax: (407) 995–0930

6159

Business Information: Auto Marketing Network, an indirect automobile lender, loans money for auto financing to clients who have had past credit problems. The average loan is $11,500 to $25,000 sub–prime. As Senior Vice–President, Mr. Snider is responsible for all aspects of Company operations, including marketing, training, and business development **Career Steps:** Senior Vice–President, Auto Marketing Network (1984–Present); President, Correct Course (1992–94); Vice–President, Hendrick Management (1988–92). **Associations & Accomplishments:** Thomas M. Holt Masonic Lodge; Addison Reserve Country Club; National Association of Sales Trainers; 1996 Speaker at NADA Convention, Las Vegas, Nevada. **Education:** Williams College, B.S. (1970); Attended: Chrysler Corporation Financial Training, General Motors Dealer Academy and NADA Dealer Academy. **Personal:** Married to Danna in 1980. Two children: Michael and Travis. Mr. Snider enjoys boating, golf, reading and horseback riding.

Thomas W. Steinke
President
Jordan Thomas, Inc.
P. O. Box 4842
Incline Village, NV 89450–4142
(702) 833–1414
Fax: (702) 833–2901

6159

Business Information: Jordan Thomas, Inc. is a firm specializing in mergers and acquisition in the leasing and equipment finance industry. Jordan Thomas, Inc. also handles venture and secondary capital and portfolio equity financing in the United States and Europe. As President, Mr. Steinke works with attorneys involved in the mergers or acquisitions and co–ordinates activities for the administrative staff of the companies involved. Future plans call for expansion of the firm and continued quick response to client needs. **Career Steps:** President, Jordan Thomas, Inc. (1985–Present). **Education:** Minnesota State University, B.A. (1971).

Karen Abram
Vice President
Countrywide Funding Corporation
400 Countrywide Way SV27
Simi Valley, CA 93065
(805) 520–5638
Fax: (805) 520–5415

6162

Business Information: Countrywide Funding Corporation, established in 1969, is the second largest mortgage banking institution in the United States. The Company originates and services mortgage loans for clients through 300 branches nationally or through the two service locations in Texas and California. As Vice President, Mrs. Abram directs the training activities for the service centers in California and Texas. Other responsibilities include direction of the in–house temporary services program and acting as a liaison between the two service centers and the 300 local branches. **Career Steps:** Countrywide Funding Corporation: Vice President, (1995–Present), Training Manager (1993–1995), Supervisor Customer Service (1992–1993). **Associations & Accomplishments:** American Society for Training and Development; International Society for Performance and Instruction. **Education:** University of Southern California, B.A. (1987). **Personal:** Married to Rick Abram, Sr. in 1994. Three children: Rick Abram, Jr., George Abram and Kaelen Abram. Mrs. Abram enjoys watching sports with her husband, swimming and quiet reading time.

Reinaldo Agostini

Vice President and Manager
Levitt Mortgage
Call Box 2119 Caparra Heights Station
San Juan, Puerto Rico 00922
(809) 781–9292
Fax: (809) 782–6650

6162

Business Information: Levitt Mortgage is a full–service mortgage banking institution with the ability to search, originate and close loans. Established in 1986, Levitt Mortgage currently employs over 50 people. As Vice President and Manager, Mr. Agostini is reponsible for the oversight of all banking operations. With hard work, a high amount of intelligence, dedication, enthusiasm, and the ability to never say no, Mr. Agostini has held a successful position with the Company for over six years, and hopes to do some consulting work after he retires. **Career Steps:** Vice President and Manager, Levitt Mortgage (1990–Present); Vice President and Production Manager, Puerto Rico Home Mortgage (1983–1989); Regional Director, Mortgage Guaranty Insurance Corporation (1973–1975). **Associations & Accomplishments:** Chapter President, Mortgage Loan Officers Association of Puerto Rico (1995); Chapter Member and Governor, Mortgage Bankers Association of Puerto Rico (1985); President, Puerto Rico Realtors Association; President, Bay Area Board of Realtors; President, Private Industry Council of San Juan. **Education:** University of Puerto Rico, B.B.A. (1959); Numerous professional certificates. **Personal:** Married to Elsa Escobar in 1960. Two children: Reinaldo and Ricardo. Mr. Agostini enjoys farming, and ornamental plants and flowers.

Carolyn J. Altobello
Production Manager
RBMG, Inc.
2700 Westhall Lane, Suite 110
Maitland, FL 32751
(407) 660–0300
Fax: (407) 660–9511

6162

Business Information: RBMG, Inc. specializes in mortgage banking which consists primarily of the purchase, sale, and servicing of residential first mortgage loans and the purchase and sale of servicing rights associated with such loans. As Production Manager, Ms. Altobello coordinates and supervises the sales and underwriting departments of the wholesale branch, evaluates production, and acts as a liaison between the brokers, wholesale office, and corporate office. **Career Steps:** Production Manager, RBMG, Inc. (1995–Present); Marketing Director, Seminole Title (1995); Sales & Underwriting Specialist, AmSouth Bank (1994–1995); Junior Underwriter, Fortune Bank (1993–1994); Mortgage Trader, Mortgage Funding Corporation of America. **Associations & Accomplishments:** Sigma Sigma Sigma; MBA; FAMB; APMW. **Education:** University of Michigan. **Personal:** Ms. Altobello enjoys golf, travel, and sky diving.

Steven R. Bailey
Senior Vice President
Countrywide Funding Corporation
400 Countrywide Way
Simi Valley, CA 93065–6298
(805) 520–5400
Fax: (805) 520–5416

6162

Business Information: Countrywide Funding Corporation is a mortgage loan servicing company. As Senior Vice President, Mr. Bailey is responsible for the management of customer contacts and training functions, including posting payments and managing client relations. He is also responsible for bringing automation into the Company. **Career Steps:** Countrywide Funding Corporation: Senior Vice President (1994–Present), Entry Level – 1st Vice President (1985–1994); Self–Employed (1982–1985). **Associations & Accomplishments:** Mortgage Business Association; Author of article in the "Servicing Management" Magazine (1992). **Education:** University of Southern California, Bachelors Degree in Music (1983). **Personal:** One child: Kindra. Mr. Bailey enjoys playing the guitar, recording music, golf, rollerblading, reading, and movies.

Dian D. Barker
Vice President and Manager
Bank of the Pacific
1007 Pacific Avenue
Long Beach, WA 98631
(360) 642–3777
Fax: (360) 642–3423

6162

Business Information: Bank of the Pacific is a regional, commercial, community, full–service, FDIC insured, equal housing lender. Five branches serve the residents of Pacific and Wahkiakum counties. As Vice President and Manager, Ms. Barker is the primary commercial lender, review appraiser, and main office manager at the Long Beach branch. **Career Steps:** Vice President and Manager, Bank of the Pacific (1975–Present). **Associations & Accomplishments:** Certified Appraiser in the State of Washington; Chairman, State Revolving Loan Board; Former President, Economic Development Council; Former Chair, Housing Authority. **Education:** University of California – Long Beach, B.A. in Psychology (1971). **Personal:** Two children: Ariel and Brent. Ms. Barker enjoys gardening, reading, playing piano, sports, and watching children play sports.

Shirin Behzadi, CPA
• • • ◄━━━━ ◎ ━━━━► • • •
Chief Financial Officer
The Hammond Company
4910 Campus Drive
Newport Beach, CA 92660
(714) 752–6671
Fax: (714) 724–4477

6162

Business Information: The Hammond Company is a mortgage banking company specializing in lending on residential properties. With one corporate headquarters and 13 branch offices, the Company works regionally, within five state. As Chief Financial Officer, Ms. Behzadi is responsible for all financial aspects of the Company, including budgeting, payroll, planning, and accounting. **Career Steps:** Chief Financial Officer, The Hammond Company (1993–Present); Auditor, Ernst & Young (1990–1993). **Associations & Accomplishments:** American Institute of Certified Public Accountants; California Society of Certified Public Accountants; Pending Approval for: Financial Executives Institute. **Education:** California Polytechnic University – Pomona, B.S. (1990). **Personal:** Married to Reza Madani in 1989. One child: Sam. Ms. Behzadi enjoys writing and jogging.

Mr. Kris W. Breon
Vice President
Sierra Tahoe Mortgage
690 East Plumb Lane, Suite 202
Reno, NV 89523
(702) 826–3737
Fax: (702) 826–3898

6162

Business Information: Sierra Tahoe Mortgage, a subsidiary of Truckee River Bank, is a mortgage origination company. As Vice President, Mr. Breon purchases mortgage loans and sells principal and servicing to investors. Established in 1980, Truckee River Bank employs over 120 people with Sierra Tahoe Mortgage annual sales of $60 million. **Career Steps:** Vice President of Secondary Marketing, Sierra Tahoe Mortgage (1994–Present); Assistant Vice President, Conduit Trade Desk, Shearson Lehman Mortgage (1986–1992); Secondary Marketing Manager, American Liberty Mortgage (1994). **Education:** Pepperdine University, M.B.A. (1992); California State University–Long Beach, B.S. in Finance. **Personal:** Married to Lori Breon in 1993. One child: Hayley Nicole.

Lacinda B. Cash, C.F.P.
Branch Manager
Ryland Mortgage
5500 Interstate North Parkway, Suite 240
Atlanta, GA 30328–4662
(770) 955–8555
Fax: (770) 955–7999

6162

Business Information: Ryland Mortgage is a full–service, mortgage processing and lending institution. Established in 1960, Ryland Mortgage currently employs 15 people. As Branch Manager, Lacinda Cash is responsible for all aspects of branch operations, including administration, operations, finance, public relations, marketing, human resources, strategic planning and marketing. **Career Steps:** Branch Manager, Ryland Mortgage (1994–Present); Branch Manger, Fleet Mortgage (1991–1994); Investment Officer, Mason State Bank (1988–1990). **Associations & Accomplishments:** Association of Professional Mortgage Women; Mortgage Banker's Association; 2,000 Notable American Women; World Who's Who of Women; Atlanta Board of Realtors; Home Builders Association; Cystic Fibrosis Foundation; Big Brothers/Big Sisters; Published several articles in trade magazines. **Education:** Calvin College, B.A. (1980); Certification: CFP (Certified Financial Planner) (1992); NASD Series 7. **Personal:** Ms. Cash enjoys running marathons, tennis, and water sports.

Arthur B. Clark
District Manager
Accu Banc Mortgage Corporation
1 Van de Graaff Drive
Burlington, MA 01803
(617) 270–5700
Fax: (617) 270–3100

6162

Business Information: Accu Banc Mortgage Corporation is a multi–million dollar corporation located in the New England region. An originator of mortgage loans from real estate professionals and non–traditional loan sources, the Firm also services the accounts. As District Manager, Mr. Clark oversees the operation for the four locations in New England. He is responsible for personnel concerns, department budgets, general accounting functions, marketing of services, and is involved in long–term planning for expansion and development of new services and markets. **Career Steps:** District Manager, Accu Banc Mortgage Corporation (1993–Present); Branch Manager, First Union Mortgage Corporation (1987–1993); Mortgage Loan Officer, Cityfed Mortgage Corporation (1981–1987) **Associations & Accomplishments:** Volunteer, Billerica House of Correction; Member of President's Club (seven years running). **Personal:** Married to Elizabeth in 1984. Three children: Lauren, Adam, and Alexandra. Mr. Clark enjoys boating, fishing, and swimming.

Mrs. Diana J. Clarke–Carter
Chief Executive Officer and Co–Owner
Summit Mortgage Corporation
10201 Wayzata Boulevard, Suite 350
Minnetonka, MN 55447
(612) 525–1150
Fax: (612) 525–1550

6162

Business Information: Summit Mortgage Corporation is a residential mortgage originator primarily in Minnesota, but licensed in 20 states. Established in 1992, Summit Mortgage Corporation reports annual revenue of $2 million and currently employs 30 people. As Chief Executive Officer, Mrs. Clarke–Carter is responsible for the overall direction of marketing, business development, and recruiting. She co–owns the Corporation with her husband. **Career Steps:** Chief Executive Officer and Co–Owner, Summit Mortgage Corporation (1992–Present); Mortgage Banker, Prime Mortgage (1989–1992); Mortgage Banker, Washington Square Mortgage (1989); Mortgage Banker, Investor's Mortgage (1987–1989). **Associations & Accomplishments:** Twin West Chamber of Commerce; National and Minnesota Mortgage Bankers Association. **Education:** St. Cloud State University, B.S. in Finance (1978). **Personal:** Married to Robert L. Carter in 1979. Two children: Alison and Jason. Mrs. Clarke–Carter enjoys downhill skiing, rollerblading, golf and soccer.

John J. Connelly
• • • ◄━━━━ ◎ ━━━━► • • •
Vice President
Mission Hills Mortgage Bankers
525 Wall Street
Chico, CA 95928
(800) 748–6169
Fax: (916) 894–0541

6162

Business Information: Mission Hills Mortgage Bankers is a financial lending service with offices in six western states: Washington, Idaho, California, Oregon, Nevada, and Arizona. As Vice President, Mr. Connelly is responsible for supervising employees, handling administrative duties, and customer relations. **Career Steps:** Vice President, Mission Hills Mortgage Bankers (1992–Present); Branch Manager, Guild Mortgage Co. (1981–1992). **Associations & Accomplishments:** California Association of Mortgage Bankers; Mortgage Bankers Association of America; Building Industry Association; National Association of Realtors. **Education:** California Real Estate Brokers License. **Personal:** Married to Nympha in 1986. Three children: Meagan, Sean, and Liam. Mr. Connelly enjoys aviation. He recently purchased a 4–seater Cessna 182.

Brad Coons
Wholesale Account Executive
Option One Mortgage
2020 East First Street, Suite 205
Santa Ana, CA 99706
(801) 271–0723
Fax: (714) 571–4677

6162

Business Information: Option One Mortgage is a wholesale "B–C" mortgage lender. As Wholesale Account Executive, Mr. Coons markets out the Company's products to mortgage brokers, as well as handles accounts and arranges funding. **Career Steps:** Wholesale Account Executive, Option One Mortgage (1994–Present); STM Mortgage: Account Executive (1992–1993); Underwriter (1992); Processing Manager, Prime Equity Capital (1991 and 1992). **Associations & Accomplishments:** Utah Mortgage Brokers Association; Licensed California Salesperson in Real Estate. **Personal:** Two children: Christopher and Nicholas. Mr. Coons enjoys fishing and skiing.

Karen Cox
Director of Human Resources
Instinet
875 3rd Avenue
New York, NY 10022
(212) 310–9558
Fax: (212) 832–5055
EMail: See Below

6162

Business Information: Instinet is a computer software stock brokerage firm with offices in New York, Massachusetts, Kansas, and the United Kingdom. As Director of Human Resources, Ms. Cox handles all policies and procedures, benefits, and training for nearly 700 employees. Internet users can reach her via: KCOX@Instinet.com. **Career Steps:** Director of Human Resources, Instinet (1989–Present); Recruiter, Coopers & Lybrand (1987–1988); Project Manager, Equitable Life/Equicor (1977–1987). **Associations & Accomplishments:** Society for Human Resource Management; Wall Street Compensation and Benefits Association. **Education:** Pace University.

Mr. Daniel G. Crockett
President
Franklin American Mortgage Company
P.O. Box 1011
Brentwood, TN 37027
(615) 377-1020
Fax: (615) 377-1134

6162

Business Information: Franklin American Mortgage Company is a retail and wholesale originator of conventional, FHA, and VA mortgage loans. As President, Mr. Crockett is responsible for the overall daily operations including: administrative, personnel, marketing and budget duties. Under his direction, the Company showed an increase in annual premium revenue from $400K to its current earnings of over $2 million. Established in 1993, Franklin American Mortgage Company employs 20 people. **Career Steps:** President, Franklin American Mortgage Company (1993–Present); Financial Consultant, J.H. Shoemaker (1991–1992); Account Executive, NSA (1991). **Associations & Accomplishments:** Nashville Junior Chamber of Commerce; Charter Member of Tennessee Mortgage Broker Association; Kappa Sigma Social Fraternity Alumnus. **Education:** Lambuth University, B.B.A. (1991); Pensecola Christian College Series 6 and Series 63 – Securities License. **Personal:** Mr. Crockett enjoys golf, football, softball, raquetball, tennis, weightlifting and church organizations.

Roland W. Davis
Vice President
Colonial Mortgage
2333 West Northern #8
Phoenix, AZ 85014
(602) 995-3990
Fax: (602) 995-4673

6162

Business Information: Colonial Mortgage is a financial institution primarily involved in mortgage lending and brokerage of residential properties and homes. Local in scope, the Company has four offices located throughout the state. Established in 1984, the Company employs 50 people. As Vice President, Mr. Davis is in charge of loan officer training and motivation. Additional responsibilities include administration, sales, public relations, marketing, producing articles for the Company newsletter, and strategic planning. **Career Steps:** Vice President, Colonial Mortgage (1990–Present); Loan Officer, Great Western Bank (1987–1989); Store Manager, Sub Factory (1984–1988); Store Manager, Atlantic Ritchfield (1986–1987). **Associations & Accomplishments:** President, Cliff Top Association; Co–Chairman, Society of the Arts; Scottsdale Chamber of Commerce; Phoenix Board of Realtors; National Mortgage Originator of the Month (March, 1995). **Education:** Arizona State University, B.S. (1987). **Personal:** Married to Colleen Jean in 1992. One child: Wesley Scott. Mr. Davis enjoys hiking, weightlifting, snow skiing, and going to church.

Joseph M. Dunn
Regional Sales Manager
Advanta Mortgage Corporation
500 Office Center Drive
Ft. Washington, PA 19034
(800) 446-3100
Fax: (215) 283-4650

6162

Business Information: Advanta Mortgage Corporation, established in 1951, is a wholesale mortgage lender employing 300+ people with annual revenue of $770 million. As Regional Sales Manager, Mr. Dunn is responsible for six direct and 15 indirect reports. Additionally, he is Regional Sales Manager for alternative origination such as telemarketing and computer loan originations. **Career Steps:** Advanta Mortgage Corporation: Regional Sales Manager (1995–Present), Business Development Manager (1995); Mortgage Coordinator, Mortgageling (1994–1995); Account executive, Crossland Mortgage (1992–1994). **Associations & Accomplishments:** Membership in various mortgage broker and banker associations throughout the United States; Volunteer worker with the under–privileged and unemployed. **Education:** St. Joseph's University, B.S. (1984). **Personal:** Married to Lori in 1989. Three children: Sean, Matthew and Caitlyn. Mr. Dunn enjoys a variety of sports and spending time with his family.

Ellis A. Febres
Controller
Santander Mortgage Corporation
P.O. Box 2199 Hayto Rey Station
San Juan, Puerto Rico 00919
(787) 274-7007
Fax: Please mail or call

6162

Business Information: Santander Mortgage Corporation is a mortgage banking firm that provides consumer and home-owner loans. The Corporation is located in Paymon, Puerto Rico and was established in 1982. As Controller, Mr. Febres supervises all accounting functions and is responsible for maintaining accurate corporation records. **Career Steps:** Controller, Santander Mortgage Corporation (1993–Present); Controller, INDECA (1993); Audit Supervisor, Banc Santander. **Associations & Accomplishments:** Puerto Rico Society of Certified Public Accountants; American Institute of Certified Public Accountants; Board of Director, Banco Santander Federal Credit Union. **Education:** Louisiana State University, B.S. (1983); Certified Public Accountant. **Personal:** Married to Norma in 1985. Two children: Andre and Fernando. Mr. Febres enjoys softball, tennis, and bike riding.

Sean E. Goff
Senior Account Executive
Neighborhood Mortgage Bankers
570 Taxter Road, Suite 135
Elmsford, NY 10523
(914) 347-2122 (800) 815-3220
Fax: (914) 347-2393

6162

Business Information: Neighborhood Mortgage Bankers, licensed through the State of New York, is a mortgage banking institution. They have two locations in New York and are in the process of opening two more offices, one in New Jersey and another in Connecticut. As Senior Account Executive, Mr. Goff is responsible for sales management, training new account executives, and locating and recruiting new clients and trading partners. **Career Steps:** Senior Account Executive, Neighborhood Mortgage Bankers (1996–Present); Vice President, Nexus Equity Management (1993–1996); Sales Manager, Effective Recovery Services (1990–1993); Assistant Manager, Action TV & Appliance (1988–1990). **Associations & Accomplishments:** New York Association of Mortgage Brokers; National Association of Mortgage Brokers. **Education:** Attended LaSalle University. **Personal:** Married to Jennifer in 1989. Three children: Alexander, Troy, and Maryanne. Mr. Goff is also a minister. He enjoys bicycling, cross–training, and restoring old cars.

Daniel J. Guajardo Jr.
Vice President
Martin Mortgage Corporation
1520 H Street
Modesto, CA 95354
(209) 524-1004 EXT. 1
Fax: (209) 524-1436

6162

Business Information: Martin Mortgage Corporation, established in 1982, is a family–owned, mortgage lending institution, providing the set–up of first and second mortgages and marketing trust deed investments to individuals. Succeeding the position of Vice President upon his mother's retirement, Mr. Guajardo is responsible for marketing and sales of trust deeds, as well as administration, operations, finances, sales, and public relations. Additionally, he makes personal appearances and oversees accounts receivables. **Career Steps:** Vice President, Martin Mortgage Corporation (1991–Present). **Associations & Accomplishments:** Licensed Real Estate Agent (Loan Officer); Mortgage Association of California; National Notary Association. **Personal:** Married to Sandra in 1989. Two children: Daniel, III and David. Mr. Guajardo enjoys family activities, water & snow skiing, and body building.

Melvin C. Henderson
President
First Security Mortgage Services Inc.
606 NE Boulevard
Clinton, NC 28328-2023
(910) 590-2222
Fax: (910) 590-2288
E–mail: see below

6162

Business Information: First Security Mortgage Services Inc. is a full–service mortgage lending institution providing consolidation loans and refinancing for homes and businesses for the entire state of North Carolina. Established in 1991, First Security currently employs 25 people and reports annual premium assets in excess of $36 million. As President, Mr. Henderson is responsible for all aspects of operations. **Career Steps:** President, First Security Mortgage Services Inc. (1991–Present); General Manager, Harris & Harris (1990–1991). **Associations & Accomplishments:** National Association of Mortgage Bankers; North Carolina Association of Mortgage Bankers. **Education:** Campbell University. **Personal:** Married to Ronda M. in 1984. Two children: Ashley Sue and Kailey Jill. Mr. Henderson enjoys mountain biking and spending time with his family.

Don M. Jervis

Owner and Vice President of Operations
Freedom Mortgage and Financial Services, Inc.
2825 Jewett
Highland, IN 46322
(219) 972-1918
Fax: (219) 972-0114

6162

Business Information: Freedom Mortgage and Financial Services, Inc. is a mortgage brokerage and financial services firm. Currently, the Firm has two offices in Indiana, with future plans to open ten more throughout the midwest. Established in 1993, Freedom Mortgage and Financial Services, Inc. reports annual revenue of $1 million and currently employs 15 people. As Owner and Vice President of Operations, Mr. Jervis is responsible for all aspects of operations. **Career Steps:** Owner and Vice President of Operations, Freedom Mortgage and Financial Services, Inc. (1993–Present); Loan Officer, Unity Mortgage (1990–1993); Manager, Dominick's Foods (1987–1990); Insurance Specialist, Mutual Benefit Life (1986–1987). **Education:** Loyola University of Chicago, M.S. in Marketing (1984). **Personal:** One child: Bradley Jervis. Mr. Jervis enjoys photography, basketball, and piano.

Carol Braddock Johnson

Vice President and Managing Director
GMAC Mortgage Corporation
8360 Old York Road
Elkins Park, PA 19027-1535
(215) 881-1116
Fax: (215) 881-1015

6162

Business Information: GMAC Mortgage Corporation is a mortgage banking corporation doing business in 50 states. GMAC Mortgage Corporation currently employs 3,000 people. As Vice President and Managing Director, Ms. Johnson is responsible for the development of opportunities for new business in niche markets. **Career Steps:** Vice President and Managing Director, GMAC Mortgage Corporation (1994–Present); Senior Director, Federal Home Loan Mortgage Corporation (1991–1994); President, Penn Federal Mortgage Company (1985–1987); Vice President, Federal Home Loan, Bank of Cincinnati (1973–1985). **Associations & Accomplishments:** Junior League (Sustainer). **Education:** University of Cincinnati, M.A. (1976), B.A. (1965); Indiana University, Savings & Loan Graduate Certificate (1980). **Personal:** Married to Ed Johnson in 1985. Four children: Lauren and Ryan Braddock and Meryl and Erica Johnson. Ms. Johnson enjoys tennis, cooking, and serving as a civic leader and volunteer.

Mr. Mark D. Johnson
Loan Officer
First Mortgage Corporation
19831 Governors Highway
Flossmoor, IL 60422
(708) 957-2020
Fax: (708) 957-6676

6162

Business Information: First Mortgage Corporation is a financial service company specializing in originating and closing residential mortgages in the Illinois, Michigan, and Ohio area. As a Loan Officer, Mr. Johnson handles all administrative aspects of loan origination and clos ing. Established in 1984, First Mortgage Corporation has a full–time staff of 60 and reports annual revenue of $200 million. **Career Steps:** Loan Officer, First Mortgage Corporation (1993–Present); Owner, The Right Angle (1992–19 93). **Associations & Accomplishments:** Treasurer, Alumni Board of Theta Chi Fraternity. **Education:** Illinois Wesleyan University, B.S. (1992).

Renee T. Johnson
Director
Household Bank
931 Corporate Center Drive
Pomona, CA 91769
(909) 397–3411
Fax: (909) 397–3990

6162

Business Information: Household Processing which is a subsidiary of Household Bank began operations in 1979 and currently boasts 70 employees. The business provides mortgage processing to internal and external customers (i.e. escrows, trustee, and document preparation). As Director, Ms. Johnson oversees the daily operation of the business. She is responsible for the quality of service provided, public relations, marketing of services, and strategic planning. Ms. Johnson works with her department managers on the development of departmental budgets and monitors their production and goal achievements. Other duties include management of the mortgage processing, foreclosures, collections, accounting and sales departments. **Career Steps:** Director, Household Bank (1995–Present): Director of Loan Administration, Household Financial Services (1994–1995); Household Finance Corporation: Director of Compliance (1993–1994) and Manager of Lending (1992–1993). **Associations & Accomplishments:** Mortgage Bankers Association; California Mortgage Bankers Association; Board of Directors, Pomona Valley Urban League; Foothill AIDS Project. **Education:** Ohio Institute of Technology, B.S. (1982). **Personal:** Ms. Johnson enjoys softball, reading, rollerblading, bungee jumping, volunteer work, and travel.

Todd A. Johnson
Vice President of Operations
United Mortgage Company
1700 Broadway, Suite 1208
Denver, CO 80290–1201
(303) 839–2700
Fax: (303) 863–1990
EMAIL: See Below

6162

Business Information: United Mortgage Company, a wholly–owned subsidiary of Norwest, originates and services loans to commercial clients. As Vice President of Operations, Mr. Johnson reports directly to the President and oversees the Servicing Administration Department, benefits administration, systems administration, and serves as financial controller. Internet users can also reach him via: umfindloan@aol.com **Career Steps:** Vice President of Operations, United Mortgage Company (1991–Present); Servicing Manager/Controller, Metropolitan Mortgage Company (1989–1991); Staff Accountant, HomeAmerican Mortgage Company (1985–1987). **Education:** Chadron State College, B.A. in Business Administration (1983); Various mortgage banker's continuing real estate classes and seminars. **Personal:** Mr. Johnson enjoys biking, hiking, and running.

William D. Keiper
Senior Vice President of Human Resources
Transamerica Financial Services, Inc.
1150 S. Olive St., No. T2800
Los Angeles, CA 90015
(213) 742–4428
Fax: Please mail or call

6162

Business Information: Transamerica Financial Services, Inc., the fourth largest independent real estate lender in the U.S., is a consumer lending company specializing in fixed–rate first and second mortgage loans, as well as unsecured personal loans in the U.S., Canada, and the United Kingdom. As Senior Vice President of Human Resources, Mr. Keiper is responsible for all personnel issues, including Worker's Compensation, management development, employee relations, strategic planning. **Career Steps:** Senior Vice President of Human Resources, Transamerica Financial Services, Inc. (1994–Present); The Travelers Companies: Division Vice President of Human Resources (1991–1994), Regional Vice President of Human Resources (1989–1991). **Associations & Accomplishments:** Society for Human Resource Management; Human Resource Planning Society; American Financial Services Association; Human Resources Strategy Forum. **Education:** Indiana University of Pennsylvania, B.A. (1978). **Personal:** Married to Karen in 1979. Two children: Laura and John. Mr. Keiper enjoys traveling and horseback riding.

Lyman E. King III
President
Future Financial Mortgage Corporation
5252 Sunrise Boulevard, Suite 5
Fair Oaks, CA 95628
(916) 863–6696
Fax: (916) 863–6695

6162

Business Information: Future Financial Mortgage Corporation is a full–service mortgage banking firm, an approved Federal Housing Administration Correspondent, and an Authorized Agent for the Veterans' Administration. In this capacity as President and Founder, Mr. King oversees administration of all Corporation operations, originates, underwrites, and closes mortgage loans, and also functions as Chief Financial Officer for the Corporation. Established in 1991, Future Financial Mortgage Corporation employs a full–time staff of 19 and reports annual revenue of $55 million. Mr. King has closed in excess of $20 million of personal production three different times in his career. **Career Steps:** President, Future Financial Mortgage Corporation (1991–Present); Senior Loan Officer, Western Residential Lending (1989–1991); Loan Representative, Union Bank (1988–1989); Branch Manager and Senior Loan Officer, GMAC Mortgage Corporation (1984–1988); Real Estate Agent, Heritage Homes & Investments, Inc. (1981–1984). **Associations & Accomplishments:** Citrus Heights Chamber of Commerce; Board of Directors, Association of Professional Women; Elks Club; California Association of Residential Lenders; Past Vice President and Member, Theta Delta Phi Honor Society; Student Senator (1978–1979); President's Award for Outstanding Student Leadership (1979–1980), Who's Who of College Students (1980). **Education:** Southern Oregon State College, B.S. in Criminology, B.S. in Political Science, magna cum laude (1980); Certified Instructor in Mortgage Banking, State of California Department of Real Estate (1992); Ongoing Sales Training and Education, 3–4 events annually; Officer Candidate School, U.S. Marine Corps, Quantico, Virginia, Graduated 1st in class of 268 (1978); Underwriting Training, Federal Housing Administration Schools.

Cheril D. Lee
Regional Vice President
Old Kent Mortgage Company
2545 Farmers Drive, Suite 140
Columbus, OH 43235–2705
(614) 761–8222 Ext.: 202
Fax: (614) 761–2310

6162

Business Information: Old Kent Mortgage Company provides the origination and quality control of wholesale and retail residential mortgage loans. Regional in scope with branch offices in Ohio and Michigan, Old Kent reports portfolio assets for 1995 in excess of $310 million. As Regional Vice President, Cheril Lee oversees all administrative office procedures company–wide. Managing a regional staff of 20, she is also responsible for the hiring and discipline of employees, and approves all customers, to whom she must ensure delivery and quality. **Career Steps:** Regional Vice President, Old Kent Mortgage Company (1993–Present); Vice President and Manager, Citizens Mortgage Company (1991–1993); Vice President and Manager, Mical Mortgage, Inc. (1987–1990). **Associations & Accomplishments:** Ohio Mortgage Bankers Association; Columbus Mortgage Bankers Association; Ohio Association of Mortgage Brokers; Indiana Association of Mortgage Brokers; Michigan Mortgage Brokers Association; Kentucky Mortgage Brokers Association. **Personal:** Married to Brian in 1986. Two children: Megan and Madison. Mrs. Lee enjoys interior decorating and golf.

Tracy L. Legan
Vice President of Mortgage Origination
St. Francis Bank
2360 North 124th Street
Wauwatosa, WI 53226
(414) 486–7432
Fax: (414) 476–2093

6162

Business Information: St. Francis Bank, established in 1923, is a 1–4 family mortgage lending service. As Vice President of Mortgage Origination, Ms. Legan is responsible for managing 1–4 family mortgage lending activities, directing policies and practices supporting the bank's mission, and handling the bank's mortgage processing, underwriting, closing, and correspondent lending departments. **Career Steps:** St. Francis Bank: Vice President of Mortgage Lending (1996–Present), Assistant Vice President of Mortgage Lending (1990–1996), Underwriting Manager (1989–1990), Association Underwriter (1987–1989); First Financial Bank: Senior Underwriter (1984–1987), Secondary Market/Administrative Assistant (1985–1986), Post Closing Auditor/Receptionist (1984–1985). **Associations & Accomplishments:**

WMBA; Credit Review Committee (Wisconsin Partner for Housing); Consumer Lending Section Members. **Education:** The Institute of Financial Education – Chicago (1984–1995); WCTC Small Business Classes (1990); IFE & MATC Specialized Lending Classes. **Personal:** Ms. Legan enjoys sports events, camping, and helping others to excel.

Carlos Maldonado
Senior Loan Officer
National Pacific Mortgage Corporation
7120 Hayvenhurst Avenue #320
Van Nuys, CA 91406–3813
(818) 787–7720
Fax: (818) 902–9966

6162

Business Information: National Pacific Mortgage Corporation specializes in the origination and service of mortgage loans. Mr. Maldonado has been a Senior Loan Officer at National Pacific since 1993, originating mortgage and home loans, providing customer service, and conducting various administrative activities. **Career Steps:** Senior Loan Officer, National Pacific Mortgage Corporation (1993–Present). **Personal:** Married to Maritza in 1990. Three children: Carlos Alfredo, Monica, and Eric.

Mr. Anthony J. Marciano
Vice President of Loan Production
Merrill Lynch Credit Corporation
4802 Deer Lake Dr., E.
Jacksonville, FL 32246
(904) 928–6004
Fax: (904) 998–0283

6162

Business Information: Merrill Lynch Credit Corporation, a division of Merrill Lynch – Private Client Group, is a full service mortgage and security–based lending firm. Originally established to provide services for present and potential clients of Merrill Lynch, mortgage services are now offered to the general public. Serving in supervisory capacities for Merrill Lynch Credit since 1987, Anthony Marciano was appointed Vice President of Loan Production in 1994. In this role, he oversees the unit responsible for originating various types of residential mortgage loans. **Career Steps:** Merrill Lynch Credit Corporation: Vice President of Loan Production (1994–Present), Vice President of Conforming Loans (1992–1994), Supervisor of Loan Closing (1987–92). **Associations & Accomplishments:** Young Republicans of Florida; Beta Gamma Sigma Business Fraternity; Sigma Alpha Epsilon Alumni Association. **Education:** University of Connecticut, B.S. in Finance, summa cum laude (1985). **Personal:** Married to Shannon Elaine in 1995. Mr. Marciano enjoys golf and collecting sports memorabilia.

Richard E. Maultsby
CEO of the Private Lending Division
Cornerstone NW Mortgage, Inc.
906 Everett Mall Way, Fourth Floor
Everett, WA 98208
(206) 290–9400
Fax: (206) 290–9123
EMail: See Below

6162

Business Information: Cornerstone NW Mortgage, Inc. is a wholly–owned subsidiary of Interwest Bank. The Company is the largest brokering firm in Washington. Private Lending deals with mortgage financing for commercial, land development, and residential projects. As CEO of the Private Lending Division, Mr. Maultsby is responsible for meeting, negotiating, and making deals with people. Internet users can reach him via: 75204,335@compuserve.com. **Career Steps:** Cornerstone NW Mortgage, Inc.: CEO of the Private Lending Division (1996–Present), Chief Operations Officer (1995–1996); Senior Vice President, Micon Properties, Inc. (1990–1995); President, Timberline Investment Corporation (1979–1995). **Associations & Accomplishments:** Chairman of Board of Trustees, Union Gospel Mission; Featured in "Fortune Magazine" (February 1969). **Education:** University of Washington r(1966). **Personal:** Married to Sheryl in 1968. Two children: Sara and Samantha. Mr. Maultsby enjoys ocean sail boat racing, music, and steelhead fishing.

Robert H. McCorkindale
Owner and President
Fidelity Financial Group, Inc.
105 West Berry Avenue
Foley, AL 36536
(334) 943–7640
Fax: (334) 943–2329

6162

Business Information: Fidelity Financial Group, Inc., established in 1989, is a mortgage brokerage firm with five offices located throughout Florida (2) and Alabama (3). With 25 years expertise in the hotel business industry, Mr. McCorkindale established Fidelity Financial Group in 1989, responsible for all aspects of operations. He is also Owner and President of Summerbreeze Management — d.b.a. Pink Pony Pub – the oldest beach bar and noted as a landmark in Gulf Shores, Alabama. **Career Steps:** Owner and President, Fidelity Financial Group, Inc. (1989–Present); Owner and President, Summerbreeze Management, d.b.a. Pink Pony Pub (1994–Present); President, Hospitality Consultants Corporation (1986–Present). **Associations & Accomplishments:** Kiwanis; National Association of Mortgage Brokers; Certified Hotel Administrator; Florida Mortgage Brokers Association. **Education:** Paul Smith's College, B.S. (1969). **Personal:** Married to Connie in 1983. Two children: Rob and Alison. Mr. McCorkindale enjoys golf and boating.

Lanett R. McCoy
Vice President
Credit Profile Services, Inc.
909 S. Meridian, Suite 350
Oklahoma City, OK 73108
(405) 946–2999
Fax: (405) 632–5400

6162

Business Information: Credit Profile Services, Inc. is a privately–owned company specializing in Residential Mortgage Credit Reports for mortgage bankers, brokers, and the real estate industry. The Company has six offices located throughout the U.S. Established in 1989, the Company employs 55 people and has estimated annual revenue in excess of $3 million. As Vice President, Ms. McCoy is responsible for her market area profit. Her duties include new sales, market research, customer service, new product development, and production center support. **Career Steps:** Credit Profile Services, Inc: Vice President (1993–Present); Sales Representative, CSC Mortgage Services (1990–1993); Sales Representative, Associated Credit Services (1984–1990); Assistant Manager, Professional Adjustment Bureau (1982–1984). **Associations & Accomplishments:** Mortgage Bankers Association; Association of Professional Mortgage Women; Women of the South. **Education:** University of Oklahoma, B.A. (1983). **Personal:** Married to Mike W. in 1985. One child: Michelle. Ms. McCoy is a musician, and enjoys reading and antiques.

Margy McManus
Quality Control Manager
Signet Mortgage Corporation
7125 Thomas Edison Drive
Columbia, MD 21046
(410) 312–4074
Fax: (410) 312–4077

6162

Business Information: Signet Mortgage Corporation is a medium–sized commercial banking and lending institution located in the Southeastern United States and reporting more the $12 billion in assets. As Quality Control Manager, Ms. McManus is responsible for quality standards, appraisals, keeping up with federal, state, and investor regulations, and teaching employees about mortgage banking. **Career Steps:** Quality Control Manager, Signet Mortgage Corporation (1995–Present); Atlantic Home Mortgage: Vice President (1993–1995), Assistant Vice President (1992–1993), Underwriting Manager (1988–1992). **Associations & Accomplishments:** Maryland Mortgage Bankers; National Association of Appraisers, Inc.; Volunteer, National Lacrosse Foundation; Board Member, Maryland Youth Lacrosse Association; Involved with Maryland Low Income Housing Service. **Education:** University of Maryland, B.A. in Sociology (1974). **Personal:** One child: Michael. Ms. McManus enjoys volunteer community work and children.

Richard W. Miller
First Vice President
First Town Mortgage
100 Plaza Drive
Secaucus, NJ 07094–3613
(201) 863–1200
Fax: (201) 271–0406

6162

Business Information: First Town Mortgage is a national financial institution, specializing in mortgage banking. Established in 1988, First Town Mortgage reports annual production of $1 billion and currently employs 250 people. With twelve years experience in the financial industry, Mr. Miller joined First Town Mortgage Corporation in 1992. Serving as First Vice President, he serves as Head of the National Wholesale Lending Division, responsible for all aspects of operations. **Career Steps:** First Vice President, First Town Mortgage (1992–Present); Vice President, Howard Savings Bank (1988–1992); Assistant Vice President, ICA Mortgage (1986–1988). **Associations & Accomplishments:** Chairman of Correspondent Lenders Committee, Mortgage Bankers Association of New Jersey; Contributing Writer, Perspective Magazine – Trade Group Publication; Former Big Brother of the Year, Camden County New Jersey Chapter of Big Brothers/Big Sisters of America. **Education:** Chadwick University, B.S. in Business Administration (1994). **Personal:** Married to Danielle in 1987. Two children: Justin and Ryan. Mr. Miller enjoys sports.

Edward J. O'Donnell

Vice President
Associates Financial Services
P.O. Box 604
Burlington, NJ 08016–0604
(609) 239–1188
Fax: (609) 239–1836

6162

Business Information: Associates Financial Services specializes in consumer finance, including non–conforming mortgage loans, installment loans, personal loans, retail finance, and home improvement. The Company is the fourth largest credit card issuing organization in the country. As Vice President, Mr. O'Donnell is responsible for growth and profitability of a $100 million consumer loan portfolio. He also oversees hiring, training, long and short interval planning, and reporting. **Career Steps:** Associates Financial Services: Vice President (1996–Present), Group Director (1995–1996), Regional Training Director (1994–1995). **Associations & Accomplishments:** New Jersey Consumer Finance Association; New England Consumer Finance Association; Knights of Columbus; National Association of Consumer Finance Professionals. **Education:** Fairfield University, B.A. (1987). **Personal:** Mr. O'Donnell enjoys watching and participating in sports, tennis, and running.

Mr. Donavon J. Ostrom
Senior Vice President
Express America Mortgage Corporation
9060 East Via Linda Street
Scottsdale, AZ 85258
(602) 661–4001
Fax: (602) 661–4042

6162

Business Information: Express America Mortgage Corporation is a full–service mortgage banking company. As Senior Vice President, Mr. Ostrom manages the controlled business arrangements program for the Company. He also manages the individual companies (up to 20). Established in 1991, Express America Mortgage Corporation employs a staff of 450 and reports annual sales of $5 billion. **Career Steps:** Senior Vice President, Express America Mortgage Corporation (1993–Present); Senior Vice President and National Production Manager, Matrix Financial Corporation (1992–1993); National Retail Sales Manager, FBS Mortgage Corporation (1991–1992); Senior Vice President and National Production Manager, Crossland Mortgage Corporation (1983–1991). **Associations & Accomplishments:** Domestic Policy Association. **Education:** American Graduate School of International Management, Masters of International Management (1983); Arizona State University, B.S.

Renee B. Pierce
Vice President
The Bank of Winter Park
1250 Lee Road
Winter Park, FL 32789
(407) 629–6447
Fax: Please mail or call

6162

Business Information: The Bank of Winter Park, based in Winter Park, Florida, currently operates four offices with two additional branches proposed. It is a state–chartered full–service bank offering a complete menu of services and residential mortgage lending. As Vice President, Ms. Pierce has developed a residential lending department and also continues her role as compliance officer at the bank. **Career Steps:** Vice President, The Bank of Winter Park (1996–Present); Senior Vice President, TransLand Financial Services (1995–1996); Assistant Vice President/Assistant Office Manager, Resource Bancshares Mortgage Group (1991–1995). **Associations & Accomplishments:** Habitat for Humanity – Winter Park/Maitland Affiliate; Orlando Chamber of Commerce; Winter Park Chamber of Commerce; Florida Bankers; Community Bankers of Florida; MBA of Central Florida. **Education:** Hillsborough Community College, Business (1976). **Personal:** Married to E. Earl in 1984. Ms. Pierce enjoys her pets, RVing, and walking.

Cathy Polasky
Senior Vice President
BankAmerica Mortgage Co.
8300 Norman Center Drive, Suite 1000
Bloomington, MN 55437–1027
(612) 893–5278
Fax: (612) 893–5206

6162

Business Information: BankAmerica Mortgage Co., a division of Bank of America, is a mortgage company responsible for residental mortgages for first time buyers. Established in 1995, BankAmerica Mortgage Co. currently employs 35 people. As Senior Vice President of Mortgage Operations and National Affinity Lending Manager, Ms. Polasky is responsible for sales through operations, sponsor and director lending, and through Bank of America customers. **Career Steps:** Senior Vice President, BankAmerica Mortgage Co. (1994–Present); Senior Vice President of Mortgage Operations, Prudential Home Mortgage (1983–1994). **Associations & Accomplishments:** Minnesota Mortgage Bankers Association Board; Member, Minnesota Tax Force for Financial Services Industry, established by the Governor; Board Member and Treasurer, Lake Country School; Member, Minnesota State Bar Association; Member, Hennepin County Bar Association; Published article in American Banker. **Education:** University of Minnesota, J.D. (1980); University of North Carolina, M.S.; Macalister College, B.A. **Personal:** Married to Averial Nelson, Jr. Two children: Erica and Elizabeth. Ms. Polasky enjoys spending time with her family and skiing.

James A. Racine
Vice President and Regional Production Manager
First Midwest Mortgage Corp.
2801 West Jefferson Street
Joliet, IL 60435
(815) 773–2538
Fax: (815) 773–2738

6162

Business Information: First Midwest Mortgage Corporation is a full–service mortgage banking and lending institution, inrcluding property sales. In operation since 1994, First Midwest currently employs 40 people and reports assets of over $280 million. As Vice President and Regional Production Manager, Mr. Racine is responsible for the management of the retail mortgage sales force in Illinois, Iowa and Wisconsin. **Career Steps:** Vice President and Regional Production Manager, First Midwest Mortgage Corporation (Jun. 1995–Present); Branch Manager, North American Mortgage Company (Jan. 1995 – Jun. 1995); District Sales Manager, Household Mortgage Services (1985–1995). **Associations & Accomplishments:** Mortgage Bankers Association; Southwest Suburban Builders Association; Lake County Board of Realtors. **Education:** Northern Illinois University, B.S. in Communications (1989). **Personal:** Married to Susan A. in 1990. Mr. Racine enjoys hockey, running, and music.

Christopher S. Reddick
Senior Vice President and Chief Operating Officer
Southtrust Mortgage Corporation
100 Brookwood Place, Suite 300
Birmingham, AL 35209–6830
(205) 254–8358
Fax: (205) 254–8232

6162

Business Information: As part of a 43 bank holding company, Southtrust Mortgage Corporation is a mortgage bank organization. Regional in scope, it originates loans in seven south-eastern states, lending a total of $5 billion in loans. Serving as secretary to Board of Governors, Christopher Reddick is Senior Vice President and Chief Operating Officer supervising accounting, loan servicing, quality control, information systems departments, human resources, mergers and acquisitions, and property management. **Career Steps:** Senior Vice President and Chief Operating Officer, Southtrust Mortgage Corporation (1994–Present); Senior Vice President and Chief Operating Officer, Mortgage Service America Company (1993–1994); Vice President and Chief Financial Officer, Banyan Management Corporation (1988–1993). **Associations & Accomplishments:** Mortgage Bankers Association of Alabama; Mortgage Bankers Association of America; Notre Dame Alumni Association. **Education:** University of Notre Dame, B.B.A. (1978). **Personal:** Married to Elizabeth in 1989. Two children: David Christopher and Jennifer Elizabeth. Mr. Reddick enjoys golf and photography.

Cindy W. Richardson
Director of Planning and Analysis
FT Mortgage Companies
2974 LBJ Freeway
Dallas, TX 75234
(214) 919–5506
Fax: (214) 919–5059

6162

Business Information: FT Mortgage Companies (formerly known as Sunbelt National Mortgage) is one of the top 25 mortgage banking companies in the nation. As Director of Planning and Analysis, Ms. Richardson is responsible for managing budgeting, forecasting and strategic planning processes, in addition to business analysis. She began her career with Sunbelt National Mortgage straight out of college in 1985. As Sunbelt National Mortgage grew, so did Ms. Richardson; when the Company merged and became FT Mortgage Company in 1995, she was offered her current position as Director of Planning and Analysis. **Career Steps:** Director of Planning and Analysis, FT Mortgage Companies (1995–Present); Sunbelt National Mortgage: Controller (1994–1995), Reporting Manager (1993–1994), DP Liason (1992–1993). **Associations & Accomplishments:** National Association of Female Executives; ALJI. **Education:** University of Texas at Austin, B.B.A. (1983). **Personal:** Married to Mike W. in 1990. Ms. Richardson enjoys jogging, golf, and reading.

Deirdre L. Rogers
Managing Director
PMI Mortgage Insurance
2000 Crow Canyon Place #350
San Ramon, CA 94583
(800) 678–4243
Fax: (800) 350–4764

6162

Business Information: PMI Mortgage Insurance is a mortgage insurance firm providing insurance coverage for banks, thrifts, and mortgage bankers from borrower default on residential mortgage loans in excess of 80% LTV. As Managing Director, Ms. Rogers is responsible for the Northern California and Hawaii regions. She monitors the activities of 5 account managers and is responsible for the second largest territory for PMI. Ms. Rogers handles recruiting of staff, personnel concerns, accounting functions, marketing of services, public relations, and planning for the future expansion of her territory. **Career Steps:** Managing Director, PMI Mortgage Insurance (1996–Present); Account Manager, PMI Mortgage Insurance (1994–1996); Business Development Manager, Bank of America (1993–1994); Vice President, Branch Manager, Security Pacific Bank (1989–1992). **Associations & Accomplishments:** American Business Womens Association Glendal/Verdugo Chapter; Association of Professional Mortgage Women Greater San Gabriel Valley Chapter; Southern California Mortgage Bankers Association; California Association of Mortgage Brokers San Gabriel Chapter. **Education:** Wheaton High School, GED (1975). **Personal:** Married to Larry in 1987. Ms. Rogers enjoys reading, antique hunting, and Egyptology.

Leslie R. Roper
Vice President of Administration
Ginger MAE
4041 Essen Lane
Baton Rouge, LA 70809
(504) 924–6007 Ext.2785
Fax: (800) 825–8006
E–MAIL: See Below

6162

Business Information: Ginger MAE is a secondary market for non–traditional mortgage loans via correspondent relationships with regulated financial institutions. As Vice President of Administration, Ms. Roper is involved with contract negotiations, development and implementation of budgets, and reporting on budgetary concerns. Other responsibilities include

the creation of marketing materials and general administrative duties. Internet users can reach her via: GingerMae.com. **Career Steps:** Vice President of Administration, Ginger MAE (1993–Present); Loan Securitization, Southern Mortgage Acquisition (1991–1993); Asset Manager, Oak Tree Capital (1987–1991); Banking Officer Construction Loan Administration, Hibernia National Bank (1981–1987). **Associations & Accomplishments:** Sales and Marketing Executives. **Education:** University of New Orleans; Numerous M.B.A. Conferences/Seminars, as well as seminars sponsored by University of New Orleans. **Personal:** Ms. Roper enjoys community theater, golf, and race walking.

Mrs. Linda J. Shelton
Vice President & Director of Quality Control & Investor Relations
Transworld Mortgage Corporation
13111 Northwest Freeway
Houston, TX 77040–6311
(713) 895–6615
Fax: (713) 895–6621

6162

Business Information: Transworld Mortgage Corporation is a mortgage banking firm concentrating on originating and servicing mortgage loans owned by investors, as well as subservices for two affiliated companies. Services are provided on a national scope for single family residential loans. Established in 1991, Transworld Mortgage Corporation currently employs 300 people. As Vice President and Director of Quality Control & Investor Relations, Mrs. Shelton manages a staff of six professionals who audit and train all operational departments and handles compliance requirements. **Career Steps:** Vice President and Director of Quality Control & Investor Relations, Transworld Mortgage Corporation (1991–Present); Regional Manager of Institutional Eligibility, Federal Home Loan Mortgage Corporation (Freddie Mac) (1987–1991); Assistant Vice President and Operations Manager, Lion Funding Corporation (1985–1987). **Associations & Accomplishments:** National Mortgage Bankers Association; Texas Mortgage Bankers Association; Houston Association of Professional Mortgage Women. **Education:** Navarro College (1978); American Institute of Banking. **Personal:** Married to Lynn. Two children: Matthew and Suzanne. Mrs. Shelton enjoys golf, reading, playing the piano and traveling.

John Sloop

President
Premiere Mortgage Corporation
4215 Eddison Lakes Parkway
Mishawaka, IN 46545–1424
(219) 271–1199
Fax: (219) 273–1199

6162

Business Information: Premiere Mortgage Corporation is a mortgage lender that has 150 different mortgage programs available for their clients. The Corporation has closed loans in 6 different states but primary focus is in northern Indiana and Michigan. As President, Mr. Sloop manages all facets of the Corporation. He is responsible for overseeing the day–to–day operations, strategic planning, marketing, and financial strategies. Premiere Mortgage Corporation boasts annual revenues in excess of $50 million, and new offices will be opening in Tennessee and other locations within the next two years. **Career Steps:** President, Premiere Mortgage Corporation (1995–Present); Vice President, First Franklin Financial Corporation (1994–1995); Vice President, World Wide Financial Service (1993–1994). **Associations & Accomplishments:** Mortgage Masters, as panelist and speaker; Indiana Mortgage Bankers; South Mishawaka Board of Realtors; Indiana Home Builders Association; Rotary International. **Education:** Attended; Indiana University and Notre Dame University. **Personal:** Married to Jenni in 1984. Three children: Johnathan, Josiah, and Jillian. Mr. Sloop enjoys basketball, tennis, coaching baseball and soccer, church activities, skiing, and public speaking.

Ouida J. Spencer
Vice President, Mortgage Loan Production Manager
Trust Company Bank
121 Perimeter Center West, Suite 300
Atlanta, GA 30346
(404) 551–4032
Fax: (404) 551–4167

6162

Business Information: Trust Company Bank is a financial institution, specializing in mortgage lending. Established in 1887, Trust Company Bank currently employs 57 people. With eighteen years expertise in the banking industry, Mrs. Spencer joined Trust Company Bank in 1993. Serving as Vice President and Mortgage Loan Production Manager, in an executive capacity, she is responsible for managing all as-

pects of mortgage lending activities. **Career Steps:** Vice President and Mortgage Loan Production Manager, Trust Company Bank (1993–Present); Department Vice President, Decatur Federal (1983–1993); Vice President, Tucker Federal (1979–1983); Vice President, Peach State Federal (1977–1979). **Associations & Accomplishments:** United Cerebral Palsy: Executive Committee, Board of Directors; Rosebud McCormick Foundation: Executive Committee, Board of Directors; Business and Professional Women's Association; National Association of Female Executives; Board of Realtors; Treasurer, Wyndemere Neighborhood Association; Homebuilders Association of Georgia; Atlanta Mortgage Bankers Association; Georgia Mortgage Bankers Association. **Education:** Georgia State University: M.B.A. (1985), B.B.A.; David Lipscomb College, B.S.; Young Harris College, A.S. **Personal:** Married to Dale in 1978. Mrs. Spencer enjoys sailing, scuba diving, hiking, climbing, and travel.

Kelly Starkey

Southeast Regional Vice President
Sunbelt National Mortgage
1 Centerview Drive, Suite 104
Greensboro, NC 27407–3712
(910) 299–3100
Fax: Please mail or call

6162

Business Information: Sunbelt National Mortgage is part of the First Tennessee Mortgage Services. With 151 offices in 29 states, they rank 7th in retail loan originations nationwide. FT Mortgage currently services $18.7 billion in mortgage loans. Ms. Starkey has been in the mortgage banking industry since 1977. She joined Sunbelt in May 1988 when she opened Sunbelt's first North Carolina office in Greensboro. As Southeast Regional Manager, Ms. Starkey began the expansion in her region in 1993. She now has 11 offices in North Carolina, Tennessee, Kentucky, and Florida producing $500 million annually. **Career Steps:** South East Regional Vice President, Sunbelt National Mortgage (1988–Present); Shearson Lihman (1985–1988); Manager of Virginia mortgage banking operations, The Carey Winston Company. **Associations & Accomplishments:** North Carolina Homebuilders Association; North Carolina Board of Realtors; Republicans of Guilford County. **Education:** Attending Duke University Center for Continuing Financial Education. **Personal:** Married to John in 1986. One child: Crystal, who is currently a senior at UNC majoring in accounting.

Steve Sullivan
Regional Manager
Norwest Mortgage, Inc.
1500 Pontiac Avenue
Cranston, RI 02920–4406
(401) 463–7563
Fax: (401) 463–9339
E MAIL: See Below

6162

Business Information: Norwest Mortgage, Inc. is the nation's largest originator of home mortgage loans with locations in all 50 states. As Regional Manager, Mr. Sullivan oversees the retail sales force for both Rhode Island and Connecticut. Mr. Sullivan is responsible for making Norwest the premier lender in each market they serve by offering innovative ideas and solutions to home financing needs. As of April of 1996, Norwest was ranked fourth in Rhode Island and Connecticut with 2–43% of the total market. Internet users may reach him via: aolssulli1109. **Career Steps:** Regional Manager, Norwest Mortgage, Inc. (1993–Present); Branch Manager, Comnet Mortgage Company (1988–1990); Branch Manager, Northeastern Mortgage Company (1986–1988); Loan Originator, RIHT Mortgage Corporation (1981–1986). **Associations & Accomplishments:** Rhode Island Mortgage Bankers Association; Providence College Front Court Club. **Education:** Providence College, B.A. in Political Science (1981). **Personal:** Married to Gail in 1978. Two children: Shannon and Patrick. Mr. Sullivan enjoys golf, playing the stock market, and being involved in his childrens activities.

Marco A. Torres
Director of Information Technology
Advanta Mortgage
16875 West Bernardo Drive
San Diego, CA 92127
(619) 674–3855
Fax: (619) 674–1481
E MAIL: See Below

6162

Business Information: Advanta Mortgage is a full–service mortgage banking and finance company. The Company provide mortgages and home equity loans primarily for residential clients. As Director of Information Technology, Mr. Torres is responsible for developing, implementing, and maintaining software applications for the Company. Strategic planning and designing software for future applications are some of his other responsibilities. He is a frequent speaker at MBA and CMBA conferences. He has written several articles on technology in mortgage banking. Internet users can reach him via: mtorres@advanta.com. **Career Steps:** Advanta Mortgage: Director of Information Technology (1995–Present), Manager of Information Technology (1993–1995); Manager of Information Technology, First Franklin Financial (1988–1993). **Associations & Accomplishments:** Data Processing Management Association; California Mortgage Bankers Association. **Education:** San Francisco State University, B.S. (1982). **Personal:** Married to Tammy in 1983. One child: Joseph. Mr. Torres enjoys music and playing the guitar.

Glenn Tourtellot

Vice President and Chief Financial Officer
Mortgage Central Corporation
2524 Victory Highway
Coventry, RI 02816
(401) 334–4000
Fax: (401) 334–4029
EMAIL: See Below

6162

Business Information: Mortgage Central Corporation — d.b.a. Equity Star Mortgage Company — is a financial service company specializing in originating and closing residential mortgages. With licenses in 28 states, the Company offers non–conforming, Fanny Mae, and Freddy Mac loans through direct marketing, telemarketing, and large brokers. Mortgage Central is divided into approximately ten companies in various areas, including leasing and banking, daycare centers, real estate offices, and a personal holding company. Bringing with him thirteen years expertise in the mortgage banking industry, Mr. Tourtellot joined Mortgage Central in 1992 as Vice President and Chief Financial Officer. He is responsible for managing all financial and operational aspects of the business. Internet users can reach him via: GLENTOU@IX.NETCOM.COM **Career Steps:** Vice President/Chief Financial Officer, Mortgage Central Corporation (1992–Present); Vice President/Chief Financial Officer, Century Mortgage Company, Inc. (1988–1992); Assistant Vice President/Controller, Greater Providence Deposit Corporation (1983–1988). **Associations & Accomplishments:** Rhode Island Association of Mortgage Bankers; New York Associaton of Mortgage Bankers; Massachusetts Association of Mortgage Bankers and Correspondence Lenders. **Education:** Johnson & Wales University, M.B.A. (1992); Bryant College, B.A.; Certified Novell Network Administrator **Personal:** Married to Kimberly in 1987. One child: Dominique Brianna. Mr. Tourtellot enjoys golf, skiing and landscaping.

Phillip J. Welzenbach

Vice President
Consumer First Mortgage
139 N. Main Street, Suite 101
Bel Air, MD 21014
(410) 893–6350
Fax: (410) 893–2542

6162

Business Information: Consumer First Mortgage is a mortgage banking institution, providing first mortgages and re–financing of property. Licensed in Maryland, Virginia, Delaware, Pennsylvania, and New Jersey, the Company serves clients from fifteen locations in the local area and is listed as the second largest lender in Baltimore, Maryland, as well as rated in 1993 as the number one mortgage lender in Harford County, Maryland. As Vice President, Mr. Welzenbach is responsible for originating loans and overseeing the production and processing in his office, as well as coordinating settlements. **Career Steps:** Vice President, Consumer First Mortgage (1992–Present); Vice President and Loan Officer, Fairfax Mortgage (1988–1992); Loan Officer, E.B. Mortgage (1984–1988). **Personal:** Married to Betty in 1963. Three children: Deborah, Lisa and Jeffrey. Mr. Welzenbach enjoys golf.

Gloria J. Wright

Vice President
United First Mortgage
2416 Davis Road
Waynesboro, VA 22980–2060
(540) 433–7149
Fax: (540) 433–7169

6162

Business Information: United First Mortgage is a privately–owned, Virginia–based company with at least six branch offices, providing the preparation of mortgage loans for VHA, FHA, and other mortgage services provided by Fannie Mae and Freddie Mac loans. Joining United First Mortgage as Vice President in 1984, Mrs. Wright is responsible for the direction of all operations of the Waynesboro, Virginia branch location, including administration, finances, public relations, and strategic planning. **Career Steps:** Vice President, United First Mortgage (1984–Present) **Associations & Accomplishments:** Working Women's Forum; Board of Realtors. **Personal:** Married to Guy. Three children: Kristi, Michael, Patrick. Mrs. Wright enjoys golf, bowling and windsurfing.

Mr. Ronald E. Brackett

Managing Director
Associated Growth Investors, L.P.
P.O. Box 1399
Manhasset, NY 11030
(516) 627–3200
Fax: (516) 627–3264

6163

Business Information: Associated Growth Investors, L.P. is a specialty financial and lending organization. Established in 1992, the Firm currently has three general partners and employs two consultant members. As Managing Director, Mr. Brackett is responsible for the overall day–to–day administrative management and client relations. **Career Steps:** Managing Director, Associated Growth Investors, L.P. (1992–Present); Consultant, Rogers and Wells (1992–1994); Partner, Rogers and Wells (1975–1991); Associate, Rogers and Wells (1968–1975). **Associations & Accomplishments:** American Bar Association; New York State Bar Association; Phi Beta Kappa. **Education:** University of Michigan Law School, J.D. (1967); Trinity College, B.A. (1964). **Personal:** Married to Susan in 1975. One child: Charles.

Eric J. Ferguson

Senior Business Analyst
Whirlpool Financial Corporation
3005 Lakeshore Drive
St. Joseph, MI 49085–2357
(616) 926–5618
Fax: Please mail or call
EMAIL: See Below

6163

Business Information: Whirlpool Financial Corporation is an international consumer and commercial lending establishment and consulting team. Mr. Ferguson joined Whirlpool in 1994 and now serves as Senior Business Analyst, responsible for business planning and analysis, purchase and sale of portfolios, and credit risk management. Internet users may reach him via: EFERGUSONI@AOL.COM **Career Steps:** Whirlpool Financial Corporation: Senior Business Analyst (1995–Present), Collections and Risk Analyst (1994–1995); Treasurer, Michigan Metri Tech (1990–1994). **Associations & Accomplishments:** Lambda Chi Alpha. **Education:** Western Michigan University: M.B.A. in progress, Bachelor of Business – Finance and Economics; Lake Michigan College, P.B.A. course work. **Personal:** Married to Wanda in 1994. Mr. Ferguson enjoys computer modeling, mountain biking, and golf.

Cathy Johnson

President & Owner
Banc – IV
1111 Northeast 25th Avenue, Suite 102
Ocala, FL 34470–5665
(352) 732–7979
Fax: (352) 732–7989

6163

Business Information: Banc–IV, located in Ocala, Florida is a residential lending company. Established in 1990, the Company has no brokerage fee, which allows them to provide more options on residential loans to their clients. As President & Owner, Ms. Johnson, who has been involved in real estate banking since 1975, oversees each and every account from origination. Additionally, she is responsible for the day–to–day operation of the Company and supervises a small support staff. Active in the community, it is her belief that everyone who wants to buy a house should be able to, and she strives to make her clients' dreams come true. **Career Steps:** President & Owner, Banc – IV (1990–Present); Loan Officer, Taylor Bean & Whitaker (1988–1990); Branch Manager, First Family Savings Bank (1987–1988). **Associations & Accomplishments:** Treasurer, Executive Officer, & Board of Directors, Marion County Builders Association; Ocala Marion County Board of Realtors. **Education:** Gulf Coast, B.S. (1975); Various Mortgage Banking. **Personal:** Married to Ron in 1975.

One child: Amie. Ms. Johnson enjoys crafts, gourmet cooking, and spending time with her granddaughter, Korey.

Stephan H. Koseian

Financial Consultant
Mr. Money
95 North Road
East Windsor, CT 06088
(860) 623–2717
Fax: (860) 623–9802

6163

Business Information: Mr. Money is a loan brokerage service and a purchaser of first mortgages. As Financial Consultant, Mr. Koseian is responsible for diversified administrative activities. Concurrently, Mr. Koseian serves as a Professional Organizer for Organization Plus, an organizer of files for small businesses. **Career Steps:** Financial Consultant, Mr. Money (1981–Present); Professional Organizer, Organization Plus (1995–); On–Site Administrator, Computer Processing Institute (1988–1990); Vice President, Enfield Realty Cons., Inc. (1978–1981); Broker/Office Manager, Enfield Realty Associates (1974–1981). **Associations & Accomplishments:** Association of MBA Executives; National Association of Professional Organizers; National Association of the Self–Employed; North Central Connecticut Chamber of Commerce; Masonic Fraternity; Shriners; Justice of the Peace. **Education:** American International College, M.B.A. (1978); Central Connecticut State University, B.S. (1973). **Personal:** Mr. Koseian enjoys photography and participating in local political affairs.

Deborah K. Oliver

Operations Vice President
The Associates
300 East John Carpenter Freeway, Two Plaza
Irving, TX 75062
(214) 541–3663
Fax: (214) 541–3401

6163

Business Information: The Associates is a financial services and credit card company with over 1,200 branch offices located around the world. Ms. Oliver has held various managerial positions with The Associates, serving as Assistant Vice President in 1991 before her promotion to Vice President in 1993. Moving into her current capacity as Operations Vice President in January of 1996, she is responsible for the Incentives Division, developing and managing incentive programs; Service Quality Division, developing and improving customer satisfaction and retention; Consumer Branch Services, a systems help–desk for field employees; and the Customer Communications Group, ensuring that all communications are easy to understand, answering policy inquiries, and reviewing new systems enhancements. **Career Steps:** The Associates: Operations Vice President (1996–Present), Vice President (1993–1996), Assistant Vice President (1991–1993). **Associations & Accomplishments:** American Management Association; American Society for Quality Control; Sterling's Who's Who; National Association for Female Executives. **Education:** NTSU, B.A. (1988). **Personal:** Ms. Oliver enjoys skiing, in–line skating, and racquetball.

Joan M. Olschewske

Corporate Reporting Manager
Citibank Student Loan Corporation
99 Garnsey Rd.
Pittsford, NY 14534–4532
(716) 248–7630
Fax: (716) 248–7007

6163

Business Information: Citibank Student Loan Corporation, a subsidiary of Citibank of New York State since 1992, is one of the nation's top originators of student loans, earning $160 million annually in net interest income. As Corporate Reporting Manager, Ms. Olschewske is responsible for taxes, internal controls, internal audits, audit interface, SEC reporting, accounting policies, FASB interpretation, and annual reporting. **Career Steps:** Corporate Reporting Manager, Citibank Student Loan Corporation (1993–Present); Corporate Consolidation, Frontier Corp. (1988–1993); Senior Auditor, Price Waterhouse, LLP (1983–1988). **Associations & Accomplishments:** Phi Kappa Phi National Honor Society; Member and Former Chair–Board of Directors, Foodlink, Inc.; Chairperson – Supervisory Committee, Summit Federal; New York State Society of Certified Public Accountants. **Education:** Rochester Institute of Technology, B.S. (1983); Certified Public Accountant. **Personal:** Married to Thomas in 1977. Four children: Jennifer, Stephen, Lindsay, and Andrew. Ms. Olschewske enjoys reading, travel, the outdoors, and swimming.

Gary G. Sullivan

Senior Vice President
WFS Financial Inc.
3055 West 15th Street
Plano, TX 75075
(214) 612–4200
Fax: (214) 612–0912

6163

Business Information: WFS Financial Inc. is an indirect automobile financing company, providing loans for automotive dealers on a national level from offices located throughout the U.S. The Company offers two divisions of loan services: Dealer – "A" credit which has low interest rates, and Branch – "C" credit with high interest rates. As Senior Vice President, Mr. Sullivan is responsible for directing the entire function of the Southwestern Division (Texas and Oklahoma), consisting of two regions and 21 branches. **Career Steps:** Senior Vice President, WFS Financial Inc. (1994–Present); Branch Manager, Olympic/Arcidia Financial Ltd. (1992–1994); Senior Vice President, North Park National Bank (1990–1992); Vice President & Branch Manager, Chase Auto Finance (1988–1990). **Associations & Accomplishments:** Published in newspapers and trade publications. **Education:** Texas Tech University, B.B.A. in Finance (1971). **Personal:** Married to Karen in 1971. Three children: Malcolm, Chad and Karry. Mr. Sullivan enjoys golf, college sports, and his children's school activities.

Gary T. Taylor

Vice President
AT&T Capital Corporation
44 Whippany Road
Morristown, NJ 07960–4458
(201) 397–4035
Fax: (201) 397–4342

6163

Business Information: AT&T Capital Corporation is an international equipment leasing and finance company. As the second largest full–service, multi–point distribution leasing company in the U.S., AT&T Capital offers telecommunication, automotive and real estate financing services throughout the U.S., Canada, Europe, Hong Kong, Australia and Mexico. As Vice President, Gary Taylor serves as the chief credit and operations officer, overseeing the business unit engaged in leasing/lending to small businesses. This includes Federally–sponsored Small Business Administration–backed loans. **Career Steps:** Vice President, AT&T Capital Corporation (1990–Present); Vice President, First National Bank of Chicago (1987–1990); Vice President, Chase Manhattan Bank (1981–1987). **Associations & Accomplishments:** Board of Advisors, National Housing and Neigborhood Development Services, Inc. **Education:** Columbia University, Executive Training (1994); Florida A&M University – School of Business and Industry, B.S. **Personal:** Married to Faith in 1989. Two children: Jordan and Kiyomi. Mr. Taylor enjoys music (plays keyboard, writes music – wife sings, owns own recording studio), and skiing.

Joe Tishoff

Senior Account Executive
First Capital Corporation
1401 Ocean Avenue, Suite 210
Santa Monica, CA 90401
(310) 458–0010 ext. 257
Fax: (818) 727–6759

6163

Business Information: First Capital Corporation is a residential mortgage loan brokerage and banking firm. As Senior Account Executive, Mr. Tishoff acts as a loan consultant and arranges mortgage loans. Mr. Tishoff plans to continue advancing within the Corporation and create a national presence. **Career Steps:** Senior Account Executive, First Capital Corporation (1995–Present); Senior Account Executive, Transcapital Mortgage Corporation (1993–95); Senior Account Executive, South Coast Financial (1983–1993). **Associations & Accomplishments:** Licensed Salesperson, California Department of Real Estate; Past Finance Co–Chairperson, Los Angeles Association of Realtors. **Education:** California State University, B.S. (1985). **Personal:** Single. Mr. Tishoff enjoys snow skiing and power boating.

Lawrence J. Wodarski

Chief Administrative Officer
The Money Store, Inc.
3301 C Street, Suite 100M
Sacramento, CA 95816–3300
(916) 446–5000
Fax: (916) 446–5301

6163

Business Information: The Money Store, Inc. is a commercial finance company providing residential, small business, auto, and student loans. A national lending leader, the Money Store is a major publicly held institution. As Chief Administrative Officer, Mr. Wodarski is responsible for all aspects of administrative operations of the Company. He handles human resource responsibilities, corporate learning center, information technology, lobbying, and company travel. **Career Steps:** Chief Administrative Officer, The Money Store, Inc. (1995–Present); President, The Money Store Investment Corporation (1990–1995); Vice President of Finance and Administration, Damin Avionica Corporation (1987–1989); District Director, U.S. Small Business Administration (1982–1986). **Associations & Accomplishments:** Board Member, National Association of Government Guaranteed Lenders; President, Board of Trustees, Sacramento Ballet Association. **Education:** Boston University, M.B.A. (1971); University of Detroit, B.S. (1968). **Personal:** Married to Linda in 1985. Two children: Lauren and Jason. Mr. Wodarski enjoys golf.

Felix Joel Zambrana–Ortiz

Assistant Staff Attorney
Norwest Island Finance
P.O. Box 71504
San Juan, Puerto Rico 00936
(787) 759–7044
Fax: (787) 759–8455

6163

Business Information: Norwest Island Finance offers small and home equity loans with financing. As Assistant Staffing Attorney, Mr. Zambrana–Ortiz handles legal counseling and notarial responsibilities. He represents the Company in all Puerto Rico courts (federal, district, superior, and U.S. District) and handles investigations, contracts, and corporate law. **Career Steps:** Assistant Staffing Attorney, Norwest Island Finance (1992–Present); Administration of Corrections Government of Puerto Rico: Director of Investigations Office (1990–1992), Vice President, Board of Directors of Managing Affairs (1992), Examiner Board of Appeals of Construction and Lotifications (1990–1991). **Associations & Accomplishments:** Puerto Rico Bar Association, Rio Piedras Chapter; American Bar Association; Puerto Rico Notary Association. **Education:** Interamerican University – School of Law, J.D. (1989); University of Puerto Rico, B.A. **Personal:** Married to Shelia M. in 1992. One child: Felix Antonio.

Diann R. Shelton

Financial Service Manager
Nissan Motor Acceptance
416 16th Street
Hunnington Beach, CA 92648
(800) 777–5101 Press 3
Fax: (714) 536–0419

6191

Business Information: Nissan Motor Acceptance is an international financial subsidiary of Nissan Motor Corporation, accommodating Nissan dealers in retail, leasing, and wholesale functions. As Financial Service Manager, Ms. Shelton is the eyes and ears for Nissan Motors and sub–dealers in the industry. She deals with attorneys, contractors, and consultants on financial matters. She is also responsible for assisting new dealerships with inventories, buildings, and establishing finance procedures. In 1976 Ms. Shelton was one of the first women to successfully enter the automotive sales field, a field predominantly male up to that point. **Career Steps:** Financial Service Manager, Nissan Motor Acceptance (1990–Present); Executive Manager, Infiniti (1988–1990); Sales Manager, Mercedes Benz (1984–1988); Sales Manager, Toyota (1976–1984). **Associations & Accomplishments:** Police Reserve. **Education:** Western Law, Paralegal Certificate (1993). **Personal:** One child: daughter, Tarrah and granddaughter Darrian. Ms. Shelton enjoys church, sewing, housekeeping, and gardening.

6200 Security and Commodity Brokers

6211 Security brokers and dealers
6221 Commodity contracts brokers, dealers
6231 Security and commodity exchanges
6282 Investment advice
6289 Security and commodity services, NEC

Lewis H. Aaron

Executive Director
SBC Warburg
19 Pembridge Crescent
London, United Kingdom W11 3DX
(44171) 860–05
Fax: (44171) 382–40
EMAIL: See Below

6211

Business Information: SBC Warburg specializes is a merchant bank and stock brokerage firm specializing in closed–end funding for investors. International in scope, the Company serves over 1,000 companies, spanning 45 markets and 45 different currencies. As Executive Director, Mr. Aaron is responsible for leading all research. He locates companies, develops strategies, and allocate assets. Mr. Aaron also consults with potential companies. Internet users can reach him via: lewis.aaron@dial.pipex.com. **Career Steps:** Executive Director, SBC Warburg (1992–Present); Director, BZW (1988–1992); Director, Lehman Brothers International (1986–1988); Manager, Coopers & Lybrand (1984–1986). **Associations & Accomplishments:** American Institute of Certified Public Accountants; Republicans Abroad. **Education:** Pennsylvania State University: M.S. in Finance (1980), B.S. in Accounting (1978). **Personal:** Mr. Aaron enjoys owning a farm, horses, and fox hunting.

Mr. Thomas B. Allgood

Financial Consultant
Merrill Lynch
510 Highway A1A North
Ponte Vedra Beach, FL 32082
(904) 273–3821
Fax: (904) 273–3890
WATS: 1–800–937–0267

6211

Business Information: Merrill Lynch is a full service financial institution providing financial products and advice for achieving retirement, estate, and investment planning goals. A registered investment advisor (Maryland), Mr. Allgood and his partner manage over $80 million for seniors in retirement, young professionals, and small businesses. They use computer analysis, financial planning and research to help clients reach their financial objectives. **Career Steps:** Financial Consultant, Merrill Lynch (1987–Present); Marketing Manager, Power Generation Chemicals, Olin Corporation (1985–1987); Account Manager, NALCO Chemical Company (1984–1985); Product Specialist, Steel Industry, NALCO Chemical Company (1980–1984). **Associations & Accomplishments:** Jacksonville Chamber of Commerce; Committee of 100; Competent Toastmaster. **Education:** University of Florida, MBA in Marketing (1975); Wofford College, B.S. in Chemistry; Lieutenant, Supply Corps, U.S. Naval Reserve (1971–1975). **Personal:** Two children: Christine and Catherine. Mr. Allgood enjoys fishing, playing golf, listening to music and going to the beach.

Peter K. Aman

Vice President
APS Financial
1802 Romford Drive
Austin, TX 78704
(512) 314–4375
Fax: (512) 444–3660

6211

Business Information: APS Financial is a broker and dealer of securities. As Vice President, Mr. Aman is responsible for all aspects of Company operations, including investing,and advising client businesses regarding stocks and bonds, securities, high yield municipals, corporate bonds, etc. **Career Steps:** Vice President, APS Financial (1992–Present). **Associations & Accomplishments:** Century Club, University of Texas – Austin; 100 Club Member. **Education:** University of Texas, B.A. in Finance (1991).

William R. Baumel

Director of Telecommunications Investing
Coral Venture Group
60 South 6th Street
Minneapolis, MN 55402
(612) 335–8698
Fax: (612) 335–8668

6211

Business Information: Coral Venture Group specializes in venture capital investing. Coral buys small companies, makes them profitable, eventually takes them public, and usually sells them. As Director of Telecommunications Investing, Mr. Baumel directs the process for telecommunications firms. He studies the companies that are going to be bought and handles the investment part of the cycle. **Career Steps:** Director of Telecommunications Investing, Coral Venture Group (1995–Present); Venture Capital, Brinson Partners (1993–1995); Certified Public Accountant, Deloitte & Touche (1989–1993). **Associations & Accomplishments:** Beta Gamma Sigma; Beta Alpha Psi; Volunteer Teacher, Apples & Pears Day Care; Junior Achievement, Volunteer Award. **Education:** University of Michigan, M.B.A.; Ohio State University, B.S.B.A. summa cum laude. **Personal:** Married to Jill in 1992. Mr. Baumel enjoys tennis, skiing, and reading.

Michael Bianco
Chairman
American Capital Markets Corporation
One Sansome Street, #2000
San Francisco, CA 94104
(415) 347–3208
Fax: (415) 951–4660

6211

Business Information: American Capital Markets Corporation is an international corporation specializing in investment banking, financial advising, and assisting clients on raising debt and equity capitol. Headquartered in San Francisco, California, the Corporation has fifteen locations throughout Asia, including Hong Kong, Shanghai, and Beijing, China. Established in 1990, the Corporation employs 1,400 people, and has an estimated annual revenue of $125 million. As Chairman, Mr. Bianco manages the Corporation and formulates policy. A liaison between major clients and investors, he is also involved with a graduate program at Dominican College called Pacific Basin, which instructs students in working with Asian people and cultures. **Career Steps:** Chairman, American Capital Markets Corporation (1994–Present); Managing Director, Arthur Anderson (1991–1993); President/Chief Executive Officer, Loelo Rhoades and Company (1971–1977); Vice President, Barclays Bank (1981–1984). **Associations & Accomplishments:** Director, California Council For International Trade; Director, Korean American Chamber of Commerce; Life Member, Stanford University, Alumni Association; President's Advisory Council, Wilkes University. **Education:** University of Michigan, M.P.A. (1968); Wilkes University, A.B. (1962); Stanford University, Advanced Management Program (1992). **Personal:** Married to Marcia in 1968. Three children: Suzanne, Francesca, and Michael Joseph. Mr. Bianco enjoys golf and sailing.

Marcos Brujis
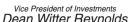

Country Manager
Midland Bank
25 De Mayo 195 – 6 Floor
Buenos Aires, BA, Argentina 1002
(541) 343–8439
Fax: (541) 343–6927

6211

Business Information: Midland Bank, a subsidiary of HSBC Group, is an international commercial and investment banking service located in 70 countries. Midland, along with the Hong Kong Bank, is the second–largest HSBC subsidiary. As Country Manager, Mr. Brujis is the HSBC Representative to Argentina, Uruguay, and Peru. As such, he is responsible for marketing, sales, handling private development funds, promoting businesses, and supervising employees. **Career Steps:** Midland Bank: Country Manager (1995–Present), Rep. for Peru/Head of Trade Finance (1986–1995); Southern Cone Representative, Bank of Nova Scotia (1985–1986). **Associations & Accomplishments:** Argentine/British Chamber of Commerce; Armchair Club. **Education:** McGill University, M.B.A. (1978); Israel Institute of Technology, B.Sc. in Industrial Engineering & Management. Mr. Brujis is mutilingual, speaking Spanish and Hebrew, as well as English. **Personal:** Married to Denise in 1976. Three children: Leon, Daniel, and Sandra. Mr. Brujis enjoys tennis and jazz music.

Graciela Cairoli

Vice President and Head of Research and Development
Capital Markets
Esmeralda 130 Piso 10
Camital Federal BA, Argentina 1035
(541) 320–1900
Fax: (541) 780–1734
E MAIL: See Below

6211

Business Information: Capital Markets is a family–owned, international investment and stock brokerage firm. Established in 1991, the Firm currently has 30 employees. As Vice President and Head of Research and Development, Ms. Cairoli directs a staff of eight and conducts research on investment opportunities for clients. Internet users may reach her via: capital@msg.smartar.com. **Career Steps:** Vice President and Head of Research and Development, Capital Markets (1994–Present); Economics Associated Professor, Universidad Di Tella (1996); Associated Professor of Economics, Universidad Catolica Argentina (1983–1994); Economic Analyst, Banco Central Argentino (1983). **Associations & Accomplishments:** Graduated Economic Association "Centro De Graduados on Econotlia de la Universidad Catolica Argentina"; Advisor, Universidad Di Tella Education Council. **Education:** University of Chicago, M.A. in Economics; Licenciado en Economica de la Universidad Catolica Argentina (1978). **Personal:** Married to Cesar Luis Ramirez–Royas in 1984. Two children: Ana Ines and Agustin. Ms. Cairoli enjoys tennis, skiing, and language studies.

Carmen Rosario Caro

Vice President of Investments
Dean Witter Reynolds
1200 Plaza Scotia Bank
San Juan, Puerto Rico 00917
(809) 759–2814
Fax: (809) 763–1108

6211

Business Information: Dean Witter Reynolds is a leading, full–service financial brokerage specializing in the sale of stocks and bonds. Established in 1913, the Company currently employs over 28,000 brokers and support staff corporatewide. As Vice President of Investments, Mrs. Caro is responsible for all contracts, investments, problem–solving, and development of new contracts. She is also a financial advisor for the Company. **Career Steps:** Vice President of Investments, Dean Witter Reynolds (1987–Present); Vice President of Marketing, Mac Kan Ericson (1979–1986). **Associations & Accomplishments:** Puerto Rico Chamber of Commerce; National Association of Female Executives. **Education:** University of Puerto Rico, M.B.A. (1977); Trinity College, Degree in Finance and Marketing, magna cum laude. **Personal:** Married to Amancio Arias–Guardialo, Esq. in 1993. Three children: Pedro L. Billoch, Paulette Arias, and Amancio Arias III. Mrs. Caro enjoys swimming, horseback riding, reading, and aerobics.

Charles M. Carrico III
Operations Manager
Fidelity Investments
200 Magellan – KN2B
Covington, KY 41015
(606) 386–4122
Fax: (606) 431–0259

6211

Business Information: Fidelity Investments is the largest mutual fund company in the United States, providing money management and investment counsel to the general public and large companies. Joining Fidelity Investments as Operations Manager in 1991, Mr. Carrico manages a team of associates responsible for the day–to–day financial operations of over 2,000 corporate retirement plans and fidelity products. **Career Steps:** Operations Manager, Fidelity Investments (1991–Present); Staff Assistant, Office of the United States Ambassador to the U.S.S.R. (1989–1991). **Associations & Accomplishments:** National Association of Securities Dealers; B.E.S.T. – Business Education Success Teams. **Education:** University of Kentucky, M.S. (1993); Rhodes College, B.A. (1989). **Personal:** Married to Michelle Williams in 1994. Mr. Carrico enjoys running.

Agnes S. Carson
Vice President/Human Resources Relationship Manager
Bankers Trust Company
Bankers Trust Company Plaza, 130 Liberty Street
New York, NY 10006
(212) 696–3797
Fax: (212) 725–2285

6211

Business Information: Bankers Trust Company, the leader in investment banking, is the world's largest investment firm. The Company provides financial services/banking to individual corporations, commercial government entities, and correspondent banks worldwide. As Vice President/Human Resources Relationship Manager, Ms. Carson is responsible for the human resource needs of 600 employees in multiple locations. She handles all general human resource functions for the Company, including hiring, benefits, and compensation. **Career Steps:** Vice President/Human Resources Relationship Manager, Bankers Trust Company (1993–Present); New York Region Director of Human Resources, Watson Wyatt Worldwide (1987–1993); Human Resources Generalist, Deloitte & Touche, L.L.P. (1985–1987). **Associations & Accomplishments:** Society of Human Resource Management; Publicity Club of New York; Former Participant/Public Service Scholar, Mayor's Office Scholarship Program; Elder, Presbyterian Church. **Education:** Pace University, M.B.A. (1987); Hunter College, B.A. in Psychology with Special Honors. **Personal:** Ms. Carson enjoys swing and tap dancing, horseback riding, running, skiing, and architecture/design.

James A. Christopher
Senior Vice President of Technology
Marketing ONE, Inc.
851 South West 6th Avenue
Portland, OR 97204
(503) 220–3308
Fax: (503) 220–0814
EMAIL: See Below

6211

Business Information: Marketing ONE, Inc., established in 1983, offers financial services, selling and investment services, and acts as a full service broker and dealer for commercial banking institutions. The Corporation currently employs 350 people. As Senior Vice President of Technology, Mr. Christopher is in charge of information systems for Marketing ONE, Inc. He handles telecommunications, technical services, and website technology. Mr. Christopher is also involved in strategic planning for the future. Internet users can reach him via: Jimc@MarketingOne.com. **Career Steps:** Senior Vice President of Technology, Marketing ONE, Inc. (1995–Present); Bank One Service Corporation: Technology Manager (1992–1995), Senior Systems Analyst (1987–1992); Self Employed Consultant, Owner (1979–1987). **Associations & Accomplishments:** Attending Meetings Of: Powerbuilder User Group, Sybase Users Group. Oregon Software Association. **Education:** Otterbein College, B.A. in Finance (1993); Ohio State University, General Studies; Marion Technical College, Data Programming Degree. **Personal:** Married to Kelly in 1981. Three children: Erin, Kaitlyn, and Andrew. Mr. Christopher enjoys golf, Internet surfing, touring wineries, and camping.

Raymond Clark

Principal
Alex Brown
601 South Figueroa Street, Suite 3650
Los Angeles, CA 90017–5741
(213) 891–2557
Fax: (213) 891–2520
EMail: See Below

6211

Business Information: Alex Brown is the nation's oldest investment firm. Established in 1800, the Firm is the 13th oldest corporation in America and has a total of 430 brokers working out of 19 offices in the U.S. as well as London, Geneva and Tokyo. As Principal, Mr. Clark works with a partner and three assistants. The team is responsible for money management. Internet users can reach him via: K401MAN.AOL. **Career Steps:** Principal, Alex Brown & Sons (1993–Present); Senior Vice President, Sutro & Company (1987–1993); Vice President, Drexel Burnham (1986–1987); Vice President, Prudential Bache (1983–1986). **Associations & Accomplishments:** Participated in United Way Corporate Fund Raiser (1988); "Broker of the Year" (1990). **Personal:** Married to Sholeh in 1988. Two children: Tiyana and Brandon. Mr. Clark enjoys tennis, snow skiing, karate, and reading.

Glenn M. Colacurci

Branch Manager/Senior Vice President
Smith Barney, Inc.
1 Sansome St., 38th Floor
San Francisco, CA 94104–4448
(415) 984–6671
Fax: (415) 984–6596

6211

Business Information: Smith Barney, Inc., one of the global leaders, specializes in financial planning and investment brokerage. International in scope, the Company currently has 10,000 brokers. A sixteen year veteran with Smith Barney, Mr. Colacurci was Promoted to Branch Manager/Senior Vice President in 1991. He is now responsible for supervising a staff of 200, performing various administrative activities, and providing executive leadership for the San Francisco branch. **Career Steps:** Smith Barney, Inc.: Branch Manager/Senior Vice President (1991–Present), Divisional Director of Sales and Marketing (1984–1991), Financial Consultant (1980–1984). **Associations & Accomplishments:** San Francisco Bond Club; Big Brothers/Big Sisters of the Peninsula Advisory Board. **Education:** Marquette University, B.A. (1972). **Personal:** Married to Glenn in 1979. Mr. Colacurci enjoys travel, sports, and collecting sports memorabillia.

Stephen R. Coma

Managing Director
Merrill Lynch
Sears Tower, 56th Floor
Chicago, IL 60606
(312) 906–6343
Fax: Please mail or call

6211

Business Information: Merrill Lynch is the world's largest financial planning, investment brokerage, and trust services company, offering a broad range of financial services for individuals and businesses. Investment instruments include stocks, bonds, mutual funds, insurance, and trust products. As Managing Director, Mr. Coma is responsible for managing the municipal public and capital markets in the Chicago office. **Career Steps:** Merrill Lynch: Managing Director (1994–Present), Director (1992–1994), Vice President (1990–1992). **Associations & Accomplishments:** Public Securities Association. **Education:** University of Chicago, M.B.A. (1985); Princeton University, A.B. (1981). **Personal:** Married to Karen Suzanne in 1989. Two children: Nicholas and Stephanie. Mr. Coma enjoys golf, tennis, and swimming.

Thomas V. Conigliaro

Director
Merrill Lynch
233 South Walker Drive, Suite 5500
Chicago, IL 60606
(312) 906–6601
Fax: (312) 906–6916

6211

Business Information: Merrill Lynch is the world's largest financial planning, investment brokerage, and trust services company, offering a broad range of financial services for individuals and businesses. Investment instruments include stocks, bonds, mutual funds, insurance, and trust products. As Director, Mr. Conigliaro is responsible for coordinating equity products and performance of the Chicago office. He manages new business development and initial public offering, and supervises a staff of ten. **Career Steps:** Director, Merrill Lynch (1987–Present). **Associations & Accomplishments:** American Institute for Management Research (AIMR). **Education:** University of South Florida, M.B.A. (1987); Widener University, B.S. (1985); Chartered Financial Analyst. **Personal:** Married to Lisa in 1987. Two children: Elizabeth and Christine. Mr. Conigliaro enjoys golf and hunting.

Thomas J. Cullen

Senior Vice President
Textron Financial Corporation
40 Westminster Street, Suite 10, 12th Floor
Providence, RI 02903–2525
(401) 621–4227
Fax: Please mail or call

6211

Business Information: Textron Financial Corporation is a wholly–owned subsidiary of Textron, Inc. – a Fortune 1000 corporation – and specializes in financial services including loans, leasing, and syndications. Mr. Cullen joined Textron Financial in 1992 as Vice President and Controller. Promoted to Senior Vice President of Finance and Treasurer in 1995, he is presently responsible for accounting, tax, and treasury management, as well as financial planning and various administrative activities. **Career Steps:** Textron Financial Corporation: Senior Vice President (1995–Present), Vice President/Controller (1992–1995); Senior Manager, Ernst & Young (1980–1992). **Associations & Accomplishments:** Rhode Island Society of Certified Public Accountants; Institute of Management Accountants; Equipment Leasing Association; Treasury Management Association; Rhode Island Good Neighbor Energy Fund; Special Olympics of Rhode Island; People in Partnership. **Education:** Stonehill College, B.S. (1970). **Personal:** Married to Shirley. Two children: Steven and Janie. Mr. Cullen enjoys skiing and golf.

John Deets

Manager of Recovery Services
GE Capital
7905 Quivira Road
Lenexa, KS 66215–2732
(913) 789–2150
Fax: (913) 676–4024
E MAIL: See Below

6211

Business Information: GE Capital, a division of General Electric, is a financial services company. As Manager of Recovery Services, Mr. Deets manages post write–offs, attorneys, and agencies involved in write–offs. Internet users can reach him via: jdeets@msn.com. **Career Steps:** GE Capital: Manager of Recovery Services (1996–Present), Account Manager (1994–1996), Portfolio Control Manager (1988–1990). **Associations & Accomplishments:** Elfun Society. **Education:** Columbia College, B.A. (1965). **Personal:** Married to April in 1965. Two children: Dawn and Tamara. Mr. Deets enjoys golf and various church activities.

Nick Dovidio

Chief Financial Officer
Vestar Capital Partners
139 West Dudley Avenue
Westfield, NJ 07090–4001
(212) 949–6423
Fax: (212) 808–4922

6211

Business Information: Vestar Capital Partners is an investment banking firm consisting of seventeen principals who invest their own money (a $260 million portfolio) into organizations. Established in 1988, Vestar Capital Partners currently employs 25 people. A financial investments and accounting executive for over fifteen years, Mr. Dovidio serves as Chief Financial Officer, responsible for the management and direction of all corporate financial activities and for consulting services to portfolio companies. **Career Steps:** Chief Financial Officer, Vestar Capital Partners (1989–Present); Chief Financial Officer, Skadden, Arps, et al (1982–1989); Manager, Ernst & Young (1977–1982). **Associations & Accomplishments:** Director, Westfield's YMCA; Director, Prestone Products Corporation; Director, International Airparts Corporation. **Education:** Stanford University, M.B.A. (1977); Fordham College, B.A. in Mathematics (1973). **Personal:** Married to Catherine in 1982. Two children: Nicholas and Thomas. Mr. Dovidio enjoys golf.

Jay A. Drummond

Loss Prevention Consultant
Motors Insurance Corporation
130 East Carpenter Freeway
Irving, TX 75062
(713) 872–6040
Fax: (713) 872–6040

6211

Business Information: Motors Insurance Corporation is an underwriter of car and truck dealership inventories, warranties and associated insurance lines for businesses. As Loss Prevention Consultant, Mr. Drummond provides loss prevention services by evaluating loss trends and exposures to vehicle inventories. He also works to improve the loss prevention services. **Career Steps:** Loss Prevention Consultant, Motors Insurance Corporation (1996–Present); Loss Prevention Consultant, Factory Mutual Engineering Associates (1988–1996); Engineering Officer, U.S. Army Corps of Engineers (1986–1987). **Associations & Accomplishments:** National Society of Professional Engineers. **Education:** Texas A&M University, B.S. (1985). **Personal:** Married to Patricia in 1991. Two children: Jay Alexander II and Patrice Jayne. Mr. Drummond enjoys gardening and family.

Manuel Escobar, Ph.D., C.F.A.

Vice President of Investments
Dean Witter Reynolds
1200 Plaza Scotiabank
Hato Rey, Puerto Rico 00917
(809) 766–0170
Fax: (809) 763–1108

6211

Business Information: Dean Witter Reynolds is one of the world's leading, full–service financial brokerage and consulting firms, specializing in the sale of stocks and bonds. With extensive experience in the pension investment area, Mr. Escobar joined Dean Witter Reynolds Hato Rey, Puerto Rico office as Vice President of Investments in 1989. He is responsible for providing investment consulting services to institutions, universities, and high–net worth individuals. Career milestones include the structuring of the Puerto Rico Teacher's Association portfolio – the largest pension fund in Puerto Rico. He also has legislative experiences regarding the laws and regulations that govern the investment of the Puerto Rico public funds. He has also served as a consultant to the Puerto Rico Teachers Retirement Board, the Puerto Rico Department of Labor, The Puerto Rico Telephone Company and currently serves as a consultant to the Catholic University of Puerto Rico Pension Fund and the Panama Canal Group Insurance Board. **Career Steps:** Vice President of Investments, Dean Witter Reynolds (1989–Present); Vice President of Investments, Kidder Peabody (1982–1989); Investment Consultant, Merrill Lynch; Teacher of Finance and Investment Courses, University of Puerto Rico – Graduate School of Business; Credit Officer, Citibank in San Juan and New York. **Associations & Accomplishments:** Association Investment Management and Research; International Association of Investment Management and Research; Institute of Chartered Financial Analysts; Former Member, American Finance Association; Conducted advanced seminars for the Board of the Puerto Rico Electric Power Retirement System in the areas of asset allocation, internatiol investments, policy design, implementation and performance evaluation; Author of book, "The 936 Market: An Introduction"; Author of numerous articles for the San Juan Star and El Nuevo Dia; Lectured before professional groups in Puerto Rico, Panama, the United States, and Spain. **Education:** Wharton School – University of Pennsylvania: M.A., Ph.D. in Finance and Investments (1974); Chartered Financial Analyst (1995); Attends numerous professional seminars annually. **Personal:** Married to Maria Teresa Piazza. Two children: Philip and Maritere. Dr. Escobar enjoys tennis, history, and philosophy.

Antonio A. Figueroa Alvarado, CPA

Assistant Vice President of Administration/Economic Advisor
PROSAD–COOP
P O Box 195449
San Juan, Puerto Rico 00919
(787) 765–7179
Fax: (787) 281–6965

6211

Business Information: PROSAD–COOP is a government insurance company for cooperatives established in 1990 and currently has 48 employees. As Assistant Vice President of Administration, Mr. Figueroa Alvarado functions as an Economic Advisor to the Company President on investment matters. He is involved in administrative duties, and personnel and budgetary concerns. **Career Steps:** Economic Advisor, PROSAD–COOP (1994–Present); Senior Auditor, Central Hispano Bank (1990–1994); Auditor, KPMG Peat Marwick (1988–1990). **Associations & Accomplishments:** Board of Directors, Almira Padera; Puerto Rico Society of Certified Public Accountants; National Dean's List. **Education:** University of Puerto Rico, B.B.A. in Accounting (1987); Certified Public Accountant (1990). **Personal:** Married to Noelia Ocasio in 1989. Three children: Janice, Christian, and Anthony. Mr. Figueroa Alvarado enjoys volleyball and music.

Joan V. Fiore, Esq.

Managing Director and Counsel
Furman Selz, L.L.C.
237 Park Avenue, Suite 910
New York, NY 10017
(212) 808–3905
Fax: Please mail or call

6211

Business Information: Furman Selz, L.L.C. is a diversified investment banking and securities firm, focusing on corporate finance, merchant banking, institutional research, trading, sales, capital management, and mutual fund administration. As Managing Director and Counsel, Miss Fiore oversees compliance by Furman's Mutual Funds Division with the Federal and state securities laws. The Mutual Funds Division serves as an administrator and distributor of mutual funds whose assets currently exceed $25 billion. Established in 1973, Furman Selz, L.L.C. currently employs over 800 people. **Career Steps:** Managing Director and Counsel, Furman Selz, L.L.C. (1991–Present); Attorney, U.S. Securities and Exchange Commission (1986–1991). **Associations & Accomplishments:** New York Bar Association; The Don Monti Memorial Research Foundation; American Museum of Natural History; National Wildlife Federation. As a law student (Who's Who Among American Law Students, 1982 ed.), Miss Fiore studied International Law with Professor Richard Arens who selected her petition against the Haitian government, alleging human rights violations, for submission to the U.N. (1982). **Education:** University of Bridgeport School of Law, J.D. (1982); Mount Holyoke College, A.B. (1978). **Personal:** Miss Fiore enjoys travel, photography, sports, music, reading, and theatre.

Gladys Flores

Chief Executive Director
Jose G. Flores, Inc. / Emelia Industrial Development
P.O. Box 2695
San Juan, Puerto Rico 00902–2695
(809) 793–2400
Fax: (809) 782–2044

6211

Business Information: Jose G. Flores, Inc./Emelia Industrial Development is a United States customs brokerage firm. Established in 1975, the Firm currently employs 52 people and has an estimated annual revenue of $2.5 million. As Chief Executive Director, Ms. Flores is a licensed Customs Broker. She is responsible for all aspects of operations for the Company. **Career Steps:** Chief Executive Director, Jose G. Flores, Inc. / Emelia Industrial Development (1975–Present); Chief Recruitment Section, Government Office (1972–1975); Customs Technical Aid, United States Customs (1969–1972). **Associations & Accomplishments:** Puerto Rico Chamber of Commerce. **Education:** University of Puerto Rico, B.A., magna cum laude (1969). **Personal:** Married to Jose G. in 1969. Two children: Jose G. and Francisco L. Flores. Ms. Flores enjoys travel.

Robert F. George

Chairman/Chief Executive Officer
Lummens International
P.O. Box 325
Fortson, GA 31808–0325
(706) 322–5447
Fax: (706) 323–5170

6211

Business Information: Lummens International is an international consultant and trader for joint ventures in China. As Chairman/Chief Executive Officer, Mr. George is responsible for all aspects of Company operations, including overall management and negotiating deals in China. **Career Steps:** Chairman/Chief Executive Officer, Lummens International (1988–Present); Chairman, Lummens Industries, Inc. (1949–1993). **Associations & Accomplishments:** Atlanta District Export Council; Advisory Council, Hubee Province Agriculture Council, People's Republic of China; Former President, Rotary Club #200; Vice Chairman, Leadership Morality Institution; Former Board Member, Barnett Bank of Southwest Georgia; United Way; Columbus, Georgia Chamber of Commerce. **Education:** Correspondence Courses: LaSalle, Wharton Business School. **Personal:** Married to Sara Craus in 1954. Two children: Angela Marie George Bacon and Sandra Gayle George Frey. Mr. George enjoys reading, woodworking, and international travel.

Steven M. Gorman

Director of Systems Development
Spires Financial, L.P.
5847 San Felipe Street, Suite 4545
Houston, TX 77057
(713) 783–5000
Fax: (713) 783–0370

6211

Business Information: Spires Financial is a top regional investment banking firm specializing in mortgage securities. As Director of Systems Development, Mr. Gorman is responsible for the direction and development of fixed–income portfolio–level financial analytics for allowing institutional investors to meet their financial oobjectives. Internet users can reach him via: gorman@spiresfin.com. **Career Steps:** Director of Systems Development, Spires Financial L.P. (1995–Present); Vice President, Westcap Corporation (1995); Vice President, MMAR Group, Inc. (1991–1994); Vice President, Bear Stearns (1986–1991). **Associations & Accomplishments:** Membership Director of VisDev, Visual Developers Group, Inc. **Education:** Self–taught in Computer Programming.

Carol B. Gray

Principal
Physician Financial Network
800 South St, Suite 600; P.O. Box 1088
Waltham, MA 02154
(617) 899–2190
Fax: (617) 899–5829

6211

Business Information: Physician Financial Network is a financial services firm, providing insurance and investment services for physicians throughout six states. Services include investment ventures counseling, financial strategies, money management, and budget management solutions. As Principal, Ms. Gray is responsible for all financial ventures for physicians, including investments, planning out financial strategies, money management, and creating budgets. **Career Steps:** Principal, Physician Financial Network (1991–Present); Commercial Real Estate Broker, Hunneman Real Estate (1988–1991); National Sales Manager, Velo–Bind Inc. (1975–1988). **Associations & Accomplishments:** Boston Life Underwriters Association; National Association Life Underwriters; Million Dollar Roundtable; Chairman's Council, New York Life; Boys and Girls Club of Boston; Wellness Community Volunteer; Big Sister Organizations. **Education:** Penn State University, B.A. (1968). **Personal:** Ms. Gray enjoys helping people in financial matters, volunteer activities, golf, and going sailing.

J. Russell Hunsaker

Quality Director
Fidelity Investments
175 East 400 South, Suite 200
Salt Lake City, UT 84111–2368
(801) 537–2016
Fax: (801) 537–2884

6211

Business Information: With over 200 funds, Fidelity Investments is the world's largest provider of mutual funds. Mr. Hunsaker started at Fidelity Investments in 1987 as a Sales Representative, and since has gained the position of Quality Director. In his current capacity, Mr. Hunsaker is responsible for the quality process in the Western Region. This includes the measurement of customer satisfaction, process improvement, and facilitation in the building of a world class organization. **Career Steps:** Fidelity Investments: Quality Director (1993–Present), Sales Manager (1989–1993); Sales Representative (1987–1989); Insurance Claims Adjuster, Utah All Claims (1985–1987). **Associations & Accomplishments:** American Society of Quality Control – Salt Lake City Chapter; State of Utah Quality Award – Public Relations Committee; Scout Master, Boy Scouts of America. **Education:** Westminster College, M.B.A. (1996); University of Utah, B.S. in Economics (1987). **Personal:** Married to Rosemary in 1988. Two children: Ellis and Jessica.

Mr. David V. Hunt

Financial Consultant
Merrill Lynch
1299 Ocean Avenue
Santa Monica, CA 90401
(310) 458–3616
Fax: (310) 451–0726

6211

Business Information: Merrill Lynch is a full service financial institution providing financial products and advice for achieving retirement, estate, and investment planning goals. Established in 1926, the Firm currently employs 20,000 people corporate–wide. As Financial Consultant, Mr. Hunt is responsible for all aspects of consultation, as well as purchasing and marketing investments and conducting educational seminars at the Santa Monica, California branch office. **Career Steps:** Financial Consultant, Merrill Lynch (1993–Present); Financial Consultant, Columbus Financial (1991–1993); President, RDW, Inc. (1989–1990). **Associations & Accomplishments:** Lion's Club; Southwest Texas State University Alumni Association; Phi Delta Theta Alumni Association. **Education:** Southwest Texas State University, B.B.A. in Marketing (1990). **Personal:** Mr. Hunt enjoys golf, sailing, horseback riding, fishing and hunting.

William B. Jackson

President
A.B. Culbertson & Company
777 Main Street, Suite 1250
Ft. Worth, TX 76102–5316
(817) 335–2371
Fax: (817) 335–2379

6211

Business Information: A.B. Culbertson & Company is an underwriting brokerage, specializing in the sale of mortgage–backed securities specifically for non–profit religious organizations. As President, Mr. Jackson is responsible for all aspects of Company operations, including finance, public relations, and strategic planning. **Career Steps:** President, A.B. Culbertson & Company (1994–Present); Consultant, The Office of William B. Jackson, P.C. (1991–1994); President, Centre Savings Associates (1989–1991); Executive Vice President, First City Bank (1980–1989). **Associations & Accomplishments:** American Institute of Certified Public Accountants; Texas Society of Certified Public Accountants; Securities Industry Association; National Association of Securities Dealers; Chicago Stock Exchange; Rotary Club. **Education:** University of Texas – Austin, B.B.A. (1978). **Personal:** Married to Sally L. in 1976. Mr. Jackson enjoys carpentry, renovating, and older residential properties.

Mr. Michael J. Jeweler

Owner
Jeweler International Consultancy
P.O. Box 11614
Shawnee Mission, KS 66207–4614
Fax: (913) 381–0919

6211

Business Information: Jeweler International Consultancy, a newly established entity in the Kansas City Metropolitan area, provides international and domestic corporate security consulting. Mr. Jeweler and his affiliates, both domestic and foreign, provide policy guidance to clients through foreign resources and on–the–scene operational coordination in the continental United States and foreign countries relating to all aspects of client security consulting, including due diligence, executive protection, and risk assessment. **Career Steps:** Owner, Jeweler International Consultancy (1996–Present); Director and Vice President of International Affairs, Intertel, a corporate consulting company established in 1970 (1986–90; 1992–96); Corporate Manager, Asset Protection (international), SBC Communications, Inc. (1990–1992); Consultant to the Hellenic National Police on terrorism matters; Legal Attache, U.S. Embassy, Rome, Italy; Special Agent, Federal Bureau of Investigation (1962–86); Senior Partner, Law Offices of Cashin, Jeweler and Blake (1960–62). **Associations & Accomplishments:** Overseas Security Advisory Council, U.S. Department of State; Society of Former Special Agents of the Federal Bureau of Investigation; Men's Club of Rome; American Society of Industrial Security; Officers Club, Ft. Myer Military District of Washington, D.C.; Masonic (32nd Degree) and Shriner Affiliations; American Legion FBI Post, Washington, D.C.; Unit Commissioner, Boy Scouts of America, Rome, Italy; Association of Former Legats; International Trade Club, Kansas City, MO; Kansas Bar Association; Fluent in Greek, Italian, and French. **Education:** University of Missouri, Kansas City, J.D. (1960); University of Missouri, Kansas City, B.B.A. (1957). **Personal:** Married to Peggy J. nee Kallos in 1962. Mr. Jeweler enjoys hunting and fishing.

Lisa M. Jones

Senior Vice President
MFS Fund Distributors
500 Boylston Street, 13th Floor
Boston, MA 02116
(617) 954–6977
Fax: (617) 954–6621

6211

Business Information: MFS Fund Distributors is a wholesale distributor of mutual funds, variable annuities, and qualified plans. MFS Fund Distributors is the sales company of MFS, the oldest mutual fund company in America. As Senior Vice President, Ms. Jones is responsible for all sales and marketing as related to the financial division. In addition to this assignment, she is also the Director of the Financial Institution Division within MFS Fund Distributors. **Career Steps:** MFS Fund Distributors: Senior Vice President/Director (1993–Present), Regional Vice President/Wholesaler (1988–1993); Product Liaison, EF Hutten & Company (1984–1988). **Associations & Accomplishments:** Trinity College Alumni Association.

Education: Trinity College, B.A. in Economics (1984). **Personal:** Married to Dan in 1988. One child: Samantha. Ms. Jones enjoys travel.

Kirk C. Kinsman

Senior Account Representative
Security First Group
11415 Northwest 60th Terrace
Alachua, FL 32615–7415
(800) 763–2838
Fax: (904) 462–0756

6211

Business Information: Security First Group is a retirement planning and counseling firm that works with state, university, county school systems, counties, hospitals, and small businesses. As Senior Account Representative, Mr. Kinsman meets with clients and helps them with their investment and retirement choices. **Career Steps:** Senior Account Representative, Security First Group (1990–Present); Representative, Multi–Financial/ Investment (1988–1990); Account Representative, AMS Financial/Insurance (1989–1990). **Associations & Accomplishments:** Big Brothers; United Way (1994–Present); Security First Group; Presidents Club, 1991 and 1993–1995 – #1 Representative nationally for the 457 in 1993 and 1994, and #1 Representative nationally for the 403B in 1995. **Education:** University of Minnesota, B.S. in Economics (1987). **Personal:** Married to Liana in 1993. One child: Kameron. Mr. Kinsman enjoys golf, networking, reading, and softball.

Claudio P. Larrain

Head Trader of International Equities
Larrain Vial S.A., Corredora de Bolsa
Av. El Bosque Norte 0177, Piso 3
Santiago, Chile
(562) 339–8562
Fax: (562) 332–0018
EMAIL: See Below

6211

Business Information: Larrain Vial S.A., Corredora de Bolsa, a family–owned business and a subsidiary of Larrain Vial S.A., is a securities brokerage house handling U.S. investment firms which conduct business in Chile and Chilean companies doing business in the U.S. As Head Trader, Mr. Larrain is responsible for the management and trade of international equities. Internet users may reach him via: cplarra@chilepac.net. **Career Steps:** Head Trader, Larrain Vial S.A., Corredora de Balsa (1991–Present); Foreign Trade Supervisor, Koplik & Sons (1989–1991). **Associations & Accomplishments:** Beacon Council; University of Miami International Student Association; International Council. **Education:** University of Miami, M.B.A. (1993); University of Chile, B.B.A. (1989). **Personal:** Mr. Larrain enjoys rugby, racquetball, computers, and conducting technical analysis of stocks.

Mr. James D. Lauter

Senior Vice President of Investments
Dean Witter Reynolds
55 South Lake Avenue, Suite 800
Pasadena, CA 91109
(818) 405–9361
Fax: (818) 584–1251

6211

Business Information: Dean Witter Reynolds is a leading, full–service financial brokerage specializing in the sale of stocks and bonds. Established in 1913, the Company currently employs 28,475 people. As Senior Vice President of Investments, Mr. Lauter counsels clients in regards to planning for retirement and the protection of their economic stability throughout retirement. **Career Steps:** Senior Vice President of Investments, Dean Witter Reynolds (1993–Present); Branch Manager, Dean Witter Reynolds (1974–1993); Vice President of Market Research, Germain's Inc. (1956–1961). **Associations & Accomplishments:** President, Pasadena Bond Club; Member, University of California at Los Angeles Alumni Association; Bruin Bench; Recipient, Sammy Award; Los Angeles Sales Executive Club; AARP; Member, UCLA Chancellor Associates and L.A. World Affairs Council. **Education:** University of California at Los Angeles, B.S. (1956); Wharton Business School; Attended the three year Securities Industries Association Education Program conducted at Wharton Business School. **Personal:** Married to Neima in 1973. Two children: Gary and Walter (deceased); and two grandchildren: Michael and Rachael. Mr. Lauter enjoys tennis, golf and the athletic club.

Evan F. Ling, Ph.D.

Assistant Vice President/Financial Consultant
Merrill Lynch
23504 Ridgeline Road
Diamond Bar, CA 91765
(818) 965–6691
Fax: (909) 861–1134

6211

Business Information: Merrill Lynch is the nation's largest brokerage firm providing full financial services to their clientele. As Assistant Vice President/Financial Consultant, Dr. Ling oversees management and operations of the office, as well as serves as financial consultant to the major clientele, assisting them in their investments (diversifying assets, buying stocks, mutual funds, money market funds, etc). He finds it especially rewarding helping Taiwanese–American people with their investments. Dr. Ling was a professional engineer for twenty years prior to switching careers and owns the patent on a copper alloy for automotive radiators. He also published over 25 research papers and edited a book on copper alloys. **Career Steps:** Assistant Vice President/Financial Consultant, Merrill Lynch (1988–Present); Research Manager, Revere Copper & Brass (1980–1987); Research Supervisor, St. Joe Minerals Corporation (1974–1979). **Associations & Accomplishments:** Board of Director, Taiwanese–American Chamber of Commerce, Los Angeles; Board of Director, Taiwanese Association for Public Affairs (FAPA); Founder, Professor Chen Wen Chen Memorial Foundation; Founder, Taiwanese Association of America Atlanta Chapter; Member, Taiwanese American Lyon Club of San Gabriel Valley, California. **Education:** Georgia Tech, Ph.D. in Metallurgy (1970); Auburn University, M.S. in Mechanical Engineering. **Personal:** Married to Elena Huang. Three children: Felix, Alvina and Benjamin. Dr. Ling enjoys tennis and gardening.

Ms. Maria Mallamaci

First Vice President
Waterhouse Securities, Inc.
55 Water Street
New York, NY 10004–3299
(212) 428–8718
Fax: (212) 968–0466

6211

Business Information: Waterhouse Securities, Inc. is a discount brokerage firm. Currently there are over 90 branch offices nationwide. As First Vice President, Ms. Mallamaci is responsible for the Retirement Plans Department, which includes IRA's, SEP, SAR–SEP, and Qualified Plans. **Career Steps:** First Vice President, Waterhouse Securities, Inc. (1994–Present); Retirement Plans, A.O., Kidder Peabody & Company Inc. (1993–1994); Supervisor of Retirement Plans, Prudential Securities, Inc. (1985–1993). **Associations & Accomplishments:** American Cancer Society; Attends all town meetings; Numerous Corporate recognition awards. **Education:** Pace University, B.B.A. (1988). **Personal:** Married to Gino in 1992. Ms. Mallamaci enjoys bowling, softball, calligraphy and playing the piano.

Carolina Martinez Santos, CPA

Financial Operations Principal/Compliance Officer
RD Capital Group, Inc.
Royal Bank Center, Suite 305
Hato Rey, Puerto Rico 00917
(787) 282–0303
Fax: (787) 282–0356

6211

Business Information: RD Capital Group, Inc., established in 1994, is a small, local brokerage firm with six employees. As Financial Operations Principal, Ms. Martinez Santos is responsible for the Group's financial operations, including all accounts relating to the Company, and overall financial management. **Career Steps:** Financial Operations Principal, RD Capital Group, Inc. (1993–Present); Financial Analysis/Accounts Payable Manager, Baxter Healthcare Corporation (1990–1993); Financial Analysis/Budget Manager, Coca–Cola Bottling Company of Puerto Rico, Inc. (1983–1989). **Associations & Accomplishments:** Colegio de Contadores Publicer Assciados de Puerto Rico: Convention Committee, Cultural Committee, Ethics Committee; American Institute of Certified Public Accountants. **Education:** Interamerican University: M.B.A. in Finance (1994), B.B.A. in Accounting; Certified Public Accountant License; Investment Broker License; Life and Disability Insurance Broker License; Financial and Operations Principal, Compliance Officer. **Personal:** Ms. Martinez Santos enjoys speed walking, aerobics, playing guitar, and wine–related activities.

Helen M. Ng, P.E

Associate
BZW/Barclays Banking
170 West 74th Street #406
New York, NY 10023
(212) 412–1173
Fax: (212) 412–6709

6211

Business Information: BZW/Barclays Bank is an international investment banking firm specializing in the management of project financial structures, transportation, airports, water systems, roadways, and telecommunications. As Associate, Ms. Ng oversees all administration and is responsible for handling all negotiations, managing travel requirements, and modeling financial structures. Additional duties include research of all marketing aspects/backgrounds and strategic planning. **Career Steps:** Associate, BZW/Barclays Bank (1996–Present); Transport Industry Analyst, U.S. Department of Transportation, Federal Railroad Administration (1995–1996); Civil Engineer, Deledin, Cather & Company (1991–1992); Civil Engineer, Morrison, Knudsen Engineers, Inc. (1989–1991). **Associations & Accomplishments:** Rotary Foundation "Ambassador of Goodwill."; First American Scholar Sent to Russia; Student of Classical Piano at the Conservatoire Rimsky–Kobsaloep, St. Petersburg, Russia; Women's Transportation Seminar. **Education:** Massachusetts Institute of Technology, M.B.A. (1995); Stanford University: B.S. in Civil Engineering (1988)m, A.B. in International Relations (1988). **Personal:** Ms. Ng enjoys piano, architecture and languages (French, Russian, and Chinese).

LLOYD®

Ricardo O'Rourke M.

Chairman of the Board/Chief Executive Officer
Operadora de Fondas Lloyd, S.A.
Mariano Otero 1915–A
Guadalajara, Jalisco, Mexico 44560
52–3–121–9050
Fax: 52–3–647–2128
EMAIL: See Below

6211

Business Information: Operadora De Fondos Lloyd, S.A. is an international investment brokerage and banking firm providing financial services to clients. The Firm operates four money market funds, two are fixed income funds for individuals, one fixed income fund for companies, and one common fund for companies and individuals. Operadora De Fondos Lloyd S.A., with over 16,000 clients and a financial portfolio of $150 million, currently employs 102 people. Operadora de Fondos Lloyd, S.A. is the Manager and Distributor of four LLOYD Funds: two Money Market Funds for Individuals, one Money Market Fund for Corportations, and a Common Stock Fund for Individuals or Corporations. It currently handles more than $150 million dollars of over 16,500 clients from all over the world. Mr. O'Rourke, as C.E.O., leads 102 employees and 8 Branch Offices throughtout Mexico. Mr. O'Rourke also manages Lloyd Intermediacion S.A. de C.V., which is a Banking Investment Broker within Mexico. Internet users can readh him at his E–mail address: lloyd@lloyd.com.mx and can obtain further information about this firm via Internet: http://www.lloyd.com.mx **Career Steps:** Chairman of the Board and C.E.O. of Operadora De Fondos Lloyd, S.A. (1988–Present); Director/Manager of Allen W. Lloyd y Asociados S. A. de C.V. (1970–1988); SFE7, U.S. Navy (1957–1970). **Associations & Accomplishments:** Former President, Chamber of Commerce of Chapala, A.C. **Education:** Several Educational Courses in the U.S. Navy; administration and financial seminars in Mexico. **Personal:** Married to Delia O'Rourke in 1973. Six children: Rose, Ann, Richard, Delia, Omar, and Ivan. Mr. O'Rourke M. enjoys having a mechanic's workshop at home and also diving.

Richard M. Orr

Division General Manager
Noble Drilling
10370 Richmond Avenue, Suite 400
Houston, TX 77042
(713) 974–3131
Fax: (713) 974–3181

6211

Business Information: Noble Drilling is an international oil drilling contractor providing offshore and onshore drilling services. Established in 1921, Noble Drilling reports annual revenue of $360 million and currently employs 2,500 people. As Division General Manager, Mr. Orr is responsible for the management of the Venezuela Division, including expanding and creating his region, and managing four offshore drilling rigs. **Career Steps:** Division General Manager, Noble Drilling (1993–Present); Western Oceanic: Area Manager (1985–1993), Drilling Supervisor (1980–1985). **Associations**

& Accomplishments: Vice President, School Board of Directors – Escuela Bella Vista, Maracaibo; Founder, IADC Chapter Venezuela. **Education:** Stanford University, B.S. in International Relations (1968). **Personal:** Married to Janette in 1987. Four children: Tucker, Julian, Ansel, and Mia. Mr. Orr enjoys photography and sailing.

Scott A. Orr

Vice President and Branch Manager
Dean Witter Reynolds
2419 East Commercial Boulevard
Ft. Lauderdale, FL 33308–4042
(954) 493–6621
Fax: (954) 493–6677

6211

Business Information: Dean Witter Reynolds Co., Inc. is a leading, full–service financial brokerage specializing in the sale of stocks and bonds. Established in 1913, the Company currently employs over 28,000 brokers and support staff corporate–wide. Joining Dean Witter Reynold's Ft. Lauderdale offices in 1987 as a regional insurance coordinator, Scott Orr was appointed as Vice President and Branch Manager in 1992. He has full executive administration over a staff of 75 brokers and 40 support staff at the Ft. Lauderdale and Plantation, Florida offices. **Career Steps:** Dean Witter Reynolds: Vice President and Branch Manager (1992–Present), Regional Insurance Coordinator (1987–1992); Brokerage Manager, Travelers Insurance Company (1985–1987). **Associations & Accomplishments:** Pompano Bead Exchange Club. **Education:** Florida Atlantic University: Masters of Education (1978), B.S. in Education. **Personal:** Married to Pam in 1984. Two children: Brittany and Brett. Mr. Orr enjoys running, golf, and tennis.

Carmen Orvananos

President
Khepra, Inc.
40 East 80th Street #25A
New York, NY 10021–0237
(212) 599–6100
Fax: (212) 879–5285

6211

Business Information: Khepra, Inc. is a full–service, international financial services firm specializing in product planning, development, investment ventures and market distribution; currently focusing on trade and venture investments in Mexico. As President, Mrs. Orvananos oversees all company operations, with primary duties involving sales force training and development; product development; sales methodology and automation; policies and procedures; and motivation. She also manages corporate accounts, partnerships, and alliances. **Career Steps:** President, Khepra, Inc. (1992–Present); President, Khepra South America (1972–1992). **Associations & Accomplishments:** Glaucoma Association; Association for the Blind; Greenpeace; ASPCA. **Education:** Universidad Autonoma de Mexico, B.A. (1972); New York School of Interior Design. **Personal:** Married to Byron in 1979. Two children: Alexander and Jean Marc. Mrs. Orvananos enjoys going to the beach, water skiing, and auto racing.

Jacques Pacquin

Chairman
Cogesfonds, Inc.
45 Dalhousie Rue
Montreal, Quebec G1K 8S3
(514) 844–9381
Fax: (514) 843–5217

6211

Business Information: Cogesfonds, Inc. is an investment corporation primarily involved in the management of high dollar portfolios. As Chairman, Mr. Pacquin oversees all aspects of the Corporation, including administrative and operational functions, customer service, and strategic planning. **Career Steps:** Chairman, Cogesfond, Inc. (1983–Present); Vice President, Societe General du Financement du Quebec (1983). **Personal:** Mr. Pacquin enjoys running, cycling, skiing, and other sports.

Marilyn W. Rathbun

Vice President of Sales and Marketing
Walnut Street Securities
670 Mason Ridge Center, Suite 300
St. Louis, MO 63141
(314) 878–1010
Fax: (314) 878–2411

6211

Business Information: Walnut Street Securities is a securities broker/dealer (NASD and SIPC) founded in 1985 to service life insurance agents engaged in the selling of securities. The Firm currently has 2,700 representatives throughout the United States and expect annual sales in excess of $40 million in 1996. As Vice President of Sales and Marketing, Ms. Rathbun oversees the activities of 1,800 representatives throughout the United States. She is involved in the design and implementation of new marketing and sales techniques and the restructuring of existing marketing and sales programs. Ms. Rathbun works with branch offices in developing training techniques. **Career Steps:** Vice President of Sales and Marketing, Walnut Street Securities (1995–Present); Vice President Program Director, First Bank/Locust Street Securities (1994–1995); Regional Sales Manager, Farm & Home Savings/Wall Street Securities (1992–1994). **Associations & Accomplishments:** Corporate Member, I.A.F.P.; Corporate Member, S.I.A. **Education:** Xavier University, M.B.A. (1983), Master's in Education (1970), and B.S. in Education (1970). **Personal:** Married to Gary M. in 1970. Ms. Rathbun enjoys skiing, antiques, and gardening.

Bruce Reeves

Clinical Manager
Human Affairs International
P.O. Box 57986, 10150 South Centennial Parkway
Sandy City, UT 84070
(801) 256–7367
Fax: (801) 256–7663

6211

Business Information: Human Affairs International, a Division of Aetna Life Insurance Company, provides managed care for behavioral disorder health care patients in the area of ensuring that the treatments received are cost effective. Established in 1973, Human Affairs International currently employs 500 people. As Clinical Manager, Mr. Reeves is responsible for all aspects of E.A.P. products, by directing the operations throughout the Company so that they are consistent. **Career Steps:** Human Affairs International: Clinical Manager (1995–Present), Acting Director (1995), Clinical Supervisor (1988–1995). **Associations & Accomplishments:** National Association of Social Workers; American Public Health Association; Board of Directors, Ririe – Woodbury, a local dance company. **Education:** University of Utah: M.S.W. (1983), B.A. (1979). **Personal:** Married to Michael Crooks–Reeves in 1993. Four children: Christopher, Jonathan, Brian and Jennifer. Mr. Reeves enjoys gardening, literature, the theatre and dance.

Lawrence J. Richardson

Vice President
A.G. Edwards and Sons, Inc.
1 Gateway Center, Suite 1002
Newark, NJ 07102–5311
(201) 622–2300
Fax: (201) 622–6130
EMAIL: See Below

6211

Business Information: A.G. Edwards and Sons, Inc. is the 4th largest national brokerage and investment banking firm in the United States, providing valued services to retail and institutional investors, as well as municipal and corporate issuers. As Vice President, Mr. Richardson focuses on providing debt financing services to corporations and municipalities. Internet users can reach him via: LJR43@AOL.COM **Career Steps:** Vice President, A.G. Edwards and Sons, Inc. (1990–Present); Director, City of St. Louis, Missouri, Economic Development Corporation (1988–1990); Program Coordinator/Project Finance, Illinois Development Finance Authority (1985–1988). **Associations & Accomplishments:** National Association of Securities Professionals, Urban League; Swarthmore College Alumni; A Better Chance Alumni Council; Former Board of Directors, St. Louis Public Libraray; Government Finance Officers Association; National Association of Black County Officials; Council Development Finance Agencies. **Education:** Wharton Graduate School, M.B.A. (1980); Swarthmore College, B.A. in Economics; Attended Cranbrook School. **Personal:** Married to Jacqueline in 1981. Two children: Ashley Nicole and Courtney Louise. Mr. Richardson enjoys basketball, football, golf, travel, politics, and reading.

Mr. Larry Santoro

Director
Merrill Lynch
245 North Maple Avenue
Greenwich, CT 06830
(212) 449–8559
Fax: (203) 629–6187

6211

Business Information: Merrill Lynch is the nation's leading investment brokerage and trusted global advisor, offering a broad range of financial services for individuals and businesses. With over 600 offices worldwide, Merrill Lynch has locations in England, Germany, France, China, Japan, Hong Kong, Italy, Canada, and Mexico. As Director, Mr. Santoro is responsible for client coverage for eastern U.S. technology companies. Established in 1885, Merrill Lynch currently employs 44,000 people and has annual portfolio assets in excess of $18 billion. **Career Steps:** Director and Investment Banker, Merrill Lynch (1987–Present); Engineer, Intel Corporation (1982–1985). **Associations & Accomplishments:** Soaring Society of America; Aero Club Albatross; New York Athletic Club; March of Dimes; Harvard Alumni; Dartmouth Alumni; Published in the Journal of Air Pollution Control Society; Had several papers published while at Harvard; Lecturer, Dartmouth College and Harvard Business School. **Education:** Harvard College Business School, M.B.A. (1987); Dartmouth College, B.E. **Personal:** Married to Elizabeth in 1985. Two children: Jack and Helen. Mr. Santoro enjoys hiking, camping, hunting, skiing, reading, fishing, and flying.

Anmar K. Sarafa, CFA

President and Chief Executive Officer
Zaske, Sarafa & Associates, Inc.
355 South Woodward Avenue #200
Birmingham, MI 48009
(810) 647–5990
Fax: (810) 647–0537

6211

Business Information: Zaske, Sarafa & Associates, Inc. is an investment management firm for liquid securities and mutual funds, specializing in the management of funds and advising high net worth individuals and small institutional investors. Co–founding the Firm in 1988, Mr. Sarafa serves as its President and Chief Executive Officer. He is responsible for numerous duties related to investment management, strategic planning, marketing and sales, and client services. **Career Steps:** President and Chief Executive Officer, Zaske, Sarafa & Associates, Inc. (1988–Present); Account Executive, Drexel Burnham Lambert (1986–1988); Summer Intern, Eli Lilly and Company (1985). **Associations & Accomplishments:** Investment Council Association of America; Financial Analysts Society of Detroit; Association for Investment Managment and Research; Association of Investment Management Sales Executives; Investment Management Consulting Association; Founder, "4 U Kid" – a program to raise funds for the promotion of educational and social values for Inner City children (1993). **Education:** University of Michigan, M.B.A. (1986), B.B.A. (1982); Certified Financial Analyst – Institute for Chartered Financial Analysts (1990). **Personal:** Mr. Sarafa enjoys coaching volleyball, sports, reading, music and spending time with friends and family.

Dr. Hector L. Scasserra

Vice President
Mercado Abierto S.A.
Avda Corrientes 415 Piso 6
Buenos Aires, Argentina 1043
(541) 348–7436
Fax: (541) 394–7501

6211

Business Information: Mercado Abierto S.A. is the Argentina stock exchange and over–the–counter market. As Vice President, Dr. Scasserra is in charge of the day–to–day operations of the stock exchange. His duties include, staff administration, general operations, financial planning, and public relations. **Career Steps:** Vice President, Mercado Abierto S.A. (1991–Present); Director, Banco Nacional Desarrollo (1982–1983); Asesor, Ministerio Economia (1980–1982); Controller, Pargues Interama S.A. (1978–1980). **Associations & Accomplishments:** Bolsa de Comercio de Buenos Aires S.A.; Instituto Agentino de Ejecutivos de Finanzas; Club Atletico boca Juniors. **Education:** Universidad Buenos Aires, Public Accounting (1969); Cursos y Seminarios Post Grado en Finanzas. **Personal:** Married to Marta Alicia in 1972. Four children: Maria Victoria, Maria Mercedes, Juan Pablo, and Luis Francisco. Dr. Scasserra enjoys tennis and soccer.

Richard A. Schaefer

First Vice President
Rauscher Pierce Refsnes
3561 East Sunrise Drive, Suite 125
Tucson, AZ 85718–3204
(520) 299–4444
Fax: (520) 299–3671

6211

Business Information: Rauscher Pierce Refsnes specializes in investments such as asset allocation, money management, bond portfolio development, stocks, mutual funds, and retirement plans. As First Vice President, Mr. Schaefer develops appropriate custom portfolios for high net worth individuals and institutions (including retirement plans). In addition, he owns two restaurants – the Milagro Bistro and the Old Town Restaurant. **Career Steps:** First Vice President, Rauscher Pierce Refsnes (Present); Owner, Milagro Bistro (Present); Owner, Old Town Restaurant (Present). **Associations & Accomplishments:** Father's Day Council, Tucson – Vice Chairman to Benefit Juvenile Diabetes; Southwest School of Music

& Dance; Southern Arizona Restaurant Association. Education: University of Arizona: B.S. in Finance (1981), B.S. in Economics (1981). **Personal:** Married to Stella V. in 1981. Two children: Richard II and Roy. Mr. Schaefer enjoys Tae Kwon Do (2nd Degree Black Belt), tennis, golf, reading, and gardening.

Douglas L. Singer
Regional Manager
NatCity Investments
1965 East 6th Street, #3015
Cleveland, OH 44114
(216) 575-3145
Fax: (216) 575-9288

6211

Business Information: NatCity Investments, a wholly-owned brokerage firm, is a subsidiary of National City Corporation. The Firm is a full-service brokerage company, offering a full array of financial products and services, serving Cleveland and the surrounding communities. As Regional Manager, Mr. Singer is directly responsible for nineteen brokers. Additional duties include developing and training the sales staff, personnel management, profit and loss ratios, and ensuring compliance with all Company policies. **Career Steps:** NatCity Investments: Regional Manager (1995–Present), Senior Investment Consultant (1992–1995); Account Executive, Ameritrust Investor Services (1990–1992). **Education:** University of Michigan, School of Business Administration, B.B.A. (1985). **Personal:** Married to Lisa L. in 1987. Two children: Lindsey and Jacob. Mr. Singer enjoys tennis, golf, and travel.

Carlos Solorzano
Vice President
Coutts & Co (USA) International
701 Brickell Avenue, 23rd floor
Miami, FL 33131
(305) 789-3711
Fax: (305) 789-3724

6211

Business Information: Coutts & Co (USA) International, headquartered in London, is a full-service financial institution specializing in international investments. As Vice President, Mr. Solorzano is responsible for marketing matters and related customer service for the Andean Region. (Colombia, Peru & Ecuador). **Career Steps:** Vice President, Coutts & Co (USA) International (1971–Present). **Associations & Accomplishments:** Greater Miami Chamber of Commerce. **Education:** University of Wisconsin, M.S. in Banking; Universidad del Valle – Cali, Colombia, B.S.; American Institute of Banking. **Personal:** Mr. Solorzano enjoys gardening.

Jonathan de Leighton Squires
Director and Co-Head of Investment Banking
Kleinwort Benson North America
200 Park Avenue, Floor 25
New York, NY 10166-2599
(212) 351-5500
Fax: (212) 983-5988

6211

Business Information: Kleinwort Benson and its affiliates is a global investment–banking firm, providing advisory banking, investment and trust services to individuals, corporations, government entities and correspondent banks around the world. As Director and Co-Head of Investment Banking, Mr. Squires specializes in advisory services to the technology, aerospace and telecommunications industries, as well as oversees all aspects of operations and services, including corporate finance and equity raising for the North American market. **Career Steps:** Director and Co-Head of Investment Banking, Kleinwort Benson North America (1993–Present); Director of Equity Research, Kleinwort Benson USA (1988–1990); General Partner, Conning International (1983–1988); Financial Planning, Charter Consolidated (Anglo American Corporation of South Africa) (1975–1978); Personal Assistant to the Chairman, Charter Consolidated (1974–1975). **Associations & Accomplishments:** New York Stock Exchange; Director, Singletrac Entertainment Technologies, Inc. **Education:** University of Rhodesia, M.A. in Industrial Psychology (1973); University of Cape Town, B.A. in Economics. **Personal:** Married to Gail in 1974. Two children: Ashley and Grant. Mr. Squires enjoys hiking, skiing, and automobile racing.

Mary T. Sullivan
Vice President and Branch Manager
Charles Schwab Company, Inc.
250 Munoz Rivera #104
Hato Rey, Puerto Rico 00918
(787) 281-2260
Fax: (787) 281-2299

6211

Business Information: Charles Schwab Company, Inc. is an international securities brokerage firm offering 24–hour service to clients. As Vice President and Branch Manager, Ms. Sullivan oversees the Caribbean and Puerto Rico operations. She takes care of the day–to–day administrative and operational duties of the Puerto Rico Branch office. Ms. Sullivan assists clients in investment choices, purchase and sales of stocks and bonds, and advises on risk management issues. Developing new business opportunities in the Caribbean arena is another of her responsibilities. **Career Steps:** Vice President and Branch Manager, Charles Schwab Company, Inc. (1987–Present). **Associations & Accomplishments:** San Juan Rotary Club; Puerto Rico Chamber of Commerce; San Juan Bankers Club. **Education:** St. Louis University: M.A. (1983), M.A. in Spanish, B.A. in Political Science and Spanish; Security License, Series 63, 7, 8. **Personal:** One child: Christopher. Ms. Sullivan enjoys soccer, travel, reading, and golf.

John R. Turbeville
Vice President of Investments
Prudential Securities
900 South Faulkner
Little Rock, AR 72212
(501) 221-4045
Fax: (501) 221-4090

6211

Business Information: Prudential Securities, a subsidiary of Prudential Insurance Company of America, is the largest financing company in North America and a major national brokerage firm, providing investment and retirement instruments such as mutual funds and annuities worldwide. Based at the Little Rock, AR branch, as Vice President of Investments John Turbeville provides investment management advice, as well as managing investments, pension and retirement assets for institutions and individuals. **Career Steps:** Vice President of Investments, Prudential Securities (1994–Present); Vice President, Smith Barney (1988–1994); Vice President/Branch Manager, Dean Witter (1980–1988). **Associations & Accomplishments:** Institute for Investment Management Consultants; Registered/Licensed with all major exchanges. **Education:** University of Central Arkansas. **Personal:** Married to Jan in 1981. Two children: Cavan and Mark. Mr. Turbeville enjoys hunting, fishing, and flying.

Carlos V. Ubinas–Taylor
Executive Vice President
Paine Webber – Puerto Rico
Pacific Place #10, 250 Munoz Rivera Ave,
Hato Rey, Puerto Rico 00918
(809) 250-2246
Fax: (809) 250-2218

6211

Business Information: Paine Webber – Puerto Rico is one of the world's leading financial planning, investment brokerage, and trust services company, offering a broad range of financial services for individuals and corporate clients. As Executive Vice President, Mr. Ubinas–Taylor oversees all investment banking activities for the Firm's Puerto Rican and Latin American sectors. His extensive experience in governmental banking and legal expertise has given him the necessary edge to keep Paine Webber at the top in the international investment arena. **Career Steps:** Executive Vice President, Paine Webber – Puerto Rico (1989–Present); Senior Executive Vice President, Government Development Bank (1986–1989); Attorney, O'Neill & Borges (1981–1986). **Associations & Accomplishments:** Puerto Rico Securities Industry Association; Public Securities Association; Chamber of Commerce **Education:** University of Puerto Rico School of Law, J.D. (1981); George Washington University, B.A. (1978). **Personal:** Married to Nilsa Davila in 1974. Two children: Gianna Patricia and Paola Carolina. Mr. Ubinas–Taylor enjoys tennis and sailing.

Hiromi Ukegawa
Executive Vice President
Nikko Securities Co., International, Inc.
1 South Wacker Drive #2760
Chicago, IL 60606
(312) 726-7037 Ext.434
Fax: (312) 726-7256

6211

Business Information: Nikko Securities Co., International, Inc. is a major international securities brokerage firm with headquarters in New York City. Since 1987, NSI has operated Chicago Branch, engaged in the trade of financial futures and options. As Executive Vice President, Mr. Ukegawa manages the Chicago Branch and is in charge of approximately 35 employees. He handles strategic planning, personnel concerns, oversees financial activities, and makes sure transactions comply with state, federal and international regulations. **Career Steps:** Nikko Securities Co., International: Executive Vice President and General Manager of Chicago Branch (1995–Present); General Manager – New York Equity (1993–1995); Deputy General Manager, Nikko Securities Co., Ltd. – Tokyo (1989–1993). **Associations & Accomplishments:** Japan Chamber of Commerce of Chicago; Mr. Ukegawa has been published in various local newspapers and magazines. **Education:** Osaka University of Foreign Languages, B.A. (1974). **Personal:** Married to Yuko in 1976. Two children: Jun and Itsumi. Mr. Ukegawa enjoys golf.

Mr. Gene C. Valentine
Chief Executive Officer
Financial West Group, Inc.
600 Hampshire Road, Suite 200
Westlake Village, CA 91361
(805) 497-9222
Fax: Please mail or call

6211

Business Information: Financial West Group, Inc. is a national and international securities and investment dealer. Established in 1985, the Firm currently employs 225 people. As Chief Executive Officer, Mr. Valentine is responsible for all aspects of operations, including administration, finances, marketing, strategic planning and servicing institutional clients for investment banking. **Career Steps:** Chief Executive Officer, Financial West Group, Inc. (1985–Present); Vice President of Marketing, Christopher Weil & Company (1981–1985); Vice President of Real Estate, Windfarms Ltd, subsidiary of Chevron (1979–1981); Lieutenant, U.S. Navy (1970–1978). **Associations & Accomplishments:** National Association of Securities Dealers; Securities Industry Association. **Education:** Bethany College, West Virginia, B.S. (1972). **Personal:** Mr. Valentine enjoys equestrian activities, sailing, golf and skiing.

Juan Carlos Virreira
Investment Banker
BHN Multibanco
Casilla 4824
La Paz, Bolivia
(591) 243-2323
Fax: (591) 243-0528
EMail: See Below

6211

Business Information: BHN Multibanco is a general financial institution specializing in securities trading, investment banking, and business research. As Investment Banker, Mr. Virreira handles international placement of securities in foreign markets. He pioneers capital markets to locate investment opportunities and acts as an economist for his business clients. Internet users can reach him via: VIRREIRA@UTAMA.BOLNET.BO. **Career Steps:** Investment Banker, BHN Multibanco (1995–Present); Financial Analyst, Inversiones Portfolio (1994–1995). **Education:** Catholic University of Chile, M.S. in Economics (1993). **Personal:** Mr. Virreira enjoys reading, racquetball, physical fitness, and continuing his education.

Victor Wang
Chairman of the Board
Duke & Company, Inc.
909 3rd Avenue, Fl 7
New York, NY 10022-4731
(212) 355-3535
Fax: (212) 355-7970

6211

Business Information: Duke & Company, Inc. is an international investment banking firm, providing services to small– to mid–capitalization companies with emerging growth potential. Joining Duke & Company as Chairman of the Board in 1993, Mr. Wang is responsible for the oversight of all aspects of operations, including administration, finances, sales, public relations, accounting, legal and tax matters, marketing, and strategic planning. **Career Steps:** Chairman of the Board, Duke & Company, Inc. (1993–Present) **Education:** Johns Hopkins University, B.A. (1989) **Personal:** One child: Dara. Mr. Wang enjoys golf.

Mr. Thomas J. Welling

President
Gallagher Benefit Services of NY, Inc.
4 Orchard Place
Bronxville, NY 10708–2510
(914) 476–3000
Fax: (914) 476–3122

6211

Business Information: Gallagher Benefit Services of NY, Inc. is a retirement plan broker and consultant specializing in 403(b) retirement plans, which are available only for non–for–profit organizations and educational institutions. Established in 1978, Gallagher Benefit Services of NY, Inc. currently employs 12 people. As President, Mr. Welling is responsible for all aspects of operations, including the supervision of staff which services Company clientele, marketing efforts, and providing consultation to institutions. **Career Steps:** President, Gallagher Benefit Services of NY, Inc. (1993–Present); President, Welling Associates, Inc. (1978–1993); President, RBH Equities, Inc. **Associations & Accomplishments:** American Society of Chartered Life Underwriter (CLU) and Chartered Financial Counselor (ChFC); International Association of Financial Planners; Former Treasurer, Bronxville PTA; Member, Finance Committee of Siwaney Country Club. **Education:** Manhattan College, B.S. (1965); American College of Life Underwriters, CLU & ChFC. **Personal:** Married to Helen in 1979. Three children: Kurt, Thomas Jr., and Kathryn. Mr. Welling enjoys golf, skiing, and fishing.

Kevin M. White

Associate
Schroder Wertheim & Company
787 Seventh Avenue
New York, NY 10019
(212) 492–6000
Fax: Please mail or call

6211

Business Information: Schroder Wertheim & Company is an investment banking firm serving Fortune 500 companies and individuals in investments. Joining the Firm upon the conferral of his law degree in 1996, Mr. White serves as Associate in the Corporate Finance Department, responsible for investing the funds of large companies, as well as managing accounting matters and legal issues. **Career Steps:** Associate, Schroder Wertheim & Company (1996–Present); Financial Analyst, Wertheim Schroder & Company (1990–1992). **Education:** Harvard Law School, J.D. (1996); Princeton University, A.B. in Economics (1990). **Personal:** Married to Anne Revel in 1996. Mr. White enjoys Alpine mountaineering, bicycling and skiing.

Faith Witryol

President/Director
Beacon Cap Company
131 East 83rd Street 7F
New York, NY 10028
(212) 396–9785
Fax: (212) 734–9472
EMAIL: See Below

6211

Business Information: Established in 1991, Beacon Cap, Inc. is an investment banking corporation, specializing in merchant banking, leveraged finance, venture capital, and investment valuation advisory. As President/Director, Ms. Witryol is responsible for all aspects of banking operations, including administration, finance, public relations, marketing, and strategic planning. Internet users can reach her via: krowitt@interramp.com **Career Steps:** President/Director, Beacon Cap, Inc. (1991–Present); Morgan Stanley: Corporate Finance Associate (1990–1991), Fixed Income Analyst (1989–1990); Fixed Income Trader, Kidder Peabody (1988–1989). **Associations & Accomplishments:** Financial Women's Association of New York; Women's Bond Club of New York; Association of Investment Management and Research; New York Society of Securities Analysts; MIT Alumni Association; National Aeronautical Association; American Society of International Lawyers Association of America; University

Women in Communications. **Education:** MIT Sloen School of Management, M.S./MBA (1988); Brown University, B.A. (1977). **Personal:** Ms. Witryol enjoys flying and skiing.

Juan Pablo Zegarra

Vice President of International Investments
Vascal S.A.
P.O. Box 14175
La Paz, Bolivia
(5912) 412–929
Fax: (5912) 413–558

6211

Business Information: Vascal S.A. specializes in the beverage and poultry industries, as well as real estate and stock market investment. After serving as Minister of Finance in Bolivia from 1992 to 1993, Mr. Zegarra was named Vice President of Risk Management at Banco Boliviano Americano. In 1995 he joined Vascal S.A. as Vice President of International Investments, lending his extensive experience and corporate leadership to the Firm. **Career Steps:** Vice President of International Investments, Vascal S.A. (1995–Present); Vice President of Risk Management, Banco Boliviano Americano (1994–1995); Bolivian Ministry of Finance: Minister of Finance (1992–1993), Undersecretary (1991–1994). **Associations & Accomplishments:** American Management Association. **Education:** Loyola University of Chicago, M.B.A. (1989); Universidad de Catolica Boliviana, B.A. in Business Administration. **Personal:** Married to Vivian Lonsdale in 1987. Four children: Adriana, Ana Valeria, Pablo A., and Felipe. Mr. Zegarra enjoys soccer, bridge, and music.

Mohammed S. Al Salah

Managing Director
Salah Trading Agencies
P.O. Box 5287
Manama, Bahrain, Saudi Arabia
(0973) 223952 223986/223995
Fax: (0973) 214191 223979

6221

Business Information: Salah Trading Agencies, established in 1974, is an international commodities marketing firm, providing the import sale of products to the local market, exploring the need of merchants, and finding the sources for what they need. Additional services include searching for good international trade opportunities for local businesses. Products marketed include Wood and Lumber, Wooden Products, Electrical Lights, Fittings and Fixtures, Construction Supplies, Interior Decoration Items, Machines, Medical Equipment, Government Supplies, Crockery, Glassware, and Cutlery. International in scope, Salah Trading Agencies has trade presence in the U.S., Japan, and other international countries. Establishing Salah Trading Agencies in 1974, Mr. Al Salah serves as Managing Director, managing and overseeing the general running of the Company, including the outside sales force and general manager. He also ensures compliance of his policies, as well as serving as a problem solver. Concurrent with his position at Salah Trading Agencies, he also oversees and owned two other companies: SAFA Company, Ltd. – 1) a building, construction material and supplies outlet, 2) Hardware, Industrial, Hand & Power Tools, D.I.Y., Wood Working machines, etc., having self–service outlet franchises at four locations in Bahrain, and Alsalah Furniture Factory – a custom–made interior decoration items firm, providing middle class to above quality vs. quantity, not discounted furniture. **Career Steps:** Managing Director, Salah Trading Agencies (1974–Present); President, Safa Company, Ltd. (1977–Present); Owner, Al Salah Furniture Factory (1983–Present). **Associations & Accomplishments:** Bahrain Society of Accountants; American Management Association; Member of Accredited Experts of the Ministry of Justice – State of Bahrain. **Education:** BAU University – Lebanon, B.Com. **Personal:** Married to Mrs. Ferdous Aladham. Four children: Rima, Wael, Raed, and Basel. Mr. Al Salah enjoys reading, and spending time with his grandsons.

Asaad Y. Alnajjar, P.E.

President
Atlas International Trading
12021 Wilshire Boulevard, Suite 355
Los Angeles, CA 90025
(310) 207–8212
Fax: (310) 207–8122
EMAIL: See Below

6221

Business Information: Atlas International Trading specializes in industrial operations and the general trading and exports of several commodities worldwide, mainly clothing & denim products. The Company markets different products trough offices in the USA, Canada, Mexico, Egypt, Iraq, and Jordan. Incorporated in 1993, as a branch of the Middle–Eastern company "Atlas Paper Products Industries," the Company employs eighteen people and has an estimated annual revenue of U.S. $3.2 million. As President, Mr. Alnajjar supervises all operations, oversees all contracts and negotiations, and is responsible for customer recruitment and products development. A founding member, Mr. Alnajjar also handles all public relations, strategic planning, and administration. Concurrent with his present position, he is President of Florida based Platinum Associates, Inc., an investment and general commodity trading company dealing in Sugar, Rice,and other food items. Mr. Alnajjar is also a Civil Engineer for the City of Los Angeles Public Works and supports several projects including "LADOT ATSAC Projects, " a large scale automated traffic surveillance and control. Internet users can reach him via: atlasinter@aol.com. **Career Steps:** President, Atlas International Trading (1993–Present); President, Platinum Associates, Inc. (1991–Present); Civil Engineer, City of Los Angeles (1989–Present). **Associations & Accomplishments:** American Society of Civil Engineers; Chi Epsilon Honor Society of Civil Engineers; Professional Engineer License for Civil Engineering; Arab Trade And Business Organizations; International Trading Association. **Education:** University of Southern California: M.S.C.E. (1989), B.S.C.E. (1987), Ph.D. (In Progress).

Joseph M. Bissanti

President/CEO/CFO
Millennium 2000, Inc.
30 Eastbrook Road, Suite 201
Dedham, MA 02026
(617) 329–7776
Fax: (317) 326–8222

6221

Business Information: Millennium 2000, Inc. is a fiduciary–financial consulting and commodities brokerage firm, providing financial consulting and "deal–making" on an international level and between governments. As President/CEO, Mr. Bissanti is responsible for all aspects of operations, including marketing, fiduciary administration, investment & financial consulting, and transaction finance. An entrepreneur for over 20 years, Mr. Bissanti is also the President and Founder of JMB & Associates. **Career Steps:** President/CEO, Millennium 2000, Inc. (1991–Present); Chief Financial Officer/Member, Board of Directors, Liresco, Inc. (1995–Present); Consultant, Laz, Inc. (1992–Present); President/Owner/CEO, Mercury & Diana Festa Tours (1985–1991); Vice President/ General Manager/Co–Owner, Brigham's Restaurant (1982–1985); General Manager, Montilio's Pastry Shops/ Boston Brownie Shops (1979–1982); Hairstyling (1965–1972). **Associations & Accomplishments:** Boy Scouts of America: Chairman of Board, Finance Committee, 1996 Recipient – Certificate of Merit; Insurance Underwriters Association; NASD; Retail Manager of the Year, 1982; Salesman of the Year, 1977; Million Dollar Roundtable–President's Club; "Best of Boston" Cake Decorating Award; Football "Pop Warner" Coach – 7 years (State Champs, 1989); Assistant Baseball Coach – 2 years; Scoutmaster – 8 years; Church Lector/Minister – 8 years **Education:** Northeastern University, B.S; Hairstyling/Barber School. **Personal:** Married to Diane M. in 1974. Three children: Nicholas, Vincent and Alicia. Mr. Bissanti enjoys gourmet cooking, classical music, the arts, sports and photography.

Nellie M. Davis

Branch Manager

F.W. Myers, Inc.

34 Spur Drive
El Paso, TX 79906
(915) 771–7077
Fax: (915) 771–7788

6221

Business Information: F.W. Myers, Inc. is a customs brokerage concern established in 1925. The Company prepares all customs paperwork for the import and export of goods across international borders. As Branch Manager, Ms. Davis is responsible for the El Paso branch operations. She oversees the activities of 16 people and is in charge of all administrative duties for the location. Other responsibilities include public relations, development and implementation of new marketing techniques for services offered, and strategic planning for the future. **Career Steps:** Branch Manager, F.W. Myers, Inc. (1995–Present); Imports Manager, Intertrans Corporation (1993–1995); Operations Manager, Wickstead Brokerage (1983–1993); Operations Vice President, Preferred Transportation. **Associations & Accomplishments:** Hispanic Chamber of Commerce; El Paso Customs Brokers Association; National League of Families for MIA's and POW's (Husband still listed as MIA). Ms. Davis is the recipient of several sales awards. **Education:** University of Texas at El Paso, Attended; Licensed Customs Broker. **Personal:** Six children: Renee, Regina, Relynn, Renell, Robin, and Michael.

Patrick B. Deely, CM, CNE

Chief Information Officer

Linden Trading Company, Inc.

2139 Highway 35
Holmdel, NJ 07733
(908) 264–7000
Fax: (908) 264–8800
EMAIL/Pager: See Below

6221

Business Information: Linden Trading Company, Inc. is the export arm of the Sinar Mas Group, serving as its source to pulp, pulp substitute and secondary fiber requirements for the Group's mill operations in Indonesia, China and India. Joining the corporate parent company (Sinar Mas) in 1994 as general manager of information systems for the Pulp, Paper and Stationary division, Mr. Deely was appointed to his current position in April of 1995. As Chief Information Officer for Linden Trading Company, he oversees all computer and systems operations corporate–wide. In addition, he also serves as Personnel and Office Manager for the New Jersey headquarters' Secondary Fibers Division. Mr. Deely can also be reached through the Internet as follows: LTCNJ@EXIT109.COM and his Pager: (908) 304–0598. **Career Steps:** Chief Information Officer, Linden Trading Company, Inc. (1995–Present); General Manager of Information Systems, Sinar Mas – Pulp & Paper Stationary Division (1994–1995); Technical Advisor, Indah Kiat Pulp & Paper Company (1992–1994). **Associations & Accomplishments:** MENSA; Institute of Certified Professional Managers; Certified Netware Engineer; American Management Association. **Education:** Kansas State University, M.B.A. (1990); Kansas State University, B.S.; Campbell University, A.A. **Personal:** Married to Nicole in 1990. Mr. Deely enjoys bowling, golf and "surfing" the Internet.

Pierre Dolbec

President

Dolbec Logistics International, Inc.

Parc Industriel Vanier 361 Rue Lavoie
Quebec City, Quebec G1M 1B4
(418) 688–9115
Fax: (418) 688–3399

6221

Business Information: Headquartered in Quebec City, Dolbec Logistics International, Inc. specializes in customs brokerage, freight forwarding, and third party logistics. Established in 1960 and with an estimated annual revenue of $1.5 million, the company presently employs 18 people. As President, Mr. Dolbec manages all aspects of company operations including marketing of services, profit and loss responsibilities, public relations, and strategic planning for the future. **Career Steps:** Dolbec Logistics International, Inc.: President (1993–Present), Vice President/Logistic Director (1982–1992); Physical Distribution Manager, All Steel Canada Limited (1980–1982); Traffic Senior Analyst, Domtar, Inc. (1975–1980); Operation Manager, Transol, Inc. (1972–1975). **Associations & Accomplishments:** Vice President, Board of Directors, World Trade Center Quebec City; Secretary, Board of Directors, La Societe des Relations Internationales de Quebec; Director of Administration Board, Quebec Chamber of Industry and Commerce of the Major Quebec Area; Montreal Traffic Club; Quebec Traffic Club; C.I.T.T.; Centre du Transport International; President of the International Trade Committee, Quebec Chamber of Industry and Commerce; Training course instructor, Canadian Purchasing Management Association; Director–Eastern Division, Canadian Institute of Customs Brokers; APEQ (Quebec); Co–chairman of the Export Promotion Committee of the Quebec Chamber of Industry and Commerce; Quebec/Brazil Chamber of Commerce; Director–Administration Board, Canadian Society of Customs Brokers. **Education:** Canadian Institute of Traffic and Transportation; **Personal:** Two children: Jean–Philippe and Pierre–Yann. Mr. Dolbec enjoys scale models, hockey, and landscaping.

Victor H. Gamas

Chief Executive Officer

Gamas Warehouse, Inc.

2439 N. Grand Avenue
Nogales, AZ 85621
(520) 281–4501
Fax: (520) 281–4175

6221

Business Information: Gamas Warehouse, Inc. is a customs brokerage concern with 40 to 50 trailers available for the transportation of goods. The Company also boasts 8 acres of outside and 45,000 sq.ft. of available warehouse storage area. The Company prepares all customs paperwork for the import and export of goods across international borders. Established in 1942, the Company has two locations in the United States and seven in Mexico. As Chief Executive Officer, Mr. Gamas is responsible for general oversight of the Company. He is involved in all financial planning, budgetary matters, business development, and strategic planning for future expansion. **Career Steps:** Gamas Warehouse, Inc.: Chief Executive Officer (1995–Present), Treasurer (1994–1995), Accounting Manager (1991–1993), Accountant (1990–1991). **Associations & Accomplishments:** National Association of Mexican Customs Brokers; Mexican Transport Association; State Finance Executives. **Education:** Tecnologico Monterrey, Certified Public Accountant (1991), Master in Finance. **Personal:** Married to Erika in 1995. Mr. Gamas enjoys playing golf and scuba diving.

Joel E. Kanter, Esq.

President and Chief Executive Officer

Allied Trading & Capital Group

224 Southport Woods Drive
Southport, CT 06490
(203) 256–1191
Fax: (203) 256–9757

6221

Business Information: Allied Trading & Capital Group specializes in international commodity trading. Established in r1993, Allied Trading & Capital Group currently employs 10 people and has an estimated annual revenue of over $100 million. As President and Chief Executive Officer, Mr. Kanter is responsible for all aspects of operations, including public relations and fund raising. **Career Steps:** President and Chief Executive Officer, Allied Trading & Capital Group (1993–Present); Attorney, Owens, Schine & Nicok (1990–1993); Attorney, Penzer, Kanter & Seely (1983–1987); Attorney, Blawic, Belinkier, Kanter & Vargue. **Associations & Accomplishments:** Former Member, Financial Advisory Committee, City of Bridgeport; Former Chairman, Commercial Law Center; Board of Education, City of Bridgeport; Bridgeport Bar Association; Former President, Virginia Bar Association; Former Member, City of Bridgeport Trust Advisory Board. **Education:** Boston University, J.D. (1958); Ohio State University, B.S. in Economics (1955).

Ms. Barbara Kendrick, J.D.

Finance Manager and Controller

Budd Mayer Company of Alabama, Inc.

2100 Riverchase Center, Suite 400
Hoover, AL 35244–1855
(205) 987–1876
Fax: (205) 985–7331

6221

Business Information: Budd Mayer Company of Alabama, Inc. is a full–service grocery brokerage firm. As Finance Manager and Controller, Ms. Kendrick is responsible for all aspects of financial operations. **Career Steps:** Finance Manager and Controller, Budd Mayer Company of Alabama, Inc. (1991–Present); Secretary, National Bank of Commerce, Birmingham (1990–1991); Corporate Secretary and Office Manager, Patton–Harris Company, Inc. (1960–1990). **Associations & Accomplishments:** Two Thousand Notable American Women; American Association of University Women; Secretary and Treasurer, Nu Epsilon Delta; Secretary, Sigma Delta Kappa (1987–1991); National Association for Female Executives; Alabama Association of Legal Assistants; National Association of Legal Assistants; Governor's Board of the Kentucky Colonels; Christian Children's Foundation; Samford University Representative to Southern Women's Show (1986); The World's Who's Who of Women; Who's Who of University Women. **Education:** Birmingham School of Law, J.D. (1991); Samford University, B.S. in Paralegal Studies (1986); Birmingham–Southern College, B.A. in Business Administration and Accounting (1981).

Mr. Hal Loevy

President and Chief Executive Officer

SGS Government Programs, Inc.

42 Broadway, 20th Floor
New York, NY 10004
(212) 804–5263
Fax: (212) 968–1570

6221

Business Information: The SGS Group is the World's largest control and inspection organization, providing an international network of independent third–party evaluations of quantity, quality and price to trade, industry and government. SGS Government Programs, Inc. (SGS GPI) conducts physical inspection and documentary verification of all types of goods, materials and commodities destined for export from the U.S. to countries whose governments have contracted with SGS. Established in 1919, SGS GPI currently employs 900 people, including field inspectors and full–time staff. As President and Chief Executive Officer, Mr. Loevy is responsible for all operational, financial and administrative aspects for U.S. operations. **Career Steps:** President and Chief Executive Officer, SGS Government Programs, Inc. (1994–Present); President and Director, SGS Qualitech Perdana and other international positions (1990–1994); Marketing Manager – China, Schlumberger Ltd. and other international positions (1980–1990). **Associations & Accomplishments:** American Society of Mechanical Engineers; Society of Petroleum Engineers; Society of Professional Well Log Analysts; American Chambers of Commerce, Waterfront Commission of New York (Stevedore License); International lecturer. **Education:** Cornell University, B.S. in Mechanical Engineering (1980). **Personal:** Married to Lina in 1988. Two children: Jennifer and Natasha. Mr. Loevy enjoys his family, golf and swimming.

John F. O'Brien

Director

Fritz Canada, Inc.

5200 Miller Road, Suite 17
Richmond, British Columbia V7B 1K6
(604) 270–9449
Fax: (604) 270–9860
E MAIL: john.obrien@frit

6221

Business Information: Fritz Canada, Inc. is Canada's largest customs brokerage firm with 80 locations throughout Canada. The Company provides logistics, supply chain engineering and transportation services for international clients. As Director, Mr. O'Brien is responsible for handling international transportation and customs brokerage for the Western Region of Canada. **Career Steps:** Director, Fritz Canada, Inc. (1995–Present); vice President, Danzas Canada, Ltd. (1989–1994); President, Behring Canada Ltd. (1984–1988); General Manager, Inter Traffic, Ltd. (1980–1984). Born in London U.K. Twelve years experience at London airport as Director, handling international air and ocean forwarding, as well as European Distribution. Has travelled exstensively in Asian Pacific Market. **Associations & Accomplishments:** Director, Canadian Logistics Institute; Past Chairman, Canadian Air Freight Forwarders Council; National Director, Canadian Freight Forwarders Association; Western Director, Canadian International Freight Forwarders Association. **Education:** St. Hughs College, Nottingham, England. **Personal:** Married to Dorothy in 1970. Two children: Julia–Marie and Kathleen. Mr. O'Brien enjoys hiking, painting, mountain biking, and travel.

Richard M Redash

Energy Analyst

New York Mercantile Exchange

4 World trade Center – Research Department
New York, NY 10048
(212) 748–3412
Fax: (212) 742–5336

6221

Business Information: New York Mercantile Exchange is a company dealing in commodities, specifically energy futures and options. Established in 1872, New York Mercantile Exchange presently employs 525 people. As Energy Analyst, Mr. Redash oversees day–to–day operations, performs marketing research, handles new futures contract development and existing contract maintenance. **Career Steps:** Energy

Analyst, New York Mercantile Exchange (1994–Present); Consolidated Edison of New York: Associate Analyst (1992–1994), Assistant Analyst (1990–1992). **Education:** New York University, M.B.A. Candidate; Pace University, B.B.A. Summa Cum Laude (1990) . **Personal:** Mr. Redash enjoys equities analysis and investing.

Ronald S. Winter

President
Delta Fibre, Inc.
209 Goshen Road
Cape May Court House, NJ 08210–1809
(609) 465–7406
Fax: (609) 465–3456

6221

Business Information: Delta Fibre, Inc. is a commodities brokerage/export company, engaged in the sale of recycled secondary fibre. As one of two Founding Partners of Delta Fibre, Mr. Winter currently serves as President. He is responsible for the coordination of all sales, including domestic and abroad, as well as overseeing all sales, staff, and office accountability for expansion and direction. Concurrent with his present position, he still serves as Acting Vice President of Sales at Raff's Recycling Company. **Career Steps:** Founding Partner and President, Delta Fibre, Inc. (1995–Present); Acting Vice President of Sales, Raff's Recycling Company (1983–Present). **Education:** Atlantic Community College, A.S. (1992). **Personal:** Married to Tammy Lynn in 1977. Two children: Christopher Michael and Daniel James. Mr. Winter enjoys all sports and hiking.

Edson Abrao

President
Papylon International Trade
P.O. Box 6629, 11515 Rochester Ave, Ste 203
Beverly Hills, CA 90025–7805
(310) 477–8164
Fax: (310) 479–7707

6231

Business Information: Papylon International Trade is an international trade consultant, providing international trade of commodities (food, grain, metal, precious metal, precious & semi–precious gems) and international investment venture consultations. Establishing Papylon International Trade in 1989, as President Mr. Abrao is responsible for all aspects of operations, including research, analysis, development, commodities marketing, client services, and venture assessments. **Career Steps:** President, Papylon International Trade (1989–Present); Director of Marketing, Forpam Ltds – Brazil (family business – food); Director of Marketing, Gendados Ltds – Brazil (family business – computer/electronics). **Education:** Attended: Brazilian University (1984) **Personal:** Married to Marguerite Abrao in 1989. Two children: Annabella and Gabriella. Mr. Abrao enjoys soccer, camping, and racing cars.

Eric J. Rosen

Vice President and Managing Director
Onex Corporation
712 5th Avenue, 40th Floor
New York, NY 10019–4108
(212) 582–2211
Fax: (212) 582–0909

6231

Business Information: Onex Corporation provides investments and leveraged buyouts. International in scope and headquartered in Canada (Toronto), Onex Corporation spans the U.S. (Sky Chefs, based in Dallas, TX, the largest airline caterer; ProSource, based in Miami, FL, a major food service distribution company, and a number of automotive component companies based in Michigan), United Kingdom, Germany, South America, Europe, and Australia. Joining Onex Corporation in 1989, Mr. Rosen is now Vice President and Managing Director, responsible for the management of the New York Office/U.S., identifying new acquisitions and monitoring existing investments. **Career Steps:** Vice President and Managing Director, Onex Corporation (1989–Present); Kidder, Peabody & Company: Associate Merchant Banking (1987–1989), Analyst Mergers and Acquisitions (1983–1985). **Associations & Accomplishments:** Wings Club; Various other trade organizations. **Education:** Stanford University, M.B.A. (1987); University of Pennsylvania – Wharton School, B.S. in Economics (1983). **Personal:** Mr. Rosen enjoys tennis, running, movies, and travel.

Anthony M. Sanfilippo

President and Chief Executive Officer
Tradetech Securities, L.P.
227 W. Monroe St. Suite 5000
Chicago, IL 60606
(312) 553–8340
Fax: (312) 553–8345

6231

Business Information: Tradetech Securities, L.P. is one of the leading third–market trading firms outside of New York. Based in Chicago, it provides broker/dealers with immediate access to the third market with its exclusive automated price discovery mechanism which electronically executes trades in all securities listed on the New York Stock Exchange. This provides customers with the best qualities of both the primary market as well as the third market. In addition to this advanced technology, Tradetech's team of risk management specialists apply their expertise and experience to personally manage the trades requiring special attention, (i.e., large share blocks, wide bid–offer spreads and other special orders). Anthony M. Sanfilippo is president, CEO and a registered principal of Tradetech Securities, L.P. Before founding Tradetech in 1993 he spent five years as Executive Vice President at Mesirow Financial, managing its Institutional Equity Division and their Chicago Stock Exchange Specialist Operation. Sanfilippo created and managed a new relationship between Mesirow and third–market trading firms. His strong interests in off–exchange execution developed in 1980, when he piloted the 19C3 market–making operation for Jefferies & Co., a pioneer in third market trading. His trading and management skills were further amplified through positions at Bateman Eichler, Dillon Read, and William Blair & Co. This extensive experience proved to be critical to the development of Tradetech's unique trading protocol. He incorporated two critical elements into Tradetech's operations, the first of which is the realization of the importance of sophisticated risk management to the success of off–exchange trading. He also recognized that genuine concern for the customer was essential to the technological efficiencies of automated trading. His vision and results–oriented goal of implementing the latest advances in high technology is what has positioned Tradetech Securities at the leading edge of the third market's evolution. **Career Steps:** President and Chief Executive Officer, Tradetech Securities, L.P. (1993–Present); Executive Vice President, Mesirow Financial (1989–1993); Vice President of Trading, Bateman, Eichler, Hill, Richards (1987–1989); Vice President, Jefferies & Co., Inc. (1980–1986). **Associations & Accomplishments:** National Organization of Investment Professionals (NOIP) — this exclusive organization of 200 professionals is a dynamic force within the investment industry, dedicated to educating and promoting dialogue on issues directly affecting the National Market System. President, Security Traders Association of Chicago (STAC); Securities Industry Association (SIA); Member (while student), Golden Key National Honor Society; Beta Gamma Sigma. **Education:** DePaul University, Finance Major; University of Illinois. **Personal:** A native of Chicago, Anthony and his wife Briget reside in Winnetka with their two children, Rachel and Neva. Mr. Sanfilippo enjoys golf, snow skiing and softball in his leisure time.

Jesus M. Martinez

General Manager of Latin American Operations
ABS Global, Inc.
6908 River Road Box 459
Deforest, WI 53532
(608) 846–6338
Fax: (608) 846–6392

6279

Business Information: ABS Global, Inc., with 15 business units, is the world's largest agribusiness and information technology company. ABS artificially inseminates cattle for genetic research. As General Manager of Latin American Operations, Mr. Martinez is responsible for managing Latin American business operations, setting strategic objectives, supervising fiscal matters, and directing business development and acquisitions. **Career Steps:** General Manager of Latin American Operations, ABS Global, Inc. (1995–Present); Vice President of Carissean Operations, Protein Genetics, Inc. (1994–1995); Director of Human Resources, ABS Global, Inc. (1994); Director of Human Resources, Baller & Taylor Books (1991–1992). **Education:** University of Wisconsin, M.S. in Policy & Administration (1986), B.A. in Sociology (1984). **Personal:** Married to Tresa F.. Two children: Marissa and Riley. Mr. Martinez enjoys baseball and basketball.

Barbara M. Aaron

Vice President of Finance, Administration, and Operations
Sturdivant & Company
223 Gibbsboro Road
Clementon, NJ 08021
(609) 627–4500
Fax: (609) 627–4500

6282

Business Information: Sturdivant & Company is an investment management firm primarily involved with assisting institutions dealing with retirement funds. Focusing on the private and public sector as well as state institutions, the Company invests primarily in the Standard and Poor 500. As Vice President of Finance, Administration, and Operations, Ms. Aaron is responsible for the operation and administration of the firm. Her duties include accounts payable and receivable, compliance, and oveseeing registered financial operations principals. Additionally, she is directly responsible for a staff of eight, handles customer relations, and manages thirty four accounts. **Career Steps:** Vice President of Finance, Administration, and Operations, Sturdivant & Company (1996–Present); Duke Management Company: Investment Administrator (1995), Operations Manager, Administrative Manager (1981). **Associations & Accomplishments:** Chairperson, Scarborough School (United Way Agency); Volunteer for Homeless Shelter Feeding Project. **Education:** Shaw University, B.S. (1993). **Personal:** Married to Walter H. in 1977. Two children: Dorjan Sef and Michael Antoan Aaron. Ms. Aaron enjoys sketching and reading.

Kenneth L. Bright

President
Financial Strategies, Inc.
301 College Street, Suite 801
Greenville, SC 29601
(803) 271–6968
Fax: (803) 271–7361

6282

Business Information: Financial Strategies, Inc. is a business consulting firm providing financial, capital, and investment planning services. Established in 1985, Financial Strategies, Inc. employs four persons and reports revenue in excess of $6 million. As President, Mr. Bright is responsible for the administration and direction of all corporate functions. **Career Steps:** President, Financial Strategies, Inc. (1985–Present); Engineering Director, Duke Power Company (1969–1982). **Associations & Accomplishments:** Better Business Bureau; Greenville Chamber of Commerce; International Association of Financial Consultants. **Education:** American College, M.S. (1994); Furman University: M.S., B.S.; American College, Chartered Financial Consultant Degree. **Personal:** Two children: Patrick and Michael.

Jeffrey G. Butler

President
Senior Information Services
33552 Coral Reach Street
Dana Point, CA 92629
(800) 732–8130
Fax: (714) 493–6427

6282

Business Information: Senior Information Services provides financial services including trust management, reverse mortgages, and insurance products, with thirty–eight independent contractors in California. As President, Mr. Butler oversees all employees, sales representatives, marketing companies, and law firms, coordinating all areas and activities to ensure operating efficiency. **Career Steps:** President, Senior Information Services (1994–Present). **Associations & Accomplishments:** Elks; Who's Who in the Southwest. **Personal:** Married to Peggy W. in 1986. Two children: Hayden Andrew and Jarrod Matthew. Mr. Butler enjoys golf, fishing, and basketball.

Mr. Daniel J. Candura

Vice President – Financial Planning Quality
American Express Financial Advisors Inc.
T4/49 IDS Tower 10
Minneapolis, MN 55440
(612) 671–5870
Fax: (612) 671–4768

6282

Business Information: American Express Financial Advisors Inc., provides investment, money management, pension planning, and personal financial advisory services to individuals, small businesses and institutions worldwide. Established in 1894, and owned by American Express, the corporation currently employs 13,000 business professionals. As Vice President – Financial Planning Quality, Mr. Candura oversees quality initiatives for 8,000 staff members within the Sales Department. He reviews financial services and investments offered to clients and ensures customer satisfaction. **Career Steps:** Vice President – Financial Planning Quality, American Express Financial Advisors Inc. (1994–Present); Vice President of Field Marketing, IDS Financial Services (1992–1994); Vice President, American Express Personal Planning (1989–1992); IDS: Regional Director (1987–1989), Financial Planner (1982–1987); Principal, Braintree Public School (1971–1982). **Associations & Accomplishments:** Member, IAFP (1983–1995); Member, ICFP (1983–1995); Chairman, Conference Board Sales Marketing Quality Council; Member, Braintree, MA School Board (1986–1992). **Education:** Bridgewater State College, M.A. (1975); Stonehill College, B.A. (1971). **Personal:** Married to Marie MacDonald in 1972. Four children: Christopher, Brandon, Jeffery and Devon.

Stephan Carlquist

President
ABB Financial Services Inc.
P.O. Box 120071, One Stamford Plaza
Stamford, CT 06912–0071
(203) 961–7800
Fax: (203) 961–7860

6282

Business Information: ABB Financial Services is one of four Business Segments of the ABB Group. Worldwide, the Segment consists of seven Business Areas: Treasury Centers, Leasing & Financing, Insurance, Investment Management, Project & Trade Finance, Structured Finance, and Energy Ventures. Mr. Carlquist was appointed President in 1993, for ABB Financial Services Inc. Concurrent with his executive position at ABB Financial Services, he serves as President of ABB Treasury Center (USA) Inc. The Company offers products and services to ABB group companies in the U.S. in asset/liability management, cash management, foreign exchange, and treasury consulting. The Company is also active in risk management in interest rate and foreign exchange areas. The Company offers their services to more than 100 ABB companies in the U.S. Mr. Carlquist is one of three members in the Business Area Management team of the Business Area Treasury Center. Appointed to this position in June of 1991, he oversees all Western Hemisphere sectors within the Business Area Division — currently encompassing 14 countries. **Career Steps:** President, ABB Financial Services Inc. (1993–Present); Business Area Manager, Treasury Centers in America (1991–Present); President, ABB Treasury Center (USA) Inc. (1990–Present); Executive Vice President, ABB World Treasury Center, Zurich (1988–1990); President, Asea Capital Corporation – Geneva (1986–1988); Manager of International Cash Management, ASEA AB (1983–1986); Foreign Exchange/Cash Manager, Atlas Copco AB, Stockholm, Sweden (1980–1983). **Associations & Accomplishments:** Executive Committee, SACC Board of Directors. **Education:** Lunds University, Sweden, Degree in Civilekonom (M.B.A.) (1980); Helsingborg College, Sweden, Degree in Electrotechnical Engineering (1976). **Personal:** Married to Margareta. Three children: Max, Charlotta, and Jenny. Mr. Carlquist enjoys tennis and jogging, as well as being a wine enthusiast.

Robert J. Case

Senior Training Analyst
VALIC
2919 Allen Parkway
Houston, TX 77066
(713) 831–4981
Fax: (713) 831–4359

6282

Business Information: VALIC specializes in providing retirement planning for the non–profit and government market. Established in 1950, the Company employs 2,000 people and has estimated annual revenue of $1 billion. As Senior Training Analyst, Mr. Case develops, designs, and instructs training programs regarding Company hardware and software. **Career Steps:** Senior Training Analyst, VALIC (1990–Present); Teacher, Houston I.S.D. (985–1990); Director of Safety and Training, Champaign–Urbana M.T.D. (1972–1985). **Associations & Accomplishments:** American Society of Training Developers; National Safety Council; Computer teacher of the year. **Education:** University of Illinois, B.S. (1985); Parkland Jr. College, A.A. (1983). **Personal:** Married to Janice Faye in 1969. One child: Heather Melissa. Mr. Case enjoys golf, outdoor activities, family, and reading.

Ted Christianson

President
Adam Smith Company
P.O. Box 965
Alexandria, MN 56308–0965
(612) 763–3886
Fax: (612) 763–3615
EMAIL: See Below

6282

Business Information: Adam Smith Company is a portfolio management and business development firm. Serving primarily private and family–based business clients throughout the Midwest U.S., the Firm provides diversified investment counsel in the areas of real estate development and venture capital. A financial investment specialist with over ten years expertise, Ted Christianson was appointed President of the Firm in 1992. He is directly responsible for the management of over $5 million in active and passive investments. Internet users can reach him as follows: TED0333@AOL.COM **Career Steps:** President, Adam Smith Company (1992–Present); Chief Financial Officer/Treasurer (1990–1992); President, Packaged Intelligence, Inc. (1986–1990); Analyst, Cherry Tree Investment, Inc. (1984–1986). **Associations & Accomplishments:** Minnesota Software Association; World Trade Center Association; St. Mary's Catholic Church: Lecturer and Sunday school teacher. **Education:** Norht Dakota State University, M.S. (1983), B.S. in Business Administration and Agricultural Economics; Attended: St. John's University. **Personal:** Married in 1982, Mr. Christianson has three children. Mr. Christianson enjoys racquetball, hunting, skiing, golf, and art.

Richard M. Cott

Chief Financial Officer
The Free Methodist Foundation
P.O. Box 580
Spring Arbor, MI 49283–0580
(517) 750–2727
Fax: (517) 750–2752

6282

Business Information: The Free Methodist Foundation (FMF), a non–profit 501(C)3 organization, provides individual and institutional investment management funding in the areas of pension, trust and endowment funds and managed accounts. FMF also provides counsel in the areas of estate planning, planned giving, mortgage lending, and capital campaigns. Established in 1987, the Foundation employs 15 support staff and investment counselors; reporting premium assets in excess of $100 million. As Chief Financial Officer, Mr. Cott is responsible for the oversight of strategic planning, investment/real estate property holdings, accounting, budgeting, auditing and human resource management. In addition to his duties with The Free Methodist Foundation (FMF), Mr. Cott is an adjunct instructor at Spring Arbor College, teaching undergraduate courses in Management and Organizational Development. **Career Steps:** Chief Financial Officer, The Free Methodist Foundation (FMF) (1992–Present); Registered Representative, The Prudential (1992); Fighter Pilot, Captain, U.S. Air Force (1984–1992). **Associations & Accomplishments:** Chairman – Board of Finance, Spring Arbor Free Methodist Church; Spring Arbor College: Investment Committee Advisor, Board of Trustees; Board of Trustees Advisor, Fellowship of Christian Athletes; Teaches undergraduate Management and Organizational Development. **Education:** California Coast University, working towards Ph.D. in Finance; Webster University, M.B.A. (1992); Hope College, B.A. (1984). **Personal:** Married to Lori Cott in 1985. Three children: Corey, Casey, and Carly. Mr. Cott enjoys golf, and music.

John R. Dean

President
National Marketing & Finance
1971 F Street
South Lake Tahoe, CA 96150–3636
(916) 761–1661
Fax: (916) 541–2601

6282

Business Information: National Marketing & Finance is a consulting firm providing assistance to clients in placing their assets into Asset Investment and Management programs. As President, Mr. Dean serves as a negotiator between clients and their financial programs, conducting all financial transactions and monitoring associates' activities. Concurrently, he is President and Director of both Sierra Note, Inc. and High Sierra Marketing, Inc. **Career Steps:** President, National Marketing & Finance (1993–Present); President and Director, Sierra Note, Inc. (1990–Present); President and Director, High Sierra Marketing (1993–Present); President and Director, Sierra Construction Services, Inc. (1968–1993). **Education:** Lawrence Institute of Technology, B.S.E.E. (1995); Post graduate studies at UCLA and various schools in Real Estate, Securities, and Insurance. **Personal:** One child: Leslie Kim Dean. Mr. Dean enjoys hiking, backpacking, cross–country skiing, and investments.

Mr. Isaac Devash

Managing Director
The Renaissance Funds
18 Belinson Street
Holon, Israel 58320
972–3–6414498
Fax: 972–3–6416910

6282

Business Information: The Renaissance Funds are the largest international private equity fund ($157 million) established for investing in Israel to date. Mr. Devash is responsible for managing the fund's day to day activities including deal souring, conducting due diligence, and structuring and negotiating investments. During his tenure, the Renaissance Funds have invested approximately $200 million, including co–investments and third party debt, in some of the leading companies in Israel. **Career Steps:** Prior to joining the Renaisance Funds, Mr. Devash worked for BEA Asociates (Credit Suisse Asset Management) in international private equity investments. Prior to BEA Associates, he worked at Credit Suisse First Boston at their Mergers and Acquisitions Department in NY, London and Tokyo, where among other projects, he worked on the Master Privatization Plan for the Israeli economy. From 1981–1985 Mr. Devash served as an officer at the Israeli Defense Forces. **Associations & Accomplishments:** Regional representative of the Harvard Business School in Israel; Founding Editor, VISION: HARVARD STUDENTS LOOK AHEAD — a yearly mult–disciplinary publication; Co–founder, "Israeli Forum on Wall Street". **Education:** Harvard Graduate School of Business Administration, M.B.A. (1991–1993); Wharton School of Business, B.A summa cum laude **Personal:** Mr. Devash enjoys martial arts, reading, and philosophy in his leisure time.

J. W. (Jack) Diamond

Founder, Executive Vice President & Registered Licensed Principal
City Commerce Corporation
P.O. Box 241446
Anchorage, AK 99524–1446
(907) 563–9683
Fax: (907) 563–6984

6282

Business Information: City Commerce Corporation is a Registered Investment Advisor with both the United States Securities and Exchange Commissions under the Investment Advisors Act of 1940, and the Securities and Banking Division of the State of Alaska; a Fiduciary under the ERISA Act of 1974; and a mortgage banking and mortgage brokerage firm. Mr. Diamond has served as Founder, Executive Vice President & Registered Licensed Principal and Member of the Board of Directors of City Commerce Corporation since its founding in 1992. He is responsible for all aspects of Operations, as well as serving as the Registered Licensed Principal, responsible for contracts, legal compliance, and marketing to pension funds. Concurrent with his responsibilities at City Commerce Corporation, he serves as Executive Vice President and Registered Licensed Principal at Crawford Diamond Roderick Insurance Agency, Inc.; as Real Estate Associate Broker for Commercial Real Estate at Crawford Real Estate Corporation; and as Chairman of the Board of Directors of the Better Business Bureau of Alaska, Inc. **Career Steps:** Founder, Executive Vice President & Registered Licensed Principal, City Commerce Corporation (1992–Present); Executive Vice President and Registered Licensed Principal, Crawford Diamond Roderick Insurance Agency, Inc. (1993–Present); Real Estate Associate Broker, Crawford Real Estate Corporation (1991–Present); Chairman of the Board of Directors, Better Business Bureau of Alaska, Inc. (1995–Present); Member, Alaska Teamsters Union, Local 959 (1974–Present); Senior Vice President, Investors Life of Nebraska (1991–1994); Senior Vice President, Primerica (1988–1991); Chairman, Last Frontier Financial, Inc. (1988–1989); Chief Operating Officer, Koch Properties (1987–1988). **Associations & Accomplishments:** Professional Licenses: State of Alaska: All Lines Insurance License, Real Estate Associate Broker License, Securities License (NASD) – Series: 6,26,63,65 and Registered Principal; Associations: International Foundation of Employee Benefit Plans (1992–Present); Anchorage Board of Realtors (1991–Present), Mediator (1992–Present); Multiple Listing Service (1991–Present); Boards and Commissions: Municipality of Anchorage, Investment Advisory Board (1996–Present); Better Business Bureau of Alaska, Inc.: Board of Directors (1991–Present), Chairman (1995–Present), Vice Chairman (1992–1995), Senior Arbitrator (1985–Present); Volunteer and Donor Activities: American Red Cross, South Central Alaska Chapter (1986–Present); Active Donor: Anchorage Blood Bank (1981–Present); Puget Sound Bone Marrow Donor Program, Seattle, WA (1989–Present). **Education:** Alaska Pacific University – Anchorage, Alaska, M.B.A. and Labor Management Relations Certificate (Pending); University of Denver – Denver, Colorado, B.S. in Business Administration, with majors in Real Estate & Construction Management. **Personal:** Married to Kathleen A. Roderick with two children: Kimberly and Kaylynne. Mr. Diamond enjoys travel, golf, and relaxing with his family during his leisure time.

Lynn O. High

President
National Institute for Estate Planning, Inc.
14785 Preston Road, Suite 350
Dallas, TX 75240–7881
(214) 991–3101
Fax: (214) 991–2966

6282

Business Information: The National Institute for Estate Planning, Inc. provides estate planning services to high networth customers of banks throughout a seven state area. An insurance and investment planning executive with over ten years expertise, Mr. High founded the agency in 1988. As President and Chief Operating Officer, he is the corporate executive responsible for the overall development and strategies, with primary focus in the management and development of local staff, marketing plans, design developments, and personnel training of regional planning staff. **Career Steps:** President, National Institute for Estate Planning, Inc. (1993–Present); Executive Vice President, OBA Insurance Agency, Inc. (1988–1993); Consultant, Lear Siegler Inc. (1987–1988); Commissioned Officer, U.S. Air Force (1966–1986). **Associations & Accomplishments:** Published in trade journals, Author of: "Pay Your$elf First" and "Ten Commandments of Wealth". **Personal:** Married to Susan in 1993. Mr. High enjoys playing bridge and flying (private pilot).

Carolyn M. King
President
King Financial Services
3053 Carlton Court
Westchester, IL 60154–5603
(708) 562–1046
Fax: (708) 562–1104

6282

Business Information: King Financial Services is an independent financial planning firm, accepting clientele on a referral basis. Having entered financial services in the early 1980's, Ms. King is responsible for all aspects of operations. Serving as advisory agent of Advisors' Mutual Service Center, Inc. (a Registered Investment Advisor) securities are offered through Mutual Service Corp. Member NASD and SIPC. While she specializes in working with pre–retirees, clients of all ages are provided with quality service. **Career Steps:** President, King Financial Services (1982–Present). **Associations & Accomplishments:** International Association for Financial Planners; American Association of Individual Investors; Involved in various charity activities; Recipient: "Women in Management", "Woman of Achievement", and "Woman of the Year" awards; Leader, Women's Choral Group (23 years); Published in various local newspapers and periodicals; Former teacher of Adult Education Courses at Lyons Township High School (11 years) and Triton College and College of DuPage. **Education:** Loyola University, B.S. magna cum laude (1957). **Personal:** Ms. King enjoys being a grandparent, photography, gardening, and music.

Ralph W. Kydd, M.O.I., I.A.F.P.
Chairman of the Board
The Corporate Group
357 Bay Street, #900
Toronto, Ontario M5H 2T7
(416) 362–9949
Fax: (416) 362–1628

6282

Business Information: The Corporate Group is an international group of financial management companies dealing with offshore investments, corporations, and trusts in 14 countries throughout the world. As Chairman of the Board, Mr. Kydd oversees all aspects of the group. **Career Steps:** The Corporate Group: Chairman of the Board (1995–Present), President and CEO (1987–1995), General Manager (1981–1987), Manager of Accounting and Tax (1974–1981). **Associations & Accomplishments:** The Offshore Institute; International Association of Financial Planners; The Board of Trade; Canadian Federation of Tax Consultants; President's Association of the American Management Association of New York. **Education:** University of Toronto. **Personal:** Married to Zorana in 1996. Mr. Kydd enjoys travel and music (formerly taught as a Professor of music at George Brown College).

Gregg Lipsitz

Managing Partner
L & M Financial Services
270 Essjay Road
Buffalo, NY 14221–8215
(716) 626–5200
Fax: (716) 962–5486

6282

Business Information: L & M Financial Services is a financial services firm, providing financial planning (payroll deduction for employees), insurances, investments, etc. An eighteen–year veteran of the Company, Mr. Lipsitz joined L&M in 1977. Appointed as Managing Partner in 1995, he is responsible for all aspects of management operations in New York and surrounding areas, in addition to his own client base. **Career Steps:** L & M Financial Services: Managing Partner (1995–Present), Vice President (1990–1994), Sales (1977–1990). **Associations & Accomplishments:** Coach, Amherst Soccer Association; Planned Giving Committee, Temple Beth America; Planned Giving Committee, United Jewish Federation; American Association Society; Charted Life Underwriters & Chartered Financial Consultants; National Association of Life Underwriters; International Association of Financial Planners. **Education:** American College: M. of Financial Services (1994), Chartered Life Underwriter (1984), Chartered Financial Consultant (1984); SUNY – Binghamton, B.S. in Business. **Personal:** Married to Ruth in 1982. Three children: Daniel, Joey, and Max. Mr. Lipsitz enjoys golf, tennis, and coaching soccer.

Mr. Mark E. Lisnyansky
Director of Investment
Silvinit J.S.C.
Naberezhnaya Srednei Nevki 6
St. Petersburg, Russia 197022
7(503)956–7950 7(812)234–3377
Fax: 7(095)250–9815 1(201)696–0995
1(888) 626–8585

6282

Business Information: Silvinit manufactures potassium chloride fertilizer and salt in the Perm Region of the City of Solikamsk, Russia. In addition to the plant in the City of Solikamsk, Silvinit has two offices in Russia (Moscow and St. Petersburg). Established in 1927, Silvinit reports annual revenue of $150 million and currently employs 9,800 people. Future plans include taking the Company public in the U.S. through ADR's and taking advantage of investment growth into Russia. Sharing the ownership in the Company and serving on the Board of Directors, Mr. Lisnyansky (a.k.a. Mark Allin) also serves as Director of Investments and is responsible for asset management through a subsidiary, SILVEL S.A. He previously developed transshipping operations in St. Petersburg Port. **Career Steps:** Director of Investment, Silvinit J.S.C. (1992–Present); President, Ello J.S.C., Moscow (1989–1992); Director of Operations, EE Development Co., New Jersey (1987–1989). **Associations & Accomplishments:** VIP Club, Moscow; Investors Rights Association, Moscow; Public Diplomacy Foundation (Board Member) with Vladimir Pozner; Foreign Policy Association (Chairman – Edward Shevardnadze); Mandated Placement Agent and Advisor for LUKOIL, Moscow; Speaker at Geonomics Conference in New York (1995), sponsored by the Geonomics Institute; Guest lecturer at Columbia University on privatization in Russia; Member of the Board of the Russia Growth Fund. **Education:** New Jersy Institute of Technology, Newark, New Jersey, B.S. in Electrical Engineering (1987); The Professional School of Business, Millburn, Money Management (1987). **Personal:** Mr. Lisnyansky enjoys horses and collecting antique Russian awards and badges.

James Monroe Marx
Chairman
Claremont Equities
"Westover"
Bernardsville, NJ 07924
(908) 953–9600
Fax: (212) 838–7600

6282

Business Information: Claremont Equities, established in 1984, is an investment banking and consulting firm providing financial and private investment services. In his current capacity, Mr. Marx oversees all aspects of operations for the investment establishment, as well as originate, structure and negotiate complex, sizeable financial transactions. **Career Steps:** Chairman, Claremont Equities (1984–Present); President, Claremont Holdings, Inc. (1986–1989); Principal, Law Offices of James M. Marx, Esq. (1980–1986); Mr. Marx practiced law in New York City with Satterlee, Warfield & Stephens; Holtzman, Wise & Shepard; and Jacobs, Persinger & Parker,

before establishing his own New York City law firm in 1980. Mr. Marx has acted as attorney for a wide range of well–known individuals, corporations and partnerships, among them, Doubleday; Holt, Rhinehardt & Winston; Fairchild Publications; Allen & Company; and Aristotle S. Onassis. As an attorney representing underwriters, he has been involved in public and private debt and equity offerings of Fortune 500 companies and others. He has served as Director of Aeicor, Inc. (now Doskocil Companies) and Oppenheimer Industries, Inc., as well as various private corporations. At the end of 1977, Mr. Marx commenced his career as an entrepreneur by arranging for, and participating in, the acquisition of 22 apartments at the Pierre Hotel, NYC, for approximately $2.1 million. From 1979 through 1986 Mr. Marx originated a variety of financial transactions for one of Texas' wealthiest families; the most celebrated of these was the successful acquisition in 1981 for approximately $200K in equity and a guarantee of $2.6 million in debt of Gtech Corporation, a company now listed on the New York Stock Exchange which became the nation's largest manager of state lottery systems, with a market value in excess of $300 million. **Associations & Accomplishments:** Mr. Marx is a member of the Council of the Rockefeller University, New York City; First Vice President, Director, and Member, Executive Committee of the Soldiers' Sailor's and Airmen's Club, Inc.; Director, Trees for Life; Director, New Jersey Congressional Award Council; Member of the Finance Committee of the Downtown Lower Manhattan Association; Member, West Point Association and of the Ends of the Earth (a private club that includes most present and former members of the Joint Chiefs); Former Director of the American Paralysis Association and of Sadler's Wells Association (U.S.); Former Trustee of the Congressional Medal of Honor Society; Trustee of the Heart Research Foundation, Mr. Marx raised more than $1 million for heart disease research. Sponsored major fundraisers for Republican candidates for Governor, U.S. Senate and Congress; Member of Doubles International Club; Member of the Finance Committee, India House, NYC; Acted as attorney and advisor to President Regan's Chief Arms Control negotiator, and has served with the U.S. Department of State in Washington D.C. **Education:** Mr. Marx is a graduate of The Pingry School (1960), Dartmouth College (A.B., 1964) and Stanford University School of Law at Stanford, CA (J.D., 1967).

Larry A. Medin
Senior Vice President of Sales
Fortis Financial Group
P.O. Box 64284, 500 Belinburg
St. Paul, MN 55164
(800) 800–2638
Fax: (612) 696–0092

6282

Business Information: Fortis Financial Group is one of the operating companies of Fortis, Inc. in New York. The Company is a manufacturing and marketing company primarily geared toward investment–based products (i.e., variable annuities). As Senior Vice President of Sales, Mr. Medin works with independent broker and dealer networks to secure meaningful alliances and provides sales and marketing support while implementing quality assurance. **Career Steps:** Senior Vice President of Sales, Fortis Financial Group (1994–Present); Senior Vice President, Colonial Investment Services (1991–1994); Regional Vice President, Alliance Capital (1990–1991); Senior Vice President, MetLife (1986–1991). **Associations & Accomplishments:** International Financial Planners; Hospice; United Way. **Personal:** Married to Renee in 1970. Two children: Nathan and Noah. Mr. Medin enjoys fly fishing, scuba diving, and flying.

Frank Messa
Senior Vice President
The Ayco Company, L.P.
One Wall Street
Albany, NY 12205
(518) 464–2306
Fax: (518) 464–2112

6282

Business Information: Ayco Company, L.P. is one of the world's leading tax and financial consulting firms. An attorney specializing in tax law, Frank Messa has held various corporate executive roles with Ayco since he joined the firm in 1976. He was promoted from Account Manager to Regional Vice President in 1981 and the following year he established and managed the Texas Regional Office. In 1987 he returned to Headquarters as the Chief Operating Officer of the Encompass Group. In 1989 he was promoted to Senior Vice President and currently has responsibility for the Encompass Department, technical and support services, information systems, and the firm's income tax practice. In 1994 Mr. Messa was one of the partners who participated in a management buy–out of the firm from the American Express Company which had acquired Ayco in 1983. **Career Steps:** Ayco Corporation: Senior Vice President (1989–Present), Chief Operating Officer of Encompass Group (1987–Present), Regional Vice President (1981–1986). **Associations & Accomplishments:** Board of Trustees, Union College; Board of Trustees, United Way of Northeastern New York; Board of Trustees,

Saint Gregory's School for Boys; Elected to Phi Beta Kappa (1973). **Education:** Albany Law School, J.D. (1976); Union College, B.A (1973). **Personal:** Married to Colleen Ann in 1978. Three children: Christopher, Peter, and Keri.

Joseph O. Miles
Managing Director – Business Development
Moody's Investors Service
99 Church Street
New York, NY 10007–2701
(212) 553–3682
Fax: (212) 553–4000

6282

Business Information: Established in 1900, Moody's Investors Service is a bond rating and financial services company. The Agency analyzes the financial strength of each bond's issuer, whether a corporation or a government body. Currently Moody's employs 1000 people. As Managing Director of Business Development, Mr. Miles is responsible for marketing, planning and sales in the Public Finance Division. **Career Steps:** Moody's Investors Service: Managing Director of Business Development (1994–Present); Vice President of Planning (1993–1994); Dun and Bradstreet: Assistant Vice President of Marketing (1992–1994), Assistant Vice President of Sales (1989–1992). **Education:** Seton Hall University: M.B.A. (1975), B.S. (1973); Dartmouth Amos Tuck School of Business Administration, Executive Management Certification; Wharton School, Executive Management Certification. **Personal:** Married to Lana in 1971. Mr. Miles enjoys tennis and reading.

Rodney Mitchell
President and Chief Executive Officer
Mitchell Group, Inc.
1100 Louisiana Street, Suite 4810
Houston, TX 77002–5211
(713) 759–2070
Fax: (713) 759–2079

6282

Business Information: The Mitchell Group, Inc. is a registered investment adviser, particularly focusing on the energy industry sector. Established in 1989, The Mitchell Group currently employs 6 people. As President and Chief Executive Officer, Mr. Mitchell provides the overall direction and vision for the company's continued growth, quality advice to customers, and strategic developments. An expert in his field, Mr. Mitchell has been interviewed by the Wall Street Journal, Business Week and the Houston Chronicle. **Career Steps:** President and Chief Executive Officer, Mitchell Group, Inc. (1989–Present); President and Chief Executive Officer, Tallasi Management Company (1970–1989); Vice President, Kidder Peabody and Company (1963–1970). **Associations & Accomplishments:** Trustee, Hampden Sydney College; Trustee, SENA Foundation. **Education:** Harvard College (1960). **Personal:** Married to Michele in 1988. Five children: Clay, Larkin, Bradley, Angus, and Callum. Mr. Mitchell enjoys reading, golf, and basketball.

David M. Miyoshi

Chairman of the Board
Miyoshi & Kitamura, Inc.
3250 Wilshire Blvd., Suite 1610
Los Angeles, CA 90010–1610
(213) 387–1081
Fax: (213) 384–3519
EMAIL: See Below

6282

Business Information: Miyoshi & Kitamura, Inc. is an international business consulting firm. Mr. Miyoshi established Miyoshi & Associates in 1982 (becoming Miyoshi & Kitamura in 1995), specializing in offshore investments for foreign and American corporations. Internet users may reach him via: DMIYOSHI@IX.NETCOM.COM **Career Steps:** Chairman of the Board, Miyoshi & Kitamura, Inc. (1995–Present); President, Miyoshi & Associates (1982–1995); Attorney, Morgan, Lewis, & Bockius (1980–1982). **Associations & Accomplishments:** Los Angeles Baptist City Missions Society; Pales Verdes Baptist Church; Japanese Evangelical Missions Society. **Education:** Harvard, M.B.A. (1978); University of California Hastings Law School, J.D.; University of Southern California, B.S.; Waseda University, Certificate of Completion. **Personal:** Married to Teruko in 1977. Two children: Mark and Brandon. Mr. Miyoshi enjoys skiing and reading. He is also a private pilot.

Gerard P. (Jerry) Mlinar, CFA
Owner/Founder
Mlinar Advisory
P.O. Box 150
Ord, NE 68862–0150
(308) 728–5532
Fax: (308) 728–5426

6282

Business Information: Mlinar Advisory is an investment advisory firm, providing money management services combined with insurance and financial planning. As Owner/Founder, Mr. Mlinar is responsible for managing client investment portfolios and helping clients complete proper insurance and financial plans. **Career Steps:** Owner/Founder, Mlinar Advisory (1995–Present); Founder/Manager, United Advantage Investments (1990–1995); Retail Broker, FirsTier Securities, Inc. (1989–1990); Retail Broker, Kirkpatrick, Pettis, Smith, Polian, Inc. (1988–1989). **Associations & Accomplishments:** Local Jaycees; Past Member, Local Toastmasters. **Education:** University of Nebraska – Lincoln, B.A. (1986); Securities Licenses: Series 7, Series 63, Series 24, and Series 65; Securities and Exchange Commission, Investment Advisor; Chartered Financial Analyst. **Personal:** Married to Michele Janee in 1987. Three children: Janee Leigh, Brenna Nicole, and Zachary Gerard. Mr. Mlinar enjoys sail boarding and horseback riding.

Michael A. Molitor, CFP

President
Molitor, Inc.
5550 Merrick Road, Suite 305
Massapequa, NY 11758–6238
(516) 798–9252
Fax: (516) 798–5437

6282

Business Information: An SEC–registered advisory firm, Molitor, Inc. provides financial counsel and assistance for individuals, assisting them in obtaining college financial aid resources, as well as money management assistance. Founding the company and all subsidiaries in 1988, Michael Molitor serves as President. Overseeing all aspects of administration and operations, he also meets with customers to address the financial aid issue and evaluate their income, assets and expenses. **Career Steps:** President, Molitor, Inc. (1980–Present); President, Molitor College Aid Council (1988–Present); President, Molitor Money Management, Inc. (1992–Present); President, Molitor Money Management Registered Investment Advisory, Inc. (1995–Present). **Associations & Accomplishments:** National Association of Securities Dealers, Inc.; National Association of Student Aid Administrators; New York State Financial Aid Administrators Association; Consultant, Alive to Thrive; Advisory Board, Orphans Aid Society. **Education:** Sierra College, B.A. (1987); CERTIFICATIONS: Certified Financial Planner – College for Financial Planners and Institute for Certified Mutual Fund Specialists **Personal:** Married to Michele in 1995. Mr. Molitor enjoys track, driving, golf, and skiing.

Nora Jean Moore
Vice President
Pension & Tax Planning Services, Inc.
1615 Bonanza Street, Suite 324
Walnut Creek, CA 94596–4531
(510) 932–3050
Fax: (510) 938–8411

6282

Business Information: Pension & Tax Planning Services, Inc. is a third party administrator, providing retirement and tax planning consultations. The Company meets with the owners of other businesses to create specific retirement plans, catering to the needs of the business and their employees. Additionally, the Company handles life insurance, estate planning, and retirement and tax planning for tax shelters. As Vice President, Ms. Moore is responsible for all aspects of Company operations, including sales and marketing, client relations, reports, and client communications. **Career Steps:** Vice President, Pension & Tax Planning Services, Inc. (1992–Present); Vice President/Co–Owner, Don Olin Spas/Rent–a–Spa (1987–1992); Controller/CEO, Spa Broker/Cal Spa's (1982–1987); Controller/CEO, Ron Carter Realty (1992–1993). **Associations & Accomplishments:** Childrens Hospital Fund raising; Clipped Wings; National Institute of Pension Administrators. **Education:** St. Mary's College (1982). **Personal:** Two children: Timothy and Daniel Sacks. Ms. Moore enjoys sports, fund raising, and learning.

Peter Norton
President
Outsource Financial Services Center Inc.
1929 West Broadway, Suite 201
Vancouver, British Columbia V6J 1Z3
(604) 736–8358
Fax: (604) 736–8359
PETER_NORTON@MINDLINK.bc.

6282

Business Information: Outsource Financial Services Center Inc. is an international cross–border (Canada/U.S.) financial services firm, providing financial planning, accounting, and taxation services for individuals and corporations. A practicing CMA in Canada and a Certified Public Accountant in Washington State with thirty–one years of experience, Mr. Norton established Outsource Financial Services Center Inc. in 1965 and serves as its President. He is responsible for all aspects of operations, including administration, finances, public relations, marketing, and strategic planning. Career milestones include being the first person to hold the Denver C.F.P. (Certified Financial Planner) and the Canadian R.F.P. (Registered Financial Planner) certifications. Internet users can also reach him via: PETER_NORTON@MINDLINK.bcca or through the Web Site via: http://www.corpinfohub.com/norton.htm **Career Steps:** President, Outsource Financial Services Center Inc. (1965–Present). **Associations & Accomplishments:** Treasurer, Pacific Corridor Enterprise Council–Seattle; Vancouver Board of Trade; MENSA. **Education:** Simon Fraser University, M.B.A. (1985). **Personal:** Married to Susan in 1984. Mr. Norton enjoys travel, crossword puzzles, running, and hiking.

Christopher J. O'Donnell, C.F.P.
First Vice President
Howe Barnes Investments, Inc.
135 South La Salle Street, Suite 1500
Chicago, IL 60603–4398
(312) 655–2936
Fax: (312) 930–1467

6282

Business Information: Howe Barnes Investments, Inc. is a financial advising, portfolio management, and retirement planning brokerage service. Established in 1925, Howe Barnes Investments, Inc. currently employs 98 people. As First Vice President, Mr. O'Donnell is responsible for the development of clients' financial strategies, as well as the monitoring of investment portfolios. **Career Steps:** First Vice President, Howe Barnes Investments, Inc. (1990–Present); Vice President and Division Manager, Continental Bank, NA (1966–1990); Lecturer, FFIEC, Washington D.C. (1985–Present); Faculty Member, American Bankers Association (1985–Present); Instructor of Economics, DePaul University (1970–1974); Instructor of Economics, East Carolina College, Greenville (1963–1963); Personal Money Management Advisor, PACE Institute (1968–1971); Colonel (Retired), United States Marine Corps Reserve. **Associations & Accomplishments:** Institute of Certified Financial Planners (CFP); Sacred Heart Parish, Winnetka IL: Chairman of Stewardship Committee (1988–1990), President of Religious Education Board (1988–1990), Eighth Grade Religious Education Teacher (1994–1995); Who's Who in Finance and Industry (1990–Present). **Education:** Marquette University, M.A. in Economics (1962); Regis University, B.S. in Economics; Securities Licensed with National Association of Securities Dealers (1991); Licensed in Life, Health, Disability, Property and Casualty Insurance (since 1990); Certified Financial Planner (1987); Mortgage Banking School, Michigan State University (1973); The American College (1992–1995). **Personal:** Married to Patricia in 1962. Three children: Erin, Meghan and Kelly. Mr. O'Donnell enjoys running, skiing, woodworking and playing the piano.

James P. Pavanelli

Vice President/Chief Executive Officer
Gruppo Triad–FFC S.A.
Representative Office Via A. Gramsci #12
Turin, Italy 10123
3911–560–7611
Fax: 3911–517–8384

6282

Business Information: Gruppo Triad–FFC S.A. is a division of Gruppo Triad–FFC, which was founded in Brussels, Belgium in 1980 by a group of businessmen with financial and banking background intent on starting financial activities that would support commercial transactions, joint ventures and investments on a medium– and long–term basis. Reorganized and incorporated in Panama in 1987, the Company has boosted its activity by creating various independent organizations. These groups include: Credito Mercantile S.A., which deals mainly with financing and investments and specializes in the management of private portfolios of important clients whether institutional or private; Colonial Export Company, Inc. which deals with credit instruments to help small and medium companies to export manufactured goods between Europe and Latin America; Export Credit Company, Inc., which assists all commercial transactions in import–export areas; Societa Per IL Commercio Estero S.A., deals with perfectly defined operations that require buying and selling merchandise to Latin America; Italian Trade Center Corporation, which acts as a private Chamber of Commerce by developing interchange between Italy and Latin America (and also has a division in Dallas, Texas); Triad Hotels and Resorts, Inc; Triad Finanzaria S.A., whose main objective is to find necessary means and capital needs for investing in all the corporation companies; and Triad Pharmacosmetic Srl; C.M. Spa. Other subsidiaries include: Triad Wold Television, Inc.; Triad Pictures Production, Inc.; Triad Publimedia Corporation; Triad Development Corporation; and Triad Art Investment S.A. International in scope, the Company has representative offices in London, Wien, Munich, Geneva, Lugano, Beiruth, New York, Dallas, San Francisco, Mexico, Panama, Caracas, Rio De Janeiro, Buenos Aires, Montevideo, Santiago De Chile, Lima, Bogota, Milan, Turin, and Rome. Leaving Italy (he was born in Ferrara, near Bologna) in 1964, Mr. Pavanelli established residence in England, where he worked as a Personal Assistant to the Peruvian Ambassador. In 1966 he worked as a correspondent for the leading Italian newspaper "Corriere della Sera", and was appointed Developing Director by the National Tourist Board of Novara Region in Northern Italy, where he consulted for Wintersports Holiday in the "Val D'Ossola Province for Novara." During the same period he worked as the official representative for a tour operator company called Leroy Travel a subsidiary of British United Airways of London. Between 1966 and 1967, Mr. Pavanelli visited the U.S. for the first time, promoting ski tours in northern Italy to some twenty–one Universities on the East coast, and became involved in developing new tourist areas in the Italian Alps and the Spanish Costa Brava/Costa del Sol areas. Due to the economic situation in England during 1970, Mr. Pavanelli sold his assets in three corporations and returned to Italy where he accepted a position with Security Management Company of Geneva, a subsidiary for John P. Chaser of Boston. Upon completion of an intensive course, he became a financial advisor for private investors in real estate, mutual funds, and private banking which led him to join a private banking group in Lebanon. Forced to abandon the country in 1975 due to the onset of war, Mr. Pavanelli returned to Italy, where he was appointed financial consultant of a subsidiary of the Italian Giant Oil Group. His financial career continued, affiliating him with such prestigious groups as FCC Brokers (which he helped found), FCC American Corporation, and FCC Security Corporation Limited. Presently he is the Vice President and Chief Executive Officer of Gruppo Triad–FCC where he oversees all phases of the European operation. Fluent in French, Spanish, Italian, German, and English, Mr. Pavanelli also has a fair knowledge of Portuguese and has participated in several monetary and currency exchange conferences in Paris and London with the International Herald Tribune. He has also served as financial consultant to several international corporations and governments. In the past twenty years he has traveled extensively in forty countries located in Europe, the Middle East, Africa, and North and South America. **Career Steps:** Vice President/Chief Executive Officer, Gruppo Triad–FFC S.A. (1980–Present). **Education:** Naval Institute, Graduated (1964); Participated in Various Banking, Financing, and other Educational Subjects. **Personal:** Two children: Lara and Emma. Mr. Pavanelli enjoys languages, politics, classical music, travel, skiing, and reading.

Robert W. Petrie

Senior Vice President
Everen Securities, Inc.
651 East Butterfield Road, Suite 506
Lombard, IL 60148
(708) 963–8750 (800) 962–8750
Fax: (708) 963–8269

6282

Business Information: Everen Securities, Inc. is a financial consulting firm specializing in qualified and non–qualified retirement plans, business succession and transition, financial planning and brokerage services. As Senior Vice President, Mr. Petrie oversees all portfolio management and overall operations for the Lombard office. **Career Steps:** Senior Vice President, Everen Securities, Inc. (1995–Present); Senior Vice President, Kemper Securities, Inc. (1990–1995); Vice President, Paine Webber; Vice President, Thomson McKinnon. **Associations & Accomplishments:** Investment Management Consultants Association; ESOP Association; Prostar Network; Kemper Executive Council; Did a Wall Street Radio Show (1984 & 1985); Interviewed and appeared in U.S. News & World Report Magazine (May 1985); Published in the book "Personal Finance" – written by Dr. Jack Kapoor, Les Dlabay, and J. Hughes, the book was published in 1988 by the Richard D. Irwin Company and used as a textbook at the College of Dupage, Lake Forest College, and Richland College. **Education:** Attended: Prairie State College (1973). **Personal:** Mr. Petrie enjoys scuba diving, snow skiing, and golf.

Michael S. Prior

Executive Director
Financial Planning Ministry
2555 E. Chapman Avenue, Suite 415
Fullerton, CA 92631
(714) 871–4900
Fax: (714) 871–1006
EMail: See Below

6282

Business Information: Financial Planning Ministry provides financial planning, specifically estate planning, dealing with wills and trusts only. Sponsoring eight non–profit organizations, the Company has 1,800 trust clients and writes 200 trusts a year. The Company also provides educational seminars on estate planning for their clients. As Executive Director, Mr. Prior is responsible for staffing, goal setting, deciding priorities, and acting as a liaison to the Board of Directors. Internet users can reach him via: MSPRIOR@AOL.COM. **Career Steps:** Executive Director, Financial Planning Ministry (1993–Present); Business Administrator, Central Christian Church (1985–1993). **Associations & Accomplishments:** Chairman of Personnel – Board of Directors, Angeles Crest Christian Campaign. **Education:** University of Phoenix, Bachelor of Science in Business Administration (1993). **Personal:** Mr. Prior enjoys skiing and travel.

Jacqueline Reeves

Vice President
Janney Montgomery Scott
26 Broadway, 8th Floor
New York, NY 10004
(212) 510–0844
Fax: (212) 425–1358
Email: See Below

6282

Business Information: Janney Montgomery Scott, established in 1846 and headquartered in Philadelphia, is a brokerage firm with over 700 employees. The Firm has clients from as far North as Boston, Massachusetts, as far South as Washington, DC, and as far West as Ohio. The Firm, a wholly-owned subsidiary of Pennsylvania National, analyzes financial companies, providing opinions to both institutional and retail investors. As Vice President, Ms. Reeves provides detailed financial analysis on more than 20 banks and thrifts to investors. Also, Ms. Reeves provides broad financial information of a hundred additional banks and thrifts in a quarterly publication, BankTalk. Ms. Reeves is responsible for analyzing financial market trends of the Banking industry for her institutional and retail client base. Internet users can reach her via: JReeve367. **Career Steps:** Vice President, Janney Montgomery Scott (1995–Present); Analyst, CS First Boston (1992–1995); Junior Analyst, Rothschild, Inc. (1992). **Associations & Accomplishments:** Bank Financial Analysts Association. **Education:** Cedar Crest College, B.S. (1988). **Personal:** Married to Jason in 1993. Ms. Reeves enjoys golf, boating, sky and scuba diving.

Kim D. Rostovsky

Vice President
Lyster Watson and Company
230 Park Avenue, Suite 2828
New York, NY 10169–2899
(212) 599–7430
Fax: (212) 599–7432

6282

Business Information: Lyster Watson and Company is an investment advisor company, serving approximately 150 clients nationwide, primarily in venture capital investment opportunities. As Vice President, Ms. Rostovsky serves as the Chief Financial Officer and Head of Operations and Administration. Her duties include directing all operations, including regulations, finances, and legal work, in addition to providing clientele support. **Career Steps:** Vice President, Lyster Watson and Company (1993–Present); Trading and Sales Assistant, Bear Stearns (1992–1992). **Associations & Accomplishments:** American ORT, Young Professionals Division. **Education:** University of California at Berkeley, B.A. (1990). **Personal:** Ms. Rostovsky enjoys tennis.

James M. Singleton

Vice President
GNA Corporation
8750 West Bryn Mawr Avenue, Suite 550
Chicago, IL 60631
(312) 380–4550
Fax: (312) 380–4558
EMail: See Below

6282

Business Information: GNA Corporation offers financial services in the area of annuities, securities, and insurance. Owned by GE Capital, the Company has $40 billion in assets through five different divisions. As Vice President, Mr. Singleton oversees production management, the field regional offices, and the wholesale of products in banks. He also has direct supervision of a staff of 60 to 70 field personnel. Internet users can reach him via: SINGLM@aol.com. **Career Steps:** Vice President, GNA Corporation (1983–Present); Vice President, H.C. Copeland & Associates (1980–1983); Regional Marketing Manager, Security First Group (1975–1980). **Education:** University of Texas – Austin, B.A. (1965). **Personal:** Married to Carol in 1985. Three children: David, Celeste, and Adrae. Mr. Singleton enjoys golf and paleontology.

Larry Jay Smith

Regional Vice President
CIGNA Financial Advisors
1360 Post Oak Boulevard, Suite 2500
Houston, TX 77055
(713) 552–7907
Fax: (713) 552–0891

6282

Business Information: CIGNA Financial Advisors is a subsidiary of CIGNA Corporation and offers financial planning, insurance and investments to the affluent market place. Established in 1940, the Houston Agency currently employs 52 people. A 23 year veteran, Mr. Smith joined CIGNA Financial Advisors (formerly Connecticut General) in 1972 and was appointed Assistant Manager of the Pittsburgh Region in 1974. Currently serving as Regional Vice President of the Houston Region (since 1992), he is responsible for overall operations of the Houston Region which encompasses Southeast Texas and Louisiana. Additional responsibilities include the oversight of finances, sales, profit, strategic planning, human resources, compliance with regulatory entities, etc. **Career Steps:** CIGNA Financial Advisors: Regional Vice President – Houston (1992–Present), Regional Vice President – Kansas City (1987–1992), Sales Manager – Detroit (1980–1987), Assistant Manager – Pittsburgh (1972–1979). **Associations & Accomplishments:** National Association of Life Underwriters; Board of Directors – Houston Chapter, General Agents and Managers Association (1994–Present); National Association of Estate Planners; Institute of Certified Financial Planners; American Society of Chartered Life Underwriters and Chartered Financial Consultants; International Association of Financial Planners; Houston Business and Estate Planning Council; Deacon, Memorial Drive Christian Church; Former Chairperson, Swope Parkway Health Center Foundation Board (1990–1991). **Education:** American College, M.S. in Financial Service (1991); Bethany College, B.S. (1971). **Personal:** Married to Marsha L. in 1973. Three children: Jason D., Tyler A., and Matthew J. Mr. Smith enjoys spending time with his family, hunting, snow skiing, water skiing, boating, fishing, and jogging.

Mr. Brian K. Speers

Financial Consultant/Attorney
Merrill Lynch
2001 Spring Road
Oak Brook, IL 60521
(708) 954–6396
Fax: (708) 954–6271

6282

Business Information: Merrill Lynch offers financial services worldwide for individuals, corporations, and governments. Mr. Speers, a Financial Consultant and Attorney, has formed a partnership with a First Vice President within Merrill Lynch. The focus of this partnership is on individual executive clients. Mr. Speers provides estate, financial, and tax planning. He also consults with small business owners on succession and retirement planning. **Career Steps:** Financial Consultant/Attorney, Merrill Lynch (1992–Present); Financial Consultant, part time, Merrill Lynch (1988–1992). **Associations & Accomplishments:** Member, Illinois Bar Association; Member, Chicago Bar Association; Member, American Bar Association; Co–Chair of Community Board, Ronald McDonald House of Loyola; Member, Phi Kappa Phi. **Education:** Loyola Law School, J.D. (1993); University of Illinois, Finance Degree (1990). **Personal:** Single. Mr. Speers enjoys golf.

A. Richard Thiernau
Vice President
Thiernau Financial Services Inc.
1910 Ridge Road
Homewood, IL 60430–1725
(708) 798–5828
Fax: (708) 798–5962

6282

Business Information: Thiernau Financial Services was founded in 1957 and offers financial planning services to local individuals and business concerns. As Vice President, Mr. Thiernau assists established clients with their financial needs and recruits new clients for the Company. He is responsible for personnel matters, marketing Company services, advertising, financial concerns of the Company, budget requests, and public relations. **Career Steps:** Vice President, Thiernau Financial Services (1984–Present). **Associations & Accomplishments:** International Association for Financial Planning; Chicago Chapter of Chartered Life Underwriters; Chicago Chapter, Chartered Financial Counselor; Homewood Chamber of Commerce; Chicago Sutherland Chamber of Commerce; Homewood Rotary Club. **Education:** Bradley University, B.S. (1983); Professional Designations: Chartered Life Underwriter; Chartered Financial Consultant; Certified Fund Specialist. **Personal:** Married to Donna in 1992. One child: Steven. Mr. Thiernau enjoys snow and water skiing, working with volunteer community activities, and model railroading.

John C. Wilbur Jr.
Executive Vice President
FNF Ventures, Inc.
17911 Von Karman Avenue, Suite 500
Irvine, CA 92614
(714) 622–4590
Fax: (714) 622–4159

6282

Business Information: FNF Ventures, Inc., a wholly–owned subsidiary of Fidelity National Financial, Inc., is a Small Business Investment Company (SBIC) and is licensed by the Small Business Association (SBA). The Company provides equity capital to small businesses and middle market companies in fields such as transportation, software, services, and distribution. As Executive Vice President, Mr. Wilbur serves as co–manager of the fund and is responsible for all day–to–day operations of the business. **Career Steps:** Executive Vice President, FNF Ventures, Inc. (1995–Present); Managing Partner, The Powell Group Limited (1992–1995); Vice President, Citicorp (1988–1992); Vice President, Bank IV (1982–1986). **Associations & Accomplishments:** The Anderson Alumni Association; The U.C.L.A. Alumni Association; The Colorado College Alumni Association; The Orange County Business Council. **Education:** Anderson Graduate School of Management, U.C.L.A., M.B.A. (1988); The Colorado College, B.A. (1982). **Personal:** Married to Ellen F. in 1991. Two children: Sam and Molly. Mr. Wilbur enjoys skiing, golf, basketball, running, and fishing.

Joseph Clarke Williams, CLU
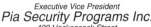

Executive Vice President
Pia Security Programs Inc.
429 Hackensack Street
Carlstadt, NJ 07072
(201) 438–7500
Fax: (201) 405–1920 (201) 438–8781

6282

Business Information: Pia Security Programs Inc. is a consulting firm, providing estate planning, financial planning and employee benefit services for commercial clients of a large property and casualty insurance agency. Established in 1975, Pia Security Program Inc. reports annual revenue in excess of $2 million. As Executive Vice President, Mr. Williams is responsible for all aspects of sales and management, in addition to conducting in excess of fifteen seminars a year. **Career Steps:** Executive Vice President, Pia Security Programs Inc. (1993–Present); Brokerage Manager, AETNA Life Insurance

and Annuity Co. (1974–1993). **Associations & Accomplishments:** American Society of CLU and ChFC; National Association of Life Underwriters; International Adjudicator for drum and bugle corps and bands. **Education:** Seton Hall, B.A. (1964). **Personal:** Married to Diane in 1968. Two children: Joseph, Jr. and Marcie Ellen Williams.

Shalisa G. Pierce
Director
Prudential Preferred
710 South Broadway, Suite 200
Walnut Creek, CA 94596
(510) 933–5111
Fax: (510) 933–1237

6283

Business Information: Prudential Preferred specializes in providing financial advice and related services to clients. As Director, Ms. Pierce oversees all day–to–day operations of the Company. She is responsible for administration, budget, personnel, marketing, sales, and strategic planning. **Career Steps:** Prudential Preferred: Director (1996–Present), Human Resources Director (1992–1996); Representative, New York Life (198–1991). **Associations & Accomplishments:** Vice President/LUTC Chairman, Mt. Diablo Association of Life Underwriters; Graduate Assistant, Dale Carnegie; Special Olympics Volunteer; Youth Sports League. **Education:** Fresno State University, B.S. (1987); American College: C.L.U., C.H.F.C. **Personal:** Two children: Jordan and Ryan. Ms. Pierce enjoys skiing, white water rafting, and fitness.

Carol Bessette
Accounting Director
Bombardier Capital Inc.
1600 Mountain View Drive
Colchester, VT 05446
(802) 654–8379
Fax: (802) 654–8423

6289

Business Information: Bombardier Capital Inc., a captive finance company, provides leasing and financial plans to corporations in the following areas: marine, RV's, manufactured housing, equipment leasing. As Accounting Director, Carol Bessette oversees all corporate accounting areas, which includes the preparation of monthly financial statements, internal customer accountability, coordination of annual external audit processes, and payroll. **Career Steps:** Accounting Director, Bombardier Capital Inc. (1989–Present); Controller, Independent Food Company (1988–1989); Accounting Manager, J. Lamson & Associates (1982–1988). **Associations & Accomplishments:** Vermont Society Certified Public Accountants; Zonta; American Institute of Certified Public Accountants. **Education:** Ithaca College, B.A. in Mathematics (1971); University of Vermont, CPA Certification. **Personal:** Married to James R. in 1983. Ms. Bessette enjoys sailing and reading.

Peter T. Davis

Principal
Peter Davis & Associates
1881 Yonge Street, P.O. Box 48033
Toronto, Ontario M4S 3C6
(416) 440–1622
Fax: (416) 440–8473
EMAIL: pdavis@can.net

6289

Business Information: Peter Davis & Associates, established in 1993, is an international consulting firm providing security, audit and control training and consulting to management. International in scope, Peter Davis & Associates span the U.S., Canada, Asia, and Europe. As Principal, Mr. Davis is responsible for all aspects of operations, including management, administration, finances, marketing, strategic planning, public relations, client relations, and writing books on security and audits for businesses. **Career Steps:** Principal, Peter Davis & Associates (1993–Present); Director of IS Audit, Office of the Provincial Auditor (Ontario); Principal, Ernst & Young; Canadian Sales Manager, Digital Pathways. **Associations & Accomplishments:** Treasurer (Voluntary), Metropolitan Toronto Association for Community Living – supporting the developmentally handicapped; Advisory Council, Computer Security Institute; Author and co–author of four books published by McGraw Hill & Sams; Speaker at professional seminars. **Education:** Carleton University, Bachelor of Commerce (honours) (1974); Certifications: CISA, CMA, CDP, CSP, CISSP, CCP, and CNA V3. **Personal:** Married to Janet in 1989. One child: Kelly.

Gregory Francis Guido
Regional Director
Foster & Dunhill
2 Urban Center, 4890 West Kennedy Boulevard, Suite 140
Tampa, FL 33609
(800) 418–9996
Fax: (708) 483–2799

6289

Business Information: Foster & Dunhill is the largest offshore financial planning provider in the U.S., with 2,500 offshore clients. The Firm provides asset protection, income, and estate tax savings. As Regional Director, Mr. Guido is responsible for the design and structuring of services, collecting information on clients, and developing strategy for service needs. **Career Steps:** Regional Director, Foster & Dunhill (1995–Present); Senior Manager, R.J. Augustine & Associates (1991–1995); Senior Manager, KPMG Peat Marwick (1981–1990). **Associations & Accomplishments:** Secretary, Institute of Certified Financial Planners – Chicago Society; American Institute of Certified Public Accountants – Tax and Personal Financial Specialist Sections; Illinois Certified Public Accountants Society. **Education:** DePaul University, M.S.T. (1982); Loyola University, B.B.A. **Personal:** Married to Denise in 1992. Mr. Guido enjoys spending time with his wife and family.

Ali S. Habib
Trade and Investment Coordinator – China
Al – Alamah Trading Cont. (KSA)
1291 Ballantrae Farm Drive
McLean, VA 22101–3027
(703) 821–5030
Fax: (703) 893–0535
EMAIL: See Below

6289

Business Information: Al – Alamah Trading Cont. (KSA), a privately–owned company, specializes in international trade. Based in Washington D.C., primary trade ventures are conducted with the Middle East, China and Korea. An international trade counselor since 1980, Mr. Habib joined the agency in 1992. As Trade and Investment Coordinator – China, he serves as liaison for all market ventures and project negotiations in the Chinese sector. Prior projects he was involved in include the implementation of a granite quarry operation in Egypt, as well as serving as liaison between China and Saudi Arabia in the import of earth moving equipment manufactured in China. Concurrent with his assignment with Al–Alamah, Mr. Habib is the President of a technology trade company — Marketing Technology. **Career Steps:** Trade and Investment Coordinator – China, Al – Alamah Trading Cont. (KSA) (1995–Present); Executive Vice President, Executive Services, Inc. (1986–1992); Marketing Manager, CCA (1983–1986). **Associations & Accomplishments:** American Management Association; World Affair Council of Washington, D.C. **Education:** Attending: John Hopkins University; West Coast University, Mechanical Engineer. **Personal:** Married to Layla in 1988. Two children: Habib and Ala'a. Mr. Habib enjoys tennis and chess.

Al Hidalgo
Vice President of Sales and Marketing
International Marketing Systems
301 Almeria Avenue, Suite 4
Coral Gables, FL 33134
(305) 529–5104
Fax: (305) 529–9242

6289

Business Information: Specializing in the Latin American market, International Marketing Systems, is a multi–functional, marketing, promotions, sales and representation company. I.M.S. has access to contacts in travel industry related fields, who are instrumental in marketing and promoting our client's products. Based in Coral Gables, Florida and with offices in Buenos Aires, Caracas, Mexico City, Santiago and Sao Paulo, I.M.S. has an established in–country General Sales Agent network that serves all of Central and South America. As Vice President of Sales and Marketing, Mr. Hidalgo interacts with the Latin American tourism industry and is responsible for overseeing and managing Latin American tourism development for all of International Marketing Systems accounts. **Career Steps:** Vice President of Sales and Marketing, International Marketing Systems (1995–Present); Director of Sales – Latin America, Greater Miami Convention & Visitors Bureau (1992–1995); Market Analyst, Carnival Cruise Lines (1988–1991). **Associations & Accomplishments:** Southeast USA Chapter Secretary, C.O.T.A.L., Federation of Latin American Travel Agencies Association; American Marketing Association; American Management Association. **Education:** Barry University, B.S. (1988). **Personal:** Mr. Hidalgo enjoys tennis, racquetball, and volunteer work.

Mr. Stephen G. Macklem
President
Arauca General, Inc.
70 East Scott Street
Chicago, IL 60610
(312) 664–2757
Fax: (312) 360–1630

6289

Business Information: Arauca General, Inc. is an international corporate risk arbitrage and securities firm providing a full range of services to include mergers, acquisitions, public offerings, reporting and more. As President of the Firm, Mr Macklem provides all aspects of administrative management with particular focus in the management of evaluation, analysis, review and assistance in risk arbitrage positions by the Firm. Established in 1991, Arauca General, Inc. employs 12 persons. **Career Steps:** President, Arauca General, Inc. (1991–Present); President, Yon, Macklem and Elliot (1985–1990); Chief Engineer, Occidental Petroleum (1978–1985). **Associations & Accomplishments:** American MENSA; Chicago Stock Exchange. **Education:** West Virginia University, B.A. (1989).

Burnett Marus, RFC
Executive Vice President
U.S. Tangible Investment Corporation
100 Highland Park Village
Dallas, TX 75205–2722
(214) 528–3500
Fax: (214) 520–6968

6289

Business Information: U.S. Tangible Investment Corporation provides specialized investment portfolios of rare coins to financial planner clientele around the world — the largest and oldest firm in this area of trade. Burnett Marus has been active in the financial planning field since 1972, where he started as a professional life agent in Michigan. He then began to specialize in tangible investment portfolios in 1975 and formed North American Investment Management Corporation in 1976. Under his guidance as President, he managed investment portfolios in rare coins, rare stamps and art objects, as well as traditional investments in excess of $7 million. From 1976 to 1980, Mr. Marus was the leading representative in sales for two major international firms dealing in rare coins and rare stamps. In 1980, he sold his interest in North American Investment Management and continued in private practice as a consultant in tangible asset investments. In 1981, Mr. Marus accepted the position of President of U.S Numismatic Investment Group, Inc., one of the nation's largest rare coin investment firms and an affiliate of Heritage Capital Corporation. Heritage Capital Corporation entities include Heritage Rare Coin Galleries and Heritage Numismatic Auctions, Inc. During his tenure, he changed the corporation name to U.S. Tangible Investment Corporation, and added specialized services and support to the investment community. Promoted to his present position as Executive Vice President of Investment Sales in January 1985 for the parent company, Heritage Capital Corporation, his responsibilities include the representation of all Heritage companies to the financial planning community, as well as the recruiting and training of sales representatives for U.S. Tangible Investment Corporation. Mr. Marus expanded company operations into Canada in 1986 and was named as the advisor to the first limited partnership in rare U.S. coins in Australia in 1991. **Career Steps:** Executive Vice President, Heritage Capital Corporation (1985–Present); President, U.S. Tangible Investment Corporation (f.k.a. – U.S. Numismatic Investment Corporation) – an affiliate of Heritage Capital Corporation (1981–Present); Private Tangible Investment Consultant, Burnett Marus Associates, Ltd. (1980–1981); President and Founder, North American Investment Management Corporation (1976–1980); Professional Life Agent, State of Michigan (1972–1976); MILITARY: Captain, U.S. Army, Military Police Corps — Active Duty in NATO (1969–1972); Active Reserves (1972–1981). **Associations & Accomplishments:** International Association for Financial Planning – Practitioner Division; International Association of Registered Financial Consultants; Texas Investment Management Council; Canadian Association of Financial Planners; American Numismatic Association; American Philatelic Society; Life Member, Reserve Officers Association; Recipient: U.S. Tangible Investment Corporation 'Salesperson of the Year' (1985, 1988, 1991, 1992); 1986 Alumni Achievement Award – Eastern Michigan University. **Education:** Eastern Michigan University, B.S. (1969); LICENSED CERTIFICATIONS: NASD Registered Representative — Texas & Michigan; Life, Health and Disability Insurance — Michigan, Ohio, Florida & Indiana; Real Estate Agent — Michigan; Registered Financial Consultant. **Personal:** Resides in Dallas, Texas with his wife, Shirley and their son, David.

Maria McCabe
Marketing Director
J.J. Kenny
65 Broadway
New York, NY 10006–2503
(212) 770–4589
Fax: (212) 269–3584

6289

Business Information: J.J. Kenny — a division of major publishing conglomerate McGraw–Hill — is a financial service specializing in municipal securities information and pricing services. Working in various marketing managerial roles for McGraw–Hill subsidiaries since 1982, Maria McCabe was transferred to J.J. Kenny in July of 1989. As Marketing Director for J.J. Kenny, Ms. McCabe is responsible for diversified activities, including promotions and all marketing aspects of the company. **Career Steps:** Marketing Director, J.J. Kenny, a Division of McGraw–Hill (1989–Present); Business Week, a Division of McGraw–Hill: Marketing Manager – International (1983–1989), Marketing Manager of Executive Programs (1982–1983). **Associations & Accomplishments:** American Marketing Association; Advertising Club of New York. **Education:** Hunter College. **Personal:** Married to Frank in 1979. Ms. McCabe enjoys gourmet cooking, real estate, and the theater.

Michael J. Onders
Vice President/Chief Technology Architect
Key Services Corporation
2025 Ontario MS#OH – 01 – 00 – 0601
Cleveland, OH 44115
(216) 689–6370
Fax: (216) 689–8982
EMAIL: See Below

6289

Business Information: Key Services Corporation is a financial services Company, providing information and technology processing. Key Services is a division of KeyCorp Bank, one of the 10 largest banking institutions in the United States. As Vice President/Chief Technology Architect, Mr. Onders manages the Architecture Services Division, whose mission is to facilitate the creation and evolution of an IT architecture framework, create and maintain an IT architecture repository, facilitate a Technology Steering Committee, and provide consulting to project teams. Internet users can reach him via: Monders@en.com **Career Steps:** Vice President/Chief Technology Architect, Key Services Corporation (1992–Present); Vice President, Peabody's Toys That Teach (1991–1992); Manager, Ernst and Young (1987–1991); Senior Analyst, Hughes Aircraft (1984–1987). **Education:** Ohio State University, M.S. in Computer Science (1989); Miami University, B.S. in Applied Science. **Personal:** Married to Debra in 1992. One child: Matthew. Mr. Onders enjoys basketball and jogging.

Kathy Orr

President
National Institute for Estate Planning, Inc.
14785 Preston Road, Suite 350
Dallas, TX 75240
(214) 991–3101 Ext. 228
Fax: (214) 991–2966

6289

Business Information: National Institute for Estate Planning, Inc. is a national institute specializing in estate planning for high net–worth clients through endorsements from bankers' associations. The Company additionally conducts seminars through financial institutions. Endorsements are found throughout the United States, including Texas, Oklahoma, Illinois, Indiana, Florida, California, Wisconsin, Michigan, and Minnesota. As President, Ms. Orr oversees the entire operation of the Company, including training, marketing, sales, accountability, and systems. **Career Steps:** National Institute for Estate Planning, Inc.: President (1996–Present), Executive Vice President (1991–1996); Senior Account Executive, UNUM Life Insurance Company (1986–1990). **Associations & Accomplishments:** Dallas Estate Planning Council; Dallas Association of Life Underwriters; North Dallas Chamber of Commerce. **Education:** SMU, Bachelor's in Business Administration (1980). **Personal:** Ms. Orr enjoys sports, competitive skeet shooting, and dog training & shows.

Dean R. Schiernbeck

President/Founder
Mutual Bancorp
3737 Camino Del Rio South, Suite 202
San Diego, CA 92108
(619) 283–8668
Fax: (619) 283–2838
EMAIL: See Below

6289

Business Information: Mutual Bancorp, the largest Company of its kind in the nation, is a privately owned company who purchases lottery payments and structured settlement annuity payments for lump sums of cash. As President/Founder, Mr. Schiernbeck oversees the day–to–day operations of the company, handles public relations, media advertising, and the marketing of the Company's services. He is responsible for obtaining funds to purchase the lottery payments and structured settlement annuities. Mr. Schiernbeck plans for the company to soon become a publicly–held corporation. **Career Steps:** President, Mutual Bancorp (1992–Present); Senior Vice President/Senior Credit Officer, 1st Western Bank (1988–1992); Golf Course Partner and General Manager, 7–Hills Golf Course (1983–1987); President and Chief Executive Officer, Mutual Funding Corporation (1979–1983). **Associations & Accomplishments:** Member and Vice President, Uptown Optimist Club of San Diego; Member and Former President, Progressive Toastmasters. **Education:** National University, B.S. in Business Administration (1979); University of Washington – Pacific Coast Banking School Graduate. **Personal:** Married to Sandra in 1977. Five children: Todd, Lynn, Jon, Paige, and Paul. Mr. Schiernbeck enjoys golf and reading.

Ronald F. Schmitt
National Sales Director
Primerica Financial Services
69 North Street, Suite 2
Danbury, CT 06810
(203) 790–1533
Fax: (203) 791–9839

6289

Business Information: Ron is an independent representative of Primerica Financial Services Insurance Marketing of Connecticut, Inc., which is a financial services company representing Primerica Life Insurance Company, the largest underwriter of individual life insurance in North America, National Benefit Life of New York which is a sister company to Primerica Life, Commercial Credit and numerous mutual fund companies including Select Mutual Funds of Smith Barney. As a company, our philosophy is to teach people how to solve the fundamental problems of how money works. As National Sales Director, Mr. Schmitt is responsible for diversified operational and administrative activities, including hiring, training and developing individuals to own and operate their own businesses under the Financial Giant Travelers Group. **Career Steps:** National Sales Director, Primerica Financial Services (1989–Present); Pilot, Trans World Airlines (1966–1989). **Associations & Accomplishments:** Chamber of Commerce; Good Friend/Big Brother Program. **Education:** American Academy of Funeral Service: Licensed Funeral Director, Ph.D. in Life. **Personal:** Married to Pamela in 1979. Two children: Ron Jr. and Daniel. Mr. Schmitt enjoys flying, boating, fishing, and skiing.

6300 Insurance Carriers

6311 Life insurance
6321 Accident and health insurance
6324 Hospital and medical service plans
6331 Fire, marine and casualty insurance
6351 Surety insurance
6361 Title insurance
6371 Pension, health and welfare funds
6399 Insurance carriers, NEC

Judy R. Bernett
Administrative Vice President
American Founders Life Insurance
2720 East Camelback Road
Phoenix, AZ 85016–4317
(602) 957–0778 Ext. 6213
Fax: (602) 224–6884

6311

Business Information: American Founders Life Insurance is primarily an individual life and disability company. Established in 1954, American Founders Life Insurance currently employs 30 people. As Vice President of Administration, Ms. Bernett provides the direction and overall management for the departments of Underwriting, Policy Issue, Claims, Customer Service, and Clerical. **Career Steps:** Vice President of Administration, American Founders Life Insurance (1991–Present); Assistant Vice President, Legacy Life Insurance Company (1989–1991); Manager of Claims, Lifeshares (1987–1989). **Associations & Accomplishments:** President, Phoenix Life and Health Claims Association. **Education:** Designations include ACS from LOMA and ALHC from the International Claims Association Program. **Personal:** Two children: Carey and Jonathan. Ms. Bernett enjoys tennis, reading, and snow skiing.

Norman P. Blake Jr.
Chairman, President, and Chief Executive Officer
USF&G Corporation
100 Light Street
Baltimore, MD 21202
(410) 547–3000
Fax: (410) 625–5682

6311

Business Information: USF&G Corporation is a leading national insurance company providing all types of insurance to include property/casualty, life, and reinsurance services, selling their products through independent agents. Established in 1896, USF&G Corporation employs over 6,700 persons throughout their 30 branch offices. As Chairman, President, and Chief Executive Officer, Mr. Blake is responsible for all aspects of Corporate operations. **Career Steps:** Chairman, President, and Chief Executive Officer, USF&G Corporation (1990–Present); Chairman & Chief Executive Officer, Heller International Corporation (1984–1990); Executive Vice President, General Electric Credit Corporation (1981–1984); Vice President and General Manager, General Electric Credit Corporation (1979–1981). **Associations & Accomplishments:** President of the Dean's Advisory Council, Purdue University (1987–Present); President, American Insurance Association (1990–Present); President (1992–Present) and Director, Owens Corning Fiberglass Corporation; Director, Enron Corporation (1993–Present); Member, Community Partnership for Education–Baltimore, MD. **Education:** Purdue University, M.S. (1967); Purdue University, B.S. (1966). **Personal:** Married to Karen in 1965. Three children: Kellie, Kim, and Adam.

Susan M. Blum
Policy Services Manager
MBL Life Assurance Corporation
520 Broad Street
Newark, NJ 07102–3111
(201) 481–8635
Fax: (201) 268–4331

6311

Business Information: MBL Life Assurance Corporation, formerly Mutual Benefit Life, is a major life insurance company located in Newark, New Jersey. As Policy Services Manager, Susan M. Blum is responsible for the training of all customer service representatives, the disbursing of loan and surrender proceeds, and the management and implementation of changes to the administrative and processing systems. **Career Steps:** MBL Life Assurance Corporation: Policy Services Manager (1991–Present), Field Training Manager (1988–1991); Customer Support Representative, Market Focus Technologies, Inc. (1985–1988); Public School Teacher, Chatham Township, NJ (1983–1987). **Associations & Accomplishments:** Board Member, Summit Chorale; Maplewood Strollers Community Theatre. **Education:** Carnegie-Mellon University, M.F.A. (1980). **Personal:** Married to Frank W. in 1990. Ms. Blum enjoys music, singing, and theater.

Manuel L. Corcuera
· · • · ━━◣ ◎ ◢━━ · • · ·

Chief Executive Officer
Muechener de Mexico
Jose Maria Velasco 30
Mexico City, Mexico
(5) 651–9388
Fax: (5) 680–0388

6311

Business Information: Muechener de Mexico is the largest re–insurance company in the world. A subsidiary of a German–based parent company, Muechener de Mexico deals primarily in Central America and the Caribbean. Internationally known in 150 countries, the Company has just acquired the third largest insurance company in the U.S. as part of its corporation. Established in 1964, the Company employs 42 people, and has an estimated annual revenue of $100 million. As Chief Executive Officer, Mr. Corcuera oversees all aspects of the Company. His duties include administration, operations,

public relations, and strategic planning. **Career Steps:** Muechener de Mexico: CEO (1986–Present), General Manager (1967–1986). **Associations & Accomplishments:** Mexican Association of Insurance; Instituto Panamericano de Alta Direccion de Empressa (IPADE); Camara Mexicano–Alemana de Comercio e Industria, A.C. (CAMEXA). **Education:** Insurance Business School, Munich, Germany (1967). **Personal:** Two children: Daniela and Manuel. Mr. Corcuera enjoys hunting, golf, horseback riding, and shooting.

Joseph W. Hamer Jr.
Vice President of Human Relations
Protective Life Corporation
P.O. Box 2606
Birmingham, AL 35202
(205) 868–3120
Fax: (205) 868–3196

6311

Business Information: Protective Life Corporation is a financial insurance institution providing life and group insurance, and annuities. As Vice President of Human Relations, Dr. Hamer is responsible for diversified administrative operations, in addition to overseeing the physical and human capital resources of the company. **Career Steps:** Vice President of Human Relations, Protective Life Corporation (1981–Present); University of Monvallo: Dean, Division of Student Affairs (1976–1981), Professor and Director of Counseling (1973–1976). **Associations & Accomplishments:** Society Human Resources Management; LOMA, Executive Human Resources Panel; Project Corporate Leadership; Board Member, INROADS Birmingham; Lay Leader, Methodist Church. **Education:** University of Georgia, Ed.D. (1973); Memphis State University, Med. (1967); Lambuth College, B.A. (1966); Harvard University, post doctoral study in Management (1978). **Personal:** Married to Elizabeth Bond in 1966. Two children: Richard and Elizabeth. Dr. Hamer enjoys water sports, various forms of spectator sports, and church and civil involvement.

Frank J. Jones, Ph.D.
Executive Vice President and Chief Investment Officer
The Guardian Life Insurance Company of America
201 Park Avenue South
New York, NY 10003
(212) 598–8232
Fax: (212) 777–6715

6311

Business Information: The Guardian Life Insurance Company of America is a mutual insurance company providing individual life insurance, group life and health insurance, and disability insurance coverages. With three regional offices in Pennsylvania, Wisconsin and Washington, The Guardian also offers their own family of mutual and annuity funds throughout the U.S. As Executive Vice President and Chief Investment Officer, Dr. Jones is responsible for stocks, bonds and real estate portfolio management, as well as funds management in the pension trust for the company and its subsidiaries. He also oversees investments for mutual funds and annuities. Established in 1860, The Guardian Life Insurance Company of America employs 5000 people and reports assets of approximately $10 billion. **Career Steps:** Executive Vice President and Chief Investment Officer, The Guardian Life Insurance Company of America (1991–Present); First Vice President and Director of Global Fixed Income Research and Economics, Merrill Lynch & Company (1989–1991); Director, Barclays de Zoete Wedd, G.S.I. (1988–1989); Managing Director, Kidder, Peabody & Company, Inc. (1983–1988). **Associations & Accomplishments:** American Economics Association; American Finance Association; Author of numerous books and articles including: The International Government Bond Markets; The Futures Game: Who Wins? Who Loses? Why?; Macro Finance: The Financial System and the Economy; Insurance Company Performance Measurement; Yield Curve Strategies; Stock Index Trading: Techniques and Applications in such journals and books as Portfolio & Investment Management; Investment Management; The CFA Digest; and The Handbook of Fixed Income Securities. **Education:** Stanford University, Ph.D. (1971); University of Pittsburgh, M.B.A. (1965); Cornell University, M.S. (1963); University of Notre Dame, B.S. (1961); University of Notre Dame, B.A. (1960).

Anne Katcher
Vice President and Senior Actuary
Equitable Life Assurance Society
787 Seventh Ave. 43N
New York, NY 10019–6018
(212) 554–2865
Fax: (212) 554–2866
E–mail: see below

6311

Business Information: Equitable Life Assurance Society — an entity of AXA Groupe which has companies in the U.S., Canada, Europe, Asia and Australia — provides life insurance services, financial analysis, and business planning for individuals. Established in 1859, Equitable currently employs over 7,000 agents and over 4,300 staff personnel. As Vice President and Senior Actuary, Ms. Katcher is responsible for individual life insurance, financial analysis, strategic planning and profitability. Ms. Katcher can also be reached through the Internet as follows: 73462,274@compuserv.com **Career Steps:** Vice President and Senior Actuary, Equitable Life Assurance Society (1991–Present, 1982–1989); Assistant Vice President, Aetna Life & Casualty (1989–1991); Associate Actuary, New York Life Insurance Company (1977–1982). **Associations & Accomplishments:** Board of Directors, Society of Actuaries; Academy of Actuaries; Chartered Financial Consultant. **Education:** SUNY – Albany: M.B.A. (1977), B.S. in Mathematics (1976).

Bankers Reserve Life
Insurance Company
Established 1959

Lois Rakus Keefe, C.L.U.
Vice President
Bankers Reserve Life Insurance Company
201 E. Pine St., Ste. 600
Orlando, FL 32801
(407) 422–1332
Fax: (407) 423–7808

6311

Business Information: Bankers Reserve Life Insurance Company, a subsidiary of Atlantic Financial Corporation, is a national insurance company providing annuities in eleven states in the Mountain Area. As Vice President, Ms. Keefe serves as the Corporate Secretary and Vice President of Operations and Administration for all of the Companies. She also teaches and lectures on hospital, health, and ambulatory care services. **Career Steps:** Vice President, Bankers Reserve Life Insurance Company (1993–Present); Assistant Broker Manager, Metropolitan Life (1985–1991); Instructor, Trinity University (1979–1983); Assistant/Associate Administrator, George Washington Medical Center (1972–1979). **Associations & Accomplishments:** American Society of Chartered Life; Underwriters and Chartered Financial Consultants; Fellow, American College – Health Care Executives (1982); Fellow, National Association of Life Underwriters (1989). **Education:** American College, C.L.U. (1995); University of Pittsburgh, M.S. (1966); Pennsylvania State University, B.S. (1962). **Personal:** Married to Thomas in 1965. Ms. Keefe enjoys sailing, walking, reading, theater, and family.

Donald K. Lawler, Esq.
Assistant General Counsel
Mutual Protective and Medico Life Insurance Companies
1515 South 75th Street
Omaha, NE 68124
(402) 391–6900
Fax: (402) 391–9106

6311

Business Information: Mutual Protective and Medico Life Insurance Companies is a full service insurance brokerage and financial services business, providing business insurance, bonds, personal insurance, life insurance, employee benefits programs, and health insurance. Established in 1930, the Agency employs 150 insurance brokers and related administrative support staff, reporting over $200 million in premium assets. A litigation attorney admitted to Nebraska and Iowa state and federal courts, Mr. Lawler serves as Assistant General Counsel, representing the Agency in all litigation and personal injury claims and arbitration matters. **Career Steps:** Assistant General Counsel, Mutual Protective and Medico Life Insurrance Companies. **Associations & Accomplishments:** Phi Alpha Delta; Chapter Justice, Sir Thomas More Chapter (1991–1992); American Bar Association; Iowa Bar Association; Nebraska Bar Association; Omaha Bar Association. **Education:** Creighton University Law School, J.D. (1992); Buena Vista College, B.A. (1989); Creighton University School of Business, MBA candidate. **Personal:** Married to Naomi in 1985. Two children: Patrick and Michael. Mr. Lawler enjoys spending time with his children.

Kaye F. Lindsey
Assistant Vice President – BI Claims
State Farm Insurance
1 State Farm Plaza E. 4
Bloomington, IL 61710–0001
(309) 766–5677
Fax: (309) 766–6690

6311

Business Information: State Farm Insurance is one of the major national full–line insurance providers. Serving both commercial and individual customers, product lines include health, life, property and auto insurance. Headquarters are located in Bloomington, Illinois. Joining State Farm Insurance in 1987, Ms. Lindsey was appointed as Assistant Vice President of Bodily Injury Claims in 1994. She is responsible for providing a resource to all regional personnel (28 regions) for bodily injury claims, which includes training, and assistance in policy and contract questions. With total responsibility for the Bodily Injury Group, she is also responsible for the development and instruction of in–house corporate programs. **Career Steps:** State Farm Insurance: Assistant Vice President – BI Claims (1994–Present), Claim Manager (1989–1994), Divisional Claim Superintendent (1987–1989). **Associations & Accomplishments:** National Women's Association; Vice President, Bethel – AME; Women's Missionary Society. **Education:** Western State Univeristy, J.D. (1989); Pacific Christian College. **Personal:** Married to Roosevelt in 1969. Two children: Daphney and Ross. Ms. Lindsey enjoys reading and golf.

Uwe Lobbert
General Manager
CALOMEX
Horacio 1844 PB Desp. "B"
C.P. 11510 Mexico, D.F., Mexico
(525) 281–5191
Fax: (525) 281–4637
EMAIL: See Below

6311

Business Information: CALOMEX is a public company specializing in reinsurance brokering and consulting placing reinsurance programs with international reinsurance marketers. Established in 1996, the Company has estimated annual revenue of $50 thousand. As General Manager, Mr. Lobbert is responsible for all marketing plans, administration, operations, and coordination with re–insurance companies. Internet users can reach him via: 74052.732@compuserve.com. **Career Steps:** General Manager, CALOMEX (1996–Present); Vice President, International, Grupo Cardinal, Mexico City (1995–1996); Vice President, International, Afianzadora Insurgentes, Mexico City (1993–1994); Manager, Credit and Bonding, Hannover Re, Hannover, Germany (1990–1992); Manager for the Underwriting in Spain, Hannover Re, Hannover, Germany (1987–1990). **Education:** University of Heidelberg, Germany, Diploma (equivalent to a Master's Degree in the US) Volkswirt (Economist) (1980). **Personal:** Married to Claudia Gongora in 1994. One child: Marco Lobbert Gongora. Mr. Lobbert enjoys computers.

William F. Logan

Vice President of Sales & Marketing
Anthem Life
5115 Briarstone Trace
Carmel, IN 46033–9605
(317) 484–3464
Fax: (317) 484–3518

6311

Business Information: Anthem Life is a national insurance company providing life and related ancillary coverages (i.e., interest sensitive whole life, UL, STD, LTD, annuities, and senior market products). Anthem Life is licensed and has significant marketing representation in 49 states. Established in 1956, Anthem Life reports estimated annual revenue of $60 million and currently employs 100 people. As Vice President of Sales & Marketing, Mr. Logan is responsible for the oversight of product development and national distribution. **Career Steps:** Vice President of Sales & Marketing, Anthem Life

(1995–Present); Vice President of Endorsed Markets Group Division, AON Corporation (Combined Insurance Company Subsidiary) (1989–1995); Brokerage Manager, Manufacturer's Life Insurance (Indiana Branch) (1986–1989); Vice President, Merchants Capital Corporation (1982–1986). **Associations & Accomplishments:** National and Indiana Associations of Life Underwriters (LUTCF designation); Charter Member, Association of Health Insurance Agents; Patron of: Big Brothers, Hillcrest Country Club, Indianapolis Athletic Club, Indianapolis Children's Museum, and Indiana Sports Corporation. **Education:** Indiana University, B.S. in Business (1983). **Personal:** Married to Marcie in 1985. Three children: Shannon, Nicholas, and Madison. Mr. Logan enjoys golf, basketball, and travel.

Kirk J. Oborn
Director of Product Marketing
B M A
1 Penn Valley Parkway
Kansas City, MO 64108
(816) 751–5314
Fax: (816) 751–7754
E/M: quakie@ix.netcom.com

6311

Business Information: Business Men's Assurance, or BMA as the Company prefers to be called, was formed in 1909. In 1990, BMA became a member of the Generali Group of Companies, one of the largest insurance organizations in the world. BMA is headquartered in Kansas City, MO and concentrates on individual, agriculture, and small business life and disability insurance. As Director of Product Marketing, Mr. Oborn is responsible for implementing and marketing of products, and training field producers. **Career Steps:** Director of Product Marketing, B M A (1992–Present); Director of Franchise Consulting, Help–U–Sell Real Estate (1987–1992); Director of Market Research, USLife Life Insurance (1985–1987). **Associations & Accomplishments:** Volunteer with local Boy Scouts; Politically active–delegate to state convention; published articles on industry concerns. **Education:** University of Utah. **Personal:** Married to Sharlene in 1981. Five children: Erin, Dane, Taylor, Allyx, and Jessie. Mr. Oborn enjoys golf, attending the symphony, theatre, and camping.

Michael J. Poulos, CLU

Chairman, President & Chief Executive Officer
Western National Corporation
5555 San Felipe, Suite 900
Houston, TX 77056
(713) 888–7888
Fax: (713) 888–7892

6311

Business Information: Western National Corporation is one of the 50 largest life insurance companies in the United States, the second largest in Texas, and one of the largest providers of retirement annuities. Mr. Poulos began his life insurance career in 1958 with the United States Life Insurance Company in New York City where he held various key sales and management positions prior to joining American General Corporation in 1970. At American General, he served as a senior officer of a subsidiary, California–Western States Life Insurance Company, until his promotion to President and Chief Executive Officer of Cal–Western in 1975. In 1979, he was named Senior Vice President in charge of American General's life insurance subsidiaries. He served as President of American General Corporation from 1981 to 1991 and Vice Chairman from 1991 until October of 1993 when he joined Western National. A Chartered Life Underwriter and NASD registered principal, Mr. Poulos presently serves as Chairman, President & Chief Executive Officer of Western National Corporation and Western National Life. With his expertise, he made Western National a public company in 1994 and is now responsible for the maintenance of shareholder and investor relations, strategic planning, selection of key personnel, and management of overall banking relations. **Career Steps:** Chairman, President & Chief Executive Officer, Western National Corporation (1993–Present); American General Corporation: Vice Chairman (1991–1993), President (1981–1991), Senior Vice President of Life Insurance Subsidiaries (1979–1981), California–Western States Life Insurance Company: President and Chief Executive Officer (1975–1979), Senior Officer (1970–1975); Various Positions, United States Life Insurance Company (1958–1970). **Associations & Accomplishments:** Director of Sam Houston Area Council, Boy Scouts of America; Former Director, Houston Symphony Society; American Management Association; American Society of Certified Life Underwriters; National Association of Life Underwriters; Houston Association of Life Underwriters; Director, Texas Association of Life Insurance Companies. **Education:** Colgate University, B.A. (1953); New York University, M.B.A. (1963); Chartered Life Underwriter; NASD Registered Principal; Certified Model–Netics Instructor; Graduate, Life Insur-

ance Marketing Research Association School for Senior Marketing Officers. **Personal:** Married to Mary Kay in 1984. Two children: Denise and Peter.

Randall H. Riley
Chief Executive Officer/Vice Chairman of the Board
Citizens, Inc.
400 East Anderson Lane
Austin, TX 78752
(512) 837–7100
Fax: (512) 836–9334

6311

Business Information: Citizens, Inc. is a full–service life insurance company. In operation since 1953, Citizens Inc. currently employs 63 people domestically and more than 1,400 representatives world wide. Citizens reports assets of more than $200 million and gross income of more than $65 million. As Chief Executive Officer, Mr. Riley is responsible for all aspects of operations of the Company. **Career Steps:** Chief Executive Officer, Citizens, Inc. (1994–Present); General Manager, Negocios Savoy, S.A. (1988–1993); Self employed (1977–1987). **Associations & Accomplishments:** Texas House of Representatives. **Education:** Baylor University (1973–1976). **Personal:** Married to Monique in 1993. Two children: Macy and Rhett. Mr. Riley enjoys hunting, golf and flying airplanes.

Scott A. Sloan
Team Leader
Texas Worker's Compensation Insurance Fund
Dallas, TX 75247
(214) 689–8452
Fax: (214) 689–8292

6311

Business Information: Texas Worker's Compensation Insurance Fund is a worker's compensation insurance company, licensed to write privately but existing as a governmental corporation. Sweeping worker's compensation reform legislation created the Company in 1992 as a solution to the ailing workers' compensation system. The Company became the largest writer of workers' compensation insurance in Texas in its' first 18 months of business. It currently serves more than 45,000 policy holders and divides its' operations in four separate regions. As Team Leader, Scott Sloan manages the Loss Prevention department of 35 safety and health professionals for the Dallas Region. The Loss Prevention department provides high quality consultative services to its policyholders in the field of occupational safety and health, and industrial hygiene. **Career Steps:** Team Leader, Texas Workers Compensation Insurance Fund (1993–Present); Safety Consultant, Occupational Safety Service, Inc. (1992–1993); Meterman #1, Oklahoma Gas & Electric (1982–1992). **Associations & Accomplishments:** American Society of Safety Engineers; Associate Safety Professional as certified by the Board of Certified Safety Professionals. **Education:** University of Central Oklahoma, B.S. Degree in Occupational Safety and Health. **Personal:** Married to Brenda in 1988. Two children: Shane and Rachel. Mr. Sloan enjoys water skiing, snow skiing, and scuba diving.

Timothy R. Sutter
Area Manager
American Republic Insurance
P.O. Box 648, 1145 School Bus Road
Springerville, AZ 85938
(520) 333–2944
Fax: (520) 333–2765

6311

Business Information: American Republic Insurance is a life, health, and senior care products insurance company. As Area Manager, Mr. Sutter is responsible for the management, education, and training of agents. He oversees the operation of over 30 staffed offices, employing over 700 active agents. **Career Steps:** American Republic Insurance: Area Manager (1995–Present), Assistant Manager (1992–1995); Regional Manager, DuPont Fiber Division (1987–1992). **Associations & Accomplishments:** Professional Insurance Agents of Arizona; Chamber of Commerce; Community Liaison for two local Hospitals; Community Service and over 20 hours of volunteer work each month. **Education:** Georgia Tech. (1988); University of Arizona, Business Management; Pima Community College, Marketing, Business Management, and Accounting. **Personal:** Married to Monica J. in 1990. Mr. Sutter enjoys golf, sailing, and tennis.

Robert A. Wilgus Jr.

Director of Marketing Communications
Lafayette Life Insurance Company
1905 Teal Road
Lafayette, IN 47903
(317) 477–3232
Fax: (317) 477–3235
EMAIL: See Below

6311

Business Information: Established in 1905, Lafayette Life Insurance Company is a national insurance company with regional offices across the United States. Insurance product lines include life, annuities, pensions, and group insurance. As Director of Marketing Communications, Mr. Wilgus is responsible for national advertising, field sales promotions, awards and recognitions, seminars, conventions, conference planning, and writing corporate communications and materials development. Internet users can reach him via: LLIC@AOL.COM. **Career Steps:** Director of Marketing Communications, Lafayette Life Insurance Company (1994–Present); Manager of Communications, Phoenix Home Life (1989–1994); Marketing Communication Coordinator, United Way (1986–1989). **Associations & Accomplishments:** Life Communication Association; Phi Sigma Alpha; Ad Club of Lafayette, IN; Ad Club of Indianapolis; Public Relations Society of America. **Education:** Westfield State College, B.S. (1985). **Personal:** Married to Lisa in 1986. One child: Zachary. Mr. Wilgus enjoys being a professional musician and golf.

Lorri Wilson

President
Elliott Wilson Insurance
225 Saddler Road
Grasonville, MD 21638
(410) 827–5514
Fax: (410) 827–7335

6311

Business Information: Elliott Wilson Insurance is a full–service insurance agency, specializing in the provision of insurance policies for the trucking industry. Coverage includes life, health, automobile, fire, and home insurance. Joining Elliott Wilson Insurance as President in 1987, Ms. Wilson is responsible for all aspects of operations, including management, finances, sales, and customer service. **Career Steps:** President, Elliott Wilson Insurance (1987–Present); Controller, Elliott Equipment Company (1984–1987). **Associations & Accomplishments:** Professional Insurance Agents; Chamber of Commerce of Queen Anne's County; Licensure: Maryland, Delaware, Virginia, and Pennsylvania. **Education:** Salisbury State (1982); Delaware Technical and Community College (1980). **Personal:** Married to Raymond Clarke in 1993. Three children: Johathan, Anthony, and Derin. Ms. Wilson enjoys boating, fishing, and tennis.

Todd R. Adams

Sales Manager
LTC, Inc.
601 Union Street, Two Union Square, Floor 22
Seattle, WA 98101–2327
(206) 827–5889
Fax: (206) 515–7299

6321

Business Information: LTC, Inc. specializes in the sale for nursing home and home health care facilities insurance. Part of GE Capital Insurance, the Company presently has 53 offices across the United States. As Sales Manager, Mr. Adams handles the region of Washington, Northern Idaho, and Montana. He is responsible for training, coaching, and advising new employees, recruiting new members, marketing, and advertising. **Career Steps:** LTC, Inc: Sales Manager (1996–Present), National Director of Sales Training (1990–1996), National Sales Trainer/Agent (1987–1990). **Education:** Washington State University, B.S. in Education (1987). **Personal:** Married to Holly Renee in 1994. Mr. Adams enjoys scuba diving, tennis, golf, travel, and wine collecting.

Terry E. Bichlmeier

Vice President
Bichlmeier Insurance Services, Inc.
P.O. Box 929
Hermosa Beach, CA 90254
(310) 376–8852
Fax: (310) 379–9272

6321

Business Information: Bichlmeier Insurance Services, Inc. is a full–service property and casualty, and life insurance agency and brokerage service. The Company currently employs 10 people and reports sales of over $5 million. As Vice President, Mr. Bichlmeier is responsible for the direction of marketing and production of all lines of insurance, as well as new business development. He is a Certified Insurance Counselor and was recently elected as the Vice President of the Professional Insurance Agents Association of California. Mr. Bichlmeier's father is the Founder of the Company, in operation since 1961. **Career Steps:** Bichlmeier Insurance Services, Inc.: Vice President (1995–Present), Sales Manager (1993–1995); Commercial Sales Agent, Jerry Bichlmeier Insurance Agency (1988–1993). **Associations & Accomplishments:** Vice President, Professional Insurance Agents of California and Nevada (1994–1995); Rotary International, Redondo Riviera Club; Director, Torrance – South Bay Family YMCA Celebrity Golf Tournament; Golden Key Honor Society, California State University – Long Beach, School of Business; Society of Certified Insurance Counselors. **Education:** California State University – Long Beach, B.S. with honors (1986); El Camino Community College, A.A. **Personal:** Married to Kristen N. in 1991. One child: Joseph L. Mr. Bichlmeier enjoys golf, skiing, computers, and collecting wine.

Mrs. Judith G. Bond

Asst. Vice President–Information Systems & Facilities Securities
Blue Cross and Blue Shield of Kansas City, Missouri
2301 Main Street
Kansas City, MO 64108
(816) 395–2601
Fax: (816) 395–2605

6321

Business Information: Blue Cross and Blue Shield of Kansas City, Missouri is a health insurance company. In her capacity as Assistant Vice President of Information Systems and Facilities Services, Mrs. Bond directs a staff of 150 employees in the acquisition, building and maintenance of computer systems and company facilities. Established in 1938, Blue Cross and Blue Shield of Kansas City, Missouri employs over 1,200 and reports annual revenue in excess of $500 million. **Career Steps:** Assistant Vice President of Information Systems and Facilities Services, Blue Cross and Blue Shield of Kansas City, Missouri (1987–Present); Director, Systems Design & Programming, Blue Cross and Blue Shield of Kansas City, Missouri (1985–1987); Manager, Systems Design & Programming, Blue Cross and Blue Shield of Kansas City, Missouri (1984–1985); Supervisor, Blue Cross and Blue Shield of Kansas City, Missouri (1983–1984). **Associations & Accomplishments:** Data Processing Management Association; Advisory Board Member, Community Living Opportunities, Overland Park, Kansas. **Education:** Benedictine College, B.A. in Math (1970).

William Cleary

Director
Blue Cross/Blue Shield of Massachusetts
100 Hancock Street
North Quincy, MA 02171
(617) 745–7880
Fax: (617) 745–7828

6321

Business Information: Blue Cross/Blue Shield of Massachusetts is a mutual insurance company whose primary business is health insurance and health benefits management. They also have HMO managed health care programs providing complete medical, dental, surgical, and pharmacy services, as well as life insurance products to their members. Established in 1942, the Quincy division employs 118 people. As Director of Operations, Mr. Cleary oversees all scanning and imaging activities related to claims processing. He is directly responsible for seven supervisors, and manages all additional personnel. **Career Steps:** Blue Cross/Blue Shield of Massachusetts: Director of Operations (1987–Present), Director of National Accountants (1984), Director of Claims (1980). **Associations & Accomplishments:** Plymouth Chamber of Commerce. **Education:** Northeastern University, B.S. (983); Suffolk University, M.B.A. Candidate. **Personal:** Married to Betsy in 1967. Two children: Christine and Cindy. Mr. Cleary enjoys being a commercial helicopter pilot.

Susan Lee Fisher, ACS, ALHC

Quality Improvement Specialist
Nationwide HMO
5525 Parkcenter Circle
Dublin, OH 43017–3685
(614) 854–3096
Fax: (614) 854–3422

6321

Business Information: Nationwide HMO is a subsidiary of Nationwide Insurance Enterprise, a large multi–line insurance enterprise offering Automobile, Homeowner, Fire, Commercial, Life Insurance and Investment Products. Nationwide HMO offers a variety of health insurance products ranging from HMO to point of service individual indemnity health plans. Established in 1992, Nationwide HMO employs 120 people. As Quality Improvement Specialist, Susan designs, generates, and analyzes reports necessary to evaluate the quality of care delivered by the plan. She also utilizes Patterns of Treatment and Episodes Profiler software to monitor appropriateness and frequency of services rendered to the plan's participants by the network's providers. Other responsibilities include compiling data for the Plan's HEDIS Report Card and Provider Profile. **Career Steps:** Quality Improvement Specialist, Nationwide HMO (1996–Present); Senior Business Analyst, InHealth (1995–1996); Quality Improvement and Risk Management Network Information Management Specialist, InHealth (1994–1995); Hearing Officer, Nationwide Insurance – Medicare (1991–1994); Claims Unit Supervisor, Nationwide Insurance – Medicare (1989–1991); Claims Examiner, Nationwide Insurance – Medicare & Group Insurance (1983–1989). **Associations & Accomplishments:** Board of Trustees (President 1992–1994, Treasurer, 1995, Member 1989–1995) – Nationwide Insurance Activities Association. Susan has earned the following designations: Associate in Customer Service (ACS) from the Life Office Management Association; Associate in Life Health Claims (ALHC) from the Internal Claims Association. Susan was also a member of the Business Advisory Committee at Goodwill Rehabilitation Center. This committee helped develop programs that helped retrain individuals for other vocations who were physically or mentally challenged. **Education:** Columbus State Community College: Associate's in Business Administration (1996), Associate's in Graphic Communications (1983).

Jim Jang

Planning & Analysis Manager
Toyota Motor Insurance Services
19001 South Western Avenue
Torrance, CA 90509–2916
(310) 787–3799
Fax: (310) 787–3899

6321

Business Information: Toyota Motor Insurance Services supplies automotive insurance–related products and services to Toyota dealers across the United States. A former Planning Administrator for Toyota Motor Sales, Mr. Jang joined Toyota Motor Insurance Services in 1985. Promoted to Planning & Analysis Manager in 1990 after serving in various supervisory positions, he is presently responsible for analyzing product pricing, monitoring profitability, and performing various actuarial functions. **Career Steps:** Toyota Motor Insurance Services: Planning & Analysis Manager (1990–Present), Systems Development Manager (1985–1990); Planning Administrator, Toyota Motor Sales – Parts (1980–1985). **Education:** California State University at Los Angeles: M.B.A. (1976), B.S. in Math. **Personal:** Married to Lily in 1979. Two children: Justin and Timothy. Mr. Jang enjoys running, bicycling, and family–oriented activities.

Mr. John W. Keithler

Cash and Investment Manager
Group Health, Inc.
441 Ninth Avenue, 7th Floor
New York, NY 10001–1681
(212) 615–0970
Fax: (212) 563–8684

6321

Business Information: Group Health, Inc. is a health insurance company servicing New York state. As Cash and Investment Manager, Mr. Keithler is responsible for managing the Company's cash flow and cash reserves, investment portfolio, and banking relationships. Established in 1937, Group Health, Inc. employs over 2,000 people and reports annual premiums in excess of $1.3 billion. **Career Steps:** Cash and Investment Manager, Group Health, Inc. (1987–Present); Cash Manager, American Brands, Inc. (1980–1986); Corporate Banking, Chase Manhattan Bank, N.A. (1970–1980). **Associations & Accomplishments:** Certified Cash Manager; Treasury Management Association of New York; National Corporate Cash Management Association; Member, Rider University Presidents Club. **Education:** Rider University, B.S. in Commerce (1970).

Edgardo J. Lebron de la Cruz, CPA

Finance Director
La Cruz Azul de Puerto Rico
C4 Calle 8, Parque de Torrimar
Bayamon, Puerto Rico 00959–8952
(787) 272–7874
Fax: (787) 272–7867

6321

Business Information: La Cruz Azul de Puerto Rico (Blue Cross), provides health insurance (traditional plan and managed care business) to area residents. As Finance Director, Mr. Lebron de la Cruz oversees accounting, billing, collection, and coordination of work with other departments. **Career Steps:** Finance Director, La Cruz Azul de Puerto Rico (1995–Present); Senior Auditor, Arthur Andersen LLP

(1988–1995). **Associations & Accomplishments:** American Institute of Certified Public Accountants; Puerto Rico Association of Certified Public Accountants. **Education:** University of Puerto Rico, B.B.A. (1988). **Personal:** Married to Amarilis in 1992. One child: Adrianna Nicole. Mr. Lebron de la Cruz enjoys helping his wife with her own business and spending time with his family.

Sharon McGregor

Regional Vice President
Great States Insurance Company
4275 Executive Square, Suite 800
La Jolla, CA 92037
(619) 546–2940
Fax: (619) 453–2812

6321

Business Information: Greater States Insurance Company is a nation–wide insurance agency, providing Worker's Compensation and health–life insurance benefits throughout five states. The first female to run a branch office in California, Ms. McGregor is the Regional Vice President, serving as Branch Manager of the San Diego office and territory. She is responsible for overseeing all aspects of operations for the office and a territory covering four counties. **Career Steps:** Regional Vice President, Greater States Insurance Company (1994–Present); Assistant Vice President, Republic Insurance Company (1982–1994); Underwriter Manager, Insurance Company of the West (1979–1982). **Associations & Accomplishments:** IBA of San Diego; Most Loyal Gander, Blue Goose International; Professional Insurance Agency Association; City of Hope Insurance Council; American Red Cross; "1991 Insurance Professional of the Year"; San Diego Insurance Adjusters Association; San Diego YMCA; Insurance Council of San Diego. **Education:** Colorado State College (1961). **Personal:** One child: Scott. Ms. McGregor enjoys golf, travel, reading, and needlepoint.

Trevor C. Reeves

Vice President and Controller of Health Plans
Aetna Life and Casualty
151 Farmington Avenue MB65
Hartford, CT 06156
(203) 636–4130
Fax: Please mail or call

6321

Business Information: Aetna Life and Casualty is a provider of health care and group insurance to planned sponsors (Fortune 500 and 1000 companies). Aetna Life & Casualty is the largest shareholder–owned insurance company in the country and one of the most recognized insurance companies in the world. They provide managed health care products such as Managed Choice and Select Choice HMO's and PPO's, property–casualty insurance, group life insurance and other diversified financial services. With Corporate headquarters in Hartford, Connecticut, Aetna Life & Casualty reports annual revenue of $8 billion and currently employs 23,000 people company–wide. Joining Aetna in 1990 as an Assistant Vice President of Internal Audits for Aetna Life & Casualty, Mr. Reeves was appointed as Vice President and Controller for Aetna International in 1992. Currently serving as Vice President and Controller of Health Plans for Aetna Life & Casualty since 1994, he oversees the administrative operations for associates and a staff of 160, in addition to handling financial and management reports, and SEC reporting. He is also responsible for tax planning, compliance and treasury functions, as well as overseeing all controlling functions. **Career Steps:** Aetna and its Subsidiaries: Vice President and Controller of Aetna Health Plans – Aetna Life & Casualty (1994–Present), Vice President and Controller – Aetna International (1992–1994), Assistant Vice President of Internal Audit – Aetna Life & Casualty (1990–1992); Senior Director of Internal Audit, RJR Nabisco (1987–1989). **Associations & Accomplishments:** Leadership Greater Hartford Alumni Association: Treasurer, Board Member. **Education:** London School of Economics, B.S. in Economics (1976). **Personal:** Married to Diana in 1983. Three children: Scott, Elizabeth, and Caitlin. Mr. Reeves enjoys coaching soccer.

Sherry Snow

Territory Office Supervisor
Physician's Mutual Insurance Company
3501 NW 63rd Street, Suite 204
Oklahoma City, OK 73116–2202
(405) 840–9010
Fax: (405) 843–8247

6321

Business Information: Physician's Mutual Insurance Company, headquartered in Omaha, Nebraska is involved in the sale of health, long–term care, life, and annuity products for individuals. The Company was established in 1902 and currently has over 1,700 employees nationwide. As Territory Office Supervisor, Ms. Snow supervises all support staff for 18 Division offices in the Western Territory. Other responsibilities include training support staff, coordinating seminars, tracking production counts, coordinating and planning for regional and territorial meetings, and assisting in divisional management in the absence of the division manager. Ms. Snow prepares input for the preparation of division budgets and monitors division use of budgeted funds. **Career Steps:** Territory Office Supervisor, Physician's Mutual Insurance Company (1995–Present); Administrative Assistant to Regional Food Director, Target Stores (1990–1992); Administrative Assistant, US Attorney's Office, Western District of Oklahoma (1987–1990). **Associations & Accomplishments:** Beta Sigma Phi; National Association of Female Executives; South Oklahoma City Chamber of Commerce. **Education:** Oklahoma University. **Personal:** Two children: Allen Manley and DeeAnne Lopez. Ms. Snow enjoys golf, attending automobile races, and anything concerning her grandchildren (Ryon and Heather Lopez and a third expected January 1997).

Kim J. Thompson

Senior Account Manager
Prudential Insurance Company
8425 Woodfield Crossing Boulevard
Indianapolis, IN 46240–2495
(317) 469–7410
Fax: (317) 469–8058

6321

Business Information: Prudential Insurance Company of America is an international personal lines insurance company, also providing investment and retirement instruments such as mutual funds and annuities. Prudential of Indianapolis, Indiana sells group health insurance plans (managed care) to businesses within the state of Indiana. Managing Prudential's existing group insurance contracts for the state of Indiana as Senior Account Manager, Kim Thompson focuses on the executive sales aspects and accounting department of the company. Responsible for all new sales, he represents clients such as Purdue University, Subaru and Isuzu. **Career Steps:** Senior Account Manager, Prudential (1994–Present); District Account Manager, Travelers Insurance Company (1976–1993). **Associations & Accomplishments:** Indiana Group Underwriters Association. **Education:** University of Indianapolis, M.B.A. (1992); Indiana State University, B.A. in Business Management. **Personal:** Married to Linda in 1971. Two children: Eric and Ryan. Mr. Thompson enjoys boating, spending time with his family and working with youth at church.

Nicolas Touma Correa

Vice President of the Agencies
Trans–Oceanic Life Insurance
P.O. Box 363467
San Juan, Puerto Rico 00936–3467
(809) 782–2680
Fax: (809) 793–6953

6321

Business Information: Trans–Oceanic Life Insurance is an insurance company specializing in the payroll deduction market, selling Cancer, Accident, and Credit Life programs to individuals and corporations within the region. Products are marketed by 100+ in–house agents at five locations in Puerto Rico. Established in 1959, Trans–Oceanic Life Insurance reports premium assets in excess of $15 million and currently employs 70 people. Starting as a General Agent for Trans–Oceanic in 1983, Mr. Touma has risen in the corporate ranks to his current position. As Vice President of the Agencies, he is engaged in the creation and supervision of the agencies. **Career Steps:** Trans–Oceanic Life Insurance: Vice President of the Agencies (1990–Present), Agencies Director (1988–1990), General Agent (1983–1988). **Associations & Accomplishments:** Association of Domestic Insurance Companies (ACODESE); Association of Food Marketing and Distribution (MIDA); Association of Health Insurance Agents (AHIA); Association of Interamerican Business Men (AIHE) **Education:** University of Puerto Rico, B.B.A. (1975); Sacred Heart University, Marketing & Motivation Courses. **Personal:** Married to Carmen Taveras in 1979. Four children: Minette, Humberto, Christian, and Edrick. Mr. Touma Correa enjoys golf and reading.

Dr. Youssef S. Towliati

Director
Blue Cross of California
2450 East Del Mar, #2
Pasadena, CA 91107
(818) 703–2969
Fax: (818) 703–4848

6321

Business Information: Blue Cross of California is a provider of health insurance coverage to individuals and groups. They have recently merged with HealthNet in California with 13 million members. Established in 1934, Blue Cross reports annual revenue in excess of $1 million and currently employs 2,000 people. As Director, Dr. Towliati is responsible for all aspects of PC applications, new technology development and strategic planning. **Career Steps:** Director, Blue Cross of California (1991–Present); Technical Supervisor, Jet Propulsion Laboratory (1987–1991). **Associations & Accomplishments:** Published articles at Institute of Electricity and Electronical Engineers (IEEE). **Education:** University of Wisconsin, Ph.D. (1972). **Personal:** Dr. Towliati enjoys reading, playing chess and working with PC computers.

Bernard F. Webber

President and Chief Executive Officer
Facility Association
20 Richmond Street, East
Toronto, Ontario M5C 2R9
(416) 361–7177
Fax: (416) 868–0894

6321

Business Information: Facility Association is a national auto reinsurance organization servicing most jurisdictions in Canada. Facility Association reinsures approximately $600 million worth of policies annually. As President and CEO, Mr. Webber is responsible for all aspects of Association operations, including administration, compliance, public relations, and strategic planning. **Career Steps:** President and CEO, Facility Association (1994–Present); Deputy Commissioner, Ontario Insurance Commission (1990–1994); Ministry of Consumer and Commercial Relations: Acting Deputy Minister (1989–1990), Assistant Deputy Minister (1987–1989). **Associations & Accomplishments:** Royal Canadian Military Institute; Chairman, Salvation Army National Advisory Council on Corrections; President, The Other Club of Ontario an affiliate of the International Churchill Society. **Education:** Waterloo Lutheran University, B.A. (1964); Althouse College of Education, Secondary School Teaching Specialist (1968). **Personal:** Married to Jeanette in 1962. Three children: Jeanine, Bernard, and Michelle. Mr. Webber enjoys hockey, football, baseball, and military history.

Kevin Williams

Director of Administrative Services
Blue Cross of Northeastern Pennsylvania
70 N. Main Street
Wilkes Barre, PA 18711
(717) 829–6141
Fax: (717) 829–6008

6321

Business Information: Blue Cross of Northeastern Pennsylvania is an organization primarily concerned with the advancement of health care. As Director of Administrative Services, Mr. Williams directs the administration of Facility operations and services (i.e., capital expenditures, planning, etc.). He is additionally responsible for corporate real estate, including new building renovations. **Career Steps:** Director of Administrative Services, Blue Cross of North Eastern Pennsylvania (1986–Present); Operations Manager, Commonwealth Communications (1983–1986); Commonwealth Telephone Company: Staff Manager (1981–1983), Senior Buyer (1979–1981). **Associations & Accomplishments:** Pennsylvania Chamber – Business and Industry; International Facility Management Association; Philadelphia Area Council of Excellence. **Education:** College Miserieordia, Bachelor of Science. **Personal:** Married to Darlene in 1974. One child: Ryan. Mr. Williams enjoys golf, skiing, and reading.

Julie I.K. Anderson

Business Unit Manager – Federal Employees Program
Blue Cross Blue Shield of Maryland
10455 Mill Run Circle
Owings Mills, MD 21117
(410) 561–4013
Fax: (410) 561–7933

6324

Business Information: Blue Cross Blue Shield of Maryland administers all health coverage and claims for members and businesses within the state of Maryland. Joining BCBSM in 1989 as a systems analyst, Ms. Anderson was promoted to her current position in November of 1995. As Business Unit Manager for the Federal Employees Program she oversees all claims and customer service operations areas for all Maryland Federal employee programs. **Career Steps:** Blue Cross Blue Shield of Maryland: Business Unit Manager – Federal Employees Program (1995–Present); Supervisor (1992–1995); Systems Analyst (1989–1992). **Associations & Accomplishments:** Chairperson, "Homebase" (local community daycare center). **Education:** De Paul University, B.S. (1981). **Personal:** Married to Todd in 1992. Two children: Meghann and Rachel. Ms. Anderson enjoys interior decorating, tennis and baking.

Jeffrey A. Baumeister

Vice President of Provider Services

Foundation Health Plan

3400 Data Drive
Rancho Cordova, CA 95670–7956
(916) 631–5970
Fax: (916) 631–5152

6324

Business Information: Foundation Health Plan, a California HMO, is a health maintenance organization. Established in 1978, Foundation Health Plan reports an operating budget of $3 billion and currently employs 8,000 people. Reporting directly to the Senior Vice President of Provider Network Development, Mr. Baumeister serves as Vice President of Provider Services. He is responsible for directing the activities of six managers and 84 staff in Provider Relations, Provider Inquiry and Provider Education Departments. Additionally, he controls an annual budget of $4 million, and monitors provider compliance with contractual arrangements, such as access, claims payment, and utilization. **Career Steps:** Foundation Health Plan: Vice President of Provider Services (1995–Present), Director of Provider Relations (1992–1995); Blue Cross & Blue Shield of Ohio: Corporate Director of Provider and Professional Relations (1988–1992), Manager of Program Development (1986–1988), Manager of Professional Relations (1985–1986); Community Mutual Insurance Company (Blue Shield): Area Manager of Professional Relations (1983–1985), Area Representative of Professional Relations (1979–1983); AETNA Life & Casualty, Sales Representative (1976–1979). **Associations & Accomplishments:** American College of Health Care Executives; Toledo Jaycees; Volunteer, Account Executive, United Way; Member, Phi Alpha Theta Honorary Society. **Education:** Bowling Green State University, B.S. in Education, cum laude graduate (1975); Completed two year program of study and earned Life Underwriters Training Council (LUTC) designation (1978); National Provider and Professional Relations School, Blue Cross & Blue Shield Association (1980); Purdue University, Krannert Graduate School of Business, Certified Health Consultant (C.H.C.) designation and scored in the top ten nationally (1985); Total Quality Management (Deming Philosophy) Institute, Ernst & Young (1990); Lee DuBois Selling Skills courses; Xerox Selling Skills courses, PSS I, II. **Personal:** Mr. Baumeister enjoys golf and tennis.

The UNIVERSITY *of* WESTERN ONTARIO

Alvin L. Beers, M.D.

Physician

Colorado Group Kaiser–Permanente

2005 Franklin Street
Denver, CO 80205
(303) 861–3459
Fax: (303) 861–3498

6324

Business Information: Colorado Group Kaiser–Permanente is an integrated health care system and management corporation (HMO) providing complete medical, surgical, and psychiatric services to its members. A Board–certified Oncologist and practicing physician for 17 years, Dr. Beers joined Kaiser–Permanente's Colorado group in 1989. He specializes in the diagnosis and treatment for adult patients in the areas of cancer and other blood diseases. **Career Steps:** Physician, Colorado Group Kaiser–Permanente (1989–Present); Physician, Cigna Health Plan, California (1985–1989); Physician, The Office of Dr. Alvin L. Beers, M.D. **Associations & Accomplishments:** American College of Physicians; American Society of Clinical Oncology. **Education:** Kansas University Medical Center, M.D. (1972); Kansas University, B.A. (1968). **Personal:** Married to Laura A. Haupenthal, Ph.D. in 1985. Two children: Stephen L. and Jeffrey C. Beers. Dr. Beers enjoys tennis, water sports, snow skiing, music, reading, travel, and playing the piano, clarinet, and saxophone.

L. J. (Ben) Benson

Director of Facilities Services

Kaiser Permanente Medical Center

9961 Sierra Avenue
Fontana, CA 92335
(909) 427–5646
Fax: (909) 427–4095

6324

Business Information: Kaiser Permanente is a leading health maintenance organization (HMO), providing complete medical, surgical, and psychiatric services to its members throughout the U.S. A Certified Healthcare Engineer for over ten years, Ben Benson was recruited to his current position with Kaiser Permanente in 1989. As Director of Facilities Services for the Fontana, California branch, he provides the overall supervision and direction of a staff of 42 clerical and health care engineers, as well as six junior managers for the service provision to facilites and user systems for the 13 million sq. ft. hospital and twelve outlet facilities. This also includes the supervision of six biomedical technicians for support of equipment and grounds maintenance at all locations. **Career Steps:** Director of Facilities Services, Kaiser Permanente Medical Center (1989–Present); Director of Facility Services, Martin Luther Hospital (1987–1989); Director of Facility Services, South Coast Medical Center (1983–1987). **Associations & Accomplishments:** California Society for Healthcare Engineering (CSHE); American Society for Healthcare Engineering (ASHE); National Fire Protection Association (NFPA); Professional Bowlers Association (PBA). **Education:** University of Phoenix, B.S. in Health Services Administration (1982). **Personal:** Married to Patricia A. in 1973. Two children: Brian Keith and Cynthia D. An avid bowler, Ben formerly competed on the Pro Bowlers Tour. He also enjoys restoring classic cars, travel, and spending time with his family.

Lisa K. Blume, C.P.A. (K)

Accounting Manager

Ochsner Health Plan

1 Galleria Boulevard, Suite 1224
Metairie, LA 70001
(504) 836–6614
Fax: (504) 836–5536

6324

Business Information: Ochsner Health Plan is primarily engaged in providing health insurance (specifically managed care) throughout the state of Louisiana. Owned and operated by two major shareholders, the Company operates in six regions. Established in 1985, Ochsner Health Plan employs 320 people. As Accounting Manager, Ms. Blume manages all general financial accounting and reporting. She is also responsible for budgetary concerns, accounts payable, and internal financial analysis and reports. **Career Steps:** Accounting Manager, Ochsner Health Plan (1994–Present); Financial Manager, Advocate Title Corporation (1993–1994); Senior Auditor, Charlet & Smith, C.P.A.'s (1992–1993); Staff Accountant, Guenther, Guenther, & Gillane, C.P.A.'s (1989–1992). **Associations & Accomplishments:** Society of Louisiana Certified Public Accountants; American Institute of Certified Public Accountants; American Society of Women Accountants; Local Chapter President, Business and Professional Women U.S.A. **Education:** University of New Orleans, B.A. in Accounting (1990). **Personal:** Married to Rudolph O. in 1994. One child: Benjamin Charles. Ms. Blume enjoys outdoor activities.

Thad E. Bond

Project Manager

M.A. Mortenson Company

44–120 Kauinohea Place
Kaneohe, HI 96744–4500
(808) 275–0038
Fax: (808) 524–0182

6324

Business Information: Blue Cross and Blue Shield of Kansas City, Missouri is a health insurance company. In her capacity as Assistant Vice President of Information Systems and Facilities Services, Mrs. Bond directs a staff of 150 employees in the acquisition, building and maintenance of computer systems and Company facilities. Established in 1938, Blue Cross and Blue Shield of Kansas City, Missouri employs over 1,200 and reports annual revenue in excess of $500 million. **Career Steps:** Assistant Vice President of Information Systems and Facilities Services, Blue Cross and Blue Shield of Kansas City, Missouri (1987–Present); Director, Systems Design & Programming, Blue Cross and Blue Shield of Kansas City, Missouri (1985–1987); Manager, Systems Design & Programming, Blue Cross and Blue Shield of Kansas City, Missouri (1984–1985); Supervisor, Blue Cross and Blue Shield of Kansas City, Missouri (1983–1984). **Associations & Accomplishments:** Data Processing Management Association; Advisory Board Member, Community Living Opportunities, Overland Park, Kansas. **Education:** Benedictine College, B.A. in Math (1970).

Jan M. Bowman

Director of Member Management Services

United Healthcare of Florida, Inc.

800 North Magnolia Avenue, Suite 600
Orlando, FL 32803–3250
(407) 428–2455
Fax: (407) 478–2340

6324

Business Information: United Healthcare of Florida, Inc. is part of United Health Care. As Director of Member Management Services, Ms. Bowman is responsible for member relations, enrollment and medical underwriting departments for the Orlando region. **Career Steps:** United Health Care of Florida, Inc.: Director of Member Management Services (1996–Present), Underwriting Manager (1995–1996); Director of Health Services, PCA (1994–1995); National Director of Managed Care, Acting, AIG (1994). **Associations & Accomplishments:** Diplomat, American Board of Quality Assurance and Utilization Review Physicians. **Education:** Indiana University, B.S.N. (1978); Purdue Univesity, A.S.D. in Nursing (1975). **Personal:** Married to Carter in 1985. One child: Joseph. Ms. Bowman enjoys travel and boating.

Dianne L. Brady

Senior Business Analyst

United HealthCare Corporation

Mail Route MN12–N188, P.O. Box 1459
Minneapolis, MN 55440–1459
(612) 992–5352
Fax: (612) 992–7480
EMAIL: See Below

6324

Business Information: United HealthCare Corporation is the nation's leading managed health care organization. Established in 1974, the organization is headquartered in Minneapolis and employs 28,000 people nationwide, with $8 billion in revenues. As Senior Business Analyst, Ms. Brady is responsible for two of the corporations health plans, assessing business needs and system solutions development. Internet users can reach her via: dbrady1@ccmail.uhc.com. **Career Steps:** United HealthCare Corporation: Senior Business Analyst (1994–Present), Business Analyst (1992–1994), Project Analyst (1990–1992). **Associations & Accomplishments:** American Institute of Certified Public Accountants; Nebraska Society of Certified Public Accountants; Past President and Chartered Member, Toastmasters International. **Education:** University of Minnesota, M.B.A. (1996); Iowa State University, B.B.A. in Accounting (1985); Certified Public Accountant Certificate (1986). **Personal:** Ms. Brady enjoys walking, running, cross–country skiing, sewing, reading, and rollerblading.

Ronald E. Brown

Vice President

Trigon Blue Cross Blue Shield

2015 Staples Mill Road
Richmond, VA 23230–3119
(804) 354–3303
Fax: (804) 354–4550

6324

Business Information: Trigon Blue Cross Blue Shield is Virginia's largest managed health care company with 1.7 million members. Trigon's family of related business offers an array of innovative programs and services that include managed care programs and comprehensive health care financing, employee benefits products, health and wellness programs, life, accident and disability coverage, and information technologies. With over twenty years of experience in a wide variety of disciplines, as Vice President Ronald Brown is responsible for corporate–wide operational and regulatory compliance, consumer affairs, customer service activities, leadership, decision–making, development, implementation, and guidance to ensure company objectives meet or exceed local, state and federal statutes governing the health care industry. In addition, he serves as the organization's expert and spokesperson on strategic matters regarding consumer affairs and compliance business plans. He is responsible for total development and implementation of new division, organizational structure, and processes directly related to compliance and customer service as a core corporate value. Additional responsibilities include: budgetary management of division; research; trend analysis for company and industry; public speaking at forums, workshops, and conferences; and acting as a consultant for other Blue Cross Plans concerning the development of consumer affairs and corporate compliance programs. **Career Steps:** Vice President, Trigon Blue Cross Blue Shield (1995–Present); Director of Customer Service, Hasbro, Inc. (1989–1995); Manager of Consumer Affairs, Kellogg Company (1987–1989); Customer Relations Representative, The People's Natural Gas Company (1980–1987); Director, Huntington Station Youth Department Association (1975–1980). **Associations & Accomplishments:** Chairman, Board of Directors, Urban League of Rhode Island; Executive Board of United Way of Southeastern New England; Board of Directors, Pawtucket YMCA; Rhode Island Congressional Black Legislators Economic Advisory Committee; Providence Chamber of Commerce School Mentors Speakers Program; Board of Directors, Rhode Island Anti–Drug Coalition; Chariman, United Way "Homers for Kids" Campaign; Rhode Island Hospital Trust–First Community Bank of Rhode Island, Advisory Committee; Board of Directors, National Society of Consumer Affairs Professional in Business; Greater Battle Creek Area Urban League: Board of Directors, Vice Chairman (1989); United Way of Battle Creek, Community Relations Committee. **Education:** Penn State University, B.S. in Human Development (1974); University of Pittsburgh, graduate coursework in Human Development and Industrial Administration. **Personal:** Married to Patricia Rose in 1973. Two children: Ronald E. II and Alexandria C. Mr. Brown enjoys travel, reading, photography, and public speaking.

Vivian A. Bryant

Director, Performance and Improvement
Alliant Health Systems
P.O. Box 35070
Louisville, KY 40232
(502) 629–8359
Fax: (502) 629–8688

6324

Business Information: Alliant Health Systems is a multi–hospital corporation comprised of two privately–owned, and one for profit hospital. As Director, Performance and Improvement, Ms. Bryant directs and performs management engineering (i.e. analysis, reengineering projects), and other operational improvement efforts. **Career Steps:** Director, Performance and Improvement, Alliant Health Systems (1993–Present); Jewish Hospital Health Care Services: Senior Management Engineer (1991–1993), Management Engineer (1987–1991). **Associations & Accomplishments:** Institute of Industrial Engineers; Society for Health Systems Division; Healthcare Information Management Systems Society; Kappa Delta Alumni Association; Young Women of the Year Award (1989). **Education:** University of Louisville: Master of Engineering (192), Bachelor of Applied Science (1987). **Personal:** Married to Terry in 1985. One child: Meredith Rose.

Alfredo J. Burlando, M.D., F.A.C.C.

Staff Cardiologist
Kaiser Permanente
2025 Morse Avenue
Sacramento, CA 95825–2115
Fax: Please mail or call

6324

Business Information: Kaiser Permanente is a leading health maintenance organization (HMO), providing complete medical, surgical, and psychiatric services to its members throughout the U.S. A practicing physician since 1960 and a Board–Certified Cardiologist, Dr. Burlando joined Kaiser Permanente in 1967 and became Assistant Chief of Medicine in 1978, advancing to Chief of Medicine in 1982. Although Dr. Burlando has retired to a part–time medical practice serving as a staff Cardiologist and consultant for Kaiser, he remains involved with the MINERVA Group, conducting drug–related research studies for pharmaceutical and drug companies. Concurrent with his medical research and practice, he serves as Clinical Associate Professor of Medicine at the University of California. During his tenure with Kaiser Permanente, he was the instrumental leader in the implementation of the Sacramento center's Cardiac Rehabilitation Program. **Career Steps:** Kaiser Permanente: Staff Cardiologist (1967–Present); Chief of Medicine (1982–1986); Assistant Chief of Medicine (1978–1982). **Associations & Accomplishments:** Sacramento–El Dorado County Medical Society; California Medical Association; American College of Cardiology. **Education:** University of Buenos Aires, M.D. (1960). **Personal:** Married to Rose Marie in 1963. Five children: Angela, Monica, Gabriella, Daniel and Andrea. Dr. Burlando enjoys tennis, basketball, jogging and reading.

Catherine M. Camp

Facilities Services Manager
Kaiser Permanente
432 Keawe Street
Honolulu, HI 96813
(808) 597–5208
Fax: (808) 533–3737

6324

Business Information: Kaiser Permanente, the nation's leading HMO, is a health maintenance organization providing complete medical, surgical, and psychiatric services to over 6 million members throughout the U.S. Serving in various management roles for Kaiser Permanente's Hawaii operations since 1991, Catherine Camp was recently promoted as the Honolulu base Facilities Service Manager. In this capacity, she oversees all areas regarding real estate, facility design, and construction, as well as the maintenance, security, communications, capital equipment, and the purchasing and maintenance of equipment for twenty–two facilities on three islands. **Career Steps:** Kaiser Permanente: Facilities Services Manager (1996–Present), Manager of Planning & Strategic Services (1992–1995), Director of Program Planning (1991–1992). **Associations & Accomplishments:** Hawaii Society of Corporate Planners; International Facility Management Association; Business Consultant, Junior Achievement of Hawaii; Board of Directors, March of Dimes Hawaii Chapter; Board of Directors & Mediator, Neighborhood Justice Center; Board of Directors, Obedience Training Club of Hawaii; Organization for Women Leaders; Governor–Appointed Council Member, Hawaii State Health Planning & Development Agency; Published in the Journal of Eurology. **Education:** Central Michigan University, Masters of Health Sciences Administration (1989); University of Pittsburgh, B.A., B.S. **Personal:** Married to Gary in 1990. Ms. Camp enjoys scuba diving, basketry, canine competitions, traveling abroad, ceramics and triathalons.

A. Bruce Campbell, Ph.D., M.D., F.A.C.P.

Chief Medical Officer
Aetna Health Plans
151 Farmington Avenue
Hartford, CT 06156–0001
(203) 636–3322
Fax: (203) 636–7148

6324

Business Information: Aetna Health Plans, a subsidiary of Aetna Life & Casualty, is a provider of health care and group insurance to planned sponsors (Fortune 500 and 1000 companies). Aetna Life & Casualty is the largest share–holder owned insurance company in the country and one of the most recognized insurance companies in the world. They provide managed health care products such as Managed Choice and Select Choice HMO's and PPO's, property–casualty insurance, group life insurance and other diversified financial services. With Corporate headquarters in Hartford, Connecticut, Aetna Life & Casualty reports premium assets of $8 billion and currently employs 23,000 people corporate–wide. A practicing physician since 1977 and a Board–Certified Clinical Oncologist, Dr. Campbell joined Aetna Health Plan's Hartford managed care center as Chief Medical Officer in 1994. **Career Steps:** Chief Medical Officer, Aetna Health Plans (1994–Present); Vice President of Medical Programs, Scripps Health (1991–1994); President, Specialty Medical Clinic (1989–1991). **Associations & Accomplishments:** American Medical Association; American College of Physicians; American Society of Clinical Oncology. **Education:** University of Vermont, M.D. (1977); University of Chicago, Ph.D. (1973); Williams College, B.A. (1969). **Personal:** Married to Jo Ann in 1989. Three children: Jese, Ian and Dana. Dr. Campbell enjoys skiing and kayaking in his leisure time.

Andrew Castle

Executive Director
AvMed Health Plan
6363 NW Sixth Way, Suite 350
Ft. Lauderdale, FL 33309
(305) 462–2520
Fax: (305) 492–9761

6324

Business Information: Established in 1969, AvMed Health Plan is a managed health care provider, currently insuring approximately 300,000 members throughout eight regional locations in Florida. As Executive Director, Mr. Castle directs all commercial sales for Broward/Palm Beach counties and acts as Regional Head for all business and public relations functions. **Career Steps:** AvMed Health Plan: Executive Director (1995–Present); Sales Manager (1993–1995); Associate Sales Manager, HUMANA Medical Plan (1987–1993); Senior Sales Associate, Blue Cross/Blue Shield of Florida (1985–1987). **Associations & Accomplishments:** Career Education Council of Broward County; Health Education Council of the Palm Beaches; Health Care Committee, Fort Lauderdale, and Palm Beaches Chamber of Commerces; Member, South Florida Health Care Coalition. **Education:** University of Massachusetts at Amherst, Bachelors (1983). **Personal:** Mr. Castle enjoys tennis, golf, softball, and basketball.

Bonnie Conley, CPCS

Director of Credentialing
Harris Methodist Select
611 Ryan Plaza Drive, Suite 700
Arlington, TX 76011
(817) 462–6614
Fax: (817) 462–6613

6324

Business Information: Harris Methodist Select, an entity of Harris Methodist Health System, is a managed–care insurance agency for the health care industry. As Director of Credentialing, Ms. Conley handles a network of over 5,000 providers, where–in she oversees the managed care providers' credentialing. **Career Steps:** Director of Credentialing, Harris Methodist Select (1993–Present); Physician Services Coordinator, EPIC Healthcare Group (1988–1992). **Associations & Accomplishments:** Texas Society of Medical Staff Services; National Association Medical Staff Services. **Education:** Attending, Tarrant County Junior College. **Personal:** Two children: Brian and Jennifer.

Gary C. Daugherty Sr.

Director of Marketing
Health Partners, Inc.
365 North Parkway, Suite 100
Jackson, TN 38305
(901) 661–0634
Fax: (901) 661–0176

6324

Business Information: Health Partners, Inc. specializes in the market and sale of insurance products, including health, life, disability and PPO network coverage. In operation since 1994, Health Partners, Inc. currently employs 12 people and reports an annual revenue of $4 million. As Director of Marketing, Mr. Daugherty is responsible for the market and sale of all insurance products, as well as administers the PPO plans — self–funded plans in which a policy holder pieces together insurance coverage to suit his own personal needs. **Career Steps:** Director of Marketing, Health Partners, Inc. (1994–Present); Manager, St. Elizabeth's Catholic Bookstore; General Agent, Life Investors Insurance Company (1986–1994); Independent Agent, Equitable Life Assurance Society (1976–1988); Non–Commissioned Officer, United States Navy (1967–1976). **Associations & Accomplishments:** Former President, Bartlett Lions Club; Published by several insurance companies. **Personal:** Married to Valerie in 1969. Two children: Gary Jr. and Cynthia Dawn. Mr. Daugherty enjoys golf and working with church missions.

Denise Matthews Dickson

Director of Membership Services
Rush Prudential Health Plan
233 East Wacker Drive
Chicago, IL 60606
(312) 234–7587
Fax: (312) 234–7001

6324

Business Information: Rush Prudential Health Plan, a Health Maintenance Organization, is a joint venture between Prudential Insurance Company and Rush Presbytery St. Lukes Hospital. The Company serves the needs of patients in the regional Chicago area. As Director of Member Services, Ms. Dickson oversees the services of over 300,000 members of the Health Plan with benefit, eligibility, and claims information. **Career Steps:** Director of Member Services, Rush Prudential Health Plan (1995–Present); Executive Director – Healthy Moms/Healthy Kids, First Health Services Corporation (1993–1995); Director of National Service Center, Assured Health Systems (1989–1993). **Associations & Accomplishments:** National Association of Social Workers; National Association of Black Social Workers; 1993 Crain's 40 Under 40. **Education:** University of Illinois – Jane Adams College of Social Work, M.S.W. (1989); Chicago State University, B.A. in Liberal Arts (1974). **Personal:** Married to Douglas in 1994. Two children: Chrystina and Charles. Ms. Dickson enjoys swimming, family, and gardening.

Robert E. Edmondson

President and CEO
Omni Healthcare
2450 Venture Oaks Way, Suite 300
Sacramento, CA 95833–3292
(916) 921–4189
Fax: (916) 921–4044

6324

Business Information: Omni Healthcare, owned by Sutter Health and Catholic Health Care West, is an integrated Health Maintenance Organization (HMO) providing complete health and medical insurance coverage to its members. Established in 1985, Omni Healthcare currently provides services to over 125,000 members throughout 22 counties in Northern California. As President and CEO, Mr. Edmondson provides the overall vision and strategies for the Company's continued development, quality service, and overall regional scope. **Career Steps:** President and CEO, Omni Healthcare (1993–Present); Executive Vice President, QualMed California (1992–1993); President and CEO, Bridgeway Plan for Health (1987–1991); Vice President, Health Plan of America (1985–1987). **Associations & Accomplishments:** California Bar Association; Nevada Bar Association; Founding Member and Board Member, California Association of HMO's; National Health Lawyer's Association; Board Member, Sacramento Community Theater. **Education:** Stanford Law School, J.D. (1970); Stanford University, A.D. (1965). **Personal:** Married to Susan in 1981. Three children: Matthew, Michael, and Stephen. Mr. Edmondson enjoys skiing.

Jo Elliott–Blakeslee

Chief of Staff, Tahoma District North Family Practice
Group Health Cooperative of Puget Sound
301 South 320th Street
Federal Way, WA 98003
(206) 874–7016
Fax: (206) 874–7019

6324

Business Information: Group Health Cooperative of Puget Sound is a staff model HMO rated in the top five in the United States. Established in the 1940's, the Cooperative currently has over 500 thousand patients. As Chief of Staff, Dr. Elliott–Blakeslee, who is licensed in the state of Washington and was Board–certified in Family Practice in 1988 and 1994, manages a medical staff comprised of 25 physicians, psychiatrists, physicians assistants, psychologists, and optometrists. Concurrently she is an Assistant Professor at the the University of Washington School of Medicine and is on staff at the College of Osteopathic Medicine of the Pacific. She is also the Chief of Staff, Federal Way Clinic and Chief of Staff, Tacoma Medical Center Family Practice, both Group Health of Puget Sound facilities. **Career Steps:** Chief of Staff, Tahoma District North Family Practice of Group Health Cooperative of Puget Sound (1994–Present); Assistant Clinical Professor, University of Washington School of Medicine (1989–Present); Assistant Clinical Professor, College of Osteopathic Medicine of the Pacific (1985–Present); Private Practice (1983–1985); Chief of Staff of Missionary Hospital in Cameroon (1981–1983); Commissioned Officer, US Naval Reserve (1983–1991). **Associations & Accomplishments:** King County Medical Society; American College of Physician Executives; Phi Kappa Phi Honor Society, Idaho State University; Outstanding Provider–Manager Award for South Region, Group Health Cooperative of Puget Sound (1994); P.A. Preceptor of the Year Award for South Region, Group Health Cooperative of Puget Sound (1992); Recipient of the Naval Achievement Award with in the Navy Reserves; Listed in Who's Who Among Students in American Colleges and Universities (1970 and 1971). In 1972 Dr. Elliott–Blakeslee had published "Ikon of the Twentieth Century", Project Text for Public Speaking. **Education:** Residency, Group Health Cooperative of Puget Sound (1985–1987); Internship, Sacred Heart Medical Center (1979–1980); University of Washington School of Medicine, M.D. (1979); Idaho State University, M.S. in Zoology (1975); Idaho State University, B.A. in Biology (1971); Management Training courses: Practicing Systems Thinking (1996), Advanced Leadership Seminar Series (1995–1996), Executive Symposium on Health Care Management (1995), Team Performance Training (1995), Physicians in Management, Part II (1995), Integrating Physician Leadership with Administration (1995), Physicians in Management, Part I (1994), Learning from Disagreement and Conflict (1994). **Personal:** Dr. Elliott–Blakeslee enjoys gardening, cooking, beachcombing, and reading.

Harry M. Feder

Senior Vice President/COO
IPRO
1979 Marcus Avenue, Floor 1
New Hyde Park, NY 11042–1002
(516) 326–7767
Fax: (516) 326–7791

6324

Business Information: IPRO is dedicated to healthcare quality development and oversight for the state of New York. The Company supervises the actions, policies, and business practices of all Health Maintenance Organizations (HMO), Managed Care Companies (PPO, EPO), and nursing homes within their jurisdiction. As Senior Vice President/COO, Mr. Feder oversees the day–to–day operations of IPRO. Other responsibilities include administrative concerns, financial concerns, marketing of new and existing services, and public relations. Coordinating with other members of the management staff, Mr. Feder develops annual budgets and long term strategic plans for IPRO. **Career Steps:** Senior Vice President/COO, IPRO (1987–Present); Executive Vice President, Comprehensive Medical Review (1984–1987); Executive Director, Bronx PSRO (1975–1984). **Associations & Accomplishments:** Health Care Executives Club; President, Bronx/Riverside YMCA. **Education:** New York University, M.P.A. (1976); Long Island University, B.A. (1972). **Personal:** Married to Faith in 1975. Two children: Jeremy and Rebecca. Mr. Feder enjoys swimming and political activities.

John Foley

Director of Operations
Delta Dental Plan of Massachusetts
10 Presidents Landing
Medford, MA 02155–5148
(617) 393–1183
Fax: (617) 393–1199
EMAIL: See Below

6324

Business Information: Delta Dental Plan of Massachusetts, the largest provider of pre–paid dental care in its state, is a managed care company for dental insurance. As a member of Delta Dental Plans Association, it is the market share leader in the United States. Delta provides dental plans for local and national accounts, providing payments for services performed throughout the world. With two offices (Charlestown and Medford), Delta employs over 300 employees and services over 1,000,000 members within the states. Employed with Delta Dental Plan of Massachusetts since 1987, Mr. Foley was appointed as Director of Operations in 1992. He is responsible for the direction of all aspects of claim processing, enrollment, and customer service. Mr. Foley can also be reached through the Internet via: JFOLEY7481@AOL.COM **Career Steps:** Delta Dental Plan of Massachusetts: Director of Operations (1992–Present), Underwriting Manager (1991–1992), Accounting Manager (1988–1991), Senior Accountant (1987–1988). **Associations & Accomplishments:** Northeastern University Alumni Association. **Education:** Northeastern University, M.B.A. (1995). **Personal:** Married to Carol H. Carfagna–Foley in 1988. Mr. Foley enjoys fly fishing and golf.

Mike Friedman

Owner
Satmed, Inc.
2318 Pal Booker
Universal City, TX 78148–1338
(210) 659–0323
Fax: (210) 659–7668

6324

Business Information: Satmed, Inc. is a health maintenance organization. With fourteen years experience in the healthcare industry, Mr. Friedman joined Satmed, Inc. in 1992. Serving as Owner, he is responsible for all aspects of operations, including overseeing administrative operations for associates and a support staff of 16. **Career Steps:** Owner, Satmed, Inc. (1992–Present); Physicians Assistant, DOD – Randolph Air Force Base Texas (1987–1992); Physicians Assistant, United States Air Force –Randolph Air Force Base Texas (1982–1987). **Associations & Accomplishments:** American Association of Physician Assistants; Sexar County Physician Assistant Society; Texas Physician Assistant Society. **Education:** University of Nebraska, B.S. (1978). **Personal:** Married to Amy A. in 1985. Five children: Kelli K., Stephanie A., Michael, Stephen, and Sharon. Mr. Friedman enjoys golf and is a basketball official.

Mr. Jon H. Friesen

President
HealthCare Oklahoma
3030 NW Expressway Street, Suite 1500
Oklahoma City, OK 73112
(405) 951–4700
Fax: (405) 951–4701

6324

Business Information: HealthCare Oklahoma is a managed care organization serving HMO, PPO, EPO, POS, Worker's Compensation, and Medicare products. The Organization has over 15,000 members and will be merging with Oklahoma Health Alliance, the state's largest PPO organization, with over 200,000 members. As President, Mr. Friesen is responsible for the overall leadership and strategic business plan for all products, reporting to the Board of Directors. **Career Steps:** President, HealthCare Oklahoma (1995–Present); Physician Corporation of America: Vice President of Finance/Chief Financial Officer – Florida Operations (1991–1995), Controller – Texas Operations (1987–1991). **Education:** Friends University, B.S./B.B.A. (1985). **Personal:** Married to LeeAnn in 1984. Two children: Jeremy and Justin. Mr. Friesen enjoys golf, racquetball, and boating.

Mr. John F. Fritz, F.S.A., M.A.A

President, CEO and Senior Vice President
FHP Life Insurance Company (FHP International)
3515 Harbor Boulevard
Costa Mesa, CA 92626
(714) 513–6183
Fax: (714) 513–6299

6324

Business Information: FHP International is a holding company of several Health Maintenance Organizations and insurance companies. The Company's HMO system Is the fifth largest in the United States. In his current capacity, Mr. Fritz serves as the Chief Actuary and Senior Vice President for FHP International, President and Chief Executive Officer of FHP Life Insurance Company, and has overall responsibility for all other insurance operations. Established in 1973, FHP has about 14,000 employees and annual premium revenue of about 4 billion dollars. 90 to 95 percent of revenues are derived from the HMOs and the remainder is insurance premium revenue. **Career Steps:** President and Chief Executive Officer, FHP Life, Senior Vice President and Chief Actuary, FHP International (1994–Present); Vice President and Chief Actuary, FHP Life and FHP, International (1991–1994); Vice President and Principal, Tillinghast (1976–1991); Assistant Actuary, Gulf Life Insurance Company (1973–1976); Research Assistant, Underwriting, Northwestern Mutual Life (1968–1973). **Associations & Accomplishments:** Fellow of the American Society of Actuaries (FSA); Member of the American Academy of Actuaries (MAAA); Fellow of the Conference of Actuaries (FCA). **Education :** University of Wisconsin, B.B.A. (1967). **Personal:** Married to Kathy in 1968. Four children: Amy, Jennifer, William, and Mary.

Roy S. Gabryl Jr., D.D.S.

National Dental Director
United Dental Care, Inc.
14755 Preston Road, Suite 300
Dallas, TX 75240
(214) 770–5205
Fax: (214) 458–7963

6324

Business Information: United Dental Care, Inc. is a managed dental care plan, providing mediation of dental benefits between provider networks and employee benefit packages. From 21 offices, United Dental Care has a presence in 26 states, the majority being West of the Mississippi. As National Dental Director, Dr. Gabryl is responsible for quality assurance, delivery care systems and development of performance standards for dentists and plans, as well as providing the oversight of all professionally–related activities in the Company. **Career Steps:** National Dental Director, United Dental Care, Inc. (1995–Present); Dental Officer, U.S. Air Force (1972–1995). **Associations & Accomplishments:** American Dental Association; Fellow and Master, Academy of General Dentistry; Council Member, Academy of Managed Care Dentistry; Provider Relations Council Member, National Association of Dental Plans. **Education:** Webster University, M.A. (1994); Georgetown University, D.D.S. (1972); University of Texas at Austin, B.A. (1968); Wilford Hall Medical Center, Certificate in General Dentistry Residency (1983). **Personal:** Married to Betty in 1987. One child: Michelle. Dr. Gabryl enjoys travel, reading, and history.

Kerry A. Garrigan

Senior Vice President of System Human Affairs
Mount Carmel Medical Center
793 W. State Street
Columbus, OH 43222–1551
(614) 234–2689
Fax: (614) 234–1359

6324

Business Information: Mount Carmel Medical Center is an integrated health care delivery system, running 23 businesses, 3 acute care hospitals, one medical center, and a home health care center. As Senior Vice President of System Human Affairs, Ms. Garrigan is responsible for public relations, human resources, organizational development, training, and employee and clinical education. **Career Steps:** Senior Vice President of System Human Affairs, Mount Carmel Medical Center (1994–Present); Cathedral Health Care System: Corporate Vice President (1991–1994), Corporate Director of Training & Education; District Manager of Human Resource Systems, AT&T (1970–1987). **Associations & Accomplishments:** Society for Human Resource Management; Human Resources Association of Central Ohio; Human Resources Roundtable Forum. **Education:** George Washington University, currently working on Doctorate degree; AT&T's Master's Program, Master's degree in Business (1978); State University of New York, B.A. in English and Philosophy (1968). **Personal:** Married to Matthias in 1989. Ms. Garrigan enjoys golf, reading, and travel.

Keith A. Givens
Account Executive
Alliance BlueCross/BlueShield
1831 Chestnut Street
St. Louis, MO 63103
(314) 923–8528
Fax: Please mail or call

6324

Business Information: Alliance BlueCross/BlueShield is a mutual insurance company whose primary business is health insurance and health benefits management. They also have HMO managed health care programs, providing complete medical, dental, surgical, and pharmacy services, as well as life insurance products to its members, As Account Executive, Mr. Givens is responsible for sales and marketing to large groups, 100 plus businesses, and other corporations. **Career Steps:** Account Executive, Alliance BlueCross/BlueShield (1995–Present); Vice President of Marketing and Public Relations, St. Louis Gateway Foundation (1994–1995); Executive Director and President, Teamwork, Inc./City of St. Louis (1991–1994). **Associations & Accomplishments:** St. Louis Ambassadors; National Black MBA Association – St. Louis Chapter; Public Relations Society of America; International Business Communicators. **Education:** University of Phoenix, M.B.A. (1990); University of Missouri, Bachelor of Science in Journalism. **Personal:** Married to Crystal Y. in 1983. Two children: Ashley Denise and Brittney Nicole. Mr. Givens enjoys sports, music, travel, and cooking.

Ralph D. Hayes, C.H.C.
Director of Marketing
NCAS Mountain Plains
4000 House Avenue
Cheyenne, WY 82001–1446
(307) 638–3825
Fax: (307) 634–7611

6324

Business Information: NCAS Mountain Plains is a third–party administrator of self–funded medical benefit programs, serving clients from two locations in Montana and Wyoming. With fourteen years of experience in the insurance industry, Mr. Hayes joined NCAS Mountain Plains as Director of Marketing in 1990. He is responsible for the development of proposals, renewal and marketing activities, and maintaining insurance company relations. **Career Steps:** Director of Marketing, NCAS Mountain Plains (1990–Present); Blue Cross Blue Shield of Wyoming: Executive Staff Position (1986–1990), District Sales Position (1984–1986), Marketing Management Trainee (1982–1984). **Associations & Accomplishments:** Cheyenne Young Professionals; Toastmasters. **Education:** Chadron State College, B.A. in Business (1982); Certified Health Consultant (1988). **Personal:** Three children: Ralph III, Vanessa, and Melissa. Mr. Hayes enjoys spending time with his children, archery, cycling, dancing, and camping.

Janie Houston
Claims Director
HealthLink
788 Office Parkway
St. Louis, MO 63141
(314) 872–9611
Fax: (314) 872–9681

6324

Business Information: HealthLink is a preferred provider organization. As Director of the Claims Department, Ms. Houston is responsible for more than 270,000 claims per month. In addition, she oversees daily operations for the Customer Service Department (108 personnel). **Career Steps:** Claims Director, HealthLink (1989–Present); Claims Supervisor, Metropolitan Life Insurance (1987–1989); Auditor, General American Life Insurance (1976–1989). **Associations & Accomplishments:** Missouri Botanical Gardens; President – Life, Health, Accident Claims Association of Greater St. Louis; Maeystown, Illinois, Historical Society. **Personal:** Married to Dwight in 1987. One child: Cheri Kay Langsdorf. Ms. Houston enjoys gardening, wine–making, and spending time with her granddaughter, Amber.

Geraldine S. Koppenaal, R.N., M.S., C.S.
Chief of Nursing
Harvard Pilgrim Healthcare – Cambridge Center
1611 Cambridge Street
Cambridge, MA 02138–4302
(617) 661–5550
Fax: (607) 661–5595

6324

Business Information: Harvard Pilgrim Healthcare, formerly Harvard Community Health Plan, is a Health Maintenance Organization (HMO) that provides inpatient/outpatient services to clients. Regional in scope, the Company has been Board certified since 1988, and plans to expand by developing their private practice, and increasing support of nurses in the organization. As Chief of Nursing, Ms. Koppenaal supervises twenty nurse practitioners and registered nurses, handles administrative duties, and participates in mental health training. A practicing psychotherapist, she also spends approximately twenty five hours a week counseling clients. **Career Steps:** Chief of Nursing, Harvard Pilgrim Healthcare Cambridge Center (1978–Present); Nursing Instructor, Massachusetts General Hospital (1976–1978); Psychotherapist, Advanced Practice Nurse, Human Resource Institute (1974–1975). **Associations & Accomplishments:** Massachusetts Nurses Association; Innovative Training Association; Rutgers University Alumni Association; Boston College Alumni Association; Rutgers University Alumni Association; Nurses United for Responsible Services (NURS); Published the article "Time Effected Group Psychotherapy Patients with Personal Disorders", in International Journal Group Psychotherapy (1996). **Education:** Boston College, M.S.N. (1974); Rutgers University, B.S.N. (1970). **Personal:** Ms. Koppenaal enjoys teaching and consulting on a national basis.

Roger A. Lewis
Purchasing Manager
Blue Cross Blue Shield
10455 Mill Run Circle
Owings Mills, MD 21117
(410) 998–9727
Fax: (410) 998–6657

6324

Business Information: Blue Cross Blue Shield is a mutual insurance company whose primary business is health insurance and health benefits management. They also have HMO managed health care programs, providing complete medical, dental, surgical, and pharmacy services, as well as life insurance products to its members, As Purchasing Manager for BCBS–Maryland, working from the Owings Mills office, Mr. Lewis is responsible for negotiating with vendors, handling returns, meeting clients' needs, and attending trade shows. In addition, he is responsible for the mailroom, and in–house print shop. **Career Steps:** Purchasing Manager, Blue Cross Blue Shield (1995–Present); Purchasing Manager, Columbia Medical Plan (1993–1995); Senior Buyer, University of Maryland Medical Systems (1991–1993). **Associations & Accomplishments:** The Maryland Society for Healthcare Materials Management; Board of Directors, Maryland/DC Minority Supplier Development Council; Purchasing Advisory Committee of Prime; National Association of Purchasing Managers. **Education:** Dyke College, B.S. in Business Administration (1976). **Personal:** Mr. Lewis enjoys jogging and exercising.

Jim D. Loving
Vice President of Sales
Blue Cross of California
2000 Corporate Center Drive
Newbury Park, CA 91320–1400
(805) 379–8033
Fax: (805) 495–7315

6324

Business Information: Blue Cross of California is a provider of health insurance coverage to individuals and groups, serving five counties in Southern California. After joining Blue Cross in 1989 as Director of Small Group Sales, Mr. Loving was promoted to Vice President of Sales in 1994. He currently specializes in individual, small group, life, dental, and worker's compensation insurance. **Career Steps:** Blue Cross of California: Vice President of Sales (1994–Present), Director of Small Group Sales (1989–1994); Regional Sales Manager, VIBA Insurance Administrators (1981–1989). **Associations & Accomplishments:** Los Angeles Association of Health Underwriters. **Education:** Abilene Christian University, B.S. (1968); University of Texas, A.A. in Aerotechnology (1964). **Personal:** Married to Becky in 1967. Mr. Loving enjoys motorcycle riding, working in the yard, and reading.

Clifford T. Maesaka Jr.

President and Chief Executive Officer
Delta Dental Plan of Kentucky
9901 Linn Station Road
Louisville, KY 40223–3808
(502) 327–5706
Fax: (502) 327–5715

6324

Business Information: Delta Dental Plan of Kentucky is a member of the Delta Dental Association, the largest dental benefits provider in the United States. Dr. Maesaka joined Delta Dental in 1995 as Senior Vice President and Chief Operating Officer. He moved into his present position as President and Chief Executive Officer in early 1995, overseeing all aspects of operations. **Career Steps:** Delta Dental Plan of Kentucky: President and Chief Executive Officer (Oct.1995–Present), Senior Vice President and Chief Operating Officer (Feb.1995–Oct.1995); Regional Director, Prudential (1991–1995); President, C.T. Maesaka, D.D.S., P.A. (1986–1989). **Associations & Accomplishments:** American Dental Association. **Education:** University of St. Thomas Acquinas, M.B.A. (1992); Indiana University School of Dentistry, D.D.S.; University of Minnesota, B.A. **Personal:** Married to Cheryl Ann in 1994. Two children: Leigh and Thompson. Dr. Maesaka enjoys golf and skiing.

Diane H. Malcolm
Network Director
Mercy Health Plans
2000 Hogback Road, Suite 15
Ann Arbor, MI 48105
(313) 971–7667
Fax: (313) 971–7455

6324

Business Information: Mercy Health Plans is a managed care organization which offers an HMO, PPO, Medicaid, TPA, Pre–price, and Medicare Risk product. As Network Director, Mrs. Malcolm is responsible for the recruitment, contracting, and servicing for all medical providers, including physician/hospital organizations. **Career Steps:** Network Director, Mercy Health Plans (1994–Present); Associate Administrator, Poudre Valley Hospital (1993–1994); Vice President, Lima Memorial Hospital (1991–1993); Director, Blue Cross and Blue Shield (1986–1990). **Associations & Accomplishments:** Community Service Award. **Education:** University of Michigan, M.B.A. (1985); Purdue University, B.S. (1971). **Personal:** One child: Andrew H.

Jere C. Manning, D.D.S.
Sole Practitioner
The Office Of Dr. Jere C. Manning, D.D.S.
121 Belle Forest Circle
Nashville, TN 37221–2103
(615) 646–2453
Fax: Please mail or call

6324

Business Information: The Office of Dr. Jere C. Manning, D.D.S. is a general practice dental facility. Establishing his private practice in 1992, Dr. Manning directs a support staff of five, in addition to his daily patient practice. He has a winning sense of humor and utilizes it to speak at elementary schools about good dental habits and preventive medicine. **Career Steps:** Sole Practitioner, The Office of Dr. Jere C. Manning, D.D.S. (1992–Present); Retail Consultant, G.A. Wright, Inc. (1987–1988). **Associations & Accomplishments:** Bellevue Chamber of Commerce; Crievewood United Methodist Church; Foster Care Review Board. **Education:** University of Tennessee, D.D.S. (1992). **Personal:** Married to Kristin Marie in 1987. One child: Kendall Marie. Dr. Manning enjoys golf and boating.

Michele L. Manning
Western Regional Sales Director
Intracorp
6 Inverness Court East, Suite 100
Englewood, CO 80112–5518
(303) 799–0500
Fax: (303) 792–9007

6324

Business Information: Intracorp, a wholly–owned subsidiary of CIGNA Corporation, offers financial planning, insurance and investments to the affluent market place; particularly focusing on managed health care and cost containment. As Western Regional Sales Director, Ms. Manning is responsible for sales and account management for 16 western states. In addition, she is responsible for establishing and maintaining a positive leadership role in local and regional home offices. **Career Steps:** Western Regional Sales Director, Intracorp (1993–Present); Vice President of Administration, National Insurance Administration (1984–1989). **Associations & Accomplishments:** Board of Directors, Indian Hills Improvement Association. **Education:** Colorado State University, B.A. (1979). **Personal:** Ms. Manning enjoys horseback riding, skiing, golf, and gardening.

Patricia C. Mashburn
Nurse Manager
Coastal Government Services
Pensacola Naval Hospital, 6000 West Highway 98
Pensacola, FL 32512–0001
(904) 453–6244
Fax: (904) 453–3858

6324

Business Information: Coastal Government Services at Pensacola Naval Emergency Department and Ambulatory Care is a subsidiary of Coastal Government Services, Inc. As a civilian government contractor of ER Departments and Ambulatory Clinics at Pensacola Naval Hospital, Coastal Government Services employs 80 people. As Nurse Manager, Ms. Mashburn is responsible for the 24 hour operation of a level II ER and Ambulatory Care Clinic that sees 60,000 patients annually on a multi–million dollar contract. **Career Steps:** Nurse Manager, Coastal Government Services (1994–Present); Nurse Manager Contract Administrator, EMA Limited Partnership (1989–1994). **Education:** Providence School of Nursing, Diploma (1978); Springhill College. **Personal:** One child: Shannon Nicole Mashburn. Ms. Mashburn enjoys boating.

Raymond McDermott Jr., M.D.
Medical Director
HealthNetwork, Inc.
1420 Kensington Road, Suite 203
Oak Brook, IL 60521–2146
(312) 346–6330
Fax: (312) 346–5940

6324

Business Information: HealthNetwork, Inc. is a health maintenance organization, providing a health care network of HMO's and PPO's throughout Illinois. A practicing physician since 1947 and Board–Certified in Obstetrics and Gynecology, Dr. McDermott joined HealthNetwork as Medical Director in 1988. Concurrent with his executive position at Healthnetwork, he has served as a practicing physician at Chicago Obstetrics & Gynecology Associates Ltd. for the past eight years, and as Assistant Professor at Northwestern University School of Medicine for the past thirty years. **Career Steps:** Medical Director, HealthNetwork, Inc. (1988–Present); Practicing Physician, Chicago Obstetrics & Gynecology Associates Ltd. (1987–Present); Assistant Professor, Northwestern University School of Medicine (1955–Present); President, Bouer, McDermott & Rapoport Sr. (1960–1988). **Associations & Accomplishments:** American Association of University Professors of Obstetrics and Gynecology. **Education:** Loyola University – Chicago, M.D. (1947). **Personal:** Dr. McDermott enjoys sailing (race sailboats).

Charles R. Mitchell Jr., O.D.

Chief of Optometry
Humana Group Health Plan
2100 Pennsylvania Avenue
Washington, DC 20037
(202) 872–7100
Fax: Please mail or call

6324

Business Information: Humana Group Health Plan, one of the oldest health maintenance organizations (HMO) in the U.S., provides multi–specialty health services to patients in 10–12 plans. A practicing optometrist since 1972, Dr. Mitchell joined Humana Group Health Plan as Chief of Optometry in 1974. He is responsible for the oversight of the optometrists serving the Metropolitan Washington, D.C., Virginia and Maryland locale, including evaluating the services of the optometrists, providing scheduling, and overseeing the delivery of care, in addition to his own patient case load. **Career Steps:** Chief of Optometry, Humana Group Health Plan (1974–Present). **Associations & Accomplishments:** National Optometric Association; Omega Psi Phi Fraternity, Inc. **Education:** New England College of Optometry, O.D. (1972); Morgan State College, B.S. (1968). **Personal:** Married to Muriel Giles in 1969. Three children: Milonda, Cherla, and

Charles Anthony. Dr. Mitchell enjoys reading, basketball, and gardening.

Maureen C. Mondor
Director of Risk Management
Pro Mutual Group
101 Aich Road
Boston, MA 02205
(617) 526–0210
Fax: (617) 330–1748

6324

Business Information: Pro Mutual Group is a health maintenance organization specializing in clinical risk management. The primary mission of the Group is to keep health insurance companies from paying medical organization/Doctor's claims when a malpractice suit is involved or may arise. As Director of Risk Management, Mrs. Mondor supervises all business operations regarding clinical risk management. She is responsible for supervising a staff of 22. **Career Steps:** Director of Risk Management, Pro Mutual Group (1992–Present); Supervisor, Risk Management, MMPIA (1989–1992); Director, Staff Development, Worcester Hahvemarr Hospital (1973–1982). **Associations & Accomplishments:** Massachusetts Society of Hospital Risk Managers; American Heart Association. **Education:** Worcester State College, B.S.N. (1976); Peter Brent Brigham School of Nursing, Diploma; Insurance Institute of America, Associate in Risk Management. **Personal:** Married to Steven in 1971. Two children: Nicole and Michelle.

Nelda H. Neal
Program Director
Genesis Health Care Management Company at Lackey Hospital
P.O. Box 428
Forest, MS 39074
(601) 469–4151
Fax: (601) 469–3681

6324

Business Information: Genesis Health Care Management Company at Lackey Hospital is a resident program specializing in the mental disorders and physical problems of the elderly. Affiliated with Lackey Hospital, a full service medical facility, the Program is regional in scope and is located in four states. As Program Director, Ms. Neal supervises all the employees on the unit, interviews potential patients, and oversees all quality assurance and daily operations. She is also responsible for personnel management, employee relations, benefits and training, and handles all patient records. **Career Steps:** Program Director, Genesis Health Care Management Company at Lackey Hospital (1995–Present); Marketing Consultant, Parkview Regional Medical Center (1993–1995); Regional Director, March of Dimes (1992–1993). **Associations & Accomplishments:** Business and Professional Women of Scott County; The University of Southern Mississippi Eagle Club; Sunday School Teacher of five year olds, Park Place Baptist Church, Pearl. **Education:** Mississippi College, Master's in Community Counseling (1988); University of Southern Mississippi, B.S. in Home Economics with an emphasis in Child Development and a minor in Family Life Studies (1987). **Personal:** Married to John R., Jr. in 1996. Two children: Jessica and Jake. Ms. Neal enjoys getting involved with her children's activities such as swimming, cheerleading and gymnastics, being a school mom, and football games.

Sheri L. Nida
Director of Facilities
CareAmerica
6300 Canoga Avenue
Woodland Hills, CA 91367
(818) 228–2114
Fax: (818) 228–5114

6324

Business Information: CareAmerica is a Southern California based health maintenance organization that provides health benefits, worker' compensation, and related insurance products. Established in 1988, CareAmerica presently employs over 700 people. As Director of Facilities, Ms. Nida is responsible for real estate negotiation, construction contract review, and tenant improvement activities. She is also responsible for the management of the facilities and related support services, distributed output, mail, and reprographics. **Career Steps:** Director of Facilities, CareAmerica (1990–Present); Office Manager, Sunset Builders (1985–1990). **Associations & Accomplishments:** International Facilities Management Association. **Education:** Criss Business College, Certificate (1984). **Personal:** Married to Christopher in 1991. Two children: Keli and Kyle. Ms. Nida enjoys camping, playing with her children, and riding a Harley Davidson motorcycle.

Alan Nussbaum
Director of Information Services
Healthchoice
2301 Lucien Way, Suite 440
Maitland, FL 32751
(407) 481–7182
Fax: (407) 481–7190
EMail: See Below

6324

Business Information: Healthchoice is a managed healthcare organization. As Director of Information Services, Mr. Nussbaum is responsible for all informational needs, including hardware, software, and application development to support the business. He also oversees the implementation of technologies with all external partners. Internet users can reach him via: Alann@ORHS.org. **Career Steps:** Director of Information Services, Healthchoice (1995–Present); Systems Specialist, Orlando Regional Healthcare System (1993–1995); Systems Analyst, Sony Corporation of America (1989–1993); Operations Research Analyst, The CIT Group (1986–1989). **Education:** Seton Hall University, M.B.A. in Finance (1991); University of Connecticut, B.S. in Mathematics (1986). **Personal:** Mr. Nussbaum enjoys golf and personal fitness.

Cheryl Odom

President
Alliance Health Providers
1518 Warwick
Mansfield, TX 76063
(817) 492–1006
Fax: (817) 496–3305

6324

Business Information: Alliance Health Providers is a Preferred Provider Organization that has 150 hospitals under contract and 100,000 covered lives. The Company, established in 1986 and employing 13 people, serves the Dallas/Fort worth area. As President, Ms. Odom oversees all operations of the Company focusing mainly on marketing and developing the networks. Concurrently, Ms. Odom has her own Company that offers consulting services in healthcare management. **Career Steps:** President, Alliance Health Providers (1995–Present); President/Owner, Healthcare Management Solutions (1992–Present); Vice President, Provider Network of America (1989–1992). **Associations & Accomplishments:** Dallas/Fort Worth Peer Forum; North Texas Business Women's Council. **Education:** Texas A&M University, B.S. (1974). **Personal:** Married to Jim. Two children: Athena and John. Ms. Odom enjoys polo, reading, and skiing.

Edward Joseph Pecikonis II

Owner/Vice President
Hen Pec Health Corporation/Central Back Care, Inc.
9830 North Central, Suite 400
Dallas, TX 75231–3338
(214) 987–9790
Fax: (214) 987–9114

6324

Business Information: Hen Pec Health Corporation is an in-house management corporation offering services to health care providers. Services offered include administrative, operational, and general accounting/billing services. The Company also produces a line of 100% organic haircare/skin care products and an analgesic cream. As Owner of Health Management Corporation, Mr. Pecikonis has oversight of all aspects of company management. He is involved in new company and product development, marketing of new and existing services and products, public relations, and strategic planning for future expansion. Concurrently, Mr. Pecikonis is Vice President of Central Back Care, Inc., a rehabilitation center for pre– and post–surgical rehabilitation outpatient services. As Vice President, Mr. Pecikonis is responsible for the day–to–day administration of the Center and is directly involved in strategic planning. **Career Steps:** Owner/Vice President, Hen Pec Health Corporation/Central Back Care, Inc. (1995–Present); CBO Collection Manager, Methodist Hospital of Dallas (1991–1993). **Education:** Regis Jesuit University, B.B.A. (1983); Red Rocks Community, Associate P.A. **Personal:** Married to Nidja in 1994. Three children: Edward Joseph III, Dakarai, and Dominic. Mr. Pecikonis enjoys politics, music, and sports.

Jowina Person
Director of Administration
United HealthCare Corporation
2929 Express Drive North
Hauppauge, NY 11788–5315
(516) 348–5714
Fax: (516) 348–5959

6324

Business Information: United Healthcare Corporation is a health maintenance organization, providing its members with all aspects of medical treatment care. A health provider management executive with over ten years expertise, Jowina Person was recently promoted to the newly created role as Director of Administration in June of 1995. In this capacity, she oversees all aspects of personnel administration, benefits and training corporate–wide. **Career Steps:** Senior Team Developer, United Healthcare Corporation (1995–Present); Metlife: Director of Administration (1995), Manager of Customer Business Unit (1991–1995), Manager of New Business Installation (1991). **Associations & Accomplishments:** National Association of Female Executives. **Education:** St. Joseph's College: Human Resources Management (1996), Certificates in Leadership and Supervision (1995); Adelphi University, B.A. in Communications (1983). **Personal:** Ms. Person enjoys travel, bowling, crocheting, and volunteer work.

George C. Phillips Jr.
President and Chief Executive Officer
HealthNetwork, Inc.
1420 Kensington Road, Suite 203
Oak Brook, IL 60521–2106
(708) 472–4107
Fax: (708) 472–4115

6324

Business Information: HealthNetwork, Inc., a subsidiary of Blue Cross/Blue Shield of Iowa and Blue Cross of South Dakota, is a managed health care organization (PPO). Established in 1985, HNI covers a twelve–state region, primarily in the Midwest U.S. As President and Chief Executive Officer, Mr. Phillips is responsible for all aspects of Company operation. **Career Steps:** President and Chief Executive Officer, HealthNetwork, Inc. (1985–Present); Executive Director, Illinois Health Facilities Authority (1977–1985); Consultant, Ponder and Company (1977); President, Memorial Medical Center (1972–1976). **Associations & Accomplishments:** Board Member and Treasurer, American Association of Preferred Provider Organizations; American College of Health Care Executives; Group Health Association of America/ American Managed Care Review Organization; American Hospital Association; Group Health Association of America; American Managed Care Review Association. **Education:** Duke University, M.H.A. (1965); Ohio State University, B.S. in Zoology (1959); Attended: Guilford College; Bowman–Gray School of Medicine; South Dakota State College. **Personal:** Married to Linda Miller in 1993. Three children: Laurie, Melissa, and Tiffany.

Christine M. Pontius
Regional Director
Universal Care
2068 Orange Tree Lane Ste. 224
Redlands, CA 92374
(909) 792–7027
Fax: (909) 793–4185

6324

Business Information: Universal Care is a health insurance company which monitors insurance claims to verify services billed were actually incurred. Universal Care works closely with HMO providers on the verification processes. As Regional Director, Ms. Pontius coordinates with medical providers on contracts and claims that come up for review. She administers a satellite office for Universal Care and is responsible for quality management in the region, reporting discrepancies in insurance claims, and conducting audits of regional HMO's and IPA's. **Career Steps:** Regional Director, Universal Care (1993–Present); Manager, Utilization Management Department, American Health, Inc. (3 Years). **Education:** Licensed Vocational Nurse. **Personal:** Married to W.G. in 1991. Ms. Pontius enjoys gardening, writing, and motorcross.

Robert G. Pope, M.D.
Medical Director
United Healthcare of Georgia
2970 Clairmont Drive, Suite 300
Atlanta, GA 30219
(404) 982–8800
Fax: (502) 982–8318

6324

Business Information: United Healthcare of Georgia is a health maintenance organization, providing its members with all aspects of medical treatment care. As Medical Director, Dr. Pope oversees all clinical and medical operations, responsible for strategic planning and implementation, member relations and medicare/medicaid product development. **Career Steps:** Medical Director, United Healthcare of Georgia (1994–Present); President and Chief Executive Officer, Corporate H.E.A.L.T.H. (1992–1994); Chief Medical Officer, Blue Cross of Kentucky (1990–1992). **Associations & Accomplishments:** Who's Who Worldwide; Named Top 50 of Health Care Professionals in Louisville; Former Chairman, Wellnes Forum in Kentucky; American Board Quality Assurance Utilization of Physicians; Lecturer and published author in medical journals. **Education:** University of Louisville School of Medicine, M.D. (1970–1974). **Personal:** Married to Georgia in 1981. Two children: Sarah and Becca. Dr. Pope enjoys skiing and model trains.

Alan B. Puzarne
Senior Vice President and Regional Chief Executive
Blue Shield of California
4401 Elder Avenue
Seal Beach, CA 90740
(310) 568–6460
Fax: (310) 670–2329

6324

Business Information: Blue Shield of California is a mutual insurance company whose primary business is health insurance and health benefits management. Blue Shield's HMO and PPO managed health care programs provide complete medical, dental, and pharmacy services to its members (residents of California). With nine years experience in managed health care plans, Mr. Puzarne joined Blue Shield of California in 1994 as Vice President of Provider Relations, and in 1995 was promoted to Senior Vice President and Regional Chief Executive. Overseeing a team of directors in charge of sales, marketing, and strategic planning, he is responsible for profit and loss for managed care insurance products in the Southern California markets. **Career Steps:** Blue Shield of California: Senior Vice President and Regional Chief Executive (1995–Present), Vice President of Provider Relations (1994–1995); FHP Healthcare: Regional Vice President (1993–1994), Associate Regional Vice President (1990–1993). **Associations & Accomplishments:** Board of Directors, Therapeutic Living Centers for the Blind (1986–1994); Adaptive Business Leaders Organization; Recipient of Award of Commendation from the City of Los Angeles for his work with developmentally disabled individuals. **Education:** California State University – Northridge, M.B.A. (1985); California State University – San Francisco, M.E.; University of California – Los Angeles, B.A. **Personal:** Married to Wendy in 1981. Two children: Aaron and Megan. Mr. Puzarne enjoys running.

Thomas Raffio
President and Chief Executive Officer
Northeast Delta Dental Plan
6 Loudon Road
Concord, NH 03301
(603) 223–1300
Fax: (603) 223–1199

6324

Business Information: Northeast Delta Dental Plan is an administrative management plan, providing dental healthcare insurance to company employees residing in New Hampshire, Vermont, and Maine. With seventeen years expertise in the insurance industry, Mr. Raffio joined Northeast Delta Dental Plan as President and Chief Executive Officer in 1995. He is responsible for all aspects of operations, as well as the growth and success of the Company. **Career Steps:** President and Chief Executive Officer, Northeast Delta Dental Plan (1995–Present); Senior Vice President, Delta Dental Plan of Massachusetts (1985–1995); Director, John Hancock Mutual Life Insurance Company (1978–1985). **Associations & Accomplishments:** Board of Directors: Wellness Community, Massachusetts Quality Council, New Hampshire Quality Council, and Christa McAuliffe Foundation. **Education:** Harvard University, B.A. (1978); Babson College, M.B.A. **Personal:** Married to Lisa in 1980. Four children: Jenna, Matthew, Brian, and Gabrielle. Mr. Raffio enjoys sports and coaching youth soccer.

Marlene P. Richter
State & Federal Program Manager
PacifiCare of Texas
8200 Ih 10 West, Suite 1000
San Antonio, TX 78230
(210) 524–2142
Fax: (210) 344–1165

6324

Business Information: PacifiCare of Texas is a rapidly growing multi–regional managed care organization, with 1.5 million HMO members in six states and over $3 billion in revenue. In addition to its core HMO product line and its position as the largest Medicare risk contractor in the country, the Company operates nine subsidiaries managing such specialized product areas as behavioral health, prescription drugs, military health, national benefit integration, workers' compensation, dental, wellness, senior care and other insurance products. Serving in various accounting management roles for PacifiCare of Texas since 1991, Marlene Richter was appointed to her current position as State & Federal Programs Manager in 1993. In this capacity, she is responsible for managing regional marketing for two large markets in San Antonio and Dallas/ Houston, as well as reviewing and renewing accounts, customer service, managing state and governmental accounts, presentations and education for members, benefit coordination, and rewarding money to quality organizations. **Career Steps:** PacifiCare of Texas: State & Federal Program Manager (1993–Present), National Accounts Manager (1994–1995), Superintendent Commercial Accounts Services (1991–1993). **Associations & Accomplishments:** PacifiCare Foundation Committee; Southside Chamber of Commerce – San Antonio. **Education:** Southwest Texas State University, B.S. in Education (1978). **Personal:** Married to Rick in 1980. Three children: Tommy, Josh, and Allison. Ms. Richter enjoys collecting unique antiques.

Patricia A. Russell
Director of Operations
Acordia of Louisville
1901 Campus Place
Louisville, KY 40299
(502) 261–2109
Fax: (502) 261–2257

6324

Business Information: Acordia of Louisville is a health insurance administration agency. As Director of Operations, Ms. Russell is responsible for the direction of all operations, including customer service, claims, enrollment, client services, and interaction with all client operations. **Career Steps:** Acordia of Louisville: Director of Operations (1995–Present), Director Client Services (1994–1995); Alternative Health: Manager Claims (1992–1994), Prepayment Analysis (1990–1992). **Education:** Jefferson Community College (1983). **Personal:** Ms. Russell enjoys sports and reading.

Dean L. Sadler, M.D.
Senior Medical Director
Sloans Lake Managed Care
1355 South Colorado Boulevard, Suite 902
Denver, CO 80222–3305
(303) 759–7264
Fax: (303) 753–4649

6324

Business Information: Sloans Lake Managed Care, the largest organization similar to an HMO in the country, is a preferred provider organization, networked with 5,000 physicians. Established in 1978, Sloans Lake Managed Care currently employs 300 people. A practicing physician since 1954, Dr. Sadler joined Sloans Lake Managed Care in 1978 as Senior Medical Director. He is responsible for all aspects of medical management, in addition to his daily patient practice. **Career Steps:** Senior Medical Director, Sloans Lake Managed Care (1978–Present); Chairman of the Board and Chief of Staff, Prevant Hospital Systems. **Associations & Accomplishments:** Clear Creek Valley Medical Society; Colorado Medical Society; Humana Medical Association; International Model Aircraft Association. **Education:** University of Colorado, M.D. (1954). **Personal:** Married to Virginia in 1992. Four children: Michael, Karen, Stephen, and Carol. Dr. Sadler enjoys radio–controlled model aircraft.

Iraj Salour
Director of Systems
Wellpoint Pharmacy Management
27001 Agoura Road, Suite 325
Agoura Hills, CA 91301
(818) 878–2708
Fax: (818) 880–6730

6324

Business Information: Wellpoint Pharmacy Management, headquartered in Los Angeles, is a subsidiary of Blue Cross of California. The Firm began operations in 1992 and offers pharmacy insurance to over 10 million clients nationwide. As Director of Systems, Mr. Salour is in charge of the data processing department of Wellpoint Pharmacy Management. He is responsible for updating and developing data processing systems and software for the Company. **Career Steps:** Director of Systems, Wellpoint Pharmacy Management (1994–Present); Blue Cross of California: Director of Systems (1988–1994), Manager of Systems (1987–1988). **Education:** University of Tampa, M.B.A. (1981); University of Cardiff, Wales, M.S.E.E. (1971). **Personal:** Married to Massi in 1973. Two children: Maryam and Kamran. Mr. Salour enjoys biking and chess.

Susan J. Scheufele
President/Chief Executive Officer
Roseburg Health Enterprises Health Plan
1813 West Harvard Avenue, Suite 432
Roseburg, OR 97470
(541) 673–1462
Fax: (541) 672–1324

6324

Business Information: Roseburg Health Enterprises Inc. Health Plan (RHEI) is an insurance company and health care administration responsible for management of an individual practice association and its health plan subsidiary. With two locations in Oregon, the Organization is a subsidiary of Douglas County Independent Practice Association (DCIPA). Wholly–owned, RHEI Health Plan is comprised of rural physicians who provide healthcare services in Commercial, Medicaid, Workers' Compensation Managed Care, and Integrated Health Care Markets. Established in 1993, the Company employs 62 people. As President/Chief Executive Officer, Ms. Scheufele serves as a key executive representative for DCI-PA/RHEI Health Plan to various constituencies including insurance companies, managed care organizations, business activities, federal and state agencies, professional groups, and the general public. She is also responsible for personnel management, budgeting, strategic planning, and finance. **Career Steps:** President/Chief Executive Officer, Roseburg Health Enterprises Health Plan (1993–Present); Supervisor of Government Office of Medical Assistance Programs, Capital Health Care, Blue Cross/Blue Shield (1992–1993); Provider Field Liaison (1987–1989). **Associations & Accomplishments:** Oregon Health Association; National Rural Health Association; MGMA; AMGA; AAHP; Chamber of Commerce. **Education:** Whitman College; Certified Managed Care Executive. **Personal:** Married to Larry Caldwell. Mrs. Scheufele enjoys taking care of her 93–acre ranch.

Betty Schneider

• • • ━━━ ◉ ━━━ • • •

Vice President
Donco Transportation
1921 NE 58th Avenue
Des Moines, IA 50313
(515) 265–2741
Fax: (515) 265–0928

6324

Business Information: Donco Transportation is a contract carrier transportation company. Established in 1983, Donco Transportation currently employs 36 people. As Vice President, Ms. Schneider is responsible for the oversight of all accounting, management, and office operations. Concurrent with her position, she serves as President of General Commodities Brokerage, Office Manager of North Iowa Express, and Vice President of Siouxland Cartage. All businesses are co-owned by Mrs. Schneider and her husband. **Career Steps:** Vice President, Donco Transportation (1983–Present); President, General Commodities Brokerage (1983–Present); Vice President, Siouxland Cartage (1993–Present); Office Manager, North Iowa Express (1982–Present). **Associations & Accomplishments:** Eastern Star; Recipient of a craft award in her silk flower business. **Personal:** Married to Donald E. Schneider. Three children: Christie Lathrum, Jerry and Jeffrey Schneider. Ms. Schneider enjoys her five grandchildren, decorating, crafts, and her silk flower business.

George A. Schneider, CPA
Vice President and Chief Financial Officer
OSF Health Plans, Inc.
300 Southwest Jefferson Avenue
Peoria, IL 61602–1413
(309) 677–8216
Fax: (309) 677–8330

6324

Business Information: OSF Health Plans, Inc. is a licensed Illinois insurance company, a wholly–owned subsidiary of the OSF Health Care System. The Sisters of the Third Order of St. Francis own and operate health care facilities and own and manage over 100 physician practices in north central Illinois and Michigan. OSF Health Plans, Inc. has developed HMO, PPO and TPA products to offer to fully insured and self insured employer groups and offers access to its integrated health care delivery system to other insuring agencies. As Vice President and Chief Financial Officer, George Schneider's responsibilities in this start–up enterprise include financial systems and controls, management information systems, planning, facilities construction and purchasing as well as participation in development of strategic directions, benefit plans, work flows and operation policies of the Health Plan. A native of Indianapolis, Indiana, Mr. Schneider has an impressive national and international health care professional background. His areas of expertise include: rating and underwriting, financial analysis, customer service, quality improvement, provider contracting, medicare contracting, new product development, wage administation, information systems, materials management, regulatory compliance, income tax, planning/forecasting, claims processing, liability/lag analysis, facilities construction, cash management and general accounting. **Career Steps:** Vice President and Chief Financial Officer, OSF Health Plans, Inc. (1994–Present); Senior Vice President, Managed Health Care Division, American International Group, Inc. (1993–1994); Senior Vice President, Chief Financial & Administrative Officer, Group Health Plan, Inc. (1990–1993); Vice President, Finance, Physicians Health Services, Inc. (1988–1990); Vice President of Finance & CFO, Healthcare, Inc. (1987–1988); Regional Controller, HealthAmerica, Inc. (1985–1987); St. Vincent Hospital & Health Care Center, Inc.: Director of Finance & Administrative Services – Stress Center (1981–1985), Manager of Financial Planning – Hospital (1979–1981), Medicare Reimbursement Analyst – Hospital (1978–1979); Medicare Auditor, Indiana Blue Cross (1976–1978); Junior Accountant, Howard Nixon, CPA (1975–1976); Staff Accountant, Statesman Insurance Group (1974–1975); Assistant Manager, National Tea Company (1969–1974). **Associations & Accomplishments:** GHAA (HMO Industry Group); Healthcare Financial Management Association; Indiana Hospice Association: Treasurer, Former Board Member; Board Member, Pond Athletic Association; Cantor/Soloist at local church; National Hospice Organization; Frequent lecturer at international, national, state and local conferences and institutional symposia and proceedings. **Education:** Indiana University, B.S. in Accounting (1976); Certified Public Accountant. **Personal:** Married to Carole in 1979. Four children: David, Patrick, Christopher, and Lisa Marie. Mr. Schneider enjoys civic, church and childrens activities.

Sheila K. Shapiro
Vice President of Finance and Administration
FHP Health Care
410 North 44th Street
Phoenix, AZ 85072
(602) 244–8200
Fax: (602) 681–7680

6324

Business Information: FHP Health Care is a managed health care organization. As Vice President of Finance and Administration, Ms. Shapiro is responsible for all operations, including the oversight of revenue ($550 million) and the operational expense budget ($18 million). **Career Steps:** FHP Health Care: Vice President of Finance and Administration (1991–Present), Human Resource Supervisor, Safeway Stores (1980–1987); Compensation & Benefits Analyst, Dillard's Department Stores (1979–1984). **Associations & Accomplishments:** American College of Healthcare Executives; Phoenix Sister Cities Program. **Education:** University of Phoenix, M.B.A. (1989–1990). **Personal:** Ms. Shapiro enjoys golf and cooking.

Keith K. Sherwood
Controller and Director of Finance
Priority Health
1231 East Beltline Avenue North East
Grand Rapids, MI 49505–4501
(616) 975–8130
Fax: (616) 942–7916

6324

Business Information: Priority Health is a provider–owned Health Maintenance Organization that provides health insurance (HMO, POS, TBA, PPO). As Director of Finance, Mr. Sherwood is responsible for diversified administrative activities, including purchasing, financial analysis, and pricing. **Career Steps:** Controller and Director of Finance, Priority Health (1995–Present); Manager, Blue Cross Blue Shield of MI (1984–1995); Controller, Facet Enterprises (1982–1984). **Associations & Accomplishments:** Health Care Financial Management Association; National Management Association; Economic Club of Grand Rapids. **Education:** Walsh College: M.B.A. in Finance (1989), Bachelor of Accounting (1982). **Personal:** Married to Alice in 1981. Five children: Melissa, Stephen, Daniel, Matthew, and Elizabeth. Mr. Sherwood enjoys hiking, biking, travel, and skiing.

Samuel D. Shipley
Director of Operations
Medimetrix Group
1001 Lakeside Avenue East, Suite 1500
Cleveland, OH 44114–1151
(216) 523–1300
Fax: (216) 523–1811
EMAIL: See Below

6324

Business Information: Medimetrix Group, established in 1987, specializes in providing healthcare consulting services to practitioners nationwide. Headquartered in Cleveland, Ohio, the Company has offices in Colorado, Massachusetts, Illinois, and throughout Ohio. As Director of Operations, Mr. Shipley has overall responsibility for information systems, administration, facilities, and operations at all Company sites. Additional duties include direct supervision of twenty–two employees, contract negotiations, and information systems strategic planning. Internet users can reach him via: sshipley@mx.com. **Career Steps:** Director of Operations, Medimetrix Group (1993–Present); Assistant Director of Operations, Ernst & Young (1990–1993); Assistant Vice President of Human Resources, Ameritrust Bank (1988–1990). **Associations & Accomplishments:** Society of Human Resource Management (SHRM). **Education:** Muskingum College, B.A. in Education (1979). **Personal:** Married to Amy in 1979. Six children: Emily, Benjamin, Adam, Abigail, Amanda, and Annabelle. Mr. Shipley enjoys travel and home remodeling.

Larry L. Sigle
Director of Sales
Delta Dental Plan of Kansas
P O Box 49198
Wichita, KS 67201–9198
(316) 264–8413
Fax: (316) 264–5912

6324

Business Information: Delta Dental Plan of Kansas is a provider of group dental insurance. As Director of Sales, Mr. Sigle markets and sells group dental plans to clients. He is responsible for the activities of the Sales Department (i.e. staff recruitment, training, evaluating, counseling, etc.). and works closely with other management staff in the development of departmental and Company–wide budgets. **Career Steps:** Director of Sales, Delta Dental Plan of Kansas (1995–Present); Marketing Superintendent, Mid Continent Life (1990–1994); Advanced Sales Specialist, Alliance Life Insurance Company (1985–1990). **Associations & Accomplishments:** Health Committee Chairman, Wichita Association of Life Underwriters; Kansas Association of Life Underwriters; National Association of Life Underwriters. **Education:** Kansas State University, M.B.A. (1983) and B.S. (1975); The American College: Chartered Life Underwriter (CLU) and Chartered Financial Counsultant (CLFC). **Personal:** Married to Susan in 1973. One child: Tara. Mr. Sigle enjoys flying, travel, and scuba diving.

Robert Wayne Smith
Director of Systems Support
Healthsource Provident
2 Fountain Square
Chattanooga, TN 37402–0300
(423) 755–1994
Fax: (423) 755–1531
EMAIL: See Below

6324

Business Information: Healthsource Provident — a wholly–owned subsidiary of Healthsource, Inc. — is a group medical insurance and managed care services firm. With corporate offices located in New Hampshire, HP has satellite locations in 25 offices throughout the U.S. As Director of Systems Support, Mr. Smith is responsible for the management and oversight of all personnel within the Systems Support Department, in addition to security administration for all systems (setting up users, profiles, and ID's). He also implements computer systems training for users, including user documentation, testing and all troubleshooting. Internet users can reach him via: SMITHRO@HLTHSRC.COM. **Career Steps:** Director of Systems Support, Healthsource Provident (1995–Present); Provident Insurance Company: Director of Systems Support (1986–1995), Claims Conversion Administrator (1980–1986). **Associations & Accomplishments:** Alpha Kappa Psi Professional Business Fraternity. **Education:** Middle Tennessee State University, B.S. (1971). **Personal:** Married to Beverly in 1973. Two children: Kimberly and Elaine. Mr. Smith enjoys fishing, sports, and computers.

Susan M. Sobczak–Chandler
Vice President – Claims Administration
Prime Health/Med One
2073 East Sahara, Suite #B
Las Vegas, NV 89104
(702) 731–1878
Fax: (702) 796–5528

6324

Business Information: Prime Health is the parent company for Silver State Medical Administrators, a third party administration company, administering claims for self funded groups. Under Med One, it is also a managed health care corporation for HMO, PPO, and EPOs, comprised of a third party administrator, a utilization review company, and has a provider network division. There are three offices located in Las Vegas, Reno, and Laughlin, Nevada. Joining the Corporation as Director of Business Operations in 1992, Ms. Sobczak–Chandler was appointed as Vice President in 1993. She oversees all claims administration, customer service, and the day–to–day operations of all three offices. Additionally, she oversees all administrative operations for associates and has a support staff of 40. **Career Steps:** Vice President, Silver State Medical Administrators (1993–Present); Director of Business Operations (1992–1993); Controller Assistant, Womens Hospital (1991–1992); Manager, Physicians Office (1990–1991). **Associations & Accomplishments:** Medical Group Management Association; Healthcare Finance Management Association; American College of Healthcare Executives; Self Insured Insurance Association; National Speedboat and Waterski Association. **Education:** College of St. Francis, M.H.A. (1995); University of Nevada – Las Vegas, B.H.A. **Personal:** Married to David in 1981. Three children: Jason, David, and Stefanie. Ms. Sobczak–Chandler enjoys water skiing, and water activities.

Nathaniel Toro
Marketing Manager – Medicaid
PCA Family Health Plan, Inc.
2002 North Lois Avenue, Suite 300
Tampa, FL 33607–2366
(813) 872–3073
Fax: (813) 872–3005

6324

Business Information: PCA Family Health Plan, Inc. is a Health Maintenance Organization providing health insurance to patients. As Marketing Manager – Medicaid, Mr. Toro helps develop strategic marketing ideas that will increase membership. He is also responsible for the monitoring of sales for each representative, helping each department reach their goals, and reporting regional and budget forecasts. **Career Steps:** Marketing Manager – Medicaid, PCA Family Health Plan, Inc. (1993–Present); Assistant Director of Admissions, International Technical Institute (1991–1993); Director of Admissions, Harding Business College (1985–1989). **Education:** Ponce Technical College, Graduate (1982). **Personal:** One child: Angelica Maria. Mr. Toro enjoys hunting, fishing, travel, and dancing.

Anne Owen Troyan

Director of Professional Services
Columbia Hoffman Estates Medical Center
1555 Barrington Road
Hoffman Estates, IL 60194
(708) 884–4790
Fax: (708) 490–2532

6324

Business Information: Columbia Hoffman Estates Medical Center is a managed healthcare organization with 335 facilities located domestically, and in Europe and Switzerland. Established in 1979, Columbia Hoffman Estates Medical Center currently employs 709 people. As Director of Professional Services, Mrs. Troyan is responsible for physician integration, recruitment, practice enhancements, communications, and business development. **Career Steps:** Director of Professional Services, Columbia Hoffman Estates Medical Center (1994–Present); Physician Services, Sherman Hospital (1994); Business Manager, Rush Occupational Health – Copley (1991–1994); Physician Services, Med First Physicians (1990–1991); Education Coordinator, ACHE (1989–1990). **Associations & Accomplishments:** National Association of Female Executives; National Association of Physician Recruiters; Chicago Health Executive Forum. **Education:** Attending: Illinois Benedictine; Wallbonser College, Nursing (1993); Southwest Texas State University, B.S. in Healthcare Administration (1988). **Personal:** Married to John Troyan in 1995.

Thomas J. Walsh

Chief Financial Officer
Preferred Care Inc.
6 Neshaminy Interplex, Suite 205
Trevose, PA 19053
(215) 639–6208
Fax: (215) 639–2674

6324

Business Information: Preferred Care Inc. is a managed health care organization that owns a preferred provider organization, third party administrator, and a reinsurance facility. As Chief Financial Officer, Mr. Walsh is responsible for all financial and accounting functions for the entire Company, as well as directs all Human Resource areas. **Career Steps:** Chief Financial Officer, Preferred Care Inc. (1989–Present). **Education:** Philadelphia College of Textiles, M.B.A. in International Business (1995); Temple University, B.A. in Accounting (1987). **Personal:** Married to Lillian T. in 1990. Two children: Jillian Marie and Connor Thomas. Mr. Walsh enjoys golf, ice hockey, coaching soccer, exploring information technology and spending time with his family.

Jessie (Jay) Ward
Technology Manager
Premier, Inc.
P.O. Box 671, 31094 Boggs Road
Exmore, VA 23350–0671
(757) 442–8237 (704) 529–3300
Fax: (704) 529–5434
E MAIL: See Below

6324

Business Information: Premier, Inc. is a multi–functional healthcare service provider. The Company provides purchasing services, physicians, consulting services, and equipment maintenance to hospitals and other healthcare facilities. Established in 1969 as Sun Health, the Company merged and became Premier, Inc. in 1996. With estimated annual revenue of $10 billion, the Company presently employs over 800 people in fifty states. As Technology Manager, Mr. Ward is responsible for the maintenance of the clinical and biomedical equipment in various hospitals. His duties include scheduling of maintenance and preventive maintenance on all clinical and biomedical equipment for clients. His duties also include contract negotiations, pre–purchase evaluations on capital equipment, and providing technology assessment reports on new technologies in the medical industry. Internet users can reach him via: Jay.Ward@premierinc.sprint.com. **Career Steps:** Technology Manager, Premier, Inc. (1996–Present); Biomedical Equipment Technician, Sun Health (1990–1995). **Associations & Accomplishments:** Moose Lodge #683. **Education:** DeVry Institute of Technology, A.A.S. Electronics (1989); Several medical equipment manufacturer service schools; Technology management classes. **Personal:** Mr. Ward enjoys concerts, swimming, and being a disc jockey.

Judith A. White
Health Services Director
Healthcare U.S.A.
8705 Perimeter Park Boulevard, Suite 3
Jacksonville, FL 32216
(904) 565–2903
Fax: (904) 646–3871
E–mail: see below

6324

Business Information: The first Medicaid HMO in Florida, Healthcare U.S.A. is an integrated health care system and management corporation (HMO) providing complete medical, surgical, and psychiatric services to its members. The Company also provides and assists patients with Medicaid and Medicare, as well as providing services to the commercial sector. Established in 1993, Healthcare U.S.A. currently employs 150 physicians and medical support staff. As Health Services Director, Mrs. White is responsible for the direction of utilization management, quality management, and network development. Mrs. White can also be reached through the internet as follows: AOL_JAWCAP **Career Steps:** Health Services Director, Healthcare U.S.A. (1994–Present); Director of Medical Operations, Humana Health Plans (1992–1994); Director of Professional Services, Av–Med Health Plans (1990–1992); Operations Director, Humana Health Plans (1984–1990). **Associations & Accomplishments:** Jacksonville Wellness Council; First Coast Executive Association; Diplomat, American Board of Quality Assurance and UR, Inc.; First Coast Physician Management Association; Healthy Family Coalition of Northeast Florida. **Education:** Southern Illinois University, B.S.H.A. (1992); St. Lukes School of Nursing, R.N. (1966). **Personal:** Married to Delbert in 1968. Two children: Keith and Dean. Mrs. White enjoys reading, biking, gardening and camping.

Gene Whobrey, C.C.M., M.R.C., C.R.C., C.V.E.
Regional Manager
Comprehensive Rehabilitation Association Managed Care, Inc.
1140 Hammond Drive, Suite A–1200
Atlanta, GA 30328
(770) 804–1119
Fax: (770) 804–1121

6324

Business Information: Comprehensive Rehabilitation Association (CRA) Managed Care, Inc. assists clients to offset the cost of lengthy hospital and skilled nursing facility stays. The Corporation has 160 offices in 48 states and employs over 2,500 people nationwide. As Regional Manager, Mr. Whobrey is responsible for the operation of offices in Georgia, South Carolina and North Carolina. His duties include staff recruitment, training, scheduling, and evaluating. Other responsibilities include public relations and strategic planning for regional expansion. **Career Steps:** CRA Managed Care, Inc.: Regional Manager (1996–Present), Manager (1994–1996), Supervisor (1992–1994). **Associations & Accomplishments:** Certified Rehabilitation Counselor; Certified Vocational Evaluator; Certified Case Manager; National Rehabilitation Association. Mr. Whobrey is the recipient of several awards relating to managed care and has been published in various trade magazines and journals. **Education:** Wright State University, Masters in Rehabilitation Counseling (1989). **Personal:** Mr. Whobrey enjoys golf.

David A. Williams
Director of Sales
Health Star, Inc.
7257 North Lincoln Avenue
Lincolnwood, IL 60646
(708) 673–3113 Ext. 2253
Fax: (708) 673–3117

6324

Business Information: Health Star, Inc. is a nationally–managed health care organization, providing health and managed care products to insurance companies. As Director of Sales, Mr. Williams is responsible for the efforts of ten sales representatives over sixteen states, including administration, public relations, sales, and marketing. **Career Steps:** Director of Sales, Health Star Inc. (1995–Present); Director of Sales, American HMO (1994–1995); Brokerage Manager, Healthstar Brokerage (1992–1994); Regional Manager, Central Benefits (1988–1992). **Associations & Accomplishments:** National Association of Health Underwriters. **Education:** Miami University, B.S. (1983). **Personal:** Two children: Ashley and Alyse. Mr. Williams enjoys sports and computers.

Robert G. Zed, C.H.E.

Chief Executive Officer
Morrison Crothall Support Services
5475 Spring Garden Road, Suite 301
Halifax, Nova Scotia B3J 3T2
(902) 422–6277
Fax: (902) 422–6715
EMAIL: robzed@istar.ca

6324

Business Information: Morrison Crothall Support Services is a health care management facility specializing in consulting and contracted care for hospitals, universities, and health care facilities. Established in 1991, the Company employs 250 people and has an estimated annual revenue of $10 million. As President, Mr. Zed oversees the day–to–day operation and marketing of the Company. His responsibilities include strategic planning, public relations, and customer service. **Career Steps:** CEO, Morrison Crothall Support Services (1992–Present); IWK Children's Hospital: Vice President (1990–1992), Director of Hospital Services (1986–1990). **Associations & Accomplishments:** Canadian College of Healthcare Executives; American College of Health Care Executives; Vice Chair, Bluenose Chapter, Canadian College; Past President, Dalhousie University World Wide Alumni; Member of Several University and Agency Boards. **Education :** Dalhousie University: M.H.S.A. (1986), B.A. (1982), C.P.A. (1984). **Personal:** Married to Dr. Joanna Zed in 1989. Two children: William Gregory Lewis and Geoffrey Robert Lewis. Mr. Zed enjoys skiing, sailing, golf, and cooking.

Robert A. Abramski

Vice President
CIGNA International
1601 Chestnut Street, #55
Philadelphia, PA 19192–0003
(215) 761–6732
Fax: (215) 761–5480

6331

Business Information: CIGNA International underwrites industrial property and casualty exposures of major U.S. multi–national companies. Originally established in 1793, under the name INA, the Company also deals in healthcare, financial, and employee benefits insurance. Located in Philadelphia, Pennsylvania, the Company hopes to expand to include overseas interests. As Vice President, Mr. Abramski is responsible for administrative and operational duties, including strategic planning and marketing. Additionally, he oversees a field staff of twenty, and handles the basic management of the U.S. market. **Career Steps:** CIGNA International : Vice President (1993–Present), European Property Manager (1989–1993), Director, Underwriting Administration (1986–1989). **Education :** Villanova University, B.S. in Physics (1971). **Personal:** Married to Mary Ann in 1972. Mr. Abramski enjoys golf, hiking, and gardening.

John C. Adiletti, PDM

Director of Marketing
Nationwide Insurance
919 NE 19th Avenue
Portland, OR 97232–2202
(503) 238–4205
Fax: (503) 797–4815

6331

Business Information: Nationwide Insurance, the fifth largest automobile insurance company in the U.S. as well as one of the leading global insurance products providers, offers a wide range of insurance services and financial products through corporate subsidiaries in the U.S. and Europe. Headquartered in Columbus, Ohio, Nationwide Insurance operates 100 offices throughout the U.S. A direct marketing insurance executive with over twenty years expertise, John Adiletti has served as Nationwide's Marketing Director since 1991. Working from the Western District Headquarters in Portland, Oregon, he directs all marketing, sales, advertising, and group sales functions covering the 21 western states. **Career Steps:** Director of Marketing, Nationwide Insurance (1991–Present); Senior Vice President, Merastar Insurance Company (1986–1991); Vice President, Balboa Insurance Group (1982–1986). **Associations & Accomplishments:** Direct Marketing Association; Direct Marketing Insurance Council; Oregon Direct Marketing Association. **Education:** University of Missouri, PDM (1994); Merrimack College, B.A. in Humanities (1966). **Personal:** Married to Linda in 1967. Mr. Adiletti enjoys golf, running and travel.

Margaret F. Anderson

Vice President of Diversity
USAA
9800 Fredericksburg Road
San Antonio, TX 78288
(210) 498–2288
Fax: (210) 498–4169

6331

Business Information: USAA is a reciprocal inter–insurance exchange offering property and casualty insurance coverage to active and retired military officers and their dependents. As Vice President of Diversity, Ms. Anderson is responsible for programs regarding cultural diversity and other related matters. **Career Steps:** USAA: Vice President of Diversity (1996–Present), Assistant Vice President of Policies and Programs (1995–1996), Assistant Vice President of Human Resource Special Programs (1994–1995), Director of Corporation Contributions (1991–1994). **Associations & Accomplishments:** Society for Human Resource Management; Life Office Management Association; EEO/AA/Diversity Committee; San Antonio Area Foundation; Junior Achievement Consultant; Texas Lyceum Alumni Board; Leadership San Antonio Alumni; San Antonio Business Forum; First Presbyterian Church; D.A.R.; Monte Vista Historical Association; D.R.T. **Education:** Texas A&M University, M.Ed. (1985); University of Texas – Austin, Bachelor of Journalism. **Personal:** Married to William Crow. Ms. Anderson enjoys movies, antiques, theater productions, and travel.

Raymond B. Aston

Chief Operating Officer
First Security Casualty Company
30775 Barrington
Madison Heights, MI 48071–1833
(810) 588–9500
Fax: (810) 588–3232

6331

Business Information: First Security Casualty Company is a property and casualty insurance company specializing in both personal and commercial lines of business, including personal, automotive, liquor liability, and commercial package products. As Chief Operating Officer, Mr. Aston is responsible for all aspects of company operations, including claims, general management, accounting, sales, customer service, and systems management. In addition to his duties as Chief Operating Officer of First Security Casualty Company, he is Chief Executive Officer of Pinnacle Underwriting Management Associates, Ltd., a start–up company offering a non–standard automobile product for the State of Michigan. Mr. Aston is involved in the development of this new product, as well as a secondary product soon to be released. **Career Steps:** Chief Operating Officer, First Security Casualty Company (1995–Present); Chief Executive Officer, Pinnacle Underwriting Management Associates Ltd. (1996–Present); Vice President and General Manager, AAA of Missouri (Auto Club of Missouri Group) (1985–1995); Vice President Underwriting and Vice President of Operations, Northwest Farm Bureau Insurance Company (1980–1985). **Associations & Accomplishments:** Board of Trustees, Oregon Fair Plan; Executive Committee Board of Directors, Missouri Insurance Underwriting Association; CPCU Society: Secretary, Treasurer of St. Louis Chapter, Junior Achievement Coalition – St. Louis, Holt Jaycees; Michigan Association of Independent Agents; Michigan Insurance Federation; Board of Directors, Missouri Joint Underwriting Association. **Education:** Michigan State University, B.S. (1970); Insurance Institute of America – Philadelphia, PA, Associate in Underwriting/Risk Management. **Personal:** Married to L. Denise in 1969. One child: Julie. Mr. Aston enjoys golf, tennis, walking, snorkling, reading, music, and autos.

Joseph L. Barnes

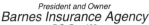

President and Owner
Barnes Insurance Agency
P.O. Box 468
Gatlinburg, TN 37738–0468
(423) 436–5807
Fax: (423) 436–2863

6331

Business Information: Barnes Insurance Agency is a national insurance company, representing all major companies (i.e., AETNA), providing property, casualty, and life insurance coverages. Co–establishing Barnes Insurance Agency in 1962 as Vice President with his brother, Mr. Barnes succeeded him as President and Owner in 1980. He is responsible for all aspects of operations, including administration, finances, sales, public relations, accounting, taxes, marketing, and strategic planning. **Career Steps:** Barnes Insurance Agency: President and Owner (1980–Present), Vice President and Co–Owner (1962–1980). **Associations & Accomplishments:** Gatlinburg Elks – BPOE; Independent Agent Association. **Education:** Travelers – Hartford. **Personal:** One child: Kathy Jo Soehn. Mr. Barnes enjoys golf and breeding Tennessee Walking Horses.

Mark C. Barry

Vice President of Administration and Finance
State Compensation Insurance Fund
5 South Last Chance Gulch
Helena, MT 59601
(406) 444–6494
Fax: (406) 444–7796

6331

Business Information: State Compensation Fund is a state agency providing insurance for Workers' Compensation benefits. A Certified Public Accountant with sixteen years of experience, Mr. Barry joined State Compensation Fund as Vice President of Finance in 1994. Working from the Helena, Montana office, he functions as the chief financial officer, responsible for all aspects of financial matters, as well as operations, strategic planning, budgeting, and administration of support services. Concurrently, he co–owns Allegro School of Dance with his wife. The School instructs students (ages 3–Adult) in dance, and conducts Spring performances annually. Specialized dance programs are also offered for persons with disabilities. **Career Steps:** Vice President of Finance, State Compensation Fund (1994–Present); Co–Owner, Allegro School of Dance (Present); Senior Auditor, Legislative Audit Division – Montana (1988–1994); Credit Representative, General Motors Acceptance Corporation (1980–1984). **Associations & Accomplishments:** Certified Public Accountant; AICPA. **Education:** Montana State University – Billings, B.S.B.A. (1988); University of Minnesota, B.A. in Psychology. **Personal:** Married to Beth Barry in 1989. Two children: Kim and Sydney. Mr. Barry enjoys hunting and fishing.

Christine A. Bernhard

Director, Office of General Counsel
AAA Michigan
1 Auto Club Drive
Dearborn, MI 48126–4213
(313) 336–1795
Fax: (313) 336–1245

6331

Business Information: AAA Michigan is an automotive club/travel service operating on a membership basis for the promotion of the interests of their members. AAA is the largest U.S. travel services organization with 36 million members. Each club provides certain basic member benefits – emergency road service, auto travel assistance and a member publication. Other benefits offered vary according to club size and location. With nearly two million members, AAA Michigan provides travel, financial, insurance (property & casualty), and auto–related services resulting in $1 billion in revenue. Special member values include fee–free American Express Traveler Cheques, savings on hotels, motels, car rentals and attraction admission discounts and more. Through legislative and educational activities, AAA is a staunch advocate for all motorists and travelers. A practicing attorney since 1978, Ms. Bernhard joined AAA Michigan in 1986. Appointed as Director for the Office of General Counsel in the Corporate Legal Department in 1994, she manages all legal aspects on behalf of AAA Michigan, serving the Michigan and Wisconsin areas. Career milestones include establishing the automation and organizational functions of the office and reducing the amount of employment litigation. **Career Steps:** AAA Michigan: Director, Office of General Counsel (1994–Present), Assistant Corporate Secretary & Counsel (1988–1994), Manager of Employment Unit (1990–1994); Staff Attorney (1986–1988). **Associations & Accomplishments:** President of Michigan Chapter (1994–1995), American Corporate Counsel Association; Mayor Pro Tem (1986–1989), Birmingham City Commissioner; Birmingham Board of Zoning Appeals (1989–1991). **Education:** New England School of Law, J.D. (1978); Newton College, B.A. (1975). **Personal:** Two children: Alexander and Jennifer. Ms. Bernhard enjoys spending time with her family and is learning to play golf.

Claudio Bietolini

President Director
Generali Do Brasil
Avenue Rio Branco, 128 – 7.0 And
Rio De Janeiro, Brazil 20042–900
55–02–12920144
Fax: 55–02–12249836

6331

Business Information: Generali Do Brasil provides life, fire, and auto insurance to the general public. As President Director, Mr. Bietolini is responsible for all aspects of Company operations, including administration, finance, public relations, and strategic planning. **Career Steps:** Generali Do Brasil:

President Director (1989–Present), Executive President (1989), President and General Manager (1982); Managing Director, Central Hispano Generali Holding (1992–1995). **Associations & Accomplishments:** Curator's Council Museum of the Republic – Rio de Janeiro; Consulting Board, National Federation of Insurers of Brazil "Fenaseg"; Board Member, Italian Brazilian Chamber of Commerce; President, Italian Peruvian Chamber of Commerce. **Education:** Catholic University – Milan: Doctorate in Political Science (1995), Doctorate in Economics (1985). **Personal:** Married to Paola in 1968. One child: Hilary. Mr. Bietolini enjoys golf and Philosophy.

Mr. David R. Bradley
President
Hartford Specialty Company
Hartford Plaza
Hartford, CT 06115
(203) 547–4834
Fax: Please mail or call

6331

Business Information: Hartford Specialty Company is a full-service insurance company, providing property and casualty risk coverage to large Fortune 2000 or "unusual" companies. The Company currently employs 600 professionals and reports annual premium revenue in excess of $800 million. As President, Mr. Bradley serves as the chief operating officer, responsible for all aspects of operations. **Career Steps:** President, Hartford Specialty Company (1990–Present); Senior President, ITT Hartford Insurance Group (1991–Present); Assistant Vice President, ITT Hartford Insurance Group (1984–1991); Actuary, ITT Hartford Insurance Group (1981–1984). **Associations & Accomplishments:** Member, Casualty Actuarial Society; Member, American Academy of Actuaries; Past Peresident, Casualty Actuaries of New England; Hartford Chapter of American Guild of Organists. **Education:** Brown University, B.S.C. (1971). **Personal:** Married to Janet Stulting in 1975. Two children: James and Eleanor. An accomplished keyboard musician, Mr. Bradley enjoys performing on piano and pipe organ.

Jose E. Burgos
MIS Vice President
Cooperativa Seguros Multiples
P.O. Box 363846
San Juan, Puerto Rico 00936–3846
(787) 753–7967
Fax: (787) 759–9961

6331

Business Information: Cooperativa Seguros Multiples is a property and casualty insurance company. The tenth largest firm in Puerto Rico, the Company concentrates on personal insurance. As MIS Vice President, Mr. Burgos handles all information systems and identifies and acquires technology to make the Company more competitive. **Career Steps:** Cooperativa Seguros Multiples: MIS Vice President (1990–Present); Corporate Planning Director (1982–1990); Accounting Manager (1976–1982). **Associations & Accomplishments:** Insurance Accounting Systems Association; Insurance Accountants for Cooperatives; Treasurer, Board of Directors, Little League, Venus Garden Community. **Education:** University of Puerto Rico, B.B.A. (1973); SMP, Program Forum Scandia Reinsurance – Sweden; College of Insurance, New York, Courses in Reinsurance; Interamerican University of Puerto Rico, MBA Courses. **Personal:** Married to Maria H. Rios in 1979. Two children: Edwin and Maricarmen. Mr. Burgos enjoys electronics, music, sports, and fishing.

Katherine R. Caldwell, P.T.
Worker's Compensation Services Director
Willis Corroon Corporation
1300 East 9th Street, Suite 1700
Cleveland, OH 44114
(216) 781–2587
Fax: (216) 861–6126

6331

Business Information: Willis Corroon is an international insurance brokerage firm with a network of over 300 offices in more than 70 countries, headquartered in the United Kingdom. A licensed Physical Therapist with over eighteen years of clinical experience in orthopedic and musculoskeletal injuries, Ms. Caldwell joined Willis Corron as Worker's Compensation Services Director in 1995. She works with companies to obtain quality medical care for injured employees with a strong emphasis on education and early return to work using modified work programs. **Career Steps:** Worker's Compensation Services Director, Willis Corroon Corporation (1995–Present); Manager, Case Management and Rehabilitation, Figgie International (1992–1995); Working Manager and Physical Therapist, University Hospital of Cleveland (1979–1992); Physical Therapist, Lutheran Hospital (1974–1979). **Associations & Accomplishments:** American Physical Therapy Association, Orthopedic Section with special interest in Industrial Work Injury; Cleveland Physical Therapy Orthopedic Study Group. **Education:** Ohio State University, B.S. (1973); Physical Therapy Certificate (1974). **Personal:** Married to R. Caldwell. Ms. Caldwell enjoys competing in equestrian events (hunter/jumper) with her horse, Rosie.

Eduardo G. Camareno Jr, J.D.
• • • ◀▬▬▬◉▬▬▬▶ • • •

Administration Services Director
Puerto Rican–American Insurance Company
Condo Galeria #1 Apt.406 Hostos Ave. Hato Rey
San Juan, Puerto Rico 00918
(787) 250–5386
Fax: (787) 250–5338

6331

Business Information: Puerto Rican–American Insurance Company, the oldest insurance company in Puerto Rico, provides property and casualty insurance to clients, while another branch provides life insurance. As Administration Services Director, Mr. Camareno is responsible for the day–to–day operations of the Company and for all administrative duties of the office. He works closely with other members of management in strategic planning for the Company. Mr. Camareno is also setting the groundwork for the opening of his own micrographics and information technology consulting firm. Concurrently, he conducts seminars and conferences, publishes articles for magazines and journals, and is working on his second micro graphics and imaging systems text. **Career Steps:** Administration Services Director, Puerto Rican–American Insurance Company (1988–Present); Corporate Systems Director, Puerto Rico Marine Management, Inc. (1965–1985). **Associations & Accomplishments:** Puerto Rico Bar Association; Founding Member and Past President, Association for Information and Image Management, Puerto Rico Chapter; Ancient and Accepted Scottish Rite 32 Shriner, Patria Lodge #61, San Juan; Past Worshipful Master of Patria Lodge; Scottish Rite Research Society; Royal Order of Jesters, B.P.O. Elks. **Education:** InterAmerican University of Puerto Rico, Juris Doctor (1975) and Bachelor of Arts in Sociology and Anthropology (1970) Cum Laude. **Personal:** Married to Lucy in 1988. Three children: Eduardo, George, and Erika. Mr. Camareno enjoys public speaking and writing.

Frank Ceraolo
Senior Vice President
California Compensation Insurance Company
21700 East Copley Drive, Suite 300
Diamond Bar, CA 91765
(909) 396–6311
Fax: (909) 396–6367

6331

Business Information: California Compensation Insurance Company is an insurance company, specializing in Worker's Compensation Insurance for California and a multi–state region. CalComp and its family of companies currently generate over $500 Million of annual premium. With twenty–two years experience in the insurance industry, Mr. Ceraolo joined California Compensation Insurance Company as Vice President in 1989, advancing to Senior Vice President in 1993. He is responsible for the management of the Diamond Bar Regional operations, including assisting the Chief Operating Officer with regional operational issues for the Company and broker relations. Mr. Ceraolo has been very successful in developing small insurance offices into large and profitable regional operations throughout his career. **Career Steps:** Senior Vice President, California Compensation Insurance Company (1989–Present); Executive Vice President, Pacific States Casualty (1988–1989); Senior Vice President, Beaver Insurance Company (1979–1988). **Education:** Ambassador College: M.A. (1974), B.A. (England & California campuses); Montclair State College, New Jersey. **Personal:** Married to Marie in 1968. Two children: Eric and Tania. Mr. Ceraolo enjoys art, music, history, current affairs, and world travel.

Ross J. Davidson Jr.
Vice President of Risk Management
USAA
9800 Fredericksburg Road, E–3–E
San Antonio, TX 78288
(210) 498–0876
Fax: (210) 498–0883

6331

Business Information: USAA, a Fortune 200 company, is an insurance brokerage providing insurance products nationwide, including property and casualty insurance benefits. As Vice President of Risk Management, Mr. Davidson is responsible for the financial management of the Agency, including asset liability. **Career Steps:** USAA: Vice President of Risk Man-

agement (1995–Present), Vice President of Capital Management 91993–1995), Assistant Vice President of Capital Management (1989–1993). **Associations & Accomplishments:** Financial Executives Institute; Treasury Management Association; Chair, P&C Subcommittee Advising National Association of Insurance Commissioners (NAIC) on Model Investment Law; Coordinate Industry Advise on Investment Law and Holding Company Acts to the NAIC; Committee on State Regulation of Investments; American Council of Life Insurers; Executive Board of Alamo Area Council of Boy Scouts of America. **Education:** Brigham Young University: M.B.A. in Finance (1976), B.A. in Economics (1974). **Personal:** Married to Jolene in 1972. Seven children: Pamela, Christena, Carmen, Ross III, Joseph, JoDell and Dawn Leigh. Mr. Davidson enjoys spending time with his family.

Renee M. Engman
Vice President
Oakley Underwriting Agency, Inc.
10 North Dearborn Street
Chicago, IL 60602–4209
(312) 357–3511
Fax: (312) 357–3525

6331

Business Information: Oakley Underwriting Agency, Inc. is a property and casualty insurance company, handling specialty lines of casualty insurance and claims. Established in 1993, Oakley reports estimated premium assets in excess of $35 million. Appointed as Vice President in 1993, Ms. Engman brings with her over ten years of underwriting expertise. As Vice President working from the Chicago office, she manages corporate and non–profit directors and officers in the liability underwriting units. **Career Steps:** Vice President, Oakley Underwriting Agency, Inc. (1993–Present); Assistant Vice President, Virginia Surety Company (1988–1993); Senior Underwriter, Crum & Forster Managers (1984–1988). **Associations & Accomplishments:** Professional Liability Underwriting Society; Volunteer, Chicago Cares. **Education:** Northwestern University – Kellogg Graduate School of Management, M.A. in Management (1995); Valparaiso University, B.S. in Business Administration (1984). **Personal:** Ms. Engman enjoys hiking, weightlifting, golf and biking.

Gregory J. Erickson, CIC
Vice President
Professional Insurance Services, Inc.
120 Bishops Way, Suite 158
Brookfield, WI 53005–6214
(414) 784–0863
Fax: (414) 784–2996

6331

Business Information: Professional Insurance Services, Inc. provides commercial property and casualty insurance coverage plans. Regional in scope, PIS has offices throughout a 15–state region encompassing the midwest U.S. sectors. A Certified Insurance Counselor with over twenty years in the insurance industry, Greg Erickson joined PIS in 1985. As Vice President, he oversees all agents and administrative support staff located at the Brookfield, Wisconsin branch; as well as spends a major portion of his time as a commercial sales agent. **Career Steps:** Vice President, Professional Insurance Services, Inc. (1985–Present); Account Representative, Wausau Insurance Company (1979–1984). **Associations & Accomplishments:** Professional Insurance Agents Association; Independent Insurance Agents Association; Society of Certifed Insurance Counselors. **Education:** University of Wisconsin – Milwaukee, B.S. (1975); Society of Certified Insurance Counselors (CIC). **Personal:** Married to Jan A. in 1974. Three children: Christin, Melissa, and Rebecca. Mr. Erickson enjoys woodworking, fishing, and hiking.

Rosemary R. Ferrero, C.P.A.
Vice President and Chief Financial Officer
Penn–America Insurance Company
420 S. York Road
Hatboro, PA 19040
(215) 443–3600
Fax: (215) 443–3603

6331

Business Information: Penn–America Insurance Company, established in 1975, is a property and casualty insurance writer which writes insurance in all 50 states. In 1993 the holding company, Penn–America Group, went public and presently has over 4 million shares traded under PAGI on the NASDAQ listings. As Vice President of the holding company and Chief Financial Officer of the subsidiary, Ms. Ferrero oversees all aspects of the businesses relating to financial matters. Other responsibilities include oversight of budgets, investor relations, and public relations. **Career Steps:** Vice President and Chief Financial Officer, Penn–America Insurance Company (1994–Present); Senior Financial Services Manager, Cooper & Lybrand (1977–1994). **Associations & Accomplishments:** Board of Directors, Ancilla Assumption Academy;

Board of Directors, Hatboro YMCA; American Institute of Certified Public Accountants; Pennsylvania Institute of Certified Public Accounts; Bank Administration Institute; National Association of Insurance Women; Junior Achievement, visiting professor for the past 5 years. Awarded YMCA Women of the Year in 1988. **Education:** Boston College, B.A. Summa Cum Laude (1977). **Personal:** Married to Emmanuel in 1980. Two children: Jennifer and Gina. Ms. Ferrero enjoys reading, gardening, wallpapering and stenciling, and snow skiing.

Hillary Grzebien–Myers
Service Manager
Liberty Mutual Insurance
P.O. Box 1157
Portsmouth, NH 03802–1157
(603) 431–3350
Fax: (603) 431–3425

6331

Business Information: Liberty Mutual Insurance is an international insurance agency, providing insurance sales and customer service in the property–casualty insurance and personal market. Working in various administrative capacities for Liberty Mutual since 1985, Hillary Myers was promoted to her current position in November of 1992. As Service Manager, she oversees all new business sales activities, as well as manages all customer service functions and related support staff for all New Hampshire sectors. **Career Steps:** Liberty Mutual Insurance: Service Manager (1992–Present), Supervisory Service Representative (1989–1992), Service Representative (1985–1989). **Associations & Accomplishments:** Rotary International; Missions Committee, Lee Church Congregational; New Hampshire Technical College Business Advisory Board; Phi Tau Beta Honor Society. **Education:** New England College, B.A. magna cum laude (1984). **Personal:** Married to James M. in 1987. Mrs. Grzebien–Myers enjoys community theater, travel, literature, music and theological studies.

Carla Marlene Hampton
Management Development Specialist
USAA
5800 Northhampton Boulevard
Norfolk, VA 23502–5513
(804) 893–4834
Fax: (804) 893–5508

6331

Business Information: USAA is an auto, property, and casualty insurance company providing insurance to military officers and dependents. As Management Development Specialist, Ms. Hampton is responsible for development and training in the mid–Atlantic region, including North Carolina, Virginia, and Maryland. She provides all Management Development curriculum. Additionally, she has developed more than 20 leadership/management classes such as Conflict Decision Making. **Career Steps:** Management Development Specialist, USAA (1994–Present); Public Relations Services, Temple–Inland Corporation (1993–1994); Manager, B.C. Harris Publishing Company (1990–1993); Legal/Political Research Analyst, Regent University Law School (1986–1990); Public Assistance Representative, Department of Social Services (1984–1986); Director of Admissions and Social Services, Towers Corporation (1982–1984). **Associations & Accomplishments:** Public Relations Society of America; Women's Network of Hampton Roads; CCC Chairperson. **Education:** Regent University, M.A. in Public Policy (1989); University of Virginia, B.A. in Sociology (1981). **Personal:** Ms. Hampton enjoys travel, outdoor activities, and community involvement.

Douglas M. Helzer
•••◄━━●━━►•••

President and Owner
Centennial Agency, Inc.
1123 North Elizabeth Street
Pueblo, CO 81003–2233
(719) 544–1111
Fax: (719) 545–5120

6331

Business Information: Centennial Agency, Inc. is an independent insurance agency, concentrating on property and casualty insurance benefits. Seventy percent of the business focuses on commercial insurance, with thirty percent on personal insurance lines. Centennial Agency, Inc. consists of two offices in Colorado (Pueblo and Denver) covering ninety percent of the state and has a current clientele enrollment of 4,500. Purchasing the Agency in 1985, Mr. Helzer serves as President and Owner. He is responsible for all aspects of operations, including sales and management, in addition to overseeing all administrative operations for associates and a support staff of 11. **Career Steps:** President and Owner, Centennial Agency, Inc. (1985–Present); Underwriter,

USF&G Insurance Company (1980–1982). **Associations & Accomplishments:** Independent Insurance Agents; Parkview Hospital Medical Board; Former President, Parkview Hospital Foundation Board; Council Member, County Planning and Zoning; Published articles in trade journals. **Education:** University of San Diego, B.A. (1980). **Personal:** Married to Jacqueline in 1983. Mr. Helzer enjoys golf, fishing, and ice hockey.

Del O. Hirsch
Regional Marketing Manager
Federated Insurance
P.O. Box 39850
Minneapolis, MN 55439–0850
(612) 831–4300
Fax: (612) 820–2388

6331

Business Information: Federated Insurance specializes in providing commercial property and casualty insurance products. Established in 1903, Federated Insurance currently employs 73 people and reports assets of $134 million. As Regional Marketing Manager, Mr. Hirsch is responsible for all sales results in 4 states. At present, there are 8 managers and 65 marketing representatives reporting directly to him. **Career Steps:** Regional Marketing Manager, Federated Insurance (1971–Present); Coordinator of Special Education, Whitman County Schools (1969–1971); Administrative Specialist, United States Army (1967–1969). **Associations & Accomplishments:** American Management Association; American Legion; First Methodist Church. **Education:** Washington State University, Psychology (1971); University of Arizona; University of Minnesota; Moorehead State University. **Personal:** Married to Carolyn. Four children: Troy, Kelsey, Andrew, and Matthew. Mr. Hirsch enjoys hunting, fishing, skiing, tennis, and doing carpentry.

Lisa C. Hiser–Busto, CPCU, AAM
Operations Manager
Lupfer–Frakes Insurance
222 Church Street
Kissimmee, FL 34741
(407) 847–2841 Ext. 117
Fax: (407) 847–0567

6331

Business Information: Lupfer–Frakes Insurance specializes in property and casualty insurance, as well as employee benefits sales. A Chartered Property & Casualty Underwriter and Associate in Automation Management, Ms. Hiser–Busto joined Lupfer–Frakes in 1994 as a Commercial Sales Agent. Promoted to Operations Manager in 1996, she is presently responsible for the management of facilities and support staff for a three–location retail insurance agency, including oversight of the Human Resources Department, quality control, and accounting activities. **Career Steps:** Lupfer–Frakes Insurance: Operations Manager (1995–Present), Commercial Sales Agent (1994–1995); Seibels Bruce Insurance: Territorial Sales Manager (1991–1993), Underwriter (1989–1991). **Associations & Accomplishments:** Director, Central Florida Chapter – Society of Chartered Property & Casualty Underwriters; Former President, Redeemer Lutheran Church; Speaker, Insurance Women of Winterpark; Vice President, Business Network International; Speaker and Chair, Women's Endeavors. **Education:** Ball State University, B.A. (1983); Insurance Institute of America: Chartered Property & Casualty Underwriter, Associate in Automation Management. **Personal:** Married to Alex in 1985. Ms. Hiser–Busto enjoys running, reading, gardening, bird–keeping, and Hatha Yoga.

James B. Holler
Vice President of Support Services
BOAT/U.S. Marine Insurance
880 South Pickett Street
Alexandria, VA 22304–4606
(703) 823–9550
Fax: (703) 461–2840

6331

Business Information: BOAT/U.S. Marine Insurance provides recreational boat and yacht insurance marketed to the Boat Owners Association of the United States. With over 500,000 members across the United States, the Association provides services and products (boating accessories). The Company has 36 marine centers, and provides additional travel services, boat financing, a foundation for boat safety, and a consumer and government affairs department. As Vice President, Mr. Holler is in charge of planning and analysis on a financial level, fixing rates, and analysis of claims and handling. Additionally, he oversees the day–to–day operations of the Marine Insurance Division and 110 employees. **Career Steps:** Vice President, BOAT/U.S. Marine Insurance (1992–Present); Comptroller, Alton Insurance Agency (1989–1992); Vice President, Crown Insurance Agency

(1975–1988). **Associations & Accomplishments:** United States Power Squadron; Antique & Classic Boat Society, Inc. **Education:** Canisius College, B.S. (1976). **Personal:** Mr. Holler enjoys antique and classic boat collecting, golf, and being a private pilot.

Andre G. Howell
Government and Community Relations Manager
Allstate Insurance Company
601 Lee Rd.
Wayne, PA 19087–5607
(601) 640–0952
Fax: (601) 648–8855

6331

Business Information: Allstate Insurance Company is the second largest property and casualty insurer in the United States. Allstate is also the number one insurer of African Americans and Hispanics. Established in 1731, Allstate Insurance Company employs 2700 people in Pennsylvania, New Jersey, Delaware, and West Virginia. As Industry Relations Manager, Mr. Howell lobbies for legislation for the advancement of the company and against legislation that has a negative effect on the insurance industry. He is a registered lobbyist in both Pennsylvania and New Jersey and also serves as the primary contact on media inquiries. **Career Steps:** Allstate Insurance Company: Industry Relations Manager (1980–Present), Human Resources Division Manager (1988–1990), Market Claim Manager (1985–1988), Casualty Unit Claim Manager (1983–1985), Casualty Claim Analyst (1981–1983), Claim Representative (1980–1981); Willingboro Board of Education (1977–1980). **Associations & Accomplishments:** Auto Theft Prevention Authority (1995); Urban Market Task Force (1995); Awards: Good Hands, Allstate Insurance Company (1986); Young Men of America, Who's Who (1986); Student Citizen of the Year, The King's College (1976); Student Athlete of the Year/MVP, The King's College (1974); Vice President Sophomore Class, The King's College (1974). **Education:** New York University, B.S. in Economics and Business Administration (1977); Antioch Division of Temple Unviversity, 20 credits in Public Administration. **Personal:** Three children: David, Tiffany, and Christina. Mr. Howell enjoys sports, reading, and relaxing.

Jimmie Hunsinger, B.S.N., M.S.
Director of Medical Administration
FCCI Mutual
2601 Cattleman Road
Sarasota, FL 34232–6214
(941) 951–3799
Fax: (941) 993–3401

6331

Business Information: FCCI Mutual is a workers' compensation insurance service company, administering self insured, funds indemnity, and medical management. As Director of Medical Administration, Mrs. Hunsinger is responsible for quality assurance, utilization reviews, and payment of medical claims. **Career Steps:** Director of Medical Administration, FCCI Mutual (1988–Present); Director of Nursing, Pine Brook Health (SNF) (1986–1988); Director of Nursing, Venice Hospital (1980–1983). **Associations & Accomplishments:** Ordained in the Episcopal Church; Board of Trustees, Hospice South West Florida; Clergy Association; Certified Case Manager. **Education:** Rhode Island College, M.S. (1973); University of Vermont, B.S.N. (1955); Diocese South West Florida, Master's of Theology. **Personal:** Married to Vern in 1994. Mrs. Hunsinger enjoys raising and riding horses.

Russell L. Jamieson
President
Florida Highway and Marine Insurance
72 South Orlando Avenue
Cocoa Beach, FL 32931–4721
(407) 799–3313
Fax: (407) 799–0045

6331

Business Information: Florida Highway and Marine Insurance provides non–standard auto, commercial, marine, and general liability insurance. As President and Owner, Mr. Jamieson focuses on market and strategic planning in addition to overseeing daily operations and administrative responsibilities. Concurrently, he serves as President of Puritan Budget Plan–Premium Finance Company. **Career Steps:** President, Florida Highway and Marine Insurance (1994–Present); President, Puritan Budget Plan–Premium Finance Company (Present); Vice President, Friendly Auto Insurance of Cocoa (1992–1994); Business Manager, Hatteras of Lauderdale, Inc. (1987–1991). **Associations & Accomplishments:** Chamber of Commerce Cocoa Beach; Specialty Insurance Agents. **Education:** Brevard Community College, Associates Degree (1994); Continuing Education for 2–20

Property & Casualty Insurance. **Personal:** Mr. Jamieson enjoys bicycling, skiing, boating, water sports, and rollerblading.

Michael R. Johnson

Senior Vice President/Claims Manager
Acceptance/Redland Insurance Company
535 West Broadway
Council Bluffs, IA 51502
(712) 329–6601
Fax: Please mail or call
6331

Business Information: Acceptance/Redland Insurance Company is a multi–line insurer in 42 states and with eight branches regionally. Some lines of insurance are truckers, high–risk, property and casualty, and events coverage. The Company's specialty is crop production insurance, and its function is on the claims end as a marketing general agency. As Senior Vice President/Claims Manager, Mr. Johnson is responsible for all aspects of Company operations, including supervising claims payment and adjustments, ensuring the adjusters get adequate training, ensuring timely insurance, providing direction for the Company, and strategic planning. **Career Steps:** Acceptance/Redland Insurance Company: Senior Vice President/Claims Manager (1994–Present), Regional Claims Supervisor (1990–1993), Field Supervisor/Training Supervisor (1988–1990). **Associations & Accomplishments:** National Crop Insurance Board of Ethics; American Agricultural Association of Insurers. **Education:** University of NE (1966–1968); Doane College, Crete, NE (1964–1966). **Personal:** Married to Virginia in 1975. Three children: Cory Michael, Scott Alan, and Adam Todd. Mr. Johnson enjoys fishing, gardening, and platform speaking.

Hale Johnston

Vice President Group Operations
Dodson Group
9201 State Line Rd.
Kansas City, MO 64114
(816) 760–5454
Fax: (816) 760–5544
EMAIL: See Below
6331

Business Information: As one of the largest private businesses in Missouri, Dodson Group consists of three national commercial lines insurance companies, and other affiliated companies in related areas. Affiliated insurance entities of Dodson Group include: Reciprocal Exchange, founded in 1900; Casualty Reciprocal Exchange, founded in 1912; and Equity Mutual, founded in 1933. Kapstone Systems, Inc., founded in 1995, is a technical services provider and business software developer/marketer. As Vice President of Group Operations, Mr. Johnston has oversight responsibility for stategic and tactical coordination among all affiliated companies,and is in charge of special project implementation. Internet users can reach him via: halej@dodsongroup.com **Career Steps:** Dodson Group: Vice President – Group Operations (1996–Present), Assistant Vice President (1991–1996). **Associations & Accomplishments:** Advisory Board, International Diabetes Center's Kansas City Affiliate; Licensed P/C Insurance Agent. **Education:** William Jewell College, B.A. in History (1995), B.A. in Political Science; JCCC, A.A. **Personal:** Married to Christina in 1991. One child: Jessica. Mr. Johnston enjoys backpacking.

Mr. John S. Lovette

Regional Claim Manager
Anthem Casualty Insurance Group
175 Mansfield Avenue
Shelby, OH 44875
(419) 347–1880 Ext. 8396
Fax: (419) 347–3636
6331

Business Information: Anthem Casualty Insurance Group is a holding company for insurance agencies. Members of Anthem Casualty Insurance Group include: The Shelby Insurance Company, Anthem Casualty Insurance Company, Insura Property and Casualty Insurance Company, Affirmative Insurance Company, and Mound Agency, Inc. Established in 1880, Anthem Casualty Insurance Group reports $360 million in written premiums and currently employs 52 people in the Regional Claims Division. As Regional Claim Manager, Mr. Lovette is responsible for claims handling throughout Ohio and oversight of more than 300 independent agents. **Career Steps:** Regional Claim Manager, Anthem Casualty Insurance Group (1987–Present); Unit Claim Manager, AllState (1977–1987). **Associations & Accomplishments:** Society of Claim Law Associates; Former Board Member of United Way of Richland County; Chairman of Administration Committee; Volunteer Worker for Red Cross – Richland County; Boy Scouts of America; Worked with TAG (talented & gifted) students in Mansfield City Schools (Odyssey of the Mind). **Education:** Southern Illinois University, B.A. in Government (1973). **Personal:** Married to Althea Lovette in 1976. Two children: Kiaisha and Avi. Mr. Lovette enjoys music, The Arts and card collecting.

Angela M. McLean

Human Resource Administrator
Meemic
691 North Squirrel Road, Suite 200
Auburn Hills, MI 48321–7019
(810) 373–5700
Fax: (810) 377–8571
6331

Business Information: Meemic is a property and casualty insurance company. As Human Resource Administrator, Ms. McLean manages the daily activities of the Human Resource Department. She is directly responsible for one person in her office. **Career Steps:** Human Resource Administrator, Meemic (1993–Present); Human Resource Assistant, First State Bank (1991–1993). **Associations & Accomplishments:** Society for Human Resource Management, American Payroll Association, Human Resource Association of Greater Detroit, Michigan State University Alumni Association. **Education:** Wayne State University, M.B.A. (1996); Michigan State University, B.A. in Business Management (1990). **Personal:** Married to Thomas in 1992. Ms. McLean enjoys golf and inline skating.

Mary Elizabeth McNinch, CPCU, AIAF

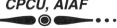

Chief Operating Officer
Davis Baldwin Insurance – Risk Management
5521 West Cypress Street
Tampa, FL 33607–1755
(813) 287–1936
Fax: (813) 286–7164
6331

Business Information: Davis Baldwin Insurance – Risk Management is the largest privately–held insurance company in the State of Florida. The Company has a full range of benefits, such as commercial benefits to claims and loss control and third party administration. With only one location, Davis Baldwin Insurance services contracts all over the world (i.e., The Outback Steakhouse). an insurance executive with over ten years expertise, Ms. McNinch joined Davis Baldwin Insurance in May of 1995. As Chief Operating Officer, she is responsible for all aspects of operations, including directing the strategic and financial operations. **Career Steps:** Chief Operating Officer, Davis Baldwin Insurance – Risk Management (1994–Present); Aetna Life & Casualty: Florida Underwriting Manager (1990–1994), Corporate Underwriting Officer (1987–1990). **Associations & Accomplishments:** The Council of Insurance Agents and Brokers; Chartered Property & Casualty Underwriters – Suncoast Chapter; Voted "Female Professional of the Year" in Buffalo, New York. **Personal:** Ms. McNinch enjoys tennis and golf.

Rick Miller

Owner – Secretary/Treasurer
Petro General Agency
P.O. Box 200428
Arlington, TX 76006–0428
(817) 640–7890
Fax: (817) 633–6860
6331

Business Information: Established in 1988, Petro General Agency is involved in the market of surplus line insurance rproducts, providing commercial, property, and casualty insurance to the oil and gas industry. Petro General is licensed in Oklahoma, Texas, and Louisiana. As Owner – Secretary/Treasurer, Mr. Miller is responsible for diversified administrative activities and all aspects of Company operations. Concurrent with his duties at Petro General, he is also the Owner and Secretary/Treasurer for two other subsidiary insurance companies: Petrosurance Casualty and McCollum, Miller & Lovelace, Inc. **Career Steps:** Owner – Secretary/Treasurer, Petro General Agency (1988–Present); Owner – Secretary/Treasurer, Petrosurance Casualty Company (1990–Present); Owner – Secretary/Treasurer, McCollum, Miller, and Lovelace, Inc. (1983–Present). **Associations & Accomplishments:** Independent Insurance Agents of Texas; Association of Oilwell Servicing Contractors; Member, Texas State Teachers Association; Sponser: Cancer Auxiliary of Texas, Arlington Theater, Arlington Creative Arts Theater and School. **Education:** Texas A&M University: M.Ed. (1975), B.A. **Personal:** Married to Lynda F. in 1967. One child: Lyndsey M. Mr. Miller enjoys golf and travel.

Judith M. Moyes–Fries

Loss Control Consultant
EBI Companies
P.O. Box 14077
Madison, WI 53714
(608) 244–8022
Fax: (608) 244–2102
6331

Business Information: EBI Companies, a subsidiary of Orion Capital Companies, is a national Worker's Compensation insurance carrier, providing services through independent agents. Headquartered in Milwaukee, Wisconsin, EBI has over 30 branches throughout 20 states (5 are in Wisconsin). As Loss Control Consultant, Ms. Moyes–Fries is responsible for working jointly with insured clientele to address Worker's Compensation programs to reduce the frequency and severity of injuries, and conducts training and education on hazards. **Career Steps:** Loss Control Consultant, EBI Companies (1993–Present); Review Program Consultant, Wisconsin Peer Review Org. (1991–1993); Utilization Review Coordinator, University of Wisconsin Hospital & Clinics (1990–1991). **Associations & Accomplishments:** American Nurses Association; National Association for Health Care Quality; EBI Team member that conducts seminars; Coordinates statewide speaking and conducts speaking at the local technical colleges and local universities. **Education:** Cardinal Stritch College, B.S. in Nursing (1988). **Personal:** Married to Gregory T. Fries in 1991. Ms. Moyes–Fries enjoys biking of all kinds, hiking, running, and tennis.

Mary Ellen Norton

Claims Specialist
Maryland Insurance Group
P.O. Box 5084
Hartford, CT 06102–5084
(203) 257–6844
Fax: (800) 378–2891
6331

Business Information: The Maryland Insurance Group provides processing of property and casualty insurance claims. Currently the Maryland Insurance Group employs 150 people. As a Claims Specialist, Ms. Norton investigates and negotiates complex claims to conclusion immediately following a major company re–organization. She also assists with jurisdictional training for co–workers. **Career Steps:** Claims Specialist, Maryland Insurance Group (1994–Present); Senior Litigation Specialist, Fireman's Fund (1994); Unit Manager, American International Adjusting Corporation (1990–1994); Field Training Manager, Supervisor and Claims Representative, Metropolitan Property and Liability Insurance (1984–1990); Case Controller and Benefit Analyst/Course Instructor (1982–1984); Substitute Teacher, East Windsor Board of Education (1981–1982); Program Advisor, Coordinator and House Director, Western Illinois University, Office of Student Activities (1980–1981). **Associations & Accomplishments:** Knitters Guild; Green Chimmneys Home for Troubled Children; Astrological Society; Volunteer, Special Olympics World Games. **Education:** Western Illinois University, M.S. in Recreation Management, magna cum laude (1981); Central Connecticut State University, B.S. in Elementary Education, cum laude (1980). **Personal:** Ms. Norton enjoys knitting, golf, hiking, yoga and reading.

Blaine Palmer

Executive Vice President and Chief Operating Officer
Missouri Employers Mutual Insurance
P.O. Box 1810
Columbia, MO 65205–1810
(573)499–9714
Fax: (573)499–4303
6331

Business Information: Missouri Employers Mutual Insurance (MEM) is a Worker's compensation insurance firm which was started from scratch in March 1995. A law was passed in the Missouri Legislature in 1993 authorizing the formation of MEM to bring stability to the worker's compensation market, increase competition, and to provide high quality coverage for small and mid–sized Missouri businesses. The Company has grown from its first policy in 1995 to over 14,000 policy holders and $115 million in annualized premium in mid–1996, making it the largest worker's compensation insurer in Missouri. With twelve years experience in the insurance industry, Mr. Palmer was invited in mid–1994 to assist in establishing Missouri Employers Mutual Insurance. As Executive Vice President and Chief Operating Officer, he is responsible for all underwriting, loss prevention, field audit, customer service, administration, claims, legal services, fraud, human resources, training and development. Career milestones include starting a similar company in Louisiana with $300 million premium and 31,000 policyholders within a year, serving as the President and CEO of the Utah Worker's Compensation Fund of Utah and being responsible for passing legislation privatizing that company after it had been a state agency for 70 years. He currently serves as national president of the American Association of

State Compensation Insurance Funds, a group of 27 state companies and 10 Canadian provinces, with annual premium income of over $20 billion per year. Mr. Palmer has been invited by many organizations, states, and insurance companies to share his experiences and successes and is very much in demand as a speaker on a national level. **Career Steps:** Executive Vice President and Chief Operating Officer, Missouri Employers Mutual Insurance (1995–Present); Executive Vice President and Chief Executive Officer, Louisiana Workers Compensation Corporation (1992–1994); President and Chief Executive Officer, Workers Compensation Fund of Utah (1985–1992); Director of International Human Resource Management, Bourns, Inc. (1983–1985); Adjunct Professor, University of Utah. **Associations & Accomplishments:** President, American Association of State Compensation Insurance Funds; Former President, Salt Lake Society for Human Resource Management; Former President, Utah Association of Civil Service Commissioners. **Education:** Brigham Young University, B.S. in Industrial Management (1963). **Personal:** Married to Shari in 1964. Mr. Palmer enjoys opera, baroque music, and off road motorcycling.

Claudette A. Paulsen
Vice President of Administration
J.E. Murphy Company
6440 Northwest Fifth Way
Ft. Lauderdale, FL 33309
(954) 776–5519
Fax: (954) 776–7595

6331

Business Information: J.E. Murphy Company provides insurance and general liability for mobile homes and mobile home parks throughout the state of Florida. Claudette Paulsen, as the Vice President of Administration, is responsible for all administration aspects including state and rate filings, and overseeing all management and personnel. **Career Steps:** J.E. Murphy Company: Vice President of Administration (1994–Present), Office Manager (1994); Supervisor, Mobile Home Departments, MHDA, Inc. (1992–1994). **Associations & Accomplishments:** National Womens Insurance Association. **Education:** Broward Community College, A.S. (1985). **Personal:** Married to Darren in 1995. One child: Jillyan Nichole. Ms. Paulsen enjoys camping, boating, and snorkeling.

Mrs. Jane E. Pell
Claim Vice President
CIGNA Property & Casualty Group
401 North White Horse Road
Voorhees, NJ 08043
(609) 782–4301
Fax: (609) 782–4601

6331

Business Information: CIGNA P & C Group is the property and casualty arm of the CIGNA insurance companies, handling fire, marine, and casualty insurance and claims. CIGNA corporate headquarters are located in Philadelphia, Pennsylvania. As Claim Vice President, Mrs. Pell manages all aspects of operations for the New Jersey Claims Division with 110 employees. **Career Steps:** Claim Vice President, CIGNA Property & Casualty Group, (1977–Present); Regional Supervisor, PMA Insurance (1970–1977); Claims Representative, Maryland Casualty (1967–1970). **Associations & Accomplishments:** National Association for Female Executives. **Education:** Casualty Claims Law Association Degree (1983); General Insurance Degree, Insurance Institute of America. **Personal:** Married to Richard in 1986.

Eugene M. Petrone
Regional Claims Vice President
CIGNA Property & Casualty Group
#1 Beaver Valley Road
Wilmington, DE 19850
(302) 479–6299
Fax: (302) 479–6079

6331

Business Information: CIGNA Property & Casualty Group is the property and casualty arm of the CIGNA Insurance Companies, handling fire, marine, and casualty insurance and claims for Fortune 500 companies. CIGNA corporate headquarters are located in Philadelphia, Pennsylvania. Established in 1792, CIGNA currently employs 110 people in the Wilmington, Delaware office. As Regional Claims Vice President, Mr. Petrone is responsible for the administration of Workers Compensation benefits in the states of Pennsylvania, New Jersey, and Delaware. **Career Steps:** CIGNA Property & Casualty Group: Regional Claims Vice President (1994–Present), Claims Manager (1992–1994), Product Management Superintendent (1990–1991); Claims Supervisor, Liberty Mutual Insurance (1985–1987). **Education:** University of Northern Colorado, B.A. (1982). **Personal:** Married to Mary K. in 1982. One child: Tiffany N. Mr. Petrone enjoys golf, basketball, softball, and reading.

Anthony L. Pyle
Sales Manager
Badger Mutual Insurance Company
1635 West National Avenue
Milwaukee, WI 53204
(414) 383–1234
Fax: (414) 383–4339

6331

Business Information: Badger Mutual is a property and casualty insurance company, providing automobile and home insurance benefits in Wisconsin and property and commercial insurance in Illinois, Minnesota, and Michigan. Established in 1871, Badger Mutual has offices in four states. With seventeen years of experience in insurance, Mr. Pyle joined Badger Mutual as Sales Manager in 1995. He is responsible for the management of all aspects of marketing, advertising, and agency contracts, in addition to overseeing a staff of 6. **Career Steps:** Sales Manager, Badger Mutual Insurance Company (1995–Present); District Sales Manager, Farmers Insurance Group (1994–1995); American Family Insurance: Sales Training Manager (1986–1994), Agent and District Sales Manager. **Associations & Accomplishments:** Independent Insurance Agents of America; Professional Insurance Agents; Publisher of numerous articles in local newspapers; Recipient of several company awards; Public speaker at professional organizations. **Education:** Northeast Missouri State University, B.S.E. (1977). **Personal:** Mr. Pyle enjoys hunting, fishing, and golf.

Ronald L. Ramsey
Regional Property Supervisor
Anthem Casualty Insurance
P.O. Box 50405
Indianapolis, IN 46250
(800) 777–0054 Ext 156
Fax: (800) 424–1082

6331

Business Information: Anthem Casualty Insurance, established in 1880, is a regional property and casualty insurance company with offices in 14 states. As Regional Property Supervisor, Mr. Ramsey supervises all property losses, both personal and commercial in Indiana, Illinois, Iowa and Wisconsin. **Career Steps:** Anthem Casualty Insurance: Regional Property Supervisor (1995–Present), Branch Casualty Supervisor (1993–1995), Auto Supervisor (1992–1993); Resident Adjuster, Cincinnati Insurance Company (1983–1992). **Associations & Accomplishments:** Akron Claims Association; Society of Claims Law Associates; Former President, Brunswick Ohio Lions Club. **Education:** Ohio University, B.Sc. (1973); Attended, LOTC, Property School, GAB Intermediate Casualty, Branch Managers School, AEI. **Personal:** Married to Dorothy in 1978. Two children: Lindsay and Jennifer. Mr. Ramsey enjoys cars, golf, and racing.

Jay Rose

• • • ◖━━━◗◉◖━━◗ • • •

Owner
Lighthouse Agency
1730 North Highway
South Hampton, NY 11968
(516) 283–7000
Fax: (516) 283–7037

6331

Business Information: Lighthouse Agency is an insurance agency whose primary focus is automobile insurance, but also markets property and casualty insurance. Currently located solely in New York, the Agency intends to expand to Florida in the very near future. One of three Owners, Mr. Rose oversees all operations and strategic planning of the Company. He is also involved with marketing and underwriting all policies. **Career Steps:** Lighthouse Agency: Owner (Present), Office Manager (1993); Congressional Staffer/Intern, U.S. House of Representatives (1992–1993). **Associations & Accomplishments:** Board Member, Greater Selden Chamber of Commerce; Advisory Member of Board, Senior Citizens Aide Association; Republican Party Committeeman, Election District 76; Board Member, Brookhaven Town Republican Club. **Education:** Attended, George Washington University (1993); Leadership Institute – Washington, D.C. **Personal:** Mr. Rose enjoys writing, graphic arts design, skiing, biking, reading, and debatting.

Azmi H. Salaymeh
Vice President
State Compensation Insurance Fund
1624 Cannon, Suite 31
Helena, MT 59601
(406) 444–1907
Fax: (406) 444–5963

6331

Business Information: State Compensation Insurance Fund is a quasi–state agency providing worker's compensation insurance services to employers throughout the State of Montana. As Vice President, Mr. Salaymeh is responsible for the Loss Control and Premium Audit departments and oversight of state fund activities. **Career Steps:** Vice President, State Compensation Insurance Fund (1994–Present); USF&G Insurance: Senior Loss Control Manager – Seattle Division (1993–1994), Loss Control/Premium Audit – Seattle Division (1992–1993), Loss Control/Premium Audit – San Jose Division (1989–1992). **Associations & Accomplishments:** A.S.S.E. **Education:** Central Missouri State University, M.S. (1977); Mankato State University, B.S. (1975). **Personal:** Mr. Salaymeh enjoys reading and travel during his leisure time.

Susan M. Saraceno
Director of Fiscal Reporting
OSF Health Plans, Inc.
300 SW Jefferson Street
Peoria, IL 61602–1413
(309) 677–8284
Fax: (309) 677–8338
EMail: See Below

6331

Business Information: OSF Health Plans, Inc. is licensed to sell accident and health insurance, and transact business as a health maintenance organization. A wholly–owned subsidiary of OSF Health Care System, the Company conducts business in Central and North Central Illinois. As Director of Fiscal Reporting, Ms. Saraceno directs the preparation of financial reports, directs accounts receivable and payables, billing, and filing tax returns and statutory reports. She can be reached by Internet users via: 76732.1102@compuserv.com **Career Steps:** Director of Fiscal Reporting, OSF Health Plans, Inc. (1995–Present); Financial Analyst, Covenant Medical Center (1994–1995); Manager of Accounting, PersonalCare Health Management Company (1990–1994); Vice President and Treasurer, Balloons by Terry, Inc. (1983–1988). **Associations & Accomplishments:** Peoria Noon Ambucs; Healthcare Financial Management Association; Balloon Federation of America. **Education:** University of Illinois, B.S. in Accounting (1974); Southern Illinois University; Sanford Community College; Valencia Community College. **Personal:** Married to H. Dale DeFord in 1992. Ms. Saraceno enjoys being a hot air balloon commercial pilot.

Kirk D. Simmons
Vice President of Claim Operations
Citizens Security Group
P.O. Box 3500
Red Wing, MN 55066
(612) 388–7171 Ext. 234
Fax: (612) 388–0538

6331

Business Information: The Citizens Security Group provides Property and Casualty insurance products. Established in 1914, Citizens Security Group currently employs 22 people, and reports annual premium assets of $50 million. As Vice President of Claim Operations, Mr. Simmons is responsible for all aspects of claims control and field operations. **Career Steps:** Vice President of Claim Operations, Citizens Security Group (1993–Present); Regional Specialist, CNA Insurance (1988–1993); Claims Specialist, Home Insurance (1986–1988); Property Claims Representative, American Family (1983–1986). **Associations & Accomplishments:** Claims Manager Association; Worker's Compensation Subcommittee, State of Minnesota; Published in trade magazines. **Education:** Drake University, B.S. in Business Administration (1983); Presently working on Master's degree in Business Administration. **Personal:** Married to Raschell in 1986. Two children: Jacob and Raschon. Mr. Simmons enjoys all outdoor activities, and military history.

Sheryl M. Simmons

• • • ◖━━━◗◉◖━━◗ • • •

Vice President/Assistant Treasurer
PHICO Insurance Company
1 PHICO Drive
Mechanicsburg, PA 17055–0085
(717) 766–1122
Fax: (717) 766–2837

6331

Business Information: PHICO Insurance Company is a property and casualty insurance company, specifically targeted for medical malpractice insurance across the United States. As Vice President/Assistant Treasurer, Ms. Simmons is responsible for investments, cash management, planning, and financial analysis of mergers and acquisitions. She is additionally responsible for the management of the Tax Department. **Career Steps:** PHICO Insurance Company: Vice President/Assistant Treasurer (1994–Present), Director of Taxation (1990–1994); Senior Tax Manager, KPMG Peat Marwick (1983–1990). **Associations & Accomplishments:** Tax Executives Institute; American Institute of Certified Public Accountants; Pennsylvania Institute of Certified Public Accountants; American Institute of Chartered Property and Casualty Underwriters. **Education:** Villanova University, M.T. (1991); Pennsylvania State University, B.B.A. (1980); Certified Public Accountant (1982); Chartered Property and Casualty Underwriter (1995). **Personal:** Married to Bruce K. Darkes in 1995. Ms. Simmons enjoys golf, music, gardening, and art galleries.

R. Stephen Trosty
Director of Risk Management
Michigan Physicians Mutual Liability Company (MPMLC)
1301 North Hagadorn Road
East Lansing, MI 48823
(517) 351–1150
Fax: (517) 333–2800

6331

Business Information: Michigan Physicians Mutual Liability Company (MPMLC), a subsidiary of the Sratton–Cheeseman Management Company, is a provider of insurance to entities and individuals with professional liability, general liability, managed care and/or stop loss coverage and workers' compensation insurance in Michigan, Minnesota, Illinois, Ohio, Kentucky, Indiana, and Tennessee. Having extensive experience in healthcare risk management, quality improvement, utilization management, medical staff affairs, and legal matters since 1981, Mr. Trosty, as Director of Risk Management is responsible for the provision and direction of all risk management services for insured physicians, clinics, managed care organizations, hospitals, nursing homes, transitional facilities, and small and medium size businesses. He manages a staff of 18 professionals including consultants, support staff, and data coordinators. In addition, he is responsible for program development, evaluation and implementation; proposal preparation and implementation; selection and direction of third party administrator services that are used to augment employed staff; seminar development and presentation; staff representative to Risk Management and Continuing Medical Education Committees of Board of Directors; new product identification and development, and provision of related legal services. **Career Steps:** Director of Risk Management, Michigan Physicians Mutual Liability Company (MPMLC) and Stratton–Cheeseman Management Company (1994–Present); Continental Insurance Health Care, Senior Health Care Consultant (1993–1994); Vice President of Quality, Risk and Insurance Management; Senior Vice President of MSJ Insurance Company; Vice President, Novare Services, Inc. (1987–1993); Director of Risk Management and Quality Assurance, Lutheran Hospitals and Homes Society (1986–1987); Director of Risk Management and Safety, and In–House Legal Counsel, MultiCare Medical Center (1985–1986); Director of Risk Management and Environmental Services, Ohio Hospital Association (1983–1985); Administrative Assistant, University of Cincinnati Hospitals (1982–1983); City of Cincinnati: Director/Founder (1976–1981), Coordinator/Supervisor (1974–1976); Attorney, Pharmacy and Hospital Employees Local (1972–1974); Reginald Heber Smith Legal Fellow, Nassau County Legal Services (1970–1972). **Associations & Accomplishments:** American Society for Healthcare Risk Management: Past President, Recipient, Distinguished Service Award for Risk Management; American Hospital Association, Task Force on Tort Reform and Risk Management Legislation; National Infusion Safety Consortium; National Anesthesia Information Consortium; Editorial Review Board, "Anesthesia Malpractice Protector"; Editorial Advisory Board, "Hospital Risk Management"; American College of Emergency Physicians, Risk Management Task Force and Publication Committee; Catholic Health Association, Quality Assurance and Risk Management Task Force; Who's Who Worldwide; Panelist, American Hospital Association Teleconference; American Society of Law and Medicine; Risk and Insurance Management Society; American Association of Hospital Attorneys; National Association of Healthcare Quality; American College of Healthcare Executives; Frequent publisher and lecturer at international, national, state and local conferences and institutional symposia and proceedings. **Education:** University of Cincinnati, M.S. in Health Administration/Planning (1983); Washington College of Law at American University, J.D. (1970); Harpur College, B.A. (1967). **Personal:** Mr. Trosty enjoys tennis, antiquing, and racquetball.

Marcia L. Ward, C.P.C.U.
Associate Manager
Prudential Property and Casualty Insurance Company
814 Commerce Drive
Oak Brook, IL 60521–1965
(708) 572–8431
Fax: (708) 368–4525

6331

Business Information: Prudential Insurance Company is an international personal lines insurance company, also providing investment and retirement instruments such as mutual funds and annuities. Prudential Property and Casualty Insurance Company, a subsidiary of Prudential, is rated in the top 15 Property and Casualty insurers. With twenty–three years of experience in the insurance industry, Ms. Ward joined Prudential Insurance in 1972. Currently serving as Associate Manager for the region, she is responsible for the design of field training and materials and conducting training (specific and groups) in eighteen states, in addition to overseeing underwriting compliance of state insurance regulations for ten states. A current project includes developing a business continuation plan for disaster planning. Additionally, Ms. Ward has taught insurance classes for the Insurance School of Chicago since 1989. **Career Steps:** Associate Manager, Prudential Insurance (1972–Present). **Associations & Accomplishments:** Society of Insurance Trainers and Educators; Former President, Hinsdale, IL Junior Woman's Club; Volunteer, Philanthropic Organization; American Institute of Insurance, CPCU designation. **Education:** Augustana College, B.A. in English (1971); Attended John Marshall Law School. **Personal:** Two children: Sarah and Barbara. Ms. Ward enjoys travel and reading.

Todd Zalucha
Assistant Manager
State Farm Insurance
100 State Farm Place
Ballston Spa, NY 12020–3722
(518) 884–5402
Fax: Please mail or call

6331

Business Information: State Farm Insurance is a full–service health, life, property and auto insurance company. Established in 1922, the State Farm Office serving upper New York State and all of the New England States currently employs 32 people. As Assistant Manager, Mr. Zalucha is responsible for the management of technical support for all data processing systems, operations, claims, and agency sales in the region, as well as all in–house training and lecturing. Like his father who was also in the Insurance business, Mr. Zalucha wanted a career that would change daily and always provide a challenge. **Career Steps:** State Farm: Assistant Manager (1994–Present), Supervisor (1988–1994), Management Trainee (1987–1988), Computer Technician (1986–1987). **Education:** University of Northern Colorado, B.S. in Management Information Systems (1986). **Personal:** Married to Kristy in 1989. Mr. Zalucha enjoys running, skiing, biking, weightlifting, and basketball.

Dianne L. Hrehor
Secretary/Treasurer
BDH Associates, Inc.
620 Hillcrest Road, Suite 400
Lilburn, GA 30247
(770) 564–2999
Fax: (770) 564–9327
EMAIL: See Below

6351

Business Information: BDH Associates, Inc. is a self–contained insurance agency specializing in fidelity and surety bonding. The Company provides its services throughout Georgia. As Secretary/Treasurer, Ms. Hrehor is responsible for all office work and accounting, supervising staff, banking relationships, and underwriting bond risks. Internet users can also reach her via: BDH @ mindspring.com. **Career Steps:** Secretary/Treasurer, BDH Associates, Inc. (1991–Present); Office Manager and Accountant, Trosby, Inc. (1988–1991); Office Manager and Accountant, King Hardware, Inc. (1985–1988). **Associations & Accomplishments:** Surety Association of Georgia. **Education:** Aurora University, B.A. in Business Administration and Computer Programming (1985); Waubonsee Community College: A.S. in Early Childhood Development, A.S. in Computer Science. **Personal:** Married to Robert G. in 1967. Two children: Donald J. and Robert M. Ms. Hrehor enjoys reading, sewing, and home decoration.

John Knox Jr.
Owner and President
Universal Surety of America
P.O. Box 1068
Houston, TX 77251–1068
(713) 722–4646
Fax: (713) 722–4684

6351

Business Information: Universal Surety of America is an insurance brokerage specializing in property surety bonding. Established in 1984, Universal Surety of America reports assets of $18 million and currently employs 52 people. As Owner and President, Mr. Knox is responsible for all aspects of operations, including the oversight of the insurance companies that insures properties. Concurrent with his position at University Surety of America, he is the owner of a variety of businesses. **Career Steps:** Owner and President, Universal Surety of America (1984–Present). **Associations & Accomplishments:** Former Chairman and Board Member, National Association of Independent Sureties; Texas Coalition of Independent Sureties. **Education:** East Texas State University. **Personal:** Married to Linda S. Knox in 1985. Three children: JT, Stephen, and David.

Serge L. Poisson
Executive Assistant to the CEO
The Canadian Surety Company
2200 Yonge Street, Suite 1200
Toronto, Ontario M4S 2C6
(416) 440–7780
Fax: (416) 489–3821

6351

Business Information: Canadian Surety is a Canadian insurance company, specializing in providing a wide range of non–life products. A subsidiary of the global insurance conglomerate – AGF Group (based in Europe), Canadian Surety Company reports annual revenues of $200 million and currently employs 400 people. As Executive Assistant, Mr. Poisson reports directly to the Chief Executive Officer and is responsible for Shareholder's reporting, corporate planning, major reports coordination, and board preparation. He also serves as liaison between the Toronto office and the European corporate headquarters, as well as other NAFTA groups in Mexico, U.S. and Canada. **Career Steps:** Executive Assistant, Canadian Surety Company (1994–Present); Management Controller, AGF International (1992–1994). **Associations & Accomplishments:** Friends of the Canadian Opera Company; United Way; Interviewed in European business magazines; Fluent in English, French, German, and Italian (learning). **Education:** European Management Programme (Spain, France, U.K.), M.B.A. (1991); University of Paris – Dauphine, B.B.A., M.S. in General Management. **Personal:** Mr. Poisson enjoys jogging, biking, skiing, opera, and concerts.

Patrick H. Ballog
Area Sales Manager
G.E. Mortgage Insurance Company
445 Hutchinson Avenue, Suite 970
Columbus, OH 43235–5677
(614) 438–5248
Fax: (614) 523–1416

6361

Business Information: G.E. Mortgage Insurance Company, a wholly–owned subsidiary of G. E. Capital, is a mortgage insurance provider. Mr. Ballog began his career with G.E. Mortgage in 1978. Promoted to Area Sales Manager, he now supervises 12 sales representatives in Ohio, Michigan, Indiana, and Kentucky branches. He is also responsible for training new representatives, administrative advisement, and customer service functions. **Career Steps:** Area Sales Manager, G.E. Mortgage Insurance Company (1978–Present); President, Peoples Savings and Loan (1974–1978); Vice President, Community National Bank (1969–1974). **Associations & Accomplishments:** Masonic Lodge; Ohio Mortgage Brokers; Colorado Mortgage Brokers; Toledo Mortgage Brokers; Cleveland Mortgage Brokers; Dayton Mortgage Brokers; Cinncinati Mortgage Brokers; Trustee, Ohio Mortgage Brokers Liaison Committee; Former Basketball Official – Ohio Valley; Former City Council Member – Flushing, Ohio. **Education:** Ohio University, Business Administration; Ohio School of Banking; Ohio State Loan School; Various courses through work: IBM, PSS, GE's and MPG–Advanced Mortgage Banking. **Personal:** Married to Vikki in 1966. Three children: Lynn, Jamie and Jason. Mr. Ballog enjoys reading, golf and outdoor activities.

Nancy Short Ferguson

Attorney
Lawyers Title Insurance Corporation
*1713 Madison Avenue
Greensboro, NC 27403
(910) 370–4496
Fax: (910) 370–4650*

6361

Business Information: Lawyers Title Insurance Corporation is a title insurance firm issuing insurance policies, insuring status of title to real estate, insuring lenders, owners, leasees and others. Established in 1926, Lawyers Title Insurance Corporation reports premium assets in excess of $5 million and currently employs 50 people. The Greensboro office was established in 1986, reports premiums of $1.2 million and currently employs 8 people. Admitted to practice in North Carolina state courts, Ms. Ferguson joined the Firm in 1990 as Attorney. She is responsible for providing legal advice regarding insurability of title problems and affirmative coverages available. **Career Steps:** Attorney, Lawyers Title Insurance Corporation (1990–Present); Counsel, Woodlake Partners/Development (1987–1990); Attorney, Short Campbell & Ferguson (1986–1987); Attorney, McLawhorn & Short (1983–1987). **Associations & Accomplishments:** Professional Women's Consortium; Quota International; North Carolina State Bar; North Carolina Bar Association – Real Property and Environmental Sections; Greensboro Bar Association: Chair of Community Involvement–Habitat for Humanity Committee, Past Chairman of Real Property Section; Speaker at various CLE functions; Articles published in internal corporate newsletters. **Education:** University of North Carolina at Chapel Hill, J.D. in Law (1983), B.S. (1980); Wake Forest University, currently in M.B.A. Executive Program – expected graduation in 1996. **Personal:** Married to Alan Earl Ferguson in 1986. Ms. Ferguson enjoys hiking, reading, travel, and gardening.

James Litwiller

Director of Marketing
Land Title of Nevada
*720 South 7th Street
Las Vegas, NV 89101
(702) 227–8579
Fax: (702) 251–7973*

6361

Business Information: Land Title of Nevada specializes in providing escrow services and title insurance to lenders and individuals to protect real property investments. Regional in scope, the Company has six locations which market the importance of title policies, and prepares preliminary reports and tax information for real estate agencies. Established in 1976, the Company employs 140 people. As Director of Marketing, Mr. Litwiller oversees all sales and marketing activities and handles all applicable administration and operational duties. He is also responsible for public relations, customer service, and strategic planning. **Career Steps:** Director of Marketing, Land Title of Nevada (1981–Present). **Associations & Accomplishments:** National Association of Home Builders; Southern Nevada Home Builders; Southern Nevada Mortgage Brokers; Southern Nevada Mortgage Bankers; Association of Professional Mortgage Women; Women's Council of Realtors. **Education:** Bluffton College, B.Sc. (1968). **Personal:** Mr. Litwiller enjoys golf, hockey, football, and Company functions.

Jorge E. Rodriguez

Founder and Director
International Land Title Company
*9051–C Siempre Viva Road, Suite 40–465
San Diego, CA 92173
52–114–30830
Fax: 52–114–31008*

6361

Business Information: International Land Title Company, established in 1990, is a title insurance company providing U.S. title insurance through Lawyer's Title Insurance Corporation throughout the country of Mexico. As Founder and Director, Mr. Rodriguez is responsible for all aspects of operations. **Career Steps:** Founder and Director, International Land Title Company (1988–Present); Administrator, Rancho San Lucas (1985–1988). **Associations & Accomplishments:** Presidential Task Force for President Ronald Reagan's Re–Election Campaign; International Students Board; Former professional tennis player. **Personal:** Mr. Rodriguez enjoys tennis, golf, and soccer.

Lance Rubachko, CFP, CLU, ChFC

Senior Partner
Tax and Financial Group
*4001 MacArthur Boulevard
Newport Beach, CA 92660
(714) 223–8100
Fax: (714) 223–8101*

6361

Business Information: Providing a full range of insurance services to clients throughout Southern California, Tax and Financial Group specializes in estate planning and protection. Established in 1965 and currently employing 140 people, the Agency has total premium sales of $30 million. Consulting primarily with wealthy clients on behalf of their estate, Mr. Lance Rubachko serves as Senior Partner of the Agency. He offers clients the best method of discounting their estate taxes and protect the estates for future generations. **Career Steps:** Senior Partner, Tax and Financial Group (1982–Present). **Associations & Accomplishments:** National Association of Life Underwriters; Chartered Life Underwriter Association; College For Financial Planning; Make A Wish Foundation. **Education:** California State University – Fullerton, B.S. in Finance (1982); CERTFICATIONS: Certified Financial Planner – Denver, CO; Chartered Life Underwriter – Bryn Mawr, PA; Chartered Financial Consultant – Bryn Mawr, PA.. **Personal:** Married to Crystal in 1985. Two children: Russell and Robin. Mr. Rubachko enjoys spending time with his family.

W. Jeffry Stein

Counsel for Central Florida Area
Lawyers Title Insurance Corp.
*130 South Orange Avenue, Suite 200
Orlando, FL 32801–3230
(407) 425–3431
Fax: (407) 841–9313*

6361

Business Information: Lawyers Title Insurance Corporation, established in 1925, is a title insurance underwriter. Admitted to practice in Florida, Mr. Stein joined Lawyers Title Insurance Corporation as Counsel for the Central Florida Area in 1995. He is responsible for providing support to branches and agents with questions on business and underwriting issues. Concurrent with his position, he does mediation on a pro bono basis for the Orange County Bar Association and is a certified Circuit Court Mediator. **Career Steps:** Counsel for Central Florida Area, Lawyers Title Insurance Corporation (1995–Present); Claims Counsel, Chicago Title/Ticor Title (1986–1995); Commonwealth Land Title: Claims Council (1985–1986), Underwriting Counsel (1984–1985). **Associations & Accomplishments:** Central Florida President, American Corporate Counsel Association; Orange County Bar Association; Florida Bar Association; American Bar Association; Published numerous trade publications and oral presentations. **Education:** Florida State University, J.D. (1980); University of Florida, B.A.; Indian River Community College, A.A. **Personal:** Married to Daryl Bean in 1985. Mr. Stein enjoys breeding, training and riding horses (wife is a farrier and owns a horse farm), building & racing cars, and photography.

Aletha L. (Campbell) Waller

Vice President and District Manager
Southeast Title Group, Inc.
*500 SE Fort King Street
Ocala, FL 34471–2238
(352) 351–3600
Fax: (352) 351–1969*

6361

Business Information: Southeast Title Group, Inc. is a State–wide Independent Real Estate Title Insurance Agency. Ms. Waller joined the Company as a Manager in 1994, moving into her present positions as Vice President and District Manager in January of 1996. She is responsible for the supervision of five district offices in Gainesville, Jacksonville, Invernes, Ocala, and Keystone Heights, Florida. Reporting directly to the corporate leadership, she administers all staff hiring activities, growth enhancement practices, and marketing functions. **Career Steps:** Southeast Title Group, Inc.: Vice President and District Manager (1996–Present), Manager (1994–1996); Mortgage Production Manager, Mid–State Federal Savings Bank (1989–1993); Branch Manager, Citizens Federal Savings and Loan, Pinellas County (1981 – acquired by Glendale Federal Savings and Loan in 1984). **Associations & Accomplishments:** Secretary, Women's Council of Realtors – Ocala Chapter; Chamber of Commerce – Ocala, Florida; Affiliate Member, Board of Realtors Marion County; Former Board Member, Chamber of Commerce – Pinellas County; March of Dimes (Coordinator of Activities, 1984). **Education:** Attended, Rio Grande College – Rio Grande Ohio, Education Major. **Personal:** Married to Curtis W. in 1991. Two children: Dustin Shane Campbell and Curtis Reed Waller. Ms. Waller enjoys fishing, hunting, reading, and walking.

Linda K. Wharton

Operations Manager
United States Title
*11 North Brentwood Boulevard
Clayton, MO 63105
(314) 727–2900
Fax: (314) 727–7414*

6361

Business Information: U.S. Title is the largest independent title insurance company in St. Louis. The Company specializes in closing both residential and commercial real estate transactions. As Operation Manager, Ms. Wharton is responsible for managing the Company's largest customer account, as well as daily operations of all 13 satellite offices and 44 employees. **Career Steps:** Operation Manager, U.S. Title (1993–Present); Escrow Manager (1986–1993); Membership Director, Equitable Relocation (1984–1986); Assistant Vice President & District Manager, Steuart Title Guarity (1982–1984). **Associations & Accomplishments:** St. Louis Board of Realtors; Missouri Land Title Association; American Land Title Association; Habitat for Humanity; Realtors Assistant Housing Fund. **Education:** UMKC, B.A. (1986); Real Estate School. **Personal:** Two children: Jake and Nick. Ms. Wharton enjoys snow skiing, golf, and being a church youth group sponsor.

Donald W. Fuller, CLU

Director of Training
VALIC
*2919 Allen Parkway L6–01
Houston, TX 77019
(713) 831–6074
Fax: (713) 831–4939*

6371

Business Information: VALIC is a financial services organization providing retirement programs to employees of not–for–profit organizations, including universities, hospitals, schools and municipal government offices. As Director of Training, Mr. Fuller is responsible for the training and development of field sales representatives and managers. **Career Steps:** Director of Training, VALIC (1994–Present); Vice President of Marketing Services, Banner Life Insurance Co. (1993–1994); Assistant Vice President of Field Development, Acacia Group (1977–1992). **Associations & Accomplishments:** American Society of CLU; American Society of Training & Development. **Education:** George Mason University (1972); LIMRA Leadership Institute Fellow.

Jane K. Hatton

Chief Financial Officer
United Services Advisors, Inc.
*7900 Callaghan Road
San Antonio, TX 78229–2327
(210) 308–1234
Fax: (210) 308–1220*

6371

Business Information: United Services Advisors, Inc. is a mutual fund and investment advice firm. Established in 1968, the Firm currently employs 100 people. As Chief Financial Officer, Ms. Hatton is responsible for all aspects of accounting and financial statements, internal and external. In the future Ms. Hatton would like to utilize her talents in business and accounting to teach aspiring young minds. **Career Steps:** United Services Advisors, Inc.: Chief Financial Officer (1994–Present), Accounting Manager (1992–1994); Senior Auditor, Price Waterhouse LLP **Associations & Accomplishments:** American Institute of Certified Public Accountants; Texas Society of Certified Public Accountants; Executive Women's Golf Association. **Education:** Trinity University, B.S. in Business (1989). **Personal:** Married to Peter Jr. in 1989. Ms. Hatton enjoys golf, racquetball, basketball, reading and shopping.

Cynthia L. Lambert

Vice President/Team Leader
W.E. Stanley & Company
*300 E. Wendover Avenue
Greensboro, NC 27401
(910) 273–9492
Fax: (910) 273–9491
EMail: See Below*

6371

Business Information: W.E. Stanley & Company is a third–party administrator of Employee Benefit Plans, specifically Defined Contribution, Defined Benefit, Section 125, and Non–qualified Plans. As Vice President/Team Leader, Ms. Lambert supervises three analysts, reviews allocations, acts as a client liaison, as well as administering her own clients' allocations. Additionally, she is active in the decisions of the Defined Contribution Department. Internet users can reach her via: CLLAMBERT@prodigy.com. **Career Steps:** W.E. Stanley & Company: Vice President/Team Leader (1996–Present), Team Leader (1994–Present), Senior Analyst (1989–Present). **Associations & Accomplishments:** Currently pursuing Qualified Pension Administrator designation though American Society of Pension Actuaries. **Education:** Appalachian State University, B.S. in Mathematics (1982). **Personal:** Ms. Lambert enjoys travel, calligraphy, and reading.

William Miller
President
First Financial Resources
13910 Laurel Lakes Avenue
Laurel, MD 20707–5084
(301) 470–2220
Fax: (301) 490–1341

6371

Business Information: First Financial Resources is an independent insurance and benefit planning company. The Company works closely with Owners, Boards, and Senior Officers to establish business succession, Executive benefits and employee benefits. First Financial represents over 1,000 private and 32 public companies providing executive benefit planning. Mr. Miller has represented the firms clients in consulting and negotiating acquisition and expansion plans in Europe and throughout North America. As President and Chief Executive Officer, Mr. Miller is responsible for all aspects of operations, including working directly with a team of professionals to serve the clients in the best manner possible. Concurrent with his position at First Financial, Mr. Miller is also the president and Chief Executive Officer of Benefits Resources, Inc., an employee benefit company. Established in 1978, First Financial Resources employs 25 people. **Career Steps:** President, First Financial Resources, Inc. (1978–Present); President and Chief Executive Officer, Benefits Resources, Inc. (1987–Present); Board of Directors, Providence Hospital, Washington, D.C. (1983–1992). **Associations & Accomplishments:** Colonial Williamsburg Foundation, Honorary Citizen; National Historic Trust, Patron; Rotary International; Civitan International; Committee of 100, Florida State University (1972–1975); Antique Collectors Society; Chair, Life Underwriters Training Council; Published in Financial Planner Magazine and Life Insurance Selling Magazine; Numerous speaking appearances. **Education:** Florida State University (1969); Dale Carnegie: Course (1968), Instructor (1969–1975); Purdue University, Advanced Insurance Program (1987); The American College; Hubener School (1992). **Personal:** Married to Margaret McPhail in 1981. Five children: Tammy, Jodi, Brian, Chris and Ray II. Mr. Miller enjoys collecting antiques and vintage cars, golf, walking, racquetball, and travel.

Kay Adam
Vice President and Counsel
Great–West Life and Annuity Insurance Company
8515 East Orchard Road, Tower 2
Englewood, CO 80112
(303) 689–3816
Fax: (303) 689–3827
EMAIL: See Below

6399

Business Information: Great West Life and Annuity Insurance Company, a wholly–owned Canadian–based agency, is the U.S. arm providing commercial insurance products as follows: Group Life, Health Care Plans, HMO and cafeteria packages. A practicing attorney since 1976, Kay Adam serves as Associate Vice President and Counsel with GWLI's Englewood, Colorado law division. Her duties involve all legal transactions, representing U.S. interests in agency acquisitions, personnel litigation and intellectual property matters. Internet users can reach her via: KAAD@GWZ.COM. **Career Steps:** Great West Life and Annuity Insurance Company: Vice President and Counsel (1992–Present), Assistant Vice President and Associate Counsel (1989–1992); Associate Counsel, Security Benefit Life (1985). **Associations & Accomplishments:** American Bar Association; Colorado Bar Association; Girl Scouts. **Education:** Washburn School of Law, J.D. (1976); Kansas State University: M.S. (1968), B.A. (1964). **Personal:** Married to Fred B. in 1961. Two children: Jared and Lindsey.

Larry Andreano, CMA, ARM, MBA
National Accounts Executive
Liberty Mutual Group
26200 Town Center Drive, Suite 200
Novi, MI 48375–1233
(800) 537–0822
Fax: Please mail or call

6399

Business Information: Liberty Mutual Group is an international insurance and financial services company, providing insurance, claims services, managed care, loss control consulting, and financial services. International in scope, the Liberty Mutual Group has over 100 locations around the globe. As a National Accounts Executive, Mr. Andreano is responsible for the sales and management of large accounts which usually fall into the Fortune 500 or Fortune 1000 rankings. **Career Steps:** Liberty Mutual Group: National Accounts Executive (1994–Present), Director of Special Projects (1992–1994), Division Financial Manager (1990–1992); Corporate Finance Analyst (1988–1990), Financial Analyst (1986–1988); Strategic Planning Analyst, Standard Oil of Ohio (BP) (1985–1986); Air Traffic Controller, Federal Aviation Administration (1980–1981); Air Traffic Controller, U.S. Air Force (1976–1980). **Education:** Case Western Reserve University, M.B.A. (1986); Youngstown State University, B.S. in Business Administration; University of Albuquerque, A.S. in Air Traffic Control. **Personal:** Married to Nancy in 1988. Two children: Tom and Jacqueline. Mr. Andreano enjoys spending time with his family, sailing, woodworking, and investing activities.

Jorge R. Anglada Lasa
Attorney
El Fenix
12 Ave. Parque De Los Ninos, Cond Chalets #153
Guaynabo, Puerto Rico 00969
(809) 793–7290
Fax: (809) 782–2858

6399

Business Information: El Fenix provides diversified insurance products to commercial and professional individuals and companies throughout Puerto Rico, primarily focusing in the area of professional liability coverages. A practicing attorney since 1990 in Puerto Rico, Mr. Anglada Lasa provides all legal support for the Corporation. Areas of expertise include litigation, malpractice defense, business law, personal injury law, insurance law, torts and arbitration. **Career Steps:** General Counsel, El Fenix (1993–Present); Sole Practitioner, Rafael Anglada Lopez Law Office (1991–1993). **Associations & Accomplishments:** Puerto Rico Bar Association. **Education:** InterAmerican University, J.D. (1990); University of Puerto Rico, B.A. in Political Science, magna cum laude. **Personal:** Married to Maria M. Acevedo in 1991. Mr. Anglada Lasa enjoys tennis and scuba diving.

Teresa Bohne
In–House Counsel
TIG Insurance Company
5205 O'Connor
Irving, TX 75039–3712
(214) 831–5123
Fax: (214) 831–5177

6399

Business Information: TIG Insurance Company is a national insurance company, providing insurance coverage from ten locations nationwide. TIG Insurance Company's home office is located in Irving, Texas. A practicing attorney in Texas courts since 1990, Ms. Bohne joined TIG Insurance Company as In–House Counsel in 1993. She is responsible for analyzing, assisting, researching, and counseling the Company representatives, regarding litigation of insurance coverage and other large exposure cases, as well as providing assistance and counseling in underwriting. Her practice concentrates on commercial general liability, commercial excess, and sport/entertainment, personal, and professional liability. **Career Steps:** In–House Counsel, TIG Insurance Company (1993–Present); Associate, Cowles & Thompson (1990–1993). **Associations & Accomplishments:** Tort and Insurance Practice Association, American Bar Association; Co–Chair, Racial Awareness Committee, Dallas Young Lawyer's Association; Author, Speaker, Continuing Legal Education Programs; Author, Speaker, In–House Seminars; Assistant Coach (1990–1993), SMU Moot Court Teams. **Education:** Baylor Law School, J.D. (1990); Baylor University, B.B.A. (1986). **Personal:** Ms. Bohne enjoys running, lifting weights, and her cocker spaniel.

Angelica T. Cantlon
Vice President Human Resources
Orion Capital Companies
9 Farm Springs Drive
Farmington, CT 06032
(203) 674–6610
Fax: Please mail or call

6399

Business Information: Orion Capital Companies is an international insurance company focusing on specialty markets. As Vice President Human Resources, Mrs. Cantlon is responsible for restructural design, downsizing, compensation and benefits, all general functions, staff relations, and payroll. She is on the Orion Leadership Team along with eleven of her co-workers. **Career Steps:** Vice President Human Resources, Orion Capital Companies (1994–Present); Director of Human Resources North America, Avon Products, Inc. (1985–1994); Manager of Health Cost Benefits, Southern New England Telephone (1982–1985); Director of Health Promotions, American Health Foundation (1975–1982). **Associations & Accomplishments:** Human Resource Planning Society; Board Member, Junior Achievement of Connecticut, Greater Hartford. **Education:** New York University, M.A. (1975); Marymount College, B.S. (1973). **Personal:** Married to Edward J. in 1973. Two children: Lauren and Matthew. Mrs. Cantlon enjoys hiking, running, and spending time with her children.

Matthew J. Chrupcala
Vice President of Personal Insurance Division
Kaplan–Walker Insurance Services
2719 Sheraton Drive
Macon, GA 31298
(912) 746–4921 (800) 334–2761
Fax: (912) 745–2442

6399

Business Information: Kaplan–Walker Insurance Services is an insurance sales agency providing insurance of all types, including underwriting accident, life, and health insurance. Established in 1945, Kaplan–Walker Insurance Services currently employs 42 people. As Vice President of Personal Insurance Division, Mr. Chrupcala is responsible for all aspects of personal insurance matters, as well as accounting responsibilities. **Career Steps:** Vice President of Personal Insurance Division, Kaplan–Walker Insurance Services (1994–Present); Travelers Insurance Companies: Managing Consultant (1992–1994), Financial Control Examiner (1990–1992). **Associations & Accomplishments:** Professional Insurance Agents (PIA); Young Professional Council (YPC). **Education:** Roger Williams University, B.S. (1985); Insurance Institute of America, Accredited Advisor of Insurance. **Personal:** Married to Kerrin Chrupcala in 1993. Mr. Chrupcala enjoys athletics, reading, and travel.

Ms. Catherine J. Colburn
Senior Vice President
Colburn – Bertholon – Rowland
200 East State Street
Media, PA 19063
(610) 565–3450
Fax: (610) 565–0711

6399

Business Information: Colburn – Bertholon – Rowland is a professional association which provides insurance administration to professionals. As Senior Vice President, Ms. Colburn is responsible for all aspects of operations and she serves as a political figurehead for the organization. Established in 1936, Colburn – Bertholon – Rowland employs 200 people with annual sales of $200 million. **Career Steps:** Senior Vice President, Colburn – Bertholen – Rowland (1984–Present); Corporate Sales, CIGNA (INA) (1980–1984). **Associations & Accomplishments:** AIPA-GIA (1995–1996); President, American Institute of Professionals; Member, Association Group Insurance Administrators; Board Member, PIMA – Professional Insurance Mass Marketing Association. **Education:** Wharton Business School University of Pennsylvania, M.B.A.; Dickinson College at Carlisle, PA, B.A.(1977); Lancaster University at Lancaster, England (1975–1976). **Personal:** Ms. Colburn enjoys golf, sailing, theatre, and travel.

Salvador DaCunha
Vice President
CIGNA International
One Datran Center, Suite 1807, 9100 South Dadeland Boulevard
Miami, FL 33156
(305) 670–9935
Fax: (305) 670–3106

6399

Business Information: CIGNA International is an insurance company specializing in individual life, accident, and health insurance. As Vice President, Mr. DaCunha is responsible for business transactions involving life, accident or health insurance and specializes in direct marketing of insurance products and services, corporate accident, and payroll deduction. **Career Steps:** Vice President, CIGNA International (1994–Present); Regional Manager – Latin America, American International Group (1988–1994). **Associations & Accomplishments:** Direct Marketing Association. **Education:** Bentley College, B.S. in Marketing Management – Minor in International Business (1982). **Personal:** Married to Roslyn in 1986. Two children: Thiago and Stefano. Mr. DaCunha enjoys tennis, water skiing, and snow skiing.

William R. Ennenbach

General Manager
Arab Commercial Enterprises
P.O. Box 2474
Safat, Kuwait 13025
(965) 241–2613
Fax: (965) 240–9450
6399

Business Information: Arab Commercial Enterprises is an international insurance brokerage agency with 17 offices throughout the Middle East, Greece, and France. Established in 1959, the Kuwaiti headquarters employs 10 people and reports estimated premium revenue of $2.5 million corporate–wide. As General Manager, Mr. Ennenbach is responsible for the operation of the Kuwait office, including diversified administrative and operations activities. **Career Steps:** General Manager, Arab Commercial Enterprises (1991–Present); Sedgwick James of New York: New Business Development (1989–92), International Department (1985–89); Instructor, University of Colorado – Boulder (1979–84). **Associations & Accomplishments:** President, American Business Council (1995–Present); New York Brokers Association (1988–92); Western Political Science Association (1980–84); Foreign Policy Advisor, Carlos Lucero Senatorial Campaign (1983–84). **Education:** University of Colorado, Fellowship (1979–84); Eastern Illinois University: M.A. (1979), B.A. (1979). **Personal:** Married to Hiba Lamia in 1990. Two children: Joanna Aida and Mounir William. Mr. Ennenbach enjoys jogging, tennis, and reading.

Melanie S. Evans

Vice President
Leader Services, Inc.
P.O. Box 275
Memphis, TN 38101
(901) 578–4392
Fax: (901) 578–4348
6399

Business Information: Leader Services, Inc., a subsidiary of Leader Federal Bank and Savings, provides insurance benefits and services for LFBS' customers, (both private individual and corporate). Recently merging with Union Planters Bank, Leader Federal Bank and Savings operates throughout the state of Tennessee, reporting assets in excess of $3 billion. As Vice President with the Memphis branch location, Melanie Evans is responsible for diversified administrative activities, primarily focusing in the areas of sales and operations management, product development and strategies. **Career Steps:** Vice President, Leader Services, Inc. (1986–Present). **Associations & Accomplishments:** Professional Insurance Agents Association; Sustaining Member and Former President, Institute of Financial Education; Professional Insurance Marketing Association; Financial Institute of Insurance Associates. **Education:** University of Memphis, M.B.A. (1994); Arkansas State University, B.S. in Finance. **Personal:** Ms. Evans enjoys music and vocal performing.

Mr. Joseph F. Goellner, Sr.

Vice President
Boynton Brothers & Company, Inc.
200 Jefferson Street
Perth Amboy, NJ 08862
(908) 442–3300
Fax: (908) 442–3813
6399

Business Information: Boynton Brothers & Company, Inc., in operation since 1892 as a specialist in professional insurance services, represents many insurance carriers. In his current capacity, Mr. Goellner is responsible for Company operations in the areas of Finance and Electronic Data Processing. Mr. Goellner has a diverse background in many industries including Manufacturing, Banking, EDP, and Professional Service. He has extensive experience in Management and Systems Consulting, as well as Mergers & Acquisitions and is a licensed Property & Casualty and Group Health Producer. **Career Steps:** Vice President, Boynton Brothers & Company, Inc. (1987–Present); Vice President of Finance, New Jersey Educational Computer Network, Inc. (1983–1987); Vice President of Marketing, Hypertek, Inc. (1981–1983). **Associations & Accomplishments:** MENSA; MENSA – SIG Central Jersey Chapter; Data Processing Management Association; National Accountants Association; Rider University Alumni Association; Registered Republican. **Education:** Rider University, M.B.A. Degree in Finance (1974); Rider University, B.S. Degree in Finance (1972). **Personal:** Married since 1990 to Diana. Four children: Joseph Jr., Nadine, Nicole, and Arielle. Mr. Goellner enjoys weightlifting, chess, classical music, and application program in his leisure time.

Arthur C. Harris

Claims Attorney
General Reinsurance Corporation
95 Lafayette Street, #11
Stamford, CT 06902–3846
(203) 328–5397
Fax: (203) 328–6420
6399

Business Information: General Reinsurance Corporation provides insurance to various types of insurance companies. A licensed attorney since 1984, Mr. Harris joined GRC in 1990. As Claims Attorney, he concentrates on claims involving litigation of environmental and mass torts, as well as reinsurance coverage issues. **Career Steps:** Claims Attorney, General Reinsurance Corporation (1990–Present); Claim Legal Counsel, Bituminous Insurance Companies (1987–1990); State Farm Insurance Companies: Claim Specialist (1983–1987), Personal & Commercial Lines Underwriter (1975–1983). **Associations & Accomplishments:** Chartered Property Casualty Underwriters; Chartered Life Underwriters; American Bar Association; Missouri Bar Association. **Education:** University of Missouri at Columbia, J.D. (1983); University of Arkansas at Pine Bluff, B.S. (1975). **Personal:** Mr. Harris enjoys tennis, reading, basketball, movies, concerts, and karate.

Efthemia S. Hinman

Ergonomics and Industrial Hygiene Technical Specialist
Atlantic Mutual Company
3 Giralda Farms
Madison, NJ 07940
(201) 408–6115
Fax: (201) 408–6132
6399

Business Information: Atlantic Mutual Company is an insurance provider. An ergonomics specialist with over ten years expertise working with some of the nation's leading petroleum industries and insurance brokerages, Ms. Hinman was appointed to her current position at Atlantic Mutual in 1993. As Ergonomics and Industrial Hygiene Technical Specialist, Mrs. Hinman designs and implements policies regarding physical hazards, hygiene, and ergonomics. Additionally, she is responsible for 72 field representatives, develops and conducts training programs, and provides executive leadership. **Career Steps:** Economics and Industrial Hygiene Technical Specialist, Atlantic Mutual Company (1993–Present); Ergonomics Specialist, Marsh & McLennan (1991–1993); IN/Ergonomist, Exxon Biomedical Sciences, Inc. (1989–1992); Occupational Health & Safety Representative – Consumer Products, Chevron Chemical Company (1988–1989). **Associations & Accomplishments:** American Industrial Hygiene Association; American Standards Testing and Materials; Human Factor and Ergonomics; American Society of Safety Engineers. **Education:** West Virginia University: M.S.E. (1988), B.S.Ch.E. (1985). **Personal:** Married to Mark in 1992. One child: Anna Maria. Mrs. Hinman enjoys violin, piano, and designing clothes and crafts.

Lance S. James

Director, Business Management
Empire Insurance & Financial Service
1425 East Dublin Granville Road, Suite 102
Columbus, OH 43203–2079
(614) 436–5480
Fax: (614) 436–5481
6399

Business Information: Empire Insurance & Financial Services is a full–service insurance provider, specializing in Bona–fide fringe benefits to Federal contractors and their employees. As Director of Business Management, Mr. James is responsible for all functions of Company operations, including budget and payroll management, staff supervision, client interface, and special projects administration. He also holds a seat on the Board of Trustees. **Career Steps:** Director, Business Management, Empire Insurance & Financial Service (1994–Present); Assistant Manager/Bartender, Marble Gang Restaurant (1992–1994); Supervisor, AmeriFlora '92 (1992). **Associations & Accomplishments:** Work for Hunger; Tutors High School and College English. **Education:** Ohio State University, Business Administration (1995). **Personal:** Mr. James enjoys working out.

Mr. Marvin Kelly

Executive Director
Texas Property and Casualty Insurance Guaranty Association
9420 Research Boulevard, Suite 100
Austin, TX 78759
(512) 345–9335
Fax: (512) 795–0447
6399

Business Information: Texas Property and Casualty Insurance Guaranty Association is a private, nonprofit, unincorporated association of all Texas licensed property and casualty insurers. The guaranty fund system was created to protect the majority of claimants from loss when an insurance company fails. It provides insurance coverage up to a limit of $100,000, and pays statuatory workers compensation benefits. Texas has had a guaranty fund since 1970 operating under the state control of the Texas Department of Insurance Liquidation Division. It was privatized in 1992 under the direction of Marvin Kelly. Mr. Kelly reports to a 9–member board composed of 5 insurance company executives and 4 public members. His current operational budget is $6.7 million, with a claims budget of $270 million. His management team consists of 5 directors, 1 manager, 1 public affairs officer, an internal auditor, and an executive secretary. **Career Steps:** Executive Director, Texas Property and Casualty Insurance Guaranty Association (1992–Present); Risk Manager, City of Austin (1989–1992); Risk Manager, City of Beaumont (1986–1989); Commercial Lines Underwriter, Chubb & Son Insurance (1985–1986); Senior Casualty Underwriter, Transamerica Insurance Company (1980–1985). **Associations & Accomplishments:** Society of Chartered Property Casualty Underwriters; National Forum of Black Public Administrators; National Association of Insurance Commissioners; National Conference of Insurance Guaranty Associations; United States Army Reserve Program; Citizen Ambassador Program; Participant 1993 First Risk Management Delegation to Russia; 1995 First Education Science and Technology Delegation to South Africa; Developed First Owner Controlled Insurance/Surety Program in the Country for City of Austin (1990); Developed First Preferred Provider Program for the City of Beaumont (1989) and the City of Austin (1991); Active lecturer. **Education:** University of Hartford, B.S. (1979); Insurance Institute of America, obtained CPCU (1991), AU (1984); Finance Officers Basic Course, Diploma (1979). **Personal:** Married to Jacqueline H. Kelly in 1987. Two children: William and Marixa Kelly. Mr. Kelly enjoys family, church, and civil activities in his spare time.

Thomas M. Kerwin, C.P.C.U.

Risk Manager
Farmers Insurance Group
4680 Wilshire Boulevard
Los Angeles, CA 90010–3807
(213) 930–4269
Fax: (213) 936–8479
6399

Business Information: Founded in 1927, Farmers Insurance Group is now the fourth largest multi–line insurance company in the United States. With 14,000 current employees, it has estimated annual sales of $5 billion. Insurance product lines primarily consist of personal lines, home, auto, life, and commercial. As Risk Manager, Thomas Kerwin is responsible for the negotiation and acquisition of corporate insurance, identifying exposures and implementing corporate safety programs. **Career Steps:** Farmers Insurance Group: Risk Manager (1995–Present), Project Manager (1991–1995), State Agency Manager (1987–1990). **Associations & Accomplishments:** Society of Chartered Property and Casualty Underwriters; Risk and Insurance Management Society. **Education:** North Central College, B.A. in Accounting (1980); Chartered Property and Casualty Underwriter (1987); Insurance Institute of America, Certificate in Insurance. **Personal:** One child: Michelle. Mr. Kerwin enjoys golf, auto racing, and go–cart racing.

Maria A. Knowles

Director of Life and Health Underwriting and Issue
USAA Life Insurance Company
9800 Fredericksburg Road
San Antonio, TX 78288
(210) 498–6845
Fax: (210) 498–0364
6399

Business Information: USAA Life Insurance Company is a life and health insurance agency. Established in 1963, USAA currently employs 25 people. As Director of Life and Health Underwriting and Issue, Ms. Knowles manages all activities of the life and health underwriting staff, as well as researching industry trends to determine the impact of new products on underwriting, evaluating performances, and initiating actions to improve productivity and efficiency. **Career Steps:** USAA Life Insurance Company: Director of Life and Health Underwriting and Issue (1993–Present), Director of Service & Issues (1989–1993), Research Administrator (1989). **Associations & Accomplishments:** Fellow of Life Management Institute;

Central Texas Home Office Life Underwriters Association; Institute of Home Office Underwriters; Home Office of Life Underwriters Association. **Education:** Southwest Texas State University, B.A.A.S. (1985); Associate of the Academy of Life Underwriters. **Personal:** Married to Raymond in 1974. Three children: John, Thomas, and Raymond. Ms. Knowles enjoys golf, reading, camping, and gardening.

Thomas M. Kuzma, ARM
Vice President of Underwriting
Nautilus Insurance Company
7273 East Butherus Drive
Scottsdale, AZ 85260
(602) 951–0905
Fax: (602) 951–9730

6399

Business Information: Established in 1985, Nautilus Insurance Company, national in scope, is a commercial liability and property insurance provider specializing in Excess and Surplus Lines business. A 20–year veteran in the insurance industry, Mr. Kuzma was appointed Vice President in 1994. In his current capacity he is responsible for setting underwriting standards for coverages, pricing and product lines. To maximize returns, Company underwriting results need constant monitoring with periodic adjustments to those standards. Business is marketed through general agents nationwide. Effective communication to the general agent and maintaining underwriting controls are critical factors that have made Nautilus Insurance one of the top Excess and Surplus Lines carriers in the industry. Nautilus, with revenues over $60 million, is part of the W.R. Berkley Corporation of Greenwich, Connecticut, with group revenues over $1 billion. **Career Steps:** Nautilus Insurance Company: Vice President of Underwriting (1994–Present), Assistant Vice President (1989–1994); Great Southwest Insurance Company: Commercial Lines Manager (1984–1986), Agency Manager (1983–1984), Commercial Underwriter (1977–1983). **Associations & Accomplishments:** Arizona Insurance Information Association. **Education:** Arizona State University, B.S. (1977); Northern Illinois University; St. Joseph's College; Associate in Risk Management (ARM), Insurance Institute of America; College of Insurance Management Program. **Personal:** Married to Dana Lynn in 1983. Two children: Carly and Caty. Mr. Kuzma enjoys golf and reading in his leisure time.

Robert W. Lawrenz
Accounting Manager
American Agricultural Insurance Company
225 West Touhy Avenue
Park Ridge, IL 60068–4202
(312) 399–5700
Fax: (312) 399–5965

6399

Business Information: American Agricultural Insurance Company provides professional reinsurance to farmers. As Accounting Manager, Mr. Lawrenz is responsible for oversight of all aspects of accounting, including account management, supervision of sales representatives, and client interface. **Career Steps:** Accounting Manager, American Agricultural Insurance Company (1994–Present); Accounting Manager, Virginia Farm Bureau Mutual Insurance Company (1986–1994); Senior Accountant, Main Hurdman (1984–1986). **Associations & Accomplishments:** Kansas Society of Certified Public Accountants; American Institute of Certified Public Accountants. **Education:** Virginia Commonwealth University, M.B.A. (1993); Emporia State University, B.S. in Accounting. **Personal:** Married to Brenda in 1980. Two children: Brian and Lucas. Mr. Lawrenz is also a private pilot.

Mr. John T. Lensi, CLU, ChFC, RHU, RFC
Coporate Field Developer and Registered Securities Principal
Prudential Insurance Company of America
432 Washington Ave.
North Haven, CT 06473
(203) 234–7117 Ext. 114
Fax: (203) 234–9330

6399

Business Information: Prudential Insurance Company of America is a personal life insurance company, also providing investment and retirement instruments such as mutual funds and annuities. In his capacity as a "Field Developer" Mr. Lensi is responsible for the training and development of sales representatives and field sales management. Established in 1875, Prudential Insurance Company of America in South Windsor employs a staff of 60. **Career Steps:** Prudential Insurance Company of America, General Manager (1991–1996), Regional Field Developer–Corporate Training and Development

(1996–Present); Vice President of Mass Marketing, Corporate Benefit Systems, Lincoln National Life Insurance Company (1989– 1991); Regional Sales Director & Assistant Vice President, Security Connecticut Life Insurance Company (1987–1989); Vice President, Agency Operations, Banner Life Insurance Company (1986); Metlife Insurance (1974–1985). **Associations & Accomplishments:** General Agent and Managers Association; National Association of Life Underwriters; Society of Chartered Life Underwriters/Chartered Financial Consultants; International Association of Registered Financial Planners. **Education:** Central Connecticut State University, B.S. in Business Administration (1974); Chartered Financial Consultant, Certified Insurance Consultant, Chartered Life Underwriter, Registered Financial Consultant; Registered Health Underwriter.

Howard Lynch
• • • ◉ • • •
President
National Administrators, Inc.
2001 Marcus Avenue
Lake Success, NY 11042
(516) 352–7000
Fax: (516) 352–3135

6399

Business Information: National Administrators, Inc. is a marketer and administrator of associations and health insurance products. National Administrators, Inc. has four locations throughout the U.S. — New York (2), Vermont, and Nevada. Established in 1974, National Administrators, Inc. currently employs 26 people. As President, Mr. Lynch oversees all areas of Corporate operations. **Career Steps:** President, National Administrators, Inc. (1974–Present); President, The Lynch Group (1974–Present); Agent, Prudential (1964–1974). **Personal:** Married to Sharon in 1964. Three children: Marcy, Larry, and Alison. Mr. Lynch enjoys antique automobiles and sports.

Dan F. Middleton
Executive Director
a/e ProNet
2913 Pine Club Drive
Plant City, FL 33567
(813) 754–9299
Fax: (813) 754–9299
EMAIL: See Below

6399

Business Information: a/e ProNet is a national association of Insurance Agents and Brokers specializing in providing professional liability and risk management insurance for Architects, Engineers, and Surveyors. As Executive Director, Mr. Middleton manages the Association, plans and conducts meetings, and writes a quarterly newsletter bringing the membership up to date with industry changes. As an active insurance broker and Association member, Mr. Middleton was extremely successful in Ohio. After retiring as a broker, Mr. Middleton was honored to be chosen by the membership to become Executive Director. His long range plans are to expand the Association to all 50 of the United States. Internet users can reach him via: 76453.1153@Compuserve.com. **Career Steps:** Executive Director, a/e ProNet (1993–Present); Vice President/Sales, Willis Corroon Corporation (1955–1993). **Associations & Accomplishments:** Society of Chartered Property Casualty Underwriters; Plant City Historic Resources Board; Jaguar Association of Central Ohio; Member, Jaguar Drivers' Club, United Kingdom; Licensed Judge, Jaguar Clubs of North America for Concours de Elegance shows. **Education:** Ohio State University; Chartered Property and Casualty Underwriter (1963); Associate in Risk Management (1967). **Personal:** Married to Marilyn J. in 1958. Two children: Timothy I. and Suzanne M. Mr. Middleton enjoys historic preservation, restoration, and judging of vintage autos.

Richard R. Mourey
Director
ITT Hartford
200 Hopmeadow Street #C1
Weatogue, CT 06089–9625
(203) 843–8885
Fax: (203) 843–3221

6399

Business Information: ITT Hartford is a Fortune 500 company, providing insurance and employee benefit services nationally and internationally from two locations on the East and West Coast. Joining ITT Hartford in 1986, Mr. Maurey was appointed as Director in 1991, responsible for managing all operations, including customer service and satisfaction, financial accounting, cash flow, taxes, and a staff of 75. **Career Steps:** ITT Hartford: Director (1991–Present), Department Director (1990–1991), Manager of Operations (1986–1990). **Associations & Accomplishments:** American Management

Association; Director – UOC, United States Amateur Snowboard Association. **Education:** University of Hartford, M.A. in Management in progress; Roger Williams College, B.S. in Management and Marketing. **Personal:** Married to Theresa in 1987. Mr. Mourey enjoys mountain biking and snow boarding.

Keith Rasmussen
President
The Insurance Group (NM)
2015 Yale Boulevard Southeast Box 3
Albuquerque, NM 87106–4139
(505) 242–1960
Fax: (505) 247–2109
EMAIL: See Below

6399

Business Information: The Insurance Group is the administrative office of health care purchasing cooperatives for the food industry and medical fund raising. Multi–state in scope, The Insurance Group operates in Texas, New Mexico, Colorado, and Oklahoma. Starting The Insurance Group (NM) in 1994, Keith Rasmussen is responsible for all aspects of operations, in addition to overseeing all administrative operations for associates and a support staff of five. He can be reached through the Internet as follows: 71172,2061@compuserv.com. **Career Steps:** President, The Insurance Group (NM) (1995–Present); President, Trinity Agencies (1988–1995); Agent Consultant, New England Financial Group (1987–1995); Research Technologist, Immunobiology Division UNM School of Medicine (1977–1980). **Associations & Accomplishments:** Food Industry Association Executives; Texas Food Industry Association; New Mexico Food Industry Association. **Education:** UCI, B.S. (1974). **Personal:** Married to Lynne Page in 1975. Two children: Cheryl and Lauren. Mr. Rasmussen enjoys spending time with his daughters, photography, and mountain hiking.

Robert T. Rondeau
Manager of Information Systems
New Mexico Physician's Mutual
7770 Jefferson Street, NE #410
Albuquerque, NM 87109–4368
(505) 821–9485
Fax: (505) 821–6202
EMAIL: See Below

6399

Business Information: New Mexico Physician's Mutual is a medical malpractice insurance company, owned by physicians. As Manager of Information Systems, Mr. Rondeau supervises information processing, design and implementation of programs, and business processing. Internet users can reach him via: US006804@INTERAMP.COM. **Career Steps:** Manager of Information Systems, New Mexico Physician's Mutual (1992–Present); Vice President of Commercial Systems, M2C5 Systems, Inc. (1989–1992); Senior Analyst, Bryan Technologies (1987–1989); President, Friendly Software (1986–1987). **Associations & Accomplishments:** Association of Information and Image Managers; American Management Association. **Education:** Albuquerque Technical/Vocational Institute. **Personal:** Married to Johanna in 1990. One child: Roseanna Catherine Fisher. Mr. Rondeau enjoys reading. He is also a ballooning enthusiast and student.

Mr. James Ryan
President and Chief Executive Officer
Market Finders Insurance Corporation
P.O. Box 6549, 9117 Leesgate Road
Louisville, KY 40206
(502) 423–1800
Fax: (502) 426–7970

6399

Business Information: Market Finders Insurance Corporation is an international wholesale insurance broker specializing in insurance coverages to include: aviation, medical malpractice, commercial auto, and professional liability. They are renowned for handling unique professional performance clients with coverage such as: dancers' legs, concert pianists' hands, singers' voices, etc. Established in 1972, Market Finders Insurance Corporation employs 57 persons in the home office and reports having estimated premiums in excess of $43 million. In his current capacity, Mr. Ryan oversees all aspects of managing the home office and five branch offices including client negotiations and public relations. **Career Steps:** President and Chief Executive Officer, Market Finders Insurance Corporation (1972–Present). **Associations & Accomplishments:** Board of Directors, American Association of Managing General Agents (AAMGA); President, Kentucky Lloyd's Agents Associations; Board of Directors, National Association of Professional Surplus Lines Offices (NAPSLO); President, Kentucky Surplus Lines Association (KSLA); Advisory Council, The Hamilton, The Colony, and The Cardinal Insurance Companies (1991–1993); Advisory Council Essex Insurance Company and Evanston Insurance Company (1993);

Kentucky Thoroughbred Owners & Breeders; Honorary Order of Blue Goose; Kosair Shrine Temple; Honorary Order of Kentucky Colonels. **Education:** University of Pittsburgh; University of Louisville; Certified Insurance Wholesaler through AAMGA (1994). **Personal:** Married to Marlene in 1973. Mr. Ryan enjoys golf and the breeding and racing of thoroughbred horses.

Victor J. Salgado Sr.

Chairman of the Board
INTEGRAND Assurance Co.
P. O. Box 70128
San Juan, Puerto Rico 00936–8128
(809) 781–0707
Fax: (809) 793–7714
6399

Business Information: INTEGRAND Assurance Company is a full–service general insurance company providing services to clients in Puerto Rico and The Virgin Islands. Originally established in 1972 under the name of CNA Casualty of P.R., INTEGRAND acquired the company in 1989. INTEGRAND Assurance Company currently employs 211 people and reports assets of over $79 million. As Chairman of the Board of Directors and Chairman of the Executive Committee, Mr. Salgado provides the overall direction and vision for the company's continued growth, quality delivery of service to customers, and strategic development. Mr. Salgado is also the Majority Shareholder in the Company. **Career Steps:** Chairman of the Board of Directors, Chairman of the Executive Committee, INTEGRAND Assurance Company (1994–Present); Director, Chairman and Chief Executive Officer, CNA Casualty of Puerto Rico (1973–1993). **Associations & Accomplishments:** Director, Puerto Rico Investors Tax Free–Fund, Inc. **Education:** Temple University, B.S. (1949). **Personal:** Married to Eva Gloria Micheo in 1953. Three children: Eva G. Salgado–Micheo, Ana Maria Salgado–Micheo, and Victor J. Salgado–Micheo.

Thomas J. Smith

Chief Financial Officer
Texas Hospital Insurance Company
PO Box 14626
Austin, TX 78761
(512) 451–5775
Fax: (512) 451–3101
6399

Business Information: Texas Hospital Insurance Company is a health care industry insurance provider, with product lines covered to include property and casualty, life and employee benefit products. As Chief Financial Officer, Mr. Smith is responsible for all investment, budget, cash receipts and cash disbursement activity. **Career Steps:** Chief Financial Officer, Texas Hospital Insurance Company (1991–Present); Controller / Treasurer, American Service Life (1990–1991); Senior Manager, Price Waterhouse (1981–1990) **Associations & Accomplishments:** Texas State Society of CPAs; American Institute of Chartered Property Casualty Underwriters; Insurance Accounting and Systems Association. **Education:** Texas Christian University, BBA in Accounting and Finance (1981); St. Edwards University, working towards MBA. **Personal:** Married to Mary in 1981. Two children: Alexandra and Ian.

Christine L. Starkweather, CIC, ARM

Senior Account Manager
Hamilton Dorsey Alston Company
3350 Cumberland Circle Northwest, Suite 100
Atlanta, GA 30339–3332
(770) 850–6672
Fax: (770) 850–9375
6399

Business Information: Hamilton Dorsey Alston is an employee–owned independent insurance agency providing its business and personal clients a full range of property, liability, employee benefits, and life insurance products. Working in various account management roles for Hamilton Dorsey Alston since 1988, Christine was appointed as Senior Account Manager in 1993. In this capacity, she is responsible for the marketing, and account management of the largest book of business in the agency, as well as the supervision of the support staff for her team. Christine is also a member of the Automation Committee, and had an integral role in converting the agency to a new computer system. **Career Steps:** Hamilton Dorsey Alston Company: Senior Account Manager (1993–Present), Account Manager (1989–1993), Assistant Personal Risk Manager (1988–1989), Commercial/Personal CSR (1983–1988). **Associations & Accomplishments:** Society of Certified Insurance Counselors; Volunteer, Atlanta Union Mission; Volunteer, Special Olympics; Volunteer, Red Cross; Awards: William H. Rauschenberg Professional Development Award (1995), Pathfinder Award (1993), Pride Award (1996). **Education:** Kennesaw College; University of Akron; Hammel Business College (1983); CIC Designation (1993); ARM Designation (1996). **Personal:** Married to Rick in 1983. One child: Luke. Ms. Starkweather enjoys running, hiking, and spending time with her husband and son.

Randy Bernard Stimmell

AVP and Area Manager for National Accounts Division
The Liberty Mutual Group
555 West Pierce Road, Suite 300
Itasca, IL 60143–2691
(708) 250–7100 Ext. 270 or 25
Fax: (708) 250–9003
6399

Business Information: The Liberty Mutual Insurance Group is a Fortune 500 organization that provides insurance, risk management services and financial products for businesses and individuals on a global scope. The National Accounts Division is based in twelve major metropolitan areas in the U.S. (Atlanta, Boston, Charlotte, Chicago, Dallas, Kansas City, Los Angeles, Minneapolis, New York, Philadelphia, Pittsburgh, San Francisco). As the Illinois Area Manager for the National Accounts Division, Mr. Stimmell is responsible for managing the marketing efforts targeted towards the property and casualty needs of larger business and governmental entities. He also leads a staff of eleven professionals in supporting the objective. **Career Steps:** Liberty Mutual Insurance Group: AVP and Area Manager for National Accounts Division (1994–Present), Risk Financial Analyst (1989–1994), Systems Marketing Representative (1987–1989); Registered Representative, Metropolitan Life Insurance Company (1985–1987). **Associations & Accomplishments:** Society of Chartered Property Casualty Underwriters; American Association of Individual Investors; Former Board Member, United Way of Northern DuPage; **Education:** Western Illinois University: M.B.A. in Finance (1985), B.A. in Marketing (1983); American Institute for Chartered Property Casualty Underwriters/Insurance Institute of America: Associate in Research and Planning, Chartered Property Casualty Underwriter, Associate in Risk Management. **Personal:** Married to Sue–Ellen in 1988. One child: Danielle. Mr. Stimmell enjoys golf, fishing, personal computing, and investing/personal finance.

John E. Swanton

President
IPBS
22917 Pacific Coast Highway
Malibu, CA 90265
(310) 317–6310
Fax: (310) 317–6300
6399

Business Information: IPBS is a commercial finance company providing financial insurance premiums to agents and agencies all over the United States. As President, Mr. Swanton is responsible for all aspects of Company operations, as well as diversified Corporate administrative activities. **Career Steps:** President, IPBS (1993–Present); President/CEO, Anthem Premium Finance, Inc. (1993–Present); President/ CEO, Premium Finance Corporation (1988–1993). **Associations & Accomplishments:** Western Association of Insurance Brokers; Malibu Chamber of Commerce; Woodland Hills Country Club; Palm Valley Country Club. **Education:** Wittenburg University, Business (1966); American Institute of Banking. **Personal:** Married to Nancy in 1971. Two rchildren: Amy and Jill. Mr. Swanton enjoys golf, reading, and travel.

Jesse J. (Jim) Thomas

Vice President – Claims
CompSource, Inc.
PO Box 25700, 5800 Executive Center Drive
Charlotte, NC 28212
(704) 531–6764 Ext: 118
Fax: (704) 531–6842
6399

Business Information: CompSource, Inc. is an administrator of a Worker's Compensation self–insurance group for the North Carolina area. Future plans include expanding into other states. Established in 1992, CompSource, Inc. currently employs 60 people. With nine years expertise in the insurance industry, Mr. Thomas joined CompSource in 1994. Serving as Vice President of Claims, he is responsible for all management of the Claims Department. **Career Steps:** Vice President – Claims, CompSource, Inc. (1994–Present); Claims Supervisor, Consolidated Administrators (1993–1994); Claims Supervisor, Liberty Mutual (1986–1992). **Associations & Accomplishments:** N.C. Association of Self Insurers; Quoted in the 1994 issue of "Business N.C." about legislative changes on Worker's Compensation. **Education:** North Carolina State University, B.A. in Business Management (1986); Insurance Institute of America, Associate in Claims. **Personal:** Mr. Thomas enjoys fishing during his leisure time.

Mr. James W. Townley, CPCU

President and Chief Executive Officer
MSO, Inc.
139 Harristown Road
Glen Rock, NJ 07452
(201) 447–6900
Fax: (201) 447–9468
6399

Business Information: MSO, Inc. is an insurance rating advisory bureau operating in the Mid–Atlantic region of the U.S., specializing in property and casualty insurance. They also serve as a service bureau developing insurance programs and rates for small to mid–size insurance companies. Evolving from a rigid bureau of just forms and rates, the Company now provides more customized consulting for its clients. As President and Chief Executive Officer, Mr. Townley oversees all operations, including the financial activities. Established in 1944, MSO, Inc. employs 24 people with annual sales of $2 million. **Career Steps:** MSO, Inc.: President and Chief Executive Officer (1991–Present); Vice President and Corporate Secretary (1984–1991); General Services Manager (1981–1984); Assistant District Manager of Insurance Services Office (1978–1981); Supervisor of Insurance Services Office (1972–1978). **Associations & Accomplishments:** Society of State Filers; Society of Chartered Property & Casualty Underwriters (CPCU); Society of Fire Protection Engineers; Society of Insurance Research; USSF Soccer Referee. **Education:** Attending, Thomas Edison State College, Business Administration; Union College, Engineering and Business Administration (1 year); University of Maryland, Engineering (2 years). **Personal:** Married to Anne in 1972. Two children: Megan and George. Mr. Townley enjoys golf and refereeing soccer.

Antonio E. Vallecillo

President
Seguros de Vida Triple–S, Inc.
Avenida Roosevelt 1441
San Juan, Puerto Rico 00920
(809) 749–4949
Fax: (809) 749–4086
6399

Business Information: Seguros de Vida Triple–S, Inc. is an insurance company, offering life and disability insurance products. Seguros de Vida Triple–S is a subsidiary of Blue Cross/ Blue Shield in Puerto Rico, known as Triple–S, which is the largest insurance company located in Puerto Rico, as well as the second largest domestic company in Puerto Rico. As President, Mr. Vallecillo is responsible for all aspects of strategic planning and direction, and operations, in addition to overseeing all administrative operations for associates and a support staff of 21. **Career Steps:** Seguros de Vida Triple–S, Inc.: President (1995–Present), General Manager (1992–1995); Assistant Vice President of Finance, Triple–S, Inc. (1987–1992). **Associations & Accomplishments:** Puerto Rico's Society of Certified Public Accountants; American Institute of Certified Public Accountants; Society for Human Resource Management; Puerto Rico Chapter, National Association of Life Underwriters. **Education:** University of Puerto Rico, B.A. (1978); Computer Programming Diploma (1985); Certification: Certified Public Accountant (1983). **Personal:** Married to Myrsa Batista in 1986. Three children: Antonio, Javier, and Sofia. Mr. Vallecillo enjoys tropical music, dominoes, and professional basketball.

Ronald K. Young

Vice President of Field Operations
American States Insurance Company
500 North Meridian Street
Indianapolis, IN 46204
(317) 262–6033
Fax: (317) 262–6616
6399

Business Information: American States Insurance Company is an insurance carrier. Established in 1925, American States Insurance Company employs 4,274 people and has revenue in excess of $2 billion. As Vice President of Field Operations, Mr. Young is one of the managers of the Company. **Career Steps:** American States Insurance Company: Vice President of Field Operations (Present), Montgomery Division Vice President, Fort Scott Assistant Division Manager, Springfield Sales Manager. **Associations & Accomplishments:** Member, Society of CPCU; Member, American Society of Chartered Life Underwriters; Board of Directors, Dance Kaleidoscope; IRT Board of Directors (as of June 1992). **Educa-**

tion: Indiana Central University, B.S. (1971); CPCU and CLU. **Personal:** Married to Susan in 1983. Two children: Laura and Kristin. Mr. Young enjoys tennis and golf in his leisure time.

6400 Insurance Agents, Brokers and Services

6411 Insurance agents, brokers and service

Sahira J. Abdool Sorrells
Regional Director of Claims
Healthsource Provident Administrator, Inc.
16225 Park 10 Place
Houston, TX 77084
(713) 579–5820
Fax: (713) 579–0730

6411

Business Information: Healthsource Provident Administrator, Inc. is an insurance firm dealing with total health care and health management organizations. As Regional Director of Claims, Ms. Abdool Sorrells supervises the Corporation's administrative functions, serves the clients and handles their claims, manages records and reports, and oversees budgetary matters. **Career Steps:** Regional Director of Claims, Healthsource Provident Administrator, Inc. (1993–Present); Human Resource Manager, Provident Life (1988–1993); Director of Student Development, Cleveland State Community College (1984–1988); Guidance Counselor, Cleveland City Schools (1981–1984). **Associations & Accomplishments:** American Society of Public Administrators; International Customer Service Association; American Management Association; Junior League of Houston. **Education:** UTC – Chattanooga, M.P.A. (1988); Tennessee State University, B.S. in Psychology (1981). **Personal:** Married to Bill Jr. in 1981. Three children: Billy, Johanne, and Brittaney. Ms. Abdool Sorrells enjoys family activities and volunteering to feed the homeless.

Steven B. Allen
Regional Claims Manager
St. Paul Insurance Company
5821 Fairview Road, Suite 500
Charlotte, NC 28209
(704) 556–8703
Fax: (704) 556–8718

6411

Business Information: St. Paul Insurance Company is the largest medical insurance company in the United States. The Company provides medical malpractice insurance to physicians, surgeons, dentists, and other healthcare professionals. As Regional Claims Manager, Mr. Allen manages claim handling for medical professional claims in North Carolina, South Carolina, and Tennessee. **Career Steps:** St. Paul Insurance Company: Regional Claims Manager (1995–Present), Claim Manager (1994–1995), Senior Claim Supervisor (1990–1994). **Associations & Accomplishments:** 100 Black Men of America; Alpha Kappa Mu Honor Society; National Association for the Advancement for Colored People. **Education:** North Carolina Central University, B.B.A. (1979). **Personal:** Married to Angela A. in 1992. Mr. Allen enjoys basketball, tennis, weightlifting, golf, and bowling.

Lucy E. Allison
Vice President
Willis Corroon of South Carolina
P.O. Box 2007
Greenville, SC 29602–2007
(803) 232–9999
Fax: (803) 271–9555

6411

Business Information: Willis Corroon of South Carolina is a full–service, international insurance brokerage, providing insurance coverage to primarily Fortune 500 companies. Joining Willis Carroon of SC in 1993, Mrs. Allison was appointed as Vice President in 1995. She manages the support staff and handles the profile articles and claims for major clients. **Career Steps:** Willis Corroon of South Carolina: Vice President (1995–Present), Assistant Vice President (1993–1994); Manager of Claims and Personal Lines (1988–1993). **Associations & Accomplishments:** Piedmont Claims Association; South Carolina Claims; Greenville Association of Insurance Women; South Carolina Claims Management Association; March of Dimes; M.A.D.D.; Red Ribbon Campaign; Works in

the nursery for her church; Recipient of Willis Carroon of South Carolina "I Make a Difference" Award (1991); Insurance Woman of the Year (1989); Greenville Association of Insurance Women (1993). **Education:** Certified Insurance Counselor, CIC (1974). **Personal:** Married to Zack in 1985. Mrs. Allison enjoys reading.

Albert W. Amandolare, ChFC, CLU
Owner and Broker
Albert W. Amandolare Insurance Agency, Inc.
220 Forbes Road, Suite 209
Braintree, MA 02184
(617) 356–5040
Fax: (617) 843–9174

6411

Business Information: Albert W. Amandolare Insurance Agency, Inc. provides insurance and investment products relative to estate planning, as well as specializing in fixed and variable annuities, both deferred and immediate. Clientele includes physicians, corporations and law firms Establishing his own business in 1990, Mr. Amandolare is the Owner and Broker. As such, he is reponsible for insurance sales and investment products as needed for development of a model estate plan. He is a registered representative with the New England Securities. Mr. Amandolare has developed his practice through the establishment of quality, long–term relationships with physicians, lawyers, high–net–worth individuals and corporations. Mr. Amandolare credits his success to persistence in his work and diligence in continuing his education and development. "A society as dynamic as ours warrants constant growth in order to remain both productive and competitive." **Career Steps:** Owner and Broker, Albert W. Amandolare Insurance Agency, Inc. (1990–Present); Unit Manager, New England Life (1975–1982); Agent, New York Life (1971–1974); Teacher, Regis High School, New York, NY (1970–1972). **Associations & Accomplishments:** Active Member, Boston Chapter of the CLU. **Education:** College of the Holy Cross, B.A. in Philosophy (1970); American College Designations: Chartered Life Underwriter, Chartered Financial Consultant; Currently taking Masters courses in Financial Services. **Personal:** Married to Camilla in 1971. One child: Bryan. Mr. Amandolare enjoys golf and reading novels.

Bar–Cochua Ben–Gera

Chief Executive
Hadar Insurance Co., LTD
1 Ben Yehuda S.E.
Tel–Aviv, Israel 61019
(03) 510–3880
Fax: (03) 516–2797

6411

Business Information: Hadar Insurance Co., LTD specializes in life and other types of insurance. A subsidiary of a London based company, the Agency conducts business primarily in Israel. Established in 1957, the Company employs 314 people and has estimated annual revenue in excess of $334 million. As Chief Executive, Mr. Ben–Gera also serves on the Board of Directors. He is responsible for all functions of the Company including administration, operations, finance, sales, marketing, and strategic planning. **Career Steps:** Chief Executive, Hadar Insurance Co., LTD (1985–Present); Branch Manager, Israel Phoenix. **Education:** Hebrew University, B.A. (1964). **Personal:** Married to Ofra in 1963. Two children: Liat and Ronit. Mr. Ben–Gera enjoys football.

Nancy Ann Blastic
Corporate Counsel/Corporate Secretary
PCA Solutions
260 Wekiva Springs Road
Longwood, FL 32779
(407) 788–1717
Fax: (407) 788–8648

6411

Business Information: PCA Solutions is a third party administrator for insurance products throughout the Southeastern U.S. A practicing attorney in Florida state courts since 1985, Ms. Blastic joined PCA Solutions as Corporate Counsel/Corporate Secretary in 1994. She is responsible for all legal contracts for the Corporation and its sister company, PCA Property and Casualty Insurance Company. **Career Steps:** Corporate Counsel/Corporate Secretary, PCA Solutions (1994–Present); O'Rioden, Mann, et al: Managing Partner/Naples (1993–1994), Attorney (1991–1993); Attorney, Thomas Moore P.A. (1988–1991). **Associations & Accomplishments:** Junior League of Greater Orlando. **Education:** Mercer University, J.D. (1988); Florida State University, B.A. (1985).

Ms. Jacqueline D. Douglas Brown
Executive Director
Conferences of the United Church of Christ Insurance Advisory Board
6001 Montrose Road, Suite #700
Rockville, MD 20852
(301) 984–0011
Fax: (301) 984–3427

6411

Business Information: Conferences of the United Church of Christ Insurance Advisory Board specializes in the administration, management and generation of financial insurance for the Churches of Christ and Disciples of Christ congregations world–wide. As President of the Association, Ms. Brown is responsible for the management of all financial and operational aspects. With over 80 service agents and administrative staff personnel, Conferences of the United Church of Christ Insurance Advisory Board currently serves 7,000 Churches of Christ and 8,000 Disciples of Christ congregational members. **Career Steps:** Executive Director, Conferences of the United Church of Christ Insurance Advisory Board (1991–Present); Risk Manager, Washington Metro Transit Authority (1987–1992); Specialist, U.S. Department of Defense (1985–1987); Broker, Marsh & McLennan, Inc. (1977–1985). **Associations & Accomplishments:** APRRD; United Church of Christ; Girl Scouts of America. **Education:** Lehman College, B.A. (1984). **Personal:** Four children: La–Trina Brown Cunningham, Randy Brown, Ashley Hargro and Alexis Hargro.

Patricia L. Burgess
Branch Administrator
The Standard Life Assurance Company
2 Sheppard Avenue East, Suite 310
Willowdale, Ontario M2N 5Y7
(416) 590–1015
Fax: (416) 590–1016

6411

Business Information: Standard Life is an assurance company founded in Edinburgh, Scotland in 1825, and serving Canadian customers since 1833. It has a AAA rating from both Moody's and Standard and Poor's. It provides group savings and retirement products, group life and health products, individual pensions, annuities and savings, individual life products, and investment management. As Branch Administrator, Ms. Burgess is responsible for handling daily operations, interacting with the head office and suppliers, managing budgetary concerns, training, overseeing staff, and human resources requirements of the Toronto Group Life and Health Customer Service Office. **Career Steps:** Branch Administrator, Standard Life (1994–Present); Executive Director, Morrison Residence Foundation (1990–1993); Human Resources Associate, TV Ontario (1986–1990); Assistant Director of Personnel, Central Hospital (1982–1986); Office Manager, Million$ Magazine (1981); Personnel Consultant, Opportunities Unlimited (1980). **Associations & Accomplishments:** Fund–raising, Royal Ontario Museum; Toronto Symphony Orchestra and TV Ontario; Chair, Volunteer Outreach Committee (1993–1994); Board Member, Community Housing Committee; Volunteer career counseling and image consulting on a referral basis. **Education:** University of Toronto, B.A. in English Honorable (1977).

Leopoldo Camara Hagen

Vice President Reinsurance
Zurich Compania de Seguros, S.A.
Guillermo Prieto No. 76
Col. San Rafael, Mexico 06470
(525) 629–2820
Fax: (525) 705–1973
E MAIL: See Below

6411

Business Information: Zurich Compania de Seguros, S.A. is the Mexican affiliate company of the Zurich Insurance Group, that operates as an international insurance firm with over 35,000 employees worldwide. As Vice President of Reinsurance, Mr. Camara Hagen has oversight of all reinsurance, large industrial accounts, treaties and organization of reinsurance against natural disaster for the Company in Mexico. Presently, Mr. Camara Hagen is part of a seven person natural catastrophe risk management team operating worldwide. Internet users can reach him via: mxzurich@ibmmail.com. **Career Steps:** Vice President of Reinsurance, Zurich, Compania de Seguros, S.A. (1994–Present); Head of Reinsurance Vigilance, Mexican Insurance Authority (1993); International Account Executive, Gerling Mexico (1990–1992). **Associations & Accomplishments:** Mexican Insurance Company Association, Member of the Reinsurance Expert Committee. **Education:** Instituto Tecnologico Autonomo de Mexico, Economist (1995); German School in Mexico City, Mexican and German Baccalaureate; Insurance Professional; Chamber of Industry and Commerce, Cologne, Germany. **Personal:** Married to Dennise Villarreal in 1996. Mr. Camara Hagen enjoys reading, tennis, and playing the piano.

Joseph A. Carabillo

Chief Legal Officer and Corporate Secretary
ULLICO Inc.
111 Massachusetts Avenue, NW
Washington, DC 20001–1461
(202) 682–4900
Fax: (202) 682–6784

6411

Business Information: Established in 1925, ULLICO Inc. is a diversified insurance and financial service company. As Chief Legal Officer and Corporate Secretary, Mr. Carabillo is responsible for all aspects of legal functions, as well as administration and finance. **Career Steps:** Chief Legal Officer and Corporate Secretary, ULLICO Inc. (1987–Present); Assistant General Counsel, The Prudential Insurance Company of America (1977–1987). **Associations & Accomplishments:** American Bar Association; Society of Financial Examiners; Defense Research Institute; Association of Life Insurance Counsel; ACCA. **Education:** New York University, LL.M. (1982); Seton Hall University Law Center, J.D. (1977); William Paterson College, B.A. (1968). **Personal:** Married to Karin in 1992. Mr. Carabillo enjoys golf.

Scott A. Carmilani

Senior Vice President – Middle Market Division
National Union Fire Insurance Co.
70 Pine Street
New York, NY 10270
(212) 770–5532
Fax: (212) 747–0488

6411

Business Information: National Union Fire Insurance Co., a subsidiary of American International Group (AIG), is the leading U.S. provider of directors and officers liability and professional liability coverages. (AIG) is the leading U.S.–based international insurance organization and the nation's largest underwriter of commercial and industrial coverages. Holding various underwriting and management positions with National Union since 1987, Scott Carmilani was appointed as Senior Vice President of the Middle Market Division in 1995. He is responsible for the management of all aspects of the Middle Market division which includes Directors and Officers Liability, Fiduciary Liability and Commercial Fidelity for middle market accounts as well as non–profit accounts for all of the U.S. branches, and is also responsible for National Unions regional company operations. **Career Steps:** Vice President of Middle Market Division, American International Group (AIG) (1995–Present); Treaty Broker, Guy Carpenter Insurance (1986–1987). **Associations & Accomplishments:** Finance Committee, New York University Board of Metro Center for Continuing Education; Member of Board of Directors, Illinois National Insurance Co. **Education:** University of Scranton, B.S. (1986). **Personal:** Mr. Carmilani enjoys golf, basketball, and sports in general.

Thomas J. Casserly Jr.

Chief Executive Officer
Thomas J. Casserly, Jr Insurance Agency–Nationwide
P.O. Box 186
Fredericksburg, VA 22404
(540) 786–6111
Fax: (540) 786–4948

6411

Business Information: Thomas J. Casserly, Jr. Insurance Agency–Nationwide, the fifth largest automobile insurance company in the U.S. as well as one of the leading global insurance product providers, offers a wide range of insurance services and financial products, through corporate subsidiaries, in the U.S. and Europe. Headquartered in Columbus, Ohio, Nationwide Insurance operates 100 offices throughout the U.S. As Chief Executive Officer, Mr. Casserly handles the day–to–day operations and management of his Agency. **Career Steps:** Chief Executive Officer, Thomas J. Casserly, Jr. Insurance Agency–Nationwide (1973–Present). **Associations & Accomplishments:** Fredericksburg Host Lions Club; Fredericksburg Auxiliary Police Department. **Education:** Marian College. **Personal:** Married to Carolyn in 1968. Two children: Charles and Kimberly.

C. Peter Cimoroni

Executive Vice President
Fedeli Group
5005 Rockside Road, Floor 5
Independence, OH 44131
(216) 328–8080
Fax: (216) 328–8081

6411

Business Information: Fedeli Group is a regional insurance firm specializing in business, health, life, home, and auto insurance, and surety and financial services. As Executive Vice President, Mr. Cimoroni heads all sales and marketing efforts, and personally handles all large accounts. Additionally, Mr. Cimoroni is starting two companies to market products (infant care products to ease teething and colic, and adult sore throat/cough drops) he has invented. **Career Steps:** Executive Vice President, Fedeli Group (1993–Present); Vice President, Bell South (1992–1993); Vice President, Ross Roy Adv. (1990–1992); President and Owner, CPCV Media (1986–1990). **Associations & Accomplishments:** NCAA; OHSAA; GEWCOA. **Education:** John Carroll University: B.A. (1980), M.A. (1983). **Personal:** Married to Valerie A. in 1983. Two children: Carmine Peter and Christian Michael. Mr. Cimoroni enjoys golf, charity work, writing, and wrestling.

Mr. Lawrence A. Cohen

President
Ringler Associates Boston, Inc.
21 Custom House Street, Suite 740
Boston, MA 02110–3525
(617) 737–8678
Fax: (617) 738–8688

6411

Business Information: Ringler Associates Boston, Inc. is the nation's leading structured settlement annuity brokerage firm, providing tax free annuity benefits to injured persons in personal injury litigation. A practicing litigation attorney since 1975, and a claims expert with over 27 years experience, Lawrence Cohen heads Ringler's New England operations from the Boston office. He is responsible for all aspects of operations, including administration, public relations, marketing, and strategic planning. **Career Steps:** President, Ringler Associates, Inc. (1983–Present); Cigna: Assistant Vice President – Northeast Area Claims (1982–1983), National Director of Claims Litigation (1980–1982), Manager – Hartford Regional Office / Manager – Philadelphia Regional Office / Multi–Lines Claims Representative (1969–1981); Claims Representative. Aetna Insurance Company (now dba CIGNA) (1969. **Associations & Accomplishments:** Pennsylvania Bar Association; Connecticut Bar Association; National Association of Life Underwriters; National Structured Settlements Trade Association; Phi Kappa Phi. **Education:** University of Delaware School of Law, J.D., magna cum laude (1975); University of Connecticut, B.A. in Economics (1969). **Personal:** Married to Ruth in 1969. Two children: Tracy and Stephanie. Mr. Cohen enjoys golf, skiing, music, and travel.

Louis M. Cohen, CIC

Vice President
Sullivan Insurance Group, Inc.
370 Main Street
Worcester, MA 01608
(508) 791–2241
Fax: (508) 797–3689

6411

Business Information: A regional, full–service insurance agency, Sullivan Insurance Group, Inc. specializes in commercial, personal, life, health and disability insurance. Founded in 1957, The Sullivan Insurance Group has built its business on knowing its clients and their changing needs. At Sullivan, the Agency will work with its clients to make the most appropriate insurance protection and risk management recommendations. Sullivan's experience and scope of expertise is the client's assurance that he/she is making the right choice. As Vice President of Marketing, Louis Cohen's principle responsibilities involve the marketing to various property/casualty insurance companies of large, complex or sophisticated commercial accounts, including specialized coverages such as HPuerto Rico property, large deductible, retention or retrospectively rated General Liability, Automobile and/or Worker's Compensation for this $35 million agency. Additional coverages, such as Directors & Officers Liability, Errors & Omissions, Professional Liability, Credit Insurance, Product Recall, Pollution/Environmental Liability, etc. are also placed; as well as coordination of in–house or off–site meetings with insurers and potential new markets, performing the necessary application procedures in securing new markets, and maintaining day–to–day relationship with the various markets with whom he does business, on either an agency or brokerage basis. Mr. Cohen has earned the Certified Insurance Counselor designation and is a Notary Public for the Commonwealth of Massachusetts. Prior to joining Sullivan, he served as an insurance underwriting manager for various major insurance carriers. **Career Steps:** Sullivan Insurance Group, Inc.: Vice President of Marketing (1995–Present), Vice President and General Manager (1986–1994); Assistant Vice President, Integrity Insurance Company (1985–1986); GECC Insurance Operations, Puritan Insurance Companies: Project Manager (1984–1985), Manager of Casualty Underwriting (1982–1984); Executive Underwriter, Falcon Insurance Company (1981–1982); Assistant Vice President and Casualty Manager, Swett & Crawford Insurance Agency of Massachusettes, Inc. (1980–1981); Product Line Manager – General and Excess Liability, Insurance Company of North America (1976–1980); Commercial Casualty Underwriter and Lead Line Worker's Compensation Underwriter, Fireman's Fund American Insurance Companies (1973–1976); Assigned Risk Technician, Massachusetts Workmen's Compensation Rating and Inspection Bureau (1967–1973). **Associations & Accomplishments:** Vice President, Sullivan Insurance Group, Inc.; Licensed Insurance Broker; Licensed Real Estate Broker; Notary Public; Certified Insurance Counselor; Certified Arbitrator, American Registry of Arbitrators; Society of Certified Insurance Counselors; American Institute of Chartered Property Casualty Underwriters. **Education:** Northeastern University, B.S. in Business Administration (1971); Certified Insurance Counselor; Certificate from General Insurance Institute of America. **Personal:** Mr. Cohen enjoys computers, photography, and collecting wine.

Mr. Richard F. Connell

Chief Information Officer
Seguros Monterrey Aetna, S.A.
Presidente Masaryk #8
Mexico City, Mexico 11588
(525) 326–9205
Fax: (525) 326–9008

6411

Business Information: Seguros Monterrey Aetna, S.A. is a full–line insurance agency specializing in life, medical, auto, property and bonds for companies and individuals. The Agency has 35 branch offices throughout Mexico, with Aetna owning 44% of the major interest. Established in 1940, Seguros Monterrey Aetna, S.A. reports premium assets of $1 million and currently employs 2,500 people. As Chief Information Officer, Mr. Connell is responsible for computing, telecommunications, systems development and business process re–engineering. **Career Steps:** Chief Information Officer, Seguros Monterrey Aetna, S.A. (1993–Present); Aetna Life and Casualty Insurance: Vice President (1990–1993), Assistant Vice President (1986–1990), Director (1984–1986). **Associations & Accomplishments:** President of Central New LEngland Chapter, Society for Information Management; Workgroup for Electronic Data Interchange (WEDI) (1993); Chairman, National Electronic Information Corporation (NEIC) (1993); Interviewed by "New York Times" and in 1992 by "Best" Magazine. **Education:** Central Connecticut State University, B.S. (1969). **Personal:** Married to Jeanne Somsen Connell in 1972. Two children: Megan Elizabeth and Katherine Anne Connell. Mr. Connell enjoys tennis and jogging.

James J. Consolati, FLMI

Director of Pension Trust
Berkshire Life Insurance Company
700 South Street
Pittsfield, MA 01201
(413) 499–4321
Fax: (413) 499–4831

6411

Business Information: Berkshire Life Insurance Company provides qualified retirement, and insurance plan sales and administration to small businesses (i.e. CPA's physicians, attorneys, etc.) via forty offices located throughout the U.S. Established in 1851, the Company has over $12 billion of individual insurance in force. Berkshire employs 800 people in combination with home office and field offices. The pension department employs 12. Annual Sales is comprised of: Life – $8.5 million; Disability – $4 million; Pension – $2 million; and Annuity – $36 million. As Director of Pension Trust, Mr. Consolati markets and administers pension plans, and is responsible for administration, and strategic planning. **Career Steps:** Berkshire Life Insurance Company: Director of Pension Trust (1995–Present); Assistant Director (1988–1995), Various (1976–1988); Computer Services (1976–1982); Pension Trust (1982–1988). **Associations & Accomplishments:** Life Office Management Association; Small Employers and Individual Pension Committee; Finance Committee Chairman, Town of Tyringham, MA. **Education:** Bentley College, B.S. in Accounting with High Honors (1974). **Personal:** Married to Karen in 1984. Four children: Benjamin, Austin, Darren, and Evan. Mr. Consolati enjoys boating, snowmobiling, volleyball, and woodworking.

Douglas B. Cressey, C.I.C.

•••━━◉━•••

President/Insurance Division
Aspen Associates, Inc.
2605 Coachmans Circle
Atlanta, GA 30202
(770) 431–1506
Fax: (770) 436–4742

6411

Business Information: Aspen Associates, Inc. is a full service insurance agency offering financial services, and commercial and personal insurance. Regional in scope, the Company is a division of the Torrey Group, the largest homebuilding firm in Atlanta. Aspen, established in 1994, was formed for the benefit of home buyers and employees. As President/Insurance Division, Mr. Cressey is responsible for risk management, and oversees the entire insurance department, including employee benefits, workers compensation, liability, and sexual harassment issues. **Career Steps:** President/Insurance Division, Aspen Associates, Inc. (1994–Present); Rollins Hudig Hall: Executive Vice President/Georgia (1991–1994), Executive Vice President/Colorado (1989–1991); Senior Vice President, Van Glider Insurance Corporation (199–1989). **Associations & Accomplishments:** Independent Insurance Agents of Georgia; Professional Insurance Agents of Georgia; Homebuilders Association of Atlanta and North Carolina; Society of Certified Insurance Counselors; Governors Task Force on Tort Reform. **Education:** Colorado State University, B.S. (1969). **Personal:** Married to C. Jill in 1987. Mr. Cressey enjoys golf, tennis, and foreign travel.

Sharon A. Dankowski, HIAA

Director of Administrative Services
Central Reserve Life
17800 Royalton Road
Strongsville, OH 44136
(216) 572–2400
Fax: (216) 572–8896

6411

Business Information: Central Reserve Life, established in 1976, offers small to mid–size business insurance plans to clients. The plans include life, annuity, accident, health, major medical, and long–term disability insurance. The Company is currently licensed in 35 states and has more than 14,000 independent agents throughout the country. As Director of Administrative Services, Ms. Dankowski oversees the following departments: mail, supply, claim preparation, and policy booklet issue. **Career Steps:** Director of Administrative Services, Central Reserve Life (1991–Present); Prescott, Ball & Turben (1985–1991); Teacher, Brooklyn Schools (1968–1982). **Associations & Accomplishments:** HIAA, Health Insurance Associate; President, Country Club Condominium Association; ARMA. **Education:** Ohio State University, B.S.Ed. (1966) **Personal:** Ms. Dankowski enjoys photography, spectator sports, and computer programming.

Juliana Deans

•••━━◉━•••

Marketing Director
Creditor Resources, Inc.
1100 Johnson Ferry Road, NE, Suite 300
Atlanta, GA 30342–1709
(404) 257–8348
Fax: (404) 257–0159
EMAIL: See Below

6411

Business Information: Creditor Resources, Inc. is the marketing division of Life Investors Insurance Company of America, a division of AEGON. Specializing in the sale of credit and mortgage insurance, as well as PC–based automation technologies to credit unions in North America, the Company was established in 1969 and employs 200 people. As Marketing Director, Ms. Deans oversees all advertising, public relations, and marketing communications involving the Company. She is responsible for trade shows, publicity, collateral materials, graphic designs, training documentation, etc. She also supervises a support staff of five, in addition to coordinating with advertising, public relations agencies and freelance writers outside the Company. Internet users can reach her via: Jdeans@aegonusa.com. **Career Steps:** Marketing Director, Creditor Resources, Inc. (1992–Present); Marketing Director, The Professional Image (1990–1992); Marketing Manager, BellSouth Information Systems (1987–1990); Sales Contract Manager, G.E. Major Appliance Division (1985–1987); Training Specialist, IBM (1983–1985). **Associations & Accomplishments:** Volunteer, 1996 Summer Olympic Games (Dignitary Level); Mentor for Company Employees; Restaurant Marketing Consultant; Speaker on Effective Advertising Campaigns and Trade–show Marketing. **Education:** Emory University, M.B.A. (1985); George Washington University, B.A. in

International Affairs. **Personal:** Married. Ms. Deans enjoys collecting red wine, scuba diving, travel, and gourmet cooking.

Bruce E. Dennis

Project Director
Mass Transit Group
523 West 6th Street, Suite 1234
Los Angeles, CA 90014
(213) 624–7617
Fax: (213) 624–0399

6411

Business Information: Mass Transit Group is a construction insurance company, specifically owner–controlled insurance programs for mega construction projects. On its current project, the Company acts as insurance consultants to the LA County Metropolitan Transportation Authority and Southern California Regional Rail Authority, handling the owner–controlled insurance programs for Metrorail subway and Metrolink commuter rail construction. As Project Director, Mr. Dennis supervises and manages the risk management, safety/loss control, claims, contracts administration, and oversees the general office staff of the wrap–up team of the Company. **Career Steps:** Project Director, Mass Transit Group (1994–Present); General Manager, Insurance Consultants, Inc., a subsidiary of Layne & Associates (1993–1994); Corporate Risk Manager, Tutor Saliba Corporation, Engineering and Contracting (1991–1993); Vice President/Risk Management Officer, Valley Capital Corporation/Valley Bank of Nevada (1988–1991); Risk Manager, Imperial Palace, Inc. Hotel/Casino (1986–1988); Assistant Secretary/International Manager of Treaty Facultative and LMX Department, Willcox Incorporated (1983–1985); Management and Department Head Positions American International Underwriters (1978–1983) **Associations & Accomplishments:** Appointed by University of Nevada Las Vegas Board of Regents to Advisory Committee for School of Insurance and Risk Management; Founder, Inaugural President and Society Director, RIMS, Nevada Chapter; Society Director, Risk and Insurance Management Society (RIMS), Nevada; Chairperson, Hotel Industry Session for National RIMS Convention; Guest lecturer for risk management classes and industry seminars. **Education:** Southampton College, B.A. in Biology (1974); Texas Lutheran College, Candidate for B.A. degree; College of Insurance, General Courses; Formerly licensed Insurance Agent in State of Nevada. **Personal:** Mr. Dennis enjoys fishing, photography, and writing.

Edward F. Denny

Broker
Marsh & McLennan, Inc. – Global Brokering
9000 Central Parkwest, Suite 400
Atlanta, GA 30328
(770) 481–7886
Fax: (770) 481–7840

6411

Business Information: Marsh & McLennan, Inc. is an insurance brokerage firm for a diversified clients base, including national and international exposures. With twenty–three years experience in the insurance industry, Mr. Denny joined Marsh & McLennan as Broker in 1996. He is responsible for evaluating and marketing casualty and property insurance programs, as well as negotiating cash flow programs. **Career Steps:** Broker, Marsh & McLennan, Inc. (1996–Present); Marketing and Brokering Executive, Alexander & Alexander, Inc. (1986–1996); Commercial Lines Manager, Maryland Casualty Company (1983–1986); Senior Casualty Underwriter, Hartford Insurance Group (1977–1983); Senior Underwriter, Nationwide (1973–1977). **Associations & Accomplishments:** Greater Richmond Chapter, CPCU; Skipper (1989–1990), Mariners Club of Greater Richmond; Church Choir; Church Refugee Program; Continuing Education Instructor, Insurance Testing Corporation. **Education:** Pennsylvania State University, B.S. in Economics (1968); Insurance Institute of America: CPCU Program (1994); ARM Program (1991); AAI Program (1988); Associate in Underwriting (1987). **Personal:** Married to Judy in 1968. Two children: Laura and Janice. Mr. Denny enjoys gardening, home and appliance repairs, church work, and boating.

Pamela N. Dufour

Senior Vice President of Operations
World Access Service Corp.
6600 West Broad Street
Richmond, VA 23230–1702
(804) 673–1465
Fax: (804) 673–1587

6411

Business Information: World Access Service Corporation is a privately–held international service company that offers insurance and assistance products to the financial services, travel, health care and consumer products industries. Established in 1985, World Access Service Corporation currently

employs 300 people. As Senior Vice President of Operations, Ms. Dufour is responsible for Information Systems and Service Delivery. **Career Steps:** World Access Service Corporation: Senior Vice President of Operations (1995–Present), Vice President of Service Delivery (1992–1995), Director of Marketing (1992); Assistant Vice President of Product Development, Crestar Bank (1989–1992). **Associations & Accomplishments:** Member, Direct Marketing Association. **Education:** Virginia Commonwealth University, M.S. (1990); James Madison University, B.B.A. **Personal:** Married to Robert M. Dufour in 1989. One child: Alexandra Marie Dufour. Ms. Dufour enjoys jogging and weight training.

Jeffrey R. DuFresne

Vice President
Dutch Institutional Holding Company (DIHC)
4550 Woodland Brook Drive
Atlanta, GA 30339
(770) 984–0600
Fax: (770) 952–8269

6411

Business Information: Dutch Institutional Holding Company (DIHC) is a wholly–owned subsidiary of PGGM – the largest private pension fund in the Netherlands – and provides real estate advisory services to Dutch and other foreign investors. As Vice President for the Southern United States, Mr. DuFresne is responsible for real estate acquisitions, investment management, dispositions, and redevelopment. **Career Steps:** Vice President, DIHC (1993–Present); Regional Asset Manager, Greystone Realty Corporation (1988–1993); Investment Manager, Prudential Realty Group (1983–1988). **Associations & Accomplishments:** President Elect, Real Estate Group of Atlanta; Founder of Cigar Aficiondo Literary Society; Georgia Trust for Historic Preservation; Atlanta Symphony Orchestra. **Education:** Trinity College, B.A. (1978); Deerfield Academy; Columbia University. **Personal:** Married to Jodi in 1985. Mr. DuFresne enjoys international travel, oil painting, skiing, tennis, jogging, and golf.

Charles D. Eaton

Executive Director
Maryland Insurance Group
P.O. Box 11615, 6100 Fairview Road, Suite 1200
Charlotte, NC 28220
(704) 551–3479
Fax: (704) 551–3488

6411

Business Information: Maryland Insurance Group is a commercial property and casualty insurance company. Focusing exclusively on industrial groups, the Company operates in strategic business units through independent agents. Established in 1898, the Charlotte unit employs eight people and has estimated annual corporate revenue of $16 million. As Executive Director, Mr. Eaton directs operations of the middle market business units for North and South Carolina. He is also responsible for marketing and underwriting, administration, operations, and strategic planning. **Career Steps:** Maryland Insurance Group: Executive Director (1990–Present), Assistant Commercial Underwriting Manager (1988–1990), Regional Commercial Lines Administrator (1987–1988), Commercial Underwriter (1986–1987). **Associations & Accomplishments:** North Carolina Wholesalers Association; South Carolina Hospitality Association; Charlotte Mecklenburg Hospitality and Tourism Association; Former President, United Methodist Men, University City, UMC. **Education:** University of North Carolina, Greensboro, B.S. (1980). **Personal:** Married to Trudy Nicholson in 1980. Two children: Sara and Ross. Mr. Eaton enjoys golf, reading, and his children's activities.

Robert J. Frcek, C.P.A.

Corporate Audit Director
HealthPlan Services, Inc.
5455 Sylmar Avenue, Unit 1905
Sherman Oaks, CA 91401–5115
(818) 575–2555
Fax: (818) 448–7089
frcek@aol.com

6411

Business Information: HealthPlan Services, Inc. (HPS) is the parent company to Consolidated Group, Inc. (CGI) and Harrington Services Corporation (HSC), which is the parent company to American Benefit Plan Administrators (ABPA). These Corporations administer health and pension plans for small businesses, unions, school districts, corporations, trade associations, and other business and professional organizations. Clients also include managed care organizations, integrated health care delivery systems, insurance companies, and health care purchasing alliances. They have over 80 offices throughout the United States and approximately 3,500 employees. As Corporate Audit Director, Mr. Frcek is responsible for the claims audit group, which audits health, dental, disability, and flex claims plans, and the operational audit group which does branch audits, financial audits, pension audits, data processing audits, and audits of regulatory filings, premium accounting, underwriting, COBRA billing, vacation plans, annuity plans, and accounting controls. He makes sure all staff members are up–to–date on all applicable state and federal regulations. **Career Steps:** Corporate Audit Director, HPS/HSC / ABPA (1984–Present); Vice President, Systems and Procedures, Southern California Savings (1982–1984); Senior Auditor, City Investing Company (1979–1982). **Associations & Accomplishments:** American Institute of Certified Public Accountants; California Society of Certified Public Accountants; Institute of Internal Auditors (IIA); MENSA; Treasurer (1983–1984), Southern California Savings Political Action Committee; Campaign Manager (1981), Park Commissioner Candidate; Press Manager (1980), State Assembly Candidate, Candidate (1979), School Board. **Education:** University of Illinois, Certified Public Accountant (1980); Roosevelt University, B.S. in Business Administration (1978). **Personal:** Mr. Frcek enjoys the various media, computers, reading, fitness, travel, and exploring new interests.

L. Peter Freisinger
Vice President
Freisinger & Stuckert, Inc.
236 South 6th Street
La Crosse, WI 54601
(608) 784–2587
Fax: (608) 784–2259

6411

Business Information: Freisinger & Stuckert, Inc., established in 1883, is a diversified insurance agency providing commercial and personal insurance products such as annuities, mutual funds, life and health coverages. The Agency specializes in serving clients in the following sectors: Day Care, Medical, Hospitality Industries, General Contractors, Religious Organizations, Boutiques, Horse Breeders, Apartment and Condominium Associations. With over 28 years in the insurance industry, Mr. Freisinger joined Freisinger & Stuckert in 1973 and was appointed Vice President and a Principal with the firm in 1980. As Vice President, he oversees all administrative office management, commercial sales, risk management and computer systems divisions. He is involved with claims dispute resolution, conducts computer training and maintenance to both Company personnel and clients, as well as conducts seminars on Safety and Risk Management, Insurance Coverages, and Insurance and the Law. With his extensive background in computer development, he was instrumental in the formation of Freisinger Associates in 1983. Serving as Partner, he designs and develops computer prospecting and proposal programs for insurance agents, as well as serves as consultant in all areas of insurance. Concurrent to his duties for Freisinger, he also serves as an adjunct instructor of Insurance and Risk Management courses at Western Wisconsin Technical College, teaching IIA continuing education courses to agents. He is a Certified Instructor for Continuing Education for Agents in the states of Minnesota, Iowa, California, New Mexico, Indiana, Missouri, Colorado and Michigan. He also provides testimony as an expert witness involving insurance coverages, interpretations and agent responsibilities. Other related areas of expertise include the development of Inland Marine forms that are in use in part or entirely by certain insurance agencies; participation in the development of the St. Paul Company's Pace Restaurant Program; and developed and continues to participate in the development of forms and rates for Capitol Indemnity Corporation on Day Care insurance matters. **Career Steps:** Freisinger & Stuckert, Inc.: Vice President (1973–Present), Principal (1980–Present); Partner and Consultant, Freisinger Associates (1983–Present); Insurance Instructor, Western Wisconsin Technical College (1970–Present); Risk Management Instructor, University of Wisconsin – La Crosse (1980–1982) Safety Engineer and Auditor, General Casualty Company (1970–1972). **Associations & Accomplishments:** Independent Insurance Agents of Wisconsin; Past Environmental Chairman, Wisconsin Jaycees; La Crosse Chamber of Commerce; American Warmblood Association; La Crosse Camara Club; Published with Independent Insurance Agent Magazine, Country Today, ComminQue; Given numerous seminars and workshops; **LICENSES:** Wisconsin: Property & Casualty & Excess, Surplus Lines; Non–resident Property & Casualty: Minnesota, Iowa, Michigan and Missouri. **Education:** University of Wisconsin – La Crosse: M.S. in Education, 12 Credits of Post–Masters Courses (1977), B.S. in Business Administration with Insurance and Accounting emphasis (1970); University of Wisconsin – Madison; Risk Management University of Iowa – Ames; Aetna Home Office School (1974); 700 hours of continuing education in certified courses from various other providers. **Personal:** Married to Joline K. in 1968. One child: Kristine. Mr. Freisinger enjoys photography, horse breeding and stable operations, and computer software design.

Mr. Donald W. Glaspey
Executive Vice President
North American Insurance Agency
P.O. Box 25928, 3800 Classen Boulevard
Oklahoma City, OK 73118
(405) 523–2100
Fax: (405) 556–2332

6411

Business Information: North American Insurance Agency is a full service insurance brokerage firm. Established in 1959, North American Insurance Agency employs 89 persons. Mr. Glaspey has been in the insurance industry since 1958. He was responsible for agency development in the states of Missouri and Kansas and in 1964 became Manager of Sales and Underwriting for the state of Oklahoma. **Career Steps:** Executive Vice President, North American Insurance Agency (1965–Present); Branch Manager, Transamerica Insurance Company (1964–1965); Sales and Marketing, Transamerica Insurance Company (1958–1964). **Associations & Accomplishments:** President, Oklahoma Association of Insurance Agents; Past President, Independent Insurance Agents of Greater Oklahoma City; Independent Insurance Agents of America; Council of Insurance Agents and Brokers; Past Chairman, Oklahoma Advisory Council–CNA Insurance Company; Past Chairman, Jonathan Trumbul Council–Hartford Insurance Company; Oklahoma City Chamber of Commerce; State of Oklahoma Chamber of Commerce; Past President, Civic Music Association; President, Oklahoma City Council of The Tulsa Opera Company; Elder, Central Presbyterian Church; various National insurance company councils. **Education:** University of Missouri, B.S. (1955); Kansas City Conservatory of Music; Captain, U.S. Air Force, Jet Pilot in Tactical Air Command. **Personal:** Married since 1960 to Judy. Two daughters and two grandsons. Mr. Glaspey, an oratorio soloist, enjoys participating in the performing arts, in particular the Tulsa Opera Company. He also enjoys golf in his leisure time.

Harold E. Goodman
Owner/Agent
Harold Goodman Insurance Agency
1302 6th Street
Bedford, IN 47421
(812) 275–6338
Fax: Please mail or call

6411

Business Information: Harold Goodman Insurance Agency is an auto, homeowners, life, health, and business sales and service agency. As Owner/Agent, Mr. Goodman is responsible for all aspects of Company operations, including sales and service, filing of claims and consulting with insurance companies on the client's behalf. **Career Steps:** Owner/Agent, Harold Goodman Insurance Agency (1975–Present). **Associations & Accomplishments:** Insurance Institute of America; Gideons International; Local and District Exchange Club. Mr. Goodman has held many positions of authority with the local and district exchange clubs, and is a three–time recipient of the Exchangite of the Year Award. Mr. Goodman attributes his success to his father, who taught him to be honest, work hard, and treat others with respect and kindness. **Education:** Purdue University, B.S. (1973). **Personal:** Married to Deborah F. in 1977. Three children: Jenia, A.J. and Nikki. Mr. Goodman enjoys hunting, fishing, reading, and helping others.

Diane Grogan
Vice President of Customer Service
Universal Insurance
585 Waughtown Street
Winston–Salem, NC 27114–5687
(910) 771–0400 Ext. 205
Fax: (910) 771–0401

6411

Business Information: Universal Insurance is a nonstandard automobile insurance carrier providing high–risk insurance. Established in 1962, Universal Insurance reports annual revenue of $32 million and currently employs 80 people. As Vice President of Customer Service, Ms. Grogan oversees customer service operations, including all policy activities. **Career Steps:** Vice President of Customer Service, Universal Insurance (19–Present); General Manager and Underwriting Supervisor, Premium Budget Plan. **Associations & Accomplishments:** Member, Pilot Mountain Jaycees (2 years); NAIW, a national and local organization. **Education:** University of North Carolina – Chapel Hill, B.A. in Sociology (1985); North Carolina Property/Casualty License; CPIW. **Personal:** Ms. Grogan enjoys cross–stitching, golf, and other outdoor sports.

J. Max Gutterman, C.F.A.
President
Performance Partners Insurance Marketing, Inc.
22231 Mulholland Highway, Suite 203
Calabasas, CA 91302
(818) 225–7194 (800) 559–1295
Fax: (818) 225–7197

6411

Business Information: Performance Partners Insurance Marketing, Inc. is a highly–specialized national financial services consultancy serving Investment Advisors, Certified Financial Planners, Asset Managers, Insurance Professionals, and Registered Representatives. The Firm specializes in the design and implementation of tax mitigations, investments, and retirement strategies. Its founder, Mr. Gutterman, is a Certified Financial Advisor, and serves as the Company's President and CEO. Max, and his staff, work with 2,500 professionals across the U.S. with sales currently $1.5 million and growing at a very rapid pace. A 20–year veteran of the financial services industry, Mr. Gutterman started his sales career at age 16 with Colliers, becoming the # I salesman in the Los Angeles Region. Opening three retail businesses by the age of 21, he then went on to market telemarketing automation equipment at the infancy of the industry. In addition, he developed original scripting and new methods of distribution. Beginning his career in financial services and insurance with Bankers Life in 1977, he became the Top Agent in the first three years, as well as a member of the President's Cabinet, and New Agent of the Year. Opening an independent general agency in 1981, he recruited, trained, and managed 50 full–time professional agents which resulted in sales of $600,000 per year. As Regional Recruiter and Director for a major insurer between 1985–1990, he developed his assigned region from $500,000 to $3 million in sales. **Career Steps:** President and CEO, Performance Partners Insurance Marketing, Inc. (1996–Present); Regional Vice President, Programmed Insurance Marketing Inc. (1990–1996); Regional Director, Kentucky Central Life Insurance Company (1985–1990); President, Metronet Insurance Services (1981–1985). **Personal:** Married to Jean. Three children: Mark, Johnathan, and Michael.

Mr. Jim H. Hall
President & Chief Executive Officer
HCM Benefits, Inc. (formerly Cal–Surance Group Benefits, Inc.)
P.O. Box 2807
Torrance, CA 90509–2807
(310) 543–9995
Fax: (310) 543–9905

6411

Business Information: HCM Benefits, Inc. is an insurance brokerage, providing the design, implementation and service of employee benefits programs to corporate clientele. As President and Chief Executive Officer, Mr. Hall is responsible for all aspects of operations. In 1974, Jim Hall joined the original Cal–Surance companies to manage the one person Group Department. The Department grew dramatically under Mr. Hall's direction. In 1986, Hall bought controlling interest of the Group Benefits division from the parent company. Today, HCM Benefits, Inc. employs 35 people with annual sales of $6.1 million. **Career Steps:** President & Chief Executive Officer, HCM Benefits, Inc. (1986–Present); Senior Vice President, Cal–Surance Group Benefits, Inc. (1980–1986); Vice President, Cal–Surance Benefit Plans, Inc. (1974–1976); Account Executive, Equitable Life Assurance Society (1968–1974). **Associations & Accomplishments:** Pru-Care Public Policy Board; Blue Shield Corporate Members; Blue Cross Broker Advisory Council; MetLife Broker Advisory Council; Unum Western Region Broker Forum; MHN Public Policy; Rotary Club of South Bay; TEC (The Executive Committee); The President's Committee on Employment of People with Disabilities; Recipient of the "Outstanding Young Men of America" Award; "Who's Who in U.S. Executives"; "International Who's Who"; Board of Directors, Palos Verdes Peninsula Booster Club; President, Panther Touchdown Club; School of Management Advisory Board, California State University at Dominguez Hills. **Education:** Susquehanna University, B.S. in Business Administration (1968); Chartered Life Underwriter (CLU), The American College (1977). **Personal:** Married to Pamela in 1968. Three children: Jennifer, Christine and Gregg. Mr. Hall enjoys golfing, softball and skiing. He and his family reside in Palos Verdes Estates, California.

Fathi H.F. Hamam
Technical Consultant
Kuwait Reinsurance Company
P.O. Box 21929
Safat, Kuwait 13080
(965) 244–1438
Fax: (965) 242–7823

6411

Business Information: Kuwait Reinsurance Company provides all types of insurance and reinsurance to businesses worldwide. As Technical Consultant, Mr. Hamam supervises all technical aspects of the Company. He also acts in a consultant capacity, assisting the new General Manager with any problems he may encounter. **Career Steps:** Kuwait Reinsurance Company: Technical Consultant (1996–Present), General Manager (1985–1996), Manager – London Office (1980–1985); Manager – London Office, Egyptian Reinsurance Company (1974–1980). **Associations & Accomplishments:** Chartered Insurance Institute, London. **Education:** Cairo University, B.Com (1960), Insurance Diploma (1964); ACII, London (1976). **Personal:** Married to Sayeda A. in 1967. Three children: Inas, Mohammed and Iman. Mr. Hamam enjoys swimming and reading.

Nick J. Harris
System Programmer
American–Amicable Life Insurance Company of Texas
425 Austin Avenue
Waco, TX 76701
(817) 753–7311
Fax: (817) 750–7733
EMail: See Below

6411

Business Information: American–Amicable Life Insurance Company of Texas provides life insurance to the military, government employees, and their dependents. As System Programmer, Mr. Harris maintains main–frame hardware and software as well as technical support to programmers and end users. Internet users can reach him via: nharris@mail.hotl.net. **Career Steps:** System Programmer, American–Amicable Life Insurance Company of Texas (1988–Present); Computer Operations, Texas State Technical College (1985–1988); Quality Analyst, General Tire (1977–1985). **Associations & Accomplishments:** Former Secretary/Treasurer, FLMI Society of Central Texas. **Education:** Texas State Technical College, A.A.S. (1987); CLU–American College, FLMI. **Personal:** Married to Jamie in 1990. Two children: Nicholas and Hope. Mr. Harris enjoys golf and racquetball.

Alan R. Hart
Vice President of Commercial Line
Great River Insurance Company
4909 Great River Drive
Meridian, MS 39302
(601) 482–6816
Fax: (601) 485–1129

6411

Business Information: Great River Insurance Company is a regional property and casualty insurance company licensed in the state of Mississippi. The Company is owned by W. R. Berkley Corporation of Greenwich, Connecticut and is now licensed in Tennessee and Louisiana. As Vice President of Commercial Lines, Mr. Hart is responsible for all operations of that section. **Career Steps:** Vice President of Commercial Lines, Great River Insurance Company (1993–Present); USF&G: Commercial Lines Manager (1992–1993), Commercial Lines Assistant Manager (1985–1986), Underwriter (1982–1986). **Associations & Accomplishments:** Chartered Property and Casualty Underwriters; Rotary Club. **Education:** Florida State University, M.B.A. (1975); University of Notre Dame, B.A. (1973). **Personal:** Married to Lou in 1976. Mr. Hart enjoys golf, travel, and reading.

Keith E. Heerdegen
Senior Project Manager
Allstate Insurance Company
1500 W. Shure Drive
Arlington Heights, IL 60004
(847) 632–8870
Fax: (847) 632–8622
Email: See Below

6411

Business Information: Allstate Insurance Company is a leading insurance company offering auto, home, renters, and life insurance products. As Senior Project Manager, Mr. Heerdegen is currently responsible for supervising all application development for customer related document production for the property and casualty company. Responsibilities include strategic planning, hardware and software evaluations related to electronic document printing and finishing, and support and maintenance activities. Internet users can reach him via: KHAK4@ALLSTATE.COM. **Career Steps:** 22+ years with Allstate, has developed and managed significant projects in claim and policy issuance systems. Present title: Sr. Project Manager of Electronic Document Processing Systems. **Associations & Accomplishments:** XPLOR International since (1980–Present); Named to OCE' Printing Systems Joint Technology Council in 1994; Named to Gunther International User Advisory Council in 1996. **Education:** Northern Illinois University, B.S. Degree in Business (1974). **Personal:** Married to Jo Ann in 1976. Three children: Kevin, Christopher, and Keith. Mr. Heerdegen enjoys community service activities which include being Commissioner of the Libertyville, Illinois Boys Club Football Program.

Julio A. Heng
Vice President of Sales and Marketing
Inservices, Inc.
2402 West Willow
Enid, OK 73703
(405) 233–2000
Fax: (405) 242–6703

6411

Business Information: Inservices, Inc. is an independent insurance agency, concentrating on commercial property and casualty insurance coverages. Established in 1927, Inservices, Inc. currently employs 20 people. As Vice President of Sales and Marketing, Mr. Heng serves as Marketing Manager, responsible for acquisitions in marketing and contracts, as well as conducting direct–mail marketing. **Career Steps:** Vice President of Sales and Marketing, Inservices, Inc. (1994–Present); Senior Multi Line Underwriter, Gulf Insurance Company (1994); CNA Insurance Company: Senior Multi Line Underwriter (1993–1994), Casualty Underwriter (1990–1993). **Associations & Accomplishments:** Oklahoma Association of Independent Agents. **Education:** University of Missouri – Kansas City, B.A. in History (1989). **Personal:** Married to Cynthia in 1985. One child: Terry. Mr. Heng enjoys golf, fishing, bowling, and exercising.

Sharon M. Holahan, Esq.
•••────◉────•••

Vice President
Associated Aviation Underwriters
51 John F. Kennedy Parkway
Short Hills, NJ 07078
(201) 379–0942
Fax: (201) 379–0923

6411

Business Information: Associated Aviation Underwriters requires that all product liability and general aviation staff members be licensed pilots. As AAU Vice President, Ms. Holahan manages the Product Liability Claims section. As a practicing attorney since 1982, she has represented numerous clients in catastrophe litigation arising out of airline, military, and general aviation accidents. She has the distinction of being AAU's first women officer. **Career Steps:** Assistant Editor, Aviation International News (1980–1982); Associated Aviation Underwriters: Attorney (1983–1988), Assistant Vice President (1988–1993), Vice President and Product Liability Claims Manager (1993–Present). **Associations & Accomplishments:** Founder and Former President, International Aviation Womens Association; American Bar Association: Aviation and Space Law Committee, Program Co–Chair (1996). **Education:** Western New England School of Law, J.D. (1982); Ohio University, A.B. in Political Science. **Personal:** Married to Mark Gertner in 1985. Two children: Philip Holahan Gertner and Elliot Holahan Gertner.

Patricia A. Hollenbeck
Vice President
Despot Nelson & Co.
6312 South Fiddlers Green Circle #435
Englewood, CO 80111
(303) 796–0200
Fax: (303) 796–0055

6411

Business Information: Despot Nelson & Co. is an insurance brokerage, owning and managing two independent agencies throughout the U.S. With twenty–one years experience in the insurance industry, Ms. Hollenbeck joined Despot Nelson & Co. in 1994. Serving as Vice President, she is responsible for all aspects of daily operations for the Sales Department, including administration, finances, sales, public relations, and marketing. **Career Steps:** Vice President, Despot Nelson & Co. (1994–Present); Vice President, Rollins Hudig Hall (1976–1994). **Associations & Accomplishments:** Business and Professional Women of Denver; Toastmasters International.; Insurance and Risk Management Institute. **Education:** Colorado State University; Accredited Advisor in Insurance; Pursuing Associate in Risk Management; CPCU. **Personal:** Married to Terry in 1974. Ms. Hollenbeck enjoys golf.

Mark A. Holzwart, CPCU, ARM, ARe
President
Lakeland Mutual Insurance Company
P.O. Box 68
Cleveland, WI 53015–0068
(414) 693–8131
Fax: (414) 693–8919

6411

Business Information: Lakeland Mutual Insurance Company is a premium provider of agri/business insurance and personal lines coverage throughout the State of Wisconsin. Established in 1871, Lakeland Mutual Insurance Company reports annual premiums in excess of $3 million and currently employs seven people. With over nineteen years of experience in the insurance industry, Mr. Holzwart joined Lakeland Mutual Insurance Company in 1995. Serving as President, he is responsible for formulating direction in strategic and operational matters. **Career Steps:** President, Lakeland Mutual Insurance Company (1995–Present); Manager of Reinsurance, Wausau Insurance Company (1992–1995); Supervisor of Reinsurance, Kemper Re (1987–1992); Supervisor of Claims, Shand Morahan (1985–1987). **Associations & Accomplishments:** Chartered Property Casualty Underwriter; United Way Allocations; NAMIC CEO Roundtable. **Education:** University of Wisconsin, B.S. (1976); Chartered Property Casualty Underwriter; ARM; ARE. **Personal:** Married to Lisa in 1978. Two children: Amanda and Allison. Mr. Holzwart enjoys music, guitar, sports, and gardening.

Michael G. Intagliata
Regional Director of Group Sales
Fortis Benefits Insurance Company
5251 Denver Technical Center Parkway, Suite 1120
Englewood, CO 80111–2740
(303) 796–7990
Fax: (303) 796–2769

6411

Business Information: Fortis Benefits Insurance Company, established in 1957, is involved in marketing employee benefits and group insurance plans through insurance brokers. Joining the Firm as Regional Manager in 1972, Mr. Intagliata was promoted to National Sales Manager in 1984 and to his present position as Regional Director of Group Sales in 1986. He is responsible for the direction of all sales activities for a five–state Rocky Mountain region, in addition to overseeing all administrative operations for associates and a support staff of ten. **Career Steps:** Fortis Benefits Insurance Company: Regional Director of Group Sales (1986–Present), National Sales Manager (1984–1986), Regional Manager (1972–1984). **Associations & Accomplishments:** Life Underwriters National Association; Health Underwriters National Association; Association of Chartered Life Underwriters. **Education:** Southeast Missouri State University, B.A. (1971). **Personal:** Married to Nancy in 1974. Three children: Kimberly, Nicolas, and Adam.

Rich Jones
Owner and District Manager
Rich Jones – District Manager
9033 East Easter Place, Suite 102
Englewood, CO 80112
(303) 771–7820
Fax: (303) 771–7946
E–MAIL: See Below

6411

Business Information: Rich Jones – District Manager is a sales and marketing office of Farmers Insurance Group Products. As District Manager, Mr. Jones leads, coaches, trains, and mentors a district of 25 insurance agents in the metro Denver area. Internet users can reach him via: RICH0747@AOL.COM. **Career Steps:** District Manager, Rich Jones – District Manager (1988–Present); Agent, Rich Jones Insurance Agency (1978). **Associations & Accomplishments:** NALU, DALU, GAMA, Kiwanis, Board of Directors (Secretary) of Rocky Mountain GAMA, Board of Directors of Highlands Ranch Kiwanis. **Education:** Colorado State University, B.S. (1972). **Personal:** Married to Marilyn E. in 1970. Two children: Christopher D. and Mollie Jo. Mr. Jones enjoys mountain biking, road biking, climbing, hiking, skiing, and running.

George J. Kalopsis

Vice President of Claims
PAFCO Insurance Company Limited
1243 Islington Avenue, Suite 300
Etobicoke, Ontario M8X 2Y3
(416) 231–1300
Fax: (416) 231–2612

6411

Business Information: PAFCO Insurance Company Limited specializes in high risk insurance, including auto and property. Established in 1970, the Company has offices in Toronto, Montreal, Vancouver, and Edmonton with estimated coverage of $200 million. As Vice President of Claims, Mr. Kalopsis oversees the technical and administrative functions of the Company. He is responsible for all technical decisions and approves all claims. He also provides support for other areas and helps maintain the Company's philosophy. **Career Steps:** PAFCO Insurance Company Limited: Vice President of Claims (1992–Present), Canadian Claims Manager (1987–1989); Partner, Norton, Kalopis, & Fuller Adjusters (1989–1992). **Associations & Accomplishments:** Insurance Institute of Canada; Association of Canadian Insurers; Claims Managers Association, Canada. **Education:** University of Western Ontario, Bachelor of Arts With Honors (1979); Associate of the Insurance Institute of Canada. **Personal:** Married to Gail Copeland in 1989. Two children: Christopher and Alexander. Mr. Kalopsis enjoys golf.

David A. Kapauan
Senior Technical Consultant
Manulife Financial
200 Bloor Street East
Toronto, Ontario M4W 1E5
(416) 926–3466
Fax: (416) 926–5454
EMAIL: See Below

6411

Business Information: Manulife Financial is the largest provider of insurance and financial services in Canada, specializing in high–end life insurance policies, estate planning, and pensions. As Senior Technical Consultant, Mr. Kapauan is responsible for the technology development, overseeing network administration, computer design architecture, and research and development. Internet users can reach him via: KAPAUAN@FTN.NET or DAVID_KAPAUAN@MANULIFE.COM **Career Steps:** Senior Technical Consultant, Manulife Financial (1990–Present); Consultant, Sequel Concepts (1987–1990); Systems Engineer, IBM (1983–1987). **Associations & Accomplishments:** Co–Founder and Co–Owner, Sequel Concepts and Sequel Net, a network consulting and service provider; Deacon, Lighthouse Baptist Church of Toronto. **Education:** University of the Philippines, B.S. (1982); Level 1, LOMA. **Personal:** Married to Marie Belle in 1984. One child: Nathaniel. Mr. Kapauan enjoys computers and scuba diving.

Sam Kashanchi
General Manager
MetLife
1 Penn Plaza, Suite 400–K
New York, NY 10119
(212) 560–4536
Fax: (212) 560–4552
EMail: See Below

6411

Business Information: MetLife is one of the world's largest underwriters of life policies and financial contracts. As General Manager, Mr. Kashanchi is responsible for day–to–day operations, administration, customer service, and daily company operations. Internet users can reach him via: WWW.LILI-LI.COM. **Career Steps:** MetLife: General Manager (1995–Present), Agency Manager (1989–1995); Financial Consultant, Sherson Lehman Brothers (1984–1988). **Associations & Accomplishments:** New York Association of Life Underwriters; National Association of Life Underwriters. **Education:** Northeastern University, M.B.A. (1973); University of California – Berkeley, B.S. **Personal:** Mr. Kashanchi enjoys bridge and tennis.

Ryan Kennedy
President
Liberty Benefit Insurance
13980 Blossom Hill Road
Los Gatos, CA 95032
(408) 445–3770
Fax: (408) 445–3789

6411

Business Information: Liberty Benefit Insurance is a full–service insurance consulting and brokerage firm, specializing in managed care. Established in 1989, the Company employs 42 people and has an estimated annal revenue of $32 million. As President, Mr. Kennedy oversees every aspect of the Company. He is responsible for administration, operations, sales, public relations, marketing, and strategic planning. Mr. Kennedy also manages all large client transactions and serves as senior consultant. **Career Steps:** President, Liberty Benefit Insurance (Present); Consultant, CBIS. **Associations & Accomplishments:** Heritage Foundation; Self–Funding Academy; Self Insurance Association of America. **Education:** Westmont, B.A. in Economics; International Business Certificate. **Personal:** Married to Diane in 1991. Mr. Kennedy enjoys fishing, motorcycles, and golf.

Craig A. Knepp
President
C.S. Claims Group, Inc.
401 Huehl Road, Suite 1–E
Northbrook, IL 60062
(708) 559–0670
Fax: (708) 559–0672

6411

Business Information: C.S. Claims Group, Inc. is an insurance investigation firm, employing 45 people and specializing in medical, disability and life insurance cases. As President, Mr. Knepp is responsible for all aspects of operations, including administration and sales, as well as directing the operations of larger, sensitive cases. **Career Steps:** President, C.S. Claims Group, Inc. (1991–Present); Regional Director, J. Thomas & Associates (1986–1991); Vice President, Northern Service Bureau (1984–1986). **Associations & Accomplishments:** General Chairperson, Midwest Claim Conference; Vice President, Chicago Claim Association. **Education:** DePaul University School of Commerce (1988); University of Michigan, B.F.A. (1977). **Personal:** Married to Margaret in 1985. Two children: Stacey and Amanda. Mr. Knepp enjoys fishing, golf, and computers.

Kurt A. Kohout
Director of Claims
American Express Property and Casualty Company
1400 Lombardi Avenue
Green Bay, WI 54304–3922
(414) 496–5180
Fax: (414) 496–5334

6411

Business Information: American Express Property and Casualty Company is a wholly–owned subsidiary of American Express. The Company focuses primarily on providing homeowner and auto insurance through direct market to card members, financial planning clients, and the general public. Established in 1984, the Company employs 125 people and has estimated annual revenue of $125 million. As Director of Claims, Mr. Kohout oversees all national claims adjusting for his division (both auto and home). He also supervises a support staff of 200. **Career Steps:** Director of Claims, American Express Property and Casualty Company (1994–Present); Regional Director of Claims, Sentry Insurance Company (1987–1994); Claims Superintendent, Home Insurance Company (1985–1987); Commercial Claims Manager, Commercial Union Insurance Company (1979–1985). **Associations & Accomplishments:** Boy Scouts of America; Local Veterans of Foreign Wars; Optimist Club; Toastmasters; C.P.C.U. **Education:** Illinois State University, B.A. (1979). **Personal:** Married to Lana in 1978. Two children: Brett and Tyler. Mr. Kohout enjoys sports, running, photography, coaching, Boy Scouts, and being a Sunday school teacher.

Edward J. Kuiper

Chairman of the Board
United Underwriters, Inc.
P.O. Box 400
Exeter, NH 03833–0400
(603) 778–0555
Fax: (603) 772–8840

6411

Business Information: United Underwriters, Inc. is an insurance and benefits brokerage house consisting of 2,000 independent insurance agents marketing insurance throughout 27 states. Founding United Underwriters, Inc. in 1974, Mr. Kuiper serves as Chairman of the Board, responsible for the oversight of the entire operations of the Company. Concurrent with his position at United Underwriters, he is the Founder and President of Benefit Council of America, a marketer of insurance benefits to individuals who are not insurance agents (i.e. credit cards, life insurance). Career milestones include taking an agency (Lincoln National) from scratch to being in the Top 25 agencies in the U.S. and making the 5 Million Dollar Roundtable by the age of 26 (after selling insurance for only three years). He has been published in insurance periodicals and journals, as well as local and national newpapers for his accomplishments. He has also taught various insurance seminars and given presentations for insurance companies and national conventions. **Career Steps:** Chairman of the Board, United Underwriters, Inc. (1974–Present); Founder, Benefit Council of America (1992–Present); National Director of Life Sales, Paul Revere Life Insurance Company (1972–1974); Regional Vice President, Reserve Life Insurance Company (1971–1972). **Associations & Accomplishments:** National Association of Life Underwriters; Sub Centers, Inc.; New Hampshire Association of Life Underwriters; Chamber of Commerce; General Agents and Managers Association; National Association of Securities Dealers; Founder, Brokers Heath Insurance Network; National Association of Independent Life Brokerage Agencies. **Education:** University of Pennsylvania, B.S. in Economics (1964). **Personal:** Married to Pamela in 1993. Seven children: Kristen, Nicole, Heather, Stephen, Jonathan, Michael, and Mark. Mr. Kuiper enjoys snow & water skiing and travel.

Sharon La Shure
Executive Vice President
Walt Szadzinski and Associates Ltd.
340 West Butterfield Road
Elmhurst, IL 60126–5069
(708) 832–3222
Fax: (708) 832–3284

6411

Business Information: Established in 1977, Walt Szadzinski and Associates Ltd. is an insurance brokerage providing a full–scope of insurance product lines including: personal life, disability, medical, benefit, retirement and executive compensation packages to individuals and corporations. As Executive Vice President, Ms. La Shure is responsible for all aspects of insurance sales and overall corporate administration. **Career Steps:** Executive Vice President, Walt Szadzinski and Associates Ltd. (1987–Present); Office Manager, Mustardi – Platt & Associates (1983–1987); Collection Manager, Paysaver Credit Union (1980–1983). **Associations & Accomplishments:** National Association of Life Underwriters; National Association of Health Underwriters; Association of Health Insurance Agents; DuPage Association of Health Underwriters. **Education:** Wright Junior College; Associates in Business (1980), Certified Professional Secretary; Northeastern University, Registered Underwriter. **Personal:** Married to Robert in 1964. Two children: Evelyn Ann and Christian Robert.

Warren L. Landry
Executive Vice President
Pauls Agency, Inc.
P.O. Drawer R
Morgan City, LA 70381
(504) 384–4450
Fax: (504) 384–9805

6411

Business Information: Established in 1904, Pauls Agency, Inc. is an independent insurance agency servicing oil related industries, a restaurant chain in 32 states, and financial institutions. As Executive Vice President, Mr. Landry is involved in all aspects of Company operations, including claims and sales. **Career Steps:** Executive Vice President, Pauls Agency, Inc. (1971–Present); Claims Manager, Harlan – LA, Inc. (1968–1971); Claims Adjuster, Crawford and Company

(1965–1968). **Associations & Accomplishments:** Professional Insurance Agents of Louisiana; Independent Agents of Louisiana; Morgan City Rotary; St. Mary Life Agent Association; Past President, Kiwanis Club; St. Mary Agents Association; Central High School Board. **Education:** University of Northwestern Louisiana, B.S. (1963). **Personal:** Married to Barbara in 1965. Three children: Donna, Robin, and Catherine. Mr. Landry enjoys fishing.

Rene Langlois
Executive Director
Professional Liability Insurance Fund, Quebec Bar Association
445 Boulevard St.–Laurent, Suite 550
Montreal, Quebec H2Y 3T8
(514) 954–3452
Fax: (514) 954–3454

6411

Business Information: Professional Liability Insurance Fund, Quebec Bar Association, is a service providing attorneys with professional liability insurance. Affiliated with the Canadian Bar Association, an attorney's membership is mandatory. Established in 1988, the Company employs fifteen people and has estimated annual revenue of $15 million. As Executive Director, Mr. Langlois, who assisted in founding the Organization, oversees the management, investment, claims and legalities of the Company. His duties include administration, operations, finance, public relations, and strategic planning. **Career Steps:** Executive Director, Professional Liability Insurance Fund, Quebec Bar Association (1988–Present); General Counsel, La Capitale, Compagnie d'assurance (1986); Trial Lawyer, Desjardins Ducharme (1983); Chartered Insurance Broker (1976). **Associations & Accomplishments:** Barreau du Quebec (Canadian Bar Association); Director, Quebec General Insurance Council; National Association of Bar Related Insurance Companies (Nabrico); Past President/Governor, The Insurance Institute of Quebec; Co–President, Quebec Diabetes Association Funding Campaign; United Nations Conference on Trade and Commerce (UNCTA). **Education:** Barreau du Quebec, L.L.L. (1983); Universite de Montreal, Law; Ecole des hautes etudes commerciales de Montreal, Management; Concordia University, Pedagogy; The Insurance Institute of Canada, Fellowship and Chartered Insurance Broker (1976). **Personal:** Married to Manon Lebeau. Three children: Guillaume, Etienne, and Renaud. Mr. Langlois enjoys skiing and mountain climbing.

Michael A. Lillie, R.H.U., R.E.B.C.
Regional Vice President
Allianz Life
1750 Hennepin Avenue
Minneapolis, MN 55403–2115
(612) 337–6261
Fax: (612) 337–6203

6411

Business Information: Allianz Life helps insurance companies and large producers through three areas: individual and group reinsurance, product manufacturing, and annuity products. The parent company, Allianz AG, was incorporated in Germany a hundred years ago and is located in forty countries with 125 locations. As Regional Vice President for Allianz Life, Mr. Lillie is responsible for three areas: 1) Reinsurance activity and product development, 2) Long term care, 3) Editor of National health publication for life underwriters. He works mainly in the Northeastern United States with the senior management of insurance companies. **Career Steps:** Regional Vice President, Allianz Life Insurance (1982–Present); Principal, Lillie, Eppinger, & Jones (1988–1992); Vice President of Marketing, Blue Cross/Blue Shield (1979–1988). **Associations & Accomplishments:** National Association of Health Underwriters: Former National President, Former State President; Former Board Member, Washington Continuing Education Board; Board Member, Long Term Care Committee – Health Insurance Association of America. **Education:** Central Washington University, B.A. (1970); Professional Degrees: Registered Health Underwriter, Registered Employee Benefits Consultant; Northeastern University. **Personal:** Married to Lawrie in 1968. Two children: Michael Jr. and Miaenn. Mr. Lillie enjoys snow skiing, golf, and boating.

Bruce I. Lipton

Vice President
Hillis Adjustment Agency, Inc.
1 Neshaminy Interplex, Suite 310
Trevose, PA 19053
(215) 245–5600
Fax: (215) 245–7101

6411

Business Information: Hillis Adjustment Agency, Inc. provides adjustment services for clients who have had property damage due to storms, floods, and other natural damage–causing events. The Company, which covers home and business owners in the Pennsylvania and New Jersey areas, was established in 1987 and currently has 28 employees. As Vice President, Mr. Lipton oversees the day–to–day operations of the Agency, provides support to field agents, assists in financial and long–term planning, and also serves as a public adjuster. **Career Steps:** Vice President, Hillis Adjustment Agency, Inc. (1991–Present); Director of Operations, International Technology Sourcing, Inc. (1987–1989); Assistant Director, Camp Ramah in the Poconos (1984–1985). **Associations & Accomplishments:** American Management Association; Le Tip International; Camp Ramah Alumni Association; Greater Philadelphia Chamber of Commerce; Philadelphia Israel Chamber of Commerce; Lower Bucks County Chamber of Commerce Better Business Bureau; VIP Member, CHASE (Chambers Association of Small Enterprises). **Education:** Temple University, B.B.A. (1979). **Personal:** Married to Meryl S. Sussman in 1992. One child: Rachel Penina Sussman Lipton. Mr. Lipton enjoys boxing and coaching Golden Gloves.

Robert B. Manley Jr., C.P.C.U.
Vice President
McCrea and Gallen
P.O. Box 311
Wayne, PA 19087
(610) 964–9250
Fax: (610) 964–0548
EMAIL: RManley844@AOL.COM

6411

Business Information: McCrea and Gallen is an independent insurance agency specializing in business insurance for medium and large companies. Established in 1981, the Company handles $40 million in sales annually. As Vice President, Mr. Manley oversees all aspects of his clients' risk management needs. He tends to areas such as finances, personnel, and strategic planning. Mr. Manley ensures that everything is in proper order for the Company and its clients. **Career Steps:** Vice President, McCrea and Gallen (1985–Present); Manager of Sales Support, Wausau Insurance Company (1981–1985). **Associations & Accomplishments:** Society of Chartered Property Casualty Underwriter; C.B.M.C.; Restoration of Historic Muhlenberg House; Active in Church. **Education:** Pennsylvania State, B.B.A. Graduated with highest honors (1981), C.P.C.U. **Personal:** Married to Paula in 1984. Two children: Stephen and Jennifer. Mr. Manley enjoys spending time with his family.

Damian Danny Martinez
President and Owner
Seguros Danny D. Martinez
Apartado 386
Caguas, Puerto Rico 00626
(809) 746–3333
Fax: (809) 746–6500

6411

Business Information: Seguros Danny D. Martinez is a full–service insurance agent, primarily serving commercial clientele throughout Puerto Rico. With thirty years of experience in the insurance industry, Mr. Martinez founded the agency in 1981 and serves as President and Owner. He is responsible for all aspects of operations, including administration and sales and services. **Career Steps:** President and Owner, Seguros Danny D. Martinez (1981–Present); Executive Vice President, Futura Insurance Agency (1978–1981); Manager, The Travelers Insurance Company (1974–1978). **Associations & Accomplishments:** Rotary International; Alpha Sigma Gamma; Professional Insurance Agent Association; Voluntarios Contra El Sida; Parent Teacher Association, Notre Dame High School; Association of Catholic Laymen; National Catholic Educational Association; Puerto Rico Life Underwriters Association. **Education:** World University, B.S. (1971); School of Insurance Certifications; LUTC. **Personal:** Married to Maria T. Ayala in 1970. Two children: Maressa and Denise. Mr. Martinez enjoys golf, tennis, snorkeling, karate, and playing the guitar and organ.

Edgardo R. Martinez Sr.
Executive Vice President – Director
National Life Insurance Company
P.O. Box 366107
San Juan, Puerto Rico 00936–6107
(787) 758–8080
Fax: (787) 764–7687

6411

Business Information: National Life Insurance Company is a locally owned company specializing in providing life insurance to clients. A leading insurance company in Puerto Rico, National Life Insurance Company has an A.M. Best & Standard & Poors' rating and is located throughout Puerto Rico and Florida. Established in 1969, the Company employs 98 people, and has an estimated annual revenue in excess of $2 million. As Executive Vice President – Director, Mr. Martinez oversees all Company departments. He directs the supervision of the Vice Presidents, handles marketing strategies, manages incentive and convention traveling, and is responsible for strategic planning and customer service. **Career Steps:** National Life Insurance Company: Executive Vice President – Director (1977–Present), Vice President (1975–1977), Assistant Vice President (1972–1975). **Associations & Accomplishments:** Puerto Rican Association of Life Underwriters; Professional Insurance Agents of Puerto Rico and the Caribbean; Counselor, Private Industry Council; Former President, Puerto Rico Chamber of Commerce; Former President, Puerto Rico Heart Association, Puerto Rico Red Cross; General Agents Management Association; Mortgage Bankers Association; Recipient of "Top Management Award" 1977. **Education:** University of Puerto Rico: B.S. in Marketing, Two Years of Law and related education in insurance and marketing courses (1968–Present). **Personal:** Married to Carmen. Three children: Edgardo, Jr., Jessica and Ricardo Javier. Mr. Martinez enjoys golf.

Marwan M. Matraji
Chairman – General Manager
Strikers Insurance & Reinsurance Company
113–6320
Beirut, Lebanon
961–1868670
Fax: 961–1868675 001–2124781183

6411

Business Information: Strikers Insurance & Reinsurance Company is a national insurance and reinsurance company, directing business in the Lebanese and Arab countries' markets. Established in 1991, Strikers Insurance and Reinsurance Company reports annual revenue of $10 million and currently employs 107 people. As General Manager, Mr. Matraji is responsible for all aspects of management activities of the Company, including overall responsibility of P & L, marketing, and strategic planning. He also serves as Chairman of the Board. **Career Steps:** Chairman – General Manager, Strikers Insurance & Reinsurance Company (1994–Present); Claims Manager, Arab Universal Insurance Company (1990–1994); Managing Director, Al–Mostasharoon Consultant Company (1981–1990); Consultant Broker, Codicom Consult Company (1981). **Associations & Accomplishments:** Association des Compagnies d'Assurances au Liban (ACAL) **Education:** Lebanese University, License in Economy (1978) **Personal:** Married to Maya Safa in 1978. Three children: Ziad, Zeina and Nour. Mr. Matraji enjoys swimming during his leisure time.

Pat B. McCoy
Owner
McCoy & Associates
3304 Richmond Road
Texarkana, TX 75503
(903) 832–7483
Fax: (903) 832–7632

6411

Business Information: McCoy & Associates is a corporate benefits and personal financial services firm, assisting business owners and top tier executives in obtaining insurance benefits. McCoy & Associates business spans a four–state region (Texas, Arkansas, Oklahoma, Louisiana), covering a 200–mile radius. Established in 1995, McCoy & Associates reports annual revenue of $2.25 million. Establishing the Firm in 1995, Mr. McCoy serves as Owner and Manager. He is responsible for all aspects of daily operations, overseeing the administrative operations for associates and a support staff of four, in addition to working with individual clientele to develop insurance and financial plans. **Career Steps:** Owner and Manager, McCoy & Associates (1995–Present); Account Manager, Offenhauser & Company (1982–1995); Account Manager, Jordache Enterprises (1977–1982). **Associations & Accomplishments:** National Association of Life Underwriters; International Association of Financial Planners; Leadership Texarkana. **Education:** Texas A&M University, Economics (1974). **Personal:** Married to Marsha in 1990.

One child: Evan. An avid computer "hacker" and active in sports.

Mr. Charles W. Miller
Executive Vice President
Bratrud Middleton Insurance Brokers
4701 South 19th Street
Tacoma, WA 98405
(206) 759–2200
Fax: (206) 752–8659

6411

Business Information: Bratrud Middleton Insurance Brokers is a full service insurance brokerage and financial services business, providing business insurance, bonds, personal insurance, life insurance, employee benefits programs, and health insurance. As Executive Vice President, Mr. Miller is responsible for managing sales and marketing, and commercial accounts. In January of 1996, Mr. Miller will become the Firm's President. One of the largest insurance brokerage firms in the state of Washington, Bratrud Middleton Insurance Brokers has five offices: Auburn, Tacoma, Longview, Olympia, Puyallup. The Company reports annual revenue of $12 million and has 140 full–time employees. **Career Steps:** Executive Vice President, Bratrud Middleton Insurance Brokers, (1989–Present); Marketing Director, Sedgwick James (1985–1989); Sales Manager, CNA Insurance Company (1982–198 5). **Associations & Accomplishments:** Independent Insurance Agents of Washington; Professional Insurance Agents Association; American Bar Association. **Education:** University of Puget Sound School of Law, J.D. (1978); Seattle University, B.A. (1974).

Carlos Mirabal–Pargas, CLU, ChFC
Chairman
Mirabal, Gigante & Asociados, Inc.
P.O. Box 191786
San Juan, Puerto Rico 00919–1786
(809) 756–5050
Fax: (809) 756–5075

6411

Business Information: Mirabal, Gigante & Asociados, Inc. is a full service life, health, property and casualty insurance agency, servicing clients throughout Puerto Rico. Established in 1989, the Firm currently employs more than 30 people and reports $7 million in property and casualty premium assets, consisting primarily from direct business and that of in–house associates. The associates are housed and provided with all type of services, including that of our own property and casualty inspector, claims handling as well as other technicians in all fields of the insurance and securities business. Thus, the "Financial Team Concept" motto, since its business philosophy is also to coordinate with other professionals in the client's best interest being a problem solver and coordinator. Mirabal, Gigante & Asociados, Inc. is currently undergoing a full scale automation program. **Career Steps:** Chairman, Mirabal, Gigante & Asociados, Inc. (1989–Present); President, Insurance Tax Planning Services, Inc. (1981–1989); Independent Insurance Agent (1975–1981). **Associations & Accomplishments:** Chartered Life Underwriter and Chartered Financial Consultant, Puerto Rico Chapter; PIA; Boys Club; Club Nautico de Puerto Rico; Instrumental in the Conceptualization and design of insurance products for insurance companies; Lectured on insurance taxation, pensions, securities and compensation arrangements in insurance and securities companies conventions in the US and Europe. **Education:** Catholic University of Puerto Rico; American College of Pennsylvania: Chartered Life Underwriter, Chartered Financial Consultant. **Personal:** Married to Aida Mirabal in 1971. Three children: Bernice, Tony and Suzette. Mr. Mirabal–Pargas enjoys sailing and tennis.

Robert L. Monte
President/Chief Executive Officer
North Waterloo Insurance Company
100 Erb Street E.
Waterloo, Ontario N2J 1L9
(519) 886–4530
Fax: (519) 746–0222

6411

Business Information: North Waterloo Insurance Company specializes in farm, rural and agri–commercial risks. A property and casualty insurance firm, the Company is regional in scope, providing service through independent brokers for the entire province of Ontario. Established in 1874, the Company employs 50 people and has an estimated annual revenue of $24 million. As President/CEO, Mr. Monte provides insight for the Company's future. His duties include administration, operations, strategic planning and public relations. **Career Steps:** President/Chief Executive Officer, North Waterloo Insurance Company (1992–Present); Executive Vice Presi-

dent, Toronto Real Estate Board (1990–1992); Vice President, Insurance Operations, Insurance Bureau of Canada (1975–1990). **Associations & Accomplishments:** Board Member, Ontario's Rural Heritage Preservation; Ontario Agricultural Museum; Canadian Bar Association; Law Society of Upper Canada; Metropolitan Toronto Board of Trade; NAMC; Published in "Canadian Insurance" Magazine; Author of "Brokers Survival Handbook". **Education:** University of Western Ontario, Diploma in Executive Management (1985); University of Toronto, LL.B. (1972); University of Guelph, B.A. (1969). **Personal:** Married to Joan in 1983. Two children: Jennifer and Rebecca. Mr. Monte enjoys being a member of the Lionhead Golf and Country Club.

Garry W. Nelson
General Adjuster
Toplis & Harding, Inc.
2601 Elm Hill Pike, Suite I
Nashville, TN 37214–3155
(615) 391–5929
Fax: (615) 391–5853

6411

Business Information: Toplis & Harding, Inc. is a provider of commercial insurance adjusting services for large losses to property and serious bodily injuries, including marine surveying. Clients are serviced by independent adjusters throughout North America. With twenty–six years of experience in the insurance industry, Mr. Nelson joined Toplis & Harding, Inc. as General Adjuster in 1984. He is responsible for the investigation, evaluation, and resolution of large claims. He recently directed the investigation of an area covering five states in the Mid–South. His largest account to date was a $44 million claim. **Career Steps:** General Adjuster, Toplis & Harding, Inc. (1984–Present); Branch Claims Manager, Lumbermans Mutual Insurance (1979–1984); Regional Adjuster, Commercial Union Insurance (1970–1979). **Associations & Accomplishments:** Treasurer of Nashville Claims Association; Member of Atlanta Claims Association; Member of Southern Loss Association; National Association of Churches; Volunteer at Shelter Program. **Education:** Georgia State University, Masters of Insurance (1978); Georgia Institute of Technology, Masters of Organization (1976); Bachelors of Management (1970). **Personal:** One child: Michael. Mr. Nelson enjoys automobile restoration, and Youth Soccer League.

Mr. Kenneth L. North, Jr., CIC
Executive Vice President
Rogers & Belding Insurance Agency, Inc.
2505 East Missouri
El Paso, TX 79903
(915) 544–3111
Fax: (915) 534–9431

6411

Business Information: Rogers & Belding Insurance Agency, Inc. is a general insurance agency. Established in 1933, Rogers & Belding Insurance Agency Inc, presently employs 65 people and bills $35.5 million in premiums. In his current capacity, Mr. North specializes in casualty insurance, serves as Account Executive responsible for medium to large commercial accounts. He is involved in all marketing and sales. He serves as coordinator and manager of all aspects of insurance coverage. Mr. North also serves as the front line contact, there to answer questions or solve problems. He is qualified to evaluate exposures, recommend coverages, and to develop a plan to meet an organization's financial goals. **Career Steps:** Executive Vice President, Rogers & Belding Insurance Agency, Inc. (1977–Present); Marketing Representative, Commercial Union (1977–1992). **Associations & Accomplishments:** Southwest Regional Director of the National Young Agents Committee/Independent Insurance Agents of America (1985–1987); Member of the Young Agents Committee of the Independent Insurance Agents of Texas, (1982–1985); Four–year member of the CFCI Executive Council (1986–1990), and acted as Southwest Regional Chairman for the 1987 term; Member (12 years), Border Business Association; Other community activities included serving on the John Hancock Sun Bowl Football Host Committee (1982–1986) and on the University of Texas at El Paso's corporate Contribution Campaign Committee (1968–1990). In 1988 and 1989, he was asked to serve on the 'CEO for a Day' panel with Zurich–American, received his Risk Manager's license in Texas, was selected for Commercial Union's Producer Advisory Council/Southwest for these years, and served as Chairman during the 1990 term. In 1989 he began three–year terms on the following: CNA's Texas Pacer Panel, the Board of Directors of the Preferred Risk Organization, and the Board of Directors of the Child Crisis Center of El Paso. During 1990, Mr. North served on the CNA Regional Pacer Council and became Chairman of the Texas Pacer Panel in 1992, was reappointed to the CFCI State Producer Council for three years, and increased his role as the First Vice President of the Child Crisis Center. In 1991, he began a three year term as a selected member of Hartford's Jonathan Trumbull Council, Texas Region, and was appointed to the Finance Committee of the IIAT (Independent Insurance Agents of Texas) and was reappointed to another three year term in the Child Crisis Cen-

ter. In 1993, Ken remains for another year on the Finance Committee of the IIAT, was elected to chair the Hartford's Council and was involved as a volunteer in the 1993 United Way Campaign. In 1994, Mr. North was elected to the State Board of Directors for Texas Independent insurance agents. **Education:** Attended, University of Texas in Austin; East Texas State University in Commerce, B.S. Degree; He received his Certificate Insurance Counselor designation in 1978. **Personal:** Married to Pamela in 1976. Three children: Sean, Chad and Amanda. Mr. North enjoys tennis, running and travel in his leisure time.

Patricia O'Bannon Muse
Marketing Director
Brigham–Williams, Realtors
8 Office Park Circle
Birmingham, AL 35223
(205) 868–4570
Fax: (205) 868–4555
EMAIL: See Below

6411

Business Information: Brigham–Williams, Realtors provides real estate marketing for 225 realtors in the Birmingham area. As Marketing Director, Ms. O'Bannon Muse is responsible for oversight of creative concepts and designs, as well as management of direct mail and radio, T.V. and billboard advertising. Internet users can reach her via: lmawgirl@aol.com. **Career Steps:** Marketing Director, Brigham–Williams, Realtors (Present); Marketing Director, Birmingham Children's Theatre (1993–1996); Owner, Studio 120 (1991–1993); Communications Director, Maynor Eye Center (1986–1991). **Associations & Accomplishments:** Birmingham Ad Club; Crestwood Neighborhood Association; Service Guild; Birmingham Children's Theatre Women's Committee; PTO President, Our Lady of Sorrows Catholic School. **Education:** Mississippi University for Women, B.S. in Journalism (1979). **Personal:** Married to Lawrence in 1980. Three children: Lauren, Chloe, and Mace. Ms. O'Bannon Muse enjoys being a writer/poet, and a published playwright.

Jorge L. Padilla Rivera, C.P.A.

Chief Financial Officer
Universal Insurance Company
P.O. Box 71338
San Juan, Puerto Rico 00936
(787) 793–7202
Fax: (787) 793–4012

6411

Business Information: Universal Insurance Company is the largest property and casualty company in Puerto Rico providing auto, homeowners, personal and commercial insurance and bonds for individuals and corporations. Regional in scope, the Company has five locations throughout the island. Established in 1971, Universal Insurance Company employs 272 people and has an estimated annual revenue of $168 million. As Chief Financial Officer, Mr. Padilla Rivera oversees all investments, accounting, budgeting, payroll, taxes and MIS. He also handles all administrative duties and day–to–day operations of his department. **Career Steps:** Chief Financial Officer, Universal Insurance Company (1985–Present); Manager, Deloitte & Touche LLP (1979–1985). **Associations & Accomplishments:** Certified Public Accountant Society, Puerto Rico Chapter; Financial Analyst Association; Institute of Internal Auditors; Inter–American Businessmen's Association; American Institute of Certified Public Accountants; Spanish Chamber of Commerce; Former Director, Boy Scouts of America Puerto Rico Chapter. **Education:** University of Puerto Rico, B.B.A. in Accounting (1979); Certified Public Accountant (1980); Various Continuing Education Courses. **Personal:** Married to Hilda Dalmau in 1980. Three children: Yaniz C., Nicole M. and Camille A. Padilla. Mr. Padilla Rivera enjoys tennis, golf, and horseback riding.

Stacy M. Parker, Esq.
Vice President
Alexander & Alexander of New York, Inc.
1185 Avenue of the Americas, 17th Floor
New York, NY 10036
(212) 238–1431
Fax: (212) 238–1019

6411

Business Information: Alexander & Alexander of New York, Inc. provides professional risk management consulting, insurance brokerage and human resource management consulting services in eighty countries. As Vice President in the Financial Services Department, Ms. Parker serves as a national resource to the A&A global network, where she assists in producing, marketing, and servicing accounts. Ms. Parker's area of expertise is in Directors' and Officers' and other professional liability coverages, as well as risk management issues. Nationally-recognized in this area, Ms. Parker has lectured at several national and international programs. She has also authored several articles on her area of expertise. **Career Steps:** Vice President, Alexander & Alexander of New York, Inc. (1995–Present); Assistant Vice President, Home Insurance Company (1992–1995); Corporate Claims Officer, Chubb & Son, Inc. (1988–1992); Hogrefe, Stern & King (1988). **Associations & Accomplishments:** Chair, American Bar Association – Tort and Insurance Practice Section, Professionals', Officers', and Directors' Liability Law Committee; Former Board Member, Jewish National Fund; Professional Liability Underwriting Society; New York Lawyers' Association, Committee on Insurance; Outstanding Young Women of America. **Education:** Western New England College School of Law, J.D. (1987); Hofstra University School of Law (1986–1987); The University of Albany, B.A. (1984). **Personal:** Ms. Parker enjoys travel, reading, theater, sports, and the outdoors.

Mitula R. Patel

Controller
Sander A. Kessler & Associates
9570 West Pico Boulevard
Los Angeles, CA 90035
(310) 247–3270
Fax: (310) 278–6396

6411

Business Information: Sander A. Kessler & Associates is one of the largest insurance brokerage firms on the west coast. The Firm specializes in providing clients with customized insurance and financial services to meet specific needs. Established in 1956, the Company employs 88 people, and estimates annual revenue to be in excess of $60 million. As Controller, Ms. Patel maintains overall supervision of the Company, and specifically oversees the finances of the accounting department. She is responsible for budgeting, financial planning, and related reports. **Career Steps:** Controller, Sander A. Kessler & Associates (1993–Present); Manager, Accounting/MIS, Liberty Agencies, Inc. (1988–1992); Manager, Accounting/Re–Insurance, Kenya Arab Orient Insurance Company (1982–1984). **Associations & Accomplishments:** Chairman of Budge Committee, Los Angeles Chapter, National Association of Insurance Women; Insurance Industry; **Education:** American Insurance Institute, A.S.; Insurance Institute of Kenya, Diploma in Marine, Fire, and Accidents. **Personal:** Married to Rajendra in 1985. One child: Anisha. Ms. Patel enjoys painting, arts/crafts, cooking, sewing, and entertaining.

Barry T. Pawielski

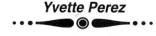

Partner
Michiana Insurance Group
P.O. Box 220
Niles, FL 49120
(616) 683–8400
Fax: (616) 683–5316

6411

Business Information: Michiana Insurance Group is a multi-line, full service insurance agency offering risk management, financial planning, and counseling to clients. Comprised of three partners, the Company was established in the 1920's, employs twelve people and has estimated annual revenue of $7 million. As Partner, Mr. Pawielski is a commercial insurance specialist and oversees sales, marketing, public relations, strategic planning, and research to increase quality and volume. **Career Steps:** Michiana Insurance Group: Partner (1994–Present); Sales (1992–1994); Partner/Vice President/Secretary/Treasurer, Rifenberg Insurance (1979–1992). **Associations & Accomplishments:** Society of Certified Insurance Counselors; Certified Professional Insurance Agents Society; Michigan Association Insurance Agents; Rotary; Babe Ruth Baseball; YMCA Fund–raising; Junior Achievement Instructor; Board, Chamber of Commerce; Board President, Orchard Hills Country Club; Board, United Way; Board, Optimist Club. **Education:** Western Michigan University, B.S. (1973); M.S.U., W.M.U., Graduate Work; Certified Insurance Counselor; Numerous Insurance Schools. **Personal:** Married to Linda S. in 1971. Two children: Christopher and Andrew. Mr. Pawielski enjoys photography, cooking, golf, fishing, working with wood.

Angel M. Perez, C.P.A.

Comptroller
Arizona General Insurance, Inc. & Subsidiaries
4120 East Kings Road
Tucson, AZ 85711
(520) 795–5555
Fax: (520) 326–4955 (520) 321–0762

6411

Business Information: Arizona General Insurance, Inc. & Subsidiaries (Certified Insurance Group, Inc. & Kelly Premium Finance, Inc.) is an insurance brokerage, providing auto, life, health, and commercial insurance coverage. With fifty–four years experience in accounting and a Certified Public Accountant since 1948, Mr. Perez joined Arizona General Insurance as Comptroller in 1988. He is responsible for all aspects of accounting functions, including banking, finances, and taxation. A native of Manila, he became a U.S. citizen in 1986. **Career Steps:** Comptroller, Arizona General Insurance, Inc. & Subsidiaries (1988–Present); In–House Certified public Accountant, American Soft Sales (Baskin & Robbins) (1987–1988); Legal Analyst, American Legal System (1987–1988); Owner, Golden Krone, Minila – wood products and wooden caskets for export to California (1971–1986); CPA Public Practice (1971–1983); Comptroller, Chesbrough Ponds, Inc. (NY and Sidney, Australia) (1969–1970); Treasurer, Inhelder Don Baxter, Inc. (1968–1969); Inhelder, Inc.: Treasurer (1960–1968), Special Assistant to the President (1957–1960), Chief Accountant (1950–1957); Internal Audit, Embassy Motors (1948–1950); Asst. Chief Accountant, Philippine Motors, Inc. (Chrysler) (1947–1948); Junior Auditor, Q.G. & Associations, a CPA firm (1945–1947); Bookkeeper & Typist, Manila Building & Loan Association (1942–1944); Office Clerk, Dean of Commerce, Ateneo de Manila (1940–1941). **Associations & Accomplishments:** Knights of Columbus – 4th Degree; Junior Chamber of Commerce; Mandaluyong Chamber of Commerce; PICPA – Certified Public Accountant Association – active in civic and politics. **Education:** Far Eastern University, B.Sc. (1947); University of the East, M.A. in Economics (1963); Certified Public Accountant – 12th Place, Board of Examination – Manila (1948). **Personal:** Thirteen children: Angel II, Angela III, George, Aurora, Liliane, Robert, Renato, Corazon, Antonio, Ernesto, Francisco, Lucy, and Victoria. Mr. Perez enjoys playing musical instruments (piano, ukelele, violin, guitar, mandolin, harmonica), bible study, and research.

Yvette Perez

Administrative Manager
Urrutia Valles, Inc.
P.O. Box 993
San Juan, Puerto Rico 00902–0993
(809) 723–3000
Fax: (809) 723–0881

6411

Business Information: Urrutia Valles, Inc. is an insurance broker, offering all lines and bonds, as well as pension and health plans for customers located in Puerto Rico. Joining Urritia Valles, Inc. as Executive Secretary and Assistant to the President in 1991, Ms. Perez was appointed as Administrative Manager in 1993. She is responsible for all aspects of operations and management of the Human Resources and Accounting departments. Her duties include the purchase of equipment and supplies, accounts payable, reporting, IRS, income tax filing, any administrative and accounting changes, hiring, and firing. **Career Steps:** Urrutia Valles, Inc.: Administrative Manager (1993–Present), Executive Secretary and Assistant to the President (1991–1993). **Associations & Accomplishments:** Society for Human Resource Management; Association of Labor Relations Practitioners; National Association of Insurance Women. **Education:** Catholic University, B.S.S. (1970); Attends seminars during the year related to her position. **Personal:** Two children: Luis R. and Carlos A. Buxo. Ms. Perez enjoys reading, music, dancing, going to the beach, movies, travel, and watching sports like football and basketball.

Christie S. Perry

Programmer Analyst
Primerica Financial Services
3120 Breckenridge Boulevard
Duluth, GA 30136
(770) 564–5290
Fax: Please mail or call

6411

Business Information: Primerica Financial Services is a financial services company representing Primerica Life Insurance Company, the largest underwriter of individual life insurance in North America, National Benefit Life of New York which is a sister company to Primerica Life, Commercial Credit and numerous mutual fund companies including Select Mutual Funds of Smith Barney. As a company, our philosophy is to teach people how to solve the fundamental problems of how money works. As Programmer Analyst, Ms. Perry is responsible for the reinsurance and valuation systems. **Career Steps:** Programmer Analyst, Primerica Financial Services (1995–Present); Programmer, Equifax (1995); DP Specialist III, State Farm (1992–1995). **Associations & Accomplishments:** Associate, Customer Service; Fellow, Life Management Institute; Alpha Kappa Alpha Sorority. **Education:** Savannah State College, B.S. in Computer Science (1992). **Personal:** One child: Brandon C. Ms. Perry enjoys bowling, music, cultural events, and spending time with her son.

Mark Alan Pilcher

Government Relations Director
State Farm Insurance
7401 Cypress Gardens Boulevard
Winter Haven, FL 33888–0001
(941) 325–3152
Fax: (941) 325–3799

6411

Business Information: State Farm Insurance, established in 1922, is a full–service health, life, property and auto insurance company. The Company offers life insurance, automobile insurance, homeowners insurance and renters insurance nationwide. As Government Relations Director, Mr. Pilcher handles all markets for the Florida department of insurance. **Career Steps:** State Farm Insurance: Government Relations Director (1995–Present), Fire Operations Manager (1993–1995), Assistant Division Manager (1992–1993). **Associations & Accomplishments:** Chartered Property and Casualty Underwriter; Florida Chamber of Commerce; Board Member, Florida Windstorm Underwriting Association; Chairman Actuary Committee, Florida Residential Joint Underwriting Association; Florida Insurance Council. **Education:** Henderson State University, B.A. (1977). **Personal:** Married to Shirley in 1977. Two children: Chad Alan and Ryan Glen.

K.C. Pitts

Human Resources Director and Compliance Administrator
PAS Financial Group, Inc.
6301 Campus Circle Drive, Suite 100
Irving, TX 75063–2791
(214) 756–0212 (800) 687–8383
Fax: (214) 756–0111

6411

Business Information: PAS Financial Group, Inc. is a third party insurance administrator providing insurance for bank and credit union members (from 6–800) throughout all fifty states. As Human Resources Director and Compliance Administrator, Mr. Pitts is responsible for all general human resource functions, policies, and procedures, in addition to payroll, recruiting, compliance administration, annual reports, ensuring compliance with licensing for all fifty states and franchise taxes for all, agent renewals, and continuing education. **Career Steps:** PAS Financial Group, Inc.: Human Resources Director and Compliance Administrator (1994–Present), Data Entry (1992–1994); Salesman, Malone & Hyde Drug Distributors (1987–1992). **Personal:** Mr. Pitts enjoys all outdoor activities.

Laura L. Podeszwa, Esq.

Claims Supervisor
State Farm Insurance
10825 Reisterstown Road
Owings Mills, MD 21117
(410) 356–8705
Fax: Please mail or call

6411

Business Information: State Farm Insurance is one of the major national full–line insurance providers. Serving both commercial and individual customers, product lines include health, life, property and auto insurance. Headquarters are located in Bloomington, Illinois. A practicing attorney in District of Columbia and Maryland courts since 1991, Ms. Podeszwa serves as Claims Supervisor at the Owings Mills office. She is responsible for providing legal advice and determining a just settlement without going to trial. **Career Steps:** Claims Supervisor, State Farm Insurance (Present). **Associations & Accomplishments:** District of Columbia Bar; Maryland Bar; American Bar Association. **Education:** Western New England College School of Law, J.D. (1991); University of Denver, B.A.; Brookdale Community College, A.A.S. **Personal:** Ms. Podeszwa enjoys rollreblading, skiing, and adding to her Mother's collection of Nantucket baskets (wood base and woven with care).

MaryEllen Presutti
Human Resources Manager
Motor Vehicle Accident Indemnification Corporation
110 Williams Street
New York, NY 10038
(212) 791–0770
Fax: Please mail or call

6411

Business Information: Motor Vehicle Accident Indemnification Corporation specializes in qualifying, investigating, and mediating claims for the uninsured motorist. A non-profit organization, the Company is funded strictly through mandatory contributions from insurance companies. As Human Resources Manager, Ms. Presutti is responsible for all aspects of personnel management including recruitment, review, benefits, and serving as liaison between Company employees and management. **Career Steps:** Human Resources Manager, Motor Vehicle Accident Indemnification Corporation (1996–Present); Human Resources Manager, Adler, Coleman, Inc. (1995); Human Resources Assistant, Continental Insurance Company (1976). **Personal:** Ms. Presutti enjoys movies, the beach, Las Vegas, gardening, and being outdoors.

ISRM

David V. Pym
President/Chief Executive Officer
International Specialized Risk Management (ISRM) Ltd
840 Howe Street, Suite 400
Vancouver, British Columbia, V6Z 2M7

(604) 669–1821
Fax: (604) 669–7762
EMAIL: See Below"

6411

Business Information: ISRM Ltd is a firm that handles risk management, litigation management and claims adjusting for individuals and business concerns in Canada and abroad. The Company was established in 1979 and has approximately 150 employees. As President/Chief Executive Officer, Mr. Pym manages the daily operation of the Company. He handles public relations duties, marketing of Company services, oversight of legal issues, and strategic planning for the future. Mr. Pym also consults with clients on issues concerning their operations. Internet users can reach him via: dpym@ISRM.com. **Career Steps:** President/Chief Executive Officer, ISRM Ltd (1979–Present). **Associations & Accomplishments:** Royal Architecture Institute of Canada; American Association of Cost Engineers; Technical Delegate, International Ski Federation (FIS); Project Management Institute; Mr. Pym has been published in various trade and professional journals and is involved in local continuing education programs and seminars. **Education:** University of New Zealand, Law (1966). **Personal:** Mr. Pym enjoys skiing and playing golf.

John William Qualls
Manager of Information Systems
Heartland Insurance
8900 Keystone Crossing, Suite 550
Indianapolis, IN 46240
(317) 844–6251
Fax: (317) 843–8049
EMail: See Below

6411

Business Information: Heartland Insurance is an insurance brokerage offering life insurance, annuities, and estate planning services. As Manager of Information Systems, Mr. Qualls maximizes the use of information systems to enhance all facets of insurance financial services. Internet users can reach him via: JOHN_QUALLS@MSN.COM. **Career Steps:** Manager of Information Systems, Heartland Insurance (1993–Present); Information Systems Director, United States Marine Corps (1987–1993). **Associations & Accomplishments:** Special Olympics; Muscular Dystrophy Association. **Education:** Metropolitan Brokerage University, Master in Brokerage (Insurance). **Personal:** Married to Jacqueline in 1991. Mr. Qualls enjoys golf and youth basketball.

Mr. David W. Restrepo
Vice President
Merrill Lynch
Two Greentree Centre, Suite 120
Marlton, NJ 08053
(609) 596–4624
Fax: (609) 596–9259

6411

Business Information: Merrill Lynch is a full-service financial institution providing financial products and advice for achieving retirement, estate, and investment planning goals. As Vice President, Mr. Restrepo is responsible for tax and retirement planning for individuals, corporate cash management, and retirement planning and design for mid-size corporate businesses and high networth individuals. **Career Steps:** Merrill Lynch: Vice President (1987–Present), Assistant Vice President (1984–1987); Branch Manager, Girard Bank (1975–1977). **Associations & Accomplishments:** Haddonfield Rotary Club. **Education:** St. Joseph's University, M.B.A. (1982); Gettysburg College, B.A. in Economics (1974). **Personal:** Married to Carol in 1977. Two children: Ryan and Randy. Mr. Restrepo enjoys golf and tennis.

Annetta Richards
Regional Sales Coordinator
AFLAC
6801 Gray Road, Suite B
Indianapolis, IN 46237–3238
(317) 782–1990
Fax: (317) 787–5203

6411

Business Information: AFLAC, the largest supplemental health insurance company in the United States is a major provider of supplemental health insurance worldwide. As Regional Sales Coordinator, Ms. Richards recruits and trains sales managers, utilizing outstanding field sales agents from among thirteen states. Additional responsibilities include administration, strategic planning, and human resources. **Career Steps:** AFLAC: Regional Sales Coordinator (1987–Present), District Sales Coordinator (1985–1986); Sales Associate (1983–1984). **Associations & Accomplishments:** National Underwriters Association; Recipient of: Top Sales Award at the National and State Convention, FAME Award (Founders Award for Management Excellence); First Advisory Council. **Education:** Clark College, Medical Business (1970). **Personal:** Married to Dennis in 1970. Two children: Kelly and Erik. Ms. Richards enjoys watersports and church activities, especially choir.

Mr. Frank W. Ridley
Vice President
R.C. Knox and Company, Inc.
One Goodwin Square
Hartford, CT 06103–4305
(203) 524–7604
Fax: (203) 240–1590

6411

Business Information: R.C. Knox and Company, Inc. is a full-service insurance agency providing commercial and personal insurance products throughout the U.S. As Vice President, Mr. Ridley is responsible for the oversight of all corporate administrative and operational functions for Personal Lines Division. In addition, he also serves as Director of Education, Public Relations and Advertising. Established in 1892, R.C. Knox and Company, Inc. employs 100 people. **Career Steps:** Vice President, R.C. Knox and Company, Inc. (1990–Present); Assistant Vice President, Manager of Sponsored Marketing Insurance Division, R.C. Knox and Company, Inc. (1987–1989); Assistant Manager, Sponsored Marketing Insurance Division, R.C. Knox and Company, Inc. (1986); Insurance Counselor, R.C. Knox and Company, Inc. (1977–1985); Various Sales and Managerial Positions, W.T. Grant Company (1970–1976). **Associations & Accomplishments:** President, Independent Insurance Agents of Connecticut, Inc.; Communications Committee, Independent Insurance Agents of America; National ASI Insurance Exam Review Committee; Patron, J.R. Heidinger Solo Ensemble; Delegate, Episcopal Diocese of Connecticut; Member, Connecticut Insurance Department Task Force on License Restructuring; State of Connecticut Insurance Exam Review Committee; Founding Member, InVest State Advisory Committee; The Executive Forum of The World Affairs Council; President, International Mass Marketing Association; State of Connecticut Insurance Department, Continuing Education Committee; American Management Association; Vice President, Board of Directors, Chamber Music Plus; Constitution Club, United Way of Greater Hartford; PAST AFFILIATIONS: Education Chairman, Secretary, Treasurer and State Director, Independent Insurance Agents of Connecticut, Inc.; Solicitor, United Way of Greater Hartford; Volunteer Fund Raiser, Hartford Hospital Capital Campaign; Meriden Refugee Committee; Lay Administrator and Advisor to the Rector, Vestryman, Junior Warden, Senior Warden, All Saints Parish, Meriden, CT; Bicentennial Celebrations Committee, Episcopal Diocese of Connecticut; Vice President and Member of Board of Directors, Muscular Dystrophy Association of CT; Board of Directors, Meriden Exposition (1976–1978); Youth and Christian Education Director, Central Connecticut Region for Episcopal Diocese of Connecticut; Campaign Manager for municipal and state elections (1977–1994); AWARDS: 1995 Outstanding Service and Leadership Award in Mass Marketing; Member, [Who's Who Worldwide] (1993 & 1994 Editions); 1993 Outstanding Service Commendation by Connecticut Insurance Department License Task Force; 1992 Agent of the Year by Independent Insurance Agents of Connecticut, Inc.; 1989 Chairman's Award by American Association of Managing General Agents. **Education:** Business Administration Post College, Waterbury, CT, B.A. summa cum laude (1985). **Personal:** Mr. Ridley enjoys classical music and opera, stamp and coin collecting, gardening, reading (especially history) and charity work. He is an accomplished vocalist and performs as Tenor Soloist in regional ensemble troupes.

Antonio Rivera–Colon, A.U.

Vice President
El Fenix De Puerto Rico, Compania De Seguros
P O Box 70340
San Juan, Puerto Rico 00936–8834
(787) 782–5825
Fax: (787) 781–4922

6411

Business Information: El Fenix De Puerto Rico, Compania De Seguros is a full service insurance company offering various types of insurance to clients. Located in San Juan, Puerto Rico, the Company was established in 1976 and currently employs 37 people. As Vice President, Mr. Rivera–Colon supervises all underwriting matters. He is in charge of marketing services and policies to new and existing clients. Mr. Rivera–Colon works with other members of the management staff to develop an annual budget and to make sure the company does not practice deficit spending. He is involved in the strategic planning for the future expansion of the Firm. Concurrently, Mr. Rivera–Colon is a Professor of Insurance at the Faculty of Business Administration, Department of Finance, of the University of Puerto Rico. He also teaches insurance courses at other institutes, on occasion. **Career Steps:** Vice President, El Fenix De Puerto Rico, Compania De Seguros (1994–Present); Actuary/Underwriting Manager, Corporation Insular De Seguros (1987–1992); Chief of Complaints Division, Office of the Commissioner of Insurance of Puerto Rico (1982–1984). **Associations & Accomplishments:** Institute of Actuaries of Puerto Rico, Inc.; Latin American Actuaries Association; Profession Insurance Agents of Puerto Rico and the Caribbean. **Education:** University of Puerto Rico, B.S. in Mathematics; Insurance Institute of America, Associate degree in underwriting. **Personal:** Married to Maria Del C. Rodriguez in 1972. Three children: Yadira Rivera, Omar Antonio, and Enid Yanil. Mr. Rivera–Colon enjoys reading, playing dominoes, and horse racing.

Richard W. Rockwood
Assistant Vice President
Holden Insurance
1101 Tower Avenue
Superior, WI 54880
(715) 394–7741
Fax: (715) 394–7502

6411

Business Information: Holden Insurance specializes in the provision of property and casualty insurance coverage for personal and commercial clientele. In his current capacity, Mr. Rockwood is presently active as Assistant Vice President of the Firm and engages in sales of commercial lines insurance. Established in 1936, Holden Insurance employs 25 people. **Career Steps:** Assistant Vice President, Holden Insurance (1980–Present); Loan Officer, Superior Community Credit Union (1976–1980); Branch Collections Manager, Gamble-Skogmo, Inc. (1973–1976); Assistant Manager, Gables Home Center (1969–1973). **Associations & Accomplishments:** Former President, Superior Douglas County Chamber of Commerce; Former President, Superior Douglas County Development Association; Former President, Superior Jaycees; District Director, Wisconsin Jaycees; Vice President, Tau Kappa Epsilon Fraternity; Board of Directors, KIDS Network; Vice President, Douglas County Fish and Game League; Board of Directors, BID District; One of "Ten Outstanding Young Wisconsinites" by the Wisconsin Jaycees; Statesman Award by Wisconsin Jaycees; "Citizen of the Year" by City of Superior, Wisconsin. **Education:** University of Wisconsin – Superior, B.S. (1973). **Personal:** Married to Michelle in 1985. Three children: Rocky, Paul and Bradley. Mr. Rockwood enjoys playing the guitar, water skiing, and camping during his leisure time.

John A. Ross
Chief Marketing Officer
Programmed Insurance Marketing, Inc.
24422 Avenida De La Carlota
Laguna Hills, CA 92653
(714) 855–6991
Fax: (714) 859–4620

6411

Business Information: Programmed Insurance Marketing, Inc. is a national insurance marketing organization, responsible for recruiting, training, and supporting independent agents and negotiating contracts with carriers. As Chief Marketing Officer, Mr. Ross coordinates his capable staff in packaging products and advanced markets concepts, recruiting and training agents and regional vice presidents on a national basis, and designing marketing and sales material. **Career Steps:** Chief Marketing Officer, Programmed Insurance Marketing, Inc. (1995–Present); National Marketing Director, National Annuity Programs (1993–1995); Regional Director, Life Partners Group (1991–1993); Regional Director, First Capital Life (1987–1991). **Associations & Accomplishments:** American Society of Chartered Life Underwriters/Chartered Financial Counselors. **Education:** University of Iowa, B.B.A. (1983); Chartered Life Underwriter (1989). **Personal:** Mr. Ross enjoys basketball, golf, tennis, and water skiing.

Jim Rzepecki
District Manager
United Group Association
17207 453rd Avenue SE
North Bend, WA 98045
(206) 228–3858
Fax: (206) 831–6256

6411

Business Information: United Group Association is a non–profit organization providing health, dental, disability and life insurance to small businesses and the self–employed. National in scope, the Company has fifty locations throughout the U.S. with over 3,500 representatives. As District Manager, Mr. Rzepecki oversees training, personnel recruitment and sales for his district. Additional duties include motivation, customer relations and strategic planning. **Career Steps:** District Manager, United Group Association (1993–Present); Risk Consultant, Pettit–Murry Company (1990–1993); Risk Consultant, Rollins, Burditch & Hunter (1986–1990); Risk Consultant, Chubb & Sons Insurance Company (1978–1986). **Associations & Accomplishments:** National Association for the Self Employed (NASE); American Society of Safety Engineers (ASSE). **Education:** West Wakesha City Technical Institute, Associate (1976); A.R.M. Associate in Risk Management (1992). **Personal:** Married to Mary Gulgenbach in 1986. One child: Kelsey. Mr. Rzepecki enjoys golf, skiing, biking, softball, hiking, and being a professional sports fan.

Emilio J. Saldana
• • • ◉ • • •
President
Urrutia Valles, Inc.
P.O. Box 993
San Juan, Puerto Rico 00902–0993
(809) 723–3000
Fax: (809) 722–1102

6411

Business Information: Urrutia Valles, Inc., the third largest insurance company in Puerto Rico, is an insurance broker for all lines of insurance, focusing on commerical and personal insurance in the San Juan area. Established in 1980, Urrutia Valles, Inc. reports premium revenue of $2.5 million and currently employs 25 people. As President, Mr. Saldana is responsible for all aspects of operations, including office management and working with clients on the production side. **Career Steps:** President, Urrutia Valles, Inc. (1993–Present); Vice President, Saldana & Associates, Inc. (1984–1993); Senior Auditor, Laventhol & Horwath (1980–1984). **Associations & Accomplishments:** Rotary Club. **Education:** University of Puerto Rico, B.B.A. (1980). **Personal:** Married to Lizette Rexach in 1983. Mr. Saldana enjoys fishing.

Valinda L. Sanders
Application Systems Analyst
Crawford & Company
4680 N. Royal Atlanta Drive
Tucker, GA 30084
(770) 621–3289
Fax: (770) 496–3921

6411

Business Information: Crawford & Company provides risk management and related insurance services to clients. As Application Systems Analyst, Ms. Sanders provides technical support for AS400 midrange computers. **Career Steps:** Crawford & Company: Application Systems Analyst (1995–Present), Network Hardware Installer (1992–1995), Network Hardware Coordinator (1992). **Associations & Accomplishments:** Project Impact; Who's Who in America. **Education:** Bowling Green State College, B.A. in MIS (1986). **Personal:** Ms. Sanders enjoys reading, bike riding and bowling.

Lee Schaffer
• • • ◉ • • •
President
Focus Insurance Services
1200 S. Church Street, Suite 6
Mt. Laurel, NJ 08054–2936
(609) 596–2866
Fax: (609) 234–4468

6411

Business Information: Focus Insurance Services is an Insurance Brokerage Operation, providing Life Insurance, Substandard–Impaired Risk LIfe Insurance, group and individual disability insurance, and group and individual health insurance. With twelve years of experience in insurance sales, Mr. Schaffer joined Focus Insurance Services as Vice President in 1986. Appointed as President in 1990, he serves as the Principal Agent and Director of sales and marketing activities. **Career Steps:** Focus Insurance Services: President (1990–Present), Vice President (1986–1990); Sales, Life Insurance Sales (1984–1986). **Associations & Accomplishments:** Rotary International; Board of Trustees, Garden State Rotary Club of Cherry Hill; Board of Advisors, Small Business Association of Delaware Valley; Board of Directors, The Alternative School. **Education:** Rutgers University, M.B.A. (1976); The American College, R.H.U. **Personal:** Married to Rhonda in 1986. One child: Samantha. Mr. Schaffer enjoys sports, reading, and spending time with his family.

Caroline M. Schluntz
Underwriting Manager
St. Paul Insurance Company
700 5th Avenue, Suite 4200
Seattle, WA 98104–5000
(206) 442–2202
Fax: (206) 442–2273

6411

Business Information: St. Paul Insurance Company is a division of St. Paul Fire and Marine Insurance Company. As Underwriting Manager, Ms. Schluntz is responsible for underwriting construction policies in the Northwest territory and Southern California . **Career Steps:** Underwriting Manager, St. Paul Insurance Company (1968–Present). **Associations & Accomplishments:** C.F.M.A.; A.G.C. **Personal:** Married to Edward in 1974. One child: Dawn Fischer. Ms. Schluntz enjoys travel.

Larry Schmaltz
Senior Director of Sales
Epic Life Insurance
702 Dearholt Road
Madison, WI 53711
(608) 223–2162
Fax: (608) 223–2179

6411

Business Information: Epic Life, a subsidiary of WPS Insurance, provides a full portfolio of ancillary products, to include group health and life, dental, optical, weekly disability, and emergency insurance to businesses. Established in 1985, the Epic Life Insurance estimates annual sales in excess of $130 million. As Senior Director of Sales, Mr. Schmaltz is responsible for all advertising, marketing and distribution in the U.S. **Career Steps:** Senior Director of Sales, Epic Life Insurance (1993–Present); District Director of Sales, Employees Health Insurance (1990–1993); President, Schmaltz Brokerage (1979–1990). **Associations & Accomplishments:** National Health Underwriters; Edgewood College Hall of Fame. **Education:** Edgewood College. **Personal:** Married to Cathy Lee in 1976. Four children: Kyle, Kam, Konnor, and Kenzie.

Mr. Schmaltz enjoys golf and coaching his children's sports programs.

Brian H. Seborg
Manager of Security Services
USF&G Corporation
5801 Smith Avenue, 1 EFF
Baltimore, MD 21209
(410) 578–4044
Fax: (410) 578–7368
EMail: See Below

6411

Business Information: USF&G Corporation is a large insurance company providing personal, commercial, fidelity bonding, and underwriting for private and business sectors. As Manager of Security Services, Mr. Seborg is responsible for ensuring the security of all automated and a portion of the non–automated corporate information. Internet users can reach him via: bseborg@usfg.com. **Career Steps:** Manager of Security Services, USF&G Corporation (1995–Present); PC/LAN Security Program Director, FDIC (1991–1995); UMBC IFSM Department: Lecturer/IS Manager (1987–1991), Research Associate (1986–1987). **Education:** University of Maryland – Baltimore County: M.S. (1990), B.S. in Computer Science. **Personal:** Married to Kimberly Kay in 1984. Three children: Brandon, Brittany, and Christi. Mr. Seborg enjoys camping, canoeing, and being an Assistant Cub Master.

Jack P. Serina
Account Executive and Registered Representative
Financial Services
27906 Blythdale Rd.
Agoura, CA 91301
(818) 991–8302
Fax: Please mail or call

6411

Business Information: Financial Services include real estate, qualified retirement plans, non–qualified plans, securities and life, health and disability insurance. Mr. Serina is responsible for recruiting, sales, and conducting seminars. **Career Steps:** Has worked in every phase of the security business from the floor of the Pacific Coast Stock Exchange to Merrill Lynch (member N.Y.S.E.). Employed also as an associate Real Estate Broker for Mike Glickman Realty, Century 21, and Gold Star Realty. **Associations & Accomplishments:** Member, National Association of Securities Dealers; San Fernando Valley Association of Realtors; Department of Insurance and Toastmasters International Communication and Leadership. **Education:** Los Angeles City College, A.A.; Real Estate Brokers License; N.A.S.D. Series 7 and 63 License; Life, Health, and Disability Insurance License. **Personal:** Married to Donna Jean in 1954. Five children: Deborah, Brian, Kathleen, Nancy, and Paul. Mr. Serina enjoys public speaking, traveling, and is a connoisseur of epicurean delite.

Randall J. Silberquit
Operations Manager
Sternberg Kozera & Gileicher
200 North Central Avenue
Hartsdale, NY 10530–1925
(914) 761–9000
Fax: (914) 761–3749
EMAIL: See Below

6411

Business Information: Sternberg Kozera & Gileicher is an independent insurance agency, marketing insurance to insurance carriers, such as mutual funds and personal & property insurance services. With twenty years of experience in the insurance industry, Mr. Silberquit joined the Agency as Operations Manager in 1990. He is responsible for the direction of all operations systems and the training of new employees. **Career Steps:** Operations Manager, Sternberg Kozera & Gileicher (1990–Present); Commercial Lines Manager, Spadaccia Ryan and Haas (1979–1982); HPuerto Rico Underwriter, IRM Insurance (1976–1979). **Associations & Accomplishments:** State Broker License. **Personal:** Married to Susan in 1981. One child: Ryan. Mr. Silberquit enjoys computers, baseball and skiing.

Larry H. Smith
Deputy Director
Armed Forces Insurance
550 Eisenhower Road
Ft. Leavenworth, KS 66048
(913) 727–4503
Fax: (913) 727–1413
EMAIL: See Below

6411

Business Information: Armed Forces Insurance provides property, casualty, and automotive insurance to military personnel only. The service is offered to active duty, Reserve, National Guard, and retired officers and senior non–commissioned officers only. As Deputy Director, Mr. Smith is responsible for all research and development, training, and marketing of the Company's services. He reviews processes and procedures and eligibility studies and also works on program automation. Mr. Smith is currently working on a study where–by the Company may be able to provide their services to junior enlisted military personnel. Internet users can reach him via: Internetafird@aol.com. **Career Steps:** Deputy Director, Armed Forces Insurance (1994–Present); United States Army: Command Sergeant Major, Combined Arms Command, Fort Leavenworth (1991–1994), Command Sergeant Major, 3rd Infantry Division, Wurzburg, Germany (1989–1991), Command Sergeant Major, 2nd Support Command Stuttgart, Germany (1988–1989). **Associations & Accomplishments:** Lifetime Member, Army Museum Association; Board of Directors/Lifetime Member, Non Commissioned Officers Association; Lifetime Member, Veterans of Foreign Wars; Association United States Army. **Education:** City College of El Paso, Associate (1981). **Personal:** Married to Barbara in 1967. One child: Michele. Mr. Smith enjoys golf, Civil War history and gardening.

Robert A. Soveran
Vice President – Marketing
The Co–operators
PO Box 3608, STN Main
Guelph, Ontario N1H 6P8
(519) 767–3077
Fax: (519) 837–0231
6411

Business Information: The Co–operators is one of Canada's leading full–line insurance brokerages. Joining the Agency in 1981 as a regional manager, Mr. Soveran was appointed to his current role in 1992. As Vice President of Marketing, he provides the overall administrative direction for all media relations, and the overall strategies for the Agency as a whole. **Career Steps:** The Co–operators: Vice President – Marketing (1992–Present); Vice President – Field Operations (1987–1992); Vice President – West Division (1984–1987); Region Manager (1981–1984). **Associations & Accomplishments:** LIMRA; LIMAC; Guelph Chamber of Commerce; Insurance Institute of Canada. **Education:** Insurance Institute, AIIC certification (1972). **Personal:** Married to Jo Anne in 1965. Two children: Terry and Tammy. Mr. Soveran enjoys fishing and model railroading.

Joyce M. Spizer
Vice President
Insurance Investigations, Inc.
5252 Orange Ave, Suite 208
Cypress, CA 90630
(714) 761–9513
Fax: (714) 761–2634
EMAIL: See Below
6411

Business Information: Insurance Investigations, Inc. provides independent adjusters, investigators, negotiators, and mediators in the California, Texas, and Nevada areas. The Company handles trademark infringements, contract disputes, and construction defects. As Vice President, Ms. Spizer is responsible for all aspects of Company operations, including administration, finances, and strategic planning. Internet users can reach her via: ININING@aol.com. **Career Steps:** Vice President, Insurance Investigations, Inc. (1979–Present). **Associations & Accomplishments:** Optimist, International; Board Member, National Kidney Foundation of Southern California; Former Board Member, UCI; Habitat for Humanity; Election Committee to re–elect former Mayor HB; Former President, Nail Odyssey; Boys & Girls Club of HB; Reporter, Local News; Mystery Writer, Sisters–In–Crime; National Writers Association; Romance Writers of America; National Criminal Justice Association. **Education:** California Coast University, MBA (1991); Attended, University of Houston (1964). **Personal:** Married to Harold B. in 1981. Four children: Robin, David, Charles, and Scott. Ms. Spizer enjoys writing, golf, travel, and charity work.

Kenneth S. Stewart
Vice President of Operations
A.F. Stewart and Associates
107–A Corporate Boulevard
South Plainfield, NJ 07080
(908) 755–6000
Fax: (908) 757–1199
6411

Business Information: A.F. Stewart and Associates is a national marketing firm specializing in health insurance products. As Vice President of Operations, Mr. Stewart is responsible for all aspects of operations, including marketing, strategic planning, desktop publishing, and ensuring Company compliance with state and federal laws. **Career Steps:** Vice President of Operations, A.F. Stewart and Associates (1991–Present); Manager, Brocorp, Inc. (1990–1991) **Associations & Accomplishments:** National Association of Health Underwriters; Volunteer, New Jersey Cares **Education:** Rutgers University, B.A. (1990); Attended: Duke University **Personal:** Mr. Stewart enjoys baseball, football, fishing, camping, travel and backpacking in his leisure time.

Philip L. Stone
Director of Investor Relations
Barry Nussbaum Company
2775 Via De La Valle Suite 205
Del Mar, CA 92014
(619) 481–3000
Fax: (619) 481–3373
6411

Business Information: Barry Nussbaum Company (BNC) is a 19–year–old investment real estate firm which has, for the past seven years, purchased large apartment properties at significantly under market value throughout the state of Texas. BNC renovates each property at cost to its limited partners and then manages them for a flat fee. Every effort is made to refinance as quickly as possible so that a return of capital can be achieved plus a dramatic profit to each partner. Over the past seven years BNC has been averaging over 30% return to its limited partners. As Director of Investor Relations, Mr. Stone is responsible for implementing strategic plans to reach new clients, interfacing with existing investors and is intimately involved with marketing and website creation and maintenance. Mr. Stone also remains involved with network television sports broadcasting. He has been the voice of NFL football for NBC, Pacific 10 Conference football and basketball for Prime Sports, he has called major league baseball for the Giants, Rangers, and Padres, as well as PGA and LPGA tournaments and numerous Olympic sports including track & field, and the Los Angeles and San Diego marathons. **Career Steps:** Investor Relations, Barry Nussbaum Company (1995–Present); Play–by–Play, Prime Sports/ESPN (1979–Present); Play–by–Play, NBC Sports (1979–1996); Sports Director, KNSD–TV San Diego (1976–1984). **Associations & Accomplishments:** Board Member, San Diego Center of Children; Board Member, Palomar–Pomerado Health Foundation; Tournament Director, San Diego Chamber of Commerce Insights Golf Classic; Director of Golf, San Diego Center For Children Charity Golf Classic. **Education:** Ohio University: M.B.A. Summa Cum Laude (1973), B.S (1972). **Personal:** Two children: Brent and Lindsay. Mr. Stone enjoys golf, snow skiing, and tennis, but says raising his two marvelous children is his greatest joy. He feels any man can be a father but it takes a dedication of time and a loving heart to be a real dad.

Monica L. Swink
Treasurer
North American Insurance Agency
3800 Classen Boulevard
Oklahoma City, OK 73125–0920
(405) 523–2100 Ext.207
Fax: (405) 556–2332
6411

Business Information: North American Insurance Agency is a national company located in several states which offers a book of personal, commercial, property and casualty insurance, with some residential lines available. As Treasurer, Ms. Swink is responsible for accounting, financial reporting, personnel, and information systems. **Career Steps:** North American Insurance Agency: Treasurer (1995–Present), Controller (1994–Present); Vice President/Treasurer, First Life Assurance Company (1989–1994). **Associations & Accomplishments:** National Association of Executive Females; Insurance Accountants and Systems Association; Allocation Committee, United Way of Greater Oklahoma City; F.L.M.I. Society of Oklahoma; Recognized as one of "Two Thousand Notable American Women" by the American Biographical Institute, (1995). **Education:** University of Central Oklahoma, B.S. (1988); Oklahoma City University, B.A. (1974). **Personal:** Married to Harold in 1984. One child: Hope C. Warrener. Ms. Swink enjoys being active in Epworth United Methodist Church.

Luis A. Torres–Olivera, Esq.
Deputy Director
Puerto Rico Health Insurance Administration
253 Tetuan
Old San Juan, Puerto Rico 00901
(787) 725–9252
Fax: (787) 725–9248
6411

Business Information: Puerto Rico Health Insurance Administration is a public corporation established by law to purchase health insurance coverage for the medically indigent. Established in 1993, the Corporation currently employs over 60 people. As Deputy Director, Mr. Torres–Olivera assists in the daily management of operations. He is involved in working with insurance carriers to establish medical coverage and contracting legal matters. Mr. Torres–Olivera works closely with the Director on the administration of the health care policies and procedures established by the Corporation. Internet users can reach him via: yvonne@caribe.net. **Career Steps:** Puerto Rico Health Insurance Administration: Deputy Director (1996–Present), Special Aide to Executive Director in Legal and Operational Affairs (1994–1996), Acting Executive Director (1996), Legal Affairs Director (1993–1994); Law Clerk, Lasa, Escalera & Reichard (1992–1993); Law Clerk, Sanchez Betances & Sifre (1991). **Associations & Accomplishments:** Federal Bar Association; Puerto Rico Bar Association; Volunteer, Children's Hospital; Certified Tutor by the College Reading and Learning Association; President, University of Puerto Rico Law School Class of 1993. **Education:** University of Puerto Rico Law School, J.D. cum laude (1993); Tulane University, B.A. (1990). **Personal:** Married to Yvonne in 1995. Mr. Torres–Olivera enjoys reading, tennis, travel, and art.

Su Liang Tran, CLU
Managing Partner
New York Life Insurance Company
Suite 800, 6901 Rockledge Drive
Bethesda, MD 20817–1817
(703) 908–8900 Ext. 8990
Fax: (703) 908–8424
6411

Business Information: New York Life Insurance Company is a life insurance company specializing in full life insurance coverage, health insurance, and funds sales. As Managing Partner, Ms. Tran manages an office of approximately 60 agents and three managers. She is also responsible for recruiting and training new agents. **Career Steps:** Managing Partner, New York Life Insurance Company (1992–Present); Associate General Manager, New York Life Insurance Company (1989–1992); Sales Manager, New York Life Insurance Company (1986–1989). **Associations & Accomplishments:** GAMA; Suburban Maryland Life Underwriters; Taiwanese Association; Chinese–American Association; Chinese Chamber of Commerce. **Education:** University of Maryland, B.A. (1980). **Personal:** Married to Say Tran in 1986. Three children: Sarah, Crisna, and Stephanie.

Sheridan B. Vogel
Vice President and Property Loss Control Engineer
Johnson and Higgins
333 South 7th Street, Suite 1600
Minneapolis, MN 55402–2427
(612) 349–9712
Fax: (612) 349–9776
6411

Business Information: Johnson and Higgins is an insurance brokerage firm for large clients, providing a full array of services, including life, casualty, property, fire, aviation, etc. International in scope, Johnson & Higgins serves clients from 50 worldwide locations. As Vice President and Property Loss Control Engineer, Mr. Vogel is responsible for interfacing with clients and insurance companies to reduce losses and keep premiums low, including focusing on fire protection and minimizing payments. **Career Steps:** Vice President and Property Loss Control Engineer, Johnson and Higgins (1987–Present); Senior District Engineer, Protection Engineer (1977–1987); Senior Field Engineer, Factory Mutual (1971–1977). **Associations & Accomplishments:** N.S.P.E.; American Institute of Chemical Engineers; N.F.P.A.; Minnesota Fire Protection Council; Assistant Boy Scout Leader. **Education:** University of North Dakota, B.S.E.E. (1971). **Personal:** Married to Marie in 1975. Three children: Jeremy, Matthew and Samuel. Mr. Vogel enjoys fishing, camping, hunting, archery and shooting.

James F. Young
Senior Vice President
Symons International Group
5900 North Andrews Avenue
Ft. Lauderdale, FL 33309–2367
(800) 448–6626
Fax: (305) 772–9873
6411

Business Information: Symons International Group specializes in insurance brokerage and company underwriting. As Senior Vice President, Mr. Young is responsible for obtaining underwriting contracts and authorities, designing and servicing underwriting facilities in the United States and London, and overseeing the day–to–day operation of the firm. **Career Steps:** Senior Vice President, Symons International Group (1985–Present); Main Board Director, C.T. Bowring NA London (1977–1986); Managing Director, Wigham Richardson BVF, London (1965–1977); Price Forbes (1948–1965). **Associations & Accomplishments:** Professional Insurance Agents; F.S.L.A.; N.A.P.L.S.O.; Two Years Royal Air Force Instructor. **Education:** Bachelors Equivalency in Insurance. **Personal:** Four children: Hazel, Karen, Keith, and Tracy. Mr. Young enjoys golf, most sports, and being a grandfather.

James G. Zack Jr.
Managing Director
High–Point Rendel
*4199 Campus Drive, University Tower, Suite 650
Irvine, CA 92715
(714) 854–5237
Fax: (714) 854–5239*

6411

Business Information: High–Point Rendel, a division of Rendel Palmer Tritton, is an international construction claims consulting firm, generally representing owners. As Managing Director, Mr. Zack is responsible for the day–to–day administrative, marketing, and operational concerns of the firm. Other responsibilities include public relations and strategic planning. **Career Steps:** Managing Director, High–Point Rendel (1995–Present); Senior Claims Consultant, CH2M Hill, Inc. (1978–1995); Director, Budgets & Claims Administration, South Carolina Department of Health & Environmental Center (1972–1978); Captain, United States Army (1968–1972). **Associations & Accomplishments:** American Arbitration Association; American Association of Cost Engineers; American Society of Civil Engineers; Construction Management Association of America; Project Management Institute; Boy Scouts of America: Eagle Scout, Scoutmaster; Certified Construction Manager. **Education:** University of South Carolina, Masters of Public Administration (1976); Assumption College, B.A. in Political Science. **Personal:** Married to Yvonne Beezley in 1970. Four children: Jennifer, Stacy, James, and Trevor. Mr. Zack enjoys Boy Scouts of America, backpacking, and camping.

6500 Real Estate

6512 Nonresidential building operators
6513 Apartment building operators
6514 Dwelling operators, exc. apartments
6515 Mobile home site operators
6517 Railroad property lessors
6519 Real property lessors, NEC
6531 Real estate agents and managers
6541 Title abstract offices
6552 Subdividers and developers, NEC
6553 Cemetery subdividers and developers

Dr. Marta Sein Coll
Administrative Assistant
Plaza San Francisco, S.E.
*P.O. Box 21346
San Juan, Puerto Rico 00928
(787) 763–3170
Fax: (787) 764–5813*

6512

Business Information: Plaza San Francisco, S.E. is a national real estate development firm, specializing in the management and administration of shopping centers and commercial real estate ventures throughout Puerto Rico. A family–owned enterprise originally established in 1970 as Sein Enterprises, current holdings include the Plaza San Francisco, S.E., and Plaza Puerto Rico shopping centers. As Administrative Assistant, Dr. Coll is the executive director over all administrative areas, with primary duties involving trouble shooting, insurance, supplies, equipment, tenants, office personnel coordination. In addition, she manages all information systems technology and tenant databases. Prior to entering the corporate world, Dr. Coll served as an Associate Professor of Office Systems Administration with the University of Puerto Rico, spanning the years 1967–1979 and as Department Chairperson during 1978. **Career Steps:** Administrative Assistant, Plaza San Francisco, S.E. (1992–Present); Administrative Assistant, Faith Lutheran Church (1985–1992); Associate Professor, University of Puerto Rico (1967–1979). **Associations & Accomplishments:** Delta Pi Epsilon, National Honorary Business Education Fraternity; Association of Business Education Professors; American Red Cross, Blood Donor Program Coordinator; Child Sponsor, Christian Children Fund; Outstanding Young Woman of America (1978). **Education:** Nova University, Ed.D. (1976); New York University, Master in Education (1970); T.I.R.I Real Estate Training Institute, Puerto Rico Broker License (1994). **Personal:** Married to Daniel Jr. in 1967. Two children: Marta Ivette and Francisco Daniel. Dr. Coll enjoys Bible study, tennis, and computers.

Mr. Tim L. Conner
Chief Engineer
Steinemann & Company
*600 West Peachtree Street, Suite 1870
Atlanta, GA 30308
(404) 872–9200
Fax: (404) 876–0652*

6512

Business Information: Steinemann & Company is a commercial real estate development and management enterprise. Regional in scope, the company owns and manages shopping complexes and office buildings throughout metropolitan Atlanta, GA and surrounding cities. As the Chief Engineer, Mr. Conner is responsible for all engineering and maintenance of high–rise office complexes, ensuring tenant safety and comfort. Established in 1977, Steinemann & Company employs four administrative support staff. **Career Steps:** Chief Engineer, Steinemann & Company (1991–Present); Chief Engineer, Kern & Company (1983– 1991); Lead Engineer, Carter & Associates (1979–1983). **Associations & Accomplishments:** National Association of Power Engineers; President–Elect, Nebo Place Home Owners Association. **Education:** Auburn University College of Engineering, B.S. (1991); Licensed Engineer 1st Class, Power Engineers, Inc.; Honeywell Institute for Energy Efficiency Improvement; Ferris State University, Refrigerant Transition and Recovery Certification Type II, III, IV; The Trane Company CentraVac Owner Operation and Maintenance Degre e.

Frank Fabish
President
Executive Office Place
*438 East Wilson Bridge Road #200
Worthington, OH 43085
(614) 888–2992
Fax: (614) 431–8258*

6512

Business Information: Executive Office Place provides office leasing, administrative support, and telephone answering services to the Columbus, Ohio, area. Mr. Fabish established the Company in 1989 and is presently responsible for overseeing all administrative, financial, sales, and marketing functions. **Career Steps:** President, Executive Office Place (1989–Present); Vice President of Marketing, Mentor Technologies (1987–1989); President and General Manager, Cellular One (1985–1986); Regional Manager, Norrell Services (1982–1985). **Associations & Accomplishments:** Board of Directors, Executive Suite Association. **Education:** Baldwin Wallace College, E.M.B.A. (1985); United States Military Academy, B.S. in Engineering. **Personal:** Married to Gail in 1967. Two children: Troy David and Todd Jared.

Ron Glover
General Manager – Pueblo Mall
The Hahn Company
*6 Stanford Avenue, Apartment B
Pueblo, CO 81005–1659
(719) 544–3454
Fax: (719) 545–5404*

6512

Business Information: The Hahn Company is the ninth largest shopping center management company in the United States. Established in 1976, the Company has an estimated annual sales of over $100 million. As General Manager – Pueblo Mall, Mr. Glover oversees all areas of operations, including marketing, leasing, security, maintenance, customer service and sales, press relations, and construction. **Career Steps:** General Manager – Pueblo Mall, The Hahn Company (1989–Present); General Manager, First Union Management (1984–1989); Marketing Manager – Magic Valley Mall, Price Development (1980–1984). **Associations & Accomplishments:** International Council of Shopping Centers; Colorado Association of Realtors; Pueblo Association of Realtors. **Education:** Montana State University, Bachelor's (1980); Real Estate Graduate and Licensed; ICSC School of Professional Development, Lifetime Designation of Shopping Mall Manager. **Personal:** Married to Karen M. in 1984. One child: Kalina Marie. Mr. Glover enjoys karate, Kung–Fu, and Tae Kwon Do.

Sally F. Gonzalez
Vice President
Laredo National Bank
*700 San Bernardo, P.O. Box 59
Laredo, TX 78042
(210) 723–1151
Fax: (210) 791–0145*

6512

Business Information: Laredo National Bank is a full service financial institution offering telephone banking services. As Vice President, Ms. Gonzalez is responsible for marketing, advertising, directing special promotions, managing special production sales, training, and guiding profitability analysis for customers. **Career Steps:** Vice President, Laredo National Bank (1994–Present); Manager of Home Loan Sales, USAA Federal Savings Bank (1986–1991); Investment Manager, Bank of the West (1983–1986); Administrative Assistant of Installment Loans, First National Bank (1979–1982). **Associations & Accomplishments:** United Way Volunteer (3 Years); Membership Chair, Women's City Club; Board Member, Laredo Chamber of Commerce; Board Member, Women's City Club (3 Years); Board Member, Junior Achievement of Laredo. **Education:** Laredo Junior College (1977). **Personal:** Married to Guillermo E. Jr., Ph.D. in 1978. Three children: Guillermo III, Sarah Elizabeth, and Matthew. Ms. Gonzalez enjoys spending time with her children.

William C. Hanson
President
James Hanson, Inc.
*235 Moore Street
Hackensack, NJ 07601–7417
(201) 488–5800
Fax: (201) 488–0249*

6512

Business Information: James Hanson, Inc., affiliated with New American Network, is a full–service, international commercial real estate firm with 150 affiliates located throughout the world. Assuming the chief executive position for the Firm in 1995 upon the death of his father, James (Founded Firm in 1955), as President, William Hanson provides the overall direction and vision strategies. His primary focus is on sales management, in addition to representing major clientele. **Career Steps:** James Hanson, Inc.: President (1995–Present), Sales Associate (1986–1995). **Associations & Accomplishments:** IOREBA; NAIOP; Published in New Jersey Business News in an article, called "40 under 40" (1994); Member of the Semi–Pro Baseball League "Ramsey White Sox" – playing center field. **Education:** Colgate University, B.A. (1986). **Personal:** Mr. Hanson enjoys playing semi–pro baseball.

Russel B. Icenoggle
Branch President
Rocky Mountain Bank
*P.O. Box 788
Plains, MT 59859–0788
(406) 826–3662
Fax: (406) 826–3236*

6512

Business Information: Rocky Mountain Bank is a regional, full service banking institution offering checking, savings, lending, and investment services to customers. As Branch President, Mr. Icenoggle administers the operations of the Plains, Montana branch. He is responsible for customer satisfaction, personnel concerns, scheduling of staff, employee reviews, and making sure his staff is trained. Mr. Icenoggle is involved in decisions regarding customer loans and investments and must be current on Federal Reserve rules and regulations. **Career Steps:** Branch President, Rocky Mountain Bank (1994–Present); President, First National Bank (1990–1994); Executive Director, Clark Fork Valley Hospital (1977–1983). **Associations & Accomplishments:** Former President, Lions Club; Former President, Chamber of Commerce; Chairman, Western Montana District Hospital Association; Board of Directors, Montana Hospital Association. **Education:** Montana State University, B.S. (1968); Numerous American Institute of Banking Schools. **Personal:** Married to Polly in 1994. Two children: Marty Radd and Deri L. Icenoggle and three stepchildren – Mellissa, Jessi, and Allison. Mr. Icenoggle enjoys various outdoor activities and working on his ranch.

Wendy D. Keck
Marketing Director
Killeen Mall
*2100 W.S. Young Drive
Killeen, TX 76543
(817) 699–2211
Fax: (817) 690–2073
EMAIL: See Below*

6512

Business Information: Killeen Mall is a full–service shopping facility providing numerous retail establishments to serve customer needs. As Marketing Director, Ms. Keck is responsible for all promotions, media advertising, special events, and public relations associated with the mall. She oversees all administration of the department, and coordinates all merchant relations. Internet users can reach her via: mall@centraltx.net. **Career Steps:** Marketing Director, Killeen Mall (1995–Present); Marketing Director, Sunrise Mall (1994–1995); Administrative Assistant, Fashion Place Mall (1991–1994). **Associations & Accomplishments:** International Council of Shopping Centers; Central Texas Ad League; ICSC Merit Award; Best in show Addy Award; Print Campaign Addy

Award; Television spot Addy Silver. **Education:** University of Utah, Commercial Recreation and Tourism (1991); American Hotel/Motel Association, Hospitality Management Certificate. **Personal:** Ms. Keck enjoys skiing, computers and cooking.

Josue D. Leon–Rodriguez

Director of the Contracts Department
Puerto Rico Development Company
Q11 Calle 21
Trujillo Alto, Puerto Rico 00976
(809) 764–3675
Fax: (809) 764–5028

6512

Business Information: Puerto Rico Industrial Development Company is a real estate company, specializing in sales and lease agreements for industrial activity. As Director of the Contracts Department, Mr. Leon–Rodriguez is responsible for all lease agreement documents for the Industrial Parks. A practicing attorney in Puerto Rico courts since 1985, he joined the District Attorney's Office in November 1995. Serving as Assistant District Attorney, he is a trial attorney for the prosecution of criminal cases. **Career Steps:** Assistant District Attorney (Nov. 1995–Present); Director of Contracts Department, Puerto Rico Develoment Company (1995); Legal Counselor, Economic Development Administration – Puerto Rico (1989–1995); Legal Defender, Office of the Legal Defender – Puerto Rico (1987–1989). **Associations & Accomplishments:** Baptist College of Carolina: Former President (1994), Vice President of Board of Directors; Board of Directors, W.I.D.A. Radio Station; Puerto Rico Bar Association. **Education:** Interamerican University of Puerto Rico School of Law, J.D. (1985); University of Puerto Rico: B.A. in Economics (1982), M.A. in Public Administration (1986); Catholic University of Puerto Rico School of Law, M.A. in Law and Economics (1993). **Personal:** Married to Milagros Cruz in 1988. Three children: Josue, Monica and Maria de Leon. Mr. Leon–Rodriguez enjoys classic guitar, violin, and basketball.

Wilbur Marvin

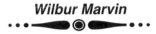

President
Commercial Properties Development Corporation
P.O. Box 1693
Baton Rouge, LA 70821
(504) 924–7206
Fax: (504) 924–1235

6512

Business Information: Commercial Properties Development Corporation is an owner and developer of commercial property used for shopping centers and other retail operations. Established in 1952, Commercial Properties Development Corporation currently employs 20 people and has an estimated annual revenue of $12 million. As President, Chief Executive Officer and Founder, Mr. Marvin provides the overall direction and vision for the Company's continued growth, quality delivery to customers and strategic development. **Career Steps:** President, Commercial Properties Development Corporation (1952–Present). **Associations & Accomplishments:** International Council of Shopping Centers; Baton Rouge Chamber of Commerce. **Education:** Harvard University, B.A. (1941); P G School, United States Naval Academy. **Personal:** Married to Livia S. Marvin in 1980. Five children: Charles, Eric, Michael, Anne and Richard. Mr. Marvin enjoys tennis.

Jose M. Nolla Jr.

Senior Vice President
Manley–Berenson Associates PR, Inc.
P.O. Box 360771
San Juan, Puerto Rico 00936–0771
(809) 795–6490
Fax: (809) 795–4890

6512

Business Information: Manley–Berenson Associates P.R., Inc. is a developer, owner and manager of major shopping center complexes throughout Puerto Rico. Established in 1975, Manley–Berensen currently employs 30 people. As Senior Vice President, Mr. Nolla is responsible for the oversight of all properties located in Puerto Rico, currently consisting of six shopping centers, with two more under construction at this writing. **Career Steps:** Senior Vice President, Manley–Berenson Associates P.R., Inc. (1994–Present); Regional General Manager, TJAC (1992–1994); Operations and Assistant General Manager, Plaza Las Americas (1988–1992); General Manager, Cueato Mall (1988–1992). **Associations & Accomplishments:** ICSC, State Operations Chairman for Puerto Rico and the Virgin Islands; Puerto Rico Chamber of Commerce; Former President, Arecibo Country Club; Treasurer, Puerto Rico Fishing Association; Published in local papers and a Caribbean Business publication. **Education:** Puerto Rico Catholic University, B.B.A. (1966); ICSC: Management I (1986), Management II (1988), Maintenance Institute (1990). **Personal:** Married to Veronica Seda in 1987. Three children: Maribel, Karen and Jose M. Mr. Nolla enjoys fishing and participating in fishing tournaments.

Jose Alonso

Resident Manager
Condado Beach Trio
P.O. Box 41226
San Juan, Puerto Rico 00940–1226
(809) 721–6090
Fax: (809) 723–4018

6513

Business Information: Condado Beach Trio is a tourist and corporate–focused resort with an ocean view. Within the resort is a convention center, restaurant, hotel, and casino. As Resident Manager, Mr. Alonso is responsible for daily operations, administrative duties, financial matters, public relations, payroll, and budget reports. Established in 1992, Condado Beach Trio employs 600 people, and boasts annual sales of $20 million. **Career Steps:** Resident Manager, Condado Beach Trio (1995–Present); Assistant to the President, Carnicon Puerto Rico Management Associates (1992–1995); Hotel Consultant, Puerto Rico Industrial Development Company (1988–1992); General Manager, Salvador Praia Hotel (1980–1981). **Associations & Accomplishments:** Cornell Society of Hotelmen; Puerto Rico Tourism & Hotel Association; Puerto Rico Chamber of Commerce; Association of Puerto Rico Products; Condado in Action Association. **Education:** Cornell University, B.S. (1978); University of Puerto Rico, Bachelors in Business (1971); Puerto Rico Hotel School; Associate Degree in Hotel Administration (1976). **Personal:** One child: Daniel. Mr. Alonso enjoys numismatics and running.

Mr. John J. Aquilina

Vice President
Eddingston Court, Inc.
P.O. Box 2544
Port Arthur, TX 77643
(409) 985–2433
Fax: Please mail or

6513

Business Information: Eddingston Court, Inc. is an apartment complex with 24 units, operated by Mr. Aquilina and his family. In his position as Vice President, Mr. Aquilina is responsible for overseeing all operations for the Complex. In his personal life, Mr. Aquilina and his family are well–known in Port Arthur as city builders and top flight citizens, giving generously of their time and assets to local charities and civic projects. Established in 1943, Eddingston Court, Inc. employs a full–time staff of two. **Career Steps:** Vice President, Eddingston Court, Inc. (1990–Present); Vice President, Holiday Motor Court, Inc. (1977–1990); President, Aquilina Realtors (1964–1977); Supervisor, Aquilina Food Store (1939– 1964); **Associations & Accomplishments:** Former Member, Board of Directors, Our Lady of Guadalupe Church; Past President of Port Arthur Evening Lion's Club – Voted Outstanding Club of the City for that year; Past President, Port Arthur Board of Realtors; Former Member of the Board of Directors, Our Lady of Guadalupe Church; Former Member of the Board of Directors, Hughen School for Crippled Children; Outstanding Lion of the Year; Outstanding Realtor of the Year. **Education:** Saint Edwards, Honorary Degree; Port Arthur High School.

Linda Dover

Director of Nursing
Barkley Place ALF
36 Barkley Circle
Ft. Myers, FL 33907
(941) 939–3553
Fax: (941) 939–2327

6513

Business Information: Barkley Place ALF is a rental retirement community/assisted living facility with 156 apartments (196 maximum capacity) and a 24–hour nursing staff. The average age of residents is 84 years. As Director of Nursing, Ms. Dover supervises health services throughout the facility, determines placement appropriateness and alternatives, and coordinates interdepartmental services. **Career Steps:** Director of Nursing, Barkley Place ALF (1988–Present); Assistant Director of Nursing, Cross Key Manor (1987–1988); Nursing Supervisor, Kane Ross Regional LTC Facility (1984–1987). **Associations & Accomplishments:** Southwest Florida Association of Health and Social Services: Vice President, Former President, Former Secretary; Southwest Florida Directors of Nursing in Long Term Care; Assisted Living Facilities Administrator's Certification. **Education:** University of Pittsburgh, B.S.N. (1984). **Personal:** Married to Larry in 1994. Ms. Dover enjoys music and playing the piano.

Mary P. Gallivan

Director of Sales
Classic Residence by Hyatt
8100 Connecticut Avenue
Chevy Chase, MD 20815
(301) 907–8895
Fax: Please mail or call

6513

Business Information: Classic Residence by Hyatt is a retirement community providing upscale living to senior citizens. Activities provided include: German and French clubs, water exercise, and poetry reading. Additionally, housekeeping and transportation services are included. Established in 1990, Classic Residence by Hyatt currently employs 120 people. As Director of Sales, Ms. Gallivan is responsible for assisting in marketing of the community and maintenance of 100% occupancy of 337 apartments. Concurrent with her position, she is a vocal performer at the Kennedy Center. **Career Steps:** Director of Sales, Classic Residence by Hyatt (1990–Present); Coordinator for Technology Transfer, Industrial Development Authority, Ireland (1979–1986). **Associations & Accomplishments:** President, University College Dublin Alumni Association – Washington–Baltimore Chapter. **Education:** University College, Dublin, Ireland, B.A. (1973); Institute of Certified Accountants, Certifed Accounting & Finance. **Personal:** Ms. Gallivan enjoys singing, art and volunteer work.

Terry Howard

Chief Operations Officer
Kisco Retirement Communities
2700 Coltsgate Road
Charlotte, NC 28211–3503
(704) 442–0888
Fax: (704) 442–0490

6513

Business Information: Kisco Retirement Communities specializes in the development of full service retirement properties. Owners of eight full–service retirement communities, predominantly on the east coast, the Company offers assisted and independent living facilities with such options as transportation, utilities, foodservice, housekeeping, activities, and twenty–four hour health care. Established in 1993, the Company employs 250 people and has an estimated annual revenue of $15 million. As Chief Operations Officer, Mr. Howard is responsible for the day–to–day operations for the East Coast Division. These include overseeing strategic planning and growth, finance, public relations, marketing, human resources, and identifying new opportunities. **Career Steps:** Chief Operating Officer, Kisco Retirement Communities (1995–Present); Executive Vice President, Birtcher Senior Properties (1990–1995); Senior Director, The Forum Group (1985–1990); Vice President of Marketing, Retirement Inns of America (1983–1985). **Associations & Accomplishments:** NASLI. **Education:** Belmont University, B.B.A. (1981); University of California – Irvine Health Care Development Institute, Graduate School of Management. **Personal:** Married to Lisa in 1986. Two children: Boston and Savannah. Mr. Howard enjoys golf, reading, skiing, and coaching soccer.

Nancy Anne Lorenz

MIS Manager
Inns By The Sea
P.O. Box 101
Carmel, CA 93921
(408) 625–9703
Fax: (408) 624–2967
EMAIL:

6513

Business Information: Inns By The Sea is a Hospitality Industry Management Company, providing seven inns in Carmel and two in Monterey, California. All locations in Carmel are 3 to 4 Diamond–rated, as well as AAA–rated, with a full line of amenities, including fireplaces, pools, continental breakfasts, etc. With twenty years experience in the computer programming industry, Ms. Lorenz joined Inns By The Sea as MIS Manager in 1987. She is responsible for creating the Company's own in–house front desk and reservation system on UNIX, as well as directing corporate administration PC's, telephone systems, and Homepage. Concurrent with her position, she operates a wedding consulting business with her partner Elena Young of Special Moments. Internet users can reach her via: RESERVE @ INNSBYTHESEA.COM **Career Steps:** MIS Manager, Inns By The Sea (1987–Present); Systems Analyst, Pro–Log Corporation (1976–1987). **Education:** Attended: Monterey Peninsula Community College; Institute for Certification of Computer Professionals (ICCP), Certificate in Data Processing (C.D.P.). **Personal:** Ms. Lorenz enjoys astronomy, science, and photography.

Manuel N. Rabell, CCP
Director of Information Systems
Palmas Del Mar Resort
P.O. Box 2020
Humacao, Puerto Rico 00792
(809) 852–6000
Fax: (809) 852–6311

6513

Business Information: Palmas Del Mar Resort, a subsidiary of Maxxam out of Houston, Texas, is a 2,750 acre full–destination resort and integrated residential community developer on the Southeast coast of Puerto Rico. The Resort consists of developed lands, a 350–room hotel, 18–hole golf course, 20 tennis courts, restaurants, and a marina. As Director of Information Systems, Mr. Rabell is responsible for the management of all electronic information resources to provide guests, property owners, and employees with quality service. **Career Steps:** Director of Information Systems, Palmas Del Mar Resort (1992–Present); Systems Consultant, Micro Teks (1985–1992). **Associations & Accomplishments:** Asociacion de Directores de Sistemas Electronicos de Informacion (Directors of Electronic Information Systems Association). **Education:** University of Puerto Rico, B.B.A. (1985); Held CDP Certification. **Personal:** Married to Katherine Negron in 1995. One child: Cesar Andres. Mr. Rabell enjoys golf, tennis and astronomy.

Michael S. Shimoda
General Manager
Yacht Harbor Towers
1600 Ala Moana Boulevard
Honolulu, HI 96815–1427
(808) 947–1855
Fax: (808) 942–0124
EMAIL: See Below

6513

Business Information: Yacht Harbor Towers is a management office for luxury condominiums, consisting of 457 apartments at three community units. With nineteen years of experience in property management, Mr. Shimoda joined Yacht Harbor Towers in 1992 as General Manager. He is responsible for the management of four major departments, including security, office, maintenance, and custodial, in addition to overseeing a support staff of 40. Internet users can reach him via: 76563,3554.com **Career Steps:** General Manager, Yacht Harbor Towers (1992–Present); Property Manager, Hawaiiana Management (1988–1992); Property Manager, Certified Management (1985–1988); Property Manager, Paradise Management (1977–1985). **Education:** University of Hawaii, M.A. in Political Science (1975); University of Oregon, B.A. in Political Science (1973). **Personal:** Mr. Shimoda enjoys travel and cooking.

Jill VanWagoner
Administrative Services Manager
Owners' Resorts & Exchange, Inc.
404 East 4500 South, Suite A34
Murray, UT 84107
(801) 269–1322
Fax: (801) 269–0169

6513

Business Information: Owners' Resorts & Exchange, Inc. is a timeshare condominium property management company for 25 different homeowner associations in the Western United States, Hawaii, and Mexico. As Administrative Services Manager, Ms. VanWagoner is responsible for human resources, payroll, in–house collections, corporate document signing, billing, scheduling, and acting as office manager. **Career Steps:** Administrative Services Manager, Owners' Resorts & Exchange, Inc. (1987–Present); Human Resource Director, RUTI–sweetwater, Inc. (1975–1987). **Associations & Accomplishments:** American Compensation Association; Intermountain Compensation and Benefits Association; Society for Human Resource Management; American Resort Development Association; USA Hockey; Utah Amateur Hockey Association. **Education:** LDS Business College, Certificate (1975). **Personal:** Married to Bradley F. in 1975. Two children: BJ and Andrew. Ms. VanWagoner enjoys coaching and managing youth hockey teams, travel, reading, and cocker spaniel dogs.

Christina P. Alletto

Executive Director
Signature Housing Solutions, Inc.
4575 Lake Avenue
Rochester, NY 14612
(716) 865–7550
Fax: (716) 621–6448

6514

Business Information: Signature Housing Solutions, Inc. is a real estate management company, specializing in providing quality, affordable housing to low–income residents from Niagra Falls to Harlem, New York, as well as Lynchburg, VA. Affiliated with the Finch Group, the agency also provides tax credit counseling and compliance. As Executive Director, Ms. Alletto oversees all areas of the Company, serving as liaison with the parent company and prospective clientele. **Career Steps:** Executive Director, Signature Housing Solutions, Inc. (1994–Present); Vice President, TFG Management Company (1981–1994); Regional Manager, CWC Management Company (1976–1981). **Associations & Accomplishments:** Rochester Real Estate Board; NYSARHO; Greater Syracuse Tenants Network; New York State Tenants and Neighbors Coalition. **Education:** IREM, C.P.M. (1988). **Personal:** Married to Louie in 1984. Two children: Alisha and LJ. Ms. Alletto enjoys Tae Kwon Do (intermediate greenbelt) and horseback riding.

Jaime L. Purcell
President
L & P Management, Inc.
P.O. Box 7759
Ponce, Puerto Rico 00732–7759
(809) 842–5333
Fax: (809) 843–5364

6514

Business Information: L & P Management, Inc. is a management firm for subsidized housing projects throughout Puerto Rico. L & P Management, Inc. currently manages six projects: three sectionized subsidized projects through partnerships in the U.S., and three government–owned projects. Established in 1983, L & P Management reports annual revenue of $1.5 million and currently employs 32 people. Establishing the Company with his partner in 1983, Mr. Purcell serves as President and is responsible for the oversight of the day–to–day operations, including involvement in the physical aspects of maintenance improvement of the buildings. **Career Steps:** President, L & P Management, Inc. (1990–Present); President, Purcell Construction Corporation (1982–1994); Vice President, Loubriel & Purcell Construction Company (1970). **Associations & Accomplishments:** Colegio Ingenieros y Agrimensores de Puerto Rico; American Society of Civil Engineers; Distinguished Executive – Construction Award by Society of Marketing and Sales Executives (1986). **Education:** University of Puerto Rico, B.S. in Civil Engineering (1954), Continuing Education courses: Design Reinforcement Concrete Structures, Estimating Construction Costs, Contracts, Labor Law, Accounting for Engineers, EEO Law. **Personal:** Married to Maria M. in 1954. Six children: Jaime Jr., Jaime R., Jaime F., Jaime E., Jaime A., Anna Maria, seven grandchildren and four great–grandchildren. Mr. Purcell enjoys sailing and power boating.

William C. Torres
Physical Properties Manager
Twin Rivers Community Trust
92 Twin Rivers Drive West
East Windsor, NJ 08520
(609) 443–1113
Fax: (908) 446–4664

6514

Business Information: Twin Rivers Community Trust, New Jersey's first and leading planned unit development company, is a community management firm for 2,773 units. Established in 1968, Twin Rivers Community Trust reports annual operational budget of $2.7 million and currently employs 48 people, with some seasonal assistance. As Physical Properties Manager, Mr. Torres is responsible for planning and managing all maintenance, including landscaping, mowing, street & parking lot maintenance, purchasing, and hiring of personnel. **Career Steps:** Physical Properties Manager, Twin Rivers Community Trust (1980–Present); Owner, Lawn Service Company (Lawn Kare) (1968–1977); Print Shop Supervisor, Lily Tulip, Owens, Illinois (1977–1979). **Associations & Accomplishments:** Professional Lawn Care Association of America; New Jersey Turf Grass Association; Community Association Institute – New Jersey Chapter; Past President, Middletown Area Chamber of Commerce; Retired Rooster, United States Jaycees; Recipient, 1993 Employee of the Year, Twin Rivers Homeowners Association. **Education:** Rutgers University, Cook College (1994); Monmouth College, Business Management; Cook College, Turf courses; Rockhurst College, Continuing Education courses. **Personal:** Three children: Marc

Andrew, Michele Lynn, and Matthew Alexander. Mr. Torres enjoys auto racing.

Dan McShane
Vice President of Acquisitions and New Venture Development
Railtex
4040 Broadway, Suite 200
San Antonio, TX 78209–6300
(210) 841–7621
Fax: (210) 841–7693

6517

Business Information: Railtex is the operator of 25 railroads across North America. As Vice President of Acquisitions and New Venture Development, Dan McShane is held responsible for acquiring new railroads, transportation related businesses, business development, and venture acquisitions. **Career Steps:** Railtex: Vice President of Acquisitions and New Venture Development (1995–Present), Vice President of Sales (1991–1995); Union Pacific Railroad: Senior Manager Rail Line Planning (1986–1991), District Sales Manager (1985–1986). **Associations & Accomplishments:** Life Member, University of Missouri Alumni Association. **Education:** University of Missouri, B.S. (1975). **Personal:** Married to Sherri in 1975. Two children: Sara and Patrick. Mr. McShane enjoys fishing, reading, history, and geography.

Suzanne Barton
Facilities Administrator
Amresco
1845 Woodall Rodgers Freeway
Dallas, TX 75201
(214) 953–7867
Fax: (214) 754–4903

6519

Business Information: Amresco, formerly part of Nations Bank, is a financial real estate service. As Facilities Administrator, Mrs. Barton is responsible for moving coordination, purchasing and leasing, and space design and implementation. Additionally, she supervises the efforts of over 400 employees through five separate offices. **Career Steps:** Facilities Administrator, Amresco (1991–Present); Loan Administrator, Nations Bank (1974–1991). **Associations & Accomplishments:** International Facility Management Association. **Education:** Oklahoma University (1963). **Personal:** Married to Jack in 1982.

Steven B. Berman
Part–Owner, Vice President, & Chief Executive Officer
FIRM Realty
3990 Sheridan Street, Suite 209
Hollywood, FL 33021–3661
(954) 981–7744 Ext. 27
Fax: (954) 966–7444
EMAIL:ZIPPY.68.ADL.CDM

6519

Business Information: FIRM Realty, a family–owned business, is a real estate development and management office for commercial and residential property. As Part–Owner, Vice President, and Chief Executive Officer, Mr. Berman is responsible for day–to–day operations, generating new business and managing the existing business. **Career Steps:** Part–Owner, Vice President, and Chief Executive Officer, FIRM Realty (1990–Present); Tax Associate, Coopers & Lybrand (1989–1990). **Associations & Accomplishments:** Broward County Bicycling Advisory Committee; City of Hollywood Capital Improvements Program Committee; Greater Hollywood Chamber of Commerce; Cystic Fibrosis Foundation; Multiple Sclerosis Foundation; American Heart Association; American Lung Association; American Diabetes Association; Named one of Ft. Lauderdale's "50 Finest" for fundraising for civic foundations. **Education:** University of Georgia, Master of Accounting (1989); University of Florida, B.S. in Accounting. **Personal:** Married to Dalia Spavak in 1996. Mr. Berman enjoys scuba diving, bicycling, yoga, and photography.

Joanne F. Bradley, P.C.
Associate Broker
Realty Executives
8787 East Pinnacle Park, Suite 125
Scottsdale, AZ 85255
(602) 585–0101
Fax: (602) 585–1571

6519

Business Information: Realty Executives is an international real estate franchisor, owning independent brokerage agencies throughout North America. Joanne Bradley, one of Realty Executives' top ten agents in North America, joined the Scottsdale, Arizona agency in 1992. Her clientele listing base consists of luxury homesites and golf course resort home properties, ranging in price from $500K to over $3 million. Concurrent to her brokerage, she also publishes a monthly magazine — "Arizona Exclusive Golf Properties and Luxury Homes." **Career Steps:** Associate Broker, Realty Executives (1992–Present); Broker DBWF, John Hall & Associates (1985–1992); Manager, Tom Adam Realty, Inc. (1980–1985). **Associations & Accomplishments:** FIABCI–USA; Arizona Cancer Society; Scottsdale Association of REALTORS; Arizona Kidney Foundation; National Association of REALTORS; Creative Women of Pinnacle Peak; Board of Directors, Biltmore Investors Bank; Two Thousand Notable Women (1996); **Awards:** Realty Executives Third Ranked Agent in Arizona (1995), Realty Executives Fifth Ranked Agent in North America (1995); Annually produces and publishes Arizona Exclusive Golf Properties and Luxury Homes magazines. **Education:** Phoenix College, Business Administration (1993); Scottsdale Community College. **Personal:** Married to Jim in 1985. Two children: Dean Benigno and Diane Bouhouch. Ms. Bradley enjoys charity fundraising events, golf, travel, and language studies.

John T. Finley
President
F & W Realty, Inc. and J & J F Enterprises, Inc.
6 W. 5th Street, Suite 700
St. Paul, MN 55102
(612) 266–8350
Fax: (612) 266–8370

6519

Business Information: F & W Realty, Inc. and J & J F Enterprises, Inc. are real estate development agencies, renting and leasing commercial and residential properties in the Minneapolis/St. Paul area. Establishing both companies in 1974, as President, Mr. Finley handles all aspects of the company's operations and administration. He is also an elected County Commissioner (7th term) for Ramsey County, and a practicing attorney. **Career Steps:** President, F & W Realty Inc. and J & J F Enterprises, Inc. (1974–Present); Commissioner, Ramsey County, Minnesota (1970–Present); Attorney, (1969–Present). **Associations & Accomplishments:** American Bar Association; Minnesota Bar Association; Ramsey County Bar Association; American Trial Lawyers Association; Minnesota Trial Lawyers Association. **Education:** University of Minnesota Law School, J.D. (1969); University of St. Thomas, B.A. **Personal:** Married to Jackie in 1965. Three children: Bridget, John and Michele. Mr. Finley enjoys playing golf and racquetball, and boating.

Michael Hill
Director
Oakwood Corporate Housing
8834 North Capital of Texas Highway, Suite 270
Austin, TX 78759
(512) 343–2340
Fax: (512) 343–7270

6519

Business Information: Oakwood Corporate Housing is a nationwide temporary housing agency, offering a variety of housing services, such as setting up phones, cable, and other utility services for individuals before anyone moves in. Services are provided for individuals temporarily living away from home, due to business or training activities. As Director, Mr. Hill is responsible for all agency activities, including the creation of housing, set-ups, and coordination of houses. **Career Steps:** Director, Oakwood Corporate Housing (1993–Present); General Manager, Corporate Lodging (1988–1993); Partner, E.M.D.C. (1982–1988); Regional Sales Manager, Dyonics (1978–1982). **Associations & Accomplishments:** Texas Apartment Association; Austin Apartment Association; National Interim Housing Network; Published in local business journals. **Education:** Houston Baptist University, Business Management (1978). **Personal:** Married to Jeanne in 1975. Two children: Shannon and Kaci. Mr. Hill enjoys golf and guitar.

Alice Oakley
Marketing Manager
Lewis Homes Management Company
1156 North Mountain Avenue
Upland, CA 91786–3633
(909) 946–7545
Fax: Please mail or call

6519

Business Information: Lewis Homes Management Company is a builder, developer, and real property manager. Holdings include homes, apartments, shopping centers, and planned communities. Lewis Homes has four regions of development: Las Vegas and Reno, Nevada; and Sacramento and Upland, California. Ms. Oakley joined Lewis Homes Management Company's subsidiary, Lewis Homes of California, as an Administrative Assistant in 1976. She was then appointed as Marketing Assistant at Lewis Homes Management Company and promoted to Marketing Manager in 1986, upon the conferral of her Certificate in Marketing. In this capacity, she is responsible for all advertising and public relations for the Southern California Region. **Career Steps:** Lewis Homes Management Company: Marketing Manager (1986–Present), Marketing Assistant (1978–1986); Administrative Assistant, Lewis Homes of California (1976–1978). **Associations & Accomplishments:** Institute of Residential Marketing – Washington, DC; Sales & Marketing Council – Southern California; MENSA – National Organization. **Education:** Chaffey College, A.A. (1989); University of California at Irvine, Certificate in Marketing (1986). **Personal:** Married to Roger in 1970. Ms. Oakley enjoys reading, music, and water sports.

Jeffrey Thomas Randolph
Vice President of Consulting Services
Trammell Crow Company
695 East Main Street #407
Stamford, CT 06901
(203) 359–2222
Fax: Please mail or call

6519

Business Information: Trammell Crow International, established in 1947, is the leading real estate development firm in the U.S. An international development firm, Trammell Crow specializes in commercial and residential trade marts (special projects) at 77 U.S. offices and 7 foreign offices located throughout Europe, Latin America and Asia. As Vice President of Consulting Services, Mr. Randolph is responsible for client development and transition of new customers, helping to ensure that the Company maintains growth and leadership in the industry. **Career Steps:** Vice President of Consulting Services, Trammell Crow Company (Present); Consultant, Apgar and Company; Staff Architect, Gruzen Samton Architects **Education:** Stern School, New York University, M.B.A.; University of Pennsylvania, M.A. in Architecture; University of Chicago, B.A. with honors. **Personal:** Mr. Randolph enjoys outdoor sports, cross country and downhill skiing, and spending time with his family and dog.

John H. Wilson
President
Wilson Real Estate & Development Company, Ltd.
P.O. Box E.E.–16315
Nassau, Bahamas
(809) 356–6882
Fax: (809) 356–6888
EMAIL: See Below

6519

Business Information: John H. Wilson, co-founder and one of the largest shareholders of the United Bank of Philadelphia, established Wilson Real Estate & Development Company, Ltd. in 1978. He is in the process of developing 1,500 acres of land in the Bahamas. In 1984, he became the first Bahamian to establish a local insurance company as an "Insurer," thereby creating Bahamas Commercial & Life Insurance Co. Ltd. (insurer). In addition, he serves as President of Grand Bahama Beach LTD. As President, he provides financial consulting and executive direction to the companies under his leadership, promoting quality and efficient service. **Career Steps:** President, Wilson Real Estate & Development Company, Ltd. (1978–Present); President, Bahamas Commercial Life & Inc. (1984–Present); President, Grand Bahama Beach LTD (1986–Present). **Associations & Accomplishments:** Scholarship Contributor, College of the Bahamas; Contributor to Charity; Contributor to Religious Sector. **Education:** University of North Carolina: Bachelor of Science (1972), M.B.A.; Attended Harvard University. **Personal:** Married to Arlene L. in 1971. Four children: Rochelle M., Zoie N., Jovan H., and Jamere J. Mr. Wilson enjoys golf, dominos, acting, reading, and lecturing.

Lawrence C. Zeigler
Director of Real Estate
Aetna Pro Management Corp.
95 Glastonbury Boulevard
Glastonbury, CT 06033–4412
(860) 652–2141
Fax: (860) 652–2268

6519

Business Information: Aetna Pro Management Corporation is a real estate development firm, providing leasing, purchasing and sale of ambulatory health care facilities. As Director of Real Estate, Mr. Zeigler is responsible for the development and management of group practice, MSO, and IPA Primary Care Networks, as well as sales, marketing, and strategic planning. **Career Steps:** Director of Real Estate, Aetna Pro Management Corporation (1994–Present); Director of Real Estate, Aetna Life and Casualty (1991–1994); Vice President of Technical R/E Services, Connecticut Housing Investment Funds (1988–1991). **Associations & Accomplishments:** IDRC; Published articles in Forbes and ASAP magazines; Black Belt Karate Instructor – Sensei. **Education:** University of Hartford. **Personal:** Married to Martha C. in 1967. Two children: Troy and Samantha. Mr. Zeigler enjoys karate, restoring classic cars, and music.

Keyla Alba
Financial Administrator/In–House Counsel
Century Group
901 SW 69 Avenue
Miami, FL 33144
(305) 261–4731
Fax: (305) 261–4805

6531

Business Information: Century Group is a real estate investment and development firm consisting of twenty companies. As Financial Administrator/In–House Counsel, Ms. Alba manages the financial operations of the Group's subsidiary companies and oversees any legal claims that arise. **Career Steps:** Financial Administrator/In–House Counsel, Century Group (1995–Present); Director of Administration, Foundation for Florida's Future (1995); Dade County Office Manager, Jeb Bush Gubernatorial Campaign (1994). **Associations & Accomplishments:** Florida Bar Association; Volunteer, Kids Voting; Volunteer, Dade County Republican Party; Society of Bar and Gavel; National Hispanics for Bob Dole. **Education:** University of Miami Law School, J.D. (1993); University of Miami, Bachelor of Business Administration in Accounting, with honors (1990). **Personal:** Ms. Alba enjoys volunteering with different youth organizations.

Barbara G. Alden
District Vice President
Premisys Real Estate Services, Inc.
1200 K Street, NW, Suite 1010
Washington, DC 20005
(202) 842–1200
Fax: (202) 842–1269

6531

Business Information: Premisys Real Estate Services, Inc. is a national commercial property management firm, providing services to corporate facilities, commercial offices, and property owned by its parent company — Prudential, consisting of approximately 70 million square feet. Premisys, formed in 1989 to manage Prudential real estate and 30% of non–Prudential properties, currently employs more than 1,000 people. As District Vice President, Mrs. Alden is responsible for the oversight of portfolio performances in Virginia, Maryland, and the District of Columbia. **Career Steps:** District Vice President, Premisys Real Estate Services, Inc. (1993–Present); Smithy Braedon Property Company: Vice President of Commercial Management (1990–1992), Asset Manager – Commercial Property Management (1989–1990). **Associations & Accomplishments:** Institute of Real Estate Management; International Facilities Management Association. **Education:** University of North Texas: M.B.A. (1986), B.B.A. **Personal:** Married to John W. in 1966. Two children: Gregory and Jennifer. Mrs. Alden enjoys sailing, scuba diving, fitness and reading during her leisure time.

Miguel A. Alvarez–Lebron
Sales Manager
Ramos Izquierdo Realty, Inc.
Villas de San Francisco Plaza Edir II, Suito 217, Ave De Diego #8
San Juan, Puerto Rico 00927
(787) 753–8570
Fax: (787) 753–8570

6531

Business Information: Ramos Izquierdo Realty, Inc., a subsidiary of Ramos Izquierdo & Associates, is the leading real estate agency in Puerto Rico, providing the marketing and sales of residential, industrial, and commercial property. As

Sales Manager, Mr. Alvarez–Lebron is responsible for the direction of all sales activities, including the oversight of fifteen agents and numerous administrative staff. He has developed important and innovative projects and programs including the development of sales methods leading to a 60% increase in sales; establishment of procedures and organizational policies to comply with government law and professional ethics; the redesign of the corporate logo and promotional materials in conjunction with selected advertising firms to position the Company identity in the marketplace; establishment of bonus, incentive, and special compensation programs in promoting production; securement of financing for clients with major financial institution officials; and directing the task force in charge of office automation. **Career Steps:** Ramos Izquierdo Realty, Inc.: Sales Manager (1992–Present), Sales Associate (1991–1992); Real Estate Agent – Trainee, Isla del Sol Real Estate, Inc. (1990–1991). **Associations & Accomplishments:** National Association of Realtors; Puerto Rico Association of Realtors; San Juan Board of Realtors; Fluent in English and Spanish; Computer literate. **Education:** Inter-American University – Rio Piedras, Puerto Rico, B.A. in Finance **Personal:** Mr. Alvarez–Lebron enjoys computing.

Chromilo B. Amin
Programmer/Analyst
Condo Tech Incorporated
1270 Ala Moana Boulevard
Honolulu, HI 96814–4217
(808) 593–6896
Fax: (808) 593–8994
E–MAIL: SEE BELOW

6531

Business Information: Condo Tech Incorporated is a real estate and marketing firm responsible for over 200 properties and resorts locally and nationally. As Programmer/Analyst, Mr. Amin manages the Company's LAN of three Netware file servers with over 100 PC workstations running on DOS, Windows 3.1, and Windows 3.11 and Windows 95. He writes accounting and administrative software packages for their client/server SQL database using progress programming language. He uses powerbuilder development tool to develop maintenance applications. Internet users can reach him via: 102130.1353@compuserv.com **Career Steps:** Programmer/Analyst, Condo Tech Incorporated (1994–Present); Systems Analyst, C.H.K. Ching & Associates (1994); Software Engineer, UH Hamilton Library (1993). **Associations & Accomplishments:** Network Professional Association (NPA) **Education:** University of Hawaii – Monoa, B.S. in Computer Science (1993); Certified Netware Administrator (1995–); Certified Netware Engineer (1995). **Personal:** Mr. Amin enjoys basketball, swimming, and reading.

George A. Arias
Executive Director
Palatka Housing Authority
PO Box 1277
Palatka, FL 32178–1277
(904) 329–0132
Fax: (904) 328–1333

6531

Business Information: Palatka Housing Authority is the municipal governmental office administering all housing assistance, home ownership and self–sufficiency programs throughout Palatka and surrounding communities. As Executive Director, Mr. Arias is the chief administrative officer directing all areas of administrative operations, as well as the management for all maintenance coordination for PHA–managed housing. **Career Steps:** Executive Director, Palatka Housing Authority (1995–Present); Executive Director, Bexar County Housing (1980–1995); Consultant, Flores & Associates (1981–1993). **Associations & Accomplishments:** Rotary International; National Association of Housing & Redevelopment Officials; Florida Association of Housing & Redevelopment Officials. **Education:** Southwest Texas State University, B.A. (1984). **Personal:** One child: Allyson Catarina. Mr. Arias enjoys working with disadvantaged youth and community assistance programs.

Richard G. Asares

President
Sterling Home Realty & Financial
P.O. Box 476
Artesia, CA 90702–0476
(310) 981–3288
Fax: (310) 981–3289

6531

Business Information: Sterling Home Realty & Financial originates loans and lists, and sells real estate in Southern California, focusing on residential property. Mr. Asares founded Sterling in 1996, overseeing all aspects of business operations, new business development, agent training, and administrative activities. **Career Steps:** President, Sterling Home Realty & Financial (1996–Present); Loan Originations/Realtor, American 2001 Realty & Financial (1991–1996); Loan Originations/Processing/Realtor, Pacific Investments Company (1990–1991). **Associations & Accomplishments:** Filipino American Chamber of Commerce – Long Beach; Long Beach Board of Realtors; National Association of Realtors; California Association of Realtors. **Education:** De La Salle University – Manila, Philippines: Marketing and Management Degree. **Personal:** Mr. Asares enjoys music and playing the piano.

Jo Anne Baggerly
Sales Associate
Coldwell Banker
2603 Holly Hill St.
Burlington, NC 27215–5156
(910) 584–0376
Fax: (910) 584–7710

6531

Business Information: Coldwell Banker is a real estate company involved in the listing and selling of residential properties. As Sales Associate, Ms. Baggerly is responsible for listing and selling real estate to customers in the Burlington, NC metro. **Career Steps:** Coldwell Banker: Sales Associate (1987–Present), Receptionist (1986–87); Secretary, Babcock and Wilcox, NNFD (1970–75). **Associations & Accomplishments:** North Carolina Association of Realtors; Alamance County Board of Realtors; North Carolina Tennessee Walking Horse Association, Tennessee Walking Horse Breeder's Association, Williams High School PTA. **Education:** Liberty Baptist College; Realtor Association: Graduate Realtor Institute, Certified Residential Specialist, Corporate Property Specialist. **Personal:** Married to Barry L. in 1978. One child: Craig J. Ms. Baggerly enjoys horseback riding and reading.

Karen S. Baker
Director of Finance
Baybriar Management Services Limited
P.O. Box 1450
Bellville, Ontario K8N 5J1
(613) 967–2904
Fax: (613) 967–2928

6531

Business Information: Baybriar Management Services Limited is a commercial real estate transportation and warehousing company, specializing in management of shares for subsidiary U.S. and Canadian companies. Established in 1976, the Company employs 300 people, and has an estimated annual revenue of $20 million. As Director of Finance, Ms. Baker oversees all financial aspects of the Company, including budget, taxes, accounting, and profit/loss ratios. She is also responsible for customer service, and acts as liaison between the Company and clients' banks and attorneys. **Career Steps:** Director of Finance, Baybriar Management Services Limited (1994–Present); Corporate Accountant, Wilkinson Company (1988–1994); Accountant, Peat, Marwick, and Thorne (1986–1988). **Associations & Accomplishments:** Treasurer, United Way of Quinte; Chairman, Junior Achievement of Hastings, Prince Edward; Past Chair, Quinte District Chartered Accountants Association. **Education:** Queen's University: M.B.A. (1986), B.A. (1983); CICA (1983). **Personal:** Married to Wayne Reid in 1994. Four children: Martha, Mark, Erie, and Abigail.

Susan K. Bakes
Controller
Hawkins Smith Management, Inc.
727 Belmont Avenue
Boise, ID 83706
(208) 376–8521
Fax: (208) 376–6804

6531

Business Information: Hawkins Smith Management, Inc. is a real estate investment and development firm for shopping centers, consisting of 27 partnerships in the areas of brokering, property, development, and investments. Hawkins Smith Management, Inc. has three satellite offices in the regional area of this office and center locations in Idaho, Nevada, Washington, Arizona, Oregon, Oklahoma, and New Mexico. A Licensed Idaho Real Estate Agent and a Certified Public Accountant, Ms. Bakes joined the Corporation in 1993. Serving as Controller, she oversees all administrative operations of a professional and clerical staff of 12, in addition to analyzing financial statements and cash flow controls. **Career Steps:** Controller, Hawkins Smith Management, Inc. (1993–Present); Vice President of Finance and Administration, Talboy Construction, Inc. (1989–1993); Consultant (1987–1989). **Associations & Accomplishments:** Idaho Society of Certified Public Accountants; Boise State University: Board of Directors, Alumni. **Education:** Boise State University, B.B.A. in Accounting (1984); Licensed Idaho Real Estate Agent (1995). **Personal:** Ms. Bakes enjoys piano, travel, and baking.

Tooraj Bakhtiari
Fine Homes/Commercial Specialist
The Prudential Arizona Realty
6590 North Scottsdale Road
Scottsdale, AZ 85253
(602) 991–3300
Fax: (602) 443–8085

6531

Business Information: The Prudential Arizona Realty provides residential and commercial real estate sales to the Phoenix area. Comprised of 450 employees, the Company has eight locations throughout the Arizona area. Established in 1986, The Prudential Arizona Realty has an estimated annual revenue of $1 billion. As Fine Homes/Commercial Specialist, Mr. Bakhtiari specializes in the sale of fine luxury homes, and all aspects of commercial real estate and joint venture. He is responsible for coordination of all residential and commercial real estate, handles out of state transactions and sales, and oversees all prospective clients and customer service. A member of the president's circle, Mr. Bakhtiari is already counted among the top 3% of all real estate specialists in the country. **Career Steps:** Fine Homes/Commercial Specialist, The Prudential Arizona Realty (1992–Present). **Associations & Accomplishments:** National Association of Realtors; Arizona Association of Realtors. **Education:** University of Phoenix, M.B.A. (1990); Arizona State University, Electrical Engineering. **Personal:** Mr. Bakhtiari enjoys jet skis, reading business and mystery books, stocks and skiing.

Mr. Robert M. Bohlen
Board Chairman and Sales Associate
Prudential Preview Properties
130 West Grand River
Brighton, MI 48116
(810) 220–1500
Fax: (810) 220–1512

6531

Business Information: Prudential Preview Properties is a commercial and residential real estate brokerage firm with offices in Novi, Northville, Ann Arbor, and Brighton, Michigan. Prudential Great Lakes (established in 1970) employ a full–time staff of 250 and report annual sales of $250 million. As Board Chairman, Mr. Bohlen is the Chief Executive Officer overseeing management of the Company's operations, and having full strategic planning responsibilities. In 1994–1995, Mr. Bohlen was the Top Sales Associate in the Prudential system out of more than 32,000 agents, based on closed income. **Career Steps:** Board Chairman, Prudential Preview Properties (1986–Present); President, Progressor Farms Company (1979–1986); President, Premier Corporation, (1969–19 79). **Associations & Accomplishments:** National Association of Realtors; Michigan Association of Realtors; Sunshine Kids. **Education:** University of Illinois, B.S. (1961).

Benedicto Bonilla Bonilla
President/Appraiser
Bonilla Real Estate Services
Cond. El Senorial Office 414, #10 Salud Street
Ponce, Puerto Rico 00731
(787) 844–1390
Fax: (787) 843–4359

6531

Business Information: Mr. Bonilla has been appraising real estate in Southern Puerto Rico through Bonilla Real Estate Services since establishing the Firm in 1974. His clients include private individuals, banks, government agencies, mortgage corporations, and financial services such as Fannie Mae, Banco Popular (the largest bank in Puerto Rico), the Department of the Treasury, Citibank of Puerto Rico, First City Mortgage Association, First Financial Services Corporation, Merrill Lynch, The Prudential, and Coldwell Banker. As President, he is responsible for overall Company management, real estate appraisal, and personal client consultations. **Career Steps:** President/Appraiser, Bonilla Real Estate Services (1974–Present); Valuation Specialist I, Treasury Department (1958–1974); Appraiser, First National Real Estate (1967–1973); Fondo de Pensiones, Banco de Ponce (1967). **Associations & Accomplishments:** Puerto Rico Professional Real Estate Appraiser Board; Puerto Rico Institute of Real Estate Appraiser; Puerto Rico Real Estate Appraiser Evaluations College; National Association of Review Appraisers Certified Real Estate Appraisers; Institute of Business Appraiser, Inc.; National Association of Real Estate Appraisers; Ponce Board of Realtors; Puerto Rico Associates of Realtors; National Association of Realtors; National Association of Review Appraisers; Puerto Rico Federal Appraisers Association; Club Rotario El Vigia; Camara de Comercio de Puerto Rico; Caballeros De Colon; Qualified Expert Witness in Real Estate Valuation. **Education:** Catholic University of Puerto Rico, Civil Engineer Studies; University of Puerto Rico, Course in Real Estate Appraising; Professional Real Estate Academy Graduate; Puerto Rico Institute of Real Estate Appraisers. **Personal:** Married to Josefina Rivera Guzman. Six children: Gloria Luz, Jose B., Maria de los Angeles, Edgardo, Jessica, and Glorimar. Mr. Bonilla enjoys basketball, dominos, softball, and baseball.

Judy M. Bosniadis, Sales & Marketing Executive

Executive Sales Director
Howard Perry & Walston
1600 E. Franklin Street
Chapel Hill, NC 27514–2885
(919) 967–9234
Fax: (919) 942–9343

6531

Business Information: Howard Perry & Walston Realtors, a division of Better Homes and Gardens, is a real estate brokerage firm specializing in residential sales and commercial leasing. With sixteen years in real estate, Ms. Bosniadis joined Howard Perry & Walston Realtors as Executive Sales Director in 1995. She is responsible for executive sales and marketing, including broker real estate transactions and facilitating and coordinating of real estate. **Career Steps:** Executive Sales Director, Howard Perry & Walston (1995–Present); Jon Douglas Company (1992–1995): Director of New Housing, Northern California Sales and Market Coordinator; CPA Administrator, Peat Marwick – San Francisco, CA; Staff Member, OU–Interests; Post International Sales Representative and Marketing Director (For 72–unit luxury high rise), Taiwan Company – San Francisco, CA. **Associations & Accomplishments:** Chamber of Commerce; Chapel Hill Board of Realtors; Board of Realtors of California, North Carolina and Virginia; California Realtors Society; University of North Carolina Alumni Association; Orange County Home Builders Association; National Association of Women Executives. **Education:** University of North Carolina; University of California, B.A. (1974); Hastings College–San Francisco, CA; Anthony School of Real Estate; Howard Perry Walston School of Real Estate. **Personal:** Two children: Ryan and Joey Ragan. Ms. Bosniadis enjoys interior design and architectural design. She also travels extensively internationally, particularly between Paris, France and the U.S.

Kathie Brewer

Realtor
Phillips Realty – Better Homes and Gardens
4021 Keith Street
Cleveland, TN 37312
(423) 472–7171
Fax: (423) 339–1399

6531

Business Information: Phillips Realty – Better Homes and Gardens, a branch of Better Homes and Gardens Realty, is a full–service real estate firm, specializing in the listing and selling of residential properties and property management, as well as providing appraisals of property for future sales. Joining the Agency as Realtor in 1994, Ms. Brewer serves as a sales agent, responsible for the listing and selling of real estate. **Career Steps:** Realtor, Phillips Realty – Better Homes and Gardens (1994–Present); Office Manager, Blue Ridge Psychiatry (1985–1994). **Associations & Accomplishments:** Kiwanis Civitan Club; Medical Alliance; Cleveland Mainstreet; Cleveland Symphony Guild. **Education:** San Francisco State, M.S. (1979); Middle Tennessee State University. **Personal:** Married to Randall in 1974. Two children: Rebecca and Adam. Ms. Brewer enjoys golf, dance, and reading.

Catherine A. Brown, Esq.

Real Estate Associate
Berger Realty
32nd & Asbury Avenue
Ocean City, NJ 08226
(609) 399–0076 (609) 398–3398
Fax: (609) 398–6883

6531

Business Information: Berger Realty is a full–service real estate firm, specializing in the listing and selling of residential properties and property management. As a Real Estate Associate, Ms. Brown is responsible for all aspects of operations, including showing and selling properties. Currently licensed in District of Columbia and Virginia state and federal courts, she plans to continue her law practice in New Jersey in the near future. Her area of practice is in civil, criminal, arbitration, and corporate law in federal and state courts. **Career Steps:** Real Estate Associate, Berger Realty (1995–Present); Sole Practitioner, Law Offices of Catherine A. Brown (1980–1995). **Associations & Accomplishments:** American Bar Association; Virginia Bar Association; District of Columbia Bar Association; World Affairs' Council; Published Treatise on State Law, also on various landmark cases. **Education:** Detroit College of Law, J.D. (1979); Marquette University, B.A. in Journalism; Loyola University of Chicago, Rome, Italy Center; College of William and Mary, Exeter, England Summer International Law Center. **Personal:** Ms. Brown enjoys photography and travel.

Rene L. Carter

Vice President
ExecuStay, Inc.
7595 Rickenbacker Drive
Gaithersburg, MD 20879
(301) 212–9660
Fax: (301) 212–9665

6531

Business Information: ExecuStay, Inc. provides fully–furnished temporary housing nationwide for those executives and their families who are relocating or working away from home. This offers the executives an alternative to staying in a hotel. The apartments and houses are fully furnished, have electrical power, local phone, and cable. Currently, ExecuStay, Inc. has eight regional offices, and plans to open one new office every year. As Vice President, Ms. Carter is responsible for marketing and advertising in foreign service journals, yellow pages, and welcome magazines. **Career Steps:** Vice President, ExecuStay, Inc. (1991–Present); Corporate Sales Representative, Oxford Management (1986–1991); Marketing Representative, Burt Hill Kosar Rittelmann Associates (1982–1986). **Associations & Accomplishments:** Society for Human Resource Managers; Outstanding Jaycee of the Year, Downtown Jaycees of Washington D.C.; State Chairman for the District of Columbia Junior Miss Pageant (1986); Senior Volunteer, Alexandria Hospital in Virginia. **Education:** George Mason University, B.S. (1985); Brevard Community College, A.A. (1980). **Personal:** Married to Dr. Norbert R. Myslinski in 1992. One child: Matthew Ryan. Ms. Carter enjoys needlework, cake decorating, reading, step aerobics, plants, and flowers.

Robert W. Carter Jr.

Vice President
LFC Nationwide, Inc.
45240 Business Court
Sterling, VA 20166
(703) 742–8200 Ext. 510
Fax: (703) 435–7427

6531

Business Information: LFC Nationwide, Inc. is a property field service management company providing services for the mortgage lending industry. As Vice President, Mr. Carter is responsible for business development and technical operations for LFC's environmental services division. **Career Steps:** Vice President, LFC Nationwide, Inc. (1990–Present); Senior Exploration Geophysicist, Western Geophysical (1981–1990). **Associations & Accomplishments:** American Association of Petroleum Geologists; Houston Geological Society; Mortgage Bankers Association. **Education:** James Madison University, B.S. in Geology (1979). **Personal:** Married to Donna in 1980. Two children: Nicholas and Sara. Mr. Carter enjoys competitive swimming via United States Masters Swimming.

Roger H. Clark

Vice President
ARES, Inc. (ARES Realty Capital Services)
1333 Butterfield Road, Suite 400
Downers Grove, IL 60515
(708) 663–4622
Fax: (708) 663–4615

6531

Business Information: ARES, Inc. (ARES Realty Capital, Inc.) is a wholly–owned subsidiary of Mutual of New York. This a full service real estate corporation with offices in Denver, Dallas, Atlanta, Chicago, Stamford, and Irvine, CA. As Vice President, Mr. Clark asset manages 6 properties containing over 1 million square feet of rentable area and acts as Director of Property Services for the Midwest Region, handling all operational details for the Midwest. These details include coordinating regional training, hiring, and implementing policies and procedures. Mr. Clark also is responsible for generating new business. **Career Steps:** Vice President, ARES, Inc. (ARES Realty Capital, Inc.) (1993–Present); Vice President/Regional Head Midwest, First Office Management (1991–1993); Property Manager, Rubloff (1986–1991). **Associations & Accomplishments:** Chicago Real Estate Organization; Association of Industrial Real Estate Brokers; Habitat for Humanity; "Real Estate Magazine" has published articles written by Mr. Clark. **Education:** Michigan State University, B.A. (1981). **Personal:** Married to Sara in 1981. Mr. Clark enjoys the outdoors, fishing, hunting, camping, cross–country skiing, and spending time with his family.

Carol E. Cook

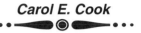

President, Chief Executive and Chief Operations Officer
Century 21 Advantage, Inc.
6320 Allentown Road
Camp Springs, MD 20748–2609
(301) 449–9100
Fax: (301) 449–5324

6531

Business Information: Century 21 Advantage, Inc. is a real estate, property management, mortgage lending, and title service firm. As President, Chief Executive and Chief Operations Officer, Ms. Cook is responsible for overseeing daily operations, performs various administrative activities, and provides executive leadership. Concurrently, she serves as President, Chief Executive and Chief Operations Officer of three other companies: Century 21 Advantage Property Management, Executive Title & Escrow, and Executive Funding, Inc. **Career Steps:** President, Chief Executive and Chief Operations Officer, Century 21 Advantage, Inc. (1994–Present); President, Chief Executive and Chief Operations Officer, Century 21 Advantage Property Management (1994–Present); President, Chief Executive and Chief Operations Officer, Executive Title and Escrow (1994–Present); President, Chief Executive and Chief Operations Officer, Executive Funding, Inc. (1994–Present). **Associations & Accomplishments:** Prince George's Association of Realtors; National Association of Realtors; Southern Maryland Association of Realtors; Real Estate Brokerage Management Council. **Education:** CRB Management (1986); Graduate of Real Estate Institute. **Personal:** Two children: Steven Michael and Sandra Lynn. Ms. Cook enjoys water, boats, horses, and dogs.

Kevin J. Cooke

Chief Executive Officer/Founder
The Cooke Organization
305 Spagnoli Road
Melville, NY 11747–3506
(516) 293–0100 Ext. 101
Fax: (516) 293–4520

6531

Business Information: The Cooke Organization is comprised of eight separate companies primarily focused on full service property management. Other services offered are real estate brokerage, commercial and private real estate inspection, general contracting, and a full–service investigation firm. As CEO/Founder, Mr. Cooke oversees the general operations of the eight companies involved in the Cooke Organization. He works with his management staff on developing and implementing marketing techniques for new and existing services, developing business plans for the various companies, and strategic planning for the future. Having a strong background with the New York Police Department, Mr. Cooke has a strong interest in with the investigative side of the Company. **Career Steps:** CEO/Founder, The Cooke Organization (1975–Present). **Associations & Accomplishments:** Founding Chair and Past President, National Association of Mortgage Field Services; Chairman–Development Committee, St. Paul's Center; National Association of Realtors; Mortgage Bankers Association of America. **Education:** Fordham University, Diploma (1988). **Personal:** Married to Jean in 1970. Five children: Kevin, Kimberly, Keith, Katherine, and Kristin. Mr. Cooke enjoys golf and skiing.

Tim E. Crockett

General Manager
Swig Weiler and Dinner Development
815 Walker, Suite 1147
Houston, TX 77002–5716
(713) 224–1663
Fax: (713) 224–0510

6531

Business Information: Swig Weiler and Dinner Development is a 70–year old real estate company, owning a portfolio of 30 high–rise office buildings located around the country and the Fairmont Hotel chain. As General Manager, Mr. Crockett is responsible for the development and implementation of marketing plans and budgets. He also is responsible for negotiating office leases, overseeing the architectural planning, and construction of leasehold improvements. **Career Steps:** Swig Weiler and Dinner Development: General Manager (1995–Present), Director of Marketing and Leasing (1989–1994); Account Management, Pandick Technologies Facility Management (1988–1989). **Associations & Accomplishments:** Aviation Committee, Houston World Trade

Association; Downtown Houston Association: Board Member, Vice President, Executive Committee, Gala Chair; Life Member, Houston Chamber of Commerce; Houston Livestock Show and Rodeo Association: Life Member, Parade Committee Vice Chairman; Leadership Houston: Former Board Member, Sustained Member; Interfaith Ministries of Greater Houston: Former Board Member, Vice President of Executive Committee. **Education:** Texas A&M University, B.B.A. in Finance (1979). **Personal:** Married to Cheryl F. in 1981. Four children: Camille, Rachel, Meredith, and Evelyn. Mr. Crockett enjoys coaching youth sports, skiing, reading, wilderness camping, and civic involvement.

John Daoud

President
E. Khashoggi Industries
1555 Roble Drive
Santa Barbara, CA 93110–2441
(805) 967–2553
Fax: (805) 683–4853

6531

Business Information: E. Khashoggi Industries is a privately-held job partnership providing international investment ventures and real property development strategies. As President, Mr. Daoud provides the overall vision and strategy for the Company, ensuring customer satisfaction, and overall growth development to keep the Company a viable presence in the international market. Concurrent with his duties at E. Khashoggi Industries, he is also president of Condas International, a property management and investment firm. **Career Steps:** President, E. Khashoggi Industries (1994–Present); Controller, America The Elegant (1980–1983); Financial Manager, Triad Condas International (1972–1978). **Education:** College education in Alexandria, Egypt, B.A. (1961). **Personal:** Married to Yvette in 1964. Three children: Michael, Rita, Natalie. Mr. Daoud enjoys photography.

Carlos A. De Araujo

Managing Director
World Trade Center
Rua Cassio Da Costa Vidigal, 70#1 And
Sao Paulo, Brazil 01456–040
55–11–8937007
Fax: 55–11–8937001

6531

Business Information: One of the 305 World Trade Centers world–wide, the Sao Paulo, Brazil Center has a hotel, trade show center, shopping center, air terminal, business club, telecommunications systems center, and inside parking area. The World Trade Center was established in Brazil in 1995. As Managing Director, Mr. De Araujo supervises and coordinates all of the business units inside the facility. He is additionally responsible for all the financial aspects of the World Trade Center and handles all monthly reports for the Board of Directors. **Career Steps:** Managing Director, World Trade Center (1995–Present); Vice President, ISS (1993–1994); Marketing Director, Johnson & Johnson Professional Products Division (1984–1988); New Business Development Manager, Bunge & Born (1983–1984). **Associations & Accomplishments:** World Trade Center – Business Club; Japan Junior Chamber of Commerce – Economy & Finance Committee. **Education:** Hull University – England, M.B.A. (1991); Saint Olaf College, B.A. with honors in Anthropology, Political Science, and Sociology (1976–1980). **Personal:** Married to Carina Edenburg. Two children: Nicholas and Stephanie. Mr. De Araujo enjoys tennis, theater, and 19th Century painting.

Jackie L. Deimel

Director of Administration & Human Resources
The Voit Companies
21600 Oxnard Street, Suite 300
Woodland Hills, CA 91367–4976
(818) 593–6243
Fax: (818) 593–6274

6531

Business Information: The Voit Companies is a full–service real estate company, specializing in property management, asset services, development, commercial brokerage, and construction. Headquartered in Woodland Hills, CA, the Company has several offices throughout California and one in Arizona. As Director of Administration & Human Resources, Ms. Deimel oversees personnel, benefits, office management, Company policy and procedure, employee relations, wellness and safety programs, and compliance with federal and state laws. **Career Steps:** Director of Administration & Human Resources, The Voit Companies (1991–Present); Executive Administrator, Munici Corporation of California (1981–1991); Showroom Manager, Maharam Fabric Corporation

(1979–1981). **Associations & Accomplishments:** Valley Wellness Association; PIHRA; Warner Center Association Inter Company Involvement; Volunteer, San Fernando Boys and Girls Club. **Education:** Ferris State College (1979); Kendall School of Design, Commercial Art Certificate; Learning Tree Univ., currently working to a Certificate in Human Resource Management. **Personal:** Married to Fred in 1981. One child: Justin. Ms. Deimel enjoys reading, aerobics, running, and art.

Mr. Randall J. DeVries

Vice President
Wiersma–DeVries Real Estate, Inc.
1029 Providence Road
Whitinsville, MA 01588
(508) 234–6441
Fax: (508) 234–0005

6531

Business Information: Wiersma–DeVries Real Estate, Inc. specializes in real estate sales, leasing, and development. Wiersma–DeVries Real Estate, Inc. has been established for 23 years. In his current capacity, Mr. DeVries is responsible for Sales, Management, and Advertising. He has over 11 years of Real Estate Sales experience, 9 years of Real Estate Management and 3 years of Construction experience to offer clients. **Career Steps:** Vice President, Wiersma–DeVries Real Estate, Inc.; Sales Associate, Century 21 Bec–Line, Chicago; Production Manager, Elim Sheltered Workshop; Mr. DeVries started his career in real estate working for a multi–million dollar company in Chicago. In 1984, he moved to Massachusetts to join the family business. He has been a top producer for Wiersma–DeVries Real Estate, Inc. and has received recognition from his peers for his integrity, honesty and professionalism in the field of real estate. **Associations & Accomplishments:** National Association of REALTORS; Massachusetts Association of REALTORS ; Greater Worcester Board of REALTORS ; National Association of Real Estate Appraisers; The Small Business Service Bureau, Inc.; Whitinsville Society for Christian Instruction; Whitinsville Christian School, School Board; Pleasant Street Christian Reformed Church in Whitinsville; Blackstone Valley Chamber of Commerce; Mr. DeVries holds the designation GRI (Graduate of Realtors Institute) and CREA (Certified Real Estate Appraiser); He is committed to continuing education to stay abreast of the latest trends in the market. **Education:** Uxbridge High School, graduate; Calvin College in Grand Rapids, MI, Alumnus; Davenport College, Grand Rapids, MI, Associates Degree (1982). **Personal:** Mr. DeVries lives in the town of Northbridge, with his wife; Shirley and two children, Cara and Ryan. He has made a successful career in real estate for over 11 years, helping hundreds of people buy, sell and invest in real estate.

Daniel T. Ditto

Chief Operating Officer
Hawaii Reserves, Inc.
55 510 Kamehameha Highway
Laie, HI 96762–1119
(808) 293–9201
Fax: (808) 293–6456

6531

Business Information: Hawaii Reserves, Inc. is a property management firm, concentrating on public facilities, such as wastewater treatment plants and agricultural and forestry commodities with 6,000 acres of land for development. Joining Hawaii Reserves, Inc. as Senior Vice President in 1994, Mr. Ditto was appointed as Chief Operating Officer in 1995. He is responsible for the overall day–to–day operations including administration, P&L, public relations, accounting, legal and tax matters, marketing and development strategies. **Career Steps:** Hawaii Reserves, Inc.: Chief Operating Officer (1995–Present), Senior Vice President (1994–1995); Manager of Operations Audits, Church of Jesus Christ of Latter–Day Saints (1992–1993); Partner, Kirton, McConkie & Poelman (1986–1987). **Associations & Accomplishments:** Utah and Nevada Bar Associations; U.S. Supreme Court Bar; Bars of the U.S. Ninth and Tenth Circuit Court of Appeals. **Education:** J. Reuben Clark Law School, J.D. (1985); Brigham Young University, B.A. in American Studies. **Personal:** Married to Laura in 1982. Six children: Daniel, Jonathan, Mary, Matthew, Samuel, and Sara. Mr. Ditto enjoys reading and golf.

Mr. Richard W. Donohue

Managing Director of New York Offices
Cushman & Wakefield, Inc.
51 West 52nd Street, Thirteenth Floor
New York, NY 10019
(212) 841–7579
Fax: (212) 841–7914

6531

Business Information: Cushman & Wakefield, Inc. is the largest commercial real estate company in the world, with offices in all major U.S. markets and partnerships and alliances globally. The Company provides commercial real estate services including brokerage, financial consulting, appraisals,

market research, tax consulting, and third–party real estate management of over 100 million square feet in the U.S.. In his capacity as Managing Director of New York Offices, Mr. Donohue is responsible for all operations and services generated by two offices, including Cushman & Wakefield, Inc. world headquarters. The New York Offices manage 45 million square feet of commercial real estate. Established in 1917, Cushman & Wakefield, Inc. New York offices employ over 900 people. **Career Steps:** Managing Director of New York Offices, Cushman & Wakefield, Inc. (1993–Present); Broker, Cushman & Wakefield, Inc. (1973–1993); Hotel Development, ResortAmerica (1971–1973); Assistant Engineer, Cushman & Wakefield, Inc. (1970–1971). **Associations & Accomplishments:** Real Estate Board of New York; NACORE International; New York Chamber of Commerce; East Side Association; Fifth Avenue Association; Sixth Avenue Associaiton; New York University Real Estate Roundtable; IDRC; Interviewed by trade journals and magazines. **Education:** City College of New York, B.A. (1970).

Beverly Whitener Eckard

Real Estate Broker
Sam W. Moore and Associates
2430 South Church Street, Suite A
Burlington, NC 27215
(910) 226–1131
Fax: (910) 226–1134
E MAIL: See Below

6531

Business Information: Sam W. Moore and Associates is a real estate firm located in Burlington, North Carolina. The Firm currently has as staff of 15. Mrs. Eckard is an independent real estate broker specializing in residential and commercial properties. Internet user may reach her via: milesbev@netpath.net. **Career Steps:** Real Estate Broker, Sam W. Moore and Associates (1977–Present). **Associations & Accomplishments:** National Association of REALTORS; Committee Member, North Carolina Association of REALTORS; President, Burlington–Alamance Association of REALTORS (1993); Trustee, St. Paul's United Methodist Church. **Education:** Gaston College; Alamance Community College; Graduate of REALTORS Institute at the University of North Carolina at Chapel Hill. **Personal:** Married to Miles in 1959. Three children: Tim, William, and Lynette. Mrs. Eckard enjoys singing in the choir, traveling the world, being a certified Koh–I–Noor art instructor, and playing tennis.

Cindy R. Essenburg, CRP

Manager
M.J. Peterson Real Estate, Inc.
1244 Niagara Falls Boulevard
Tonawanda, NY 14150–8924
(800) 268–4569
Fax: (716) 862–9761

6531

Business Information: M.J. Peterson Real Estate, Inc. is a real estate sales and services firm, selling residential and commercial real estate, and operating 3,000 rental units. Services include relocating and home building from five offices. With twenty years of experience in real estate, Ms. Essenburg joined M.J. Peterson Real Estate, Inc. as Director of Housing in 1986 and then as Director of Relocation in 1990. She was appointed as Manager in 1995, responsible for overseeing the day–to–day operations of residential sales. **Career Steps:** M.J. Peterson Real Estate, Inc.: Manager (1995–Present), Director of Relocation (1990–1995), Director of Housing (1986–1990). **Associations & Accomplishments:** American Business Womans Association: Selected as Woman of the Year; National Association of Realtors; New York Association of Realtors; Buffalo Association of Realtors; Womans Council of Realtors; Certified Exchange Advisor; North Tonawanda Board of Assessment Review Member; Sunset Island Womans Auxiliary; Sunset Island Association; Employee Relocation Council; Articles in focus (NTL Board to Broker Magazine) and in local papers; Recipient of numerous awards for advertising. **Education:** Real Estate, CRP (1995); Realtors Institute GRI; Certifications: Exchange Advisor, CEA, Relocation Professional CRP. **Personal:** Married to George in 1975. Two children: Chad and Adam. Ms. Essenburg enjoys all water sports, swimming, snorkeling, jet–skiing, fishing, water skiing, volleyball, tennis, and reading.

Joe Feliciano

President
Joe Feliciano Realty
Ave. Munoz Rivera C–9, Apartado 7467
Ponce, Puerto Rico 00732
(787) 843–6635
Fax: (787) 840–9789

6531

Business Information: Joe Feliciano Realty is a real estate office specializing in the buying and selling of property mainly in Southern Puerto Rico. Currently, the Company has eight vendors. As President, Mr. Feliciano is responsible for managing daily business operations, handling business expansion, supervising employees, and customer satisfaction. **Career Steps:** President, Joe Feliciano Realty (1971–Present). **Associations & Accomplishments:** San Juan Board of Realtors; Vice President (1980), (1981), (1982), Puerto Rico Association of Realtors; President (1980), (1981), (1993), Ponce board of Realtors; Vie President (1993), (1994), Sales & Marketing Executive Association; President (1994–), Puerto Rico Real Estate Examination Board; Realtor of the Year – Puerto Rico (1980); Realtor of the Year – Ponce (1980); Executive of the Year in Real Estate – Ponce (1980), (1993); Distinguished Person in Real Estate – Ponce (1993). **Education:** Currently attending Catholic University Law School – Ponce; Professional Real Estate Academy; Graduate Realty Institute; Catholic University – Puerto Rico, Bachelors in Business Administration. **Personal:** Married to Virgen Cardona in 1973. Three children: Joseph, Jessika, and Natasha. Mr. Feliciano enjoys basketball, billiards, checkers, and music.

J. Michael Flynn
Senior Vice President
Meredith & Grew, Inc. ONCOR International
160 Federal Street
Boston, MA 02110
(617) 330–8017 Ext. 5017
Fax: (617) 330–8130
EMail: See Below

6531

Business Information: Meredith & Grew, Inc. ONCOR International is a full–service (management, consulting, and brokerage services) real estate firm. The Company is an industrial and commercial real estate broker offering financial and developmental services. As Senior Vice President, Mr. Flynn provides leasing and sales of commercial real estate services. Internet users can reach him via: mail@m–g.com. **Career Steps:** Senior Vice President, Meredith & Grew, Inc. ONCOR International (1974–Present). **Associations & Accomplishments:** Society of Industrial and Office Realtors; Commercial Industrial and Investment Council; Urban Land Institute. **Education:** Boston College, B.S. (1969). **Personal:** Married to Suzanne in 1992. Three children: Christine, Brian, and Patrick. Mr. Flynn enjoys golf, hockey, tennis, and rollerblading.

Terry E. Golden
New Home Sales and Marketing Director
The Prudential Hubbell Real Estate Company
1020 South Crayts Road
Lansing, MI 48917–3016
(517) 321–1000 Ext. 323
Fax: (517) 321–5999

6531

Business Information: Consistently ranked in the top 5 out 1,400 Prudential franchises and with a share of over 25% of the local market, The Prudential Hubbell Real Estate Company distinguishes itself as a nationwide leader. Prudential Hubbell has been ranked in the top 300 real estate companies by two independent reporting services. In the past two years the National Association of Home Builders Sales & marketing Council has awarded Prudential Hubbell the highest honors available. Ms. Golden, as New Home Sales & Marketing Director has created a dramatic turn around in the new homes development area by assisting builders and developers with a complete marketing services package. This turn around has created a 160% in sales. Services include comprehensive market research, innovative approaches to marketing and a hands–on sales effort. Ms. Golden has assumed a leadership role in several professional organizations which help her provide the best and most current information for her clients as well as sharing and networking information with her peers in the real estate industry. **Career Steps:** New Home Sales and Marketing Director, The Prudential Hubbell Real Estate Company (1991–Present); Vice President, Fairmont Builders, Inc. (1984–1991); Sales Coordinator, Dunn and Fairmont (1979–1984). **Associations & Accomplishments:** National Assn. of Realtors – CRB, CRS; National Assn. of Home Builders– CSP, MIRM Candidate; Michigan Assn. of Home Builders – Board of Directors; Greater Lansing Assn. of Home Builders – Board of Directors; Institute of Residential Marketing; Builder Marketing Society. **Personal:** Married to James in 1965. Two grown sons – J. Michael and Jeffrey P. Hobbies include photography, camping, canoeing, and reading.

Thomas W. Goss

Divisional President
BlueGreen Corporation
P.O. Box 1413
Monument, CO 80132
(719) 260–5566
Fax: (719) 481–0395

6531

Business Information: Blue Green Corporation, the nation's most successful recreational land sales company which sells and finances land used for hiking, camping, fishing, hunting, and for building their primary, vacation, or retirement homes. Formerly known as Patten Corporation West, BlueGreen Corporation buys the right land at the right price, sells and finances at affordable prices, and provides superior customer service. Traded on the New York Stock Exchange as BXG, operations have expanded to include the west, southwest, midwest, and southeast, as well as the northeast region of the country, where Patten began. Corporate headquarters is located in Boca Raton, Florida, providing leadership and support to 28 regional offices located across the U.S., with one in Canada. The West Division office is located in Colorado Springs, Colorado and employs 40 people. As Divisional President, Mr. Goss is responsible for the oversight of all aspects of operations in the West Division, including property identification, acquisitions, staff, and marketing. **Career Steps:** Divisional President, Blue Green Corporation, formerly Patten Corporation (1994–Present); Patten Corporation: Regional President (1989–1994), Regional Vice President (1987), Regional Manager (1985–1987). **Education:** Attended Berkshire Community College and North Adams State College. **Personal:** Married to Julie George in 1988. Three children: Alexandra, Victoria, and Connor. Mr. Goss enjoys boating, scuba diving, and hunting.

Carl R. Haaf
Vice President
Fox & Lazo, Inc.
1020 Black Horse Pike, Suite #6
Turnersville, NJ 08012
(609) 227–8900
Fax: (609) 232–2020
EMAIL: See Below

6531

Business Information: Fox & Lazo, Inc. is a multi–state independent real estate company with thirty offices in Pennsylvania, Delaware, and New Jersey. One of the top twenty–five independent realtors in the U.S., the Turnersville office has been the largest volume office since 1986, and has the largest number of million dollar producers in the Company. As Vice President, Mr. Haaf is responsible for overseeing the largest office in the Company, as well as the one with the most volume. Entering real estate as a sales associate in 1977, he built on his background in sales and believed he could provide quality service to home buyers and sellers based on honesty, integrity and hard work. The determination and commitment paid off, and he was named to manage his own office within three years. Upon joining Fox & Lazo, Mr. Haaf bought with him a management style that reflected his confidence, personality, and strong dedication to subordinates. His ability to recruit and motivate makes him one of the most respected managers in the Company. Internet users can reach him via: fox49@foxandlazo.com. **Career Steps:** Fox & Lazo, Inc: Vice President (1986–Present), Manager, Hadenfield (1981–1986); Sales Manager, Paparone Realty (1978–1981). **Associations & Accomplishments:** Past President, Gloucester County Board of Realtors; Life Member Award, Realtor Political Action Committee; Top Office Award, Fox & Lazo (1987–1995). **Education:** Temple University; Spring Garden Institute of Technology, Associate Degree in Electrical Engineering. **Personal:** One child: Lisa. Mr. Haaf enjoys golf and fishing.

Dolores J. Hall
Broker
Coldwell Banker
City of Hollyvilla, 10714 Charlene Drive
Fairdale, KY 40118–9316
(502) 361–9441
Fax: (502) 366–8683

6531

Business Information: Coldwell Banker Foremost, Realtors, an independently owned and operated member of Coldwell Banker Residential Affiliates, Inc., is a holding company concentrating in brokerage and real estate sales. As Broker and Realtor, Mrs. Hall is responsible for the listing and sale of real estate properties. She is a member of the Million Dollar Club and Louisville Board of Realtors. Concurrently, she has served as Councilwoman for the City of Hollyvilla since 1990 and Clerk/Treasurer since 1986. **Career Steps:** Broker and Realtor, Coldwell Banker Foremost (1977–Present); City of

Hollyvilla: Councilwoman (1990–Present), Clerk/Treasure (1986–Present). **Associations & Accomplishments:** Genealogy Society, Kentucky and Tennessee Chapters; Fairdale Community Club; Honorable Order of Kentucky Colonels; Board, Farnsley Moremen Historical Home. **Education:** Brokers License, State License (1980); Real Estate License, State License (1977). **Personal:** One child: William H. (deceased). Mrs. Hall enjoys travel, and genealogy.

Janis C. Harrison
President
Action Property Management
701 South Parker Street, Suite 1600
Orange, CA 92668–4720
(714) 285–2600
Fax: (714) 285–1167

6531

Business Information: Action Property Management is a homeowners association (H.O.A.) and property management firm, providing management services to over 15,000 units in both Orange and Riverside Counties from two offices. Founding Action Property Management in 1984, Ms. Harrison serves as its President and Sole Owner, responsible for all aspects of operations, including Corporate planning and management. Concurrently, she is owner and operator of two other companies, including an APM data processing company and a publishing company — Community Association Publishing Services (CAPS). **Career Steps:** President, Action Property Management (1984–Present); District Manager, Professional Management Service (1983–1984); Manager, Mercury Property Management (1980–1983); Public Relations, State Bank (1970–1980). **Associations & Accomplishments:** American Water Ski Association; Track and Field Association; Former Board of Directors, AIDS Walk. Orange County; California Association of Community Managers; Community Associations Institute; Building Industry Association. **Education:** Ventura College. **Personal:** Two children: Kristi and Nicole. Ms. Harrison enjoys running marathons, century bike rides, and tournament water skiing.

Valerie Haynal
Sales Associate
RE/MAX
23480 Sunset Drive
Los Gatos, CA 95030
(408) 353–6261
Fax: (408) 353–6214

6531

Business Information: RE/MAX is a broker–owned commercial, residential, and investment property real estate franchise. Unlike other real estate brokerages, RE/MAX employees are entitled to 100 percent of their commissions. Established in 1985, RE/MAX operates 2400 offices worldwide. As Sales Associate, Mrs. Haynal is responsible for assisting clients in purchasing luxury homes, relocating, or selling their present home. Concurrent with her present position, Mrs. Haynal is a working artist specializing in oils done in the "old master" style. She is also a partner of Haynal Studios International which markets antique and contemporary fine art. **Career Steps:** Sales Associate, RE/MAX (1994–Present); Sales Associate, Partner, Contempo Real Estate Corporation (1993–1994); Sales Executive, Referral Realty (1987–1990); Partner, Haynal Studios International (Present). **Associations & Accomplishments:** Founding Member of the Mountain Artists Association; **Education:** O'Buda Festo Iskola, Hungary, Bachelor of Fine Arts (1993); Folk Art Academy, Budapest, Master of Folk Art Certificate; Cabrillo College, Associate Degree. **Personal:** Married to Rudolf Haynal, Baron Uhlyarik von Rico in 1980. Mrs. Haynal enjoys travel and being a practicing and exhibiting artist.

Alberto Hernandez
President
Alberto Hernandez Real Estate
1603 Loiza Street
San Juan, Puerto Rico 00911
(809) 728–6124
Fax: (809) 728–3670

6531

Business Information: Alberto Hernandez Real Estate, a part of Century 21's international family of realtors, provides all areas of commercial and residential property management, land development and real estate sales throughout Puerto Rico. Established in 1963, Alberto Hernandez Real Estate currently employs 25 people at its two offices in the greater San Juan–metro area. With 32 years expertise in the real estate industry, Mr. Hernandez established his private real estate office in 1963. He is responsible for all aspects of operations, with the assistance of his daughter and son–in–law. Career milestones include: acquiring a Juris Doctorate and selling the largest condominium in Puerto Rico, as well as other large multi–family residences [i.e. River Park (500 units), Candado del Mar (411 units), San Juan East La Verda (320 units) in

Playa Dorrada]. **Career Steps:** President, Alberto Hernandez Real Estate (1963–Present). **Associations & Accomplishments:** Puerto Rico Association of Realtors, Inc.; San Juan Board of Realtors, Inc.; The Wine and Food Society. **Personal:** Married to Hilda Pujol in 1957. Four children: Ligia G., Brigitte M., Alex A., and Ingrid D. Hernandez Pujol. Mr. Hernandez enjoys bicycling, travel, and the gym.

Randy J. Holihan

Senior Vice President
Trammell Crow Company
1120 Paladin Court
Orlando, FL 32812
(407) 422–8400
Fax: (407) 422–5533

6531

Business Information: Trammell Crow Company, a subsidiary of Trammell Crow International – established in 1947, is the leading real estate development, management, and leasing firm in the U.S. An international development firm, Trammell Crow specializes in commercial and residential trade marts (special projects) at 77 U.S. offices and 7 foreign offices located throughout Europe, Latin America and Asia. Established in 1920, Trammell Crow Company currently employs 1,600 nation–wide. With eleven years experience in executive positions, Mr. Holihan joined Trammell Crow Company in 1994. Serving as Senior Vice President, he is responsible for the oversight of retail real estate operations for the Company in Central and North Florida. **Career Steps:** Senior Vice President, Trammell Crow Company (1994–Present); Senior Vice President, The Brandon Company (1989–1994); Senior Vice President, Lake Nona Corporation (1989–1986); Director of Operations, Ellesmere (Cayman), Ltd. (1984–1986). **Associations & Accomplishments:** Government Affairs Committee, International Council of Shopping Centers; PAC State of Florida; Advisor, Orange County Comp. Plan; Director, Florida Hospital Foundation; Board of Directors, CMS. **Education:** Eastern Kentucky University, B.B.A. (1977). **Personal:** Married to Carolyn in 1990. One child: Ryan. Mr. Holihan enjoys water sports.

Richard A. Hrabe

General Manager
MS Management Services
205 North Michigan Avenue, Suite 3900
Chicago, IL 60601
(312) 819–4474
Fax: (312) 819–4473

6531

Business Information: MS Management Services is a national real estate management company, specializing in high–rise commercial office buildings and residential apartments. A Licensed Stationary Engineer, Mr. Hrabe has served in various supervisory positions with MS, most recently promoted to General Manager in 1992. He is presently responsible for monitoring and directing the performance, profitability, and asset protection for a 1 million square foot office tower in the City of Chicago, Illinois. His responsibilities include oversight of accounting functions, supervision of security and contract service personnel, clerical staff, carpenters, and engineers. **Career Steps:** MS Management Services: General Manager (1992–Present); Building Manager (1988–1992), Project Manager (1984–1988). **Associations & Accomplishments:** Chief Engineers Association of Chicago; Building Owners Management Institute; RPA Candidate; International Union of Operating Engineers Local 399, Licensed Stationary Engineer. **Education:** Prosser High School, Diploma (1964). **Personal:** Married to Luba in 1973. Two children: Kimberly and Chantel. Mr. Hrabe enjoys antique cars, museums, bowling, travel, and spending time with his family.

Jeffery J. Keim

President
RDI Resort Services Corp.
12995 South Cleveland Avenue, Suite 164
Ft. Myers, FL 33907–3875
(941) 936–5800
Fax: (941) 936–5604
EMAIL: See Below

6531

Business Information: RDI Resort Services, established in 1982, is a family–owned business providing management services for 38 resorts. The Company has four divisions, resort property management, time share resales, condo rentals, and a travel agency. As President, Mr. Keim is responsible for resort services and ovesees all services in addition to conducting the association meetings. He is involved in expansion planning, establishing budgets, maintaining cost control, and construction completed in a timely manner. Internet users can reach him via: rdi@coconet.com. **Career Steps:** RDI Resort Services: President (1986–Present), Vice President of Operations (1983–1986). **Associations & Accomplishments:** Licensed Florida Real Estate Broker; Licensed Community Association Manager in Florida; ARDA Resort Owners Coalition; ARDA Property Management Committee. **Education:** Ball State University. **Personal:** Married to Barbara in 1990. Two children: Carley and Emily. Mr. Keim enjoys fishing, camping, and golf.

Kevin L. Kelly, CPA

Controller
Pardoe Pardoe & Graham Real Estate
1307 Dolley Madison Boulevard, #4B
McLean, VA 22101
(703) 442–5025
Fax: (703) 442–8122

6531

Business Information: Pardoe Pardoe & Graham Real Estate is a full–service, real estate brokerage with a small number of commercial leases. As Controller, Mr. Kelly is responsible for six companies, for which he handles all financial statements, tax returns, statistics on home sales, network administration, troubleshooting, and a large support staff. **Career Steps:** Controller, Pardoe Pardoe & Graham Real Estate (1995–Present); Supervisor, Bond, Beebe, A Professional Corporation (1987–1995). **Associations & Accomplishments:** American Institute of Certified Public Accountants; Virginia Society of Certified Public Accountants. **Education:** George Mason University, B.S. in Accounting (1987). **Personal:** Married to Paula in 1992. Three children: Kevin Jr., Erin, and Hope. Mr. Kelly enjoys golf, skiing, and basketball.

EQUITABLE REAL ESTATE
INVESTMENT MANAGEMENT INC.

Michael P. Kercheval

Senior Vice President
Equitable Real Estate
787 7th Avenue
New York, NY 10019
(212) 554–3439
Fax: (212) 315–2916

6531

Business Information: Equitable Real Estate, a subsidiary of The Equitable Life Assurance Society, is one of the world's largest and most diversified real estate organization and the nation's leading real estate manager for institutions. As Senior Vice President, Mr. Kercheval is responsible for all aspects of the Company's commercial mortgage portfolios. He may be reached via e–mail: mkercheval@equitre.com. **Career Steps:** Equitable Real Estate: Senior Vice President (1992–Present), Vice President (1990–1992); Senior Economist, Equitable Life Assurance (1982–1986). **Associations & Accomplishments:** National Association of Business Economists; American Real Estate Society; National Council of Real Estate Investment Fiduciaries; Chairman Working Group on Mortgages, American Council of Life Insurance. **Education:** Columbia University, Ph.D. (ABD) (1982), M.A. Degree in Economics; University of Colorado, B.A. in International Affairs. **Personal:** Married to Dana in 1986. Two children: Jacquelyn and Adam. Mr. Kercheval enjoys spending time with his family.

Avis L. King

Director of Human Resources
Greenbelt Homes, Inc.
Hamilton Place
Greenbelt, MD 20770
(301) 474–4161
Fax: (301) 474–4006

6531

Business Information: Greenbelt Homes, Inc. is one of the oldest housing cooperatives in the U.S. with roots dating back to the "New Deal" era of Franklin Roosevelt. With a staff of 80 and an annual budget of over $6 million, it provides a variety of services to its 1,600+ membership. As Director of Human Resources, Ms. King is the senior advisor to the General Manager in the areas of strategic planning, organizational change and human resource management. **Career Steps:** Director of Human Resources, Greenbelt Homes, Inc. (1995–Present); Employee Development Specialist, General Accounting Office (1992–1995); Human Resources Manager, Goodwill Industries International (1989–1992). **Associations & Accomplishments:** Society for Human Resource Management (SHRM), national and county chapters, Former Commissioner, Frederick County Commission for Women; Certified Senior Professional in Human Resources (SPHR); Certified Mediator. **Education:** Johns Hopkins University, M.S. in Applied Behavioral Sciences (1996); University of Maryland, B.A. in Psychology Organizational Cultures. **Personal:** Married to Jay in 1981. Two children: Kimberly and Lisa Bugash. Ms. King enjoys boating, walking, and writing.

Helen M. Kocemba

Controller
Highcrest Management Co.
7550 Janes Avenue
Woodridge, IL 60517
(708) 985–3303
Fax: (708) 985–2101

6531

Business Information: Highcrest Management Company is a condominium and townhome management firm. As Controller, Miss Kocemba is responsible for all aspects of accounting and personnel, as well as administrative matters. **Career Steps:** Controller, Highcrest Management Company (1986–Present). **Associations & Accomplishments:** Better Business Contacts. **Education:** Illinois Benedictine College, B.A. in Accounting (1990); Illinois Real Estate Sales Broker.

Mr. Richard S. Lalla

Vice President
Trammell Crow International
2001 Ross Avenue, Suite 3200
Dallas, TX 75201
(214) 978–4494
Fax: (214) 978–4499

6531

Business Information: Trammell Crow International, established in 1947, is the leading real estate development firm in the U.S. An international development firm, Trammell Crow specializes in commercial and residential trade marts (special projects) at 77 U.S. offices and 7 foreign offices located throughout Europe, Latin America and Asia. As Vice President, Mr. Lalla is responsible for all aspects of operations, including development (design, finance, building and operating) and management of projects on a worldwide level, concentrating in Japan and Asia. He specializes in trade mart development. **Career Steps:** Vice President of Trade Center Development, Trammel Crow International (1992–Present); Director of International Sales and Marketing, Japan Market Center Co. — a joint venture of Trammel Crow Intl. and Sumitomo Trust & Bank, Ltd. (1988–1992); Dallas Market Center Company: Vice President of International Development (1985–1988), General Manaer of Menswear Mart (1984–1985), Director of Leasing (1982–1984); Senior Trade Specialist, U.S. Department of Commerce – International Trade Administration (1978–1982). **Associations & Accomplishments:** Chairman, Pacific Rim Committee, International Trade Advisory Board; Board of Directors, Dallas Council on World Affairs; Board of Directors, State Fair of Texas/Pan American Council; Board of Directors, International Society of Dallas/Fort Worth; Past Chairman and President, International Trade Association of Dallas/Fort Worth; International Committee Member, North Texas Commission; Special Member, Consular Corps of Dallas/Fort Worth; International Committee Member, Greater Dallas Chamber of Commerce; Alumni, Leadership Dallas; Conducts seminars on International Real Estate; Numerous personal and professional awards, including national recognition for trade promotion achievements from Secretary of Commerce–Malcolm Baldridge in 1982. **Education:** American Graduate School of International Management–Thunderbird, M.I.M. (1974); Texas Tech University, B.B.A. (1972). **Personal:** Married to Judi in 1973. Two children: Alicia and Olivia.

Robert Love

President
Love Enterprises
301 East Broadway
Alton, IL 62002–2402
(618) 462–3155
Fax: (618) 462–3156

6531

Business Information: Love Enterprises is a commercial and residential real estate sales and property management firm; owner of the Mineral Springs Mall in Alton, Illinois. Established in 1995, Love Enterprises reports annual revenue of $4 million. With fifteen years experience in the industrial and administrative management industry, Mr. Love established Love Enterprises in 1995. He is responsible for all aspects of operations and management of Mineral Springs Mall. **Career Steps:** President, Love Enterprises (1995–Present); Realtor, Bryants Real Estate Group (1989–1994); Operations Manager, Echlin Inc. (1980–1989); Manager of Customer Services, Gould (1978–1980). **Associations & Accomplishments:**

National Association of Realtors; Illinois Association of Realtors; Recipient, Alton/Wood River Board of Realtors Homer Adams Citizenship Award (1993); Former President, Alton Landing Betterment District; Small Business Council; Riverbend Growth Association. **Education:** Southern Illinois University, M.B.A. (1978); Washington University at St. Louis, B.S. in Business Administration and Industrial Management (1974). **Personal:** Married to Brenda in 1992. Three children: Michael, Eric, and Jennifer. Mr. Love enjoys antiques, boating, and motor home travel.

Mrs. Mary Ann W. Lundy
Vice President of Finance
Ev Cochrane and Associates
207 Stanton, P.O. Box 1099
Ames, IA 50014
(515) 292–4562
Fax: (515) 292–2603

6531

Business Information: Ev Cochrane and Associates specializes in real estate development and apartment rentals throughout Ames, Iowa and surrounding communities. Currently the Association employs 25 people and rents over 500 apartment homes. As Vice President of Finance, Mrs. Lundy is responsible for all aspects of accounting operations and for developing sources of financing. **Career Steps:** Vice President of Finance, Ev Cochrane and Associates (1989–Present); Accounting Manager, Mishler, Lyden and Company (1986–1989); Staff Accountant, Mishler, Moore and Company (1985–1986); Staff Accountant, Dougherty and Company (1981–1985). **Associations & Accomplishments:** Iowa Society of Certified Public Accountants; Chair of Program Committee, Ames Chamber of Commerce; Beta Gamma Sigma – Honor Society for Collegiate Schools of Business; Treasurer and Board Member, Alzheimers Association – Heart of Iowa Chapter; Treasurer and Administrative Board Member, Collegiate United Methodist Church; Phi Kappa Phi; Member, City of Ames Historic Preservation Committee. **Education:** Iowa State University, M.B.A. (1994), B.S. in Industrial Administration (1981), Certified Public Accountant (1985). **Personal:** Married to Paul in 1967. Two children: Erik and Karl. Mrs. Lundy enjoys traveling, reading and aerobic exercise.

Patti J. McDonald, CPM
Divisional Vice President
Property Asset Management
237 South Westmonte Drive #240
Altamonte Springs, FL 32714
(407) 865–7400
Fax: (407) 865–9611

6531

Business Information: Property Asset Management, a subsidiary of AIMCO (Apartment Investment and Management Company), is a public–held company on the New York Stock Exchange. Headquartered in Denver, Colorado, the Company specializes in the management of apartment communities. The 12th largest property management company in the United States, Property Asset Management oversees 36,000 units. As Vice President of the Florida Division, Ms. McDonald utilizes her expertise in the field of personal administration to administer 10,000 units in Florida. **Career Steps:** Property Asset Management: Divisional Vice President Florida (1996–Present), Vice President (1991–1995), Regional Property Manager (1986–1990). **Associations & Accomplishments:** National Apartment Association; Treasurer, Apartment Association of Greater Orlando; Board Member, Florida Apartment Association; CAM and CAPS Instructor, AAGO. **Education:** Lamar University, B.A. (1984); Institute of Real Estate Management, CPM Designation (1992).

Tammy McDonald Anderson
Division Administrator
Lennar Homes, Inc.
12230 Forest Hill Boulevard
West Palm Beach, FL 33414
(407) 790–0202
Fax: (407) 790–4825

6531

Business Information: Lennar Homes, Inc. is the largest real estate developer in Florida and one of the top ten in the United States. As Division Administrator, Mrs. McDonald Anderson is responsible for fiscal management, new community planning, establishment of HOA/POAs, and management for the Palm Beach County operations. **Career Steps:** Division Administrator, Lennar Homes, Inc. (1986–Present); Director of Internal Audit, Windmere Corporation (1983–1986); Senior Auditor, International Multi Foods Corporation (1981–1983). **Associations & Accomplishments:** Advisory Council for State of Florida, Community Association of Managers; Sunday School Superintendent & Vestry Member, St. Matthews Episcopal; Zeta Phi Beta; National Association for the Advancement of Colored People. **Education:** Florida A&M

University, B.S. in Accounting (1980). **Personal:** Married to Seth. Two children: Robyn and Spenser.

Mrs. Mary E. McGuire
• • • ◄━━━━◉━━━━► • • •
Owner/Broker
McGuires Inc. d.b.a. Century 21 Pioneer Valley Associates
26 Crafts Avenue
Northampton, MA 01060
(413) 586–5401
Fax: (413) 585–9633

6531

Business Information: McGuires Inc. d.b.a. Century 21 Pioneer Valley Associates, established in 1986, is a full service real estate firm serving the Franklin and Hampshire counties population with services including: residential sales, commercial sales and leasing, and relocation. As Owner and Broker of McGuires Inc., Mrs. McGuire is responsible for overall operations. Established in 1986, McGuires Inc. employs 11 sales associates and clerical staff personnel. **Career Steps:** Owner/Broker, McGuires Inc. d.b.a. Century 21 Pioneer Valley Associates (1986–Present); Pharmaceutical Sales, CIBA–Geigy Company, Summitt, NJ (1981–1986); Secondary School Teacher, Enfield High School and Cathedral High School (1970–1981). **Associations & Accomplishments:** Franklin–Hampshire Board of Realtors (1986–Present); Greater Springfield Board of Realtors (1986–Present); Massachusetts Association of Realtors (1986–Present); National Association of Realtors (1986–Present). **Education:** Western New England University, M.B.A. (1986); Massachusetts College of Pharmacy, M.S. in Therapeutic Pharmacology (1979); Elms College, B.A. in Liberal Arts and Secondary–School Teaching Certificate (1970).

Bonnie A. Meisner
Vice President
Continental Properties Corporation
1064 Laskin Road, Suite 25C
Virginia Beach, VA 23451–6337
(804) 491–2460
Fax: (804) 422–5062

6531

Business Information: Continental Properties Corporation is a real estate agency, providing real estate development, sales, leasing, and property management. As Vice President, Ms. Meisner is responsible for the oversight of day–to–day operations and directing financial activities. **Career Steps:** Vice President, Continental Properties Corporation (1988–Present); Field Administrator, Bally/Holiday Health and Fitness (1983–1988); Traffic Controller, International Contractors Supply (1981–1982). **Associations & Accomplishments:** Community Association Institute; Tidewater Builders Association; Tidewater Multi–Family Council; American Payroll Association; Former Treasurer, Cape Henry Optimist Club. **Education:** Bethany College: B.A. in Education (1977), minors in Math and Psychology. **Personal:** Ms. Meisner enjoys reading, crafts, computers, and bike riding.

Olivia C. Merlin
• • • ◄━━━━◉━━━━► • • •
Commercial Specialist
Century 21 – Aa Carnes Inc.
382 State Road 434 West
Longwood, FL 32750
(407) 767–1234
Fax: (407) 332–1320

6531

Business Information: Century 21 – Aa Carnes Inc., affiliated with the international real estate chain, Century 21, is a real estate, property management, residential and commercial brokerage firm serving Florida, the U.S. and the world. As Commercial Specialist, Ms. Merlin serves as an Income Producing Properties Sales Agent at the Longwood office. Concurrently, she serves as President and Chief Executive Officer with AGEFI (France), an investment corporation located in France which is involved in the Stock Exchange, property portfolios, and property management. At this location, a manager and three sales representatives operate the office in her absence. In addition, she serves as Executive Manager of I.I.C.I., an international investment consultation firm. **Career Steps:** Commercial Specialist, Century 21 – Aa Carnes Inc. (Present); President and Chief Executive Officer, AGEFI – France (Present); Executive Manager, I.I.C.I.– Longwood, FL (Present). **Associations & Accomplishments:** F.I.A.B.C.; NAR International; FAR International; World Trade Center. **Education:** Task Academy of Real Estate, Sales License

(1994); Sorbonne – France, Post Graduate (1979); ASSAS Law School – Paris, France, Post Graduate. **Personal:** Ms. Merlin enjoys amateur photography, tennis, reading, and Ice Figure Skating.

William F. Morris III
Vice President
First American Real Estate Information Services
1400 Corporate Dr.
Irving, TX 75038–2420
(214) 580–8712
Fax: (214) 714–5611

6531

Business Information: Established in 1889, First American Real Estate Information Services is the leading provider of property data and services for real estate sales credit and loan information. As Vice President, Mr. Morris is responsible for all aspects of Company operations, and is the Western Regional Sales Manager. **Career Steps:** Vice President, First American Real Estate Information Services (1989–Present); Assistant Vice President, Lomas Mortgage (1985–1989); Operations Manager, Cigma Insurance (1981–1985). **Associations & Accomplishments:** Dallas Mortgage Bankers Association; Texas Association of Assessing Officers; Mission Arlington; United Cerebral Palsy of Dallas. **Education:** University of Northern Colorado, M.A. (1977); Texas A&M University, B.S. (1974). **Personal:** Married to Barbara in 1972. Two children: Alace and Will. Mr. Morris enjoys running, reading, and tennis.

Ms. Tina K. Morrow
Senior Vice President
Insignia
5665 New Northside Dr. Suite 350
Atlanta, GA 30326–1022
(770) 916–9090
Fax: (770) 916–9066

6531

Business Information: Insignia, a division of Insignia Finance, is a commercial real estate firm with four divisions: Commercial, Residential, Mortgage and Finance. Established in 1993, Insignia reports annual revenue of $25 million and currently employs 1,200 employees. As Senior Vice President, Ms. Morrow is responsible for supervision of all property and corporate transitions, developing standard operating procedures, training and providing compliance audits, risk management, administration, and engineering services. **Career Steps:** Senior Vice President, Insignia (1994–Present); Vice President and District Manager, Balcor Property Management (1987–1994); Senior Property Manager, Gerald Hines Interests (1984–1987). **Associations & Accomplishments:** Institute of Real Estate Management (IREM); Commerce Real Estate Women (CREW); Building Owner Manager Association (BOMA); United Way Organization; Habitat for Humanity – WWF (World Wildlife Fund); Published in internal newsletter that is sent to customers (10,000 copies quarterly). **Education:** Institute of Real Estate Management (IREM), CPM achieved in 1985. **Personal:** Married to Brian in 1990. Ms. Morrow enjoys golf, ballet, cooking and her pets (6 cats).

Barbara S. Payton
Owner and Broker
W. V. Goodfellow
RR 2 Box 425
Ridgeley, WV 26753–9639
(304) 726–4313
Fax: (304) 726–4574

6531

Business Information: W. V. Goodfellow, formerly a branch of ERA Goodfellow, is primarily a rural real estate company serving a two–county area. They concentrate in the marketing of homes with acreages and recreational properties. With twelve years experience in real estate and a West Virginia State Certified Restate Specialist, Mrs. Payton joined ERA Goodfellow in 1984, buying out the branch in 1991. Serving as Owner and Broker, she is responsible for all aspects of operations, including the direction of office activities and marketing real estate. **Career Steps:** Owner and Broker, W. V. Goodfellow (1991–Present); Associate Broker, ERA Goodfellow (1984–1991). **Associations & Accomplishments:** President, Potomac Highland Board of Realtors; Director, West Virginia State Association of Realtors; Vice President, West Virginia State Certified Residential Specialist; Junior High Sunday School Teacher, Assembley of God Church. **Education:** Certified Residential Specialist (CRS) (1995). **Personal:** Married to Wayne B. in 1965. Two children: Melissa McLaughlin and Daniel Payton. Mrs. Payton enjoys painting and bass fishing.

Russ Peterson, CPM

Vice President
Summit Real Estate Management
500 Northeast Multnomah Street, Suite 950
Portland, OR 97232–2039
(503) 238–7700 Ext.: 105
Fax: (503) 238–7750

6531

Business Information: Summit Real Estate Management is a full–service real estate management firm. Summit provides professional management for multifamily housing with approximately 55% of their portfolio managed for third party clients. Functions and services of Summit include multi–family property management, property development, single–family home development, as well as property development counsel. Summit currently manages 4,000 units. A Certified Property Manager, Mr. Peterson joined Summit Real Estate Management as Vice President in 1995. He is responsible for the daily supervision of the Real Estate Management Division, including overseeing 1,000 units himself and three property managers. Mr. Peterson was recently charged with the oversight of an exterior renovation of one of their properties. **Career Steps:** Vice President, Summit Real Estate Management (1995–Present); Regional Vice President, Premiere Management Company (1992–1995); Vice President – Marketing, CTL Management (1987–1992). **Associations & Accomplishments:** Institute of Real Estate Management; Portland Board of Realtors; St. Mark's Lutheran Church; Chair, FOCUS newsletter; Associate Real Estate Broker, State of Oregon. **Education:** University of North Dakota, Bachelors (1983). **Personal:** Mr. Peterson enjoys rollerblading, reading, hockey, and going to the movies.

Darlene West Reynolds

Marketing Director and Vice President
Douglas Real Estate and Insurance
45 Wintonbury Avenue
Bloomfield, CT 06002
(860) 242–2205
Fax: (860) 286–8820

6531

Business Information: Douglas Real Estate and Insurance is a real estate and insurance agency, providing the sale, rental, and property management of real estate and the sale of casualty and property insurance. With sixteen years of experience in the insurance industry, Ms. Reynolds joined Douglas Real Estate and Insurance in 1995 as Marketing Director and Vice President. Her primary duties include oversight of real estate and insurance sales activities, sales staff recruitment and training. **Career Steps:** Marketing Director and Vice President, Douglas Real Estate and Insurance (1995–Present); Senior Employee Communications Consultant, Mass Mutual Life Insurance (1993–1995); Area Director, ITT Hartford (1984–1993); Senior Underwriter, The Travelers (1980–1984). **Associations & Accomplishments:** Health Insurance Association of America; United Way Allocations Committee; National Association fo Realtors; Editor's Choice Poetry Award; Charlotte Bass Award for Publications. **Education:** Simmons College, B.A. (1980); Rensselaer Polytechnical Institute, Masters Degree (anticipated completion 1996). **Personal:** Married to Larry E. Reynolds, Sr. Three children: Alysse, Shannon and Larry Jr. Ms. Reynolds enjoys skiing and writing during her leisure time.

Donald W. Richardson

Vice President
Stonemark Management
6640 Powers Ferry Road, Suite 250
Atlanta, GA 30339
(770) 952–9400
Fax: (770) 955–6729
EMAIL: See Below

6531

Business Information: Stonemark Management is a residential property management firm for 8,000 apartment units located throughout the southeastern U.S. With eleven years experience in management and a Certified Public Accountant in the State of Tennessee, Mr. Richardson joined the Firm in 1995. Serving as Vice President, he is responsible for managing accounts, personnel, and support services. **Career Steps:** Vice President, Stonemark Management (1995–Present); Controller, Homecorp Management (1993–1995); Controller/Treasurer, Property Dynamics, Inc. (1989–1993); Assistant Vice President/Accounting Manager, Jacques–M.Mer, Inc. (1984–1988). **Associations & Accomplishments:** Deacon of Communications, Smyrna Church of Christ. **Education:** David Lipscomb College, B.S. (1981); Certified Public Accountant – Tennessee. **Personal:** Married to Susan in 1990. One child: Davis. Mr. Richardson enjoys golf, gardening, going to church, and spending time with his family.

Edith Dolores Roman

Owner
Roman Realty
17978 Knight Drive
Castro Valley, CA 94546
(510) 886–8853
Fax: (510) 886–8853 (call first)

6531

Business Information: Roman Realty is a full–service, real estate brokerage. Ms. Roman is a remarkable woman considering her rough background – orphaned at 11 years old, sent to the Youth Guidance Center for shelter, later became a ward of the court, and then into a foster home. She was married at age 18 and divorced five years later with the responsibility of two small children. At a low point in her life in 1973, she found herself as a recipient of welfare and only able to obtain menial jobs to support herself and her children. Wanting more out of life and for her children, she decided to study real estate. With a dream of becoming a millionaire, a goal she reached at age 29, Edie Roman set off to start her million. Though she was not successful the first year, she reached her goal in 1975 and was admitted to membership in the Million Dollar Club – a result of selling $1 million in real estate. She opened up her own real estate brokerage firm in 1978, serving as Owner and Broker. She is responsible for all aspects of operations, including administration, finances, sales, public relations, client relations, accounting, marketing, and strategic planning. Upon her successes, she has been able to repay all welfare monies paid to her, purchase new homes, and new vehicles. Believing that owning real estate is the way to acquire real wealth, she tries to accumulate as much as possible. **Career Steps:** Owner, Roman Realty (1975–Present); Peach Canner, Del Monte (1972–1973); Clerical Work, Macy's (1967–1969); Part–Time Sales Representative, Small Lingerie Store (1960–1967). **Associations & Accomplishments:** Featured on the front page of Oakland Tribune "Rags to Riches"; Modeling School, L.A. International – Awarded three Honorable Mentions; Toastmasters National Speakers Association; Volunteer at Chabot College – motivated from a welfare recipient to become the owner of a Rolls Royce and a half–a–million dollar ($500,000) custom home in a prestigious neighborhood. Spoke in various seminars in Hawaii, Claremont Hotel, Oakland, CA, Phoenix, AZ, and other parts of the world. Appeared in a real estate publication by a famous author. **Education:** Chabot College, Real Estate Courses (1972); Certified Real Estate Agent, Real Estate Broker, and Notary. **Personal:** Two children: Francisco and Cassandra. Ms. Roman enjoys dancing, motivating others, public speaking. She also enjoys travel, experiencing sunrises and sunsets, time at the beach, and time spent working in her garden surrounded by angels. Her present goal is to write a book about her experiences and how it is possible to change our scars into rainbows. It is one thing to be good, and another to be great, and only through the intervention of our one true Lord is this possible, which is a miracle in itself.

WE CARE ABOUT YOU — SUSAN A. RYAN REAL ESTATE LTD. — SERVICE • ATTITUDE • RESULTS

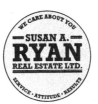

Susan A. Ryan

President
Susan A. Ryan Real Estate, Ltd. and SAR Group, Inc.
4316 Village Centre Court
Mississauga, Ontario L4Z 1S2
(800) 359–9917 (905) 566–9166
Fax: (905) 566–9368
EMail: See Below

6531

Business Information: Susan A. Ryan Real Estate, Ltd. specializes in real estate sales and marketing for home purchase, home sale relocation orientation, and destination. The Company specializes in relocation services and helping senior citizens and others who have not been well taken care of by others in the real estate industry. The Company is the leading independent real estate company in Mississauga and carries 3–5% of the market share at any given time. After getting burned in real estate many years ago, Ms. Ryan decided to make a difference and change the field. She is President of the real estate Company, and her duties include administration, operations, sales and marketing, client relations, and strategic planning. Concurrently, she is President of SAR Group, Inc., a small company that takes care of snow removal, construction, and painting for senior citizens and others who need assistance. SAR Group, Inc. also has its own relocations services department. Ms. Ryan has a national trademark – S.A.R. (Service.Attitude.Results: Service + Attitude = Results). Internet users can reach her via: SUERYAN@IDIRECT. **Career Steps:** President, Susan A. Ryan Real Estate, Ltd. (1988–Present), Susan A. Ryan Real Estate, Ltd. is a network broker for PHH since 1989; Residential Department, Nordale Real Estate (1986); Agent, Montreal Trust (1979–1986). **Associations & Accomplishments:** Director, Mississauga Real Estate Board; Toronto Real Estate Board; Mississauga Board of Trade; Port Credit Yacht Club; Canadian Relocation Council; Ronald E. Sanderson Community Service Award (1995). **Education:** Sheridan College, Real Estate Broker (1988). **Personal:** Married to Lawrence K. in 1972. Ms. Ryan enjoys boating, golf, reading, and cooking.

Juliet I. San Martin

Managing Broker
RE/MAX St. Croix
5 Company Street
Christiansted, VI 00820–4965
(809) 773–1048
Fax: (809) 773–1917

6531

Business Information: RE/MAX St. Croix, the only international franchise in St. Croix, is a real estate brokerage and an active referral agency, specializing in the sales and management of rental properties. The St. Croix office has technological advances which are not available to other real estate offices. As Managing Broker, Ms. San Martin is responsible for the oversight of all sales, marketing, and public relations for the Agency, including the provision of training to agents. **Career Steps:** Managing Broker, RE/MAX St. Croix (1984–Present); Construction Manager/Estimator, Self–Employed, Tucson, Arizona, (1978–1984); Plumbing Contractor, Self–Employed, Tucson Arizona, (1973–1978); Systems Analyst, TRW Systems, Manned Space Craft Center, Houston TX (1968–1972). **Associations & Accomplishments:** Fleet Captain– St. Croix Yacht Club; Treasurer, St. Croix Board of Realtors; Yacht race scorekeeper. **Education:** Duke University, B.A. in Mathematics, (1968) **Personal:** Married to Joseph in 1973. One child: George.

Isabella Scott, CCIM, CRB, CIPS, GRI, CBR

Broker Associate
Arvida Realty Sales, Ltd.
1 West Camino Real, Suite 203
Boca Raton, FL 33432–5966
(407) 750–3100
Fax: (407) 393–3651
EMAIL: See Below

6531

Business Information: Arvida Realty Sales, Ltd., affiliated with local, national, and international marketing affiliations and networks, is a real estate agency, marketing general real estate, resort properties, luxury homes, and commercial properties, as well as providing leasing of properties through strong national and international networks. Arvida Realty Sales' national and overseas marketing systems include: Boca Raton Resort & Club; referral organizations; marketing presentations and programs; and network affiliations, including the World Trade Centers, National Association of Real Estate Executives, International Real Estate Federation (FIABCI), Marche International Des Professionels De L'immobilier, Employee Relocation Council, Boca Raton Association of Realtors, Florida Association of Realtors, National Association of Realtors, Chambers of Commerce (Boca Raton, Florida, U.S., British–American, Brazilian–American), Business Development Board–Palm Beach County, and the Japan Society of South Florida. With twenty years of experience in real estate commercial and luxury home sales and a Licensed Mortgage Broker, Ms. Scott joined Arvida Realty Sales, Ltd. as Broker Associate in 1993. Working primarily from referrals, she is responsible for general real estate sales, with emphasis on luxury residential, commercial, and international markets. In addition to the membership associations and educational designations, she participates in ongoing business development programs for Referrals and Customer Service. Internet users can reach her via: PARAFL@IBM.NET. **Career Steps:** Broker Associate, Arvida Realty Sales, Ltd. (1993–Present); Owner and President, International Realty and Financial Services Corporation (1990–Present); Sales Associate, Equity Marketing (1988–1990). **Associations & Accomplishments:** National Association of Realtors and Affiliates (NAR): Commercial Investment Real Estate Institute, Real Estate Brokerage Managers Council, International Section of NAR, Residential Sales Council; Womens Council of Realtors, Real Estate Appraisal Section of NAR; Real Estate Management Section of NAR; Realtors Land Institute; Graduate Realtor Institute (GRI); Certified Buyer Representative (CBR); Registered Real Estate Appraiser and Licensed Mortgage Broker; Recipient of Real Estate Association Honor Society Awards for involvement on committees, involvement and attendance at association conferences and events, and educational advancements. Recipient of Award in 1995 for Best Real Estate Deal of the Year for a Land Deal (a $23 million transaction), given by South Florida Business Journal and Ernst & Young. **Education:** Twenty years experience in Real Estate sales;

Completed extensive real estate specialty courses and sales criteria to obtain certification and designations, Commercial Sales (CCIM); Brokerage Management (CRB); International Sales (CIPS); Residential Sales (GRI, CBR), Property Management, Appraisal (Appraiser), and Financing (Mortagage Broker). **Personal:** One child: Megan. Ms. Scott enjoys tennis and health clubs, reading, art and antique shows, museums, home design and decorating shows.

Craig R. Seal
Senior Vice President
Barbara Sue Seal Properties
4103 Mercantile Drive
Lake Oswego, OR 97035
(503) 241–5505
Fax: Please mail or call

6531

Business Information: Barbara Sue Seal Properties is a regional real estate company dealing primarily in residential sales. Established in 1983, the Company has 250 employees and posted revenues in excess of $750 million dollars in 1995. The Company handles properties in parts of Canada and Oregon. As Senior Vice President, Mr. Seal is in charge of operations. He oversees and assists in the accounting functions of the Company. Personnel concerns, information technology, and the purchasing and closing on properties are his areas of concern. Mr. Seal works with developing marketing strategies for the Company and developing information systems for the Firm. **Career Steps:** Barbara Sue Seal Properties: Senior Vice President (1995–Present), Director of Marketing; Counselor, Bunker Hill Community College; Employment Training Specialist, Goodwill Industries. **Education:** Boston College, M.A. Degree in Counseling and Psychology (1995); Santa Clara University, B.A. Degree in Psychology. **Personal:** Married to Christine in 1993. Mr. Seal enjoys reading, gaming, computers, and basketball.

William G. Shepherd
Vice President of Design and Construction
Littlefield Real Estate Company
106 East 6th Street #530
Austin, TX 78701
(512) 476–7100
Fax: (512) 476–5498

6531

Business Information: Littlefield Real Estate Company is a real estate agency specializing in commercial real estate. Established in 1984, Littlefield Real Estate Company reports annual revenue of $10 million and currently employs 140 people. With sixteen years experience in real estate, Mr. Shepard joined Littlefield Real Estate Company in 1991. Serving as Vice President of Design and Construction, he manages the design and construction or rehabilitation of commercial real estate. **Career Steps:** Vice President of Design and Construction, Littlefield Real Estate Company (1990–Present); Development Manager, Steiner Ranch Development Company (1987–1991); Development Manager, Rust Properties (1979–1984). **Associations & Accomplishments:** American Institute of Architects; Texas Society of Architects; Heritage Society of Austin; Air Force Association. **Education:** University of Texas – Austin, M.S. Architecture (1976), B.S. in Architecture; United States Air Force Academy, Engineering. **Personal:** Married to Barbara in 1969. Three children: Trent, Todd, and Mark. Mr. Shepherd enjoys antique auto restoration.

Cres Shields
Owner, Chief Executive Officer & President
The Shields Corporation
7222 Commerce Center Drive
Colorado Springs, CO 80919
(719) 593–1000
Fax: (719) 548–9357
EMAIL: See Below

6531

Business Information: The Shields Corporation is a residential homes and land real estate agency working hand in hand with Shields Connections In Relocation, a subsidiary of The Shields Corporation, providing a referral business on a national level. Founding The Shields Corporation in 1985, Mr. Shields serves as Owner, Chief Executive Officer and President of both companies. He is responsible for all aspects of operations, including administration and strategic planning. With over 40 brokers and a support staff of 25, Shields generates sales in excess of $150 million. Mr. Shields attributes the company's phenomenal growth to the emphasis placed on personal and professional development of skilled brokers and to their commitment to the community. The Shields Corporation, an independent company, was recently selected as "Preferred Broker" by PHH Corporation. The recognition, given by one of the world's largest mortgage/ relocation firms, reflects the trust Shields has earned among leaders in the industry. Internet users can reach him via: cres@shieldscorp.com. **Career Steps:** Owner, Chief Executive Officer & President,

Shields Corporation (1984–Present); President and Broker, The Shields Corporation (1985–1994); President, Excalibur Research Corporation (1980–1981); Lt. Colonel, United States Air Force (1960–1980). **Associations & Accomplishments:** National Association of Realtors; Colorado Association of Realtors; Pikes Peak Association of Realtors; Economic Development Corporation; Broadmoor Golf Club; Housing and Building Association; USAF Academy Association of Graduates;, Colorado Springs Symphony Board of Directors; Colorado Springs Chamber of Commerce. **Education:** Arizona State University, Ph.D. (1975); North Carolina State University, M.S. (1968); United States Air Force Academy, B.S. in Military Science (1960). **Personal:** Married to Mary in 1984. Four children: Creston, Nicole, Trent, and Alissa. Mr. Shields enjoys golf, photography, squash, and strength and fitness building.

Marianne Simek
Vice President
Action Property Management
701 S. Parker Street, Suite 1600
Orange, CA 92865–4720
(714) 285–2600
Fax: (714) 285–1167

6531

Business Information: Action Property Management is a homeowner's association specializing in oversight of approximately 16,000 homes in California. Regional in scope, the Company has three locations throughout the Orange, California area and employs forty–two people. As Vice President, Ms. Simek oversees management operations of the Association and is responsible for a management staff of fifty. Additional duties include new client services, ensuring compliance with state and federal regulations, and oversight of new associations. **Career Steps:** Action Property Management: Vice President (1991–Present), Association Manager (1987–1990); Association Manager, PCM, Inc. (1984–1987). **Associations & Accomplishments:** Board of Directors, California Association of Community Managers (ACM); Board of Directors/Past President, Community Associations Institute (CAI). **Education:** California State University, Fresno, A.A. (1980). **Personal:** Married to Michael in 1989. Ms. Simek enjoys boating and snow skiing.

Ronald J. Smith
Sales and Marketing Director
Picerne Properties
75 Lambert Lind Highway
Warwick, RI 02886
(401) 732–3700
Fax: (401) 738–6452

6531

Business Information: Picerne Properties is a real estate development firm, providing the development and construction of homes and management of apartments and commercial properties. Picerne Properties is active in fourteen states with Corporate offices in Rhode Island, Arizona, and Florida. Established in 1925, Picerne Properties currently employs 500 people company–wide. With nine years expertise in the real estate industry, Mr. Smith joined Picerne Properties in 1991. Serving as Sales and Marketing Director, he is responsible for the management of the new home sales force and development of marketing plans for 100–125 new homes a year, having seven sites a year under construction at one time. Additional responsibilities include involvement with product development and customer complaints. **Career Steps:** Sales and Marketing Director, Picerne Properties (1991–Present); New Home/Condo Salesperson, Trammel Crow Company (1987–1990); Home Salesperson, Plaza West Realty (1986–1987). **Associations & Accomplishments:** Rhode Island Association of Realtors; National Association of Realtors. **Education:** University of Rhode Island, Economics (1984). **Personal:** Mr. Smith enjoys boating.

Lynny Snider

Owner and Broker
ERA Oak Manor Realty, Inc.
128 Sumner Road
Fayetteville, GA 30214
(770) 461–0090
Fax: (770) 461–5593

6531

Business Information: ERA Oak Manor Realty, Inc., one of ERA's 2,800 national realty franchises, serves the southern crescent of Atlanta, Georgia, and was named #1 in service. Ms. Snider joined ERA in 1988 as a Licensed Real Estate Agent and became a full owner in 1993. She currently supervises 13 licensed agents, oversees daily operations and sales, and is responsible for varied administrative activities and strategic planning. **Career Steps:** ERA Oak Manor Realty, Inc.: Owner and Broker (1993–Present), Real Estate

Agent (1988–1993); Sales Agent, Coldwell Banker (1986–1988). **Associations & Accomplishments:** Fayette County Board of Realtors. **Education:** Southwest Texas University, B.S. (1986); Dental Hygiene Degree. **Personal:** Married to Paul. Six children: Michelle, Paul, Keith, Tricia, Kate, and Leigh Margaret. Ms. Snider enjoys horses, reading, and swimming.

Helen V. Sosso
Executive Vice President and Partner
The Prudential Preferred Realty
0401 McKnight Road
Pittsburgh, PA 15237
(412) 367–8028
Fax: (412) 367–2718

6531

Business Information: The Prudential Preferred Realty is primarily a real estate, mortgage, title, and insurance company. Established in 1991, The Prudential Preferred Realty presently employs 501 people, and has an estimated annual revenue in excess of $17 million. As Executive Vice President and Partner, Mrs. Sosso is responsible for the overall company performance, including the management of 14 branches, the Marketing Department, and new homes operation. **Career Steps:** Executive Vice President and Partner, The Prudential Preferred Realty (Present); Merrill Lynch Realty: Regional Vice President, Branch Manager. **Associations & Accomplishments:** Board of Directors, Family Health Council; Former Director, YMCA; Director, Realtors Association of Metropolitan Pittsburgh; Mrs. Sosso has been quoted in numerous real estate publications. **Personal:** Married to Daniel in 1971. Two children: Mark and Scott.

Lori M. Steave
Real Estate Agent
Realty Executives – Bettye Harrison & Associates
3837 Hixson Pike
Chattanooga, TN 37415
(423) 870–9388
Fax: (423) 842–6883

6531

Business Information: Realty Executives – Bettye Harrison & Associates is a real estate agency, marketing residential and commercial property. Mrs. Steave is a licensed real estate agent in the states of Tennessee and Georgia, marketing residential and commercial properties part–time, focusing primarily on residential properties. Concurrently, she serves as a full–time Nuclear Security Officer for TVA's Chattanooga, Tennessee nuclear facility. She is responsible for controlling access to and from the nuclear plant (motor and foot passage), as well as checking out barriers, alarms, and individuals entering the facility. Future plans include changing to real estate full–time. **Career Steps:** Realty Estate agent, Realty Executives – Bettye Harrison & Associates (1994–Present); Nuclear Security Officer, Tennessee Valley Authority (1983–Present); Sales, Lovemans (1983); Receptionist, Manpower, Inc. (1978). **Associations & Accomplishments:** National Association of Realtors; Tennessee Association of Realtors; Women's Council of Realtors; Ducks Unlimited. **Education:** Chattanooga State Tech., currently attending; University of Tennessee–Chattanooga; Tennessee Real Estate License. **Personal:** Married to David Lewis in 1992. One child: Caitlin. Mrs. Steave enjoys spending time with her family, skiing (water & snow), going to the beach, rollerblading, and reading.

Amy L. Stoehr
Marketing Partner
The Cathy Russell Team/CBSR
120 Sagamore Parkway West
West Lafayette, IN 47906–1569
(317) 463–7000
Fax: (317) 497–5681
E–mail: see below

6531

Business Information: The Cathy Russell Team, Coldwell Banker Sycamore Realty is a full–service real estate company specializing in residential sales. In 1994, Cathy Russell and her team were number 2 in Coldwell Banker internationally. Established in 1989, The Cathy Russell Team currently employs seven people and reports over $35 million in sales. As Marketing Partner, Ms. Stoehr is responsible for all aspects of staff hiring and training, office management, bookkeeping, the annual budget, projections, revising and tracking of systems, and the oversight of a newly–formed marketing sub–company. Ms. Stoehr can also be reached through the Internet as follows: fksb14a@prodigy.com **Career Steps:** Marketing Partner, The Cathy Russell Team/CBSR (1993–Present); Assistant Manager, Maurices, Inc. (1992–1993); Fashions Supervisor, K–Mart Corporation (1988–1992). **Associations & Accomplishments:** National Association of Realtors; Indiana Association of Realtors; Howard Brinton Star Power Club; National Organization of Real Estate Assistants. **Education:** Purdue University, B.A. (1992); Licensed Realtor, State of Indiana (1992). **Personal:** Married to Jeffrey in 1994. Ms. Stoehr enjoys rendering and writing poetry.

Michael J. Sullivan

Realtor
RE/MAX Associates Plus, Inc.
3351 Round Lake Boulevard
Anoka, MN 55303
(612) 581–8881 (800) 568–5818
Fax: (612) 323–6223
EMAIL: REALTORMM@aol.com

6531

Business Information: RE/MAX Associates Plus, Inc. is a real estate sales agency serving clients from three local offices in the Anoka, Minnesota area. The Agency offers realtors an opportunity to work as an independent agent on a contractor–basis, providing office space and necessities to conduct business. Obtaining his Realtors License in November 1992, Mr. Sullivan became an independent contractor with RE/MAX Associates Plus, Inc. in 1994. Conducting $10 million in real estate sales per year, he is responsible for administration, operations, sales, marketing, and strategic planning activities. He also publishes his own magazine on a quarterly basis for his 3,500 client base. Internet users can reach him via: REALTORMM@aol.com **Career Steps:** Realtor, RE/MAX Associates Plus, Inc. (1994–Present); Realtor, Edina Realty (1992–1994); Hotel Manager, Nicollet Island Inn (1991–1993). **Associations & Accomplishments:** National Association of Realtors; Minnesota Association of Realtors; Anoka County Association of Realtors. **Education:** Attended: University of Minnesota (1987), Iowa State University, Normandale Community College. **Personal:** Married to Michelle in 1993. Mr. Sullivan enjoys golf, camping and travel.

Michelle A. Sullivan

Chief Executive Officer
Gloria Dei Outreach Corporation
570 Welsh Road
Huntingdon Valley, PA 19006–6427
(215) 947–7362
Fax: (215) 947–4089

6531

Business Information: Gloria Dei Outreach Corporation is a real estate management and development firm, providing residential independent living facilities for the elderly. Established by the Lutheran Church (from donations by members), Gloria Dei Outreach Corporation consists of six buildings (568 units) presently built, with three new locations (450 units) planned for the near future. As Chief Executive Officer, Ms. Sullivan is responsible for all aspects of operations, including preparing budgets for the six present buildings, preparing financial statements, tax planning, all human resource functions, and coordinating with contractors, engineers, attorneys, and financial agents. **Career Steps:** Chief Executive Officer, Gloria Dei Outreach Corporation (1994–Present); Commonwealth of Pennsylvania: Auditor III (Audit Supervisor) (1993–1994), Auditor I (Auditor) (1990–1993); Waitress/Hostess, Red Lobster Restaurants (1988–1990). **Associations & Accomplishments:** Sponsor and Fund–Raising Volunteer, Big Brothers/Big Sisters; Pennsylvania Non–Profit Homes for the Aging (PANPHA); Feltonville–Olney Betterment Alliance (FOBA). **Education:** Lebanon Valley College, B.S. in Accounting & Management (1990); Philadelphia College of Textiles & Science, Working towards M.A. in Taxation; H&R Block Tax School. **Personal:** Ms. Sullivan enjoys snow skiing, international travel, and Latin dancing during her spare time.

Kenneth A. Swanson

President
OXBOW Realty, Inc.
725 Canton Street
Norwood, MA 02062
(617) 769–2222
Fax: (617) 769–8186

6531

Business Information: OXBOW Realty, Inc. is a real estate asset management company providing development, commercial brokerage, and property management services. As President, Mr. Swanson is responsible for administrative duties, development, consulting, and asset management. **Career Steps:** President, OXBOW Realty, Inc. (1993–2001); Project Manager, OXBOW Realty, Inc. (1988–1993); Development Project Manager, Meredith & Grew (1984–1987); President, The Swanson Company (1987–1988); President, Swanson Construction, Inc. (1979–1983). **Associations & Accomplishments:** U.L.I.; BOMA; NAIOP; International Marina Institute; University of Wisconsin Real Estate Alumni Association; Massachusetts Board of Realtors. **Education:** University of Wisconsin, M.S. (1983), B.A. Economics. **Personal:** Married to Patricia in 1989. Mr. Swanson enjoys fly-fishing and skiing.

Phillip Taylor

Chief Executive Officer and Executive Director
Opelika Housing Authority
P.O. Box 786
Opelika, AL 36803–0786
(334) 745–4171
Fax: (334) 745–6783

6531

Business Information: Opelika Housing Authority provides federal government housing to low–income families in the Opelika, Alabama locale. As Chief Executive Officer and Executive Director, Mr. Taylor is responsible for all aspects of operations, such as maintenance, finances, and residential services. In addition, he oversees all administrative operations for associates and a support staff of 52. **Career Steps:** Chief Executive Officer and Executive Director, Opelika Housing Authority (1994–Present); Area Housing District Manager, Augusta Housing Authority (1991–1994); Public Housing Manager, Savannah Housing Authority (1984–1991); Librarian Assistant, Chatham County Public School (1982–1984). **Associations & Accomplishments:** Board of Directors, Boys and Girls Club of Lee County; Board of Directors, Harvest Food Bank; Advisory Council, United Way; Board of Directors, Alabama Council of Human Relations; East Alabama Personnel Association; Kiwanis; Leadership Lee County; National Association of Housing Redevelopment Officials. **Education:** Savannah State College, B.A. in Business Administration (1982); Draughon's Business College, Computer Science (1983). **Personal:** Mr. Taylor enjoys reading, investing, and sports.

Michael W. Thacker, CDP

President
Home Connections
528 Holiday Drive
Macon, NC 27551–9529
(919) 257–2563
Fax: (919) 257–5602
EMAIL: see below

6531

Business Information: Home Connections provides computerized listings of residential and commercial properties to real estate agents and the buying public via the Internet nationwide. Joining Home Connections as President in 1995, Mr. Thacker is responsible for all aspects of operations, including marketing and quality assurance. Internet users can reach him via: mthacker@ihomes.com , as well as on the worldwide web via: URL: www.ihomes.com **Career Steps:** President, Home Connections (1995–Present); President, Simply the Best, Inc. (1989–1995); President, Professional Systems (1982–1989). **Associations & Accomplishments:** Data Processing Management Association; President (1995–1996), Warrenton Rotary Club; District Drug Abuse Committee; Warren County Schools Technology Committee. **Education:** Arizona State, M.S. in Computer (1973); Institute for Certification of Computer Professionals, Chicago, IL, Certi-

fied Data Processor (CDP). **Personal:** Married to Connie in 1989. Two children: Julie and Rodney. Mr. Thacker enjoys snow skiing and competing in professional fishing tournaments (walleye pike).

Byron P. Travis

Real Estate Agent
Century 21
546 South Washington Street
Papillion, NE 68046–2632
(402) 339–2001
Fax: (402) 339–0021
EMail: See Below

6531

Business Information: Century 21 is a real estate, property management, mortgage lending, and title service firm. As Real Estate Agent, Mr. Travis serves as an independent contractor for Century 21, and is responsible for the showing and selling of real estate for others. Internet users can reach him via: ByronT@aol.com. **Career Steps:** Real Estate Agent, Century 21 (1992–Present); U.S. Air Force: Department Chief of Staff, MWR & Services–HQ Pacific Air Forces (1991–1992); Director of Housing & Services–HQ Pacific Air Forces (1989–1991); Commander, Army & Air Force–Exchange Service, Okinawa, Japan (1988–1989); Active Duty (1966–1992). **Associations & Accomplishments:** Society for the Preservation & Encouragement of Barbershop Quartet Singing in America; Air Force Association; The Society of the Strategic Air Command; National Realtors Association; National Residential Sales Council; Nebraska Realtors Association; Defense Housing Association. **Education:** Embry–Riddle Aeronautical University, M.B.A. (1986); University of Nebraska – Lincoln, B.S. in Business (1966). **Personal:** Married to Susan in 1969. Two children: Kimberly and Paul. Mr. Travis enjoys barbershop singing, recreational flying, travel, hiking, camping, and snow skiing.

Felix H. Tseng, CMA, CPA

Chief Financial Officer
Benebase Invesment, Inc.
108 North Ynez Avenue, Suite 209
Monterey Park, CA 91754–1680
(818) 288–2098
Fax: (818) 288–2199

6531

Business Information: Benebase Invesment, Inc., a subsidiary of Benebase Enterprises – headquartered in Hong Kong, is a real estate investment and management firm. A Certified Public Accountant, Mr. Tseng joined the Firm in 1991 as Chief Financial Officer. He is responsible for investment and financial decisions for the Monterey Park, California office, including budgeting and allocation of funds for project investments. Concurrent with his position as CFO at Benebase, he is Partner at Lilly Property Management. **Career Steps:** Chief Financial Officer, Benebase Investment, Inc. (1991–Present); Partner, Lilly Property Management (1995–Present); Certified Public Accountant, Ronald A. Stein, CPA (1989–1991). **Associations & Accomplishments:** President (1995–1996), Institute of Management Accountants – Los Angeles; American Institute of Certified Public Accountants; Southern California Society of Certified Management Accountants; California Society of Certified Public Accountants. **Education:** Pepperdine University, M.B.A. (1989), B.S. (1985). **Personal:** Married to Rachel W. in 1992. Two children: Walter F. and Riley F. Mr. Tseng enjoys sports, fishing, and bridge.

Aida D. Turbow, GRI, CIPS

Director of Business Development
Arvida Realty Sales, Ltd.
501 East Camino Real
Boca Raton, FL 33432
(561) 391–9201
Fax: (561) 338–5321
arvida@gate.net

6531

Business Information: Arvida Realty Sales, Ltd. is a full service real estate firm with an international outreach. The Company is one of the largest realty companies in the Southeast. Arvida Realty has offices in Georgia, South Carolina, Florida (12 locations), North Carolina, and California. Offices are also located in Japan, France and other European countries, and in South America. As Director of Business Development, Ms. Turbow manages two locations in Florida and assists in the development and coordination of new business opportunities on both domestic and international levels. **Career Steps:** Arvida Realty Sales, Ltd.: Director of Business Development (1991–Present), International Relocation Director (1987–1991); President of Parkeast 56, Parkeast Executive Center (1981–1987). **Associations & Accomplishments:** National Association of Realtors: Chairperson for International Section, Education & Publication subcommittee, Chairperson for CIPS (Certified International Property Specialist), Presidential Advisory Board for International Operations, Reciprocal Director for Brazil and Argentina; International Real Estate Federation (FIABCI); Florida Association of Realtors; Realtor Association of South Palm Beach County; Business Development Board of Palm Beach County; Japan Society of South Florida; NACORE International; FIRA (Federacion Inmobiliaria de la Republica de Argentina). **Education:** Venezuelan University, B.A. (1964). **Personal:** Married to Morton in 1986. Two children: Felix and Daniel Martinez. Ms. Turbow enjoys studying Japanese culture and language, reading, music, and travel.

Trinita R. Tyus

President
Town Square Realty
304 Priceton Parkway
Birmingham, AL 35211
(205) 780-7000
Fax: (205) 780-7022

6531

Business Information: Town Square Realty is a locally-owned, residential, commercial, and new construction real estate firm. The Firm also has plans to open a real estate school in Birmingham, Alabama. Town Square Realty has two offices in Birmingham with plans expanding to seven offices in the next few years. As President, Ms. Tyus manages all operations of Town Square Realty including staffing the office, planning an annual budget, cash management, customer service, and personnel/human resource management. As a qualifying broker, Ms. Tyus handles sales and brokerage of real estate properties for resale and investment purposes. **Career Steps:** President, Town Square Realty (1995–Present); President, Town Square Realty (1995–Present); with over 10 years of experience in Real Estate and management. **Associations & Accomplishments:** Birmingham Association of Realtors; Birmingham Ad Club; First Commercial Bank Advisory Board; Christian Service Mission Advisory Board. **Education:** Alabama School of Real Estate, Certified Residential Specialist, Graduate of Real Estate. **Personal:** Married to Andre in 1984. Three children: Andre'a Latrice, Lanitra Shawnte', and Andre' Jr. Ms. Tyus enjoys reading and playing the piano.

Stephen M. Verba

Chief Information Officer/Senior Vice President
Realty One Corporate Center
6000 Rockside Woods Boulevard
Cleveland, OH 44131-2350
(216) 328-2500
Fax: (216) 328-5030

6531

Business Information: Realty One is one of the nations largest real estate companies (ranked no. 11 in the residential market), with offices serving 20 northern counties. As Chief Information Officer/Senior Vice President, Mr. Verba has been involved with all aspects of the development and implementation of the Company's strategic plan and initiatives, with direct responsibility for both the Information Services Department and the Marketing Department. **Career Steps:** Chief Information Officer/Senior Vice President, Realty One Corporate Center (1994–Present); President, MarketWyse, Division of Wyse Advertising Inc. (1980–1994); Software Products Manager, Neoterics, Inc. (1976–1980). **Associations & Accomplishments:** American Real Estate Society (ARES); American Anthropological Association; Psychometric Society; Semiotic Society; American Marketing Association; Gestalt Institute of Cleveland. **Education:** Cleveland State University, Bachelor's degree (1974); Gestalt Institute of Cleveland, Organization and Systems Development Program (1995). **Personal:** Married in 1972, Mr. Verba and his wife, Betty, have four children. Mr. Verba enjoys amateur astronomy and contemporary poetry.

Russell W. Wolfertz Jr., GRI

Owner
ERA Cousens Realty
310 Main Street
Rockland, ME 04841-2533
(207) 596-6433
Fax: (207) 596-6779
EMAIL: See Below

6531

Business Information: ERA Cousens Realty is a real estate sales and management company specializing in residential, seasonal, and commercial properties encompassing the greater Rockland, Maine and surrounding counties area. As Owner, Mr. Wolfertz is responsible for all aspects of Company operations, as well as brokerage activities. Internet users can reach him via: WOLFDUCK@MIDCOAST.COM. **Career Steps:** Owner, ERA Cousens Realty (1956–Present).

Associations & Accomplishments: Pen Bay Board of Directors; Rockland–Thomaston Chamber of Commerce; National Director for ERA Commercial Industrial Broker Network. **Education:** University of Maine, B.A. (1970). **Personal:** Married to Nancy in 1971.

William E. Young

Vice President
NationsBank
5121 Maryland Way, Ste. 203
Brentwood, TN 37027
(615) 371-3036
Fax: (615) 371-1960

6531

Business Information: NationsBank Real Estate Banking Group provides real estate services for single family construction. As Vice President, Mr. Young is responsible for generating builders and developers, and maintaining their requests. **Career Steps:** Vice President, NationsBank (1976–Present). **Associations & Accomplishments:** Middle Tennessee Builder's Association; Masonic Lodge; Served with the 9th Infantry in Viet Nam and was awarded the Bronze Star Medal. **Education:** Draughon's Junior College, A.A. (1966); Middle Tennessee State University; University of Colorado; University of Oklahoma; Vanderbilt University. **Personal:** Married to Jo Ann in 1975. Mr. Young enjoys reading, travel, and working on PCs.

Michael S. Yu

President
I. Max Realty, Inc.
21400 International Boulevard, Suite 105
Seattle, WA 98198
(206) 824-4933
Fax: (206) 824-4802

6531

Business Information: I. Max Realty, Inc., international in scope, is a commercial and residential brokerage company. As President, Mr. Yu is responsible for all aspects of Company operations, including appraising of real estate and business opportunities, and consulting about investment and financing. **Career Steps:** President, I. Max Realty, Inc. (1994–Present); Manager/Broker, Park Realty, Inc. (1990–1994). **Education:** University, B.A. **Personal:** Married to Mary in 1982. Two children: Michelle and Christein. Mr. Yu enjoys vacationing and travel.

Joseph A. Rizk

President
Sargents Abstract and Title Company
625 South Grand Traverse Street
Flint, MI 48502
(810) 767-2355
Fax: (810) 767-2430

6541

Business Information: Sargents Abstract and Title Company is a title insurance and complete escrow service with two locations in Flint, MI. As President, Mr. Rizk is responsible for all administrative duties, training, marketing and acts as chief problem solver for the Company. **Career Steps:** President, Sargents Abstract and Title Company (1994–Present). **Associations & Accomplishments:** Director, Flint Area Association of Realtors; Former Treasurer, Montrose Board of Education; Downtown Flint Kiwanis Club; Former Director, Eastern Michigan Mortgage Bankers; Director, Little League Baseball Operations. **Personal:** Married to Vicki in 1972. Two children: Jennifer and Joseph. Mr. Rizk enjoys golf, hunting, fishing, and reading.

Phil R. Acuff

President
Acuff Homes
P.O. Box 6507
Leawood, KS 66206
(913) 888-7514
Fax: (913) 888-7947

6552

Business Information: Acuff Homes specializes in land development and home building, primarily single family homes approximately 2,700 square feet and larger. Established in

---

1961, Acuff homes currently employs 15 people and has an estimated annual revenue of $10 million. As President, Mr. Acuff is responsible for all aspects of operations, including finance and land assembly. **Career Steps:** President, Acuff Homes (1961–Present). **Associations & Accomplishments:** Director, National Association of Home Builders; Former Chairman, Overland Park Planning Commission; Executive Committee, University of Missouri Conservatory of Music; Director, Shawnee Mission Medical Center; Former Campaign Chairman, Cancer Society; University of Missouri Faculty Alumni Award (1995). **Education:** University of Missouri, B.S. in Business Administration (1953). **Personal:** Married to Gail in 1955. Three children: Russ, Ann and Laura Tongate. Mr. Acuff enjoys reading, tennis, walking, hiking and canoeing.

Mr. Jack L. Atkins

Vice President and Treasurer
Atkins Development Co., Inc.
101 Old Short Hills Road
West Orange, NJ 07052
(201) 325-7900
Fax: (201) 325-2361

6552

Business Information: Atkins Development Co., Inc. specializes in real estate development (town houses, office buildings, and more). In his current capacity, Mr. Atkins is responsible for all financial activities for the company as well as operations. Established in 1990 (in other partnerships since 1970), Atkins Development Co., Inc. presently employs 10 people and has an estimated annual revenue in excess of $15 million. **Career Steps:** Vice President and Treasurer, Atkins Development Co., Inc.; General Partner, Atkins–Kent Motel, Ltd. (1982–Present); General Partner, Lenat Development Company (1984–Present); General Partner, Atkins Associates (1970–1982); Former Partner in Ford, Chrysler, Plymouth, Dodge and Chevrolet auto dealerships; Presently Partner in Infiniti and three Saturn Auto Dealerships. **Education:** Bucknell University, B.S.M.A. (1970).

Gordon Price Cantwell

Director of Site Development
Fibrebond Resources
1300 Davenport Drive
Minden, LA 71055
(405) 755-8886
Fax: (405) 755-8938

6552

Business Information: Fibrebond Resources is a comprehensive site development company dedicated to the telecommunications industry. As Director of Site Development, Mr. Cantwell oversees site development, marketing, contract negotiations, and is responsible for reporting to the Board of Directors. **Career Steps:** Director of Site Development, Fibrebond Resources (1993–Present); Associate Director of Site Development, Steven Bernstein & Associates (1992–1993); Senior Engineering Technician, Kleinfelder (1990–1992); Superintendent, Robert Sorenson Construction (1987–1989). **Associations & Accomplishments:** American Concrete Institute; International Conference Building Officials; International Association of Electrical Inspectors; International Association of Plumbing and Mechanical Officials; American Construction Inspection Association; Boy Scouts of America. **Education:** Butte College, Building Inspection Technology Program (1989). **Personal:** Married to Jean in 1975. Three children: Christopher, Jamie, and Gregory. Mr. Cantwell enjoys camping, hunting, and fishing.

J. R. de Jesus Chantengco

Principal/Senior Project Director
Landquest Development
4550 Kearney Villa Road, Suite 219
San Diego, CA 92123
(619) 569-7000
Fax: (619) 569-7779
EMAIL: See Below

6552

Business Information: Landquest Development is a real estate development firm involved in three areas: Affordable Housing, Land Development, and Commercial Redevelopment. As Principal/Senior Project Director, Mr. Chantengco is responsible for contract negotiations, proposals, supervising day–to–day activities, project selection, and team development. Currently, the Firm is involved in a portfolio of ongoing development projects in California valued between $50 to $60 Million. Examples of projects include a 1500 residential unit master planned community; an urban mixed–use hotel and retail development; and an inner–city hospital with expansion plans for long–term care (LTC) facilities. Internet users can reach him via: 102222.430@compuserve.com. As Principal/Senior Project Director, Mr. Chantengco is responsible for contract negotiations, proposals, supervising day–to–day activities, project selection, and team development. Internet users can reach him via: 102222.430@compuserve.com. **Career Steps:** Principal/Senior Project Director, Landquest

Development (1995–Present); Senior Realty Advisor, The TriWest Group (1990–Present); Vice President, Monolithic Building Systems (1995–Present); Lease Auditor/Abstractor, CB Commercial (1995); Legal Consultant for Real Estate Issues, Law Offices of Carlos A. Batara (1994–Present); President of Hotel Management and Operations, Pacific Rim Century, Inc. (1989–1992); Manager/Trainer of Sales Division, ERA – Chantengco Realty, Inc. (1988–1992); Legislative Aide, California State Legislature (1987–1988). **Associations & Accomplishments:** A consummate professional, Mr. Chantengco is the first Asian American entrepreneur and real estate broker in California to ever serve on a housing commission, a tax assessment appeals board, and a city redevelopment loan committee all in the same county (San Diego). He has appeared in publications about international business and politics, and has written numerous articles about commercial real estate, development, and sophisticated lending stategies. Mr. Chantengco is a licensed real estate broker, a Realtor member, a certified commercial investment member, and a real estate appraiser. He later undertook legal studies at WSU/Thomas Jefferson Law School after earning a Pro Bono Scholarship. He utilizes his background in the real estate and the legal professions to structure deals. Active in politics, Mr. Chantengco has served as a national speaker for the Rev. Jesse Jackson for President Campaign (1988); field director for President Bill Clinton (1992); and San Diego Congressmember Bob Filner (1996). Most importantly, Mr. Chantengco is involved in many civic, cultural and humanitarian affairs in his community, and he has equally received numerous recognitions, awards, and citations of merit. **Education:** University of California – San Diego, B.S. in Biochemistry and Cell Biology; Western State University – Thomas Jefferson School of Law, J.D. studies. **Personal:** Mr. Chantengco enjoys golf, scuba diving, mountain biking, walking, and travel.

Angelica Fernandez

Project Director
Grupo Situr
1551 Shelter Island Drive
San Diego, CA 92106–3102
(619) 222–1581
Fax: (619) 226–7891

6552

Business Information: Grupo Situr — A public Mexican owned company and one of the largest development companies in Mexico. The Company is a developer of a variety of public resort and hospitality properties, including hotels, marinas, golf courses and tourist real–estate villas and condominiums, etc. As Project Director for Situr–Kona Kai Inc., Ms. Fernandez oversees the direction of different projects, including strategic planning, coordination of all areas, for example design, finances, administration, development, supervision and profitability of the final project. She is currently working on two projects: the first one, a $20 million dollar Resort in San Diego, CA, with an additional second Phase worth $17 million dollars. The second project is a hotel renovation in Los Angeles. Joining Situr Kona Kai, Inc. as Project Director in 1984, Ms. Fernandez oversees the direction of all projects, including administration, finances, strategic planning, hiring, profitability, and design. She is currently working on two projects: the first one, a $20 million hotel in the second phase of development in San Diego and the second, a hotel renovation in Los Angeles. **Career Steps:** Grupo Situr (1984–Present), construction of seven large different Hotels and Resorts; 4 years in charge of design involved in 35 different hospitality projects through Mexico; Project Director, Situr–Kona Kai Inc. (1992–Present). **Associations & Accomplishments:** Federal Offices Oturban Development; Ecology Guad; Mey 1984; Colege of Architect Guad; MEX; National Association of Female Executives; Crew S.D. **Education:** National Autonomous University Otguad, B.S. in Architecture (1979–1983); Diploma on Business Administration; Technologico of Monterrey; Toefl English as a Foreign Language. **Personal:** Ms. Fernandez enjoys sports, including going to the gym, biking, rollerblading, hiking, etc.

Natalia V. Galindo, CPA

Project Controller
A H Development, S.E.
Montehiedra
San Juan, Puerto Rico 00926
(787) 731–2100 Ext. 204
Fax: (787) 731–2111

6552

Business Information: A H Development, S.E. is a Miami–based real estate development firm engaged in the development of exclusive residences. These houses primarily range from $300,000 to $575,000, and the total project exceeds $75,000,000. The Company is a local and regional firm with locations in Miami, FL and Puerto Rico. Established in 1990, A H Development, S.E. employs 25 people. As Project Controller, Mrs. Galindo communicates with subcontractors and is responsible for all financial and accounting information related to each project. **Career Steps:** Project Controller, A H Development, S.E. (1992–Present); Tax Senior & Audit Semi–Se-

nior, Arthur Andersen (1987–1992). **Associations & Accomplishments:** Puerto Rico Society of Certified Public Accountants; American Institute of Certified Public Accountants. **Education:** Univ. Sagrado Corazon, BBA (1987). **Personal:** Married to Paul Barreras–Diaz, CPA in 1990. Mrs. Galindo enjoys reading, walking, and water and beach activities.

Francisco Gelpi Martin

Owner/Developer
Inbersiones Reales
Urb Torrimar, Building 11–1, Calle Cordova
Guaynabo, Puerto Rico 00966
(787) 792–0947
Fax: Please mail or call

6552

Business Information: Inbersiones Reales specializes in high end real estate development of exclusive properties in prestigious neighborhoods. Comprised of 200 acres on the West side of the island, the Company is developing residential, commercial, and industrial locations for clients, and will retain ownership of an agricultural house, bakery, and gas station. As Owner/Developer, Mr. Gelpi Martin directs, organizes, and develops plans for the sites, as well as oversees all financial and tax matters. Concurrent with his present position, Mr. Gelpi Martin also breeds and shows Paso Fino horses. **Career Steps:** Owner/Developer, Inbersiones Reales (1991–Present); Controller/Director of Finance, St. Jude Medical, Puerto Rico, Inc. (1987–1991); Financial Consultant, Puerto Rico Cryogenics Corporation (1983–1987); Director of Finance, C.W. Caribe, Inc. (1980–19863). **Associations & Accomplishments:** College of Certified Public Accountants, Puerto Rico State Society; American Institute of Certified Public Accountants; Asociacion Nacionse Deporte Caballes de Paso Fino de Puerto Rico, Inc. **Education:** Inter American University of Puerto Rico, M.B.A. in Finance (1989); University of Puerto Rico, B.B.A. in Economics and Accounting; Certified Public Accountant (1984). **Personal:** Married to Rosalina in 1973. Two children: Francisco Jose and Marie Christine. Mr. Gelpi Martin enjoys tennis, reading, and riding and competing Paso Fino horses.

Antonio A. Giordano

Office Manager and Director of Project Development
Consultants Inc.
190 Broad Street
Providence, RI 02903–4029
(401) 331–5454
Fax: (401) 831–2540

6552

Business Information: Consultants Incorporated is a Real Estate Investment and Development, Consulting Firm founded in 1970. Consultants Incorporated is responsible for the processing, financing, development, construction, and management of Nursing Homes and Affordable Housing Projects. This is accomplished through utilizing current Federal Programs under Housing and Urban Development and State Programs available for project development. Consultants Incorporated, since its existence, has developed hundreds of millions of dollars in Nursing Homes and Multifamily Housing Projects. Serving in managerial and project analyzing/feasibility roles with the Firm since 1989. Antonio A. Giordano currently serves as office manager and director of project development. In these capacities, he directs and monitors daily activities, accounting information, attorneys, architects, engineers, and customer relations, as well as, computer systems. **Career Steps:** Consultants Incorporated: Office Manager/Director of Project Development (1995–Present), Director of Project Development (1993–1995), Financial Analyst (1989–1993). **Associations & Accomplishments:** Nursing Home Administrator's License (1995); Real Estate Sales License (1994); The Greater Providence Board of Realtors; State of Rhode Island Contractor's License (1993); Rhode Island Builder's Association (1987–Present); National Association of Home Builders (1987–Present); Notary Public (1995). **Education:** New York University, M.A. in Real Estate Development (1992); Catholic University of America, B.A. in Financial Management (1989); Home Builder's Institute, Graduate Master Builder (1996). **Personal:** Mr. Giordano enjoys karate, skiing, fishing, and movies.

Sally A. Goodnow

Regional Manager
Realty One Builder Marketing
4368 Dressler Rd., N.W.
Canton, OH 44718
(216) 493–2549
Fax: (216) 493–8012

6552

Business Information: Realty One Builder Marketing is a builder marketing servicer, providing sales and marketing for new construction and land development. As Regional Manag-

er, Mrs. Goodnow manages the builder and developer accounts, as well as oversees the sales agents throughout Southern Ohio. She is also responsible for creating builder and developer materials and advertising. **Career Steps:** Regional Manager, Realty One Builder Marketing (1995–Present); Custom Home Consultant, Petros Homes (1994–1995); Vice President of Sales and Marketing, Georgetown Homes, Inc. (1990–1994). **Associations & Accomplishments:** National Sales and Marketing Council; Home Builder Association of Akron; Home Builder Association of Wayne and Holms County; BIA of Cleveland; BIA of Stark County; Recipient, Gold Sales Master Award; Recipient, Gold Award NSMC (1994). **Education:** St. Thomas University, B.S. in Marketing (1988). **Personal:** Married to Joseph Berardelli in 1995. One child: Meggie. Three step children: Rebecca, John, and Don. Mrs. Goodnow enjoys attending seminars, step aerobics, spending time with her children and traveling.

Teri Hagadorn

Vice President
California Factory Stores
5959 Topanga Century Boulevard, Suite 285
Woodland Hills, CA 91367
(818) 346–7700 Ext. 16
Fax: (818) 346–7400
EMAIL: See Below

6552

Business Information: California Factory Stores specializes in factory outlet development and management. Yehuda Netanel, Inc. dba California Factory Stores was founded in 1978 to develop luxury apartments and condominiums. In 1990, California Factory Stores was founded to develop, lease and manage architecturally appealing Shopping Centers featuring brand name merchandise at discount prices. Ms. Hagadorn has been involved in all facets of Outlet Center development and management. Currently, she oversees Leasing, Marketing and Management. Internet users can reach her via: factorystores@earthlink.com **Career Steps:** Vice President, California Factory Stores (1994–Present); Director of Leasing and Marketing (1992–1994); Assistant to the Leasing Department, California Factory Stores (1990–1991); Manager, Aunt Bonnie's Cookies, Northern and Central California (1985–1990). **Associations & Accomplishments:** Developers of Outlet Centers, Factory Outlet Marketing Association; National Association of Female Executives; 1995 Savvy Award, Honorable Mention **Education:** University of San Francisco, B.S. Organizational Behavior (1989). **Personal:** Ms. Hagadorn enjoys traveling, sports events, and learning about cultures around the world.

Isaac Hanono M.

President
Inmobiliaria El Faro S.A.
Apartado 8580 Zona
Panama City, Panama
(507) 227–1054
Fax: (507) 227–1064

6552

Business Information: Inmobiliaria El Faro S.A. is real estate developing company specializing in developing, building projects, and the rental of apartment buildings. Owners of twelve apartment complexes, the Company deals in residential and commercial properties. Established in 1983, the Company employs ten people and has estimated annual revenue in excess of $2 million. As President, Mr. Hanono oversees all aspects of the Company. He is responsible for administration, operations, sales, marketing, public relations, and strategic planning. **Career Steps:** President, Inmobiliaria El Faro S.A. (1983–Present); Republic of Panama: Ambassador to Taiwan (1994–1996), Minister of Commerce (1989); President, Sesamo Internacional (1979–1984); President, Confecciones Levisak (1964–1979). **Associations & Accomplishments:** Coronado Golf Club; Apede; Chamber of Commerce; Club Cultural Hebreo; President of Albert Einstein Institute of Panama; Former member of Board of largest Jewish Organization, Shevet Ahim. **Personal:** Married to Paulette in 1967. Four children: Moises, Salomon, Sara, and Esther. Mr. Hanono enjoys reading and golf.

Stephen A. House

Property Manager
Park Tower Management, Inc.
1001 19th Street North, Suite 1000
Rosslyn, VA 22209
(703) 525–4455
Fax: (703) 841–2459

6552

Business Information: Park Tower Management, Inc. is a national and international commercial real estate development and management firm, managing nine million square feet of property in the New York City area, as well as sites both nationally and internationally. As Property Manager, Mr. House is responsible for all portfolio projects outside the New York City area, particularly emphasizing the Southeast U.S. locale. **Career Steps:** Property Manager, Park Tower Management, Inc. (1988–Present); Director of Engineering Services, Legum & Norman, Inc. (1985–1988). **Associations & Accomplishments:** National Association of Power Engineers; National Association of Power Engineers Educational Foundation; Apartment and Office Building Association; Published in trade journals and condominium and cooperative publications. **Education:** Concord Carlisle High School (1971); Numerous courses through: Building Owners and Managers Institute (BOMA), National Association of Power Engineers Educational Foundation (NAPEEF), Community Associations Institute (CAI). **Personal:** Married to Lynn in 1988. Three children: Christina, Katherine, and Arthur. Mr. House enjoys golf and rugby.

Charles E. Knox Jr.

President
The Knox Group, Inc.
P.O. Box 32821
Charlotte, NC 28232–2821
(704) 896–1911
Fax: (704) 896–7499

6552

Business Information: Knox Group is a commercial real estate development and brokerage firm. Co–founding the Firm in 1991, Mr. Knox serves as Vice President, managing all projects under development by the Firm, including public relations. **Career Steps:** Vice President, Knox Group (1991–Present); Project Manager, Oliver McMillan, Inc. (1986–1991). **Associations & Accomplishments:** Director, North Mecklenburg Chamber of Commerce; Charlotte Chamber of Commerce; Capital Campaign Committee, YMCA; Cornelius Land Use Task Force. **Education:** Davidson College, B.A. (1986); University of California – San Diego, Professional Courses in Real Estate Development. **Personal:** Married to Colette in 1995. Mr. Knox enjoys writing and golf.

Monica J. Kurbursky
Director of Financial Operations
Simon Property Group
115 W. Washington St.
Indianapolis, IN 46204
(317) 263–2326
Fax: (317) 263–2339

6552

Business Information: Simon Property Group is a retail real estate development and management firm. They have properties located in 28 states. The SPG portfolio is comprised of 122 properties that include regional malls, community shopping centers, and mixed use properties. SPG is responsible for the development/management of the Mall of America and The Forum, shops in Las Vegas. New projects include the 1995 openings of Circle Centre (Indianapolis, IN), Seminole Town Center (Sanford, FL), and Lakeline Mall (Austin, TX). Newest is the opening of Cottonwood Mall in Albuquerque, NM, expected July 31, 1996. As Director of Financial Operations, Ms. Kurbursky is responsible for the direction of all financial operations, including management of rental collections, legal collections, cash, applications, accounts payable, and property audits and analysis. **Career Steps:** Simon Property Group: Director of Financial Operations (1996–Present), Senior Manager of Financial Operations (1994–1996), Manager of Accounts Receivable (1992–1994). **Associations & Accomplishments:** Secretary, Avon Junior Athletic Association. **Education:** Indiana University. **Personal:** Married to Dan E. in 1982. Five children: Erin, Brandin, Morgan, Allison, and Jacquelyn. Ms. Kurbursky enjoys spending time with her children, basketball, bicycling, reading, and coaching soccer and basketball.

Marge Landry
Senior Vice President
Vista Group
2295 A Renaissance Drive
Las Vegas, NV 89119
(702) 798–7970
Fax: (702) 798–1029

6552

Business Information: Vista Group is a commercial real estate development firm with one location in Las Vegas. Although located in Nevada, the Group buys, sells, and leases properties in Nevada, Utah, and California. Established in 1975, Vista Group now employs approximately 30 people. As Senior Vice President, Mrs. Landry handles the marketing and leasing of approximately 3 million square feet of retail and office space throughout the Group's marketing area. She negotiates and prepares all lease documents and media re-

leases for print, radio, and television. Mrs. Landry directly supervises 5 employees and handles all personnel, training, scheduling, and budgetary concerns for the department. **Career Steps:** Senior Vice President of Marketing, Vista Group (1992–Present); Senior Property Manager, Koll Management (1990–1992); Vice President, Sanborn Development (1987–1990). **Associations & Accomplishments:** Certified Commercial Investment Member Candidate; International Council of Shopping Centers; National Association of Industrial Office Parks; National Association of Women Business Owners. **Education:** University of Texas – El Paso, B.A. in Journalism (1972). **Personal:** Married to Ray in 1995. Mrs. Landry enjoys reading and travel.

Randall S. Leferink
Purchasing Manager
McCoy Development
28000 Spanish Wells Boulevard
Bonita Spring, FL 34135–9943
(941) 992–5529
Fax: (941) 992–0218

6552

Business Information: McCoy Development, established in 1978, is a regional commercial and residential land development company. The Company is also involved in the construction of new buildings and the sale of the completed structures. As Purchasing Manager, Mr. Leferink develops construction budgets via estimating, bidding and negotiating activities with sub–contractors and material suppliers. Other duties include monitoring quality, costs and scopes of work as contracted. **Career Steps:** Purchasing Manager, McCoy Development (1995–Present); Purchasing and Estimating Manager, Centex Homes (1993–1995); Estimator, Dugan's Inc. (1990–1993); Sergeant, US Air Force (1976–1980). **Associations & Accomplishments:** Rotary International; Collier Building Industry Association; Guadeloupe Center Thanksgiving Benefit. **Education:** University of Southwestern Louisiana, B.S. (1989); Certified General Contractor, State of Florida (1993). **Personal:** Married to Vickie in 1989. Three children: Crystal, Melissa, and Lauren.

Stanley Loewenthal
Controller
LCOR Incorporated
245 Park Avenue 25th Floor
New York, NY 10167
(212) 972–5510
Fax: (212) 697–1701

6552

Business Information: LCOR Incorporated is a real estate development firm engaged primarily in commercial construction and management doing business in all of New York City, Northern New Jersey, and some of Connecticut. LCOR has five offices in New York, Pennsylvania, Illinois, and Florida. Starting his career as a Social Studies teacher in 1968, Mr. Loewenthal was certified as a Public Accountant in 1979. Joining LCOR as Controller in 1991, he is responsible for all aspects of accounting functions for the corporation. **Career Steps:** Controller, LCOR Incorporated (1991–Present); Cost Comptroller, Tishman Construction Corporation (1984–1991); Controller, Morse/Diesel International (1976–1984); Staff Accountant, Liesure Technology Corporation (1975–1976); Staff Accountant, Arthur Anderson & Company (1973–1975). **Associations & Accomplishments:** American Institute of Certified Public Accountants; New Jersey Society of Certified Public Accountants; Construction Management Financial Association; Treasurer, Temple Neve Shalom. **Education:** Rutgers University: M.B.A. in Accounting (1973), M.A. in History (1970), B.A. in History (1968); New Jersey Secondary School Teaching Certificate. **Personal:** Married to Marilyn in 1971. Two children: Elana and Carrie. Mr. Loewenthal enjoys tennis and bike riding.

Edgardo L. Martinez Nazario
Assistant General Counsel/Director of Litigation
Puerto Rico Industrial Development Company
P.O. Box 362350
San Juan, Puerto Rico 00936–2350
(787) 764–6966
Fax: (787) 754–7131

6552

Business Information: Puerto Rico Industrial Development Company is an establishment primarily engaged in industrial real estate development and the leasing and selling of real estate property. Established in 1941, the Company employs 495 people. As Assistant General Counsel, Mr. Martinez Nazario is responsible for directing all litigation, specifically real estate, tort, environmental, and bankruptcy law. **Career Steps:** Assistant General Counsel, Puerto Rico Industrial Company (1990–Present); Puerto Rico Legal Services Corporation: (1986–1990); Director, Service Center (1983–1986). **Educa-**

tion: University of Puerto Rico School of Law, J.D. (1975); University of Puerto Rico School of Public Administration, M.A.; University of Puerto Rico, B.A. in Economics and Political Science. **Personal:** Five children: Omar E., Edgardo L., Hjamil A., Edwin and Isabel A.. Mr. Martinez Nazario enjoys stamp collecting and swimming.

Bahram Motamedian
Acquisition Manager
Hines
2800 Post Oak Boulevard
Houston, TX 77056
(713) 966–7872
Fax: (713) 966–2636

6552

Business Information: Hines is an international real estate developer with 42 offices in the United States and offices in nine other countries. As Acquisition Manager, Mr. Motamedian is responsible for seeking new international real estate acquisitions and development opportunities, market contacts with Fortune 500 companies, and the monitoring of market conditions. **Career Steps:** Acquisition Manager, Hines (1995–Present); Real Estate Finance, Kidder Peabody – New York (1994); Consultant, Rosen Consulting Group (1990–1993). **Associations & Accomplishments:** Board of Directors, University of California–Berkeley Alumni Association (1993–1996); International House Council Chairperson (1990) . **Education:** University of California–Berkeley: M.B.A. in Finance/Real Estate, B.A. in International Economics

Juan F. Ortega

President
Inverdec, Inc.
P.O. Box 193138
San Juan, Puerto Rico 00919–3138
(787) 753–8783
Fax: (787) 758–6015

6552

Business Information: Inverdec, Inc. is an establishment primarily engaged in the design, development, and consultation of real estate, specifically housing sub–divisions, including streets and lighting. Regional in scope, the Company also provides investment opportunities to clients, managing construction and development of properties. As President, Mr. Ortega is involved in all aspects of the business and oversees all projects and developments. He is also responsible for consulting with clients and investors, strategic planning, and recruiting new markets. **Career Steps:** President, Inverdec, Inc. (1992–Present); Vice President, Empresas Nativas, Inc. (1985–1992); Project Coordinators, James L. Tate & Associates (1975–1984). **Associations & Accomplishments:** Construction Specification Institute; National Association of Home Builders; Puerto Rico Association of Home Builders; San Juan Board of Realtors. **Education:** New Hampshire College, Bachelors Degree (1986); Licensed Architectural Draftsman; Licensed Real Estate Broker. **Personal:** Married to Alison Torres in 1987. Two children: Alison Marie and Linarys. Mr. Ortega enjoys bowling and Lifesprint LP–15.

F.W. (Freddie) Schinz
President
Tiforp Development Corporation
P.O. Box 1568
Destin, FL 32541
(904) 654–4884
Fax: (904) 654–4662

6552

Business Information: Tiforp Development Corporation provides commercial, industrial and shopping center development with a primary focus on high rise resorts. Certified general contractors, the Company has designed and developed resorts for major locales along the Florida coast, including current projects involving Jade East Towers (an 18 story luxury beach resort), Windancer, Tranquillity on the Beach, and Krystle Sands in Clearwater, Florida. Established in 1982, the Company employs three people, and has an estimated annual revenue of $40 million. As President, Mr. Schinz is the original founder of the Company and oversees all administration and operational functions. Additional duties include finance and budget, sales, public relations, marketing and strategic planning. **Career Steps:** President, Tiforp Development Corporation (1982–Present). **Associations & Accomplishments:** American Institute of Constructors; Sunday School Teacher; Special Deputy Sheriff. **Education:** Florida International University, B.S. (1976). **Personal:** Married to Sharon in 1974. Two children: Zac and Krystle. Mr. Schinz enjoys skiing, boating, water activities and flying.

Sirdar (Mark) Shah

President
Professional Wealth Builders of America
P.O. Box 675570
Rancho Santa Fe, CA 92067
(619) 792–0077
Fax: (619) 792–6855
6552

Business Information: Professional Wealth Builders of America conducts seminars on business opportunities, and motivates, trains, and develops leaders in free enterprise. As President, Mr. Shah motivates, trains, and sells courses designed to assist clients in the development of leadership skills to succeed in free enterprise. Concurrent with his Professional Wealth Builders of America position, Mr. Shah is also President of Empire Estates, a real estate development company. **Career Steps:** President, Professional Wealth Builders of America (Present); President, Empire Estates. **Associations & Accomplishments:** Self Made Millionaires of America; Eagle Scout, Boy Scouts of America; Elks Club; Honorably Discharged From the U.S. Navy and U.S. Air Force; Thalians Presidents Club; Direct Descendent of the Mogul Empire of India, The Exiled Shah of Kashmir; Member of Grolier's Greats. Education: Maryland University, M.S.; Securities Insurance Real Estate License; Trained Matador, Fought Bulls in Mexico. **Personal:** Married to Liliane in 1958. Four children: Karmin, Kim, Lord, and Mark. Mr. Shah enjoys sports, travel, charity, real estate and company acquisition, and his seven grandchildren.

Elliott John Talgo Sr.

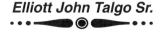

General Manager
San Carlos Lake Development Corporation
HCR1 Box 24
Peridot, AZ 85542
(520) 475–2756
Fax: (520) 475–2535
6552

Business Information: San Carlos Lake Development Corporation is a retail store and trailer park centered around the beauty of San Carlos Lake. The San Carlos Lake Development Corporation is also the fund–raiser and promoter of the projected recreational developments for the area. Established in 1988, the Corporation currently employs 12 people. As General Manager, Mr. Talgo is responsible for the management of the retail store and the trailer park and is personally involved in seeking funding for the recreational developments. He also serves as a member of the Board of Directors, wherein all strategic developments and long–range goals are initiated. **Career Steps:** General Manager, San Carlos Lake Development Corporation (1993–Present); San Carlos Housing Authority: Collection Supervisor (1986–1993), Collection Officer (1983–1986); Emergency Medical Technician, San Carlos Apache Tribe (1982–1983). **Associations & Accomplishments:** Arizona Interscholatic Association; Our Saviors Lutheran Church Council; American Sportsfishing Association. **Education:** Eastern Arizona College; Certification: Hotel Management. **Personal:** Married to Beverly in 1980. Four children: Elliott Jr., Loreal, Ashley, and Lesley. Mr. Talgo enjoys basketball, softball, coaching youth and fishing.

Esther Don Tang

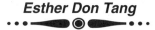

Vice Chair
Netwest Development Corporation
2221 East Broadway Boulevard Suite 211
Tucson, AZ 85719
(520) 624–5511
Fax: (520) 624–9007
6552

Business Information: Netwest Development Corporation constructs, owns, and operates rental businesses for multi–family living for special populations such as elderly, women, minorities, and children. Developed by 35 original stock holders and $750,000, the Company's philosophy is to earn an "honest dollar" and build good communities. The Company did extensive research in the state of Arizona to determine exactly where their facilities were most needed. They work in cooperation with federal, state, and local government regarding ideas and community involvement. Above all else, the Company designs and builds their structures as if their own mothers were going to live in them — every one is built with love, caring, and beauty. As Vice Chair, Ms. Tang is responsible for handling public relations, performing research, and introducing new innovative ideas. Additionally, she is the Owner of Markets & Rentals. **Career Steps:** Vice Chair, Netwest Development Corporation (1984–Present); Executive Director, Pio Decimo Neighborhood Center (1965–1985); 1955–: Co–Owner, D & B Market; Business Woman & Co–Owner, Dave's One Stop Market; Co–Owner, Dave's Beverages; Co–Owner, Business Properties in Tucson; Landowner, Dateland, Marana, & Tucson; Co–Owner, Campbell & Grant Shopping Strip; 1965–1985: Executive Director, Pio Decimo Neighborhood Center; 1985–1996: Board Member & Stockholder, Netwest Development Company, Inc., Vice Chairman, Netwest Development Company, Inc. Board, Limited Partner, 7 Netwest Building Projects in Casa Grande, Yuma, Peoria, Kingman, & Bullhead City, Co–General Partner, Inn at the Amethyst – Peoria, Foreign Trade Development Association, Inc. **Associations & Accomplishments:** Civic Boards & Committees: Co–Chair 30th Anniversary, St. Thomas More Center and Chapel (1993–1994); Delegate for White House Conference on Aging – Pima County (1993–1994); Chair, Official Visit of Director General of Taiwan Economic and Cultural Office – Los Angeles (1993–1994); Co–Chair, Sister CIties Association of Tucson Fundraiser; Honorary Co–Chair, NAACP Banquet Fundraiser (1993–1994); Selection Committee, Tucson Unified School District Supervisor of High Schools (1993–1994); Nominating Committee, Tucson Airport Authority (1975–1996); Chair, Roots & Wings Fundraiser Honoring Dennis DeConcini (1993–1994); Honorary Chairman, Anne Frank 1995 Diary Exhibit; Women's Anti–discrimination Task Force (1993–1994); Women's Coalition on Harassment (1993–1994); Sponsor, Diane Newsome's "The Mandate" Fundraiser (1993–1994); Co–Chair, Andy Nichols 1994 Re–election Fundraiser (1993–1994); Pima Community College Action Committee (1933–1994); Chair, Tucson/Taichug Sister Cities (1984–1996); Arizona Civil Rights Advisory Board (1993–1994); Chair, Maria Urquides Scholarship Fund for Children – La Frontera (1993–1994); Arizona Historical Society Nomination Committee, Now & Then Council, Marshall Foundation (1993–1994); (1975–1985) Pima Community College Board, Honorary Doctorate University of Arizona, Human Letters (1992); Dedicated Nash Elementary School Senior Wellness Center for Pima Council on Aging (1993–1994); Honors & Awards: Y.W.C.A. Lifetime Achievement Award (1993); Emeritus Club, University of Arizona Alumni Association (1993); The Old Pueblo Civitan Foundation "Para Los Ninos" Award (1994); St. Thomas More Center & Chapel 30th Anniversary Award (1994); Kente Cloth, Martin Luther King Jr. Center at U of A (1994); St. Thomas Newman Club University of Arizona Award (1994); Publications: Tucson Magazine, "78 of the Most Influential People in Tucson" (1978); Hembra, One of 23 Successful Career Women Serving as Minority Models by Arizona Women's Commission (1979); October/November Tucson Magazine, International Book of Honor, First World Edition (1985); "Who Runs Tucson:Minorities with Power, Women with Power (1989); Tucson Life Style Magazine:"Profile Feature on Business" (1989); Who's Who of American Women – 17th Edition (1991); Pima Community College Board (1975–1985); University of Arizona Humane Letters, Honorary Doctorate. **Education:** University of Arizona, Foods and Nutrition, Sociology; Draughons Business College; Doctor of Humane Letter (May 1992). Fluent in Two Languages: Chinese (Cantonese) & Spanish. **Personal:** Married to David Wing Tang Sr. Four children: David Jr., Patricia, Diana, and Elizabeth. She also has six grandchildren: David III, Catherine and Brian Crowley, Shane Herrick, Darren, and Andre Simoes. Ms. Tang enjoys extensive travel to China, Taiwan, and the Mideast.

Paul M. Thrift

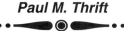

Partner
Thompson–Thrift Development
1100 Spruce Street
Terre Haute, IN 47807–2152
(812) 235–5959
Fax: (812) 235–8122
6552

Business Information: Thompson–Thrift Development, initially a construction company, is a real estate development and construction firm. The Company also provides management of a 150–unit apartment complex, as well as single family housing and commercial real estate. Mr. Thrift co–established Thompson–Thrift Development with his partner upon their high school graduation in 1986. Currently serving as Co–owner and Partner, he is responsible for the overall financial operations for new business development, in addition to office management functions. **Career Steps:** Partner, Thompson–Thrift Development (1986–Present). **Associations & Accomplishments:** Board Member (Chair), Wabash Valley Red Cross; Board Member, Terre Haute Homebuilders Association; Member, Terre Haute Chamber of Commerce. **Education:** Indiana State University, B.S. (1991). **Personal:** Married to Angie in 1994. Mr. Thrift enjoys water skiing and boating.

Gregory S. Tibbot

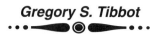

Controller
Colson & Colson
2250 McGilchrist SE, Suite 200
Salem, OR 97302
(503) 370–7071 Ext: 7156
Fax: (503) 370–4205
6552

Business Information: Colson & Colson is an international real estate investment, development and construction firm. Established in 1963, the Firm currently employs 50 people. As Controller, Mr. Tibbot supervises all accounting and administrative functions, as well as working with lenders, cash management, budgeting, and cost analysis. **Career Steps:** Controller, Colson & Colson (1989–Present); Controller and Treasurer, Red Hat Construction, Inc. (1985–1989); Accountant, Electronic Superstore (1985). **Associations & Accomplishments:** Institute of Management Accountants; American Financial Association; Troop Treasurer, Boy Scouts of America; Beta Alpha Psi. **Education:** Oregon State University, B.S. in Business, major Accounting and Finance, minor Behavioral Sciences (1994); Oregon State Real Estate License. **Personal:** Married to Mary in 1982. Three children: James, Steven, and Kevyn. Mr. Tibbot enjoys model trains, sports, martial arts, and travel.

Allen W. Warren

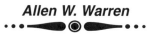

President
New Faze Development, Inc.
777 Campus Commons Road, Suite 200
Sacramento, CA 95825–8309
(916) 924–9906
Fax: (916) 565–7691
6552

Business Information: New Faze Development, Inc. is a real estate developer, providing conceptual designs for all types of property, conducting feasibility studies, and erecting infrastructures, as well as building residential and commercial structures. Founding New Faze Development as President in 1990, Mr. Warren is responsible for the development of the land, including interfacing with local municipal government offices, such as the City Counsel, County Board of Supervisors, City and County Planning, and Public Works Department. **Career Steps:** President, New Faze Development, Inc. (1990–Present); Credit and Assistant Branch Manager, Northwest Financial, Inc. (1991); Account Executive and Stock Broker, Dean Witter Reynolds (1989–1990); Professional Baseball Player, New York Yankees (1987–1988). **Associations & Accomplishments:** 100 Black Men; 1995 Developer of the Year; National Association for the Advancement of Colored People; Urban League. **Education:** California State University – Hayward, B.A. in Political Science and Option Affairs Administration (1989); Certified Series VII Exam; Certified Life Insurance Program. **Personal:** Mr. Warren enjoys outdoor activities (i.e. fishing and hiking).

THE MILLS CORPORATION
THE NEXT GENERATION OF RETAILING

Barry H. Young

Senior Vice President
Mills Corporation
1300 Wilson Blvd., Ste 400
Arlington, VA 22209
(703) 526–5081
Fax: (703) 526–5201
6552

Business Information: Mills Corporation is a developer of shopping centers, specializing in the development of mega–value oriented shopping malls, such as the Potomac Mills Mall in Washington, D.C. The Corporation also owns 12 power centers and three other Mills projects. Future plans include branching out into the entertainment field through joint ventures and by expanding the Mills concept. Joining Mills Corporation as Vice President in 1988, Mr. Young is responsible for the operation of the Specialty Leasing Department's existing and new projects in Florida and Illinois, as well as on the West Coast. Concurrent with his position at Mills Corporation, Mr. Young is a Professional Magician (since age 8), working with charitable organizations, and is a member of the International Brotherhood of Magicians. He is also a Professional Sculptor, conducting numerous expositions/exhibitions and one–man shows. **Career Steps:** Senior Vice President, Mills Corporation (1988–Present); Vice President Director Real Estate, S & A Restaurant Corporation (1985–1988); Vice President Real Estate and Development, Beefsteak Charlies (1982–1985); President and Chief Executive Officer, Young Food Corporation (1971–1982). **Associations & Accomplishments:** ICSC; Life Member of IBM, International Brotherhood of Magicians; Society of American Magicians; Washington Fencing Society. **Education:** Michigan State University, B.A. (1964); George Washington University, B.A. (1960); Howard Community College, Real Estate (1987). **Personal:** Married to Gayle in 1971. Three children: Zachary, Jeremy, and Melissa. Mr. Young enjoys skiing, fencing, kendo, racquetball, and sculpting (has his own work featured in office buildings, colleges and private collections).

S. Ralph Gerbie

Senior Vice President
Equis Corporation
161 North Clark Street, Suite 2700
Chicago, IL 60302
(312) 424–8125
Fax: (312) 424–0150
EMAIL: See Below

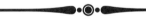

6574

Business Information: Equis Corporation provides real estate advisory and facilities outsource services to national and international corporate clients. Established in 1984, the Corporation employs 180 people. As Senior Vice President, Mr. Gerbie is responsible for directing account service programs throughout the United States and internationally. He has been involved in all aspects of commercial real estate including corporate relocation, renewal, build–to–suit, building purchase and sale, lease disposal, master planning, alternative workplace advisory and consulting. He has completed commercial real estate transactions in more than 100 cities, with a total value in excess of $750 million. Mr. Gerbie further acts as Principal of HomeSpace Properties, an enterprise which focuses on acquisition, renovation, and management of vintage residential investment property. Internet users can reach him via: rgerbie@equiscorp.com. **Career Steps:** Equis Corporation: Senior Vice President: (1990–Present), Vice President – National Accounts (1987–1990), Director of Research and Financial Services (1984–1987); Principal and Founder, HomeSpace Properties (1988–Present). **Associations & Accomplishments:** Village of Oak Park, IL – Zoning Board of Appeals; Building Owners and Managers Association; Historic Preservation Award; International Real Estate Development Council; National Trust for Historic Preservation; Licensed Real Estate Broker, various states. Published articles – Real Estate Review, Business Facilities, Area Development. Various other articles, lectures, awards, etc. **Education:** The University of Michigan M.B.A. (1984); Winner – Pryor Entrepreneurial Award, General Motors Case Competition; University of Colorado, B.A. in Economics (1981). **Personal:** Married to Jody in 1986. Two children: David and Danielle. Mr. Gerbie enjoys family activities, the arts, and travel.

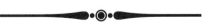

6700 Holding and Other Investment Offices

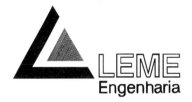

- 6712 Bank holding companies
- 6719 Holding companies, NEC
- 6722 Management investment, open–end
- 6726 Investment offices, NEC
- 6732 Educational, religious, etc. trusts
- 6733 Trusts, NEC
- 6792 Oil royalty traders
- 6794 Patent owners and lessors
- 6798 Real estate investment trusts
- 6799 Investors, NEC

LEME Engenharia

Flavio M. L. Campos

Chief Executive Officer/Director General
Leme Engenharia, Ltd.
Rua Guajajaras, 43 Belo Horizonte
Minas Gerais, Brazil 30180–909
55–31–273–3200
Fax: 55–31–273–3602
EMAIL: See below

8711

Business Information: Leme Engenharia, Ltd. is primarily engaged in engineering consulting, construction management and design, providing services to clients worldwide. Established in 1965, the Company employs 212 people and has an estimated annual revenue of $18 million. Its aim is to offer international customers the experience it has developed and consolidated in large scale projects in the Energy, Sanitation, Environment, Industry, Regional and Urban Planning, Transportation and Infrastructure Fields. As CEO/Director General, Mr. Campos is responsible for providing leadership to the Firm, ensuring work ethic of a quality and nature that will result in growth, profitability and continuance. His duties include quality assurance, profit and growth ratios, and all administrative functions. Mr. Campos also worked with Elektrowatt Engineering Services, Switzerland where he was responsible for hydraulic analysis and design calculations for several hydroelectric power plants in Switzerland, Turkey, and Morocco. Internet users can also reach him via: lemeng@net.em.com.br. **Career Steps:** Leme Engenharia Limited: CEO/Director General (1994–Present), Technical Director (1988), Project Manager (1976); Hydraulic Engineer, Elektrowat Engineering Services (1974–75). **Associations & Accomplishments:** Board of Advisors, Brazilian Society of Consulting Engineers (ABCE); Former President, President of Auditing Council, Minas Gerais State Society of Engineers (SME); President, International Chamber of Commerce of Brazil–CIC BR, (1996–1998). **Education:** School of Civil Engineering, Federal University of Minas Gerais, Civil Engineer (1973). **Personal:** Married to Vera Perez Campos in 1978. Three children: Laura, Julia and Henrique. Mr. Campos enjoys sports, travel, and time with his family.

Mr. Tieman Henry Dippel Jr.

Chairman and President
Brenham Bancshares, Inc.
2211 S. Day Street, Suite 401
Brenham, TX 77833
Fax: Please mail or call

6712

Business Information: Brenham Bancshares, Inc. is a bank holding company. Chairman of the Board and President of Brenham Bancshares, Inc., Chairman of the Board, Brenham National Bank, President and Registered Investment Adviser of Dippel, Winston & Associates, Chairman and President of Dippel Venture Capital Corporation, Partner of Dippel & Alfred Interests, Mr. Dippel is well–known in his community and in the state of Texas as an influential thinker and political independent. His knowledge in the four major areas of influence, (politics, economics, media and information), is both comprehensive and far ranging. Tim Richardson, editor of the highly regarded Austin political newsletters Quorum Report, reports, "Tieman Henry Dippel, Jr. is often listed as one of the state's most influential leaders, but his power does not lie in being what one would call 'the networker's networker ... Far more important, he is a philosophical leader...a political independent who understands the importance of ideas in a state that any presidential candidate must win to have any hope of success. Dippel realizes that we get the government we elect and our level of consciousness and sense of responsibility are the real keys to our future success." His highly acclaimed book, The New Legacy (Taylor Publishing, 1987), has been proclaimed "a map to the future" by Texas Governor Ann Richards, and a "prescription for life and government all wrapped in one" by his friend, Senator Phil Gramm. Fellow Texan Treasury Secretary Lloyd Bentsen comments, "in today's world where roots are often shallow...it is refreshing to find someone who is so firmly grounded in his native heritage." Tim Richardson writes that The New Legacy "could be a singularly influential book to the future of Texas...it is the synergism of the masterful perspective of life, of responsibility, and of history that blend with the vacuum that presently exists in Texas. This book is an inspiration to a sense of destiny because it gives Texans a choice between two futures...increasingly partisan politics and a muddling through, or a vision of Texas being a third coast of thought for a common good with coordinated goals...one of the few recent works that I have seen that has a sense of vision, integrity, and values that could hopefully inspire popular involvement in the process." Mr. Dippel has contributed articles on education, economics, politics, and Texas to many distinguished publications, and has been listed in Who's Who in Finance & Industry (1977/78), Who's Who in American Law (First Edition), and Who's Who in the World (Fifth Edition 1980/81). He has been profiled by Texas Business four times in "The Rising Stars of Texas" (1980), "Who Really Rules Texas" (1983), "Twenty Who Hold the Power in Texas" (1986), and "Be the Best" (1987); and twice in Ultra in "Texas CEOs, Young & Powerful" (1984), and "Texas Trailblazers" (1986). Tieman Henry Dippel, Jr. is a distinguished American, and a visionary leader in politics, economics, and the media. Established in 1933, Brenham Bancshares, Inc. employs over 50 people and reports assets in excess of $100 million. **Career Steps:** Chairman of the Board and President, Brenham Bancshares, Inc. (1983–Present); President, Dippel, Winston & Associates (1991–Present); Chairman of the Board and President, Dippel Venture Capital Corporation (1983–Present); Chairman of the Board, Chairman of the Executive Committee, Brenham National Bank (1972–Present); Partner, Dippel & Alfred Interests, Real Estate Development Partnership. **Associations & Accomplishments:** Former President, Texas State Chamber of Commerce; Former Chairman and President, Texas Lyceum Association; Former Chairman, Texans for Quality Education; Former Commissioner and Legislative Chairman, Texas Commission of the Arts; Former President, East Texas Chamber of Commerce; Recipient, John Ben Shepperd Forum "Outstanding Texas Leader" Award (1990); Director and Charter Committee Member, Texas Business Roundtable; Nominating Committee, Texas Research League; Director, Federal Reserve Bank of Dallas–Houston Branch; Executive Committee, Blue Cross & Blue Shield of Texas; Chaired statewide committees of independents for various statewide candidates; Former Director, Covenant House of Texas; Present Director, Caring for Children Foundation; Active in Boy Scouts of America, Eagle Scout with cluster; Methodist Church; University of Texas Centennial Commission; Development Board, University of Texas Health Science Center (Houston). **Education:** University of Texas at Austin, B.B.A. Class Valedictorian (1968); University of Texas at Austin, J.D., Chancellor Society (1971); U.S. Naval Justice School, LTCDR Naval Reserve, Certified Trial & Defense Counsel; Admitted to Practice: United States Supreme Court, United States Tax Court, United States Court of Claims, United States Court of Military Appeals, United States District Court (Western District of Texas), United States Fifth Circuit Court of Appeals, State of Texas Bar; Series 7 Securities License; Real Estate License – Texas; Insurance Licenses – Texas.

Pen Hollist

First Vice President
First Chicago NBD
320 E. Big Beaver 5th Floor
Troy, MI 48083
(810) 619–4511
Fax: (810) 619–4260

6712

Business Information: First Chicago NBD is the 7th largest bank holding company in the United States with $110 billion in total assets, domestic operations in Illinois, Michigan, Indiana, and Florida, as well as international operations. As First Vice President, Mr. Hollist is responsible for data base administration, data warehousing, data mining, change management, testing, quality assurance, and year 2000 conversion. **Career Steps:** First Vice President, First Chicago NBD (1994–Present); Vice President, Holland Systems Corporation (1992–1994); Senior Manager, Deloitte and Touche (1989–1992); Lieutenant Colonel, U.S. Army (1969–1989). **Education:** Kansas State University, M.S. (1980); University of Southern California, M.S. (1978); Utah State University, B.S. (1969). **Personal:** Married to Julie in 1968. Five children: Japen, Lisa, Tiffany, Sharri, and Tyler. Mr. Hollist enjoys church leadership, skiing, golf, and gardening.

Peter N. Horne

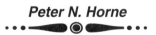

President
Midstates Bankshares, Inc.
P O Box 271
Harlan, IA 51537–0271
(712) 755–7738
Fax: (712) 755–7739

6712

Business Information: Midstates Bankshares, Inc. is a multi–bank holding company started in 1989. The holding company currently operates three banks in four separate locations in western Iowa and employs 60 people. As President, Mr. Horne oversees the general operation of three subsidiary banks. Individual CEOs give day–to–day operational reports to Mr. Horne, who in–turn assists the bank CEOs on the development of individual budgets and monitors bank compliance to set budgets. Internet users can reach him via: Midstates@NetIns.Net. **Career Steps:** Midstates Bankshares, Inc.: President (1996–Present), Vice President (1989–1996); Vice President, Harlan National Company (1981–1989). **Education:** University of Nebraska at Lincoln, B.S. (1980). **Personal:** Married to Penny in 1987. Two children: Cassandra Lynn and Peter Jr. Mr. Horne enjoys hunting, fishing, golf, trap shooting, and tennis.

Janine K. Pinel, C.P.A.

Chief Financial Officer
Eastern Bancorp
282 Williston Road
Williston, VT 05495
(802) 879–9002
Fax: (802) 879–9247

6712

Business Information: Eastern Bancorp is a bank holding company with 25 branches in Vermont and New Hampshire. As Chief Financial Officer, Ms. Pinel is responsible for all SEC regulations reporting, investor relations, and office administrative activities. **Career Steps:** Chief Financial Officer, Eastern Bancorp (1995–Present); Royalty Accountant, Schering–Plough (1992–1993); Senior Auditor, Ernst & Young (1988–1992). **Associations & Accomplishments:** Financial Executives Institution; National Association of Female Executives; Vermont Society of Certified Public Accountants; American Institute of Certified Public Accountants. **Education:** Clemson University, B.S. (1988). **Personal:** Married to Robert in 1995. Ms. Pinel enjoys religion, exercising, watersports, cooking, reading, travel, and quality family time.

Kevin E. Rushing

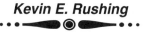

Vice President of Operations
Banc One Financial Services
P.O. Box 50417
Indianapolis, IN 46250–0417
(317) 595–8117 (800) 796–7363
Fax: (317) 595–8298

6712

Business Information: Banc One Financial Services Inc. is a subsidiary of Banc One Corporation based in Columbus, Ohio. The Corporation offers all banking services, to include lending, selling, collecting, litigation, etc. and has been in operation since 1902. As Vice President of Operations, Mr. Rushing is involved with all facets of the Corporation. He is responsible for strategic planning, cost analysis, evaluation of a wide variety of departmental functions and financial consulting. Mr. Rushing's long–term plans change as changes occur in the world financial markets. There are always new opportunities to seek out. His most important career milestone was the change from a legal to financial career. **Career Steps:** Banc One Financial Services: Vice President of Operations, (1996–Present), Department Manager Vice President (1994–1996), Assistant Vice President of Audit and Compliance (1992–1994), Branch Manager (1990–1992). **Associations & Accomplishments:** United States Army Officer; Coach, Police Athletic League; Indiana State University Alumni Association; United Way Volunteer; Fully Licensed Insurance Agent; Indiana Notary Association; American Financial Services Association; National Second Mortgage Association. **Education:** Indiana State University, B.S. (1986); Enrolled in Masters of Science and Management Program, Indiana Wesleyan University (Completion – 1998); United States Army Basic and Advanced Infantry Officer School / Commissioned Officer (1985); United States Army Command and Staff School; American Financial Services Association Management Development Program Graduate. **Personal:** Married to Frances in 1983. Five children: Stephanie, Sarah, Anthony, Samantha, and Zachary. Mr. Rushing enjoys karate, scuba diving, and all sports.

Mr. Luiz Andrade

President
Luna's U.S.A. Inc.
5850 Lakehurst Drive, #205
Orlando, FL 32819
(407) 352–0100
Fax: (407) 351–9643

6719

Business Information: Luna's U.S.A. Inc. is an exporter of diversified durable goods (i.e., chocolate, toys, BMW and Jaguar automobiles), as well as the management holding company for hospitality concerns in Portugal and Brazil (i.e., hotels and steak house restaurants). Established in 1991, Luna's U.S.A. currently employs four people and has an estimated annual revenue of $1.2 million. As President, Mr. Andrade oversees all aspects of commercial operations. **Career Steps:** President, Luna's U.S.A. Inc. (1991–Present); Financial Director, Luna's Brazil (1984–1991). **Associations & Accomplishments:** Director, Association of Hotels in Brazil; Treasurer, Brazilian Association of Central Florida; Member, FGBMFI, Orlando, Florida. **Education:** University – Business Administration Degree (1990). **Personal:** Married to Daniela in 1985. Mr. Andrade enjoys automobiles.

Claye W. Atcheson

Vice President, Operations
Marriott Golf
7001 Lake Ellenor Drive
Orlando, FL 32809
(407) 850–0077 ext 2810
Fax: (407) 850–2092

6719

Business Information: Marriott Golf, a wholly–owned subsidiary of Marriott Hotels International, is the management holding company for premier golf courses and related golf operations development. International in scope, present holdings include 18 national courses, and international courses located in Spain, Morroco, Costa Rico and New Delhi. Joining Marriott Golf in 1987 as the director of the Camelback Golf Club, Mr. Atcheson was appointed to his current position as Vice President of Operations in 1993. He has overall corporate executive charge for operational aspects at all national golf facilities, as well as the administrative direction of one international location. **Career Steps:** Marriott Golf: Vice President, Operations (1993–Present), Director of Operations (1989–1993), Director of Golf, Camelback Golf Club (1987–1989). **Associations & Accomplishments:** Professional Golfers Association; Golf Course Superintendents Association of America; Club Managers Association; Various articles in golf media publications. **Education:** Arizona State University, B.S. in Management (1978). **Personal:** Married to Patti in 1978. Three daughters. Mr. Atcheson enjoys running.

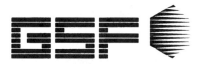

Lionel Bernard

Executive Vice President of European Business
GSF, S.A.
BP 25
Sophia Antipolis Cedex, France 06901
33–93957300
Fax: 33–92969456

6719

Business Information: GSF, S.A. is a holding company for industrial cleaning services with subsidiaries in the U.S., United Kingdom, Canada, and all over Europe. GSF provides cleaning services to industrial offices, food processing plants, technical plants, roads, supermarket chains, and other retail chains. Joining GSF as Executive Vice President of European Business in 1995, Mr. Bernard is responsible for the existing European relationships, as well as business development in the area, from opening new offices to developing the market. Additionally, he is responsible for sales, human resources, and management. **Career Steps:** Executive Vice President of European Business, GSF, S.A. (1995–Present); Vice President of Finance and Administration, GSF Safeway (1992–1995); Executive Vice President, GSF Auriga (1987–1992); Audit, Aluminium Alcan (1983–1987). **Education:** Ecole Polytechnique de Lausanne – Switzerland, Engineer (1983). **Personal:** Married to Santa in 1987. Two children: Vianney and Pierre–Alexis. Mr. Bernard enjoys golf, skiing, and antiques.

Christine E. Borger

Executive Vice President/Chief Financial Officer
The Holt Corporation
961 Marcon Boulevard, Suite 400
Bethlehem, PA 18017
(610) 264–4040
Fax: (610) 266–6464
E MAIL: See Below

6719

Business Information: The Holt Corporation is a multi–faceted, international broadcasting corporation. The Corporation owns and operates radio stations, functions as a brokerage company for the rental, sales, and appraisal of broadcasting stations, and handles national and international consulting projects. As Executive Vice President/CFO, Mrs. Borger oversees corporate financial activities, various special projects, accounting matters, and payroll. Other responsibilities include developing and implementing departmental budgets, overseeing project budgets, and strategic planning for the future. Internet users can reach her via: cbwtkz@aol.com. **Career Steps:** Executive Vice President/CFO, The Holt Corporation (1986–Present); Director of Corporate Accounting, Holt Corporation PA (1982–1986); Business Manager, WZZO (1979–1982). **Associations & Accomplishments:** Broadcast Cable Financial Management; National Association of Broadcasters; Chamber of Commerce. **Education:** Clarion University, B.S. (1978). **Personal:** Married to Jeffrey in 1980. Two children: Kayla Marie and Nathaniel Adam. Mrs. Borger enjoys swimming, reading, gardening, exercising, and volunteering work at Notre Dame school.

Walid Faiz Boustany

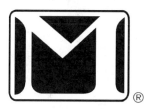

Chief Financial Officer
Corpalmar
1101 Brickell Avenue – Suite 401
Miami, FL 33131
(582) 206–7186
Fax: (582) 206–7119

6719

Business Information: Corpalmar (Vollmer Group) is a leading Venezuelan investment holding group with interests in sugar, foods, forestry, real estate and financial services. Established in the 1940's, Corpalmar currently employs over 3,000 people Corporate–wide. As Chief Financial Officer, Mr. Boustany, a British citizen and native of Lebanon, is responsible for overall Corporate financial management, acquisitions and restructuring, Corporate treasury, strategy and technology. Mr. Boustany is a Board Director of all operating subsidiaries and the group holding company. The Caracas headquarters are located at: Corpalmer, Torre Banco del Orinoco, Av. F. de Miranda, Caracas, Venezuela 1060. **Career Steps:** Chief Financial Officer, Corpalmar (1994–Present); Managing Director, Boustany & Co. (1993–Present); Principal, Booz Allen & Hamilton (1991–1993); Partner, Spicer Oppenheim Consultants (1986–1991); Senior Associate, Booz Allen & Hamilton (1983–1986). **Associations & Accomplishments:** Fluent in English, Arabic, Spanish, French and German. **Education:** Columbia University, M.B.A. (1983); American University, B.Sc. (1980); Cornell University School of Architecture; American University of Beirut. **Personal:** Married to Veronica in 1980. Two children: Faiz and Hilda Sofia. Mr. Boustany enjoys travel, investment, real estate, jazz music, and politics.

David C. Carrithers

Vice President – Individual Awards Division – Strategic Planning,
Maritz Performance Improvement Company
1309 North Highway Drive
St. Louis, MO 63099
(314) 827–2375
Fax: (314) 827–8437
EMAIL: see below

6719

Business Information: Maritz, Inc. is a 100 plus years old, privately held company, serving as the parent company to four companies, including Maritz Performance Improvement Company, Maritz Travel Company, Maritz Marketing Research, Maritz Europe. Maritz provides a wide range of services for their multi–national clients including, but not limited to, incentives programs, cost reduction programs, training, communications, tracking, database, teleservices, direct mail, loyalty management, group, individual and corporate travel services, fulfillment services, awards and relationship management. Maritz clients come from the ranks of America's top corporations – the Fortune 500. Maritz is committed to helping its clients improve their performance in critical areas such as sales, marketing, quality, customer satisfaction and cost reduction. As Vice President of Strategic Planning, Development and Marketing, Mr. Carrithers is responsible for one of the largest divisions with Maritz, Individual Awards, include people and resource management, strategic planning, market and competitive research, new product development, existing product management and enhancements, customer satisfaction, market research, technology applications development for product marketing and distribution (i.e. online services, Internet strategies, CD–ROM development, etc.), marketing communications, award catalog development and production, and he also drives the division's mission, values and objectives. Mr. Carrithers has involvement and input into operations, customer service, merchandising, warehousing, partnership and supplier alliances, systems, etc. Maritz has over 50 U.S. locations and 20 worldwide locations (including Canada, Mexico, and Europe) and sales over $1.9 billion. Internet users can reach him via: carritdc@maritz.com. **Career Steps:** Executive Roles with subsidiaries: Vice President Strategic Planning, Development & Marketing, Maritz Performance Improvement Company (1996–Present); Vice President – Strategic Planning & Development, Maritz Performance Improvement Company (1995–1996); Director of Business Development, Maritz Travel Company (1993–1995); Program Manager, Maritz Performance Improvement Company (1992–1993); Project Director, Maritz Performance Improvement Company (1990–1993); Manager of International Marketing Communications – Semiconductor Division, Air Products & Chemicals (1987–1990); Product Information & Publicity Manager, American Cyanamid (1985–1987). **Associations & Accomplishments:** American Marketing Association; Sigma Phi Epsilon; Supporter: Ronald McDonald House, Our Little Haven, United Way. **Education:** Northwestern University: Advanced Certification in Art of Venturing Within a Corporate Environment (1995), Advanced Certification in Finance (1994); Washington Univeristy, M.B.A. in International Affairs and Business (in progress); American Management Association Certification in Accounting (1987); Loyola University, B.A. in Marketing Communications (1995). **Personal:** Married to Kristy Kloster in 1985. One child: Carolyn Regina. Mr. Carrithers collects information on Winston Churchill (books, articles, photographs) and enjoys sailing.

Rose M. Culbertson

Tax Director
ARM Financial Group, Inc.
239 S. 5th Street, Floor 12
Louisville, KY 40202–3213
(502) 582–7928
Fax: (502) 582–7995
E MAIL: See Below

6719

Business Information: ARM Financial Group, Inc. is an insurance holding company whose subsidiaries sell annuities and other retirement/investment products. As Tax Director, Ms. Culbertson is responsible for federal and state tax compliance, product and tax reporting to the Internal Revenue Service, financial reporting, and monitoring examinations conducted by tax authorities. Other responsibilities include review of all tax returns, product taxation, and financial reports. Current projects include determination of tax provisions regarding the acquisition of other insurance companies. Internet users can reach her via: Rculber@armfinancial.com. **Career Steps:** Tax Director, ARM Financial Group, Inc. (1994–Present); Tax Manager, Cooper and Lybrand (1990–1993); Tax Manager, Providian Corporation (1988–1990). **Associations & Accomplishments:** Kentucky Society of Certified Public Accountants; Committee for Goals for Greater Louisville; Tax Executive Institute; National Tax Study Group Five–A. **Education:** Walsh College, Bachelor of Accountancy (1978). **Personal:** Married to Paul in 1986. Two children: Benjamin and Meredith. Ms. Culbertson enjoys golf, running, and spending time with her family.

Sidney O. Davis Sr.

President, Chief Executive Officer, Chairman of the Board
Sid Davis Enterprises
114 5 Oaks Avenue
Dayton, OH 45405–4350
(513) 222–2674
Fax: Please mail or call

6719

Business Information: Sid Davis Enterprises is an entrepreneurial establishment that handles a wide variety of business fields. The Company deals with property investment, redevelopment, management, photography, promotions, music productions, and innovation seminars. Founded in 1971, Sid Davis Enterprises focuses on the "6 M's" – money, materials, machines, manpower, methods, and morale. As President, Chief Executive Officer, and Chairman of the Board, Mr. Davis is responsible for Company finances and accounting, maintaining and updating materials and machines, personnel, and long–range planning. **Career Steps:** President, Chief Executive Officer, Chairman of the Board, Sid Davis Enterprises (1971–Present); Technology Planner, AF Wright Aeronautical Labs (1960–1989); Design Mechanical Engineer, GoodYear Atomic Corporation (1957–1960); Aviator (Navigator), United States Air Force (1954–1957). **Associations & Accomplishments:** Former Member, American Society of Mechanical Engineers; ASTM; American Society of Metals, Professional Societies. **Education:** Ohio State University, M.S. in Metallurgical Engineering (1971); Tennessee State University, B.S. in Mechanical Engineering (1954); Attended: Massachusetts Institute of Technology, University of Minnesota, Shephard's Behavioral Institute, University of Denver, Sinclair College, University of Dayton, Special Studies. **Personal:** Seven children: Anita, Lillian, Karen, Mark, Sidney Jr., Miracle, and Precious. Mr. Davis enjoys golf, bowling, and physical fitness.

Mohsen El Badramany

Group Vice President
Salim Al Moosa Group
P.O. Box 24775
Dubai, United Arab Emirates
(971) 4–371274 or 371270
Fax: (971) 4–353251
EMAIL: See Below

6719

Business Information: Salim Al Moosa Group is an international conglomerate of diversified businesses, including 10 subsidiaries and 10 affiliates in the construction, trading, publishing, shipping, travel, and tourism industries. As Group Vice President, Mr. El Badramany is in charge of the International Business relations and has a supervisory role over several divisions. In addition, he serves as a member of the Group Board. He can be reached through the Internet via: bdrmny95@emirates.net.ae **Career Steps:** Group Vice President, Salim Al Moosa Group (1986–Present); General Manager, The United Arab Emirates Contractors Association (1985–1986); General Manager, SKYWAY Insurance Company (1982–1985). **Associations & Accomplishments:** International Advertising Association; American Management Association; World Organization of Building Officials; The Institute of Professional Managers; AIAPA. **Education:** Cairo University, B.S.C. (1973); Secondary School; Computer Programming; Quality Seminars. **Personal:** Married to Ann in 1985. Mr. El Badramany enjoys classical music, gym workout, travel, and the Internet.

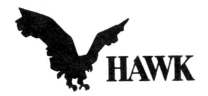

John Andrew Geishecker III

Director of International Marketing
Hawk Resorts International L.P.
Route 100
Plymouth, VT 05056
(802) 672–3811
Fax: (212) 808–0163
EMail: See Below

6719

Business Information: Hawk Resorts International L.P. is the holding company for Hawk Inn and Mountain Resort, a luxury resort and vacation home community in Plymouth, Vermont. Hawk Resorts International L.P. also maintains offices in Manhattan. As Director of International Marketing, Mr. Geishecker is responsible for all international advertising and marketing programs. he is additionally responsible for special overseas programs. Mr. Geishecker is also the Producer of "Doing Business Internationally", a television series that airs on the Discovery Channel in the United States and has international distribution on USA Networks. The show profiles investment opportunities in foreign countries for international business professionals and corporations, and is filmed on–location in the subject country. Doing Business Internationally Inc. is a joint venture of Financial Programming Productions and Langa Communications Corporation **Career Steps:** Director of International Marketing, Hawk Resorts International L.P. (1996–); Producer, Doing Business Internationally, Inc. (1996–); Director of Market Development, Leaders Magazine (1994–1996); Assistant for Latin American Affairs, Center for Democracy, Washington DC (1994); Assignment Desk, WCVB–TV, Boston (1993); News Anchor & Producer, WDIS Radio (1993). **Education:** Georgetown University, B.S. in Foreign Service. **Personal:** Mr. Geishecker enjoys snow skiing, sailing, and getting away from the city.

Mr. Ronald N. Goldstein

Vice President
MacAndrews and Forbes
35 East 62nd Street
New York, NY 10021
(212) 572–8618
Fax: please mail or

6719

Business Information: MacAndrews and Forbes is an international holding company for Fortune 500 companies to include: Revlon, Coleman, National Health Labs, Marvel, and New World Entertainment. As Vice President of the Firm, Mr. Goldstein is responsible for the administration of all merger and acquisition functions for the Firm. Established in 1975, MacAndrews and Forbes, with offices located across the U.S., employs over 50,000 persons and reports estimated revenue in excess of $4 billion. **Career Steps:** MacAndrews and Forbes: Vice President (1984–Present), Director (1982–1984); Director, Pitney Bowes (1979–1982). **Associations & Accomplishments:** American Jewish Congress; Wharton Business School Alumni Association; YIVO, Eastern European Jewish Historical Society. **Education:** Wharton Graduate Business School, M.B.A. (1977); Stanford University, M.S. in Operations Research; City College of New York, B.S. **Personal:** Married to Olgo in 1982. Two children: Carrie and Dara.

Samir Gustavo Jerez

Chief Executive Officer and General Partner
Go 2 Group
P.O. Box 700731
Miami, FL 33170–0731
(305) 235–6183
Fax: (305) 235–6146

6719

Business Information: Go 2 Group is the general holding company for diversified medical commercial trade and ethnic business ventures. Entities include as follows: Bio–Behavioral Corporation — a pain and stress management services clinic; Bio–Behavioral International Seminars — provides training and counseling seminars throughout the world; The 9th Wave — a facsimile broadcast operation focused on marketing and research; Ink Master Studios — professional skin artistry studio and cosmetic surgery. As Chief Executive Officer and General Partner, Mr. Jerez serves in executive roles for all entities of the organization. A specialist in pain management and behavioral counseling, he focuses the majority of his time in managing the biofeedback and medical services entities of the Corporation. **Career Steps:** Chief Executive Officer and General Partner, Go 2 Group (1996–Present); Psychophysiologist and President, Bio–Behavioral Diagnostics & Rehab., Inc., Miami, FL (1994–1995); Psychologist, Austin Neurological Institute, P.A., Austin, TX (1993–1994); U.S. Marine Corps.: Sergeant (1986–1993), Press Chief – Community Relations Chief – Combat Photojournalist, MCAS El Toro, CA – Operation Desert Shield/Storm (1990–1993), Assistant to Chaplain – Collateral Duty (1986–1993), Defense Information School (1990), Data Processing Chief, MCB Camp Pendleton (1986–1990). **Associations & Accomplishments:** Psi Chi National Honor Society; Pepperdine University Alumni Association; National University Alumni Association; Association for Muslim Social Scientists; American Counseling Association; American Rehabilitation Counseling Association; Association for Applied Psychophysiology and Biofeedback; American Pain Society; Disabled American Veterans Association; Greater South Dade Chamber of Commerce; National Youth Sports Coaches Association; YMCA; American Mental Health Counselors Association; Association for Assessment in Counseling; Association for Multicultural Counseling & Development; Association for Specialists in Group Work; Association for Spiritual, Ethical, Religious & Value Issues in Counseling; Military Educators and Counselors Association; Biofeedback Society of Texas; Community Health Services – Miami, FL; Florida Department of Vocational Rehabilitation, Tallahassee, FL; Volunteer: Mental Health Care – Extended Care Unit at Austin State Hospital, Project Together – Orange County Mental Health Care Agency, Group Home Worker with Cerebral Palsy Association; Numerous presentations and publications on Islamic writings, psychological theories and Islamic discrimination; Fluent in English and Spanish; AWARDS: Meritorious Unit Commendation (2); Good Conduct Medal; National Defense Service Medal; Rifle Expert (4th Award); Pistol Expert; Secretary of the Navy–Letter of Commendation; Certificate of Appreciation (15). **Education:** Pepperdine University, M.A. in Psychology; National University, B.A. in Behavioral Science (1992); National University, A.A. in General Studies (1988); Robert Morgan Vocational Technical Institute, C.C. in Criminal Justice (1981); Post–Graduate Training: Miami Pain & Stress Clinic, Biofeedback Internship (1994); University of Houston – Victoria, Counseling–Education Practicum (1994); Austin Neurological Institute, P.A., Psychology Internship (1993–1994); Extensive courses and seminars taken for career counseling and pain assessment studies.

Mark S. Joseph

President
The MJM Entertainment Group
P.O. Box 1731
Los Angeles, CA 90637–1731
(310) 921–1330
Fax: (310) 921–1338
EMAIL: See Below

6719

Business Information: The MJM Entertainment Group, originally formed as Pacific Promotions, is an international multi–media holding company, owning television and radio production interests, recording industries, and book publication concerns throughout Japan. Entity holdings include: MJM Entertainment, MJM Broadcasting, MJM Records, MJM Associates, and Renaissance Recordings. MJM Entertainment has produced numerous special programs for NHK Television in addition to its work with all of the major Japanese television networks. MJM Records releases have included releases by American rock acts such as Jet Circus, Magdallan, Mozart, Angelica, Recon, Ken Tamplin, Holy Soldier, Jon Gibson and others. 1993 found the release of MJM's first U.S.

record by the rock group Tamplin. The son of American missionaries living in Japan, Mark Joseph grew up in an ordinary Japanese neighborhood. Thanks to his Japanese playmates and a near addiction to Japanese television, by the age of four he was speaking fluent Japanese. Beginning his career as a print journalist writing a column on American music for Japanese magazines at the age of thirteen and moving into the radio/television career at the age of fifteen, his career in television began upon signing with the Bazaar Talent agency in Tokyo, working in numerous television programs and commercials. He has served as a television anchor with the CNN–owned Turner Entertainment Report, which then led to his appointment as host/producer of a new interview program for the Japanese television network NHK in 1994. With a viewership of 10 million, this program features one–on–one interviews with American cultural figures such as Los Angeles Mayor Richard Riordan, Broadcaster Larry King, Actor Charlton Heston, and Comedian Jay Leno among others. While still in college, Mark formed Pacific Promotions with the goal of introducing new U.S. artists to the Japanese market, and assisting in the production of Japanese record and television projects in the U.S. In 1991, Pacific Promotions became MJM Entertainment Group Inc. Currently, Mark is hosting and producing the NHK television program, developing a television program for Korean television stations KBS and SBS, and continuing to develop MJM Records. Internet users can also reach him via: 72263.1561.compuserve. **Career Steps:** President, The MJM Entertainment Group (formerly known as – Pacific Promotions) (1988–Present); News Commentator, Tokyo FM (1993–Present); Television Talk Show Host, NHK (Japan Broadcasting) (1994–Present); Anchor, CNN– Turner Entertainment (1992–1994); Entertainment News Anchor (1992–1994); News Commentator, FM Yokuhama (1991–1993). **Associations & Accomplishments:** Board of Directors, Reap Missions Inc.; Profiled in 350 newspapers worldwide. **Education:** Biola University, B.A. in Communications, with radio, television, film emphasis (1990) **Personal:** Mr. Joseph enjoys basketball, baseball, rollerblading, travel, and long walks.

Mr. Thomas E. Kohut

Vice President and Controller

Meridian Sports Incorporated

625 Madison Avenue
New York, NY 10022
(212) 527–4421
Fax: (212) 527–4094

6719

Business Information: Meridian Sports Incorporated is a publicly–held company which markets and manufactures active recreation products in the marine recreation field. Entities include: Master Craft boats, O'Brien waterski products and scuba equipment. Meridian Sports, reports annual revenue of approximately $100 million and currently employs 800 people. Sixty–five percent of Meridian Sports is owned by MacAndrews & Forbes Group. As Vice President and Controller, Mr. Kohut is responsible for all aspects of operations focusing primarily on acquisitions, divestitures and financings, as well as the Company's 1994 IPO. **Career Steps:** Vice President and Controller, Meridian Sports Incorporated (1993–Present); Assistant Controller, MacAndrews & Forbes Group (1987–1993); Senior Auditor, Ernst & Young (1984–1987). **Education:** Lehigh University, B.S. (1984). **Personal:** Married to Rita Iannicelli in 1991. Mr. Kohut enjoys bicycling, hiking and traveling.

Tim K. Light

Director of Planning & Analysis

CSW International, Inc.

1616 Woodall Rodgers Freeway
Dallas, TX 75202
(214) 777–1749
Fax: (214) 777–1700

6719

Business Information: CSW International, Inc. is the subsidiary of Central and Southwest Corporation involved in the electric power industry outside of the United States. As Director of Planning & Analysis, Mr. Light is responsible for development and negotiation of electric power project agreements. **Career Steps:** Director of Planning & Analysis, CSW International, Inc. and CSW Energy, Inc. (1994–Present); Fifteen years of electric power industry experience, primarily in contract negotiation and strategy development. **Personal:** Mr. Light enjoys golf and water sports.

Tony Lloyd

Chief Financial Officer

Targus Group International, Inc.

6180 Valley View Street
Buena Park, CA 90620–1030
(714) 523–5429
Fax: (714) 661–4135

6719

Business Information: Targus Group International, Inc. is a holding company for groups designing and marketing carrying cases (vinyl and leather) for electronic equipment and portable computers. As Chief Financial Officer, Mr. Lloyd is responsible for the financial operations of the Company, including accounting and taxes. **Career Steps:** Chief Financial Officer, Targus Group International, Inc. (1993–Present); Financial Analyst, WPP Group PLC (1992–1993); Group Finance Director, McColl Group International PLC (1988–1992); Audit Manager, Arthur Andersen (1982–1988). **Associations & Accomplishments:** Institute of Chartered Accountants of England and Wales. **Education:** Liverpool University – England, Bachelor of Commerce (1982). **Personal:** Married to Fiona in 1983. Two children: Peter and Alastair. Mr. Lloyd enjoys soccer, squash, reading and travel.

June Mullins

Comptroller

Burmont, Inc.

7150 Gantt Access Road
Azle, TX 76020–5638
(817) 444–2516
Fax: (817) 444–5443

6719

Business Information: Burmont, Inc. is a holding company primarily engaged in owning and operating nursing homes, assisted living complexes, and commercial cattle operations. Established in 1964, the Company operates five nursing homes, one assisted living complex, and 700– 800 head of cattle, destined for slaughter. Plans for the future include the building of two more nursing homes and an additional assisted care facility. As Comptroller, Ms. Mullins oversees a multi–corporation complex. She is responsible for all accounting, financing, and related administration, including budget, payroll, taxes, and accounts payable and receivable. **Career Steps:** Burmont, Inc.: Comptroller (1995–Present), Chief Accountant (1989–1995), Office Manager/Accountant (1985–1989). **Associations & Accomplishments:** Mayor Pro–tem, City of Azle (1995–Present); City Council Place 5, City of Azle (1994–Present); Past President, Azle Chamber of Commerce; Past President, Azle Ambassador. **Education:** Henderson State University; American Institute of Management. **Personal:** One child: Kenneth White. Ms. Mullins enjoys reading and being an aerobics instructor.

William J. Opper

Chairman and Chief Executive Officer

Rattlesnake Holding Company, Inc.

3 Stamford Landing, Suite 130
Stamford, CT 06902
(203) 975–9455
Fax: (203) 975–7973

6719

Business Information: Rattlesnake Holding Company, Inc. is the management parent company for Southwestern Grill restaurants. Currently operating eight locations in Connecticut, New York and New Jersey, future plans include expanding throughout the U.S. With twenty–seven years expertise in the restaurant industry, Mr. Opper established the Corporation in 1992 and serves as Chairman and Chief Executive Officer. He is responsible for all aspects of operations, including administration, finances, sales, public relations, accounting, marketing, and strategic planning. A highly successful restauranteur, for the period spanning 1986 to 1991, he owned several well–known franchises, such as TGIF, Hard Rock Cafe, and Bennigans. **Career Steps:** Chairman and Chief Executive Officer, Rattlesnake Holding Company, Inc. (1992–Present); President, Atlantic Professional Resources, Inc., d.b.a. APuerto Rico (1988–1992); Executive Vice President of Marketing, NCI Foodservice, Inc. (1982–1988). **Associations & Accomplishments:** National Restaurant Association; Published in Business Week and the Boston Globe Financial. **Education:** St. Bonaventure University, B.A. (1966). **Personal:** Married to Anne Johnson–Opper in 1995. Mr. Opper enjoys travel, sailing and scuba diving.

Ricardo P. Pacheco

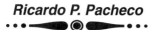

Legal Advisor

Merci–Coop of Puerto Rico

Urb El Vedado 211 Padre Las Casas
San Juan, Puerto Rico 00918–3003
(809) 736–4553
Fax: (809) 736–4563

6719

Business Information: Merci–Co–op of Puerto Rico is the management holding company for diversified financial and retail concerns throughout Puerto Rico. Entities include credit union operations, drug stores and convenience store gas stations. A practicing attorney in Puerto Rico courts since 1993, Mr. Pacheco joined Merci–Coop of Puerto Rico in 1994. Serving as Legal Advisor, he provides legal counsel to the President and represents the Credit Union in all legal matters. **Career Steps:** Legal Advisor, Merci–Coop of Puerto Rico (1994–Present); Legal Advisor, Right to Employment Administration (1992–1994). **Education:** Interamerican University School of Law, J.D. (1993); University of Puerto Rico B.A. in Political Sciences and Labor Relations. **Personal:** Married to Astrid O'Neill in 1990. One child: Ricardo Jose Pacheco O'Neill. Mr. Pacheco enjoys music, baseball, tennis, basketball, and reading.

Mr. Stan C. Pennock

Vice President of Operations

Redley Enterprises Inc.

13635 Bel–Red Road
Bellevue, WA 98005
(206) 641–1104
Fax: (206) 643–2883

6719

Business Information: Redley Enterprises Inc. is the management holding company for twelve (12) McDonald's restaurant franchises in the Bellevue, Washington and surrounding communities. As Vice President of Operations, Mr. Pennock has the direct responsibility for the administration and oversight of seven (7) of the Company's twelve franchises. Established in 1975, Redley Enterprises Inc. employs over 600 persons and has annual revenues in excess of $20 million. **Career Steps:** Vice President of Operations, Redley Enterprises Inc. (1975–Present); Hourly Manager, McDonald's Corporation (1972–1975). **Associations & Accomplishments:** Chamber of Commerce of Auburn, WA; Chamber of Commerce of Kent, WA; Seattle Ronald McDonald House; Sponsor, Washington State Special Olympics. **Education:** Shoreline Community College (1977); Shoreline High School (1976) .

Richard Romer

First Vice President

Calista Corporation

601 West 5th Avenue, Suite 200
Anchorage, AK 99501–2226
(907) 279–5516
Fax: (907) 272–5060

6719

Business Information: Calista Corporation, an Alaska Native Corporation, is the second largest of the twelve regional corporations formed under the Alaska Native Claims Settlement Act of December 18, 1971, functioning as a business corporation and land holding company. Calista, designated as a minority–owned enterprise, is a for–profit corporation, concentrating on investing in businesses and developing its land and resources granted to it under the Alaska Native Claims Settlement Act, as well as earning revenues for the benefit of Calista shareholders. The Calista Corporation headquarters are located in Anchorage, Alaska, with a satellite office located within the Calista Region in Bethel, Alaska. Its land holdings total more than 6.5 million acres of subsurface estate and 250,000 acres of surface estate. Calista also has numerous active business enterprises and subsidiaries, including: Yulista Management Services, d.b.a. Village Management Services, providing business and consulting services; Bilista Contractors, Inc., d.b.a. Calista Enterprises, a business entity capable of pursuing and completing construction projects in Southwest Alaska; Tunista Properties, Inc., a holding and investment company which includes contract management and real estate holdings; Ookichista Drilling Services, Inc., d.b.a. Calista Well Services, Inc. a joint venture of Nordic Well Servicing, Inc. and Calista Corporation, forming Nordic–Calista Well Services, Inc., providing work–over and completion services at the Prudhoe Bay oil fields; Ilakista Ventures, Inc., a holding company for various joint ventures and businesss partnerships; and Bista Expediting Service, a provider of camp and expediting services to support rural mineral exploration camps and camp services to mining companies. As

First Vice President, Mr. Romer assists the President in developing and seeking new corporate development opportunities, including new investments and new business ventures. **Career Steps:** Calista Corporation: First Vice President (1995–Present), Special Assistant of Rural Affairs, Office of the Governor (1991–94); Principal, Romer & Associates (1988–91). **Associations & Accomplishments:** Board Member, Bethel Native Corporation; Junior Achievement Statewide Boad; Resource Development Council. **Education:** University of Alaska – Fairbanks (1974). **Personal:** Three children: Jennifer, Brandy, and Roxanna. Mr. Romer enjoys golf, hunting, and fishing.

Myron J. Salz

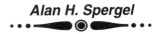

Controller
Rochester Economy Lodging
501 6th Avenue, NW
Rochester, MN 55901–2673
(507) 288–7069
Fax: (507) 288–4335
6719

Business Information: Rochester Economy Lodging is a hotel management holding company, overseeing a total of thirteen hotels with 970 rooms and 250 employees located throughout the regional area of Rochester, Minnesota. A Certified Public Accountant with seven years of experience, Mr. Salz joined Rochester Economy Lodging as Controller in 1994. He is responsible for all finance and accounting functions for thirteen hotels, including cash flow, statistics, financial correspondence, financial reporting, and spending authorizations. **Career Steps:** Controller, Rochester Economy Lodging (1994–Present); Senior Accountant, Smith, Schafer & Associates (1991–1994); Staff Accountant, Coffman, Nehring & Christopherson (1989–1991). **Associations & Accomplishments:** American Institute of Certified Public Accountants; Minnesota Society of Cerfitied Public Accountants; Institute of Management Accountants, Inc. **Education:** St. Mary's University, B.A. in Accounting and Finance (1989). **Personal:** Married to Michelle in 1993. One child: Abigail. Mr. Salz enjoys golf, basketball, and hunting.

Ray E. Sanchez

Safety Director
Kort Investment
P.O. Box 15007
Casa Grande, AZ 85230
(520) 836–8228
Fax: (520) 421–0832
6719

Business Information: Kort Investment is an international holding company for a variety of companies, such as: Arizona Grain, Inc. (grains), Eagle Milling Company, Inc. (feeds), VALPAR (research), and VERCO Manufacturing Company (steel fabricators). As Safety Director, Mr. Sanchez is responsible for traveling to all subsidiaries to inspect for safety and to certify employees. He gets involved with all safety issues from the ground up. Milestones include helping set up government standards in the decontamination of plants. **Career Steps:** Safety Director, Kort Investment (1996–Present); Corporate Safety Manager, Eagle Milling Company, Inc. (1996); Safety/Environmental, Strick Corporation (1990–1996); Safety–Matt Team, Frito–Lay (1985–1990). **Associations & Accomplishments:** National Safety Council; Arizona State Safety Engineer; Herpetology (study of reptiles – lizards). **Education:** Pima College (1993–1996); Attended Arizona State Environmental Technology Training Center. **Personal:** Married to Deborah in 1985. Two children: Shannan and Shelby. Mr. Sanchez enjoys studying reptiles.

Alan H. Spergel

President
Mandelbaum Spergel Group
505 Consumers Road
North York, Ontario M2J 4V8
(416) 497–1660 Ext. 128
Fax: (416) 494–7199
EMAIL: See Below
6719

Business Information: Mandelbaum Spergel Group is a holding company comprised of three main divisions: Mandelbaum and Partners, a chartered accounting firm; Mandelbaum Spergel Inc., a personal bankruptcy holding firm; and Spergel and Associates, a strategic planning firm specializing in advisory services, consulting, liquidation, forensic accounting, and mediation. Established in 1987, the Company employs 35 people and has estimated annual revenue of $3 million. As President, Mr. Spergel oversees all aspects of the Company. He is responsible for administration, operations, finance, sales, public relations, marketing, and strategic planning. Internet users can reach him via: spergel@trustee.com. **Career Steps:** President, Mandelbaum Spergel Group (1987–Present). **Associations & Accomplishments:** President, York District Chartered Accountants Association; Canadian Insolvency Practitioners Association Task Force; Re Amendments to the Bankruptcy and Insolvency Act; Director, Wishbone Foundation; Board of Trustees: Toronto Area Discussion Group, Community Hebrew Academy of Toronto; Author of various articles that have been published. **Education:** University of Guelph, Bachelors of Communications (1976); CA; C.F.E.; C.I.P. **Personal:** Married to Julie in 1976. One child: Gillian. Mr. Spergel enjoys bicycling, squash, tennis, and rollerblading.

Mr. Henry R. Szabo

Chief Financial Officer
Private Corporations
37 East Hudson Street
Columbus, OH 43202
(614) 447–9100
Fax: (614) 447–9119
6719

Business Information: Mr. Szabo controls all financial aspects of three corporations, to include the oversight of personnel matters and supervisory management. One company, formed in 1993, is a professional waste management firm that negotiates with waste haulers for the most financially feasible service contracts and consolidation of billings and services. It specializes in serving major retail establishments, and industrial clientele across the U.S. (e.g., drug stores, restaurants). The second company, established in 1987, is a franchise of a national restaurant company (Rally's). It currently operates 78 restaurants, mainly in Ohio, employing over 2,200 people. The third company, established in 1993, is a franchise of a national pizza company (Papa John's). It currently operates 9 restaurants in South Florida. **Career Steps:** Chief Financial Officer, Private Corporations (1992–Present); Vice President of Finance, Rax Restaurants, Inc. (1983–1992); Senior Auditor, Deloitte–Touche (1978–1983); Specialist 5, U.S. Army (1972–1975). **Education:** Ohio University, B.A. in Accounting (1978); Terra Technical Institute, Fremont, OH, A.A. in Accounting (1972).

Richard Tyler

Chief Executive Officer
Tyler International, Inc. – Family of Companies and Services
P.O. Box 630249
Houston, TX 77273–0249
800–800–EXCEL
Fax: (713) 974–2672
6719

Business Information: Tyler International, Inc. – Family of Companies and Services is the corporate management company which include Richard Tyler International, Inc. – providing education, consulting, marketing, and seminars; Tyler International Travel – specializing in domestic and international travel; Food Brokers International, Inc. – a brokerage, distribution, and marketing company; Smart Business Strategies (TM) – a small business consulting firm; Leadership for Tomorrow (TM) – provides youth education programs; and EXCELLENCE EDGE (TM) – providing personal and professional products. As Chief Executive Officer, Mr. Tyler is responsible for all aspects of Company operations. **Career Steps:** Chief Executive Officer, Tyler International, Inc. – Family of Companies and Services (Present); Vice President of Sales and Marketing, Superior Bedrooms; Vice President of Sales and Marketing, ARC Publishing. **Associations & Accomplishments:** Outstanding Young Men in America (1984); Member, Republic Senatorial Inner Circle (1991); Who's Who Worldwide of Global Business Leaders; Who's Who in American Education; Who's Who in Executives and Professionals; Member, International Platform Association; Member, American Society for Training and Development; Member, National Speakers Association. **Personal:** Mr. Tyler enjoys sports, theater, deep–sea fishing, and amateur wrestling.

Mr. Rong Yang

Chairman and President
Brilliance China Automotive Holdings, Ltd. (NYSE listed company)
65–F Bank of China Tower
1 Garden R, Hong Kong
(852) 523–7227
Fax: (852) 526–8472
6719

Business Information: Brilliance China Automotive Holdings, Ltd. owns and manages several rapidly growing corporations in China. The company is listed on the New York Stock Exchange (since October 9, 1992) and is registered with the U.S. Securities and Exchange Commission as well as being registered in Bermuda as a holding company. Operating companies produce minibuses, heavy–duty and medium– duty trucks, bulldozers, excavators and road rollers in China. In his current capacity, Mr. Yang manages the operations for the entire company. Established in 1992, Brilliance China Automotive Holdings, Ltd. (NYSE listed company) presently employs 10,000 people and has an estimated annual revenue in excess of $235 million (U.S.). **Career Steps:** Chairman and President, Brilliance Group Holdings (1990–Present); Chairman and General Manager, Broadsino Finance Company, Ltd. (1988–1990); Director and Vice President, Broadsino Industries (1985–1988). **Associations & Accomplishments:** Adjunct Professor, Finance Institute of China; Deputy Director of Research, Center for Special Economic Zones in China; Executive Director and Vice Chairman of the Chinese Financial Education Development Foundation; Academic Advisor to the ++++Economist++++ (China). **Education:** South West University of Finance, China, Ph.D. (1994).

Richard C. Agnew

Chief Executive Officer
ARC Capital Management
977 Albion Street
San Diego, CA 92106
(602) 588–8207
Fax: (602) 588–8207
EMail: See Below
6722

Business Information: ARC Capital Management provides international money management services. Mr. Agnew started this Company in 1995 because he enjoyed the challenge of running his own company. As Chief Executive Officer, he manages and advises clients regarding pension funds on international equity and capital markets. Internet users can reach him via: AGNEWRC@t–bird.edu. **Career Steps:** Chief Executive Officer, ARC Capital Management (1995–Present); Associate, NatWest Capital Markets (1994); Sales Associate, LGT Capital Management (1991–1994). **Associations & Accomplishments:** California Foreign Affairs Association; Thunderbird Investment and Finance Club; Boys Club of San Diego; Everyone is a Reader/Rollins Reader. **Education:** The American Graduate School of International Management – Thunderbird, M.I.M. (1997); University of California – Los Angeles: B.A. in International Economics, Minor in International Studies, Minor in French. **Personal:** Mr. Agnew enjoys tennis, golf, soccer, art history, and philosophy.

Thelma Alane

Market Representative
Insight Capital Research and Management, Inc.
225 Coggins Drive
Pleasant Hill, CA 94523
(510) 274–5000
Fax: Please mail or call
6722

Business Information: Insight Capital Research and Management, Inc. provides investment management services to individuals, corporations, and institutions. As Market Representative, Ms. Alane specializes in providing investment services to clients. Concurrently, she is a General Partner of Sword Play Enterprises, a private competitive fencing school where she manages daily operations, coaches juniors, and promotes fencing in the local community. She is also in the process of creating a non–profit foundation that relies on sports to provide self–confidence to children and adults. **Career Steps:** Market Representative, Insight Capital Research and Management, Inc. (1996–Present); General Partner, Sword Play Enterprises (1988–Present); Investment Specialist, Charles Schwab and Co., Inc. (1993–1996). **Associations & Accomplishments:** United States Fencing Association; National Association of Securities Dealers; Mentioned in New York Times Article for excellent service to special needs customers. **Education:** Georgetown University, B.S. in Foreign Service (1980); Humanistic Hypnosis Center, Master Hypnotist and Hypnotherapist (1988). **Personal:** Married to George in 1990. Ms. Alane is a nationally ranked fencing athlete. She also enjoys computer programming.

Stephen A. Bradley

Chairman and Chief Executive Officer
Bradley Int'l Group Inc.
1605 Lucas Valley Road
San Rafael, CA 94903
(415) 472–0750
Fax: (415) 499–8484
E–mail: see below
6722

Business Information: Bradley Int'l Capital is an investment management company utilizing a value style that manages portfolios on a fee only basis for high net worth individuals and institutions. Bradley Capital is also a Special Limited Partner of Millenium Technology partners which invest in private companies that develop computer software and technology in the USA and Europe. Currently, Mr. Bradley is Senior Vice President, investments with Dean Witter. In his present position he advises individuals and institutional investors. He can also be reached through the Internet as follows: sbrad64103@aol.com **Career Steps:** Chief Executive Officer, Bradley Int'l Group, Inc. – Special Limited Partner Millenium Technology Investment Fund, LP (1996–Present); Dean Witter: Senior Vice President and Investment Manager (1993–1996), Senior Vice President and District Manager (1976–1993); Institutional Sales, Merrill Lynch (1971–1976); Board of Directors, Hillsdale Group (1980–Present); UDI Software (1995–Present). **Associations & Accomplishments:** Board, Family Service, Marin Symphony Vincents; Association of Investment Consultants; Rotary International. **Education:** Wharton Business School – University of Pennsylvania; University of San Francisco, B.S. (1988); San Jose State University. **Personal:** Married to Kathleen H. in 1969. One child: Stephen Jr. Mr. Bradley enjoys tennis, skiing, sailing, fox hunting, running, and restoring antique foreign cars.

Mr. William N. Brown

Senior Vice President, Chief Financial Officer and Treasurer
American Capital Management & Research, Inc.
2800 Post Oak Boulevard
Houston, TX 77056
(713) 993–4261
Fax: (713) 993–4360

6722

Business Information: American Capital Management & Research, Inc. is a full–service mutual fund management and service company, serving Fortune 500 companies and other business concerns with open–end funding. National in scope, the Firm has offices in Kansas City, KS and Houston, TX. As Senior Vice President, Chief Financial Officer and Treasurer, Mr. Brown is responsible for all aspects of the company, particularly focusing in the areas of technical components, portfolios, investment trust, retail distribution, and shareholder services. Established in 1926, American Capital Management & Research, Inc. employs 500–700 people. **Career Steps:** Senior Vice President, Chief Financial Officer and Treasurer, American Capital Management & Research, Inc. (1988–Present); Assistant Controller, Gordon Jewelry (1986–1988); Manager of Financial Report, Sonat (Birmingham & Houston) (1975–1986). **Associations & Accomplishments:** M.B.A.; C.P.A; C.M.A. **Education:** University of Alabama, M.B.A. Degree of Finance (1985); Auburn University, B.S. Degree of Accounting. **Personal:** Married to Julee. One child: William N. Brown Jr.

Ms. Agnes J. Bundy

Sr. Vice President & Director of Corporate Community Development
Fleet Financial Group
50 Kennedy Plaza, 16th Floor
Providence, RI 02906
(401) 278–6783
Fax: (401) 278–3278

6722

Business Information: Fleet Financial Group is a $48 billion diversified financial services company listed on the New York Stock Exchange (NYSE–FLT) with approximately 1,200 offices nationwide. Its lines of business include commercial and consumer banking, mortgage banking, consumer finance, asset–based lending, equipment leasing,investment management, and student loan processing. In her capacity as Senior Vice President and Director of Corporate Community Development, Ms. Bundy manages all corporate community development, specifically an $8 billion three year venture called Fleet INCITY. Established in 1791, Fleet Financial Group employs over 21,000 people and reports annual revenue in excess of $48 billion. **Career Steps:** Senior Vice President and Director of Corporate Community Development, Fleet Financial Group (1993–Present); Counsel, U.S. Budget Committee (1989–1993); Law Clerk, Miller, Cassidy, Larroca & Lewin (1987–1989); Manager, Congressional Liaison, Fairchild Republic Company (1984–1987). **Associations & Accomplishments:** American Bar Association; Pennsylvania Bar Association; Bar of Supreme Court of Pennsylvania; Women's Bar Association of District of Columbia; Washington Lawyers for the Arts; Chair, Nominating Committee, Alumni Association of Smith College; Advisory Board Member, Dorcas Place Literacy Center; Trustee, National Conference of Christians & Jews; Camp Atwater Capital Campaign Committee Member; MLLE Career Board Member. **Education:** Georgetown University Law Center, J.D. (1989); Smith College, B.A. (1979).

Mr. Franklin A. Burke

President and Treasurer and Senior Partner
Venture Securities Corporation and Burke, Lawton, Brewer & Burke
926 Bethlehem Pike, P.O. Box 150
Flourtown, PA 19319
(215) 836–7200
Fax: (215) 836–1098

6722

Business Information: Venture Securities Corporation is an investment management company, and Burke, Lawton, Brewer & Burke is an investment securities firm. Mr. Burke is Director of Research and Portfolio Management at both companies. Venture Securities Corporation was established in 1971. Burke, Lawton, Brewer & Burke was founded in 1964. The Companies employs a staff of 19 and report revenues in excess of $22 million. **Career Steps:** President and Treasurer, Venture Securities Corporation (1971–Present); Senior Partner, Burke, Lawton, Brewer & Burke (1964–Present); Director of Contract Management and Pilot, U.S. Air Force, American Embassy London (1962–1964). **Associations & Accomplishments:** Treasurer, Board of Trustees, Williamson School; Board of Trustees, Lancaster Theological Seminary; Board of Trustees, Wyncote Church Home; Chairman, Investment Committee, Pennsylvania Southeast Conference; Board of Trustees, Upper Perkiomen Manor; President, Omega Institute. **Education:** London School of Economics, University of London (1962–1964); University of Colorado School of Management, M.B.A. (1960); Kansas State University, B.S. in Business and Finance.

Luiz A. Cardoso

Executive Manager
Sao Paulo Corporation
5850 Lakehurst Drive, Suite 150–25
Orlando, FL 32819–8386
(407) 248–3414
Fax: (407) 248–3415
EMAIL: See Below

6722

Business Information: Sao Paulo Corporation is an international venture investment firm, serving executive clientele in the U.S. and Brazil in venture trading venues involving all areas of industrial, financial and real property investments counsel. With ten years expertise in financial and international trade markets, Mr. Cardoso founded Sao Paulo Corporation in 1995. Serving as Executive Manager, he provides the overall vision and strategies to keep the Corporation a viable and quality concious firm; also serving as counsel to major clientele — primarily in financial investments areas. Mr. Cardoso can also be reached through the Internet via: 74763,625.compuserv **Career Steps:** Executive Manager, Sao Paulo Corporation (1995–Present); Chief Executive Officer, PreviPlan Investments, Inc. USA (1994–1995); Dealing Desk Manager, West L/B – Bank (Brazil) (1988–1994); Branch Manager, Crefisul Bank (Citibank associate in Brazil) (1987–1988). **Associations & Accomplishments:** Treasurer, USA–Brazilian of Central Florida; The Brazilian American Chamber of Commerce; International Association of Professional Financial Consultants, Inc.; Brazilian Economic Accreditation Council **Education:** Catholic University of Sao Paulo, M.B.A. (1991); MacKenzie University, Sao Paulo, Brazil, B.S. in Economics (1982). **Personal:** Four children: Flaviana, Luiz Gustavo, Jennifer and Janaina F. Mr. Cardoso enjoys chess and walking.

Linda M. Corujo–Ramsey

Financial Planner
Successful Money Management
35 Calle Mayaquez
Hato Rey, Puerto Rico 00917–4917
(809) 754–7487
Fax: (809) 754–7494

6722

Business Information: Successful Money Management specializes in financial planning concentrating mainly on money and risk management for both private individuals and corporate clientele throughout Puerto Rico. As Financial Planner, Mrs. Corujo–Ramsey locates equity investment opportunities in private companies. She also serves as coordinator and trainer for financial planning seminars sponsored by the firm. **Career Steps:** Financial Planner, Successful Money Management (1987–Present). **Associations & Accomplishments:** International Association of Financial Planners; Woman of the Year, San Juan City (1992–1993). **Education:** University of Puerto Rico. **Personal:** Married to Wilton I. Perez in 1995. She enjoys reading, tennis and horseback riding during her leisure time.

Sergio Langarica

Treasurer
Four X Corporation
5479 Penfield Avenue
Woodland Hills, CA 91364
(818) 888–2169
Fax: (818) 888–6158

6722

Business Information: Four X Corporation is a foreign currency investment consulting company, buying and selling currency on an international level, and offering consultation services to clients on the business of hedging and risk management protecting businesses and individuals from currency fluctuation. As Treasurer, Mr. Langarica is responsible for buying and selling, recruiting international corporations, foreign currency trading, and consulting. **Career Steps:** Treasurer, Four X Corporation (1996–Present); President, Mexico Business Promotion; Researcher, ITESM Center for Strategic Studies; International Projects, San Diego Economic Development Corporation. **Associations & Accomplishments:** National Society of Hispanic MBA's; Latin Business Association; Frente Juvenile Revelucionario; Published an Article for Mexican Research on Facing Realities. **Education:** ITESM Campus Guadalajaro, M.B.A. (1995); University of California – San Diego, B.A. Degree in Economics. **Personal:** Mr. Langarica enjoys yoga, mountain bicycling, hiking, and camping.

Tejinder Singh

Vice President
Unterberg Harris
10 East 50th Street, 22nd Floor
New York, NY 10001
(212) 572–8069
Fax: (212) 888–8678
EMAIL: See Below

6722

Business Information: Unterberg Harris specializes in investment banking, venture capital, and worldwide acquisitions and mergers of public companies. As Vice President, Mr. Singh provides investigations and research into companies, and eventually makes recommendations whether or not to buy or sell the companies. He also handles equity research and private venture investing. Internet users can reach him via: tsingh@unterberg.com. **Career Steps:** Vice President, Unterberg Harris (1995–Present); Marketing Project Manager, INTEL Corporation (1993); Senior Computer Engineer, Sun Microsystems (1991–1992). **Associations & Accomplishments:** Supervisory Committee, American Electronics Association Credit Union; Institute of Electrical and Electronics Engineers. **Education:** Northwestern University, M.B.A. (1994); University of Michigan – Ann Arbor, M.S. in Electrical Engineering; University of Roorkee, India, Bachelor of Electrical Engineering. **Personal:** Mr. Singh enjoys skiing, tennis, windsurfing, and travel.

Winston T. Wei

Agency Manager
Equitable
120 West 45th Street – 3rd Floor
New York, NY 10036
(212) 356–1900
Fax: (212) 356–1929

6722

Business Information: Equitable is a national distributor of variable life and annuity products, mutual funds, and other investment products and services. They also provide Financial Planning Fitness Strategies for personal markets, business markets, and estate planning. Mr. Wei is mainly responsible for hiring and developing top quality agents and District Managers. He is also responsible for financial supervision, budgetary concerns, employee relations, and client services. **Career Steps:** Equitable: Agency Manager (1996–Present), Senior District Manager (1984–1996), Agent (1978–1996). **Associations & Accomplishments:** Director, Philippine Chinese American Association; National Association of Life Underwriters; General Agents and Managers Association; Lifetime Member, Million Dollar Round Table; Equitable Hall of Fame; Equitable Distinguished Service Award. **Education:** Seton Hall University, B.S. in Business Administration (1978). **Personal:** Married to Angel in 1989. Mr. Wei enjoys basketball, tennis, and stamp collecting.

Ronald A. Adelhelm

Vice President of Finance and Chief Financial Officer
WLD Enterprises, Inc.
1 East Broward Boulevard, Suite 1101
Ft. Lauderdale, FL 33301–1872
(954) 523–7771
Fax: (954) 760–9845

6726

Business Information: WLD Enterprises, Inc. is an investment management firm with investments in marketable securities, income–producing real estate, and a management buy-out portfolio of operating companies. As Vice President of Finance and Chief Financial Officer, Mr. Adelhelm is responsible for all financial, treasury, tax reporting, risk management, and investment monitoring activities. **Career Steps:** Vice President of Finance and Chief Financial Officer, WLD Enterprises, Inc. (1995–Present); Vice President of Finance and Chief Financial Officer, KSL Florida Holdings, Inc. (1994–1995); Vice President of Finance and Chief Financial Officer, Mesa Holdings Corporation (1990–1994); Senior Manager, Arthur Andersen & Company (1981–1989). **Associations & Accomplishments:** American Institute of Certified Public Accountants; Board Member of Finance Committee, American Hotel & Motel Association. **Education:** San Diego State University, M.B.A. in Finance (1981); University of California at Los Angeles, B.A. in Economics (1979). **Personal:** Married to Heather in 1980. Two children: Stirling and Victoria. Mr. Adelhelm enjoys basketball, running, and watersports.

Tsilah B. Burman

Senior Research Director
Westmark Realty Advisors
865 S. Figueroa Street, Suite 3500
Los Angeles, CA 90017–2543
(213) 683–4200
Fax: (213) 683–4301

6726

Business Information: Westmark Realty Advisors, formally TCW Realty Advisors, works with companies interested in investing pension funds into commercial real estate. As Senior Research Director, Ms. Burman works with acquisition directors and portfolio managers giving strategic advice on properties and markets, developing strategic and business plans for new products and client marketing. **Career Steps:** Senior Research Director, Westmark Realty Advisors (1996–Present); Partner, TCW Realty Advisors (1986–1996); Real Estate Analyst, CB Commercial (1984–1986); Assistant Director, Hollywood Revitalization Committee (1980–1982). **Associations & Accomplishments:** Urban Land Institute; International Council of Shopping centers; Westside Urban Forum; Los Angeles Urban Consortium; Field Representative for California State Senator Herschel Rosenthal. Ms. Burman has been published in trade journals. **Education:** University of Southern California, Masters in Planning (1985); Brandeis University, B.A. in Politics (1979). **Personal:** Married to Jeff in 1987. Two children: Zipporah and Jacob. Ms. Burman enjoys being a Girl Scout leader and staying active.

Gregory V. Clarke

Executive Vice President
Washington Investment Corporation
1010 Wisconsin Avenue NW, Suite 300
Washington, DC 20007
(202) 342–7400
Fax: (202) 338–3521

6726

Business Information: Washington Investment Corporation is a full service investment firm specializing in the areas of business retirement plans and investment management consulting. As the Executive Vice President, Mr. Clarke oversees the Retirement Planning Group and the Consulting Services Division. Established in 1989, Washington Investment Corporation employs 38 people. **Career Steps:** Executive Vice President, Washington Investment Corporation (1989–Present); Financial Consultant, E.F. Hutton/Shearson Lehman Jutton (1986–1989); Municipal Bond Specialist, DeRand Investment (1985–1986). **Associations & Accomplishments:** Institute for Investment Management Consultants; Friends of the Kennedy Center. **Education:** Shephard College, B.S. in Business and Finance (1984); Accredited Investment Management Consultant **Personal:** Mr. Clarke enjoys golf, shooting, rock climbing and running.

Barry L. Dennis

Principal
Price Waterhouse
1801 K Street, NW
Washington, DC 20006
(202) 861–6265
Fax: (202) 296–2785

6726

Business Information: Price Waterhouse is one of the 'Big Six' financial investment and economic consultancy firms in the world, with branch firms located internationally. Dealing with major corporate clientele, products include investment, stocks, bonds and securities, financial accounting, group financing, taxation and administration. As Principal and a Partner with the Washington branch, Barry Dennis manages all domestic practice relations for the Finance and Economics Group. Established in 1850, Price Waterhouse employs in excess of 14,000 principals and administrative support worldwide people with annual sales of in excess of $2 billion. **Career Steps:** Principal, Price Waterhouse (1991–Present); Senior Manager, Price Waterhouse (1986–1991); Manager, Price Waterhouse (1984–1986). **Associations & Accomplishments:** National Economics Association; National Tax Association; Society of Government Economists. **Education:** University of Maryland, M.A. (1979); Ball State University, B.A. **Personal:** Married to Jo Ellen in 1974. Two children: William and Megan. Mr. Dennis enjoys sailing and biking.

Maureen Farrow, FCMC

Executive Vice President and Research Director
Loewen, Ondaatje, McCutcheon Limited
55 Avenue Road, Suite 250, Hazelton Lanes, East Tower
Toronto, Ontario M5R 3L2
(416) 964–4486
Fax: (416) 964–4490

6726

Business Information: Loewen, Ondaatje, McCutcheon Limited is an institutional brokerage firm. As Executive Vice President and Research Director, Ms. Farrow provides the overall vision and strategy for the Firm's continued success, as well as represents major clients in all areas of business investment and consumer trading ventures. During her career, she has specialized in applied economics, forecasting, and policy development. Her professional experience includes a wide range of engagements spanning 25 years and, in particular, she has acquired an in–depth knowledge of the consumer products sector, retailing, metals and minerals sector, steel industry, insurance industry, financial markets, telecommunications, real estate and construction. She is widely–recognized for her frequent public speaking engagements on global economic trends, the new economy, Canadian and regional economics, demographics, competitiveness and the environment. **Career Steps:** Executive Vice President and Research Director, Loewen, Ondaatje, McCutcheon Limited (1994–Present); Partner and Chief Economist, Coopers & Lybrand – Canada (1980–1992); President, C.D. Howe Institute (1987–1989). **Associations & Accomplishments:** Director, National Trustco, Inc.; Trustee, Imperial Oil's Pension and Savings Plans; Director, The Equitable Life Insurance Company; Director, Schnieider Corporation; Director, Dylex Limited; Director, Penreal Advisors Ltd.; Director, Canadian Chamber of Commerce; British North American Committee; C.D. Howe Policy Committee; Public Governor, Toronto Stock Exchange (1993–1994); Board Member (1985–1991), Social Sciences and Humanities Research Council of Canada; Ontario Round Table on the Environment and the Economy (1991); Current Member and Former President, Canadian Association of Business Economics; Current Member and Former President, Toronto Association of Business Economists; Fellow, Institute of Management Consultants. **Education:** Hull University, England, B.Sc. in Economics (1966); York University, Ontario, Post–graduate work.

Bruce C. Grant

Senior Vice President
Quorum Funding Corporation
1177 West Hastings Street, Suite 2415
Vancouver, British Columbia V6E 2K3
(604) 681–9048
Fax: (604) 685–9002

6726

Business Information: Quorum Funding Corporation is a private, equity investor in Canadian technology companies, as well as serving as a fund manager. Joining Quorum Funding Corporation as Senior Vice President in 1992, Mr. Grant is responsible for managing a portfolio of investments in the Western Canada market. **Career Steps:** Senior Vice President, Quorum Funding Corporation (1992–Present); Account Manager, Bank of Montreal (1988–1992); Project Engineer, Shaw Industries (1985–1987); Project Manager, Fording Coal Ltd. (1980–1985). **Associations & Accomplishments:** Association of Professional Engineers of Ontario; Director/President, Not–for–Profit Housing. **Education:** Queens University: M.B.A. (1988), B.Sc. (1979). **Personal:** Married to Dori Antolin in 1987. Mr. Grant enjoys golf, hockey, and skiing.

A. Javier Hamann

Economist
International Monetary Fund
700 19th, N.W.
Washington, DC 20431
(202) 623–4154
Fax: (301) 933–1749
EMail: See Below

6726

Business Information: International Monetary Fund is a diversified investment banking and securities firm, focusing on corporate finance, merchant banking, institutional research, trading, sales, capital management, and mutual fund administration, primarily for international entities. As Economist, Mr. Hamann directs all foreign financial assessment ventures and research reporting. Currently his strategy focus is targeting venture capital acquisitions in Italy and Greece. Internet users can reach him via: AHAMANN@IMF.ORG **Career Steps:** Economist, International Monetary Fund (1991–Present); Instructor, Boston University (1989–1991); Visiting Research Fellow, Grade – Lima, Peru (1989). **Associations & Accomplishments:** American Economist Association; Greenpeace. **Education:** Boston University: Ph.D. (1991), M.A. in Political Economy. **Personal:** Married to Pamela Henderson in 1990. Two children: Annika and Phoebe. Mr. Hamann enjoys soccer.

Todd W. Mugford

President
Milestone Financial Group, Inc.
175 Hegeman Avenue
Colchester, VT 05446
(802) 655–6515
Fax: (802) 656–6520

6726

Business Information: Milestone Financial Group, Inc. is an investment counseling concern established in 1996. The Group manages investments for companies and individuals, provides investment counseling, insurance sales, pension planning, retirement planning, financial counseling, and investment management. As President, Mr. Mugford is also the owner of the Firm and makes all major decisions regarding client accounts. He personally recruits, trains, evaluates, and counsels employees. Mr. Mugford develops and implements new techniques for marketing offered services, handles public relations, and does strategic planning. Other responsibilities include being up–to–date on changes in the investment market and on SEC regulations. **Career Steps:** President, Milestone Financial Group, Inc. (1996–Present); Advanced Sales, Vermont Benefit Planning Group (1990–1996); Sales Representative, Massachusetts Mutual (1985–1990); Shareholder/Manager, M & W Publishing (1984–1985). **Associations & Accomplishments:** Vermont Life Underwriters; Burlington Life Underwriters; National Association of Life Underwriters; First Baptist Church of Barre, Vermont. Mr. Mugford received several awards while in college and sales awards from employers. He has been published in several trade publications. **Education:** American International College A.I.C., B. A. (1984); Guardian Career Development, 1990); Massachusetts Mutual, 57th Career Development School. **Personal:** One child: Matthew Wayne. Mr. Mugford enjoys hunting, fishing, eating, skiing, and weightlifting.

Carl H. Otto

Managing Director
AMI Partners Inc.
1130 Sherbrooke Street, West, Suite 900
Montreal, Quebec H3A 2S7
(514) 286–4503
Fax: (514) 286–6145

6726

Business Information: AMI Partners Inc. is an investment counseling firm dealing with international corporate entities providing assistance with financial investment, pension, mutual funds, government and endowment funds. AMI has over 70 group locations, with partnerships in the United States, Canada, and Hong Kong. A Partner with the Firm since 1968, Mr. Otto currently serves as Managing Director for overall administration, as well as research consultant to major clients. Established in 1959, AMI Partners Inc. employs 70 people with annual sales of $10 million in assets worldwide. **Career Steps:** Managing Director, AMI Partners Inc. (1990–Present); Managing Director, AMI Asset Management International (1986–1990); Chairman, Montreal Investment Management, Inc. (1975–1986). **Associations & Accomplishments:** Former President and Current Member, Montreal Society of Financial Analysts; Member, Institute of Chartered Financial Analysts; Former Chairman and Current Member, Montreal Children's Hospital Foundation; Director, Montreal Children's

Hospital Corporation; Former Governor, McGill University Montreal Children's Hospital Research Institute. **Education:** University of Freiburg, West Germany: Doctorate in Law (1959), LL.B. (1955); Post graduate work carried out at the Bank for International Settlement, London Institute of Bankers and Oxford University; Institute of Chartered Financial Analysts, Virginia, CFA (1968). **Personal:** Married to Michaela C. in 1961. Three children: Christina H., Valerie B., and Caroline E. Mr. Otto enjoys history, time studies and farming.

Ross S. Rennie

Executive Vice President, Sales
Investors Group
447 Portage Avenue
Winnipeg, Manitoba R3C 3B6
(204) 956–8714
Fax: (204) 956–1446

6726

Business Information: Investors Group offers a wide range of financial services to clients. These services include tax preparation, mortgage funding, brokerage services, and insurance. Investment products offered include mutual funds, GIC's and certificates of deposit. Established in 1940, Investors Group estimates revenue of $7 billion and presently employs over 4,500 people throughout Canada. As Executive Vice President, Sales, Mr. Rennie is responsible for all management and administrative duties associated with the direction of the Company's sales force. He oversees development of sales techniques, develops compensation and recognition programs, monitors policy and procedure compliance, and develops training programs. Mr. Rennie is involved in planning for future increases in Company portfolios and the utilization of new business technologies. **Career Steps:** Investors Group: Executive Vice President, Sales (1996–Present), Senior Vice President, Ontario (1994–1996), Regional Vice President, Ontario (1991–1994); President, Rennie Consulting (1988–1991). **Associations & Accomplishments:** Board Member, "The Canadian Stage Company". Mr. Rennie has written a series a books on National Hockey League teams. **Education:** McMaster University, M.B.A. (1974); University of Toronto, B.A. (1967). **Personal:** Married to Patti Lee in 1977. Three children: Scott, Chad, and Adam. Mr. Rennie enjoys golf, reading, and walking.

Heidi S. Steiger

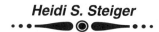

Individual Asset Management
Neuberger & Berman
605 Third Avenue
New York, NY 10158
(212) 476–5750
Fax: (212) 476–5757

6726

Business Information: Neuberger & Berman is an independent, entrepreneurial–minded investment advisory firm with more than a 55 year history in money management. As Individual Asset Manager, Ms. Steiger has oversight of the Individual Asset Management Group. Her Group is responsible for sales, marketing, client administration, and performance of individual and smaller institutional accounts having a minimum investment of $250,000. Other responsibilities include product development, budegtary concerns, strategic planning and overall management of a staff of 30 plus six branch offices. Concurrently, Ms. Steiger writes a regular column for "Physician's Financial News". **Career Steps:** Managing Director, Neuberger & Berman (1986–Present); Senior Vice President, Herzfeld & Stern (1983–1985); Director of Marketing, Fidelity Group (1977–1983). **Associations & Accomplishments:** Board Member, Foundation House; Board Member, The Children's Aid Society; Board Member, The Women's Campaign Fund; Business Committee and Major Gifts Committees of the Metropolitan Museum of Art; Financial Women's Association; Alumni Counseling Board Member, Columbia University. **Education:** Columbia University, M.B.A. in Finance (1985); Boston College, B.A. (Summa Cum Laude and Phi Beta Kappa) (1975). **Personal:** Married to Paul in 1985. Two children: Isabelle and William. Ms. Steiger enjoys skiing, tennis, piano, collecting art and is fluent in French.

Marycatherine Yeagley

Senior Vice President of Human Resources
GNA
601 Union Street, Suite 5600
Seattle, WA 98101
(206) 516–2880
Fax: (206) 516–2800

6726

Business Information: GNA is a wholly–owned subsidiary of GE Capital involved with investment products. The Company has over $40 billion in assets, over 3,500 employees located in Washington, California, Florida, and Virginia, and has regional offices throughout the United States. As Senior Vice President of Human Resources, Ms. Yeagley heads the human resource functions for all of their companies, including compensation, benefits, staffing, and compliance. She also does due diligence on all acquisitions. **Career Steps:** GNA: Senior Vice President of Human Resources (1995–Present), Vice President of Human Resources (1987–1995); Director of Human Resources, PACCAR, Inc. (1987–1994). **Associations & Accomplishments:** Society for Human Resource Management. **Education:** University of Washington, B.A. (1969); Northwestern University, Executive Program (1985). **Personal:** Ms. Yeagley enjoys racquetball and flowers.

Jenny C. Frayer

Vice President and Treasurer
University of Nevada Reno Foundation
Mail Stop 162
Reno, NV 89557
(702) 784–6622
Fax: (702) 784–1394

6732

Business Information: University of Nevada Reno Foundation, the fundraising arm of the University of Nevada Reno, administers all fund–raising activities and the dispersal of funds raised to be used for scholarships, research, and university programs. Established in 1981, the Foundation reports annual revenues of $10 million. As Vice President and Treasurer, Ms. Frayer is responsible for all financial, personnel, administration, accounting, legal matters, taxes, and aspects of the operations. She also handles all investments (up to $29 million) and reports to the Board of Trustees on all activities. **Career Steps:** Vice President and Treasurer, University of Nevada Reno Foundation (1990–Present); Associate Dean for Finance Administration, University of Nevada College of Agriculture (1982–1990); Audit Manager, Grant Thornton, CPA's (1977–1982). **Associations & Accomplishments:** American Institute of Certified Public Accountants; Nevada Society of Certified Public Accountants; Reno Wheelmen. **Education:** University of Nevada Reno: M.B.A. (1987), B.S. (1977). **Personal:** Ms. Frayer enjoys cycling, hiking, and cross–country skiing.

Elaine L. Gould

Project Coordinator
Massachusetts Caring for Children Foundation
P.O. Box 393
Lawrence, MA 01842–0793
(508) 681–4335
Fax: (617) 832–7616

6732

Business Information: Massachusetts Caring for Children Foundation is a charitable organization dedicated to children's healthcare. Programs include free health insurance and mobile medical unit programs. As Project Coordinator, Ms. Gould is responsible for the mobile medical unit offering free dental and medical exams to inner–city children in a predominantly Latino community. Ms. Gould handles the day–to–day administration of the medical unit including recruitment and scheduling of medical and dental providers, scheduling of children, selection of service locations, communication with school nurses to coordinate services, maintaining communication with community partners, healthcare providers and parents, referral follow–up, maintaining records, driving the vehicle, producing reports, and promoting programs with the community. **Career Steps:** Project Coordinator, MA Caring for Children Foundation (1995–Present); Health Educator, Greater Lawrence Family Health Center (1994–1995); Chief Polysomnographic Technician, Carlisle Hospital Sleep Disorders Center (1992–1993). **Associations & Accomplishments:** American Medical Technologists (1986–Present); Christian Service Corps Volunteer in Mexico and Guatemala (1982–1986). **Education:** Pennsylvania State University, M.Ed. in Health Education (1991); The King's College, B.S. (1981); The Academy of Medical Arts and Business, Medical Assistant diploma (1986). **Personal:** Ms. Gould enjoys hiking, camping, bicycling, skiing, reading, and foreign and domestic travel.

Wayne H. Koike

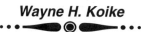

Director of Finance
CPMCF
3700 California Street, 1st Floor
San Francisco, CA 94118
(415) 750–2415
Fax: (415) 387–7817
EMAIL: See Below

6732

Business Information: CPMCF is the fund raising foundation for California Pacific Medical Center, the largest non–profit medical center in Northern California, with 1,000 registered beds. Responsible for raising approximately $8–12 million a year, the Foundation also advises potential benefactors on taxes and other issues. As Director of Finance, Mr. Koike oversees all financial and accounting operations for the Foundation. He is also responsible for information systems and handles all financial matters, including taxes, financial statements, and coordination of funding and fund–raising. Internet users may contact him via: harry53@aol.com. **Career Steps:** Director of Finance, CPMCF (1992–Present); Director of Finance/Controller, Bridgeway Plan for Health (1991–1992); Director of Financial Planning & Analysis, CIGNA Health Plan of Northern California (1990–1991); Controller, Take Care Corporation (1985–1990). **Associations & Accomplishments:** Association for Healthcare Philantrophy; Northern California Planned Giving Council; Sensei Organization. **Education:** Chicago State University, B.S. (1976); Sophia International University, Certificate in Japanese Studies. **Personal:** Married to Frances in 1985. Two children: Michelle and Melissa. Mr. Koike enjoys golf.

Lokelani Lindsey

Trustee
Kamehameha Schools Bishop Estate
P.O. Box 3466
Honolulu, HI 96801
(808) 523–6208
Fax: (808) 536–6895

6732

Business Information: Kamehameha Schools Bishop Estate is a non–profit educational trust with an established pre–school system and K–12 facilities. Comprised of 1,080 students in the pre–school level and 3,080 in grades K–12, its students come from all over Hawaii to a 600–acre campus on Oahu and two new 100–acre campuses on the islands of Maui and Hawaii. The Trust was established by Bernice Pauahi Bishop (1831–1884), a beloved Hawaiian princess. Awarding approximately $20 million in scholarships annually, the School has investments in the Upper Peninsula of Michigan, Goldman Sachs Co. in New York, a bank in China, and owns a golf course in Washington, D.C. Established in 1884, the Trust employs 1,350 people and has an estimated asset value in excess of $1.9 billion. Ms. Lindsey is one of five trustees who oversee all administrative, fiscal, and educational operations of the Trust. **Career Steps:** Trustee, Kamehameha Schools Bishop Estate (1993–Present); Superintendent of Education – Maui, State of Hawaii Department of Education (1982–1993); Kaimuki High School: Principal (1981–1982), Vice Principal (1977–1981), Teacher (1966–1977). **Associations & Accomplishments:** Trustee, Public Schools Foundation of Hawaii; Board Member, Native Hawaiian Cultural and Arts Program; Board Member, Maui United Way; Maui Community Arts and Cultural Center; Mayor's Committee for the Betterment of Youth; Executive Board, Boy Scouts of America; Committee Member, Year of the Hawaiian; Executive Committee, Maui Symphony Orchestra; Board of Governors, Nissan Hawaii High School Hall of Honor; Police Commissioner, County of Maui. **Education:** University of Hawaii, Master's (1975); Brigham Young University, Hawaii, B.S. in Physical Education; Professional Teacher's Certificate (1966); Professional Administrator's Certificate (1975). **Personal:** Married to Stephen B. in 1961. Two children: daughters, Kuuipo Peggy Lee Lindsey Barrows and Kananioaliiluka Harriet Lindsey Omalza; and eleven grandchildren.

Mrs. Margaret H. Maddox

Managing Trustee
Maddox Foundation
3833 Cleghorn Avenue, Suite 400
Nashville, TN 37215
(615) 269–7389
Fax: (615) 269–7389

6732

Business Information: The Maddox Foundation is a private foundation which focuses on dividing charitable contributions among conservation, education, religious, cultural, medical, and welfare organizations. Special emphasis is given to education which includes providing scholarships for undergraduate students; also in the field of conservation. Maddox

Foundation also works with underprivileged kids through special YMCA programs. With a background in the finance industry and retiring as a Financial Vice President of Associates Capital Corporation, Mrs. Maddox has served as Managing Trustee of Maddox Foundation since 1969. She is responsible for interviewing grant applicants to see if they meet Foundation qualifications, as well as spending many hours providing community services. Mrs. Maddox believes in promoting programs on prevention for underprivileged children and providing them with education. **Career Steps:** Managing Trustee, Maddox Foundation (1969–Present); Retired Financial Vice President, Associates Capital Corporation. **Associates & Accomplishments:** One of the early recipients of the Certified Professional Secretary rating; Selected as Tennessee's Secretary of the Year (1960); Active in Covenant Presbyterian Church; Chairman of the Board of Directors, Executive Committee, YMCA of Metropolitan Nashville and Middle Tennessee; Member of Advisory Board, YMCA's Y–Cap Program; Headed a $20 million "Agenda for Greatness" campaign and was inducted into the Belmont University collegiatus in 1986; Member, Board of Regents, Belmont University; Advisory Board of the Jack C. Massey School of Business; Member, Historic Travellers Rest, Historic Belmont Association; Member, Heritage Society Member, National Historic Preservation Society; Life Member, Blair School of Music; Member, Shikar Safari Club International; Recipient, Best Record Book Mountain Nyala ever taken by a woman from Ethiopia; Collected, Grand Slam of North American Sheep; Recipient of two Shikar Safari Club area awards for the Outstanding Trophy of the Year; Board of Minnie Pearl Cancer Foundation. **Education:** George Peabody College for Teachers, Certified Professional Secretary rating; Institute of Banking, Watkins Institute; East High School Graduate (1947). **Personal:** Married to Dan in 1969.

Donald R. Zook, Ed.D.

Chief Executive Officer
Jacob Engle Foundation, Inc.
PO Box 290
Grantham, PA 17027–0290
(717) 697–2634
Fax: (717) 697–7714
6732

Business Information: Jacob Engle Foundation, Inc. is a private foundation which focuses on dividing monies invested or donated to specific ministries of the Brethren in Christ Church. Established in 1972, Jacob Engle Foundation, Inc. reports annual revenue of $2 million and currently employs ten people. As Chief Executive Officer, Dr. Zook is responsible for all major decisions relating to the ongoing ministry and effectiveness of the organization. **Career Steps:** Chief Executive Officer, Jacob Engle Foundation, Inc. (1990–Present); Area Director, Person/Wolinsky CPA Review Courses; Brethren in Christ Church: Executive Director – Board for Stewardship Services (1990–1994), Executive Director – World Missions (1982–1990). **Associations & Accomplishments:** American Accounting Association; American Institute of Certified Public Accountants; Pennsylvania Institute of Certified Public Accountants; American Management Association; Institute of Certified Financial Planners; Chair – Board of Trustees, Ministers Pension Fund of Brethren in Christ Church; National Association of Security Dealers (1989); Ordained Minister, Brethren in Christ Church (1957). **Education:** Temple University, Ed.D. (1980); Pennsylvania State University, M.S. in Business Administration (1972); Elizabethtown College, B.A. in Business Administration (1955); Certifications: Certified Internal Auditor (1981); Certified Financial Planner (1981); Certificate in Management Accounting (1979); Certified Public Accounting (1973); Academic Achievements: Straight A average in Temple University doctoral program; Highest GPA of all those graduating with Ed.D. in Business Education from Temple University (May 1980); Highest GPA of all those graduating with M.S. in Business Administration from Penn State (March 1972); Summa cum laude and highest GPA in graduating class at Elizabethtown College (1955); Passed all five parts of Certified Financial Planner examination at first sitting of each (1980–1981); Passed all four parts of Certified Internal Auditor examination at first sitting (1981); Top score in Pennsylvania, among twelve highest nationwide, CMA exam (June 1979); Passed all four parts of CPA examination at first sitting (1973). **Personal:** Married to Anna in 1957. Dr. Zook enjoys collecting sermon materials and resource information; he is also intensely interested in investment return and safety.

Barbara C'De Baca

Executive Director
Desert State Life Management
320 Central Avenue, Southwest, Suite 200
Albuquerque, NM 87102
(505) 843–7535
Fax: (505) 243–1052
6733

Business Information: Established in 1987, Desert State Life Management is a corporate non–profit, guardianship and conservatorship trust company — the only non–profit trust company in the U.S. Estimating one million dollars in annual profits and employing 55 persons, Desert State now occupies four New Mexico cities, including Santa Fe, Las Cruces and Roswell. Appointed as Chief Executive Officer in September 1993, Barbara C'De Baca provides the overall executive leadership and direction for administrative operations and staff. **Career Steps:** Chief Executive Officer, Desert State Life Management (1993–Present); Director of Frail Elderly Programs, City of Albuquerque – Office of Senior Affairs (1986–1993). **Associations & Accomplishments:** Kiwanis Club of Greater Albuquerque; National Guardianship Association; National Institute of Aging; Published Author on Abuse, Neglect and Exploitation of the Elderly. **Education:** University of New Mexico, M.F.A. (1979).

Renee L. Cook

Vice President, Manager – Investment Technologies
United States Trust Company of New York
114 West 47th Street
New York, NY 10036–1510
(212) 852–1909
Fax: (212) 852–1833
6733

Business Information: United States Trust Company of New York is a full–service investment banking institution. With seven locations in the U.S. (Louisiana, Florida, Texas, New Jersey, Connecticut, New York, and Oregon), U.S. Trust Company of New York plans to branch out into other technology areas to provide individual services, to educate the consumers on investment products, and expand more on money management skills. Established in 1853, U. S. Trust Company of New York reports assets of $40 million and currently employs 1,400 people. Starting out in the banking industry in 1972 while attending college, Ms. Cook joined U.S. Trust Company of New York as Assistant Vice President in 1984. Appointed as Vice President and Manager of Investment Technologies Department in 1987, she is responsible for performance measurement functions, with the assistance of a support staff of nine. **Career Steps:** United States Trust Company of New York: Vice President and Manager of Investment Technologies (1987–Present), Assistant Vice President (1984–1987); Pension Trust Officer, Marine Midland Bank (1982–1984); Manager of Trust and Investment Division, Morgan Guaranty Trust (1978–1982). **Associations & Accomplishments:** Treasurer, Trust Universe Comparison Services; Board of Global Ministries; Board of Richmond Children's Center; Director, Avodah Dance Ensemble. **Education:** City College of New York, B.A. (1972); University of Wisconsin – Bank Administration Institute; Smith College, Management Program. **Personal:** Married to Dr. Leonard G. Meggs in 1980. Ms. Cook enjoys travel, reading, and tennis.

Russell Johnson

Vice President and Regional Trust Manager
U.S. Bancorp
P.O. Box 52172
Idaho Falls, ID 83405–2172
(208) 525–1667
Fax: (208) 525–8249
6733

Business Information: U.S. Bancorp is an international trust administration and investment firm, providing services for individual and corporate trusts and all aspects of investments. As Vice President and Regional Trust Manager, Mr. Johnson heads the Regional Trust Department, responsible for all aspects of management of the regional activities in Montana, Washington, and Oregon, as well as managing all CPA's, CFA's, and CFP's. Career milestones include beginning the movement to push a new law through Idaho legislature to enable attorneys, overseeing a trust account, to be paid according to what they do, instead of receiving a certain fee regardless of what duties they perform. With the passing of the law in Idaho, he has been asked to start the movement in California. **Career Steps:** Vice President and Regional Trust Manager, U.S. Bancorp (1991–Present); Vice President and Trust Marketing, First Intersate Bank (1983–1991). **Associations & Accomplishments:** President, Utah Bankers Association; Former Chair, Board of Primary Children's Medical Center; National Association of Estate Planners; Rocky Mountain Pension. **Education:** College For Financial Planning, C.F.P. in progress; Brigham Young University, B.S. (1991); Utah Technical, A.A. (1989). **Personal:** Mr. Johnson enjoys fly–fishing, and mountain biking in his leisure time.

Calvin Kubota

Comptroller
Alaska Permanent Fund Corporation
P.O. Box 25500
Juneau, AK 99802–5500
(907) 465–3171
Fax: (907) 586–2057
E–Mail: See Below
6733

Business Information: Alaska Permanent Fund Corporation is a government corporation managing an investment trust for the State of Alaska. The Company manages about $19 billion in assets for the State. As Comptroller, Mr. Kubota manages all accounting functions, identifies policy issues, and procures new accounting and investment systems. Internet users can reach him via: ckubota@alaskapermfund.com. **Career Steps:** Alaska Permanent Fund Corporation: Comptroller (1992–Present), Accounting Manager (1990–1992); Senior Timber Accountant, Klukwan Forest Products, Inc. (1988–1990). **Education:** University of Washington: M.B.A. (1986), B.S. (1976). **Personal:** Married to Barbara in 1979. Four children: Ryan, Michael, Matthew, and Stephen. Mr. Kubota enjoys fishing, and coaching and refereeing soccer.

Dr. Rene Navarro–Gonzalez

Executive Vice President/Partner
Global Finance Trust Corporation
P.O. Box 5177
La Paz, Bolivia
(591) 231–7256
Fax: (591) 237–304
6733

Business Information: Global Finance Trust Corporation is an international finance firm. A former Minister Counselor of the Bolivian Embassy in Great Britain/Northern Ireland, Dr. Navarro–Gonzalez joined the Corporation in 1984. As Executive Vice President, he is responsible for all financial operations, monitoring economic and long term profitability, with presence in the United States, Canada, England, Germany, Japan, Taiwan, and Russia. **Career Steps:** Executive Vice President, Global Finance Trust Corporation (1984–Present); Report Systems Analyst, Inter–American Development Bank (1979–1984); Credit Manager, Bank of America N.T. & S.A. (1974–1979); A Former Minister Counselor of the Bolivian Embassy in Great Britain/Northern Ireland (1994–1995); Former Consultant, The World Bank and United Nations; Former Program Economist, USAID/Bolivia. **Associations & Accomplishments:** President, Yale Club of Bolivia – Delegate to the Association of Yale University Alumni; New York Academy of Sciences; Fellow Member, Canadian Management Association; Former State Advisor to The United States Congressional Advisory Board. **Education:** Columbia State University, Ph.D. in Economics (1993); Yale University–Som–91–EMP, M.A., B.A.; Columbia Pacific University, Graduated Law School; Universidad Mayor de San Andres, LaPaz, Bolivia, Masters in Bolivian Politics (In Progress). **Personal:** Two children: Paola and Valeria Navarro–Zalles. Dr. Navarro–Gonzalez enjoys academic research, economics, finance, politics, racquetball and golf.

Robert Whitten

Data Processing Manager
LACERA
300 North Lake Avenue, Suite 750
Pasadena, CA 91101–4199
(818) 564–2422
Fax: (818) 564–6180
6733

Business Information: LACERA is a public employee's retirement trust fund. Joining LACERA as Data Processing Manager in 1985, Mr. Whitten is responsible for all data processing activities, including working with IBM mainframes, 250 Node Novell/Windows Network, and RS6000. **Career Steps:** Data Processing Manager, LACERA (1985–Present); Computer Operations Manager, Los Angeles County Facilities Management (1983–1985); Data Center Manager, Los Angeles County Data Processing Department (1974–1983). **Associations & Accomplishments:** Mason: Sustained Member, Former Master; U.S. Constitution Observ.; Public Schools. **Education:** California Polytechnic State University, B.S.E.E. (1974). **Personal:** Married to Melanie in 1978. One child: Aaron. Mr. Whitten enjoys electronic equipment design/construction and wood working.

Chris Kopp

Chief Financial Officer
Total Car Franchising Corp.
P.O. Box 1549
Conway, SC 29526
(803) 347–8818
Fax: (803) 347–0349
6794

Business Information: Total Car Franchising Corp., d.b.a. Colors on Parade, is a franchisor of mobile automotive paint repair units, consisting of 150 franchises located in 20 states. As Chief Financial Officer, Mr. Kopp is responsible for financial management and computer program development. **Career Steps:** Chief Financial Officer, Total Car Franchising Corp. (1992–Present); Manager, Insty–Prints (1988–1992); Purchasing Agent, Sheriar Press (1985–1988). **Associations & Accomplishments:** Automotive Service Association; Institute of Management Accountants. **Education:** Horry–Georgetown Technical College, working toward Accounting Degree (to be completed in 1997). **Personal:** Married to Rachel in 1988. Mr. Kopp enjoys water activities, athletics, and the outdoors.

Mrs. Maybelle R. Ashland
Vice President
Aladdin Investments, Inc.
5500 Rushmore Road
Rapid City, SD 57701
(605) 343–6477
Fax: Please mail or call
6798

Business Information: Aladdin Investments, Inc. is a private investment firm, specializing in real estate investments and stocks and bond trading. Co–owner with her husband Paul, Mrs. Ashland acts as Vice President for Aladdin Investments. She handles supervisory functions. Successful entrepreneurs, she and her husband also own retail venture establishments which include the following: Black Hills Flea Market, Iron Kettle Snack Shop and Aladdin Rock and Gift Shop. The Gift Shop specializes in the sale and trade of lapidary supplies and products (e.g., rocks, semi–precious stones, fossils, artifacts), as well as miscellaneous collectibles and antiques. Aladdin Investments, Inc. was established in 1974 and employs 10 people in the various satellite ventures. **Career Steps:** Vice President, Aladdin Investments, Inc. (1974–Present); Co–Owner and Manager, Black Hills Flea Market (1974–Present); Owner and Manager, Iron Kettle Snack Shop (1974–Present); Owner and Manager, Aladdin Rock and Gift Shop (1974–Present); President, Bluebird, Inc. (1996–Present); Co–Owner and Broker, A A Realty (1964–1974). **Associations & Accomplishments:** Rapid City Area Chamber of Commerce; Black Hills, Badlands and Lakes Association; Old West Trail Foundation; Disabled American Veterans Auxiliary; Moose Lodge Auxiliary; Fraternal Order of Eagles Auxiliary; Canyon Lake Senior Citizen Center; Minneluzahan Senior Center; American Association of Retired Persons. **Education:** Dakota Wesleyan University; University of South Dakota. **Personal:** Married to Paul R. (President and Co–Owner) in 1945. Two children: Bruce A. Ashland and Deborah K. Cooley. Mrs. Ashland enjoys coin collecting, gardening and lapidary.

Mr. Paul R. Ashland
President
Aladdin Investments, Inc.
5500 Rushmore Road
Rapid City, SD 57701
(605) 343–6477
Fax: Please mail or call
6798

Business Information: Paul R. Ashland, President of Aladdin Investments Inc., is primarily involved in local real estate investments, as well as handling limited stocks & bonds and retail sales. Mr. Ashland, seventy–four years young, oversees all aspects of Aladdin and subsidiary entities. **Career Steps:** President, Aladdin Investments Inc. (1974–Present); Vice President, Bluebird, Inc. (1996–Present); Co–Owner (with his wife Maybelle) and Manager, Black Hills Flea Market & Aladdin of the Black Hills (1974–1995); Vice President, A&E Development Company (1969–1979); Co–Owner (with his wife Maybelle) and Real Estate Broker, AA Realty (1964–1974). **Associations & Accomplishments:** Rapid City Area Chamber of Commerce; Black Hills Badlands & Lakes Association; Old West Trail Foundation; Masonic Lodge; Moose Lodge; Fraternal Order of Eagles; Disabled American Veterans; Veterans of Foreign Wars; American Legion; Canyon Lake Senior Citizen Center; Minneluzahan Senior Center; AARP. **Education:** Hamilton School of Commerce, Business Accounting Diploma (1940). **Personal:** Married to Maybelle R. Ashland in 1945. Two children: Bruce A. Ashland and Deborah K. Cooley. Mr. Ashland enjoys coin and stamp collecting, gardening, forestry, investments and running his flea market.

Margot I. Bogert
Division Head
Sanwa Bank
601 South Figueroa Street
Los Angeles, CA 90017
(213) 896–7082
Fax: Please mail or call
6798

Business Information: Sanwa Bank is the second largest trust and investment banking service in the world. The Institution deals with investment, real estate, tax, and private institu-

tions. As Division Head, Ms. Bogert is responsible for performing administrative duties, managing reports, and supervising marketing and functions and advertising. **Career Steps:** Division Head, Sanwa Bank (1991–Present); Deputy Division Head, Sanwa Bank (1992–1995); Chief of Staff, TSA, Inc. (1982–1992); Trust Officer, Title Insurance & Trust Co. (1975–1982). **Education:** Edinburch University, B.A. (1973); CTFA September (1991). **Personal:** Married to John in 1975. Three children: Caitlin, Rachael, and Ian. Ms. Bogert enjoys running, reading, and golf.

Randle W. Case II
President and General Counsel
Case International Company
102 East Pikes Peak Avenue, Suite 601
Colorado Springs, CO 80903–1823
(719) 634–2273
Fax: (719) 634–2274

6798

Business Information: Case International Company is a regional, national and international investment agency, primarily in the areas of real estate. Established in 1953, Case International currently employs 65 people, including contracts and affiliates, and reports assets of over $6.5 million. As President and General Counsel, Mr. Case oversees all Company operations, acquisitions and sales. A trial lawyer admitted to practice in Colorado courts since 1988, he also represents the Company in all legal matters, as well as continues to serve in an Of Counsel capacity concurrently with the firm of Paul Hamilton Company. **Career Steps:** President and General Counsel, Case International Company (1988–Present); Attorney and Broker Associate, Paul Hamilton Company (1984–1989); Ambulance Technician, A–1 Paramedics Company (1980–1985); Driver Engineer, Ivywild Cheyenne Canon Fire Protection District (1980–1982). **Associations & Accomplishments:** Chairman, Pikes Peak Avenue Business Improvement District; Government Representative, Pikes Peak Association of Realtors and Housing and Building Association; El Paso County Association of Realtors; Colorado Association of Realtors; National Association of Realtors; El Paso County Bar Association; Colorado Bar Association; American Bar Association; Colorado Trial Lawyer's Association; American Trial Lawyer's Association. **Education:** University of Denver, J.D. (1988); University of Colorado – Colorado Springs, B.S. (1983); Jones Real Estate College, Sales and Brokers License (1979, 1984). **Personal:** Married to Jill D. in 1991. Two children: Brennan and Kurt. Mr. Case enjoys outdoor sports, including football, skiing, scuba diving, running, and boating, as well as church activities, local and international travel, and spending time with his family.

Richard F. Cavenaugh

President and Chief Operating Officer
Ambassador Apartments, Inc.
77 West Wacker Drive, Suite 4040
Chicago, IL 60601–1629
(312) 917–4410
Fax: (312) 917–9910
EMail: See Below

6798

Business Information: Ambassador Apartments, Inc. is a real estate investment trust specializing in multi–family acquisitions and management. The Company owns and operates 12,000 middle income apartments across the nation, 39 complexes in Texas, Arizona, Colorado, Tennessee, Georgia, Florida, and Illinois. As President and Chief Operating Officer, Mr. Cavenaugh is responsible for day–to–day operations and management. Internet users can reach him via: rfc@aah.com. **Career Steps:** President and Chief Operating Officer, Ambassador Apartments, Inc. (1994–Present); Senior Vice President, The Prime Group (1990–1994); Partner, Embrey Investments (1989–1990); Executive Vice President, Pacific Realty Corporation (1983–1988). **Associations & Accomplishments:** Young Presidents Organization; National Multi–Housing Council; National Apartment Association; Lake County Affordable Housing Commission. **Education:** University of Illinois, B.S.C.E. (1982). **Personal:** Married to Elizabeth in 1990. One child: John. Mr. Cavenaugh enjoys golf and travel.

John Y.Y. Cheng

Chief Financial Officer
Caesars Investment, L.L.C.
700 E. Main Street
Stamford, CT 06901–2111
(203) 961–9909
Fax: (212) 864–3424
6798

Business Information: Caesars Investment, L.L.C. is a real estate investment and hotel management firm with international affiliates. A Certified Public Accountant, Mr. Cheng joined Caesars Investment as Chief Financial Officer in 1991. He oversees all financial operations of the Company and its affiliates. **Career Steps:** Chief Financial Officer, Caesars Investment, L.L.C. (1991–Present); Senior Tax Consultant, Kenneth Leventhal & Company (1991) **Associations & Accomplishments:** American Institute of Certified Public Accountants; Golden Eagle Club of Tamkanj University – Taiwan **Education:** Banich College/CUNY, M.B.A. (1987). **Personal:** Mr. Cheng enjoys music, sports, travel and reading during his leisure time.

Gerard S. Donohue
Vice President of Operations Services
SCG Realty
2455 North East Loop 410, Suite 230
San Antonio, TX 78217–5650
(210) 655–0979
Fax: (210) 599–0740
6798

Business Information: SCG Realty is a subsidiary of Security Capital Group, which is itself a subsidiary of Security Capital Pacific Trust. The Company owns and manages 45,000 units of multiple family properties. As Vice President of Operations Services, Mr. Donohue is responsible for 8,000 properties in Texas and is involved in research and development. He assists other management personnel in setting Company policy, developing budgets, and marketing new and existing services. **Career Steps:** Vice President of Operations Services, SCG Realty (1995–Present); Regional Vice President, Insignia Property Management (1994–1995); Vice President, Balcor Property Management (1990–1994); Director of Operations, Clark Financial Corporation (1982–1990). **Associations & Accomplishments:** Board Member, San Antonio Apartment Association. **Education:** Southern Utah University, B.S. in Business (1981); Institute of Real Estate Management, Certified Professional Manager; Colorado Real Estate Broker. **Personal:** Married to Julie in 1976. Three children: Jason, Ryan, and Amber. Mr. Donohue enjoys mountain biking, travel, and continuing his education.

Dorrie Green
Vice President of Administration
Merry Land and Investment Company
624 Ellis Street
Augusta, GA 30901–1417
(706) 722–6756
Fax: (706) 722–0002
6798

Business Information: Merry Land and Investment Company is a real estate investment trust. Publicly–owned and traded on the NYSE, it is the third largest apartment real estate investment trust in the nation. Current holdings encompass over 22,000 multi–residential units throughout the southern U.S. Bringing with him over fifteen years in financial and real estate investment management expertise, Dorrie Green joined MLI's Augusta, Georgia operations in 1994. As Vice President of Administration, he provides the overall executive administration for property tax, insurance, corporate budgeting and reporting, corporate tax and S.E.C. filing matters. He also serves as liaison for rating agency, debt and investor relations matters. **Career Steps:** Vice President of Administration, Merry Land and Investment Company (1994–Present); Chief Financial Officer, JG Financial Management (1991–1994); Chief Financial Officer, Trammell Crow Residential – Orlando, FL (1988–1991); Vice President, Guaranty Service Corporation (1985–1988). **Associations & Accomplishments:** Easter Seals of East Georgia. **Education:** University of Georgia: M.A. in Accounting (1980), B.B.A. **Personal:** Married to Cindy in 1984. Two children: Katy and Sara. Mr. Green enjoys tennis and golf.

Berthold K. Koester, J.D.
Chairman and Certified Real Estate Broker
Finvest Corporation
6201 East Cactus Road, P.O. Box 15674
Phoenix, AZ 85060–5674
(602) 840–0414
Fax: (602) 951–9271 (602) 840–0476
6798

Business Information: Finvest Corporation is a real estate trustee and brokerage service specializing in land holdings in the Republic of Germany. In his current capacity as Chairman, Dr. Berthold is responsible for all aspects of operations. **Career Steps:** Chairman and Certified Real Estate Broker, Finvest Corporation (1990–Present); Board of Directors, Arizona Partnership Air Transportation (1988–1992); Chairman and Chief Executive Officer, Arimpex Hi–Tec, Inc. (1988–1992); Honorary Consultant, Federal Republic of Germany for Arizona (1982–1992); Chief Executive Officer and Chairman of the Board, German Consultants in Real Estate Investments, Phoenix (1989–Present); Beucler Real Estate Investments (1986–1988); Applewhite, Laflin & Lewis: Real Estate Investments (1981–1986), Partner (1986–1988); Professor of International Business Law, American Graduate School of International Management (1978–1981); Attorney and Trustee International Corps, Tancer Law Offices, Phoenix (1978–1986); President, Bremer Tank University, Kuehlschiffahartsges (1964–1972); Vice President of J.H. Vogeler & Co. Bank, Duesseldorf (1960–1964); Attorney, Courts of Duesseldorf Federal Republic of Germany (1960–1982); Assistant Professor of Civil and International Law, University of Muenster (1957–1960). **Associations & Accomplishments:** President, Parents Association of Humboldt Gymnasium, Duesseldorf; Active German Red Cross; Member, Duesseldorf Chamber of Lawyers; Association of Tax Lawyers; President, Bonn German–Saudi Arabian Association (1976–1979); Bonn German–Korean Association; President, Association for German–Korean Economic Development (1974–1978); Secretary and Treasurer, Arizona Consular Corps (1988–1989); German–American Chamber of Commerce; Phoenix Metropolitan Chamber of Commerce; Rotary International. **Education:** University of Muenster, J.D. (1957); Certified Real Estate Broker, State of Arizona. **Personal:** Married to Hildegard M. in 1961. Three children: Georg W., Wolfgang F. and Reinhard B. Mr. Koester enjoys hunting, languages and studying Art History.

Peter Laurens Kreeger

President
KFI Investments
9000 Bronson Drive
Potomac, MD 20854
(202) 338–3550
Fax: (301) 299–7215

6798

Business Information: KFI Investments is a privately owned, real estate and venture capital investment firm specializing in financial management and development consultation. As President, Mr. Kreeger is responsible for all aspects of operations. He oversees financial investments and reviews opportunities for the Firm's clientele. KFI Investments was established in 1989 and has a staff of five people. **Career Steps:** President, KFI Investments (1993–Present); President and Legal Counsel, Main Street Partners (1990–1993); Vice President and Staff Counsel, Michael SwerdPow Companies (1986–1989); President, Florida Properties (1979–1986); General Counsel's Staff Attorney, Waste Management, Inc.(1977–1979). **Associations & Accomplishments:** Member, American Bar Association; Member, District of Columbia Bar Association; President, The Kreeger Foundation; Board of Trustees, The Kreeger Museum; Board of Directors, Washington Performing Arts Society; Member, The Metropolitan Club, Washington, D.C.; Member, Woodmont Country Club, Rockville, MD. **Education:** Indiana University, J.D. (1973); Indiana University, B.A. in Government (1969); Mercersburg Academy (1965). **Personal:** Married to Ineke Davis Kreeger in 1968. Three children: Alisha Rebecca, Joshua Laurens and Andrea Lynn. Mr. Kreeger enjoys tennis, golf, skiing, boating, travel and hiking.

Donald W. Phillips

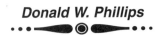

Chairman
Equity Institutional Investors, Inc.
2 North Riverside Plaza
Chicago, IL 60606–2600
(312) 466–4044
Fax: (312) 454–0157

6798

Business Information: Equity Institutional Investors, Inc., a division of Equity Group Investments, Inc., is the world's leading owner of office buildings and real estate. With offices around the world, EGI's corporate revenue is in excess of $12 billion, employing over 70,000 people corporate–wide. As Chairman of Equity Institutional Investor's Inc. located in its Boston headquarters, Mr. Phillips is responsible for maintaining and establishing relationships with institutional investors, as well as overall operational direction and supervision of a staff of eleven. Concurrent with his position, he serves as Executive Vice President of Equity Group Investments, Inc. **Career Steps:** Chairman, Equity Institutional Investors, Inc. (1990–Present); Executive Vice President, Equity Group Investments, Inc. (1990–Present); Chief Investment Officer, Ameritech (1984–1990); Director of Employee Benefits, Beatrice Companies, Inc. (1974–1984); Chairman, Consolidated Fibres Company; President, Nucorp, Inc.; Military Policeman, U.S. Army (1970–1972). **Associations & Accomplishments:** Board of Director Memberships: Capsure Holdings Corporation, United Capitol Insurance Company, Great American Management Company, Sit "New Beginnings" Mutual Fund Group, Larimer and Company. **Education:** Northern Illinois University, M.B.A. (1974); Western Illinois University, B.A. (1970). **Personal:** Married to Karen in 1970. Two children: David and Ryan.

Saeed A. Al–Khabaz

Managing Director
Al–Khabaz International Trading Company
P.O. Box 10764
Dhahran, Saudi Arabia 31311
966–3–873–7691
Fax: 966–3–824–0538

6799

Business Information: Al–Khabaz International Trading Company is a commission agent that acts as the middleman and manufacturer's representative for various manufacturing companies. As Managing Director, Mr. Al–Khabaz is responsible for strategic planning, decision making, and business development. A successful entrepreneur, he also holds executive positions with the British venture company AJC Trading & Engineering, Ltd. (U.K.), as well as Saudi Aramco. Career Steps: Managing Director, Al–Khabaz International Trading Company (1991–Present); Chairman and Chief Executive Officer, AJC Trading and Engineering, Ltd. (1994–Present); Training Superintendent, Saudi Aramco (1992–Present). **Associations & Accomplishments:** Board Member, Gulf Institute for Human Resources Development; Life Board Member, The Center for Gulf Studies; Commercial Arbitrator, The Abu Dhabi Commercial Arbitration Center; Commercial Arbitrator, GCC Commercial Arbitration Center; Board Member, Arabian Society For Human Resource Management (ASHRM); Expert, GCC Commercial Arbitration Center; Chairman, 1996 ASHRM Conference. **Education:** Arizona State University, B.S.B.A. (1980). **Personal:** Married to Suad in 1972. Four children: sons, Ramzi and Mohammed; and daughters, Khulood and Areej. Mr. Al–Khabaz enjoys reading and travel.

Robert Alvine

Chairman, President and Chief Executive Officer
I–Ten Management Corporation
55 North Racebrook Road
Woodbridge, CT 06525
(203) 387–1550
Fax: (203) 389–5153

6799

Business Information: I–Ten Management Corporation, established in 1987 along with the Aim Capital Group, are establishments primarily focusing on broad–based management and board level consulting, investments and acquisitions. As Chairman, President and Chief Executive Officer, Mr. Alvine is responsible for all aspects of Corporation operations, including investments. **Career Steps:** Chairman, President and Chief Executive Officer, I–Ten Management Corporation (1987–Present); Board Member and Head of the Executive Committee and Investor, Wedge Computers (1987–1991); Principal, Charterhouse Group International, Inc. (1988–1995); Chairman, CEO and major investor of Charter Power Systems (1988–1993); Vice Chairman, CEO and Major Investor, A.P. Parts Manufacturing Co., Inc. (1988–1992); Principal, Uniroyal Holdings, Inc. – CDU Liquidating Trust (1986–Present); Chief Executive of Engineered Products and Services Worldwide and President of Uniroyal Plastics and Power Transmission Companies – Corporate Senior Officer for Mergers and Acquisitions and Member of the Corporate Management Committee and Various Boards (1982–1987); Leader in the management buy out of Uniroyal in 1985; President, Uniroyal Development Company – President, Uniroyal Merchandising Company – Member, Corporate Management Committee and various boards (1980–1982); Vice President and General Manager of Uniroyal Tire Company, Inc. and President of Uniroyal Merchandising Company, Inc. (1979–1980); Vice President of Corporate Planning and Development, Uniroyal, Inc. – Director of Strategic Planning and Business Development, Uniroyal Chemical Company, Inc. (1977–1979); Vice President (Commercial), Coatings & Specialties Company (1975–1976); Director of Marketing and Operations, Celanese Piping Systems & Fabricated Products Company (1972–1974); Business Manager of Polyolefins, Celanese Plastics Company (1969–1972); Product Manager, Nylon Products (1967–1968); Military: United States Army Reserve (1962–1968); Other directorships include: Board of Directors E.O.O. Corporation; Jackson Laboratories; Wildlife Conservation Society; LongWharf Theater; National Theater of the Deaf; Advisor Board, Polaris Fund; Board of Advisors for Rutgers University. **Associations & Accomplishments:** National Association of Corporate Directors; National Association for Corporate Growth; President's Association; American Management Association; Business Week 100; North American Planning Society; Society of Automotive Engineers; Battery Council of America; Society of Plastics Industry; Council of the Americas; World Affairs Council; American Association for the Advancement in Science; Newcomen Society; Honorable Order of Kentucky Colonel; Statue of Liberty Foundation, Inc.; National Maritime Historical Society; Rutgers and Harvard Alumni Associations; Harvard Business School Club of New York & Southern CT; Citizens Against Government Waste; The Presidential Task Force; The Legion of Merrit; The Chi Phi Fraternity Alumni Association; Oaklane Country Club; Renaissance Club; Among numerous business, biographical and civic recognitions, received an Outstanding Achievement in Business and Distinguished Leadership Awards and a proclamation and inclusion in the Book of Honor selected for supreme achievement within the International Community from the American Biographical Institute and among a variety of recognitions, listed in Who's Who in the World, Who's Who in America, Who's Who in the East, Who's Who in Finance and Industry, Who's Who in Society, International Who's Who of Intellectuals, Who's Who in U.S. Executives, Men and Women of Distinction, The Book of Honors, International Register of Profiles, and Men of Achievement over the past eight years. **Education:** Rutgers University, B.A. in Chemistry and Chemical Engineering (1960); Syracuse University Graduate School, Sales and Marketing Management, SMEI (1967–1968); Harvard Business School, Graduate PMD 23 (1972); South Eastern Signal School, honor graduate (1962); Numerous management development and corporate governance programs. **Personal:** Two children: Robert James and Laurie Anne. Mr. Alvine enjoys reading, entrepreneurial business enterprising, sailing, golf, tennis, gardening, art, music, travel and cooking.

Mr. Franz R. Brand

General Counsel – Asia Pacific Region
ABB Energy Ventures
202 Carnegie Center, Suite 100
Princeton, NJ 08540
(609) 243–7575
Fax: (609) 243–9168

6799

Business Information: ABB Energy Ventures, part of the ABB Group – a Swedish/Swiss/American conglomerate, is a development and project financing firm for power generation and transmission projects. Established in 1989, ABB currently employs 60 people. As General Counsel for the Asia Pacific Region, Mr. Brand is responsible for all aspects of legal representation, as well as strategic planning, business development, finance and negotiations of all legal documentation, including project documents, credit agreements, and security documents. **Career Steps:** Associate General Counsel, ABB Energy Ventures (1994–Present); Finance Consultant, Union Bank of Switzerland (1994); Business Consultant, EKA, Finland (1993); Attorney, Lewis, D'Amato, Brisbois & Bisgaard (1988–1992). **Associations & Accomplishments:** American Bar Association, International Section; Wisconsin Bar Association; California Bar Association; Washington, D.C. Bar Association; Wisconsin & California District Courts of Appeals. **Education:** IMD Business School, International M.B.A. (1993); University of Wisconsin Law School, J.D. (1987); University of Wisconsin, B.S with Honors (1982). **Personal:** Mr. Brand enjoys traveling, reading, participating in sport activities, music (plays guitar and piano).

David Del Bianco

Owner, President, and Chief Executive Officer
Euro–Am Pacific Enterprises, Ltd.
1324–11th Avenue, SW, Suite 308
Calgary, Alberta T3C 0M6
(403) 228–1345
Fax: (403) 229–3279

6799

Business Information: Euro–Am Pacific Enterprises, Ltd. is an international commodities trading agency. Products traded include cement and sugar. Established in 1986, Euro–Am Pacific Enterprises employs 25 agents. Establishing the Firm in 1985, Mr. Del Bianco serves as Owner, President, and Chief Executive Officer. He is responsible for all aspects of operations, in addition to overseeing all administrative operations for associates and a support staff of 12. He also meets with agents who serve as buyers and sellers and is responsible for procuring contracts. **Career Steps:** Owner, President, and Chief Executive Officer, Euro–Am Pacific Enterprises, Ltd. (1985–Present). **Associations & Accomplishments:** Chamber of Commerce; Rotary International; Arda; Hotel Association. **Personal:** Mr. Del Bianco enjoys collecting stamps, soccer, hockey, and yachting.

Charles J. Diodosio
Chairman of the Board
TMGC Ltd. (The Meadow Gold Investment Company, Ltd.)
822 West Oakdale
Chicago, IL 60657
(312) 871–0453
Fax: (312) 871–5263

6799

Business Information: TMGC Ltd. (The Meadow Gold Investment Company, Ltd.) is a venture capital company, focusing on investments in the People's Republic of China. China's largest ice–cream maker, the Company is currently involved in at least eleven joint venture operations in cities throughout China. Distributed widely throughout China, TMGC currently has operations in Tianjin, Nianjing, Xi'an, Beijing, Chengdu, Liaoning, Harbin, Shanghai, Wuhan, Hangzhou, and Changsha — resolved to become one of China's leading companies by bringing 21st Century technology and conciousness into Company operations, environmental workplace designs, customer service and product quality. Senior plant management is imported to make operations and personnel management techniques modern, investment recovery periods rapid, and advertising and marketing impact extremely effective. Custom advanced ice–cream making equipment is imported directly from Denmark and the United States. In July of 1994, Australian diversified manufacturer Pacific Dunlop Ltd. (PacDun) invested to buy a half share of Meadow Gold, taking a quantum leap into China's fast growing markets. PacDun will provide Meadow Gold with new product development, technology, funding and marketing initiatives, as well as management input. As Chairman of the Board, Mr. Diodosio oversees all aspects of Company operations. Established in 1988, TMGC Ltd. and subsidiaries employ 3,000 people. **Career Steps:** Chairman of the Board, TMGC Ltd. (1988–Present); Vice President, Asia Development, Beatrice Company (1984–1988); International Counsel, Beatrice Company (1980–1984); Associate, McDermott, Will & Emery (1976–1980). **Associations & Accomplishments:** American Bar Association. **Education:** Northwestern University Law School, J.D., cum laude (1976); University of Colorado, B.S. in Chemical Engineering, magna cum laude (1973).

A. Martin Erim
Chairman, Chief Executive Officer
First Renaissance Ventures
11601 Rolling Meadow Drive
Great Falls, VA 22066
(703) 404–0330
Fax: (703) 404–8428

6799

Business Information: A. Martin Erim is the Chairman and Chief Executive Officer for international investment and venture capital firms as follows: First Renaissance Ventures and Overseas Partners, Inc. (located in Washington, D.C.). Mr. Erim oversees all aspects for both firms, focusing on portfolio development, financial advice, international project development, investments strategies and risk capital funding. **Career Steps:** Chairman, Chief Executive Officer, First Renaissance Ventures (1994–Present); Chairman, Overseas Partners, Inc. (1994–Present); Senior Vice President, CACI, Inc. (1992–1994); President and CEO, American Legal Systems (1980–1992). **Associations & Accomplishments:** Chapter Officer, Young Presidents' Organization; Board Member, National Association of Legal Vendors; Interviewed and written in trade journals and magazines ("FORBES"). **Education:** The American University, J.D. (1977); Penn State University, B.A. (1973).

Ivy Gilbert–Vigue
Senior Vice President and Chief Financial Officer
Firstmark Corporation
1 Financial Place, 222 Kennedy Memorial Drive
Waterville, ME 04901
(207) 873–0691
Fax: (207) 873–5999

6799

Business Information: Firstmark Corporation is a venture capital financial services corporation. As Senior Vice President and Chief Financial Officer, Ivy Gilbert–Vigue is responsible for all financial transactions and accounting operations. She also specializes in advising women in estate planning. **Career Steps:** Senior Vice President and Chief Financial Officer, Firstmark Corporation (1981–Present) **Associations & Accomplishments:** Financial Advisor, Women & Investing (1991–Present); Chief Executive Officer, The Hamilton Foundation (1989–Present). **Education:** Thomas College; College for Financial Planning. **Personal:** Married to James Vigue. Two children: Kristopher and Kailyn. Mrs. Gilbert–Vigue enjoys being with her children.

Ernesto Haberer, Ph.D.

President
Promex International, Inc.
7500 San Felipe Street
Houston, TX 77063–1707
(713) 782–8081
Fax: (713) 782–8177

6799

Business Information: Promex International, Inc. is an international trading company, supplying raw material to most countries world–wide. Products include petrochemicals, chemicals, plastics, and metals. International in scope, Promex has offices in the U.S., Mexico, Brazil, Malaysia, and Indonesia. Joining Promex International as one of five partners in 1978, appointed President in 1994, Dr. Haberer is responsible for all aspects of operations, including administration, finances, sales, public relations, accounting, legal matters, taxes, marketing, and strategic planning. **Career Steps:** President, Promex International, Inc. (1994–Present); Chairman, IRC Group (1992–1994); President, Hanex S. A. (1984–1992); Managing Director, Interco (1978–1984). **Associations & Accomplishments:** Greater Houston Partnership; Mexican Business Council for International Affairs; American Chemical Society; National Petroleum Refiners Association. **Education:** University of Paris, Ph.D. (1965); University of Montevideo: M.S. in Engineering, B.Sc. **Personal:** Married to Irene in 1973. Five children: Monica, Daniel, Elizabeth, Jacqueline and Miriam. Dr. Haberer enjoys golf, music, tennis and travel during his leisure time.

Mohan C. Imbuldeniya
President
MCI Enterprises
23350 Kewsick Street
West Hills, CA 91304–5304
(818) 884–2514
Fax: (818) 884–2928

6799

Business Information: MCI Enterprises is an international company involved in import and export; trade and countertrade; marketing new products for foreign manufactures and exporters; and consulting for foreign government tenders for electrical power plants. Founding MCI Enterprises in 1991 and serving as its President and Owner, Mr. Imbuldeniya is responsible for all aspects of operations. **Career Steps:** President, MCI Enterprises (1991–Present); Controller, Arkas Properties, Inc. (1986–1991); Accountant, Starr, Judson – CPA's (1982–1986). **Education:** Woodbury University, M.S. (1980). **Personal:** Married to Sunitha K. in 1972. Two children: Dilini and Mayanthi. Mr. Imbuldeniya enjoys travel, reading, and skiing.

Mr. Howard M. Jacobson
Director, Ventures
Corporate Research & Technology Group/Hoechst A.G.
86 Morris Avenue
Summit, NJ 07901
(908) 522–7964
Fax: (908) 522–7754

6799

Business Information: Corporate Research & Technology (CRT) has prime responsibility for corporate renewal and business development for Hoechst A.G. globally. CRT currently employs over 2,000 professionals. As Director, Ventures, Mr. Jacobson is responsible for the acquisition of companies and technologies to support the extension of current businesses or the development of new business. **Career Steps:** Director, Ventures, Corporate Research & Technology/Hoechst A.G. (1996–Present); Director, Ventures, Advanced Technology Group/Hoechst Celanese Corporation (1994–Present); Business Director, Sunett (1990–1994); Director of Strategic Development (1988–1989); Manager of Business Diversification (1986–1988). **Associations & Accomplishments:** Trustee, Morris County Urban League; Member, Commercial Development Association. **Education:** Hofstra University, M.B.A. (1974); Long Island University, B.S. in Finance. **Personal:** Married to Sheryl in 1970. Two children: Melissa and Gregg. Mr. Jacobson enjoys reading, golf, skiing and travel.

David S. Lobel

Chairman and Managing Partner
Sentinel Capital Partners
245 Park Avenue, 41st Floor
New York, NY 10167
(212) 490–5945
Fax: (212) 682–0082
EM:102161.332@CompuServe

6799

Business Information: A private equity, principal investment firm, Sentinel Capital Partners specializes in buying and building middle market companies throughout the United States in partnership with management. The Firm's investments focus primarily on the consumer sector. Investments typically take the form of management buyouts, growth equity, and restructurings. A principal investment executive for the past 16 years, Mr. Lobel founded the Firm in 1995. As Chairman and Managing Partner, he directs all aspects of the Firm's operations. **Career Steps:** Smith Barney: Managing Director (1988–1992), Vice President (1983–1987), Associate (1981–1982). **Education:** Stanford University: M.B.A. (1979), M.S. (1978); University of The Witwaterstrand: B.Sc (Hons) (1975), B.Sc (1974). **Personal:** Married. Born and raised in South Africa. U.S. citizen.

Mr. Donald J. Mucha
Chairman
MMP Investments, Inc.
6318 West Rawson Bridge Road
Cary, IL 60013
(708) 516–9028
Fax: (708) 516–9844

6799

Business Information: MMP Investments, Inc. specializes in international investing opportunities with a primary focus on Eastern Europe. As Chairman, Mr. Mucha is responsible for searching out good investments. Established in 1989, MMP Investments, Inc. employs a full–time staff of 10. **Career Steps:** Chairman, MMP Investments, Inc. (1989–Present); Chairman, Unitronex Corporation (1974– Present); Chairman, AESI (1976–Present). **Associations & Accomplishments:** Vice Chairman, U.S. Polish Economic Council; Vice President, American Polish Chamber of Commerce. **Education:** University of Chicago, M.B.A. (1969); University of Illinois, B.S. in Engineering; Kent College of Law.

Luis F. Rodriguez Rodriguez

Vice President
Caribbean Produce Exchange
P.O. Box 11990
San Juan, Puerto Rico 00922–1990
(809) 793–0750
Fax: (809) 781–7776

6799

Business Information: Caribbean Produce Exchange, a family–owned business, is the largest producer and importer of fruits and vegetables in the Caribbean. They are in the Top 100 of 200 locally–owned companies in Puerto Rico, marketing produce to supermarket chains and cash–n–carry stores in Puerto Rico, as well as exporting to other islands in the Caribbean. Products are imported from the U.S., Canada, Chile, and Central America. Established in 1960, Caribbean Produce Exchange reports annual revenue of $57 million and currently employs 120 people. Joining the Company in 1975, Mr. Rodriguez Rodriguez was appointed as Vice President in 1984. Besides holding the position as Vice President, he is also the buyer for all produce imported from Central America and directs the entire garlic business world–wide. **Career Steps:** Caribbean Produce Exchange: Vice President (1984–Present), Marketing (1975–1984). **Associations & Accomplishments:** Board of Directors, Wholesaler Chamber of Commerce; Former Director, MIDA; Honorary First Lieutenant Police Department. **Education:** University of Puerto Rico, Marketing (1975); Colegio San Jose, Production and Cannery. **Personal:** Married to Maritza F. de Rodrigrez in 1979. Two children: Nanette Marie Rodriguez Franceschini and Fernando Luis Rodriguez Franceschini. Mr. Rodriguez Rodriguez enjoys collecting antique toys & general antiques, cars, and off–road activities.

Juan N. Velasco

Vice President of Special Projects
Intergrated Trade Systems
2500 Citywest Boulevard, #2400
Houston, TX 77042
(713) 430-3162
Fax: (713) 430-3318

6799

Business Information: Intergrated Trade Systems is an international trading company, providing procurement and logistics services for the oil industry. Products traded include equipment, parts telecommunications equipment, etc. As Vice President of Special Projects, Mr. Velasco is responsible for the implementation of different multi-million dollar projects, including reengineering, quality system, learning organization, and knowledge management. He is also involved in a project to give access to customers in Mexico, enabling companies to order directly from them. **Career Steps:** Vice President of Special Projects, Intergrated Trade Systems (1994-Present); International Purchasing Manager, PEMEX in Houston (1991-1994); Commercial Director, Turborreactores in Mexico (1990); General Manager, Turbotex, Inc. in Dallas (1988-1989). **Associations & Accomplishments:** American Production and Inventory Control Society; Institute of Industrial Engineers; American Society for Quality Control; National Association of Purchasing Management. **Education:** UNAM – Mexico, B.S. in Industrial Engineering (1987); University of Houston. **Personal:** Married to Leticia B. in 1983. Two children: Monica and Moutserrat. Mr. Velasco enjoys sports, music and reading.

Tony W. Vick
Accountant
Toyota Tsusho America, Inc.
1125 Cherry Blossom Way
Georgetown, KY 40324-9565
(502) 868-3442
Fax: (502) 868-3475

6799

Business Information: Toyota Tsusho America, Inc. is an international trading company whose largest client is Toyota Motor Manufacturing. The company provides services in warehousing steel coils; logistics (just–in–time deliveries); importing and exporting machinery, steel, and autoparts; recycling; slitting services (steel coils), and engineering services and consultancy. Established in 1986, the Company estimates revenue to exceed $1.7 billion and presently employs 500 people. As Accountant, Mr. Vick is responsible for processing payroll and related taxes for employees. Other responsibilities include working with general tax accounting, such as, sales taxes and accounts payable. **Career Steps:** Toyota Tsusho America, Inc.: Accountant (1993-Present), Accounting Assistant (1992-1993); Assistant Administrator, Royal Manor, Inc. (1989-1991). **Associations & Accomplishments:** American Payroll Association; Notary Public, State at Large (KY). **Education:** Western Kentucky University, B.S. Accounting (1988) **Personal:** Mr. Vick enjoys music, dancing, biking, running, and hiking.

7000 – 8999
SERVICES

7000 Hotels and Other Lodging Places

7011 Hotels and motels
7021 Rooming and boarding houses
7032 Sporting and recreational camps
7033 Trailer parks and campsites
7041 Membership–basis organization hotels

Jeffrey C. Abel
Director of Construction
Grand Casino, Inc.
2909 13th Street
Gulfport, MS 39501-1949
(601) 870-5129
Fax: (601) 864-6969

7011

Business Information: Grand Casino, Inc. is a riverboat casino operation with a full range of entertainment facilities, including restaurant, gambling, lounge, and sports entertainment. Grand Casino, Inc. currently has six regional locations. As Director of Construction, Mr. Abel is responsible for the coordination and supervision of the four additional properties in progress of being built, two locations in Mississippi and two in Louisiana. **Career Steps:** Director of Construction, Grand Casino, Inc. (1994-Present); Director of Construction, Casino Resource Corporation (1978-1994). **Personal:** One child: Brandon William. Mr. Abel enjoys hunting, fishing, camping, boating, and real estate.

Dwayne L. Allen
Director of Lodging Systems
Marriott International
1 Marriott Drive
Washington, DC 20058
(301) 380-2469
Fax: (301) 380-2003

7011

Business Information: Marriott International is a conglomerate service and hospitality company. The company's revenue for 1994 was $8.4 billion and the total employee base was 180,000. Marriott's two primary businesses are centered around its internal lodging and service groups which earned revenues of $4.8 and $3.6 billion respectively. The Marriott Lodging group's portfolio of products starts with its full service hotel. This division is commonly called Marriott full service hotels, resorts, and all suite hotels. The Lodging group also has a limited lodging group which includes Courtyard by Marriott — moderately priced hotels targeted towards business travelers, and Residence Inn — designed for the extended stay market. Also included in this group is Fairfield Inn, Marriott's economy market product. All totaled, the Marriott Lodging group has 880 hotels in 40 countries providing over 185,000 rooms plus conference and meeting facilities. As a compliment to the traditional properties, the Lodging group also has a vacation time share division called Marriott Ownership Resorts. This division has 28 properties totaling 1,950 units and has the ability to sell up to 95,000 vacation weeks to owners. The internal counterpart to the Marriott Lodging group is the Marriott Service Group. This group is made up of Marriott Management Services (MMS), Marriott Senior Living Services (SLS), and Marriott Distribution Services (MDS). The Marriott Management Services division manages health care, corporate, higher education, secondary school, and facilities management accounts. They have over 3,000 accounts under contracts in these highly competitive markets. Most of these contracts can be terminated with only 30 days notice. The Senior Living Services division has retirement community for the elderly. through 19 senior living communities offering 5,600 apartments. The final business in the Marriott Service group is its Distribution Services division. This Division acts as the food, cleaning, and disposable products provider to over 1,600 Marriott properties and external distribution customers. From its seven warehouses, the Division supplies more than 8,000 different products to internal and external customers. Marriott International is the result of the division of Marriott Corporation holdings in the Fall of 1993. This special stock dividend produced two companies, Marriott International and Host Marriott. Host Marriott, with revenues of approximately $1.5 billion in 1995, operates concessions and restaurants in seventy (70) U.S. and three (3) international airports, operates merchandise and concessions at five (5) U.S. arenas, manages and operates 37 entertainment and tourist facilities across the country, performs real estate development, owns $300 million in undeveloped real estate, and operates 93 travel plazas on fourteen U.S. toll roads. As Director of Lodging Systems, Mr. Allen manages an applications development staff of seven, plus expanded staff on a project basis. Responsibilities include: preparation of project time and cost estimates. liaison between I/S senior management and corporate clients, compilation and draft of performance appraisals and training plans, annual budget preparation, contract consulting services, and conduct senior management presentations. He oversees over $85 million in internal computer and telecommunication processing charges, accuracy of 33,000 unique charging units, support for 5,000 report management system users, over 600 FOCUS data base users, and Marriott's electronic commerce requirements. Accountable for the following areas: Electronic Data Interchange (EDI); Reengineering; Computer billing; Telecommunications billing; Marriott Communications Network; Report Management Expert System; FOCUS Data Base Support; Production migration process. In 1988 Mr. Allen was the recipient of the Marriott Information Systems Distinguished Service Award. **Career Steps:** Director of Lodging Systems and Director of Corporate Systems, Marriott International; Manager, Roy Rogers Systems. **Associations & Accomplishments:** Heritage Fellowship United Church of Christ, Reston, VA – served as a Deacon and was a member of the Pastoral Search Committee; Greater Washington Cultural Alliance – business volunteers for the Arts program (offered consulting services free of charge for local arts organizations); Fairfax County Juvenile & Domestic Court – volunteer mentor for minority youths on probation. **Education:** George Washington University, Washington, D.C., Masters Degree in Business Administration (executive program) – Concentration: Global Commerce (current, 1996); Yale University, New Haven, CT, Leadership Program, School of Organization and Management (1993); University of Virginia, Charlottesville, VA, Bachelor of Arts Degree in Communications (1984); **Personal:** Married to Jennifer in 1992. Mr. Allen enjoys travel, sports, theater, art, and people.

Carol J. Balfour
General Manager
Dixie Management II
2500 West State Street
Alliance, OH 44601-5605
(330) 821-5555
Fax: (330) 821-4919

7011

Business Information: Dixie Management II is a hotel and hospitality establishment. As General Manager, Ms. Balfour is responsible for diversified administrative duties, payroll, and bookkeeping functions. Ms. Balfour also serves as Sales Manager. **Career Steps:** General Manager, Dixie Management II (1996-Present); Administrative Manager, Comfort Inn (1989-1996); Front Desk and Night Auditor, Best Western (1988-1989); Manager, General Nutrition Center (1986-1988). **Associations & Accomplishments:** Former President, West Branch Elementary PTO; Former President, Alliance Chapter Sweet Adelines. **Personal:** Three children: Cindy Ashwal, Bobbi Balfour, and Jamie Balfour. Ms. Balfour enjoys crochet, tole painting and cooking.

Nancy C. Berger
Income Auditor
Holiday Inn Riverfront
200 North 4th Street
St. Louis, MO 63102
(314) 621-8200 Ext.6108
Fax: (314) 621-8073

7011

Business Information: Holiday Inn Riverfront is a 454 room hotel that is part of the Holiday Inn chain, a full–service hospitality and accommodation operation, providing full–scale lodging and dining facilities for many corporate travelers, government personnel, and social groups. As Income Auditor, Ms. Berger is responsible for the accounting department, the night audit crew, balances the income journal, and manages computer installation and maintenance. **Career Steps:** Income Auditor, Holiday Inn Riverfront (1990-Present). **Education:** Southwest Missouri State University, B.S. in Management/Minor In Computers (1990). **Personal:** Ms. Berger enjoys reading and cross–stitch.

Carla C. Block
Vice President of Marketing Systems
Trump Taj Mahal Hotel and Casino
1000 Boardwalk
Atlantic City, NJ 08401
(609) 449-6381
Fax: (609) 449-6794

7011

Business Information: Trump Taj Mahal Hotel and Casino is an international hotel and casino, providing overnight accommodations, gambling, various entertainment, and pleasure–fun shows. As Vice President of Marketing Systems, Ms. Block is responsible for all aspects of marketing systems analysis and design, data entries, and direct mail functions pertaining to the casino industry. She may be reached through the Internet via: cblock@trumptaj.com **Career Steps:** Trump Tau Mahal Hotel & Casino: Vice President of Marketing Systems (1993-Present); Casino Host/PD Specialist (1990-1993), Executive Assistant to Vice President of Player Development, Showboat Hotel & Casino (1989-1990). **Associations & Accomplishments:** National Organization for Female Executives; National Organization for Women; Mainland Chamber of Commerce. **Education:** Monmouth University, M.B.A. (1993); Stockton State College, B.A.; Angelina College, Associates Degree in Data Processing. **Personal:** Married to Jeffrey S. Ropiecki in 1994. Ms. Block enjoys reading, skiing, and golf.

George S. Broadwell
Vice President
Geo Hotel Corporation, Inc.
70 East First Street
Oswego, NY 13126
(315) 343-1600
Fax: (315) 342-1222

7011

Business Information: Geo Hotel Corporation, Inc. is a hotel management company, owning and operating Econo Lodge and River Front Hotels in Oswego, New York. As Vice President, Mr. Broadwell is responsible for all aspects of Hotel operations for both Hotels, as well as managing the lounge and banquet facilities. **Career Steps:** Vice President, Geo Hotel Corporation, Inc. (1992–Present); General Manager, Best Western Captain's Quarters Hotel (1991–1992); Banquet, Floor Manager, Captain's Lounge (1990–1991). **Education:** Rochester Institute of Technology, Degree in Hotel Technology (1990); Syracuse University – Utica Colleges Branch, Restaurant Management. **Personal:** Mr. Broadwell enjoys golf, skiing, softball, and swimming.

Suzanne B. Chambers
Director of Human Resources
Orlando Marriott
8001 International Drive
Orlando, FL 32819
(407) 351–2420
Fax: (407) 352–7054

7011

Business Information: Orlando Marriott is a full–service, accommodation with full–scale dining and lodging facilities. The Marriott has 1,100 rooms, one full service restaurant, one dinner only restaurant, one pool side restaurant, three pools, and 600 employees. As Director of Human Resources, Ms. Chambers is in charge of all recruitment, benefits, training, and career development. **Career Steps:** Director of Human Resources, Orlando Marriott (1995–Present); Director of Human Resources, Charlotte Marriott (1990–1995); Director of Human Resources, Adams Mark Hotel (1988–1990). **Associations & Accomplishments:** Acting Secretary, Hotel Personnel Association; Society of Human Resource Management. **Education:** East Tennessee State University. **Personal:** Married to Landon David in 1977. Three children: Colby, Darrin, and Katie (Anna Kathryn). Ms. Chambers enjoys horseback riding, computers, and reading.

Ronald Lee Coley
Executive Director
AQUAREN SPRINGS
Southwest Texas State University, P.O. Box 2330
San Marcos, TX 78667–2330
(512) 245–7575
Fax: Please mail or call

7011

Business Information: AQUAREN SPRINGS, recently purchased by Southwest Texas State University, is a resort complex centered on a 12,000 year old archaeology site located on 90 acres – the last Spanish mission to be built in Texas. The complex consists of a resort, conference center, hotel, theme park, and a nature center. Joining AQUAREN SPRINGS as Executive Director in 1994, Mr. Coley is responsible for all aspects of operations for the Center, in addition to overseeing all administrative operations for associates and a support staff of 350. **Career Steps:** Executive Director, AQUAREN SPRINGS (1994–Present); Vice President of Marketing, Ocean Edge (1990–1994); National Sales Manager, TEKNA (1989–1990); Director of Advertising, SeaQuest (1986–1989). **Associations & Accomplishments:** Board of Directors, Texas Hill Country Tourism Association; Board of Directors, Texas Nature Tourism Association; Board of Directors, San Marcos Chamber of Commerce. **Education:** University of Tulsa, B.S. (1973); Brook Institute of Photography; University of Southern California – Marine Biology Lab, Catalina Island; University of California – Los Angeles, Diving Physiology. **Personal:** Married to Deborah Ann in 1986. One child: Stephen Ray. Coley enjoys scuba diving, sailing, and photography.

Wanda J. Costi
Controller
Red Lion Jantzen Beach
909 North Hayden Island Drive
Portland, OR 97217
(503) 283–4466
Fax: (503) 978–4550

7011

Business Information: Red Lion Jantzen Beach is a 320–room hotel and convention facility, providing 32,000 square feet of banquet and convention space. Red Lion Jantzen Beach is a part of Red Lion Company, owning and operating 53 hotels in the Northwestern U.S. Established in 1978, Red Lion Jantzen Beach reports annual revenue of $15 million and currently employs 260 people. As Controller, Ms. Costi is responsible for all accounting functions at this site, including accounts receivable, accounts payable, and payroll. She also handles the annual budget, monthly forecasts, and all computer upgrades. **Career Steps:** Controller, Red Lion Jantzen Beach (1992–Present); Controller, Red Lion Inn at the Quay (1990–1992); Westin Benson: Controller (1979–1990), Information Clerk (1967–1979). **Associations & Accomplishments:** Vice President, International Association of Hospitality Accountants; Soroptimist International of Portland; Miss Washington Scholarship Pageant; Beta Sigma Phi. **Education:** Clark College, A.A. (1992); American Hotel and Motel

Association, CHAE Certificate. **Personal:** Married to Dennis G. in 1986. Ms. Costi enjoys music, golf, walking, and travel.

Angela Culmer
Controller
Sun International Bahamas
915 NE 125th Street
Miami, FL 33161–5713
(809) 363–3000
Fax: (809) 363–2493

7011

Business Information: Sun International Bahamas, Ltd., is a 1,300–room hotel and casino resort located in the Bahamas with a recently opened water park. Sun International Bahamas has three hotel properties and currently employs more than 3,000 people. As Controller, Ms. Culmer is responsible for the daily operations of the finance office in the Bahamas. **Career Steps:** Sun International, Bahamas: Controller (1995–Present), Assistant Controller (1992–1995), Accounting Manager (1991–1992), Internal Auditor (1984–1991). **Associations & Accomplishments:** International Association of Hospitality Accountants; Chartered Association of Certified Accountants – Scotland; Bahamas Association of Chartered Accountants. **Education:** London School of Accounting, A.C.C.A. (1981); St. Augustine's College, Nassau, Bahamas. **Personal:** One child: Doyle Anton Rolle. Ms. Culmer enjoys basketball, track & field, swimming, and sewing.

Jay Dearing
Director of Sales and Marketing
Henry VIII Hotel
4690 North Lindbergh Boulevard
St. Louis, MO 63044
(314) 731–3040
Fax: (314) 731–0246

7011

Business Information: Henry VIII Hotel is a hospitality facility comprised of 400 rooms (1/2 suites), 37,000 square feet of meeting space, as well as conference rooms and banquet facilities. Established in 1964, the Company employs 200 people and has estimated annual revenue of $8 million. As Director of Sales and Marketing, Mr. Dearing is responsible for the generation of all revenues into all areas of the Company. **Career Steps:** Director of Sales and Marketing, Henry VIII Hotel (1989–Present); Founder and President, Rebuild, Inc. NFP (1993–Present); President, Experience Travel, Inc. (1982–1989). **Associations & Accomplishments:** Grace United Methodist Church; Christian Businessmen's Committee; Kiwanis; Chamber of Commerce; Neighborhood Associations; SKAL Club. **Education:** University of Miami, B.A. (1977); Certified Travel Counselor Degree; Licensed Real Estate Agent. **Personal:** Married to Susan Costello in 1989. One child: Grace Anne. Mr. Dearing enjoys sports, charitable giving and deeds, travel, and being foster parents.

Pamela Lyn Dorneden
Director of Hotel Marketing and Development
BTI Americas, Inc.
400 Skokie Boulevard
Northbrook, IL 60062–2816
(847) 486–8607
Fax: (847) 480–3027

7011

Business Information: BTI Americas, a market leader, specializes in providing managed travel business solutions. Established in 1975, the Company has an estimated annual sales of over $3.2 billion and is a founding partner of Business Travel International (BTI), a joint venture partnership of leading travel management companies worldwide. With fourteen years of extensive experience in travel industry sales, marketing, and customer service management, Ms. Dorneden joined BTI Americas, Inc. as Director of Hotel Marketing and Development in 1994. She is responsible for sales, marketing, new business development, and operations of BTI Americas' Worldwide Hotel Center. Duties include overseeing all vendor relations, development, production and fulfillment of annual global hotel program and directory; MIS and database management; new technology product development; commission reconciliation; and the consulting services group. In addition, she manages an annual budget of $1.5 MM and a staff of 28 in the Northbrook and Dallas offices. Career highlights include successfully integrating all hotel functions into one streamlined department; directing and implementing a merger of the former USTravel Hotel Department into BTI Americas' organization; launching BTI Americas' Hotel Consulting Services Group with a focus on strategic development of client specific lodging programs; designing, developing and launching InnQuery, a software companion to the BTI printed hotel directory; establishing and implementing preferred vendor marketing partnerships. **Career Steps:** Director of Hotel Marketing and Development, BTI Americas, Inc. (1994–Present); Director Travel Agency Sales, Hilton Hotel Corporation (1992–1994); Director, US Travel (1989–1992); Director of Sales, Omni

Morton Hotel (1988–1989); Corporate Sales Manager, The Palmer House Hilton (1987–1988); Corporate Sales Manager, Sheraton International at O'Hare (1985–1987); Incentive Sales Manager, The Sheraton Corporation (1984–1985). **Associations & Accomplishments:** Business Travel International: Purchasing Committee, Hotel Working Group, GDS Committee; National Business Travel Sales Person of the Year, Hilton Hotels Corporation (1993); Travel Advisory Board Member, Westin Hotels and Resorts (1994–1996); Hilton Hotels Corporation (1994–1995); Holiday Inn Worldwide (1994–1996); Ritz Carlton Hotels (1994–1996); Hotel Clearing Corporation (1994–1996). **Education:** Triton Junior College, Psychology (1981); Professional selling Skills III/ITT Sheraton Corporation (1984); Priority One Guest Satisfaction/Hilton Hotels Corporation (1988); Apollo/SABRE Training (1991); Customer Focused Selling – Cirriculum I & II/Hilton Hotels Corporation (1992–1993); Consulting Skills & Development/Professional Development Institute (1994). **Personal:** Married to Gregory. Three children: Jason, Emily, and Guenevere.

Ellis J. Etter

Director of Food and Beverage
Herco Inc. d.b.a. Hotel Hershey
Hotel Road
Hershey, PA 17033
(717) 534–8848
Fax: (717) 534–8888

7011

Business Information: Located in Hershey, PA, Herco Inc. d.b.a. Hotel Hershey is a 241–room award winning resort hotel. Hotel amenities include a formal dining room, fountain cafe, seasonal club house cafe and cocktail lounge. Established in 1934, Hotel Hershey employs 200 restaurant professionals with estimated annual sales of $18.5 million. A longtime resident of Hershey, PA and a graduate of Hershey High School, Mr. Etter has been an employee with Herco Inc. for over 18 years. As Director of Food and Beverage, he is responsible for the direction of food and beverage operations for this resort property in Central Pennsylvania. **Career Steps:** Herco Inc. d.b.a. Hotel Hershey: Director of Food and Beverage (1994–Present); Banquet Manager (1993–1994); Assistant Director of Food and Beverage (1992–1993); Beverage Manager (1988–1992); Assistant Beverage Manager (1987–1988); Bartender (1977–1987). **Associations & Accomplishments:** Pennsylvania Restaurant Association, Central Chapter. **Education:** Dauphin County Vocational Technical School. **Personal:** Married to Kim B. in 1986. Mr. Etter enjoys hunting, fishing, hiking, scuba diving, and motorcycle touring.

Becky L. Fowler
Senior Human Resource and Benefits Specialist
Silver Star Resort & Casino
P.O. Box 6048, Hwy 16 West
Philadelphia, PA 39350–6048
(601) 650–1215 1–800–557–0711
Fax: (601) 650–1250

7011

Business Information: Silver Star Resort & Casino is the most successful land–based casino in Mississippi. A development of the Mississippi Band of Choctaw Indians, the Casino is operated by Boyd Gaming of Las Vegas. As Senior Human Resource and Benefits Specialist, Ms. Fowler is responsible for diversified administrative activities, including employee benefits and customer relations. **Career Steps:** Senior Human Resource and Benefits Specialist, Silver Star Resort & Casino (1994–Present); Assistant Human Resource Manager, Kilgore Operations (1990–1994); Office Manager, Wells Lamont Corporation (1975–1988). **Associations & Accomplishments:** Philadelphia/Nebosha County Arts Council; West Tennessee Personnel Association. **Education:** University of Mississippi. **Personal:** Two children: Jason and Derek Russell. Ms. Fowler enjoys travel, golf, and music.

Michel P. Garnier
General Manager
Crowne Plaza
Hwy. 187, Kilo 1.5
San Juan, Puerto Rico 00979
(787) 253–2929
Fax: (787) 253–0079

7011

Business Information: Crowne Plaza is one of the busiest corporate hotels in Puerto Rico. Its El Tropical Casino is the second largest and the only themed Casino on the Island. Located across from the airport directly on Isla Verde Beach minutes from Downtown San Juan. It is the most successful hotel in the area and has the highest occupancy. Established in 1992, the Hotel provides its mostly executive clientele with a variety of exclusive packages including discounts, travel miles, Club floors, and many other benefits. As General Manager, Mr. Garnier oversees all aspects of the operation, including guest relations, administration, and public relations. During his one year with the Hotel, he has concentrated on focusing on new programs and expanding corporate clientele. **Career Steps:** Crowne Plaza: General Manager – San Juan (1995–Present), General Manager – Ottawa, Ontario (1991–1995); General Manager, Ramada Hotel – Montreal, Quebec (1989–1991); Assistant General Manager, C.P. Hotels – Mirabel, Quebec (1988–1989). **Associations & Accomplishments:** Board of Directors, SKAL Club of Ottawa; Board of Directors, Interdelegations; President, Ottawa–Hull Hotel Association; Board of Directors, Greater Montreal Hotel Association. **Education:** I.T.H.Q. Hotel Administration (1980); Certified Hotel Administrator (CHA); American Hotel and Motel Association. **Personal:** Married to Monique Sabella in 1989. Two children: Philippe–Alexandre and Camille. Mr. Garnier enjoys fishing and teaching.

Wolfgang D. Geckeler, C.E.C., A.A.C.

Executive Chef
Showboat Hotel and Casino
801 Boardwalk
Atlantic City, NJ 08401–7509
(609) 343–4229
Fax: (609) 345–2334

7011

Business Information: Showboat Hotel and Casino is an 800–room hotel and casino located in Atlantic City, New Jersey, providing twelve food outlets, a commissary, and a banquet room. Showboat Hotel and Casino's parent company is located in Las Vegas, Nevada, with a sister company in Sidney, Australia. As Executive Chef, Mr. Geckeler is responsible for the oversight of all food production and food outlets (gourmet and fast food), as well as banquet activities and a staff of 25 chefs and 200 food preparation cooks. Duties include overseeing the budget, food costs, labor costs, purchasing, and equipment selection. **Career Steps:** Executive Chef, Showboat Hotel and Casino (1988–Present); Executive Sous Chef, Bally's Park Place Casino Hotel (1982–1988); Chef/Owner, Black Horse Tavern and Hotel (1979–1982); Executive Chef, Otto's Biergarten Restaurant (1976–1979). **Associations & Accomplishments:** ACF Professional Chef's Association of South Jersey; German Chef's Association of Frankfurt, Germany; American Academy of Chefs; American Culinary Federation. **Education:** The Culinary Institute of Bad Ueberkingen, Germany, B.S. (1965); Certified Chef – The American Culinary Federation. **Personal:** Married to Maria in 1973. Three children: Heidi, Nicole and Jason. Mr. Geckeler enjoys spending time with his family, swimming, horseback riding, flying and travel.

Melhem Hage

Managing Director
Byblos–Sur–Mer
B.P. 22
Port De Byblos–Jbeil, Lebanon
09–940356
Fax: 961–9944859

7011

Business Information: Byblos–Sur–Mer is a hotel and beach resort located in the oldest city in history, dating back to 5000 BC. The Resort offers special corporate and group rates, as well as a four–star restaurant. Future plans include providing a ground and light show for the Town of Byblos, similar to the one in Egypt at the Giza Pyramids. Established in 1979, Byblos–Sur–Mer reports annual revenue of $2 million and currently employs 60 people. As Managing Director, Mr. Hage is responsible for all aspects of management and direction of operations. **Career Steps:** Managing Director, Byblos–Sur–Mer (1979–Present); General Manager, S.E.T.I. Oman (1976–1979); Senior Accountant, Joseph Tasso (1972–1976). **Associations & Accomplishments:** Secretary General, St. Jacques Parish in Byblos; Member, Board of the Syndicate Hotel Owners of Lebanon (1995–Present); Member, The Skal International, the Professionals of Tourism; Fluent in French, Arabic, and English; Active member of community activities. **Education:** Pigier, Char. Account (1973), Baccalaureate in Philosophy. **Personal:** Married to Marilyn in 1984. Mr. Hage enjoys swimming, reading, and collecting antiques.

Veeann R. Hamon

Director of Human Resources
The Georgian Hotel
1415 Ocean Avenue
Santa Monica, CA 90401
(301) 395–9945
Fax: (310) 451–3374

7011

Business Information: The Georgian Hotel, Santa Monica's gracious hotel by the sea, is a premiere hotel offering comfortable rooms to fit everyone's needs. As Director of Human Resources, Ms. Hamon is responsible for the oversight of personnel, staffing, and legal human resource functions at the Corporate level for five hotels. **Career Steps:** Director of Human Resources, Georgian Hotel (1996–Present); Assistant Manager, The Gap; Assistant Manager, Ross. **Associations & Accomplishments:** Santa Monica Convention & Visitors Bureau. **Education:** University of Arizona, B.S. (1992); Pima Community College, Associates Degree. **Personal:** Married to Jeremy W. in 1977. Ms. Hamon enjoys hiking, reading, and running.

David L. Harju

Vice President of Sales
Forte Hotels, Inc.
1973 Friendship Drive
El Cajon, CA 92020–1140
(619) 258–6597
Fax: (619) 562–0901

7011

Business Information: Forte Hotels, Inc. is the international corporate management office of the hotel and motel chain operating 500 Travelodge and Thriftlodge hotels throughout North America. The hotels range from two story facilities with outside corridors to high–rise business hotels. Future plans include expanding their sales force. With over 23 years experience in sales and marketing, Mr. Harju joined Forte Hotels, Inc. as Vice President of Sales in 1994. He is responsible for all aspects of operations of the North American sales effort. **Career Steps:** Vice President of Sales, Forte Hotels, Inc. (1994–Present); Regional Director, Worldwide Sales, Holiday Inn Worldwide (1991–1994); National Sales Development, Premier Cruise Lines (1987–1991). **Associations & Accomplishments:** A.S.T.A.; N.T.A.; N.B.T.A.; H.S.M.A.I.; T.I.A. **Education:** Miami University (1967–1971). **Personal:** Married to Diane in 1987. Two children: Zachary, and Madison. Mr. Harju enjoys marathon running and golf.

Robert E. Harmon

General Manager
Holiday Inn Northglenn
10 East 120th Avenue
Northglenn, CO 80233–1002
(303) 452–4100
Fax: (303) 457–1741

7011

Business Information: John Q. Hammons Hotels was developed in 1969. The Springfield, Missouri–based company is a leading independent owner, manager and developer of upscale hotels in secondary, tertiary and airport market areas. Operating under the brand names of Holiday Inn and Embassy Suites, JQH owns forty–two hotels in eighteen States ranging from the West Coast of Oregon to the East Coast of North Carolina. One of the properties owned by JQH, the Holiday Inn Denver Northglenn currently employs a staff of 150 and reports an estimated annual revenue of $5 million. As General Manager, Mr. Harmon is responsible for all aspects of operations at the Northglenn, Colorado site. **Career Steps:** General Manager, Holiday Inn Northglenn (subsidiary of John Q. Hammons, Inc.) (1994–Present); Regional Food & Beverage Director, Prime Hospitality (1988–1994); District Manager, Campbell Soup dba Campbell Hospitality (1980–1988). **Associations & Accomplishments:** Knights of Columbus 3rd Degree; Knights of Columbus, 4th Degree Man of the Year (1988); Denver Metro and Northglenn Chamber of Commerce. **Education:** Niagara University, B.A. in Biology and Sociology (1974); University of Phoenix, M.B.A., in progress. **Personal:** Married to Mary in 1978. Three children: Robert, Jessica and Nicole. Mr. Harmon enjoys skiing, tennis, bike riding and cooking.

Thomas R. Haufe

General Manager
Sofitel Hotels
1914 Connecticut Avenue Northwest
Washington, DC 20009
(202) 797–2000
Fax: (202) 328–1984

7011

Business Information: Sofitel Hotels, a wholly–owned subsidiary of Accor Hotels, is a four–star French hotel chain with 110 establishments in 40 countries worldwide. As General Manager of the Sofitel Hotel in Washington, D.C., Mr. Haufe oversees a staff of 75 in daily operations, public relations, customer service, and administrative activities. **Career Steps:** General Manager, Sofitel Hotels (1988–Present); General Manager, Doubletree Hotel (1986–1988). **Associations & Accomplishments:** Director, Washington Hotel Association. **Education:** Florida International University, B.A. (1971). **Personal:** Married to Lynne in 1991. Four children: Marialice, Jocelyn, Norah and Thomas. Mr. Haufe enjoys tennis, travel and photography.

Clifford C. Hay

Director of Rides and Attractions
Circus Circus Enterprises
3900 Las Vegas Boulevard South
Las Vegas, NV 89119–1004
(702) 262–4565
Fax: (702) 262–4567

7011

Business Information: Circus Circus Enterprises is a parent company, providing rides and attractions in a casino/hotel environment through a series of hotels, including Excaliber Hotels, Circus Circus Hotel, Luxor Hotel & Casino, and Monte Carlo Hotel – all of which have affiliated theme (or theme–type) parks behind or in their hotels. Joining Circus Circus Enterprises as Director of Rides and Attractions in 1993, Mr. Hay is responsible for the direction of all activities in the Rides and Attractions Department, conducting his business from Luxor Hotel in Las Vegas. The attractions include motion rides, The Nile River Ride, and a museum designed like King Tut's Tomb. Career milestones include designing and building Nickelodeon Studios Tours at Universal Studios, Orlando and serving as Project Manager on "Back to the Future", also at Universal Studios, Orlando. Prior to this, he spent 13 years with Paramount Pictures in Hollywood. **Career Steps:** Director of Rides and Attractions, Circus Circus Enterprises (1993–Present); Technical Director, The Trumbull Company (1992–1993); Project Manager, Universal Studios Florida (1989–1992); Director of Operations, Paramount Pictures (1977–1989). **Associations & Accomplishments:** IAAPA; SMPTE; AES; IAFEC. **Education:** USIU, SPA, M.A. (1991). **Personal:** Married to Sandi in 1987. Two children: Greg and Libby. Mr. Hay enjoys working and golf.

Daniel (Dan) Higgins

Senior Sales Manager
Renaissance Hotels
11 E. Ocean Boulevard
Long Beach, CA 90802
(310) 437–5900
Fax: (310) 499–2512

7011

Business Information: Renaissance Hotels offers accommodations at 72 properties worldwide. The Renaissance Long Beach is a 374–room hotel with 15,000 sq. ft. of meeting and function space. The Hotel employs over 300 people and has estimated annual revenue over $16 million. As Senior Sales Manager, Mr. Higgins oversees scheduling of conventions and other events. He is also responsible for contract negotiations and many hotel promotions. **Career Steps:** Senior Sales Manager, Renaissance Hotels (1994–Present); National Sales Manager, Long Beach Convention Bureau (1991–1994); Convention Sales Manager, Palm Springs Desert Resorts C.V.B. (1989–1990). **Associations & Accomplishments:** Society of Government Meeting Professionals (SGMP); Board of Directors, Sacramento Chapter Meeting Professionals International (MPI); Southern and Northern California Chapter, American Society of Association Executives (ASAE); Toastmasters International; Sierra Club. **Education:** University of Massachusetts, B.A. (1989). **Personal:** Mr. Higgins enjoys sports, fitness, art, music, and travel.

Geraldine M. Hodgkins, CPA, MBA
Controller
The Ritz Carlton Hotel—Pentagon City
1250 South Hayes Street
Arlington, VA 22202
(703) 412–2750 (703) 415–5000
Fax: (703) 415–5846

7011

Business Information: The Ritz Carlton Hotel is one of the premier, leading luxury hotel chains in the world. The Pentagon City branch, established in May of 1990, employs over 400 support and administrative staff. A Certified Public Accountant with over ten years expertise in hospitality audit and financial management, Ms. Hodgkins was appointed as Controller of the Pentagon City location in November of 1992. Her primary functions involve the overall administration of financial aspects, including budget allocations, forecasting, future projections, analysis and accounting. She also serves as advisor and consultant to the 8–member Executive Committee. **Career Steps:** Controller, The Ritz Carlton Hotel—Pentagon City (1992–Present); Senior Auditor, ITT Sheraton Corporation (1989–1992); Audit Supervisor, Alan Edelstein & Company, CPA's (1985–1989). **Associations & Accomplishments:** International Association of Hotel Administrators; American Institute of Certified Public Accountants; District of Columbia Institute of Certified Public Accountants. **Education:** Suffolk University, M.B.A. (1983); University of California – San Diego, B.A.

Tamre Grace M. Hoover
Human Resources and Benefits Manager
Argosy/K O A R Group, Inc.
12016 Turtle Cay Circle
Orlando, FL 32830–2069
(407) 238–2800 Ext.328
Fax: (407) 238–2511

7011

Business Information: Argosy/K O A R Group, Inc. specializes in timeshare sales of major resorts such as Signature Resorts in Orlando and South Beach, Florida, California, South Carolina, Branson, Missouri, Hawaii, and St. Martin. Headquartered in Orlando, the Company was established in 1993 and employs 500 people. As Human Resources and Benefits Manager, Mrs. Hoover handles all benefits and human resource issues. She oversees insurance, profit sharing, payroll, personnel management, and training. **Career Steps:** Argosy/K O A R Group, Inc: Human Resources and Benefits Manager (1996–Present), National Payroll Manager (1995–1996); Personnel Coordinator, Human Services Associates, Inc. (1993–1995). **Education:** Florida Southern, B.A. in Business Administration/Human Resources (1996); University of Central Florida, B.S. in Education. **Personal:** One child: Jessica Leigh L. Sprecher. Mrs. Hoover enjoys reading, sewing, woodcrafts, and being active in church.

Mr. Thomas J. Huegel
Director of Market Planning & Strategy
Hilton Hotel Corporation
1645 Village Center Circle, Suite 170
Las Vegas, NV 89134
(702) 243–3024
Fax: (702) 243–3073

7011

Business Information: Hilton Hotel Corporation is the management operations for the Hilton chain of hotel resorts and casino operations most well known in the United States and abroad. As Director of Market Planning & Strategy, Mr. Huegel is responsible for strategic planning and research for hotel and casino development projects. **Career Steps:** Director of Market Planning & Strategy, Hilton Hotel Corporation (1988–Present); Director of Development and Planning, Laurenthol & Horwath (1984–1988). **Associations & Accomplishments:** Apparel Institute; Canyon Ridge Christian Church; Featured in "Business Geographics." **Education:** Florida State University, M.S. in Market Research (1983); University of Wisconsin at Madison, B.S. (1981). **Personal:** Married to Mary Jane in 1985. Two children: Emory and Madison. Mr. Huegel enjoys sports, primarily golf and skiing.

Joann Y. Jackson
Human Resource Director
Philadelphia Marriott Hotel
1201 Filbert Street
Philadelphia, PA 19107
(215) 625–6080
Fax: (215) 625–6105

7011

Business Information: Philadelphia Marriott Hotel is a luxury hotel located in downtown Philadelphia. The Hotel offers a wide range of amenities to both the business and vacation traveler. The downtown location has 1,200 rooms with a large conference center, while the airport facility has 419 rooms. As Human Resource Director, Ms. Jackson is responsible for employment, benefits, payroll, worker's compensation, employee relations, and training for two full service hotels. In addition, Ms. Jackson is the regional trainer for a number of Corporate courses, including diversity training. **Career Steps:** Philadelphia Marriott Hotel: Director of Human Resources, Director of Community/Associate Relations (1994–Present); Director of Human Resources, Marriott's Harbor Beach Resort (1992–1994); Director of Human Resources, Marriott's Minneapolis City Center (1989–1992). **Associations & Accomplishments:** Multi–Cultural Affairs; Marriott's Network Group; Hotel/Motel Association; African American Human Resources Hotel Council; Philadelphia High School Hospitality; National Association of Black Meeting Planners; Marriott's Human Resource Advisory Council; Greater Philadelphia Urban Affairs Coalition; Marriot Greater Delaware Valley Business Council. Awards received include: Most Diverse Hotel of the Best of the Best in Human Resources (1996); Hotel of the Year and Innovative Hotel of the Year (1995). **Education:** Governor State University, Bachelor of Science; Jocelyn Ryan Modeling School. **Personal:** One child: Amber. Ms. Jackson enjoys reading, travel, interior decorating and repairs, and gardening.

George Jacobs Negron

Casino Director
Ponce Hilton and Casino
P.O. Box 7419
Ponce, Puerto Rico 00732
(809) 721–0303
Fax: (809) 722–8750

7011

Business Information: Ponce Hilton and Casino, a subsidiary of Caribe Hilton Hotel and Casino, is a casino and resort hotel with 156 suites, convention rooms, sports and spa facilities. Serving in various supervisory roles for Caribe Hilton Hotel subsidiaries in 1985, George Negron was appointed to the Ponce Hilton position in 1992. As Casino Director, he was responsible for all casino administration, including marketing and customer service. In September of 1995, He was transferred from the Ponce Hilton to the Caribe Hilton, as Casino Director. The Caribe Hilton, with 671 rooms, was the first hotel in Puerto Rico to boast a casino. **Career Steps:** Casino Director, Caribe Hilton (1995–Present); Ponce Hilton and Casino (1992–1995); Casino Director, Mayaguez Hilton (1987–1992); Casino Supervisor, San Juan Hotel (1985–1987). **Education:** Colegio Universitario Metropolitano, Bachelors (1985). **Personal:** Mr. Jacobs Negron enjoys basketball and exercise.

Mohamed Abdullah Jammal
Managing Director and Shareholder
Marble Tower Hotel
113
Beirut, Lebanon 6452
(961) 134–6260
Fax: (961) 134–6262
EMAIL: See Below

7011

Business Information: Marble Tower Hotel, located in the center of Beirut, is a totally refurbished business hotel with a 70% occupancy rate, offering 60 rooms and suites. Joining Marble Tower Hotel as Managing Director and Shareholder in 1992, Mr. Jammal is responsible for the general management of the hotel, including administration, finances, public relations, and oversight of a staff of 46. **Career Steps:** Managing Director and Shareholder, Marble Tower Hotel (1992–Present); General Manager, Fresh Meat and Milk Company (1987–1991); General Manager, New Jersey (1984–1987). **Associations & Accomplishments:** SKAL – Association de Professionals du Tourism. **Education:** Beirut Arab University, M.S. in Sociology (1972). **Personal:** Married to Dina Hammoud in 1978. Three children: Babii, Rami, and Rima. Mr. Jammal enjoys collecting stamps.

Peggy Johnson
Assistant Comptroller
Exchange Club of Beatty
604 North Main Street
Beatty, NV 89003
(702) 553–2368
Fax: (702) 553–2441

7011

Business Information: Exchange Club of Beatty is a 24–hour, full–service bar, restaurant, casino, and 44 room motel. As Assistant Comptroller, Mrs. Johnson has oversight of all financial aspects of the operation including payroll, accounts receivable, cash management, gaming compliance, and cage reports. **Career Steps:** Assistant Comptroller, Exchange Club of Beatty (1992–Present); Office Manager, Stagecoach (1990–1992); Head Teller, RMFS&L (1988–1990). **Associations & Accomplishments:** Board Member, Beatty Chamber of Commerce; Board Member, Beatty Historical Society; Chair of Several Committees; Beatty Lions Club. **Education:** Utah Tech, Associates (1984). **Personal:** Married. Three children: Anthony, Aubrey, and Samantha. Mrs. Johnson enjoys crafts.

Shelly J. Kalins
Marketing Director
Vacation Charters
1 Lake Drive
Lake Harmony, PA 18624
(800) 255–7625
Fax: (717) 722–8831

7011

Business Information: Vacation Charters, d.b.a. Split Rock Resort, is a family–owned and operated business located on Lake Harmony, Pennsylvania. As Marketing Director, Ms. Kalins oversees all marketing strategies and services offered to individuals and groups. She develops all special event programs as well. **Career Steps:** Marketing Director, Vacation Charters (1995–Present); Marketing Coordinator, MacFarlane Partners, S.F.,CA (1994–1995); Special Events Coordinator, The Resort at Split Rock (1993–1994). **Associations & Accomplishments:** Pocono Mountains Vacation Bureau; Carbon County Chamber of Commerce. **Education:** George Washington University, M.B.A. (1993) and B.A. (1990). **Personal:** Ms. Kalins enjoys snowboarding, mountain biking, tennis, hiking, music, and waterskiing.

Vipin K. Khullar
Executive Chef
La Guardia Marriott
10205 Ditmars Boulevard
East Elmhurst, NY 11369–1327
(718) 533–3025
Fax: (718) 899–0764
EMAIL: See Below

7011

Business Information: La Guardia Marriott, part of Marriott International, is an international hotel chain conglomerate, providing full service hotels, resorts, and all suite hotels. Marriott provides moderately–priced hotels targeted towards business travelers and vacationers, as well as offering restaurant, airline catering, food, and beverage services. Marriott has 1003 hotels in 40 countries, providing over 185,000 rooms plus conference and meeting facilities. The La Guardia Marriott is located adjacent to La Guardia International Airport. With twenty–one years experience in the food preparation industry and a Culinary Expert, Mr. Khullar joined Marriott Corporation as Executive Chef in 1989. He is responsible for directing total food operations, including menus, food quality, purchase of foods, and controlling and costing of food served. Throughout his career he has worked in the Far East, Middle East, Europe, and U.S. Internet users can reach him via: VKHULLAR@AOL.COM. **Career Steps:** Executive Chef, La Guardia Marriott (1989–Present); Owner and Chef, Bombay Brasserie (1986–1989); Executive Chef, Indian Hotels Company (1975–1986). **Associations & Accomplishments:** American Culinary Federation; National Executive Chef Association. **Education:** Institute of Hotel Management – India (1975); Delhi University – India, Bachelor's of Commerce. **Personal:** Married to Indu Khullar. Two children: Onkar and Aarti. Mr. Khullar enjoys computers and camping.

Theresa R. King, CMP
Director of Catering
Hyatt Fair Lakes
12777 Fair Lakes Circle
Fairfax, VA 22033
(703) 818–3161
Fax: (703) 818–3140

7011

Business Information: Hyatt Fair Lakes, is a member of the Hyatt Resorts, one of the world's leaders in premier and mid–

level economy hospitality facilities. As Director of Catering, Ms. King is responsible for sales, marketing, public relations, and generating revenue for the hotel by soliciting social events. **Career Steps:** Director of Catering, Hyatt Fair Lakes (1995–Present); Catering Manager /Restaurant, Hyatt Regency: Washington (1986–1990), Crystal City, Catering Manager (1990–1992); Senior Catering Manager, Grand Hyatt – Washington (1992–1995). **Associations & Accomplishments:** National Council of Negro Women; Certified Meeting Planner; Coalition of 100 Black Women; National Association of Catering Executives. **Education:** Marshall University, Bachelors (1985). **Personal:** Married to Eric in 1995. Ms. King enjoys tennis, gardening, cooking, and volunteering for charity organizations.

Kelli L. Kitzman
General Manger
Superior Shores Resort and Conference Center
10 Superior Shores Road
Two Harbors, MN 55616
(218) 834–5671
Fax: (218) 834–5677

7011

Business Information: Superior Shores Resort and Conference Center is comprised of 150 privately owned units, standard motel suites, condos, indoor/outdoor pool, 2,000 foot pebble beach, and related recreational facilities. Located on the north shore of Lake Superior, the Resort provides services to both business and vacationing clientele. As General Manger, Ms. Kitzman performs all human resource functions, handles personnel and guests, and serves as a liaison between the resort, owners, and guests to ensure smooth operation and client satisfaction. **Career Steps:** General Manger, Superior Shores Resort and Conference Center (1995–Present); Office Manager, Crow Wing County Extension Service (1992–1995). **Associations & Accomplishments:** Dale Carnegie Graduate; 4H Adult Volunteer; Project 4 Teens Adult Advisor; Past Member of Brainerd Daily Dispatch Advisory Board; Regional Future Farmers of America (FFA) Alumnae Officer; Crisis Line Volunteer. **Education:** St. Cloud Business College. **Personal:** One child: Adam. Ms. Kitzman enjoys softball and playing on the shore of Lake Superior with her son.

D. J. Kot
Executive Director – Customer Development
The Grand Casino
Boston At Pacific Ave.
Atlantic City, NJ 08401
(609) 236–4142
Fax: (609) 340–7128

7011

Business Information: The Grand Casino, a Bally's Casino Resort, provides marketing to high level casino patrons, in addition to organizing and planning customer parties and off-site events. Working as a casino executive with some of the country's premier resorts for the past ten years, Mr. Kot has served in various managerial roles with The Grand Casino since 1992. Appointed Executive Director of Customer Development in 1995, he aggressively pursues, acquires and maintains high–level Casino players by treating guests with "First Class" amenities (i.e., limousine and private jet services, premier events and shows tickets, penthouse accomodations). **Career Steps:** The Grand Casino: Executive Director of Customer Development (1995–Present), Director of Customer Service (1993–1995), Executive Host (1992–1993); Executive Marketing Representative, Showboat Hotel and Casino (1992); Casino Host, Trump Castle Hotel and Casino (1987–1992). **Education:** Watauga High, Diploma (1986); Hotel Marketing, Advertising, Trump Castle Management Skills I, II, and III. **Personal:** Married to Linda–marie in 1993. Two children: Noel–marie and Michael D. Mr. Kot enjoys golf, wrestling, football, hunting, and fishing.

Darelynn Lehto
Vice President
Prairie Island Tribal Council
3272 Camelot Drive
Woodbury, MN 55125
(612) 385–4108
Fax: (612) 388–1576

7011

Business Information: Prairie Island Tribal Council is a government policy maker and tribally–owned casino. The profits gained through the casino are used to develop the community economically, socially, and culturally. The Council develops community infrastructure such as a clinic, school, and land acquisition. As Vice President, Miss Lehto governs or makes laws for the community and oversees the management of the multi–million dollar casino. She also serves as the Council Representative for various committees, including Business, Constitution Re–Vision, Environment, Education, and Enroll-

ment. **Career Steps:** Elected Vice President, Prairie Island Tribal Council (1993–1997); Owner, Founder, Computer Search, Inc. (1993–1995); Founder, Owner, Golden Palace Casinos (1992–1994). **Associations & Accomplishments:** National Congress of American Indians; Minnesota Indian Gaming Association; Minnesota Indian Chamber of Commerce; Red Wing Racism Committee; National Association of Female Executives; Sheldon Theatre Association of Red Wing; American Management Association; National Council of Urban Economic Developers. **Personal:** Two children: Jo-Dee and Nicole. Miss Lehto enjoys golf, travel, and fishing.

Mr. Niklaus J. Leuenberger
General Manager
The Peninsula New York
700 Fifth Avenue
New York, NY 10019
(212) 247–2200
Fax: (212) 903–3974

7011

Business Information: The Peninsula New York – affiliated with The Peninsula Group, an international hotel/resort holding corporation – is a full–service luxury hotel establishment. Purchased in 1988 by Peninsula, the hotel was totally renovated to its present status as a four–star luxury hotel which encompasses 2 full–service restaurants, 2 lounges, 6 meeting rooms and a 242 rooms and suites hotel. Coming to Peninsula New York in 1992 from executive positions with The Peninsula Group's Manila and Hong Kong operations, Mr. Leuenberger now serves as General Manager for New York concerns. He is responsible for the overall administrative direction of the hotel's operations, focusing primarily on sales, marketing strategies, public relations and customer service. Originally established in 1905 and purchased in 1988 by The Peninsula Group, The Peninsula New York employs approximately 280 staff personnel. **Career Steps:** General Manager, The Peninsula New York (1992–Present); General Manager, The Peninsula Manila, The Peninsula Group (1988–1992); General Manager, The Kowloon Hotel, The Peninsula Group (1987–1988); General Manager, The Garden Hotel, The Peninsula Group (1984–1987). **Education:** Pacific Western University, M.B.A. (1988); School of Hotel Management, Lucerne, Switzerland.

Diana L. Lovejoy
Director of Sales and Marketing
Royal River Casino and Bingo
P. O. Box 326, Veteran Street
Flandreau, SD 57028
(605) 997–3746 (800) 833–8666
Fax: (605) 997–9998

7011

Business Information: Royal River Casino and Bingo is a Las Vegas–style gaming and entertainment facility. Operated on the local Indian reservation, the Company also offers several restaurants and lounges and is in the process of building a $17 million dollar expansion that includes a hotel and other facilities (scheduled completion is June 1997). As Director of Sales and Marketing, Ms. Lovejoy oversees all advertising, public relations, sales, and promotion for the Casino. She is responsible for the entertainment, bussing, and guest services departments, as well as the gift shop. **Career Steps:** Director of Sales and Marketing, Royal River Casino and Bingo (1990–Present); Contract Administrator, Flandreau Santee Sioux Tribe (1980–1990); Finance Clerk, Bureau of Indian Affairs (1976–1980). **Associations & Accomplishments:** Sales and Marketing Executives for Sioux Falls, South Dakota; President of Glacial Lakes Tourism Association of South Dakota; Sioux Falls, Pipestone, MN, and Flandreau, Chambers of Commerce. **Education:** Dakota State University, Associate (1979); South Dakota State University; Pipestone Vo Tech School; Travel Industry Specialist Program; Purdue University; Brown County University. **Personal:** Four children: Della Haus, Lisa Weston, Ricky and Tevia Long. Ms. Lovejoy enjoys reading, working, and spending time with her family and seven grandchildren.

Carla G. Macknin
Director of Human Resources
The Ritz Carlton Hotel
600 Stockton Street
San Francisco, CA 94108–2305
(415) 296–7465
Fax: (415) 362–4427

7011

Business Information: The Ritz Carlton Hotel is one of the premier, leading luxury hotel chains in the world. As Director of Human Resources, Ms. Macknin is responsible for diversified administrative activities and company operations. In addition, she selects and trains employees and is responsible for benefit administration. **Career Steps:** Director of Human Resources, The Ritz Carlton Hotel (1992–Present); Director of Human Resources, Guest Quarters (1989–1992); Director of Human Resources, Checkers Hotel (1988–1989). **Associa-**

tions & Accomplishments: Northern California Human Resources Council; Society for Human Resource Management. **Education:** Southern California College, B.A. (1982); California State – Long Beach, Training Certificate Program. **Personal:** Married to Gary in 1992.

Penny McCoy Booth
Administrator of Training and Employee Relations
Mammoth Mountain Ski Area
P.O. Box 24
Mammoth Lakes, CA 93546
(619) 934–2571
Fax: (619) 934–0602

7011

Business Information: Mammoth Mountain Ski Area is a full–service ski resort offering accommodations and winter and summer activities to clients. The Resort has seven mountains, a climbing wall, concerts, and an adventurous ropes course. As Administrator of Training and Employee Relations, Ms. McCoy Booth oversees all areas of human resources. She is responsible for handling all phases of personnel management including recruitment, reviews, benefits, and troubleshooting for 2,000 employees. Concurrently, she serves on the Board of Directors for the Mammoth Mountain Ski Area facility. **Career Steps:** Mammoth Mountain Ski Area: Administrator of Training and Employee Relations and Member of the Board of Directors (1994–Present), Special Events Coordinator (1990–1994), Ambassador of Skiing (1990–1994). **Associations & Accomplishments:** Church Activities; World Champion Skier. **Personal:** Married to George in 1990. Three children: David, Melissa, and Stanton. Ms. McCoy Booth enjoys mountain biking, writing, hiking, triathlons, and skiing.

Nicholas Naples
Manager
Four Seasons Hotel
1 Logan Square
Philadelphia, PA 19103
(215) 963–2742
Fax: (215) 963–1439

7011

Business Information: Four Seasons Hotel is a five diamond accommodation establishment. Offering a restaurant and banquet facility, a pool, and a gym for patrons, the Hotel has earned the highest rating attainable for hotels and restaurants. As Manager, Mr. Naples manages a diverse 550 member staff and management work force. He is responsible for setting and maintaining the standards of the establishment, to include training and developing employees and future managers. Mr. Naples personally assures that customers receive quality assistance and enjoy their visit to the Hotel. **Career Steps:** Four Seasons – Ritz Carlton: Manager (1992–Present), Rooms Division Executive, Chicago (1992–1995), Executive Assistant Manager, Mauna Lani (1991–1992), Executive Assistant Manager, Lagunaniguel (1988–1991). **Associations & Accomplishments:** Cornell Society of Hotelmen; United States Figure Skating Association. **Education:** Cornell University, Masters (1984); University of Albany, B.A. in Business Administration. **Personal:** Married to Deborah in 1994. Mr. Naples enjoys hotel and restaurant design, skiing, ice skating, travel, and tennis.

W.A. Colin Noble,, F.S.C.A, M.H.C.I.M.A.
President and Chief Executive Officer
Noble Hospitality, Inc.
1641 Anderson Avenue
Manhattan, KS 66502
(913) 539–3800
Fax: (913) 539–1155

7011

Business Information: Noble Hospitality, Inc. is the parent management compan for five hotel chain entities. Established in 1991, Noble Hospitality, Inc. employs approximately 800 staff and reports estimated annual revenue in excess of $15 million. In his current capacity, Mr. Noble is responsible for all aspects of Corporate operations. **Career Steps:** President and Chief Executive Officer, Noble Hospitality, Inc. (1991–Present); President and Chief Executive Officer, Emerald Hotels (United Kingdom) (1980– 1991); President, Northern Group (United Kingdom) (1966–1980). **Associations & Accomplishments:** Member, Northern Ireland Chamber of Commerce (1985–1991); Fellow, Society of Company Accountants (F.S.C.A.); Member, Hotel and Catering Institute Management Association (M.H.C.I.M.A.). **Education:** Degree in Accountancy (United Kingdom), F.S.C.A. (1965); Certification M.H.C.I.M.A. in United Kingdom. **Personal:** Mr. Noble enjoys all types of sports and music during his leisure time.

Deborah Enari Noerper
Director of Human Resources and Quality
Sheraton Princess Kaiulani
120 Kaiulani Avenue
Honolulu, HI 96815–3227
(808) 931–4637
Fax: (808) 931–4656

7011

Business Information: Sheraton Princess Kaiulani is a 1150 room luxury hotel located in the heart of Waikiki. A member of the Sheraton chain of hotels, the Princess Kaiulani was established in 1955, and employs 500+ people. As Director of Human Resources and Quality, Ms. Noerper is responsible for recruitment, community outreach, employee job satisfaction, management development, and total quality management. **Career Steps:** Director of Human Resources and Quality, Sheraton Princess Kaiulani (1996–Present); Employment/ Benefits Manager, Sheraton Washington Hotel, D.C. (1994–1996); Housekeeping Operations Manager, Sheraton Carlton Hotel, D.C. (1993–1994); International Human Resources Coordinator, ITT Sheraton Headquarters, Boston (1990–1993). **Associations & Accomplishments:** Society for Human Resource Management (SHRM); American Business Women's Association. **Education:** Loyola University, M.S.I.R. (1991); Eastern Illinois University, Bachelor's Degree in Psychology (1986). **Personal:** Married to Dr. Stephen E. in 1989. Ms. Noerper enjoys Japanese culture and being an English riding instructor (hunters/jumpers).

Mr. Kevin E. O'Brien, CHA
Vice President and General Manager
**Holiday Inn O'Hare International
d.b.a. O/K Associates, Ltd.**
5440 North River Road
Rosemont, IL 60018
(708) 671–6350
Fax: (708) 671–1378

7011

Business Information: Holiday Inn O'Hare International dba O/K Associates, Ltd. is the operator of the world's largest Holiday Inn Hotel, with 507 rooms, 3 restaurants, 2 lounges, 55,000 square feet of meeting space, a health club, and an indoor/outdoor pool. As Vice President and General Manager, Mr. O'Brien is the chief operating officer responsible for overseeing management of all hotel functions, strategic planning, and business development. Established in 1972, Holiday Inn O'Hare International dba O/K Associates, Ltd. employs 350 people and reports annual revenue of $20 million. **Career Steps:** Vice President and General Manager, Holiday Inn O'Hare International dba O/K Associates, Ltd. (1990–Present); General Manager, Ramada Renaissance (1988–1990); General Manager, Ramada, Inc. (1986–1988); F & B Director, Ramada, Inc. (1984–1986). **Associations & Accomplishments:** Illinois Hotel Association; Chicago Convention Bureau. **Education:** University of Minnesota, B.A. (1980); Mankato State University.

Helma O'Keefe
General Manager
Tremont Suite Hotels
222 Saint Paul Street
Baltimore, MD 21202–2045
(410) 727–2222
Fax: (410) 685–4216

7011

Business Information: The Tremont Suite Hotels is a hospitality and accommodation establishment, as well as a restaurant and banquet facility. The Tremont Suite Hotels operates two all–suite hotels, including a 230–suite and a 60–suite facility, two restaurants, and a Deli. As General Manager, Ms. O'Keefe is responsible for all aspects of operations for the hotel chain, including personnel, payroll, and all administrative functions. With Tremont Hotels for eleven years, Ms. O'Keefe supervises a staff of 150. **Career Steps:** Tremont Suite Hotels: General Manager (1990–Present), Director of Housekeeping (1987–1990), Payroll and Personnel Manager (1985–1987). **Associations & Accomplishments:** Downtown Partnership; Motel/Hotel Management Association; Former Secretary 15th Street Improvement Association, now defunct. **Education:** Received Associates degree in 1959, and attended post–secondary Secretarial School all in Berlin, Germany. **Personal:** Seven children: James (deceased), Vincent Michael, Jacqueline, Roger, Kerry, Tony, and Kathleen. O'Keefe enjoys travel, reading, and study of foreign languages.

Ms. Ora S. Oaks
President
Oaks Properties, Inc.
P.O. Box 26
Panacea, FL 32346
(904) 984–5370
Fax: Please mail or call

7011

Business Information: Oaks Properties, Inc. is the management corporation for the commercial establishment known to the public as the Oaks Restaurant & Motel (family–run business). As President, Ms. Oaks is responsible for all aspects of operations for the restaurant/motel. Established in 1953, Oaks Properties, Inc. employs 60 people with annual sales of $1 million. **Career Steps:** President, Oaks Properties, Inc. – Buys, then offers tracts of land for sale to individuals offering owner financing. **Associations & Accomplishments:** Wakulla Chamber of Commerce; Florida Restaurant Association; Florida Sheriffs Association. **Personal:** Three children: Clayton, Evalinda, and Sonja Lynn. Ms. Oaks enjoys listening to music, reading and watching movies.

Steve Perroots
Operations Manager
Marriott International
10401 Fernwood Road, Suite 300A
Bethesda, MD 20817–1110
(301) 380–5318
Fax: (301) 380–3787

7011

Business Information: Marriott International, Inc. is a conglomerate service and hospitality company. Marriott's two primary businesses are centered around its internal lodging and service groups. The Marriott Lodging group's portfolio of products starts with its full service hotel. This division is commonly called Marriott full service hotels, resorts, and all suite hotels. All totaled, the Marriott Lodging group has 880 hotels in 40 countries providing over 185,000 rooms plus conference and meeting facilities. The internal counterpart to the Marriott Lodging group is the Marriott Service Group — made up of Marriott Management Services (MMS), Marriott Senior Living Services (SLS), and Marriott Distribution Services (MDS). The Marriott Management Services division manages health care, corporate, higher education, secondary school, and facilities management accounts. Marriott International is the result of the division of Marriott Corporation holdings in the Fall of 1993. This special stock dividend produced two companies, Marriott International and Host Marriott. Serving in a managerial capacity for various subsidiary locations of Marriott Corporation since 1983, Steve Perroots was appointed as Marriott International's first Operations Manager in 1991. In this capacity, he is responsible for self–insured and self–administered claims for the Eastern Region sector. One of six regional offices, Mr. Perroot's regional division consists of thirty claims support staff, including seventeen adjusters and 4 supervisors. The Eastern Region Claims Office processes over 7,500 Workers' Compensation and liability claims annually for an 8–state area. **Career Steps:** Operations Manager, Marriott International (1991–Present); Marriott Corporation: National Examiner (1987–1991), Supervisor – California Office (1983–1987); Senior Adjuster, Liberty Mutual Insurance Company (1980–1983). **Associations & Accomplishments:** American Management Association; New York Self–Insured Association; Maryland Self–Insured Association; Participant, Marriott Mentoring Program and Peer Review Panel Program. **Education:** West Virginia University, B.S. (1979). **Personal:** Married to Diana in 1990. Two children: Jessica and Katherine. Mr. Perroots enjoys volunteering for the Catholic youth ministry.

John B. Powers
Facilities Manager – Chief Engineer
Penn Tower Hotel
Civic Center Blvd., 34th Street
Philadelphia, PA 19104
(215) 387–8333
Fax: (215) 573–2040

7011

Business Information: Penn Tower Hotel, owned and operated by the University of Pennsylvania, located on the campus, is a 175 room, 21 story multi–use building. The Penn Tower houses medical offices, as well as hotel rooms, lounges, dining areas, and a 300–seat ballroom. As Facilities Manager – Chief Engineer, Mr. Powers is responsible for overseeing the building, hotel budget, all scheduling, purchasing, and working with contractors. **Career Steps:** Facilities Manager – Chief Engineer, Penn Tower Hotel (1988–Present); Vice President, Inncorp Management (1978–1988); Assistant General Manager, Sheraton Rolling Green (1967–1978). **Associations & Accomplishments:** Philadelphia Hotel Engineers Association. **Personal:** Mr. Powers enjoys taking an annual trip to Mexico.

Ms. Kay A. Reece
General Manager
Holiday Inn Express
641 South Cumberland Street
Lebanon, TN 37087
(615) 444–7020
Fax: (615) 443–4185

7011

Business Information: Holiday Inn Express is a streamlined version of the traditional Holiday Inn (without restaurant/ lounge facilities), offering inexpensive accommodations with complimentary jacuzzi and sauna facilities, and a small meeting facility. The Hotel has been rated #1 for guest satisfaction. As General Manager, Ms. Reece manages all aspects of Hotel operations, administration and staffing. Established in 1992, Holiday Inn Express employs a staff of 15. **Career Steps:** General Manager, Holiday Inn Express (1992–Present); General Manager, Hampton Inn (1991– 1992); Public Housing Manager, Gallatin Housing Authority (1990–1991). **Associations & Accomplishments:** Chamber of Commerce.

Kimberly Sawyer–Chavez
Director of Catering
Sheraton Four Points
3535 Quebec Street
Denver, CO 80207
(303) 333–7711
Fax: (303) 329–9642

7011

Business Information: Sheraton Four Points is a full–service accommodation operation offering full–scale lodging and dining services. As Director of Catering, Ms. Sawyer–Chavez oversees all catering functions, including marketing, advertising, and soliciting new business. **Career Steps:** Sheraton Four Points: Director of Catering (1996–Present), Banquet Manager (1994–1996). **Associations & Accomplishments:** Association of Professional Wedding Planners; Rocky Mountain Chapter of Meeting Professionals International. **Education:** University of Northern Colorado. **Personal:** Married to Joseph in 1986. Two children: Shaina and Joshua. Ms. Sawyer–Chavez enjoys skiing and hiking.

Al Sikirdji
Director of Table Games
Harrah's Casino
151 North Joliet Street
Joliet, IL 60432–4018
(815) 740–7808
Fax: (815) 774–2659

7011

Business Information: Harrah's Casino is an adult entertainment gaming facility. In operation 22 hours a day, 7 days a week, the Casino offers craps, roulette, Caribbean stud poker, black jack and slot machines. With 15 locations in the United States, and one casino in New Zealand. Harrah's is a multi–billion dollar corporation. As Director of Table Games for the Joliet riverboat concern, Mr. Sikirdji manages the riverboat operation and a staff of 550 people. He is responsible for daily operations, customer relations, budgetary concerns, payroll, and strategic planning for the Joliet operation. **Career Steps:** Harrah's Casino–Joliet: Director of Table Games (1995–Present), Casino Manager (1993–1995); Harrah's Casino–Atlantic City: Dual Rate Shift Manager (1989–1993), Pit Boss (1985–1989). **Education:** William H. Taft High School. **Personal:** Married to Karen in 1976. Two children: Alan and Marissa. Mr. Sikirdji enjoys weightlifting and bicycling.

Hermann Simon
General Manager
The Cliff Bay Resort Hotel
Estrada Monumental 147, 9000 Funchal
Madeira, Portugal
(351) 91761818
Fax: (351) 91762524

7011

Business Information: The Cliff Bay Resort Hotel, an Inter–Continental and Global Partner Resort, is a 201–room, 5–Star resort hotel, providing three restaurants, an indoor/outdoor fresh water heated pool, fitness activities, four fully–equipped conference and banqueting rooms, and numerous other luxury amenities. The Cliff Bay Resort Hotel accommodates mainly the luxury tourist market in Funchal, Madeira–Portugal. With over 25 years experience in the hotel industry and a Certified Hotel Administrator, Mr. Simon joined The Cliff Bay Resort Hotel as General Manager in 1994. He is responsible for all aspects of operations, including administration, finances, sales, and marketing. Career milestones include being associated with the Sheraton chain for 16 years, as well as serving at the Kuwait International Hotel (formerly Kuwait Hilton), the world–renowned Imperial Hotel in Vienna, the Montreux Palace Hotel in Switzerland, and at the Berlin and London Hiltons. **Career Steps:** General Manager, The Cliff Bay

Resort Hotel (1994–Present); General Manager, Kuwait International Hotel (1988–1993); General Manager, Abu Dhabi Sheraton (1988); General Manager, Dhaka Sheraton (1984–1988). **Associations & Accomplishments:** Chaine Des Rotisseurs (1983–Present); President, International Hotel Association of Bangladesh; CHA; Global Hoteliers Club; Recipient, Sheraton President's Award for outstanding performance (1983); Nominatee, ITT Harold S. Geneen Award (1987); Awardee, Golden Insignia of Merit of The Republic of Austria by the President of Austria for his contributions to the Hotel industry (1990); Fluent in three languages; Full Member, MHCIMA by the British–based Hotel Catering an Institutional Management Association. **Education:** CHA (1992); Hotel Management School – Berlin; The Educational Institute of the American Hotel & Motel Association, Certified Hotel Administrator's Degree. **Personal:** Married to Monica in 1972. Mr. Simon enjoys golf, tennis, chess, gardening, and collecting vintage radios and televisions.

Richard B. Simzak, CHA

General Manager
Greenville Inn Inc.
851 Martin Street
Greenville, OH 45331–1860
(513) 548–3613
Fax: (513) 548–5851

7011

Business Information: Greenville Inn, Inc. is a full–service, hotel, food, and beverage operation located in Greenville, Ohio. Established in 1985, Greenville Inn, Inc. reports annual revenue of $2.5 million and currently employs 48 people. A Certified Hotel Administrator with over seventeen years expertise in the hotel and restaurant industries, Mr. Simzak joined Greenville Inn, Inc. in 1993. Serving as General Manager, he has total financial profit and loss responsibility for the Corporation. **Career Steps:** General Manager, Greenville Inn Inc. (1993–Present); Vice President Food & Beverage, MMI Hotel Group – Jackson, MS (1983–1993); Area Director, Poole Associates – Charleston, WV (1981–1983); Food & Beverage Director, Radisson Hotel Corporation (1978–1981). **Associations & Accomplishments:** National Restaurant Association; Board of Directors, Darke County Chamber of Commerce; Ohio Hotel & Motel Association; Vice Chairman, Darke County Visitors Bureau American Hotel & Motel Association; Better Business Bureau; National Institute of Food & Beverage; Civitan; Kiwanis; Miami Restaurant Association; National Food Service Panel (1984–1993). **Education:** Michigan State University (1953–1956); 4th U.S. Army Food Service School; Holiday Inn University; Central Michigan University; CERTIFIED: CHA (Certified Hotel Administrator) (1985). **Personal:** Married to Joyce in 1985. Four children: Gary, Deborah, Danny and Richard B II. Mr. Simzak enjoys reading, walking, travel and collecting unusual recipes and menus.

Sharon M. Sing

Director of Reservations
Hyatt Hotels & Resorts
9805 Q Street
Omaha, NE 68127
(402) 593–5108
Fax: (402) 593–9838

7011

Business Information: Hyatt Hotels & Resorts is one of the world's leaders in premier hospitality facilities. The National Sales Office, located in Omaha, Nebraska, is the managerial administrative office for in–bound reservation service for all hotels and resorts operated by the Hyatt Corporation. As Director of Tele–Services, Ms. Sing is responsible for Frequent Travel Operations in Omaha, private label contract negotiation and management for both clients and vendors, strategic planning and oversight of the Customer Service Group. In addition, she is responsible for ensuring quality performance and service in all areas, as well as coordinating account support services. **Career Steps:** Director of Reservations, Hyatt Hotels & Resorts (1995–Present); Manager of Customer Service Operations, Marriott International (1990–1995); Manager of Quality Control, Marriott Hotels, Resorts, and Suites (1989–1990). **Associations & Accomplishments:** Society of Consumer Affairs Professionals; International Association of Reservation Executives; Association of Quality Participation; International Quality & Productivity Center: Guest Speaker on Self–Directed Work Teams, Service Strategies, and Total Quality Management. **Education:** Development Dimensions International, Certified Trainer; Attended: University of Nebraska – Omaha, Institute of Financial Education – Omaha. **Personal:** Married to John in 1971. Two children: Jamie Jo and Jason John. Ms. Sing enjoys gardening, playing piano, reading, and travel.

Daniel P. Smith

Food & Beverage Director
Holiday Inn
6515 International Drive
Orlando, FL 32819
(407) 351–3500
Fax: (407) 351–5727

7011

Business Information: Holiday Inn, International Drive, Orlando, Florida, is a full service, 652 room resort and convention center with multiple food and beverage outlets. As Food & Beverage Director, Mr. Smith is responsible for consulting six Holiday Inns in Florida, rendering his expertise in the food and beverage service. **Career Steps:** Food & Beverage Director, Holiday Inn (1989–Present); F & B Director, HIID (1995–Present); F & B Director, Sheraton Park South (1993–1995); Reg. General Manager, Imaginative Operations, Inc. (1991–1993). **Associations & Accomplishments:** South Orange Little League. **Education:** University of Florida (1975–1977); Certified Food & Beverage Executive by American Hotel Motel Assn.; Certified Food & Beverage Manager; Holiday Inn University; Microsoft Extension Courses; Valencia Community College. **Personal:** Married to Julie Renae. Four children: Michael, Danielle, Michelle, and Sean. Mr. Smith enjoys sports.

Kathaleen J. (K.J.) Smith

Credit/Cage Manager
Clarion Hotel Casino
3800 South Virginia Street
Reno, NV 89502
(702) 825–4700
Fax: (702) 825–1409

7011

Business Information: Clarion Hotel Casino is an over 900 room facility providing luxury accommodations to clients in the Reno, Nevada area. A member of Clarion, one of the world's leaders in premier and mid–level economy hospitality facilities, the Clarion Hotel Casino employs over 1,500 people. As Credit/Cage Manager, Ms. Smith is responsible for the Casino's credits and collections, and for controlling the cash flow. In addition to supervising a staff of 40, Ms. Smith designs and implements training programs for the cage, vault, credit, and hard count operations, as well as regulation 6A and budgeting resources. She is responsible for planning and programming, and for building good team skills. **Career Steps:** Credit/Cage Manager, Clarion Hotel Casino (1992–Present); Manager, Vault, Cage, Credit Departments, Pioneer Inn Hotel/Casino (1988–1992); Sales Representative, Trans Union Credit Information Company (1987–1988); Credit Collection Manager, California Video Sales (1986–1987); Credit Collection Cage Manager, John Ascuaga's Nugget (1971–1986). **Associations & Accomplishments:** Past President, International Credit Association Local Chapter; Board of Directors, ICA District 11; Charter Member SNCA, CWI; NCCCIA; Special Olympics; Trindy Church Alter Guild. **Education:** TMCC; University of Nevada, Hotel Management; Portland State, Business Administration Major; Trackee Meadows Community College; Numerous Seminars pertaining to business management and related subjects. **Personal:** Two children: Tasha Smith Lowrey and Douglas A. Ms. Smith enjoys walking, camping, boating, reading, and gardening.

Ms. Stephanie Sonnabend

Executive Vice President
Sonesta International Hotels Corporation
200 Clarendon Street
Boston, MA 02116
(617) 421–5400
Fax: (617) 421–5402

7011

Business Information: Sonesta International Hotels Corporation is a hotel management company that owns and operates 18 hotels in the United States and other areas such as the Caribbean, South America, Egypt and Israel. As Executive Vice President, Ms. Sonnabend oversees the marketing, information technology and design divisions. She is also involved in strategic planning and development. Established in 1956, Sonesta International Hotels Corporation employs 4000 people. **Career Steps:** Executive Vice President, Sonesta International Hotels Corporation (1993–Present); Vice President, Marketing, Sonesta International Hotels Corporation (1983–1993). **Associations & Accomplishments:** Member, Young Presidents Organization; Member, The Boston Club; Member, American Marketing Asociation; Member, American Society of Travel Agents; Member, Meeting Professionals International; Member, Business Executives for National Security; Board Member, Cambridge Chamber of Commerce; Young Presidents Organization. Education: MIT, Sloan School of Management, M.B.A.; Harvard University, B.A. **Personal:** Married to Gregory Ciccolo in 1985. Two children: Antonia and Nicholas."

Grace Soo, C.G.A.

Director of Finance/Treasurer
Great Canadian Casino Company Ltd
13775 Commerce Parkway, Suite 350
Richmond, British Columbia V6V 2V4
(604) 303–1000 (604) 303–1025
Fax: (604) 279–8505

7011

Business Information: Great Canadian Casino Company Ltd. is a charity casino management company providing casino gaming fund–raising opportunities for non profit organizations. Regional in scope, the Company has seven locations throughout British Columbia, Canada. As Director of Finance/Treasurer, Ms. Soo is accountable for the preparation of the consolidated group's annual budget and overall integrity and effective operation and management of the Company's accounting, financial management and reporting systems including its payroll and employee benefits and casino accounting systems. She is responsible for preparation of the consolidated group's financial statements and related income tax and Company filings, advising the President and Chairman on financing, financial matters and maintaining a close liaison with the Company's auditors and other related regulatory bodies. She supervises a support staff of eight. **Career Steps:** Great Canadian Casino Company Ltd.: Director of Finance/Treasurer (1995–Present), Controller (1987–1995); Financial Advisor, Goldrush Casino & Mining Corporation (1994); Senior Accountant, Canadian Western Bank (1984–1987); Batch Auditor/Customer Service, Bank of Montreal (1980–1984). **Associations & Accomplishments:** The Certified General Accountants Association of British Columbia; International Association of Hospitality Accountants, Inc.; Tutor for various courses offered by the Certified General Accountants Association. **Education:** The Certified General Accountants Association of British Columbia, Certified General Accountant (1987); The Certified General Accountants Association of Canada, Certified General Accountant (1987); British Columbia Institute of Technology, Diploma of Technology, Financial Management (1983); Vancouver Community College (1981); The Canadian Securities Institute, The Canadian Securities Course (1994). **Personal:** Ms. Soo enjoys bowling, cycling, rollerblading, and reading.

Bernard J. Strackhouse

Beverage Manager
Hotel Hershey
P. O. Box 400
Hershey, PA 17033
(717) 533–2171
Fax: (717) 534–8888

7011

Business Information: Hotel Hershey has been called the hotel that "out–palaces the palaces of the Maharajas of India." With elegant Mediterranean touches, formal gardens, and Four–Diamond luxury, the Hotel is dedicated to personal, attentive and friendly service. The Facility offers 241 guest rooms, many with views of the golf course or gardens and two of Central Pennsylvania's most renowned restaurants. As Beverage Manager, Mr. Strackhouse oversees all aspects of beverage selection for the Hotel. He is responsible for assuring all functions (i.e. banquets, conferences, meetings, etc.) are properly supplied, and ensures the Hotel restaurant and other Company facilities are well stocked with a premier selection of alcoholic and non–alcoholic beverages. **Career Steps:** Beverage Manager, Hotel Hershey (1994–Present); General Manager, Italian Oven, Mechinburg (1992–1994); General Manager, Italian Oven, Scott Township (1990–1994). **Associations & Accomplishments:** Pennsylvania Restaurant Association; Boy Scouts of America. **Education:** Pennsylvania State University, B.S. (1986). **Personal:** Mr. Strackhouse enjoys golf, biking, and being a wine enthusiast.

Wayne F. Swanson

President
Island Romance Holidays
4928 Lejeune Road
Coral Gables, FL 33146–2208
(305) 668–0008
Fax: (305) 668–0111

7011

Business Information: Island Romance Holidays is a hotel and resort marketing firm, representing hotels and resort properties throughout Florida and the Caribbean. As President, Mr. Swanson is responsible for all aspects of Company operations, including sales, public relations, marketing, strategic planning, hiring and firing, securing hotels and tours, and tour operator contracting. **Career Steps:** President, Island Romance Holidays (1994–Present); Senior Vice President, Sandals Resorts (1982–1993). **Associations & Accomplishments:** Jamaica–American Chamber of Commerce; Caribbean Hotel Association; Coral Gables Chamber of Commerce. **Education:** Boston University, B.F.A. (1966); University of Maryland, B.A. in Psychology (1964). **Personal:** Married to Cynthia in 1996. Mr. Swanson enjoys collecting art and exotic cars.

Mohammed Tarique
Director and Assistant Secretary
Servico Hotel and Resorts
1601 Belvedere Road
West Palm Beach, FL 33406
(407) 689–9970
Fax: (407) 689–5666

7011

Business Information: Servico Hotel and Resorts is a hotel owner and operator. Currently Servico owns the second largest Holiday Inn franchise, as well as 34 other hotels in 19 states. Servico operates an additional 20 hotels throughout the United States and is always expanding their venture by merging with other hotel owners. Established in 1956, Servico Hotel and Resorts currently employs 98 people in the headquarters office. As Director and Assistant Secretary, Mr. Tarique is responsible for property procurement and acquisition, credit card processing, and the oversight of all operations. In his first five years with the Company, Mr. Tarique has saved Servico over $4 million and has used his expertise to determine the most useful data base for credit card processing. **Career Steps:** Director and Assistant Secretary, Servico Hotel and Resorts (1990–Present); Controller, Hyatt Corporation (1983–1990); Manager, Dixie Hotel (1981–1983). **Associations & Accomplishments:** National Association of Credit Management, Florida Chapter; Treasurer, MC Palm Beach County Association. **Education:** Glasgow College of Technology, B.S. (1979). **Personal:** Married to Habiba in 1989. Two children: Emad and Nabeel. Mr. Tarique enjoys basketball, chess and watching movies.

Bruce A. Taylor
General Manager
Palms at Palm Springs
572 N. Indian Canyon Drive
Palm Springs, CA 92262–6030
(619) 325–1111
Fax: (619) 327–0867

7011

Business Information: Palms at Palm Springs is a full–service, 40–room hotel, resort and spa facility, offering a full–line of exercise programs, workshops, and seminars, as well as a variety of food and beverages. Joining Palms at Palm Springs as General Manager in 1994, Mr. Taylor is responsible for all administration and supervision of daily operations, including financial matters, food, and beverages. **Career Steps:** General Manager, Palms at Palm Springs (1994–Present); President, Sports Leisure Group (1991–1994); Operating Officer, Nakano Ltd (1987–1991); Resort Administrator, LaCosta Resort & Spa (1985–1987). **Associations & Accomplishments:** Palm Springs Hotel Association; Hospitality Golf Association; Desert Resorts Association; Chamber of Commerce. **Education:** University of California – Los Angeles: M.S. and B.S. (1980); LMT, Mueller/San Diego **Personal:** Married to June in 1985. Mr. Taylor enjoys golf, hiking, and fitness training.

Kenneth R. Taylor
••• —◉— •••

Chief Engineer
Courtyard by Marriott – Medical Center
5601 Peachtree–Dunwoody Road
Atlanta, GA 30342
(404) 843–2300
Fax: (404) 851–1938

7011

Business Information: Courtyard by Marriott is a conglomerate service and hospitality company. Marriott's two primary businesses are centered around its internal lodging and service groups which earned $4.8 and $3.6 billion respectively in annual sales last year. The Marriott Lodging group's portfolio of products starts with its full service hotel. This division is commonly called Marriott full service hotels, resorts, and all suite hotels. The Lodging group also has a limited lodging group which includes Courtyard by Marriott — moderately priced hotels targeted towards business travelers, and Residence Inn — designed for the extended stay market. Also included in this group is Fairfield Inn, Marriott's economy market product. All totaled, the Marriott Lodging group has 880 hotels in 40 countries providing over 185,000 rooms plus conference and meeting facilities. As Chief Engineer, Mr. Taylor is responsible for maintenance of the 128 room hotel. He also travels to other Marriott hotels in his region to help with their maintenance programs. **Career Steps:** Chief Engineer, Marriott Corporation (1995–Present); Winegardner & Hammons: Maintenance Supervisor – Best Western (1995), Maintenance Department Lieutenant – Radisson (1991–1995). **Associations & Accomplishments:** Refrigeration Service Engineers Society; Radisson Hotels International Corporate Employee of the Year (1993). **Education:** Pinellas Technical Education Center: H.V.A.C. (1992), Building Maintenance

(1994). **Personal:** Mr. Taylor enjoys travel, exercise, shopping, and reading.

Paula Taylor
Food and Beverage Director
Best Western, Shelton Inn
450 E. Pershing Road
Decatur, IL 62526
(217) 877–2073
Fax: (217) 875–4085

7011

Business Information: Best Western, Shelton Inn is an independently–owned and operated 150 room hotel, with a full restaurant and banquet hall. A member of the Best Western chain of hotels, the Inn was established in 1959 and employs eighty people. As Food and Beverage Director, Mrs. Taylor also serves as General Manager of the Hotel. She is responsible for oversight of all aspects of the Inn including human resources and personnel management, administration, operations, customer service, reservations, and inventory control. **Career Steps:** Food and Beverage Director, Best Western, Shelton Inn (1986–Present). **Associations & Accomplishments:** Treasurer, Illinois Restaurant Association. **Education:** Richland Community College, Associate (1981). **Personal:** Four children: Vicky Gagnon, Jon, Pam, and Marc Taylor. Mrs. Taylor enjoys college basketball.

Roger C. Turvey Jr.
Chief Maintenance Engineer
Culver Properties d.b.a. Quality Inn
3301 Market Street NE
Salem, OR 97301–1819
(503) 370–7888
Fax: (503) 370–6305

7011

Business Information: Culver Properties d.b.a. Quality Inn is a 150–room hotel with a convention center and 13 meeting rooms. Established in 1980, the hotel/convention center currently employs 110 people. As Chief Maintenance Engineer, Mr. Turvey oversees all renovations to the hotel/convention center. Other duties include oversight of hotel security, the maintenance department, room renovations and general and sub–contractors. **Career Steps:** Chief Maintenance Engineer, Culver Properties DBA Quality Inn (1995–Present); Engineer, Radisson Hotels (1992–1993); Superintendent, Nico.mgt. and Gholon Industries (1988–1992). **Education:** Middletown High School (1986). **Personal:** Mr. Turvey enjoys scuba diving, rappeling, and renovating custom houses.

Marsha Van
Director of Catering
Hyatt Regency Reston
1800 Presidents Street
Reston, VA 22090
(703) 709–1234
Fax: (703) 709–6244

7011

Business Information: Hyatt Regency Reston is a four–star premier and mid–level economy hospitality facility with reception and convention centers. Ms. Van started her catering career with Hyatt in 1991 as Assistant Director of Catering at the O'Hare Hyatt Regency. Promoted in the interim to Director of Catering at the Minneapolis Hyatt, she transferred to her present position in Reston, Virginia, in 1994. She is now part of a nine member Executive Management Team, supervising catering and convention services, public relations, and various administrative activities. **Career Steps:** Hyatt Hotels and Resorts: Director of Catering, Hyatt Regency Reston (1994–Present), Director of Catering, Hyatt Regency Minneapolis (1993–1994), Associate Director of Catering, Hyatt Regency Ohare (1991–1993). **Associations & Accomplishments:** National Association of Catering Executives; Area Chamber of Commerce. **Education:** Certified Meeting Planner; LES–Learning Enviroment. **Personal:** Two children: Jill Gildea and Terri Gordon. She also has four grandchildren. Ms. Van enjoys fundraising, outdoors, and spending time with family and friends.

Joanne Witmer
Director of Payroll
MGM Grand Hotel
3799 Las Vegas Boulevard South
Las Vegas, NV 89109–4319
(702) 891–3745
Fax: (702) 891–3760

7011

Business Information: MGM Grand Hotel, the world's largest casino hotel, is a full–service accommodation operation,

with full–scale lodging and dining facilities. As Director of Payroll, Ms. Witmer is responsible for directing the payroll department in the payment of over 8,000 employees. **Career Steps:** Director of Payroll, MGM Grand Hotel (1995–Present); Payroll Supervisor, Caesars Palace (1986–1995); Payroll Administrator, EG&G Special Projects (1984–1986). **Associations & Accomplishments:** American Payroll Association: Government Liasion, Membership Coordinator. **Personal:** Married to David in 1982. Two children: Jamie and Joshua. Ms. Witmer enjoys writing payroll newsletter "PayDirt".

Paul D. Anderson
Director of Marketing and Operations
Shammineau Camp and Conference Center
P O Box 244
Motley, MN 56466
(218) 575–2240
Fax: (218) 575–2371

7032

Business Information: Shammineau Camp and Conference Center is a year 'round camp and conference center hosting over 14,000 guests annually. Established in 1958, the Center estimates 1996 revenue at $1 million, employing 100 people during the summer season and 20 full–time employees during the rest of the year. As Director of Marketing and Operations, Mr. Anderson oversees the day–to–day operations of the campground/conference center. Other responsibilities include developing and implementing new marketing techniques for the services offered, public relations, and fund raising. **Career Steps:** Director of Marketing and Operations, Shammineau Camp and Conference Center (1991–Present); Owner, Homes Today (1986–1991); Store Manager, Ashland Oil (1978–1985). **Associations & Accomplishments:** Motley Minnesota School Board. **Education:** Northwestern College, B.Sc. (1993); Normandale Junior College, A.A. Lib.Ed., A.A. Orthopedic Physician's Assistant. **Personal:** Married to Janet in 1979. Four children: Laura, Gabriel, Joshua, and Wade. Mr. Anderson enjoys fishing, reading, music, and spending time with his family.

Amy F. Pattee
Revenue System Director
Denali Park Resorts
241 West Ship Creek Avenue
Anchorage, AK 99501–1670
(907) 279–2653
Fax: (907) 258–3668

7032

Business Information: Denali Park Resorts is made up of three resort hotels and a tour operation for Denali National Park. The Park is situated near Mt. McKinley in the Alaska's interior. As Revenue System Director, Ms. Pattee is responsible for inventory control, ranking wholesalers, and client rate negotiations. As Systems Administrator, Ms. Pattee assists in the training of staff members on the in–house software system and has written a software manual for the system. Other duties include public relations for the Park and strategic long– and short–term planning for her departments. **Career Steps:** Aramark–Denali Park Resorts: Revenue System Director (1995–Present); Hotel Manager, Denali Park Hotel (1995), Front Office Manager (1992–1995); Assistant Hotel Manager, Aramark–Lake Quinault Lodge (1991–1992). **Education:** University of Puget Sound, B.A. (1989); University of Otago, New Zealand, Graduate Diploma. **Personal:** Ms. Pattee enjoys backpacking, mountain, biking and reading.

Sallie T. Ransom
Director of Promotions
Camp Seagull / Camp Seafarer
RR 65 Box 1
Arapahoe, NC 28510
(919) 249–1111
Fax: (919) 249–1266
EMAIL: See Below

7032

Business Information: Camp Seagull / Camp Seafarer are YMCA resident camps serving families, corporate groups, school children, and church organizations. As Director of Promotions, Ms. Ransom is responsible for the design of all promotional literature and videos, media relations, publication of the newsletter, and travel to more than 60 cities to promote the camps and programming. Internet users may reach her via: SGSF.promo@coastalnet.com **Career Steps:** Director of Promotions, Camp Seagull / Camp Seafarer (1995–Present); Manager, Black Dog Cafe; Advertising Associate, Sally Johns Design. **Associations & Accomplishments:** American Camping Association; Craven County Leadership Association; Pledge Advisor – UNC Chapel Hill, Chi Omega Sorority; Committee Chamber Member – Jobs and Teens; Associate Member, North Carolina Museum of History; Camps featured in 'Family Life' magazine. **Education:** Auburn University,

B.A. (1991). **Personal:** Ms. Ransom enjoys being outside, tennis, mountain biking, and skydiving.

7200 Personal Services

7211 Power laundries, family and commercial
7212 Garment pressing and cleaners' agents
7213 Linen supply
7215 Coin–operated laundries and cleaning
7216 Drycleaning plants, except rug
7217 Carpet and upholstery cleaning
7218 Industrial launderers
7219 Laundry and garment services, NEC
7221 Photographic studios, portrait
7231 Beauty shops
7241 Barber shops
7251 Shoe repair and shoeshine parlors
7261 Funeral service and crematories
7291 Tax return preparation services
7299 Miscellaneous personal services, NEC

Randol F. Bartsch

President/Chief Executive Officer
Act One Textile Service Cos
P.O. Box 2094, 2448 Townline Road
Clearbrook, British Columbia V2T 3X8
(604) 854–4106
Fax: (604) 852–8681

7213

Business Information: Act One Textile Service Cos is an industrial and commercial textile maintenance and linen supply company. The Company offers its services to hotels, hospitals, and industrial and commercial businesses in Western Canada. As President/Chief Executive Officer, Mr. Bartsch is responsible for all aspects of Company operations, including administration, growth, and market expansion. **Career Steps:** President/Chief Executive Officer, Act One Textile Service Cos (1988–Present); President/Chief Executive Officer, Interwest Sport Promotions (1980–198n4); World Cup Freestyle Ski Competitor, Canadian Ski Team (1976–1982). **Associations & Accomplishments:** Former President, Rotary; Director, Western Canada Summer Games; Trustee, British Columbia Sports Hall of Fame; Chapter Executive, Y.P.O. **Personal:** Married to Patsy in 1980. Two children: E. Brendon and Bryan John Randol. Mr. Bartsch enjoys skiing, racquetball, and target shooting.

Mr. Nick M. Granato

Franchise Director
Coit Services, Inc.
897 Hinckley Road
Burlingame, CA 94010
(415) 697–5471 ext 121
Fax: (415) 697–6117

7217

Business Information: Coit Services, Inc. is an international home cleaning service specializing in drapery, carpet and upholstery cleaning. The Company currently has offices located throughout the United States, London, Canada and Thailand. As Franchise Director, Mr. Granato is responsible for all activities regarding the sale of new franchise units, as well as the servicing of 52 current franchise operations. Established in 1950, Coit Services, Inc. employs 1,000 people with annual sales of $65 million. **Career Steps:** Franchise Director, Coit Services, Inc. (1992–Present); President, Cleaning Systems Inc. (1992–1987); Vice President of Operation, Coit Services (1987–1985); General Manager, Cleanol Services (1980–1985); Sales Representative, Cleanol (1978–1980). **Associations & Accomplishments:** Certified – Institute of Inspection, Cleaning and Restoration; Association of Specialty Cleaning and Restoration. **Education:** East York Collegiate – Canada (1976); Mr. Granato has received diversified certificates within the cleaning industry. **Personal:** Married to Jean in 1980. Three children: Erinn, Anthony and Justin. Mr. Granato enjoys sports, camping and coaching.

J.A. (Bud) Granger

Vice President of Overall Cleanroom Division
Overall Laundry Services, Inc.
7200 Hardeson Road
Everett, WA 98206–9040
(800) 926–6996 Ext. 261
Fax: (206) 682–1254
EMail: See Below

7218

Business Information: Overall Laundry Services, Inc. provides cleanroom laundry and consulting services. The cleanroom services are provided to businesses in the semiconductor industry and other industrial companies. As Vice President of Overall Cleanroom Division, Mr. Granger is responsible for the design of garments, training on laundered products use, change rooms, and the selection of new fabrics. Internet users can reach him via: overallsv@aol.com **Career Steps:** Vice President of Overall Cleanroom Division, Overall Laundry Services, Inc. (1981–Present); Executive Recruiter, Executive Suite (1980–1981); Marketing Representative, IBM (1976–1980); Major (Pilot), U.S. Marine Corps (1970–1976). **Associations & Accomplishments:** Institute of Environmental Sciences; Uniform and Textile Services Association. **Education:** United States Naval Academy, B.S. (1970); Pepperdine University, Graduate work in Business. **Personal:** Married to Laurel in 1979. Two children: Patrick and Meghan. Mr. Granger enjoys piano and golf.

Derrick G.A. Miller

Vice President
UFI Inc.
129–01 Jamaica Avenue
Richmond Hill, NY 11418
(718) 846–2900
Fax: (718) 849–9316

7218

Business Information: UFI Inc. is a leading national industrial laundry and health aids supplier. Products offered include rrental uniforms, linens, and diapers; serving hospitals, nursing homes, banks, industrial plants, airlines and other commercial enterprises. Established in 1934, UFI distributes throughout the tri–state area of New York, Connecticut and New Jersey, and reports annual revenue in excess of $20 million. As Vice President, Mr. Miller is responsible for plant, engineering and fleet operations, as well as the oversight of all sales and distribution activities. **Career Steps:** UFI Inc.: Vice President (1986–Present), Engineering Manager (1984–1986); Engineering Manager, Eutectic Inc. (1980–1984); Plant Manager, Colgate–Palmolive Company (1970–1979); Project Engineer, Seagrams Company (1965–1970). **Associations & Accomplishments:** Institute of Mechanical Engineers; Association of Energy Engineers; American Management Institute; Plant Engineering Institute; Published in "Institute of Mechanical Engineers Journal"; Lectured at APEC Technical College, he was Adjunct Professor. **Education:** New York University, M.B.A. (1978); University of Birmingham – England, B.Sc. (1964); London Imperial College, B.Sc. (1962). **Personal:** Married to Dorothy in 1991. Mr. Miller enjoys flying, golf, and playing chess.

Peter S. Andreas

Production Manager
Alfa Color Lab
535 West 135th Street
Gardena, CA 90248–1505
(310) 532–2532
Fax: Please mail or call

7221

Business Information: Alfa Color Lab is one of the leading portrait labs in the country, printing custom portraits for high–end portrait studios. Established in 1967, the Company employs 150 people and has an estimated annual revenue of $7.5 million. As Production Manager, Mr. Andreas oversees all aspects of the Lab, ensures production schedules are met, and is responsible for quality assurance, equipment maintenance, and training. **Career Steps:** Alfa Color Lab: Production Manager (1994–Present), Lab Manager (1978–94); Vice President/Lab Manager, Stikich Colour Lab (1978). **Education:** Brook Institute, B.A. (1977). **Personal:** Mr. Andreas enjoys working on cars, hiking, hunting, fishing, horseback riding, and cycling.

Kevin Boyles

Owner
Expose International
1155 Coast Village Road #E
Santa Barbara, CA 93108–2744
(805) 969–1941
Fax: (805) 969–7503

7231

Business Information: Expose International is a full–service hair salon and spa with two locations. As Owner, Mr. Boyles is responsible for all aspects of Company operations, to include staffing; hiring, employee motivation, scheduling, hair cutting, styling and the oversight of all spa activities. **Career Steps:** Owner, Expose International (1988–Present); Artistic Director, Philip Sitron (1984–1988); Artistic Telecommunications Manager, Alen International (1980–1984). **Associations & Accomplishments:** World Federation of Superior Hair Dressers; President, Art & Fashion Group; Local Businessmen of Santa Barbara. **Education:** Belmont Abby, Graduate (1977). **Personal:** Four children: James, Sophie, Maxwell, and Sara. Mr. Boyles enjoys cars, biking, boating, and travel.

Mitiko Yanagui

Owner
Mitiko's Hairdresser and Boutique
Conselneiro Moreira De Barros 515 Sta–Tergeinha
Sao Paulo, Brazil 02018
(011) 290–2780
Fax: (011) 298–9650

7231

Business Information: Mitiko's Hairdresser and Boutique is an establishment offering hairdressing and related services, as well as clothing, jewelry, and accessories. Established in 1970, the Company employs ten people, and has an estimated annual revenue of $80 thousand. As Owner, Ms. Yanagui is responsible for all aspects of the Company. Her duties include, administration, customer service, finance and budgetary concerns, and strategic planning. She is also fluent in French, English, and Italian. **Career Steps:** Owner, Mitiko's Hairdresser and Boutique (1970–Present); Rural Worker; Chore Girl; Dressmaker. **Associations & Accomplishments:** Commercial Associates; ICD Intercoiffure. **Personal:** Ms. Yanagui enjoys swimming and travel.

D. A. Naegelin

Regional Sales Vice President
The Loewen Group
1133 N. Robinson Avenue
Oklahoma City, OK 73103
(405) 236–2067
Fax: (405) 239–5148

7261

Business Information: The Loewen Group provides management services to funeral homes and cemeteries. Established in 1990, the Group supervises over 1,000 funeral homes and 330 cemeteries throughout Canada and the United States. With estimated revenue of $16 million, the Group is the largest of its kind in Canada and second largest in the United States. As Regional Sales Vice President, Mr. Naegelin has oversight of the midwest region, one of nine in North America. Other responsibilities include recruiting, training, motivating, and evaluating sales staff. Mr. Naegelin is involved in the establishment of budgets, sales quotas, and sales training and incentive programs. **Career Steps:** Regional Sales Vice President, The Loewen Group (1990–Present); Accountant Representative, The Forethought Group (1988–1990); Sales Director, Schooler Gordon Funeral Homes (1986–1988). **Education:** Amarillo College, Associate degree (1986); Various industry – funeral service – seminars and schools. **Personal:** Married to Lori in 1988. Two children: Danielle and Desiree. Mr. Naegelin enjoys golf, spending time with his family, and attending school events with his children.

Janice L. Rhodus

Vice President of Sales and Marketing
Stewart Enterprises, Inc.
2860 Sunset Point Road, Sylvan Abbey Memorial Park
Clearwater, FL 34619–1605
(813) 796–1992
Fax: (813) 726–6460

7261

Business Information: Sylvan Abbey Memorial Park, established in 1853, is part of Stewart Enterprises, Inc. the 3rd largest provider of death care products and services in the world. A NASDAC listed company, holdings in Pinellas County, Florida include Sylvan Abbey Memorial Park, Memorial Park Funeral Home and Cemetery, Woodlawn Memory Gardens,

Woodlawn Funeral Home, Beach Memorial Chapel, and Lakeview Chapel Funeral Home. As Vice President of Sales and Marketing, Ms. Rhodus oversees the activities of over 50 sales counselors who work through direct response mail and multimedia advertising. She has seven sales managers who report directly to her. **Career Steps:** Vice President of Sales and Marketing, Stewart Enterprises, Pinellas County (1996–Present); Vice President of Sales and Marketing, Baldwin Fairchild Cemeteries and Funeral Homes, Orlando (1989–1996); Analytical Chemist, Louis C. Herring Company **Education:** University of Kentucky (1970). **Personal:** Two children: Joanne Carol and Donnie Wayne.

George L. Henzel
Chief Executive Officer and President
AES Corporate Services, Inc.
640 Airport Rd.
Winchester, VA 22602
(540) 667–2696
Fax: Please mail or call

7299

Business Information: AES Corporate Services, Inc., established in 1979, is a multi–division company providing temporary help, janitorial services and supplies, airport and limousine services, and is a Thrifty Car Rental licensee operating offices in the Shenandoah Valley. Mr. Henzel provides the overall direction and vision to assure the Company's continued growth and diversification into related services to meet the changing needs of its corporate clients. **Career Steps:** Chief Executive Officer and President, AES Corporate Services, Inc. (1979–Present); Sales and Marketing Manager, Dorsey Corporation (1976–1978); Sales Manager, Metro Glass (1973–1975). **Associations & Accomplishments:** Campaign Chairman and President, Local United Way; Board Member, Wayside Theater; 1989–1990 Boss of the Year Award; 1995 Entrepreneur Award; Rotarian; OIC Business Advisory Council; President, Fairport, NY Jaycees; 1983 Small Business Award; Board of Directors, BSCAI. **Education:** Bucknell University, B.A. in Economics (1966); American University, M.B.A. in Marketing (1969). **Personal:** Married to Victoria L. in 1966. Two children: Christopher and Cheryl. Mr. Henzel enjoys boating and tennis.

Peggy S. Isakson
Assistance and Investigation Specialist
Office of the Inspector General – Fitzsimons Army Medical Center

Aurora, CO 80045–5001
(303) 361–3813
Fax: (303) 361–3609

7299

Business Information: Fitzsimmon Army Medical Center, a counterpart of the Office of the Inspector General, conducts non–criminal investigations and inspections into allegations of misconduct and assists clients with various complaints. Serving in various executive administrative roles for the U.S. Federal Government Civil Services since 1969, Peggy Isakson has served the Inspector General's Office as Assistance and Investigation Specialist at the Fitzsimons Army Medical Center since 1994. Her primary functions in this role include investigation procedures, counseling assistance to clients in resolving medical maltreatment, standards of conduct protocols, and management complaints. **Career Steps:** Assistance and Investigation Specialist – Fitzsimons Army Medical Center, Office of the Inspector General (1992–Present); U.S. Federal Government, Civil Services: Conference Coordinator, Protocol and Administration Officer (1969–1992). **Associations & Accomplishments:** Sustaining Member and Former President, Society of Government Meeting Planners – Colorado Chapter; Meeting Planners International; Qualife Wellness Association; Multiple Sclerosis Society – National and State chapters. **Education:** University of Phoenix: B.S.B.A. (1996), Certificate Program/Human Resources (1996); Inspector General Certificate Program, Ft. Belvoir, VA (1992) **Personal:** Four children: Paula Jo, Viki Luanne, Jill Renae and Jonna Kay. Ms. Isakson enjoys horseback riding, reading, and providing assistance to other people with Multiple Sclerosis.

Mr. Dan J. Monaghan
Chief Executive Officer
Diamond Destinies International, Inc.
190 Attwell Drive, Suite 301
Toronto, Ontario M9W 6H8
(416) 798–2299
Fax: (416) 798–2292

7299

Business Information: Diamond Destinies International, Inc. specializes in the manufacture of personal development training products such as books, cassettes, seminars, CD ROM and software products. Mr. Monaghan co–founded Diamond Destinies International with his brother Paul Monaghan. Prior to founding DDI, Inc., at ages 23 and 25, both brothers were attending college. As Chief Executive Officer, Dan Monaghan is responsible for the companies international operations. As President, Paul Monaghan is responsible for all aspects of the operations for the company. Established in 1991, Diamond Destinies International, Inc. employs 38 people with annual sales of $14 Million. **Career Steps:** Chief Executive Officer, Diamond Destinies International, Inc. (1991–Present). **Associations & Accomplishments:** Mr. Dan Monaghan, along with his brother, developed an outreach program as a part of the Company and speaks alongside Olympic athletes and celebrities to high school students teaching them prinicples of success. They also authored the best selling book, "Why Not Me?" **Personal:** Married to Tasha in 1992. Two children: Karly and Austin. Mr. Monaghan enjoys youth outreach programs and being a Dixieland Jazz musician.

Steven A. Tulk

President
Card Systems International, LLC
11250 Louise Avenue
Granada Hills, CA 91344–4105
(800) 860–3567
Fax: (818) 308–1062
EMAIL: See Below

7299

Business Information: Card Systems International, LLC is a provider of national ID card systems for foreign countries. Establishing the Company in 1995, Mr. Tulk is responsible for leading the future strategy of this technology–based company. He also oversees all administrative operations for associates and a support staff of eleven, as well as defining new methods and processes. He can also be reached through the Internet via: Steve_tulk@msn.com **Career Steps:** President, Card Systems International, LLC (1995–Present); Vice President of Technical Development, A M Systems, LLC (1995–Present); Owner, Steven Tulk Consulting, Inc. (1986–Present); Director of Information Systems, Pharmacia Ophthalmics (1988–1995). **Associations & Accomplishments:** Heal the Bay Foundation; Independant Computer Consultants Association. **Education:** University of California – Riverside, B.S. (1990). **Personal:** Married to Yafit in 1992. One child: Ariel. Mr. Tulk enjoys water skiing, golf, and spending time with family.

Darin Voss
Senior Sales Representative
Delphax Systems
1 N. 19th Street, Suite 2E
Richmond, VA 23223
(804) 643–4167
Fax: (804) 643–4858
EMAIL: See Below

7299

Business Information: Delphax Systems specializes in the international manufacture of digital imaging systems via its four plants located throughout the world. Established in 1980, the Company has an estimated annual revenue of $70 million. As Senior Sales Representative, Mr. Voss oversees all domestic sales and marketing and is responsible for approximately 80% of the market in the U.S. Internet users can reach him via: dvoss@ccmail.delphax.com. **Career Steps:** Senior Sales Representative, Delphax Systems (1994–Present); Investment Officer, Signet Bank (1993); Product Specialist, Avery Dennison (1988–1993). **Associations & Accomplishments:** Blue Key National Leadership Society; Trout Unlimited Preservation Society; United States Golf Association; Republican Presidential Task Force; United States Rowing Association. **Education:** University of Richmond, B.A.

(1987). **Personal:** Mr. Voss enjoys fly fishing, golf, and rowing.

7300 Business Services

7311 Advertising agencies
7312 Outdoor advertising services
7313 Radio, TV, publisher representatives
7319 Advertising, NEC
7322 Adjustment and collection services
7323 Credit reporting services
7331 Direct mail advertising services
7334 Photocopying and duplicating services
7335 Commercial photography
7336 Commercial art and graphic design
7338 Secretarial and court reporting
7342 Disinfecting and pest control services
7349 Building maintenance services, NEC
7352 Medical equipment rental
7353 Heavy construction equipment rental
7359 Equipment rental and leasing, NEC
7361 Employment agencies
7363 Help supply services
7371 Computer programming services
7372 Prepackaged software
7373 Computer integrated systems design
7374 Data processing and preparation
7375 Information retrieval services
7376 Computer facilities management
7377 Computer rental and leasing
7378 Computer maintenance and repair
7379 Computer related services, NEC
7381 Detective and armored car services
7382 Security systems services
7383 News syndicates
7384 Photofinishing laboratories
7389 Business services, NEC

Christopher B. Allison
Senior Vice President of Retail Account Services
Stone and Ward Advertising
225 East Markham, Suite 450
Little Rock, AR 72201–1629
(501) 375–3003
Fax: (201) 375–8314

7311

Business Information: Stone and Ward Advertising is a full–service advertising, marketing, and public relations firm. As Senior Vice President of Retail Account Services, Mr. Allison is responsible for the direction and supervision of all retail account services, including strategic development, planning, and agency management. **Career Steps:** Senior Vice President of Retail Account Services, Stone and Ward Advertising (1990–Present). **Education:** University of Arkansas, B.A. in Journalism (1987). **Personal:** Married to Dee Dee in 1990. Mr. Allison enjoys playing guitar, fishing and the outdoors.

Debbie Alonso
President
ADCOM Group
BBV Plaza, 11th Floor, Office A, Ave. F.D. Roosevelt, Suite 1510
Caparra, Puerto Rico 00968
(809) 781–1700
Fax: (809) 781–3314

7311

Business Information: ADCOM Group is an advertising and public relations agency serving business, civic and governmental entities throughout the Carribbean regions. Established in 1993, ADCOM Group reports annual revenue of $2.5 million and currently employs five people. As President and Chief Executive Officer, Ms. Alonso provides the overall operational direction and vision strategies for the Firm's continued growth and development. **Career Steps:** President and Chief Executive Officer, ADCOM Group (1993–Present); Advertising Manager, Mr. Special Supermarkets (1988–1993). **Associations & Accomplishments:** American Marketing Association (AMA); Direct Marketing Association (DMA); Proyecto Amor; Published in Caribbean Business, was recognized as the Youngest Business Woman of the Year. **Education:** Interamerican University, M.B.A. (1992); Sacred Heart University, B.A. (1988). **Personal:** Married to Salvador Vilella in 1991. One child: Stephanie M. Vilella. Ms. Alonso enjoys reading, aerobics and jogging.

Stephen E. Atkins
Senior Vice President of Operations Management
Dab Row Radio, Inc.
20311 SW Birch Street, Suite 180
Newport Beach, CA 92660
(714) 252–9191
Fax: Please mail or call

7311

Business Information: Dab–Row Radio is an agency specializing in radio and television advertising, with an emphasis on automotive accounts. Others include auctions and financial institutions. Mr. Atkins began his broadcast career in 1964 in Los Angeles and was a Co–Founder of Dab–Row Radio in 1988. He supervises the physical operation of office and studio facilities in Southern California and Las Vegas, Nevada. His voice is heard each week in many cities across the country. **Career Steps:** Senior Vice President/Operations Management, Dab–Row Radio (1988–Present); Owner/OPerator, SEA_PRO Communications (1990–Present); Producer/Director of Syndication Division, Interstate Satellite Network (1987–1989); Owner/Operator, Viz–Com Video Productions (1983–1985); Instructor, Nation College (1984); Owner/Operator, Audio Marketing Concepts (1972–1976). **Associations & Accomplishments:** AFTRA, SPERDVAC, FCC License, Electro–Acoustic certificate, "Creative Excellence" Award by the San Francisco Ad Club. **Education:** Pasadena College, Don Martin School of Radio/TV, Syn–Aud–Con seminars. **Personal:** Married to Linda in 1968. Three children: Andrea, Stephen Jr., and Scott. In his spare time, Mr. Atkins is a consultant, writer, narrator, and engineer in the communications industry.

Gustavo Bastos

President and Creative Director
Gr 3 Propaganda S/A
R. Lauro Muller, 116–Grupo 806 T. Rio Sol
Rio De Janeiro, RJ, Brazil 22290–160
(021) 542–4040
Fax: (021) 275–7795
EMAIL: See Below

7311

Business Information: Gr 3 Propaganda S/A is an advertising agency specializing in magazines, newspapers, and television. Mr. Bastos co–founded the agency in 1993, serving as President and Creative Director. His present responsibilities include supervision of daily operations in every department, financial oversight, and Corporate leadership. Internet users can reach him via: GR3@UNIKEY.COM.BR **Career Steps:** President and Creative Director, Gr 3 Propaganda S/A (1993–Present); Vice President and Creative Director, J. Wagner Thompson (1991–1993); Creative Director, DPZ Propaganda (1987–1990). **Associations & Accomplishments:** Brazilian Advertising Association; Member and Former President (1990–1992), Creative Club of Rio de Janeiro. **Education:** Faculdade Hsuo Rwnso University, Degree (1986). **Personal:** One child: Clara. Mr. Bastos is a part–time DJ at private parties.

Marcelo Bastos

Financial Director
Gr 3 Propaganda S/A
R. Lauro Muller, 116–Grupo 806–T. Rio Sol
Rio De Janeiro, Brazil 22290–160
(021) 542–4040
Fax: (021) 275–7795
EMAIL:See Below

7311

Business Information: Gr 3 Propaganda S/A is an advertising agency specializing in magazines, newspapers, and television. Mr. Bastos co–founded the company in 1993, serving as Financial Director. He presently supervises a staff of seven in financial oversight, bookkeeping, and accounting duties. Internet users can reach him via: GR3@UNIKEY.COM.BR **Career Steps:** Financial Director, Gr 3 Propaganda S/A (1993–Present); Lawyer Assistant, MFR Advogados (1991–1994); Director, Brasita Commercio E Industria (1989–1991); Trainee, Advogados Associados (1984–1989). **Education:** Universidade Catolica, Degree (1989). **Personal:** Married to Raquel Parga Bastos in 1995. Mr. Bastos enjoys computers.

Ruba T. Batayneh
General Manager/Owner
Profess Graphics
P O Box 930072
Amman, Jordan 11193
(9626) 822–770
Fax: (9626) 822–770

7311

Business Information: Profess Graphics is an advertising agency headquartered in Amman, Jordan. The Company prepares television and print ads, commercials, graphic designs, and market research. Profess Graphics also organizes international exhibitions, motor shows, and fairs. As General Manager/Owner, Ms. Batayneh provides the overall operational direction and vision strategies for the Firm's continued growth and development. She organizes exhibits, develops new business markets, and markets Company services to an international client base. **Career Steps:** General Manager/Owner, Profess Graphics (1991–Present); Marketing Researcher, Jordan Export Development Company (JEDCO) (1990–1991); Assistant General Manager, Jerash Festival for Culture and Arts (1986–1989). **Associations & Accomplishments:** Jordanian Humanum Forum; Jordan Rally; World Trade Center Association; Author of a book titled "Jerash Festival". **Education:** State University of New York, M.A. (1990); Yarmouk University, Irbid, Jordan, B.A. (1986). **Personal:** Ms. Batayneh enjoys writing, swimming, and playing the organ.

Karen A. Boyce
Director of Recruitment
J. Walter Thompson
1 Detroit Center, 500 Woodward
Detroit, MI 48226
(313) 964–2705
Fax: (313) 964–3191

7311

Business Information: J. Walter Thompson is an international advertising agency serving large corporations, including the Ford Motor Company. As Director of Recruitment, Ms. Boyce is responsible for all hiring decisions, from secretaries to executives; conducting campus recruiting, selecting and interviewing applicants, and offering positions. In addition, she supervises the Human Resources Department and monitors internal employee relations. **Career Steps:** Director of Recruitment, J. Walter Thompson (1994–Present); Recruitment Manager, Campbell Edward (1988–1994). **Associations & Accomplishments:** Adcraft Club; American Managers Association. **Education:** Walsh College, B.A. (1987). **Personal:** Married to Andy in 1987. One child: Benjamin. Ms. Boyce enjoys spending time with her son.

William Scott Boyer
Advertising Director
Unique Travel Services
7265 Estapona Circle, Suite 201
Fern Park, FL 32730–2349
(407) 767–8100
Fax: (407) 767–0941
EMAIL: See Below

7311

Business Information: Unique Travel Services is an in-house advertising agency for Unique Travel Services, Inc. and Dreamquest International. As Advertising Director, Mr. Boyer negotiates advertising contracts for newspapers, radio, and television. Internet users can reach him via: admanbb@magicnet.net **Career Steps:** Advertising Director, Unique Travel Services (1992–Present); Owner/Operator, Orlando Home Journal (1989–1991). **Education:** Seminole Junior College, A.A. (1969). **Personal:** Married to Doris E. in 1976. Mr. Boyer enjoys computers and golf. He is also interested in environmental concerns.

Rachel C. Buckley
President and Chief Executive Officer
Carolina Media Professionals, Inc.
111 Wall Street, Suite 302
Spartanburg, SC 29301
(864) 582–6842
Fax: (864) 597–0435

7311

Business Information: Carolina Media Professionals, Inc. is a national advertising agency, specializing in the provision of media placement services on the radio. In addition to serving as a media buying service, the Corporation purchases and acquires radio air time for clients ranging from syndicated talk shows to 30–second spots, managing 60 clients per week. As President and Chief Executive Officer, Mrs. Buckley is responsible for all aspects of operations, including administrative functions, overseeing the sales staff, and managing all client relations. **Career Steps:** President and Chief Executive Officer, Carolina Media Professionals, Inc. (1992–Present); Assistant Sales Manager, Select Radio and Television (1983–1992). **Associations & Accomplishments:** National Female Executives Association. **Education:** Hallie Turner Private School – High School. **Personal:** Married to Lawrence in 1985. Two children: Neal and Lawson. Mrs. Buckley enjoys spending time with her children and going to movies.

David R. Castle
President
Castle and Associates
1299 Prospect Street
La Jolla, CA 92037
(619) 456–0708
Fax: (619) 456–2606
E MAIL: See Below

7311

Business Information: Castle and Associates, established in 1987, is a marketing, advertising, and communications company for colleges, hotels, credit companies, and auto dealer groups. With estimated annual revenue of $5 million, the Company presently employs 10 people. As President, Mr. Castle oversees the day–to–day operations of the Company. Other responsibilities include marketing of services, financial concerns, cash management, human resource concerns, payroll, public relations, and planning for Company growth. Internet users can reach him via: castle777@aol.com. **Career Steps:** President, Castle and Associates (1987–Present); District Sale Manager, General Motors Corporation (1983–1987). **Associations & Accomplishments:** Fairbanks Ranch Country Club; San Diego Hall of Champions; American Advertising Federation; San Diego Advertising Golf Association. **Education:** Northwood University, Bachelor of Business and Finance (1987). **Personal:** Married to Lisa in 1995. Mr. Castle enjoys golf, theater, and spending time with his family.

Tony Chapman
President
CAPiTAL C
256 Adelaide Street East
Toronto, Ontario M5A 1N1
(416) 777–1124
Fax: (416) 777–0060

7311

Business Information: CAPiTAL C is a Toronto based advertising agency with clients in Europe, the United States and Canada. Their focus is on strategic planning, new product development and creative production, including new media. Clientele includes Pepsi–Cola, Rubbermaid and Thomas Cook. Established in 1992, CAPiTAL C reports revenue of $8 million. Prior to establishing CAPiTAL C, Mr. Chapman was the founder and president of Communique, one of North America's leading communication agencies, which he sold to a British Advertising Agency in 1988. As the President of CAPiTAL C he is responsible for strategic and creative direction. In addition to his executive position, Mr. Chapman is a recognized business speaker and an active member in the Young Presidents' Organization. **Career Steps:** President, CAPiTAL C (1992–Present); President, Communique (1979–1992). **Associations & Accomplishments:** Former Executive, Young Presidents' Organization (Ontario Chapter); Former

Board Member, Metro Toronto Convention & Visitors Association, Technicomp, Cleveland. **Education:** Sir George Williams University, Honors in Marketing and Finance (1979). **Personal:** Married to Ann Horton in 1984. Two children: Alexandra and Michaella. Mr. Chapman enjoys golf, skiing, and history.

Antonio Calil Cury

Financial, Administrative, & Computer System Director
Fischer, Justus Comunicacoes, Ltda.
R. Prof. Alceu Maynard de Araujo #698
Sao Paulo, Brazil 04717–004
55–11–246–1411
Fax: 55–11–548–3991

7311

Business Information: Fischer, Justus Comunicacoes, Ltda. is an advertising agency specializing in television, radio, and newspapers with two locations in Brazil and one each in Venezuela and Argentina. As Financial, Administrative, & Computer System Director, Mr. Cury is responsible for financial and administrative oversight of all four locations. **Career Steps:** Financial, Administrative, & Computer System Director, Fischer, Justus Comunicacoes, Ltda. (1989–Present); Financial and Administrative Vice President, Fischer, Justus, Young & Rubican (1988–1989); Financial Director, Castelo Branco & Associados Propaganda (1971–1988). **Associations & Accomplishments:** Former Director, Advertising Agencies Brazilian Association (1988–1994); Advertising Agencies of State of Sao Paulo Union: Director and Economic, Financial, and Work Consultant (1984–Present); Advertising Professional Association (1980–1982). **Education:** Uberlandia University, Economy (1970); FGV – Administration for Executives; Price Waterhouse – Auditor (1970). **Personal:** Married to Maria Aparecida Zago in 1976. Three children: Leonardo, Fabricio, and Tatiane Zago Cury. Mr. Cury enjoys sports and playing soccer.

Ruth Drury

President
Drury Marketing Services, Inc.
1914 Maple Avenue
Palmyra, NY 14522
(315) 597–9290
Fax: Please mail or call

7311

Business Information: Bringing with her a vast experience in direct marketing strategies and multi–level marketing organizational planning, Ruth Drury recently sold a successful MLM organization to focus her career as a seminar leader. She provides consulting with corporations or professionals who are faced with various marketing challenges of the 90's. In addition, she leads seminars on various topics, including: How to Get Your Bills Paid Without Dunning Letters or Phone Calls, Making Your Goals Become a Reality, Creating Your Own Destiny Through Niche–Marketing, How to Recognize Your Talents and Use Them to Build Your Self–Confidence, and How to Have Your Employees Excel at Customer Service. **Career Steps:** President, Drury Marketing Services, Inc. (1992–1996); Sales Coordinator, Shaklee Corporation (1973–1992); Office Manager, Xerox Corporation (1969–1974); Secretary to Advertising Manager, Garlock, Inc. (1964–1969); Welcome Wagon Hostess for Palmyra, New York (1961–1964); Customer Service Representative and Office Manager, Various Western Union Offices in New York State (1945–61). **Associations & Accomplishments:** National Speakers Association, Writers & Books; Palmyra–Macedon Church Women; First Baptist Church of Palmyra, New York; Minister, Associated with The Second Spiritual Science Church of Rochester, New York; Published Author: "Tapping Into Prosperity," Prosperity Times Publishing Company (1992); Special Talents: Heal Hands ability, locating missing people via intuition, character analysis, developing visions of new products, determining the credibility of bondability of a person. **Education:** University of Science & Philosophy (1987). **Personal:** Ms. Drury enjoys writing poetry and short stories, swimming, reading, and hiking.

Francisco Fernandes C.

Finance Director
DDB Needham
Rua Gumercindo Saraiua 54
Sao Paulo, SP, Brazil 01449–070
55–11–883–7222
Fax: 55–11–853–1511

7311

Business Information: Established in Latin America in 1990 and headquartered in New York, DDB Needham is a full service advertising agency located in over 50 countries. The Company handles advertising for such clients as American Airlines. As Finance Director, Mr. Fernandes is responsible for administrative duties, handling fiscal matters, and supervising 12 employees. **Career Steps:** Finance Director, DDB Needham (1995–Present); Finance Director, Leo Burnett Company (1979–1995); Finance Manager, Young & Rubicam Advertising (1975–1979). **Associations & Accomplishments:** Business Administration Union. **Education:** Faculdade Santana, B.M.A. (1982). **Personal:** Married to Elza in 1981. One child: Mariana M.F. Mr. Fernandes C. enjoys swimming.

Stephen Graham

President
Lowe SMS
2 St. Clair Avenue East, 8th Floor
Toronto, Ontario M4T 2T5
(416) 961–3817
Fax: (416) 961–5818

7311

Business Information: Allwest Fire and Sound provides sales, service, and installation of fire safety and specialty electronics systems (e.g., fire alarms, nurse–calling systems, prison electronics systems). Mr. Graham has held various supervisory positions within Allwest, to include Operations Manager and Project Manager, and as Vice President of Operations. Promoted to Executive Vice President of Allwest Fire and Sound in 1994, Mr. Graham presently supervises the Operations Department, responsible for project management, engineering, technical design, and drafting areas. He is also a member of the Executive Committee, which oversees all Company operations. Internet users can reach him via: allwest@abwam.com **Career Steps:** Allwest Fire and Sound: Executive Vice President (1994–Present), Operations Manager (1992–1993), Project Manager (1991–1992); Vice President Operations, Allwest Systems (1993–1994). **Associations & Accomplishments:** Purdue University, B.S. (1983). **Education:** American Correctional Association. **Personal:** Married to Debbie in 1986. Mr. Graham enjoys camping, sailing, and bicycling.

Gilberto Guasp Gutierrez

President/General Manager
Ammirati Puris Lintas
268 Munoz Rivera, Suite 800
Hato Rey, Puerto Rico 00918
(787) 754–8810
Fax: (787) 751–1522
EMAIL: See Below

7311

Business Information: Ammirati Puris Lintas is the world's seventh largest advertising agency, with 155 office in 58 countries and 7,200 employees. In Puerto Rico, the Company handles advertising for major corporations including: Hanes, Johnson & Johnson, R.J. Reynolds, General Motors, Pfizer Corp., Penzoil, and Banco Bilbao Vizcaya, among others. As President/General Manager, Mr. Guasp is in charge of the daily operations of the Puerto Rico location. Internet users can reach him via: pomlinternet/lpuertoric/esantiag. **Career Steps:** Ammirati Puris Lintas: President/General Manager (1994–Present), Vice President/General Manager (1992–1994); Badillo, Saatchi & Saatchi: Vice President Account Supervisor (1988–1992), Assistant to the President (1986–1988), Account Executive (1984–1988); Product Manager, Colgate–Palmolive (1983–1984). **Associations & Accomplishments:** Sales and Marketing Executive Association; Chamber of Commerce of Puerto Rico; Board of Directors, Junior Achievement; President, Advertising Agencies Association; Board of Directors, Ford Foundation; Phi Delta Gamma Fraternity; Better Business Bureau; Advertising Professor, University of Sacred Heart. **Education:** Syracuse University, M.A. in Advertising (1981); University of Puerto Rico, B.A. in Marketing (1980). **Personal:** Married to Lizzie Perez in 1982. Three children: Gerardo Manuel, Gabriel Andre, and Guillermo Javier. Mr. Gutierrez enjoys community involvement and being an advertising and marketing professor.

Daniel F. Hunt

Systems Manager
WT Quinn Inc.
285 Davidson Avenue
Somerset, NJ 08873
(908) 563–6900
Fax: (908) 563–6933

7311

Business Information: WT Quinn Inc. is a nationwide advertising agency for high–end malls and retailers, specializing in direct mail, radio, television, and magazine advertising. As Systems Manager, Mr. Hunt is responsible for system and software maintenance, installation and administration of all computer systems and networks (e.g., Mac, Novell, and Windows for Workgroups), and designing training programs for Windows users, Mac artists and art directors. Additionally, he evaluates, selects, and interfaces with vendors, identifying new cost–effective sources. Daniel has over sixteen years in production, production management and sales of graphic and prepress services to the advertising and publishing industries. His expertise ranges from graphic design to extensive knowledge of prepress and desktop video production to systems/LAN architecture and administration. During his tenure with WT Quinn, he implemented and supervised the restructure of the Company's network system, installing three new Mac networks, one new Novell network, two Windows for Workgroups networks and two major upgrades of a Novell network totalling over 100 nodes at three sites. **Career Steps:** Systems Manager, WT Quinn Inc. (1993–Present); Director of Print Services/Systems Manager, The Carlino Group Inc. (1991–1993); Account Executive/General Manager, L&B Typo, Inc. (1988–1991); Shift Manager, Dimensional Graphics (May 1988–Dec. 1988); Special Agent & Registered Representative, Prudential Insurance Co. (1987–1988); Freelance Graphic Design Consultant (1986–1988); Account Executive / General Manager / Shift Manager / Typographer, David E. Seham Associates (1979–1988); Typographer & Proofreader, Elizabeth Typesetting Co., Inc. (1977–1979). **Associations & Accomplishments:** National Association of Desktop Publishers. **Education:** Rutgers University, B.S. in Computer Science. **Personal:** Two children: Kacey and Kieran. Mr. Hunt enjoys reading sci–fi, computers, and spending time with his children.

Mrs. Lorraine Hurd Placey

Owner
Lyndonville Printing Company
Depot Street, P.O. Box 944
Lyndonville, VT 05851
(802) 626–9072
Fax: (802) 626–9072

7311

Business Information: Lyndonville Printing Company specializes in general commercial printing, both offset and letterpress. The Company currently has the only complete operating letterpress department in the state of Vermont. Since its inception by Mrs. Placey in 1972, she has made all decisions pertaining to its operations (20 years). The Company employs 5 people and has been established since May 1972. **Career Steps:** After graduating High School, she worked for Safeway Heating Elements, Middletown, CT as the Engineering department secretary. Also Raymond Engineering Laboratory, Westfield, CT in the blueprint and printing department. International Business Machines, (IBM), Poughkeepsie, N.Y. blueprint department controller. **Associations & Accomplishments:** Member, Lyndon Area Chamber of Commerce; Past Member, National Federation of Independent Businesses; Mrs. Placey also works closely with her local police department on programs for local youths. **Education:** Graduated Woodrow Wilson High School, Middletown, CT class of 1956. Attended correspondence school courses, attended several printing shows and business seminars.

Patricia A. Kemmer

President
AAA Internet Advertising
900 Meridian East, Suite 19–366
Edgewood, WA 98371
(206) 840–5189
Fax: (206) 840–5196
Email: See Below

7311

Business Information: Established in 1995, AAA Internet Advertising is an international advertising agency specializing in internet advertising, marketing, design, and broadcasting. The Company has independent contractors, and combines computer technology and advertising making its services a rare commodity. With an estimated annual sales gross of $1.2 million, AAA International currently employs over 200 people. As President, Ms. Kemmer is responsible for recruiting retail business personnel, managing and operating all Company functions including consulting, business planning, marketing, and advertising. Additionally, she is the Company's Chief Executive Officer. Internet users can reach her via: LIFEWRKS@NWRAIN.COM. **Career Steps:** President, AAA Internet Advertising (1995–Present); Commercial Account Manager, Commonwealth Land Title/Reliance (1993–1995); Vice President of Sales & Marketing, World Tech (1992–1993); Commercial Director, Realty One (1989–1992). **Associations & Accomplishments:** Zoological Society; Master Builders Association; Gig Harbor/Peninsula Chamber of Commerce; Chairman, Gig Harbor Parade Committee; Numerous Charity & Civic Chairmanships. **Education:** Pierce College, Associates (1985); Commercial Real Estate License; Numerous Specialty Seminars in Advertising, Marketing, and Sales. **Personal:** Ms. Kemmer enjoys being devoted to training disabled persons to be financially independent, emotionally strong, and respected.

Daniel R. Kerns
President and Owner
Kerns Commerce
3605 Horizon Drive
Lancaster, PA 17601–1115
(717) 285–5566
Fax: (717) 464–3250

7311

Business Information: Kerns Commerce is an advertising agency providing contracted services to small and large businesses in Pennsylvania. As Owner, President, and Marketing and Sales Director, Mr. Kerns is responsible for all aspects of operations, including administration, finances, sales, public relations, accounting, marketing, and strategic planning. Concurrently, he serves as a Financial Advisor and Marketing and Sales Consultant for Pri–America, a finance company which provides financial consulting to businesses in Pennsylvania. Future plans include opening a new recreation center by converting two vacant warehouses, to feature an "extreme" skating park, arcade, snack shop, and dance hall. **Career Steps:** Owner, President, and Marketing and Sales Director, Kerns Commerce (1994–Present); Marketing and Sales Director, A.L.P. Corporation (1994–Present); Business Consultant, Trails End Enterprise (1995–Present); Disbursement Manager, Wagner Enterprises (1995–1996). **Personal:** Mr. Kerns enjoys collecting foreign– and domestic–proof bills and coins and custom–bound novels.

Pierre Serge Khouri
Group Chairman
Impact/BBDO
Zabeel Road, 2nd Floor of Carrera Building
Dubai, United Arab Emirates 19791
(9714) 34–7147
Fax: (9714) 36–6038

7311

Business Information: Impact/BBDO, a Lebanese/American–owned company, is a full–service advertising firm operating in the Middle East, offering a full range of services to various corporations. Founding Impact in 1971, which then merged with BBDO in 1979, Mr. Khouri serves as Group Chairman and is responsible for strategic planning and direction of the Company. **Career Steps:** Group Chairman, Impact/BBDO (1979–Present); General Manager, Impact (1971–1979); General Manager & Co–Founder, Publigraphics (1968–1971). **Associations & Accomplishments:** International Advertising Association. **Education:** ENSAAV – Brussels, Advertising (1966). **Personal:** Married to Joumana in 1975. Three children: Mylene, Karim, and Nadim. Mr. Khouri enjoys reading and travel.

Malak Khukhaji

Sales and Marketing Executive
Fortune Promoseven
Sami Solh Avenue, George Yonis Building
Badaro, Lebanon
(961) 360–6001
Fax: Please mail or call

7311

Business Information: Fortune Promoseven is a full–service advertising and marketing agency. Clients include Coca–Cola Lebanon, a manufacturer and distributor of carbonated soft drinks, such as Coca–Cola, Fanta, and Sprite. Joining Fortune Promoseven as Managing Director in 1990, Mr. Khukhaji was appointed as the Sales and Marketing Executive Manager in 1995. His duties include the exclusive responsibility for the Coca–Cola Lebanon account. **Career Steps:** Fortune Promoseven: Sales and Marketing Executive Manager of the Coca–Cola – Lebanon Account (1995–Present), Managing Director (1990–1995); Account Manager, Procter & Gamble (1982–1989). **Associations & Accomplishments:** Syndicate of Advertising in Lebanon. **Education:** American University of Beirut, B.B.A. (1980). **Personal:** Mr. Khukhaji enjoys swimming, reading, and walking.

Linda Kohlhagen
General Manager
CableRep Advertising
1901 Oak Street
Myrtle Beach, SC 29577–3142
(803) 448–9984
Fax: (803) 946–9970

7311

Business Information: CableRep Advertising, a subsidiary of Cox Communications in Atlanta (a branch of Cox Enterprises), is a cable television advertising sales agency serving the Horry County, SC area, including South Myrtle Beach, Myrtle Beach and surrounding locations. As General Manager, Ms. Kohlhagen is responsible for the oversight of all aspects of budgeting, personnel administration and benefits, P & L, future revenue growth, and the vision of the Company. **Career Steps:** General Manager, CableRep Advertising (1985–Present); Account Executive, WRUF AM/FM (1982–1984); D.J., Local Radio Station (during college). **Associations & Accomplishments:** Rotary International; Board of Directors, American Heart Association; Coastal Advertising and Marketing Professionals. **Education:** University of Florida, B.S. in Communications (1982). **Personal:** Married to Gerald Graham in 1983. Two children: Graham and Cody. Ms. Kohlhagen enjoys boating, music (piano), and cake decorating.

Enrique Bernardo Mariano

Sales and Marketing Manager
Reuters
Av. Eduardo Madero 940 Piso 25
Buenos Aires, Argentina 1106
(541) 318–0680
Fax: (541) 382–7420

7311

Business Information: Reuters is the world's largest news agency, handling 70% of the industry's business. Based in Britain, the Agency works with trade groups such as Merrill Lynch, on a global basis. As Sales and Marketing Coordinator, Mr. Mariano is responsible for the coordination of all sales and marketing operations throughout Argentina, Uruguay, and Paraguay, in addition to overseeing a support staff of 17. **Career Steps:** Sales and Marketing Coordinator, Reuters (1994–Present); Financial Analyst, First National Bank of Boston (1993–1994); Financial Analyst, Investment Banking Services (1991–1993); Professor of Econometrics, Universidad de Belgreno. **Associations & Accomplishments:** Energy Institute of Argentina; Economics Graduates Center; International Honor Society in Economics. **Education:** University of Illinois, M.S. (1993); Erdsmus University – The Netherlands, International M.S. (1992); Universidad de Belgrano, Licenciado en Economics (1991). **Personal:** Mr. Mariano enjoys tennis.

R. Mark Miller
Vice President – Support Services
CS&A Advertising
808 El Dorado Road
Bloomington, IL 61704
(309) 664–0707
Fax: (309) 663–9589
EMAIL: See Below

7311

Business Information: CS&A Advertising is a full–service, national marketing and communications firm, providing sales support, new product information, and incentive and general marketing programs to business–to–business customers. Promoted in 1991 to the position of Vice President of Support Services, Mr. Miller is primarily responsible for accounting and financial reporting, Human Resources, employee benefits, building maintenance/equipment, and PC network administration. He also performs the function of Controller, as well as being responsible for all legal matters, real estate transactions, property management, and assists in strategic planning. Internet users can reach him via: ThinkCSA@AOL.com **Career Steps:** CS&A Advertising: Vice President – Support Services (1991–Present); Controller (1989–1991); Plant Data Manager/Trainee, Purina Mills Inc. (1988–1989); Accountant, Shell Western E&P, Inc. (1985–1987). **Associations & Accomplishments:** Mclean County Chamber of Commerce: Leadership Development Program, Healthcare Coalition; Society for Human Resource Management; Second Wind Advertising Agency. **Education:** Pensacola Christian College, B.S. (1985); Snead State Junior College, A.S. (1982). **Personal:** Married to Lori in 1985. Three children: Kristin, Micheal and Jared. Mr. Miller enjoys reading, participating in and watching sports and Andy Griffith reruns, preparing personal income tax returns, and church involvement.

William F. Napier, Strategic Marketer

President and Chief Executive Officer
PMA Network, Inc.
5091 Alameda Street
Shoreview, MN 55101–1202
(612) 223–8200
Fax: (612) 223–8288

7311

Business Information: PMA Network, Inc. is a national advertising agency. Over the past 15 years, Bill Napier has established a reputation in the business development and promotional marketing arena for creating and executing innovative promotional programs that deliver quantitative results. Prior to forming PMA Network in 1993, he spent many years in various high level management positions on both the client and agency side of the business, developing a diverse expertise in general management that is focused on business growth, proprietary product development and in production innovation. **Career Steps:** President and Chief Executive Officer, PMA Network, Inc. (1993–Present); Vice President, Wessel Company (1990–1993); President and Chief Executive Officer, CDI Associates (1987–1990); Director of Marketing, Meyers Printing (1983–1987). **Associations & Accomplishments:** Creator of World Color's "MarkeTalkers" Patent; 1994 Pinnacle Finalist For New Product Development (Market Talkers); 1994 Direct Marketing Association's Echo Award Finalist; 1993 Pro Award Finalist For Consumer Choice Check Program; 1993 First Place Tempo Award For Most Innovative Production Technique For Space Advertising; 1993 Second Place Tempo Award For Business Space Advertising. **Personal:** Married to Diane in 1980. Three children: Alexandra, Ryan, and Brady. Mr. Napier enjoys sports, tennis, skiing, and golf.

Sebastian R. Pastor

President and Chief Executive Officer
Delfos Y&R
P.O. Box 25320
Miami, FL 33102–5320
504–399066
Fax: 504–327732

7311

Business Information: Delfos Y&R is an advertising agency, providing marketing, political consultations, and strategic planning to clientele in Honduras and other countries in Central America. Founding Delfos Y&R in 1993, Mr. Pastor serves as its President and Chief Executive Officer. He is responsible for all aspects of operations, including administration, finances, public relations, and strategic planning. His primary mission is to ensure that the Company continues on the same path of growth. **Career Steps:** President and Chief Executive Officer, Delfos Y&R (1993–Present); Ministry of Foreign Affairs: International Organization Department (1988–1990), Analyst of Foreign Affairs (1990–1992). **Associations & Accomplishments:** United Nations Organization of the United States of America; Political Science Association of the United States of America; Alumni Association of the University of New Orleans; Center for the Study of the Presidency. **Education:** University of New Orleans, B.A. in Political Science r(1988); Universidad Nacional Autonoma (in progress); XXI Cooperation and Integration Latin American and Caribbean Regional Course – Honduras. **Personal:** Married to Rosina Ferrari de Pastor in 1993. Mr. Pastor enjoys reading and sports.

Laura J. Pemberton
Director of Employee Benefits
Saatchi & Saatchi North America, Inc.
375 Hudson Street
New York, NY 10014
(212) 463–2189
Fax: (212) 463–2962
Email: See Below

7311

Business Information: Saatchi & Saatchi North America, Inc. is an international advertising agency. As Director of Employee Benefits, Ms. Pemberton is responsible for designing, implementing, and managing employee benefits plans including 401K, health and life plans, maternity/paternity and vacation leave. She is currently building a merger between Employee Benefits and Payroll, in order to pull more responsibility to the Administration office. Internet users can reach her via: LPEMBERTON@S&SNY.COM. **Career Steps:** Director of Employee Benefits, Saatchi & Saatchi North America, Inc.

(1992–Present); Group Insurance Manager, Saatchi & Saatchi Holdings USA (1989–1991); Benefits Administrator, Bates USA (1983–1989). **Associations & Accomplishments:** WEB; CEBS; American Payroll Association. **Education:** Various Courses: CEBS Classes, AMA Seminars, Benefit Specific Seminars, Institute of Employee Benefit Training. **Personal:** Married to Robert in 1994. Ms. Pemberton enjoys reading, walking, and relaxing on the beach.

Mr. Richard D. Proffer
Regional Marketing Director
TCI Media Services – Mid Northern Region
955 Century SW
Grand Rapids, MI 49503
(616) 452–3951
Fax: (616) 452–5435

7311

Business Information: TCI Media Services specializes in the preparation of advertising, including writing copy, artwork, graphics and other creative work to be shown on cable television. As Regional Marketing Director, Mr. Proffer is responsible for the marketing, management and implementation of revenue producing programs for his region covering Illinois, Michigan, Indiana, and Wisconsin. **Career Steps:** Regional Marketing Director, TCI Media Services – Mid Northern Region (1995–Present); Division Co–op/Vendor Manager, TCI Media Services (1993–1995); Media Director, Godfrey and Associates (1992–1993); Faculty, Southeast Missouri State University (1992–1993). **Associations & Accomplishments:** Chairs the Corporate Committee on Coop/Vendor Development for TCI Corporate Ad Sales; Jaycees; Peoria Area Chamber of Commerce; Freemasonry, DeMolay; Published numerous articles; Featured on the cover of "Co–opportunities Communique" (twice); Legion of Honor – DeMolay; Member, CAB's Communications Committee. **Education:** Southeast Missouri State University, B.A. (1988). **Personal:** Mr. Proffer enjoys reading, music, singing and theatre.

Daniel W. Rhee
Senior Vice President /Treasurer
Cheil Communications America, Inc.
105 Challenger Road
Ridgefield Park, NJ 07660–2106
(201) 229–6055
Fax: (201) 229–6058
EMAIL: See Below

7311

Business Information: Cheil Communications America, Inc. is a subsidiary of the Samsung Group in Korea. The Samsung Group is a conglomerate involved in electronics, semiconductors, and other fields. Cheil Communications is an advertising agency which handles public relations, outdoor advertising, marketing consulting, media exposure, and creative consulting for clients. As Senior Vice President /Treasurer, Mr. Rhee assists clients, handles public relations, instigates mid and long term managerial plans, and plans business enhancement. In his duties as Treasurer, Mr. Rhee handles corporate financial matters and personnel functions. Internet users can also reach him via: CCAIDANIEL@AOL.COM **Career Steps:** Senior Vice President /Treasurer, Cheil Communications America, Inc. (1992–Present); Partner, KPMG Peatmarwick LLP (Present); President, Arden Sutherland DoDo – UK Company (Present); Lawyer, Steven, Dunnington Barthow & M (Present). **Education:** Korea University – Seoul, Korea, B.A. in Arts and Economics (1989). **Personal:** Married to Jung Hwa in 1990. One child: Eun JT. Mr. Rhee enjoys golf, travel, driving, and collecting stamps.

Timothy J. Roehl
Principal
Forte Communication Corporation
3310 University Avenue, Suite 202
Madison, WI 53705
(608) 231–1166
Fax: (608) 231–1476
EMAIL: See Below

7311

Business Information: Forte Communication Corporation is a full service advertising firm involved in print, radio, television, and world wide web advertising. As Principal, Mr. Roehl is responsible for sales, marketing, and consulting. Mr. Roehl has won various Cable Advertising Bureau awards. Internet users can reach him via: TIM@NETFORTE.COM. **Career Steps:** Principal, Forte Communication Corporation (1995–Present); Regional Advertising Manager, Telecommunications, Inc. (1989–1995); Sales Manager, Jones Intercable (1984–1989). **Associations & Accomplishments:** Exchange Club of Madison; Exchange Club of East Madison/Monona. **Education:** University of Wisconsin at Whitewater (1983); University of Wisconsin at Rock County, Rock County Leadership Council. **Personal:** Married to Amy L. in 1991. Two children: Douglas Cameron and Nicole Marie. Mr. Roehl enjoys golf and politics.

Glenn Rosen
Regional Training and Development Manager – Asia/Pacific
Young & Rubicam, Inc.
331 North Bridge Road, #16–01/03
Odeon Towers, Singapore 188720
(65) 334–5557
Fax: (65) 334–0368
EMAIL: See Below

7311

Business Information: Young & Rubicam, Inc. provides commercial communications (i.e., advertising, public relations, identity and design, sales promotion, direct marketing) to build leverage, protect, and manage client's brands. Joining Young & Rubicam, Inc. in 1990, Mr. Rosen was appointed as Regional Training and Development Manager – Asia/Pacific in 1996. He is responsible for the design and delivery of training and development opportunities to improve the technical, professional and managerial skills of the in–house work force. He attributes much of his success to his father. Internet users can reach him via: Glenn_Rosen@yr.com. **Career Steps:** Young & Rubicam, Inc.: Regional Training and Development Manager – Asia/Pacific (1996–Present), Human Resources Development Manager (1993–1996), Senior Management Development Associate (1992–1993). **Associations & Accomplishments:** Metropolitan Association of Applied Psychology; American Society for Training and Development; Recreational Therapist, Pilgram State Psychiatric Hospital (1984–1987); Drug Counselor, NYS Division of Substance Abuse (1990). **Education:** CUNY – Baruch College, M.B.A. (1995); SUNY – Stony Brook, B.S. **Personal:** Married to Alysa Rosen in 1995. Mr. Rosen enjoys camping, fishing, basketball, studying mandirin, and managing the company softball team.

Nancy Ruiz
Administrative Assistant
Arteaga & Arteaga
Calle 57 AK 18, Rexville
Bayamon, Puerto Rico 00957–4229
(809) 250–0006
Fax: (809) 759–9580

7311

Business Information: Arteaga & Arteaga, an affiliate of DMB&B, is a global advertising agency, providing publicity, marketing, and public relations services. As Administrative Assistant, Ms. Ruiz assists the account executives in the coordination of local and international accounts, in addition to serving as a liaison between the Company's management and international offices. **Career Steps:** Administrative Assistant, Arteaga & Arteaga (1995–Present); Executive Secretary, DMB&B (1994–1995); Executive Secretary, Royal Bank of Canada (1989–1994); Administrative Assistant and Licensed Agent, Freeman–Matsen Insurance (1986–1994). **Associations & Accomplishments:** Professional Secretaries International; Organizer of blood drives at RBC (three years). **Education:** University of Puerto Rico, B.A. (1981). **Personal:** Ms. Ruiz enjoys athletics (aerobics, weights, in–line skating).

salles
DMB&B

Paulo Salles
President and Chief Executive Officer
Salles/DMB&B Publicidade S.A.
P.O. Box 3138
Sao Paulo, Brazil 04038–904
(011) 575–2722
Fax: (011) 571–0410

7311

Business Information: Salles/DMB&B Publicidade S.A., the third largest company in Brazil, is a full–service advertising agency working with a variety of companies and industries in Brazil. The Agency was founded by Mr. Salles' father and aunt in 1966. As President and Chief Executive Officer, Mr. Salles is responsible for all aspects of operations, including management and strategic planning. **Career Steps:** Salles/DMB&B Publicidade S.A.: President and Chief Executive Officer (1992–Present), Executive Vice President (1990–1992), Vice President (1985–1990), Director (1980–1985). **Associations & Accomplishments:** Associacao Brasileira de Esclerose Multipla; Vice President, Brazilian Association of Advertising Agents; The International Advertising Association. **Education:** Business Administration (1978) **Personal:** One child: Isabella Galliez Pinto Salles. Mr. Salles enjoys car racing, tennis, and snow & water skiing.

Kevin J. Scharnek
Vice President/Partner
Wild Promotions, Inc.
16925 West Victor Road
New Berlin, WI 53151
(414) 796–1188
Fax: (414) 796–8686

7311

Business Information: Wild Promotions, Inc. is an international premiums and advertising specialist providing products to top name companies. The Company was nominated for Future 50 for Wisconsin in 1996. As Vice President/Partner, Mr. Scharnek is responsible for playing a major role in the promotion of all sales, marketing, and sales management, in addition to planning and developing new promotions for sales to companies. **Career Steps:** Vice President/Partner, Wild Promotions, Inc. (1994–Present); Sales Representative, FM Marketing (1992–1994). **Associations & Accomplishments:** Theta Delta Chi; Author, "Hot Growth Companies – Four Firms That Really Sizzle" (1996); University of Wisconsin Men's Varsity Track & Field Team. **Education:** University of Wisconsin, B.S. in English (1992). **Personal:** Married to Tracey L. in 1995. Mr. Scharnek enjoys spending time with his family and water skiing.

Lana Sobolnitsky
Account Coordinator
Lerner Advertising
19940 Sunnyslope Drive
Beverly Hills, MI 48025
(810) 645–1200
Fax: (810) 645–1362

7311

Business Information: Lerner Advertising is a privately–owned establishment primarily engaged in retail advertising and related services. As Account Coordinator, Ms. Sobolnitsky plans, coordinates, and directs advertising campaigns. She is also responsible for interviewing and guiding media representatives, artists, typesetters, and printers to develop estimates, produce, and implement specific projects. Additional duties include: handling and coordinating advertising campaigns, budgetary concerns, customer service, and direction of media events. **Career Steps:** Account Coordinator, Lerner Advertising (1995–Present); Loan Processor, AAA Mortgage (1994–1995); Marketing Assistant, Rock Financial (1993); Research Intern, WJBK–TV 2 (1992). **Associations & Accomplishments:** The Adcraft Club of Detroit; Young Adult Division of the Jewish Federation of Metropolitan Detroit; Hillel of Metropolitan Detroit. **Education:** Michigan State University, B.A. in Advertising (1992). **Personal:** Ms. Sobolnitsky enjoys drawing, painting, reading mystery novels, hiking, camping, and swimming.

Roy Tattersall
Vice President of Finance
Marketing Communication, Inc.
633 Colborne Street
London, Ontario N6B 2V3
(519) 660–8460
Fax: (519) 660–8474
EMAIL: See Below

7311

Business Information: Marketing Communications, Inc. is a full–service, international advertising agency, with major business focus generated in the U.S. With ten years experience in finance and a Certified Management Accountant in Ontario, Mr. Tattersall joined Marketing Communications as Vice President of Finance in 1985. He is responsible for all financial analysis and strategic management. Mr. Tattersall can also be reached through the Internet via: ROY@MCLONDON.FTN.NET **Career Steps:** Vice President of Finance, Marketing Communications, Inc. (1985–Present). **Associations & Accomplishments:** Society of Management Accountants of Ontario (SMAO); Canadian Mental Health Association. **Education:** Society of Management Accountants of Ontario, C.M.A. (1992). **Personal:** Married to Deborah in 1987. Three children: Christopher, Graham, and Suzanne. Mr. Tattersall enjoys gardening, music, computers, golf, and future markets.

John Van Osdol
Managing Partner, Broadcast Production
Bozell Worldwide
1000 Town Center, Suite 1500
Southfield, MI 48075–1217
(810) 746–8314
Fax: (810) 354–5429

7319

Business Information: Bozell Worldwide is a global, full–service advertising agency serving such companies as Cellular One, Chrysler–Plymouth Jeep Eagle, and Hugh Puppies. As Managing Partner of Broadcast Production, Mr. Van Osdol oversees the Broadcast Production Department and Audio/Visual Department, supervising all aspects of commercial production. **Career Steps:** Managing Partner of Broadcast Production, Bozell Worldwide (1994–Present); Senior Producer, CME–KHBB (1990–1994); Producer, Ross Rox, Inc. (1986–1990); Freelance, First Chicago Telemedia (1985–1986). **Associations & Accomplishments:** Interviewed in Big Idea Magazine; 1994 Cannes Award for Yukon Commercial. **Education:** Northwestern University, B.S. (1986). **Personal:** Married to Amy in 1991. Mr. Van Osdol enjoys golf, scuba diving, skiing, rollerblading, sailing, mountain biking, hunting, and general outdoor activities.

Dulce MA. Parra Hernandez

Marketing Director
Grupo S.P.S.
Golfo de San Jorge #48 Col. Jacuba
Mexico City, Mexico 11410
(525) 399–2115
Fax: (525) 399–6202
EMail: See Below

7312

Business Information: Grupo S.P.S. is an outdoor advertising company, placing advertisements on billboards, POP materials, and awnings for clients including Corona Beer, Coca-Cola, and Nestle. Established in 1985 by Ms. Parra's father, the Company is now run by herself and her two brothers. As Marketing Director, Ms. Parra is responsible for international trade and public affairs as well as administration and strategic planning. Internet users can reach her via: 74054,46@compuserve.com. **Career Steps:** Grupo S.P.S.: Marketing Director (1991–Present), Commercial Director (1985–1991); Associated Creative Director, McCann Erickson (1983–1985). **Associations & Accomplishments:** Outdoor Association of America, Inc.; Young Entrepreneurs Organization; Asociacion Mexicana de Publicidad Exterior. **Education:** Universidad Iberoamericana, B.A. (1985). **Personal:** Married to Nicolai A. Saitcevsky G. in 1992. One child: Tamara. Ms. Parra Hernandez enjoys car racing.

Mr. Andrew S. Bernstein
Vice President and Director of Finance
AFGL International, Inc.
850 Third Avenue
New York, NY 10022
(212) 508–3415
Fax: (212) 508–3542

7319

Business Information: AFGL International is a full–service advertising agency. In his current capacity, Mr. Bernstein, reporting directly to the Chief Operating Officer, has the supervision responsibility for a staff of ten persons. He is responsible for all financial reporting to insure the compliance of SEC regulations. Established in 1872, AFGL International employs 60 persons and reports having an estimated revenue in excess of $50 million. **Career Steps:** Vice President and Director of Finance, AFGL International (1986–Present); Supervisor, Laurenthol and Horwath, CPA (1983–1986); Senior Accountant, Herman J. Dobkin, CPA (1980–1983). **Associations & Accomplishments:** New York State Society of Certified Public Accountants; American Institute of Certified Public Accountants; National Society of Tax Professionals. **Education:** State University of New York–Binghamton, B.S. in Accounting (1980). **Personal:** Married to Randi in 1985. Two children: Rachel and Erica. Mr. Bernstein enjoys tennis, swimming, and jogging during his leisure time.

William P. Coyne
Chief Executive Officer
Coyne Beahm Inc.
8518 Triad Drive
Colfax, NC 27235–9765
(910) 996–1255
Fax: Please mail or call

7319

Business Information: Coyne Beahm Inc. is a marketing and advertising agency. As Chief Executive Officer, Mr. Coyne is responsible for all aspects of operations, including artwork and creative thinking. **Career Steps:** Chief Executive Officer, Coyne Beahm Inc. (1979–Present). **Associations & Accomplishments:** Frequent public speaking appearances. **Personal:** Seven children. Mr. Coyne enjoys photography, golf and contemporary Christian graphics.

Robert L. Foss
Advertising Director
Central Tractor Farm & Country
3915 Delaware Avenue
Des Moines, IA 50313
(515) 266–3101
Fax: (515) 266–2952

7319

Business Information: Central Tractor Farm & Country is a national manufacturer and supplier of farming equipment and supplies. Established in 1939, Central Tractor Farm & Country reports annual revenue of $260 million and currently employs 2,600 people companywide. As Advertising Director, Mr. Foss is responsible for directing all advertising and MAC prepress activities and supervising creative and conceptual production of Company advertising. **Career Steps:** Advertising Director, Central Tractor Farm & Country (1993–Present); Director of MAC Research/Designer, Gannett Corp./Des Moines Register (1990–1993); Lee Ent./The Lincoln Star: Editorial Art Director (1986–1990), Advertising Designer (1984–1986). **Associations & Accomplishments:** Des Moines MAC PrePress User Group; Illustrators of Omaha. **Education:** Des Moines Community College (1997); University of Nebraska, Art/Advertising; Southeast Community College, Graphic Arts Degree (1984); Digital Technology – Orem Utah, Masters Degree. **Personal:** Married to Mary in 1990. Three children: Jordan, Bronte, and Honor. Mr. Foss enjoys woodworking and restoring old houses.

Kathy D. Fountain
Chief Financial Officer
Cotton & Company
2081 E. Ocean Boulevard, Suite 2–B
Stuart, FL 34996–3382
(407) 287–6612
Fax: (407) 286–6268
EMAIL: See Below

7319

Business Information: Cotton & Company is an advertising agency, with focus on upper–end real estate accounts and banking industry clientele throughout the southern sector of Florida. Producing advertising materials in–house, Cotton & Company provides advertising on radio, television, billboards, and newspapers. As Chief Financial Officer, Ms. Fountain is in charge of all accounting activities, including financial statements and consults with the Company's President on investments issues. She can also be reached through the Internet via: Cottonstep@AOL.com **Career Steps:** Chief Financial Officer, Cotton & Company (1988–Present); Bookkeeper, O. Franklin Wolfe Inc. (1987–1988); Accounting Clerk, Miami University (1981–1987). **Associations & Accomplishments:** Secretary and Board of Directors, Florida Oceanographic Society. **Education:** Monroe Community College, A.S. (1980). **Personal:** Ms. Fountain enjoys scuba diving and conducting undersea research.

Gary R. Gress
Director of Engineering & Creative Services
CDA Industries Limited
1430 Birchmount Road
Scarborough, Ontario
(416) 752–2301
Fax: Please mail or call
EMAIL: See Below

7319

Business Information: CDA Industries Limited, established in 1954, is a creative design company that designs and manufactures merchandising displays for retail stores and exhibit. The Company also manufactures custom architectural products. As Director of Engineering & Creative Services, Mr.

Gress is the head of design and engineering projects and departments and the director of design solutions. Internet users can reach him via: grhino@idirect.com. **Career Steps:** Director of Engineering & Creative Services, CDA Industries Limited (1994–Present); Project Engineer, Metalumen Manufacturing Limited (1985–1993); Performance Analyst, Pratt and Whitney, Canada (1978–1984). **Associations & Accomplishments:** Canadian Aeronautics and Space Institute; Visual Arts, Ontario. **Education:** University of Toronto, B.A.Sc. in Mechanical Engineering; Ontario College of Art. **Personal:** Married to Sylvie in 1987. Mr. Gress enjoys painting and aircraft propeller research and development.

Farid J. Hakim, CPA

Vice President of Finance
CSI International Corporation
800 2nd Avenue, 8th Floor
New York, NY 10017
(212) 687–5600
Fax: (212) 867–6113

7319

Business Information: CSI International Corporation is a worldwide corporate barterer for various products and services as well as a media buying service. As Vice President of Finance, Mr. Hakim is responsible for all aspects of financial operations of the Company, including accounting and strategic planning. **Career Steps:** Vice President of Finance, CSI International Corporation (1983–Present); Controller, Tarrab Export Corporation (1979–1983); Cost Accountant, Grumbacher (1977–1979). **Education:** New York University, B.S. in Accounting (1979). **Personal:** Married to Doris in 1975. Five children: Cristina, Natasha, Sarah, Emil, and Elizabeth. Mr. Hakim enjoys boating.

Robert M. Lassen
Owner and Chief Executive Officer
Graphic Art Resource Associates
257 West 10th Street, #5E
New York, NY 10014–2508
(212) 929–0017
Fax: (212) 929–0017
Call First Before Fax

7319

Business Information: Graphic Art Resource Associates is a graphic communications firm, providing design, editorial, photographic, print production, and advertising agency services. Establishing Graphic Art Resource Associates in 1980, Mr. Lassen serves as Owner and Chief Executive Officer. He is responsible for all aspects of operations, including design and art direction, writing, editing, editorial and creative direction, photography, overall project supervision, planning and quality control, cost estimating, evaluation and selection of subcontractors; general business management, sales and purchasing. **Career Steps:** Owner and Chief Executive Officer, Graphic Art Resource Associates (1980–Present); Owner and Chief Executive Officer, Lassen Advertising (1968–1980); Studio Manager, Ben Lassen Studios (1950–1968). **Associations & Accomplishments:** Biography, Who's Who in America (1996); Biography, Who's Who in the World (1996–1997); Recipient of "American Graphic Design Award: 1995"; Represented in photographic group shows at Gallery on the Green, Canton, Connecticut and The Salmagundi Club, New York, NY. **Education:** Germain School of Photography, Certificate (1978); City College of New York and Hunter College of New York, Graduate Studies (1965–1968); City College of New York, B.A. (1959). **Personal:** Mr. Lassen enjoys scenic photography, chess, crossword puzzles, military history of the U.S. Civil War, and natural philosophy.

Miss Jean M. Owen
President
Jean Owen Agency
594 Broadway #408
New York, NY 10012
(212) 334–4433
Fax: (212) 965–0675

7319

Business Information: Jean Owen Agency represents photographers, hair stylists, and make–up artists working in the fashion and entertainment industry. Revlon, Covergirl, Mademoiselle, and The Gap are just a few of the accounts that the agency works with. As President, Miss Owen oversees management of all agency operations. In her role as an artist's Agent, she designs portfolios of her clients' work; markets these to magazines, advertising companies, record companies, and department stores; negotiates contracts; and arranges bookings. Established in 1989, Jean Owen Agency employs a full–time staff of 2. **Career Steps:** President, Jean Owen Agency (1989–Present); Artist Representative, Judy Casey & Company (1986–1989); Artist Representative, Dan Brennan & Associates (1983–1986). **Education:** Amherst Regional High School (1980).

Joseph R. Paolino

Vice President and Controller
DDB Needham Worldwide Europe
12 Rue Mederic
Paris, France 75017
33–1–40–53–613
Fax: 33–1–47–64–475

7319

Business Information: International in scope, DDB Needham Worldwide Europe is the European headquarters of an advertising and communications company with offices in 23 European capitals. The corporate headquarters of DDB Needham Worldwide Inc. are in New York. DDB Needham Worldwide Inc. is owned 100% by Omnicom Group Inc., an American communications group traded on the New York stock exchange. As Vice President and Controller, Mr. Paolino is responsible for all aspects of financial operations, including mergers, acquisitions, financial control, strategy and development in Europe, South Africa and the Middle East. **Career Steps:** Vice President and Controller, DDB Needham Worldwide Europe (1992–Present); Associate Airspace Finance, Credit National–Jet Finance (1991–1992); Manager, MONY Financial Services (1988–1990); Business Analyst, ATT Microelectronique (1986–1988). **Associations & Accomplishments:** Toastmasters International; Republicans Club Abroad France; Association of American Residents Overseas; Speaks English and French. **Education:** New York University, M.A. (1989); Manhattanville College, B.A. (1986); Universite de Paris IV, La Sorbonne Certificat. **Personal:** Married to Anne in 1991. Two children: Laura Anne Marie and James Joseph Robert. Mr. Paolino enjoys running and bicycling.

Brad Richdale

Chairman
Health Tec, Inc.
455 South Nova
Ormond Beach, FL 32174–6138
(904) 677–5405
Fax: (904) 677–0040

7319

Business Information: Health Tec, Inc. is a global direct marketing corporation specializing in direct response television production. As Chairman, Mr. Richdale oversees the general operations of the Corporation. His responsibilities include public relations, marketing of services and products, and strategic planning for the future. Mr. Richdale is responsible for increasing the Corporations revenues from $ 0 to $78 million dollars within two years. Concurrently, Mr. Richdale owns National Direct Corporation, a direct marketing service on television on how to be successful. **Career Steps:** Chairman, Health Tec, Inc. (1993–Present); Chairman, PVG America (1987–1990); President, Richdale Hewitt Group (1990–1992). **Associations & Accomplishments:** Direct Marketing Association. **Education:** Southern Methodist University. **Personal:** Married to Deborah in 1983. Two children: Andrew and Derek. Mr. Richdale enjoys golf.

Phillip E. Stimpson

Vice President – New York Market Manager
Transportation Displays, Inc.
275 Madison Avenue
New York, NY 10016–1101
(212) 599–1100
Fax: (212) 599–0672

7319

Business Information: Transportation Displays, Inc. (TDI) is one of the nation's preeminent out–of–home media advertising companies, as well as one of the world's largest. TDI provides advertisers displays on transit systems, primarily bus posters and rail posters, across the nation. Additionally, TDI sells other out–of–home media, like billboards, telephone kiosks, and beach media. TDI has more than 100 franchises in 26 cities in the U.S. and the U.K. TDI's presence is focused in the largest markets, including: New York, Los Angeles, Chicago, San Francisco, Philadelphia, Dallas, Washington DC, Atlanta, and London. Joining TDI in 1990 and rising to Vice President of Sales in 1994, Mr. Stimpson directs the sales and marketing of TDI's New York Media properties, which include: bus posters, bulletins, 30 sheets, commuter rail advertising, terminal displays, and telephone kiosks. **Career Steps:** TDI:

Vice–President, New York Market Manager (1995–Present), Vice President of Sales (1994–1995), National Account Executive (1990–1994); Account Executive, Winston Network (1985–1989); Sales Representative, Katz Television (1981–1985). **Education:** University of Vermont, B.A. (1981); The Choate School.

Ms. Margot Teleki

President and Chief Executive Officer
TAL International Marketing, Inc.
65 Madison Avenue
Morristown, NJ 07960
(201) 504–8333
Fax: (201) 540–0475

7319

Business Information: TAL International Marketing, Inc., formed in New York City in the early 1970s, is an international marketing firm that serves blue chip corporations in the areas of promotion and market research. In the 1970s, TAL helped introduce GREY POUPON MUSTARD in the U.S. The TAL Program increased GREY POUPON sales 25 percent in its first year, and its success was written up in the Heublein Annual Report of 1979, as well as in the Heublein House Organ, HEUBLEIN TODAY. Over the years, TAL has worked with over 300 brands being marketed in the U.S., covering such categories as health and beauty, food, household cleaning products, pet products, beverages, automobiles, etc. In 1982, the Company moved to Morristown, New Jersey. From its inception, TAL conducted interactive relationship marketing programs by generating word–of–mouth recommendation networks as a tool. This was a good 25 years before the marketing world adopted interactive relationship marketing as a selling technique. In her current capacity, Ms. Teleki is responsible for all aspects of operations, with administration, finance, accounting, and legal personnel reporting to her. **Career Steps:** Founder, President, and CEO, TAL International Marketing, Inc. (1975–Present); Former Editor, MEDIA/SCOPE, a leading marketing publications (two years); Contributing Editor, VIERTELJAHRESHEFTE FUR MEDIA PLANUNG, a German marketing publication (six years); Media Executive, J. Walter Thompson; Research Executive, Young & Rubicam; Account Executive, N.W. Ayer. **Associations & Accomplishments:** Former Trustee, Morris Animal Foundation (five years); Serves on the Board of Trustees, St. Hubert's Giralda, an animal welfare organization established by Geraldine Rockefeller Dodge; Member, Yale Club; Contributor of articles to advertising/marketing publications; Continuing contributor to the Audubon Club, World Wildlife Federation, Greenpeace, etc. **Education:** New England Conservatory of Music Graduate; Harvard Extension and Radcliffe, Special Student matriculating toward Political Science degree; New York University, Marketing courses.

Ned S. Curtis III, Ed.D.

President
Organizational Challenges
402 East Saginaw Street
Lansing, MI 48906
(517) 346–8324
Fax: (517) 346–7785
EMAIL: See Below

7322

Business Information: Organizational Challenges, a division of MeccaTech, Inc., is a unique contracted services organization providing third–party educational and medical billing and related services. A public educator and administrator for the past twenty years, Ned S. Curtis III established Organizational Challenges in 1992. As President he oversees all operational and administrative areas. A widely acknowledged expert in educational improvement and management, Dr. Curtis implemented a series of seminars entitled "Leadership Skills for School Improvement," which he presents 6–8 times a year to civic and educational parties throughout the United States. Internet users can also reach him via: NVCURTIS@MSN.COM **Career Steps:** President, Organizational Challenges, Inc. (1992–Present); Superintendent of Education, School District City of Holland – Michigan (1992–1995); Superintendent of Education – Lakeshore Public Schools, Michigan (1985–1992); Superintendent of Schools – Fulton, Michigan (1981–1985). **Associations & Accomplishments:** American Association of School Administrators; Association for Quality and Participation; AASA – Total Quality Network; Michigan Association of School Administrators; Michigan State Chamber of Commerce; Illinois Association of School Administrators; Rotary International, District 6. **Education:** Western Michigan University: Ed.D. (1996), S.P.A.D.A. (1991); Central Michigan University: Ed.S. (1985), M.A. in Leadership (1979), B.S. in Education (1976). **Personal:** Married to Verna M. in 1974. Two children: Mackenzie K. and Kyle S. Dr. Curtis enjoys reading, research, hockey, basketball, running, swimming, and family.

Robert L. DiGennaro

Vice President/Director of Collections
Household Credit Services, Inc.
1111 Town Center Drive
Las Vegas, NV 89134
(702) 243–1011
Fax: (702) 243–1251

7322

Business Information: Household Credit Services, Inc., a wholly–owned entity of Household International, specializes in the collections of Bunkland and private label retail collections on open and bad debt accounts. Holding various executive management positions with Household International Canadian Division since 1992, Robert DiGennaro was appointed to his current Corporate position with the U.S. national office in 1995. As Vice President for the Virginia Beach Headquarters, he oversees all external collection activities, marketing, sales, acquisitions, and related support staff Corporate–wide. **Career Steps:** Household Recovery Services: Vice President/Director of Collections, Household Credit Services, Inc. (1996–Present); Household Recovery Services: Vice President (1995–1996), Vice President/National Director Collections – Toronto, Canada (1994–1995), Vice President/Director Collections – Montreal, Canada (1992–1994); Vice President – Recovery Group, First Card Services Inc. (1988–1992); Assistant Vice President – Collection Group, First Interstate Bancard, N.A. (1986–1988); Assistant Vice President – Fraud and Credit Departments, Citibank N.A. (1982–1986). **Associations & Accomplishments:** National Collection and Recovery Association; American Banker Association; Who's Who Among Rising Young Americans; Advisory Board member, Rothenberg Recovery System Group. **Education:** C.W. Post College, M.P.A. (1982); S.U.N.Y. – Stony Brook, NY, B.S. (1980). **Personal:** Married to Dorina C. in 1982. One child: Vincent. Mr. DiGennaro enjoys football, baseball, golf, chess, fishing, and travel.

William Montgomery Norbeck

Director
Central Healthcare Services, Inc.
P.O. Box 1300, 300 Hospital Drive, Suite 132
Glen Burnie, MD 21061
(410) 760–1925
Fax: (410) 766–3489

7322

Business Information: Central Healthcare Services, Inc. is a specialized business services management company, serving healthcare professionals and institutions with a full scope of financial services including receivables management, insurance claims, collections and medical assistance programs. National in scope with headquarters in Atlanta, GA, the Company also has offices in Baltimore, MD; Cleveland, OH; Orlando, FL; Houston, TX; and Las Vegas, NV. As Director of the Baltimore offices, William Norbeck has direct responsibility for the oversight of administrative operations and staff, program development and governmental regulatory compliance. **Career Steps:** Director, Central Healthcare Services, Inc. – Baltimore, MD (1989–Present); Supervisor, Government of the District of Columbia (1976–1989). **Associations & Accomplishments:** American Public Welfare Association; American Public Health Association; American Guild of Patient Accounts Management; Healthcare Financial Management Association; People–to–People Citizen Ambassador Program; Crofton Athletic Council. **Education:** The Johns Hopkins University, B.S. (1976). **Personal:** Mr. Norbeck enjoys golf, and coaching: lacrosse, football, and basketball during his spare time.

Gabrielle Rogge, C.P.A.

Director
Intrastate Medical Collections
1230 Rosecrans Avenue, Suite 2020
Manhattan Beach, CA 90266
(310) 297–8699
Fax: (310) 297–8630

7322

Business Information: Intrastate Medical Collections specializes in collections for a 402 bed hospital owned by Orinda Health Care Agency. The Company focuses primarily on physician accounts, clinics, and gift shops within the Facility, as well as insurance, HMO, and Medicaid/Medicare collections. Established in 1985, the Company employs twenty–five people. As Director, Ms. Rogge oversees all aspects of the Company. She is responsible for managing special directives assigned by the Chief Financial Officer, managing all problem accounts, and providing support to the legal department in referring out cases. She is also directly responsible for a staff of twenty–five. **Career Steps:** Director, Intrastate Medical Collections (1996–Present); Continela Hospital: Business Office Director (1995–1996), Director of Internal Audit (1994–1995), Business Office Director (1993–1994). **Associations & Accomplishments:** California Society of Certified Public Accounts; American Institute of Certified Public Accountants; American Collectors Association, Inc.; California Association of Collectors. **Education:** California

State University, Northridge, B.S. in Accounting (1986); C.P.A. License (1990).

Marg Arland
Vice President of Marketing
Equifax Canada, Inc.
60 Bloor Suite West, Suite 1200
Toronto, Ontario M4W 3C1
(416) 964–5361
Fax: (416) 964–1869

7323

Business Information: Equifax Canada, Inc. specializes in consumer credit reporting services. An affiliate of Equifax, Inc. – one of the world's leading credit reporting agencies – Equifax Canada, Inc. provides businesses throughout the Canadian provinces with diverse credit and financial recovery report services including: consumer credit and business information services, financial recovery services, cheque guarantee and insurance services. Established in 1899, Equifax Inc. reports annual revenue of $1.5 billion and currently employs 14,000 people worldwide. Joining Equifax in 1989 as Manager of Marketing, Ms. Arland was appointed as Vice President of Marketing in June of 1994. She is responsible for all Corporate marketing functions, including market research, communications, product management, and statistical analysis. **Career Steps:** Equifax Canada, Inc.: Vice President of Marketing (1994–Present), Vice President Sales and Marketing, Insurance Division (1991–1994), Director of Corporate Development (1990–1991), Manager of Marketing (1989–1990). **Associations & Accomplishments:** Board of Trade, Sales & Marketing Executives Toronto. **Education:** Seneca College, Business (1987). **Personal:** Married to Garvin William in 1972. Three children: David, Gordon, and Sean. Ms. Arland enjoys curling, reading, and boating.

Mike F. Gardiner
Project Manager
Equifax
3660 Mcquire Boulevard, Suite 300
Orlando, FL 32803
(407) 897–4767
Fax: (407) 895–4723

7323

Business Information: Equifax is one of the three largest credit reporting agencies in the world. The Corporation, headquartered in Atlanta, Georgia, has numerous offices in the United States and other locations internationally. Equifax does pre–screening for pre–approved credit lists. As Project Manager, Mr. Gardiner co–ordinates projects between clients, and technical support from implementation to completion. His position requires an understanding of complex cross–referencing and computer referencing. One of his primary functions is to be the liaison between Equifax and their clients. **Career Steps:** Equifax: Project Manager (1995–Present), Accounting Manager (1988–1995), Customer Service Manager (1986–1988), Tape Manager (1984–1986). **Education:** Dekalb College. **Personal:** Married to Carmen in 1988. One child: Ana. Mr. Gardiner enjoys fishing, hunting, and sports.

Alberto Rosado Ruiz, J.D.

President
International Reporting Service
P. O. Box 192281
San Juan, Puerto Rico 00936
(787) 753–7950
Fax: (787) 753–7977

7323

Business Information: International Reporting Service is a credit reporting agency for mortgage lenders, property and life insurance reports, and personnel selection reports. As President, Mr. Rosado Ruiz serves as Chief Executive Officer in charge of all operations, ensuring quality services and customer satisfaction. **Career Steps:** President, International Reporting Service (1994–Present); HUD Caribbean Office: Director, FHA Program (1991–1994), Chief, Mortgage Credit (1984–1991). **Associations & Accomplishments:** President, Education Committee–Mortgage Bankers Association of Puerto Rico; Mortgage Loan Officers Association of Puerto Rico; Puerto Rico Bar Association. **Education:** University of Puerto Rico Law School, J.D. Cum Laude (1977); University of Puerto Rico School of Business, B.B.A. **Personal:** Married to Dinorah Negroni in 1979. Four children: Alberto, Alberto F., Marco, and Lucia. Mr. Rosado Ruiz enjoys travel, reading, and swimming.

Shivraj Anand
Chief Financial Officer
Package Fulfillment Center, Inc.
1401 Lakeland Avenue
Bohemia, NY 11716–3317
(516) 567–7000 EXT: 121
Fax: (516) 567–7803

7331

Business Information: Package Fulfillment Center, Inc. (PFC) is a full–service direct marketing company, providing complete support services for direct marketing domestically and internationally. Services include caging–deposits, data entry, product fulfillment, collating and package assembly, polybagging, shrinkwrapping, warehousing and distribution, customer service, Group 1 merge/purge and postal presorts, laser and impact printing, lettershop and mailing services, printing, layout and design, and planning and budgeting. A Certified Public Accountant, Mr. Anand joined PFC as Chief Financial Officer in 1994. He is responsible for performing all aspects of accounting functions, including cost accounting, budgeting, cash flow, liaison with banks and outside auditors, etc. **Career Steps:** Chief Financial Officer, PFC (1994–Present); Corporate Controller, Letts of London (1990–1993); Accounting Manager, Barron's Edu. Series, Inc. (1989–1990). **Associations & Accomplishments:** American Institute of Certified Public Accountants; New York State Certified Public Accountants Association. **Education:** Adelphi University, M.B.A. in Taxation; Hofstra University, B.B.A. in Public Accounting; Certified Public Accountant – New York. **Personal:** Married to Prachi Anand, M.D. in 1990. Mr. Anand enjoys golf and tennis.

Roger J. Homan
National Franchise Director
Mailhouse, Inc.
180 Bodwell Street
Avon, MA 02322–1177
(508) 580–4340
Fax: (617) 698–6660

7331

Business Information: Established in 1983, Mailhouse, Inc. is a cooperative direct mail company. Involved in numerous entrepreneurial enterprises, Roger Homan serves as National Franchise Director for "Super Coups" a franchise of Mailhouse, Inc. Additional businesses he owns and manages also include: Homan Enterprises — serves as holding company for various business enterprises such as travel, satellite communications and sporting goods/monogramming; as well as the operation of seasonal radio broadcasting stations – WBET/ WCAV–FM/ and WHTD–FM. **Career Steps:** National Franchise Director, "Super Coups" – Mailhouse, Inc. (1991–Present); President, Homan Enterprises (1989–Present); Broadcaster, WBET/WCAV–FM/WATD–FM (1978–Present); Sub Franchiser, Val–Pak (1983–1991). **Associations & Accomplishments:** High School Freshman Basketball Coach; AMVET; President, Milton Men's Softball; President, Thursday Night Mixed Bowling League; President, Milton Boosters; Town Meeting Member. **Education:** Quincy College (1973); Career Academy School of Broadcasters (1972). **Personal:** Married to Susan in 1970. Three children: Richard Christopher, Roger John Jr. and Sandra Marie. Mr. Homan enjoys golf, baseball, fantasy sports, basketball, football, tennis and racquetball.

Rob Laird
Client Services Director
Tabs Direct
1002 FM 2234 Road
Stafford, TX 77477–6482
(713) 386–7230
Fax: (713) 261–5020

7331

Business Information: Tabs Direct is a full–service, direct mail marketing company. The Company provides laser and data base design. As Client Services Director, Mr. Laird is responsible for design, implementation, and suggestion for modification of systems. He works daily with customers, handles system analysis, and manages a large support staff of data processing professionals. **Career Steps:** Tabs Direct: Client Services Director (1991–Present), Client Services Manager (1988–1991), Account Coordinator (1987–1988); Computer Operator/Programmer, Al's Formal Wear (1984–1987). **Associations & Accomplishments:** Xplor. **Education:** Clarion State College, B.C. in Business (1981). **Personal:** Married to Tammy in 1987. One child: Katie. Mr. Laird enjoys golf and boating.

C. Jay LaRue
Vice President/Controller
Output Technologies Incorporated
2534 Madison Avenue
Kansas City, MO 64108
(816) 435–3029
Fax: (816) 435–1413

7331

Business Information: Output Technologies Incorporated is a public, international holding company for design print and mail business communications. Established in 1991, Output Technologies Incorporated reports annual revenue of $150 million and currently employs 2,000 people. With seventeen years experience in accounting and financial matters, Mr. LaRue joined the Corporation in 1989. Serving as Vice President/Controller, he is responsible for the management of the Company and support staff, as well as serving as Chief Financial Officer, responsible for all aspects of financial activities. **Career Steps:** Vice President/Controller, Output Technologies Incorporated (1989–Present); Audit Manager, Grant Thornton (1983–1989); Senior Auditor, Main Hurdman (1978–1983). **Associations & Accomplishments:** Kansas Society of Certified Public Accountants; Missouri Society of Certified Public Accountants; American Institute of Certified Public Accountants. **Education:** Kansas State University, B.S. (1978). **Personal:** Married to Anita in 1974. Three children: Megan, Caleb, and Nathaniel. Mr. LaRue enjoys travel and spending time with his children.

Terri J. Marvel
President
Information Connection, Inc.
738 NW State Route 7
Blue Springs, MO 64014
(816) 228–1722
Fax: (816) 224–0419

7331

Business Information: Information Connection, Inc., one of three subsidiaries of family–owned Data and Mailing Services, Inc., provides business services, marketing, graphic design, direct mailings, database maintenance, and design to retail consumers. As President, Ms. Marvel is responsible for all aspects of Company operations, including design and marketing for all three subsidiaries. **Career Steps:** President, Information Connection, Inc. (1980–Present); Vice President of Operations, Data & Mailing Services, Inc. (1990–Present); Chief Executive Officer, Parcel Depot, Inc. (1985–Present); 8th grade Algebra Teacher, Kansas City, MO School District (1990–1996). **Associations & Accomplishments:** Blue Springs Chamber of Commerce. **Education:** University of Missouri – Kansas City, B.S. in Education (1992); Southwest Missouri State. **Personal:** Ms. Marvel enjoys volleyball, biking, reading, and family.

Giselle Torres
Account Executive/Assistant Manager/Writer
Casiano Communications
P.O. Box 6253
San Juan, Puerto Rico 00914
(787) 728–3000
Fax: (787) 728–3000 Ext. 409

7331

Business Information: Casiano Communications is the pioneer in Puerto Rico in the creation of targeted, upscale publications and direct response marketing services. Through its nine targeted publications and three directs marketing services, Casiano Communications can develop a customized integrated marketing program to sell various products or services. From the strategic brainstorming, to the design and production, Casiano is the "one–stop" targeted marketing center in Puerto Rico. The Company produces business publications, consumer publications, direct marketing services, promotions, market research, custom publishing, multimedia, and interactive technologies. Ms. Torres has several functions and title with the Company, and works with two divisions. First, she is the Assistant Manager and an Account Executive of the Integrated Marketing Department. She works directly with the COO and President of the Company. She prepares Integrated Marketing campaigns for clients utilizing the publications, direct mail, telemarketing, and other services. Ms. Torres coordinates projects from the initial brainstorming to executive of the programs. Second, she is a writer for one the Casiano's monthly publications: Buena VIDA. The publication targets five areas: Beauty, Exercise, Nutrition, Health, and Family. She works directly with the CEO of the company to compile articles regarding exercise and fitness. **Career Steps:** Account Executive/Assistant Manager/Writer, Casiano Communications (1992–Present); Production Supervisor/Direct Mail Coordinator, Clipper, Inc./Cox Enterprises (1990–1992); Advertising Coordinator, D.H. Jones Real Estate Group (1988–1989). **Associations & Accomplishments:** Direct Mail Association; Involved with her church. **Education:** University of Massachusetts – Amherst, B.A. in Communications

(1988); Continuing **Education:** Advanced English Grammar, Advanced Writing, Creative Writing, Real Estate, and others. **Personal:** Ms. Torres enjoys body building, fitness, writing, and reading.

Sharon Rachel Cahn, C.P.A.
Senior Accountant
K–Graphics, Inc. dba Kinko's Copies
2555 55th Street, Building D, Suite 200
Boulder, CO 80301–5729
(303) 449–9247
Fax: (303) 449–5432
EMAIL: See Below

7334

Business Information: K–Graphics, Inc. provides commercial printing and business services, such as copying, faxing, computer services, and photos. Regional in scope, K–Graphics primarily serves the midwestern United States from three divisional offices, and is a subsidiary of a larger international corporation, Kinko's Copies. As Senior Accountant, Ms. Cahn prepares financial statements, performs analysis, and manages the fixed assets and lease accounting functions of the Company. Internet users can reach her via: sharcahn@kinkos.com. **Career Steps:** K–Graphics, Inc: Senior Accountant (1995–Present), Staff Accountant (1994–1995). **Associations & Accomplishments:** American Institute of Certified Public Accountants; Colorado Society of Certified Public Accountants. **Education:** University of Denver: M.A.C.C. (1994); B.S.A.C. **Personal:** Ms. Cahn enjoys swimming and skiing.

Linda Cano–Rodriguez
General Manager
Jackson Sound
3301 W. Hampden Avenue, Unit C
Englewood, CO 80110
(303) 761–7940
Fax: (303) 789–0557

7334

Business Information: Jackson Sound is a duplicator of audio cassettes, producing up to a million copies of one tape. The Company also provides a studio for the original production of audio cassettes. As General Manager, Ms. Cano–Rodriguez is responsible for all aspects of Company operations, including personnel issues, hiring, purchasing equipment, and sales and marketing. **Career Steps:** General Manager, Jackson Sound (1974–Present). **Personal:** Married to Adalberto in 1991. Three children: Jesse, Sam, and Mark. Ms. Cano–Rodriguez enjoys camping, fishing, and outdoor sports.

Mr. Michael F. Guerchon
Director of Human Resources
NightRider, Inc. – A Division of ALCO Office Products
14405 Walters Road, Suite 800
Houston, TX 77014
(713) 587–4171
Fax: (713) 587–4182

7334

Business Information: NightRider, Inc. – A Division of ALCO Office Products is the world's largest litigation support service. They provide photocopying, imaging, digital printing and management services. Established in 1987, the multi–million dollar company currently employ approximately 3,000 professionals throughout 57 locations. As Director of Human Resources, Mr. Guerchon directs all recruiting, strategic planning, training and development for the Company. **Career Steps:** Director of Human Resources, NightRider, Inc. – A Division of ALCO Office Products (1993–Present); Regional Director, Elliot Associates, Inc. (1991–1993); Director of Recruiting and Training, Mr. Gatti's Restaurants (1989–1991); Director of Training, Bennigans Restaurants (1985–1989). **Associations & Accomplishments:** Houston Human Resource Management Association; Council of Hotel and Restaurant Trainers; American Management Association. **Education:** Northern Arizona University, B.F.A. (1983). **Personal:** Married to Susan Lee Guerchon in 1987. One child: Victoria Grace Guerchon. Mr. Guerchon enjoys skiing, fishing, camping and boating.

Donna Michele Kuchwara
Human Resources Manager
K–Graphics, Inc. d.b.a. Kinko's Copies
2555 55th Street, Building D, Suite 200
Boulder, CO 80301–5729
(303) 449–9247
Fax: (303) 447–2268

7334

Business Information: Kinko's Copies provides a full scope of photocopy services, binding, desktop publishing services, and miscellaneous stationery items. As Human Resources Manager, Ms. Kuchwara is responsible for implementing and administrating policies and programs related to the effective management of human resources. Primary duties involve: benefits administration, implementation and compliance of policies and procedures, Company occupational safety and health programs, implement and administer wage and salary policies and structures, employee relationships and all governmental regulatory matters. **Career Steps:** Kinko's Copies: Human Resources Manager (1989–Present), Branch Office Manager (1984–1989); U.S. Air Force: Health Services Administrator (1987–1995), Medical Specialist (1984–1987). **Associations & Accomplishments:** Boulder Area Human Resources Association; American Payroll Association; National Association for Female Executives. **Education:** National University, M.A. in Management (1992); California State Polytechnic University – Pomona: B.A. in Behavioral Science (1982), Certificate in Gerontology (1983). **Personal:** Miss Kuchwara enjoys reading, baking, volleyball, and spending time with her family.

Bernard K. Perrine

Partner & Vice President
Kinkos Copies
2502 Hillmeade Lane
Nashville, TN 37221–3920
(800) 247–9237
Fax: (615) 297–8002

7334

Business Information: Kinkos Copies is an international electronic printing, copying, and retailing company. The Company markets a line of high–speed copiers, and video, duplication, and office product supplies. As Partner & Vice President, Mr. Perrine is responsible for visiting the four stores for which he is Vice President, overseeing operations, supervising employees, and handling customer relations. **Career Steps:** Kinkos Copies: Partner & Vice President (1995–Present), Partner (1992), Regional Manager (1989). **Education:** University of Akron, Accounting (1985).

June Anderson
Owner and President
June Anderson & Associates, Inc.
4245 Sentinel Post Road, NW
Atlanta, GA 30327
(404) 261–9226
Fax: (404) 841–1022

7336

Business Information: June Anderson & Associates, Inc. is an international planning and design firm, geared specifically to promote and sell products or services, as well as providing consultants to manufacturers and retail customers. Founding June Anderson & Associates, Inc. in 1972, Ms. Anderson serves as its Owner and President. She is responsible for all aspects of operations, including administration, oversight of support staff, designing, consulting, and writing. **Career Steps:** Owner and President, June Anderson & Associates, Inc. (1972–Present); Head Interior Designer, Drexel–Heritage (1969–1972). **Associations & Accomplishments:** The British American Business Group; The Buckhead Business Association; American Society of Interior Designers; Friends of the Atlanta Opera; Chairman, Cathedral of St. Philip Welcoming Committee; Member, St. Julian Guild; Served on Board of Directors, Atlanta Ballet (4 years); Charter Member, The World Trade Club; Delegate, Andrew Young's Business Mission to Paris. **Education:** Greensboro College, B.A. (1969); Virginia Commonwealth University, major in Architecture and Interior Design. Attended: Social Research NYC. **Personal:** One child: Alexander Anderson Gussin. Ms. Anderson enjoys music, films, sports car racing, literature, gardening, art, and sailing.

Diana Beach
Co–Owner
Moon Tree Visions
HC 30, Box 1772
Lawton, OK 73501
(405) 246–3360
Fax: (405) 429–3384

7336

Business Information: Moon Tree Visions provides American Indian and Equine art and professional picture framing. The Company employs two artists, painters, and sculptors for the commercial industry. As Co–Owner with her husband George, Ms. Beach and her husband are the two artists for the Company. She has outside employees who are responsible for marketing, financing, and other duties. She handles the supervision of those employees, runs the framing business, and paints full time. **Career Steps:** Co–Owner, Moon Tree Visions (1972–Present). **Associations & Accomplishments:** Recipient of over one hundred fifty major awards including twenty Grand and seven Peoples Choice Awards. She founded and organized the Seven Cherokee Women Legends Show which traveled to museums and galleries throughout the U.S. from January, 1988 to January, 1990. She is listed in Indian Arts of Oklahoma, Who's Who of the American Indian and the American Artists Illustrated Survey of Leading Contemporaries; AMBUCS. **Education:** North Texas State University, Master of Fine Arts (1976). **Personal:** Married to George C. in 1990. Three children: Doug, Amber, and Talana. Ms. Beach enjoys skiing, boating, fishing, sculpting, and horseback riding.

Raymond L. Gauvin
Vice President/General Manager
Baldwin Dampening Systems
141 Sheridan Drive
Naugatuck, CT 06770–2034
(203) 729–4455
Fax: Please mail or call

7336

Business Information: Baldwin Technology Company, Inc. is a worldwide manufacturer and supplier of equipment to the Graphic Arts Industry. Mr. Gauvin currently serves as Vice President/General Manager of Baldwin Dampening Systems, a division of Baldwin Technology, located in Connecticut. Baldwin Dampening Systems products are sold throughout the Americas – North, South, and Central and distributed to Asia–Pacific and Europe. Mr. Gauvin is responsible for all facets of the Connecticut Divisions Operations **Career Steps:** Vice President/General Manager, Baldwin Dampening Systems (1994–Present); Vice President/Sales, Oxy–Dry Corporation (1992–1994); Executive Vice President, Fimag, Inc. (1988–1992); Engineering Director, Hantscho, Inc. (1984–1988). **Associations & Accomplishments:** Research and Engineering Council of Graphic Arts; Graphic Arts Technical Foundation; Speaker at selected Graphic Arts Conferences. **Education:** University of Florida, M.B.A. (1982); University of New Hampshire, B.S.E.E. (1974). **Personal:** Married to Lillian. One child: Raegan. Mr. Gauvin enjoys talking about and playing golf.

Louis Guidette
Owner and President
Golden Silk
P.O. Box 3209
Palm Desert, CA 92261–3209
Fax: (619) 346–1959

7336

Business Information: Golden Silk is a commerical and fine art computer graphics business. Established in 1987, Golden Silk currently employs 12 people. As Owner and President, Mr. Guidette is responsible for all artistic and creative aspects of the business. **Career Steps:** Owner and President, Golden Silk (1987–Present); Chief Operations Officer, Training Technology (1985–1987). **Associations & Accomplishments:** The Gurdjieff Foundation; Art Work in the White House Collection. **Education:** San Diego State University, B.A. (1968). **Personal:** Mr. Guidette enjoys reading.

John M. Hall
Executive Vice President
Spectrum Design Services, Inc.
17629 El Camino Real, Suite 140
Houston, TX 77058–3051
(713) 286–5265
Fax: (713) 286–5805

7336

Business Information: Spectrum Design Services, Inc. (SDS) is a national corporation providing contract design and personnel services and management of international projects. Eighty percent of their clients are Fortune 500 companies. SDS is pre–qualified as a 1996 "INC. 500 Fastest Growing Private Companies in America." As Executive Vice President, Mr. Hall is executive director for all Company projects, as well as corporate administrative and financial issues. **Career Steps:** Executive Vice President, Spectrum Design Services, Inc. (1990–Present); Senior Project Manager and Manager of Project Controls, CDI/Stubbs Overbeck (1979–1990); Manager of Special Projects, Woodward, Inc. (1976–1978). **Associations & Accomplishments:** Founding Member, Forum Club of Houston; American Association of Cost Engineers; American Institute of Industrial Engineers. **Education:** Dupont Scholar at the University of Virginia. **Personal:** Married to Lucy in 1979. Mr. Hall enjoys travel, golf, and fishing.

Janice Jaworski
Creative Director
Lipson, Alport, Glass & Associates
666 5th Avenue Floor 36
New York, NY 10103
(212) 541–3946
Fax: (212) 541–3947
EMAIL: See Below

7336

Business Information: Lipson, Alport, Glass & Associates is the leading packaging design company in the United States, specializing in brand identity development for Fortune 500 consumer products companies. An international marketing consulting firm, the Company has offices in New York City, Cincinnati, and Chicago. As Creative Director for the New York Office, Ms. Jaworski oversees all strategic and creative work being executed against specific client objectives. She has created programs for renowned companies, such as Borden, Mattel, Mazda, and Godiva Chocolates. Ms. Jaworski is also the recipient of many awards for creative excellence in product and industry areas. Internet users can reach her via: jjaworski.LAGA_NYC@mcimail.com. **Career Steps:** Creative Director, Lipson, Alport, Glass & Associates (1996–Present); Creative Director/Partner, The Benchmark Group (1982–1996); Senior Design Director, Interbrand (1989–1992); Senior Designer, Landor Associates (1988–1989). **Associations & Accomplishments:** Package Design Council International; Design Management Institute; Museum of Modern Art – New York City; Whitney Museum of American Art; LAG&A – Winner of Grand Cleo Award for Best Package Design. **Education:** University of Rhode Island, B.F.A. (1984); Philadelphia College of Art (1979). **Personal:** Ms. Jaworski enjoys music, dance, aerobics, rollerblading, and entertaining.

Carol J. Jenkins
Owner
CD Graphics Presents
P.O. Box 57
Argenta, IL 62501–0057
(217) 795–3325
Fax: (217) 795–3325

7336

Business Information: CD Graphics Presents specializes in graphic production for texts and educational material for industrial and educational facilities, including DePaul University business department. Plans for the future include expansion through the use of high end equipment and colorization. As Owner, Ms. Jenkins is responsible for oversight of twelve contracts, one of which is for a standards book for utilities. A certified professional secretary, drafter, and layout artist, she is also responsible for administration, operations, finance, sales, public relations, accounting, and strategic planning. **Career Steps:** Owner, CD Graphics Presents (1989–Present); Church Secretary; Secretary to Department Manager, Firestone; Caterpillar, Inc.; Private Consultant. **Associations & Accomplishments:** Phi Beta Kappa. **Personal:** Married in 1961. Ms. Jenkins enjoys travel, computers, and spending time with her two children.

William P. Johnson
Chief Financial Officer/Controller/H.R. Director/MIS Director
Digital Photographic Imaging
6085 Barfield Road North East, Suite 206
Atlanta, GA 30328–4403
(404) 843–2050
Fax: (404) 847–0302
EMAIL: See Below

7336

Business Information: Digital Photographic Imaging is a photographic imaging company specializing in pre–press service bureau, digital printing, digital photography, and graphic design. Established in 1992 with 22 employees, the Company expects estimated annual sales in excess of $2 million. As Chief Financial Officer/Controller/H.R. Director/MIS Director, Mr. Johnson is responsible for all aspects of company opera-

tions, including human resources, MIS direction, financial aspects, accounting, employee relations, and information services. Internet users can reach him via: WJOHN1657@AOL.com. **Career Steps:** Chief Financial Officer/Controller/H.R. Director/MIS Director, Digital Photographic Imaging (1992–Present); Pilot Instructor, United Airlines (1991–1994); Supply Officer, U.S. Navy (1986–1991). **Associations & Accomplishments:** AOPA: Big Brothers. **Education:** Iowa State University, B.S. (1986). **Personal:** Married to Jennifer in 1985. Mr. Johnson enjoys flying.

Molly M. Scanlon
Director of Client Services
Ayres Group Animation
750 B Street, Suite 42
San Diego, CA 92101
(619) 696–6800
Fax: (619) 696–6868
EMAIL: See Below

7336

Business Information: Ayres Group Animation designs three–dimensional visualization techniques using animation and multimedia techniques for architecture, real estate, litigation, military defense, health care, education, and training simulation. These services help the companies present complex issues to a wide variety of audiences. As Director of Client Services, Ms. Scanlon is responsible for marketing, national public speaking, and project management for animation services. Additionally, she handles marketing for the Architecture Division, case work, proposal writing, client response, and payment response from clients. Internet users can also reach her via: mmm_scanlon@prodigy.com **Career Steps:** Director of Client Services, Ayres Group Animation (1995–Present); Director of Health Care Design, Tucker Sadler & Associates (1990–1995); Health Facility Specialist, Anderson DeBartolo Pan (1985–1990). **Associations & Accomplishments:** Registered Architect, State of Arizona; Board of Directors, San Diego Multimedia Association; American Institute of Architects; Fellow, Health Facility Institute; Nominated for Outstanding Young Citizen Award, Junior Chamber of Commerce (1993). **Education:** Clemson University: Master of Architecture (1985), B.S. in Design (1983). **Personal:** Married to James Gordon in 1996. Ms. Scanlon enjoys golf, tennis, and gardening.

Ratree C. Smith
Owner/Graphic Designer
Ratree's Desktop Publishing
7914 Charter Oak Ln.
Charlotte, NC 28226–4790
(704) 343–6975
Fax: (704) 554–0640

7336

Business Information: Ratree's Desktop Publishing is a free–lance, desktop publishing company, providing high quality, professional looking documents and eye–catching designs typesetting, brochures, newsletters, menu–forms, booklets, manuals, reports, presentation and resume packages for individuals and businesses. Establishing Ratree's Desktop Publishing in 1996, Ms. Smith serves as Owner and Graphic Designer. She is responsible for the oversight of all functions of the Company, including design and production. Concurrently, she serves as an Administrative Secretary for three offices within the Charlotte–Mecklenburg School District. **Career Steps:** Owner/Graphic Designer, Ratree's Desktop Publishing (1996–Present); Administrative Secretary – Charlotte–Mecklenburg Schools (1981–Present); Real Estate Agent, Kennedy Realty (1991). **Education:** Sheffield School of Interior Design, currently attending; Krirk's College – Bangkok, Thailand, Business Administration; Bryman School of Medical Assistant, Certified Medical Assistant; Century 21 Academy, Licensed Real Estate Agent. **Personal:** One child: Erica Marie. One grandchild: Bria Nicole. Ms. Smith enjoys tennis and weightlifting. She attends various software workshops, home–based seminars, any seminars that help with business as well as personal growth. Life is subject to change.

Lori J. Waknin
Production Manager
Design & Image Communications
1900 Wazee Street, Suite 200
Denver, CO 80202–1259
(303) 292–3455
Fax: (303) 292–3424
EMAIL: See Below

7336

Business Information: Design & Image Communications is a nationally–based, graphic design firm, specializing in identifying systems, environmental signage, annual reports, and

corporate collateral. Clientele include national companies, such as Santa Fe Pacific Gold (mining), William Mercer Hyatt & Hewitt, Transplant Banks (organ donors), National Renewal Energy Lab, and international clients. Joining Design & Image as Production Manager in 1991, Mrs. Waknin is responsible for the management of all jobs in–house, including budgeting, financial functions, monthly reports, and overseeing a staff of five designers and the Corporate Secretary. She also conducts seminars and communicates with clientele. Internet users can reach him via: DandiLW **Career Steps:** Production Manager, Design & Image Communications (1991–Present); Office Manager, Skyline Fasteners (1988–1991). **Associations & Accomplishments:** American Institute for Graphic Arts (non–profit – AIGA); Graphic Arts Production Club (GAPC); Former volunteer for Big Sisters, Neighborhood Clean–up, and Habitat for Humanity (painting). **Education:** Aimes Community College (1985). **Personal:** Married to Scott in 1988. Mrs. Waknin enjoys reading, biking, crocheting, sewing, and listening to live music at clubs.

Scott L. Yaw

Managing Director
Deskey Associates
145 East 32nd Street
New York, NY 10016–6002
(212) 447–9400
Fax: (212) 447–0020

7336

Business Information: Deskey Associates is a graphic design company focusing on brand identification, package and product design, and corporate identity. Clientele include Fortune 100 and 500 companies, as well as new product companies and joint ventures spanning nationally and internationally. Deskey Associates consists of two offices located in New York (New York) and Ohio (Cincinnati). A seventeen–year veteran of Deskey Associates, Mr. Yaw joined the Company in 1978. Appointed as Managing Director in 1991, he is responsible for the oversight of all aspects of operations in the New York office, in addition to overseeing all administrative operations of a support staff of 80. **Career Steps:** Deskey Associates: Managing Director (1991–Present), Vice President of Sales (1986–1991), Operations Manager (1978–1991). **Associations & Accomplishments:** American Marketing Association; Package Design Council; Design Management Institute. **Education:** Central Academy Commercial Art Academy, B.A. **Personal:** Married to Debra in 1974. Two children: Jessica and Nickolous. Mr. Yaw enjoys boating, fishing, and historic preservation.

Khalid Saleh Al Fraiji

General Manager
Mace Pest Control
P.O. Box 16565
Riyadh, Saudi Arabia 11474
9661–465–3070
Fax: 9661–464–0779

7342

Business Information: Mace Pest Control is a pest control service with branches in Beirut and Riyadh, serving 6,000 customers with a staff of eight agricultural engineers and twelve technicians. As General Manager, Mr. Al Fraiji performs research, administrative functions, and is currently supervising a government pest control project. Four other companies are administered by Mr. Al Fraiji. The Kumma Food Factory, acquired in 1994, is a wholesaler of baked goods throughout Saudi Arabia and Lebanon. Riyadh Development, Ltd. is a contract construction company specializing in tourist attraction and accommodation construction. Al–Fraiji Engineering & Construction Company designs and constructs residential and commercial property, including hospitals, schools, and hotels. Al–bayan Education Foundation was established in 1986 as an alternative education option for Mr. Fraiji's children. The school now caters to 2,000 students. **Career Steps:** General Manager, Mace Pest Control (1984–Present); Director of Engineering, Sysorex Int., California (1985); D.D.G. Facilities, Saudi Arabia Public Transit (1983). **Associations & Accomplishments:** American Society of Civil Engineers (1980). **Education:** Northrop University, M.S.MT (1983); University of North Carolina, Civil Engineer (1982); Wye University, London presently preparing for a Ph.D. in Pesticides; University of California at Irvine, Civil Engineering (1982). **Personal:** Married to Nabbilla in 1980. Four children: Fahad, Fawaz, Faris and Moh'd. Mr. Al Fraiji enjoys reading, flying, and languages (French and Dutch).

Richard Amstutz

Vice President
United States Service Industries
721 Sligo Avenue
Silver Spring, MD 20910–4745
(301) 587–6900
Fax: (301) 588–7563

7349

Business Information: United States Service Industries is a full–service building maintenance and janitorial service company. USSI has operations in four states (Florida, Washington DC, Maryland, Virginia), providing janitorial and building maintenance services, etc. to businesses. As Vice President, Mr. Amstutz is responsible for all aspects of the Maryland operations, including administration, P & L, finances, public and client relations. Future plans include opening his own company in 1997 called, Gator Gear – a retail sports gear store. **Career Steps:** Vice President, United States Service Industries (1987–Present); Major (retired), United States Army (1966–1987). **Education:** University of Toledo, B.E. (1966). **Personal:** Married to Betty in 1987. Three children: James, Erik, and Michelle. Mr. Amstutz enjoys golf and racquetball.

Edward N. Bradshaw

Vice President
Synergy Services
137 Tanner Road
Greenville, SC 29606–6148
(803) 234–6083
Fax: (803) 297–9219

7349

Business Information: Synergy Services is a full–service maintenance company, performing industrial contract maintenance and providing maintenance consultation of maintenance programs. Established in 1991, Synergy Services performs contract maintenance in the Southeast and employs 150 people. As Vice President, Mr. Bradshaw provides leadership and direction of the Company in marketing and project management. **Career Steps:** Vice President, Synergy Services (1991–Present); Manager of Projects, Fluor Daniel (1983–1991); Division Engineer and Maintenance Manager, Sara Lee (1977–1983); Production Manager, Abbott Laboratories (1974–1977); Burlington Industries (1967–1974); Dan River (1963–1967). **Associations & Accomplishments:** American Institute of Plant Engineers; Southern Textile Association. **Education:** North Carolina State University, B.S. in Industrial Technology (1963); ICS, Power Plant Engineering; Licensed General Contractor Unlimited; Certified Plant Engineer. **Personal:** Married to Judy E. Two children: Neal and Lisa.

Ellen R. Chardon Bermudez
Vice President of Operations & MIS
National Building Maintenance Company
Hostos Avenue, #45 Playa
Ponce, Puerto Rico 00731
(809) 843–5305
Fax: (809) 848–0930

7349

Business Information: National Building Maintenance Company (NBM) is a group of interrelated companies specialized in building maintenance, sanitation, recycling, personnel training and property management for industries such as: pharmaceuticals, electronics, office buildings, educational institutions, hospitals, and banks. Established in 1967, NBM currently employs 1,000 people. As Vice President of Operations & MIS, Ms. Chardon Bermudez is responsible for planning, developing, organizing, coordinating and directing the Company's operational standard methods, procedures and activities as to achieve specified cost and profit, sales and return on investments. **Career Steps:** National Building Maintenance Company (NBM): Vice President of Operations & MIS (1990–Present), System Consultant & Project Manager (1987–1989), Trainee (1981–1985). **Associations & Accomplishments:** Building Service Contractor Association International; Asociacion Alumni del Colegio de Agricultura & Artes Mecanicas – Mayaguez, Puerto Rico; The Institute of Electronics and Electrical Engineers, Inc.; Data Processing Management Association (DPMA). **Education:** University of Puerto Rico – Mayaguez Campus, B.S.C.P.E. in Computer Engineering (1987); Certified Building Service Executive

(CBSE) (1995). **Personal:** Married to Samuel Pulliza in 1989. Ms. Chardon Bermudez enjoys beach activities, sports, tennis, volleyball, and basketball.

Carol A. Cohea
President
Dexter Enterprises, Inc.
5235 Mission Oaks Boulevard #356
Camarillo, CA 93012–5400
(805) 388–2875
Fax: (805) 987–2258
E MAIL: See Below

7349

Business Information: Dexter Enterprises, Inc. As President, Ms. Cohea Internet users may reach her via: DexterEnt.@DexterEnt.com. **Career Steps:** President, Dexter Enterprises, Inc. (1982–Present). **Associations & Accomplishments:** AAUW. **Education:** California Lutheran University, M.B.A. (1996); University of California at Los Angeles, B.S. in Geology; Diablo Valley Junior College, A.A. in Business Administration. **Personal:** Married to Dennis in 1975. Ms. Cohea enjoys hiking and travel.

Alfredo L. Didier, Jr.

Operations Manager
ISS Cleaning
P.O. Box 9600
Caguas, Puerto Rico 00726
(787) 743–0210
Fax: (787) 743–1712

7349

Business Information: ISS Cleaning, number one in the world in its field, provides cleaning and janitorial services for pharmaceutical companies and commercial buildings. The Company also provides electrical and mechanical services. As Operations Manager, Mr. Didier is responsible for the finances, general operations, and customer relations for the Company. **Career Steps:** Operations Manager, ISS Cleaning (1991–Present); Store Manager, Round Tree Stores (1990–1991); U.S. Navy Officer, U.S. Department of Defense (1980–1990). **Associations & Accomplishments:** Muscular Dystrophy Association Volunteer; Building Service Contractors Association; Rotary Club International; Naval Officers Club. **Education:** Catholic University, B.B.A. (1991); University of Phoenix, A.S.B. **Personal:** Married to Rosemary in 1985. Two children: Rosemary Leanette and Sheila Marie. Mr. Didier enjoys computers, horseback riding, and swimming.

Alexander W. Elliott
President/Chief Executive Officer
PAA of California, Inc.
909 S. Glendora Avenue
West Covina, CA 91790
(818) 966–1203
Fax: (818) 858–9930

7349

Business Information: PAA of California, Inc. is a privately–held corporation engaged in janitorial maintenance concentrating on commercial buildings and health care facilities. Established in 1952 by William Alexander Elliott, Sr., the Corporation estimates revenue of $1 million and presently employs 75 people. In 1994, Mr. Elliott became partial owner of PAA of California, Inc., and by 1995 was the sole shareholder in the Corporation. As sole owner, Mr. Elliott is responsible for daily operations, job bidding, and strategic planning for the future. Other responsibilities include developing and implementing marketing strategies for the development of new business, public relations, and all financial concerns of the business. **Career Steps:** PAA of California, Inc.: President/CEO (1995–Present), Marketing Consultant (1994–1995); Lecturer and Instructor, Mt. San Antonio College (1979–1994); Sun American Financial Services: Investment Advisory Representative (1989–1995), Registered Representative (1983–1989); Registered Tax Preparer, State of California (1979–Present); Financial Planning Representative, James G. Freeman (1977–1979); Agent Metropolitan Life Associates (1976–1977). **Associations & Accomplishments:** PABSCO since 1995; Government Affairs Committee since 1995; BSCAI since 1995; CMI since 1995; Member Speaker's Bureau, Internal Association of Financial Planners (1980–1985); Pomona Chamber of Commerce – Treasurer,

Board of Directors, Executive Committee, Chairman of Business Development Committee, Finance Committee (1983–1989); Cal Poly University Music Association (1983–1989); Pomona Valley YMCA – Past Member, Board of Directors (1983–1989); Pomona Urban League, TECH Center – Past Chairman, Advisory Board (1983–1989); Los Angeles Urban League – Past Member, ETAC Committee (1983–1989); Past Member, Westside Action Group (1983–1989); Saturday Academy – Member, Advisory Committee (1983–1989). Creator and host of Financial Corner on the T.C.I. cable stations (1987–1989). **Education:** California Polytechnic University, B.A. (1974); Internal Revenue Service: Taxation Course (1975), Tax Planning and Preparation (1978); Sun America: Continuing Education (1975), Registered General Securities Representative (NASD) (1983); State of California: Life and Disability Insurance (1976), Registered Tax Preparer (1979); Investment Training Institute, Graduate (1982); Risk Management Planning (1982). **Personal:** Mr. Elliott enjoys tennis and gardening.

Terry M. Fenstad
Assistant Director of Operations
Amherst College Physical Plant
P.O. Box 2247
Amherst, MA 01004–2247
(413) 542–2262
Fax: (413) 542–5789

7349

Business Information: The Amherst College Physical Plant is responsible for all buildings, grounds, operations, and maintenance for the private, four–year college, including construction projects, renovations, campus beautification and structure climate control. Established in 1821 when the college was founded, the physical plant currently employs 120 people and has an operational budget of $6 million. As Assistant Director of Operations, Mr. Fenstad oversees all aspects of facility operations and maintenance. **Career Steps:** Assistant Director of Operations, Amherst College Physical Plant (1993–Present); Senior Vice President of Facility Management, NATO, Naples, Italy (1990–1992); Director of Physical Plant, United States Air Force, Beale Air Force Base, CA (1988–1990). **Associations & Accomplishments:** Society of American Military Engineers; American Institute of Plant Engineers; American Planning Association; Association of Physical Plant Administrators; American Society for Healthcare Engineering; Certified Plant Engineer. **Education:** Texas A & M University, Masters of Urban Planning (1974). **Personal:** Married to Carolyn in 1970. Two children: Jonathan and Gregory. Mr. Fenstad enjoys model railroading, and studying history and architectural history.

Darren G. Fields
President
W.D. Enterprise
P.O. Box 8804
Wichita, KS 67208–0804
(316) 686–0069
Fax: Please mail or call

7349

Business Information: W.D. Enterprise provides janitorial services to commercial, residential, and retail businesses in the Kansas area. As President, Mr. Fields is responsible for overseeing management of all company operations, concentrating on public relations, finance, and contract management and negotiations. **Career Steps:** President, W.D. Enterprise (1991–Present); Construction Analyst, Thorn Enterprise, (1989–1991). **Associations & Accomplishments:** Building Service Contractors Association International; Kappa Alpha 2 PSI Fraternity; Wichita Minority Business Development Council. **Education:** Wichita State University **Personal:** Married to LaWanda Holt in 1994. One child: Danae. Mr. Fields enjoys weightlifting and basketball.

Mr. Earl Fuhrmann
Vice President
Hugo's Cleaning Service, Inc.
5401 West Lake Street
Chicago, IL 60644
(312) 921–7050
Fax: (312) 921–5585

7349

Business Information: Hugo's Cleaning Service, Inc. is a janitorial and facilities management services firm providing services to commercial, industrial, health care and governmental agencies. Established in 1970, the Firm has two offices (Chicago, Illinois and Miami, Florida) servicing customers nationally and currently employs 350 people. As Vice President, Mr. Fuhrmann is responsible for all aspects of operations, including project management, administration, finances, sales, legal matters, marketing and strategic planning. **Career Steps:** Vice President, Hugo's Cleaning Service, Inc. (1983–Present); Executive Housekeeper, International Total Services (1979–1983); Regional Manager, ServiceMaster (1973–1979). **Associations & Accomplishments:** National

Executive Housekeepers Association, Inc.; Society for the Preservation and Encouragement of Barbershop Quartet Singing in America; Active member of Barbershop Quartet. **Education:** Mankato State University, B.S. in Biology (1973). **Personal:** Married to Beth in 1973. Four children: Robert, Amy, Rebecca and Andrew. Mr. Fuhrmann enjoys gardening, remodeling, fishing and singing.

Manuel E. Garcia
General Manager
Puerto Rico LINC Service
65th Infantry Avenue Marginal Empresas Diaz Building, 3rd Floor
Rio Piedras, Puerto Rico 00928
(809) 250–7400
Fax: (809) 250–6178
EMAIL: See Below

7349

Business Information: Puerto Rico LINC Service is a general contracting firm, providing HVAC industrial/commercial mechanical service and maintenance throughout Puerto Rico. A Professional Engineer with nine years experience, Mr. Garcia joined Puerto Rico LINC Service as General Manager in 1994. He is responsible for the oversight of all aspects of operations for his division, including sales, public relations, accounting, marketing, and strategic planning. Internet users can reach him via: 102440,3562@compuserve.com. **Career Steps:** General Manager, Puerto Rico LINC Service (1994–Present); Project Manager, Cobian, Agustin & Ramos (1992–1994); Design Engineer, Juan L. Cardet & Associates (1989–1992). **Associations & Accomplishments:** Puerto Rico Board of Professional Engineers. **Education:** University of Bridgeport, B.S.M.E. (1989). **Personal:** Married to Maria E. Margarida in 1992. Mr. Garcia enjoys scuba diving, photography, tennis, and fishing.

Jack D. Hamel
Vice President
Southwestern Building Services
7800 Bissonnet, Suite #145
Houston, TX 77074
(713) 995–7744
Fax: (713) 995–8835

7349

Business Information: Southwestern Building Services provides janitorial services to commercial and industrial companies. Established in 1977, Southwestern Building Services currently employs 189 people and has an estimated annual revenue of $2.2 million. As Vice President, Mr. Hamel is responsible for all aspects of management, including sales, personnel and policy. A successful entrepreneur, he also manages the companies SBS Building Services, and Texas Cleaning, Inc. **Career Steps:** Vice President, Southwestern Building Services (1992–Present); Environmental Director, Fort Bend Hospital (1990–1992); Assistant Environmental Director, Memorial Hospital (1988–1990). **Education:** Marine Corps Logistics Academy, Logistics Certification (1986). **Personal:** Mr. Hamel enjoys weightlifting, tennis and racquetball.

Dennis Hooper
Regional Vice President and General Manager
ABM Janitorial
5200 Eastern
Los Angeles, CA 90040
(213) 720–4020
Fax: (213) 727–7493

7349

Business Information: ABM Janitorial is a commercial and industrial janitorial services industry, providing janitorial, security, maintenance, and engineering services for complete commercial properties, including parking lots and elevator lighting. Established in 1909, ABM Janitorial currently employs 4,000 company–wide. As Regional Vice President and General Manager, Mr. Hooper is responsible for all aspects of operations for his division, including the supervision of all personnel. His division spans Southern California, Hawaii, Arizona and Nevada. **Career Steps:** Regional Vice President and General Manager, ABM Janitorial (1977–Present); Vice President, National Cleaning Company (1969–1977). **Associations & Accomplishments:** Building Owners and Managers Association (BOMA); Central City Association (CCA); Los Angeles Headquarters Association; Los Angeles Beautiful; Burbank on Parade. **Education:** California State University – Los Angeles, B.S.; Los Angeles Valley College, A.A. **Personal:** Married to Sally in 1965. Three children: Denny, Michael, and Diane. Mr. Hooper enjoys golf, tennis, softball, camping, and fishing.

Clyde F. Mayhew
Senior Vice President
Kanon Service Corporation
10011 Overbrook Lane
Houston, TX 77042–3103
(713) 789–2707
Fax: (713) 789–2560

7349

Business Information: Kanon Service Corporation is an airline contracting services company, providing building maintenance, janitorial, aircraft cleaning, airline support services, and consulting to airlines. Services provided range from interior cabin cleaning to janitorial services for airlines, and the cleaning of office buildings to malls. National in scope, Kanon Service Corporation provides services from sixteen locations throughout the U.S., such as New England and Florida. Founding Kanon Service Corporation in 1986, Mr. Mayhew serves as its Senior Vice President. Taking the Company from zero in 1986 to eight million dollars in 1996, he is responsible for all contract negotiations, proposal preparations and submissions, financial planning, market trend forcasting, labor contracts, I & E, P & L, and management training. **Career Steps:** Senior Vice President, Kanon Service Corporation (1986–Present); Vice President and General Manager, World Service Corporation (1980–1985); Regional Director, Braniff Airlines (1965–1980). **Associations & Accomplishments:** Volunteer (1985–Present), Houston Livestock Show; Windfern Gardens Civic Association (1985–1990): President, Treasurer; BOMA; BSCAII; Builders/Owners Management Association. **Education:** Kansas State University, B.S.; Rice University; Cornell University, Management Assessment/Transactual Analysis (1975). **Personal:** Two children: Gregory A. and Shawna A. Mayhew Rocha. Mr. Mayhew enjoys horses, sailing, golf, and travel.

Erin L. McLean
Personnel Manager
United Building Services
2939 Lockport Road
Niagara Falls, NY 14305–2307
(716) 284–2676
Fax: (716) 284–9748

7349

Business Information: United Building Services provides contract commercial cleaning services for other companies. As Personnel Manager, Ms. McLean is responsible for diversified administrative activities, including recruitment, selection and training of employees, orientation of new hires, unemployment, workers compensation, and disability claims. **Career Steps:** Personnel Manager, United Building Services (1994–Present); Assistant Service Manager, Mike Smith Buick, Inc (1990–1992); Warranty Claims Administrator, Beatty Pontiac, Olds GMC (1988–1990). **Associations & Accomplishments:** Society for Human Resource Managers; United Way Loaned Associate (1995–1996); Employer of the Year, Center for Vocational Rehabilitation (1995); Mobile Works Job Work Shop. **Education:** Alfred State University, A.O.S. (1986); Certificate in Recruit, Select and Train Program. **Personal:** One child: Victoria. Ms. McLean enjoys family time, reading, teaching church school, and crafts.

Thomas J. Morgan Jr.
Director of Engineering
Premier Manufacturing Support Services, Inc.
4790 Red Bank Expy., Ste. 128
Cincinnati, OH 45227–1509
(513) 561–0808
Fax: (513) 561–7997

7349

Business Information: Premier Manufacturing Support Services, Inc., a privately–held company, provides manufacturing support services, primarily paint shop cleaning and janitorial services to automobile assembly plants. Established in 1984, the Company operates from locations throughout the United States, Canada, Mexico, and Europe. The Company's focus is on long term support contracts with minimum terms of one year. Contracts currently held include GM, Ford, Chrysler, NUMMI and Saturn. An automotive engineer with over fifteen years expertise, Thomas Morgan joined Premier in 1992 and has had multiple responsibilities for both operational and technical aspects of the business. In his current capacity as Director of Engineering, he directs all aspects of technical support to field operations, including safety and technical training. **Career Steps:** Director of Engineering, Premier Manufacturing Support Services, Inc. (1992–Present); Senior Manufacturing Engineer, General Motors Corporation (1985–1992); Plant Engineer, Caterpillar Tractor Company (1981–1985). **Education:** Purdue University, B.S. in Engineering (1981). **Personal:** Married to Christina in 1991. Two children: Nicholas and

William. Mr. Morgan enjoys rebuilding antique radios & audio equipment and reading about automotive and WWII history.

Yvonne M. Pico
Vice President
Glenn Company
1040 New York Drive
Altadena, CA 91001–3118
(818) 398–8000
Fax: (818) 398–1290

7349

Business Information: Glenn Company, a small janitorial company, is a professional building maintenance services firm for commercial and residential clientele. Established in 1987, Glenn Company reports annual revenue of $1.5 million and currently employs 100 people. Joining the Firm in 1990 while still a student, Ms. Pico was appointed as Vice President in 1995. Participating in all major Company decisions in financial matters and otherwise, she is also responsible for sales and marketing functions, and customer service. **Career Steps:** Vice President, Glenn Company (1990–Present). **Associations & Accomplishments:** Building Owners and Managers Association; Pasadena Chamber of Commerce; Hillsides Home for Children's Young Professionals. **Education:** California State University – Dominion Hill, B.A. (1991). **Personal:** One child: John Thomas Pico–Nicoloro.

Mr. Jose Sampedro
President
C.P.F. Corporation
1724 Kalorama Road N.W., #200
Washington, DC 20009
(202) 265–7356
Fax: (202) 483–6328

7349

Business Information: C.P.F. Corporation is a provider of complete janitorial and custodial services to government buildings in Washington, DC, Maryland and Virginia (government contracts only). They also provide maintenance services, including painting and painting supply distribution. In his current capacity, Mr. Sampedro oversees all aspects of Corporate operations. C.P.F. Corporation presently employs 479 people, has estimated annual revenue in excess of $7.4 million, and was established 198 3. **Career Steps:** President, C.P.F. Corporation (1986–Present); Corporate Secretary, Diplomatic Painting Services (1984–1991); General Manager, Apollo XI (1980–1984). **Associations & Accomplishments:** Mr. Sampedro has been interviewed for magazines and newspapers. **Education:** University of Oviedo, Spain, Accounting Degree (1979).

Joseph Joe Scott
President and Chief Executive Officer
World Technical Services, Inc.
1603 South W.W. White Road, Suite 605
San Antonio, TX 78220–4762
(210) 333–1514
Fax: (210) 333–3433

7349

Business Information: World Technical Services, Inc. is a provider of janitorial and ground maintenance services for commercial customers, but primarily focusing on government PX's and commissaries from five locations in Texas. Services include stocking shelves and janitorial services. As President and Chief Executive Officer, Mr. Scott is responsible for all aspects of operations, including administration, finances, budgeting, and strategic planning. His career highlights include working closely with President Johnson. **Career Steps:** President and Chief Executive Officer, World Technical Services, Inc. (1981–Present). **Associations & Accomplishments:** United States Chamber of Commerce; Life Member, American Legion; National Association for the Advancement of Colored People; Alabama Chamber of Commerce; Veterans of Foreign Wars; Omega Psi Phi Fraternity; N.I.S.H.; T.I.B.H.; Disabled American Veterans; N.A.A.C.P.; St. Joseph's Grand Lodge. **Education:** Our Lady of the Lake University, M.Ed. (1954). **Personal:** Married to Cecilia A. in 1950. Three children: Cynthia A. Warrick, Joseph A. III, and Cecily A. Mr. Scott enjoys golf and church activities.

Ms. Ann Urbach
President
Metro Maintenance Service, Inc.
3939 Oakton Street
Skokie, IL 60076
(708) 677–8113
Fax: Please mail or

7349

Business Information: Metro Maintenance Service, Inc. is a janitorial service, serving commercial, industrial and government facilities in the Chicagoland area. In her capacity as President, Ms. Urbach is responsible for overseeing management of all Company operations, concentrating on public relations, finance, and contract management and negotiations. Established in 1979, Metro Maintenance Service, Inc. employs a staff of 50. **Career Steps:** President, Metro Maintenance Service, Inc. (1992–Present); Bookkeeper, Michael Silver & Company (1990–1991); Trust Assistant, Devon Bank (1980–1986). **Education:** University of Illinois, B.A. (1975).

Dawn R. Vande Berg

Controller
Indy Lube
6515 East 82nd Street
Indianapolis, IN 46250
(317) 845–9444
Fax: (317) 577–3169

7349

Business Information: Indy Lube is a provider of quick lubes and services. As Controller, Ms. Vande Berg is responsible for the overall financial presentation of operations and daily financial activities. **Career Steps:** Controller, Indy Lube (1995–Present); Staff Accountant, Crowe Chizek & Company (1992–1995); Marketing Assistant, Cardiovascular Credentialing International (Summers of 1991 & 1992); Sales Assistant, Archer Daniels Midland (Summer of 1990). **Education:** University of Dayton, B.S. in Accounting (1992). **Personal:** Married to Tom in 1995. Ms. Vande Berg enjoys aerobics, golf and outdoors.

Philip Vicinanza III

Financial Manager/Systems Administrator
Pritchard Industries Incorporated
1120 Avenue of the Americas, Floor 17
New York, NY 10036
(212) 382–2295 Ext. 312
Fax: (212) 382–0710

7349

Business Information: Pritchard Industries Incorporated is a full service cleaning firm providing janitorial services to 70% of Manhattan's buildings. National in scope, the Company has branch offices in Massachusetts, Connecticut, Texas, Virginia and Washington, D.C. Established in 1986, the Company currently employs 5,000 people. As Financial Manager/Systems Administrator, Mr. Vicinanza serves as network/remote site administrator. He is responsible for the local, Virginia and Washington D.C. networks, and coordinates all customer and corporate data. Additional duties include management of accounts payable/receivable and the current drafting of policy and procedure manuals. **Career Steps:** Financial Manager/Systems Administrator, Pritchard Industries Incorporated (1996–Present). **Associations & Accomplishments:** Phi Theta Kappa Society. **Education:** Pace University, B.B.A. (1996). **Personal:** Mr. Vicinanza enjoys travel.

Mr. Barry R. Wentland

Vice President
Crowder & Associates, Inc.
109 Derby Woods Drive
Lynn Haven, FL 32444
(904) 265–0740
Fax: (904) 265–6810

7349

Business Information: Crowder & Associates, Inc. is a maintenance management software and consulting company. The Company provides a software product called the Work Information Management System (WIMS) to corporations with large physical plants to better enable them to effectively manage their maintenance requirements. In addition to providing automated solutions to maintenance management, the Company also offers a complete spectrum of consulting services, including training requirements analyses, technical writing, programming, and conversions. As Vice President, Mr. Wentland is responsible for strategic planning, technical writing, software implementations, training and demonstrations. His position requires extensive travel. Established in 1988, Crowder & Associates, Inc. employs 6 people with annual sales of $500K. **Career Steps:** Vice President, Crowder & Associates, Inc., (1992–Present); United States Air Force Chief of Engineering Computer Applications and Development (1986–1992), Headquarters Pacific Air Forces Chief of Engineering Management Systems (1983–1986). **Associations & Accomplishments:** Mr. Wentland is the individual that conceived, designed, developed, implemented and managed the Air Force automated maintenance management system. He is a member of the Society of American Military Engineers (S.A.M.E.), Association of Physical Plant Administrators (A.P.P.A.), the American Institute of Plant Engineers (A.I.P.E.), and the International Maintenance Institute (A.M.I.). **Education:** University of Northern Colorado, M.B.A. (1980); Rensselaer Polytechnic Institute, M.E. (1973); B.S. (1972). **Personal:** Married to Audrey in 1990. Mr. Wentland enjoys home construction projects, travel, and golf.

Patricia A. Purser

National Accounts Director
Hill–Rom Company
1061 Trumbull Avenue, Unit G
Girard, OH 14420–3490
(330) 629–6408
Fax: (330) 629–6409

7352

Business Information: Hill–Rom Company, a Hillenbrand Industry, is an international distributor of health care products, specializing in specialty beds, hospital beds, overbed tables and other hospital equipment (low air–loss, air–fluidized, irrigation and lateral rotation therapies). As National Accounts Director, Mrs. Purser is responsible for negotiating contracts with LTC corporations, implementing the contracts, and determining field strategy. **Career Steps:** National Accounts Director, Hill–Rom Company (1994–Present); Support Systems International, Territory Sales Manager (1992–1994), Nurse Consultant, Support Systems International (1991–1992). **Associations & Accomplishments:** Former Member Board of Directors, Easter Seal Society (Trumbull–Mahoning Counties); Former Member, Youngstown Panhellenic; Former Member, Warren Area Chamber of Commerce. **Education:** Youngstown State University: B.S.N. (1989–1991), A.A.S. (1976); Attending University of Akron, working towards M.S.N. **Personal:** Married to Joseph R. in 1963. Two children: Jeffrey and Traci Purser Boyce. Mrs. Purser enjoys travel, reading, decorating, and needlework.

Timothy E. Shaw

MIS Director
Aggregate Equipment Supply
1601 N. Main Street
East Peoria, IL 61611–2149
(309) 694–6644
Fax: (309) 694–6648
EMAIL: See Below

7353

Business Information: Aggregate Equipment Supply sells, leases, and services for all types of construction, air lift equipment, and retail supplies. Headquartered in Peoria, Illinois, the Company is national in scope, with twenty–two locations in eight states. Established in 1958, the Company employs 350 people. As MIS Director, Mr. Shaw is responsible for all MIS activities including driving the Company's growth via technology. Additional responsibilities include handling customer service, company voice and data communication, system hardware and software, and overseeing personnel management and training. Internet users can reach him via: TSHAW@cyberdesic.com. **Career Steps:** MIS Director, Aggregate Equipment Supply (1994–Present); Manufacturing Specialist, Veltri Internaltron (1993–1994); Systems Engineer, EDS Corporation (1991–1993); Manufacturing Engineer, McDonnell Douglas (1981–1991). **Associations & Accomplishments:** Local Computer Associations; School Support Functions. **Education:** Southern Illinois University, Edwardsville, B.S. (1992); Lewis and Clark Community College, A.A.S. (1981). **Personal:** Married to Renae in 1981. Two children: Nicole and Lauren. Mr. Shaw enjoys golf, fishing, and working around the house.

Larry Armstrong

President and Chief Executive Officer
Ponder Industries, Inc.
5005 Riverway, Suite 550
Houston, TX 77056
(713) 965–0653
Fax: (713) 965–0047

7359

Business Information: Ponder Industries, Inc. specializes in the rental of oil fields and fishing tool service. The Company rents high pressure blow prevention equipment. Mr. Armstrong started with the industry at the age of 14 with his father. By the age of 24, he owned his own tool company with seven franchised stores. He sold that Company to Petroleum Equipment Tools, Inc. in 1978. Later, he joined Ponder Industries, Inc. Since he has been with Ponder, the stock and net worth of the Company has increased dramatically. As President and Chief Executive Officer, Mr. Armstrong handles all aspects of Company operations, including finance, administration, and strategic planning for the expansion of the Company. **Career Steps:** President and Chief Executive Officer, Ponder Industries, Inc. (1995–Present); President, Armstrong Tool, Inc. (1983–1995); Executive Vice President and Chief Operating Officer, Petroleum Equip Tools, Inc. (1978–1983). **Associations & Accomplishments:** American Petroleum Institute; Society of Petroleum Engineers; International Association of Drilling Contractors; American Association of Well Servicing Contractors; Chairman, Petroleum Equipment Supplier Association; Fishing and Rental Committee, Chamber of Commerce; President, School Board Association. **Personal:** Married to Gail in 1957. Three children: Edward, Leslie Quick, and Angela.

Bob Bogardus

Division Manager
Brambles Equipment Service, Inc.
3351 Brecksville road
Richfield, OH 44286
(216) 659–7272
Fax: (330) 659–0972

7359

Business Information: Brambles Equipment Service, Inc. is an equipment rental, equipment asset management, and construction and industrial equipment maintenance firm. The Richfield location was established in 1994 and is part of a 30–location company headquartered in Australia. The Richfield operation employs over 110 people. As Division Manager, Mr. Bogardus handles the administrative duties and daily operations for a multi–branch division. **Career Steps:** Division Manager, Brambles Equipment Service, Inc. (1995–Present); Vice President/General Manager, Kirkpatrick & O'Connell (1993–1995); District Manager, Link Belt Construction Equipment (1990–1993); Marketing Representative, Lehigh Portland Cement Company (1980–1990). **Education:** Xavier University, M.B.A. (1990); University of Indianapolis, Bachelor of Arts (1980). **Personal:** Married to Linda in 1991. Three children: Amanda, Sean, and Austin. Mr. Bogardus enjoys golf and being with his children.

Brian K. Burns

Vice President
Wellington Equipment Corporation
4230 North 126th Street
Brookfield, WI 53005–1817
(414) 790–0500
Fax: (414) 790–0505

7359

Business Information: Wellington Equipment Corporation, a free–standing spin–off company of Wellington Management Corporation, specializes in aerial lift sales, rental, service, and parts. The Retail Division negotiates directly with contractors while the Wholesale Division markets re–rentals for large projects (hotels, airports, dams). As Vice President, Mr. Burns reports directly to the Chief Executive Officer of Wellington Management and is responsible for overseeing all aspects of operations and business development for Wellington Equipment. **Career Steps:** Vice President, Wellington Equipment Corporation (1993–Present); General Manager, State Equipment Corporation (1990–1993). **Associations & Accomplishments:** AED; ARA. **Personal:** Married to Pamela in 1981. Two children: Steven and Joshua. Mr. Burns enjoys spending time with family.

Carol Sue Cornett

Respiratory Clinical Director
Community Home Care Services
RR 2 Box 350B
Cedar Bluff, VA 24609–9611
(540) 964–7448
Fax: (540) 963–3549

7359

Business Information: Community Home Care Services is a JCAH Clinically Accredited Durable Medical Equipment Company. As Respiratory Clinical Director, Mrs. Cornett provides and supervises patient home therapy, oversees daily operations of the Therapy Division, and performs various administrative functions. **Career Steps:** Respiratory Clinical Director, Community Home Care Services (1991–Present); Respiratory Therapy Director, Appalachian Regional Hospital (1987–1990); Respiratory Therapy Director, Family Pharmacy (1982–1987). **Associations & Accomplishments:** American Association of Respiratory Care; Virginia Black Lung Association; National Association of Medical Equipment; Virginia Association of Durable Medical Equipment Companies. **Education:** Eden Trace Scoring School, Certified (1994); Southwest Virginia Community College; National Association of Respiratory Care, Respiratory Care Practitioner. **Personal:** Married to Michael. Mrs. Cornett performs with a locally–known female gospel quartet as a drummer and singer.

George Fore
Vice President of Marketing
Advanta Business Services
1020 Lorrel Oak Road
Voorhees, NJ 08043–1228
(609) 782–7300
Fax: Please mail or call

7359

Business Information: Advanta Business Services, a wholly–owned subsidiary of Advanta Corporation, provides Mastercard or other credit card services for business purposes. Additionally, the Company leases commercial equipment to small companies. As Vice President of Marketing, Mr. Fore is responsible for new product development, developing strategic alliances, and enterprising wide market research projects. **Career Steps:** Vice President of Marketing, Advanta Business Services (1991–Present); Vice President of Marketing, Cigna Corporation (1986–1991); Vice President of Marketing, Automatic Business Center–Cigna Corporation (1983–1986). **Associations & Accomplishments:** American Marketing Association; Direct Marketing Association. **Education:** Temple University, M.B.A. (1971); Rutgers University, B.A. in Psychology. **Personal:** Married to Christina in 1975.

James G. Froberg
General Counsel
The LINC Group
303 Wacker Drive
Chicago, IL 60601
(312) 946–7363
Fax: Please mail or call
Email: See Below

7359

Business Information: The LINC Group, a financial provision firm, specializes in the leasing of medical equipment as well as the lease or lending of industrial and business equipment. Primarily serving corporate and medical professionals throughout the U.S., the firm also serves some international clientele. With over 18 years expertise in corporate legal services, James Froberg serves as General Counsel. As the chief legal counsel, he oversees all support staff in the Legal Department, as well as represents the Firm in all major legal transactions and litigation proceedings. He can also be reached through the Internet via: jimfro@aol.com **Career Steps:** General Counsel, The LINC Group (1991–Present); Associate General Counsel, Heller Financial Inc. (1984–1991); Senior Counsel, Associates Commerical Corp. (1982–1984). **Associations & Accomplishments:** Chicago Bar Association; American Bar Association; Equipment Leasing Association; American Corporate Counsel Association. **Education:** Northwestern University, MBA (1989); Loyola University School of Law, J.D. (1977); Loyola University College of Arts and Sciences, A.B. (1974). **Personal:** Married to Julie in 1984. One child: John. Mr. Froberg enjoys golf, staying fit, and being an outside corporate director.

Juan Ramon Gutierrez
Vice President of Sales
Popular Leasing and Rental
P.O. Box 50045
San Juan, Puerto Rico 00903
(809) 759–4900
Fax: (809) 759–4940

7359

Business Information: Popular Leasing and Rental specializes in the leasing of vehicular equipment. The Company serves 22,500 customers in six regions throughout Puerto Rico. In operation for 32 years, Popular Leasing and Rental currently employs 209 people and has an estimated annual revenue of $240 million. As Vice President of Sales, Mr. Gutierrez is responsible for all aspects of sales, directing a staff of 54 sales representatives. Under his guidance, sales have increased from $25 million to over $200 million, with over 32,000 units being leased. **Career Steps:** Vice President of Sales, Popular Leasing and Rental (1995–Present); Vice President of Sales, Velco Popular Leasing (1982–1995); Leaseway of Puerto Rico (1977–1982); Captain (Ret.), National Guard. **Associations & Accomplishments:** National Association of Fleet Administrators; United States Officers Association; Sales and Marketing Executive Association; Published in local newspapers. **Education:** University of Puerto Rico, B.A. (1971); Catholic University of Puerto Rico Law School. **Personal:** Married to Wanda E. Rovira in 1975. Three children: Beatriz, Juan Ramon and Jose Antonio. Mr. Gutierrez enjoys reading and golf.

Dennis Mastry
Marketing Manager
Rent–A–Center
26319 Dancing Bear
San Antonio, TX 78258–5817
(210) 497–8901
Fax: (210) 497–7292

7359

Business Information: Rent–A–Center is one of largest rent–to–own business in the United States. The Company provides household supplies such as furniture, appliances, and electronic equipment on a weekly or monthly payment basis. As Market Manager, Mr. Mastry handles all hiring, training, recruiting, marketing, advertising, ordering, and inventory of ten stores in San Antonio and Austin. **Career Steps:** Market Manager, Rent–A–Center (1994–Present); Owner/Director, The Telephone Warehouse (1993–1994); Managing Director of Operations, Radio Shack de Mexico (1973–1993); Store Manager, District Manager & Managing Director of Caribbean, Tandy Corporation (1973–1992). **Associations & Accomplishments:** Former Member: Rotary, MENSA, Society of Manufacturing Engineers (Corpus Christi). **Education:** Corpus Christi State (1991); Stetson University, B.B.A. in Business and Accounting; Texas A&M Univ., Post Graduate Courses; Numerous specialized training (business and management) courses. **Personal:** Married to Marga in 1974. Mr. Mastry enjoys computers, photography, and golf.

Ruth A. Morey, Ed.D.
Senior Vice President and Corporate Resource Officer
AT&T Capital Corporation
44 Whippany Road
Morristown, NJ 07925
(201) 397–4116
Fax: (201) 397–3220

7359

Business Information: AT&T Capital Corporation is an international equipment leasing and finance company. As the second largest, full–service, multi–point distribution leasing company in the U.S., AT&T Capital offers telecommunication, automotive and real estate financing services throughout their operations in the U.S., Canada, Europe, Hong Kong, Australia and Mexico. As Senior Vice President and Corporate Resource Officer, Dr. Morey is responsible for information technology, human resources, quality and corporate communications. Established in 1985, AT&T Capital Corporation employs over 2,500 people. **Career Steps:** Senior Vice President and Corporate Resource Officer, AT&T Capital Corporation (1989–Present); Vice President Of Human Resources, AT&T Capital Corporation, (1987–1989); Regional Director of Stock Transfer Services, AT&T TransTech (1983–1987). **Associations & Accomplishments:** United Way; Equipment Leasing Association; Sponsor and Fund Raiser at numerous local community programs. **Education:** Temple University, Ed.D. (1973); Indiana University at Bloomington, M.S.; S.U.N.Y.at Cortland, B.S. **Personal:** Dr. Morey enjoys golf and swimming.

Maria Teres Ruiz Mendez

President/Owner
Equity Leasing
Calle Parque de Los Ninos KM 5.2 Los Frailes
Guaynabo, Puerto Rico 00969
(787) 789–0208
Fax: (787) 272–2140

7359

Business Information: Equity Leasing, established in 1988, provides medical, industrial, and office equipment on a lease basis. As President/Owner, Mrs. Ruiz Mendez is responsible for negotiation and approval of all lease contracts. Concurrently, she is the President/Owner of Real Cleaners, a laundry and dry cleaning concern. As President of Real Cleaners, she is responsible for staff recruitment, staff evaluation, and supervision, payroll, customer service, and strategic planning and public relations for both companies. **Career Steps:** President/Owner, Equity Leasing (1988–Present); President/Owner, Real Cleaners (1992–Present); Attorney, Municipality of San Juan, Financial Department (1982–1986). **Associations & Accomplishments:** Commission for Public and Cultural Acts of the Puerto Rico Bar Association. **Education:** Puerto Rico University: Juris Doctor, Cum Laude (1979), Art B.A., Magna Cum Laude (1976); Passed the Bar Exam (1979). **Personal:** Three children: Ricardo, Garbiel, and Natalia Abreu. Mrs. Ruiz Mendez enjoys spending time with her family and attending their ball games (volleyball and basketball).

Frank Russo
General Manager
Burch–Lowe, Inc.
145 Providence Oaks Circle
Alpharetta, GA 30201
(404) 363–7770
Fax: (404) 285–9207

7359

Business Information: Burch–Lowe, Inc. is a distributor of Nissan products (rental, leasing, and buying). The Company has eight branches throughout Georgia. Each branch has three subdivisions: Highway Heavy, Industrial Construction, and Materials Handling. As General Manager, Mr. Russo handles all operations of the Materials Handling Division. Additionally, he has a strong computer background, so he plays a role in all information systems, as well as strategic planning. **Career Steps:** General Manager, Burch–Lowe, Inc. (1993–Present); General Manager, Western Carolina Forklift (1989–1993). **Associations & Accomplishments:** MHEDA; American Management Association; Nissan Advisory Board. **Education:** B.S. in Business (1963). **Personal:** Married to Mary in 1985. Two children: Michael and Daniella. Mr. Russo enjoys sports.

Charles R. Stevens Jr.
National Accountant Executive
New England Capital Corporation
30 Avon Meadow Lane
Avon, CT 06001
(860) 677–9423
Fax: (860) 674–8478

7359

Business Information: New England Capital Corporation is a nationwide commercial equipment leasor employing approximately 50 people, and estimating annual sales in excess of $50 million. As National Accountant Executive, Mr. Stevens is responsible for bringing new business into the Company, and loan and lease originations. **Career Steps:** National Accountant Executive, New England Capital Corporation (1996–Present); Center Capital Corporation, AVP Senior Credit Manager (1991–1996); Director of Operations, Concord Commerce Corporation (1988–1990); Portfolio Operations Manager, Unisys Finance Corporation (1986–1988); National Credit Manager, Wang Finance Corporation (1986–1987). **Education:** Suffolk University, M.B.A. in Finance (1986); University of Massachusetts, B.S. in Mathematics (1972). **Personal:** One child: Laura Ann Stevens. Mr. Stevens enjoys tennis and the Worship Team at the First Church of Christ.

Peter J. Boswick
Marketing Director
DRAKE International
181 Bay Street, Suite 2030 BCE Place
Toronto, Ontario
(416) 216–1005
Fax: (905) 470–2346

7360

Business Information: DRAKE International is an international outsourcing company, providing staff and process productivity staffing (i.e., flexible, permanent, contracted, etc.) to companies nationwide and internationally. As Marketing Director, Mr. Boswick is responsible for the direction of all national accounts and client's special projects, including human resources, productivity, hiring, and outplacement. **Career Steps:** Marketing Director, DRAKE International (1984–Present); Vice President of Systems, Olinetti Canada (1987–1990); President, Anwser Computer Centres (1984–1987); Manager, Channel Strategies, IBM Canada Ltd. (1969–1984). **Associations & Accomplishments:** Canadian Professional Sales Association; Ontario Real Estate Association; Canadian Franchise Restaurant Association. **Education:** Attended, Ryerson University, Business Administration; Significant courses in Sales Management, Business Processes, Communications and Systems Applications with IBM; Mr. Boswick was the Canadian on the IBM Personal Computer Team in 1981. **Personal:** Married to Maureen in 1969. Three children: Justin, Mandy and Melissa. Mr. Boswick enjoys car racing, skiing, racquetball and woodworking.

V. Ricardo Alvar

Director of Business Development – Latin America
Kelly Service
12000 Biscayne Boulevard #105
Miami, FL 33181
(305) 892–6426
Fax: (305) 893–9430

7361

Business Information: Kelly Service, established in 1946, provides temporary employment and total staffing solutions and services for all corporate levels and industries. As Director of Business Development – Latin America, Mr. Alvar is responsible for the expansion of operations throughout Latin America. Her duties include senior–level decision–making, sales, negotiation, and strategic planning. **Career Steps:** Director of Business Development – Latin America, Kelly Service (1994–Present); Group Manager, Todays Temporary (1990–1994); Executive Director, Chase Choice (1987–1990). **Associations & Accomplishments:** Society for Human Resource Management; Society for Advancement of Management. **Personal:** Married to Torry in 1988. Mr. Alvar enjoys soccer, music, and travel.

Richard A. Assunto

Director of Payroll Services
Norrell Corporation
3535 Piedmont Road
Atlanta, GA 30305–4535
(404) 240–3731
Fax: Please mail or call

7361

Business Information: Norrell Corporation, established in 1969, is an international provider of managed staffing employees throughout the U.S., Canada, and Puerto Rico. As Director of Payroll Services, Mr. Assunto is responsible for the overall Corporate payroll of approximately 200,000 employees per year. **Career Steps:** Director of Payroll Services, Norrell Corporation (1994–Present); Manager of Payroll, AlliedSignal (1992–1994); Aetna Life: Manager Acquisitions (1992–1994), Manager of Payroll (1981–1992), Administrator (1973–1981). **Associations & Accomplishments:** American Payroll Association; Cowboy Artists of America Museum; American Society of Payroll Managers; Who's Who in Business Leaders (1992); Who's Who Worldwide (1990, 1992); Who's Who in Finance Industry (1996, 1997); Published in Fortune and Business Week magazines. **Education:** University of Hartford, M.B.A. (1987); Biola University, B.A. **Personal:** Mr. Assunto enjoys bicycling, swimming, art collecting, basketry, and reading.

Staffing Services Tele Ressources
your employment partner

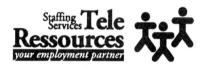

Johanne Berry

President/Chief Executive Officer
Tele–Resources Staffing Services Limited
2021 Rue Union, Suite 815
Montreal, Quebec H3A 2C1
(514) 842–0066
Fax: (514) 842–8797

7361

Business Information: Tele–Resources Staffing Services Limited provides recruitment and placement of temporary and/or permanent personnel as stipulated in an agreement with a client and or an outsourcing contract. Founded in 1985, the Firm was awarded the prestigious "Total Quality Mercuriades" trophy in 1995, and received the international certification ISO 9002 in 1996. A major partner of Canadian Personnel Services, Inc., a firm that includes the best independent staffing firms in Canada, the Company now has access to every province and major city in the country. As President/Chief Executive Officer, Ms. Berry oversees all aspects of the Company. Assisted by her Vice President and Executive Assistant, she is responsible for administration, sales, recruitment, public relations, and strategic planning. The Company's founder, she was honored as "Woman Entrepreneur" by the Comite Action Femmes d'Affaires (CAFA) of the Montreal Chamber of Commerce in 1996, in addition to winning the title "Woman of Merit in the Business, Profession, and Entrepreneurship Category" by the YWCA. **Career Steps:** President/Chief Executive Officer, Tele–Resources Staffing Services Limited (1985–Present). **Associations & Accomplishments:** Nominated as "Personality of the Week", by La Presse Newspaper; Business Women Association of the Province of Quebec; Canadian Personnel Staffing Services (CPSI); City of Saint Laurent Chamber of Commerce; Quebec Employers Council Association of Quebec; Greater Montreal Chamber of Commerce; Human Resources Professionals; Montreal Executives Association (MA); National Association of Personnel Consultants (NAPS); National Association of Staffing Services (NASS); Young President Organization (YPO); Board of Directors, Cegep Andre–Laurendeau Foundation; Vice President/Board of Directors, Jules and Paul–Emile Leger Foundation. **Education:** Certified Personnel Consultant. **Personal:** Ms. Berry enjoys golf, skiing, reading, music and theater.

Mike G. Boyce

President/Owner
Interim Personnel
711 Executive Place, Suite 403
Fayetteville, NC 28305
(910) 323–2777
Fax: (910) 323–3588

7361

Business Information: Interim Personnel is an employment agency assisting regional businesses in locating permanent and temporary employees. Established in 1993, the Company currently has two locations, nine full–time employees, and a pool of 450 temporary employees. As President/Owner, Mr. Boyce is accountable for all operations of the firm, including personnel recruitment, marketing of services, financial concerns, and strategic planning for the future. **Career Steps:** President/Owner, Interim Personnel (1993–Present); Manager, Personnel Pool/Interim (1992–1993); Sales Manager, Stone's School Supply (1990–1992); Pilot/Crew Scheduler, US Air Force (1982–1990). **Associations & Accomplishments:** Board Member, Fayetteville Chamber of Commerce Ambassador; Kiwanis Club; American Racquetball Association; Member of the Professional Racquetball Tour; AUSA; Human Resources Association; Affiliated with National Association of Temporary and Staffing Services. **Education:** Park College, B.S. (1990); East Carolina University, Accounting; US Air Force Academy, Electronic Technology. **Personal:** Two children: Nicholas and Jessica. Mr. Boyce enjoys racquetball (has participated on the Professional Tour), fishing, and basketball.

Faye Carter

Vice President of Operations
Talent Tree Staffing/Bradruss, Inc.
440 Mall Boulevard, Suite M
Savannah, GA 31406–4823
(912) 354–9675
Fax: (912) 354–0894

7361

Business Information: Talent Tree Staffing/Bradruss, Inc. is an employment service and staffing company. Established in 1990, the Company has an estimated annual revenue of $3 million. As Vice President of Operations, Ms. Carter is responsible for the training and management of all operation personnel, as well as the administrative and financial functions of the Company. **Career Steps:** Vice President of Operations, Talent Tree Staffing/Bradruss, Inc. (1993–Present); Office Manager, Norrell Services, Inc. (1990–1992); Controller, Quality Broadcasting, Inc. (1987–1990). **Associations & Accomplishments:** Business and Professional Women's Club; Volusia Manufacturers Association. **Personal:** Ms. Carter enjoys reading and boating.

Gerald Clark

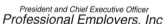

President and Chief Executive Officer
Professional Employers, Inc.
720 Wackerly Street
Midland, MI 48641
(517) 839–4837
Fax: (517) 839–4124

7361

Business Information: Professional Employers, Inc. is a technical personnel service providing contracting and consulting. Included in the Company's contracting services are composite thermoset molding compounds, chemical process design, specialty organics, weathering stabilizers, vinyl plastics, quality assurance systems, and quality control manuals. Established in 1994, with 47 employees, the Corporation has an estimated annual revenue in excess of $1.3 million. Mr. Clark has over 31 years of experience as an industrial chemist, ranging from analytical chemist to organic chemicals process development to chemical production management. Following retirement from The Dow Chemical Company, he has been involved with the formation and growth of two start–up technical companies. **Career Steps:** President and Chief Executive Officer, Professional Employers, Inc. (1994–Present); Manager of Engineering and Technology Development, Omni Tech International Ltd. (1990–1994); Executive Vice President, Manteo International (1986–1990); Manager of Manufacturing Engineering, Quantum Composites (1984–1986); Senior Research Manager, Dow Chemical (1951–1982). **Associations & Accomplishments:** Past President, Rotary Club of Midland Morning, MI; American Legion; American Chemical Society. **Education:** Michigan State University: M.S. (1951), B.S. (1949). **Personal:** Married to Cheryl L. in 1975. Five children: Christine Molick, Barbara Dietz, Nancy John, Robin Koss, and Derek Sanders. Mr. Clark enjoys tennis, boating, fishing, and hunting.

Camilla Clark–Garlock

Principal and Vice President – Business Development
Clarks' & Associates
1400 Millgate Drive, Suite D
Winston–Salem, NC 27103–1336
(910) 765–7377
Fax: (910) 765–9958

7361

Business Information: Clarks' & Associates is a national staffing and recruitment service firm, specializing in administrative and executive recruiting for businesses. Clients include the Sara Lee Corporation and other Fortune 500 companies. Established in 1994, Clarks' & Associates reports annual revenue of $5 million. As Principal and Vice President of Business Development, Ms. Clark–Garlock is responsible for the oversight of all aspects of business development. **Career Steps:** Principal and Vice President – Business Development, Clarks' & Associates (1993–Present); Director of Business Development, Golden Staffing Services (1991–1993); Operations Manager, Todays Temporary (1989–1991). **Associations & Accomplishments:** Advisory Board, Goodwill Industries; Sponsor, Family Services for Battered Women; Chamber of Commerce; Fomer Member, American Advertising Association; Leadership Winston–Salem National Association Staffing Services. **Education:** Salem College (1980). **Personal:** Married to David Garlock in 1994. One child: Rebecca. Ms. Clark–Garlock enjoys competitive equestrian activities and collecting antiques.

ERS

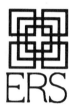

Tammy R. Cohen, PHR

Vice President
Employer's Reference Source
1950 North Park Place, Suite 550
Atlanta, GA 30339
(770) 984–2727
Fax: (770) 984–8997

7361

Business Information: Employer's Reference Source is a pre–employment screening company conducting background investigations on applicants for prospective employers, including criminal and credit history investigations, as well as drug testing. Established in 1989, the Company currently employs 30 people and has an estimated annual revenue of $2.7 million. As Co–owner, Ms. Cohen is responsible for the oversight of the departments of Accounting, Human Resources, Customer Service and Investigations. **Career Steps:** Vice President, Employer's Reference Source (1989–Present). **Associations & Accomplishments:** Public Speaker: High Schools, County and State Education Departments, and Employers on the subject of Workforce 2000; Board of Directors, YWCA of Cobb County; Chairperson, Entrepreneur Panel, Hugh O'Brian Youth Foundation; Cobb County Georgia Award for Occupational Leadership; Chairperson, Cobb Chamber of Commerce Youth Apprenticeship Program; Member, Cobb County Business and Education Steering Committee; Member, Cobb County Public Schools Business Advisory Board; Society of Human Resource Management; National Association of Female Executives; Cobb Executive Women. **Education:** University of Texas. **Personal:** Married to Blair. Two children: Courtney and Alyssa. Ms. Cohen enjoys public speaking, writing, and being a Girl Scout Leader.

Laura de Acha

General Manager
Resource
Calle Uno # 527, Urb. Corpac
San Isidro, Lima 27, Peru
(511) 224–2366
Fax: (511) 224–1082
EMail: See Below

7361

Business Information: Resource is a human resource consulting company providing employee recruitment for middle management positions for both multi–national and local companies. As General Manager, Ms. de Acha is responsible for all aspects of Company operations, including commercial and client attendance, marketing, and operations. She handles final interviews, presentations, and reference checks for her clients. Internet users can reach her via: resource@amauta.rcp.net.pe. **Career Steps:** General Manager, Resource (1991–Present); Operations Manager, Intex S.A. (1985–1991). **Associations & Accomplishments:** Society for Human Resource Management; Association of PADES–ESAN. **Education:** Lima University, B.A. in Business Administration (1983); ESAN, specialized in Operations Management. **Personal:** Married to Gerardo in 1985. Two children: Gerardo and Laura Isabel. Ms. de Acha enjoys reading, cooking, time with her children, and social meetings.

Elissa M. DeMartini
••• ━━━◉━━━ •••

Vice President, Regional Manager
Kelly Services
120 Route 17 North, Suite 211
Paramus, NJ 07652
(201) 261–9350
Fax: (201) 262–3679

7361

Business Information: Established in 1946, Kelly Services provides temporary and total staffing solutions, and management services for businesses and corporations throughout the U.S. Kelly Services, serving clients in Northern New Jersey, employs 57 people in 14 branches, and has an estimated annual revenue of $40 million. As Regional Manager, Mrs. DeMartini is responsible for all aspects of operations for the region, including strategic planning, senior level decision–making, sales, negotiations, customer service and operations. **Career Steps:** Vice President, Regional Manager, Kelly Services (1994–Present); Chief Operating Officer, INITIAL Contract Services; Vice President of Sales, Pitney Bowes Management Services. **Associations & Accomplishments:** National Association of Female Executives; Various industry and commerce organizations; Juvenile Diabetes Foundation; Published in corporate newsletters and NAFE publications. **Education:** Adelphi University, M.S. (1976); Lady Cliff College, B.A. (1974). **Personal:** Married to Joseph in 1986. Mrs. DeMartini enjoys swimming, reading, and cross country skiing.

David Dubinsky
Executive Director of West Region
NISH, Inc.
4615 First Street, Suite 100
Pleasanton, CA 94566–7367
(510) 417–6880
Fax: (510) 417–6888
EMAIL: See Below

7361

Business Information: NISH, Inc. is a national not–for–profit organization in business to create employment opportunities for people with disabilities. Joining NISH, Inc. as Executive Director for the West Region in 1981, Mr. Dubinsky is responsible for the management and direction of all affairs encompassing the states of Hawaii and the Western U.S., as well as the provinces of Guam and American Samoa. He is also directly responsible for managing over $100 million in federal contracts being performed by people with severe disabilities. Internet users can reach him via: Ddubinsky@NISH.ORG **Career Steps:** NISH, Inc.: Executive Director of West Region (1993–Present), Assistant Vice President of Regulatory Assistance (1986–1993), Operations Manager (1986–1991). **Associations & Accomplishments:** American Management Association; National Contract Management Association. **Education:** Clemson University: M.A. in Economics (1981), B.S. in Administrative Management. **Personal:** Married to Sofia in 1984. Four children: Emily, Alison, Anna, and Gloria. Mr. Dubinsky enjoys tennis, gourmet cooking, and gardening.

Jeniece Carter Fiola
District Sales Manager
Paychex Business Solutions
1177 Louisiana Avenue, Suite 208
Winter Park, FL 32789
(407) 647–3399
Fax: (407) 647–2343

7361

Business Information: Paychex Business Solutions pools all different types of companies together to form a benefits buying group. In doing this, the Company is able to help businesses get better rates on health insurance, workers' with compensation, 401 (k) plans, and helps them attract and retain employees. Paychex is typically able to save a company money on their overall benefits costs while offering more and better benefits to employees. As a District Sales Manager, Ms. Fiola manages the sales requirement of the branch. She helps solve client problems, coordinates all the departments, and

assists in closing meetings with sales representatives. Ms. Fiola's biggest responsibility is accessing the areas of risk for the Company and making decisions on what business is healthy for the organization. **Career Steps:** District Sales Manager, Paychex Business Solutions (1994–Present); Vice President of Sales/Marketing, TW Tele–Management (1993–1994); Sales Manager, Wiltel Communications (1990–1993). **Associations & Accomplishments:** Downtown Orlando Partnership; Orlando Chamber of Commerce; Osecola Children's Home Society. **Education:** Lake Sumter Community College, 2 year Accounting (1986); Continuing Education for Powerful Communicating, Women in Business. **Personal:** Married to Michael in 1992. Two children: Megan and Marissa (twins). Ms. Fiola enjoys a modeling and movie career with children, and working out.

Beth A. Gifford
••• ━━━◉━━━ •••

President
United Staffing Services, Inc.
246 East 4th Street, Suite 502
Mansfield, OH 44902
(419) 524–6209
Fax: (419) 524–7423
EMail: See Below

7361

Business Information: United Staffing Services, Inc. is an independent personnel staffing, project management, and employee leasing company. The Company offers its services in a four county radius and is primarily involved in the manufacturing and home health care industries. As President, Ms. Gifford is responsible for all aspects of Company operations, including legal and risk management, taxes, OHSA training, and all decision making. Internet users can reach her via: HIREU@AOL.COM. **Career Steps:** President, United Staffing Services, Inc. (1994–Present); President, Access Personnel Systems (1987–1994); Manager, The Olsten Corporation (1989–1994). **Associations & Accomplishments:** Former Board of Directors, Ohio Temporary and Staffing Services Association; Former Member of Services Committee, National Association of Temporary and Staffing Services. **Education:** Franklin University (1983–1984); Georgetown College, B.Me. **Personal:** Married to Thad in 1984. Three children: Scott, Steven, and Christopher. Ms. Gifford enjoys golf, downhill skiing, travel, and volunteer work.

Wendy P. Hall
Division Service Manager
Norrell Services
3030 Old Ranch Parkway
Seal Beach, CA 90740–2752
(310) 299–0080 Ext. 12
Fax: (310) 799–0841

7361

Business Information: Norrell Services is a national contingent staffing and outsourcing service, providing temporary personnel to Fortune 500 companies and outsourcing for United Parcel Service. Established in 1961, the Company is headquartered in Atlanta, Georgia. As Division Service Manager, Ms. Hall develops and manages all operations of the West Division, performing administrative functions and providing organizational leadership. **Career Steps:** Division Service Manager, Norrell Services (1993–Present); Regional Vice President, Apple One Services (1983–1993). **Associations & Accomplishments:** National Association of Staffing Services. **Education:** University of Southern California, M.B.A. (1994); Carnegie–Mellon University, B.F.A. **Personal:** Ms. Hall enjoys working out.

Michele R. Harman
Market Manager
Portfolio
1730 K Street Northwest, Suite 1350
Washington, DC 20006–3868
(202) 293–5700
Fax: (202) 293–9025
EMAIL: See Below

7361

Business Information: Portfolio is an international staffing agency, specializing in temporary and permanent placement within the creative industry (graphic design, illustrating, copywriters). Portfolio serves their clientele from eight national locations. Joining Portfolio as Assignment Manager in 1992, Ms. Harman was appointed as Market Manager in 1995. She manages the Washington, DC market, as well as being responsible for sales, P & L, marketing, management, creating and initiating all advertising, media contacts, and reporting directly to the headquarters in Cambridge, Massachusetts. In-

ternet users can reach her via: mharman@portfolio.skill.com **Career Steps:** Portfolio: Market Manager (1995–Present), Assignment Manager (1992–1995); Assistant Account Executive, Eisner,Petron & Associates (1991–1992). **Associations & Accomplishments:** Art Directors Club of Metropolitan Washington; Ad Club of Metropolitan Washingon; American Institute of Graphic Arts; Board of Directors, University of Maryland, University College Graduate Studies in Marketing; Alumnae Advisor, Kappa Delta – University of Maryland; Published in Washington Business Journal. **Education:** University of Maryland, B.S. (1992); University of Maryland, University College, Towards Master's in General Administration. **Personal:** Ms. Harman enjoys skiing, volleyball, and tennis.

Dianne Lovell Henderson, R.N.
Nurse Manager – Operating Room
Onslow Memorial Hospital
317 Western Boulevard
Jacksonville, NC 28546–6338
(910) 577–2299
Fax: (910) 577–2469
EMAIL: See Below

7361

Business Information: Onslow Memorial Hospital is a 150–bed community hospital serving Jacksonville, North Carolina, and rural Onslow County. As Nurse Manager of the Operating Room, Ms. Henderson is accountable for all aspects of staffing, budgeting, public relations, and conflict resolution 24–hours a day. **Career Steps:** Nurse Manager – Operating Room, Onslow Memorial Hospital (1996–Present); Clinical Manager – Operating Room, New Hanover Regional Medical Center (1991–1996); Orthopedic Head Nurse – Operating Room, Durham Regional Hospital (1987–1991); Duke University Medical Center, Operating Room: Head Nurse (1985–1987); Staff Nurse, (1983–1985), Licensed Practical Nurse (1981–1983); Licensed Practical Nurse/Certified Surgical Technologist, Operating Room, Memorial Hospital, Martinsville, VA (1975–1981). **Associations & Accomplishments:** Association of Operating Room Nurses; Member and Former Secretary and Member of Board of Directors of local chapter of the Association of Surgical Technologists (1975–1983). **Education:** University of State of New York–Regents, Bachelor's Degree in Nursing, in progress; Alamance Community College, Associate Applied Science in Nursing (1983); Memorial Hospital of Martinsville & Henry County School of Practical Nursing, Licensed Practical Nurse (1975). **Personal:** Married to Robert L. in 1992. Three children: Jerri Elizabeth, Jason Cameron, and Stephen Davis. Ms. Henderson enjoys cross–stitching, fishing, camping, backpacking, boating, and studying.

David H. Hinze
Vice President
OutSource International
3420 NW 26th Avenue
Boca Raton, FL 33434–3422
(407) 997–5000
Fax: (407) 995–7650
EMAIL: see below

7361

Business Information: OutSource International is an employment firm, providing staffing, temporary help, and employee leasing. OutSource International has 104 locations throughout the U.S. Established in 1974, OutSource International reports annual revenue of $330 million and currently employs 245 full–time and 22,000 temporary and leased employees. As Vice President, Mr. Hinze is responsible for all aspects of growth issues, finances and strategic planning. He began his career as a self–employed Certified Public Accountant and served as a consultant to President Nixon's White House. He can be reached through the Internet as follows: 102121,2342@compuserve.com **Career Steps:** Vice President, OutSource International (1993–Present); Vice President, E.K. Williams & Co. (1972–1993); Owner, Hinze Management Company (1962–1972). **Associations & Accomplishments:** Director, Florida Franchise Association; Member, International Franchise Association; Member, National Association of Temporary & Staffing Services; Past Vice President of South Carolina Jaycees; Listed in 1969 Edition of Outstanding Young Men of America; Listed in 1970 Edition of Outstanding Personalities in the South; Kids In Distress – a program in Southern Florida for abused and neglected children, 3% of OutSource International's profits go to this program and other children's programs; Lobbying in areas that affect the business primarily through letters and phone calls; Published articles in trade magazines. **Education:** University of South Carolina; East Carolina University. **Personal:** Married to Margaret in 1964. Three children: Keith, Leanne, and Gregory. Mr. Hinze enjoys spending time with his family, music, sports, and reading.

Myra Hunter

Regional Manager
Darrell Walker Personnel
515 Two Mile Pike, #210
Goodlettsville, TN 37072–1830
(615) 859–1153
Fax: (615) 859–1162

7361

Business Information: Darrell Walker Personnel is a full service employment agency providing permanent and temporary placement services. Established in 1953, the Company has 13 offices in Tennessee, Alabama, and Missouri. As Regional Manager, Ms. Hunter manages four offices in Tennessee, and is responsible for the oversight of all operations, financial records, in addition to the supervision of 20 employees. **Career Steps:** Regional Manager, Darrell Walker Personnel (1980–Present); Assistant Cashier, Capital City Bank (1970). **Associations & Accomplishments:** Rotary: Board Member, Paul Harris Fellow; Goodlettsville & Nashville Chamber; Advisory Board, Hunter's Lane Adult Education; Board Member, Expressway to Learning. **Personal:** Two children: Terry Davis and Paula Raper. Ms. Hunter enjoys gardening, reading, and travel.

Lissa Inzer

Operations Manager
Interim Personnel
2615 Pacific Highway, Suite 120
Hermosa Beach, CA 90254
(310) 318–1561
Fax: (310) 318–1776

7361

Business Information: Interim Personnel specializes in the temporary and full–time placement of employees, primarily for large and Fortune 500 companies. Previously doing operations as OnCall Personnel since 1978, Interim Personnel acquired the Hermosa, California company as a wholly–licensed entity in 1993. The Hermosa facility, joining the over 800 Interim nationwide locations, employs over 300 full–time and temporary staff. As Operations Manager, Ms. Inzer is responsible for all management and sales operations, including the interviews and placement of client employees, and the solicitation of new business throughout California. **Career Steps:** Operations Manager, Interim Personnel (1992–Present); General Manager, Entervest Management (1990–1992). **Associations & Accomplishments:** Manhattan Beach Chamber of Commerce; Redondo Beach Chamber of Commerce. **Education:** Rancho Santiago College, A.S. (1992). **Personal:** Married to Brent in 1992. One child: Zachary. Ms. Inzer enjoys aerobics, ice skating and spending time with her family.

Jeffrey A. Kapelus, CPA

President of Temporary Staffing
The Execu–Search Group
675 Third Avenue
New York, NY 10017
(212) 922–1001
Fax: (212) 922–0033

7361

Business Information: The Execu–Search Group is a specialized temporary placement firm, providing staffing of financial and accounting professionals serving the tri–state area. Established in 1992, The Execu–Search Group currently employs 22 people. As President of Temporary Staffing, Mr. Kapelus is responsible for various administrative functions, the supervision and training of staff, client relations, and to personally fill difficult and high level positions. **Career Steps:** President of Temporary Staffing, The Execu–Search Group (1992–Present); Placement Counselor, Robert Half International (1990–1992); Self–Employed Certified Public Accountant (1987–1990); Senior Accountant, KPMG Peat Marwick (1983–1986). **Associations & Accomplishments:** New York State Society of Certified Public Accountants; American Institute of Certified Public Accountants; National Association of Temporary Services; New York Association of Temporary Services. **Education:** Baruch College – CUNY, M.B.A. (1983), B.B.A. **Personal:** Married to Phyllis in 1994. One child: Max. Mr. Kapelus enjoys tennis, softball, and coordinating charitable functions such as the Special Olympics.

William E. (Gene) King III

Executive Vice President
Employee Resource Management, Inc.
147 Wappoo Creek Drive, Suite 503
Charleston, SC 29412
(803) 795–9751
Fax: (803) 795–0591

7361

Business Information: Employee Resource Management, Inc. is a Professional Employer Organization specializing in professional employment, staff leasing, contract staffing, and temporary employment for small to large companies. As Executive Vice President, Mr. King is responsible for implementing the business plan of the Company and making sure that the Company reaches the goals set by each division. Established in 1990, Employee Resource Management, Inc. employs over 2,000 people with annual gross revenues exceeding $25 million. **Career Steps:** Executive Vice President, Employee Resource Management, Inc. (1993–Present); Vice President, Marketing & Sales, Employee Resource Management, Inc. (1991–1993); Broker, Prudential Securities (1987–1991); Broker, Dean Witter (1986–1987); Personal Finance Officer, South Carolina Federal Savings Bank (1984–1986); Self Employed Contractor (1975–1984). **Associations & Accomplishments:** Blue Chip Initiative Award Winner, U.S. Chamber of Commerce (1995); Entrepreneur of the Year, Emerging Growth Companies, Ernst & Young/Inc. Magazine (1994); SC Governor's Individual Initiative Award for Rural Development (1994); Founder/Past President, Tri–County Regional Chamber of Commerce (1992); Founder/President/Chairman of the Board, The Charleston Regatta, Inc., a Rowing Sports Marketing firm managing 2 annual sporting events (1993 was first year); Board Member to 5 companies; Leadership South Carolina (1995–1996); Managing Partner, Rhino Sales Training Institute (1995). **Education:** The Citadel (1993–1995); Business Management, Marketing and Sales Schools. **Personal:** Married to Doris Hutto in 1990. One child: Doris Bryant King. Mr. King enjoys raising his daughter, being a good father, golf and books.

Mrs. Wilma I. Lopez–Ocasio

Vice President
Kelly Services
American International Plaza Suite 704, 250 Munoz Rivera Avenue
Hato Rey, Puerto Rico 00918
(809) 754–0060
Fax: (809) 759–9710

7361

Business Information: Kelly Services, established since 1964, is a temporary employment company. In 1974, Kelly Services' one office operation consisted of a volume in hours of 1,000 and 25 temporary employees. In 17 years, Kelly Temporary Services with its eight branches islandwide, has grown to be the leader of the industry by employing almost 5,147 temporary employees, producing a volume of more than 205,363 hours weekly with a payroll of almost $872,793.00 weekly and a gross sales volume of almost $1,221,926.00 and administering a budget of $8,000,000.00. On March 23, 1993 the Hispanic Association on Corporate Responsibility distributed their Corporate HACR Study 1993 from the Fortune 500 Industries and 500 Services representing the leading sector of Corporate America. For year end 1991, the Industrial 500 accounted for $2.26 trillion in sales, $55 billion in profits and almost 12 million employees. Almost as impressive was the Service 500, which accounted for $450 billion in sales, $67 billion in profits and 2.5 million employees. In 1994, Kelly Services was named as recipient of the "1994 Customer Satisfaction Excellence Award – Service Industry" which was given by P.R. 2000, Inc. and P.R. Manufacturers Association and received the award of PRIVATE EMPLOYER OF THE YEAR 1–299 from the Governors Committee of Employment of People with Disabilities in 1995. In her current capacity, Mrs. Lopez–Ocasio serves as Hispanic Executive Officer and one of 11 female executive officers in the industry. She directs and manages nine offices in Puerto Rico assuring that consistent quality and value added services are provided by all offices islandwide. **Career Steps:** Kelly Services: Vice President (1989–Present), Regional Manager (1986–1989); District Manager (1982–1986), Resident Branch Manager (1974–1982); Personnel Manager, IBEC (1973–1974); Record Manager, San Juan City Hall (1970–1973); Real Estate Broker, Mackle Brothers (1966–1970); Sales Manager, Empresas Diaz (1962–1966); Personnel Supervisor, F.W. Woolworth (1960–1962). **Associations & Accomplishments:** American Business Women Association; Association of Labor Relations; Camara de Comercio Espanola; Club Zonta; Honorary President Hall of Fame of Puerto Rican Sports; Greater San Juan Committee; Labor Relations Practitioners Network; PRATS–P.R. Association of Temporary Services; Puerto Rico Golf Association; P.R. Manufacturers Association; P.R. Chamber of Commerce; SHRM–Society of Human Resources; Muscular Dystrophy Association; Awarded the "Vista Corporate Achievement Award" (1994); Fluent English and Spanish. **Education:** University of Puerto Rico at Rio Piedras, Puerto Rico, B.A. Degree in Arts – Major: Psychology/Economics (1959). **Personal:** Married to Rafael Ocasio in 1992. Two children: Rene and Angel Aviles. Mrs. Lopez–Ocasio enjoys enjoys spelunking, music, and golf in her leisure time.

Amy Beth Lurier

President
Techfind, Inc.
3 Whitridge Road
South Natick, MA 01760
(508) 647–0111
Fax: (508) 647–0110

7361

Business Information: Techfind, Inc. provides executive search services for executive level technical people and human resource consulting. Ms. Lurier founded Techfind, Inc. in 1987, consulting with clients regarding all their search and human resource requirements. **Career Steps:** President, Techfind, Inc. (1987–Present); Senior Scientist, ICI Americas (1983–1987). **Associations & Accomplishments:** Association for the Advancement of Science; American Chemical Society; American Association for Clinical Chemistry; RAPS. **Education:** University of Massachusetts, B.S./M.S. in Organic Chemistry. **Personal:** Married to Eliot in 1984. Two children: Emily and Hannah.

Donald A. Marr Jr.

Vice President
Brewer Personnel Services
P.O. Box 1687
Fayetteville, AR 72702
(501) 973–6000
Fax: (501) 973–6019
EMAIL: See Below

7361

Business Information: Brewer Personnel Services provides employment staffing of professional, medical, and technical clients on a temporary or permanent basis, and offers companies and corporations the opportunity to screen prospective employees before hiring. Established in 1988, the Company has 187 full time, and over 10,000 staffing employees. With twenty–six locations, the Company has an estimated annual revenue of $75 million. As Vice President, Mr. Marr oversees all branch operations, is responsible for human resources and training, manages the MIS, Risk Management, and Safety Departments, and handles all marketing. Internet users can reach him via: dmarr@brewerstaff.com. **Career Steps:** Vice President, Brewer Personnel Services (1990–Present); Human Resources Manager, Magnatek (1987–1990). **Associations & Accomplishments:** National Association of Temporary Staffing Services (NATSS); Board Member, Arkansas State Council Human Resource Managers; Board Member, Humane Society of the Ozarks; President, North West Arkansas Society of Human Resource Management. **Education:** Radford University, B.S. in Management (1986). **Personal:** Mr. Marr enjoys tennis, basketball, reading, exercise, and gardening.

Mary McDonough Glatt, R.N., B.S.N.

Vice President/Secretary
Nightingale Nurses
12801 North 28th Drive, Suite 7
Phoenix, AZ 85029
(602) 504–1555
Fax: (602) 504–1552

7361

Business Information: Nightingale Nurses is a totally self–funded organization providing staffing for registered nurses, licensed practical nurses and certified nursing assistants. State licensed and Medicare certified, the Company provides skilled professionals to medical facilities private duty clients, and clients requiring intermittent skilled visits in the home. Established in 1994, the Company employs 300 people and has an estimated annual revenue of over $1 million. As Vice President/Secretary, Ms. McDonough Glatt oversees the private duty division, and serves as Director of Nursing. In conjunction with her partner, Susan Van Wie, also a nurse, Ms. McDonough Glatt plans to expand the Company slowly, to avoid compromising quality of care. **Career Steps:** Vice President/Secretary, Nightingale Nurses (1994–Present); Home Health Field Nurse/R.N., Olston Kimberly Quality Care (1990–1994); Respite Pediatric Nurse, R.N., AZ DES DDD (1988–1990); Staff R.N., North Lincoln Hospital (1984–1986). **Associations & Accomplishments:** North American Small Business Association; Sigma Theta Tau; Phi Kappa Phi. **Education:** Arizona State University, B.S.N. (1990); University of Phoenix, Masters in Nursing (In Progress). **Personal:** Married to

Thomas in 1990. One child: Ian. Ms. McDonough Glatt enjoys spending quality time with her newly–adopted six–year old son.

Timothy J. Minard

President
Epic Staff Management
10701 West North Avenue, Suite 100
Milwaukee, WI 53224
(414) 476–8050
Fax: (414) 771–4848

7361

Business Information: Epic Staff Management leases and contracts skilled professionals into their trade, sometimes managing the entire staff of a client company from payroll to legal issues to workman's compensation. As President and Partner, Mr. Minard is responsible for providing strategic direction and coordinating business growth. **Career Steps:** President, Epic Staff Management (1996–Present); Information Solutions, Inc: Vice President (1994–1996), National Sales Manager (1993–1994), Sales Manager (1992–1993). **Associations & Accomplishments:** Wisconsin Automation Users Group – Keynote Speaker; International Graphics Users Group; National Association of Technical Services; P.E.O.; COSBE–MMAC; Future 50; Numerous Speaking Engagements on Technology; Awarded a Breakfast with Then British Prime Minister Margaret Thatcher; Numerous Sales and Achievement Awards; One of the Top 50 Growing Companies in New Jersey. **Education:** University of Wisconsin, B.S. in Finance/Marketing (In Progress). **Personal:** Mr. Minard enjoys tennis, volleyball, chess, table tennis, billiards, reading, travel, and Volunteering for the Special Olympics.

Randall H. Nelson

President
Career Network – Division of Orion Consulting
512 Windstream Way
Cary, NC 27511–9038
(919) 851–3309
Fax: (919) 851–0129

7361

Business Information: Career Network – Division of Orion Consulting specializes in recruiting military personnel for future careers with Fortune 500 companies. In operation since 1991, Orion Consulting currently employs 33 professionals. As President and Co–founder, Mr. Nelson is responsible for the overall operations of the Career Network Division, the Division that recruits Enlisted and Non–Commissioned Officers for career placements in technical positions. The Orion division places Junior Military officers. He is also the Vice President and Member of the Orion Board of Directors, involved with strategic planning and overall decision–making for the Company. **Career Steps:** President, Career Network – Division of Orion Consulting (1995–Present); Vice President, Orion Consulting (1991–Present); Salesman, Lucas Associates (1989–1990). **Associations & Accomplishments:** President and Board of Directors, Raleigh Swimming Association; Raleigh Recruiting District Assistance Council; Navy League. **Education:** Miami University – Ohio, B.S. in Accounting (1983); Naval Nuclear Training, Equivalent of Masters in Nuclear Engineering. **Personal:** Married to Marijo in 1983. Three children: Nicole, Shannon, and Matt. Mr. Nelson enjoys sports and travel.

Sharon A. O'Connor

Director of the Information Systems Division
MRC Resources Group, Inc.
5728 LBJ Freeway, Suite 460
Dallas, TX 75240–6308
(214) 458–7880
Fax: (214) 458–0465

7361

Business Information: MRC Resources Group, Inc. is a national, full–service, permanent and contract information systems technical staffing firm. Clients include Fortune 500 and Fortune 1000 companies. Established in 1985, MRC Resources Group, Inc. reports annual revenue $16 million and currently employs 300 people. As Director of the Information Systems Division, Ms. O'Connor is responsible for directing sales, operations and administration of the $16 million organization in data processing staffing. **Career Steps:** Director of the Information Systems Division, MRC Resources Group, Inc. (1995–Present); Senior Technical Staffing Manager, Decision Consultants Inc. (1989–1995); Senior Recruiter, Omni Search (1987–1989). **Associations & Accomplishments:** National Association of Female Executives (NAFE). **Education:** Carl Sandburg Junior College (1971); Morris Catholic High School. **Personal:** Ms. O'Connor enjoys cultural events such as ballet and art galleries.

Gene Obermeyer

President/Chief Operation Officer, Franchise Division
Norrell Corporation
3535 Piedmont Road
Atlanta, GA 30305
(404) 240–3310
Fax: (404) 240–3014
EMAIL: See Below

7361

Business Information: Norrell Corporation provides administrative, general clerical, light industrial, information technologists, out–sourcing and financial (i.e. controllers, accountants, etc.), staffing to Fortune 100 companies, local small businesses, and major corporations such as IBM, UPS, and MCI from 5/400 locations across the nation. Established in 1963, the Company employs 1,500, and has an estimated annual revenue of $1 billion. As President/Chief Operation Officer, Franchise Division, Mr. Obermeyer oversees all aspects of the Franchise division which accounts for half of Norrells operations. His responsibilities include administration, public relations, strategic planning, and management of corporate accounts. Internet users can reach him via: gene1145@postoffice.Worldnet.att.net. **Career Steps:** Norrell Corporation: President/Chief Operation Officer, Franchise Division (1991–Present), President of Company Operations (1990–1991), Division Vice President and General Manager (1984–1990). **Associations & Accomplishments:** International Franchise Association; United Way; Alpha Kappa Psi. **Education:** Florida State University, B.S. in Marketing (1967). **Personal:** Married to Barbara in 1967. Two children: Roger and Brian. Mr. Obermeyer enjoys golf.

Julia M. Ortega

President
Reliable Employment Agency, Inc.
628 Park Avenue
Cranston, RI 02910–2144
(401) 467–8606
Fax: (401) 467–5320

7361

Business Information: Reliable Employment Agency, Inc., is a full service agency specializing in providing employment for factory, office, and maintenance workers. Established in 1992, the Agency has one location in Cranston, Rhode Island, with plans for an additional branch to open soon. As President, Ms. Ortega is responsible for all aspects of the Agency, including sales, accounting, payroll, and administration. Concurrently, she is the owner of Reliable Guiding Services, an interpretation, translation, and paging company. **Career Steps:** President, Reliable Employment Agency, Inc. (1992–Present); Personnel Manager, Jobs For Progress (1990–1992); Sales Representative, Sears Service Center (1989); Teacher's Aid, Little People's Playhouse (1988–1989). **Associations & Accomplishments:** United States Chamber; Who's Who; Providence Chamber; MBE/WBE/DBE; Notary Public; State of Rhode Island Notary Public. **Education:** Bunker Hill Community College; Humphrey Center Degree, Advance Business Management. **Personal:** Married to Juan in 1984. One child: Edna J. Ms. Ortega enjoys exercise, computers, and work.

Ms. Catherine E. Palmiere

Director
Advice Personnel, Inc.
230 Park Avenue, Suite 903
New York, NY 10169
(212) 682–4400
Fax: (212) 697–0343

7361

Business Information: Advice Personnel, Inc. is an executive search firm, providing business clientele in two distinct human resource areas: Accounting/Financial and Secretarial/Bookkeeping. In her current capacity, Ms. Palmiere is the Director of the Secretarial/Bookkeeping Division. She is the "hands–on" manager who is responsible for the recruitment and placement of all qualified candidates for this division. In addition, she manages a team of recruiters. Ms. Palmiere is a Certified Personnel Consultant (CPC), a Certified Temporary Staffing Specialist (CTS), and a Certified International Personnel Consultant (CIPC), and a Certified Search Specialist (CSS). Established in 1984, Advice Personnel, Inc. employs 8 recruiters and 3 administrative support staff. **Career Steps:** Director, Advice Personnel, Inc. (1992–Present); Vice President, Adam Personnel Inc. (1981–1992). **Associations & Accomplishments:** National Association of Personnel Services; The International Confederation of Personnel Services; Delta Mu Delta. **Education:** Manhattan College, M.B.A. (May 1995); Manhattan College, B.S.

Jeffrey W. Pettegrew

Vice President – Insurance and Risk Management
Western Staff Services
301 Lennon Lane
Walnut Creek, CA 94598–2418
(510) 930–5308
Fax: (510) 256–1563

7361

Business Information: A temporary service industry leader for over 46 years, Western Staff Services is one of the largest, privately–owned, worldwide staffing service companies. With 350 offices in eight countries, Western provides approximately 200,000 employees to over 10,000 corporations and governmental agencies in all areas of work, including professional, medical, technical and industrial segments. As Vice President of Insurance and Risk Management at Western Staff Services' Walnut Creek, California headquarters, Mr. Pettegrew manages all corporate self–insured programs in workers' compensation programs, general liability, medical malpractice, fidelity, and employee benefit programs. He has full directional management over corporate loss control and safety programs, including the design of safety manuals, safety training programs, compilation and narration of loss control videos. With more than 17 years in the risk management field, he is a nationally–recognized authority in the risk management industry, also recognized for pioneering risk management education and his dedicated unselfishness in the sharing of his knowledge with others. With his innovations, Jeff has been instrumental in developing some of the nation's first self–insured public agency risk management pools; his articles on risk management have run in numerous professional journals; and he is a frequent lecturer and keynote speaker for universities, governmental agencies and employment industry activities. **Career Steps:** Vice President – Insurance and Risk Management, Western Staff Services (1991–Present); Chief Executive Officer and Risk Manager, Contra Costa Municipal Risk Manager Insurance Authority (1980–1991); Risk Manager, City of Sunnyvale, CA (1979–1980). **Associations & Accomplishments:** Risk and Insurance Management Society (RIMS): Board of Director (since 1992), President, and Member of National Nominating Committee; Public Agency Risk Managers Association (PARMA): President, Board of Directors and Lifetime Member; California Association of Joint Powers Authorities (CAJPA): President, Board of Directors, Chairperson for Risk Management Accreditation Program; Board of Directors, State of California's Local Agency Self–Insurance Authority; Life Member, Risk Management Forum; Awarded Risk Manager of the Year in 1989 by "Business Insurance" magazine; Co–Authored "Self–Funding Employee Benefits, Institute of Local Self–Government" (1982), "Controlling the Risks of Using the Alternative Workforce", Journal of Worker's Compensation (1995), and the Employee Benefits Self–Funding Handbook; Frequent lecturer throughout the U.S. on a variety of risk management topics; Appeared as spokesperson on "60–Minutes" and "CNN"; Expert witness in risk management cases. **Education:** California State University–Hayward, M.P.A. in Public Administration, magna cum laude (1976); Denison University, B.A. in Communications (1968), voted Outstanding Graduate by faculty. **Personal:** Married to Valerie in 1991. Three children: Jenna, Jonathan, and Joya. Mr. Pettegrew enjoys music. Prior to the Vietnam War, he sang with John Denver and can play many stringed instruments and the piano.

Mark Rivard

Vice President
Placement Pros
27 Maiden Lane, Suite 301
San Francisco, CA 94108–5415
(415) 397–3384
Fax: Please mail or call

7361

Business Information: Placement Pros provides temporary placement of professionals in legal, technical and administrative positions, serving the San Francisco and surrounding areas. Established in 1991, Placement Pros reports annual revenue of $4 million and currently employs 155 people. As Vice President, Mr. Rivard is responsible for all aspects of operations, including administration, client relations, sales, recruiting, and marketing. **Career Steps:** Vice President, Placement Pros (1991–Present); Operations Manager, White Collar Temps Services (1989–1991); Branch Manager, Yanker Contract Services (1986–1990); Sales Manager, Lowell Honda (1981–1985). **Associations & Accomplishments:** American Motorcycle Road Racers Champion (1981); World Ironman Triathalon Championships Finisher (1994); 1994 Triathalon All American Honorable Mention Status. **Personal:** Mr. Rivard enjoys biking (100 miles every Saturday), running (25 miles every Sunday), and swimming (every day).

Alfred P. Roach
Founder, Chief Executive Officer, President
Dunhill del Caribe
Call Box 2134
San Juan, Puerto Rico 00922
(809) 782–2096
Fax: (809) 782–4885
EMail: See Below

7361

Business Information: Dunhill del Caribe is an international professional recruiting services agency, providing temporary, executive searching, and management staffing throughout the Caribbean, North and South America, and Europe. The Agency's focus is in the placement of executives and managers into temporary positions, primarily in Southern and Mid–State Florida. Founding Dunhill del Caribe in 1992, Mr. Roach serves as Chief Executive Officer and President. He is responsible for the overall operations of the Company, including recruiting and placements of prospects, administration, finances, public relations, and strategic planning. Internet users can reach him via: alroach@msn.com. **Career Steps:** Founder, Chief Executive Officer and President, Dunhill del Caribe (1992–Present); United States Air Force (1967–1970). **Associations & Accomplishments:** United States Chamber of Commerce; Puerto Rico Chamber of Commerce; Knights of Columbus; Republican Presidents Club; Society for Human Resource Management. **Education:** University of Notre Dame: Ph.D. candidate, M.A. (1971); Fairfield University, B.A. (1965) **Personal:** Three children: Alfred, Michael and Michele. Mr. Roach enjoys fishing, swimming, playing chess, boating and model trains.

Jerry Robinson
Senior Vice President
Power Industry Consultants
1165 Northchase Parkway, 4th Floor
Marietta, GA 30067
(770) 850–0100
Fax: (770) 850–0102

7361

Business Information: Power Industry Consultants is a group of companies operating within the staffing industry, with primary focus in technical placement, both temporary and permanent. The Company has locations in Texas, Georgia, and Malaysia, with operating Companies throughout the world. As Senior Vice President, Mr. Robinson is responsible for the development, growth, and diversification. **Career Steps:** Senior Vice President, Power Industry Consultants (1993–Present); Vice President of Sales, Hopeman Industries; National Sales Manager, Besteel; National Accounts Department Manager, API. **Education:** Long Beach State (1976). **Personal:** Married in 1977. Mr. Robinson enjoys golf, reading, and group social activities.

Pamela Ruebusch
Co–Owner and Director
TSI Group
5045 Orbitor Drive, Building 8 Suite 400
Mississauga, Ontario
(905) 629–3701
Fax: (905) 629–0799
Email: See Below

7361

Business Information: TSI Group is Canada's leading recruitment firm, specializing in logistics, transportation, and supply chain management. As Co–Owner and Director, Ms. Ruebusch is responsible for overseeing daily operations and managing Company functions. Internet users can reach her via: TSIGroup@Inforamp.Net. **Career Steps:** Co–Owner and Director, TSI Group (1990–Present); Recruitment Consultant, PRN Transportation Careers (1988–1990); Sales Executive, Manpower Temporary Services (1986–1988). **Associations & Accomplishments:** Board of Directors, Canadian Association of Logistics Management. Education: Wilfrid Laurier University, B.A. (1987). **Personal:** Ms. Ruebusch enjoys competitive precision figure skating."

Jennifer F. Ryan, CPC
Senior Consultant/Partner
Ryan Executive Search
PH 1615 Marcantil Plaza
San Juan, Puerto Rico 00918
(787) 766–1666
Fax: (787) 766–1467

7361

Business Information: Ryan Executive Search is an executive search and related employment service. As Senior Consultant/Partner, Ms. Ryan is responsible for interviewing professionals for permanent employment to determine their qualifications based on Skills, Knowledge, and Abilities and other employment factors. She refers candidates to different openings through all type industries in the job market, assists employers in the preparation of compensation packages, and recommends correct selection of personnel based on EEO and applicable labor laws. She is also in charge of salary surveys, outplacement programs, and other special projects. **Career Steps:** Senior Consultant/Partner, Ryan Executive Search (1987–Present); Public Relations & Personnel, Estee Lauder (1985–1987); Sales/Marketing Consultant, Elizabeth Arden (1983–1985); Personnel Assistant, Careers, Inc.; Model, Norma Kamali and Edo Penna. **Associations & Accomplishments:** Board of Directors/Professor, Society of Human Resource Managers; Senior Human Resource Professional and Human Resource Professional; Teacher of Recruitment Course for Society of Human Resource Management. **Education:** University of Sacred Heart, B.B.A. in Management (1985); Target Selection Administrator; Advanced School of Personnel Management; National Association of Personnel Consultants, Certified Personnel Consultant; Certified to Administer Myers Briggs Type Indicator. **Personal:** Married to Andres Arias in 1994. Ms. Ryan enjoys water sports, dancing, reading, and studying continually on Human Resource subjects.

Debbie Sze Schiro
Director of Research
McCann, Choi, & Associates
590 Madison Avenue, 26th Floor
New York, NY 10022
(212) 755–7051
Fax: (212) 355–2610

7361

Business Information: McCann, Choi, & Associates is an established New York–based executive search firm specializing in the recruitment of senior and middle level executives to investment banks. The Firm has been published by Executive Recruiter News as being one of the forty largest retained search firms in the U.S. The Company was established in 1991 and has grown to approximately 14 personnel, including professionals. As Director of Research, Ms. Schiro is responsible for the collection and upkeep of current data resources enabling search consultants to accurately target potential candidates. Additionally, Research conducts competitive market analysis in the financial services industry. **Career Steps:** Director of Research, McCann, Choi, & Associates (1995–Present); Financial Analyst, CS First Boston (1990–1995); Internal Consultant Administrator, Shearson Lehman Hutton (1988–1990). **Associations & Accomplishments:** Research Roundtable; Author of a children's book. **Education:** SUNY Stony Brook, B.A. in Political Science (1987). **Personal:** Married to Lawrence Schiro in 1993. Ms. Schiro enjoys sculpting, piano, and writing.

Franklin A. Shaffer
Vice President/Education
Cross Country Staffing
118 Perry Street, Suite J–39
New York, NY 10014
(212) 255–2356
Fax: (212) 255–1864
EMAIL: See Below

7361

Business Information: Cross Country Staffing is a supplemental staffing service dedicated to providing the highest trained, best quality nurses in the industry to institutions throughout the world. As Vice President/Education, Dr. Shaffer is responsible for the development and quality of education and training for nursing staff members. Dr. Shaffer's plan for the next few years is to continue working with nurses to insure continued training and education, provide them with services that will enable them to become certified in various specialties, and to utilize career mapping. It is also in Dr. Shaffer's long term plans to continue development of the "Ask the Professor" information services and world wide web page enhancement on Cyberspace Internet. One of the most important mile-

stones in Dr. Shaffer's career was receiving an Honorary Doctorate of Science from his peers. This honor restates his favorite quote "Blessed are the flexible, for they can not be bent out of shape". Dr. Shaffer is concurrently Director of Professional Affair for Springfield House, Inc. Springfield House, Inc. is a division of Reed Publishing the world's largest publisher of scientific journals. Internet users can reach him via: fshaffer@crosscountry.com. **Career Steps:** Vice President/Education, Cross Country Staffing (1986–Present); Executive Director, Springhouse Corporation (1994–Present); Corporate Director/Education Resources, S.N. Publications (1991–1994); Senior Vice President, National League for Nursing (1981–1991). **Associations & Accomplishments:** American Nurses Association; Sigma Theta Tau International; National League for Nursing; National Organization Nurse Practitioner Faculty; American College of Nurse Practitioners. **Education:** Columbia University, Honorary Doctorate (1983): Columbia University Teachers College: Ed.M., M.A.; East Strasbug University, B.S. **Personal:** Dr. Shaffer enjoys surfing the Internet, reading, walking, and country dancing.

Opal M. Teague
Manager III
Oklahoma Employment Security Commission
P.O. Box 9
Poteau, OK 74953
(918) 647–3123
Fax: Please mail or call

7361

Business Information: Oklahoma Employment Security Commission is a job service agency, providing assistance to employers and people seeking employment throughout the state of Oklahoma. Employed by the Oklahoma Employment Security Commission for the past seventeen years in many capacities, Mrs. Teague was appointed Manager III (second in charge) in 1992 for the Poteau, Stilwell and Sallisaw local offices. She is responsible for directing all programs on unemployment insurance & employment service functions as required by federal and state laws and regulations, as well as: Assigning staff to positions in the office in such a manner as to facilitate the day–to–day operations of the local office as it pertains to its mission; Training & evaluating staff on new ES, UI, special programs, procedures and refresher training; Supervising and monitoring the Veteran's Program and Employer Relations Program; Conducting all local office administration; Conducting Job Service Employer Council meetings; Serving as Youth Coordinator; Attending conferences on a local and statewide basis; Attending civic meetings; and Community affairs participation. Future plans include retiring in the near future and establishing a not–for–profit organization on an old Indian Reservation; creating a historical site for church groups and schools to bring needy children; providing education and recreation, such as camping, fishing, sports, hiking, horseback riding, as well as a petting farm. **Career Steps:** Manager III, Oklahoma Employment Security Commission (1978–Present). **Associations & Accomplishments:** Director, Employer Advisory Council – Poteau & Stilwell local offices; Board of Directors, Economic Enhancement Foundation, Inc. – Poteau (1993–1994); Advisory Committee for "New Direction Center" at Kaimichi Area Vo–Tech School (1993–1994); Executive Board of Directors, Poteau Chamber of Commerce (1993–1995); Spiro Chamber of Commerce; Poteau Rotary Club; International Association of Personnel in Employment Security (IAPES): Institutes & Convention Chairperson (1992–1994), President Elect, Southeast District – IAPES (1993), President, Southeast District – IAPES (1994–1995); Board of Directors, Economic Assessment Council (EAC) – Poteau (1994); "Pride in Poteau" Committee (1995); Chairperson, Hospitality Committee – Poteau – (Welcomes new businesses & residents as they come to town); Manager's Advisory Committee – to the Executive Director of Employment Security Commission; "Manager of the Year" Award (1993); "State Merit Award" (1994); Hostess to foreign exchange students. **Education:** Draughon's Business College, Muskogee, OK; Connors State College, Warner, OK; East Central University, Ada, OK; Continuing Education courses thru various Institutions with O.E.S.C. on Leadership and Supervisory skills. **Personal:** Mrs. Teague enjoys sewing, gardening, travel, civic organization activities, outdoor activities (camping, hiking, fishing, volleyball, swimming, horseback riding), reading, crafts, volunteer work, and writing poetry.

Rob Vitters

Director of Randstad Automatiserings Diengtens of Diemen
Automatiserings Diengten
Diemermere 25 1112 TC
Diemen, The Netherlands
31–2056–95047
Fax: 31–2056–95590

7361

Business Information: Automatiserings Diensten is a supplier of temporary employees and contract business services in the Information Technologic industry. As Director, Mr. Vitters is responsible for the day–to–day operations of the Company, including administration, finances, and strategic planning. **Career Steps:** Director, Automatiserings Diensten (1992–Present); Director, Microlite/HCS (1990–1992); Manager, Municipal Amsterdam (1973–1990); Manager, Philips (1960–1973). **Education:** High Technical School (1966). **Personal:** Married to Jozien Vitters–de Zeeuw in 1967. Two children: Brent and Lars. Mr. Vitters enjoys tennis, sailing, and skiing.

Mr. Kevin G. Attar
President
Surge Resources, Inc.
136 Harvey Road, Hilltop Center
Londonderry, NH 03053
(603) 623–0007
Fax: (603) 624–7007

7363

Business Information: Surge Resources, Inc. is an employment agency providing employment services, leased and temporary employees on a contract and fee basis. The Company takes all employees from a company then leases them back; processing and providing employee benefits, payroll, and taxes. They work in conjunction with their clients human resource divisions in the implementation of hiring process and compensation reviews. As President and Founder, Mr. Attar is responsible for all aspects of operations, focusing in the areas of customer relations, compliance guidelines for employment regulations, recruiting, sales, and marketing. Concurrent with his duties at Surge Resources, Inc., he is serving his first term as an elected District Representative for the New Hampshire House of Representatives. He currently serves as a member of the House's Labor, Industrial and Rehabitation Services Committee. Established in 1989, Surge Resources, Inc. and Surge Temp, Inc. currently employs 1,500 people and has an annual revenue in excess of $12 million. **Career Steps:** President, Surge Resources, Inc. and Surge Temps, Inc. (1989–Present); State Representative, New Hampshire House of Representatives (1995–Present). **Associations & Accomplishments:** Board of Directors, Rotary Club International; Board of Directors, Chamber of Commerce; State Representative, District 29, New Hampshire House of Representatives; Vice President, New Hampshire Association of Temporary and Employee Services; Vice President, New Hampshire Technical Services Association (2 years); Offense Coordinator, Londonderry Football Team; Town Budget Committee. **Personal:** Married to Ann L. in 1987. One child: Alyssa Marie. Mr. Attar enjoys all types of sports, gardening, boating, and coaching.

Pamela E. Breier
General Manager
Legal Network
600 North Pearl Street, Suite 2100
Dallas, TX 75201
(214) 777–6400
Fax: (214) 777–6477

7363

Business Information: Legal Network is a full–service staffing company, specializing in providing support personnel for the legal industry. Legal Network serves clientele from three locations in Texas (Dallas, Irving, Bedford). Joining the Company as General Manager in 1993, Mrs. Breier oversees and manages the day–to–day operations of the Company, including marketing and payroll. In addition to overseeing all administrative operations for associates and a support staff of 25, she is also actively involved with overall operations and management of the Sales Personnel. **Career Steps:** General Manager, Legal Network (1993–Present); Human Resource Coordinator, Thompson & Knight (1986–1993); Administrator, Brunn McColl McCullough & McCurley (1982–1986). **Associations & Accomplishments:** Association of Legal Administrators (1983–1993); Texas Association of Staffing (1994–Present); Women's Service League (1989); Junior League of Dallas, Inc. (1990); Published articles for Association of Legal Administrators on Hazardous Waste. **Education:** Baylor University, B.F.A. in Design (1977). **Personal:** Married to Mitch G. in 1981. Mrs. Breier enjoys Harley Davidson motorcycles, gardening, and volunteering.

Ms. Kim Dawson
• • •───◉───• • •
President
Kim Dawson Agency, Inc.
P.O. Box 585060
Dallas, TX 75258–5060
(214) 638–2414
Fax: Please mail or call

7363

Business Information: Kim Dawson Agency, Inc. is a modeling and talent agency in the Dallas, Texas area. As President, Ms. Dawson is responsible for all aspects of operations. Her career milestones include modeling internationally and opening up her own modeling agency. **Career Steps:** President, Kim Dawson Agency, Inc. (1962–Present); Fashion Director, Dallas Apparel Mart (1964–1990); Model, Neiman Marcus (1950–1961). **Associations & Accomplishments:** Fashion Group of Dallas; Women in Film – Dallas; Dallas Communications Council; Board Member, Dallas Chamber of Commerce; Board Member, Dallas Theater Center; Board Member, K.D. Studio. **Personal:** Married to George in 1952. Three children: Kim Vernon, M.D. (OB/GYN Specialist); Lisa (soon to be taking over management of the Agency); and Tiger (Youth Minister). Ms. Dawson enjoys reading, water aerobics, travel and spending time with her grandchildren.

Don Doster
• • •───◉───• • •
Vice President
Medical Doctor Associates
3495 Holcomb Bridge Road
Norcross, GA 30092
(770) 246–9194
Fax: (770) 246–0882

7363

Business Information: Medical Doctor Associates provides physician placement, both temporary and permanent positions, for physicians in outpatient primary care, pediatrics, and allied care for therapists and nurses. The Company is the second largest physician placement service in the nation. As Vice President of Operations, Mr. Doster is responsible for four team leaders in the area of emergency medicine, primary care, allied health, and pediatrics. He handles 49% of the Company, including 30 employees and $14 million in annual revenue/sales. **Career Steps:** Medical Doctor Associates: Vice President of Operations (1994–Present), Director of Primary Care (1992–1994), Regional Manager (1990–1992). **Associations & Accomplishments:** Deacon, First Christian Church Disciples of Christ; Elon Society – Chairman, Reunion Committee; Sigma Phi Epsilon Fraternity. **Education:** Elon College, B.A. (1986). **Personal:** Married to Lenore in 1991. Mr. Doster enjoys tennis, golf, softball, basketball, running, water and snow skiing, and fishing.

Lisa N. Dussault
Regional Vice President
Prudential Resources Management
1100 Woodfield Road, Suite 520
Schaumburg, IL 60173
(708) 706–4730
Fax: (708) 513–5724

7363

Business Information: Prudential Resources Management provides relocation, real estate, human resources and related consulting services to individuals and institutions globally. Established in 1964, Prudential Resources Management reports annual revenue of $15 million and currently employs 1,200 people. With twelve years experience in sales, Ms. Dussault joined Prudential in 1990. Serving as Regional Vice President, she is responsible for all aspects of sales and marketing. **Career Steps:** Regional Vice President, Prudential Resources Management (1990–Present); Sales Consultant, Baird & Warner (1985–1990); Sales Representative, United Van Lines (1983–1985). **Associations & Accomplishments:** Corporate Relocation Council: Board Member (1993–1995), Chair (1995), Recording Secretary (1994–1995); Soccer Coach, Geneva High School–Geneva, IL; Team Member, Illinois Women's State Soccer League; Democratic National Committee. **Education:** Aurora University, working towards M.B.A. (expected completion date Dec. 1996); Cedar Crest College, (1983). **Personal:** Married to Gerald Hubka in 1992.

Cecilia J. Knauf, CPA
International Controller
Spencer Stuart
401 North Michigan Avenue, Suite 3456
Chicago, IL 60611–4208
(312) 822–0088
Fax: (312) 822–0117

7363

Business Information: Spencer Stuart is an international executive search firm with locations in Europe, Asia, South Africa, and the United States. The Firm employs 350 people throughout the world. As International Controller, Miss Knauf receives financial reports from the various office locations world wide. She consolidates the information and reports to upper management and the Board of Directors on the results of the international operations. **Career Steps:** International Controller, Spencer Stuart (1994–Present); Supervising Senior Accountant, KPMG Peat Marwick (1990–1994). **Associations & Accomplishments:** Illinois Certified Public Accountant Society; American Institute of Certified Public Accountants. **Education:** Illinois State University, B.S. in Accounting (1990). **Personal:** Miss Knauf enjoys outdoor activities.

Robert J. Luciano
Director/Management Information Systems
Butler Service Group, Inc.
110 Summit Avenue
Montvale, NJ 07645
(201) 476–5455
Fax: (201) 573–9360
E MAIL: See Below

7363

Business Information: Butler Service Group, Inc. provides contract services in a variety of industries to companies nationally and internationally. As Director, Management Information Systems, Mr. Luciano is responsible for the development and maintenance of all major software systems. Internet users can reach him via: RLuciano@ButlerIntl.com. **Career Steps:** Butler Service Group, Inc.: Director/Management Information Systems (1991–Present), Database Administrator (1989–1991), Technical Support Specialist (1986–1989), Senior Analyst (1984–1986). **Education:** Fairleigh Dickinson University, M.S. in Computer Science (1984); Providence College, B.A. in Mathematics Education. **Personal:** Married to Linda in 1978. Mr. Luciano enjoys gardening, painting with oils, softball, and biking.

Thomas D. Sabourin, Ph.D
Vice President
Pro–2–Serve
10294 Osprey Trace
West Palm Beach, FL 33412–1542
(407) 694–1548
Fax: (407) 694–0325
EMAIL: See Below

7363

Business Information: Pro–2–Serve is a professional project staffing organization providing scientists and engineers for environmental and product development projects. The Company contracts out to large and small companies. As Vice President, Dr. Sabourin is responsible for management and marketing, as well as technical consulting, strategic business planning, and customer service. Dr. Sabourin teamed with an old colleague to start this business because of the trend in companies work processes to projectizing. Internet users can reach him via: TDSABO@AOL.com. **Career Steps:** Vice President, Pro–2–Serve (1996–Present); Director of Corporate Technical Services, Toxikon Corporation (1994–1995); Vice President/Director of Agrochem Product Development, Battelle Memorial Institute (1982–1994). **Associations & Accomplishments:** American Chemical Society; Society of Environmental Toxicology and Chemistry – Europe; Society of Toxicology. **Education:** Louisiana State University, Ph.D. (1981); California State University–Hayward, M.S.; University of Michigan–Ann Arbor, B.S. **Personal:** Married to Josanne in 1974. Dr. Sabourin enjoys golf, basketball, tennis, hiking, fishing, and skiing.

Thomas J. Shaw
Vice President of International Marketing & Operations
Dun & Bradstreet Information Services
One Diamond Hill Road
Murray Hill, NJ 07974–1218
(908) 665–5823
Fax: (908) 665–5361

7363

Business Information: Dun & Bradstreet Information Services, a company of The Dun & Bradstreet Corporation, is a worldwide provider of financial and business information services. Mr. Shaw currently serves as Vice President for Dun & Bradstreet information Services International in the U.S. The international group is a supplier of commercial marketing and credit information with operations in 39 countries and a worldwide database of more than 41 million businesses. As Vice President of International Marketing and Operations, he is responsible for the management activities of international sales, marketing and operations of the Company's global products to the U.S. market. Career milestones include the establishment of new Dun & Bradstreet operating subsidiaries in Japan, Tawan and Puerto Rico China. **Career Steps:** Dun & Bradstreet Information Services: Vice President of International Marketing & Operations (1995–Present); Vice President of Asia Pacific & Latin American Region – International Performance Quality and Operations (1993–1995); General Manager Venezuela C.A. (1992–1993); Director of Operations – Japan K.K. (1988–1992) **Associations & Accomplishments:** Information Industry Association (IIA); National Association Credit Managers (NACM); Japan Society; Japanese American Lions Club. **Education:** St. Johns University, Accounting (1971). **Personal:** Married to Toshiko in 1995. Mr. Shaw enjoys tennis, skiing and spectator soccer.

Vern C. Vokus

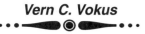

Vice President, General Manager, & Chief Operating Officer
Sprint Staffing Inc. Work Force USA
5444 Bay Center Drive, Suite 200
Tampa, FL 33679–8385
(813) 286–2860
Fax: (813) 287–2647

7363

Business Information: Sprint Staffing Inc. Work Force USA is a temporary staffing agency specializing in light industrial and skilled construction positions. As Vice President, General Manager, & Chief Operating Officer, Mr. Vokus oversees the running of the Company and assists in strategic planning for the future. He is involved in developing marketing techniques for new and existing services. Mr. Vokus was instrumental in increasing company revenues from $11 million to $30 million dollars in the last two years. **Career Steps:** Vice President, General Manager, & Chief Operating Officer, Sprint Staffing Inc. Work Force USA (1993–Present); President, Hoover Services (1985–1986); Vice President Security, Securex (1978–1984). **Associations & Accomplishments:** NATS; FLASSA. **Education:** Florida State University. **Personal:** One child: Justin. Mr. Vokus enjoys running, weightlifting, and reading.

Wayne A. Voris

General Manager
Aim Executive, Inc.
445 Byers Road
Miamisburg, OH 45342–3662
(513) 859–8896
Fax: (513) 859–1767

7363

Business Information: Aim Executive, Inc. is a human resources consultancy, providing executive search and recruitment, corporate outplacement, contract staffing and human resources counseling. Headquartered in Toledo, the Firm has over 22 office locations across the U.S. As General Manager, Mr. Voris oversees all regional offices in the Ohio sector. **Career Steps:** General Manager, Aim Executive, Inc. (1990–Present); Director of Human Resources, AM Graphics (1986–1990); Manager of Human Resources, PMI – Food Equipment Group (1982–1986). **Associations & Accomplishments:** International Association of Career Management Professionals. **Education:** Marshall University, M.B.A. (1981); Glenville State College, B.A. (1979). **Personal:** Married to Della Kay in 1981. Two children: Shayne and Casey.

Deborah L. Weaver

National Sales Manager
CIC, Inc.
2941 W. Bay Road
Belleair Bluffs, FL 33770
(813) 559–0034 Ext. 126
Fax: (813) 559–0232

7363

Business Information: CIC, Inc. provides pre–employment background checks for companies on potential employees. CIC, Inc. offers clients information to aid in employee retention and create a safer workplace. As National Sales Manager, Ms. Weaver is responsible for overseeing the sales department she founded, monitoring of all systems, advertising and market research, and various aspects of human resources including recruitment, training and employee review. Instrumental in developing the program for the Company to aid in–house and sales functions, Ms. Weaver also supervises a staff of five. **Career Steps:** National Sales Manager, CIC, Inc. (1995–Present); Long & Foster Realtors (1992–1994): Sales Manager (1992–1994), Realtor/Top Producer (1985–1992). **Associations & Accomplishments:** International Hospital and Security (IAHSS); American Society for Industrial Security (ASIS)' Sun Coast Human Resource Management Association (SHRMA); St. Petersburg Chamber of Commerce. **Personal:** Married to David in 1981. Two children: Joshua and Michael. Ms. Weaver enjoys being a prayer counselor, gourmet cooking, reading, and gardening.

Andrew Aird

Senior Vice President
WILCO Systems
347 West 57th Street, Apt. 15D
New York, NY 10019–3173
(212) 269–3970
Fax: (212) 269–3925

7371

Business Information: WILCO Systems, a division of ADP, is a software development company. The Company develops and markets computer software settlement, accounting, and communications programs for the securities industry. The parent company, ADP, has offices in Hong Kong, England, and the United States. Established in 1970, WILCO Systems now employs 450 people throughout national and international locations. As Senior Vice President, Mr. Aird manages and works with teams of analysts on the development of computer software and deals directly with a number of clients to develop customer relations. On the management side of his position, he handles staff recruitment, staff training, manages work sites, establishes budgets, and other financial concerns. Mr. Aird works closely with other management staff in planning for the future of WILCO Systems and in developing and marketing new and existing products and services. **Career Steps:** Senior Vice President, WILCO Systems (1995–Present); Assistant Director, Natwest Markets (1989–1995); Vice President, Security Pacific Hoare Govett (1986–1989). **Associations & Accomplishments:** Association of MBAs (United Kingdom). **Education:** City University, London, M.B.A. (1992); Edinburgh University, M.A. in Economics (1983). **Personal:** Mr. Aird enjoys rugby, baseball, arts and music, and his vacation home in Pennsylvania.

Vickie L. Bair

Director of Operations
Baseview Products
333 Jackson Plaza
Ann Arbor, MI 48103
(313) 662–5800
Fax: (313) 662–5204

7371

Business Information: Baseview Products, a subsidiary of Harris Corporation, provides computer software for the newspaper and publishing industry. Established in 1989, Baseview Products reports annual revenue of $9.5 million and currently employs 81 people. As Director of Operations, Mrs. Bair directs all aspects of marketing, sales, support, installation, and training. Mrs. Bair started with Computype/Harris Corporation in 1977 and has come full circle back to Harris Corporation via Baseview. In the interim, she has worked for other newspaper vendors such as Xitron (now Triple III), Deucalion Resources Group, Lorenz Publishing, and Ctext. She has come up through the ranks and has held such positions as an award winning technical writer, engineering technician, technical support, manager of educational resources, trainer, senior QC/documentation engineer, sales manager, and sales director. **Education:** Western Michigan University, B.S. (1972); Eastern Michigan University, graduate courses. **Personal:** Married to Charles H. in 1980. Three children: Melissa, Matthew and Nicole. Mrs. Bair enjoys reading, swimming and softball.

Cynthia Marie Barcelone

Senior Director, Global Business Team
Fastech, Inc.
450 Parkway Drive
Broomall, PA 19446
(610) 359–5823
Fax: (610) 544–3695

7371

Business Information: Fastech, Inc. is a sales force automation company, providing custom software and consulting services. Mrs. Barcelone joined Fastech in 1988, serving in various supervisory positions before being promoted to Senior Director of the Global Business Team in 1995. Her present responsibilities include business development, project management, and support resources. **Career Steps:** Fastech, Inc.: Senior Director, Global Business Team (1995–Present), Director of Account Management (1994–1995), Account Manager (1990–1994). **Associations & Accomplishments:** American Management Association. **Education:** St. Joseph's University, B.S. in Food Marketing (1988). **Personal:** Married to Joseph in 1992. Mrs. Barcelone enjoys skiing, reading, gardening, and exercise.

Stephen H. Benedict

President
Micro Star
2245 Camino Vida Roble
Carlsbad, CA 92009
(619) 931–4949
Fax: (619) 931–4950

7371

Business Information: Micro Star specializes in the publishing and distribution of prepackaged computer software. Sales market includes retail operations in the United States, Latin America, England, Australia and Europe. The Company also offers a software club and caters to the home computer market, offering entertainment and educational software and shareware. Established in 1987, Micro Star currently employs 70 people and has an estimated annual revenue of $6 million. As President and Chief Executive Officer, Mr. Benedict provides the overall direction and vision for the company's continued growth, quality delivery to customers and strategic development. **Career Steps:** President, Micro Star (1987–Present). **Education:** University of Florida, B.S. in Business Administration (1976). **Personal:** One child: Justin.

Ramakrishna Bhupatiraju

Project Manager
E–Z Data, Inc.
1723 Kerry Court
West Covina, CA 91792–2339
(818) 810–7771
Fax: (818) 810–5779
EMAIL: See Below

7371

Business Information: E–Z Data, Inc. designs and develops DOS and Windows applications for the insurance and financial industries. As Project Manager, Mr. Bhupatiraju conducts home office client consulting in data modeling and data integrity. Additionally, he is responsible for supervising the design and development of applications software. Internet users can reach him via: DILIP@IX.NETCOM.COM **Career Steps:** Project Manager, E–Z Data, Inc. (1990–Present). **Education:** New York Institute of Technology, M.S. in Computer Science (1990). **Personal:** Married to Radha G. in 1993. Mr. Bhupatiraju enjoys tennis and reading.

Plamen I. Bliznakov

Senior Software Engineer
Parametric Technology Corporation
128 Technology Drive
Waltham, MA 01254
(617) 398–5712
Fax: (617) 398–5633
EMail: See Below

7371

Business Information: Parametric Technology Corporation specializes in the development of comprehensive CAD/CAM/CAE software systems. As Senior Software Engineer, Mr. Bliznakov is responsible for software development and implementation. Internet users can reach him via: Plamen@PTC.com. **Career Steps:** Senior Software Engineer, Parametric Technology Corporation (1995–Present); Graduate Assistant, Arizona State University (1992–1995); Research Assistant, Technical University – Sofia (1987–1991), (1984–1985). **Associations & Accomplishments:** American Society of Mechanical Engineers; Association of Computer Manufacturers. **Education:** Arizona State University, Ph.D. candidate (1996); Technical University – Sofia: Graduate Program (1988–1991), Mechanical Engineer (1980–1985). **Personal:** Married to Luba D. in 1988. One child: Yana P. Mr. Bliznakov enjoys judo – placed second in state finals.

Karen S. Brooks

Assistant Vice President
Affiliated Computer Services, Inc.
2828 N. Haskell Ave.
Dallas, TX 75204–2909
(214) 841–6397
Fax: (214) 821–2874
Email: See Below

7371

Business Information: Affiliated Computer Services, Inc. is a nationwide provider of information technology solutions to commercial, financial, and government markets, with client representation in all major industries. In addition, ACS owns and operates Money Maker, one of the largest ATM networks in the United States. As Assistant Vice President, Ms. Brooks is currently responsible for Corporate business continuity and business resumption planning. Internet users can reach her via: karen_brooks@acs–inc.com. **Career Steps:** Affiliated Computer Services, Inc.: Assistant Vice President (1981–Present), Business Continuity (1996–Present), New Product Development Manager (1992–1995), Financial Services Account Manager (1988–1992); First Texas Computer Corp.: Vice President, Manager of Client Services (1986–988), Manager/Business Analyst (1982–1986). **Associations & Accomplishments:** Association of Contingency Planners; International Network of Women in Technology; Administrative Board Member, Highland Park United Methodist Church. **Education:** University of Texas, B.A. in English (1974). **Personal:** One child: Jordan. Ms. Brooks enjoys her son and being a mother, theater, classical music, arts and crafts, reading, teaching elementary Sunday School, and volunteering for various community events.

Alexis Castro

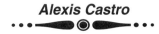

President
MACOM
P.O. Box 70793
Caracus, Venezuela 1070
58–22–672989
Fax: 58–22–640196
EMAIL: See Below

7371

Business Information: MACOM services, installs, and maintains commercial computers in Venezuela and the Caribbean islands. The Company handles all computer types and brands for large companies and industries. They also provide outsourcing and help desk services. As President, Mr. Castro is responsible for all aspects of Company operations, including administration, finance, and strategic planning. Internet users can reach him via: ALEXISCS@ELDISH.LAT.NET. **Career Steps:** President, MACOM (1983–Present); Data Processing Manager, Ceprochoca (1980–1983); System Analyst, Navy (1975–1980); Programmer, C.A.D. Center – England (1971–1973). **Associations & Accomplishments:** Rotary Club; Director, Cavedatos Computer Association; Director, Conintel Telecommunications Association. **Education:** Kennedy Western University, M.B.A. (1985); Attended, Cambridgeshire College of Arts and Technology – England, Computer Science. **Personal:** Married to Ana in 1970. Three children: Alexis, Alejandro, and Ana Carolina. Mr. Castro enjoys sailing.

Mr. John R. Costanza

President and Chief Executive Officer
Jc–I–T Institute of Technology, Inc.
6825 South Galena Street
Englewood, CO 80112
(303) 792–8300
Fax: (303) 792–8335

7371

Business Information: Jc–I–T Institute of Technology, Inc. specializes in the development of manufacturing educational material and manufacturing software (The Demand Flow). As President and Chief Executive Officer, Mr. Costanza is responsible for all aspects of Company operations. Established in 1984, Jc–I–T Institute of Technology, Inc. employs 140 people. **Career Steps:** President and Chief Executive Officer, Jc–I–T Institute of Technology, Inc. (1984–Present); Corporate Manufacturing, Hewlett–Packard (1984–Present); Director of Manufacturing, Johnson & Johnson (1977). **Associations & Accomplishments:** American Society of Quality Control; American Society of Manufacturing Engineering; American Society of Certified Public Accountants; Numerous publications, including "The Demand Flow Manufacturing Concept." **Education:** University of Southern Colorado (1971); University of Colorado at Boulder. **Personal:** Married to Linda. One child: Melissa. Mr. Costanza enjoys antique auto's and skiing.

Charles B. Daniels

Director, Solutions Development
UNISYS–HIM
12010 Sunrise Valley Drive
Reston, VA 22091
(703) 620–7989
Fax: (703) 620–7966
E MAIL: ddaydan@aol.com

7371

Business Information: UNISYS–HIM provides computing hardware and software solutions for the health care industry internationally. As Director of Solutions Development, Mr. Daniels manages and directs a geographically diverse group of 150 software engineering professionals in the design, develop, and delivery of health care information systems to support state, federal government, and commercial business requirements. He is accountable for executive customer interface, budgeting, monitoring, and control and review for all development activities. **Career Steps:** Director, Solutions Development, UNISYS–HIM (1996–Present); Director, Quality, UNISYS–GSG (1994–1996); Director, MSSS, UNISYS (1993–1994). **Associations & Accomplishments:** American Society of Quality Control; Board of Senior Examiners, Malcolm Baldridge National Quality Award; Fluent in Russian. **Education:** Saint Joseph's University, M.B.A. candidate; State University of New York, B.S.; Attended: University of Houston and George Washington University. **Personal:** Married to Cindy Lou in 1982. Mr. Daniels enjoys sailing, bridge, exercising, and wine tasting.

Edward J. Donnelly

Account Executive – Southern Region
VISTA Information Solutions
5060 Shoreham Place, Suite 300
San Diego, CA 92122
(619) 450–6100
Fax: (619) 450–6195
EMail: See Below

7371

Business Information: VISTA Information Solutions licenses data and software applications to produce environmental information reports for corporations, bankers, engineers, and various other industries. As Account Executive – Southern Region, Mr. Donnelly handles all accounts in the southern region of the United States, and serves as an industry specialist for electronics, waste management, telecommunications, and food industry. Internet users can reach him via: aggie@mail.adnc.com. **Career Steps:** Account Executive – Southern Region, VISTA Information Solutions (1996–Present); Territory Sales Manager, VISTA Environmental Information (1993–1996); Business Development Manager, Blackwell Environmental, Inc. (1992–1993). **Associations & Accomplishments:** Society of Texas Environmental Professionals; Habitat for Humanity Volunteer. **Education:** Texas A&M University, Bachelor's degree (1991). **Personal:** Mr. Donnelly enjoys golf, soccer, tennis, running, and softball.

George E. Durtler

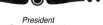

President
Graphicode
6608–216th Street, SW
Mount Lake Terrace, WA 98043
(206) 672–1980
Fax: Please mail or call

7371

Business Information: Graphicode is an international developer of software for electronics manufacturing. Future plans include leading a shift in focus from a technology–driven company to a market–driven company and to accelerate growth. Joining Graphicode as Vice President of Sales and Marketing in 1994, Mr. Durtler was appointed as President in 1995. He oversees all administrative operations for associates and a support staff of 25, primarily providing the overall strategies and vision to keep the company a growing and viable presence in the technology marketplace. **Career Steps:** Graphicode: President (1995–Present), Vice President of Sales and Marketing (1994–1995); General Manager of Technical Imaging, Escher–grad, Inc. (1990–1993); International Sales Manager, Matrox Graphics, Ltd. (1985–1990). **Associations & Accomplishments:** Washington Software Association (WSA). **Education:** Concordia University, B.Sc. in Physics, honors, with distinction (1984). **Personal:** Married to Patricia in 1994. Mr. Durtler enjoys reading, golf, skiing, hiking, and growing bonsai trees.

Juan Carlos Esteche

Latin American Client Manager
J.D. Edwards & Company
800 Douglas Entrance
Coral Gables, FL 33134
(305) 442–7806
Fax: (305) 442–7850
EMAIL: See below

7371

Business Information: J.D. Edwards & Company is a software development and consultancy, specializing in the sales and implementation of commercial software. International in scope, the company has offices in Europe, Asia and Latin America, as well as numerous locations in the United States. As Latin American Client Manager, Mr. Esteche is responsible for large global accounts originating from Latin America. In this capacity, he oversees the engineering department, providing support and vision, as well as strategy development. He can be reached through the internet via: juan_esteche@jdedwards.com **Career Steps:** Latin American Client Manager, J.D. Edwards (1992–Present); International Project Manager, Burger King Corporation (1992); International Project Leader, DHL (1987–1992). **Education:** Universite de Paris, M.S. (1983); Western Washington University: B.A., B.S.; Civilization Francaise La Sorbonne. **Personal:** Mr. Esteche enjoys playing piano, horseback riding and skiing.

Herbert Fenkhuber

Chief Executive Officer
ITEC– CompCom–Systems
1842 Avenue De Templiers
Vence, France 06140
33–(4) 93–5885
Fax: 33–(4) 93–5864

7371

Business Information: ITEC– CompCom–Systems is a complete computer/communication systems supplier for architects, construction companies, attorneys, notaries, real estate, and tourism agencies. Mr. Fenkhuber founded ITEC–CompCom – an SW R&D–oriented company on the cutting–edge of technology – in 1993. As Chief Executive Officer, he is responsible for general operations management and supervision of strategic key account projects. **Career Steps:** Chief Executive Officer, ITEC– CompCom–Systems; Vice President, General Electric; Executive Director, Texas Instruments, Muich, Paris, Milano, Bedford; Director, Siemans Semiconductor Products, Munich, S. Jose California, Mega Projects. **Associations & Accomplishments:** Member, IEEE, ISCC, and foundation member of FEFA Foundation; Embedded in the Executives Network of Global Semiconductor; Communication and Computer Industries/Companies; Assistant Professor, Technical Highschool TGM, Vienna. **Education:** Technical University of Vienna, Ph.D. (1976); Technical Highschool HTL Steyr/TGM Vienna, B.S. in Electrical Engineering (1970). **Personal:** Dr. Fenkhuber enjoys avionics and nautical sports.

David Foster

Vice President
J.P. Brown and Associates
780 Gordon Baker Road
North York, Ontario M2H 3B4
(416) 494–0472
Fax: (416) 494–0504
EMAIL: See Below

7371

Business Information: J.P. Brown and Associates is a computer software distribution company specializing in products to enhance clients existing systems. Importing products from manufacturers worldwide, the Company then markets the software through independent dealers and wholesalers, focusing exclusively on the Canadian market. Established in 1971, the Company employs 20 people and has estimated annual revenue of $2.5 million. As Vice President, Mr. Foster oversees all import and export of software, and manages all aspects of the operation. He is responsible for communicating with suppliers, establishing product lines, and serving as a liaison between J.P. Brown and Associates and other companies. Internet users can reach him via: dfoster@inforamp.net or davef@jpbrown.com. **Career Steps:** Vice President, J.P. Brown and Associates (1984–Present); Vice President of Finance and Administration, Wm. E. Taylor Canada Ltd. (1967–1984). **Education:** Ryerson University, Business Administration (1972). **Personal:** Married to Sandy in 1968. Three children: Jeffrey, Katherine, and David. Mr. Foster enjoys power boating.

Helmuth E. Freericks

Vice President of Research and Development
Command Software Systems, Inc.
1061 East Indiantown Road, Suite 500
Jupiter, FL 33477–5143
(407) 575–3200 Ext. 148
Fax: (407) 575–3026
EMAIL: HFREERICKS@COMMAN

7371

Business Information: Command Software Systems, Inc. is a manufacturer of anti–virus and PC security software. As Vice President of Research and Development, Mr. Freericks manages the development, technical support, MIS, and shipping departments. Currently, he is directly responsible for 24 people. Internet users can reach him via: HFREERICKS@COMMANDCOM.COM. **Career Steps:** Vice President of Research and Development, Command Software Systems, Inc. (1995–Present); Director of Research & Development, Peerless Systems Corporation (1990–1996); Manager Communications Services, Quotron Systems, Inc. (1985–1990); Technical Director, Microcomputer Business, Ltd. (1981–1985). **Associations & Accomplishments:** Institute of Electronics and Electrical Engineers; A.C.M. **Education:** Technical University – Eindhoven, Bachelor of Computer Science (1980). **Personal:** Married to Ishraq in 1984. Four children: Rania, Sara, Kyle, and Tiana. Mr. Freericks enjoys martial arts.

Mr. Patrick P. Gelsinger

Vice President & General Manager, Personal Conferencing Division
Intel
JF2–01 2111 North East 25th Avenue
Hillsboro, OR 97124
(503) 696–8600
Fax: (503) 696–6181

7371

Business Information: Intel, established in 1894, is the world's leading marketer of semiconductors. Intel's Personal Conference Division designs, manufactures, and markets video and data conferencing software and hardware components. As Vice President & General Manager of the Personal Conferencing Division, Mr. Gelsinger is responsible for all aspects of Division operations, focusing primarily with strategic development, architecture design and innovations, sales and marketing, and overall supervision for a staff of 450 people. **Career Steps:** Vice President & General Manager of the Personal Conferencing Division, Intel (1993–Present); General Manager of Processor (486 & P6) Development, Intel (1991–1993); General Manager of CAD/Architecture, Intel (1990–1991); Manager of Processor (286, 386 and 486) Development, Intel (1987–1989). **Associations & Accomplishments:** Institute of Electrical and Electronic Engineers; Tau Beta Pi; Active Member and Committee Member of the Singing Hills Christian Church – leads home Bible study, teaches Sunday School classes. **Education:** Stanford University, M.S in Electrical Engineering and Computer Science (1985); Santa Clara University, B.S in Electrical Engineering and Computer Science (1983); Lincoln Technical Institute, A.A. (1979). **Personal:** Married to Linda in 1983. Four children: Elizabeth, Josiah, Nathan, and Micah. Mr. Gelsinger enjoys racquetball, gardening, and wood working.

Gary L. Gibbs

Regional Vice President
Intersolv
1040 Crown Pointe Parkway, Suite 840
Atlanta, GA 30338–4724
(770) 551–5078
Fax: (770) 551–5089
EMAIL: See Below

7371

Business Information: Intersolv is a software products company specializing in client/server applications, enablement, and development, and Internet solutions. As Regional Vice President, Mr. Gibbs is responsible for the Chicago to Atlanta region. He manages $30 million in sales revenue, recruitment, training, and cross–manages telesales operations in Oregon, North Carolina, and Maryland. Internet users can reach him via: GARY–GIBBS@INTERSOLV.COM. **Career Steps:** Regional Vice President, Intersolv (1993–Present); Senior Sales Manager, Must Software International (1989–1993); Technical Support, Unisys (1988–1989); Programmer/Analyst, Lockheed/Martin Marietta (1985–1988). **Associations & Accomplishments:** American Management Association; Phi Sigma Kappa. **Education:** Georgia State University, B.B.A. (1990); Georgia Institute of Technology, B.S. in Management (1984–1988). **Personal:** Married to Kristen in 1991. Mr. Gibbs enjoys golf.

David P. Goad

Manager Sales Support
Sterling Commerce
4600 Lakehurst Court
Dublin, OH 43016–3255
(614) 793–7088
Fax: (614) 793–7092

7371

Business Information: Sterling Commerce, established in 1996, is a branch–off of Sterling Software. The Company provides electronic movement of business information, both by physical network and software. As Manager Sales Support, Mr. Goad is responsible for diversified operational activities, including administration, sales, marketing, and strategic planning. He oversees and monitors 100 people, and is responsible for sales training, on–site consultation, sales awareness seminars, and coordinating the Automation Sales Committee. **Career Steps:** Sterlilng Software: Manager Sales Support (1990–Present), Manager Healthcare Sales (1987–1990); Vice President Sales, Pulse Computer Systems (1982–1987). **Associations & Accomplishments:** President, Home Owners Association; United Way; NWDA; Private Industry Council. **Education:** University of Evansville (1960). **Personal:** Married to Sheila in 1989. Four children: Michael, Dianna, Jason and Adam. Mr. Goad enjoys golf and travel.

Regina G. Hall

Senior Technical Consultant
Parker Management Consultants, Ltd.
695A Main Street
Laurel, MD 20707
(800) 335–4465
Fax: (301) 617–9778

7371

Business Information: Parker Management Consultants, Ltd. (PMC) is a leading provider of technical consulting services to manufacturing clients throughout the U.S. and the world. PMC provides services to support the following functional areas: Application Audit Reviews, ISO 9000 Implementation and Training, System Customization and Modification, Software Development, Functional Area Consulting and Training, Business Process Reengineering, System Management and Audits, UDMS Programming and Training, MRP II Implementation, and System Security. A system's analyst with over 20 years of expertise, Regina Hall serves as one of PMC's senior technical consultants. Her duties involve the management and execution of various consulting projects for a wide range of manufacturers. Internet users can reach her via: PMCLTD@AOL.COM. **Career Steps:** Senior Technical Consultant, Parker Management Consultants, Ltd. (1996–); Director of Customer Services, Peripheral Software Concepts, Inc. (1985–96); Regional Technical Manager, ASK Computer Systems, Inc. (1980–1985); MIS Manager, ARKAY Packaging Corporation (1978–1980); MIS Manager, Hoerbiger Corporation of America (1972–1978).

Lisa D. Hargiss

Vice President
CPS Systems, Inc.
5005 West Laurel Street, Suite 215
Tampa, FL 33607–3836
(813) 288–9880
Fax: (813) 288–9791

7371

Business Information: CPS Systems, Inc. provides comprehensive data processing solutions to Counties, Cities, Appraisal Districts or Property Appraisers, Regulated Utilities and Commercial Markets. These solutions operate as multi–user multi–tasking systems for UNIX/AIX and NT based mini-computer leaders such as IBM, HP, Altos, and NCR. The company consists of five divisions: Collections, CAMA, Cities, RPS and Field Engineering. Founded in 1975, CPS Systems, Inc., is an $8 million plus revenue company providing quality software and service to over 400 customers nationally. With a strong history of excellence and commitment to the customer, CPS Systems, Inc. is endeavoring to provide state–of–the–art systems competitively priced with outstanding after–the–sale support with a single point contact for software, hardware, service and training. Ms. Hargiss currrently serves as Vice President of the Collections Division in charge of Software Development, Client Support and Sales. **Career Steps:** CPS Systems, Inc.: Vice President, Collections Division (1995–Present), Regional Manager, Collections Division (1993–1995), Senior Analyst, CAMA Division (1992–1993), Client Support Manager, Collections Division (1990–1992), Client Support Analyst, Appraisal Division (1987–1989). **Associations & Accomplishments:** Member of IAAO, Tax Collectors Association, NACO, NAFE, and Epsilon Delta Pi. **Education:** Texas A&M – Commerce, B.S. (1985); Southwestern Junior College, A.A.(1983). **Personal:** Ms. Hargiss enjoys golf, reading, and collecting Southwestern Art.

Jonathan Haverly

Chief Financial Officer and Controller
Sorian Systems, Inc.
1420 Providence Hwy.
Norwood, MA 02062–4662
(617) 769–2189
Fax: (617) 769–7154
EMAIL: See Below

7371

Business Information: Sorian Systems, Inc. is a national computer software development firm. With ten years expertise in financial management consulting, Mr. Haverly established the firm with two friends in 1993. Serving as Co–Owner, Chief Financial Officer, and Controller, he is responsible for all aspects of financial matters, as well as sharing business responsibilities with his partners. **Career Steps:** Co–Owner, Chief Financial Officer, and Controller, Sorian Systems, Inc. (1993–Present); Business Consultant, Independent (1990–1993); Contact Officer, DMR (1985–1990). **Education:** Northeastern University, M.B.A. (1990); Clark University, B.A. **Personal:** Mr. Haverly enjoys skiing.

Jerome L. Haynesworth

Vice President of Human Resources
Hughes Information Services
1768 Business Center Drive
Reston, VA 22090
(703) 759–1749
Fax: (709) 757–1403
EMAIL: See Below

7371

Business Information: Hughes Information Services provides professional services, including data base software design for federal and civil government and information technology. As Vice President of Human Resources, Mr. Haynesworth facilitates strategic planning and coordination of human assets/resources with the goal of contributing to shareholder equity. Internet users can reach him via: jlhaynesworth@ccgate.hac.com. **Career Steps:** Vice President of Human Resources, Hughes Information Services (1994–Present); Principal Consultant, HR Solutions, Inc. (1991–1994); Director of Human Resources, The Interface Group (1987–1991); Group Human Resource Manager, Honeywell Information Systems (1980–1987). **Associations & Accomplishments:** Washington Technical Personnel Association; National Human Resources Association; President, Middlesex, MA – National Association for the Advancement of Colored People; Urban League; Various Professional Organizations. **Education:** Ohio University, B.S. (1971). **Personal:** Married to Patricia in 1973. One child: Kendall J. Mr. Haynesworth enjoys golf.

David W. Hoy

Vice President of Operations
Terraglyph Interactive Studio
1375 Remington Road
Schaumburg, IL 60173–4813
(847) 781–4100
Fax: (847) 781–1558
EMail: See Below

7371

Business Information: Terraglyph Interactive Studio specializes in family entertainment and multi–media CD roms. The Company deals primarily with store chains and educational facilities. As Vice President of Operations, Mr. Hoy handles administration, operations, and facility management. He goes over checks and balances for payments, oversees human resources, and handles the maintenance and leasing of the facility. Internet users can reach him via: DHOY@MSN.COM. **Career Steps:** Vice President of Operations, Terraglyph Interactive Studio (1994–Present); Vice President of Operations, Viacom Nem Media (1993–1994); Vice President of Publishing, ICOM Simulations (1990–1993); Business Analyst, Severn Companies (1990). **Education:** United States Military Academy – West Point, NY, B.S. (1977). **Personal:** Married to Debra in 1989. Mr. Hoy enjoys reading.

Bryant Ingram

President
Programming by Design
6011 North West 63rd, Suite F1
Oklahoma City, OK 73132
(405) 773–1313
Fax: (405) 773–1314

7371

Business Information: Programming by Design is a computer consulting and programming firm, offering programming and networking solutions to various clients. Used as a Beta Test Site for Microsoft's Visual Foxpro, most of Programming by Design programming is performed using Foxpro for Windows and/or Borland's C++. A Networking Consultant and a Certified Novell Engineer, Mr. Ingram provides computer services to local businesses, as well as a few out of the state. As President and Owner, he is responsible for all aspects of operations, including administration, finances, programming, consulting and strategic planning. His experiences include having the opportunity to work with Sprint's MIS Department located in Dallas, Texas for several months, learning additional information on system design and development. Career highlights include being responsible for the release of "Project Manager" – a time–tracking and billing package for computer consultants, to the Shareware market and the development of educational software which was sold in well–known software stores throughout the U.S. **Career Steps:** President and Owner, Programming by Design (1994–Present); Software Development and Network Administrator, Access Unlimited (1995); Senior Foxpro Programmer and Network Administrator, Candid Color Systems (1992–1994); Software Developer, Software/Hardware Support and Networking Consultant, The American Education Corporation (1990–1992). **Associations & Accomplishments:** Certified Novell Engineer (CNE); The Association of Network Service Professionals; Microsoft Certified Systems Engineer Candidate (MCSE); The Association of Shareware Professionals (ASP); The International Who's Who; Published several articles in Foxpro Advisor. **Education:** Attended numerous computer related classes: Microsoft (Foxpro Developers Conference), Precision Computer Services (Novell); Attended: University of Science & Arts of Oklahoma, Computer Programming/Software Engineering, University of Central Oklahoma, Computer Programming, University of Texas–Arlington, Pascal. **Personal:** Married to Stacy Ingram in 1993. Mr. Ingram enjoys writing and Karate.

Edward L. Irvin
Senior Business Consultant
Cincinnati Bell Information Systems
600 Vine Street
Cincinnati, OH 45202
(513) 723-7190
Fax: (513) 241-4826
EMAIL: See Below

7371

Business Information: Cincinnati Bell Information Systems (CBIS) provides customer care and billing solutions for two communications industries, through specialized software specifically suited to their needs. Located in Cincinnati, Ohio, the Company services telephone companies and cellular phone distributors. Established in 1983, the Company has five locations nationally, and plans to expand through training. As Senior Business Consultant, Mr. Irvin trouble–shoots any problems that arise, maintaining a high quality of customer service. Additionally, he is responsible for all administrative and marketing duties, including training, and oversight of development and delivery. Internet users can reach him via: Ed.Irvin@CBIS.com **Career Steps:** Senior Business Consultant, CBIS (1992–Present); President, Organizational Quality Systems (1992–Present); Senior Internal Consultant, Mead Corporation (1987–1992); Manager, Corporate Quality Systems, Owens Corning Fiberglas (1967–1986). **Associations & Accomplishments:** Senior Member, American Society for Quality Control; Executive Board of Madisonville Education And Assistance Center; Managing Coordinator of Knox Interpath Hospitality Network. **Education:** University of Cincinnati, B.S. in Chemistry (1971); University of Tennessee, George Washington University, Advanced Studies. **Personal:** Married to Marla in 1994. Two children: Heather and William. Mr. Irvin enjoys golf, softball, and classical music.

Robert A. Kelley
Chief Technical Officer
Kapre Software
4775 Walnut Street, Suite D
Boulder, CO 80301
(303) 546-8803
Fax: (303) 938-9053
EMAIL: See Below

7371

Business Information: Kapre Software develops financial software for large multinational companies. Focusing primarily on package solutions and custom–created programs, the Company also offers object–oriented programs, distributed client servers, and worldwide web access. Established in 1992, the Company employs forty people. As Chief Technical Officer, Mr. Kelley is responsible for product design, assisting with solutions and engineering problems, and strategic planning. One of the Company's founders, Mr. Kelley also handles sales and marketing, and evaluates and develops technological solutions. **Career Steps:** Chief Technical Officer, Kapre Software (1992–Present); Consulting, Independent (1989–1992); Vice President, Pyramid Technology Corporation (1981–1988); Senior Computer Scientist, Stsc, Inc. (1979–1981). **Education:** University of Colorado, Graduate Student; Stanford University: B.S. (1976), M.A. (1977); College for Financial Planning, Certified Financial Planner (CFP). **Personal:** Married to Colleen in 1989. Two children: Jonathan and Benjamin. Mr. Kelley enjoys martial arts, computerized trading, and investing in wine.

Patrick G. Lamp
Senior Software Engineer
Logica–Cynercom
1817 Park
Houston, TX 77019
(713) 954-7050
Fax: (713) 521-7074
EMail: See Below

7371

Business Information: Logica–Cynercom specializes in multi vendor software consulting, utility management software, and Internet application development. As Senior Software Engineer, Mr. Lamp is responsible for a team of systems and software engineers, field work with specific software, work management, and information systems. Internet users can reach him via: pglamp@netropolis.net. **Career Steps:** Senior Software Engineer, Logica–Cynercom (1996–Present); Senior Systems Analyst/MIS Director, Anheuser Busch, Inc. (1994–1996); CIO/Senior Systems Consultant, Premier Industries (1990–1994). **Associations & Accomplishments:**

Information Systems, American Management Association; University of High School of Music Board; Houston Grand Opera Board; American Suicide Foundation Board; Houston Council on Alcoholism. **Education:** University of Miami: M.S. Degree in Industrial Psychology (1979), B.S. Degree in Business Psychology (1975); American University, M.B.A. Degree in Business Administration (1984). **Personal:** Mr. Lamp enjoys music, classical piano, composing, tenor 1, and musical theatres.

Todd McCarthy
Vice President of Worldwide Sales & Operations
Restrace, Inc.
8 Barn Lane
Westford, MA 01886–2071
(617) 320-5384
Fax: (617) 320-5630
EMAIL: See Below

7371

Business Information: Restrace, Inc. is a provider of human resource staff software solutions. As Vice President of Worldwide Sales and Operations, Mr. McCarthy is responsible for the promotion of the business on a global basis. Internet users can reach him via: Toddm@Restrac.com **Career Steps:** Vice President of Worldwide Sales, Restrace, Inc. (1995–Present); Vice President and General Manager, Padrom, Inc (1994–1995); North East Regional Director, Software 2000 Inc. (1993–1994). **Associations & Accomplishments:** United States Marine Corps Association. **Education:** Merrimack College, B.S. in Computer Science (1984). **Personal:** Married to Pam in 1984. Two children: Meghan and Sean. Mr. McCarthy enjoys golf and skiing.

Chuck W. McDonald
Vice President
Spectrum R&D
2261 West 9 Mile Road
Pensacola, FL 32534
(904) 969-9701
Fax: (904) 969-9705
EMail: See Below

7371

Business Information: Spectrum R&D, established in 1995, is a systems integration and software development firm for data acquisition and system control products, related to government registration development research. With five facilities located throughout Florida and New Jersey, Spectrum R&D employs field engineers that work mostly out of their homes. As Vice President, Mr. McDonald is responsible for the engineering and conceptual design of projects and project management. He can be reached through the Internet via: SPECRD@Gulf.Net. **Career Steps:** Vice President, Spectrum R&D (1995–Present); Spectrum Systems, Inc.: Vice President of Manufacturing (1993–1995), Vice President of Operations (1989–1993), National Service Manager (1987–1989). **Associations & Accomplishments:** Air and Waste Management Association; Instrument Society of America. **Education:** Devry Technical Institute, 3–year A.E.E.T. (1993); Pensacola Junior College, 2 years attended in Pre–Engineering. **Personal:** Married to Kay M. in 1972. Three children: Suzanne, John, and Mike. Mr. McDonald enjoys boating and scuba diving.

Daniel R. Menudier
Controller
Intellicorp
1975 El Camino Real
Mountain View, CA 94041
(415) 965-5500
Fax: Please mail or call

7371

Business Information: Intellicorp, a publicly–traded business, is an international software development firm, designing and developing software objects to improve other software products. Established in 1983, Intellicorp currently employs 130 people. As Controller, Mr. Menudier is responsible for the management of all accounting and finance functions. **Career Steps:** Controller, Intellicorp (1993–Present); Assistant Controller, Smurfit France (1992–1993); Manager, Ernst & Young, Paris (1958–1991); Senior, Ernst & Young, San Francisco (1986–1988). **Associations & Accomplishments:** Chamber of Commerce in Paris. **Education:** California Polytechnic State University, B.S. in Economics (1983). **Personal:** Mr. Menudier enjoys snow skiing and sailing.

Frank L. Mighetto
President
Mighetto & Associates
1260 NE 69th Street
Seattle, WA 98115
(206) 525-1458
Fax: (206) 525-1458
EMAIL: See Below

7371

Business Information: Mighetto & Associates, established in 1988, is an international computer software development firm. With twelve years of experience in the information systems consulting field, Mr. Mighetto serves as President. He is responsible for the oversight of all operations, including consulting with major health care facilities and serving as the primary developer. Mr. Mighetto can also be reached through the Internet via: mighetto@eskimo.com **Career Steps:** President, Mighetto & Associates (1991–Present); Chair, Information Systems, City University (1989–1991); Consultant, Executive Consulting Group (1984–1987); Consultant, Arthur Andersen (1983–1984); Co–founded, CHEC Medical Centers (1982). **Associations & Accomplishments:** Washington Software Association; Diplomat, American College of Healthcare Executives; Institute for Certification of Computing Professionals; Published in "Wall Street Journal" and several other publications. **Education:** University of Washington, Masters (1983); University of California, Santa Barbara, B.A. (1978). **Personal:** Married to Lisa in 1981. Mr. Mighetto enjoys classical guitar, and classic car restoration.

John C. Mockus
Vice President of Marketing and Sales
QC Data, Inc.
777 Grant Street, Suite 500
Denver, CO 80203–3501
(303) 837-1444
Fax: (303) 220-5145

7371

Business Information: QC Data, Inc. is a builder of digital map databases for automated mapping/facilities management (AM/FM) computer systems. Projects have included working with major Telephone, Electric, and Gas Utilities around the world. As Vice President of Marketing and Sales, Mr. Mockus is responsible for the marketing and sales activities for all of the Corporation's companies worldwide. He may also be reached through the Internet via: JMOCKUS.AOL.COM **Career Steps:** Vice President of Marketing and Sales, QC Data, Inc. (1992–Present); Vice President/General Manager – USA, GeoVision (1987–1992); Senior Vice President/General Manager – USA, EASINET – Australia (1984–1987); Senior Vice President, Butler Computer Graphics (1978–1987). **Associations & Accomplishments:** Member, AM/FM International – served on AM/FM Executive Management Symposium Board; Board of Directors, two companies in Australia. **Education:** E.C.P.I., Associate's (1967); Attended numerous courses: Extensive Management/Executive Leadership Training, Strategic Selling, Finance for Executives. **Personal:** Married to Linda in 1972. Two children: Michael and Mandy. Mr. Mockus enjoys sports cars, street rods, electronics, and personal computers.

Blake G. Modersitzki
World Wide Channel Marketing Manager
Novell, Inc.
387 E. 1890 N.
Orem, UT 84057
(801) 861-5956
Fax: (801) 861-2717
EMAIL: See Below

7371

Business Information: Novell, Inc. is an international computer networking and service provider with locations in Utah and California. The Company designs, develops, and markets computer network software throughout the world. As World Wide Channel Marketing Manager, Mr. Modersitzki manages all channel marketing and programs worldwide for Novell's small networks business unit. He also oversees quarterly marketing promotions and determines venues for marketing of new products. Internet users can reach him via: bmockrs.tzki.@novell.com. **Career Steps:** Novell, Inc: Senior Marketing Manager, Small Business Unit (1996–Present), Channel Marketing and Programs Manager, Business Applications (1994–1996), International Product Marketing Manager (1993–1994); Distribution Sales Manager, Corel, Inc. (1996); Word Perfect: Channel Accounting Manager (1992–1993), Regional Sales Manager (1992), Advertising Analyst (1991–1992). **Associations & Accomplishments:** Who's Who Among Outstanding Students Award; Open Water Diver, Scuba School International; Economic History Thesis Finalist; Volunteer Leader, Boy Scouts of America; Volunteer, American's Freedom Festival. **Education:** Brigham Young University, Bachelor of Arts and Economics m(1992); Kellogg School of Management, Northwestern University, Communicating with the Japanese Business Wold; TAGS

Channel, Inc., TAGS Channel Marketing Training. **Personal:** Married to Sandy in 1989. Two children: McCall and Allyson. Mr. Modersitzki enjoys travel, sports, and outdoor activities.

Lea A. Moncier

Chief Financial Officer
Quick Pen International
384 Inverness Drive South, Suite 200
Englewood, CO 80112–5810
(303) 799–6500 Ext: 223
Fax: (303) 799–6547

7371

Business Information: Quick Pen International is a software development and consultancy, specializing in the sales and implementation of commercial software, primarily utilized in construction industry applications (i.e., CAD, Estimating, Project Management). A management accountant with over ten years expertise, Ms. Moncier serves as Chief Financial Officer, responsible for all financial and treasury operations. **Career Steps:** Chief Financial Officer, Quick Pen International (1989–Present); MIS Consultant and Staff Accountant, Holben, Boak, Cooper & Company CPA's (1985–1989); Accounting Manager, Thorsen & Company (1984–1985). **Associations & Accomplishments:** Board Member (1991–Present), Institute of Management Accountants. **Education:** University of Denver, M.B.A. (1988); Fresno State College, B.A. (1969). **Personal:** Married to Raymond M. in 1972. Ms. Moncier enjoys gourmet cooking.

Michele Morris

Director of Marketing
Antalys
1687 Cole Boulevard
Golden, CO 80401
(303) 274–3125
Fax: (303) 274–3030

7371

Business Information: Antalys specializes in software development and implementation for sales force operations. As Director of Marketing, Ms. Morris is responsible for all aspects of marketing for the Company, including telemarketing, research, materials, partnerships, and press relations. **Career Steps:** Director of Marketing, Antalys (1995–Present); IBM: Business Unit Executive (1992–1994), Marketing Manager (1987–1992), Marketing Representative (1981–1987). **Associations & Accomplishments:** Influence of Denver. **Education:** Bucknell University, B.A. in Biology and Political Science (1981). **Personal:** Married to Gregory W. in 1985. Three children: Christopher, Jonathan, and Jennifer. Ms. Morris enjoys skiing, golf, gardening, biking, cooking, and sewing.

Richard C. Perkinson

Director of Product Management
Liant Software
959 Concord Street
Framingham, MA 01701–4682
(508) 872–8700
Fax: (508) 626–2221
EMAIL: See Below

7371

Business Information: Liant Software develops applications for UNIX, Windows NT, and Windows '95 operating systems. As Director of Product Management, Mr. Perkinson is responsible for product specifications, release management, and marketing materials. Internet users can also reach him via: DickP@LIANT.COM **Career Steps:** Director of Product Management, Liant Software (1994–Present); Product Manager, Intersolv (1985–1994); Vice President, QED Information Sciences (1980–1985); DBA, TJ Maxx Corporation (1977–1980); Senior Program Analyst, John Hancock Mutual Life (1973–1977). **Associations & Accomplishments:** Author of "Data Analysis: The Key To Database Design." **Education:** Boston University: M.S. in Computer Science (1984), B.S. in Biology (1972). **Personal:** Married to Diane in 1991. Three children: David, Stephanie, and Abigail. Mr. Perkinson enjoys golf.

Deborah Susan Porter

Financial Analyst
Cambridge Technology Group
219 Vassar Street
Cambridge, MA 02139–4310
(617) 876–2338
Fax: Please mail or call
EMAIL: See Below

7371

Business Information: A national executive educator of technology, Cambridge Technology Group manufactures software and hardware to help new businesses set and meet all goals. As Financial Analyst, Deborah Porter works in conjunction with the Controller and Chief Financial Officer in analysts of revenue, gross product management, budgeting, financial statements, conducting yearly audits and maintaining the financial status of Cambridge. Internet users can reach her via: dporter@ctgroup.com. **Career Steps:** Financial Analyst, Cambridge Technology Group (1992–Present); Credit Analyst, Augat, Inc. (1991–1992). **Associations & Accomplishments:** United Nations Volunteers of America; Amnesty International. **Education:** New Hampshire College – Graduate School of Business, M.B.A. in progress; Bentley College, B.S. in Economics and Finance (1991). **Personal:** Ms. Porter enjoys running, classical music, museums, and modern art.

Carl E. Reid

President
NetTECH Systems Reid & Associates, Inc.
66 Romaine Avenue, Suite 7
Jersey City, NJ 07306
(201) 222–5390
Fax: (201) 222–5391

7371

Business Information: NetTECH Systems Reid & Associates, Inc. is a professional computer consulting firm, specializing in the design, installation and support of Novell Networks, Windows and Lotus Notes. As Founder and President, Mr. Reid spearheads all system designs and installations in a project manager capacity and acts as liaison between NetTECH and clients. **Career Steps:** President, NetTECH Systems Reid & Associates, Inc. (1991–Present); Adjunct Professor, Hudson County Community College (1994–Present); Manager, Computer Services, The Door (1990–1992). **Associations & Accomplishments:** American Seminar Leaders Association (ASLA) Certification; Gives seminars to schools & universities teaching them how to interview to market themselves. **Education:** Fordham University, B.S. in Computer Science. **Personal:** One child: Tiana K. Mr. Reid enjoys assisting people with resume preparation and job interview skills.

Judith G. Ribble, Ph.D.

Vice President of Education
Safeware, Inc.
9010 Ayrdale Crescent
Philadelphia, PA 19128
(215) 509–7513 (215) 487–0117
Fax: (215) 487–0117
EMAIL: See Below

7371

Business Information: Safeware, Inc. is a national provider of multimedia products for healthcare education. As Vice President of Education, Dr. Ribble provides strategic and tactical direction for multimedia educational products relating to certification requirements of healthcare professionals. She is responsible for the design of the CME screens for The Virtual Physician, a CD–ROM series whose first module prepares physicians and trauma teams for ACLS recertification. Responsible for the implementation of joint sponsorship with the American College of Emergency Physicians, she also initiates and maintains collaborative alliances for the education and training of allied emergency medical personnel and for the consumer marketplace. Internet user can reach her via: judyribb@aol.com. **Career Steps:** Vice President of Education, Safeware Inc. (1995–Present); Director, Continuing Education, Reuters Health Information Services, GeoMedica Networks, Lifetime Medical Television (1991–1995); Director, Department of Medical Education, American College of Physicians (1987–1991); Vice President, Professional Education, Arthritis Foundation (1984–1986); Associate Director, Office of Continuing Medical Education, Jefferson Medical College, Thomas Jefferson University (1983–1984); Director, Division of Continuing Mental Health Education, Research Assistant, Medical College of Pennsylvania (1979–1983); Adjunct Assistant Professor, Department of Psychiatry, Emory University School of Medicine; Assistant Professor (Psychology), Department of Psychiatry, Jefferson Medical College, Thomas Jefferson University; Medical College of Pennsylvania: Assistant Professor, Department of Psychiatry, Research

Instructor, Department of Community and Preventive Medicine. **Associations & Accomplishments:** Member, Board of Directors and Chair, External Relations Committee, Alliance for Continuing Medical Education; American Medical Inforrmatics Association; United States Distance Learning Association; Founding Member, Continuing Health Education Exchange Network; Union Institute Graduate School, Adjunct Faculty; Advisory Board, Medical Books for China International; National Task Force on CME Provider/Industry Collaboration; Center for Literacy, Tutor; Various Publications, Presentations and Publications. **Education:** The Medical College of Pennsylvania, Ph.D. in Social Sciences; Temple University, course work in Psychology and Education; University of Pennsylvania, B.A. with Honors in German, minors in Biology and French; Honors: Delta Phi Alpha, German Honor Society (Secretary); Pi Delta Phi, French Honor Society; Pi Sigma Alpha, Mortarboard; President, Women's Student Union; Vice President, Alpha Chi Omega. **Personal:** Married to Clark E. Bussey in 1994. Three children: Darrah, Glenn and Anna. Dr. Ribble enjoys collecting Chinese export porcelain and American quilts.

Victor L. Rice, Ph.D.

Chief Technology Officer
Simulation Sciences, Inc.
2950 North Loop West, Suite 830
Houston, TX 77092
(713) 683–1710
Fax: Please mail or call
EMAIL: See Below

7371

Business Information: Simulation Sciences is a leading provider of software and services to the process industry. Established in 1967, the Company employs over 250 people and serves over 500 customers worldwide. The Company's software is used at more than 400 universities to help educate chemical and petroleum engineers. Simulation Sciences is best known for it's open architecture and easy to use, standards–based graphical user interface. As Chief Technology Officer, Dr. Rice is responsible for developing programs for new and innovative software and services. Additional duties include operations, public relations, and apprising the board of directors on the Company's financial investments. **Career Steps:** Simulation Sciences, Inc: Chief Technology Officer (1996–Present), General Manager, ROM Division (1994–1996); Consulting Manager of Technology, Litwin Process Automation (1989–1994). **Associations & Accomplishments:** AICHE; ISA. **Education:** Oklahoma State University: Ph.D. in Chemical Engineering (1988), M.C.H.E. (1977), B.S. (1976). **Personal:** Married to Donna S. in 1974. Four children: Sarah, Adam, Haley, and Andrew. Dr. Rice enjoys gourmet cooking.

Erick Rivas

Vice President of the Clear Lake Lab
Platinum Technology, Inc.
17629 El Camino Real, Ms: 400
Houston, TX 77058
(713) 480–3233 Ext. 6020
Fax: (713) 480–6606
EMAIL: See Below

7371

Business Information: Platinum Technology, Inc. offers software solutions for professionals who are building and managing multi–tiered enterprise–wide software systems. Platinum acquired Protosoft, Inc. in 1995 and is currently the 9th fastest growing high–technology company in the U.S., employing over 3,000 people and located in over 50 locations worldwide. As Vice President of the Clear Lake Lab, Mr. Rivas oversees daily operations, serving as chief architect and providing product vision and strategic leadership. Internet users can reach him via: rivas@platinum.com. **Career Steps:** Vice President of the Clear Lake Lab, Platinum Technology, Inc. (1995–Present); Co–Founder/Vice President of Engineering, Protosoft, Inc. (1985–1995). **Associations & Accomplishments:** Speaker at conferences and seminars on object technology and component–based software development. OMG and EIA–CDIF Commitee; Chief Architect, Paradigm Plus software. **Education:** University of Houston, B.S. in Computer Science (1990). **Personal:** Mr. Rivas enjoys the internet, skiing and bicycling.

James W. Ruprecht

Director of World Wide Information Technology
Seagate Technology, Recording Head Operations
7801 Computer Avenue
Edina, MN 55435–5412
(612) 844–7801
Fax: (612) 844–8284
EMail: See Below

7371

Business Information: Seagate Technology manufactures data technology–oriented hardware and software; the principle product is hard disc drives. As Director of Information Technology for Seagate's worldwide Recording Head Operations, Mr. Ruprecht provides IT services within his division. **Career Steps:** Director of Information Technology, Seagate Technology (1993–Present); Director of Systems Services, Star Tribune Newspaper (1985–1993); Group Manager of Planning and Systems, Medtronic (1980–1985); IS Audit Supervisor, 3M (1974–1980). **Associations & Accomplishments:** Society for Information Management; Institute of Electronic and Electrical Engineers, Computer Chapter; Certified Information Systems Auditor, EDP Auditors Association; Security, Auditability, and Control, Stanford Research Institute, IBM and the Institute of Internal Auditors; Mounds Park Academy: Board of Directors, Executive Committee Vice Chair, Academic Committee Chair, Buildings and Grounds Committee, Parents Association Board Representative; Minnesota 100 Mentor Program; Venue Media Chief, International Special Olympics (1991); Venue Media Chief, U.S. Olympic Festival (1990); Chair, Cowles Media Corporation/Star Tribune United Way Campaign (1989–1990). **Education:** University of St. Thomas, B.S. (1974). **Personal:** Married to Barbara in 1976. Two children: Rebecca and Jessica. Mr. Ruprecht enjoys private piloting, reading, theater, and baseball.

Nancy J. Sauer
Director of Data and Distribution
Standard & Poor's Compustat
6138 East Hinsdale Court
Englewood, CO 80112
(303) 721–4410
Fax: (303) 721–4443
EMAIL: See Below

7371

Business Information: Standard & Poor's Compustat, affiliated with Standard & Poor's and owned by McGraw–Hill, provides financial information and software to prospective buyers. As Director of Data and Distribution, Ms. Sauer collects fundamental financial information, packages it into software, and sells to prospective clients. Internet users can reach her via: SAUERN@MGH.COM. **Career Steps:** Standard and Poor's Compustat: Director of Data and Distribution (1995–Present), Regional Sales Manager (1994–1995), Account Executive (1990–1994). **Associations & Accomplishments:** President, Virginia Tech Alumni Association. **Education:** College of William and Mary, MBA (1994); Virginia Tech, B.S. in Industrial Engineering and Operations Research (1984). **Personal:** Married to Ronald B. in 1994. Ms. Sauer enjoys skiing, swimming, travel, and tennis.

Ricardo A. Schaffner
Project Manager
Perceptron, Inc.
23855 Research Drive
Farmington Hills, MI 48335–2628
(810) 478–7710
Fax: (810) 478–7059
EMAIL: See Below

7371

Business Information: Perceptron Inc. is an international company providing vision systems for quality and process control in the automotive industry. Established in 1984, Perceptron Inc. has offices in Europe, Korea, and Japan. As Project Manager, Mr. Schaffner is responsible for installation, customer support, and development of software for data analysis and historical reporting. Internet users can reach him via: ricardo@perceptron.com **Career Steps:** Perceptron Inc.: Project Manager (1995–Present), Project Engineer (1994–1995); Software Engineer, Miami Systems (1993–1994). **Education:** Case Western University, Masters (1993); B.S. in Electrical Engineering. **Personal:** Mr. Schaffner enjoys swimming and car modeling.

Gregory A. Sherrill
• • • ━━━◉━━━ • • •
Vice President of Sales
Silicon Valley Research
300 Ferguson Drive, #300
Mountain View, CA 94043
(415) 254–4328
Fax: (415) 962–3001

7371

Business Information: Silicon Valley Research is a manufacturer of electronic design automation software that actually designs chips. Established in 1984, Silicon Valley Research reports annual revenue of $12 million and currently employs 60 people. With eleven years experience in computer technology sales and management, Mr. Sherrill joined Silicon Valley Research in 1992. Serving as Vice President of Sales, he is responsible for world–wide sales and marketing. **Career Steps:** Vice President of Sales, Silicon Valley Research (1992–Present); Sun Micro Systems: General Man-

ager (1990–1992), Director of Sales (1988–1990), Field Regional Director (1984–1988). **Education:** University of California – Los Angeles, MBA (1973); Whittier College, B.A.; Orange Coast College, A.A. **Personal:** Married to Teressa Fay in 1987. Two children: Ethan and Ashley.

Mrs. Donna J. Stokes
Director of Quality Assurance
EDR Technologies Inc.
4640 South Arville, Suite G
Las Vegas, NV 89103
(702) 253–1120
Fax: (702) 253–1145

7371

Business Information: EDR Technologies Inc. specializes in software research and development. Established in 1989, the Company currently employs 20 people. As Director of Quality Assurance, Mrs. Stokes is responsible for organizing software testing, verifying data and software maintenance, as well as providing assistance and technical support to clientele. **Career Steps:** Director of Quality Assurance, EDR Technologies Inc. (1994–Present); Executive Assistant, Westwood Studios (1991–1993); Lab Assistant, University of Nevada, Las Vegas (1989–1990); Assistant Manager, Cloth World, Inc. (1989). **Associations & Accomplishments:** Member, (NAFE) National Association of Female Executives; Member, Aircraft Owners & Pilots Association. **Education:** University of Nevada, Las Vegas, B.S. (1990). **Personal:** Married to Bill in 1994.

Cynthia M. Wagner
Manager of Employee Benefits
Computer Data Systems, Inc.
1 Curie Drive
Rockville, MD 20850
(301) 921–7000
Fax: (301) 921–0795

7371

Business Information: Computer Data Systems, Inc. provides innovative applications of information technology to enhance business processes which enable the Company's customers to realize cost efficiencies, better service, and introduce new capabilities. As Manager of Employee Benefits, Ms. Wagner is responsible for management, planning, and administration of corporate 401(K) retirement and benefits plans and finances. **Career Steps:** Benefits Manager, Computer Data Systems, Inc. (1993–Present); Division Manger – Benefits and Human Resources, Coca–Cola Enterprises, Inc. (1988–1992); Human Resources Administrator/ Benefits Specialist, Thomson – Car Medical Corporation (1988–1992). **Associations & Accomplishments:** Maryland Health Care Coalition; International Benefits Foundation; Washington Technical Personnel Forum. **Education:** Wharton School of Business, CEBS Program; Catonsville Community College, Human Resources Coursework; Pursuing Certification – Employee Benefits Specialist. **Personal:** Married to Frank E. Jr. in 1984. Two children: Danielle Lauren and Paige Larissa. Ms. Wagner enjoys interior decorating, crafts, landscaping, and gardening.

Zvi I. Weiss
Senior Advisory Analyst
ADP/BISG
2 Journal Square
Jersey City, NJ 07306
(201) 714–8589
Fax: (201) 714–8004
EMail: See Below

7371

Business Information: International in scope, ADP–BISG designs, codes, and markets back–office and front–office computer services for brokerage firms. As a Senior Advisory Analyst, Mr. Weiss supports and mentors members of the systems and programming department. Similarly, he develops standards to be followed within that department of the Firm. He handles desktop troubleshooting, customizes applications for various colleagues within the Department, and does product evaluations. Internet users can reach him via: WeissZ@JSQstrat.bis.adp.com. **Career Steps:** Senior Advisory Analyst, ADP/BISG (1984–Present); Advisory Programmer, ETS (1980–1984); Member of Technical Staff, Bell Telephone Laboratories (1974–1980). **Associations & Accomplishments:** Association of Orthodox Jewish Scientists; Mensa. **Education:** New York University, M.S. (1974); Yeshiva College, B.S. cum laude (1971). **Personal:** Married to Devorah in 1975. Three children: Netanel, Avital, and Baruch J. Mr. Weiss enjoys reading, relaxing, and spending time with his family.

Njai Wong
Director of Product Development
Empress Software Inc.
3100 Steeles Avenue East
Markham, Ontario L3R 8T3
(905) 513–8888
Fax: (905) 513–1668
e–mail: See Below

7371

Business Information: Empress Software Inc. develops and markets relational database management systems. Originally specializing in systems for scientific engineers, the Company has expanded to provide a database for the Internet as well. Headquartered in Ontario, Canada, the Company is international in scope, with a majority of sales being in North America and Japan. As Director of Product Development, Ms. Wong is responsible for overseeing and directing new product development, coordinating efforts with the sales team. She also manages product marketing and product support. She can be reached through e–mail: njai@empress.com. **Career Steps:** Empress Software Inc.: Director of Product Development (1990–Present), Manager of Product Development (1986–1990). **Associations & Accomplishments:** Harvard Business School Alumnus. **Education:** University of Toronto, B.Sc. in Computer Science (1979). **Personal:** Married to John Kornatowski in 1981. Two children: Alexander and Sean. Ms. Wong enjoys reading, music, ballet, and jazz.

Chris E. Zahlmann
• • • ━━━◉━━━ • • •
Vice President of Client Services
Summit Information Systems
P.O. Box 3003
Corvallis, OR 97339
(800) 937–7500
Fax: (503) 758–9211

7371

Business Information: Summit Information Systems, a subsidiary of Fiserv, is a national data processing firm, providing development, marketing, implementation, and support of turn–key software packages for credit unions and other financial institutions. Future plans include improving support mechanisms, opening up a bulletin board system, and providing more electronic means for software support. With over eleven years experience in financial institutions, Mr. Zahlmann joined Summit in 1992. Serving as Vice President of Client Services, he is responsible for the management and oversight of customer service areas and client relationships. **Career Steps:** Vice President of Client Services, Summit Information Systems (1992–Present); Vice President of Operations, Clark County Credit Union (1990–1992); Controller, FAA Employees Credit Union (1984–1990). **Associations & Accomplishments:** Boy Scouts; Little League; Soccer; Speaks at annual conferences and audit seminars using their software packaging. **Education:** Brigham Young University, B.S. (1977). **Personal:** Married to Dolores in 1975. Eight children: Chris, Scott, Robin, Renee, Kari, Todd, Trevor, and Kymberlee. Mr. Zahlmann enjoys golf, church activities, and youth sports.

M. Susan Zwickel
Vice President
Computron Software, Inc.
301 State Route 17
Rutherford, NJ 07070
(201) 935–3400
Fax: (201) 939–6955
EMail: See Below

7371

Business Information: Computron Software, Inc. specializes in the development and sales of software. As Vice President, Ms. Zwickel is responsible for sale operations and corporate contracts worldwide. Internet users can reach her via: szwickel@ctronsoft.com. **Career Steps:** Vice President, Computron Software, Inc. (1994–Present); Director, Information Builders, Inc. (1991–1994); Manager, Timiplex, Inc. (1987–1991). **Associations & Accomplishments:** Executive Women of New Jersey; American Management Association; Contract Management Branch of American Bar Association. **Personal:** Married to Jay in 1967. Three children: Alan, Erica, and Richard. Ms. Zwickel enjoys tennis, gardening, and gourmet cooking.

Mr. Eugen M. Bacic
President and Chief Executive Officer
Texar Software Corporation
56 Castlethorpe Crescent
Nepean, Ontario K2G 5R1
(613) 724–9577
Fax: (613) 723–0603

7372

Business Information: Texar Software Corporation develops software packages for a variety of computer systems. As

President and Chief Exective Officer, Mr. Bacic is responsible for all aspects of Company operations, including designing and overseeing the development of the software packages. Established in 1994, Texar Software Corporation employs 2 people. **Career Steps:** President and Chief Exective Officer, Texar Software Corporation (1994–Present); Senior Information Security Research Scientist, Communications Security Establishment, Government of Canada (1987–1994); Senior Analyst, Carleton University (1985–1987); AI Researcher, BNR (1984). **Associations & Accomplishments:** Chief Architect of the Canadian Trusted Computer Product Evaluation Criteria; Member, Institute of Electronics and Electrical Engineers; Member, Institute of Electronics and Electrical Engineers – Computer Society; Member, ACM. **Education:** Carleton University, Master of Computer Science candidate (1995); Carleton University, Bachelor of Computer Science (1984), Honours. **Personal:** Married to Jagoda in 1987. Two children: Ariana and Goran. Mr. Bacic enjoys reading, computers, and music.

Rowena Cheng

Vice President
BIDM Corporation
241 West 17th Street
New York, NY 10011
(212) 620–5847
Fax: (212) 620–5845

7372

Business Information: BIDM Corporation is a certified IBM distributor specializing in software packages for the shipping and cargo transport industries. International in scope, the Corporation has offices in New York, Dubai, Delhi, and Hong Kong, and assists clients with customized system design and implementation. Plans for the future include expansion into areas such as placement services, Electronic Data Interchange (EDI), and a certified service bureau for electronic customer filing. Established in 1987, the Corporation employs 50 people worldwide, and has an estimated annual revenue of $1.7 million. As Vice President, Ms. Cheng oversees daily operation of the New York headquarters. She is responsible for customer relations, coordination with other branch offices around the world, and technical development within the Corporation. **Career Steps:** Vice President, BIDM Corporation (1986–Present); Project Manager, Procom Leasing and Management (1981–1986). **Education:** State University of New York, Albany, B.S. (1980). **Personal:** Married to Dr. Lap Yan Cheng in 1983. Two children: Lorraine and Vivian.

Mr. Andrew R. Cohen

Senior Director of Development
Micrografx, Inc.
1303 Arapaho Road
Richardson, TX 75081
(214) 994–6086
Fax: (214) 994–6475

7372

Business Information: Micrografx, Inc. is an independent software vendor (ISV) of Windows and Macintosh software products, especially graphics applications. Three major areas of development are business applications, technical engineering, and the "at home market" (education and entertainment). Products are distributed to Europe, Japan, Canada, and Australia. As Senior Director of Development, Mr. Cohen directs software development activities. Established in 1982, Micrografx employs a staff of 305 and reports annual revenue of $65 million. **Career Steps:** Senior Director of Development, Micrografx, Inc. (1992–Present); Manager, Systems Development, American Airlines (1985–1992); Staff Engineer, InteCom Inc. (1984–1985). **Associations & Accomplishments:** President, International Sybase Users Group; B'nai B'rith International; Board Member, B'nai B'rith Senior Citizens Council; Long Horn Council for the Boy Scouts; Columnist for Data Base Monthly; Distinguished Service Award, Micrografx; Engineering Excellence Award, General Dynamics. **Education:** University of Central Florida, Candidate for B.S. in Computer Science; Seminole Community College, A.S.

Mr. Paul Covelo

Vice President
JD Edwards & Company
8055 East Tufts Avenue
Denver, CO 80237
(303) 488–4875
Fax: (303) 488–4696

7372

Business Information: JD Edwards & Company is one of the leading manufacturers and distributors of computer software serving the electric and construction industry. Established in 1977, JD Edwards and Company currently employs 1,500 individuals. As Vice President, Mr. Covelo is responsible for international growth and market strategies. **Career Steps:** JD Edwards & Company: Vice President and General Manager – Latin America; Manager – Newport Beach (1988–Present). **Education:** Loyola Maymount, B.A. (1979). **Personal:** Married to Laurie in 1988. Two children: Stephen and Kevin.

Brad Norman Craig

Vice President of Business and Market Development
Forte Technologies, Inc.
2615 West Henrietta Road
Rochester, NY 14623
(716) 427–8595
Fax: (716) 292–6353
EMAIL: See Below

7372

Business Information: Forte Technologies, Inc. manufactures virtual reality hardware and software, sound board chips, and motion platforms. As Vice President of Business and Market Development, Mr. Craig is responsible for business and product development, clientele maintenance, and Corporate leadership. Internet users can reach him via: CRAIG0126@aol.com **Career Steps:** Vice President of Business and Market Development, Forte Technologies, Inc. (1995–Present); Director of Market and Business Development, Gravis (1991–1995); Manager of Consumer Products Division, Ingram Micro (1986–1991). **Associations & Accomplishments:** Software Publishers Association; Published in: PC Gamer, PC Review, Retail Week, PC Format. **Education:** Georgian College, B.A. in Marketing; Humber College, Advanced Marketing Studies. **Personal:** Mr. Craig enjoys golf, fishing, and baseball.

Patricia Day Stein

Vice President, Editor–in–Chief, and Chief Financial Officer
Writepro Corporation
43 South Highland Avenue
Ossining, NY 10562–5226
(914) 762–1255
Fax: (914) 762–5871
EMAIL: See Below

7372

Business Information: Writepro Corporation is an international computer software publishing company, providing creative writing software programs. Trademark products include: WritePro — for business creative writing, and FictionMaster — for private individual needs. One of the founders of the Company in 1989, Ms. Day Stein serves as Vice President, Editor–in–Chief, and Chief Financial Officer. She is responsible for editing programs, writing basic texts, and managing all finances on behalf of the Company. Internet users can reach Patricia via: rightpro@pipeline.com **Career Steps:** Vice President, Editor–in–Chief, and Chief Financial Officer, Writepro Corporation (1989–Present); Vice President, Stein and Day, Inc. (1962–1987); Vice President, Mid–Century Book Society (1959–1962). **Education:** Columbia University, Post–Graduate Work (1962); State University of Iowa, M.A.; Barnard College, B.A. **Personal:** Three children: Elizabeth and David Day Stein, and Robert Bruce Bennett.

Daniel A. Derin

Vice President
Caleo Software, Inc.
5255 Triangle Parkway, Suite 150
Norcross, GA 30092
(404) 453–9680 Ext.327
Fax: (404) 453–9686
E–mail: See below

7372

Business Information: Caleo Software, Inc. specializes in the manufacture of computer software, enabling computers and telephones to share information. The focus is on Collaborative communications which allow teams and work groups to better communicate with each other. With the advent of Telecommuting, remote communications will change and challenge the way people do business today. By enhancing communication with Caleo tools, people can achieve results faster without compromising inclusion of key people. This translates to a competitive advantage for customers. Established in 1990, Caleo Software currently employs 40 people. As Vice President, Mr. Derin is responsible for the oversight of all sales, marketing and operations. Mr. Derin can also be reached through the Internet as follows: dand@caleo.com **Career Steps:** Vice President, Caleo Software, Inc. (1995–Present); Regional Sales Manager, S2 Systems, Inc. (1992–1995); Account Executive, Dun & Bradstreet Software (1989–1992). **Associations & Accomplishments:** Vice President of the Board of Directors, Unity North Atlanta. **Education:** Wayne State University, B.S. in Business Administration, major in management and marketing with honors (1980), Deans list. **Personal:** Married to Pamela in 1983. Two children: Ashley and Austin. Mr. Derin enjoys tennis, boating, biking, and attending concerts and the theatre.

JETFORM®

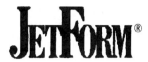

Bradford C. DuPont

Director of Sales
Jetform Corporation
894 White Point Boulevard
James Island, SC 29412
(803) 406–1759
Fax: (803) 406–1760

7372

Business Information: Jetform manufactures electronic form software used to streamline business procedures at Fortune 1000 companies. Mr. DuPont is responsible for the managing and training senior sales executives and systems engineers, as well as vendor relations, distribution, developing product promotions and following emerging technology. Mr. DuPont and his team are responsible for maintaining a 130% annual growth rate in product and consulting services business. Internet users can reach him via: bdupont@jetform.com. **Career Steps:** Director of Sales, Jetform (1991–Present); Director of Sales, NBI, Inc. (1988–1991); Director of Inside Sales, Alloy Computer Products (1986–1988); Regional Sales Manager, MicroAmerica, Inc. (1980–1986). **Associations & Accomplishments:** Harvard Business School; American Management Association; EMA; BFMA. **Education:** Pennsylvania State University, M.B.A. (1990); University of Massachusetts, B.S. **Personal:** Married to Mary in 1981. One child: Alexis Jeanne. Mr. DuPont enjoys skiing, fishing, and travel.

Paul K. Erickson

Vice President
Sterling Wentworth Corporation
57 West 200 South, Suite 500
Salt Lake City, UT 84101
(801) 355–9777
Fax: (801) 355–9792

7372

Business Information: Sterling Wentworth Corporation is the market leader in the design, development, and marketing of rule–based sales software for the financial services industry (i.e., banks, insurance companies, brokerage firms). Joining Sterling Wentworth Corporation as a Project Manager in 1994, Mr. Erickson was promoted to Vice President in 1995. Mr. Erickson is currently responsible for the design and development of computer software and management of multiple software development projects. **Career Steps:** Sterling Wentworth Corporation: Vice President (1995–Present), Project Manager (1994–1995); Client Representative, IBM (1991–1994); Financial Executive, Multiserve Corporation (1987–1990); Financial Consultant, Brock and Associates (1986–1987). **Associations & Accomplishments:** The Church of Jesus Christ of Latter Day Saints, Honolulu, Hawaii: Voluntary Representative (1983–1984), President of a Church Men's Organization (1994–Present); Software Development Project highlighted in December 4, 1995 issue of Forbes magazine. **Education:** Brigham Young University, B.S. in Accounting (1990). **Personal:** Married to Stephanie in 1984. Four children: Nicole, Matthew, Melissa and Tiffany. Mr. Erickson enjoys golf, tennis, basketball, and snow skiing.

Denise M. Fields

Vice President, Sales and Marketing
Research Systems, Inc.
2995 Wilderness Place
Boulder, CO 80301
(303) 413–3948
Fax: (303) 786–9909
EMAIL: See Below

7372

Business Information: Research Systems, Inc. is an international, privately owned software company specializing in technology software to earth scientists, engineers, and research professionals. The Company has two locations and 10 distributors. As Vice President, Sales and Marketing, Ms. Fields is responsible for the development of new markets and products, public relations issues, and establishing contacts with prospective customers. Internet users can reach her via: Denisef@rsinc.com. **Career Steps:** Vice President, Sales and Marketing, Research Systems, Inc. (1993–Present); Vice President, Marketing, Altia, Inc. (1993–1994); Director of Sales, Visual Numerics, Inc. (1990–1993); Director of Marketing, Lotus Development Corporation (1986–1990). **Education:** Northeastern University, M.B.A. (1981); Boston College, B.S. in Business (1979). **Personal:** Ms. Fields enjoys mountain hiking, bicycling, and running.

David K. Garver
Executive Vice President
Genelco
P.O. Box 14490
St. Louis, MO 63178
(314) 525–5273
Fax: (314) 525–5892

7372

Business Information: Genelco is an international provider of insurance–related software products and third–party outsourcing services for life, medical, annuity, and pension plans. Genelco has six locations and serves clientele in 15 countries. Joining Genelco as Vice President of Sales and Marketing following the completion of his master's degree in 1989, David Garver was appointed as Executive Vice President in 1995. He is responsible for the direction and management of all activities of two divisions: Life Administration and Medical TPA Self–Funded Medical Plans. **Career Steps:** Genelco: Executive Vice President (1995–Present), Vice President of TPA Services (1992–1995), Vice President of Sales & Marketing (1989–1992). **Associations & Accomplishments:** Vice President, St. Louis FLMI Society; Board Member, Literary Service Center of Greater St. Louis; Consultant, Management Assistant Center, United Way of Greater St. Louis; Former President, Galveston, Texas Jaycees; Outstanding Young Men of America (1981, 1986); Author of articles on health care cost outsourcing and government involvement in health care; Public speaking and conducting workshops and seminars. **Education:** University of Arkansas at Little Rock, M.B.A. (1988); Harding University, B.B.A. **Personal:** Married to Lori in 1993. Mr. Garver enjoys reading, hunting, and fishing.

Kevin D. Graham, Ph.D.
Director of Project and Product Development
Medication Management Systems
12910 Automobile Boulevard
Clearwater, FL 34622
(813) 573–7647
Fax: (813) 573–1677

7372

Business Information: Medication Management Systems is a developer of medical software for nursing and pharmaceutical systems, such as automated medical dispensing, performance pharmacy and data management. Joining Medication Management Systems as Director of Project and Product Development in 1992, Dr. Graham is responsible for directing projects and program developments, new products programs, and systems network implementation. **Career Steps:** Director of Project and Product Development, Medication Management Systems (1992–Present); Patient Centering Coordinator, Tampa General Hospital (1980–1992). **Associations & Accomplishments:** Florida Society of Hospital Pharmacy Technicians; Men's Senior Baseball League. **Education:** University of South Carolina, Ph.D. (1979); Attended: Southern Connecticut State California, St. Leo's College. **Personal:** Married to Teresa in 1994. One child: Candice. Dr. Graham enjoys playing baseball.

Michael Hayes
Director, Worldwide Marketing, Lotus Services Group
Lotus Development Corporation
55 Cambridge Parkway
Cambridge, MA 02142
(617) 693–8773
Fax: (617) 693–8617
EMAIL: See Below

7372

Business Information: Lotus Development, international in scope, is a manufacturer and seller of information technology software, including Lotus Notes, Lotus Smartsuite, and CC: Mail. Recently, the Company has merged with IBM. As Director, Mr. Hayes is responsible for marketing Lotus support around the world. Internet users can reach him via: Michael_Hayes@CRD. Lotus.com **Career Steps:** Director, Lotus Development (1994–Present); Manager of Marketing, Digital Equipment Corporation (1981–1994); Manager of Distribution, Ford Motor Company (1978–1981). **Associations & Accomplishments:** Association for Service Management International; American Management Association; Commissioner, Industrial Development Commission, Town of Hopedale, MA; Boston Fellows The Partnership. **Education:** University of Lavern, B.A. (1977). **Personal:** Married to Diana L. in 1970. Three children: Michelle Lynn, Denise Nicole, and Michael Lawrence. Mr. Hayes enjoys long distance running, reading and golf.

Randal Hoff
Vice President of United States Operations
FairCom Corporation
4006 W. Broadway
Columbia, MO 65203
(573) 445–6833 Ext. 105
Fax: (573) 445–9698
E MAIL: See Below

7372

Business Information: FairCom Corporation, established in 1979, is a software manufacturer and distributor of cross–platform application development tools. Products include B+tree Indexed Data Access (1980), C–tree File handler (1984), R–tree Report Generator (1987), D–tree Development Toolbox (1988), and the first portable FairCom database server (1987). In 1992, the second generation FairCom Server, built on a multi–threaded kernel allowing higher data concurrency while insuring a system can grow and change as needed, was released. FairCom has continued to focus on technology, and the results are evident with faster throughput and more flexibility. The Company now has a presence in over 100 countries worldwide with corporate offices in the United States, Europe, Japan, and Brazil. Some of the major corporate users of FairCom products include Alcatel, Auto–Soft Corporation, Computer Associates International, Federal Express, The Follett Software Company, McGraw–Hill School Systems, and Winnebago Software Company. As Vice President of United States (U.S.) Operations, Mr. Hoff oversees the daily operations and international communications for the U.S. operations. He is responsible for all legal and business contracts, developing and implementing marketing strategies and techniques for new and existing products, and strategic planning for the future. Internet users can reach him via: faircom@faircom.com. **Career Steps:** FairCom Corporation: Vice President of U.S. Operations (1996–Present), Director of Technical Operations (1993–1996). **Associations & Accomplishments:** Institute of Electronics and Electrical Engineers; Boy Scouts of America, Eagle Scout. Mr. Hoff was published in Dr. Dobbs' Journal in 1994. **Education:** University of Missouri, B.S. Electrical Engineering and B.S. Computer Engineering (1991). **Personal:** Married to Maryane in 1990. Mr. Hoff enjoys hiking, mountain biking, and other outdoor activities.

Douglas M. Krebs
Regional Vice President
Cerver Corporation
2800 Rock Creek Parkway
Kansas City, MO 64117
(816) 221–1024 Ext. 2142
Fax: (916) 221–0539

7372

Business Information: Cerver Corporation is a developer and service provider of computer software for the health care industry. Services include developing software, implementing, consulting, on–going reports and support. A national corporation with international business in Europe, United Kingdom, Australia, and Saudi Arabia (9%), Cerner Corporation has a 91% national business with a client base consisting of large multiple health systems (i.e., hospitals, outpatient care, clinics, HMOs, etc.). As Regional Vice President, Mr. Krebs serves as the General Manager of the South East United States operations, which covers seven states and over 100 current clients. In his region, he oversees the activities of 82 employees throughout the region, as well as directing the Profit Center and all other activities, with the exception of product development. He also directs marketing, client relations, and client satisfaction. **Career Steps:** Regional Vice President, Cerver Corporation (1994–Present); IBM Corporation – U.S.: Director Distribution Strategy (1992–1994), U.S. Manager Product Distribution (1991–1992), Branch Manager – Cincinnati Office (1989–1991). **Associations & Accomplishments:** Past Board Member, Council of Growing Companies, Washington, D.C.; Harvard University Alumni Association; Illinois State University Alumni Association; Healthcare Industry Management Systems Society; Soup Kitchen Volunteer; Publisher of trade publications, interviews, quotes, and representing IBM during his employment. **Education:** Harvard University Business School, P.M.D. (1991); Illinois State University, B.S. (1979). **Personal:** Married to Susan H. in 1983. Two children: Natalie and Daniel. Mr. Krebs enjoys golfing, jogging, bicycling, music and reading.

Konstantin V. Malkov, Ph.D.
Technical Director
MTI/PWI – Planning Works Institute
6663 Huntley Road, Suite R & S
Columbus, OH 43229
(614) 436–5300
Fax: (614) 436–7108

7372

Business Information: MTI/PWI – Planning Works Institute is a high–tech software development and scientific research facility. Established in 1991, the organization reports annual revenue of $2 million and currently employs 12 people. As Technical Director, Mr. Malkov is responsible for all aspects of projects management and research. **Career Steps:** Technical Director, MTI/PWI – Planning Works Institute (1991–Present); Professor of Applied Mathematics, Physics and Computer Science, Moscow State University (1990–1991); Researcher, Moscow State University (1986–1990). **Associations & Accomplishments:** Who's Who in the World; International Biographic Center, England; International Pen Research Committee. **Education:** Moscow State University, Ph.D. (1986). **Personal:** Married to Olga V. Pushkin in 1994. One child: Dennis. Mr. Malkov enjoys music and piano.

David C. Mello
Vice President
DNS Worldwide
6 New England Executive Park
Burlington, MA 01803
(617) 272–4252 Ext. 4411
Fax: (617) 272–5820
E/M: USNBPB89@IBMMAIL.com

7372

Business Information: DNS Worldwide is an international software development company specializing in – EDI– Edge – for electronic data interchanges. The Company markets products through direct and distributor sales. As Vice President of Operations and Administration, Mr. Mello is responsible for the management of all operations and administration of the Company. His responsibilities include overseeing, directing, and coordinating all sales, production development, technical support, education, production & administration departments, in addition to strategic planning. **Career Steps:** DNS Worldwide: Vice President of Operations and Administration (1995–Present), Vice President of Customer Services (1992–1995), Director of Technical Services (1988–1992). **Associations & Accomplishments:** Published article in "E.D.I. World" magazine regarding "Electronic Data Interchange (EDI)" (1993). **Education:** Bentley College, B.S. in Computer Information Systems (1985). **Personal:** Mr. Mello enjoys physical training and spending time with his girlfriend.

Natalie A. Nutter

Major Account Manager
Rasnacorp
3310 Miriam Drive
Emmaus, PA 18049
(610) 398–3138
Fax: (610) 965–7131

7372

Business Information: Rasnacorp specializes in mechanical computer–aided engineering software for the mechanical design automation industry. Joining Rasnacorp as Eastern Regional Account Manager in 1992, Ms. Nutter was appointed as Major Account Manager in 1995. She is responsible for managing all activities for AT&T worldwide. **Career Steps:** Rasnacorp: Major Account Manager (1995–Present), Eastern Region Manager (1993–1995), Eastern Region Account Manager (1992–1939); Account Manager, SDRC (1990–1992). **Associations & Accomplishments:** American Society of Mechanical Engineering. **Education:** Purdue University, B.S. in Mechanical Engineering (1983).

Borra R.K. Pavan Kumar
Senior Systems Engineer
WIPRO Systems
333 Cobalt Way, Ste 107
Sunnyvale, CA 94086
(617) 760–3046
Fax: (617) 760–3850
E/M: Pavan_Kumar@Putnami

7372

Business Information: WIPRO Systems is a software developer, maintenance and support company offering specialized services worldwide. Established in 1984, the Company's headquarters are located in Sunnyvale California. As a Senior Systems Engineer, Mr. Pavar Kumar is responsible for all aspects of design, development and support for application software. Working as a Consultant for Putnam Investments, Franklin, his long term goal is to attain a unique position in his Company and help the Company to achieve higher standards. **Career Steps:** WIPRO Systems – Sunnyvale, CA: Senior Systems Engineer (1996–Present), Systems Engineer (1994–1996). **Associations & Accomplishments:** Mathematics Olympiao Association, A.P. India; Engineers – Institute of Engineers, India; National Geographic Association; Harvard Business Association. **Education:** R.E.C. – Warangal, India, Bachelor's in Technology (1994); Obtained Gold Medal for securing university first in Electronics and Communications Engineering. **Personal:** Mr. Pavan Kumar enjoys reading technical and business magazines and cricket.

INTEGRATED SUPPLY
CHAIN MANAGEMENT

Raj Ponnuswamy

Managing Partner
Shamrock Computer Resources
800 36th Avenue
Moline, IL 61265–7159
(309) 762–7626
Fax: (309) 762–9542
EMAIL: See Below

7372

Business Information: Shamrock Computer Resources is a software development and systems integration firm with five branches in seven different states in the Midwest. The Company also helps with the post support, training, and contract services. As Managing Partner, Mr. Ponnuswamy is responsible for service delivery and technology. Internet users can reach him via: RAJP@SRock.com. **Career Steps:** Managing Partner, Shamrock Computer Resources (1990–Present); Systems Engineer, IBM (1983–1990). **Associations & Accomplishments:** DPMA; Institute of Electronic and Electrical Engineers. **Education:** University of Iowa, M.B.A. (1982); University of Madras, B.S. (1979); Coe College, B.A. (1980). **Personal:** Married to Akila in 1985. Two children: Naveen and Josh. Mr. Ponnuswamy enjoys tennis and reading.

Mr. Gary Quinn

Senior Vice President
Computer Associates International, Inc.
One Computer Associates Plaza
Islandia, NY 11788–7000
(516) 342–2484
Fax: (516) 342–6864

7372

Business Information: Computer Associates International, Inc., the second largest integrated software developer in the world, develops, licenses and supports more than 300 integrated products. Products include: systems and database management, application development, financial and manufacturing applications and consumer solutions. CA application development and database management tools offer software clients worry–free migration to client/server computing, including creation of entirely new client/server systems; CA systems management solutions provide integrated and secure administration of complex client/server systems; CA full–function business applications simplify customization to meet the special needs of individual businesses. This successful strategy is based on adherence to a unique software blueprint, CA90s : Computing Architecture For The 90s. Through CA90s, CA developers create modular software designed to be continually and consistently improved. As Senior Vice President, Mr. Quinn is responsible for the global marketing of all Computer Associates International, Inc. (CA) software solutions. Mr. Quinn joined CA in 1985 as an MVS Systems Programmer. Prior to his current position, he served in sales, technical and management capacities including: sales representative, regional technical manager, technical director, vice president – professional services and vice president research and development. With his experience encompassing many critical aspects of the corporation, Quinn serves as a barometer for CA's position in the software arena. It is this expertise that defines him as an industry catalyst propelling CA's marketing strategies well into the next decade. Established in 1976, Computer Associates International, Inc. employs over 8,000 people corporate wide and has annual gross revenue in excess of $2.1 billion. Attuned to client needs at all levels, CA supports over 300 user groups worldwide, offers extensive conference programs for both technicians and executives, and remains in constant touch with specialized client councils. **Career Steps:** Senior Vice President, Computer Associates International, Inc. (1994–Present); Vice President Research and Development, Computer Associates (1992–1994); MVS Systems Programmer, Computer Associates International (1985–1992). **Education:** Hofstra University, B.S. in Computer Science (1983).

Murrali Rangarajan

President and Chief Operating Officer
Logistix
48021 Warm Sprrings Boulevard
Fremont, CA 94539–7497
(510) 498–7010
Fax: (510) 438–9486
EMAIL: See Below

7372

Business Information: Logistix, the world's largest independent turnkey software manufacturer, provides software manufacturing and outsourcing services for high–technology companies. An integrated supply chain management firm providing a global network of OPS Centers, Logistix provides consulting, project management, supply base management, hardware configuration, printing, disk duplication, CD–ROM replication, Microsoft Authorized Replication, localization, packaging, fulfillment and distribution, third–party licensing and royalty management, telemarketing, telesales, and complete call center services. In November 1995, Logistix and Hewlett–Packard announced a strategic outsourcing partnership, where Logistix will provide all warehousing, fulfillment and distribution services to Hewlett–Packard's Software & Information Delivery Operation (SIDO). Joining Logistix in 1993, Mr. Rangarajan has served in several key business management positions. Appointed as President and Chief Operating Officer in October of 1995, he has maintained responsibility for the Company's P&L management, operations, and business planning. He has been instrumental in Logistix growing its services base broadening to 12 worldwide locations and has seen significant revenue growth, achieving annual growth over the last four years of nearly 500% (1995 run rate revenue reported over $350 million). Internet users can reach him via: MURALI@LGX.LOGISTIX.com **Career Steps:** Logistix: President and Chief Operating Officer (1995–Present), Served Several Key Business Management Positions (1993–1995); West Coast Materials Manager, Digital Equipment Corporation; Corporate Inventory Manager, Ford Motor Company – Europe. **Associations & Accomplishments:** SMA; IITMNAAI; SIPA. **Education:** University of California – Los Angeles, M.B.A.; Arizona State University, M.S. in Engineering; Indian Institute of Technology – Madras India, B.S. in Engineering. **Personal:** Mr. Rangarajan enjoys classical music, tennis, basketball, and spending time with his daughters.

John Reina

Director of Client Support
SCT Corporation
3000 Ridge Road East
Rochester, NY 14622
(716) 467–7740
Fax: (716) 467–8046
EMAIL: See Below

7372

Business Information: SCT Corporation is a manufacturer of administrative software products for colleges and universities, providing information technology outsourcing for higher education and local government jurisdictions. Joining SCT Corporation in 1982, Mr. Reina was appointed as Director of Client Support in 1995. He is responsible for the day–to–day operations of the Support Services Department in the Rochester and San Diego offices, offering technical help desk–type activities. Internet users can reach him via: JREINA@SCTCORP.com. **Career Steps:** SCT Corporation: Director of Client Support (1995–Present), Senior Manager, Client Support (1987–1995); Teacher of Emotionally Disturbed Children, BOCES #1, Monroe County (1971–1978). **Associations & Accomplishments:** Director at Large, Association of Quality and Participation; Monroe County – Perinton Democratic Committee; Who's Who Among Students in American Colleges and Universities (1971). **Education:** Nazareth College of Rochester, M.S. in Education (1975); St. John Fisher College, B.A. in Math (1971). **Personal:** Married to Kathleen J. in 1974. One child: Aron J. Mr. Reina enjoys golf and snow skiing.

Bradley C. Rode

Senior Vice President
Teknekron Software Systems
587 Sleeper Avenue
Mountain View, CA 94040
(415) 325–1025
Fax: Please mail or call

7372

Business Information: Teknekron Software Systems is a software design firm, specializing in distributed systems software utilized in the finance, manufacturing and telecommunication sectors. As Senior Vice President, Mr. Rode is responsible for the overall management for software development and technology. **Career Steps:** Senior Vice President, Teknekron Software Systems (1987–Present); Technical Staff Member, AGS Computers (1983–1987); Technical Staff Member, Alberta Government Telephones (1980–1983). **Education:** University of Alberta, B.S. (1982). **Personal:** Married to Judy in 1985. Three children: Timothy, Madeleine, and Nicholas. Mr. Rode enjoys music and outdoor sports.

Ardis C. Schultz

Vice President of Sales & Marketing
Comdel, Inc.
1601 Carmen Drive, Suite 103
Camarillo, CA 93010–3103
(800) 858–9154
Fax: (805) 388–2483

7372

Business Information: Comdel, Inc. specializes in software development of Crescendo Planned Gifts Marketing Software and educational seminars for Crescendo users. As Vice President of Sales & Marketing, Ms. Schultz is responsible for software marketing and advertising, product support, sales, and teaching seminars for professionals. **Career Steps:** Vice President of Sales & Marketing, Comdel, Inc. (1983–Present); Administrator, CBS (1988–1990); Teacher, Cornerstone School (1987). **Associations & Accomplishments:** National Committee on Planned Giving; Planned Giving Roundtable of Ventura County. **Education:** California Lutheran University, M.A. (1991); University of Michigan, Graduate Studies; Northern Michigan University, B.A. (1973). **Personal:** Married to A. Charles in 1970. Two children: Kristen Kaye and Laurie Leigh. Ms. Schultz enjoys being a community volunteer, reading, and singing.

Jack M. Taylor

President
Edukeep Company
RR 16, Box 652
Bedford, IN 47421–9806
(812) 275–8111
Fax: (812) 275–8118

7372

Business Information: Edukeep Company specializes in the manufacture of computer software for tracking employees training records. The Company supplies completed packages for city governments, health care facilities, State agencies, and organizations such as OSHA. Established in 1982, Edukeep currently employs 5 people. As President, Mr. Taylor is responsible for sales, technical support, and on–site and class training. **Career Steps:** President, Edukeep Company (1992–Present); President, JMI Enterprises (1984–1992); Partner and Technician, Medcomp Data (1982–1984). **Education:** De Vries Technical Institute (1978). **Personal:** Married to Pauline in 1949. Four children: Greg M., Kevin (deceased), Denise, and Debra Ann Strunk. Mr. Taylor enjoys woodworking, building and repairing computers, and electronic devices.

James R. Trial

Director of Finance
Electric Image, Inc.
117 East Colorado Boulevard, Suite 300
Pasadena, CA 91105
(818) 577–1627
Fax: (818) 577–2426
EMAIL: See Below

7372

Business Information: Electric Image, Inc. develops 3D animation software for computer and video games. As Director of Finance, Mr. Trial is responsible for accounting and finances, payroll, purchasing, personnel management, and various administrative functions. Internet users can also reach him via: Jim.Trial@ElectricImg.com **Career Steps:** Director of Finance, Electric Image, Inc. (1994–Present); Controller, Norton Simon Museum (1989–1994); Director of Cash Reporting, Public Storage (1985–1989); Staff Accountant, Price Waterhouse (1983–1995). **Associations & Accomplishments:** Pasadena Tournament of Roses (1989–Present). **Education:** Pacific Union College, B.S.B.A. (1983); Walla Walla College, B.A. **Personal:** Married to Janet in 1983. Two children: Erica and Jeff. Mr. Trial enjoys skiing.

Joan Ziegler
President/Chief Executive Officer
Jazz Interactive Learning
1735 Tiburon Boulevard
Tiburon, CA 94920
(415) 435–5000
Fax: (415) 435–5153
E MAIL: See Below

7372

Business Information: Jazz Interactive Learning, established in 1995, is a manufacturer and distributor of results–oriented educational software. The software is available in English, Spanish, German, Chinese, Japanese, and the United Kingdom version of English. With estimated revenue of $3 million, the Company presently employs 12 people. As President/Chief Executive Officer, Ms. Ziegler oversees the day–to–day operation of the Company. She looks for strategic partners, identifies countries ready for product distribution, and creates partnerships with other curriculum companies. **Career Steps:** President/Chief Executive Officer, Jazz Interactive Learning (1995–Present); Senior Vice President, Mindscape (1994–1995); Senior Vice President, Hi Tech Expressions (1983–1994); Staff Psychologist, Psychological and Family Consultants (1976–1981). **Associations & Accomplishments:** Bay Area Multimedia Technology Alliance; Digital Village; Tiburon Chamber of Commerce; St. Hilary Lector. **Education:** Florida State University, M.S. Psychology (1981); Florida Atlantic University, B.S. Psychology (1976). **Personal:** One child: Daniel Ziegler. Ms. Ziegler enjoys skiing, mountain biking, and boxing aerobics.

M. Susan Zwickel

Vice President of Worldwide Corporate Contracts
Computron Software, Inc.
301 Route 17, North
Rutherford, NJ 07070
(201) 935–3400 Ext. 477
Fax: (201) 393–6955
EMail: See Below

7372

Business Information: Established in 1979, Computron Software, Inc. is an international developer and distributor of software for financial institutions with ten major locations around the world. As Vice President of Worldwide Corporate Contracts, Mrs. Zwickel is responsible for contract negotiation and revenue recognition, varied administrative activities, and executive leadership. Internet users can reach her via: SZWICKEL@CTRONSOFT.COM. **Career Steps:** Computron Software, Inc.: Vice President of Worldwide Corporate Contracts (1994–Present), Director of Corporate Contracts (1994–Present); Director of Coporate Contracts, Information Builders (1991–1994). **Associations & Accomplishments:** National Association of Female Executives; Executive Women of New Jersey; Executive Board Member, Gratitude House – Newton, NJ. **Personal:** Married to Jay in 1967. Three children: Alan, Erica, and Richard. Mrs. Zwickel enjoys gardening, antiqueing, and decorating.

Mr. David Ambrose

President
Ambrose Research Corporation
68 Redondo Drive
Thornhill, Ontario
(905) 889–6552
Fax: Please mail or call
EMAIL: see below

7373

Business Information: Ambrose Research Corporation is an international system integration consulting and software development firm, focusing primarily on providing PeopleSoft to Fortune 1000 companies throughout the U.S. and Canada. Established in 1993, Ambrose Research Corporation currently employs seven people. As President, Mr. Ambrose is responsible for all aspects of operations, including administration, sales, marketing, strategic planning, client relations, recruitment, and budgeting. He can be reached through the Internet as follows: 73474.2104@compuserv.com

Career Steps: President, Ambrose Research Corporation (1993–Present); Senior System Analyst, Ontario Hydro (1991–1993); Senior Consultant, Andersen Consulting (1987–1991). **Associations & Accomplishments:** Community and animal related activities. **Education:** University of Waterloo, Mathematics and Computer Science (1986). **Personal:** Married to Margot Ambrose in 1987. One child: Kira.

Brian (Keoki) Andrus
Director, Corporate Marketing
Novell, Inc.
122 East 1700 South
Provo, UT 84606–7379
(801) 228–4846
Fax: (801) 228–5078
EMAIL: Kandrus@novell.co

7373

Business Information: Novell, Inc. is an international computer networking and service provider with locations in Utah and California. The Company designs, develops, and markets computer network software throughout the world. As Director of Corporate Marketing, Mr. Andrus directs the development and implementation of marketing strategies and plans targeted at specific industries. **Career Steps:** Novell, Inc.: Director of Corporate Marketing (1996–Present), Product Line Manager (1995–1996), Product Manager (1994–1995); Senior Program Manager, Microsoft Company (1988–1994). **Associations & Accomplishments:** United Way Crisis Center Volunteer; boy Scouts of America. **Education:** Seattle University, WIP–MBA and BS Statistic, Magna Cum Laude (1987). **Personal:** Married to Linda in 1985. Four children: Aden, Austin, Skyler, and Dawnika. Mr. Andrus enjoys golf, racquetball, vocal music, and reading.

Barbara A. Babcock
Vice President of Commercial Marketing
UNISYS Corporation
P.O. Box 500, Mail Stat A–8
Blue Bell, PA 19422
(215) 986–6515
Fax: (215) 986–3889

7373

Business Information: UNISYS Corporation provides computing hardware and software solutions for high volume business transactions internationally. UNISYS Corporation reports annual revenue of $7 billion and currently employs 25,000 people Corporation–wide. As Vice President of Commercial Marketing, Ms. Babcock is responsible for commercial and federal government marketing. She has extensive expertise in market research, strategic expansions and planning. **Career Steps:** Vice President of Commercial Marketing, UNISYS Corporation (1994–Present); Vice President of Marketing of Enhanced Business Services, Ameritech (1993–1994); Vice President of Marketing, Stratus Computer (1991–1993); Vice President and Service Director, Gartner Group (1988–1991). **Associations & Accomplishments:** Northeastern University, M.B.A. (1982); HBS, PMD–53 (1987); Carleton College, B.A. (1970). **Personal:** Ms. Babcock enjoys golf, playing the piano, reading, and writing.

Mr. Rick K. Bacchus
President
Associated Software Consultants, Inc. (ASC)
7251 Engle Road, Suite 300
Middleburg Heights, OH 44130
(216) 826–1010
Fax: (216) 826–1140

7373

Business Information: Associated Software Consultants, Inc. (ASC) specializes in the design and development of software utilized in lending institutions, including banks, credit unions, thrifts and savings & loans establishments. Established in 1978, Associated Software Consultants, Inc. employs 45 people with annual sales of $6 million. ASC's products include UNI–FORM(R), PowerSeller(R), and PowerLender(TM). **Career Steps:** Associated Software Consultants, Inc.: President (1996–Present), Vice President of Product Development and Strategic Planning (1992–1996); Senior Management Consultant, Benton International (1990–1992); Director of Finance, Shared Health Network Services, Toronto, Canada (1988–1990); Senior Accountant and Consultant, Price Waterhouse (1986–1988). **Associations & Accomplishments:** Mortgage Banking Association. **Education:** York University, M.B.A. (1988); York University, Toronto, Canada, B.B.A. (1986) with combined honors in Accounting and Computer Science **Personal:** Married to Cathy

in 1990. One child: Ryad. Mr. Bacchus enjoys reading, writing, music, and all sports.

Zack Bajin
President
Lexis Interactive Corporation
284 Hickory Circle
Oakville, Ontario
(905) 338–0608
Fax: (905) 338–0609
EMAIL: See Below

7373

Business Information: Lexis Interactive Corporation, established in 1991, is located in Oakville, Ontario. The Corporation offers online and professional development and training to clients in the computer and energy (conservation and alternative) industries. Lexis Interactive is a registered developer and solutions provider on the PowerPC computer platform (POWER – Performance Optimization With Elimination of RISC, RISC – Reduced Instruction Set Computing). As President, Mr. Bajin oversees all operational aspects of the Corporation, concentrating on the areas of strategic marketing and business development. Internet users may contact Mr. Bajin via: zack@ipgnet.com, zack@interlog.com, or at AppleLink: LEXIS.Corp. **Career Steps:** President, Lexis Interactive Corporation (1991–Present); Education Director, International Programmers Guild (1996); George Brown College: Coordinator of Interactive Studies (1991–1995), Professor of Computer Science and Engineering (1989–1991); Professor of Math and Science (since 1974). **Associations & Accomplishments:** President, Consortium of Canadian User Groups; Club Mac, Toronto: Education Coordinator – Two years, President – Three years. **Education:** University of Stuttgart, Master in Physics (1970). **Personal:** Married to Ilse in 1967. Two children: Christine and Markus.

Louis Birk
President
Moonface, Inc.
P.O. Box 201
Sumneytown, PA 18084–0201
(215) 234–8399
Fax: (215) 234–0736
EMAIL: See Below

7373

Business Information: Mr. Birk established Moonface, Inc. in 1994, specializing in software development for mid–sized companies in the United States and abroad. He is responsible for various administrative activities, daily operations, sales and marketing. A former software engineer with General Electric, his expertise led to the recent development of Moonface's Majestic HTML Viewer. He may be reached via email: birk@moonface.com or the web: http://www.moonface.com or http://www.avantext.com **Career Steps:** President, Moonface, Inc. (1994–Present); Software Development Engineer, General Electric (1984–1994). **Education:** University of Maryland, B.S. in Computer Science (1984). **Personal:** Married to Maria in 1984. One child: Charles. Mr. Birk enjoys travel, golf, and music.

David S. Buck
President
Advanced Information Solutions, Inc.
268 Summer Street Floor 7
Boston, MA 02210–1108
(617) 350–8818 Ext: 102
Fax: (617) 350–7696
EMAIL: See Below

7373

Business Information: Advanced Information Solutions, Inc. (AIS), named as one of the 55 fastest growing companies, is a computer systems development and integration corporation, specializing in object–oriented and client–server systems. Established in 1993, AIS currently employs fifteen people. With nine years expertise in the management and engineering industry, Mr. Buck founded AIS in 1993. Serving as President and Chief Executive Officer, he is responsible for all aspects of operations, including administrative, finances, and strategic planning. **Career Steps:** President, Advanced Information Solutions, Inc. (1993–Present); Systems Engineer, Next Computer, Inc. (1990–1993); Sales Engineer, Symbolics, Inc. (1988–1990); Management Consultant, Deloitte, Haskins & Sells (1986–1988). **Associations & Accomplishments:** Chief Executive Network; Young Entrepreneurs Organization; Boston Computer Society. **Education:** University of Dayton, B.S. (1986). **Personal:** Mr. Buck enjoys skiing, golf, and running.

Donna Jones Cox
Director of Support and Services
Liant Software Corporation
8911 Capital of Texas Highway North
Austin, TX 78759
(512) 343–1010 Ext. 5591
Fax: (512) 835–0501
EMAIL: See Below

7373

Business Information: Liant Software is a provider of Cobol Compilers and technology tools for the computer software industry. As Director of Support and Services, Mrs. Cox manages five departments, including Technical Support, QA & Porting, Consulting and Training, Technical Publications, and London Support Group. She was personally responsible for the development of the Technical Support Group in Austin. Internet users can reach her via: donna@rm1.liant.com. **Career Steps:** Director of Support and Services, Liant Software (1992–Present); Vice President of Correspondent Banking, First City National Bank – Austin (1990–1992); Support & Services Manager for DP – Correspondent Banks, EDS – Austin (1988–1990). **Education:** Texas State Technical College, Associate of Computer Science (1973). **Personal:** Married to Thomas A. in 1994. One child: Daniel. Mrs. Cox enjoys cats, collectibles, and cats.

Mr. Reginald G. Daniel
President
Scientific & Engineering Solutions
12138 Central Avenue, Suite 274
Mitchellville, MD 20721
(800) 820–2012
Fax: (301) 390–3127
EMAIL: rdaniel338@aol.com

7373

Business Information: Scientific & Engineering Solutions is a computer systems integration firm. Established in 1994, SES currently employs 5 people. As President, Mr. Daniel is responsible for the management direction and management of the Company. **Career Steps:** President, Scientific & Engineering Solutions (1994–Present); Vice President, ECS Technologies (1991–1994); Silicon Graphics: Account Manager (1989–1991), Systems Analyst Cray Research (1984–1989). **Education:** Loyola College, M.B.A. candidate (1996); University of Maryland, B.S. in Computer Science. **Personal:** Married to Audrey B. Daniel in 1989. Father to daughter, Regina Vashti, born October 1995. Mr. Daniel enjoys tennis and coaching basketball.

Rodney L. Drummond

President
Dynamic Computer Concepts, Inc.
8201 Corporate Drive, Suite 730
Landover, MD 20785
(301) 731–4393 (800) 346–0256
Fax: (301) 731–3224

7373

Business Information: Dynamic Computer Concepts, Inc. (DCC) is a provider of computer services, such as LAN/WAN installation, software development, systems and personal computer sales and maintenance. A minority–owned business certified by the Federal Government's 8(a) program and Minority Certified by the states of Maryland and Virginia, Dynamic Computer Concepts, Inc. reports annual revenue of $2.5 million and currently employs 25 people. Founding the Company in 1987, as President, Mr. Drummond provides all necessary leadership to plan, organize, direct, coordinate, and control the business operation. **Career Steps:** President, Dynamic Computer Concepts, Inc. (1987–Present); Manager, Techmatics Technologies (1986–1988); Manager, Advance, Inc. (1982–1986). **Associations & Accomplishments:** MBOC, Coach, Boys & Girls Club; Oldtimers Basketball Association. **Education:** Attended: Kensington University; University of Maryland; Computer Learning Center. **Personal:** Married to Beverly A. in 1976. Two children: Ronique M. and Rodney L. Jr.

Moustafa A. El Gabaly, Ph.D.
Chairman and Managing Director
AITeC Consulting
7 Okasha St., Messaha Square, P.O.Box 288
Dokki, Cairo, Egypt Giza 12211
(202) 348–7799
Fax: (202) 348–7822

7373

Business Information: AITeC Consulting is an international advanced information technology, consulting and service provider. AITeC offers a wide range of services in the areas of management and technology, including feasibility studies, design, development and management of engineering and industrial projects. Special emphasis is given to telecommunications, internetworking, energy and software engineering. AITeC is helping investors from U.S. and Europe to operate in Egypt (high–tech companies) and provide consulting on automation of companies and organizations such as hospitals and educational institutes in Egypt, Kuwait and other locations in the Mid East. Joining AITeC as Chairman and Managing Director in 1991, Dr. El Gabaly is responsible for setting policies, strategic planning, conducting engineering projects, and design consultancy work. **Career Steps:** Chairman and Managing Director, AITeC Consulting (1991–Present); Chairman and Professor, Department of Electronic and Computer Engineering – Kuwait University (1984–1990); Professor of Electronics, University of Michigan – Ann Arbor (1982–1983). **Associations & Accomplishments:** Institute of Electronics and Electrical Engineers: Senior Member – MTT Society, Senior Member – Communications Society, Senior Member, Computer Society, Senior Member, Electronic Device Society; International Solar Energy Society; Professional Engineer – Alberta, Canada and Egypt. **Education:** University of Alberta, Canada, Ph.D. in Electrical Engineering (1974); Cairo University – Egypt: B.Sc. in Electrical Engineering (1965), M.Sc. in Electrical Engineering (1967), B.Sc. in Mathematics (1969). **Personal:** Married to Nagwa M. El–Gabaly in 1970. Three children: Daughters: Abeer, Heba, and Mona. Dr. El Gabaly enjoys tennis, swimming, and reading history and novels.

Ms. Wanda B. Fesnak
Manager of the Executive Briefing Center
IBM Global Network
1311 Mamaroneck Avenue
White Plains, NY 10605
(914) 684–4669
Fax: (914) 684–4253

7373

Business Information: IBM Global Network, a wholly–owned entity of IBM Corporation, is a networking service provider specializing in network outsourcing and network centric computing. As Manager of the Executive Briefing Center, Ms. Fesnak manages a marketing and support briefing center for customers and prospects. This Center provides marketing programs designed to close businesses and capture incremental revenue). Established in 1992, IBM Global Network employs 5,000 people with annual sales of $4 billion. **Career Steps:** Manager of the Executive Briefing Center, IBM Global Network (1992–Present); Marketing Manager, IBM Corporation (1991–1992); Marketing Representative, IBM Corporation (1987–1991); Marketing Support/Contracts Specialist, IBM Corporation (1983–1987). **Associations & Accomplishments:** Junior League. **Education:** College of Mount St. Joseph, B.A. Degree (1987). **Personal:** Married to Frank in 1992. Ms. Fesnak enjoys golf and snow skiing.

Scott Gannon
Regional Manager – Southwest
Equitrac Corporation
1200 Smith Street, Suite 3515
Houston, TX 77002
(800) 229–7277
Fax: (713) 759–1104

7373

Business Information: Equitrac Corporation is a small, public company providing automated computer billing systems (cost accounting system) for professional firms, such as attorney's offices. This system provides firms with an automated method of tracking costs (i.e., copies, faxes, telephone calls, other related expenses, etc.) for each client. Headquartered in Coral Gables, Florida, Equitrac Corporation services clients in all major cities throughout the U.S. A sales executive with over twelve years expertise in office equipment and computer software technology distribution, Scott Gannon joined Equitrac Corporation as Regional Manager in 1986. Reporting directly to the Vice President of Sales, he is responsible for all aspects of management for the entire Southwest Region of the U.S., including revenue base, profitability, and operations. He is also responsible for the oversight of sales and finance throughout the Southwest Region, in addition to overseeing a support staff of more than twenty people. Scott can also be reached through the Worldwide Web via: http:\\www.equi-trac.com **Career Steps:** Regional Manager, Equitrac Corporation (1986–Present); Sales Representative; Pandick Technologies, Inc. (1985–1986); Sales Representative, XE-ROX Corporation (1983–1985). **Associations & Accomplishments:** Xerox Corporation; President's Club; Six Time Winner of Equitrac's Over–Achiever Club. **Education:** University of Louisville, B.S. in Business Administration (1982). **Personal:** One child: Ryan Nicholas. Mr. Gannon enjoys golf, travel, and fitness.

Aixa M. Gonzalez
Outside Sales Representative
Anixter
7 Metro Office Pk.
Guaynabo, Puerto Rico 00968
(809) 783–6300
Fax: (809) 783–7380

7373

Business Information: Anixter is a value–added provider of integrated networking and cabling solutions that support business information and network infrastructures. Services provided include customized pre– and post–sale services, a wide range of technology products from the world's leading manufacturers, and rapid delivery through a global distribution network. As Outside Sales Representative, Ms. Gonzalez is responsible for the Puerto Rico customer base, closing major projects, customer visits, and other diversified activities. She can also be reached through E–Mail: aixa.gonzalez@anix-ter.com **Career Steps:** Outside Sales Representative, Anixter (1993–Present). **Associations & Accomplishments:** Who's Who Among Students in American High Schools. **Education:** University of Puerto Rico, B.B.A. (1992). **Personal:** Married to Genaro Perez in 1994. One child: Aisha. Ms. Gonzalez enjoys reading, cooking, and spending time with her family.

Mr. Dennis J. Grant
President and Chief Executive Officer
HighGround Systems
1300 Massachusetts Avenue, Suite 205
Boxboro, MA 01719
(508) 263–5588 Ext. 110
Fax: (508) 263–5565
E/M: See below

7373

Business Information: HighGround Systems is a software company focusing on the NT market. Providing storage resource management applications for NT networks, HighGround's SRM applications facilitates NT's emergence as an ubiquitous mission–critical server platform and provides the foundation for full–scale implementation of distributed client/server applications. As Founder, President and Chief Executive Officer, Mr. Grant is responsible for all aspects of operations, involving administrative, financial, sales, marketing and strategic planning. Internet users can reach him via: dgrant@highground.com. **Career Steps:** Founder, President and Chief Executive Officer, HighGround Systems (1995–Present); Vice President of World Wide Marketing, StorageTek (1992–1995); Chief Executive Officer, DML Computers, Ltd. (1979–1995); Engineering Manager, SMS (1973–1979). **Education:** Educated in Scotland and specialized in Electronics. **Personal:** Married to Marion. Three children: Cameron, Alistair and Sarah. Mr. Grant enjoys skiing, walking and reading.

Teresa Helgeson
Account Manager
Confer Tech International
12110 North Pecos Street
Westminster, CO 80234–2076
(303) 446–4729
Fax: (303) 633–3001
EMAIL: See Below

7373

Business Information: Confer Tech International is a telecommunications service, providing audio and video conferencing, document conferencing, and fax services to Fortune 1000 and 500 companies. As Account Manager, Ms. Helgeson is responsible for all inside sales covering the Southeastern United States sectors. Internet users can reach her via: THELG@CFER.COM. **Career Steps:** Inside Sales Manager, Confer Tech International (1995–Present); Inside Sales, Van Gilder Insurance (1992–1995); Inside Sales, BCBS of

Colorado, (1989–1992); First and Second Mortgage Consultant, Bank Western (1987–1989). **Associations & Accomplishments:** Member of Rocky Mountain Speakers Bureau; 1996 Participated in fundraising for Children's Legal Clinic – a non–profit organization; 1996 Ninth Place graduate of Tom Hopkins Boot Camp (Total graduates–600); 1992 Treasurer of the employees Association of BCBS; 1991 Coordinated Olympic Breakfast fund raiser for the Olympics on behalf of Colorado; 1991 Coordinated and hosted United Way Campaigns for BCBS; 1990 Awarded Rep of the Year at BCBS; 1981 Honorable Discharge U.S. Army. **Personal:** Married to Michael Richard in 1989. Four children: Mandy, Kristen, Amber and Jonathon. Ms. Helgeson enjoys watching NASCAR racing.

James W. Huggins
Director – Integrated Solutions Center
Encompass
1100 Crescent Green, Suite 210
Cary, NC 27511–8106
(919) 852–4200
Fax: (919) 852–4299
EMAIL: See Below

7373

Business Information: Encompass is a computer systems development firm, providing logistics information services to global corporations, primarily to Fortune 100 companies. Serving in managerial positions with Encompass since 1992, James Huggins was appointed to his current position in 1995. As Director of the Integrated Solutions Center, Mr. Huggins oversees all design, development, and installation engineering efforts, in addition to quality assurance in meeting customer design requirements, customer implementations, end–to–end testing and overall analysis. Internet users can also reach him via: Huggins@encmail.encompass.com. **Career Steps:** Encompass: Director – Integrated Solutions (1995–Present), Manager – Design & Integration (1993–1995), Manager – Database Development (1992–1993); Major, United States Air Force Reserves (1984–Present). **Associations & Accomplishments:** Phi Kappa Phi National Honor Society; Former Member – Board of Directors, St. Timothy's Middle & Hale High School; Assistant Professor, ROTC; Co–Author of an article entitled, "EDI, the Cornerstone to Supply Chain Management" with Apple Computer Company; Awarded the Defense Meritorious Service Medal; Twice Received the Joint Services Commendation Medal. **Education:** California Coast University, M.S. in Engineering (1996); Campbell University, B.S. in Math (1984); University of Colorado, Graduate Work (1986–87); Webster University, Graduate Work (1987). **Personal:** Married to Susan in 1984. Mr. Huggins enjoys golf, basketball, Corvettes, and space/astronomy.

Peter H. Johnsen
Senior Vice President and General Counsel
PRC Inc.
1500 PRC Drive
McLean, VA 22102
(703) 556–1980
Fax: (703) 556–1069

7373

Business Information: PRC Inc. is a diversified provider of systems integration and technology–based services to government and commercial customers worldwide. Currently PRC, Inc. employs 6,000 people. As Senior Vice President and General Counsel, Mr. Johnsen is responsible for all aspects of the Company's legal affairs. **Career Steps:** Senior Vice President and General Counsel, PRC Inc. (1993–Present); Vice President – Legal, CACI International, Inc. (1991–1993); Vice President of Strategic Planning and Legal Affairs, Intelligent Electronics, Inc. (1989–1990); Vice President of Legal Affairs and Sales Development, Entre Computer Centers, Inc. (1986–1988). **Associations & Accomplishments:** American Corporate Counsel Association; American Bar Association; Maryland Bar Association; Virginia State Bar Association; Professional Services Council. **Education:** University of Virginia, J.D., M.B.A. (1976); Dartmouth College, A.B. (1972). **Personal:** Married to Peggy in 1976. Six children: Henry, Thomas, Peter, Paul, Rebecca and Rachel.

Mick M. Kapetanovic
President
CompuTec Integrated Solutions Inc.
North 7134 Huntington Court
Hartland, WI 53029–9197
(414) 538–1728
Fax: (414) 538–1718

7373

Business Information: With 15 years of sales experience behind him, Mr. Kapetanovic established CompuTec Integrated Solutions Inc. in 1995, specializing in integrated hardware and software solutions for the retail and distribution industry. In only its second year, the Company now grosses approximately $3 million annually. As President, Mr. Kapetanovic is responsible for all business and financial transactions. **Career Steps:** President, CompuTec Integrated Solutions Inc. (1995–Present); Sales, Orion (1991–1994); Salesperson, ADP (1988–1991); Manager/Sales, Motorola (1985–1988). **Associations & Accomplishments:** Wisconsin Handball Association; United States Field and Track; Boston Marathon. **Education:** University of Wisconsin–Milwaukee, B.A. (1983). **Personal:** Mr. Kapetanovic enjoys marathons, reading, handball, bicycling, and skiing.

Carol Ann Kemtes
Senior Accountant
Dataworks
7441 Lincoln Way
Garden Grove, CA 92641
(714) 891–6336
Fax: (714) 897–3213

7373

Business Information: Dataworks is a retail supplier of new developments in computer software and hardware to manufacturing companies. As Senior Accountant, Ms. Kemtes is responsible for all accounting procedures related to payroll, sales and income tax, and internal audits. **Career Steps:** Senior Accountant, Dataworks (1994–Present); Accounting Manager, Madic Compufact (1989–1994); Accounting Manager, Compufact (1980–1989). **Associations & Accomplishments:** American Payroll Association. **Education:** Webster University, B.A. (In Progress); Cypress College, A.A. in Business; El Camino College. **Personal:** Ms. Kemtes enjoys bowling, reading, and school homework.

Joanne Murphy
Director of Business Development
IBM Corporation
1 Commerce Plaza
Hartford, CT
(203) 727–6000
Fax: Please mail or call

7373

Business Information: IBM Corporation designs, manufactures and markets high–tech products globally, including information systems products and services, computers, semiconductors, networking hardware and software, computer hardware and software as well as outsourcing services, multi-vendor support services and consulting. With over ten years in systems technology marketing and development, Joanne Murphy joined IBM in September of 1995. As Director of Business Development she serves as a project leader for the Legacy Transformation Group providing strategies in technology development to bring IBM's mainframe applications into the Year 2000. **Career Steps:** Director of Business Development, IBM Corporation (1995–Present); Director of Business Development, Computer Horizons Corporation (1987–1995); Sales Executive, Honeywell (1986–1987). **Associations & Accomplishments:** Finance Committee, Parent Teachers Organization (local community) **Education:** University of Massachusetts, B.S. in Marketing (1980); University of Hartford, M.B.A. in progress **Personal:** One child: Dennis F. Murphy IV. Ms. Murphy enjoys golf, skiing and community affairs.

Ronald D. Newman
Director of Business Development
Hughes Aircraft
P.O. Box 902
El Segundo, CA 90245
(310) 416–6314
Fax: (310) 416–3459
EMail: See Below

7373

Business Information: Hughes Aircraft specializes in integrated supportability solutions, automated publications and interactive electronic technical manuals (IETM), and CALS compliant data management. As Director of Business Development, Mr. Newman is responsible for strategic alliances and support/engineering services management. Internet users can reach him via: rdnewman@ccgate.hac.com. **Career Steps:** Hughes Aircraft Company: Director of Business Development (1995–Present), Manager of Marketing (1991–1995), Product/Program Marketing Manager (1989–1991). **Associations & Accomplishments:** Aerospace Industries Association; Armed Forces Communication and Electronics Association; Society of Logistics Engineers; American Society of Naval Engineers; American Management Association. **Education:** University of Redlands, B.S.B.A. (1987); Northrop University, Engineering. **Personal:** Married to Karen in 1984. Five children: James, Carie, John, Samantha, and Jaclyn. Mr. Newman enjoys golf.

Arthur M. Nutter
President and Owner
TAEUS
4308 Ridgelane Drive
Colorado Springs, CO 80918–4332
(719) 533–1375
Fax: (719) 533–1376
EMAIL: See Below

7373

Business Information: Arthur M. Nutter founded TAEUS in 1992 to provide protection to patent holders against unauthorized usage. TAEUS is primarily engaged in high–tech detective work, employing reverse engineering of electronic hardware and software systems to support patent licensing on a global scale. With a network of the best technical specialists in the world, TAEUS studies patent portfolios to discover unauthorized patent usage, producing a report for the TAEUS customer to present to the offender and pressing charges if necessary. TAEUS engineers will also serve as expert witness in the case. Concurrently, he serves on the District II El Paso County School Board – the second largest school district in Colorado – and generously invests his time in community civic efforts. Mr. Nutter may be reached via the Internet at: TAEUS@aol.com. **Career Steps:** President, TAEUS (1992–Present). **Associations & Accomplishments:** District II School Board – El Paso County, Colorado (1993–Present); Choir Director, Holy Apostles Catholic Church (1990–Present). **Education:** University of Phoenix, M.B.A. (1988); University of Akron, B.S.M.E. **Personal:** Mr. Nutter enjoys skiing, swimming, and fishing.

Darryl J. Patterson
Vice President – On Line Services
Interactivity Inc.
25 Defries Street
Toronto, Ontario M5A 3R4
(416) 364–4710
Fax: (416) 364–3616
EMAIL: See Below

7373

Business Information: Interactivity Inc. is a national multi–media production company, involved in the creation of all media from CD–ROM to the Internet, serving business–to–business, individual consumers, and governmental contracts. Joining Interactivity Inc. as Vice President of On–Line Services in 1994, Mr. Patterson is responsible for management, purchasing, invoicing, operations, and administration of all on–line services. Internet users can also reach him as follows: darryl@interactivity.com. **Career Steps:** Vice President – On Line Services, Interactivity Inc. (1994–Present); Sound Editor, The Film House (1993–1994); Sales Representative, Soo Piano (1989–1991). **Associations & Accomplishments:** CIRPA; IMAT **Education:** Harris Institute for the Arts, Production Engineering (1993); Adgoma University, Business Administration

Kimberly A. Paul
Communications Director
Integrated Data Solutions Inc.
580 Middletown Boulevard, Suite 103
Penndel, PA 19047
(215) 750–7600
Fax: (215) 750–1155

7373

Business Information: Integrated Data Solutions Inc., established in 1993, provides a consulting service regarding computer designs, marketing services, and staff training. The Company specializes in providing Computer Aided Design (CAD), Computer Aided Family Management (CAFM), and multimedia services to clients. As Communications Director, Ms. Paul is involved in project management. She creates presentations for clients and potential clients, designs and produces a Company newsletter, and sets–up and coordinates tradeshows and product–related seminars. She is involved in developing marketing and sales strategies for new and existing services and products offered to clients, and developing and implementing strategic business plans, financial and marketing plans, and marketing budgets. **Career Steps:** Communications Director, Integrated Data Solutions Inc. (1994–Present); Program Coordinator, Philadelphia Park Race Track (1990–1994). **Education:** Temple University, B.A. in Journalism (1990). **Personal:** Ms. Paul enjoys bowling and travel.

Rene' M. Potter

Vice President of Marketing
Systems & Programing Resources of Tulsa, Inc.
401 South Boston Avenue, Suite 400
Tulsa, OK 74103–4040
(918) 587–8825
Fax: (918) 587–2408

7373

Business Information: Systems & Programing Resources of Tulsa, Inc. is an information systems consultancy, providing information services for logistic systems and Year 2000 data compliance for Fortune 1000 companies. Joining the Firm as Marketing Manager in 1985, Ms. Potter was appointed as Vice President of Marketing in 1994. She is responsible for all aspects of administrative functions and marketing services. She also serves as Director of Information Systems. **Career Steps:** Systems & Programing Resources of Tulsa, Inc.: Vice President of Marketing (1994–Present), Marketing Manager (1985–1994). **Associations & Accomplishments:** Advisory Board Member, Tulsa Junior College. **Education:** University of Arkansas, Studies in Music and Business. **Personal:** Ms. Potter enjoys gardening, jazz singing, and music.

Johns F. (Jeff) Rulifson, Ph.D.

Director of Technology Department
Sun Microsystems
3785 El Centro Avenue
Palo Alto, CA 94306–2642
(415) 786–6365
Fax: (415) 857–1046

7373

Business Information: Sun Microsystems is one of the world's leading computer network systems design manufacturers, providing development and marketing of design automation software and services that accelerate and advance the process of designing electronic systems, as well as the manufacture of desktop scanners and computer work stations. An award–winning computer scientist with over thirty years expertise in computer technology, as Director of the Technology Development Group, Dr. Rulifson directs all advanced development projects involving high resolution video, video compression, distributed shared memory, security and nomadic networking systems. Dr. Rulifson has garnered numerous accolades for his pioneer ARPANET work which led to the development of Internet and the implementation of the NLS System. **Career Steps:** Director of Technology Department, Sun Microsystems (1987–Present); Scientist, Syntelligence (1985–1987); Manager, ROLM Corporation (1980–1985); Scientist, Xerox Palo Alto Research Center (1973–1980); Mathematician, SRI International (1966–1973). **Associations & Accomplishments:** Fellow, Association for Computing Machinery; Institute of Electrical and Electronics Engineers; AWARDS: System Software Award (1990) – awarded by ACM for his pioneering work on augmenting human intellect with hypertext and video conferencing utilized in the NLS System; ARPANET Pioneer (1994) – recognized by Bolt Beranek and Newman for his pioneer work, along with 34 other scientists, for packet networking which resulted in Internet. **Education:** Stanford University, Ph.D. in Computer Science; University of Washington, B.S. in Mathematics (1966). **Personal:** Married to Janet Irving in 1963. Two children: Eric Johns and Ingrid Catharine. Dr. Rulifson enjoys fine art, photography, and adventure travel.

Marvin B. Sauer

Chief Financial Officer
DataServ, Inc.
37562 Hills Technical Drive
Farmington, MI 48331
(810) 489–8400
Fax: (810) 489–8403
EMAIL: See Below

7373

Business Information: DataServ, Inc. is a systems integration firm specializing in systems integrations for the K–12 education market. Services provided include technology planning, design, implementation and support. DataServ, Inc. has four regional locations: one in Michigan, two in Ohio, and one in Indiana. As Chief Financial Officer, Mr. Sauer is responsible for overall financial management and operational management for the Michigan and Indiana operations. Duties include maintaining banking relations and insuring the Corporation has sound and accurate financial statements. Concurrently, he serves as the Director of the Indiana and Michigan Operations, responsible for monitoring and updating strategic plans and expanding the business and staff. The seventh employee to be hired within the Corporation in November 1988, he has played a key role in expansion through his strategic planning, sales and financial expertise. He may also be reached through the Internet via: MSAUER@K12.DSERV.COM **Career Steps:** Chief Financial Officer, DataServ, Inc. (1988–Present); Vice President, The Katke company (1981–1988). **Associations & Accomplishments:** American Management Association; Michigan School of Business Officials; Seventh employee to be hired within the company in November 1988. **Education:** University of Michigan, M.B.A. (1986); University of California – Los Angeles, B.S. in Mathematics/Computer Science. **Personal:** Married to Claudia in 1989. Two children: Shelby and Victoria. Mr. Sauer enjoys skiing, travel, and financial investing.

Brian A.D. Selzer

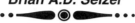

Vice President of Sales
NEXSYS Corporation
18 King Street East, Suite 1601
Toronto, Ontario N5C 1C4
(416) 364–4100
Fax: (416) 364–4041
EMAIL: See Below

7373

Business Information: NEXSYS Corporation is a cutting edge, systems solutions provider. Services include computer systems integration, networking, hardware/software reselling and providing Internet–access. As Vice President of Sales, Mr. Selzer is responsible for all sales, marketing, and promotions for NEXSYS. **Career Steps:** Vice President of Sales, NEXSYS Corporation (1994–Present); President, Casting Images (1992–1994); Chairman of the Board, Silver Screen Talent (1988–1992); Chief Executive Officer, CAN–AM Video Productions (1983–1988). **Associations & Accomplishments:** Canadian Professional Sales Association. **Personal:** Married to Norah. Mr. Selzer enjoys competitive handgun shooting and playing squash.

Toni M. Smith

Director of Product Support
Global Village Communications
1144 East Arques Avenue
Sunnyvale, CA 94086–4602
(408) 523–2360
Fax: (408) 523–2580
EMAIL: See Below

7373

Business Information: Global Village Communications is an international manufacturer of computer software and modems for personal computers, as well as providing Internet services. Established in 1989, Global Village Communications currently employs 200 people. As Director of Product Support, Ms. Smith is responsible for providing technical support and customer service. She can also be reached through the Internet via: toni_smith@globalvillage.com **Career Steps:** Director of Product Support, Global Village Communications (1994–Present); Senior Manager, Intuit (1989–1994); Customer Service Manager, Saratoga Savings and Loan (1986–1989); Technical Support/Customer Service Representative, NCR (1981–1986). **Associations & Accomplishments:** Published in service newsletter. **Personal:** Married to Tom Smith in 1979. Ms. Smith enjoys reading, gardening, and photography.

Ricardo Studart, P.E.

President
Synesis International, Inc.
555 North Pleasantburg Drive, Suite 325
Greenville, SC 29607
(803) 233–3404
Fax: (803) 233–7807

7373

Business Information: Synesis International, Inc. is a computer systems integration and operations improvement service company. Established in 1984, Synesis International, Inc. currently employs 20 people. As President, Mr. Studart is responsible for all aspects of operations, including strategic planning and marketing. With over 15 years of experience in the systems integration field, Rick has led the analysis, design, development and implementation of several small and large systems integration projects. He also has extensive end–user and customer contact — providing user training, technical consultation, project estimating and management, and functional specification. **Career Steps:** President, Synesis International, Inc. (1994–Present); Senior Systems Engineer, CRS Engineers, Inc. (1987–1994); Automation Systems Engineer, Electronic Data Systems (1983–1987); Senior Systems / Project Engineer, Jacobs–Sirrine Engineers. **Associations & Accomplishments:** American Production and Inventory Control Society; Registered Professional Engineer — state of South Carolina; Society of Manufacturing Engineers. **Education:** University of Ottawa, B.S. in Mechanical Engineering, cum laude (1983); EDS Systems Engineering Development Program (1986). **Personal:** Married to Brenda in 1983, Mr. Studart has three children. He enjoys bicycling and swimming with his family.

Craig Thomson

President
Paradon Computer Systems, Ltd.
360 Bay Street
Victoria, British Columbia V8T 1P7
(604) 360–1473
Fax: (604) 360–1182
EMail: See Below

7373

Business Information: Paradon Computer Systems, Ltd. is a computer systems integrator, taking computer systems and customizing them to meet customer's requirements. The Company is also involved in distribution and retail sales of computer components. As President, Mr. Thomson serves as the business planner, visionary, prospector, and opportunity seeker. He has total profit and loss responsibility and oversees every aspect of the business. Internet users can reach him via: CTHOMSON@PARADON.COM. **Career Steps:** President, Paradon Computer Systems, Ltd. (1991–Present); Combat Systems Engineer, Canadian Navy (1983–1991). **Associations & Accomplishments:** Board of Advisors, University of Victoria Faculty of Business; Young Entrepreneurs Organization; Victoria Chamber of Commerce – Business Achievement Committee; Canadian Guide Dogs for the Blind – Puppy Trainer. **Education:** Royal Military College, Bachelor in Engineering (1987). **Personal:** Married to Laurie–Annie in 1988. Mr. Thomson enjoys bridge and training seeing eye dogs.

Fred Van Dyk

Controller
Control Transaction Corporation
130 Clinton Road
Fairfield, NJ 07004–2914
(201) 575–9100 Ext. 218
Fax: (201) 575–1769

7373

Business Information: Control Transaction Corporation is a computer systems assembly and sales corporation, providing point–of–sale systems for the restaurant and hotel industries; utilizing customized software. Established in 1979, Control Transaction Corporation currently employs 52 people and has an estimated annual revenue of $5 million. As Controller, Mr. Van Dyk oversees all financial reporting and activities. Also duties include responsibility for receivable and payable departments, sales tax filings, commission program, treasury and investments, as well as insurance for Company and employees. **Career Steps:** Controller, Control Transaction Corporation (1993–Present); Controller, CHEMAP Division, Alfa Laval Inc. (1989–1993); Senior Financial Auditor, Hertz Rent–a–Car (1988–1989); Audit Manager, Curtiss Wright Corporation (1985–1988). **Associations & Accomplishments:** Treasurer, New Jersey Midland Railroad Historical Society; Vestry, Saint Clements Episcopal Church; Outstanding Young Man of America (1988); New Jersey and United States Jaycees, Award Winner (1988, 1989, 1990); POW/MIA National League of Families, Medal Recipient; Former Master Councilor, Order of De Molay. **Education:** Rutgers University, B.A. in Accounting (1982). **Personal:** Mr. Van Dyk enjoys photography and railroads.

Mr. Richard F. Van Praag

Consultant
RVP Group
6639 Mount Royal Drive
San Jose, CA 95120–1939
(408) 997–6858
Fax: (408) 997–6858 Ext: 11

7373

Business Information: RVP Group is a systems integration consultancy, providing data, software products and local area network (LAN) integration and installation. Mr. Van Praag serves as Senior Consultant responsible for all LAN and WAN installation and design aspects. **Career Steps:** Consultant, RVP Group (1993–Present); Senior Staff Analyst, Tandem Computers Inc. (1985–1993); Manager of Systems Development, Braegen (1983–1984); Senior Staff Consultant, Memorex (1977–1983); Software Development, IBM (retired); Officer, U.S. Army Air Defense (retired). **Associations & Accomplishments:** Network Professional Association; Campbell Moose Lodge of Loyal Order of Moose; Retired Army Officer Association. **Education:** Wayne State University, B.A. (1951); Riverside Military Academy. **Personal:** Married to Georgia L. in 1982. Six children: Richard F. Jr., Raymond K., Ralph L., Russell D., Bob Thompson and deceased son Col. Jerald L. Thompson. Mr. Van Praag enjoys motorcycle riding (BMW).

Douglas Lee Varble

National Sales Manager
Xyquad, Inc.
2921 South Brentwood Boulevard
St. Louis, MO 63144–2713
(314) 961–5995 Ext: 20
Fax: (314) 961–8094
EMAIL: See Below

7373

Business Information: Named as one of the fastest growing businesses in the Inc. 500 magazine in 1988 and 1989. Xyquad, Inc. provides personal computer–based software packages and hardware maintenance to financial industries, commercial banks, and traditional savings and loans. As National Sales Manager, Douglas Varble manages sales and growth of the company as one of the three managers, with seven employees under his authority. Internet users can reach him via: dvarble@xyquad.com **Career Steps:** National Sales Manager, Xyquad, Inc. (1988–Present); Sales Representative, Keldon, Inc. (1982–1988); Store Manager, Lettuce Leaf Restaurants (1980–1982). **Associations & Accomplishments:** Boy Scouts of America; Friends of Scouting; President, Mid-Missouri Mud Masters; The University Club. **Education:** University of Missouri – Columbia, B.S. in Recreation & Park Administration (1981). **Personal:** Married to Amy Ivey in April,1991. One child: Curtis Lee, born November, 1993. Mr. Varble enjoys trout fishing, off–road vehicles, and surfing the Internet.

Edmond J. Blausten

Chief Technical Officer
GTECH Corporation
P.O. Box 6074
Warwick, RI 02887–6074
(401) 392–7410
Fax: (401) 884–8886
EMAIL: See Below

7374

Business Information: GTECH Corporation is a provider of transaction processing systems and networks for the lottery, welfare, and other government–operated/associated automated programs. GTECH is also moving into the non–gaming side of governmental divisions — they just took on the Texas Fish and Game Department and will do licensing by computer, etc. Established in 1982, GTECH reports annual revenue of $700 million and currently employs more than 4,000 people. With over sixteen years expertise in the communications industry, Mr. Blausten joined GTECH in 1992. Serving as Chief Technical Officer of the Government Services Division, he defines the overall architecture (system and operation) from communication networks to central CPU's. **Career Steps:** Chief Technical Officer, GTECH Corporation (1992–Present); Vice President – TDS, Electronic Data Systems (1985–1992); Director of Research and Development, ITT World Communications, Inc. (1979–1985). **Associations & Accomplishments:** International Telecommunications Union; Group Chairman, CCITT; National Association of Radio and Telecommunications Engineers. **Education:** University of Phoenix, M.B.A.; Fairleigh Dickinson, M.S.E.E.; Lehigh University, B.S. **Personal:** Married to Toshiko in 1982. Mr. Blausten enjoys breeding and showing dogs.

James R. Driscoll

Division Vice President
EDS
1601 Trapelo Road
Waltham, MA 02154
(617) 487–1707
Fax: (617) 487–1898

7374

Business Information: EDS is a global information technology services company providing business information to corporations in the financial, transportation, health care, communications, retail, and government sectors. Founded in 1962 by Ross Perot, the Corporation is currently a subsidiary of General Motors and is experiencing approximately 20% annual growth. EDS employs 80,000 people and reports annual revenue of over $10 billion. An executive with EDS since 1991, Mr. Driscoll was appointed in his current position as Division Vice President in 1994. He oversees all North American operations for the Wireless Industry division. Established in 1986, the division employs over 800 people with annual sales in excess of $140 million. **Career Steps:** EDS: Division Vice President (1994–Present), Vice President of Sales (1993–1994), Vice President of Consulting (1991–1993). **Associations & Accomplishments:** Cellular Telecommunications Industry Association; Public speaker at conferences. **Education:** University of Maine, B.A. in Math (1975). **Personal:** Married to Gayle in 1977. Two children: James and Leslie. Mr. Driscoll enjoys golf, basketball, woodworking, coaching, and spending time with his family.

Patrick H. Enright

Senior Sales Consultant
Oracle Corporation
196 Van Buren Street
Herndon, VA 22070–5337
(703) 708–6599
Fax: (703) 708–7922
EMAIL: See Below

7374

Business Information: Oracle Corporation is the second largest information management software company in the world. Established in 1979, the Company provides relational databases, software tools, and services to over 93 countries. Employing over 23,000 people, the Company has an estimated annual revenue of $4 billion. As Senior Sales Consultant, Mr. Enright is responsible for all aspects of sales support. His duties include administration, operations, public relations, and strategic planning. He also manages a staff of five that provides information to the sales team. Internet users can reach him via: Penright@US.oracle.com. **Career Steps:** Senior Sales Consultant, Oracle Corporation (1993–Present). **Education:** Carisius College: B.A. in Computers, B.A. in Engineering, B.A. in Psychology, B.S. in Marketing (1993). **Personal:** Mr. Enright enjoys sky diving, fast cars, and taking risks.

Jim M. Peoples

Product Development Manager
IHS – Regulatory Products
15 Inverness Way East
Englewood, CO 80112–5776
(303) 754–4047
Fax: (303) 754–4085
EMAIL: See Below

7374

Business Information: IHS Group is a publisher of regulatory data bases in the areas of banking, engineering, and health and environmental issues, using Microsoft Base Windows. IHS primarily serves businesses in Denver, Colorado, but also serves customers from IHS Group in India. With ten years of experience in computer applications, Mr. Peoples joined IHS as Product Development Manager in 1994. He is responsible for directing the development of Federal Personnel products, as well as evaluating requirement and potential software solutions. Concurrent with his position at IHS, he is a partner with the software development firm — AFIS. In this capacity, he designs and implements database applications for personal computers. Internet users can reach him via: jim.peoples@ihs.com **Career Steps:** Product Development Manager – Regulatory Products, IHS Group (1994–Present); Partner, AFIS (software consulting firm); Project Manager / Team Leader, Jeppesen Sanderson (1990–1994); Senior Systems Analyst, Coors Brewing Company (1989–1990); Software Consultant – Federal Systems, Intergraph Corporation (1988–1989); Senior Information Systems Specialist, Martin Marietta – Astronautics Division (1981–1988); Program Control Analyst, SDC – Pittsburgh Energy Technology Center (1979–1981); Electronics Maintenance Supervisor, USAF – McClellan AFB (1973–1978). **Associations & Accomplishments:** Pilot, Civil Air Patrol – Colorado Wing, Black Sheep Squadron (1989); Aircraft Owners and Pilots Association; Association for Computing Machinery; AWARDS: President's Award for Excellence in Customer Satisfaction Improvement (1990) – by Coors Brewing Company; MVP Award (1988) and Performance Award (1984) – by Martin Marietta Corporation; Commendation for Outstanding Performance (1976) – USAF. **Education:** Metropolitan State College, Denver, CO, B.S. in Computer and Management Science, summa cum laude (1986) – President's Honor Roll, Golden Key Honor Society, Colorado Scholars Awards; Americn River College, Sacramento, CA, A.A. in Mathematics and Physical Sciences; USAF: Honor Graduate – Leadership Academy (1977) and Electronic Communications and Cryptographic Systems (1974). **Personal:** Married to Helen in 1973. Two children: Ann and Darien. Mr. Peoples enjoys aviation and sailing.

Denise Jean Richardson

Associate Site Director
SCT at Fairfield University
Bannow GR–20, North Benson Road, Fairfield University
Fairfield, CT 06430
(203) 254–4000 Ext. 2460
Fax: (203) 254–4003

7374

Business Information: SCT is an out–source data processing contract firm, specifically serving the higher education sectors. Working for SCT at various university sites since 1992, Denise Richardson was transferred to the Fairfield University site in September of 1994. Currently serving as Site Director, she manages all computer functions and support personnel. **Career Steps:** SCT at Fairfield University: Acting Site Director (1995–Present), Associate Director (1994–1995), Technical Staff, SCT – Mississippi College (1992–1994); Technical Specialist and Project Manager, Harvard University (1991–1992); Sr. Technical Consultant, PSDI (1986–1991). **Associations & Accomplishments:** Fairfield Public rSchools Mentor Program; MENSA Member; Licensed Construction Superintendent. **Education:** Harvard University, A.L.B. cum laude (1992). **Personal:** Ms. Richardson enjoys dog training (raises and trains AKC Portugese Water dogs) and community service work.

James F. Rivas

General Manager/Vice President
Demand Publishing, Inc.
1301 Friedrichs Street
Gretna, LA 70053
(504) 366–7469
Fax: (504) 368–7258
EMail: See Below

7374

Business Information: Demand Publishing, Inc. provides specialty data services and publishing for many Fortune 500 companies. The Company also handles custom work for their clients. As General Manager/Vice President, Mr. Rivas is responsible for all aspects of Company operations, including day–to–day operations, and achievement of long– and short–term goals. Internet users can reach him via: dpi@access-com.net. **Career Steps:** General Manager/Vice President, Demand Publishing, Inc. (1993–Present); President, Rivas Business Forms, Inc. (1986–1993); Assistant Plant Manager, Ball Metal Decorating, Inc. (1985–1986). **Associations & Accomplishments:** Board Member, GCCA Delta Chapter. **Education:** Rochester Institute of Technology, B.S. (1985). **Personal:** Married to Denise in 1986. Two children: Meredith and Anne. Mr. Rivas enjoys fishing and skiing.

Stephen G. Romano

Vice President
Securities Industry Automation Corporation
2 Metrotech Center
Brooklyn, NY 11201
(212) 383–6188
Fax: (212) 479–3773

7374

Business Information: Securities Industry Automation Corporation is a provider of Data Processing Services for the New York Stock Exchange, American Stock Exchange, and the National Securities Clearing Corporation and its' affiliates. Established in 1972, Securities Industry Automation Corporation has two offices in New York and currently employs 1,400 people. Joining the corporation in 1986, as Vice President Stephen Romano provides the Development and Production support of Securities Clearance and Settlement Applications. He also oversees the Administration of Financial support functions for the Clearing Corporation. **Career Steps:** Vice President, Securities Industry Automation Corporation (1986–Present); Director of Information Technology, Eastern States Bankcard (1981–1986); Manager of Development, Citicorp (1976–1981). **Associations & Accomplishments:** Securities Industry Association, Data Management Division; Wall Street Member; Cashiers' Association of Wall Street; United Way Campaign, Chairman (1994–1995); Recent Accomplishment: Implementation of the Securities and Exchange Commission T+3 Settlement Mandate for the National Securities Clearing Corporation (1993); Speaker and Sponsor of the Technical Leadership program which is part of the Corporate Wide Leadership Development system at SIAC. **Education:** SUNY (1978); U.S. Army Data Processing Instructor, Ft. Benjamin Harrison. **Personal:** Married to Patricia in 1994. Four children: Laura, Donna, Gina, and Stephen Jr. Mr. Romano enjoys golf, tennis, and doing volunteer work.

Arthur B. Smith

President/Founder
Emergent Technology
4500 County Road 351
Fulton, MO 65251
(573) 642–8802
Fax: (573) 884–5444
EMail: See Below

7374

Business Information: Emergent Technology is an independent consulting firm, providing training, analysis design, and the development of computerized data base applications. The Company's focus is on three specific areas: data base design and MUMPS; training of design and MUMPS Program; and technical writing. Founding Emergent Technology in 1995 and serving as its President, Mr. Smith is responsible for all aspects of operations, including consulting services. He is currently compiling an article for Dr. Dobbs Journal on "Object–Oriented Programming in MUMP." Internet users can reach him via: art@vets.vetmed.missouri.edu **Career Steps:** President/Founder, Emergent Technology (1995–Present); Senior Computer Programmer/Analyst, University of Missouri – Department of Veterinary Medicine and Surgery (1991–Present); Engineering Development Manager, Computerized Medical Systems (1987–1991); Senior Scientific

Programmer, Teknivent (1985–1987). **Associations & Accomplishments:** Chair, Veterinary Informatics Standards Organization; Subcommittee Chair, Mumps Development Committee; M Technology Association; Institute for Electrical and Electronics Engineers; Firefighter/EMT, Millersburg Fire Protection District; Secretary/Treasurer, Millersburg Fire Protection District; Publisher, Millersburg Mirror; Missouri Historical Society; Religious Society of Friends (Quakers); Published "M Computing" comparison on data bases, strengths and effectiveness technology in 1996; Amateur Tubist. **Education:** University of Delaware: M.S./C.I.S. (1985), M.S./Chem. (1985), B.S./Chem. (1981). **Personal:** Married to Amanda in 1983. One child: Michael. Mr. Smith enjoys playing the tuba.

Steve Taylor
General Manager
Cashflex
5201 W. Kennedy Blvd., Ste. 800
Tampa, FL 33609–1822
(813) 282–8855
Fax: (813) 289–0287
E/M: AOL.CFTAYLORS

7374

Business Information: Cashflex is a payment and data processing center providing lock box services for its customers. Cashflex operates 16 sites across the United States. As General Manager of the Tampa, Florida site, Steve Taylor is responsible for site profitability and administration of operations, customer satisfaction, as well as the supervision of 180 employees. **Career Steps:** General Manager, Cashflex (1993–Present); Operations Manager, Barnett Bank (1987–1993); Operations Manager, Telecheck Southcoast (1981–1985); Hospital Corpsman, U.S. Navy (1976–1980). **Education:** University of North Florida, B.A. in Management (1987). **Personal:** Married to Stacey Mashburn in 1996. Mr. Taylor enjoys surfing, running, and rollerblading.

Gilberto Teixeira

Customer Satisfaction Director
IBM Brazil, Limited
CP 71 CEP 13001–050
Campinas, San Paulo, Brazil
55011–8865126
Fax: 55019–8657671

7374

Business Information: IBM Brazil, Limited designs, manufactures and markets high–tech products globally. This includes information systems products and services, computers, semiconductors, networking hardware and software, and computer hardware and software. Services include outsourcing, multivendor support, and consulting. As Customer Satisfaction Director, Mr. Teixeira handles the strategic planning and customer satisfaction operations for IBM Latin American. **Career Steps:** IBM: Customer Satisfaction Director (1996–Present), Industrial/Marketing Administration Director (1990–1996), Manufacturing Operations Manager (1985–1990). **Associations & Accomplishments:** President, Association of Campinas Region Executives; Vice President, Association for Infant Protection Against Violence. **Education:** Faculdade Engineering Industrial, Electronic Engineering (1970). **Personal:** Married to Eloisa Portes in 1973. Four children: Gustavo, Elena, Fernando, and Paulo. Mr. Teixeira enjoys tennis.

Thomas York Jr.
Vice President
SCC Resources, Inc.
165 East Water Street
Sandusky, OH 44870–6061
(419) 625–1605
Fax: (419) 625–0081

7374

Business Information: SCC Resources, Inc. is a financial data processing firm comprised of three divisions: Corporate, Microcomputer, and Banking Operations. The primary focus of the company is back room financial systems services and personal computer sales and support. Established in 1966, the company serves community banks as well as other financial institutions. As Vice President, Mr. York's primary responsibility is managing and ensuring the profitability of the Microcomputer Division of SCC. Additionally, Mr. York oversees the company's strategic planning and process improvement teams, coordinates managers of the company's divisions, prepares divisional financial reports, ensures quality customer service, and implements various company policies and procedures. **Career Steps:** SCC Resources, Inc.: Vice President (1996–), Division Manager (1995–96); MIS Manager, Lear Corporation (1993–1995). **Associations & Accomplishments:** Erie County Chamber of Commerce; American Banking Association; Sandusky Jaycees; APICS; USGA.

Education: Ashland University, M.B.A. (1996); Bowling Green State University, B.S.B.A. **Personal:** Married to Lisa in 1995. Mr. York enjoys golf, basketball, baseball, and personal computers.

Francois Aird

President
CEDROM–SNI
825 Rue Querbes, Bureau 200
Outremont, Quebec H2V 3X1
(514) 278–6060
Fax: (514) 278–5415
EMail: See Below

7375

Business Information: CEDROM–SNI specializes in electronic publishing and distribution. As a result of a merger between CEDROM Technologies and SNI in 1991, CEDROM–SNI was created to distribute information products (CD–ROM) and Internet servers. As President, Mr. Aird is in charge of management and Corporate relations. He is also President of A&G Consulting Group, a general consultancy in information technology. Internet users can reach him via: aird@cedrom-sni.qc.ca. **Career Steps:** President, CEDROM–SNI (1994–Present); President, CEDROM Technologies (1989–1994); President, A&G Consulting Group (1987–1989). **Associations & Accomplishments:** Member of the Governor's Office; CPLQ (Software Association in Quebec); High Technology Advisory Committee, National Bank of Canada. **Education:** HEC; College Sean de Bribeuf. **Personal:** Married to Marieke Lemieux. One child: Marianne. Mr. Aird enjoys scuba diving, rock climbing, and cross country skiing.

Edward R. Alexander Jr.
Director of Information Technology
Infoteq
5801 Supra Place
Riverdale, MD 20737
(301) 345–9608
Fax: (301) 345–9609

7375

Business Information: Infoteq is a government contractor providing the government with information technology. Established in 1983, Infoteq reports annual revenue of $13 million and currently employs 40 people. As Director of Information Technology, Mr. Alexander is responsible for the control of all technologies, program telecommunications, computers, and information technology equipment. **Career Steps:** Director of Information Technology, Infoteq (1993–Present); Programmer Tasklead, ISSC (1991–1993); Information Developer, IBM (1988–1991). **Associations & Accomplishments:** Sterling Who's Who Executive Directory (1995). **Education:** American University, M.S. in Information Systems (1993), B.S. in Information Systems (1989). **Personal:** Mr. Alexander enjoys jazz, multi–media computers, weight training and billiards.

Gerard Blanding
Internal Systems Consultant
Equifax
Drop 410, 1505 Windward Course
Alpharetta, GA 30202–4180
(770) 740–4689
Fax: (770) 740–4653

7375

Business Information: Equifax is a credit information supplier to corporations and individuals, including vehicle records, property, health care facility records, and public records. Joining Equifax in 1983 as a Systems Programmer, Gerard Blanding was promoted to his current position as Internal Systems Consultant in 1995. He is responsible for the design, development and support of communications systems. **Career Steps:** Equifax: Internal Systems Consultant (1995–Present), Senior Systems Programmer (1987–1995), Systems Programmer (1983–1987); Data Systems Engineer, RCA (1978–1983). **Associations & Accomplishments:** DEC Users Group; Deacon, Hopewell Baptist Church. **Education:** Southern College of Technology, Electrical Engineering Technology (1981). **Personal:** Married to Veta in 1991. Two children: Alisha Jenay and Gerard Jr. Mr. Blanding enjoys photography, investing, and spending time with his family.

David R. Bornemann

President and Chief Executive Officer
DR Bornemann
8133 Leesburg Pike, Suite 500
Vienna, VA 22182–2706
(703) 821–6848
Fax: Please mail or call

7375

Business Information: DR Bornemann is an informations systems firm for the airline industry, marketing to approximately 50 airlines worldwide. The Firm develops and publishes software to provide schedules for pilot's and flight attendants, and determine how much fuel and cargo is carried for the airlines. Established in 1978, DR Bornemann reports annual revenue of $3 million and currently employs 22 people. As President and Chief Executive Officer, Mr. Bornemann is responsible for the oversight of all aspects of operations, including designing software and supervising a staff of ten computer professionals, seven customer support staff, and five administrators. **Career Steps:** President and Chief Executive Officer, DR Bornemann (1978–Present); Vice President, Planning Research Corporation (1972–1978); Manager of Operations Research, American Airlines (1967–1971). **Associations & Accomplishments:** International Aviation Club; Operations Research Society of America; Frequent lecturer on environmental issues **Education:** Harvard Business School, M.B.A. (1967); Amherst College, A.B. in Math **Personal:** Married to Carmody in 1963. Two children: Cecily and Elizabeth.

Jeffrey E. Cline
Sales Manager
Agency Management Services
7481 Eleanor Drive
Mechanicsville, VA 23111
(804) 730–1240
Fax: (804) 730–0743
EMail: See Below

7375

Business Information: Agency Management Services specializes in information systems and automation production for independent insurance agents. Located all over the United States, the Company provides software to over 350 insurance companies. As Sales Manager, Mr. Cline is responsible for the Eastern Regional Sales division. He is mainly responsible for personnel, as well as recruiting new clients and customer relations. Internet users can reach him via: ClineJe@amsrating.iix.com. **Career Steps:** Agency Management Services: Eastern Regional Sales Manager (Present), Southern Regional Sales Manager, Account Manager. **Associations & Accomplishments:** Washington Henry Masonic Lodge #334; Eastern Hanover Volunteer Fire Department: Vice President, Firefighter; EMT, Eastern Hanover Volunteer Rescue Squad. **Education:** Lasalle University, B.A. in Business Administration (1996); J. Seargent Community College, A.A.S. in Management. **Personal:** Married to Melanie in 1993. One child: Jeffrey Douglas.

Jorge D. DeCesare
Administrative Director
UniHealth Information Services
11155 Sepulveda Boulevard
Mission Hills, CA 91345–1113
(818) 837–2733
Fax: (818) 837–2880
Email: See Below

7375

Business Information: UniHealth Information Services is one of the largest healthcare information services provider in the nation, offering D.P. and WAN connectivity to over sixty sites. As Administrative Director, Mr. DeCesare is responsible for administering daily support, providing staff management services, and strategic planning. Internet users can reach him via: Decesare@mhdc.unihealth.com. **Career Steps:** Administrative Director, UniHealth Information Services (1994–Present); Vice President, R & D Technologies, Inc. (1991–1994); Account Executive, MCI Telecommunications (1989–1991); Account Executive, Pacific Bell (1984–1989). **Associations & Accomplishments:** Telecommunications Association; Microsoft Healthcare Users Group; International SL1 Users Group; Society of Telecommunications Consultants. **Education:** University of Redlands, B.S. (1988); Fiber Optics Design Certification; AT&T Certification; Northern Telecom Certification. **Personal:** Mr. DeCesare enjoys motorcycles, mountain bicycling, and writing.

Howard T. DeRemer

Director
Dun & Bradstreet Solution Center
899 Eaton Avenue
Bethlehem, PA 18025–0001
(610) 882–6060
Fax: (610) 882–6005
7375

Business Information: Dun & Bradstreet Information Services is a global information company with the world's largest 'commercial' database, specializing in business–to–business credit, marketing, and other risk management and decision support services. A management executive with Dun & Bradstreet since 1987, Howard DeRemer was appointed to his current position in 1995. As Director of D&B's Solution Center, he is responsible for planning, implementing, and directing all programs associated with an inbound/outbound call center to present, promote, and deliver Dun & Bradstreet's products and services through customer education. **Career Steps:** Dun & Bradstreet Information Services: Director – D&B Solution Center (1995–Present), Call Center Manager (1993–1995), Sales Trainer (1992–1993), Sales Manager (1991–1992), Senior Divisional Manager – Information Resources Division (1987–1991). **Education:** Moravian College, M.B.A. (1995); Shippensburg University of Pennsylvania, B.S, B.A. in Accounting. **Personal:** Married to Lisa in 1990. One child: Paige. Mr. DeRemer enjoys golf, boating, fishing, and reading.

Naheed R. Ferguson

Senior Director of Product Development
Knight Ridder Information, Inc.
One Summit Way
Woodside, CA 94062
(415) 299–9510
Fax: (415) 299–1970
EMAIL: See Below
7375

Business Information: Knight–Ridder Information, Inc. is a global leader in providing electronic publishing and on–line information technologies. A Certified Novell Network Analyst, Naheed Ferguson joined Knight–Ridder in November of 1994. As Senior Director of Product Development, she manages international and Internet/Web product development, as well as has international marketing and P&L responsibilities. Internet users can reach her via: nferg@datatools.com **Career Steps:** Senior Director of Product Development, Knight–Ridder Information, Inc. (1994–Present); Managing Director of Services, Network General (1990–1994); Director of Marketing, Microbar Systems, Inc. (1988–1990); Product Marketing Manager, Novell/Excelan (1984–1988). **Associations & Accomplishments:** Commercenet Consortium Committees; American Management Association; American Electronics Association. **Education:** Stanford University, M.B.A. (1993); OSU, B.S. in Computer Science (1982). **Personal:** Married to Roger in 1994. One child: Ariana. Ms. Ferguson enjoys swimming, The Web, and spending time with her daughter.

TITAN

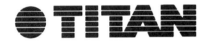

C. L. Hensel

President
Titan Systems Group
1900 Campus Commons Drive
Reston, VA 22091–1535
(703) 758–6505
Fax: (703) 758–6501
7375

Business Information: Titan Systems Group is an informations management systems firm providing design and integration services. Established in 1982, Titan Systems Group reports annual revenue of $35 million and currently employs 300 people. As President, Mr. Hensel is responsible for all aspects of operations, including operating as General Manager of Government Business. **Career Steps:** President, Titan Systems Group (1995–Present); Senior Vice President and General Manager, ARC (1988–1994); Vice President and General Management, Perkin Elmer (1985–1988). **Associations & Accomplishments:** Member of the Board of Directors, Joint Military Intelligence College Foundation (1989–Present); Member of the Board of Directors, University of Southern Connecticut Foundation (1987–1988); Member of the Board of Directors, Chamber of Commerce, Danbury, Connecticut (1985–1988). **Education:** Drexel University, M.S. in Electrical Engineering (1966); Northeastern University, B.S. in Electrical Engineering (1959). **Personal:** Married to Carole A. Hensel in 1957. Five children: Leroy Michael and John P. Hensel, Cheryl M. Gamber, Victoria L. Lascomb, and Julia A. Morgan. Mr. Hensel enjoys golf, reading, and exercise.

Michael R. Johnston

Director of Content Development
DataTimes
14000 Quail Springs Parkway, Suite 450
Oklahoma City, OK 73134
(405) 749–6334
Fax: (405) 749–7150
EMail: See Below
7375

Business Information: DataTimes is an information network of over 5,000 newspapers, newswires, trade and industry, and financial information. The Company delivers information products through online, Internet, EMail, and LAN products. As Director of Content Development, Mr. Johnston directs all activities related to licensing content for the enterprise–wide use of electronic information services. This includes the management of content acquisition, contract administration, and development of content collection procedures. Internet users can reach him via: MJOHNSTON@DATATIMES.COM. **Career Steps:** DataTimes: Director of Content Development (1996–Present), Manager of Content Acquisition (1995), Manager of Online Division (1994), East Region Manager (1992–1993), Account Executive (1989–1992). **Associations & Accomplishments:** Interactive Services Association; Special Libraries Association; University of Oklahoma Alumni Association; Ducks Unlimited; Delta Tau Delta; Excellence in Performance Award in Business Development (1995); Treasurer, Delta Tau Delta Housing Corporation; DataTimes Generator Award (July 1989, September 1989, April 1990, and June 1991). **Education:** Oklahoma University: B.S. in Public Affairs and Administration (1988), currently attending MBA program. **Personal:** Married to Jenny Monroe in 1994. One child: Abigail Jane. Mr. Johnston enjoys hunting, scuba diving, and golf.

NETCOM
Leading Internet
Service Provider

Warren J. Kaplan

Executive Vice President
Netcom On–Line Communication Services, Inc.
3031 Tisch Way
San Jose, CA 95128
(408) 556–3287
Fax: (408) 983–1550
EMAIL: See Below
7375

Business Information: Netcom On–Line Communication Services, Inc., the first Internet company to go public, is an Internet software end access and service provider and is the manufacturer of NetCruiser software. Major offices are in Dallas, Texas; Toronto, Canada; and the United Kingdom, with other locations in over 200 cities worldwide. A Certified Public Accountant with more than eight years experience in finance, Mr. Kaplan joined Netcom as Chief Financial Officer in 1994. Appointed as Executive Vice President in 1994, Mr. Kaplan is charged with expanding the Company on a global basis. Concurrent with his position as Executive Vice President, he serves as Managing Director International, Secretary, and Director. Internet users can reach him via: wjk@netcom.com. **Career Steps:** Netcom On–Line Communication Services, Inc.: Executive Vice President (1994–Present), Managing Director International (1995–Present), Secretary (1994–Present), Director (1994–Present), Chief Financial Officer (1994–1995); Vice President of Operations, Gefinor (USA), Inc. (1989–1993); Senior Vice President, Chief Financial Officer, and Interim Chief Executive Officer, Sheaffer Pen Company, a subsidiary of Gefinor (USA) Inc. (1989–1991 and 1989–1990); Chief Financial Officer, The Interface Group, Inc. (1988–1989). **Associations & Accomplishments:** Certified Public Accountant: State of New York and State of Massachusetts. **Education:** Long Island University, M.B.A. in Taxation; New York University, B.S. in Accounting. **Personal:** Married to Judy. Two children: Marc and Stuart.

Steven P. Kimmich

Vice President of Information Services
Claritas
53 Brown Road
Ithaca, NY 14850–1262
(607) 257–5757
Fax: (607) 266–0891
7375

Business Information: Claritas specializes in providing a demographic and behavioral database for market research and site selection. In operation since 1970, Claritas currently employs 240 people. Joining Claritas' information and computer services staff in 1985, Mr. Kimmich was appointed to his current executive position in 1994. As Vice President of Information Service, he is responsible for the group and processing functions for delivery of corporate data products to clients. **Career Steps:** Claritas: Vice President of Information Service (1994–Present), Director of Information Service (1993–1994), Director of Information and Computer Service (1985–1993). **Associations & Accomplishments:** American Management Association; DECUS (Digital Equipment Computer Users Group). **Education:** State University of New York – Potsdam, B.A. in Computer Science (1978). **Personal:** Married to Tammie in 1979. Mr. Kimmich enjoys motorcycles, snowmobiles, bowling and horses.

Thomas H. Maurer

Director of Communication Services
Roadway Information Technology
1077 Gorge Boulevard
Akron, OH 44309–3558
(216) 258–6264
Fax: (216) 643–6933
7375

Business Information: Roadway Information Technology is the information systems–operations arm of major transportation conglomerate Roadway Services, Inc., providing infrastructure and support to its operating entities and subsidiaries. Future plans include setting up a Frame Relay Network System for data communication, providing international contract for services in voice and data communication, as well as a single point of contact for paging in cellular telephones. Established in 1994, Roadway Information Technology currently employs 225 people. As Director of Communication Services, Mr. Maurer is responsible for the overall direction of voice/data communications, corporate systems, end user computing/ LAN services, and data administration. Additional duties include business planning, strategic planning, directing reports, developing policies, problem solving, budget development, and software and hardware implementation strategies. **Career Steps:** Director of Communication Services, Roadway Information Technology (1992–Present); Vice President, Progressive Insurance, Inc. (1984–1992); President of the Northwest Division, The Boise Company (1981–1984); General Manager of the Housing Division, Boise Cascade (1976–1981). **Associations & Accomplishments:** International Communications Association (ICA); Telecommunications Committee Conference Board, The Center for Information Systems – Kent State University; Recipient of Galen Roush Award (1993). **Education:** Wittenberg University, B.S. in Physical Science (1960). **Personal:** Married to Jacqueline in 1960. Five children: Jennifer, Kimberly, Scott, Todd, and Daniel. Mr. Maurer enjoys music, golf, and camping.

Maltee McMahon

Information Specialist
First Call for Help, Inc.
915 15th Avenue, SE
Menomonee, WI 54751–3404
(715) 235–3947
Fax: (715) 235–4881
7375

Business Information: Established in 1994, First Call for Help is an information and referral service for Health & Human Service Agencies. As Information Specialist, Ms. McMahon is responsible for the creation and maintenance of information and referral systems for five counties. She also recruits, trains, and supervises all volunteer and clerical staff, performs marketing and advertising duties, and obtains, updates, and verifies information. Concurrently, Ms. McMahon is the Owner of Ramraj Logistics, Inc., a transportation and delivery company with 51% of shares. **Career Steps:** Information Specialist, First Call for Help (1994–Present); Shift Supervisor, Microfilm Service of Rice Lake (1994–1994); Camera Operator, Micrographics Lab, University of Wisconsin–Stout (1987–1992). **Associations & Accomplishments:** Volunteer Coordinators Network; Dunn County Core Coordination Team; Secretary of Information and Referral Providers of Wisconsin; national Association of Female Executives and Eau Claires womens Network; Alliance of Information and Refferal Systems; Dunn County Food & Shelter Coalition. **Education:** University of Wisconsin–Stout: Master (1992), Bachelor of Science (1989). **Personal:** Married to Jim in 1990. One child:

Christopher. Ms. McMahon enjoys skiing, walking, reading, and golf.

Karl E. Nicosia

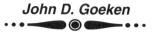

Vice President of Receivables Outsourcing
Dun & Bradstreet Information Services, N.A.
899 Eaton Avenue
Bethlehem, PA 18025
(610) 882–6620
Fax: (610) 882–6650

7375

Business Information: Dun & Bradstreet Information Services (DBIS) is the world's leading provider of business information and decision support services that help customers in marketing, commercial credit and collections reduce risk, improve cash flow, increase sales and revenues and speed payments. As Vice President of Receivables Outsourcing, Mr. Nicosia is responsible for DBIS' Receivables Management Outsourcing group which consists of more than 200 employees. This group provides a wide range of collection–related services performed in the name of the client. He is also responsible for managing the accounts receivable portfolio for DBIS. **Career Steps:** Dun & Bradstreet Information Services: Vice President of Receivables Outsourcing (1994–Present); Assistant Controller (1991–1994); Controller, D & B Business Marketing Services (1985–1991). **Education:** St. Johns' University, B.S. (1973); Attended, Pace University, General Studies in Business. **Personal:** Married to Lucille in 1976. Two children: Karl and Blake. Mr. Nicosia enjoys sports, coaching soccer, and reading.

William E. Schuler, Ph.D.

Corporate Vice President
BDM Federal
1428 Catron Avenue
Albuquerque, NM 87123–4216
(505) 848–5090
Fax: (505) 848–5120

7375

Business Information: BDM Federal, a subsidiary of BDM International, is an international technical services firm focusing on information technologies, such as systems integration, software development, and applications. Established in 1959, BDM reports annual revenue of $800 million and currently employs 7,000 people. As Corporate Vice President of Business Development and Planning, Dr. Schuler is the senior BDM corporate official in New Mexico where BDM currently has approximately 500 employees. He focuses on a wide range of business development efforts centered in BDM's Albuquerque operations, while supporting marketing across the full spectrum of the Company's business activities. He is helping strengthen the marketing by Albuquerque–based business units while also seeking to build business with the national laboratories and other valued and potential clients in New Mexico. Representing BDM to state and national political leaders, Dr. Schuler is also the senior BDM Board Member of AB Ventures, a joint venture between BDM and ARCH Venture Partners (AVP), that has available a $30M venture capital fund. AB Ventures is focused on technology transfer and commercialization from UNM, Sandia National Laboratories, and Los Alamos National Laboratory. **Career Steps:** Corporate Vice President, BDM Federal (1993–Present); Partner, Coopers & Lybrand (1988–1993); Corporate Vice President, Science Applications International Corporation (SAIC) (1985–1988). **Associations & Accomplishments:** Serves on the Boards of Directors for: Rio Grande Technology Corporation (RIOTECH), The Technical Vocational Institute Foundation, The UNM Anderson Schools of Management Foundation, The UNM Technology Development Corporation (TDC), and the New Mexico Citizens Crime Commission; Member: Governor's Business Advisory Council (GBAC), The Waste–Management Education and Research Consortium, Albuquerque Economic Forum, Greater Albuquerque Chamber of Commerce, The Alliance for Transportation Research (ATR), Industry Advisory Board (IAB), and The UNM College of Engineering Dean's Advisory Council; Highly decorated veteran of the Vietnam conflict, U.S. Air Force. **Education:** Purdue University, Ph.D. in Operations Research (1972); University of Southern California – Los Angeles, M.S. in Industrial Engineering; United States Naval Academy – Annapolis, B.S. in Engineering; Del Mar College, A.A. **Personal:** Married to Carolyn Callaway in 1981. Four children: William, James, and Michael Schuler and Sharon Von Schrader. Dr. Schuler enjoys fishing, target shooting, and golf.

Ms. JoAnn D. Suleiman

President and Head of Library Services Division
Sanad Support Technologies
11820 Parklawn Drive
Rockville, MD 20852–2529
(301) 231–5999
Fax: (301) 231–5990

7375

Business Information: Sanad Support Technologies is a library and information services company providing language training to the federal government and federal government agencies. Additional services include facility maintenance, Internet/Network/Communication services, training (electronic/ADP, management, English as a second language/ESOL), and VR applications. Established in 1990, Sanad Support Technologies reports annual revenue of $2.5 million and currently employs 49 people. As President and Head of Library Services Division, Ms. Suleiman is responsible for all aspects of operations, including directing operations in Library Services. **Career Steps:** President and Head of Library Services Division, Sanad Support Technologies (1989–Present); Project Manager of NASA, Informations/Sterling Software (1986–1989); Librarian of Advanced Engineering Division, General Electric Informations Systems Company (1983–1986); Head of Regional Medical Center Library, U.S. Air Force, Wright Patterston (1972–1982); Assistant Director of Ohio State University College of Medicine Library (1967–1972). **Associations & Accomplishments:** American Library Association; LITA Division/DC Library Association; Review for American Libraries (1968–Present); Published poetry and short fiction. **Education:** Simmons College, M.S.L.S. (1967); Boston University, B.A. (1962), M.A. in Slavic Composition & Literature (1964). **Personal:** Married to Fuad K. Suleiman, Ph.D. in 1972. Two children: Robin and Colin. Ms. Suleiman enjoys creative writing (poetry & short fiction) and classical music.

Walt J. Wikman

Vice President – Product Engineering
CCC Information Services, Inc.
444 Merchandise Mart
Chicago, IL 60654
(312) 222–4636 Ext. 3423
Fax: Please mail or call
EMAIL: See Below

7375

Business Information: CCC Information Services, Inc. is a custom designer and distributor of software and data products, providing services for insurance companies primarily with the automotive industry and automobile body shops. International in scope, CCC Information Services has two large offices in Illinois and California, with sales offices serving clientele throughout the U.S. and Canada. As Vice President of Product Engineering, Mr. Wikman develops software products on Windows, Unix, and mainframe–based platforms for several product lines within the Decision Support and Server Based Systems. **Career Steps:** Vice President – Product Engineering, CCC Information Services, Inc. (1995–Present); Vice President, Decision Support Development, A.C. Nielsen (1982–1995); Senior Software Engineer, Network Systems Corporation (1979–1982). **Education:** Nassau Community College, A.S. (1976). **Personal:** Married to Vicki in 1974. Two children: Michael and Joseph. Mr. Wikman enjoys golf, guitar, reading and travel.

David N. Gill

Director of Operations
Arcus Data Security, Inc.
P.O. Box 867
Simi Valley, CA 93062–0867
(805) 520–9452
Fax: (805) 520–9343

7376

Business Information: Arcus Data Security, Inc., established in 1971, is an off–site computer data storage and disaster recovery services company, providing contingency planning for the business community. Primarily national in scope, Arcus Data Security, Inc. has locations in all metropolitan areas in the U.S., such as New York, Newark, Philadelphia, Atlanta, Tampa/Orlando, Chicago, Cleveland, Dallas/Fort Worth, Denver, Colorado Springs, Phoenix, Las Vegas, San Diego, Los Angeles, Orange County, Sacramento, San Jose, and San Francisco, as well as one international location in London, England. Joining Arcus Data Security, Inc. in 1992, Mr. Gill serves as Director of Operations. He is responsible for the overall direction and daily activities of the Simi Valley Branch, including client relations, developing and testing disaster plans, and the administrative operations of a support staff of 19. He also serves as the Disaster Recovery Coordinator. Concurrent with his executive position at Arcus, Mr. Gill serves as Assistant Command Inspector with the rank of Major in the U.S. Marine Corps Reserves. **Career Steps:** Director of Operations, Arcus Data Security, Inc. (1992–Present); Assistant Command Inspector, United States Marine Corp Reserve – Major (1992–Present); Executive Officer, United States Marine Corps – Lt. Captain (1979–1991). **Associations & Accomplishments:** The Retired Officers Association; Marine Corps Reserve Officers Association; Marine Corps Association; Lambda Chi Alpha Corporation Board – Beta Rho: Director, Alumni Advisor; Grand Lodge of the Philippines – Okinawa #118. **Education:** California State University – Northridge, B.A. (1979); Pierce College, A.A. (1976); Marine Corps University, Completion Certificates: Amphibious Warfare School, Command and Staff College. **Personal:** Married to Eufrosa in 1984. Four children: Gina, Russell, Krystle, and David Jr. Mr. Gill enjoys organized sports, camping, and jogging.

John D. Goeken

Chairman/Chief Executive Officer
Goeken Group Corporation
1751 Diehl Road, Suite 400
Naperville, IL 60563
(708) 717–6700
Fax: (708) 717–6066

7376

Business Information: Goeken Group Corporation, an international corporation located in Naperville, Illinois, was established in 1974. The Corporation operates three divisions: Medical Data Forwarding, Personal Security, and Personal Safetyware. Mr. Goeken serves as the Corporation's Chairman and Chief Executive Officer, responsible for all aspects of operations. It is also his responsibility to promote the Group's vision for the future. Due to his fervor for busting up communications monopolies, as evidenced by his founding of MCI thirty years ago and causing the break–up of Ma Bell's monopoly, he won the title, "Jack the Giant Killer." Later, he combined computers and flowers, forming FTD Mercury Network, the world's largest online computer network; phones and airplanes, forming Airfone, Inc., the world's first commercial air–to–ground telephone service; and founded In–Flight Phone Corporation, which uses all–digital radio, video screens, and under–the–seat 386 PCs to bring noise–free communications, information and entertainment services to the skies. Mr. Goeken has always made it his goal to seek out ways to make communications possible anywhere people go – an idea that has revolutionized the telecommunications industry. As a result, the industry considers him the father of air–to–ground telephone communication. **Career Steps:** Chairman/Chief Executive Officer, Goeken Group Corporation (1974–Present); Chairman/Chief Executive Officer, In–Flight Phone Corporation (1989–1994); Chairman/Chief Executive Officer, Airfone, Inc. (1974–1989); President/Chief Executive Officer, M.C.I. (1963–1974). **Associations & Accomplishments:** Board Member Foundation, University of New Hampshire; Fellow, Radio Club of America; Board Member Foundation, Southern Illinois University; Board Member, St. Joseph College; Aircraft Owners and Pilots Association; National Business Aircraft Association. **Education:** University of New Hampshire, Honorary Doctorate of Business. **Personal:** Married to Mona Lisa in 1951. Two children: Sandra Kay Goeken Martis, and John A. Mr. Goeken enjoys flying aircraft.

INTERNET AMERICA™

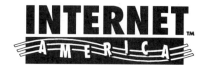

Robert Maynard Jr.

President and Chief Executive Officer
Internet America
350 North Saint Paul Street, Suite 200
Dallas, TX 75201–4240
(214) 979–9009
Fax: (214) 979–9077
EMAIL: See Below

7376

Business Information: Internet America is the largest Internet service provider in Texas, which serves basically as a phone company for computers. Experiencing fast growth, Internet America became the largest provider in Texas in just one year. Joining Internet America as President and Chief Executive Officer in 1995, Mr. Maynard is responsible for all aspects of operations, including balance sheet management, capital planning, and strategic planning. Internet users can reach Robert via: ceo@airmail.net **Career Steps:** President and Chief Executive Officer, Internet America (1995–Present); Chief Executive Officer, Paravision (1994–1995); Chief Executive Officer, Segue Investments (1991–1994); Profit Center Manager, Citibank (1987–1991); U.S. Army Special Forces (1980–1985). **Associations & Accomplishments:** Author of a book called "What Every Good Parent Needs to Know About the Internet"; Frequent speaker on censorship and the vision of the Internet; Awarded the Wall Street Journal

Award; Nominated for Harry S. Truman Scholarship; Recognized as a distinguished military graduate. **Education:** Northern Arizona University, B.S.B.A., graduated first in class (1987). **Personal:** Married to Teresa in 1989. Two children: Mariah and Molly.

Michael J. Monk

Vice President of Marketing and Technology Development
Interface Electronics Inc.
4579 Abbots Bridge Road
Duluth, GA 30155
(770) 623–1066
Fax: (770) 623–8001

7376

Business Information: Interface Electronics Inc. is an international computer networking firm, providing CD services and building computer networks for public libraries and universities. Other areas of expertise include providing networking components, custom cable assemblies, and installation accessories. Interface Electronics has designed, furnished, and installed over half of the campus network systems in the University System of Georgia. Established in 1986, Interface Electronics Inc.'s corporate headquarters is located in Duluth, Georgia. Mr. Monk joined Interface in December of 1986. In his capacity as manager of sales and of product development, he has assisted the Company in establishing a leadership position in networking in the State of Georgia. He is also responsible for directing business planning, as well as developing new markets for the Company. Career milestones include forming a television systems integration company in Atlanta, Georgia, called Technical Video Systems in 1981. He designed and installed the first pay–per–view systems in several cities around the U.S. for Cox Cable. These systems incorporated the latest in video and computer automation. The culmination of efforts in design and management of turnkey projects, consulting services, computer integration, network design, and video technology, was an order from Landmark Communications to design, furnish, and install The Weather Channel. **Career Steps:** Vice President of Marketing and Technology Development, Interface Electronics Inc. (1986–Present); Vice President of Engineering, American Health Monitoring (1984–1986); Vice President, Technical Video Systems (1981–1983); National Marketing Manager, Hitachi (1974–1981). **Associations & Accomplishments:** Columnist in Local Newspaper; Holder of a Private Pilot's License. **Education:** University of Central Florida (1972); Valencia Community College, A.A. (1971). **Personal:** One child: Michelle. Mr. Monk enjoys flying and water sports.

Jimmy D. Long

Director of Services
Bannex Corporation
2530 Electronic Lane
Dallas, TX 75220–1214
(214) 352–1764
Fax: (817) 627–6319

7378

Business Information: Bannex Corporation is an international third–party maintenance company, specializing in the repair of computers, scanners, printers, optics, and other peripheral equipment. As Director of Services, Mr. Long is responsible for the supervision of all managers and service contracts, personnel decisions, and various administrative activities. **Career Steps:** Director of Services, Bannex Corporation (1990–Present); Truck Driver, Gohmann Asphalt (1984–1990); Staff Sergeant, U.S. Army (1967–1980). **Education:** Control Data Institute, Certification (1990); Nuclear Biological Studies, Germany; Various Educational Courses through the U.S. Army; Various Management courses. **Personal:** Married to Nicky in 1968. Two children: Patty and Elizabeth. Mr. Long enjoys spending time with his family and working with kids. He is also a 1st Degree Black Belt.

Joseph C. Tran

Senior System Engineer
Compucom
4831 Winterset Drive
Hopkins, MN 55343
(612) 885–5922
Fax: Please mail or call

7378

Business Information: Compucom is a computer networking consulting, V.A.R., and service concern located in Hopkins, Minnesota. The Company was started in 1981 and currently has over 2,000 employees. As Senior System Engineer, Mr. Tran provides technical support to customers/clients on network and personal computer system problems. He oversees the activities of his department and performs as the in–house system engineer. **Career Steps:** Senior System Engineer, Compucom (1996–Present); Lead Lan Analyst, United Health Care Corporation (1995–1996); Senior Network Administrator, Wyatt Prefferchoice (1995); Lan Manager, Clinical Pharmacy (1994–1995). **Associations & Accomplishments:** Black Professional Association; Asian Professional Association. **Education:** Angsburg College, M.I.S. (1993). **Personal:** Married to Tuyet Anh in 1981. Three children: Jonathan, Anne, and Justin. Mr. Tran enjoys fishing.

Victor A. Abrahamsen

Vice President and Partner
Lansafe Network Services, Inc.
31 East 28th Street, 8th Floor
New York, NY 10016
(212) 889–8100
Fax: (212) 889–8146
E–mail: see below

7379

Business Information: Lansafe Network Services, Inc. provides computer consulting and systems integration services to businesses in the Greater New York area. Established in 1991, the Company reports an annual revenue of $1.7 million. As Vice President and Partner, Mr. Abrahamsen is responsible for assisting clients with the design and implementation of Local Area Networks and providing continuing technical support and training, as well as research and development. As a Partner with Lansafe Network Services, Mr. Abrahamsen plans to be an important part of the continued growth of the Company. **Career Steps:** Vice President and Partner, Lansafe Network Services, Inc. (1991–Present); Manager, Radio Shack (1985–1987). **Associations & Accomplishments:** American Mensa. **Education:** New York University (1984); Rensselaer Polytechnic University (1981).

DEDALUS

Jose Carlos Abrahao

Owner/President
Dedalus Informatica, Ltda.
Rua Baltazar Lisboa No 32
Rio de Janeiro, Brazil 20540–130
55–21–2644456
Fax: 55–21–2645976

7379

Business Information: Dedalus Informatica, Ltda. provides computer services, including field maintenance, training, consulting, net services, and computer sales. The Company sells "Digital" and "Data General" equipment, and offers training and consulting on basic computer use, Windows and other computer programs. As Owner/President, Mr. Abrahao is responsible for all aspects of Company operations, including operational management. **Career Steps:** Owner/President, Dedalus Informatica, Ltda. (1991–Present); Consultant, Elebra Computadores (1989–1992); Field Support Engineer, Cobra Computadores (1984–1989). **Education:** Electric Engineer (1984); Bachelor's degree in Mathematics. **Personal:** Married to Joseli B.G. in 1980. Two children: Ana Carolina and Manuela.

Patrick J. Ambrogio, P.Eng.

President
Computer Solutions Group
695 Richmond Square, Suite 1011
London, Ontario N6A 5M8
(519) 657–7202
Fax: (519) 667–0786

7379

Business Information: Computer Solutions Group is a retail microcomputer service company providing full turn–key solutions to end users including hardware selection, networking solutions, programming and training. As President, Mr. Ambrogio oversees all operational aspects including sales and technical staff, sub–contractors/associates, strategic planning and customer relations. Concurrent with his duties at Computer Solutions, Mr. Ambrogio holds top executive positions for the following diverse companies. Diodatics International, Inc. — Established in March 1991, this is an innovative fitness enterprise, currently holding several patents for fitness devices. The Company is also a national sponsor of Arnold Schwarzenneger's Ms. Fitness World '95 competition for women. Stage Four Technologies, Inc. — Established in the Summer of 1994, this Corporation functions as a sister company to Computer Solutions as a wholesale distributor of microcomputers and related technologies, but it is an independent entity which also services others in the industry. Patrizio Design International, Inc. — Established in March 1994, Patrizio is an engineering design entity serving Diodatics and other manufacturing industries, as well as professional organizations and institutions. Established in 1986, Computer Solutions Group employs 10 people. **Career Steps:** President, Computer Solutions Group, (1986–Present); Vice President, Secretary/Treasurer, Diodatics International, Inc. (March 1994–Present); President, Stage Four Technologies, Inc. (Summer 1994–Present); President, Patrizio Design International (March 1994–Present); Engineering Research, 3M Canada Inc. (1981–1986). **Associations & Accomplishments:** Professional Engineers of Ontario; Canadian Council of Professional Engineers; University of Western Ontario Alumni Association; London Community Foundation Volunteer; Former Director and Treasurer, Middlesex Condominium Corporation. **Education:** University of Western Ontario, B.E.Sc. on Dean's List (1981); Ontario Robotics Center, Robotic Studies (1984). **Personal:** Mr. Ambrogio enjoys piano, architectural design and renovation, racquet sports, fitness training and photography.

Candice J. Barker

Director, Support and Implementation
Citation Computer
424 South Woods Mill Road, Suite 200
Chesterfield, MO 63017–3428
(314) 579–7900
Fax: (314) 579–7990

7379

Business Information: Citation Computer provides health care computer systems to hospitals and laboratories. Operating internationally from over 500 sites, Citation also provides software, hardware, service and support functions. Serving in various managerial roles with Citiation since 1984, Candice Barker was appointed to her current position in 1995. As Director of Support and Implementation, she directs all operational aspects for the departments of Customer Support, Customer Training and Network Services. **Career Steps:** Citation Computer: Director, Support and Implementation (1995–Present), Senior Development Manager (1994–1995), Product Manager (1987–1994), Educational Coordinator (1984–1987). **Associations & Accomplishments:** American Society for Clinical Laboratory Science; Missouri Organization for Clinical Laboratory. **Education:** Illinois State University, B.S. (1978). **Personal:** Married to Phillip in 1981. Ms. Barker enjoys travel.

Victor P. Becker

Director of Human Resources
Entex Information Services
725 Canton Street
Norwood, MA 02062
(617) 575–8207
Fax: (6175) 755–820

7379

Business Information: Entex Information Services is a systems integration company providing computers, maintenance, outsourcing, and integrated desk top solutions to customers. With regional headquarters in Norwood, Massachusetts and Corporate headquarters in Ryebrook, New York, the Company is international in scope and has an estimated annual revenue of $2.2 billion. As Director of Human Resources, Mr. Becker is responsible for the support function for the Eastern, Southern, and Mid–Western areas of the U.S. (approximately 2500 employees). He also oversees all administrative duties, marketing, strategic planning, public relations, and management of a staff of twelve recruiters and two human resource generalists for his region. **Career Steps:** Director of Human Resources, Entex Information Services (1993–Present); Human Resources Manger, Data General Corporation (1981–1989); Human Resources Manager, Stop & Shop Companies (1976–1981). **Education:** Providence College, B.A. in Business Management (1975). **Personal:** Mr. Becker enjoys golf, reading, and sports.

Myrna F. Beilke

Director of Services
Corporate Technologies
P.O. Box 9355
Fargo, ND 58106–9355
(701) 277–0011
Fax: (701) 277–0012
EMAIL: See Below

7379

Business Information: Corporate Technologies, formerly ComputerLand of Fargo, is a franchise company of Computer Land, Inc. The Company is a computer and network sales and consulting firm with 300 global locations, headquartered in Pleasanton, California. As Director of Services, Ms. Beilke manages a team of 8 service and training managers, as well as human resources. Internet users can reach her via: mbeilke@corptechnologies.com **Career Steps:** Director of Services, Corporate Technologies (1989–Present); Sales Support Manager, Great Plains Software (1984–1989); Assistant Store Manager, Zales Jewelry (1982–1985). **Associations & Accomplishments:** Former President and board member, FM Human Resources Association; Former President, North Central Telemarketing Association. **Education:** North Dakota State University, B.A. in Business Administration and Merchandising–Retailing (1982); Attended, State University of New York. **Personal:** One child: Joshua. Ms.

Beilke enjoys karate, reading and spending time with family and friends.

Lloyd Bernhardt
Vice President of Development
GDT Softworks, Inc.
4664 Lougheed Highway, Suite 188
Burnaby, British Columbia
(604) 473–3622
Fax: (604) 291–9689
EMAIL: See Below

7379

Business Information: GDT Softworks, Inc. specializes in Macintosh software development for printers. A dominant factor in the Canadian market, the Company was named in "Profit Magazine" as one of the top 100 growing companies, three years in a row. As Vice President of Development, Mr. Bernhardt is responsible for all product development, quality assurance, and technical support. Internet users can reach him via: lloyd@gdt.com. **Career Steps:** Vice President of Development, GDT Softworks, Inc. (1994–Present); Chairman, Motion Works (1988–1992). **Associations & Accomplishments:** Winner of Macintosh Award for Best Product. Founder of "Motion Works", a Macintosh Company that specialized in multi–media software, and at age 26 took the Company public. **Education:** British Columbia Institute of Technology (1980). **Personal:** Married to Kim Schachte in 1992. Mr. Bernhardt enjoys hiking, boating, woodworking, and computers.

Magnus Birkner
President
Iridescent Systems Corporation
3450 West 22nd Avenue
Vancouver, British Columbia, V6S 1J2

(604) 250–9459
Fax: Please mail or call
70544.2216@compuserve.com"

7379

Business Information: Iridescent Systems Corporation specializes in computer software development and computer consulting for various industries. As President, Mr. Birkner is responsible for corporate direction and management, research, software development, and consulting. Internet users can reach him via: 70544.2216@compuserve.com. **Career Steps:** President, Iridescent Systems Corporation (1990–Present); Systems Analyst, BC Telephone Company (1978–1993); Systems Programmer, Bell Canada (1976–1978); Methods Analyst, Alcan (1974–1976). **Associations & Accomplishments:** Canadian Information Processing Society (CIPS); ACM First Society in Computing; Universal level member, Microsoft Developer Network; Microsoft Technical Network; Associate Member, Institute of Electrical and Electronics Engineers, Inc.; Mathematical Association of America; American Mathematical Society; Vancouver Board of Trade. **Education:** Lund University – Sweden, B.Sc. (1974); Attended numerous courses and professional development programs. **Personal:** Married to Marita in 1974. Two children: Theodore and Maximilian. Mr. Birkner enjoys swimming, sponsoring little league baseball, and coordinating church group activities.

Dominique Boisset
Chairman
Aquitaine Advanced Distribution Network
ZA De Marticot
Cestas, France 33610
(335) 621–5808
Fax: Please mail or call

7379

Business Information: Aquitaine Advanced Distribution Network provides the engineering of local and long distance networks, as well as the creation of concepts and images in 3–D with the capability of simulating any process in industrial/technical fields. One of their projects include working very closely with the Beaudaws Fire Department to simulate the different routes and buildings in the City. Their main customer is the Minister of Foreign Affairs. Founding Aquitaine Advanced Distribution Network in 1991, Mr. Boisset serves as its Chairman, President, and Director General. He is responsible for all aspects of operations, including new business development, strategic planning, and ensuring that the Company performs to its highest standards. **Career Steps:** Chairman, Aquitaine Advanced Distribution Network (1991–Present); Regional Director, CRE 2I (1986–1991). **Associations & Accomplishments:** Euro Leaders Club. **Education:** French Institute of Gestion, Naitioc di Gestion (1978). **Personal:** Two children: Florian and Marie. Mr. Boisset enjoys horseback riding.

Robert B. Brandt
Information Systems Director
Matrix Information Consulting
65 E. Route 4
River Edge, NJ 07661
(201) 488–4181
Fax: (201) 488–1867
EMAIL: See Below

7379

Business Information: Matrix Information Consulting specializes in providing computer and management consulting to Fortune 500 and entrepreneurial companies. Established in 1986, the Company employs 175 people and has estimated annual revenue of $15 million. As Information Systems Director, Mr. Brandt provides technical support to the Company. He is also responsible for market evaluations, overseeing and coordinating all software and networks, and strategic planning. Internet users can reach him via: bbrandt@matrixcc.com. **Career Steps:** Information Systems Director, Matrix Information Consulting (1987–Present); Development Manager, May Department Stores (1978–1987); Senior Programmer/Analyst, Federated Department Stores (1971–1978). **Associations & Accomplishments:** International Committees, United Methodist Church; Northern New Jersey AIDS Action Task Force. **Education:** Lebanon Valley College, B.A. (1971); United Theological Seminary. **Personal:** Married to Ruth Ann in 1970. One child: Matthew Scot. Mr. Brandt enjoys collecting sports memorabilia.

Bill Brewer
Corporate Controller
Sykes Enterprises, Inc.
100 North Tampa Street
Tampa, FL 33622–5809
(813) 274–1000
Fax: (813) 273–0148

7379

Business Information: Sykes Enterprises, Inc. provides technical support, professional services and foreign language translation to business. Established in 1977, the Company employs 2,500 people and has an estimated annual revenue of $60 million. As Corporate Controller, Mr. Brewer oversees SEC filings, investments, financial statements for forty clients, and supervises a management staff of fourteen. **Career Steps:** Corporate Controller, Sykes Enterprises, Inc. (1993–Present); Corporate Controller, Vroman Foods (1971–1973); Financial Advisory Manager, FinEx, Inc. (1972–1973); Controller, Klondike Ice Cream (1969–1971). **Associations & Accomplishments:** Past Member, American Institute of Certified Public Accountants. **Education:** University of North Florida, B.S.A. (1974). **Personal:** Married to Melinda in 1973. Two children: Darby and Linsey. Mr. Brewer enjoys golf and tennis.

William P. Bruno
Director of Service Operations
Polaris Service, Inc.
257 Cedar Hill Street
Marlboro, MA 01752
(508) 460–1800 Ext. 237
Fax: (508) 485–1113

7379

Business Information: Polaris Service, Inc. is an international provider of third party UNIX workstation services, including both hardware and software throughout the U.S. and The Netherlands. Established in 1987, Polaris Service, Inc. currently employs 130 people. As Director of Service Operations, Mr. Bruno manages field and phone support systems, as well as the customer service center. **Career Steps:** Director of Service Operations, Polaris Service, Inc. (1987–Present); Technical Support Engineer, VIA Systems (1984–1987). **Associations & Accomplishments:** AFSMI. **Education:** Apple Valley Community College, Business (1984). **Personal:** Married to Hong in 1990. Two children: Quyen and Allyson. Mr. Bruno enjoys golf and beekeeping.

Robert Buosi
Owner
Robert Buosi Enterprises
7230 Dooley Dr.
Mississauga, Ontario L4T 2S6
(905) 671–1633
Fax: (905) 612–1370
EMAIL: See Below

7379

Business Information: Robert Buosi Enterprises is a computer consulting firm providing consulting, computer resale and contracting services to companies and individuals in Southern Ontario. With ten years experience in electronics and computers, Mr. Buosi established Robert Buosi Enterprises in 1996 and is currently responsible for all aspects of operations. Internet users can reach him via: Robert_Buosi@MSN.COM **Career Steps:** Owner, Robert Buosi Enterprises (1996–Present); Programming Centre Manager, Hamilton Avnet (1986–1990). **Associations & Accomplishments:** Cadet Instructor, List–Canadian Forces. **Education:** Humber College. **Personal:** Mr. Buosi enjoys computers, hockey, chess, tennis, and collecting coins and stamps.

Richard A. Callahan, Ph.D.

Founder and President
Center for Technology Commercialization
100 North Drive
Westborough, MA 01581
(508) 870–0042
Fax: (508) 366–0101
EMAIL: See Below

7379

Business Information: The Center for Technology Commercialization is a non–profit, private technology commercialization company. Clientele include NASA, federal government and private sectors. As Founder and President, Dr. Callahan is responsible for all aspects of operations, including setting and administering company goals, managing finances, and executing and teaching others to execute new means of commercialization technology. Internet users can reach him via: rcallahan@CTC.org **Career Steps:** Founder and President, Center for Technology Commercialization (1992–Present); President and Chief Executive Officer, Idaho Research Foundation (1986–1991); President and Co–Founder, Vestar Inc. now Nexstar (1981–1985). **Associations & Accomplishments:** New York Academy of Sciences; American Association for the Advancement of Science; Board of Directors of the following corporation: CTC; Siteworks, Inc.; Advanced Hardware; Architecture, Inc. (Chairman & Co–Founder); Chromatochem, Inc.; Former Director, Vestar, Inc.; and the Idaho Research Foundation, Inc. **Education:** University of Massachusetts – Amherst, Ph.D. in Invertebrates (1969); College of the Holy Cross, B.S. Biology (1963). **Personal:** Married to Jane P., Ph.D. in 1963. Three children: Christopher A. (Ph.D), Amy E., and Matthew J. Dr. Callahan enjoys kayaking, skiing, aviculture, and cultivating Bonsai plants.

Nagib C. Callaos, Ph.D.
Chairman and Chief Executive Officer
Callaos & Associates Corporation
14269 Lord Barclay Drive
Orlando, FL 32837
(407) 856–4265
Fax: (407) 856–6274

7379

Business Information: Callaos & Associates Corporation is a systems consulting firm specializing in software development and training, cybernetics and informatics. As Chairman and Chief Executive Officer, Dr. Callaos is responsible for all aspects of Company operations, including administration, consulting, sales and marketing, and strategic planning. **Career Steps:** Chairman and Chief Executive Officer, Callaos & Associates Corporation (1989–Present); University of Simon Bolivar: Titular Professor (1976–1996), Dean of R&D (1986–1988). **Associations & Accomplishments:** Venezuelan Christian Democratic Party: Secretary of the Youth, National Secretary of Information Systems; Institute of Electronics and Electrical Engineers – Chairman of the Venezuelan Chapter; Licensing Executive Society – Founder/Chairman of the Venezuelan Chapter; Venezuelan Systems Association; Association of Computing Machinery; Venezuelan Executives Association; Technology Transfer Executives – Venezuelan Chapter. **Education:** University Central de Venezuela, Electrical Engineering (1968); University of Texas – Austin: Master of Science (1973), Ph.D. (1976). **Personal:** Married to Bekis Margarita in 1979. Three children: Leonisol Liliana, Belkis Helena, and Jorge Emeterio. Dr. Callaos enjoys jogging.

Will F. Cassell Jr.
Systems Engineer
The Electronic Lab
1511 November Circle, #102
Silver Spring, MD 20904
(301) 622–5107
Fax: (301) 840–1528
EMAIL: See Below

7379

Business Information: The Electronic Lab is a computer data communication networking company, specializing in the design, development, implementation, and integration of data communications systems. As Systems Engineer, Mr. Cassell designs, implements, integrates, supports, and trains staff in computer data communications networking. Internet users can reach him via: wfcassell@interramp.com. **Career Steps:** Systems Engineer, The Electronic Lab (1996–Present); Senior Network Engineer, New Boston At Sprint (1996); Senior Software Engineer, Microtemp at USPS (1995); Systems Engineer, AM Tech Resources at CSC (1994). **Associations & Accomplishments:** American Computing Machinery; Toast Masters. **Education:** University of St. Thomas (1991); Langston University, B.S. in Computer Science. **Personal:** Mr. Cassell enjoys electronic configuration, in–line skating, and tennis.

Alain Chaboche
President – Director General
Aston
36 Av De L'Europe
Velizy, France 78140
331 3465 79 50
Fax: 331 3465 79 40

7379

Business Information: Aston is a client/server engineering integration firm providing application's development, training, consulting, and network services. Established in 1990, Aston reports annual revenue of 30 million in French Francs and currently employs 55 people. As President and Director General, Mr. Chaboche is responsible for all aspects of operations. **Career Steps:** President and Director General, Aston (1990–Present); Division Director, Asystel (1984–1990); Chief of Products, Auchan (1983–1984); Chief of Products, Sodicam Groupe Renault (1980–1983). **Associations & Accomplishments:** Vice President, Confederation Nationale des Junior–Entreprise (CNJE) (1978–1980); President, ESC Service (Junior Entreprise ESC Montpellier) (1978–1980). **Education:** E.S.C. Montpellier, DESCAEF (1980); London Chamber of Commerce (1980); E.S.M. Saint Cyr Coetquidan E. Or. (1976); Lieutenant de reserve. **Personal:** Married to Ausset Beatrix in 1986. Four children: Aymeric, Amaury, Angelique, and Apolline. Mr. Chaboche enjoys meeting new friends, skiing, sailing, windsurfing, and bridge.

Adel Chalouhi

President and Chief Executive Officer
Integro
3, rue Saint Philippe du Roule
Paris, France 75008
Fax: 33–1–42–89–112

7379

Business Information: Integro is a telecommunications software editor, including PC mainframe and client/server integration. Clientele includes the United States Army and Navy, NATO, Groupe BULL, Alcatel, France Telecom, Deutch Telekom, Banque de France and the French Ministry of Defense and Justice. Established in 1981, Integro currently employs 100 people and has an estimated annual revenue of $18 million. As President and Chief Executive Officer, Mr. Chalouhi is responsible for all aspects of operations, including management, strategic planning, and definition of products. Mr. Chalouhi is also one of the founders of the Company. **Career Steps:** President and Chief Executive Officer, Integro (1981–Present); Mid–East Director of Operations, CII Honeywell Bull (1976–1981); Telecom Projects Manager, CII/DAS (1972–1976). **Education:** Ecole Nationale Superieure de l'Aeronautique et de l'Espace, Paris, Ingenieur (1968); Ecole Superieure d'Ingeniors de Beyrouth, ESIB (1966); Civil Engineer (1966); Electronics Engineer (1966). **Personal:** Married to Marie–Helene in 1973. Three children: Christel, Jean Charles and Olivier. Mr. Chalouhi enjoys reading, history, spiritual music and walking.

Joseph J. Chang, BA.Sc, P.E.

President
Phaselock Systems International, Inc.
1260 Old Innes Road, Ste 601
Ottawa, Ontario K1B 3V3
(613) 742–7070
Fax: (613) 742–7901
E/M: Phaselck@globalx.net

7379

Business Information: Phaselock Systems International, Inc. is a private corporation that performs computer hardware/software networking, consulting and sales. As President, Mr. Chang's responsibilities consist of project planning, high–level technical consulting, technical support, software programming and development. **Career Steps:** President, Phaselock Systems International, Inc. (1993–Present); Vice President/Shareholder, Inly Systems International Ltd. (1987–1993); Engineer, International Standards Development, Telecom Canada (1976–1988). **Associations & Accomplishments:** Association of Professional Engineers of Ontario (APEO); Ottawa Chamber of Commerce; Canadian Professional Sales Association. **Education:** University of Toronto, BA.Sc. (1976). **Personal:** Married to Wendy in 1977. Two children: Alexander and Andrew. Mr. Chang enjoys writing, reading, invention, and programming.

William J. Cloutier, Ph.D.

Chief Informations Officer
Lightner Associates, Inc.
441 Carpenter Avenue
Wheeling, IL 60090–6013
(708) 215–8888
Fax: (708) 215–8890

7379

Business Information: Lightner Associates, Inc. is a computer informations firm. Established in 1959, Lightner Associates, Inc. reports annual revenue of $10M and currently employs 60 people. As Chief Informations Officer, Mr. Cloutier is responsible for all aspects of direct data processing. **Career Steps:** Chief Informations Officer, Lightner Associates, Inc. (1985–Present); Professor, University of Illinois (1979–1985). **Associations & Accomplishments:** Electronic Industry Association. **Education:** University of St. Mary of the Lake, Ph.D. (1979); Northwestern University, M.A. (1972); Loyola University of Chicago, B.A., with honors (1971). **Personal:** Mr. Cloutier enjoys computers, classical music, and travel.

William B. Cooper
Director of Technology
Sylvest Management Systems
10001 Derekwood Lane
Lanham, MD 20706
(301) 459–2700
Fax: (301) 459–5558

7379

Business Information: Sylvest Management Systems is a national systems integration contract firm, providing development and implementation to corporate clientele. The Company has one Commercial Division (working with corporation accounts) and two Federal Divisions (working with federal government accounts). Future plans include becoming more focused on software programs and consulting services for contract customers (federal government and commercial). Established in 1987, Sylvest Management Systems reports annual revenue of $100 million and currently employs 106 people. As Director of Technology, Mr. Cooper is responsible for providing sales and marketing support, program management, and technical development for Federal Program Management. He identifies possible federal account opportunities and puts strategies in place to gain those accounts by contract, as well as conducting new business development in the federal market. **Career Steps:** Director of Technology, Sylvest Management Systems (1992–Present); Cray Research: Sales Representative (1991–1992), Sales Analyst (1984–1991); Independent Consultant (1980–1984). **Associations & Accomplishments:** National Society of Black Engineers; Association for Computing Machinery; Who's Who Among Black Americans; Outstanding Young Men of America; National Roster of Black Elected Officials; Interviewed in 1995 for article in "Federal Computer Week" on Industry in General. **Education:** University of Maryland (1976–1978). **Personal:** Married to Sandra F. Burrus in 1983. Three children: Barrington B., Charles A., and A. Maxwell. Mr. Cooper enjoys golf, participating in his church, and spending time with his family.

Dr. R. Cordeiro
Partner and Consultant
Decision Processes International
Praca Rainha D Filipa 6 4E
1600 Lisbon, Portugal
351–1–759–1987
Fax: 351–1–757–2463

7379

Business Information: Established in Portugal in 1994, DPI is a private consulting firm, based in Connecticut, comprised of 40 independent partners in 16 countries, who employ "process consulting" philosophy and procedures to improve strategic management and innovation. As Partner and Consultant, Dr. Cordeiro is responsible for all aspects of Company operations, including administration, finance, sales, public relations, accounting, legal, taxes, marketing, and strategic planning. In addition, he does the consulting, selling, and delivering of services. **Career Steps:** Partner and Consultant, D.P.I. (1994–Present); Managing Director, Auto–Sueco (1985–1993). **Associations & Accomplishments:** APEC – Portuguese Association of Economists and APM – Portuguese Management Association. **Education:** Business Administration, degree of Licenciado (1974). **Personal:** Married to Isabel Amaral. One child: Monica. Dr. Cordeiro enjoys golf.

John Neal Crossman
Graphic Artist/Owner
The Office of John N. Crossman
6 Lone Hollow Cove
Sandy, VT 84092
(801) 553–1958
Fax: (801) 553–0297

7379

Business Information: John Crossman became a freelance video editor and computer graphics animator in 1992. He specializes in video post production, computer generated graphics, and training videos for large corporate clients. **Career Steps:** Graphic Artist/Owner, The Office of John N. Crossman (1992–Present); Partner, BetaBay, Inc. (1986–1992); Chief Editor, KSLTV News (1978–1986); Staff Member/Band Director, "Up With People" (1974–1976). **Associations & Accomplishments:** Winner of Three Rocky Mountain Awards, Twelve TeleAwards for International Independent Business. **Education:** University of Utah, Bachelor's Degree (1981). **Personal:** Married to Wendy Wood. Two children: J.J. and Luke. Mr. Crossman is a musician and writes his own music, hoping to pursue it as a career in the future.

Douglas A. Cummins

President /Owner
Delphi Consulting Services, Inc.
1087 County Place Drive
Houston, TX 77079–4750
(713) 287–7840 (800) 578–3075
Fax: Please mail or call
EMAIL: See Below

7379

Business Information: Delphi Consulting Services, Inc. is a computer consulting firm specializing in Oracle systems, the number one database product in the world. They primarily do business with the petrochemical (oil and gas) industry. The Company develops new products, specialized and custom databases, and offer performance calls for their clients. As President /Owner, Mr. Cummins sees to all day–to–day operations of the Company, as well as marketing, public relations, and strategic planning. Internet users can also reach him via: dacummins@delphi.com **Career Steps:** President /Owner, Delphi Consulting Services, Inc. (1993–Present). **Associations & Accomplishments:** Board Member, International /Regional Oracle Users Groups. **Education:** University of Houston, B.S. (1989). **Personal:** Mr. Cummins enjoys martial arts, scuba diving, sky diving, and racing.

David F. Curry

Senior Vice President of Business Development
Architel Systems Corporation
190 Attwell Drive, Suite 300
Toronto, Ontario M9W 6H8
(416) 674–4078
Fax: (416) 674–2290
EMAIL: See Below

7379

Business Information: Architel Systems Corporation specializes in the development, marketing, and support of advanced operations support systems used in global telecommunications. Traded on the New York Stock Exchange, the

Company plans to be a part of NASDAQ by the end of 1996. Established in 1984, Architel Systems Corporation employs 120 people, and has an estimated annual revenue of $20 million. As Senior Vice President of Business Development, Mr. Curry is active in intrinsic product development, marketing, and sales. A co–founder, he is also responsible for administration, operations, customer service and public relations. Internet users can reach him via: d.curry @architel.com. **Career Steps:** Senior Vice President of Business Development, Architel Systems Corporation (1984–Present). **Associations & Accomplishments:** Board of Trade, Toronto, Canada; Information Technology Association of Canada. **Education:** Carleton University, Bachelors in Civil Engineering (1971). **Personal:** Married to Ellen. Mr. Curry enjoys skiing and golf.

Charles J. De Felice

Director of Field Services
Decision Consultants Incorporated
3265 Meridian Parkway, Suite 122
Ft. Lauderdale, FL 33331–3523
(305) 384–0999
Fax: (305) 389–0204

7379

Business Information: Decision Consultants Inc. specializes in providing professional computer services, including programming. Established in 1984, the Firm currently employs 85 people and has an estimated annual revenue of $7 million. As Director of Field Services, Mr. De Felice is responsible for all aspects of personnel, performance reviews, benefit administration, Company policy, sales and recruiting for all of Southern Florida. **Career Steps:** Director of Field Services, Decision Consultants Incorporated (1994–Present); Director of Mid–range Applications, CTX Systems Corporation (1993–1994); Account Information Engineer, Management Dynamics (1991–1993); Manager of Systems and Programming, Cobrite Plastics Company (1987–1991). **Associations & Accomplishments:** Toastmasters International; American Management Association; Solution Provider for Computer Associates. **Education:** Hudson County Community College, A.S. (1993); Taylor Business Institute, Certificate of Programming (1983). **Personal:** Married to Jacqueline in 1984. One child: Chip. Mr. De Felice enjoys street hockey, softball, golf, bowling, and singing.

Thomas M. Del Monte

Account Manager
SunGard
1285 Drummers Lane
Wayne, PA 19087
(610) 341–4338 (800) 276–0236
Fax: (610) 687–1756

7379

Business Information: SunGard provides disaster recovery services to computer mid–range and mainframe subscribers and offers clients alternative data centers to work out of. Established in 1978, the Company employs 450 people, and has an estimated annual revenue of $540 million. As Account Manager, Mr. Del Monte manages 500 accounts in the Southeastern United States and ensures their coverage is current with the actual configuration the customer is using. **Career Steps:** Account Manager, SunGard (1995–Present); Research Coordinator, The Vanderveer Group (193–1995); Project Director, TMR, Inc. (1990–1993); Sales Representative, Lanier Worldwide (1989). **Associations & Accomplishments:** Vice President, Haverford High School Baseball Boosters. **Education:** Penn State University: M.B.A. (1996), B.S. in Marketing (1989). **Personal:** Mr. Del Monte enjoys coaching baseball and volleyball, being an EBLA speaker, and volunteering with the National Multiple Sclerosis Society.

Patti Dock

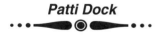

Executive Director of Object Technology Practice
IBM Corporation
Route 100, Building 1 Mail Drop 1301
Somers, NY 10589
(914) 766–1032
Fax: Please mail or call

7379

Business Information: IBM Corporation (IBM Consulting Group) is a management consulting firm, providing marketing, design, information systems, business transformation consulting, and information technology solutions. Joining IBM as Executive Director of Object Technology Practice in 1995, Ms. Dock is responsible for managing world–wide consulting and strategy of object technology for the finance industry. **Career Steps:** Executive Director of Object Technology Practice, IBM (1995–Present); President, Pillar Systems (1993–1994); Vice President, OrgWare, Inc. (1992). **Education:** Kansas State University, M.S. (1990); University of WFLA, B.A. in Mathematics and Computer Science. **Personal:** Two children: Heather and Travis. Ms. Dock enjoys volleyball.

Gregory J. Dorman

Vice President of Research and Development
Information Builders, Inc.
1250 Broadway 38th Floor
New York, NY 10001–3701
(212) 736–4433
Fax: Please mail or call
EMAIL: PGMGJD@JBI.COM

7379

Business Information: Information Builders, Inc., one of the oldest software companies in the U.S., is a privately–held business software company. Products include: Focus (decision support), EVASQL (market leaders and client server), and a new product to be released serving Fortune 500 and 1000 companies worldwide. Established in 1975, Information Builders, Inc. reports annual revenue of $250 million and currently employs 1,500 people. As Vice President of Research and Development, Mr. Dorman is responsible for the research and development of software programs for computers. **Career Steps:** Information Builders, Inc.: Vice President of Research and Development (1990–Present); Vice President of Development (1987–1990), Director of Programming (1985–1987). **Education:** Columbia University, M.S. (1982). **Personal:** Married to Marina Lebedeva in 1995. Two children: Veronica and Audrey. Mr. Dorman enjoys sky diving, reading, travel, and ancient languages.

Pamela Dunsky

Senior Director – Support Services
Lexis–Nexis
9595 Springboro Pike
Miamisburg, OH 45342–5074
(513) 865–1409
Fax: (513) 865–1655
EMAIL: See Below

7379

Business Information: Lexis–Nexis is an on–line legal information system, providing up–to–the–minute news and information to the legal professional market. Joining Lexis in 1989 as a fabrication developer, Ms. Dunsky was appointed to her current position in 1995. As Senior Director of Support Services she is responsible for the overall technical support for the Company's 200 Unix mainframe servers. **Career Steps:** Lexis–Nexis: Senior Director of Support Services (1994–1995); Director of Fabrication Development (1992–1994); Manager of Fabrication Development (1989–1992). **Associations & Accomplishments:** University of Dayton MIS Advisory Board; PMI **Education:** University of Dayton, B.S. in Computer Science (1983); North Central College, coursework being taken towards M.S. in MIS **Personal:** Married to Dr. Martin Dunsky in 1982. Three children: Karlie, Kristin and Kevin. Ms. Dunsky enjoys Taijutsu, and racquetball.

Fern Espino, Ph.D.

President
Commandtrain, Inc.
15726 Michigan Avenue
Dearborn, MI 48126–2903
(313) 846–2912
Fax: (313) 846–2736

7379

Business Information: Commandtrain, Inc., founded in 1984, is a consulting business, specializing in education and training applications, personal computer software support, including computer–aided design and office automation. Commandtrain is also an AutoDesk Authorized Autocad Training Center (ATC). Dr. Espino serves as President, Chief Executive Officer, Operating and Financial Officer. She is responsible for all aspects of operations, including administration, finances, public relations, marketing, and strategic planning. **Career Steps:** President, Commandtrain, Inc. (1984–Present); Dean of Student Development, GMI Engineering and Management Institute (1980–1992); Dean of College and Financial Services, College of the Mainland, (1976–1980); Associate Dean and Instructional Services, Pima Community College (1969–1976). **Associations & Accomplishments:** National Association of Autocad Users Group; The International Torch Club; National Association of Women Business Owners; The Greenleaf Center for Servant Leadership; Board of Directors, National Hispana Leadership Institute; Board of Trustees, Leadership Detroit; Member, Minority Economic Development; Committee of New Detroit, Inc.; Fluent in Spanish and French. **Education:** University of Arizona, Ph.D. (1976); Harvard – JFK School of Government; Harvard – Institute for Educational Management. **Personal:** Married to Thomas Short in 1990. Dr. Espino enjoys classical and opera music and dancing.

Mr. David D. Evans

Principle Systems Test and Evaluation Engineer
Excel Professional Services, Inc.
24491 Hawks Circle
Evergreen, CO 80439–5626
(303) 771–1765
Fax: (303) 771–1866

7379

Business Information: Excel Professional Services, Inc. is a computer system consulting services firm. Established in 1990, Excel Professional currently employs 170 people. As Principle Systems Test and Evaluation Engineer, Mr. Evans is responsible for large scale real time testing and evaluation services and test process reengineering services. **Career Steps:** Principle Systems Test and Evaluation Engineer, Excel Professional Services, Inc. (1994–Present); System Test Engineer Senior, Unisys Corporation (1971–1994). **Associations & Accomplishments:** International Test and Evaluation Association (ITEA); Armed Forces Communication and Electronics Association (AFCEA). **Education:** Test and Evaluation Process–International Test and Evaluation Association (1994); Software Engineering Institute – System Test, Quality Assurance, Requirements Management, and the Capacity Maturity Model (1993); Unisys – Design and Programming in "C" (1993); University of Denver, Postgraduate Ada Programming (1991); University of Phoenix, Management & Leadership (1991); Unisys – System Tests and Integration (989); Northwestern Institute of Electronics – Electronics Technology (1980); University of Minnesota – Computer Analysis & Design (1976); Inver Hills Community College – Pre–Engineering (1973). **Personal:** Married to Alta A. Evans in 1984. One child: Angela. Mr. Evans enjoys woodworking.

Margi M. Fatcheric

Owner and President
Relational Options, Inc.
100 Campus Drive, Suite 125
Florham Park, NJ 07932–1006
(201) 301–0200
Fax: (201) 301–0377
EMAIL: See Below

7379

Business Information: Relational Options, Inc. is a computer consulting firm serving large corporations, including the pharmaceutical industry, and specializing in application development, client server, and information technology. Mrs. Fatcheric founded ROI in 1988, serving as President and Chief Executive Officer. She is responsible for overseeing all administrative functions at the Corporate headquarters, sales and marketing, and personnel decisions. Internet users may reach her via: mfatcheric@roi.com **Career Steps:** Owner and President, Relational Options, Inc. (1988–Present); Director of Corporate Human Resources, Howard Systems International (1984–1988); Spectrum Technology Group: Manager of Human Resources (1980–1983), Recruiter (1983–1984). **Education:** Caldwell College, B.A. in Psychology (1995). **Personal:** Married to Jerome in 1969. Two children: Matthew John and Amy Christine. Mrs. Fatcheric enjoys in–line skating, skiing, cooking, and antiques.

Daniel J. Fitzgerald

Director of Facilities, Real Estate & Security
EMC Corporation
171 S Street
Hopkinton, MA 01748–1659
(508) 435–1000
Fax: (508) 435–3324

7379

Business Information: EMC Corporation provides large capacity disk drive storage for a variety of computers. International in scope, the Company is headquartered in Hopkinton with 60 offices throughout the United States and 20 overseas. As Director of Facilities, Real Estate & Security, Mr. Fitzgerald oversees the daily operations and activities of all 60 offices in the United States. **Career Steps:** EMC Corporation: Director of Facilities, Real Estate & Security (1989–Present), Location Manager (1984–1988). Maintenance (1979–1982). **Associations & Accomplishments:** Who's Who Worldwide (1994); A.I.P.E.; A.S.I.S.; A.F.M.A. **Education:** Boston College, B.S. in Mathematics and Computer Science (1986). **Personal:** Mr. Fitzgerald enjoys golf, basketball, boating, fishing, and rollerblading.

Enrico J. Galietta

Recovery Center Director
Comdisco Disaster Recovery Services
480 Gotham Parkway
Carlstadt, NJ 07072
(201) 896–2335
Fax: (201) 896–2001

7379

Business Information: Comdisco (NYSE:CDO) is one of the worlds leading providers of solutions that help organizations reduce technology and risk. These services include equipment leasing and remarketing; business continuity, and related consulting services, systems integration; asset mangement tools and services; and more. Joining the Company in 1990, Mr. Galietta currently serves as Director, responsible for the direction of three major recovery centers (field offices). **Career Steps:** Recovery Center Director, Comdisco Disaster Recovery Services (1990–Present); Assistant Vice President, Prudential Securities (1984–1990); Telecommunications Manager, EF Hutton & Company, Inc. (1978–1984). **Associations & Accomplishments:** Board member, Park Court Homeowners Association. **Personal:** Married to Francine in 1985. Two children. Mr. Galietta enjoys woodworking, spending time with his family, and working with charities and less fortunate people.

Douglas Getty

International Manager
Everyware Development Corporation
7145 West Credit Avenue
Mississauga, Ontario L5N 6J7
(905) 819–1173
Fax: (905) 819–9891
Email: See Below

7379

Business Information: Everyware Development Corporation is a manufacturer of software database products for intranet and internet data management solutions. As International Manager, Mr. Getty is responsible for international sales, maintaining international partners, signing new countries, and supervising 12 distributors. Internet users can reach him via: dgetty@everyware.com. **Career Steps:** International Manager, Everyware Development Corporation (1990–Present). **Education:** Sheridan College (1985); Wilfred Lavrier University Business. **Personal:** Married to Patricia in 1982. Two children: Jonathan and Carling. Mr. Getty enjoys spending time with his family.

Mr. Kevin Gordon

Vice President
Bulloch Systems
1200 Bay Street, Suite 703
Toronto, Ontario M5R 2A5
(416) 923–9255
Fax: (416) 920–9134
EMail: See Below

7379

Business Information: Bulloch Systems is an international computer company, providing computer services to the film and entertainment industry. Mr. Gordon joined Bulloch Systems in 1979, becoming Vice President in 1985. He is responsible for the programming, technical services, and research and development departments. Internet users can reach him via: Kevin@bullochmail.com. **Career Steps:** Bulloch Systems: Vice President (1985–Present), Various positions (1979–1985). **Associations & Accomplishments:** Board of Directors, North Toronto Hockey Association; Board of Directors, Willowbank School. **Education:** University of Toronto, B.A. with honors (1978). **Personal:** Married to Nathalie Laporte in 1990. One child: Adam.

Joshua L. Greer

Founder/Chairman/CEO
Digital Planet
3555 Hayden Avenue
Culver City, CA 90232–2412
(310) 287–3636
Fax: (310) 287–3642

7379

Business Information: Digital Planet is a network–based interactive multimedia production house that uses the interactive market to create exposure and publicity. The Company has brought together entertainment and technology to create interactive content for movies. Mr. Greer worked in the computer industry with communications and entertainment. He saw a need for a high tech outlook on entertainment, so he created the first interactive marketing kit and founded Digital Planet to make these services available. Digital Planet is now moving into the exciting area of original content creation. **Career Steps:** Founder/Chairman/CEO, Digital Planet (1994–Present); Director, The Berkeley Group (1994); Special Projects, Universal Pictures (1991–1993). **Associations & Accomplishments:** Who's Who in the United States; Foundation for Ileitis and Colitis. **Education:** York University (1990). **Personal:** Married to Lorraine in 1993. Mr. Greer enjoys reading, climbing, biking, photography, and computers.

David Paul Grunsted

Vice President of Operations and General Manager
Priority Data Systems, Inc.
16021 Orchard Circle
Omaha, NE 68135
(402) 592–2550 Ext: 224
Fax: (402) 592–5052
EMAIL: See Below

7379

Business Information: Priority Data Systems, Inc. is an information processing company, targeted specifically towards data conversion, data maintenance programming and product distribution in the information service industry. A privately–held company, Priority Data Systems, Inc. specializes in information management and product distribution. As Director of Operations and General Manager, Mr. Grunsted managing all operational infrastructures and computer operations, as well as strategic planning, acquisitions, and growth. Internet users can reach him via: D3909@AOL.com **Career Steps:** Director of Operations and General Manager, Priority Data Systems, Inc. (1995–Present); Director of Product Operations, Inacom Corporation (1989–1995); Sales, Connecting Point Computer Center (1987–1989). **Associations & Accomplishments:** AKSARBEN; Joslyn Museum. **Education:** Mankato State University, B.S. in Accounting and Finance (1987). **Personal:** Married to Kathy in 1994. Mr. Grunsted enjoys golf, gardening, and biking.

Russell S. Gunderson

Vice President
Baan U.S.A., Inc.
4600 Bohannon Drive
Menlo Park, CA 94025–1030
(415) 462–4949
Fax: (415) 462–4960
EMAIL: See Below

7379

Business Information: Baan U.S.A., Inc., a European company conducting business internationally, is an international client–server enterprise, providing software for Fortune 500 manufacturing companies. With sixteen years of experience in marketing, Mr. Gunderson joined Baan U.S.A., Inc. as Vice President in 1995. He is responsible for the overall strategic and tactical marketing for Baan America. **Career Steps:** Vice–President, Baan U.S.A., Inc. (1995–Present); Vice–President, Marketing and Business Development, Ascent Logic Corporation,(1994–1995); Marketing Manager, CSO, Hewlett Packard Company, (1980–1994). **Associations & Accomplishments:** American Association of Industrial Engineers, American Youth Social Organization, (AYSO). **Education:** University of California at Los Angeles, M.B.A., (1980); Stanford University, Masters in Industrial Engineering (1977); University of California at Berkeley, B.S. in Industrial Engineering and Operations Research (1976). **Personal:** Married to Mary Jo in 1982. Two children: Matt and Jenna. Mr. Gunderson enjoys hiking, skiing, water sports and woodworking.

Mr. Rusty K. Hammond

Owner
Rusty's Computer Services
418 Broadway
Larned, KS 67550
(316) 285–2879
Fax: (316) 285–3381

7379

Business Information: Rusty's Computer Services is a personal computer consulting and training firm. They teach people how to use personal computers, and also sell software. As Owner, Mr. Hammond oversees all aspects of the business, including customer relations, book keeping, marketing and strategic planning. **Career Steps:** Owner, Rusty's Computer Services (1993–Present); Service Engineer, The Lockwood Co., Inc., an IBM agent (1992–1993); Deputy County Clerk, Pawnee County, KS (1991–1992). **Associations & Accomplishments:** Member, Larned Area Chamber of Commerce; Participant, American Heart Association – Cardiac Arrest; Wrestling Coach, Larned Middle School; Den Leader, Cub Scout Pack #123. **Education:** Fort Hays State University, Degree in Mathematics with emphasis in Computer Science (1991). **Personal:** Mr. Hammond enjoys freshwater aquariums, hunting, fishing and on–line computer services.

Kathleen Handal, M.D.

Creator and President
Health–Net
8711 East Pinnacle Peak Road, #221
Scottsdale, AZ 85255
(602) 502–9736
Fax: (602) 502–9735
EMAIL: See Below

7379

Business Information: Health–Net is an on–line medical information service with sponsors whose products are health–related, including first aid kits. Dr. Handal, an Emergency Medicine Physician authored "The American Red Cross First Aid & Safety Handbook." (Little, Brown & Company) She has taken her interest in patient education to the air waves and is an active member of the National Association of Physician Broadcasters. A practicing physician since 1975, she created Health–Net in 1995 and serves as its President, responsible for all aspects of operations, including administration and strategic planning. An advocate of accident prevention, she believes that the informed lay person can play an important role in the management of emergencies and natural disasters to minimize the negative outcome. Concurrently, she practices emergency medicine at a Trauma Center in Phoenix and hosts a radio talk show, called "Health Matters." Internet users can reach Dr. Handal via: http://www.health–net.com **Career Steps:** Creator and President, Health–Net (1995–Present); Emergency Medicine Physician, Trauma Center, Phoenix, Arizona (Present); Host, "Health Matters" Radio Talk Show, Phoenix, Arizona (Present). **Associations & Accomplishments:** American Medical Association; Active Member, National Association of Physician Broadcasters; American Medical Women's Association; American Board of Emergency Medicine; Instructor in Basic and Advanced Cardiac Life Support, American Heart Association; Instructor in Advanced Trauma Life Support, American College of Surgeons Committee on Trauma; Serves on several national medical committees; Consultant, Bureau of Business Practice and The Educational Management Group; Author of several articles for popular national magazines, including Woman's Day and Glamour; Public Speaker on Emergency Medicine, EMS, Safety and First Aid Training internationally (Perth, Brisbane, Adelaide and Melbourne, Australia; Rome, Italy; Dublin and Cork, Ireland; Geneva, Switzerland; Beijing, China; Leningrad and Moscow, U.S.S.R.) and numerous cities in the U.S.; Co–authored and functioned as the on–site medical and safety consultant of a two–part consumer–oriented video, "Medicine Emergencies in the Workplace I: Life–Sustaining Response – the winner of a certificate for Creative Excellence at the 1993 International Film and Video Festival and given a medal by the prestigious CINDY and Telly awards for the second part of this video; Author and producer of a 20–minute video for Spanish and English–speaking children, called "Trauma Run," distributed nationally by United Learning (1994); Appeared on CNN, NBC's "Today Show," and other major city networks, in addition to 37 radio talk show interviews, promoting The American Red Cross First Aid & Safety Handbook and educating the public on accident prevention, the importance of emergency procedures, and a good first aid kit. **Education:** Medical College of Pennsylvania, M.D. (1975); St. Peter's College, B.S. in Biology.

A. Michael Hanna

President/Chief Executive Officer
Interpro
10600 West Higgins Road, Suite 710
Rosemont, IL 60018
(847) 299–9090
Fax: (847) 299–9095
EMAIL: See Below

7379

Business Information: Interpro is a software developing/consulting company comprised of three divisions: Interpro Consulting, which implements and designs client servers and systems integrations; Interpro Translations, which provides translation of software, technical manuals and offers web site solutions in multiple languages; and Interpro Software, which provides software development of complete client server travel and expense processing support. Established in 1989, the Company is also responsible for developing "Globiz", a software program which enables users to transfer data into a foreign language. As President/Chief Executive Officer, Mr. Hanna oversees all aspects of the Company. Fluent in Arabic, Spanish, French, and English, with degrees in mechanical and electrical engineering, he is responsible for the reconstruction of all three Company divisions, as well as developing innovative solutions for a changing world. Internet users can reach him via: Mhanna@interproinc.com, or at Web Site: http://www/interproninc.com. **Career Steps:** President/Chief Executive Officer, Interpro (1995–Present); Vice President, Infomag (1988–1994); Communication Manager, Army Corps of Engineers (1987). **Associations & Accomplishments:** Chicago Software Association (CSA); Illinois Institute of Technology Alumni; ASSET User Group; Catholic Church; International Translation Association (ITA); ITAA. **Education:** Illinois Institute of Technology: B.S.E.E., (1984), B.S. in Computer Science; Dudley College, H.N.D. in Mechanical Engineering. **Personal:** Married to Dr. Eva Hanna in 1989. Two children: Jonathan and Michael. Mr. Hanna enjoys tennis, golf, and skiing.

Mrs. Sharon Payne Hardy
Controller
Integrated Systems Technology, Inc.
1720 Regal Row, Suite 210
Dallas, TX 75235
(214) 630–4379
Fax: (214) 634–0448

7379

Business Information: Integrated Systems and Technology, Inc. is a multi–media computer–related and telecommunications consulting and equipment organization. Specializing in computer applications systems, they provide consulting and applications services to wholesalers and industrial end users, as well as provide software distribution. National in scope, IST distributes software throughout the U.S., Canada, and Puerto Rico. In her capacity as Controller, Mrs. Hardy is responsible for all administration and supervision for financial aspects of the Firm which include treasury, budget control, audit, taxes, accounting, insurance activities and personnel benefits. Established in 1982, Integrated Systems Technology, Inc. employs 50 technical and administrative support staff. Annual gross revenue for fiscal year 1994 is reported in excess of $4 million. **Career Steps:** Controller, Integrated Systems Technology, Inc. (1993–Present); Charge Accountant, Zadeck Energy Group, Inc. (1991–1993). **Associations & Accomplishments:** National Association of Female Executives; Family Outreach of America (Child Abuse Prevention). **Education:** University of Alabama–Birmingham, B.S. in Accounting (1985).

Saleh Hegazy
General Manager
Data Bank Computers
160 Emtedad Ramsis 2, P.O. Box 4 Abbassia
Nasr City, Cairo, Egypt
(202) 401–0038 (202) 401–0039
Fax: (202) 401–1984

7379

Business Information: Data Bank Computers is a fast growing company, specializing in computer assembly s/w applications, communications development and total solutions. Additional service: analysis, design, training, consultation, maintenance and implementation of special purpose equipment and control units. As General Manager, Mr. Hegazy is responsible for all management functions for the facility, including administration and design work. **Career Steps:** General Manager, Data Bank Computers (1987–Present); Senior Electronics Engineer – Saudi Arabia (1985–1987). **Associations & Accomplishments:** Associated to PTV (Project Technology Valley) related to the Cabinet of Ministries and Decision Support Center; Associated to German Arab Chamber of Commerce. **Education:** Faculty of Engineering – Cairo, Egypt (1984); Ain Shams University, Diploma in Computer Engineering; Cairo University, Master in Computer Field. **Personal:** Mr. Hegazy enjoys walking, reading, and sports.

Frank Hegyi
President & CEO
Hegyi Geotechnologies International, Inc.
707–170 Laurier Ave. W.
Ottawa, Ontario K1P 5V5
(613) 237–8055
Fax: (613) 237–1176

7379

Business Information: Hegyi Geotechnologies International, Inc. is an international software engineering firm and developer of Mobile Technical Office (MTO). The Company also focuses on research and development of wireless communication, digitized maps, Global Positioning System (GPS) interface, and sales of related products. Hegyi Geotechnologies, Inc. currently employs 17 people at its Victorian and Ottawa offices with plans to expand into Hungary in the future. Established in 1990, HGI has estimated annual revenue of $2 million. As President and CEO, Mr. Hegyi oversees the daily operations of the Company. As founder of HGI, he was the first person to mug global satellite (GS) mapping into GIS environment and showed how to geocode information. By doing this, Mr. Hegyi basically revolutionized the industry from manual drafting to computer–assisted mapping and established all the wireless communication capacities so it can be taken to the field. **Career Steps:** President & CEO, Hegyi Geotechnologies International, Inc. (1990–Present); Director, B.C. Forest Service (1977–1990); Research Scientist, Canadian Forest Service (1965–1977); Asst. Conservator of Forests, Guyana Forest Service (1961–1965). **Associations & Accomplishments:** Association of B.C. Professional Forest-

ers; American Society of Photogrammetry & Remote Sensing; Geomatics Industry Association of Canada; Past Governor, PNW District, Kiwanis International, South Vancouver Island Hockey Association; Founder, Pacific Cup for the Old–Timers Hockey Association. **Education:** University of Toronto, M.Sc. (1969); University of Edinburgh, B.Sc. (1961). **Personal:** Married to Rose in 1970. Three children: Jennifer, Randy, and Michael. Mr. Hegyi enjoys futuristic technology design, volunteer work, and hockey.

Julie Heitz
Director of Corporate Training
CyCare Systems, Inc.
700 Locust Street
Dubuque, IA 52001–6824
(319) 557–3425
Fax: (319) 557–3397
EMAIL: See Below

7379

Business Information: CyCare Systems, Inc. is a provider of information systems and services, including EDI, to the healthcare industry and professionals. As Director of Corporate Training, Ms. Heitz is responsible for the coordination and delivery of all internal employee training. Internet users can reach her via: JHEITZ@dbq.cycare.com. **Career Steps:** CyCare Systems, Inc.: Director of Corporate Training (1993–Present); Director of Quality Assistance (1991–1993); Director of Client Services (1988–1991). **Associations & Accomplishments:** Certified Quality Analyst; ASTD. **Education:** American Institute of Business, A.A. in Computer Science and Accounting (1981); Certified Instructor for Zenger Miller FRONTLINE and TEAM Leadership Modules; Certified Instructor for White Wilson, Shipley Associates Modules. **Personal:** Married to Mark in 1983. Three children: Chad, Carrie and Cody. Ms. Heitz enjoys playing the piano and gardening.

Hans P. Hermann
District Manager
Postalsoft, Inc.
1515 East Woodfield Road, Suite 92
Schaumburg, IL 60173–6046
(847) 240–1888
Fax: (847) 240–1898
EMAIL: See Below

7379

Business Information: Postalsoft, Inc. specializes in computer software solutions for postal automation, database management, and document processing, including writing, development, licensing, and marketing the software. As District Manager of a seven state area, Mr. Hermann manages client accounts, sells postal processing, database management, and document processing software, and reintroduces products to the clients. Internet users can reach him via: hans@postalsoft.com. **Career Steps:** Postalsoft, Inc.: District Manager (1994–Present), Human Resources Administrator (1993), Sales Trainer (1992). **Associations & Accomplishments:** ICP Society of Million Dollar Sellers (1995, 1996); Postalsoft Sales Representative of the Year (1995); Milwaukee World Trade Association. **Education:** University of Wisconsin – La Crosse, B.S. in Finance (1990). **Personal:** Married to Denise in 1993. Mr. Hermann enjoys acoustic guitar, song writing, and restoring automobiles.

Andrew S. Hillman
National Sales Coordinator
Digital Data Systems, Inc.
6210 North Belt Line Road
Irving, TX 75063–2655
(214) 550–0191
Fax: (214) 714–9358

7379

Business Information: Digital Data Systems, Inc. is a provider of CD–ROM software and multiple listings on compact disc. With corporate offices located in Irving, Texas, Digital Data Systems, Inc. serves clients from 15 national offices. As National Sales Coordinator, Mr. Hillman is responsible for the management of all accounts nationwide, including inventory control and overseeing a staff of 15. **Career Steps:** National Sales Coordinator (Aug. 1995–Present), Sales Associate (May–Aug. 1995) Digital Data Systems Inc.; Manager, Mid-Way Auto Supply (1992–1995); Promotions Assistant, Dallas Mavericks (1990–1992). **Associations & Accomplishments:** Leader, Boy Scouts of America; Lions Club; Church Youth Group Leader. **Education:** Southern Methodist University, B.A. (1995) **Personal:** Mr. Hillman enjoys boating, fishing, and hunting.

Mr. Bandele F. Hinton
President and Chief Executive Officer
HI Communications
240 M Street, SW
Washington, DC 20024
(202) 508–8253
Fax: (202) 484–5131

7379

Business Information: HI Communications, established in 1992, is a quality–driven high–tech company competent in delivering solutions that leverage computing technology in ways that improve how organizations do business. Innovative approaches to problem solving make them a formidable rival in today's high–tech marketplace. As the developers of Distributed Data Management Services (DDMS), their solutions are geared at developing infrastructures that will provide access to information superhighway "the NET". Product line includes: DDMS, network support services, information infrastructure planning and development, Smartech, and IT Consulting Services. Additional services include office automation, network planning and design, and systems integration. HI Communications delivers state–of–the–art design of LAN and WAN solutions, system analysis design, feasibility studies and analysis, network cabling, system development, and ongoing facilities management. All of their projects are managed through Total Quality Management (TQM) concepts; therefore, they guarantee all services with total customer satisfaction. HI Communications has partnerships established with many of the leading vendors to provide customers with total system solutions. HI can ensure that customers are offered customer–focused solutions that increase productivity and saves on the bottom–line. By using proven tools and methodologies, their solutions are customer–focused to allow organizations to benefit from high–tech. As President and Chief Executive Officer, Mr. Hinton is responsible for all aspects of operations. **Career Steps:** President and Chief Executive Officer, HI Communications (1992–Present); Senior Network Engineer, Compus Services Corporation; Senior Network Engineer, Cincinnati Bell Information Systems. **Associations & Accomplishments:** Certified Government Contractor; Certified Professional Systems Engineer (Microsoft); United Methodist Church; In 1988, Mr. Hinton entered the Olympic Trials for boxing. He was rated in the top 10 in his weight division. **Education:** American University, B.S. (1992). **Personal:** One child: Brandan Hinton. Mr. Hinton enjoys golf, photography, reading, and writing.

Phyllis R. Hoffmann
Senior Director of Marketing
Dyncorp I&ET
12750 Fair Lakes Circle
Fairfax, VA 22033
(703) 222–1500
Fax: (703) 222–1552
EMail: See Below

7379

Business Information: Dyncorp I&ET specializes in the development and integration of information technology solutions. Projects are created for special government projects and various organizations. As Senior Director of Marketing, Mrs. Hoffmann directs an integrated marketing/technical team to win new business. She is involved with business strategic planning, producing high–end technology, marketing research, and public relations. Internet users can reach her via: hoffmap@dyniet.com. **Career Steps:** Senior Director of Marketing, Dyncorp I&ET (1995–Present); Director of Proposal Management, Sprint (1992–1995); PRC, Inc.: Senior Program Development Specialist (1989–1992), Manager of Marketing Communications (1986–1988). **Associations & Accomplishments:** Board of Directors, Women in Technology; American Management Association; American Business Women's Association; Armed Forces Electronics/Communications Association. **Education:** West Virginia University, M.S. in Journalism (1983); Loyola University – Chicago, B.A. in Communications; Univ. of Maryland, M.S. candidate in Financial Management. **Personal:** Married to Richard L. in 1979. Two children: Kerry R. and Louis J. Mrs. Hoffmann enjoys photography, camping, reading, and playing the guitar.

Patrick D. Hollett, CM
Training Manager
Computer Sciences Raytheon
Building 535 Room 206
Patrick Air Force Base, FL 32925
(407) 494–5667
Fax: (407) 494–5668

7379

Business Information: Computer Sciences Raytheon is subcontracted by the United States Air Force Aerospace Division, providing support to all space shuttle missions out of Cape Canaveral. A Certified Manager, Mr. Hollett has been responsible for training space shuttle mission support personnel for CSR since 1991, first as a Training Coordinator and then as a

Certification Manager, promoted in 1994 to Training Manager. His current responsibilities include technical and management training development and training program administration. **Career Steps:** Computer Sciences Raytheon: Training Manager (1994–Present), Certification Administrator (1993–1994), Training Coordinator (1991–1993). **Associations & Accomplishments:** National Management Association; American Society for Training and Development – Space Coast Chapter; Space Coast Training Consortium; Space Business Roundtable Education Committee; Vice President, People Adopting Children Everywhere; Brevard Vision 2005. **Education:** Warner Southern College, B.A. in Organizational Management (1996); Certified Manager (ICPM) (1995). **Personal:** Married to Kathryn Liell in 1978. One child: Patrick Jr. (P.J.). Mr. Hollett, CM enjoys biking, beach volleyball and woodworking.

Oliver C. Ibe, Sc.D.

Network Architect
Cabletron Systems, Inc.
35 Industrial Way
Rochester, NH 03867
(603) 337–7047
Fax: (603) 337–7370
E–mail: see below

7379

Business Information: International in scope, Cabletron Systems, Inc. specializes in the manufacture of computer networking equipment (i.e., switches, etc.), and provides service to the same. Established in 1985, Cabletron Systems, Inc. currently employs 5,000 people. As Network Architect, Dr. Ibe is responsible for new network architecture, design and development. He was instrumental in spearheading development activities on ATM networks (integration of all network systems). He can also be reached through the Internet as follows: ibe@ctron.com. **Career Steps:** Network Architect, Cabletron Systems, Inc. (1994–Present); Visiting Scientist, Massachusetts Institute of Technology (1993–1994); Senior Member of the Teaching Staff, GTE Laboratories (1990–1993). **Associations & Accomplishments:** Institute of Electrical and Electronics Engineers; Sigma Xi; INFORMS; Who's Who in Science and Engineering; Evangelical Christian. **Education:** Massachusetts Institute of Technology, Sc.D. (1981); Northeastern University, M.B.A. (1980). **Personal:** Married to Christina in 1977. Four children: Chidinma, Ogechi, Amanze and Ugonna. Dr. Ibe enjoys table tennis, soccer and reading.

Gonzalo Jimenez

Director of Business Development
Infinity Info Systems
1560 Broadway, Suite 905
New York, NY 10036
(212) 354–4228
Fax: (212) 354–0210
EMail: See Below

7379

Business Information: Infinity Info Systems is a computer and management consultancy, specializing in sales force automation. Currently, the Company has three offices, but will be expanding in the near future. As Director of Business Development, Mr. Jimenez handles the business development of clients and partnerships, maintains and builds clients through the U.S., and engages clients with their services. He is additionally responsible for all marketing and public relations, trade shows, and seminars for the Company. Internet users can reach him via: gonzalo@infinityinfo.com **Career Steps:** Director of Business Development, Infinity Info Systems (1994–Present); Network Specialist, Skadden, Arps, Slate, Meagher & From (1992–1994); Marketing Consultant, BASYS, Inc. (1989–1992); Marketing Consultant, Fugitsu Networks Industry (1987–1989). **Associations & Accomplishments:** American Management Association; Volunteer, Childrens Welfare Fund; The Planetary Society; National Association of Sales Professionals. **Education:** Pace University, B.S. (1987). **Personal:** Mr. Jimenez enjoys flying private planes, sky diving, whitewater rafting, and reading.

Steven M. Jimmo

President
GeneSys Computing Technologies
163 Meadow Street
Chicopee, MA 01013–2230
(413) 532–1316
Fax: (413) 532–1316
EMAIL: See Below

7379

Business Information: GeneSys Computing Technologies designs and develops individual business solutions, specializing in client–server systems, network design, and systems integration. Mr. Jimmo founded GeneSys in 1994 and as President is responsible for all operations, sales and marketing, accounting functions, and Corporate leadership. Internet users can reach him via: Sjimmo@aol.com **Career Steps:** President, GeneSys Computing Technologies (1994–Present); Technical Director, Epsilon Data Management (1990–1993); Senior Systems Analyst, U.S. Army (1974–1990). **Associations & Accomplishments:** Who's Who Worldwide; Sterling's Who's Who; American Legion. **Education:** University of Maryland, Business Management (1982). **Personal:** Married to Sandra T. in 1980. Two children: George and Michael. Mr. Jimmo enjoys scuba diving and gun collecting.

Ronald Joern

Chief Executive Officer
Software Research and Development
3101 North Central Avenue, # 480
Phoenix, AZ 85012
(602) 331–0854
Fax: (602) 266–8071

7379

Business Information: Software Research and Development is a software consulting firm for major companies, including American Express and Motorola. Established in 1984, the Firm has three regional locations in Denver, Phoenix, and Orange County. As Chief Executive Officer, Mr. Joern is responsible for all aspects of Company operations, including administration, finance, public relations, and strategic planning. **Career Steps:** Chief Executive Officer, Software Research and Development (1984–Present); MIS Manager, Cahners Publishing (1986–1987); Western Regional Manager, CAP Gemini DASD (1976–1986). **Associations & Accomplishments:** Past President, Jaycee's, Madison Chapter; Eagles Club. **Education:** University of Wisconsin, Graduate Studies (1982). **Personal:** Mr. Joern enjoys flying (pilot), scuba diving, and skydiving.

Barbara B. Kernan

Partner
Data Chromatics, Inc.
9175 Guilford Road, Suite 100
Columbia, MD 21046–1844
(410) 880–0790
Fax: (410) 880–0794
EMAIL: See Below

7379

Business Information: Data Chromatics, Inc. is a high tech firm specializing in computer technology for Federal, State, and Local governments for land use and land development, and 70% for utilities and telecommunications. As Partner, Ms. Kernan is one of the founding partners of Data Chromatics, Inc. She got started in this business through her experiences in county government and her experiences with an English planning firm. When they started implementing technologies, she found it exciting and took their interests and spun off Data Chromatics, Inc. She is responsible for government relations, marketing plans, strategies, and implementations. **Career Steps:** Partner, Data Chromatics, Inc. (1989–Present); Vice President, Daft McCune Walker (1986–1989); Economic Developer, Balto County, MD (1983–1986); Legislative Aide, Balto County Council (1978–1983). **Associations & Accomplishments:** Board of Directors, Balto Association of Retarded Citizens; Chair of Board, Institute for Teaching and Research on Women; Towson State University; Member Chancellor's, Advisory Committee, University of Maryland System. **Education:** Sinai Hospital School of Radiologic Technology, Certificate of Graduation (1968). **Personal:** One child: Benjamin Polakoff. Ms. Kernan enjoys reading novels.

Donald F. King

President/Chief Executive Officer
Aquarius Disk Services
701–52A Kings Row
San Jose, CA 95112–2726
(408) 280–2255
Fax: (408) 287–0160

7379

Business Information: Aquarius Disk Services works in the hard memory disk industry, primarily within the Silicon Valley area and the affiliate offices in Singapore. The Company specializes in disk polishing, reclamation, and washing. As President/Chief Executive Officer, Mr. King is responsible for all aspects of Company operations, including strategic planning, focusing his time on new business, and development of new products. **Career Steps:** President/Chief Executive Officer, Aquarius Disk Services (1984–Present). **Associations & Accomplishments:** Chairman, East Side Union High School Desegregation Committee; Author, "Privacy and Security Under Title 28." **Education:** Wayne State University, B.S. (1957). **Personal:** Two children: Jennifer and Sharon. Mr. King enjoys skiing and tennis.

Mr. Stephen D. King

President
King's Point Software
2108 22nd Avenue, S.W.
Calgary, Alberta T2T 0S5
(403) 228–1476
Fax: Please mail or call

7379

Business Information: King's Point Software is a private software design firm, specializing in the development of emerging technologies such as CD–ROM, multimedia authoring and electronic publishing (Internet HTML, Hypertext help). Mr. King speaks to thousands of professionals yearly at trade shows and seminars concerning the use of computer technology to increase productivity. Establishing the Firm in 1995, Mr. King is responsible for all operational aspects. **Career Steps:** President, Kings Point Software (1995–Present); Vice President of Software Development, CANTAX (1988–1995); Vice President of Technical Services, Videotex Atlantic (1985–1988). **Education:** Acadia University, B.C.S. (1985). **Personal:** Married since 1992. Mr. King is also president of Optic Frog Productions, a company founded to pursue his music interests. Mr. King enjoys playing the guitar and writing and producing original songs. His digital music has recently appeared on several multimedia platforms, including CD–ROM.

JoAn A. Kitchens

Vice President of Sales and Client Relations
Access/Ability, Inc.
8000 East Prentice Avenue, Suite C4
Englewood, CO 80111–2727
(303) 220–8350
Fax: (303) 741–6483
EMAIL: See Below

7379

Business Information: Access/Ability, Inc. provides customized software training and consulting to clients on proprietary programs and customized coursewares. A totally "woman owned" company, Access/Ability, Inc. offers on–site and in–house training and specializes in assiting clients in creating web pages, network setup and programming. Established in 1990, the Company employs 20 people. As Vice President of Sales and Client Relations, Ms. Kitchens oversees sales of training and consulting programs, maintains client relations and training quality control, and is responsible for customer service. Additional duties include personnel management and reviews, and serving as a liaison between instructors/consultants and clients. Internet users can reach her via: train4future@aol.com. **Career Steps:** Vice President of Sales and Client Relations, Access/Ability, Inc. (1995–Present); Owner/Broker, Real Estate, AMX Limited & The Windham Group (1995–Present); Vice President of Operations, Western Capital Development (1985–1990). **Associations & Accomplishments:** Denver Metro Chamber of Commerce; South Metro Chamber of Commerce; Denver Metro Commercial Association of Realtors. **Education:** Oklahoma City University; Jones Real Estate Colleges, Inc., Broker License (1991). **Personal:** Two children: Bradley Scott Cooper and Teri Suzanne Tod. Ms. Kitchens enjoys golf, sailing, oil/watercolor painting, and interior decorating.

Hershel A. Kleinberg

Technical Consulting
Amber Wave Productions
P.O. Box 2004
Washington, DC 20013–2004
(703) 486–8590
Fax: (703) 486–3830
E–mail: see below

7379

Business Information: Under the sole proprietorship of Amber Wave Productions, Mr. Kleinberg provides consulting and development services in multimedia and other areas of computer technology. Such services include: priority research in patent matters, information design, interface design and development, and product development for distribution by CD–ROM or the Internet. Amber Wave Productions is a member of The Lightbeam Group, a consortium of independent designers and developers specializing in making high end content offered by museums and similar institutions accessible. Mr. Kleinberg can also be reached through the Internet as follows: amberwave1@aol.com **Career Steps:** Technical Consulting, Amber Wave Productions (1994–Present); Judicial Clerk, Federal Circuit Court of Appeals (1995–Present); General Counsel and Technical Director, Lightbeam Interactive (1994–1995); Associate Attorney, Howrey & Simon (1992–1994); Member of the Technical Staff, Bell Communications Research (1986–1989). **Associations & Accomplishments:** Tau Beta Pi; Etta Kappa Nu; Maryland Bar Association; Patent Bar; American Bar Association; AIPLA. **Education:** Georgetown University Law Center, J.D. (1992); University of Southern California, M.S. (1987); Washington University, B.S. in Computer Science and Electrical Engineering (1986). **Personal:** Mr. Kleinberg enjoys photography, graphic art and the theatre.

Rob Kolstad
President
Berkeley Software Design, Inc.
7759 DelMonico Drive
Colorado Springs, CO 80919–1050
(719) 593–9445
Fax: (719) 598–4238
EMAIL:kolstad@bsdi.com.

7379

Business Information: Berkeley Software Design, Inc. is a privately–held, international software engineering and marketing firm of Internet Gateway systems, including the design of personal computer software. Established in 1991, Berkley Software Design, Inc. reports annual revenue of $5 million and currently employs 25 people. As President, Mr. Kolstad is responsible for all aspects of operations, including administration, finances, sales, public relations, and accounting, as well as serving as the ultimate backstop for most matters. **Career Steps:** President, Berkeley Software Design, Inc. (1991–Present); Senior Staff Engineer, Sun Microsystems (1989–1991); Vice President of Software, Drisma, Inc. (1988–1989); Manager of Operating Systems, Convex Computer Corporation (1982–1988). **Associations & Accomplishments:** USENIX – Editor of a 72–page bimonthly newsletter (circulation of 6,000) and Chairman of the Board (1993); LISA; Head Judge, Pikes Peak Regional Science Fair; Deputy Director, USA Computing Olympiad; Author of 68 publications; Recipient of Lifetime Achievement Award for SAGE. **Education:** University of Illinois – Urbana, Ph.D. (1982); Notre Dame, M.S. in Electrical Engineer (1976); SMU, B.A. in Science with highest honors (1974). **Personal:** Mr. Kolstad enjoys scuba diving and photography.

Mauricio Korbman
Vice President of Research and Development
food–online.com
280 Hillside Avenue
Needham, MA 02194–1343
(617) 449–3002
Fax: (617) 449–3034
EMAIL: See Below

7379

Business Information: food–online.com is a provider of on-line grocery shopping services through the Internet. Customers build their orders by searching and selecting food items. Once a customer pays electronically for the order, the grocery store receives an electronic copy of the list, then shops and either delivers or prepares the order for pickup. As Vice President of Research and Development, Mr. Korbman is responsible for the evaluation of new technology and management of the Software Development Department, in addition to conducting research and designing software which is used on the Internet. Current projects include designing a program for corporate use. Internet users can reach him via: mauricio@food–online.com. **Career Steps:** Vice President of Research and Development, food–online.com (Present); President, SyTech (1993–1996); Senior Consultant, Feld Technologies (1989–1993). **Education:** Boston University, Masters in Information Systems (1989); Instituto Tecnologico De Estudios Superiores De Monterey, Mexico, B.S. in Computer Engineering. **Personal:** Married to Carol in 1987. One child: Avi. Mr. Korbman enjoys reading and travel.

Phyllis B. Kramer
Director of Contracts and Pricing
OAO Corporation
7500 Greenway Center Drive
Greenbelt, MD 20770–3502
(301) 220–7160
Fax: (301) 345–9669
EMAIL: See Below

7379

Business Information: OAO Corporation is a national multi–services company, providing information and technology services, aerospace engineering services, facilities management services, and robotic vehicle manufacturing. Joining OAO Corporation as Director of Contracts and Pricing in 1992, Ms. Kramer is responsible for the direction of all contracts and pricing, in addition to supervising the Purchasing Department activities and serving as in–house Legal Counsel. Additional duties include supervising a support staff of 11, drafting, negotiations, and Corporate policies. Internet users can reach her via: PKRAMER@OAO.COM. **Career Steps:** Director of Contracts and Pricing, OAO Corporation (1992–Present); Associate Council and Senior Contracts Administrator, Information Systems and Networks (1991–1992); Counsel and Contracts Manager, Science Management Corporation (1985–1991); Attorney – Advisor (Contracts), United States Army TECOM – Aberdeen Proving Ground (1979–1985). **Associations & Accomplishments:** District of Columbia Bar Association; National Contract Management Association;

Baltimore Science Fiction Society, Inc. **Education:** University of Baltimore Law School, J.D. (1977); University of Maryland, B.A. in History. **Personal:** One child: Megan T. Allen. Ms. Kramer enjoys needlecraft.

Patricia A. La Forge
Director of Engineering Services
LANSystems, Inc.
2021 Midwest Road, Suite 100
Oak Brook, IL 60521–1336
(708) 953–9900
Fax: (708) 953–6228
EMAIL:plaforge@lansystems

7379

Business Information: LANSystems, Inc. is a system integrator for both wide–area networking and local–area networking, utilizing high–end router/micro computer equipment, including Microsoft/Novell OS, as well as multiple protocols and applications. A Certified Netware Engineer, Ms. La Forge serves as Director of Engineering Services, responsible for the management of all project managers and engineering staff over multiple branches located in the Midwest/South Region. She also directs all quality assurance, job profitability, and client satisfaction activities. **Career Steps:** LANSystems, Inc.: Director of Engineering Services (1995–Present), Manager of Engineering Services (1994–1995); Senior Project Manager, Techlaw Automation Partners (1991–1994). **Associations & Accomplishments:** Certified Netware Engineer (since 1990). **Education:** Florida State University, B.S. in Marketing (1981). **Personal:** Married to Philip in 1987. Two children: Peter and Claire. Ms. La Forge enjoys ice skating, reading, roller blading, and home computing.

Evelyn Labbate
Computer Scientist
Computer Sciences Corporation
620 Tinton Avenue
Tinton Falls, NJ 07724
(908) 389–6327
Fax: (908) 389–8214
EMAIL: See Below

7379

Business Information: Computer Sciences Corporation provides computer and consulting services to the private sector and the U.S. Department of Defense. A Computer Scientist with CSC since 1990, Ms. Labbate offers guidance and assistance to the electronic publishing arena, designs prototypes and solutions, and conducts system and application development. She is presently assisting the U.S. Army in its transition from paper–based information management to digital systems management. Internet users can reach her via: elabbate@csc.com **Career Steps:** Computer Scientist, Computer Sciences Corporation (1990–Present); Senior Engineer, Analytics, Inc. (1987–1990); Owner/Manager, Computer Hospital (1984–1987). **Associations & Accomplishments:** Association of Computing Machinery; Tech Corp New Jersey (Task Force). **Education:** Nova Southeastern University, Ph.D (In Progress); Monmouth University, M.S. in Software Engineering; Thomas Edison State College, B.S. in Computer Science. **Personal:** Married to John. One child: Jamie. Ms. Labbate enjoys America Online and guitar.

Kim J. Landrum
Director of Service and Support
ZEOS International, Ltd.
1301 Industrial Boulevard
Minneapolis, MN 55413
(612) 362–1488
Fax: (612) 362–1588

7379

Business Information: ZEOS International, Ltd., a division of Micron Electronics, Inc. is a mail order technical support and service company for the home and business PC user. Established in 1982, the Company currently employs 152 technical advisors and staff members. As Director, Ms. Landrum is responsible for the management of the technical support and service department, as well as the implementation of service options. **Career Steps:** Director of Service and Support, ZEOS International. Ltd. (1993–Present); Manager of Technical Support, VTech Computer (1991–1993); Manager of Customer Service, Laser Computer (1988–1991). **Associations & Accomplishments:** National Seminar Groups. **Personal:** Ms. Landrum enjoys riding her 1977 Harley Davidson Superglide.

Karen E. Larson–Marazzi
Vice President
Caribbean Internet Service Corporation
P.O. Box 19645
San Juan, Puerto Rico 00910–1645
(8098 728–3992
Fax: (787) 726–3093
EMAIL: See Below

7379

Business Information: Caribbean Internet Service Corporation provides internet access and services to Puerto Rico. As Vice President and Co–Owner with her husband, Mrs. Larson–Marazzi is responsible for oversight of daily systems operations, web page design, planning, and management activities. Internet users can also reach her via: kmarazzi@car.be.net **Career Steps:** Vice President, Caribbean Internet Service Corporation (1994–Present); Systems Analyst, AMAZI Systems, Inc. (1993–1994). **Education:** University of Massachusetts at Amherst, B.S. in Mathematics (1993). **Personal:** Married to Carlo Marazzi in 1994. One child: Carmen Elizabeth. Mrs. Larson–Marazzi enjoys travel.

Timothy J. Layaute
Owner
AMS, Inc.
518 Dogwood circle
Summerville, SC 29485–5717
(803) 812–2532
Fax: Please mail or call

7379

Business Information: AMS, Inc. is a company specializing in international computer program, data processing, and high tech system consultation. As Owner, Mr. Layaute, as Senior Analyst, is responsible for consultation and analysis. Established in 1972, AMS, Inc. employs 5,000 people with annual sales of $600 million. **Career Steps:** Owner, AMS, Inc. (1993–Present); Charleston Naval Shipyard: Head, Programming & Analyst Branch (1993), Head, Industrial Applications (1986–1992). **Education:** LaSalle University, B.A. Degree in Computer Science (1996). **Personal:** Married to Beverly in 1981. Two children: Jessica and Aaron. Mr. Layaute enjoys education and spending time with his family.

Philippe Le Roux
President
VCDL 2, Inc.
1205 Papineau Bur. 154
Montreal, Quebec H2K 4R2
(514) 599–5712
Fax: (516) 599–5729
EMAIL: See Below

7379

Business Information: VCDL 2, Inc. provides Internet, information highway and international public speaking consulting to clients. As President, Mr. Le Roux oversees all customer strategies and speeches in relation to seminars and conferences. A founder of the Company, he also manages all administrative and operational duties. Internet users can reach him via: leroux@vdl2.ca. **Career Steps:** President, VCDL 2, Inc. (1995–Present); President, Servacom America, Inc. (1988–1995); Vice President, Imperasoft, France (1986–1988); Teacher, Universite Paris VIII. **Associations & Accomplishments:** Computer Professionals for Social Responsibility. **Education:** University of Paris XI, DEVG (1984).

Paul M. LeFrois Jr.
Controller
Millennium Computer Corporation
2851 Clover Street
Pittsford, NY 14534
(716) 248–0510
Fax: (716) 248–0538

7379

Business Information: Millennium Computer Corporation is a software engineering and ghostwriting company. Established in 1985, Millennium reports annual revenue of $6 million and currently employs 45 people. As Controller, Mr. LeFrois serves as the office manager, responsible for the management of accounting and finances, as well as payroll and personnel operations. **Career Steps:** Controller, Millennium Computer Corporation (1995–Present); Mortgage and Credit Specialist, Citibank (NYS) (1993–1995). **Associations & Accomplishments:** Volunteer, American Diabetes Association; Volunteer, New York State Special Olympics; Member, Auxiliary VFW; Notary Public – Monroe County, State of New York. **Education:** St. Bonaventure University, B.B.A. in Finance

(1993). **Personal:** Mr. LeFrois enjoys bike riding, running, reading, softball and bowling.

Bradley G. Lewis
Director of Operations/Cabling Services Division
XL Connect
295 Sutton Court
Lebanon, OH 45036
(513) 672–8050
Fax: (513) 932–0699
Email: See Below

7379

Business Information: XL Connect is a national computer service providing hardware, software, Internet services, LAN services, and WAN services. Established in 1974, the Company has progressed through several identities and now employs over 2,000 people. As Director of Operations/Cabling Services Division, Mr. Lewis is focused on how the company operates. He is in charge of the daily operations including personnel concerns, accountability, profit margins, sales, product management, and development of new services. Internet users can reach him via: BLEWIS@XLConnect.com. **Career Steps:** Director of Operations/Cabling Services division, XL Connect (1994–Present); Operations Manager, CommLine, Inc. (1992–1994); Installation Manager, Network Solutions (1987–1992). **Associations & Accomplishments:** Building Industry Consulting Services International; National Fire Protection Association; Bass Anglers Sportsman Society; Registered Communications Distribution Designer; Member, Engineering and Methods Committee for BICSI. **Education:** Oklahoma State University, Associates (1982). **Personal:** Married to Lisa in 1991. Mr. Lewis enjoys golf and fishing.

Ronald W. Loback
Founder, Owner, President and Chief Executive Officer
Sage Communications, Inc.
7373 North Scottsdale Road, Suite 8290
Scottsdale, AZ 85253–3550
(602) 905–0480
Fax: (602) 905–0719
EMAIL:RLoback@SageCom.com

7379

Business Information: Sage Communications, Inc. is an international computer systems integration and consulting firm oriented towards very large databases and providing consultations to Fortune 500 companies. The Company specializes in information warehousing. Established in 1994, Sage Communications, Inc. reports annual revenue of $6 million and currently employs 25 people. Founding the Company in 1994, Mr. Loback serves as Owner, President and Chief Executive Officer and is responsible for all aspects of operations, including administration, finances, sales, public relations, client relations, business development, and strategic planning **Career Steps:** Founder, Owner, President and Chief Executive Officer, Sage Communications, Inc. (1994–Present); Assistant Vice President, AT&T GIS (1992–1994); Assistant Vice President, Teradata (1987–1992); Director, Amdahl (1981–1987). **Associations & Accomplishments:** Frequent speaker at lectures and talks; Church leader; Owner of a Harley Davidson motorcycle. **Education:** Mesa College, B.A. (1972); BellSystem Professional Training. **Personal:** Married to Denise in 1986. Two children: Lee and Nathan. Mr. Loback enjoys boating, motorcycling, and being a church leader.

P. B. MacIntyre
President
Beacon Systems
9 Maclaughlan Drive, Suite 3–13
Charlottetown, Prince Edward Island C1B 1M2
(902) 569–4449
Fax: (902) 569–4317
EMAIL: See Below

7379

Business Information: Beacon Systems specializes in the development of computer software and related products. Working regionally with all types of industries, the Company provides turn–key consulting, training, and customized programs to serve specific client needs. As President, Mr. MacIntyre oversees all aspects of the Company. He is responsible for system program development, project management, and client relations. The Company's founder, Mr. MacIntyre also handles all marketing and strategic planning. Internet users can reach him via: 73204666@compuserve.com or petermac@isn.net. **Career Steps:** President, Beacon Systems (1993–Present); Senior Program Analyst, Province of Prince Edward Island (1989–Present). **Associations & Accomplishments:** Vice President of Local Chapter, Clipper Users Group; Contributing Author, of Two Books; Lead Author of a Work in Progress. **Education:** Holland College, Business Computers (1989). **Personal:** Married to Meredith in 1988. Two children: Charity and Simon. Mr. MacIntyre enjoys coin collecting and sports.

R. David MacKinnon

President/Founder
E–Concept
1751 Richardson Street, Suite 6600
Montreal, Quebec H3K 1G6
(514) 932–1441 Ext. 223
Fax: (514) 932–6866
EMAIL: See Below

7379

Business Information: E–Concept, established in 1984, is an "Innovation Company" specializing in interactive broadcast and interactive computer technologies. The 17–member staff develops software packages used by hotels, private apartment complex companies, telemarketing bureaus, and small cable systems. Established in 1995, E–Concept employs 17 people with annual sales of $2.2 million. As President/Founder, Mr. MacKinnon, along with his three partners, focuses on production and production management. Internet users can reach him via: David@econcept.com. **Career Steps:** President/Founder, E–Concept (1994–Present); Senior Vice President, Pelmorex Communications, Inc. (1992–1994); Vice President, Operations, Meteomedia, Inc. (1988–1992). **Education:** St. Mary's University. **Personal:** Remarried to Rosemary Gilbert in 1979, they have one child, Aletha. Mr. MacKinnon enjoys the theater.

David W. MacKnight
Director of Information Services
Open Payment Technologies, Inc.
7500 N. Dreamy Draw Drive, Suite 210
Phoenix, AZ 85020
(602) 331–2922
Fax: (602) 943–8251
EMail: See Below

7379

Business Information: Open Payment Technologies, Inc. specializes in systems development of electronic payment processing. The Company provides these services to major grocery store chains and other clientele. The Company has branched out in new categories, including electronic coupon distribution. As Director of Information Services, Mr. MacKnight is responsible for project management, facilities, personnel, design, and programming. Internet users can reach him via: david_macknight@optinc.com. **Career Steps:** Director of Information Services, Open Payment Technologies, Inc. (1995–Present); Software Development Manager, First Data Corporation (1993–1995); Anasazi: Account Manager (1993), Software Engineer (1992–1993). **Associations & Accomplishments:** Arizona Software Association. **Education:** Northern Arizona University, B.S. in Business Administration (1986). **Personal:** Married to Lynne M. in 1987. Four children: Marie, Nathan, Steven, and Michelle. Mr. MacKnight enjoys flying, guitar, piano, golf, and being with his family.

John P. Mahoney

Partner and Treasurer
The Leadership Companies, Inc.
201 Great Road
Acton, MA 01720–5700
(508) 264–2900
Fax: (508) 264–2912

7379

Business Information: The Leadership Companies, Inc. provides products and services to small, medium and Fortune 500 companies in purchasing and supplier management areas, which includes, but is not limited to, contracts and negotiation skills. Services provided include software products, training courses, management guides and assessment services. Established in 1993, Leadership Companies, Inc. reports annual revenue of $3 million and currently employs 12 people. As Co–Founder, Partner, and Treasurer, Mr. Mahoney shares responsibilities with his partner, including providing consultations. His ten years of expertise in computer contract and procurement management with some of the world's leading computer corporations has given him the necessary "edge" to provide his clients with the utmost in state–of–the–art networking and systems solutions. **Career Steps:** Partner and Treasurer, The Leadership Companies, Inc. (1993–Present); Digital Equipment Corporation: Corporate Contracts Manager (1991–1995), Purchasing Manager (1987–1990); Contract Manager, Modicon, Inc. (1986–1987). **Associations & Accomplishments:** St. Johns Nursing Home – Event/Fundraising Committee; St. Johns Men's Guild; Vice President, Belvedere Resident Association; Boston College Alumni Association; Published in Suppliers Selection & Management Report and Purchasing Magazine. **Education:** Boston College, B.A. in Economics (1981). **Personal:** Mr. Mahoney enjoys golf and squash.

David A. Manigault

Executive Vice President
COHR, Inc.
201 North Figueroa Street
Los Angeles, CA 90012–2623
(213) 250–5600
Fax: (213) 250–4863
EMAIL: See Below

7379

Business Information: COHR, Inc. is a provider of health care solutions and nationwide information services. With seventeen years in the computer industry, Mr. Manigault joined COHR, Inc. in 1992. Appointed as Executive Vice President in 1995, he is responsible for designing, implementing and integrating electronic communications systems between computer systems. Career milestones include designing computer software for the health care industry that revolutionalized the field. Internet users can reach him via: Cyberchap@AOL.COM. **Career Steps:** COHR, Inc.: Executive Vice President (1995–Present), Senior Vice President of Information Masterplan Division, Vice President of MIS. **Associations & Accomplishments:** HEDIC (Health Care EDI Corporation); Public speaker. **Education:** Attended seminars: Pace University; Harvard University. **Personal:** Married to Cynthia in 1983. Two children: Christopher and Matthew. Mr. Manigault enjoys space science.

Ben Matthews

Director of Manufacturing
Optical Data Systems, Inc.
1101 East Arapahoe Road
Richardson, TX 75081–2336
(214) 301–3694
Fax: (214) 301–3874

7379

Business Information: Optical Data Systems, Inc., an ISO9000 Certified company, is an OEM and designer of local area networks, including high–end solutions for the networking requirements of industry, government, medical, finance, and military sectors. As Director of Manufacturing, Mr. Matthews is responsible for the direction of scheduling, planning, manufacturing, and research & development interface with engineering to provide and meet revenue and delivery commitments. **Career Steps:** Director of Manufacturing, Optical Data Systems, Inc. (1988–Present); Commerical Division Quality Manager, Honeywell Optoelectronics (1981–1989); Maintenance Chief Aircraft, VMAT–203 Harrier Squadron USMC (1978–1980); NCOIC Airframes/Hydrolics Aircraft, USMC (1959–1980). **Associations & Accomplishments:** VFW of Richardson, TX; American Legion of Richardson, TX. **Education:** Webster University of Chicago, IL, M.A. in Management (1987); Southern Illinois University, B.S. (1984); Military A/C and Maintenance Schools for Supervisors/Managers; Beaufort Institute of Technology Electronics, S.C. **Personal:** Married to Patricia A. in 1964. Two children: David A. and Dana A. Mr. Matthews enjoys golf, fishing, and reading a good book.

Eric M. McCaw
Systems and Network Administrator
J.A. Jones Applied Research Company
9816 White Cascade Drive
Charlotte, NC 28269–8395
(704) 547–6090
Fax: (704) 547–6028

7379

Business Information: A software consultant with more than twelve years of data processing and networking experience, Mr. McCaw is presently employed by J.A. Jones Applied Research Company, which serves as the prime contractor for the Electrical Power Research Institute, based in Palo Alto, California. As a Systems and Network Administrator and a member of the Computer Services Group, he is primarily responsible for providing systems and network support with regards to the Digital VAX systems and HP–9000 systems, and planning/managing departmental budgetary goals. This also includes end–user, application, and network support in a client–server environment, and he serves as secondary backup for the Novell System's Administrator. Mr. McCaw is a co–owner of Trebor Consulting, Inc., which specializes in systems and network integration and installation services. Mr. McCaw is a partner and Marketing Representative with Hairston Realty & Investment Group. Which specializes in commercial real estate, franchises, and residential property. He will be sitting for the State's License exam later this year. **Career Steps:** Systems and Network Administrator, J.A. Jones Applied Research Center (1994–Present); Marketing Representative & Partner, Hairston Realty & Investment Group (1995–Present);

Co–owner, Trebor Consulting, Inc. (1996); Digital Equipment Corporation: Software Specialist III (1988–1994), Software Specialist II (1984–1988). **Education:** University of North Carolina – Charlotte, B.S. in Mathematics with Computer Science Option (May 1983); Completed over 800 hours of company–sponsored training including Effective Presentations, Time Management, and Diversity Training; Novell Netware Certified 4.x. **Personal:** Married to Angela Hill McCaw in 1986. Two children: Angelo Maurice and Erika Patrice.

Mig H. Migirdicyan
President
National Data Corporation of Canada, Ltd.
1 Concorde Gate, Suite 700
Don Mills, Ontario M3C 3N6
(416) 455–7151
Fax: (416) 445–7168

7379

Business Information: National Data Corporation of Canada, Ltd., a fully–integrated extension of National Data Corporation, provides financial transaction processing services to the Canadian marketplace, including credit card authorization, electronic draft capture, corporate cash management, information reporting, health care claims processing, and value–added services. As President, Mr. Migirdicyan is responsible for the total management of the Canadian subsidiary, including strategic planning, finance, Corporate personnel decisions, and sales. **Career Steps:** President, National Data Corporation of Canada, Ltd. (1990–Present); Group Vice President, National Business Systems (1989–1990); Vice President and General Manager, National Business Systems (1985–1989); Systems and Sales Management positions, Burroughs (Unisys) (1970–1983). **Education:** American University – Istanbul, B.S. in Mechanical Engineering (1968). **Personal:** Married to Ani in 1970. Two children: Anoush and Saro. Mr. Migirdicyan enjoys photography and tennis.

Nelu Mihai, Ph.D.
District Manager
AT&T, Bell Labs
6239 Grand Oak Way
San Jose, CA 95135
(415) 577–7739
Fax: (415) 577–7711
EMAIL: See Below

7379

Business Information: AT&T, Bell Labs is a research and development company of distributed computing environments (operating systems) and Internet technologies. As District Manager, Dr. Mihai is a software architect and manager in the area of real–time operating systems and Internet protocols. Internet users can reach him via: NELU@GEOPLEX.COM or NELU@COSMOS. ATT.COM. **Career Steps:** District Manager, AT&T, Bell Labs (1996–Present); District Manager, AT&T, Advanced Technologies (1995); Staff Software Engineer, Microtec Research, Inc. (1992–1995). **Associations & Accomplishments:** Institute of Electrical and Electronics Engineers. **Education:** University of Bucharest: Ph.D. (1992), M.S. in Computer Science (Poly Tech Institute). **Personal:** Married to Julietta in 1981. Two children: David and Gabriel. Dr. Mihai enjoys music (classical and modern), history, art, literature, and basketball.

Mary Ann Moll
President
Computer Management and More
#6 Joffre Street, Laguna Terrace, Apt 11–D
San Juan, Puerto Rico 00907-1653
(809) 722–4434
Fax: (809) 723–4434

7379

Business Information: Established in 1994, Computer Management and More specializes in computer–aided bi–weekly mortgage payment plans. Introduced in Puerto Rico by Ms. Moll herself, the plan offers individuals an opportunity to save a substantial amount of money on their mortgage by paying more frequently on the principal and reducing the amount of interest paid. As President, Ms. Moll is responsible for all aspects of operations, as well as the overall growth and success of the business. **Career Steps:** President, Computer Management and More (1994–Present); Director of Administration and Finance, Lemar Manufacturers Representative (1991–1992); Administrator, Joanne Romanacce Workshop (1986–1990); Assistant Sales Manager, Caribe Hilton International (1979–1986); Administrative Assistant, Baker & McKenzie Law Office (1976–1979); Sales Representative, Pan American Airways (1970–1976). **Education:** University of Puerto Rico, Secretarial Sciences; Marymount Junior Collge, Merchandising; Hilton International Management Training Center, Sales and Marketing. **Personal:** Two children: Carina and Carla. Ms. Moll enjoys tennis.

STANLEY COMPUTER SYSTEMS, INC.

Eric Morrison
Senior Vice President
Stanley Computer Systems, Inc.
1515 Jefferson Davis Highway, Suite 715
Arlington, VA 22202–3320
(703) 413–6040
Fax: (703) 413–0203
EMAIL:scsi@mnsinc.com

7379

Business Information: Stanley Computer Systems, Inc. is a U.S. government computer services contractor. Established in 1983, the Company serves governmental entities from office locations in Virginia and New York. Joining the Firm in 1988, Eric Morrison was promoted to Senior Vice President of the Arlington, Virginia office in 1993. His primary duties involve the management and development of business programs for the Mid–Atlantic and Southeastern regions, as well as oversees all multi–state contracts and projects. **Career Steps:** Stanley Computer Systems, Inc.: Senior Vice President (1993–Present), Vice President of Marketing (1988–1993); Project Manager, Wilkens Systems, Inc. (1986–1988). **Associations & Accomplishments:** Minority Business Enterprise Legal Defense and Education Fund, Inc. (MBELDEF); Association of Banyan Users International (ABUI); Waters House Condominium Association; Unity Christ Church of Gaithersburg, MD; Gospel Mission for the Homeless (Washington, D.C.) **Education:** Attended: New School of Social Research, New York City; New York University Graduate School of Business Administration; American Management Association; George Washington University; Courses in Computer Technology, Marketing, LAN's and Government Contracts/Procurement. **Personal:** Mr. Morrison enjoys horseback riding, guitar, saltwater fishing, computing, rollerblading, art, music, hiking, and producing videos.

Brian K. Mosbey
Chief Operating Officer
Superstar Computing
9819 Valley View Road
Eden Prairie, MN 55344
(612) 942–0919
Fax: (612) 941–3356

7379

Business Information: Superstar Computing specializes in computer training and sales using notebook computers and vertical marketing software programs nationwide. As Chief Operating Officer, Mr. Mosbey is responsible for all decision making, overseeing all departments, strategic planning, and negotiating Corporate contracts. **Career Steps:** Chief Operating Officer, Superstar Computing (1992–Present); Chief Operating Officer, Roald Marth Learning Systems (1989–1992). **Associations & Accomplishments:** Meridian Group. **Education:** Attended: University of Minnesota. **Personal:** Married to Lisa in 1994.

JoAnn L. Nagel
Manager of Information Technologies
Entex Services
4705 Duke Drive
Mason, OH 45040
(513) 336–1107
Fax: (513) 336–1890
EMAIL: See Below

7379

Business Information: Entex Services provides personal computer networking, integration, sales of hardware/software, and services to Fortune 500 companies. Established in 1993, the Company employs 5,000 people. As Manager of Information Technologies, Ms. Nagel oversees the distribution site at Erlanger, KY, as well as the service site at Mason, OH. Additional duties include management of the 4500 and AH 9000 systems and trouble–shooting. Internet users can reach her via: joann.nagel@entex.com. **Career Steps:** Manager of Information Technologies, Entex Services (1994–Present); Technical Support Analyst, Coca Cola Enterprises (1990–19994); Operations Analyst, Great American Broadcasting (1983–1990). **Associations & Accomplishments:** Dale Carnegie Graduate Assistant. Presidents Club Award (1996). **Education:** Cincinnati State and Technical College, Associate C.S. (1993). **Personal:** Married to Michael Jr. in 1988. One child: Steven. Ms. Nagel enjoys gardening, reading, swimming, and water sports.

Mohammad Nour
Vice President of Engineering
Ace Consulting Firm
28432 Rancho Cristiano # A
Laguna Niguel, CA 92677–7427
(213) 658–7080 (619) 428–2065
Fax: (714) 362–5345
EMAIL: See Below

7379

Business Information: Ace Consulting Firm provides international consulting on various types of computers including mainframe and mini, and advises clients on software and hardware selections. Established in 1986, the Company has two locations in California and plans expansion to include the Middle East and other countries. As Senior Systems Engineer, Mr. Nour oversees design and implementation of new programs and systems, schedules maintenance, and manages customer support and services. Internet users can reach him via: MNOUR@PLAYMATESTOYS.COM. **Career Steps:** Senior Systems Engineer, Ace Consulting Firm (1986–Present); Chief of Networking Engineering, Gers Retail Systems (1995); Project Leader, Children's Hospital of Los Angeles (1995); Senior Systems Engineer, BASF Corporation (1994). **Associations & Accomplishments:** Institute of Electronics and Electrical Engineers; Certified Network Engineer with UNIX; Certified Novell Engineer With Novell, Microsoft Certified Engineer with Microsoft. **Education:** California State University, Long Beach, M.S.E.E. (1987); Southern Illinois University, B.S.C.E. **Personal:** Married to Oresa F. in 1989. One child: Armand R. Mr. Nour enjoys karate, volleyball, reading, and fishing.

Antonio A. Nunes Jr.
Senior Vice President
Lomas Information Systems
1525 Viceroy
Dallas, TX 75235
(214) 879–5703
Fax: (214) 879–7309

7379

Business Information: Lomas Information Systems is a systems development management firm, providing computer software exclusively to the mortgage banking industry. Services include installing and maintaining technical and processing equipment worldwide, primarily in Canada and the U.S. Joining Lomas Information Systems as Senior Vice President in 1988, Mr. Nunes is involved in all aspects of installation, design, and implementation of products, as well as systems development management. **Career Steps:** Senior Vice President, Lomas Information Systems (1988–Present); Development Manager, Farmer Savings and Loan (1985–1988). **Education:** University of San Francisco, B.S. (1988).

W. Stephen Nye
President
Equifax National Decision Systems
P.O. Box 919027
San Diego, CA 92191
(619) 550–5700
Fax: (619) 677–9601

7379

Business Information: Equifax National Decision Systems is the reading provider of marketing information, geodemographic solutions, desk top data delivery systems and unique high value marketing data. As President, Mr. Nye is responsible for all aspects of Company operations. **Career Steps:** President, Equifax National Decision Systems (Present); President/CEO, NSSI; Senior Vice President, Computer Associates. **Education:** James Madison University: M.B.A. (1980), B.S. (1977).

Mr. David William Nyland
Vice President – Product Development
Architel Systems Corporation
190 Attwell Drive, Suite 300
Toronto, Ontario M9W 6H8
(416) 674–4007
Fax: (416) 674–2290
EMAIL: d.nyland@acrhitel.

7379

Business Information: Architel Systems Corporation is a telecommunications software company. based in Toronto, Canada with Sales & Professional Services regional offices in Washington DC, Denver and Spokane. Architel was established in 1984 and has grown substantially since 1984 to approximately 120 staff worldwide. Architel's specific focus is software solutions for Operations Support Systems (OSSs). Current product offering include Network Element Provisioning (Automatic Service Activation Program – ASAP), Workforce Management (centralized Field Access Management Information System – FAMIS, and hand–held Craft Access System – CAS) and most recently in the development of other OSS technologies based on ASAP. In his capacity as Vice President, Product Development, Mr. Nyland has established a Product Research & Development Center containing Product Marketing, Product Engineering and Product Customer Support groups in Toronto. The purpose of this operation is to investigate new market and technology opportunities, enhance and extend existing software products, research & develop entirely new software products and provide 24x7 product support for core software solutions on a global basis. Mr. Nyland has led the evolution of this group from 20 full–time staff in Q2, 1995 to over 75+ full time staff in Q2, 1996. At Mr. Nyland's previous employer, Andersen Consulting UK, he was a manager in the global Communications Industry Group and worked on many customer projects in the Government, Utilities and Telecommunications. Additional management responsibilities included designing and implementing Software Engineering and Quality Management processes and procedures to ISO standards. **Career Steps:** Architel Systems Corporation: Vice President – Product Development (1995–Present); Architel Systems Corporation: Director Software Engineering (1995–1996); Andersen Consulting: Manager – Communications Industry Group (1990–1995); BTR Industries: Manufacturing Systems Engineer (1986–1989). Education: Brunel University, London, UK, BEng (Hons) 1st Class – Manufacturing Systems Engineering & Management (specializing in Computer Integrated Manufacturing) **Personal:** Married to Jane in 1994."

Gerard J. Oberle

Senior Software Engineer
Meca Software, L.L.C., Fairfield, CT
55 Walls Drive
Fairfield, CT 06430
(203) 256–5019
Fax: (203) 375–0541
EMAIL: See Below

7379

Business Information: Meca Software, L.L.C., Fairfield, CT is a publisher of personal financial software for personal computers. The Company's main focus is helping users manage their money more efficiently. As Senior Software Engineer, Mr. Oberle is responsible for providing technical leadership to a team of engineers implementing on–line banking software, as well as strategic planning. Internet users can reach him at 102056.2331@compuserve.com. **Career Steps:** Senior Software Engineer, Meca Software, L.L.C., Fairfield, CT (1995–Present); Independent Consulting Engineer, Self Employed (1994–1995); Software Consultant, Digital Equipment Corporation–New York, NY (1990–1994). **Associations & Accomplishments:** American Bar Association; Association for Computing Machinery; Connecticut Object Oriented Users Group; Published software technical articles in the VAX Professional, the FOCUS Systems Journal, and various computer association technical journals. **Education:** New York Law School, J.D.; University of Bridgeport, M.B.A., B.E.S.; Norwalk Community College, A.S. **Personal:** Mr. Oberle enjoys photography.

Yoram Ofek, Ph.D.

Research Staff Member
IBM Research Division
T. J. Watson Research Center, P.O. Box 704
Yorktown Heights, NY 10598–0704
(914) 784–7085
Fax: (914) 784–6205
E–mail: See Below

7379

Business Information: IBM Research, a Division of IBM, conducts research in networking for multimedia communications and distributed computing. Dr. Ofek has initiated the research activities on ring local area networks with spatial bandwidth reuse, switch–based local area networks, and synchronization for supporting voice and video communications over the Internet and legacy local area networks (Ethernet and Token–ring). In particular, he has been leading the research activities on the MetaRing and MetaNet network architectures. Dr. Ofek was the general chairperson of the 7th and the program co–chairperson of the 7th IEEE Workshop on Local and Metropolitan Area Networks. Dr. Ofek has been giving tutorials world–wide on multimedia networking, and is currently writing a book on this subject. He can also be reached through the Internet via: ofek@ibm.com **Career Steps:** Research Staff Member, IBM T. J. Watson Research Center (1987–Present); Research Engineer, RAFAEL – Israel (1979–1982); Gould Electronics, Urbana, IL (1984–1986); Fermi National Accelerator Laboratory, Batavia, IL (1983–1984). **Associations & Accomplishments:** Institute of Electrical and Electronics Engineers. **Education:** University of Illinois – Urbana: Ph.D. (1987), M.Sc. (1985); Technion – Haifa, Israel, B.S. (1979), all in Electrical Engineering. **Personal:** Married in 1976. Four children: Tidhar, Gidon, Daphna and Maya. Dr. Ofek enjoys running marathons, classical music, philosophy and the Opera.

Crystel Orndoff–Kurtzberg

Technical Information Center Manager
TRW FPI/1189
One Federal Systems Park Drive
Fairfax, VA 22033–4404
(703) 803–5484
Fax: (703) 803–5479
EMAIL: See Below

7379

Business Information: TRW FPI/1189 specializes in research needs, and tracking domestic and federal standards on the Internet, CD ROM, and Online Catalog services. As Technical Information Center Manager, Ms. Orndoff–Kurtzberg produces the online catalog for the Technical Information Center. She is additionally responsible for budgeting and writing acquisitions. Internet users can reach her via: crystel.l.kurtzberg@trw.com. **Career Steps:** Technical Information Center Manager, TRW FPI/1189 (1993–Present); Supervisor – Library, Barrios Technology (Space Station) (1990–1993); Information Specialist, Council for Exceptional Children (1987–1990). **Associations & Accomplishments:** Special Libraries Association; D.C. Online Users Group. **Education:** University of North Carolina – Chapel Hill, M.S. in Library Science (1976); College of William and Mary, B.A. (1975). **Personal:** One child: David. Ms. Orndoff–Kurtzberg enjoys reading.

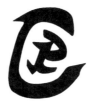

Dr. J. Luc Paquin

President
JLP Consultants
2875 Des Chenes
La Conception, Quebec J0T 1M0
(819) 686–5932
Fax: (819) 686–5377
EMAIL: See Below

7379

Business Information: JLP Consultants provides business and multimedia computer programming, graphics, and 3–D animation services to businesses and industries throughout North America. As President, Dr. Paquin is responsible for all administrative and operational functions of the Company including programming, customer relations, and marketing. Formerly a dental surgeon, he founded the Company in 1987. Internet users can reach him via: 73730.2125@compuserve.com or JLPConsultants@cil.qc.ca. **Career Steps:** President, JLP Consultants (1987–Present); Dental Surgeon, Private Practice (1983–1991). **Associations & Accomplishments:** Quebec Software Promotion Centre. **Education:** McGill University: D.D.S. (1983), B.Sc. (1981). **Personal:** Dr. Paquin enjoys cooking, shooting sports, training for the Olympics in 1976, and writing science fiction.

Carlos Paz–Soldan

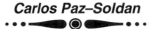

Owner and Vice President of Marketing
Tenet Computer Group, Inc.
606 Magnetic Drive
Toronto, Ontario M3J 2C4
(416) 665–3069 Ext: 205
Fax: (416) 665–2946
EMAIL: See Below

7379

Business Information: Tenet Computer Group, Inc. is a network systems integrator. Founding Tenet Computer Group, Inc. in 1984, Mr. Paz–Soldan serves as the Owner and Vice President of Technology and Marketing. He is responsible for all aspects of operations, in addition to directing technological and marketing activities. Internet users can reach him via: carlos@tenet.com. **Career Steps:** Owner and Vice President of Marketing, Tenet Computer Group, Inc. (1984–Present); Project Lender, Canadian Imperial Bank of Commerce (1980–1984); Systems Analyst, Bunge & Born Corporation (1976–1980). **Associations & Accomplishments:** Canadian Information Processing Society; Institute of Electrical and Electronic Engineers; Troop Leader, Scouts Canada. **Education:** University of Toronto, M.B.A. (1984); Universidad Nacional de Ingenieria – Lima, Peru, B.Sc. in Industrial and Systems Engineering. **Personal:** Married to Patricia in 1980. Three children: Carlos, Daniel, and Mario. Mr. Paz–Soldan enjoys cross country skiing and camping.

Terry G. Perrella

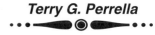

President
Terry & Associates, Inc.
8815 Harpers Point Drive
Cincinnati, OH 45249
(513) 260–3765
Fax: Please mail or call

7379

Business Information: Terry & Associates, Inc. is a computer consulting firm, providing contract programming, project supervision, and training of personnel and clientele to large firms on a national level. They also own and operate a trucking (20 long haul trucks) and construction (subdivision contracts) companies in Missouri and Kansas. As President, Mr. Perrella is responsible for all aspects of operations, including serving as a controlling stockholder and supervising consultants and a support staff of 7. Concurrent with his position at Terry & Associates, he serves as President of Perrella Enterprises. **Career Steps:** President, Terry & Associates, Inc. (1980–Present). **Associations & Accomplishments:** Loveland Chamber of Commerce; Church Council. **Education:** Southwest Missouri, M.B.A.; IBM; NCR. **Personal:** Four children: Jennifer, Aaron, Terry, and Sean.

Narendra Rana

Vice President and Managing Director
Knight Ridder Information, Inc.
2440 El Camino Real
Mountain View, CA 94040–1400
(408) 773–9261
Fax: (408) 773–9261

7379

Business Information: Knight Ridder Information, Inc. is a provider of on–line database information. Established in 1969, the Company reports annual revenue of $300 million and currently employs more than 700 people. With an extensive background in international marketing, Mr. Rana joined Knight Ridder International, Inc. as Vice President and Managing Director of the International Division in 1994. **Career Steps:** Vice President and Managing Director, Knight Ridder Information, Inc. (1994–Present); Dialog Information Services, Inc.: Vice President of Worldwide Marketing (1994), Senior Director of International Marketing (1992–1993); International Director and General Manager, Mead Data Central. **Education:** University of Cincinnati, M.B.A.; University of Colorado, M.S.; Indian Institute of Technology – Kanpur, India, B.S. with honors. **Personal:** Married to Nelle Gartner in 1993. One child: Jennifer. Mr. Rana enjoys skiing, travel, reading, and community work.

Donald J. Riley

Vice President of Management Services
IBM/ISSC
44 South Broadway
White Plains, NY 10591
(914) 288–3500
Fax: Please mail or call

7379

Business Information: IBM/ISSC, a subsidiary of IBM Corporation, is an international integrated system solutions company providing outsourcing consulting services. Established in 1991, IBM/ISSC currently employs 15,000 people companywide. As Vice President of Management Services, Mr. Riley is responsible for all aspects of management, including managing programs for Human Resources, communications and administration of 15,000 staff nationally and management of global operations of 26,000 staff for Human Resources and communications and administration locally. **Career Steps:** Vice President of Management Services, IBM/ISSC (1995–Present); IBM: Vice President of Human Resources – Latin America (1988–1995), Director of Human Resources and Marketing (1987–1988), Director of Human Resources and Real Estate (1985–1987). **Associations & Accomplishments:** Society of Human Resource Management (SHRM); Latin America Personnel Association (LAPA); New York Special Olympics; Local Chairman, IBM Blood Drive; Frequent speaker at global conferences and seminars. **Education:** College of Steubenville, B.S. in Business (1970).

Kathleen Rivera Spencer

President
Rivera Hartling Systems Limited
22 Point Crescent
Kingston, Ontario
(613) 384–0525
Fax: (613) 384–0146
EMAIL: rivera@rivera.ca

7379

Business Information: Rivera Hartling Systems Limited is an international computing consultant and software development firm specializing in international enterprise networks, smart-cards for healthcare systems, and government database systems. In 1985, Ms. Rivera Spencer co-founded the Company, which currently employs 15–20 people. Serving as President and Chief Executive Officer, Ms. Rivera Spencer's duties involve project management, systems analysis and technical design, consulting, administration, financial planning, business plans, and marketing. Recently, she was the project manager for the Ontario Encounter Card Pilot Project which integrated the SmartCare (TM) electronic patient records system with personal, portable smartcards for use by patients at hospitals, clinics, and pharmacies. Rivera Spencer and Associates, the new sister company, is now handling the smartcard and healthcare business. **Career Steps:** President, Rivera Hartling Systems Limited (1985–Present); Instructor, Queen's University (1985); Systems Engineer, Electronic Data Systems International (1980–1982); Ms. Rivera Spencer began her career in computing in Texas in 1969. **Associations & Accomplishments:** Canadian Organization for the Advancement of Computers in Healthcare (COACH); American Medical Peer Review Association (AM-PRA); Board of Directors, Advanced Card Technology Association (ACT CANADA) (1993–1994); Canadian Institute for Health Information (CIHI); Health Level Seven (HL7); EDI Council of Canada; Healthcare Information & Management Systems Society (HIMMS); Active in personal charities and "Career Day" programs; International professional publications; Conducts seminars and conferences. **Education:** Queen's University – Ontario, Canada, M.Sc. in Computing Science (1985); Inter-American University – Puerto Rico, B.A. in Business Administration (1981). **Personal:** Married to Ronald Carl Hartling in 1987. Two children: Kathleen Jones Rivera and Elizabeth Emily Rivera Hartling. Ms. Rivera Spencer enjoys music, reading, and travel.

Joseph C. Rocha

Controller & Chief Financial Officer
AEC Data Systems, Inc.
7550 Interstate 10 West Suite 400
San Antonio, TX 78229
(210) 308–9001
Fax: (210) 308–9015

7379

Business Information: AEC Data Systems, Inc. is a total solutions provider for facilities management, software development, and project management. As Controller & Chief Financial Officer, Mr. Rocha is responsible for fiscal matters, handling human resources, managing contracts, promoting the Company, and engaging in small legal issues. **Career Steps:** Controller & Chief Financial Officer, AEC Data Systems, Inc. (1995–Present); Director of MIS, Red Line Burgers, Inc. (1990–1995). **Associations & Accomplishments:** Alamo PC Users Group. **Education:** U.T.S.A., B.B.A. in Accounting (1993). **Personal:** Married to Dawn in 1995. Mr. Rocha enjoys jogging, cycling, and computers.

Nicholette Ross

Marketing Programs Manager
BMC Software
2101 City West Boulevard
Houston, TX 77042
(713) 918–5005
Fax: (713) 918–2970
EMAIL: See Below

7379

Business Information: BMC Software specializes in the development of software for user groups and vendor fairs. Established in 1980, the Company employs 1,600 people. As Marketing Programs Manager, Ms. Ross manages corporate seminars in North America and participates in regional user groups and vendor fairs. Internet users can reach her via: nicholette–ross@bmc.com. **Career Steps:** BMC Software: Marketing Programs Manager (1995–Present), Software Consultant (194–1995); Database Administrator, Harris Trust and Savings Bank (1988–1993). **Associations & Accomplishments:** Board of Directors, International DB2 User Group; Institute of Electronics and Electrical Engineers Computer Society Member. **Education:** DePaul University, B.S. in

Information Systems (1989); Missouri Southern State College, A.S. in Computer Programming. **Personal:** Ms. Ross enjoys music, theater, travel, and books.

Enzo Rossini

Manager
Micrograph, Inc.
Av Indico 66, Sala 71 Liardim Do Mar, Sao Bernardo Do Campo
Santana SP, Brazil 09750–600
551 – 14480665
Fax: 551 – 14588431

7379

Business Information: Micrograph, Inc. established in 1989, is a computer consulting company working with multi–national companies in Brazil. They consult on CAE/CAD/CAM and RISC/UNIX Environment workstations. As Manager, Mr. Rossini is a sales engineering consultant and assists companies with computer problems. He handles strategic planning for the Corporation, administrative duties, and financial accounting and planning. **Career Steps:** Manager, Micrograph, Inc. (1995–Present); Consultant, Multiple Bank (1995); Manager, Microtec/DEC (1989–1991); Lead Team, Villares Group (1985–1989). **Associations & Accomplishments:** Associacao Dos Diplomados Da Escola Superior De Guerra War College. **Education:** Mackenzie University, Electrical Engineering (1982); University of Sao Paulo: Microprocessors, Computer Graphics. **Personal:** Mr. Rossini enjoys swimming.

David A. Rothschild

President/Senior Consultant
C.I.S.S., Inc.
800 West Airport Fwy., Suite 1100
Irving, TX 75062
(214) 401–0840
Fax: Please mail or call

7379

Business Information: C.I.S.S., Inc., established in 1993, is a computer consulting company specializing in Composer by IEF(TM) software made by Texas Instruments. The Company works with several Fortune 500 companies, reporting annual sales in excess of $1 million. As President/Senior Consultant and Sole Owner, Mr. Rothschild is responsible for all management operations of, and customer relations for the Company. **Career Steps:** President/Senior Consultant, C.I.S.S., Inc. (1993–Present); Project Leader, Mobil Oil (1979–1993); Systems Analyst, FMC (1976–1979). **Associations & Accomplishments:** National Association of Self Employed **Education:** Amber University, M.S. in Professional Development (1986); McNeese State University, B.S. in Computer Science (1974). **Personal:** Married to Leila in 1995. Mr. Rothschild enjoys computers, golf, snow skiing, and photography.

Ken Rubin

Director of Sales
Source Digital
111 Presidential Boulevard, Suite 201
Bala Cynwyd, PA 19004
(610) 617–7950
Fax: (610) 617–3458
E MAIL: See Below

7379

Business Information: Established in 1990, Source Digital serves the Mid–Atlantic region from offices in McLean, Virginia, Philadelphia, and Pittsburgh, Pennsylvania, and Charlotte, North Carolina. Source Digital is a solutions provider with a focus on digital video creation and delivery systems, interactive multimedia, and Internet websites. The Company's expertise in integration and networking originated from designing cross–platform integrations production systems encompassing Macintosh, PC and Unix workstations and networks. They are the largest dealer in the world of Avid non–linear editing systems. Estimated revenue for 1996 is expected to exceed $10 million. As Director of Sales, Mr. Rubin also functions as the National Sales Manager for the Company. His responsibilities include managing the four offices in Pennsylvania, Virginia and North Carolina. Mr. Rubin is responsible for the development and implementation of new sales and marketing techniques for products and services offered by Source Digital. Other responsibilities include staff recruitment, training, and performance evaluation. Mr. Rubin is also involved in budget development and strategic planning. Internet users can reach him via: krubin@source digital.com, or Misteravid@aol.com. **Career Steps:** Director of Sales, Source Digital (1992–Present); Owner/ President, New York's Finest Wholesale (1990–1992); Crew Sales Manager, Potomac News (1989–1990). **Associations & Accomplishments:** President, Philadelphia Chapter of International Television Association; Co–founder, Metro–Mug. **Education:** Villanova University; George Mason University. **Personal:**

Mr. Rubin enjoys investing in the stock market, travel, golf, and skydiving.

Gilles E. Saint–Amant, Ph.D.

President
Image Et Forme Inc.
3929 Rue Rivard
Montreal, Quebec H2L 4H8
(514) 844–6850
Fax: Please mail or call

7379

Business Information: Established in 1985, Image Et Forme Inc. specializes in computer science research and development training for small businesses. As President, Mr. Saint-Amant is responsible for all aspects of operations, including information systems consulting. Concurrent to his position with Image Et Forme Inc., Dr. Saint–Amant is also a Professor at the University of Quebec at Montreal. **Career Steps:** President and Chief Executive Officer, Image Et Forme Inc. (1985–Present); Professor, Universite Du Quebec at Montreal (1991–1995). **Associations & Accomplishments:** Published 12 books in French and various software programs. **Education:** University of Quebec at Montreal, Ph.D. (1988). **Personal:** Mr. Saint-Amant enjoys reading and writing.

Raj Sajankila

Vice President
Softrix, Inc.
60 David Ct.
Dayton, NJ 08810
(908) 274–0073
Fax: (908) 274–0162
raj@softrix.com

7379

Business Information: Softrix, Inc. is an executive recruiting and consulting firm, specializing in engineering, telecommunications, software, and computer consulting. As President, Mr. Sajankila is responsible for all aspects of company operations, including operations management, recruiting, consulting, and marketing. Internet users can reach him via: raj@softrix.com **Career Steps:** President, Softrix, Inc. (1993–Present); Senior Consultant, Boston Group (1990–1995); Consultant (Software), Digital Equipment Corporation (1989–1990); Several years experience as Programmer and Software Engineer. **Associations & Accomplishments:** New Jersey Association of Staffing Professionals; Nationwide Interchange Service. **Education:** Mysore University – India, B.S. in Electronics Engineering (1980). **Personal:** Married to Amritha Raj in 1988. One child: Nitin Sajankila. Mr. Sajankila enjoys working with computer software.

Klaus Schneegans

President
OR Partner of North America
101 South Main Avenue, Suite 620
Sioux Falls, SD 57104
(605) 339–3074
Fax: (605) 339–2947
EMAIL: See Below

7379

Business Information: OR Partner of North America, sister company of Or Partner of Germany, is a software consulting firm, specializing in organizational consulting and software implementation of SAP software for Fortune 5000 companies. Mr. Schneegans coordinated the establishment of the U.S. location in 1994, providing corporate leadership, interfacing with major clients, and overseeing all recruiting and hiring activities. Internet users can reach him via: KLAUS@orpartner.com **Career Steps:** President, Or Partner of North America (1994–Present); Manager of Business Development, Raven Industries (1990–1993); Export Manager, Daktronics, Inc. (1984–1990); Export Sales, Technocommerz (1982–1984). **Associations & Accomplishments:** Service Corps of Retired Executives (SCORE); ACE Volunteer. **Education:** Aachen College, M.B.A. (1980). **Personal:** Married to Jill A. in 1983.

Carlton P. Schowe

Senior Vice President
IMI Systems, Inc.
100 East Pembrey Drive
Wilmington, DE 19803
(302) 478–8001
Fax: (302) 478–8005

7379

Business Information: IMI Systems, Inc., a subsidiary of Olsten Corporation, is an international professional services company, providing development, support and conversions of mainframes and client/server systems. With over fifteen years experience in the computer industry, Mr. Schowe joined IMI Systems in 1988. Serving as Senior Vice President since 1995, he is responsible for the direction of operations for the Northeastern Region (New England to Virginia), including sales, client relations, profit & losses, and problem resolution. **Career Steps:** IMI Systems, Inc.: Senior Vice President (1995–Present), Vice President of Northeast Division (1992–1995), Manager Director (1988–1991); Managing Director, Sterling Software (International Operation), London, England (1987–1988); Senior Manager, Informatics (International Operation), London, England (1982–1986). **Associations & Accomplishments:** DuPont Country Club; St. Mary Magdalens Catholic Church. **Education:** F.S.U.: M.S. (1976), Post-graduate Work Towards Doctorate (1976–1979); U.S.F., B.A. **Personal:** Married to Vicky in 1981. Two children: Heather and Devan. Mr. Schowe enjoys golf, tennis, and cycling.

Barrie Schwortz
Owner, Producer, and Director
Barrie Schwortz Productions
3003 Glendale Boulevard
Los Angeles, CA 90039–1803
(213) 665–7722
Fax: (213) 665–7722
EMAIL: See Below

7379

Business Information: Barrie Schwortz Productions is a producer of still, video and multi–media services and computer graphics for the scientific, medical and educational fields. Services include the preparation for production of photomicrocopy, still photographs, slides, video, and electronic imaging. Markets include home video, PBS, Discovery, etc. As Owner, Producer and Director, Mr. Schwartz is responsible for all aspects of operations, including shooting and directing films, editing, conducting editorial consulting, post production activities, and supervising production staff. Career highlights include serving as a member of the research team which performed the first in–depth scientific examination of the Shroud of Turin in 1978 (he was the Documenting Photographer). He is the developer and host of the largest Shroud of Turin WEB-SITE on the Internet and is currently producing a CD–ROM set and book on the Shroud. Other productions include a video with James Earl Jones, entitled "Money History In Your Hands." Internet users can reach him via: bschwortz@SHROUD.COM **Career Steps:** Owner, Producer and Director, Barrie Schwortz Productions (1985–Present); President and Founder, Educational Video, Inc. (1978–1988); Owner, Barrie Schwortz Studios (1971–1985). **Education:** Brooks Institute of Photography, B.A. (1971). **Personal:** One child: David H..

J. D. Seal
Director of Operations
Read Technologies, Inc.
5405 Alton Parkway, Building 5A, Suite 502
Irvine, CA 92604
(714) 551–2049
Fax: (714) 786–5395

7379

Business Information: Read Technologies, Inc. is a computer software solutions provider and reseller of corporate software. The Company also provides custom software solutions, consulting, and site licenses. As Director of Operations, Mr. Seal heads Marketing, Administration, and Finance. He handles all customer relations, budgeting, and strategic planning. **Career Steps:** Director of Operations, Read Technologies, Inc. (1990–Present); Director of Financial Planning, Hume Publishing, Inc. (1985–1989); Senior Financial Analyst, Electro Rent Corporation (1980–1984). **Associations & Accomplishments:** Lake Hills Community Church – Laguna Hills, CA; Indiana University Alumni Association. **Education:** Indiana University, B.S. (1979). **Personal:** Mr. Seal enjoys church activities, spending time with family and friends, and golf.

Thomas W. Shaw

Client Manager
IBM Corporation
117 Retford Avenue
Cranford, NJ 07016
(212) 493–2640
Fax: (212) 493–2188

7379

Business Information: IBM Corporation (IBM Consulting Group) is a management consulting firm, providing marketing, design, information systems, business transformation consulting, and information technology solutions. Joining IBM as Client Manager in 1994, Mr. Shaw is responsible for the direction of large Corporate relations and accounts within the financial services industry. **Career Steps:** IBM Corporation: Client Manager (1994–Present), Marketing Manager (1991–1992); Vice President, FD Consulting, Inc. (1992–1993). **Associations & Accomplishments:** Elected, Republican Councilman – Township of Cranford, New Jersey (1995) for the term 1996–1998; Commissioner of Finance for the Fresh Air Fund, Township of Cranford, New Jersey (1996); Donator to the March of Dimes; Basketball coach for 3rd and 4th graders. **Education:** Fordham University, M.A. in Public Policy in process, B.S. in Finance/Marketing (1980). **Personal:** Married to Carol in 1982. Mr. Shaw enjoys coaching youth basketball, swimming, biking, and travel.

Don Sheppard
Senior Manager
The PSC Group
145 King Street, Suite 601
Toronto, Ontario M5H 1J8
(416) 364–4275
Fax: (416) 364–4276
EMAIL: See Below

7379

Business Information: The PSC Group specializes in telecommunications and distributed systems, education, consulting, and software engineering. Established in 1985, the Company employs 200 people and has estimated annual revenue of $20 million. As Senior Manager, Mr. Sheppard manages all functions of the advanced technology consulting group. He is responsible for developing tutorials, speeches and conferences. Internet users can reach him via: dons@hookup.net or via: compuserve:73021,2613. **Career Steps:** The PSC Group: Director of Research and Technology (1994–Present), Senior Consultant (1985–1994); Senior System Manager, Canadian Imperial Bank of Commerce (1978–1985). **Associations & Accomplishments:** Professional Engineers of Ontario; Institute of Electrical and Electronic Engineers; Canadian Standards Association; Former President, Canadian Interest Group on Open Systems; more than 35 papers and conference presentations on Information Technology. Listed in International Businessman's Who's Who (1986) and Marquis' Who's Who of Computer Graphics (1984). **Education:** McGill University: Diploma in Management (1978), Bachelors in Engineering (1969); University of Toronto, M.A. Sc. (1972). **Personal:** One child: Lindsay Catherine. Mr. Sheppard enjoys wine making, skiing, and cooking.

PSSI

Alexander P. Sheyner
Principal
ProSource Systems, Inc.
186 Crescent Road
Needham, MA 02194
(617) 449–9119 Ext. 201
Fax: (617) 449–8118
EMAIL: See Below

7379

Business Information: ProSource Systems, Inc. (PSSI) is a software consulting service, specializing in data base design and development, process reengineering, client/server architecture, graphical user interface (GUI), and corporate Internet presence. As Principal, Mr. Sheyner is responsible for system and database architecture, overseeing production, strategic planning, and various administrative activities. Internet users can reach him via: ASHEYNER@AOL.COM **Career Steps:** Principal, ProSource Systems, Inc. (1992–Present); Senior Engineer – QA, EASEL Corporation (1989–1992); Engineer, Digital Equipment (1986–1989). **Associations & Accomplishments:** Institute of Electronics and Electrical Engineers. **Education:** Northeastern University, B.S. (1989).

Vivek Sinha

Vice President
System Development Bureau
50–12 Kiffena Boulevard
Flushing, NY 11355
(718) 244–0074
Fax: (718) 244–1039
E–mail: see below

7379

Business Information: System Development Bureau is a computer consulting and software development company. Established in 1986, System Development Bureau currently employs 25 people and has an estimated annual revenue of $3 million. As Vice President, Mr. Sinha is responsible for the hiring, management, development and decision–making in reference to all personnel. He can also be reached through the Internet as follows: SDBNYKATTMAIL **Career Steps:** Vice President, System Development Bureau (1990–Present); Vice President, AVS Systems, Inc. (1989–1990); Systems Engineer, Granada Systems, Inc. (1988–1989). **Associations & Accomplishments:** Member, Queens PC Users Group **Education:** New York Institute of Technology, M.S. in Computer Science (1988); B.I.T., Bangalore, ISC, B.S. in Mechanical Engineering; College Masipur, India, R.N. **Personal:** Married to Jaya in 1990. Two children: Apoorva and Sonya. Mr. Sinha enjoys reading, movies, socializing, and researching new areas and techniques in freight forwarding.

Karen L. Smiddy
Senior Marketing Program Manager
Tandem Computers, Inc.
1255 W. 15th Street
Plano, TX 75075
(214) 516–6370
Fax: (214) 516–6806
EMAIL: See Below

7379

Business Information: Tandem Computers, Inc. is a manufacturer of telecommunication and client server systems. Established in 1974, the Company employs 10,000 people and has sixty worldwide locations. As Senior Marketing Program Manager, Ms. Smiddy is responsible for communications, planning and strategy including marketing, collateral development, and publications management. Internet users can reach her via: smiddy_Karen@tandem.com. **Career Steps:** Senior Marketing Program Manager, Tandem Computers, Inc. (1995–Present); Northern Telecom: Manager, Communications and Marketing (1993–1994), Senior Specialist, Marketing and Communications (1993). **Associations & Accomplishments:** International Association of Business Communicators (IABC); Board Member/Job Counselor, North Dallas Shared Ministries; Parish Deacon, Churchill Way Presbyterian Church. **Education:** Texas A&M University, B.S. in Microbiology (1987). **Personal:** Married to Roger Kent Smiddy in 1995. Ms. Smiddy enjoys fiction writing, travel, and spending time with family.

Deborah G. Smith
Marketing Director
Sheriton Software Systems
35 Pinelawn Road, Suite 206E
Melville, NY 11747
(516) 753–0985 Ext. 193
Fax: (516) 753–3661
EMail: See Below

7379

Business Information: Sheriton Software Systems is a leader in the development and publication of add–on tools and components for visual developers. Distributing internationally, the Company focuses on companies and clientele developing Windows–based applications. Established in 1991, the Company employs 48 people, and has estimated annual revenue of $5 million. As Marketing Director, Ms. Smith is responsible for all aspects of her department including administration, operations, marketing, and strategic planning. She also oversees all public relations and manages trade shows and advertising. Internet users can reach her via: debs@shersoft.com. **Career Steps:** Marketing Director, Sheriton Software Systems (1995–Present); Events Specialist, Cheyenne Software (1994–1995); Program Executive, Travel Planners (1993–1994); Trade Show Manager, International Trade Facilitation Council (1989–1992). **Education:** Colgate University, B.A. (1987). **Personal:** Ms. Smith enjoys sports, photography, music, and dancing.

Kenneth T. Smith
President and Chief Executive Officer
Smith Computer Consulting, L.L.C.
8211 Goodwood Boulevard, Suite C1
Baton Rouge, LA 70806–7740
(504) 925–2878
Fax: (504) 926–6988
EMAIL: See Below
7379

Business Information: Smith Computer Consulting, L.L.C. is an information consulting firm specializing in computer hardware, software, and network solutions. Mr. Smith founded SCC in 1993. As President and Chief Executive Officer he is responsible for overseeing day–to–day activities, administrative functions, business development, and client management. Internet users may reach him via: SCC8211@intersurf.com **Career Steps:** President and Chief Executive Officer, Smith Computer Consulting, L.L.C. (1993–Present). **Associations & Accomplishments:** Alpha Phi Alpha Fraternity, Inc.; Kiwanis; Lions Club International; Toastmasters International – Certified Toastmaster. **Education:** Southern University, B.S. (1987). **Personal:** One child: Jasmine Alexis Smith. Mr. Smith enjoys reading sci–fi.

Willie J. Smith II
Hardware/Software Engineer
EDS/INS–ITP
800 K Street, Suite 830
Washington, DC 20001–8000
(202) 414–8242
Fax: (202) 414–8383
7379

Business Information: Electronic Data Systems (EDS/INS–ITP), an international leader in information technology, is working in partnership with the Immigration and Naturalization Service (INS) to develop and implement technology solutions to improve services and more efficiently enforce U.S. immigration policies. As Hardware/Software Engineer, Mr. Smith is responsible for the installation, configuration, and testing of LAN/WAN components. **Career Steps:** EDS/INS–ITP: Hardware/Software Engineer (1995–Present), Business Relations Analyst (1993–1995); Navigator, United States Navy (1972–1993). **Education:** University of the State of New York (SUNY), A.S. (1988); C.N.E. **Personal:** Married to Nadine in 1990. One child: Tiana. Mr. Smith enjoys reading and computer repair.

Joyce S. Snyder
Associate Director
Information Resources, Inc.
150 N. Clinton Street
Chicago, IL 60661
(312) 474–8484
Fax: (312) 474–8465
EMAIL: See Below
7379

Business Information: Information Resources, Inc. is a marketing research company specializing in consumer goods and computer industries with a field collection force of over 2,000. International in scope, the Company has 100 facilities worldwide, with corporate headquarters located in New York. Established in 1979, the Company employs over 5,000 people and has an estimated annual revenue of $330 million. As Associate Director, Ms. Snyder oversees special projects (i.e. rrre–engineering and process development). She is also responsible for direct supervision of twenty employees, interfacing with vendors Company–wide, and ensuring timely completion of all projects. Internet users can reach her via: joyce.snyder@infores.com. **Career Steps:** Associate Director, Information Resources, Inc. (1986–Present). **Personal:** Ms. Snyder enjoys swimming, going to the movies, and reading.

Erik Stearns
Founder and President
Star Blazer Enterprises
3201 Duval Road
Austin, TX 78759–3514
(512) 719–1099
Fax: (512) 719–1066
EMAIL: See Below
7379

Business Information: Star Blazer Enterprises is a computer consulting firm, targeting small businesses and home users. Future plans include expanding into other cities, such as Dallas and Houston, Texas, as well as internationally. Founding Star Blazer Enterprises in 1993, Mr. Stearns serves as its President, responsible for all aspects of operations, including finances and special projects. He also manages accounts payable, accounts receivable, administration, sales, marketing, strategic planning, etc. Most of his success is due to his expertise in diagnosing and troubleshooting customers' problems and fulfilling their needs. **Career Steps:** Founder and President, Star Blazer Enterprises (1993–Present); MIS, Dimension Graphics (1994–1995); IBM: Test Engineer (1993–1994), Systems Administrator (1993). **Associations & Accomplishments:** Central Texas Systems Operators Association. **Education:** University of Texas, B.S. in MIS (1994); RDA for CNE and MSCSE. **Personal:** Mr. Stearns enjoys music and hiking.

Ms. Sharon K. Stephens
Chief Executive Officer
Computer Applications, Etc. Inc.
5630 Crowder Boulevard, Suite 206
New Orleans, LA 70127
(504) 245–9913
Fax: (504) 245–9913
7379

Business Information: Computer Applications, Etc, Inc. is a Value–Added Reseller (VAR) for the health, legal and business industries. The Company has 4 Divisions: Research and Development, Sales (including Academic software and hardware), Service (laser cartridge recharging, electronic presentations, and desk top publishing), Service and Training. Established in 1992, the Firm currently employs six people. As Chief Executive Officer, Ms. Stephens is responsible for all aspects of operations, including administration, marketing, and strategic planning. She developed software for physician offices and has been involved in healthcare consulting work (i.e. high risk pregnancies). While employed at Bell Communications Research, she was involved with designing two key concepts: testing systems from the central office on phone installations and systems that will pinpoint trouble in the lines (TI carriers). Ms. Stephens was also heavily involved with concepts of three–way calling, call waiting, etc. Concurrent with her present position, Ms. Stephens serves as Professor at Southern University at New Orleans. **Career Steps:** Chief Executive Officer, Computer Applications, Etc. Inc. (1992–Present); Professor, Southern University at New Orleans (1993–Present); Member of Technical Staff, Bell Communications Research (1984–1993); Member of Technical Staff, Bell Laboratories (1982–1984). **Associations & Accomplishments:** National Technical Association (NTA); American Management Association (AMA); Who's Who in the Computer Industry; Pi Mu Epsilon (Mathematical Honor Society); Alpha Kappa Alpha Sorority, Inc.; Who's Who Among American High School Students; Who's Who Among Music Students; Society of Distinguished High School Students; Alpha Chi Scholarship Fraternity; Mary Kay Sales Director for 3 years; GRANTS AWARDED: NASA Minority Universities Information Network for Research and Education. **Education:** Purdue University, M.S. (1983); Southern University at Baton Rouge, B.S. in Computer Science, cum laude; Tulane University – School of Public Health, M.S. in Health Administration (1996). **Personal:** Ms. Stephens enjoys sewing, swimming, crafts, hiking, singing and bicycling.

Manfred M. Strauss
President
Testerion, Inc.
1220 Village Way
Santa Ana, CA 92705
(714) 564–9350
Fax: (714) 564–9344
7379

Business Information: Testerion, Inc. provides test systems and services for the printed circuit board and electronics industry. Established in 1980 with over $15 million in estimated annual sales, the Company is national in scope with locations in California, Minnesota, Illinois, New Hampshire, Virginia, Florida, and Texas. As President, Mr. Strauss oversees all Company operations, including human resources and marketing. **Career Steps:** President, Testerion, Inc. (1994–Present); President, ATG Test Systems (1993–1994); Division Manager, ATG Electronics (1983–1993); Sales Engineer, Ericson Information Systems (1981–1982). **Education:** GSBA – Zurich, Switzerland, M.B.A. (1993); FH Dieburg – Germany, Master of Science Degree. **Personal:** Married to Katerina in 1994. Mr. Strauss enjoys climbing, skiing, and squash.

Mark A. Sudweeks
Facility Manager
C.D.B. Infotek
6 Hutton Centre Drive, Suite 600
Santa Ana, CA 92707
(714) 708–2000 Ext. 566
Fax: (714) 708–1000
7379

Business Information: C.D.B. Infotek, established in 1986, is an online public database company with subscriber–members and twelve locations throughout the United States. Subscribers include various industries, insurance companies, attorneys, government agencies, etc. The Company presently employs over 250 people nationwide. As Facility Manager, Mr. Sudweeks is responsible for shipping and receiving merchandise and supplies, off–site storage of materials, office reconstruction, capital equipment purchases, and supply inventories. Other responsibilities include personnel concerns for his office and research/search updates for clients and staff members. **Career Steps:** Facility Manager, C.D.B. Infotek (1995–Present); General Manager, American Stores (1990–1995); Supervisor, McDonalds Corporation (1974–1992); Accounts Payable Supervisor, Carelines (1994–1995). **Associations & Accomplishments:** Fund Raiser for O.C. Ronald McDonald House; Fund Raiser for Adam Walsh for Lost Children Finders. **Education:** Cypress College, Attending; University of California at Los Angeles, B.A. Pharmaceutical Medicine; University of California at Sacramento, B.A. Marketing; California State at Long Beach, Marketing and Medicine. **Personal:** Mr. Sudweeks enjoys travel, crafts, and do it yourself jobs.

Ralph S. P. Sutton
Vice President
Gemplus International Associate
77–79 Peter Street
Toronto, Ontario M5V 2G4
(416) 593–2718
Fax: (416) 593–9686
7379

Business Information: Gemplus International Associate is the world's largest producer of Smartcards & related hardware. Joining Gemplus as an Associate, Mr. Sutton is responsible for all marketing pertaining to transportation and contactless technology and new applications. Concurrent with his executive position as a Gemplus Associate, he is also a Principal partner with the firm of Blackhall & Company. **Career Steps:** Vice President of Marketing, Gemplus International Associate (1995–Present); President, Blackhall & Company (1990–Present); Executive Vice President, Gamorenler Machineu Bau (1988–1990); Vice President, Weldo (1986–1988). **Associations & Accomplishments:** Reform Party of Canada; Royal Canadian Yacht Club; Former Member, Board of Trade. **Education:** Queen's University, MBA (1980); Ridley College; Trent University, M.A. in Archealogy. **Personal:** Married to Tara D. Charkonueau in 1988. Three children: Aja, John, and Alex. Mr. Sutton enjoys scuba diving, skiing, and karate.

Miss Carla V. Tang
Systems Consultant
Cutting Edge Computer Solutions, Inc.
Five Great Valley Parkway, Suite 314
Malvern, PA 19355
(610) 648–3881
Fax: (610) 695–9752
7379

Business Information: Cutting Edge Computer Solutions, Inc. is a computer systems consulting firm providing professional services to the Fortune 500. Cutting Edge Consultants design, develop and implement systems in client/server environments using graphical user interfaces and relational database systems. As Systems Consultant, Miss Tang is responsible for the development and oversight of all projects. Established in 1991, Cutting Edge Computer Solutions, Inc. employs 13 people. **Career Steps:** Systems Consultant, Cutting Edge Computer Solutions, Inc. (1993–Present); Student Consultant, Lehigh University Computing Center (1992–1993); Librarian, Lehigh University Libraries (1990–1992). **Associations & Accomplishments:** Association for Computing Machinery; (IEEE) Institute for Electrical and Electronic Engineers; Cultural Societies; United Way. **Education:** Lehigh University, B.S. in Computer Science (1993). **Personal:** Miss Tang enjoys playing the piano and guitar, reading, volunteering in the community, canoeing, roller blading, and outdoor activities.

Richard C. Tegge Jr.
Vice President of Business Development
Telular Canada, Inc.
9 Townsend West, Suite 1
Nashua, NH 03063
(603) 883–7371
Fax: (603) 881–5328
EMAIL: See Below
7379

Business Information: Telular Canada, Inc. is an international mobile offices computing company providing hand–held computers, wireless voice and data communications, and mobile computing. Mr. Tegge served as Executive Vice President of Portable Network Solutions for two years before the Corporation joined TCI in 1994. In his present position as Vice President of Business Development, he is responsible for personnel recruitment, strategic planning, value–added resale functions, and supervision of Corporate expansion. Internet users can reach him via: RTEGGE@GCICOM.COM **Career Steps:** Vice President of Business Development, Telular Canada, Inc. (1994–Present); Executive Vice President, Portable Network Solutions (1992–1994); Account Executive, CompuCom, Inc. (1991–1992); Account Executive, Inacom Computer Centers (1989–1991). **Education:** Northern Michigan University, B.S. in Management (1985). **Personal:** Married to Beth M. in 1985. Two children: Steven and Zackery. Mr. Tegge enjoys hockey, baseball, hunting, fishing, and spending time with his children.

Alex Tsang

Director
WestPac Technology, Inc.
361 Alden Road
Markham, Ontario L3R 3L4
(905) 940–8056
Fax: (905) 474–0954

7379

Business Information: WestPac Technology, Inc. imports and distributes personal computer products to government agencies, educational institutions, and commercial businesses in Canada. As Director and Partner, Mr. Tsang is responsible for daily operations, strategic planning, importing, financial control, and Corporate organization. **Career Steps:** Director, WestPac Technology, Inc. (1992–Present); Vice President of Marketing and Finance, PAL Systems, Inc. (1991–1992); Sales Manager, Computer Access System, Inc. (1990–1991). **Education:** Newcastle School of Management Polytechnic – United Kingdom, Post Graduate Diploma in Marketing (1973); Enfield College of Technology – United Kingdom, B.A. in Business Studies. **Personal:** Married to Mary Wong in 1975. One child: Belinda. Mr. Tsang enjoys travel, music, and sports.

Robert A. Van Cleave Jr.
President and Chief Executive Officer
Professional Technology Systems, Inc.
11341 Aegean Trace
Woodbridge, VA 22192–7105
(703) 490–5253
Fax: (703) 490–3533

7379

Business Information: Professional Technology Systems, Inc. specializes in quality systems development, ISO 9000 standard series compliance and training, process re–engineering, customer satisfaction, product development, and design process training. As President and Chief Executive Officer, Mr. Van Cleave is responsible for all aspects of Company operations, including administration, strategic planning, and finances. **Career Steps:** President and Chief Executive Officer, Professional Technology Systems, Inc. (1992–Present); Vice President, Quality Assurance and World–Wide Telecommunication, Dynatech Communications, Inc. (1989–1992); Manager, Corporate Quality Assurance, Hayes Microcomputer Products, Inc. (1985–1989). **Associations & Accomplishments:** Registered Professional Engineer; Texas Electrical–Electronic; California Quality Reliability; ISO Certified Quality Systems Auditor, IQA/RBA; Institute of Electronics and Electrical Engineers; American Society for Quality Control; American Management Association; Northern Virginia Business Leader. **Education:** University of Houston, M.S. in Electrical Engineering (1969); University of Arizona, Advanced Reliability Engineering Courses (1982–1983); Mississippi State University, B.S.in Electrical Engineering (1964). **Personal:** Married to Mary Elizabeth Eskridge in 1965. Mr. Van Cleave enjoys reading, walking, hiking, tennis, and fishing.

Richard P. Vatcher
Director of European CV Software Services
Computervision, Ltd.
Kingsmead Business Park
High Wycombe, England HP11 1JU
44–1494429529
Fax: 44–1494440303
EMAIL: See Below

7379

Business Information: Computervision Ltd. provides CAD/CAM and data management software to companies worldwide. Computervision's products and services are helping some of the largest automotive, aerospace and ship building

companies improve their competitive advantage. Joining ComputerVision's U.S. operations in 1981, Mr. Vatcher was appointed as Director of Software Services – Europe in 1995. He is responsible for all aspects of operations for Computervision's European office, which includes Eastern Europe, Middle East Africa, and parts of Asia, consisting of 70% of their customers. Internet users can reach him via: RVATCHER@UK.CV.COM **Career Steps:** ComputerVision Ltd: Director of Software Services – Europe (1995–Present); Far East Services Director – Japan (1992–1994); Various managerial roles – United States Division (1981–1992). **Education:** Harvard Business School (1992); Worcester Polytechnic Institute, B.S. in Mechanical Engineering. **Personal:** Married to Rita in 1988. Two children: Margret London, and William Tokyo. Mr. Vatcher enjoys tennis, basketball, skiing and golf.

Ms. Tracy L. Venezia
Founder and President
Computer Consultant Services
5000 Birch, West Tower, Suite 3000
Newport Beach, CA 92660
(714) 759–9137
Fax: (714) 759–9160

7379

Business Information: Computer Consultant Services is a temporary technical consultant placement and computer systems consulting firm. Established in 1982, Computer Consultant Services currently employs 50 people. As Founder and President, Ms. Venezia is responsible for all aspects of operations. **Career Steps:** Founder and President, Computer Consultant Services (1982–Present). **Associations & Accomplishments:** Immediate Former President, Community Action Division of Newport Harbor Area Chamber of Commerce; Founder of Business Assistance Workshops for the Newport Harbor Area Chamber of Commerce; Director for South Coast Repertory Supporting Cast Board of Directors. **Education:** Coleman College, A.S. in Computer Sciences (1981). **Personal:** Two children: Joshua and Brittany. Ms. Venezia enjoys shopping, the gym, cooking, and playing with her children.

Herman H. Verkade
Technical Director
CompuThoughts (UK) Limited
Audley House, Northbridge Road
Berkhamsted, Herts, United Kingdom HP4 1EH
01442–879426
Fax: 01442–879427
EMail: See Below

7379

Business Information: CompuThoughts (UK) Limited is a computer consultancy firm specializing in the management of large–scale Microsoft Windows NT networks for mission–critical applications. The Company's background as a DEC consultancy has made them the de facto specialists in migration from Open VMS to Windows NT and in the management of mixed–platform Windows NT environments (Intel, DEC Alpha, PowerPC). The Company's clients are primarily global organizations, a large portion of them are in the financial sector. The Company has developed a number of systems management tools to facilitate the large–scale deployment of Windows NT Workstation and Windows NT Server. These tools are sold alongside the consultancy services, as well as through a global network of resellers. As Founder and sole Director, Mr. Verkade was for many years responsible for all aspects of Company operations, but is now – as Technical Director – focusing more and more on the technical direction of the Company. Internet users can reach him via: Herman.Verkade@computhoughts.co.uk **Career Steps:** Computhoughts (UK) Ltd.: Technical Director (1996–Present), Director (1987–1996); Senior Software Specialist, Digital Equipment Corporation Nederland B.V. (1986); Software Engineer, Multihouse Nederland B.V. (1983–1986). **Associations & Accomplishments:** Institute of Directors; Microsoft Certified Professional; Mensa. **Education:** Attended: Technical University Delft (The Netherlands). **Personal:** Mr. Verkade enjoys and collects popular music (from 1967 to present).

Thomas J. Voshell
Professional Services Manager
Symbol Technologies
401 Hackensack
Hackensack, NJ 07601–6411
(201) 488–2001
Fax: (201) 488–0705
EMAIL: See Below

7379

Business Information: Symbol Technologies is an international manufacturer of portable data collection systems and radio interfaced systems used for collecting data and work process improvement. International in scope, Symbol

Technologies operates 50 offices globally. As Professional Services Manager, Mr. Voshell is responsible for managing the design system staff for the Mid–Atlantic Region. Career highlights include the establishment of a top quality team to meet the challenges of changing technologies. Internet users can reach him via: Voshell@Symbol.com **Career Steps:** Professional Services Manager, Symbol Technologies (1993–Present); Business Manager, FMC (1991–1993); Production Systems Manager, National Sports Daily (1990–1991); Senior Systems Engineer, The Bergen Record (1983–1990). **Associations & Accomplishments:** Former member, Society of Manufacturing Engineers. **Education:** University of Phoenix, M.B.A. (1995); Salisbury State University, B.A. **Personal:** Married to Diane in 1989. Mr. Voshell enjoys sailing, racing sailboats, biking, carpentry and remodeling.

Bryan Wahl

President/Executive Director
Bryan and Brian, Inc.: Webdirect Internet Services
P.O. Box 33045
Shoreline, WA 98133
(206) 467–1996
Fax: (206) 546–5585
EMAIL: See Below

7379

Business Information: Bryan and Brian, Inc.: Webdirect Internet Services specializes in creating, developing, and placing world wide web sites for businesses. Providing complete Internet services, the Company will maintain and market clients' sites, provide access, and general consulting. As President/Executive Director, Mr. Wahl oversees all aspects of the business including marketing, advertising, web page development, consultations, and day–to–day office procedures. Concurrent with his present position, Mr. Wahl is Executive Director of the King County, Washington, Republican Party. Internet users can reach him via: webdirect@wwwdirect.com. **Career Steps:** President/Executive Director, Bryan and Brian, Inc.: Webdirect Internet Services (1991–Present); President, Wahl and Associates (1991–Present); Executive Director, King County Republican Party (1995–Present); Executive Director, Concord Coalition of Washington (1993–1994). **Associations & Accomplishments:** Washington State Senate Republican Nominee; King County Department of Youth Services; Citizens Advisory Committee; Shoreline Parks and Recreation Commissioner; Chairman of the Board, Shoreline Business Roundtable; Founder and Chair, Shoreline Chamber of Commerce; Committee Chair, Government Affairs; Campaign Chair, Vision Shoreline Incorporation; Shoreline Rotary; Community Service Committee; Board of Trustees, Celebrate America Board of Trustees. **Education:** University of Washington, B.A. of CMU (1992); Leadership Institute: (1984, 1987, 1988), Instructor (1992,1993); Advertising and Layout Training (1988). **Personal:** Married to Maria in 1995. Mr. Wahl enjoys water and snow skiing.

Michael M. Westerheim, P.E.
Program Manager Corporate Environmental Affairs
UNISYS Corporation
3199 Pilot Knob Road, M.S. F1B05
Eagan, MN 55121
(612) 687–2887
Fax: (612) 687–2455

7379

Business Information: Unisys Corporation provides computing hardware and software solutions for high volume business transactions internationally. As Program Manager for Corporate Environmental Affairs, Mr. Westerheim serves as the official responsible for the oversight of remediation projects at hazardous waste sites. He is the liaison with governmental compliance entitites, acting on behalf of Unisys for regulatory affairs regarding environmental remediation and liability. He is responsible for design and implementation of soil and groundwater remediation systems at sites in the U.S. and Europe. Established in 1986, UNISYS Corporation employs 40,000 people. **Career Steps:** Program Manager–Corporate Environmental Affairs, Unisys Corporation (1992–Present); Project Manager, Delta Environmental Consultants (1987–1992); Environmental Engineer, Twin City Testing Corporation (1982–1987). **Associations & Accomplishments:** Association of Groundwater Scientists and Engineers; American Society of Civil Engineers; American Water Works Association. Mr. Westerheim is a registered professional engineer in California, Washington, Tennessee, New York and Puerto Rico. **Education:** University of Minnesota, B.C.E. (1984). **Personal:** Married to Marianne in 1992. One child: Nicole. Mr. Westerheim enjoys snow skiing and water skiing.

Stephen T. Wheeler
President/Chief Executive Officer
Wheeler Technologies, Inc.
P O Box 812350
Boca Raton, FL 33481–2350
(561) 375–8526
Fax: (561) 375–9185

7379

Business Information: Wheeler Technologies, Inc. established in 1990, specializes in data communications, systems consulting, outsourcing, and software development. The Corporation currently employs over 500 people and has a client base Fortune 100 companies. As President/CEO, Mr. Wheeler oversees all aspects of the business. He coordinates reports from all departments/division, detailing corporate operations and reports to the Board of Directors on the status of the Corporation. He represents the Corporation at various public functions. Mr. Wheeler is closely involved in the strategic planning for controlled growth of the Corporation in order to maintain excellent customer service and quality products. **Career Steps:** President/CEO, Wheeler Technologies, Inc. (1990–Present). **Associations & Accomplishments:** I.E.E.E.; Chamber of Commerce; Gator Alumni. **Education:** University of Florida, B.S.E.E. (1990). **Personal:** Mr. Wheeler enjoys boating, working out, running, and golf.

Mr. John E. White
Vice President of Operations
Queue Systems, Inc.
1800 St. Julian Place, Suite 304
Columbia, SC 29204
(803) 771–4100
Fax: (803) 771–0810

7379

Business Information: Queue Systems, Inc. is a computer consultancy providing computer solutions to real time users, primarily industrial facilities and power plants. Services include turn–key solutions, hardware integration, software development and training. International in scope, the headquarters are located in Columbia, SC and development facilities in Houston, TX. As Vice President of Operations, Mr. White oversees the overall daily operations of the Firm, including project manager for major contracts, customer relations liaison, technical leader, testing consultant and human resource supervision and management. Established in 1980, Queue Systems, Inc. employs 20 people. **Career Steps:** Vice President of Operations, Queue Systems, Inc., (1992–Present); Site Manager, Queue Systems, Inc. (1989–1992); Manager of Operations, Utility Software Systems (1988–1989); Manager of Development, Queue Systems, Inc. (1982–1988). **Associations & Accomplishments:** Instrument Society of America; Computer Science Curriculum Advisory Panel, Sacramento State College; Published in trade journals. **Education:** Sacramento State College, (1986); Boise State University, Chemistry and Computer Science. **Personal:** Married to Vivianne in 1986. Mr. White enjoys woodworking and outdoor activities.

Steve White
Vice President
NCR Canada Ltd.
320 Front Street, West
Toronto, Ontario M5V 3C4
(416) 351–2154
Fax: (416) 351–2181

7379

Business Information: NCR Canada Ltd. is a computer solution company selling to the financial, retail, and communications industries. Established in 1884, with approximately 1,100 employees, the Company has an estimated annual sales in excess of $225 million. As Vice President, Mr. White is responsible for all aspects of company operations, including sales, banks, credit unions, financial institute in Canada, and the sale of computer–based solutions to the Canadian financial industry. **Career Steps:** NCR Canada Ltd.: Vice President (1995–Present), Team Leader – Royal Bank (1992–1995); Marketing Manager – Asia Pacific Area, NCR Corporation Ltd. (1991–1992). **Associations & Accomplishments:** Toronto Board of Trade. **Education:** University of Santa Clara, CA, M.B.A. (1984); Queen's University, Kingston, Ontario, Honors Economics. **Personal:** Married to Linda in 1986. Three children: Christie, Loren, and Jason. Mr. White enjoys golf and tennis.

Jay T. Williamson
President/Senior Level Consultant
JCC Enterprises Inc.
11311 134 1/2 Avenue
Dayton, MN 55327
(612) 209–6714
Fax: (612) 209–6714

7379

Business Information: JCC Enterprises Inc. specializes in client server development, design and solutions. Established in 1994, the Company employs three people, and has developed applications for several Fortune 100 Companies. As President/Senior Level Consultant, Mr. Williamson oversees all aspects of the Company. He is responsible for day–to–day operations, including administration, operations, sales, marketing, and strategic planning. **Career Steps:** President/Senior Level Consultant, JCC Enterprises (1994–Present); Senior Programmer/Analyst, United Health Care Corporation (1990–1994); Systems Programmer, Fourth Shift Corporation (1988–1990). **Associations & Accomplishments:** Certified Power Builder Developer Associate; Twin Cities PowerBuilders Group; Twin Cities Sybase Group. **Education:** South Dakota School of Mines and Technology, B.C.S.C. (1988). **Personal:** Married to Donna in 1990. Three children: Jordan, Connor and Chelsea. Mr. Williamson enjoys snowmobiling, skiing, basketball, golf and is a member of the Old Apostolic Lutheran Church.

Ruth A. Woody
Vice President
ASA Solutions, Inc.
8040 East Morgan Trail, Suite 21
Scottsdale, AZ 85258–1211
(602) 922–9532
Fax: (602) 922–9536
EMAIL: See Below

7379

Business Information: ASA Solutions, Inc. provides software consulting services, to include contract service and in–house custom software development. International in scope, the Corporation focuses primarily on Fortune 100–500 companies, with clients in Hong Kong, Singapore, London, and the United States. Established in 1994, the Corporation employs 40 people and has an estimated annual revenue of $3.5 million. As Vice President, Ms. Woody is one of four founders of the Company, and is responsible for oversight of operations and management of the contract services division. Internet users can reach her via: rwoody@asasol.com. **Career Steps:** ASA Solutions, Inc: Vice President (1995–Present), General Manager (1994–1995); Manager of Contract Services, NCM A/S Phoenix B.V. (1992–1994). **Associations & Accomplishments:** Arizona Software Association; NTSA; "Pride in Performance" Award from Triple I, Inc. (1991). **Education:** Durham Business College – Houston, TX; Palomar College – San Marcos, CA. **Personal:** Married to William in 1993. Three children: Heather, Christina, and Jonathon Fourneau. Ms. Woody enjoys writing and music production.

Eric Xiao
Senior Software Engineer
WHEB Systems, Inc.
9672 Via Excelencia
San Diego, CA 92126
(619) 586–7885
Fax: (619) 271–6559

7379

Business Information: WHEB Systems, Inc. deals with automated data capture, on OCR and ICR, as well as form processing. As Senior Software Engineer, Mr. Xiao is responsible for layout system architecture, as well as system design, product development, and system integration. **Career Steps:** Senior Software Engineer, WHEB Systems, Inc. (1995–Present); Senior Software Engineer, Mitchell International (1993–1995); Software Engineer, Micro Images Inc. (1989–1993). **Associations & Accomplishments:** AIIM. **Education:** University of Nebraska–Lincoln, M.S. (1993). **Personal:** Married to Jenny Huang in 1989. One child: Laura.

Carol L. Yu
Senior Director
Knight Ridder Information, Inc.
2440 El Camino Real
Mountain View, CA 94040
(415) 254–8334
Fax: (415) 254–8541
EMAIL: See Below

7379

Business Information: Knight Ridder Information, Inc. provides on–line information services with over 500 databases, including news, medical, intellectual property, CD ROM products, delivery and documentations, etc. International in scope, Knight Ridder Information, Inc. has two of its main functional offices in Mountain View, California (Palo Alto is part of Mountain View) and Bern, Switzerland (Bern has over 300 databases in different dialogues and languages). Sales offices are located world–wide, including Europe, Asia, Switzerland, U.S., etc. Joining Knight Ridder Information as Senior Director in 1994, Ms. Yu directs all aspects of operations, including managing a unit that licenses, develops and updates databases in biomedical, pharmaceutical and social science areas. She also is responsible for supporting marketing, sales, customer service and working with issues or opportunities that need to be addressed for primary and secondary publication, sharing the information with the public. Internet users can reach her via: Carol_Yu @corp.dialog.com. **Career Steps:** Senior Director, Knight Ridder Information, Inc. (1994–Present); Dialog Information Services: Director of Business Database Development (1992–1994), Technical Manager (1990–1991), Senior Programmer Analyst (1988–1990). **Associations & Accomplishments:** Special Library Association. **Education:** University of Santa Clara, M.S.E.E.C.S. (1989); University of San Jose State, B.A. in Mathematics. **Personal:** Married to Thomas in 1985. Two children: Elaine and Andrew. Ms. Yu enjoys skiing, biking, and travel.

Phil Zaczek

President and Chief Executive Officer
Diamond Consulting, Inc.
1420 Kensington Road
Oak Brook, IL 60521–2143
(708) 586–0000
Fax: (708) 586–0023
EMAIL: See Below

7379

Business Information: Diamond Consulting, Inc. is a national computer consulting firm, providing hardware sales and business processing engineering. The Firm provides IBM Mid Ranges, PC Lands, main frames, etc. Joining Diamond Consulting as President and Chief Executive Officer in 1993, Mr. Zaczek is responsible for all aspects of operations, including administration and strategic planning. Internet users can reach him via: DYMND.com **Career Steps:** President and Chief Executive Officer, Diamond Consulting, Inc. (1993–Present); Vice President of Operations, Midwest Indemnity (1992–1993); Vice President of Information Services, Allied American Insurance (1989–1992). **Associations & Accomplishments:** President, Midrange Professional Association; Omni; Speaker at common conferences; Public speaking globally on Business Process Reengineering, Effective Communications, Project Management and Technical Projects. **Education:** Roosevelt University, B.A. (1988). **Personal:** Married to Kay Lynn in 1990. Mr. Zaczek enjoys mountain climbing and opera singing at community theaters.

Anthony G. Arcaro
U.S. Operations Manager
Intercon Security Ltd.
212 West Van Buren, 6th Floor
Chicago, IL 60607–3903
(312) 986–0200
Fax: (312) 986–0106

7381

Business Information: Intercon Security Ltd. is a private security contractor with private detective licensure, providing personal security to executives, property owners, and their families. A licensed private detective and licensed private security contractor, Mr. Arcaro has served in various capacities with Intercon, most recently promoted to U.S. Operations Manager in 1992. He is responsible for all personnel decisions in the states of Florida, Wisconsin, and Illinois. He supervises all recruiting, hiring, firing, and training procedures, and providing continuing education to present employees. **Career Steps:** Intercon Security Ltd.: U.S. Operations Manager (1992–Present), Special Services Group Operations Manager – Canada (1991–1992), Personnel Manager – Canada (1987–1991). **Associations & Accomplishments:** West Suburban Chiefs of Police Association of Western Cook County & Eastern DuPage; Illinois Police Instructor Trainers Association; International Association of Law Enforcement

Firearms Instructors; International Association of Asian Crime Investigators; International Council of Shopping Centers. **Education:** Smith and Wesson Academy, Completed Firearms Instructor and Defensive Tactics Instructor (P.P.C.T. – Pressure Points Control Tactics); Attended Sir Sanford Fleming College – Canada. **Personal:** Married to Kelly E. in 1991. One child: Anthony Joseph. Mr. Arcaro enjoys sport shooting, fishing, hunting, and camping.

Jay Burke
Owner
Protective Service of Southern California
12235 Beach Boulevard, Suite 27
Stanton, CA 90680
(714) 379–1275
Fax: Please mail or call

7381

Business Information: Protective Service of Southern California is an investigative and uniformed protection services firm for five counties in Southern California (Los Angeles, Orange, San Bernadino, San Diego, Ventura). Clientele include retail plazas, concert events, construction sites, high–rise apartment complexes, etc. As Owner, Mr. Burke is responsible for all aspects of operations, including administration, public relations, marketing, and strategic planning. He also becomes actively involved in the community by speaking at neighborhood watch programs and city–city programs. **Associations & Accomplishments:** California Robbery Association; Citizens Against Lawsuit Abuse; Better Business Bureau. **Personal:** Mr. Burke enjoys boating, scuba diving, and skiing.

Conrado Dumlao
Chairman
Truth Verifier Systems
455 Broad Avenue
Leonia, NJ 07605–1601
(201) 944–4912
Fax: (201) 944–5003

7381

Business Information: Truth Verifier Systems is a private detective agency headquartered in the Philippines. The Leonia, New Jersey, location purchases law enforcement and security products (e.g., lie–detectors, fingerprint kits, cameras) for export to the Philippine National Police and the National Bureau of Investigators. Mr. Dumlao founded Truth Verifier Systems in 1966. As Chairman, he is responsible for the procurement, purchase, and export of all products to the Philippines. In addition, he serves as the Area Governor for the World Association of Detectives. **Career Steps:** Chairman, Truth Verifier Systems (1966–Present); Area Sales Manager, Chrysler Corporation (1962–1965); Major, Armed Forces of the Philippines (1955–1959). **Associations & Accomplishments:** American Society for Industrial Security: Member and Winner of Outstanding Leadership Award; Area Governor, World Association of Detectives; Association of Certified Fraud Examiners; American Polygraph Association. **Education:** Atengo de Manila University, M.B.A. (1976); University of Santo Tomas, B.S. **Personal:** Married to Josefina F. in 1958. Seven children: Conrado Jr., Jose, Maria Rosario, Roberto, Gerardo, Luis, and Maria Teresa. Mr. Dumlao enjoys swimming.

Albert E. Johnson
District Manager
Budd Services, Inc.
310 Dalton Avenue
Charlotte, NC 28206
(704) 334–1494
Fax: (704) 334–1487

7381

Business Information: Budd Services, Inc. is a contract cleaning and uniformed security guard service. Joining Budd Service, Inc. as Director of Human Resources in 1982, Mr. Johnson was appointed as District Manager in 1988. He is responsible for all aspects of administrative operations for associates and personnel within the Charlotte sector. **Career Steps:** Budd Services, Inc.: District Manager (1988–Present), Director of Human Resources (1982–1988); Owner, Morris Cleaning Service (1969–1982). **Associations & Accomplishments:** President, Mid South Cleaning Association (2 years); President, Shallow Lakes Home Owners Association (3 years); Board of Directors, Mid South Cleaners Association (4 years). **Education:** Attended: North Carolina State University (1968). **Personal:** Married to Barbara B. in 1975. Two children: Emily and Katie. Mr. Johnson enjoys golf and yard work.

Michael G. Lutz
Chief Financial Officer
McRoberts Protective Agency
17 Batterly Place
New York, NY 10004
(212) 425–2500
Fax: (212) 785–1685

7381

Business Information: McRoberts Protective Agency is a security services firm, providing security guard services, alarm installations, and monitoring. Established in 1876, McRoberts Protective Agency reports annual revenue of $18 million and currently employs 1,000 people. As Chief Financial Officer, Mr. Lutz is responsible for the management of the financial and computer operations of four companies.

George A. Morse
President
Failure Analysis Service Technology
P.O. Box 5489
Pine Mountain, CA 93222–5489
(805) 242–0902
Fax: (805) 242–4910

7381

Business Information: Failure Analysis Service Technology is a national aviation mishap investigation firm, specializing in investigation of aircraft crashes. With twenty–three years in the aviation industry, Mr. Morse found the Company in 1990. As President he is responsible for all aspects of operations, including conducting investigations. **Career Steps:** President, Failure Analysis Service Technology (1990–Present); Department Manager, Lockheed Aeronautical Systems Corporation (1980–1990); Captain, U.S. Air Force (1972–1980). **Associations & Accomplishments:** Board of Directors, National Aerospace FOD Prevention, Inc.; International Society for Air Safety Investigators (ISASI); Antelope Valley Public Policy Officer (AIAA). **Education:** University of Alaska, M.S. in Chemistry (1980); University of Cincinnati, B.S. in Chemistry (1971). **Personal:** Married to Lorie in 1972. One child: Christopher. Mr. Morse enjoys coaching his son's soccer team and piloting aircraft.

Arthur D. Murphy
President
Inter Secure Technology, Inc.
5402 15th Avenue Building B.
Columbus, GA 31904–4466
(706) 571–8890
Fax: (706) 563–9823

7381

Business Information: Inter Secure Technology, Inc. is an international investigation, security, polygraph, and forensic testing company. As President, Mr. Murphy is responsible for diversified administrative activities. Additionally, he is President of Lanier Mortgage Company, a national real estate mortgage and financing institution, established in 1993. **Career Steps:** Inter Secure Technology, Inc./ Lanier Mortgage and Financial Services: President, (1995–Present), Vice President (1993–1995); Special Agent Supervisory, Department of the Army (1979–1993). **Associations & Accomplishments:** Teaches local college courses in Business courses; Member, American Polygraph Association; National Mortgage Banker and Broker Associations. **Education:** Jacksonville State University, M.S. (1994); Central Michigan University, M.A. in Business Management, (1983). **Personal:** Married to Donna in 1994. Mr. Murphy enjoys boating and working with computers.

Shari Ann Pheasant
Founder/Chief Executive Officer
Parent Patrol, Inc.
P O Box 20659
Sun Valley, NV 89433
(702) 359–7153
Fax: (702) 359–7153

7381

Business Information: Parent Patrol, Inc. is a non–profit organization dealing with elementary school–age children. Members of the Parent Patrol patrol the local streets before and after school in order to prevent violence to students. As Founder/CEO, Ms. Pheasant oversees all aspects of operations including utilization, recruitment, and direction of staff. **Career Steps:** Founder/CEO, Parent Patrol, Inc. (1995–Present); Fullcharge Bookkeeper, American Refrigeration (1991–1992); Manager and Bartender, Metamorphosis (1986–1989); Regional Director, Petrie Stores, Inc. (1982–1986); Regional Sales Director, Pleasant Dreams Lingerie Home Parties (1991–Present). **Associations & Accomplishments:** President, Parent Faculty Association of Rita Cannan Elementary. **Education:** University of Southern Colorado. **Personal:** Married to Jeffrey John in 1991. Two children: Shyla Marie and Gregory Warren. Ms. Pheasant enjoys camping, sewing, community work, lingerie parties, and crafts.

Dennis Reilly
Regional Director
Nation Wide Security, Inc.
4000 Hollywood Boulevard 635 South
Hollywood, FL 33021–6755
(305) 966–9088
Fax: (305) 967–8866

7381

Business Information: Nation Wide Security, Inc. is a security guard and investigation firm. Established in 1980, Nation Wide Security, Inc. currently employs 1,000 people corporate–wide. With eight years expertise in the security industry, Mr. Reilly joined Nation Wide Security, Inc. in 1992. Serving as Regional Director for the Gulf Region, he has overall responsibility of the District Office consisting of branch offices located in five states. **Career Steps:** Regional Director, Nation Wide Security, Inc. (1995–Present); District Manager, Nation Wide Security (1992–1995); Client Development Manager, Summit Security (1990–1992); Regional Sales Manager, Globe Security (1987–1990). **Associations & Accomplishments:** ASIS; Boca Square Civic Association; Hollywood, Florida Chamber of Commerce. **Education:** Attended: New York Institute of Technology (1980). **Personal:** Married to Kathy in 1986. Three children: Pat, Shannon, and Anita. Mr. Reilly enjoys golf and hockey.

Mr. Kim K. Bowers, CML
President
East Texas Safe & Lock and Kim Bowers & Associates
214/216 East Main Street
Kilgore, TX 75662
(903) 984–5707
Fax: (903) 984–5510

7382

Business Information: East Texas Safe & Lock is a provider of premise security systems, safes, and vaults. Kim Bowers & Associates is an industry specific public relations and marketing company, and is a manufacturer's representative for international physical & information high–security systems such as biometric (retinal scan) systems and devices, proximity systems (rf), intelligent controllers, host systems, and reader interface devices. As President, Mr. Bowers is responsible for overseeing management of all Company operations for East Texas Safe & Lock and Kim Bowers & Associates. Established in 1985, East Texas Safe & Lock and Kim Bowers & Associates employs a full–time professional staff of five. **Career Steps:** President, East Texas Safe & Lock and Kim Bowers & Associates (1985–Present); Marketing Director, A/S Sash & Door Manufacturing Company, Inc. (1984–1985); Service Technician, Deckelman's (1980–1984); Contract Sales, Abilene Lumber (1975–1979). **Associations & Accomplishments:** Director, Associated Locksmiths of America (ALOA); Safe & Vault Technician's Association; Door and Hardware Institute; Ark–La–Tex Locksmith's Association; Texas Locksmith's Association; Past President and Charter Member, Kiwanis International; Civic Affairs Committee, Chamber of Commerce; Amnesty International; "The ACE Award", ALOA; Instructor for many industry related courses; Published in many trade and business journals. **Education:** University of Texas (1974); Certification/Training: High Security Lock Systems: Abloy Master Keying, Miwa Factory Training, Medeco Biaxial, Schlage Primus, ALOA Instructor Training; Electronic Access Control, CCTV, Time & Attendance Database Systems: Electromechanical/Electromagnetic Devices, Industry and Manufacturer Classes, applied first retinal scan biometric recognition to safe & vault use; Safe & Vault: AMSEC, Major Safe, Allied/Gary Vault Installation and Safe servicing, Sargent & Greenleaf, Mas–Hamilton X–07, Tidel Engineering; Associated Locksmith's of America Proficiency Certification: Registered, Professional, Master, Instructor.

Ulysses J. Brualdi Jr.
President and Chief Executive Officer
ADT Security Systems, Inc.
63 Midwood Terrace
Madison, NJ 07940–2712
(201) 316–1426
Fax: Please mail or call

7382

Business Information: ADT Security Systems, Inc. is an international leader in the manufacture of security systems to residential and commercial clientele. Established in 1872, ADT Security Systems reports annual revenue of $135 million and currently employs 135 people. The Company markets, installs, maintains and monitors electronic security and fire alarm systems. Serving as President for ADT, Inc. since 1980, Mr. Brualdi also holds the titles of Chief Operating Officer (appointed 1986) and Chief Executive Officer (appointed 1988). He provides the overall vision and strategies for corporate development, quality product and service output, and international relationships. **Career Steps:** President and Chief Executive Officer, ADT Security Systems, Inc. (1988–Present); ADT, Inc.: President and Chief Operating Officer (1986–1988), President (1980–1986). **Associations & Accomplishments:** Central Station Alarm Association; National Burglar and Fire Alarm Association; Junior Achievement, Inc.; National Crime Prevention Council. **Education:** Harvard Business School, A.M.P.; City College of New York, M.B.A.; University of Connecticut, B.S. in Mechanical Engineering. **Personal:** Married to Carol in 1960. Three children: Lorene Donahue, Lisa Gotsch, and Christine Brualdi. Mr. Brualdi enjoys golf.

William F. Buttersworth
Operations Manager
Norred & Associates, Inc.
7370 Hodgson Memorial Drive
Savannah, GA 31406
(912) 354–4520
Fax: (912) 351–9472

7382

Business Information: Norred & Associates, Inc. provides corporate and domestic security and investigation as well as insurance fraud services. A former Chief of Police, Mr. Buttersworth joined Norred in 1991 and currently serves as Operations Manager, supervising security operations, corporate and private investigations, and sales for the Savannah, Georgia office. **Career Steps:** Operations Manager, Norred & Associates, Inc. (1990–Present); Chief of Police, City of Glenville, Georgia (1989–1990); Training Coordinator, Armstrong State College Criminal Justice Training Center (1986–1989). **Education:** Armstrong State College; Dale Carnegie Seminar, Graduate (1974). **Personal:** Two children: Amy and Brad. Mr. Buttersworth enjoys fishing and motorcycling.

Carl J. Calkins
President and Director of Security
Staff Control Security Services
5980 The Toledo
Long Beach, CA 90803–4147
(310) 223–1135
Fax: (310) 223–1131

7382

Business Information: Staff Control Security Services provides private security services for the home, business, and special events. Services include providing security personnel for security posts and vehicle checks. Their Motto is: "SCSS" SERVING CLIENTS WITH SUPERIOR SECURITY. Established in 1993, Staff Control Security Services currently employs 150 people. As President and Director of Security, Mr. Calkins is responsible for all aspects of operations, including the delivery of quality security service to clients, development of staffing criteria for security posts and vehicle checks specified in existing and new contracts, and guiding staffing plan development to maximize human resources and minimize costs to both client and the Company. He also establishes a continuing growth level with acceptable profitability margins. **Career Steps:** President and Director of Security, Staff Control Security Services (1995–Present); Security Consultant, Staff Control, Inc. (1995); Lecturer, Educator, and Advisor, Criminal Justice Consultant (1974–1995); Real Estate Broker, Independent, Carl J. Calkins Real Estate (1988–Present); Real Estate Broker, Managing General Partner, Tule Valley Ranch (1982–1994); Yacht Broker, Stan Miller Yachts (1980–1982); Chief of Police, Long Beach Police Department (1976–1979); Director of Department of Community Safety, City of Carson (1974–1976); Captain of Police, Commanding Officer Venice Operations, Los Angeles Police Department (1954–1974); Staff Sergeant – Korean War, United States Army (1951–1954). **Associations & Accomplishments:** Co-founder, Community Action Association Program; Long Beach Neighborhood Citizens Committee; Mayor's Advisory Council Long Beach (Public Safety Liaison); Association of Realtors, Long Beach; International Association of Police Chiefs; California Peace Officers Association; Federal Bureau of Investigation, National Executives Association; California State University – Los Angeles Alumni Club; University of Southern California Alumni Club; President (1982–1983), Rotary Club of Long Beach; American Legion Post 381 Los Angeles; St. Bartholomews Catholic Church; Long Beach Yacht Club; Long Beach Community Hospital Foundation; Volunteer, Public Schools Program; Fellow, United States Office of Law Enforcement Assistance (1968–1969); Phi Kappa Phi National Honor Society; Who's Who in the West (1987–1988); Who's Who in California (1988–1990); Member (1979), Federal Bureau of Investigation National Executive Institute (1979); Personalities of the Americas, A.B.I., USA (1989); Men of Achievement I.C.B., Cambridge, England (1989); International Biographical Society; Who's Who in American Real Estate (1990); Various

publications concering law enforcement. **Education:** University of Southern California, M.A. in Public Administration (1973); University of California – Berkeley, M.S. in Criminology (1969); California State University – Los Angeles, B.S. (1960); Los Angeles City College, A.A. (1957); Certifications: California Peace Officers Standards and Training (1954–1979), California Class D Teaching Credential (1972), Real Estate Brokers License. **Personal:** Married to Yvonne Marie in 1955. Three children: Colette, Kristina, and Mark. Mr. Calkins enjoys sailing, photography, model railroads, old books and fine art.

John J. Charles
President
Akron Security Center, Inc. (Formerly Bond Security Consultants)
3643 Copley Road
Copley, OH 44321
(216) 666–6007
Fax: (216) 666–3007

7382

Business Information: Akron Security Center, Inc. sells, installs and services residential and commercial security systems, stereo/intercom systems, and central vacuum systems. The Company, one of 150 Dynamark franchises in 38 states, is one of the top 10 Dynamark franchises nationwide. Business growth is averaging 15% annually. As President, Mr. Charles manages all aspects of Company operations, concentrating on sales, marketing, and staff training and development. Established in 1984, Akron Security Center, Inc. (Formerly Bond Security Consultants) employs 10 people. **Career Steps:** President, Akron Security Center, Inc. (Formerly Bond Security Consultants), (1984–Present); Director of Security, Akron General Medical Center (1980–1984); Chief, Cuyahoga Community College Police and Security; Corrections Officer, Summit County Sheriff's Department (1972–1973). **Associations & Accomplishments:** American Society for Industrial Security; National Association of Chiefs of Police; Professional Certification, Certified Protection Professional; Involved in programs to find lost children; [Who's Who of Security Professionals]. **Education:** University of Akron, M.S. in Education (1975); B.A. in Education; A.A.S. in Law Enforcement (1972). **Personal:** Married to Alisa. One child: Ryan. Mr. Charles enjoys racquetballl, baseball, and golf.

Robert L. Clevenger Jr.
Manfacturing Manager
BI Incorporated
6400 Lookout Road
Boulder, CO 80301–3377
(303) 530–2911
Fax: (303) 530–5349

7382

Business Information: BI Incorporated is a manufacturer of electronic home arrest and monitoring systems, serving customers from plants in Indiana and Colorado. As Manfacturing Manager, Mr. Clevenger is responsible for the overall day-to-day operations, with duties including manufacturing engineering, production, materials, purchasing, order management, field services, telecommunications and facilities. **Career Steps:** Manfacturing Manager, BI Incorporated (1993–Present); Director of Operations, Tecnetics Inc. (1991–1993); Manufacturing Manager, Prairietek Inc. (1989–1991); Operations Manager, Ball Corporation (1984–1989). **Associations & Accomplishments:** Boulder Chamber of Commerce: Chair – Manufacturing Council, Transportation Committee; National Association of Manufacturers. **Education:** Kennedy–Western University: M.B.A. (1996), B.S., B.A.; ITT Technical Institute, A.S.E.E.T.; Indiana University – Graduate School of Business. **Personal:** Married to Carol J. in 1977. Two children: Danielle Nichol and Calie Shanon. Mr. Clevenger enjoys crafts, golf, writing and family activities.

James E. Dobrovolny
Director of Operations
American Security Corporation
1717 University Avenue West
St. Paul, MN 55104–3613
(612) 637–2698
Fax: (612) 641–0523

7382

Business Information: American Security Corporation is a national security agency providing security services to malls, banks, and institutions throughout the Mid–West Region. Services include uniformed personnel, armored cars, and investigations. As Director of Operations for Contract Security Services, Mr. Dobrovolny is responsible for the oversight of contract management and negotiation, system operations and analysis, and employee relations. **Career Steps:** Director of Operations, American Security Corporation (1988–Present); Security Manager, Northwestern National Life Insurance

Company (1995–1996); Security Manager, Fravenshaw Corporation (1993–1995); Security Manager, Control Data Corporation (1991–1993). **Associations & Accomplishments:** American Philosophical Society; Eagle Scout Award Recipient; Greenpeace; American Civil Liberties Union; Planned Parenthood; Editor and Author of "ASC Today" Newsletter. **Education:** Hamline University, Masters in Applied Liberal Studies (In Progress); University of Minnesota, B.A. in Philosophy.

Jonathan Graham
Executive Vice President
Allwest Fire and Sound
5701 Logan Street
Denver, CO 80216
(303) 293–2345
Fax: (303) 293–2131
EMAIL: See Below

7382

Business Information: Allwest Fire and Sound provides sales, service, and installation of fire safety and specialty electronics systems (e.g., fire alarms, nurse–calling systems, prison electronics systems). Mr. Graham has held various supervisory positions within Allwest, to include Operations Manager and Project Manager, and as Vice President of Operations. Promoted to Executive Vice President of Allwest Fire and Sound in 1994, Mr. Graham presently supervises the Operations Department, responsible for project management, engineering, technical design, and drafting areas. He is also a member of the Executive Committee, which oversees all company operations. Internet users can reach him via: allwest@abwam.com **Career Steps:** Allwest Fire and Sound: Executive Vice President (1994–Present), Operations Manager (1992–1993), Project Manager (1991–1992); Vice President Operations, Allwest Systems (1993–1994). **Associations & Accomplishments:** Purdue University, B.S. (1983). **Education:** American Correctional Association. **Personal:** Married to Debbie in 1986. Mr. Graham enjoys camping, sailing, and bicycling.

Paul S. Holloway
President
Security Technical Services
1105 Front Street
Niles, MI 49120–1665
(616) 684–0040
Fax: (616) 684–0128

7382

Business Information: Security Technical Services is a national security and detective company, providing premises security through patrol and on–site protection with both armed and unarmed personnel. They also provide personnel for workplace and personal protection. Mr. Holloway established the Company in 1990 and became active in his current capacity as President and Chief of Operations in 1995. He is responsible for daily operations and a variety of administrative activities. **Career Steps:** President/Chief of Operations, Security Technical Services (1995–Present); President, Seventrees Corporation (1983–1995); Police Captain, Dowagiac Police Department (1966–1993). **Associations & Accomplishments:** Michigan Association of Chiefs of Police; Charter Member, Optimist Club of Dowagiac; American Society for Industrial Security; 3rd Marine Division Association. **Education:** Southwestern Michigan College (1982). **Personal:** Married to Lucille in 1982. Four children: Lisa, Yolanda, Carlos and Jerry. Mr. Holloway enjoys collecting sports cards and logo pins.

Mr. Steven M. Johner
General Manager, St. Louis Office
AAA Security Systems, Inc.
128 Hilltown Village Center
Chesterfield, MO 63017–0709
(314) 532–1927
Fax: (314) 532–1834

7382

Business Information: AAA Security Systems, Inc. is a communications systems dealer, marketing, installing and servicing security systems for residential and commercial applications. As General Manager, St. Louis Office, Mr. Johner is responsible for sales, operations, installations, engineering and service in the St. Louis office. Established in 1993, the St. Louis office employs nine technical staff and reports annual revenue in excess of $1 million. **Career Steps:** General Manager, St. Louis Office, AAA Security Systems, Inc. (1994–Present); Project Manager, Tech Electronics (1986–1994); Instructor, Henkles & McCoy (1985–1986). **Associations & Accomplishments:** Alarm Association of St. Louis; Home Builders Associaiton; Chesterfield Chamber of Commerce; U.S. Chamber of Commerce; Knights of Columbus; Former member, Jaycees. **Education:** U.S. Air Force Electronics Training; Affton High School (1972).

Gerald T. Johns Sr.

President and Chief Executive Officer
Tenco Services, Inc.
15 Park Avenue, P.O. Box 369
Ambler, PA 19002–0369
(215) 643–6930
Fax: (215) 643–0298

7382

Business Information: Tenco Services, Inc. is a security corporation, with services provided including armed guard, manned security protectors, executive protection and investigations. Currently Tenco has office locations in Pennsylvania (Ambler), Texas (Houston), and Illinois (Chicago), and is licensed in New York, New Jersey, Pennsylvania, Louisiana, Texas, and Illinois. Future plans include being functionable in all 50 states. As President and Chief Executive Officer, Mr. Johns is responsible for the overall day–to–day operations, with his primary focus in the areas of policies and procedures, bid proposals, contract negotiations and budgetary oversight. **Career Steps:** President and Chief Executive Officer, Tenco Services, Inc. (1994–Present); Administrative Assistant and Chief of Security, Systems Management America (1984–1994); Teacher, Norfolk City Schools (1977–1984); Social Work, S.T.O.P. Organization (1968–1977). **Associations & Accomplishments:** Fraternal Order of Police: District of Columbia Chapter, Pennsylvania State Lodge; American Society for Industrial Security; Nine Lives Association. **Education:** Norfolk State University: M.S. (1981), B.S.W.; University of California at Los Angeles; L.A.C.C. **Personal:** Two children: Gerald T. Jr. and Gerri P. Mr. Johns enjoys fishing, photography, weightlifting and tennis.

Ellen Koh

Art Director
Sonitrol Corporation
1800 Diagonal Road, Suite 180
Alexandria, VA 22314–2840
(703) 684–6606
Fax: (703) 684–6612
EMAIL: See Below

7382

Business Information: Sonitrol Corporation is an international security franchisor, with 170 locations nationwide and in Canada and Europe. Sonitrol prides itself on providing the most intelligent, effective, and verified loss prevention solutions. Integrated loss and preventive services include: Audio Intrusion Detection, Verification, Access Control, UL Fire Detection, Video Surveillance, and 24–Hour Security Monitoring. Corporate headquarters are located in Alexandria, Virginia. As Art Director, Ms. Koh provides advertising, sales and marketing support to the Sonitrol Franchise Network; as well as writing, editing, and designing Corporate publications, and promoting and managing internal programs. Internet users can also reach her via: EllenKoh@aol.com **Career Steps:** Sonitrol Corporation, Art Director (1995–Present), Communications Specialist (1993–1995); Image Matrix, Inc.: Account Services Representative (1991–1992), Production Control Assistant (1990–1991); Marketing Intern, Blattner/Brunner, Inc. (1989); Associate Puerto Rico Coordinator, Princeton Community Hospital (1988). **Associations & Accomplishments:** Women in Communications, Inc. (WICI); Art Directors Club of Metropolitan Washington; Graphic Artists Guild; Washington Express; Washington Women in Public Relations (WWPR); Freelance Projects: Tysons Club for Health and Fitness, '94 and '95 Toys for Tots campaign/holiday display signage, Members Appreciation Week display signage, '94 Tradeshow display signage used for a promotional event held at Nordstroms (Tysons Corner), and '95 Tradeshow display signage used for a local tradeshow at the McLean Hilton Hotel; Multiple computer skills and experience; rPublished in the Orlando Centennial on security. **Education:** Carnegie Mellon University, B.A. in Professional Writing with a concentration in Visual Design (1990). **Personal:** Ms. Koh enjoys working out, painting, travel, camping, hiking, and sports (tennis, golf).

Philip C. Lake

President
Chubb Security Systems, Inc.
5025 Burnet Road
Austin, TX 78756–2611
(512) 458–8104
Fax: Please mail or call

7382

Business Information: Chubb Security Systems, Inc. is an international marketer of security systems, such as alarms, card access, etc. Joining Chubb Security Locks, Ltd – Canada as President in 1989, Mr. Lake was appointed as President of Chubb Security Systems, Inc. in 1994. In this position, he is responsible for sales and profitability of U.S. operations. **Career Steps:** President, Chubb Security Systems, Inc. (1994–Present); President, Chubb Security Locks, Ltd. – Canada (1989–1994); Various Senior Management Positions, Honeywell Limited – Canada (1975–1989). **Associations & Accomplishments:** National Fire and Burglary Alarm Association; Building Owners and Managers Association; American Society of Industrial Security; Who's Who in Canada. **Education:** Certified General Accountant (CGA) Canada (1978); University of Toronto, Various Executive Programs. **Personal:** Married to Janet in 1971. Two children: Jennifer and Bradley. Mr. Lake enjoys golf.

James F. Lambert, CPP

President
Universal Systems Associates, Inc.
18 Clinton Drive
Hollis, NH 03049
(603) 880–4564
Fax: (603) 881–7282

7382

Business Information: Universal Systems Associates, Inc. (USA), designs, engineers, markets, sells, and maintains electronic security systems. Primarily serving the New England area, USA does establish contract companies throughout the U.S. Established in 1978, USA reports annual revenue of $3.5 million, and currently employs 35 people. USA's President, Jim Lambert, while responsible for the corporation's success, concentrates his efforts on advertising, marketing, and sales. He became interested in crime prevention while attending Graduate School at Boston University. He continues to expound on the theory that prevention is significantly less costly than incarceration. **Career Steps:** President and Treasurer, Universal Systems Associates, Inc. (1978–Present); Vice President, North American Video Corporation (1972–1977); National Sales Manager, Nashua Corporation (1969–1972); Assistant Professor, University of Massachusetts at Lowell (1965–1969). **Associations & Accomplishments:** American Society for Industrial Security (ASIS); International Association for Healthcare Safety and Security (IAHSS); Board of Directors, Boys and Girls Club of Nashua, NH; Recipient of a NASA Award for Creativity; Recipient of the American Red Cross Presidential Citation and The Humane Society of Massachusetts Bronze Medal for bravery in life saving; Inducted into the University of Massachusetts at Lowell Athletic Hall of Fame in 1977; Further, he is an accomplished writer for regional and national safety and security publications. **Education:** Certified Protection Professional (CPP) (1990); Boston University, M.Ed. (1965); University of Massachusetts at Lowell, B.S. (1960). **Personal:** Jim uses his leisure time to golf, swim, walk, fish, and enjoys doing needlepoint.

ALL SECURITY SERVICES, INC.
P.R.

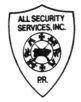

Guido Peralta

Chairman of the Board
All Security Services, Inc.
P.O. Box 13472
Santurce, Puerto Rico 00908–3472
(809) 792–4243
Fax: (809) 792–1707

7382

Business Information: All Security Services, Inc., certified by the SBA, is a security company, providing electronic security systems, closed circuits & alarm systems, security patrols, and armed & unarmed guards. A Licensed Private Detective with fifteen years experience in the security industry, Mr. Peralta established All Security Services, Inc. as President in 1980. Currently serving as Chairman of the Board since 1993, he is responsible for the operations, financing, and strategic planning for the Company. He is presently soliciting for a license to open a branch in Florida. **Career Steps:** All Security Services, Inc.: Chairman of the Board (1993–Present), President (1980–1993); Sales Manager, Puerto Rico Distillers Company (1975–1980). **Education:** La Habana University, B.A. (1950); Antilles Detective Academy, Private Detective. **Personal:** Married to Palmira in 1950. Two children: Eduardo and Guido Jr.

Oscar A. Perez

Vice President
Protective Management of America
12398 South West 82 Avenue
Miami, FL 33156
(305) 378–6933
Fax: (305) 378–6932

7382

Business Information: Protective Management of America provides statewide security and investigative services, as well as security consulting. As Vice President, Mr. Perez is responsible for the Investigative and Consulting Division of the Company. He handles all investigation and consulting matters. **Career Steps:** Vice President, Protective Management of America (1994–Present); Assistant Chief of Police, City of Sweetwater (1995); Chief Executive Officer, Del Mar S.A. (1993–1995); Sales Manager, Performance Truck Brokers (1991–1993). **Associations & Accomplishments:** Deacon, American Catholic Church. **Education:** University of North Florida (1986); South Florida Institute of Criminal Justice (1976); Numerous College Courses on Police Related Matters. **Personal:** Mr. Perez enjoys church, reading, and studying the Bible.

Mr. Frank Piper

Director of Security
Allied Security Inc.
2880 West Oakland Park Boulevard, Suite 111
Ft. Lauderdale, FL 33311
(305) 486–5608
Fax: (305) 730–2365

7382

Business Information: Allied Security Inc. provides investigations, guard services and consulting. Established in 1957, Allied Security Inc. currently employs 280 people in South Florida. As Director of Security for South Florida branches, Mr. Piper oversees all aspects of daily operations, hiring, training and placement. Mr. Piper also oversees the field supervisors to ensure that services are delivered in a quality and cost effective manner. As a second–level Manager, Mr. Piper assists the Branch Manager in most areas, including sales, and is prepared to stand in for him or his own subordinates as needed. **Career Steps:** Allied Security Inc.: Director of Security (1994–Present), Operations Supervisor (1990–1994), Utility Officer (1989–1990); Weapons Security Specialist, United States Marine Corps (1984–1985). **Associations & Accomplishments:** Civil Air Patrol, Ground Search and Rescue; National Rifle Association; Golden Eagles; USMC: Physical Fitness Award, Honor Graduate from Paris Island, Achieved E–3 in Less than 2 Years. **Education:** High School Graduate. **Personal:** Married to Heather in 1992. Two children: Christopher and Rick. Mr. Piper enjoys shooting, the Martial Arts, and spending time with his children.

Larry J. Richardson

President and Co–Owner
Crime Watch, Inc.
3227 Falcon Grove Drive
San Antonio, TX 78217
(210) 829–4357
Fax: (210) 829–4375

7382

Business Information: Crime Watch, Inc. is a residential home security retailer, providing both commercial and residential customers with the sale, installation, and service of monitored security systems. Regional in scope, with headquarter offices located in San Antonio, Texas, Crime Watch also serves customers from service offices in: Austin, Texas; Phoenix, Arizona; and Tucson, Arizona. As President and Co–Owner, Larry Richardson provides the overall direction for the Company as a whole, ensuring quality product and customer service, as well as the development and strategies needed to keep the Company a viable presence in the security marketplace. **Career Steps:** President and Co–Owner, Crime Watch, Inc. (1994–Present); Branch Manager, Protect America, Inc. (1993–1994); Branch Manager, Emergency Networks, Inc. (1989–1993); Sales Manager, Ever Fresh Foods (1985–1989). **Associations & Accomplishments:** Masonic Lodge; Shrine Club of North America; University Methodist Church – San Antonio, TX; Active Parent Sponsor, Little League Baseball; Children's Community Theater. **Education:** Cerritos Junior College (1970–1972). **Personal:** Married to Nancy in 1981. Two children: Adam and Audrey. Mr. Richardson enjoys golf, softball, the L.A. Dodgers, reading, and watching thoroughbred horse races.

Anthony J. Robbio Jr., Ph.D.

President
AAA Security Task Force
117 Beacon Street
Cranston, RI 02910
(401) 944–4443
Fax: (401) 943–0914

7382

Business Information: AAA Security Task Force is a security service, providing guard and investigation services, installation of alarm and CCTV systems. The Company has two locations in Rhode Island (Cranston and Warwick). In his capacity as President, Dr. Robbio oversees management of all Company operations. Established in 1974, AAA Security Task Force employs a staff of 50 and reports annual revenue of $1 million. **Career Steps:** President, AAA Security Task Force (1974–Present). **Associations & Accomplishments:** Past School Committee Member, Cranston School Department; U.S. Army Reserve, Chief Warrant Officer Retired; Greater Cranston Chamber of Commerce, Past President; R.I. Congress of PTA, Past Vice President, Secretary & Board Member; Cranston Community Action Program, Past Chairman & Board Member; National Alarm Association of America, Nation Vice President; Boy Scouts of America, Past Scout Master & Commissioner; American Legion, Commander & Department Chairman; The American Society for Industrial Security; National Vice President, National Association of Chiefs of Police; Life Member, Reserve Officers Association of America; Training Officer, Providence Police Department; Constable with Power, Superior, District, and Family Courts; National Association of Professional Process Servers; R.I. Security & Detective Association, Past President, Executive Board Member; Rhode Island Rifle Association; Better Business Bureau of R.I., Chairman of the Board; National Committee for Employer Support of the Guard and Reserve; Southern New England Security Alliance, Past President; Who's Who in Rhode Island 1990; Who's Who in American Law Enforcement 6th Edition; Awarded the J. Edgar Hoover Memorial Gold Medal for Distinguished Public Service Award; Awarded the American Police Hall of Fame Commemorative Legion of Honor Medal; International Intelligence & Organized Crime Investigators Association, Special Agent; National Association of Private Security Industries; RI Trade Shops Schools, Private Security and Investigation Instructor; Rotary Club of Providence. **Education:** Master of Science in Security Administration; Doctor of Science in Security Administration; Professional Certificate in Law Enforcement and Criminal Justice (1990); National Rifle Association of America, Certified Firearms Instructor & Training Counselor; Licensed Private Detective, State of RI.

Blair M. Stuart
General Manager
ADT Security Systems, Inc.
7895 Browning Road
Pennsauken, NJ 08109–4640
(609) 661–6067
Fax: (609) 661–6064

7382

Business Information: ADT Security Systems, Inc. is the world's leading provider of security alarm systems to residential and commercial customers and has the world's second largest customer service and monitoring call center located in the greater Philadelphia area. ADT Security Systems, Inc. provides services from eighteen locations in North America and several in Europe. Established in 1874, ADT Security Systems, Inc. center in the greater Philadelphia area reports annual operating budget of $7.5 million and currently employs 125 people. As General Manager, Mr. Stuart is responsible for all aspects of management and operational functions of the Pennsauken, New Jersey Customer Service and Monitoring Call Center. **Career Steps:** General Manager, ADT Security Systems, Inc.; Senior Administrative Officer, East Penn Bank. **Associations & Accomplishments:** Board of Directors, Lehigh Valley Arts Council (1995–1998); Borough of Emmaus – Parks & Recreation Commission (1992–1995); Board of Directors, Kiwanis Club of Emmaus (1992–1995); Recipient, Outstanding Young Men of America Award (1989–1990). **Education:** Bucknell University – Graduate School of Banking (1995); Dickinson College Central Atlantic School of Banking (1992); Alvernia College, B.A. in Criminal Justice Administration (1976); Allentown, PA Police Academy, Civilian Graduate (1989). **Personal:** Married to Sharon L. in 1981. Two children: Erin and Bradley. Mr. Stuart enjoys sports, music and art. He is also an Official for NCAA Volleyball.

Mr. Jon Tholen
Managing Director for the North American Call Center
ADT Security Systems
7406 Fullerton Street
Jacksonville, FL 32256–3552
(904) 363–7640
Fax: (904) 363–7641

7382

Business Information: ADT Security Systems is a provider of security systems to residential and commercial customers. Established in 1872, ADT Security Systems reports annual revenue of $135 million and currently employs 135 people. As Managing Director for the North American Call Center, Mr. Tholen is responsible for the support of the entire field operations, including sales activity (200 offices, 1,000 installers, 1,000 sales consultants), customer service, billing, and major advertising types of activities, and answering triage calls. Career milestones include establishing a telemarketing program for American Express in Germany. **Career Steps:** Managing Director for the North American Call Center, ADT Security Systems (1994–Present); Director of Marketing Services, American Express – Greensboro/Jacksonville (1984–1994);

Director of Marketing Services, American Express – Frankfurt, Germany (1989–1991). **Associations & Accomplishments:** Boy Scouts of America; Church of Jesus Christ of Latter Day Saints; American Telemarketing Association; Author of textbook chapter on Direct Marketing with New Mediums (1993) – on telemarketing in the U.S. **Education:** University of North Carolina – Greensboro, M.B.A. (1992); University of Utah, B.A. in Accounting (1986). **Personal:** Married to Holly in 1986. Three children: Jessica, Emily, and Sharron. Mr. Tholen enjoys waterskiing, boating, and team sports.

Kim Torp–Pedersen
General Manager/Chief Financial Officer
American National Security, Inc.
14711 North East 29th Place, Suite 204
Bellevue, WA 98007
(206) 883–0077
Fax: (206) 861–7438

7382

Business Information: American National Security, Inc. began operations in 1994 and currently employs 74 people. The Corporation conducts business in Idaho, Oregon, and Washington, offering residential and commercial fire and intrusion protection systems and central monitoring. As General Manager/Chief Financial Officer, Mr. Torp–Pedersen oversees the day-to-day operations and monitors service quality. As Chief Financial Officer, he is responsible for all financial affairs of the Corporation, management, strategic planning, and human resources. **Career Steps:** General Manager/Chief Financial Officer, American National Security, Inc. (1994–Present); Principal, Torp–Pedersen Group (1990–1996); Manager of National Account Marketing, Microsoft, Inc. (1987–1990); Director of Channel Marketing, Northern Telecom (1985–1987). **Associations & Accomplishments:** Chairman, 48th Legislative District Republicans; American Association of Blood Banks; American Society of Quality; Benchmark and Oversight Committee, King County Growth Management Act. **Education:** City University, M.B.A. candidate; San Diego State University, Cell Biology. **Personal:** Married to Ann L. Torp–Pedersen in 1987. Mr. Torp–Pedersen enjoys sail boat racing, civic activities, and Bible studies.

Charles P. Williams
Vice President and Director of Operations
LTC Group, Inc.
7136 Lakeview Parkway West
Indianapolis, IN 46268–4104
(317) 387–8666
Fax: (317) 387–8667

7382

Business Information: LTC Group, Inc., is a private organization specializing in providing corporate clients with top level investigations and security. Comprised of medical, business, and law enforcement professionals, including active and retired members of the Indiana State Police, the Corporation offers companies a wide variety of security and investigation services. Background investigation of prospective employees, insurance fraud, and investigation of internal or external espionage and theft are just a few of the services provided. Investigators are bonded, licensed and authorized to be armed, and are supported by a comprehensive system of computer and surveillance equipment, as well as the expertise of board of professionals. This elite group consists of accountants, psychologists, insurance consultants, board certified doctors and dentists, and other business professionals. Established in 1995, the Corporation is located in Indianapolis, Indiana. As Vice President, Mr. Williams is directly responsible for investigative and operational side of LTC. During his 30 years with the Indiana State Police, Mr. Williams, who retired with the rank of Captain, was Assistant Commander of the Enforcement Division, responsible for the Aviation Section, security for the Governor and his family, as well as SCUBA, Riot and Bomb Squad, and other specialty teams. In addition, Mr. Williams commanded two Indiana State Police Districts, overseeing investigations and traffic in 10 counties, as well as statewide drug, auto theft, and criminal investigations. Mr. Williams' long term goal is to commit himself to upholding the corporation's mission of "providing professional investigations and security to their clients through the principles of truth and honesty, preserving the integrity and values of the legal system in which we function." **Career Steps:** Vice President and Director of Operations, LTC Group, Inc. (1995–Present); Indiana State Trooper, Rising through the ranks as Sgt, First Sgt, Lt., and Captain (1962–1995). **Associations & Accomplishments:** Indiana State Police Alliance; Indiana Fraternal Order of Police. **Education:** Indiana University, Masters (1987); University of Evansville, B.S. (1976). **Personal:** Married to M. Norene in 1968. Four children: Cris Ann, Janessa Lee, Sherry Lynn, and Charles II. Mr. Williams enjoys fishing.

Bernadette S. McCormick
Regional Manager
Business Wire
100 West 6th Street, Suite 750–B
Minneapolis, MN 55403
(612) 376–7979
Fax: (612) 376–9784
EMAIL: See Below

7383

Business Information: Business Wire is a leading source of news on/for major U.S. corporations, including Fortune 500, and NASDAQ companies through the electronic dissemination of full text news releases for public and investor relations. This service allows professionals to have simultaneous access to the news media, on–line services, databases, the Internet, and the investment community, worldwide. International in scope, the Company has seventeen locations worldwide, and is one of only two companies of its type in the world, and the only one founded in the United States. Established in 1965, the Company employs 250 people, and has an estimated annual revenue of $40 million. As Regional Manager, Ms. McCormick oversees five states: Minnesota, Iowa, North and South Dakota, and Nebraska. She is responsible for public relations, sales and marketing, and customer relations. Ms. McCormick was also instrumental in starting the first office partition refurbishing business in the mid–west, which is now the third largest in the country. The granddaughter of a Thai princess, Ms. McCormick is fluent in Thai, French, and English. Internet users can reach her via: bernadette@bizwire.com. **Career Steps:** Regional Manager, Business Wire (1992–Present); Director of Sales and Marketing, A&M Business Interior Services, Inc. (1990–1992); Dayton's Commercial Interiors: Director of Sales and Marketing (1990–1992), Account Executive (1986–1990). **Associations & Accomplishments:** National Investor Relations Institute (NIRI); Minnesota Software Association (MSA); Public Relations Society of America (PRSA). **Education:** University of Minnesota, M.A. (1982); Macalester College, B.A. (1981). **Personal:** One child: Andrew Thomas McCormick. Ms. McCormick enjoys tennis, volleyball, biking, softball, classical piano, dancing, painting, and Asian and Middle East Cuisine.

Barry L. Berggren

Vice President and Treasurer
E.B. Luce Corporation
74 Chilmark Street
Worcester, MA 01604
(508) 757–6361
Fax: (508) 757–1367

7384

Business Information: E.B. Luce Corporation is a custom, commercial imaging laboratory, specializing in electronic and conventional photographic murals for trade shows, aquarium, and museum exhibits. Clientele include the National Aquarium in Baltimore, in which they processed over 700 transparencies. Future plans include seeking other technologies to enable them to process larger, faster, and inexpensive products, while at the same time, providing the highest quality. Established in 1881, E.B. Luce Corporation reports annual revenue of $3 million and currently employs 24 people. With 22 years expertise in the photography industry, Mr. Berggren joined E.B. Luce Corporation in 1973 at the age of 19. Working his way up the corporate ladder, he currently serves as 50% Shareholder of the Company (since 1976), Vice President, and Treasurer, responsible for sales, purchasing, employee reviews, technical training, support to customers and employees, and general management. Career milestones include being responsible for keeping E.B. Luce Corporation on the forefront of technology, with constant growth since 1976, and in the last two years growing 80% by the addition of digital imaging equipment. Nationally recognized as an expert in the field of High Resolution Digital Imaging, he is called upon regularly to speak on this subject — most recently at Visomm 1995 – Jacob Javits, New York, NY. **Career Steps:** Vice President and Treasurer, E.B. Luce Corporation (1973–Present). **Associations & Accomplishments:** Association of Professional Color Laboratories (APCL); Photo Marketing Association (PMA); United States and Local Chamber of Commerces. **Education:** University of Massachusetts at Amherst (1972–1973). **Personal:** Married to Christine Stratford in 1992. Mr. Berggren enjoys boating, photography, cooking, wine, and computers.

Frank M. Topinka
Vice President
McKenna Professional Imaging
P.O. Box 5600
Waterloo, IA 50704–5600
(319) 235–6265
Fax: (319) 235–1121

7384

Business Information: McKenna Professional Imaging is a professional imaging company. Joining McKenna Professional Imaging as Marketing Director in 1988, Mr. Topinka was appointed as Vice President in 1991. He is responsible for the day–to–day operations of the Company. Prior to joining McKenna, he aspired to become a teacher, but took a hiatus from his educational career and obtained a position with Fotomat as Area Manager serving 125 stores. He then became West Regional Manger of the retail side, overseeing 600 employees and 900 stores. **Career Steps:** McKenna Professional Imaging: Vice President (1991–Present), Marketing Director (1988–1991); Vice President, T–H Enterprises (1984–1988). **Education:** University of Wisconsin – La-Crosse, B.A. (1973). **Personal:** Married to Deborah in 1983. Two children: Lauren and Elise. Mr. Topinka enjoys tai–chi chuan.

Sue Weinsoff

District Sales and Marketing Director
The Darkroom
9227 Reseda Boulevard
Northridge, CA 91324
(800) 442–3873 (800) 442–DUPE
Fax: (818) 885–6030

7384

Business Information: The Darkroom is a professional, full service, custom color and black and white photographic lab and camera store. Specializing in slide duplication for professional photographers, the Company has two locations in California and serves clients worldwide. Established in 1981, the Company employs thirty people. As District Sales and Marketing Director, Ms. Weinsoff oversees sales and marketing of all stock photographers' work across the U.S. and abroad. She is also responsible for networking with clients and potential clients, and receiving and processing orders. **Career Steps:** The Darkroom: District Sales and Marketing Director (1994–Present), Store Operations Manager (1988–1994); Camera Department Manager, J.C. Penney (1986–1988). **Associations & Accomplishments:** Licensed Amateur Radio Operator. **Education:** University of California, San Diego, B.A. (1980); Emergency Medical Technician. **Personal:** Ms. Weinsoff enjoys HAM radio operation which includes disaster preparedness.

Rae Michele Rivera Ray

Freelance Paralegal
–Independent–
2102 Tecumseh Trace
Carrollton, TX 75006
(214) 242–9528
Fax: Please mail or call

7388

Business Information: As a freelance paralegal, Mrs. Rivera Ray provides office and files organization, recorded statements transcription, mail reviewing for responses and action, forms revision, documents and status requests, and oral dictation on an as needed basis. **Career Steps:** Freelance Paralegal, Rae Michele Rivera Ray (1996–Present); Secretary, City of Carrollton (1995–1996); Paralegal, Jay Kaskie, Inc. (1993–1995); Paralegal, Ferguson and Burns (Jerome H. Ferguson, P.C.) (1985–1993). **Associations & Accomplishments:** Notary Public; National Notary Association; Americas Monthly 1988 Secretary of the Year; Publication in Carrollton Chronicle (1988). **Education:** El Centro College: Legal Assistant Technology (1995), Associate of Applied Science (1994). **Personal:** Married to Lonzo J. One child: Andrea. Mrs. Rivera Ray enjoys law, computers, and hunting.

Raymond H. Ackerlund

President
Cardinal Resource Group
740 Vincent Court, #208
Stevens Point, WI 54481
(715) 342–9303
Fax: (715) 342–9303
E–mail: See below

7389

Business Information: Cardinal Resource Group provides outside resource groups for small to mid–sized companies in need of information and database acquisition in the areas of customer service, marketing, sales functions and mailing lists. Established in 1994, Cardinal Resource Group currently employs 16 people. As President, Mr. Ackerlund is responsible for all aspects of operations, as well as consulting, customer service, and organizational development. Mr. Ackerlund specializes in database and customer service functions consulting. Mr. Ackerlund can also be reached through the Internet as follows: rackerlu@coredes.com **Career Steps:** President, Cardinal Research Group (1994–Present); Consultant, University of Wisconsin – Stevens Point (1993–1994); Director of Customer Service, Linkage Communication (1992–1993). **Education:** University of Wisconsin, B.A. (1992); University of Wisconsin – Stevens Point, Marketing and Organizational Development. **Personal:** Married to Connie in 1995. Mr. Ackerlund enjoys golf and reading.

Ms. Muriel W. Adcock

President/Consultant
Adcock & Associates
929 Sir Frances Drake Boulevard, Suite C226
Kentfield, CA 94904
(415) 925–9056
Fax: (415) 925–9057

7389

Business Information: Adcock & Associates is a design and production consultancy with a primary emphasis on research. Most recently, the focus has been on developing educational media for a combination of video/print material. Topic areas include: health and environmental issues; educational systems design; general evolutionary systems theory; the transition into a free market economy; seminar planning and development; cross–cultural communications; human development and organizational development. As President/Consultant, Ms. Adcock is responsible for all aspects of operations. **Career Steps:** President/Consultant, Adcock & Associates (1993–Present); Independent Researcher/Consultant (1992–Present); Special Education Teacher/Consultant (1989–1990); Educational Research/Consultant (1988–1989); Administrator, Association Montessori Internationale–USA (1988); Course Assistant, Montessori Special Education Institute (1985–1987); Teacher/Consultant, Tenderloin Community Children's Center (1985–1987); Teacher, The Concordia School (1980–1985). **Associations & Accomplishments:** Secretary, International Forum of the World Affairs Council of Northern California, San Francisco (1990–1995); Program Chair (1993–1995), Program Committee of the World Affairs Council (Present), Member Association for Curriculum and Supervision Development; Council for Exceptional Children; National Association for the Education of Young Children; American Association on Mental Retardation; Association Montessori Internationale; North American Montessori Teachers Association; Association of Childhood Education International; Smithsonian Institute; New York Academy of Sciences; National Geographic Society; Menninger Foundation; International Systems Institute; Fellow of the American Orthopsychiatric Association; Board Member, Foundation for Cerebral Palsy and Other Disabilities; Member; International Society of Systems Scientists; Contributor of articles to professional journals. **Education:** University of California – Sonoma State, Rohnert Park, B.A. cum laude (1979); Association Montessori Internationale Primary Diploma, Mt. View, CA (1980); Association Montessori Internationale Special Education Diploma, Mt. View, CA (1985); Certificate in Educational Therapy, San Francisco, CA (1990); Currently undertaking graduate work in educational systems design and the parallels between psychological and physiological development.

Voldemar Avarlaid

Owner
V. Avarlaid
20 Crestland Avenue
Toronto, Ontario M4C 3L1
(416) 423–9703
Fax: Please mail or call

7389

Business Information: V. Avarlaid is a privately–owned company, established in 1930, specializing in the design of fine scientific instruments, including helium gas liquifiers, electron–microscopes, and high–vacuum measuring instruments. As Owner, Mr. Avarlaid is responsible for all aspects of Company operations, including the design and repair of custom–made instruments for institutions. **Career Steps:** Instrument Maker, V. Avarlaid (1974–Present); Instrument Maker, McGill University Physics, Montreal (1950–1973); Instrument Maker, V. Avarlaid, Tartu Estonia (1930–1944). **Associations & Accomplishments:** Teachers Association, Tartu, Estonia; Estonian Association of Toronto. **Education:** Attended: McGill University, Montreal, University of Tartu, Estonia. **Personal:** Mr. Avarlaid enjoys telescope–making and polishing reflector mirrors.

Thom C. Balistrieri

President/Owner
Sales Network, Inc.
245 West Roosevelt Road
West Chicago, IL 60185–4813
(708) 231–3400
Fax: (708) 231–3496

7389

Business Information: Sales Network, Inc. is an audio/video manufacturers representative, representing automotive and home theatre audio manufacturers throughout Illinois. Founding the Company in 1985, Thom Balistrieri provides the overall vision and strategies, primarily focusing on customer relations and trade development. **Career Steps:** President/Owner, Sales Network, Inc. (1985–Present); National Sales Manager, JVS Corporation (1980–1985); Sales Manager, Markal Sales (1975–1980); Manager, Playback (1972–1975). **Associations & Accomplishments:** C.A.S.A.; I.A.S.C.A.; V.S.A. **Education:** Northern Illinois University, B.A. (1973). **Personal:** Married to Susan in 1981. Three children: Stephanie, Nicole, and Christie. Mr. Balistrieri enjoys music.

Lynne V. Bartlett, C.D.

Owner/Designer
LVB Design
12 Mara Vista Court
Belvider Tiburon, CA 94920
(415) 435–5084
Fax: Please mail or call

7389

Business Information: LVB Design specializes in residential interior design for both new homes and remodeling work. The Company handles mainly kitchen and bathroom design, as well as furniture. As Owner/Designer, Ms. Bartlett is responsible for designing custom furniture for remodels and new homes. She is additionally responsible for all aspects of Company operations, including administration, finance, sales and marketing, and strategic planning. **Career Steps:** Owner/Designer, LVB Design (1983–Present); Manager, Spilsted & Associates (1980–1982); Graphics Department Administrator, Touche Ross & Company (1974–1978). **Associations & Accomplishments:** Certified California State Interior Designer; Co–Chair, Art Literacy for Reed Union School District; Former President, Pt. Tiburon Bayside Association; Published in local and regional newspapers, and the hardcover edition of "Kitchens and Baths." **Education:** Canada College, B.F.A. (1973); New York University; Ohio University, Graduate Studies in Art History.

Bliss Beasley

Vice President of Corporate Communications
American Exhibition Services
2700 2nd Avenue South
Birmingham, AL 35233
(205) 323–2211
Fax: (205) 323–2246

7389

Business Information: American Exhibition Services is the predominant trade show marketing firm in the United States, working with over 300 of the largest trade shows in the country and serving over 30,000 clients annually. As Vice President of Corporate Communications, Miss Beasley works directly with CEO and President, and is responsible for strategic planning, overseeing industry relations, and marketing public relations. **Career Steps:** Vice President of Corporate Communications, American Exhibition Services (1991–Present); Manager, 18 Carats (1990–1991); Assistant to Food and Beverage Director, Birmingham–Jefferson Convention Center. (1984–1990). **Associations & Accomplishments:** International Association of Exhibition Managers – serve on several key committees; Professional Convention Management Association; Center for Exhibition Industry Research. **Education:** University of Alabama – Birmingham – School of Business and Communication. **Personal:** Miss Beasley enjoys going to the beach.

Tammy Benedict

Vice President
Lexi International, Inc.
1645 North Vine Street, Suite 400
Los Angeles, CA 90028–8843
(213) 848–5312
Fax: (213) 848–5775

7389

Business Information: Lexi International, Inc. is a direct marketing company with emphasis on outbound telemarketing and database marketing. As Vice President, Ms. Benedict is responsible for management of Client Services and Operations Departments, including profitability and efficient process. She performs training, coordinates operations, and is a data broker. **Career Steps:** Vice President, Lexi International, Inc. (1995–Present); Telesales Manager, McKesson Water Products (1992–1995); Operations Manager, Pacific Bell/GMA Research (1990–1991). **Education:** Grace College, B.A. in Mathematics (1983). **Personal:** Two children: Brent and Nathan. Ms. Benedict enjoys rollerblading, softball, outdoor activities, camping, and going to the beach.

Mark J. Bollman
Senior Vice President
Creative Colors International
5550 175th Street
Tinley Park, IL 60477
(708) 614–7786
Fax: (708) 614–9685

7389

Business Information: Creative Colors International is a franchisor, selling franchises that repair leather, vinyl, and fabric in all markets throughout the United States. The Company has over 30 locations with 65 mobile units each, and provides services to hospitals, hotels, and a variety of businesses. As Senior Vice President, Mr. Bollman oversees the operation of all franchise outlets, training, sales, marketing, and production. **Career Steps:** Creative Colors International: Senior Vice President (1994–Present), Operations Manager (1992–1994); Merchandiser, Quality Beers (1990–1992). **Associations & Accomplishments:** Home Business Association; American Entrepreneur Association; International Franchise Association. **Education:** St. Joseph's College, B.B.A. in Marketing (1992). **Personal:** Married to Kelli in 1995. Mr. Bollman enjoys golf, skiing, and bowling.

Tracy A. Bond
Sales & Marketing Director
O.B.M.E., Inc.
224 Harrison Street, Suite 300
Syracuse, NY 13202
(315) 472–5212
Fax: (315) 475–3514

7389

Business Information: O.B.M.E., Inc., a Division of the Onondaga County Medical Society, provides a 24–hour live–operator answering service, voice mail, and pager service. As Sales & Marketing Director, Miss Bond is responsible for directing sales staff programming for all new answering service and voice mail customers, as well as the activation and service of pagers. **Career Steps:** Sales & Marketing Director, O.B.M.E., Inc. (1994–Present). **Associations & Accomplishments:** American Marketing Association; Chamber of Commerce. **Personal:** Miss Bond enjoys golf, skiing, horseback riding, and travel.

Leroy Briggs
Director– Hampton Roads Office
ISSOT, a division of FOSSAC
P.O. Box 15129
Norfolk, VA 23511
(804) 445–1720
Fax: (804) 444–0175

7389

Business Information: ISSOT (Intra–Fleet Supply Support Operations Team), a division of FOSSAC, is a provider of logistics and support services assistance to the U.S. Navy and other Department of Defense (DOD) activities. Joining FOSSAC upon his retirement from the U.S. Navy in 1982, Mr. Briggs serves as Director of the Hampton Roads base. He is responsible for the supervision of a staff of sixteen Civil Service workers and 200 contractor workers, in addition to the direct supervision of Civil Service workers involved in the support of supply functions, (i.e., inventories, material shipment, causative research, data processing, bar code systems, packaging, warehousing). **Career Steps:** Director of the Hampton Roads Office, ISSOT, a division of FOSSAC (1982–Present); Chief Petty Officer, U.S. Navy (1961–1982). **Associations & Accomplishments:** Minister, Mount Gilead Baptist Church; Civic League; Fleet Reserve Association; Licensed Minister since 1991; Published in Virginia Pilot – Daily Break (newspaper) with a front page article and comments on "Natural Born Killers." **Education:** St. Leo College, Religious studies **Personal:** Married to Sheila in 1990. Six children: Kim, Victor, Toshia, Michael, Tina, and Tia. Mr. Briggs enjoys researching and studying the Bible, fishing, and karate.

Don Brown
Systems Support Manager
NCR Information Solutions
1510 North Walton Boulevard
Bentonville, AR 72712–4138
(501) 271–2703
Fax: (501) 271–2795
EMAIL: See Below

7389

Business Information: NCR Information Solutions is one of the leading providers of business services. The Company provides systems integration, systems management, business process management, outsourcing consultation and solutions to global companies. As Systems Support Manager, Mr. Brown is responsible for coordinating service activities between the Wal–Mart home office and 3,100 stores domestically and internationally. Internet users can reach him via: DON.L.BROWN@bentonvilleAR.NCR.COM. **Career Steps:** Systems Support Manager, NCR Information Solutions (1995–Present). **Education:** University of Missouri–Rolla, B.S. (1982). **Personal:** Mr. Brown enjoys fishing and sports car restoration.

Mark S. Burns
Creative Director
Exhibit Group
180 Selig Drive South West
Atlanta, GA 30336–2033
(404) 696–7500
Fax: (404) 691–3280

7389

Business Information: Exhibit Group is an organizer of trade shows for other companies. As Creative Director, Mr. Burns is responsible for setting the direction for all phases of design in exhibit groups. **Career Steps:** Creative Director, Exhibit Group/Giltspur (1991–Present); Design Director, Exhibit Group (1984–1991); Design Director, Franklin–Jones – Chicago (1976–1984). **Associations & Accomplishments:** Industrial Design Association; Exhibit Designers and Producers Association; International Exhibitors Association. **Personal:** Married to Susan in 1984. Two children: Christopher and Julia. Mr. Burns enjoys model railroads, computers (MAC), and bikes.

Kendall W. Carpenter, CPA, CMA
Controller and Corporate Secretary
Web Technologies, L.L.C.
10816 East Newton Street, Suite 117
Tulsa, OK 74116
(918) 234–9200
Fax: (908) 234–0608
EMail: See Below

7389

Business Information: Web Technologies, L.L.C. is an Internet presence provider, focusing on corporate consulting in the area of Internet marketing and business. Co–founding the Firm in 1993, as Controller and Corporate Secretary, Ms. Carpenter is responsible for overseeing daily operations, personnel decisions, and executive leadership. Concurrently, she serves as Corporate Secretary and Controller for Global Interface Solutions, developing proprietary software and automated consoles for the airline industry. Internet users can also reach Kendall via: Kendall@MAIL.WEBTEK.COM **Career Steps:** Controller and Corporate Secretary, Web Technologies, L.L.C. (1995–Present); Controller and Corporate Secretary, Global Interface Solutions (1993–Present); Law Firm Manager, Carpenter & Carpenter (1991–1993); Chief Operating Officer, Ansa Bottle Company (1986–1987). **Associations & Accomplishments:** American Institute of Certified Public Accountants; Oklahoma Society of Certified Public Accountants; Tulsa Society of Certified Public Accountants; Institute of Management Accountants; Girl Scout Leader. **Education:** Oklahoma State University, Accounting (1978); Certified Public Accountant (1980); Certified Management Accountant (1984). **Personal:** Married to David A. in 1983. Two children: Valerie Elaine and Grant Allen. Ms. Carpenter enjoys reading and needlework. She is also a Certified Master Gardener (landscaping).

Isaac Chowrimootoo
Regional Manager
John Mini Indoor Landscape
233 Fordham Street
Bronx, NY 10464–1414
(212) 366–9004 (718) 885–2426
Fax: (718) 885–0446

7389

Business Information: John Mini Indoor Landscape is an interior landscaper, providing plants and plant accessories to Fortune 500 companies in the Tri–State (New York, New Jersey, Connecticut, and Pennsylvania) area. As Regional Manager, Mr. Chowrimootoo is responsible for New York City operations, which include 600 accounts. He handles reviews, staffing concerns, design and sales of key accounts, contract negotiations, quality control reviews, and customer service complaints. **Career Steps:** Regional Manager, John Mini Indoor Landscape (1986–Present); Guyana Government: Regional Superintendent/Member of Parliament (1980–1986), Coordinator of Workers Education Unit (1974–1986). **Associations & Accomplishments:** Lower Corenty Lions Club. **Education:** York College, G.C.E. (1973); Kuru Kuru Cooperative College – Guyana. **Personal:** Married to Bibi in 1976. Three children: Michael, Shelleza, and Annette. Mr. Chowrimootoo enjoys reading, dancing, and politics.

Mrs. M. Christina Clark
President
Speak Easy Languages
757 South Main Street
Plymouth, MI 48170
(313) 459–5556
Fax: (313) 459–1460

7389

Business Information: Speak Easy Languages is a provider of language training, interpretation and translation services. Providing language training for more than 20 major foreign languages, including the instruction of English as a Second Language, the Organization serves all ages from children to adults. They also provide interpreters for business meetings and court appearances, as well as produce manual publications and video voice–over translations. As President, Mrs. Clark is responsible for all aspects of operations for the organization. Established in 1980, Speak Easy Languages employs 75 people. **Career Steps:** President, Speak Easy Languages; Stewardess, Eastern Airlines. **Associations & Accomplishments:** U.S. Chamber of Commerce; Plymouth Chamber of Commerce; American Translators Association; People to People. **Education:** Universidad de Cuyo, Argentina, English degree (1965). **Personal:** Married to William B. in 1969. Three children: Danielle, Lisa, and Taryn. Mrs. Clark enjoys horseback riding, bird watching and traveling.

Alexander "Robb" Clawson
Marketing Manager
TRW Information Services Division
425 North Martingale Road, Suite 600
Schaumburg, IL 60173–2406
(847) 240–7621
Fax: (847) 240–0045

7389

Business Information: TRW Information Services Division provides market consumer credit and list information to medical, automotive, and various other industries. As Marketing Manager, Mr. Clawson is responsible for the creation, development, and implementation of direct marketing campaigns, interfacing with new clientele, supervising direct mail and telephone sales, and maintenance of existing accounts. **Career Steps:** Marketing Manager, TRW Information Services Division (1993–Present); Field Marketing Specialist, TAP Pharmaceuticals (1991–1993); United States Army Officer (1986–1991). **Associations & Accomplishments:** BMA – Chicago Chapter; Direct Marketers Association; Veterans of Foreign Wars; American Legion. **Education:** Attending: Northern Illinois University, M.B.A. in progress; University of Illinois, B.A. (1986); Defense Language Institute – Foreign Language Center; Attaining Native Fluency in Greek. **Personal:** Married to Lauren in 1989. Two children: Nicholas and Emma. Mr. Clawson enjoys spending time with his family, writing, and golf.

Terrence J. Coan
•••━━━◎━━━•••

Vice President
First American Records Management
5530 Bandini Boulevard
Bell, CA 90201
(213) 260–7200
Fax: (213) 260–7885

7389

Business Information: First American Records Management provides professional off–site storage (microfilming), records management and data information services to corporate and governmental agencies. Joining First American in 1989 as a sales representative, Mr. Coan was appointed to his current position in 1994. As Vice President he oversees all operational and administrative aspects for the Los Angeles branch office. **Career Steps:** First American Records Management: Vice President (1994–Present), Sales Representative (1989–1994); Records Supervisor, Glendale Federal Bank (1988–1989); Records Coordinator, Hertzberg, Jacob & Weingarton (1986–1987); Records Center, Kelly Services **Associations & Accomplishments:** Association of Records Managers and Administrators; ARMA International; Participant, 1995 California AIDS Ride **Education:** University of Phoenix, B.A. (1993); Macomb Community College, A.A. **Personal:** Mr. Coan enjoys biking, music and travel.

Harold J. Collins

Regional Sales Manager
Milton Cannon Foods
3501 Old Oakwood Road
Oakwood, GA 35066
(800) 934–3663
Fax: (704) 681–0417

7389

Business Information: Established in 1949, Asheville Packing/Cannon Foods is a food service distribution company. Mr. Collins began his career in 1959 in the Sales Department of Asheville Packing Co., promoted to his current position as Sales Manager in 1981. Milton/Cannon Foods, a subsidiary of Performance Food Group, acquired Asheville Packing Co./Cannon Foods in June 1995. Mr. Collins was promoted to Regional Sales Manager at that time. **Career Steps:** Regional Sales Manager, Milton Cannon Foods (1981–Present) **Associations & Accomplishments:** Sales Marketing Executives of Ashe; International Food Services Executives. **Personal:** Married to Gwen in 1959. Three children: Jeff, Tim, and Robin. Mr. Collins enjoys golf, fishing, and sports.

INNISBROOK WRAPS PREMIUM PRODUCTS FOR FUNDRAISING

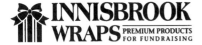

Jane D. Collins

Assistant Regional Manager
Innisbrook Wraps
309 East Maple Avenue
Merchantville, NJ 08109
(609) 662–1840
Fax: (609) 663–1070

7389

Business Information: Headquartered in Greensboro, NC, Innisbrook Wraps sells and distributes premium products as a fundraising program to schools and not–for–profit organizations. Catalog items sold include gift wraps, accessories, chocolates, tote bags, as well as other quality fundraising merchandise. Established over fourteen years ago, Innisbrook Wraps has become the biggest Division of it's parent company. As Assistant Regional Manager, Mrs. Collins is responsible for the co–management of the North East Region. An employee with the company since 1987, her duties include hiring, training, motivating and managing a staff of 35 professionals, as well as travel in the field throughout the Northeast and the country for National Conventions. **Career Steps:** Innisbrook Wraps: Assistant Regional Manager (1993–Present), District Manager (1990–1993), Sales Representative (1987–1990). **Associations & Accomplishments:** City Council Public Events Chair; Worthy Matron and Past Grand Officer, NJOES; President, Merchantville Woman's Club; State Board Member, NJSFWC; BPW; Brownie/Girl Scout Leader; Appeared in "Selling Magazine." **Education:** Averett College, Certificate (1959). **Personal:** Married to Ronald W. in 1959. Two children: R. Wayne Collins II and Monette W. Collins. Mrs. Collins enjoys travel, reading, and needlepoint.

Alayne A. Cook

Director
IUK Alumni Association
2715 South Lafountain Street
Kokomo, IN 46901
(317) 455–9411
Fax: (317) 455–9504
EMAIL: See Below

7389

Business Information: IUK Alumni Association is the support organization for all program activities for alumni members of Indiana University–Kokomo. As Director, Ms. Cook oversees all alumni contact, as well as the coordination of volunteer staff, fund–raising campaigns and special activities programs. She can also be reached through the Internet via: ACook@IUKFS1.IUK.INDIANA.EDU **Career Steps:** Director, IUK Alumni Association **Education:** Indiana University, B.A. (1964). **Personal:** One child: Betty Joyce Symphony.

Mr. Luis Cruz–Tirado

Vice President and General Manager
Telemarketing Solutions Corporation
1606 Ponce De Leon Avenue, Suite 800
San Juan, Puerto Rico 00909
(809) 289–0522
Fax: (809) 289–0528

7389

Business Information: International in scope, Telemarketing Solutions Corporation is a diversified telemarketing company that offers services to businesses that use networking strategies, working with management to determine the best telemarketing techniques for the business. With a continually updated database of more than one million names, Telemarketing Solutions has access to large target audience that can be segmented to suit the appropriate business needs. Services include: inbound telemarketing, outbound telemarketing, fulfillment, direct mail, database, segmentation, infomercial, project analysis, telecollections, sales leads, market research and surveys, client qualification, follow–up programs and solutions. Established in 1994, Telemarketing Solutions Corporation currently employs 50 people. As Executive Vice President and General Manager, Mr. Cruz–Tirado is responsible for all aspects of operations, and is a Member of the Board of Directors. **Career Steps:** Executive Vice President and General Manager, Telemarketing Solutions Corporation (1994–Present); Telemarketing Sales Manager, Casiano Communications (1991–1994); Sales Manager and Administrator, A.M. Communications (1990–1991); International Sales Manager, Computer Partners (1988–1990); Export Sales Manager and Sales Manager, Olivetti (1981–1988); Sales Representative, Kodak Caribbean (1976–1981). **Associations & Accomplishments:** Sales Marketing Executives; Direct Marketing Association; Les Amis Du Vin; Salesman of the Year, Kodak Caribbean (1980); TA Adler Performance Sales of the Year, London (1985). **Education:** University of Puerto Rico, B.S. in Biology (1981); PG International Marketing (1985). **Personal:** Mr. Cruz–Tirado enjoys outdoor sports, photography, travel and wine.

Luis Jose Cuerda

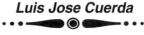

President
Tomas Cuerda, Inc.
P.O. Box 363307, Billas Commercial Center
San Juan, Puerto Rico 00936–3307
(809) 758–7830
Fax: (809) 764–8553

7389

Business Information: Tomas Cuerda, Inc. is a family–owned, manufacturer's representative and distributing company. Established in 1975, the Company reports annual revenue of $1.5 million. Joining the family business in 1965 as Vice President, Mr. Cuerda was appointed President in 1975. He provides the overall vision and strategy for the Company's continued development, quality service, and international presence. **Career Steps:** Tomas Cuerda, Inc.: President (1975–Present), Vice President (1965–1975); Project Engineer, Blythe Company (1960–1965). **Associations & Accomplishments:** Engineers College – Sports Committee; Water Environmental Association; Instrument Society of America; Ato–Prico; Club Manor of Rio Peidras; Olympic Efforts Committee; President, Centroamerica & Caribbean Bowling Confederation; President, Federacion de Bolos de Puerto Rico. **Education:** University of Puerto Rico – Mayaguez, B.S. in Civil Engineering (1960). **Personal:** Married to Sara Perez in 1962. Three children: Luis Jose, Tania Margarita, and Luis Alfredo. Mr. Cuerda enjoys sports and bowling.

Sallye Grant DiVenuti

Senior Sales and Marketing Manager
Hampton Conventions and Tourism
2 Eaton Street, Suite 106
Hampton, VA 23669–4054
(757) 722–1222
Fax: (757) 727–1310
EMAIL: See Below

7389

Business Information: Hampton Conventions and Tourism generates revenue for the city through booking conventions in local hotels, and marketing to companies, organizations, and individual customers. Local in scope, the Company has fifteen hotels throughout the Hampton, Virginia area. As Senior Sales and Marketing Manager, Ms. DiVenuti performs the director's functions in their absence, supervises the Visitor Center and convention sales and services, and oversees staff, training and special projects. She can also be reached through E–Mail via: SGRANTDI@CITY.HAMPTON.VA.US. **Career Steps:** Senior Sales and Marketing Manager, Hampton Conventions and Tourism (1994–Present); Director of Sales and Marketing, Sheraton Hotels (1992–1993); Director of Sales and Marketing, Hawthorn Suites (1990–1991); Front Office Manager, OMNI Newport News Hotel (1993); Director of Sales, Sheraton Inn Coliseum (1992–1993); Owner, Sassy Services (1991–1992); Director of Marketing, Limehouse Properties (1990); Norfolk Convention and Visitors Bureau: Convention Sales Manager (1985–1989), Operations Conventions Service Manager (1984–1985); Director of Catering, The Hotel Madison (1984). **Associations & Accomplishments:** Past President, Market Area Merchants Association; Board Member/Education Chairperson, Hospitality Sales and Marketing Executives; Harborfest; Southeastern Virginia Foodbank; Corresponding Secretary/Board Member, Port Norfolk Civic League; Colonel, Confederate Air Force; Virginia Association of Convention Bureaus; 101st Airborne Division Association; Special Forces Association; Destroyer Escort Sailors Association; American Legion; Air Weather Association; Air Force Association; Education Committee Quad State Convention and Visitors Bureau Conference; Past President, Charleston Hoteliers Exchange Club; Organizing Chairperson, Sales/Marketing Executives of Charleston; Charleston CVB Board of Governors; Charleston Travel Council; Volunteer Docent, Historic Charleston Foundation. **Education:** Old Dominion University. **Personal:** Married to Mark in 1983. Ms. DiVenuti enjoys gardening, needlepoint, and computers.

Eivind K. Djupedal

Vice President and Head of Representation
Cargill Enterprises
c/o Cargill Moscow, P.O. Box 5674
Minneapolis, MN 55440
7095 244–3311
Fax: 7095 244–3365

7389

Business Information: Cargill Enterprises, a wholly owned subsidiary of Cargill, Inc., is an organization whose primary objective is to assist the company penetrate Eastern Europe. Cargill Inc. itself is a privately held company with 70,000 employees in 70 countries in 50 different product lines, including commodity trading, agricultural processing, steel and fertilizer production as well as financial trading. It is Mr. Djupedal's challenge to transfer the skills necessary to introduce Cargill's main businesses to Russia, in which there currently are 10 in 3 different offices in the Russian Federation. An executive with Cargill, Mr. Djupedal started his career in 1981 and has since held various trading and management positions in the US and Europe. He was appointed Vice President and Head of Representation for Cargill Enterprises in Moscow in 1992 and moved to Moscow the same year. Mr. Djupedal is a native of Norway. His languages include Norwegian, Italian, and Russian. **Career Steps:** Vice President and Head of Representation, Cargill Enterprises (1992–Present); Country Manager – Italy, Cargill SrL, Milano (1990–1992); Managing Director, MLPD, Cargill PLC, London (1989–1992); Trading Manager, MLPD, Cargill, Inc., Minneapolis (1986–1989). **Associations & Accomplishments:** President/Board Member, United Way, Moscow; Board Member, American Chamber of Commerce, Russia; Board Member, Junior Achievement, Russia; Board Member, Russian National Orchestra. **Education:** University of Minnesota, M.A. (1984); University of Oslo, Norway, B.A. (1979) **Personal:** Married to Gwenn in 1980. Two children: Kristofer and Jennifer. Mr. Djupedal enjoys cross country skiing, wines, and opera.

David C. Dodd

Vice President of Sales
Sidewinder Products Corporation
850 Municipal Drive
Hoover, AL 35216–5516
(205) 979–0422
Fax: (205) 979–5118

7389

Business Information: Sidewinder Products Corporation develops, manufactures, and markets proprietary hand tools for retail chains and catalogues, as well as export to Europe, Japan, and Australia. As Vice President of Sales, Mr. Dodd coordinates all export sales and national account domestic sales, supervises the sales staff, and attends international trade shows every year. **Career Steps:** Vice President of Sales, Sidewinder Products Corporation (1987–Present); Sales Representative, Graphic Corporation (1984–1987). **Education:** Attended, University of Alabama. **Personal:** Married to Kim in 1991. Two children: Tyler and Shanan. Mr. Dodd enjoys sports.

John J. Doyle

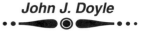

Vice President
Sound & Stagecraft, Inc.
1500 Birchwood Avenue
Des Plaines, IL 60018–3002
(708) 699–9080
Fax: (708) 699–9723

7389

Business Information: Sound & Stagecraft, Inc. is a national provider of audio–video services, setting up audio–video products needed for conferences, trade shows, and meetings. The Company prides itself on providing the total scope of stage services — from theatre lights, concert sounds, slide projectors, audio equipment, flip charts, overheads, etc., to providing all labor needed for the productions to be ready. Projects have included sporting events, product launching for companies, and the world's largest Superbowl party for players lasting for four days in 1994. Established in 1977, Sound & Stagecraft, Inc. reports annual revenue of $20 million and currently employs 100 people. As Vice President, Mr. Doyle is responsible for all aspects of events staging, including bidding, organizing, getting everything together for the operations end of the business, marketing and technical ends. **Career Steps:** Vice President, Sound & Stagecraft, Inc. (1983–Present); General Manager – Branch, Bauer Audio Video (1979–1983). **Associations & Accomplishments:** International Communications Industries Association (ICIA); Association for Multi–Image (AMI). **Education:** Penn State, B.A. (1975). **Personal:** Married to Kathleen in 1983. Two children: Sean and Shannon.

Brent B. Dupper
Vice President of Operations
J J & R Medical Data Systems, Inc.
342 Bonnie Circle Suite B
Corona, CA 91720
(909) 273–1500
Fax: (909) 273–0977

7389

Business Information: J J & R Medical Data Systems, Inc. is a national management firm, providing medical management, billing and collection services from five offices located in California and Florida. Established in 1984, J J & R currently employs 45 people. As Vice President of Operations, Mr. Dupper directs all day–to–day operations of the business, ranging from budgeting to personnel matters. **Career Steps:** Vice President of Operations, J J & R Medical Data Systems, Inc. (1990–Present); Business Manager, Family Medical Associates (1988–1990); Assistant Director Patient Business Office, White Memorial Medical Center (1986–1988). **Associations & Accomplishments:** Medical Group Management Association. **Education:** Loma Linda University, B.B.A. (1986). **Personal:** Mr. Dupper enjoys sports.

Robert E. Elam
Operations Manager
Nashville Convention Center
601 Commerce Street
Nashville, TN 37203
(615) 742–2000
Fax: (615) 742–2029

7389

Business Information: The Nashville Convention Center has provided a venue for conventions, trade shows, conferences, and meetings since 1986. Joining the Convention Center in its inaugural year, Mr. Elam moved into his present position as Operations Manager in 1987. His responsibilities include event management, engineering, security and emergency medical arrangements, reception area supervision, contract service, facilities maintenance, and personnel management. **Career Steps:** Nashville Convention Center: Operations Manager (1987–Present), Facility Services Coordinator (1986–1987); Executive Housekeeper, Nashville Sheraton Hotel (1985–1986); Maxwell Clarion Hotel: Housekeeping Supervisor, Executive Steward, Kitchen Manager, Purchasing Agent (1980–1984). **Associations & Accomplishments:** Association for Convention Operations Management; Society of Corporate Meeting Planners; Maxwell House Employee of the Month; Featured in a local minority newspaper; Featured in national Black Meeting Planners Magazine. **Education:** Attended: Fisk University, International Association of Auditorium Managers, School for Public Facility Management. **Personal:** Mr. Elam enjoys golf and soap operas.

Michael G. Feldstein
Director of Credit Systems
Eaton Credit Corporation
3 Concorde Gate, 4th Floor
Don Mills, Ontario M3C 3N7
(416) 382–5344
Fax: (416) 382–5422

7389

Business Information: Eaton Credit Corporation is a credit card issuer for T. Eaton Acceptance Company and National Retail Credit Service, their private label operations throughout Canada. Cards are issued for retail store cards, retail outlets stores, property management, and finance corporations. Established in 1990, Eaton Credit Corporation currently employs 400 people. Reporting to the Chief Operations Officer, Mr.

Feldstein serves as Director of Credit Systems. He is responsible for all aspects of systems operation and development, including all new product enhancements. He is also responsible for merchant services, which includes client point of sale support. **Career Steps:** Director of Credit Systems, Eaton Credit Corporation (1992–Present); Director of Systems Card Services, Royal Trust (1985–1992); Senior Manager Operations and Systems, Bank of Montreal (1974–1985). **Associations & Accomplishments:** Recipient of Canadian Productivity Award (company award) for 3 years in a row. **Education:** McGill University, M.B.A. (1981), Bachelor of Electrical Engineering; Sir George Williams University (1973). **Personal:** Married to Susan in 1975. Two children: Brian and Jonathan.

Ms. Barbara B. Fisher
Owner, Appraiser, and Chairman of the Board
Fisher Auction Company, Inc.
431 NE 1st Street
Pompano Beach, FL 33060
(305) 942–0917
Fax: (305) 782–8143

7389

Business Information: Fisher Auction Company, Inc. is an auctioneer and appraiser of personal property and real estate. Types of property appraised include: residential property, commercial (hotel/motel, offices, acreage, warehouses, professional offices), residential contents, antiques, jewelry, collectibles, glassware, and miscellaneous items. Established in 1971, Fisher Auction Company, Inc. reports annual revenue of $220 million and currently employs 17 people. As Owner, Appraiser, and Chairman of the Board, Ms. Fisher is responsible for all aspects of operations, including conducting appraisals, lectures and serving as office manager. **Career Steps:** Owner, Appraiser, and Chairman of the Board, Fisher Auction Company, Inc. (1971–Present). **Associations & Accomplishments:** Organization of Professional Real Estate Appraisers (OPREA): President–Elect, Past Vice President; International Society of Appraisers; National Association of Master Appraisers; National Association of Real Estate Appraisers; Pompano Beach Chamber of Commerce; Former Board of Advisors, International College of Real Estate Appraisers; Former Board of Directors, Visiting Nurses Association of Broward County; Former Board of Directors, Ladies Auxillary of the National Auctioneers Association; Former President for Ladies Auxiliary of the Florida Auctioneers Association; Board of Directors, Florida Home Health Care. **Education:** Florida Business College (1980); Gold Coast Real Estate School, Real Estate License Law, earned Real Estate Salesman License (1980); Indiana University, Certification Program for Personal Property Appraisers Course 101, 102 & 103, Course 106 Depreciable Residential Content, earned ISSA designation; International College of Real Estate Appraisers, Principles & Techniques of Real Estate Appraising, SREA Material, earned PREA (1984); Lincoln Graduate Center, earned MRA (1990); Continuing Educational courses in Real Estate and Residential Contents (1979–1990); Gem Spectrum Course, earned G.S. designation (1985). **Personal:** Married to Louis B. Fisher, Jr. in 1955. Two children: Louis B. III and Lamar Paul Fisher.

Larry D. Friedlan
President & Chief Executive Officer
National Marketing Group
1730 South College, Suite 204
Ft. Collins, CO 80525
(970) 221–0153
Fax: (970) 221–1478

7389

Business Information: Established in 1978, National Marketing Group is a business consulting service offering product marketing ideas to small companies. As President & Chief Executive Officer, Mr. Friedlan is responsible for the presentation of trade shows on behalf of his clients. Concurrent with his position at National Marketing Group, Mr. Friedlan is a Partner and President of Myatt & Associates, Inc., one of the largest mortgage brokers in the region. **Career Steps:** President and Chief Executive Officer, National Marketing Group (1987–Present); Partner and President, Myatt & Associates, Inc. (1995–Present); President and Chief Executive Officer, Friedlan & Associates, Inc. (1978–92); President, Meriam Woods Corporation (1980–86). **Associations & Accomplishments:** Who's Who in Real Estate in America (1983); Chocolatier, voted World's Best Chocolate in Chicago (1987). **Education:** Nebraska University, B.S. (1971); Various Schools of Real Estate from California, Arizona, Virginia, Missouri, and Colorado; School of Insurance from Missouri; Over 20 years in Commercial Real Estate Business; Antique Auto Appraiser. **Personal:** Married to Karen in 1995. One child: Lorrie Ann. Mr. Friedlan enjoys hiking, skiing, golf, tennis, and playing the piano.

Todd Gibson
Vice President
Unibase Direct, Inc.
3 Century Drive
Parsippany, NJ 07054
(201) 285–1700
Fax: (201) 285–9246
EMAIL: See Below

7389

Business Information: Unibase Direct, Inc. is an international database marketing and telemarketing firm established in 1992. Unibase Direct is also the largest data entry company in the United States. In addition, the Corporation offers direct marketing software products to American companies with a desire to market their products overseas. As Vice President, Mr. Gibson is responsible for the general management of the Corporation. As a part owner in the Corporation, he is also involved in contract administration and negotiating terms with prospects and clients. Mr. Gibson's plans for the future are to continue expanding the Company client base as a premier provider of multinational direct marketing services. Mr. Gibson has been published in the telecommunications and direct marketing trade press and is a regular participant in industry panels and forums. Internet users can reach him via: unibase@unibasedirect.com. **Career Steps:** Vice President, Unibase Direct, Inc. (1992–Present); Director, Value Added Services/American Business Information (1991–1992); Director, Trinet (1985–1990); Manager, Market Research, Baker Industries (1984); Senior Market Research Analyst, Rockwell International (1979–1983). **Associations & Accomplishments:** Beta Gama Sigma; Sigma Iota Epsilon; National Honor Society; Direct Marketers Association; Regular Hospital Volunteer. **Education:** Baylor University: M.B.A. in Marketing (1979), B.S. in Biology (1977). **Personal:** One child: Wendy. Mr. Gibson enjoys photography, sailing, fine wine, and snorkeling.

Marcy A. Gitterman
Chief Executive Officer
Action Business Centers
PO Box 591
Old Bridge, NJ 08857–0591
(908) 679–2225
Fax: (908) 679–2208

7389

Business Information: Action Business Centers, established in 1995, is a sales and training services firm for all aspects of business. Serving as Chief Executive Officer, Marcy Gitterman is responsible for all aspects of administrative and training functions, including serving as a trainer. **Career Steps:** Chief Executive Officer, Action Business Centers (1995–Present); President and Chief Executive Officer, Action Leasing & Sales, Inc. (1992–1995); Leasing Manager, Lease Options, Inc. (1990–1992); Teacher, Old Bridge/East Brunswick Schools (1983–1989); Cooking Instructor, East Brunswick Evening Adult School (1984–1989). **Associations & Accomplishments:** Board of Directors, NJ Chapter, National Vehicle Leasing Association (1991–Present); National Association of Female Executives. **Education:** Glassboro State University, B.A. (1983). **Personal:** Ms. Gitterman enjoys cooking, baking, skating, art, camping and antique collecting during her leisure time.

Craig G. Hannah
Executive Vice President and Managing Director
DHR International
19200 Von Karman, 5th Floor
Irvine, CA 92715
Fax: Please mail or call

7389

Business Information: DHR is the ninth largest executive search firm in the world responsible for business development, primarily on the West Coast and Hawaii. One of the unique aspects of this DHR practice is that clients can pay fees in stock to Kenmore Capital, thereby preserving working capital. As Executive Vice President and Managing Director, Mr. Hannah established the Orange County practice in late 1995, responsible for all aspects of operations. Starting his career as a CPA right out of college, he then went on to serve for fourteen years in various executive marketing positions with IBM. Following this, he bought a fitness company — Life Fitness — recently selling his share of the Company to his partner in order to establish Kenmore Capital. **Career Steps:** Sole Proprietor, Kenmore Capital, venture funds (1995–Present); Executive Vice President, Life Fitness (1991–1995); IBM: Senior Location Manager (1988–1991), Area Marketing Manager (1987–1988). **Associations & Accomplishments:** American Marketing Association; American Institute of Certified Public Accountants; Melbourne Cricket Club – Australia. **Education:** University of Hawaii, B.B.A., with Honors (1977); Certified Public Accountant. **Personal:** Married to Mary Jane in 1980. One child: Erik. Mr. Hannah enjoys golf, deep sea fishing, and coaching soccer.

Timothy S. Harrison
Director of Regional Operations
Hospitality Resources, Inc.
10505 Delta Parkway
Schiller Park, IL 60176
(847) 671–6312
Fax: (630) 671–6288
EMAIL: See Below.

7389

Business Information: Hospitality Resources, Inc. (HRI) provides professional hospitality support services to premier hotels, resorts, and convention centers. HRI has become one of the largest and fastest growing hospitality service Companies in the nation through a combination of state of the art hardware, experienced on–site professionals, full automation at the local level, a comprehensive on–going training program, and a significant package of business incentives. As Director of Regional Operations, Mr. Harrison oversees operations for the hotel Audio Visual Division. Internet users can reach him via: tharriso@hrinc.com. **Career Steps:** Director of Regional Operations, Hospitality Resources, Inc. (1986–Present). **Associations & Accomplishments:** MPI; NACE. **Personal:** Two children: Timothy and Marc. Mr. Harrison enjoys martial arts and water sports.

Boyd Michael (Mickey) Hicks
President
Eagle Printing Company, Inc.
100 S. Michigan Avenue
Coldwater, MI 49036–2013
(517) 279–7948
Fax: (517) 278–8436

7389

Business Information: Eagle Printing Company, Inc. is a consumer packaging plant offering various graphic art and printing label services for large and small businesses. As President, Mr. Hicks is responsible for all aspects of Company operations, including administration, marketing, public relations, and strategic planning. **Career Steps:** President, Eagle Printing Company, Inc. (1995–Present); Plant Manager, Fort Dearborn Lithograph (1993–1995); Plant Manager, Jefferson Smurfit (1985–1992). **Associations & Accomplishments:** Chicago Litho Club; Chaplain, State of Michigan; Deacon and Missionary Representative for his church. **Education:** MFCI; S.P.C.; T.Q.M.; RIT (Management); Research and Development; Engineer. **Personal:** Married to Peggy in 1964. Two children: Ann Michele and Michael Thomas. Mr. Hicks enjoys flying, motorcycle riding, and church activities.

Wendy Houdek Erskine
Executive Director
Jackson Convention and Tourist Bureau
6007 Ann Arbor Road
Jackson, MI 49201–8884
(517) 764–4440
Fax: (517) 764–4480

7389

Business Information: Jackson Convention and Tourist Bureau is a not–for–profit marketing organization for travel and tourism in Jackson and Jackson County, Michigan. As Executive Director, Ms. Houdek Erskine is responsible for marketing, planning, budgeting, and staffing. In addition to supervising daily operations, she also attends various trade shows and coordinates marketing through travel magazines, travel newspapers, and brochures. **Career Steps:** Executive Director, Jackson Convention and Tourist Bureau (1996–Present); Program Supervisor, Ann Arbor Public Schools (1992–1995); Administrator, Ypsilanti Recycling Project (1991–1992); Marketing Director, Recycle Ann Arbor (1990–1991). **Associations & Accomplishments:** Outstanding Staff Member – WIDR Radio (1982,1983); Who's Who Among Young Americans. **Education:** Eastern Michigan University, M.A. in Marketing (1986); Western Michigan University, B.S. in Communications (1983). **Personal:** Married to Keith Erskine in 1988. Ms. Houdek Erskine enjoys travel and photography.

Ernie Hudson
Senior Vice President, Human Resources
PSCU Service Centers
560 Carillon Parkway
St. Petersburg, FL 33716–1202
(813) 571–4608
Fax: (813) 572–8503

7389

Business Information: PSCU Service Centers is a provider of backoffice support and customer service to issuers of credit and debit cards. Established in 1988, PSCU currently employs 325 people. With ten years experience in human resources, Mr. Hudson joined PSCU in 1991 as Human Resources Manager and was promoted to Senior Vice President of Human Resources in 1992. He is responsible for all aspects of personnel administration, personnel training, and overall Corporate strategies. **Career Steps:** PSCU Service Centers: Senior Vice President of Human Resources (1992–Present); Human Resources Manager (1991–1992); Human Resources Manager, Affiliated of Florida, Inc. (1985–1991); Office Assistant, Bruno's Food Stores (1975–1985). **Associations & Accomplishments:** Former President, HR Tampa; Board Member, Franklin Christian Academy; Deacon, Bell Shoals Church of Christ. **Education:** University of Alabama, Marketing (1984); Senior Professional in Human Resources. **Personal:** Married to Jacqueline in 1983. Two children: Forrest and Hunter. Mr. Hudson enjoys scuba diving, photography, exercise, church, and family.

ncit

Serviços e Tecnologias de Informação, Lda.

Paulo Medina Igrejas
General Manager
NCIT
Alameda Antonio Sergio 7, 1 D
Linda–A–Velha, Portugal 2795
351–01–414–610
Fax: 351–01–414–613

7389

Business Information: NCIT provides traditional and value–added services to the information systems industry. Mr. Igrejas co–founded NCIT in 1995 and currently serves as General Manager, defining company strategy, providing executive leadership, and overseeing sales and marketing. **Career Steps:** General Manager, NCIT (1995–Present); Services Country Manager, Digital Equipment (1986–1995); Services Director, Compta S.A. (1985–1986); Services Director, NCR (1981–1985). **Education:** ISEL–Electronics and Telecommunications, Bachelor (1980). **Personal:** Married to Natalia Igrejas in 1976. One child: Pedro Igrejas. Mr. Igrejas enjoys scuba diving.

Mr. Michael J. Johnston
Vice President and General Manager
Philips Service Co.
P.O. Box 555
Jefferson City, TN 37760–0555
(615) 475–0020
Fax: (615) 475–0104

7389

Business Information: Philips Service Co., an affiliate of Philips Consumer Electronics (which produces Magnavox products, such as televisions, VCRs, camcorders, and audios), provides after–sale and support of consumer electronic products throughout the U.S. Philips Service Co. currently employs 1,100 people. As Vice President and General Manager, Mr. Johnston leads the business in achieving growth in sales, market share and new business development. Additionally, he is in charge of a team of 9 different field services, including extended warranties, call center, instruction manuals, training manual, parts, etc. **Career Steps:** Vice President and General Manager, Philips Service Co. (1994–Present); Vice President of Manufacturing, Black & Decker (1991–1994); Senior Vice President and General Manager, Danly Die Set (1989–1991); Site Manager, General Electric Co. (1988–1989). **Associations & Accomplishments:** Published in trade journals. **Education:** St. Joseph's University, B.S. in Chemistry (1970). **Personal:** Married to Lydia in 1978. Three children: Michael Jr., Colleen, and Laura. Mr. Johnston enjoys golf.

Charles (Chuck) P. Jones

Chief Executive Officer
NuWorld Marketing Limited
2910 Jamacha Road
El Cajon, CA 92019
(619) 670–6141
Fax: (619) 670–6230

7389

Business Information: NuWorld Marketing Limited is a promotional marketing support service primarily for packaged goods. The Company operates as a coupon redemption service and is a developer of new and innovative marketing tools. As Chief Executive Officer, Mr. Jones oversees Company administration and operations. He recruits upper management staff, does long–term planning for NuWorld Marketing, and assists in the compilation of an annual budget. Mr. Jones works closely with other management personnel in developing new markets and marketing techniques. **Career Steps:** Chief Executive Officer, NuWorld Marketing Limited (1991–Present); President/CEO, Meridian Technology (1984–1989); Chief Executive Officer, Micro Systems International Corporation (1981–1984); President, Systems Integration and Design (1978–1981). **Associations & Accomplishments:** Interactive Advertising Association; Sons of the American Revolution. **Personal:** Married to Gladys in 1991. three children: Joe, Julissa, and Katty. Mr. Jones enjoys fishing, fine wines, and his children.

Mr. Santos A. Juarez
Plant Manager – Southwest Region
Griffith Micro–Science
2400 Airport Road
Santa Teresa, NM 88008
(505) 589–9300
Fax: (505) 589–9729

7389

Business Information: Griffith Micro–Science is an international company providing sterilization of medical instruments through a chemical process. As Plant Manager – Southwest Region, Mr. Juarez is responsible for all activities associated with the Southwest region of the U.S., including profit and loss, regulatory compliance to local, state, and federal requirements, business plan development and executives. He has also established pricing strategies and developed customer marketing strategies. **Career Steps:** Plant Manager – Southwest Region, Griffith Micro–Science (1991–Present); Materials Manager, Becton Dickinson Acutecare (1988–1991); Critikon, Inc., a Johnson & Johnson Co.: Senior Materials Coordinator (1985–1988), Planner/Buyer (1983–1985); Production Supervisor, Johnson & Johnson (1980–1983). **Associations & Accomplishments:** Malcolm Baldrige Criteria Award Examiner, NM; Past Member, Toastmasters International; Chairman and Treasurer, MFBC; American Society for Quality Control. **Education:** Lewis University, B.A. in Business Administration (1980); Illinois Institute of Technology, Graduate Studies in Economics (1983–1985); Certified by the American Production and Inventory Control Society (CPIM). **Personal:** Married to Elizabeth in 1984. One child: Hannah E. Juarez. Mr. Juarez enjoys golf, snow and water skiing, reading, and non–profit organization activities.

A.W. Kilani
President
Creative Business Solutions
798 Ashwood St.
Jacksonville, FL 32605
(904) 272–8286
Fax: Please mail or call

7389

Business Information: Creative Business Solutions (CBS) is a marketing and sales company specializing in locating and qualifying distributors for businesses seeking distributors in national and international markets. Some of the services provided are: allocating markets and territories; selling distributorship rights; interviewing and qualifying potential distributors; creating sales and marketing presentations; and training sales staff. **Career Steps:** President, Creative Business Solutions (1996–Present); Marketing, Kingdom of Toys (1995–1996); Vice President of Sales and Marketing, Comex BA, International (1994–1995); Vice President of International Marketing and Sales, Silver Lake Resort (1990–1994). **Associations & Accomplishments:** Charter Member, Emergency Medical Services. **Education:** University of Columbia, M.B.A. (1975); Northwest Missouri State, B.S. in Marketing. **Personal:** Mr. Kilani enjoys tennis and computers.

Charles L. Koryda Jr.
Supervisor
U.S. Pharmacopeial Convention, Inc.
12601 Twinbrook Parkway
Rockville, MD 20852–1717
(301) 816–8102
Fax: (301) 816–8501

7389

Business Information: U.S. Pharmacopeial Convention, Inc. is a non–profit organization, promoting public health by establishing and disseminating officially–recognized standards of quality and authoritative information for use of medicines and other health care technologies. As Supervisor, Mr. Koryda is responsible for the supervision of warehouse operations, which processes and fills orders for reference guides, literature, and other related information which is bought, sold, and shipped worldwide. **Career Steps:** Supervisor, U.S. Pharmacopeial Convention, Inc. (1994–Present); Facilities Assistant, Vredenburg (1989–1994); Supervisor, Eastern Chemical Waste Systems (1986–1989). **Associations & Accomplishments:** Fairfax County Adult Softball: Division President, League Coordinator; President, Dolley Madison Stamp Club. **Education:** Northern Virginia Community College (1973). **Personal:** Mr. Koryda enjoys all sports, and collecting stamps and baseball cards.

Mehmet Koryurek
* ● ● ● ◀▬▬▶ ◉ ◀▬▬▶ ● ● ● *

Chief Operating Officer & Chairman of the Board
MA. X Global Resources, Inc.
95 Horatio Street Suite 503
New York, NY 10014
(212) 627–5220
Fax: (212) 627–8475 Voice Mail

7389

Business Information: MA.X Global Research, Inc. is an export/import brokerage firm involved in global resourcing. The Corporation matches buyers and sellers of various manufacturers around the world. As Chief Operating Officer & Chairman of the Board, Mr. Koryurek is responsible for profit/loss accountability and oversees all global business operations. Internet users can reach him via: mehmet@bway.net. **Career Steps:** COO & Chairman of the Board, MA.X Global Research, Inc. (1996–Present); Logistics Manager, Ceram Trading America, Inc. (1995–); Foreign Relations, Delta Ajans, Ltd. (1991–1995); Small Business Consultant, Wharton Small Business Development Center (1994–1995). **Associations & Accomplishments:** Penn Club; Wharton Management Club; West Village Dog Owners Club; American Management Association; Turkish American Businessmen Association. **Education:** Wharton School, University of Pennsylvania, B.B.A. (1995). **Personal:** Mr. Koryurek enjoys music, arts, history, internet, and business, but spends most of his time with his brown–spotted dalmation, PASHA.

Stewart N. Krevolin
Vice President
M. Guzman, Co.
2920 Bunkerhill Court
Bensalem, PA 19020
(215) 947–5101
Fax: (215) 947–5103

7389

Business Information: M. Guzman, Co. is an interior finishing contractor, with services including drywall, wall covering, and painting. The Company provides interior construction services in Pennsylvania, New Jersey, Maine, and Massachusetts. As Vice President, Mr. Krevolin is responsible for all aspects of Company operations including sales and estimating services and development and termination of projects. **Career Steps:** Vice President, M. Guzman, Company (1992–Present); President, S–K Builders, Inc. (1985–1992); President, Harry Krevolin Associates, Inc. (1968–1985). **Associations & Accomplishments:** National Fire Protection Association; Neshaminy Valley Town Watch; Former Director, Neshaminy Valley Athletic Association; Former Board Member, Temple Shalom; Treasurer, Interior Finish Contractors Association. **Education:** Temple University: B.S. in Engineering (1974), Associate's degree (1973); Rutgers, Construction Management Certificate (1987); Home Inspection School (1994). **Personal:** Married to Anita in 1969. Two children: Philice Cohen and Michael. Mr. Krevolin enjoys reading, opera, culture, and family.

Ms. Nancy J. Langdon
Manager of New Business Development
Power Packaging GmbH
Sieben–Steinhauser–Weg 13
Fallingbostel, Germany 29683
49 5162/978–10
Fax: 49 5162/978–99

7389

Business Information: Power Packaging GmbH, a subsidiary of Power Packaging, Inc., is an independent service provider to the fast–moving consumer goods industry, specializing in manufacturing, packaging, distribution and logistics. Established in 1968, the Company currently employs 2,500 people. As Manager of New Business Development, Ms. Langdon is responsible for marketing, research, public affairs, project coordination and human resource culture development. With the Company's committment to international expansion, it is Ms. Langdon's primary objective to realize the company's goal of providing world–class manufacturing and logistics services worldwide. **Career Steps:** Power Packaging GmbH: Manager of New Business Development, Assistant to the Directorship; Media Analyst, IFM; Copy Editor and Staff Writer, The Tennessean. **Associations & Accomplishments:** Publications include: "European Supply Chain Management," Logistics Publication (1994). **Education:** Indiana University, B.A. in Journalism, Political Science and German (1989). **Personal:** Ms. Langdon enjoys sailplaning, languages and travel.

James D. Lee
Systems Engineer
Health Management Systems
401 Park Avenue, South
New York, NY 10016–8808
(212) 685–4545
Fax: (212) 679–3692

7389

Business Information: Health Management Systems processes uncollected health insurance claims from major inner–city hospitals using proprietary matching software, sending claims to insurance companies, Medicare, and Medicaid. As Systems Engineer, Mr. Lee is responsible for inter/intra–platform connectivity, hardware reliability, application development, and coordination of disaster recovery. Additionally, he supervises client site work, interfaces with hardware vendors, and oversees LAN maintenance. **Career Steps:** Systems Engineer, Health Management Systems (1989–Present); Systems Programmer, Bankers Trust Company (1982–1989); Software Engineer, Informatics General (1981–1982); Data Processing Manager, M. Serman & Company (1971–1981). **Associations & Accomplishments:** Society for Creative Anachronism. **Education:** Attended, College of Staten Island. **Personal:** Married to Donna Rose Dalia–Lee in 1990. One child: Joylene Gabrielle Dalia. Mr. Lee enjoys spending time with his family, golf, and bowling.

Coni S. Leoni
Consultant
Corporate Sign, Inc.
1361 East Sleepy Hollow Drive
Olathe, KS 66062
(913) 782–7301
Fax: Please mail or call

7389

Business Information: Corporate Sign, Inc. is an exterior electric sign company specializing in the sale and service of signs for national retail chains. As Consultant, Ms. Leoni designed the organizational structure, formulated a strategic plan, and developed policies, procedures, budgets, etc. **Career Steps:** Co–Owner and Consultant, Corporate Sign, Inc. (1988–Present); Director Medical Records, Truman Medical Center (1984–1986). **Associations & Accomplishments:** National Health Information Management Association; Institute of Management Consultants. **Education:** Mid America Nazarene College, M.B.A. (1996); College of St. Mary's, B.S. in Medical Record Administration. **Personal:** Four children: Joseph, Sean, Blake, and Chad. Ms. Leoni enjoys dance, aerobics, and developing her four children into moral, responsible individuals.

Connie L. Licon
Executive Director
Kankakee County Convention & Visitors Bureau
1711 North State Route 50, Suite #1
Bourbonnais, IL 60914
(815) 935–7390
Fax: (815) 935–5169
EMAIL: See Below

7389

Business Information: Kankakee County Convention & Visitors Bureau solicits meetings, conventions, tours, and leisure travelers to Kankakee County's 980 hotel rooms and 16 festivals, including the nation's largest fishing derby with $315,000 in prizes and the National Boat Races. The Bureau also maintains one of the nation's first tourism education radio stations. As Executive Director, Ms. Licon coordinates all county publications, including the calendar of events and visitors guides. She sits on every major festival committee and assists in the delegation of public festival funds. In addition, she is responsible for public relations and various administrative, marketing, and operational functions. Internet users can reach her via: kccvb@colint.com **Career Steps:** Executive Director, Kankakee County Convention & Visitors Bureau (1994–Present); Director of Sales, Chicago Southland Convention & Visitors Bureau (1989–1994); National Sales Manager, El Paso Convention & Visitors Bureau (1991–1994); Flight Attendant, Continental Airlines (1969–1990). **Associations & Accomplishments:** National Tour Association; Illinois Society of Association Executives; Chicago Society of Association Executives; Society of Government Meeting Planners; Experimental Aviation Association; Kankakee River Valley Chamber of Commerce; Kankakee Historical Society; Bourbonnais/Bradley Chamber of Commerce; St. Anne Business Association; One of 75 Betty Crockers Chosen Nationally. **Education:** University of Texas (1989); Olivet Nazarene University; Kankakee Community College. **Personal:** Married to Arthur in 1985. One child: Jason. Ms. Licon enjoys quilting, baking, gardening, boating, and planning the National Boat Races every Labor Day.

Anna Maria Lobo
President/Director
AM Letras
Rua Oscar Freire 530 Andar 1
Sao Paulo, SP, Brazil 01426–000
55–11–30613004
Fax: 55–11–30611077

7389

Business Information: AM Letras proposes, plans, and carries out cultural, educational, and artistic projects in Brazil. One of the objectives of the Organization is to assist writers to publish art books, transcriptions, and translations of taped lectures, discussions, speeches, and meetings dealing with education, culture, and the arts. As President/Director, Ms. Lobo founded AM Letras in 1994. She handles all operations of the Company, including administration, sales and marketing, finances, and strategic planning. **Career Steps:** President/Director, AM Letras (1994–Present); Member of Council for the Arts, Teatro Municipal (1991–1992); Director of Teatro Municipal and four other city theaters (1979–1980); Associacao Alumni: Cultural Director (1982–1994), Member of Board of Trustees (1971–Present), Founder (1960); Secretary/Companion, Mme. Guiomar Novaes – Brazilian pianist (1953–1956). **Associations & Accomplishments:** Girl Scouts Association of Brazil – Chief Girl Scout for the state of Sao Paulo (1954–1962) Alumni Association – Founder (1961). **Education:** Catholic University, Librarian (1945); Columbia University – New York, Writing I (1952–1953). **Personal:** Ms. Lobo enjoys playing the piano and writing.

Mr. Michael P. Marcus
Chairman of the Board and Chie
Eastern Research Services
130 South State Road
Springfield, PA 19064
(610) 543–0575
Fax: (610) 543–2577

7389

Business Information: Eastern Research Services is a unique business services establishment providing data collection and tabulation for the market research industry. As Chairman of the Board and Chief Financial Officer, Mr. Marcus oversees all executive operations of the firm, as well as administer financial and accounting operations. Established in 1992, Eastern Research Services employs 230 people with annual sales of $3 million. **Career Steps:** Chairman of the Board and Chief Financial Officer, Eastern Research Services, (1992–Present); Company Director, T&N, Inc., Media, PA (1988–1992); Owner, MKB Industries, Connecticut (1980–1988); Executive, Instrial Plastics (1970–1980). **Associations & Accomplishments:** Society of Plastic Engineers; American Marketing Association. **Education:** Manchester University, United Kingdom, B.Sc. (1968). **Personal:** Married to Valerie in 1976. Three children:

Geoffrey, Michelle and Andrew. Mr. Marcus enjoys golf and coaching youth soccer.

Robert T. Marshall Jr.
Director of Sales, Marketing, and Account Services
Inter–Media Marketing
201 Carter Drive
West Chester, PA 19382–4998
(610) 429–5036
Fax: (610) 429–5137

7389

Business Information: Inter–Media Marketing is the 14th largest inbound telemarketing company in the country, employing 1,500 people at eight locations in Pennsylvania and South Carolina. Mr. Marshall has served in various executive positions within Inter–Media since 1991. Promoted to Director of Sales, Marketing, and Account Services in 1995, his current responsibilities include providing support services for clients, interfacing with prospective clients, and diversified administrative activities. Additionally, he supervises a team of five Account Executives in staff training and guideline development. **Career Steps:** Inter–Media Marketing: Director of Sales, Marketing, and Account Services (1995–Present), Senior Account Executive (1993–1995), Account Executive (1991–1993). **Education:** Widener University, A.S. (1980); Certified Radiological Technician (USAF). **Personal:** Mr. Marshall enjoys sports, reading, music, fishing, and spending time with his son.

Peter A. Mayone Sr.
President and Chief Executive Officer
Offi–Serv
P.O. Box 249
Ravena, NY 12143
(518) 756–7777
Fax: (518) 756–7700

7389

Business Information: Offi–Serv, a beverage service supplier, provides business and industrial customers with a full range of beverage and related equipment. Service products include coffee, soft drinks, juices, water coolers, coffee machines, refrigerators and microwave ovens. As President and Chief Executive Officer, Mr. Mayone oversees all of his company's activities. Established in 1984, Offi–Serv employs 25 people. **Career Steps:** President and Chief Executive Officer, Offi–Serv (1984–Present); President and CEO, Juice–Time (1984–Present); President, Capitol & Columbia Vending (1968–Present). **Associations & Accomplishments:** Past Grand Knight, Knights of Columbus; Albany Executive Club; Columbia County's Business Man of the Year (1972). Mr. Mayone gives seminars at local colleges. **Education:** Christian Brothers Academy (1954). **Personal:** Married to Peggy in 1958. Four children: Peter, Mark, Andrea and Julie.

Daniel J. Mcmahon
•••◄━━━◉━━━►•••

Director of Marketing
Network Services Company
1550 Bishop Court
Mount Prospect, IL 60056–6039
(847) 803–4888
Fax: (847) 438–4917

7389

Business Information: Network Services Company is a distribution company. As Director of Marketing, Mr. Mcmahon directs all marketing, business planning, and business development activities. **Career Steps:** Director of Marketing, Network Services Company (1993–Present); Baxtor Healthcare Group: Group Marketing Manager (1989–1993), Senior Product Manager (1984–1989); International Marketing Manager, Travenol International Services (1981–1984). **Education:** Webster University, M.A. (1993); Seattle University, B.A. **Personal:** Married to Marianne C. in 1971. Two children: Bradley and Amy.

Mr. Albert G. McWhorter
Systems Engineer
Mid South Control Systems, Inc.
3950 Pinson Valley Parkway
Birmingham, AL 35217
(205) 854–2902
Fax: (205) 854–9581

7389

Business Information: Mid South Control Systems, Inc. designs, installs and services automated energy management systems for use in commercial buildings, to achieve maximum energy efficiency and cost benefit. In his capacity as Systems Engineer, Mr. McWhorter is responsible for energy analysis of commercial buildings and consulting for changes to building automation systems. Established in 1976, Mid South Control Systems, Inc. employs a technical staff of eight. **Career Steps:** Systems Engineer, Mid South Control Systems, Inc. (1990–Present); Electronic Technician, Alabama Controls (1986–1990); Electronic Technician, Parisian's (1984–1986). **Associations & Accomplishments:** Association of Energy Engineers; Environmental Engineers & Managers Institute. **Education:** R.E.T.S. Electronics, A.A. (1983).

Jack E. Miller Jr.
Operations Manager
GATX Logistics
1312 Russell Cave Road
Lexington, KY 40505
(606) 252–7185
Fax: (606) 252–7438

7389

Business Information: GATX Logistics, a subsidiary of General American Transportation, Inc., specializes in contract logistics, distribution, packaging, transportation management, and return processing of client products. Primary clients include Grolier books and encyclopedias, Readers Digest, Ford, General Motors, Kellogg's, Rand McNally, and EMC Paradiem Shopping. International in scope, the Company has clients in Mexico, Canada, and the United States. Established in 1995, the Lexington division employs 60 people, and has an estimated annual revenue of $1.8 million. As Operations Manager, Mr. Miller manages Grolier's national returns center, and oversees packaging and shipping of Grolier books, Readers Digest Young Family returns, and EMC Shopping. He is also responsible for training coordination, and personnel management. **Career Steps:** Operations Manager, GATX Logistics (1995–Present); Captain, Artillery/Logistics, United States Marine Corps (1982–1995). **Education:** Clemson University, B.S. in Mechanical Engineering Technology (1981). **Personal:** Married to Kimberly in 1981. One child: Jack III. Mr. Miller enjoys weightlifting, spectator sports, racquetball, and various church activities.

Leszek Mokrzycki
Director
Polish National Tourist Office
275 Madison Avenue, Suite 1711
New York, NY 10016–1101
(212) 338–9412
Fax: (212) 338–9283
EMail: See Below

7389

Business Information: Polish National Tourist Office is a national tourist office promoting Poland as a travel destination and building awareness of tourists to the Polish government. Established in 1992, Polish National Tourist Office currently employs six people. As Director, Mr. Mokrzycki is responsible for planning and developing market strategies, managing personnel, and budgeting. He can be reached through the Internet via: LESMOK@aol.com **Career Steps:** Director, Polish National Tourist Office (1992–Present); Marketing Director, American Travel Abroad (1991–1992); Office Manager, Polish–American Resources Corporation (1990–1991); Account Coordinator, Sabena World Airlines (1988–1990). **Associations & Accomplishments:** ASTA; USTOA; ETC; American Management Association (AMA); Recipient, Europe Person of the Year (1994), Awarded by the Travel Agent Magazine. **Education:** Warsaw School of Economics, M.Sc. 91976). **Personal:** Married to Emilia in 1979. Two children: Joanna and Michal. Mr. Mokrzycki enjoys IBM–PC's, photography, jogging, and tennis.

Anita R. Neidert
Director of Training Program Development
ERM–SE (Georgia Pacific)
300 Chastain Center Boulevard, Suite 075
Kennesaw, GA 30144–5557
(770) 590–8383
Fax: (770) 590–9164

7389

Business Information: ERM–SE (Georgia Pacific) is an environmental consulting firm working primarily for worldwide industrial clients. As Director of Training Program Development, Mrs. Neidert develops management systems and training programs in environmental health and safety. Concurrently, she holds various supervisory training positions with several different companies, including: Project Training Director at Milliken & Company, and Principal of SCMG. **Career Steps:** Director of Training Program Development, ERM–SE (Georgia Pacific) (1993–Present); Project Training Director, Milliken & Company (1992–Present); Principal, SCMG (1995–Present). **Associations & Accomplishments:** American Society for Quality Control; N.A.I.H.; Atlanta Chamber of Commerce; Environmental Chair, Parent Teacher Association; N.E.T.A. **Education:** University of Cincinnati, M.S. (1978); Phil Crosby's Quality College. **Personal:** Married to Jerry in 1983. One child: Drew. Mrs. Neidert enjoys collecting antique American art pottery.

David J. Oliphant, CMP
Director of Sales
GES Exposition Services
8430 Terminal Road
Lorton, VA 22079
(703) 550–6211
Fax: (703) 550–5582

7389

Business Information: GES Exposition Services — a Dial Corp. company, which is a Fortune 500 company — is a trade show general service contractor, providing the set up of exhibits and trade shows – with 35 offices nation wide. Mr. Oliphant's region is Baltimore, Washington, D.C., and Philadelphia. GES was established in 1969 and has over 1600 employees nationwide. As Director of Sales, Mr. Oliphant is responsible for the oversight, direction, and facilitation of the sales and marketing program. **Career Steps:** GES Exposition Services: Director of Sales (1994–Present), Sales Executive (1991–1993); Account Executive, United Exposition Services (1991–1993); Convention Service Manager, Hyatt Hotels (1990–1991); Trans World Airlines (1985–1989). **Associations & Accomplishments:** International Association of Exposition Management (IAEM); Greater Washington Society of Association Executives (GWSAE); Professional Convention Management Association (PCMA). **Education:** University of Nevada – Reno, majored in elementary education; Certified Meeting Professional (CMP). **Personal:** Mr. Oliphant enjoys outdoor sports, water, travel, and public speaking.

Mr. David Pompis
•••◄━━━◉━━━►•••

President
Clothing Correctables Inc.
9103 NW 105th Circle
Miami, FL 33178–1306
(305) 887–9904
Fax: (305) 887–9291

7389

Business Information: Clothing Correctables Inc. specializes in the repair of imported apparel items for most major chain operations, including such well–known chains as Wal–Mart, L.L. Bean, Levis, Sears, J. Crew, Gap and others. It is not uncommon that when clothing items are imported from around the world, they are damaged, mislabeled or packed incorrectly. The purpose of Clothing Correctables is to prepare the items to store quality. One of only three companies like this in the world and the largest of the three, Clothing Correctables Inc. was established in 1993 and currently has 300 employs. The Company reports an estimated annual revenue of $38 million. As President, Mr. Pompis is responsible for all aspects of daily operations, including finance. **Career Steps:** President, Clothing Correctables Inc. (1993–Present); Chief Executive Officer, Global Group International (1984–1982); President, California Women's Wear (1973–1984). **Associations & Accomplishments:** Beacon Council of Dade County; International Imports Association; Manufacturers Association of Canada; Outstanding Development of Imported Mens Apparel, Sears, (1985–1986); Outstanding Vendor, Hudson Bay Company (1983–1988); Published featured articles in Miami Herald and Montreal Gazette; Frequent lecturer for Merrill Lynch on garmet importation. **Education:** B. Com. (1973) **Personal:** Married to Sheree in 1973. Three children: Nolan, Layne and Ilana. Mr. Pompis enjoys development of countries for import. Mr. Pompis has traveled to 52 countries teaching new production methods.

Bette Price
President and Owner
The Price Group
4114 Leadville Place
Dallas, TX 75244–3107
(214) 404–0787
Fax: (214) 980–2302

7389

Business Information: Established in 1982, The Price Group is a Professional Speaking, Training and Consulting firm based in Dallas, Texas. As President and Owner, Ms. Price offers communication and marketing–based programs to teach intrapersonal skills. She is responsible for all aspects of the business. She speaks internationally for corporations and associations, as well as providing one–on–one executive coaching. **Career Steps:** President and Owner, The Price Group (1982–Present); Society Editor, The Kansas City Star (1979–1982); Public Relations Manager, Kansas City Visitors Bureau. **Associations & Accomplishments:** National Speakers Association; National Association of Women Business Owners; North Texas Speakers Association; National Association of Female Executives. **Education:** Attended: Hunter College. **Personal:** Married to John W. in 1980. Miss Price enjoys writing.

Ms. Susan K. Pye

President
Access/Ability Inc.
8000 East Prentice Avenue, Suite C4
Englewood, CO 80111–2727
(303) 220–8350
Fax: (303) 741–6483

7389

Business Information: Access/Ability Inc. specializes in customized software training by developing curriculum around corporate structure. Established in 1990, Access/Ability currently employs 17 people. As President, Ms. Pye is responsible for all aspects of operations, particularly focusing with sotware training, courseware development, skills assessment, post performance and the evaluation of trainers and students. **Career Steps:** President, Access/Ability Inc. (1990–Present); Technical Specialist, Computer Training Concepts (1988–1990); Technical Support, Molina and Associates (1986–1988). **Associations & Accomplishments:** Volunteers of Outdoor Colorado; Writes all documentations for clients. **Education:** Glen Ellyn Community College (1981); P.S. School; Business School (1972). **Personal:** Married to Randolph E. in 1979. One child: Heather D. Ms. Pye enjoys biking and reading.

Ms. Ann C. Rhea

Owner
Design Criteria Group
P.O. Box 60841
Phoenix, AZ 85082
(602) 945–0526
Fax: Please mail or call

7389

Business Information: Established in 1983, Design Criteria Group specializes in hotel interior design. As Owner, Ms. Rhea's primary duties involve the preparation of space plans for hotels, motels, healthcare and other offices; the preparation of budgets, presentations, design concepts and specifications for clients; the supervision of installations; the preparation of written specifications; marketing and extensive consulting. Some of Ms. Rhea's major projects include Embassy Suites, Ramada Hotels and Quality Inns. A free–lance artist, she also exhibits and sells her work through Design Criteria. **Career Steps:** Owner, Design Criteria Group (1983–Present); Associate, Hauser Design, Scottsdale, AZ (1980–1982); Interior Designer, Ramada Inns Inc. (1972–1978); Interior Designer, Holiday Inn, Inc. (1970–1972). **Associations & Accomplishments:** Arizona Hotel/Motel Association Service Award (1990); Outstanding Substitute Teacher, Fowler School District (1988); Who's Who of American Women; Who's Who of Emerging Leaders in America; Who's Who in the West; Ladies of Auxilliary Scholarship, Memphis College of Arts (1964–1967); National Association of Interior Design Qualifications. **Education:** Memphis College of Arts, B.F.A. (1967); University of Mississippi, B.A. (1962); Scottsdale and Gateway Community Colleges. **Personal:** Ms. Rhea enjoys Anthropology and Archeology studies, and handicraft work.

Jamie G. Rice

Director of Tourism Sales
Greater Rochester Visitors Association
126 Andrews Street
Rochester, NY 14604
(716) 262–4241
Fax: (716) 232–4822

7389

Business Information: Greater Rochester Visitors Association is the official convention and tourist promotion agency for Rochester, New York and surrounding areas. Established in 1932, the Association employs 31 people, and has an estimated annual revenue of $2 million. As Director of Tourism Sales, Ms. Rice is responsible for direct sales to tour operators, bus companies, travel trade counselors, etc., resulting in increased leisure business for the area. During her eight years with the Association, she has been instrumental in increasing tourism in the area, assisting in bringing the Empire State Games to Rochester in 1993, and is currently working on details for their return in 1998. **Career Steps:** Greater Rochester Visitors Association: Director of Tourism Sales (1994–Present), Senior Sales Manager/Convention Sales Manager (1988–1994), Public Relations Director, Casa Larga Vineyards (1986–1988). **Associations & Accomplishments:** Local Organizing Committee, Empire State Games; Executive Committee/Marketing Chair, Celebration of Women's Sufferage National Tour Association; International Association of Convention and Visitors Bureaus; American Business Association; Ontario Motorcoach Association. **Education:** Miami University, B.S. in Marketing (1982). **Personal:** Ms. Rice enjoys skiing, playing tennis, and travel.

Dale S. Robbins Sr.

Vice President of Southeastern Region
Southex Exhibition, Inc.
6915 Red Road, Suite 228
Coral Gables, FL 33143
(305) 666–5944
Fax: Please mail or call

7389

Business Information: Southex Exhibition, Inc. is a producer of trade and consumer shows. Established in 1967, Southex Exhibition, Inc. currently employs 20 people. As Vice President, Southeastern Region, Mr. Robbins is responsible for the supervision of all aspects of management functions at ten shows in the Southeastern Region. **Career Steps:** Vice President, Southeastern Region, Southex Exhibition, Inc. (1994–Present); Regional Manager, Miami International Boat Show (1991–1994); Show Manager, Tampa International Boat Show (1981–1991); Co–op Advertising Director, Tampa Tribune (1980–1981). **Associations & Accomplishments:** President, Kendall/South Miami Division of the American Heart Association (1994–Present); Tourist and Convention Center Expansion Authority (1992–Present); Trustee Member, Greater Miami Chamber of Commerce (1992–Present); Past President, Marine Industries Association (1989–1991); Bishop, Church of Jesus Christ of Latter Day Saints (1993–1995); Boy Scouts; Public speaking. **Education:** Catauba College, Salisbury, NC (1976). **Personal:** Married to Teresa (Terri) in 1977. Five children: Dale Jr., Christina, Nikki, Billy, and Mandi. Mr. Robbins enjoys running, fiction writing, and swimming.

Christopher J. Roberts

Production Manager
Isomedix Operations Inc.
23 Elizabeth Drive
Chester, NY 10918–1367
(914) 469–4087
Fax: (914) 469–7512

7389

Business Information: Isomedix Operations Inc.is the industry Leader in contract sterilization, providing both gamma irradiation and ethylene oxide sterilization services to the healthcare and consumer goods industries. Isomelix operates a network of eleven irradiation facilities in the United States and Canada, including three combined irradiation/ethylene oxide facilities. As Production Manager, Mr. Roberts is responsible for the oversight of warehouse personnel, administration, entry level supervision and issues related to production scheduling, processing specifications, and shipment of new products. **Career Steps:** Production Manager, Isomedix Operations Inc. (1993–Present); Assistant Store Manager, Foot Locker (1992–1993). **Associations & Accomplishments:** APICS; Orange County Business and Industry Network; Job Servicer Employee Committee. **Education:** Canisius College, B.S. in Management (1992); Marist College, M.B.A. in progress. **Personal:** Mr. Roberts enjoys skiing, hunting, and golf.

Gil E. Rosado Ortiz

Controller and Accounting Manager
Teddy Diaz Fastening Systems
P.O. Box 10953
San Juan, Puerto Rico 00922–0953
(809) 781–9889
Fax: Please mail or call

7389

Business Information: Teddy Diaz Fastening Systems is a wholesaler, retailer and manufacturer's representative for heavy duty power tools and construction materials. Established in 1989, Teddy Diaz Fastening Systems currently employs 20 people and has an estimated annual revenue of $2.5 million. As Controller and Accounting Manager, Mr. Rosado Ortiz is responsible for all aspects of the accounting department, computer systems implementation, and general accounting procedures, as well as training. **Career Steps:** Controller and Accounting Manager, Teddy Diaz Fastening Systems (1992–Present); General Accountant, Alfa & Omega, S.E. (1990–1992). **Associations & Accomplishments:** Fi Sigma Alfa Fraternity. **Education:** University of Puerto Rico – Rio Piedras, B.B.A. (1990); Colegio San Ignacio de Loyola – Rio Piedras. **Personal:** Married to Gisela Feliciano in 1993. Mr. Rosado Ortiz enjoys music, tennis, outdoor activities, and sporting events.

Kevin P. Rupkey

President
Warrantech Consumer Product Services, Inc.
300 Atlantic Street
Stamford, CT 06901–3522
(203) 975–1100
Fax: (203) 356–7676

7389

Business Information: Warrantech is a consumer product service company providing extensive warranties to consumers on home appliances, consumer electronics, computers and home office equipment. Other services include database marketing, private label direct mail campaigns, telemarketing and retail sales training and motivation. Major corporate clientele include Comp USA, TOPS, and Macy's. Established in 1981, Warrantech currently employs 300 people and has an estimated annual revenue of $100 million. As President, Mr. Rupkey is responsible for all aspects of operations, particularly focusing on overall Corporate strategies, new product and venture growth development. Since his appointment as President in 1994, Warrantech's revenues have increased from $21MM to over $55MM. **Career Steps:** President, Warrantech (1994–Present); General Electric Company: Manager, Consumer Service Marketing (1990–1994), District Sales Manager (1980–1990). **Associations & Accomplishments:** Phi Kappa Sigma Fraternity; Local Church. **Education:** Adrian College, B.A. in Marketing (1980); Xavier University, Graduate Studies. **Personal:** Married to Pamela in 1982. Two children: Autumn and Colton.

Timescape™

Diana P. Russell

Executive Vice President
Timescape, Inc.
5 Swallow Wood
Sandy, UT 84092
(888) 837–2273 (TIMESCAPE)
Fax: (801) 576–1473

7389

Business Information: Timescape, Inc. provides an electronic time management database for clients. The Service provides reminder calls utilizing modern technology with beepers, E–Mail, and telephones to remind salespeople and insurance companies about appointments, contacts, etc. As Executive Vice President, Ms. Russell is responsible for the administrative duties of the Company. Other responsibilities include customer service, verification of contracts, product/service security, and public relations. **Career Steps:** Associate Broker, Drobe Realtor (1995–Present); Principal Broker, Rocky Mountain Construction and Real Estate (1993–1995). **Associations & Accomplishments:** Utah Heritage Foundation; American Association of Retired Persons. **Personal:** Married to Paul in 1984. Six children: Tracy, Lisa, Kris, Tonna, Robert, and Noel. Ms. Russell enjoys camping and backpacking.

Sasha

President/Chief Executive Officer
Savebone Music, Inc.
130 West 42nd Street, Suite 952
New York, NY 10036
(212) 997–0206
Fax: (212) 997–0481
EMAIL: See Below

7389

Business Information: Savebone Music, Inc. is a full service recording studio, video production, graphic design, and record label production facility. As President/Chief Executive Officer, Sasha is the in house producer, arranger, organizer of backup musicians, and designer of videos and graphics. He is also responsible for the day–to–day operations of the studio and record label. These duties include payment of ASCAP royalties, marketing of services, sales of products, public relations, personnel concerns, and planning to become an established household recording label. Internet users can reach him via: Sgracanin@aol.com. **Career Steps:** President/Chief Executive Officer, Savebone Music, Inc. (1994–Present); President,

Gracanin Records, Vienna (1989–1994). **Associations & Accomplishments:** Sasha Gracanin Music; Audio Engineering Society; N.A.R.A.S.; Gracanin Sounds, Limited. **Education:** Vienna Technical University, Audio Engineer (1988). **Personal:** Sasha enjoys motion pictures, computers, and videos.

Bert Schlegel
Vice President
Strategic Telecom Systems
PO Box 10165
Knoxville, IN 37939–0165
(423) 584–4460
Fax: (423) 584–7366

7389

Business Information: Strategic Telecom Systems, a wholly-owned subsidiary of Personal Choice Network — one of the nation's leading marketing agencies — serves as the marketing arm for telecommunication pre–paid calling cards utilized for long distance calling. Joining the parent company in 1992, as Vice President Mr. Schlegel oversees all day–to–day operations, as well as supervision and direction with key management staff for the telecommunications arm. He also serves on the Board of Directors with the parent company, providing strategies and overall development planning for the Company as a whole. **Career Steps:** Vice President, Personal Choice Network (Strategic Telecom Systems) (1992–Present); National Marketing Director, National Safety Associates (1989–1992); Crew Foreman, Crow Wing Power & Light Company (1975–1989). **Associations & Accomplishments:** Rough Grouse Society. **Personal:** Married to Celina Schlegel in 1991. Three children: Heidi, Totti and Megan. Mr. Schlegel enjoys reading and travel.

Stephen Schweitzer
• • • ━━◆◎◆━━ • • •

Chief Executive Officer
Apex Environmental Resources
700 West Pete Rose Way
Cincinnati, OH 45203–1892
(513) 241–9050
Fax: (513) 241–7525

7389

Business Information: Apex Environmental Resources is a general contractor, providing environmental contracting services (primarily to government and waste water treatment facilities) and general contracting services (primarily to government facilities). Covering a three–state area (Ohio, Kentucky, Indiana), Apex Environmental also contracts with schools and conducts architectural and engineering services. Joining Apex Environmental Resources as Chief Executive Officer in 1988, Mr. Schweitzer is responsible for all aspects of operations, including adminstrative and technical activities. **Career Steps:** Chief Executive Officer, Apex Environmental Resources (1988–Present); Vice President of Construction, A.D.S. (1986–1988); Project Manager, Schweitzer Construction (1984–1986); Project Manager, I.D.S. (1983–1984). **Education:** University of Cincinnati, B.A. in Architecture (1984). **Personal:** Married to Meg in 1986. Two children: Michaela and Adam.

Mr. Christopher J. Seal
Director of Strategic Customer Services
Moore Corporation
Three Hawthorne Parkway, Suite 350
Vernon Hills, IL 60061
(708) 367–3083
Fax: (708) 367–3661

7389

Business Information: Moore Corporation is an information handling solutions company, inclusive of print management and related products and services. Established in 1882, the Moore Corporation currently employs 20,000 people in 59 countries and has annual revenues of $2.4 billion. As Director of Strategic Customer Services, Mr. Seal oversees the Print Management Services organization for the U.S., Midwest Region providing consultative services around clients' print–related management needs. **Career Steps:** Moore Corporation: Director of Strategic Customer Services (1994–Present), Client Services Consultant (1992–1993), Account Representative (1990–1991), Sales Representative (1988–1989). **Associations & Accomplishments:** American Production and Inventory Control Society. **Education:** Illinois State University: M.B.A. (1987), B.S. in Marketing. **Personal:** Married to Denise M. in 1991. Mr. Seal enjoys reading and golf.

Scott B. Seaton
President
Scott Enterprises, Inc.
10547 Bondesson Circle
Omaha, NE 68122–9703
(402) 571–5115
Fax: (402) 571–1742

7389

Business Information: Scott Enterprises, Inc. is a general contractor providing commercial roofing for industrial industries. As President, Mr. Seaton is responsible for all commercial roofing operations and construction activities. **Career Steps:** President, Scott Enterprises, Inc. (1982–Present). **Education:** U.N.D., B.S. (1985). **Personal:** Married to Anne in 1988. Three children: Cody, Alexandra, and Max.

Earl W. Seitz
Marketing Consultant
E & T Innovations
120 Fair Haven Road
Fair Haven, NJ 07704
(908) 530–5424
Fax: (908) 530–5547

7389

Business Information: E & T Innovations, established in 1984, is an international design and marketing company for commercial and interior design companies on an account basis with U.S., Canada, and Mexico. As Marketing Consultant, Mr. Seitz is responsible for providing marketing consultations and marketing consumer appliances. Concurrent with his consulting position, he serves as Vice President and Director of Rahway Savings Institution (RSI). **Career Steps:** Marketing Consultant, E & T Innovations (1984–Present); Vice President and Director, Rahway Savings Institution (Present); Chairman and President, Regina Corp.– Rahway, NJ (1961–1984); Administrator of Marketing, York Corporation, York, PA (1954–1961). **Associations & Accomplishments:** Women's Center of Monmoth County; Director, Human Immunology Foundaiton; Director, Healthshares Corp., Rahway, NJ; Director, Palm Beach White House Association. **Education:** Harvard Business School, MBA (1968); Pennsylvania State University, Industrial Engineering. **Personal:** Married to Theresa I. in 1981. One child: Deborah Risuk.

Terri A. Senecal
President
Rosebudd & Associates
28935 Flanders Drive
Warren, MI 48903
(810) 771–8145
Fax: (810) 771–8145

7389

Business Information: Rosebudd & Associates promotes recording artists to the music industry. Rosebudd & Associates is a partner to Rosebudd Records, a producer of compact discs and cassettes for various artists. As President, Ms. Senecal is responsible for all aspects of Company operations and administrative activities for both Rosebudd & Associates and Rosebudd Records. In addition to her duties as President, she is the Human Resources Administrator for Pitney Bowes, an outsourcing company for mailing, copying, and office services. **Career Steps:** Human Resources Administration, Pitney Bowes (1993–Present); President, Rosebudd & Associates (1990–Present); Network 1 USA Account Clerk, Network 1 USA (1989–1990). **Associations & Accomplishments:** Songwriters Guild (1992); Metro Detroit Songwrtier Association; Society of Human Resource Mangement. **Education:** Michigan University: A.B. in Creative Writing, B.A. in Music Business. **Personal:** Ms. Senecal enjoys promoting, recording, and performing music.

Frederick G. Simpson
Senior Executive
Fred Simpson & Associates
3 Stony Brook Road
Medfield, MA 02052
(508) 359–5956
Fax: (508) 359–4141

7389

Business Information: Fred Simpson & Associates is an independent distributorship, which recruits and trains others to market products of their own selection. As Senior Executive, Mr. Simpson is responsible for recruiting internationally for Quorum International, Ltd., as well as coordinating marketing. **Career Steps:** Senior Executive, Fred Simpson & Associates (1991–Present); Real Estate Broker, Jack Conway Realtor (1987–1991); Recruiting and Placement Consultant, Robert J. Grace Associates & Independent (1977–1987); Registered Professional Engineer, The General Electric Company (1959–1970). **Associations & Accomplishments:** President and Board of Directors, Westwood Lions; Ambassador

---

and Membership Committee, Neponset Valley Chamber of Commerce; Class and Decade Chair, Northfield Mount Hermon School. **Education:** Tufts University, C.A.G.S. in Math and Science Education (1971); Northeastern University, Thermodynamics and Heat Transfer (1968); Columbia Engineering School, B.S. in Mechanical Engineering (1959); Sales Training Institute of Boston, Honor Graduate (1969). **Personal:** Married to Carol E. in 1969. Mr. Simpson enjoys cross–country skiing, tennis, swimming, travel, the Arts, and theatre.

Can (Jon) Sonat
Co-Founder
CENTER Foreign Trade
403 Circular Drive, #35
Florence, AL 35632–0001
(205) 760–4248
Fax: (205) 767–6066

7389

Business Information: CENTER Foreign Trade, a family–owned company, is the sole distributor of Nautilus and Trotter brand conditioning equipment in Turkey. Co–founding CENTER Foreign Trade in 1992, Mr. Sonat oversees the operations of the Company, as well as serving as the co–owner of two other businesses: Interyapi, Ltd. – an industrial floors and light construction company, and Intermark, Ltd. – a light contruction machinery sales and service company. **Career Steps:** Co–Founder, CENTER Foreign Trade (1992–Present); Marketing Manager, Hurriyet International Trade (1993–1995); Co–Owner, Intermark Ltd. (1990–Present); Co–Owner, Interyapi, Ltd. (1993–Present). **Associations & Accomplishments:** Professional Basketball Player, Turkish First Division (1982–1992); Basketball Player, Turkish Olympic Team (50 games); Basketball Critic, "Spor Gazetesi," Istanbul (1993–1994); Speaks fluent Japanese and English. **Education:** University of North Alabama, M.B.A., in progress; University of North Dakota, B.A. in Economics (1981). **Personal:** Married to Suna Akgul in 1986. One child: Tunahan. Mr. Sonat enjoys sports, history, music, travel, and languages.

Thomas J. Stanley
President
Summit Settlement Services
P.O. Box 7626, 8152 Whitestone Dr.
Huntington Beach, CA 92615–7626
(800) 795–1690
Fax: (714) 374–0007

7389

Business Information: Summit Settlement Services, #2 in the U.S., is a structured settlement consulting firm, providing services to customers nationally in 30 major cities. Established in 1993, Summit Settlement Services has grown to over 45 people strong. As President of California operations, Mr. Stanley is responsible for providing Structured Settlement services to Casualty insurers, public entities and self–insured corporations. **Career Steps:** President, Summit Settlement Services, California (1992–Present); Structured Settlement Consultant, Kidder, Peabody & Co., Minnesota/California (brokerage) (1987–1992); Director of Insurance Products, Engler, Budd, Inc. (brokerage) (1985–1987). **Associations & Accomplishments:** National Structured Settlement Trade Association; National Association of Security Dealers, Registered Principal. **Education:** University of Phoenix, M.B.A. (1996); University of Notre Dame, Certified Structural Settlement Consultant (1994); University of Minnesota, B.S.B. (1985). **Personal:** Mr. Stanley enjoys golf, reading, aerobics, racquetball, and being a native Minnesotan.

Betsy Steiner
Owner
Dressage Classic International
2764 Borchard Road
Newbury Park, CA 91320–3865
(310) 589–2722
Fax: (805) 499–8237

7389

Business Information: Dressage Classic International is an equestrian training academy, providing international and olympic level training of both horses and riders in the sport of dressage. A World Champion and International Dressage U.S. Team member, Betsy Steiner founded the organization in

June of 1995. She provides all training, particularly focusing on the training of horses, as well as administrative roles and the supervision of employees. **Career Steps:** Owner, Dressage Classic International (1995–Present); Director of Dressage Operations, Sandstone (1993–1995); Vice President, Steiner Dressage, Ltd. (1989–1993); Assistant Trainer/International Competitor, Friendship Farms (1971–1989). **Associations & Accomplishments:** Equestrian Representative, U.S. Olympic Committee Athletes Advisory Council ; Board of Directors, U.S. Equestrian Team; American Horse Shows Association; Chairperson, Active Riders Committee; West Coast Representative, U.S. Equestrian Team; Commentator for the Dressage World Cup (1995); Beginning production on training videos. **Education:** Reitinstitut von Neindorff, Germany (1970); Kirkland High School, Diploma (1969) . **Personal:** Two children: Jessie and Devon. Ms. Steiner enjoys theatre, music, Thai Chi, working out, reading, is writing a book on dressage training, and recently completed a dressage promo video.

Christopher R. Sturm

President

Sturm & Associates

913 Vanderbuilt Lane
Kenner, LA 70065
(504) 593–1054
Fax: Please mail or call

7389

Business Information: Sturm & Associates is an interactive distributor of products affiliated with Amway. A Distributor since 1987, Mr. Sturm is the President of his Company. As such, he is responsible for all aspects of operations. Becoming an Independent Distributor has made him financially free and provided more time to spend at home. Concurrent to his distribution business, Mr. Sturm is also a Pilot with U.S. Air, Inc. **Career Steps:** President, Sturm & Associates (1987–Present); Pilot, U.S. Air, Inc. (1986–Present); Pilot, Royale Airlines (1983–1986); Chief Pilot, Weaks Supply Company (1981–1983). **Associations & Accomplishments:** Westwood Homeowners Association; St. Charles Community Church; Airline Pilots Association; Christian Businessmens Association; National Republican Senatorial Committee; The Heritage Foundation. **Education:** Louisiana Technical University, B.S. (1981). **Personal:** Married to Yvonne Marie in 1988. One child: Matthew Pierre. Mr. Sturm enjoys flying, hunting, reading and travel.

Yvonne Sturrock

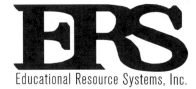

President

Unified Staffing & Associates

1776 Woodstead Court, Suite 210
The Woodlands, TX 77380–1450
(713) 363–2445
Fax: (713) 363–4506

7389

Business Information: Unified Staffing & Associates (USA), a staff leasing firm, standing out from the rest by offering personalized administrative tasks, enabling employers to select from a variety of services to suit their needs. Services include payroll, Worker's Compensation, government compliance, and W–2 forms. Established in 1994, Unified Staffing & Associates reports annual revenue of $30 million and currently employing over 2,000 people. Founding the Company in 1994, Ms. Sturrock oversees all administrative areas, as well as being responsible for all aspects of operations. **Career Steps:** President, Unified Staffing & Associates (1994–Present); Manager, CCSI (1991–1994). **Associations & Accomplishments:** Treasurer, Lions Club International – Houston Area. **Education:** Tyler Junior College (1982). **Personal:** Married to Kent in 1984. Two children: Drew and Trevor. Ms. Sturrock enjoys antique shopping.

Raymond Swinson Jr.

Director of Personnel/Human Resources

Triple P Services, Inc.

P.O. Box 151
Mt. Olive, NC 28365
(919) 658–5204
Fax: (919) 658–2402

7389

Business Information: Triple P Services, Inc. is a service contract management company which contracts on federal installations for janitorial, food service, armed guard protection, and facility maintenance. The Firm also markets its services to state and local government agencies and to commercial and private institutions. As Director of Personnel/Human Resources, Mr. Swinson is responsible for all personnel and human resource operations of the Company. He also handles labor management relations and employee benefits. Mr. Swinson is a retired US Air Force Lt. Colonel whose military career led to significant highlights. For instance, while assigned with Headquarters 21st Air Force in New Jersey, he was a member of the Command and Control element which managed the recovery and funeral airlift to the USA of the victims of the Jones Town tragedy. Years later, he was posted for duty to a Department of Defense Logistics Center in Philadelphia, PA. Here, he led a team of supply inventory management specialists providing crucial direct support to US military forces involved in hostilities in Panama and the Persian Gulf. Among other assignments, he has served in Vietnam (twice), Korea and Germany. He is the recipient of numerous military decorations and awards. **Career Steps:** Director of Personnel/Human Resources, Triple P Services, Inc. (1993–Present); U.S. Air Force: Deputy Commander of Logistics, Chanute AFB, IL (1991–1992); Chief, Item Management Division II, Defense Logistics Agency, Philadelphia (1988–1991); Chief of Supply and Commander, 410 Supply Squadron, K. I. Sawyer AFB, MI (1985–1988); Various assignments and localities (1968–1985). **Associations & Accomplishments:** American Legion; Forty and Eight; Wayne County Personnel Association; Commissioner, Goldsboro Recreation and Parks Commission. US Air Force, retired; Vietnam War Veteran. Former Second Vice President, Kiwanis (Gwinn, MI). **Education:** North Carolina A&T State University, B.S. (1968); Commission – Air Force ROTC; Northern Michigan University, Various Courses (1988–1989). **Personal:** Mr. Swinson enjoys automobiles, music, and model airplanes. Currently resides in Goldsboro North Carolina.

Kathy L. TeBrink

Vice President

TeBrink & Associates, Inc.

213 Country Hollow Court
St. Charles, MO 63304–4528
(314) 939–6901
Fax: (314) 447–0220

7389

Business Information: TeBrink & Associates, Inc. is a developer of promotional and incentive programs for corporations. The Company supplies the products (headwear, t–shirts, sweatshirts, jackets, etc.) with Corporate logos and also correlates incentive programs. Co–founding the Company with her husband Todd in 1993, Kathy TeBrink serves as Vice President, overseeing all operations. Her responsibilities include calling on a wide–range of clientele and developing a full–line of promotional goods for their Company. **Career Steps:** Vice President, TeBrink & Associates, Inc. (1993–Present); Sales Associate, Legend Marketing, Inc. (1990–1992). **Associations & Accomplishments:** National Association for Female Executives. **Education:** Northwestern College, B.A. in Business Administration and Marketing (1990). **Personal:** Married to Todd in 1987. Two children: Tyler and Kelsey. Mrs. TeBrink enjoys music, interior decorating, and snow sports activities.

ERS
Educational Resource Systems, Inc.

Gregg J. Terry

President

Educational Resource Systems, Inc.

34 Sycamore Avenue
Little Silver, NJ 07739
(908) 842–0202
Fax: (908) 842–1707

7389

Business Information: Educational Resource Systems, Inc. specializes in medical communications and pharmaceutical sales training; producing literature, software, and videos for some of the largest pharmaceutical companies in the world. Mr. Terry established ERS in 1993, providing strategic leadership to new business development, new product development, and client relations. **Career Steps:** President, Educational Resource Systems, Inc. (1993–Present); Executive Director of Sales and Marketing, Reed Elsevier Medical Group (1990–1993); Director of Visual Communications, Ortho Pharmaceutical Corporation (1982–1990). **Associations & Accomplishments:** Healthcare Marketing & Communications Council, Inc. (formerly, Healthcare Marketing and Communications Council, Inc. International Television Association. First place award for Video Production in Tri-State United Way Communications Contest. Featured in Journal Article "Procreation". Audio Visual Communications, June, 1988. **Education:** Seton Hall University, B.A. in Communications/Marketing, Dean's List. **Personal:** Married to Debra J. in 1986. Two children: Ryan and Justin. Mr. Terry enjoys sport fishing and surfing on the East Coast.

Mary C. Thompson–Furr

Trade Show Director

Miller Freeman, Inc./Interbike

310 Broadway
Laguna Beach, CA 92651
(714) 376–6161
Fax: (714) 497–3932
EMail: See Below

7389

Business Information: Miller Freeman, Inc./Interbike produces the world's largest exclusive bicycle trade show each fall in Anaheim, California, as well as a successful annual East Coast regional bicycle show in Philadelphia. As Trade Show Director, Ms. Thompson–Furr has been instrumental in the growth of Interbike over the past eleven years, experiencing its rgrowth from a small preseason show to the current status of a "top 200 trade show." Ms. Thompson–Furr has been involved in all facets of show production, including exhibit sales and floorplan management, promotions, direct mail campaigns, registration, housing, events, contractors, bureau and center relations, site selection, future dates and overall operations and budget responsibility. Internet users can reach her via: mthompson@mfi.com. **Career Steps:** Trade Show Director, Miller Freeman, Inc./Interbike (1985–Present); Tradeshow Coordinator, motorcycle, bicycle, and spa trade and consumer shows, Hester Communications (1981–84); Advertising & Special Projects Coordinator, Subaru of Co. California Distributor (1979–1981). **Associations & Accomplishments:** International Association of Exposition Managers. **Education:** University of Montana, B.A. in English/Education (1979). **Personal:** Ms. Thompson–Furr enjoys singing, piano, writing, swimming, and skiing.

David H. Tikkala

Director of Finance

International Foundation for Election Systems

1101 15th Street Northwest, Suite 3
Washington, DC 20005–5002
(202) 828–8507
Fax: (202) 452–0804

7389

Business Information: International Foundation for Election Systems is a provider of election–related services to emerging and established democracies; providing observation, technical assistance, procurement, information and education, as well as encouraging voter participation. Established in 1987, the Foundation currently employs 90 people and has an operational budget of $13 million. As Director of Finance, Mr. Tikkala is responsible for all aspects of financial operations. **Career Steps:** Director of Finance, International Foundation for Election Systems (1991–Present); Director of Internal Audit, GRC International, Inc. (1990–1991); Senior Audit Manager, KPMG Peat Marwick (1981–1990). **Associations & Accomplishments:** American Institute of Certified Public Accountants; Virginia Society of Certified Public Accountants. **Education:** College of William and Mary, B.B.A. (1980). **Personal:** Married to Patricia in 1995. Mr. Tikkala enjoys biking, birding, and the outdoors.

Hector Toledo

Director Regional para Latinoamerica

AMP/GISB

Prol. Paseo de la Reforma No. 61–3A
Torre Axis, Col. Lomas de Sant, Mexico D.F 01210
(525) 258–5522
Fax: (525) 258–5520

7389

Business Information: AMP specializes in the manufacturing of connectivity products and solutions, in addition to having nearly a 20% market share in this $25 billion market. Headquartered in Harrisburg, Pennsylvania, AMP employs 41,000 in 212 facilities, with subsidiaries in 40 countries. **Career Steps:** Regional Director for Latin America, AMP/GISB (1996–Present); Managing Director, Black Box (1994–1996); Vice President of Sales, Northern Telecom (1990–1994); Vice President of Sales, E.D.S. (1986–1990); President, Hawker Siddeley (1982–1986). **Associations & Accomplishments:** President, Asociacion Mexicana de Telematica (AMEXTEL); Co–Founder, Mexican Intelligent Building Institute; Highlander Club. **Education:** IPADE, AD–2 (1996); University of California, Los Angeles: M.B.A. (1976), Engineering B.S.C.H. (1971). **Personal:** Married to Aurora Sobrevilla in 1974. One child: Ursula. Mr. Toledo enjoys being an opera singer promoter.

Mr. Eric A. Triplett

Owner and Chairman of the Board
The Ritz Carlton Hotel
300 Town Center Drive
Dearborn, MI 48126
(313) 441–2000
Fax: (313) 441–2051
7389

Business Information: The Ritz Carlton Hotel is a promotional company, planning events, parties, fashion shows, and providing fashion coordinating services for magazines, television shows, celebrities, seasonal and travel promotions, catalog businesses, and major department stores. In his capacity as Owner and Chairman of the Board, Mr. Triplett handles all aspects of business operations as well as being the creative force behind the business, developing motion pictures and soap operas. Mr. Triplett is also a Christmas specialist for Neiman Marcus, and a Board Member of Createur a la Mode, Paris. Established in 1960, T.V. employs a full–time staff of ten. **Career Steps:** Owner and Chairman of the Board, T.V. (1960–Present). **Associations & Accomplishments:** The National Film Institute. **Education:** Paris Fashion Institute (1981); The Fashion Institute of Design Merchandising.

Joseph L. Troxtel

Creative Director
Jarob Design, Inc.
2601 Elmridge Drive NW
Grand Rapids, MI 49544
(616) 453–5419
Fax: (616) 453–6362
7389

Business Information: Jarob Design, Inc. specializes in signage, graphics, and interior decor design and fabrication for the retail and wholesale industries. As Creative Director, Mr. Troxtel is responsible for marketing, designing, managing, and coordinating all aspects of corporate advertising and commercial design. Concurrently, he manages a private firm, J.L. Troxtel & Associates. **Career Steps:** Creative Director, Jarob Design, Inc. (1985–Present); Owner, J.L. Troxtel & Associates (1982–Present); Designer/Illustrator, Ideas Unlimited, Inc. (1983–1985). **Education:** Kendall College of Art and Design, A.F.A. (1985); Attended Kellogg Community College. **Personal:** Married to Kelly in 1983. Mr. Troxtel enjoys photography, scuba diving, and computer graphic animation.

Samuel J. Tuttle

Director of Program Planning
APAC TeleServices
425 Second Street Southeast
Cedar Rapids, IA 52401–1819
(319) 369–4019
Fax: (319) 399–2447
7389

Business Information: APAC TeleServices provides telemarketing services, and inbound and outbound outsourcing services for customer service and sales solutions. APAC is in the top five of the top 50 telemarketing companies in the United States. Established in 1973, APAC currently employs 5,000 people. As Director, serving as the liaison between sales and operations, Samuel Tuttle plans and implements programs for prospective clients, including overseeing operational parameters, costs and pricing. **Career Steps:** Director of Program Planning, APAC TeleServices (1995–Present); Strategic Marketing Manager, Century Telecommunications, Inc. (1992–1994); Group Product Manager, AT&T American Transtech (1988–1992); Manager Analysis and System Design, CSX Transportation (1984–1988). **Associations & Accomplishments:** International Customer Service Association; YMCA Indian Guide Program. **Education:** Northwestern University – Kellogg Graduate School of Management, Master of Management (1984); Emory University, B.A. in Economics. **Personal:** Married to Katherine C. in 1983. Two children: William Anderson and Olivia Grace. Mr. Tuttle enjoys running and spending time with his family.

Russell S. Ussery

Plant Manager
CuTec, Inc.
310 East Frontage Road
Greer, SC 29651
(803) 879–0036
Fax: (803) 879–3517
7389

Business Information: CuTec, Inc. is a contracted packaging company for all retail products (i.e. cleaning products, vitamins, clothing, etc.) for discount stores, including Sam's Club, Wal–Mart, and K–Mart. As Plant Manager, Mr. Ussery is in charge of production and maintenance of both buildings and machinery, as well as shipping/receiving of new projects. **Career Steps:** Plant Manager, CuTec, Inc. (1987–Present). **Associations & Accomplishments:** Contract Packagers Association; Institute of Packaging Professionals. **Education:** Greenville Technical College (1986). **Personal:** Mr. Ussery enjoys sports.

Mr. John D.M. Veliquette

Senior Vice President
Brokerage Services, Inc.
26476 Verdugo
Mission Viejo, CA 92692–4147
(714) 474–6262
Fax: (714) 474–6263
7389

Business Information: Brokerage Services, Inc. specializes in food brokerage sales to all major food chain outlets in Southern California. The Corporation represents over 50 national food related brands. Established in 1988, Brokerage Services, Inc. currently employs 46 people. As Senior Vice President, Mr. Veliquette is responsible for all aspects of operations, including Corporate sales and daily business. **Career Steps:** Senior Vice President, Brokerage Services, Inc. (1994–Present); Area Director, Campbell Sales Company (1992–1994); Account Executive, Broman Southern California (1982–1992). **Associations & Accomplishments:** Illuminations (food industry club to study issues and implement programs); Fresh Produce and Floral Council. **Education:** California School of Professional Psychology, M.A. (1983); University of California – Irvine, B.A. in Biological Sciences (1981). **Personal:** One child: Nicholas. Mr. Veliquette enjoys exercise, sailing and hiking.

Sarah L. Webster

Director of Business Affairs
Morrisville Auxillary Corporation
Box 901 SUNY Morrisville
Morrisville, NY 13408
(315) 684–6047
Fax: (315) 684–6168
7389

Business Information: Morrisville Auxillary Corporation is a non–profit organization, providing services on a contractual basis to the college campus community of SUNY – Morrisville. The Corporation offers food, bookstore, cable television, garbage collection, washer and dryer, recreation, snack bar, and vending machine services. Established in 1953, Morrisville Auxiliary Corporation reports annual revenue of $5.7 million and currently employs 250 people. Joining the Corporation as an accountant in 1976, Ms. Webster was appointed as Director of Business Affairs in 1986. She oversees all financial accounting and human resource activities, as well as payroll functions. **Career Steps:** Morrisville Auxillary Corporation: Director of Business Affairs (1986–Present), Accountant (1976–1986). **Associations & Accomplishments:** Society for Human Resource Management; American Lung Association of Mid – New York: Board Member, Secretary; National Association of College Auxiliary Services; Bowling League: Member, Former President; Bowling Association: Member, Director of Board. **Education:** SUNY College of Technology – Utica/Rome, B.S. in Accounting (1990); SUNY Morrisville, A.A.S. in Accounting. **Personal:** Ms. Webster enjoys golf, cross–country skiing, canoeing, camping, and reading.

Nannette E. Wellstein

Human Resources Director
American Appraisal Associates, Inc.
P.O. Box 664
Milwaukee, WI 53201–0664
(414) 271–7240
Fax: (414) 225–1283
7389

Business Information: American Appraisal Associates, Inc. is the world's largest independent professional valuation firm. AAA and its subsidiaries provide a wide range of professional valuation, appraisal and consulting services to corporate, governmental and institutional clients on a worldwide basis. AAA is a wholly owned subsidiary of AA Management Group, Inc., which in turn is owned by approximately 70 shareholders rworldwide who are managers and employees of AAA. AAA was formed in 1896 to provide independent property valuations for use in adjustments and settlements between insurance companies and property owners. Some famous deals AAA has worked on are the RJR Nabisco merger, Elvis Presley's estate and various sports teams, including the Los Angeles Rams and Houston Astros. Joining the Corporation in 1978, Ms. Wellstein has served the Company in various capacities, from information systems, tax credits, administration, as Manager of Accounting and Contract departments, to her present position as Human Resources Director. In this capacity, she is responsible for the direction of all human resource functions, including the oversight of 310 employees, recruitment, training and development. She is currently working on her Master's Degree in International Business and hopes to serve as a liaison for AAA and it's international operations. **Career Steps:** American Appraisal Associates, Inc.: Human Resource Director (1995–Present), Manager of Contract & Accounting Departments (1992–1995), and various positions throughout the Company (1978–1992). **Associations & Accomplishments:** Troop Leader, Girl Scouts of Milwaukee Area (5th year); Published Who's Who of Colleges & Universities. **Education:** Milwaukee School of Engineering, B.S. in Management Systems (1989); University of Wisconsin – Milwaukee, currently pursuing an M.S. in International Business. **Personal:** Married to Lawrence in 1984. Ms. Wellstein enjoys family activities, baking, and singing with her family in the family church choir.

Sam Wherry

President and Chief Executive Officer
The Wherry Company
P.O. Box 687, 201 North Church Street Towns Square
Monticello, AR 71655–0687
(501) 367–0377
Fax: (501) 367–1282
EMAIL: See Below
7389

Business Information: The Wherry Company is a financial, loan broker, and community development company, responsible for identifying the specific needs of businesses and their funding. Founding the Company in 1994, Mr. Wherry serves as President and Chief Executive Officer. He is responsible for all aspects of operations, in addition to providing consultation to businesses located in South Arkansas, North East Louisiana, and Western Mississippi. Mr. Wherry can also be reached through the Internet via: AOL:Wherry Co **Career Steps:** President and Chief Executive Officer, The Wherry Company (1993–Present); Economic Consultant, Republican Party of Arkansas (1993); Marketing Consultant, Ford Motor Company/McGehee Auto (1989–1992); Economic Specialist, A.M.E. Church/12th District (1990–Present). **Associations & Accomplishments:** Angorna Consistery Valley of Pine Bluff; 32nd Degree Mason; Specialist Economic Development, A.M.E. Church/12th District. **Education:** University of Arkansas, B.S. (1973); University of Chicago, MDIV, M.B.A. **Personal:** Married to Florence in 1970. Two children: Antonio F. and Reggie D. Mr. Wherry enjoys hunting, fishing, and sports.

Jan B. Wild

Vice President of Sales and Marketing
Maintenance Automation Corporation
3107 West Hallandale Beach Boulevard
Hallandale, FL 33009
(305) 962–8800
Fax: (305) 981–9055
7389

Business Information: Maintenance Automation Corporation is a developer and distributor of computer software products. MAC consists of branch offices located throughout Minnesota, Texas, Florida, and New England. Future plans include continuing to develop and achieve opportunities to obtain markets in Germany, Thailand and Australia. Entering the sales force at the age of fourteen, Mr. Wild worked with his cousin in a stock brokerage company before establishing his own successful business. Joining Maintenance Automation Corporation as Vice President of Sales and Marketing in 1988, he is responsible for the sales processes of national and international markets, as well as the oversight of all U.S. branch offices. He also oversees the administrative operations for associates and a support staff of 47, consisting of 31 salespersons and 16 dealers. **Career Steps:** Vice President of Sales and Marketing, Maintenance Automation Corporation (1988–Present); Owner, Wild Things, Inc. (1986–1988); Owner and Vice President, Heimlich Wild Sales (1984–1986); Sales Manager/Representative, Olympic Narrow Fabrics (1980–1984). **Associations & Accomplishments:** International Facility Managers Association; American Industrial Plant Engineers; Building Operation Managers of America. **Education:** Queens College, B.A. (1976). **Personal:** Married to Barbara in 1976. Three children: Michael, Robert, and Lindsey. Mr. Wild enjoys weight lifting, golf, and basketball.

Graig H. Williams

–Independent–
1411 S. Montreal Avenue
Dallas, TX 75208
Fax: Please mail or call
7389

Business Information: Mr. Williams has experience in national sales and marketing. He has worked with Fortune 500 and 100 regional companies handling leasing programs, coordinating development for national sales efforts, and overseeing sales and referral processes. Mr. Williams assisted in developing a national vendor network, interfaced with senior management on the development of marketing strategies, identifing new market areas and expanding to explore new business opportunities to increase and revenues and ensure customer loyalty. **Career Steps:** Vice President of Marketing and Sales, Corporate Living (1993–1995); Director of Corporate Homes, Centeq Companies (1990–1993). **Associations & Accomplishments:** Texas Real Estate Commission; Dallas Relocation Professionals. **Education:** Stephen F. Austin, B.A. (1987). **Personal:** Mr. Williams enjoys horses, swimming, boating, and travel.

Siobhan Hart Willoughby

Vice President of Marketing and Sales
K. E. Service Group
201 Park Place 205
Altamonte Springs, FL 32701–3574
(407) 834–4011
Fax: (407) 834–4221

7389

Business Information: K. E. Service Group is a fast growing, full–service company, providing appraisals, closings, collateral verifications, remarketing, and recovery of property for finance companies. With Corporate offices in Altamonte Springs, K. E. Service Group spans throughout the globe, including key offices in Arizona and service agents throughout the U.S., Germany, and Puerto Rico. They also have over 850 subcontractors internationally and nationally. The Company is known for its fast turnover of service to its clients. By always looking for ways to improve their service to meet clientele needs, K. E. Service Group strives to maintain its level of excellence while widening their scope of service. Future plans may include a program that will run credit checks for finance companies, called Dataquest. As Vice President of Marketing and Sales, Ms. Willoughby is responsible for all aspects of operations within the Marketing and Sales Department, including administration, financing, public relations, sales, collections, appraisals, marketing and strategic planning. **Career Steps:** Vice President of Marketing and Sales, K. E. Service Group (1989–Present); Part Owner, Quality Wholesales (1978–Present); Assistant Manager, Carol Woods (1984–1986); Assistant Manager and Auditor, Ambassador Inns of America (1975–1980). **Education:** West Humber Collegiate (1973); West Virginia Community College; South Seminole Community College. **Personal:** Married to Kevin in 1983. Two children: Kevin Lee and Sherrod Marie. Ms. Willoughby enjoys spending time with her family.

Wayne D. Wilson

President and Chief Executive Officer
Wilson & Associates
P.O. Box 4220
Clearwater, FL 34618–4220
(813) 796–4955
Fax: (813) 796–4014

7389

Business Information: Wilson & Associates is an international executives search firm for the apparel and clothing industry. Clientele include Levi's, The Gap, The Limited, etc. The Company has two international locations, one in the U.S. (Florida) and one in Columbia, S.A. Founding Wilson & Associates in 1990, Mr. Wilson serves as its President and Chief Executive Officer. He is responsible for all aspects of operations, including administration, "hands on" activities, and management. He also founded Source–I and serves as its Owner and Operater. Source–I is an apparel manufacturing agency, providing a full package of apparel programs for U.S. clientele (i.e. the Company will do plant evaluations and approve manufacturing facilities for golf apparel, shirts and slacks, knits and woven manufacturing; negotiate prices; monitor production, and do final quality checks. The full package also consists of locating all raw materials and trim for approval, such as yarns, lables, zippers, buttons, etc. and delivering a full finished product to the Clients Distribution Center in the states). Mr. Wilson handles all documentation, shipping, customs, etc. **Career Steps:** President and Chief Executive Officer, Wilson & Associates (1990–Present); President and Chief Executive Officer, Source–I (1993–Present). **Associations & Accomplishments:** American Apparel Manufacturers Association; American Apparel Contractors Association; Screenprinters Association International; Southeastern Apparel Manufacturer and Supplier Association; Better Business Bureau; West Florida Association of Personnel Consultants; The Textile Institute; Clearwater Chamber of Commerce. **Education:** Rutgers University (1978); St. Petersburg Junior College, A.A.. **Personal:** Two children: Jed and Zach. Mr. Wilson enjoys painting, photography, fishing, camping, and gardening.

ORACLE MARKET RESEARCH

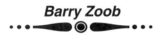

Magdalena Wong

Managing Director
Oracle Market Research, Ltd.
22/F Technology Plaza, 651 King's Road
North Point, Hong Kong
85–223760002
Fax: 85–223760307

7389

Business Information: Oracle Market Research, Ltd. is a consumer market research firm, specializing in fast–moving consumer products, fashion, and service industries. It provides a full range of research services to multinational clients in Hong Kong and China. Ms. Wong is one of the pioneers in China consumer studies. She established Oracle in 1994 after holding various supervisory positions in the research industry. She is presently responsible for managing business development, research analysis, and consultancy. **Career Steps:** Managing Director, Oracle Market Research, Ltd. (1994–Present); Director of Research, J. Walter Thompson China (1992–1993); Research Director, Survey Research Group (1983–1992); Executive, Walmsley Research, Ltd (1981–1982). **Education:** University of Hong Kong, Bachelor's Degree in Social Science (1981). **Personal:** Ms. Wong enjoys movies, reading, and travel. She has a special interest in studying developing countries..

Barry Zoob

Vice President of Sales & Marketing
Idelman Telemarketing
902 North 91st Plaza
Omaha, NE 68114–2403
(402) 393–8000
Fax: (402) 393–3454

7389

Business Information: Idelman Telemarketing is a telemarketing service agency supporting Fortune 500 companies in telecommunications, financial services, travel, and tourism industries, as well as services in fee–based products. Established in 1986, Idelman Telemarketing Agency reports annual revenue in excess of $120 million and currently employs 7,500 people company–wide. After succeeding in the apparel industry with ownership of 5 chain stores of fine women's apparel, Mr. Zoob turned over operations to his wife to join the challenging world of the telemarketing industry in 1989. Currently serving as Idelman's Vice President of Sales & Marketing, he is responsible for all activities related to client revenue, new client revenue acquisition and related marketing activities. **Career Steps:** Vice President of Sales & Marketing, Idelman Telemarketing (1993–Present); Senior Vice President, Sitel Corporation (1989–1993); President and Chief Executive Officer, Zoob's, Inc. (1969–1988). **Associations & Accomplishments:** President, NE Chapter of Cystic Fibrosis; Chad/United Way Executive Committee; Former Member, Cerebral Palsy Board; Member, Director Marketers Association (DMA); Member, American Marketing Association (AMA); Member, National Infomercial Association; Published various industry articles in Direct Magazine, Telemarketer Magazine and Teleprofessional Magazine. **Education:** University of Wisconsin, B.B.A. (1969). **Personal:** Married to Nora in 1977. Three children: Laurie, Amy, and Johnathan. Mr. Zoob enjoys golf and basketball.

Jose Rafael Zozaya Machado

General Manager
Professional Services International, Inc.
2201 Water Ridge Parkway, Suite 500
Charlotte, NC 28217
(704) 357–3311
Fax: (704) 357–3318

7389

Business Information: Professional Services International, Inc. is an international industrial procurement servicer, as well as a marketer of equipment for the iron and steel industry. PSI serves clientele in North and South America, Japan, Australia, Europe, Asia, and the Middle East. Joining PSI as Market Development Manager in 1993, Mr. Zozaya Machado was appointed as General Manager in 1994. He is responsible for the overall operations for all Latin American subsidiaries in South America. **Career Steps:** Professional Services International, Inc.: General Manager (1994–Present), Market Development Manager (1993–1994); General Manager, PSI Sur America S.A. (1994); Project Coordinator, Opco (1988–1991). **Associations & Accomplishments:** Board Member, Venezuelan Society for Spina Bifida; Venezuelan American Chamber of Commerce; Venezuelan Institute of Siderurgy. **Education:** Carnegie Mellon University, M.S. (1993); University of Florida, B.S. in Civil Engineering; Attended: Metropolitan University of Caracas, Venezuela, Construction Management Studies. **Personal:** Married to Maitane in 1990. Mr. Zozaya Machado enjoys sports, martial arts, racquetball, and reading.

Don Dea

Partner
aVn COD
46 North Avenue
Webster, NY 14580
(716) 872–1900
Fax: (716) 872–2014
EMAIL: See Below

7398

Business Information: aVn COD specializes in designing and developing conferences, events, and meetings for major leading corporations, and associations including the White House. Concentrating on meeting design, production, and technology, aVn COD produces programs that engages people's minds and hearts which facilitates knowledge and adult learning. Established in 1974, the Company is based in New York, but designs conferences worldwide. As Partner, Mr. Dea oversees the day–today operation of the Company, as well as advising on all technological aspects. His long–term goal is to continue to build the Company and its people. Internet users can reach him via: dddea@earthlink.net **Career Steps:** Partner, aVn COD (1996–Present); Vice President/Co–Founder, Alaris, Inc. (1993); Xerox Corporation: General Manager, U.S. Operations (1990), General Manager, Channel Operations (1988). **Associations & Accomplishments:** Chairman of the Board/ Vice President, Association for Blind; Board of Directors, Salvation Army; Board of Advisors, Fuqua School of Business; President, Alumni Association, Western Maryland College. **Education:** Massachusetts Institute of Technology, Sloan School, Senior Executive (1988); Fuqua School of Business, M.B.A. (1978); Western Maryland College, B.A. (1976). **Personal:** Married to Catherine in 1984. Two children: Erin and Alexander. Mr. Dea enjoys running.

Mr. Jeffrey S. Edwards

Quality Process Consultant and Educator
Philip Crosby Associates, Inc.
3260 University Boulevard
Winter Park, FL 32792
(904) 276–0067
Fax: (904) 276–0067

7399

Business Information: Philip Crosby Associates, Inc. is a leading global management consulting firm specializing in implementation support of quality management processes, providing a full array of support including employee training, executive support, qualitative research and analysis and total quality management support efforts. Global in scope, the Firm has over 200 consultants, and office locations in more than 15 countries worldwide including the United States, Canada, Mexico, Germany, United Kingdom and Japan. As a Consultant with the Firm, Mr. Edwards provides clientele with diverse services including business analysis, process reengineering, compliance audits (ISO 900 and others), curriculum development, executive education and training. Established in 1979, Philip Crosby Associates, Inc. reports management portfolio revenues in excess of $100 million. **Career Steps:** Quality Process Consultant and Educator, Philip Crosby Associates, Inc. (1989–Present); Project Manager and Systems Engineer, American Systems Corporation (1984–1989); Commissioned Officer, U.S. Navy, Warships/Submarines (1979–1984) Reserve Duty, U.S. Navy (1984–Present). **Associations & Accomplishments:** American Society for Quality Control (ASQC); American Society for Training and Development (ASTD); International Brotherhood of Magicians. **Education:** Jacksonville University, B.S. (1979); Numerous military schools for warship and submarine officer assignments; Instructor in The Quality College.

Mr. Marcus A. Hart

President and Chief Executive Officer
Hart's Food Service, Inc. d.b.a. Delta Food Service
P.O. Box 18864
San Antonio, TX 78218
(210) 657–7104
Fax: (210) 657–7166

7399

Business Information: Hart's Food Service, Inc. d.b.a. Delta Food Service – the largest minority–owned company in San Antonio – provides cafeteria, dining facilities, vending, and catering services in Texas, Louisiana, and Virginia. As President and Chief Executive Officer, Mr. Hart oversees management of all company operations. Established in 1978, Hart's Food Service, Inc. dba Delta Food Service has 532 full–time employees and reports annual revenue of $7 million. **Career Steps:** President and Chief Executive Officer, Hart's Food Service, Inc. d.b.a. Delta Food Service (1978– Present); Chief Warrant Officer (Retired), U.S. Army (1957–1977). **Associations & Accomplishments:** Member, Greater San Antonio

Chamber of Commerce; Board of Directors: Carver Community Center, East–Side San Antonio; Revitalization Agency; National Contract Management Association; Association of U.S. Army; The National Federation of Independent Business; The Retired Officers Association; Financial contributor: MD Anderson Cancer Center, Cal Farley's Boys Ranch, United Way, Children's Hospital in San Antonio, United Negro College Fund; The Hendrick Arnold Lifetime Achievement Award (1994), Texas African American Heritage Organization; San Antonio Black Achievement Award (1994), San Antonio Black Achievement Awards Association; 1993 Texas Agriculture Excellence Award; 1993 Small Businessperson of the Year, U.S. Small Business Administration; Author of two novels; Many more Awards and Recognition too numerous to name here. **Education:** University of Hawaii; University of Virginia; Warrant Officer Training Course, U.S. Army; U.S. Army Helicopter Pilot Training Course.

7500 Auto Repair, Services, and Parking

7513 Truck rental and leasing, no drivers
7514 Passenger car rental
7515 Passenger car leasing
7519 Utility trailer rental
7521 Automobile parking
7532 Top and body repair and paint shops
7533 Auto exhaust system repair shops
7534 Tire retreading and repair shops
7536 Automotive glass replacement shops
7537 Automotive transmission repair shops
7538 General automotive repair shops
7539 Automotive repair shops, NEC
7542 Carwashes
7549 Automotive services, NEC

Ms. Mary Lou Bechina

Vice President
Carmichael Leasing
2200 S. Loomis
Chicago, IL 60608
(312) 666–8500
Fax: (312) 666–7382

7513

Business Information: Carmichael Leasing is one of the largest Cartage transportation truck leasing corporations in Chicago specializing in refrigeration. Established in 1951, Carmichael Leasing currently employs 200 professionals and has an estimated annual revenue of $24 million. As Vice President, Ms. Bechina is responsible for all aspects of operations concerning customer relations, sales and marketing including special events and the company newsletter. **Career Steps:** Carmichael Leasing; Vice President (1989–Present); Director of Public Relations (1983–1989); Educator; Reavis High School (1966–1983). **Associations & Accomplishments:** Illinois Transportation Association; Rotary Club of Chicago; Executive Club of Chicago; National Association of Female Executives. **Education:** B.S. and M.S. in Education; Certificate of Advanced Study in Administration. **Personal:** One child: Kathleen McKnight. Ms. Bechina enjoys golf and travel.

Dina Hornberger
Manager
Penske Truck Leasing
RT 10
Green Hills, PA 19607
(610) 775–6106
Fax: (610) 796–6571

7513

Business Information: Penske Truck Leasing is a national truck leasor offering trucks and trailers of various sizes to customers. As Manager, Ms. Hornberger is directly responsible for a staff of eight. Her staff conducts internal audits, monitors sales, leases, rentals, and use of vehicles, compiles information for tax purposes, and complies with state and Federal tax regulations. **Career Steps:** Penske Truck Leasing: Manager (1994–Present), Tax Accountant (1992–1994); Tax Accountant, Leid & Company, L.P. (CPA) (1988–1992). **Associations & Accomplishments:** Tax Executives, Inc.; Institute of Property Taxation; Committee on State Taxation. **Education:** Pennsylvania State University, B.S. (1988). **Personal:** Married to Anthony in 1991. Ms. Hornberger enjoys golf and searching for antiques.

Paul T. Mangulis
Area Manager
Premier Car Rental
739 Smithtown Bypass
Smithtown, NY 11787–5128
(516) 724–4444 Ext. 108
Fax: (516) 724–6671

7514

Business Information: Premier Car Rental provides insurance replacement car rental. National in scope, the Company has locations in thirteen regional markets and is adding more rapidly. Established in 1990, Premier Car Rental of New York employs 140 people, and has an estimated annual revenue of $12 million. As Area Manager of the New York area, Mr. Mangulis oversight of thirteen branch offices and more on the way. He manages all rentals, sales, and marketing, and reports directly to the board of directors on development of area offices. Additional duties include public relations, administration, and strategic planning. **Career Steps:** Area Manager, Premier Car Rental (1995–Present); Area Manager, Snappy Car Rental (1987–1995). **Associations & Accomplishments:** New York Vehicle Rental Association; Long Island Association; Professional Insurance Agents. **Education:** Dowling College. **Personal:** Mr. Mangulis enjoys golf.

Salim Mattar

President/CEO/Chairman
Localiza Ltda
Ave Bernardo Monteiro 1.563–5.0 Fumcion Arios
Belo Horizonte, Brazil 30150–902
55–31–2477000
Fax: 55–31–2477003
EMail: See Below

7514

Business Information: Localiza Ltda is the largest car rental company in Brazil, renting cars for leisure, corporate, and individual use. Localiza has four divisions: Car Rental, Fleet Management, Car Sale, and Franchising, in nine countries in South America. As President/CEO/Chairman, Mr. Mattar is responsible for all aspects of Company operations, including strategic planning, global expansion, and administration. He can be reached through the World Wide Web: http://www.localiza.com.br. **Career Steps:** President/CEO/Chairman, Localiza Ltda (1973–Present). **Associations & Accomplishments:** President, Liberal Institute. **Education:** FUMEC, Business Administration (1975). **Personal:** Married to Adriana. Three children: Tatiana, Sarah, and Sophia. Mr. Mattar enjoys breeding and raising Arabian horses.

Jennifer Paauwe–Riffe

Training Supervisor/Human Resource Coordinator
Enterprise Rent–A–Car
20400 SW Teton Avenue
Tualatin, OR 97062–8812
(503) 692–8400 Ext. 585
Fax: (503) 692–8820
EMail: See Below

7514

Business Information: Enterprise Rent–A–Car is one of the nation's largest automobile rental, leasing and sales organizations, beating out 72 companies to win the Better Business Bureau's Integrity Award. Serving in various managerial roles for Enterprise since 1993, Jennifer Paauwe–Riffe was appointed as Training Supervisor and Human Resources Coordinator in March of 1995. Her primary duties involve the recruiting, hiring, interviewing, and training of new employees, as well as ensures compliance of all governmentally–mandated regulations. Internet users can reach her via: JPRIFFE@AOL.COM **Career Steps:** Enterprise Rent–A–Car: Training Supervisor/Human Resource Coordinator (1995–Present), Human Resource Coordinator (1995), Assistant Manager (1993–1995). **Associations & Accomplishments:** United Way Coordinator; Raleigh Hills Neighborhood Association; Northwest Womens Investment Club; L.E.C. Participant. **Education:** Oregon State University, B.A. (1990); Universidad Catolica de Quito. **Personal:** Ms. Paauwe–Riffe enjoys water skiing, hiking, horseback riding, theatre, and reading.

Cesar Pacheco
Retired Financial Officer
Hertz d.b.a. Puerto Ricancars, Inc.
P.O. Box 38084 Airport Station
San Juan, Puerto Rico 00937–1084
Fax: (809) 791–0797

7514

Business Information: Retired from Puerto Ricancars, Inc., a division of Hertz Rental Cars, after 32 years of dedicated service, Mr. Pacheco served as Financial Officer of the Puerto Rican chain of the national car rental firm. He was responsible for the administrative and financial matters of the Puerto Rican office. **Career Steps:** Retired (1990–Present); Hertz d.b.a. Puerto Ricancars, Inc.: Financial Officer (1980–1990), Zone Controller (1971–1880), Assistant Controller (1971). **Associations & Accomplishments:** Fraternity – Phi Delta Gamma; AARP. **Education:** Catholic University of Puerto Rico, B.B.A. in Accounting (1962). **Personal:** Married to Angela in 1954. Two children: Cesar Jr. and Robert. Mr. Pacheco enjoys golf, baseball, and tennis.

Sam S. Swaleh

Director
Thrifty Car Rental
520 Mason Street
San Francisco, CA 94102
(415) 788–5809
Fax: (415) 788–5810

7514

Business Information: Thrifty Car Rental is a Chrysler–owned conglomerate offering leisure travel with an emphasis ron local corporations. A multi–billion dollar Company, Thrifty Car Rental offers auto, RV, and corporate rentals worldwide. As Director, Mr. Swaleh oversees all sales and marketing in the San Francisco Bay area. Primarily focusing on local corporate needs, he concentrates his efforts on conventions, airports, etc. He also supervises a staff of eighty, and develops and implements promotions to entice new business. **Career Steps:** Director, Thrifty Car Rental (1995–Present); General Manager, Applebee's Restaurant (1994); District Manager, Agency Rent A Car (1991–1994); General Manager, Marriott Corporation (1988–1991). **Associations & Accomplishments:** San Francisco Conventions and Visitors Bureau; Meeting Planners International (MPI); Daly City Chamber of Commerce. **Education:** San Francisco State, B.S. in Business Administration (1979). **Personal:** Married to Melissa. One child: Samirah Montana Swaleh. Mr. Swaleh enjoys tennis.

Steven E. White

President and Chief Executive Officer
White Auto Rental, Inc.
P.O. Box 334
Glenolden, PA 19036–0334
(610) 532–0777
Fax: (610) 532–9853

7514

Business Information: White Auto Rental, Inc. specializes in the rental of automobiles and vans. The Company also provides full–service auto and truck repair. As President and Chief Executive Officer, Mr. White is responsible for all administrative functions, as well as the repair and maintenance of autos. **Career Steps:** President and Chief Executive Officer, White Auto Rental, Inc. (1987–Present); Rental Manager, Robin Ford, Inc. (1983–1987); Manager. Agency Rent–A–Car (1982–1983); Petty Officer, United States Navy (1977–1982). **Associations & Accomplishments:** Delaware County Chamber of Commerce; PADI; Tang So Do. **Education:** Delaware County Community College, Business Administration (1986). **Personal:** Married to Valerie in 1982. Two children: Kimbery and Brian. Mr. White enjoys physical fitness, fishing, outdoor activities, white water rafting, sky diving, and sailing.

Mike Worley

Controller
Enterprise Rent–A–Car
501 South 48th Street, Suite 101
Tempe, AZ 85281–2324
(602) 954–7500
Fax: (602) 954–6811

7514

Business Information: Enterprise Rent–A–Car is a nationwide automobile/truck rental concern. The Phoenix office began operations in 1981 and currently has as staff of 350 people. Enterprise offers daily rentals of vehicles, fleet services for companies with fleets of 10 to 70 vehicles, and retail automobile sales activity. As Controller, Mr. Worley is responsible for all aspects of financial operations, including accounting, financial reports, payroll, taxes, management, and projects. **Career Steps:** Enterprise Rent–A–Car: Controller (1991–Present), Corporate Accounting Supervisor (1988–1991); Staff Auditor, Touche Ross (1986–1988). **Associations & Accomplishments:** Phoenix Controllers Club. **Education:** University of Missouri at St. Louis, B.S. in Accounting (1986). **Personal:** Married to Carla in 1983. Three children: Joshua, Aryn, and James. Mr. Worley enjoys community activities, spending time with his family, sports, basketball, golf, and tennis.

Steven R. Murphy

Vice President and National Marketing Director
Westar Leasing Incorporated
P.O. Box 919
Olympia, WA 98507–0919
(360) 705–4545
Fax: (360) 705–1329

7515

Business Information: Westar Leasing Incorporated is a national financial institution for non–recourse automobile leasing which works with dealers and buys papers from dealerships. As Vice President and National Marketing Director, Mr. Murphy is responsible for the expansion of nationwide marketing activities for the Company. **Career Steps:** Vice President and National Marketing Director, Westar Leasing Incorporated (1984–Present); President and Chief Executive Officer, First Leasing Corporation (1970–1984); Group Executive, Marine Midland Automotive (1984–1988); President and Chief Executive Officer, Bank Inventory Disposal System (1989–1992). **Associations & Accomplishments:** Past President, National Vehicle Leasing Association (NVLA) (1980–1981): Recipient of the Clemens–Pender Award, the Association's highest honor. He is the namesake of "Murphy Cup," given annually to the chapter with the largest increase in memberships. **Education:** California State University, Certified Vehicle Leasing Executive (2 year program) (1964). **Personal:** Two children: Kevin and Brian. Mr. Murphy enjoys exercise, golf, and fishing.

Michael J. Sharkey
MIS Manager
Xtralease
1801 Park 270 Drive, Suite 400
St. Louis, MO 63146–4020
(314) 579–9300
Fax: Please mail or call

7519

Business Information: Xtralease specializes in over the road trailer leasing. As MIS Manager, Mr. Sharkey is responsible for all aspects of Management Information Services for the Company. **Career Steps:** MIS Manager, Xtralease (1993–Present); SCS/Compute: Manager of Manufacturing/Distribution (1993), Director of Processing Software (1990–1992), Northwest Region Manager (1988–1990). **Education:** St. Charles Community College. **Personal:** Married to Carol in 1990. One child: Marissa. Mr. Sharkey enjoys golf.

Lloyd Heck

Comptroller
Greco, Debelles, Camero, Inc. Auto Refinish
P. O. Box 598
Ocoee, FL 34761–0598
(407) 877–7344
Fax: (407) 877–8220

7532

Business Information: Greco, Debelles, Camero, Inc. Auto Refinish specializes in automobile and auto body refinishing and repair. The Company services and reconstructs various makes of automobiles for auto auction. As Comptroller, Mr. Heck is responsible for all monies that the come into and leave the Company. Other duties include, preparing all external financial data, overseeing payroll functions and human resource functions, and he is in charge of information and computer systems. **Career Steps:** Comptroller, Greco, Debelles, Camero, Inc. Auto Refinish (1994–Present); Junior Accountant, Lou Heck, C.P.A. (1986–1994). **Education:** University

of Central Florida (1996). **Personal:** Mr. Heck enjoys golf, model railroads, reading, and scuba diving.

Michael C. Kucharski

District Manager, Central Operations
Monro Muffler
200 Holleder Parkway
Rochester, NY 14615
(800) 876–7676
Fax: (716) 647–0945

7533

Business Information: Monro Muffler is a manufacturer and retailer of automotive mufflers and various other undercar care products. As a national retail chain with over 60 locations, the Company specializes in general automotive repair and undercar care. Established in 1957, the Company has an estimated annual revenue of $39 million. As District Manager of Central Operations, Mr. Kucharski oversees management of 60 retail locations, and controls profit and loss ratios for five regions. **Career Steps:** Monro Muffler: District Manager, Central Operations (1995–Present), Regional Manager, Harrisburg, Pennsylvania (1991–1995), Regional Manager, Watertown (1990–1991). **Associations & Accomplishments:** Explorer Chairman, Boy Scouts of America; NADA; PADE. **Education:** Dale Carnegie (1995); Several Business courses and clinics. **Personal:** Married to Paula in 1980. Two children: Michael and Nickole. Mr. Kucharski enjoys boating, camping, motorcycling, and his automotive collection.

Michael T. Cahillane
Director of Insurance Relations
CarStar Automotive, Inc.
157 Prospect Avenue
Northampton, MA 01060
(800) 999–0216
Fax: (413) 582–0283

7538

Business Information: CarStar Automotive, Inc. is a national automotive collision repair franchise, currently operating over 360 locations across the U.S. Joining CarStar Automotive in Franchise Development in 1990, Mr. Cahillane was appointed as Director of Insurance Relations in 1993. He is responsible for the direction of all insurance activities corporate–wide. **Career Steps:** CarStar Automotive, Inc.: Director of Insurance Relations (1993–Present), Franchise Development (1990–1993), Vice President, Cahillane Motors, Inc. (1964–1990). **Associations & Accomplishments:** Former President, Northampton Lion's Club; Former President, Hampshire County Sheriff's Association; Former President, Western Massachusetts Association of Auto Body Craftsmen. **Education:** Attended: Springfield Technologic Community College. **Personal:** Married to Florence M. in 1968. Three children: Dr. Cherie A., Michael A. and Thomas C. Mr. Cahillane enjoys Alpine skiing, sailing, and travel.

Charles T. Morrell

Vice President of Sales & Marketing
Single Source, Inc.
6399 Jimmy Carter Boulevard
Norcross, GA 30071–2320
(770) 840–7877
Fax: (770) 368–0731

7539

Business Information: Single Source, Inc. is a national distribution network organization, serving the collision repair industry. Services include sales, management, and marketing. National in scope, Single Source, Inc. operates from fifteen locations (Atlanta and Norcross, Georgia; Jacksonville and Orlando, Florida; Las Vegas, Nevada; San Antonio and Houston, Texas; Portland, Oregon; Denver, Colorado; Detroit, Michigan; St. Louis, Missouri; Long Island, New York; Greer and Columbia, South Carolina; New Jersey). Future expansion will include 50 locations by 1999. As Vice President of Sales & Marketing, Mr. Morrell is a majority shareholder of SIngle source, Inc. and his scope of responsible include: sales and marketing activities, including administration, sales, public relations, marketing, and strategic planning. **Career Steps:** Vice President of Sales & Marketing, Single Source, Inc. (1995–Present); Akzo Nobel: N.A. Manager of Organizational Development (1995), U.S. Sales Manager (1993–1995), Northern Zone Manager (1991–1993). **Associations & Accomplishments:** Director of the Junior Youth Department, Hawthorne Baptist Church. **Education:** University of South Florida, B.S. in Electrical Engineering (1986); HCC, Tampa, Florida, A.A. in Pre Medical. **Personal:** Married to Sophia in

1986. Four children: Timmy, Mikey, Stephanie and Ryan. Mr. Morrell enjoys being a good Christian husband and father. He also enjoys golf and church activities.

Tammy Lawing
Director of Operations and Marketing Manager
Gas House Car Washes
655 Craig Road, Suite 220
St. Louis, MO 63141–7170
(314) 961–4589
Fax: (314) 961–8362

7542

Business Information: Gas House Car Washes is a 50–year service organization that owns and operates full–service car wash stations, providing express and self–serve car washes; automotive detail shop; gasoline services; and a convenience store in the St. Louis, Missouri area. Joining Gas House Car Washes as Director of Operations and Marketing Manager in 1993, Ms. Lawing is responsible for all aspects of operations for the Full–Service Division, as well as serving as Marketing Manager and Fund Raiser Representative for the Company. **Career Steps:** Director of Operations and Marketing Manager, Gas House Car Washes (1993–Present); Santh Plus: Director of Operations (1983–1993), Regional Manager (1991–1993). **Associations & Accomplishments:** International Car Wash Association; St. Louis Car Wash Association. **Education:** Florissant Valley Community College. **Personal:** One child: Erick. Ms. Lawing enjoys home decorating, gardening and painting.

Alan H. Clark

Logistics Manager
APL Automotive Logistics
17197 North Laurel Park Drive, Suite 200
Livonia, MI 48152
(313) 953–8204
Fax: (313) 953–5528
EMAIL: See Below

7549

Business Information: APL Automotive Logistics is an international company specializing in automotive parts and vehicle transportation. Mr. Clark has served with various subsidiaries of APL, most recently assigned to APL Automotive Logistics as Logistics Manager for North America. His responsibilities include management of all logistics activities, cost, distribution, and site analysis, and ensuring customer satisfaction and quality service. Internet users can reach him via: Alan_Clark@ccgate.apl.com **Career Steps:** APL: Logistics Manager, APL Automotive Logistics (1994–Present), APL Distribution Services: Logistics Analyst (1993–1994), Senior Pricing Analyst (1992–1993), Logistics Analyst, APL Stacktrain Services (1990–1991). **Associations & Accomplishments:** Council of Logistics Management; Master Mason. **Personal:** Married to Alina in 1988. Three children: Alan Jr., rMitchell, and Eric. Mr. Clark enjoys hunting, fishing, rollerblading, bicycling, golf, and spending time with his family.

Michael J. Oeler

Project Manager
Starcon, Inc.
260 Market Place
Manhatten, IL 60442
(708) 385–7128
Fax: (815) 478–5532 (708) 385–7176

7549

Business Information: Starcon, Inc. is a mechanical contractor serving the petrochemical industry. With headquarters located in Manhattan, Illinois and two temporary field offices (one south of Chicago and one in Baltimore, Maryland), Starcon, Inc. serves the eastern half of the U.S. (east of the Mississippi River). As Project Manager, Mr. Oeler is responsible for all aspects of project management, including budgeting, controls, estimating, scheduling, major projects, safety, customer relations, and executing projects from $50,000 to $3 million. He also oversees employees working on projects (approximately 10–60 people, depending on project size). **Career Steps:** Project Manager, Starcon, Inc. (1986–Present); 2nd Class Petty Officer, U.S. Navy (1977–1982) **Associations & Accomplishments:** Inducted into the Baseball Hall of Fame – Babe Ruth Division (1975); Big Brothers Program through Starcon, Inc.; Coach for Little League (10 years). **Education:** Attended numerous seminar, trade schools, and personal improvement workshops. **Personal:** Married to Debra A. in 1980. Three children: Michael, Matthew and Joshua. Mr. Oeler enjoys coaching baseball, playing softball, weightlifting, music, and participating in charitable events for children through his Company.

7600 Miscellaneous Repair Services

7622 Radio and television repair
7623 Refrigeration service and repair
7629 Electrical repair shops, NEC
7631 Watch, clock, and jewelry repair
7641 Reupholstery and furniture repair
7692 Welding repair
7694 Armature rewinding shops
7699 Repair services, NEC

Scott L. Gordon
President/Owner
Tropic AC
3000 NW 77 Court
Miami, FL 33122
(305) 592-2251
Fax: (305) 592-0015

7623

Business Information: Tropic AC, a contracting company, is a marketer, servicer, and installer of air conditioning and refrigeration equipment, specializing in indoor air quality systems, optimization, and tests and balances. Services are contracted by residential (30%) and commercial (70%) businesses located throughout Southern Florida (Key West and Broward County to the West Coast of Florida). Established in 1958, Tropic AC currently employs fifteen people. Joining the Company as a part-time employee in 1974 and going full-time in 1978, Mr. Gordon worked his way up the corporate ladder to President and Owner in 1986. He is responsible for all aspects of operations, including designing and building systems, supervising commercial and industrial services, and replacement of HVAC systems. **Career Steps:** Tropic AC: President/Owner (1988-Present), Vice President/Stockholder (1984-1988), Service Manager/AC Contractor (1980-1984). **Associations & Accomplishments:** Chamber of Commerce – Homestead/Florida City; Air Conditioning Contractors of America; Refrigeration Service Engineers Society; Le Tip of Kendalls – Miami; Published in trade magazines. **Education:** Factory Training Schools: Durham Bush, Trane Carrier, RSES, and ACCA Training. **Personal:** Married to Donna Gaskell in 1977. One child: Samantha Kathleen Victoria. Mr. Gordon enjoys scuba diving, traveling with his family, and horseback riding.

Randall L. Schmitt

President
Schmitt Refrigeration
200 S. Governor
Evansville, IN 47713
(812) 424-5878
Fax: (812) 426-1267

7623

Business Information: Schmitt Refrigeration is a national provider of mechanical services, including installations and energy management of refrigeration, heating, and air conditioning equipment. Established in 1964, Schmitt Refrigeration reports annual revenue of $2.5 million and currently employs more than 25 people. As President, Mr. Schmitt is responsible for all aspects of operations, including coordinating and estimating services and supervising a staff of 22 people. **Career Steps:** Schmitt Refrigeration: President (1992-Present), Various Management Positions (1977-1992). **Associations & Accomplishments:** AOPA **Education:** Apprenticed with Plumbers & Pipefitters Association; Business Courses taken at University of Indiana-Evansville **Personal:** Three children: Natosha, Chandelle and Taleatha. Mr. Schmitt enjoys flying and scuba diving during his leisure time.

Kenneth Schwarz
Mid-Atlantic Area Manager and Stockholder
Kinetic Biomedical Services, Inc.
1310 Industrial Highway
Southampton, PA 18966
(215) 953-1590
Fax: (215) 396-1590

7629

Business Information: Kinetic Biomedical Services, Inc. provides medical equipment repair, maintenance, and technology management services to hospitals and other medial facilities. As a stockholder and Mid-Atlantic Area Manager, Mr. Schwarz is responsible for managing all Mid-Atlantic Region operations. **Career Steps:** Mid-Atlantic Area Manager and Stockholder, Kinetic Biomedical Services, Inc. (1989-Present); Biomedical Service Manager, AMSCO (1985-1989); Technical Operations Manager, COMTEL Business Systems, Medical Division (1984-1985). **Associations & Accomplishments:** Association for the Advancement of Medical Instrumentation. **Education:** Thomas Edison, BSAST; New Jersey Institute of Technology; William Patterson College; University of Maryland; Regis College. **Personal:** Mr. Schwarz enjoys boating, hunting, and physical fitness activities.

Craig Graybar
President and Chief Executive Officer
Graybar Furniture
3430 West Kimberly Avenue
Milwaukee, WI 53221-4752
(414) 258-2390
Fax: Please mail or call

7641

Business Information: Graybar Furniture specializes in building, repairing and restoring furniture, including classic pieces such as gargoyles and serpents. Established in 1979, Graybar Furniture currently employs 21 people. As President and Chief Executive Officer, Mr. Graybar provides the overall direction and vision for the company's continued growth, quality delivery to customers, and strategic developments. **Career Steps:** President and Chief Executive Officer, Graybar Furniture (1979-Present); Petty Officer, United States Navy (1974-1979). **Associations & Accomplishments:** Wisconsin Manufacturers and Commerce; West Allis Chamber of Commerce; American Business Association; Vietnam Veterans of America; Veterans of Foreign Wars; American Legion; Donor to the Milwaukee Art Museum; Milwaukee Ballet; Milwaukee Repertory Theatre; Skylight Opera Company; Who's Who in Leading Executives; Who's Who in Science and Technology; Who's Who in the Midwest; Recognized as one of the Top 100 Woodworking Shops in America by "Wood and Wood Products Trade Journal" for the last five years; Nominated for the Wisconsin Manufacturer of the Year and Entreprenuer of the Year; Winner, Chicago Excellence in Woodworking Show and the Atlanta Excellence in Woodworking Show. **Education:** University of Wisconsin, B.S. (1985). **Personal:** Married to Helen A. in 1993. Mr. Graybar enjoys scale model railroading.

Francisco Avendano
Owner
Enertec Ltd.
P.O. Box 16306
Santiago, Chile
56-2-223-6681
Fax: 56-2-225-2553

7690

Business Information: Enertec Ltd. projects, installs and maintains air conditioning systems. As Owner, Mr. Avendano is responsible for daily operations, administrative activities, sales, marketing, public relations, and accounting functions. **Career Steps:** Owner, Enertec Ltd. (1985-Present); Engineer, T. O'Connor and Sons (Austrailia) (1971-1976); Engineer, IDP (Chile) (1975-1976); Engineer, Andina (Boliva) (1976-1981). **Associations & Accomplishments:** American Society of Heating, Refrigeration, and Air Conditioning Engineers; Camara Chilena De Refrigeracion y Climatizacion. **Education:** Santiago University, Engineering (1971). **Personal:** Married to Judith in 1977. One child: Antonio. Mr. Avendano enjoys swimming.

William Lance Killmeyer
Controller
Kasunick Welding
1541 Spring Garden Avenue
Pittsburgh, PA 15212-3632
(412) 321-2715
Fax: (412) 321-2229

7692

Business Information: Kasunick Welding is an industrial welding company, providing customized design, welding, fabrication, and machinery for industrial customers. Established in 1972, Kasunick Welding currently employs 30 people. As Controller, Mr. Killmeyer is responsible for accounting, budgeting, financial planning, human resource administration, health benefits coordination, and supervision of office staff. **Career Steps:** Controller, Kasunick Welding (1994-Present); Senior Accountant, DS Financial Services (1993-1994); Associate – Audit, Coopers & Lybrand (1992-1993); Manager, The Saloon (1990-1991). **Associations & Accomplishments:** Beta Alpha Psi; National Accounting Honors Society: Secretary (1991), Member (1989-Present). **Education:** Pennsylvania State University, B.S. in Accounting (1991). **Personal:** Mr. Killmeyer enjoys bodybuilding and being a fitness consultant.

Kate M. Bast
Business Unit Controller
Acutus Gladwin Industries
200 Waydom Dr., RR #1
Ayr, Ontario N01 1E0
(519) 621-7560
Fax: (519) 622-3944

7699

Business Information: Acutus Gladwin Industries is a professional service company for the steel industry repairing continuous casters and solving other steel related needs. As Business Unit Controller, Ms. Bast is responsible for handling fiscal matters, accounting, and supervising the treasury and administration of Canadian operations. Internet users can reach her via: Kbast@Gladwin.com. **Career Steps:** Business Unit Controller, Acutus Gladwin Industries (1989-Present); A/P Administrator, Apex Metals, Inc. (1988-89); Financial Analyst, Wilfrid Laurier University (1987-88); Annual Givings Coordinator, University Development Affairs (1985-87). **Associations & Accomplishments:** Certified General Accountants; Novell User Group; Founding Member, Scubalnog Dive Club. **Education:** Wilfrid Laurier University, B.A. (1987), Diploma in Accounting; Conestoga College, Certificate in Occupational Health & Safety; Certificate in Computing. **Personal:** Married to Brian in 1987. Ms. Bast enjoys gardening and travel.

Dennie Chambers
President and Chief Operating Officer
Piano Forte, Inc.
1090 Boylston Street
Boston, MA 02215-2317
(617) 266-4933
Fax: (617) 424-7918

7699

Business Information: Piano Forte, Inc. specializes in piano restoration, sales, and technical service. Mr. Chambers created PFI in 1982 working out of his private apartment in Massachusetts as a student and Concert Piano Tuner at Berklee College of Music. Fifteen years and a 3,000 square foot showroom later, he is rebuilding and restoring classic pianos like the 1886 and 1922 Steinway. **Career Steps:** President and Chief Operating Officer, Piano Forte, Inc. (1982-Present), Concert Piano Tuner, Berklee College of Music. **Associations & Accomplishments:** Published in "The Boston Herald," "Bostonian," and "African Technological Forum." **Education:** Berklee College, B.S.in Music (1984); University of Maine, A.S. in Music (1981); Attended: Columbia University and George Washington University. **Personal:** Married to Jacqueline DiPrima in 1990. Four children: Xavier, Michael, Cassie and Serene. Mr. Chambers enjoys skiing, canoeing and world exploration.

Enrique Cortes
President
Cortes Industrial Organization, Inc.
P.O. Box 41264
Santura, Puerto Rico 00940
(809) 724-0041
Fax: (809) 724-7211

7699

Business Information: Cortes Industrial Organization, Inc., established in 1977, provides industrial repair and maintenance of rotating machinery. Services include rebuilding industrial electric motors and other rotating machinery for the commerce, shipping, and hotel industries in Puerto Rico and the Caribbean, as well as providing preventative maintenance. Founding the Company in 1977, Mr. Cortes is responsible for all aspects of operations, as well as overseeing all administrative operations for associates and a support staff of 70. **Career Steps:** President, Cortes Industrial Organization, Inc. (1977–Present). **Associations & Accomplishments:** Apparatus Service Association; Puerto Rico Manufacturing Association; United Way. **Education:** Inter–American University, B.A. (1970). **Personal:** Married to Ivette in 1969. Four children: Enrique Jr., Ariel, Monica, and Briseida. Mr. Cortes enjoys golf.

A.W. (Tony) Hooper
Senior Vice President, Marketing and Technology
Instuform Technologies, Inc.
1770 Kirby Parkway Suite 300
Memphis, TN 38138–7406
(901) 759–7473
Fax: (901) 759–7513

7699

Business Information: Instuform Technologies is the world leader in the trenchless rehabilitation of wastewater, water, gas, and industrial pipelines. As Senior Vice President, Mr. Hooper is responsible for Corporate marketing, product management, research and development, engineering and technical support, and sales and technical training. **Career Steps:** Senior Vice President, Instuform Technologies (1993–Present); President of Forming and Drying Division, Weavexx, Inc. (1991–1993); President of Pulp, Paper and Board Division, Sprout Bauer, Inc. (a subsidiary of ABB/Combustion Engineering) (1988–1991); Chief Executive Officer, S.W. Hooper Corporation (1976–1988). **Associations & Accomplishments:** Registered Professional Engineer; APWA; AWWA; WEF; TAPPI; CPPA; CPPA Certificate of Appreciation for Service to the Industry (1986); Holder of seven U.S. patents; Author of numerous papers and two chapters in industry standard textbooks. **Education:** University of Sherbrooke, B.Sc.A. (1973); Beloit College, B.A. in Physics (1973). **Personal:** Married to Cynthia in 1969. three children: . Mr. Hooper enjoys skiing, hiking, climbing, and sailing.

G. W. Kelsey

President/Owner
Compass Aviation
814 East Moore
Terrell, TX 75160
(214) 524–7811
Fax: (214) 962–4867

7699

Business Information: Compass Aviation is a Federal Aviation Association (FAA) repair station providing overhaul of interior and exterior lighting systems and accessories for commercial and military aircraft. Established in 1995, the Company employs three people and has an estimated annual revenue of $900 thousand. As President/Owner, Mr. Kelsey oversees all aspects of the Company and is responsible for administration, operations, finance, public relations and strategic planning. **Career Steps:** President/Owner, Compass Aviation (1995–Present); Production Manager, Chrysler Technologies (1994–1996); Production Supervision, E–Systems (1987–1994); Aircraft Maintenance Chief, United States Navy (1961–1987). **Associations & Accomplishments:** Public Relations Officer, Grand Lodge of Texas Masons. **Personal:** Married to Sandra in 1967. Mr. Kelsey enjoys golf and fishing.

Bruce R. Perry
Vice President of Marketing
Thomson Mechanical
19002 South Santa Fe Avenue
Compton, CA 90221–5909
(310) 639–3523
Fax: (310) 639–8217
EMAIL: See Below

7699

Business Information: Thomson Mechanical is a machinery overhaul contractor specializing in the installation, maintenance, and overhaul of rotating and reciprocating machinery. Established in 1971, the Company employs 150 people and estimates annual revenue to be in excess of $23 million. As Vice President of Marketing, Mr. Perry manages all sales and marketing activities, and oversees new client accounts. Internet users can reach him via: bperry@general.net. **Career Steps:** Vice President of Marketing, Thomson Mechanical (1988–Present); Sales Manager, Argo International (1983–1988). **Associations & Accomplishments:** Electric Club; Pacific Energy Association; Geothermal Resources Council; Northern California Congregation Association; Gey-

sers Geothermal Association; Volunteer Chaplain, California Institution for Men, Chino, California. **Education:** Cypress College. **Personal:** Married to Zeena in 1985. Two children: Allyson and Michael. Mr. Perry enjoys music and golf.

William E. Radcliffe
Director of Integration Services
ARINC Corporation
2551 Riva Road
Annapolis, MD 21401
(410) 266–2083
Fax: (410) 573–3171
EMail: wradclif@aol.com

7699

Business Information: ARINC Corporation specializes in the production and development of aircraft avionics integration and upgrades for government and commercial customers. Serving in managerial and technical engineering roles for ARINC since 1988, Bill Radcliffe was appointed Director of Integration Services in 1994. He provides the overall administration and supervision for engineering support staff in the areas of drafting, engineering, fabrication, testing, and field installation. **Career Steps:** ARINC Corporation: Director of Integration Services (1994–Present), Director of Product Development (1993–1994), Technical Director of Product Support (1988–1993). **Associations & Accomplishments:** Institute of Electronics and Electrical Engineers; American Society for Quality Control. **Education:** Ohio State Unviersity, M.S. (1981); New Mexico State University, B.S.I.E. **Personal:** Married to Pat in 1966. Five children: Cheryl, William, Mindy, Christopher, and Courtney. Mr. Radcliffe enjoys amateur radio and sailing.

Alex Santiago

Vice President and General Manager
Piezas Extra Inc.
P.O. Box 5222
Caguas, Puerto Rico 00726–5222
(809) 258–2420
Fax: (809) 258–2419

7699

Business Information: Piezas Extra Inc. is a manufacturing company specializing in heavy equipment and trailers. In addition, the Corporation sells new and used parts and equipment. Established in 1991, the Corporation currently employs 50 people and has an estimated annual sales of over $6 million. As Vice President and General Manager, Mr. Santiago is responsible for all aspects of Corporate operations, including management. Mr. Santiago holds two inventor patents on automobile and industrial equipment. **Career Steps:** Vice President and General Manager, Piezas Extra Inc. (1991–Present). **Associations & Accomplishments:** American Management Association; Society of Automotive Engineers; I.D.A. **Personal:** Married to Joanne in 1981. Three children: Alan, Bray and Alex.

Gary R. Torkelson
Vice President – Northern Division
Furmanite, Inc.
8900 Mississippi Street
Merrillville, IN 46410
(219) 769–9040
Fax: (219) 769–9079

7699

Business Information: Furmanite, Inc. is an industrial maintenance corporation serving the power, pulp and paper, steel, and food industries. Services provided include: under pressure leak sealing, field machining, concrete repair, valve and safety valve repair. International in scope, with offices across the U.S. and Canada, Furmanite's reported sales income for 1995 is in excess of $100 million. Starting with Furmanite, Inc. as a temporary employee thirteen years ago, Mr. Torkelson proceeded to work his way up the corporate ladder to his current position as Vice President of the Northern Division in 1995. He is responsible for the oversight of all operations for the Division, including budgeting, safety, training, sales, and operations, in addition to overseeing administrative operations of a support staff of 110. **Career Steps:** Furmanite, Inc.: Vice President of the Northern Division (1995–Present), Vice President, Midwest Division (1993–1995), Sales Manager, Midwest Division (1989–1993). **Education:** University of Albuquerque. **Personal:** Married to Beverly in 1971. Two chil-

dren: Eric and Zakary. Mr. Torkelson enjoys golf, camping, and auto restoration.

7800 Motion Pictures

7812 Motion picture and video production
7819 Services allied to motion pictures
7822 Motion picture and tape distribution
7829 Motion picture distribution services
7832 Motion picture theaters, ex drive–in
7833 Drive–in motion picture theaters
7841 Video tape rental

Thomas H. Axelson
Administrative Director
The Jesus Film Project
910 Calle Negocio
San Clemente, CA 92673
(714) 361–7575
Fax: Please mail or call

7812

Business Information: The JESUS Film Project is a non–profit organization centered on international distribution of the film "JESUS." The organization is affiliated with Campus Crusade for Christ. Prior to distribution, the Company first translates the film into the required language. With over 450 mission organizations as well as operations in 167 countries, the Company coordinates with local TV and video companies. As Administrative Director, Mr. Axelson is responsible for fiscal operations, computer and information services, and facility operations. **Career Steps:** Administrative Director, The JESUS Film Project (1986–Present); Financial Planner, Independent (1983–1986); General Manager, Cascade Oil Company (1979–1983). **Associations & Accomplishments:** President, Shiloh International; Director, Christian Associates, Inc. **Education:** Claremont Graduate School, M.S. (1978); Bemidji State University, B.A. **Personal:** Married to Diane Kay in 1968. Two children: Sonja and Mark. Mr. Axelson enjoys sailing, golf, skiing (water and snow).

Hamid Azize

Owner and President
Stage Crew Audiovisual, Inc.
999 Ashford Avenue
San Juan, Puerto Rico 00907
(809) 723–6398
Fax: (809) 721–1410

7812

Business Information: Stage Crew Audiovisual, Inc., established in 1984, acts as a creative and technical partner in audio visual communications, specializing in the rental and operation of professional audio visual, sound, lighting, video projection, interactive and multi–imaging equipment. Stage Crew A/V can interpret and satisfy the most complex requirements in terms of timing, logistics and aesthetic format of any activity wherever professional quality meetings, conventions, or presentation enhancement, is required. Stage Crew A/V can also provide communications systems, two–way radios, cellular telephones and beepers, and satellite teleconferencing to any place globally, and coordinate simultaneous translation services with professional interpreters for conferences. In addition, they provide the most complete and comprehensive design and mounting services for trade shows and conventions, including booths and bonded in–bound/ out–bound freight handling and storage. **Career Steps:** Owner and President, Stage Crew Audiovisual, Inc. (1984–Present); Supervisor, Puerto Rico Telecommunications (1984–1988). **Associations & Accomplishments:** Puerto Rico Hotel and Tourism; San Juan Convention Bureau; Puerto Rico Chamber of Commerce; Association of Young Executives. **Education:** Col. Tecgnologico, Associate Degree (1982); University of Puerto Rico, College of Agricultural and Mechanical Arts, Mayaquez, PR, B.S. in Electrical Engineering. **Personal:** Married to Carmen Loinaz in 1980. Two children: Hamid Khalil and Khali. Mr. Azize enjoys scuba diving, snow skiing and computers.

Howard Barish
President
Kandoo Films, Inc.
4515 Van Nuys Boulevard, Suite 100
Sherman Oaks, CA 91403
(818) 789–6777
Fax: (818) 789–2299

7812

Business Information: Kandoo Films, Inc. is a full service production and post–production facility specializing in On–Air

Promotions, Theatrical Trailers, and Film and T.V. Promotional Presentations for all of the major networks and studios. Kandoo Films has most currently working mainly with on–air promotions, marketing, and advertising presentations for the three major television networks. Kandoo Films has most recently played an active role in the production of NBC's "Must See T.V." promotion for the 1995 Fall Season prime–time line–up, the theatrical launch of Disney's upcoming "101 Dalmations", as well as CBS' May Sweeps specials including the 1996 Miss Universe Pageant. As President and Owner, Mr. Barish is charged with the oversight of all areas of the Corporation. He is heavily involved in the marketing and sales of the Corporation's services and productions and plans to continue as a major supplier of programming to the various T.V. Networks and film studios. **Career Steps:** President, Kandoo Films, Inc. (1992–Present); Vice President, Development, Planet 3 Entertainment (1991–1992); Senior Staff Producer, Directions International (1990–1991); Assistant Director, Alliance Communications (1989–1990). **Associations & Accomplishments:** Directors Guild of Canada; Academy of Canadian Cinema and Television; Kandoo Films Inc. received the 1995 Mobius Award for Best T.V. and Promotional Campaign for the CBS Twilight Zone; Nominated this year for the Promax Award. **Education:** York University, B.F.A. (1983). **Personal:** Married to Suzanne in 1989. Two children: Justin and Jacqueline.

John Eric Bogner
Director
Sony Pictures Entertainment, Inc.
10202 West Washington Boulevard
Culver City, CA 90232
(310) 280–5646
Fax: (310) 280–6808
EMAIL: See Below

7812

Business Information: Sony Pictures Entertainment, Inc., the parent company of Columbia, Tri–Star, and Merv Griffin Enterprises, is a motion picture and television production company. As Director, Mr. Bogner is responsible for diversified administrative activities, including staffing, buying, and financing. In addition, he is director of Fire/Life Safety, Emergency Preparedness, and Business Resumption. Internet users can reach him via: JBOG4ME.AOL. **Career Steps:** Director, Sony Pictures Entertainment (1991–Present); Emergency Preparedness Manager, TRW Space and Defense (1988–1991); Occupational Safety Coordinator, Chevron Corporation (1980–1988); Program Coordinator, Muscular Dystrophy Association (1977–1980). **Associations & Accomplishments:** Board of Directors, Association of Contingency Planners; Business and Industry Council on Emergency Preparedness and Planning; National Fire Protection Association; American Red Cross; The Association of Contingency Planners; Federal Emergency Agency; Electric Power Research Institute. **Education:** University of California – Irvine, Certificate in Occupational Safety (1990); Ohio State University, B.S. in Business Administration (1976). **Personal:** Mr. Bogner enjoys jogging, pencil drawing, and helping as a buddy to care for individuals that are HIV infected.

Louise A. Franicich
President/Founder
Captain Edgar's Videoworks Illinois
P.O. Box 575
Bedford Park, IL 60499–0575
(708) 458–7722
Fax: (708) 458–7768

7812

Business Information: Captain Edgar's Videoworks Illinois, founded in 1988 by Lou Ann Franicich, is a small video production company in Bedford Park, Illinois. In the past, the Company focused on filming equestrian sporting events, currently the Company is in the process of branching out to work on other creative projects including television productions. As President/Founder, Ms. Franicich handles all of the day–to–day operations including staff recruitment, financial matters, marketing of services, and planning for the future. She is directly involved in the producing, directing, editing, animating, and filming of videos. **Career Steps:** President/Founder, Captain Edgar's Videoworks Illinois (1990–Present). **Associations & Accomplishments:** Women in Film; United States Combined Training Association. **Personal:** Ms. Franicich enjoys dressage riding, being a pilot, and composing music.

Harold M. Fraser
Vice President of Operations, Home Video Division
Paramount Pictures
5555 Melrose Avenue
Los Angeles, CA 90038–3197
(213) 956–3776
Fax: (213) 862–0300
EMAIL: See Below

7812

Business Information: Paramount Pictures is a major television and motion picture production studio. The Company provides production and distribution of entertainment products worldwide. The Home Video Division oversees the manufacturing, distribution, advertising, and selling of video products for the Company. As Vice President of Operations for the Home Video Division, Mr. Fraser is responsible for managing manufacturing of the products, all applicable systems, and logistics of new and developing projects. He also oversees purchasing, customer service, and inventory management. Internet users can reach him via: HAROLD_FRASER@PARAMOUNT.COM **Career Steps:** Vice President of Operations, Home Video Division, Paramount Pictures (1990–Present); President, Fraser Logistics Services (1988–1990); Senior Manager, American Honda Motor Company (1983–1988). **Associations & Accomplishments:** Biola University Studio Task Force; Vice President, Old Baldy Council, Boy Scouts of America; Council of Logistics Management. **Education:** University of Southern California, M.B.A. (1977); Stetson University, B.A. (1970). **Personal:** Married to Julie in 1973. Two children: Anne and James. Mr. Fraser enjoys backpacking, running, and computers.

Abby Ginzberg
Producer and Director
Ginzberg Video Productions
1136 Evelyn Avenue
Albany, CA 94706–2316
(510) 528–9116
Fax: (510) 528–2810
EMAIL: See Below

7812

Business Information: Ginzberg Video Productions is a producer of educational training films and documentaries. Clientele include government agencies, legal groups, and public interest groups. An award–winning video producer, Ms. Ginzberg began her career as a lawyer and law teacher. She was in private practice as a civil and criminal trial lawyer and as a lawyer for OSHA. In 1984, she established Ginzberg Video Productions as Producer and Director. Working full–time as an educational video producer, director, and editor, she teaches hundreds of labor education classes and designs many training programs in the field of Hazardous Waste and Hazard Communication. During the past several years, Ms. Ginzberg has been working on training films designed to help the legal profession overcome discrimination within its own ranks as well as in other areas. Her recent documentary, "DOING JUSTICE: The Life and Times of Arthur Kinoy" won the Best of Festival Award and the Best of Justice and Human Rights Category from the Vermont International Film Festival. Additional awards include: CINE Gold Eagle Award, a Silver Gavel award from the American Bar Association and a Silver Apple from the National Educational Film Festival. The documentary has been screened at the Film Arts Festival in San Francisco, the Museum of Modern Art in New York, and was shown on KQED–TV in September 1995. Additional documentaries and training films in which she has produced include: "THOSE WHO KNOW DON'T TELL" – an independently produced documentary on the fight for safe working conditions in the U.S. – it has been used extensively in public health education programs (1991); "JUSTICE IS A CONSTANT STRUGGLE" – on the history of progressive lawyers over the past 50 years (1989); three videos used throughout the U.S. as the basic program for combatting racism and sexism within the legal profession include: "ALL THINGS BEING EQUAL," "A FIRM COMMITMENT," and "ALL IN A DAY'S WORK"; "INSIDE/OUT: A Portrait of Gay and Lesbian Lawyers" – a film designed to overcome sexual orientation discrimination; and "BREAKING DOWN BARRIERS" – a film geared toward increasing inclusion of disabled lawyers and legal workers in the profession. She has recently completed two dramatic training films on legal ethics entitled: "PULP ETHICS: Ethical Dilemmas for Criminal Lawyers" and "THE GUILDING HAND: Ethical Issues in Estate Planning"; "PULP ETHICS" won a 1996 Gold Award from the Houston Film Festival; Internet users can reach her via: AbbyGinz@aol.com. **Career Steps:** Producer and Director, Ginzberg Video Productions (1984–Present); Staff Attorney, California Department of Industrial Relations (1980–1982); Litigation Attorney, U.S. Department of Labor – OSHA (1979–1980); Attorney, Zaks & Harris Law Firm (1976–1979). **Associations & Accomplishments:** San Francisco Bar Association; California State Bar Association; District of Columbia Bar Association; National Lawyers Guild; Board of Directors, Meiklejohn Civil Liberties Institute (1991–Present); Active Coalition for Civil Rights (1988–Present); Former Board of Advisors, K.P.F.A.; Recipient, Certificate of Recognition, California Assembly (1988); Alice Toklas Democratic Club Award (1988); Award of Merit, Bar Association of San Francisco (1994). **Education:** Hastings College of the Law, J.D. (1975); Cornell University, B.A.

(1971); London School of Economics, attended junior year abroad (1969–1970). **Personal:** One child: Sasha Sesser–Ginzberg. Ms. Ginzberg enjoys swimming, photography, and movies.

John Harcourt
Director of Post Production
Atlantis Films Ltd.
65 Heward Avenue
Toronto, Ontario M4M 2T5
(416) 406–7242
Fax: (416) 462 0254
EMAIL: See Below

7812

Business Information: Atlantis Films Ltd. is a film and television production, post production, and distribution studio. As Director of Post Production, Mr. Harcourt supervises post production and related areas for approximately 100 hours of programming annually, overseeing a staff of five in movie and mini–series project operations. Internet users may also reach him via: HARCOURT@HOOKUP.NET **Career Steps:** Director of Post Production, Atlantis Films Ltd. (1985–Present); Freelance Editor (1982–1985). **Education:** Attended, York University (1982). **Personal:** Mr. Harcourt enjoys photography, computing, and travel.

Ms. Virginia A. Hart
Vice President of Sales and Marketing
Grace and Wild Studios, Inc.
23689 Industrial Park Drive
Farmington Hills, MI 48335
(810) 471–6010
Fax: (810) 471–6013

7812

Business Information: Grace and Wild Studios, Inc. is a sales, marketing, and training video production and post video production company providing services for corporations such as Chrysler and Ford. Established in 1985, Grace and Wild Studios, Inc, currently employs 100 people. As Vice President, Sales and Marketing, Ms. Hart is responsible for total sales and marketing for the facility. **Career Steps:** Vice President, Sales and Marketing, Grace and Wild Studios, Inc. (1990–Present); National Sales Manager, LTM Corporation of America (1986–1990); General Manager, Victor Duncan Inc. (1969–1986). **Associations & Accomplishments:** Detroit Producers Association; Adcrafters; ITVA; MIPIC; Big Brothers/Big Sisters; SMPTE. **Education:** Madonna University, B.A. (1995); University of Detroit; Detroit College of Business. **Personal:** One child: Adam. Ms. Hart enjoys scuba diving, reading, bicycling, cooking, visiting museums, travel and attending plays, concerts and movies.

Ms. Janis Nelson

Contract Service Representative, Product Distribution Services
Metro Goldwyn Mayer Inc. (MGM)
2500 Broadway Street, Suite A3270
Santa Monica, CA 90404–3061
(310) 449–3763
Fax: (310) 449–3100

7812

Business Information: Metro Goldwyn Mayer Inc. (MGM) is a major motion picture studio providing world–wide production and distribution of entertainment products, including motion pictures, television programming, home video, interactive software, music, and licensed merchandise. MGM has a 1,500 title film library, a 4,500 title home video library and a significant television library. Established in 1924, MGM currently employs more than 750 people. As a Contract Service Representative of Product Distribution Services, Ms. Nelson is responsible for reviewing sales documentation and translating terms into contract language; completing standard terms and entering contracts into the system; researching and processing Consent for Assignments; negotiations of restructures of domestic television license agreements; primary legal issues in television (including copyright, trademark, pay–or–play, exclusivity, etc.); fundamental laws and their effect on the development, acquisition, transfer and termination of rights. She is also responsible for collection of Domestic and Canadian accounts and credit analysis for new and existing clients. Ms. Nelson also served as a Member of the Official Unsecured Creditors' Committee (KDFI Chapter II Bankruptcy case) and Vice President of Riemer National Television Credit Association. **Career Steps:** Metro Goldwyn Mayer Inc.: Contract Service Representative of Product Distribution Services (1995–Present), Manager of Credit and Collections (1992–1995), Credit Administrator (Sept. 1990), Customer Service Representative for Home Video Operations (1988–1990). **Associations & Accomplishments:** Vice President, Riemer Reporting Service – a National Television Credit Association (1994–Present); Unsecured Creditors

Committee – Dallas Media Investors Corporation (Chapter II Bankruptcy Case – TV Station KDFI) (1992–1994); The West Coast Literary Circle (1993–1995); NAACP – Motion Picture Image Award Committee (1989 and 1990) and MGM S.T.A.R.S. Core Re–engineering Team (1994–Present). **Education:** UCLA Extension: Entertainment Business and Management Certificate Program (Current); Dun & Bradstreet Education Services, Certificate (1991); The University of Detroit, B.A. in Liberal Arts (1982). **Personal:** Nelson enjoys aerobic exercise, Tai Chi, fencing, and photography.

Ben (Ponz) Ponzio

Vice President/General Manager
High Technology Video
3575 Cahuenga Boulevard West #490
Los Angeles, CA 90068
(213) 969–8822
Fax: (213) 969–8860

7812

Business Information: High Technology Video is one of the premier post production companies in the country. Specializing in film transfers, the Company processes films to video tapes for consumer rentals that are pre–formatted to fit T.V. screens. Working primarily with major film studios such as MGM, Universal, Warner Brothers, Disney, 20th Century Fox, and Paramount, the Company also provides digital mastering and services clients worldwide. Established in 1995, High Technology Video employs twenty people and has estimated annual revenue of $4 million. As Vice President/General Manager, Mr. Ponzio oversees all sales, marketing, and management operations. He is responsible for all business development and contacts, and handles all public relations and strategic planning. **Career Steps:** Vice President/General Manager, High Technology Video (1996–Present); Vice President of Sales/Operations, Deluxe Laboratories (1995–1996); Vice President of Studio Sales, All Post In (1991–1995); General Manager, Stars, Inc. (19990–1991). **Associations & Accomplishments:** SMPTE; NATPE; USGA. **Education:** University of Portland, B.A. (1968). **Personal:** Married to Esther "Hank" Smith in 1988. Mr. Ponzio enjoys golf, cooking, and crossword puzzles.

Max A. Schneider, M.D., C.A.D.C.

President
Max A. Schneider, M.D., Inc.
3311 East Kirkwood Ave.
Orange, CA 92669
(714) 639–0062
Fax: (714) 639–0987

7812

Business Information: Max A. Schneider, M.D., Inc. specializes on the production of educational films concerning alcoholism and drug abuse. The videos are distributed internationally in two languages, English and Spanish. As President, Dr. Schneider is responsible for the oversight of all company operations. Concurrent with his position as President, Dr. Schneider is the Medical Director of St. Joseph's Hospital, and Deputy Chairman of the Board of Directors for the National Council of Alcoholism, as well as teaching medical students as a Clinical Associate Professor at the University of California at Irvine. **Career Steps:** President, Max A. Schneider, M.D., Inc. (1953–Present); Clinical Associate Professor, University of California – Irvine (1989–Present); Current Hospital Staff Affiliations: St. Joseph Hospital (Orange), UCI Medical Center, Children's Hospital of Orange County; Internal Medicine Practice Background: Orange County, California (1964 – Retired from private practice Jan. 1981), Buffalo, New York (1953–1964); Locum Tenens – Chatauqua, New York (1953). **Associations & Accomplishments:** Licensed to practice: New York State, California; Fellow, American College of Addiction Treatment Administrators; Board of Directors, American Academy of Addictionology; Co–Founder, American Association of Physicians for Human Rights; American Medical Association; American Society of Addiction Medicine: President (1983–1985), Member (Since 1972), Board of Directors; American Society of Internal Medicine; California Society of Internal Medicine; Orange County Society of Internal Medicine; Association for Medical Education and Research in Susbstance Abuse (AMERSA); California Society of Addiction Medicine; Medical Education and Research Foundation: Chairman of the Board (Since 1987), President (Since 1988); National Council on Alcoholism & Drug Dependence: National Board of Directors (Since 1983), Co–Chair–Medical / Scientific Committee, Secretary, Deputy Chair of the Board of Directors; National Council on Alcoholism & Drug Dependence–Orange County, California Chapter, Board Member, Treasurer; California Medical Association; Orange

County Medical Association; Co–Founder, Southern California Physicians for Human Rights; California Womens Commission on Alcohol & Drugs; Consortium of Medical Educators in Substance Abuse; Professional Education Committee, California Institute of Professional Education in Addiction; RECENT AWARDS: Physician of the Year Award (1995) – Orange County Medical Association; Golden Apple Award for Excellence in Teaching (1995) – University of California–Irvine; Lifetime Career Achievement Award (1994) – University at Buffalo Medical Alumni Association; Best Doctors in America (1992–1995); Silver Key Award (1993) – National Council on Alcoholism and Drug Dependence; Annual Distinguished Service Award (1993) – American Society of Addiction Medicine; Outstanding Contribution in the Field of Human Relations (1993) – Orange County Human Relations Commission; Man of the Year Award (1992) – Orange County Cultural Pride; Inducted into Hall of Fame – California Association of Alcoholism & Drug Abuse Counselors (1987); Certified By Examination By American Society Of Addiction Medicine (1986). **Education:** University of Buffalo: M.D. (1949), dual major in Psychology and Biology (1939–1942); Internship, Buffalo General Hospital (1949–1950); Residency, Buffalo General Hospital (1950–1952); Fellowship, Harvard Medical School/ Assistant in Medicine (1952–1953); Chemical Dependency Credentialing: Utah School of Alcoholism (1969), Georgian Mental Health Institute (1970); CERTIFICATIONS: Certified Alcoholism Counselor (1988) **Personal:** Dr. Schneider enjoys travel, stamps, birding, and classical music.

Daniel E. Stanton

Director IPSO Operations
MCA INC.
100 Universal City Plaza, 508–1
Universal City, CA 91608
(818) 777–7655
Fax: (818) 733–1523
E MAIL: destant@mca.com

7812

Business Information: MCA, INC. (MCA) is a major entertainment company who produces and distributes motion picture, television and home video products, and recorded music; publishes books; and operates theme parks and retail stores. MCA is a subsidiary of The Seagram Company Ltd. (Seagram) and is the parent company of Universal Studios, Universal Pictures, MCA TV, MCA Records, MCA Home Video, Spencer Gifts, The Putnam Berkeley Group and many other companies. As Director IPSO Operations, Mr. Stanton is responsible for all major information processing systems for MCA and Seagram worldwide. He directs a staff of 65 and is responsible for personnel, budgetary concerns, marketing of services, strategic planning of new technologies, developing and implementing new services, and re–evaluation of existing services. **Career Steps:** Director IPSO Operations, MCA, INC. (1992–Present); Project Manager, Cap Gemini of America (1987–1991); Vice President Mortgage Systems Development, Great Western Bank (1985–1987). **Associations & Accomplishments:** Rotary Club of Westlake Village Sunrise (Past President 1986–1987); Rotary Club of Simi Sunrise; Mason; AFCOM – Selected 1995 Top five Data Center Manager of the Year. **Education:** Computer Learning Center, Programming Certificate (1976); Attending, University of Phoenix Business Program. **Personal:** Married to Hannah in 1989. One child: Julie. Mr. Stanton enjoys golf, travel, reading, and family activities.

Carol L. Wiel
Vice President of Advertising
Ingram Entertainment, Inc.
2 Ingram Boulevard
La Vergne, TN 37086–3600
(615) 287–4500
Fax: (615) 287–4984
EMAIL: See Below

7812

Business Information: Ingram Entertainment, Inc. is a privately–held, video and audio distribution company, representing all studios. Ingram Design Group does all the designs for the Company. Established in 1965, Ingram Entertainment, Inc. reports annual revenue of $800 million and currently employs 820 people. Joining Ingram Entertainment as Vice President of Advertising in 1988, Ms. Wiel is responsible for all aspects of advertising activities. She also is the General Manager of Ingram Design Group. **Career Steps:** Vice President of Advertising, Ingram Entertainment, Inc. (1988–Present); Manager of Administration, Aladdin Industries (1981–1988); Owner and General Manager, Standard Sales (1978–1981). **Associations & Accomplishments:** Tennessee Art League; Nashville Advertising Federation; Visual Artists Alliance of Nashville; Maryland Farms Athletic Club; National Association of Women in the Arts; National Association of Female Executives; National Association of Video Dealers; Delta Gamma Alumnae Association. **Education:** University

of Maryland, B.A. (1964). **Personal:** Married to Thomas T. in 1964. One child: Gregory. Ms. Wiel enjoys watercolor painting, exercising, and tennis.

Mr. Alan D. Youngstein
Business Consultant
Universal Studios
100 Universal City Plaza
Universal Studios, CA 41608
(818) 777–7948
Fax: Please mail or call

7812

Business Information: Universal Studios M.C.A. is a television and motion picture production studio, as well as a universal theme park. They also distribute and exhibit motion pictures in commercially operated theaters and furnish diversified services to the motion picture industry. Mr. Youngstein currently serves as a Business Consultant for the motion picture establishment. **Career Steps:** Business Consultant, Universal Studios M.C.A. (1995–Present); Vice President of Finance and Administration, KRIV–TV, Fox Television Stations (1993–1995); Director of Finance, Skyshapers, Inc. (1992–1993); Manager of Budgeting and Forecasting, Sony Pictures Entertainment (1990–1992); Business Consultant, Fox Television (1987–1989). **Associations & Accomplishments:** Certified Public Accountant; Member, AICPA. **Education:** New York University, M.B.A. (1983); Brooklyn College, B.S. Degree in Accounting. **Personal:** Mr. Youngstein enjoys basketball and weightlifting.

Mr. Michael E. Marcus
President and Chief Operating Officer
Metro Goldwyn Mayer Pictures (MGM)
2500 Broadway Street
Santa Monica, CA 90404
(310) 449–3400
Fax: (310) 449–3055

7813

Business Information: Metro Goldwyn Mayer Pictures is a major motion picture studio, established in 1924. As President and Chief Operating Officer, Mr. Marcus has the final decision for what movies the studio makes, and profit and loss responsibility for studio operations. Established in 1924, Metro Goldwyn Mayer Pictures (MGM) employs a full–time staff of 750. **Career Steps:** President and Chief Operating Officer, Metro Goldwyn Mayer Pictures (MGM) (1993–Present); Motion Picture Agent, Creative Artists Agency (1981–1993); Co–Owner and Agent, Kohner/Levy/Marcus (1977–1981). **Associations & Accomplishments:** The Academy of Motion Pictures Arts and Sciences; Board of Directors, Environmental Media Association; Venice Family Clinic. **Education:** Pennsylvania State University, B.A. in Economics (1967).

Michael S. Keefe
Director of New Media
ICE, Integrated Communications & Entertainment, Inc.
489 Queen Street, East
Toronto, Ontario M5A 1V1
(416) 868–3295
Fax: (416) 367–8996

7819

Business Information: ICE, Integrated Communications & Entertainment, Inc., an international firm for the development of multimedia and internet content for consumers and corporate clients located in Toronto, was established in 1978 and currently employs 110 people. The Company prepares print and graphic designs, videos and television productions in Canada. As Director of New Media, Mr. Keefe works with clients to create innovative and interactive marketing programs. He is involved with strategic planning for ICE, locating and developing new media areas, and creative development. Mr. Keefe assists with the determination of where to make corporate investments to obtain the best return. **Career Steps:** Director of New Media, ICE, Integrated Communications & Entertainment, Inc. (1992–Present); Consultant, Communications, Canadian Government–Department of Communications (1988–1992); Manager, Planning and Research, First Choice Communications (1986–1987). **Associations & Accomplishments:** Interactive Media and Technology Association (IMAT); Mr. Keefe has been published in various trade journals and participated in television interviews. **Education:** York University, B.A. (1985); Canadian Junior College, Lausanne, Switzerland (OSSHGD). **Personal:** Married to Diane Patricia in 1982. Two children: Sean Ryan and Sarah Emily. Mr. Keefe enjoys travel, sports, and the movies.

Vicky M. Marlow
Director of Sales
Sigma Designs
46501 Landing Parkway
Fremont, CA 94538–6421
(510) 770–2637
Fax: (510) 656–9974 (510) 770–2918
EMAIL: See Below

7819

Business Information: Sigma Designs is a manufacturer of multimedia video compression, 2D/3D graphics chips, and M–PEG playback cards under their product name "Real Magic." As Director of Sales, Ms. Marlow is responsible for the oversight of all domestic sales of playback boards in the United States and Canada. Internet users can reach her via: Vicky_Marlow@sdesigns.com **Career Steps:** Director of Sales, Sigma Designs (1995–Present); Director of OEM Sales, Ulead Systems (1995); National Sales Manager, Creative Labs (1992–1994); General Manager of Operations, Trading Zone (1991); District Sales Manager, Atari (1985–1989). **Associations & Accomplishments:** National Association of Female Executives; National Library of Poetry; Awarded Recognition from Child Advocacy Council. **Education:** Attended: Cerritos College, Academy of Real Estate. **Personal:** Two children: Carisa and Eric Salazar. Ms. Marlow enjoys scuba diving, gourmet cooking, and charity work.

Luis Carlos Vasquez Mazzilli
Freelance Director
Independent
P.O. Box 7–0600, San Jose 1000
San Jose, Costa Rica
(506) 220–1134
Fax: (506) 220–1134

7819

Business Information: Mr. Vasquez Mazzilli is an independent director specializing in movies, videos, T.V., theater, and various other entertainment and media fields. **Career Steps:** Free Lance Director, Independent (Present); Art Director, Hangar Film Production (1996); Casting Director, Nordisk Film, Denmark (1995–1996); Director, National University Drama Theater (1989–1994); Director, Speculum Mundi Company of Dance Theater and Images; Casting Director in Costa Rica, Aoi Advertising Promotion Japan; Art Director, M.A. Production (1996); Teaching, National University in Heredia Body Movement and Introduction to Play Direction. **Associations & Accomplishments:** National Theater of Costa Rica; National Theater Company; International Festival of Arts, Costa Rica. **Education:** Licensed in Theater. **Personal:** Mr. Vasquez Mazzilli enjoys fashion, costume design, and art book collecting.

Mr. Alan D. Youngstein
Business Consultant
Universal Studios M.C.A.
100 Universal City Plaza
Universal Studios, CA 41608
(818) 777–7948
Fax: Please mail or call

7819

Business Information: Universal Studios M.C.A. is a television and motion picture production studio, as well as a universal theme park. They also distribute and exhibit motion pictures in commercially operated theaters and furnish dviersified services to the motion picture industry. Mr. Youngstein currently serves as a Business Consultant for the motion picture establishment. **Career Steps:** Business Consultant, Universal Studios M.C.A. (1995–Present); Vice President of Finance and Administration, KRIV–TV, Fox Television Stations (1993–1995); Director of Finance, Skyshapers, Inc. (1992–1993); Manager of Budgeting and Forecasting, Sony Pictures & Entertainment (1990–1992); Business Consultant, Fox Television (1987–1989). **Associations & Accomplishments:** Certified Public Accountant; Member, A.I.C.P.A. **Education:** New York University, M.B.A. (1983); Brooklyn College, B.S. Degree in Accounting. **Personal:** Mr. Youngstein enjoys basketball and weighlifting.

Sharon Wood
Executive Vice President
E.M.C.I.
24 Richmond Hill Avenue
Stamford, CT 06901–3600
(203) 327–6545
Fax: (203) 431–6121

7822

Business Information: E.M.C.I. is an international entertainment marketing company for the distribution of music, movies, video and home games worldwide. With a background in sports marketing, mass media, and advertising, Ms. Wood joined E.M.C.I. as Executive Vice President in 1993. She di-

rects all marketing efforts of a 15–member staff, as well as providing business leadership, growth, and development of marketing strategies and marketing programs for clients. **Career Steps:** Executive Vice President, E.M.C.I. (1993–Present); Director of Promotions, Barker Campbell & Farley (1989–1993); Account Executive, Guild Group (1988–1989). **Associations & Accomplishments:** Promotion Marketing Association of American (PMAA); Cable Television Advertisers (C–TAM); Listed in Who's Who in America. **Education:** Attended: University of Maryland. **Personal:** Ms. Wood enjoys tennis, baseball, and reading.

Kristin D. Bevens

Vice President of Sales and Marketing
Platinum, Inc.
3421 East Harbor
Phoenix, AZ 85034
(602) 437–9100
Fax: (602) 437–8580

7829

Business Information: Platinum, Inc. is a national company specializing in the sale and duplication of videos. Owned by Motion Pictures Laboratories, the Company is headquartered in Nashville and Memphis, TN. As Vice President of Sales and Marketing, Ms. Bevens is responsible for the direction of the Company and is currently involved in a joint effort with the Boys and Girls Club. **Career Steps:** Vice President, Sales and Marketing, Platinum, Inc. (1996–Present); Marketing, Time America (1994–1996); Director of Sales and Marketing, P.R.S. (1993–1994). **Associations & Accomplishments:** APOA; National Association of Women Business Owners. **Education:** Palmor College, Associates degree (1986). **Personal:** Ms. Bevens enjoys gardening, animals, volunteer work at the Phoenix Zoo, and road racing.

Mr. Dean C. Hallett

Vice President of Finance and Administration
Buena Vista Pictures Marketing, A Division of the Walt Disney Motion Picture Gro
500 South Buena Vista Street
Burbank, CA 91521
(818) 560–6402
Fax: (818) 557–6401

7829

Business Information: Buena Vista Pictures Marketing specializes in motion picture marketing and distribution for three production studios (Walt Disney Pictures, Touchstone Pictures, and Hollywood Pictures). As Vice President of Finance and Administration, Mr. Hallett is responsible for all financial planning, budget development, forecasting and financial control, related to the marketing and distribution of productions. He is also involved with human resource activies and facilities management. **Career Steps:** Vice President of Finance and Administration, Buena Vista Pictures Marketing, A Division of the Walt Disney Motion Pictures Group, (1994–Present); Director of Finance, Buena Vista Pictures Marketing, A Division of the Walt Disney Motion Pictures Group (1991–1994); Manager, Corporate Management Audit, The Walt Disney Company (1990–1991); Group Controller, Anthony Industries, Inc. (1988–1990); Senior Manager, Ernst & Whitney (1981–1988). **Associations & Accomplishments:** AICPA; California Society of CPA's; University of Southern California – Accounting Circle; Campus Recruiting Coordinator, University of Southern California (1985–1988); Exchange Visitor, Ernst & Whitney – London (1986–1987). **Education:** University of Southern California, B.S. Degree in Business (1980). **Personal:** Married to Kelli L. in 1983. Two children: Drew C. and Makenzie R. Mr. Hallett enjoys snow skiing and golf.

J. Kathleen Gosa
Vice President of Software Engineering
Jc–I–T Institute of Technology, Inc.
6825 South Galena Street
Englewood, CO 80112
(303) 792–8300
Fax: (303) 792–8311
E MAIL: See Below

7831

Business Information: Jc–I–T is a full solutions provider of demand flow technology for manufacturing companies. As Vice President of Software Engineering, Ms. Gosa is responsible for the development and deployment of support software products for demand flow technology, as well as management of the membership information systems. Internet users can reach her via: Kkgosa@jcit.com. **Career Steps:** Vice President of Software Engineering, Jc–I–T Institute of Technology, Inc. (1995–Present); Information Foundation: Director of Software Development and Training (1989–1995), Manager of Software Development (1986–1989); Instructor, Washburn University (1984–1986). **Associations & Accomplishments:** Member of Phi Kappa Phi; Upsilon Pi Epsilon; Pi Mu Epsilon; and Kappa Mu Epsilon honorary academic fraternities. **Education:** University of Kansas: M.S. Computer Science (1986), B.S. Mathematics; Washburn University: B.S. Computer Science, A.A. Information Science. **Personal:** Married to Bill in 1970. Two children: Laura and Melissa. Ms. Gosa enjoys outdoor activities with her family, hiking in the mountains, and reading.

John Macdonald Jentz

President and Chief Executive Officer
Spring Brook Center, Inc.
105 Billingsgate Road, Box 900
South Wellfeet, MA 02663–0900
(508) 349–2520
Fax: (508) 349–2902

7832

Business Information: Spring Brook Center, Inc. is a holding company for movie theatre locations, doing business as Wellfeet Cinemas. Regional in scope, it owns the oldest (and few remaining in the U.S.) drive–in movie theatre in the New England states, as well as an in–house 4–screen cinema mall. As President and Chief Executive Officer, Mr. Jentz oversees all operations for entity holdings, as well as presides at all board meetings providing corporate strategies and developments. **Career Steps:** President and Chief Executive Officer, Spring Brook Center, Inc. (1957–Present); President and Chief Executive Officer, Kauai Mountain Tours, Inc. (1982–); Acting Chief, Wellfleet Fire Department (1967–1995). **Associations & Accomplishments:** MIT Club of Cape Cod; Harvard Club of Cape Cod; Cape Cod Foresters and Firefighters Association; National Rifle Association; Southeastern Massachusetts Police Association; Republican Party. **Education:** Massachusetts Institute of Technology, S.M. (1956); Harvard College, A.B. in Architectural Sciences (1952). **Personal:** Mr. Jentz enjoys animals.

Donald R. Guzauckas Jr.

Director
HB Group, Inc.
222 Elm Street, Suite 4
North Haven, CT 06473–3260
(203) 234–8107
Fax: (203) 239–4882

7841

Business Information: HB Group, Inc. is an audio and video rental company offering professional presentation and video production equipment and services. Joining HB Group, Inc. in 1989, Mr. Guzauckas began in Technical Operations and has subsequently been promoted to oversee all operations. He oversees sales, administrative operations, MIS and technical operations. **Career Steps:** HB Group, Inc.: Director (1992–Present), Manager, Technical Services (1989–1992). **Associations & Accomplishments:** ICIS; CLEF. **Personal:** Married to Marianne in 1995. Mr. Guzauckas enjoys rock climbing.

Christopher S. Light
District Manager
Movie Warehouse Corporation
3536 Rochester Road
Troy, MI 48083
(810) 524–0200
Fax: (810) 524–3915

7841

Business Information: Movie Warehouse Corporation specializes in audio–video rental and retail sales. Regional in scope, the Company has twenty–five stores in Detroit, with another forty–five in the Lexington, Kentucky area. Established in 1987, Movie Warehouse Corporation employs 745 people, and has an estimated annual revenue of $27 million. As District Manager, Mr. Light oversees the day–to–day operations of three locations. Responsible for human resources, his duties include all aspects of personnel management, as well as purchasing movies, budgetary concerns, and preparing monthly reports. **Career Steps:** Movie Warehouse Corporation: District Manager (1996–Present), Store Manager (1995–1996); Store Manger, Holiday Video (1993–1995). **Associations & Accomplishments:** Delta Sigma Phi; Oakland County Health Division; Troy School District. **Education:** Ferris State University School of Business, Accounting (1992); Currently attending Oakland University, Continuing Education. **Personal:** Married to Amy Light in 1994. Two children: Identical twins Stephanie Amber and Samantha Ann. Mr. Light enjoys movies, tennis, and reading.

7900 Amusement and Recreation Services

7911 Dance studios, schools, and halls
7922 Theatrical producers and services
7929 Entertainers and entertainment groups
7933 Bowling centers
7941 Sports clubs, managers and promoters
7948 Racing, including track operation
7991 Physical fitness facilities
7992 Public golf courses
7993 Coin–operated amusement devices
7996 Amusement parks
7997 Membership sports and recreation clubs
7999 Amusement and recreation, NEC

Monica Barnett Smith
Owner/Artistic Director
Exclusively Ballet
7154 Cahaba Valley Road
Birmingham, AL 35242
(205) 995–9220
Fax: (205) 991–3954
EMAIL: See Below

7911

Business Information: A Principal Dancer with the State of Alabama Ballet from 1981–1984, Ms. Barnett Smith established Exclusively Ballet in 1991, pursuing her desire to help dancers reach their potential in the art she has loved since childhood. The prestigious school offers 240 students a year the opportunity to learn ballet, tap, jazz, piano, voice, and pageant propaganda in various skill groups, from beginner to professional. Fund–raising performances are held each year for various community organizations, including a 1996 performance for St. Jude's Children's Hospital. Ms. Barnett Smith is responsible for daily operations at the school, coordinating all activities and fund–raising. She choreographs, instructs classes, provides artistic direction, and gives individual attention to each student in the further development of their talents. She was nominated in April of 1996 to the Alabama State Ballet Board. She has also volunteered her time as a guest speaker at local schools promoting the art of dance to students and served as Teacher and Choreographer for Heather Whitestone, "Miss America 1995." Internet users can reach her via: EXBALLET@AOL.COM **Career Steps:** Owner/Artistic Director, Exclusively Ballet (1991–Present); Teacher and Choreographer for Heather Whitestone – "Miss America 1995" (1995); Principal Dancer, State of Alabama Ballet (1981–1984). **Associations & Accomplishments:** Miss America Pageant; Sponsor, Little League Baseball. **Education:** University of Alabama – Birmingham, B.A. in Arts and English with Honors (1979). **Personal:** Married to Scott R. Smith in 1984. Two children: Kenneth Blake and Matthew Jarrod. Ms. Barnett Smith enjoys spending time with her two boys and attending Little League games.

William L. Anoka
Senior Producer
Walt Disney Attractions Entertainment
P.O. Box 10,000
Lake Buena Vista, FL 32830
(407) 397–3704
Fax: (407) 397–3915

7922

Business Information: Walt Disney Attractions Entertainment, affiliated with the Walt Disney Co., providing quality live show family entertainment, is the senior producer for the new 30,000 seat amphitheater facility at Walt Disney World. With twenty–five years of experience in Disney Entertainment Management, Walt Disney World, and an Opening Day, October 1, 1971 entertainment staff member with three years of prior entertainment management and technical theme park experience with Six Flags Over Georgia, Mr. Anoka has served in his current position as Senior Producer of Walt Disney Attractions Entertainment since 1994. In this capacity, he is responsible for coordinating and implementing all entertainment aspects of show development, opening day menu, organizing and operating plans for the facility, and special events for the project. His experience includes ten years as Stage Manager and Production Manager for entertainment products for conventions, special events and WDW road tours; opening entertainment productions for conventions, special events and WDW road tours; opening entertainment staff for EPCOT Center, and eight years as EPCOT Theme Park Entertainment Man-

ager; two and a half years as Manager and two and a half years as General Manager of Resort Entertainment Productions. He has a musical, performing and technical background, including eight years of clarinet, performing gymnastics, vaulting and synchronized tumbling, circus high wire, low casting and vaulting routines, as well as college and community theater activities. **Career Steps:** Senior Producer, Walt Disney Attractions Entertainment (1994–Present); WALT DISNEY WORLD: General Manager – Resort Entertainment Prod. (1992–1994), Manager – Resort Entertainment Prod. (1989–1992), Manager – EPCOT Center Entertainment (1984–1989), Production Manager – EPCOT Center Entertainment (1982–1984), Area Stage Manager – Resort Conv./ Spec. Events (1977–1982), Stage Manager – Resort Conventions (1976–1977), Area Supervisor – Resort Conventions (1973–1976), Senior Coordinator – Resort Conventions (1972–1973), Technical Coordinator – Special Events (1972) Show Coordinator (1971–1972); MILITARY: Florida Army National Guard – Major (RET) (1971–1992); Stage Manager Positions: Miss Florida Pageant, Orlando (June 1971), Boy Scout National Conference, Atlanta, GA (May 1971); Production Stage Manager, Six Flags Over Georgia – Crystal Pistol Music Hall (1969–1971); Retail Salesperson, Schwobilt Clothiers (1967–1969). **Associations & Accomplishments:** International Association of Auditorium Managers; Florida National Guard Officers Association; I.A.T.S.E. Local 631; MILITARY HONORS: Leadership Award – OCS Class #17 FLNGMA (1978); Retention and Recruiting Badge (1979); Active Duty Acknowledgement for service during Miami riots (May 1980); Support of Battalions hosting NGOA Conference (1982, 1988, 1994); Senior Tactics Committee Member (1985); State of Florida Sumter L. Lowry Leadership Award (1987); Nominated – General Douglas MacArthur National Leadership Award (1989); Member of Military Committee sent to assist the Venezuela War College in "First Battle" tactics (1990); Member of Military Committee assigned to write The Central America "War Plan" (1990–1991). **Education:** University of Tennessee – Chattanooga, B.S. in Business Administration – Special (1971); Attended: Shorter College, Business Administration (1968–1969); Professional Development: Florida Officers Candidate School; Basic and Advance Infantry School; School for Assembly Facility Management, Phases I & II. **Personal:** Married to Gail M. in 1983. Two children: William L. II and Brittney L. Mr. Anoka enjoys watersports, tennis, coaching Little League, and participating in the YMCA Indian Guides.

R. Bradford Barton
Director of Network Advertising
NTN Communications, Inc.
91 Raymond Street
Darien, CT 06820
(203) 656–2762
Fax: (203) 656–2762

7922

Business Information: NTN Communications, Inc. is the largest provider of interactive television services to the education, home, and hospitality industries. Headquartered in the United States, the Company also maintains affiliates in South Africa, Australia, and Europe. Mr. Barton joined NTN in 1988 as Director of Network Advertising. He is presently responsible for overseeing a staff of ten in the marketing of commercial air–time and the development of new marketing and production ideas. **Career Steps:** Director of Network Advertising, NTN Communications, Inc. (1988–Present); Marketing Director and Founder, Arena Football (1985–1988); Senior Vice President, Dentsu – Young & Rubicam (1979–1985). **Associations & Accomplishments:** Interactive Television Association. **Education:** International Graduate School, Masters (1969); Attended: Parsons College, Deerfield Academy. **Personal:** Two children: Robert and Bridgitte. Mr. Barton enjoys golf, snow skiing, and sailing.

Laura Cason
Senior Manager of Corporate Sales
Opryland U.S.A.
2802 Opryland Drive
Nashville, TN 37214–1200
(615) 871–5994
Fax: (615) 871–6661

7922

Business Information: Opryland U.S.A. is the management office that oversees entertainment attractions, such as The Grand Ole Opry, Opryland Themepark, The Ryman Auditorium, General Jackson Show Boat, Nashville On Stage Concerts, and Wildhorse Saloon. Joining Opryland U.S.A. as Senior Manager of Corporate Sales in 1992, Ms. Cason is responsible for the management of corporate sales, including sales to corporations, military forces, and credit unions. **Career Steps:** Opryland U.S.A.: Senior Manager of Corporate Sales (1994–Present), Corporate Sales Account Executive (1992–94); Regional Consultant, American Red Cross (1992); Customer Contact Representative, John H. Harland Company (1989–1992). **Associations & Accomplishments:** Nashville Chamber of Commerce; CABLE; Society for Human Resource Managers; National Employee Services and Recreational Association. **Education:** Florida State Uni-

versity, B.S. (1988). **Personal:** Married to Greg in 1993. Ms. Cason enjoys pottery, reading, and gardening.

Jon Kevin Gossett
Development Director
Houston Grand Opera
510 Preston Suite 500
Houston, TX 77002
(713) 546–0274
Fax: (713) 247–0906

7922

Business Information: Houston Grand Opera is the fifth largest opera production company in America. As Development Director, Mr. Gossett is responsible for corporate grants and sponsorships, government grants, individual underwriting and annual support, special events, endowment and capital campaigns, planned giving, and board development. **Career Steps:** Development Director, Houston Grand Opera (1994–Present); Director of Development, The Guthrie Theater (1989–1994); President, Ft. Wayne Fine Arts Found (1984–1989); Executive Director, High Point Arts Council (1980–1984). **Associations & Accomplishments:** Opera America; American Council for the Arts; Theatre Development Group. **Education:** The University of Michigan – Ann Arbor, B.M.A. in Business Administration and Music Performance (1977). **Personal:** Mr. Gossett enjoys weightlifting, music, the organ, and running.

Walter D. Harmon Jr.
President
Positive Art Industries
P.O. Box 230289
Anchorage, AK 99523–0289
(907) 561–4888
Fax: (907) 561–6688
EMAIL: See Below

7922

Business Information: Positive Art Industries is a concert promoter and events specialist, coordinating concerts (e.g., adult contemporary, jazz, etc.) throughout the Northwest United States. As President, Mr. Harmon is responsible for oversight of daily operations, client interface, personnel supervision, and customer service. Internet users can reach him via: carepluse@alaska.net **Career Steps:** President, Positive Art Industries (1991–Present); President, Wal–Harm Enterprises (1989–1991). **Associations & Accomplishments:** National Association for the Advancement of Colored People; Black Caucus; Anchorage Bowlers Association; United Way; City of Hope. **Education:** Attended, Eastern Washington University; Attended, University of Alaska – Anchorage. **Personal:** Mr. Harmon enjoys martial arts, bowling, bicycling, travel, networking, and physical fitness.

Ricky D. Hawkins
Chief Executive Officer
John W. Hawkins Institute of Performing Arts Inc.
2 Ayrault Street
Newport, RI 02840–2742
(401) 841–4136
Fax: (401) 848–7484

7922

Business Information: Devoting his entire professional career to the betterment of entertainers and their education and promotion, Ricky Hawkins serves as Chief Executive Officer for various recording production and performing arts education centers as follows: John W. Hawkins Institute of Performing Arts, Inc. – for the training and education of performing arts, providing dance, vocal and musical performance and recording instruction; Chayar Productions, Inc. – provides bookings for students pursuing dance and theatrical careers; and Accord Records, Inc. – full–service recording studio. As Chief Executive Officer, Mr. Hawkins manages all programs, as well as coordinates all student scholarships and recording contracts. **Career Steps:** Chief Executive Officer, John W. Hawkins Institute of Performing Arts Inc. (1993–Present); Chief Executive Officer, Accord Records, Inc. (1995–Present); Chief Executive Officer, Chayah Productions, Inc. (1995–Present). **Associations & Accomplishments:** Scottish Rite Mason; York Rite Mason; The Order of the Eastern Star; Shriners; NAACP; Served in Desert Storm and Desert Shield campaigns. **Education:** University of Virginia, (1995); University of Alabama; Concordia College, A.A. **Personal:** Mr. Hawkins enjoys music, tennis and basketball.

Michael A. Joseph

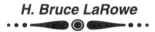

President and Chief Executive Officer
Omari Productions
22150 Stratford Street
Oak Park, MI 48237–2566
(313) 337–4008
Fax: Please mail or call
7922

Business Information: Omari Productions is an entertainment production company specializing in video, radio, and live shows. The Company provides the overall operations and management for the nationally–syndicated daily talk show — "The Michael Joseph Show". Geared towards the youth of America, topics include such timely issues as anti–drug campaigns, teenage pregnancy, abortion, gang violence, peer pressure and family relationships. As President and Chief Executive Officer, Mr. Joseph not only is the host/producer of the talk show, he also oversees all other video production and development strategies. **Career Steps:** President and Chief Executive Officer, Omari Productions (1990–Present). **Associations & Accomplishments:** National Association for the Advancement of Colored People; Save Our Sons and Daughters; Putting Dollars in Detroit, Economic Summit Organizer; Coalition of Black Trade Unionists; Junior Achievement; Domestic Violence Taskforce; Detroit Producers Association; Actors Equity; AAU Basketball; Outstanding Young Man of America (1986); Nominated Best Talk Show Host and Producer of the Year by Blacks in Advertising, Radio and Television (BART). **Education:** Wayne State University, Labor School; Central Michigan University, Radio/TV – Film. **Personal:** One child: Jamal Omari Mandela. Mr. Joseph enjoys reading, motivational workshops, and coaching youth sports.

H. Bruce LaRowe

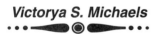

Executive Director
Children's Theatre of Charlotte
1017 East Morehead Street
Charlotte, NC 28402
(704) 376–3774
Fax: (704) 376–3774
7922

Business Information: Children's Theatre of Charlotte is a non–profit organization, designed to serve area youth from the ages of three to eighteen years old in theatre arts education. The Theatre offers afterschool programs by professional performers teaching drama, playwriting, etc. Role–playing courses on subjects such as violence prevention and substance abuse. During the year, eight different productions are presented by the youth and professional actors. In addition, a Pro–Tour company performs at local schools and in the community from Labor Day through Memorial Day. New work is also commissioned from independent writers. Future plans include hosting a national conference in 1997 for the 50th year anniversary of the American Alliance of Theatre Education. As Executive Director, Mr. LaRowe is responsible for the direction of all theatre operations, including overseeing the budget, representing the theatre in the community, and public relations. He also serves as a liaison to the Volunteer Board of Directors. **Career Steps:** Executive Director, Children's Theatre of Charlotte (1993–Present); Director of Development, Belmont Abbey College (1991–1993); Association Director, Arts & Science Council (1983–1991). **Associations & Accomplishments:** Laubach Literacy Program, tutor at local prison; Active Member and Former President, Arts North Carolina. **Education:** University of Illinois–Springfield, M.A. (1982); Millikin University, B.A. (1975). **Personal:** Married to Anita in 1983. Two children: Jonathan and Joanne. Mr. LaRowe enjoys backpacking in the North Carolina mountains and long–distance bike riding.

Victorya S. Michaels

Talent Agent
The Irv Schechter Company – Talent Agency
9300 Wilshire Boulevard, Suite 400
Beverly Hills, CA 90212
(310) 278–8070
Fax: (310) 278–6058
EMAIL: See Below
7922

Business Information: The Irv Schechter Company Talent Agency is an establishment primarily engaged in providing writers, directors, producers and actors to the television and motion picture industry. International in scope, the Agency was established in 1976, and employs twenty people. Talent agent Victorya Michaels has been with the Agency for over ten years, representing producers, directors, animation writers, as well as below–the–line talent (technicians that make the movies). In addition to agenting, Victorya Michaels is also a sought after motivational speaker, inspiring her audience to chase forgotten dreams and find happiness at every stage of life. She offers insight and inspiration to audiences of all ages. She has spoken at conventions, universities, women's retreats, churches, and high schools. Her topics include "How To Live a Thrilling Life in Spite of Reality" and "How to be Happy and Still Thrive in Your Career", among others. Annually, she teaches a twelve week course at the University of California at Los Angeles extension entitled "Your Career Path in Hollywood" and has appeared at Los Angeles Convention Center's "Show Biz Expo" for the past two years. On the agent front, Michaels' wide range of clientele has won awards across the board, including Academy Awards, Emmy Awards, Humanitas Awards, Ace Awards, and Clio Awards. She has had clients on such films as "Zorro", "Waiting to Exhale", "Crimson Tide", "Species", "The Firm", "Die Hard", "Dances With Wolves", "Batman", and "Ghost" to name a few. In the television arena, her clients produce, direct or write animation, sitcoms and reality television. She sold the television series "Extreme" for ABC and the animation series "Two Stupid Dogs" for the Turner Network. Ms Michaels' entree to the entertainment industry came as a talent liaison/coordinator for such award show ceremonies as the "Grammy Awards", "MTV Awards", "American Music Awards", "Academy of Country Music Awards", "Golden Globe Awards", and "Emmy Awards', among others. Since 1982 she has worked on more than fifty of those televised award shows. She spent a year in public relations at a small firm that handled a few well known comedians. She then moved over to The Irv Schechter Company. Starting as assistant to the President, sixteen months later she was promoted to talent agent. Raised in Garden Grove, Califronia, Ms. Michaels has resided in Los Angeles for the past ten years, where she balances her dual career as a talent agent and motivational speaker. She recently received her Master's of Theology at Fuller Theological Seminary in Pasadena, California, and was Ordained by the International Ministerial Fellowship. Internet users can reach her via: VictoryaM@aol.com or THRILLNGLFE@aol.com. **Career Steps:** The Irv Schechter Company–Talent Agency: Agent (1986–Present), Department Head: Below the Line (1988–Present), Department Head, Animation; President, Thrilling Life Seminars (1996–Present). **Associations & Accomplishments:** Associates in Media, Premiss; Academy of Television Arts & Sciences; International Ministerial Fellowship (Ordained Minister as of October, 1995). **Education:** Fuller Theological Seminary, M.A. in Theology (1996); California State University, Long Beach, Bachelor of Arts in Journalism, with a Minor in Speech (1985). **Personal:** Ms. Michaels enjoys speaking, writing, hiking, working out, and attending concerts.

Mr. Robert A. Radel

Treasurer
Ole Olsen Memorial Theatre
154 South Broadway
Peru, IN 46970
(317) 473–3214
Fax: Please mail or call
7922

Business Information: Ole Olsen Memorial Theatre is a civic theatre serving the residents of Peru, Indiana. The theatre provides 4 performances each year which includes a comedy, a drama and two musicals. As Treasurer, Mr. Radel is responsible for all financial aspects. He also assists in the productions as both set designer and cast performer. In addition to his duties with the Theatre, Mr. Radel is a partner in a licensed retail liquor establishment, Main Street Liquors. He also manages his family's 147–year operational crop production farm. **Career Steps:** Treasurer, Ole Olsen Memorial Theatre (1975–Present); Partner, Main Street Liquor (1984–Present); Bookkeeper, Dunn Auto Stop (1972–1984); Managing Farmer, Radel Farms, Inc. (1941–Present). **Associations & Accomplishments:** Indiana Theater Association; Indiana Community Theater League; Indiana Farm Bureau; Indiana State Liquor Association; Knights of Columbus; Fraternal Order of Police; Indiana Sheriff Association; President, Fair Board 4–H; Recipient: The Indiana Homestead Award and Outstanding Advocate and Volunteer Award in Community Theatre by the Indiana Theatre Association. **Education:** Peru High School, (1941). **Personal:** Married to Josephine in 1944. Four children: Robert A. Jr., Mary Jo, Anita Louise and Roger A. Mr. Radel also has nine grandchildren and four great–grandchildren. Mr. Radel enjoys community theater, computers and plate collecting.

Steven J. Ragland, CHSP

Project Manager, Administration
Opryland U.S.A.
2800 Opryland Drive
Nashville, TN 37214–1200
(615) 871–5974
Fax: (615) 871–5728
7922

Business Information: Opryland U.S.A. includes the world's largest hotel convention center and a musical themepark; other attractions include a Senior PGA golf course, showboat, and the famed Grand Ole Opry. A property of Gaylord Entertainment Company (NYSE sym. GET), Opryland U.S.A. accounted for $294.2 million of Gaylord's $707.4 million in 1995 revenues. Joining Opryland U.S.A. as Project Manager of Administration in 1995, Mr. Ragland is responsible for planning and executing projects and programs relating to technology, human resources, marketing, security, training, budgets, etc. for the Vice President of Administration. **Career Steps:** Project Manager, Administration, Opryland U.S.A. (1995–Present), Opryland Hotel: Convention Services Manager (1993–1995), Special Services (V.I.P.) Supervisor (1992–1993), Rooms Division Supervisor (1991–1992); Project Intern, Congressional Tourism Caucus, D.C. (1990). **Education:** Educational Institute, American Hotel/Motel Association, Certified Hospitality Sales Professional (CHSP) (1996); West Virginia University, B.S. in Public Relations Journalism summa cum laude (1984); University of Hawaii, Graduate Studies in Travel Industry Management (1989). **Personal:** Mr. Ragland enjoys golf and horseback riding.

Marv Smith

Owner
Visions International
1639 South 310th Street, Suite A
Federal Way, WA 98003–4955
(206) 941–3680
Fax: (206) 946–2605
EMAIL: See Below
7922

Business Information: Marv Smith, co–founder of Visions International, produces and performs international shows for the beauty industry, combining artistry in choreography, costume and wardrobe design, with forward–thinking hair designs to bring a fresh approach to product promotion, education, and sales. Recognized internationally, Mr. Smith and the Visions team offer 20 years of industry experience and 16 years of Platform Artistry to create innovative designs, powerful marketing programs, and exciting products that combine the precision of a Broadway musical and the flash of a Vegas stage show. Contracted as the premier International Show Team for Matrix in 1990, the team has traveled extensively throughout North America, Europe, Guam, Korea, Hong Kong, China, Japan, New Zealand, and Australia, orchestrating elaborate stage productions, photo sessions, television ad campaigns, marketing promotions, comprehensive education seminars, and hands–on workshops. Mr. Smith also owns and operates salons on the East and West Coast and has been published internationally. Internet users can reach him via: MARV3@IX.NETCOM.COM. **Career Steps:** Visions International: International Show Team – Matrix (1990–Present), Platform Artists/Educational Consultants – Helene Curtis (1988–1990), Platform Artists/Research and Development Consultants – Lamaur/Dow (1984–1988); Consultant, Dow Chemical (1981). **Associations & Accomplishments:** Make–A–Wish Foundation; Published in: Modern Salon, American Salon, and High Style. **Education:** Renons Beauty School; Yuki & Wendy's Salon, Apprenticeship; Vidal Sasson Sukis Academy, Roots and Wings; Landmark Education Corporation; Professional: Sasoons & Trevor Sorbie, Vivienne Mackinder. **Personal:** Married to Mary Jane in 1995. Mr. Smith enjoys scuba diving, skydiving, fly fishing, writing, and art.

Rodney J. Smith

General Manager
Denver Performing Arts Complex
950 13th Street
Denver, CO 80204–2153
(303) 640–5142
Fax: (303) 640–2397
7922

Business Information: Denver Performing Arts Complex is a performing arts facility, providing performing arts, music, art, acting, and dance from eight different performing art facilities. With over 25 years experience in the theatre industry, Mr. Smith joined the Denver Performing Arts Complex as Assistant General Manager in 1989. Appointed as General Manager in 1992, he is responsible for the general management of a multi–venue arts complex, in addition to the direction of all operations. **Career Steps:** Denver Performing Arts Complex:

General Manager (1992–Present), Assistant General Manager (1989–1992); Assistant Producing Director, Denver Center Theatre Company (1982–1989); Instructor, Loretto Heights College (1980–1982). **Associations & Accomplishments:** International Association of Auditorium Managers; International Committee, Performing Arts Managers; Rocky Mountain Section, United States Institute for Theatre Technology: Sustained Member, Former President. **Education:** San Jose State University, M.A. (1979); Fort Lewis College, B.A. (1976). **Personal:** Married to Donna E. in 1985. Two children: Chelsea Marie and Nicholas Benjamin. Mr. Smith enjoys skiing, music, travel, and spending time with family.

Ron Steinberg

Executive Director
Manistee Civic Players – Ramsdell Theatre
P.O. Box 32, 101 Maple Street
Manistee, MI 49660
(616) 723–7188
Fax: Please mail or call

7922

Business Information: Manistee Civic Players – Ramsdell Theatre displays eight productions a year, as well as children's workshops. The Theatre contains an exhibit hall, ballroom, and is a nationally registered historic site. As Executive Director, Mr. Steinberg is responsible for managing the theatre, booking acts and events, fund raising, hiring directors, and producing. **Career Steps:** Executive Director, Manistee Civic Players – Ramsdell Theatre (1991–Present); Advertising Director, Manistee News Advocate (1969–1991). **Associations & Accomplishments:** Rotary Club; Manistee Downtown Development Authority; Michigan Council for the Arts; National League of Historic Theatres. **Education:** Grand Rapids Junior College (1965). **Personal:** One child: Don. Mr. Steinberg enjoys amateur theatre and reading.

Thomas S. Taylor

Vice President of Internal Audit
EMI Music
152 West 57th Street, 42 Floor
New York, NY 10019–3310
(212) 261–3085
Fax: (212) 261–3149

7922

Business Information: EMI Music is an international producer, distributor, and marketer of music. With sixteen years expertise in a diverse background of financial management, which includes employment with Price Waterhouse, Central Soya Company, and Kraft Foods, Mr. Taylor joined EMI Music as Vice President of Internal Audit in 1995. He is responsible for the restructuring and maintaining of the auditing procedures of the Company. **Career Steps:** Vice President of Internal Audit, EMI Music (1995–Present); Vice President of Finance and Strategy, Kraft General Foods (1990–1995); Vice President and Controller, Central Soya Company, Inc. (1988–1990); Audit Manager, Price Waterhouse (1980–1988). **Associations & Accomplishments:** American Institute of Certified Public Accountants; American Management Association. **Education:** Notre Dame, M.B.A. (1990); Miami University, B.S. in Accounting. **Personal:** Married to Jennifer in 1992. One child: Zachary. Mr. Taylor enjoys sports and travel.

Joi Wilson

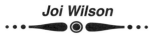

Chief Financial Officer/Controller
J. T. and Associates
7165 West Sunset Boulevard
Los Angeles, CA 90046
(213) 969–9333
Fax: (213) 969–8333

7922

Business Information: J. T. and Associates is a personal, business, and talent management company. As Controller, Ms. Wilson is responsible for all financial concerns of the Company. These responsibilities include cash management, tax reporting, accounts payable, accounts receivable, and payroll. Concurrently Ms. Wilson is Chief Financial Officer for Third Street Sound Company, an audio post production firm. Third Street Sound works on programs such as Cops, National Geographic, Public Service Television, movies, etc. **Career Steps:** Controller, J. T. and Associates (1995–Present); CFO, Third Street Sound; C.M./Controller, Sunset Post, Inc. (1990–1995); Executive Vice President for Financing, Brittinham International (1988–1990); Co–Owner, Panache–EDI (1980–1988). **Associations & Accomplishments:** AIDS Walk Project; LA Works; Association for Retarded Citizens; Doree Foundation; Toys for Tots; Humane Society; Best Friends Association; Many other charitable organizations than those listed. Ms. Wilson coordinates with organizations and assists in setting up fund raisers. **Education:** Skillpath Seminars, Conflict Skills Management (1996); IDA, General Business Management. **Personal:** Married to Glenn Ford in 1994. Ms. Wilson enjoys horseback riding, outdoor activities, and planning fund raisers.

John Klingberg

Product Engineering R & D Director
Winterland Productions
4 Bryerwood Court
Novato, CA 94947
(415) 597–9844
Fax: (415) 597–9607

7929

Business Information: Winterland Productions is a music and entertainment merchandiser with three divisions: Tour – concerts, music properties, etc.; Custom – Donna Karen, Tommy Hilfiger, etc; Wholesale – movie properties and working through mass merchandisers. As Product Engineering R & D Director, Mr. Klingberg is responsible for directing the engineering efforts into the development of new technologies and engineer designs to be incorporated into a manufacturable prototype. **Career Steps:** Product Engineering R & D Director, Winterland Productions (1993–Present); Senior R & D Chemist, Flexible Products (1990–1993). **Education:** Marshall University, B.S. & B.A. (1988). **Personal:** Married to Giselle in 1991. Mr. Klingberg enjoys mountain biking, skiing, photography, and weight lifting.

Ms. Michele C. Laurent

President
Prime Hotels & Resorts
770 Lexington Avenue
New York, NY 10021
(212) 486–2575
Fax: (212) 308–6392

7929

Business Information: Prime Hotels & Resorts is a marketing, sales, advertising, and public relations firm serving the hotel and resort industry. The Company also operates the St. James' Club–Antigua hotel/resort. Services include providing star entertainment for resorts, athletic professionals (i.e. tennis, golf) for resort athletic programs, and more. As President, Ms. Laurent is responsible for all aspects of company operations. Established in 1984, Prime Hotels & Resorts employs a full–time staff of 6. **Career Steps:** President, Prime Hotels & Resorts (1988–Present); Sales and Public Relations, Air France (1978– 1988); Teacher, High School in Germany (1975–1978). **Associations & Accomplishments:** Board of Directors, Adam Walsh Children's Fund; Other Charitable Organizations. **Education:** Hunter College, Masters (1975).

Allison B. Vulgamore

President
Atlanta Symphony Orchestra
1293 Pchtre Street Northeast, Suite 300
Atlanta, GA 30309–3527
(404) 733–4906
Fax: (404) 733–4901

7929

Business Information: Atlanta Symphony Orchestra is a group of performers on various musical instruments, playing music, symphonies, operas, popular music, or other compositions. Atlanta Symphony Orchestra will perform in their biggest event at the 1996 Olympic Games, an event that will be watched by more than 3 million people. With sixteen years experience in orchestra management, Ms. Vulgamore joined the Atlanta Symphony Orchestra in 1993. Currently serving as President, she is responsible for the overall general management and operations of the orchestra, including production and marketing. **Career Steps:** President, Atlanta Symphony Orchestra (1993–Present); General Manager, New York Philharmonic Orchestra (1987–1993); General Manager, National Symphony Orchestra – Washington (1982–1987); General Manager, Philadelphia Orchestra (1980–1982). **Associations & Accomplishments:** Rotary Club Atlanta; American Symphony Orchestra League; Board of Trustees, Oberlin. **Education:** Oberlin, B.A. **Personal:** Married to Peter M. Marshall.

Mr. Gene Thomas Giegoldt

Vice President and General Manager
Canoga Park Bowl, Inc.
20122 Vanowen Street
Canoga Park, CA 91306–4308
(818) 340–5190
Fax: (818) 340–2282

7933

Business Information: Canoga Park Bowl, Inc. is a 24–hour bowling center located on the premises of Best Western Motel, Restaurant and Lounge. Joining Canoga Park Bowl, Inc. as Vice President and General Manager in 1987, Mr. Giegoldt is responsible for all aspects of operations, including management, administration, finances, public relations, and strategic planning for both Canoga Park Bowl, Inc. and the Best Western Motel. He also serves as the Chief Operating Officer. **Career Steps:** Vice President and General Manager, Canoga Park Bowl, Inc. (1987–Present); Manager, Northrop – Electronics Division (1985–1987); Assistant Manager and Supervisor, Fairchild Industries (1978–1985). **Associations & Accomplishments:** Winnetka Optimist Club; Board of Directors, Winnetka Chamber of Commerce; Life Member, U.S. Army Non–Commissioned Officers Association; Former President and Chief Executive Officer, Los Angeles Sertoma Club; Elks Lodge #7190; Canoga Park Chamber of Commerce; Valley Industry and Commerce Association; Los Angeles Bowling Association; Written and published in the "National Birmingham Rolling Club." **Education:** Northridge University, 12 units short of B.S. (1985); Los Angeles Pierce College, A.A. (1982). **Personal:** Married to Asako in 1983. Two children: Daniel and Brian. Mr. Giegoldt enjoys raising pigeons, fishing, and travel.

Sam Abu–Nasser

General Manager
Severna Park Racquet Ball and Nautilus
8514 Veterans Highway
Millersville, MD 21108
(410) 987–0980
Fax: (410) 987–7855
EMAIL: See Below

7941

Business Information: Severna Park Racquet Ball and Nautilus is a full service health club providing aerobics instruction (55 classes), motivational and incentive training, fitness consulting, and a 30,000 square foot pool. Serving all of Anne Arundel County, Maryland, the Company is regional in scope, and plans to open a second location in the near future. Established in 1981, the Company employs 90 people, and has an estimated annual revenue of $2 million. As General Manager, Mr. Abu–Nasser oversees all aspects of the Company. His duties include reporting to the board of directors, consulting on fitness, planning future expansions, high level personnel management, implementing policies and procedures, budgetary concerns, development of new programs, and direct supervision of ten managers. Internet users can reach him via: Club4me@aol.com. **Career Steps:** General Manager, Severna Park Racquet Ball and Nautilus (1988–Present); Manager, YMCA (1986); Owner, Sam's Sports Center (1983). **Associations & Accomplishments:** Severna Park Chamber of Commerce; ADC; IRSA. **Education:** U.M.U.C., Master of International Business (In Progress); Washburn University (1986). **Personal:** Married to Sarah in 1991. Mr. Abu–Nasser enjoys racquetball, hiking, reading, and travel.

Mr. Richard P. Bellinger

President and Chief Operating Officer
Golden Bear International, Inc.
11780 U.S. Highway One
North Palm Beach, FL 33408
(407) 626–3900
Fax: (407) 626–4104

7941

Business Information: Golden Bear International, Inc. specializes in managing and developing golf and sports–related businesses (construct, maintain, and design golf courses and produces sports videos). In his current capacity, Mr. Bellinger heads up the Company's executive committee, sets Company policy, and serves as a direct link to Jack Nicklaus. Established since 1970, Golden Bear International, Inc. presently employs 150 people. **Career Steps:** President and Chief Operating Officer, Golden Bear International, Inc. (1985– Present); Senior Vice President, Chief Financial Officer and Treasurer, Golden Bear International, Inc. (1979–1985); Controller, Del Monte Corporation (1974– 1979). **Associations & Accomplishments:** Member, Economic Council of Palm Beach County; Board Member, National Football Foundation and College Hall of Fame; Member, North Carolina Outward Bound Foundation; Interviewed by the New York Times, Wall Street Journal, Forbes Magazine, and Golf Digest. **Education:** University of Miami, M.B.A. Degree (1976), B.B.A. Degree in Accounting (1973). **Personal:** Married to Laurie in 1975. Two children: Sarah and Lindsay. Mr. Bellinger enjoys golf in his leisure time.

Thomas A. Cline

General Manager
Sylvania Tam–O–Shanter
7060 Sylvania Avenue
Sylvania, OH 43560
(419) 885–1167 Ext.: 307
Fax: (419) 885–2479

7941

Business Information: Sylvania Tam–O–Shanter is an entertainment arena including 2 ice rinks, pro shop, concessions, restaurant, and a lounge. Future plans include adding another facility. As General Manager, Mr. Cline is responsible for all daily operations, management and employee supervision, and planning of future attractions. Established in 1981, Sylvania Tam–O–Shanter employs 70 people with annual sales of $2 million. **Career Steps:** General Manager, Sylvania Tam–O–Shanter (1991–Present); Controller, Schmidt Leasing (1990–1991); Controller, Tailford Associates (1990); Business Manager, George Ballas Leasing (1984–1990). **Associations & Accomplishments:** Rotary Club of Sylvania; Hockey Coach, Sylvania Midget AA. **Education:** Bowling Green State University, Bachelor's Degree (1983). **Personal:** Mr. Cline enjoys golf and skiing.

Steven M. Dauria

Vice President and Chief Financial Officer
Florida Panthers Hockey Club
100 North East 3rd Avenue, 2nd Floor
Ft. Lauderdale, FL 33301–1155
(954) 768–1900
Fax: (954) 768–1920

7941

Business Information: Florida Panthers Hockey Club is a professional hockey organization established in 1993. The Club is new to the league but in 1996, the team had great success and made it to the Stanley Cup Finals. As Vice President and Chief Financial Officer, Mr. Dauria is responsible for all organizational financial affairs, management, strategic planning, and human resources. **Career Steps:** Vice President and Chief Financial Officer, Florida Panthers Hockey Club (1994–Present); Controller, New York Yankees (1991–1993); Financial Manager, Time Warner, Inc. (1988–1991). **Education:** Bernard Baruch College, B.B.A. (1983); Certified Public Accountant (1987). **Personal:** Married to Theresa in 1989. Two children: Stefanie and Nicolas. Mr. Dauria enjoys scuba diving, skiing, and tennis.

Ernest W. Hahn II

Vice President
San Diego Sports Arena
3500 Sports Arena Boulevard
San Diego, CA 92110
(619) 225–9813 Ext. 345
Fax: (619) 224–3010

7941

Business Information: San Diego Sports Arena provides a place where spectators can watch sporting events, concerts, conventions, and other entertainment events. As Vice President, Mr. Hahn handles all aspects of business development, including scheduling, booking and contract administration for the facility, budgeting, and cash flow. **Career Steps:** Vice President, San Diego Sports Arena (1991–Present); Contract Administrator, Land Grant Development (1990–1991). **Associations & Accomplishments:** Midway Planning Group; Century Club; Presidents Circle – San Diego City College. **Education:** Santa Clara University, B.S. (1990). **Personal:** Married to Kristin in 1992. One child: Alexis. Mr. Hahn enjoys surfing, tennis, golf, and basketball.

Kathy L. Lumbard–Cobb

Assistant General Manager & Director of Merchandising
Hudson Valley Renegades
P.O. Box 661
Fishkill, NY 12524–0661
(914) 838–0094
Fax: (914) 838–0014
EMail: See Below

7941

Business Information: Hudson Valley Renegades is a Class A (short season) Minor League baseball affiliate of the Texas Rangers and the Tampa Bay Devil Rays. As Assistant General Manager & Director of Merchandising, Ms. Lumbard–Cobb handles all pre–season advertising and promotional sales, oversees part–time stadium staff hiring, handles all designs and purchases, and tracks merchandising efforts. Internet users can reach her via: info@hvrenegades.com. **Career Steps:** Assistant General Manager & Director of Merchandising, Hudson Valley Renegades (1993–Present); Assistant General Manager, Erie Sailors Baseball (1991–1993); Business Manager, Williamsport Bills Baseball (1989–1991); Student Activities Assistant, Pennsylvania College of Technology (1986–1989). **Associations & Accomplishments:** Southern Dutchess Chamber of Commerce Leadership Program, Graduate; American Heart Association; Alzheimer's Association – Mis–Hudson Chapter; National Association of Professional Baseball Leagues. **Education:** Pennsylvania College of Technology, Associate of Arts (1988). **Personal:** One child: Joel Christopher. Ms. Lumbard–Cobb enjoys speed walking, reading, and sports.

Gerald J. Connors Jr.

Director of Racing Information
Rosecroft Raceway
6336 Rosecroft Drive
Ft. Washington, MD 20744–1999
(301) 567–4000
Fax: (301) 567–9267

7948

Business Information: Rosecroft Raceway is a horse racing track and entertainment facility, specializing in harness racing and simulcasts. As Director of Racing Information, Mr. Connors is responsible for publicity, information dissemination, statistics, in–house writing, and assisting in marketing and advertising. **Career Steps:** Director of Racing Information, Rosecroft Raceway (1989–Present); Director of Publicity, Northfield Park (1987–1989); Director of Publicity, Foxboro Raceway (1986–1987). **Associations & Accomplishments:** United States Harness Writers Association, Mid–Atlantic Chapter, Secretary/Treasurer, National Director; North American Harness Publicists Association, Golden Pen Award (1996), Past President. **Education:** University of Connecticut, M.A. (1980); St. Joseph's College, B.A. (1978). **Personal:** Mr. Connors enjoys sports, soccer, music, television, movies, and reading.

Mr. Yvan C. Forest

Vice President, Finances
Hippodrome Blue Bonnets
7440 Boulevard Decarie
Montreal, Quebec H4P 2H1
(514) 739–2744
Fax: (514) 340–2025

7948

Business Information: Hippodrome Blue Bonnets is one of the major race tracks in Canada with more than $160 million in pari mutal. The Company organizes harness races and simulcasts foreign races. As Vice President, Finances, Mr. Forest is responsible for three areas: Finance (all company operations); Data Processing/Computer (MIS) Systems; and the Printing Department. He oversees the printing of race programs. Established in 1906, Hippodrome Blue Bonnets employs 430 people with annual sales of 40 million. **Career Steps:** Vice President, Finances, Hippodrome Blue Bonnets (1990–Present); Vice President, Finance and Administration, Piscines Citadelle (1988–1989); Comptroller, MD Vaillancourt Ltd. (1985–1987); Administrator, Mercure Beliveau (1983–1984). **Associations & Accomplishments:** Mr. Forest is chartered accountant and a certified management accountant. **Education:** Hautes Etudes Commercial, M.B.A. (will be complete in 1996); University of Quebec at Montreal, B.A.A. (1981). **Personal:** Married to Helene in 1987. Three children: Simon, Maxime, and Laurence. Mr. Forest enjoys alpine skiing, cross country skiing, and walking in the forest.

James H. Hunter

President
Darlington Raceway
P.O. Box 500
Darlington, SC 29532–0500
(803) 395–8900
Fax: (803) 393–3911

7948

Business Information: Darlington Raceway, established in 1950, is the oldest super speedway in the country. The Raceway, sponsered by NASCAR, promotes and stages 2 Winston Cup Series and 1 Busch Series Automobile Race Annually. As President, Mr. Hunter oversees the daily operations of the track, including ticket sales, maintenance, promotions, public relations and sponsorships. **Career Steps:** President, Darlington Raceway (1993–Present); Vice President of Marketing & Administration, NASCAR (1981–1993); Public Relations Director, Talladega Superspeedway (1974–1981). **Associations & Accomplishments:** Board Member, Coker College; Board Member, Florence Darlington Technical College; Board Member, Nations Bank; Delegate, White House Conference on Travel & Tourism. **Education:** University of South Carolina (1957–1960). **Personal:** Married to Ann in 1961. Two children: Scott Hunter and Amy Hunter McKernan. Mr. Hunter enjoys golf and spending time with family.

Mr. Lonny T. Powell

Executive Vice President and General Manager
Turf Paradise
1501 West Bell Road
Phoenix, AZ 85023
(602) 942–1101
Fax: (602) 942–8659

7948

Business Information: Turf Paradise, a Hollywood Park facility, is a horse racing track and wagering entertainment facility. Established in 1956, Turf Paradise currently employs 800 people. As Executive Vice President and General Manager, Mr. Powell is the Chief Operating Officer of the racing complex. **Career Steps:** Executive Vice President and General Manager, Turf Paradise (1994–Present); President, Multnomah Greyhound Park (1992–1994); Executive Vice President and Chief Operating Officer, Longacres Park (1990–1992); Director, University of Arizona Race Track Industry Program (1986–1990). **Associations & Accomplishments:** University of Arizona Race Track Industry Program Advisory Council; Arizona Thoroughbred Breeders Association; Washington Thoroughbred Breeders Association; American Quarter Horse Association. **Education:** University of Arizona, B.S. (1982). **Personal:** Married to Karen. Three children: Jeff, Sean and Sara. Mr. Powell enjoys reading, fishing, golf and continuing education programs.

Damon D. Thayer

Director of Communications
Turfway Park
P.O. Box 8
Florence, KY 41022–0008
(606) 647–4841
Fax: (606) 647–4730
EMAIL: See Below

7948

Business Information: Turfway Park is a horse racing track and simulcasting center specializing in the excitement and competition of racing Thoroughbred horses. Established in 1986, the Company employs 300 people and has an estimated betting handle of $250 million. As Director of Communications, Mr. Thayer oversees all marketing, public relations, advertising, promotions and media functions, and assists in race scheduling and development. Internet users can reach him via: turfway@turfway.com. **Career Steps:** Director of Communications, Turfway Park (1992–Present); Director of Media Relations, Maryland Jockey Club (1991–1992); Director of Media Relations, Thistledown Race Track (1989–1991); Publicity Assistant, Ladbroke Racing, Michigan (1985–1988). **Associations & Accomplishments:** Turf Publicists of America; Treasurer, Grant County Republican Party; Grant County Chairman, Jim Bunning for Congress Campaign. **Education:** Michigan State University, Bachelor's in Communications (1989). **Personal:** Married to Carrie M. in 1991. Mr. Thayer enjoys horseback riding, politics, and reading (Dick Francis, John Grisham, Tom Clancy, Michael Crichton, and presidential History).

Kennth N. May

Senior Vice President
Disney Vacation Development
200 Celebration Place
Celebration, FL 34747
(407) 939–3112
Fax: (407) 939–3339

7949

Business Information: Disney Vacation Development is an organization that develops family vacation products and services. Services offered include: Disney Vacation Club – a membership club for families who enjoy vacationing together. Members can stay at more than 200 resorts including Disney's Old Key West, Vero Beach, Hilton Head Island and Boardwalk Resorts. Variation experiences also include white water rafting, eco tours, etc. Joining Disney Vacation Development as Senior Vice President in 1993, Mr. May directs the vision and development of strategies for the organization. In addition, he is responsible for all resort operations, sales and marketing to finance the Club, and total operations of the Disney Vacation Club. **Career Steps:** Senior Vice President, Disney Vacation Development (1993–Present); President – Grupo Gamesa, Pepsico Foods International – Mexico (1991–1993); Vice President of Strategic Planning, Pepsico Foods International – Dallas (1989–1991); Vice President of Marketing and Sales, Colgate–Palmolive – Mexico (1986–1989). **Associations & Accomplishments:** American Resort Development Association; Leadership Orlando; Volunteer. **Education:** American Graduate School of International Management, M.A. in International Management (1975); Middlebury College – Vermont, Major in Russian (1972). **Personal:** Married to Mary in 1976. Three children: Molly, Peter, and Alexander. Mr. May enjoys skiing, sailing, scuba diving, reading, and camping.

Gordon B. Kaye

Executive Vice President
Broadway Sports and Entertainment, Inc.
102 Circular Street
Saratoga Springs, NY 12866–3225
(518) 587–1218
Fax: (518) 583–3953
EMAIL: See Below

7990

Business Information: Mr. Kaye, the Executive Vice President of Broadway Sports & Entertainment, Inc., operates and manages an entertainment complex composed of two dinner theaters, a sports bar, and a restaurant. He is responsible for overseeing the daily operation and staffing of the facilities. Internet users can reach him via: gkaye@globalone.net In addition to his work with Broadway Sports and Entertainment, Mr. Kaye also serves as the Executive Vice President of Capital Sports and Entertainment, Inc., a Sarasota Springs–based Company which owns and manages minor–league professional sports teams. **Career Steps:** Executive Vice President, Capital Sports & Entertainment, Inc. (1994–Present); Executive Vice President, Broadway Sports and Entertainment, Inc. (1996–Present); Vice President, Institute for Health and Human Services (1995–1996); Executive Vice President, Mass Marauders, Inc. (1994–1995); Executive Assistant to the Commissioner, Arena Football League (1992–1994); Director of Operations, Utica Blue Sox (1988–1989). **Education:** Indiana University, M.S. (1992); Hamilton College, B.A. (1991); Choate Rosemary Hall. **Personal:** Mr. Kaye enjoys playing hockey, reading, sports, and computers.

Donald R. Foxe

Marketing Director
Franco's Athletic Club
100 Bon Temps Roule
Mandeville, LA 70471–2555
(504) 845–2639
Fax: (504) 845–2746

7991

Business Information: Franco's Athletic Club is a health and fitness club providing physical training and related services to area residents. Established in 1988, the Company employs 160 people and has an estimated annual revenue of $3 million. As Marketing Director, Mr. Foxe oversees all marketing and sales, and serves as a consultant to other facilities. **Career Steps:** Marketing Director, Franco's Athletic Club (1995–Present); Director, Westbay Athletic Club (1991–1995); General Manager, New Life Fitness World (1989–1991). **Associations & Accomplishments:** American College of Sports Medicine; Certified Personal Trainer, American College of Exercise; Heart By Provider, American Heart Association; Numerous Magazine Articles on Health and Fitness. **Education:** University of South Carolina, B.S. (1986); King's College: B.A. in English (1980), M.Ed. (1981). **Personal:** Married to Sarah in 1990. Mr. Foxe enjoys running, biking, and landscaping.

Stephanie R. Hahn Vaughan

President
Splash Company of Virginia
155 Old Forest Circle
Winchester, VA 22602
(540) 667–3333
Fax: (540) 667–0585

7991

Business Information: The Splash Company of Virginia is an aquatic exercise company providing fitness programs, instruction, equipment sales, and lectures at state and national fitness conferences. The Company has summer and winter programs for the entire family, providing deep water and shallow water classes for all age ranges. During the winter, the Company specializes in water therapy for healthy and physically handicapped individuals. Established in 1992, The Splash Company of Virginia currently employs 15 people. As President and Founder, Ms. Hahn Vaughan is responsible for all aspects of operations, including marketing, teaching, presenting, and patenting products. She developed the program after her husband, an OB/GYN Doctor, designed a postpartum recovery program utilizing aquatic exercise. She was the first student in the program, following the birth of their first child. **Career Steps:** President, Splash Company of Virginia (1992–Present); Director of Education, Bioenergetics, Inc. (1995–Present); Purchasing and Materials Manager, Fabritek Company, Inc. (1984–1989). **Associations & Accomplishments:** United States Water Fitness Association; AEA; IDEA; USTA; UUAW; AAHPERD; VAHPERD; VRPS; AOPA; USSS; American College of Sports Medicine; Written and published books on water exercise guidelines; Published in local newspapers; Bonnie Prudent Fitness and Living Award (1994); State Water Fitness Award (1994–1995); Who's Who in American Women. **Education:** Shenandoah University: M.B.A. (1985), B.A. in Biology (1983); Lord Fairfax Community College, VPI and SU, Undergraduate in Biology. **Personal:** Married to Ward P. in 1980. Three children: Carol, Eva and Robert. Ms. Hahn Vaughan enjoys triathlons, water skiing, snow skiing, reading, flying, sewing, and smocking.

Deana Hegland

Corporate Marketing Director
Spare Time, Inc.
2399 American River Drive, Suite 2
Sacramento, CA 95825
(916) 971–8710 (916) 638–7001
Fax: (916) 971–8728

7991

Business Information: Spare Time, Inc. provides multi–recreational family fitness facilities located throughout Northern California. Each club features a variety of fitness programs and sporting events. As Corporate Marketing Director, Ms. Hegland is responsible for the marketing of each individual club and the Corporation as a whole. She designs combined ad campaigns and promotions, and provides community recognition and visibility. **Career Steps:** Corporate Marketing Director, Spare Time, Inc. (Present); Leukemia Society; A/E, Comstock's Magazine; Graphic Assistant, Anne Bruce/Trevor Cartwright. **Associations & Accomplishments:** American Marketing Association; Point West Business Association; Children's Bereavement Art Program; Sacramento Polo Association. Education: Los Angeles Technical Institute, A.A. in Marketing (1987). **Personal:** Married to Craig in 1993. Ms. Hegland enjoys polo, scuba diving, and marathon races.

Randy Robbins

Owner/Partner
Arizona Health, Inc.
P.O. Box 7269
Nogales, AZ 85268
(520) 287–8343
Fax: (520) 287–6746

7991

Business Information: Arizona Health, Inc. is a successful fitness and equipment retail store, offering fitness equipment, personal training, group training, fitness testing/evaluation, and nutrition counseling. The Corporation trains and receives endorsements from professional athletes (i.e. Sean Elliott, Byron Evans, Michael Scurlock, Ken Lofton, various Colorado Rockies, etc.), movie stars (i.e., Rene Russo, Sharon Stone, Gene Hackman, Laura Petty, etc.), corporations and/or businesses (i.e., Jim Click Ford, Arizona Bank employees, etc.) and numerous private individuals. With nine years of athletic experience in the National Football League (NFL), including eight with the Denver Broncos and one with the New England Patriots, Mr. Robbins experienced both team (AFC West Division and AFC Conference championships and a Super Bowl participant) and personal success (recipient of the Defensive Player of the Game – Broncos). Founding Arizona Health, Inc. in 1993, he serves as Partner and Vice President, owning and operating the business. He is responsible for all aspects of operations, including administration, finances, sales, public relations, accounting, client relations, marketing, and strategic planning. Concurrently, he serves as the Treasurer, Director, and Owner of Premium Produce – a wholesale distributor of fresh fruits and vegetables grown in both Mexico and Arizona; Director of Nogales Parks and Recreation Department; and Assistant Football Coach at Nogales High School. **Career Steps:** Owner/Partner, Arizona Health, Inc. (1993–Present); Director, Nogales Parks and Recreation Department (1995–Present); Assistant Football Coach, Nogales High School (1993–Present); Treasurer/Director/Owner, Premium Produce (1991–Present); Defensive Back, New England Patriots (1992–1993); Defensive Back, Denver Broncos (1984–1992). **Associations & Accomplishments:** American Football Coaches Association; Vocational Chairman, Rotary Club; District Chairman, Boy Scouts – Santa Cruz County; Secretary, Southern Arizona Sports Development Corporation; University of Arizona Hall of Fame Selection Committee; Black Coaches Association; NFL Alumni Association; Omega Psi Phi Alumni; Denver Broncos Alumni Association; Fellowship of Christian Athletes. **Education:** University of Arizona, currently working toward B.A. in General Business (1996); Denver Broncos, NFL Instructional Mini Camps (1984–1992); Pima Community College, continuing education toward Bachelor's Degree (1989); Hogan School of Real Estate: Licensed Mortgage Broker (1987), Licensed Real Estate Agent (1986); University of Arizona: continuing education toward Bachelor's Degree (1985), pursuing B.A. in Business Studies (1980–1984). **Personal:** Mr. Robbins enjoys spending time with children.

Richard A. Cary

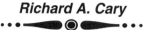

President
Capital Music, Inc.
3108 Broadwater Avenue
Helena, MT 59602–9222
(406) 442–7088
Fax: (406) 442–0098

7993

Business Information: Capital Music, Inc. specializes in coin operated amusement and gaming devices (i.e. juke boxes and gambling machines). Established in 1947, the Company is the fourth largest in the state and employs thirteen people. As President, Mr. Cary oversees all aspects of the Company. Purchasing the Company in 1975, he is responsible for administration, operations, finance, sales and marketing, public relations, and strategic planning. **Career Steps:** President, Capital Music, Inc. (1975–Present); Manager, A–1 Rentals (1962–1975); Manager, Capital Music Company (1962–1975). **Associations & Accomplishments:** Amusement and Machine Operators Association (AMOA); Treasurer and Past President, Montana Coin Machine Operators Association (MCMOA); Moose Lodge; American Legion Eagles; Founder and Treasurer, Montana State Eight Ball Tournament. **Education:** U.S. Army: Track Mechanic, Welding; Technical School, Machine Shop. **Personal:** Married to Vickie Jo in 1975. Five children: Christine, Claudene, Richard, Ryan, and Robin. Mr. Cary enjoys engraving, photography, four wheeling, and auto restoration.

Alan B. Gordon

General Manager
Soboba Casino
23333 Saboba Road, P.O. Box 817
San Jacinto, CA 92583
(909) 654–2883 Ext.: 23
Fax: (909) 654–5844

7993

Business Information: Soboba Casino is a 30,000 sq. ft. adult entertainment gaming center for the Soboba Indian tribe. In operation 24 hours a day, 7 days a week, the Casino offers bingo, poker, black jack and video gaming machines. All profits made through the Casino's business are to be used toward the expansion of the Soboba Indian Reservation, with beneficial projects including the construction of hospitals and gymnasiums. As General Manager, the Tribal Council has entrusted Mr. Gordon with the responsibility of generating new income into the community. In addition, he is responsible for the operation of the casino, as well as the supervision of key management staff. **Career Steps:** General Manager, Soboba Casino (1995–Present); Clubhouse Manager, Lake Elsinore Storm (1994); Mortgage Banker, Business West Mortgage (1989–1994); Owner, ABG & Company (1988–1989). **Education:** California State University at Long Beach (1979). **Personal:** Married to Lisa H. in 1978. Five children: Kelly, Alan, Melissa, David, and Natalie.

James P. Jackson

Senior Vice President of Gaming Operations
WMS Gaming Inc.
3401 North California Avenue
Chicago, IL 60618
(312) 961–1620
Fax: (312) 961–1025

7993

Business Information: WMS Gaming Inc. is the leading manufacturer of gaming equipment, including video lottery terminals and slot machines. Branch offices are located in Nevada, New Jersey (Atlantic City), Mississippi, Missouri, and Florida. With ten years experience in gaming industry sales and marketing, Mr. Jackson joined WMS Gaming in 1993. Serving as Senior Vice President of Gaming Operations, he oversees all administrative operations for associates and a support staff of 40, in addition to the responsibility of sales, marketing, field service, customer service, and administration. **Career Steps:** Senior Vice President of Gaming Operations, WMS Gaming Inc. (1993–Present); Sigma Game Inc.: General Manager (1993), Director of Marketing and Sales (1988–1993), Assistant Director of Operations (1986–1988). **Education:** University of Nevada, B.S. (1983). **Personal:** Married to Hope in 1988. Two children: Nikayla and Miranda. Mr. Jackson enjoys golf, tennis, and reading.

Robert E. King

Risk Manager
Bayon Caddys Jubilee Casino
P.O. Box 1777
Greenville, MS 38702–1777
(601) 335–1111
Fax: (601) 379–2510

7993

Business Information: Bayon Caddys Jubilee Casino is a riverboat casino featuring 800 slot machines and 23 gaming tables. The Casino boasts over 60,000 square feet of gaming and entertainment facilities. As Risk Manager, Mr. King, whose background includes experience in narcotics investigation, is responsible for general liabilities, workmen's compensation, adherence to OSHA requirements and regulations, and the overall safety of the casino. **Career Steps:** Risk Manager, Bayon Caddys Jubilee Casino (1996–Present); Security Supervisor, Cotton Club Casino (1993–1995); Narcotics Investigator, Central Delta Drug Task Force (1990–1993). **Education:** Delta State University, B.S. in Criminal Justice (1989). **Personal:** Married to Lea Ann in 1995. One child: Ryan L. Mr. King enjoys being a camp leader at a special education camp.

Sheila A. Morago

Director of Marketing
Gila River Casino
1201 South 56th Street, Box 5074
Chandler, AZ 85226–5113
(520) 796–7807
Fax: (520) 796–7783

7993

Business Information: Gila River Casino is an adult gaming facility that was established in 1994 by the Pima Indians. The Pima's were one of the very first tribes to open a casino. Offering Video Poker, Video Blackjack, Video Craps, Video Roulette, Slots, Keno, Bingo, and Live Poker, the Casino has broken ground for the new permanent 167,000 square foot building and has plans for a hotel and golf course in the future. As Director of Marketing and Public Relations, Ms. Morago handles all the media coverage for the Casino on television, radio, and in the two local papers. She maintains public interest and awareness through advertising and publicity. **Career Steps:** Director of Marketing, Gila River Casino (1994–Present); General Manager, O'Malley on Fourth (1993–1994); General Manager, Grand American Fare, Inc. (1988–1993). **Associations & Accomplishments:** Board of Directors, Arizona American Indian Tourism Association; East Valley Partnership; Chandler Chamber of Commerce; Rho–Mate, Alpha Gamma Rho Fraternity; National Congress of American Indians; Phi Lamba Phrateres; Former Board of Directors, West Hollywood Chamber of Commerce. **Education:** Attended, University of Arizona. **Personal:** Ms. Morago enjoys reading and camping.

Debbie Munsee

Marketing Director
Robinson Rancheria Bingo & Casino
1545 East Highway 20
Nice, CA 95464
(707) 275–9000 Ext. 11
Fax: (707) 275–9100
WWW: http://www.thrillse

7993

Business Information: Robinson Rancheria Bingo & Casino is a community–oriented Indian gaming facility, complete with black jack, poker, slot machines, and bingo. As Marketing Director, Ms. Munsee is responsible for all promotional activities for bingo and the casino, campaigns for community involvement, and the development of all advertising and marketing materials. Ms. Munsee may also be reached at: (800) 809–3636. **Career Steps:** Marketing Director, Robinson Rancheria Bingo & Casino (1994–Present); Indian Education Counselor/Tutor, Lake County Office of Education (1982–1994). **Associations & Accomplishments:** Board of Directors, Boys & Girls Club of Lake County; Redwood Empire Association; Northshore Business Association; Konocti Business Alliance; Greater Lake County, Clearlake and Sonoma County Chamber of Commerce. **Education:** Sacramento City College, A.A. E.C.E. (1980). **Personal:** Four children: Christina, Bernard, Tara, and Marcus. Ms. Munsee enjoys reading, sewing, arts & crafts, and the ocean.

Steven T. Romeyn

Controller
California Commerce Club Inc.
6131 East Telegraph Road
City of Commerce, CA 90040–2501
(213) 721–2100
Fax: (213) 728–8874
EMAIL: See Below

7993

Business Information: Established in 1983, California Commerce Club Inc. is a gaming casino, providing card and tile games, as well as entertainment. As Controller, Mr. Romeyn is responsible for payroll, financial reporting, accounts payable, internal audit, food & beverage transactions, and overseeing a staff of 25. Internet users can reach him via: CALCASINO@AOL.COM **Career Steps:** Controller, California Commerce Club Inc. (1993–Present); Senior Associate, Coopers and Lybrand (1990–1993). **Associations & Accomplishments:** American Institute of Certified Public Accountants; California Society of Certified Public Accountants. **Education:** University of Southern California, B.S. (1989). **Personal:** Mr. Romeyn enjoys hockey and sailing & racing catamarans.

Mr. Scott D. Schweinfurth

Senior Vice President, Chief Financial Officer and Treasurer
Bally Gaming International, Inc.
6601 South Bermuda Avenue
Las Vegas, NV 89119
(702) 896–7700
Fax: Please mail or call

7993

Business Information: Bally Gaming International, Inc. specializes in the manufacture, design and international distribution of gaming machines and the design and implementation of computer systems for security, accountability and player tracking for slot machines from facilities based in the U.S. and Germany. As Senior Vice President, Chief Financial Officer and Treasurer, Mr. Schweinfurth is responsible for finance, accounting and controls worldwide. Established in 1949, Bally Gaming International, Inc. presently employs 1,000 people and has an annual revenue in excess of $250 million. **Career Steps:** Senior Vice President, Chief Financial Officer and Treasurer, Bally Gaming International, Inc. (1995–Present); Partner, Ernst & Young (1976–1994). **Associations & Accomplishments:** Omni Youth Services: Board of Directors, Treasurer, and President; City Club of Chicago: Board of Directors and Vice President; Campaign Treasurer for Politician; American Institute of Certified Public Accountants; Beta Gamma Sigma; Beta Alpha Psi; Union League Club; Had articles published on media issues. **Education:** Miami University, B.S. (1976). **Personal:** Married to Margaret English in 1983. Four children: Carolyn, Andrew, Thomas and Patricia. Mr. Schweinfurth enjoys golf, gardening, and spending time with the family.

Flor M. Costa

Operating Supervisor
Six Flags California
27603 North Ronridge Drive
Saugus, CA 91350
(805) 255–4714
Fax: (805) 255–4149

7996

Business Information: Six Flags California is part of the family of Six Flags theme parks, with numerous locations throughout the United States. As Operating Supervisor, Mr. Costa provides vision, leadership, and resourcefulness in the achievement of department goals consistent with the Company's mission statement. He also manages, directs, and supervises the entire Buildings and Grounds department functions, and establishes, communicates, tracks, and meets expense objectives and budget. Additional responsibilities include establishment of training programs to ensure an effective, well informed, cost–effective work force, and supervision of a staff of 200 employees. **Career Steps:** Operating Supervisor, Six Flags (1987–Present); Executive Vice President, C.O.D. Customs Brokerage Corporation (1978–1986); Trader, LMST Securities Corporation (1971–1975). **Associations & Accomplishments:** Integrated Customs Brokers Association of the Philippines; Life Member, Omega Beta Sigma Fraternity; Ex–Director, Rotary Club of Intramuros, Manila, Philippines; Cleaning Management Institute. **Education:** University of La Verne, M.B.A. (1994); Philippines Maritime Institute, Bachelor of Science in Customs Administration (1980); University of Santo Thomas, Bachelor of Science in Business Administration (1971). **Personal:** Married to Mercedes K in 1971. Two children: Fritz K. and Joanne K. Mr. Costa enjoys reading, basketball, movies, and spending time with family.

Arthur Earnest Heisler III

Creative Design Manager
Walt Disney World Co., Inc.
P.O. Box 10000
Lake Buena Vista, FL 32830–1000
(407) 397–6285
Fax: (407) 390–5148

7996

Business Information: Walt Disney World Co., Inc. is the world's most renowned family entertainment Resort. This resort was a result of the dream an vision of Mr. Walt Disney – the creator and producer of the Disney cartoon, film and entertainment legacy. Disney Corporation currently has four resort locations throughout the world: Disneyland in California, Disney World in Florida, Tokyo Disneyland in Japan and Euro Disney, France. As Creative Design Manager, Mr. Heisler develops Store Designs from concept to final installation and contributes to the work created by his staff. He describes his position as the "Design and Approval Valve" from which the creative process flows and develops through synergy between the Visual, Products and Project management. Store Interiors cover many periods and styles. Mr. Heisler enjoys bringing the Disney Characters into the shoppers world through the use of Disney's special magic. **Career Steps:** Walt Disney World Co., Inc.: Merchandising – Store Design Manager (1994–Present); Design and Engineering – Store Design Supervisor (1989–1994), Visual Merchandising – Store Design Department Head (1984–1989). **Associations & Accomplishments:** American Society of Architects; American Society of Interior Design; Licensed Registered Member, Architects and Interior Design State of Florida; Institute of Store Planners. **Education:** Brigham Young University, B.F.A. (1978); Brevard Community College, A.A. (1975). **Personal:** One child: Amy. Mr. Heisler enjoys antique auto restoration.

Cynthia Isert Anderson

Leadership Development Representative
Walt Disney World Co.
P O Box 10000
Lake Buena Vista, FL 32890
(407) 824–4357
Fax: Please mail or call

7996

Business Information: Walt Disney World Co. is a large family entertainment park. The Park was made possible due to the vision of Mr. Walt Disney — the creator and producer of animated cartoons, motion pictures, etc. Well–known nationally and internationally, Disney Corporation currently has four locations throughout the world: Disneyland in Los Angeles, California (company headquarters); Disney World in Orlando, Florida; Tokyo Disneyland; and Euro Disney in Paris, France. Future sites are being planned. As Leadership Development Representative, Ms. Isert–Anderson oversees the training and development of the leadership membership team. Other duties include research and design of new programs, and facilities programs. **Career Steps:** Leadership Development Representative, Walt Disney World Co. (1993–Present); Attorney, Private Firm (1989–1993); Professor of Philosophy, Indiana University (1990–1993). **Education:** Indiana University School of Law, J.D. (1989); Purdue University, B.S. **Personal:** Married to William Anderson in 1990. Ms. Isert Anderson enjoys golf and reading.

Donald J. Staples

Director of Creative Entertainment
Walt Disney World Resort
P.O. Box 10000
Lake Buena Vista, FL 32830–1000
(407) 397–3218
Fax: (407) 397–3736

7996

Business Information: Walt Disney World Resort is a large family entertainment park. The Park was made possible due to the vision of Mr. Walt Disney — the creator and producer of animated cartoons, motion pictures, etc. Well–known nationally and internationally, Disney Corporation currently has four locations throughout the world: Disneyland in Los Angeles, California (company headquarters); Disney World in Orlando, Florida; Tokyo Disneyland; and Euro Disney. Future sites are being planned. Joining Disney World as Manager of Creative Development in 1988, Mr. Staples was appointed as Director of Creative Entertainment in 1993. He oversees all administrative operations for associates and a support staff of 132, as well as 95 consultants and temporaries who produce all live shows for Walt Disney World parks, resorts, and special events. **Career Steps:** Walt Disney World: Director of Creative Entertainment (1993–Present), Manager Creative Development (1988–1993); Lead Trombonist, Lawrence Welk Show (1965–1982). **Associations & Accomplishments:** Sigma Chi Alumni Association; U.C.L.A. Alumni Association;

American Federation of Musicians Local #47; ASCAP; Voting Member, N.A.R.A.S. (Grammys). **Education:** University of California – Los Angeles, B.A. (1962). **Personal:** Married to Marsha in 1988. Two children by first marriage: Sheryl Lynn and Deborah Anne Staples. Mr. Staples enjoys sailing, golf, gardening, listening to music, and travel.

Kathryn K. Sweeney
International Recruitment Representative Senior
Walt Disney World Co., Inc.
P.O. Box 10090
Lake Buena Vista, FL 32830–0090
(407) 828–5830
Fax: (407) 934–6878

7996

Business Information: Walt Disney World Co., Inc. a family entertainment business, supports the Marketing Division nationally and internationally (Hong Kong, China; Canada; Paris, France; Italy; Netherlands; Germany; U.K.; Japan; Chicago, IL; New York; Washington, D.C.; San Francisco; Seattle; and Florida). As International Recruitment Representative Senior, Ms. Sweeney oversees the human resources initiatives of cast members which includes training and development, and hiring both domestically and internationally. **Career Steps:** Walt Disney World Co., Inc.: International Recruitment Representative Senior (1994–Present), International Recruitment Representative (1991–1994), College Recruitment Representative (1989–1991). **Associations & Accomplishments:** Black Hills Regional Ski for Light; Camp Good Days and Special Times; Published in Walt Disney magazine and local papers. **Education:** Purdue University, B.S. (1985). **Personal:** Married to Brian T. in 1992. Ms. Sweeney enjoys snow and water skiing, cooking, travel, and planning parties and activities.

Denis R. Boucher
Food & Beverage Director
Woodlands Club
39 Woods Road
Falmouth, ME 04105–1153
(207) 781–3104
Fax: (207) 781–5226

7997

Business Information: Woodlands Club is a full–service, year–round golf and country club with a snack bar and two restaurants. As Food & Beverage Director, Mr. Boucher administers the Food & Beverage Department and is responsible for coordinating catering, kitchen, and dining room activities, and the recruiting, hiring, and training of all Departmental employees. He also maintains service standards, an inventory system, monthly menus changes, and member requests. **Career Steps:** Food & Beverage Director, Woodlands Club (1991–Present); Assistant Food & Beverage Director, Doral Country Club (1990–1991); Food & Beverage Director, The Biltmore Hotel (1987–1990). **Associations & Accomplishments:** Private Club Chef's Association; Kidney Foundation "Great Chef's" Dinner; Scouting Fundraising; Grand Marnier Chef's Ski Race to benefit the Food Pantry of New England. **Education:** Culinary Institute of America, Associates (1976); Florida International University, Food & Beverage Management Courses. **Personal:** Mr. Boucher enjoys singing in the community chorus, skiing, fishing, and stunt kites.

Barbara J. Brungard
General Manager
Lycoming County Recreation Authority
RR 1 Box 183
Montgomery, PA 17752
(717) 547–2825
Fax: (717) 547–2827

7997

Business Information: Lycoming County Recreation Authority is a public golf course complex consisting of two 18 hole championship courses and a nine hole executive course. Established in 1964, the Complex currently has 40 employees and posted revenues in excess of $1.3 million dollars in 1995. As General Manager, Ms. Brungard oversees the day–to–day business operations of the three golf course operations. She is responsible for making sure everything runs smoothly and efficiently, and for the general accounting functions for the Complex. Ms. Brungard coordinates information from other department heads and reports to the Board of Directors and Commissioners on items concerning the golf course operations. **Career Steps:** Lycoming County Recreation Authority: General Manager (1995–Present) and Accountant (1995); Accountant, Lock Haven Flood Protection Authority (1991–1996). **Associations & Accomplishments:** Member, Harley Owners Group – Local and International Units. **Education:** Hawkeye Institute, Associate degree in Accounting (1983); Thiel College, Attended. **Personal:** Three children: Christa, Jason, and Nathan. Ms. Brungard enjoys reading, shooting pool, and owning and riding her motorcycle.

Kirk Cavarra

General Manager
Skyland Country Club
P.O. Box 879
Crested Butte, CO 81224–0879
(970) 349–6131
Fax: (970) 349–6134

7997

Business Information: Skyland Country Club, managed by Newport Properties, Inc., is a first class, full–service, private country club. Skyland offers a beautiful, Robert Trent Jones–qualified golf course with a Four–Star rating, in addition to a John Jacobs Golf School. Other amenities include tennis, racquetball, swimming, skiing, snowshoeing, and a full–service restaurant. The Club was rated among the Top 1% of new courses in 1985, and one of the Top 100 Women–Friendly courses. As Head Golf Professional/General Manager, Mr. Cavarra oversees the entire country club operation, including the budget, insurance, monthly bills, and marketing. He also oversees the activities of five department heads, and serves as Head of the Golf Shop, responsible for the encouragement and promotion of golf. **Career Steps:** Newport Properties, Inc., d.b.a. Skyland Country Club: General Manager (1995–Present), Head Golf Professional (1990–1995). **Associations & Accomplishments:** Professional Golfers Association; Club Managers Association; National Golfers Association. **Education:** Western State College; Colorado State University. **Personal:** Married to Ranee in 1986. Two children: Christian and Nicholas. Mr. Cavarra enjoys hunting and fishing.

W.A. (Toppy) Cowen
Managing Director
Pink Beach Club
P.O. Box HM 1017
Hamilton, Bermuda
(441) 293–1666
Fax: (441) 293–8935
EMail: See Below

7997

Business Information: Pink Beach Club is a premier resort on Bermuda's south shore. The Club is nestled in 16 1/2 acres of rolling hills and lush gardens, overlooking two pink coral sand beaches, and surrounded by a barrier of coral reefs. The Club offers 93 rooms, 186 beds, two tennis courts, a dining room with seating for 200, a bar, and an ideal location (10 minutes to the airport and 15 minutes to the city of Hamilton) for vacationers. As Managing Director, Mr. Cowen oversees the total operation of the hotel, including administration, employee and maintenance supervision, guest accommodation, and public relations. Internet users can reach him via: pinkclub@ibl.bm **Career Steps:** Managing Director, Pink Beach Club (1977–Present); Golf Club Manager, Port Royal Golf Course (1975–1977); General Manager and Club Secretary, Mid Ocean Club (1965–1975); Restaurant Owner, The Windjammer (1961–1965). **Associations & Accomplishments:** Former President, Skal Bermuda; Former President, Hotel Employers of Bermuda; Former Trustee, The Bermuda Equestrian Federation "Vesey St."; Bermuda Road Safety Council; Director, Bank of N.T. Butterfield & Son; Former Rotarian. **Education:** Bermuda Commercial School (1953). **Personal:** Married to Saundra Kaaren in 1967. Three children: Ricky, Heidi, and Heather Cowen Henderson. Mr. Cowen enjoys writing, reading, and being a passionate golfer (handicap 12).

Marcelo De Rada
Marketing Director
National Soccer Federation
Top Bol No. 110, P.O. Box 52–0777
Miami, FL 33152–0777
(591) 231–6981
Fax: (591) 271–1462

7997

Business Information: National Soccer Federation is a professional association for members of the soccer industry. The Organization provides educational programs, trade shows and soccer tournaments for its members, as well as conducting national and international seminars. As Marketing Director, Mr. De Rada is responsible for the organization of the 1997 South American Soccer Cup (Copa America). He oversees the marketing and public relations of the tournament in which 12 teams from the United States, Mexico, and South America will participate. **Career Steps:** Marketing Director, National Soccer Federation (1995–Present); Master Agent, Amedex/Winter HWR (1993–Present); General Sales Manager, Bisa Seguros & Reseguros (1992–1994). **Associations & Accomplishments:** Former President, Entrepreneurs Association of La Paz; National Coordinator, National Association of Entrepreneurs; Life Member Qualifier, Million Dollar Round Table; President's Prudential Honor Guard. **Education:** Babson College, B.S., M.B.A. (1983); Harvard, Crisis Manage-

ment; Prudential Insurance Company, Insurance Advisor; Inconstrag, Advanced Risk Manager; Million Dollar Round Table, Seminar Selling Techniques. **Personal:** Married to Katia Ocampo in 1991. Three children: Sofia, Marcelo, and Anthony. Mr. De Rada enjoys speaking on advanced marketing strategies.

Steven Dondo

Chief Engineer and Director of Engineering
Jonathan Club
545 South Figueroa Street
Los Angeles, CA 90071
(213) 312–5214
Fax: (213) 488–9483

7997

Business Information: Jonathan Club is the most exclusive private club west of the Mississippi. Located in Los Angeles, the Club offers a 13–story hotel, private club and beach club. Established in 1895, Jonathan Club currently has a membership of 2,000 and employs more than 250 people. As Chief Engineer, Director of Engineering, Mr. Dondo is responsible for facilities engineering, remodeling, and construction of plant operations. His most recent project included the oversight of a $2 million remodeling project. Originally from Hungary, he arrived in the U.S. without any knowledge of English. After attending school, he worked his way up to his present position, by working in various companies in a janitorial capacity. **Career Steps:** Chief Engineer, Director of Engineering, Jonathan Club (1982–Present); Instructor, University of California – Los Angeles Extension – Facilities Management, Housekeeping Management (1992–Present). **Associations & Accomplishments:** Past President of San Fernando Valley Chapter, National Association of Power Engineers; National Fire Protection Association; Association of Professional Energy Managers; Association of Energy Engineers; Life Member, UCLA Alumni Association **Personal:** Married to Apollonia in 1961. Three children: Jeanett, Elizabeth, and Michelle.

Rick D. Graves

Controller
Newport Harbor Yacht Club
720 West Bay Avenue
Newport Beach, CA 92661
(714) 723–6850
Fax: (714) 673–3972

7997

Business Information: Newport Harbor Yacht Club is a full–service club where its 1,000 members can enjoy a dining facility, full bar, deck, boat yard, 40 moorings, 10 docking facilities, 400 boat lockers, and a dock station. As Controller, Mr. Graves handles all financial operations of the Club, including administering and controlling finances, and overseeing the internal control system. **Career Steps:** Controller, Newport Harbor Yacht Club (1996–Present); Watterson College Pacific: Vice President of Finance (1993–1996), Controller (1990–1993); Senior Accountant, Carson–Brooks Industries (1989–1990). **Associations & Accomplishments:** Club Managers Association of America; Club Controllers of Southern California. **Education:** California State University – Dominguez Hills, B.S. (1986). **Personal:** Married to Sherry in 1990. One child: Jacy Alexa. Mr. Graves enjoys fishing, camping, and travel.

Roy E. Hall
Certified Executive Chef
Little Traverse Bay Golf Club
995 Hideaway Valley Drive
Harbor Springs, MI 49740–9450
(616) 526–7800
Fax: (616) 526–9661

7997

Business Information: Little Traverse Bay Golf Club is an open membership golf and country club. A graduate of the Culinary Institute of America and a Certified Chef with more than twenty years experience, Mr. Hall joined the Little Traverse Bay Golf Club Restaurant in 1992. As Executive Chef, he is responsible for menu design, food preparation, ordering, personnel hiring and training, advertising, cost analysis, inventory and quality control, as well as directing all kitchen duties. **Career Steps:** Certified Executive Chef, Little Traverse Bay Golf Club (1992–Present); Executive Sous Chef, Birchwood Farms Golf & Country Club (1985–1992); Chef, Bartley House (1974–1984). **Associations & Accomplishments:** President, American Culinary Federation de Cuisine; Emmet County Ambulance Tending EMT; Former President, American Heart Association (1984–1985); Harbor Springs Police Reserves. **Education:** Culinary Institute of America, C.E.C. (1996). **Personal:** Married to Nancy in 1978. Three children: Scott, Jodi, and Ashley. Mr. Hall enjoys hunting, fishing, sports, volunteer work, and is an adult education instructor.

David A. Herbert, CHAE

Director of Finance
Polo Club of Boca Raton P.O.A., Inc.
5400 Champion Boulevard
Boca Raton, FL 33496–1607
(407) 995–1212
Fax: (407) 995–1232

7997

Business Information: The Polo Club of Boca Raton P.O.A., Inc. is a private country club residential community. Established in 1986, the Polo Club of Boca Raton currently employs 400 people and has an estimated annual revenue of $18 million. A Certified Hospitality Accountant Executive since 1992, Mr. Herbert serves as Director of Finance responsible for the overall administration of accounting and financial reporting. **Career Steps:** Director of Finance, Polo Club of Boca Raton P.O.A., Inc. (1993–Present); Controller, Golf and Racquet Club at Eastpointe (1991–1993); Assistant Controller, Boca West Country Club (1988–1991). **Associations & Accomplishments:** President–Elect, Florida Gold Coast Chapter of the International Association of Hospitality Accountants; Member, Community Association Institute. **Education:** Certified Hospitality Accountant Executive. **Personal:** Mr. Herbert enjoys computers, music and golf.

David H. Lynch

General Manager
Bath Club, Inc.
5937 Collins Avenue
Miami Beach, FL 33140
(305) 866–1621
Fax: (305) 866–1703

7997

Business Information: Bath Club, Inc. is a full–service, private beach club. As General Manager, Mr. Lynch is responsible for all aspects of the Club's operations, including administration, sales and marketing, and day–to–day activities. **Career Steps:** General Manager, Bath Club, Inc. (1995–Present); Assistant General Manager, The Center Club, Inc. (1985–1995). **Associations & Accomplishments:** National Association of Catering Executives; Club Managers Association of America; International Special Event Society. **Education:** Townson State College, B.S. (1973). **Personal:** Mr. Lynch enjoys the beach and travel.

Roger D. Manary

Controller
Rainier Golf and Country Club
1856 South 112th Street
Seattle, WA 98168–1733
(206) 242–2222
Fax: (206) 242–4600

7997

Business Information: Rainier Golf and Country Club is a private country club with a restaurant, bar, 18–hole golf course (72 par), and a pool. The Club presently serves 400 members and holds 17 private tournaments and social events annually. As Controller, Mr. Manary handles all finances, researching of club trends in accounting, financial statements, membership dealings, and account reconciliation. **Career Steps:** Controller, Rainier Golf and Country Club (1991–Present); Controller, Aspen Paints (1989–1991); Controller, Preservative Paints (1978–1989). **Associations & Accomplishments:** International Association of Hospitality Accountants. **Education:** University of Washington, B.A. in Finance (1978). **Personal:** Married to Linda in 1970. Two children: David and Tina. Mr. Manary enjoys golf and woodworking.

Marcell M. Mustafah

Executive Chef
Spanish Hills Country Club
999 Crestview Avenue
Camarillo, CA 93010
(805) 388–5000
Fax: (805) 484–7914

7997

Business Information: Spanish Hills Country Club is a first class, full–service, private country club. As Executive Chef, Mr. Mustafah is responsible for all aspects of the food operations for the country club. **Career Steps:** Executive Chef, Spanish Hills Country Club (1994–Present); Executive Chef, Ojai Cafe Emporium (1992–1994); Executive Chef, Ojai Valley Inn (1990–1992); Executive Sous Chef, Ma Maison – Beverly Hills (1987–1990). **Associations & Accomplishments:** Les Amis D'Escofier; Confrerie de la Chaine Des Rotisseur; Chairman of Membership of C.I.C.A.; American Culinary Federation; American Bocese D'Or Academy; US Pastry Alliance. **Education:** SESC Culinary School, Major (1987); CIA: Hyde Park, St. Helena. **Personal:** Mr. Mustafah enjoys riding his Harley Davidson.

Nancy Rawlings

Controller
Bradenton Country Club
4646 9th Avenue West
Bradenton, FL 34209
(941) 792–1602
Fax: (941) 792–5983

7997

Business Information: Bradenton Country Club, established in 1927, is a private club, currently employing 84 people. The Club has golf, tennis, swimming facilities, and a full service dining room. As Controller, Ms. Rawlings is responsible for all aspects of financial operations, including accounting, financial reports, payroll, taxes, management, and projects. Other duties include management of all automated computer systems, committee involvement, board meetings, and membership in the executive committee. Ms. Rawlings has oversight of the tennis department. **Career Steps:** Controller, Bradenton Country Club (1985–Present); Chief Accountant, Retired Corporation of America, Inc. (1983–1985); Junior Accountant, John E. Rawlings, CFP (1964–1983). **Associations & Accomplishments:** Membership Committee, International Association of Hospitality Accountants (IAHA); First Brethern Church. **Personal:** Married to John E. in 1972. Ms. Rawlings enjoys golf, bike riding, swimming, and being a choraler.

Joseph S. Whiteside, III

Executive Director
Elmhurst Family YMCA
211 West First Street
Elmhurst, IL 60126
(708) 834–9200
Fax: (708) 834–9221

7997

Business Information: Imhurst Family YMCA, is a nonprofit human services organization providing community–based services, educational and recreational programs for the western suburb of Chicago, Illinois, serving a population of approximately 100,000. The organization is part of YMCA's worldwide organization, the oldest and largest membership organization in the world. As Executive Director, Mr. Whiteside is responsible for the administrative direction of all operations for this Chapter. Primary duties include community programs, operations, program development, marketing, community leadership development and fundraising activities. The original YMCA was organized in 1874. Established in 1960, Elmhurst Family YMCA employs 200 people with annual sales of operational budget in excess of $1.5 million. **Career Steps:** Executive Director, Elmhurst Family YMCA (1993–Present); Associate Executive Director, Abington YMCA (1990–1993 & 1985–1989); Executive Director, Fox–Morris Consultants (1989–1990). **Associations & Accomplishments:** Abington Kiwanis; Elmhurst Rotary; Elmhurst Jaycees; Elmhurst Chamber of Commerce; Elm Fest; Elmhurst Youth Coordinating Council; Elmhurst Community Effort; Listed in: Who's Who in the East, Who's Who Among Young American Professionals, Who's Who of Emerging Leaders in America; Recipient of John Wanamaker Award; YMCA Metropolitan Chicago Executive Director Award; Association of Professional Directors. **Education:** Pensacola Christian College, B.S. in Education (1985). **Personal:** Mr. Whiteside enjoys activities in active sports, particularly soccer and basketball, and enjoys reading, music, and travel.

Themis J. Zymarakis

Director of Food and Beverage
Paradise Valley Country Club
7101 North Tatum Boulevard
Paradise Valley, AZ 85253
(602) 840–8100
Fax: (602) 840–2628

7997

Business Information: Paradise Valley Country Club is a full–service, members–only country club. As Director of Food and Beverage, Mr. Zymarakis is responsible for all aspects of food and beverage operations, including recruitment, training, food and labor costs, and preparations for scheduled events such as weddings, private parties, and charity dinners or functions. **Career Steps:** Director of Food and Beverage, Paradise Valley Country Club (1994–Present); Food and Beverage Consultant, CHMC Group, Inc. (1993–1994); General Manager – Restaurant, The Phoenician Resort (1991–1993). **Associations & Accomplishments:** Volunteer, American Foundation for the Blind Children. **Education:** New York Community College, Associate in Hotel and Restaraunt Management (1972); School of Visual Arts – New York City, Graphics and Advertising (1976). **Personal:** Married to Beverly in 1987. Two children: Ian and Jason. Mr. Zymarakis enjoys reading, swimming, golf, and cooking.

Charles R. Achterberg

Chief Executive Officer
Entertainment Concepts, Inc.
3044 Shepherd of the Hills Expressway, Suite 307
Branson, MO 65616
(417) 339–4405
Fax: (417) 339–4408

7999

Business Information: Entertainment Concepts, Inc. is a management company controlling six attractions. Attractions, such as "Ripley's Believe It or Not," are located in Branson, Missouri, and Orlando and Key West, Florida. Joining the Company as Chief Executive Officer in 1992, Mr. Achterberg is responsible for all budgeting, as well as complete control for the six locations operated by limited partnerships. In addition, he oversees all administrative operations for associates and a support staff of 120. **Career Steps:** Chief Executive Officer, Entertainment Concepts, Inc. (1992–Present); Inside Salesman, UNR/Rohn (1991–1993); President and Chief Executive Officer, K.G. Johnson Lusk EQ (1978–1991). **Associations & Accomplishments:** Rotary Club; Former member, Elks; American Veterans Association; United Methodist Church. **Education:** University of Wisconsin (1978). **Personal:** Married to Joyce in 1962. Three children: Karl, Kevin, and Kurt. Mr. Achterberg enjoys golf, fishing, and boating.

Gene H. Almy Jr.

Director of Sales and Marketing
Medieval Times Dinner and Tournament
1812 Market Center Boulevard
Dallas, TX 75207
(214) 761–1801
Fax: (214) 761–1805

7999

Business Information: Medieval Times Dinner and Tournament is a medieval theme attraction featuring knights on horseback competing in jousting matches and hand–to–hand combat, while spectators enjoy dinner. Established in 1992, Medieval Times Dinner and Tournament currently employs more than 180 people. As Director of Sales and Marketing, Mr. Almy is responsible for coordinating the sales and marketing efforts in the Southwest Region of the U.S., as well as managing a team of 25 sales people. **Career Steps:** Medieval Times Dinner and Tournament: Director of Sales and Marketing (1994–Present), Public Relations Manager (1992–1994). **Associations & Accomplishments:** Meeting Planners International; Hospitality Sales and Marketing Association International; International Association of Business Communicators; Public Relations Society of America. **Education:** Texas A&M University, B.S. (1991). **Personal:** Mr. Almy enjoys singing and golf.

David L. Boger

Vice President
State Dock, Inc.
6365 State Park Road
Jamestown, KY 42629–7801
(502) 343–2525
Fax: (502) 343–4793

7999

Business Information: State Dock, Inc., a subsidiary of Marina Management Services, is a marine operation on Lake Cumberland, Kentucky (63,000–acre lake, 110 miles long), whose primary focus is to provide the rental of luxury houseboats (a total of 108), as well as a selection of ski boats. Established in 1985, State Dock, Inc. is located in South Central Kentucky, reporting annual revenue of $7 million and currently employs 190 people. As Vice President, Mr. Boger serves as General Manager and is responsible for all day–to–day operations and personnel, including hiring and firing, off–season project work, and repairs, as well as controlling the budget and customer service. **Career Steps:** Vice President, State Dock, Inc. (1988–Present); Teacher/Instructor, Russell County School System (1987–1988); Auto Mechanic, Hudson Chevron (1984–1987); Sergeant, United States Army (1972–1982). **Associations & Accomplishments:** Russell County Tourist Commission; Veterans of Foreign Wars. **Education:** Campbellsville College, B.S. (1988); Lindsey Wilson College, A.A. **Personal:** Married to Karen in 1995. Two children: Charles and Stefanie. Mr. Boger enjoys classic automobiles.

Katherine R. Bouckaert

Risk Manager
President Riverboat Casinos
800 North 1st Street
St. Louis, MO 63102–2529
(314) 622–3113
Fax: (314) 622–3029

7999

Business Information: President Riverboat Casinos is an entertainment and gambling casino located on the riverfront of St. Louis, MO. The Casino operates from two boats, one being the full–service casino, and the other a reception area for weddings, etc. As Risk Manager, Ms. Bouckaert investigates, processes, and manages employees and guest inquiries. She acts as a liaison between attorneys and the Company. She is mainly responsible for maintaining the Company's compliance with Federal and State Laws. **Career Steps:** Risk Manager, President Riverboat Casinos (Present); Private Investigator, Easterling & Steinmetz; President, Buck Asphalt. **Associations & Accomplishments:** Bridgeton Chapter of Optimist International. Education: Florissant Community College, A.A.S. in Criminal Justice (In Progress); International Hair Institute, Barber's License. **Personal:** Married to Gary in 1988. Two children: Michael and Kelly. Ms. Bouckaert enjoys being a composer and musician, photography, and poetry.

Larita D. Clark

Director of Fiscal Operations
Metropolitan Pier and Exposition Authority
2301 S. Prairie Avenue
Chicago, IL 60616
(312) 791–6134
Fax: (312) 567–8040

7999

Business Information: Metropolitan Pier and Exposition Authority, established in 1955, is the largest convention center in the United States. With estimated revenue of $60 million, the Center presently employs over 1,000 people. As Director of Fiscal Operations, Ms. Clark oversees the activities of a staff of 35. Her responsibilities include staff recruitment, training, evaluating, and payroll. Other duties include accounting functions such as accounts payable, accounts receivable, general billing, collections, and other budgetary concerns. Ms. Clark prepares financial reports for upper management to assist in developing corporate planning for the future. Concurrently, Ms. Clark is a Minister of Love Center Christian Fellowship. **Career Steps:** Director of Fiscal Operations, Metropolitan Pier and Exposition Authority (1984–Present); Auditor, KPMG Peat Marwick (1982–1984). **Associations & Accomplishments:** Certified Public Accountant – Illinois (since November 1982); American Institute of Certified Public Accountants; Illinois Certified Public Accountant Society; National Association of Black Accountants; President, Board of Directors, STRIVE – a job training program for chronically–unemployed, low income adults. **Education:** Northwestern University Kellogg School of Business, Masters of Management (1993); Loyola University, Bachelor of Business Administration. **Personal:** Married to Gregory in 1988. Two children: Gregory Clark II and Kyle. Ms. Clark enjoys studying the Bible and ministering the Word of God.

Mahina Cockett

Operations Manager
Maui Tropical Plantation
1670 Honoapiilani Hwy.
Wailuku, HI 96793
(808) 244–7643
Fax: (808) 242–8983

7999

Business Information: Maui Tropical Plantation is a visitor attraction promoting commercial agriculture via tram tour, restaurant, and shopping. Ms. Cockett joined the company in 1984 as a Tour Hostess, was promoted to Guest Activities Manager in 1992, and has been Operations Manager since 1994. She oversees all aspects of operations for all departments, to include, Retail, Food & Beverage, Sales & Marketing, Tours/Guest Activities, Farm and Administration. **Career Steps:** Maui Tropical Plantation: Operations Manager (1994–Present), Guest Activities Manager (1992–1994), Tour Hostess (1984–1992). **Associations & Accomplishments:** Ahahui Ka'ahumanu, Maui Chapter; Mamakakaua, Daughters & Sons of Hawaii. **Personal:** Three children: Sheldon, Christian, and Abra Lene. Ms. Cockett enjoys reading mysteries and Hawaiian Ethnobotony.

Manuel Dipre

International Coordinator Operations
GTECH Latin American Corporation
1505 Ponce De Leon Avenue, Mercantile Plaza, Suite 807
Hato Rey, Puerto Rico 00918
(809) 766–0996
Fax: (809) 766–0995 (809) 766–4044

7999

Business Information: GTECH specializes in the installation of electronic lottery systems around the world. As International Coordinator Operations, Mr. Dipre is responsible for all aspects of lottery facilities set up. **Career Steps:** GTECH: International Coordinator Operations, (1996–Present), Computer Analyst (1993–1996), Control Room Supervisor (1991–1993). **Associations & Accomplishments:** Church of God Pentecostal International Movement. **Education:** Interamerican University, B.S. in Computer Science (1987); Managing Projects Course; Digital Systems Administrator; UNIX and Prosys Course; Labor Law Seminar. **Personal:** Mr. Dipre enjoys visiting the church, body building, and reading books and magazines.

Michael W. Donahue

Chief Executive Officer
Gila River Gaming Enterprises
1201 South 56th Street, Box 5074
Chandler, AZ 85226
(520) 796–7777
Fax: (520) 796–7712

7999

Business Information: Gila River Gaming Enterprises is the operating management company for a 90,000 square–foot casino and travel facility. Established in 1994, the Casino currently employs 1,400 people. As Chief Executive Officer and General Manager, Mr. Donahue is responsible for all aspects of operations, including marketing, strategic planning and all daily operations. A successful Manager in the gaming industry, Mr. Donahue has opened 4 casinos in 3 years, and has been quoted in the Phoenix Magazine, the Arizona Republic, Casino Player and Card Player Magazines. **Career Steps:** Chief Executive Officer, Gila River Gaming Enterprises (1994–Present); Director of Operations, Mazatzal Casino (1993–1994); Director of Slot Operations, Ft. McDowell Casino (1988–1993). **Associations & Accomplishments:** Advisory Board for Curriculum Development, Scottsdale Community College Gaming Program; Speaker at the 1994 Annual Meeting of the National Center for American Indian Enterprise Development, Phoenix, Arizona. **Education:** Indiana University, B.A. (1978). **Personal:** Married to Julie Marie in 1984. Two children: Patrick and Erin.

John A. James

Chairman
Bingo Cabazon, Inc.
84245 Indio Springs Drive
Indio, CA 92201
(619) 342–5000
Fax: Please mail or call

7999

Business Information: Bingo Cabazon, Inc., the largest employer in the Chocilla Valley, is a bingo gaming business run by the Cabazon Indian Tribe, employing 600 people. Future plans include expansion of a bowling alley and an eight–story hotel. A recognized leader of the Cabazon Tribe, Mr. James joined Bingo Cabazon, Inc. in 1988. Currently serving as Chairman, he is responsible for the overall Company operations, including supervising the count of gaming receipts and administration. **Career Steps:** Chairman, Bingo Cabazon, Inc. (1988–Present). **Personal:** Mr. James enjoys shooting sports.

John S. Kay

Director of Marketing
United States Army Morale, Welfare & Recreation
Ft. Myer Military Community, 120 Custer Road, Room 310
Arlington, VA 22211–1199
(703) 696–3817
Fax: (703) 696–6491
EMAIL: See Below

7999

Business Information: U.S. Army Morale, Welfare & Recreation (MWR) is a provider of recreational programs and services for members of the U.S. Army and their dependents, including offering hotels, marinas, tennis centers, clubs, bowling centers, etc. International in scope, MWR departments are located at military bases worldwide. Involved with the MWR for the past twenty years in Hawaii, Mr. Kay joined the Ft. Myer Army Base location as Director of Marketing in 1975. He is responsible for the direction of all marketing functions, including business marketing planning, market surveys, sales programs, newspaper production, and promotional brochures. Internet users can reach him via: ALOHAYAALL@aol.com or KayJ@McNair–EMH2.Army.mil **Career Steps:** Director of Marketing, U.S. Army Morale, Welfare & Recreation (MWR) (1975–Present); General Manager, Lahaina Treehouse Restaurant (1973–1975); General Manager, Braniff International Hotels (1971–1973). **Associations & Accomplishments:** American Marketing Association – President of Honolulu Chapter (1975–Present); Board of Directors, Sales and Marketing Executives (1975–1995); Active Member of several committees, Hawaii Hotel Association (1975–1995); Board of Directors, Pacific–Asia Travel Association (PATA) (1975–1995). **Education:** University of Arizona, B.S. (1967); Attended: Cornell University, Hotel School, three–month summer professional course, Department of Army course on Personnel Management for Executives (high level). **Personal:** Mr. Kay enjoys music, reading, boating, photography, and world travel.

Lisa A. Lavieri

Director, Software Product Support
GTECH Corporation
55 Technology Way
West Greenwich, RI 02817
(401) 392–7226
Fax: (401) 392–0476
EMAIL: See Below

7999

Business Information: With over 11 years of experience in software management in the on–line lottery industry, Ms. Lavieri currently directs the activities of the Software Product Support Group. She is responsible for developing and directing this new organization to fulfill its primary charter: transitioning the ongoing support of new products to the South West Services Organization through a mix of skill training, implementation, and ongoing support activities. This includes: working closely with the Product Development Group to determine product development team assisgnments; management of new product development activities; developing and delivering Technical Training Programs and documentation; providing Product Marketing and Sales with product liaisons and specialists to support demo, conference and sales activities. Ms. Lavieri has extensive software project implementation experience. She led the startup software project management efforts for: Ohio, California, New York, Ireland, Catalunya, Finland, Denmark, Iceland, Argentina (Provincial), and Puerto Rico, as well as serveral game and feature implementations worldwide. Internet users may reach her via: llavieri@gtech.com **Career Steps:** GTECH Corporation (1985–Present); Director, Software Product Support, Director, Latin American Software Services, Manager, European & Latin American Software Services, Manager, International Support Services, Manager, Software Projects, Software Project Manager. **Associations & Accomplishments:** Skidmore College Alumni Association, President since 1989. **Education:** Ms. Lavieri holds a Bachelor of Arts degree in English/History from Skidmore College with teaching certification, and a Master of Business Administration degree in Computer–based Management Systems from Clarkson University. Working knowledge of FORTRAN. Additional course certificates in Management and System Operations. Professional teaching experience. **Personal:** Married to Charles R. Smith in 1985. One child: Suzanne Elizabeth Smith. Ms. Lavieri enjoys biking, jogging, drawing, crafts, and various home and garden hobbies.

Deborah McBratney–Stapleton

Executive Director
Anderson Fine Arts Foundation, Inc.
226 West 8th Street
Anderson, IN 46046–1354
(317) 649–1248
Fax: (317) 649–0199

7999

Business Information: Established in 1967, Anderson Fine Arts Foundation, Inc. is a visual and performing arts museum. As Executive Director, Ms. McBratney–Stapleton oversees planning, directs operations, fiscal management, and public relations. **Career Steps:** Executive Director, Anderson Fine Arts Foundation, Inc. (1980–Present). **Associations & Accomplishments:** Legislative Chair, Midwest Museums Conference; Small Museums Administrator's Committee, American Association of Museums; Personnel Evaluation Committee; Association of Indiana Museums: First Vice President, Second Vice President in Charge of Developing Statewide Professional Workshops; Mayor's Arts and Culture Commission; Rotary International; National Society of Arts and Letters. **Education:** Ball State University, Master of Arts (1990), M.A. in Executive Development for Public Service;

Sangamon State University – Sangamon Institute for Arts Administration (1982). **Personal:** Ms. McBratney–Stapleton enjoys puzzles, aqua aerobics, entertaining, and travel.

Patricia A. Misher
Assistant to the Director of Community Centers
Kansas City Parks & Recreation
1008 Locust
Kansas City, MO 64106–2621
(816) 871–5786
Fax: (816) 871–3138

7999

Business Information: The Community Centers division of Kansas City, MO Parks & Recreation provides programs for pre–schoolers through senior citizens. Currently operating through nine separate center sites, program offerings include sports leagues, crafts, social services, among others. Working in various directional roles for Kansas City Parks & Recreation since 1970, Patricia Misher has served in her current position since 1984. As Assistant to the Community Centers Director, she is responsible for providing assistance in the following areas, as well as act on behalf of the Director in his/her absence. Duties include the supervision of staffing, oversight of the total operations of nine community centers (soon to be 12), budgetary management and dispersals, and materials procurement. **Career Steps:** Kansas City, MO. Parks & Recreation: Assistant to the Director of Community Centers (1984–Present), Recreation Director II (1973–1984), Recreation Director I (1970–1973). **Associations & Accomplishments:** Missouri Parks and Recreation; Recipient, "Black Women in City Government" award for 25 years or more of service service from City Hall. **Education:** University of Kansas, B.S. (1970). **Personal:** One child: Ivy. Ms. Misher enjoys sewing and travel.

Mr. Ivan R. Orlandi

Executive Director
Puerto Rico Bid Committee
3 Ponce De Leon Avenue, Stop #1
San Juan, Puerto Rico 00902
(809) 723–2004
Fax: (809) 268–2004

7999

Business Information: Puerto Rico Bid Committee, established in 1987 for the 2004 Summer Olympics is charged with the bidding for the Olympics. The Committee consists of a Board of Directors (20 people), directing technology, telecommunications, consultants, and architectures. The decision will be made on September 5, 1997 as to the location of the 2004 Olympics. As Executive Director, Mr. Orlandi oversees all procedures, studies, compiling of studies, lobbying process, and traveling all over the world to meet with the National Bid Committee. **Career Steps:** Executive Director, Puerto Rico Bid Committee (1993–Present); Executive Director, Grand Regatta Columbus (1988–1992); Government Affair Director, Puerto Rico Telephone Company (1985–1988). **Associations & Accomplishments:** Jaycees; Puerto Rico Manufacturing Association; Marketing Superstar of the World (1993). **Education:** University of Puerto Rico, B.B.A. (1962). **Personal:** Married to Socorrito Orlandi in 1962. Three children: Natasha, Ivan, and Annushka. Mr. Orlandi enjoys taking care of his lawn and banana & orange trees.

Yulita Osuba
Director of Sales and Marketing
Ocean Center
19 North Atlantic Avenue
Daytona Beach, FL 32118–4203
(904) 254–4500
Fax: (904) 254–4512

7999

Business Information: Ocean Center is a multi–purpose convention, sports, and entertainment facility. As Director of Sales and Marketing, Ms. Osuba is responsible for the direction of convention sales and marketing, as well as directing sales and bookings for large groups of 500–10,000 people for conventions. Concurrent with her duties for Ocean Center, she is an adjunct instructor with the Hospitality Management program at Daytona Beach Community College. **Career Steps:** Director of Sales and Marketing, Ocean Center (1988–Present); Adjunct Instructor, Hospitality Management Degree Program, Daytona Beach Community College. **Associations & Accomplishments:** American Society Association of Executives; Florida Society Association of Executives; Religious Conference Management Association; Professional Convention Management Association; ACME. **Education:** Daytona Beach Community College, A.S. (1981), A.A. (1996); Attending: California Coast University for B.A. in Business Administration. **Personal:** Married to Henry

in 1981. Two children: Brannon and Amber. Ms. Osuba enjoys working out in the gym daily and sewing.

Sandra L. Poulson
President and CEO
Tempe Convention & Visitors Bureau
51 West 3rd Street #105
Tempe, AZ 85281–2833
(602) 894–8158
Fax: (602) 968–8004
Email: See Below

7999

Business Information: Tempe Convention & Visitors Bureau, founded in 1988 by Ms. Poulson, specializes in tourism promotion for the City of Tempe, AZ. As President and CEO, Ms. Poulson is responsible for all aspects of Bureau operations, including administration, sales and marketing, public relations, and strategic planning. The City of Tempe successfully hosted the 1996 Super Bowl and there is talk of a return in 2000. In 1994, she successfully started a new event that has attracted over 2 million people to Tempe's Fantasy of Lights, held annually between Thanksgiving and New Years. The downtown area glows and sparkles with hundreds of thousands of lights and animated displays. **Career Steps:** President and CEO, Tempe Convention & Visitors Bureau (1988–Present); Vice President, Mission Travel (1981–1988); Public Relations Manager, Phoenix Convention & Visitors Bureau (1977–1981); Sales Manager, Pointe Resorts (1977). **Associations & Accomplishments:** IACVB; ASAE; MPI; JDF; Mill Avenue Merchants Association; SKAL; Grand Canyon State Games; Fiesta Bowl Committee; Who's Who in the West; Who's Who in America. **Education:** University of Arizona, B.F.A. (1970); University of Calgary, Certified Destination Management Executive (1996). **Personal:** Married to Michael R. Hecomovich in 1993. Ms. Poulson enjoys golf, skiing, camping, hiking, tennis, and her dog Ruff, Yorksuperior.

Janna Jo Shisler
General Counsel
Hoosier Lottery
201 South Capitol Avenue, Suite 1100
Indianapolis, IN 46225
(317) 264–4990
Fax: (317) 264–4908

7999

Business Information: The Hoosier Lottery was established by the Indiana General Assembly in 1989 for the purpose of raising significant additional money for the citizens of the State of Indiana through the sale of lottery tickets. The Lottery is a body politic and corporate, separate from the State, and operates as an entrepreneurial business enterprise. In fiscal year 1995, the Lottery generated an annual revenue of $615 million. As General Counsel, Ms. Shisler acts as a resource with regard to legal issues and is responsible for drafting and negotiating contracts and leases, pursing minor litigation, monitoring outside counsel, responding to legal filings, and drafting and reviewing administrative procedures and rules. She is admitted to practice before all Indiana state and federal courts, as well as the United States Court of Appeals for the Seventh Circuit. **Career Steps:** General Counsel, Hoosier Lottery (1992–Present); Staff Attorney, Indiana State Teachers' Retirement Fund (1990–1992); Law Clerk, United States District Court, Southern District of Indiana (1988–1990). **Associations & Accomplishments:** Indianapolis Bar Association; Indiana State Bar Association; American Bar Association; Governor's Planning Council for People with Disabilities; Indiana Rehabilitation Hospital Foundation Board; Julian Center Board of Directors (services for abused women). **Education:** Indiana University School of Law – Indianapolis, J.D. (1988); Indiana University – Purdue University, Indianapolis, B.A. (1984). **Personal:** Ms. Shisler enjoys reading. theater, and travel.

Larry R. Smith
Director of Operations
Kentucky Lottery Corporation
3899 Produce Road
Louisville, KY 40218
(502) 966–9574
Fax: (502) 964–0136

7999

Business Information: Kentucky Lottery Corporation produces and provides lottery games of the highest quality and integrity, which are consistent with good public policy and social responsibility. The Company is regional in scope, with eleven locations throughout the Kentucky area. Established in 1989, the Company employs 220 people and has an estimated annual revenue of $530 million. As Director of Operations, Mr. Smith oversees the proper functions of fleet management, shipping and receiving, warehousing, and vending machine operations. **Career Steps:** Director of Operations, Kentucky

Lottery Corporation (1989–Present); General Manager, Naish–Mayflower Moving and Storage (1984–1989); Traffic Manager, Indiana Grain Corporation (1980–1984); Manager of Transportation, Louisville and Nashville Railroad Corporation (1966–1980). **Education:** Sullivan College: Marketing (1996), Business Management (1989). **Personal:** Three children: Kasey, Nicholas, and Kory. Mr. Smith enjoys golf and coaching youth league football.

Robert L. Sokolowski
Corporate Officer & Vice President of Program Development
Sports Challenge International, Inc.
4707 140th Avenue North
Clearwater, FL 34622
(813) 524–2933
Fax: (813) 524–2868
EMAIL: See Below

7999

Business Information: Sports Challenge International, Inc. is an international youth sports travel company, providing competition and travel activities for youth athletes and coaches through the fundraising efforts of the children, aged 13 to 19 years old. These seven–day trips offer them the opportunity to learn other cultures, socialize, and compete with other children their age on an international level. As Corporate Officer & Vice President of Program Development, Mr. Sokolowski is responsible for athlete and tour research, as well as maintaining Corporate records and providing guidance to group leaders. Internet users can also reach Robert via: BOBSOKS@AOL.COM. **Career Steps:** Corporate Officer & Vice President of Program Development, Sports Challenge International, Inc. (1992–Present); Pinellas County Schools – Florida: Elementary School Principal (1981–1992), Assistant Principal (1979–1980), Elementary School Teacher (1971–1978). **Associations & Accomplishments:** Board of Directors and Former President, Boys and Girls Clubs of the Suncoast – St. Petersburg, Florida; Former Chairman, Florida Area Council of Boys and Girls Club; Chi Chi Rodrigues Foundation; Recipient, Lamons Award for Service and Gold Medalion from Boys and Girls Clubs of America; Post Graduate Award, FICAPA Gold Key Award for Education Leadership; Outstanding Layman Award. **Education:** Loyola University – Chicago, M.Ed. (1970); St. Louis University, A.B. in Political Science (1968); He has more than 36 hours of Educational Leadership Graduate Work from University of South Florida and Nova University (1986–1990). **Personal:** Married to Claudia in 1970. Two children: Douglas and Matthew. Mr. Sokolowski enjoys golf, hiking, and travel.

Lorin D.M. Stewart
General Manager
Old Town Trolley Tours
2115 Kurtz Street
San Diego, CA 92110
(619) 298–8687
Fax: (619) 298–3404

7999

Business Information: Old Town Trolley Tours, a wholly–owned entity of Historic Tours of America, provides guided tours of various locations throughout San Diego, CA and surrounding areas. Tours include a variety of historical and entertainment destinations such as restaurants, shopping areas, naval bases and city tours. Established in 1989, Old Trolley Tours currently employs a staff of 100. Mr. Stewart joined Old Town Trolley Tours as a Driver/Tour Guide in 1989. As Safety Officer in 1990, he was inspired to create and implement a national program, "Safety in the Workplace," which was based on Senate Bill 198. Promoted to Operations Manager and most recently to General Manager, he has attained an exclusive permit with the United States Navy to give historic tours of various Naval bases in San Diego. An accomplished magician and entertainer, Mr. Stewart performs regularly in hotels, restaurants, country clubs and on cruise ships. He has performed during receptions in Hollywood, Paris and England for the film industry. An aspiring actor, Mr. Stewart was featured in Billy Idol's rock video, "LA Woman," and most recently was hired by United Artist's/MGM as the Head of the Department for Magic Design, where he is responsible for designing the illusions in Clive Barker's full–length feature film, "Lord of Illusions." Mr. Stewart also played Scott Bakula's sidekick, Billy Who in the film. **Career Steps:** Old Town Trolley: General Manager (1994–Present), Operations Manager (1993–1994), Safety Officer (1990–1993), Tour Guide and Driver (1989–1990); Department Head – Magic Design, United Artist's/MGM "Lord of Illusions." **Associations & Accomplishments:** International Rotary Club #33; Old Town Chamber of Commerce; San Diego Chamber of Commerce; San Diego Port Tennants Association; The National Trust; San Diego Historical Society; Screen Actor's Guild; British Actor's Equity; Awarded San Diego Chamber of Commerce's "Best Small Business" (July 1994); Awarded Save Our Heritage Organization "Historic Preservation Award" (1995). **Education:** University of Santa Clara, B.A., cum laude (1980); Guildhall School, London, U.K. **Personal:** Mr. Stewart enjoys gardening, music, sculpting, swimming, sailing, and designing magic and illusions for feature films.

Dorothy A. Thompson
Housekeeping Department Manager
Treasure Island Casino
*P.O. Box 75, 5734 Sturgeon Lake Road
Red Wing, MN 55066–0075
(800) 222–7077 ext 2595
Fax: (612) 385–2560*

7999

Business Information: Established in 1983, Treasure Island Casino is owned and operated by the Mdewakanton Sioux tribe of Welch, MN. Treasure Island Casino encompasses 186,544 square feet and employs 1,400 people. With nine years experience in management, Ms. Thompson joined Treasure Island Casino in 1992. Dorothy serves as Housekeeping Department Manager and is responsible for 120 employees. She is responsible for assuring that cleanliness is maintained throughout the complex, maintaining supplies, institutes and maintains budget, she also serves as a member of the Safety, Task Force, and Employee committees. Ms. Thompson is also a member of the National Association for Female Executives and Building Owner & Managers Association of St. Paul, MN. **Career Steps:** Housekeeping Department Manager, Treasure Island Casino (1992–Present); General Manager, Super 8 Motel – St. Louis, MO (1990–1992); General Manager, Super 8 Motel – Okawvill, IL (1986–1990). **Education:** Belleville College; Super 8 Management Training; Motels of America Management Training; Red Wing Technical College (currently). **Personal:** Married to Ronald Dean in 1964. Four children: Ronald Jr., Joy Ann, James Thomas, and Roger Dale. Ms. Thompson enjoys outdoor sports, making crafts, and sewing.

Anita Tornyai
Community Activities Director
MWR Department
*P.O. Box 109, Building 200
NAS Cecil Field, FL 32215–0109
(904) 778–6116
Fax: (904) 778–6636*

7999

Business Information: MWR Department is a morale, welfare, and recreation department serving the members of the Armed Forces at NAS Cecil Field, Florida. As Community Activities Director, Ms. Tornyai is responsible for the planning and administration of a comprehensive recreation program for a base community of 29,000. Duties include serving as liaison for college students and conducting commercial sponsorships for television, radio, and movie theaters. She also serves as the Intern Coordinator for the Department and Sponsorship Coordinator for the base. **Career Steps:** Community Activities Director, MWR Department (1990–Present); Flight Attendant, Delta Air Lines (1989–1990); College Intern–Athletics, MWR Department – NAS Bermuda (Fall 1988). **Associations & Accomplishments:** Esprit de Corps, a support group for Hospice; National Recreation and Parks Association; Jacksonville Jaycees; Former Member, Southern Scholarship Foundation; Rho Phi Lambda, an honorary leisure services and recreation fraternity; Selected to be a member of the Golden Key National Honorary Fraternity; Published in the military newsletter, ASAP; Guest speaker for the Navy Armed Forces Recreation Society. **Education:** Florida State University, Bachelors Degree, cum laude (1988). **Personal:** Ms. Tornyai enjoys water sports and athletic activities (water skiing, scuba diving, fishing, cycling, aerobics, etc.).

Ms. LaRue M. Tyndall
Director – Health, Physical Education and Recreation
South Mississippi Regional Center
*1170 West Railroad Street
Long Beach, MS 39560
(601) 867–1390
Fax: (601) 865–9364*

7999

Business Information: The South Mississippi Regional Center Health, Physical Education and Recreation Department provides physical education, leisure and recreation activities for clientele. Established in 1978, South Mississippi Regional Center currently employs 420 people, with 13 in the department. As Director, Ms. Tyndall is responsible for the supervision of 12 staff members, numerous administrative functions, and acting as a facilitator between her department and others within the Center. **Career Steps:** Director, South Mississippi Regional Center Health, Physical Education and Recreation Department (1994–Present). **Associations & Accomplishments:** United States Tennis Association. **Education:** William Carey College, M.B.A. (1995); University of Mississippi, B.A. in Recreation; Supervisory Management Certification; Certified Public Manager Program, Level V. **Personal:** As a

member of the U.S.T.A., Ms. Tyndall enjoys competing in the Volvo Tennis Challenge.

8000 Health Services

8011 Offices and clinics of medical doctors
8021 Offices and clinics of dentists
8031 Offices of osteopathic physicians
8041 Offices and clinics of chiropractors
8042 Offices and clinics of optometrists
8043 Offices and clinics of podiatrists
8049 Offices of health practitioners, NEC
8051 Skilled nursing care facilities
8052 Intermediate care facilities
8059 Nursing and personal care, NEC
8062 General medical and surgical hospitals
8063 Psychiatric hospitals
8069 Specialty hospitals exc. psychiatric
8071 Medical laboratories
8072 Dental laboratories
8082 Home health care services
8092 Kidney dialysis centers
8093 Specialty outpatient clinics, NEC
8099 Health and allied services, NEC

Asiru Abu–Bakare, M.D.
Physician
The Office of Asiru Abu–Bakare, M.D.
*Medical Arts Building, 115 Hazen Street
St. John, New Brunswick E2L 3L3
(506) 652–7930
Fax: (506) 849–3860*

8011

Business Information: The Office of Asiru Abu–Bakare, M.D. is a private practice endocrinology clinic. As Physician, Dr. Abu–Bakare oversees all administrative operations for the Clinic, in addition to his daily patient practice. Dr. Abu Bakare currently sees 8–16 patients per day, each having been referred by a General Practitioner. He is affiliated with several hospitals in the area, including St. Johns Regional, Charlotte Hospital, and Sussex Health Center. **Career Steps:** Physician, The Office of Asiru Abu–Bakare, M.D. (1995–Present); Senior Staff Consultant, King Fahad National Guard Hospital (1989–1995); Senior Consultant, Hamad General Hospital (1985–1989). **Associations & Accomplishments:** American College of Physicians; Royal College of Physicians and Surgeons of Canada; American College of Clinical Endocrinologists; New Brunswick College of Physicians and Surgeons. **Education:** University of Toronto, M.D. (1970); Morehouse College, B.S.; Liverpool School of Trop. Medicine and Hygiene, DTM&H. **Personal:** Married to Amina in 1986. Four children: Ayesha, Tahira, Farida, and Amal. Dr. Abu–Bakare enjoys squash.

Said Abuhasna, M.D.
President
Critical Care Consultants
*23260 Beechcrest St.
Dearborn Heights, MI 48127
(313) 361–8081
Fax: Please mail or call*

8011

Business Information: Critical Care Consultants is a medical care consultancy firm, providing hospitals with the services of more than fourteen physicians specialized in critical care. A practicing physician since 1987 and Certified as an Internal Medicine and Critical Care Physician, Dr. Abuhasna established the Firm in 1994. Serving as President, he is responsible for all aspects of operations, as well as the administrative operations for associates and a support staff. Concurrent with his consultancy firm, he serves as Medical Director at Michigan Hospital and Medical Center. **Career Steps:** President, Critical Care Consultants (1994–Present); Medical Director of Intensive Care Unit, Michigan Hospital and Medical Center (1994–Present). **Associations & Accomplishments:** American College of Physicians; American College of Chest Physicians; Society of Critical Care Medicine. **Education:** Wayne State Univ., M.D. (1993); Ross School of Medicine, M.D. (1987). **Personal:** Married to Aysha in 1987. Three children: Iyas, Inas, and Isra. Dr. Abuhasna enjoys travel.

Elbert R. Acosta II, M.D.

Director
Acosta & Associates
*3128 Wilmington Road
New Castle, PA 16105–1132
(412) 658–3020
Fax: (412) 658–6094*

8011

Business Information: Dr. Acosta established his internal medicine practice in 1988, specializing in trauma and critical care. Concurrently, he serves as Director of three local clinics and teaches medical students in residency. **Career Steps:** Director, Acosta & Associates (1988–Present); Director, Noble House Clinic (1988–Present); Emergency Room Doctor, Jameson Hospital (1985–1988); Resident, Cleveland Clinic/St. Vincent's (1983–1986). **Associations & Accomplishments:** American Medical Association; PMS; FACIP; Chamber of Commerce; ACEP; Cleveland Clinic Compre Care; AFS; Lawrence County Medical Society. **Education:** Ross School of Medicine, M.D. (1983); University of California, B.S. in Biological Science (1977). **Personal:** Married to Beth Ann in 1990. Two children: Jonathan and Maria. Dr. Acosta enjoys golf, skiing, Arabian horses, music, boating, and dancing.

Tony Adamo

Business Manager
Coral Ridge Surgical Associates
*6405 North Federal Highway, Suite 401
Ft. Lauderdale, FL 33308–1414
(954) 491–0900
Fax: (954) 491–1306
EMAIL: See Below*

8011

Business Information: Coral Ridge Surgical Associates is a general surgery group practice consisting of three physicians and affiliated with six hospitals in the county. With twenty–one years experience in business management, Mr. Adamo joined Coral Ridge Surgical Association as Business Manager in 1994. He is responsible for the overall administration and strategical planning for the practice, including setting up budgets, negotiating managed care contracts, and setting monthly physician–staff meeting agendas. Internet users can reach him via: www.antapanther.msn.comm. **Career Steps:** Business Manager, Coral Ridge Surgical Associates (1994–Present); Store Manager, Circuit City Stores (1992–1994); General Manager, Standard Brand's (1980–1992); Business Owner, Bagel Break (1975–1980). **Associations & Accomplishments:** Broward County Economic Development Council. **Education:** University of Miami, M.B.A. (1997). **Personal:** Married to Lynn in 1982. One child: John. Mr. Adamo enjoys biking and golf.

Julian F. Adams, M.D.
Physician
Niagara Medical Professional Centre
*P.O. Box 10
Virgil, Ontario L0S 1T0
(905) 468–3275
Fax: (905) 468–7960*

8011

Business Information: Niagara Medical Professional Centre is a family medical center with five physicians providing care and treatment to the Ontario area since 1956. A Family Practitioner at the Centre since beginning his career in 1969, Dr. Adams is responsible for patient care and clinic administration. **Career Steps:** Physician, Niagara Medical Professional Centre (1969–Present). **Associations & Accomplishments:** Ontario Medical Association; College of Physicians & Surgeons, Ontario. **Education:** Queen's University, Northern Ireland: M.B., B.Ch., (1966). **Personal:** Married to Emma in 1969. Two children: Mark and Clara. Dr. Adams enjoys tennis, gardening, bicycling, and skiing.

Timothy E. Adkins
Administrator
Cabin Creek Health Center
*P.O. Box 70
Dawes, WV 25054–0070
(304) 595–5006
Fax: (304) 595–5007
EMAIL: See Below*

8011

Business Information: Cabin Creek Health Center is a primary health care facility providing services to the rural community of Dawes, West Virginia. An Administrator at Cabin Creek since 1993, Mr. Adkins is presently responsible for daily administrative operations, budget oversight, grant writing, and personnel management. Internet users can reach him via: tadkins@muvm56.1.mu.wvnet.edu **Career Steps:** Administrator, Cabin Creek Health Center (1993–Present); Administrator, Humana Hospital – Lewisburg, WV (1991); Administrator, Family Guidance Center (1981–1990). **Associations & Accomplishments:** Jaycees Outstanding Young Businessman Award (1977); Kiwanis Club, Clinch Valley, Virginia. **Education:** Ohio University: M.P.A. (1990), B.B.A. in Accounting (1984); Emmanuel College, A.A. Pastoral Studies. **Personal:** Married to Susan F. in 1976. Mr. Adkins enjoys spectator sports, tennis, and swimming.

Rahmat Afrasiabi, M.D.

Sole Practitioner
The Office of Rahmat Afrasiabi, M.D.
251 Cohasset Road, Suite 110
Chico, CA 95926
(916) 896–7450
Fax: (916) 896–1717

8011

Business Information: The Office of Rahmat Afrasiabi, M.D. is a full–service, private practice medical office, providing diagnosis and treatment to patients suffering from allergies, asthma, rheumatoid arthritis, and other related complaints. A practicing physician since 1977 and a Board–Certified Clinical and Laboratory Immunologist and Allergist, Dr. Afrasiabi oversees all administrative operations for associates and a support staff of seven, in addition to his daily patient practice. **Career Steps:** Sole Practitioner, The Office of Rahmat Afrasiabi, M.D. (1994–Present); Private Practice, Cameron Park Allergy Medical Clinic (1990–1994); Medical Director, Ministry of Health Hospital – Shiraz, Iran (1981–1983); Physician, Marshall Hospital (1990–1995); Physician, Enloe Hospital (1990–Present); Physician, Chico Community Hospital (1990–Present). **Associations & Accomplishments:** American Academy of Allergy, Asthma, and Immunology; American College of Allergy, Asthma, and Immunology; American College of Rheumatology; California Medical Association; Diplomate, American Board of Internal Medicine; Diplomate, American Board of Diagnostic Laboratory Immunology; Diplomate, American Board of Allergy and Immunology; National Specialty Examination Certification of Ministry of Culture; American College of Physicians; Butte–Glenn Medical Society; California Medical Association; Frequent publications and presentations at various associations and symposia in his area of specialty. **Education:** Pahlavi University Medical School, M.D. (1977); Pahlavi University School of Arts and Sciences, B.A. in Premedicine (1971); University of California – Los Angeles School of Medicine: Clinical Fellowship in Allergy and Clinical Immunology (1988–1990), Residency in Pathology (1985–1986), Clinical and Laboratory Immunology Rotation (1976); Yale–affiliated St. Mary's Program, Residency in Internal Medicine (1986–1988); University of California – Los Angeles Center for Interdisciplinary Research in Immunologic Diseases, Postdoctoral Scholar in Immunology (1983–1985) (Dr. Afrasiabi's research at UCLA between 1983 and 1985 was focused in AIDS–Kuposis Sarcoma, which lead to the discovery of a sub–group of patients with negative HIV serology, and raised the question for the role of Alternative Viruses. This finding was brought to World Medical News Attention.); University of Chicago, Elective Research in Immunopathology (1975–1976); Pahlavi University Medical Center: Residency in Internal Medicine (1977–1980), Rheumatology Electives in Rheumatology (1978–1979), Straight Internship in Internal Medicine (1975–1977). **Personal:** Married to Sima. Two children: Dena and Arman. Dr. Afrasiabi enjoys travel, fishing, movies and spending time with his family.

Joan P. Agnetti

Administrator
Laser and Skin Surgery Center
317 E. 34th Street, 11 North
New York, NY 10016
(212) 686–7306
Fax: (212) 686–7305
E MAIL: See Below

8011

Business Information: Laser and Skin Surgery Center is a dermatologic surgery practice specializing in laser surgery, dermatologic surgery and MOHS micrographic surgery. The practice was established in 1983 and presently employs 35 people. As Administrator, Ms. Agnetti oversees staff assignments and coverage, billing, accounts payable, and monitors the monetary value of accounts receivable. Other responsibilities include supply and materials inventories, marketing of services and procedures offered by the practice, and working with one of the surgeons on legislature for new Practice procedures. Internet users can reach her via: laser@mail.laser_ny.com. **Career Steps:** Administrator, Laser and Skin Surgery Center (1994–Present); Consultant, Roth/Danish Associates (1991–1994); Office Manager, Donald Wood–Smith, MD,PC (1980–1990); Secretary, John– Marquis Converse, MD (1974–1980). **Associations & Accomplishments:** Medical Group Management Association; Membership Committee, Association of Dermatology Administrators and Managers. **Personal:** Married to John in 1976. One child: Jamison. Ms. Agnetti enjoys exercise, running, and spending time at the beach.

Ahmad Y. Al–Shash, M.D.

Physician
Allergy Institute, P.C.
1701 22nd Street, Suite 207
West Des Moines, IA 50266–1443
(515) 223–8622
Fax: (515) 223–5324

8011

Business Information: Allergy Institute, P.C. — serving patients from two locations in West Des Moines, IA — is a multi–associate medical group specializing in allergic and immunological diseases and disorders. A practicing physician since 1977, Board–certified in Internal Medicine and a Fellow in Allergies and Immunology, Dr. Al–Shash is founder and President of the Group. He oversees an administrative and medical support staff of sixteen, as well as serves as Senior Practitioner. His particular medical practice focus is on asthmatic disorders. **Career Steps:** President, Founder and Senior Practitioner, Allergy Institute, P.C. (1977–Present). **Associations & Accomplishments:** American Medical Association; American College of Physicians; American Academy of Allergy and Immunology; West Des Moines Rotary Club; American College of Asthma, Allergy and Immunology. **Education:** University of Iowa, Fellowship in Allergy (1977); University of Damascus, M.D. (1972). **Personal:** Married to Sahar in 1977. Four children: Ammar, Farrah, Hania, and Masa. Dr. Al–Shash enjoys tennis, golf, chess, travel, art, and antiques.

Sharon Albright, D.D.S.

Dental Director
Cabot Westside Clinic
1810 Summit Street
Kansas City, MO 64108
(816) 471–0900 (816) 471–7707
Fax: (816) 471–3150

8011

Business Information: Cabot Westside Clinic is a community health center comprised of two general physicians, three nursing practitioners, and two dental hygienists. The Clinic, established in 1906, provides health and related services to the community. As Dental Director, Dr. Albright handles all dental aspects of the program. She is responsible for bookkeeping, management of medical records, patient care and diagnosis. **Career Steps:** Dental Director, Cabot Westside Clinic (1993–Present); Accounting Analyst, Rockwell International (1983–1985); Accounting Management Trainee, Republic Steel Corporation (1981–1983). **Associations & Accomplishments:** National Dental Association; American Dental Association; Missouri Dental Association; California Dental Association; Rinehart Foundation, University of Missouri, Kansas City School of Dentistry. **Education:** University of Missouri, Kansas City, D.D.S. (1991); University of California, Los Angeles School of Dentistry, AEGD Certificate (1992); Florida A&M University, B.S. in Accounting.

Larry M. Allen, M.D.

Physician
Diagnostic Center – Internal Medicine
2010 Goldring Avenue #100
Las Vegas, NV 89106
(702) 366–0640
Fax: (702) 366–9075

8011

Business Information: Diagnostic Center – Internal Medicine is a private, group medical practice, consisting of 16 physicians providing treatment to patients with internal medicine complaints. A practicing physician since 1985, Dr. Allen joined Diagnosis Center – Internal Medicine in 1990. He practices internal medicine on adults not requiring surgery. He also serves as the Director of Physician Relations. **Career Steps:** Physician, Diagnostic Center – Internal Medicine (1990–Present); Chief of Staff, Rehab Hospital – Las Vegas (1993–1995); Physician, Family Medical Center (1988–1990); Physician in Training, University of Nevada (1985–1988). **Associations & Accomplishments:** Board Director, American Heart Association; Chairman, Internal Medicine Program – Valley Hospital, Las Vegas (1985–1988). **Education:** University of Nevada, M.D. (1985); University of Iowa, B.S. (1990). **Personal:** Married to Kim Mandelbaum in 1986. One child: Blake Allen. Dr. Allen enjoys hunting, fishing, and wine collecting.

James M. Andrews, M.D.

Physician
Medical Associates of Northern Georgia
320 Hospital Road
Canton, GA 30114–2410
(770) 479–5535
Fax: (770) 479–8821

8011

Business Information: Medical Associates of Northern Georgia is a large multi–specialty physicians group practice consisting of Family Practitioners, Internists (Internal Medicine), Gastroenterologists and Pulmonologists. Expansion plans include opening a center for sleep disorders and adding a Neurologist and a Pediatrician to the Practice. A Board–certified Pulmonologist and Thoracic Surgeon, Dr. Andrews joined the Group in 1994. He specializes in critical care treatment and pulmonary diseases and dysfunctions, particularly focusing on sleep disorders. **Career Steps:** Physician, Medical Associates of Northern Georgia (1994–Present). **Associations & Accomplishments:** American Thoracic Society; American College of Chest Physicians; American Sleep Disorders Association; American College of Physicians. **Education:** University of Tennessee – Memphis, M.D. (1985); University of Tennessee – Knoxville, B.A. in Chemistry. **Personal:** Married to Susie Cho Andrews in 1993. One child: Grayson Cho Andrews. Dr. Andrews enjoys spending time with his family, church activities, music and photography.

C. Annerud, M.D.

Emergency Medicine Physician
–Independent–
446 G Avenue
Coronado, CA 92118
(619) 437–0486
Fax: Please mail or call

8011

Business Information: As Emergency Medicine Physician, Dr. Annerud is affiliated with three hospitals in the San Diego area, providing diagnosis and treatment of patients in emergency environments. Her experience includes practicing international travel medicine in primitive areas. **Career Steps:** Emergency Medicine Physician (Present). **Associations & Accomplishments:** Conducted a conference in Cambridge on medicine in the Polar Regions.

Andre K. Artis, M.D.

President
Andre K. Artis, M.D., P.C.
3130 London Drive
Olympia Fields, IL 60461
(219) 884–9180
Fax: (219) 884–9280

8011

Business Information: Andre K. Artis, M.D., P.C. is a medical practice specializing in cardiovascular diseases and interventional cardiology. Establishing the practice in 1992, Dr. Artis oversees all administrative operations, in addition to his patient care. Concurrent with his private practice, he serves as Director of the Cardiac Catheterization Lab at Methodist Hospital and is also an Assistant Professor of Medicine at Indiana University – Northwest. **Career Steps:** President, Andre K. Artis, M.D., P.C. (1992–Present); Director of Cardiac Catheterization Lab, Methodist Hospital (1990–Present); Assistant Professor of Medicine, Indiana University – Northwest (1991–Present); Assistant Professor of Medicine Cardiology, University of Missouri (1988–1989). **Associations & Accomplishments:** Board Member, American Heart Association; National Medical Association; American College of Physicians; Urban League of Northwest Indiana. **Education:** University of Missouri, Cardiology Fellow (1986–1988); Meharry Medical College, M.D.; Oakwood College, B.A. **Personal:** Married to Neva in 1981. Three children: Ashley, Adrianne, and Andre. Dr. Artis enjoys biking, boating, and weightlifting.

John D. Ashley Jr., M.D.

Physician
Newport Hospital and Clinic
2000 McClain Street
Newport, AR 72112–3661
(501) 523–9865
Fax: (501) 523–9132

8011

Business Information: Newport Hospital and Clinic is a tertiary care hospital, also providing multi–specialty primary and ambulatory care services. Board–certified in Internal Medicine, Dr. John Ashley founded the Hospital's Clinic in 1949. The Clinic consists of six multi–specialty physicians, all providing private practice services in addition to their association with the Group. Dr. Ashley serves as Senior Physician responsible for the overall administrative direction, as well as his daily patient practice. **Career Steps:** Physician, Newport Hospital and Clinic (1949–Present); United States Army, Retired in the grade of Lt. Col. (1944–1949). **Associations & Accomplishments:** Jackson County Medical Society; Arkansas Medical Society; American Medical Society; Southern Medical Society; American Board of Internal Medicine; American College of Medicine; Faculty, University of Arkansas Medical College. **Education:** Medical College of Virginia, M.D. (1940); University of Missouri: B.S. in Medicine (1938), B.S. in Zoology and Chemistry (1936); University of Oklahoma, Medical Internship and Residency (1944). **Personal:** Widower. Three children: Jerry, Avey Edward, and Thomas Eugene. Dr. Ashley enjoys flying, art, painting, music, boating, photography, medical conventions, and travel.

Jonathan E. Askew, M.D.

President
Jonathan E. Askew, M.D., P.C.
6304 South Price Road
Tempe, AZ 85283
(602) 820–6966
Fax: (602) 820–6970

8011

Business Information: Jonathan E. Askew, M.D., P.C. is a clinical medical practice, providing obstetrics, gynecology, and infertility services. A practicing physician since 1969 and Board–Certified in Obstetrics and Gynecology, Dr. Askew established his solo practice of medicine in 1980. He is responsible for all aspects of operations, in addition to his daily patient practice. Concurrent with his private medical practice, he serves as Consultant in the OB/GYN Resident's Primary Care Clinic at Good Samaritan Hospital in Phoenix, Arizona. **Career Steps:** President, Jonathan E. Askew, M.D., P.C. (1989–Present); Consultant, OB/GYN Resident's Primary Care Clinic at Good Samaritan Hospital (1993–Present); Assistant Professor of OB–GYN, University of Oklahoma (1975–1976); U.S. Public Health Service: Chief of Surgery (1974–1979), Medical Director (1969–1974). **Associations & Accomplishments:** Maternal/Child Health project, Kosova, Serbia, Mercy Corps (1995–1996); Diplomate, American Board of Obstetrics & Gynecology (1977); Fellow, American College of Obstetricians and Gynecologists (1978); American Medical Association (1969–Present); Arizona Medical Association (1976); Maricopa County Medical Society (1976); Phoenix OB/GYN Society (1976–Present); Former President, East Valley OB/GYN Society; National Delegate and President, Christian Medical Dental Society – Phoenix (1978–1993), Board of Trustees (1993–1997); Board of Directors, Frontiers Mission (1993–Present); National Council on International Health; State of Arizona Licensure; Christian Family Care Agency (largest adoption/foster care agency in Arizona): Founding Member (1982–1985), Board of Reference (1990–Present); Board of Directors, INA Healthplan (now CIGNA) (1977–1980); World Vision: Cambodian Refugee Relief (1980), Romanian Medical Relief, CMDS, Food for the Hungry, Medical Assistance Programs (1986–Present); Board of Directors, Enterprise Development International, Washington, D.C. (micro–enterprise development); Governor's Committee on Children – Arizona (1987–1988); Executive Committee, International Christian Medical Dental Association (1994–Present); Relief and Development, Romania, church–based clinics (1984–Present). **Education:** Indiana University School of Medicine, M.D. (1969); Taylor University, Upland, IN, A.B. in Chemistry (1965); **Personal:** Married to Harriet in 1965. Four children: Gretchen, Jeffrey, Greg, and Holly. Dr. Askew enjoys hunting, fishing, and breeding/raising Tennessee Walking Horses.

Paramjit S. Aulakh

Sole Practitioner
Office of Paramjit S. Aulakh, M.D.
8675–120 Street
Delta, British Co V4C 6R4
(604) 599–6909
Fax: (604) 599–4192

8011

Business Information: Paramjit S. Aulakh established his private practice in 1986, specializing in family medicine and obstetrics. The Practice employs one additional physician and is affiliated with Surrey Memorial Hospital, a 500–bed acute care medical facility. **Career Steps:** Sole Practitioner (1986–Present). **Associations & Accomplishments:** Canadian Medical Association; British Columbia Medical Association; Surrey Memorial Hospital: Active Staff, Executive Committee, OB/GYN Committee; IndoCanadian Bone Marrow Registry; Canadian Council of Family Physicians. **Education:** M.B.B.S. – India, M.D.; M.C.F.P. – Canada, L.M.C.C., Flex. **Personal:** Married to Cindy in 1982. Three children: Rajni, Arpan and Ajay. Dr. Aulakh enjoys travel and table tennis.

Dr. H. Thompson Avey

Physician
The Office of H. Thompson Avey, M.D.
3435 Northwest 56th Street
Oklahoma City, OK 73112
(405) 946–0786
Fax: (405) 946–2361

8011

Business Information: The Office of H. Thompson Avey, M.D., affiliated with the Baptist Medical Center, specializes in the practice of internal medicine. As Physician, Dr. Avey is responsible for all aspects of operations, including the care and treatment of patients. **Career Steps:** Physician, The Office of H. Thompson Avey, M.D. **Associations & Accomplishments:** American College of Physicians; Member of numerous Oklahoma State and County Medical Associations. Education: University of Wisconsin, M.D. (1939). **Personal:** One child: Carl T. Avey. Dr. Avey enjoys walking and gardening.

Stephen W. Baker, M.D., FACC

Cardiologist
Coast Cardiology Center
1104 Broad Avenue
Gulfport, MS 39501–2414
(601) 864–1161
Fax: (601) 864–1969

8011

Business Information: Coast Cardiology Center is a group medical practice specializing in cardiology. Established in 1988, the Center currently maintains 3 staff physicians. As a Cardiologist, Dr. Baker focuses on Invasive Cardiology, performing such procedures as catheterization, coronary angioplasty, pacemaker therapy, thrombolysis, surgical evaluation and follow up, cardiovascular drug investigations, stents, rotoblator, and nuclear cardiology. He provides healthcare to his patients on a daily basis in addition to overseeing administrative duties and operations, handling public relations and strategic planning for the Center. **Career Steps:** Cardiologist, Coast Cardiology Center (1990–Present). **Associations & Accomplishments:** American College of Cardiology; American Medical Association; American Society for Cardiac Angiography and Intervention. **Education:** Mt. Carmel Medical Center – Cols. OH, Fellowship Cardiology (1990); Indiana University School of Medicine, B.A.; Board Certified in Internal and Cardiovascular Medicine.

John Balfour Cowan, M.D.

Physician in Charge
Wasaga Beach Medical Centre
P O Box 460
Collingwood, Ontario L9Y 3Z4
(705) 429–3482
Fax: (705) 429–3484

8011

Business Information: Wasaga Beach Medical Centre is a full service medical facility providing health and related services to area residents. As Physician in Charge, Dr. Balfour Conway has been actively involved in general/family practice since 1971. During this time, he has performed over 40 locums, including practices which involved the health care of Glasgow University Teaching Staff, Diplomatic Corps in Glasgow, and regular health/disease examination of all crew members arriving on foreign ships on the River Clyde. Dr. Balfour Cowan's current patient load is approximately 2,500 patients, which includes all stages of pregnancy, neonates, infants, pediatrics, teenagers, early adults, and geriatrics. In his capacity as a family practitioner, he has given numerous presentations and demonstrations to school children of all ages, as well as to numerous service clubs on a broad variety of topics. Currently the Medical Advisor to the Wasaga Beach Branch, Arthritis Society, and Medical Coordinator of the Flood Disaster Team, Dr. Balfour Cowan is also the past advisor to the Canadian Cancer Society of Collingwood. Having been a dispensing physician for six years, responsible for all prescription processing for his patients, he was instrumental in recruiting and bringing a pharmacy to the area when the volume of perscriptions became unmanageable. During his years as a dispensing physician, Dr. Balfour Cowan sat on the Ontario Medical Association Committee on Physician Dispensing, resigning the position when the pharmacy became operational. **Career Steps:** Physician in Charge, Wasaga Beach Medical Centre (1972–Present); Regimental Medical Officer, Grey and Simcoe Forester Militia (1985–1990); Coroner, Solicitor General of Ontario (1972–Present). **Associations & Accomplishments:** Manito Lodge; Canadian Society of Aviation Medicine; Collingwood District Medical Society; Ontario Medical Association; Canadian Medical Association; Canadian Medical Protective Association; American Society of Geriatrics; Canadian Arthritis Society; Grey and Simcoe Foresters; Defence Medical Association of Canada; Glasgow University Union; Manitoba Medical Association. Past Association: Collingwood Rotary Club; Kinsmen Club of Collingwood; Board Member, General and Marine Hospital. **Education:** Glasgow University Medical School, M.B., Ch.B. (1965). **Personal:** Married to Judith in 1986. Five children: Aaron, Amy, Andrew, Laura, and Garry. Dr. Balfour Cowan enjoys gardening, fishing, power/sail boating, forensic medicine and geriatrics.

Bradley C. Banks, M.D.

Cardiologist
Ochsner Medical Institutions
1514 Jefferson Highway
New Orleans, LA 70121
(504) 842–3000
Fax: (504) 838–8853

8011

Business Information: Ochsner Medical Institutions is a tertiary care medical center, widely known as a regional referral facility. As Chief Fellow in Cardiovascular Medicine, Dr. Bradley Banks is a Consultant and Primary Physician for patients with cardiac and peripheral vascular disease; performing invasive and non–invasive diagnostic studies, as well as coronary and peripheral angioplasty, cardiac pacing and hemodynamic support devices. **Career Steps:** Cardiologist, Ochsner Medical Institutions (1992–Present); Emergency Department Physician (1989–Present); Medical Attendant, Jefferson Parish Correctional Center (1989); General Internist, Ochsner Hospital (1989–1992); Medical Student, Louisiana State University Medical Center (1984–1989); Nurse Aide, Baton Rouge General Hospital (1982). **Associations & Accomplishments:** American Medical Association; American College of Physicians; American College of Cardiology; Phi Delta Epsilon Fraternity; Sigma Nu Fraternity; Kiwanis; License for Medicine and Surgery, Louisiana State Board of Medical Examiners; Diplomate, American American Board of Internal Medicine (1992), Federal Licensure Examination (1989), Certified ACLS; Chief Fellow in Cardiovascular Diseases, Ochsner Medical Institutions (1994–1995); LSUMC Student Research Fellowships (1987, 1988); Phi Eta Sigma; American Legion Scholarship Award; Captain John Adrien Martin Memorial Collegiate Scholarship; Oral Presentations at American Federation of Clinical Research (1993) and American College of Chest Physicians (1992); Abstracts: 'High Hostility in Married Patients with Acute Coronary Syndromes" (1993), "Age and Gender Related Differences in Psychosocial Variables in Acute Coronary Syndromes" (1993), "Analysis of Risk Status in Elderly & Young Inpatients with Acute Coronary Syndromes" (1992); Articles: " 'Snare Loop' technique utilizing a wire basket for removing intravascular foreign bodies", Critical Care Medicine. **Education:** Louisiana State University Medical Center, M.D. (1989), Clinical Research Assistant (1987); Louisiana State University, B.S. in Mathematics (1984). **Personal:** Married to Robin Baber Banks in 1987. Two children: Sarah Ashley and Emily Katherine. Dr. Banks enjoys carpentry and fishing.

David H. Barad, M.D.

Director – Division of Reproductive Endocrinology & Infertility
Fertility and Hormone Center of the Montefiore Medical Center
20 Beacon Hill Drive
Dobbs Ferry, NY 10522–2402
(914) 693–8820
Fax: (914) 693–5428
EMAIL: See Below

8011

Business Information: A practicing physician since 1978 and a Board Certified Obstetrician and Gynecologist, Dr. Barad joined Montefiore Medical Center as Director of Reproductive Endocrinology & Infertility in 1984. Dr. Barad has published extensively and is a recognized authority in his field. In addition to his daily practice of reproductive endocrinology and infertility, Dr. Barad directs all of the activities of his Division at the Montefiore Medical Center and the Albert Einstein College of Medicine. He can also be reached via: barad@aecom.y.edu. **Career Steps:** Director – Division of Reproductive Endocrinology & Infertility, Montefiore Medical Center (1985–Present); Associate Professor, Albert Einstein College of Medicine (1984–Present); Private Practice OB/Gyn (1978–Present) **Associations & Accomplishments:** American College of Obstetrics and Gynecology; New York Obstetrical Society; American Society of Reproductive Medicine; American Medical Association; American Association of Gynecological Laparoscopy; Numerous publications in medical journals, as well as appearances and interviews on media broadcasts. **Education:** University of Medical and Dentistry of New Jersey, M.D. (1978); Boston University, M.A.; Rutgers University, B.A. **Personal:** Married to Iris Sarah in 1974. Three children: Alexis, Justin and Ashely. Dr. Barad enjoys sailing, reading, music performance (stringed instruments), and computers (particularly "surfing" the Internet) in his leisure time.

Kathy Bastianelli

Imaging Manager
East Range Clinics, Ltd.
910 N. 6th Avenue
Virginia, MN 55792–2311
(218) 741–0150
Fax: (218) 741–0539

8011

Business Information: East Range Clinics, Ltd. is a multi–specialty medical clinic, including primary care, OB/GYN, Urology, Neurology, Orthopedics, Pediatrics, Ophthalmology, Surgery, Industrial Medicine, Oncology, ENT, and Pulmonary clinics. As Imaging Manager, Ms. Bastianelli administers all "imaging" modalities within the clinic, including Radiology, ECG, EEG, Ultrasound, and Mammography. Additionally, she represents management in union issues and negotiations. **Career Steps:** East Range Clinics, Ltd.: Imaging Manager (1989–Present), Radiologic Technologist (1984–1989); Radiology Supervisor, Eveleth Fitzgerald Community Hospital (1969–1984). **Associations & Accomplishments:** American Society of Radiology Technicians; ARRT; AHRA; Minnesota Society of Radiology Technicians; AFSCME Stewart; Former President, Ladies Elks; Former President, Curling Club **Education:** Mesabi Community College; St. Mary's School of Radiologic Technology, ARRT. **Personal:** Married to Pat in 1965. Three children: Tina, Tammy, and Tony. Ms. Bastianelli enjoys family, flowers, reading, theatre, musicals, shopping, and curling.

Vincent Bayarri, M.D.

Pediatrician
The Office of Dr. Vincent Bayarri, M.D.
421 Deer Park Avenue
Babylon, NY 11702–2313
(516) 661–3693
Fax: Please mail or call

8011

Business Information: The Office of Dr. Vincent Bayarri, M.D. is a full–service pediatric and adolescent practice. The Practice is affiliated with two area hospitals: Southside Hospital and Good Samaritan Hospital. Founding the private practice in 1961, Dr. Bayarri serves local patients and those residing within a 50–mile radius of Babylon, NY. His practice is limited to the diagnosis and treatment of infants and children. **Career Steps:** Pediatrician, The Office of Dr. Vincent Bayarri, M.D. (1961–Present). **Associations & Accomplishments:** New York State Medical Society; Suffolk Pediatric Society; Suffolk Medical Society; American Academy of Pediatrics; President, Suffolk County Pediatric Society (1977); Chief of Pediatrics, Lakeville Hospital, Copiague, NY – now closed (1970's); Licensed to practice medicine in Florida (1970); Educated in Spain where he studied French, German, Greek and Latin languages, he is fluent in composition and translation of French and has an understanding of Portuguese. **Education:** Valencia Medical School – Spain, M.D. (1952); Foreign Graduate Exam Diploma (1960); Poly Clinic Medical School, New York (1958–1960); Psychiatric Residencies (1956–1958 and 1960) – Central Islip State Hospital, Central Islip, New York. **Personal:** Married to Phyllis in 1956. Dr. Bayarri enjoys reading, languages and swimming activities.

LaNoard M. Bayouth II, M.D.

Interventional Cardiologist
Cardiology Associates of Lubbock
3514 21st Street
Lubbock, TX 79410
(806) 792–5105
Fax: (806) 796–0703

8011

Business Information: The Cardiology Associates of Lubbock is a full–service, cardiology clinic specializing in the treatment of patients with heart diseases and disorders. Currently, the practice employs 150 physicians and medical support staff. As Interventional Cardiologist, Dr. Bayouth is responsible for the care and treatment of patients. Board–certified in Cardiology, he has been with the clinic for two and a half years. **Career Steps:** Interventional Cardiologist, Cardiology Associates of Lubbock (1993–Present). **Associations & Accomplishments:** Fellow, American College of Cardiology; American College of Chest Physicians; American College of Physicians; American Medical Association; Texas Medical Association. **Education:** University of Texas Medical Branch, M.D. (1987); Scott and White Memorial Hospital: Internal Medicine Residency and Cardiology Fellowship. **Personal:** Dr. Bayouth enjoys golf, tennis, hunting, camping, and skiing.

Lowery Beck, M.D.

Owner and Pediatrician
Apache Drive Children's Clinic
P.O. Box 19069
Jonesboro, AR 72402–9069
(501) 935–1800
Fax: (501) 935–2917

8011

Business Information: Apache Drive Children's Clinic is a full–service, general practice medical clinic, specializing in the diagnosis and treatment of children (i.e., colds, shots, casts, broken bones, etc. no surgeries). The Practice is affiliated with two local hospitals. A practicing physician since 1988 and a Board–Certified Pediatrician, Dr. Beck established Apache Drive Children's Clinic in 1991 and serves as its Owner and Pediatrician. He oversees all administrative operations for associates and a support staff of six, in addition to his daily patient practice. **Career Steps:** Owner and Pediatrician, Apache Drive Children's Clinic (1991–Present); Staff Physician, Children's Mercy Hospital (1988–1991). **Associations & Accomplishments:** American Medical Association; American Academy of Pediatrics; Arkansas Medical Society; Crainhead County Medical Society. **Education:** University of Arkansas Medical School, M.D. (1988) University of Arkansas, B.S. in Zoology (1984). **Personal:** Married to Teresa in 1988. Two children: Stephen and David. Dr. Beck enjoys travel, sports, and fishing.

Melody L. Bell, A.S.N.

Nurse
Orthopaedics Indianapolis
8402 Harcourt, Suite 430
Indianapolis, IN 46260
(317) 338–9250
Fax: (317) 338–9256

8011

Business Information: Orthopaedics Indianapolis is a private practice medical facility specializing in orthopaedic surgery. As Nurse, Ms. Bell is responsible for assisting Dr. Timothy E. Dicke in the operating room, the office and with rounds on the floor. Ms. Bell has a great deal of contact with the patients, and therefore tries to put herself in their place, making her more conscious of the patient's needs. She enjoys what she does and plans to continue to assist Dr. Dicke as long as possible. **Career Steps:** Nurse, Orthopaedics Indianapolis (1995–Present); St Vincent's Hospital: Clinical Instructor and SDC (1987–1995), CST (1986–1987). **Associations & Accomplishments:** AST; AORN; CPR Instructor; ACLS Certified. **Education:** University of Indianapolis, A.S.N. (1994); Technical Certificate for Surgical Technology (1985); Indiana Vocational Technical College. A.S.N. (1995). **Personal:** Married to Jeffrey in 1976. One child: Crystal Lynn. Ms. Bell enjoys scuba diving, water skiing, snow skiing, racquetball, and circuit training.

Wesley Stewart Bennett, M.D.

Cardiologist
Internal Medicine Clinic
2113 11th Street, 2nd Floor
Meridian, MS 39301
(601) 483–5322
Fax: (601) 693–8080
EMAIL: See Below

8011

Business Information: Internal Medicine Clinic is a group medical clinic consisting of ten physicians, two of whom are Cardiologists performing physician services for the public. Future plans include adding one more cardiologist and strive to be recognized as a referral center. A practicing physician since 1984, Dr. Bennett joined Internal Medicine Clinic as Cardiologist in 1990. Choosing the cardiology field because of his interest in human dynamics and cardiovascular disorders, he is responsible for the diagnosis and treatment of patients with cardiac complaints using the latest technological equipment for diagnosis, as well as performing surgeries. His practice is also affiliated with Jeff Anderson Regional Medical Center and Rielly Memorial Hospital. Concurrently, he conducts presentations on Congenitive Heart Failure. Internet users can reach him via: BENWE58@Eclmtlinlsnet **Career Steps:** Cardiologist, Internal Medicine Clinic (1990–Present). **Associations & Accomplishments:** Board of Trustees, Meridan Grand Opera House; First Vice President, Piley Hospital Medical Staff. **Education:** University of Missouri Medical Center, M.D. (1984); Tulane University, B.S. and Departmental Honors (1980). **Personal:** Married to Lallie Owens in 1986. Three children: John Jenning, Wesley Stewart Jr. and Lallie Elisa. Dr. Bennett enjoys golf, sailing and water sports.

Frederick A. Berger, M.D.

Pediatrician
Frederick A. Berger, M.D., P.A.
28 Riverview Street, Suite 114
Franklin, NC 28734–2651
(704) 369–4241
Fax: Please mail or call

8011

Business Information: Frederick A. Berger, M.D., P.A. is a private, general pediatric practice. Founding the solo practice in 1975, Dr. Berger oversees all administrative aspects, as well as patient care, focusing his practice in adolescent medicine. Concurrent with his private practice, he serves as Physician for the Lyndon B. Johnson Job Corps Center and lecturer at local schools on various first aid procedures. **Career Steps:** Pediatrician, Frederick A. Berger, M.D., P.A. (1975–Present). **Associations & Accomplishments:** Fellow, American Academy of Pediatrics; North Carolina Pediatric Society; North Carolina Medical Society; Franklin Rotary Club; Active in the Community Theater (performed in Oklahoma and Babes in Toyland); Frequent lecturer and speaker at professional presentations. **Education:** St. Louis University, M.D. (1972); Duke University, A.B. (1968). **Personal:** Married to Lee in 1971. Three children: Jennifer, Amy, and Stephanie. Dr. Berger enjoys acoustic guitar, running, biking, swimming, and landscape work.

Arthur J. Berman, M.D.

Physician
Arthur J. Berman, M.D.
One Pondfield Road, West
Bronxville, NY 10708
(914) 779–7700
Fax: (914) 779–4642

8011

Business Information: Arthur J. Berman, M.D. is a private practice specializing in internal medicine and gastroenterology. Establishing the practice in 1959, Dr. Arthur J. Berman is responsible for all aspects of operations, including diagnosis and treatment of patients. **Career Steps:** Physician, Arthur J. Berman, M.D. (1959–Present). **Associations & Accomplishments:** Fellow, American College of Physicians; Fellow, American College of Gastroenterology; Former Fulbright Fellow; Emeritus Director, Department of Medicine, Lawrence Hospital; Emeritus Director of Gastroenterology Lawrence Hospital, Assistant Clinical Professor of Medicine, A.E.C.O.M.; Assistant Clinical Professor of Medicine, Columbia Presbyterian; President, Deerhill Civic Association; Published in medical journals. **Education:** New York University College of Medicine, M.D. (1951); New York University College of Arts and Sciences, B.S. **Personal:** Married to Carol in 1959. Three children: Douglas, Judith and Susanne. Dr. Berman enjoys computers.

Abha U. Bernard

Vice President of Operations and Chief Operating Officer
Progressive Health Network
5600 Long Island Drive
Atlanta, GA 30327
(404) 851–1833
Fax: (404) 319–9684

8011

Business Information: Progressive Health Network is a managed–care organization and medical practice, consisting of 50 medical professionals and staff. As Vice President of Operations and Chief Operating Officer, Ms. Bernard is responsible for all aspects of operations, as well as acting as the organization's General Counsel. Concurrent with her position at Progressive Health Network, Ms. Bernard is also the Director of Legal Administration with the Georgia Department of Medical Assistance and General Counsel with the Georgia Spine and Sports Physicians, P.C. **Career Steps:** Vice President of Operations and Chief Operating Officer, Progressive Health Network (1995–Present); General Counsel, Georgia Spine and Sports Physicians, P.C. (1995–Present); Director of Legal Administration, Georgia Department of Medical Assistance. **Associations & Accomplishments:** Georgia Bar Association; Amerian Bar Association. **Education:** University of Alabama: J.D. (1990), B.S. **Personal:** Married to Scott in 1992. One child: Kierin.

Bernard Bernhardt, M.D.

Hematology/Oncology Physician
Bernard Bernhardt, M.D.
150 Lockwood Avenue
New Rochelle, NY 10801
(914) 632–5397
Fax: (914) 632–5450

8011

Business Information: Dr. Bernard Bernhardt, a private practitioner since 1968 and Board–Certified in Internal Medicine, Hematology, and Medical Oncology, provides treatment and diagnosis of cancer and other blood disorders to private and referral patients from New Rochelle, New York and surrounding communities. Concurrent with his private medical practice, he teaches and conducts research at the New York Medical College in Valhalla, New York and CALGB. Dr. Bernhardt also serves as Chief of Hematology/Oncology Services at the New Rochelle Hospital Medical Center. **Career Steps:** Private Practice, Hematology/Oncology Physician, (1968–Present); Chief of Hematology/Oncology Services, New Rochelle Hospital Medical Center (1973–Present); New York Medical College: Clinical Professor of Medicine (1991–Present), Clinical Associate Professor of Medicine (1978–1991). **Associations & Accomplishments:** Fellow, American College of Physicians; American Society of Clinical Oncology; American Society of Hematology; New York State Medical Society; Westchester County Medical Society; Westchester County Academy of Medicine; Numerous publications in medical journals and frequent presentations at medical conference proceedings and symposia on his clinical research findings in Leukemia, Chemotherapy treatments, and other Carcinogenic diseases. **Education:** Northwestern University, M.D. (1961); Queens College–New York, B.S. (1957); Intern and Residency Training: D.C. General Hospital–Washington, DC: Intern (1961–1962), Resident in Internal Medicine (1962–1963); New York Medical College, Resident in Internal Medicine (1965–1966); Montefiore Hospital, Bronx, New York: Chief Resident in Internal Medicine (1966–67), Resident in Hematology (1967–1968). **Personal:** Married to Roberta. Three children: Pamela, Cindy and Erica.

Raakesh C. Bhan, M.D.

Critical Care Physician
Critical Care Pulmonary Medicine, P.C.
126 College Street
Battle Creek, MI 49017
(616) 969–6100
Fax: (616) 969–6102

8011

Business Information: Critical Care Pulmonary Medicine, P.C. is a multi–associate group practice specializing in the treatment of pulmonary disorders and critical care patients. A practicing physician since 1980, Board–certified in Critical Care Medicine and Pulmonology, Dr. Bhan joined the Group's Battle Creek, Michigan location as an associate in 1986. Appointed President in 1991, he oversees all administrative support staff and associates, in addition to his daily patient practice. Concurrent to his private medical practice, he also serves as Director of Critical Care Units for Battle Creek Health Systems. **Career Steps:** Critical Care Pulmonary Medicine, P.C.: Critical Care Physician Associate (1980–Present), President (1991–Present); Director – Critical Care Units, Battle Creek Health System (1991–Present). **Associations & Accomplishments:** Society of Critical Care Medicine; American College of Chest Physicians. **Education:** Wayne State University, M.D. (1986); Fellowship in Critical Care Medicine. **Personal:** Married to Harriet in 1987. Two children: Chetan J. and Chantal J. Dr. Bhan enjoys music (Mozart and Jazz) and painting during his leisure time.

Michael Joseph Bishop, M.D., M.B.A., F.A.A.P.

Owner/Practitioner
Michael J. Bishop, M.D. Pediatrics
1111 Highway 6 #155
Sugarland, TX 77478–4913
(713) 494–8687
Fax: (713) 491–3866

8011

Business Information: Michael J. Bishop, M.D. Pediatrics is a private medical practice specializing in the care of children. Affiliated with five hospitals, the Office is comprised of two Pediatricians, five full–time and one part–time employee. As Owner/Practitioner, Dr. Bishop is responsible for all aspects of the Practice. His responsibilities include administration, operations, finance, strategic planning, and office– based research. Concurrent to his position as Owner/Practitioner, Dr. Bishop is also a clinical instructor at the University of Texas. **Career Steps:** Owner/Practitioner, Michael J. Bishop, M.D. Pediatrics (1991–Present). **Associations & Accomplishments:** Board Certified, American Board of Pediatrics; Board Member, West Fort Bend County Chapter of American Heart Association; Texas Medical Association; Houston Pediatric Society; Harris County Medical Society; Chairman, Department of Pediatrics and Child Health at Memorial Southwest Hospital; Alumnus, University of Minnesota; Alumnus, University of Illinois; Alpha Tau Omega Fraternity; Phi Kappa Phi Fraternity; Who's Who in Executive Professionals (1993–1994). **Education:** University of Illinois: M.D., M.B.A. (1986); University of Minnesota, B.S.B. With Distinction. **Personal:** Married to Patricia in 1981. Three children: Michelle, Nicole, and Danielle. Dr. Bishop enjoys fishing, golf, tennis, and reading.

Jerome E. Block, M.D., FACP

Physician
Southeast Kansas Internal Medicine Associates
1501 West 4 Street
Coffeyville, KS 67337
(316) 251–2400
Fax: (316) 251–1619

8011

Business Information: Southeast Kansas Internal Medicine Associates is a private practice medical facility. A practicing physician since 1964, Board–certified in Internal Medicine, Dr. Block focuses his research attention on longevity in addition to his daily patient practice. **Career Steps:** Internal Medicine Associate, Southeast Kansas Internal Medicine Associates (1990–Present); Consulting Staff, Mercy Hospital – Independence, KS (1990–Present); Cotteyville Regional Medical Center – Cotteyville, KS: President of Medical Staff (1990–1992), Executive Committee (1988–1993), Chief of Staff (1989–1990), Vice President of Medical Staff (1988), Chief of Medicine (1987–1988), Secretary of Medical Staff (1987–1988), Cardiorespiratory Dept. (1985–1988), Medical Advisor (1985–1987), ICU–CCU Chairperson (1985–1987); Chief of Medicine, Truman Medical Center – Kansas City, MO (1982–1985); Staff Physician, Baptist Memorial Hospital – Kansas City, MO (1982–1985); Staff Physician, Fitzgibbon Memorial Hospital – Marshall, MO (1972–1978); Director of Cardiorespiratory Dept., Windsor Hospital – Windsor, MO (1970–1979); Bothwell Memorial Hospital – Sedalia, MO: Cardiorespiratory Dept. (1971–1979), Medical Advisor (1971–1979), Chief of Internal Medicine (1971–1979), ICU–CCU Chair (1969–1979), Staff Physician (1969–1982). **Associations & Accomplishments:** Who's Who in Missouri; Who's Who in America; Outstanding American; Outstanding Teacher Vocational Education; American Board of Internal Medicine; American College of Physicians; American Medical Association; Missouri Medical Association; Pettis County Medical Society; Vienna Society of Medicine; Southeast Kansas Medical Society; Kansas Medical Society; Licensed in California, Missouri, and Kansas; American Heart Association; Missouri Heart Association; Private Pilot Licensure; Publication in Journal of Clinical Psychiatry and Medical Audio Cassette; Frequent lecturer of international, national, state, and local conferences and institutional symposia and proceedings. **Education:** New Jersey College of Medicine, M.D. (1964); Muhlenberg College, B.S. (1960); Los Angeles County General Hospital: Internship (1964–1965), Residency (1965–1967). **Personal:** Married to Brunhilde Wilhelm. Eight children: Vici Janis, Deborrah Ann, Dorlisa Ann, Michael Alan, Debra Jill, Erika Luisa, Karl Wilhelm, and Steven Jeffery. Dr. Block enjoys jogging.

Michael John Bloudoff, M.D.

Sole Practitioner
Office of Michael J. Bloudoff, M.D.
4576 Yonge Street, Suite 506
North York, Ontario M2N 6N4
(416) 223–2349
Fax: (416) 223–1307

8011

Business Information: Office of Michael J. Bloudoff, M.D. is a private medical practice, specializing in addictive medicine. Counseling is offered to patients suffering from addiction disorders, such as drug, alcohol, gambling, etc., on a one–on–one, group, or family basis. A practicing physician since 1969, Dr. Bloudoff established his private practice in 1987, overseeing all administrative operations for associates and support staff, in addition to his daily patient practice. Concurrently, he consults with companies, such as Park Medical Systems, on business issues. **Career Steps:** Sole Practitioner, Michael J. Bloudoff, M.D. (1987–Present); Medical Director, Hospital Corporation of America (1990–1991); Assistant Director, Bellwood Health (1988–1991). **Associations & Accomplishments:** Director, Canadian Association of Compulsive Gamblers; Consultant, Park Medical Systems; Director, Business for Gene Screen. **Education:** University of British Columbia: M.D. (1969), B.Sc.; American Society of Addiction Medicine, Certification. **Personal:** One child: Douglas. Dr. Bloudoff enjoys sailing, fishing, reading, working out regularly, and travel.

Kwabena Appenteng Boateng, M.D., F.A.C.O.G.

Physician
Kwabena A. Boateng OB/Gyn
4610 Ryehill Drive
Joliet, IL 60435
(815) 744–4320
Fax: (815) 744–5137

8011

Business Information: Kwabena Boateng OB/Gyn is a private medical practice, providing specialized care to women. Board–Certified in Obstetrics and Gynecology, Dr. Boateng obtained his medical degree in 1983. Establishing his private medical practice in 1995, he provides clinical care to women with gynecology complaints and specialized medical care in obstetrics. **Career Steps:** Private Practice Physician, Kwabena Boateng OB/Gyn (1995–Present); Attending Physician, St. Joseph Medical Center (1994–1995); Physician, Glenwood Medical Group (1992–1994); Resident Physician, Interfaith Medical Center (1988–1992). **Associations & Accomplishments:** American Cancer Society; American College of Obstetrics and Gynecology; American Board of Obstetrics and Gynecology. **Education:** University of Ghana, M.B., Ch.B. (1983). **Personal:** Married to Florence in 1986. Two children: Ama Marie and Michael. Dr. Boateng enjoys reading, art, and sports.

Loretta Bobo–Mosley, M.D.

President, Chief Executive Officer, & Chief Physician
Lorretta Bobo–Mosley, M.D., P.C.
1750 Madison Avenue, Suite 300
Memphis, TN 38104
(901) 278–2452
Fax: (901) 722–5774

8011

Business Information: Lorretta Bobo–Mosley, M.D., P.C., established in 1995, is a private, full–service, general internal medicine and primary care practice. A practicing physician since 1980, Dr. Bobo–Mosley established the sole practice internal medicine office in 1995, serving as President, Chief Executive Officer & Chief Physician. She is responsible for all aspects of operations, primarily providing quality health care to patients in internal medicine. She also conducts research in the intracultural aspects of medicine and chronic medical problems, as well as in women's health issues. Concurrent with her private medical practice, she serves as Clinical Associate Professor at University of Tennessee. **Career Steps:** President, Chief Executive Officer, & Chief Physician, Lorretta Bobo–Mosley, M.D., P.C. (1995–Present); University of Tennessee – Memphis: Associate Professor of Medicine (1991–1994), Assistant Professor of Medicine (1986–1991). **Associations & Accomplishments:** Bluff City Medical Society; Society of General Internal Medicine; American College of Physicians; Published various articles in medical journals. **Education:** University of Tennessee – Memphis, M.D. (1980); LeMoyne Owen College – Memphis, B.S. (1976). **Personal:** Married to Eddie Mosley, III in 1993. Two children: Eddie IV and Jason. Dr. Bobo–Mosley enjoys writing and reading.

Victoria Bojanowski, M.D. FRCSC

Urologist and Surgeon
Victoria Bojanowski, M.D. FRCSC
206–4949 Bathurst Street
Willowdale, Ontario M2R 1Y1
(416) 222–6755
Fax: Please mail or call

8011

Business Information: A Urologist and Surgeon with seven years practical and surgical experience, Victoria Bojanowski, M.D. FRCSC established her private urological surgery practice (affiliated with North York Branson Hospital in Ontario) in 1991. **Career Steps:** Urologist and Surgeon, Victoria Bojanowski, M.D. FRCSC (1991–Present). **Associations & Accomplishments:** Canadian Urological Association; Society of Urologic Surgeons of Ontario; Ukrainian Medical Association; Board of Interstitial Cystitis Association of Canada; Ontario Medical Association; Interest in male infertility. **Education:** University of Toronto, FRCSC (1990); University of Kingston, M.D. (1982); American Board of Urology Certification (1993). **Personal:** Married to Dr. Craig Fielding – Plastic Surgeon in 1993. Dr. Bojanowski enjoys scuba diving, trekking, travel, cave climbing, gardening, kayaking, and furniture refinishing.

Jeffrey Bomze, M.D.

Sole Practitioner
The Office of Dr. Jeffrey Bomze, M.D.
1201 County Line Road
Bryn Mawr, PA 19010
(610) 525–3335
Fax: (610) 527–2773

8011

Business Information: The Office of Dr. Jeffrey Bomze, M.D. is a private practice specializing in Pediatrics and Adolescent Sports Medicine. Establishing the private practice in 1993, as Sole Practitioner Dr. Jeffrey Bomze provides all patient care, as well as oversees an administrative staff of three. **Career Steps:** Sole Practitioner, The Office of Dr. Jeffrey Bomze, M.D. (1993–Present); Private Practice Pediatrics Practitioner (1991–1993); Pediatrician, Philadelphia Health Associates (1984–1988); Sports Medicine Physician, Graduate School, University of Pennsylvania (1988–1991). **Associations & Accomplishments:** American Academy of Pediatrics; Society for Adolescent Medicine; American College of Sports Medicine; Main Line Physician Organization; Numerous community and hospital lectures and seminars; Multiple hospital committees. **Education:** University of Pennsylvania School of Medicine: M.D. (1975), Infectious Disease training; Nonsurgical Sports Medicine. **Personal:** Married to Dr. Melanie Wilson in 1994. Dr. Bomze enjoys sports, tennis, reading, and staying fit.

Carolyn J. Boone, M.D.

Sole Practitioner
The Office of Carolyn J. Boone, M.D.
700 West Grace Street, Suite 103
Richmond, VA 23220–4118
(804) 783–8788
Fax: Please mail or call

8011

Business Information: A practicing physician since 1980, Board–certified in Pediatrics, Dr. Carolyn Boone established her private pediatric practice in 1986. She oversees all administrative operations for associates and a support staff of 6, in addition to her daily patient practice. Her practice is affiliated with five city hospitals, providing diagnosis and treatment of children, as well as serving as a mentor to adolescent mothers, and as a volunteer in the Projects. **Career Steps:** Sole Practitioner, The Office of Carolyn J. Boone, M.D. (1986–Present). **Associations & Accomplishments:** Fellow, American Academy of Pediatrics. **Education:** Medical College of Virginia, M.D. (1980). **Personal:** Married to Melvin Todd in 1985. Two children: Melvin and Bridget.

Don R. Bosse, M.D.

Chief Executive Officer and Lab Director
Bellville Clinic L. C.
235 West Palm Street, #105
Bellville, TX 77418–1300
(409) 865–3124
Fax: (409) 865–9193

8011

Business Information: A practicing physician since 1982, Dr. Bosse joined the Bellville Clinic L.C. in 1992. Currently serving as Chief Executive Officer, concurrent with his executive duties, he specializes in the medical treatment of patients suffering from internal medicine, geriatrics, and cardiology complaints. He also serves as Lab Director at Bellville Clinic Clinical Lab and Director at Austin County Medical Clinic. **Career Steps:** Director, Austin County Medical Clinic (1995–Present); Chief Executive Officer, Bellville Clinic L. C. (1992–1995); Lab Director, Bellville Clinical Lab (1992–1995). **Associations & Accomplishments:** Texas Medical Association; President, Austin, Waller, Grimes Medical Society; American Society of Internal Medicine. **Education:** University of Texas Medical School – San Antonio, M.D. (1982); Texas A&M University, B.S. (1978). **Personal:** Married to Adrienne in 1980. Two children: Jason Terrell and Kyle Brandon. Dr. Bosse enjoys flying, hunting, fishing, and golf.

Charles J. Brook, M.D.

Pulmonary Physician and Corporate Vice President
Kansas City Pulmonary Clinic
6420 Prospect, Suite 303T
Kansas City, MO 64132
(816) 333–1919
Fax: (816) 333–2614

8011

Business Information: Kansas City Pulmonary Clinic is a medical group practice specializing in pulmonary, critical care, and sleep disorders medicine. Kansas City Pulmonary Clinic currently employs eight physicians and nine office support staff. As Pulmonary Physician and Corporate Vice President, Dr. Brook is responsible for providing health care to patients, as well as administrative operations oversight. **Career Steps:** Pulmonary Physician and Corporate Vice President, Kansas City Pulmonary Clinic (1977–Present); Pulmonary Fellow, University of Michigan Medical Center (1975–1977); Major, U.S. Air Force, Ellsworth Air Force Base (1973–1975); Internal Medicine Resident, University of Michigan Medical Center (1969–1973). **Associations & Accomplishments:** Fellow, American Thoracic Society; Fellow, American College of Chest Physicians; Fellow, American College of Physicians; American Sleep Disorders Association; Society of Critical Care Medicine. **Education:** University of Chicago, M.D. (1969); Carleton College, B.A. **Personal:** Married to Judy in 1968. Two children: Braden Paul and Dana Katherine. Dr. Brook enjoys running, biking, swimming, tennis, skiing, sailboarding, fishing, and reading.

Dale Brown Jr., M.D.

President
Dale Brown Jr., M.D. & Associates
6624 Fannin Street, #2180
Houston, TX 77030–2333
(713) 797–1144
Fax: (713) 797–0556

8011

Business Information: Dale Brown Jr., M.D. & Associates is a group medical practice, specializing in OB/Gyn practices. A practicing physician since 1964, Board–certified in Obstetrics and Gynecology, Dr. Brown established the practice in 1977. He oversees all physician associates and support staff, as well as provides patient care. Concurrent to his private medical practice, he serves as Chief of Staff at St. Luke's Episcopal Hospital. **Career Steps:** President, Dale Brown Jr., M.D. & Associates (1977–Present) **Associations & Accomplishments:** American Medical Association; Texas Medical Association; American Board of Obstetrics and Gynecology; President, International Society for the Study of Vulvovaginal Disease **Education:** University of Texas Medical School, M.D. (1964); University of New Mexico, B.S. (1959). **Personal:** Married to Eleanor Bartlett Moore in 1965. Two children: Stephen and Chris. Dr. Brown enjoys hunting, fly–fishing and skiing.

Claire–Lucie Brunet

Physician
Mary Berglund Health Center
P.O. Box 390, 204 Beaverton, Ignace
Toronto, Ontario P0T 1T0
(807) 934–2251
Fax: (807) 934–6552

8011

Business Information: Mary Berglund Health Center is a community health center offering primary care only. The Center is especially busy during the summer months due to the transient tourist and summer resident population. Affiliated with Dryden Hospital, the Center employs three physicians and 12 support personnel. As Physician, Dr. Brunet is responsible for various administrative activities at the Center, as well as her daily patient load. **Career Steps:** Physician, Mary Berglund Health Center (1992–Present); Medical Consultant, Ministry of Health, Ontario (1989–1992); Physician in Private Practice, Dr. Claire–Lucie Brunet (1985–1989). **Associations & Accomplishments:** Fellow, College of Family Physicians of Canada; Ontario College of Family Physicians; Canadian Medical Association; Physicians for Global Survival; Association des Medecins de Langue Francaise du Canada. **Education:** University of Ottawa, M.D. (1983); Laurentian University: B.Sc. with honors, M.Sc. **Personal:** Dr. Brunet enjoys photography, handicrafts, sewing, travel, and collecting wildflowers.

Michael J. Butler, M.D.

Cardiologist
Lewis–Gale Clinic
1802 Braeburn Dr.
Salem, VA 24018
(540) 776–2001
Fax: (540) 776–2080

8011

Business Information: Lewis–Gale Clinic is a multi–specialty medical clinic, providing diagnosis and treatment of patients. A practicing physician since 1984 and a Board–Certified Cardiologist, Dr. Butler joined Lewis–Gale Clinic as Cardiologist in 1993. He provides health care to patients suffering from heart problems. **Career Steps:** Cardiologist, Lewis–Gale Clinic (1993–Present); Cardiology Fellow, Geisinger Medical Center (1989–1993); Physician, United States Air Force (1984–1992). **Education:** St. Louis University – School of Medicine, M.D. (1984); University of Notre Dame, B.S. (1979). **Personal:** Dr. Butler enjoys golf, fishing, and travel.

Russell B. Butler, M.D.

President
Russell B. Butler, M.D., P.C.
730 John Cuming Bldg.
Concord, MA 01742
(508) 369–7812
Fax: (508) 369–3353

8011

Business Information: The Office of Neurologist Russell B. Butler, M.D., P.C. deals with diseases of the nervous system. As President, Dr. Butler handles the daily operations of his pri-

vate practice, including all financial aspects, public relations, the marketing of his services, and attending to his patients. Dr. Butler is also an Associate Professor at a local university. **Career Steps:** President, Russell B. Butler, M.D., P.C. (1975–Present); President of Medical Staff, Emerson Hospital (1994–1996). **Associations & Accomplishments:** Fellow American Heart Association – Stroke Council; American Academy of Neurology; President, Massachusetts Medical Society District; Former President, Massachusetts Neurologic Association. **Education:** University of Chicago, M.D. (1967); Cornell University, B.S. **Personal:** Married to Carole in 1966. Three children: Kathylynn, Lauranne, and Genevieve. Mr. Butler enjoys skiing, sailing, and gardening.

Lea Ann Camp, R.N.

Director of Nursing
A. P. & S. Clinic, L.L.C.
221 South 6th Street
Terre Haute, IN 47807–4214
(812) 232–0564 Ext. 492
Fax: Please mail or call

8011

Business Information: A. P. & S. Clinic, LLC is a physician and surgeons clinic offering specialty medical care (i.e., laboratory, x–ray, EKG, CAT scans, mamography, echos, eye exams). The Clinic is comprised of 57 physcians and 3 surgeons, and recently merged with Union Hospital. As Director of Nursing, Ms. Camp is responsible for the supervision of 55 nurses, as well as the oversight of scheduling, personnel hiring, OSHA and other federally–regulated policies compliance, and infectious control training. **Career Steps:** Director of Nursing, A. P. & S. Clinic, LLC (1994–Present); HIV/STD Nurse, Vanderburgh County Health Department (1993–1994); RN Charge Nurse – Emergency Room, Humana University of Louisville (1990–1993); RN Supervisor, Scott County Memorial Hospital (1986–1990). **Associations & Accomplishments:** Indiana Association for Healthcare Quality. **Education:** University of Evansville, B.S.N. (1981). **Personal:** Married to Rev. Melvin D. Camp in 1981. Two children: Jennifer Ann and Elizabeth Ann. Ms. Camp enjoys church activities and music."

Joan T. Campagna, M.D.

Private Practitioner
Joan T. Campagna, M.D.
750 Las Gallinas Avenue
San Rafael, CA 94903
(415) 491–0713
Fax: Please mail or call

8011

Business Information: Joan T. Campagna, M.D., established in 1989, is a private medical practice specializing in rheumatology. As Private Practitioner, Dr. Campagna is responsible for all aspects of operations including administration, diagnosis and treatment of patients, as well as conducting research in rheumatology. **Career Steps:** Private Practitioner, Joan T. Campagna, M.D. (1989–Present); Rheumatologist Internist, Marin Medical Group (1987–1989); Rheumatologist, Ross Valley Clinic (1984–1987); General Internist, Kaiser Hospital (1982); General Physician, North of Market Senior Citizens Clinic (1979–1980). **Associations & Accomplishments:** APPOINTMENTS: Chairwoman of the Board of Directors of the Northern California Branch Arthritis Foundation (1992–1993); Board of Directors, Marin County Branch Arthritis Foundation (1988–1991); Assistant Clinical Professor of Medicine, General Arthritis Clinic, University of California – San Francisco; ACTIVITIES OF FELLOWSHIP: Outpatients – six clinics per week: one at Stanford, five at Valley Medical Center; Inpatients – Consultations; Responsibilities as a teacher: Stanford Medical Students – formal sections every six weeks, noon conferences for Housestaff – monthly, conferences for Housestaff on service – weekly, Radiology rounds – weekly; Case presentation – Stanford Immunology Grand Rounds; Journal Clubs: Stanford – weekly; her presentations included articles from the "Proceedings of the National Academy of Sciences" and from the "Journal of Clinical Investigation"; Research – clinical, as previously listed; Numerous publications and presentations on Arthritis and Lyme Disease manifestation; CLUB MEMBERSHIPS: American College of Rheumatology; California Medical Association; Marin Medical Society; EXTRACURRICULAR ACTIVITIES DURING EDUCATION: Notre Dame – Counselor to Freshmen; Loyola Medical – Advisor to First Year Students; Presbyterian Hospital – Resident Selection Committee. **Education:** Stanford at Santa Clara Valley Medical Center, Fellowship, Board Certification in Rheumatology (1984); Presbyterian Hospital of Pacific Medical Center, Internship and Residency in Internal Medicine (1982); Loyola University Stritch School of Medicine, honors in Evaluation in Medicine, Pediatrics (1978); University of Notre Dame, B.S. with honors (1975) **Personal:** Dr. Campagna enjoys Italian and German languages, sailing, theatre, oil painting and music.

James P. Capo Jr., M.D.
President and Physician
Internal Medicine Associates of Atlanta
5505 Peachtree Dunwoody, #650
Atlanta, GA 30342–1713
(404) 256–2444
Fax: (404) 256–0321

8011

Business Information: Internal Medicine Associates of Atlanta, affiliated with St. Joseph's Hospital in Atlanta, is a specialized medical practice, concentrating on the diagnosis and treatment of internal medicine complaints. A practicing physician since 1977, Dr. Capo joined Internal Medicine Associates of Atlanta as President and Physician in 1984. His practice concentrates on internal medicine with a sub–specialty in pulmonary disease. **Career Steps:** President and Physician, Internal Medicine Associates of Atlanta (1984–Present); Staff Physician, Smyrna Emergency Care (1983–1984); Resident Physician, Pensacola Educational Program (1979–1983). **Associations & Accomplishments:** American Medical Association; Southern Medical Association; American Society of Internal Medicine; American Society of Hypertension; American College of Physician Executives; Trustee, St. Joseph Health Care System; Board Member, Atlanta Health Partners; Blue Cross – Blue Shield. **Education:** University Autonomous of Guadalara, Mexico, M.D. (1977); Belmont Abbey College, B.S. (1972). **Personal:** Married to Roberta M. in 1974. One child: James. Dr. Capo enjoys scuba diving, travel, and golf.

Jose P. Cariaga, M.D.
Physician
Hodges – Cariaga Medical Partnership
13801 Bruce B. Downs Boulevard, Suite 102
Tampa, FL 33613
(813) 971–8520
Fax: (813) 971–3249

8011

Business Information: Hodges – Cariaga Medical Partnership, established in 1993, is a full–time, medical practice, consisting of two primary care physicians who provide health care to patients of all ages. A practicing physician since 1982 and Board–Certified in Geriatrics, Dr. Cariaga co–founded this medical practice in 1993, sharing all aspects of operations with his partner, as well as providing diagnosis and treatment to patients. **Career Steps:** Physician, Hodges – Cariaga Medical Partnership (1993–Present); Physician, Trelles Clinic (1992–1993); Physician, Forest Hills Clinic (1991–1992) **Associations & Accomplishments:** American College of Physicians; American Geriatric Society; Ethics Committee, University Community Hospital – Tampa. **Education:** University of Santo Tomas College of Medicine and Surgery, M.D. (1982); Loyola University – Los Angeles, B.S. (1976). **Personal:** Married to Maria–Luisa in 1984. Two children: Jennifer and Jillianne. Dr. Cariaga enjoys tennis, basketball, chess, football, and ping pong.

William M. Carr, M.D., FAAP
President
Stafford Pediatrics Inc.
385 Garrisonville Road #209
Stafford, VA 22554
(540) 659–6272
Fax: (540) 720–5867
EMAIL: See Below

8011

Business Information: Stafford Pediatrics Inc. is a multi–associate medical group, providing all areas of medical diagnosis, treatment and counsel in pediatric medicine, serving patients ranging from birth to 18 years of age. A practicing Pediatrician since 1981, Dr. William Carr founded Stafford Pediatrics in October of 1990. As President, Dr. Carr oversees all administrative support staff and associates, in addition to his daily patient practice. As the only full–time pediatrician on staff, Dr. Carr focuses his private practice in the field of ADD (Attention Deficit Disorder), as well as asthma and other allergy disorders. Internet users can reach him via: BILL705479 **Career Steps:** President, Stafford Pediatrics Inc. (1990–Present); Pediatrician, Pediatric Associates of Manassas (1985–1990) **Associations & Accomplishments:** American Medical Association; American Academy of Pediatrics, National and Virginia Chapters; Medical Society of Virginia; Prince William County Medical Society; American Heart Association; Special Olympics, State and Local Chapters. **Education:** Medical College of Georgia, M.D. (1981); Emory University, B.A. in Chemistry (1977); Residency and Internships: Medical College of Georgia (1981–1984). **Personal:** Married to Jeri Carr, M.D. (Neurologist) in 1981. Dr. Carr en-

joys golf, bowling, softball, hiking, bicycling, and Olympic pin collecting.

Jose V. Castellanos, M.D.
Attending Physician
MonteFiore Medical Center
305 East 161 Street
Bronx, NY 10451
(718) 579–2500
Fax: (718) 579–2599

8011

Business Information: MonteFiore Medical Center is a private medical group, providing full service medical and health related services to patients. As Attending Physician, Dr. Castellanos is responsible for patient diagnosis and treatment, oversight of quality of care, and management of administrative and operational functions pertaining to his department. **Career Steps:** MonteFiore Medical Center: Attending Physician (Present), Medical Director (1993–1996), In–Patient Associate Medical Director Family Practice (1992–1993), Comprehensive Health Care Center/Full Time Attending Physician (1990). **Associations & Accomplishments:** American Medical Association. **Education:** University of Dominica, M.D. (1981). **Personal:** Married to Maria in 1980. Three children: Jose Victor, Michael and Karla. Dr. Castellanos enjoys target shooting and cigars.

Richard L. Chalal, M.D.
••• ◉ •••
Physician and President
The Office of Richard L. Chalal, M.D., P.A.
535 Gandy Street, NE
Russellville, AL 35653
(205) 332–3544
Fax: (205) 332–5178

8011

Business Information: The Office of Richard L. Chalal, M.D., P.A. is a general practice medical facility specializing in Internal Medicine. Established in 1981, the Office currently employs three medical support staff. As President and Physician, Dr. Chalal is responsible for all aspects of operations, including the care and treatment of patients. **Career Steps:** Physician and President, The Office of Richard L. Chalal, M.D., P.A. (1981–Present). **Associations & Accomplishments:** Council Member, American Society of Internal Medicine; American College of Physicians; American College of Physician Executives; American Society of Addiction Medicine; Certified, American Board of Internal Medicine and American Society of Addiction Medicine; Optimist Club, Palm Beach County, Florida; Member, Opera Chorus, Palm Beach County, Florida; Published in medical magazines and local newspapers. **Education:** Hahnemann University, M.D. (1976); Muhlenberg College, B.S. (1971). **Personal:** Married to Betsy in 1989. Two children: Lauren and Samantha. Dr. Chalal enjoys golf, travel, movies and the arts.

Diane L. Charon–Silvia
R.N.
Hawthorne Medical Associates
94 Country Road
East Freetown, MA 02717
(508) 996–3991
Fax: Please mail or call

8011

Business Information: Hawthorne Medical Associates is a full–service, family practice medical office, providing general and specialty health care. As R.N., Ms. Silvia is responsible for the Coumadin Program, where–in the drug Warfarin is used as an anticoagulant in control of various human blood disorders. **Career Steps:** R.N., Hawthorne Medical Associates (1995–Present); Employee Health, St. Luke Hospital (1993–1995); New Bedford – MA: Cardiac Rehabilitation Patient Education (1987–1993), Critical Care (1980–1987); Medical–Surgical (1973–1980). **Associations & Accomplishments:** American College of Sports Medicine; Board of Directors, Alumni Services, Bristol Community College; National Association of Female Executives; Public Speakers Bureau, American Heart Association; Bristol Community College Nursing Advisory Committee. **Education:** Attending, Lesley College – Cambridge, MA; University of Massachusetts – Dartmouth, Bachelors Degree in Nursing; Bristol Community College, Associates Degree in Nursing. **Personal:** Two children: Melissa and Jason. Ms. Charon–Silvia enjoys travel and walking.

Barton A. Chase III, M.D.
Owner/Physician
Dr. Barton Chase Family Practice Health Center
Highway 57, P O Box 99
Ramer, TN 38367
(901) 645–6118
Fax: (901) 645–8424
E MAIL: See Below

8011

Business Information: Dr. Barton Chase Family Practice Health Center, established in 1990, is a private family practice office. With estimated revenue of $700,000, the Center presently has eight employees. As Physician, Dr. Chase is certified in family and forensic medicine. His practice is affiliated with McNairy County General Hospital, where he is Chief of Staff. On occasion, he teaches the Hospital's Certified Nursing Assistant course. Internet users can reach him via: B3Chase@aol.com. **Career Steps:** Physician, Dr. Barton Chase Family Practice Health Center (1990–Present); Physician/Chief of Staff, McNairy County General Hospital (1995–Present); Physician, Medical Arts Clinic (1988–1990); Physician, St. Martinsville Infirmary (1985–1990). **Associations & Accomplishments:** American Medical Association; Tennessee Medical Association; Board of Family Practice; American Association of Family Physicians; Aircraft Owners and Pilots Association. **Education:** Howard University College of Medicine, M.D. (1982); Rensselaer Polytechnic Institute. **Personal:** One child: Tiffany Yvonne. Dr Chase enjoys aviation and being a commercial pilot.

Doyle E. Chastain, M.D.
••• ◉ •••
President
D.E. Chastain, M.D., P.A.
1309 Garden Street
Titusville, FL 32796
(407) 267–4700
Fax: (407) 383–3057

8011

Business Information: D.E. Chastain, M.D., P.A. is a private medical practice concentrating in internal medicine. Board–Certified in Internal Medicine, Dr. Chastain has been practicing medicine since 1960. Opening his private practice in 1966, Dr. Chastain serves as President and is responsible for all aspects of operations, including the diagnosis and treatment of patients. Additionally, he has obtained seven patents for natural and environmentally–safe biodegradable bactericides and fungicides. **Career Steps:** President, D.E. Chastain, M.D., P.A. (1966–Present). **Associations & Accomplishments:** American Medical Association; Florida and Brevard County Medical Associations; American Society of Internal Medicine; Southern Medical Association; American College of Physicians; Director, First Union National Bank of Brevard. **Education:** University of Miami School of Medicine, M.D. (1960); Harvard School of Medicine, Internal Medicine Reviews. **Personal:** Married to Jackie in 1965. Two children: John and David. Dr. Chastain enjoys golf, personal computer work, and reading.

Anthony W. Cheng, M.D., F.C.C.P., F.A.C.A.
Physician
South Atlantic Pulmonary & Critical Care Associates
483 Upper Riverdale Road #A
Riverdale, GA 30274–2538
(770) 991–3888
Fax: (770) 994–0278

8011

Business Information: South Atlantic Pulmonary & Critical Care Associates is a full–service medical practice, specializing in pulmonary disorders and critical care practices. A practicing physician since 1984 and a Board–Certified Chest Physician, Dr. Cheng joined South Atlantic Pulmonary & Critical Care Associates as one of three physicians in 1991. His practice specializes in internal medicine, pulmonary medicine, and critical care. **Career Steps:** Physician, South Atlantic Pulmonary & Critical Care Associates (1991–Present); Pulmonary Fellow, New York Medical College (1989–1991); Medical Resident, Harbor Hospital Center (1986–1989). **Associations & Accomplishments:** Fellow, American College of Chest Physicians; American College of Physicians; Fellow, American College of Angiology; Experimental Aircraft Association; Private Pilots License. **Education:** Universidad Autonoma de cd Juarez, Chih, Mexico, M.D. (1984); Florida State University, B.S. **Personal:** Married to Shiow Jen in 1986. Two children: Andrew P. and Bernard P. Dr. Cheng enjoys flying.

Anbukili (Anne) Chetty, M.D.
Pediatric Pulmonologist
Children's Hospital
16845 Windwood Court
Brookfield, WI 53005–6828
(414) 266–6730
Fax: (414) 266–2653
EMAIL: see below

8011

Business Information: Children's Hospital, in affiliation with the Medical College of Wisconsin, provides comprehensive acute and critical care to infants through adolescence, as well as clinical research and residency instruction. As a Pediatric Pulmonogist, Dr. Chetty is responsible for conducting research and clinical treatment. Concurrent with her position, she serves as Assistant Professor at the Medical College of Wisconsin. She can be reached through the Internet as follows: AChetty@MCW.edu **Career Steps:** Pediatric Pulmonologist, Children's Hospital (1993–Present); Assistant Professor, Medical College of Wisconsin (1993–Present); NIH Sponsored Research Fellow, CWRU, Cleveland, Ohio (1991–1993); Faculty of Pediatrics, All India Institute of Medical Sciences, New Delhi, India (1976–1988). **Associations & Accomplishments:** Member, American Thoracic Society; Fellow, American Academy of Pediatrics; National Institute of Health – recipient of a training grant fellowship (1991); Published several publications. **Education:** Madura Medical College, Madras University, India, M.B.B.S. (1962). **Personal:** Married to V. K. Chetty in 1962. Three children: Malathy, Shanthy, and Nadaraj. Dr. Chetty enjoys music and gardening.

Naoki Chiba
Gastroenterologist
Office of Dr. Naoki Chiba
Suite 105–21 Surrey Street West
Guelph, Ontario N1H 3R3
(519) 836–8201
Fax: (519) 766–0754
EMail: See Below

8011

Business Information: Surrey GI Clinic is a community–based medical clinic specializing in research into ulcer disease, dyspepsia, and bacterial infection of the stomach with Helicobacter pylor, which is associated with ulcers. Dr. Chiba, a gastroenterologist in private practice, certified in Internal Medicine and affiliated with McMaster University as an Assistant Clinical Professor, is concurrently Head of the Surrey GI Clinic. Dr. Chiba's main research interests focus on disorders of the upper GI tract, namely reflux and ulcer disease. He is considered an expert in the treatment of H. pylori infections using meta–analytical techniques to summarize medical literature. Internet users can reach him via: chiban@fhs.csu.mcmaster.ca. **Career Steps:** Gastroenterologist, Surrey GI Clinic (1992–Present); Assistant Clinical Professor, McMaster University – Hamilton (1992–Present). **Associations & Accomplishments:** American Gastroenterology Association; American College of Gastroenterology; Canadian Association of Gastroenterology; American College of Physicians; Canadian Medical Association; Fellow, Royal College of Physicians of Canada; Alpha Omega Alpha; Cochrane Collaboration for Dyspepsia. **Education:** McMaster University – Hamilton: FRCP(c) (1990,1991), presently working toward M.Sc. in Clinical Epidemiology; University of Western Ontario, M.D. (1986). **Personal:** Married to Christina Louise in 1990. Two children: Kentaro Connor and Seiji Alexander. Dr. Chiba enjoys research, choral singing, and skiing.

Jean M. Chin, M.D.
OB/GYN Physician
Offices of Jean Chin, M.D. and Joyce Kim, M.D.
1130 Park Avenue
New York, NY 10128–1255
(212) 348–2525
Fax: Please mail or call

8011

Business Information: Offices of Jean Chin, M.D. and Joyce Kim, M.D. is a specialty medical practice, providing all aspects of obstetrics and gynecology practice delivery. A practicing physician since 1976, Board–Certified in Obstetrics and Gynecology, Dr. Chin co–founded the Practice in 1980. **Career Steps:** OB/GYN Physician, Offices of Jean Chin, M.D. and Joyce Kim, M.D. (1980–Present). **Associations & Accomplishments:** Phi Beta Kappa; Alpha Omega Alpha; Sigma Phi. **Education:** Coulumbia P&S, M.D. (1976) **Personal:** Married to Ken Williams in 1977. Two children: Kerrie and Germane.

George Chu, M.D.
Physician
Mid–South Internal Medicine
6027 Walnut Grove, Suite 206
Memphis, TN 38120–2127
(901) 767–5000
Fax: (901) 767–6000

8011

Business Information: Mid–South Internal Medicine is a private medical practice, providing quality family practice medical care. A practicing physician since 1989, Dr. Chu opened Mid–South Internal Medicine as one of two practitioners in 1001. **Career Steps:** Physician (1909–Present). **Associations & Accomplishments:** Diplomate, American Board of Internal Medicine (1989); American College of Physicians; Tennessee Medical Association; Shelby County Medical Society. **Education:** University of Tennessee: M.D. (1986), B.A. (1981). **Personal:** Married to May in 1987. Two children: Benjamin and Jason.

Lindy Lee Cibischino, M.D.

Pediatrician
Madison Pediatric Associates, PSC
789 Eastern Bypass, Suite 17
Richmond, KY 40475
(606) 624–2020
Fax: Please mail or call

8011

Business Information: Madison Pediatric Associates, PSC is a full–service, private pediatrics practice. A Board–certified Pediatrics specialist since 1993, Dr. Cibischino established her private practice in July 1995, following her teaching and residency fellowship with the University of Medicine & Dentistry of New Jersey and the Children's Hospital of New Jersey. **Career Steps:** Pediatrician, Madison Pediatric Associates, PSC (1995–Present); University Medicine & Dentistry of New Jersey/Children's Hospital of New Jersey: Teaching Pediatrician (1994–1995), Pediatrics Chief Resident (1993–1994), Pediatrics Resident (1990–1993). **Associations & Accomplishments:** American Medical Association; American Academy of Pediatrics; American Medical Women's Association; Alpha Omega Alpha Honor Society. **Education:** New Jersey Medical School, M.D. (1990); Rutgers University, B.A. **Personal:** Married to Maurizio in 1990. Dr. Cibischino enjoys golf, riding bicycles and swimming.

Donald W. (Don) Clary, M.D.
Family Physician
Pulaski Medical Arts Building
101 1st Street NW, Box 1641
Pulaski, VA 24301–5603
(540) 980–0555
Fax: (540) 980–9141

8011

Business Information: Pulaski Medical Arts Building is a full–service, general family practice medical clinic. Serving a regional area around Pulaski, Virginia, Pulaski Medical Arts was established in 1991 and currently has employment of 14. As Family Physician, Dr. Clary has various administrative duties, as well as treating patients on a daily basis. **Career Steps:** Family Physician, Pulaski Medical Arts Building (1991–Present); Medical Assistant, SVMS (1984–1988). **Associations & Accomplishments:** Diplomate, American Board of Family Practice; Sigma Xi; Omicron Delta Kappa; American Medical Association; Phi Beta Kappa; Medical Society of Virginia. **Education:** Eastern Virginia Medical, M.D. (1988); Hampden–Sydney College, B.S.; Residency: Roanoke Memorial Hospital (1988–1991); Certifications: Certified A.C.L.S. Director; Certified N.A.L.S. and A.T.L.S. **Personal:** Married to Marie B. in 1994. Four children: Jaime and Michael Barnes, and Clayton and Carolyn Clary. Dr. Clary enjoys woodworking and computer games.

Rosa Coca, M.D.
Physician
The Office of Rosa Coca, M.D.
P.O. Box 762
Cayey, Puerto Rico 00737–0762
(809) 263–3040
Fax: Please mail or call

8011

Business Information: A practicing physician since 1986, Dr. Coca established her sole practice medical office in 1990, specializing in internal medicine. **Career Steps:** Physician, Dr. Rosa Coca, M.D. (1990–Present); Director of the Medical Department, Hospital Menonita Cayey (1993). **Associations &**

Accomplishments: American Medical Association. **Education:** University of Central Caribe, School of Medicine, M.D. (1986); Cabrini Medical Center, New York City, Internal Medicine Specialist. **Personal:** Two children: Rafael H. Gil de Rubio and Ricardo Diaz. Dr. Coca enjoys painting and drawing.

Carol Lynn Coglianese, M.D.
Internist and Pediatrician
MED–PEDS Associates – Riverside Health System
122 East Washington St.
Momence, IL 60954–1518
(815) 472–3923
Fax: (815) 472–2816

8011

Business Information: MED–PEDS Associates – Riverside Health System is a hospital–based medical practice, providing a full–range of diagnosis and treatment services to patients in the Momence, Illinois community, in addition to the Hopkins Park and Kankakee areas. Board–certifed in Internal Medicine and Pediatrics, Dr. Coglianese joined MED–PEDS Associates upon completion of her residency fellowship in 1991. She specializes in the care of premature babies and children with developmental delays, as well as handicapped children. As an Internist, she provides services in intensive care unit management and hospital management. **Career Steps:** Internist and Pediatrician, MED–PEDS Associates – Riverside Health System (1991–Present); Medical Resident and Doctor, University of Tennesse – College of Medicine (1991–1995); Instructor of Life Sciences, Parkland College (1985–1987); Teaching Assistant, University of Illinois – College of Veterinary Medicine (1982–1984). **Associations & Accomplishments:** American Medical Association; Illinois Medical Society; Kankakee Medical Society; American College of Physicians; American Academy of Pediatrics; Silver Medal of American Dairy Science Association; AIDS Education Coordinator; Chapter Vice President, American Medical Association; American Medical Women's Association; Treasurer, Golen's Medical Society; Has ten years of experience in the veterinarian field. **Education:** University of Illinois: College of Medicine, M.D. (1991), College of Agriculture, B.S. (1992), College of Veterinary Medicine, M.S. (1984). **Personal:** Dr. Coglianese enjoys fiber artistry (quilting, tatting, embroidery, lace making), painting, reading, and studying Russian and medical histories.

Jacob H. Colarian, M.D.
Sole Practitioner
Westwood Medical Park
Westwood Medical Park #10
Bluefield, VA 24605
(540) 322–2513
Fax: (540) 322–2513

8011

Business Information: Westwood Medical Park is a private practice medical care facility, specializing in gastroenterology and fiberoptic surgical procedures. Upon the conferral of his medical degree in 1985, Dr. Colarian established a private practice for himself, later opening the Westwood Medical Park office in 1991. As Sole Practitioner, he oversees all administrative areas and support staff, in addition to his daily patient practice. **Career Steps:** Sole Practitioner, Westwood Medical Park (1991–Present). **Associations & Accomplishments:** Fellow, American College of Physicians and Gastroenterology. **Education:** Wayne State University, M.D. (1985); Internal Medicine Residency & Gastroenterology Fellowship (1991); American University of Beirut, B.S. (1980); Board Certified Internal Medicine and Gastroenterology. **Personal:** Married to Susan in 1995. Dr. Colarian enjoys reading non–medical novels, travel, international cuisine, jazz, opera, and playing the guitar.

Col. (Retired) Jean Colimon, M.D.
Private Physician
–Independent–
2046 Elk Spring Drive
Brandon, FL 33511
(813) 689–0091
Fax: Please mail or call

8011

Business Information: A recently retired U.S. Air Force physician, Col. Colimon established his private medical practice in 1992, providing diagnosis and non–surgical treatment of diseases to patients. **Career Steps:** Private Physician (1992–Present); Chief Medical Services, MacDill AFB, Florida (1989–1992); Chief Hospital Services, Shaw AFB, South Carolina (1984–1989). **Associations & Accomplishments:** Military Surgeons of the U.S.; Retired Officers Association. **Education:** Air University, Air Command and Staff Air War (1980). **Personal:** Married. Two children: Kenya Chenelle and Sonya Michelle. Col. Colimon enjoys travel.

Andrew R. Conn, M.D.

Gastroenterologist
Burlington County Internal Medical Group
651 J F Kennedy Way
Willingboro, NJ 08046
(609) 871–7070
Fax: (609) 835–4510

8011

Business Information: Burlington County Internal Medical Group is a multi–specialty group of 9 physicians. Established in 1992, and located in Willingboro, New Jersey, the group offers a full range of medical specialities. As Gastroenterologist, Dr. Conn is responsible for providing diagnosis and treatment to patients suffering from stomach and intestinal disorders. **Career Steps:** Gastroenterologist, Burlington County Internal Medical Group (1992–Present). **Associations & Accomplishments:** American College Gastroenterology; American College of Physicians; American Medical Association. **Education:** Yale Medical School, M.D. (1986); Temple University Hospital, Internship, Residency, Internal Medicine; University of Pennsylvania Hospital, Gastroenterology Fellowship; Rutgers University, M.S. in Nutrition (1982); Kenyon College, B.A. (1979). **Personal:** Married to Leslie Coney in 1983. One child: Alixe Coney. Dr. Conn enjoys fishing and wine collecting.

Thomas A. Cook, M.D.

Sole Practitioner
Office of Thomas A. Cook, M.D.
344 University Boulevard West
Silver Spring, MD 20901
(301) 593–9074
Fax: (301) 593–3962

8011

Business Information: Office of Thomas A. Cook, M.D. is an obstetrics and gynecology practice. Dr. Cook has been in private practice since 1955, responsible for patient care, administrative activities, and staff supervision. Concurrently, he is Senior Attending Physician at both Holy Cross Hospital and George Washington University Hospital, as well as an Associate Clinical Professor at George Washington University. **Career Steps:** Sole Practitioner, Office of Thomas A. Cook, M.D. (1955–Present). **Associations & Accomplishments:** Former President, Wheaton–Kegington Rotary Club; Former Senior Warden, Grace Episcopal Church of Silver Springs; American Medical Association; Washington GYN Society. **Education:** University of Virginia, M.D.(1949); University of Puerto Rico, Pre–Medical (1945). **Personal:** Married to Clara in 1949. Three children: Vyvian, Randolph and Steven. Dr. Cook enjoys travel, golf and fishing.

Andrew Coronato, M.D., F.A.C.P., F.A.C.G.

President
Medical Diagnostic Associates, P.A.
417 West Broad Street
Westfield, NJ 07090–4104
(908) 233–0895 Ext. 113
Fax: (908) 233–3873

8011

Business Information: Medical Diagnostic Associates, P.A. is a 22–physician multi–specialty group practice with expertise in internal medicine, cardiology, gastroenterology, oncology, immunology, nephrology, and family medicine. The Practice has grown from 14 to 22 physicians in the past year. Established in 1971, Medical Diagnostic Associates, P.A. currently employs 110 people. Board–Certified in Gastroenterology and Internal Medicine, Dr. Coronato joined the Practice as President in 1971. He is responsible for all aspects of operations, including providing health care to patients. His hospital affiliations include: Rahway Hospital and Overlook Hospital. Concurrent with his medical practice, he serves as Instructor at Columbia Medical School, instructing medical students, interns, and residents in Clinical Medicine and Gastroenterology. **Career Steps:** President, Medical Diagnostic Associates, P.A. (1971–Present); Instructor in Clinical Medicine, Columbia University College of Physicians and Surgeons; Rahway Hospital: Attending, Former Chief of the Department of Medicine, Former Chief of Section of Gastroenterology; Overlook Hospital: Attending, Former Chief of Section of Gastroenterology. **Associations & Accomplishments:** Diplomate of the American Board of Internal Medicine; Diplomate of the American Board of Gastroenterology; Alpha Omega Alpha Honor Society; Recipient, American Gastroenterological Association Award, Merck Manual Award, and Mead Johnson Residency Scholar Award; Recipient, Governor's Appointment to the New Jersey Essential Health Services Commission (1992–Present); Chairman, Judicial Committee of Union County Medical Society (1986–1991); Chairman, Council on Public Relations Medical Society of New Jersey (1990–Prsent); Treasurer, Union County Medical Society; New Jersey Gastroenterological Society; American Gastroenterological Association; American Society for Gastrointestinal Endoscopy; Fellow of American College of Physicians; Fellow of American College of Gastroenterology; American Medical Association. **Education:** Metropolitan Hospital, New York Medical College Center, Residency in Internal Medicine and Fellowship in Gastroenterology (1967–1971); Bellevue Hospital, Cornell Division, New York, Medical Internship (1966–1967); New York Medical College, M.D. (1966); Georgetown University, B.S. in Biology (1962). **Personal:** Married to Paulette in 1962. Four children: Sabina, Cecile, Anthony, and Wilfred. Dr. Coronato enjoys golf and woodworking.

Louis H. Andres Cox, M.D.

President and Physician
The Office of Louis H. Cox, M.D., Inc.
4140 West Memorial Road, Suite 207
Oklahoma City, OK 73120–8300
(405) 749–4220
Fax: (405) 749–4221

8011

Business Information: The Office of Louis H. Cox, M.D., Inc. is a general practice medical facility specializing in Internal Medicine. Establishing the sole practice in 1990, as President and Physician, Dr. Andres Cox is responsible for the care and treatment of patients, as well as the administrative functions of the Office. Concurrent with his private practice, Dr. Cox is also the Co–Director of the Mercy Hospital Rehabilitation Unit. As such, he oversees speech, cognitive and physical therapies, as well as hematology research. **Career Steps:** President and Physician, The Office of Louis H. Cox, M.D., Inc. (1990–Present). **Associations & Accomplishments:** Board Member, Rehabilitation Medical Foundation; American Medical Association; ACP; Physicians Inc.; Board Member, Oklahoma State Medical Association; Oklahoma County Medical Association; Published in "Blood" and "Psychology" magazines. **Personal:** Married to Kathryn Denson in 1986. Three children: Michael, Sarah and Caroline.

Andrew C.S. Crichton, M.D.

Ophthalmologist
Calgary Medical Center
Suite 333–933 17th Avenue, South West
Calgary, Alberta T2T 5R6
(403) 245–3730
Fax: (403) 233–8252

8011

Business Information: Calgary Medical Center, established in 1988, is a health care facility that specializes in the structure, functions, and diseases of the eye. As Ophthalmologist, Dr. Crichton sees patients on a day–to–day basis focusing on the treatment of ocular diseases, i.e. glaucoma. **Career Steps:** Ophthalmologist, Calgary Medical Center (1988–Present). **Associations & Accomplishments:** Canadian Ophthalmolic Society; American Academy of Ophthalmology; Ophthalmological Society of Alberta. **Education:** University of Toronto, Fellowship in Ophthalmology (1987); University of British Columbia: Bachelor of Science, Medical Degree, Fellowship in Glaucoma. **Personal:** Married to Michele in 1995.

William J.R. Daily, M.D.

Medical Director
Neonatology Associates, Ltd.
300 West Clarendon, Suite 375
Phoenix, AZ 85013
(602) 277–4161
Fax: (602) 274–3394

8011

Business Information: Neonatology Associates, Ltd. is a private practice medical association specializing in neonatology. Established in 1967, the Association currently employs 14 physicians, all of which have a strong belief that the health of children and mothers should come before all else. The Association is based on the genuine care of patients and faith in the profession, thus making it a successful service. As Medical Director, Dr. Daily is responsible for the care and treatment of patients, as well as clinical instruction. It is Dr. Daily's belief that clinical medicine and academics go hand in hand. **Career Steps:** Medical Director, Neonatology Associates, Ltd. (1970–Present). **Associations & Accomplishments:** American Academy of Pediatrics and District VIII Perinatal Pediatric Section; American Medical Association; Arizona Medical Association; Arizona Perinatal Society; California Perinatal Society; Maricopa County Medical Society; Phoenix Pediatric Society; Society for Pediatric Research; Western Society for Pediatric Research; European Society for Pediatric Research; Published article for Clinical Pediatrics. **Education:** Stanford University, M.D. (1961). **Personal:** Married to Sasa Fait Johnson in 1988. Six children: Barclay Ann, Leif Eric, Stacy Lynn, Kimberly Diane, Andrew Joseph Johnson and Joseph David Johnson. Dr. Daily enjoys skiing, and incorporating Native American Culture into his daily life.

Zuhdi M. Dajani, M.D.

Physician
Office of Zuhdi M. Dajani, M.D.
248 Allegheny Boulevard
Brookville, PA 15825–2608
(814) 849–6767
Fax: (814) 849–3158

8011

Business Information: Office of Zuhdi M. Dajani, M.D. is a private medical practice, providing diagnosis and treatment to patients suffering from cardiac and internal medicine complaints from two offices. A practicing physician since 1987, Board–certified in Internal Medicine with a sub–specialty in Cardiology, Dr. Dajani founded the practice in 1991. Serving as Owner and Head of the Office, he oversees all administrative operations for associates and support staff for two locations, in addition to his daily patient practice. **Career Steps:** Physician, Office of Zuhdi M. Dajani, M.D. (1991–Present). **Associations & Accomplishments:** Pennsylvania Medical Society; American College of Cardiology; Arab–American Medical Association. **Education:** Georgetown Hospital, M.D. (1987) **Personal:** Married to Alia A. in 1980. Four children: Ruba, Lana, Deema, and Mohamed. Dr. Dajani enjoys travel, horseback riding, and classic music.

Caroline G. Dale, M.D.

Physician
Forbes Medical Associates
6039 Saltsburg Road
Pittsburgh, PA 15147
(412) 795–8070
Fax: Please mail or call

8011

Business Information: Forbes Medical Associates is a full–service, medical practice, providing diagnosis and treatment of patients. A practicing physician since 1989 and a Board–Certified Medical Internist, Dr. Dale joined Forbes Medical Associates as Staff Physician in 1994. Her practice concentrates on internal medicine. **Career Steps:** Physician, Forbes Medical Associates (1994–Present); Physician, Comphealth–Kron, Inc. (1993–1994). **Associations & Accomplishments:** American Medical Association; American College of Physicians; Pennsylvania Medical Society; Women's Medical Association; Recipient: Mary Mildred Sullivan Award (1983). **Education:** Medical University of South Carolina, M.D. (1989); Converse College, B.A. in Biology and Chemistry; University of Pittsburgh, Residency in Internal Medicine. **Personal:** Married to Ken Rothfield in 1995. Dr. Dale enjoys horseback riding, running, music, and travel.

Terri Daugherty

Marketing Director/Patient Education
MidWest EyeCenter
4452 Eastgate Boulevard, Suite 305
Cincinnati, OH 45245–1584
(513) 752–5700
Fax: (513) 752–5716

8011

Business Information: MidWest EyeCenter is a publicly–owned ophthalmology clinic, providing eye surgery (i.e. refractive, cataract, and radio kerotatomy) to the area. Affiliated with the national company of Physicians Resource Group (P.R.G.), the Clinic has three locations. As Marketing Director/Patient Education, Ms. Daugherty places and writes media ads, handles patient education, and addresses any questions they may have regarding their surgeries. **Career Steps:** Marketing Director/Patient Education, MidWest EyeCenter (1989–Present); Regional Secretary, Rent–A–Center (1987–1989); Opthalmolic Surgical Assistant, David M. Schneider, M.D., Inc. (1984–1989); Pharmacist's Assistant, Kreinder Medical Center (1982–1984). **Associations & Accomplishments:** Lion's Club; Wagon Master's Holiday Committee; B–T 200; Bethel Historical Society; Clermont County Historical Society; Recipient of the "Tenth Annual Health Care Advertising Award" (1993). **Education:** University of Cincinnati. **Personal:** Married to Howard in 1969. Two children: Paul and Amy. Ms. Daugherty enjoys volunteer work and spending time with her grandchildren.

Thea Kay Davies, M.D.
Physician
Medical Specialists
2200 North 3rd Street
Phoenix, AZ 85004–1401
(602) 258–6634
Fax: (602) 258–3411

8011

Business Information: As a private practice physician, specializing in Internal Medicine, Dr. Davies has been providing medical care to the Phoenix, AZ area for two years. Her practice, established in 1965, employs 14 medical and administrative support staff. **Career Steps:** Physician, Medical Specialists (1993–Present). **Associations & Accomplishments:** Arizona Medical Association; American College of Physicians; Maricopa Medical Society; Southern Medical Association. **Education:** Tulane Medical School, M.D. (1990); Cedar Sinai Medical Center, Internship and Residency (1990–1993); USC/LAC Hospital, Fellowship Pulmonary and Critical Care Medicine (1993–1994). **Personal:** Dr. Davies enjoys aerobics, sailing, water skiing, and ice skating.

Thomas P. Davis, M.D.
Cardiologist
Eastlake Cardiovascular
25990 Kelly Road
Roseville, MI 48066
(810) 771–3400
Fax: (810) 641–8782

8011

Business Information: Eastlake Cardiovascular, organized in 1993, boasts seven cardiologists who serve the needs of their patients in St. John's Hospital, Bon Secour Hospital, and College Hospital, with whom they are affiliated. In addition to his daily patient practice, Dr. Davis oversees all administrative operations for associates and support staff. He also serves as Director of the Cardio Intensive Care Unit at St. John's Hospital. **Career Steps:** Cardiologist, Eastlake Cardiovascular (1993–Present); Henry Ford Hospital: Cardiology Fellow (1990–1993), Resident Physician (1987–1990). **Associations & Accomplishments:** American Heart Association; American College of Cardiology; Wayne County Medical Society. **Education:** St. Georges University, M.D. (1986); Michigan State University, B.S. **Personal:** Married to Barbara Lynn in 1989. Two children: Meagan Nicole and Jessica Morgan. Dr. Davis enjoys golf and tennis.

Dr. J. Lance Defoa
General Practitioner
Wawa Medical Center
96 Broadway Avenue, Box 1217
Wawa, Ontario P0S 1K0
(705) 850–1313
Fax: (705) 856–1330
EMAIL: See Below

8011

Business Information: Wawa Medical Center is a private medical practice offering medical and related services to area residents. As General Practitioner, Dr. Defoa is responsible for patient care and diagnosis, training and research. Internet users can reach him via: Jldefoa@sympatico.ca. **Career Steps:** General Practitioner, Wawa Medical Center (1993–Present); Surgical Assistant, Shourones Hospital (1993); Intern, North York General Hospital (1992–1993). **Associations & Accomplishments:** Canadian Medical Association (CMA); Canadian Owners and Pilots Association (COPA); Ontario Medical Association (OMA); Christian Medical and Dental Society (CMDS); Experimental Aviation Association (EAA). **Education:** Queens University: M.D. (1992), B.Sc. in Life Sciences, With Honors. **Personal:** Dr. Defoa enjoys being a pilot, kayaking, sailing, and skiing.

Rekha J. DeSai, M.D.
Internal Medicine Physician
Gwinnett Internal Medicine Associates
601 Old Nor Crossroads, # A
Lawrenceville, GA 30245
(770) 963–2474
Fax: (770) 963–2476

8011

Business Information: Gwinnett Internal Medicine Associates is a private, general practice of medicine, consisting of two partners (both internal medicine physicians). A practicing physician since 1970, Dr. DeSai joined Gwinnett Internal Medicine Associates in 1985. Currently the owner of the practice, she focuses on internal medicine and minor surgeries. **Career Steps:** Internal Medicine Physician, Gwinnett Internal Medicine Associates (1985–Present); Internist, Prucare Health Care (1982–1985); Private Practice, Toccoa

Clinic Medical Associates (1980–1982). **Associations & Accomplishments:** American College of Physicians; American Association of Physicians of India; Indian–American Cultural Association; International Club of Atlanta; Professional Indian Network. **Education:** B.J. Medical College: M.B.B.S. / M.D. (1970); St. Xaviers College (1964). **Personal:** Married to Jay in 1972. Two children: Pankti and Palak. Dr. DeSai enjoys music, painting, creative writing, rafting, and snow skiing.

Derrick M. DeSilva Jr., M.D.
Physician
The Medical Offices of Derrick M. DeSilva Jr., M.D.
760 Amboy Avenue
Edison, NJ 08837–3224
(908) 738–8080
Fax: (908) 738–4228

8011

Business Information: A practicing physician since 1982 and a Medical Internist, Dr. De Silva established his sole practice medical office in 1988. He oversees all administrative operations for associates and a support staff, in addition to his daily patient practice. Concurrent with his private practice, he hosts a nationally syndicated radio talk show, regarding general medical information and authors a national column in the Globe Syndicate. **Career Steps:** Physician, Self–Employed (1988–Present). **Associations & Accomplishments:** American Medical Association; Internal Medicine Society; American Heart Association; American Diabetes Association; Naitonal Association of Radio Talk Show Hosts; National Association of Broadcasters; Published article on "Coping with Lyme Disease." **Education:** University Central Del Este – Dominican Republic, M.D. (1982). **Personal:** Married to Susan Carole in 1982. Two children: Derrick Michael, III and Travis Michael. Dr. DeSilva enjoys tennis, running, and having fun.

James E. Dickson, M.D.
President
Geneva Medical Group, L.L.P.
324 West North Street
Geneva, NY 14456–1559
(315) 789–6111
Fax: (315) 789–3020

8011

Business Information: Geneva Medical Group, L.L.P. is a group medical practice consisting of four OB/GYN physicians, one gynecologist, six pediatricians, and seven internists. The Practice is affiliated with Upstate Medical School and the University of Rochester Medical School, as well as Geneva General and F.F. Thompson hospitals. The practice is also associated with Soldiers & Sailors Hospital. A practicing physician since 1969 and Board–Certified in Obstetrics and Gynecology, Dr. Dickson oversees all administrative operations for associates and a support staff of 85, in addition to his daily patient practice in obstetrics and gynecology. **Career Steps:** President, Geneva Medical Associates (1975–Present). **Associations & Accomplishments:** Buffalo OB/GYN Society; Norman Miles Society; Robert Wilson Society; American Association of OB/GYN. **Education:** Wayne State University, M.D. (1969); University of Michigan, B.S. (1968). **Personal:** Married to Joan in 1968. Two children: Alison and Andrew. Dr. Dickson enjoys astronomy, water skiing, and travel.

Eduardo A. Dijamco, M.D.
Cardiologist
Vineland Medical Associates
1100 East Chestnut Avenue
Vineland, NJ 08360–5002
(609) 696–0108
Fax: (609) 691–1106

8011

Business Information: Vineland Medical Associates is a private physician group practice, providing general medical diagnosis and treatment to patients. A practicing physician since 1980 and a Cardiologist, Dr. Dijamco joined Vineland Medical Associates as Cardiologist in 1987. His practice specializes in the diagnosis and treatment of patients suffering from heart problems, as well as conducting surgery to place pacemakers and catheters. Concurrent with his private medical practice, he is affiliated with Newcomb Hospital and South Jersey Hospital. **Career Steps:** Cardiologist, Vineland Medical Associates (1987–Present); Fellow, St. Francis Medical Center (1985–1987); Resident, Atlantic City Medical Center (1982–1985). **Associations & Accomplishments:** Cumberland County Medical Society. **Education:** U.E.R.M.M.M.C., M.D. (1980); St. Joseph's University, B.S. in Biology (1974). **Personal:** Married to Neolita in 1980. Two children: Manuel and Jonathan. Dr. Dijamco enjoys golf and basketball.

J. Crawford Dobson, M.D.
Orthopaedic Surgeon
Dr. J. Crawford Dobson
471 Burke Street
Timmins, Ontario P4N 7A7
(705) 268–7344
Fax: (705) 268–6743

8011

Business Information: Dr. Dobson has been in private practice as an Orthopaedic Surgeon since 1990. He is also Medical Director of the surgical program at Timmins Hospital and District Hospital, and runs a sports clinic where he is Chief of Surgery. As the Medical Director at the Hospitals, he is responsible for the surgery floor, OR area, all surgeons, anesthesiologists, OB/GYN physicians, nurses, paramedics, and all other personnel. He handles all program direction and physician disputes. **Career Steps:** Orthopaedic Surgeon, Dr. J. Crawford Dobson (1990–Present); Timmins and District Hospital: Medical Director of Surgical Program (1995–Present), Chief of Surgery (1993–Present); Clinical Teacher, Queen University – Department of Family Medicine (1992–Present). **Associations & Accomplishments:** Porcupine District Medical Society: Former President, Former Vice President; Ontario Medical Association; Canadian Medical Association; Ontario Orthopaedic Association; Florida West Arthroscopy Association. **Education:** University of Ottawa: FRCS(c) in Orthopaedic Surgery (1989), Sports Medicine Fellowship (1990); University of Western Ontario, M.D. (1984); American Board of Orthopaedic Surgery Certified (1995). **Personal:** Two children: Christopher Marshal and William Crawford. Dr. Dobson enjoys golf and hockey.

T. Anthony Don Michael, MD, PhD, FACC, FACP, FRCP
• • • ━━◆◉◆━━ • • •

Senior Managing Partner
Central Cardiology Medical Clinic
2110 Truxtun Avenue
Bakersfield, CA 93301
(805) 323–8384
Fax: (805) 323–7218

8011

Business Information: Dr. Don Michael has been a Clinical Professor of Medicine at the University of California in Los Angeles since 1982. As the Founder and Senior Partner of the Central Cardiology Medical Clinic, one of the larger cardiology clinics in Southern California, he directs the activities of the clinic with eight cardiologists and a support staff of 42. A highly–esteemed cardiologist, he is affiliated with major hospitals and universities throughout California, as well as a recruiter of the majority of the cardiologists into the Central Valley. Dr. Don Michael has published 150 publications and has 14 inventions to his name, including: Angioplasty Catheter with a Second Balloon – for carotid angioplasty, protected; Regional Perfusion Catheter – a similar device for treatment of acute myocardial infarction involving the catheter for controlling the biological environment between two balloons; Mini–Environment Catheter – treating the patients locally with biological substances, including drugs; A device for dissolution of clots between two balloon catheters with the means of providing blood supply to the organ; HIV Resistant Kiss of Life Mask – HIV resistant mask while doing CPR, the first and only one in the world; Emboli Removal Catheter – for the prevention of clots thrown into the brain during angioplasty or ultrasonic ablation; and the Ultrasonic Ablation Catheter – which is a coreometer, opening totally obstructive arteries in the heart and in peripheral arteries. He has also invented a language of the heart called, "cardiophonics," which translates heart sounds into phonics. A native of Sri Lanka, where he served his internship in Forensic Medicine, Dr. Don Michael is now serving as an Honorary Consul for California on behalf of Sri Lanka, as well as providing medical treatment to prominent persons from the State Department, in a totally honorary capacity, including a multitude of prime ministers and presidents from his own country, among ordinary persons. He has also extended himself as a philanthropist, teacher, and writer. **Career Steps:** President, Central Cardiology Medical Clinic (1973–Present); University of California–Los Angeles: Clinical Professor of Medicine (1982–Present), Clinical Associate Professor of Medicine (1974–1982); Clinical Professor of Clinical Sciences, California State University–Bakersfield (1986–Present); Academic Director, Cardiac Interventional Center–Bakersfield (1987–Present); Director of Education and Research, Central California Heart Institute–Bakersfield (1989–1992); Director of Cardiology, Kern Medical Center (private practice) (1973–1974); Director of Cardiology and Chair of Department of Internal Medicine, Kern General Hospital (1972–1973); Fellow and Staff in Cardiology, Cedars–Sinai Medical Center (1971–1972); Fellow in Cardiology–Cleveland Clinic, Educational Foundation Cardiac Lab (1970–1971); Professor of Medicine, University of Gundishpoor, Iran (1965–1970); Chief of Internal Medicine, Abadan, Iran (1963–1965). **Associations & Accomplishments:** British Medical Association; Ceylon Medical Association; Royal Society of Medicine; Postgraduate Medical Association; Fellow, Royal College of Physicians – London; Royal College of Physicians – Edinburgh; Fellow, American College of Cardiology; International Society of Internal Medicine; Fellow, American College of Physicians; American Society of Ultrasound; American Society for Geriatrics; California Society Internal Medicine; Fellow, American College of Chest Physicians; National and International Committee Member, American Heart Association CPR Committee; Panelist, Emergency Airway Control – National Academy of Scientists; Vidyajothi (1990) – equivalent to Knighthood, Government of Sri Lanka; 1992 Who's Who Award as American Inventor of the Year; Who's Who of Global Business Leaders; Fellow, Clinical Council of the American Heart Association; BOARD CERTIFICATIONS: Diplomate, American Boards of Internal Medicine; Diplomate, Subspeciality Board Cardiovascular Diseases; MRCP, Member of Royal College of Physicians–London (equivalent to Diplomate Internal Medicine); MRCP, Member of Royal College of Physicians–Edinburgh (equivalent to Diplomate Cardiology). **Education:** University of Ceylon: MBBS with honors/distinctions in Medicine and Forensic Medicine (1957), M.D. (1957), B.S. in Physics, Biology and Chemistry (1951); INTERNSHIP: University of Ceylon, Lady Ridgeway Hospital and General Hospital, Colombo, Ceylon (1957–1958); Clinical Assistant Kings College Hospital (1958); RESIDENCIES: Registrar, St. Stephen's Hospital–University of London Cardiac Department (1958–1961); Registrar, St. George's Hospital, University of London Cardiac Department (1961–1962); Registrar, London Hospital, University of London (1962–1963). **Personal:** Dr. Don Michael enjoys ballroom dancing, lecturing, and travel. He is an accomplished vocalist, and enjoys performining in operas.

Joseph C. Dougherty, M.D.

Vice President/Physician
Valley Diagnostic Clinic
2200 Haine Drive
Harlingen, TX 78552
(210) 421–5016
Fax: Please mail or call

8011

Business Information: Valley Diagnostic Clinic is a full–service health care facility specializing in the diagnosis, and treatment of patients (outpatient clinic). Established in 1954, Valley Diagnostic Clinic presently employs 120 people and has an estimated annual revenue in excess of $12 million. In his current capacity, Dr. Dougherty is responsible for all aspects of operations for the Clinic. **Career Steps:** Vice President/Physician, Valley Diagnostic Clinic. **Associations & Accomplishments:** President, Texas Society of Internal Medicine (1994); Chairman of the Council of Medical Education, Texas Medical Association (1994); Published 25 scientific articles. **Education:** Cornell University Medical School, M.D. (1960). **Personal:** Married since 1959 to Katherine. Four children: William R., Suzanne V., Timothy J., and Laura E. Dr. Dougherty enjoys art collection in his leisure time.

James T. Dove, M.D.

President
Prairie Cardiovascular Consultants, Ltd.
301 North 8th Street, Suite 3B 301
Springfield, IL 62794–9420
(217) 788–0706
Fax: (217) 525–2535

8011

Business Information: Prairie Cardiovascular Consultants, Ltd. is a private practice of doctors in the field of cardiology. Located next to St. John's Hospital, they treat over 15,000 patients a year, handling all areas of cardiology. A practicing physician since 1965 and a Board–Certified Cardiologist, Dr. Dove joined Prairie Cardiovascular Consultants, Ltd. as President in 1973. He is responsible for the oversight of all patient care, consultation, diagnostic study, administration, and one–on–one teaching for residents. **Career Steps:** President, Prairie Cardiovascular Consultants, Ltd. (1973–Present); Southern Illinois University School of Medicine: Clinical Professor of Medicine and Chief of the Division of Cardiology (1990–Present), Clinical Associate Professor of Medicine (1976–1990), Clinical Assistant Professor (1973–1976); Instructor in Medicine, University of Rochester School of Medicine (1971–1973); Assistant in Medicine, Mt. Sinai School of Medicine (1966–1969); St. Johns Hospital: Administrative Director of Cardiovascular Services (1984–Present), President of Medical Staff (1988–1989), President–Elect of Medical Staff (1986–1987), Department of Cardiology Chairman (1982–1984, 1977–1979); Sangamon County Heart Association: President (1976–1977), Vice President (1975–1976). **Associations & Accomplishments:** American College of Physicians: Fellow, Governor–Elect Downstate Illinois (1987–1988), Governor Downstate Illinois (1988–1992), Governor's Financial Advisory Committee (1988–1989), Governor's Regional Meeting and Chapter Advisory Committee (1989–Present); Fellow, American Heart Association Council on Clinical Cardiology; American College of Cardiology: Fellow, Councilor of Illinois Chapter (1991–Present), Chairman of Government Relations Committee – Illinois Chapter (1991–1994), Chairman of Membership Committee – Illinois Chapter (1994–Present), Governor and President–Elect – State of Illinois (1996–1997); Fellow, American College of Chest Physicians; Fellow, American Society of Cardiovascular Interventionists; American Heart Association; American Medical Association; Sangamon County Medical Society; Illinois Heart Association: Fund Raising Council (1977–1978), Board of Directors (1977–1983), Research and Review Committee (1977–1978); International Who's Who in Medicine, Second Edition (1994); Sterling Who's Who, Executive Edition (1994); AWARDS: Mead Johnson Award for Graduate Training in Internal Medicine (1968–1969) and Laureate Award (1992) by American College of Physicians; Research Interests: Acute Myocardial Dysfunctions and Thrombolytic Therapy; Frequent lecturer at local, national, and state medical associations and symposia. **Education:** Case–Western Reserve University, M.D. (1965); Wittenberg University, B.A. in Chemistry cum laude (1961); Mt. Sanai Hospital: Intern (1965–1966), Residency (1966–1968), Chief Resident (1968–1969); USPHS, Georgetown University Military, Lt. Cmdr. (1969–1971); University of Rochester, Cardiology Trainee (1971–1973); Certification: National Board of Medical Examiners Part I, II, and III (1966); Diplomate, American Board of Internal Medicine (1971); Diplomate, American Board of Cardiovascular Diseases (1975). **Personal:** Married to Carol in 1960. Two children: Laura and Steven. Dr. Dove enjoys hunting, fishing, and travel.

Mary Anne Doyle–Hirschenbein, R.N.

Administrator
Personal Physicians
1685 East Main Street, Suite 202
El Cajon, CA 92021
(619) 579–8681
Fax: (619) 579–0759

8011

Business Information: Personal Physicians, a subsidiary of Neil W. Hirschenbein, M.D. a Medical Corporation, is a multi–specialty, primary care physician group practice, providing diagnosis and treatment to patients. With thirty–four years expertise in the health care field and a Registered Nurse since 1961, Mrs. Doyle–Hirschenbein joined Personal Physicians as Administrator in 1994. She oversees all administrative operations of associates and a support staff of 23, in addition to identifying and responding to the needs of affiliate physicians. This has included establishing a medical assistant pool; developing a nurse–practitioner recruiting and retention program, and identifying offices as preceptor sites; implementing a physician recruitment and retention program; and generating a physician marketing and development plan. **Career Steps:** Administrator, Personal Physicians (1994–Present); Director of Network's Physician Development, UCSD (1993–1994); Administrator, Neil W. Hirschenbein, M.D. (1993); Director of Marketing – ORNDA, Harbor View Medical Center (1992–1993); Associate Administrator, Valley Medical Center (1989–1992); Director of Physician Services, Mission Bay Hospital (1989); Director of Marketing, Harbor View Medical Center (1986–1989); Director of Marketing and Sales, Western Mood and Sleep Disorders Institute, Inc. (1986); Coordinator, South Coast Physician's Group, Harbor View Medical Center (1985–1986); Director of Marketing, Harbor View Medical Center (1983–1986); Director of Marketing Services, California Health Plan (1982); Head Nurse, Main Street Emergency Center (1981–1982); Head Nurse – Back Office Manager, Whitelock – Williams Medical Group (1980–1982). **Associations & Accomplishments:** National Association of Female Executives; National Charity League; San Diego Society for Hospital Marketing and Public Relations; Executive Board – Secretary, Preferred Provider Organization for Plastic Surgery; Executive Committee, Women's Opportunity Week (1988); Greater San Diego Chamber of Commerce, Small Business Committee; Central City Association, Marketing Committee; Advisory Board, Downtown Marketing Study. **Education:** Mercy College of Nursing, R.N. (1961); University of San Diego (1961); San Bernardino Valley College (1958); Certified Nurse Specialist Substance Abuse Nursing: Part 1 (Sept. 1987), Part 2 (Dec. 1987). **Personal:** Married to Neil W. Hirschenbein, M.D. in 1992. Three children: Sean Patrick, Colleen, and Megan. Mrs. Doyle–Hirschenbein enjoys power walking, weight lifting, skiing, and bicycling.

Dr. Christiaan Dreyer

Physician
Medical Office of Dr. Christiaan Dreyer
P.O. Box 97
Emerson, Manitoba R0A 0L0
(204) 373–2504
Fax: Please mail or call

8011

Business Information: Medical Office of Dr. Christiaan Dreyer is located in Emerson, Canada. Established in 1994, it is a full–service family medical practice. Choosing to be a family physician because he didn't want to specialize in any one area, Dr. Dreyer is responsible for all aspects of the medical office, including administrative and financial duties, as well as public relations and strategic planning. Concurrent with the duties of his private practice, Dr. Dreyer is the Chief of Staff for all the physicians within his Health District. **Career Steps:** Physician, Medical Office of Dr. Christiaan Dreyer (1994–Present); Anesthetist/Emergency Medical Officer, Thompson General Hospital (1993–1994); Anesthetist, Self Employed (1992–1993); General Practitioner, Self Employed (1989–1992). **Associations & Accomplishments:** Canadian Medical Association. **Education:** University of Pretoria, M.B.C.H.B. (1984); College of Medicine, South Africa, Diploma in Anesthesiology (1993). **Personal:** Married to Ronel in 1985. Five children: Geral, Christel, Tiaan, Nicolaas, and Etienne. Dr. Dreyer enjoys playing the piano, Christian religious activities, and is a distributor in an International Network Marketing business.

Rafael Ducos, M.D.

Physician
Ochsner Clinic of New Orleans
1514 Jefferson Highway
New Orleans, LA 70121–2429
(504) 842–5200
Fax: (504) 842–3676

8011

Business Information: The Ochsner Clinic of New Orleans specializes in the care and treatment of pediatric patients with cancer and blood disorders. Specializing in Pediatric Oncology and Hematology, Dr. Ducos established his private practice in 1988. He attends to patients suffering from blood disorders such as Anemia, and provides chemotherapy for children fighting cancer. Dr. Ducos was also on the Board of Directors for the Ronald MacDonald House in its opening years, and received "The Loving Award" in 1994. **Career Steps:** Physician, Ochsner Clinic of New Orleans (1988–Present); Director, Division of Pediatrics, Hematology, and Oncology, Louisiana State University (1976–1988); Instructor in Pediatrics, Washington University – St. Louis (1974–1976). **Associations & Accomplishments:** American Society of Hematology; American Society of Clinical Oncology; Pediatric Oncology Group. **Education:** University of Chile, M.D. (1961). **Personal:** Married to Lilian in 1961. Two children: Luis and Consuelo.

William Henry Dufendock, B.S., M.D.

Physician
Office of William Henry Dufendock, B.S., M.D.
909 Main Street
Genoa, OH 43430
Fax: Please mail or call

8011

Business Information: Office of William Henry Dufendock, B.S., M.D. is a private, general medicine practice. As Physician, Dr. Dufendock established his practice in 1939 and provided patient care for over 50 years. He retired in 1990. **Career Steps:** Physician, Office of William Henry Dufendock, B.S., M.D. (1939–Present). **Associations & Accomplishments:** Alpha Omega Alpha Honorary Medical Society; Honorary Member, St. Charles Hospital, Oregon, Ohio, Staff Medical Honorary. **Education:** University of Louisville Medical College, M.D. (1938); University of Toledo, B.S. (1935). **Personal:** Three children: William Charles, Jon Phillip, and Kay Ann (Deceased). Dr. Dufendock enjoys reading, history, photography, medicine and travel.

Navneet W. Dullet, M.D.

Cardiologist
Kaiser Permanente
411 North Lakeview Avenue
Anaheim, CA 92807
(213) 667–5850
Fax: (213) 667–8974

8011

Business Information: Kaiser Permanente is a leading Health Maintenance Organization (HMO), providing complete medical, surgical, and psychiatric services to its members throughout the U.S. As Cardiologist, Dr. Dullet specializes in the diagnosis and treatment of patients suffering from cardiac problems. **Career Steps:** Cardiologist, Kaiser Permanente (1989–Present). **Associations & Accomplishments:** American College of Cardiology; North American Society of Pacing and Electrophysiology. **Education:** University of California at San Francisco, Cardiac Electrophysiology Fellowship (1988); Board Certification in Cardiology, Cardiac Electrophysiology, Internal Medicine. **Personal:** Married to Sukajit in 1981. Two children: Suneet and Navjit. Dr. Dullet enjoys dancing.

Michael M.H. Duong, M.D.

President
Westmount Cosmetic and Laser Dermatology Clinic
5025 West Sherbrooke Street, Suite 320
Montreal, Quebec H4A 1S9
(514) 488–4873
Fax: (514) 488–4873

8011

Business Information: Dr. Duong established his private dermatology practice, Westmount Cosmetic and Laser Dermatology Clinic, in 1984. He is responsible for patient care, office administration, and supervision of support staff. In addition, he is a practicing dermatologist at both Saint Mary's Hospital and Montreal Chinese Hospital. **Career Steps:** President, Westmount Cosmetic and Laser Dermatology Clinic (1984–Present); Dermatologist, Saint Mary's Hospital (1984–Present); Dermatologist, Montreal Chinese Hospital (1985–Present). **Associations & Accomplishments:** Quebec Medical Association; Canadian Medical Association; Quebec College of Physicians; Quebec Association of Dermatologists; Published in Canadian Medical Journal; Active member of New York Academy of Sciences. **Education:** University of Montreal, Board of Dermatology (1984); McGill University, Montreal, American Board of Family Practice; University of Saigon, Vietnam, M.D. (1975). **Personal:** Married to Lienchi Tonnu, M.D. in 1975. Two children: Christina and Silvia. Dr. Duong enjoys music, tennis, reading, and travel.

William T. Durkin, Jr., M.D., FACEP

Emergency Physician
William T. Durkin, Jr., M.D., Inc.
P.O. Box 3880
Rancho Santa Fe, CA 92067
(619) 756–1259
Fax: Please mail or call

8011

Business Information: William T. Durkin, Jr., M.D., Inc., established in 1992, is a medical practice specializing in emergency medicine consulting and quality assurance. As Emergency Physician, Dr. Durkin serves as a consultant in emergency medicine and an expert medical witness. He is affiliated with Sharp–Cabrillo Hospital, Hemet Valley Hospital System and Villa View Hospital. **Career Steps:** Emergency Physician, William T. Durkin, Jr., M.D., Inc. (1992–Present); Emergency Physician, Sharp–Cabrillo Hospital (1995–Present); Emergency Physician, El Centro Regional Medical Center (1994–1995); Emergency Physician, Villa View Hospital (1993–Present); Emergency Physician, Paradise Valley Hospital (1987–1993); Lieutenant Commander, U.S. Navy (1984–1987). **Associations & Accomplishments:** American Medical Association; Fellow, American College of Emergency Physicians; Fellow, American Academy of Emergency Medicine; New York Academy of Sciences; San Diego Zoological Society; Conducted workshops; Diplomate, American Board of Emergency Medicine; Vice President, Co–founder of AccuQual/Super Doc Systems, Inc. **Education:** Resident Physician, Harvard Surgical Service, New England Deaconess Hospital, Boston, MA (1981–1983); Intern, Georgetown University Medical Center (1980–1981); Georgetown University, M.D. (1980); Georgetown University, B.S. (1975). **Personal:** Married to Patricia Karen Sung in 1994. Dr. Durkin enjoys sailing, skiing, traveling, gardening and tennis.

Ahmad Ellini, M.D.

President and Pediatrics Physician
Annandale Pediatric Associates Ltd.
7501 Little River Turnpike #202
Annandale, VA 22003–2923
(703) 256–7200
Fax: Please mail or call

8011

Business Information: Annandale Pediatric Association Ltd. is a pediatric practice consisting of one full–time and two part–time pediatricians, providing diagnosis and treatment to children. A practicing physician since 1970 and a Board–Certified Pediatrician, Dr. Ellini joined Annandale Pediatric Associates in 1990. Appointed as President in 1995, he oversees administrative operations for associates and a support staff of eleven, in addition to his daily patient practice. Dr. Ellini also is affiliated with Fairfax and Alexandria hospitals. **Career Steps:** Annandale Pediatric Associates Ltd.: President (1995–Present), Pediatrician (1990–1996); Pediatrics Associate, Prinius Clinic (PHP) (1987–1995). **Associations & Accomplishments:** American Academy of Pediatrics; Virginia Medical Society; Northern Virginia Pediatric Society; Fairfax Medical Society. **Education:** Tehran Medical School, M.D. (1970). **Personal:** Married to Parvin in 1967. Three children: Parisa, Ahmad Reza, and Arash. Dr. Ellini enjoys swimming, reading, and travel.

Leslie Ellison, C.M.M.

Practice Administrator
Columbia Gastroenterology Associates
2739 Laurel Street, Suite 1–A
Columbia, SC 29204–2028
(803) 799–4800
Fax: (803) 252–0052

8011

Business Information: Columbia Gastroenterology Associates is a full–service, specialized physician group practice and ambulatory surgical center, providing diagnosis, treatment, and ambulatory surgical services to patients suffering from gastroenterologic complaints. A Certified Medical Manager with over ten years expertise, Leslie Ellison serves as CGA's Practice Administrator. She is primarily responsible for the administration and oversight of all office and administrative functions of the seven–physician practice and ambulatory surgical center. **Career Steps:** Practice Administrator, Columbia Gastroenterology Associates (1995–Present); Office Manager, S. Clay Miller, M.D. (1993–1995); Medical Director – Medical Division, Columbia Health Care (1990–1993); Office Manager, South Carolina Cardiovascular Associates (1983–1988). **Associations & Accomplishments:** Certified Medical Manager; Professional Association of Health Care Office Managers; Medical Group Management Association; American Academy of Procedural Coders; Board of Directors, South Carolina Medical Management Association. **Education:** Midlands Technical College, currently working toward B.S. degree. **Personal:** Married to Douglas E. in 1983. Two children: Brittany and Andrew. Ms. Ellison enjoys reading and tennis.

Anne C. Epstein, M.D.

Internal Medicine Practitioner
–Independent–
3502 9th Street, Suite 360
Lubbock, TX 79415
(806) 743–2885
Fax: (806) 743–1579

8011

Business Information: Dr. Epstein became a sole practitioner in 1995, leaving her position as Associate Professor at Texas Tech University's Health Science Center to pursue an interest in internal medicine. Her current practice focuses specifically on chronic fatigue syndrome, complex and difficult diagnoses, primary care, and consultation. **Career Steps:** Private Internal Medicine Practitioner (1995–Present); Associate Professor, Texas Tech University Health Science Center (1985–1994). **Associations & Accomplishments:** Senior Professor, Medical School Association; American College of Physicians. **Education:** Baylor College of Medicine, M.D. (1981); University of Texas at Austin, B.A. (1977). **Personal:** Married to Dr. Howard J. Curzer in 1981. One child: Mirah Epstein Curzer. Dr. Epstein enjoys the study of medical ethics.

T. Horace Estes, M.D.

Physician
Women's Care
1 Medical Park Drive, Suite 1C
Chester, SC 29706
(803) 581–5100
Fax: (803) 581–5102

8011

Business Information: A Practicing Physician since 1965, Dr. Estes established the Women's Care obstetrics and gynecology clinic in 1992. He is responsible for patient care, office administration, and supervision of support staff. **Career Steps:** Physician, Women's Care (1992–Present); Physician, Carolina Women's Center (1983–1992); Physician, OB–GYN Associates P.C. (1972–1983); Physician, U.S. Army (1969–1972). **Associations & Accomplishments:** South Carolina Obstetrical and Gynecological Society; Rotary; American Society of Reproductive Medicine; The Retired Officers Association; Society of Laparoscopic Surgeons; American Associates of Gynecological Laparoscopy; American Medical Association; Southern Medical Association. **Education:** University of Tennessee, M.D. (1965); Vanderbilt University, B.A. **Personal:** Married to Patricia in 1966. Three children: Eric, Gregory, and Sean.

Walter H. Eversmeyer, M.D.

Chair – Department of Medicine
Browne McHardy Clinic
4315 Houma Boulevard
Metairie, LA 70006
(504) 889–5357
Fax: (504) 889–5408

8011

Business Information: Browne McHardy Clinic, the second largest clinic in Louisiana, is a clinical medical practice consisting of 75 physicians. The Practice is limited to just rheumatology. Joining the Browne McHardy Clinic in 1978, after serving a year on the faculty at LSUMC, Dr. Eversmeyer serves as Chair of the Department of Medicine. He is a Board–Certified Rheumatologist, responsible for providing quality health care to patients suffering from painful conditions of the joints and muscles. **Career Steps:** Chair – Department of Medicine, Browne McHardy Clinic (1991–Present) **Associations & Accomplishments:** Fellow, American College of Rheumatology; American College of Physicians; Secretary, Arthritis Foundation – New Orleans; Louisiana Medical Society; Jefferson Parish Medical Society; American Congress of Rehabilitation. **Education:** University of Mississippi, M.D. (1970) **Personal:** Married to Pam in 1967. Three children: Jenny, Katie and Melissa. Dr. Eversmeyer enjoys golf, reading, and music during his leisure time.

Dr. Marita M. Fallorina, M.D.

Pediatrician and Family Practice
Dr. Marita Fallorina, M.D.
1 Catherine Street, Route 273
New Castle, DE 19720
(302) 322–6847
Fax: (302) 322–6909

8011

Business Information: Dr. Marita Fallorina, M.D. is a pediatrics and general practice where Dr. Fallorina is the primary physician. The practice currently employs 4 people and has been established for 18 years. **Career Steps:** Dr. Fallorina has been a self–employed physician for 19 years. Dr. Fallorina has also worked part–time at St. Francis Hospital for the past 19 years, and worked at public health clinics during her first two years in Delaware. **Associations & Accomplishments:** Member, William Newcastle Pediatric Association. **Education:** Manila Central University, Doctor of Medicine degree (1965); Internship at St. Barnabas Medical Center; Residency in Pediatrics, Harrisburg Hospital, St. Barnabas Medical Center. **Personal:** Five children: Jessmar, Marie Chona, Victor, Katherine and Don Felix. Dr. Fallorina enjoys ballroom dancing and karate.

Nadir R. Farid, MBBS

Professor of Medicine
Nadir R. Farid, MBBS, FRCP(Lon), FRCP(c), FACP
157 Grand Avenue West
Chatham, Ontario N7L 1B9
(519) 351–3397
Fax: (519) 351–8680

8011

Business Information: Nadir R. Farid, MBBS, FRCP(Lon), FRCP(c), FACP specializes in consulting in molecular endocrinology, genetics, metabolism, and internal medicine. Along with private practice of medicine, Dr. Farid is affiliated with two major hospitals, St. Joseph's and Public General Hospital. **Career Steps:** Professor of Medicine, Nadir R. Farid, MBBS, FRCP(Lon), FRCP(c), FACP (1995–Present). **Associations & Accomplishments:** American Association for the Advancement of Science; American College of Physicians; American Federation for Clinical Research; American Thyroid Association; American Society of Clinical Investigation; Canadian Medical Association; Canadian Society of Immunology; Canadian Society of Clinical Investigation; Canadian Society of Endrocrinology and Metabolism; Endocrine Society; New York Academy of Sciences; Newfoundland Medical Association; Ontario Medical Association; Royal College of Physicians, London; Royal College of Physicians and Surgeons, Canada; Sigma Xi; Grants Committee, Canadian Diabetic Association; Study Section Special Reviewer, NIH, Bethesda; MRC Fellowship Committee; Reviewer Panel, Arizona Health Commission; Advisory Committee on Endocrinology, U.S. Pharmacopoeia; American Thyroid Development Committee; Men and Women of Science in America; Who is Who in the World; International Who's Who of Contemporary Achievement; 5000 Personalities of the World; Faculty of Medicine Representative, American Federation for Clinical Research, Eastern Section; Councillor, Canadian Society for Clinical Investigation; Councillor, Canadian Society of Endocrinology and Metabolism; Frequent publisher/lecturer at international, national, state, and local conferences and institution symposia and proceedings. **Education:** Comboni College (1956–1960); University of Khartoum Medical School, M.B.B.S. (1961–1967); Degrees: M.R.C.P. (U.K.) (1971), F.R.C.P.(C) (1973); Qualifications: F.A.C.P. (1981), F.R.C.P.(Lon.) (1989). **Personal:** Married to Behnaz Shahedian in 1996. Two children: Claire Inger and Emma Louise (children are 24 and 22 years old from a previous marriage).

Bruce A. Feldman, M.D.

President
Feldman Oringher Otolaryngology, P.C.
1145 19th Street Northwest, Suite 402
Washington, DC 20036–3701
(202) 884–2398
Fax: (301) 299–3892
8011

Business Information: Feldman Oringher Otolaryngology, P.C. is a private practice health care facility specializing in ear, nose and throat disorders which include: Pediatric and Adult Otolaryngology, Head and Neck Surgery, Otology, Endoscopic Sinus Surgery, Otolaryngic Allergy, Sleep Apnea and Snoring Surgery, Neurotology, Audiology, and Laser Surgery. Currently, the Practice employs six physicians and 28 medical support staff in its three satellite office locations (2–Washington, DC; 1–Chevy Chase, MD). As President and Physician, Dr. Feldman is responsible for the care and treatment of patients, as well as the administrative functions of the Practice. Board–certified in Otolaryngology since 1971, he is licensed to practice in the District of Columbia, Maryland and Pennsylvania — staff physician in afffiliation with five Washington, D.C.–metro hospitals. **Career Steps:** Feldman Oringher Otolaryngology, P.C.: President (1990–Present), Physician (1972–Present); LCDR, MC, USNR – Otolaryngologist, Naval Hospital, Camp Lejeune, NC (1970–1972); Clinical Professor of Surgery (Otolaryngology), Pediatrics, and Health Care Sciences, George Washington University School of Medicine. **Associations & Accomplishments:** American Board of Otolaryngology; Diplomat, National Board of Medical Examiners; Phi Beta Kappa; Mosby Scholarship Award; Alpha Omega Alpha; Mosher Award, The American Laryngological, Rhinological and Otological Society, Inc.; Children's Hospital Physicians Recognition Award for Distinguished Service; Who's Who in the East; Who's Who in American Jewry; Who's Who in the World; Top Doctors in Washington; The Best Doctors in America; American Medical Association; Fellow, American Academy of Otolaryngology; Centurions of the Deafness Research Foundation; Medical Society of the District of Columbia; President, Washington Metropolitan Ear, Nose and Throat Society; President, Jacobi Medical Society; Montgomery County Medical Society; Fellow, American College of Surgeons; Fellow, Charter Member, Society of Ear, Nose and Throat Advances in Children; Fellow, American Academy of Pediatrics – Section of Otolaryngology and Bronchoesophagology; President, Washington D.C. Graduate Club, Phi Delta Epsilon Medical Fraternity; American Laryngological, Rhinological, and Otological Society; Montgomery–Prince George's Pediatric Society; Prosper Menier's Society; American Sleep Disorder Society; National Hearing Association; American Neuro–Otologic Society; Pan–American Association of Otorhinolaryngology Head and Neck Surgery; American Academy of Otolaryngic Allergy; American Rhinological Association; Southern Medical Association; Over 17 Publications and Presentations for Medical Journals Symposia Proceedings. **Education:** Harvard Medical School, M.A., M.D. (1965); Dartmouth College: A.B. (1962), B. Med. Science (1963); Clinical Fellow in Otolaryngology (1969–1970); Hospital of the University of Pennsylvania: Internship (1965–1966), Residency (1966–1967); Massachusetts Eye and Ear Infirmary, Residency (1967–1970). **Personal:** Married to Sharon P. in 1966. Two children: Kathryn and Michael. Dr. Feldman enjoys golf, tennis, and travel.

Andrea Ferrara, M.D.

Surgeon
Colon and Rectal Clinic of Orlando
110 Underwood Street
Orlando, FL 32806–1112
(407) 422–3790
Fax: (407) 425–4358
8011

Business Information: Colon and Rectal Clinic of Orlando, established in 1965, is a surgical facility specializing in the diagnosis, treatment, and care of colon and rectal disease. As Surgeon, Mr. Ferrara's practice is limited to colon and rectal surgery, with special interests in the surgical treatment of inflammatory bowel disease, laparoscopic surgery, pelvic floor physiology, anorectal manometry, electromyography, biofeedback, and the treatment of incontinence and constipation. **Career Steps:** Surgeon, Colon and Rectal Clinic of Orlando (1992–Present). **Associations & Accomplishments:** American Board of Colon and Rectal Surgery; American Board of Surgery; American Medical Association (1984); Association for Academic Surgery (1985); Associate Fellow, American College of Surgeon (1990); Mayo Alumni Association (1992); The Priestly Society (1992); Florida Medical Association (1992); Orange County Medical Society (1992); Southern Medical Association (1993); American Society of Colon and Rectal Surgeons (1993); Frequent publisher and lecturer at international, national, state and local conferences and institutional symposia and proceedings. **Education:** University of Rome Medical School, M.D. (1979); Mayo Clinic, Fellow in Colon and Rectal Surgery (1990–1992); Yale Regional Surgical Program, Chief Resident in General Surgery (1989–1990); Departments of Surgery Yale University and Bridgeport Medical Center, Research Fellow (1988–1989); State University of New York – Brooklyn, New York, Resident in General Surgery (1985–1988); Department of Surgery State University of New York – Brooklyn, New York, Research Fellow (1983–1985); State University Hospital: Resident in General Surgery (1980–1983), Internship in General Surgery (1980). **Personal:** Married to Carla Bruschi in 1976. Three children: Marco, Luca Andrea, and Guilia Benedetta. Mr. Ferrara enjoys history, astronomy, collecting Roman coins, and classical music.

Jacqueline W. Fincher, M.D.

Physician
McDuffie Medical Associates
505 Mount Pleasant Road, P.O. Box 300
Thomson, GA 30824
(706) 595–1461
Fax: (706) 597–9824
8011

Business Information: McDuffie Medical Associates is a full–service, primary care practice medical office, providing diagnosis and treatment of patients. A practicing physician since 1988, Dr. Fincher joined McDuffie Medical Associates in 1988 as an Internal Medicine Physician. **Career Steps:** Physician, McDuffie Medical Associates (1988–Present). **Associations & Accomplishments:** President (1995), American Heart Association – Georgia Affiliate; Board Member, American Lung Association; Board Member, American Cancer Society; Charter Member, Leadership McDuffie; Public speaker on health related topics; Founder, McDuffie County Breast Cancer Support Group; Olympic Torchbearer for being a community hero. **Education:** Medical College of Georgia, Internal Medicine Residency (1988), M.D. (1985); Oral Roberts University, Biology (1981). **Personal:** Married to James L. Lenley, M.D. in 1987. One child: Laura. Dr. Fincher enjoys playing the piano, reading, and speaking.

Philip Fleishman, M.D.

Physician
East Islip Medical Associates, P.C.
45 Montauk Highway
East Islip, NY 11730–2502
(516) 581–0737
Fax: (516) 581–0729
8011

Business Information: Established in 1970, The East Islip Medical Associates, P.C. is a full–service, private practice medical organization. As Physician, Dr. Fleishman concentrates his practice in the area of Internal Medicine with a subspeciality in Diabetes. As such, he is reponsible for the care and treatment of patients. In practice for 28 years, Dr. Fleishman has been published several times and enjoys being a Doctor. **Career Steps:** Physician, East Islip Medical Associates, P.C. (1967–Present). **Personal:** Married to Anita in 1965. Three children: David, Beth and Rachael. Dr. Fleishman enjoys jogging and attending the theatre.

Theodore L. Folkerth, M.D.

Cardiovascular Surgeon
–Independent–
3998 Vista Way
Oceanside, CA 92056–4500
(619) 726–2500
Fax: (619) 632–0167
8011

Business Information: Dr. Theodore Folkerth, a Board–certified cardiovascular surgeon in California for the past eighteen years, provides private and referral care from his private medical practice in all areas of cardiac needs. Utilizing the latest technological advances in cardiovascular surgery, Dr. Folkerth performs such procedures as: coronary by–passes and heart valve replacements. **Career Steps:** Cardiovascular Surgeon, Theodore Folkerth, M.D. (1977–Present). **Associations & Accomplishments:** Society of Thoracic Surgeons; Western Thoracic Surgical Association. **Education:** Indiana University: M.D. (1965), M.S. in Biochemistry (1962); Earlham College, A.B. in Chemistry (1959). **Personal:** Married to Jean in 1995. Three children: Wesley, Elizabeth, and Geoffrey. Dr. Folkerth enjoys woodworking and breeding thoroughbred horses.

Pierre Forgacs, M.D.

Physician
Lahey–Hitchcock Medical Clinic
41 Mall Road
Burlington, MA 01805
(617) 273–8608
Fax: (617) 273–5243
8011

Business Information: Lahey–Hitchcock Medical Clinic is a private, large group medical practice and health service establishment specializing in Internal Medicine and Surgery. Currently, the Clinic employs 800 physicians and medical support staff. As Physician, Dr. Forgacs concentrates his practice in the area of infectious diseases. As such, he is responsible for the care and treatment of patients, as well as some clinical instruction and research. **Career Steps:** Physician, Lahey–Hitchcock Medical Clinic (1977–Present). **Associations & Accomplishments:** Infectious Diseases Society of America; American Society for Microbiology; Massachusetts Infectious Diseases Society; Published in medical journals. **Education:** University of Sherbrouke, M.D. (1971). **Personal:** Married.

Thomas J. Forlenza, M.D.

Physician
Thomas J. Forlenza, M.D.
29 Brenton Place
Staten Island, NY 10314
(718) 816–4949
Fax: (718) 273–5504
8011

Business Information: Thomas J. Forlenza, M.D. is in private medical practice, specializing in oncology and hematology. A practicing physician since 1977 and Board–Certified in Internal Medicine, Pathology, Hematology, and Oncology, Dr. Forlenza established his solo practice medical office in 1983. Concurrent with his private medical practice, he serves as Clinical Assistant Professor of Medicine at New York University; Assistant Attending Physician at Bellevue Hospital in New York; Faculty of the Physicians Assistance Training Program and Chief of Hematology and Oncology at Bayley Seton Hospital in Staten Island, New York; Clinical Affiliate Faculty at St. John's University – Wagner College at the College of Staten Island; and Member of the Teaching Faculty; Director of Oncology at St. Vincent's Medical Center of Richmond; and Medical Director of Pax Christi Hospice at St. Vincent's Medical Center – Bayley Seton Hospital. **Career Steps:** Private Practice Physician (1983–Present); Clinical Affiliate Faculty: St. John's University, Wagner College, College of State Island (1995–Present); Faculty for Physicians Assistance Training, Bayley Seton Hospital (1995–Present); Asst. Attending Physician, Bellevue Hospital (1989–Present); Clinical Faculty Member, St. Vincent's Medical Center (1983–Present); Director of Oncology, St. Vincent's Medical Center of Richmond (1988–Present); Medical Director, Pax Christi Hospice–St. Vincent's Medical Center–Bayley Seton Hospital (1988–Present); Chief of Hematology/Oncology, Bayley Seton Hospital (1994–Present); Associate Director of Oncology, Woodhull Medical Center (1983–1988); Medical Director–Blood Bank, Bayley Seton Hospital (1984–1987). **Associations & Accomplishments:** Diplomate, American Board of Internal Medicine (1981); Diplomate, Blood Banking – American Board of Pathology (1984); American Board of Internal Medicine: Diplomate in Hematology (1984), Diplomate in Oncology (1985); Fellow, American College of Physicians; Richmond County Medical Society; New York State Medical Society; Bell Society – St. Vincent's Medical Center of Richmond; Bayley Seton Society – Council of Hospital Blood Disorders of the Greater New York Region, Inc.; Cooley's Anemia Foundation – Staten Island Chapter; American Society of Hematology; American Medical Association; Board of Directors, National Cooley's Anemia Foundation; American Society of Clinical Oncology; Society for the Study of Blood; American Association Sovereign Military Order of Malta; Executive Committee, New York State Society of Medical Oncologists & Hematologists; Academy of Hospice Physicians; New York Metropolitan Breast Cancer Group; HONORS: Scholar – College in Psychology (1973); Hourglass Award – Cooley's Anemia Foundation (1986); Honoree – Sword of Hope Ball Am. Cancer Society St. Island Chapter (1988); Who's Who in the East; Honoree, Leukemia Society of America, Staten Island Unit (1995); Phi Beta Kappa (1973); Frequent lecturer and numerous papers presented at Medical Conference and Symposia Proceedings on his research in Leukemia, Breast Cancer and other cancer–related diseases; Author: "Malignant Lymphomas", "Renal Cell Carcinoma" and "Supportive Care of the Cancer Patient". **Education:** Boston University School of Medicine, M.D. (1977); Boston College, A.B. summa cum laude (1973); Internship: Straight Medicine – St. Vincent's Medical Center (1977–78); Residency: Internal Medicine – University of Kentucky at Lexington (1978–80); Fellowships: Clinical – Div. Hematology, New York University School of Medicine; Clinical – Div. Oncology, Downstate/Kings County Medical Center (1982–83); Research – Div. Hematology, New York University School of Medicine (1981–82); Blood Bank – Div. Pathology, New York University School of Medicine (1981–82). **Personal:** Married to Lucille Coniglione. Two children: Thomas Joseph, Jr. and Rebecca Suzanne. An accomplished musician, he studied piano at the Mannes College of Music. Dr. Forlenza is also fluent in French, Conversational

Spanish, and has reading knowledge of Greek, Latin, and Italian. Dr. Forlenza enjoys playing the piano (accompanying singers), going to the opera, reading non–medical books, and volunteering with the American Cancer Society. Lecture interests also include "Issues in the Final Phase of Life" and "Pain Management".

Earl Foster, M.D.

President of Medical Staff
Scott Orthopedic Center
2828 1st Avenue
Huntington, WV 25701
(304) 525–6905
Fax: (304) 525–9643
EMail: See Below

8011

Business Information: Scott Orthopedic Center is a private practice medical clinic with nine physicians specializing in orthopedics and two specializing in hands, of whom Dr. Foster is one. He is the Senior Partner in his own medical clinic, overseeing all administrative duties and support staff, as well as his daily patient load. Concurrently, he is the President of Medical Staff for Cabell Huntington Hospital. There he sees patients and sits on the Board. Internet users can reach him via: YUUB76A@prodigy.com. **Career Steps:** President of Medical Staff, Scott Orthopedic Center (1980–Present); Hand Fellow (1979–1980); Orthopedic Resident, Syracuse University (1975–1979). **Associations & Accomplishments:** American Academy of Orthopedic Surgery; American Society for Surgeons of the Hand; American Board of Orthopedics; Fellow, American College of Surgeons. **Education:** University of Iowa: M.D. (1974), B.S. in Science (1970). **Personal:** Married to Carol in 1975. Two children: Taryn Leigh and Kyle Brandon. Dr. Foster enjoys flying, running, mountain biking, and skiing.

Barbara Anne Foxwell, MB, BS, LRCP, MRCS

Physician
Dr. Barbara Foxwell, Ltd.
103–8843 204th Street
Langely, British Co V1M 2K4
(604) 882–9027
Fax: (604) 882–9028

8011

Business Information: Dr. Barbara Foxwell, Ltd. is a full service, family practice medical office, providing general medical care to patients of all ages. As Physician, Dr. Foxwell oversees all administrative operations for associates and support staff, in addition to her daily patient practice. Dr. Foxwell is also a staff member at Langley Memorial Hospital. **Career Steps:** Physician, Dr. Barbara Foxwell, Ltd. (1993–Present); Workers Compensation Board of British Columbia: Assistant Director – Rehabilitation Center (1991–1993), Senior Medical Advisor (1989–1991). **Associations & Accomplishments:** Director, Langley Stepping Stones Society for psychiatrically disabled adults; Director, Ishtar Transition House Society; Vice Chairman, Langley School District; Commissioner, Langley Parks and Recreation Commission; Co–Chair, Langley Stepping Stones Fundraising Campaign; Langley Memorial Hospital Board; Chairman, Community Health Education Committee; Provincial President, Social Credit Women's Auxiliary; Soroptomists International of the Langleys. **Education:** University of London, UK: LRCP, MRCS, M.B., B.S. (1965), B.Sc. first class honours in Anatomical Sciences (1963); LMCC, Canada (1966). **Personal:** Three children: Mark, Stephanie, and David. Dr. Foxwell enjoys reading, music, art, and needlework.

Timothy D. Francis, M.S., D.C., F.I.A.C.A., N.D.

Sole Practitioner
Tri–Chiropractic Kinesiology
3750 South Jones
Las Vegas, NV 89103
(702) 221–8870
Fax: (702) 367–7809

8011

Business Information: In private practice since 1985, Dr. Timothy D. Francis, M.S., D.C., F.I.A.C.A., N.D. is a Diplomate to the International Board of Applied Kinesiology and a Diplomate to the American Academy of Pain Management. As Sole Practitioner of Tri–Chiropractic Kinesiology, Dr. Francis specializes in research as well as the care and treatment of patients. Dr. Francis is also an Instructor for the International College of Applied Kinesiology responsible for teaching the 100–hour Kinesiology Certification Course. **Career Steps:** Physician, Tri–Chiropractic Kinesiology (1985–Present); Chairman, Syllabus Review Committee and Instructor, International College of Applied Kinesiology (1991–Present); Joint Study Participant, National Olympic Training Center, Beijing, China (1990); Adjunct Faculty Member, The Union Institute's College of Undergraduate Studies (1993); Los Angeles College of Chiropractic: Teaching Assistant, Department of Principles and Practice, Teaching Assistant, Department of Diagnosis and Full–time Faculty, Department of Principles and Practice (1983–1985); Professional Faculty, Department of Recreation and Physical Education, University of Nevada–Reno (1976–1980). **Associations & Accomplishments:** American Chiropractic Association; Nevada State Chiropractic Association; National Strength and Conditioning Association; ACA, Councils on Sports Injuries, Nutrition, Roentgenology, Technic and Mental Health; International College of Applied Kinesiology; International Chiropractic Association, Council of Chiropractic Pediatrics; Gonstead Clinical Studies Society; Foundation for Chiropractic Education and Research; National Institute of Chiropractic Research; National Academy of Research Biochemists; American Naturopathic Medical Association; Scholar of the Year, University of Nevada (1980); National Dean's List (1984); Who's Who in California; Who's Who in the West; Men of Achievement; Community Leaders of America; Five Thousand Personalities of the World; Who's Who Among Rising Young Americans; International Book of Honor; Biographical Institute's Medal of Honor; Recipient of the Golden State Award, Who's Who Historical Society; International Directory of Distinguished Leadership; Recipient of the Key Award; International Who's Who of Intellectuals; Man of the Year (1990); Dictionary of International Biography; International Cultural Diploma of the Year; Who's Who of Emerging Leaders in America; Personalities of America; Who's Who in the World; Who's Who Among Young American Professionals; Who's Who in Science and Engineering; Man of the Year, International Centre, England (1992); Personalities of America; Who's Who, The Elite Registry of Extraordinary Professionals; Who's Who in the Registry of Rising Young Americans; Dictionary of International Biography; American Biographical Institute, Lifetime Achievement Award; Two Thousand Notable American Men; Distinguished Men in Southern Nevada; U.S. Registry's Who's Who Among Outstanding Americans; Vice President and Scholar of the Year (1980), National Honor Society of Phi Kappa Phi. **Education:** British Institute of Homeopathy: Fellow (1994), Di. Hom. (1993); American Naturopathic Medical Certification and Accreditation Board, N.M.D. (1993); American Academy of Pain Management, D.A.A.P.M. (1990); International College of Applied Kinesiology, D.I.C.A.K. (1990); International Academy of Clinical Acupuncture, F.I.A.C.A. (1989); International College of Applied Kinesiology (1988); Clark County Community College, Certified E.M.T. (Present); University of Bridgeport, M.S. in Nutrition and Biology (1990); Los Angeles College of Chiropractic: D.C. magna cum laude (1984), B.S. (1982); Western Nevada Community College (1978). **Personal:** Dr. Francis enjoys karate.

Diane H. Freeman, M.D.

Partner
Arkansas Pediatric Clinic
500 South University Avenue #200
Little Rock, AR 72205–5304
(501) 664–4117
Fax: (501) 664–1137

8011

Business Information: Arkansas Pediatric Clinic is a full–service, general practice medical office, specializing in the diagnosis and treatment of children. The Practice consists of four other partners, Drs. Gil Buchanan, H. Frazier Kennedy, Thomas Smith, and Anthony Johnson. A practicing physician since 1985 and a Board–Certified Pediatrician, Dr. Freeman joined Arkansas Pediatric Clinic as Equal Partner and Pediatrican in 1991. Her practice consists of providing general pediatric care, as well as hospital care of children. Concurrent with her private medical practice, she serves as Co–Director of St. Vincent's Ready Care Clinic. **Career Steps:** Partner, Arkansas Pediatric Clinic (1991–Present); Co–Director, St. Vincent's Ready Care Clinic (1993–Present). **Associations & Accomplishments:** Board Certified, AAP; Central Arkansas Pediatric Society; Board Member, Junior Deputy Babe Ruth Booster Club; Board Member, Forest Park Elementary Parent Teachers Association; Girl Scout Leader for Brownie Troop; Delegate, Ouachita Girl Scout Council. **Education:** University of Texas – Houston Medical School, M.D. (1985); Texas A&M University, B.S. (1981). **Personal:** Married to Tom W. Freeman, M.D. in 1984. Three children: Aaron Kenneth, Shannon Helene, and Ryan Donald. Dr. Freeman enjoys activities with her children, reading, and crafts.

Robert I. Fulmer, M.D.

President
Robert I. Fulmer, M.D. & Associates
805 East 32nd Street, #203
Austin, TX 78705–2529
(512) 477–3322
Fax: (512) 477–2826

8011

Business Information: Robert I. Fulmer, M.D. & Associates is a gynecological medical facility. Dr. Fulmer established his private practice in 1976. As President, he is responsible for personnel decisions, administrative activities, and patient care. **Career Steps:** President, Robert I. Fulmer, M.D. & Associates (1971–Present); Medical Doctor, Gynecologist Associates (1972–1976); Major, Chief OB/GYN, Medical Corp U.S. Air Force (1970–72). **Associations & Accomplishments:** President–Elect, South Central OB/GYN Association; Austin Fertility Association; Austin College of OB/GYN – Austin OB/GYN South; Texas OB/GYN Society; American Medical Association; Travis County Medical Society. **Education:** Baylor University – College of Medicine: M.D. (1966), Master of Science (1963); Rice Institute, B.A. (1959). **Personal:** Married to Patricia Seidenberg Fulmer in 1995. Four children: Robert Paul Fulmer, Thomas Scott Fulmer, Michael Seidenberg, and Philip Seidenberg. Dr. Fulmer enjoys golf, photography, tennis, and skiing.

Gordon L. Fung, M.D., M.P.H.

Physician
Gordon L. Fung, M.D., M.P.H., Inc.
789 Vallejo Street
San Francisco, CA 94133–3834
(415) 982–6691
Fax: (415) 982–0914
EMAIL: See Below

8011

Business Information: Gordon L. Fung, M.D., M.P.H., Inc. is a cardiology consultation and clinical medical practice with two locations in San Francisco, providing diagnosis and treatment to patients suffering from cardiovascular problems. A practicing physician since 1979, a Board Certified Cardiologist and Critical Care specialist, Dr. Fung established his private practice in 1985. He oversees all administrative operations for associates and support staff, in addition to his daily patient practice. Internet users can reach him via: G7L12F6@mem.po.com. **Career Steps:** Physician, Gordan L. Fung, M.D., M.P.H., Inc. (1985–Present); QA/UR Chief, Chinese Hospital – San Francisco (1994–Present). **Associations & Accomplishments:** President Elect (1995–1996), American Heart Association California Affiliate; President (1992–Present), Ding Sum, Inc.; "Friends of ..." (1989–Present). **Education:** University of California – San Francisco School of Medicine, M.D. (1979); University of California – Berkeley School of Public Health: M.P.H. (1979), B.A. in Economics (1973); California Institute of Integral Studies, Ph.D. Candidate. **Personal:** Married to Peggy in 1980. Three children: Kelly Ann, Everett Paul, and Jana Marie. Dr. Fung enjoys composing and performing music.

Hosny S. Gabriel, M.D.

President
Huntington Anesthesiology Group
P.O. Box 528
Huntington, WV 25710–0528
(304) 526–1087 (304) 523–0169
Fax: (304) 523–1514

8011

Business Information: Huntington Anesthesiology Group provides services to St. Mary's Hospital & Huntington Hospital in West Virginia with ten anesthesiologists, thirty–five Certified Registered Nurses, and ten support personnel. As President, Dr. Gabriel is responsible for patient care, budget oversight, management of employee benefits, medical and support staff recruitment and hiring decisions. He is also a Professor of Clinical Anesthesiology at Marshall Medical School. **Career Steps:** President, Huntington Anesthesiology Group (1988–Present). **Associations & Accomplishments:** American Medical Association; American Society of Anesthesia; American Society of Pain Management; Cardio Vascular Anesthesia Society. **Education:** School of Medicine, M.D. (1968); American Board of Anesthesia (1988); American Academy of Pain Management (1990). **Personal:** Married to Aida A. in 1975. Two children: Alexandra and Michael. Dr. Gabriel enjoys swimming, soccer, gardening, boating, outdoor activities, and fishing.

Maria Galainena–Johnson

Area Vice President
Baxter Renal Therapy Services
1200 South Pine Island Road, Suite 200
Plantation, FL 33324
(954) 476–3721
Fax: (954) 723–7510
EMAIL: See Below

8011

Business Information: Renal Therapy Services, a new affiliate of Baxter Healthcare Corporation, manages and or acquires dialysis treatment centers in key foreign markets. Concentrating primarily in Europe, Latin America, and the Far East, the Company plans on aggressive growth for this newly formed division by providing physicians / dialysis centers with the tools to deliver improved patient care in the most cost effective manner. As Area Vice President, Ms. Galainena–Johnson oversees all aspects of the Latin American operation, and is responsible for budgets, customer bases, and client/doctor services. Internet users can reach her via: johnsome@baxter.com. **Career Steps:** Area Vice President, Baxter Renal Therapy Services (1995–Present), Director, Market Development, Baxter World Trade, Eastern Europe & The Mediterranean (1994–1995), Director, Business Development, Baxter World Trade, Latin America (1992–1994). **Associations & Accomplishments:** American Institute of Certified Public Accountants. **Education:** DePaul University Masters in Accounting (1985); Kellog/Northwestern University, M.B.A. in International Business Management (In Progress). **Personal:** One child: Eric. Ms. Galainena–Johnson enjoys snow skiing, white water rafting and scuba diving.

Leanne E. Gallison

Health Resources Manager
Pacific Medical Clinics
1200 12th Avenue South – Quarters 8–9
Seattle, WA 98144
(206) 621–4710
Fax: Please mail or call

8011

Business Information: Pacific Medical Clinics is a full–service, community and associated–based, health care facility serving 40,000 patients from six locations. The Clinic consists of 85 primary care physicians and 50 specialists, as well as providing a multi–cultural center and a translator program. As Health Resources Manager, Ms. Gallison is responsible for the operations of three areas of the clinic: referral authorization processes, case management, and data analysis. **Career Steps:** Health Resources Manager, Pacific Medical Clinics (1995–Present); Utilization Management Manager, Pacific Health Plans (1990–1995); Utilization Management Supervisor, Blue Cross of Washington and Alaska (1985–1989); Post Anesthesia Recovery Nurse, Swedish Hospital (1979–1984). **Education:** University of Washington, B.S. in Nursing. **Personal:** Married to Mark. Ms. Gallison enjoys spending time with her family, decorating her home, aerobics, and snow skiing.

John E. Gamboa, M.D.

Medical Director – Radiation Oncology
St. Alphonsus Cancer Treatment Center
1055 North Curtis Road
Boise, ID 83706–1309
(208) 378–3131
Fax: (208) 378–3174

8011

Business Information: St. Alphonsus Cancer Treatment Center is a private practice radiation oncology clinic. As Medical Director – Radiation Oncology, Dr. Gamboa is a Board Certified Radiation Oncologist treating both adult and pediatric cancer patients. **Career Steps:** Medical Director – Radiation Oncology, St. Alphonsus Cancer Treatment Center (1992–Present); Medical Director – Radiation Oncology, Southern Idaho Regional Cancer Center (1990–1992). **Associations & Accomplishments:** American Society for Therapeutic Radiology and Oncology; American College of Radiology; American College of Radiation Oncology; American Medical Association; Idaho Medical Association; Ada County Medical Society; Idaho Society of Clinical Oncologists; Clinical Assistant Professor, University of Washington; " The Best Doctors in America–Pacific Region" (1996–1997 edition). **Education:** University of Washington, Completed Residency in Radiation Oncology (1990); University of Utah, M.D. (1984); Creighton University, B.S. in Chemistry (1977); General Surgery Residency (1984–1986). **Personal:** Married to Susan C. Thackaberry in 1978. Three children: Christina, Joseph, and Nicholas. Dr. Gamboa enjoys snow skiing, running, weightlifting, and spending time with his family. Dr. Gamboa is of Basque nationality.

Andrew M. Garfinkle

Ophthalmologist
Cornwall
Suite 226, 820 McConnel Avenue
Cornwall, Ontario K6H 4M4
(613) 938–0868
Fax: (613) 930–2478

8011

Business Information: Cornwall specializes in cataract and refractive surgery. As Ophthalmologist, Dr. Garfinkle offers assistance to patients with general eye problems, cataracts, and those in need of refractive surgery. He is currently focusing his analytical efforts on cataract problems. **Career Steps:** Ophthalmologist, Cornwall (1989–Present); Assistant Professor, McGill University (1990–Present). **Associations & Accomplishments:** American Society of Cataract and Refractive Surgery; Canadian Society of Cataract and Refractive Surgery; Association for Research in Vision and Ophthalmology; Canadian Ophthalmology Society; American Academy of Ophthalmology; Society for Biomaterials. **Education:** University of Washington, M.D., Ph.D. (1984); McGill University, Specialty Training Ophthalmology (1989). **Personal:** Married to Dr. Irena Danys in 1979. One child: Nathalie. Dr. Garfinkle enjoys fishing, skiing, and travel.

Sylvia Garnis–Jones, MSC,MDCM,FRCP(C)

Dermatologist
Dr. Sylvia Garnis–Jones, MSC, MDCM, FRCP(C)
#1 Highway 20 East
Fonthill, Ontario L0S 1E0
(905) 892–8850
Fax: (905) 892–5578

8011

Business Information: Dr. Sylvia Garnis–Jones, MSC, MDCM, FRCP(C) runs a full–service dermatology clinic specializing in rejuvenation, psycho–cutaneous medicine and skin cancer. As a Dermatologist, Dr. Garnis–Jones oversees all administrative operations for associates and support staff, in addition to her daily patient practice. **Career Steps:** Dermatologist, Dr. Sylvia Garnis–Jones, MSC, MDCM, FRCP(C) (1995–Present); Director, Psycho–Dermatology Clinic, McMaster University (1995–Present); Ottawa University: Director, Psycho–Dermatology Clinic/Photo–Biology Clinic, Ottawa (1994–1995), Clinical Assistant Professor (1987–1995). **Associations & Accomplishments:** Association for Psycho–Cutaneous Medicine of North America: Treasurer and Newsletter Editor; President, Ottawa Branch – Federation of Medical Women of Canada; Fellow of the Royal College of Physicians and Surgeons of Ontario; Ontario Medical Association; Canadian Medical Association; Canadian Dermatology Association; Director of Melanoma Research Laboratory (1987–1992); recipient of several grants for Cancer Research; Rotary Club. **Education:** McGill University: M.D. (1980), M.Sc. (1976), B.Sc. (1974); Specialty Training in Dermatology (1982–1986); Boston University, Internship (1981–1982). **Personal:** Married to Dr. Barry Jones in 1974. Two children: Brendan and Saundra.

Alan Anthony Garvin, M.D.

Director of Nuclear Medicine and Stress Testing
Valley Heart Associates Medical Group
3600 Columbine Drive, #8
Modesto, CA 95356
(209) 577–5557
Fax: Please mail or call
E-mail: see below

8011

Business Information: Valley Heart Associates Medical Group is a medical facility specializing in the care and treatment of patients with cardiovascular disease. Established in 1970, Valley Heart Associates Medical Group currently employs 100 physicians and medical support staff. As Director of Nuclear Medicine and Stress Testing, Dr. Garvin is responsible for the oversight of the Nuclear Medicine Department, performs stress testing, and instructs medical residents. He can also be reached through the Internet as follows: TGarv@AOL.COM **Career Steps:** Director of Nuclear Medicine and Stress Testing, Valley Heart Associates Medical Group (1993–Present). **Associations & Accomplishments:** American Medical Association; American College of Physicians; American College of Cardiology; Society of Nuclear Medicine; Association of Black Cardiologists; American Society of Nuclear Cardiology. **Education:** University of California – Los Angeles, M.D. (1985); Los Angeles County – University of Southern California Medical Center, Internal Medicine Residency; University of Chicago, Cardiology Fellowship; Emory University, Nuclear Medicine Fellowship. **Personal:** Dr. Garvin enjoys playing the jazz trombone, snow skiing, photography and travel.

William H. George, M.D.

Staff Physician
Medical Arts Group
520 Cobb Street
Cadillac, MI 49601–2541
(616) 775–6521
Fax: Please mail or call

8011

Business Information: Medical Arts Group is a multi–specialty medical facility, consisting of eighteen physicians (3–surgeons, 2–pediatricians, 2–OB/GYN, 6–family practitioners, 1–oncologist, 4–internal medicine practitioners), serving the rural community of Cadillac, Michigan. A practicing physician since 1977, Dr. George joined Medical Arts Group as Staff Physician in 1991, providing primary care to patients. He is an Internal Medicine Specialist, operating a small town practice where patients sometimes have to travel from 20–40 miles away to be treated by him. One to two days a week, he travels to Hotten, Michigan to treat some long–time patients as well. **Career Steps:** Staff Physician, Medical Arts Group (1991–Present); Staff Physician, Audable Medical Associates (1981–1991). **Associations & Accomplishments:** Cadillac Symphony Orchestra (trumpeter); First Michigan Light Artillery, Battery D. **Education:** Michigan State University: M.D. (1977), B.S. in Medicine. **Personal:** Married to Carol in 1977. Three children: Tim, Betsy, and Lauren. Dr. George enjoys trumpet, civil war artillery, and water sports.

G. Leonard Gioia, M.D.

President
The Office of G. Leonard Gioia, M.D., P.A.
255 Fortenberry Road, Suite A1
Merritt Island, FL 32952–3601
(407) 453–2440
Fax: (407) 454–4914

8011

Business Information: A practicing physician since 1960 and a Board–Certified Obstetrician, Gynecologist, and Surgeon, Dr. Gioia established his private medical practice in 1965. He oversees all administrative operations for associates and a support staff of five, in addition to his daily patient practice. Dr. Gioia's practice specializes in gynecology, gynecological surgery, infertility, and reproductive endocrinology. Concurrent with his private practice, he serves as an active staff member at Cape Canaveral Hospital in Cocoa Beach, Florida, as well as participating in "Health First," a new three–hospital program. Career milestones include designing an 18–wheel trailer medical unit, with all types of medical equipment, including an X–Ray unit and all technical aspects to provide physical examinations and medical service for incoming National Guard members. He also provides medical support for the Democratic and Republican National Conventions conducted in Miami. **Career Steps:** President, The Office of G. Leonard Gioia, M.D., P.A. (1965–Present); Staff Member, Cape Canaveral Hospital (1965–Present). **Associations & Accomplishments:** Cape Canaveral Hospital – Cocoa Beach, Florida Committees: Chairman, Nursing Liason; Pharmacy; Surgical Practice; Diasaster Planning; Chairman, Department of Obstetrics and Gyneclogy; Credentials; Chairman, AIDS Committee; Chairman, Medical Records; Infection Control; Utilization Review; Chairman, Ethics; Civic Memberships: TICO Airport Authority, Brevard County; Director, American Bank of the South (1974–Present); Aircraft Owners and Pilots Association; Flying Physician Association; Experimental Aircraft Association; Board of Directors, Center for Health Imaging. **Education:** Bucknell University – Lewisburg, Pennsylvania, B.S. (1956); Albert Einstein College of Medicine – New York, M.D. (1960); Orange Memorial Hospital – Orlando, Florida: Internship (1961), Residency (1961–1965). **Personal:** Married to Dorothy in 1962. Four children: Camille, Christopher, Cathryn, and Jason. Dr. Gioia enjoys inventing, scuba diving, photography, woodworking, and scientific reading.

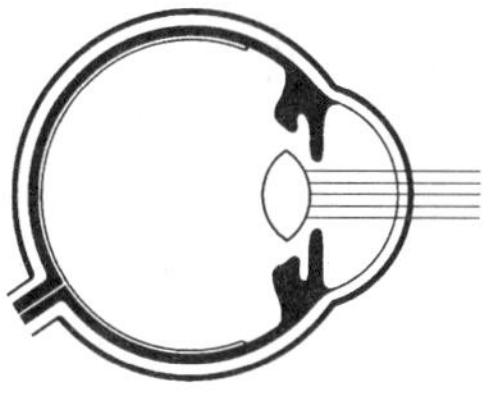

Dr. Frank J. Goes

Medical Director
Antwerp Ophthalmologic Centre
Willem Klooslaan 6 B–2050
Antwerp, Belgium
0032–32193925
Fax: 0032–32196667

8011

Business Information: Antwerp Ophthalmologic Centre is focused on the surgery of the anterior eye–segment, especially cataract and refractive surgery (surgery of myopia, farsightedness and astigmatism). The Centre is equipped to practice ophthalmology in a complete and perfect way. The equipment of the Centre can be adapted to the new requirements of modern technology instantaneously. This way of working means a clear decrease in expenses for society and, indirectly, for every citizen. It does not require hospitalization nor round the clock supervision. Members of the family can follow the operations "live" on a video screen. The Centre provides a relaxed and safe environment for those undergoing eye surgery and their families. After obtaining his medical degree with highest distinction in 1965, Dr. Goes began his private practice in 1969. He developed the Antwerp Ophthalmological Centre for outpatient ophthalmologic surgery (the first in Belgium, Netherlands, Luxemburg, Benelux) in 1984. In the Polyclinic Department, he works with the collaboration of five other ophthalmologists. He is currently the Medical Director at the Center, responsible for administration, patient care, and surgery. **Career Steps:** Medical Director, Antwerp Ophthalmological Centre (1984–Present); Solo Practitioner (1969–Present). **Associations & Accomplishments:** American Academy of Opthalmology; American Society of Cataract and Refractive Surgery; Board of Directors, Belgian Association of Outpatient Surgery; Board of Directors, Belgian Ophthalmological Society; Board of Directors, Belgian Professional Society of Ophthalmology; Founding Member, Belgian Ophthalmic Outpatient Society; International Refractive Surgery Club; International Society of Refractive Surgery; European Society of Ophthalmic Echography; European Society for Phaco–laser Surgery; Excimer Laser European Society; Ophthalmic Anesthesia Society; Outpatient Ophthalmic Surgery Society; Societas Internationalis Diagnoctioa Ultra sonica in Ophthalmolgia; Jules Francois Foundation – Belgium; Sobeveco – Society of Contact Lenses and Refractive Surgery; Societe Francaise d' Ophtalmologie. **Education:** University of Louvain, M.D. Highest Distinction (1965); Fellowships: University of Ghent (1965–1969). **Personal:** Married to Merckx Rita in 1966. Three children: Carl, Frank Jr., and Tom. Dr. Goes enjoys travel.

Martin S. Goldstein, M.D.

Sole Practitioner
Martin S. Goldstein, M.D.
1192 Park Avenue
New York, NY 10576
(212) 996–0400
Fax: (212) 369–8376

8011

Business Information: Martin S. Goldstein, M.D., established in 1963, is a full–service medical practice, providing diagnosis and treatment of women with gynecologic disorders. A practicing physician since 1966 and Board–Certified in Obstetrics, Gynecology, Gynecologic Laparoscopy, Urogynecology, and Fertility, Dr. Goldstein established his sole practice office in 1973. He is responsible for all administrative operations, including providing health care to patients, conducting surgery in gynecologic disorders, and overseeing a staff of four. **Career Steps:** Sole Practitioner, Martin S. Goldstein, M.D. (1973–Present). **Associations & Accomplishments:** New York Obstetrical Society; American College of Ob/Gyn; American Fertility Society; American Society for Laser Medicine and Surgery; American Association of Gynecologic Laparoscopists; American Urogynecologic Society. **Education:** SUNY Upstate Medical Center – Syracuse, M.D. (1966); New York University, B.A. (1962). **Personal:** Married to Susan in 1989. Five children: Lauren, Eric, Todd, Margo, and Karen. Dr. Goldstein enjoys golf, historical novels & biographies, and antique collecting.

Glenn M. Gomes, M.D.

Pulmonary Physician
Ochsner Clinic of Baton Rouge
16777 Medical Center Drive
Baton Rouge, LA 70816
(504) 755–5271
Fax: (504) 755–5011

8011

Business Information: Ochsner Clinic of Baton Rouge is a multi–specialty, acute, primary and tertiary referral care medical center. Board–certified in Internal and Critical Care Medicine and Pulmonary Diseases, with a sub–specialty in Pulmonary Diseases, Dr. Glenn Gomes is a Staff Physician with the Clinic's Pulmonary Disease Department. Concurrent with his daily practice at Ochsner Clinic, Dr. Gomes is on the staffs of Ochsner Medical Institutions, Medical Center of Baton Rouge, Baton Rouge General Hospital, and Rehabilitation Hospital of Baton Rouge. He is also involved with extensive research, currently researching occupational lung disease, chronic bronchitis and manifestations of community–acquired pneumonia. **Career Steps:** Pulmonary Physician, Ochsner Clinic of Baton Rouge (1993–Present); Clinical Assistant Professor, Department of Internal Medicine, Pulmonary Division, University of Texas Medical School (1989–1993); Private Practice, Pulmonary Medicine Group, White Wilson Medical Center (1987–1989); Physician, Elmwood Industrial Clinic, Emergency Medicine, Occupational and Industrial Medicine (1981–1983, 1985); Microbiology Lab Assistant, Methodist Hospital (1972–1973); Respiratory Care Technician, Baptist Hospital and Charity Hospital (1975–1976). **Associations & Accomplishments:** Alpha Omega Alpha, American Medical Association; American Thoracic Society; American College of Chest Physicians; Diplomate: American Board of Internal Medicine, Subspecialty Board of Pulmonary Disease, Critical Care Medicine; Treasurer and Board of Directors, Physicians Home Care, Inc.; Current Research Projects: as Principal Investigator — "PRI Acute Exacerbation of Chronic Bronchitis," "PRI Community Acquired Pneumonia"; NIOSH certified "B" reader of chest radiographs. **Education:** Louisiana State University Medical School, M.D. (1980); University of New Orleans, B.A. (1975); Louisiana State University, Earl K. Long Memorial Hospital, Internal Medicine Internship (1980–1981); Louisiana State University, Charity Hospital of New Orleans, Pathology Residency (1981–1983); Ochsner Foundation Hospital, Pulmonary Fellowship (1985–1987). **Personal:** Married to Sally in 1983. Three children: Nyssa, Michael and Jason. Dr. Gomes enjoys "Shotokan" Karate.

Dolores Cruz Gomez

Clinic Director
Clinica Del Valle
850 Freedom Boulevard
Watsonville, CA 95076–3814
(408) 761–1588
Fax: (408) 761–1677

8011

Business Information: Clinica Del Valle is a non–profit clinic offering medical services to migrant farm workers and other low income families within a 15 mile radius of Monterey and Brundale Counties. Staff members assist patients with language difficulties and those who need transportation in order to visit the Clinic. The Clinic currently has two physicians on staff and will be adding a third in 1996. As Clinic Director, Ms. Cruz Gomez administers the daily operations of the Clinic. She is responsible for recruiting staff members, employee reviews, scheduling of staff, financial concerns, and planning the expansion of Clinic services. Ms. Cruz Gomez is also a member of the Board of Directors for the Clinic and assists in obtaining funds to continue operations. **Career Steps:** Clinic Director, Clinica Del Valle (1993–Present); Project Director, Migrant Media Education Program (1991–1994); Clinic Director, Salud Para La Gente (1991–1994); Project Co–Coordinator, Food & Nutrition Services (1979–1991). **Associations & Accomplishments:** Founder and Coordinator, Grupo Adelante; Founder and Coordinator, Trabajadores Lastimados; Defendant in Successful Suit Changing At–Large Elections to District Elections; Ms. Gomez is a contributing author to the children's book "Mr. Sugar Comes To Town". **Education:** University of California – Santa Barbara, Teaching Credit (1972), B.A.; Santa Barbara City College. **Personal:** Two children: Cynthia and Jennifer Coates. Ms. Gomez enjoys dancing, cooking, nature, music, crafts, and weaving.

Gale L. Gordon, M.D.

Pediatric Nephrologist
South California Permanente Medical Group
4700 Sunset Boulevard
Los Angeles, CA 90027–6082
(213) 667–8830
Fax: (213) 667–5367

8011

Business Information: South California Permanente Medical Group is an integrated health care system and management corporation (HMO) providing complete medical, surgical and psychiatric services to its members. Currently, the Medical Group employs 1,500 physicians. A Board–certified Pediatrician with a sub–specialty in Pediatric Nephrology, Dr. Gordon is responsible for the care and treatment of children with kidney diseases and dysfunctions. **Career Steps:** Pediatrician and Nephrologist, South California Permanente Medical Group (1976–Present); Pediatric Nephrologist, Children's Hospital of Los Angeles (1975–1976). **Associations & Accomplishments:** Alpha Omega Alpha. **Education:** Temple University, M.D. (1971); Vassar College, B.A. (1967). **Personal:** Two children: Jonathan and Ari.

Lisa Faith Gould

Ophthalmologist
Winnipeg Clinic
425 Saint Mary Avenue
Winnipeg, Manitoba R3C 0N2
(204) 957–3252
Fax: (204) 943–2164

8011

Business Information: Winnipeg Clinic is a multi–specialty clinic located in downtown Winnipeg. Among other areas, the Clinic offers the talents of seven ophthalmologists to the public. As Ophthalmologist, Dr. Gould has special interest in Glaucoma and Cataracts. **Career Steps:** Ophthalmologist, Winnipeg Clinic (1991–Present). **Associations & Accomplishments:** Canadian Glaucoma Society; Canadian Medical Association; Manitoba Medical Association; Ontario Medical Association; American Academy of Ophthalmology; ARVO. **Education:** University of Toronto, FRCS (1991); Fellowship in Glaucoma, University of Toronto (1991); University of Manitoba, M.D. (1986). **Personal:** Dr. Gould enjoys golf, music, and playing the flute and piano.

Patricia J. Grena, D.O.

Medical Director
Emergency Physicians Medical Group
746 South Grand
Fowlerville, MI 48836
(517) 223–7900
Fax: Please mail or call

8011

Business Information: Emergency Physicians Medical Group, established in 1993, is a multi–physician group practice and private corporation that contracts physicians out to hospitals and clinics. As Medical Director, Dr. Grena provides primary care in a small, rural Michigan community and oversees patient care concerns and other everyday problems. **Career Steps:** Medical Director, Emergency Physicians Medical Group (1993–Present); Urgent Care Physician, SelectCare (1992–1993). **Associations & Accomplishments:** American Medical Association; Michigan State Medical Society; Golden Key National Honor Society; Phi Kappa Phi National Honor Society; Diplomate, National Board of Osteopathic Medical Examiners. **Education:** Michigan State University, D.O. (1986), B.S. with high honors (1982); Internship, Botsford Hospital – Farmington Hills, MI; Residency: Henry Ford Hospital. **Personal:** Two children: Rebekah Plagens and Sarah Tryon. Dr. Grena enjoys gardening, reading, yoga, travel, history and spending time with her children.

Margaret Grenison, M.D.

Medical Director and Chairman
Franciscan Skemp Clinic, Center for Women's Health
800 West Avenue South
La Crosse, WI 54601
(608) 791–9891
Fax: (800) 535–9055

8011

Business Information: Franciscan Skemp Clinic, Center for Women's Health is an acute care community medical facility. As Medical Director and Chairman, Dr. Grenison is responsible for patient care, medical and support staff supervision, and various administrative activities. **Career Steps:** Franciscan Skemp Clinic: Medical Director and Chairman, Center for Women's Health (1993–Present), Family Practice Physician (1992–1993); Staff Physician, United States Army (1985–1992). **Associations & Accomplishments:** American Academy of Family; LaCross County Medical Association; Board Member, "Break the Cycle." **Education:** Medical College of Wisconsin, M.D. (1984); Viterbo College, B.A. and B.S. **Personal:** Married to John Cochran in 1981. Three children: Caitlin, Luke, and Madeline. Dr. Grenison enjoys reading, piano, travel, tennis, and spending time with her family.

Dr. Dante R. Guinhawa, M.D., F.R.C.P.C.

Consulting Psychiatrist
Dante R. Guinhawa Professional Corporation
Suite 703, 10731 Saskatchewan Drive
Edmonton, Alberta T6E 6H1
(403) 477–4567
Fax: (403) 477–4797

8011

Business Information: Dante R. Guinhawa Professional Corporation is a private medical office specializing in the treatment and counseling of patients with psychiatric and related mental health problems. As a Consulting Psychiatrist, Dr. Guinhawa oversees all aspects of his practice and is responsible for patient care and diagnosis. He is also involved with community psychiatry as a clinical coordinator of the Home Support Team for the Royal Alexandre Hospital. The team supports patients and their families in their homes without necessitating hospital admissions. Concurrent with his present position, Dr. Guinhawa is a staff member of the Royal Alexander Hospital and Surgeon Community Health Center, where he performs psychiatric consultations. He is an Assistant Clinical Professor of the Department of Psychiatry at the University of Alberta Hospital. Educated throughout the world, Dr. Guinhawa has studied medicine in the Philippines, England, and Saudi Arabia. He did his early training in Internal Medicine at the United States Air Force Hospital, Clark Air Base. **Career Steps:** Consultant Psychiatrist, Dante R. Guinhawa Professional Corporation (1985–Present); Consultant Psychiatrist, Royal Alexander Hospitals (1985–Present); Consultant Psychiatrist, Alberta Hospital Ponoka (1985–1987); Consultant Psychiatrist, Glenrose Rehabilitation Hospital (1993–Present); Consultant Psychiatrist, Sturgeon Community Health

Center (1995–Present). **Associations & Accomplishments:** American Psychiatrist Association; Canadian Psychiatrist Association; Alberta Medical Association; Royal College of Physicians and Surgeons of Canada; Academy of Psychosomatic Medicine of America; Association of General Hospital Psychiatry. **Education:** University of Alberta, Fellow, Royal College of Physicians, Canada (FRCP) (1985); University of Santo Tomas, Faculty of Medicine and Surgery, Manila, Philippines, M.D. (1974). **Personal:** Dr. Guinhawa enjoys painting, art collecting, and travel.

Gerard M. Guiraudon, M.D.
Staff Surgeon and Professor
London Health Sciences Centre – University Campus
P.O. Box 5339 Station B, 339 Windermere Road
London, Ontario N6A 5A5
(519) 663–3621
Fax: (519) 663–8806

8011

Business Information: London Health Sciences Centre – University of Western Ontario is an acute care medical facility and university learning environment. A Staff Surgeon and Professor at L.H.S.C. since 1981, Dr. Guiraudon is responsible for instructing residents and medical students, patient care, and conducting research in cardiac surgery. **Career Steps:** Staff Surgeon and Professor, London Health Sciences Centre – University Campus (1981–Present); Professor, St. Antoine–Paris, France (1975–1981). **Associations & Accomplishments:** Anatomic Society of Paris; Association of Anatomists; French Speaking Society of Thoracic and Cardiovascular Surgery; French Society of Transplantation; European Society of Cardiovascular Surgery; Paris Association of the Academy of Surgeons; French Society of Cardiology; Fellow, Royal College of Surgeons of Canada; College of Physicians and Surgeons of Ontario; London & District Academy of Medicine; Society of Thoracic Surgeons; Ontario Medical Association; American College of Cardiology; Council Member, American Heart Association; Canadian Cardiovascular Society; International Society for Heart Transplantation; North American Society of Pacing and Electrophysiology; New York Academy of Sciences; European Association for Cardio–Thoracic Surgery; Chancellor's Society, University of Western Ontario; Chief Editor, La Vie Medicale; Editorial Board, Journal of Clinical Cardiology; Editorial Board, Anatomia Clinica; Review and Development Review Committee, Heart and Stroke Foundation of Ontario; Board of Trustees, North American Society of Pacing and Electrophysiology; Editorial Board, Kluwer Academic Publishers; Editorial Board, New Trends in Arrhythmias. **Education:** Lycee Henri IV, Baccalaureat (1950); Faculty of Science, P.C.B. (1951); Faculty of Medicine, M.D. (1965). **Personal:** Married to Colette M–J. in 1956. Three children: Valerie, Nicolas, and Virginie. Dr. Guiraudon enjoys skiing, sailing, literature, reading, and biking.

Madhu Guliani, M.D.
Family Practice Physician
–Independent–
2740 West Foster Street, Suite 210
Chicago, IL 60625
(312) 728–0929
Fax: Please mail or call

8011

Business Information: A practicing physician since 1985, Board–certified in Internal Medicine, Dr. Madhu Guliani serves the greater Chicago–metro with all aspects of general family medicine practices. **Career Steps:** Sole Internal Medicine Practitioner, Madhu Gulliani, M.D. (1985–Present). **Associations & Accomplishments:** American College of Physician; Chicago Medical Society; Illinois State Medical Association. **Education:** Snt. N.H.L.M.M. College – Ahmedabad, Gujrat, India (1978); INTERN TRAINING: Grant Hospital (1980–1981); RESIDENCY: Illinois Masonic Hospital (1983–1985). **Personal:** Married to Dr. Rajinder Guliani. One child: Gaurav. Dr. Guliani enjoys reading, tennis, music, spending time with family and friends and cooking.

Rajinder K. Guliani, M.D.
President
Guliani Medical Associate
2740 West Foster Avenue
Chicago, IL 60625
(312) 728–0929
Fax: (312) 728–3524

8011

Business Information: Guliani Medical Associate, established in 1980, is a full–service, general medical practice. As President, Dr. Guliani is responsible for all aspects of operations, including providing patient care. Concurrent with his private medical practice, he serves as Director of Cardiology at Sweedish Covenant Hospital. **Career Steps:** President, Guliani Medical Associate (1980–Present); Swedish Covenant

Hospital: Director of Cardiology (1989–Present), Director of Intensive Care Unit (1983). **Associations & Accomplishments:** American Medical Assocation; Faculty at Rush Pres St. Lukes Medical Center and Chicago Medical School. **Education:** Rush Pres St. Lukes Medical Center, M.D. (1977–1979). **Personal:** Married to Madhu in 1978. One child: Gaurav. Dr. Guliani enjoys tennis, music, and comparative religion.

Thomas Gullatt, M.D.
Physician
Pulmonary and Internal Medicine Associates
102 Thomas Road, Suite 104
West Monroe, LA 71291
(318) 323–1559
Fax: Please mail or call

8011

Business Information: Pulmonary and Internal Medicine Associates is a private practice specializing in the care and treatment of patients with lung diseases and disorders. Currently the practice employs three Pulmonologists and an Internist. As Physician, Dr. Gullatt devotes half of his time attending to patients in local hospitals and the other half of his time with the patients in his office. He also now serves as the Chief of Staff for Glenwood Regional Medical Center, appointed in 1995. **Career Steps:** Physician, Pulmonary and Internal Medicine Associates (1989–Present). **Associations & Accomplishments:** Northeast Lousiana University Booster Club. **Education:** Louisiana Medical Center, M.D. (1984); Northeast Louisiana University, B.S. (1981). **Personal:** Married. Dr. Gullatt enjoys basketball, jogging and domestic travel.

Ebru Gultekin, M.D.
Physician
The Office of Ebru Gultekin, M.D.
5 Lyndon Medical Building – 8013 New LaGrange Road
Louisville, KY 40222–4707
(502) 426–2548
Fax: Please mail or call

8011

Business Information: The Office of Ebru Gultekin, M.D. is a private pediatrics practice. In his current capacity, Dr. Gultekin is responsible for all aspects of operations, including the care and treatment of patients. **Career Steps:** Physician, The Office of Ebru Gultekin, M.D. (1995–Present); Endocrinology Fellow, Children's Hospital Medical Center – Cincinnati, OH (1993–1995). **Associations & Accomplishments:** American Medical Association; American Academy of Pediatrics. **Education:** University of Louisville, M.D. (1990). **Personal:** Dr. Gultekin enjoys reading and swimming.

Richard Guthrie, M.D.
President and Medical Director
Mid–America Diabetes Associates, P.A.
200 South Hillside Street
Wichita, KS 67211–2127
(316) 687–3100
Fax: (316) 687–0286

8011

Business Information: Mid–America Diabetes Associates, P.A. is a group medical practice, specializing in the diagnosis and treatment of patients suffering from carbohydrate metabolic disorders (diabetes). A practicing physician for the past thirty–five years and Board–Certified in Pediatrics and Pediatric Endocrinology and Metabolism, Dr. Guthrie founded Mid–America Diabetes Associates in 1985. Serving as President and Medical Director, he is responsible for all aspects of operations, including the medical direction and strategic planning of the Practice and providing health care to children and adults suffering from diabetes. Concurrent to his private practice, he serves as Medical Director of the Diabetes Treatment Center at Via Christi Medical Center St. Joseph Compor, and Director of the Robert L. Jackson Diabetes Research Institute. **Career Steps:** President and Medical Director, Mid–America Diabetes Associates, P.A. (1985–Present); University of Kansas School of Medicine – Wichita: Clinical Professor of Pediatric Family Community Medicine (1985–Present), Professor (1982–1985), Professor and Chairman – Department of Pediatrics (1973–1982); Associate Professor, University of Missouri Medical Center (1968–1973); Intern, United States Navy (1961–1963). **Associations & Accomplishments:** Board of Directors (1972–1977, 1994–Present), American Diabetes Association; American Academy of Pediatrics; American Medical Association; Kansas Medical Society; American Association of Diabetes Educators. **Education:** University of Missouri Medical Center: Fellowship in Endo-

crinology (1968), M.D. (1960); Pediatric Residency (1965). **Personal:** Married to Diana in 1957. Three children: Laura, Joyce, and Tamara. Dr. Guthrie enjoys photography, stamps, skiing, and music.

Susan S. Haack, M.D.
Physician
Tulare Pediatric Group, Inc.
1008 North Cherry St.
Tulare, CA 93274
(209) 686–3824
Fax: (209) 686–3741

8011

Business Information: Tulare Pediatric Group, Inc. is a full–service, medical practice, specializing in the diagnosis and treatment of children. A practicing physician since 1978 and Board–Certified in Pediatrics, Dr. Haack joined Tulare Pediatric Group, Inc. in 1992. She provides health care to patients, specializing in pediatrics. **Career Steps:** Physician, Tulare Pediatric Group, Inc. (1992–Present). **Associations & Accomplishments:** American Medical Association; American Academy of Pediatrics. **Education:** University of Santo Tomas, M.D. (1978), B.S. (1974); Texas Tech University Health Sciences Center, Pediatric Internship and Residency (1989–1992); Manila Doctors Hospital, Manila, Philippines, Pediatric Residency (1980–1984). **Personal:** Married to Kenneth in 1988. Dr. Haack enjoys travel.

Scott E. Hallgren, D.O.
Physician
The Medical Office of Scott E. Hallgren, D.O.
9405 Beachberry Place
Pinellas Park, FL 34666
(813) 544–1600
Fax: (813) 546–9071

8011

Business Information: The Medical Office of Scott E. Hallgren, D.O. is a full–service, medical practice, providing diagnosis and treatment of gastroenterology, internal medicine, and hepatology disorders. A practicing physician since 1980 and Board–Certified in Osteopathic Medicine and Surgery, Dr. Hallgren established his sole practice medical office in 1990. He oversees all administrative operations for associates and a support staff of 15, in addition to his daily patient practice. **Career Steps:** Physician, The Medical Office of Scott E. Hallgren, D.O. (1990–Present); U.S. Army – Fitzsimons Army Medical Center: Assistant Chief Gastroenterology (1988–1990), Chief of Endoscopy Services (1986–1988). **Associations & Accomplishments:** American College of Physicians; Florida Osteopathic Medical Association. **Education:** College of Osteopathic Medicine and Surgery, D.O. (1980); University of Maryland, B.S. (1977). **Personal:** Married to Toni in 1980. Two children: Jessica and Jeffrey. Dr. Hallgren enjoys basketball, softball, golf, and bicycling.

Gerald Lee Hamilton, M.D.
Physician
OB–GYN Unlimited
35 West Street
Concord, NH 03301–3596
(603) 224–0000
Fax: Please mail or call

8011

Business Information: OB–GYN Unlimited is a general practice obstetrics and gynecology facility. Dr. Hamilton established his private practice in 1979, specializing in innovative medical practices. He opened a free–standing birthing center and favors drug–free labor. **Career Steps:** Physician, OB–GYN Unlimited (1979–Present); Physician, Concord Clinic (1974–1979). **Associations & Accomplishments:** New Hampshire Medical Society; Memmock County Medical Society; American Laser Society; American Society of Colposcopy and Cervical Pathology; Obstetrical Respresentative, Law Midwifery Advisory Committee to Director of Public Health; American College of Obstetrics and Gynecology; American Board of Ob–Gyn Certified. **Education:** Columbia University College of Physicians and Surgeons, M.D. (1966); Hamilton College, B.A. (1962); Internship, Strong Memorial Hospital – Rochester, New York (1966–1967); Residency, The Presbyterian Hospital in New York City (1967–1972). **Personal:** Married to Christine F. Kuhlman, CNM, MPH in 1980. One child: Christopher I. Dr. Hamilton enjoys tennis and skiing. He also collects fossils, coins, and skulls.

Gregory S. Handel, Ph.D.

Program Director
Rapha
350 Memorial Drive
Chicopee, MA 01020–5000
(413) 594–2211
Fax: (413) 592–9753

8011

Business Information: Rapha is a national medical facility specializing in behavioral services on an in–patient and out–patient basis. The Clinic was founded in Houston in 1986 and a second location was established in Chicopee in 1995. As Program Director, Dr. Handel provides Christian psychiatric services, combining his faith and his profession to aid patients with behavioral problems. He also oversees program marketing to church communities in New England and Mid–Atlantic states. Concurrently, he maintains a private practice where he tends to patients and deals with their psychological and spiritual needs. **Career Steps:** Program Director, Rapha (1995–Present); Psychologist, Private Practice (1986–Present); Associate Pastor, Agape Community Church (1991–Present). **Associations & Accomplishments:** Board of Director, Family Empowerment Program; Secretary, Board of Directors, Pioneer Valley Pop Warner Football League; Ordained Minister, Alliance for Renewal Churches; American Psychological Association. **Education:** Washington State University: Ph.D (1983), M.S. (1981); Boston University, B.A. (1978). **Personal:** Married to MaryAnn in 1981. Four children: Nicole, Stuart, Johnny, and Jacob. Dr. Handel enjoys coaching youth sports, fishing, and playing Saxophone.

James R. Hanley III, M.D.

Pediatrician
The Office of James R. Hanley III, M.D.
28 West Macclenny Avenue, #5
Macclenny, FL 32063–2078
(904) 259–5766
Fax: Please mail or call

8011

Business Information: The Office of James R. Hanley III, M.D., the only pediatrician office in the county, is a full–service, general practice medical office, specializing in the diagnosis and treatment of children. Entering into Pediatrics because of a childhood fear of physicians, Dr. Hanley has been a practicing physician since 1988 and is Board–Certified as a Pediatrician, Emergency Physician, and Family Physician. He oversees all administrative operations for associates and a support staff of six, in addition to his daily patient practice. **Career Steps:** Owner and Pediatrician, The Office of James R. Hanley III, M.D. (1991–Present); Resident Physician, University of Florida Health Science Center (1988–1991); Naval Officer, U.S. Navy (1979–1983). **Associations & Accomplishments:** American Academy of Pediatrics; American College of Emergency Physicians; Florida Medical Association; Duval County Medical Society; American Medical Association; Civil Area Pastor; American Academy of Family Physicians; National Association of EMS Physicians. **Education:** Eastern Virginia Medical, M.D. (1988); Auburn University, B.S. in Chemistry; Old Dominion University, Matriculated Graduate Student. **Personal:** Married to Denise in 1995. Two children: Christopher and Nathaniel. Dr. Hanley enjoys hiking, camping, deep sea fishing, and reading.

Gerald E. Hanson, D.D.S., M.P.H.

Owner/Oral & Maxillofacial Surgeon
Dr. Gerald E. Hanson, Limited
2585 South Jones Boulevard
Las Vegas, NV 89102
(702) 367–6666
Fax: (702) 367–9555

8011

Business Information: Gerald E. Hanson, Limited is the office of a private practice physician specializing in oral and maxillofacial surgery. Dr. Hanson performs reconstructive surgery for patients and is affiliated with several hospitals in the Las Vegas area. As Owner/Oral & Maxillofacial Surgeon, Dr. Hanson handles all administrative and operational decisions for his private practice. **Career Steps:** Owner/Oral & Maxillofacial Surgeon, Gerald E. Hanson, Limited (1973–Present). **Associations & Accomplishments:** President, Western Society of Oral and Maxillofacial Surgeons; Board of Directors, Oral and Maxillofacial Surgery Foundation; Division Chief, Oral and Maxillofacial Surgery/Dental Division, Sunrise Mountainview Hospital; Clark County Aviation Association; Las Vegas Executives Association. **Education:** University of Minnesota, Certification in Oral & Maxillofacial Surgery (1976); Loma Linda University, D.D.S., M.P.H. (1973). **Personal:** Dr. Hanson enjoys being a commercial instrument pilot, collecting and restoring antique airplanes, music, snow skiing, sailing, and being a certified diver.

Kathleen P. Hanson, R.N., PSC

Patient Service Coordinator
Wichita Clinic
3311 East Murdock
Wichita, KS 67208–3054
(316) 689–9717
Fax: (316) 689–9182

8011

Business Information: Wichita Clinic, the largest ambulatory clinic in the state of Kansas with 12 locations and 150 physicians, offers day surgery, immediate care, dental, and primary care. As Patient Service Coordinator, Ms. Hanson works with 19 physicians and coordinates the hiring, firing, and counseling 45 employees. She is also responsible for annual budgets, client complaints, and all the meetings and conferences inherent to keeping a clinic running smoothly. Ms. Hanson has been a nurse for 15 years, and attributes her success to her parents' guidance, her strong ethics and her willlingness to take risks. **Career Steps:** Patient Service Coordinator, Wichita Clinic (1994–Present); Registered Nurse/Staff Mentor, Columbia HCA Wesley Medical Center (1985–1994); Registered Nurse – Home Health, Olsten Kimberely Quality Care (1993–1994). **Associations & Accomplishments:** Current Lay Minister Gloria Dei Lutheran Church; Active Girl Scout Leader, 1988–1991, in Augusta, KS, and took 14 girls to Washington, DC and met Senators Bob Dole and Nancy Kasebaum; Delta Delta Sorority Alumnus; Fund Raising Team, American Heart Association. **Education:** Rapid City Regional Hospital School of Nursing, R.N. Diploma (1983). **Personal:** Married to David Jay in 1986. Three children: Laura K. Martin, Heather D. and Jonathan R. Hanson. Ms. Hanson enjoys painting, camping, swimming, gardening, and family oriented activities.

Dr. Jayshree C. Haribhai

Physician
Fraserview Medical Associates
665 Front Street, Suite 32
Quesnel, British Co V2J 5J5
(604) 992–3636
Fax: (604) 992–7587

8011

Business Information: Fraserview Medical Associates is a full service medical clinic serving the Quesnel, Canada area. Established in 1980, the clinic has a staff of ten physicians. As Physician, Dr. Haribhai is responsible for all phases of patient care including diagnosis, treatment, and follow up. **Career Steps:** Physician, Fraserview Medical Associates (1995–Present); Physician, Greene Clinic (1994–1995). **Education:** University of Natal, South Africa, M.B.C.A.B. (1983). **Personal:** Dr. Haribhai enjoys reading, walking, and music.

Charles F. Harvey, D.O.

Doctor of Osteopathy
Peach Tree Health Center
1100 North Mustang Road
Mustang, OK 73064
(405) 376–5000
Fax: (405) 376–1831

8011

Business Information: Peach Tree Health Center, established in 1991, is a full–service family medical practice. As Doctor of Osteopathy, Dr. Harvey is responsible for patient care, supervision of a 5–person office support staff, and diversified administrative activities. **Career Steps:** Doctor of Osteopathy, Peach Tree Health Center (1990–Present) **Associations & Accomplishments:** Okalahoma Osteopathic Association; American Osteopathic Association; American College of Osteopathic Family Practioners. **Education:** Oklahoma State University College of Osteopathic Medicine, D.O. (1990). **Personal:** Married to Teresa in 1989. One child: Phillip. Dr. Harvey enjoys fishing and teaching and training in Tae Kwon Do.

Eva L. Haskell

Psychiatrist
Howesound Mental Health Centre
P.O. Box 2199, 38075 2nd Avenue
Squamish, British Co V0N 3G0
(604) 892–9215
Fax: (604) 892–9279

8011

Business Information: Howesound Mental Health Centre is a full service medical facility providing diagnosis and treatment of patients. Dr. Haskell was lured from her private psychiatric practice by the University of British Columbia in 1984. As part of her staff duties, she is the primary psychiatrist working the University's "Outreach" program, where–in she, once a month, travels to different towns and consults with University referred physicians and patients. She is also responsible for the day–to–day operations of Howesound, providing psychiatric services and consulting to her private clientele. **Career Steps:** Psychiatrist, Howesound Mental Health Centre (1992–Present); Outreach Psychiatrist, University BC (1984–Present); Psychiatrist, Vancouver BC; Private Practice, Eva Haskell, MD, Inc. (1984–1990); Community Psychiatrist, Greater Vancouver Mental Health (1983–Present). **Associations & Accomplishments:** British Columbia Medical Association; College of Physicians & Surgeons of BC; Fellow, Royal College of Physicians & Surgeons of Canada; Published in Canadian Journal of Psychiatry (1984). **Education:** McMaster University, M.D. (1978); University of Western Ontario, B.Sc.N. (1969). **Personal:** One child: Sean Peter. Dr. Haskell enjoys music, swimming, and literature.

Dr. Robert S. Hauptman

Physician
Associate Medical Clinic
25 St. Michael Street
St. Albert, Alberta T8N 1C7
(403) 961–3991
Fax: (403) 460–7941

8011

Business Information: Associate Medical Clinic, composed of six doctors, is a primary care family practice medical clinic. As Physician, Dr. Hauptman specializes in asthma and allergies. **Career Steps:** Physician, Associate Medical Clinic (1995–Present); Family Physician, Lauidem Medical Clinic (1992–1995); Family Physician, Haig Medical Clinic (1989–1990). **Associations & Accomplishments:** Chairperson, Family Physician Asthma Group of Canada. **Education:** University of Alberta, M.D. (1987), B.M.Sc. (1985). **Personal:** Married to Marg in 1990. Two children: Christopher and Joshua. Dr. Hauptman enjoys camping, photography, hiking, reading, and spending time with his family.

Bruce L. Henschen, M.D.

Pulmonary and Critical Care Physician
Knoxville Pulmonary Group, PA
1932 Alcoa Highway, Suite 480
Knoxville, TN 37920–1517
(423) 524–7471
Fax: (423) 544–6563

8011

Business Information: Knoxville Pulmonary Group, PA is a multi–physician specialty practice, specializing in the evaluation and treatment of lung diseases and critical care medicine in the outpatient and inpatient setting. A practicing physician since 1982, Board–certified in Internal Medicine, Pulmonary and Critical Care Medicine, Dr. Henschen joined KPG upon completion of his specialty fellowship in 1987. **Career Steps:** Physician, Knoxville Pulmonary Group, PA (1987–Present) **Associations & Accomplishments:** Fellow, American College of Chest Physicians; American Thoracic Society; American College of Physicians; Board Member, Knox County Air Pollution Control. **Education:** East Carolina University Medical School, M.D. (1982); Davidson College, B.S. (1977); Board Certified in: Internal Medicine (1985), Pulmonary Medicine (1988), Critical Care Medicine (1989); RESIDENCY: University of Kentucky (1982–1985); FELLOWSHIP: Medical College of Georgia (1985–1987). **Personal:** Married to Catherine in 1982. Two children: Bruce Jr. and Charlie. Dr. Henschen enjoys soccer, golf, tennis and choral singing.

Jane Hernandez–Ing, M.D., P.A.

President
Jane B. Hernandez–Ing, M.D., P.A.
777 East 25th Street, Suite #306
Hialeah, FL 33013
(305) 696–0701
Fax: (305) 696–1239

8011

Business Information: Jane B. Hernandez–Ing, M.D., P.A., established in 1995, is a private, full–service, general practice, medical office specializing in Rheumatology. The Practice operates as a private practice within a medical office group. Board Certified in Internal Medicine, Dr. Hernandez–Ing serves as President and is responsible for all aspects of operations, including providing health care to patients. **Career Steps:** President, Jane B. Hernandez–Ing, M.D., P.A. (1995–Present); Primary Care Physician/Rheumatology, WIL–MED, Inc. (1994); Rheumatologist, New York Medical Associates (1993–1994); Rheumatologist, National Care Center, Inc. (1993–1995); Primary Care Physician, South Florida Internal Medicine Associates (1992–1993); Teaching Attending Episcopal Hospital (1989–1990). **Associations & Accomplishments:** American Board of Internal Medicine Diplomate (1991); Federal Licensure Examination (1987/1988); Educational Commission Foreign Medical Graduates (1984); Licensure: Pennsylvania (1988), Florida (1989), New Jersey (1992); American College of Rheumatology; American Medical Association; Florida Society of Internal Medicine; Author of publications: Prolonged Activated Partial Thromboplastin Time in Systemic Lupus Erythematosus Overlap Syndrome; Fatal Bleeding Due to Factor VII Inhibitor, Journal of Clinical Rheumatology (1995). **Education:** Fellowship in Rheumatology, Cooper University Medical Center/UMDNJ (1990–1992); Residency in Internal Medicine, Episcopal Hospital, Temple University Affiliate (1986–1989); American University of the Caribbean, M.D. (1985); University of Miami (1981); Miami Dade College, A.A. **Personal:** Married to Albert Ing, M.D. in 1984. Three children: Jonathan, Christopher, and Ileana. Dr. Hernandez–Ing enjoys golf, swimming, and travel.

Roger C. Hill, M.D.

Physician Executive
PHP Healthcare
15 West Third Street
Sterling, IL 61081
(815) 626–2170
Fax: (815) 626–2260

8011

Business Information: PHP Healthcare is the healthcare facility for Northwestern Steel and Wire Company. The facility provides healthcare to current employees, retired employees, and family members on an out–patient basis. As Physician Executive, Dr. Hill is a member of the Board of Directors and handles the day–to–day operations. One of three physicians on staff, Dr. Hill treats patients for a variety of medical problems and recommends specialized treatment as necessary. **Career Steps:** Physician Executive, PHP Healthcare (1995–Present); Partner, Medical Arts Center (1981–1995); Medical Practitioner, Whittaker Corporation (1979–1981). **Associations & Accomplishments:** American College of Physicians; American College of Physician Executives; American Society of Gastrointestinal Endoscopy. **Education:** University of Illinois, M.D. (1967), D.V.M. (1962), B.S.)1960). **Personal:** Married to Mary Ann in 1967. Two children: Erik and Nathan. Dr. Hill enjoys farming, flying, and fly fishing.

Nabil Hilwa, M.D.

President
Associated Florida Urologists
6388 Silver Star Road, Suite 2A
Orlando, FL 32818–3235
(407) 298–6950
Fax: (407) 578–2354

8011

Business Information: Associated Florida Urologists is a private urological disorder and disease practice, serving patients throughout greater Orlando, Florida and surrounding communities. A practicing physician since 1969, Board–Certified in Urology with particular subspecialty in Urological Cryosurgery, Dr. Hilwa founded Associated Florida Urologists in 1979. He oversees all administrative operations for associates and a support staff of four, in addition to his daily patient practice. He concentrates his practice in the treatment of urological cancer, and is a pioneer in the state of Florida in utilizing the latest surgery technique for cancer treatment — Cryosurgery (freezing technique). Within the past three years he has treated over 130 patients utilizing this technique. **Career Steps:** President, Associated Florida Urologists (1979–Present); Chief of Staff – Urology, Princeton Hospital (1994–1996). **Associations & Accomplishments:** Fellow, International College of Surgeons; Society of Urological Cryosurgeons; American Association of Clinical Urologists, Inc.; Past President and Sustaining Member, Arab–American Medical Association – Florida Chapter. **Education:** Damascus University, M.D. (1969). **Personal:** Married to Guada Hilwa in 1972. Two children: Danny and Steve. Dr. Hilwa enjoys swimming, boating, soccer, and computing.

Katherine A. Hoover, M.D.

Physician Associate – Myer's Clinic
Little Ragged Island Co.
Rt. 2 Box 203
Lost Creek, WV 26385
(304) 457–2800
Fax: (304) 457–4011

8011

Business Information: Myer's Clinic, established in 1930, is a family practice medical clinic consisting of three physicians, specializing in medical and cardiac rehabilitation. Located at 112 N. Woods Street in Phillipi, WV, the clinic serves the rural community of Phillipi and surrounding counties. A practicing physician since 1975, Dr. Hoover joined Myer's Clinic in 1995. Serving as Physician Associate, she is responsible for diagnosis and treatment of patients with internal medicine problems. Concurrent with her position at Myer's Clinic, she also serves as Medical Director of a nursing home. Her future plans include establishing a diving resort on an island in the Bahamas that she and her husband own. **Career Steps:** Physician Associate, Myer's Clinic (1993–Present); Development Director, Little Ragged Island Company (1993–Present); Director and Owner, Sunbelt Medical Center (1985–1993). **Associations & Accomplishments:** American Medical Women's Association; American Pain Society, Author of Book: "An Orgasm a Day Keeps the Doctor Away." **Education:** Michigan State University, M.D. (1975); University of Michigan, B.S. (1971). **Personal:** Married to John Tomasic in 1976. Two children: Michael and Stephen.

Judy Howard

Practice Manager
Women's Health Specialists
1818 North Meade Street
Appleton, WI 54911
(414) 749–4000
Fax: (414) 749–4015

8011

Business Information: Women's Health Specialists is a specialized medical practice, providing obstetric and gynecological care. Comprised of six physicians, two assistants, and a nurse practitioner, the Clinic also has an in–house lab and ultrasound facility. Established in 1988, the Clinic has two locations, one in Appleton and the other in Neenah, Wisconsin. As Practice Manger, Ms. Howard manages all aspects of the practice. Her duties include: billing, accounts payable and receivable, HMO contracts, and business development and administration. **Career Steps:** Practice Manager, Women's Health Specialists (1989–Present); Controller, Moe Northern Company (1986–1989); Assistant Controller, Mid American Tag and Label (1984–1986); Assistant Controller, Valley School Suppliers (1981–1984). **Associations & Accomplishments:** Wisconsin Association of Certified Public Accountants; Advancement Chairman, Boy Scouts of America Troop #1; Stewardship Committee, St. Mary's Church. **Education:** University of Wisconsin, Osh–Kosh: B.A. in Accounting (1976), B.A. in Manpower Management (1978). **Personal:** Married to Robert in 1978. Two children: Michael and Daniel. Ms. Howard enjoys time with her children.

E. W. Hudson, M.D.

Consultant Radiologist/Nuclear Medicine Physician
Diagonostic Imaging International
606 Dorset Park
Windsor, Ontario N8N 3L2
(519) 979–0853
Fax: (519) 979–4314

8011

Business Information: An Independent Radiology Consultant and Nuclear Medicine Physician, Dr. Hudson is presently under contract with Diagnostic Imaging International, a provider of diagnostic medical imaging, radiology, x–ray, scanning, and ultrasound services. **Career Steps:** Consultant Radiologist/Nuclear Medicine Physician, Diagnostic Imaging International (1993–Present); Consultant Radiologist, Belleville General Hospital (Jul.1989–Jun.1991); Medical Officer/Flight Surgeon, Canadian Armed Forces (1979–1984). **Associations & Accomplishments:** Canadian Association of Radiologists; Canadian Medical Association; Society of Nuclear Medicine; Royal College of Physicians and Surgeons of Canada; Voluntary Assistant Instructor of Youth Aikido. **Education:** Memorial University of Newfoundland, Canada, M.D. (1978); Diplomate of the American Board of Radiology (1989); Diplomate of the American Board of Nuclear Medicine (1992); Fellow of The Royal College of Physicians and Surgeons of Canada, Radiology (1989), Nuclear Medicine (1992). **Personal:** Married to Janet in 1979. Two children: Sarah and Rachel. Dr. Hudson enjoys music and the Japanese martial art of Aikido.

Dr. Joseph E. Huggins

Director/Physician
Don Mills Eglinton Medical Centre
797 Don Mills Road, Main Floor West
North York, Ontario M3C 1V1
(416) 429–2323
Fax: (416) 429–8017

8011

Business Information: Don Mills Eglinton Medical Centre is a general medical practice and research center located in North York, Ontario. The Center's focus is on Autism, with emphasis placed on diagnosis and treatment. The Facility's research into the treatment of severe aggressive and rage behavior will soon become a model for treatment centers worldwide. As Director/Physician, Dr. Huggins oversees the operations of the Medical Centre and operates a large primary and consultative autistic/PDD outpatient and residential practice. He is the originator of a model treatment plan for patients with abnormal behavior. In May of 1996, Dr. Huggins was the recipient of the Gerry Bloomfield Award, presented by the Autism Society of Ontario in recognition of his contributions in the treatment of people with autism. He has developed a Diagnostic and Treatment Model that is reported to have made a significant change in the lives of people with autism. Dr. Huggins has had 20 published articles on such diverse subjects as medicine, computers and wine. **Career Steps:** Director/Physician, Mony Life Tower (Present); Director/General Manager, Don Mills Eglinton Medical Centre (1975–1996); Medical Director, Kerry's Place Autism Services (1990–1996). **Associations & Accomplishments:** Alpha Omega Alpha Honor Medical Association; Ontario Medical Association; College of Physicians and Surgeons of Ontario; The Gerry Bloomfield Award (1995–1996). **Education:** University of Toronto, M.D. (1972); University of Windsor, B.Sc. (1968). **Personal:** Married to Mei Ching in 1968. Three children: Jonathan, Joanne, and Jason. Dr. Huggins enjoys wine, computers, car restoration, and fly fishing.

Dawn Huggins–Jones, M.D.

Physician
Queens–Long Island Medical Group
116–65 233rd Street
Cambria Heights, NY 11411–1835
(718) 262–5870
Fax: (718) 262–7045

8011

Business Information: Queens–Long Island Medical Group is a full–service healthcare institution specializing in the diagnosis, treatment, and rehabilitation of patients (i.e., corporate drug screening, inoculations, etc.). As Physician, Dr. Huggins–Jones specializes in the Obstetrical/Gynecological area of the practice, and is responsible for patient and pre–natal care, diagnosis, and follow up. **Career Steps:** Physician, Queens–Long Island Medical Group (1989–Present); Attending Physician, Health & Hospitals Corporation (1987–1989); Clinical Assistant Professor, Dunnstate Medical Center (SUNY) (1988–1989). **Associations & Accomplishments:** American College of Obstetricians and Gynecologists; American Association of Gynecologic Laproscopics. **Education:** Hahneman Medical College, M.D. (1981); Lincoln University. **Personal:** Married to Vincent W. in 1982. Two children: Sydney and Lindsey. Dr. Huggins–Jones enjoys singing and dancing.

John I. Hughes, M.D., F.A.C.P., F.A.C.G.

Associate Medical Director
Kelsey–Seybold Clinic
6624 Fannin Street, St. Luke's Medical Tower
Houston, TX 77030–2311
(713) 791–8700
Fax: (713) 799–2738

8011

Business Information: Kelsey–Seybold Clinic is a large, multi–specialty clinic established in 1949. A practicing physician for the past twenty years and Board–Certified in Gastroenterology, Dr. Hughes was appointed as Medical Director of the Vercellino Gastrointestinal Institute in 1983. He is responsible for the direction of all medical and administrative functions of the Clinic, including physician management, patient care, and strategic planning. Concurrent with his position at the Clinic, he serves as Senior Staff Gastroenterologist, Associate Medical Director of medical specialties, and is an elected member of the Board of Directors for the Kelsey–Seybold Medical Group. **Career Steps:** Associate Medical Director, Kelsey–Seybold Clinic (1983–Present); Kelsey–Seybold Medical Group: Board of Directors (1992–Present), Associate Medical Director (1994–Present); Clinical Associate Professor – Dept. Internal Medicine/Gastroenterology Section, Baylor College of Medicine, Houston, TX (1988–Present); Staff Physician – Dept. Internal Medicine/Gastroenterology Section, St. Luke's Episcopal Hospital (1981–Present); Affiliate Physician – Dept. Internal Medicine/Gastroenterology Section, The Methodist Hospital (1981–Present); MILITARY SERVICE: Paratrooper, U.S. Army Airborne (1965–1968) – Combat Tour of Duty in South Vietnam (1966–1967). **Associations & Accomplishments:** American Board of Internal Medicine (1980); American Board of Internal Medicine–Subspecialty Gastroenterology Board (1983); American College of Physicians: Fellow (F.A.C.P.), Board of Directors – Texas Academy Chapter (1993–1996); The American College of Gastroenterology: Fellow (F.A.C.G.), Ad Hoc Committee on Practice Parameters, National Patient Care Committee; Medical Advisory Board – Houston Chapter, United Ostomy Association, Inc.; American Gastroenterological Association; American Medical Association; The American Society for Gastrointestinal Endoscopy; Harris County Medical Society; Houston Gastroenterological Society; Texas Medical Association; Leonidas Berry Society for Gastroneterology; American Society of Internal Medicine; Medical Advisor to the Governing Board, Greater Houston Society of Gastroenterology Nurses & Associates; Houston Philosophical Society; HONORS & AWARDS: Baylor College of Medicine: "Best Teacher Award" by Class of 1987, "Outstanding Clinical Faculty Member Award" (1984–1985); "Best Scientific Research Paper" by American College of Gastroenterology (1990); American Cancer Society Award "Colorectal Health Check" Achievement in Public Education (1985); Extensive research in the fields of gastrointestinal and colorectal cancers; Pulished author of over 40 articles, books, chapters and abstracts – some of which include: "The American Journal of Gastroenterology", "Clinical Chemistry", "Gastroenterology"; Frequent speaker at conferences and symposia proceedings. **Education:** University of South Florida College of Medicine, M.D. (three–year accelerated program) (1975); Florida A&M University, B.S. in Biology magna cum laude (1972); Fellowship in Clinical Gastroenterology, University of Texas Health Science Center (combined program, M.D. Anderson Cancer Hospital and Tumor Institute and the U.T. Medical Center) (1979–1981); RESIDENCY TRAINING: Internal Medicine Residency, Los Angeles County Hospital, Martin Luther King, Jr. General Hospital (UCLA affiliated) (1977–1979), Family Medicine Residency, University of South Florida College of Medicine – Bayfront Medical College (1976–1977); INTERNSHIP: Rotating, Bayfront Medical Center, University of South Florida College of Medicine (1975–1976) **Personal:** Married to Joan Barnett. One child: Andrea Denise. Dr. Hughes enjoys photography, Cont. Jazz, and classic autos.

J. Milton Hutson, M.D.
Physician and Partner
Hutson & Edersheim
523 East 72nd Street, Floor 9
New York, NY 10021
(212) 472–5340
Fax: (212) 737–0358
E MAIL: See Below

8011

Business Information: Hutson & Edersheim is a private Obstetrics and Gynecology practice, comprised of two Partners and specializing in high risk obstetrics and multiple pregnancies. As Physician, Dr. Hutson treats patients with high–risk pregnancies and various other medical concerns affecting women. As Partner, he handles the general administrative responsibilities of the practice and works with his partner in the development of long–term plans. Internet users may reach him via: jmhutson@msn.com. **Career Steps:** Physician and Partner, Hutson & Edersheim (1990–Present). **Associations & Accomplishments:** Fellow, American College of OB/GYN; New York Obstetrical Society; Society of Perinatal Obstetricians. **Education:** University of Alabama School of Medicine, M.D. (1975). **Personal:** Married to Jennifer I. Downey in 1984. One child: Sophia. Dr. Hutson enjoys sailing and computers.

John J. Iacuone, M.D.
••• ◦◦•═━⬤━•◦◦ •••
Pediatrician
The Office of Dr. John J. Iacuone, M.D.
3606 21st Street, Suite 107
Lubbock, TX 79410
(806) 796–1251
Fax: (806) 796–0161

8011

Business Information: The Office of Dr. John J. Iacuone, M.D. is a pediatric medical facility specializing in Hematology and Oncology. Established in 1977, the Office currently employs 9 medical support staff. As Pediatrician, Dr. Iacuone is responsible for the care and treatment of patients. Concurrent with his private pediatric practice, Dr. Iacuone is also the Chief of Staff and Director of Pediatric Oncology at the Methodist Children's Hospital. **Career Steps:** Pediatrician, The Office of Dr. John J. Iacuone, M.D. (1977–Present); Chief of Staff and Director of Hematology and Oncology, Methodist Children's Hospital (1994–Present); Director of Hematology and Oncology, Texas Tech University Health Science Center (1977–1995). **Associations & Accomplishments:** Fellow, American Academy of Pediatrics; Responsible Investigator, Children's Cooperative Group; American Society of Pediatric Hematology and Oncology; Published several peer reviews. **Education:** Indiana University School of Medicine, M.D. (1973). **Personal:** Married to Connie in 1971. Three children: Paul, Joshua and James. Dr. Iacuone enjoys golf, tennis and skiing.

Sultana Ikramullah, M.D.
Shareholder
Citrus Psychiatric Medical Clinic
315 North Third Avenue #300
Covina, CA 91723
(818) 859–2686
Fax: (818) 859–2685

8011

Business Information: A practicing physician since 1963 and a Board–Eligible Psychiatrist, Dr. Ikramullah joined Citrus Psychiatric Medical Clinic as Shareholder in 1994. Concurrently, she operates a private psychiatric practice in psychopharmacology (70%) and psychotherapy (30%). The Practice

provides treatment to children, adults, and geriatrics from an in– and out–patient facility. She also serves as Co–Service Director at Charter Behavior Health System. **Career Steps:** Shareholder, Citrus Psychiatric Medical Clinic (1994–Present); Psychiatrist, Private Practice (Present); Chairman, Department of Psychiatry, Inter Community Medical Center (1994–1995); Co–Service Director, Charter Behavioral Health System (1994– present); Medical Director, Optimum Care, Day Treatment (1992–1993); Chief Resident, Cooper Hospital University Medical Center (1985). **Associations & Accomplishments:** American Psychiatric Association; Southern California Psychiatric Society; Medical Director, Dial For Care; Conducted presentation at the Charter Behavioral Health Systems, Laguna, California; Islamic Society of Orange County. **Education:** Fatima Jinnah Medical College, M.B.B.S. (1963); Psychiatric Residency, Cooper Hospital, University Medical Center – New Jersey; Affiliate of Rutgers University. **Personal:** Married to Mahammad in 1966. Three children: Rubina, Aasim, and Samina. Dr. Ikramullah enjoys reading, travel, and sightseeing.

Glenn R. Irani, M.D., F.A.A.P.
Physician
Irani & Irani
5525 Etiwanda Avenue, #212
Tarzana, CA 91356–3645
(818) 344–7600
Fax: (818) 996–9709

8011

Business Information: Irani & Irani is a private physicians practice specializing in pediatrics and adolescent medicine. Co–founding the practice with his wife Kristine (also a board–certifed pediatrician) in 1987, Dr. Glenn Irani shares administrative duties, in addition to his daily patient practice. Concurrent with his private practice, Dr. Irani also teaches at Cedars–Sinai Medical Center. **Career Steps:** Physician, Irani & Irani (1987–Present). **Associations & Accomplishments:** Chairman of Pharmacy and Therapeutics Committee, Encino–Tarzana Regional Medical Center (1992–Present). **Education:** George Washington University School of Medicine, M.D. (1983); University of Connecticut, B.S. in Chemistry (1978). **Personal:** Married to Kristine Kern Irani, M.D. in 1980. Two children: Shannon and Megan. Dr. Irani enjoys travel, exercise, and reading.

Larry W. Irvin, M.D.
Assistant Medical Director
East Dallas Health Center
408 North Haskell, Suite 115
Dallas, TX 75246–1426
(214) 670–8937
Fax: (214) 670–5108

8011

Business Information: East Dallas Health Center, a satellite location of Parkland Memorial Hospital, is a community–oriented primary care facility providing indigent care to patients in the Dallas County Hospital District. East Dallas Health Center currently employs more than 60 people. As Assistant Medical Director, Dr. Irvin is responsible for administration, public relations, strategic planning, and providing health care in Internal Medicine at the East Dallas Health Center and several geriatric outreach centers. **Career Steps:** Assistant Medical Director, Dallas County Hospital District, East Dallas Health Center (1990–Present); Managed Care Practice, Kaiser Permanente (1989–1990); Private Practice Medical, Larry Wayne Irvin, M.D. (1983–1989). **Associations & Accomplishments:** Dallas County Alcohol and Drug Abuse Council; Expansion of Parkland's Geriatric Community Outreach; Establishment of Parkland's Geriatric Assessment Program; Establishment of Refugee Care Medical Outreach; Establishment of Geriatric Care Medical Outreach in Brady Center. **Education:** University of Texas: M.D. (1980), B.S. (1975): Registered Pharmacist (1976). **Personal:** Three children: Alana, Anthony, and Brian. Dr. Irvin enjoys backpacking, cycling, walking, and music.

J. P. Jackson, M.S., M.D., F.A.C.P.
General Internal Medicine Physician
Little Rock Diagnosis Clinic, P.A.
10001 Lile Drive
Little Rock, AR 72205
(501) 227–8000
Fax: (501) 221–5856

8011

Business Information: Little Rock Diagnosis Clinic, P.A. is a provider of general internal medicine, treatment consultancy and a tertiary referral center. Established in 1961, the Group currently has 26 physician associates. As a Physician Associate in Internal Medicine, Dr. Jackson concentrates his medical practice in the treatment and referral of hypertension and its resultant conditions. Concurrent with his medical practice, he serves as an Assistant Clinical Professor of Medicine

at University of Arkansas Medical Center. **Career Steps:** General Internal Medicine Physician, Little Rock Diagnosis Clinic, P.A. (1978–Present); Assistant Clinical Professor of Medicine, University of Arkansas Medical Center (1978–Present); Ochsner Clinic and Hospital: General Internist (1977–1988), Intensive Care Director (1975–1976). **Associations & Accomplishments:** American College of Physicians; American Medical Association; Southern Medical Association; Arkansas Medical Society; Pulaski County Medical Society; Chairman, Nutritional Support Committee, Baptist Medical Center; Baptist Medical Center: Medical Educational Committee, Intensive Care Unit Committee; Little Rock Racquet Club; Westside Tennis Center; Elected to Fellowship of the American College of Physicians (1989); Antibiotic Task Force for Dovolopmont of the Antibiotic Formulary, Baptist Medical Center (1992); Pharmacy & Therapeutics Committee for Arkansas Blue Cross/Blue Shield Managed Health Care Companies (1990); Member Board of Directors & Secretary for Central Arkansas' Managed Care Company (AMCO): the AMS Statewide PPO Managed Care Plan; Numerous publications: "Dimensions of humoral recognition factor depletion in cardinomatous patients" (1972), "Comparative evaluation of particulate and baterical opsonization by plasma of normal and neoplastic individuals" (1973), "Serum Opsonic Activity in Patients with Carinoma," and "Home Intravenous Antibiotic Therapy in Arkansas." **Education:** Tulane University: M.D. & M.S. (combined) in Physiology, B.S. in Chemistry, Mathematics and Physics. **Personal:** Married to Courtney Carmichael Jackson. Two children: Jessica and Tanner. Dr. Jackson enjoys church activities, tennis, and racquetball.

Barkat A. Jaferi, M.D.
Physician
Office of Barkat A. Jaferi, M.D.
941 White Horse Avenue, Suite #3
Trenton, NJ 08610–1407
(609) 581–1515
Fax: (609) 581–0665

8011

Business Information: The Office of Barkat A. Jaferi, M.D. is a full service, private practice medical office specializing in internal medicine. A native of Pakistan, where he received his medical degree in 1983, Dr. Jaferi emigrated to the U.S. in 1988, whereupon he opened his private practice in Trenton, New Jersey. As sole practitioner, he oversees all administrative areas, in addition to his family patient practice. Concurrent to his private practice, Dr. Jaferi is also a staff physician for St. Mary's Hospital ICU unit. **Career Steps:** Physician, Office of Barkat A. Jaferi, M.D. (1988–Present); ICU Physician, St. Mary's Hospital (1988–Present). **Associations & Accomplishments:** American College of Physicians; New Jersey Medical Association; Association of Pakistani Physicians. **Education:** Trenton Affiliated Hospitals, Residence (1987); M.B.B.S., (M.D.) in Pakistan; Certifications: Internal Medicine Board; Advanced Life Support; Advanced Trauma. **Personal:** Married to Zahida in 1980. Five children: Sania, Zafar, Fatima, Tahira and Jaferi. Dr. Jaferi enjoys spending time with his family.

Jai K. Jalaj, M.D.
Physician
Office of Jai K. Jalaj, M.D., F.C.C.P.
97 Main Street, Suite A
Fishkill, NY 12524–1700
(914) 897–3210
Fax: (914) 897–3290

8011

Business Information: A practicing physician since 1980 – Board–certified in Internal Medicine and Pulmonary Diseases – Dr. Jalaj established his sole practice medical office in 1990. He oversees all administrative operations for associates and a support staff of four, in addition to his daily patient practice. **Career Steps:** Physician, Office of Jai K. Jalaj, M.D., F.C.C.P. (1990–Present). **Associations & Accomplishments:** Fellow, American College of Chest Physicians. **Education:** Prince of Wales, M.B.B.S. (1980). **Personal:** Married to Suman in 1980.

John J. Janick, M.D., F.A.C.P., F.A.C.E.
Physician/President
Diabetes Treatment and Learning
4369 Tamiami Trail
Port Charlotte, FL 33980
(941) 629–3366
Fax: (941) 629–7729

8011

Business Information: Diabetes Treatment and Learning is a private medical practice specializing in the fields of endocrinology and metabolism. Regional in scope, the Practice has a sister location in Punta Gorda, Florida. Established in 1978, the Office, employing 25 people, is part of the Janick Medical Group. As Physician/President, Dr. Janick oversees all aspects of the Practice. His duties include administration, operations, strategic planning, and patient care and diagnosis. **Career Steps:** Physician/President, Diabetes Treatment and Learning (1978–Present); Medical Director/Board of Trustees, ResCare Home Health Agency (1978–Present); Medical Director, Lifeline, Home Health Center (1994–Present); President, Physician's IV Therapy (1992–Present). **Associations & Accomplishments:** Program Chairman, Florida Endocrine Society; Member, Board of Directors/Program Chairman, American Association of Clinical Endocrinologists; Hospital Committees: Medical Care Evaluation Committee/Utilization Review Committee, St. Joseph Hospital, Medical Care Evaluation Committee/Utilization Review Committee/Pharmacy Committee, Medical Center Hospital; American Society of /Contemporary Medicine and Surgery; American Fertility Society; American Medical Association; Florida Medical; Association; American Society of Internal Medicine; Florida Society of Internal Medicine; Charlotte County Medical Society; American College of Medicine; New York Academy of Sciences; Royal Society of Medicine; Advisor, Charlotte County Diabetes Foundation; Advisor, Diabetic Insulin Pump Foundation; American Diabetes Association; Kiwanis; Elks; Orlando Endocrine Discussion Group; American College of Physicians; American College of Physician Executives; American College of Endocrinology; Selected Honored Member: Who's Who in Executives and Professionals, Who's Who of Outstanding Americans, The Best Doctors in America, Southeast Region; Author of Numerous publications and presentations; Assistant Clinical Professor, University of South Florida. **Education:** SUNY, Graduate Magna Cum Laude (1967); Cornell University, M.D. (1971); Internship and Assistant Physician, The New York Hospital (1971–1973); Fellowship in Endocrinology, The National Institutes of Health and Joint Endocrinology Training Program (1973–1976); Board Certified in Internal Medicine (1989); Board Eligible in Endocrinology; Licensed Radionuclide Investigator, Atomic Energy Commission **Personal:** Married to Dawn in 1990. Five children: Christine, Elaina, John Jr., Jeffrey and Justin. Dr. Janick enjoys fishing and hunting.

Gregory K. Jenkins, M.D.

Physician
Gregory K. Jenkins, M.D.
6027 Walnut Grove, Suite 303
Memphis, TN 38120
(901) 685–1804
Fax: (901) 685–0453

8011

Business Information: Gregory K. Jenkins, M.D. is a private, medical practice specializing in the diagnosis and non–surgical treatment of diseases. A practicing physician since 1986 and Board–Certified in Internal Medicine, Dr. Jenkins established his private medical practice in 1989, providing quality health care to patients. **Career Steps:** Physician, Gregory K. Jenkins, M.D. (1989–Present); Resident Physician, Baptist Memorial Hospital (1986–1989). **Associations & Accomplishments:** American College of Physicians; Tennessee Medical Association; Chairman of the Board of Directors, Baptist and Physicians Integrated Delivery System; Clinical Assistant Professor of Medicine, University of Tennessee. **Education:** University of Mississippi, M.D. (1986), B.A. in Biological Science (1982). **Personal:** Married to Susan in 1984. Three children: Tyler, Trent, and Matthew. Dr. Jenkins enjoys playing the piano.

William L. Johnson, M.D.

Chief Executive Officer/Physician
William L. Johnson, M.D., P.C.
289 Union Street Prince Edward Square Mall
St. John, New Brunswick E2L 1B4
(506) 634–1719
Fax: (506) 634–0463

8011

Business Information: William L. Johnson, M.D., P.C. is a general practice medical clinic providing general medical services to patients of all ages. Dr. Johnson established his private practice upon conferral of his medical degree in 1963. In addition to his private practice, Dr. Johnson is a staff physician at two local hospitals, Saint John Regional Hospital and St. Josephs' Hospital. **Career Steps:** Chief Executive Officer/Physician, William L. Johnson, M.D., P.C. (1963–Present); Teaching Program, Family Practice Unit – Saint John Regional Hospital, Emergency Department of the Regional St. Josephs' Hospital on a rotation basis (1970–1976, 1978–1994); Staff, Department of Family Medicine, Saint John Regional Hospital and St. Josephs" Hospital (1978–Present); Director of Ambulatory Care, Department of Family Medicine, Saint John Regional Hospital (1983–1986); Associate Professor, Department of Family Medicine, University of Tennessee Center for Health Sciences (1976–1978); Associate Director, Family Practice Residency, St. Josephs" Hospital – East, Memphis Tennessee (1976–1978); District Medical Officer, Air Canada, Canadian National & Via (1974–1976); Atomic Energy of Canada – Saint John New Brunswick Area (1978–Present). **Associations & Accomplishments:** President, New Brunswick Ski Association (1981–1985); Board of Directors, Canadian Ski Association (1981–1985); Host Chairman, Canadian Ski Association National Convention (1985); Poley Mountain Development Association (1986–1991); President, Poley Mountain Development Association (1991–1994); Honorary Fellowship College of Family Physicians (1988); Deputy Head, Department of Family Medicine (1990–1992); New Brunswick Medical Society; Saint John Medical Society; Canadian Medical Association; Canadian Medical Protective Association; Serves on various committees; Clinical Department Head Family Medicine, Region II New Brunswick (1992–Present). **Education:** Dalhousie University, M.D. (1963); Mt. Allison University, B.A. (1957); Internship, Saint John General Hospital, recipient of the Senator Emmerson Award for interning with distinction; Certification: Canadian College of Family Physicians (1972), American Boards – Family Medicine (1978), re – certification (1984). **Personal:** Married.Two Children. Dr. Johnson enjoys skiing, sailing,hiking, and reading.

Helen L. Jones, M.D.

Director of X–Ray and Lab
Linder Quinn Medical Group
210 East Hawes
Fresno, CA 93706–3022
(209) 449–5777
Fax: Please mail or call

8011

Business Information: Linder Quinn Medical Group, established in 1992, is a group medical practice consisting of 11 physician associates, all specializing in internal medicine. As Founding Partner and Director of X–ray and Lab, Dr. Jones is responsible for all aspects of the X–ray and laboratory operations, as well as diagnosis and treatment of patients and setting guidelines and procedures for the Practice. **Career Steps:** Director of X–Ray and Lab, Linder Quinn Medical Group (1992–Present); Sole Proprietor, Helen Jones, M.D. (1988–1992). **Associations & Accomplishments:** Board of Governors Fresno–Madera Medical Society; Instructor, University of California–Davis Physician Assistant Program; Member, American College of Physicians; National Delegate and Local Secretary, American Medical Women's Association; Keynote Speaker, City of Fresno Martin Luther King Celebration; California State University–Fresno Ethnic Studies Advisory Board. **Education:** University of California – San Francisco, M.D. (1985); University of California – Berkeley, B.A.; University of California – Riverside; Clark College – Atlanta, Georgia. **Personal:** Married to Vernon Lee Jones, Jr. in 1988. Three children: Arielle Kiah, Vernon III, and Bryce Hosea. Dr. Jones enjoys playing the cello and bowling on the UCB Women's Team. She is fluent in Spanish.

Victoria Jones, M.D.

Psychiatrist
North York Medical Arts Building
141–1333 Sheppard Avenue East
North York, Ontario M2J 1V1
(416) 491–4318
Fax: Please mail or call
EMAIL: See Below

8011

Business Information: North York Medical Arts Building is a private psychiatric practice specializing in psychotherapy, abuse, eating disorders, infertility/reproductive problems, and adolescent psychiatry. As Psychiatrist, Dr. Jones is responsible for the day–to–day operation of the practice, in addition to prescribing medications, and overseeing patient care. Concurrent with her private practice, Dr. Jones is also a consulting psychiatrist on the staff of North York General Hospital. Internet users can reach her via: vjones@cycor.ca. **Career Steps:** Psychiatrist, North York Medical Arts Building (1985–Present); Consulting Staff, North York General Hospital (1985–Present); Staff Psychiatrist, Queen Elizabeth Hospital, Montreal (1983–1985). **Associations & Accomplishments:** Ontario Medical Association; Canadian Medical Association; Ontario Psychiatric Association; Canadian Psychiatric Association; National Board of Turner's Syndrome Society of Canada. **Education:** McGill University, Certified in Psychiatry (1983); University of Western Ontario, M.D. (1977). **Personal:** Dr. Jones enjoys piano, fitness, yoga, reading, spending time with nieces and nephews, and synagogue membership.

Stephanie L. Joseph, CPA

Controller
Herbert H. Joseph, M.D.
11921 Rockville Pike, Suite 404
Rockville, MD 20852–2737
(301) 770–5884
Fax: (301) 770–3788
EMAIL: Prodigy@BSHY37A

8011

Business Information: Herbert H. Joseph, M.D. is a private orthopaedic medical practice. As Controller, Ms. Joseph prepares all financial statements and tax returns. **Career Steps:** Controller, Herbert H. Joseph, M.D. (1992–Present); Controller, We Care Projects, Inc. (1990–1992); Senior Accountant, Laventhol & Horwath (1986–1990). **Associations & Accomplishments:** American Institute of Certified Public Accountants; District of Columbia Institute of Certified Public Accountants; Crohn's and Colitis Foundation of America. **Education:** George Washington University, B.A. in Accounting, graduated summa cum laude and valedictorian (1986). **Personal:** Ms. Joseph enjoys collecting comic books and trading cards. She is also active in her synagogue and the Washington, D.C. Jewish Healing Network.

Richard G. Judelsohn, M.D.

Managing Partner
Buffalo Pediatric Associates
909 Amherst Manor Drive
Williamsville, NY 14221
(716) 634–0744
Fax: (716) 634–1954

8011

Business Information: Buffalo Pediatric Associates is a medical group practice specializing in pediatric diagnosis and treatment. Established in 1935, Buffalo Pediatric Associates reports annual revenue of $1.8 million and currently employs 21 people, including six physicians and two nurse practitioners. As Managing Partner, Dr. Judelsohn oversees the overall administrative aspects of the Group, in addition to his daily patient practice. Concurrent with his private patient practice, he serves as Medical Director at Erie County Health Department and teaches classes on immunization around the community for the Department. He is also a Clinical Associate Professor of Pediatrics at the State University of New York–Buffalo School of Medicine; and a jazz disc jockey for WBF0 Radio Station. **Career Steps:** Managing Partner, Buffalo Pediatric Associates (1972–Present); Medical Director, Erie County Health Department (1974–Present); Clinical Associate Professor of Pediatrics, State University of New York at Buffalo School of Medicine (1972–Present); Jazz Disc Jockey, WBF0 Radio Station (1976–Present); EIS Officer, U.S. Public Health Service (1970–1972). **Associations & Accomplishments:** American Medical Association; American Public Health Association; New York State Medical Society; Chairman, Public Health Committee and Member of Executive Committee, Medical Society of the County of Erie; American Academy of Pediatrics; Member of Board of Directors, Blue Cross and Blue Shield of Western New York; Broadcasting: Health issues on all local radio and TV stations, and Be-Bop & Beyond – jazz disc jockey WBF0 (1976–Present); Published in American Journal of Public Health and JAMA. **Education:** State University of New York Medical School, M.D. (1967). **Personal:** Married to Antoinette in 1988. Three children: David, Amy, and Alexandra. Dr. Judelsohn enjoys jazz broadcasting and teaching.

Fred J. Kader, M.D.

Pediatric Neurologist
Fred J. Kader, M.D.
8601 West Dodge Road #238
Omaha, NE 68114–3495
(402) 354–8150
Fax: (402) 390–0321

8011

Business Information: A practicing physician since 1964, Dr. Kader established his private practice in 1978. As a Pediatric Neurologist, he oversees all administrative operations for associates and support staff, in addition to his daily patient practice. Concurrently, he serves as Assistant Clinical Professor at Creighton University School of Medicine and University of Nebraska College of Medicine, in addition to serving as Courtesy Staff and Consulting Staff at numerous local hospitals and serving on numerous medical committees. Born in Antwerp, Belgium, he is a refugee of the Holocaust Era — one of the "hidden children" — who spent five years in an orphanage in Belgium during the war. Only having dim recollections of what happened to him during that time, he attended the First International Gathering of Children Hidden During World War II in May 1991. During the two day conference, he was able to ascertain that he had wandered off from his parents' convoy (at four years old), which was en route from Antwerp to Malines and then onto Auschwitz (Malines was the primary gathering spot for those headed to Nazi death camps). He was found later in a room in Malines, with six other children, by several Jewish orphans who were part of a group of 53 Jewish orphaned children who had been saved from certain death by the Queen of Belgium. The six children were placed with the group and sent to Wezembeek, a children's orphanage near Brussels. He was found there at age nine by an uncle, who had hidden in Belgium during the war, looking for surviving family members. Living with his uncle for a short time, he eventually became a part of his great aunt's family in Montreal, Quebec. He took his aunt's last name, Kader, as his own and went on to receive his education and become a naturalized Canadian citizen in 1960. He trained in the U.S. as of 1966 and continued his post graduate training in Maryland and New York hospitals, such as Johns Hopkins Hospital in Baltimore and Albert Einstein College of Medicine of Yeshiva University and Affiliated Hospitals in New York City. Completing his training in 1971, he served in academic and hospital appointments before starting in private practice in 1978. Making his new home in the U.S., he became a naturalized U.S. citizen in 1995. **Career Steps:** Pediatric Neurologist, Fred J. Kader, M.D. (1978–Present); Pediatric Neurologist, Staff, University of Nebraska Medical Center (1974–1978); Staff, Creighton University School of Medicine (1974–1978). **Associations & Accomplishments:** Medical Licensure: States of Nebraska (1975–Present), Iowa (1981–Present), California (1992–Present); Licentiate of the Medical Council of Canada; Certification as a Diplomate by the Nationa Board of Medical Examiners U.S.A.; Neurology, College of Physicians and Surgeons of the Province of Quebec, Canada; Neurology with Special Competence in Child Neurology, American Board of Neurology & Psychiatry; Fellow, American Academy of Pediatrics; Fellow, American Academy of Neurology; National Child Neurological Association; Publisher of numerous articles of pediatric neurology issues. **Education:** McGill University: M.D.C.M. (1964), B.Sc. Honors in Psychology (1960). **Personal:** Married to Sarah in 1964. Three children: Howard A.I., Darrin J., and Eileen R.B. Dr. Kader enjoys reading Civil War literature, music (Klezmer and Cantorial), and stamp collecting.

David J. Kahan, M.D.

Emergency Physician
Professional Emergency Physicians
10163 Bracken Drive
Ellicott City, MD 21042–1675
(410) 368–2000
Fax: Please mail or call

8011

Business Information: Professional Emergency Physicians provides emergency medical care physicians to area hospitals throughout Maryland. An Associate with the Group, Dr. David Kahan is currently assigned to the Emergency Services Division, providing all emergency patient care at St. Agnes Hospital in Baltimore, MD. **Career Steps:** Emergency Physician, Professional Emergency Physicians (1994–Present); Emergency Physician, EMSA (1991–1993); Emergency Physician, Emergency Service Systems (1989–1991). **Associations & Accomplishments:** Association of Emergency Physicians; National Rifle Association. **Education:** University of Maryland School of Medicine, M.D. (1985); University of Maryland at College Park, B.S., cum laude (1979). **Personal:** Married to Kristina in 1985. Three children: Aaron, Rachel, and Allison. Dr. Kahan enjoys music (specifically guitar playing), homebrewing, weightlifting, and shooting.

Vijay Kalidindi, M.D., F.A.A.P.

Pediatrician
Offices of Vijay Kalidindi, M.D.
1701 Main Street
Baton Rouge, LA 70810
(504) 343–1624
Fax: Please mail or call

8011

Business Information: Offices of Vijay Kalidindi is a full service pediatric practice providing health care to children. Dr. Kalidindi is board certified in Pediatrics and board eligible in Cardiology. Dr. Kalidindi, besides working full time at Eden Park Health Center, also serves on staff at Woman's Hospital, and Our Lady of the Lake Regional Medical Center at Baton Rouge, LA. **Career Steps:** Pediatrician, Eden Park Health Center (1996–Present); Children's Hospital of Michigan/ Wayne State University School of Medicine, Detroit, MI: Fellow in Pediatric Cardiology (1992–1995), Resident in Pediatrics (1989–1992). **Associations & Accomplishments:** Fellow, American Academy of Pediatrics; Member, American College of Cardiology; Licensed to practice Medicine in Michigan and Louisiana; Published in Pediatric Journals. **Education:** Osmania Medical College, M.B., B.S.; Board Certified in Pediatrics. **Personal:** Dr. Kalidindi enjoys travel, photography and dancing.

Dorothy H. Kelly, M.D.

Associate Director and Clinical Professor of Pediatrics
University of Texas Medical Branch
301 University Boulevard
Galveston, TX 77555
(409) 772–1011
Fax: (409) 297–4202

8011

Business Information: Dr. Dorothy Kelly — a Board–certified Pediatrician, with a sub–specialty in Pediatric Pulmonology — is currently assigned to the University of Texas' Southeast SIDS Research Institute. As Associate Director, she conducts extensive research for treatment and cause of infants predisposed to pulmonary disorders. Concurrent to her research work, she also is a Staff Physician and Clinical Professor of Pediatrics with the University of Texas at Houston, Brazos Port Memorial Hospital – Lake Jackson, Texas and the Univeristy of Texas Medical Branch. **Career Steps:** University of Texas Medical Branch: Associate Director of Southeast SIDS Research Institute (1994–Present), Associate Clinical Professor of Pediatrics (1995–Present), Associate Clinical Professor of Ambulatory Division – Dept. of Pediatrics (1995–Present); Associate Clinical Professor of Pediatrics, University of Texas at Houston (1995–Present); Harvard Medical School: Associate Professor of Pediatrics (1989–1995), Assistant Professor of Pediatrics (1981–1989); Massachusetts General Hospital: Associate Director of Pediatric Pulmonary Unit (1988–1995), Assistent Pediatrician (1979–1984), Pediatric Group Practice (1975–1995); Health Consultant, Research Council of New Zealand. **Associations & Accomplishments:** American Medical Women's Association; American Board of Pediatrics; American Academy of Pediatrics; American Thoracic Society; International Pediatric Society; Association for the Psychophysiological Study of Sleep; Society for Pediatric Research; Massachusetts Thoracic Society; The Eastern Society for Pediatric Research; American Autonomic Society; Professional Organization Society for Pediatric Research; Who's Who in American Colleges and Universities; Phi Beta Kappa; Alpha Omega Alpha; Awarded: "Woman of Vision" award from National Society for Prevention of Blindness, Massachusetts Affiliate (1981); Fitchburg State College first person awarded "Distinguished Alumni" (1984); MAJOR RESEARCH INTERESTS: Control of Ventilation, Sudden Infant Death Syndrome (SIDS), Sleep Apnea, Autonomic Nervous System Dysfunction in Infants & Children with Apnea; Numerous lectures and publications in the field of SIDS and other Pediatric Pulmonary disorders. **Education:** Wayne State University School of Medicine, M.D. with distinction (1972); Wayne State University, B.S. with distinction; Fitchburg State College, B.S.N. magna cum laude (1966); INTERNSHIP: Massachusetts General Hospital, Department of Pediatrics (1972–1973); RESIDENCIES: Resident in Pediatrics, Massachusetts General Hospital; Teaching Fellow – Harvard Medical School (1973–1975). **Personal:** One child: Jonathan.

Judy McPherson–Kelly, D.C.

Clinical Director
CliniCorp Medical Center
2661 Midway Road, Suite 102
Carrollton, TX 75006
(214) 713–6496
Fax: (214) 248–7559

8011

Business Information: CliniCorp Medical Center, established in 1992, is a health care clinic providing care in chiropractic medicine. As Clinical Director, Dr. Kelly is responsible for all clinical operations of the Center and providing health care in Chiropractic medicine. **Career Steps:** Clinical Director, CliniCorp Medical Center (1992–Present); Accident & Injury Chiropractic, Private Practice (1991–1992). **Associations & Accomplishments:** State Alumni Representative, Life College. **Education:** Life College, D.C. (1988). **Personal:** Married to Joseph in 1991. Two children: James and Christopher. Dr. Kelly enjoys spending time with her two little boys.

Andrea B. Kent, D.O.

Physician
Tallahassee Endocrine Associates
1330 Miccosukee Road, Suite 201
Tallahassee, FL 32308–5069
(904) 877–7387
Fax: (904) 656–3376

8011

Business Information: Tallahassee Endocrine Associates is a health care practice specializing in endocrine and metabolism problems. Established in 1985, Tallahassee Endocrine Associates consists of two physician associates, one nurse practitioner and twelve administrative support staff. Board–certified in Osteopathy and Internal Medicine, Dr. Kent provides diagnosis and treatment in metabolic and endocrine disorders (i.e., diabetes, Thyroid dysfunction, hormonal imbalance). **Career Steps:** Physician, Tallahassee Endocrine Associates (1993–Present); Endocrine Fellow, Medical College of Georgia (1991–1993); Medical Director, The Diabetes Center at Tallahassee Memorial (1993–Present); Internal Medicine Resident, Cabrini Medical Center (1988–1991); Intern, Massapequa General Hospital (1987–1988). **Associations & Accomplishments:** Board of Governors, Capital Medical Society; Capital Medical Society; American Medical Association; American Osteopathic Association; Florida Medical Association; American Association of Clinical Endocrinologists; Diplomate of the American Board of Osteopathic Medical Examiners (1988); Diplomate of the American Board of Internal Medicine (1991); Licensure: Georgia and Florida; Florida Endocrine Society; House Staff Association, Cabrini Medical Center: President (1990–1991), Vice President (1989–1990); Student Osteopathic Medical Association – President (1984–1985); Coordinator and President, Birth Control Clinic of the State University of New York at Binghamton (1982–1983); Clinical Assistant, University Health Center of the State of University of New York at Binghamton (1979–1983); Presentation at the Meeting of the Southern Society for Clinical Investigation of an abstract, "Osteoclastic Activation Causes Hypercalcemia in Acute Myleloblastic Leukemia," (1992); Numerous research experiences; Numerous publications. **Education:** New York College of Osteopathic Medicine, D.Osteo. (1987); State University of New York–Binghamton, B.A with honors. **Personal:** Married to Graydon R. Kent in 1991. Dr. Kent enjoys hiking, running, boating, and collecting antiques.

Algimantas S. Kerpe, M.D.

Primary Care Physician
Dreyer Medical Clinic, S.C.
1870 West Galena Boulevard
Aurora, IL 60506
(708) 879–2110
Fax: (708) 879–2155

8011

Business Information: Dreyer Medical Clinic, S.C. is an establishment of licensed medical practitioners engaged in the practice of general and internal medicine. A practicing physician since 1980, Dr. Kerpe joined the medical clinic in 1989. As a Primary Care Physician, Dr. Kerpe provides quality, general medical care to patients. **Career Steps:** Primary Care Physician, Dreyer Medical Clinic, S.C. (1994–Present); Clinical Instructor, University of Chicago (1988–1989); Clinical Instructor, University of Illinois (1983–1988); Instructor in Internal Medicine, L.A. Weiss Memorial, a University of Chicago affiliate (1983–1989). **Associations & Accomplishments:** American College of Physicians; American Medical Associations; American Society of Internal Medicine; Published article in Archives (1980). **Education:** University of Illinois, M.D. (1980); Illinois Benedectine College, B.S.

Steven R. Kilgore

Program Director of Biofeedback and Psychological Services
Georgia Neurology Associates, P.C.
4500 North Shallowford Road, Suite 200
Atlanta, GA 30338–6404
(770) 390–9001
Fax: (770) 698–8979

8011

Business Information: Georgia Neurology Associates, P.C. is the leading neurology facility in Georgia, currently operating from six satellite offices throughout the greater Atlanta metro. Joining Georgia Neurology Associates as Program Director of Biofeedback and Psychological Services upon the request of a psychologist friend in 1992, Mr. Kilgore is responsible for numerous functions within the facilities, including the oversight of bio–feedback therapy, massage therapy, EEG testing, and others. He also provides direct patient care and hypnotherapy as a licensed Clinical Hypnotherapist. **Career Steps:** Program Director of Biofeedback and Psychological Services, Georgia Neurology Associates, P.C. (1992–Present); Program Director, Georgia Center For Headaches (1992–1995); Clinical Director and Administrator, Dekalb Pain Management & Rehabilitation Center (1982–1992). **Associations & Accomplishments:** Newsmagazine Editor (1991–1995), Association for Applied Psychophysiology & Biofeedback; National Association of Social Workers; American Board of Medical Psychotherapists. **Education:** University of Georgia, M.S.W. (1982); Emory University, B.A. (1977). **Personal:** Two children: Judson and Kevin. Mr. Kilgore enjoys fitness, aerobics, reading, and spending time with his children.

David B. King, BSC, MD, FRCP(c)

Neurologist
David B. King, BSC, MD, FRCP
5523 Spring Garden Road, Suite 208
Halifax, Nova Scotia B3J 3T1
(902) 425–7344
Fax: (902) 423–0879
EMAIL: See Below

8011

Business Information: David B. King, BSC, MD, FRCP is a full–service, neurological practice for adult patients. Dr. King has been practicing medicine since receiving his degree in 1971. Seventy–five percent of his time is spent with patients, and the rest is divided into doing research, teaching, and administrating. Internet users can reach him via: LITCH33@aol.com. **Career Steps:** Neurologist, David B. King, BSC, MD, FRCP (1971–Present). **Associations & Accomplishments:** Canadian Neurologic Society; American Academy of Neurology; World Society of Movement Disorders; Canadian Society of Movement Disorders; Royal College of Physicians and Surgeons of Canada; Canadian Headache Society; Medicolegal Society of Nova Scotia; Atlantic

Clinical Neurosciences Society. **Education:** University of Toronto, FRCP(c) (1975); Dalhousie University: B.Sc., M.D. cum laude (1971). **Personal:** Married to Gillian in 1985. One child: Daniel. Dr. King enjoys history and wine.

Douglas H. Kirkpatrick, M.D.

President
Douglas Kirkpatrick, M.D., P.C.
4200 West Conejos Place, Suite 516
Denver, CO 80204
(303) 571–1821
Fax: (303) 875–5001

8011

Business Information: Douglas Kirkpatrick, M.D., P.C. is a private practice medical office, specializing in obstetrics and gynecology. A practicing physician since 1969 and a Board–Certified Obstetrician and Gynecologist, Dr. Kirkpatrick established his private medical practice in 1976. He is responsible for the oversight of all administrative operations for associates and a support staff of nine, in addition to his daily patient practice. Concurrent with his medical practice, he teaches to residents at the University of Colorado Health Science Center. **Career Steps:** President, Douglas Kirkpatrick, M.D., P.C. (1976–Present); Clinical Assistant Professor, University of Colorado Health Science Center. **Associations & Accomplishments:** American College of Obstetricians/Gynecologists, Colorado Section: Secretary of District VIII (Western USA) and Vice Chair Elect for District VIII (1996), Chair and Vice–Chair (1986–1991); President, Colorado GYN/OB Society (1989); American College of Obstetricians/Gynecologists, Colorado Section Chair & Vice Chair (1986–1991); Published in numerous medical journals and other Who's Who publications and directories. **Education:** Cornell College, A.B. (1965); University of Iowa, M.D. (1969); University of Michigan Medical School, Residency OB/GYN (1972–1975). **Personal:** Married to Joan Mae Landquist in 1966. Three children: Scott, Kristin, and Brooke. Dr. Kirkpatrick enjoys downhill and cross country skiing, mountain biking, and mountain climbing. He has climbed all of Colorado's 14,000 feet+ peaks (a total of 54).

Joseph W. Kittinger, M.D.

Gastroenterologist
Wilmington Health Associates
1202 Medical Center Drive
Wilmington, NC 28401
(910) 341–3345
Fax: (910) 341–3419

8011

Business Information: Wilmington Health Associates is a multi–specialty, group medical practice consisting of 45 physicians. Specialties are in allergy/pulmonary, cardiology, dermatology, endocrinology, gastroenterology, general medicine, infectious diseases, neurology, neuropsychology, oncology/hematology, and general surgery. Established in 1970, Wilmington Health Associates operates three offices located in Wilmington, including a surgery office and currently employs 170 people. As Gastroenterologist, Dr. Kittinger is responsible for providing diagnosis and treatment of patients suffering from stomach and intestinal disorders. Concurrent with his medical practice, he serves as an Associate Professor at the University of North Carolina – Chapel Hill. **Career Steps:** Gastroenterologist, Wilmington Health Associates (1985–Present); Associate Professor, University of North Carolina – Chapel Hill (1985–Present). **Associations & Accomplishments:** Ameircan Gastroenterological Association; American College of Physicians. **Education:** University of Arkansas, M.D. (1980); University of North Carolina – Chapel Hill, Fellowship in Gastroenterology (1985). **Personal:** Married to Sandra in 1975. Dr. Kittinger enjoys participating in triathlons and marathons.

Neil C. Klein, M.D.

Physician
Stamford Medical Group
1450 Washington Boulevard
Stamford, CT 06902–2451
(203) 327–9321
Fax: (203) 967–2140

8011

Business Information: Stamford Medical Group is an association of internists established in 1966. Dr. Klein practices internal medicine with a subspecialty interest in gastroenterology. **Career Steps:** Physician, Stamford Medical Group (1967–Present). **Associations & Accomplishments:** Fellow of the American College of Physicians (FACP); Fellow of the American College of Gastroenterology (FACG); American Gastroenterology Association (AGA); ASGE; Past President, Cornell University Medical School Alumni Association; Past President, Fairfield County Medical Association; Past President, Stamford Medical Society; Past Associate, Chief Dept. of Medicine, Stamfrod Hospital; Past Chairman, Section of Gastroenterology, Stamford Hospital; Member, Board of Trustees, Officer, Insurance Company; Member of Board, Chairman, Finance Committee, Stamford Health Network; Clinical Professor of Medicine, New York Medical College. **Education:** Cornell University, M.D. (1960); Columbia University, A.B. (1956). **Personal:** Married to Phyllis in 1989. Three children: Lisa, Susannah, and David; and two stepchildren: Emily and Oliver.

Kevin J. Kollman, M.D.

Site Director
Geisinger Medical Group – Tyrone
2 Hospital Drive
Tyrone, PA 16686
(814) 684–2438
Fax: (814) 684–0461

8011

Business Information: Geisinger Medical Group – Tyrone is a full–service, general medicine practice consisting of three full–time physicians and five part–time physicians. Geisinger Medical Group in Tyrone is a part of the Geisinger System – a health care organization which provides health care in rural Pennsylvania. In addition to Geisinger System owning and operating a tertiary care facility in Danville, a community hospital in Wilkes–Barre and a substance abuse center in Waverly, the System provides other medical services such as home infusion through Vitaline and health care and medical insurance products through the Geisinger Health Plans. Geisinger is a system of over one hundred (100) offices throughout Central and Northeastern Pennsylvania. The Geisinger Health Plans provide for managed care programs, point of service options, worker's compensation coverage and wellness programs, in addition to providing third party administrative services for organizations who want to self–insure the health care and well–being of their employees. The Geisinger Health Plans division was established in 1985, employs approximately 200 people serving approximately 200,000 members. A practicing physician for eleven years, Dr. Kollman joined Geisinger Medical Group in 1992. Serving as Site Director, he is responsible for the direction of all operations at the Tyrone site, including administration, finances, public relations, accounting, marketing, and strategic planning. **Career Steps:** Site Director, Geisinger Medical Group – Tyrone (1995–Present); Staff Physician, Brookville Hospital (1988–1992); Tyrone Hospital: Chief of Medicine, Director of ICU, Director of Respiratory Services, Director of Medical Education (1994–Present). **Associations & Accomplishments:** American College of Physicians; Diplomat, American Board of Internal Medicine (1987). **Education:** Ross University School of Medicine, M.D. (1984); Internal Medicine Residency: St. Thomas Medical Center, Akron, OH (1984–1988). **Personal:** Married to Yvonne Patterson, M.D. in 1985. Three children: Kera, Kristopher and Kayla. Dr. Kollman enjoys camping, boating, and fishing during his leisure time.

R. Michael Kough

Executive Director
Echo Health Center
713 North Second Avenue
Evansville, IN 47710–1592
(812) 421–9850
Fax: (812) 421–9855

8011

Business Information: Echo Health Center is the only free clinic in Southern Indiana, providing medical treatment of uninsured, underinsured, or low–income individuals. Joining Echo Health Center as Executive Director in 1995, Mr. Kough is responsible for all facets of operations, including writing grants, budgets, hiring, and supervision of personnel. **Career Steps:** Executive Director, Echo Health Center (1995–Present); Principal Broker, River City Realty (1989–1996); President, Northstar Electronic Systems, Inc. (1983–1992); Field Consultant, Indiana Office of Social Services (1976–1983). **Associations & Accomplishments:** United Way Allocations Panel (1979–1983); Co–Chairperson (1995), Partners in Caring Subcommittee Health, Mental Health and Substance Abuse; Steering Committee, Foundation for Community Health; Crisis Line Volunteer; Eagle Scout; Parish Council; Outstanding Young Men of America (1979). **Education:** University of Evansville: M.A. (1976), B.S. (1970). **Personal:** Married to Barbara in 1967. One child: Thomas. Mr. Kough enjoys boating, skiing and piloting (private pilot).

Michael A. Kozer

Executive Director
Preferred Primary Care Physicians
2101 Greentree Road
Pittsburgh, PA 15220–1400
(412) 429–7727
Fax: (412) 429–9466

8011

Business Information: Preferred Primary Care Physicians is a multi–specialty managed care physicians group practice. Established in 1995, Preferred Primary Care Physicians currently employs 20 physicians and 85 medical support staff in 11 offices. As Executive Director, Mr. Kozer is responsible for all aspects of corporate operations, including human resources and training. **Career Steps:** Executive Director, Preferred Primary Care Physicians (1994–Present); Assistant Administrator, Tri–State Orthopedics (1986–1994); Regional Support Manager, Computerland (1982–1986). **Associations & Accomplishments:** Medical Group Management Association; Management Professionals in Healthcare. **Education:** Duquesne University, B.S. (1981). **Personal:** Mr. Kozer enjoys golf, boating, hunting, and skiing.

Patricia A. Kroken

Executive Director
Radiology Associates of Albuquerque
P.O. Box 3130
Albuquerque, NM 87190–3130
(505) 292–8485
Fax: Please mail or call

8011

Business Information: Radiology Associates of Albuquerque is a large radiologic practice consisting of seventeen physician associates also offering medical management services and medical–legal consultants. A Certified Medical Practice Executive, Ms. Kroken joined Radiology Associates as Business Development Director in 1990. Appointed as Executive Director in 1993, she is responsible for the oversight of all financial and operational functions, as well as strategic planning, contract negotiations, business expansion, and marketing planning. In addition, she oversees all administrative operations for associates and a support staff of 55. **Career Steps:** Radiology Associates of Albuquerque: Executive Director (1993–Present), Business Development Director (1990–1993); Marketing Director, X–Ray Associates (1989–1990); Adjunct Professor of Advertising, University of New Mexico (1982–1994). **Associations & Accomplishments:** Publications Committee, Radiology Business Management Association; New Mexico Medical Group Management Association: President (1995) and Board of Directors; Medical Group Management Association. **Education:** Northern Michigan University, B.S. in Education (1970); American College of Medical Practice Executives, Medical Practice Executive Certification. **Personal:** Married to Bruce in 1967. Two children: Christina and Jennifer. Ms. Kroken enjoys horseback riding, writing, music, and reading.

Michael L. Kudla, M.D.

Owner/Physician
Dr. Michael Kudla, OB/Gyn
2770 2nd Avenue, Suite 203
Lake Charles, LA 70601–8902
(318) 477–7871
Fax: Please mail or call

8011

Business Information: Dr. Kudla has been a practicing physician since obtaining his degree in 1973. He has been the Owner and Sole Practitioner of his medical office, Dr. Michael Kudla, OB/Gyn since 1978. Affiliated with three hospitals in the Lake Charles area, Dr. Kudla specializes in women's health and prenatal care. **Career Steps:** Owner/Physician, Dr. Michael Kudla, OB/GYN (1978–Present). **Associations & Accomplishments:** Chairman, Board of Directors, Children's Shelter; Chairman, State Medical Society – Physician's Health Committee. **Education:** University of Texas Southwestern – Medical School, M.D. (1973); Louisiana State University, P.A. **Personal:** Married to Joellen in 1968. Two children: Jeff and Colleen. Dr. Kudla enjoys sailing, climbing, and literature.

Sharda Kumar, M.D.

Pediatrician
Stanocola Medical
1401 North Foster Drive
Baton Rouge, LA 70806
(504) 926–7200
Fax: (504) 928–6797

8011

Business Information: Stanocola Medical is a full–service, multi–specialty acute and primary care medical facility. Established in 1924, the Clinic currently employs 130 people. Board–certified in Pediatrics, and also with a background in OB/Gyn specialties since 1966, Dr. Kumar joined the Pediatrics staff at Stanocola in 1983. **Career Steps:** Pediatrician, Stanocola Medical (1983–Present); Pediatric Consultant, Mental Health (1978–1982); Instructor of Pediatrics, Louisiana State University Medical Hospital (1976–1978). **Associations & Accomplishments:** American Medical Association; Louisiana State Medical Society; American Board of Pediatrics; Louisiana State Pediatric Society; Baton Rouge Pediatric Society. **Education:** Patna University, M.S. in Obstetrics and Gynecology (1966); Prince of Wales College Patna, Bihar, India, M.B.B.S. **Personal:** Married to Dr. M.B. Kumar in

1965. Two children: Madhuresh and Vinita. Dr. Kumar enjoys gardening and working with special needs children.

David L. Kyger, M.D.

Physician
Muskogee Regional Medical Center
3332 West Okmulgee
Muskogee, OK 74401–5069
(918) 682–2482
Fax: Please mail or call

8011

Business Information: The Office of Dr. David L. Kyger, M.D. is a full–service, private practice medical facility. Board–certified in Internal Medicine, Dr. Kyger is affiliated with the Muskogee Regional Medical Center. Re–establishing the Muskogee, Oklahoma office in 1985, Dr. Kyger oversees an office staff of four, as well as his daily patient practice. **Career Steps:** Private Practice Physician, Muskogee, OK (1985–Present, 1971–1976); Private Practice Physician, Santa Fe, NM (1976–1985). **Associations & Accomplishments:** American Society of Internal Medicine; East Central Oklahoma Medical Society; Oklahoma State Medical Association; American Medical Association; Thoroughbred Owners and Breeders Association. **Education:** Washington University School of Medicine, M.D. (1967); Resident in Medicine, University of Oklahoma, Health Sciences Center (1970–1971); Resident in Medicine, St. John's Mercy Hospital (1968–1970); Rotating Internship, St. John's Mercy Hospital, St. Louis, MO (1967–1968).. **Personal:** Married to Susan Masters in 1984. Seven children: Christine, Robert, John George, Laura Elizabeth, Danielle Wong, May Yen, and John Paul Yen. Dr. Kyger enjoys breeding thoroughbreds, organizing racing partnerships, and breeding poultry.

Anne R. LaForte–Moore, M.D.

Consultant Psychiatrist
Beaver County Psychiatric Services
219 3rd Street
Beaver, PA 15009
(412) 775–9150
Fax: (412) 775–9153

8011

Business Information: Beaver County Psychiatric Services, established in 1991, provides mental health services to adults and children. As Consultant Psychiatrist, Dr. LaForte–Moore is responsible for providing assessments for children and family psychiatric programs. Concurrent with her position at Beaver County Psychiatric Services, Dr. LaForte–Moore is a consultant physician at University of Pittsburgh Medical Center – Beaver Valley, Sarnia General Hospital, and The Pearson Centre, Chatam (Ontario, Canada), and is Director and Speaker at ADHD Educational Seminars. **Career Steps:** Consultant Psychiatrist, Beaver County Psychiatric Services (1994–Present); Consultant Psychiatrist, University of Pittsburgh Medical Center (1994–Present); Consultant Psychiatrist, Sarma General Hospital (1988–Present); Lecturer, Department of Psychiatry, University of Western Ontario (1985–1990); Director of Child and Family Services, Woodstock General Hospital (1985–1988). **Associations & Accomplishments:** Fellow of the Royal College of Physicians and Surgeons of Canada; Canadian Academy of Child and Adolescent Psychiatrists; American Society of Adolescent Psychiatrists. **Education:** University of the West Indies, M.D. (1980); FRCPC/CABAP, (Canadian and American Board Certification in Adult and Adolescent Psychiatry). **Personal:** Married to Gordon B. Moore in 1994. Three children: Shona, Zonia, and Zariq. Dr. LaForte–Moore enjoys travel and reading for pleasure.

Dinesh K. Lahoti, M.D.

Sole Practitioner
The Office of Dinesh K. Lahoti, M.D.
#E –2636, West State Street
Olean, NY 14760
(716) 373–5801
Fax: (716) 373–5802

8011

Business Information: The Office of Dinesh K. Lahoti, M.D. is a private practice medical facility specializing in Internal Medicine for adults and the elderly. Established in 1985, the Office currently employs three medical support staff. As Sole Practitioner, Dr. Lahoti provides all administrative direction and patient treatment. Board–certified in Internal Medicine, Dr. Lahoti is affiliated with area hospitals as a Staff Internist. He plans to return to India in the next five years, open a private practice to help the underprivileged, and write a book on the subject of unconventional medicine. **Career Steps:** Sole Practitioner, The Office of Dinesh K. Lahoti, M.D. (1985–Present). **Associations & Accomplishments:** New York State Medical Society; Cattaraugus County Medical Society. **Education:** New York Medical College, M.D. (1975). **Personal:** Married to Manju in 1981. Two children: Neha and Mayauk. Dr. Lahoti enjoys reading.

Jules Y.T. Lam, M.D.

Cardiologist
Montreal Heart Institute
5000 Belanger Street East
Montreal, Quebec H1T 1C8
(514) 376–3330
Fax: (514) 672–8900

8011

Business Information: Montreal Heart Institute is a subspecialty medical practice specializing in cardiology, currently employing 60 physicians, 35 of whom are cardiologists. A practicing physician and Cardiologist since 1979, Dr. Lam practices a non–invasive treatment in cardiology, treating patients through lifestyle modification, as well as drug therapy. In addition, he is involved in clinical and laboratory research which is funded by the Medical Research Center, the Canadian government, and the Institute. He has written articles on the work–related effects of nitroglycerine on thrombosis in numerous cardiology journals. **Career Steps:** Cardiologist, Montreal Heart Institute (1989–Present); Associate Professor of Medicine, University of Montreal (1987); Cardiologist, Montreal (1987). **Associations & Accomplishments:** American College of Cardiology; American Heart Association, Thrombosis Council; Canadian Cardiovascular Society. **Education:** McGill University: M.D, C.M. (1979); Mayo Clinic, and Mayo Graduate School of Medicine. **Personal:** Married to Teresa.

Elaine L. Lambert, RN, CNOR, BPS

Director
Orthopedic Surgery Center
HC 64 Box 698 Kersarge Valley Road
Wilmont, NH 03287–9801
(603) 228–7211
Fax: Please mail or call

8011

Business Information: Established in 1995, Orthopedic Surgery Center is a health care facility specializing in orthopaedic surgery and rehabilitative medicine, including orthopaedic surgery, sports medicine, and rheumatology. A registered nurse with over twenty–five years of administrative nursing, Elaine Lambert was appointed as Director of the Center in 1994. She planned, staffed and opened the entire Center. She has the responsiblilty for the entire operation of the Center including daily operations, patient care, human resources, medical records, and a variety of administrative functions. **Career Steps:** Director, Orthopedic Surgery Center (1994–Present); Director, Senior Manager of Operating Room, Rutland Medical Center (1991–1994); Valley Regional Hospital Director of Operating Room (1982–1991), Charge Nurse for ICU and House Supervisor (1972–1982). **Associations & Accomplishments:** National Association of Orthopedic Nurses; Association of Operating Room Nurses; National Association of Female Executives; National Organization of Nurse Executives; Federated Ambulatory Sugery Association. **Education:** University of New Hampshire, B.P.S. (1993); Association of Operating Room Nurses Certified; Presbyterian/ Univeristy of Pennsylvania – Philadelphia, PA, Diploma in Nursing. **Personal:** Married to Dennis in 1989. Two children: Brenda and Bruce. Ms. Lambert enjoys travel, antiquing and reading.

Preston R. Lamberton, M.D.

Physician
Diabetes and Endocrinology Associates, Inc.
180 Central Avenue
North Scituate, RI 02857–2117
(401) 351–7100
Fax: (401) 751–6179

8011

Business Information: Diabetes and Endocrinology Associates, Inc. is a specialty medical group providing care and treatment for patients with Diabetes and endocrinology disorders. As Physician, Dr. Lamberton is responsible for the care and treatment of patients. Concurrent to his position as a Physician, Dr. Lamberton is also a Clinical Associate Professor of Medicine at the Brown University School of Medicine. **Career Steps:** Physician, Diabetes and Endocrinology Associates, Inc. (Present); Associate Professor, Brown University School of Medicine (Present). **Associations & Accomplishments:** Former President, Rhode Island Affiliate, American Diabetes Association; Chairperson, Diabetes Professional Advisory Council, Rhode Island Department of Health; Endocrine Society; American Diabetes Association; American Medical Association; American Thyroid Association. Education: Yale University School of Medicine, M.D. (1978); University of Vermont, B.A. (1974). **Personal:** Married to Deborah Ann in 1980. Three children: Robert Ryan, Jennifer and Jill. Dr. Lamberton enjoys his family and the time he spends as the Scituate High School boy's varsity assistant soccer coach.

Randall C. Lanier, M.D.

Physician Associate
Affinity Health Group
712 East 18th Street
Tifton, GA 31794
(912) 382–3814
Fax: (912) 382–8474

8011

Business Information: Affinity Health Group is a multi–specialty medical clinic, serving patients in Tifton, Georgia and surrounding counties. A Physician Partner with the Group since 1990, Dr. Lanier specializes in the treatment and care of pulmonary diseases and critical care. Established in 1960, Affinity Health Group employs 16 physicians and 80 physician associates and administrative support staff people. **Career Steps:** Physician Partner, Tifton Medical Clinic, P.A., (1990–Present). **Associations & Accomplishments:** American Thoracic Society; Fellow, College of Chest Physicians; American Medical Association; Tifton Medical Society; Director, Tifton Hospice; Task Force for Tuberculosis; Education for the American Lung Association. **Education:** Medical College of Georgia, M.D. (1985); University of South Carolina Medical School, Fellow of Pulmonary and Critical Care (1990). **Personal:** Married to Kathy in 1984. Three children: Martin, Amanda and Callie. Dr. Lanier enjoys hunting, fishing, and golf.

Michael J. Larkin Jr., M.D.

New Castle Orthopedic Associates
2602 Wilmington Road
New Castle, PA 16105–1594
(412) 652–7702
Fax: (412) 652–4489

8011

Business Information: Dr. Larkin has been in private orthopedic practice in New Castle, Pennsylvania, since ending his orthopedic surgery residency at Temple University Hospital and Shriner's Hospital for Crippled Children in 1982. In addition, he presently serves as President of the Medical and Dental Staff at Jameson Memorial Hospital, a 250–bed full–service, community hospital, and a staff orthopedic surgeon at St. Francis Hospital. **Career Steps:** Orthopedic Surgeon, New Castle Orthopedic Associates (1982–Present); Jameson Memorial Hospital: Orthopedic Staff (1982–Present), President of Medical and Dental Staff (1995–1996); Orthopedic Staff, St. Francis Hospital (1982–Present). **Associations & Accomplishments:** Pennsylvania Orthopedic Society; Fellow, American Academy of Orthopedic Surgeons; Eastern Orthopedic Society; Former President, Lawrence County Medical Society; Pennsylvania Medical Society; Former President, Interstate Orthopedic Society; Fellow, American College of Physicians. **Education:** St. Louis University, B.S. (1969); University of Padua, School of Medicine – Padua, Italy (1970–1974); Temple University School of Medicine, M.D. (1977); Temple University Hospital, General Surgery Internship (1977–1978); Shriner's Hospital for Crippled Children/ Temple University Hospital, Orthopedic Surgery Residency (1978–1982); National Board of Medical Examiners, Certificate; American Board of Orthopedic Surgery, Certificate (1984); Licensed, State of New Jersey; Board Certified Orthopedic Surgery, American Board of Orthopedic Surgery (1984). **Personal:** Married to Gabriela in 1972. Three children: Tanya, Karen and Katie. Dr. Larkin enjoys tennis and golf, and is a member of the New Castle Country Club.

German Lasala, M.D.

Physician
Arizona Community Physicians
6365 East Tanque Verde #200
Tucson, AZ 85715
(520) 298–3000
Fax: (520) 296–6695

8011

Business Information: Arizona Community Physicians is a full–service medical group practice, specializing in primary care. Established in 1994, there are currently 12 physician associates in five locations throughout Arizona. Dr. German Lasala, Board–certified in Internal Medicine since 1992, provides medical care and administrative direction for the group. **Career Steps:** Physician, Arizona Community Physicians (1994–Present); Physician, Canjon Internal Medicine (1991–1994). **Associations & Accomplishments:** American College of Physicians; American Medical Association; Latin American Medical Society; Received state and national recognition for group and himself. **Education:** Universidad Central del Caribe, M.D. (1988); Board certified since 1992;

Fully bilingual in English and Spanish. **Personal:** Married to Brenda in 1988. Three children: Gabriella, Adriana, and Andrea. Dr. Lasala enjoys spending time with his family, travel, and scuba diving.

Paul M. Latonero, M.D.
Pediatrician
Paul M. Latonero, M.D. P.C.
310 Fullerton Avenue
Newburgh, NY 12550
(914) 561–5227
Fax: Please mail or call

8011

Business Information: Paul M. Latonero, M.D. P.C. is a private medical practice specializing in pediatric and adolescent medicine, affiliated with St. Luke's and Cornwall hospitals. A Board–Certified Pediatrician in the U.S., United Kingdom and Canada, Dr. Latonero established his private pediatric practice in 1975. Concurrent with his private pediatrics practice, he serves as an attending physician and Chairman of the Department of Pediatrics at St. Luke's Hospital; where he is currently involved in the implementation of a Level II Neonatal critical care unit. **Career Steps:** Pediatrician, Paul M. Latonero, M.D. P.C. (1975–Present); Attending Physician (1975–Present) and Chairman of the Department of Pediatrics (1990–Present), St. Luke's Hospital; Assistant Professor of New Jersey College of Medicine. **Associations & Accomplishments:** Fellow of the American Academy of Pediatrics; Board Certified American Board of Pediatrics; Member, New York State Medical Society. **Education:** New Jersey College of Medicine, Pediatrics (1972). **Personal:** Married to Manolita in 1970. Three children: Tina, Mark, and Jeff. Dr. Latonero enjoys skiing, movies, and fitness programs.

Kadie E. Leach, M.D.

Sole Practitioner
Kadie Elaine Leach, M.D., P.A.
9500 Annapolis Road #A1
Lanham, MD 20706
(301) 577–5819
Fax: (301) 577–4120

8011

Business Information: A practicing physician since 1975 and an Internal Medicine Physician, Dr. Leach established her private, sole practice medical office in 1985. Her practice is 85% focused on internal medicine (i.e., cardiovascular disease, arthritis, renal disease, etc.), with 15% of the practice concentrating on emergency medicine and trauma. In addition to being certified in Flexible Sigmoidoscopy, Dr. Leach concurrently serves as an active staff member of Internal Medicine at Doctor's Community Hospital, Prince George's General Hospital, and Washington Hospital Center. **Career Steps:** Sole Practitioner, Kadie Elaine Leach, M.D. (1985–Present); Claims Review Board, American Postal Worker's Union Insurance Company (1991–1993); Associate Medical Director, Patuxent Naval Emergency Department (1989–1991); Consultant in Internal Medicine, D.C. Correctional Facilities (1987–1989); Emergency Room Physician, Bowie Health Center (1985–1987); Medical Director, Calvert Memorial Hospital (1983–1984); Instructor/Emergency Room Physician, Prince George's General Hospital (1982–1985). **Associations & Accomplishments:** Doctor's Community Hospital: Peer Review Committee (1990–1991), Credentials Committee (1989–1990); Arbitration Board – State of Maryland (1993). **Education:** Johns Hopkins University, Certification in Flexible Sigmoidoscopy (1994); University of Maryland – Prince George's General Hospital, Internal Medicine Board Eligible (1980–1983); Kingston Regional Hospital, Intern (1979–1980); University of the West Indies, MB.BS. (1975–1979); Howard University, B.Sc. in Chemistry (1968–1970). **Personal:** Married to Wilson. Two children: Diana and Robert. Ms. Leach enjoys scrabble.

Zina Darcel Lee, M.D.
Physician Associate
Southwest Mississippi Internal Medicine Clinic
150 Marion Drive
McComb, MS 39648
(601) 249–0706
Fax: (601) 249–0971

8011

Business Information: Established in 1990, the Southwest Mississippi Internal Medicine Clinic is a multi–specialty medical group practice, offering a variety of treatment options to patients throughout southwestern Mississippi. Board–certified in Internal Medicine, Dr. Lee joined the Clinic following her res-

idency fellowship in 1993. **Career Steps:** Internal Medicine Specialist, Southwest Mississippi Internal Medicine Clinic (1993–Present). **Associations & Accomplishments:** American Medical Association; Board Certified in Internal Medicine; National Medical Association; ACP. **Education:** University of Mississippi Medical Center, M.D. (1990); Jackson State University, B.S. in Biology (1986); Howard University Hospital, Internship and residency in Internal Medicine (1990–1993). **Personal:** One child: Zinnette Cheryln Lee. Dr. Lee enjoys spending time with family.

Marianne J. Legato, M.D.
Sole Practitioner
The Office of Marianne J. Legato, M.D.
962 Park Avenue
New York, NY 10028–0313
(212) 737–5663
Fax: (212) 737–6306

8011

Business Information: The Office of Marianne J. Legato, M.D. is a full–service, private practice medical office, providing diagnosis and treatment to patients. A practicing physician since 1972, Dr. Legato established her sole medical practice in 1993. Thirty percent of her time is dedicated to her private practice, whereas the rest is devoted to women's health issues. In addition, she is an Associate Professor of Clinical Medicine and serves as Associate Attending Physician at the Presbyterian Hospital in the City of New York and Director of Marketing and Fund Raising for the Center For Women's Health at the Columbia Presbyterian College of Physicians and Surgeons. **Career Steps:** Sole Practitioner, The Office of Marianne J. Legato, M.D. (1993–Present); Director of Marketing and Fundraising, Columbia Presbyterian Medical Center, Center for Women's Health (1993–Present); St. Luke's–Roosevelt Hospital Center: Senior Attending Physician (1980–Present), Attending Physician (1970–1980), Assistant Attending Physician (1969–1970), Director, Postgraduate Medical Education (1985–1993), Director, Continuing Medical Education (1981–1993), Course Director, Subinternships (1985–1993), Course Director, Third Year Clerkship (1972–1993), Preceptor, Introduction to the Patient (1967–Present); The Presbyterian Hospital in the City of New York: Associate Attending Physician (1980–Present), Associate Physician (1977–1980), Assistant Physician (1973–1977); Columbia University College of Physicians and Surgeons: Associate Professor of Clinical Medicine (1977–Present), Assistant Professor of Medicine (1973–1977), Assistant Clinical Professor of Medicine (1970–1973), Associate in Medicine (1969–1970), Instructor in Medicine (1968–1969). **Associations & Accomplishments:** American Association for Advancement of Science; American Federation for Clinical Research; International Society for Heart Research; New York Academy of Sciences; New York County Society of Medicine; New York Society of Internal Medicine; New York Academy of Medicine: Committee on Medical Education (1979–1986), Vice Chairman (1982), Committee on Admissions (1981–1982), Committee on Resources and Development (1985–1987), Trustee (1984–1987), Nominating Committee (1991–1993); American Heart Association: Criteria Committee (1979–1980), Director (1978–1982), Fund Raising Committee (1979–1982), Task Force on Women's Health (1992–Present); Chairwoman of Quality Assurance Committee of the Medical Board (1989–1993), St. Luke's–Roosevelt Hospital Center; Chairwoman of Medical Advisory Board, Women's Heart Research Foundation (1992–Present); Advisory Board of the Office of Research on Women's Health, National Institutes of Health (1995–Present); Long Island Heart Council: Director, Honorary Board Member (1993–Present); Diplomate, American Board of Internal Medicine; Fellow, American College of Physicians; AWARDS: New York Heart Association: Martha Lyon Slater Fellowship (1965–1968), Senior Investigator (1968–1972), J. Murray Steele Award (1971); Research Career Development Award, National Institutes of Health (1972–1977); Blakeslee Award, The American Heart Association (1992); "Women With Heart" Award, Long Island Heart Council (1993); Leadership in Action Award, Women's Action Alliance (1994); Winner, Best in Category of Women's Health for "Shattering the Myths: The Truth About Women and Coronary Artery Disease", International Medical Film Festival (1995), "1,000 Women for the Nineties", Marabella Fifth Anniversary Issue (1994); RESEARCH INTERESTS: Arrythmias, Myocardial Disorders, Physiologic Pharmacology; EDITORSHIPS: Health Columnist, Woman's Day (1992–1994); Editorial Board, Cardiovascular Risk Factors (1993); The Female Patient: Editor in Chief (1993), Associate Editor (1992–1993). **Education:** New York University College of Medicine, M.D. (1962); Manhattanville College, A.B. (1956); Visiting Fellow, Columbia University College of Physicians and Surgeons (1965–1968); Senior Assistant Resident, The Presbyterian Hospital of the City of New York, Columbia–Presbyterian Medical Center (1964–1965); Bellevue Hospital First (Columbia) Division: Junior Assistant Resident (1963–1964), Intern (1962–1963).

Maurice N. Leibman, M.D.
Partner/Physician
Southwest OB/GYN Associates
7500 Beechnut Street #366
Houston, TX 77074–4326
(713) 270–0527
Fax: (713) 270–1591

8011

Business Information: Southwest OB/GYN Associates is a group practice with nine doctors and fifty employees. The Clinic specializes in specialty medical care for women. As Partner/Physician, Dr. Leibman oversees all administrative operations for associates and support staff, in addition to his daily patient practice. **Career Steps:** Partner/Physician, Southwest OB/GYN Associates (1995–Present); Owner, Maurice Leibman, M.D. & Associates (1981–1995). **Associations & Accomplishments:** American College of Obstetricians and Gynecologists; American College of Surgeons; American Fertility Society; Texas Association of Obstetricians and Gynecologists. **Education:** University of Pretoria, South Africa, B.Sc., M.B.Ch.B., M.Sc.; Albert Einstein College of Medicine, NY, F.A.C.O.G., F.A.C.S. **Personal:** Married to Suzanne in 1975. Dr. Leibman enjoys martial arts, scuba diving, and underwater photography.

Charles F. Leinberry, M.D.
Vice President
Commonwealth Orthopaedic Associates
11 Fairlane Road
Reading, PA 19606–9567
(610) 779–2663
Fax: (610) 779–3367

8011

Business Information: Commonwealth Orthopaedic Associates, the largest orthopaedic practice in Reading, is a multi–specialty group practice, specializing in orthopaedics. The Practice consists of four regional offices. A practicing physician since 1984 and an Orthopaedic Surgeon, Dr. Leinberry joined Commonwealth Orthopaedic Associates as Partner in 1990, following his fellowship in Hand Orthopaedics at the University of New Mexico. He is responsible for providing quality orthopaedic care to patients. **Career Steps:** Commonwealth Orthopaedic Associates: Vice President (1994–Present), Partner (1990–Present); Teaching and Research Assistant, Drexel University (1975–1979); Thomas Jefferson University Hospital: Orthopaedic Residency (1985–1989), Hand Fellowship (1989); Hand Fellowshiop, University of New Mexico (1990). **Associations & Accomplishments:** American Society of Surgery of the Hand; American Academy of Orthopaedic Surgeons; Pennsylvania Orthopaedic Society; Philadelphia Orthopaedic Society; American Medical Association; Pennsylvania Medical Society; Berks County Medical Society; RESEARCH: Distal Radius Fracture Study – Norian; Endoscopic Carpal Tunnel Release; Prospective Research on Carpal Tunnel Sundrome; Patellofemoral Complication Following Total Knee Arthroplasty; Cemented vs. Uncemented Total Hips and the Incidence of Pulmonary Emboli; Lunotriquetral Fusions – Complications and Results; Trigger Finger – Resuts of Injections; He has presented his research work on Carpal Tunnel Syndrome at numerous local, national and international medical symposia and conference proceedings. **Education:** Thomas Jefferson University Jefferson Medical College, M.D. (1984); Drexel University: M.S. in Environmental Sciences (1977), B.S. in Chemistry (1975) cum laude, Dean's List; Allentown Affiliated Hospitals, Internship (1984–1985). **Personal:** Married to Beth in 1988. Two children: Alex and Morgan. Dr. Leinberry enjoys skiing, cycling, skydiving, and outdoor activities.

A. Martin Lerner, M.D.
Internist
Dr. A. Martin Lerner, M.D.
31000 Lahser
Birmingham, MI 48025
(810) 540–9866
Fax: (810) 540–0139

8011

Business Information: Dr. A. Martin Lerner, M.D. is a private, general practice medical office providing diagnosis and treatment of patients in internal medicine. Establishing his private practice in 1982, Dr. Lerner is an Internist providing medical care to his patients, as well as subspecializing in infectious diseases. He is affiliated with William Beaumont Hospital, providing health care services and instruction to medical students. Concurrent with his private practice, he conducts research – currently in chronic fatigue syndrome. **Career Steps:** Internist, Dr. A. Martin Lerner, M.D. (1982–Present); Former Professor of Medicine and Director of Division Infectious Diseases, Wayne State University (1963–1982). **Associations & Accomplishments:** American College of Physicians (Michigan Chapter) Governor (1990–1994); Member, Association American Physicians; Member, American Society for Clinical Investigation; Charter Member, Infectious Diseases Society of America. **Education:** Washington School of Medicine, M.D. (1954). **Personal:** Married to Lueva in 1989. Three children: Joshua, Joel, and Liz. Dr. Lerner enjoys swimming, research studies, and his family.

Pierre Levesque

Obstetrician/Gynecologist
La Clinique St. Germain
101–180 Rue Des Gouverneurs
Rimouski, Quebec G5L 8G1
(418) 722–4333
Fax: (418) 736–4637
EMAIL: See Below

8011

Business Information: La Clinique St. Germain is a clinic of six physicians specializing in the obstetrics and gynecology. As Obstetrician/Gynecologist, Dr. Levesque oversees all administrative operations for associates and support staff, in addition to his daily patient practice. Internet users can reach him via: plevesqu@sie.qc.ca. **Career Steps:** Obstetrician/Gynecologist, La Clinique St. Germain (1981–Present). **Associations & Accomplishments:** Royal College of Surgeons, Canada; Society of Obstetricians and Gynecologists of Canada. **Education:** Laval University, Gynecology/Obstetrics (1978). **Personal:** Married to Carole in 1971. Three children: Simon, Julie, and Daniel. Dr. Levesque enjoys equitation and farming.

Warren M. Levin, MD

Physician
Physicians for Complementary Medicine
24 West 57th Street, #701
New York, NY 10019
(212) 397–5900
Fax: (203) 762–9905
E MAIL: See Below

8011

Business Information: Physicians for Complementary Medicine is a private medical practice, comprised of two physicians, offering both conventional and alternative methods of treatment. Treatment is usually accomplished by combining the two methods. As Physician, Dr. Levin, known as the "Dean of holistic medicine in New York City," treats patients through nutrition and other non–conventional methods (help the body heal itself rather than using medication). Dr. Levin finds it rewarding to create health in patients who have come to him as a last resort. Internet users can reach him via: WMLEVIN@REUTERSHEALTH.COM. **Career Steps:** Physician, Physicians for Complementary Medicine (1994–Present); Medical Director, World Health Medical Group (1979–1994); Medical Director, Heights Holistic (1974–1979). **Associations & Accomplishments:** Board of Governors, International College of Applied Nutrition; Board of Directors/Treasurer, American Academy of Medical Preventives; Board of Trustees/Vice President, American Society of Bariatric Physicians. Dr. Levin has numerous articles published in medical journals. **Education:** Jefferson Medical College, M.D. (1956); Ursinus College, B.S. (1952). **Personal:** Married to Frances in 1982. three children: Beth Ann, Julie Ruth, and Erika Alexandra. Dr. Levin enjoys ice skating, sailing, and swimming.

John O. Levine, M.D.

Physician
Cole Harbour Family Medicine Centre
920 Cole Harbour Road
Dartmouth, Nova Scotia B2V 2J5
(902) 435–6312
Fax: (902) 462–3331

8011

Business Information: Cole Harbour Family Medicine Centre is a full–service, family practice, with staff providing general and emergency medical care, in addition to obstetrics. A practicing physician since 1988 and a Certified Family Physician, Dr. Levine joined Cole Harbour Family Medicine Centre as one of four partners in 1993. He is responsible for providing family medical care to patients of all ages. Dr. Levine maintains privileges at Dartmouth General Hospital and the one–week Grace Health Centre in Halifax, Nova Scotia. **Career Steps:** Physician, Cole Harbour Family Medicine Centre (1993–Present); Physician, Inverness Medical Clinic (1989–1993). **Associations & Accomplishments:** Canadian Medical Association; College of Family Physicians of Canada; Canadian Medical Protective Association; Medical Society of Nova Scotia; Nova Scotia College of Physicians and Surgeons; Dartmouth Medical Society; Phi Rho Sigma Medical Society; Canadian Numismatic Association; Atlantic Provinces Numismatic Association; Japan Karate Association World Federation; Musical Heritage Society. **Education:** Dalhousie University: Rotating Internship (1989), M.D. (1988), B.Sc. (1983). **Personal:** Married to Kelly in 1989. One child: Matthew. Dr. Levine enjoys karate (Black Belt, 1996), numismatics, home computing, and classical music.

Marie A. Lewandowski, M.D.

Owner/Practitioner
Parkside Family Practice
1235 Taraval Street
San Francisco, CA 94116
(415) 753–6553
Fax: (415) 341–7359

8011

Business Information: Parkside Family Practice is a private medical office comprised of two physicians and a nurse practitioner. Affiliated with two local hospitals, the Office, established in 1994, specializes in general family practice medicine. As Owner/Practitioner, Dr. Lewandowski oversees all aspects of the Practice and is responsible for administration, operations, patient care, diagnosis and follow–up, and strategic planning. **Career Steps:** Owner, Practitioner, Parkside Family Practice (1993–Present); Physician, Urgent Care, Emergency Department, and Trauma Follow Up, Kaiser Permanente (1992–Present); Physician, Atwater Medical Group (1992–1993). **Associations & Accomplishments:** American Medical Association; American Association of Family Practitioners. **Education:** Medical Academy, Poland, M.D. (1982). **Personal:** Married to Edmund S. in 1983. Dr. Lewandowski enjoys travel, playing the piano, and outdoor activities.

Dr. Donald H. Lewis, M.D.

President
Mountain Region Pediatrics, P.C.
1201 North Wilcox Drive
Kingsport, TN 37660
(615) 246–8700
Fax: (615) 246–3857

8011

Business Information: Mountain Region Pediatrics, P.C., affiliated with Holston Valley Hospital and Indian Path Hospital, is a general pediatric primary care medical practice. Patients range from infants to college students. Established in 1995 (merger), Mountain Region Pediatrics currently employs 50 people, including 10 physicians. As President, Dr. Lewis is responsible for all aspects of operations, including the oversight of administrative activities, as well as general practice of pediatrics with a patient load of 30–40 a day. **Career Steps:** Mountain Region Pediatrics, P.C.: President (1996–Present), Vice President (1995–1996); Chair of Pediatrics Department, Holston Valley Hospital (1988–1989). **Associations & Accomplishments:** Fellow of the American Academy of Pediatrics – Board Certified; Tennessee Chapter of American Academy of Pediatrics; Member, First Assembly of God Church; Assists with Royal Rangers Program. **Education:** University of Tennessee, M.D. (1979); Children's Medical Center, Pediatric Specialty Training; The University of Texas – Southwestern Medical School, Department of Pediatrics (1982). **Personal:** Married to Estenia. Three children: Benjamin, Rebeca and Laura. Dr. Lewis enjoys gardening, birdwatching and hiking.

EA'thel G. Lewis

Risk and Quality Manager
West End Medical Centers, Inc.
868 York Avenue, S.W.
Atlanta, GA 30310
(404) 752–1400
Fax: (404) 758–1231

8011

Business Information: West End Medical Centers, Inc. is a primary care medical center with a patient population of 55,000, providing health care through seven primary care medical centers in urban settings throughout the Atlanta, Georgia. Established in 1976, West End Medical Centers, Inc. currently employs 110 people. As Risk and Quality Manager, Mrs. Lewis is responsible for the management of security, bio–hazardous wastes, patient focus, auditing, property management, site evaluation, and police agency activities. She is also the Operations Coordinator for Choice Health Care – the result of a collaborative effort between Southside Medical System and Georgia Baptist Health Care System. **Career Steps:** West End Medical Centers, Inc.: Risk/Quality Manager (1979–Present), Medical Records Administrator (1980–1983); System Administrator, Georgia Baptist Medical System (1983–1986); Medical Records Director, Alton/Park Health Center (1968–1979) **Associations & Accomplishments:** Sister–Sister – (a network of Black Women who act as mentors to high school drop–out females trying to get them into adult programs or night schools); Supporter, Atlanta Union Mission; Frequent speaker on managed care issues and liabilities to medical and non–medical groups. **Education:** Shorter College: Studies in pursuit of Masters, B.S. Art; American Medical Records Academy; Attended: Morris Brown College, Atlanta, GA; Spelman College, Atlanta, GA; Atlanta Technical College, License in Barber/Cosmetology – graduated with honors and was appointed VICA representative **Personal:** Married to Arthur in 1972. Five step children: Valerie, Valancia, Arthur, Carl and Eric. Mrs. Lewis enjoys computers, reading and writing romance novels and stories for publication.

Nicholas A. Leyland, M.D.

Head, Division of General Obstetrics/Gynecology
N. Leyland, M.D., F.R.C.P.S.(c)
655 Bay Street, 10th Floor, Suite 1007
Toronto, Ontario M5G 2K4
(416) 979–1162
Fax: (416) 979–1371

8011

Business Information: N. Leyland, M.D., F.R.C.P.S.(c) is a health care facility that specializes in Gynecologic surgery and Endoscopic/Laser surgery. As Head, Division of General OB/GYN, Dr. Leyland performs clinical research/studies, endoscopic laser surgery, and administrative functions. Additionally, he is an instructor at the University of Toronto, teaching first year Medical students and Interns. **Career Steps:** Head, Division of General OB/GYN, N. Leyland, M.D., F.R.C.P.S.(c) (1983–Present); Assistant Professor, OB/GYN Faculty Medicine, University of Toronto. **Associations & Accomplishments:** Alpha Omega Alpha Medical Honor Society; Society of Obstetricians and Gynecologists of Canada; Fellow of Royal College of Surgeons, Canada. **Education:** University of Toronto, M.D. (1983); University of Guelph, B.A.Sc. **Personal:** Married to Carol in 1976. Four children: Alistair, Whitney, Andrew, and Aidan. Dr. Leyland enjoys biking and foreign travel.

Chung K. Lin, M.D., F.A.C.P.

Partner
Atlantic Hematology – Oncology Group
415 South Chris Gaupp Drive, Unit D
Absecon, NJ 08201
(609) 652–6750
Fax: (609) 652–2306

8011

Business Information: Atlantic Hematology – Oncology Group, established in 1985, is a full–service, medical practice for diagnosis and treatment of blood disease and cancers. The Practice, consisting of four physicians, conducts chemotherapy on the premises and is affiliated with one hospital and provides consultation to another. A practicing physician since 1969, Dr. Lin joined Alantic Hematology – Oncology Group in 1994. He is responsible for treating patients and diagnosing problems on call and by consultations with hospitals. Concurrent with his private practice, he serves as Attending Physician at Ruth Newman Shapiro Regional Cancer Center – Atlantic City Medical Center in New Jersey. **Career Steps:** Partner, Atlantic Hematology – Oncology Group (1994–Present); Attending Physician, Ruth Newman Sharpiro Regional Cancer Center – Atlantic City Medical Center, New Jersey (1994–Present); Director of Hematology Division, Veterans General Hospital – Taipei, Taiwan (1987–1994); Associate Professor in Medicine, Yang–Ming Medical University – Taipei, Taiwan (1987–1994); Chief of Hematology – Oncology Section, Chang–Gung Memorial Hospital (1986–1987). **Associations & Accomplishments:** Fellow, American College of Physicians; International Society of Hematology; Cancer Community of Oncology Practice in New Jersey; Associate Member, Cancer and Leukemia Group B; Publication of 43 Academic papers in American and international journals. **Education:** National Taiwan University, M.D. (1969). **Personal:** Married to Su in 1972. One child: Steve S.

Claudio E. Linares, M.D.

Obstetrician/Gynecologist
Navarre Avenue OB/GYN
2735 Navarre Avenue, #101
Oregon, OH 43616–3275
(419) 691–5716
Fax: (419) 691–3340

8011

Business Information: Navarre Avenue OB/GYN is a private obstetrics and gynecology practice, providing all normal testing and birthing services. A practicing physician since 1984, Board–certified in Obstetrics and Gynecology with his concentrated specialty in Gynecologic Laparoscopic surgery, Dr. Linares founded his private practice in November of 1993. As the sole practitioner, he provides the overall administration for medical and clerical support staff, in addition to his daily patient practice. **Career Steps:** Obstetrician/Gynecologist, Navarre Avenue OB/GYN (1993–Present); Medical Director, Toledo Family Health Center (1994–Present); Major, US Air Force Medical Corps (1989–1993). **Associations & Accomplishments:** American College Obstetrician and Gynecology; American Medical College; Ohio State Medical Association; The American Association of Gynecologic Laparoscopists; The Society of Laparoendoscopic Surgeons. **Education:** Universidad Central Del Este, Dominican Republic, M.D. (1984). **Personal:** Married to Madeline in 1987. Five children: Claudio, Rhannyel, Madelyn, Anthony, and Alexandra. Dr. Linares enjoys travel, sports, and music.

Alfred J. Lines, FRCS (Edin)
Physician
Dr. Alfred J. Lines, FRCS (Edin)
222 – 3rd Avenue West, Suite 3
Prince Rupert, British Co V8J 1L1
(604) 624–3331
Fax: (604) 624–9464

8011

Business Information: Dr. Alfred J. Lines, FRCS (Edin) is a full–service, family practice medical office, providing general medical care to patients of all ages. As Physician, Dr. Lines oversees all administrative operations for associates and support staff, in addition to his daily patient practice. **Career Steps:** Physician, Dr. Alfred J. Lines, FRCS (Edin) (1990–Present); D. Napier & Son (1953–1955); Iraq Petroleum Co. (1949–1953) **Education:** Bart's Hospital: M.B.B.S. (1961), MRCS LRCP (1961), FRCS (Edin) (1968); St. John's College – Cambridge, B.A. **Personal:** Married to Ann in 1963. Seven children: Mark, Joanne, Rachel, Catherine, Amy, Jolyon, and Alfred. Dr. Lines enjoys selling blue–green algae, ocean kayaking, model shipbuilding, and nutrition.

Sheree B. Lipkis, M.D.
Physician
Sheree B. Lipkis, M.D., S.C.
2150 Pfingsten Road, Suite 2260
Glenview, IL 60025
(708) 729–8833
Fax: (708) 729–8852

8011

Business Information: Established in 1995, Sheree B. Lipkis, M.D., S.C. is an Internal Medicine practice, serving patients of all ages throughout the greater Chicago–metro area. Affiliated with Evanston and Glenbrook hospitals, the Clinic employs an administrative and support staff of six. A practicing Physician since 1980, Dr. Lipkis specializes in Internal Medicine, with a sub–interest in adolescent and women's health care. Sharing the practice with her husband, together they oversee all aspects of the Clinic. **Career Steps:** Physician, Sheree B. Lipkis, M.D., S.C. (1995–Present); Urgent Care Center – Med First (1983–1991): Medical Director, Medical Quality Assurance. **Associations & Accomplishments:** American Medical Association; American Women's Medical Association; American Society of Internal Medicine; Mother's Against Drunk Driving; Evanston Hospital Professional Staff, Women's Group Committee. **Education:** Northwestern, M.D. (1980), Residency (1980–1983). **Personal:** Married to Evan L. Lipkis, M.D. in 1979. One child: Aimee K.

Mitchell E. Lipton, M.D.
Cardiologist
Lipton & Greenberg
2035 Ralph Avenue #A2
Brooklyn, NY 11234–5315
(718) 763–1116
Fax: (718) 763–1902

8011

Business Information: Lipton & Greenberg is a private cardiology practice. A native of New York, Dr. Lipton established his private practice in 1982. As Senior Physician, he oversees all adminstrative aspects, in addition to his daily patient practice. **Career Steps:** Cardiologist, Lipton & Greenberg (1982–Present). **Associations & Accomplishments:** Fellow, American College of Cardiology. **Education:** Autonomous University – Guadalajara Medical School, M.D. (1976). **Personal:** Married to Rena in 1978. Two children: Allyson and Jason. Dr. Lipton enjoys golf, music, and playing the guitar.

Stephen E. Litman, M.D.
Sole Practitioner
The Office of Stephen E. Litman, M.D.
200 Pennsylvania Avenue
Oreland, PA 19075–1261
(215) 887–7422
Fax: (215) 887–4830

8011

Business Information: Board–certified in Internal Medicine, Dr. Stephen E. Litman established his private medical practice in 1986 following his residency affiliation with Abington Memorial Hospital. Overseeing a staff of five medical and administrative support staff, he provides all aspects of general family medicine diagnosis, treatment and counsel to the rural community of Oreland, Pennsylvania. **Career Steps:** Internal Medicine Sole Practitioner, The Office of Stephen E. Litman, M.D. (1986–Present); Resident Physician, Abington Memorial Hospital (1983–1986); Construction Supervisor, Litman Construction Corporation (1971–1978). **Associations & Accomplishments:** American Society of Internal Medicine; Diplomate, American Board of Internal Medicine. **Education:** Universidad del Noreste, M.D. (1982); University of Medicine and Dentistry of New Jersey (1983); Temple University, B.A. (1971). Internship: Abington Memorial Hospital; Residency: Prince George Hospital and Abington Memorial Hospital. **Personal:** Married to Karen Lynn in 1973. Two children: Kimberly and Courtney. Dr. Litman enjoys sportsfishing and gardening.

Alan B. Loren, M.D., Ph.D.

· · · ◆━━◉━━◆ · · ·

President
Kinney Loren & Conway, S.C.
500 North Hicks Road, Suite 250
Palatine, IL 60067–3614
(708) 705–9500
Fax: Please mail or call

8011

Business Information: Kinney Loren & Conway, S.C., established in 1987, provides medical services at two local offices in the Palatine, Illinois area. As President, Dr. Loren is responsible for all aspects of operations, including providing physical care in general surgery. Licensed to practice General Surgery in Illinois since 1982, Dr. Loren is an attending physician/surgeon with Northwest Community Hospital and Alexian Brothers Medical Center. **Career Steps:** President, Kinney Loren & Conway, S.C. (1987–Present). **Associations & Accomplishments:** American Medical Association (1981); Chicago Medical Society (1981); Illinois State Medical Society (1981); New York Academy of Sciences (1982); Chicago Committee of Trauma (1986); American Society of Gastroenterology (1987); Midwest Surgical Society (MWSS) (1989); Illinois State Surgical Society (ISSS); Fellow of the American College of Surgeons (1989); Society of American Gastrointestinal Endoscopic Surgeons (1991); American Society of Abdominal Surgeons (1991); Founding Member, Metropolitan Chicago Minimally Invasive Surgery Group (1992); American Society of General Surgeons (SGS); Society of Laparoendoscopic Surgeons (SLS); National Board of Medical Examiners (1982); Diplomate of the American Board of Surgery (1987); Recertification of the American Board of Surgery (1995); Licensee: Illinois, Physician/Surgeon (1982), Certified Instructor – Advanced Trauma and Life Support (1987); Illinois State Scholar (1973); Phi Eta Sigma, Freshman Honor Society (1974); Scholarship from Bio–Rad for Work with Immunobeads, $1,000.00 (1980); Peustow Surgical Society, Life Member (1986); Board of Directors, Elk Grove PHO (1988); Council Member, American College of Surgeons, Chicago Chapter (1991–1996); Illinois Representative Young Surgeons of American College of Surgeons (1993); American College of Surgeons, Committee on Applicants (1993); Medicare Advisory Board, American College of Surgeons Representative (1994–1996); Vice Chief General Surgery, Northwest Community Hospital (1994); Author of numerous presentations of papers and bibliographies. **Education:** University of Illinois of Medical Center, Ph.D. in Immunopathology (1981); Loyola University, M.D. (1981); University of Illinois, B.S. in Biology (1977).

Evelyn J. Lorenzen, Ph.D., M.D.
Pediatrician
–Independent–
2303 Bellefontaine
Houston, TX 77030–3203
(713) 529–9144
Fax: Please mail or call

8011

Business Information: Dr. Evelyn J. Lorenzen, Ph.D., M.D. was a private practice Pediatrician from 1954 until 1991, operating her own office and providing loving care for her children

---

patients. In 1991, she became a member of the staff of the Children's Protective Service of Harris County in Houston, Texas. Dr. Lorenzen remained a Pediatrician with the Service until 1994. **Career Steps:** Pediatrician, Children's Protective Services of Harris County, Texas (1991–1994); Pediatrician, The Office of Evelyn J. Lorenzen, Ph.D., M.D. (1954–1991); Lecturer, University of Houston (1963–1966); Instructor, Charity Hospital, New Orleans; Instructor, Cook County School of Nursing; Instructor in the Department of Surgery and Department of Pediatrics, University of Illinois College of Medicine; Instructor of Infant and Child Nutrition, Cornell University (1942–1946). **Associations & Accomplishments:** Fellow, American Academy of Pediatrics; American Medical Association; Texas Medical Association; Houston Pediatric Society; Texas Pediatric Society; Phi Beta Kappa; Sigma Xi; Who's Who of American Women; Who's Who in American Men and Women of Science; Who's Who in America; Who's Who in Texas; Who's Who in the South and Southwest; International Who's Who of Women; Men and Women of Distinction; World's Who's Who of Women; Personalities of the South; Gave the Lidia J. Robert Memorial Lecture in Puerto Rico on two subjects, Teenage pregnancy and Pediatric Nutritional problems (1989); Various lectures and presentations; Numerous committee appointments. **Education:** Cornell University, Ph.D. in Nutrition with minor in Biochemistry (1946); Harvard Medical School, Research Fellow of Medicine (1946–1947); University of Illinois College of Medicine, M.D. (1951); University of Oklahoma, B.S. (1942); Charity Hospital: Rotating Internship (1951–1952), Pediatric Residency (1952–1954); Certified by the American Board of Pediatrics and the American Board of Nutrition. **Personal:** Married to W. James Tuscany in 1980. Dr. Lorenzen enjoys needlepoint, reading, cooking and travel.

Randall A. Loy, M.D.
Physician/Co–Director
Center for Fertility and Reproductive Medicine, P.A.
3093 Timpana Point
Longwood, FL 32779
(407) 740–0909
Fax: (407) 740–7262
EMAIL: See Below

8011

Business Information: Center for Infertility and Reproductive Medicine, P.A. is a private medical practice specializing n the diagnosis and treatment of infertility, including In Vitro Fertilization, laser surgery, etc. Established in 1985, the Facility is comprised of two physicians and is affiliated with several Florida hospitals. As Physician/Co–Director, Dr. Loy specializes in endoscopic surgery and concurrent with his daily patient–related duties, he is also responsible for the day–to–day operation of the facility. Internet users can reach him via: Cirm@aol.com. **Career Steps:** Physician/Co–Director, Center for Infertility and Reproductive Medicine (1989–Present); Medical Director, Orlando Surgery Center (1996–Present); Co–Chairman, American Reproductive Medicine Specialists (1996–Present). **Associations & Accomplishments:** American Society for Reproductive Medicine; Society for Assisted Reproductive Technologies; Society of Reproductive Endocrinologists; Florida OB/GYN Society; Central Florida OB/GYN Society; Florida Medical Society; Alpha Omega Alpha; Chief Administrative Resident (1987–1988); Sigma Xi; American Board of Obstetricians and Gynecologists; Numerous Publications and Abstracts; Various Presentations and Speaking Engagements; Listed in Best Doctors in America (1996–1997). **Education:** Medical College of Georgia: M.D. (1983); Memphis State University: University of California, Los Angeles, B.A. in English (1978); Medical College of Georgia Hospitals and Clinics, Residency; Beth Israel Hospital (Boston)/Yale New Haven Hospital, Fellowships in Reproductive Endocrinology; National Board of Medical Examiners, Diplomate (1984); American Board of Obstetrics and Gynecology: Diplomate (1990), Subspecialty Certification in Reproductive Endocrinology (1992). **Personal:** Married to Julie Ann Gooding. One child: Jonathan Asher Gooding Loy. Dr. Loy enjoys travel, snow skiing, and cooking.

Kathleen E. Lucas, M.D.
Pediatrician
Kathleen E. Lucas, M.D., P.A.
1209 Magnolia Street
Greensboro, NC 27401
(910) 274–0106 Ext. 11
Fax: (910) 274–3068

8011

Business Information: Kathleen E. Lucas, M.D., P.A., established in 1994, is a private pediatrics practice. A Board–certified Pediatrician since 1987, Dr. Lucas is Sole Practitioner responsible for all aspects of operations, including administration, public relations, strategic planning, and diagnosis and treatment of children's diseases. **Career Steps:** Pediatrician, Kathleen E. Lucas, M.D., P.A. (1994–Present); Pediatrician, Wendover Pediatrics (1987–1994). **Associations & Accomplishments:** North Carolina Pediatric Society; American Academy of Pediatrics: Board Certified (1987–1995) and renewed certification (1995–2002); Council for Children's Health; Appointed to North Carolina State Infant Specialist Task Force; Guilford Health Care Fact Finding Committee (HFFC). **Education:** Marshall University School of Medicine, M.D. (1984). **Personal:** Married to J. Laurence Ransom, M.D. in 1989. Four children: Matthew and Jason Lucas, and Carla and Amy Ransom. Dr. Lucas enjoys lecturing on child advocacy, and hiking.

Martin J. Luria, M.D.
Sole Practitioner
Martin J. Luria, M.D., P.A.
170 Morris Avenue, Suite F
Long Branch, NJ 07740–6660
(908) 222–8256
Fax: (908) 222–8584

8011

Business Information: Martin J. Luria, M.D., P.A. is a private medical practice specializing in Endocrinology. Established in 1976, the office employs four medical professionals. As Sole Practitioner, Dr. Luria is responsible for all day–to–day operations of his medical office and concurrently treats patients through his practice as an Endocrinologist. **Career Steps:** Sole Practitioner, Martin J. Luria, M.D., P.A. (1976–Present). **Associations & Accomplishments:** American Association of Clinical Endocrinologists; Endocrine Society; American Diabetes Association; American College of Physicians; American Society of Internal Medicine. **Education:** New York University, M.D. (1971); Rutgers University, A.B. (1967). **Personal:** Married to Joyce Luria in 1970. One child: Hal. Dr. Luria enjoys reading and sports.

Barry A. S. Lycka, M.D., F.R.C.P.
Cosmetic Surgeon/Dermatologist
First Edmonton Place
10665 Jasper Avenue, Suite 920
Edmonton, Alberta T5J 3S9
(403) 424–4440
Fax: (403) 424–2534

8011

Business Information: Located in First Edmonton Place is a medical practice focusing on dermatology and cosmetic surgery. The practice was established in 1989 and has a staff of four physicians and fifteen nursing/administrator employees. As Cosmetic Surgeon/Dermatologist, Dr. Lycka performs Mohs micrographic surgery, liposuctions, glycolic acid peels, and laser surgery. Dr. Lycka was among the first surgeons in Canada to develop these techniques. As a partner in the medical practice some of his other duties include general administrative tasks, public relations, and planning for future expansion. **Career Steps:** Cosmetic Surgeon/Dermatologist, First Edmonton Place (1989–Present). **Associations & Accomplishments:** ASTRA; Knights of Columbus. **Education:** University of Minnesota, Fellowship in Dermatology (1989); University of Alberta, M.D. (1983); University of Calgary, B.Sc. with Honors in Psychology (1978). **Personal:** Married to Lucie Marie Bernier in 1987. Four children: Michelle, Christine, Jacqueline, and Stephanie. Dr. Lycka enjoys golf, theatre, and writing.

Dr. Ian Ma
Physician
Office of Dr. Ian Ma
3809 Main Street
Vancouver, British Co V5V 3Pl
(604) 872–4025
Fax: (604) 872–2252

8011

Business Information: Office of Dr. Ian Ma is a full–service, family practice medical office, affiliated with Mount Saint Joseph Hospital, providing general medical care to patients of all ages. As Physician, Dr. Ma oversees all administrative operations for associates and support staff, in addition to his daily patient practice. Every year Dr. Ma networks with other physicians and medical groups to plan a mission trip to China to help with the medical needs of people abroad. **Career Steps:** Physician, Office of Dr. Ian Ma (1976–Present). **Associations & Accomplishments:** Canadian Medical Association; Director and Medical Missionary, China West Mission; Evangelical Medical Aid Society. **Education:** University of British Columbia: M.D. (1975), B.Sc. **Personal:** Married to Pauline in 1975. Two children: Praise and Alvin. Dr. Ma enjoys table tennis, reading, and spending time with his family.

Ethel L. MacIntosh, M.D.
Surgical Oncologist
Winnipeg Clinic
425 Saint Mary Avenue
Winnipeg, Manitoba R3C 0N2
(204) 957–3214
Fax: (204) 943–2164

8011

Business Information: Winnipeg Clinic is a multidisciplinary medical office employing 60 doctors. As Surgical Oncologist, Dr. MacIntosh is responsible for providing medical care with a specialization in surgical oncology. Additionally, she became an Associate Staff Surgeon in August of 1995 at Grace General Hospital, and in January of 1996 at Victoria General Hospital. **Career Steps:** Surgical Oncologist, Winnipeg Clinic (1995–Present); Associate Staff Surgeon, Grace General Hospital (1995–Present); Associate Staff Surgeon, Victoria General Hospital (1996–Present). **Associations & Accomplishments:** Society of Surgical Oncology; American College of Surgeons; Canadian Association of General Surgeons; Canadian Medical Association; Physicians For A Smoke Free Canada. **Education:** University of Manitoba, M.D. (1986), M.Sc.; University of Winnipeg, B.Sc. **Personal:** Dr. MacIntosh enjoys marathon running and golf.

Ranbir S. Mann, M.D.
Physician
Dr. Ranbir Mann Family Medicine Clinic
6690 Fraser Street
Vancouver, British Co V5X 3T5
(604) 273–6051 Direct Line
Fax: (604) 625–0070
(604) 325–4907

8011

Business Information: Dr. Ranbir Mann Family Medicine Clinic is a private medical office providing family medical care and services. Established in 1994, the Clinic employs three people, and is geared towards broad–based holistic medicine. As Physician, Dr. Mann specializes in traumatic brain injuries and cross–cultural medicine (mostly Asian). He is responsible for all administrative duties related to the practice, and handles all strategic planning. **Career Steps:** Physician, Dr. Ranbir Mann Family Medicine Clinic (1985–Present). **Associations & Accomplishments:** American Academy of Family Physicians; Ontario Medical Association; Canadian College of Family Physicians; Royal Canadian Medical Association; Canadian Medical Association; Ontario College of Physicians and Surgeons; British Columbia College of Physicians and Surgeons. **Education:** University of Manitoba: M.D. (1985), B.Sc. (1981) **Personal:** Married to Sunilam in 1985. Dr. Mann enjoys Judo and being a musician.

David C. Marsh, M.D.
Medical Consultant
Addiction Research Foundation
33 Russell Street
Toronto, Ontario M5S 2S1
(416) 595–6858
Fax: (416) 595–6619
EMAIL: dmarsh@arf.org

8011

Business Information: Addiction Research Foundation is an academic health sciences centre affiliated with the University of Toronto. As Medical Consultant, Dr. Marsh seeks to integrate pharmacological and psychological treatments for individuals with substance abuse or dependence. His particular interests are a harm reduction approach to methadone maintenance and psychotherapy for those affected by HIV. **Career Steps:** Medical Consultant, Addiction Research Foundation (1995–Present); General Psychotherapist, Private Practice (1994–Present); Medical Research Council, Canada Studentship (1986–1990). **Associations & Accomplishments:** American Society of Addiction Medicine; Board Member, General Practice Psychotherapy Association; Amnesty International; Christian Medical Dental Society of Canada; Board Member, College of Physicians and Surgeons of Ontario; Participant, Project CREATE (Curriculum Renewal and Evaluation of Addiction Training and Education). **Education:** Memorial University of Newfoundland: M.D. (1992), B.Med.Sci. (1986). **Personal:** Married to Teresa N. in 1994. Three children: Shireen, Riaan and Cathy. Dr. Marsh enjoys travel, photography, philosophy, good books, and close friends.

John C. Mason Jr., M.D.
Physician
Carle Clinic Association
2300 North Vermilion Street
Danville, IL 61832–1735
(217) 431–7850
Fax: Please mail or call

8011

Business Information: Carle Clinic Association is a full–service, general practice medical clinic consisting of 100 medical and administrative support staff and 15 doctors. Carle Clinic operates five main branches located in Danville, Mohammed, Robano, and Bloomington, Illinois. A practicing physician since 1955 and Board–Certified in Obstetrics and Gynecology, Dr. Mason is responsible for providing specialized medical diagnosis and treatment to women. Concurrent with his private medical practice, he teaches medical students at the University of Illinois and conducts volunteer work as a member of the medical staff at a Danville hospital. **Career Steps:** Physician, Carle Clinic Association (1984–Present); Physician, Private Practice (1961–1984); Captain, United States Army (1959–1961). **Education:** University of Illinois, M.D. (1955). **Personal:** Married to Donna in 1957. Four children: John, Jeffrey, Steven, and Michael. Dr. Mason enjoys travel.

Manapurathu V. Mathew, M.D.
Physician
Drs. Mathew & Natarajan Limited
990 Grand Canyon Parkway, Suite 417
Hoffman Estates, IL 60194–1737
(708) 882–0988
Fax: (708) 882–1282

8011

Business Information: Drs. Mathew & Natarajan Limited is a private medical practice, specializing in internal medicine and cardiology areas. Board–certified in Internal Medicine, with a sub–specialty in cardiovascular diseases, Dr. Mathew shares administrative duties with his practicing partner for a support staff of six, in addition to his daily patient practice. He also serves as a Staff Physician and Non–Invasive Cardiologist with Alexian Professional and Hoffman Estates Medical Centers. **Career Steps:** Physician, Drs. Mathew & Natarajan Limited (1973–Present); Attending Physician and Non–Invasive Cardiologist, Alexian Professional Medical Center (1973–Present); Attending Physician and Non–Invasive Cardiologist, Hoffman Estates Medical Center (1978–Present). **Associations & Accomplishments:** American College of Physicians; American Medical Association; Chicago Medical Society; Illinois Medical Society; Board Certified, Internal Medicine and Cardiovascular Disease. **Education:** Bangalore Medical – India, M.B.B.S. (M.D.) (1963); Internship, Residency, and Fellowship in U.S.A. (1965); Board Certified in Internal Medicine (1971) and Re–Certified (1977); Certified in Cardiovascular Diseases (1985). **Personal:** Married to Mary in 1964. Three children: Verghese, Thomas, and Joseph. Dr. Mathew enjoys church choir, social services, tennis, exercise, and hospital committees.

Teodulo R. Mationg, M.D., P.A.
Sole Practitioner, Internal Medicine & Geriatrics
Mationg Medical Clinic
8820 State Road 52
Hudson, FL 34667–6741
(813) 862–8800
Fax: (813) 868–8642

8011

Business Information: Mationg Medical Clinic is a primary care medical clinic, providing health care to mostly internal medicine and geriatrics through HMO and private practices. A practicing physician since 1967, Dr. Mationg opened Mationg Medical Clinic in 1991 as a Primary Care Physician. He oversees all administrative operations for associates and a support staff of six, in addition to his daily patient practice. **Career Steps:** Sole Practitioner, Mationg Medical Clinic (1991–Present); Lt. Colonel, Medical Corps, U.S. Army Reserve (1976–1991); Primary Care Physician, HUMANA Health Care Plan – Florida (1990–1991). **Associations & Accomplishments:** American Medical Association; Association of Military Surgeons of the U.S.; U.S. Army Medical Corps – Active Duty (7 years), Reservist (13 years); Lt. Col. – Medical Corps, U.S. Army Reserve. **Education:** Manila Central University, M.D. (1967). **Personal:** Five children: Thomas, Emily, Krysia, Stefan, and Eugenia. Dr. Mationg enjoys playing the violin, swimming, tennis, reading, and aerobic exercise.

Susie Matulis, M.D.
Private Practitioner
–Independent–
3100 MacCorkle Avenue, Suite 906
Charleston, WV 25304
(304) 345–6700
Fax: (304) 345–1034

8011

Business Information: Susie Matulis, M.D. is a private practice of internal medicine with a subspecialty in infectious diseases, providing diagnosis and treatment of patients. As Private Practitioner, Dr. Matulis is responsible for all aspects of operations, including providing health care of internal medicine to her patients. Concurrent with her private medical practice, she serves as Clinical Faculty at University of West Virginia Medical School. **Career Steps:** Private Practitioner, (1992–Present); Clinical Faculty, University of West Virginia Medical School; Internship and Residency, Charleston Area Medical Center, University of West Virginia; Fellowship, Marshall University at Huntington, West Virginia. **Associations & Accomplishments:** American Medical Association; Kanawha Medical Society; West Virginia State Medical Association; American College of Physicians; Alpha Omega Alpha; Published several articles on Clinical Infectious Disease and Annals of Internal Medicine. **Education:** West Virginia University School of Medicine, M.D. (1985), summa cum laude; University of College, R.N. (1969). **Personal:** Married to Steve Matulis, M.D. Three children: Missy, Lisa, and Shannon. Dr. Matulis enjoys spending time with her family, reading, jazzercize and shopping.

Joseph H. Matusic Jr., M.D.

Pediatrician
Care Point, Inc.
830 Pennsylvania Avenue, Suite 200
Charleston, WV 25302
(304) 343–1863
Fax: (304) 344–1755

8011

Business Information: Care Point, Inc. is a primary care, group practice providing health care to patients (pediatrics to geriatrics). Established in 1995, Care Point, Inc. has 10 locations throughout Charleston, West Virginia and surrounding counties and currently employs 11 pediatricians and 15 family practice physicians. As Pediatrician, Dr. Matusic is responsible for providing health care to pediatric patients. **Career Steps:** Pediatrician, Care Point, Inc. (1995–Present); Pediatrician, Private Practice (1992–1995); Resident, Charleston Area Medical Center (1989–1992). **Associations & Accomplishments:** Fellow of the American Academy of Pediatrics; American Modelers Association. **Education:** West Virginia University, M.D. (1989). **Personal:** Married to Kelley in 1992. One child: Lauren Aileen. Dr. Matusic enjoys skiing and model airplanes.

Cornell McCullom, D.D.S., M.D.

Oral and Maxillofacial Surgeon
Cornell McCullom, D.D.S., M.D.
820 East 87th Street, Suite 201
Chicago, IL 60619–6204
(312) 488–3738
Fax: (312) 874–6575

8011

Business Information: Dr. Cornell McCullom, a Board–eligible Oral and Maxillofacial Surgeon provides patients in the greater Chicago–metro area with all medical treatments in relation to facial cosmetic and reconstructive surgery. Establishing his private practice upon the completion of his residency fellowship in 1988, Dr. McCullom oversees all administrative operations for a support staff of three, in addition to his daily patient practice. **Career Steps:** Oral and Maxillofacial Surgeon, Cornell McCullom, D.D.S., M.D. (1988–Present); Clinical Instructor, Northwestern University (1988–1992); Assistant Professor, University of Illinois (1988–1991); Resident, Howard University (1985–1988). **Associations & Accomplishments:** American Association of Oral and Maxillofacial Surgeons; Illinois Society of Oral and Maxillofacial Surgeons; American Medical Association; American Society of Anesthesiologists. **Education:** Northwestern University, M.D. (1994); Howard University: D.D.S., Oral and Maxillofacial Surgery Residency; Yale University, B.A.; Cook County Hospital, Anesthesiology and Critical Care Residency. **Personal:** Married to Yetta in 1987. Three children: Kristyn, Cornell IV, and Noelle. Dr. McCullom enjoys scuba diving, jogging, and Kung Fu.

Mary A. McRae, M.D.

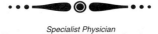

Specialist Physician
Reproductive Endocrinology Associates, S.C.
340 West Miller Street
Springfield, IL 62702
(217) 523–4700
Fax: (217) 523–9025

8011

Business Information: Reproductive Endocrinology Associates, S.C. provides comprehensive evaluation and treatment of infertility and other reproductive endocrinologic disorders. The range of expertise of the associates includes infertility, menstrual problems, endometriosis, reproductive surgery, hormone replacement, menopause, recurrent abortions, and problems of puberty. The Clinic provides special surgeries including in vitro fertilization, GIFT/ZIFT, micromanipulation, cyrobank, intrauterine insemination, laparoscopic laser surgery, myomectomy, and tubal ligation reversal. Their Assisted Reproductive Technology Program is registered with the Society for Assisted Reproductive Technologies, and complies with all regulatory agencies. After completing her medical training and residency in OB/GYN at Ohio State University in Columbus, Mary Ann McRae established a busy practice in reproductive endocrinology and infertility. In 1986, she joined Dr. Phillip Galle on the faculty of SIU School of Medicine where she was active in teaching, research, and medical care for the next seven years. Dr. McRae and Dr. Galle established Reproductive Endocrinolgoy Associates, S.C. for the private care of patients in 1992. **Career Steps:** Specialist Physician, Reproductive Endocrinology Associates, S.C. (1992–Present); Associate Professor, Reproductive Endocrinology, Southern Illinois University (1986–1992); Honorary Research Registrar, Obstetrics and Gynecology, Welsh National School of Medicine, Cardiff, Wales (1984–1985); Community Health Plan, Albany Medical Center – Albany, New York (1981–1984, 1986). **Associations & Accomplishments:** American Association of Gynecologic Laparscopists; American College of Obstetricians and Gynecologists; American Federation for Clinical Research; American Society of Reproductive Medicine; American Medical Association; Association of Professors of Gynecology and Obstetrics; Society of Reproductive Endocrinologists; The Endocrine Society; Society of Reproductive Surgeons; American Association of Gynecological Laparoscopists; American Society of Andrology; American Institute of Ultrasound Medicine; Society of Assisted Reproductive Technology; International Menopause Society; Illinois State Medical Society; Sangamon County Medical Society; Laboratories of Reproductive Biology – SIU; Central Association of Obstetricians and Gynecologists; American Fertility Society Sessions Management Committee; American Society of Andrology Program Local Arrangements Committee; American Medical Association Diagnostic and Therapeutic Technology Assessment Group; Consultant, Illinois Department of Public Health; SIU, Student Progress Committee; SIU Admissions Committee; SIU Grievance Committee; SIU Search Committee for Molecular Pharmacology; Director, Division of Reproductive Endocrinology Laboratory, Department of Obstetrics and Gynecology; Memorial Medical Center Hysteroscopic Surgery Guidelines Committee; Memorial Medical Center IVF Project Development Committee; Memorial Medical Center Quality Assessment Committee; Director, Artificial Insemination by Donor Program, Division of Reproductive Endocrinology, Department of Obstetrics and Gynecology; Director, IVF Program, Memorial Medical Center and SIU Division of Reproductive Endocrinology, Department of Obstetrics and Gynecology; Medical Director, Reproductive Endocrinology Associates Laboratories; Medical Director, Reproductive Endocrinology Associates Laboratories; Medical Director, Reproductive Endocrinology Associates, Assisted Reproductive Technologies Program. Frequent publisher, lecturer at international, national, state and local conferences and institutional symposia and proceedings. **Education:** University of Pennsylvania, (Reproductive Endocrinology) – Philadelphia (1981); Ohio State University – Columbus: M.D. (1975), Obstetrics and Gynecology (1975–1979); University of Dayton, B.S. (1970); Licensure: American Board of Obstetrics and Gynecology, Certification of Special Competence in Reproductive Endocrinology – American Board of Obstetrics and Gynecology, Voluntary Recertification in Obstetrics and Gynecology, Voluntary Recertification in Reproductive Endocrinology. **Personal:** Married to Kim J. Hodgson, M.D. in 1982. Dr. McRae enjoys pets, water skiing, snow skiing, and scuba diving.

Malti Mehta, M.D.

Psychiatrist
Piedmont Psychiatric Association
1040 X Ray Drive
Gastonia, NC 28054
(704) 867–9601
Fax: (704) 868–3939

8011

Business Information: Piedmont Psychiatric Association is a general psychiatric practice offering family counseling, group therapy, and marital counseling. As Psychiatrist, Dr. Mehta and her husband, Dr. Praful Mehta, operate a private practice for patients coping with mental diseases and/or disorders. She handles all aspects of the Practice including finances, administration, and operations. **Career Steps:** Psychiatrist, Piedmont Psychiatric Association. **Personal:** Married to Praful C. Mehta, M.D. in 1973. Four children: Nupur, Parin, Rupan, Milap. Dr. Mehta enjoys painting, hand–painting, coloring, cooking, ceramics, macrame, knitting, crocheting, and playing bridge.

James W. Melenchuk, M.D

Family Physician
Pleasant Hill Plaza Medical Centre
1623 20th Street West
Saskatoon, Saskatchewan S7M 0Z7
(306) 384–9888
Fax: (306) 384–1565
EMAIL: See Below

8011

Business Information: Dr. Melenchuk has been in private practice in Saskatoon, Saskatchewan, since 1981. He built a large family medicine practice with special emphasis on paediatrics, obstetrics, and long–term care. In 1993, he received his certification in Family Medicine by examination. Concurrent with his private practice, Dr. Melenchuk teaches residents at the University of Saskatchewan College of Medicine, and also serves as Vice President of Saskatchewan's Liberal Party, networking with medical professionals on a worldwide scale in an effort to revise the Canadian health care system. To highlight his varied and colorful background, Dr. Melenchuk is the Secretary/Treasurer of Pleasant Hill Plaza, Inc., a real estate operating company, as well as being the staff manager for Paradox Management Ltd. He also sits on the Medical Operations Committee of Parkridge Centre, a regional special care home. Internet users can reach him via: J.Melenchuk@sasknet.sk.ca **Career Steps:** Family Physician, Pleasant Hill Plaza Medical Centre (1988–Present); Clinical Professor of Family Medicine, University of Saskatchewan College of Medicine (1993–Present). **Associations & Accomplishments:** Vice President, Saskatchewan Liberal Party; Former President, Saskatchewan Medical Association; Certified Specialist in Family Medicine; Award of Merit, Saskatchewan Medical Association, Outstanding Leadership (1995); Silver Medal, Outstanding Graduate in Paediatrics, University of Saskatchewan, College of Medicine (1980); Saskatchewan Medical Association; Canadian Medical Association; College of Family Physicians of Canada; College of Physicians and Surgeons (Saskatchewan); Chairman, Health Care Steering Committee, Her Majesty's Loyal Opposition (Liberal Caucus) (1995–Present); Vice President of Finance, Saskatchewan Liberal Association; Task Force on the Ethical Allocation of Resources – Saskatoon District Health Board (1995–1996). **Education:** University of Saskatchewan, M.D. (1980); University of Regina: B.A. in Psychology (1977), B.Sc. with Honors in Biology (1975). **Personal:** Married to Donna L. in 1974. Three children: Jennifer, David, and Jared. Dr. Melenchuk enjoys golf, curling, photography, history of medicine, politics, and spending family time, especially summers together at their cottage at Last Mountain Lake.

Joe Mendiola Jr., M.D.

Neonatologist
Rio Grande Valley Neonatal Associates
P.O. Box 5115
McAllen, TX 78502
(210) 686–3401
Fax: (210) 686–5398

8011

Business Information: Established in 1989, The Rio Grande Valley Neonatal Associates is a group of four Neonatologists providing medical care and treatment to infant patients in the McAllen, Texas area. A Board–certified Neonatologist, Dr. Mendiola joined the Group in 1991. Concurrent with his private patient practice, he serves as the Chief of Pediatrics at the McAllen Medical Center, a position he has held for the past year. He is also a Clinical Professor at the University of Texas Health Sciences Center, providing family practice methodology instruction to pediatric residents. **Career Steps:** Physician, Rio Grande Valley Neonatal Association (1991–Present); Chief of Pediatrics, McAllen Medical Center (1991–Present); Assistant Chief of Newborn Medical Services, Walter Reed Army Medical Center (1989–1991). **Associations & Accomplishments:** Texas Medical Association; American Academy of Pediatrics; Texas Pediatric Society; Hidalgo Starr Counties Medical Society. **Education:** University of Texas Health Science Center at San Antonio: M.D. (1980), Residency (1981–1983), Internship (1980–1981); University of Texas Medical School at Houston, Neonatal Fellowship (1987–1989); **Personal:** Married to Norma Somohano in 1994.

Arnold B. Meshkov, M.D., M.B.A.

President
Philadelphia Cardiology Group, P.C.
8 Huntington Pike
Rockledge, PA 19046
(215) 379–4700
Fax: Please mail or call

8011

Business Information: Philadelphia Cardiology Group, P.C., established in 1982, is an eleven doctor practice of cardiology, with four regional offices serving primarily suburban Philadelphia. As President, Dr. Meshkov oversees administrative operations for associates and support staff in addition to his daily patient practice. **Career Steps:** President, Philadelphia Cardiology Group, P.C. (1995–Present); President, Philadelphia Cardiology Group, P.C. (1994–1995); President, Suburban Cardiovascular Specialists, Ltd. (1982–1994). **Associations & Accomplishments:** American College of Cardiology; American Heart Association. **Education:** Temple University, M.B.A. (1995); University of Pennsylvania: M.D. (1975), B.A. (1971). **Personal:** Married to Norma in 1970. Two children: Adam and Karen. Dr. Meshkov enjoys skiing and golf.

Philip S. Metz, M.D.

President
Plastic Surgical Arts
801 South 48 Street
Lincoln, NE 68510
(402) 483–2573
Fax: (402) 483–2619

8011

Business Information: Plastic Surgical Arts serves the populace of Lincoln, Nebraska with all aspects of reconstructive and cosmetic/aesthetic surgery. A practicing surgeon since 1969, Dr. Metz founded the practice in 1982. As President, he oversees all administrative operations and a support staff of five, in addition to his daily patient practice. Concurrent to his private medical practice, Dr. Metz is a member of the Nebraska Board of Medical Examiners. A retired Medical Officer with the U.S. Navy serving during the Vietnam Era, prior to entering private practice, Dr. Metz was the Chairman of the Plastic Surgery Unit at Bethesda Medical Hospital. **Career Steps:** President, Plastic Surgical Arts (1982–Present). **Associations & Accomplishments:** Nebraska State Board of Medical Examiners; American College of Surgeons; International College of Surgeons; Officer, U.S. Navy Reserves. **Education:** University of Nebraska, M.D. (1969). **Personal:** Married to Dianne in 1970. Four children: Amy, Wendy, Stephanie, and Robb.

Jeffrey S. Metzger, M.D.

Family Practice Physician
–Independent–
30 Prospect Street #200
Ridgefield, CT 06877–4514
(203) 438–8081
Fax: (203) 435–0774

8011

Business Information: A family practice physician since 1981, Dr. Jeffrey Metzger is one of three physicians, all operating as independent practitioners, serving the community of Ridgefield, CT. A Board–certified Internist, he treats patients of all ages, focusing primarily on geriatric care and counsel. **Career Steps:** Physician (1984–Present). **Associations &**

Accomplishments: Fairfield County Medical Society. **Education:** Hahnemann University School of Medicine, M.D. (1981); Danbury Hospital: Medical Intern and Resident (1981–1984); Wilkes College, B.S. in Biology. **Personal:** Married to Nancy in 1986. Two children: Dana and Alison. Dr. Metzger enjoys bike riding, skiing, gardening, and photography.

Beth Meyer

Director of Marketing
The Eye Center Group
200 N. Tillotson Avenue
Muncie, IN 47304–3988
(317) 286–8888
Fax: (317) 747–7962

8011

Business Information: The Eye Center Group is an ophthalmology practice specializing in medical and surgical eye care. Comprised of thirteen doctors, the practice has five clinics and two ambulatory surgery centers in East Central Indiana. As the Director of Marketing, Mrs. Beth Meyer oversees all aspects of the practice's marketing, public relations, outreach, optometric co–management programs, and advertising including radio, T.V., print, and outdoor for all five locations. **Career Steps:** Director of Marketing, The Eye Center Group (1995–Present); Account Coordinator, Caldwell VanRiper (Advertising Agency), Indianapolis, IN (1994–1995); Marketing Consultant, Business Connections, Indianapolis, IN (1993–1994); Director of Advertising and Internal Promotions, Val Corporation (15 store retail chain), New Castle, IN (1987–1993). **Associations & Accomplishments:** American Marketing Association; American Advertising Federation; Chamber of Commerce; American Business Women Association; Chi Omega Social Sorority; Alpha Lambda Delta Honorary Fraternity. **Education:** Ball State University, B.S. in Marketing with Honors (1993). 1993 Top 10 Marketing Students at Ball State University. **Personal:** Married to William Shayne Meyer in 1994. Mrs. Meyer enjoys golf, volleyball, travel, and music.

Dr. Jean–Marie C. Michel

Sole Practitioner
Office of Dr. Jean–Marie C. Michel
C.P. 800
Shippagan, New Brunswick E0B 2P0
(506) 336–8653
Fax: (506) 336–1911

8011

Business Information: Dr. Michel established his private practice in 1972, providing quality family healthcare to the community of Shippagan, New Brunswick. **Career Steps:** Sole Practitioner, Office of Dr. Jean–Marie Michel (1972–Present). **Associations & Accomplishments:** Canadian College of Family Physicians. **Education:** Universite De Strasbourg, Doctorat D'Etat (1968); LMCC (1975). **Personal:** Married to Doris Mallet in 1978. Six children: Florence, Bobby, Pascal, Christian, Maud, and Myriam. Dr. Michel enjoys yachting and flying.

David J. Miller, M.D.

Physician Associate and Partner
Rocky Mountain Pediatric Cardiology, P.C.
1601 East 19th Avenue, Suite 5600
Denver, CO 80218
(303) 860–9933
Fax: (303) 838–5844

8011

Business Information: Rocky Mountain Pediatric Cardiology, P.C. is a Pediatric Cardiology specialty group practice, consisting of three Physician Associate partners. A Board–certified Pediatric Cardiologist, Dr. Miller joined as a Partner in 1994. He specializes in interventional cardiology. **Career Steps:** Physician Associate and Partner, Rocky Mountain Pediatric Cardiology, P.C. (1994–Present). **Associations & Accomplishments:** Fellow, American Academy of Pediatrics; American College of Cardiology; American Heart Association. **Education:** University of Nebraska College of Medicine. M.D. (1988); University of Wisconsin, B.S. with honors (1984); Baylor College of Medicine: Pediatrics Residency (1991), Pediatric Cardiology Fellowship Training (1994). **Personal:** Dr. Miller enjoys golf, sailing and skiing.

Deborah Miller–Lopez

Administrator
Cranial Facial Institute/Ian T. Jackson, M.D.
16001 West 9 Mile Road
Southfield, MI 48075
(810) 424–5473
Fax: (810) 424–5881

0011

Business Information: Cranial Facial Institute/Ian T. Jackson, M.D. is a joint venture with a local hospital for plastic and reconstructive surgery. The primary surgeon, Ian T. Jackson, M.D. (one of the top five cranial facial surgeons in the world), is world reknowned for his surgical skills and serves as advisor, guest speaker, and guest surgeon to hospitals and clinics worldwide. Affiliated with the Institute are a cleft palette clinic, a research department, and a residency program. As Administrator, Ms. Miller–Lopez is responsible for personnel, accounts payable and receivable, billing, charity programs, resident and fellowship programs, new program development, and grant writing. **Career Steps:** Administrator, Cranial Facial Institute/Ian T. Jackson, M.D. (1993–Present); Consultant/ Owner, D.L. Miller, Inc. (1990–1993); Business Manager, Internal Medicine Consultants, PC (1986–1990); Unit Clerk, McLaren Regional Medical Center (1974–1986). **Associations & Accomplishments:** Annual Conference Development Board Member, Plastic Surgery Administrative Association; Medical Group Management Association. **Education:** University of Michigan, Associate (1985). **Personal:** Married to Jorge Lopez in 1994. Three children: Jay and Patrick Miller, and David Lopez. Ms. Miller–Lopez enjoys camping, gardening, and being a Cub Scout leader.

Robert L. Minor Jr. M.D., F.A.C.C.

Cardiologist/Cardiovascular Interventionist
Rockford Cardiology Associates, Ltd.
5668 East State Street
Rockford, IL 61108–2443
(815) 348–3000
Fax: (815) 398–3041

8011

Business Information: Rockford Cardiology Associates, Ltd., a part of Saint Anthony Medical Center, is a full–service medical practice, specializing in diagnosis and treatment of patients suffering from coronary artery and peripheral vascular disease. A practicing physician since 1986 and a Board–Certified Cardiologist, Dr. Minor provides cardiovascular intervention to patients, with heavy emphasis on the use of NE endovascular technologies and stents. He also serves as Director of the Cardiac Catheterization Laboratory and Director of the Multidisciplinary Center for Peripheral Vascular Disease. **Career Steps:** Cardiologist, Rockford Cardiology Associates, Ltd. (1993–Present). **Associations & Accomplishments:** Fellow, American College of Cardiology; American Medical Association; American College of Physicians. **Education:** Duke University: M.D. (1986), B.A. (1982); University of Iowa Hospitals: Internship and Residency in Internal Medicine, Chief Resident (1989), Fellowship in Cardiovascular Diseases (1992). **Personal:** Married to Margaret Lande. Two children: Sarah Margaret and Elizabeth Anne. Dr. Minor enjoys snow skiing, scuba diving, tennis, and golf.

Frank A. Monteleone, M.D.

President
Frank A. Monteleone, M.D., PC
173 Mineola Boulevard
Mineola, NY 11501
(516) 741–4131
Fax: (516) 294–4301

8011

Business Information: Frank A. Monteleone, M.D., PC is a general surgery medical practice. A practicing physician since 1971, and a Board–certified General Surgeon, Dr. Monteleone founded his U.S. practice in 1980. As President he oversees all associates and administrative operations, in addition to his daily patient base. He concentrates his practice in the fields of laparoscopic and breast surgery. **Career Steps:** President, Frank A. Monteleone, M.D., PC (1980–Present). **Associations & Accomplishments:** Fellow, American College of Surgeons; Fellow, American Abdominal Surgery; American Society of Breast Surgery; Society of Endo–Laparoscopy; New York State Medical Society; Nassau County Medical Society; Nassau Surgical Society; Nassau Academy of Medicine; Assistant Clinical Professor in General Surgery, SUNY – Stonybrook, NY. **Education:** University of Padua,

Italy, M.D. (1971). **Personal:** Married to Rosemary in 1971. Three children: Andrew, Grace, and Marie. Dr. Monteleone enjoys tennis, golf, and travel.

Charles B. Moore, M.D.
Partner and Cardiologist
Ochsner Clinic of New Orleans
1514 Jefferson Highway
New Orleans, LA 70121–2429
(504) 842–4135
Fax: (504) 842–4131

8011

Business Information: The Ochsner Clinic of New Orleans is a large, multi–specialty medical clinic and training facility. Currently the Clinic employs 450 Physicians and has over 650 trainees. Affiliated with the Ochsner Foundation Hospital 525–bed, free–standing private hospital), the Clinic offers 26 training programs. Board–certified in Cardiology, Dr. Moore is responsible for the care and treatment of patients with heart diseases and disorders. In addition to his patient practice, he is the Director of the Electro–Cardiography Department and is an Instructor of Medical Ethics at Tulane University. Dr. Moore studied Theology at the Catholic University of America and received a Master's degree in 1974. He was then ordained to the Priesthood in the Episcopal Church. **Career Steps:** Partner and Cardiologist, Ochsner Clinic of New Orleans(1958–Present); Heart Fellowship; Internship, United States Navy (1952–1954). **Associations & Accomplishments:** Former President, Rotary Club; Paul Harris Fellow; Chaplain. Military Order of St. Lazarus of Jerusalem; FACC; EACC; FACP; International Cardiovascular Society. **Education:** University of Tennessee: M.D. (1952), B.S. in Chemistry (1949); Catholic University of America, M.S. in Moral Theology (1974). **Personal:** Married to Cuqui Moore in 1990. Six children: Gilda, Mark, Kirk, Lillian, Ray and Frank.

Richard J. Moore, M.D.
••• ◄━━━━◉━━━━► •••

Internal Medicine Physician
The Office of Richard J. Moore, M.D.
3838 California Street, Suite 416
San Francisco, CA 94118
(415) 387–8800
Fax: (415) 387–5204

8011

Business Information: The Office of Richard J. Moore, M.D. is a private Internal Medicine practice. Sharing his office space with four other multi–specialty physicians, and affiliated with California Pacific Medical Center and St. Mary's Hospital, Dr. Moore established his solo practice in 1989. Dr. Moore is Board Certified in both Internal Medicine and Geriatric Medicine. **Career Steps:** Solo Practice Physician, The Office of Richard J. Moore, M.D. (1989–Present); Chief Resident of Internal Medicine, Children's Hospital of San Francisco (1988–1989). **Associations & Accomplishments:** San Francisco Medical Society; California Medical Society; Japanese Medical Society of America; French Foundation for Medical Research and Education; American College of Physicians; Published two articles. **Education:** University of Nevada School of Medicine, M.D. (1986); University of Nevada – Reno, B.S. in Zoology, with Distinction. **Personal:** Married to Eileen in 1993. Dr. Moore enjoys golf, tennis, biking and fishing.

William S. Morgan, M.D.
Partner and Pediatrician
Pediatric Associates
1941 Johnson Avenue, Suite 201
San Luis Obispo, CA 93401–4157
(805) 541–6030
Fax: (805) 541–4905

8011

Business Information: Pediatric Associates is a full–service, private medical facility specializing in pediatric medicine. Established in 1980, Pediatric Associates currently employs 6 physicians and 25 medical support staff. As Partner and Pediatrician, Dr. Morgan is responsible for all aspects of operations, as well as some clinical instruction. An active supporter of civic and community needs, he serves in pro bono capacities as a team physician for a local football team, as well as provides medical treatment for families in need. **Career Steps:** Partner and Pediatrician, Pediatric Associates (1992–Present); Partner, Encino Pediatrics (1986–1992); Attending Staff, Children's Hospital of Los Angeles (1985–1992). **Associations & Accomplishments:** American Academy of Pediatrics; Member, Adolescent Section, American Academy of Pediatrics; Sigma Xi Scientific Research Society; Partnership for the Children; Numerous community service lectures. **Education:** Washington University: M.D. (1980), A.B. (1976). **Personal:** Married to Roxanne in

1987. One child: Isabel Lila. Dr. Morgan enjoys skiing, biking and golf.

J. Guy Morissette, M.D.
Sole Practitioner
Office of J. Guy Morissette, M.D.
214 Boul Cite Des Jeunes
Hull, Quebec J8Y 6S9
(819) 777–2719
Fax: (613) 837–4925
EMAIL: jgmoris@comnet.ca

8011

Business Information: Office of J. Guy Morissette, M.D. is a full–service medical office, providing specialized diagnosis and treatment of bone disorders. Services include transplants, bone marrows, etc. Establishing his sole practice upon the conferral of his medical degree in 1955, Dr. Morissette is a Medical Physician and Board–Certified Bone Specialist, overseeing all administrative operations for associates and support staff, in addition to his daily patient practice. His practice is now mainly directed to orthopedic legal expertise. **Career Steps:** Sole Practitioner, Office of J. Guy Morissette, M.D. (1955–Present). **Associations & Accomplishments:** President, Pantheon des Sports L'Outaouais; President, Quebec Junior/Major Hockey League; President, Quebec Ice Hockey Federation; Hall of Fame Award for Contributions as President; Wrote a 400 page book on his ancestors titled: ON PREND TOUJOURS UN TRAIN. **Education:** University of Ottawa: M.D. (1955), B.A.; Trained in Orthopedic Surgery at Cleveland, Columbus, Ohio and at The Royal Victoria Hospital of Montreal, Canada. **Personal:** Married to Marcelle in 1987. Five children: Guy, Andree, Elaine, Carole, and Michel. Dr. Morissette enjoys trout fishing, boating, and traveling abroad with his wife.

H. Lee Morton, M.D.
Private Practice Physician
H. Lee Morton, M.D.
P.O. Box 6
Anthony, NM 88021
(915) 886–2117 (915) 886–2362
Fax: Please mail or call

8011

Business Information: H. Lee Morton, M.D. is a private, general medical practice. Established in 1957, the office employs 2 to 4 staff members. As Sole Practitioner, Dr. Morton is responsible for all aspects of administrative operations and medical care. **Career Steps:** Private Practice Physician, General Medical Practice, H. Lee Morton, M.D. (1957–Present); Consultant, Federal Prison of LaTuna, Texas (1957–1979). **Associations & Accomplishments:** Association of Physicians and Surgeons; American Geology Association; Musicians Union; National Rifle Association; Consultant, LaTuna Federal Correctional Institute; Various bands and symphonies; Gemology and Fossil Groups; Who's Who in Southwest (1976). **Education:** University of Texas, Galveston, M.D. (1956); University of Texas at El Paso, B.A.; New Mexico State University, undergraduate work. **Personal:** One child: Michael Cody. Dr. Morton enjoys paleontology, geology, gemology (jewelry maker), electronics, music and is a competitive Trap and Target Shooting participant.

Faranak Motaghian, M.D.
Pediatrician
Memphis Children's Clinic
1129 Hale Road
Memphis, TN 38116–6373
(901) 396–0390
Fax: (901) 396–3728

8011

Business Information: Memphis Children's Clinic is a full–service, multi–specialty pediatrics group practice. Established in 1966, the Clinic is affiliated with the University of Tennessee–Memphis Medical Center and currently employs 50 physicians and medical support staff. As Pediatrician, Dr. Motaghian is responsible for the care and treatment of patients, as well as instructing parent training programs for children with asthma. **Career Steps:** Pediatrician, Memphis Children's Clinic (1988–Present); Pediatric Resident, University of Tennessee (1985–1988); Physician in Charge, Iran Health Department (1980–1985). **Associations & Accomplishments:** Fellow, American Academy of Pediatrics; Memphis Pediatric Society; Mid South Pediatric Society. **Education:** University of Tennessee, Pediatrics (1988); Shiraz University, M.D. **Personal:** Married to Feridoon Parsioon, M.D. One child: Maryam Parsioon. Dr. Motaghian enjoys reading, writing, walking and tennis.

Assaad Mounzer, M.D.
President
URO–EXCEL
#7 St. Lukes Professional Building
Bluefield, WV 24701
(304) 325–5451
Fax: (304) 327–6667

8011

Business Information: URO–EXCEL, affiliated with Bluefield Regional Medical Center, is a private practice, medical clinic, specializing in urology, prostate and bladder diseases (cancer, infections, etc.), and surgery. The Clinic also provides free prostate cancer screening. Dr. Mounzer established the Clinic upon the completion of his residency (where he decided to specialize in Urology) in 1988. As President, Dr. Mounzer is responsible for all aspects of the Clinic's operations, including treating patients and administrative activities. In addition to his doctorate degree, Dr. Mounzer received a Masters in Psychology to gain insight into human nature and to assist him in working with cancer patients. He is also the founder of the first Prostate Cancer Support Group in Virginia and West Virginia. **Career Steps:** President, URO–EXCEL (1988–Present).

Robert Mueller, M.D.
Medical Director
Sierra Medical Clinic
9375 San Fernando Road
Sun Valley, CA 91352–1418
(818) 768–3000
Fax: Please mail or call

8011

Business Information: Sierra Medical Clinic is a multi–specialty group medical practice, consisting of 15 practicing partners and 40 physician associates. Areas of medical specialty include private family care, Orthopedic, Pediatrics, HMO patient coverage, Neurology, OB/Gyn, Opthalmology, Cardiology, etc. Practicing in Internal Medicine and specializing in diabetic disorders and disease, Dr. Mueller has been at Sierra since it was founded in 1975. As Medical Director, he serves as the executive administrator over all associates and support staff, providing the vision and strategy for the clinic for the ensurance of quality patient care and delivery; all this in addition to his daily patient practice. Concurrent with his private medical practice, Dr. Mueller also serves as Chief of Staff at Pacifica Valley Hospital — a 240–bed acute care hospital. **Career Steps:** Sierra Medical Clinic: Medical Director (1992–Present), Internal Medicine (Diabetes) Associate (1975–Present); Chief of Staff, Pacifica Valley Hospital (1992–Present). **Associations & Accomplishments:** Unified Medical Group Association. **Education:** University of Illinois–Chicago Medical School, M.D. (1971); University of Illinois – Champaign–Urbana, B.S. (1967); Northwestern University Medical School, Internship (1971–1972); University of California–Los Angeles, Wadsworth Residency in Internal Medicine (1972–1974). **Personal:** One child: Vallerie. Dr. Mueller enjoys art, and collecting sports memorabilia.

Jorge A. Mundo, M.D.
Physician/Owner
Medical Offices of Dr. Jorge Mundo, M.D.
Barcelona #17
Torrimar, Guaynago, Puerto Rico 00966
(787) 850–6005
Fax: (787) 852–5449

8011

Business Information: Medical Offices of Dr. Jorge Mundo, M.D. is a full–service. family practice medical office providing rheumatology care to patients. As Physician/Owner, Dr. Mundo oversees all administrative operations for associates and support staff, in addition to his daily patient practice. **Career Steps:** Physician/Owner, Medical Offices of Dr. Jorge Mundo, M.D. (1991–Present). **Associations & Accomplishments:** Fellow, American College of Rheumatology; American Medical Association. **Education:** University of Puerto Rico, M.D. (1981). **Personal:** Married to LyLy in 1991. Two children: Sebastian and George Andrew. Dr. Mundo enjoys boating.

Albert A. Musca, M.D.
President
Rockport Medical Center
3665 West 117th Street
Cleveland, OH 44111
(216) 251–5464
Fax: (216) 251–5963

8011

Business Information: Rockport Medical Center is a medical/surgical provider. As President, Dr. Musca oversees operations, and serves as a physician and general surgeon in private practice. Rockport Medical Center employs a staff of 11

and reports annual revenue of $300K. **Career Steps:** President, Physician and Surgeon, Rockport Medical Center (1973–Present); Physician and Surgeon, United States Steel Corporation (1972–1973); Physician and Surgeon, Los Angeles Coroner's Office (1969–1972). **Associations & Accomplishments:** American Medical Association; Cleveland Surgical Society; Cleveland Academy of Medicine; Ohio State Medical Society; Fellow in the American College of Surgeons; American College of Surgeons. **Education:** Case–Western Reserve Medical School, M.D. (1961).

Harold Narain, M.D., F.A.C.O.G.
Sole Practitioner
Harold Narain, M.D.
75 Piedmont Avenue Northeast #508
Atlanta, GA 30303–2507
(404) 522–7700
Fax: (404) 522–9900

8011

Business Information: Harold Narain, M.D., established in 1985, is an obstetrics, gynecology and infertility practice, serving patients throughout the greater Atlanta–metro and suburbs. A practicing physician since 1976 and a Board–Certified Obstetrician and Gynecologist, Dr. Narain established his private OB–GYN practice in 1985. He particularly focuses his practice in the treatment of infertility disorders. A native of Surinam, South America, where he served his residency, as well as served as staff physician for various hospitals in the country, Dr. Narain emigrated to the U.S. to continue his specialty education in 1979. Upon the completion of his fellowship at Allegheny General Hospital, he moved to Atlanta in 1985 to open his current private practice. **Career Steps:** Private Practice OB/GYN Physician (1985–Present); PGY II–IV, Allegheny General Hospital – Pittsburgh, PA (1982–1985); PGYI OB/GYN, Elmhurst Hospital – Queens, NY (1981–1982); PGYI – II General Surgery, Brooklyn–Cumberland Medical Center (1979–1981); Family Practice and Emergency Room Physician, Paramaribo, Surinam, S.A. (1977–1979); House Staff OB/GYN, Academic Hospital – Surinam (1976–1977). **Associations & Accomplishments:** Board of Directors, Atlanta Peach Caribbean Carnival; Fellow, American College of Obstetrics/Gynecology; Diplomate, American Board of Obstetrics/Gynecology; Languages: Surinamese, Dutch, English, German, French, Spanish; Surgery Skills: Laser/Microsurgery, Laparoscopic Assisted Vaginal Hysterectomy. **Education:** Thorbecke Lyceum – Utrecht, Diploma (1969); University of Leyden Medical School – The Netherlands, Diploma (1972); Medical School of Surinam, Doctorate Arts Diploma (1976). **Personal:** Married to Ruby in 1977. Four children: David, Daniel, Naomi, and Timothy. Dr. Narain enjoys tennis, chess, and jungle safaris hunting large game.

Munir E. Nassar, M.D.
Physician
–Independent–
176 Holly Brook Road
Brockport, NY 14420
(716) 637–0049
Fax: (716) 637–0049

8011

Business Information: Dr. Munir E. Nassar, a respected internal medicine physician and Tropical Medicine Diplomate, currently serves as a physician with the New York branch of the Veteran Affairs Department. In this capacity, he specializes in internal medicine, cardiology and general patient care. Dr. Nassar is qualified in internal medicine and cardiology. **Career Steps:** Physician, Veteran Affairs Department (1986–Present); Major, United States Air Force (1975). **Associations & Accomplishments:** American Medical Association; Member, New York Cardiological Society; American Society of Internal Medicine; Fellow, Royal Society of Medicine; Easter Seal Society; Church Activities; Lectureship in the Department of Medical History; Recipient, Editor's Choice Award for Outstanding Achievement in Poetry from the National Library of Poetry. **Education:** School of Medicine A.U.B., B.S., M.D.; Fellow, American College of Physicians (1987), Diplomate Tropical Medicine (DMT). **Personal:** Married to Leila in 1959. Two children: Ramzi M. Nassar, M.D. and Rania M. Nassar, B.S. Dr. Nassar studied at Uppsala, Sweden, enjoys tennis, walking, classical music, philosophy, literature and the history of medicine.

Louay K. Nassri, M.D.
Pediatric Pulmonologist
Holt–Krock Clinic – Department of Pediatrics
2901 S. 74th Street
Ft. Smith, AR 72903
(501) 452–7500
Fax: (501) 452–7900

8011

Business Information: Holt–Krock Clinic is a private multispecialty clinic with 156 physicians. It was established in Fort Smith, Arkansas in 1921. In 1980, Dr. Nassri established the Pediatric Department. Currently, the department has 20 employees. In addition to being Chief of Department, Dr. Nassri practices both general and pulmonary Pediatrics. His major interests are Asthma, Cystic Fibrosis, and care for children who need or have already received lung transplants. He also instructs residents in his area of subspecialty. **Career Steps:** Chief of Department of Pediatrics and Senior Pediatrician, Holt–Krock Clinic (1980–Present); Assistant Clinical Professor of Pediatrics, University of Arkansas (1980–Present); Associate Professor of Pediatrics, Damascus University (1980); Assistant Professor of Pediatrics, Damascus University (1976–1980); Private Pediatric Practice (1973–1976). **Associations & Accomplishments:** American Academy of Pediatrics; American Thorasic Society; American College of Chest Physicians; International Union Against Tuberculosis; Islamic Medical Association of America; Frequent speaker and lecturer at Sparks Regional Medical Center and St. Edward Medical Center. **Education:** Damascus University, Syria, M.D. (1967); Tulane University; Board Certified in General Pediatrics (1972), Board Certified in Pediatrics Pulmonology (1994). **Personal:** Two children: Tameem and Leila. Dr. Nassri enjoys tennis, swimming, traveling, and classical music.

Neil Nedley, M.D.
Physician
The Medical Offices of Neil Nedley, M.D.
1010 14th Avenue Northwest
Ardmore, OK 73401–1807
(405) 223–5980
Fax: (405) 223–1108

8011

Business Information: A practicing physician since 1986, Dr. Nedley began his thriving solo practice from scratch in Internal Medicine in July 1989. Affiliated with local hospitals, he performs many colonoscopies, gastroscopies (including percutaneous G–tube placements, control of hemorrhage, esophageal dilatations, polypectomies, etc.), as well as placing cardiac pacemakers, Swan–Ganz catheters, interpreting 2D–Echocardiograms, carotid ultrasounds, venous and arterial ultrasounds, and stress exercise testing with or without thallium/echo. Concurrent with his daily patient practice, he is involved as Medical Director in the planning and development of a Health Conditioning Center (a 42–bed inpatient unit), emphasizing nutrition, exercise and other lifestyle measures in the treatment of heart disease, diabetes, hypertension, obesity and other degenerative diseases. Scheduled to open in the Spring of 1996, he will be leaving the Presidency of the Medical Staff to be actively involved in this project. He is currently authoring a textbook on Nutrition, Lifestyle and Preventive Medicine, scheduled to be published in late 1996. A CD–ROM version, including hundreds of illustrations that can be printed in educational transparency form will soon follow. Lecturing extensively in North America and Europe to large audiences on nutrition and preventative medicine, he also conducts numerous nutrition and cooking courses, stop smoking seminars, stress seminars, etc. **Career Steps:** Physician, Neil Nedley, M.D. (1989–Present); Ardmore Institute of Health: Medical Director (1992–Present), Instructor, Community Health Education; Ardmore Adventist Hospital: Director and Chairman of Medical/Surgical Department (1991–1992), Intensive Care Director (1990–1992), Director of Cardiopulmonary Department (1989–1992), Community Health Education and Advanced Cardiac Life Support Instructor (1989–1992); Instructor of Medicine, Wright State University (1986–1989); Instructor of Medicine, Physician Assistant Program, Kettering College of Medical Arts (1986–1989); Memorial Hospital of Southern Oklahoma: President of Medical Staff (1994–Present), Chief of Medicine (1992–1993) **Associations & Accomplishments:** American Medical Association; Physicians Recognition Award (1989, 1991, 1994); American College of Physicians; American Society of Internal Medicine; Oklahoma State Medical Association; Carter County Medical Association; Alpha–Omega–Alpha Honor Medical Society; Adventist International Medical Society; Griggs Award, Loma Linda University (1986); Board Member, Ardmore Adventist Church Board; Constitution and By–Laws Committee, Oklahoma Conference – SDA; Kettering Medical Center Resident's Association; Publications: Journal of Health and Healing, Cancer Prevention, and Three Angels Broadcasting Network; Frequent lecturer at international, national, state and local conferences and institutional symposia and proceedings. **Education:** Loma Linda University, M.D. (1986); Andrews University, B.A. Major: Biochemistry, Minor: Religion

(1982); Kettering Medical Center and Wright State University: Internship in Internal Medicine (1986–1987); Residency (1986–1989); BOARD CERTIFICATION: American Board of Internal Medicine (1989); Diplomate, National Board of Medical Examiners (1987); LICENSURE: Ohio (1987); Oklahoma (1989). **Personal:** Married to Erica. Two children: Joel and Allen. Dr. Nedley enjoys tennis and mountain biking.

Kenneth K. Newton
President
Office of Kenneth K. Newton, M.D., P.C.
15252 Gratiot Avenue
Detroit, MI 48205
(313) 371–2416
Fax: (313) 371–6865

8011

Business Information: A practicing physician since 1955, Dr. Newton established his private practice internal medicine office in 1962. He oversees all administrative operations for associates and a support staff of five, in addition to his daily patient practice. Born in what is now Gorzow Wielkopolski, Poland in 1927, Dr. Newton was brought up in a war–torn country, living through events that some people have only read about — starting with his family being expelled by the Nazi Party from Landsberg/Warthe in 1938 to his escape to Berlin in March 1945. During that time, he and his family were evicted from their home by the family of Reinhard Heydrich, a protector of Bohemia and Moravia who was killed by Czech Resistance Fighters, when the family attended the state funeral of Heydrich in Berlin; Expelled from high school the same month; Arrested by the Gestapo and released; Lost another home, this time to an air raid by RAF; Subpoenaed by the Gestapo and transported to Paris; Marched throughout France, Belgium, and Germany building underground facilities for airplane construction; and escaped to Berlin during a battle at Ruhr Pocket. After walking to Berlin and arriving there ten days later, he was liberated by the Russian Infantry during the Battle of Berlin and moved to what was to become the U.S. sector of Berlin. While he was there, he had the opportunity to attend a special high school, affiliated with Humboldt University, to finish his secondary education. He was then transported to Bremerhaven in June 1946 and immigrated to the U.S., arriving in New York on June 18, 1946. In September 1946, he joined the U.S. Army and was shipped to his first military assignment, in Korea with the 51st Field Artillery Battalion, 6th Infantry Division in December of the same year. In spite of his hardships, Dr. Newton went on to finish his education in the U.S., obtaining a Bachelors Degree in 1951, a Doctorate of Medicine in 1955, and attending other continuing education courses throughout the years. Concurrent with his private medical practice, he serves as a Delegate to a NATO organization, participating in national security; travels to Europe (three times in 1995); serves as Preceptor in the Department of Family Medicine at three universities: Wayne State University, Michigan State University, University of Michigan; serves as Associate in the Department of Family Medicine and Clinical Professor of Medicine at Wayne State University; serves as Instructor and Course Director of Advanced Cardiac Life Support for the American Heart Association; and as Instructor and Course Director of Advanced Cardiac Life Support in the Department of Joint Medical Readiness Training for the Academy of Health Sciences, U.S. Army. **Career Steps:** President, Office of Kenneth K. Newton, M.D., P.C. (1962–Present); Wayne State University: Preceptor in the Department of Family Medicine (1960–Present), Associate in the Department of Medicine (1976–Present), Clinical Associate Professor of Medicine (1995–Present); Preceptor in the Department of Family Medicine, Michigan State University (1960–Present); Receptor in the Department of Family Medicine, University of Michigan (1960–Present); Instructor and Course Director for Advanced Cardiac Life Support, American Heart Association (1977–Present); Instructor and Course Director for Advanced Cardiac Life Support, Department of Joint Medical Readiness Training, Academy of Health Sciences, U.S. Army, Ft. Sam Houston (1992–Present); Holy Cross Hospital: President of the Governing Board (1990), Member of the Governing Board (1988–1992), President of the Medical–Dental Staff (1982–1983), Chief of the Department of Medicine (1977–1979 and 1991), Director of Medical Education (1976–1988). **Associations & Accomplishments:** Society of Medical Consultants to the Armed Forces: Committee on Graduate Medical Education; American College of Chest Physicians: Section on Coronary Artery Disease; American Society of Internal Medicine: Trustee; Society of Hospital Medical Education; Aerospace Medical Association; Deutsche Gesellschaft fuer Wehrmedizin; Deutsche Gesellschaft fuer Luft und Raumfahrtmedizin; Association of Military Surgeons of the United States; Confederate Interalliee Des Officiers Medicaux de Reserve: Judge – Military Life Saving Competition, Delegate, Vice–Chief Delegate; American Heart Association; Michigan Heart Association: Advanced Cardiac Life Support Subcommittee; Reserve Officers Association: National Surgeon (1992–1993); Reserve Officers Association – Department of Michigan: Vice President – 70th Division Chapter, Department Surgeon (1988–Present); Licensure: Ohio and Michigan; Special Invitation, Governing Mayor of the City of Berlin (Regierender Buergermeister) (1990); Special Tribute, Senate Resolution No. 314, Michigan Senate (1985); Distinguished Service Medal, State of Michigan (1985), Meritorious Service Medal, Department of the Army (1982 and 1992); Active Teacher Recognition, American Academy of

Family Physicians (1980); Army Commendation Medal, Department of the Army (1978); Legion of Merit, State of Michigan (1977); Letter of Appreciation, President of the United States (1973); Certificate of Public Service, Governor of New York (1958). **Education:** Western Reserve University, M.D. (1955); University of Buffalo, B.A. (1951); Henry Ford Hospital: Internship (1955–1956), Residency in Internal Medicine (1956–1959), Residency in Physical Medicine and Rehabilitation (1959), Residency in Internal Medicine (1959–1960); U.S. Army Command & General Staff College, Honor Graduate (1968–1972); U.S. Army Aviation School, Flight Surgeon Training (1974); Advanced Cardiac Life Support Instructor Course (1977); Deployment Medicine Course Instructor Course (1993); Pre–Hospital Trauma Life Support Instructor Course (1994). **Personal:** Mr. Newton enjoys photography and travel.

Richard Kim–Thean Ng, M.D., F.A.C.P.

Sole Practitioner
–Independent–
929 Clay Street, Suite 105
San Francisco, CA 94108
(045) 989–1228
Fax: (415) 989–1227

8011

Business Information: A Board–certified Internal Medicine and Medical Oncologist, Dr. Ng provides all aspects of medical diagnosis, treatment, and referral for cancer patients and other blood disorders. A native of Malaysia, he received his medical degree in Taiwan and served his residency in the United States, Dr. Ng established his U.S. private practice in 1984. In conjunction with his private medical practice, Dr. Ng also conducts clinical research in the fields of breast, head, and neck cancers. **Career Steps:** Private Practice Internal Medicine and Oncology Physician (1984–Present). **Associations & Accomplishments:** Fellow, American College of Physicians; American Society of Clinical Oncology. **Education:** Taipei Medical College, M.D. (1973).

Ivan P. Nohel, M.D., F.R.C.P.C.

Doctor of Internal Medicine
Medical Offices of Dr. Ivan P. Nohel, M.D., F.R.C.P.C.
511 East 15th Avenue
Vancouver, British Co V5T 4S4
(604) 876–3683
Fax: (604) 876–2421

8011

Business Information: Medical Offices of Dr. Ivan P. Nohel, M.D., F.R.C.P.C. is a private medical practice specializing in the area of internal medicine. Affiliated with St. Paul and Delta hospitals, the Business was established in 1972 and is a solo practice. As Doctor of Internal Medicine, Dr. Nohel oversees all administrative and operational functions relating to the Office. He is responsible for patient care and diagnosis, finance, and strategic planning. **Career Steps:** Doctor of Internal Medicine, Medical Offices of Dr. Ivan P. Nohel, M.D., F.R.C.P.C. (1972–Present). **Associations & Accomplishments:** Canadian Medical Association; Czech and Slovak Association of Canada. **Education:** Charles University, Prague, M.D. (1960); Fellow, Royal College of Physicians and Surgeons of Canada (1972); U.S.A., E.C.F.M.G. (1969); L.M.C.C., Canada (1970). **Personal:** Two children: Ivana and Christopher. Dr. Nohel enjoys being a car enthusiast.

Egon Novak, M.D., Ph.D.

Chief Executive Officer
B.I. Forbes Medi–Tech
Com El Medical Bldg., Ste. 302–2620 Commercial Dr.
Vancouver, British Co V5N 4C4
(604) 873–5561
Fax: (604) 873–5529

8011

Business Information: Forbes Med–Tech is a biotech company involved in cardiovascular research. As Chief Executive Officer, Dr. Novak is a physician with thirty–one years of medical experience, responsible for research with Forbes Meditech. Concurrently, he operates a private medical practice with emphasis in geriatrics. **Career Steps:** Academy of Science, Prague, Czechoslovakia (1965–69); Dept. of Pharmacology, U.B.C. Vancouver, Canada (1969–1972); Chief Executive Officer, Forbes Meditech (1993–Present); Physician, Private Practice (Present). **Associations & Accomplishments:** Postgraduate Fellowship in the Department of Pharmacology at University of British Columbia (1969–72); Fluent in six languages: Hungarian, Croatian, Russian, Czech, English and Slovak. **Education:** Conenius University, M.D. (1965); Academy of Science, Ph.D. in Pharmacology (1969). **Personal:** Married to Zeljka in 1975. One child: Gabrielle.

Richard Novick, M.D.

Cardiothoracic and Transplant Surgeon
London Health Sciences Center, University Campus
P.O. Box 5339
London, Ontario N6A 5A5
(519) 663–3159
Fax: (519) 663–3858
EMAIL: See Below

8011

Business Information: London Health Sciences Center, on the campus of the University of Western Ontario, is a medical research facility. A Cardiothoracic and Transplant Surgeon at the Center since 1988, Dr. Novick also conducts scientific research at the Robarts Research Institute. Internet users can reach him via: rnovick@julian.uwo.ca **Career Steps:** Cardiothoracic and Transplant Surgeon, London Health Sciences Center, University Campus (1988–Present); Scientific Researcher, Robarts Research Institute (Present); Fellow in Cardiac Surgery, Stanford University (1987–1988); Resident in Cardiothoracic Surgery, McGill University (1985–1987). **Associations & Accomplishments:** American Association for Thoracic Surgery; Society of Thoracic Surgeons; International Society for Heart and Lung Transplantation. **Education:** McGill University: M.D. (1980), MSc. (1983); Brandeis University, B.A. (1976). **Personal:** Married to Terri in 1981. Two children: Jason and Daniel.

William R. Nuessle, M.D.

Partner and Surgeon
Clinic for Colon and Rectal Surgery
303 Williams Avenue, #1011
Huntsville, AL 35801
(205) 533–6070
Fax: (205) 533–4839
E/M: wrn@traveller.com

8011

Business Information: Clinic for Colon and Rectal Surgery is a specialty medical center for the care and treatment of patients with disorders and diseases of the colon and rectum. The Clinic has a staff of three physicians. As a Partner and Surgeon, Dr. Nuessle oversees management of the clinic's operations. Dr. Nuessle is a Board –Certified surgeon specialist. Established in 1976, Clinic for Colon and Rectal Surgery employs 5 people. **Career Steps:** Partner and Surgeon, Clinic for Colon and Rectal Surgery (1990–Present); Surgeon and Partner, Q&R Clinic, Bismarck, ND (1983–1990). **Associations & Accomplishments:** American Board of Surgery; American Board of Colon and Rectal Surgery; Fellow, American College of Surgeons; Fellow, American Society of Colon and Rectal Surgery; Southern Medical Association; Published articles in American Journal of Surgery, American Journalist, and Journal for Diseases of Colonary Surgery. **Education:** University of Alabama, M.D. (1977); University of North Dakota, B.S. **Personal:** Married to Anna Maria in 1982. Three children: Aaron, Alexa and Matthew. Dr. Nuessle enjoys fishing, tennis, golf and traveling.

Mary H. O'Brien, M.B., F.R.C.P.(C)

Medical Internist
Health Care Corporation St. John's
198 Lemarchant Road
St. John's, Newfoundland A1C 2H6
(709) 778–3534
Fax: Please mail or call

8011

Business Information: Health Care Corporation St. John's is a healthcare facility specializing in internal medicine and critical care of patients. As Medical Internist, Dr. O'Brien is responsible for providing medical service to patients. Additionally, she holds the offices of Teacher at the University of Newfoundland, Director of Intensive Care Unit at St. Clares Mercy Hospital, and Staff Intensivist ICU at Health Science Center. Career Steps: Medical Internist, Health Care Corporation St. John's (1993–Present); Director of ICU St. Clare's, Mercy Hospital (1993–); Staff Intensivist – ICU, HSC, ST. John's (1993–Present). **Associations & Accomplishments:** Canadian Society of Internal Medicine; American Thoracic Society; Canadian Medical Association; New Foundland & Labradore Medical Association; American College of Physicians. **Education :** University College Colk, M.B., BAD, BCh (1986); University College Colk – Ireland, B.S. in Physiology with Honors (1993). **Personal:** Married to Brendan J. Barrett in 1988. Two children: Stephen Patrick and Michael Brendan.

Gene L. O'Kelley

Office Manager
The Office of Dr. Robson and Dr. Griggs
331 South Meridian
Puyallup, WA 98371–5913
(206) 841–4241
Fax: Please mail or call

8011

Business Information: Affiliated with Pellette Family Health Care Systems, the Office of Dr. Robson and Dr. Griggs is a private general medical practice. Established in 1973, the Office currently employs 9 people, including Ms. O'Kelley who is the Office Manager. She is responsible for all aspects of personnel, bookkeeping, patient relations and acting as an insurance advocate. Ms. O'Kelley ran the clinic for over 16 years and was rewarded for her leadership and ability by being offered the Office Manager position. She has been a guest speaker for numerous social groups and has written flyers for women's organizations. A fighter and survivor of cancer, Ms. O'Kelley is involved in cancer support groups. **Career Steps:** Office Manager, Dr. Robson & Dr. Griggs (1991–Present); Receptionist and Coordinator, Valley Internal Medicine (1987–1991); Receptionist and Bookkeeper, The Office of Dr. Blackburn (1984–1987). **Education:** Fort Steilacoom Community College, Secretary Science (1975). **Personal:** Two children: Thomas and Michael. Ms. O'Kelley enjoys fishing, dog training, sewing, reading, gardening and home decorating.

J. David Ogilby, M.D.

Professor of Medicine
Medical College of Pennsylvania / Hanehan University Hospital
222 Orchard Way
Wayne, PA 19807
(215) 662–9020
Fax: (215) 662–9217

8011

Business Information: Medical College of Pennsylvania is dedicated to instructing students and professionals in the intricacies and skills of the medical profession. Hanehan University Hospital, affiliated with the Medical College, offers residencies, internships, and fellowships to medical students and professionals. The Hospital, aids these students in their studies, while providing diagnosis, treatment, and quality service to all patients. As Professor of Medicine, Dr. Ogilby is responsible for instructing courses each semester to students. A Board–Certified Cardiologist, Dr. Ogilby specializes in teaching subjects regarding diseases and surgeries regarding the human heart. Concurrently, he serves as Director of the Cardiac Cath Lab for the Philadelphia Heart Institute. In this capacity, Dr. Ogilby oversees and performs cardiac catheterization and angioplasties. He attributes his success to taking great pride in his work. **Career Steps:** Professor of Medicine, Medical College of Pennsylvania / Hanehan University Hospital (Present); Philadelphia Heart Institute: Director Cardiac Center Lab (1993–Present), Associate Director Cardiac Center Lab (1989–1993). **Associations & Accomplishments:** American Heart Association. **Education:** Boston University School of Medicine, M.D. (1979); Harvard University, B.S. (1974). **Personal:** Married to Katrina in 1983. Three children: Kate, John and Sally. Dr. Ogilby enjoys skiing, tennis, sailing and jogging.

W. P. Olszynski, M.D.

Physician/Associate Professor
Rheumatology Associates
Midtown Medical Center, 39 23rd Street East
Saskatoon, Saskatchewan S7K OH6
(306) 244–2277
Fax: (306) 244–6755

8011

Business Information: Rheumatology Associates is an internal medicine practice, specializing in the field of rheumatology and immunology with a specific interest in metabolic bone diseases. A Physician/Associate Professor at the University of Saskatchewan, Dr. Olszynski is responsible for patient care, student teaching, and various administrative functions. **Career Steps:** Physician/Associate Professor, University of Saskatchewan (1989–Present); Visiting Professor, Royal Free Hospital – London, England (1982–1983); Associate Professor, Institute of Hematology–Warsaw, Poland (1974–1982). **Associations & Accomplishments:** Canadian Medical Association; Saskatchewan Medical Association; American College of Rheumatology; Polish Rheumatology Society; Osteoporosis Society of Canada; American Society of Bone and Mineral Research; Royal College of Physicians and Surgeons of Canada. **Education:** Medical Academy – Warsaw, Poland, M.D. (1974); Institute of Hematology – Warsaw, Poland, Ph.D. (1980); Royal College of Physicians and Surgeons of Canada, Specialist Certificate in Internal Medicine (1987). **Personal:** Married to Ewa in 1973. Three children: Magdalena, Paul, and Martin. Dr. Olszynski enjoys history.

Sang Kee Pahk, M.D., Ph.D.

Gastroenterologist
The Office of Sang Kee Pahk, M.D., P.C.
136–30 Maple Avenue, Suite 1–D
Flushing, NY 11355
(718) 939–8705
Fax: Please mail or call

8011

Business Information: The Office of Dr. Sang Kee Pahk, M.D., P.C. is a private medical practice specializing in Internal Medicine and Gastroenterology. A native of Seoul, Korea where he practiced for over 20 years specializing in Internal Medicine and Gastroenterology, Dr. Pahk established his private medical practice in the U.S. in 1979. In addition to his private patient practice, he is also a staff physician with Parson and St. John's Queens hospitals in New York. **Career Steps:** Gastroenterologist, The Office of Dr. Sang Kee Pahk, M.D., P.C. (1979–Present); Gastroenterologist, Parson Hospital (1979–Present); Gastroenterologist, St. John's Queens Hospital (1981–Present); Director of Medicine, Maryknoll Hospital Korea (1969–1971); Associate Clinical Professor of Medicine, Catholic Medical College (1969–1971); Assistant Clinical Professor of Medicine, College of Medicine, Seoul National University (1967–1969); Clinical Lecturer of Medicine, College of Medicine, Seoul National University (1966–1967); Associate Director of Medicine, Department of Internal Medicine, Seoul Red Cross Hospital (1964–1969); Director of Medicine, Korean Air Force Hospital (1961–1962); Medical Officer, Korean Air Force (1957–1964). **Associations & Accomplishments:** Diplomate, American Board of Internal Medicine and Gastroenterology; Diplomate, Korean Board of Internal Medicine; Councillor,Korean Association of Gastroenterology; American Society for Gastrointestinal Endoscopy. **Education:** Seoul National University: Ph.D. (1963), M.S. (1958); Seoul National University College of Medicine, M.D. (1956). **Personal:** Married to Hong Ja in 1973. Two children: Albert and Patricia. Dr. Pahk enjoys photography and golf.

Nuzhath Parveen–Jawadi, M.D.

Pediatrician
Med – Net
500 Walter Street Northwest, Suite 404
Albuquerque, NM 87102–2563
(505) 242–4944
Fax: (505) 242–4956

8011

Business Information: Med – Net is an administrative medical group of six pediatricians affiliated with four local hospitals. As Pediatrician, Mrs. Parveen–Jawadi is responsible for clinical care and patient relations. Concurrent with her duties as Staff Pediatrician, Dr. Parveen–Jawadi provides an in–service program for nurses, and also serves as a mentor to students considering a career in pediatrics. **Career Steps:** Pediatrician, Med – Net (1992–Present). **Associations & Accomplishments:** American Academy of Pediatrics; New Mexico Pediatric Society; New Mexico Medical Society. **Education:** Kansas University Medical Center, M.D. Degree in Pediatrics (1992); Osmania Medical College – India, M.B.B.S. (1982). **Personal:** Married to Mohammad S. in 1979. One child: Sumayya S.. Mrs. Parveen–Jawadi enjoys listening to music.

Bharat Kumar Patel, M.D.

Internal Medicine Physician
The Medical Office of Bharat Kumar Patel, M.D.
23501 Jefferson Avenue
St. Clair Shores, MI 48080–1985
(810) 776–8200
Fax: (810) 775–0091

8011

Business Information: The Medical Office of Bharat Kumar Patel, M.D., affiliated with four hospitals, is a private, general practice medical office, concentrating on internal medicine complaints. A practicing physician since 1972, Dr. Patel oversees all administrative operations for associates and a support staff of 4, in addition to his daily patient practice. He also conducts public speaking at hospital lectures. **Career Steps:** Physician, The Medical Office of Bharat Kumar Patel, M.D. (1989–Present); Resident Physician, Bon Secours Hospital (1986–1989); Resident Physician Mercy Hospital (1985–1986). **Associations & Accomplishments:** Wayne County Medical Society; Michigan State Medical Society; American College of Physicians; American Society of Addiction Medicine; Certified in Addiction Medicine. **Education:** Grant Medical College, M.D. (1972). **Personal:** Dr. Patel enjoys photography and travel.

Dilip G. Patel, M.D., F.A.C.O.G.

OB/GYN Physician
The Medical Office of Dilip G. Patel, M.D.
10411 Vacco Street #A
South El Monte, CA 91733–3350
(818) 448–9882
Fax: (818) 448–9877

8011

Business Information: The Medical Office of Dilip G. Patel, M.D. is a full–service, private medical practice, specializing in obstetrics and gynecology. A practicing physician since 1981 and a Board–Certified Obstetrician and Gynecologist, Dr. Patel established his private practice in 1989. He oversees all administrative operations for associates and support staff, in addition to his daily patient practice. His practice includes pre– and post–natal care, as well as performing surgeries and delivering babies. **Career Steps:** Sole Practitioner, The Medical Office of Dilip G. Patel, M.D. (1989–Present); Physician, General Medicine (1982–1989). **Associations & Accomplishments:** Fellow, American College of Obstetricians and Gynecologists. **Education:** Rutgers Medical School (1981); Medical College of Baruda, M.B.B.S., D.A.O., M.D. **Personal:** Married to Nilam D. in 1975. Two children: Herschel and Poonam. Dr. Patel enjoys reading, sightseeing, tennis, volleyball and Far Eastern sports.

Mahendra M. Patel, M.D.

Physician
Boston Road Medical
3454 Boston Road
Bronx, NY 10469
(718) 798–2236
Fax: Please mail or call

8011

Business Information: Boston Road Medical is a private, medical practice providing diagnosis and treatment of patients. The Practice is affiliated with two hospitals: Our Lady of Mercy and Mt. Vernon Hospital. Established in 1983, Boston Road Medical currently consists of four physician associates and employs six support staff. Practicing medicine for the past 20 years, Dr. Patel serves as physician and is responsible for all aspects of operations, including providing health care to patients. His practice includes the areas of internal medicine, cardiovascular diseases, endocrinology, G.I., G.V. & C.N.S. disorder and dermatology. **Career Steps:** Boston Road Medical: Physician (1995–Present), Secretary (1995), Vice President (1994–1995), President (1993–1994). **Associations & Accomplishments:** AAPI; Bronx Medical Society; New York Medical Society; B.SS. **Education:** Grant Medical College, M.B.B.S. (1974), M.D.; Residency training at Mt. Vernon Hospital and Montefiore Hospital. **Personal:** Married to Purnima in 1975. Two children: Alpesh and Mayur.

Thomas M. Patton

Director, Materials Management
First Coast Medical Group
2005 Riverside Avenue
Jacksonville, FL 32204–4441
(904) 387–7605
Fax: (904) 388–4577

8011

Business Information: First Coast Medical Group, a division of Phycor, is a multi–group medical practice. The parent company, Phycor, is an organization of forty facilities and approximately 85 physicians in the United States. As Director, Materials Management, Mr. Patton has an annual multi–million dollar budget and is responsible for the courier system, telecommunications, maintenance of equipment and building, and the bidding on capital expense items. He has a staff of eight and handles all personnel functions of the department. **Career Steps:** Director, Materials Management, First Coast Medical Group (1987–Present); Plant Facilities Supervisor, Winter Haven Hospital (1978–1986). **Associations & Accomplishments:** American Society for Healthcare Materials Management; Jacksonville Purchasing Agency; American Hospital Association. **Education:** University of Southern Florida, B.A. (1978). **Personal:** Married to Debbie in 1992. One child: Michelle Lee Alford.

W. Allen Paul, M.D.

President and Senior Physician
Rheumatology Associates, P.C.
2145 Highland Avenue South, Suite 200
Birmingham, AL 35205
(205) 933–0320
Fax: (205) 933–6400

8011

Business Information: Rheumatology Associates, P.C. is a private general medical practice, specializing in rheumatology and arthritic disorders. A practicing physician since 1980, Board–certified in Internal Medicine with a subspecialty in Rheumatology, Dr. Paul founded Rheumatology Associates in 1987. As President, he oversees all administrative and medical support staff, in addition to his daily private patient practice. Concurrent to his private practice, Dr. Paul is a staff physician affiliate with St. Vincent Hospital, Brookwood Hospital, and Healthsouth Medical Center. **Career Steps:** President and Physician, Rheumatology Associates, P.C. (1987–Present); Physician, St. Vincent Hospital (Present); Physician, Brookwood Hospital (Present); Physician, Healthsouth Medical Center (Present); Physician, University of Alabama (1984–1987); Physician, University of Kentucky (1980–1984). **Associations & Accomplishments:** American Society of Internal Medicine; American Medical Association; American College of Rheumatology; Alabama Society of Rheumatic Disease; Best Doctors in America, Southwest Region. **Education:** Medical College of Georgia, M.D. (1980); University of Georgia, A.B. summa cum laude (1974); University of Kentucky, Internship and Residency (1980–1984); University of Alabama at Birmingham, Fellowship in Rheumatology (1987). **Personal:** Married to Ruth in 1984. Three children: Drew, Lauren, and Rebecca. Dr. Paul enjoys running and playing the guitar and mandolin in his leisure time.

Elsa P. Paulsen, M.D.

Physician
Elsa P. Paulsen, M.D., P.C.
316 10th Street, NE
Charlottesville, VA 22902–5317
(804) 293–8207
Fax: (804) 295–9123

8011

Business Information: Elsa P. Paulsen, M.D., P.C., established in 1991, is a full–service, private medical practice concentrating on the diagnosis and treatment of diabetes in pediatrics, adolescents, and young adults. As Physician, Dr. Paulsen is responsible for all aspects of operations, including providing patient care for 700 patients. Concurrent with her position, she conducts research in diabetes. Future plans include conducting more research in toxemia in pregnancy. **Career Steps:** Physician, Elsa P. Paulsen, M.D., P.C. (1991–Present); Associate Professor, University of Virginia School of Medicine (1970–1991); Fellow, Instructor, and Associate Professor, Einstein College of Medicine (1960–1970). **Associations & Accomplishments:** American Medical Association; National Organization of Women; American Academy of Science; Published book entitled, "Kidney Int'l." **Education:** University of Minnesota, M.D. (1954); Indiana University, M.A.; University of Illinois, A.B. **Personal:** Married to former Monrad G. Paulsen (who was Dean of University of Virginia Law School prior to his death) in 1955. Two children: Peter William and Christopher Monrad. Dr. Paulsen enjoys opera and traveling to foreign countries.

France Perron, M.D.

General Practitioner
Clinique Medicale Lac Megantic
102–5256 Rue Frontenac
Lac Megantic, Quebec
(819) 583–3344
Fax: Please mail or call

8011

Business Information: Clinique Medicale Lac Megantic is a clinic offering a wide range of medical services. As General Practitioner, Dr. Perron treats patients with standard medical problems, conducts physicals, and refers patients to specialists as needed. **Career Steps:** General Practitioner, Clinique Medicale Lac Megantic (1985–Present). **Education:** Laval University, M.D. (1979). **Personal:** Dr. Perron enjoys travel, scuba diving, and bicycling.

Terilyn C. Perry, M.D.

Pediatrician
The Office of Terilyn C. Perry, M.D.
705 17th Street, Suite 300
Columbus, GA 31901–1976
(706) 660–1205
Fax: (706) 660–0600

8011

Business Information: The Office of Terilyn C. Perry, M.D. is a private, full–service medical practice specializing in pediatrics. A practicing physician since 1989 and a Board Certified Pediatrician, Dr. Perry oversees all administrative operations for associates and a support staff of 8, in addition to her daily patient practice and consulting services. **Career Steps:** Pediatrician, The Office of Terilyn C. Perry, M.D. (1992–Present); Pediatric Resident Physician, University of South Florida – Tampa (1989–1992); Biological Science Research Assistant, Maharry Medical College (1986–1987). **Associations & Ac-**

complishments: National Medical Association; American Medical Association; MAG; Columbus Fort Benning Medical Association; AKA. **Education:** Meharry Medical College, M.D. (1989); Austin Peay State University, B.S. (1984). **Personal:** Dr. Perry enjoys art, playing the piano, singing, dance, and reading.

Joann Pfundstein, M.D.

Physician
–Independent–
3289 Woodburn Road, Suite 200
Annandale, VA 22003
(703) 560–7900
Fax: (703) 560–8408

8011

Business Information: Dr. Joann Pfundstein specializes in diagnosing and treating adults and children with infectious diseases. Her areas of interest include infectious diseases in transplant patients and AIDS. A member of the Infectious Disease Society of America, Dr. Pfundstein combines patient practice with clinical research and teaching. Her perseverance and the need to help people has lead to her success as a physician. **Associations & Accomplishments:** American College of Physicians; American Society of Microbiology; Infectious Diseases Society of America. Education: University of Medicine and Dentistry of New Jersey – Robert Wood Johnson Medical School, M.D. (1990); Columbia University, M.S. in Nutrition (1986); Bucknell University, B.S. in Biology (1984).

Clifford M. Phibbs, M.D.

President
Oxboro Clinics
600 West 98th Street
Bloomington, MN 55420
(612) 885–6052
Fax: (612) 885–6022

8011

Business Information: Oxboro Clinics specializes in health care employing 107 people. Established in 1953, Oxboro Clinics has an estimated annual revenue of $7 million. As President, Dr. Phibbs oversees all aspects of operations for the clinics. He is also a General Surgery Specialist. **Career Steps:** President, Oxboro Clinics (Present); Surgeon Specialist, U.S. Army Corps; Medical Director, Minnesota Protective Life Insurance Company. **Associations & Accomplishments:** Hennipin County Medical Society; Minnesota State Medical Association; American Medical Association; American College of Surgeons; Minnesota Surgical Society; American Board of Surgery; Pan Pacific Surgical Association; Minnesota Chapter of American College of surgeons; Association for Surgical Education; Royal Society of Medicine; American College of Sports Medicine; Member of 10 different Bloomington City committees over the years; Member, Board of Directors, Washington State University Foundation, Pullman, Washington; Board of Directors, Bloomington Minnesota Chamber of Commerce Chairman (1984–1985); Dr. Phibbs has also been published in numerous medical journals. **Education:** University of Washington, M.D. (1955); University of Minnesota Medical School, M.S. in Surgery (1960); Washington State University, B.S. in Zoology (1952); **Personal:** Married to Pat for 41 years. Three children: Wayne Robert, Marc Stuart, and Nancy Louise.

Marvin Thomas Phillips III, M.D.

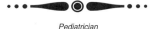

Pediatrician
The Longstreet Clinic, PC
650 Broad Street SE
Gainesville, GA 30505
(770) 535–3611
Fax: (770) 535–7092

8011

Business Information: The Longstreet Clinic, PC is a multi–discipline medical clinic, providing pediatrics; neonatology; OB/GYN; family, internal and rehabilitation medicine; and general surgery practices. All physician associates operate as private entities in their respective specialties. A Board–certified Pediatrician, Dr. Phillips is one of seven physician associates with the Clinic's Pediatric Department. In addition to his private practice, Dr. Phillips is also on the staff of the Northeast Georgia Regional Medical Center and associated with Egleston Children's Hospital in Atlanta. **Career Steps:** Pediatrician, The Longstreet Clinic, PC (1995–Present); Pediatrician, Northeast Georgia Pediatric Group (1990–1995). **Education:** Medical College of Georgia, M.D. (1987); University of Georgia, B.S. in Chemistry (1983). **Personal:** Married to Rachel in 1987. Two children: Cameron and Aaron. Dr. Phillips enjoys skiing and computers.

Zaiga Alksne Phillips, M.D.

Pediatrician
Pediatric Associates
2700 Northrup Way
Bellevue, WA 98004
(206) 827–4600
Fax: (206) 828–2256

8011

Business Information: Pediatric Associates is a full–service, pediatric care practice, providing diagnosis and treatment of children through three satellite offices in the Bellevue, Washington area. Established in 1967, Pediatric Associates consists of 17 pediatricians and over 50 medical and administrative support staff. As a practicing pediatrician for over thirty years, Dr. Phillips joined Pediatric Associates in 1977. She is responsible for providing quality health care to children, particularly focusing on those patients suffering from allergic disorders. Concurrent with her private medical practice, Dr. Phillips provides medical assistance through the Bellevue, WA – Liepaja, Latvia Sister City Association and "Healing the Children" organization to children and physicians in Latvia. Dr. Phillips was the initiator of the Bellevue, WA and Liepaja, Latvia Sister City Association. She also serves as a Clinical Instructor with the University of Washington's Department of Pediatrics. **Career Steps:** Pediatrician, Pediatric Associates (1977–Present). **Associations & Accomplishments:** American Association of Pediatricians; Washington State Pediatricians; King County Medical Society; Washington State Medical Association; North Pacific Pediatricians Association AAFA; Washington State Chapter Board AAFA; Bellevue Sister City Association; Board Member, Bellevue School District Stay In School Program; Board Member, Bellevue Citizens Stay in School Program; Board Member, Medical Center American Latvian Association; Board Member, American Latvian Association; Latvian Association of Dentists and Physicians. **Education:** University of Washington: M.D. (1959); B.S. (1956). **Personal:** Three children: Albert L., Lisa K., and Cynthia Lynn. Dr. Phillips enjoys travel and skiing.

Stuart B. Pink, M.D., FACC, FACCP

Cardiologist Associate
Associated Cardiologists, P.C.
856 Century Drive
Mechanicsburg, PA 17055
(717) 697–3304 (800) 845–1742
Fax: (717) 697–3929

8011

Business Information: Associated Cardiologists, P.C. is a full–service, cardiology practice, providing diagnosis and treatment to patients suffering from heart problems. A practicing physician since 1980 and a Board–Certified Cardiologist, Dr. Pink is an Interventional Cardiologist, providing quality medical care to patients and specializing in the prevention of heart problems. **Career Steps:** Cardiologist Associate, Associated Cardiologists, P.C. (1988–Present); Assistant Clinical Professor of Medicine, Pennsylvania State University Medical School (Present); Staff Cardiologist, Medical West Community Health Plan – Chicopee, MA (1985–1988); Emergency Medicine Physician, Shady Grove Adventist Hospital – Rockville, MD (1984–1985); Emergency Medicine Physician, Gary Langston, M.D.–Dept. of Emergency Medicine (1984–1985); Emergency Medicine Physician, DePaul Hospital – Bridgeton, MO (1983–1984); Emergency Medicine Associate, Anthony P. Friedrich, M.D., Chair–Dept. of Emergency Medicine (1983–1984). **Associations & Accomplishments:** American Heart Association; American College of Cardiology; American College of Physicians; American College of Chest Physicians; American Medical Association; Pennsylvania Medical Society; Dauphin County Medical Society; Society of Diplomates of Harrisburg; American Society of Echocardiography; Fellow, American College of Cardiology; Fellow, American College of Chest Physicians; Recipient, Kline Family Practice "Outstanding Teaching Award" (1991); Extensive research, publications and presentations in the fields of Myocardial Infarction, Cardiac Catheterization and other Coronary–related procedures. **Education:** Cornell University Medical College, M.D. (1980); City College of New York, B.S. in Pre–Medicine (1973–1975); Hamilton College, B.A. (1971); POST GRADUATE TRAINING: Washington Hospital Center, Washington, D.C. (George Washington University): Internship in Internal Medicine (1980–1981), Residency in Internal Medicine (1981–1983); Baystate Medical Center, Springfield, MA (Tufts University): Fellowship in Cardiovascular Diseases (1985–1987), Fellowship in Interventional Cardiology (1987–1988). **Personal:** Married to Patrice Jacqueline Pink, R.N. Five children: Brian, Caitlin, Melissa, Kevin and Carrie. Dr. Pink enjoys golf, skiing, reading, tennis and playing the guitar during his leisure time.

Daniel J. Pipoly, M.D.

Physician
Toledo Pulmonary & Sleep Specialists, Inc.
2109 Hughes Drive, Suite 760
Toledo, OH 43606–5111
(419) 479–2676
Fax: (419) 479–2696

8011

Business Information: Toledo Pulmonary & Sleep Specialists, Inc. is a private medical practice, specializing in pulmonary, critical care, and sleep medicine. A practicing physician since 1981 and a Certified Thoracic and Chest Physician, Dr. Pipoly joined Toledo Pulmonary and Sleep Specialists, Inc. as Physician in 1993. He is one of three doctors, responsible for providing quality medical care to patients suffering from pulmonary, critical care, and sleep disorders. **Career Steps:** Physician, Toledo Pulmonary & Sleep Specialists, Inc. (1993–Present); Physician, Eastern Ohio Pulmonary Consultants, Inc. (1987–1993); Physician, Washington University of St. Louis (1986–1987). **Associations & Accomplishments:** American Thoracic Society; American College of Chest Physicians. **Education:** University of Cinninnati, M.D. (1981); Ohio State University, B.S. (1977). **Personal:** Married to Cynthia J. Pipoly in 1987. Four children: Mathew, Julianne, George, and Josef. Dr. Pipoly enjoys running and golf.

James D. Piscioneri, P.A.– C.

Physician Assistant
Smokey Point Family Medicine
16410 Smokey Point Boulevard
Arlington, WA 98223–8415
(360) 653–4569
Fax: (360) 659–9834

8011

Business Information: Smokey Point Family Medicine, affiliated with Cascade Valley Hospital, is a medical clinic specializing in family practice and emergency medicine. With over 21 years of experience as an Emergency Technician, a Paramedic and a Board–Certified Physician Assistant and board certified in primary care and surgery, James Piscioneri joined Smokey Point Family Medicine as Physician Assistant in 1991. He provides diagnostic and therapeutic health care, serving as a member of the health care team. Additional duties include performing physician examinations, interpreting medical testing, providing treatment of an array of medical abnormalities, working with physicians on complicated cases and serving as First Assistant in the operating room suites. Due to his natural ability with children, he has a strong drive toward the pediatric aspect of medicine. Concurrent with his physician assistant duties, James is using his inventive desire to start a business venture, resulting from his on–the–job injury as a firefighter/paramedic. He has invented a concept for stopping the panic aspect of high–rise fires, as well as currently working on a concept for other safety features, such as seatbelts and flares. **Career Steps:** Physician Assistant, Smokey Point Family Medicine (1991–Present); Physicians Assistant – Certified, Northwest Emergency Physicians (1990–1991); Physician Assistant–Student, University of Washington (1989–1990); Firefighter/Paramedic, City of Ontario Fire Department (1983–1987); Firefighter/Paramedic, City of Redlands Fire Department (1981–1983); Firefighter Reserve, Monclair Fire Department (1980–1981); E.M.T. Chief Paramedic, B&B Medevac (1975–1980); Emergency/Orthopedic Technician, San Antonio Hospital (1975–1980). **Associations & Accomplishments:** American Academy of Physicians Assistants; National Commission of Certified Physicians Assistants; Washington Academy of Physicians Assistants; Washington State Medical Association; National Registry of Emergency Medical Technician/Paramedics; University of Washington School of Medicine Affiliate Faculty, PA Student Trainer; Physician Assistant – Board Certified in Primary Care and Surgery; Paramedic; California State Firefighter; FBI–trained S.W.A.T. Member; Advanced Cardiac Life Support; Advanced Trauma Life Support; Helitac Certified; Medal of Valor (1981). **Education:** University of Washington, Physician Assistant Program (1990); Crafton Hills College, Yucaipa, California, Paramedicine/Premedicine; Chaffey College, Alta Loma, CA, General Studies (1977). **Personal:** Married to Lori in 1995. Two children: Darik and Anna. Mr. Piscioneri, a Christian, enjoys fishing, camping, inventing, and skiing.

John H. Powers III, M.D.

Physician
John F. Reinhart, P.A.
311 Llanfair Road
Wynnewood, PA 19096
(302) 731–0800
Fax: (302) 731–7888

8011

Business Information: John F. Reinhart, P.A. is a full–service, medical practice, providing care for patients relating to the prevention and treatment of infectious diseases. A practicing physician since 1988, Dr. Powers joined the Practice in

1995, providing quality medical care to patients. In addition to his practice, he serves as Attending Physician in Infectious Diseases for the Department of Medicine at the Medical Center of Delaware. Concurrent with his private practice, he is a Clinical Instructor at Thomas Jefferson School of Medicine. **Career Steps:** Physician, John F. Reinhart, P.A. (1995–Present); Physician in Infectious Diseases, Department of Medicine, Medical Center of Delaware (1995–Present); Clinical Instructor, Thomas Jefferson School of Medicine (1995–Present). **Associations & Accomplishments:** Medical Society of Delaware; American College of Physicians; Infectious Society of America; American Society for Microbiology. **Education:** Temple University School of Medicine, M.D. (1988). **Personal:** Dr. Powers enjoys art, music, and basketball.

Jyothi Puram, M.D.

Physician
Dr. Jyothi Puram, M.D.
2440 East High Street
Springfield, OH 45505–1324
(513) 325–5583
Fax: (513) 325–8113

8011

Business Information: Dr. Jyothi Puram, M.D., established in 1994, is a private family medical practice. Board–certified in Internal Medicine, Dr. Puram established the private medical practice in 1994. A native of India, Dr. Puram completed his residency there, as well as practiced General Medicine for two years prior to immigrating to the United States. **Career Steps:** Physician, Dr. Jyothi Puram, M.D. (1994–Present); Physician, Mt. Carmel Medical Center (1991–1994). **Associations & Accomplishments:** Member of American College of Physicians; American Medical Association; AAPI; OSMA; Clark County Medical Society. **Education:** Madras Medical College, M.D. & B.S. (1984); Bangalore Medical College – Board Eligible in Anesthesiology. **Personal:** Married to Chandra Y. Sekharudu in 1986. One child: Priyanka Puram Sekhar. Dr. Puram enjoys painting, writing poetry, and travel.

Steven W. Queen, M.D.

Internist
Sylva Medical Center
48 Hospital Road
Sylva, NC 28779–2794
(704) 586–8971
Fax: (704) 586–4083

8011

Business Information: Sylva Medical Center is a full–service health care facility specializing in internal medicine and HIV/AIDS research with 3TC. As Internist, Dr. Queen spends most of his time doing clinical practice and AIDS research searching for new medications. Concurrently, he also serves as a clinical instructor to 3rd year medical students from the University of North Carolina–Chapel Hill. **Career Steps:** Internist, Sylva Medical Center (1991–Present); Internist, US Government IHS (1988–1991). **Associations & Accomplishments:** AIDS Coordinator, Southern Medical Association; American Foundation for AIDS Research; American Cancer Society. **Education:** East Carolina University, M.D. (1984); University of North Carolina, (1980); University of Texas, Resident/Intern Programs (1987). **Personal:** Dr. Queen enjoys hiking, weight training, cooking, and photography.

Robert L. Quigley, M.D., D.Phil.

Cardiothoracic Surgeon
Guthrie Clinic, Ltd.
Guthrie Square
Sayre, PA 18840
(717) 882–2306
Fax: (717) 882–2290

8011

Business Information: Guthrie Clinic, Ltd., adjacent to Robert Packer Hospital, is a multi–specialty clinic with over 200 physicians, providing diagnosis and treatment to patients. A practicing Cardiothoracic Surgeon since 1992, Dr. Quigley joined Guthrie Clinic, Ltd. in 1995. Serving as an Associate with the Cardiothoracic Surgery Department, he performs open heart and valve by–pass surgeries and treats patients with lung and esophageal cancer. **Career Steps:** Cardiothoracic Surgeon, Guthrie Clinic, Ltd. (1995–Present); Evanston Hospital, Northwestern University: Assistant Professor of Surgery, Department of Surgery, Cardiothoracic Division – Co–Director Surgical Research Laboratory, Attending Surgeon (1992–1994), Senior Attending Surgeon, Director Surgical Research Laboratory (1994–1995). **Associations & Accomplishments:** The Irving Heward Cameron Undergraduate Scholarship in Surgery (1982); Tau Omicron Phi Chi Scholarship (1985–1987); Overseas Research Student Award (1985–1988); Horatio Symonds Studentship in Surgery (1986–1987); Irving Cameron Scholarship (1986); Golden Apple Award (1989) – The American Medical Student Association; Alpha Omega Alpha (1990); Thomas Baffes MD Research Award (1995); Licentiate, Medical Council of Canada (1983); Diplomat, National Board of Medical Examiners of the USA (1983); American Board of Surgery, Diplomat (1992), Certificate of Added Qualifications in Critical Care (1993); Diplomat, The American Board of Thoracic Surgery (1994); Fellow, American College of Chest Physicians (1995); Fellow, American College of Surgeons (1995); Fellow, International College of Surgeons (1996); RESEARCH INTERESTS: Endothelium, Hemostatsis, Transplant Rejection and Related Disorders; Frequent publisher and lecturer at international, national, state and local conferences and institutional symposia and proceedings. **Education:** University of Toronto, M.D. cum laude (1982); Oxford University, D.Phil. in Transplantation Immunology (1988); Dalhousie University, B.S. cum laude (1978); Rotating Internship, St. Michael's Hospital – University of Toronto; (1982–1983); Resident, Department of Surgery, University of Toronto (1983–1985); Research Fellow, Nuffield Department of Surgery, Oxford University (1985–1988); Duke University Medical Center: Senior Resident (1988–1990), Chief Resident (1990–1991), Teaching Scholar (1991–1992) . **Personal:** Married to Debra Kristine Crumb, registered nurse/attorney. Dr. Quigley enjoys Harley Davidson riding, running, skiing, and playing tennis.

Virginia M. Quinones, M.D.

President and Physician
Minden Pediatrics Inc.
Number 2, Medical Plaza
Minden, LA 71055
(318) 377–7116
Fax: (318) 377–9979

8011

Business Information: Minden Pediatrics Inc. is a full–service, multi–specialty pediatric and neonatology facility. Established in 1990, Minden Pediatrics currently employs six medical support staff. As President and Physician, Dr. Quinones is responsible for the care and treatment of patients, as well as all administrative decisions. Concurrent with her private practice, she also serves as Director of Pediatrics at Minden Medical Center, responsible for establishing policies for Pediatrics and the Nursery. She also attends Cesarean Sections, complicated and premature deliveries, and provides intensive neonatal care when necessary. Dr. Quinones also serves as a Courtesy Clinical Faculty member with the Louisiana State University Medical Center. As Chief Neonotologist at Caguas Regional Hospital she directs teaching and supervision of Pediatric residents and Neonatal residents, interns, nurses and third and fourth year medical students. **Career Steps:** President, Pediatrician, Minden Pediatrics Inc. (1990–Present); Director of Nursery and Pediatrics, Minden Medical Center (1990–Present); Chief Neonatologist, Caguas Regional Hospital, Puerto Rico (1981–1990); Private Practice, Neonatology, Mayaguez Pediatric Center, Puerto Rico (1983–1990). **Associations & Accomplishments:** Fellow, American Academy of Pediatrics; Member, Puerto Rico Chapter, AAP; Member, Louisiana Chapter, AAP; American Medical Society; Webster Parish Medical Society; Southern Medical Association; Beta Beta Beta Biological Society; Minden–South Webster Chamber of Commerce; Board of Directors, Pregnancy Aid Center; Minden Medical Center: Chairman of Pharmacy and Therapeutics Committee, Quality Assurance and Risk Management Committee, Chairman of Nursery Subcommittee, Medical Staff Committee; Caguas Regional Hospital: Total Parenteral Nutrition Committee, Control of Infectious Diseases Committee, Research and Investigation Studies Approval Committee, Drugs and Therapeutic Committee, Pediatric Department Acceptance and Promotion of Residents Committee; Control of Infectious Diseases Committee, Ashford Memorial Community Hospital; Awards and Honors include: Bausch & Lomb Honor Award Medal, Outstanding Young Women of America; Who's Who in Hispanic America; American Academy of Family Physicians Recognition as Active Teacher in Family Practice; Quien es Quien in U.S. Medical Care; Sterling Who's Who; EXCEL from College of American Pathologists, Excellence in Laboratory Testing; Who's Who in Leading Professionals and Executives; Numerous speaking engagements and publications; Fluent in Spanish and English. **Education:** University of Puerto Rico School of Medicine, M.D. (1976); University of Puerto Rico – Rio Piedras Campus (1972); Caguas Regional Hospital, Residency in Pediatrics (1976–1979); Fellowship in Neonatology, University Pediatric Hospital (1979–1981). **Personal:** One child: Jessica M. Milan–Quinones. Dr. Quinones enjoys reading, music, poetry, sewing, cooking, bowling and walking.

John J. Raleigh, M.D.

Medical Director
Fresh Start, Inc.
6510 Schneider Drive
Middletown, MD 21769–7018
(301) 371–6569
Fax: Please mail or call

8011

Business Information: Fresh Start, Inc., established in 1962, is a full–service medical practice, specializing inobstetrics and gynecology. A practicing physician since 1957 and Board–Certified in Gynecology, Dr. Raleigh joined Fresh Start, Inc. in 1993. Serving as Medical Director and Clinician, he provides diagnosis and treatment in obstetrics and gynecology. He also conducts surgery on gynecology diseases. His subspecialty is in sexually–transmitted diseases and addiction medicine. **Career Steps:** Medical Director, Fresh Start, Inc. (1993–Present); Clinician, Washington County Health Department (1991–1993); Private Practice (1962–1968). **Associations & Accomplishments:** American Medical Association; University of Maryland School of Medicine Alumni Association; Holy Family Community Church; American Legion. **Education:** University of Maryland School of Medicine, M.D. (1957); Roanoke College, B.S. (1952); C.B.S. Schools – Limerick City, Ireland. **Personal:** Three children: Kevin, Michael, and Kathleen. Dr. Raleigh enjoys reading, gardening, trout fishing, and H.I.V. studies.

Keith F. Rawlinson, M.D.

Maternal–Fetal Medicine Consultant
Great Neck Women's Medical Center
1010 Northern Boulevard, Suite 106
Great Neck, NY 11021–5306
(516) 466–3663
Fax: (516) 773–3201

8011

Business Information: Great Neck Women's Medical Center is an international women's health care facility, providing care in obstetrics and gynecology. Available services include mammography, OB/GYN ultrasounds, and prenatal diagnosis. A practicing physician since 1962, Dr. Rawlinson joined Great Neck Women's Medical Center as a Maternal–Fetal Medicine Consultant in 1993. He is responsible for providing consultative care to patients, in addition to conducting obstetric sonography and prenatal diagnosis. **Career Steps:** Maternal–Fetal Medicine Consultant, Great Neck Women's Medical Center (1993–Present); Chief of Maternal–Fetal Medicine, North Shore University Hospital – New York (1986–1993); Chief of Obstetrics, Harlem Hospital – Manhattan, New York (1980–1986); Perinatologist and Associate Professor, University of Alberta Hospital – Canada (1975–1980). **Associations & Accomplishments:** Fellow, American College of OB/GYN; Fellow, Society of Perinatal Obstetricians; Fellow, Royal College of OB/GYN of the United Kingdom; Fellow, Royal College of Physicians and Surgeons of Canada. **Education:** Medical College of St. Bartholomew's Hospital, University of London – United Kingdom, M.D. (1962–1967); University of Southern California, M.F.M. Board Certification (1975); University of Edinburgh, M.R.C.O.G. (1968–1973). **Personal:** Married to Ann in 1966. Five children: Caroline Emma, Simon Alexander, Jeremy, Rebecca, and Rachel. Dr. Rawlinson enjoys all types of sports.

Sherry L. Reagan

Director of Staffing and Personnel
East Tennessee Medical Group
P.O. Box 5358
Maryville, TN 37802
(423) 681–1972
Fax: (423) 984–3420

8011

Business Information: East Tennessee Medical Group is a multi–specialist group of oncology, neurology, and pulmonary specialists. As Director of Staffing and Personnel, Ms. Reagan is responsible for diversified administrative activities, including handling all hiring, firing, salary, and employee discipline. **Career Steps:** Director of Staffing and Personnel, East Tennessee Medical Group (1994–Present); East Tennessee Internal Medicine: Office Manager (1990–1994), Billing and Insurance (1989–1990); Transcriptionist, Blount Memorial Hospital (1985–1989). **Associations & Accomplishments:** Hospice Volunteer. **Personal:** Two children: Dusty and Holly. Ms. Reagan enjoys church activities, watching University of Tennessee sports & Atlanta Braves, and reading.

William J. Reed, M.D., F.A.A.P.

Sole Practitioner
Office of William J. Reed, M.D., F.A.A.P.
2900 North Street, Suite 408
Beaumont, TX 77702–1542
(409) 892–8362
Fax: (409) 892–1660

8011

Business Information: An esteemed physician with twenty–eight years of experience, Dr. Reed has been a practicing physician since 1968. Board–Certified in Pediatrics, he established his private practice in 1979, specializing in the diagnosis and treatment of children. Concurrently, he serves as Clinical Assistant Professor of Pediatrics at the University of Texas at Houston and the University of Texas Medical Branch at Galveston, providing direct patient care and instruction to students. **Career Steps:** Sole Practitioner, Office of William J. Reed, M.D., F.A.A.P. (1979–Present); Clinical Assistant Professor of Pediatrics, University of Texas – Houston (1992–Present); Clinical Assistant Professor of Pediatrics; University of Texas Medical Branch (1991–Present); Director of Neonatal Intensive Care Unit, Rush Foundation Hospital (1978–1979); Co–Director of Pediatric and Neonatal Intensive Care Units, South Georgia Medical Center (1972–1975); Chief of Pediatrics, U.S. Naval Hospital (1972–1975). **Associations & Accomplishments:** Executive Committee, Baptist Hospital, Beaumont, Texas; Fellow, American Academy of Pediatrics (Secion on Child Abuse), International College of Pediatrics; Texas Medical Association; Texas Pediatric Society; Southeast Texas Pediatric Society; Jefferson County Medical Society; Southern Medical Society; Director, Child Abuse Team – St. Elizabeth Hospital; AHEC Professor of Pediatrics; Board of Directors, St. Elizabeth PHO; Co–Founder, The Mickey Mettaffrey Child Advocacy Center; Medical Director, The Joseph B. Rogers Southeast Texas Community Health Clinic. **Education:** University of Texas Medical School, M.D. (1968); Lamar University, B.S. (1965); U.S. Navy Internship; U.S. Navy Residency in Pediatrics with rotations at the University of North Carolina; Medical College of Virginia; Cornell (1972); Certified Pediatrics: (1973), (1987). **Personal:** Married to Ruth in 1980. Six children: Randy, Rusty, Nick, Tami, Sean, and Christian. Dr. Reed enjoys golf, flying, Karate, child advocacy, and teaching.

Eugene P. Reese Jr., M.D.

• • • ━━━◉━━━ • • •

Physician Associate
Jackson Clinic, P.A.
616 West Forest Avenue
Jackson, TN 38301–3902
(901) 422–0339
Fax: (901) 422–0442

8011

Business Information: The Jackson Clinic, P.A. is a full–service, multi–specialty medical group practice. Established in 1952, the Jackson Clinic currently has 90 physician associate members and employs over 300 medical support staff. Dr. Eugene Reese is an Oncology/Hematology Associate with the Group, specializing in the diagnosis and treatment of cancer and blood diseases. Concurrent with his patient practice, Dr. Reese provides consultation and treatment with the staff of Jackson Madison County General Hospital. **Career Steps:** Physician, Jackson Clinic, P.A. (Present). **Associations & Accomplishments:** American Society of Clinical Oncology; American Society of Hematology; American College of Physicians; American Medical Association. **Education:** University of Louisville School of Medicine, M.D. (1967); United States Military Academy, West Point, B.S. (1960). **Personal:** Married to Eliane in 1965. Father of two children: Gene and Maria. Dr. Reese enjoys swimming, photography, reading and sports.

Ronald G. Rehn

Chief Administrative Officer
Northeast Washington Medical Group
1200 East Columbia Avenue
Colville, WA 99114–3354
(509) 684–3701
Fax: (509) 684–5817

8011

Business Information: Northeast Washington Medical Group is a multi–specialty medical group practice. With the main location in Colville, Washington, there are also satellite offices in Kettle Falls and Chewelah. Bringing with him an extensive background in laboratory technology, Ronald Rehn was appointed to his current position in 1994. As Chief Administrative Officer, he provides the overall executive direction for all administrative operations at all locations. **Career Steps:** Northeast Washington Medical Group: Chief Administrative Officer (1994–Present), Ancillary Services Manager (1985–1994); Managing Member, Colville PHO (1995–Present); Laboratory Technician, Mt. Carmel Hospital (1978–1985); Laboratory Technician, Dr. James Stageman (1977–1978). **Associations & Accomplishments:** Medical Group Management Association; Clinical Lab Management Association; American Society of Clinical Pathologists; Board of Directors, Colville Chamber of Commerce; Vocational Technology Advisory Board, Kettle Falls High School; Boy Scouts of America Troop 904. **Education:** Eastern Washington University, B.A. (1994); Wenatchee Valley College, A.A.A. in Medical Laboratory Technology. **Personal:** Married to Jamie L. in 1978. Three children: Jess, Jake, and Andrew. Mr. Rehn enjoys hunting, fishing, and sailing.

Robert L. Reid, M.D.

Orthopedic Surgeon
Mckinney Centre
510 Ingersoll Ave, Suite 107
Woodstock, Ontario N4S 4X9
(519) 539–7444
Fax: (519) 539–7445

8011

Business Information: Dr. Reid established Mckinney Centre, his private orthopedic practice, upon conferral of his orthopedic surgery licensure in 1970. In addition to patient care, he is also responsible for all administrative and financial activities. **Career Steps:** Orthopedic Surgeon, Mckinney Centre (1970–Present). **Associations & Accomplishments:** Rotary Club of Woodstock; Canadian Medical Association; Canadian Orthopedic Association; Ontario Orthepedic Association; Order of St. Luke. **Education:** University of Ontario: M.D. (1963), FRCS(C) in Orthopedic Surgery (1970). **Personal:** Married to Marjorie in 1960. Four children: Graham, Brian, Barbara, and Bonnie. Dr. Reid enjoys fishing, windsurfing, and scuba diving.

Abraham D. Reinhartz

Physician
Abraham D. Reinhartz, M.D.
960 Lawrence Avenue West, Suite 303
North York, Ontario M6A 3B5
(416) 781–6199
Fax: (416) 781–4515

8011

Business Information: Proctor & Gamble, headquartered in Cincinnati, Ohio, is a major consumer products manufacturer distributing globally. Products include health and beauty aids; liquid, dry, and flaked soaps; dental care products; household cleaners; and much more. As At–Large Representative, Mr. Acevedo–Vila is responsible for representing constituent needs in various areas. His current term is over this year, and he is hoping to be re–elected for another four years. Though a freshman democratic legislator in a primarily republican government, he has had a very effective term of office, with the republican Governor responding well to his concerns. **Career Steps:** At–Large Representative, House of Representatives (1993–Present); Advisor of Legislative Affairs, Puerto Rico Governor's Office (1988–1992); Law Clerk, Judge Campbell–US Court of Appeals 1st Circuit of Boston (1987–1988); Law Clerk, Justice Hernandez Denton – PR Supreme Court (1985–1986). **Associations & Accomplishments:** Board of Directors, Popular Democratic Party. **Education:** Harvard University, LLM (1987); University of Puerto Rico School of Law, J.D. (1985); University of Puerto Rico, B.A. in Political Science (1982). **Personal:** Married to Luisa Gandara in 1987. Two children: Gabriela and Juan Carlos. Dr. Reinhartz enjoys reading.

Edward Gerald Reis, M.D.

Physician
McKee & Shepard Medical Associates
4631 Baltimore Avenue
Philadelphia, PA 19143–2116
(215) 726–8299
Fax: Please mail or call

8011

Business Information: McKee & Shepard Medical Associates is a private medical office, providing patient care for adults and the elderly. A practicing physician since 1992, Dr. Reis joined McKee & Shepard Medical Associates in 1995. His practice specializes in internal medicine and pulmonary diseases. **Career Steps:** Physician, McKee & Shepard Medical Associates (1995–Present); Emergency Medical Attending, Presbyterian – HUP Medical Center (1994–Present); Primary Care Physician, Philadelphia Health Department (1994–1995); T.B. Consultant, Bucks County Health Department (1994–1995).. **Associations & Accomplishments:** American Medical Association; American Thoracic Society; American College of Physicians; Published three articles in the University of the Philippines on "learning and memory"; Presented an article on "Oral Vitamin K vs. IM Vitamin K." **Education:** University of Santo Tomas – Philippines, M.D. (1987); University of California – Santa Cruz, B.A. in Psychology. **Personal:** Married to Cynthia Venegas, M.D. in 1994. Dr. Reis enjoys tropical fish and art.

Michi Relvas

Director of Operations
Palm Beach Orthopedic Institute
3401 P.G.A. Boulevard, Suite 500
Palm Beach Gardens, FL 33410
(561) 694–7776
Fax: (561) 694–3099
E MAIL: See Below

8011

Business Information: Palm Beach Orthopedic Institute provides orthopaedic services to residents of North Palm Beach and Martin Counties in Florida. Palm Beach Orthopedic Institute has eleven orthopedic surgeons on staff and a support group of forty people. As Director of Operations, Ms. Relvas is responsible for supply inventory, quality improvement, and developing, implementing and monitoring budgets. Other duties include staff recruitment, training, scheduling, and evaluating. Internet users can reach her via: micster_b@aol.com. **Career Steps:** Director of Operations, Palm Beach Orthopedic Institute (1995–Present); Manager of Printing & Forms, JFK Medical Center (1994–1995); Forms Coordinator, Cedars–Sinai Medical Center (1985–1994). **Education:** Palm Beach Atlantic College, Masters candidate; Pepperdine University, B.A. (1982). **Personal:** Ms. Relvas enjoys travel and photography.

Santuccio Ricciardi, M.D.

Physician and Partner
Primary Care Associates, Inc.
7355 California Avenue, Suite 4
Boardman, OH 44512–5602
(216) 726–4500
Fax: (216) 726–5931

8011

Business Information: Primary Care Associates, Inc. is a private medical practice, providing primary care for adolescent, adult, and geriatric patients. With two offices in Ohio (Boardman and Youngstown), Primary Care Associates, Inc. is affiliated with St. Elizabeth and Western Reserve Care Systems. A practicing physician since 1988 and a Board–Certified Internal Medicine Physician, Dr. Ricciardi co–established Primary Care Associates, Inc. as one of two physicians. He is responsible for providing quality primary care to patients. **Career Steps:** Physician and Partner, Primary Care Associates, Inc. (1991–Present). **Associations & Accomplishments:** American Medical Association; American Society of Internal Medicine; American Geriatric Society. **Education:** Northeastern Ohio College of Medicine, M.D. (1988). **Personal:** Married to Lynda Marie in 1994. Dr. Ricciardi enjoys sports, tennis, and travel.

Sherrie D. Richey, M.D.

Physician
Maternal – Fetal Medicine of Alaska
2841 DeBarr Road, #45
Anchorage, AK 99508–2945
(907) 272–6772
Fax: (907) 272–8033

8011

Business Information: Dr. Sherrie Richey specializes in Maternal – Fetal Medicine caring for high risk pregnant women and their fetuses. High–resolution ultrasounds and intrauterine fetal therapy are a few of the technologies used by Dr. Richey. As President of Maternal–Fetal Medicine of Alaska, Dr. Richey is responsible for all aspects of operations for the Corporation she formed. A physician since 1988, she enjoys gaining the respect and trust of parents and referring physicians. Strategic plans for the future include collaboration with other perinatologists in setting up outcome–based research to improve the quality, and lower the cost of high–risk care. **Career Steps:** Physician, Maternal – Fetal Medicine of Alaska (1994–Present); Physician Fellow, University of Texas Southwestern Medical School (1992–1994); Staff Physician, St. Paul Hospital (1992–1994); Resident Physician, Parkland Memorial Hospital (1988–1992). **Associations & Accomplishments:** American Medical Association; Alaska State Medical Association; American College of Obstetricians/Gynecologists; Society of Perinatal Obstetricians; American Institute of Ultrasound in Medicine. **Education:** University of Texas – Southwestern Medical School, M.D. (1988); University of Texas Health Science Center, B.S. in Biology. **Personal:** Married to Mark E. Richey, M.D. in 1985. Three children: Christopher Andrew, Jonathan Mark, and Ian James. Dr. Richey enjoys piano, reading, and skiing.

Daniel L. Ridout III, M.D.

Physician
Crozer Chester Medical Center
Building One, Suite 401
Chester, PA 19013–3995
(610) 872–8857
Fax: (610) 872–2257

8011

Business Information: Crozer Chester Medical Center is a privately–owned and incorporated medical practice, providing diagnosis and treatment of patients. A practicing physician since 1979 and a Gastroenterologist, Dr. Ridout established Crozer Medical Center as Physician in 1988. His practice specializes in gastroenterology and associated cancer. **Career Steps:** Physician, Crozer Chester Medical Center (1988–Present); University of Pennsylvania – Affiliation Graduate Hospital: Private Practive Gastroenterology (1986–Present), Attending Full–time (1983–1984), Attending Part–time (1984–1986, 1982–1983); Chief GI Division, Veterans Administration (1987–1989); General Internist via Independent Contract, Methadone & Alcohol Rehabilitation Clinic – Thomas Jefferson University Hospital (1981–1983); University of Pennsylvania: Clinical Instructor and Full–time Attending in Emergency Medicine (1983–1984), Chief Medical Resident and Instructor of Internal Medicine (1982–1983). **Associations & Accomplishments:** American Medical Association; Pennsylvania Medical Society; Philadelphia County Medical Society; The American Professional Practice Association; New Castle County Medical Society; Board of Directors (1995–1996), Delaware Medical Society; Medical Society of Eastern Pennsylvania; American Society for Gastrointestinal Endoscopy; Philadelphia College of Physicians; American College of Physicians; Pennsylvania Society of Gastroenterology; American Society of Internal Medicine; Crohns and Colitis Foundation of America; Paper Presentation American College of Physicians: Eastern and Western Pennsylvania and West Virginia Scientific Meeting (1986); Who's Who in the East (1995–1995); Achievement and Service in Medicine Award, Afro–American Historical Society of Delaware (1989). **Education:** University of Cincinnati College of Medicine, M.D. (1979), Dartmouth College, B.A. in Music (1975); University of Pennsylvania Graduate Hospital: Intern (1979–1980), Residency (1980–1982), Fellowship in Gastroenterology and Nutrition (1984–1986); Specialty Certification: American Board of Internal Medicine (1982); Subspecialty Certification: Gastroenterology and Nutrition (1987). **Personal:** Dr. Ridout enjoys music.

Theodore J. Robinson, M.D.

Chief Executive Officer
Mardan Management, Ltd.
Suite 703–625 Fifth Avenue
New Westminster, British Columbia V3M 1X4
(604) 522–2917
Fax: (604) 524–3263

8011

Business Information: Involved in Private Practice since 1971, Dr. Robinson, as Chief Surgeon and only Plastic Surgeon on–staff, performs all types of cosmetic and three types of laser surgery. Concurrently, he serves as the CEO of Mardan Management, Ltd. a company involved in investment management. He also works as Secretary for INTIRMAC, a Firm involved in the recycling of old tires to manufacture such products as bricks, tennis shoe soles, new tires, and various other items. Dr. Robinson is one of the Founders of EPI, a Company which has just patented the first biodegradable plastic. He is involved as well in Trenchless Technologies, Inc., a Company which specializes in repairing old sewage pipes without digging up roads and highways. **Career Steps:** Chief Physician/CEO, Mardan Management Ltd. (1971–Present); Chief Executive Officer, Bison Petroleum (1978–1980); Chief Executive Officer, Aquarius International, Inc. (1986–1990); Secretary, INTIRMAC (1995–Present). **Associations & Accomplishments:** Founding Member, Environmental Protection, Inc.; Founding Member, Trenchless Technologies, Inc. **Education:** University of Manitoba, M.D. (1963); Royal College of Surgeons of Canada, F.R.C.S.(c) (1972). **Personal:** Two children: Daniel and Marni. Dr. Robinson enjoys running, photography, and travel.

Zoltan P. Rona, M.D., M.Sc.

Physician and Author
Clairhurst Medical Centre
1466 Bathurst Street, Suite 305
Toronto, Ontario M5R 3S3
(416) 534–8880
Fax: (416) 534–6723
EMAIL: See Below

8011

Business Information: Clairhurst Medical Centre is a medical practice specializing in nutritional medicine. He best describes his clinic as office–based and a blend of conventional general practice with preventive medical counseling. A practicing physician since obtaining his degree in 1985, Dr. Rona established his private practice in 1978. Internet users can reach him via: zrona@wwonline.com. or through the Internet wide site: http://www.selene.com/selene/healthlink/zpr.html; http / /www.wwonline.com/rona.zpr.htm; http: / / www.natural-link.com/business_hp/zoltan_rona_bhp/index.html; http: / /www.yorku.ca/admin/wellness/articles.htm **Career Steps:** Physician and Author, Clairhurst Medical Centre (1978–Present). **Associations & Accomplishments:** President, Canadian Holistic Medical Association; Advisory Board, Dominion Herbal College – Vancouver and Toronto; Consultant to Motherisk Program, Department of Pharmacology – The Hospital for Sick Children – Toronto, Canada; Consultant, Health Provider's Choice; York University, Wellness Medicine Section Advisor, Internet web site; Author/Co–Author of 4 medical related books and over 200 articles; Appearances on several radio and television talk shows; Speaker and Lecturer at numerous medical seminars and conventions. **Education :** University of Bridgeport, CT, Master of Science in Biochemistry and Clinical Nutrition (1985); McGill University, Montreal: M.D.C.M. (1977), B.Sc. (1973); Completed rotating internship at Toronto East General and Orthopaedic Hospital (1978). **Personal:** Married to Sharon Elizabeth in 1977. Two children: Matthew and Darcy. Dr. Rona enjoys tennis, jogging, writing, computers, and teaching.

Larry I. Rubin, M.D.

Physician
Passaic Internal Medicine Group
200 Gregory Avenue
Passaic, NJ 07055
(201) 473–2597
Fax: (201) 473–5958

8011

Business Information: Passaic Internal Medicine Group is a private general practice medical organization. In operation since 1940, the Group currently employs 20 physicians and medical support staff. As a Board–certified Internist, sub–specializing in Gastroenterology, Dr. Rubin provides diagnosis, care and treatment to patients with digestive disorders and disease, as well as overall general family medical care. **Career Steps:** Physician, Passaic Internal Medicine Group **Associations & Accomplishments:** American College of Physicians; American Association of Gastroenterology; American Society of Internal Medicine; American Society of Gastroenterology Endoscopy; Alpha Omega Alpha Medical Honor Society. **Education:** Chicago Medical University, M.D. (1994); Rutgers College, B.A. (1965). **Personal:** Married to Linda in 1971. Two children: Jodi and Seth. Dr. Rubin enjoys reading, running marathons and travel.

Deborah K. Rufner, M.D.

Pediatrician
Group Health Associates
55 Progress Place
Cincinnati, OH 45246–1715
(513) 346–5050
Fax: (513) 671–8348

8011

Business Information: The Group Health Associates is a full–service, multi–specialty group practice. Currently, Group Health Association employs 80 people. As a Pediatrics Associate, Dr. Rufner is responsible for the care and treatment of primary and acute pediatric problems. **Career Steps:** Pediatrician, Group Health Associates (1991–Present). **Associations & Accomplishments:** Fellow, American Academy of Pediatrics; Board Certified, American Board of Pediatrics. **Education:** Ohio State University, M.D. (1975). **Personal:** One child: Britt Larson. Dr. Rufner enjoys the theatre, concerts, some outdoor activities, and travel.

Theodore J. Robinson, M.D.

Chief Executive Officer
Mardan Management, Ltd.
Suite 703–625 Fifth Avenue
New Westminster, British Columbia V3M 1X4
(604) 522–2917
Fax: (604) 524–3263

8011

Business Information: Involved in Private Practice since 1971, Dr. Robinson, as Chief Surgeon and only Plastic Surgeon on–staff, performs all types of cosmetic and three types of laser surgery. Concurrently, he serves as the CEO of Mardan Management, Ltd. a company involved in investment management. He also works as Secretary for INTIRMAC, a Firm involved in the recycling of old tires to manufacture such products as bricks, tennis shoe soles, new tires, and various other items. Dr. Robinson is one of the Founders of EPI, a Company which has just patented the first biodegradable plastic. He is involved as well in Trenchless Technologies, Inc., a Company which specializes in repairing old sewage pipes without digging up roads and highways. **Career Steps:** Chief Physician/CEO, Mardan Management Ltd. (1971–Present); Chief Executive Officer, Bison Petroleum (1978–1980); Chief Executive Officer, Aquarius International, Inc. (1986–1990); Secretary, INTIRMAC (1995–Present). **Associations & Accomplishments:** Founding Member, Environmental Protection, Inc.; Founding Member, Trenchless Technologies, Inc. **Education :** University of Manitoba, M.D. (1963); Royal College of Surgeons of Canada, F.R.C.S.(c) (1972). **Personal:** Two children: Daniel and Marni. Dr. Robinson enjoys running, photography, and travel.

Stephen J. Ryzewicz, M.D.

Medical Director
Meadows Medical Associates
200 North Main Street
East Longmeadow, MA 01028
(413) 525–4555
Fax: (413) 525–4898

8011

Business Information: Meadows Medical Associates is a medical practice specializing in internal medicine. As Medical Director, Dr. Ryzewicz is responsible for the overall administrative direction, in addition to his patient care practice. Concurrent to his private patient practice, Dr. Ryzewicz is a consulting physician on staff at Baystate Medical Center and formerly at St. Vincent Hospital and The Fallon Clinic; serving as mentor, teacher and supervisor to medical residents and students in ambulatory care settings. Additionally he is also a faculty member with the University of Massachusetts and Tufts University School of Medicine. He is board certified in Internal Medicine. He is also certified by The American Society of Addiction Medicine in the treatment of alcoholism and other drug dependencies. **Career Steps:** Medical Director, Meadows Medical Associates (1995–Present); Staff Internist, Baystate Medical Center (1995–Present); Assistant Clinical Professor of Medicine, Tufts University School of Medicine (1995–Present); Fallon Clinic, Inc.: Staff Internist (1987–1995), Medical Director for Substance Abuse Services (1990–1995); Saint Vincent's Hospital: Preceptor, Ambulatory Care Clinic (1/2 day weekly) (1990–1995), Staff Internist (1987–1995); University of Massachusetts Medical School: Instructor of Medicine (1992–1994), Assistant Professor of Medicine (1994–1995); Resident in Internal Medicine, Maine Medical Center (1984–1987). **Associations & Accomplishments:** American Medical Association; American College of Physicians; American Society of Addiction Medicine – Certified in Alcoholism and other Drug Dependencies; Massachusetts Medical Society; Licensure in Commonwealth of Massachusetts; Hamden District Medical Society; American College of Forensic Examiners; American Board of Internal Medicine (1988); Phi Beta Kappa Society (1980); Worcester District Medical Society; University of Massachusetts Alumni Council (1990–Present); Numerous teaching activities at Saint Vincent's Hospital; Contributor to questions to American Board of Internal Medicine Program and Recertification Program; Selected by American Board of Internal Medicine as "Relevance Reviewer in Internal Medicine" (1994); Conducted research on hematology at Saint Vincent's Hospital (1979–1981) and on electron microscopy at Worcester Foundation for Experimental Biology (1982). **Education:** University of Massachusetts Medical School, M.D. (1984); College of The Holy Cross, A.B. in Biology, cum laude (1980).

John T. Sack, M.D.

President and Surgeon
Seattle Hand Surgery Group, P.C.
600 Broadway, Suite 440
Seattle, WA 98122–5371
(206) 292–6252
Fax: (206) 292–7893

8011

Business Information: Seattle Hand Surgery Group, P.C. specializes in surgery of the hand and the upper extremities. Established in 1950, the Seattle Hand Surgery Group, P.C. currently employs 22 people. As President and Surgeon, Dr. Sack is responsible for the care and treatment of patients, as well as the administrative functions of the office. Concurrent with his private medical practice, Dr. Sack is also a Clinical Professor in the Department of Orthopaedics at the University of Washington. **Career Steps:** President and Surgeon, Seattle Hand Surgery Group, P.C. (1978–Present); Private Practice, General Orthopaedics and Surgery of the Hand and Upper Extremity, Tacoma, WA (1974–1984); Attending Physician, Harborview Medical Center Hand Clinic (1978–Present); Attending Physician, University of Washington Hospital Hand Clinic (1978–Present); Clinical Assistant Instructor, Department of Orthopaedics, University of Pennsylvania (1969–1973); University of Washington: Clinical Instructor (1978–1982), Clinical Assistant Professor, Department of Orthopaedics (1982–1984), Clinical Associate Professor, Department of Orthopaedics (1984–1989). **Associations & Accomplishments:** American College of Sports Medicine; Washington State Orthopaedic Association; American Medical Association; Overseas and Corresponding Member, British Society for Surgery of the Hand; American Society for Surgery of the Hand; Fellow, American Academy of Orthopaedic Surgeons; Western Orthopaedic Association; Tacoma Surgical Society; Seattle Surgical Society; King County Medical Society; Pierce County Medical Society; Washington State Medical Association; Elected Offices include: Chairman, Surgical Committee, Puget Sound General Hospital (1975–1977), Secretary, Medical Staff, Tacoma General Hospital (1977), Northwest Regional Representative, Sports Medicine Committee, United States Rowing Association (1976–Present), Team Physician, United States Rowing Association (1978), Consultant Team Physician, United States Rowing Association (1983); Numerous presentations and publications. **Education:** University of Edinburgh – Scotland, Hand Fellowship (1974); Jefferson Medical College, M.D. (1966); University of Pennsylvania, Orthopaedic Residency (1969–1973); University of Wisconsin, Internship

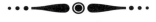

(1967–1969); Bowdin College, B.S. **Personal:** Five children: Eric, Kristen, John, Mary and Richard.

Anthony G. Saleh, M.D.
Physician
The Office of Dr. Anthony G. Saleh, M.D.
7510 4th Avenue
Brooklyn, NY 11209
(718) 745–1156
Fax: Please mail or call

8011

Business Information: The Office of Dr. Anthony G. Saleh, M.D. is a private medical practice specializing in Pulmonary medicine. Working in conjunction with Methodist Hospital, where his offices are located, Dr. Saleh is a Board–certified specialist in Pulmonary and Internal Medicine. He provides diagnosis and treatment to his private patients, as well as serves as Staff Pulmonologist at Methodist for referral patients with chest trauma and lung disorders. **Career Steps:** Physician, The Office of Dr. Anthony G. Saleh, M.D. (1988–Present) **Associations & Accomplishments:** Fellow, American College of Chest Physicians; American College of Physicians; American Board of Internal Medicine; Brooklyn Lung Association; American Medical Association. **Education:** St. George's University, M.D. (1985); State University of New York – Oneonta, B.S. (1981). **Personal:** Married to Theresa in 1993. Dr. Saleh enjoys basketball and running.

Marcella Salib, M.D.
Owner
St. Luke Medical Clinic
4160 John R Street #817
Detroit, MI 48201–2014
(313) 832–4818
Fax: (810) 478–3430

8011

Business Information: St. Luke Medical Clinic is a full–service, internal medical office, providing primary care and adult medicine. A practicing physician since 1969, Dr. Salib established St. Lukes Medical Clinic in 1983. She oversees all administrative operations for associates and a support staff of 7, in addition to her daily patient practice. Her medical services are offered to the community in the area of geriatrics to churches, hospices, and other geriatric communities. Dr. Salib's special interests are in preventive medicine and patient education. **Career Steps:** Owner, St. Lukes Medical Clinic (1983–Present). **Associations & Accomplishments:** American Medical Association; AMWA; ACP; ASIM; MSMS; WCMS; St. Paul Lutheran Church. **Education:** Ain Shams University – Cairo, Egypt, M.D. (1969); Wayne State University (1982). **Personal:** Married to Kamal in 1971. Two children: Suzy and Christina. Dr. Salib enjoys reading, aerobics, swimming, and stress management.

D. Skip Sallee, M.D.
Chairman/Chief Executive Officer
Team Health Radiology Services
1900 Winston Road, Suite 300
Knoxville, TN 37919
(423) 539–8000
Fax: (423) 539–8030

8011

Business Information: Team Health Radiology Services is a physician practice management company. A subsidiary of Medpartners, the Practice provides radiology and teleradiology to patients via seventy locations nationwide. Established in 1993, the Corporation has estimated annual revenue of $12 million. As Chairman/Chief Executive Officer, Dr. Sallee oversees all management, operations, growth and development, strategic planning and supervision of clinic facilities. **Career Steps:** Chairman/Chief Executive Officer, Team Health Radiology Services (1993–Present); Assistant Professor of Radiology, Duke University Medical Center (1991–1993). **Associations & Accomplishments:** American Medical Association; Society for Cardiovascular and Interventional Oral Radiology; American College of Radiology; American College of Radiology Executives; Radiological Society of North America; Author of several publications. **Education:** University of Missouri, Kansas City, M.D. (1985). **Personal:** Dr. Sallee enjoys scuba diving, golf, reading, and sports.

Rene Salvador–Charles, M.D.

Physician
Visalia Ob–Gyn Medical Associates
419 West Murray Street
Visalia, CA 93291
(209) 738–5970 Ext: 419
Fax: (209) 627–1535

8011

Business Information: Visalia Ob–Gyn Medical Associates is a full–service, private medical practice, specializing in obstetrics and gynecology. A practicing physician since 1987 and Board–Certified in Ob–Gyn, Dr. Salvador–Charles co–established the Practice in December 1995. He is responsible for providing Ob–Gyn services and managing the administrative aspects of the Practice. **Career Steps:** Physician, Visalia Ob–Gyn Medical Associates (1995–Present); Partner, Kaweah–Sierra Medical Group (1991–1995); Resident, Texas Tech – El Paso (1987–1991). **Associations & Accomplishments:** Alpha Omega Alpha; American College of Ob–Gyn; American Medical Association; California Medical Association; Officer, Tulare County Medical Society; American Association of Gynecologic Laparoscopists. **Education:** University of Minnesota, M.D. (1987); Texas Tech – El Paso Ob–Gyn Residency (1991). **Personal:** Married to Lupe in 1972. Three children: Ramon, Joaquin, and Miguel. Dr. Salvador–Charles enjoys backpacking, hiking, fishing, and running.

Syed A. Samad, M.D.

President
Arkansas Surgery & Endoscopy Center
4800 Hazel
Pine Bluff, AR 71603
(501) 536–4800 (501) 534–5533
Fax: (501) 536–1609

8011

Business Information: Founded by Dr. Samad in 1995, Arkansas Surgery & Endoscopy Center is the only out–patient surgical facility serving the South Arkansas region and catering to all out–patient procedures. A Board Certified Gastroenterologist, Dr. Samad has his private medical practice in Digestive Care, P.A. In addition, Dr. Samad also serves as an Assistant Professor of Medicine at the University of Arkansas at Little Rock. **Career Steps:** President, Arkansas Surgery & Endoscopy Center (1995–Present); President, Digestive Care, P.A. (1994–Present); Assistant Professor of Medicine, University of Arkansas at Little Rock (1993–Present). **Associations & Accomplishments:** American College of Physicians; Crohn's & Colitis Foundation of America; American College of Gastroenterology "Speakers Forum"; National Motility "Speakers Forum"; American Gastroenterology Association; American Liver Foundation; American Society of Gastrointestinal Endoscopy; AWARDS: Outstanding Gastroenterology Fellow in North America (1992); Resident of the Year (1990); Best Teacher of the Year (1995) – University of Arkansas; ACP Research Award; NACGF Research Award; Marshall University Foundation Award (1991). **Education:** Dow Medical College, M.D. (1983); University of Texas Medical School – Internal Medicine Residency; Wright State University, Gastroenterology Fellowship. **Personal:** Married to Ayesha M. in 1983. Three children: Ahmed, Rabiya and Ahad. In her leisure time, Dr. Samad enjoys hunting and fishing.

Olga T. Sanabria–Torres, M.D.
Physician
Office of Dr. Olga T. Sanabria–Torres
Urb. Monte Carlo 125, Box 1056
Vega Baja, Puerto Rico 00694
(809) 858–0763
Fax: Please mail or call

8011

Business Information: Office of Dr. Olga T. Sanabria–Torres, established in 1987, specializes in the practice of general medicine and surgery. As Physician, Dr. Sanabria–Torres is responsible for all aspects of operations for the solo practice, including the diagnosis, treatment and rehabilitation of patients (2,000 patients). **Career Steps:** Physician, Office of Dr. Olga T. Sanabria–Torres (1987–Present). **Associations & Accomplishments:** Honorary Member, Paralyzed Vet of American; American Medical Association; Commander Club (DAV); American Professional Practice Association; Supporting Member, American Red Cross; Cystic Fibrosis Foundation; Gold Member, Missionary Association of Mary Immaculate; College of Surgeons & Physicians; Chairman of a group of 25 practitioners at a teleconference at the University of Florida. **Education:** University of Nac Pedro H. Urena, M.D. (1979). **Personal:** Married to Anibal Morales Rubero in 1984.

Two children: Jose Anibal and Carlos Manuel Morales. Dr. Sanabria–Torres enjoys reading, music, and sewing.

Paul L. Sandler

Chief Operating Officer
Shady Grove Radiological Consultants
19650 Club House Road, Suite 201
Gaithersburg, MD 20879
(301) 948–5700
Fax: (301) 590–8961

8011

Business Information: Shady Grove Radiological Consultants is a radiology practice that provides services to physicians throughout Maryland. Having started with Shady Grove Radiological Consultants in 1980, Mr. Sandler has been given increased responsibility over the years. Reporting directly to the Board of Directors, Mr. Sandler currently serves as Chief Operating Officer. He is responsible for all operations, finance, accounting, and taxes for all locations. **Career Steps:** Chief Operating Officer, Shady Grove Radiological Consultants (1980–Present). **Associations & Accomplishments:** Radiology Business Managers Associations; Medical Group Management Association; American Group Practice Administrators; American Hospital Radiology Association; U.S. Coast Guard Auxiliary; Local Chamber of Commerce; Chesapeake Bay Foundation; Chesapeake Bay Yacht Clubs Association; Fraternal Order of Police. **Education:** George Washington University, M.H.A. (1983); Old Dominion University, B.S.B.A (1966). **Personal:** Married to Dianne in 1968. Two children: Howard and Shari. Mr. Sandler enjoys boating, boating safety education, diving, golf, and racquetball.

Dr. Suzan Sandor
Psychiatrist
Office of Dr. Zsuzsanna Sandor
Suite C–1500 Royal York Rd.
Etobicoke, Ontario M9P 3B6
(416) 249–6677
Fax: Please mail or call

8011

Business Information: A graduate of Semmelweis Medical University and the University of Toronto, Dr. Sandor has been a practicing psychiatrist since 1987, establishing her private practice in 1995. **Career Steps:** Psychiatrist, Office of Dr. Zsuzsanna Sandor (1995–Present); Senior Psychiatrist, Queen Street Medical Health Centre (1986–1995); Psychiatrist Resident at various Toronto hospitals (1980–1986). **Associations & Accomplishments:** Royal College of Physicians and Surgeons of Canada; The College of Physicians and Surgeons of Ontario; Ontario Psychiatric Association; Canadian Medical Protective Association. **Education:** Semmelweis Medical University, M.D. (1979); University of Toronto: F.R.C.P.(C) Specialist Certificate in Psychiatry (1988), B.A. (1972). **Personal:** Dr. Sandor enjoys reading, writing, tennis, golf, theatre, opera, ballet, and travel.

James B. Sauers, M.D.
Sole Practitioner
James B. Sauers, M.D., Inc.
1801 East Perkins Avenue
Sandusky, OH 44870–4200
(419) 626–0023 (216) 464–3280
Fax: Please mail or call

8011

Business Information: James B. Sauers, M.D., Inc. is a private medical practice, specializing in allergies and immunological disorders. A Board–Certified Pediatrician, Allergist and Immunologist, Dr. Sauers has been a practicing physician since 1958. He established his private medical practice in 1963, providing medical care to a second generation of patients suffering from asthma, hay fever, and eczema. **Career Steps:** Sole Practitioner, James B. Sauers, M.D., Inc. (1963–Present). **Associations & Accomplishments:** American Academy of Pediatrics; American Academy of Allergy and Immunology; Cleveland Allergy Society. **Education:** Ohio State Medical School, M.D. (1958); University of Colorado, Fellowship in Allergy/Immunology (1961–1963); Ohio Wesleyan University, B.A. in Pre–Medicine (1952). **Personal:** Dr. Sauers enjoys antique collecting, farming, and orchards.

Michael D. Savarese, M.D.

General Practice Physician
Naugatuck Valley Medical Associates
687 Straits Tpke. #1C
Middlebury, CT 06762–2846
(203) 758–8645
Fax: (203) 598–7616

8011

Business Information: Naugatuck Valley Medical Associates is a general practice medical clinic providing quality healthcare services and treatment to patients in the greater Middlebury, CT communities since 1973. Joining Naugatuck Valley Medical Associates upon completion of his residency in 1992, Dr. Savarese specializes in Internal Medicine, providing diagnosis, treatment and counsel in general family practices. **Career Steps:** General Practice Physician, Naugatuck Valley Medical Associates (1992–Present). **Associations & Accomplishments:** NMS. **Education:** University of Connecticut School of Medicine, M.D. (1989); University of Notre Dame, Premedical Student (1981–1985). Residency: Hospital of St. Raphael (1989–1992); **Personal:** One child: Patrick. Dr. Savarese enjoys snow skiing, wind surfing, tennis, and triathlons.

Edgar C. Schick Jr., M.D.

Physician
Lahey–Hitchcock Medical Clinic
41 Mall Road
Burlington, MA 01805
(617) 273–8840
Fax: (617) 273–5246

8011

Business Information: Lahey–Hitchcock Medical Clinic is a private clinic for multiple specialties for adults, including a small pediatric facility. A practicing physician since 1970 and a Board–Certified Cardiologist, Dr. Schick joined Lahey–Hitchcock Medical Clinic in 1989. His practice focuses on non–invasive cardiology surgery. He also directs the operations of the Endocardiography Laboratory. **Career Steps:** Physician, Lahey–Hitchcock Medical Clinic (1989–Present). **Associations & Accomplishments:** American Heart Association; American College of Cardiology; American Society of Echocardiography; Published articles in various medical journals. **Education:** Cornell University, M.D. (1970); Holy Cross College, B.S. in Biology (1966). **Personal:** Married to Constance in 1969.

Katherine Schlotfeldt

Administrator
Medical Park Family Care
2211 East Northern Lights Boulevard
Anchorage, AK 99508–4142
(907) 257–8121
Fax: (907) 257–8180

8011

Business Information: Medical Park Family Care is a full–service medical practice consisting of nine physicians, providing diagnosis and treatment to patients. As Administrator, Ms. Schlotfeldt is responsible for managing all aspects of the business for physicians, including operations, finances, public relations, and strategic planning. **Career Steps:** Administrator, Medical Park Family Care (1993–Present); Vice President of Human Resources, Denali Group Companies – Anchorage, Alaska (1991–1993); Hotel Manager, Pinacle Club, Sun Valley, Idaho (1989–1991); Self–Employed, Business Owner National Fast Food Franchises (1971–1989). **Associations & Accomplishments:** Anchorage South Rotary; Anchorage Chamber of Commerce; Board of Directors, Crime Stoppers; Medical Group Management Association; Certified Scuba Diver (1996). **Personal:** Married to Walt in 1995. Two children: Kristin and Rodney Ledbetter. Ms. Schlotfeldt enjoys fishing, flying, skiing, and diving.

Mike Schweitzer, M.D.

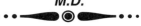

President
Billings Anesthesiology, P.C.
1302 24th Street West #331
Billings, MT 59102
(406) 655–4658
Fax: (406) 656–5869
EMAIL: See Below

8011

Business Information: Billings Anesthesiology, P.C. is a private practice medical clinic providing anesthesia, chronic pain management, and critical care services. Established in 1993, the Facility employs 12 people, and has an estimated annual revenue of $3,000,000. Plans for the future include continued educational development, possible international contracts, development of cost containment programs for cardiac surgery, and development and implementation of an HMO for area residents. As President, Dr. Schweitzer oversees the day–to–day management of the facility, negotiates medical care and employee contracts, and manages billings and collections. Internet users can reach him via: Mswitz@imt.net. **Career Steps:** President, Billings Anesthesiology, P.C. (1993–Present); President, Montana Society of Anesthesiologists (1996–Present); President, Schweitzer Anesthesiology Clinic, Inc. (1989–1993); Co–Owner, M&J Enterprises, Inc. (1995–Present). **Associations & Accomplishments:** Chair, Montana Medical Association Managed Care Committee; Member Executive Committee, Montana Medical Association; President–Elect, Yellowstone Valley Medical Association; Delegate, American Society of Anethesiologists; Fund–Raising Chair, Eagle Mount (1992–195); Steering Committee for Heal Montana; American College of Physicians and Surgeons; American Medical Association; Montana Society of Anesthesiologists; Anesthesiology Society of America; Society of Cardiovascular Anesthesiologists; American Academy of Pain Management; National Federation of Independent Business; Numerous Hospital Committees; Over five publications on patient cost reduction and anesthesia related topics. **Education:** University of Colorado School of Medicine, M.D. (1980); The Colorado College, B.A. (1976); University of Michigan Post Graduate Anesthesiology (1984). **Personal:** Married to Jolyn in 1992. Four children: Bryan, Frederick, Joy, and Hans. Dr. Schweitzer enjoys snow boarding, tennis, hiking, camping, and scuba.

Michael J. Seely

Administrator
Craig Medical Center
580 Pershing Street
Craig, CO 81625
(970) 824–3213
Fax: (970) 824–6476

8011

Business Information: Craig Medical Center is a private, family medical practice, providing diagnosis and treatment to patients in the Craig, Colorado locale. The Center is comprised of primary care physicians, neurologists, internist specialists, and a physician's assistant. Future plans include expansion into a new building and development into a multi–specialty clinic to meet all the local community's needs. As Administrator, Mr. Seely is responsible for the overall operations of the Center, including finances, all human resources for staff and physicians, all administrative duties, fee schedules and office management. **Career Steps:** Administrator, Craig Medical Center (1995–Present); Ranch Manager, Double E Livestock (1994–1995); Ranch Manager, Del Mesa Farms (1991). **Associations & Accomplishments:** American College of Medical Practice Executives (Nominee). **Education:** Colorado State University, B.S. in Arts and Science (1990); University of Phoenix, M.B.A. in progress. **Personal:** Married. One child: Bryce Michael. Mr. Seely enjoys hunting, rodeo, horseback riding, and reading.

William L. Semler, M.D.

Sole Practitioner
Office of William L. Semler, M.D.
2350 W. Villard Avenue #106
Milwaukee, WI 53209–5080
(414) 462–2272
Fax: Please mail or call

8011

Business Information: Office of William L. Semler, M.D. is the office of a private practice gynecologist. Dr. Semler has been in practice since 1950 and has had a private practice since 1985. As Sole Practitioner, Dr. Semler is a physician specializing in the treatment of diseases and medical problems suffered by women. **Career Steps:** Sole Practitioner, Office of William L. Semler, M.D. (1949–Present). **Associations & Accomplishments:** American Medical Association; State of Wisconsin Medical Society; Milwaukee County Medical Society; Milwaukee Gynecology Society; Wisconsin Society of OB–GYN; American Menopause Society; Society of Laser Endoscopic Surgeons; American Society of Physician Executives; Medical Director, Chicago and Milwaukee Region SCCA; Cendiv Medical Representative; SCCA. **Education:** University of Wisconsin, M.D. (1949), B.S. (1944). **Personal:** Married to Ellen in 1950. Three children: David, Karen, and Barbara. Dr. Semler enjoys golf, skiing, water sports, jewelry, photography, stained glass, and his eight grandchildren.

Florence Maria Battle Shafiq, M.D.

Medical Director and Associate Professor of Internal Medicine
Morehouse Medical Associates, Inc.
75 Piedmont Avenue, Suite 700
Atlanta, GA 30303
(404) 756–1418
Fax: (404) 756–1495

8011

Business Information: Morehouse Medical Associates, Inc. is a full–service, multi–specialty physician group practice, providing diagnosis and treatment to patients throughout the greater Atlanta–metro locale. A practicing physician since 1976 and Board–Certified in Internal Medicine since 1980, Dr. Shafiq joined Morehouse Medical Associates, Inc. in 1987. Serving as Medical Director and Senior Internist, she spends eighty percent of her time on administrative functions, such as establishing policies and procedures related to the infrastructure of the organization, initiating the continuing Quality Improvement protocols, and preparing and presenting the annual Medical Director's report. Other duties include organizing and presiding at Informational Update meetings for the physicians; maintaining proper liaison between dissatisfied customers and the physician, staff, or organization and between HMO's and the Practice; and approving arrangements for departmental clinical research trials. She also serves as a vital member on the governing body of the organization as Presiding Officer in the absence of the Chair; on the interview team for the selection and hiring of the Chief Executive Officer, Administrator, Clinical Nurse Coordinator, Medical Records Technician, members of the nursing staff and medical reception staff, and Chair for the Department of Medicine, Pediatrics and Surgery; on the decision–making team relative to daily operations (CORE Administrative Group); on the Strategic Planning Council as Facilitator of the Service Focus Group (Subcommittee of the Strategic Planning Council); and a vital member on several committees (i.e., Clinical Research, Infectious Disease/OSHA Guidelines, Answering Service Search, Managed Care). Affiliated with Southwest Hospital and Medical Center, Crawford W. Long Hospital, Dekalb Medical Center, and Grady Memorial Hospital since 1987, she spends the balance of her time providing health care to patients. Concurrent with her administrative duties and medical practice, she serves as Associate Professor at the Morehouse School of Medicine in Atlanta, and as Attending Physician at the Morehouse School of Medicine of Internal Medicine Residents at Grady Memorial Hospital. Dr. Shafiq also presents monthly CME's (General Medicine Topics) – sponsored by Southside HealthCare, pharmaceutical companies, and Morehouse School of Medicine; as well as attending Managed Care seminars. Major accomplishments while serving as Medical Director of Morehouse Medical Associates include: Establishing the "Expected Physicians' Behavior" and "Quality Assurance" manuals; Supervising the nursing and front office staff prior to the hiring of the Clinical Nurse Coordinator and the front office manager; Serving as Co–chair of bi–monthly clinical staff meeting; Preparing annual evaluations of the nursing staff; Organizing a successful Team–Building retreat; Being featured on a CNN television advertisement for the CDC–supported 1994 influenza immunization of the elderly; Developing job descriptions for the position of Radiology Technician; Developing the "Physician's Policies and Procedures Manual"; Developing a Primary Care Focused HealthCare Delivery Model; and Developing the policies and procedures for Worker's Compensation for employees of the institution, the surrounding institutions of higher learning, as well as the general population. During her employment as Course Director for Ambulatory Medicine, she created and developed the curriculum and syllabus for the course via a combination of academic facts from her fellowship program with practical experiences; motivated students to a higher level of learning with a focus of integrating facts of basic science within the clinical arena of medicine; depicted on a pictorial advertisement in a marketing brochure for Morehouse School of Medicine; featured in the marketing video of Morehouse School of Medicine – displayed at the National Medicine Association in 1991; and selected by the graduating senior class as "Teacher of the Year" for 1989, 1990, 1991, and 1992. **Career Steps:** Administrative Medical Director and Senior Internist, Morehouse Medical Associates, Inc. (1987–Present); Morehouse School of Medicine: Associate Professor (1993–Present), Assistant Professor (1987–1992); Attending Physician, Humana MedFirst Stone Mountain (1985–1987); Medical Director, Humana MedFirst Snapfinger (1982–1985); Physician, Federal Employee's Health Clinic (1980–1982); Fan Physician, Atlanta Falcons (1981–1982); Emergency Room Physician, Button–Gwinnett Hospital and Sylvan Grove Hospital (1977–1982); Attending Physician, DeKalb–Grady Clinic (1980–1981); Assistant Professor, Emory University (1980–1981); Consultant, Social Security Administration – Regional Office of Disability Analysis Branch, Atlanta, GA (1980–1987). **Associations & Accomplishments:** Diplomate, American Board of Internal Medicine (1980); Georgia State Medical Association; National Medical Association; Fellow and Member of Community Affairs Committee, Atlanta Medical Association; Association of Black Cardiologists; American College of Physician Executives; Society of Physician Executives; Board Member, Arbor Montessori School (1990); PTA Memberships: Farrington High School, Snapfinger High School, Kittredge High School,

Chamblee High School, Henderson Mill Elementary; Co–Chair – Hospital Subcommittee, Atlanta Committee for the Olympic Games; Co–Negotiator, Correctional Medicine Contract; Georgia Better Health Care Committee (Georgia's Medicaid Managed Care Product); Integrated Service Network Planning Committee; RESEARCH: Clinical studies on Hypertension and Kidney Disease in African–Americans, LST Study, a Merck– sponsored clinical study based on the effectiveness and tolerability of Losartan – an anti–hypertensive drug treatment. **Education:** University of Iowa School of Medicine, M.D. (1976); University of Iowa, M.S. (1972); Coe College, B.A. (1970); Emory University School of Medicine: Internship (1976–1977), Residency (1977–1979), Fellowship in Ambulatory Medicine (1979–1980). **Personal:** Two children: Aaliyah and Malikah. Dr. Shafiq enjoys swimming, dancing, photography and travel during her leisure time.

Manjula S. Shah, M.D.

Gynecologist
Shah Medical Associates, Inc.
629 South Main Street
Du Bois, PA 15801
(814) 371–0240
Fax: (814) 371–5351

8011

Business Information: Shah Medical Associates, Inc. is a full–service medical practice, providing gynecological services on a part–time basis. With a staff of 6, the Practice focuses on patient care. As Gynecologist and General Surgeon, Dr. Shah divides her time between disciplines, with general surgery receiving the lion's share. She also devotes a great deal of her spare time to volunteer efforts at the DuBois Senior Citizen's Center, where she serves on the Governing Board. **Career Steps:** Gynecologist, Shah Medical Associates, Inc. (Present). **Associations & Accomplishments:** American Association of College Women; DuBois Area Association on Aging; Trained Tutor for the Mid–State Literary Council; AAUW; Governing Board, DuBois Senior Citizen Center; Volunteer, Meals – On– Wheels; Make a Wish Foundation; DuBois Regional Medical Center Auxiliary; American Association of Women Physicians. **Personal:** Married to Shirish M. Shah, M.D. in 1965. Three children: Susie, Shirley, and Sushrut. Dr. Shah enjoys travel and reading.

Joseph G. Shami, M.D.

Vice President
Passaic County Gastroenterology P.A.
535 Union Boulevard
Totowa, NJ 07512
(201) 595–5505
Fax: (201) 595–5412

8011

Business Information: A Board–certified Gastroenterology specialist, Dr. Joseph Shami joined Passaic County Gastroenterology, P.A. in 1984 following his residency and fellowship training with St. Joseph's Medical Center. Serving as Vice President, he shares administrative direction duties for the supervision of a support staff of eight, in addition to his daily patient practice. His practice consists of 80% diagnosis and treatment for digestive disorders and the remaining in general internal medicine treatment. **Career Steps:** Vice President, Passaic County Gastroenterology P.A. (1983–Present); President–Medical Staff, St. Joseph's Medical Center, Paterson, NJ (1993–Present); Chief Medical Resident, St. Joseph's Medical Center, Paterson, NJ (1981–1982). **Associations & Accomplishments:** Passaic County Medical Society; American Gastroenterological Association; American Society of Gastrointestinal Endoscopy; American College of Physicians. **Education:** Universita Cattolica, Rome, Italy, M.D. (1978); St. Peter's College, Jersey City, NJ, B.Sc.; University of London, England, "A" level GCE, Biology, Chemistry. **Personal:** Married to Ilona in 1981. Four children: Anne, Richard, Stephen, and Michael.

Souhail G. Shamiyeh, M.D., F.A.C.P.

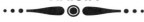

Physician
Medical Associates of Norton
280 Virginia Avenue
Norton, VA 24273
(540) 679–9177
Fax: (540) 679–9156

8011

Business Information: Medical Associates of Norton, affiliated with Bristol Regional Medical Center, is a full–service, primary care facility providing general family medical practices. A practicing physician since 1989 and an Internal Medicine Specialist, Dr. Shamiyeh joined Medical Association of Norton as Physician in 1989. He is responsible for providing quality medical care, particularly focusing in the diagnosis, treatment and medical counsel to geriatric patients. **Career Steps:** Physician, Medical Associates of Norton (1989–Present). **Associations & Accomplishments:** American Medical Association; American College of Physicians; Massachusetts Medical Society; Wise County Medical Society. **Education:** American University of Beirut, M.D. (1985); Internal Medicine Training (1986–1989). **Personal:** Married to Dany in 1986. Two children: George and Caline. Dr. Shamiyeh enjoys basketball and collecting coins.

Dr. Lalitha Shankar

Diagnostic Radiologist
St. Joseph's Health Centre
30 The Queensway
Toronto, Ontario M6R 1B5
(416) 530–6701
Fax: (416) 246–9798

8011

Business Information: St. Joseph's Health Centre is a group practice of seven physicians, all diagnostic radiologists. The Centre uses the latest techniques including X–Rays, Ultrasound, and Magnetic Resonance, and also performs diagnosis for therapy. As Diagnostic Radiologist, Dr. Shankar is a clinical imaging specialist in CT, MR, and Ultrasound imaging. She is also a subspecialist in ear, nose, and throat radiology. **Career Steps:** Diagnostic Radiologist, St. Joseph's Health Centre (1984–Present); Attending Radiologist, St. Michael's Hospital (1992–Present); Courtesy Staff Radiologist, Plummer & General Hospitals (1995–Present). **Associations & Accomplishments:** Radiology Society of North America; American Roengen Ray Society; American Society of Head & Neck Radiology; Canadian Association of Radiologists; Ontario Association of Radiologists; Canadian Association of Physicians of Indian Origin; Author of "An Atlas of Imaging of Paranasal Sinuses" and several articles in peer reviewed journals. **Education:** University of Toronto, FRCP(c) (1983); American Board of Radiology (1983); University of Calcutta, M.B.B.S. (1975). **Personal:** Two children: Samantha and Meghana. Dr. Shankar enjoys painting, reading, music, and playing the guitar.

Terry L. Sharpe, M.D.

Physician/Owner
South Fulton Medical Arts Center
1136 Cleveland Avenue, Suite 615
East Point, GA 30344–3618
(404) 763–0609
Fax: (404) 763–0609

8011

Business Information: A practicing physician since 1979, Dr. Sharpe established South Fulton Medical Arts Center, a private dermatology practice, in 1986. In addition to the responsibilities of her practice, she is also an Assistant Professor at Emory University where she was the school's first black female dermatology resident. **Career Steps:** Physician/Owner, South Fulton Medical Arts Center (1986–Present); Assistant Professor, Emory University (Present). **Associations & Accomplishments:** Former Consultant, Essence Magazine. **Education:** University of California at San Francisco, M.D. (1979); Stanford University, B.A. (1974). **Personal:** One child: Maliu. Dr. Sharpe enjoys movies, theater, modern art and dance.

Dr. Ketankumar Sheth

Attending Cardiologist
Lewistown Cardiologist Associates
299–1/2 Logan Boulevard
Burnham, PA 17009–1825
(717) 248–5431
Fax: (717) 248–5038

8011

Business Information: Lewistown Cardiologist Associates is a full–service, specialized group practice, concentrating in cardiology. As Attending Cardiologist, Dr. Sheth is responsible for providing specialized health care to patients with cardiac disease. Concurrent with his position at Lewistown Cardiology Associates, he serves as Attending Cardiologist at Lewistown Hospital and Polyclinic Medical Centre. **Career Steps:** Attending Cardiologist, Lewistown Hospital (1993–Present); Attending Cardiologist, Polyclinic Medical Centre (1993–Present). **Associations & Accomplishments:** Fellow, American College of Cardiology; Fellow, American College of Chest Physicians; Published numerous publications in medical journals; Amateur musician: Harmonica and an Indian instrument. **Education:** M.S. University, India, M.B.B.S. (1984). **Personal:** Married to Kalpana Sheth in 1985. Two children: Suchir and Suruchi Sheth. Dr. Sheth enjoys reading and music.

Joseph D. Shomo

Chief Financial Officer/Director of Finance
Augusta Community Care
Rt. 1, Box 254A
Swoope, VA 24479
(540) 886–9111
Fax: (540) 886–7890

8011

Business Information: Augusta Community Care, located in Staunton, VA is a local multi–million dollar outpatient only health care provider working with local physicians and Medicare. The company offers services in home health care, DME, hospice care, wellness centers, and other related health fields. Augusta Community Care provides physical therapy, speech therapy, and occupational therapy for local patients. As Chief Financial Officer/Director of Finance, Mr. Shomo handles all financial matters for August Community Care. He has oversight of all accounting functions, cash management, payroll, purchasing, MIS/CIS, operating and capital budgets, and all human resource management concerns. **Career Steps:** Chief Financial Officer/Director of Finance, Augusta Community Care (1993–Present); President and Owner, Lawn Doctor of Augusta (1986–1992). **Associations & Accomplishments:** Local Chapter of Parent–Teacher Association; Supporter of the Area Habitat for Humanity. **Education:** James Madison University, B.B.A. (1992). **Personal:** Married to Carolyn H. in 1988. Three children: Kristin, Kaitlyn, and Hunter. Mr. Shomo enjoys spending time with his children, public speaking, skiing, cycling, golf, and financial planning for the under–privileged.

Hari Krishna Shukla, M.D.

Owner/Director/Physician
Children's Medical Center
42–72 Kissena Boulevard
Flushing, NY 11355
(718) 359–6767
Fax: (718) 445–5658

8011

Business Information: Children's Medical Center is a pediatric, neonatal, and perinatal healthcare facility. As Owner/Director, Dr. Shukla is responsible for all operations, as well as direction of the medical center. Concurrently, he also serves as a practicing physician. **Career Steps:** Residency training at N.Y. Medical College (1980–1982); Fellowship training at N.Y. University Medical Center (1982–1984); Research Fellow (1984–1985); Assistant Professor at N.Y. University School of Medicine (1988–Present); Started Practice in 1985 in Flushing Queens. He was first physician in whole Queens to use surfactant for premature infants. He established Children's Medical Center in 1995. He has published several research article in Medical Journals and has been quoted for his research in several books. **Associations & Accomplishments:** Received award for Rotary Foundation of Rotary International in 1980. Has received several Youth Leadership Awards; Actively involved in community service with Red Cross and Rotary Club; Received Special Achievement Award from Chemical Bank for Community Service; Fellows of American Academy of Pediatrics; American Society of Contemporary Medicine and Surgery and New York Prenatal Society; Life Member of American College of Forensic Examiner, Red Cross Society, St. John Ambulance. He is treasurer with Queens Pediatric Society; Received best Teacher award in 1992. **Education:** M.B.B.S. (1975); D.Ped. (1976); M.D. (1977); Diplomat American Board of Pediatrics (1985); Diplomat American Board of Neonatal Perinatal Medicine (1988); Diplomat American Board of Forensic Examiner (1996); Forensic Medicine (1966). **Personal:** Married to Kirti in 1979. Two children: Mrugank and Mehool. Dr. Shukla enjoys photography, target shooting, and tennis.

John A. Shull, M.D.

Physician/Owner
John A. Shull, M.D., OB/GYN
929 Spring Creek Road, Suite 203
Chattanooga, TN 37412–2975
(423) 855–0357
Fax: (423) 855–4917

8011

Business Information: John A. Shull, M.D., OB/GYN is a private medical office specializing in the care and diagnosis of pregnancy and related women's health services. Established in 1979, the Practice employs four people. As Physician/Owner, Dr. Shull oversees all aspects of the Practice, and is responsible for all administrative and operational functions. Additional duties include patient care and diagnosis, ensuring quality service, and strategic planning. **Career Steps:** Physician/Owner, John A. Shull, M.D., OB/GYN (1979–Present). **Associations & Accomplishments:** American Medical Association; Tennessee Medical Association; Chattanooga and Hamilton County Medical Societies; Chattanooga OB/GYN Society. **Education:** Loma Linda University, M.D. (1974). **Personal:** Married to Anne in 1978. Two children:

Paige and Hunter. Dr. Shull enjoys snow skiing and being an avid University of Tennessee football fan.

Edwina E. Simmons, M.D.
Physician
Church Square Medical Associates
7963 Euclid Avenue
Cleveland, OH 44103–4226
(216) 229–1322
Fax: (216) 229–1088

8011

Business Information: Church Square Medical Associates, associated with Mt. Sinai Medical Center in Cleveland, Ohio, is a full–service, multi–specialty group medical practice. A practicing physician since 1984 and Board–Certified in Obstetrics and Gynecology, Dr. Simmons joined Church Square Medical Associates in 1994. Serving as Physician, she is responsible for providing health care to women in obstetrics and gynecology with the assistance of midwives and support staff. **Career Steps:** Physician, Church Square Medical Associates (1994–Present); Cleveland Neighborhood Health Services: Chief OB/GYN (1992–1994), Staff Physician (1988–1992). **Associations & Accomplishments:** Cleveland OB/GYN Society; Board Certified, American College of Obstetrics and Gynecology (1990); Antioch Baptist Church (1989–Present); Published: "Immunoregulatory activity in supernatants from cultures of normal human trophoblasts of the first trimester." Morinal K. Sanyal, Ph.D., Charles J. Brami, Paul Bischof, Ph.D., Edwina Simmons, M.D., Erylan R. Barnes, M.D., John M. Dwyer, M.D., Ph.D., Frederic Naflolia, M.D., D.Phil. – American Journal of Obstetrics and Gynecology, Vol. 161, No 2pp, 446–453, August 1989. **Education:** Yale University School of Medicine, M.D. (1984); Wichita State University, Bachelor of General Studies. **Personal:** One child: Myles. Dr. Simmons enjoys knitting, reading, and travel.

William C. Simon, D.C.
Chiropractor
Riverside Health Systems
1245 N. West Street
Wichita, KS 67203
(316) 945–6910
Fax: (316) 945–3514

8011

Business Information: Riverside Health Systems is a family medical practice focusing on complementary medicine for preventive care. Affiliated with Riverside Health Systems and involved with most local HMO's, the Company is comprised of eight other general practice medical offices and a full service hospital. As Chiropractor, Dr. Simon is assisted in patient care by one other physician and two interns. His duties include providing general medicine to patients, natural counseling, vitamins, and homeopathic practices, including acupuncture. **Career Steps:** Chiropractor, Riverside Health Systems (1991–Present); D.O. Physician, Macks Creek Clinic; Chiropractor, Chiropractic Clinic. **Associations & Accomplishments:** ACOPF; AOA; Kansas Osteopathic Association; American Academy of Medical Acupuncture; Sedgwick County Osteopathic Society; American Academy of Osteopathy. **Education:** UHS–COM, D.O. (1989); Park College, B.S. in Nutrition; Trom Chiropractic College, D.C.; State Fair Community College, A.A.; Fellow in International Academy of Clinical Acupuncture. **Personal:** Married to Elizabeth in 1982. One child: Peder. Dr. Simon enjoys golf and collecting flashlights and pens.

Lalendra K. Sinha, M.D.
President
South Island New Health Associates
1731 Seagirt Boulevard
Far Rockaway, NY 11691
(718) 471–5400
Fax: Please mail or call

8011

Business Information: South Island New Health Associates is a full–service, medical practice, offering extensive medical care (diagnostic and therapeutic) to the community. A practicing physician since 1960, Dr. Sinha established South Island New Health Associates in 1975. Serving as President, he oversees the administrative operations for five full–time and eight part–time physicians and a support staff of forty, in addition to his private medical practice. **Career Steps:** President, South Island New Health Associates (1975–Present). **Associations & Accomplishments:** American Medical Association; American College of Physicians; New York State Medical Society; Kings County Medical Society. **Education:** Prince of Wales Medical College, M.D. (1960). **Personal:** Married to Lalmani in 1960. Four children: Keisha, Lena, Aimee, and Oneil. Dr. Sinha enjoys tennis, bicycling, gardening, reading, and designing art.

Abraham J. Sklar, M.D.
OB/GYN Physician
–Independent–
100 High Street
Buffalo, NY 14203
(716) 859–2114
Fax: (716) 859–2250

8011

Business Information: Entering into private practice upon the conferral of his medical degree in 1984, Dr. Sklar joined with two other physicians to specialize in obstetrics and gynecology. In addition to his practice, he serves as an instructor at the State University of New York at Buffalo School of Medicine, teaching students about high risk obstetrics. **Career Steps:** Private Practice (1984–Present). **Associations & Accomplishments:** Buffalo Ob/GYN Society; Association of Certified Obstetrics and Gynecology; Christian Management Association; SOGC; AAGL; SLS. **Education:** University of Toronto, M.D. (1984).

Janet Smith
Office Manager
Methodist Neuroscience Clinic
731 South Pear Orchard
Ridgeland, MS 39157–4800
(601) 952–0480
Fax: (601) 952–0493

8011

Business Information: Methodist Neuroscience Clinic, affiliated with Methodist Medical Center, is a specialized medical clinic concentrating in neurology and neurosurgery with two clinics located in Jackson, Mississippi. The Clinic provides diagnosis, treatment, and surgery to patients suffering from neurology, neuro–oncology and neuro–surgical problems. Established in 1994, Methodist Neuroscience Clinic reports annual revenue in excess of $1 million and currently employs 10 people, including three neurosurgeons, one neurologist, and one neuro–oncologist. Entering the workforce after her high school graduation in 1982, Ms. Smith has held various positions in the medical field, such as purchasing clerk, customer service representative, and operating room inventory coordinator. Currently, she serves as Office Manager and is responsible for all aspects of administration, management and oversight of daily activities of both clinics, as well as supervision of 10 employees. **Career Steps:** Office Manager, Methodist Neuroscience Clinic (1994–Present); Operating Room Inventory Coordinator, Methodist Medical Center (1988–1994); Customer Service, Healthcare Suppliers (1987–1988); Purchasing Clerk, Hinds General Hospital (now Methodist Medical Center) (1982–1987). **Education:** Wingfield High School, Diploma (1982). **Personal:** Married to Hank Smith in 1990. One child: Clinton Gregory Smith. Ms. Smith enjoys reading, computers, fishing, and listening to music.

Jo Carroll Smith, M.P.A.
Staff and Community Developer
West Oakland Health Council, Inc.
2730 Adeline Street
Oakland, CA 94607
(510) 465–1800
Fax: (510) 465–1508
EMail: See Below

8011

Business Information: West Oakland Health Council, Inc. is a grassroots, non–profit organization providing primary health care, mental health, and substance abuse treatment services for over 25 years. The Council has residential programs for adults alone or with families. It also provides transitional housing for homeless families. As Staff and Community Developer, Miss Smith is responsible for the development of staff training programs, provisions of training, and public relations and networking in the community. Internet users can reach her via: JSMITH1283@AOL.COM. **Career Steps:** Staff and Community Developer, West Oakland Health Center, Inc. (1992–Present); Program Director, Oakland Housing Authority (1991–1992); Deputy Probation Officer II, Alameda County Probation Department (1989–1991). **Associations & Accomplishments:** Twelve year commitment to mentor young girls through Simba, Inc. **Education:** California State University: Master's degree in progress (1997), B.A. in Political Science (1988). **Personal:** Miss Smith enjoys reading, writing, fashion design, and illustration. She also enjoys teaching Internet navigation.

Paul A.S. Smith, M.D.
Physician
Riverside Medical Clinic
186 Lincoln Road
Fredricton, New Brunswick E3B 2A3
(506) 339–7650
Fax: (506) 454–9358

8011

Business Information: Riverside Medical Clinic is a medical practice with two physicians on staff. As Physician, Dr. Smith is a general practitioner, whose practice emphasizes wholistic and complementary medicine, immunology, allergy and environmental testing, nutritional analysis, electro–diagnostics, and live blood analysis. **Career Steps:** Physician, Riverside Medical Clinic (Present). **Associations & Accomplishments:** NBMS. Education: Dalhousie University (1978); University of New Brunswick, B.Sc. **Personal:** Dr. Smith enjoys skiing, hiking, and outdoor activities.

Maurus L. Sorg, M.D., M.P.H.
Owner/Partner
Keystone Medical Associates
136 State Street
St. Marys, PA 15857
(814) 781–6758
Fax: (814) 834–1038

8011

Business Information: Keystone Medical Associates is a private family practice. Comprised of two doctors and a per diem associate, the Association specializes in primary care. Affiliated with two hospitals, they also handle sports and occupational medicine. With the help of his wife Rosemaria, who is also a practicing physician with the Associates, Dr. Sorg, oversees the day–to–day operation of the Facility, including patient care and diagnosis, as well as instructing medical students, physician assistants, and nurse practitioners in his fields of medicine. Concurrently, he works as a part–time Emergency Physician. **Career Steps:** Owner/Partner, Keystone Medical Associates (1982–Present). **Education:** Medical College of Wisconsin, M.P.H. (1980); Penn State, M.D.; Diplomate American Boards of Family Medicine and Emergency Medicine; Has Masters Degree in Public Health and Occupational Medicine; Certified in Sports Medicine. **Personal:** Married to Rosemarie in 1979. Three children: Sarah, Rebecca, and Rachael. Dr. Sorg enjoys being a private pilot, mountain biking, cross–country skiing, downhill skiing, horseback riding, hunting, and fishing.

Marilyn June Stewart, M.D., CCFP
Medical Doctor
Moosonee Health Center
9 ATIM Road
Moosonee, Ontario P0L 1Y0
(705) 336–2341
Fax: (705) 336–3715
EMAIL: See Below

8011

Business Information: Moosonee Health Center is a community–based general health care facility. The Center is located in an isolated and remote portion of the Province of Ontario. The Center serves mostly Northern Canadian Indians (Cree) and unemployed. As Medical Doctor, Dr. Stewart is the only physician in a remote and isolated area of Ontario. Her practice provides general family medicine, emergency services, and obstetrical services for approximately 3,000 people. Internet users can also reach her via: lymnal.stewart@sympatico.ca **Career Steps:** Medical Doctor, Moosonee Health Center (1992–Present). **Associations & Accomplishments:** Ontario Medical Association; Canadian Medical Association; La Leche League; Canadian Palliative Care Association; Cirum Polar Health Organization; Society For Rural Physicians; Alpha Omega Alpha Honor Medical Society. **Education:** Queen's University, CCFP (1992); Dalhousie University Medical School, M.D. (1990); University of Western Ontario, Microbiology and Immunology Degree in Honorous Standing; Althouse College of EDM, HSA II; Trent University, B.S. in Chemistry. **Personal:** Married to Allan in 1972. Two children: Robin and Terrence. Dr. Stewart enjoys gardening and computers.

J. W. Stucki, D.C.
Chairman and Chief Executive Officer
American HealthChoice
1300 Walnut Hill Lane, Suite 275
Irving, TX 75038
(214) 751–1900
Fax: (214) 751–1901

8011

Business Information: American HealthChoice Inc. owns and operates 26 primary care clinics in Texas, Georgia, and

Louisiana. American HealthChoice Inc. Nasdaq AHIC went public March 1,1994. Dr. Stucki has served as Chairman, Chief Executive Officer, and President since that time. **Career Steps:** Chairman and Chief Executive Officer, American Health Choice (1994–Present); President, Chief Executive Officer/Founder, United Chiropractic Clinics (1982–Present); President/Chief Executive Officer, Innovative Diagnostic Labs, Inc. (1990–94); Consultant, Clinic Group, Inc. (1992–93); Managing Partner, Back Pain Chiropractic Clinics (1985–88,1990–91); Director and Shareholder, Health Dental Plans (1990–Present); President/Chief Executive Officer, United Franchise (1986–90); President, Business Industrial Chiropractic Services (1986–Present). **Associations & Accomplishments:** International Chiropractic Association; American Chiropractic Association; Parker Chiropractic Research Foundation; Chiropractic Association of Louisiana; Diplomate National Board of Chiropractic; Board Member, Chiropractic Association of Louisiana (1987–89); Texas Chiropractic Association; Indiana Chiropractic Association; Republican Executive Committee (1983–86); International Who's Who of Professionals (1995–96); Advisory Board of Texas Civil Justice League (1996–Present); Advisory Board, Medical Research Industries, Inc. (1996–Present); Republican Executive Committee; Kiwanis Club; American Chiropractic Association. **Education:** Logan College of Chiropractic: D.C. (1982), B.S. (1980); Ricks College, Associates Degree in Pre–Med (1979); Licensure: State of Texas, State Louisiana, State of Illinois, State of Missouri. **Personal:** Married to Juanita in 1976. Six children: Afton, Chad, Kade, Jake, Tyler, and Anna. Dr. Stucki enjoys fishing and all sports.

Michael Sugarman, M.D.

Staff Physician

St. Jude Heritage Medical Group

433 W. Bastanchury Road
Fullerton, CA 92635
(714) 879–7050
Fax: (714) 992–1135

8011

Business Information: St. Jude Heritage Medical Group, affiliated with St. Jude's Hospital, is a full–service, multi–specialty group medical practice. Affiliated medical groups, consisting of 52 physicians on staff, provide health care from seven locations throughout Orange County. A practicing physician since 1970 and Board–Certified in Rheumatology and Internal Medicine, Dr. Sugarman joined the staff of St. Jude Heritage Medical Group in 1994. Serving as Staff Physician, he provides diagnosis and treatment to patients suffering from arthritic conditions, as well as general medical diagnosis and treatment. He also serves on the Board of Trustees of the Heritage Medical Foundation and on the Advisory Board of the Southern California Lupus Foundation. **Career Steps:** Staff Physician, St. Jude Heritage Medical Group (1994–Present); Physician, Fullerton Internal Medicine Center (1976–1994). **Associations & Accomplishments:** Advisory Board, Southern California Lupus Foundation; Fellow, American College of Rheumatology; Board of Trustees, St. Jude Hospital; Board of Trustees, St. Jude Heritage Medical Fund; Fellow, American College of Internal Medicine; Published articles on Lupus Kidney Disease at the 4th Regional Conference of the Arthritis Foundation, as well as articles on Palm Thorn Arthritis and Pasteurella Multicida (Arthritis Rheumatology). **Education:** University of California–San Francisco, M.D. (1970); Fellowship in Rheumatology, University of Southern California–Los Angeles County Hospital **Personal:** Married to Hilda in 1967. Two children: Jason and Steven. Dr. Sugarman is an avid golfer during his spare time.

Sudha Sur, M.D., F.A.C.O.G.

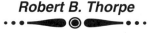

President

Sudha Sur, M.D., P.A.

7777 Southwest Highway, #306
Houston, TX 77074–1809
(713) 779–3100
Fax: (713) 779–6962

8011

Business Information: Sudha Sur, M.D., P.A., affiliated with Southeast Memorial Hospital, is a private medical practice, specializing in obstetrics and gynecology. A practicing physician since 1973 and a Board Certified Obstetrician and Gynecologist, Ms. Sur oversees all administrative operations for associates and support staff, in addition to her daily patient practice. **Career Steps:** Sudha Sur, M.D., P.A.: President of Houston Office (1989–Present), President of Pasadena Office (1984–1988), President of Orange Office (1974–1984). **Associations & Accomplishments:** Associated Professional; American Medical Association; TMA; AAGL; ACOA Cultural Association; Tajore Society & Balaca in Houston; Orange Hosspital, Chairman, Ob/Gyn (1983); Jefferson County Medical Society: President (1982), Secretary (1981). **Education:** American College of Ob–Gyn, Board–Certified (1975), Re–Certified (1983), F.A.C.O.A. (1976); Burdwan (Indian) School Final College, Intermediate Science Medical School; NRS Medical College, M.B.B.S.; Calcutta University, Diploma in Ob–GYN; Master in Obstetrics, M.O. – U.S.A. **Personal:** One child: Mrs. Sutapa Sur, M.B.A. Ms. Sur enjoys music, sports, politics, and business.

Roberto Talamantes, M.D.

Physician, Developmental Pediatrics

Roberto Talamantes, M.D.

1250 Hillrise Circle
Las Cruces, NM 88011
(505) 521–1378
Fax: (505) 522–2318

8011

Business Information: Established in 1986, The Office of Roberto Talamantes, M.D. is a private practice medical facility specializing in Developmental Pediatrics. A Board–certified Pediatrician, Dr. Talamantes is responsible for the care and treatment of patients, as well as Pediatric research in the areas of normal and abnormal defects in children. Concurrent to his private medical practice, Dr. Talamante is also a member of the Board of Directors for Cimarron HMO, an integrated healthcare system and management corporation providing complete medical, surgical, and psychiatric services to its members. Dr. Talamantes also serves as President of the Independent Physicians Association (a professional association encompassing 150 Doctors in seven area counties), and President of the Medical Staff for Memorial Medical Center. **Career Steps:** Physician, the Office of Roberto Talamantes, M.D. (1986–Present); President of the Medical Staff, Memorial Medical Center (1994–Present); Member of the Board, Cimarron HMO (1992–Present). **Associations & Accomplishments:** President, New Mexico Independent Physicians Association (Present); Fellow, American Academy of Pediatrics; American Professional Society on the Abuse of Children; American Board of Pediatricians; New Mexico Pediatrics Society; American College of Executive Physicians; New Mexico Medical Society; Fellow, Society for Developmental Pediatrics; Member, Section Child Abuse, American Academy of Pediatrics; Member, Section Developmental Disabilities, American Academy of Pediatrics. **Education:** Baylor College of Medicine, M.D. in Pediatric Developmental Fellowship (1979). **Personal:** Married to Bianca Y. in 1972. Two children: Christian and Steven. Dr. Talamantes enjoys chess and playing the guitar.

Robert B. Thorpe

Owner/Physician

South Hill Medical Clinic

450 Lillooet Street West
Moose Jaw, Saskatchewan S6H 7T1
(306) 691–0030
Fax: (306) 694–5666

8011

Business Information: South Hill Medical Clinic provides family health care with five physicians, a lab facility, and on–site x–ray services. A Licensed Physician in Canada, South Africa, and Great Britain, Dr. Thorpe joined the Clinic in 1989. In addition to patient care, he is also responsible for various administrative functions. **Career Steps:** Owner/Physician, South Hill Medical Clinic (1989–Present); Owner/Physician, South Hill Medical Care Centre (1993–1996); Physician, Hamiota Health Centre (Jul.1992–Dec.1992); Emergency Room Physician, Regina Regional General Hospital (Jan.1992–May 1992). **Associations & Accomplishments:** Saskatchewan Medical Association; Canadian Medical Association; South African Medical Association; General Medical Council – Britain; Moose Jaw–Thundercreek District Medical Association. **Education:** University of Witwatersrand – South Africa, M.B.B.Ch. (1989); F.L.E.X. (U.S.A.); M.C.C.E.E. (Medical Council of Canada); L.M.C.C.I. (Medical Council of Canada). **Personal:** Dr. Thorpe enjoys golf, skiing, squash, bridge, piano, guitar, and drama.

Sushil Tibrewala, M.D.

Staff Gastroenterologist

Carbondale Clinic

2601 West Main
Carbondale, IL 62901–1031
(618) 549–5361
Fax: (618) 457–4542

8011

Business Information: Carbondale Clinic is a full–service, multi–specialty medical facility, providing quality and complete health care at Carbondale. Dr. Tibrewala joined the Carbondale Clinic as a staff Gastroenterologist in 1992. He is responsible for providing quality care to patients suffering from gastrointestinal disorders. Currently, he holds the chairmanship for the department of medicine at Memorial Hospital of Carbondale, and serves as clinical assistant professor of medicine at Southern Illinois University School of Medicine. **Career Steps:** Staff Gastroenterologist, Carbondale Clinic, Memorial Hospital of Carbondale (1992–Present); Fellowship in Gastroenterology, University of Health Sciences/The Chicago Medical School (1990–1992); Chief Resident, Department of Medicine, University of Health Sciences/The Chicago Medical School (1989–1990). **Associations & Accomplishments:** American Medical Association; American Gastroenterological Association; American College of Gastroenterology; American Society of Gastrointestinal Endoscopy; American College of Physicians; Publications on various Gastroenterological topics in peer review journals; Speaker in various Gastroenterological meeting and seminars; Certified by American Board of Internal Medicine in the fields of Internal Medicine and subspecialty of Gastroenterology. **Education:** Grant Medical College/University of Bombay: MBBS (M.D.) (1977), M.S. (1980). **Personal:** Married to Neelam in 1981. Two children: Anjan and Neha. Dr. Tibrewala enjoys swimming and tennis.

Tim Tieken

Director of Operations

Radnet

1516 Cotner Avenue
Los Angeles, CA 90025–3303
(310) 445–5666 Ext. 7190
Fax: (310) 478–5810

8011

Business Information: Radnet, the largest imaging network chain in California, is a network of twenty free–standing radiology imaging centers located in California. Reporting an estimated annual revenue of $100 million, Radnet currently employs more than 300 people. Reporting directly to the Chief Executive Officer, as Director of Operations, Mr. Tieken manages all radiology imaging centers, in addition to strategical planning and information systems development and implementation. **Career Steps:** Owner and Director of Operations, Radnet (1995–Present); Director of Client Services, Medaphis (1994–1995); Administrator, Rothman Chafetz Medical Group (1990–1994); Director of Ambulatory Care Services, National Medical Enterprises – Dominguez Medical Center (1988–1990). **Associations & Accomplishments:** Rradiology Business Management Association; Medical Group Management Association. **Education:** California State Unviersity – Long Beach, Masters in Healthcare Administration (1991); University of LaVerna, California, Bachelors Degree in Healthcare Management; Santa Rosa Junior College, A.A. in Radiology Technology. **Personal:** Married to Shonda in 1987. One child: Bentley. Mr. Tieken enjoys water skiing, snow skiing, speed boating, and golf.

Mary B. Tierney, M.D.

Physician and Medical Director

Health Services for Children With Special Needs, Inc.

1654 D Beekman Place, NW
Washington, DC 20009
(202) 466–7474
Fax: (202) 466–8514

8011

Business Information: Health Services for Children with Special Needs, Inc. is a non–profit medical facility and health service establishment providing services for children with special needs and their families. Established in 1993, Health Services for Children with Special Needs currently employs 36 people. As Physician and Medical Director, Dr. Tierney is responsible for the care and treatment of patients, as well as administrative functions, credentialing of Physicians, setting medical policies, and acting as second in charge of the entire operation. **Career Steps:** Physician and Medical Director, Health Services for Children with Special Needs, Inc. (1994–Present); Medical Director, Office of Medical Affairs for Social Services (1990–1994); Assistant Medical Director, Chesapeake Health Plan (1983–1990); Director, Office of Child Health, Health Care Financing Administration (1978–1981). **Associations & Accomplishments:** American Academy of Pediatrics; American Women's Medical Association; Amnesty International; Advisory Committee, Robert F. Kennedy Memorial; Juvenile Justice Reform, Washington, D.C.; Published numerous articles on the subject of children with special needs. **Education:** University of Minnesota, M.D. (1970); Marquette University, B.A. (1966); Pediatrics Residency, Children's National Medical Center (1970–1971), and Columbia–Presbyterian Hospital (1972–1974). **Personal:** Married to Thomas Quinn in 1983. One child: Thomas Quinn. Dr. Tierney enjoys horseback riding, scuba diving, and swimming.

Wilhelm Tietke, M.D.

Physician
Huntsville Gastroenterology Associates
119 Longwood Drive SE
Huntsville, AL 35801–4548
(205) 533–6488
Fax: (205) 533–6495

8011

Business Information: Huntsville Gastroenterology Associates, affiliated with two local hospitals, is a full–service, private medical practice, specializing in the diagnosis and treatment of diseases in the digestive system. Born and raised in Germany, Dr. Tietke obtained his Medical Doctorate in the U.S. and is Board–Certified in Gastroenterology. Joining the Practice in 1975, he is responsible for providing medical care to patients. **Career Steps:** Physician, Huntsville Gastroenterology Associates (1975–Present). **Associations & Accomplishments:** Published in local newspapers. **Personal:** Married to Imme. Two children: Isabel and Cornelia. Dr. Tietke enjoys tennis and photography.

John Ul Ting, M.D.

Physician
Medical Office of Dr. John Ul Ting, M.D.
9914 Morrison Street, Suite 203
Ft. McMurray, Alberta T9H 4A4
(403) 743–5414
Fax: (403) 743–5605

8011

Business Information: Medical Office of Dr. John Ul Ting, M.D. is a family medical practice with two physicians on staff. As Physician, Dr. Ting sees patients with a variety of medical problems. He has oversight of the daily operations of the Practice and handles recruitment of staff, employee benefits, financial concerns, and strategic planning. **Career Steps:** Doctor, Medical Office of Dr. John Ul Ting, M.D. (1978–Present); Resident, University of Alberta Hospital (1976–1978); Resident, University of Saskatchewan Hospital (1974–1976). **Associations & Accomplishments:** Canadian Medical Association; Alberta Medical Association; Fort McMurray Chinese Canadian Cultural Society. **Education:** University of Singapore, M.D. (1972). **Personal:** Married to Joy in 1974. Two children: Gabriel and Rosalind. Dr. Ting enjoys prayer meetings and cultural studies.

Sandra Eisele Tinley, M.D.

Pediatrician
Dr. Sandra Eisele Tinley, M.D., Pediatric Medicine
510 Washington Avenue
Sandersville, GA 31082
(912) 552–7001
Fax: Please mail or call

8011

Business Information: A practicing physician since 1977 and a Board–Certified Pediatrician, Dr. Tinley serves as Pediatrician in a small rural town with her husband, a certified Physician's Assistant. She is responsible for providing quality patient care to children. Concurrent with her private practice, she serves as a staff member of a local hospital and physician for the Regional Youth Detention Center (1986–Present). **Career Steps:** Pediatrician, Dr. Sandra E. Tinley, M.D., Pediatric Medicine (1980–Present); Regional Youth Detention Center (1986–Present). **Associations & Accomplishments:** Board of Health (1983–Present); Child Abuse Protocol Committee (1993–Present); Washington County Medical Society; Adolescent Committee (1991–1992), Georgia Chapter, American Academy of Pediatrics.; Medical Association of Georgia (1982–1994); Washington County Alliance for Children (1982–1989); Board Member, Mental Retardation Training Center (1982–1989); Liaison for Medical Association and Organized Annual Teen Health Forum Medical Association of Georgia Auxillary (1994). **Education:** Medical College of Georgia, M.D. (1977); Jacksonville University – Florida, B.A. in Math (1968); Pediatric Residency in Jacksonville, Florida. **Personal:** Married to Jim in 1976. One child: Jason (attends Presbyterian College). Dr. Tinley enjoys tennis, skiing, gardening, geneology research, crafts, and church activities. Dr. Tinley and her husband are members of Annie S. Page Baptist Church.

Andrew A. Toledo, M.D.

Partner
Southeastern Fertility Institute
5505 Peachtree – Dunwoody Road, Suite 400
Atlanta, GA 30342
(404) 257–1900
Fax: (404) 257–0792

8011

Business Information: Southeastern Fertility Institute is a group medical practice of five partners/physicians and four additional physicians, specializing in all clinical problems of infertility in couples. The Practice consists of two locations serving patients throughout the State of Georgia, with satellite offices in Athens, Savannah and Columbus. A practicing physician since 1979 and a Board–Certified Reproductive Endocrinologist, Dr. Toledo joined Southeastern Fertility Institute as Partner in 1990. He is responsible for dealing with reproductive organ problems in women (from infertility to thyroid problems). Future plans include getting more involved in immunological disorders (repeated pregnancy losses). Concurrent with his private practice, he serves as Partner at Reproductive Biology Associates (RBA) Invitro Fertilization Center which was the first to successfully inject sperm directly into an egg in the U.S. (baby was born and is doing fine). He also serves as Assistant Clinical Professor in OB/GYN at Emory University, Active Staff Member at Northside Hospital, and as Consulting Staff Member at Piedmont Hospital and Dunwoody Medical Center. **Career Steps:** Partner, Southeastern Fertility Institute (1990–Present); Active Staff Member – OB/GYN, Northside Hospital (1991–Present); Consulting Staff – OB/GYN, Piedmont Hospital (1991–Present); Consulting Staff – OB/GYN, Shallowford Hospital (1991–Present); Emory University – Department of Obstetrics and Gynecology: Assistant Clinical Professor (1991–Present), Assistant Professor (1985–1991); Physician, Emory Clinic (1985–1990). **Associations & Accomplishments:** Active Member and Society Development Committee, The American Fertility Society (1987–Present); The Louisville Obstetrical and Gynecological Society; Founding Fellow, North American Society for Pediatric and Adolescent Gynecology; International Correspondence Society for Obstetricians and Gynecologists; The Association of Professors of Gynecology and Obstetrics (APGO); Founding Member, Yussman Society; The South Central Obstetrical and Gynecology Society; Diplomate, American Board of Obstetrics and Gynecology (1986) – Division of Reproductive Endrocrinology (1987); Fellow, American College of Obstetricians and Gynecology; American Society of Reproductive Medicine; Society of Reproductive Endocrinologists; Society for Reproductive Surgeons; Medical Association of Georgia; Atlanta Obstetrical and Gynecological Society; Georgia Obstetrical and Gynecological Society; Phi Beta Phi National Honor Society; Omicron Delta Kappa National Leadership Society; Founding President, Alpha Epsilon Delta National Pre–Medical School, University of South Florida; Recipient of numerous teaching and paper presentation awards; Author and presenter of numerous publications. **Education:** University of South Florida Medical School, M.D. (1979); Attended: University of South Florida (1976); University of Louisville: Categorical Internship (1979–1980), Residency in the Department of Obstetrics and Gynecology (1980–1983), Fellowship in the Division of Reproductive Endrocrinology, Department of Obstetrics & Gynecology (1983–1985); Licensure: Kentucky (1980) and Georgia (1985). **Personal:** Married to Cindy. Three children: Jason Andrew, Joshua Evan, and Chelsea Elizabeth. Dr. Toledo enjoys snow skiing, tennis, and water sports.

Joseph E. Trader, M.D.

Chief of Medical Staff
Holy Family Memorial Medical Center
P.O. Box 1450
Manitowoc, WI 54221–1450
(414) 682–6376
Fax: (414) 682–6778

8011

Business Information: Holy Family Memorial Medical Center is a full–service, general practice medical office, specializing in orthopaedics and orthopaedic surgeries. A practicing physician since 1971 and a Board–Certified Orthopaedic Surgeon, Dr. Trader joined Holy Family Memorial Medical Center as Chief of the Medical Staff in 1987. He is responsible for the direction of the medical staff within the Center, including administration, personnel functions, and budgeting, in addition to his daily patient practice. Concurrently, he serves as Partner and Vice President of Orthopedic Associates of Manitowoc. **Career Steps:** Chief of the Medical Staff, Holy Family Memorial Medical Center (1978–Present); Partner and Vice President, Orthopedic Associates of Manitowoc (Present); Member, Executive Committee (1985–Present); Emergency Room Physician, Columbia Hospital; Emergency Room Physician, St. Joseph's Hospital; LCDR, U.S. Navy. **Associations & Accomplishments:** American Academy of Orthopaedic Surgeons; American College of Surgeons; American Medical Association; Society of Medical Surgeons of Wisconsin; Wisconsin State Orthopaedic Society; Milwaukee Orthopaedic Society; Midwest Orthopaedic Society; Holy Innocents Men's Choir; Manitowoc Yacht Club; YMCA; Cantor and Songleader at his Church. **Education:** Medical College of Wisconsin, M.D. (1971); Attended: Marquette University (1964–1967); Milwaukee County General Hospital, Internship (1972); Orthopaedic Residency (1972–1976). **Personal:** Married to Rhonda Sue in 1990. Three children: James Edward, Jonathan Michael, and Ann Elizabeth. Dr. Trader enjoys sailing, snorkeling, scuba diving, biking, rollerblading, snow skiing, tennis, golf, and music (piano & voice).

Brian C. Turrisi, M.D., F.C.C.P.

Physician
The Office of Brian C. Turrisi, M.D., F.C.C.P.
1601 18th Street, Suite 1
Washington, DC 20009
(202) 667–0134
Fax: (202) 667–0148

8011

Business Information: The Office of Brian C. Turrisi, M.D., F.C.C.P. is a private practice specializing in Internal Medicine and Pulmonary Diseases. Establishing the private specialty practice in 1984, Dr. Turrisi oversees a support staff of five, as well as provides quality care to patients. An active pilot, he also conducts medical exams for persons seeking aviation licensing. **Career Steps:** Physician, The Office of Brian C. Turrisi, M.D., F.C.C.P. (1984–Present). **Associations & Accomplishments:** American College of Chest Physicians; American Medical Association; American Thoracic Society; District of Columbia Medical Society; American Society of Internal Medicine; House of Delegates, American Medical Association; Christmas Seals; Numerous Community Associations; Published articles as a Fellow; Listed twice in the "Washingtonian" as one of D.C.'s Top Physicians. **Education:** Georgetown University, M.D. (1978); College of the Holy Cross–Worcester, MA, B.A. in Biology, cum laude (1974). **Personal:** Dr. Turrisi enjoys flying.

John Urbanetti, M.D.

Chief Executive Officer
Southeastern Pulmonary Associates
155 Montauk Avenue
New London, CT 06320
(860) 444–2223
Fax: (860) 440–3153

8011

Business Information: Southeastern Pulmonary Associates is a pulmonary medical services practice. Established in 1980, Southeastern Pulmonary Associates reports annual revenue of $2 million and currently employs 10 people. As Chief Executive Officer, Dr. Urbanetti is responsible for all aspects of operations, including providing health care to patients. Concurrent with his position, he serves as Clinical Assistant Professor at Yale University and as Consultant for the U.S. government. **Career Steps:** Chief Executive Officer, Southeastern Pulmonary Associates (1980–Present); Clinical Assistant Professor, Yale University (1980–Present); Assistant Professor of Medicine, Tufts University (1974–1980). **Associations & Accomplishments:** Fellow, Royal College of Physicians & Surgeons – Canada; Fellow, American College of Physicians; Fellow, American College of Chest Physicians. **Education:** Johns Hopkins University School of Medicine, M.D. (1967); Johns Hopkins University, A.B. (1964). **Personal:** Two children: Andrew and Alexis. Dr. Urbanetti enjoys swimming, travel, and reading.

Roberto Uriel, M.D.

Sole Pediatrics Practitioner
South Florida Pediatrics, Inc.
5590 W. 20th Ave., Suite 300
Hialeah, FL 33016–7061
(305) 821–3388
Fax: (305) 821–3116

8011

Business Information: South Florida Pediatrics, one of Hialeah, Florida's largest pediatric practices, is a private pediatric practice, providing diagnosis and treatment of children from birth to eighteen years of age. A practicing physician since 1986, Dr. Uriel oversees all administrative operations for associates and a support staff of six, in addition to his daily patient practice. **Career Steps:** Sole Pediatrics Practitioner, South Florida Pediatrics (1991–Present). **Associations & Accomplishments:** American Academy of Pediatrics; American Medical Association; Greater Miami Pediatric Society; Florida Pediatric Society; Holder of a 2nd Degree Black Belt in Karate and 2nd degree Black Belt in Jiu Jitsu. **Education:** Central Eastern University, M.D. (1986). **Personal:** Married to Ileana in 1977. Three children: Jacklyn, Daniel J., and Deborah. Dr. Uriel enjoys spending time with his family, martial arts, and playing the guitar.

Laurie J. Vassos, BSc., M.D.
Physician
Dr. L. J. Vassos, BSc., M.D.
3510 8th Street East
Saskatoon, Saskatchewan S7H 0W6
(306) 373–6000
Fax: (306) 477–5000

8011

Business Information: Dr. L. J. Vassos, BSc., M.D. is a family physician and medical hypnotherapist providing hypnotherapy sessions for stress related disorders and for personal growth and development using visualization techniques. In 1997, Dr. Vassos will be establishing a center dedicated to research in parapsychology. **Career Steps:** Medical Doctor, Dr. L. J. Vassos, BSc., M.D. (1982–Present); President, L. J. Vassos Enterprises (1985–1994); President, L. J. Vassos Research (1997). **Associations & Accomplishments:** Rhine Research Centre – Institute for Parapsychology; Association for Research & Enlightenment – Virginia; Published in Various Works. **Education:** University of Saskatchewan, M.D. (1980), B.Sc. in Physiology (1975). **Personal:** Married to Colleen in 1981. Two children: Alyssa and Nicholas. Dr. Vassos enjoys paranormal research and studies, travel, and snow skiing.

Dr. Fedde (Fred) Veenstra, M.D., C.C.F.P. (EM)
Sole Practitioner
Office of Fedde Veenstra, M.D., C.C.F.P. (EM)
888 15th Street, AE
Owen Sound, Ontario N4K 1Y1
(519) 376–5700
Fax: (519) 376–1592

8011

Business Information: Office of Fedde Veenstra, M.D., C.C.F.P. (EM) is a private, general practice medical office providing health care to patients. A practicing physician since 1976, Dr. Veenstra established his private practice in 1985. He is responsible for all administrative operations for associates and support staff, in addition to his daily patient practice. **Career Steps:** Sole Practitioner, Office of Fedde Veenstra, M.D., CCFP (1985–Present); Locum Tenums, Ordyzon Community Health (1984–1985); Medical Doctor, Christian Reformed World Mission (1978–1984). **Associations & Accomplishments:** Christian Reformed Church; Ontario Medical Service Association; College of Physicians and Surgeons of Owzards; OWFN Sound Flying Club; Licensed Pilot. **Education:** College of Family Physicians, CCRP (1992); University of Western Ontario, M.D. (1976). **Personal:** Married to U.R. Lynn in 1978. Dr. Veenstra enjoys music (playing the piano) and flying.

Sarita Verma, LL.B., M.D., CCFP
Physician
Family Medicine Centre – Kingston
220 Bagot Street
Kingston, Ontario K7L 3G2
(613) 549–4480
Fax: (613) 544–9899
EMAIL: See Below

8011

Business Information: Family Medicine Centre – Kingston is a full-service medical facility offering medical care, treatment, and rehabilitation to patients. As a Physician, Dr. Verma is responsible for diversified administrative activities, research, and her patient practice. Concurrently, Ms. Verma is an assistant professor at Queen's University in Kingston. She is responsible for instructing undergraduate and postgraduate students. Internet users can reach her via: sv3@post.queensu.ca. **Career Steps:** Physician, Family Medicine Centre – Kingston (1994–Present); Physician, Queen's University – Kingston (1994–Present); Country Representative, World University Service of Canada (1986–1988); Canadian Government (1982–1985). **Associations & Accomplishments:** College of Physicians and Surgeons; College of Family Physicians; Law Society of Upper Canada. **Education:** McMaster University, M.D.; Ottawa University, LL.B. **Personal:** Ms. Verma enjoys international law and international health.

Colin Mark Verrier–Jones
Sole Practitioner
Office of Dr. Colin Mark Verrier–Jones
Suite 106–520 17th Street
West Vancouver, British Columbia V7V 3S8
(604) 922–2912
Fax: (604) 926–1633

8011

Business Information: Office of Dr. Colin Mark Verrier–Jones is a full service pediatric practice located in West Vancouver, Canada. Established in 1996, the Company has one location, and plans to expand in the future. As Sole Practitioner, Dr. Verrier–Jones is responsible for overseeing the total operation of the Office, as well as patient care and diagnosis. Affiliated with four hospitals, Dr. Verrier–Jones also performs consultations. **Career Steps:** Sole Practitioner, Office of Dr. Colin Mark Verrier–Jones (1996–Present); Infections Diseases Fellow, British Columbia Children's Hospital (1991–1994); Hospice Physician, Canuck Place (1995–1996). **Associations & Accomplishments:** Canadian Pediatric Society; Canadian Infectious Diseases Society; International College of Palliative/Hospice Care. **Education:** Royal Free Medical School: M.B.B.S. (1985), F.R.C.P. (c). **Personal:** Married to Amanda in 1988.

Andrew C. Villa Jr., M.D.
Physician OB/GYN
Women's Health Care Associates
4545 East Chandler Blvd., Suite #208
Phoenix, AZ 85044–7645
(602) 592–9330
Fax: (602) 592–9499

8011

Business Information: Women's Health Care Associates is a group medical practice located at ten locations in Arizona, providing specialized health care to women. Dr. Villa joined Women's Health Care Associates, after completing his training, as Administrative and Academic Chief Resident in 1991. Currently serving as Partner and OB/GYN Physician, he specializes in the diagnosis and treatment of women with gynecological and obstetric complaints, in addition to developing a personal relationship with the patients and their families. **Career Steps:** Vice President, Arizona Women's and Children's Health Care Network (1995–Present); Partner, Women's Health Care Associates (1991–Present). **Associations & Accomplishments:** American College of OB/GYN; American College of Surgeons; International College of Surgeons; Board of Trustees for Maricopa Foundation; Chairman Department OB/GYN/PEDS Tempe St. Luke Hospital; Board Certified in Obstetrics and Gynecology; Who's Who in Health and Medicine **Education:** University of South Florida, M.D. (1987); University of Miami, B.S. (1983) **Personal:** Married to Renee M. Villa in 1984. Two children: Michael and David. Dr. Villa enjoys sports, fitness, and his family.

Dulce Villacampa, M.D.
Pediatrician
Associates in Pediatric and Adolescent Medicine
1008 Goodlette Road, N., Suite 100
Naples, FL 33940–5406
(941) 262–8226
Fax: (941) 262–4302

8011

Business Information: Associates in Pediatric and Adolescent Medicine is a full-service medical office, specializing in the diagnosis and treatment of children, from newborns to teenagers. A practicing physician since 1982 and a Board-Certified Pediatrican, Dr. Villacampa established her private pediatric practice in 1988. She oversees all administrative operations for associates and a support staff of seven, in addition to her daily patient practice. **Career Steps:** Pediatrician, Associates in Pediatric and Adolescent Medicine (1988–Present); Fellow, American Academy of Pediatrics (1991); PGY3 of Pediatric Residency, Miami Childrens Hospital (1987–1988); PGY1 and PGY2 of the Pediatric Residency, St. Luke's Medical Center – Chicago, IL (1985–1987). **Associations & Accomplishments:** Florida Medical Association; American Academy of Pediatrics; Collier County Medical Society; Pediatric Boards (1989), Re–certified (1995). **Education:** University Central del Este, M.D. (1982). **Personal:** Dr. Villacampa enjoys reading, jogging, rollerblading, social interaction, and being a pediatrician.

Alan R. Vinitsky, M.D.
President and Physician
Vinitsky and Mizrahi Associates, Inc.
902 Wind River, Suite 207
Gaithersburg, MD 20878
(301) 840–0005
Fax: (301) 417–0262

8011

Business Information: Vinitsky and Mizrahi Associates, Inc. is a private, general practice medical facility specializing in primary care and internal medicine; currently consisting of five multi–specialty physician associates. A Board–certified Pediatrician and Internist, Dr. Vinitsky founded the group practice initially as a sole practice in 1982, incorporating in 1992. As President, he is responsible for the overall administrative direction of all physician associates and support staff, in addition to his daily patient practice. **Career Steps:** President and Physician, Vinitsky and Mizrahi Associates, Inc. (1980–Present). **Associations & Accomplishments:** Montgomery County Medical Society; State Medical Society. **Education:** University of Pennsylvania, M.D. (1976); University of Maryland, B.S. **Personal:** Married to Ruth in 1971. Three children: Emily, Seth and Ariel. Dr. Vinitsky enjoys sports, physical fitness, computers and gardening.

Prabha Katta Viralam, M.D.
•••━◀█▶━◉━━•••

Physician
Gardens Family Practice, P.A.
3365 Burns Road, Suite 217
Palm Beach Gardens, FL 33410–4312
(407) 627–7433
Fax: (407) 775–1055
EMAIL: See Below

8011

Business Information: Gardens Family Practice, P.A., affiliated with Palm Beach Gardens Medical Center and Jupiter Hospital, is a full–service, family practice medical office, providing diagnosis and treatment to patients over the age of three years old. A practicing physician since 1980, Dr. Viralam established her private family practice in 1995. She oversees all administrative operations for associates and support staff, in addition to her daily patient practice. Internet users can reach her via: PUIRALAM@mem.po.com. **Career Steps:** Physician, Gardens Family Practice, P.A. (1995–Present); Physician, Wellington Healthcare Associates (1993–1994); Resident, Family Practice, Lutheran Medical Center – New York (1991–1993); Resident, Family Practice, Brookhaven Medical Center – New York (1990–1991). **Associations & Accomplishments:** American Association of Family Physicians; Florida Medical Association; American Academy of Family Physicians. **Education:** Kurnool Medical College, M.B.B.S. (1980). **Personal:** Married to Setry in 1978. Three children: Vinay, Munish, and Suneel.

Tejinder Virdee, M.D.
•••━◀█▶━◉━━•••

Pediatrician
Southern Tier Health Associates
428 Canisteo Street
Hornell, NY 14843–2154
(607) 324–0811
Fax: (607) 324–6554

8011

Business Information: Southern Tier Health Associates, affiliated with the local community hospital, is a group practice medical office, providing diagnosis and treatment to patients. A practicing physician since 1979, Dr. Virdee serves as a family physician and pediatrician, providing quality primary care to patients of all ages. **Career Steps:** Pediatrician, Southern Tier Health Associates (1993–Present); Family Physician, Bacon Lane Surgery, Edgeware, Middlesex, United Kingdom (1988–1993). **Associations & Accomplishments:** Royal College of General Practitioners – United Kingdom. **Education:** St. Andrews University, B.S.C. (Med/Sc.) (1976); Manchester University – United Kingdom: MBCHB, MRCGP. **Personal:** Married to Maninder Kaur in 1981. Three children: Sanjiv, Sarena, and Rohan. Dr. Virdee enjoys squash, tennis, reading, and skiing.

Ngoc Dien Vu, M.D.
Physician
Centre Medical Fleury
Suite 211, 2157 East Rue Fleury
Montreal, Quebec H2B 1K1
(514) 384–8556
Fax: Please mail or call

8011

Business Information: Centre Medical Fleury is an acute care medical facility, specializing in the diagnosis, treatment, and rehabilitation of patients. A Family Physician since 1978, Dr. Vu maintains an established private practice and concurrently treats patients at the Centre Medical Fleury. **Career Steps:** Physician, Centre Medical Fleury (1978–Present); Sole Practitioner (1978–Present). **Associations & Accomplishments:** Canadian College of Family Physicians; Quebec Federation of General Practioners. **Education:** M.D. (1978); E.C.F.M.G.; F.L.E.X. **Personal:** Married to Kim Loan Nguyen in 1970. Two children: Catherine and Anne–Marie. Dr. Vu enjoys music, literature, and gardening.

Jo Ann Walker, RN, CPHQ

Director of Nursing
Premier Medical Management/Holt–Krock Clinic
Route #1, Box 229–3
Muldrow, OK 74948
(501) 784–5020 Ext.: 6641
Fax: (501) 788–5911
(918) 875–3115

8011

Business Information: Newly formed Premier Medical Management LLC is 50% owned by Holt–Krock Clinic and 50% owned by Sparks Medical Center. Premier Medical Management is a general practice medical clinic and health care system. Responsible for quality, utilization, and medical management of physician services and the credentialing of physicians and all ancillary staff. Jo Ann Walker serves as the Director of Nurses. She is currently setting up another new managed care health system. This is the third implementation of a start–up organization for managed care with which she has assisted. **Career Steps:** Director of Nursing, Holt–Krock Clinic/ Managed Care (1995–Present); Manager of Medical Services, University of Texas – Southwestern Health Systems (1994–1995); Manager of Champus Quality Assurance, Harris Methodist Health Systems (1993–1994); Lead Coordinator – Manager of Pre–Admission Program, St. Joseph's Hospital (1992–1993). **Associations & Accomplishments:** Educational Team Member (1995–1996), National Association for Healthcare Quality; Board Member and Program Chair, American Diabetic Association; Mayor's Council for Drug Awareness; President, Jaycee–ette's. **Education:** RKFD College/ SAH School of Nursing, RN (1962); Certified Professional in Healthcare Quality. **Personal:** Married to George E. in 1986. Three children: Timothy J., Jeffrey J., and Kimberly Ann Corirossi. Ms. Walker enjoys machine knitting, designing sweaters and dresses on computers, gardening, camping, sewing, and crafts.

Hsinn–Hong Wang, M.D.

Pediatrician
Pediatric Care
30 Medical Park, Suite 202
Wheeling, WV 26003
(614) 695–1210
Fax: (304) 243–1518

8011

Business Information: Pediatric Care is a full–service, general practice in newborn, children, and adolescent; consisting of three board–certified pediatricians, three qualified pediatric nurses, one office manager, and four support personnel. A Board–Certified Pediatrician and Neonatologist, Dr. Wang oversees the administrative operations in addition to the daily patient care. **Career Steps:** Practice in neonatology, pediatric and adolescent since 1975. **Associations & Accomplishments:** Board–certified in Pediatrics and Neonatal–Perinatal Medicine; American Academy of Pediatrics; National Perinatal Association; Yale Club at Pittsburgh. **Education:** Medical College of National Taiwan University, M.D. (1967); Residency in pediatrics at National Taiwan University (1968–1970) and Maimonides Medical Center, NY (1970–1973); Fellowship in neonatology at Downstate Medical Center (1973–1975). **Personal:** Married to Janet in 1970. Two children: Philip (studying computer science at Columbia University, NY) and Jennifer (studying biology at Yale University, CT). Dr. Wang enjoys classical music, racquetball, and swimming. Dr. Wang is active in community activities. He is pediatric advisor at Northern Panhandle Head Start, Early Intervention Service Coordination, Medi–Home Health Agent, and library Committee at Wheeling Hospital.

Teresa L. Watts, M.D.

Sole Practitioner
The Office of Teresa L. Watts, M.D.
5325 Greenwood Avenue, Suite 301
West Palm Beach, FL 33408–1909
(407) 845–9234
Fax: (407) 848–7380

8011

Business Information: A practicing physician since 1985, and a Board–certified Pediatrician and Pediatric Pulmonologist, Dr. Watts established her private practice in pediatric pulmonology (respiratory diseases in children) in 1991. She oversees all administrative operations for associates and support staff, in addition to her daily patient practice. Concurrently, she serves as Medical Director of Pediatric Pulmonary Services and Assistant Director for the Cystic Fibrosis Clinic at St. Mary's Hospital in West Palm Beach, Florida. **Career Steps:** Sole Practitioner, The Office of Teresa L. Watts, M.D. (1991–Present); St. Mary's Hospital, West Palm Beach: Medical Director of Pediatric Pulmonary Services (1991–Present), Assistant Director for the Cystic Fibrosis Clinic (1991–Present); University of Florida College of Medicine – Department of Pediatrics: Instructor in Pediatrics – Division of Pulmonary Disease/Cystic Fibrosis (1990–1991), Pediatric Pulmonary Fellow – Division of Pulmonary Disease/Cystic Fibrosis (1988–1990), Pediatric Residency (1986–1988), Pediatric Internship (1985–1986). **Associations & Accomplishments:** Licensure: State of Florida (1986); American Thoracic Society; American Academy of Pediatrics; Palm Beach County Medical Society; Palm Beach County Pediatric Society; Numerous medical presentations and publications. **Education:** University of Kentucky College of Medicine, M.D. (1985); Emory University, B.S. (1980); Board–Certified in General Pediatrics (1991), Board Eligible in Pediatric Pulmonology; **Personal:** Married to Kenneth Steely in 1985. Two children: Adam and Peter. Dr. Watts enjoys exercising and going to the beach.

Arnold Wax, M.D.

Physician
The Office of Arnold Wax, M.D.
3920 South Eastern Avenue #202
Las Vegas, NV 89119–5171
(702) 369–4604
Fax: (702) 369–8530

8011

Business Information: The Office of Arnold Wax, M.D. is a private medical office specializing in Oncology and Hematology. A practicing physician since 1976, Board–certified in Internal Medicine with specialities in Oncology and Hematology, Dr. Wax established his private Las Vegas practice in 1985. He provides the overall administration for medical and clerical support staff, in addition to his daily patient practice. He also serves as an affiliate physician with eight Las Vegas area hospitals, and continues in cancer research through funding with the Southern Nevada Cancer Research Foundation. **Career Steps:** Private Practice, The Office of Arnold Wax, M.D. (1985–Present); Current Staff Physician (Las Vegas area): Sunrise Hospital, Desert Springs Hospital, Nathan Adelson Hospice, Valley Hospital, University of Las Vegas Medical Center, St. Rose Dominican Hospital – Henderson, Nevada; University of North Dakota School of Medicine: Clinical Assistant Professor of Medicine (1982–1985), Director – Internal Medicine Program (1982–1983); Instructor of Medicine, University of Rochester (1979–1981); Clinical Assistant Instructor of Medicine, State University of New York–Buffalo (1977–1979). **Associations & Accomplishments:** Licensed to Practice: Florida, California, North Dakota, Minnesota, New York, Nevada and Arizona; American Board of Internal Medicine; American Board of Internal Medicine–Subspecialty of Medical Oncology; American Board of Quality Assurance & Utilization Review Physicians; American Academy of Pain Management; Rho Chi Honor Society; American Medical Association; American College of Physicians; American Society of Clinical Oncology; Nevada State Medical Society; Clark County Medical Society: Sustaining Member, Board of Trustees, Peer Review Committee; Nevada Peer Review Organization; "I Can Cope" Support Group – American Cancer Society Las Vegas Chapter; University of Nevada–Las Vegas Foundation; Nevada Dance Theater; Nevada Opera Theater; Las Vegas Symphony; Nevada Institute of Contemporary Art; Lied Museum; Allied Arts Council; James Platt White Society – University of Buffalo Foundation; Board of Trustees, Clark County Medical Society; AWARDS and HONORS: Bronze Medal (1979) – Rho Chi Honor Society; Alumni Association of Columbia University (1971); Who's Who in American Colleges and Universities (1971); Physician Recognition Award (1979, 1982, 1985, 1988) – American Medical Association; Postdoctoral Fellowship Award (1979) – American Cancer Society; Postoloff Award (1979) – Milard Fillmore Hospital; Publication: "Cancer Patient Accessions Into Clinical Trials: A Pilot Investigation into some Patient and Physician Determinants of Entry", published in the American Journal of Clinical Oncology, April, 1982. **Education:** State University of New York–Buffalo, M.D. (1976); Columbia University, B.S. in Pharmaceutical Sciences, cum laude (1971).

William H. Wenmark

Founder, President, and Chief Executive Officer
NOW Care Medical Centers
9800 Shelard Parkway, Suite 210
Plymouth, MN 55441
(612) 593–9818
Fax: (612) 593–0079

8011

Business Information: NOW Care Medical Centers, a group of four medical centers in the Twin Cities area, is an ambulatory care medical facility with locations in Minnetonka, Roseville, Eagan, and Plymouth, Minnesota. Future plans include building 4 to 6 more. As Founder, President, and Chief Executive Officer, Mr. Wenmark initiated the concept of ambulatory care medical facilities for the Minnesota Twin Cities area in 1983. He is responsible for all aspects of operations, including overseeing all administrative and management of the Centers. Career milestones include being one of the first in the country to develop a comprehensive Home Care Program for Adults and Children with Respiratory Disease and to develop an educational curriculum on Home Monitoring for Sudden Infant Death Syndrome (SIDS) – a program allowing mothers and fathers to care for their children at home on apnea and cardiac monitoring equipment. **Career Steps:** Founder, President, and Chief Executive Officer, NOW Care Medical Centers (1983–Present). **Associations & Accomplishments:** President, National Association for Ambulatory Care (NAFAC); Founder and President, American Lung Association Running Club (ALARC), the largest running club in the State of Minnesota and author of a 13–week training program for people who desire to run their first marathon. Conducts two programs of 45 students each: Grandma's Marathon and Twin Cities Marathon. Noted as the most successful Marathon Coach in the U.S. – only 6 out of 1,331 students running the marathon not finishing; President, American Lung Association, Hennepin County; President, Minnesota Society for Respiratory Care; Vice President, U.S.A. Track & Field – Minnesota; Former Vice President, U.S.A. Track & Field, the National Governing Body for Athetics in the U.S.; Member, Governors Council on Sport and Fitness – active on issues of fitness and nutrition for children grades K–12; Congressional Health Care Advisory Committee – both for the Senate and House; Race Director, Edmund Fitzgerald UltraMarathon (Duluth, MN); Participant, Race Across the Sky—The Leadville Trail 100 mile mountain race – a run that is all above 10,000 feet, taking up to 30 hours of non–stop running to complete; Written and lectured across the country on his Health Care Reform concept called "The Solutions Plan"; Frequent speaker on Managed Health Care Systems, Health Care Financing, and Retail Medicine; First non–physician (third year) to be elected as President of the National Association for Ambulatory Care – an organization representing all Ambulatory Practices of Medicine in the U.S.; One of the most decorated Combat Corpsman in Vietman; Lectured extensively on the prevention and treatment of Lung Disease; Taught Quit Smoking programs for the Cancer Society; Frequently featured on radio, television, newspapers, and magazines promoting healthy lifestyles, motivation, and health care; Had a weekly radio program on WCCO Radio called "Your Health"; An entire chapter of "The Marathon" by Hal Higdon, Senior Editor for Runners World, is dedicated to Bill Wenmark called "The Man Who Coached 1000 Marathoner's"; Awarded the Distinguished Service Award from the Minnesota Distance Runners Association; Recognized as one of "Minnesota's Natural Resources in Running" in an article in the Star & Trib newspaper in January 1995. **Education:** Completed medical training and two years in the U.S. Navy as a Hospital Corpsman (1968). **Personal:** Married to Monica in 1981. Four children: Scott, Eric, Jake, and Jena. Mr. Wenmark enjoys fitness, running, marathons, mountain racing (100 mile race).

Steven Reynolds West, M.D.

Cardiologist
Southwest Florida Heart Group
8540 College Parkway
Ft. Myers, FL 33919
(941) 433–8862
Fax: (941) 433–8863

8011

Business Information: Southwest Florida Heart Group is a full–service cardiology group consisting of 13 physician associates, providing diagnosis and treatment of patients with heart problems. Joining the medical group upon the completion of his medical training in 1985 and Board–Certified in Cardiology, Dr. West is responsible for the diagnosis and treatment of patients with heart disease and other cardiac disorders. **Career Steps:** Cardiologist, Southwest Florida Heart Group (1985–Present). **Associations & Accomplishments:** Fellow, American College of Cardiology; Fellow, American Heart Association; Fellow, American College of Physicians; Fellow, American College of Chest Physicians; Past President, Lee County Medical Society; Medical Director, Edison Community College Cardiovascular Technical Program; Past President, Board of Directors, American Heart Association Lee County; Leadership Lee County Class (1993). **Education:** Indiana University School of Medicine, M.D. (1979), B.A. (1975), Internship and Residency Internal Medicine (1979–1982); Indiana University and The Krannert Institute of Cardiology, Fellowship Cardiovascular Disease (1982–1985). **Personal:** Married to Jane in 1979. Five children: Kathleen, Patrick, Samuel, Nicholas, and Daniel. Dr. West enjoys tennis, golf, and spending time with his children.

Richard K. Westerdoll

Executive Administrator

Vista Del Mar Medical Group

1200 West Gonzales Road
Oxnard, CA 93030
(805) 983–0691
Fax: (805) 983–2026

8011

Business Information: A multi–entrepreneurial group employing 70 multi–specialty physician associates, Vista Del Mar Medical Group offers other medical offices a chance to pull their practice back up before bankruptcy. As Executive Administator, Mr. Richard Westerdoll has direct supervision over three companies that have come to Vista Del Mar for help. He helps provide strategy for the company in the community and works with HMO's and the federal government. **Career Steps:** Executive Director, Vista Del Mar Medical Group (1995–Present); Vice President IPA, Greater Valley IPA (1994–1995); Administrator, Alta California IPA and Simi Hills Medical Group (1989–1994). **Associations & Accomplishments:** Medical Group Managers Association; Rend Physicians Association; American Academy of Medical Administrators. **Education:** University of California–Irvine, B.S. (1972). **Personal:** Married to Kathryn in 1986. Four children: Elysse, Celeste, Hannah, and Miranda. Mr. Westerdoll enjoys sailing.

C. Ross Westley, M.D.

Staff Allergist

Colorado Permanente Medical Group

c/o Kaiser Permanente, 8383 West Alameda Parkway
Lakewood, CO 80005
(303) 239–7342
Fax: (303) 239–7509

8011

Business Information: Colorado Permanente Medical Group is a group health care office providing diagnosis and treatment of patients. As Staff Allergist, Dr. Westley is responsible for providing patient care in allergies. **Career Steps:** Staff Allergist, Colorado Permanente Medical Group (1986–Present); Officer, United States Public Health Service (1963–1986). **Associations & Accomplishments:** American Academy of Allergy, Asthma and Immunology; American College of Allergy, Asthma and Immunology; American Academy of Pediatrics; American Medical Association; American Thoracic Society; Author of numerous abstract papers and publications. **Education:** Temple University School of Medicine, M.D. (1962); Ursinus College, B.S. **Personal:** Married to Mary in 1962. Dr. Westley enjoys jogging, race competition, skiing, and model railroading.

Dr. John Paul Whelan

Urologic Surgeon

Medical Office of Dr. John P. Whelan

Suite 419–1 Young Street
Hamilton, Ontario L8N 1T8
(905) 528–1266
Fax: (905) 529–3383

8011

Business Information: Dr. J. Paul Whelan operates a private practice in urology academically affiliated with McMaster University. His clinical interests are in urinary stone disease, transplantation, and urologic oncology. Dr. Whelan also operates a research group testing new drugs in all facets of urologic care. **Career Steps:** Urologic Surgeon, Medical Office of Dr. John P. Whelan (1987–Present). **Associations & Accomplishments:** American Urologic Association; Canadian Urologic Association; Ontario Medical Association; Head of Urology and Transplantation, St. Joseph's Hospital; Clinical Associate Professor of Surgery, McMaster University – Hamilton, Ontario; Author of numerous articles in peer reviewed journals. **Education:** McMaster University, M.D. (1981); Fellow of Royal College of Surgeons FRCS (1987). **Personal:** Married to Dr. Angela Mazza in 1982. Three children: Lauren, Jordan, and Kaitlyn. Dr. Whelan enjoys golf, tennis, and skiing.

Anne Margaret White, M.D.

Physician

Office of Anne Margaret White, M.D.

Suite 601–1 Young Street
Hamilton, Ontario L8N 1T8
(905) 523–0277
Fax: (905) 523–4566
EMAIL: See Below

8011

Business Information: Dr. Anne Margaret White began her private practice of Internal Medicine in 1995. An affiliate of McMaster University, the Office of Anne Margaret White, M.D. has an interest in Neurology, Addiction Medicine, Gastroenterology, Physical Medicine, Behavioral Medicine, and teaching problem–based learning. She also serves as an Assistant Clinical Professor of Medicine at McMaster University. Dr. White went to medical school at age 42, after 10 years as a Physiotherapist and raising three children. Internet users can reach her via: amwhite@netinc.ca. **Career Steps:** Physician, Office of Anne Margaret White (1995–Present); McMaster University: Assistant Clinical Professor of Medicine (1989–Present), Internist (1988–1990), Chief Resident (1986), Internship and Residency (1983–1988); Staff Physician, Homeward Healthcare (1990–1994). **Associations & Accomplishments:** Fellow, Royal College of Physicians of Canada; American Society of Addiction Medicine, Canadian Medical Society for Alcohol and Other Drugs; Chartered Society of Physiotherapists; Numerous committees; Frequent lecturer and publisher at international, national, state, and local conferences and institutional symposia and proceedings; Ontario Thoracic Society grant (1987); Regional Medical Associates Scholarship (1987); McMaster University Graduate Scholarship (1979); Chairman Section of Addiction Medicine, Ontario Medical Association (1996–1997). **Education:** McMaster University: M.D. (1980–1983), M.Sc. (1979–1980); Lakehead University, B.Sc. in Biology (1976); Bristol School of Physiotherapy (1960–1964) **Personal:** Three children: Christopher, Nicholas, and Sara. Dr. White enjoys scuba diving.

S. Gayle Widyolar, M.D.

President

S. Gayle Widyolar, M.D., Inc.

23961 Calle de Magdalena, Suite 403
Laguna Hills, CA 92653
(714) 452–3814
Fax: (714) 855–1007

8011

Business Information: S. Gayle Widyolar, M.D., Inc. is a medical office specializing in dermatology and sub–specializing in dermopathology (skin cancer). Established in 1976, S. Gayle Widyolar, M.D., Inc. currently employs four full–time and two part–time support staff. Purchasing the practice in 1976, Dr. Widyolar serves as President and is responsible for all aspects of operations, including diagnosis and treatment of patients. **Career Steps:** President, S. Gayle Widyolar, M.D., Inc. (1976–Present). **Associations & Accomplishments:** Past President, Dermatologic Society of Orange County; President, Opera Pacific; Member, Center Club; Balboa Bay Club; Orange County Medical Association; California Medical Association; American Medical Association; Pacific Dermatologic Association; American Academy of Dermatology; American Society Dermatopathology. **Education:** Howard University, M.D. (1972); Loma Linda University, B.S. (1962). **Personal:** One child: Keith Widyolar.

Delores J. Williams, M.D.

President and Treasurer

Williams Medical Associates

1245 Whitehorse Mercerville Road #A418
Trenton, NJ 08619–3831
(609) 581–8111
Fax: (609) 581–4673

8011

Business Information: Williams Medical Associates is a full–service, group medical practice, providing primary care in all sectors of medical practices. A practicing physician since 1981 and Board–Certified in Obstetrics and Gynecology, Dr. Williams established the group practice in 1991. Serving as President and Treasurer, she oversees all administrative operations for associates and a support staff of eight, in addition to her daily OB–GYN patient practice. **Career Steps:** President and Treasurer, Williams Medical Associates (1991–Present). **Associations & Accomplishments:** American Medical Association; Medical Society of Eastern Pennsylvania. **Education:** Thomas Jefferson Medical College, M.D. (1981); Swarthmore College, B.A. in Biology (1977). **Personal:** Married to Ulysses Williams Jr., M.D. in 1979. Four children: Aisha Louise, Ulysses III, Brandon Ajene, and Ayana Delores. Dr. Williams enjoys tennis, activities and sponsorship with NMF Mentoring Program, and lectures on community education programs.

Sandra Willingmyre, M.D.

Physician and Clinical Director

CAMcare Health Corporation

3 Cooper Plaza, Suite 104
Camden, NJ 08103
(609) 541–3270
Fax: (609) 541–4611

8011

Business Information: CAMcare Health Corporation is a multi–specialty, community health care facility, providing health care services in adult medicine, rheumatology, pediatrics, obstetrics, and geriatrics. Established in 1978, CAMcare Health Corporation currently employs 150 people. A practicing physician since 1987, Dr. Willingmyre joined CAMcare Health Corporation in 1990. Serving as Physician and Clinical Director of Adult Medicine, she directs all administrative and operational activities of the Adult Medicine Department, as well as providing diagnosis and treatment to patients. **Career Steps:** Physician and Clinical Director, CAMcare Health Corporation (1990–Present); Associate Medical Director, Wiley Nursing Home (1988–1990); Chief Resident, Cooper Hospital (1986–1987); Private Practice Physician, Rykiel/La Monaco (1987–1980). **Education:** Jefferson Medical College, M.D. (1979); University of Pennsylvania, B.A. in Natural Science. **Personal:** Married to Steven Adamson in 1989. Three children: Daniel, Spencer and Grant. Dr. Willingmyre enjoys scuba diving, travel, reading, history, stamp collecting and playing the piano during her leisure time.

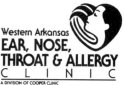

Western Arkansas
EAR, NOSE, THROAT & ALLERGY
C L I N I C
A DIVISION OF COOPER CLINIC
Helping you look and feel your best since 1950

Paul I. Wills, M.D.

Otolaryngologist

Western Arkansas Ear, Nose, Throat & Allergy Clinic

P.O. Box 3528
Ft. Smith, AR 71913–3528
(501) 478–3540
Fax: Please mail or call

8011

Business Information: Western Arkansas Ear, Nose, Throat & Allergy Clinic is an otolaryngology practice providing head and neck surgery, diagnosis and treatment of ear, nose, throat, and allergy problems. Established in 1950, the Clinic is a division of Cooper Clinic. A Board–Certified Otolaryngologist, Dr. Wills is responsible for diagnosis and treatment of patients. **Career Steps:** Otolaryngologist, Western Arkansas Ear, Nose, Throat & Allergy Clinic; Military Service: Holiman Air Force Base, New Mexico (1970–1972). **Associations & Accomplishments:** Licensures: State of Arkansas (1975), State of Arizona (1969), State of Texas (1968); American Board of Otolaryngology (1975); Sebastian County Medical Society: Vice President (1993), President (1992), Secretary (1987–1989); Councilor, Arkansas Medical Society District #10 (1992); American Academy of Otolaryngology–Head and Neck Surgery: Chairman, Board of Governors (1991–1992), Subcommittee on Relative Value Scale (1990–1993); Chairman, Sebastian County Legislative Liaison Committee; Secretary, Arkansas Chapter, American College of Surgeons (1988–1989); American Academy of Otolaryngology – Head and Neck Surgery: Board of Governors, Arkansas Representative (1983–1985 and 1986–1988), Secretary, Board of Governors (1987–1988, 1988–1989, 1989–1990); Fellow, American College of Surgeons; Fellow, American Society for Head and Neck Surgery (1982); Numerous contributions to medical literature; Numerous academic, hospital, and committee appointments; Honor Awards Recipient, American Academy of Otolaryngology–Head and Neck Surgery (1994); Board of Directors, Chamber of Commerce, City of Fort Smith, Arkansas (1992–1995); Board of Directors, St. Edward Mercy Medical Center, Fort Smith, Arkansas (1993–Present); Editorial Board, American Journal of Otolaryngology (1992–1995); Numerous seminar presentations. **Education:** Baylor College of Medicine, Houston, Texas, M.D. (1968); John Brown University, Siloam Springs, Arkansas, B.A., summa cum laude (1964); Numerous continuing education courses. **Personal:** Married to Margaret Harrell Wills. Two children: Alan A. and Shawn S. Wills.

Edward R. Winga, M.D.
Physician
Gundersen Clinic, Ltd.
1836 South Avenue
La Crosse, WI 54601–5429
(608) 782–7300 Ext: 2325
Fax: (608) 791–4466

8011

Business Information: Gundersen Clinic, Ltd. is a multi–specialty clinic consisting of more than 300 physicians and 28 satellite locations. Gundersen Clinic provides diagnosis and treatment of patients, as well as providing a Residency Teaching Program for medical residents. A practicing physician since 1962 and a Board–Certified Chest Physician, Dr. Winga joined Gundersen Clinic as Physician in 1969. He provides medical care in pulmonary medicine and critical care to patients. **Career Steps:** Physician, Gundersen Clinic, Ltd. (1969–Present); Southwestern Texas Medical School: Pulmonary Fellowship (1968–1969), Internal Medicine Residency (1965–1968); Physician and Captain, United States Army (1963–1965). **Associations & Accomplishments:** American Thoracic Society; Wisconsin Thoracic Society; American College of Chest Physicians; Sleep Disorders Association; American College of Physicians; American Medical Association; Elder, First Presbyterian Church; Foundation Board, La Crosse Lutheran Hospital; Foundation Board, American Lung Association of Wisconsin; Foundation Board, Western Wisconsin Technical College. **Education:** University of Iowa: M.D. (1962), B.A. (1958). **Personal:** Married to Sharon in 1963. Three children: Daniel, Julie, and Andrew. Dr. Winga enjoys running, and woodworking.

Anne E. Winkler, M.D., Ph.D.
Physician
Springfield Clinic
3231 South National
Springfield, MO 65807
(417) 883–7422
Fax: (417) 883–0171

8011

Business Information: Springfield Clinic is a multi–specialty health care clinic, providing diagnosis and treatment of patients. A Board–Certified Rheumatologist, Dr. Winkler has been a practicing physician since 1981. Joining the Clinic as Physician in 1989, she provides health care to patients suffering from arthritis, lupus erythematosus, and scleroderma. **Career Steps:** Physician, Springfield Clinic (1989–Present); University of Missouri – Columbia: Physician and Fellow (1984–1989), Physician and Resident (1981–1984). **Associations & Accomplishments:** American College of Physicians (ACP); American College of Rheumatologists (ACR); AMWA; American Association for the Advancement of Science (AAAS); Author of 12 publications. **Education:** University of Missouri – Columbia: M.D. (1981), Ph.D. in Microbiology (1989); University of Pennsylvania, B.A. (1974). **Personal:** Married to Dennis Lathrop in 1991. Two children: Nathaniel and Tobias. Dr. Winkler enjoys competing in equestrian activities, particularly Dressage competition.

Michael P. Woods, M.D.
Physician
Bluffs Gynecology Associates
1 Edmunson Place
Council Bluffs, IA 51503–4643
(712) 328–1827
Fax: (712) 328–1911

8011

Business Information: Bluffs Gynecology Associates is a private medical office specializing in obstetrics and gynecology. Comprised of three physicians and one physician's assistant, the Practice has three outlying clinics and is affiliated with seven hospitals, two of which are in Nebraska. As Physician, Dr. Woods is responsible for all phases of patient care. He is responsible for oversight and care of maternity patients, including delivery, ensures proper treatment and follow–up of clients, and is responsible for providing quality care. Dr. Woods is also involved on a national level with managed care, ensuring that quality is not sacrificed. Concurrent with his present position, Dr. Woods teaches at the University of Nebraska and works with handicapped children. Dr. Woods has special interest in developing maternity outreach clinics in rural areas. **Career Steps:** Physician, Bluffs Gynecology Associates (1989–Present). **Associations & Accomplishments:** American College of Obstetricians and Gynecologists; Central Association of Obstetrics and Gynecology; American Society of Reproductive Medicine; American Association of Gynecologic Laproscopists; Iowa State Medical Society; Associate Clinical Professor, Department of Obstetrics and Gynecology, University of Nebraska Medical Center; Selected for the McCain Fellowship; Medical Director and Founder, Southwest Iowa Maternal Care Clinic. **Education:** Loyola State School of Medicine, M.D. (1985); Knox College, B.A. (1981); Residency in Obstetrics and Gynecology at the University of Nebraska Medical Center. **Personal:** Married to

Anne in 1988. Four children: Rachel, Leah, Monica, and Anna. Dr. Woods enjoys volleyball, fishing, and antique refinishing.

Leonard C. Wright
Chief Financial Officer
Lindora, Inc.
3505 Cadillac Avenue, Suite N2
Costa Mesa, CA 92626
(714) 979–5680
Fax: (714) 668–9341

8011

Business Information: Lindora, Inc. is a national bariatric medical practice, specializing in the control and treatment of obesity and allied diseases. Established in 1970, Lindora, Inc. currently employs 180 people. As Chief Financial Officer, Mr. Wright is responsible for all financial affairs of organization, management, strategic planning, and human resources. **Career Steps:** Chief Financial Officer, Lindora, Inc. (1992–Present); Chief Financial Officer, Manderin Cigma of California (1989–1992); Auditor, Kruse Menillo & Seko (1987–1989). **Associations & Accomplishments:** California Society of CPAs; American Institute of CPAs; Health Care Financial Management Association. **Education:** California State University at Fullerton, B.S. (1984). **Personal:** One child: Andrew Steven Wright. Mr. Wright enjoys wild caving and hiking.

James R. Yates, M.D.
Physician
Jacksonville Medi–Plex
1460 Second Avenue, SW, Suite #A
Jacksonville, AL 36265
(205) 435–2180 Ext. 10
Fax: (205) 435–9525

8011

Business Information: Jacksonville Medi–Plex, an affiliate of Norwood Clinic, is the largest multi–specialty group in Birmingham, Alabama. Physicians serving the Clinic are all Board Certified. A practicing physician since 1978 and Board–Certified in Internal Medicine and Geriatrics, Dr. Yates joined the Jacksonville Medi–Plex in 1989. He is responsible for seeing and evaluating patients and administering treatment. **Career Steps:** Physician, Jacksonville Medi–Plex – Norwood Clinic Affiliate (1989–Present). **Associations & Accomplishments:** Fellow, American College of Physicians; Board of Directors: ALMDA, HEA, and PHO of Calhoun County; Member: AMA, AMDA, ASIM, AGS, SAGM, AQAF, SMA, & AHA; MASA; SMA; ACP; Calhoun County Medical Society; Westside Baptist Church: Deacon and Sunday School Director; Past President, Exchange Club; Past Chief–of–Staff, Jacksonville Hospital; Certified Medical Director by AMDA; Affiliate Faculty for ACLS by AHA. **Education:** University of Alabama – Birmingham – Medical School, M.D. (1978); University of Alabama – Birmingham, B.S. (1974). **Personal:** Married to Phyllis in 1972. Two children: Melissa and Brian. Dr. Yates enjoys karate and church activities.

Ming–Neng Yeh, M.D.
Physician
Ming–Neng Yeh, M.D.
161 Fort Washington Avenue
New York, NY 10032
(212) 305–5239
Fax: (212) 305–1159

8011

Business Information: Ming–Neng Yeh, M.D. is an obstetrics and gynecology medical practice specializing in high risk pregnancy. As Physician, Dr. Yeh has a private practice in obstetrics and gynecology, specializing in high risk pregnancy care. Concurrently, Dr. Yeh is a full time faculty member at Columbia University. **Career Steps:** Physician, Ming–Neng Yeh, M.D. (1973–Present); Columbia University: Clinical Professor in Obstetrics/Gynecology (1987–Present), Associate Professor (1982–1987), Assistant Professor (1974–1982). **Associations & Accomplishments:** Fellow of American College of Obstetricians and Gynecologist; Fellow of New York Academy of Medicine; Fellow of New York Academy of Science; American Fertility Society; American Institute of Professionals in Medicine; New York Obstetrical Society; New York Gynecological Society. **Education:** National Taiwan University, M.D. (1964). **Personal:** Married to Lisa in 1965. Four children: Angela, Rubina, Noreen, and Janet. Dr. Yeh enjoys classical music, reading, and swimming.

Florencio E. Yuzon, M.D.
President and Owner
F. E. Yuzon, M.D., Inc.
3885 Oberlin Avenue
Lorain, OH 44053–2842
(216) 282–9367
Fax: (216) 282–1302

8011

Business Information: F. E. Yuzon, M.D., Inc. is a private, multi–specialty practice affiliated with three hospitals in Lorain, Ohio. A practicing physician since 1964 and Board Certified in Internal Medicine, Dr. Yuzon established his private practice in 1974 and serves as its President and Owner. He oversees all administrative operations for associates and a support staff of 16, in addition to his daily patient practice. His practice concentrates on the diagnosis and treatment of patients suffering from gastroenterologic complaints. **Career Steps:** President and Owner, F. E. Yuzon, M.D., Inc. (1974–Present); New Jersey College of Medicine and Dentistry: Instructor (1972–1973), Fellow – Internal Medicine/Gastroenterology (1970–1972). **Associations & Accomplishments:** Lorain County Medical Society; American Medical Association; American Society of Internal Medicine; Association of Philippine Physicians in Ohio; Association of Philippine Practicing Physicians in America. **Education:** University of St. Thomas, M.D. (1964). **Personal:** Married to Lily T. in 1965. Four children: Maria Isabel, Maria Teresa, Lily Ann, and Florencio John. Dr. Yuzon enjoys travel and reading.

Lee M. Zehngebot, M.D.
Hematologist/Oncologist
Hematology/Oncology Consultants
255 Moray Lane
Winter Park, FL 32792–4122
(407) 628–5594
Fax: (407) 628–9529

8011

Business Information: Hematology/Oncology Consultants provides all aspects of cancer therapy and treatment to patients throughout Winter Park, and surrounding Orange and Seminole County communities. One of four partners with the practice, and a Board–certified Hematologist and Oncologist since 1976, Dr. Zehngebot provides treatment and consultation to patients. **Career Steps:** Hematologist/Oncologist, Hematology/Oncology Consultants (1976–Present). **Associations & Accomplishments:** American Society of Clinical Oncology. **Education:** University of Pennsylvania, M.D. (1976); Union College, B.S. (1972). **Personal:** Married to Wendy in 1976. Two children: Corey and Jay. Dr. Zehngebot enjoys tennis and scuba diving.

Manfred Ziesmann, M.D., FRCSC
Chief of Plastic Surgery
Health Sciences Centre
820 Sherbrook Street, Room GC411
Winnipeg, Manitoba R3A 1R9
(204) 787–1485
Fax: (204) 787–4837

8011

Business Information: Health Sciences Centre is a tertiary medical center of 1,100 beds, affiliated with the University of Manitoba Medical School. In the area of plastic surgery, the Center offers microsurgery, cosmetic surgery, hand surgery, and reconstructive surgery for children and adults. As Chief of Plastic Surgery, Dr. Ziesmann provides care in all four areas. Currently, Dr. Ziesmann is on staff at the University of Manitoba Medical School as Chief of Plastic Surgery. **Career Steps:** Health Science Centre: Chief of Plastic Surgery (1991–Present), Director of Microsurgery (1988–Present); Chief of Plastic Surgery, University of Manitoba (1991–Present). **Associations & Accomplishments:** Canadian Medical Association; Manitoba Medical Association; Canadian Society of Plastic Surgeons; Royal College of Surgeons of Canada; Midwestern Association of Plastic Surgeons; Group For Advancement of Microsurgery; Western Society of Clinical Surgeons; Board of Directors, Burn Foundation of Manitoba; Nucleus Committee, Royal College of Physicians and Surgeons of Canada. **Education:** University of Manitoba, M.D. (1980); Fellow of Royal College of Surgeons of Canada (FRCSC) (1986); University of Toronto, Fellowship in Microsurgery (1987). **Personal:** Married to JoAnn in 1979. Three children: Michael, Markus, and Matthew. Dr. Ziesmann enjoys model building, sports, and music.

Emeline B. Abay
Sole Practitioner/Orthodontics
Office of Emeline Belen Abay, D.M.D., M.S.
3305 East Douglas, Suite 201
Wichita, KS 67218
(316) 686–4321
Fax: (316) 685–2122

8021

Business Information: Office of Emeline Belen Abay, D.M.D., M.S. is a full–service orthodontic practice. A practicing orthodontist since 1982, Dr. Abay established her sole practice office in Wichita in 1994. She oversees all administrative operations for associates and a support staff of four, in addition to her daily patient practice. **Career Steps:** Sole Practitioner/Orthodontist, Office of Emeline Belen Abay, D.M.D., M.S. (1994–Present); Professional Lecturer (1982–1984); Sole Practice – Orthodontics (1982–1984); Instructor, University of the Philippines (1974–1976); Private Practice – General Dentistry (1974–1976). **Associations & Accomplishments:** American Cancer Society; American Association of Orthodontists; American Dental Association; Kansas Dental Society; Wichita District Dental Society; Southwestern Society of Orthodontist; Kansas Society of Orthodontists; Author of article for the Philippine Dental Journal. **Education:** Mayo Graduate School of Medicine, Residency in Orthodontics (1982); St. Louis University, M.S. in Orthodontics; University of the Philippines, D.M.D. **Personal:** Married to Eustaquio O. Abay II, M.D. Six children: Christine, Michael, Erl, Casey, Ian, and Emily. Dr. Abay enjoys gourmet cooking.

Dianne D. Applegate, D.D.S.
Sole Practitioner
Dianne Applegate, D.D.S.
3362 Loma Vista Road
Ventura, CA 93003
(805) 654–1961
Fax: Please mail or call

8021

Business Information: Dianne Applegate, D.D.S., established in 1992, is a full–service, family practice dentistry office, providing general dentistry to patients of all ages. A practicing dentist since 1987, Dr. Applegate established her sole practice in 1992. She oversees a support staff of three, as well as her daily patient practice — focusing primarily on children's dental care. **Career Steps:** Sole Practitioner, Dianne Applegate, D.D.S. (1992–Present); Dentist, Dr. Michael Potts (1989–1992); Dentist, Dr. Robert Turner (1988–1990). **Associations & Accomplishments:** American Dental Association; California Dental Association; Santa Barbara Ventura County Dental Society; Ventura County Professional Womens Network. **Education:** Loma Linda University, D.D.S. (1987); Attending: California Lutheran University, M.B.A. Program. **Personal:** Married to Jeffrey Zoria in 1989. Dr. Applegate enjoys mountain biking, camping, hiking, and gardening.

Lawrence Avramenko, D.D.S.

Dentist
Lawrence Avramenko, D.D.S.
501 Brighton Beach Avenue
Brooklyn, NY 11235
(718) 332–0900
Fax: (718) 332–2185

8021

Business Information: Dr. Lawrence Avramenko is a family practice dentistry practitioner, providing cosmetic, general dentistry, periodontics, endodontics and oral surgery. Establishing his sole practice upon conferral of his doctorate in dentistry in 1977, Dr. Avramenko oversees all administrative operations for associates and support staff, in additiion to his daily patient practice. **Career Steps:** General Dentistry Practitioner, Lawrence Avramenko, D.D.S. (1977–Present). **Associations & Accomplishments:** American Dental Association; Black Belt, Kung Fu. **Education:** New York University, D.D.S. (1976). **Personal:** Married to Clara in 1972. Two children: Michael and Eugenia. Dr. Avramenko enjoys Kung Fu.

Michael Ayzin, D.D.S.
Sole Practitioner
Michael Ayzin, D.D.S.
1160 N. East Street
Anaheim, CA 92805–1428
(714) 535–7373
Fax: Please mail or call

8021

Business Information: Michael Ayzin, D.D.S. is a full–service, family practice dentistry office, providing cosmetic, general dentistry, and oral surgery. A practicing physician since 1988, Dr. Ayzin established his sole practice in 1991. **Career Steps:** Sole Practitioner, Michael Ayzin, D.D.S. (1991–Present); Managing Dentist, Dr. Lum's Dental Office (1989–1991); Dentist, Dr. Kutner (1988–1989). **Associations & Accomplishments:** American Dental Association; California Dental Association; Academy of General Dentistry; Orange County Dental Society; Federation Dentaire Internacionale; Wrote numerous articles in community papers on dental topics. **Education:** University of Southern California, D.D.S. (1988). **Personal:** Married to Inna in 1994. One child: J. Ronald Michael. Dr. Ayzin enjoys travel, movies, and dining out.

Joelle Balmir–Thevenin, D.D.S.
Dentist
Dr. Joelle Balmir Thevenin, D.D.S.
10621 North Kendall Drive, Suite 102
Miami, FL 33176
(305) 271–0510
Fax: (305) 271–3532

8021

Business Information: Dr. Joelle Balmir–Thevenin, D.D.S. is working in a private, general dentistry practice providing diagnosis, treatment, and preventative dental care. Established in 1993, the Practice currently employs 8 people. As Dentist, Dr. Thevenin is responsible for providing all aspects of dental care to patients. **Career Steps:** Dentist, Dr. Joelle Balmir–Thevenin, D.D.S. (1995–Present); Dentist, Phanord & Associates (1993–Present); Dentist, Smile America (1989–1992). **Associations & Accomplishments:** Florida Dental Association; American Dental Association; East Coast District Dental Society; United States Dental Institute; National Society of Dental Practitioners; Who's Who Among Rising Young Americans (1992); Taught English at Haitian–American Institute while obtaining her degree; United Negro College Fund. **Education:** Faculte D'Odontologie, P–AU–P, Haiti, D.D.S. (1986); New York University Institute for Foreign–Trained Dentists, Certificate (1988); College Classique Feminin, Haiti, Baccalaureats Parts I and II (1981). **Personal:** Married to Joseph Thevenin, Jr. in 1985. Two children: Jean–Sebastien (son) and Anouk (daughter). Dr. Balmir-Thevenin enjoys crafts, cooking, and reading.

Santiago Batres, D.D.S.
Sole Practitioner
The Dental Office of Santiago Batres, D.D.S.
2150 Trawood Drive #A200
El Paso, TX 79335–3322
(915) 593–7229
Fax: Please mail or call

8021

Business Information: The Dental Office of Santiago Batres, D.D.S. is a full–service, family practice dentistry office, providing cosmetic, general practice, oral surgery, and dental laboratory services. A practicing dentist since 1974, Dr. Batres oversees all administrative operations for associates and a support staff of seven, in addition to his daily patient practice. **Career Steps:** Sole Practitioner, Santiago Batres, D.D.S. (1975–Present); Biology Teacher, Ysleta Independent School District (1966–1970). **Associations & Accomplishments:** American Dental Association; Texas Dental Association; President (1993–1994), El Paso District Dental Society; Fellow, Academy of General Dentistry; Texas Academy of General Dentistry; El Paso Academy of General Dentistry. **Education:** Creighton University Dental School, D.D.S. (1974); Texas Western College, B.B.S. (1966). **Personal:** Married to Barbara Jean in 1976. Five children: Brian, Christina, Jennifer, Rebecca, and Christopher. Dr. Batres enjoys basketball, golf, travel, and spending time with his family.

Robert A. Baysa, D.D.S.
Owner/Dentist
Dental Arts
95–720 Lanikuhana Avenue #290
Mililani, HI 96789
(808) 625–6300
Fax: (808) 623–6810

8021

Business Information: Dental Arts is a full–service, family practice dentistry office, providing cosmetic, general dentistry, periodontics, and maxillofacial surgery. A practicing dentist since 1986, Dr. Baysa founded the seven–chair dental office in 1988. He oversees all administrative operations for associates and a support staff of nine, in addition to his daily patient practice. Concurrent with his private dentistry practice, he serves as Dental Officer (rank of Captain) for the Hawaii Air National Guard and a Dental Examiner for the Hawaii State Boards. **Career Steps:** Owner/Dentist, Dental Arts (1988–Present); Dental Officer – Capt., Hawaii Air National Guard (1992–Present); Dental Examiner, Hawaii State Boards (1992–Present). **Associations & Accomplishments:** American Dental Association; Hawaii Dental Association; Academy of General Dentistry. **Education:** Creighton University, D.D.S. (1986), B.S. in Pharmacy (1982). **Personal:** Married to Lora A.C. Baysa in 1986. One child: Zachary A.K. Baysa. Dr. Baysa enjoys golf and tennis.

Elton Dale Behner, D.D.S.
Owner
Lakewood Dental Group
5987 East 71st Street, Suite 103
Indianapolis, IN 46220
(317) 842–2337
Fax: (317) 842–1640

8021

Business Information: Lakewood Dental Group is a full–service, private practice dentistry office, providing cosmetic, general dentistry, oral and endodontic surgery. A practicing dentist since 1984, Dr. Behner established his sole practice dental office in 1985. He is responsible for all administrative operations for associates and a support staff of four, in addition to his daily patient practice. **Career Steps:** Owner, Lakewood Dental Group (1985–Present); Medical Technologist, Indiana University Medical Center Hospital (1982–1984); Medical Technologist, Loma Linda University Medical Center Hospital (1976–1979). **Associations & Accomplishments:** American Dental Association; Indiana Dental Association; Indianapolis District Dental Society; Fellow, Academy of General Dentistry; Aircraft Owners and Pilots Association. **Education:** Indiana University School of Dentistry, D.D.S. (1984); Loma Linda University, B.S. in Medical Technology (1976). **Personal:** Married to A. Lynn Behner in 1984. Three children: Nicolas, Ryan, and Tadd. Dr. Behner enjoys flying, woodworking, auto restoration, boating, camping, and fishing.

John A. Behrmann, D.D.S.
Sole Practitioner – General Dentistry
The Dental Office of John A. Behrmann, D.D.S.
425 Maple Avenue, Rt. 9
Saratoga Springs, NY 12866
(518) 587–3625
Fax: Please mail or call

8021

Business Information: The Dental Office of John A. Behrmann, D.D.S. is a full–service, family practice dentistry office, providing cosmetic, general dentistry, orthodontics, and oral surgery. Dr. Behrmann established his sole practice dentistry office upon the conferral of his dental degree in 1960. He oversees all administrative operations for associates and a support staff of three, in addition to his daily patient practice. **Career Steps:** Sole Practitioner, The Dental Office of John A. Behrmann, D.D.S. (1960–Present). **Associations & Accomplishments:** United States Trotting Association (USTA); Historical Society of Saratoga Springs; New York Dental Society; Chamber of Commerce. **Education:** McGill University School of Dentistry – Montreal, Canada, D.D.S. (1960); Wake Forest University, B.S. (1956). **Personal:** Married to Jane R. in 1982. Two children: Christina and Lisa Jane. Dr. Behrmann enjoys harness racing, tennis, racquetball and handball during his spare time.

Jean L. Beninato, D.M.D.
Dentist
Drs. Boisselle & Beninato
122 Kenoza Avenue
Haverhill, MA 01830–4139
(508) 374–7942
Fax: Please mail or call

8021

Business Information: Drs. Boisselle & Beninato is a full–service general dental practice, providing dental services to include restorative, cosmetic and implantology. Joining the practice following the completion of her clinical residency in 1990, Dr. Beninato shares administrative duties with her associates, in addition to her daily patient practice. She also serves as a dental consultant with Palace Health Care Center and also provides dental services to several area nursing home, rehabilitation, and mentally ill patients. **Career Steps:** Dentist, Drs. Boisselle & Beninato (1990–Present); Course Director and Instructor, Tufts University School of Dental Medicine (1989–1990). **Associations & Accomplishments:** Adult Sponsor, Big Brother/Big Sister Association of America; Former President, Royal Oaks Condo Association; Adult Sponsor, Girls Club, Inc. – Take Your Daughter to Work Day. **Education:** Boston University, D.M.D. (1989); Merrimack College, B.S. in Biology. **Personal:** Dr. Beninato enjoys tennis, and music in her leisure time.

Nathan S. Birnbaum, D.D.S.

Dentist
The Office of Dr. Nathan S. Birnbaum
1 Washington Street, #306
Wellesley, MA 02181–1706
(617) 431–9999
Fax: (617) 431–9195 (617) 332–8575

8021

Business Information: The Office of Dr. Nathan S. Birnbaum is a private, general dentistry practice, specializing in prosthodontics, including reconstructive, restorative and aesthetic dentistry. In private practice for 23 years, Dr. Birnbaum directs an administrative and medical support staff of four, in addition to providing all areas of dental treatment. Dr. Birnbaum is also a Clinical Instructor at Harvard University School of Dental Medicine and an Assistant Clinical Professor at Boston University School of Graduate Dentistry, as well as a Clinical Evaluator for the Aesthetic Dentistry Research Group. Dr. Birnbaum enjoys what he is currently doing and hopes that his practice continues to grow. Concern for quality, a good work ethic, integrity, and the crown of a good name are his personal keys to success. **Career Steps:** Dentist, The Office of Dr. Nathan S. Birnbaum (1973–Present). **Associations & Accomplishments:** International College of Dentists; Omicron Kappa Upsilon Honorary Dental Society; American Academy of Pain Management; American Academy of Fixed Prosthodontics; Academy of Osseointegration; American Academy of Cosmetic Dentistry; Former International Marshal, Regent and Treasurer of Foundation, Alpha Omega International Dental Fraternity; State of Israel Bonds, Boston Cabinet Member; Overseer, Combined Jewish Philanthropies; Editorial Board, "Current Opinion in Cosmetic Dentistry;" American Dental Association; Published six articles in trade magazines. **Education:** Boston University School of Graduate Dentistry, Certificate of Advanced Graduate Studies (1974); Northwestern University Dental School, D.D.S. (1972); Harvard College, A.B. (1968). **Personal:** Married to Robin Lappe in 1979. Three children: Daniel, Heidi and Erica. Dr. Birnbaum enjoys computers, golf, and collecting stamps.

B. Keith Black, D.D.S., M.S., P.A.

Chief Executive Officer
B. Keith Black, D.D.S., M.S.
5 Yorkshire Street
Asheville, NC 28803
(704) 277–7103
Fax: (704) 277–1142

8021

Business Information: B. Keith Black, D.D.S., M.S. is in the private practice of orthodontics, providing for the prevention and correction of tooth and jaw irregularities. In addition to private orthodontics, Dr. Black also teaches at the University of North Carolina–Chapel Hill and travels an international lecture circuit on Practice Management and non–compliance treatment in orthodontics. **Career Steps:** Chief Executive Officer, B. Keith Black, D.D.S., M.S. (1986–Present); Teacher, University of North Carolina–Chapel Hill; International Lecturer for Ormco Corporation, Progressive Concepts Corporation, and Professional Business Management Incorporated. **Associations & Accomplishments:** American Association of Orthodontists; American Dental Association; North Carolina Association of Orthodontists; North Carolina Dental Association; President, Big Brothers/Big Sisters of Western North Carolina; Small Business Leader of the Year, Western North Carolina (1994); Employer of the Year, Buncombe County (1994). **Education:** University of North Carolina: M.S. in Orthodontics (1986), School of Dentistry, D.D.S. (1983); Emory University, B.S. in Chemistry (1979). **Personal:** Married to Susan in 1986. Two children: Michelle and Kathryn. Dr. Black enjoys golf, tennis, and spending time with his daughters.

Paul R. Boecler, D.M.D., M.S.

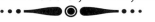

Orthodontist
Dental Office of Paul R. Boecler, D.M.D., M.S.
958 Joe Frank Harris SE #A104
Cartersville, GA 30120–2151
(770) 386–2442
Fax: Please mail or call

8021

Business Information: The Dental Office of Paul R. Boecler, D.M.D., M.S. is a full–service, dentistry office, specializing in orthodontics, treating children and adults five days a week. Establishing his private dentistry practice upon the conferral of his dental degree in 1985, Dr. Boecler oversees all administrative operations for associates and a support staff of 5, in addition to his daily patient practice. **Career Steps:** Orthodontist, Dental Office of Paul R. Boecler, D.M.D., M.S. (1985–Present). **Associations & Accomplishments:** American Association of Orthodontists; Southern Association of Orthodontists; Fellow, World Association of Orthodontists; American Dental Association; Georgia Dental Association; Phi Beta Kappa; Eagle Scout. **Education:** University of Detroit – Mercy, M.S. in Orthodontics (1985); Medical College of Georgia, D.M.D. (1983); University of Georgia, B.S. (1979). **Personal:** Married to Robyn in 1995. Dr. Boecler enjoys golf, landscaping, and classical music.

William L. Bowles Jr., D.D.S.

Dentist
Dental Offices of W.L. Bowles Jr., D.D.S.
249 Paine Avenue
New Rochelle, NY 10804
(914) 576–7604
Fax: (914) 633–0943

8021

Business Information: The Dental Offices of W.L. Bowles, Jr. is a private, general dentistry practice, with a primary focus on cosmetic work. Major clientele include athletes, film and theatrical performers. Establishing the private practice in 1984, Dr. Bowles is involved in all areas of administration and patient practices. Board–certified in Anesthesiology as well, he also serves as Director of the medical clinic at Richard Allen Center on Life — a multi–specialty, primary and acute care medical group consisting of 40 physician associates. **Career Steps:** Sole Practitioner, Dental Office of W.L. Bowles, Jr., D.D.S. (1984–Present); Director–Medical Clinic, Richard Allen Center on Life (1992–Present); Owner and Practitioner, Medical and Dental Arts Center (1974–1993); Owner and Practitioner, Various women's clinics and medical and dental clinics (1974–1984). **Associations & Accomplishments:** American Association of Dental Anesthesiology; American Academy of Dental Therapeutics; American Academy of Cosmetic Dentistry; New York Academy of Sciences; American Dental Association; National Dental Association. **Education:** Columbia University College of Physicians and Surgeons, Anesthesiology (1973); Meharry Medical College, D.D.S. (1970); Winston–Salem State University, B.S. (1963). **Personal:** One child: William L. III. Dr. Bowles enjoys hunting, fishing, scuba diving, and collecting coins and art.

Thomas B. Braun, D.D.S., M.S.

Sole Practitioner
Thomas B. Braun, D.D.S., M.S.
2312 Plainfield Road
Crest Hill, IL 60435
(815) 744–7175
Fax: (815) 744–7196

8021

Business Information: Thomas B. Braun, D.D.S., M.S., established in 1990, is a practice limited to periodontics. Certified in Periodontics, Dr. Braun is responsible for all aspects of operations, including production, marketing, management, and leadership. **Career Steps:** Sole Practitioner, Thomas B. Braun, D.D.S., M.S. (1990–Present). **Associations & Accomplishments:** American Dental Association; Illinois State Dental Society; Will County Dental Society; American Academy of Periodontics; Midwest Society of Periodontists; Illinois Society of Periodontists; Will County Chamber of Economic Development; Will – Grundy Free Dental Clinic. **Education:** University of Illinois: Master of Science/Certificate in Periodontics (1988), D.D.S. (1985); Illinois Wesleyan University, B.A. in Biology and Chemistry. **Personal:** Dr. Braun enjoys golf, landscaping, and outdoor activities.

Alexander L. Bretos, D.M.D., P.A., F.A.G.D.

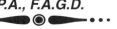

Owner
Royal Oaks Dental Office
15502 NW 77th Court
Hialeah, FL 33016–5804
(305) 822–7332
Fax: (305) 822–9490

8021

Business Information: Royal Oaks Dental Office is a general practice dental office providing cosmetic and general dentistry, and oral surgery care. Establishing the practice in 1992, Dr. Bretos is responsible for all aspects of operations, including management, accounting, staff supervision, and providing general dentistry. **Career Steps:** Owner, Royal Oaks Dental Office (1992–Present); Contracted General dentist, Howard Levine, D.D.S. (1991–1992); General Dentist, Steven Aaron, D.D.S. (1991–1992). **Associations & Accomplishments:** American Dental Association; Fellow, Academy of General Dentistry; Tau Kappa Epsilon Fraternity; Psi Omega Dental Fraternity; Florida Dental Association. **Education:** University of Florida Dental School, D.M.D. (1989); University of Miami, Pre–Med Bachelor of Science. **Personal:** Dr. Bretos enjoys weightlifting, gymnastics, aerobics and snow skiing.

James P. Brown, D.D.S.

Sole Practitioner
James P. Brown, D.D.S.
P.O. Drawer 407 Route 55
Craigsville, WV 26205
(304) 742–5085
Fax: (304) 742–3871

8021

Business Information: James P. Brown, D.D.S. is a full–service, full practice dentistry office, providing cosmetic, general dentistry, periodontics, and implants. The Practice also handles emergency procedures and accepts referrals. A practicing dentist for the past eleven years, Dr. Brown established the Craigsville, West Virginia office in 1989. As sole practitioner for the two–chair practice, he is responsible for all aspects of operations, as well as providing dental care to patients. **Career Steps:** Sole Practitioner, James P. Brown, D.D.S. (1989–Present). **Associations & Accomplishments:** New River Valley Dental Association; American Dental/ Association; Academy of General Dentistry. **Education:** West Virginia University School of Dentistry, D.D.S. (1984); John Tyler Community College, A.A.S. **Personal:** Married to Gloria Nicholas–Brown in 1993. Dr. Brown enjoys woodworking.

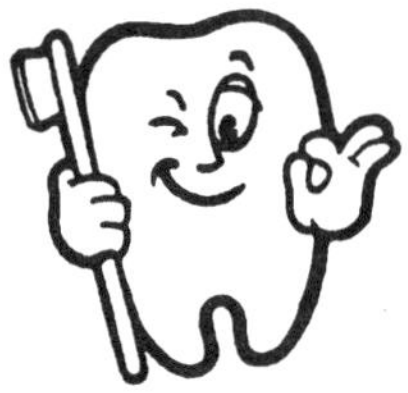

Anthony Scott Browning, D.M.D.

President and Owner
Vicco Dental Center
Highway 15
Vicco, KY 41773
(606) 476–8121
Fax: Please mail or call

8021

Business Information: Vicco Dental Center is a six–chair, full–service dental center providing dental care from braces to surgical extractions. Established in 1993, Vicco Dental Center currently employs five people. As President and Owner, Dr. Browning is responsible for all aspects of operations, including patient care. Marrying his high school sweetheart, Dr. Sandra H. Browning, they both went on to train in dentistry and now share their own dental practice. They were the first married couple to attend the University of Kentucky College of Dentistry. **Career Steps:** President and Owner, Vicco Dental Center (1993–Present); Associate, Jim Caudill, P.S.C. (1992–1993). **Associations & Accomplishments:** The Sons of the American Revolution; The Key to the City of Hazard; Veterans of Foreign Wars Award; American Dental Association; Kentucky Dental Association; Phi Theta Kappa; Health Career Opportunity Program at University of Kentucky; Published in local newspaper, "Hazard Herald" and "Perry County News." **Education:** University of Kentucky; D.M.D. (1992), A.S. **Per-**

sonal: Married to Dr. Sandra H. Browning in 1985. Dr. Browning enjoys oil painting, Little League activities, and local church.

Sandra Holbrook Browning, D.M.D.
Dentist
Vicco Dental Center
Highway 15
Vicco, KY 41773
(606) 476–8121
Fax: Please mail or call

8021

Business Information: Vicco Dental Center is a six–chair, full–service dental center providing dental care from braces to surgical extractions. Established in 1993, Vicco Dental Center currently employs five people. As Dentist, Dr. Browning is responsible for all aspects of operations, including patient care. Marrying her high school sweetheart, Dr. Anthony Scott Browning, at age 18, they both went on to train in dentistry and now share their own dental practice. They were the first married couple to attend the University of Kentucky College of Dentistry. **Career Steps:** Dentist, Vicco Dental Center (1993–Present). **Associations & Accomplishments:** American Dental Association; Kentucky Dental Association; American Orthodontic Society; Phi Theta Kappa; Health Careers Opportunity Program at The University of Kentucky. **Education:** Leatherwood Elementary; Dilce Combs High School; Hazard Community College; University of Kentucky; University of Kentucky College of Dentistry. **Personal:** Married to Anthony Scott Browning, D.M.D. in 1985. Dr. Browning enjoys stamp collecting, photography, and community service.

Dr. Anne Bui
Dental Surgeon
The Office of Dr. Anne Bui
5025 Rue Sherbrooke, Suite 330
Montreal, Quebec H4A 1S9
(514) 485–3999
Fax: (514) 485–8580

8021

Business Information: The Office of Dr. Anne Bui is a full–service, family practice dentistry office, providing general dental care to patients of all ages, including implants, bridges, and dentures. As Dental Surgeon, Dr. Bui oversees all administrative operations for associates and support staff, in addition to her daily patient load. **Career Steps:** Dental Surgeon, The Office of Dr. Anne Bui (1991–Present). **Associations & Accomplishments:** National Dental Examining Board of Canada; Association des Chirurgiens Dentistes du Quebec; Ordre des Dentistes du Quebec. **Education:** University of Montreal, D.M.D. (1991) **Personal:** Dr. Bui enjoys fishing, playing the piano, and pottery.

Thuong Tran Bui, D.D.S.
Dentist
The Dental Office of Thuong Tran Bui, D.D.S.
9191 Bolsa Avenue, Suite 103
Westminster, CA 92683
(714) 891–6769
Fax: Please mail or call

8021

Business Information: The Dental Office of Thuong Tran Bui, D.D.S. is a full–service, family practice dentistry office, providing cosmetic, general dentistry, and oral surgery. A practicing dentist since 1971, Dr. Bui established the two–chair dental practice in 1993. He oversees the administrative operations for associates and a support staff of nine, in addition to his dentistry practice. **Career Steps:** Dentist, The Dental Office of Thuong Tran Bui, D.D.S. (1994–Present); General Dentist, Bui Viet Can, D.D.S. Corp. (1992–1993); General Dentist, Hospital of Saigon – South Vietnam (1979–1990); Captain – Dentist, Republic of Vietnam Army Dental Corps (up to 1975). **Associations & Accomplishments:** American Dental Association. **Education:** School of Dental & Medicine, University of Saigon, Degree in Dental Surgery (1971). **Personal:** Married to Phuong Dang in 1971. Two children: Han and Ninh Bui. Dr. Bui enjoys tennis and volleyball.

Henry H. Bunch Jr., D.M.D.
Dentist
Associated Family Dental Care
2134 Nicholasville Road, # 8
Lexington, KY 40503–2521
(606) 276–4345
Fax: (606) 276–4346

8021

Business Information: Established in 1977, Associated Family Dental Care is a general practice family dental facility. Joining the practice in 1992, Dr. Bunch shares the responsibility of directing a staff of 8, in addition to his daily patient practice — focusing on orthodontic treatments. **Career Steps:** Dentist, Associated Family Dental Care (1992–Present); Dentist, Dental Care of Knoxville (1989–1995); Dentist, Dr. Henry Bunch (1983–1992). **Associations & Accomplishments:** American Dental Association; Academy of General Dentistry; American Orthodontic Society; Bluegrass Dental Society; Bluegrass Dental Study Club. **Education:** University of Louisville Dental School, D.M.D. (1983); Cumberland College (1976–1977); University of Kentucky (1977–1979). **Personal:** Married to Kaki in 1982. Three children: Leslie Lane, Charles Kendrick, and Kelli Lynn. Dr. Bunch enjoys golf, boating, and horseback riding.

Dr. J. Bruce Burley
Sole Practitioner
The Dental Office of J. Bruce Burley, D.D.S.
201 South Cleveland Avenue #105
Hagerstown, MD 21740–5745
(301) 739–7003
Fax: Please mail or call
EMAIL: See Below

8021

Business Information: The Dental Office of J. Bruce Burley, D.D.S. is a full–service dentistry practice, providing cosmetic (for ages 18 and older) and general dentistry. Establishing the sole practice, four–chair dental office upon the conferral of his dental degree in 1986, Dr. Burley oversees all administrative operations, in addition to his daily patient practice. He can also be reached through the Internet via: JBBDDS@AOL.com **Career Steps:** Sole Practitioner, The Dental Office of J. Bruce Burley, D.D.S. (1986–Present). **Associations & Accomplishments:** American Dental Association; Washington County Dental Society: Sustained Member, Former President; Academy of General Dentistry; Gorgas Odontological Honor Society; Local Club President, Rotary International. **Education:** Baltimore College of Dental Surgery, D.D.S. (1986); Wake Forest University, B.A. in Biology cum laude (1982). **Personal:** Married to Connie in 1986. Two children: Brandon and Allison. Dr. Burley enjoys cycling, golf, tennis, and basketball.

Craig J. Butler, D.D.S.
Sole Practitioner
Hanover Park Family Dentistry
7201 Hanover Parkway #A
Greenbelt, MD 20770–2006
(301) 220–0690
Fax: (310) 220–3550

8021

Business Information: Hanover Park Family Dentistry is a general dentistry facility. Establishing the sole practice in 1993, Dr. Butler provides all administrative duties and patient care. Concurrent with his private general dentistry practice, he is also a faculty member at Howard University College of Dentistry, and will also be joining the practice of Drs. Abraham Ingber and Prestipino to develop his subspecialty in Prosthodontics treatment. **Career Steps:** Sole Practitioner, Hanover Park Family Dentistry (1993–Present); Faculty Member, Howard University College of Dentistry (1993–Present); Dental Resident, Albert Einstein Medical Center (1992–1993); Dental Technician, Abraham Ingber, D.D.S. (1986–1988). **Associations & Accomplishments:** Bi–County Medical Study Club; American Dental Association; Chi Delta Mu Fraternity. **Education:** Howard University, D.D.S. (1992). **Personal:** Married to Demetris in 1986. Three children: Courtney, Ashley and Shauna. Dr. Butler enjoys playing the piano and the organ.

Christopher A. Buttner, D.D.S.
Oral Surgeon
Oral and Maxillofacial Surgery
6800 Montgomery Boulevard Northeast #A
Albuquerque, NM 87109–1425
(505) 881–1130
Fax: (505) 881–2081

8021

Business Information: Established in 1994, Oral and Maxillofacial Surgery is a full–service dental surgery group. Currently the Group employs two Dentists, but will be expanding to four when the office moves to the west side of Albuquerque. As Oral Surgeon, Dr. Buttner is responsible for the care and treatment of patients. **Career Steps:** Oral Surgeon, Oral and Maxillofacial Surgery (1994–Present). **Associations & Accomplishments:** American Association of Oral and Maxillofacial Surgeons; American Dental Associaton; New Mexico Dental Association; New Mexico Society of Oral and Maxillofacial Surgeons. **Education:** University of Illinois – Chicago, Oral and Maxillofacial Surgery (1994); University of Missouri – Kansas City, D.D.S.; University of New Mexico, B.S. in Biology. **Personal:** Married to Jayne in 1989. Dr. Buttner enjoys running, skiing, hiking and racquetball.

William V. Byrne, D.M.D.
Sole Practitioner
William V. Byrne, D.M.D., PC
148 Main Street
Watertown, MA 02172–4409
(617) 924–1220
Fax: Please mail or call
EMAIL: See Below

8021

Business Information: William V. Byrne, D.M.D., PC, established in 1990, is a full–service, family practice dentistry office, providing cosmetic, general dentistry, bridges, and oral surgery. As Sole Practitioner, Dr. Byrne is responsible for all aspects of operations, including providing general dental care to patients. Concurrent with his private dental practice, he teaches one day a week at Tufts University. He can also be reached through the Internet via: WVBDMD@AOL.COM **Career Steps:** Sole Practitioner, William V. Byrne, D.M.D., PC (1990–Present); Assistant Clinical Professor, Tufts University (1990–Present) **Associations & Accomplishments:** American Dental Association; Massachusetts Dental Society; Middlesex District Dental Society; Omicron Kappa Upsilon; Completed a 10K race; Published research paper in 1986 at University of Notre Dame. **Education:** Tufts University, D.M.D. (1990); University of Notre Dame, B.A. in Psychology **Personal:** Married to Patricia Keenan in 1992. One child: Emma. Dr. Byrne enjoys golf and volunteer activities in his leisure time.

C. Aydin Cabi, D.D.S.
Dentist and President
The Office of Dr. C. Aydin Cabi, D.D.S.
215 West Garfield Road, #210
Aurora, OH 44202–8849
(216) 562–1644
Fax: Please mail or call

8021

Business Information: The Office of Dr. C. Aydin Cabi, D.D.S. is a general dentistry practice, serving families in two locations in Aurora and Stowe, Ohio. Establishing both practices in 1992, as Dentist and President Dr. Cabi is responsible for all aspects of operations, as well as the administrative functions for the office. Concurrent with his private practice, Dr. Cabi is also a Clinical Instructor at Case Western Reserve University Dental School, focusing on crown and bridge reconstructive dentistry. **Career Steps:** Dentist and President, The Office of Dr. C. Aydin Cabi, D.D.S. (1992–Present); AEGD Resident, Case Western Reserve University Dental School (1991–1992). **Associations & Accomplishments:** American Dental Association; Ohio Dental Association; Greater Cleveland Dental Society; Aurora Chamber of Commerce; Kiwanis Club. **Education:** Case Western Reserve University, D.D.S. (1991); Ohio State University. **Personal:** Married to Jeannie in 1993. One child: Austin. Dr. Cabi enjoys golf, the outdoors, and travel.

Dwaine E. Cales, D.D.S.
Dentist
The Dental Office of Dwaine E. Cales, D.D.S.
908 East 7th Street
Joplin, MO 64801–2230
(417) 623–4424
Fax: Please mail or call

8021

Business Information: The Dental Office of Dwaine E. Cales, D.D.S. is a full–service, general practice dentistry office, providing cosmetic, general dentistry, and oral surgery. Establishing his private dentistry practice upon the conferral of his law degree in 1975, Dr. Cales oversees all administrative operations for associates and a support staff of 4, in addition to his daily private practice. **Career Steps:** Dentist, The Dental Office of Dwaine E. Cales, D.D.S. (1975–Present). **Associations & Accomplishments:** Academy of General Dentistry; Board Member, Amazon Mission Organization; Board Member, Teen Challenge. **Education:** Creighton University, D.D.S. (1975); University of Kansas, B.A.; Pratt Community College, A.A. **Personal:** Married to Margaret in 1972. Four children: Jessica, Joshua, Joy, and Joseph. Dr. Cales enjoys tennis and boating.

Dustine Cameron, D.M.D.
Sole Practitioner
The Office of Dr. Dustine Cameron, D.M.D.
1015 Madison Street
Oak Park, IL 60303–4404
(708) 848–0014
Fax: (708) 848–0415

8021

Business Information: The Office of Dr. Dustine Cameron, D.M.D. is a full–service dental practice. Establishing the private practice in 1993, Dr. Cameron is responsible for all aspects of operations, including the care and treatment of patients. **Career Steps:** Sole Practitioner, The Office of Dr. Dustine Cameron, D.M.D. (1993–Present). **Associations & Accomplishments:** American Dental Association; Chicago Dental Society; Illinois State Dental Society; Academy of General Dentistry, **Education:** Washington University Dental School, D.M.D. (1990); Lewis University, B.S. (1983). **Personal:** Married to Alice Gail in 1994. Three children: Alexis, Terrance and Shantae. Dr. Cameron enjoys basketball, baseball, football, hockey and bowling.

Elio A. Cardenas, D.D.S.
Dentist
The Office of Elio A. Cardenas, D.D.S., P.A.
6791 West Flagler Street
Miami, FL 33144–2923
(305) 261–0633
Fax: Please mail or call

8021

Business Information: The Office of Elio A. Cardenas, D.D.S., P.A. is a general practice dental facility. Establishing the sole practice in 1992, Dr. Cardenas oversees the administration of a staff of three, in addition to his daily patient practice. **Career Steps:** Dentist and President, The Office of Elio A. Cardenas, D.D.S., P.A. (1992–Present); Dentist and President, New Height Dental Office (1991–1992); Dentist and Clinical Instructor, New York University College of Dentistry (1991–1992). **Associations & Accomplishments:** Director and Editor of the Bi–monthly bulletin, CEOCA (Latin American dental study club); West Dade Dental Society; Academy of General Dentistry. **Education:** New York University, D.D.S. (1991). **Personal:** Married to Soraya in 1983. Two children: Elio Jr. and Stephanie. Dr. Cardenas enjoys reading and softball.

J. Edward Carroll, D.M.D.
Sole Practitioner
The Dental Office of J. Edward Carroll, D.M.D.
2000 East Edgewood Drive, Suite 111
Lakeland, FL 33803–3639
(941) 665–5201
Fax: (941) 668–9713

8021

Business Information: The Dental Office of J. Edward Carroll, D.M.D. is a full–service, family practice dentistry office, providing treatment of all types of dental work, including dental implants. His patients range in ages from 5 years old and up, with the oldest patient so far being 106 years old. A practicing dentist since 1985, Dr. Carroll established his private dentistry office in 1989. He oversees all administrative operations for associates and a support staff of five, in addition to his daily patient practice. **Career Steps:** Sole Practitioner, The Dental Office of J. Edward Carroll, D.M.D. (1989–Present); Dentist,

United States Air Force (1985–1988). **Associations & Accomplishments:** President, Polk County Dental Society; Delegate, Florida Dental Association. **Education:** University of Florida, D.M.D. (1985). **Personal:** Married to Vivien M. in 1976. Two children: Paul and Leah. Dr. Carroll enjoys tennis and motorcycling.

Dennis L. Carter, D.D.S.
Sole Practitioner
The Dental Office of Dr. Dennis L. Carter, D.D.S.
530 West Indiana Avenue
South Bend, IN 46613
(219) 233–8255
Fax: Please mail or call

8021

Business Information: Dennis L. Carter, D.D.S. is a general practice Sole Practitioner specializing in on–site and in–home services for the Homeless Center, the Migrant Clinic and two County jails within the South Bend vicinity. He also runs a four–chair, private practice with one partner. Devoting the majority of his time providing dental care to the needy, Dr. Carter was instrumental in developing a dental apparatus for people who are otherwise bedridden. **Career Steps:** Sole Practitioner, Dennis L. Carter, D.D.S. (1972–Present). **Education:** Indiana University, D.D.S. (1972); Alma College, B.S. **Personal:** Married to Emma Doris in 1982. Three children: Joe, Melanie, and Monique. Dr. Carter enjoys writing short stories and poems, fishing and golf.

Keith Casella, D.M.D.
Prosthodontist
The Office of Keith Casella, D.M.D.
637 Beulah Road
Wilkins Township, PA 15145
(412) 829–7010
Fax: Please mail or call

8021

Business Information: The Office of Dr. Keith Casella, D.M.D. is a general dental facility specializing in Prosthodontics. Establishing his private specialty practice following his fellowship in Prosthodontics in 1994, Dr. Casella administers all areas of operations and patient treatment. He also serves as a Clinical Instructor of Prosthodontics at the University of Pittsburgh School of Dental Medicine. **Career Steps:** Prosthodontist, The Office of Dr. Keith Casella, D.M.D. (1995–Present); University of Pittsburgh School of Dental Medicine: Clinical Instructor (1994–Present), Advanced Prosthodontic Fellow (1993–1994). **Associations & Accomplishments:** American Dental Association; American College of Prosthodontics; Western Pennsylvania Dental Society. **Education:** University of Pittsburgh, Certified Implant Prostnodontics (1994); University of Pittsburgh School of Dental Medicine: Certified in Prosthodontics (1993), D.D.S. (1991); University of Pittsburgh School of Health Related Professions/Clinical Dietetics and Nutrition (1983). **Personal:** Married to Bernice in 1985. Two children: Kristen Marie and Colin Bryce.

Chuck A. Casey
Dentist
The Office of Dr. Chuck A. Casey
4695 Sherbrook Street, West
Montreal, Quebec H3Z 1G2
(514) 937–7221
Fax: Please mail or call

8021

Business Information: The Office of Dr. Chuck A. Casey is a full–service, family practice dentistry office, providing general dental care to patients of all ages. As Dentist, Dr. Casey oversees all administrative operations for associates and support staff, in addition to his daily patient practice. **Career Steps:** Dentist, The Office of Dr. Chuck A. Casey (1962–Present). **Associations & Accomplishments:** International Dental Academy. **Personal:** Dr. Casey expects his son, Patrick, to join his practice in June of 1996.

Lee Chamoun, D.M.D., M.S.
Dentist
The Office of Dr. Lee Chamoun, D.M.D., M.S.
1413 Thompson Circle, Suite D
Gardendale, AL 35071–2514
(205) 631–0340
Fax: (205) 631–0828

8021

Business Information: The Office of Dr. Lee Chamoun, D.M.D., M.S. is a private practice dental facility that provides treatment of most dental diseases. Establishing this private, family dental practice in 1993, Dr. Chamoun directs an administrative and dental support staff of five, in addition to his daily patient practice. He is planning to expand his business by bringing in additional associates as well as building an ultra–modern facility. Dr. Chamoun enjoys what he does and attributes his success to his father who taught him strong work ethics. In addition to his dental doctorate, Dr. Chamoun has extensive engineering expertise, completing a Master's degree in Biomedical Engineering, with research toward his Doctorate in this field also being completed. His dental practice skills combined with his extensive engineering skills have allowed him to provide his patients with state–of–the–art technology treatments. The topic of his dissertation research, his research studies have led to his development of an electronic bone–growth stimulator, as well as the design of orthopedic and dental implants utilized to study bone growth with applied electrical fields. **Career Steps:** Private Practice, (1993–Present); Associate Dentist, Dr. Larry Cox, D.M.D. (1992–1993); Consultant, Oratronics, Inc. (1985–1989); Research Associate, University of Alabama–Birmingham (1982–1989). **Associations & Accomplishments:** Academy of General Dentistry; Vice President and also 1995 "Member of the Year", Gardendale Chamber of Commerce; Sigma Psi dental fraternity; Alumni Association; American Dental Association; Bioelectric Repair and Growth Society; Sigma Xi; Engineering Society; Biomedical Engineering Society (former President); Numerous lectures and publications presented in journals and conference symposia on his electrical stimulation research findings and dental implant studies. **Education:** University of Alabama–Birmingham: M.D. (1992), M.S. in Biomedical Engineering, Course curriculum for Doctorate in Biomedical Engineering; American University of Beirut, B.S. in Chemistry. **Personal:** Married to Rhonda in 1988. Two children: Alex Christopher and Danielle Christine. Dr. Chamoun enjoys running, tennis and playing the flute.

Edward C. L. Chang, D.D.S.
Dentist
Dr. Edward Chang, D.D.S.
4616 Vegas Road Northwest
Calgary, Alberta T3A 0N1
(403) 276–7226
Fax: Please mail or call

8021

Business Information: A graduate of the University of the Philippines, Dr. Chang established his private family dental practice – specializing in orthodontistry – after arriving in Canada from Hong Kong in 1986. **Career Steps:** Sole Practitioner, Dr. Edward Chang, D.D.S. (1986–Present). **Associations & Accomplishments:** Alberta Dental Association; Calgary Dental District Association. **Education:** University of the Philippines, D.D.M. (1986). **Personal:** Married to Stella in 1989. One child: Samuel.

Edward H. Chappelle Jr., D.D.S.
Sole Practitioner
The Dental Office of Edward H. Chappelle, Jr., D.D.S.
12164 Central Avenue, Suite 221
Mitchellville, MD 20721–1944
(301) 249–8885
Fax: (301) 249–0761

8021

Business Information: The Dental Office of Edward H. Chappelle, Jr., D.D.S. is a full–service, family practice dentistry office, providing quality dental care to patients of all ages. A practicing dentist since 1979, Dr. Chappelle established the sole practice dental office in 1983. He oversees the administrative operations for a support staff of three, in addition to his daily patient practice. **Career Steps:** Sole Practitioner, The Dental Office of Edward H. Chappelle, Jr., D.D.S. (1983–Present). **Associations & Accomplishments:** Academy of General Dentistry; Treasurer, Robert T. Freeman Dental Society; International Association for Orthodontics; President, Washington, D.C. Chapter of Meharry Medical College Alumni Association; Omega Psi Phi Fraternity, Inc. **Education:** Meharry Medical College, D.D.S. (1979); Rutgers University, B.A. in Mathematics (1975); Eastman Dental Center, Certificate of General Practice Residency (1980); The Genessee Hospital, Certificate of General Practice Residency (1981). **Personal:** Married to Sherra Hicks in 1982. Two children: Edward III and April Nicole. Dr. Chappelle enjoys sports, coaching football, basketball & baseball, computers, and photography.

George K. Chew, D.D.S.
Oral Surgeon
George K. Chew, D.D.S.
132 South Mission Drive
San Gabriel, CA 91776-1102
(818) 282-9108
Fax: (818) 282-1943

8021

Business Information: George K. Chew, D.D.S. is a private dental practice specializing in oral maxillofacial surgery. Services includes: facial defects, facial trauma implants, TMJ surgery, dental alveolar surgery, impacted wisdom teeth, and general anesthesia. Established in 1992, the Practice reports annual revenue of $500K and currently employs five people. A Board-eligible Oral/Maxillofacial Surgeon, Dr. Chew opened the practice with his wife Vickie (an Orthodontist) in 1992, following his residency fellowship. **Career Steps:** Oral Surgeon, George K. Chew, D.D.S. (1992-Present); Chief Resident, Harlem Hospital (1988-1992). **Associations & Accomplishments:** American Dental Association; California Dental Association; American Association of Oral and Maxillofacial Surgeons; California Association of Oral and Maxillofacial Surgeons. **Education:** Columbia University, Oral & Maxifacial Surgery (1992); Northwestern University, D.D.S. **Personal:** Married to Dr. Vickie Greenberg in 1992. One child: Alisa Chew. Dr. Chew enjoys saltwater fishing and collecting plants (coral).

Jady L. Chiakowsky, D.D.S., M.S.
Orthodontist
The Dental Office of Jady L. Chiakowsky, D.D.S., M.S.
2209 Coffee Road # I
Modesto, CA 95355-2359
(209) 524-8381
Fax: (209) 524-1909

8021

Business Information: The Dental Office of Jady L. Chiakowsky, D.D.S., M.S., with offices in Modesto and Oakdale, California, specializes in Orthodontics. Orthodontist and Owner, Dr. Chiakowsky manages all aspects of the practice. As the sole practitioner, he divides his attention between offices seeing over 60 patients a day. **Career Steps:** Orthodontist, The Dental Office of Jady L. Chiakowsky, D.D.S., M.S. (1992-Present). **Associations & Accomplishments:** American Association of Orthodontists; Pacific Coast Society of Orthodontists; American Dental Association; California Dental Association. **Education:** Loma Linda University: M.S. (1992), D.D.S., B.S. **Personal:** Married to Connie in 1992. Dr. Chiakowsky enjoys golf, hockey, softball, and skiing.

Gary L. Cohen, D.M.D.
Dentist
Dr. Gary L. Cohen
30 E. 38th St., Suite 1D
New York, NY 10016-2515
(212) 684-3794
Fax: Please mail or call

8021

Business Information: The Dental Offices of Dr. Gary Cohen is a full-service, family practice dentistry office, providing cosmetic, general dentistry and oral surgery. A practicing dentist since 1989, Dr. Cohen established his dental practice in 1993. He shares the practice with his wife, Marsha Rubin, a dental surgeon, and is responsible for providing general dentistry to patients of all ages. **Career Steps:** Dentist, Dr. Gary Cohen (1993-Present); Dentist, Jamacia Hospital (1989-1990). **Associations & Accomplishments:** Fellow Academy of General Dentistry. **Education:** Fairleigh Dickenson, D.M.D. (1989); Wittenberg University, Philosophy Degree. **Personal:** Married to Marsha Rubin, D.D.S. in 1992. One child: Jessica. Dr. Cohen enjoys reading, sports, and movies.

Bobby L. Collins, DDS
Sole Practitioner
The Office of Dr. Bobby L. Collins, DDS, PC
4466 Elvis Presley Boulevard #241
Memphis, TN 38116-7100
(901) 396-7097
Fax: (901) 396-8214

8021

Business Information: The Office of Dr. Bobby L. Collins, DDS, PC is a general practice dental facility. Establishing his private practice in 1976, Dr. Collins oversees an administrative and medical support staff of six, in addition to his daily patient practice. **Career Steps:** Sole Practitioner, The Office of Dr. Bobby L. Collins, DDS, PC (1976-Present); Instructor, University of Tennessee College of Dentistry (1975-1977); Administrator and Teacher, Memphis City Schools (1965-1972). **Associations & Accomplishments:** American Dental Society; Tennessee Dental Society; Memphis Dental Society; Pan-Tennessee Dental Society; Shelby County Dental Society; American Associaiton of Deans and Dental Examiners; Member and Former President, Tennessee Board of Dentistry; Academy of General Dentistry; FAGD. **Education:** University of Iowa, DDS (1975); University of Memphis: M.S.T., B.S. **Personal:** Two children: Valerie Joy and Kim E. Collins Presley. Dr. Collins enjoys tennis, reading and golf.

John P. Craig, D.M.D.
President and Dentist
Family and Cosmetic Dentistry of North Florida
310 North Ohio Avenue
Live Oak, FL 32060
(904) 362-6800
Fax: (904) 364-5199

8021

Business Information: Family and Cosmetic Dentistry of North Florida is a general practice, specializing in Orthodontics and Implant Dentistry which features root form, blade form, and the Ramus frame implant. These are used in conjunction with a variety of bone grafting procedures including maxillary sinus lifts. Combining orthodontics, implant dentistry and cosmetic dentistry procedures, the highest quality of patient satisfaction can be obtained in the areas of aesthetics and function. As President, Dr. Craig is also reponsible for the overall direction and growth of the practice. Active in the community, Dr. Craig and his Associates are the sponsors of a city league softball team. **Career Steps:** President, Family and Cosmetic Dentistry of North Florida (1990-Present). **Associations & Accomplishments:** American Orthodontic Society; American Academy of Implant Dentistry; Boys Club Ranch. **Education:** University of Florida College of Dentistry, D.M.D. (1989); University of Florida, B.S. in Microbiology and Cell Science. **Personal:** Married to Ivy in 1993. Dr. Craig enjoys travel and outdoor activities.

Theresa Y. Crawley, D.D.S.
Sole Practitioner
The Dental Office of Theresa Y. Crawley, D.D.S.
1701 Fall Hill Avenue
Fredericksburg, VA 22401-3510
(540) 371-1090
Fax: (540) 371-5230

8021

Business Information: Establishing her five-chair, full-service, dentistry office upon the conferral of her dental degree, Dr. Crawley operates as a sole-practitioner concentrating on cosmetic, general dentistry, and periodontics. **Career Steps:** Sole Practitioner, Theresa Y. Crawley, D.D.S. (1983-Present). **Associations & Accomplishments:** Rappahannock Valley Dental Society; Northern Virginia Dental Society; Virginia Dental Association; American Dental Association; Mary Washington College Alumni Association: President-Elect (to assume Presidency July 1996). **Education:** Medical College of Virginia: D.D.S. (1983), M.S. in Anatomy (1979); Mary Washington College, B.S. in Biology (1977). **Personal:** Married to William B. in 1979. Dr. Crawley enjoys boating, gardening, reading, cooking, running, and aerobics.

Cheryl L. Cushman, D.D.S
Sole Practitioner
Dental Office of Cheryl L. Cushman, D.D.S.
1680 Mulkey Road #A
Austell, GA 30001-1118
(770) 739-5097
Fax: Please mail or call

8021

Business Information: The Dental Office of Cheryl L. Cushman, D.D.S. specializes in Periodontics and Implantology. Establishing her private practice in 1993, Dr. Cushman performs peridontal therapy and places dental implants, as well as follows through on all administrative functions of the practice. **Career Steps:** Sole Practitioner and Periodontist, The Dental Office of Cheryl L. Cushman, D.D.S. (1993-Present); General Dentist, Evans Family Dental (1991-1993); General Dentist, Employee Dental Services (1989-1991). **Associations & Accomplishments:** American Dental Association; Georgia Dental Association; American Academy of Periodontology. **Education:** Medical College of Georgia, Certificate in Periodontics (1993); Case Western Reserve University School of Dentistry, D.D.S. (1988); University of Michigan, B.S. in Biology (1983); Emory University, General Practice Residency (1989). **Personal:** Married to William Claybrook in 1993.

John C. Daire, D.D.S.
Orthodontist and Partner
Drs. Horaist and Daire, Orthodontics
1615 Kerr Street, Suite 103
Opelousas, LA 70570-7825
(318) 948-3491
Fax: Please mail or call

8021

Business Information: Established in 1993, Drs. Horaist and Daire, Orthodontics is a full-service Orthodontics practice. Currently there are 2 Orthodontists and 8 support staff in 2 offices. As Orthodontist and Partner, Dr. Daire is responsible for the care and treatment of patients. Dr. Daire returned to school to specialize in Orthodontics after 10 years in the general dentistry practice. **Career Steps:** Orthodontist and Partner, Drs. Horaist and Daire, Orthodontics (1993-Present); Orthodontist Associate, Dr. Noel Dragon, Orthodontist (1991-1993); Dentist and Owner, Dr. John C. Daire, D.D.S., General Dentistry (1979-1989). **Associations & Accomplishments:** American Association of Orthodontics; Southwestern Society of Orthodontics; American Dental Association; Louisiana Dental Association; Former Treasurer, Acadiana District Dental Association; Evangeline Dental Study Club; Deacon, Southside Bible Chapel, Lafayette, LA. **Education:** Louisiana State University: Orthodontics (1991), Dental (1979), B.S. in Microbiology (1975). **Personal:** Married to Debbie in 1976. Two children: Hannah and Katie. Dr. Daire enjoys golf, hunting, and fishing.

Robert S. Dame, D.D.S.
Owner
Robert S. Dame, D.D.S.
422 North Park Street NE
Grand Rapids, MI 49505-2580
(616) 361-7265
Fax: Please mail or call

8021

Business Information: Robert S. Dame, D.D.S. is a full-service, general dentistry practice providing cosmetic, family dentistry, and oral surgery services. Services include aesthetics, root canals, fillings, dentures, and orthopedics. Establishing his sole-practice in 1994, Dr. Dame provides comprehensive dental treatment of patients, marketing the practice, and managing day-to-day business activities in a modern office setting. **Career Steps:** Owner, Robert S. Dame, D.D.S. (1994-Present); Associate Dentist, Charles F. Cole, D.D.S. (1992-1994); Customer Service Representative, Zin-Plas Corporation (1983-1987). **Associations & Accomplishments:** American Dental Association; Michigan Dental Association; West Michigan Dental Society; Academy of General Dentistry; National Association of Doctors; Kent County Dental Society; Conducts seminars for eight schools, K-2nd grades on oral hygiene. **Education:** University of Michigan, D.D.S. (1992); Calvin College, B.S. (1987). **Personal:** Married to Darcy J. Dame in 1990. Dr. Dame enjoys softball, basketball, choral singing, and spending an evening with friends.

Miriam Levitan Dani, D.D.S.
Sole Practitioner
Miriam Levitan Dani, D.D.S.
716 Elm Street
Winnetka, IL 60093
(708) 884-1200
Fax: Please mail or call

8021

Business Information: Miriam Levitan Dani, D.D.S., established in 1992, is a full-service, family practice dentistry office with two locations, providing cosmetic, general dentistry, and oral surgery. A practicing dentist since 1991, Dr. Dani established this sole practice dental office in 1992, responsible for all aspects of operations. **Career Steps:** Sole Practitioner, Miriam Levitan Dani, D.D.S. (1992–Present); Dentist, Rush Presbyterian St. Lukes Hospital (1991–1992). **Associations & Accomplishments:** Junior League – Evanston – North Shore; Chicago Dental Society; American Dental Association; American Association of Women Dentists. **Education:** University of Illinois: D.D.S. (1991), B.S. **Personal:** Married to Michael in 1993. Dr. Dani enjoys tennis, paddle tennis, horseback riding, and skiing.

Rockwell F. Davis, D.D.S.

Sole Practitioner
Dental Office of Rockwell F. Davis, D.D.S.
16 Center Street
Brunswick, ME 04011–1504
(207) 729–3571
Fax: (207) 725–2801

8021

Business Information: The Office of Rockwell F. Davis, D.D.S. is a general practice family and cosmetic dental facility. In operation since 1850, the Office has changed ownership over the years but has continued to provide quality services throughout. The Owner of the practice for two years, Dr. Davis directs a support staff of four, in addition to his daily patient practice. An experienced Dentist since 1968, Dr. Davis provided services for the top executives of Arabian–American Oil Company and their family members. As such, he has spent a lot of time overseas and is very familiar with foreign cultures. Dr. Davis was also offered the position of Chief of the Outpatient Dental Clinic in Washington, D.C. where he would have provided services for Congress and the President. He choose to decline the position and enter into private practice. **Career Steps:** Sole Practitioner, The Office of Rockwell F. Davis, D.D.S. (1993–Present); General Dentist, Arabian–American Oil Company (1981–1993); Sole Practitioner, Drs. Davis and Savage, Ltd. (1974–1981); Dentist, United States Public Health Service (1969–1972). **Associations & Accomplishments:** American Dental Association; President, Duke Alumni Association of Tidewater Virgina; Main Dental Association; Virginia Dental Association; Former Director, Dental Emergency Service, Virginia Beach Hospital; American Legion; Eagle Scout; Scout Master, Saudi Arabia. **Education:** Georgetown University School of Dentistry, D.D.S. (1968); Duke University, A.B. (1964); USPHS Hospital General Residency (1968–1969); **Personal:** Married to Mary in 1980. Three children: Amy, Brant, and Chris. Dr. Davis enjoys foreign languages, tourism, video photography, sailing, and skiing. He is such an avid skier that he recently underwent arthoscopic surgery to his knee, just to be ready for the 1995–1996 ski season.

Amy De Groat, D.D.S.

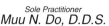

Dentist
Bayshore Dental Office
3351 Plainview Street #A1
Pasadena, TX 77504
(713) 943–0064 (713) 261–8258
Fax: (713) 943–1554 (713) 261–7859

8021

Business Information: Bayshore Dental Office is a full–service, general dentistry practice with two offices in the local area. Established in 1992, the Practice currently employs four people. As Dentist, Dr. De Groat is responsible for providing dental care to patients. Concurrent with her position, she serves as Dentist at Dentists at Lexington Colony. **Career Steps:** Dentist, Bayshore Dental Office (1992–Present); Dentist, Dentists at Lexington Colony (1994–Present); Dentist, Reed Dental Implant Institute (1989–1992). **Associations & Accomplishments:** Academy of General Dentistry; Greater Houston Dental Society; American Dental Association; Texas Dental Association; Academy of Dental Excellence. **Education:** University of Texas Health Science Center – Houston, D.D.S. (1989).

Marielena Diakogiannis, D.D.S.

Periodontist
The Dental Offices of Diakogiannis & Baron, D.D.S.
3443 213 Street
Flushing, NY 11361–1500
(718) 224–6656
Fax: (718) 767–7951

8021

Business Information: The Dental Offices of Diakogiannis & Baron, D.D.S. is a full–service, family practice dentistry office, specializing in periodontics, implants, and surgery on gums. Co–founding the Practice upon conferral of her dental degree in 1991, Miss Diakogiannis is a Board–Certified Periodontist. She is responsible for administrative operations for associates and a support staff of four, in addition to her daily patient practice. She specializes in periodontics and implant dentistry, as well as conducting research for an implant program. Articles will be published on the program in the next year. **Career Steps:** Periodontist, The Dental Offices of Diakogiannis & Baron, D.D.S. (1991–Present); Resident Surgeon, Veterans Administration Medical Center (1991–1994); New York University Advanced Education Implant Dentistry, New York University Dental Center (1995–1997). **Associations & Accomplishments:** American Dental Association; Academy of General Dentistry; American Academy of Periodontics; Northeast Society of Periodontics; Long Island Society of Periodontics; Helenic Dental Society. **Education:** New York University Dental Center, D.D.S. (1991); Veterans Administration Medical Center, Surgical Training and Specialty in Periodontics and Implants (1991–1994). **Personal:** Miss Diakogiannis enjoys travel, physical training, and weight training.

Muu N. Do, Ph.D., D.D.S.

Sole Practitioner
Muu N. Do, D.D.S.
9010 Bolsa Avenue
Westminster, CA 92683–5531
(714) 892–5710
Fax: Please mail or call

8021

Business Information: Muu N. Do, D.D.S. is a full–service, family dental practice. Services provided include: cosmetic, restorative and denture work, as well as basic dentistry care. Establishing his private practice in 1992, Dr. Do is responsible for all aspects of operations, including providing treatment to dental patients. **Career Steps:** Owner and Dentist, Muu N. Do, D.D.S. (1992–Present); Dentist, M. L. Glossman, D.D.S. (1992–1993); Research Chemist, M. D. Anderson Hospital – Texas (1987–1988). **Associations & Accomplishments:** American Dental Association; California Dental Association; Orange County Dental Association; Recipient of past awards as a research chemist, searching for new drugs for beating diseases. **Education:** University of California – Los Angeles Dental School, D.D.S. (1992); Clark University, M.A., PH.D. (1982). **Personal:** Married to Sandy in 1980. Three children: Tom, Jeannie, and Jessica. Dr. Do enjoys reading and travel.

Vicky Domondon, D.M.D.

Dentist
Professional Dental Care
2100 West 3rd Street, Suite 320
Los Angeles, CA 90057–1922
(213) 484–2919
Fax: (213) 484–2132

8021

Business Information: Professional Dental Care is a full–service family dental practice. Establishing her private practice in 1983, Dr. Domondon oversees all administrative operations, in addition to patient treatment. **Career Steps:** Owner and Dentist, Professional Dental Care (1983–Present); Hospital Administrator, Children's Medical Center, Phil. Inc. (1964–1969); Practicing dentist in Philippines (1952–1969). **Associations & Accomplishments:** American Dental Association; California Dental Association; Los Angeles Dental Society; Fellow, Academy of Dentistry International; Academy of General Dentistry; National Association of Filipino Dentists in America; Secretary, Filipino American Republican Council of California; Board of Asian Battered Women. **Education:** D.M.D. (1952); College of Oral and Dental Surgery, Manila Philippines (1952); University of the Philippines, Hospital Administrator (1964). **Personal:** Married to Oscar Domondon, D.D.S., a practicing dentist in Long Beach, CA (1964–Present) in 1983. Four children: Grace Michaelman, Reiner de los Santos, Mariza Gatdula and Victor (a practicing dentist in her office) and five grandchildren. Dr. Domondon enjoys reading, playing the piano, and bowling. Dr. Domondon is a native of Bulacan, Philippines.

Gregory P. Doroski, D.M.D.

Sole Practitioner
The Dental Office of Gregory P. Doroski, D.M.D.
887 Old Country Road
Riverhead, NY 11901
(516) 727–0770
Fax: Please mail or call

8021

Business Information: The Dental Office of Gregory P. Doroski, D.M.D. is a general practice dental facility, including cosmetic dentistry, crowns, bridges, and implants. Establishing the practice in 1980, Dr. Doroski directs a support staff of five, in addition to his daily patient practice. **Career Steps:** Sole Practitioner, The Dental Office of Gregory P. Doroski, D.M.D. (1980–Present). **Associations & Accomplishments:** American Dental Association; Former Church Trustee; Former Trustee and Vice President, Local Library; Former Secretary, Rotary Club **Education:** Fairleigh Dickinson: D.M.D. (1980), B.S. in Biology (1976). **Personal:** Married to Robin in 1989. Five children: Stacey, Leigh, Gregory Jr., Elizabeth, and Matthew.

John T. Doyle, D.D.S.

Dentist and Owner
The Office of Dr. John T. Doyle, D.D.S.
6451 Chippewa Street
St. Louis, MO 63109–2104
(314) 752–3123
Fax: Please mail or call

8021

Business Information: The Office of Dr. John T. Doyle, D.D.S. is a general practice dental facility. Establishing his private practice in 1990, Dr. Doyle specializes in the surgical removal of prosthetics, including bridges and implants. Concurrent to his private dental practice, Dr. Doyle is a Colonel in the United States Air Force Reserves. As such, he spent ten years on active duty and has spent the last ten years providing his services to the government one weekend a month and for two weeks during the summer. **Career Steps:** Dentist and Owner, The Office of Dr. John T. Doyle, D.D.S. (1990–Present); Elementary Science Teacher (1974–1976). **Associations & Accomplishments:** American Dental Association; Academy of General Surgeons; Association of Military Surgeons of the United States; Former President and Vice President, Webster University Alumni Association; Member of the School Board, 8 years; IMA Assistant, Command Dental Surgeon, 5 years; Published in local papers regarding dental health. **Education:** Webster University, M.S. in Management (1985); Indiana University School of Dentistry, D.D.S. (1976); Academy of General Dentistry, Fellowship (1983); St. Meinrad College, B.S. in Biology (1970). **Personal:** Married to Marilyn L. in 1970. Three children: Rebecca, Amy and Marianne. Dr. Doyle enjoys snow skiing, hiking, photography and painting.

Jim F. Drake, D.D.S.

Oral and Maxillofacial Surgeon
Jim F. Drake, D.D.S.
12665 Garden Grove Boulevard, #204
Garden Grove, CA 92643–1916
(714) 530–5290
Fax: (714) 530–4543

8021

Business Information: Jim F. Drake, D.D.S. is a private dental practice specializing in oral and maxillofacial surgery. He performs surgical intervention of jaws and surrounding parts in children and adults. Established in 1964, the Practice currently employs eight people. As Oral and Maxillofacial Surgeon, Dr. Drake is responsible for all aspects of operations. Concurrent with his practice, he teaches Graduate Oral Surgery to residents at the University of Southern California School of Dentistry. Dr. Drake is also President of Better Life International, Inc., a health and nutrition company. He also lectures internationally. **Career Steps:** Oral and Maxillofacial Surgeon, Jim F. Drake, D.D.S. (1964–Present); Assistant Clinical Professor, Department of Oral and Maxillofacial Surgery, University of Southern California School of Dentistry (1968–Present); Oral Surgeon, Crown Dental Group (1991–1993); Oral Surgeon, DHA Dental Group (1986–1990); Private Practice of Oral and Maxillofacial Surgery, Yucaipa, California (1979–1985); Assistant Professor of Surgical Sciences, Department of Anesthesia and Medicine, University of Southern California School of Dentistry (1979–1985); Private Practice of Oral and Maxillofacial Surgery, Los Angeles, California (1971–1978); Associate of Dr. Ralph O'Brien in Practice of Oral and Maxillofacial Surgery, South Gate, California

(1968–1970); Private Practice of Oral and Maxillofacial Surgery, Norman, Oklahoma (1964–1967); Instructor in Oral and Maxillofacial Surgery Department, University of Oklahoma School of Medicine. **Associations & Accomplishments:** Hospital – past and present active staff memberships: USC/LA County Hospital, Garden Grove Hospital, St. Bernadine Hospital, Redlands Community Hospital, St. Francis Hospital, Downey Community Hospital, Huntington Park Community Hospital, Mission Hospital, Norman Municipal Hospital; American Dental Association; California Dental Association; Orange County Dental Society; American Dental Society of Anesthesiology; American College of Oral and Maxillofacial Surgeons; Southern California Society of Oral and Maxillofacial Surgeons; International Society of Maxillo Facial Surgery; American Society of Osseointegration; International Congress of Oral Implantologists; American College of Oral Implantology; Beta Theta Pi Social Fraternity; Xi Psi Phi Dental Fraternity; Who's Who in California; Who's Who in the West; Men of Achievement; Noteworthy American and Community Leaders; International Who's Who of Intellectuals; California Dental License; General Anesthesia Permit; Articles published: "The Granular Cell Ameloblastoma" (1964), "Malignant Mixed Tumor of the Palate" (1965), "Massive Oral Hemangioma with Phlebolithiasis" (1966), and "Granular Cell Ameloblastoma with Remarkable Mucin Production" (1966). **Education:** John Gaston Hospital – Oral & Maxillofacial Surgery: Residency (1962–1964), Internship (1961–1962); University of Tennessee, College of Dentistry, D.D.S., President of Freshman Class, President of Xi Psi Phi Dental Fraternity (1957–1961); University of Oklahoma (1954–1957). **Personal:** Married to Karen in 1975. Two children: John Michael and Rhonda Drake and a foster son, Brian Minert. Dr. Drake enjoys golf and spectator sports.

Timothy H. Droege, D.M.D.
Sole Practitioner
Timothy H. Droege, D.M.D.
111 N. Main St.
Breese, IL 62230
(618) 526–2020
Fax: Please mail or call

8021

Business Information: The Dental Offices of Timothy H. Droege, D.M.D. is a full–service, family practice dentistry office, providing cosmetic, general dentistry, and orthodontics. A practicing dentist for the past eight years and Board–Certified in Orthodontics, Dr. Droege established the Practice in 1987. He oversees the administrative operations for associates and a support staff of nine, in addition to his daily patient practice. **Career Steps:** Sole Practitioner, Timothy H. Droege, D.M.D. (1987–Present). **Associations & Accomplishments:** President (1995), Breese Lions Club; President (1990–1991), Chamber of Commerce; President (1995), Clinton County Health Board; American Dental Association; International Association of Orthodontics; Academy of General Dentistry. **Education:** SIU – Acton Dental School, D.M.D. (1987). **Personal:** Married to Kathryn in 1985. Three children: Kelly, Jessica, and Scott. Dr. Droege enjoys golf and hunting.

Daniel A. Duran, D.D.S.
Dentist
The Dental Office of Daniel A. Duran, D.D.S., P.A.
2909 Hillrise Drive
Las Cruces, NM 88011
(505) 521–1664
Fax: Please mail or call

8021

Business Information: The Dental Office of Daniel A. Duran, D.D.S., P.A. is a full–service, family practice three–chair dentistry office, providing cosmetic, general dentistry, and limited oral surgery. Establishing his private dental practice upon conferral of his doctorate in dentistry in 1989, Dr. Duran oversees all administrative operations for a support staff of six, in addition to his daily patient practice. **Career Steps:** Dentist, The Dental Office of Daniel A. Duran, D.D.S., P.A. (1989–Present). **Associations & Accomplishments:** American Dental Association; New Mexico Dental Association; Academy of General Dentistry; Delta Sigma Delta Dental Fraternity. **Education:** University of Colorado, D.D.S. (1988); New Mexico State University, B.S. in Biology. **Personal:** Married to Debra in 1988. Two children: Craig Anthony and Kacie Lyn Duran. Dr. Duran enjoys golf, and coaching children's sports.

Andrew M. Eisenberg, D.D.S.
Owner and Dentist
The Office of Andrew M. Eisenberg, D.D.S., P.A.
601 North Flamingo Road, #415
Pembroke Pines, FL 33028
(305) 438–4444
Fax: Please mail or call

8021

Business Information: The Office of Andrew M. Eisenburg, D.D.S., P.A. is a general practice dental facility, primarily focusing on cosmetic dentistry. Establishing the sole practice in 1979, Dr. Eisenberg oversees an administrative and hygienist support staff of five in two locations (Miami and Hollywood), in addition to his daily patient practice. A special note of interest is that one of his patients — Barbara Bann — was the winner of the 1986 Star Search Model competition. In concurrence with his dental practice, he is Board Chairman of a large poultry export farming concern — Cypress Farms, Inc. Upon graduating from Georgetown University Dental School, Dr. Eisenberg served as a military dentist with the U.S. Marine Corps, stationed at Parris Island, S.C. and also Beaufort Marine Corp Air Station, S.C. **Career Steps:** Owner and Dentist, Andrew M. Eisenberg, D.D.S., P.A. (1979–Present). **Associations & Accomplishments:** American Dental Association; Florida Dental Association; East Coast District Dental Association. **Education:** Georgetown University School of Dentistry, D.D.S. (1975); Adelphi University, B.A. **Personal:** Married to Joyce in 1980. Three children: Tiffany, Brittany and Michael. Dr. Eisenberg enjoys snow skiing, working out and collecting Disney memorabilia.

Saleh A. Elahwal, D.D.S.

Senior Associate
Dental Art Center
481 83rd Street, Floor 2
Brooklyn, NY 11209–4512
(718) 748–1122
Fax: Please mail or call

8021

Business Information: The Dental Art Center, established in 1990, is a full–service, family practice dentistry office, providing cosmetic, general dentistry, orthodontics, periodontics, and oral surgery consisting of one full time dentist and two part–time associates. Establishing his sole practice dental office in 1990, Dr. Elahwal serves as Senior Associate, responsible for all aspects of operations, including providing dental care to patients. **Career Steps:** Senior Associate, Dental Art Center (1990–Present). **Associations & Accomplishments:** Chamber of Commerce. **Education:** New York University, D.D.S. (1989) **Personal:** One child: Camillia. Dr. Elahwal enjoys reading, light music and travel during his leisure time.

William W. Eng, D.D.S, P.C.
Dentist
The Office of William W. Eng, D.D.S., P.C.
2101 Crawford Street, #107
Houston, TX 77002–8941
(713) 655–8100
Fax: (713) 655–8109

8021

Business Information: The Office of William W. Eng, D.D.S., P.C. is a general and cosmetic family dental practice providing the most updated and technological services available, including invisible fillings, teeth whitening, and implants that look and feel natural. Established in 1994, the Office currently employs four people. As a dentist, Dr. Eng is responsible for the care and treatment of patients. Dr. Eng is always involved with hundreds of hours of Continuing Education in order to be current with the latest dental procedures. His goal is to provide patients with preventive measures and restoration to last a lifetime. **Career Steps:** Dentist, The Office of William W. Eng, D.D.S., P.C. (1994–Present); Assistant Professor, Baylor College of Dentistry (1993–1994). **Education:** Baylor College of Dentistry, graduated with honors (1993). **Personal:** Married with two children. Dr. Eng enjoys reading, travel, stamp collecting and a variety of sports.

Cayetano L. Farcon, D.M.D.
Dentist
Dental Image
42 Parsonage Road
Edison, NJ 08837–2416
(908) 494–6161
Fax: (908) 494–3504

8021

Business Information: Dental Image is a full–service, general dentistry practice providing cosmetic, family dentistry and oral surgery. Establishing the practice in 1993, Dr. Farcon oversees a support staff of five, in addition to his daily patient practice. **Career Steps:** Dentist, Dental Image (1993–Present). **Associations & Accomplishments:** American Dental Association; New Jersey Dental Association; Academy of General Dentistry; Middlesex County Dental Association. **Education:** Tufts University School of Dental Medicine, D.M.D. (1992); Tufts University, B.S. in Biology (1987); JFK Medical Center, Edison, NJ, General Practice Residency (1992–1993). **Personal:** Married to Dr. Armie B. Farcon in 1994. Dr. Farcon enjoys ballroom dancing and travel.

Kenneth P. Ferentchak, D.D.S.
President and Owner
Kenneth Ferentchak, D.D.S., S.C.
827 North 68th Street
Wauwatosa, WI 53213
(414) 476–2243
Fax: Please mail or call

8021

Business Information: Kenneth Ferentchak, D.D.S., S.C., established in 1990, is a private, full–service, general practice dental office, providing cosmetic, family dentistry, and oral surgery. A practicing dentist since 1988, Dr. Ferentchak established his sole practice dentistry office in 1990, providing all aspects of dental care to patients. Concurrent with his private dental practice, he serves as Dentist at West Allis Dental Care and Bayview Dental Care. **Career Steps:** President and Owner, Kenneth Ferentchak, D.D.S., S.C. (1990–Present); Dentist, West Allis Dental Care (1992–Present); Dentist, Bayview Dental Care (1993–Present); Dentist, Dr. Michael Costello (1989–1990). **Associations & Accomplishments:** Academy of General Dentistry; American Academy of Cosmetic Dentistry; Interviewed in local paper. **Education:** Marquette University Dental School, D.D.S. (1988); University of Illinois, B.S. in Biology. **Personal:** Married to Pamela in 1991. One child: Kevin. Dr. Ferentchak enjoys spending time with his family and all sports.

Richlyn D. Fernandes, D.D.S.
Sole Practitioner
Richlyn D. Fernandes, D.D.S.
8127 Mariner's Drive, Suite 301
Stockton, CA 95219
(209) 476–1001
Fax: Please mail or call

8021

Business Information: Richlyn D. Fernandes, D.D.S. is a full–service, private practice dentistry office, providing general and cosmetic dentistry. A practicing dentist since 1988, Dr. Fernandes established her sole practice dentistry office in 1989. She is responsible for providing diagnosis and treatment to patients of all ages — the majority of her patients include adults age 55 and older and children — in general and cosmetic dentistry. Concurrent with her private dentistry practice, she serves as Ship Dentist for the Holland America Line – Westours, Inc. and as Site Auditor for Dental Benefit Providers of California, Inc. **Career Steps:** Sole Practitioner, Richlyn D. Fernandes, D.D.S. (1989–Present); Ship's Dentist, Holland American Line – Westours, Inc. (1995–Present); Site Auditor, Dental Benefit Providers of California, Inc. (1995–Present) **Associations & Accomplishments:** San Joaquin Dental Society; California Dental Association; American Dental Association; National Health Reform Advocate; Xi Psi Phi; National Headache Institute; Independent Dentists of America; Former Board Member, The American Red Cross **Education:** University of the Pacific School of Dentistry, D.D.S. (1988); University of the Pacific, B.A. in Biological Sciences, English Grammatics and Linguistics (1985); Chabot College – Hayward, CA, A.A. in General Education and Pre–Dental Academia. **Personal:** Dr. Fernandes enjoys painting, cooking and crafts.

Debra M. Ferraiolo, D.M.D.
Partner
The Dental Offices of David J. Martin, D.D.S., F.A.G.D.
336 Union Boulevard
Totowa, NJ 07512
(201) 942–6467
Fax: (201) 942–7763

8021

Business Information: The Dental Offices of David J. Martin, D.D.S., F.A.G.D. is a full–service, family practice dentistry office, providing cosmetic, general dentistry, and oral surgery. A practicing dentist since 1987, Dr. Ferraiolo joined the Practice as Associate in 1988. Currently serving as one of two partners since 1992, she is responsible for providing quality dental care to patients. **Career Steps:** The Dental Offices of David J. Martin, D.D.S., F.A.G.D.: Partner (1992–Present), Associate (1988–1992). **Associations & Accomplishments:** American Dental Association; Academy of General Dentistry; New Jersey Dental Association – Passaic County Chapter. **Education:** Fairleigh S. Dickinson, Jr. College of Dental Medicine, D.M.D. (1987); Fordham University, B.S. in Biology/A.A. in Italian. **Personal:** Dr. Ferraiolo enjoys travel, shopping, and exercise.

Stephanie H. Foster, D.M.D., FAGD

Dentist, Owner and Partner

Dr. Stephanie H. Foster, D.M.D.

P.O. Box 904
Concordville, PA 19331–0904
(610) 558–0416
Fax: (610) 558–1005
E-mail: see below

8021

Business Information: The Office of Dr. Stephanie H. Foster, D.M.D. is a general practice dental facility. Established in 1993, the Office currently employs 2 Dentists and 10 support staff. As Dentist, Owner and Partner, Dr. Foster practices advanced cosmetic dentistry, dentures, oral photos, bleaching, and porcelain procedures. The only female partnership in the area, Dr. Foster and her associate — Marie G. Scott — are proud of being a comprehensive practice. Dr. Foster hopes to become more involved in the local and Pennsylvania dental associations and plans to write a humorous yet informative book on the trials and tribulations of the dental profession. She can also be reached through the Internet via: TWISTATWRK@AOL.COM **Career Steps:** Dentist, Owner and Partner, The Office of Dr. Stephanie H. Foster, D.M.D. (1993–Present); Dentist, Private Practice (1989–1993); Dentist, Prison Health Services (1988–1989). **Associations & Accomplishments:** Xi Psi Phi Dental Fraternity; Life Member, Alpha Phi Omega National Service Fraternity; Fellowship Recipient, Academy of General Dentistry; Published in local newspapers; Occasional public speaking appearences. **Education:** Temple University, D.M.D. (1987); Academy of General Dentistry, Fellowship Award (1995). **Personal:** Married to Paul E. in 1984, she has two sons. Dr. Foster enjoys Tai Kwan Do and spending time with her sons.

Christopher J. Fotinos, D.D.S.

Sole Practitioner

Dental Office of Christopher J. Fotinos, D.D.S.

605 East Chapman Avenue
Orange, CA 92666–1604
(714) 538–5182
Fax: (714) 675–6753

8021

Business Information: Dental Office of Christopher J. Fotinos, D.D.S. is a general dental practice specializing in restorative dentistry for professional team athletes, and is on the medical staff's of the Anaheim Mighty Ducks and California Angels. Establishing his private practice in 1990, Dr. Fotinos directs a support staff of six, in addition to his daily patient practice. **Career Steps:** Sole Practitioner, The Dental Office of Christopher J. Fotinos, D.D.S. (1990–Present). **Associations & Accomplishments:** American Dental Association; California Dental Association; American Academy of Implantology; Academy of Professional Team Dentistry; Orange County Dental Society. **Education:** University of the Pacific, D.D.S. (1990); San Diego State University, B.S. in Biology. **Personal:** Dr. Fotinos enjoys studying architecture and photography and is an avid athlete.

Salvatore L. Franco, D.M.D.

Dentist

The Office of Dr. Salvatore L. Franco, D.M.D.

8 –A East 63rd Street
New York, NY 10021–7210
(212) 888–6214
Fax: (212) 688–7735

8021

Business Information: Established in 1993, the Office of Dr. Salvatore L. Franco, D.M.D. is a private practice general and cosmetic dentistry facility. As Dentist, Dr. Franco is responsible for the care and treatment of patients. Concurrent to his private dental practice, Dr. Franco also does some volunteer instructing at Columbia University. **Career Steps:** Dentist, The Office of Dr. Salvatore L. Franco, D.M.D. (1993–Present); Faculty, Columbia University School of Dentistry, (1991–1993). **Associations & Accomplishments:** International Dental Federation; Academy of General Dentistry; Dental Study Club of New York; American Dental Association; Pennsylvania Dental Alumni Association and Club; American Association of French Speaking Health Professionals; Dr. Franco is fluent in five languages. **Education:** Columbia University School of Dentistry: A.E.G.D. II (1993), A.E.G.D. I (1992); University of Pennsylvania, D.M.D. (1990); Emory University, B.S. in Chemistry (1981); Collegio San Gabriele, Rome, Italy, Maturita Scientifica (1976). **Personal:** Dr. Franco enjoys golf, fencing, philately (stamp collecting), and international travel.

Karen E. Franklin, D.D.S.

Dentist

Cody Dental Center

18113 West Chicago Avenue
Detroit, MI 48228–1836
(313) 837–4700
Fax: Please mail or call

8021

Business Information: Cody Dental Center is a general practice dental facility for adults and children. Established in 1993, the Cody Dental Center currently employs 4 support staff. A practicing Dentist for over 15 years, Dr. Franklin bought Cody Dental Center in 1993. She practices all areas of general family dentistry. **Career Steps:** Dentist, Cody Dental Center (1993–Present); Associate Dentist, Private Practice (1987–1992); Staff Dentist, Samaritan Health Center (1984–1987); Dentist, U.S.P.H.S. (1982–1984). **Associations & Accomplishments:** American Dental Association; Michigan Dental Association; Detroit Dental Society; National Dental Association; National Association of Female Executives; Wolverine Dental Society; Zonta International; National Association of Women Business Owners. **Education:** Meharry Medical College, School of Dentistry, D.D.S. (1982); Wayne State University. **Personal:** Three children: Chris, Ingrid and Alison. Dr. Franklin enjoys reading, gardening, collecting dolls and angels, and travel.

Robert E. Gan, D.M.D.

Dentist

Cherry Ridge Dental Center

RR 2 Box 3145
Honesdale, PA 18431–9600
Fax: Please mail or call

8021

Business Information: Cherry Ridge Dental Center is a full–service, general dentistry group practice, providing cosmetic, general dentistry, and oral surgery. Established in 1965, the Practice currently employs 10 people. Joining the Group upon the conferral of his dental degree in 1985, Dr. Gan provides all areas of general dentistry care. **Career Steps:** Dentist, Cherry Ridge Dental Center (1985–Present). **Associations & Accomplishments:** American Dental Association; Pennsylvania Dental Association; Scranton District Dental Society. **Education:** Fairleigh Dickinson University, D.M.D. (1985), B.S. **Personal:** Married to Mary J. Gan in 1988. Two children: Stephen Robert and Alicia Marie Gan. Dr. Gan enjoys sports, gardening, and travel.

Anjani Gandhi, MDS, DMD

Endodontic Associate

Dr. T.P. Doolittle, P.C.

638 Western Avenue
Albany, NY 12203
(518) 482–0403
Fax: (518) 482–0135

8021

Business Information: Dr. T.P. Doolittle, P.C. is a private dental practice specializing in Endodontics (root canal therapy). Established in 1972, the Office currently employs 8 Dentists and support staff. As Endodontic Associate, Dr. Gandhi is responsible for the care and treatment of patients. Attending Dental School in India. She is a Volunteer with the Tri City India Association and also the Secretary of the 3rd District Dental Society. From a family of Dentists, she is very dedicated to his work. **Career Steps:** Endodontic Associate, The Office of Dr. T.P. Doolittle, P.C. (1992–Present); Clinical Instructor, Department of Endodontics, Tufts School of Dental Medicine (1988–1991); Chief Resident, Nair Hospital Dental College (1985–1987); Board Certified, Diploma of american Board of Education. **Associations & Accomplishments:** Secretary and Chairman Council of Relief, Third District Dental Society of New York (1993–1996); Representative, Third District to New York State Association of Endodontics and the American Association of Endodontics; Secretary and Treasurer, Albany County Dental Study Club (1994–1995); Secretary, Treasurer and Founder, Capital District Women's Dental Study Group; President, Albany County Dental Club (1995–1996). **Education:** Tufts University School of Medicine: DMD (1991), Endodontics Specialty; Nair Dental College – Bombay, India, BDS, MDS. **Personal:** Dr. Gandhi enjoys racquetball, and music appreciation.

Donatienne Gilain, D.M.D.

Owner

Dentoclinic

600 Rue–Pierre–Caisse
St–Jean–Sur Richelieu, Quebec J3A 1M1
(514) 348–4956
Fax: (514) 348–4956

8021

Business Information: Dentoclinic is a general practice dental clinic. Established in 1985, the Clinic is comprised of four dentists, with required support staff. Establishing his private practice upon the conferral of his dental degree in 1987, Dr. Gilain serves as Owner, responsible for all aspects of the Clinic's day–to–day operations, including the treatment of patients and administration. **Career Steps:** Owner, Dentoclinic (1987–Present). **Associations & Accomplishments:** Societe Dentaire du Hout Richelieu; Association Dentaine Canadienne; Odre des Dentistes du Quebec; Association des Chirogiens Dentistes du Quebec. **Education:** University of Montreal, D.M.D. (1987). **Personal:** Three children: Nicolas, Christian, and Laetitia. Dr. Gilain enjoys skiing and horseback riding.

David H. Gisborne, D.M.D.

Dentist

The Office of Dr. David H. Gisborne, D.M.D.

146 SW 2nd Avenue
Canby, OR 97013
(503) 266–5596
Fax: Please mail or call

8021

Business Information: The Office of Dr. David H. Gisborne, D.M.D. is a general practice dental facility. Establishing his private practice in 1983 in a small Oregon community, Dr. Gisborne is responsible for the care and treatment of his dental patients. He chose the dental profession because it seemed to have a unique blend of arts and science, and Dr. Gisborne plans to continue to serve the community with current dental needs for a long time. After completing his degree in Dentistry, Dr. Gisborne acquired a General Practice Residency at Los Angeles County Hospital where he improved his diagnostic and operating skills dramatically. **Career Steps:** Dentist, The Office of Dr. David H. Gisborne, D.M.D. (1983–Present). **Associations & Accomplishments:** American Dental Association; Oregon Dental Association; Multnomah Dental Society; Academy of General Dentistry. **Education:** Oregon Health Sciences University, D.M.D. (1983); Los Angeles County Hospital and the University of Southern California, General Practice Resident in Dentistry (1988). **Personal:** Married to N. Jo Collins in 1979. Dr. Gisborne enjoys golf and travel.

Rose Gonzales–Mugaburu, D.M.D.

Sole Practitioner

Soft Touch Dentistry

545 Island Road, Suite 1A
Ramsey, NJ 07446
(201) 818–6565
Fax: (201) 818–6555

8021

Business Information: Soft Touch Dentistry is a full–service, family practice dentistry office, providing cosmetics (laminates, bleaching, tooth–colored restorations), periodontics, fillings, crowns, etc. — the major portion of its patient focus is for pediatrics. Establishing his sole practice dentistry office upon the conferral of his dental degree in 1989, Dr. Gonzales–Mugaburu oversees all administrative operations and support staff, in addition to his daily patient practice. **Career Steps:** Dentist, Soft Touch Dentistry (1989–Present). **Associations & Accomplishments:** American Dental Association; American Academy of Cosmetic Dentistry; New Jersey Dental Association; Bergen County Dental Association; Academy of General Dentistry; American Society of Dentistry for Children; Mahwah Chamber of Commerce; Allendale Chamber of Commerce. **Education:** Fairleigh Dickinson University Dental School, D.M.D. (1989); Fairleigh Dickinson University, B.S. (1983). **Personal:** Dr. Gonzales–Mugaburu enjoys dogs, tennis, and racquetball.

Steven Gorman, D.D.S.

Sole Practitioner
The Office of Steven A. Gorman, D.D.S., P.A.
700 Village Center Drive, #100
North Oaks, MN 55127–3020
(612) 483–5134
Fax: (612) 483–2923

8021

Business Information: The Office of Steven A. Gorman, D.D.S., P.A. is a private practice dental facility with an emphasis on cosmetic and restorative dentistry. In private practice since 1981, Dr. Gorman is being accredited by the American Academy of Cosmetic Dentistry and is a member of the American Academy of General Dentistry. **Career Steps:** Sole Practitioner, The Office of Steven A. Gorman, D.D.S., P.A. (1981–Present). **Associations & Accomplishments:** American Dental Association; Academy of General Dentistry; American Academy of Cosmetic Dentistry; Minnesota Dental Association; Former President, Little Lakes Little League; Board Member, South St. Paul Education Foundation; President, Minnesota Alliance of Concerned Dentists; Interviewed on healthcare review issues. **Education:** University of Minnesota: D.D.S. (1981), B.S. (1979); University of Notre Dame, B.A. (1977). **Personal:** Married to Connie M. in 1988. Three children: Emily, Anna and Madeline. Dr. Gorman enjoys baseball, golf, basketball, running and reading.

Marie–Kateri Goulet, D.M.D.

Dentist
Marie–Kateri Goulet, D.M.D.
1376 Sainte–Catherine West, Suite 206
Montreal, Quebec H3G 1P8
(514) 861–6106
Fax: Please mail or call

8021

Business Information: Marie–Kateri Goulet, D.M.D. is a general practice dental office specializing in cosmetic dentistry and "smile design". Established in 1988, the Practice employs three people. As a Dentist, Dr. Goulet spends most of her time making beautiful smiles, including full mouth rehabilitation. She enjoys creating remarkable smiles. Additional duties include performing all dental and related services on patients, and maintaining quality of care and service. Dr. Goulet also holds an industry related patent, was the first dentist in Canada to design her own office and office uniforms following the current trend in fashion, and consults with other dentists regarding her ideas. **Career Steps:** Dentist, Marie–Kateri Goulet, D.M.D. (1988–Present). **Associations & Accomplishments:** American Academy of Cosmetic Dentistry; Recipient of Smile Contest Award, American Academy of Cosmetic Dentistry (1995); Smile Design Council; Author of a chapter in: "Current Opinion in Cosmetic Dentistry" and is an editor for a dental publication. Numerous reports were made about her in health & beauty magazines, television interviews and talk shows. "LaPresse", the most important French newspaper in America gave a two full page report on her. **Education:** University of Montreal, D.M.D.; McGill University, Multi–disciplinary Residency Program. **Personal:** Dr. Goulet enjoys fashion, sports, tennis, rollerblading, swimming, skiing, going to the gym, mountain biking, cycling, and jogging.

Alex M. Greenberg, D.D.S.

Sole Dental Practitioner
Dentofacial Associates of New York, L.L.P.
30 East 60th Street, Suite 1504
New York, NY 10022
(212) 319–9700
Fax: (212) 319–9778

8021

Business Information: Dentofacial Associates of New York, L.L.P. is a specialty dentistry practice, providing oral and maxillofacial surgery — particularly focusing on dental implantology, cleft palate, jaw fractures, and corrective jaw surgery. A practicing dentist since 1983, Dr. Greenberg established Dentofacial Associates of New York in 1987. As Sole Practitioner, he oversees all administrative operations for associates and a support staff of eight, in addition to his daily patient practice. **Career Steps:** Sole Practitioner, Dentofacial Associates of New York, L.L.P. (1987–Present) **Associations & Accomplishments:** American Dental Association; American Association of Oral and Maxillofacial Surgeons; New York Academy of Dentistry; Textbook Author, Craniomaxillofacial Fractures: Principles of Internal Fixation Using the AO/ASIF Technique, Springer–Verlag, New York. **Education:** Columbia University, D.D.S. (1983); Lafayette College, B.S.; Mt. Si-

nai School of Medicine, Oral and Maxillofacial Surgery Residency; University of Basel, Basel, Switzerland, Maxillofacial Fellowship. **Personal:** Dr. Greenberg enjoys marathon running.

Kristal Greniuk–Wioncek, D.D.S.

Dentist
Singelyn & Greniuk, D.D.S., P.C.
5640 West Maple Road, Suite 203
West Bloomfield, MI 48322–3718
(810) 851–6430
Fax: (810) 851–1617

8021

Business Information: Singelyn & Greniuk, D.D.S., P.C. is a full–service, family practice dentistry office, specializing in orthodontics and dental implants. Established in 1994, the Practice currently employs 12 people. With nine years experience in the dentistry field, Dr. Greniuk–Wioncek joined Singelyn & Singelyn in 1992. Currently serving as Dentist, she provides family dental services, concentrating in general dentistry and orthodontics. Concurrent with her dental practice, she provides pro bono dental hygiene community services in schools and health centers, as well as conducts lectures on dental hygiene at hospitals. **Career Steps:** Singelyn & Greniuk, D.D.S., P.C.: Dentist (1994–Present), Associate Dentist (1992–1993); Orthodontic Assistant, University of Detroit (1986–1988). **Associations & Accomplishments:** Polish National Alliance; American Dental Association; Michigan Dental Association; Oakland County Dental Society; Vice President, Detroit District Dental Society; St. Robert's Catholic Church; Academy of General Dentistry; Polish Dental National Arts Group. **Education:** University of Detroit – Mercy, D.D.S. (1992); Completed several Continuing Education courses since graduation, as well as extensive training in the field of Orthodontics. **Personal:** Married to John M. Wioncek, Jr. in 1993. One child: Katrina Louise. Dr. Greniuk–Wioncek enjoys family activities.

Dr. Dean Paul Gresko

Dental Surgeon
Northwood Family Dental
509 Edward Street, North
Thunder Bay, Ontario P7C 4R1
(807) 475–7500
Fax: (807) 475–7690

8021

Business Information: Northwood Family Dental is a general practice, dental clinic run by two dentists. The Clinic presently employs two dentists and ten employees overall. A practicing dentist since 1992, Dr. Gresko oversees all administrative operations for associates and support staff, in addition to his daily patient practice. **Career Steps:** Dental Surgeon, Northwood Family Dental (1992–Present). **Associations & Accomplishments:** Commanding Officer, 18 (Thunder Bay) Medical Company – Canadian Armed Forces; St. John Ambulance – District Dental Surgeon; Order of St. Lazarus Society; Canadian Ski Patrol Systems – Patroller. **Education:** University of Minnesota, D.D.S. (1992); Lakehead University: H.B.Sc., B.Adm. **Personal:** Dr. Gresko enjoys sailing and being a member of the local art gallery.

Randall O. Grill, D.D.S.

Dentist
Gentle Dentistry Group
119 East Lincoln Avenue
Wellington, KS 67152–3046
(316) 326–7983
Fax: (316) 326–8086
Email: Dr2step@aol.com

8021

Business Information: The Office of Randall O. Grill, D.D.S. is a general practice dental facility. Establishing the private family dental practice in 1991, Dr. Grill directs a support staff of seven, in addition to his daily patient practice. A Dentist since 1976, Dr. Grill decided upon his career after spending time on the golf course with his father and fellow golfers who were in the dental field. Choosing his career when he was in ninth grade, Dr. Grill loves what he does. In addition to being a Dentist, he is also an independent Disc Jockey providing his services for dances and parties, and a professional dancer. He is a Bronze 3 Ballroom dancer and teaches a variety of dance in the community, including Line Dancing and Latin Dancing, one of his favorites. **Career Steps:** Dentist, The Office of Randall O. Grill, D.D.S. (1991–Present); Associate Professor of Clinical Operative Dentistry, UMKC Dental School (1987–1988); Dentist, United States Air Force (1975–1979). **Associations & Accomplishments:** President, Wellington Chamber of Commerce (1995); Rotary International; Board of

Directors, Wellington Senior Center (1994, 1995); Sons of American Legion; Life Member, Christian Dental Association; Argonia Wesleyan Church; Eagle Scout (1964); Sigma Chi; Private pilot and certified scuba diver. **Education:** UMKC Dental School, D.D.S. (1976); Kansas State University, B.S. (1972); Pankey Institute (1987). **Personal:** Married to Pam in 1994. Three children: Amy, Ashley, and Aaron. Dr. Grill enjoys dancing, reading, walking, and being a disc jockey for local dances.

Robert E. Grill Jr., D.M.D.

General Dentistry Practitioner
–Independent–
905 Westfield Road
Scotch Plains, NJ 07076–2123
(908) 889–5271
Fax: (908) 889–7244

8021

Business Information: Dr. Robert Grill Jr., a practicing dentist since 1986, is an associate in his father's general dentistry practice. He concentrates his practice in the field of family dentistry, and has future plans to expand his field of expertise into dental anesthesia. This would be a pioneer endeavor in this field of specialty for the state of New Jersey. **Career Steps:** General Dentistry Practitioner, Robert E. Grill, D.M.D. Family Dentistry (1986–Present) **Associations & Accomplishments:** American Dental Association; New Jersey Dental Association; Central Dental Society **Education:** University of Pittsburgh: D.M.D. (1986); B.S. (1982) **Personal:** Married to Mary Louise in 1987. Three children: Sarah, Robert John (B.J.) and August. Dr. Grill enjoys tropical fish (particularly African Cichlids) and motorcycling.

Robert A. Grollman, D.D.S., F.A.G.D.

Chief Executive Officer and General Dentistry Practitioner
Dental Offices of Robert A. Grollman, D.D.S., F.A.G.D.
160 N. Main Street
Alpharetta, GA 30201–1623
(770) 475–4300
Fax: Please mail or call

8021

Business Information: Dental Offices of Robert A. Grollman, D.D.S., F.A.G.D. is a general dentistry practice, providing family dentistry, orthodontics, and oral surgery. A practicing dentist since 1967, Dr. Grollman established the practice in 1972. As Chief Executive Officer he oversees all associates and an administrative support staff of four, in addition to his daily patient practice. **Career Steps:** Chief Executive Officer and General Dentistry Practitioner, Dental Offices of Robert A. Grollman, D.D.S., F.A.G.D. (1972–Present) **Associations & Accomplishments:** Fellow, Academy of General Dentistry (1991); American Dental Association; Georgia Dental Association; Alpha Omega Dental Fraternity. **Education:** Emory University, D.D.S. (1967). **Personal:** Married to Dinah in 1972. Two children: Jenny and Robbie.

Gerald B. Grossman, D.D.S.

Partner
Ganz & Grossman
1600 Stewart Avenue
Westbury, NY 11590–6611
(516) 683–0888
Fax: (516) 683–0892

8021

Business Information: Ganz & Grossman is a prestigious, group dental practice specializing in quality treatment of difficult dental problems, usually on a referral basis, such as dental implantology, cosmetics and bridges. Ganz & Grossman currently employs four dentists, specializing in surgical implants, prosthetic implants, periodontology, and an associate who serves as an instructor at Stoneybrook University. As Partner, Dr. Grossman is responsible for providing patient care, specializing in prosthetic implants. Career milestones include the presentation of a paper on Aesthetics in Toronto for the Academy of General Dentistry Meeting and was the recipient of an award for the Best Clinic. Concurrent with his position, he is a frequent lecturer across the U.S. and Canada and an Instructor at Nassau County Medical Center. He previously taught for fifteen years at the Long Island Jewish Hillside Medical Center. **Career Steps:** Partner, Ganz & Grossman; Instructor, Nassau County Medical Center. **Associations & Accomplishments:** Academy of Osseointegration; Implants Certified; Fellow, American Society of Dental Aesthetics; Published numerous articles in dental journals. **Education:** New York University, D.D.S. (1969). **Personal:** Married to Cheryl in 1965. Two children: Michelle and David. Dr. Grossman enjoys golf, photography and gourmet cooking.

Lawrence P. Hale, D.D.S.

Owner and Dentist
Lawrence P. Hale, D.D.S.
5558 Colerain Avenue
Cincinnati, OH 45239–6802
(513) 542–2070
Fax: (513) 741–0134

8021

Business Information: Lawrence P. Hale, D.D.S. is a private, solo practice family dentistry office, including orthodontics and implants. Established in 1987, the Practice operates three offices locally and currently employs five people. A new multi–clinical practice opened in 1995 with all the latest technological advances available. As Owner and Dentist, Dr. Hale is responsible for all administrative operations, in addition to his daily patient practice. **Career Steps:** Owner and Dentist, Lawrence P. Hale, D.D.S. (1987–Present). **Associations & Accomplishments:** American Orthodontic Society; Midwest Implant Institute; Eagle Scout and Volunteer for the Boy Scouts of America; Mason 32; Scottish Rite Lodge; Frequent lecturer to professional associations on implants, gum tissue and others. **Education:** Case Western Reserve, D.D.S. (1986); Northeast Regional Board Clinical Exam, scored perfectly (100). **Personal:** Married to Patricia in 1994. Four children: Andy, Ashley, Julie, and Patty. Dr. Hale enjoys computer games, reading, tennis, and golf.

Douglas R. Hamill, D.D.S.

President
The Dental Office of Douglas R. Hamill, D.D.S., P.C.
407 University Avenue #104
Syracuse, NY 13210–1834
(315) 476–3552
Fax: Please mail or call

8021

Business Information: The Dental Office of Douglas R. Hamill, D.D.S., P.C. is a full–service, private practice dentistry office specializing in crowns, bridges and cosmetic bonding. Established in 1985, the dental practice employs five dental professionals. Attaining his dental degree in 1983, Dr. Hamell established his own private dental practice in 1985. As President, he is responsible for all aspects of operations and provides general dentistry services to patients. **Career Steps:** President, The Dental Office of Douglas R. Hamill, D.D.S., P.C. (1985–Present); Dentist, Howard P. Roswick, D.D.S., P.C. (1983–1985). **Associations & Accomplishments:** Former President, Syracuse Host Lions Club; American Dental Association; New York State Dental Association; 5th District Dental Society; Academy of General Dentists; Onandaga Dental Society; Volunteer Dental Instructor, St. Joseph Hospital. **Education:** University of Buffalo School of Dentistry, D.D.S. (1983); University fo Vermont, B.S. in Economics. **Personal:** Married to Pamela K. in 1985. Two children: Jeremy and Tyler. Dr. Hamill enjoys hockey, karate, tennis, and coaching children's hockey & soccer team.

Day Cursons Hannah

Dentist
Dr. Day Cursons Hannah, D.D.S.
120 Jarvis Street
Ft. Erie, Ontario L2A 2S4
(905) 871–5652
Fax: Please mail or call

8021

Business Information: Dr. Day Cursons Hannah, D.D.S. is a full–service dentistry practice. As Dentist, Dr. Hannah is responsible for all daily operations of his practice pertaining to patient dental care. Established in 1970, Dr. Day Cursons Hannah, D.D.S. employs 5 people. **Career Steps:** Dentist, Dr. Day Cursons Hannah, D.D.S. (1970–Present). **Associations & Accomplishments:** Former President, Niagara Peninsula Dental Association; Director, Kinsman Minor Hockey Association of Fort ON; Assistant Hockey Coach, University of Buffalo; Director of North End Businessman Association–Fort Erie. **Education:** SUNY at Buffalo, D.D.S. (1970). **Personal:** Married to Sue in 1973. Three children: Julie Ann, Katie, and Jamie. Dr. Hannah enjoys hockey, golf, and gardening. He has scaled his practice back to four days a week, to allow more time for hockey management.

Alan D. Hecht, D.D.S.

Senior Dental Practitioner
The Dental Office of Alan D. Hecht
5838 Main Street
New Port Richey, FL 34652–2714
(813) 849–5696
Fax: (813) 849–0405

8021

Business Information: The Dental Office of Alan D. Hecht is a full–service, family practice dentistry office, providing cosmotic, general dentiatry, and oral surgery. The Practice consists of two dentists and two hygienists. Establishing his dental practice upon the conferral of his dental degree in 1987, Dr. Hecht is responsible for overseeing all administrative operations for associates and support staff, in addition to his daily patient practice. **Career Steps:** Senior Dental Practitioner, The Dental Office of Alan D. Hecht (1987–Present). **Associations & Accomplishments:** West Coast Dental Association; West Pasco Dental Association; Florida Dental Association; American Dental Association. **Education:** University of Texas Health Science Center–San Antonio, D.D.S. (1987); Southwestern Adventist College, B.S. in Chemistry. **Personal:** Dr. Hecht enjoys collecting toys and playing the guitar. Dr. Hecht occasionally attends the sporting events in Tampa Bay including, the Tampa Bay Buccaneers, Lightning, and Storm.

Philip N. Heinecke, D.D.S, F.A.G.D.

Sole Practitioner
The Dental Office of Philip N. Heinecke, D.D.S., F.A.G.D.
103 Bell Avenue
Brooksville, FL 34601–2603
(904) 796–3380
Fax: Please mail or call

8021

Business Information: The Dental Office of Philip N. Heinecke, D.D.S., F.A.G.D. is a full–service family practice dentistry office, providing cosmetic, general dentistry, and oral surgery. Establishing his sole dental practice upon the conferral of his degree in 1986, Dr. Heinecke oversees all administrative operations of a staff of three, in addition to his daily patient practice. Additionally, he is responsible for finances, sales, public relations, and strategic planning. **Career Steps:** Sole Practitioner, The Dental Office of Philip N. Heinecke, D.D.S., F.A.G.D. (1987–Present). **Associations & Accomplishments:** Fellow, Academy of General Dentistry. **Education:** University of Nebraska, D.D.S. (1986); Kansas State University, B.S. magna cum laude (1982); University of Florida, General Practice Residency (1987). **Personal:** Married to Charlene in 1989. Four children: Tommy, Katie, Ashley, and Nathaniel. Dr. Heinecke enjoys hunting, fishing, tennis, and Nebraska football.

S. Dale Hibbert, D.D.S.

Dentist
Pediatric Dentistry
2112 Hillfield #1
Layton, UT 84041–4711
(801) 774–0770
Fax: (801) 774–9939

8021

Business Information: Pediatric Dentistry is a full–service dental practice exclusively for children and teenagers, specializing in providing cosmetic, general dentistry, oral surgery and orthodontics. They serve patients at two locations, one in Layton, Utah and the other in Southwest Salt Lake. A practicing dentist since 1992, Dr. Hibbert oversees all administrative operations for associates and a support staff of 16, in addition to his daily patient practice. **Career Steps:** Dentist, Pediatric Dentistry (1992–Present). **Associations & Accomplishments:** American Dental Association; American Association of Pediatric Dentists; ASDC; UDA; Weber District Dental Society; Salt Lake District Dental Society; Speaker/Lecturer. **Education:** Children's Hospital of Michigan in Detroit (1992); University of Michigan, Pediatric Dentistry (1991); Brigham Young University, B.S. (1986); Creighton University, D.D.S. (1990). **Personal:** One child: Caitlin. Dr. Hibbert enjoys scuba diving, skydiving, water skiing, basketball, racquetball, and snow skiing with his daughter.

Dilshad Hirji–Kara, PSC, DMD

Dentist
The Office of Dilshad Hirji–Kara, PSC, DMD
930 North Park Drive
Brampton, Ontario L6S 3Y5
(905) 791–7520
Fax: Please mail or call

8021

Business Information: The Office of Dilshad Hirji–Kara, PSC, DMD is a full–service, family practice dentistry office, providing general dental care to patients of all ages. As Dentist, Dr. Hirji–Kara oversees all administrative operations for associates and support staff, in addition to his daily patient practice. **Career Steps:** Dentist, The Office of Dilshad Hirji–Kara, PSC, DMD (1994–Present); Resident, State University of New York – Buffalo (1993–1994). **Associations & Accomplishments:** American Dental Association; Ontario Dental Association; Academy of General Dentistry; Delta Sigma Delta; World Wildlife Fund. **Education:** State University of New York – Buffalo, A.E.G.D. (1993–1994); Tufts University, D.M.D. (1993); McGill University, B.Sc. (1989). **Personal:** Married to Shanif Kara in 1992. Dr. Hirji–Kara enjoys running, reading, and writing.

Paul F. Hofer, D.D.S.

Sole Practitioner
–Independent–
8137 Parallel Parkway
Kansas City, KS 66112–2010
(913) 299–8900
Fax: (913) 299–2022

Business Information: A practicing dentist since 1988, Dr. Paul Hofer established his private dental practice in 1989. He oversees a support staff of 9, in addition to his daily patient practice providing all areas of general family and cosmetic dentistry services. **Career Steps:** Sole Practitioner, Paul F. Hofer, D.D.S. (1989–Present); Dentist, Guy Gronniger, D.D.S. (1988–1990). **Associations & Accomplishments:** American Dental Association; Kansas Dental Association; First District Dental Association; Wyandotte County Dental Society; Past Grand Knight, Knights of Columbus. **Education:** University of Missouri–Kansas City, School of Dentistry, D.D.S. (1988); Pittsburgh State University, B.S. **Personal:** Married to Gena in 1985. One child: Alexis. Dr. Hofer enjoys boating and flying during his leisure time.

James Percy Hood III, D.D.S.

Partner
Post Office Lake Associates
603 Post Office Road, Suite 208
Waldorf, MD 20602–1914
(301) 705–7552
Fax: Please mail or call

8021

Business Information: Post Office Lake Associates is a full–service, family practice dentistry office consisting of one oral surgeon and two orthodontists, providing cosmetic, general dentistry, oral surgery, and orthodontics. A practicing dentist since 1990, Dr. Hood joined Post Office Lake Associates as Partner in 1991. He is responsible for providing quality dental care to patients. **Career Steps:** Partner, Post Office Lake Associates (1991–Present); Dentist, R.I.C.A. (November 1991); Dentist, Maryland Boot Camp (November 1994). **Associations & Accomplishments:** Charles County Chamber of Commerce; Health Board Advisory Committee, Charles County Board of Education; NAACP; Group Practices Association; Maryland Boot Camp; Staff Member, Boy's Village. **Education:** Meharry Medical College, D.D.S. (1990); Virginia State University, B.S. (1983). **Personal:** Married to Brenda Wilson Hood in 1995. Dr. Hood enjoys all kinds of sports.

H. Mikel Hopkins, D.D.S., FICCMO

Sole Practitioner
Tampa Bay TMJ Pain Center
1952 Bayshore Boulevard
Dunedin, FL 34698–2500
(813) 738–6105
Fax: (813) 734–7702

8021

Business Information: The Tampa Bay TMJ Pain Center is a general practice dental facility specializing in the treatment of

Temporal Mandibular Joint Syndrome. A Dentist and Sole Practitioner since 1976, Dr. Hopkins established the TMJ Pain Center in 1981. As such, he provides care and treatment for patients suffering from degenerative jaw disorders. Dr. Hopkins directs a support staff of eight, in addition to his daily patient practice. **Career Steps:** Sole Practitioner, Tampa Bay TMJ Pain Center (1981–Present); Sole Practitioner, Dental Office of Dr. H. Mikel Hopkins, D.D.S. (1976–Present). **Associations & Accomplishments:** Upper Pinellas County Dental Association; West Coast Dental Association; Florida Dental Association; American Dental Association; Fellow, International College of Craniomandibular Orthopaedics; International College of Oral Implantology. **Education:** West Virginia University School of Dentistry, D.D.S. (1976); Fellow, International College of Craniomandibular Orthopaedics. **Personal:** Married to Rebecca in 1971. Two children: Amy and Christopher.

Larry G. Hubbard, D.D.S.
Sole Dentistry Practitioner
The Dental Office of Larry G. Hubbard, D.D.S.
4 Lester Road
Statesboro, GA 30458–5020
(912) 764–9891
Fax: Please mail or call

8021

Business Information: The Dental Office of Larry G. Hubbard, D.D.S. is a full–service dentistry practice specializing in cosmetic dentistry. Establishing his private practice upon completion of his residency fellowhip in 1979, Dr. Hubbard oversees all adminstrative operations for a support staff of five, in addition to his daily patient care. Concurrently, he is also an Associate Professor with the Department of Restorative Dentistry at the Medical College of Georgia's School of Dentistry. **Career Steps:** Owner, The Dental Office of Larry G. Hubbard, D.D.S. (1979–Present). **Associations & Accomplishments:** Rotary Club; Fellow, Academy of General Dentistry; American Dental Association; Georgia Dental Association; Southeast District Dental Society; Former President, Coastal Dental Study Group. **Education:** Emory University School of Dentistry, D.D.S. (1979); Emory University, B.S. in Biology (1975). **Personal:** Married to Lynn in 1985. Dr. Hubbard enjoys travel, snorkeling in the Caribbean, fly fishing, and cooking.

Patricia A. Hunter, D.M.D.
Dentist
Dental Office of Patricia A. Hunter, D.M.D.
Suite 110, 821 Ackroyd Road
Richmond, British Co V6X 3K8
(604) 273–6011
Fax: (604) 273–6016

8021

Business Information: Dental Office of Patricia a. Hunter, D.M.D. is a private practice general dentistry office. Comprised of five chairs, an associate dentist and two hygienists, the practice offers basic dental care as well as some orthodontic work. As Dentist, Dr. Hunter is responsible for the overall operation of the Practice, including all administrative and operational functions. Additional duties include monitoring patient's dental health and promoting good oral hygiene. **Career Steps:** Dentist, Dental Office of Patricia a. Hunter, D.M.D. (1987–Present). **Associations & Accomplishments:** Omicron Kappa Upsilon Dental Fraternity; College of Dental Surgeons; Canadian Dental Association; Tucker Gold Study Club; Greater Vancouver Crown and Bridge Study Club; Canadian Powersail Squadron; Bluewater Cruising Association. **Education:** University of British Columbia, D.M.D. (1983); Diploma in Dental Hygiene (1972). **Personal:** Married to Lewis Andrew Hilts in 1991. Two children: Jackson and Rachel. Dr. Hunter enjoys sailing and skiing.

Randy L. Hunter, D.D.S.
• • • ◼◆◼ ◎ ◼◆◼ • • •

Chief Executive Officer
Hunter Dental Care
91 South Washington Street
Oxford, MI 48371–4979
(810) 628–2540
Fax: (810) 969–0677

8021

Business Information: Hunter Dental Care is a full–service, family practice dentistry office, providing cosmetic, periodontic, dental surgery, implantology and general dentistry. Establishing Hunter Dental Care upon the conferral of his dental degree in 1982, Dr. Hunter serves as Chief Executive Officer. He

oversees all administrative operations for associates and a support staff of 13 (3 dentists), in addition to his daily patient practice. Concurrent with his dental practice, he is a 50% shareholder of a retail pizza sales business (Little Caesars) and serves as Chief Financial Officer and Vice President. **Career Steps:** Chief Executive Officer, Hunter Dental Care (1982–Present); Vice President and Chief Financial Officer, Lynn Enterprises, Inc. (Little Caesars franchise) (1985–Present). **Associations & Accomplishments:** American Dental Association; Michigan Dental Association; Oakland County Dental Society; American Academy of Cosmetic Dentistry; Crown Council; Chamber of Commerce; Heritage Foundation's Physician Council; Rotary Club International; National Restaurant Association. **Education:** University of Detroit, D.D.S. (1982); Michigan State University, B.S. in Physiology (1978). **Personal:** Married to Marie Hunter, D.D.S. in 1976.

James T. Hutta, D.D.S.
Orthodontist
James T. Hutta, D.D.S.
555 Officenter Place, Suite 118
Gahanna, OH 43230–5315
(614) 475–7800
Fax: (614) 475–7326

8021

Business Information: James T. Hutta, D.D.S., established in 1992, is a specialty dental office, limited to the practice of Orthodontics. A practicing Orthodontist for the past six years, Dr. Hutta oversees the administrative functions and a support staff of five, in addition to his daily patient practice. He continues to pursue clinical research in the latest technological advances in orthodontic practices, particularly focusing on TMJ disorders. **Career Steps:** Orthodontist, James T. Hutta, D.D.S. (1992–Present); Eastman Dental Center: Orthodontist (1990–1992), Adjunct Faculty and Clinical Instructor (1990–1992), Associate General Dentistry Practitioner (1989–1990); Orthodontic Assistant and Lab Assistant, J. Lawrence Hutta, D.D.S. (1986–1989). **Associations & Accomplishments:** American Dental Association; Columbus Dental Society; Chicago Dental Society; Ohio State Alumni Member; Ohio State University College of Dentistry Alumni Member; Ohio Dental Association; Rochester Study Group; American Association of Orthodontics; Young Professionals in Medicine and Dentistry; Chairman, Children Dental Health Month; American Lingual Orthodontic Association; International Association of Esthetic Orthodontists; Gahanna Rotary; Licensure: Northeast Regional Board Certification (1989); National Board Certification (1989); Ohio License to Practice Dentistry (1989); New York State License to Practice Dentistry (1990); Numerous professional presentations and research in the fields of Sports Medicine and TMJ findings. **Education:** Eastman Dental Center – Rochester, New York: Department of Orthodontics, Certificate (1992), Advanced Education in General Dentistry, Certificate (1990); Ohio State University College of Dentistry, D.D.S. (1989); Ohio State University College of Biological Sciences, B.S. in Microbiology (1985). **Personal:** Married to Lori (she serves as a Dental Hygienist in his practice) in 1988. One child: Christopher James. Dr. Hutta enjoys golf.

J. Fletcher Jernigan Jr., D.D.S.
Sole Practitioner
J. Fletcher Jernigan, Jr., D.D.S.
3280 Howell Mill Road, Suite 237
Atlanta, GA 30327
(404) 355–8120
Fax: (404) 355–9280

8021

Business Information: J. Fletcher Jernigan, Jr., D.D.S., established in 1979, is a full–service, specialized dentistry practice, concentrating on restorative and rehabilitative (cosmetic) dental care. A practicing dentist for sixteen years, Dr. Jernigan established his sole practice dental office in 1979, providing specialized dental care to patients. **Career Steps:** Sole Practitioner, J. Fletcher Jernigan, Jr., D.D.S. (1979–Present). **Associations & Accomplishments:** American Dental Association; Georgia Dental Association; Northern District Dental Society; Buckhead Business Association; Buckhead Business Network. **Education:** Emory University School of Dentistry, D.D.S. (1979); Vanderbilt University, B.S. **Personal:** Married to Cordelia in 1978. Three children: Gray, Caroline, and Jay. Dr. Jernigan enjoys spending time with his children, golf, and tennis.

T. M. Jimison
Director of Human Resources
Compdent Corporation
1840 Summerbrook Drive
Dunwoody, GA 30350
(770) 998–8936 Ext. 241
Fax: Please mail or call

8021

Business Information: Compdent Corporation is a dental managed care facility. The Company currently provides benefits in 16 states and is still growing. They are the third largest independent DMO in the nation. Joining Compdent Corporation in 1995 as Director of Human Resources, Ms. Jimison has changed the department dramatically in the time she has been there. She is mainly responsible for consolidation, staff, managing payroll, benefits, and employee training. She oversees 40 inside sales representatives and 60 customer service employees. **Career Steps:** Director of Human Resources, Compdent Corporation (1995–Present); Benefits Manager, President Baking Company (1993–1995); Independent Consultant, Self–Employed (1992–1993); Regional Employee Relations Director, CIGNA/Intacorp (1989–1992). **Associations & Accomplishments:** Society of Human Resource Management; Big Brothers/Big Sisters; Certified Human Resource Generalist. **Education:** University of Illinois, B.S. in Business, Minor in Psychology (1985). **Personal:** One child: Megan Marie. Ms. Jimison enjoys golf, pool, and water sports.

Lionel A. Jones, D.M.D.
Dentist
Lionel A. Jones, D.M.D.
5660 Chew Avenue
Philadelphia, PA 19138–1742
(215) 848–5848
Fax: (215) 848–5886

8021

Business Information: Lionel A. Jones, D.M.D. is a private, general dentistry practice, providing cosmetic, family–care dentistry, and oral surgery. In the practice of General Dentistry since 1987, Dr. Jones established his sole practice office in 1990. **Career Steps:** Owner and Dentist, Lionel A. Jones, D.M.D. (1990–Present); Dentist, Dr. Chauthry, D.D.S. (1989–1990); Dentist, Dr. Usmani, D.D.S. (1988–1989). **Associations & Accomplishments:** National Society of Dental Practitioners. **Education:** Temple University Dental School, D.M.D. (1987); Temple University, B.A. in Biology. **Personal:** Married to Teresa in 1990. Two children: Shadaria and Avatar. Dr. Jones enjoys boxing and motorcycling.

Paula S. Jones, D.D.S.
Dentist
Paula S. Jones, D.D.S.
610 East Roosevelt Road, Suite 101
Wheaton, IL 601875575
(708) 653–9002
Fax: (708) 653–7403

8021

Business Information: Paula S. Jones, D.D.S. is a general dentistry practice. Establishing the practice in 1984, Dr. Jones is responsible for all administrative operations, as well as patient care. **Career Steps:** Dentist, Paula S. Jones, D.D.S. (1984–Present). **Associations & Accomplishments:** American Dental Association; Illinois State Dental Association; Chicago Dental Society; Fellow, Academy of General Dentistry; Fellow, Academy of Dentistry International; Membership Council Chairman, Academy of General Dentistry; Recipient of Distinguished Service Award (Peer Recognition); Published in "Illinois Advisor" concerning Women in Dentistry in the Fall of 1993; Speaker at Membership Council of Dentistry; Assisted with a video on "How to Introduce Young Dentists into AGD Membership." **Education:** Case Western Reserve University, D.D.S. (1984), B.S.; Indiana University, A.S. in Dental Hygiene. **Personal:** Married to Matthew in 1980. Two children: Meghan and Heather.

Sivi E. Jones, D.D.S.
Sole Practitioner
Sivi Jones, D.D.S.
1070 Springfield Avenue
Irvington, NJ 07111
(201) 375–5575
Fax: (201) 375–7217

8021

Business Information: Sivi Jones, D.D.S., established in 1990, is a family practice dentistry office, providing cosmetic, general dentistry, and oral surgery. A practicing dentist for eight years, Dr. Jones established his sole practice dental office in 1990. He is responsible for all aspects of operations and management of the practice, as well as providing treatment to patients. **Career Steps:** Sole Practitioner, Sivi Jones, D.D.S. (1990–Present); Staff Dentist, Washington Park Dental Association (1989–1991); Associate Dentist, Maureen Frazer Family Dentistry (1987–1989). **Associations & Accomplishments:** Commonwealth Dental Association. **Education:** Howard University, D.D.S. (1987). **Personal:** Married to Jacqueline in 1990. One child: Nicole. Dr. Jones enjoys jogging, walks, and video tapes.

Sabah Kalamchi, D.D.S.
Oral and Maxillofacial Surgeon
Arizona Institutes – Oral Maxillofacial Institute
3501 North Scottsdale Road, Suite 110
Scottsdale, AZ 85251–5649
(602) 945–2310
Fax: (602) 947–3991

8021

Business Information: Arizona Institutes – Oral Maxillofacial Institute is a specialty medical group practice, specializing in oral and maxillofacial surgery and the treatment of facial deformity caused by traumatic injury to the face. A practicing dentist and a Board–Certified Oral and Maxillofacial Surgeon for over ten years, Dr. Kalamchi joined the Arizona Institutes – Oral Maxillofacial Institute in 1993. Additionally, he also serves as a Consultant and Maxillofacial Surgeon at Scottsdale Memorial Hospital. **Career Steps:** Oral and Maxillofacial Surgeon, Arizona Institutes – Oral Maxillofacial Institute (1993–Present); Consultant Maxillofacial Surgeon, Scottsdale Memorial Hospital (1990–Present); Lecturer, University of London Eastman Dental Hospital, England (1984–1986); Registrar, Newcastle Upon Tyne Hospital, England (1981–1983). **Associations & Accomplishments:** Fellow Faculty of Dentistry, The Royal College of Surgeons, Ireland; British Association of Oral Surgeons; Fellow, American Association of Oral and Maxillofacial Surgeons. **Education:** Creighton School of Dentistry, D.D.S.; Royal College of Surgeons – Ireland F.F.D.R.C.S. (1985); Royal College of Surgeons – Edinburgh L.D.S.R.C.S. (1984); Certification: American Board of Oral and Maxillofacial Surgery. **Personal:** Married to Samr in 1991. Three children: Michael, Tamarra, and Louay. Dr. Kalamchi enjoys reading, writing, and skiing.

Thomas E. Karr, D.D.S.
Dentist
The Office of Thomas E. Karr, D.D.S.
3501 Soncy Road, Suite 123
Amarillo, TX 79121–1748
(806) 352–2800
Fax: (806) 352–8592
E–mail: see below

8021

Business Information: The Office of Thomas E. Karr, D.D.S. is a full–service dentistry practice. Establishing the office in 1984, Dr. Karr oversees all administrative operations, in addition to his daily patient practice. Dr. Karr can also be reached through the Internet as follows: tkarr@arn.net. **Career Steps:** Dentist, The Office of Thomas E. Karr, D.D.S. (1993–Present); Partner and Dentist, Cassada & Karr, D.D.S., Inc. (1985–1993). **Associations & Accomplishments:** American Dental Association; Texas Dental Association; Panhandle District Dental Society; Texas Academy of General Dentistry – Panhandle Chapter: Membership Chairman (1995–Present), Board of Directors and Delegate, President (1994–Present), Vice President (1992–1994); Academy of General Dentistry; Kiwanis Club of Amarillo – South; Sunday School Teacher, Paramount Terrace Christian Church (1992–Present); Advisory Board, Amarillo Area Crisis Pregnancy Center; Member and holder of various office positions, Porsche Club of America; Board of Directors and Volunteer, High Plains Epilepsy Association; Member and Committee Chairman, Amarillo Chamber of Commerce; Golf Tournament Co–Chairman and Volunteer, American Diabetes Association — Potter–Randall Chapter. **Education:** University of Texas Dental School – San Antonio, D.D.S. (1984); Texas Tech University (1977–1980). **Personal:** Married to Shirley Ann Russell in 1981. Three children: Jessica Rochelle, Randall Elliot and Rebecca Janelle. Dr. Karr enjoys snow skiing, hunting, fishing, tennis, golf, computers and playing the guitar.

Mark B. Kelchner, D.D.S.
Dentist and Managing Partner
Mark B. Kelchner – Family Dentistry
132 E. Front Street
Berwick, PA 18603–4818
(717) 752–2230
Fax: Please mail or call

8021

Business Information: Mark B. Kelchner – Family Dentistry, established in 1960, is a full–service, family practice dental office, providing cosmetic and general dentistry to patients of all ages. With the office location housed in one of Berwick's oldest buildings, dating back to circa 1800's, extensive remodeling is planned to accommodate the growing practice services and associates. A practicing dentist for four years, Dr. Kelchner joined the Practice in 1991 and is in the process of buying out the senior partner. He currently serves as Dentist and Managing Partner, providing dental care to patients and handling all administrative duties of the business. He also conducts state–mandated dental examinations on children ranging from kindergarten to junior high school. **Career Steps:** Dentist and Managing Partner, Mark B. Kelchner – Family Dentistry (1991–Present). **Associations & Accomplishments:** American Dental Association; Academy of General Dentistry; Pennsylvania Dental Association; Berwick Dental Society; Board of Directors, Berwick Rotary Club; Board of Directors – Local Chapter, American Red Cross; Advisory Board Member, Salvation Army; Trustee, Bower Memorial United Methodist Church. **Education:** Baltimore College of Dental Surgery, D.D.S. (1991); Albright College, B.S. (Majors: Biology, Pre–Med, Pre–Dental). **Personal:** Married to Betsy K. in 1987. One child: Katelyn E. An avid fisherman, Dr. Kelchner also enjoys racquetball and photography.

Peter P. Korch, D.M.D.
Sole Practitioner
The Dental Office of Peter P. Korch, D.M.D.
P.O. Box 338
Barnesboro, PA 15714
(814) 948–9650
Fax: Please mail or call
EMAIL: GamLam9@aol.com

8021

Business Information: The Dental Office of Peter P. Korch, D.M.D. is a full–service, family practice dentistry office, providing cosmetic and general dentistry. Inheriting his father's dental practice upon the conferral of his dental degree in 1991, Dr. Korch serves as Sole Practitioner. He oversees all administrative operations for his support staff, in addition to his daily patient practice. **Career Steps:** Sole Practitioner, The Dental Office of Peter P. Korch, D.M.D. (1991–Present). **Associations & Accomplishments:** American Dental Association; American Academy for the History of Dentistry; Academy of Dental Therapeutics and Stomatology; Academy of General Dentistry; Cambria County Dental Society; Pennsylvania Dental Association; Entomological Society of Washington; Education Chairman, Allegheny Plateau Audubon Society; Adjunct Associate Professor, University of Pittsburgh at Johnstown; C. F. Reynolds Medical History Society. **Education:** University of Pittsburgh, D.M.D. (1991); Southern Illinois University, M.A.; University of Pittsburgh – Johnstown, B.S. **Personal:** Dr. Korch enjoys insect biology and music.

James M. Kornegay, D.D.S.

• • • ◀━━● ◉ ●━━▶ • • •

Dentist
The Office of James M. Kornegay, D.D.S.
1617 Catalina Boulevard
Deltona, FL 32725–9699
(904) 789–7990
Fax: (904) 789–4503

8021

Business Information: The Office of James M. Kornegay, D.D.S. is a full–service, family dental practice. Establishing the practice in 1987, Dr. Kornegay is responsible for the care and treatment of patients, as well as the administrative functions. **Career Steps:** Dentist, The Office of James M. Kornegay, D.D.S. (1987–Present); Sales Manager, John Hancock Insurance Company (1980–1982); Sales Manager, Prudential Insurance Company (1976–1979); Electronics Technician, United States Air Force (1967–1976). **Associations & Accomplishments:** American Dental Association; Florida Dental Association; Central District Dental Association; Volusia County Dental Association; West Volusia Study Club; Academy of General Dentistry; Outstanding Young Men of America (1985). **Education:** University of Missouri, D.D.S. (1986); Troy State University, B.S. in Management, cum laude (1976); Allan Hancock College, A.S. **Personal:** Married to Beth. Four children: James, Jennifer, Julie and Tim. Dr. Kornegay enjoys fishing, reading, and woodworking.

D. Bartholomew Kreiner, D.D.S.
Owner
The Dental Office of D. Bartholomew Kreiner, D.D.S.
10 West Broadway Street
Bel Air, MD 21014–3555
(410) 879–1730
Fax: Please mail or call

8021

Business Information: The Dental Office of D. Bartholomew Kreiner, D.D.S. is a full–service, general practice dentistry office, providing cosmetic, general dentistry, and oral surgery. Establishing the solo practice upon the conferral of his dental degree, Dr. Kreiner is responsible for all aspects of operations, in addition to his daily patient practice. **Career Steps:** Owner, The Dental Office of D. Bartholomew Kreiner, D.D.S. (1990–Present); Clinical Instructor, University of Maryland Dental School – Baltimore College of Dental Surgery (1989–1995). **Associations & Accomplishments:** Voluntary Dental Mission to Dominican Republic (1989, 1990, 1993); Volunteer Firefighter, Bel Air Volunteer Fire Company (1992–Present); Academy of General Dentistry (1989–Present); American Dental Association (1989–Present); Maryland State Dental Association (1990–Present); Harford–Cecil County Dental Association (1990–Present): President (1995–1996), Treasurer (1994–1995), Secretary (1993–1994). **Education:** University of Maryland Dental School – Baltimore College of Dental Surgery, D.D.S. (1989), Certificate in Advanced General Dentistry. **Personal:** Married to Martha in 1991. Dr. Kreiner enjoys firefighting, crabbing, and bull's–eye shooting.

David J. Krynauw, D.D.S.
Dentist
Flagler Dental Associates
901 North Flagler Drive
West Palm Beach, FL 33401–3707
(407) 659–3277
Fax: (407) 659–3278
E–mail: see below

8021

Business Information: Established in 1985, Flagler Dental Associates is a full–service, cosmetic and laser dental practice, consisting of two dentists and seven support staff. A general dentistry practitioner since 1985, Dr. Krynauw joined Flagler Dental Associates in 1993. He shares the responsibility of managing the support staff, in addition to his daily patient practice. Dr. Krynauw can also be reached through the Internet as follows: Davidk@Flinet.com **Career Steps:** Dentist, Flagler Dental Associates (1993–Present); Director and Dentist, Welgemoed Dental (1991–1993); Dentist, Tring Dental (1989–1991); Dentist, Brixton Cosmetic (1986–1989). **Associations & Accomplishments:** American Dental Association; British Dental Association; Florida Dental Association; South African Dental Association. **Education:** Witwatersrand, B.D.S. (1985); SAMS, Fakkel School. **Personal:** Married to Karen in 1985. Two children: Maxine and Sasha. Dr. Krynauw enjoys golf, squash, and computer programming.

Sonya L. Kummer, D.D.S.
Dentist
Sonya L. Kummer, D.D.S.
119 North 8th Street
Nebraska City, NE 68410–2441
(402) 873–3111
Fax: Please mail or call

8021

Business Information: The Dental Offices of Sonya L. Kummer, D.D.S. is a general dentistry practice providing family practice and cosmetic dentistry. In the private practice of dentistry since 1988, Dr. Kummer established her sole practice in 1992. She is responsible for the administration of a staff of three, as well as her daily patient care. **Career Steps:** Dentist, Sonya L. Kummer, D.D.S. (1992–Present); Associate Dentist, Dr. Steven Rallis, D.D.S. (1988–1991); General Practice Resident, VA Medical Center (1987–1988). **Associations & Accomplishments:** American Dental Association. **Education:** University of Nebraska, D.D.S. (1987). **Personal:** Married to Randy in 1986. One child: John. Dr. Kummer enjoys cross–stitching, jazzercise, and reading.

Ronald F. Lambert, D.D.S.

• • • ◀━━● ◉ ●━━▶ • • •

Dentist
Louisville Dental Associates
1760 Centennial Drive
Louisville, CO 80027–1302
(303) 665–7505
Fax: Please mail or call

8021

Business Information: Louisville Dental Associates is a full–service general practice dental facility. The Office also provides cosmetic dentistry and enjoys providing family dentistry. Established in 1982, Louisville Dental Associates currently employs 2 Dentists and 8 support staff. As Dentist, Dr. Lambert is responsible for the care and treatment of patients. Dr. Lambert is also on faculty at the University of Colorado School of Dentistry where he teaches Dental Anatomy and Morphology. **Career Steps:** Dentist, Louisville Dental Associates (1992–Present); Resident University of Washington (1991–1992); Student, University of Colorado (1987–1991). **Associations & Accomplishments:** American Dental Association; Academy of Operative Dentistry; Academy of General Dentistry; Colorado Prosthodontic Society; Published two Dental articles. **Education:** University of Colorado, D.D.S. (1991); University of Washington, Certificate in Hospital Dentistry (1992). **Personal:** Married to Candace J. in 1987. Four children: Robert Kyle, Aaron Michael, Christopher Daniel and Joshua Thomas. Dr. Lambert enjoys skiing, leatherworking, and racquetball.

Edward L. Lamoreaux, D.D.S.
Dentist
Springcrest Family Dentistry
2424 Spring Arbor Road
Jackson, MI 49203
(517) 787–2226
Fax: (517) 787–1256

8021

Business Information: Springcrest Family Dentistry is a full–service, family practice dentistry office, providing cosmetic and general dentistry for the entire family. A practicing dentist since 1987, Dr. Lamoreaux founded Springcrest Family Dentistry in 1993. He is responsible for overseeing all administrative operations for associates and a support staff of 9, in addition to his daily patient practice. **Career Steps:** Dentist, Springcrest Family Dentistry (1993–Present); Owner, Ed Lamoreaux, D.D.S. (1987–1993); President, CELT Laundries, Inc. (1975–1983). **Associations & Accomplishments:** American Dental Association; Michigan Dental Association; Jackson District Dental Society; Academy of General Dentistry; Sleep Disorders Dental Society; Former Newsletter Editor, Clark Lake Lions Club. **Education:** University of Michigan, D.D.S. (1987); Spring Arbor College, B.A. **Personal:** Married to Linda in 1971. Two children: Amy O'Lynn and Nicolas. Dr. Lamoreaux enjoys singing in gospel quartet, coaching a men's basketball team and playing softball.

J. Monty Lang, D.D.S.
Dentist
J. Monty Lang, D.D.S.
913 Holland Avenue
Philadelphia, MS 39350
(601) 656–7410
Fax: (601) 656–0636

8021

Business Information: J. Monty Lang, D.D.S., established in 1994, is a general practice dental office concentrating in family dentistry. As Owner and Dentist, Dr. Lang is responsible for all aspects of operations, including providing comprehensive dental care to all patients. **Career Steps:** Owner and Dentist, J. Monty Lang, D.D.S. (1994–); GPR Resident, Veteran's Administration Hospital, Birmingham, Alabama (1992–1993); Private practitioner (1990–). **Associations & Accomplishments:** American Dental Association; Mississippi Dental Association; Psi Omega Fraternity; Pi Kappa Alpha; Theta Nu Epsilon; Member, Lion's Club; Member, Philadelphia Downtown Development; First United Methodist Church member; Mississippi Economic Council; Chamber of Commerce Member; Rotary Club Member. **Education:** University of Tennessee – Memphis, D.D.S. (1990); University of Mississippi, B.A. **Personal:** One child: James Keaton Lang. Dr. Lang enjoys hunting, snow & water skiing, boating, fishing, and all sport activities.

Tomas H. Lang, D.D.S.
Dentist
Offices of Tomas H. Lang, D.D.S.
10811 East Garvey Avenue
El Monte, CA 91733
(818) 442–6115
Fax: (818) 442–3422

8021

Business Information: Offices of Tomas H. Lang, D.D.S. is a full–service, family practice dentistry office, providing cosmetic, general dentistry, and oral surgery. A practicing dentist for the past thirty–five years, Dr. Lang established the El Monte, California office in 1987. As sole practitioner for the four–chair practice, he oversees all administrative functions and support staff in addition to his daily patient practice. **Career Steps:** Private Practice Dentistry, throughout Florida (1961–Present). **Associations & Accomplishments:** American Dental Association; Florida Dental Association; East Coast District Dental Society; Latin–American Dental Society; Academy of General Dentistry; Pankey Institute Alumnis Group; San Fernando Valley Dental Association. **Education:** U.N.A.M.,

D.D.S. (1960). **Personal:** Married to Alba in 1960. Three children: Tomas A. Lang, Alba M. Ocon, and Sandra E. Balon. Dr. Lang enjoys reading and watching movies.

Edwin D.Y. Lee, D.M.D.
Prosthodontist
–Independent–
70 Grand Avenue
Englewood, NJ 07631–3506
(201) 567–8088
Fax: Please mail or call

8021

Business Information: The Office of Edwin D.Y. Lee, D.M.D. is a dental practice specializing in Restorative Dentistry, Full Mouth Rehabilitation, Prosthodontics, and Implant Prosthodontics. **Career Steps:** Private Practice in Restorative and Prosthetic Dentistry (1993–Present). **Associations & Accomplishments:** American Dental Association; American College of Prosthodontists. **Education:** Columbia University School of Dentistry and Oral Surgery, Speciality Certificate (1986–1988); University of Pennsylvania School of Dental Medicine, D.M.D. (1982–1984). **Personal:** Dr. Lee enjoys skiing and watching movies.

Robert Leedy, D.D.S.
Managing Partner
Abilene Dental Associates
3001 South Danville Drive
Abilene, TX 79605–6454
(915) 692–3344
Fax: Please mail or call

8021

Business Information: Abilene Dental Associates is a full–service, general practice dentistry office, providing cosmetic and reconstructive dentistry. Established in 1992, Abilene Dental Associates reports annual revenue of $1.3 million and currently employs 14 people. A practicing dental practitioner for the past eleven years, Dr. Leedy joined Abilene Dental Associates in 1992. Currently serving as Managing Partner, he is responsible for all aspects of operations and management of the Practice, as well as providing general dentistry. **Career Steps:** Managing Partner, Abilene Dental Associates (1992–Present); Dentist, Self–Employed (1984–Present). **Associations & Accomplishments:** American Academy of Cosmetic Dentists; American Dental Association; Texas Dental Association; AGD. **Education:** University of Texas Health Science Center at San Antonio, D.D.S. (1984). **Personal:** Married to Christie Leedy, D.D.S. in 1984. Two children: Corey and Jace. Dr. Leedy enjoys golf and coaching children's sports.

Rudolph R. Leidl, D.M.D.
Dentist and President
The Office of Dr. Rudolph R. Leidl, D.M.D.
2 Mountain View Avenue
Long Valley, NJ 07853–3122
(908) 876–3458
Fax: Please mail or call

8021

Business Information: The Office of Dr. Rudolph R. Leidl, D.M.D. is a general dentistry practice. Established in 1978, the Office currently employs 4 dentists and 13 support staff. As Dentist and President, Dr. Leidl is responsible for the care and teatment of patients, as well as some administrative functions. **Career Steps:** Dentist and President, The Office of Dr. Rudolph R. Leidl, D.M.D. (1978–Present); Captain and Dentist, United States Air Force (1974–1976). **Associations & Accomplishments:** Fellow, Academy of General Dentistry; American Dental Association; Fellow, Academy Dentistry International; Academy of General Dentistry; Who's Who in America. **Education:** University of New Jersey School of Dentistry, D.M.D. (1974); Seton Hall University, B.A. in Biology (1971). **Personal:** Married to Mary Lynn in 1992. Five children: Daniel, Erin, Melissa, Matthew, Kaitlyn. Dr. Leidl enjoys tennis, skiing, and spending time with his family.

Dr. Eric Lessard
Dentist
Clinique Dentaire Eric Lessard
C.P. 640 950 Ave Champlain
Disraeli, Quebec G0N 1E0
(418) 449–1800
Fax: (418) 449–1798

8021

Business Information: Clinique Dentaire Eric Lessard is a local dental clinic with six employees. The clinic offers minor oral surgery and general and hospital dentistry. As Dentist, Dr. Lessard attends to patient needs in both the hospital and the clinic offices. He is the founder of Clinique Dentaire and handles daily management of the clinic. Dr. Lessard is responsible for recruiting, hiring and evaluating staff members, and all financial concerns of the clinic. He acts as public relations director and does the planning for expansion of the dental practice. Dr. Lessard is concurrently on staff at Thetford Mines General Hospital. **Career Steps:** Dentist, Clinique Dentaire Eric Lessard (194–Present); Dentist, Dental Clinic Doyon–Gagnon (1993–1994); Dentist, Thetford Mines General Hospital (1993–Present); Dentist, North Coast (1994–1995). **Associations & Accomplishments:** Academy of General Dentistry; American Association of Hospital Dentists; Ordre Des Dentistes Du Quebec; Academy of Special Care Dentistry; Canadian Dental Association; Association Des Chirugiens Dentistes Du Quebec. **Education:** Montreal University, Certified GDR; Laval University, DmD; McGill University, Certified Geriatric Dentistry. **Personal:** Married to Judith Lecours in 1995. Dr. Lessard enjoys fishing, travel, fitness, hockey, and reading.

William Q. Lim, D.D.S.
President, Manager, and Owner
Centennial Square Dental Associates
10316 Baltimore National, Suite A
Ellicott City, MD 21042–2195
(410) 313–9483
Fax: (410) 313–9482

8021

Business Information: Centennial Square Dental Associates, is a full–service general denistry group practice, consisting of three independent dental practitioners. Dental services provided include general dentistry, cosmetic (crowns & veneers), and trauma work. Future plans include serving more patients, primarily targeting the elderly (i.e., denture, bridge work) and expanding offices throughout the state. As President, Manager, and Owner, Dr. Lim is responsible for all aspects of operations and dental practice. **Career Steps:** President, Manager, and Owner, Centennial Square Dental Associates (1994–Present). **Associations & Accomplishments:** The Honor Society of Phi Kappa Phi; American Dental Association; Maryland State Dental Association; Baltimore County Dental Association. **Education:** University of Maryland Dental School, D.D.S. (1992); University of Maryland, B.A. **Personal:** Dr. Lim enjoys martial arts and exotic fishes.

Arnelle A. Lloyd, D.D.S.
Sole Practitioner
Arnelle A. Lloyd, D.D.S, P.C.
651 Church Lane
Yeadon, PA 19050
(610) 622–2077
Fax: (610) 622–2068

8021

Business Information: Arnelle A. Lloyd, D.D.S, P.C. is a full–service, family practice dentistry office, providing cosmetic, general dentistry, and oral surgery at two locations, Dr. Lloyd's home in Yeadon and a practice in Philadelphia, Pennsylvania. A practicing dentist since 1982, Dr. Lloyd established the in 1985 and opened a second practice in her home in 1994. She oversees the administrative operations for associates and a support staff of three (two full–time and one part–time), in addition to her daily patient practice. Dr. Lloyd also visits local schools, giving talks, pertaining the dentistry, to students. **Career Steps:** Sole Practitioner, Arnelle A. Lloyd, D.D.S, P.C. (1985–Present). **Associations & Accomplishments:** New Era Dental Society; National Dental Association; Bright Smiles/Bright Futures Dental Volunteer; Who's Who in Dentistry; Delta Sigma Theta Sorority, Inc. **Education:** Howard University, D.D.S. (1982); Fisk University, B.S. in Chemistry (1978). **Personal:** Dr. Lloyd enjoys swimming, boating, golf, reading, and travel.

David C. Mace, D.D.S.
Dentist and Partner
Precision Dental Care
1825 South 324th Place
Federal Way, WA 98003–8505
(206) 838–2018
Fax: (206) 838–9175

8021

Business Information: Precision Dental Care, established in 1993, is a full–service, family practice dentistry office, consisting of two dentists providing cosmetic and general dentistry. Established in 1993, the Practice serves patients residing in Tacoma, Auburn, Federal Way, and Seattle. As Dentist and Partner, Dr. Mace joined the Practice in 1993 and is responsible for providing general dental care to patients. **Career Steps:** Dentist and Partner, Precision Dental Care (1993–Present). **Associations & Accomplishments:** American Dental Association; Washington State Dental Association; Seattle – King County Dental Society; Academy of General Dentistry; Recipient, Teledyne Hanau Prosthodontics Award. **Education:** University of Washington: D.D.S. (1993), B.S. (1989). **Personal:** Dr. Mace enjoys water skiing and golf.

Sandra Madison, D.D.S.
Endodontist
The Office of Dr. Sandra Madison, D.D.S.
5 Yorkshire Drive
Asheville, NC 28803–2751
(704) 277–7668
Fax: (704) 277–0277

8021

Business Information: The Office of Dr. Sandra Madison, D.D.S. is a private dental practice specializing in Endodontics. Diplomate of the American Board of Endodontics, Dr. Madison established her solo practice in 1992, following her faculty appointment with the Department of Endodontics at the University of North Carolina School of Dentistry. Her practice involves the procedures of root canals, endodontic surgeries, and management of traumatic injuries. **Career Steps:** Endodontist, The Office of Dr. Sandra Madison, D.D.S. (1992–Present); Associate Professor and Department Chair, Department of Endodontics, University of North Carolina School of Dentistry (1986–1992); Assistant Professor and Graduate Program Director, Department of Endodontics, University of Iowa College of Dentistry (1981–1986). **Associations & Accomplishments:** American Association of Endodontists; Diplomate and Director, American Board of Endodontics; American Dental Association; International Assocaiton of Dental Research; Tarheel Endodontic Association. **Education:** University of Iowa, M.S. (1981); University of North Carolina – Chapel Hill: D.D.S. (1978); M.P.H. (1972); B.S. (1971). **Personal:** Married to Richard D. Jordan, DDS in 1976. Three children: Joshua, Christopher, and Abigail. Dr. Madison stays busy with her family, practice and professional commitments. She enjoys traveling and tennis.

Robert Maimone, D.D.S.
Sole Practitioner
The Office of Robert Maimone, D.D.S, P.C.
71 Broadway, Suite 1415
New York, NY 10006–2601
(212) 514–8600
Fax: (212) 809–6835

8021

Business Information: The Office of Dr. Robert Maimone, D.D.S, P.C. is a full–service, oral and Maxillofacial surgery practice. A Sole Practitioner since 1990, Dr. Maimone is Board Certified in Oral and Maxillofacial Surgery, Dental Anesthesiology, Carbon Dioxide Laser Surgery, and Interpore and Branemark endosteal titanium dental implants. Currently, Dr. Maimone is utilizing a Nd:YAG laser and has experience with CO2, Argon and Ruby lasers. His practice is affiliated with the Montefiore and Beth Israel Medical Centers in New York City, and he is also an Instructor of Dental Medicine. Dr. Maimone is personally responsible for founding PULSE, the Professional Updating Lecturers Series, and is a firm believer in continuing education. **Career Steps:** Sole Practitioner, The Office of Dr. Robert Maimone, D.D.S, P.C. (1990–Present). **Associations & Accomplishments:** American College of Oral Implantology; American Academy of Laser Dentistry; American Society for Laser Medicine and Surgery; Who's Who Among Rising Young Professionals; Founder, Professional Updating Lecturers Series; Captain of the Lacrosse Team, Johns Hopkins University; Actively involved in Church functions and reponsible for implementing the Men's and Women's Ministries. **Education:** New York University College of Dentistry, D.D.S.; Johns Hopkins University, B.A. in Natural Sciences; Residency, Montefiore–Albert Einstein Medical Center. **Personal:** Married to Ali in 1992. One child: Matthew. Dr. Maimone enjoys church activities and lacrosse.

Ben Manesh, D.D.S.
Dentist
The Office of Dr. Ben Manesh, D.D.S.
5542 Norbeck Road
Rockville, MD 20853–2441
(301) 369–0000
Fax: (301) 369–0032

8021

Business Information: The Office of Dr. Ben Manesh, D.D.S. is a private dental practice, currently employing 17 dental support staff. Establishing the private practice in 1991, Dr. Manesh is responsible for the care and treatment of patients, as well as the administrative functions of the office. **Career Steps:** Dentist, The Office of Dr. Ben Manesh, D.D.S. (1993–Present). **Associations & Accomplishments:** American Dental Association; AGD; SMDS; ACP. **Education:** Dental School, D.D.S. (1993). **Personal:** Married to Nadia in 1988. One child: Keon. Dr. Manesh enjoys volleyball.

Nelson R. Marques, D.D.S.

Owner and Dentist
Nelson R. Marques, D.D.S.
141 NE 3rd Avenue, Suite 401
Miami, FL 33132–2238
(305) 938–4599
Fax: (305) 938–9879

8021

Business Information: Nelson R. Marques, D.D.S. is a general practice dental office providing cosmetic, general dentistry and implants to patients. Established in 1989, the Practice currently provides dental care at two offices located in Fort Lauderdale and Miami, Florida. As Owner and Dentist, Dr. Marques is responsible for all aspects of operations, including providing dental care to patients. **Career Steps:** Owner and Dentist, Nelson R. Marques, D.D.S. (1989–Present). **Associations & Accomplishments:** Associate Fellow, American College of Oral Implantology; Associate Fellow, American Society of Osseointegration; Member, International Congress of Oral Implantologists; Broward County Dental Association. **Education:** New York University (1994); FDA–UNESP, D.D.S. (1975). **Personal:** Married to Denise Marques in 1994. Dr. Marques enjoys chess, fishing, and karate.

Julie A. Martinez, D.D.S
Pediatric Dentist
North Main Dental Center
1925 Studewood Street
Houston, TX 77008–4410
(713) 367–6558 (713) 861–8466
Fax: Please mail or call

8021

Business Information: The North Main Dental Center is a full–service pediatric dental facility. A general dentistry practitioner since 1988, and completing her pediatric dental residency in 1990, Dr. Martinez shares administrative duties with her associate, Dr. David Hernandez, in addition to her daily patient practice. **Career Steps:** Pediatric Dentist, North Main Dental Center (1994–Present); Clinical Assistant Professor, The University of Texas Health Science Center – Houston (1991–1994); Fellow, Indiana University United Cerebral Palsy Foundation (1990–1991). **Associations & Accomplishments:** American Academy of Pediatric Dentistry; Hispanic Dental Association; Lulac Young Woman of the Year, Houston Council District (1982). **Education:** The University of Texas Health Science Center – Houston Dental School, D.D.S. (1988); University of St. Thomas, B.A. in Biology (1984); Indiana University, Pediatric Dentistry Resident (1988–1990). **Personal:** Married to Dr. David Hernandez in 1987. Three children: Jonathan, Catherine, and Daniel. Dr. Martinez enjoys camping.

Rosanna U. Masciadri, D.M.D.
Family Dental Practitioner
Rosanna U. Masciadri, D.M.D., P.C.
1010 Brookview Place
Athens, GA 30606
(706) 546–8480
Fax: (706) 546–6055
EMail: See Below

8021

Business Information: Rosanna U. Masciadri, D.M.D., P.C. is a full–service, family dentistry practice. As Dental Associate and co–founder of the practice, Dr. Masciadri serves in all areas of administrative operations direction, dental treatment and procedures. She can also be reached through the Internet as follows: MMAS-CIAD@uga.cc.uga.edu **Career Steps:** Dental Associate, Rosanna U. Masciadri, D.M.D., P.C. (1992–Present). **Associations & Accomplishments:** Georgia Dental Association; American Dental Association; Hispanic Dental Association; Partners of Americas. **Education:** Tuft Dental School, D.M.D. (1992); State University of Uruguay, D.D.S. (1989); Fluently speaks Spanish, Portuguese and Italian. **Personal:** Married to Milton Masciadri in 1986. Two children: Daniel and Nicholas. Dr. Masciadri enjoys aerobics, cooking, sports and listening to classical music.

Michael S. Matz, D.M.D., F.A.G.D.
Dentist
The Office of Dr. Michael S. Matz, D.M.D., F.A.G.D.
Cedarbrook Hill Apartments, Suite 1, 8460 Limekiln Pike
Wyncote, PA 19095
(215) 576–1770
Fax: Please mail or call

8021

Business Information: The Office of Dr. Michael S. Matz, D.M.D., F.A.G.D. is a general practice dental facility. Establishing the sole practice in 1992, Dr. Matz oversees all administrative support staff, in addition to his daily patient treatment practice. **Career Steps:** Dentist, The Office of Dr. Michael S. Matz, D.M.D., F.A.G.D. (1992–Present). **Associations & Accomplishments:** American Dental Association; Pennsylvania Dental Association; Philadelphia County Dental Society; Fellow, Academy of General Dentistry; Who's Who Among Colleges and Universities (1983–1984); Alpha Omega International Dental Fraternity. **Education:** Temple University School of Dental Medicine, D.M.D. (1988); Armstrong State College, B.S. in Biology, cum laude (1984). **Personal:** Married to Ellen Horowitz in 1988. Two children: Joshua and Zachary. Dr. Matz enjoys tennis, golf, swimming and softball.

John J. McCarty, D.M.D.
Dentist
Family Dentistry
379 Egg Harbor Road
Sewell, NJ 08080
(609) 582–0090
Fax: Please mail or call

8021

Business Information: Family Dentistry, established in 1980, is a full–service, family practice dentistry office, providing cosmetic, general dentistry and oral surgery. A practicing dentist since 1992, Dr. McCarty joined the Practice in 1993. Serving as Dentist, he is responsible for providing general dental care to patients. **Career Steps:** Dentist, Family Dentistry (1993–Present); Dentist, Monmouth Medical Center (1992–1993); Dentist, Centra State Medical Center (1992–1993). **Associations & Accomplishments:** American Dental Association; New Jersey Dental Association; Monmouth/Ocean County Dental Association; Academy of General Dentistry; National Society of Dental Practitioners; St. George's Oral Cancer Society. **Education:** University of Pennsylvania, D.M.D. (1992); Ursinus College, B.S. in Biology (1988). **Personal:** Dr. McCarty enjoys team sports, music, and science fiction.

Ligaya Deleon McFarlane, D.M.D.
Sole Practitioner
Dental Office of Dr. Ligaya Deleon McFarlane
110 West 34th Street, Suite 1203
New York, NY 10001
(212) 947–6418
Fax: Please mail or call

8021

Business Information: The Dental Office of Ligaya Deleon McFarlane is a general practice dental facility. Establishing her private practice in 1989, Dr. McFarlane is responsible for the care and treatment of patients, as well as all administrative functions for the Office. **Career Steps:** Sole Practitioner, The Dental Office of Ligaya Deleon McFarlane (1989–Present); Dental Reviewer, New York State Department of Health (1979–1991). **Associations & Accomplishments:** American Dental Association; New York State Dental Society; First District Dental Society, Mangaldan New York, New Jersey, and Eastern Region. **Education:** New York University, American Licensure (1983); University of the East – Philippines, D.M.D. **Personal:** Married to Val in 1978. Dr. McFarlane enjoys painting and helping disadvantaged people.

Kimberly McNeal, M.S., D.M.D.
Orthodontist and Chief Executive Officer
–Independent–
8737 Dunwood Place, #1
Atlanta, GA 30350–2985
(770) 594–7090
Fax: (770) 594–7191

8021

Business Information: A practicing dentist since 1987 and a Board–certified Orthodontist, Dr. McNeal established her private orthodontics practice in 1992. A four–chair practice, the office has the utmost in state–of–the–art systems utilized in orthodontic and dentofacial treatments. A family–oriented practice, services include lingual and invisible braces, retaining treatments, dentofacial and cranial facial treatments, and TMJ disorders. It also provides treatment and preparation of patients for maxillofacial surgery referrals. **Career Steps:** Orthodontist and Chief Executive Officer, (1992–Present); Practicing Resident and Instructor, Emory University (1987–1989); Instructor – Department of Emergency Medicine, University of Kentucky (1985–1987). **Associations & Accomplishments:** American Association of Orthodontists; American Dental Association; Georgia Dental Association; Board of Directors, Atlanta Women's Medical Alliance; American Cleft Palate and Craniofacial Association; Foundation for Craniofacial Education Seminars (F.A.C.E.S.). **Education:** Emory University, Orthodontics Certification (1989); University of Kentucky, D.M.D. (1987); Eastern Kentucky University, M.S. (1981); Angelo State University, B.S. (1978). **Personal:** Married to Dr. Ralf Poineal in 1993.

Promila Mehan, D.D.S.
Sole Practitioner
Dr. Promila Mehan Dental Office
800 Franklin Boulevard, Unit 2
Cambridge, Ontario N1R 7Z1
(519) 740–1407
Fax: (519) 658–5164

8021

Business Information: Dr. Promila Mehan Dental Office is a part–time, family practice dentistry office, conducting general dental care and surgeries. A practicing dentist since 1988, Dr. Mehan established her sole practice dental office in 1994. She oversees all administrative operations for associates and support staff, in addition to her daily patient practice, which also includes surgical procedures. **Career Steps:** Sole Practitioner, Dr. Promila Mehan Dental Office (1994–Present); Associate Dentist, Various Offices (1988–1991). **Associations & Accomplishments:** Ontario Dental Association; Canadian Dental Association; Soroptomist International of the Americas – Cambridge, Ontario. **Education:** University of Toronto, D.D.S. (1988). **Personal:** Married to Upender in 1989. Two children: Prayrna and Divya. Dr. Mehan enjoys family activities, reading, sewing, cooking, crafts, fitness activities, and gardening.

Thomas J. Meyer, D.D.S.
Dentist
Thomas J. Meyer
1200 East Woodhurst Drive #200H
Springfield, MO 65804–3742
(417) 881–6000
Fax: Please mail or call

8021

Business Information: Thomas J. Meyer is a general practice dental facility. Co–founding the practice in 1984, Dr. Meyer shares administrative responsibilities for the direction of a staff of six, as well as his daily patient practice. Once a year, Dr. Meyer takes his knowledge of dentistry and good oral hygiene to the local elementary schools to encourage the children to brush their teeth and see a dentist frequently. **Career Steps:** Dentist, Thomas J. Meyer (1984–Present). **Associations & Accomplishments:** American Dental Association; Missouri Dental Association; Past President, Springfield Dental Society; Southwest Missouri Society of Oral Implantologists; International Congress of Oral Implantologists; American College of Oral Implantology; American Society of Osseointegration; Chairman of Missouri Dental Political Action Committee; Received Outstanding Young Dental Leader Award, Missouri Dental Association. **Education:** University of Missouri, D.D.S. (1984); Southwest Missouri State University, B.S. in Biology (1979). **Personal:** Married to Susan D. in 1983. Two children: Ashley and Nicole. Dr. Meyer enjoys water skiing and snow skiing.

Daniel K. Miller, D.D.S.
Sole Practitioner
Family Dental Clinic
1104 West Sam Houston Street #A
Pharr, TX 78577–5104
(210) 781–0031
Fax: (210) 781–0202

8021

Business Information: Family Dental Clinic is a full–service, family practice dentistry office, providing orthopedics, periodontics, and aesthetic dentistry through two locations. A practicing dentist since 1985, Dr. Miller established his sole practice, five–chair dental office in 1985. He oversees all administrative operations for associates and a staff of six, in addition to his daily patient practice. He provides comprehensive dentistry through a wide network of specialists and expert laboratories. Concurrent with his private practice, he serves in the U.S. Army Reserves as a Dental Specialist. **Career Steps:** Sole Practitioner, Family Dental Clinic (1988–Present); Dental Hygienist, Daniel K. Miller, R.D.H. (1988–1994); Dental Specialist, United States Army Reserve (1985–Present). **Associations & Accomplishments:** American Dental Association; Texas Dental Association; Rio Grande Valley Dental Society; Supreme Chapter Xi Psi Phi Fraternity; Phi Theta Kappa; Golden Key National Honor Society; American Society for Geriatric Dentistry; Who's Who Among Students in American Junior Colleges; Wharton Junior College Alumni Association; Southwest Texas State University Renegade Rugby Association; University of Texas Health Science Center – San Antonio Alumni Association; South Texas Off Road Mountain Bike; National Rifle Association. **Education:** University of Texas Health Science Center – San Antonio, D.D.S. (1994); Southwest Texas State University, B.S. (1990); Wharton County Junior College, A.A.S., R.D.H. **Personal:** Married to Diane Shodrock in 1994. Dr. Miller enjoys golf, off–road biking, country dancing, performing arts, acoustic guitar, and hunting.

Joseph G. Mirci, D.D.S., MAGD
Dentist
Dr. Joseph G. Mirci, D.D.S., MAGD
2286 East 2100 South
Salt Lake City, UT 84109
(801) 487–3836
Fax: Please mail or call

8021

Business Information: Dr. Joseph G. Mirci, D.D.S., MAGD is a general practice dental office, providing all aspects of general dental care including, orthodontics and gum surgery, but with the exception of placing implants. As Dentist, Dr. Mirci oversees all aspects of the office, performing all aspects of general dentistry except implant placement. **Career Steps:** Dentist, Dr. Joseph G. Mirci, D.D.S., MAGD (1983–Present); Associate Clinical Professor, University of Utah (1987–Present). **Associations & Accomplishments:** Master Plan Chairman, Secretary, and Vice President, Utah Academy of General Dentistry; Utah Dental Association; Fellow, Pierre Fauchard Academy; Achievement Award, American Orthodontic Society; Fellow, Academy of Dentistry International; Master in Academy of General Dentistry; American Dental Association; Fellow, Academy of Dentistry International. **Education:** Case Western Reserve, D.D.S. (1982); University of Utah, B.S. in Medical Biology (1978); Youngstown Hospital Association, General Practice Residency (1982–1983). **Personal:** Married to Bonnie L. in 1975. Five children: Joseph J., Curtis, Daniel, Michael, and Michelle. Dr. Mirci enjoys racquetball, skiing, woodworking, and Scouting.

Charles L. Mitnyan, D.M.D.
Dental Physician
Clinique Familiale St. Vincent
250 King Est, Suite 205
Sherbrooke, Quebec J1G 1A9
(819) 563–4848
Fax: (819) 563–4849

8021

Business Information: Dr. Mitnyan established Clinique Familiale St. Vincent, a family dental practice, upon conferral of his dental licensure in 1974. The Clinic is a 3–chair facility providing a wide range of dental services including cleanings, check–ups, fillings, extractions, bridgework and cosmetic dentistry. **Career Steps:** Dental Physician, Clinique Familiale St. Vincent (1974–Present). **Associations & Accomplishments:** Dental Surgeons of Eastern Quebec; Active member of Centre Hospitalier of St–Vincent Paul; Counsel member of the C.H.U.S. Pediatry Department of Sherbrooke; Member, The Order of Dentistry of Quebec; Member, The Canadian Dental Association; Member, The American Academy of Cosmetic Dentistry; Member, The Institute of Erikson Therapie and Hypnosis of Quebec. **Education:** University of Medicine,

Budapest, Faculty of Stomatologie (1965); Licence Province of Quebec, Canada 1974. **Personal:** Three children: Erika, Coralie, and Manuel. Dr. Mitnyan enjoys skiing and travel.

Nitin O. Mody, D.D.S.
Partner
Friendly Dental Center
5422 Woodruff Avenue
Lakewood, CA 90713–1533
(310) 867–6453
Fax: (310) 804–7261

8021

Business Information: Friendly Dental Center is a full–service, general practice dentistry office, providing cosmetic and general dentistry from three locations. A practicing dentist since 1980, Dr. Mody joined Friendly Dental Center as Partner and Dentist in 1992. Partnered with two other dentists, he provides general dentistry to children and adults. **Career Steps:** Partner, Friendly Dental Center (1992–Present); Dentist, Family Dentistry (1989–1992); Dentist, Dr. Beauchamp (1988–1989). **Associations & Accomplishments:** International Dental Association. **Education:** Nair Dental College, B.D.S. (1980). **Personal:** Married to Bela in 1983. Two children: Karan and Ronak. Dr. Mody enjoys travel, hiking, movies, and gardening.

Lyle D. Monger, D.D.S.
Sole Practitioner
The Dental Office of Lyle D. Monger, D.D.S.
131 Belle Forest Circle
Nashville, TN 37221
(615) 662–0256
Fax: (615) 662–2993

8021

Business Information: The Dental Office of Lyle D. Monger, D.D.S. is a full–service, family practice dentistry office, providing cosmetic, bridges, general and aesthetic dentistry. A practicing dentist since 1983, Dr. Monger established his sole practice dentistry office in 1986. He oversees all administrative operations for associates and a support staff of five, in addition to his daily patient practice. **Career Steps:** Sole Practitioner, The Dental Office of Lyle D. Monger, D.D.S. (1986–Present). **Associations & Accomplishments:** American Society for Dental Aesthetics; American Academy of Cosmetic Dentistry; Nashville Dental Society; American Academy of General Dentistry; American Dental Association; Omicron Kappa Upsilon Dental Fraternity; Lion's Club. **Education:** University of Tennessee Dental School, D.D.S. (1983); University of Arkansas, B.A. in Zoology and Chemistry. **Personal:** Married to Carol in 1978. Dr. Monger enjoys golf, travel, horses, skiing, camping, and spending time with family.

Ray A. Morse, DMD
Sole Practitioner
The Dental Office of Ray A. Morse, DMD
510 South Ohio Avenue
Live Oak, FL 32060
(904) 362–1408
Fax: (904) 362–1319

8021

Business Information: The Dental Office of Ray A. Morse, DMD is a general dentistry practice providing cosmetic, restorative and full family dental services. In the general practice of dentistry since 1993, Dr. Morse established his private practice in 1995. He oversees an adminstrative and dental support staff of six, in addition to his daily patient practice. **Career Steps:** Sole Practitioner, The Office of Ray A. Morse, DMD (1995–Present); Dentist, Mayo Family Dental Services (1993–1995). **Associations & Accomplishments:** American Dental Association; Academy of General Dentistry; Florida Dental Association; National Society of Dental Practitioners; American Association of Public Health Dentistry; Live Oak Rotary; Suwanee County Chamber of Commerce. **Education:** University of Florida College of Dentistry, DMD

(1992); Florida State University; North Florida Junior College. **Personal:** Dr. Morse enjoys tennis, teaching volleyball, and computer science.

Alan Choong K. Mun, D.D.S

President and Dentist and Implantologist
Dental Implant and Cosmetic Center
791 Central Park Avenue
Scarsdale, NY 10583–2522
(914) 472–6611
Fax: (914) 725–6460

8021

Business Information: The Dental Implant and Cosmetic Center is a comprehensive dental practice with an emphasis on implants and cosmetic dentistry. A comprehensive dentistry practitioner since 1981, Dr, Mun established his specialty restorative practice in 1987, directing a staff of eight, in addition to his patient practice. Always on the leading edge of dental technology, he continually pursues post–graduate training in the latest dental procedures and breakthroughs, and is also in the process of writing consumer guides on the subject of dental implants. **Career Steps:** President and Dentist, Dental Implant and Cosmetic Center (1991–Present); Owner, President and Dentist, Group Health Dental Associates (1981–1991). **Associations & Accomplishments:** Fellow, International Congress of Oral Implantologists; Fellow, American Society of Osseointegration; Associate Fellow, American College of Oral Implantologists; American Dental Association; American Academy of Cosmetic Dentistry; Dental Society of the State of New York. **Education:** New York University: D.D.S. (1981); Postdoctoral Training leading to Certificates of Achievement; University of Rochester, B.A. in Biology and Psychology (1978). **Personal:** Married to Doris C. in 1976. Three children: Laura, Amanda, and Alex. Dr. Mun enjoys skiing, watersports, travel and spending time with his family.

Anthony Musella, D.D.S.
Oral & Maxillofacial Surgeon
Wheat Ridge Oral Surgery
4485 Wadsworth Boulevard, Suite 201
Wheat Ridge, CO 80033–3310
(303) 421–4010
Fax: (303) 423–9051

8021

Business Information: Wheat Ridge Oral Surgery, established in 1963, is an oral and maxillofacial surgery practice, specializing in correction of dento–facial deformities and infections, temporomandibular joint derangements, jaw implants, and reconstruction of regional trauma and pathology. As an Oral and Maxillofacial Surgeon, Dr. Musella is responsible for providing all aspects of his specialty to patients. **Career Steps:** Oral and Maxillofacial Surgeon, Wheat Ridge Oral Surgery (1991–Present); Oral & Maxillofacial Surgeon, U.S. Air Force (1981–1991); General Dentist, U.S. Air Force (1981–1988). **Associations & Accomplishments:** Fellow, American Association of Oral and Maxillofacial Surgery; Diplomate, American Board of Oral and Maxillofacial Surgery; Member, Colorado Society of Oral and Maxillofacial Surgery; Member, American Dental Association; Member, Colorado Dental Association; Member and Officer of Affiliate Chapter, Metropolitan Denver Dental Society; Member, Rocky Mountain Dental Society; Chairman, Department of Oral and Maxillofacial Surgery – Lutheran Medical Center, KIND – Kids in Need of Dentistry; "Dentists with a Heart"; Handicapped Children's Dentistry. **Education:** David Grant Medical Center, Travis Air Force Base, California, Specialty in Oral and Maxillofacial Surgery (1988); Ehrling Berquist Regional Medical Center, Offutt Air Force Base, Nebraska, General Practice Residency (1982); University of Colorado, D.D.S. (1981); University of Northern Colorado, B.A. (1977). **Personal:** Married to Eileen in 1976. Dr. Musella enjoys playing the piano and sports including skiing, tennis, swimming, and hiking.

Mark T. Musgrave, D.D.S.
Associate
Musgrave & Musgrave
98 West William Street
Delaware, OH 43015–2305
(614) 362–6952
Fax: (614) 363–5670

8021

Business Information: Musgrave & Musgrave is a full–service, general practice dentistry office, specializing in orthodontics and TMJ disorders. With two locations in Ohio, the Practice consists of an eight–chair practice in Delaware and a six–chair practice in Waldo. Co–founding the Practice with his father in 1992 and a Certified Orthodontist, Dr. Musgrave is responsible for his daily patient practice, including reducing jaw discrepancies and straightening teeth through braces. He

also treats patients with Temporomandibular Joint Disorders and facial pain. **Career Steps:** Associate, Musgrave & Musgrave (1992–Present). **Associations & Accomplishments:** American Dental Association (1988–Present); American Association of Orthodontists (1992–Present); Assistant Soccer Coach, Delaware Christian High School (1992). **Education:** Eastman Dental Center: Certificate in Orthodontics (1992), Certificate In Temporomandibular Joint Disorders (1990); University of Michigan, D.D.S.; Ohio Wesleyan University, B.A. **Personal:** Dr. Musgrave enjoys weightlifting, skiing, piano, and soccer.

Rolando G. Naraval, D.D.S.

Partner
Modern Dental Center
2080 York Road, Suite 265
Timonium, MD 21093–4251
(410) 560–2616
Fax: (410) 560–2016

8021

Business Information: Modern Dental Center, established in 1992, is a full–service, group, family dental practice, providing cosmetic, oral surgery, and general dentistry services. Co–founding the dental practice in 1992, Dr. Naraval serves as Partner, providing basic dental, cosmetic surgical and non–surgical procedures, reconstruction, replacement of implants, and preventative dentistry. Future plans include expanding the practice, doubling the size, and moving into a management role. Concurrent with his dental practice, he serves as Supervisor and Teacher at Medix School and as Associate at Fallston Dental Care. **Career Steps:** Partner, Modern Dental Center (1992–Present); Supervisor and Teacher, Medix School (1994–Present); Associate, Fallston Dental Care (1994–Present); Cardio–Pulmonary Technician/EMT, St. Joseph's Hospital (1985–1990). **Associations & Accomplishments:** American Dental Association; Maryland State Dental Association; Baltimore County Dental Association; Philippine Relief Fund; Frequent public community speaking. **Education:** University of Maryland at Baltimore, D.D.S. (1992); Juniata College, B.S. in Biology and Pre–Dental. **Personal:** Dr. Naraval enjoys travel, skiing, and restoring cars.

Donka Neimar, D.O.S., D.D.S.

Owner
Dr. Donka Neimar, D.O.S., D.D.S., P.C.
2850 Artesia Boulevard, Suite 210
Redondo Beach, CA 90278–3413
(310) 371–0316
Fax: (310) 542–1488

8021

Business Information: Dr. Donka Neimar, D.O.S., D.D.S., P.C., established in 1993, is a full–service, general dental practice. As Owner, Dr. Neimar is responsible for all aspects of operations, including providing patients with dental care. A native of Yugoslavia, she arrived seven years ago in the U.S. and during this time, she married, had two children, went through dental school, and started her own dental practice. Through her involvement with the International Rescue Committee (IRC), she provides former Yugoslavians with free dental care as a contribution to the Cause. **Career Steps:** Owner, Dr. Donka Neimar, D.O.S., D.D.S., P.C. (1993–Present); Clinical Instructor, University of Southern California School of Dentistry (1992–1993); Associate, R. Mokbel, D.O.S., D.D.S. (1992–1993). **Associations & Accomplishments:** Western Los Angeles Dental Society; California Dental Association; American Dental Association; University of Southern California Alumni working with International Rescue Committee (IRC) on special refugee program from the former Yugoslavia. **Education:** University of Southern California School of Dentistry, D.D.S. (1991); University of Belgrade, Yugoslavia, D.O.S. (Doctor of Stomatology). **Personal:** Married to Jeffrey in 1987. Two children: Tiffany Ann and Oscar Harrison. Dr. Neimar enjoys gourmet cooking, volunteer work in the community, reading, and listening to classical music.

Bruce L. Nelson, D.D.S.
President
The Dental Office of Bruce L. Nelson, D.D.S., P.C.
1776 East Glendale Avenue
Phoenix, AZ 85020–5505
(602) 678–4500
Fax: Please mail or call

8021

Business Information: The Dental Office of Bruce L. Nelson, D.D.S., P.C. is a full–service, family practice dentistry office, with emphasis on cosmetic dentistry, including orthodontics. A practicing dentist since 1977, Dr. Nelson established the four–chair dentistry practice in 1982. Serving as President, he oversees the administrative operations for associates and a staff of seven, in addition to his dental practice. **Career Steps:** President, The Dental Office of Bruce L. Nelson, D.D.S., P.C. (1993–Present); Owner, Bruce L. Nelson, D.D.S. (1982–1993); Shareholder and Board of Directors, Arizona Dental Health Associates, P.C. (1978–1982). **Associations & Accomplishments:** American Dental Association; Arizona State Dental Association; Central Arizona Dental Society; Optimist Club of Phoenix: Former President, Former Vice President, Sustained Member; National Dental Electronic Interchange Council: Board of Trustees, Vice Chairman; Member and Former Commander, Maricopa County Sheriff's Office Executive Posse. **Education:** Northwestern University, D.D.S. (1977); University of Arizona, B.S. (1972). **Personal:** Married to Sheryl in 1976. Two children: Krystine and Kandice. Dr. Nelson enjoys fly fishing, skiing, four–wheeling, shooting, and computers.

Thomas P. Niedermeier, D.D.S.
President and Sole Practitioner
The Office of Thomas P. Niedermeier, D.D.S.
119 West 3rd Street
Oakboro, NC 28129
(704) 485–3306
Fax: (704) 485–3306

8021

Business Information: The Office of Thomas P. Niedermeier, D.D.S. is a full–service general dental facility, with a primary focus on crowns and bridges. Establishing the private, individual practice in 1973, as President and Sole Practitioner Dr. Niedermeier oversees an administrative and medical support staff of three, in addition to his daily patient practice. **Career Steps:** Dentist and President, The Office of Thomas P. Niedermeier, D.D.S. (1973–Present). **Associations & Accomplishments:** American Dental Association; North Carolina State Dental Society; Third District Dental Society; Stanly County Dental Society; Secretary and Treasurer, L. D. Pankey Study Club; Kiwanis International; Former Baseball Umpire and Football Official. **Education:** Loyola Dental School, D.D.S. (1971); Indiana University; University of Evansville, B.S. **Personal:** Married to Linda J. in 1967. Two children: Timothy H. and Deanna L. Dr. Niedermeier enjoys sports.

Marta L. Nieto, D.D.S.
President
Marta L. Nieto, D.D.S., P.A.
5511 SW 8th Street, Suite 201
Miami, FL 33134
(305) 262–4499
Fax: (305) 262–6004

8021

Business Information: Marta L. Nieto, D.D.S., P.A. is a full–service, family practice dentistry office, providing cosmetic, general dentistry, and oral surgery. Establishing her sole practice dentistry office upon the conferral of her dental degree in 1992, Dr. Nieto oversees all administrative operations for associates and a support staff of six, in addition to her daily patient practice. **Career Steps:** President, Marta L. Nieto, D.D.S., P.A. (1992–Present). **Associations & Accomplishments:** East Coast Dental Association; American Dental Association; Florida State Association; CEOLA; HELO. **Education:** Florida State Board of Dentistry (1992). **Personal:** One child: Dayron. Dr. Nieto enjoys movies, restaurants, beach activities, and dancing.

Thomas P. Nordone, D.M.D.
Oral & Maxillofacial Surgeon
Thomas P. Nordone, D.M.D.
295 Saint James Place
Philadelphia, PA 19106
(215) 592–1755
Fax: (215) 592–1757

8021

Business Information: Thomas P. Nordone, D.M.D., a Board–Eligible Oral and Maxillofacial surgeon since 1983, was part of a group practice for nine years before establishing his sole practice office in 1992. He is responsible for all aspects of operations, overseeing a support staff of four, in addition to his daily patient practice and teaching responsibilities. **Career Steps:** Oral and Maxillofacial Surgeon, Thomas P. Nordone, D.M.D. (1983–Present). **Associations & Accomplishments:** American Associaton of Oral and Maxillofacial Surgeons; American Dental Association; All State and Local Societies; International Association of Oral and Maxillofacial Surgeons; Currently President–Elect of Philadelphia County Dental Society. **Education:** Villanova University, B.S. (1975); Temple University, D.M.D. (1980); University of Pennsylvania, Certificate in Oral and Maxillofacial Surgery (1983). **Personal:** Married to Christine in 1985. Three children: Laura, Tommy, and Nathan. Dr. Nordone enjoys sailing and bicycle riding.

Steven B. Oken, D.D.S.
Periodontal Practitioner
The Dental Office of Steven B. Oken, D.D.S.
1550 Pelham Parkway
Bronx, NY 10461–1105
(718) 597–8457
Fax: Please mail or call

8021

Business Information: The Dental Office of Steven B. Oken, D.D.S. is a high–tech, modern periodontics and dental implantology practice. Operating with one full–time dentist and a part–time associate dentist, the Office accepts most insurance carriers for its patients. Founding the practice in 1987, Dr. Steven Oken oversees all administrative and associate support staff, in addition to his daily patient base. Concurrent to his private dental practice, he also teaches at several local hospitals in and around the greater Bronx burroughs. **Career Steps:** Owner, Steven B. Oken, D.D.S. (1987–Present). **Associations & Accomplishments:** American Dental Association; Northeast Society of Periodontists; Bronx County Dental Society; New York Dental Society; American Academy of Periodontology; Academy of Osseointegration. **Education:** University of Tennessee, Periodontal Specialty Certificate (1984); SUNY– Stony Brook Dental School, D.D.S.; SUNY– Buffalo, B.A. **Personal:** Married to Sharon in 1987. Two children: Melisa and Adam. Dr. Oken enjoys tennis, skiing, scuba diving, stain glass work and photography.

Hasan Sami Osseiran, D.D.S., M.S.

Dentist
Watergate Dental Associates
2506 Virginia Avenue, NW, Suite 2506
Washington, DC 20037–1902
(202) 965–5400
Fax: (202) 298–7760

8021

Business Information: Watergate Dental Associates is a full–service, private dental practice providing general dentistry, cosmetic and oral surgery to patients. Establishing the private practice in 1975, Dr. Osseiran is responsible for all aspects of operations, including providing general dentistry care with a dual specialty in TMJ (joints of the jaw – grinding teeth and headaches) management and prosthetics (replacement of missing parts, both simple & complex matters) dentistry. A highly–esteemed expert in dental prosthetics and procedures, he has been appointed to provide dental counsel to both the United Arab Emirate and Saudi Arabia. **Career Steps:** Dentist, Watergate Dental Associates (1990–Present); Dental Consultant, United Arab Emirate and Saudi Arabia (1993–Present); Teacher Assistant, Georgetown University School of Dentistry (1985–1988). **Associations & Accomplishments:** American Dental Association; American Academy of Implant Dentistry; American Academy of General Dentistry; American College of Prosthodontists; American Academy of Cosmetic Dentistry; Published in Journal of American Dental Association. **Education:** Georgetown University, D.D.S., M.S. (1985–1988). **Personal:** Dr. Osseiran enjoys scuba diving, martial arts, hiking, and biking.

John W. Pak, D.D.S.
Dentist
The Office of Dr. John W. Pak, D.D.S.
900 East Almond Avenue
Madera, CA 93637–5642
(209) 674–5477
Fax: (209) 674–5476

8021

Business Information: The Office of Dr. John W. Pak, D.D.S. is a full–service dental practice. Establishing the practice in 1994, Dr. Pak is responsible for all administrative aspects, the care and treatment of patients, and the education of proper dental hygiene practices. **Career Steps:** Dentist, The Office of Dr. John W. Pak, D.D.S. (1994–Present); Associate Dentist, Valley Dental Center (1992–1994); Dental Student, Loma Linda University (1987–1991). **Associations & Accomplishments:** Fresno–Madera Dental Society; California Dental Association; American Dental Association. **Education:** Loma Linda University, D.D.S. (1991). **Personal:** Married to Susan in 1992. Dr. Pak enjoys golf, snow skiing, tennis, reading, and spending time with his wife.

John J. Paterno II, D.D.S.

Dentist
The Dental Office of John J. Paterno II, D.D.S.
14102 Sullyfield Circle, #500
Chantilly, VA 22021–1615
(703) 378–4004
Fax: (703) 378–6921

8021

Business Information: The Dental Office of John J. Paterno II, D.D.S. is a comprehensive dental practice, exclusively providing aesthetic and cosmetic dentistry. A practicing dentist since 1984, Dr. Paterno established his sole practice dentistry office in 1986. He oversees all administrative operations and a support staff of 4, in addition to his daily patient practice. **Career Steps:** Dentist, The Dental Office of John J. Paterno II, D.D.S. (1986–Present). **Associations & Accomplishments:** American Academy of Cosmetic Dentistry; American Society for Dental Aesthetics; Fellow, Academy of General Dentistry; American Dental Association; Virginia Dental Association; Dulles Area Chamber of Commerce. **Education:** Georgetown University School of Dentistry, D.D.S. (1984); University of Buffalo, Postgraduate Program in Cosmetic and Aesthetic Dentistry (1995); New York University, B.A. (1979); **Personal:** Married to Beverly in 1991. Two children: Samantha and Brooke.

Harry J. Pearsall, D.D.S.
Sole Practitioner
The Office of Harry J. Pearsall, D.D.S.
404 Shearer Building
Bay City, MI 48732
(517) 895–5481
Fax: Please mail or call

8021

Business Information: The Office of Harry J. Pearsall, D.D.S. is a general practice dental facility. Establishing his private practice in 1945, Dr. Pearsall, D.D.S. oversees all aspects of office operations focusing on the care and treatment of his older patients. **Career Steps:** The Office of Harry J. Pearsall, D.D.S. (1945–Present); Dentist with 107th Medical Battalion, 32nd Infantry Division from October 1940 to December 1945 – three years in Australia and New Guinea. **Associations & Accomplishments:** Michigan Dental Association; Former President and Delegate, American Dental Association; Saginaw Valley Dental Association; American College of Dentists; International College of Dentists; Chamber of Commerce; American Legion; Elks Lodge; Former Member, Michigan National Guard. **Education:** Marquette University, D.D.S. (1939); Marquette University, B.S. **Personal:** Widower. One child: Paul R. Dr. Pearsall enjoys fishing and hunting.

Hector Luis Perez, DDS

Sole Practitioner
Westchester Family Dental Care, P.C.
1840 Westchester Avenue, #B
Bronx, NY 10472–3016
(718) 931–2000
Fax: (718) 931–2000

8021

Business Information: Westchester Family Dental Care, P.C. is a full–service, general dental facility providing such services as cosmetic dentistry, crown and bridge placement, and dentures. Establishing his private dental practice in 1994, Dr. Perez oversees all administrative aspects, in addition to his patient practice. An expert in his field, Dr. Perez has experience and knowledge in all levels of dental care from the laboratory and materials to the actual procedures. **Career Steps:** Dentist, Westchester Family Dental Care, P.C. (1994–Present). **Associations & Accomplishments:** Hispanic Dental Association; American Dental Association; Phi Eta Mu Fraternity. **Education:** New York University, D.D.S. (1991); Universidad Central Del Este, D.M.D. (1980); Texas Dental Technology School, M.D.T. (1988). **Personal:** Married to Dr. Linda E. Velez in 1989. Two children: Alice and Zormarie Perez. Dr. Perez enjoys breeding and training Paso Fino horses.

Than T. Pham, D.D.S.
President and Owner
Monterey Park Dental Group
933 South Atlantic Boulevard
Monterey Park, CA 91754–4715
(818) 308–0943
Fax: Please mail or call

8021

Business Information: Monterey Park Dental Group is a full–service, family practice dentistry office, providing cosmetic, general dentistry, and oral surgery. A practicing dentist since 1959, Dr. Pham established Monterey Park Dental Group in 1982 and currently serves as President and Owner. He is responsible for all administrative operations for associates and a support staff of three, in addition to his daily patient practice. **Career Steps:** President and Owner, Monterey Park Dental Group (1982–Present). **Education:** Vietnam, D.D.S. (1959). **Personal:** Dr. Pham enjoys photography and gardening.

Robert J.G. Piedalue, D.M.D.
Sole Practitioner
Office of Robert J.G. Piedalue, D.M.D.
4822 50 Street, Suite 301
Red Deer, Alberta T4N 1X4
(403) 346–9122
Fax: (403) 341–6969

8021

Business Information: Office of Robert J.G. Piedalue, D.M.D. is a full–service, family practice dentistry office, providing general dentistry and TMJ care to patients. Establishing his sole practice dentistry office upon the conferral of his doctorate degree in 1988, Dr. Piedalue oversees all administrative operations for associates and support staff, in addition to his daily patient practice. Concurrently, he operates an independent distributorship for Oxyfresh Worldwide. **Career Steps:** Sole Practitioner, Robert J.G. Piedalue, D.M.D. (1988–Present). **Associations & Accomplishments:** Alberta Dental Association; Canadian Dental Association; Knights of Columbus; Piper Creek Optimist Club. **Education:** University of Manitoba: D.M.D. (1988), B.Sc. in Dental Research; Simon Fraser University, B.Sc. in Kinesiology. **Personal:** Married to Gillian in 1991. 2 children: Kirstan Elizabeth, and Katherine Ann. Dr. Piedalue enjoys golf and downhill skiing.

Jack Piermatti, D.M.D.
Dentist
The Dental Office of Jack Piermatti, D.M.D.
205 White Horse Road
Voorhees, NJ 08043
(609) 783–5777
Fax: (609) 435–6506

8021

Business Information: Established in 1986 as a solo general practice, Dr. Piermatti has developed his office into one of the most successful private practices in South Jersey. This quality–oriented practice emphasizes adult reconstructive dentistry, including crown and bridge, and removable prosthodontics, as well as implant surgery and restoration. Dr. Piermatti is responsible for overseeing all operations, including that of associate dentists, lab technicians, and administrative staff, as well as providing direct patient care. **Career Steps:** Founder and Dentist, The Dental Office of Jack Piermatti, D.M.D. (1986–Present). **Associations & Accomplishments:** American Dental Association; New Jersey Dental Association; Southern Dental Society; Academy of General Dentistry; American Academy of Implant Dentistry. **Education:** New York University School of Dentistry, Implantology Training (1996); St. Joseph's Hospital and Medical Center, Internship (1980); Fairleigh Dickinson University School of Dentistry, D.M.D. (1979); Fairleigh Dickinson University, B.S. (1975). **Personal:** Married to Carol in 1978. Three children: Laura, Valerie, and John.

Craig O. Preis, D.D.S.
General Dentistry Practitioner
Preis & Stein
541 Chester Pike
Prospect Park, PA 19076–1406
(610) 532–0984
Fax: (610) 532–0869

8021

Business Information: Preis & Stein is a full–service general dentistry practice, providing family dental care, oral surgery and cosmetic dental procedures. A practicing general dentist since 1980, Dr. Preis purchased the practice in March, 1996 from Leo J Stein his partner since 1987. Besides providing administrative duties for a support staff of six, he practices all areas of family and cosmetic dentistry. **Career Steps:** General Dentistry Practitioner, Preis & Stein (1987–Present) **Associations & Accomplishments:** American Dental Association; Chester/Delaware Dental Society; Philadelphia County Dental Society. **Education:** Case Western Reserve University Dental School, D.D.S. (1980); Case Western Reserve University, B.S. (1978) **Personal:** Married to Maureen (nee' Walton) in 1993. Two children: Sean and Bradley. Dr. Preis enjoys fishing, biking and reading.

Steven G. Press, D.D.S.

Oral and Maxillofacial Surgeon
Northern Virginia Oral
2508 Columbia Pike, Suite B
Arlington, VA 22204–4408
(703) 278–8916
Fax: Please mail or call

8021

Business Information: Northern Virginia Oral is a specialized group dental practice concentrating in oral and maxillofacial surgery with five offices in Northern Virginia. A practicing oral and maxillofacial surgeon since 1989, Dr. Press joined the Group in 1993, serving patients from Arlington, Virginia and Washington, D.C. areas. **Career Steps:** Oral and Maxillofacial Surgeon, Northern Virginia Oral (1993–Present); Oral and Maxillofacial Surgeon, Washington Hospital Center (1989–1993). **Education:** Medical College of Virginia, D.D.S. (1989); Washington Hospital Center in Oral and Maxillofacial Surgery, Certificate. **Personal:** Dr. Press enjoys golf and travel.

Danny W. Qualliotine, D.D.S.
Dentist
Aesthetic Dental Care
107 Oakmont Drive
Greenville, NC 27858–5937
(919) 321–2500
Fax: (919) 321–0248

8021

Business Information: Aesthetic Dental Care is a general dental practice focusing on cosmetic reconstruction. The practice has served some North Carolina candidates for various beauty pageants. As Dentist, Dr. Qualliotine is responsible for all aspects of operations, including providing dental care to patients with an emphasis on cosmetics. His practice started in Greenville in 1977, expanding in 1991 to provide enhanced cosmetic services. Dr. Qualliotine is also an expert in computer–generated restorations on CEREC CAD–CAM. **Career Steps:** Dentist, Aesthetic Dental Care (1977–Present). **Associations & Accomplishments:** American Dental Association; Academy of General Dentistry; Academy of Computerized Dentistry; Graduate of Institute for Advanced Dental Aesthetics; Sunday school teacher and Deacon, Hooker Memorial Christian Church; Black Belt in Gama Goju Karate. **Education:** University of North Carolina – Chapel Hill School of Dentistry, D.D.S. (1976), B.S. in Dentistry (1974). **Personal:** Married to Paula Stokes Qualliotine in 1986. Two

children: Rachel Marie and Ryan Danielle. Dr. Qualliotine enjoys karate, carpentry, and his family.

Catharine C. Quartapella Goodson, D.D.S.

Owner
Island Dental Associates
6821 Stewart Road
Galveston, TX 77551
(409) 744–5253
Fax: (713) 474–1208

8021

Business Information: Island Dental Associates is a full service, general practice dental office, providing comprehensive dental services. With two locations in Texas (Galveston and League City), the Practice consists of six general dentists and specialists, and 21 employees. A practicing dentist since 1985, Dr. Quartapella Goodson is responsible for providing quality dental care to patients. Dr. Quartapella Goodson's areas of special interest include interceptive orthodontics and treatment of temporomandibular joint dysfunction. She also participates in on–going education in local elementary schools, career days in the high schools and sponsors programs assisting disabled and abused children. **Career Steps:** Owner, Island Dental Associates (1994–Present); Clinical Director, Castle Dental Center (1992–1994); Clinical Director, Dental World (1989–1992). **Associations & Accomplishments:** American Dental Association; Texas Dental Association; American Orthodontic Society; Mid–American Orthodontic Society; Academy of General Practitioner Orthodontics; Ninth District Dental Society. **Education:** University of Texas Dental School – Houston, D.D.S. (1985); University of Houston, B.S. in Biology. **Personal:** Married to Timothy Goodson in 1990. One child: Timothy Daniel. Dr. Quartapella Goodson enjoys antiques, piano, and ceramics.

Carlos Quilichini, D.D.S.
Dentist
All Dental & Denture Service
1869 North 66th Avenue
Hollywood, FL 33024–4017
(305) 983–3992
Fax: Please mail or call

8021

Business Information: All Dental & Denture Service, established in 1992, is a full–service, general practice dental office providing cosmetic, family–care dentistry, oral surgery, and denture services. Establishing his private practice in 1992, Dr. Quilichini directs a dental staff of five, in addition to his daily patient practice. **Career Steps:** Dentist, All Dental & Denture Service (1992–Present). **Associations & Accomplishments:** American Dental Association; South Broward Dental Association; West Dade Dental Association. **Education:** Marquette University, D.D.S. (1987); University of Puerto Rico, B.S. **Personal:** Married to Maribel Quilichini in 1993. One child: John Carlos Quilichini. Dr. Quilichini enjoys baseball, golf, and basketball.

Jeffrey L. Rajchel, D.D.S.
Dental Surgery Associate
Miller Oral Surgery
400 Nationwide Drive
Harrisburg, PA 17110–9752
(717) 657–2660
Fax: (717) 657–5774

8021

Business Information: Miller Oral Surgery is a full–service oral and maxillofacial surgery facility. In operation since 1940, Miller Oral Surgery currently employs 15 Dental Associates and support staff. Specializing in oral, head and neck surgery, Dr. Rajchel joined as an Associate with Miller Oral Surgery in 1992. **Career Steps:** Dental Surgery Associate, Miller Oral Surgery (1992–Present); Private Practice Surgeon, Asheville, North Carolina (1988–1990); Assistant Professor, Baylor College of Dentistry (1985–1988). **Associations & Accomplishments:** American Board of Oral and Maxillofacial Surgery; American Association of Oral and Maxillofacial Surgery; American College of Oral and Maxillofacial Surgeons. **Education:** University of Michigan, M.S. (1985); University of Notre Dame, B.S.; Marquette University, D.D.S. **Personal:** Married to Nancy Lee in 1986. Two children: Todd Matthew and Lauren Elizabeth. Dr. Rajchel enjoys tennis and golf.

Dr. Dan H. Rathgeber
President
Dan H. Rathgeber, D.D.S., PC
5637 Telegraph Road
St. Louis, MO 63129–4219
(314) 892–4445
Fax: (314) 892–5972

8021

Business Information: Dan H. Rathgeber, D.D.S., PC is a full–service general dentistry practice. Establishing the private practice upon his retirement from the U.S. Air Force in 1978, Dr. Rathgeber provides the overall direction for the 3 chair practice, in addition to his daily patient base. **Career Steps:** President, Dan H. Rathgeber, D.D.S., PC (1978–Present); Dentist, U.S. Air Force (1976–1978). **Associations & Accomplishments:** American Dental Association; Missouri Dental Association; Greater St. Louis Dental Association; Academy of General Dentistry; Association of Military Surgeons; Mehlville Optimist Club; Volunteer: Probation & Parole **Education:** University of Missouri–Kansas City, D.D.S. (1976); University of Missouri–Columbia, B.A. **Personal:** Married to Carla in 1991. Dr. Rathgeber enjoys boating, horses, jogging and hunting.

Susan G. Rifkin, D.D.S.
Dentist
Alan M. Kuehn D.D.S., P.C. and Susan G. Rifkin, D.D.S.
1000 Abernathy Road Northeast #330
Atlanta, GA 30328–5613
(770) 393–0800
Fax: (770) 668–8075

8021

Business Information: Alan M. Kuehn D.D.S., P.C. and Susan G. Rifkin, D.D.S. is a full–service, family practice dentistry office, providing cosmetic and general dentistry. A practicing dentist since 1982, Dr. Rifkin co–established the group practice in 1984 with her partner, Dr. Kuehn. She shares administrative operations of a staff of ten, in addition to her daily patient practice. **Career Steps:** Dentist, Alan M. Kuehn D.D.S., P.C. and Susan G. Rifkin, D.D.S. (1984–Present). **Associations & Accomplishments:** American Dental Association; Northern District Dental Society; Hinman Dental Society; Alpha Omega Dental Fraternity; Rotary Club of Sandy Springs; Women's American ORT; Haddassah; Congregation Etz Chaim Sisterhood. **Education:** SUNY – Buffalo School of Dentistry, D.D.S. (1982); SUNY – Buffalo, B.S. in Economics (1978). **Personal:** Married to David L. in 1987. Two children: Zachary and Dani. Dr. Rifkin enjoys travel and art classes.

Melinda W. Robertson, D.D.S.
Sole Practitioner
The Office of Melinda W. Robertson, D.D.S.
10022 Robious Road, Robious Hall Shopping Center
Richmond, VA 23235
(804) 320–2009
Fax: Please mail or call

8021

Business Information: The Office of Melinda W. Robertson, D.D.S. is a full–service family dentistry practice. Establishing the private practice in 1994, Dr. Robertson is responsible for the care and treatment of her dental patients, as well as the administrative aspects of office operations. **Career Steps:** Dentist, The Office of Melinda W. Robertson, D.D.S. (1994–Present). **Associations & Accomplishments:** Virginia Dental Association; Richmond Dental Society; American Dental Association. **Education:** Medical College of Virginia, D.D.S. (1992); Eastern Mennonite College, B.A. **Personal:** Married to Walter in 1993. Dr. Robertson enjoys racquetball, art, linguistics, and playing the piano, trumpet and violin.

M. Arlena Roshel, D.D.S.

Dentist
The Dental Office of M. Arlena Roshel, D.D.S.
4246 South 7th Street
Terre Haute, IN 47802–4358
(812) 299–1113
Fax: Please mail or call

8021

Business Information: The Dental Office of M. Arlena Roshel, D.D.S. is a full–service, family practice dentistry office, providing cosmetic and general dentistry. Establishing her sole–practice, six–chair dentistry practice upon the conferral of her dental degree in 1979, Dr. Roshel oversees all administrative operations for associates and a support staff of eight, in addition to her daily patient practice. **Career Steps:** Dentist, The Dental Office of M. Arlena Roshel, D.D.S. (1979–Present). **Associations & Accomplishments:** American Dental Association; Indiana Dental Association; Western Indiana Dental Association. **Education:** Indiana University, D.D.S. (1979).

Glen Scott Ruben, D.D.S.

Dentist
Glen S. Ruben, D.D.S
308 Main Street
Port Washington, NY 11050
(516) 944–3400
Fax: (516) 944–3403

8021

Business Information: Glen S. Ruben, D.D.S., established in 1990, is a full–service, state–of–the–art family dental practice, providing cosmetic and general dentistry. The Practice also conducts research in all areas of patient awareness by using video cameras to log information. Future plans include expanding the practice to include an associate and three chairs. A practicing physician since 1985, Dr. Ruben established his three–chair, sole practice dental office in 1990. He is responsible for all aspects of operations, including providing quality dental care to patients and supervising a support staff of four. **Career Steps:** Dentist, Glen S. Ruben, D.D.S. (1991–Present); Dentist (1985). **Associations & Accomplishments:** American Dental Association; National Society of Dental Practitioners; New York State Dental Society; Nassau County Dental Society; Port Washington Chamber of Commerce. **Education:** University of Buffalo School of Dentistry, D.D.S. (1985); SUNY – Binghamton, B.A. in Psychology. **Personal:** Married to Tami in 1993. One child: Nina. Dr. Ruben enjoys exercising, and spending time with his family.

Louis F. Rubino Jr., D.M.D.

Periodontist
–Independent–
135 Nutt Rd.
Phoenixville, PA 19460–3905
(610) 933–1236
Fax: (610) 933–4675

8021

Business Information: Louis F. Rubino Jr., D.M.D. is a private, full–service dental specialist, whose office is limited to periodontology, with services in dental implantology. Dr. Rubino maintains a satellite office in Drexel Hill, Pennsylvania as well. A practicing dentist since 1989, Dr. Rubino completed his periodontal training in 1991, at which time he established his periodontal practice. He oversees all administrative operations, as well as a support staff of six, in addition to his daily patient clinical practice. Dr. Rubino is also involved in teaching at both Albert Einstein Medical Center in Philadelphia, Pennsylvania and Marcum College in Bryn Mawr, Pennsylvania. He has lectured locally at the Liberty Dental Conference held in Philadelphia, where the latest topic was "Smoking and Periodontal Treatment". Dr. Rubino serves on the active staff at Phoenixville Hospital. He is also a member of the Phoenixville Chamber of Commerce. **Career Steps:** Periodontist, The Dental Office of Louis F. Rubino Jr., D.M.D. (1989–Present); Active Visiting Teaching Staff, Albert Einstein Medical Center (1995–Present); Instructor, Harcum College, (1993–Present). **Associations & Accomplishments:** American Dental Association; American Academy of Periodontology; Pennsylvania Society of Periodontists; Philadelphia Society of Periodontology; Academy of Osseointegration; Pennsylvania Dental Association; 2nd District Dental Association; Board of Governors, Dental Society of Chester County and Delaware County; Philadelphia County Dental Society; Temple University Dental Alumni Association: Secretary, Board of Directors. **Education:** Temple University, D.M.D. (1989), Temple University, Certificate in Periodontics (1991); Ursinus College, B.S. **Personal:** Married to Elizabeth Ann in 1986. Two children: Matthew Quinn and Annamarie Grace. Dr. Rubino enjoys golf.

Sergio Rubinstein, D.D.S.

President and Dentist
Oral Rehabilitation Center, P.C.
64 Old Orchard Shopping Center, Suite #420
Skokie, IL 60077
(708) 673–9292
Fax: (708) 674–4696

8021

Business Information: Oral Rehabilitation Center is a dental office limited to restorative and reconstructive dentistry. Established in 1992, the Center currently employs ten people. As President and Dentist, Dr. Rubinstein co–founded the Center with his partner, Dr. Alan J. Nidetz. He is responsible for all aspects of operations from laboratory work (waxing, casting, milling and ceramics) along with Dr. Nidetz and one of the finest laboratory technicians in the world, Mr. Masayuki Hoshi. Dr. Rubinstein provides optimum dental care to patients in the areas of cosmetics, bonding, prosthetics, full mouth reconstructions and dental implants. Career milestones include the invention of the Rubinstein–Hoshi Abutment in 1991. This is a one piece screw and angle post prosthetic abutment to correct misaligned implants. Dr. Rubinstein has also published articles on adhesive dentistry, restoration of hemisected teeth and implant prosthetics. **Career Steps:** President and Dentist, Oral Rehabilitation Center (1992–Present); President and Dentist, Sergio Rubinstein, D.D.S., P.C. (1986–1992); Assistant Professor, University of Illinois (1983–1992). **Associations & Accomplishments:** Chicago Academy of Dental Research (1989–Present), currently President; Academy of Osseointegration (1994–Present); American Academy of Cosmetic Dentistry (1994–Present); American Prosthodontic Society (1994–Present); Chicago Dental Society (1988–Present); American Dental Association (1988–Present); Illinois State Dental Society (1988–Present); Alpha Omega Fraternity (1984–Present); Who's Who Among Young Rising Americans; American Society & Business (1992); Attendee of numerous meetings, courses, and lectures; Conducted numerous lectures internationally including U.S.A., Mexico, Argentina and Israel. **Education:** University of Illinois, Certificate of Proficiency (1980–1982); Universidad Tecnologica de Mexico, D.D.S. (1976–1980); Michigan State Dental License (1987); Illinois State Dental License/Private Practice (1986); Part I and Part II of the U.S. National Boards (1985); Dental License – Mexico. **Personal:** Married to Anat in 1986. Two children: Michelle Lynn and Alissa Jill. Dr. Rubinstein enjoys racquetball, soccer, tennis, horseback riding and camping.

Joseph A. Rubulotta, D.M.D.

Dentist
The Dental Office of Joseph A. Rubulotta, D.M.D.
650 Washington Street
Toms River, NJ 08753
(908) 505–2005
Fax: Please mail or call

8021

Business Information: The Dental Office of Joseph A. Rubulotta, D.M.D. is a full–service, family practice dentistry office, providing cosmetic, dentistry, and oral surgery. A practicing dentist since 1988, Dr. Rubulotta established his sole practice dentistry office in 1992. He oversees all administrative operations for associates and a support staff of 4, in addition to his daily patient practice. **Career Steps:** Dentist, The Dental Office of Joseph A. Rubulotta, D.M.D. (1992–Present). **Associations & Accomplishments:** Fellow, Academy of General Dentistry; T.M.J. Alumni Society, University of Medicine and Dentistry of New Jersey; Rutgers University Alumni Association; University of Medicine and Dentistry of New Jersey Alumni Association. **Education:** University of Medicine and Dentistry of New Jersey, D.M.D. (1988); Rutgers University, Newark College of Arts and Sciences, B.A. (1984). **Personal:** Married to Lisa in 1993. Dr. Rubulotta enjoys scuba diving and trap/skeet competition.

Nicholas J. Russo, D.M.D.

Dentist
The Dental Office of Nicholas J. Russo, D.M.D.
300 Foulk Road #101
Wilmington, DE 19803–3819
(302) 652–3775
Fax: Please mail or call

8021

Business Information: The Dental Office of Nicholas J. Russo, D.M.D. is a full–service, family practice dentistry office, providing cosmetic and general dentistry. Establishing the general family dentistry office upon the conferral of his dental degree in 1992 with his father, Dr. Russo oversees all administrative operations for associates and a support staff of ten, in addition to his daily patient practice. **Career Steps:** Dentist, The Dental Office of Nicholas J. Russo, D.M.D. (1992–Present). **Associations & Accomplishments:** Chairman, New Dentist Committee – Delaware, American Dental Association; Membership Chairman for Delaware Academy of General Dentistry; Rotary International. **Education:** Temple University School of Dentistry, D.M.D. (1992); High Point University, B.S. **Personal:** Married to Cynthia Scolis Russo, D.M.D. in 1994. Dr. Russo enjoys golf, hiking, and biking.

Valeri Sacknoff, D.D.S.

Sole Practitioner
Valeri Sacknoff, D.D.S.
16766 Bernardo Center Drive, Suite #105
San Diego, CA 92128–2501
(619) 673–1001
Fax: Please mail or call

8021

Business Information: Valeri Sacknoff, D.D.S. is a full–service, family practice dentistry office located in Rancho Bernardo, providing general dental care, cosmetic, restorative, and denture work. As the Owner of a space–shared dental practice since January 1996, Dr. Sacknoff specializes in cosmetic and reconstructive oral surgery, such as venire, bleaching, implants, and crowns. Concurrently, she practices in a second dental practice in San Diego. **Career Steps:** Dentist, Valeri Sacknoff, D.D.S. (1996–Present); Dentist, Paul Davis, D.D.S.; Dentist, Ronald Aanerrud, D.D.S. **Personal:** Married to Larry.

Gerardo Santiago, D.D.S.

President
Children's Dentistry of Naples
3699 Airport Road North
Naples, FL 33942
(941) 262–3898
Fax: (941) 263–1035

8021

Business Information: Children's Dentistry of Naples is a full–service, general practice dental office, specializing in dentistry for children, infants, teens, and the handicapped. A practicing dentist since 1991 and a pediatric dental specialist, Dr. Santiago established his private dental practice in 1994. Serving as its President, he oversees all administrative operations for associates and a support staff of five, in addition to his daily patient practice. Concurrent with his dental practice, he serves as a Pediatric Dentist volunteer with the Public Health Unit of Collier County, Florida, as well as serving on the staff at Naples Community and North Collier hospitals. **Career Steps:** President, Children's Dentistry of Naples (1994–Present); Pediatric Dentist, Public Health Unit – Collier County (1996–Present); Pediatric Dentist, Public Health Unit – West Palm Beach (1994–1995); Pediatric Dentist, Interfaith Medical Center (1991–1994). **Associations & Accomplishments:** Co–Sponsor with the Senior PGA Tour–Free dental services for disadvantaged kids; American Academy of Pediatric Dentistry; American Society for Dentistry for Children; American Dental Association; Florida Dental Association; West Coast Dental Association; Collier County Dental Association. **Education:** New York University College of Dentistry, D.D.S. (1991); Interfaith Medical Center, Pediatric Dental Specialty. **Personal:** Married to Meylenid in 1992. One child: Paola Cristina Santiago. Dr. Santiago enjoys golf, fishing, boating, bicycle riding, and rollerblading.

Lawrence A. Saunders, D.M.D., M.S.

Surgeon
Palo Alto Oral Surgery
703 Welch Rd # 5
Palo Alto, CA 94304–1710
(415) 328–2322
Fax: (415) 328–JAWS

8021

Business Information: Palo Alto Oral Surgery is a full–service, general practice dental office, specializing in oral and maxillofacial surgery and implantology. A practicing dentist since 1965, Dr. Saunders joined Palo Alto Oral Surgery in 1981. He specializes in surgical treatments for facial and neck deformities, as well as facial deformities resulting from traumatic injuries. **Career Steps:** Surgeon, Palo Alto Oral Surgery (1981–Present); Assistant Professor of Oral/Maxillofacial Surgery, University of Pennslyvania (1977–1981); Private Practice, Petaluma, California (1970–1977). **Associations & Accomplishments:** Diplomate, American Board of Oral and Maxillofacial Surgeons; Fellow, American and International Association of Oral and Maxillofacial Surgeons; Founding Fellow, American College of OMS; American Dental Association; California Dental Society; Fellow, International Congress of Oral Implantologists; American Society of Laser Dentistry; Petaluma, California: Trustee, Board of Education, City Council; Lions Club; Rotarian; Toastmasters International. **Education:** Temple University, D.M.D. (1965), A.B. (1961); University of Pennsylvania, GM Graduate Medicine (1967); University of Pacific Graduate School, M.S. **Personal:** Married to Laura Anne in 1965. Three children: David, Deborah, and Jonathan. Dr. Saunders enjoys golf, tennis, boating and fishing. Dr. Saunders is an accomplished jazz musician and stained glass artist.

Charles J. Schildroth, D.M.D., P.A.

Owner and Operator
Perdido Dental Center
13020 Sorrento Road
Pensacola, FL 32507–8701
(904) 492–0533
Fax: (904) 492–5299

8021

Business Information: Perdido Dental Center is a full–service, general dental practice, concentrating in cosmetic, general dentistry, and oral surgery. Establishing the sole practice in 1993, Dr. Schildroth manages a staff of ten administrative, dental aide and hygienist staff, in addition to his daily patient care practices. Concurrent with his dental practice, involved in entrepreneurial concerns he is President of Great Southern Entertainment, Inc. – a restaurant and bar business. **Career Steps:** Owner and Operator, Perdido Dental Center (1993–Present); Dentist, Defuniak Dental Clinic (1992–1995); Dentist, U.S. Navy (1988–1992). **Associations & Accomplishments:** American Dental Association; Pirates of Lost Treasure (Donational Program); Member of Chamber of Commerces: Pensacola and Perdido Keys, Florida, and Orange Beach, Alabama; Big Brothers; Okalossa Dental Society; Sponsor, Ball Park Team Softball, Perdido Keys; Patron of Big Lagoon State Park; Sponsor for S.T.A.R. Program, Walton Middle School; Member, General Academy of Dentistry. **Education:** University of Southern Illinois, B.S. (1987), D.M.D., P.A.

Adolph K. Schmidt, D.D.S.

Sole Practitioner
–Independent–
1435 French Road
Depew, NY 14043–4867
(716) 668–9001
Fax: Please mail or call

8021

Business Information: Adolph K. Schmidt, D.D.S. is a full–service, general dentistry practice providing cosmetic, family dentistry and oral surgery. Specialties include orthodontics, periodontics, implants, and maxillofacial surgery. With 33 years expertise in the dentistry field, Dr. Schmidt established his private dental practice in 1962 and is responsible for all aspects of operations, as well as providing patient care. **Career Steps:** Sole Practitioner, Adolph K. Schmidt, D.D.S. (1962–Present). **Associations & Accomplishments:** Erie County Dental Society; Eighth District Dental Society; New York State Dental Society; American Dental Society; Phi Kappa Psi Fraternity; Delta Sigma Delta Dental Society; Concordia 143 Masonic Blue Lodge; Schriner's. **Education:** University of Buffalo: D.D.S. (1962), B.S. in Biology (1958). **Personal:** Three children: Bradley, Jeffrey, and Wesley. Dr. Schmidt enjoys travel and visiting the sick in hospitals.

Dr. Shih Lin Shieh

Dentist
Queenston Mall
686 Queenston Road
Hamilton, Ontario L8G 1A3
(905) 561–7310
Fax: (905) 561–0505

8021

Business Information: Dr. Shieh, who has been in private practice since 1987, joined the private dental practice at the Queenston Mall in 1994, specializing in general/family dentistry, including some orthodontics and implant restoration surgery. In addition to patient care, he is also responsible for office management and various administrative duties. **Career Steps:** Dentist, Queenston Mall (1994–Present). **Associations & Accomplishments:** Ontario Dental Association; Canadian Dental Association. **Education:** Mangalore University, B.D.S. (1987); Continuing Dental Courses from the University of Western Ontario, University of Toronto, and other North American universities. **Personal:** Married to Shawna Banh in 1991. Dr. Shieh enjoys yard work and landscaping.

Dennis R. Smith, D.D.S.

Sole General Dentistry Practitioner
The Dental Office of Dennis R. Smith, D.D.S.
106 College Street
Gordon, GA 31031
(912) 628–2142
Fax: Please mail or call

8021

Business Information: The Dental Office of Dennis R. Smith, D.D.S. is a full–service, family practice dentistry office, providing cosmetic, general dentistry, oral surgery, and an In–house dental laboratory. A practicing dentist since 1985, Dr. Smith oversees all administrative operations for associates and a support staff of 6, in addition to his daily patient practice. **Career Steps:** Dentist, The Dental Office of Dennis R Smith, D.D.S. (1985–Present). **Associations & Accomplishments:** American Dental Association; Georgia Dental Association; Central District Dental Association. **Education:** Emory University Dental School, D.D.S. (1985); Mercer University, B.S. **Personal:** Married to Tina in 1984. Three children: Tripp, Jenna, and Logan. Dr. Smith enjoys golf, coaching baseball, and football.

Gary D. Smith, D.D.S.

Dentist
The Dental Office of Gary D. Smith, D.D.S., P.C.
118 North Main Street
Altus, OK 73521–3102
(405) 482–4873
Fax: (405) 482–4895

8021

Business Information: The Dental Office of Gary D. Smith, D.D.S., P.C. is a full–service, family practice dentistry office, providing a complete range of general dental procedures performed with the exception of comprehensive orthodontics. Services include restorative, preventative, surgery of jaw and gums, dentures, crowns, and bridges dentistry. After graduating in 1981, Dr. Smith served in a General Practice Residency at the University of Chicago hospitals and clinics. He established his sole dental practice in 1982, designing and contracting the construction project. He oversees all administrative operations for associates and a support staff of 3, in addition to his daily patient practice. **Career Steps:** Dentist, The Dental Office of Gary D. Smith, D.D.S., P.C. (1982–Present); Resident of General Dentistry, University of Chicago Hospitals and Clinics (1981–1982); Public Relations Department Head, Resco Enerprises (1972–1981). **Associations & Accomplishments:** Leadership Altus; Oklahoma Republican Committeeman; Republican National Committee: Presidential Trust, Presidential Task Force – Campaign Advisor; Personalities of the South; County Coordinator (1994) for Frank Keating – Governor of Oklahoma, Mary Fallin – Lt. Governor of Oklahoma, J. C. Watts – Member of Congress, Jim Inhofe – U.S. Senator; Bob Dole for President, Member, Presidential Circle; American Dental Association; Oklahoma Dental Association; Board of Directors, Delta Dental Plan of Oklahoma (7 years). **Education:** University of Oklahoma, D.D.S. (1981); University of Chicago, Certificate in General Dentistry (1982). **Personal:** Married to Linda in 1991. One child: Renee. Dr. Smith enjoys flying – Private Pilot, politics, golf, automobiles, gardening, renovation, and photography.

Teresa Lambert Smith, D.D.S.

Owner
Dr. Teresa Lambert Smith, Family Dentistry
3142 West Vista Way, Suite 203
Oceanside, CA 92056
(619) 439–6425
Fax: (619) 439–4863

8021

Business Information: Dr. Teresa Lambert Smith, Family Dentistry, established in 1991, is a full–service, general practice dentistry office, providing cosmetic, family dentistry, and oral surgery. A practicing dentist since 1991, Dr. Smith established her sole practice dentistry office in 1995. She is responsible for all aspects of operations, including performing general dentistry, as well as dental surgeries and procedures. **Career Steps:** Owner, Dr. Teresa Lambert Smith, Family Dentistry (1995–Present); Dentist, Dr. Barry Reder (1991–1995). **Associations & Accomplishments:** San Diego County Dental Society; California Dental Society; American Dental Association; Soroptimist International of the Americas (Oceanside); Board Member, Santa Margarita YMCA. **Education:** University of California – Los Angeles School of Dentistry, D.D.S. (1990); Mesa Community College, A.A.; Attended: San Diego State University. **Personal:** Married to J. Ken in 1991. Dr. Smith enjoys community service, outdoors, golf, skiing, and jogging.

Mila Sorkin, D.D.S.

President
Smile Again
2667 Coney Island Avenue
Brooklyn, NY 11223–5502
(718) 934–0070
Fax: (718) 891–8949

8021

Business Information: Smile Again is a full–service family dentistry practice. Establishing her private dental practice upon conferral of her dental degree in 1988, Dr. Sorkin shares administrative duties with her daughter Diana, in addition to providing all dental treatment to patients. **Career Steps:** President, Smile Again (1988–Present) **Associations & Accomplishments:** American Dental Association; DSSNY **Education:** New York University, D.D.S. (1987); Moscow Medical Dental Institute (1970). **Personal:** One child: Diana Sorkin. Dr. Sorkin enjoys gardening, painting, interior decorating, poetry, alpine skiing, snorkeling and teaching.

Philip Spector, D.D.S.

President
Spector & Goldstein, P.C.
159–05 92nd Street
Howard Beach, NY 11414–3123
(718) 848–6944
Fax: (718) 843–1677

8021

Business Information: Spector & Goldstein, P.C. is a full–service, dentistry practice, specializing in orthodontic dentistry. The Practice currently has two offices in New York (Howard Beach, and Brooklyn). A practicing dentist since 1974 and an Orthodontist, Dr. Spector co–established the practice as Altman, Arnold & Spector in 1975. Established as Spector & Goldstein in 1993, Dr. Spector serves as President, overseeing all administrative operations for associates and a support staff of 6, in addition to his daily patient practice. **Career Steps:** President, Spector & Goldstein, P.C. (1993–Present); President, Spector & Bobrow (1986–1993); Vice–President, Arnold, Spector & Bobrow (1983–1986). **Associations & Accomplishments:** Queens County Dental Society; New York State Dental Society; Northeastern Society of Orthodontists; American Association of Orthodontics. **Education:** New York University College of Dentistry, Certificate in Orthodontics (1974), D.D.S. (1970); CCNY, B.S. (1966). **Personal:** Married to Linda in 1990. Three children: Debra, Rachel, and Heather. Dr. Spector enjoys coin collecting and computing.

Silvia Stambler, D.D.S.

Owner and Dentist
Silvia Stambler, D.D.S.
2040 NE 163rd Street, Suite 206
North Miami Beach, FL 33162–4941
(305) 949–4352
Fax: Please mail or call

8021

Business Information: Silvia Stambler, D.D.S., established in 1986, is a full–service, family practice dental office, providing cosmetic, general dentistry, root canals, and oral surgery. Purchasing the existing practice in 1985 upon the conferral of her dental doctorate, Dr. Stambler virtually rebuilt the practice from "scratch". **Career Steps:** Owner and Dentist, Silvia Stambler, D.D.S. (1985–Present). **Associations & Accomplishments:** East Coast District Dental Society; North Dade Dental Society; Florida Dental Association; American Dental Association. **Education:** New York University Dental School, D.D.S. (1985); Brown University, B.A. in Economics. **Personal:** Married to Andrew Stern in 1991. One child: Isaac Michael Stern.

Lawrence M. Stanleigh, D.D.S.

Dentist
Larry M. Stanleigh, D.D.S.
4th Street SW, Suite 1601–1800
Calgary, Alberta T2S 2S5
(403) 228–3783
Fax: (403) 228–2114
EMAIL: See Below

8021

Business Information: Dr. Stanleigh acquired the practice and established Lawrence M. Stanleigh, D.D.S. in 1994. Focusing on quality dental care for his patients, he has brought the practice into the top 20% of Canadian dental practices. Internet users can reach him via: drlarry@spots.ab.ca **Career Steps:** Dentist, Larry M. Stanleigh, D.D.S. (1994–Present); Dentist, Dentrix Inc (1990–1994); Dental Officer, Canadian Forces (1984–1990). **Associations & Accomplishments:** Alpha Omega International Dental Fraternity; Academy of General Dentistry; American Association of Implant Prosthodontics; Canadian Dental Association; Alberta Dental Association; Calgary District Dental Society. **Education:**

University of Toronto: D.D.S. (1987); M.S.C. (1983); B.S.C. (1981). **Personal:** Married to Pratibha (Tina) in 1994. One child: Isabel Rupa. Dr. Stanleigh enjoys Star Trek, science fiction, baseball, skiing, golf, cycling, and reading.

Tom B. Styles, D.D.S.
Owner/Dentist
Churchill Dental Associates
11819 Blanco Road   Suite A
San Antonio, TX 78216–5435
(210) 344–0101
Fax: (210) 344–0109

8021

Business Information: Churchill Dental Associates, established in 1988, is a general practice dental clinic. The Clinic currently offers 1 associate, 4 chairs, and 7 rooms to its clients. A practicing dentist since 1969, Mr. Styles is responsible for all aspects of the Clinic's operations, including tending to patients and various office requirements. **Career Steps:** Owner, Churchill Dental Associates (1988–Present); Solo Dental Practice (1973–1988); Major, Officer in Charge (Clinic Director), Butzbach, Germany, United States Army Dental Corps (1969–73). **Associations & Accomplishments:** Helotes Masonic Lodge #1429 (Past Master); Scottish Rite of Free Masonry, York Rite of Free Masonry; Delta Sigma Phi, Delta Sigma Delta Dental Fraternity. **Education:** University of Texas – Dental Branch, Houston, D.D.S. (1969); St Mary's University of Texas, B.A. (1963). **Personal:** Married to Mary Katherine. Two children: Eric and Kelly. Dr. Styles enjoys hunting, fishing, horseback riding, and photography, and is a devout Republican and Presbyterian.

Steven D. Sudbrink, D.M.D.
President
Oral Surgery Associates
800 Grandview Drive
Ephrata, PA 17522
(717) 733–8645
Fax: (717) 733–9172

8021

Business Information: Oral Surgery Associates is a practice specializing in oral and maxillofacial surgery. Dr. Sudbrink provides surgery in the full scope of oral and maxillofacial surgery as well as administrative direction. **Career Steps:** Oral Surgery Associates: President (1995–Present), Associate (1993–1995); Resident in Surgery, Long Island Jewish Medical Center in New York (1989–1993). **Associations & Accomplishments:** Board Certified and Diplomate, American Board of Oral and Maxillofacial Surgery; Fellow, American Association of Oral and Maxillofacial Surgery; Fellow, American College of Oral and Maxillofacial Surgery; Member, Pennsylvania Society of Oral and Maxillofacial Surgery. **Education:** Tufts University, D.M.D., summa cum laude, valedictorian (1989); State University of New York at Stonybrook, B.S. in Biochemistry. **Personal:** Married to Susan in 1991. Two children: Eric and Lindsay. Dr. Sudbrink enjoys astronomy and reading.

Eric Swainston, D.D.S.
Sole Practitioner
The Dental Office of Eric Swainston, D.D.S.
12828 Harbor Boulevard #340
Garden Grove, CA 92640–5807
(714) 530–9754
Fax: (704) 638–8622

8021

Business Information: The Dental Office of Eric Swainston, D.D.S. is a full–service, family practice dentistry office, providing general and cosmetic dentistry to patients. A practicing dentist since 1991, Dr. Swainston established his sole practice dentistry office in 1994. He oversees all administrative operations for a staff of four, in addition to his daily patient practice. **Career Steps:** Sole Practitioner, The Dental Office of Eric Swainston, D.D.S. (1991–Present). **Associations & Accomplishments:** American Dental Association; California Dental Association; Orange County Dental Society; Academy of General Dentistry; Volunteer as Part–time Faculty, University of Southern California Dental School. **Education:** University of Southern California, D.D.S. (1991); University of North Las Vegas, B.S. **Personal:** Dr. Swainston enjoys scuba diving, gourmet cooking, and attending church.

Thomas P. Sweeney, D.D.S.

Periodontal Surgeon
Periodontics Northwest
2111 North Northgate Way, #215
Seattle, WA 98133
(206) 367–6767
Fax: (206) 367–4788

8021

Business Information: Periodontics Northwest is a full service dental facility specializing in Periodontics, Implants and Esthetic Periodontal Surgery. The practice was established in 1987. The Practice continually sponsors and provides continuing education opportunities for the dental community. **Career Steps:** Periodontal Surgeon, Periodontics Northwest (1987–Present); Assistant Clinical Insuctor, The University of Washington (1988–Present); Past President, Washington State Society of Periodontists (1992–1993); Board of Directors, Western Society of Periodontology (1988–1989). **Associations & Accomplishments:** Washington Society of Periodontics; Western Society of Periodontology; American Academy of Periodontics; American Dental Association; Seattle King County Dental Society; Washington State Dental Association; Academy of Osseointegration; Woodland Park Zoological Society; Pacific Science Center; Published in dental journal. **Education:** University of Washington: Residency in Periodontics (1986), D.D.S. (1984); Foothill College, RDH (1979); California State University, Masters Candidate (1977); University of California – Davis, B.S. (1975). **Personal:** Married to Christine Lentz, D.D.S.. Three children: Sean, Kendall and Brianna. Dr. Sweeney enjoys horseback riding, skiing and spending time with his family.

Russell K. Tankersley, D.D.S.

Dentist
The Office of Dr. Russell K. Tankersley, D.D.S.
8305 Walnut Hill Lane, #230
Dallas, TX 75231–4203
(214) 368–5224
Fax: Please mail or call

8021

Business Information: The Office of Dr. Russell K. Tankersley, D.D.S. is a full–service, general practice dental facility specializing in the restoration of implants. Admitted to practice General Dentistry since 1988, Dr. Tankersley established his individual practice in 1992. **Career Steps:** Dentist, The Office of Dr. Russell K. Tankersley, D.D.S. (1992–Present); Associate Dentist, The Office of Dr. Stan Ashworth & Associates (1989–1992); Associate Dentist, Aspen Dental (1988–1989). **Associations & Accomplishments:** American Dental Association; Texas Dental Association; Dallas County Dental Society. **Education:** Baylor College of Dentistry, D.D.S (1988); University of Texas – Austin, B.A. in Biology (1984). **Personal:** Married to Elizabeth Shafton in 1993. Dr. Tankersley enjoys all sports, photography, and gardening.

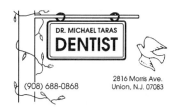

DR. MICHAEL TARAS
DENTIST
(908) 688-0868
2816 Morris Ave.
Union, N.J. 07083

Michael Taras, D.M.D., F.A.G.D.
Sole Practitioner
The Office of Dr. Michael Taras, D.M.D., F.A.G.D.
2816 Morris Avenue
Union, NJ 07083–4842
(908) 688–0868
Fax: Please mail or call

8021

Business Information: The Office of Dr. Michael Taras, D.M.D., F.A.G.D. a is full–service, general dentistry facility. A General Dentistry practitioner since 1988 and recently awarded Fellowship with the Academy of General Dentistry, Dr. Taras established his private practice in 1993. In addition to general dentistry, he also counsels patients on lifestyle and dietary alternatives to prevent oral disease and enjoy health.

Career Steps: Some of Dr. Taras' career steps include the work experience of dental offices in Berkeley Heights, Mountainside, Little Falls, Somerset, Union, Edison, Newark, South Orange, East Orange, Milltown, Passaic, Irvington, Woodbridge and East Brunswick. **Associations & Accomplishments:** Union County Dental Society; New Jersey Dental Association; American Dental Association; Garden State Dental Study Club; Essex County Dental Study Club; Essex County Dental Society; East Essex Dental Study Club; Middlesex County Dental Society; Federation Dentaire Internationale; Academy of General Dentistry and the Newark Dental Study Club; Third Degree member of the Union Knights of Columbus council 4504. **Education:** University of Medicine and Dentistry of New Jersey, D.M.D. (1988); Fellowship, Academy of General Dentistry (1994). **Personal:** Married to Linda in 1988. Two children: Kevin and Elizabeth. Dr. Taras enjoys reading, computers, exercising, hiking, travel and family activities.

James H. Taylor, D.D.S.

Owner and Dentist
James H. Taylor, D.D.S.
115 Bradford Avenue
Fayetteville, NC 28301–5401
(910) 484–2166
Fax: Please mail or call

8021

Business Information: James H. Taylor, D.D.S. is a full–service, general dentistry practice, concentrating in cosmetic, family dentistry and oral surgery. Establishing his private general dentistry practice upon conferral of his dental doctorate in 1991, Dr. Taylor oversees an administrative and medical support staff of five, in addition to his daily patient practice. **Career Steps:** Owner and Dentist, James H. Taylor, D.D.S. (1991–Present); Assistant Sailing Master, YMCA, Raleigh, North Carolina (1984–1987). **Associations & Accomplishments:** Commodore, Southeastern District of International Lightning Class Association; American Dental Association; North Carolina Dental Association. **Education:** University of North Carolina – Chapel Hill, D.D.S. (1991). **Personal:** Married to Ashley Arthur Taylor in 1995. Dr. Taylor enjoys sailing and golf.

Mark L. Teach, D.D.S.
Owner
The Dental Office of Mark L. Teach, D.D.S.
1281 Union Road
West Seneca, NY 14224–2916
(716) 675–3163
Fax: Please mail or call
EMAIL: See Below

8021

Business Information: The Dental Office of Mark L. Teach, D.D.S. is a full–service, family practice dentistry office, providing cosmetic, general dentistry, orthodontics, and oral surgery. Establishing his dentistry office upon the conferral of his dental degree in 1976, Dr. Teach oversees all administrative operations for associates and a support staff of 6, in addition to his daily patient practice. Internet users can reach him via: SOCR61334 **Career Steps:** Dentist, The Dental Office of Mark L. Teach, D.D.S. (1976–Present). **Associations & Accomplishments:** American Dental Association; Dental Society State of New York; Eighth District Dental Society; Academy of General Dentistry; American Orthodontic Society; Erie County Dental Society; Niagara Frontier Dental Practitioners Association; Metropolitan Dental Study Club; West Seneca Chamber of Commerce; Active in many functions of local parish, Queen of Heaven Church. **Education:** SUNY – Buffalo, D.D.S. (1976); Ithaca College, B.A. in Chemistry. **Personal:** Married to LuAnn in 1976. Three children: Andrew, Zachary, and Gannon. Dr. Teach enjoys indoor soccer, bicycling, golf, photography, and boating.

Ernest R. Thompson, D.M.D.
Owner and President
Ernie Thompson, D.M.D., P.C.
Aloha Professional Plaza, 3895 SW 185th Avenue, Suite 130
Aloha, OR 97007
(503) 649–5900
Fax: Please mail or call

8021

Business Information: Ernie Thompson, D.M.D., P.C., is a full–service, general dental practice, providing cosmetic, aesthetics, and general dentistry to children and adults. Established in 1983, the Practice currently employs seven people. As Owner and President, Dr. Thompson is responsible for all aspects of operations, including providing general dentistry care to patients. **Career Steps:** Owner and President, Ernie Thompson, D.M.D., P.C. (1983–Present). **Associations &**

Accomplishments: American Dental Association; Fellow, Academy of General Dentistry; Oregon Dental Association; Washington County Dental Society; Outstanding Young Americans (1984); Public speaking at his church; Volunteer with the Boy Scouts of America for the past twelve years. **Education:** Oregon Health Sciences University, Medical School, D.M.D. (1983); Portland State University; Brigham Young University, B.S. **Personal:** Married to Jennifer in 1977. Five children: Scott, Jared, Katelyn, Kelsie, and Jessica. Dr. Thompson enjoys golf, camping, hiking, and bicycling.

Anthony L. Tortorich, D.D.S.

Oral and Maxillofacial Surgeon
Anthony L. Tortorich, DDS, P.A.
8500 W. Markham, Suite 330
Little Rock, AR 72205
(501) 224–8332
Fax: (501) 219–8003

8021

Business Information: Anthony L. Tortorich, DDS, P.A. is a full–service, dental practice, specializing in oral and maxillofacial surgery. A practicing dentist since 1983 and an Oral and Maxillofacial Surgeon, Dr. Tortorich is the founding partner of his private oral and maxillofacial surgery practice since 1986. He oversees all administrative operations for associates and a support staff of 4, in addition to his daily patient practice. **Career Steps:** Oral and Maxillofacial Surgeon, Anthony L. Tortorich, DDS, P.A. (1986–Present). **Associations & Accomplishments:** Fellow, American Association of Oral and Maxillofacial Surgery; Diplomate, American Board of Oral and Maxillofacial Surgery; Fellow, American College of Oral and Maxillofacial Surgery; American Dental Association; American Society of Dental Anesthesiology; Arkansas Society of Oral and Maxillofacial Surgeons; Pierre Fuchard Academy; Arkansas State Dental Association. **Education:** University of Tennessee College of Dentistry, D.D.S. (1983); Arkansas State University, B.S.; Residency in Oral and Maxillofacial Surgery, Vanderbilt University Medical Center. **Personal:** Married to Torre in 1995. Three children: Joseph W., Jordan A., and Andrew Collin.

Debbie Tranmer, D.D.S.

Sole General Dentistry Practitioner
Debbie Tranmer, D.D.S.
353 North 4th Suite 102
Pocatello, ID 83201
(208) 232–3205
Fax: (208) 232–0305

8021

Business Information: Starting in her father's general family dental practice in 1979 as a hygienist, Debbie Tranmer has carried on the tradition and respect the practice acquired while under his direction. Taking over the practice upon the conferral of her dental doctorate in 1989 and sadly, upon the death of her father, Dr. Arthur D. Tranmer, she provides all administrative direction for a support staff of twelve, in addition to her daily patient care base. Inspired by his tireless devotion to the community, Debbie provides considerable low cost services to the less fortunate, as well as serves as a forensic expert for the County, and expert testimony in trials on behalf of abused children with the Bannock County Child Abuse Task Force. **Career Steps:** Sole General Dentistry Practitioner, Debbie Tranmer, D.D.S. (1989–Present); Dental Hygienist, Arthur Tranmer, D.D.S. (1979–1986); Owner, The Entertainer – Dancewear and Dance Instruction (1980–1986). **Associations & Accomplishments:** American Dental Association; Academy of General Dentistry; American Association of Women Dentists – Creighton Chapter: Sustaining Member, President (1993), Vice President (1992), Treasurer (1991); Pocatello Dental Society; President, Kasai Foundation; Vice President and Instructor, Pocatello Tae Kwon Do Association; Affiliate, Bannock County Child Abuse Task Force. **Education:** Creighton University Boyne School of Dentistry, D.D.S. (1989); Idaho State University, B.S. in Dental Hygiene. **Personal:** One child: Michael Brandon Monroe. Dr. Tranmer enjoys dance (i.e. ballet, tap, jazz, flamenco), tae kwon do, skiing, animal care and photography.

Robert J. Ueber, D.D.S.

Owner
The Dental Office of Robert J. Ueber, D.D.S.
6216 Fairfield Avenue
Ft. Wayne, IN 46807–3618
(219) 456–1310
Fax: (219) 745–3838

8021

Business Information: The Dental Office of Robert J. Ueber, D.D.S. is a full–service, family practice dentistry office, providing cosmetic, general dentistry, and orthodontics. Establishing the six–chair solo practice upon the conferral of his dental degree in 1987, Dr. Ueber oversees all administrative operations for associates and a support staff of 13, in addition to his daily patient practice. **Career Steps:** Owner, The Dental Office of Robert J. Ueber, D.D.S. (1987–Present); Lab Technician, Indiana Univrsity Medical Center (1983–1987); Tool and Die Maker, General Electric (1980–1982). **Associations & Accomplishments:** Isaac Knapp District Dental Society; Indiana Dental Association; American Dental Association; Functional Orthodontic Association; American Orthodontic Society; Academy of General Dentistry. **Education:** Indiana Univesity, D.D.S. (1987). **Personal:** Married to Susan in 1980. Four children: Jill, Paul, Don, and Drew.

Alexandra Ukmar, D.D.S.

General Dentistry Practitionor
–Independent–
27127 Chardon Road
Cleveland, OH 44143–1115
(216) 943–0071
Fax: (216) 943–9513

8021

Business Information: The Dental Office of Alexandra Ukmar, D.D.S. is a full–service, family dentistry practice, providing complete dental care to adults and children. Establishing her private dentistry office upon the conferral of her dental degree in 1988, Dr. Ukmar oversees all administrative operations in addition to her daily patient practice. **Career Steps:** General Dentistry Practitioner (1988–Present). **Associations & Accomplishments:** American Dental Association; Ohio Dental Association; Greater Cleveland Dental Society; Academy of General Dentistry; American Association of Women Dentists; American Academy of Implant Dentistry; Slovenian–American Heritage Foundation; Euclid Jaycees. **Education:** Case Western Reserve University, D.D.S. (1988); Cleveland Institute of Music North Coast Ballet Company; MetroHealth Medical Center, General Practice Residency; Midwest Implant Institute, Endosseous & Prosthetic Externship; Boston University, Trustee Scholar. **Personal:** Dr. Ukmar enjoys Performing Arts (she is an accomplished ballet performer), travel and skiing.

Borasmy N. Ung, D.D.S.

Dentist
The Office of Dr. Borasmy N. Ung, D.D.S.
3112 North Federal Highway
Lighthouse Point, FL 33064
(305) 782–3271
Fax: (305) 782–0021

8021

Business Information: The Office of Dr. Borasmy N. Ung, D.D.S. is a general practice dental facility specializing in endodontics and root canal therapy. Establishing her private practice in 1994, Dr. Ung is the Dentist for a growing office. Through persistance and patience, she practices good dentistry and maintains her position in her professional associations. **Career Steps:** Dentist and Endodontist, The Office of Dr. Borasmy N. Ung, D.D.S. (1994–Present); Dentist and Endodontist, Dental Care Group (1993–1994). **Associations & Accomplishments:** American Association of Endodontics; Florida Endodontic Association. **Education:** Loma Linda University, Associates Degree in Endodontics (1989); University of Maryland, D.D.S.; Virginia Commonwealth University, B.S.

Elizabeth Van Landschoot, D.D.S., FAGD

General Dentist
–Independent–
760 West Washington Street
Marquette, MI 49855–4138
(906) 228–4646
Fax: (906) 228–4166

8021

Business Information: The Office of Dr.'s James P. and Elizabeth D. Van Landschoot, D.D.S. is a full–service, family practice dentistry office, providing cosmetic, general dentistry, and oral surgery. A practicing dentist since 1984, Dr. Van Landschoot joined the dental practice in 1990, providing general dentistry care to patients, mainly in endodontics, crowns, and bridges. **Career Steps:** Dentist, The Office of Dr.'s James P. and Elizabeth D. Vanlands School (1990–Present); General Dental Officer, United States Air Force (1984–1990). **Associations & Accomplishments:** American Dental Association; Michigan Dental Association; Fellow, Academy of General Dentistry (1995); American Association of Women Dentists; Phi Beta Kappa; Whitman School Organizaton. **Education:** Baltimore College of Dental Surgery University of Maryland: D.D.S. (1984), B.S. in Zoology (1979). **Personal:** Married to James in 1989. Two children: Megan and Ryan. Dr. Van Landschoot enjoys cross–country skiing, boating, snowmobiling, reading, and crafts.

Mitchell A. Vance, D.D.S.

Owner/Dentist
The Dental Office of Mitchell A. Vance, D.D.S.
805 Frederick Road
Catonsville, MD 21228
(410) 747–1130
Fax: Please mail or call

8021

Business Information: The Dental Office of Mitchell A. Vance, D.D.S. is a full–service, family practice dentistry office, providing cosmetic, general dentistry, and oral surgery. The Practice was established in 1970 and purchased by Dr. Vance in 1995. A practicing dentist since 1990, Dr. Vance oversees all administrative operations for the two–chair office, in addition to his daily patient practice. **Career Steps:** Owner/Dentist, The Dental Office of Mitchell A. Vance, D.D.S. (1995–Present); Associate Dentist, John K. Hart D.D.S. (1991–1995); Associate Dentist, Richard A. Weiler D.D.S. (1990–1991); Security Officer, Howard County General Hospital (1980–1990). **Associations & Accomplishments:** ADA; MSDA; AGD; BCDA; Greater Catonsville Dental Study Club; Howard County Chamber of Commerce. **Education:** University of Maryland Dental School, D.D.S. (1990); Loyola College, Baltimore, MD, B.A. in Psychology. **Personal:** Married to S. Michele in 1986. Two children: Christina and Aaron. Dr. Vance enjoys golf, vacationing, and spending time with his wife and children.

Eduard D. Vayman

Dentist
The Dental Office of Eduard D. Vayman, D.D.S., Ltd.
3414 West Peterson Avenue #B
Chicago, IL 60659–3447
(312) 583–9045
Fax: Please mail or call

8021

Business Information: The Dental Office of Eduard D. Vayman, D.D.S., Ltd. is a full–service, family practice dental office, providing cosmetic, general dentistry, and oral surgery. A practicing physician in the Ukraine since 1971 and in the U.S. since 1992, Dr. Vayman established his private dental practice in 1993, providing quality dental care to patients. **Career Steps:** Dentist, The Dental Office of Eduard D. Vayman, D.D.S., Ltd. (1993–Present); Dentist, 5th Dental Clinic, Kharkov, Ukraine (1971–1989). **Education:** Northwestern University (1991–1992); Poltara Medical Dental School, D.D.S.; Kharkov Medical Dental School. **Personal:** Married to Lisa in 1971. One child: Marina. Dr. Vayman enjoys music (classical and jazz).

George J. Walters, D.D.S.

President
The Office of George J. Walters, D.D.S., P.A.
2202 State Avenue, Suite 200
Panama City, FL 32405
(904) 763–8585
Fax: Please mail or call

8021

Business Information: The Office of George J. Walters, D.D.S., P.A. is a private practice dental facility specializing in oral and maxillofacial surgery. A Board–eligible Oral/Maxillofacial Surgeon since 1989, Dr. Walters established his private practice in 1995. As President he oversees all administrative operations, in addition to his patient practice. Concurrent to his private practice, he is also a Staff Physician with two Panama City hospitals. **Career Steps:** President and Surgeon, The Office of George J. Walters, D.D.S., P.A. (1995–Present); Oral/Maxillofacial Surgeon, Walters and Grantham (1991–1995); Oral/Maxillofacial Surgeon, Miller Oral Surgery (1989–1991); Oral/Maxillofacial Surgery Resident, University of Maryland Hospital (1985–1989). **Associations & Accomplishments:** American Association of Oral/Maxillofacial Surgery; Florida Society of Oral/Maxillofacial Surgery; American Dental Association; Northwest Florida Dental Association; Bay County Dental Society; Middle Atlantic Society of Oral/Maxillofacial Surgery; Rotary International;

Civil War Roundtable of Bay County. **Education:** University of Maryland, D.D.S. (1985); University of Maryland Hospital and Shock Trauma Center, Certificate, Oral/Maxillofacial Surgery; Medical College of Pennsylvania, Anesthesiology Certificate; York Hospital, General Practice Residency Certificate; Loyola College, B.S. in Chemistry. **Personal:** Married to Melanie Goodreau in 1989. One child: Christopher Parker. Dr. Walters enjoys sports memorabilia, golf, history, aircraft, sports and reading.

Scott A. Walters, D.D.S.
Owner and Dentist
Scott A. Walters, D.D.S.
724 West Center Street
Kingsport, TN 37660-3163
(423) 247-6521
Fax: Please mail or call

8021

Business Information: Scott A. Walters, D.D.S., established in 1992, is a full–service, family practice, providing cosmetic, general dentistry, and oral surgery to adults and children; serving the Tri–city area of Johnson City, Bristol, and Kingsport, Tennessee. As Owner and Dentist, Dr. Walters is responsible for all aspects of operations, including providing dental care to patients. **Career Steps:** Owner and Dentist, Scott A. Walters, D.D.S. (1992–Present); Assistant Dental Officer, U.S. Navy (1987–1992). **Associations & Accomplishments:** American Dental Association (ADA); Past President, Downtown Kingsport Optimist Club; East Tennessee Academy of Dental Practice Administration. **Education:** University of Tennessee, D.D.S. (1987); University of Tennessee – Knoxville, B.A. **Personal:** Married to JoAnna Walters in 1983. Three children: Christopher, Elizabeth, and Nicholas. Dr. Walters enjoys fishing, collecting, and reading.

Mark C. Waring, D.D.S.
Periodontist
The Dental Office of Mark C. Waring, D.D.S.
2080 East Southern Avenue #E102
Tempe, AZ 85282-7521
(602) 820-4342
Fax: (602) 820-0754

8021

Business Information: The Dental Office of Mark C. Waring, D.D.S. is limited to periodontics with services in dental implants. A practicing dentist since 1987 and a Certified Periodontist, Dr. Waring established his sole–practice dentistry office in 1989. He oversees all administrative operations of a staff of three, in addition to his daily patient practice. **Career Steps:** Periodontist, The Dental Office of Mark C. Waring, D.D.S. (1989–Present). **Associations & Accomplishments:** American Academy of Periodontics; American Academy of Oral Medicine; Arizona State Dental Association; American Dental Association; Arizona Society of Periodontists; International Congress of Oral Implantologists; Omicron Kappa Upsilon. **Education:** Louisiana State University, Certificate in Periodontics (1989); Northwestern University Dental School, D.D.S. (1987). **Personal:** Married to Francene in 1981. Four children: Ciera, Kyra, Slater, and Brennan. Dr. Waring enjoys running and water sports.

Arnold Watkin, D.D.S., M.Sc.D.
President
Watkin Dental Associates
60 Federal Street
Boston, MA 02110
(617) 423-6165
Fax: (617) 426-0006

8021

Business Information: Watkin Dental Associates is a full–service, multi–specialty dental practice, providing everything but pedodontics (children dentistry). A practicing dentist since 1969, Dr. Watkin established the Practice in 1982. He oversees the administrative operations for associates and a support staff of 28, in addition to his daily patient practice, specializing in prosthodontics. Concurrent with his private dental practice, he is involved with First Dental Associates – a cluster of multi–specialist practices, now with twelve locations, is expected to reach up to forty locations within a year, with offices all over Massachusetts. The practices will be acquired through mergers and acquisitions. **Career Steps:** President, Watkin Dental Associates (1982–Present). **Associations & Accomplishments:** Greater Boston Dental Society. **Education:** Boston University, M.Sc.D. (1972); University Witwatersrand – South Africa, D.D.S. (1969). **Personal:** Married to Marcelle in 1969. Two children: Heath and Charla. Dr. Watkin enjoys skiing.

Jennifer L. Watters, D.D.S.
Periodontist
Stultz & Watters, D.D.S.
666 3rd Street, Suite 280
San Rafael, CA 94901
(415) 454-1064
Fax: Please mail or call

8021

Business Information: Stultz & Watters, D.D.S. is a full–service dental facility specializing in Periodontics and Oral Implantology. Established in 1980, Stultz & Watters currently employs 15 support staff. As Partner and Periodontist, Dr. Watters is responsible for the care and treatment of patients. **Career Steps:** Partner and Periodontist, Stultz & Watters, D.D.S. (1980–Present). **Associations & Accomplishments:** American Academy of Periodontology; American Association of Women Dentists; American Dental Society of Anesthesiology; American Dental Association; California Dental Association; California Society of Periodontist; International Congress of Oral Implantologists. **Education:** University of California – San Francisco, B.S., D.D.S. (1991); University of Washington, Certificate of Speciality in Periodontics; California State University – Sacramento, B.A., Chemistry. **Personal:** Dr. Watters enjoys gardening, cooking and her home.

Mark E. Weitzman, D.D.S.
Dentist
Offices of Mark E. Weitzman, D.D.S.
178 South Victoria Avenue, Suite #B
Ventura, CA 93003
(805) 650-0700 (805) 388-3319
Fax: Please mail or call

8021

Business Information: Offices of Mark E. Weitzman, D.D.S. is a full–service, general cosmetic dental practice concentrating in cosmetic and aesthetic dentistry for adults and children. Establishing his private dental practice upon conferral of his dental doctorate in 1991, Mark Weitzman is responsible for all aspects of operations, including providing dental care. **Career Steps:** Dentist, Offices of Mark E. Weitzman, D.D.S. (1991–Present). **Associations & Accomplishments:** California Dental Association; American Dental Association; Academy of Cosmetic Dentistry. **Education:** University of the Pacific, D.D.S. (1991); Carroll College, B.S.; U.O.D. Dental School. **Personal:** Dr. Weitzman enjoys the outdoors, surfing, biking, and dentistry.

Steven R. Wert, D.D.S
Sole Practitioner
Steven R. Wert, D.D.S.
1910 St. Joe Center Road, Suite 21
Ft. Wayne, IN 46825
(219) 483-4588
Fax: Please mail or call

8021

Business Information: Steven R. Wert, D.D.S. is a full–service, family practice dentistry office, providing cosmetic, general dentistry, and oral surgery. A practicing dentist for the past nine years, Dr. Wert established the Fort Wayne, Indiana office in 1986. As a sole practitioner for the four–chair practice, he responsible for all aspects of operations, including providing general dentistry to patients. **Career Steps:** Sole Practitioner, Steven R. Wert, D.D.S. (1986–Present). **Associations & Accomplishments:** American Dental Association; Indiana Dental Association; Isaac Knapp Dental Association; Board of Directors, Lutheran Homes, Inc. **Education:** Indiana University School of Dentistry, D.D.S. (1986); Valparaiso University, B.S. in Biology & Chemistry. **Personal:** Married to Eunice in 1982. One child: Daniel. Dr. Wert enjoys golf.

Cheryl A. Widdis, D.D.S.
Sole Practitioner
The Dental Office of Cheryl A. Widdis
450 Sutter Street, Suite 2021
San Francisco, CA 94108-4104
(415) 981-4960
Fax: (415) 981-4963

8021

Business Information: The Dental Office of Cheryl A. Widdis is a full–service, general practice dentistry office, providing general dentistry and surgery, with emphasis on facial cosmetic dentistry (i.e., bleaching, crowns). Establishing the sole practice dentistry office upon the conferral of her dental degree in 1985, Dr. Widdis oversees all administrative operations and a support staff of five, in addition to her

daily patient practice. **Career Steps:** Sole Practitioner, The Dental Office of Cheryl A. Widdis (1985–Present). **Associations & Accomplishments:** American Dental Association; California Dental Association; San Francisco Dental Society. **Education:** University of the Pacific, D.D.S. (1985). **Personal:** Married to Dr. Robert E. Jarvis, II in 1995. Dr. Widdis enjoys ballet, opera, charity benefits, and travel.

Dr. Merle L. Yaneza–Danov
Dentist
Office of Merle L. Yaneza, D.D.S.
12319 East Imperial Highway
Norwalk, CA 90650-8303
(310) 868-1739
Fax: (310) 946-4787

8021

Business Information: Office of Merle L. Yaneza, D.D.S. is a full–service, family practice dentistry office, providing general dentistry and surgery to patients. There are two offices which collectively house five dentists. Establishing his private practice upon the conferral of his dental degree in 1979, Dr. Yaneza–Danov oversees all administrative operations for associates and support staff, in addition to his daily patient practice. **Career Steps:** Dentist, Office of Merle L. Yaneza, D.D.S. (1979–Present). **Associations & Accomplishments:** Ordained Minister, Holy Spirit Divine Ministry. **Education:** University of California – Los Angeles: D.D.S. (1979), B.A. in English and Dental Hygienist. **Personal:** Married to Paul B. Danov in 1989. Dr. Yaneza–Danov enjoys serving our most high God.

Juliana B. Young, D.D.S.
Sole Practitioner
The Dental Office of Juliana B. Young, D.D.S., Inc.
81 Casa Buena
Corte Madera, CA 94925
(415) 924-5300
Fax: (415) 924-7909

8021

Business Information: The Dental Office of Juliana B. Young, D.D.S., Inc. is a full–service, family practice, dentistry office providing cosmetic, general dentistry, and oral surgery. Establishing her sole practice dentistry office upon the conferral of her dental degree in 1986, Dr. Young oversees all administrative operations for associates and a support staff of 4, in addition to her daily patient practice. **Career Steps:** Dentist, The Dental Office of Juliana B. Young, D.D.S., Inc. (1986–Present). **Associations & Accomplishments:** International Lecturers in Japan 1972; California State Board of Dental Examiners; American Dental Association; California Dental Association; Marin County Dental Society; Academy of General Dentistry; Academy of Cosmetic Dentistry. **Education:** University of the Pacific, D.D.S. (1986); Idaho State University, R.D.H. (1965). **Personal:** Married to Walter Grevesmuhl in 1989. One child: Juliana Grevesmuhl. Dr. Young enjoys painting, diving, travel, and photography.

Keith Leung Young, D.D.S.
Owner and Dentist
Keith L. Young, D.D.S.
37070 Newark Boulevard
Newark, CA 94560
(510) 797-6211
Fax: (510) 797-9828

8021

Business Information: Keith L. Young, D.D.S., established in 1965, is a five–chair, full–service, family practice dentistry office, providing cosmetic, general dentistry, and oral surgery at two locations in California (Fremont and Newark). Future plans include adding several associates and concentrating on advanced dentistry. A practicing dentist for the past thirty years, Dr. Young established this sole practice dentistry office in 1965. Operating as Owner and Dentist, he is responsible for all aspects of operations, including providing dental care to children and adults. **Career Steps:** Owner and Dentist, Keith L. Young, D.D.S. (1965–Present). **Associations & Accomplishments:** American Dental Association (ADA); Southern Alameda Dental Society; Fellowship, Academy of Dentistry International; Fellowship, Pierre Fauchard Academy; Mission Valley Dental Study Group; Served on the CDA Council on Dental Health and Education which published a sugarless cookbook, made a video on the dangers of smokeless tobacco, and other dental health publications. **Education:** University of California – San Francisco, D.D.S. (1965); City College of San Francisco, A.A. **Personal:** Married to Aileen in 1980. Three children: Karen, Deena, and Bradley. Dr. Young enjoys photography, hiking, camping, and writing.

Sami I. Youssef, D.D.S.

•••—◆—•••

Managing Doctor
Dr. Beauchamp–Western Dental
751 West Shaw Avenue
Clovis, CA 93612–3217
(209) 323–5500
Fax: Please mail or call

8021

Business Information: Dr. Beauchamp–Western Dental is a renowned dental group practice with offices in California, Oregon and Arizona. Established in 1962, the Clovis, California office currently employs 24 people. As Managing Doctor, Dr. Youssef is responsible for all aspects of management, as well as conducting minor oral surgery and general dentistry at the Clovis facility. **Career Steps:** Managing Doctor, Dr. Beauchamp–Western Dental (1994–Present). **Associations & Accomplishments:** American Dental Association (ADA); California Dental Association. **Education:** University of Southern California School of Dentistry, D.D.S. (1994); School of Dentistry, Alexandria, Egypt. **Personal:** Married to Dina Youssef in 1993. Dr. Youssef enjoys reading, fishing, and soccer.

Ronald J. Zokol, D.M.D., D.A.B.O.I.

Dentist, Board Certified in Implant Dentistry
Camgara Dental Group
7575 Cambie Street
Vancouver, British Co V6P 3H6
(604) 322–3250
Fax: (604) 322–3045
Email: See Below

8021

Business Information: As a dentist, Board Certified in Implant Dentistry, Dr. Zokol focuses his practice in advanced reconstructive dentistry. His special interest is in implant surgery, where–in orthopedic devices are placed into the jawbone to create new "roots" for prosthetic teeth. Dr. Zokol is the founder and director of the Pacific Institute for Implant Dentistry located in Vancouver, British Columbia. Internet users can reach him via: ZOKOLRJ@VANCOUVER.ARK.COM **Career Steps:** Dentist, Private Practice (1974–Present). **Associations & Accomplishments:** Diplomate, American Board of Oral Implantology; Diplomate, International Congress of Oral Implantologists; Director, Canadian Society of Oral Implantology; American Academy of Implant Dentistry; Canadian Academy of Restorative Dentistry & Prosthodontics; Past President, Vancouver & District Dental Society; Chief Examiner, College of Dental Surgeons of B.C.; Founder & Director, Pacific Institute of Implant Dentistry. **Education:** University of British Columbia, Faculty of Dentistry, D.M.D. (1974); Misch Implant Institute. **Personal:** Married to Marie in 1992. Three children: Ryan, Richard, and Robert. Dr. Zokol enjoys aviation, scuba diving, and computer technology.

Lisbeth L. Baird, D.C., F.I.A.C.A.

Sole Practitioner
Baird Holistic Health Center
1779 East Alosta Avenue
Glendora, CA 91740–3813
(818) 963–9463
Fax: Please mail or call

8041

Business Information: Baird Holistic Health Center is a provider of natural health care to patients suffering from musculo–skeletal–neurologic and organ problems. Baird offers their patients an alternative to drugs and surgery with the use of acupressure, herbal therapy, and emotional clearing. A Certified Clinical Acupressurist, Dr. Baird established her sole practice chiropractic office upon the conferral of her doctorate degree in 1978. She oversees all administrative operations for associates and support staff, in addition to her daily patient practice. Duties include examining, diagnosing, and treating patients, as well as recommending diet changes, supplements, herbal botanical formulas, homeopathic remedies, balancing and strengthening exercises. **Career Steps:** Sole Practitioner, Baird Holistic Health Center (1978–Present). **Associations & Accomplishments:** Fellow, International Association of Clinical Acupressurists; World Council of Women Chiropractors; ICA Council of Chiropractic Pediatrics. **Education:** Cleveland Chiropractic, Los Angeles, California, D.C. (1978). **Personal:** Two children: Devin Vincent and Justin Steven. Dr. Baird enjoys metaphysics, theology, organic gardening and herbal studies, and researching alternative techniques to improve health.

Darryl V. Bauer, D.C.

Owner
North Calcasieu Chiropractic Centre
102 McNeese Street
Dequincy, LA 70633
(318) 786–4691
Fax: (318) 786–4693

8041

Business Information: North Calcasieu Chiropractic Centre' is a general, full–service family chiropractic facility. Services provided include: therapeutic spinal manipulation, sports related injuries rehabilitation, trauma injury rehabilitation, as well as full nutritional and health wellness counseling. Establishing his private practice upon the conferral of his chiropractic degree in 1977, Dr. Bauer oversees all administrative operations for associates and a support staff, in addition to his daily patient practice. Board–Certified in Pediatric Chiropractic, his practice specializes in athletic injuries in children and adults with the assistance of his brother who also is a chiropractor. **Career Steps:** Owner, North Calcasieu Chiropractic Centre' (1977–Present). **Associations & Accomplishments:** American Chiropractic Association; International Chiropractic Association; Louisiana Chiropractic Association; Former President, DeQuincy Chamber of Commerce (1980–1981); Listed in Who's Who of Executives & Professionals. **Education:** Palmer College of Chiropractic, D.C. (1977); McNeese State University, Pre–Med. **Personal:** Dr. Bauer enjoys fishing and casino gaming on local riverboats.

Cynthia A. Becker, D.C.

Chiropractor
Becker Chiropractic Clinic
1114 Meriden St.
Mendota, IL 61342
(815) 538–2182
Fax: Please mail or call

8041

Business Information: Becker Chiropractic Clinic is a general, full–service chiropractic facility specializing in the therapeutic system based primarily upon the interactions of the spine and nervous system, the method of treatment usually being to adjust the segments of the spinal column. Dr. Becker has been a practicing Chiropractor since establishing the Clinic in 1991. Her current responsibilities include accounting functions, administrative activities, and patient care. **Career Steps:** Chiropractor, Becker Chiropractic Clinic (1991–Present). **Associations & Accomplishments:** Illinois Prairie State Chiropractic Association; President–Elect, Mendota Business and Professional Womens Association; Board of Directors, Mendota Civic Center; Mendota Women's Softball League. **Education:** Palmer College of Chiropractic, D.C., B.S. (1991). **Personal:** Married to John in 1990. Dr. Becker enjoys softball.

James A. Beebe, D.C.

•••—◆—•••

Chiropractor
Millville Chiropractic Health Center
1014 North High Street
Millville, NJ 08332–2527
(609) 327–0320
Fax: (609) 825–4183

8041

Business Information: Millville Chiropractic Health Center is a private practice general chiropractic clinic using holistic healing methods. Comprised of 4,000 square feet with six therapy, two treatment, an exam and x–ray room, the Clinic has a staff of three physicians, and a support staff of five. Local in scope, the Clinic plans to expand by including additional physicians. As Chiropractor, Dr. Beebe is responsible for patient care, administrative duties, operations, public relations, marketing, and strategic planning. **Career Steps:** Chiropractor, Millville Chiropractic Health Center (1977–Present). **Associations & Accomplishments:** American Chiropractic Association; New Jersey Chiropractic Society; Cumberland County Chiropractic Association. **Education:** Logan College of Chiropractic: B.S., D.C. (1977); Glassboro State College. **Personal:** Married to Barbara in 1988. Two children: Zachary and Tiffani. Dr. Beebe enjoys being an international adventurer and a large and small game hunter.

D. Richard Bellamy, D.C., D.A.C.A.N.

Chiropractor
The Chiropractic Offices of D. Richard Bellamy D.C.
1800 Saint James Place, #308
Houston, TX 77056–4109
(713) 623–0956
Fax: (713) 623–6380

8041

Business Information: The Chiropractic Offices of D. Richard Bellamy D.C. is an exciting, full–service chiropractic facility specializing in the therapeutic system based primarily upon the interactions of the spine and nervous system, the method of treatment usually being to adjust the segments of the spinal column. A practicing Chiropractic physician since 1985, Dr. Bellamy established his sole practice chiropractic office in 1986. He is responsible for all aspects of operations, including administration, public relations, marketing, and strategic planning, in addition to his daily patient practice. He also conducts seminars on positive mental wellness and personal development on a worldwide level, as well as providing consultations to individuals in business industry and government. **Career Steps:** Chiropractor, The Chiropractic Offices of D. Richard Bellamy D.C. (1986–Present). **Associations & Accomplishments:** American Chiropractic Association; Texas Chiropractic Association: Member, Former Board of Directors; Texas Chiropractic Association. **Education:** Texas Chiropractic College, D.C. (1985); Fellow, International Academy of Acupuncture; Diplomate, American Academy of Pain Management; Diplomate, American Chiropractic Academy of Neurology. **Personal:** Dr. Bellamy enjoys what he does and does what he loves for a living so his personal life blends with his professional life. He inspires others with talking about his book "Manifesting With Vision Inspiration and Purpose". He also is an accomplished guitarist. He enjoys visiting ancient sites, such as the ruins of Mexico, Peru and Egypt.

Ronald R. Bernardini, D.C.

•••—◆—•••

Owner and Director
Lake Chiropractic
375 Portion Road
Lake Ronkonkoma, NY 11779
(516) 981–1333
Fax: (516) 981–1335

8041

Business Information: Lake Chiropractic is a full–service, 5,500 square foot chiropractic, nutritional and holistic facility, specializing in the treatment of patients using all techniques of chiropractic treatment. Establishing Lake Chiropractic upon the conferral of his chiropractic degree in 1981, Dr. Bernardini serves as its Owner and Director. Licensed to practice in New York and Florida, he is responsible for all aspects of operations, in addition to the examination and treatment of patients and overseeing all administrative operations for associates and a support staff of 20. His specialty practice areas include: lumbar flexion distraction, thermography, full spine diversification, and adjunctive therapy. **Career Steps:** Owner and Director, Lake Chiropractic (1981–Present). **Associations & Accomplishments:** New York State Chiropractic Association: Distinguished service citation (1985–1989), Board Appointment (1994–1995), District 7, Suffolk County, Appointment and voted for Second term (1995–1996), Chairman, State Chapter Membership Committee (1984–1985); Vice President of New York Chiropractic College Alumni Association; Liaison to Clinic Advisory Committee to President of New York Chiropractic College, Dr. Ernest Napolitano; President of Chamber of Commerce of Lake Ronkonkoma (1983–1985); Chiropractic Lay Lecture Committee (1980); Who's Who in Universities and Colleges; Vice President of Lake Grove Lions; Award for Donation; American Chiropractic Association; New York State Chiropractic Association; Council on Diagnostic Injuries; Parker Chiropractic Research Foundation; Foundation for Chiropractic Education and Research; Alumni New York Chiropractic College. **Education:** New York Chiropractic College, Doctorate in Chiropractic (1981); State University of New York – Stony Brook, B.S. in Biology, Pre–Med (1978); Licensed Chiropractor, State of New York; Licensed Chiropractic Physician State of Florida; National Board of Chiropractic Examiners; Diplomate Status of Chiropractic; Examinations Part one and two–including x–ray; Mt. Sinai School of Medicine, Clinical Thermography; Internship at Greenvale and Levittown Clinics. **Personal:** Married to Cynthia in 1990. One child: Robert.

Michael N. Bernhardt, D.C.

Chiropractor
Albany Central Chiropractic
706 Madison Avenue
Albany, NY 12208–3013
(518) 465–3331
Fax: (518) 462–6697

8041

Business Information: Albany Central Chiropractic is a general, full–service chiropractic facility specializing in the therapeutic system based primarily upon the interactions of the spine and nervous system, the method of treatment usually being to adjust the segments of the spinal column. Dr. Bernhardt established his private practice in 1983 and is currently responsible for administrative functions, daily operations, and patient care. A New York State Certified Paramedic since 1990, he also responds to EMS calls in the Town of Guilderland. **Career Steps:** Chiropractor, Albany Central Chiropractic (1983–Present); Civilian Paramedic, Town of Guilderland (1990–Present); Chiropractor, Barile Chiropractic (1982–1983). **Associations & Accomplishments:** New York State Chiropractic Association; Board Member, Western Turnpike Rescue Squad; Peer Support Person, Albany County Critical Incident Stress Debriefing Team; Emergency Medical Services Lecturer; Lecturer for Support Groups in St. Peter's Hospital. **Education:** Hudson Valley Community College, Paramedic (1990); Life Chiropractic College, State University of New York College at Farmingdale. **Personal:** Married to Kathleen in 1981. Three children: Christopher, Caitlyn, and Lyndsay. Dr. Bernhardt enjoys bowling, billiards, camping, and autos.

SPINAL REHABILITATION CENTER

Darrell M. Blain, D.C.

Chiropractor
Spinal Rehabilitation Center
914 South Gloster Street
Tupelo, MS 38801
(601) 840–7600
Fax: (601) 840–8008

8041

Business Information: Spinal Rehabilitation Center is a full–service, general practice chiropractic office, providing treatment for personal injuries due to car accidents and other injuries. Services include pain management, thermography, kinesiology, legal procedures, and disability analysis. A practicing chiropractor, Senior Disability Analyst and a Certified Clinical Thermographist, Dr. Blain directs all administrative operations for associates and support staff, in addition to his daily patient practice. **Career Steps:** Director, Spinal Rehabilitation Center (1976–Present); Founder and Director, Chiropractic Diagnostic and Treatment Center of St. Louis; Chiropractor, Lindell Hospital; Exiting Board Examiner, Logan College Faculty Board; Clinical Research Scientist, United States Center for Musculoskeletal Research; **Associations & Accomplishments:** Licensed in Missouri and Mississippi; International Chiropractic Association; American Chiropractic Association; Missouri State Chiropractic Association; Mississippi Associated Chiropractors; Parker Chiropractic Research Foundation; National Academy of Research Biochemists; National Association of Wholistic Medicine; Cleveland College Alumni Association; Lindell Hospital Committee on Communicable Disease Control; American Academy of Pain Management; American Academy of Spinal Biomechanical Engineering; Founding Member, United States Health Association; Charter Member, Chiropractic Institute of Thermography; Fellow, American Back Society; International Biocranial Institute; Who's Who in Executives and Professionals; Who's Who in Excellence; AWARDS: Outstanding Student Award (1975); Leviathon Award (given for outstanding accomplishments in the chiropractic profession and the health of mankind); US Coast Guard Certificate of Appreciation; Frequent publisher and lecturer on the international, national, state and local levels at civic, association and institutional conferences, symposia and proceedings. **Education:** Cleveland Chiropractic College – Kansas City, MO; US Army: Nuclear, Biological and Radiological School, Engineer Officer Candidate School; Newport News School of Naval Architecture and Design; College of William and Mary; University of Florida; Pinellas Institute of Technology; DIPLOMATE: American Academy of Pain Management; American Board of Disability Analysts; CERTIFICATION: Kinesiology and Thermography – Palmer College of Chiropractic; Radiology Disc Disorders, Physiological Therapeutics, Orthopedics Diagnosis – National College of Chiropractic; Radiology – Logan College of Chiropractic; Acupuncture – International Academy of Clinical Acupuncture; Paraspinal E.M.G. – Life College; Protocol and Hospital Administration – Lindell Hospital; Clinical Thermography – Chiropractic Institute of Thermography. **Personal:** Married to Wilma. Seven children: Lewis, Chamilla, Stacey, Wendy, Leah, Sarah and Matthew. Dr. Blain enjoys martial arts, sailing and writing.

Goar Blanco, D.C.

Chiropractor
Chiropractic Offices of Dr. Goar Blanco
Winston Church #138, Mail Box #655
San Juan, Puerto Rico 00926
(809) 751–9147
Fax: Please mail or call

8041

Business Information: The Chiropractic Offices of Dr. Goar Blanco is a full–service private practice chiropractic center servicing both adults and children for a range of problems, ranging from stress to work related injuries. As Sole Chiropractor, Dr. Blanco is responsible for the daily operations of the office, in addition to his daily patient practice. **Career Steps:** Chiropractor, Dr. Goar Blanco (1989–Present). **Associations & Accomplishments:** President, Puerto Rico Chiropractic Association; American Chiropractic Association; Ballet Concerto Directory. **Education:** Life College: D.C. (1986), B.S. in Chemistry, cum laude (1976). **Personal:** Married to Virginia F. in 1981. One child: Marta Irene. Dr. Blanco enjoys painting, traveling, and collecting.

Aaron Blossom, D.C.

Owner
de Flores Chiropractic Clinic
5065 Miller Road
Flint, MI 48507–1037
(810) 732–6780
Fax: (810) 733–7246

8041

Business Information: de Flores Chiropractic Clinic is a general, full–service family practice chiropractic facility specializing in the therapeutic system based primarily upon the interactions of the spine and nervous system, the method of treatment usually being to adjust the segments of the spinal column. A practicing chiropractor for the past forty years, Dr. Blossom established de Flores Chiropractic Clinic as Owner, Operator, and Primary Physician in 1990. He oversees all administrative operations for associates and a support staff of four, in addition to his daily patient practice. **Career Steps:** Owner, de Flores Chiropractic Clinic (1990–Present); Blossom Chiropractic Clinic: Owner and Chief Executive Officer – Michigan office (1969–1987), Owner and Chief Executive Officer – Indiana office (1959–1969). **Associations & Accomplishments:** Grostic Research Association; Parker Chiropractic Research Association; Gonstead Research Association; International Chiropractic Association; Michigan Chiropractic Society; Vice President, New Horizons Youth Ministries; Caribe Vista Program; Professional Photographer; Teacher of Continuing Education. **Education:** Palmer College, D.C., certified in post graduate/continuing education 40 years. **Personal:** Married to Mary in 1953. Seven children: Paul, Mike, Daniel, Mary, Sara, James, and Matthew, as well as 23 grandchildren. Dr. Blossom enjoys photography.

Steven H. Centner, D.C.

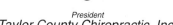

President
Taylor County Chiropractic, Inc.
1301 N. Jefferson Street
Perry, FL 32347
(904) 584–5214
Fax: Please mail or call

8041

Business Information: Taylor County Chiropractic, Inc. is a full–service chiropractic services clinic, providing family services including manipulation, massage and physical therapy, as well as nutritional counseling. A practicing chiropractor since 1982, Dr. Centner founded the clinic in 1991. As President he oversees all administrative operations for a support staff of three, as well as his daily patient practice. **Career Steps:** President, Taylor County Chiropractic, Inc. (1991–Present); Physician, Pavlik Chiropractic Group (1989–1990); Affiliate Physician, Doctors on Call (1990–1991). **Associations & Accomplishments:** Florida Chiropractic Association; Kiwanis International; Sustaining Member and Secretary, Elks Club; Secretary, Optimist International Local Chapter. **Education:** Palmer College of Chiropractics, D.C. (1982); Michigan State University, B.S. **Personal:** Married to Diane in 1982. Three children: Michelle, Steven and Cassandra.

HERESCO CHIROPRACTIC & ASSOCIATES
Advanced Spinal Health Care

Ronald A. Clifton, D.C.

Chiropractic Physician
Heresco Chiropractic & Associates
408 NW 7th Street
Corvallis, OR 97330–6308
(541) 757–9933
Fax: (541) 757–7713

8041

Business Information: Heresco Chiropractic is a private chiropractic office, specializing in advanced spinal health care and health wellness nutritional counseling. A practicing chiropractor since 1992, Dr. Clifton is one of three chiropractic associates. As the senior staff clinician, he focuses his patient therapy by utilizing the latest in intersegmental and wholistic practices. **Career Steps:** Chiropractic Associate, Heresco Chiropractic (1994–Present); Chiropractor, Mt. Angel Chiropractic (1992–1993); Senior Credit Analyst, Sears (1984–1993). **Associations & Accomplishments:** American Chiropractic Association; Chiropractic Association of Oregon; National Eagle Scout Association; Boy Scouts of America; Rotary International. **Education:** Western States Chiropractic College: D.C. (1992), B.S. in Human Anatomy; Spokane Falls Community College, A.A. **Personal:** Married to Tonya I. in 1989. Three children: Michelle, Raquel and Christopher. Dr. Clifton enjoys snow skiing, jet skiing, and rebuilding old cars.

Roger R. Coleman, D.C.

Chiropractor
Coleman Chiropractic Clinic
1344 East Main Street
Othello, WA 99344
(509) 488–9679
Fax: Please mail or call

8041

Business Information: Coleman Chiropractic Clinic, established in 1975, is a full–service chiropractic clinic. A practicing Chiropractor since 1974, Dr. Coleman established his chiropractic clinic in 1975, responsible for all aspects of operations. **Career Steps:** Chiropractor, Coleman Chiropractic Clinic (1974–Present). **Associations & Accomplishments:** Former Master of Paul Revere Masonic Lodge; Former Worthy Patron, The Order of the Eastern Star; International Chiropractic Association; Charter Member, Washington State Chiropractic Association; Published four papers in the American Journal of Clinical Chiropractic; Lecturer to medical specialists in South Korea on chiropractic care. **Education:** Palmer College of Chiropractic, D.C. (1974). **Personal:** Married to Jean in 1974.

Kyzor M. Dahdah–Ramirez, B.S.D.C.

Chiropractic Physician
–Independent–
1802 North University Drive, Suite 100B
Plantation, FL 33322–4115
(305) 474–3919
Fax: (309) 474–3958

8041

Business Information: Establishing his private chiropractic practice in 1992, Dr. Kyzor Dahdah–Ramirez provides services to patients throughout Plantation, Florida and surrounding communities. Utilizing a holistic approach to therapy, services are offered in spinal manipulation, injury rehabilitation and nutritional wellness counseling. Concurrent to his private chiropractic practice, Dr. Dahdah also served as the Director of Rehabilitation Services at the Medical Rehabilitation Center in Miami. **Career Steps:** Chiropractic Physician, Kyzor M. Dahdah– Ramirez, B.S.D.C. (1992–Present); Director Rehabilitation Services, Medical Rehabilitation Center (1991–1995). **Associations & Accomplishments:** American Chiropractic Association; International Chiropractic Association; Spine Society; Childrens Crime Prevention Unite; Florida Chiropractic Association; Institute of Quantum and Molecular Medicine. **Education:** New York Chiropractic College, Doctor (1990); Attended, University of Puerto Rico; Biology Honor Society. **Personal:** Married to Dr. Teri H. Dahdah in 1990. Two children: Erica Michele and Evan Philip. Dr. Dahdah–Ramirez enjoys tennis, scuba diving and skiing.

Rowena M. de Jesus, D.C.

Chiropractic Associate
Degenhart Chiropractic Health Center
1749 E. Broad Street, #A
Hazleton, PA 18201–5650
(717) 454–2474
Fax: (717) 454–0097

8041

Business Information: Degenhart Chiropractic Health Center is a general, full–service chiropractic facility specializing in the therapeutic system based primarily upon the interactions of the spine and nervous system, the method of treatment usually being to adjust the segments of the spinal column. Dr. de Jesus specializes in a family care practice utilizing cranial and meningeal adjustments to her technique. A practicing chiropractor since 1989, Dr. de Jesus established her sole practice chiropractic office in 1990. She oversees all administrative operations for associates and a support staff of three, in addition to her daily patient practice. **Career Steps:** Chiropractic Associate, Degenhart Chiropractic Health Center (1990–1995); Private Chiropractic Practitioner (1990–1995). **Associations & Accomplishments:** Sustaining Member, Secretary, Chiropractic Fellowship of Pennsylvania; Board of Regents, Sherman College of Straight Chiropractic. **Education:** Sherman College of Straight Chiropractic, D.C. (1989); Temple University (1984–1986). **Personal:** Dr. de Jesus enjoys skiing, golf, hiking and tennis during her leisure time.

Kevin Doan, D.C.

Chiropractor
Doan's Chiropractic Centre
2201 West 32nd Avenue
Denver, CO 80211
(303) 433–1219
Fax: (303) 433–5953

8041

Business Information: Doan's Chiropractic Centre is a general, full–service chiropractic facility specializing in the therapeutic system based primarily upon the interactions of the spine and nervous system, the method of treatment usually being to adjust the segments of the spinal column. A chiropractor since 1988, Dr. Doan established his private practice in 1993, specializing in the treatment of pulled muscles, nerve damage, and broken bones. **Career Steps:** Chiropractor, Doan's Chiropractic Centre (1993–Present). **Associations & Accomplishments:** Colorado Chiropractic Association. **Education:** Palmer College of Chiropractic, Doctorate (1988). **Personal:** Married to Deborah A. in 1982. Three children: Tara, Megan and Alexandra.

David J. Dobson, D.C., DABCO

Sole Practitioner
Dobson Chiropractic Clinic
102 First Street Northwest
De Smet, SD 57231–2249
(605) 854–9141
Fax: (605) 854–3355

8041

Business Information: Dobson Chiropractic Clinic is a general, full–service chiropractic facility providing all aspects of traditional chiropractic treatments, as well as nutritional and health wellness counseling. A practicing chiropractor since 1981, Dr. Dobson established his sole practice chiropractic office in 1982. He oversees all administrative operations for associates and support staff, in addition to his daily patient practice. Receiving patients primarily on a referral basis, Dr. Dobson specializes in orthopedics, adjustments, and nutritional counseling. He believes in the use of herbs, minerals, and organic extracts to treat patients. Concurrent with his private practice, he serves as a Nutrition Consultant for a nutrition consulting and mail order business; Manager of a landscape tree farm business; and an active builder of a network marketing business. **Career Steps:** Chiropractor, Dobson Chiropractic Clinic (1982–Present). **Associations & Accomplishments:** South Dakota Chiropractors Association; Amway Distributors Association. **Education:** Northwestern College of Chiropractic: D.C. (1981), DABCO (1986); Pillsbury College, B.A.; Control Data Institute, Computer Science. **Personal:** Married to Yvonne in 1969. Five children: Janie, James, Jeremy, Jennifer, and Julie. Dr. Dobson enjoys farming, hunting, fishing, skiing, and reading.

Michele M. Doone, D.C.

Chiropractic Physician
Mullican Chiropractic Center
4021 Belt Line Road, Suite 201
Dallas, TX 75244–2330
(214) 980–4848
Fax: (214) 490–5858

8041

Business Information: Mullican Chiropractic Center is a full–service, group practice chiropractic facility. A practicing chiropractor since 1986 and a Licensed Chiropractor in the states of Texas and California, Dr. Doone joined Mullican Chiropractic Center in 1991. She is one of four chiropractic associates with the Group. **Career Steps:** Chiropractic Physician, Mullican Chiropractic Center (1991–Present); Clinic Director, Back Pain Chiropractic (1988–1991); Doctor/Manager, Accident Centers of America (1987); Parker College of Chiropractic – Dallas, TX: Clinic Staff Doctor / Associate Professor (1986–1987), Radiology course Instructor / Chief Radiologic Technologist (1983–1985); Associate Doctor, Margolies Chiropractic Center (1986). **Associations & Accomplishments:** Texas Chiropractic Association; American Chiropractic Association; Sustaining Member and Board of Directors Member, Parker College of Chiropractic Alumni Association; Licensures: State of Texas (1986) and State of California (1988); Certifications: Paramedical Examiner – Health Systems (1970), Certified Radiologic Technologist – State of California – Bureau of Radiologic Health (1971), Diplomate – National Board of Chiropractic Examiners (1986), Management of the Post–Surgical Patient – Metroplex Neurospinal Diagnostic Medical and Surgical Association (1987), Certified in Impairment Rating – Utilizing the AMA "Guides to the Evaluation of Permanent Impairment" (1991), Diplomate – American Academy of Pain Management (1992); Board Eligible, American Board of Chiropractic Orthopedists (1993); Who's Who of Women Executives; LeBaron Blue Book; International Book of Honor; Who's Who of American Women; Doctor of the Year, Parker College of Chiropractic Alumni Association; The World Who's Who of Women; International Directory of Distinguished Leadership; Personalities of the South; Who's Who in Science and Engineering; International Who's Who of Intellectuals; Who's Who in the World; 2000 Notable American Women; World Intellectual of 1993; International Who's Who of Professional and Business Women; Who's Who in the South and Southwest; 500 Leaders of Influence; Staff Privileges, Tri–City Hospital (1995–Present); Texas Chiropractic Association – Radiology Committee. **Education:** Parker College of Chiropractic, D.C. summa cum laude (1986); Brookhaven, Mountain View, and Northlake Community Colleges, Pre–Med (1984); Los Angeles Valley College, Pre–Med (1963); Valley College of Medical and Dental Careers, C.M.A. (1962).

Russell C. Doyle, D.C.

Chiropractor
The Office of Millville Chiropractic Center
1014 N. High Street
Millville, NJ 08332–2527
(609) 327–0320
Fax: (609) 825–4183

8041

Business Information: The Office of Millville Chiropractic Center is a general, full–service chiropractic facility specializing in the therapeutic system based primarily upon the interactions of the spine and nervous system, the method of treatment usually being to adjust the segments of the spinal column. A practicing chiropractor since 1983, Dr. Doyle founded his private practice in 1984. He oversees all administrative and medical support staff, in addition to his daily patient caseload. **Career Steps:** Chiropractor, The Office of Millville Chiropractic Center (1990–Present); Chiropractor, Canton Center Chiropractic Clinic (1984–1989); Chiropractor, O'Conner Chiropractic Clinic (1984). **Associations & Accomplishments:** Former Board Member, New Jersey Chiropractic Society; Ethics Chairman, Cumberland County Chiropractic Association; American Chiropractic Association; 1988 Chiropractor of the Year. **Education:** Palmer College of Chiropractic, D.C. (1983); Henry Ford College. **Personal:** Four children: Christopher, Lindsey, Stephanie and Mallory. Dr. Doyle enjoys golf, bowling, and gardening.

Philip M. Epstein, D.C.

Chiropractor
Chiropractic Office of Philip M. Epstein, D.C.
1 Dorothea Street
Plainview, NY 11803
(516) 932–1616
Fax: Please mail or call

8041

Business Information: The Chiropractic Office of Philip M. Epstein, D.C. provides full–service family chiropractic services, including health wellness and nutritional counseling. A

practicing chiropractor since 1990, Dr. Epstein established the Plainview, New York practice in 1995. As Sole Practitioner, he is responsible for the overall operations, dividing his time between the administration of the Clinic and daily patient care. **Career Steps:** Chiropractor, Chiropractic Office of Philip M. Epstein, D.C. (1995–Present); Clinic Director, Optimum Chiropractic (1992–1995); Clinic Director, Gilbertson Chiropractic H.C. (1990–1992). **Associations & Accomplishments:** New York Chiropractic Council; New York State Chiropractic Association; American Chiropractic Association; International Chiropractic Association. **Education:** Logan College of Chiropractic, D.C. (1989). **Personal:** Married to Tarra in 1993. Dr. Epstein enjoys golf, tennis, football. An avid musician, Dr. Epstein is a back–up vocalist and plays keyboard & guitar.

Dr. Scott Featherstone

Chiropractor/Owner
Featherstone Chiropractic
1182 Grimes Bridge Road, Suite 200
Roswell, GA 30075
(770) 587–2900
Fax: (770) 587–1058

8041

Business Information: Featherstone Chiropractic is a private medical office providing chiropractic care (i.e. therapy, adjustments, x–ray, and physical exam) to patients. Seeing approximately twenty patients a day, the Office is comprised of two employees and a chiropractic assistant. As Chiropractor/Owner, Dr. Featherstone oversees all aspects of the Office, and is responsible for providing nutritional consulting, therapy and manual spinal adjustments, taking radiographs, and performing physical examinations. **Career Steps:** Chiropractor/Owner, Featherstone Chiropractic (1995–Present); Chiropractor, Advanced Chiropractic (1995); Chiropractic Assistant, Dr. Michael Vandersluis (1994). **Associations & Accomplishments:** American Chiropractic Association; Georgia Chiropractic Association; Atlanta Executive Network; Certified in Carpal Tunnel Syndrome and Cumulative Trauma Disorders, Sports and Industrial Diagnosis, Treatment and Rehabilitation, Extremity–Related Injuries. Certified in Spinal Pelvic Stabilization, Custom–molded Foot Orthotics. **Education:** Life College, D.C. (1993). **Personal:** Dr. Featherstone enjoys jet skiing, snow skiing, scuba diving, and hiking.

Joseph D. Flowers, D.C.

Chiropractor
Goleta Valley Chiropractic
6831 Hollister Avenue, #A
Goleta, CA 93117–3015
(805) 685–8400
Fax: (805) 685–9001

8041

Business Information: Goleta Valley Chiropractic is a full–service, chiropractic office, providing the restoration of patient's health by restoring proper nerve functions (removing subluxations). A practicing chiropractor since 1989, Dr. Flowers joined Goleta Valley Chiropractic as Chiropractor in 1990. He oversees all administrative operations for associates and a support staff of three, in addition to his daily patient practice. His practice concentrates on removing nerve interference and assists individuals in the elimination of pain without the use of drugs. **Career Steps:** Chiropractor, Goleta Valley Chiropractic (1990–Present); Assistant, Freemont Chiropractic (1989–1990); Assistant, Curry Chiropractic (1987–1988); Second Class Petty Officer, U.S. Navy (1969–1973). **Associations & Accomplishments:** Toastmasters; International Chiropractic Association; Gonstead Clinical Studies Society; U.S. Navy: Riverboat Vietnamese Advisor, awarded Bronze Star with combat 'V', Navy Commendation with combat 'V', Presidential Unit Citation, Purple Heart (2), Vietnamese Cross of Gallentry. **Education:** Life West Chiropractic College, D.C. (1989); El Camino College, A.A. **Personal:** Dr. Flowers enjoys piano, surfing, mountain biking and scuba diving.

Chris J. Frogley, D.C.

Director
Frogley Chiropractic, P.C.
1605 West Kimberly Road
Davenport, IA 52806
(319) 386–4798
Fax: (319) 386–0903

8041

Business Information: Frogley Chiropractic, P.C. is a managed health care practice providing quality, cost–effective chiropractic and nutritional counseling. As Director, Dr. Frogley manages all aspects of the Practice, including the care and treatment of patients. Established in 1961, Frogley Chiropractic, P.C. employs four people. **Career Steps:** Director, Frogley Chiropractic, P.C. (July, 1994 to Present); Mission President, Church of Jesus Christ of Later Day Saints (1991–1994); Physician, Frogley Chiropractic Office (1985–1991); Physician, Centro Chiroterapico Umbro–Italy (1982–1985). **Associa-**

tions & Accomplishments: Palmer Alumni Association; American Chiropractic Association. **Education:** Palmer College, D.C. (1981); In process of certification as Certified Chiropractic Sports Physician. **Personal:** Married to Sharol in 1977. Four children: Jessica, David, Jami and Ian. Dr. Frogley enjoys horseback riding, hiking, camping, basketball, playing with his kids and traveling.

Anastasia F. Fry, D.C.

Sole Practitioner
The Chiropractic Office of Anastasia F. Fry, D.C.
812 West Broad Street
Bethlehem, PA 18018
(610) 867–6386
Fax: Please mail or call

8041

Business Information: A practicing Chiropractor since 1958, Dr. Anastasia Fry provides the overall administrative direction for her private practice office, in addition to her daily patient base. Her practice involves consulting, adjusting, analyzing, and providing natural remedies, and homeopathy and acupuncture treatments. **Career Steps:** Sole Practitioner, The Chiropractic Office of Dr. Anastasia F. Fry (1958–Present); Librarian, Logan Basic College (1954–1958); Inventory Controller, Bethlehem Steel (1945). **Associations & Accomplishments:** American Dowsing Society; British Radionics Society; Pennsylvania Chiropractic Association; YMCA; YWCA; Sun Inn Historical Society. **Education:** Logan Chiropractic University, D.C. (1958); Moravian College; Saint Luke's School of Nursing. **Personal:** Widow of Mervin Fry (married 1941, deceased 1990). Two children: Barry James and Mervin John. Dr. Fry enjoys golf, radionics, dowsing, music, art, fitness activities, and writing.

William H. Gearhart Jr., D.C.

Doctor of Chiropractic
Gearhart Chiropractic Center
66 West Valley Avenue
Elysburg, PA 17824
(717) 672–3295
Fax: (717) 672–9414

8041

Business Information: Gearhart Chiropractic Center was established in 1982. As Doctor of Chiropractic, Dr. Gearhart treats patients for sprains, strains, shoulder adjustments, physical therapy, and rehabilitation without the use of drugs or surgery. He seeks to relieve pain, illnesses, and disability by skillful manipulation of the spine and joints. **Career Steps:** Doctor of Chiropractic, Gearhart Chiropractic Center (1982–Present). **Associations & Accomplishments:** Secretary, Pennsylvania Chiropractic Federation; Board eligible, Diplomat – American Board Chiropractic Orthopedics. **Education:** Pennsylvania College of Chiropractic, D.C. (1981); Pennsylvania State University, B.S.; Parker College of Chiropractic, Diplomate American Board Chiropractic Orthopedics. **Personal:** Married to Beth Ann in 1980. Two children: Megan and Ryan. Dr. Gearhart enjoys bow hunting, fishing, and camping.

Hutan Ghojallu, D.C.

Associate Chiropractor
Strong Chiropractic
1040 South Koeller Street
Oshkosh, WI 54901
(414) 426–9898
Fax: (414) 426–9810

8041

Business Information: Strong Chiropractic is a private clinic focusing on specific upper cervical chiropractic and holistic health care, including physical therapy, musculoskeletal rehabilitation, and nutritional consulting. Diagnostic procedures include case history review, spinal exams, and x–rays. A practicing Chiropractor since the conferral of his degree in 1994, Dr. Ghojallu serves as an Associate Chiropractor of Strong Chiropractic, providing care to a wide variety of patients. **Career Steps:** Associate Chiropractor, Strong Chiropractic (1994–Present). **Associations & Accomplishments:** Delta Sigma Chi Fraternity of Straight Chiropractic; Wisconsin Chiropractic Association. **Education:** Palmer College of Chiropractic, D.C. (1994); Springfield College, B.S. in Biology (1990). **Personal:** Dr. Ghojallu enjoys amateur kickboxing and Jiujitsu.

Joseph A. Grauso, D.C.

Chiropractic Physician
Berkeley Heights Chiropractic Center
492 Springfield Avenue
Berkeley Heights, NJ 07922–1112
(908) 665–0770
Fax: (908) 665–0002

8041

Business Information: Berkeley Heights Chiropractic Center is a full–service group practice family chiropractic facility. Joining the Center upon the conferral of his chiropractic degree in 1989, Dr. Grauso is one of six chiropractors in private practice. He is responsible for the examination and treatment of patients, as well as conducting monthly lectures, classes, and workshops at libraries, hospitals, homes, and adult schools. **Career Steps:** Chiropractic Physician, Berkeley Heights Chiropractic Center (1989–Present). **Associations & Accomplishments:** American Chiropractic Association; New Jersey Chiropractic Society; International College of Applied Kinesiology; Trout Unlimited. **Education:** New York Chiropractic College, D.C. (1989); University of Bridgeport, Connecticut, M.S. in Nutrition; Boston College, B.S. in Biology and Theology; Academy of Health Sciences, C.O.T.A. in Occupational Therapy; Various continuing education seminars in Health, Nutrition and Sports Medicine. **Personal:** Dr. Grauso enjoys fly–fishing, rugby, basketball, football, and boating.

A. David Gutierrez, D.C.

Chiropractor
Spine and Health Institute
701 San Pedro
San Antonio, TX 78212–5247
(210) 354–2020
Fax: Please mail or call

8041

Business Information: Spine and Health Institute specializes in chiropractic and rehabilitative health care, nutrition, and exercise. As Chiropractor, Dr. Gutierrez diagnosis injuries and conditions, examines, and treats patients. **Career Steps:** Chiropractor, Spine and Health Institute (1995–Present); Doctor of Chiropractic, First Chiropractic (1992–1995); Doctor of Chiropractic, Angel Chiropractic (1990–1991). **Associations & Accomplishments:** Texas Chiropractic Association; Associate Pastor of Spanish Christian Church. **Education:** Texas Chiropractic, Doctor of Chiropractic (1988). **Personal:** Married to Barbara in 1989. One child: Samuel. Dr. Gutierrez enjoys reading, playing guitar, and arcade games.

Kathryn J. Hafer, D.C.

Sole Practitioner
Office of Kathryn J. Hafer, D.C.
611 Howard Street
Kalamazoo, MI 49008–1919
(616) 381–0737
Fax: (616) 381–5120

8041

Business Information: Office of Kathryn J. Hafer, D.C. is a general, full–service chiropractic facility specializing in the therapeutic system based primarily upon the interactions of the spine and nervous system, the method of treatment usually being to adjust the segments of the spinal column. A practicing chiropractor since 1985, Dr. Hafer established her sole practice chiropractic office in 1991. She oversees all administrative operations for associates and support staff, in addition to her daily patient practice. She specializes in Palmer Package and Low Force techniques, osteos manipulation, soft tissue manipulation, sports rehabilitation and chronic conditions. She also provides nutrition and workout programs and consultations regarding home and work habits. **Career Steps:** Sole Practitioner, Office of Kathryn J. Hafer, D.C. (1991–Present); Chiropractor, Abies Chiropractic Clinic (1989–1991); Chiropractor, Bangor Chiropractic Clinic (1986–1989). **Associations & Accomplishments:** Michigan Chiropractic Society. **Education:** Palmer College of Chiropractic, D.C. (1985); Western Michigan University, B.S.

Edward J. Hartman, D.C.

Chiropractor
Hartman Family Chiropractic Center
4355 New Falls Road
Levittown, PA 19056
(215) 949–3300
Fax: (215) 949–3347
E MAIL: See Below

8041

Business Information: Hartman Family Chiropractic Center is a healthcare office focused on treatment for spinal and neck problems through the manipulation of the spine and other joints. Establishing his practice in 1989, Dr. Hartman directs a staff of two. He seeks to relieve pain, illness and disability by providing skillful manipulation of the spine and other joints, utilizing other clinical procedures as necessary. Internet users can reach him via: Xbwn62A@prodigy.com. **Career Steps:** Chiropractor, Hartman Family Chiropractic Center (1989–Present); Office Manager, Oxford Chiropractic Center (1983–1988); Medical Examiner, World Wide Health Services (1976–1983). **Associations & Accomplishments:** Pennsylvania Chiropractic Society; Pennsylvania State University Alumni Association. **Education:** Pennsylvania College of Chiropractic, D.C. (1988); Pennsylvania State University, B.S. (1975). **Personal:** Married to Margo in 1993. Two children: Edward III and Amanda. Dr. Hartman enjoys hockey, computers, and business.

Dr. Jeffrey D. Heimensen

Chiropractor
Stange Chiropractic Clinic
111 Arizona Avenue Northwest
Orange City, IA 51041
(712) 737–3850
Fax: (712) 737–3859

8041

Business Information: Stange Chiropractic Clinic is a full–service chiropractic practice, providing services to patients ranging from newborns to geriatrics on a referral basis. A practicing chiropractor since 1992, Dr. Heimensen joined the Clinic in 1994 as Chiropractor and is responsible for providing patient care in chiropractic medicine. **Career Steps:** Chiropractor, Stange Chiropractic Clinic (1994–Present); Pastor, Center Baptist Church (1993–1994). **Associations & Accomplishments:** Iowa Chiropractic Society. **Education:** Parker Chiropractic College, D.C. (1992). **Personal:** Married to Laura in 1989.

Alison F. Henderson, D.C.

Owner and Chiropractor
Neurohealth Chiropractic Center
1234 19th Street, Suite 710
Washington, DC 20036
(202) 293–2225
Fax: (202) 293–7694

8041

Business Information: Neurohealth Chiropractic Center, established in 1992, is a full–service, health care facility providing care in chiropractic medicine and physical therapy. As Owner and Chiropractor, Dr. Henderson founded the Center in 1992 and is responsible for all aspects of operations, including providing chiropractic care to patients and supervision of a staff of four. Concurrent with her private chiropractice practice, she and her husband run a Tae Kwon Do school. She was a previous Olympic candidate, but never competed due to an automobile accident. **Career Steps:** Owner and Chiropractor, Neurohealth Chiropractic Center (1992–Present); Medical Technician and Research Assistant, Life College Clinic (1988–1992); Medical Technologist, D.C. General Hospital (1983–1988). **Associations & Accomplishments:** American Chiropractic Association; International Chiropractic Association; Alpha Delta Upsilon – Women's Chiropractic Honor Society; United States American Athlete Representative, Tae kwon do Union. **Education:** Life Chiropractic College, D.C. (1992); Howard University, B.S. in Zoology. **Personal:** Married to Darryl in 1982. Four children: Ayanna, Jared, Jenna, and Jasmine. Dr. Henderson enjoys Tae Kwon Do (black belt holder), yoga, and tennis.

Michael D. Herzberg, D.C.

Chiropractor
Herzberg Family Chiropractic
5323 Brainerd Road 101
Chattanooga, TN 37411–5305
(423) 954–9818
Fax: (423) 954–1196

8041

Business Information: Herzberg Family Chiropractic is a general, full–service chiropractic facility specializing in the therapeutic system based primarily upon the interactions of the spine and nervous system, the method of treatment usually being to adjust the segments of the spinal column. A practicing chiropractor since 1991, Michael Herzberg established his private practice in 1993. He provides the overall direction for administrative and medical support staff, in addition to his daily patient practice. **Career Steps:** Chiropractor, Herzberg Family Chiropractor (1993–Present); Chiropractic Associate, Backpain Clinics (1992–1993); Chiropractic Associate, Lensgraf Clinics (1991–1992); Micro Lab Technician, Deaconess Medical Center (1988–1991). **Associations & Accomplishments:** American Chiropractic Association; International Chiropractic Association; Jaycees; Southeast Tennessee Chiropractic Association; Chamber of Commerce; Better Business Bureau; Multiple Sclerosis Society; Mustang Club of America; Acupuncture International; UTC Mocs Athletic Program; Chattanooga Lookouts Baseball, and various other sport clubs. **Education:** Logan College of Chiropractic, D.C. (1991); Eastern New Mexico University: M.S. in Microbiology (1986), B.S. in Biology/Chemistry . **Personal:** One child: Brandon. Dr. Herzberg enjoys space program, fast cars, martial arts, writing, and water sports.

Michael E. Johnson, D.C.
Sole Practitioner
Office of Michael E. Johnson, D.C., D.C.C.C.
11034 Westheimer Road
Houston, TX 77042–3206
(713) 974–0390
Fax: (713) 784–7902

8041

Business Information: Office of Michael E. Johnson, D.C., D.C.C.C. is a private practice chiropractic office, consisting of a chiropractic physician, physical therapists, and X–ray services, receiving patients on a referral basis, including Worker's Compensation cases. The Practice specializes in diagnostic and rehabilitation of neuro–muscular and acute chronic back complaints. Establishing his sole practice chiropractic office upon the conferral of his degree, Dr. Johnson oversees all administrative operations for associates and a support staff of four, in addition to his daily patient practice. **Career Steps:** Sole Practioner, Office of Micheal E. Johnson, D.C., D.C.C.C. (1979–Present). **Associations & Accomplishments:** Diplomate Congress of Chiropractic Consultants; American Chiropractic Association; Texas Chiropractic Association; TCCAA; Education Committee,Texas Board of Chiropractic Examiners; West Houston Chamber of Commerce. **Education:** Texas Chiropractic College, D.C. (1979); Post Graduate, C. Diplomate Congress of Chiropractic Consultants, D.C.C.C. **Personal:** Married to Wendy in 1988. Two children: Michael E. Johnson Jr. and Kory William. Dr. Johnson enjoys fishing, boating, hiking, water skiing and scuba diving.

Neil F. Kolle, D.C.
Chiropractor
Neil F. Kolle, D.C.
25726 West Chicago
Bedford, MI 48239
(313) 937–1414
Fax: Please mail or call

8041

Business Information: Neil F. Kolle, D.C. is a private practice medical office specializing in chiropractic care and services for the surrounding community. Established in the 1960s, the Company employs two people. Plans for the future include expanding the Practice to include another chiropractor. As Chiropractor, Dr. Kolle is responsible for the day–to–day operation of the office, including diagnosis, referrals, and administrative duties. **Career Steps:** Chiropractor, Neil F. Kolle, D.C. (1978–Present). **Associations & Accomplishments:** Diplomate, National Board of Chiropractor Examiners; American Chiropractic Association; Michigan Chiropractic Society; National College Alumni Association. **Education:** National College of Chiropractic, D.C. (1978). **Personal:** One child: Melissa Ann. Dr. Kolle enjoys golf and bowling.

Elizabeth C. Kressin, D.C.
Sole Practitioner
Chiropractic Arts Clinic
P.O. Box 800
Spencer, IA 51301
(712) 262–3517
Fax: (712) 262–2357

8041

Business Information: Chiropractic Arts Clinic is a general, full–service chiropractic facility specializing in the therapeutic system based primarily upon the interactions of the spine and nervous system, the method of treatment usually being to adjust the segments of the spinal column. A practicing chiropractor since 1986, Dr. Kressin established her private office in 1987. As Sole Practitioner, she oversees all administrative functions and support staff, in addition to her daily patient practice. **Career Steps:** Chiropractic Arts Clinic: Sole Practitioner (1987–Present), Chiropractic Assistant (1979–1983); Chiropractic Assistant, Zelm Chiropractic Clinic (1976–1979). **Associations & Accomplishments:** Iowa Chiropractic Society; American Chiropractic Association; President, Business and Professional Womens Organization; Board Member, Iowa Board of Chiropractic Examiners; Board Member, First English Lutheran Church; Counselor, Pinnacle Chiropractic Organization; Former Vice–President, Spencer Area Association of Business and Industry; Advisor for Medical Assistant, Medical Secretary, and Chiropractic Technician curriculums for Spencer College which merged with Iowa Lakes Community College. **Education:** Palmer University, D.C. (1986); Iowa State University. **Personal:** Married to Dr. Rex Jones in 1980. Dr. Kressin enjoys power boating, flying, and mentoring recent graduates.

Douglas R. Larsen, D.C.
Sole Practitioner
Larsen Chiropractic, Inc.
2548 East 7th Avenue
Flagstaff, AZ 86004
(520) 576–8533
Fax: (520) 527–4000

8041

Business Information: Larsen Chiropractic, Inc. is a full–service, general chiropractic practice. Establishing his private practice in 1993, Dr. Larsen is responsible for the care and treatment of patients with back and neck disorders, as well as all administrative functions for the office, including business decisions and finances. **Career Steps:** Sole Practitioner, Larsen Chiropractic, Inc. (1993–Present); Realtor, Century 21 (1985–1989); Landscaper, Larsen Landscape, Construction and Design (1984–1985). **Associations & Accomplishments:** First Class Scout and Former Senior Patrol Leader, Boy Scouts of America Troop 3. **Education:** Cleveland Chiropractic College, D.C. (1992); Moorpark College, CA., A.A. **Personal:** Dr. Larsen enjoys snow and water skiing, reading books and attending seminars related to health, nutrition, and spiritual enlightenment.

Seth Lederman, D.C.

Owner
Lederman Back & Neck Center
7050 Austin Street
Forest Hills, NY 11375–4703
(718) 575–0300
Fax: (718) 575–3559

8041

Business Information: Lederman Back & Neck Center specializes in chiropractic and rehabilitative health care, nutrition, and exercise (personal injury clinic). As Owner, Dr. Lederman is responsible for all aspects of Company operations and the treatment of patients. **Career Steps:** Owner, Lederman Back & Neck Center (1990–Present) **Associations & Accomplishments:** Young Entrepreneurs Organization (YEO). **Education:** New York Chiropractic College, D.C. (1988); State University of New York – Albany, B.A. (1985). **Personal:** Dr. Lederman enjoys personal development through books, tapes, videos and seminars, exercising and skiing.

Benson K. Lee, D.C.
Associate Clinic Director
Chan Chiropractic Clinic
4339 West Kennewick Avenue
Kennewick, WA 99336
(509) 735–0311
Fax: (509) 783–1206

8041

Business Information: Chan Chiropractic Clinic is a group chiropractic health care practice. A practicing chiropractor since 1983, Dr. Lee joined Chan Chiropractic Clinic as Associate Clinic Director in 1984. Aside from his administrative function, he is also responsible for the diagnosis and treatment of children and adults with chiropractic methods. He is a certified Bio–Energetic Synchronization Technique Practitioner. **Career Steps:** Associate Clinic Director, Chan Chiropractic Clinic (1984–Present); Assistant Manager, Alitalia (1972–1973); Air Freight Officer, Cathay Pacific Airway (1969–1972). **Associations & Accomplishments:** Washington State Chiropractic Association; Morter Health System; Knights of Columbus. **Education:** Palmer College of Chiropractic, D.C. (1983); University of Michigan, B.B.A. **Personal:** Married to Souvannary in 1978. Three children: Alexander, Christina, and Jonathan.

Asher Z. Leeder, D.C.
Owner
Commonwealth Chiropractic
1216 Commonwealth Avenue #1
Allston, MA 02134–4638
(617) 739–0046
Fax: (617) 738–9441
EMAIL: See Below

8041

Business Information: Commonwealth Chiropractic is a general, full–service chiropractic facility, specializing in the therapeutic system based primarily upon the interactions of the spine and nervous system, the method of treatment usually being to adjust the segments of the spinal column. A practicing chiropractor since 1980, Dr. Leeder established his solo practice in 1982. He is responsible for all aspects of opera-

tions, in addition to his daily patient practice. **Career Steps:** Owner, Commonwealth Chiropractic (1982–Present). **Associations & Accomplishments:** Council on Sports Injuries, American Chiropractic Association; Massachusetts Chiropractic Society; Ordained Rabbi; Black Belt First Dan, Tora Dojo Association. **Education:** New York Chiropractic College, D.C. (1980); Isaac Elchanan Theological Seminary, Rabbinic Ordination; Yeshiva University, M.S. in Education; Yeshiva College, B.A. in Biology and Chemistry. **Personal:** Married to Shira in 1977. Five children: Leah, Daniel, Avrum, Suri, and Yehuda.

Michelle A. Legault, D.C.

Owner
Lifestyle Chiropractic Clinic
2405 San Pedro Northeast
Albuquerque, NM 87110
(505) 888–1186
Fax: Please mail or call

8041

Business Information: Lifestyle Chiropractic Clinic is a general chiropractic facility specializing on the family and preventative aspects of chiropractic care. Conducting complete neuro and ortho exams, Dr. Michelle Legault treats all patients from the ages of one to ninety. Believing the more the patient knows, the better the treatment given, she is a flexible risk taker who will bring her work to the personal level. **Career Steps:** Owner, Lifestyle Chiropractic Clinic (1993–Present); Bartender, Bugsy's (1991–1993); Bartender, Champps (1989–1991). **Associations & Accomplishments:** American Chiropractic Association; New Mexico Chiropractic Association; Women Entreprenuers. **Education:** Northwestern College of Chiropractic, D.C. (1993). **Personal:** Dr. Legault enjoys fishing, reading, public speaking, tennis, ergonomics and consulting for companies. Dr. Legault also believes herbs and nutritional supplements are necessary for health and the healing process.

Harvelee H. Leite–Ah Yo, RPT, DC
Physical Therapist/Chiropractor
Hawaii Physical Therapy & Chiropractic Clinic, Inc.
41 Laimana Street
Hilo, HI 96720–2542
(808) 961–5663
Fax: (808) 969–3767

8041

Business Information: Hawaii Physical Therapy & Chiropractic Clinic, Inc. offers physical therapy, massage therapy, aerobics instruction, and chiropractic treatment for patients. Dr. Leite–Ah Yo spent over 20 years as a physical therapist and through natural progression, became a chiropractor. As a chiropractor, she provides care and treatment for patients with back and neck disorders. A believer in holistic methods of treatment, Dr. Leite–Ah Yo also offers her patients alternative treatments. She is also responsible for all aspects of administration, marketing, and public relations for the Practice. **Career Steps:** Physical Therapist/Chiropractor, Hawaii Physical Therapy & Chiropractic Clinic, Inc. (1993–Present); Keaau Chiropractic Center (1992); St. Mary's spine Center (1992); Physical Therapist, APEX Physical Therapy (1989–1992). **Associations & Accomplishments:** American Physical Therapy Association; American Chiropractic Association; American Society for Psychoprophylaxis in Obstetrics; Alpha Sigma Nu–Jesuit Honor Society; Hawaii State Chiropractic Association. Listed in Who's Who Among Students in American Universities and Colleges (1991). **Education:** Life Chiropractic College West, D.C. Summa Cum Laude (1991); University of California: B.S. in Physical Therapy (1976), B.A. Psychology Cum Laude (1975), Certificate in Lamaze Childbirth Education (1982). **Personal:** Married to Casmir K. Ah Yo in 1980. Three children: Kanani J., Kaahukane G., and Healani K.. Dr. Leite–Ah Yo enjoys spending time with her children.

Dwight B. Lewis, D.C.
President
Chiropractic Outreach Inc.
7032 US Highway 431
Albertville, AL 35950
(205) 878–1432
Fax: Please mail or call

8041

Business Information: Chiropractic Outreach Inc. is a private general practice specializing in chiropractic care. A practicing chiropractor since 1949, Dr. Lewis established COI in 1984. As President and sole practitioner, he oversees an administrative and chiropractic support staff of five, in addition to his daily patient practice. **Career Steps:** President, Chiropractic Outreach Inc. (1984–Present); Doctor of Chiropractic,

Dwight B. Lewis, D.C. (1949–1984). **Associations & Accomplishments:** Masonic Lodge Scottish Rite Shrine; Chiropractic Society of Alabama; American Chiropractic Association; United Methodist Church. **Education:** Bebout College of Chiropractic: Ph.C. (1951), D.C. (1949); Rio Grande College; Denison University; Ohio State University. **Personal:** Two children: Sherry and Pamela. Dr. Lewis enjoys golf and fishing.

Dr. J. Kevin Martin
Chiropractic Associate
River Parish Chiropractic Clinic
1108 W. Airline Highway
La Place, LA 70068
(504) 652–7904
Fax: Please mail or call

8041

Business Information: River Parish Chiropractic Clinic is a full–service, health care facility specializing in chiropractic medicine. Established in 1988, River Parish Chiropractic Clinic currently employs 10 people. One of two practicing chiropractic associates, Dr. Martin shares responsibility for the overall administrative operations, in addition to his daily patient practice. **Career Steps:** Chiropractic Associate, River Parish Chiropractic Clinic **Associations & Accomplishments:** American Chiropractic Association: Council on Nutrition, Council on Sports Activities & Physical Fitness, Council on Radiographic Imaging; California Chiropractic Association; International Brotherhood of Magicians; Society of American Magicians; Academy of Magical Arts & Sciences. **Education:** Cleveland Chiropractic College, D.C. (1988); Nicholls State University, B.A. in Psychology (minor in Chemistry) **Personal:** Dr. Martin is a professional magician and musician, devoting his leisure time to performing.

Dr. Kevin F. McCabe
Chiropractor
Chiropractic Associates, S.C
1647 South 108th Street
West Allis, WI 53214–4018
(414) 476–6300
Fax: (414) 476–6319

8041

Business Information: Chiropractic Associates, S.C is a multidisciplinary practice with four chiropractors, offering medical care, physical therapy, and massage therapy. A practicing chiropractor since 1989 and a Certified Chiropractic Sports Practitioner, Dr. McCabe joined Chiropractic Associates, S.C. in 1991. He is responsible for providing high quality care and services to his patients. His background includes serving as a research biologist in wildlife science prior to pursuing his chiropractic practice. **Career Steps:** Chiropractor, Chiropractic Associates, S.C (1991–Present); Associate Doctor, North Grand Back and Neck Care Center (1989–1991); Photographer, McCabe Custom Photography (1987–1989). **Associations & Accomplishments:** Wisconsin Chiropractic Association; American Chiropractic Association; Palmer College Alumni Association; The Wildlife Society; Master Gardener (UW Extension); Citizens for a Better Environment; Published in South Dakota Conservation Digest and Proceedings of the 5th National Wild Turkey Symposium. **Education:** Palmer College of Chiropractic, D.C. (1989); South Dakota State University (1984); University of Wisconsin–Madison (1981). **Personal:** Married to Dr. Laurie McCabe in 1987. Dr. McCabe enjoys photography, golf, hunting, dog training, skiing, windsurfing and reading.

John J. McEachron, D.C.
Chiropractor
McEachron Chiropractic Clinic
1905 4th Avenue East, Suite A
Olympia, WA 98506
(360) 943–8370
Fax: Please mail or call
E MAIL: See Below

8041

Business Information: McEachron Chiropractic Clinic is a managed health care practice providing quality, cost–effective chiropractic care. Dr. McEachron treats patients of all ages for spinal and back problems. As Chiropractor, Dr. McEachron seeks to relieve pain, illness and disability by providing skillful manipulation of the spine and other joints, with other clinical procedures as necessary. Concurrently, Dr. McEachron is a computer consultant for the Washington State County Road Administration Board and provides expert advise to businesses statewide. Internet users can reach him via: drjohn@crab.wa.gov. **Career Steps:** Chiropractor, McEachron Chiropractic Clinic (1993–Present); Computer Information Consultant, Washington State County Road Administration Board. **Associations & Accomplishments:** American Chiropractic Association; Washington State Chiropractic Association; South Puget Sound Chiropractic Association. **Education:** Western States Chiropractic College: D.C.

(1992), B.S. in Human Biology; Pacific Lutheran University, B.S. in Computer Science. **Personal:** Dr. McEachron enjoys mountain biking, soccer, skiing, and scuba diving.

Eric Miller, D.C.
Clinic Director and Partner
Midwest Chiropractic Care Center
9441 West 144th Place
Orland Park, IL 60462
(708) 403–2727
Fax: (708) 403–2770

8041

Business Information: Midwest Chiropractic Care Center is a full service healthcare practice specializing in providing chiropractic and rehabilitation services. A practicing chiropractor since 1991, Dr. Miller joined the Midwest Chiropractic Care Center as Clinical Director and Partner in 1993. He is responsible for the direction of all clinical activities in addition to his daily patient practice. **Career Steps:** Clinic Director and Partner, Midwest Chiropractic Care Center (1993–Present); Clinical Director, Daniels Chiropractic (1992–1993); Nuclear Medicine Technician, Virginia Medical Center (1985–1988). **Associations & Accomplishments:** American Chiropractic Association; Texas Chiropractic Society. **Education:** National College of Chiropractic, D.C. (1991); Eastern Illinois University, B.S. in Human Biology; Certified Injury Prevention Consultant. **Personal:** Married to Stephanie L. in 1994. Dr. Miller enjoys collecting antique furniture and playing golf.

James G. Moellendorf, D.C.

Chiropractor
Moellendorf Chiropractic Office, Ltd.
1140 Egg Harbor Road
Sturgeon Bay, WI 54235
(414) 743–2126
Fax: (414) 743–1145

8041

Business Information: Moellendorf Chiropractic Office, Ltd. is a general, full–service chiropractic facility specializing in the therapeutic system based primarily upon the interactions of the spine and nervous system, the method of treatment usually being to adjust the segments of the spinal column. Establishing his private chiropractic practice upon the conferral of his doctorate degree in 1983, Dr. Moellendorf oversees all administrative operations for associates and a support staff of three, in addition to his daily patient practice. **Career Steps:** Chiropractor, Moellendorf Chiropractic Office, Ltd. (1983–Present). **Education:** Palmer College of Chiropractic, D.C. (1983). **Personal:** Married to Sharon in 1984. Two children: Pamela and Matthew. Dr. Moellendorf enjoys building model railroads.

Donald C. Myren Jr., D.C.
Chiropractic Physician
–Independent–
41750 Winchester Road, Suite M
Temecula, CA 92590–4898
(909) 699–6226
Fax: (909) 699–6210

8041

Business Information: A licensed chiropractor since 1987, Dr. Donald C. Myren established his private practice office in 1989. As President, he oversees all administrative operations for a support staff of three, in addition to his daily patient practice. His practice involves physiotherapy, general chiropractic treatments, and nutritional wellness counseling. **Career Steps:** Clinical Director, D.C. Myren Chiropractic Offices (1989–Present); Clinic Director, MCO Chiropractic (1988–1989) **Associations & Accomplishments:** American College of Sports Medicine; Temecula Valley Chapter – Kiwanis Club; Former President, Doctors Speaker Bureau of Temecula. **Education:** Los Angeles College of Chiropractic, B.S., D.C. (1987); California Community College Teaching Credential; Licensed Chiropractor in California and Oregon; Diplomate, National Board of Chiropractic Examiners **Personal:** Married to Lorrie in 1983. Two children: Carolyn and Wendy. Dr. Myren enjoys family trips, golf, tennis and exercise.

Daniel L. Nelson, D.C.
Chiropractor
Olympic Spinal Care
711 N. Northlake Way
Seattle, WA 98103
(206) 548–1522
Fax: Please mail or call

8041

Business Information: Olympic Spinal Care is a full–service, alternative health care practice specializing in the re–alignment of the spine and subluxations – helping the body to heal itself internally. The Clinic added the services of a physical therapist in 1996 and hopes to eventually add a medical doctor. As Chiropractor, Dr. Nelson founded the Center in 1992 and is responsible for all aspects of operations, including providing chiropractic care to patients. Concurrent with his private chiropractic practice, Dr. Nelson is a full–time Seattle firefighter and is a Post Graduate Lecturer at several Chiropractic Colleges in the area. **Career Steps:** Chiropractor, Olympic Spinal Care (1986–Present); Post Graduate Lecturer, Los Angeles Chiropractic College (1988–Present); Firefighter, City of Seattle (1995–Present). **Associations & Accomplishments:** Professional Chiropractic Association: Board of Directors, Swim Club; Board of Directors, Seattle Executives Association. **Education:** Los Angeles Chiropractic College, Chiropractic Orthopedist (1988); Western States Chiropractic College, D.C. (1985); University of Washington: M.Sc in Exercise Physiology (1982), B.S. in Biology (1977). **Personal:** Married to Catherine in 1979. Four children: Liz, Joe, Kelly and Mark. Dr. Nelson enjoys tennis, swimming, hiking, weight training, volleyball, biking, gardening, woodworking, climbing, soccer, and cross country skiing.

Robert C. Nelson, D.C.

President
The Chiropractic Office of Robert C. Nelson, D.C., P.C.
10576 West Alameda Avenue
Lakewood, CO 80226–2602
(303) 969–0884
Fax: (303) 969–0019

8041

Business Information: The Chiropractic Office of Robert C. Nelson, D.C., P.C. is a private practice chiropractic office, specializing in the provision of chiropractic health services to families and individuals with sports injuries. A practicing chiropractor since 1986, Dr. Nelson established his sole practice chiropractic office in 1987. Serving as President, he oversees all administrative operations for associates and a support staff of four, in addition to his daily patient practice. Prior to entering the health field, he suffered an injury while serving as a Sheriff's detective, prompting him to give up his law enforcement career at the age of 31 and study chiropractic medicine. **Career Steps:** President, The Chiropractic Office of Robert C. Nelson, D.C., P.C. (1987–Present); Detective Sergeant, Boulder County Sheriff's Department (1975–1983); Police Officer, Louisville Police Department (1972–1975). **Associations & Accomplishments:** Board of Directors, Colorado Chiropractic Association; Jefferson County Chiropractic Society: Sustaining Member, Former President and Vice President; Fellow, International Academy of Clinical Acupuncture; Colorado Chiropractic Sports Council. **Education:** Logan College of Chiropractic, D.C. (1986); Metropolitan State College: B.S., A.A.S. **Personal:** Married to Sharron D. Williams, RN in 1991. One child: Heather. Dr. Nelson enjoys scuba diving and snow skiing.

Ai Duy A. Nguyen, D.C., O.M.D., Ph.D.
Doctor of Chiropratic & Owner
Pain Clinic of Westminister
9302 Bolsa Avenue
Westminster, CA 92683
(714) 897–7424
Fax: Please mail or call

8041

Business Information: Pain Clinic of Westminster is an establishment which seeks to relieve pain and restore health in human being through analytical and holistic approaches. Dr. Ai Nguyen is not only a chiropractic physician, but also a biochemist and pharmacist. He combines his knowledge in biochemist of the spine, biochemical intermaxiliary metabolism in the body and acupuncture principles in the treatment of his patients. **Career Steps:** Doctor of Chiropratic & Owner, Pain Clinic of Westminster (1987–Present); President, Natico, Inc. (1982–Present); Faculty, Saigon Medical School (1965–1975). **Associations & Accomplishments:** American Chiropractic Association; California Chiropractic Association; Board of Directors, Vietnamese Pharmacists Association; Vietnamese American Independent Pharmacists Group. **Education:** Los Angeles College of Chiropractic, D.C. (1985); Saigon Pharmacy School – Saigon University, Pharmacist Degree (1965); Nebraska University Medical School, Ph.D. in Biochemistry (1975); University of Oriental Medicine, O.M.D. (1985); Extensive research on carbohydrate metabolism, growth hormone like factor, fatty liver and cancer in rats. **Personal:** Married to Phuong Anh S. in 1969. Three children: Phuong–Thao, An Duy, and Pamela. Mr. Nguyen enjoys pingpong and singing.

Charlie Nguyen, D.C.
Sole Practitioner
Charlie Nguyen, D.C.
6060 Richmond Avenue, Suite 207
Houston, TX 77057
(713) 266–8493
Fax: (713) 266–8494

8041

Business Information: Established in 1992, Charlie Nguyen, D.C. is a private general practice and healthcare facility specializing in chiropractic care. As Sole Practitioner, Dr. Nguyen is responsible for all aspects of company operations, including administrative activities and patient practice. **Career Steps:** Sole Practitioner, Charlie Nguyen, D.C. (1992–Present); Chiropractor, Chiropractic & Acupuncture Clinic (1989–1992). **Associations & Accomplishments:** Texas Chiropractic Association; American Back Society; Texas Acupuncture Association. **Education:** Los Angeles College of Chiropractic, D.C. (1987); South Baylo University, Oriental Medicine Doctor (1987). **Personal:** Married to Thu–Hong in 1981. Two children: Charles and Helen. Dr. Nguyen enjoys swimming, table tennis, and fishing.

Dr. Tuan Duc Nguyen
Chiropractor
Good Samaritan Chiropractic
15563 Brookhurst Street
Westminster, CA 92683
(714) 531–6867
Fax: (714) 531–6867 Please Call
Before Faxing

8041

Business Information: Good Samaritan Chiropractic is a private, chiropractic healthcare facility. Establishing his practice in 1994, Dr. Nguyen directs a staff of two, and seeks to relieve pain, illness and disability by providing skillful manipulation of the spine and other joints, with other clinical procedures as necessary. **Career Steps:** Chiropractor, Good Samaritan Chiropractic (1994–Present); Associate Doctor of Chiropractic (1993–1994). **Associations & Accomplishments:** American Chiropractic Association; California Chiropractic Association; Executive Board, Hiep Nhat Magazine Non–Profit Organization; Executive Board, Vietnamese Catholic Community of Diocese of Orange. **Education:** Los Angeles College of Chiropractic: D.Chir. (1992), B.S. in Biology. **Personal:** Married to Tamminh Dang, Pharm. D., in 1986. One child: Tuan Viet Kevin Nguyen. Dr. Nguyen enjoys tennis, watching football, and social and church activities.

Dr. Glen P. Oemcke
Doctor of Chiropractic
Middlebury Chiropractic Group
60 Lakeside Blvd. West
Waterbury, CT 06708
(203) 755–7610
Fax: (203) 755–0679

8041

Business Information: Middlebury Chiropractic Group, established in 1957, is a full–service chiropractic clinic, offering diversified techniques as well as nutritional counseling and health wellness treatment. As Doctor of Chiropractic, Dr. Oemcke has been treating people with various illnesses from faulty metabolism, cancer, hand/wrist problems and low back syndromes since 1992. **Career Steps:** Doctor of Chiropractic, Middlebury Chiropractic Group (1992–Present). **Associations & Accomplishments:** American Chiropractic Association; International Chiropractic Association; Connecticut Chiropractic Association; Currently doing TV show once a month; 2 Radio programs twice a month. **Education:** New York Chiropractic College, D.C. (1992); Villanova University, Pre-chiropractic. **Personal:** Married to Kathleen in 1991. One child: Evan. Dr. Oemcke enjoys golf, outdoors, basketball, snow mobiling, skiing, and spending time with his son.

Alice Holm Ogawa, D.C.
Doctor of Chiropractic
Ogawa Chiropractic
956 Kuhio Highway
Kapaa, HI 96746
(808) 822–7113
Fax: (808) 823–0810

8041

Business Information: Ogawa Chiropractic is a full–service chiropractic office, providing quality health care for the entire family. The clinic offers: spinal rehabilitation, therapeutic modalities, as well as nutritional and fitness counseling. Sharing the practice with her husband, Dr. Alice Ogawa concentrates her practice in the treatment of children. **Career Steps:** Doctor of Chiropractic, Ogawa Chiropractic (1987–Present); Chiropractic Physician, Kiropraktisk Klinik, Denmark (1984–1987). **Associations & Accomplishments:** Hawaii State Chiropractic Association; Dansk Kiropractiks Forening. **Education:** Palmer College of Chiropractic, D.C. (1981); Denmark: Helsingor Gymnasium, Holte Gymnasium: HF and GSK **Personal:** Married to Dr. R. Ogawa in 1987. Two children: Sean and Cyrus. Dr. Ogawa enjoys swimming, yoga, and body building.

Debra A. Owens, D.C.
President
Owens Chiropractic Center, P.C.
1013 Business Hwy. 60 West
Dexter, MO 63841
(314) 624–1935
Fax: (314) 624–1935

8041

Business Information: Owens Chiropractic Center, P.C. is a full–service, chiropractic office, with emphasis in family chiropractic care, nutrition counseling, and acupuncture. A practicing chiropractor since 1991, Dr. Owens established the Owens Chiropractic Center in 1992. As Owner and President, she oversees the administrative operations for associates and a support staff of two, in addition to her daily patient practice. **Career Steps:** President, Owens Chiropractic Center, P.C. (1992–Present). **Associations & Accomplishments:** International Chiropractors Association; American Chiropractic Association; Missouri State Chiropractors Association; World Congress of Women Chiropractors; Logan College Alumni Association; Board of Directors, Dexter Kiwanis; Dexter Chamber of Commerce: Board of Directors – President (1995), First Vice President (1994), Second Vice President (1993). **Education:** Logan College of Chiropractic, D.C. (1991); Southeast Missouri State University, B.S. in Education (1975). **Personal:** One child: Jacqueline. Dr. Owens enjoys watersports and quilting.

Lloyd S. Paredes, D.C.
Chiropractor
Better Health Chiropractic Center, Inc.
128 Hamakua Drive, Suite J
Kailua, HI 96734–2825
(808) 262–5555
Fax: (808) 262–6611

8041

Business Information: Better Health Chiropractic Center, Inc. specializes in chiropractic and rehabilitative care, nutrition, and exercise. As Clinical Director, Dr. Paredes oversees all administrative operations for associates and support staff, in addition to his daily patient practice. **Career Steps:** Clinical Director, Better Health Chiropractic Center, Inc. (1995–Present); Associate Doctor, Health and Accident Clinic (1994–1995); Associate Doctor, Morelli and Mililani Clinics (1993–1994). **Associations & Accomplishments:** Secretary, Hawaii State Chiropractic Association (1995–1996); Former Sports Chairman, Makakilo Community Association (1994–1995). **Education:** Palmer West College of Chiropractic, D.C. (1992); American River College, A.S. in Physical Sciences. **Personal:** Married to Janet in 1986. Three children: Parker, Corey, and Garrett. Dr. Paredes enjoys olympic weightlifting, hunting, and auto repair.

James V. Pertree, D.C.
• • • ━━━◉━━━ • • •
Chiropractor
Back and Joint Medical Clinic
9220 South Pennsylvania Avenue
Oklahoma City, OK 73139
(405) 799–7246
Fax: Please mail or call

8041

Business Information: Back and Joint Medical Clinic specializes in medical, chiropractic treatment, physical rehabilitation, and therapy. The Clinic seeks to relieve pain, illness and disability by providing skillful manipulation of the spine and other joints, with other clinical procedures as necessary. As Chiropractor, Dr. Pertree is responsible for all administrative duties. Concurrent to his position at Back and Joint Medical Clinic, Dr. Pertree is also the owner of Silverleaf Chiropractic, and Back and Joint Chiropractic. **Career Steps:** Chiropractor, Back and Joint Medical Clinic (1986–Present) **Associations & Accomplishments:** Honorary Attorney General of Oklahoma; Recommended by the U.S. Army for the Medal of Honor. **Education:** North Georgia College, B.A. in Science; Oklahoma City Community College, History and Psychology. **Personal:** Married to Charlotte in 1972. Two children: Tyler and Courtney. Dr. Pertree enjoys scuba diving, fishing, sailing, parachuting, and sky diving.

John J. Pizzo, D.C.
Chiropractic Physician
Barre Chiropractic Center
108 Washington Street
Barre, VT 05641
(802) 479–3206
Fax: (802) 479–3348

8041

Business Information: Frogley Chiropractic, P.C. is a managed health care practice providing quality, cost–effective chiropractic and nutritional counseling. Establishing the Clinic in 1983, Dr. Pizzo is involved with all aspects of its operation, particularly focusing in team sports treatment and rehabilitation. He currently serves as the team physician for Spaulding High School in Barre, Vermont. Barre Chiropractic Center currently employs one chiropractic associate and four administrative support staff. **Career Steps:** Chiropractic Physician, Barre Chiropractic Center (1983–Present). **Associations & Accomplishments:** Member, Vermont Board of Chiropractic Examination and Registration (1985–Present); President, Vermont Board of Chiropractic Examination and Registration (1988–1992); Member, American Chiropractic Association; Member, Vermont Chiropractic Association (1993); Recipient, "Chiropractor of the Year;" State Delegate, National Board of Chiropractic Examiners (1988–1992); Fellow, International College of Chiropractors. **Education:** New York Chiropractic College, D.C. (1982); S.U.N.Y. at Buffalo, NY, B.A. (1972). **Personal:** Married to Lynda in 1972. Two children: Richard and Melissa. Dr. Pizzo enjoys skiing and golf. He has a special interset in lobbying for health care reform and chiropractic inclusion..

Victor Poletajev, D.C.
Director
West Chester Chiropractic and Rehabilitation Center
P.O. Box 1788, 1606 Locust Avenue
Fairmont, WV 26554
(304) 366–3695
Fax: (304) 366–3695

8041

Business Information: West Chester Chiropractic and Rehabilitation Center is a full–service accident/injury treatment facility, specializing in muscloskelatal care, complete physical medicine, and certified impairment ratings. A fully–equipped rehabilitation center, with accupuncture and nutritional counseling is also available. A practicing chiropractor since 1986, Dr. Poletajev established his sole practice chiropractic office in 1990. He oversees the administrative operations of a staff of three, in addition to his daily patient practice. Serving as Director of the Clinic, he specializes in rehabilitation, impairment, and disability evaluations. Dr. Poletajev has also developed and currently markets his own line of nutritional products, under the copyrighted name "Myostar." **Career Steps:** Director, West Chester Chiropractic and Rehabilitation Center (1990–Present); Sales, Myostar Vitamin Company (1982–Present). **Associations & Accomplishments:** Foundation of Chiropractic Education and Research, and past or present member of West Virginia, Tennessee, Pennsylvania, International, and American Chiropractic organizations; Served as treating Doctor for Natural Athletes Strength Association and The United States Power Lifting organization; Authored numerous research articles on the treatment of injuries and nutrition; Set numerous records and currently holds a 1981 National Collegiate Record of 540 pounds. **Education:** Palmer College of Chiropractic, Doctor of Chiropractic; New

York University, Bachelor of Science; Montgomery County College, Associates of Science, Masters programs in Impairment Rating, Accident Injury Care, and Rehabilitation. **Personal:** Married with one child.

Christopher Ragan, D.C.

Director and Chiropractic Associate
Bennett Chiropractic
1205 E. 11th Place
Big Spring, TX 79720
(915) 267–6753
Fax: Please mail or call

8041

Business Information: Bennett Chiropractic is a full–service chiropractic clinic, serving patients in three locations throughout the greater Big Spring, Texas metro and surrounding counties. A practicing chiropractor since 1989, Mr. Ragan joined Bennett Chiropractic as Director of the Big Spring location and Chiropractic Associate in 1991. He is responsible for the overall administrative direction of associates and support staff, in addition to his daily patient case load. **Career Steps:** Director of the Clinic and Chiropractic Associate, Bennett Chiropractic (1991–Present); Chiropractic Associate, Health Star Chiropractic (1990–1991); Chiropractic Associate, Rolling Hills Chiropractic (1989–1990) **Associations & Accomplishments:** Board Member, Heritage Museum; Ambassadors Club **Education:** Parker College of Chiropractic, D.C. (1989) **Personal:** Married to Diane E. in 1994. Two children: Bethany and Nicholas. Dr. Ragan enjoys bowling, and is an avid Martial Arts participant.

Steven Craig Read, D.C.

Chiropractor
Monahan Chiropractic Clinic
4022 Blanding Boulevard
Jacksonville, FL 32210–5417
(904) 778–7963
Fax: (904) 779–1329

8041

Business Information: Monahan Chiropractic Clinic is a general, full–service chiropractic facility consisting of two physician/partners, specializing in the therapeutic system based primarily upon the interactions of the spine and nervous system. Located in Jacksonville and Orange Park, Florida, the Practice uses their diversified techniques in the chiropractic field mostly for accident victims, trauma cases, and automobile or work related cases. A practicing chiropractor since 1987, Dr. Read co–founded the Practice in 1989. He is responsible for all administration, operations, public relations, and strategic planning, in addition to his daily patient practice at both locations. **Career Steps:** Chiropractor, Monahan Chiropractic Clinic (1989–Present); Chiropractor, Kingsley Chiropractic Clinic (1987–1989). **Associations & Accomplishments:** International Chiropractic Association; Florida Chiropractic Association; Sertoma; Former President, Pi Kappa Chi. **Education:** Palmer College of Chiropractic, D.C. (1987); Attended: Pennsylvania State University; Indiana University of Pennsylvania. **Personal:** Married to Lori in 1993. Two children: Wesley Ashton and Ansley Elizabeth. Dr. Read enjoys U.S. history and politics.

Phil E. Roberts, D.C.

Chiropractor
Roberts Chiropractic Center
302 North Greenwood Avenue
Ft. Smith, AR 72901
(501) 782–9505
Fax: (501) 782–7505

8041

Business Information: Roberts Chiropractic Center is full–service chiropractic practice, providing chiropractic services and health care. Establishing his private practice upon the conferral of his chiropractic degree, Dr. Roberts oversees all administrative operations for associates and support staff, in addition to his daily patient practice. **Career Steps:** Sole Practitioner, Roberts Chiropractic Center (1986–Present). **Associations & Accomplishments:** Arkansas Chiropractic Association: Chairman of Insurance Committee, Ethics and Grievance Committee, Constitution/Bylaws Committee. **Education:** Cleveland Chiro College, Chiropractic, magna cum laude graduate (1986); Westark Community College – Fort Smith, Pre–Med. **Personal:** Three children: Jeremy, Jennifer, and Jessica. Dr. Roberts enjoys boating.

Randall W. Robirds, D.C.

Sole Practitioner
Chiropractic Specialty Centers
1201 North Decatur Boulevard, #109
Las Vegas, NV 89108–1213
(702) 646–1150
Fax: (702) 646–9216

8041

Business Information: Chiropractic Specialty Centers is a general, full–service chiropractic facility specializing in the holistic treatment of the musculoskeletal system. A practicing chiropractor since 1990, Dr. Robirds oversees all administrative operations for associates and a support staff of three, in addition to his daily patient practice. **Career Steps:** Sole Practitioner, Chiropractic Specialty Centers (1992–Present). **Associations & Accomplishments:** International College of Applied Kinesiology; Council on Internal Diagnosis; O.N.E. Foundation. **Education:** Los Angeles College of Chiropractic, D.C. (1990); San Diego State University, B.S. in Marketing; Saddleback College, A.A.

Nicholas John Ruggiero, D.C.

President
Ruggiero Chiropractic Center
756 Riverside Drive
Pompano Beach, FL 33071–7008
(305) 753–3910
Fax: (305) 753–3857

8041

Business Information: Ruggiero Chiropractic Center is a general, full–service chiropractic facility specializing in the therapeutic system based primarily upon the interactions of the spine and nervous system, the method of treatment usually being to adjust the segments of the spinal column. The practice consists of chiropractors, a medical doctor, and an orthopedist, with a neurologist as a consultant. Establishing his private practice upon the conferral of his chiropractic degree, Dr. Ruggiero oversees all administrative operations for associates and a support staff of eight, in addition to his daily patient practice. **Career Steps:** Chiropractor, Ruggiero Chiropractic Center (1988–Present). **Associations & Accomplishments:** American Chiropractic Association; Century Pac, Florida Chiropractic Association; Cleveland Chiropractic College Alumni Association; Broward Chiropractic Association; Medical Legal Association; American Association of Non–Invasive Diagnosticians; American Association of Clinical Nutritionist; AWARDS: Who's Who Among Students in American Universities and Colleges (1988), Outstanding Patient Care while in clinic (1988). **Education:** Cleveland Chiropractic College, D.C. (1988); University of Miami, B.S. in Human Biology (1985); Broward Community College (1985); Certification: Physical Therapy (1988); Phlebotomy (1988); Manipulation Under Anesthesia (1992); Impairment Ratings and Disability (1992–1995); National Board of Chiropractic Examiners (1988); Worker's Compensation Doctor (1995); Musculoskeletal Diagnostic Ultrasound (1995); POSTGRADUATE STUDIES: Sports Medicine (1994), Master's Program of Cervical Whiplash (1995), Impairment Rating's and the Law (1995), Manipulation Under Anesthesia, Personal Injury (1995), Musculoskeletal Diagnostic Ultrasound (1995), American Chiropractic Council on Clinical Nutrition. **Personal:** Married to Kelly in 1992. One child: Amanda. Dr. Ruggiero enjoys body building.

Parrish T. Skrien, D.C.

Chiropractor/President
Chiropractic Family Clinic of Nicollet, P.A.
312 Pine Street, P.O. Box 50
Nicollet, MN 56074
(507) 225–3925
Fax: (507) 225–3925

8041

Business Information: A practicing Chiropractor since 1993, Dr. Skrien recently opened his private practice facility, the Chiropractic Family Clinic of Nicollet, P.A., in 1996, specializing in the Gonstead Procedure. **Career Steps:** Chiropractor/President, Chiropractic Family Clinic of Nicollet, P.A. (1996–Present); Partner/Doctor, Southwest Chiropractic Clinic (1994–1996); Associate/Doctor, Bentz Chiropractic Clinic (Apr.1994–Oct.1994); Exam Doctor, McConlley, Quandt Chiropractic (1993–1994). **Associations & Accomplishments:** Minnesota Chiropractic Association; International Chiropractic Association; Palmer Alumni Association; Nicollet Chamber of Commerce; Lions Club of Nicollet. **Education:** Palmer College of Chiropractic, D.C. (1993); Worthington Community College, A.S. **Personal:** Married to Cynthia in 1991. Two children: Anastacia and Katelyn. Dr. Skrien enjoys golf, hunting, camping, and family activities.

A. B. Smith, D.C.

Chiropractor
Northbrook Offices
810 W. Bristol Street, Suite M
Elkhart, IN 46514–2954
(219) 264–4300
Fax: Please mail or call

8041

Business Information: Dr. Smith started his wage earning career in 1915 at age 15 as a Railroad Telegrapher on the B&O Railroad. In 1918 he started telegraphing nights at the Western Union office to enable him to enroll in the Progressive Chiropractic College in Chicago from which he graduated in 1922. He opened his practice in Elkhart, Indiana where he is still practicing six days a week. **Career Steps:** Chiropractor, Northbrook Offices (1922–Present); Telegrapher, Western Union (1918); Railroad Telegrapher, B&O Railroad (1915–1917). **Associations & Accomplishments:** Elk Lodge; Lion's Club; Louisville State Convention presented him with a plaque for dedication to service (1995). **Education:** Progressive College (1922). **Personal:** Dr. Smith enjoys golf.

Arlen L. Smith, D.C.

Sole Practitioner
A. A. Chiropractic
3270 Market Street Northeast
Salem, OR 97301–1815
(503) 364–9910
Fax: (503) 375–3897
EMAIL: See Below

8041

Business Information: A. A. Chiropractic is a general, full–service chiropractic facility, specializing in the therapeutic system based primarily upon the interactions of the spine and nervous system, the method of treatment usually being to adjust the segments of the spinal column. A practicing chiropractor since 1986, Dr. Smith established his sole practice chiropractic office in 1992. He serves as a primary care physician, specializing in sports injuries and biomechanical functions by using manual manipulation of the spine and/or related structures. **Career Steps:** Sole Practitioner, A. A. Chiropractic (1992–Present); Chiropractic Physician, Stayton Chiropractic (1990–1991); Chiropractic Physician, Pacific Chiropractic & Physical Therapy (1987–1990). **Associations & Accomplishments:** Former President, Oregon Doctors of Chiropractic; Texas Chiropractic Association; Licensed in Victoria by Licensing Board of Chiropractors and Osteopaths, Australia; Also Licensed in Colorado, Texas, and Oregon. **Education:** Western States Chiropractic College, D.C. (1986); Attended: Oregon State University; Eastern Oregon State College; Portland State University. **Personal:** Dr. Smith enjoys mountain biking, raquetball, computers, music, and travel.

Martin A. Smith

Chiropractor
Smith Chiropractic, P.C.
6610 East Main Street
Farmington, NM 87402–5124
(505) 324–1111
Fax: (505) 324–0139

8041

Business Information: Smith Chiropractic, P.C. is a general, full–service chiropractic facility specializing in the therapeutic system based primarily upon the interactions of the spine and nervous system, the method of treatment usually being to adjust the segments of the spinal column. Dr. Smith has been a practicing Chiropractor since 1990. He established his private practice in 1992, specializing in manual manipulation and activated methods. **Career Steps:** Chiropractor, Smith Chiropractic, P.C. (1992–Present); Assistant Manager, Lionel Playworld (1981–1982); Office Assistant, Summa Corporation (Hughes) (1970–1977). **Associations & Accomplishments:** New Mexico Chiropractic Association; Farmington Rotary Club; Secretary, Former President, S.P.E.B.S.Q.S.A., Inc., Barbershop Quartet Singing Society, San Juan Chapter. **Education:** Parker College of Chiropractic, D.C. (1990); Brigham Young University, B.A. (1978); Pierce College, A.A. (1976). **Personal:** Married to Margie L. in 1970. Nine children: Tim, Mary Anne, Lynne, Sherry, Robert, Melissa, Amanda, Marc and Craig, all adopted. Dr. Smith enjoys fishing, camping, and woodworking.

Keith Allan G. Srch, D.C.

Partnership Practice
Office of Srch Chiropractic Clinic
2340 South 6th Street
Klamath Falls, OR 97601–4340
(541) 882–7401
Fax: (541) 883–1102

8041

Business Information: Office of Keith Allan G. Srch, D.C. is a general, full–service Chiropractic facility specializing in the system based primarily upon the interation of the spine and nervous system, joints and their associated structures. The method of treatment usually being to manually manipulate the affected osseous structures of the patient. Establishing his Chiropractic practice upon the conferral of his Doctorate degree in 1984, Dr. Srch attends to the Administrative operation for his partnership and staff, in addition to his daily patient practice. Concurrently, he operates a home-based international marketing business. **Career Steps:** Chiropractic Practitioner, Office of Srch Chiropractic Clinic (1985–Present). **Education:** Palmer College of Chiropractic, D.C. (1984); Incarnate Word College, B.S. in Psychology (1980). **Personal:** Married to Debra in 1983. Two children: Heather and Alysha. Dr. Srch enjoys water skiing and horseback riding.

Harvey W. Stern, D.C., D.A.B.C.O., D.A.C.N.B.

The Office of Harvey W. Stern, D.C.
296 Ridgebury Road
Slate Hill, NY 10973–9784
(914) 355–8080
Fax: Please mail or call

8041

Business Information: The Office of Harvey W. Stern, D.C. is a general, full–service chiropractic facility specializing in the therapeutic system based primarily upon the interactions of the spine and nervous system, the method of treatment usually being to adjust the segments of the spinal column. Establishing his sole practice chiropractic office upon the conferral of his chiropractic degree, Dr. Stern oversees all administrative operations for associates and a support staff, in addition to his daily patient practice. His practice specializes in orthopedics and neurology and provides clinical examinations, x–rays, and ordering bloodwork, which is sent to a lab for special testing. **Career Steps:** Sole Practitioner, The Office of Harvey W. Stern, D.C. (1982–Present). **Associations & Accomplishments:** American Chiropractic Association; Foundation for Chiropractic Education and Research; New York State Chiropractic Association; Aircraft Owners Pilot Association; Boy Scouts of America; Cessna Owners Organization; Diplomate, American Board of Chiropractic Orthopedists; Diplomate, American Chiropractic Neurology Board. **Education:** National Chiropractic College, D.C. (1982). **Personal:** Married to Ellen in 1989. Dr. Stern enjoys hunting, piloting, karate, and backpacking.

Jerry R. Szych, DC, MS, CCN, CCSP

Chiropractor/Nutritionist
Tall Pines Chiropractic Center
120 Cedar Grove Lane
Somerset, NJ 08873
(908) 469–6005
Fax: (908) 469–0915

8041

Business Information: Tall Pines Chiropractic Center is a multi–specialty group facility. Serving the community of Somerset, New Jersey and surrounding counties, the Group consists of three chiropractors and two acupuncturists. A practicing chiropractor with five years experience in a multi–disciplinary out–patient clinic working alongside M.D.'s, R.N.'s, O.M.D.'s and D.C.'s, Dr. Szych treats patients of all ages with a wide variety of ailments. His particular areas of specialty include: Applied Kinesiology, Sacro–Occipital Technique, Meridian Therapy, Proprioceptive Neuromuscular Facilitation, Spray and Stretch, Nutritional Counseling, Muscle and Joint Rehabilitation. **Career Steps:** Chiropractor/Nutritionist, Tall Pines Chiropractic Center (1990–Present); Teaching Assistant, New York Chiropractic College (1989–1990); Pharmacist Technician, Parkview Pharmacy (1985–1987). **Associations & Accomplishments:** American Chiropractic Association; American College of Sports Medicine; National Association of Sports Medicine; Foundation for Chiropractic Education and Research; New Jersey Chiropractic Society; American Academy of Pain Management; American College of Nutrition; American Preventive Medical Association; Chiropractic Rehabilitation Association; Fellow, American Board of Disability Analysts; Fellow, International Academy of Clinical Acupuncture. **Education:** New York Chiropractic College, D.C. with honors, Awarded Distinguished Service Certificate (1990), University of Bridgeport, M.S. in Nutrition (1994); Fairleigh Dickinson University, B.S. in Biology (1987); Certifications: Certified Chiropractic Rehabilitation Doctor; Certified Chiropractic Sports Physician; Certified Clinical Nutritionist, Applied Kinesiology – New York Chiropractic College; Certified in CPR for Community, Professional Rescuer and Community First Aid and Safety **Personal:** Married to Suzan in 1992. Dr. Szych enjoys going to the Islands to snorkel. He credits his success in life to the support of his wife, and the values instilled in him by his parents and grandparents.

John S. Virga, D.C.

Chiropractor
Virga Family Chiropractic Center
489 Hialeah Drive #11
Hialeah, FL 33010
(305) 889–0889
Fax: (305) 889–1749
EMAIL: See Below

8041

Business Information: Virga Family Chiropractic Center is a general, full–service chiropractic facility, specializing in the therapeutic system based primarily upon the interactions of the spine and nervous system, the method of treatment usually being to adjust the segments of the spinal column. A practicing chiropractor since 1989, Dr. Virga established the solo practice in 1995. He is responsible for all aspects of operations, in addition to his daily patient practice. Dr. Virga can also be reached through the Internet via: DrJohn289@AOL.com **Career Steps:** Chiropractor, Virga Family Chiropractic Center (1995–Present); Clinic Director, Doctors Network of South Florida (1990–1995); Clinic Director, Tri–County Injury Consultants (1992–1995). **Associations & Accomplishments:** Florida Chiropractic Association; Dade County Chiropractic Association; International Chiropractic Association; International Rotary Club; Kappa Sigma Fraternity Alumni Association; Palmer College of Chiropractic Alumni Association. **Education:** Palmer College of Chiropractic, D.C. (1989); Eastern New Mexico University. **Personal:** Dr. Virga enjoys music, computers, and cooking.

David B. Waggoner, D.C.

Chiropractic Physician
Edwards Clinic of Chiropractic
163 SE 33rd
Edmond, OK 73013–4602
(405) 340–0007
Fax: (405) 340–0266
EMAIL: See Below

8041

Business Information: Edwards Clinic of Chiropractic is a general, full–service chiropractic facility specializing in the therapeutic system based primarily upon the interactions of the spine and nervous system, the method of treatment usually being to adjust the segments of the spinal column. Joining Edwards Clinic of Chiropractic upon the conferral of his Chiropractic degree in 1993, Dr. Waggoner is responsible for the diagnosis and treatment of patients. He may be reached through the Internet via: SUDV@MSN.COM **Career Steps:** Chiropractic Physician, Edwards Clinic of Chiropractic (1993–Present); Sergeant, Army National Guard (1985–1991). **Associations & Accomplishments:** American Chiropractic Association; International Chiropractic Sports Federation; Oklahoma SCA; American Chiropractic Sports Council; Wrangler Sports Chiropractic; Ambassador Edmond Chamber of Commerce. **Education:** National College of Chiropractic: D.C. (1993), B.S. Human Biology (1991); Los Angeles College of Chiropractic, Certified Chiropractic Sports Physician (1994). **Personal:** Married to Dr. Susan Chung in 1995. Dr. Waggoner enjoys camping and fishing.

Jack VanArsdel Waters, D.C., DABCO, CCSP

Chiropractor
Offices of Jack V. Waters, D.C.
1500 North Washington
Roswell, NM 88201
(505) 622–8118
Fax: (505) 622–8118

8041

Business Information: Offices of Jack V. Waters, D.C., established in 1986, is a general, full–service chiropractic facility specializing in the therapeutic system based primarily upon the interactions of the spine and nervous system, the method of treatment usually being to adjust the segments of the spinal column. A practicing chiropractor for the past nine years and a Certifed Chiropractic Orthopedist, Dr. Waters established the practice in 1986. He oversees the administrative operations for associates and a support staff of four, in addition to his daily patient practice. **Career Steps:** Chiropractor, Offices of Jack V. Waters, D.C. (1986–Present). **Associations & Accomplishments:** American Chiropractic Association; Vice President, New Mexico Chiropractic Association; Rotary Club; Council on Chiropractic Orthopedics; Council on Chiropractic Sports Medicine; Diplomate, American Board Chiropractic Orthopedist; Certified Chiropractic Sports Physician. **Education:** Cleveland Chiropractic College, D.C. (1987); Texas Tech University, B.S. **Personal:** Married to Dr. Lisa R. Reinecke, D.C. One child: Austin. Dr. Waters enjoys team roping, flyfishing, quail hunting, snowskiing, and waterskiing.

Daniel White, D.C.

Sole Practitioner
The Chiropractic Offices of Daniel White, D.C.
590 West End Avenue, Suite 2B
New York, NY 10024–1749
(212) 877–5726
Fax: Please mail or call

8041

Business Information: The Chiropractic Offices of Daniel White, D.C., highly–known in the dance community, is a private chiropractic practice, specializing in the treatment of dancers and the education of dancers for injury prevention, as well as treating other types of patients. Appointing one day a week to be "dancers day", the Practice treats dancers for a reduced rate, as well as treating young people in sports, who often overbuild one side of their body, thereby causing imbalances that can become a problem over a long period of time. X–rays are not done unless static palpation, motion palpation, and muscle examination results show that they are needed. A practicing chiropractor since 1986, Dr. White established his sole practice chiropractic office in 1987. Responsible for treating patients, as well as providing instruction and education on injury prevention techniques and rehabilitative exercises, he treats neuromuscular–skeletal problems (necks, backs, pelvis, hips, knees, ankles) through an examination using static palpation (feeling joints), motion palpation (checking motion), and muscle examination (bone misalignment can be located by weaknesses in muscles). Dr. White has been offered a second office space by the world renowned ballet instructor, David Howard (taught Patrick Swayze, Mikhal Barishinokov, and Mary Tyler Moore), in his new studio. Future plans include teaching injury prevention classes, writing, and conducting research in the vein of Clinical Research. **Career Steps:** Sole Practitioner, The Chiropractic Offices of Daniel White, D.C. (1987–Present); Masseuse, Private Practice (1981–1987); Exercise Teacher (Pilades–based technique), Fran Lehew Studio (1980–1983). **Associations & Accomplishments:** American Chiropractic Association; Foundation for Chiropractic Education and Research; New York Chiropractic College Alumni Association. **Education:** New York Chiropractic College, D.C. (1986). **Personal:** Dr. White enjoys yoga (every day), reading, playing the guitar, racquetball, gym activities, weightlifting, rollerblading, and movies.

Jonathan J. Widenbaum, D.C.

Sole Practitioner
Widenbaum Chiropractic Offices
7450 San Ramon Road
Dublin, CA 94568
(510) 829–8484
Fax: (510) 829–1806

8041

Business Information: Widenbaum Chiropractic Offices is a private chiropractic practice, specializing in automobile and work–related accidents, as well as the treatment of children and adults. A practicing chiropractor since 1988, Dr. Widenbaum oversees all administrative operations for associates and a staff of 6, in addition to his daily patient practice. His practice is based on his belief in chiropractic adjustments and natural healing as opposed to surgery and drugs. **Career Steps:** Sole Practitioner, Widenbaum Chiropractic Offices (1991–Present). **Associations & Accomplishments:** Director, Dublin Chamber of Commerce; Former Director, Dublin Lions Club; California Chiropractic Association; American Chiropractic Association. **Education:** Cleveland Chiropractic College, D.C. (1988); Wayne State University, B.S. **Personal:** Married to Diane in 1993. One child: Jared Seth. Dr. Widenbaum enjoys golf.

Nila T. Wipf

Corporate Director/Owner
Wipf Chiropractic Center
1100 West Tyler Street
Harlingen, TX 78550
(210) 423–2000
Fax: (210) 421–2565

8041

Business Information: Wipf Chiropractic Center is a group of six chiropractic clinics in the Rio Grande region of Texas. Established in 1988, the six clinics now have a combined staff of 43 people. As Corporate Director/President, Ms. Wipf is responsible for the daily operations of the clinics and developing innovative ways of marketing services. She also handles the research into the statistical collection rate. **Career Steps:** Wipf Chiropractic Clinics: Corporate Director/President (1996–Present), Continuing Educational Coordinator (1988–1996); Resource RN, Central DuPage Hospital (1984–1988). **Associations & Accomplishments:** National Association of Self Employed; National Association of Female Executives; Texas Chiropractic Association Auxiliary; Philippine Nurses Association of Illinois. **Education:** University of the Philippines, M.Ed. (1978); University of Santo Tomas, B.S.N. **Personal:** Married to R. Jay in 1973. Two children: Jason Renaldo and Jasmin Roxanne. Ms. Wipf enjoys travel, exercising, quilting, and fishing.

Steven G. Yeomans, D.C., F.A.C.O.

Owner & Chiropractor
Yeomans Chiropractic Center, S.C.
404 Eureka Street
Ripon, WI 54971–1192
(414) 748–3644
Fax: (414) 748–3642
EMail: See Below

8041

Business Information: Yeomans Chiropractic Center is a general practice chiropractic clinic specializing in neuromusculoskeletal complications, sports medicine care, on the job accidents, and legal matters relating to disabilities and impairments. As Owner & Chiropractor, Dr. Yeomans oversees all administrative operations for associates and support staff, in addition to his daily patient practice. Internet users can reach him via: BYeomans1@Aol.Com. **Career Steps:** Owner & Chiropractor, Yeomans Chiropractic Center (1979–Present). **Associations & Accomplishments:** Vice President, Northeast District Wisconsin Chiropractic Association; President, Northeast District; Chairperson, WCA Clinical/Advisory Committee; Peer Review Committee, Medicaid, State of Wisconsin; Selected as Member of a Five Member Insurance Review Panel for DILHR; Documentation Committee; Post Graduate Faculty Positions: National College of Chiropractic, Northwestern College of Chiropractic, Los Angeles College of Chiropractic, Canadian Memorial College of Chiropractic; Faculty Position, Joint Conference between WCA and Complete Source; Faculty, Wisconsin Back Society; Achievement Award in Anatomy; Who's Who Among Students in American Universities and Colleges; National College of Chiropractic; Who's Who Among Rising Young Americans; President's Award for Outstanding Work and Achievement in the WCA, Chiropractor of the Year (1994); Published in Various Medical Journals and Books; Lectures on Chiropractic Matters and Medical Procedures. **Education:** North Central College (1973–1975); National College of Chiropractic (1975–1979); Cook County Hospital, Clerkship in Orthopedics–Back & Foot Service (1977); National College of Chiropractic, Bachelor of Science degree (1977), Doctor of Chiropractic (1979), Postgraduate Division 300 plus Hours in Chiropractic Orthopedics (1979–1985); 100 Hour Course in Acupuncture and Meridian Therapy (1979); Board Certified in Chiropractic Orthopedics (1985); State License, Wisconsin and North Carolina. **Personal:** Married to Brigid in 1978. Three children: Adam, Rachel, and Abigail. Dr. Yeomans enjoys music and sports.

Monica A. Young, D.C.

Chiropractor
Forever Young
231 Old Bernal, Suite 3
Pleasanton, CA 94566
(510) 462–1100
Fax: Please mail or call

8041

Business Information: Established in 1995, Forever Young is a private, full–service chiropractic office. As Chiropractor, Dr. Young is responsible for finding subluxations (misalignments) and realigning the spine to promote optimal health. **Career Steps:** Chiropractor, Forever Young (1995–Present); Teacher for Chiropractic Review Company, National Board Specialists (1994–Present). **Associations & Accomplishments:** Member, ACA. **Education:** Life Chiropractic College–West, D.C. (1992). **Personal:** Married to John C. Ross II in 1994. One child: Stephanie. Dr. Young enjoys playing on a co–ed softball team.

Dr. Marguerite E. Ball

Optometrist
Eye Associates of Winter Park
1928 Howell Branch Road
Winter Park, FL 32792–1013
(407) 671–5445
Fax: (407) 671–2899

8042

Business Information: Eye Associates of Winter Park is a full–service, private optometric group practice specializing in ocular disease, specialty contact lenses and pediatric optometry. Established in 1984, Eye Associates of Winter Park consists of three Optometric Associates and 12 medical support staff. A Board–certified Optometrist since 1989, Dr. Ball joined as an Associate with the Eye Associates in 1994. She focuses her practice in the diagnosis and treatment of ocular diseases. **Career Steps:** Optometrist, Eye Associates of Winter Park (1994–Present); Neuro–Ophthalmology Clinical Supervisor, Bascom Palmer Eye Institute (1989–1993). **Associations & Accomplishments:** Fellow, American Academy of Optometry; Member, American Optometric Association; Florida Optometric Association; Central Florida Optometric Association; Member and Board of Directors, Rotary Club. **Education:** Southern College of Optometry, O.D. (1989); Stetson University, B.S. in Biology. **Personal:** Dr. Ball enjoys wind surfing, biking and scuba diving.

Phyllis S. Chisholm

Chief Executive Officer
The Ophthalmic Group
2808 M.L. King Blvd., W.
Tampa, FL 33607
(813) 876–1331
Fax: (813) 872–0647

8042

Business Information: The Ophthalmic Group, established in 1964, is a full–service medical and surgical practice specializing in ophthalmology. As Chief Executive Officer, Mrs. Chisholm is responsible for administration, finances, accounting, and marketing. She also serves as Executive Director of the Eye Surgery Facility, Inc. **Career Steps:** Chief Executive Officer, The Ophthalmic Group (1991–Present); Executive Director, Eye Surgery Facility, Inc. (1988–Present). **Associations & Accomplishments:** Development Committee, College of Arts & Sciences – University of South Florida; Former President, County Medical Association Auxiliary; American Society of Ophthalmic Administrators; Florida Society of Ophthalmic Administrators; American Society of Ophthalmic Registered Nurses; Tampa, Florida Chamber of Commerce; U.S. Chamber of Commerce. **Education:** University of South Florida: M.A. (1985), B.A. (1975); University of Nebraska, R.N. (1955); Attended: University of Omaha, Dayton University, Nebraska Wesleyan; University of Pennsylvania Wharton School of Business, Executive Training for Ophthalmic Administration (1995). **Personal:** Married to Leslie L. Chisholm, Jr., M.D. in 1955. Three children: Leslie III, Douglas, and Philip. Mrs. Chisholm enjoys skiing, performing arts, music, exotic cars, travel, reading and gardening during her leisure time.

Sonia M. Colon, O.D.

Optometrist
S.M. Colon Optometry
164 Delfin Olmo Avenue
Arecibo, Puerto Rico 00612
(809) 878–5895
Fax: (809) 878–3186

8042

Business Information: A practicing optometrist since 1984, Dr. Sonia Colon established her private, full–service Optometry practice to provide eye exams, contact lens and eyeglass dispensal to patients in Arecibo, Puerto Rico. She oversees all aspects of business operations, in addition to her daily patient practice. Concurrent with her private optical practice, she serves as Senior Partner and President of Optica Robles Corporation, (managed by her son Jose Garcia – a practicing Optician), as well as serves as President of Colegio de Optometras de Puerto Rico. **Career Steps:** Private Practice Optometrist (1984–Present); President and Senior Partner, Optica Robles Corporation (1984–Present); President, Colegio de Optometras de Puerto Rico **Associations & Accomplishments:** Recipient: 1970 Economy Award by Junior Chamber of Commerce; "Premio Vision" 1994 Highest Recognition in Optometrist; Licensed Optician #19, Puerto Rico Board of Opticians; Association of Optical Laboratory (1985); Former President, Optometric Society; First President, Colegio de Optometras (formerly Optometric Society); Lecturer for Optometry Association of the Dominican Republic (1993); American Optometric Association; Magna Cum Laude Assemble of God Bible Institute; Licensed Preacher (1987), Defenders of the Christian Faith Church; WERR, Rio Piedras Puerto Rico: Director of Public Relations, Department of Communications, Defenders of the Christian Movement, Editor of Bulletins "Misiones" and "Omega"; Board of Directors, Luces de Vida Institute at Venzuala. **Education:** Interamerican University School of Optometry (1984); Interamerican University: B.B.A. cum laude, B.S. **Personal:** Two children: Sr. Jose Garcia and Dra. Yelitza Garcia.

John D. Falcon

Executive Administrator
South Texas Eye Consultants
2222 Morgan Avenue, Suite 101
Corpus Christi, TX 78405–1909
(800) 728–1831
Fax: (512) 884–0649

8042

Business Information: South Texas Eye Consultants (STEC) was established as an ophthalmology group practice in 1972. John Falcon was hired by STEC in 1993 to perform the group's chief executive functions and to re–organize and expand the company. By 1995, Mr. Falcon merged four corporations which included three medical practices, five M.D.'s, one O.D., thirty–two employees, and six clinic locations in three different counties. This increased the group's annual revenues by 1.4 million. Resourceful and innovative, Falcon created a "resource based" capitation fee system, a highly marketable "vision plan", a well–balanced "profit distribution plan", a state–of–the–art "cost accounting system" (that compartmentalizes each physician), an advanced eye care delivery system for "self–insured industries", a "co–management network" with optometrists, and a corporate information system that communicates accurate and timely reports to stock holders. His non–medical experiences include assignments as Commissioned Officer/Pilot in the military, and as Inspector General in the Federal system. While working for the Army Deputy Under Secretary and traveling 100,000 miles annually, his performance was commended for administration and logistics which spanned several states. Elected County Tax Commissioner in Georgia, Mr. Falcon was later hired by Nueces County, Texas to merge 29 taxing jurisdictions into one billing and collection activity. His success lead to a third county assignment to "design", "install", and "manage" the county's first Civil Service/Human Resource Management System for 1300 employees. A respected administrator and property tax expert, he was invited to write an editorial column in the Corpus Christi newspaper on public service efficiency. **Career Steps:** Executive Administrator, South Texas Eye Consultants (1993–Present); Director of Human Resources, Nueces County, Texas (1989–1993); Elected Tax Commissioner, Webster County, Georgia (1985–1988); Commissioned Officer, United States Army (1964–1984). **Associations & Accomplishments:** Pi Gamma Mu; Georgia Bicentennial Commission; Vice President, Ada Wilson Children's Center Foundation; Corpus Christi Civitan; Chairman, Corpus Christi Cathedral Finance Council; Retired Military Officers Association. **Education:** Columbus College, M.S.A. (1989); William Carey College, B.A. in Social Science. **Personal:** Married to Irma in 1966. Two children: Christopher Paul and Monica. Mr. Falcon enjoys church, family, golf, fishing, and hunting.

Christie Geiger

Accounting Manager
Jervey Eye Group, P.A.
20 Medical Ridge Drive
Greenville, SC 29605–5605
(864) 271–6951 Ext: 314
Fax: (864) 232–6195
EMAIL: See Below

8042

Business Information: Jervey Eye Group, P.A. is a multi–specialty eye care group with 17 doctors and a staff of 100+. Serving in five locations from Greenville, S.C. to Easley, S.C., Jervey specializes in surgery and diseases of the eye with special emphasis on corneal implants, neuro–ophthalmology, ophthalmic plastic surgery, and pediatric ophthalmology. As Accounting Manager, Christie Geiger is responsible for the preparations of all financial reports and statements, as well as preparing annual budget information for the Board of Directors. Internet users can reach her via: 103327.3404@compuserve.com **Career Steps:** Accounting Manager, Jervey Eye Group, P.A. (1994–Present); Accounting Manager, Denture Care, Inc. (1992–1994); Staff Accountant, Coopers & Lybrand (1990–1992); Staff Accountant, Boyd & Company (1989–1990). **Associations & Accomplishments:** Zantas Charities (shelters for battered, homeless, and pregnant women). **Education:** University of South Carolina, B.S. in Accounting (1989). **Personal:** Married to Allen A. Jr. in 1990. Mrs. Geiger enjoys physical fitness, crafts, and church activities.

Eddie L. Golden, O.D.

Associate Doctor of Optometry and Orthokeratology
Memphis Eye and Cataract Associates
10336 Shrewsbury Run West
Collierville, TN 38017
(901) 853–7918
Fax: (901) 853–7918

8042

Business Information: Memphis Eye and Cataract Associates is a medical practice specializing in the eye with special emphasis on cataract removal and intraocular lens implants, refractive surgery, laser, and orthokeratology–corneal molding – a technique for correcting refractive errors in vision by changing the shape of the cornea with the temporary use of progressively flatter oxygen permeable contact lenses. Memphis Eye and Cataract Associates currently employs over 60 people. As a Doctor of Optometry and Orthokeratology, Dr. Golden is responsible for general optometry and eye examinations, as well as advanced orthokeratology, precise corneal moldings, and post–operative care. **Career Steps:** Associate Doctor of Optometry and Orthokeratology, Memphis Eye Cataract Associates (1994–Present); Partner & Associate Doctor of Optometry and Orthokeratology, Mid–South PCM Group, Inc. (1994–1995); Owner and Doctor, Golden Eye Clinic (1983–1994); Owner and Doctor, Clover Leaf Eye Clinic (second office) (1991–1993). **Associations & Accomplishments:** American Optometric Association: Contact Lens Section, Sports Vision Section, Optometric Recognition Award (11 years consecutively – this year 126 received this award out of over 37,000 ODs); Southern Council of Optometry; Mississippi Optometric Association; National Eye Research Foundation; International CKR Society; International Computerized Orthokeratology Society; Who's Who in Mississippi; Who's Who in the South and Southwest; Who's Who Among Outstanding Americans; Deacon, Temple

Baptist Church; International Rotary Club; University of Southern Mississippi Eagle Club; Pi Kappa Alpha; Listed in Dictionary of International Biography; Named "Mr. ECJC" while attending East Central Junior College, was also Freshman Class Favorite and Student Body Vice–President; Tennessee Optometric Association; West Tennessee Optometric Society; Who's Who of American Professionals (1995); International Who's Who of Professionals (1996). **Education:** Southern College of Optometry, O.D. (1982); University of Mississippi (1977); East Central Junior College, A.A. (1975). **Personal:** Married to Kathy Davis in 1982. Four children: Jonathan, Heather, Jeremy and Matthew. Dr. Golden enjoys golf, fishing, sports events and yardwork.

Daniel J. Karr, M.D.
Physician
Children's Eye Clinic
4540 Sand Point Way NE #100
Seattle, WA 98105–3941
(206) 526–5222
Fax: (206) 526–0341

8042

Business Information: Children's Eye Clinic is a private practice Pediatric Ophthalmology clinic offering medical and surgical eye care. A practicing physician since 1978, Dr. Karr is a Board–certified Ophthalmologist and fellowship–trained Pediatric Ophthalmologist, and one of three physician partners at Children's Eye Clinic. **Career Steps:** Physician, Children's Eye Clinic, and Clinical Assistant Professor Ophthamology, University of Washington (1991–Present); Chief Ped. Ophthalmology, University of Washington/Children's Hospital (1986–1991); Assistant Professor Ophthalmology, West Virginia University (1985–1986). **Associations & Accomplishments:** Volunteer – Nepal (1968–1970), Peace Corps; Fellow, American Academy of Ophthalmology; Fellow, American Academy of Pediatrics; Washington Academy of Eye Physicians and Surgeons; Washington State Medical Association; King County Medical Association. **Education:** University of Miami Medical School, M.D. (1978); Florida Presbyterian College, B.A. (1968); University of Washington, Pediatric Residency (1978–1981), Ophthalmology Residency (1981–1984). University of Iowa, Pediatric Ophthalmology Fellowship (1984–1985). **Personal:** Married to Susan J. in 1971. Two children: Emilia and Eli. Dr. Karr enjoys music, locksmithing, gardening, backpacking and camping.

Joseph C. Kim, M.D., F.A.C.S.
President and Physician
North Shore Ophthalmologists, Inc.
585 Main Street
Malden, MA 02148
(617) 322–1725
Fax: (617) 322–2202

8042

Business Information: NSO, Inc. is a multi–specialty group specializing in cataract and lens implant surgery, glaucoma and retina therapy and laser treatments, as well as the diagnosis and treatment of eye disorders and diseases. Established in 1968, North Shore Ophthalmologists, Inc. currently employs 6 support staff. As President and Physician, Dr. Kim is responsible for all aspects of operations, as well as the care and treatment of patients. **Career Steps:** President and Physician, North Shore Ophthalmologists, Inc. (1968–Present); Academic Appointments: Clinical Instructor in Ophthalmology, Harvard Medical School (1976–Present); Assistant Clinical Professor in Ophthalmology, Tufts University School of Medicine (1993–Present); Hospital Appointments: Chief of Ophthalmology, The Malden Hospital (1973–Present); Surgeon in Ophthalmology, Massachusetts Eye and Ear Infirmary/Harvard Medical School (1984–Present). **Associations & Accomplishments:** American Medical Association; American College of Surgeons; New England Ophthalmological Society; Korean–American Ophthalmological Society; American Academy of Ophthalmology; Has published many articles as well as having been guest lecturer at numerous symposiums around the world. **Education:** Harvard Medical School, M.D. (1964); St. Anselm's College, A.B.; University of Illinois, Research and Educational Hospital, Rotating Internship; Massachusetts Eye and Ear Infirmary/HMS Resident. **Personal:** Married to Mija Kim in 1978. Three children: Michelle, Jennifer and Anthony. Dr. Kim enjoys golf.

Nelsa Chacon Losada, O.D., PA
Optometrist
Nelsa Chacon Losada, O.D., PA
6001 Vineland Road, Suite 105
Orlando, FL 32819
(407) 370–6800
Fax: Please mail or call

8042

Business Information: The Office of Nelsa Chacon Losada, O.D., PA performs eye exams and fits glasses and contact lenses for clients/patients. As Optometrist, Dr. Losada performs eye exams and oversees the daily operations of the office. Other responsibilities include budgetary concerns, fiscal matters, personnel and payroll. Concurrently, Dr. Losada is a member of the State Board of Examiners for Florida. **Career Steps:** Optometrist, Nelsa Chacon Losada, O.D., PA (1992–Present); Optometrist, Levin Eye Center (1991–1992). **Associations & Accomplishments:** American Optometric Association; Florida Optometric Association; Central Florida Optometric Society; Sociedad Cubana de Orlando. **Education:** University of Houston, O.D. (1991); University South Florida, B.S. in Biology. **Personal:** Married to Prudencio Losada in 1984. One child: Janel. Dr. Losada enjoys golf, going to the beach, and shopping.

Jeffrey R. Lose, OD, CCHP
Owner
Institutional Eye Care/Senior Eye Care
41 South Third Street
Lewisburg, PA 17837–1944
(717) 524–4489
Fax: (717) 524–2817

8042

Business Information: Institutional Eye Care/Senior Eye Care (IEC/SEC) is a unique optometry, eyeglass, and vision care practice, specializing in the provision of contracted on-site vision care to correctional inmates (IEC) and nursing home patients (SEC). They currently serve 100 institutions (78,000 patients) throughout 26 states. Establishing IEC/SEC upon the conferral of his optometric doctorate in 1983, Dr. Lose is responsible for all aspects of operations, including administration and the oversight of the administrative operations for associates and a support staff of 40. Concurrent with his ownership of IEC/SEC, he operates a private optometry practice. Career milestones include being the only Optometrist in the U.S. who holds the distinction of a CCHP certification. **Career Steps:** Owner, Institutional Eye Care/Senior Eye Care (1983–Present). **Associations & Accomplishments:** American Public Health Association; American Jail Association; American Correctional Association; American Correctional Health Services Association; American Optometric Association; American Association of Homes and Services for the Aging; National Commission on Correctional Health Care Certified Professional; Pennsylvania Optometric Association; Pennsylvania Association Non–Profit Homes for the Aging. **Education:** Pennsylvania College of Optometry, O.D. (1983). **Personal:** Married to Janice in 1980. Dr. Lose enjoys boating.

Antonia M. Orfield, O.D., FCOVD
Optometrist
New England Eye Institute and Harvard University Health Service
678 Massachusetts Ave. Suite 205
Cambridge, MA 02139
(617) 868–8742
Fax: Please mail or call

8042

Business Information: A Board–certified Optometrist and Fellow of the College of Optometrists in Vision Development, Dr. Antonia Orfield specializes in Binocular Vision and Vision Therapy for adults and children. She has a private vision therapy practice in Cambridge, Massachusetts, and is also a Staff Optometrist with the New England Eye Institute and the Harvard University Health Services. As an Assistant Adjunct Professor of Optometry at the New England College of Optometry, she is responsible for clinical instruction in the graduate training program for binocular vision and pediatrics. Dr. Orfield is currently the Chief Investigator and Grant Administrator for the Mather School Vision Research Project, conducting research on inner–city youth, relating vision problems to problem symptoms such as learning disabilities, slow learners and dropouts. Publishing articles and lecturing on myopia reduction, she treats patients with myopic disorders with exercise therapy as opposed to radical surgical procedures. Dr. Orfield works in collaboration with a local chiropractor conducting research on

cervical spine and sacral adjustment effects on vision. **Career Steps:** Assistant Professor of Optometry, New England Eye Institute and Optometrist, Harvard University Health Service (1991–Present); Chief Investigator and Grant Administrator, Mather School Vision Research Project (1995–Present). **Associations & Accomplishments:** Parent Member, Kenwood Academy High School Council under the school reform plan in Chicago (1989–1991); Fellow, College of Optometrists in Vision and Development; American Academy of Optometry; Neuro Optometric Rehabilitation Association; International College of Applied Kinesiology; International Academy of Sports Vision; American Optometric Association; Massachusetts Society of Optometrics. **Education:** Illinois College of Optometry, O.D. (1989); University of Chicago, M.A.T. (1966); Smith College, B.A. (1963). **Personal:** Married to Gary Orfield in 1963. Three children: Amy, Sonia, and Rosanna. Dr. Orfield enjoys swimming and spending time with her family.

Kathleen M. Ploszaj
Administrative Director
California Eye Institute
1360 East Herndon, Suite 240
Fresno, CA 93720
(209) 449–5000
Fax: (209) 449–5090

8042

Business Information: California Eye Institute is a state–of–the–art comprehensive ophthalmology facility, consisting of fifteen ophthalmologists and a joint venture with the leading area hospital. The Institute has satellite offices located throughout the city. Established in 1988, California Eye Institute is currently owned by three autonomous ophthalmology groups and employs over 150 support staff. With fourteen years experience in health care administration and a Certified Ophthalmic Assistant, Ms. Ploszaj joined the Institute in 1988. Serving as Administrative Director, she is responsible for the direction of all joint California Eye Institute activities, as well as serving as Property Manager of the 60,000 square foot, four–story building and Chief Financial Officer of the $1.5 million medical group. Career milestones include organizing and coordinating the public relations and surgical programs, as well as the managed care contracts for the Institute. **Career Steps:** Administrative Director, California Eye Institute (1988–Present); Director of Public Relations and Surgical Programs, Fogg & Maxwell Eye Care (1981–1988). **Associations & Accomplishments:** Joint Commission on Allied Health Personnel in Ophthalmology (1986–Present); American Society of Ophthalmic Administrators (1989–Present); California Association of Ophthalmology (1989–Present); Windsor National Associates (1991–Present); Medical Group Management Association (1994–Present); Ophthalmic Photographers Society (1993–Present). **Education:** California State University – Fresno, B.S. (1982); Certified Ophthalmic Assistant. **Personal:** One child: Brett. Ms. Ploszaj enjoys water & snow skiing, biking, cooking, aerobics, and dancing.

Walter S. Ramirez, O.D.
Optometrist
Optiland
P.O. Box 363551
San Juan, Puerto Rico 00936
(809) 744–6468
Fax: (809) 767–2828

8042

Business Information: Optiland is a vision care office, providing all aspects of eyecare treatment and eyewear dispensing. With ten years experience in Optometry, Dr. Ramirez established his sole practice in 1993. Dr. Ramirez is responsible for all administrative operations, in addition to his daily patient practice. Concurrent with his private optometry practice, he serves as Clinical Supervisor at the Inter–American University School of Optometry, teaching continuing education classes. **Career Steps:** Optometrist, Optiland (1993–Present); Clinical Supervisor, School of Optometry – InterAmerican University (1992–Present); Optometrist, Pearle Vision Express. **Associations & Accomplishments:** Treasurer, Colegio De Optometras de Puerto Rico (1985–Present); Fundacion SIDS de Puerto Rico – AIDS Foundation; Iniciativa Comunitaria Investigacion (ICI) – providing pro bono visual examinations for AIDS patients; Volunteer, Red Cross of America. **Education:** Inter–American University, School of Optometry, O.D. (1985); University of Puerto Rico, B.S. in Biology, with minors in Sociology, Theater/Drama, Mathematics. **Personal:** Dr. Ramirez enjoys traveling to Venezuela.

Richard L. Sanchez

Senior Vice President
Vision 21
7209 Bryan Dairy Road
Largo, FL 34647–1505
(813) 545–4300
Fax: (813) 545–5116
EMAIL: See Below

8042

Business Information: Vision 21 is a physician practice management company. The Company acquires and manages eye care physicians and practices. As Senior Vice President, Mr. Sanchez is responsible for all aspects of Company operations. This Company also provides services to major HMO's. Internet users can reach him via: info@vision 21.com. **Career Steps:** Senior Vice President, Vision 21 (1992–Present); Exxon Company USA: Marketing Services Manager (1990–1992), Western Area Distribution Manager (1987–1990), Midwest Market Manager (1985–1987). **Associations & Accomplishments:** American Society of Ophthalmic Administrators. **Education:** Florida State University, B.S. in Chemistry (1975); Temple University, MBA Program. **Personal:** Married to Sharon in 1976. Three children: Ryan, Ross, and Rendall. Mr. Sanchez enjoys reading, golf, and tennis.

Lesley A. Spektor

Administrator
Center for Excellence in Eye Care
8940 North Kendall Drive – 4th Floor
Miami, FL 33176
(305) 598–2020
Fax: (305) 274–0426

8042

Business Information: Center for Excellence in Eye Care is a multi–doctor ophthalmology practice, created by a merger of five medical practices. Changing her career from Physical Therapist to Administrator ten years ago, Ms. Spektor joined the Center for Excellence in Eye Care (fka, Southeast Eye Associates) as Administrator in 1986. She is responsible for all administrative functions for the office. **Career Steps:** Administrator, Center for Excellence in Eye Care (1996–Present); Administrator, Southeast Eye Associates (1986–1996); Physical Therapist, Groote Schuur Hospital (1972–1975). **Associations & Accomplishments:** American Society of Ophthalmic Administrators; Member, Phi Kappa Phi Honor Society. **Education:** University of Miami, B.C.S. (1997); University of Cape Town, Diploma in Physiotherapy (1972). **Personal:** Married to Frank in 1973. Two children: Jonathan and Steven.

Stephen E. Owusu, D.P.M.

Chief Executive Officer and Attending Podiatrist
Mount Zion Podiatry, PC
106 Pennsylvania Avenue
Brooklyn, NY 11207–2427
(718) 385–2085
Fax: (718) 385–2085

8043

Business Information: Mount Zion Podiatry, PC is a medical facility specializing in the care and treatment of foot and ankle ailments. A Podiatrist since 1992, Dr. Owusu now serves as Chief Executive Officer and Attending Podiatrist at Mount Zion. His present responsibilities include patient care, medical and support staff supervision, and various administrative activities. **Career Steps:** Chief Executive Officer and Attending Podiatrist, Mount Zion Podiatry, PC (1993–Present). **Associations & Accomplishments:** Asanteman Association; Christian Fellowship; American Podiatric Medicine Association; National Podiatric Medicine Association. **Education:** Pennsylvania College of Podiatric Medicine, D.P.M. (1992); City College of New York: M.A., B.S. **Personal:** Married to Grace in 1983. Four children: Stephen Jr., Victoria, Daniella and David. Dr. Owusu enjoys tennis, Bible study and reading.

Ketan Patel

Operations Manager
Regional Health Supply
1220 East Corporate Drive
Arlington, TX 76006
(817) 640–0600 Ext. 111
Fax: (817) 640–0476
EMAIL: See Below

8047

Business Information: Regional Health Supply specializes in the national distribution of medical and surgical supplies to hospitals, research institutes, and universities. National in scope, the Company has three other branches located throughout Texas. Established in 1988, the Company employs 45 people, and has an estimated annual revenue of $36 million. As Operations Manager, Mr. Patel oversees all aspects of the Company. His duties include administration, finance, public relations, and strategic planning. Internet users can reach him via: ketanRHS@aol.com. **Career Steps:** Regional Health Supply: Operations Manager (1995–Present), National Sales Manager (1994–1995); Executive Accounts Manager, AT&T/NCR Corporation (1992–1993). **Education:** University of Texas: M.B.A. (1995), B.B.A. (1991). **Personal:** Mr. Patel enjoys going to musicals, Jazz festivals, and world travel.

Jeannette Acrea, Ph.D.

Psychotherapist
Christian Psychological Services
1635 Rancho Avenue
Glendale, CA 91201–2905
(818) 247–6644
Fax: Please mail or call

8049

Business Information: Christian Psychological Services is a private psychotherapist office, providing marriage, family, and child counseling services, primarily for abusive relationships. A practicing psychotherapist since 1969, Dr. Acrea oversees all administrative operations for associates and support staff, in addition to her daily patient practice. **Career Steps:** Psychotherapist, Christian Psychological Services (1969–Present); Psychologist, Narramore Christian Foundation – Rosemead, California (1961–1969); Psychologist and Marriage, Family & Child Counselor, American Institute of Family Relations – Los Angeles (1953–1961). **Associations & Accomplishments:** American Psychological Association; California Psychological Association; Glendale Area Mental Health Professionals Association; Promoted and hosted a witnessing group; Deacon in Protestant Church (20 years); Led a grief group after the death of her husband. **Education:** Southern California Institute of Psychology, Ph.D. (1969); Occidental College – Los Angeles, M.A. (1953); University of California – Berkeley, B.A. (1932). **Personal:** Married to Ivan (deceased) in 1944. One child: Douglas and one foster son, Steven Dean. Dr. Acrea enjoys tennis and church activities.

Van Austin, Ph.D.

Psychotherapist
Van Austin, Ph.D.
871 S. Lucerne Blvd.
Los Angeles, CA 90005
(213) 930–2412
Fax: (213) 930–2412

8049

Business Information: Van Austin, Ph.D. specializes in result–oriented integral psychotherapy. Dr. Austin guides clients through negative experiences and consequent emotions. He assists them in reframing these experiences to uncover potential for growth, understanding, and empowerment through a variety of techniques, including hypnotherapy and unaided visualization, clients reconnect to the "authentic" selves – the source of all self–esteem and inner peace. Dr. Austin also conducts seminars and produces motivational tapes. **Career Steps:** Psychotherapist, Van Austin, Ph.D. (1985–Present). **Education:** Ryokan College, Ph.D. in Human Behavior (1993); Antioch University M.A. in Clinical Psychology (1988); Trinity College, B.A. in English Literature (1971). **Personal:** Married to Mirian in 1995. One child: Vanessa. Mr. Austin enjoys songwriting, eastern philosophy and religion, and running.

Michael P. Baker, Ph.D.

Physician
Associates for Psychological and Therapy Services
1551 Indian Hills Drive #221
Sioux City, IA 51104–1800
(712) 252–1473
Fax: (712) 252–5672

8049

Business Information: Associates for Psychological and Therapy Services is a multi–associate family counseling practice, offering the services of psychologists, social workers, mental health workers, and addiction counselors. A practicing psychologist since 1983, Dr. Baker established Associates for Psychological and Therapy Services in 1986, providing therapy and psychological evaluations of patients, as well as supervising staff and overseeing administrative functions. **Career Steps:** Psychologist, Associates for Psychological and Therapy Services (1986–Present) Psychologist, A.P.M. (1985–1986); Psychologist, C.M.H.I. (1979–1985); Psychologist Technician, V.A.M.C. – Miami, Florida (1978–1979). **Associations & Accomplishments:** Iowa Psychological Association; American Psychological Association. **Education:** University of South Dakota, Ph.D. (1983); University of Miami, M.S.; University of Northern Iowa, B.A. **Personal:** Married to Susan in 1973. Four children: Dylan, Aaron, Noah and Michele. Dr. Baker enjoys computers and reading.

Susan J. Borninski

Business Development Director
Ortho Care Physical Therapy
30695 Little Mack Avenue, Suite 600
Roseville, MI 48066–1781
(810) 294–9030
Fax: (810) 294–9033

8049

Business Information: Ortho Care Physical Therapy is an outpatient physical therapy clinic established in 1992 and currently employing 10 people. The Clinic services parts of Wayne and Macomb counties and participates with Medicare, Blue Cross/Blue Shield, Private Insurances, PPOM, Worker's Compensation, Auto Accidents, and can accept self–pay. Ortho Care Physical Therapy accepts referrals from any M.D. or D.O. including Sports Medicine Specialists, Family Practice Physicians, Internists, Orthopaedic Surgeons, Physical Medicine and Rehabilitation Physicians, Neurologists, Neuro Surgeons, Rheumatologists, and Podiatrists. Individuals can also call and be referred to a physician. As Business Development Director, Ms. Borninski facilitates all promotional efforts and manages the clinic. She develops and implements new marketing strategies to promote the clinic and stays abreast of all changes in insurance regulations. **Career Steps:** Ortho Care Physical Therapy: Business Development Director (1992–Present), Development Director, Rehabilitation, Inc./Rehability Orthopedic (1990–1992); Director of Guest Relations, Bon Secours Senior Community (1988–1990); Director of Staffing/Administration, St. John Medical Center (1981–1987). **Associations & Accomplishments:** Ethics Committee, St. John–Bon Secours Senior Community; Executive Board Member, Tri–County Dental Health Council; Fund Raising/Fund Appropriation Representative, Alpha Phi Alumni Fraternity; Fontbonne Auxilliary; Grosse Point Historical Society; Grosse Pointe Hunt Club. **Education:** Wayne State University, M.S. (1989); Michigan State University, B.S. (1978). **Personal:** Ms. Borninski enjoys music, cycling, swimming, sailing, tennis, golf, food, reading, and travel.

Clive E. Brewster

Physical Therapist/Administrator
Health South Sports Medicine and Rehabilitation
23220 Cass Avenue
Woodland Hills, CA 91364
(310) 674–5213
Fax: (818) 222–4205
EMAIL: See Below

8049

Business Information: Health South Sports Medicine and Rehabilitation is a private medical facility specializing in the sports medicine and rehabilitation of professional athletes such as the Los Angeles Lakers, Angels, etc. Employing fifty people, the Facility is regional in scope with four locations throughout the area. As Physical Therapist/Administrator, Mr. Brewster is responsible for all administrative aspects of the Facility and its three satellite offices. He is also a practicing physical therapist with a full caseload of clients, thereby involving him in diagnosis, treatment and follow–up care. Internet users can reach him via: cliveeb@aol.com. **Career Steps:** Physical Therapist/Administrator, Health South Sports Medicine and Rehab (1995–Present); Director of Physical Therapy, Kerlan–Jobe Orthopedic Clinic (1976–1995). **Education:** University of Nevada, Reno: B.Sc. (1974), M.S (1975); Childrens Hospital School of Physical Therapy, Registered Physical Therapist. **Personal:** Mr. Brewster enjoys his work.

Dorothy Thomas Catalano

Director
Therapy Specialists of North Florida, Inc.
3334 Capital Medical Boulevard
Tallahassee, FL 32308–4470
(904) 877–4205
Fax: (904) 878–0784

8049

Business Information: Therapy Specialists of North Florida, Inc. specializes in hand and upper extremity rehabilitation, employing two hand, two part–time occupational, one part–

1–651

time physical, and one licensed massage therapist. Serving as Director and Certified Hand Therapist, Ms. Dorothy Catalano has administrative responsibilities in the office and provides extensive therapy to her patients. **Career Steps:** Director, Therapy Specialists of North Florida, Inc. (1985–Present); OT Consultant, Hand Rehabilitation of North Florida (1980–1984); Occupational Therapy Consultant, Tallahassee Memorial Regional Medical Center (1978–1979); Occupational Therapist, Easter Seal Rehabilitation Center (1975–1978). **Associations & Accomplishments:** American Society of Hand Therapists; American Occupational Therapy Association; Worker's Compensation Liaison, Florida Occupational Therapy Association; Founding Member, Florida Hand Society; Hand Therapy Certification Commission, Inc.; Legislative Impact Team; Florida Occupational Therapy Association; Florida Chapter, American Society of Hand Therapists; HONORS AND AWARDS: Award of Appreciation (1983), Distinguished Service Award (1987)– Florida Chapter of the Arthritis Foundation; Award of Recognition (1990, 1993); Florida Occupational Therapy Association; Occupational Therapy Consultant (1990) – Florida State Bureau of Workers' Compensation Insurance; Frequent lecturer at conference and institutional symposia proceedings in her field of specialty. **Education:** University of Florida, B.S.in Occupational Therapy with honors (1975); CERTIFICATION: American Occupational Therapy Association (1975); Hand Therapy Certification Commission, Inc. (1991). **Personal:** Married to Robert Stephen in 1984. Two children: Thomas Joseph and John Benton. Ms. Catalano enjoys gardening, body conditioning, and beach activities.

Linda C. Crow, M.A.
Sole Practitioner
The Office of Linda C. Crow, M.A.
130 East State Street
Media, PA 19063–3431
(610) 565–5221
Fax: Please mail or call
EMAIL: See Below

8049

Business Information: Establishing her private practice in 1989, Ms. Crow's practice focuses on the treatment of neuropsychology. Her patients include neurotics and accident victims, in addition to treating victims of domestic abuse, anxiety, and depression in and around the Philadelphia area in individual therapy, usually involving hypnosis. Internet users can reach her via: ARXM13A@Prodigy.com **Career Steps:** Sole Practitioner, The Office of Linda C. Crow, M.A. (1989–Present); Systems Analyst, Continental American Life Insurance Company (1967–1977); Teacher, Smyrna Special School District (1964–1967). **Associations & Accomplishments:** American Psychological Association; Pennsylvania Psychological Association; Neuro–Linguistic Programming Association; Milton Erickson Association; Executive Board, Academy of Community Music. **Education:** West Chester University, M.A. (1981); Rollins College, B.S. (1960). **Personal:** Ms. Crow enjoys sailing and computers.

Ceola Digby–Berry, Ph.D., HSPP
Licensed Psychologist
–Independent–
1111 West Jackson Street and 3
Muncie, IN 47304
(317) 284–0879
Fax: (317) 284–1480

8049

Business Information: A Licensed Psychologist and Health Service Provider in Psychology, Dr. Digby-Berry serves as Director of Psychology at New Castle State Developmental Center. She is responsible for the management of the department, specializing in psychological services to the developmentally delayed, mentally retarded and mentally ill. Dr. Digby–Berry also maintains private practices as Owner and Chairperson of the Board of Associates in Mental Health (AMH), Inc. in Muncie, Indiana, and as Owner of Anchor Behavioral Counseling (ABC), Inc. in New Castle, Indiana. AMH, Inc. and ABC, and LLC each provide psychological services to adults, children, couples, families, corporations and government sectors specializing in depression, teenage motherhood, sports psychology and chronic pain management. Dr. Digby–Berry is the only private practice licensed psychologist in the State of Indiana who is fluent in the language of sign. Dr. Digby–Berry serves and holds office on numerous state and local community service boards, as well as serving as a frequent guest lecturer for national conventions. **Career Steps:** Director of Psychology, New Castle Development Center (Present); Owner and Chairman of the Board, Associates in Mental Health, Inc. (Current); Owner, Anchor Behavioral Counseling, Inc. (Current). **Associations & Accomplishments:** Founding Member, Indiana Sports Psychologist Association; Co–Chairperson, National Mental Health Association; Licensed Psychologist – Indiana; Health Service Provider in Psychology (HSPP) – Indiana; National Council of Negro Women's Mary McLeod Bethune Community Service Award (1990); Recipient, Daughters of the American Revolution Award; Recipient, New York State Regents Scholarship; Governor's ap-

pointee to the State Licensure Board for Psychologists; Vice Chair of Licensure Board for Psychologists. **Education:** Ball State University – European Campus: Ph.D. in Psychological Counseling & Guidance Service, HSPP, M.A. in Guidance and Counseling; California Baptist College – Riverside, B.A. in Social Welfare; National Tech. Institute for the Deaf, Sign Language studies. **Personal:** Dr. Digby–Berry enjoys horseback riding, bridge, scrabble, and dancing.

Kathleen S. Fuller
Director/Owner
Center of Life
49 West Seminole Street, #203
Stuart, FL 34994
(407) 220–4556
Fax: Please mail or call

8049

Business Information: Center of Life provides hypnotherapy and psychotherapy counseling to individuals and families. Specializing in depression, anxiety and stress, poor self–esteem, eating disorders, and smoking and alcohol dependency. The Center also counsels couples on communication, expressing tenderness, finding the joy in relationships, and listening to each others' needs. Established in 1992, the Center strives to assist clients in discovering how to make "deep assessments to find and be content with one's inner self and higher being." As Director/Owner, Ms. Fuller 's work as counselor, lecturer, and author has helped countless individuals find the happiness that has eluded them. Finding her own "power to change," Ms. Fuller has become a recognized authority on dysfunctional behaviors and she has found personal accomplishment in sculpture, children's books, and academic research. A teacher at Indian River Community College, a professional liaison for La Leche International, and establisher of Mommie and Me lab schools in St. Lucie and Martin Counties, Florida, Ms. Fuller has also shared her "power" with others through various workshops on nutrition, art, and creativity. **Career Steps:** Director/Owner, Center of Life (1992–Present); Director, Circle C Ranch For Dressage (1987–1991); Director, Mommie and Me Lab Schools (1982–1985); LLL Leader, Leche League International (1979–1985). **Associations & Accomplishments:** American Counseling Association; American Mental Health Counselors Association; Florida Ethical Hypnosis Society; American Institute for Hypnotherapy and Psychotherapy; Fellow, Nova University; Board Certified Nationally in Hypnosis; Diplomat, Board Licensed by the State of Florida; American Association of Professional Hypnotherapists; Ethical Hypnosis Society; American Mental Health Association; American Association of Behavioral Therapists; Sunday School Teacher; Founded Sunnyfield Farms Boarding Stables and at the age of fifteen managed the books, mucked stalls, and trained top–level show horses; Author "I Feel Great Without Sugar."; Two National Dressage Championships at Training Level; Recognized and exhibited in many art shows presenting Fibre Sculpture, Children's Illustrations, and "Emotions in Art"; Planned and Implemented Several workshops on nutrition; Author of numerous research papers; Co–Lead a Therapy Group with Marlene Pharr, M.S.W. **Education:** Nova University, M.S. (1992); University of Puget Sound, B.A. in Education and Art; Extensive Leadership Training for La Leche League International. **Personal:** Two children: Danielle Marie and Shannon Noel Crouch. Ms. Fuller enjoys mediating and working as a counselor with non–profit organizations.

Graham D. Glancy, ChB, MRC Psych, FRCP(c)
Psychiatrist
The Psilex Group
205 Richmond Street West, Suite 702
Toronto, Ontario M5V 1V3
(416) 408–3000
Fax: (416) 408–3002

8049

Business Information: The Psilex Group is a private practice in forensic psychiatry. The staff psychiatrists assist law enforcement agencies in developing psychological profiles on the criminal mind. As Psychiatrist, Dr. Glancy is a medical doctor specializing in the treatment of mental diseases or disorders. Concurrently, Dr. Glancy is a part–time consultant at the METFORS, Clarke Institute of Psychiatry. He is an Assistant Professor in the Department of Psychiatry at the University of Toronto and assists the Ontario Ministry of Corrections as a consultant to several regional jails and correctional centers. Dr. Glancy has been a member of the the Ontario Criminal Code Review Board since 1989. **Career Steps:** Psychiatrist, The Psilex Group (1991–Present); Clarke Institute of Psychiatry: Consultant, METFORS, (1991–Present), Chief Psychiatrist/Forensic Service (1988–1991), Forensic Inpatient Service (1987–1988); Consultant, Ontario Ministry of Corrections (1991–Present); Psychiatric Member, Ontario Criminal Review Board (1989–Present). **Associations & Accomplishments:** President, Canadian Academy of Psychiatry and The Law; Ontario Psychiatric Association; Canadian Psychiatric Association; Canadian Medical Association; American Academy of Psychiatry and The Law; Royal College of Physicians, England; Association of Manchester Psychiatrists in Training;

Numerous publications in referred and non–refereed journals; Several Presentations at Juried Conferences; Recipient of Two Grants from Ontario Mental Heath Foundation; Invited Teacher at various Associations and Committee Seminars; Board of Directors, Regeneration House, Inc; Great Britain Swimming Team, Ex–Holder of six national records (1969–1972); British Universities Water Polo Team (1976). **Education:** University of Toronto, Diploma in Post Graduate Studies (1982); Victoria University of Manchester: M.B., Ch.B. (1976); Fellow, Royal College of Physicians and Surgeons of Canada, FRCP(C) (1985); Royal College of Psychiatrists, England, M.R.C. Psych (1980); Indiana University, Pre–Medicine. **Personal:** Married to Dr. C. Regehr. Dr. Glancy enjoys squash, playing soccer, and coaching his son's soccer team.

Roberta D. Granger, Ph.D.
Licensed Clinical Psychologist
The Spectrum Center
1550 Spring Road #215
Oak Brook, IL 60521–1362
(708) 782–5050
Fax: Please mail or call

8049

Business Information: The Spectrum Center is a full–service, general group practice, consisting of psychologists, licensed social workers, art therapists, and career consultants. A practicing clinical psychologist since 1986, Dr. Granger founded The Spectrum Center in 1993. She oversees all administrative operations for associates and a support staff of 10, in addition to her daily patient practice. **Career Steps:** Psychologist, The Spectrum Center (1993–Present); Northwestern Medical School: Clinical Psychologist (1991–1995), Professor (1991–1995); Clinical Psychologist, University of Illinois Hospital (1986–1989). **Associations & Accomplishments:** American Psychological Association; Illinois Psychological Association; Union Church of Hinsdale, teach adult classes on spirituality. **Education:** University of Illinois: Ph.D. (1986), M.S. in Developmental Psychology (1982); Purdue University, M.S. in Clinical Psychology (1976). **Personal:** Married to Bruce in 1977. Dr. Granger enjoys gardening, reading, traveling, and sailing.

Rolanda Moore Haycox
Manager, Clinical & Reimbursement Regulation
NovaCare, Inc.
11595 North Meridian Street, Suite 400
Carmel, IN 46032
(800) 753–2867 Ext. 270
Fax: (317) 575–3465

8049

Business Information: NovaCare, Inc. is a rehabilitative services company providing physical, occupational, and speech therapy to nursing homes (Contract Services Division). Facilities provided include outpatient clinics providing orthopedic and support services nationally (Outpatient Services Division), and 125 orthotic and prosthetic laboratories which specialize in the manufacture of artificial limbs. NovaCare, Inc. currently has the number one market share in the U.S. for all three divisions. Using her experience in nursing and law, Mrs. Haycox joined NovaCare, Inc. as Region Director of Clinical Analysis & Compliance/Division Manager of Clinical & Reimbursement Regulation in August of 1995. Her primary duties involve the analysis of reimbursement trends; coordination of appeals for denied claims; compliance audit program administration; regulatory advice and monitoring; interpretation of state practice acts and professional association guidelines compliance assurance; the development and administration for the document review program; and development of educational materials for management personnel and direct care providers. **Career Steps:** Region Director of Clinical Analysis & Compliance/Division Manager of Clinical & Reimbursement Regulation, NovaCare, Inc. (1995–Present); Associate Attorney, Baker & Daniel (1991–1995); Associate, McDermott, Will & Emery (1994); Research Assistant – Legal Writing Faculty, Indiana University School of Law (1990–1992); Community Hospital, East – Indianapolis: Critical Care Staff Nurse (1986–1990), Relief Charge Nurse (1990–1991); Critical Care Registry, St. Francis Hospital (1990); Student Nursing Assistant, Wishard Memorial Hospital (1985–1986); Nursing Assistant/Qualified Medication Aide, Norrell Health Care (1984–1986); Nursing Assistant, Northwest Manor Health Care (1981–1985) **Associations & Accomplishments:** American Bar Association; Indiana Bar Association; Indianapolis Bar Association; American College of Healthcare Executives; National Health Lawyers Association; American Academy of Healthcare Attorneys; Medical Group Management Association; American Academy of Healthcare Attorneys; American Society of Writers on Legal Subjects; ABA Forum on Health Law; Member, Board of Directors, Alpha Home Association of Greater Indianapolis; Professional Advisory Council, Hospice of Indianapolis; Volunteer, Methodist Hospital Hospice; Frequent publications and papers presented. **Education:** Indiana University – Indianapolis: School of Law, J.D. (1992), School of Public and Environmental Affairs, M.H.A. (1992), School of Nursing, B.S.N. (1986). **Personal:** Married to James W. in 1986.

Robert G. Hlasny, Ph.D.
Clinical Psychologist
–Independent–
401 Gilford Avenue, Suite 105
Gilford, NH 03246–7536
(603) 528–6106
Fax: (603) 528–2257

8049

Business Information: The Private Practice of Robert G. Hlasny, Ph.D. provides a full scope of psychological services for drug & alcohol, depression, grief, relationship, adjustment, stress, and anxiety problems in adolescents, adults and elderly. A practicing psychologist since 1979, Dr. Hlasny established his private practice in 1989. He provides treatment to individuals, families, and groups through psychotherapy, psychological evaluations, and consultations. **Career Steps:** Clinical Psychologist, Private Practice (1989–Present); Lakes Region General Hospital: Part–Time Psychologist (1989–1991), Psychologist, Director of Outpatient Services, Lakes Region Mental Health Center (1979–1989); Psychological Associate, Dayton Mental Health and Developmental Center (1974–1976); Psychological Consultant, Bureau of Social Security Disability Determination (Since 1996). **Associations & Accomplishments:** American Psychological Association; New Hampshire Psychological Association; New Hampshire Certified Psychologist since 1981; National Register of Health Service Providers in Psychology; Past President, Gilford Professional Park Association; Coach, Laconia Little League Baseball and Soccer Leagues; co–authored articles regarding values, trust and warmth in therapy and regarding the meaning of dreams. **Education:** University of Ottawa, Ph.D. (1979); Xavier University, M.A. (1974); Boston College, B.A. cum laude (1972). **Personal:** Married to Linda in 1977. Two children: Adam and Evan. Dr. Hlasny enjoys skiing, hiking, raquetball and boating.

Jeffrey S. Kahn, Ph.D.
Founder, President, and Clinical Director
Summit Psychological Services, P.A.
47 Summit Avenue
Summit, NJ 07901–3613
(908) 273–5558
Fax: Please mail or call

8049

Business Information: Summit Psychological Services, P.A. is a community–based, private practice that provides comprehensive, professional services designed to facilitate personal growth for adults, adolescents and children. Dr. Kahn, a licensed psychologist, heads a staff of ten professionals who provide psychotherapy for individuals, couples and families; psychological testing; career counseling and vocational testing; stress management and hypnosis; specialized group therapies for men, women and adolescents; as well as creative arts therapies. With two locations in New Jersey (Summit and Montclair), the group includes clinical, counseling and school psychologists, family therapists, creative arts therapists and a consulting nutritionist. The team approach at SPS provides an opportunity for optimal treatment combinations that can be individually designed, helping to bring recovery to the whole fmaily system affected. Career milestones for Dr. Kahn include founding SPS in 1990, founding the Partial Hospitalization Program at Fair Oaks Hospital in 1984, and, as Director of Hudson House, securing a grant to purchase a community residence that enabled hospitalized psychiatric patients to return to a supportive community. A specialist in the treatment of addictive behaviors and group psychotherapy, Dr. Kahn has been published on subjects including the creation of therapeutic environments, addictions, eating disorders, anxiety and mood disorders. **Career Steps:** Founder, President, and Clinical Director, Summit Psychological Services, P.A. (1990–Present); Supervising Psychologist, STEPS Recovery Centers (1988–1990); Psychologist and Team Leader, Fair Oaks Hospital (1984–1986); Director of Hudson House, Catholic Community Services (1979–1984). **Associations & Accomplishments:** American Psychological Association; New Jersey Psychological Association; Trustee, Society of Psychologists in Private Practice; Alcoholism Counselor Certification Board of New Jersey; National Registry of Certified Group Therapists. **Education:** New York University, Ph.D.; St. John's University, M.S.; Hunter College, A.B. **Personal:** Married to Rona in 1972. One child: David. Dr. Kahn enjoys tennis, skiing, cycling, and guitar.

Thomas A. Lorren III
• • • ━━━◉━━━ • • •

President/Owner
Restore Physical & Industrial Rehabilitation
2324 A Judson Road
Longview, TX 75605
(903) 236–3566
Fax: (903) 236–3185

8049

Business Information: Restore Physical & Industrial Rehabilitation — the leading physical therapy spine – specific practice in East Texas — specializes in the prevention and physical restoration of spine and orthopedic injuries, particularly those involving injuries sustained in industrial accidents. A licensed Physical Therapist in several states since 1978, Mr. Lorren established the practice in 1992. Serving as Managing Partner, he oversees all administrative functions, as well as provides daily patient care. Widely acknowledged by his peers, he was nominated by the East Texas Chapter of Ambucs in May of 1995 for the Therapist of the Year Award. He lectures extensively throughout the U.S. and Europe, has taught at California's Loma Linda University, and is currently a guest lecturer in Physcial Therapy at Kilgore College. **Career Steps:** President/Owner, Restore Physical & Industrial Rehabilitation (1992–Present); Director of Rehabilitation, Texas Back Institute (1989–1992); Director of Education/Sales, Loredan Biomedical (1985–1989); Director of Physical Therapy, Woodland Memorial Hospital (1982–1985). **Associations & Accomplishments:** Ambucs; Longview Leadership; Texas Physical Therapy Association – Treasury, East Texas District; Board of Directors, Loredan Biomedical (since 1992); Published in various medical journals. **Education:** Loma Linda University, B.S.in Physical Therapy (1978); Pacific Union College, B.S. in Science. **Personal:** Married to Linda in 1988. Three children: Amanda, Talena, and Alisha. Mr. Lorren enjoys water skiing, snow skiing, softball, and hunting.

Deborah A. Madanayake
Senior Geriatric Physical Therapist
Rehab Dynamics, Inc.
9096 Fox Run Circle
Eden Prairie, MN 55347
(612) 948–7914
Fax: (612) 942–6556
EMAIL: See Below

8049

Business Information: Rehab Dynamics, Inc. provides rehabilitation services to clinics, hospitals, nursing facilities, and home bound individuals on a contract basis. As Senior Geriatric Physical Therapist, Ms. Madanayake is board certified in geriatric physical therapy. One of only 170 geriatric specialists in the U.S., she is responsible for clinical resources, management of administrative duties, handling training, and serving as student mentor. She also directly supervises a staff of nine. Internet users can reach her via: samm@sihope.com. **Career Steps:** Senior Geriatric Physical Therapist, Rehab Dynamics, Inc. (1995–Present); Rehab Manager, Novacare, Inc. (1988–1995); Physical Therapist, Creative Rehab, Inc. (1988). **Associations & Accomplishments:** American Physical Therapy Association; Geriatric Section, American Physical Therapy Association; Clinical Site Instructor, St. Catherine's College Physical Therapy Program; Travels to Sri Lanka every three years bringing equipment and knowledge to a physical therapist in Colombo. **Education:** College of St. Scholastica, B.A. in Physical Therapy (1986); University of Minnesota, Graduate **Personal:** Married. Ms. Madanayake enjoys long distance running.

Lawrence N. Metz, M.D.
Physician
Neurosurgical & Neurological Group, Inc.
80 Congress Street
Springfield, MA 01104
(413) 781–5050
Fax: (413) 734–6524

8049

Business Information: Neurosurgical & Neurological Group, Inc. is a medical group practice, with 8 physicians – 4 neurologists and 4 neurosurgeons. Dr. Metz is a Neurologist with the group practice. Established in 1967, Neurosurgical & Neurological Group, Inc. employs a staff of 28. **Career Steps:** Physician, Neurosurgical & Neurological Group, Inc. (1967–Present); Solo Practice, (1964–1966). **Associations & Accomplishments:** Fellow, American Academy of Neurology; Fellow, North American Neuroophthalmology Society. **Education:** University of Michigan, M.D. (1959); Dartmouth College, A.B.

Stephen G. Meyer, Ph.D.
Director of Psychological Services
A Child's Life
1111 South Grand Avenue #J
Diamond Bar, CA 91765–1044
(909) 861–7150
Fax: (909) 861–0194

8049

Business Information: A Child's Life is a behavioral and family counseling practice, primarily targeting the needs of children and adolescents. A practicing psychologist since 1976, Stephen Meyer joined A Child's Life in 1988. Serving as Director of Psychological Services, he oversees all associates and administrative operations, in addition to his regular patient practice. Additionally, as a specialist in Forensic Psychology, he provides expert testimony as requested. **Career Steps:** Director of Psychological Services, A Child's Life (1988–Present); Co–Director, Associated Psychologists of Diamond Bar (1978–1988). **Associations & Accomplishments:** American Psychological Association; Numerous articles in National Journal of Perinatology in the area of children's brain injuries and the related disorders encountered. He is now in the process of writing a book on parenting skills, soon to be published. **Education:** Fuller Graduate School of Psychology, Ph.D. (1976); Fuller Theological Seminary, M.A. (1976); Massachusetts Institute of Technology, B.S. (1964). **Personal:** Married to Ardith in 1972. One child: Elisa Eileen. Dr. Meyer enjoys sailing and photography.

Collin A. Myers, Ph.D.
• • • ━━━◉━━━ • • •

Owner/Director
Fairhaven Counseling, Inc.
3570 Executive Drive, Suite 101
Union Town, OH 44685
(330) 896–2820
Fax: (330) 896–2849

8049

Business Information: Fairhaven, Inc. is a private counseling agency with a moral and ethically–based practice. The Center provides seven therapists in four clinics for patients of all ages. Programs are geared toward those suffering from abuse, depression, anxiety, attention deficit disorder, gay and lesbian issues, and spiritual issues. As Owner/Director, Dr. Myers is involved with long–term strategic planning, public relations, as well as being a therapist to his daily clients. He is heavily involved in associations and with the Board of Advisors. Fairhaven also offers the Highlands Program, a national career and life planning process. He is also a founding board member of a regional behavioral health management service, Woodland Reserve Behavioral Health System, Inc. **Career Steps:** Owner/Director, Fairhaven Counseling, Inc. (1992–Present); Counselor, Human Development and Counseling Association (1981–1995); Chair and Associate Professor, Walsh University (1981–1987); Associate Professor, Notre Dame College of Ohio (1976–1981). **Associations & Accomplishments:** American Counseling Association; Ohio Counseling Association; National Board of Certified Counselors; American Association of Marriage and Family Therapists; Professional Association on Retardation of Ohio; American Association of Christian Counselors. **Education:** Kent State University: Ph.D. (1980), M.Ed.; Walsh University, M.A.; Houghton College, B.A. **Personal:** Married to Rebecca Tatter in 1970. Two children: Sara and Andrew. Dr. Myers enjoys Scottish history, church, and music.

Samuel M. Ricks, CDP, CSP
Chief Information Officer
Health Info Designs
9302 Lee Hiway, Suite 600
Fairfax, VA 22031–1214
(703) 218–5845
Fax: (703) 218–5810
EMAIL: See Below

8049

Business Information: Health Information Designs Inc. is one of several companies that make up the Value Health Corporation. It is a specialty–managed health care provider, providing all aspects of specialty–managed care benefit programs such as Pharmacy Benefit Management and Mental Health and Substance Abuse, Provider Profiling and many more. It provides services to more than 78 million people. As

Chief Information Officer, Mr. Ricks is responsible for all computer systems and related staff support. He can also be reached through the Internet via: SMRICKS@HID.VRX.VHI.COM **Career Steps:** Chief Information Officer, Health Info Designs (Present); President, Facilities & Systems, Inc.; Director Information Systems, Group Health Inc.; Director Information Systems, Warner Amex Cable. **Associations & Accomplishments:** Association of Systems Managers; Data Processing Management Association; Independent Computer Consultants Association. **Education:** Long Island University, BSAE (1979). **Personal:** Married in 1972. Two children: Iresha and Samuel III. Mr. Ricks enjoys being active in community activities.

Dr. Efrain Rodriguez Malave

Owner
Efrain Rodriguez Malave, N.D.
P.O. Box 4396
San Juan, Puerto Rico 00919
(809) 751–4682
Fax: (809) 767–4148

8049

Business Information: With eleven years of clinical experience and nine years of private practice experience in Naturopathic Medicine, Dr. Rodriguez Malave established his private practice office in Natural Medicine in 1987. His practice concentrates on the provision of naturopathic medicine through clinical nutrition, medicinal herbs, life style changes, homeopathy, etc. Patients suffering from stress, asthma, sinusitis, respiratory problems, prostate problems, arthritis, etc. are treated by this method. In addition, he serves as a frequent speaker, lobbyist (six years experience), and an educator of legislators and professionals on the benefits and services of naturopathic medicine. He also has ten years of theorical and practical organizational experience in environmental sciences. In Puerto Rico, Dr. Rodriguez Malave is recognized by the media as an expert in the theme of alternative medicine. **Career Steps:** Owner, Efrain Rodriguez–Malave, N.D. (1987–Present) **Associations & Accomplishments:** American Association of Naturopathic Physicians; Puerto Rico Association of Naturopathic Physicians; International Homeopathic Foundation; Homeopathic Academy of Naturopathic Physicians; National Center for Homeopathy; Published studies on "Mixed Modality Outcome Study of Adult and Pediatric Asthma" in the Journal of Naturopathic Medicine; Author of book, "Medicina Natural: Retorno a nuestra esencia." **Education:** National College of Naturopathic Medicine – Portland, Oregon, N.D. (1986); Interamerican University, B.S. in Biology (1981); Colegio Regional de Aguadilla – University of Puerto Rico, A.D. in Environmental Technology (1978); Dale Carnegie Institute: Strategies on Public Speaking (1991), Communication and Human Relations (1991).

Lillian T. Saavedra, M.D.
Doctor of Psychiatry
Orlando Psychiatric Group, PA
1315 South Orange Avenue, Suite 3–E
Orlando, FL 32806
(407) 849–0227
Fax: (407) 843–6095

8049

Business Information: Orlando Psychiatric Group, PA specializes in the practice of psychiatry. The Practice has been established since 1986. As Doctor of Psychiatry, Dr. Saavedra is one of the practicing psychiatrists with the Group. **Career Steps:** Doctor of Psychiatry, Orlando Psychiatric Group, PA (Present); Medical Director of Partial Hospitalization, Glenbeigh Hospital (1990–Present); Medical Director of Inpatient Psychiatry (1984–Present); Residency in Psychiatry, 9th University of Florida, Gainesville, FL (1982–1985); St. Frances Hospital, Peoria, Illinois: Internship in Medicine (1979–1990), Internship in Pathology (1978–1979); Senior House Officer, North Halerton, England (1972); House Officer, Bremen, West Germany (1971); Intern in Straight Neurology, Moscow, U.S.S.R. (1969–1970). **Associations & Accomplishments:** Member, American Medical Association; Member, American Physician Association; Member, F.P.A.; Member, W.M.A.; Member, O.C.M.S.; Award for Excellence, Psychiatric Residency (1985); Licensure: ECFMG #167–605–5 and FLEX #45693. **Education:** University of Moscow, Moscow, U.S.S.R., M.D. (1969); Lycee Razi, Tehran, Iran, B.S. in Biology; Attended high school and college in Tehran, Iran (1960–1962). **Personal:** Married to Oswald T. Saavedra, M.D. with two children.

Sherwood M. Smith Jr., Ph.D.
President, Psychologist
S.M. Smith Jr., Ph.D., P.C.
P.O. Box 29782
Atlanta, GA 30359
(770) 934–3963
Fax: (770) 934–2090

8049

Business Information: S.M. Smith Jr., Ph.D., P.C. is a clinical psychology practice, providing assessment, treatment and consultation in all aspects of mental–behavioral health issues. A Board–certified Clinical Psychologist in practice since 1969, Dr. Smith established the Cartersville office in 1981. As President he provides the overall administrative direction for a support staff of five, in addition to sharing clinical practices with one other associate, serving as the Senior Clinician. **Career Steps:** President and Senior Clinician, S.M. Smith Jr., Ph.D., P.C. (1981–Present); Chief Psychologist, Georgia Mental Health Institute (1971–1976). **Associations & Accomplishments:** American Psychological Association; Georgia Psychological Association; American Hellenic Educational Progressive Association; Psi Chi Honor Society; Fellow, American Board of Disability Analysts; Atlanta Hypnosis Society; Hellenic – American Who's Who; Archon of the Eastern Orthodox Ecumenical Patriarchate. **Education:** University of South Carolina: Ph.D. (1971), M.S. (1969), B.A. (1967) **Personal:** Married to Eugenia K. in 1969. Two children: Andrea R. and S. Manning, III.

Joseph C. Stankus, Ph.D.
Clinical Psychologist
Arbor Heights Mental Health Clinic, P.C.
8801 West Center Road, # 304
Omaha, NE 68124–2072
(402) 390–9894
Fax: (402) 390–6058

8049

Business Information: Arbor Heights Mental Health Clinic, P.C. is a full–service mental health clinic, providing a wide spectrum of therapeutic services to promote wellness in body, mind, and spirit. Purchasing a private practice from a psychiatrist in August 1991, Dr. Stankus formed Arbor Heights Mental Health Clinic, quadrupling the size of the professional staff from two to eight clinicians, including two psychiatrists, three clinical social workers (all LCSW's), and two counselors. Serving as President and Owner, he manages the entire clinic, in addition to serving as Clinical Psychologist, seeing patients and treating them for whatever problems they present. **Career Steps:** Clinical Psychologist, Arbor Heights Mental Health Clinic, P.C. (1991–Present); Clinical Psychologist, Outpatient Mental Health Clinic – Ehrling Bergquist Strategic Hospital, Offutt Air Force Base (1988–1991); Health Promotion Coordinator and Clinical Psychologist, 341st Strategic Hospital, Malmstrom Air Force Base (1985); Clinical Psychologist, USAF Regional Hospital Langley Air Force Base (1982–1985); Clinical Psychologist, USAF Clinic Kadena Air Base (1979–1982); Clinical Psychology Resident and APA Approved Internship, USAF Medical Center Wright–Patterson Air Force Base (1978–1979); Graduate Student in Residence, University of Minnesota (1977–1978); Instructor of Counseling Psychology Program, Far East Division University of Maryland – Camp Butler Okinawa, Japan (1981–1982); Chief, Test Construction Teamforce, USAF Occupational Measurement Center Lackland Air Force Base (1974–1977); Assessment Adjudicator, 3700 Personnel Resources Group Lackland Air Force Base (1971–1974); Research Assistant, University of Minnesota (1970–1971); Vocational Rehabilitation Counselor, Cooperative Vocation Rehabilitation Program Anoka Stake Hospital (1970); Research Assistant, University of Minnesota (1970); Counselor, Neighborhood Youth Corps (1969). **Associations & Accomplishments:** American Society of Clinical Hypnosis; International Society of Hypnosis; American Association for the Advancement of Science; Association of Private Practice Therapists. **Education:** University of Minnesota – Department of Psychology: Ph.D. (1982), M.A. (1972). **Personal:** Two children: Nicholas J. and Christina J. Dr. Stankus enjoys jogging, weightlifting, skiing, camping, choir, and landscaping.

Terry Varney Freerks, Ph.D.
Clinical Supervisor
Liss & Associates, Inc.
1353 Jeffco Boulevard
Arnold, MO 63010
(314) 296–1600
Fax: (314) 296–7685

8049

Business Information: Liss & Associates, Inc. provides comprehensive psychiatric and psychological services. Joining Liss & Associates, Inc. as Clinical Supervisor in 1974, Dr. Varney Freerks is responsible for the supervision of clinical staff and activities, in addition to her daily patient practice and oversight of counseling services. **Career Steps:** Clinical Supervisor, Liss & Associates, Inc. (1974–Present); Team Director, Clayton Shaw Parks Swimming Team (1974–Present); Private Practice (1990–1991); Adjunct Professor, Lindonwood College (1992–1995). **Associations & Accomplishments:** American Psychological Society; American Association for Marriage and Family Therapy; Association for Psychological Type; American Swimming Coaches Association – Level 5; National Board of Certified Counselors; American Association of Psychology; Licensed Counselor, State of Missouri; United States Swimming Committee; Education and Abuse Prevention. **Education:** Saint Louis University, Ph.D. (1989); University of Missouri: M.A. in Education, B.A. in History. **Personal:** Married to Stanley A. Freerks in 1979. Dr. Varney Freerks enjoys travel, reading, and competitive swimming.

Arlene Cupo, B.S.N.
Director of Nursing
Manor Care Nursing & Rehabilitation Center
6931 West Sunrise Boulevard
Ft. Lauderdale, FL 33313–4406
(954) 583–6200
Fax: (954) 584–8521

8050

Business Information: Manor Care Nursing & Rehabilitation Center, a part of Manor Health Care Corporation, is a full–capacity, long–term, skilled nursing care facility with 120 residents and a nursing staff of 85 people. As Director of Nursing, Ms. Cupo is responsible for diversified administrative activities, including managing all nursing staff, running the facilities, educational needs for the staff, and the maintenance of nursing standards. **Career Steps:** Director of Nursing, Manor Care Nursing & Rehabilitation Center (1994–Present); Nursing Director, Teaneck Nursing Center (1992–1993); Assistant Director of Nurses, Dunrover Nursing Center (1988–1992). **Associations & Accomplishments:** FADONA; NADONA; Florida Healthcare Association; South Florida Nurse Executives; Broward County Director of Nurses Association. **Education:** Felician College: B.S.N. (1991), A.A.S. (1974); Certification as Director of Nursing/LTC (1995). **Personal:** Married to Anthony in 1988. One child: Sandra. Ms. Cupo enjoys marine fishing, planting/gardening, and reading.

Irene H. Kawashima
Director of Nursing
Keiro Nursing Home
2221 Lincoln Park Avenue
Los Angeles, CA 90031–2920
(213) 225–1393
Fax: (213) 225–7267

8050

Business Information: Keiro Nursing Home is a provision of nursing care in the long–term care setting, specializing in meeting the physical, mental, and psychosocial well–being of the Japanese population. As Director of Nursing, Mrs. Kawashima is responsible for the organization and management of Nursing Services in the 300–bed facility. She is actively involved in the development, and growth and coordination of new programs and services. **Career Steps:** Director of Nursing, Keiro Nursing Home (1995–Present); Clinical Educator/Practitioner, Kaiser Permanente Hospital (1989–1995); Director of Nursing Services, Visiting Nurses Association (1983–1988). **Associations & Accomplishments:** California Nurse Association; AIDS Trainer; Sigma Theta Tau International Nursing Honor Society: Charter Member, President Elect, Nominations and ByLaws Committee; Oncology Nurse Society; NAVAN; NNSDO; Dean's List; Who's Who Among Students; American Nurses Association, Certification in Staff Development; Alpha Chi Omega Sorority. **Education:** California State University – Los Angeles: Master of Nursing (1994), B.S.N.; University of California – Los Angeles, B.A. in Economics. **Personal:** Married to Fred in 1984. Two children: Tracy and Michael. Mrs. Kawashima enjoys cooking and music.

David R. Adam
Executive Vice President
Simpson House
2101 Belmont Ave.
Philadelphia, PA 19131–1628
(215) 878–3600
Fax: (215) 878–6701

8051

Business Information: Established in 1865, Simpson House is a retirement community providing independent living, personal care, and nursing assistance for its 350–bed occupancy. With an annual budget of $10 million, the company presently employs 190 people. As Executive Vice President, Mr. Adam is responsible for overseeing and directing daily operations. **Career Steps:** Executive Vice President, Simpson House (1984–Present); Director of Resident Services, Ralston House (1977–1984); Director of Resident Services, Evangelical Manor (1976–1977). **Associations & Accomplish-**

ments: Bala Cynwyd–Narberth Rotary Club; Sons of the American Revolution; Published a booklet on Simpson House. **Education:** Eastern College, A.B. (1967); Eastern Seminary; Licensed Nursing Home Administrator. **Personal:** Mr. Adam enjoys public speaking, historical research, writing, genealogy, and antique restoration.

Charlene M. Akina

Activities Director
Convalescent Center of Honolulu
1900 Bachelot Street
Honolulu, HI 96817–2431
(808) 531–5302
Fax: (808) 537–1573

8051

Business Information: Convalescent Center of Honolulu is a 182 bed long–term care nursing facility with a specialized respiratory unit. As Activities Director and Consultant, Ms. Akina is responsible for administering therapeutic recreation programs and designing new rehabilitation and maintenance activities. Concurrently, she serves as Coordinator for Culinary and Health Arts at Kapiolani Community College, an educational institution best known for its culinary program. In this capacity, she implements creative international programs bridging both fields. **Career Steps:** Activities Director and Consultant, Convalescent Center of Honolulu (1994–Present); Kapiolani Community College: Coordinator for Culinary and Health Arts (1994–Present), Culinary Ethnic and Fine Arts Coordinator (1992–1994); Elderhostel Coordinator, University of Hawaii (1989–1991). **Associations & Accomplishments:** National Association of Activity Certified Professionals; Hawaii Association of Activity Coordinators; National Organization of Volunteer Leaders; YMCA; Boy Scouts of America; Hawaii Intergenerational Network; Hawaii Pacific Gerontological Association. **Education:** University of Hawaii: M.P.H. (1989), B.A. in Anthropology/History. **Personal:** Five children: Shane, Chelsi, Koryn, C. Jay, and Riann.

Virginia G. Alagano, R.N., B.S.N.

Charge Nurse
Debary Manor
1703 Creekwater Terrace #209
Lake Mary, FL 32746
(407) 324–7854
Fax: Please mail or call

8051

Business Information: Mrs. Alagano is currently employed in De Bary Manor, 60 North Hwy 17–92, De Bary, FL, which is a 120–bed skilled nursing facility providing care for geriatric patients. The Manor has a long–term care setting and a short–term care (rehabilitation) section. Mrs. Alagano is the Head Nurse in the short–term care section. She is responsible for diversified operational activities including administration, strategic planning, and care planning. She also filled in the position of Assistant Director of Nursing in the absence of the said person in charge. **Career Steps:** Head Nurse, De Bary Manor, FL (1995–Present); LPN–GN–Registered Nurse, Winter Park Memorial Hospital, FL (1991–1995); King Khaled Eye Specialist Hospital, Riyadh, Saudi Arabia: Infection Control Coordinator (1988–1991), Utilization Review Nurse Coordinator (1985–1987), Infection Control Nurse (1983–1985); Royal Globe Professional Placement Services, Inc., Philippines: Administrative Officer, Utilization Review Coordination Nurse, Training Coordinator (1987–1988); Santo Tomas University Hospital – Manila, Philippines: Infection Control Coordinator, Clinical Nurse Supervisor, Head Nurse (1980–1982), Staff Nurse (1977–1980); Staff Nurse, Pampanga E.E.N.T. and General Hospital – Pampanga, Philippines (1977). **Associations & Accomplishments:** Association of Practitioners in Infection Control; Philippine Nurses Association; National Orthopedic Nursing Association; National Association of Physician Nurses. **Education:** Manila Central University – Philippines, B.S. in Nursing (1979); St. Catherine Colleges – Quezon City, Philippines, Graduate in Nursing (1976); Santo Tomas University Hospital: Post Graduate Training Courses in Critical Care Nursing, Psychiatric Nursing, and Maternal & Child Nursing; Certification: IV Therapy, CPR. **Personal:** Married to Edwin V. in 1982. Two children: Gierwin Ian and Jayne Wingie. Ms. Alagano enjoys dancing, parties, tennis, and swimming.

Suzanne L. Alford

Senior Director of Quality Management
Beverly Enterprises
5111 Rogers Avenue
Ft. Smith, AR 72919–3324
(501) 452–6712
Fax: (501) 484–8402

8051

Business Information: Beverly Enterprises, Inc. is the nation's leading provider of long–term health care. Headquartered in Ft. Smith, Arkansas, Beverly Enterprises currently operates over 780 facilities across the U.S. (all operating under private names), providing services through Rehabilitation Centers, Nursing and Assisted Living Facilities, Retirement Centers, Sub–Acute Units, and Home Health Care Centers. As Senior Director of Quality Management, Ms. Alford is responsible for all aspects of the Quality Management Program and its field staff, as well as measuring the quality of services provided by the company. **Career Steps:** Senior Director of Quality Management, Beverly Enterprises (1986–Present); State Surveyor, Missouri – Division of Aging (1983–1986); Director of Nursing, Pemiscot County Memorial Hospital (1969–1983). **Associations & Accomplishments:** American Nurses Association; National League for Nursing; Board Member, Missouri League for Nursing; National Association of Health Care Quality. **Education:** St. Joseph College, B.S. (1983); Methodist Hospital School of Nursing. **Personal:** Married to John in 1961. Two children: Christie Lewis Curtis and Kale Walsh. Ms. Alford enjoys antique furniture and gardening.

Gary K. Atchley

President/Chief Executive Officer
Country Woods Care Facility
P O Box 427
Festus, MO 63028–0427
(314) 937–3150
Fax: (314) 937–3989

8051

Business Information: Country Woods Care Facility an 81–bed, regional, skilled nursing facility with an 18–bed Alzheimers unit. The Facility, established in 1992, is located in Festus, Missouri. With estimated annual revenue of $5 million, the Facility presently employs 61 people. As President/Chief Executive Officer, Mr. Atchley oversees the day–to–day operations of the Facility. His responsibilities include cash management, general financial concerns, marketing of services, public relations, and strategic planning for the future. Concurrently, Mr. Atchley is the owner of Investigations Unlimited, a private investigation firm specializing in workman's compensation, fraud, missing persons, and accident reconstruction cases. **Career Steps:** President/Chief Executive Officer, Country Woods Care Facility (1993–Present); Chairman/Owner, Investigations Unlimited (1984–Present). **Education:** School of Mortuary, Associate Degree (1979); Degree in Mortuary Science; Law Enforcement Degree, 36 weeks State Police Academy. **Personal:** Married to Linda in 1988. Four children: Gary K. Jr., Tina, Tracey, and Mellisa. Mr. Atchley enjoys fishing, camping, hunting, water skiing, and skeet shooting.

Paul E. Bachschneider

Administrator
Golden Crest Healthcare Center
2413 1st Avenue
Hibbing, MN 55746–2101
(218) 262–1081
Fax: (218) 262–4976

8051

Business Information: Golden Crest Healthcare Center is an 84–bed, regional, skilled nursing care facility in Hibbing, Minnesota. The Center specializes in sub–acute care and has a 40% rehabilitation rate. As Administrator, Mr. Bachschneider is responsible for all aspects of operations for the Center, including administrative support for a staff of 120. **Career Steps:** Administrator, Golden Crest Healthcare Center (1991–Present); Administrator, Colonial Manor of Balaton (1987–1991). **Associations & Accomplishments:** Care Providers of Minnesota; Secretary, Hibbing/Chisholm Breakfast Rotary. **Education:** University of Minnesota, B.G.S. (1986). **Personal:** Mr. Bachschneider enjoys retreating to his cabin.

W. Christine Bangtson

Director of Social Services
Hearthstone
2901 East Barnett
Medford, OR 97504–8308
(541) 779–4221
Fax: (541) 779–8294

8051

Business Information: Hearthstone is one of the largest long–term care facilities in the state of Oregon. A non–profit organization, Hearthstone is a 161–bed facility for functionally and mentally–impaired individuals. With thirteen years experience in the healthcare field, Ms. Bangtson joined Hearthstone as Director of Social Services in 1989. She is responsible for the admission and discharge of residents, ensuring the psychosocial needs of all residents are addressed, overseeing all residents' rights, managing any complaints or concerns from families or residents, and evaluating residents' mental health needs. Ms. Bangston was very instrumental in establishing the Alzheimer's Unit at Hearthstone, which was the forerunner of such units in the valley. Other duties include managing all the Social Services staff, and support in the area of family counseling. **Career Steps:** Hearthstone: Director of Social Services, Director of Recreation; Rogue Valley Medical Center: Director of Senior Services, Director of Social Work (1989–Present); Elderbridge Agency on Aging: Caregiver Support Coordinator (1986–1989), Nutrition Supervisor (1983–1986); Teacher, Lyons Township High School and Junior College (1968–1970).. **Associations & Accomplishments:** Oregon Long Term Care Social Worker Association; Southern Oregon Alzheimer Board; Ascension Lutheran Church and Senior Choir; Phi Upsilon Omicron. **Education:** Iowa State University, M.S.F.E. (1983); Ohio University, B.S. in Home Economics. **Personal:** Married to Edward in 1985. Three children: Laura Dolan, and Keith and Todd Brown. Ms. Bangtson enjoys travel, art work (pen & ink), crafts, stitchery, gardening, hiking, and reading.

Steven K. Booth, RS, BSN

Director of Nursing
Johannas Courtyard Care Center
433 East 2700 South
Salt Lake City, UT 84115–3325
(801) 487–2248
Fax: (801) 466–7262

8051

Business Information: Johannas Courtyard Care Center is a 41–bed nursing home facility specializing in providing inpatient nursing and rehabilitative services to patients who require continuous healthcare. As Director of Nursing, Mr. Booth is directly responsible for all nursing services and personnel. **Career Steps:** Director of Nursing, Johannas Courtyard Care Center (1993–Present); Director of Staff Education, Horizon Health Care (1992–1993); Assistant Director of Nursing, Doxey Hatch Medical Center (1989–1992). **Associations & Accomplishments:** National Association of Nursing; Utah Long Term Care Association, 1994 Nurse of the Year, Long Term Care. **Education:** Webster State University, B.S.N. (1992); University of Utah, B.A. in Business Management (1984). **Personal:** Two children: Matthew and Mark. Mr. Booth enjoys horseback riding, gardening, and reading.

Cindy G. Briggs, RN

Director of Nursing
Starmount Villa Nursing Center
109 South Holden Road
Greensboro, NC 27407
(910) 292–5390
Fax: (910) 852–5479

8051

Business Information: Starmount Villa Nursing Center is a long–term care 126–bed facility. The facility has a mostly geriatric, in–patient population and also contains a health rehabilitation department. Starmount Villa is part of Beverly Enterprises, one of the nation's largest health and nursing care management concerns. As Director of Nursing, Ms. Briggs oversees all administrative operations for all nursing and support staff. She is responsible for recruitment, training, evaluating, and scheduling of the nursing staff. Other duties include quality assurance, financial concerns, and budgetary concerns. Ms. Briggs acts as a liaison between the nursing staff and the medical staff. **Career Steps:** Starmount Villa Nursing Center: Director of Nursing (1996–Present), RN Assessment Coordinator (1995–1996); RN Unit Manager, Wilmac Corporation (1992–1995); Program Coordinator–RN, Chandler Hall Nursing Services (1989–1992). **Education:** Presbyterian Nursing School, RN (1982); Attended: Bucks County Community College and Camdon County Community College. **Personal:** Married to Dale in 1981. Three children: Randi–Marie, Kelleye, and Raymond. Ms. Briggs enjoys reading, gardening, cooking, and being with her family.

Melinda Cade Brockwell

Director of Nursing
Connecticut Hospice
61 Burban Drive
Branford, CT 06405–4003
(203) 481–6231 Ext. 302
Fax: (203) 483–9539

8051

Business Information: Connecticut Hospice is a palliative and supportive care program designed for patients with an advanced irreversible illness and their family members. Established in 1974, it is the first American hospice and presently employs over 300 people. In addition to extensive home care services, Connecticut Hospice has its own inpatient facility. As Director of Nursing, Ms. Brockwell is responsible for quality, utilization, and leadership development in the management of patient care services and nursing personnel. Ms. Brockwell can be reached on the World Wide Web via: http:\\www.hospice.bom. **Career Steps:** Director of Nursing, Connecticut Hospice (1993–Present); Director of Medical Oncology Patient Support Services, Norwalk Hospital (1977–1993); Oncology Nurse, Norwalk Medical Group P.C. (1974–1977). **Associations & Accomplishments:** Oncology Nursing Society; Sigma Theta Tau, National Nursing Honor

Society; National Hospice Organization; Advanced Practice Certification in Oncology Nursing (1995). **Education:** College of New Rochelle, M.S. Nursing; Pace University, B.S.N.; Norwalk Hospital School of Nursing, Diploma; Attended the University of Connecticut. **Personal:** Married to James in 1986. Four children: Carin Cade, Mark, Greg, and Kurt Brockwell. Ms. Brockwell enjoys running, biking, and gardening.

Cynthia A. Brown

Director of Nursing Services
Community Nursing and Rehabilitation Center
850 West Poe Road
Bowling Green, OH 43402–1219
(419) 352–7558
Fax: (419) 352–8719

8051

Business Information: Community Nursing and Rehabilitation Center, owned by Beverly Enterprises, is a long–term care and rehabilitation service facility with 100 beds (75 – long term, 25 – skilled care). Current staffing includes: 25 skilled nurses, 60 nurses aides, a medical director, 8 physicians with attending privileges, and a full rehabilitation team. Joining Community Nursing Home as Director of Nursing Services in 1994, Ms. Brown serves as the second in command of the Facility, overseeing all nursing services, including administration, evaluations, training, policy and procedures, reviewing medical records, infection control, and ensuring quality assurance surveys go smoothly. She attributes her success to a strong work ethic instilled in her by her parents. **Career Steps:** Director of Nursing Services, Community Nursing Home, a subsidiary of Beverly Enterprises (1994–Present); St. Francis Health Care Center: MDS + Coordinator (1992–1994), Long Term Coma Floor Unit Manager (1991–1992), Assistant Unit Manager (1988–1991). **Associations & Accomplishments:** Rehabilitation Nurses Association; Rehabilitation Hospital Association; International Member, La Leche League; Member, St. Thomas Moore Catholic Church; Teaches nursing; Public Speaker. **Education:** Marion Technological College, A.S. in Nursing (1988); Certification in Rehabilitative Nursing; ACLS Certified, Basic Life Support Instructor; Certification in Restorative Nursing; Certified as a Substitute Instructor for School of Practical Nursing. **Personal:** Married to Ronald L. in 1988. Three children: Daniel, Matthew, and Jamie. Ms. Brown enjoys reading, crafts, and baking.

Patricia C. Buckley

Manager
VNACJ Foundation
625 Bangs Avenue
Asbury Park, NJ 07712
(908) 502–5122
Fax: (908) 774–6006

8051

Business Information: VNACJ Foundation is a management company of long–term care community–based programs for the elderly, disabled, and special need population (AIDS patients). They have four locations in New Jersey and are the fifth largest home health care Company in the United States. As Manager, Mrs. Buckley's responsibilities include management of ten programs of long– term care for New Jersey Department of Health and NJDHS along with a Ryan White Title II AIDS Consortium. She does all grant writing for programs and is involved in establishing and implementing annual budgets for the various programs. Mrs. Buckley organizes 14 BSN's and MSW Nurses' schedules and does case management for 200 clients at any given time. **Career Steps:** Manager, VNACJ Foundation (1988–Present); Director, Private Care Services of MCOSS (1983–1988); Director HHA Services, CHC of North Jersey (1976–1983); Supervisor of Nursing, CNS of Essex and West Hudson (1972–1976). **Associations & Accomplishments:** Governor's Advisory Council on AIDS; Chapter President, Association of Nurses in AIDS Care; N.J.SNA and HIV Forum. **Education:** Georgetown University, B.S.N. (1956). **Personal:** Married to Thomas T. in 1958. Four children: Brian, Catherine, Michael, and Ellen. Mrs. Buckley enjoys playing bridge, walking on the beach, and her grandchildren.

Paul Burrowes III

Director of Projects
United Methodist Homes of New Jersey
3311 State Route 33, P.O. Box 0667
Neptune, NJ 07754–0667
(908) 922–9802
Fax: (908) 922–9375

8051

Business Information: United Methodist Homes of New Jersey provides housing and skilled nursing care for 1,100 elderly men and women. The Homes specialize in all forms of care, assisted living, residential, rehabilitation, and provides low income housing for elderly residents. As Director of Projects, Mr. Burrowes oversees planning, design, and construction of all new facilities. He also handles job site preparation, interior design, renovations, oversight of construction with engineers, and architectural design review. **Career Steps:** Director of Projects, United Methodist Homes of New Jersey (1989–Present); Construction Manager, Lakeside Homes (1987–1989); Owner, WB Construction (1973–1987). **Associations & Accomplishments:** New Jersey Association of Non–Profit Homes for the Aged; National Fire Protection Association; American Association for Healthcare Engineers; President, Hospital Engineers Association of Southern New Jersey. **Education:** Teterburo School of Aeronautics, Aircraft and Powerplant Mechanic. **Personal:** Married to Dolores in 1960. Three children: Angel Somers, Paul IV, and Kimberly Berlen.

Jamie E. Campbell

Administrator
Beverly Enterprises Blue Ridge Haven East
3625 North Progress Avenue
Harrisburg, PA 17110–9690
(717) 652–2345
Fax: (717) 652–3034

8051

Business Information: Blue Ridge Haven East, a 95–bed nursing home, is one of 700 long term care facilities in Pennsylvania owned by Beverly Enterprises. Ms. Campbell joined Beverly Enterprises upon conferral of her law degree in 1993. She served as an Assistant Administrator at Sleepy Hollow Nursing Facility until 1994, accepting an Administrative position at Mansion Nursing Facility in April of 1994, and moving into her present position at Blue Ridge Haven East in November of 1994. Her duties at Blue Ridge include oversight of daily operations, budget management, accounts payable and receivable, and ensuring compliance with all applicable state and federal laws. **Career Steps:** Beverly Enterprises: Administrator, Blue Ridge Haven East (1994–Present), Administrator, Mansion Nursing Facility (Apr.1994–Nov.1994), Assistant Administrator, Sleepy Hollow Nursing Facility (1993–1994) **Associations & Accomplishments:** Pennsylvania Health Care Association: Government Relations Committee, Legal Task Force. **Education:** Widener Law School, J.D. (1993); Indiana University of Pennsylvania: B.A. in Psychology, B.A. in History. **Personal:** Ms. Campbell enjoys travel and scuba diving.

Mr. Timothy B. Cassidy

President
Elder Care, Inc.
901 Ernston Road
South Amboy, NJ 08879
(908) 721–8788
Fax: (908) 721–2932

8051

Business Information: Elder Care, Inc. provides management and consulting services for long–term care facilities, assisted living, retirement housing and rehabilitation programs in New Jersey, Connecticut, New York, Michigan and Virginia. As President, Mr. Cassidy oversees management of all company operations, administration and regulatory compliance, and quality assurance. Established in 1990, Elder Care, Inc. employs a professional staff of over 180 and reports annual revenue in excess of $9 million. **Career Steps:** President, Elder Care, Inc. (1990–Present); President, G.C. Management, Inc. (1988–Present); Executive Director, Preventive Care Centers, Inc. (1993–Present); President, Meg Management Corporation (1983–1990). **Associations & Accomplishments:** Co–Founder, Preventive Aging Center, Inc., a non-profit senior wellness provider of free health care screenings and professional lectures on senior and health care issues, and developer of intergenerational programs reaching and benefitting thousands of people. **Education:** Rutgers University (1976)

Dayna Colaizzi

Administrator
Sidney Square Convalescent Center
2112 Sidney Street
Pittsburgh, PA 15203–1911
(412) 481–5566
Fax: (412) 481–5640

8051

Business Information: Sidney Square Convalescent Center, a regional chain of Grane Health Care, is a long–term nursing care facility specializing in providing in–patient nursing and rehabilitative services to patients who require continuous healthcare. Services include, but are not limited to subacutes and telemetry programs. As Administrator, Ms. Colaizzi is responsible for the administration of all aspects of Company operations. **Career Steps:** Grane Health Care: Administrator (1991–Present), Director of Nursing (1989–1990); Director of Nursing, Kane (1990). **Associations & Accomplishments:** Taught CCD and volunteer work with her local school and church. **Education:** Shadyside Hospital School of Nursing, Nursing (1976). **Personal:** Married to Donald in 1978. Two children: Gina and Jeff.

Catherine M. Congo

Administrator
Wingate at Reading
1364 Main Street
Reading, MA 01867
(617) 942–1210
Fax: (617) 942–7251

8051

Business Information: Wingate at Reading is a 123–bed skilled nursing and rehabilitation facility that is Medicare certified and Joint Commission accredited. As Administrator, Ms. Congo oversees the daily operation of the Facility. Her responsibilities include overall operations and fiscal management, development and implementation of patient care programs, and public relations. Ms. Congo is involved in maintaining the quality of the care patients receive while they are at Wingate at Reading. **Career Steps:** Wingate at Reading: Administrator (1994–Present), Director of Social Services (1993–1994); Social Worker, Holy Family Hospital and Medical Center (1987–1993); Social Worker, Whittier Rehabilitation Hospital (1982–1987). **Associations & Accomplishments:** American College of Health Care Administrators; Merrimack Valley Health Care Social Workers; Methuen Conservation Commission (1994–1995). **Education:** Suffolk University, M.P.A. (1992); Merrimack College, B.S. (1977). **Personal:** Two children: Jeffrey and Brian. Ms. Congo enjoys gardening, golf, cooking, reading, boating, travel, spending time with family and friends and is a facilitator of a Breast Cancer Support Group.

Yvette Crespo

Director of Administration/Senior Staff Executive
The Meadows of Napa Valley
1800 Atrium Parkway
Napa, CA 94559–4800
(707) 257–7885
Fax: (707) 257–6915

8051

Business Information: The Meadows of Napa Valley is a retirement community providing assisted–living units and a skilled–nursing center for 300 residents. As Director of Administration, Ms. Crespo is responsible for human resource functions and serves as Assistant to the Executive Director. **Career Steps:** Director of Administration, The Meadows of Napa Valley (1994–Present); Executive Assistant, Embarcadero Center (1991–1993); Executive Assistant, Tri Realtors (1988–1993). **Associations & Accomplishments:** National Notary. **Education:** Attended, Napa College. **Personal:** Four children: Peter, Jaime, Michael, and Christopher. Ms. Crespo enjoys reading, computers, and increasing her knowledge.

Linda L. Csiza, PT

Physical Therapy Director
Cherry Hills Health Care Center
3575 South Washington Street
Englewood, CO 80110–3807
(303) 789–2265
Fax: (303) 781–8808

8051

Business Information: Cherry Hills Health Care Center is a long–term care facility with a subacute rehabilitation department. The 91–bed Center, an affiliate of Vencore Corporation, offers all forms of therapy, including IV, Physical, Occupational, and Speech. As Physical Therapy Director, Ms. Csiza is responsible for patient care, physical therapy administration duties, staffing issues, education, human resource functions, and program development. **Career Steps:** Physical Therapy Director, Cherry Hills Health Care Center (1995–Present); Pediatric Lead Therapist, The Well Mill, PC (1992–1995); Lead Physical Therapist, Arlington Memorial Hospital (1991–1992); Physical Therapist, Mid Cities Back and Neck Clinic (1990–1991); Physical Therapist, Parkland Memorial Hospital (1989–1990). **Associations & Accomplishments:** American Physical Therapy Association; Texas Physical Therapy Association; IDF. **Education:** Texas Women's University, B.S. in Physical Therapy (1989). **Personal:** Married to Gyula in 1974. Three children: Cristina, Veronica, and Steven. Ms. Csiza enjoys dancing, gymnastics, Tae Kwon Do, and running.

Diana J. Curzon, R.N.
Director of Nursing
Southminster, Inc.
8919 Park Road
Charlotte, NC 28210–7610
(704) 551–7119
Fax: Please mail or call

8051

Business Information: Southminster, Inc. is a private retirement community located on twelve acres in Charlotte, North Carolina, providing long–term care to residents. Governed by a Board of Directors, including members from two churches and local business owners, the Facility provides more than 200 one– and two–bedroom apartments and cottages and a 80–bed rest home (67–beds are in a skilled nursing unit). With thirty–five years of experience in nursing and over twelve years expertise in skilled nursing, Mrs. Curzon joined Southminster in 1995. Serving as Director of Nursing, she is responsible for all aspects of in–house and on campus nursing activities. **Career Steps:** Director of Nursing, Southminster, Inc. (1995–Present); Owner/Operator of Rest Home, D. Curzon, Inc. (1992–1994); ADON, Beverly Enterprises (1990–1992); Ventilator Unit Manager, Hawthorne Nursing Center (1988–1990). **Associations & Accomplishments:** Adult Choir, First Baptist Church; Union County Red Cross Disaster Team. **Education:** Queen Elizabeth Hospital School of Nursing – Birmingham, England, B.S.N. (1960). **Personal:** Four children: John, Sarah, Iain, and Caroline. Mrs. Curzon enjoys reading, crafts, and her grandchildren.

Danna L. Daily, R.N.
Director of Nursing
Medicalodge of Columbus
101 North Lee
Columbus, KS 66725
(316) 429–2134
Fax: (316) 429–2246

8051

Business Information: Medicalodge of Columbus is a 89–bed, long–term geriatric nursing care facility. As Director of Nursing, Ms. Daily oversees all aspects of the Facility. Her duties include staff supervision, direct resident care, acting as House Supervisor, monitoring wound and skin coordination, infection control coordination, staff education, serving as Hospice Contact Person, and serving as liaison between the Facility and occupational, physical, and speech consultants, podiatrists, and pharmaceutical consultants. Additional duties include Acting Resource Person for other professional nursing staff, and writing policies and procedures. **Career Steps:** Director of Nursing, Medicalodge of Columbus (1996–Present); Assistant Director of Nursing, St. Lukes Nursing Center (1995–1996); Staff Nurse, Visiting Nurse Association of South West Massachusetts (1994–1995); Clinical Nurse, Department of Justice, B.O.P. (1987–1994). **Associations & Accomplishments:** Methodist Church; Eastern Star, Bethel Chapter; Tenth Missouri (C.S.A. and U.S.A.) Civil War Re–Enactment Unit; National Association of Directors of Nursing Administration and Long Term Care (NADONALTC/LTC). **Education:** Belleville Area College, A.A.S. in Nursing (1983). **Personal:** Two children: Anne Michelle and Catherine Marie Zellmer. Ms. Daily enjoys Civil War re–enacting, gardening, and music of all kinds.

Maurice M. Dalton Jr.
Executive Director
Riddle Village Lifecare Community
1048 West Baltimore Pike
Media, PA 19063–5149
(610) 891–3784
Fax: (610) 891–3671

8051

Business Information: Riddle Village Lifecare Community is a continuing care retirement community, providing independent living services, assisted living services, and skilled nursing services to senior citizens over the age of 65. Currently the facility has 300 units, all of which are occupied, and a waiting list of 100 potential residents. In operation since 1988, Riddle Village currently employs 200 medical professionals and staff members. As Executive Director, Mr. Dalton is responsible for all aspects of operations, including new residents, budget functions and daily operations. **Career Steps:** Executive Director, Riddle Village Lifecare Community (1993–Present); Executive Director, CRSA – Memphis, TN (1986–1993); Vice President and General Manager, Babe's Ace Hardware – Venice, FL (1973–1986). **Associations & Accomplishments:** Columbus College Alumni; Fraternal Order of Masons; Rotary Club; American Association of Homes and Services for the Aging; Pennsylvania Association of Homes and Services for the Aging; Colorado Gerontological Society; Who's Who of American College Athletes (1973); Bass Anglers Sportsmans Society. **Education:** Columbus College at Georgia: B.S. in Education (1973), B.S. in Social Studies, B.S. in Business. **Personal:** Married to Robin in 1977. Two children: Holly and Matthew. Mr. Dalton enjoys baseball, golf, the sym-

phony orchestra, bass fishing, and spending time with his family.

Mary L. Deane
Director of Health Services
Sunnyside Center
1824 South Van Buren Street
Enid, OK 73703–7903
(405) 233–6422
Fax: (405) 242–4322

8051

Business Information: Sunnyside Center is an intermediate care facility for developmentally disabled adults. As Director of Health Services, Ms. Deane is responsible for the supervision of all Nursing and Medical Services, Interdisciplinary Team Members, personnel hiring, and various administrative activities. **Career Steps:** Director of Health Services, Sunnyside Center (1995–Present); Consultant/Administrator, County Health Services (1971–1986 and 1989–1995); Consultant/Administrator, Oklahoma Nursing Homes Ltd. (1988–1989); Consultant/Administrator, Amity Care Corporation (1986–1988). **Associations & Accomplishments:** Enid Civilian Club; State Board, Oklahoma Development Corporation; Industrial Board Eastern Oklahoma County Vo–Tech; President's National Council of Women in the Work Place. **Education:** Western Oklahoma State College, Sociology (1981); Wordward Hospital School of Nursing; Oklahoma School of Nursing Home Administration; Oklahoma School of Preceptor for Nursing Home Administration. **Personal:** Two children: Curtis Deane and Louise Deane Dunn. Ms. Deane enjoys antiques, physical fitness, and fishing.

Donna M. Deitch
Administrator
Grant Street Health and Rehabilitation Center
425 Grant Street
Bridgeport, CT 06610–3222
(203) 366–5255
Fax: (203) 368–4389
E MAIL: See Below

8051

Business Information: Grant Street Health and Rehabilitation Center, established in 1975, is a skilled nursing and rehabilitation center for Medicare/Medicaid, managed care and private insurance patients. The center presently has 250 employees. As Administrator, Ms. Deitch has oversight of the day–to–day operations of the Center. She works closely with department heads on recruiting, scheduling, training, and evaluating staff. Other duties include developing, implementing, and monitoring budgets for the Center. Internet users can reach her via: ddeitch782@aol.com. **Career Steps:** Grant Street Health and Rehabilitation Center: Administrator for several multi–facility corporations (1987–Present). **Associations & Accomplishments:** Vestry Member, St. Peter's Episcopal Church. **Education:** Hartford Graduate Center, M.S.; Quinnipiac College, B.S. in Health Administration. **Personal:** Married to Barry in 1984. Three children: Dan and Paul Terrill and Wendy Deitch. Ms. Deitch enjoys weaving, sewing, and Civil War history.

Kandi L. Dye
Administrator
Parkway Manor Care Center (Texas Health Enterprises)
114 Cherry Avenue
Lubbock, TX 79403
(806) 765–8608
Fax: (806) 765–9323

8051

Business Information: Parkway Manor Care Center (Texas Health Enterprises) is a long–term care facility with 59 beds. The Center provides speech, physical, occupational, respiratory, and IV therapies for Medicare, Medicaid, and private paying patients. As Administrator, Ms. Dye oversees the daily operation of the Facility. She works with staff to develop and implement programs beneficial to residents and strives to improve the quality of care provided. Other responsibilities include public relations and strategic planning for the future. **Career Steps:** Administrator, Parkway Manor Care Center (Texas Health Enterprises) (1995–Present); Assistant Administrator, Grapevine 400 (1994–1995). **Associations & Accomplishments:** Former Member of Texas Health Care Association. **Education:** Southwestern Adventist College, B.B.A. (1993). **Personal:** Ms. Dye enjoys basketball, volleyball, and reading.

Ruth Eddy

Administrator/President
Forester Nursing Home
524 Canton Road
Wintersville, OH 43952–3909
(614) 264–7788
Fax: (614) 264–7765

8051

Business Information: Forester Nursing Home. established in 1947, is a private, 50–bed, skilled nursing facility. As President, Ms. Eddy oversees the day–to–day operations of the Facility. Her responsibilities include patient care and welfare, staff recruitment and training, marketing of facility services, and public relations. **Career Steps:** Forester Nursing Home: Administrator/President (1996–Present), Administrator/Vice President (1985–1996), Administrator (1956–1985). **Associations & Accomplishments:** Jefferson County Nursing Home Administration Association; Advisory Committee, Jefferson County Joint Vocational School; Advisory Member, Jefferson Community College: EMT Program, Medical Assistant Program. **Personal:** Married to George in 1949. Two children: Denise and George. Ms. Eddy enjoys gardening (in 1971 was awarded Outstanding Gardener of the Year by the Jefferson County Garden Club, Region 12), fishing, and camping.

Rochelle M. Faber, R.N.
Director of Nursing
Community Care of America at La Villa Grande
2501 Little Bookcliff Drive
Grand Junction, CO 81501–8802
(970) 245–1211
Fax: (970) 245–4437

8051

Business Information: Community Care of America at La Villa Grande is a 104–bed, skilled, residential nursing facility for the aged and infirm. With twelve years experience in nursing, Ms. Faber joined the Community Care of America at La Villa Grande as Director of Nursing in 1995. She is responsible for the direction of all nursing activities, including hiring, firing, scheduling, and supervision of a staff of 70 RNs and LPNs. **Career Steps:** Director of Nursing, Community Care of America at La Villa Grande (1995–Present); House Supervisor, IHS of Mesa Manor (1993–1995); Allergy Nurse, Colorado West Otolaryngologist (1992–1993); Director of Nursing, Unicare (1991–1992). **Education:** Madisonville Community College, A.S.N. (1984). **Personal:** Married to Terry Lee in 1994. Five children: Candace, Stephanie, Joseph, Anastassia, and Lance. Ms. Faber enjoys crocheting, reading, and fishing.

Alda H. Forte, RN, MS
Director of Administration
Herbert Gregg Home
24 AA Estate Kings Hill
St. Croix, Virgin Islands 00850
(809) 778–1323
Fax: Please mail or call

8051

Business Information: The Herbert Gregg Home is a federally–subsidized 98–bed nursing home facility. The Home provides nursing and medical services to patients ranging in age 60 years and older. As Director of Administration, Mrs. Forte is responsible for a staff of 73, the total management of the nursing home, and diversified administrative activities. **Career Steps:** Herbert Gregg Home: Director of Administration (1987–Present), Nursing Supervisor (1973–1981); Nursing Instructor, University of the Virgin Islands (1984). **Associations & Accomplishments:** Association of Seventh Day Adventist Nurses; Clerk, Seventh Day Adventist Church; Judge St. Croix Orchid Society. **Education:** Loma Linda University: M.S. (1971), B.S. (1966); Atlantic Union College/New England Sanitarium & Hospital School of Nursing, Nursing degree. **Personal:** Married to Hugh in 1965. Two children: Marcel and Dwane. Mrs. Forte enjoys gardening, orchidology, camping, swimming, travel, and floral designing.

Harriett M. Fredericksen, R.N.
Director of Nursing
Gaspard Nursing Care Center
2689 65th Street
Port Arthur, TX 77640
(409) 736–1541
Fax: (409) 736–2030

8051

Business Information: Gaspard Nursing Care Center is a long–term skilled nursing facility with 102 beds. Established in 1973, the Facility has 65 employees and is located in Port Arthur, Texas. As Director of Nursing, Ms. Fredericksen is in charge of a staff of 40 people. She handles recruiting of staff, verification of credentials, scheduling, and training. Ms. Fredericksen develops and updates job descriptions, handles personnel concerns, establishes budgets, and maintains quality service while ensuring low overhead. She is responsible for planning, organizing, directing, coordinating, reporting, budgeting and management of facilities, people, supplies and equipment. She is responsible for nursing 24 hours a day. **Career Steps:** Director of Nursing, Gaspard Nursing Care Center (1995–Present); Charge Nurse, Byrd Hospital (1994–1995); Staff R.N. Psyche Unit, Lake Charles Memorial Hospital (1995); Charge Nurse, DeQuincy Hospital (1993–1994). **Associations & Accomplishments:** American Nurses Association; Donaset. **Education:** Lamar University: A.D.R.N. (1993), L.V.N. (1992), A.S. in Academic Studies, Concentration in Psychology, A.S. in Academic Studies, Concentration in Sociology. **Personal:** One child: Rayne B.. Ms. Fredericksen enjoys gardening and reading.

Mary J. Gernetzke

Director of Admissions
Middleton Village Nursing & Rehabilitation Center
6201 Elmwood Avenue
Middleton, WI 53562–3319
(608) 831–8300
Fax: (608) 831–4253

8051

Business Information: Middleton Village Nursing & Rehabilitation Center is a 97–bed skilled nursing facility and member of PersonaCare family of centers based in Atlanta, GA. The Center offers long–term, rehabilitative, sub–acute, and Alzheimers care on specially designed and dedicated hallways. As Director of Admissions, Ms. Gernetzke is directly responsible for facilitating admissions and hospitality services. She researches and supplies the Facility continuously with ways to improve the conditions of the Village. **Career Steps:** Director of Admissions, Middleton Village Nursing & Rehabilitation Center (1992–Present); Admissions Director, Leader Nursing & Rehabilitation Center (1990–1992); Vocational Specialist, New Medico, Inc. (1989–1990); Director of Vocational Training, Goodwill Industries (1986–1989). **Associations & Accomplishments:** President, Dane County Committee on Aging; Continuity of Care; Wisconsin Nursing Home Social Workers Association; Task Force for Dane County Commission of Aging Resource Fair; Middleton Chamber of Commerce; Available as public speaker on topics related to aging issues. **Education:** University of Wisconsin – Whitewater, B.A. in Social Work (1974); Numerousworkshops, conferences, and seminars. **Personal:** Two children: Sarah and Michael. Ms. Gernetzke enjoys sports and politics.

Nora Gregoire, R.N.

In–Service/Education Director
Thunderbird Healthcare Center
8825 South 7th Street
Phoenix, AZ 85040
(602) 243–6121
Fax: Please mail or call

8051

Business Information: Thunderbird Healthcare Center, a part of SUNRISE Healthcare Corporation, is a long– term care nursing home. As In–Service/Education Director, Ms. Gregoire instructs all CNA classes. She also oversees all continuing education and in–service education for Thunderbird's staff. **Career Steps:** Inservice Education Director, Thunderbird Healthcare Center (1994–Present); DON Director of Nursing, Park Regency Health Care Center (1993–1994); RN Staff Nurse, Hearthstone of MESA (1991–1993). **Education:** Phoenix College, RN (1991); Orem Valley Community College, LPN. **Personal:** Two children: Kelly and Bradley Willes. Ms. Gregoire enjoys water skiing, fast cars, and boats.

Jeanne Guddee

Administrator
Pleasant Care Napa
630 Ross Court
Sonoma, CA 95476
(707) 996–2781
Fax: (707) 255–1015

8051

Business Information: Pleasant Care Napa is a 62–bed skilled nursing facility that is Medicare certified, has HMO and Hospice contracts, and offers rehabilitation services (respiratory, IV, and speech). As Administrator, Ms. Guddee oversees all aspects of the facility, including medical records, social services, nurses, staff development, dietary needs, and all business functions. **Career Steps:** Administrator, Pleasant Care Napa (1995–Present); Regency Health Services: Director of Nursing Services (1994–1995), Administrator (1993–1994), Care Home Health Case Manager (1989–1996). **Associations & Accomplishments:** National Nurses Association; Former Member: Sonoma Chamber of Commerce, Sister Cities Association of Sonoma. **Education:** Medical University of Southern California School of Nursing, R.N. (1966). **Personal:** Three children: Allison, Matthew, and Lindsay.

Edith Haber

Director of Nursing Services
Latah Health Services
510 West Palouse River Drive
Moscow, ID 83843
(208) 882–7586
Fax: (208) 883–4473

8051

Business Information: Latah Health Services is a long–term health care facility providing skilled nurses in homehealth, subacute, and Alzheimer's. As Director of Nursing Services, Ms. Haber is responsible for 20 nurses, 50 nursing assistants, and 84 patients. Her responsibilities include overseeing patient care and managing daily operations. **Career Steps:** Latah Health Services: Director of Nursing Services (1996–Present), Staff Development Coordinator (1992–1996); Staff Development Coordinator, Palouse Hills Nursing Center (1990–1992); Director of Nursing Service, Palouse Hills Nursing Center (1988–1990). **Associations & Accomplishments:** Womens Chapel Guild – Concordia Lutheran Church. **Education:** Lutheran Hospital School of Nursing (1954). **Personal:** Married to Donald in 1956. Five children: Kristin, Daniel, Kimberly, Tricia, and Dawn. Ms. Haber enjoys cooking, gardening, and outdoor activities with her family.

Elson P. Hargrove

Administrator
Oklahoma Methodist Manor
4134 E. 31st Street
Tulsa, OK 74135–1511
(918) 743–2565
Fax: (918) 743–1782

8051

Business Information: Oklahoma Methodist Manor is a retirement housing and health care facility. The Manor has 300 residents and 157 apartments over a 40–acre landscape. As Administrator, Mr. Hargrove is responsible for all aspects of the Manor's operations including budget, employee management, finance, and program administration. **Career Steps:** Administrator, Oklahoma Methodist Manor (1984–Present); Pastor, First United Methodist (1980–1984). **Education:** Southern Methodist, B.D. (1961). **Personal:** Married to Joyce in 1958. Two children: Steven and Belinda. Mr. Hargrove enjoys fishing and camping.

Amber L. Harris

Administrator
Westview Nursing Home
P.O. Box 80
Center, MO 63436–0080
(573) 267–3920
Fax: (573) 267–3216

8051

Business Information: Westview Nursing Home is a 60–bed skilled nursing facility providing medical care to low income persons. As Administrator, Ms. Harris is responsible for overseeing daily operations. **Career Steps:** Administrator, Westview Nursing Home (1990–Present); Clerk, K–Mart (1988–90). **Associations & Accomplishments:** Missouri League of Nursing Home Administrators; Ralls County Human Services Council. **Education:** Hannibal La–Grange, A.S. (1994). **Personal:** Ms. Harris enjoys boating and crafts.

Carolyn A. Hartley

Chief Executive Officer/Administrator
Abbiejean Russell Care Center
700 S. 29th Street
Ft. Pierce, FL 34947
(561) 465–7563
Fax: (561) 465–5619

8051

Business Information: Abbiejean Russell Care Center is a non–profit, 79–bed skilled nursing facility. As Chief Executive Officer, Ms. Hartley is responsible for all aspects of Company operations, including administration, strategic planning, patient care, and finances. **Career Steps:** Chief Executive Officer, Abbiejean Russell Care Center (1975–Present); Accountant, Star Radio Washington D.C. (1972–1975); Supervisory Accountant, U.S. Air Force (1969–1972). **Associations & Accomplishments:** Florida Health Care Association; American Health Care Association; Pilot International. **Education:** University of South Florida, Humanities Area (1986). **Personal:** Married to James A. Sr. in 1956. Two children: Patty Sweat and James A. Jr. Ms. Hartley enjoys collecting antique glassware and reading.

Jeffrey N. Heinze, MHA

Administrator–Heritage Hall South Nursing & Rehabilitation Center
Genesis Elder Care
100 Harvey Johnson Drive
Agawam, MA 01001–2169
(413) 786–8000
Fax: (413) 786–8505

8051

Business Information: Heritage Hall South Nursing & Rehabilitation Center, a section of Genesis Elder Care, is a 122–bed Level II and Level III skilled nursing center. Genesis maintains numerous therapy centers on the East Coast, specializing in speech, physical, and IV therapy, as well as providing physician services, home health care, a pharmacy, and a vendor group. Mr. Heinze joined Genesis in 1994 after attaining his Masters in Health Administration from Clark University. He served as Assistant Administrator of Heritage Hall East Nursing & Rehabilitation Center before being named Administrator in 1995. His present responsibilities include personnel management, overseeing daily operations, budgeting, and accounting functions. **Career Steps:** Genesis Elder Care: Administrator, Heritage Hall South Nursing & Rehabilitation Center (1995–Present), Assistant Administrator, Heritage Hall East Nursing & Rehabilitation Center (1994–1995). **Education:** Clark University, M.H.A. (1993); Quinnipiac College, B.S. in Health Services Administration (1991). **Personal:** Mr. Heinze enjoys bowling, softball, skiing, and bicycling.

Vickie L. Henderson, ADM

Administrator
Walnut Hill Nursing Center
2720 East 12th Avenue, P.O. Box 845
Winfield, KS 67156–4114
(316) 221–9120
Fax: (316) 221–4611

8051

Business Information: Walnut Hill Nursing Center, established in 1973, is a family–owned, 54–bed nursing home providing long–term care to patients in the Winfield, Kansas locale. As Administrator, Ms. Henderson is responsible for all aspects of operations for the Center, including administration, management, staff oversight, and overseeing day–to–day activities. In addition, she serves as the Resident Advocate, opening her doors for suggestions, complaints, etc. on a daily basis. Concurrently, she serves on the Board of Directors with her parents (owners) and brother. **Career Steps:** Walnut Hill Nursing Center: Administrator (1995–Present), Administrative Assistant (1994–1995); Administrative Assistant, Mental Health Consortium (1991–1993); Administrative Assistant, Parallax (1988–1991). **Associations & Accomplishments:** Kansas Professional Nursing Home Administrators Association. **Education:** Southwestern College, B.S. (1983). **Personal:** Two children: Michael and Roy. Ms. Henderson enjoys spending time with her children, reading and sports.

Mary Louise Howell

Director of Nurses
Plantation Health Care Center
204 Oak Drive South
Lake Jackson, TX 77566
(409) 297–0425
Fax: (409) 297–1073

8051

Business Information: Plantation Health Care Center is a skilled nursing facility providing medical and related services to clients. Established in 1990, the Center employs 75 people. As Director of Nurses, Ms. Howell oversees all functions relating to the nursing staff. Her duties include scheduling and supervision of staff, coordinating care for patients, ordering and receiving supplies, and responsibility for all administrative aspects including monitoring of patient charts and preparing reports concerning Facility regulations. **Career Steps:** Plantation Health Care Center: Director of Nurses (1991–Present), R.N. Program Coordinator (11991–Present); Assistant Director of Nurses, Lake Jackson Nursing Home (1988–1991). **Education:** Alvin Community College, Associate of Applied Science in Nursing (1983). **Personal:** Married to Kenneth in 1978. One child: Marcus. Ms. Howell enjoys reading, sewing, and crafts.

Georgiana Hsu
Employment Manager
St. Mary's Hospital For Children
29–01 216th Street
Bayside, NY 11360–2810
(718) 281–8965
Fax: (718) 428–5936

8051

Business Information: Operating as a pediatric skilled nursing care facility and pediatric long–term home health care service, St. Mary's Hospital For Children provides home healthcare to 600 to 700 children, as well as a medical day care program for special needs children. Established in 1876, St. Mary's currently employees 470 and extends services throughout New York's five Burroughs, as well as Suffolk, Nassau, and Westchester counties. Responsible for the recruitment for clinical positions and services, Georgiana Hsu has been with St. Mary's since 1992. In her current position as Employment Manager, Ms. Hsu's duties include employee relations, setting policies and procedures, the printing of a newsletter, as well as training the staff in Human Resources. **Career Steps:** St. Mary's Hospital For Children: Employment Manager (1995–Present), Human Resources Specialist (1992–1995); Recruiter, New York Founding Hospital (1991–1992). **Associations & Accomplishments:** Society for Human Resource Management. **Education:** Columbia University, M.A. (1991); Barnard College, B.A. (1988). **Personal:** Married to John Luk in 1994. Ms. Hsu enjoys reading.

L. Alan James
Facility Administrator
Westfield Village Nursing Center
776 North Union Street
Westfield, IN 46074–9421
(317) 896–2515
Fax: (317) 896–3978

8051

Business Information: Westfield Village Nursing Center, an 80–bed long–term health care facility, is one of 360 such facilities managed by Vencor Corporation nationwide. As Facility Administrator, Mr. James is responsible for overseeing daily operations, business marketing, and management of patient care programs. **Career Steps:** Facility Administrator, Vencor Corporation/Westfield Village Nursing Center (1995–Present); Assistant Administrator, Hillhaven Corporation (1993–1994); Marketing Director, Columbus Convalescent Center (1990–1993). **Associations & Accomplishments:** Indiana Healthcare Association; American College of Healthcare Administrators; Bylaws Choir Indiana Chapter. **Education:** Indiana Wesleyan University, M.B.A. (1994); Wheaton College, B.A. (1986). **Personal:** Mr. James enjoys golf, sports, and church activities.

Jesse Jantzen
Administrator
Littlefield Hospitality House
P.O. Box 589
Littlefield, TX 79339
(806) 385–4544
Fax: (806) 385–4229

8051

Business Information: Littlefield Hospitality House is a long–term health care facility providing medical and related services for the elderly. As Administrator, Mr. Jantzen leads a team of professional staff in delivering professional, dependable, and quality care to the residents. **Career Steps:** Administrator, Littlefield Hospitality House (1995–Present); B.T. Health Care, Inc. (1994–Present). **Associations & Accomplishments:** President Elect, Littlefield Rotary Club; Golden Key National Honor Society; Lubbock Jaycees. **Education:** Texas Tech University: M.B.A. (In Progress), B.B.A. Cum Laude. **Personal:** Married to Shannon in 1995. Mr. Jantzen enjoys scuba diving, reading, watching football, and travel.

Martha J. Jenness
Administrator
Valley West Health Care Center
2300 Warren Street
Eugene, OR 97405
(541) 686–2828
Fax: (541) 686–9093

8051

Business Information: Valley West Health Care Center is a 121–bed skilled and ICF facility, with a 16–bed secured Alzheimer's Unit. The Center provides skilled nursing care and rehabilitation to continuous care patients. As Administrator, Ms. Jenness is responsible for the total operation of the Facility, including employee supervision, patient care, and budgeting. **Career Steps:** Administrator, Valley West Health Care Center – a part of Life Care Centers of America (1995–Present); Administrator, Beverly Enterprises (1987–1995). **Associations & Accomplishments:** Oregon Health Care Association; The Alzheimers Association – Education Committee; Eugene Chamber of Commerce. **Education:** University of Oregon, graduate studies (1990); Southern Nazarene University, B.A. **Personal:** Married to David in 1987. Two children: Gene and Anthony Knippers. Ms. Jenness enjoys scuba diving, reading, and family activities.

Anne Marie Jette
Director of Nursing Services
Jewish Health Care Center
629 Salisbury Street
Worcester, MA 01609–1120
(508) 798–8653
Fax: (508) 753–2668

8051

Business Information: Jewish Health Care Center provides various health care services, including a 60–bed long–term care unit, a 40–bed secured Alzheimer's care unit, and 25–bed transitional care unit. The Center has attained a (D.P.H.) Department of Public Health Deficiency–Free Survey 2 years in a row. As Director of Nursing Services, Ms. Jette is responsible for personnel functions, planning nursing operations, education about healthcare changes, developing and coordinating continuing education programs for staff and colleagues, strategic planning, and cost containment. **Career Steps:** Director of Nursing Services, Jewish Health Care Center (1994–Present); Greenery Extended Care: Supervisor (1992–1994), Nurse Manager (1990–1992). **Associations & Accomplishments:** Massachusetts Organization of Nurse Executives; National Association of Director of Nursing Administration; Massachusetts Nurses Association; Scholarship Committee, David Prouty High School; 4–H Leader. **Education:** Anna Maria, B.S.N. (1996); Becker College, R.N. – A.S.N. (1989); David Hale Fanning, L.P.N. (1974). **Personal:** Married to Ronald Jr. in 1974. Two children: Michael John and Carolyn Claire. Ms. Jette enjoys golf, horses, snowmobiling, and skiing.

Vijay V. Khatiwala, M.D.
••• ⬤ •••

Medical Director
Shalom Nursing Home
10 Claremont Avenue
Mount Vernon, NY 10550–1609
(914) 699–1600 Ext. 348
Fax: (914) 699–1015

8051

Business Information: Dr. Khatiwala divides his time between various positions with different companies. He serves as Medical Director at Park Avenue Health Care and Shalom Nursing Home. He is also an attending physician with the Park Avenue Health Care system and Our Lady of Mercy Medical Center. At New York Medical College, Dr. Khatiwala is a Clinical Instructor specializing in Internal Medicine working mainly with geriatric patients. **Career Steps:** Medical Director, Shalom Nursing Home (1993–Present); Park Avenue Health Care: Medical Director (1995–Present)l Attending Physician–Internist: Watrenburg Home (1995–Present), Workmen's Circle Geriatric Center (1994–Present), Florence Nightingale Nursing Home (1994), Grand Manor Nursing Home (1994); Our Lady of Mercy Medical Center: Voluntary Attending Physician–Internal Medicine (1994–Present), Attending Physician, Internal Medicine (1993–1994); New York Medical College, Clinical Instructor in Internal Medicine (1993–Present) **Associations & Accomplishments:** Associate, American College of Physicians; American Medical Association; Medical Registration: New York State Board of Medicine and New Jersey State Board of Medicine; World Wildlife Association; World Wildlife Fund; Automobile Association of America. **Education:** Our Lady of Mercy Medical Center, affiliate of New York Medical College, M.D. in Internal Medicine (1993); Osmania Medical College, M.B.B.S. (1984). **Personal:** Married to Rita in 1990. One child: Roshni. Dr. Khatiwala enjoys tennis, golf, swimming, and travel.

Susan J. Korman, N H A
Administrator
Health Center at Brentwood
2333 North Brentwood Circle
Lecanto, FL 34461–8536
(352) 746–6611
Fax: (352) 746–6690

8051

Business Information: Health Center at Brentwood, owned and operated by Beverly Health & Rehabilitation Services, Inc., a subsidiary of Beverly Enterprises, is a 60–bed skilled nursing facility affiliated with a local retirement community. The Facility was established in 1984 and provides respiratory, occupational, speech, and physical therapy programs as well as a long–term placement program. As Administrator, Ms. Korman oversees the daily operations of the Facility and the various programs offered. She is also responsible for personnel, finances, budgetary, and administrative concerns. Ms. Korman develops and implements long–term plans for the Facility. **Career Steps:** Administrator, Health Center at Brentwood (1993–Present); Nurse, Harborside Health Care, Inc. (1987–1993). **Education:** St. Petersburg Junior College, A.S. (1992); Licensed Practical Nurse. **Personal:** Ms. Korman enjoys reading and tennis.

Vicki Krick, A.D.C.
Activity Director
Mifflin Center, Genesis ElderCare Network
500 East Philadelphia Avenue
Shillington, PA 19607–2799
(610) 777–7841
Fax: (610) 775–7198

8051

Business Information: Mifflin Center, Genesis ElderCare Network, is a skilled nursing and rehabilitation facility with 136 beds. The Center was established in 1985 and has approximately 150 employees. As Activity Director, Ms. Krick plans, organizes, and directs all activities for short– and long–term rehabilitation patients. She is responsible for the overall operation of the activities programs and works with medical and nursing staff members to develop therapeutic activities. **Career Steps:** Activity Director, Mifflin Center, Genesis ElderCare Network (1992–Present); Berks County Home: Activity Director (1983–1992), Social Worker (1978–1981); Workshop Director, Tarsus, Inc. (1981–1982). **Associations & Accomplishments:** National Association of Activity Professionals; Pennsylvania Activity Professionals Association; Certified as Activity Director by National Certification Council for Activity Professionals. **Education:** Albright College, B.A. (1976); Alvernia College; Reading Area Community College.

Traci A. Lane, RN, BSN, DON
Director of Nursing
Wheatland Manor, Health Care of Iowa
Wheatland, IA 52777
(319) 374–1295
Fax: (319) 374–1107

8051

Business Information: Wheatland Manor, Health Care of Iowa is a local nursing home affiliated with the Jackson County Hospital and currently serving 51 patients. The nursing home began operations in 1966 and has a staff of 53 physicians, nurses and support personnel. As Director of Nursing, Ms. Lane works closely with her nursing staff. She acts as liaison between the medical, administrative, and nursing staffs. Ms. Lane is in charge of all facets of the nursing staff and is responsible for staff recruitment, credential verification, hiring, employment counseling, and evaluations. She works with staff physicians in the scheduling of nursing staff and developing plans for patient care. Additional duties may include conducting conferences on patient care and planning for the future. **Career Steps:** Director of Nursing, Wheatland Manor, Health Care of Iowa (1995–Present); RN, Jackson County Public Hospital (1991–1995). **Associations & Accomplishments:** US Army Reserves; Sigma Theta Tau, International Honor Nursing Society. **Education:** University of Dubuque, B.S.N. (1996); Clinton Community College, A.D.N. (1991). **Personal:** Married to Kenneth in 1993. One child: Ryne James. Ms. Lane enjoys reading and gardening.

Sharon Billion Laro
Director of Nursing
Mary Lyon Nursing Home
34 Main Street
Hampden, MA 01036–9642
(413) 566–5511
Fax: (413) 566–8488

8051

Business Information: Mary Lyon Nursing Home is a 100–bed, long–term care facility, providing skilled nursing services. As Director of Nursing, Ms. Laro is responsible for directing all nursing services, including overseeing certified nursing staff. **Career Steps:** Director of Nursing, Mary Lyon Nursing Home (1988–Present); Administrative Nursing Supervisor, Ludlow Hospital (1981–1988); Supervisor and Charge Nurse, Baystate Medical Center, Wesson Memorial Hospital Division (1968–1981). **Associations & Accomplishments:** Veterans of Foreign Wars. **Education:** Lynn Hospital School of Nursing – Diploma in Nursing (1968). **Personal:** Married to Edward in 1991. Two children: Arthur (25 years of age) and Shaun (22 years of age).

Donna Zepp Leister

Director of Care Management
Manor Health Care
10770 Columbia Pike
Silver Spring, MD 20901
(301) 905–3651
Fax: (301) 905–3489
EMAIL: See Below

8051

Business Information: Manor Health Care is one of the nation's leading skilled long– and short–term health care providers, also recognized for its home health services. National in scope, Manor Health Care has over 180 nursing centers in more than 28 states. As Director of Care Management, Donna Leister is responsible for strategic planning related to clinical/management program development that positions Manor Care at the forefront of long term care. The Program includes the development of clinical pathways, IV therapy, wound care systems, restorative nursing, information control practices, care delivery reengineering, and discharge planning. Internet users can reach her via: DONNA_LEISTER@manorcare.com. **Career Steps:** Director Care Management, Manor Health Care (1995–Present); Director of Clinical Services, Genesis Health Ventures (1994–1995); Quality Improvement Coordinator, Meridian Healthcare (1992–1994); Deaton Hospital and Medical Center of Christ Lutheran Church: Vice President for Nursing (1987–1992), Director, Geriatric Nursing Assistant School (1990–1992), Coordinator Ventilator Unit (1987–1987); Clinical Nurse Critical Care Unit, Baltimore County General Hospital (1981–1984); Clinical Nurse Coronary Care and Progressive Care Units, Saint Joseph's Hospital (1977–1981); Private Duty Nurse and Medial Surgical Clinical Nurse, Sinai Hospital of Baltimore (1968–1974). **Associations & Accomplishments:** Maryland Organization of Nurse Executives, Program Committee; Maryland Nurses Association; American Association of Critical Care Nurses, Chesapeake Bay Chapter; Sigma Theta Tau National Honor Society, Pi Chapter; Maryland Hospital Association; Task Force on Temporary Agencies; Shawan Valley Association, Inc.: Association Member (1981–Present), Architectural Review Committee (1991–1993) Chairman (1993–1994), Activities Committee (1981–1983; 1986–1987), Vice President (1983–1984), Board of Directors (1980–1981; 1983–1984); Falls Road Community Association; Publications: Journal of Nursing Administration (1992), A Clinical Evaluation, Nursing Informatics (1991), Resource Manual, Trauma/Critical Care Resource Library at the University of Maryland at Baltimore (1986). **Education:** University of Maryland at Baltimore: M.S. (1987), B.S.N. (1977); Maryland General Hospital School of Nursing, Diploma in Nursing (1968). **Personal:** Married to Lewis F. in 1968. One child: Mark Franklin. Ms. Leister enjoys piano, church choir, crosswords, and tennis.

Mother Mary Anthony Lemire

Superior
St. Elizabeth Home
502 St. Lawrence Avenue
Janesville, WI 53545
(608) 752–6709
Fax: (608) 752–1724

8051

Business Information: St. Elizabeth Home is a 43–bed, regional nursing home specializing in providing inpatient nursing and rehabilitative services to patients who require continuous heatlhcare. As Mother Superior, Sister Mary Anthony is responsible for all areas of operations, management, and supervision of all the Sisters and staff. **Career Steps:** Superior, St. Elizabeth Home (1988–Present). **Associations & Accomplishments:** Eastern Connecticut State University Alumni Association. **Education:** Eastern Connecticut State University, B.S. (1976). **Personal:** Mother Lemire enjoys religious activities, meetings, and reading.

Wayne D. Locke, CA

Vice President and Treasurer
Tendercare (Michigan) Inc.
209 East Portage Avenue
Sault Ste Marie, MI 49783–2053
(906) 635–0020
Fax: (906) 635–0212

8051

Business Information: Tendercare (Michigan) Inc. is the owner of thirty long–term care nursing homes and a rehabilitation hospital in Michigan, providing care for 3,000 patients. With twenty–one years of expertise in public accounting, acquisitions, and financial management, Mr. Locke joined the Company in 1990 as General Manager of Finance. He was appointed as Vice President and Treasurer in 1993 and is responsible for finance and business development. **Career Steps:** Tendercare, Inc.: Vice President and Treasurer (1993–Present), Director of Finance (1990–1993); General Manager of Finance, Algoma Steel Corporation (1974–1990). **Associations & Accomplishments:** Member, Canadian Institute of Chartered Accountants; Board of Directors, Economic Development Corporation of Sault Sainte Marie; Chairman of the Board of Directors, Sault College of Applied Arts and Technology (1980–1989). **Education:** Laurentian University, B.A. in Economics (1972); Canadian Institute of Chartered Accountants, Chartered Accountant (1974). **Personal:** Married to Wendy in 1963. Two children: Piper Lee and Andrew. Mr. Locke enjoys sailing, golfing, skiing, and bicycling.

Gloria B. Loudermilk

Administrator
Guardian Care Nursing Home
1212 Sunset Drive East
Monroe, NC 28112
(704) 283–8548
Fax: (704) 283–4664

8051

Business Information: Guardian Care Nursing Home provides long–term care services at a 174–bed facility with a Skilled Nursing Unit, Assisted Living, Alzheimer's Unit, Managed Care and Sub–Acute Unit. Administrator of Guardian Care since 1994, Ms. Loudermilk is responsible for management of overall facility operations. **Career Steps:** Administrator, Guardian Care Nursing Home (1994–Present); Hillhaven: Assistant Administrator (1992–1994), Marketing Coordinator (1990–1992), Social Services Director (1986–1989). **Associations & Accomplishments:** National Association for Female Executives; American Association of University Women; Federated Women's Club; North Carolina Association of Long Term Care Facilities. **Education:** Berea College, B.A (1971). **Personal:** Married to Phillip in 1969. Two children: Brian and Joella. Ms. Loudermilk enjoys reading, cross–stitch, and gardening.

Rodney E. Mason

President
Peter Becker Community
800 Maple Avenue
Harleysville, PA 19438–1032
(215) 256–9501
Fax: (215) 256–9768

8051

Business Information: Peter Becker Company is a long–term care facility providing housing for 400 retired persons. The Center has 94 skilled beds, 45 personal care, and 168 independent living (cottages, units, and apartments) facilities. As President, Mr. Mason oversees the day–to–day operations of the Facility. He is also President of Community Home Services, a home health agency. **Career Steps:** Peter Becker Community: President (1992–Present), Assistant Administrator (1986–1992); Assistant Director, Bridgewater Healthcare Foundation (1985–1986). **Associations & Accomplishments:** Indian Valley Chamber of Commerce; Association of Brethren Caregivers; Pennsylvania Association of Non–Profit Homes for the Aging; American Association of Health Services for the Aging; Civic 1st Vice President and Deputy Chief of Harleysville Community Fire Company; Indian Creek Church of the Brethren; Who's Who Among Students in American University and Colleges (1982–1983); Outstanding Young Men of America (1987–1988). **Education:** Bridgewater College, B.A. (1983). **Personal:** Married to Laurie in 1988. Mr. Mason enjoys firefighting, sports, and music.

Lisa A. Maxberry, R.N.

Director of Nursing Services
Hillcrest Healthcare Center
3740 Old Hartford Road
Owensboro, KY 42303–1727
(502) 684–7259
Fax: (502) 684–3004

8051

Business Information: Hillcrest Healthcare Center is a local long–term care facility containing 156 beds, with rehabilitation and Alzheimer's disease units. As Director of Nursing, Ms. Maxberry directs and trains her staff of 95 nurses and CNAs. She evaluates residents to ensure their medical and nursing needs are met, meets weekly with unit managers and unit coordinators, and checks medical orders for the Center residents. **Career Steps:** Hillcrest Healthcare Center: Director of Nursing (1994–Present), R.N.A.C. (1992–1994), Supervisor (1984–1992). **Associations & Accomplishments:** N.A.D.O.N.A.; K.N.A. District 8. **Education:** Henderson Community College, Associates (1992); Owensboro Vocational School, L.P.N. **Personal:** Two children: Samantha, and Jessica. Ms. Maxberry enjoys camping, travel, home remodeling, and gardening.

Daisy Murphy

Administrator
Macon Health Care Center
P.O. Box 465
Macon, MO 63552–0465
(816) 385–5797
Fax: (816) 385–5814

8051

Business Information: Macon Health Care Center is a 120 bed skilled nursing facility. Privately–owned, the Center is supervised by the National Health Care LP. A Medicare and Medicaid contract center, the Facility focuses primarily on the care and rehabilitation of geriatric patients. As Administrator, Ms. Murphy oversees all aspects of the Centers operations, to include administration, strategic planning, and public relations. **Career Steps:** National Health Care LP: Administrator, Macon Home Health Care Center (1985–Present), Assistant Administrator (1994–1995), Regional Consultant (19991–1994). **Associations & Accomplishments:** American College of Health Care Administrators; Missouri Health Care Association; Rotary Club; Chamber of Commerce Board Member; Certified Trainer of Customer Relations Trainers; Certified Supervisory Trainer (3 levels); Overall Census Development Award (1991). **Education:** Lindenwood College; Indian Hills Community College, Licensed Practical Nurse (1982). **Personal:** Married to Randy in 1995. Two children: Rod Gray and Cory Murphy. Ms. Murphy enjoys boating.

Debbie Neff

Director of Admissions and Marketing
The Oakridge Home
26520 Center Ridge Road
Westlake, OH 44145–4033
(216) 871–3030
Fax: (216) 871–3036

8051

Business Information: The Oakridge Home is a skilled and intermediate care nursing facility. The Home is part of Life Care Centers of America and offers long–term care, with 25–30 doctors on consultation call. As Director of Admissions and Marketing, Ms. Neff is responsible for the marketing of the facility for prospective admissions. She handles all admissions and conducts tours of the facility. **Career Steps:** Oak Ridge Homes: Director of Admissions and Marketing (1988–Present), Secretary (1986–1988); Secretary, Republic Steel (1968–1974). **Associations & Accomplishments:** Ethics Committee, St. John's West Shore Hospital. **Personal:** Married to Ralph in 1972. Three children: Douglas, Brian, and John. Ms. Neff enjoys reading and sewing.

Theresa O'Connell

Social Services Director
Manor Care Health Services
14 Lincoln Avenue
Yeadon, PA 19050
(610) 626–7700
Fax: (610) 626–7690

8051

Business Information: Manor Care Health Services, formerly known as Leader Nursing and Rehabilitation Center, is a skilled nursing facility (172 skilled nursing patients) and Alzheimer's division (26 Alzheimer patients). A privately–owned Company, the Facility was established in 1963, and employs 250 people. As Social Services Director, Ms. O'Connell interfaces with residents and families, provides death and dying counseling, MDS, care plans, and assists the restorative committee. Additional duties include training staff, psycho–social assessments, discharge planning and case management. **Career Steps:** Social Services Director, Manor Care Health Services (1995–Present); Program Instructor, Allegheny Valley School (1991–1995); Counselor, Devereux Foundation (1989–1994); Program Director, Jenny Craig (1990–1991). **Associations & Accomplishments:** Sigma Phi Delta Sorority; Social Workers Association for Nursing Homes; Certification in Mental Health and Aging. **Education:** Millersville University, B.A. (1989); Certification in Mental Health and Aging, PCA. **Personal:** One child: Brennan. Ms. O'Connell enjoys spending time with her son, camping, cross–stitch, and cooking.

Varena (Willi) O'Neal, R.N., M.S.N.

Director of Nursing
Oakwood Nursing and Rehabilitation Center
5520 Indian River Road
Virginia Beach, VA 23464–5217
(804) 420–3600
Fax: (804) 424–5076

8051

Business Information: Oakwood Nursing and Rehabilitation Center is a long– and short–term acute care facility for the injured and elderly. As Director of Nursing, Ms. O'Neal is responsible for all patient pre– and post–admission reviews and evaluations, personnel interviews, and quality assurance procedures. **Career Steps:** Director of Nursing, Oakwood Nursing and Rehabilitation Center (1993–Present); Administrative Supervisor, Sentara Bayside Hospital (1990–1993); Nursing Supervisor, PHP Healthcare Corporation (1991); Director of Nursing and Critical Care Services, DePaul Medical Center (1989–1989). **Associations & Accomplishments:** Virginia Association of Directors of Nursing; National Directors of Nursing Association; Chaplain, Ocean View Democratic and Social Club. **Education:** Col. Pacific University: M.S.N. (1984), B.S.N.; College of William and Mary; Old Dominion University; Norfolk State; T.C.C. **Personal:** Married to Nathan "Pete" in 1959. Three children: Nathan, Patrick and Kimberly. Ms. O'Neal enjoys mentoring to high school students and reading.

Carla B. Olena
Director of Nursing
DePaul Adult Care Community
420 Main Street
E. Rochester, NY 14445
(716) 586–8010
Fax: (716) 586–6151

8051

Business Information: DePaul Adult Care Community is a 169–bed facility located in East Rochester, New York. An adult home community for the elderly and mentally ill, the facility was established in 1973, and is regulated by the state's Department of Social Services. As Director of Nursing, Ms. Olena is the only nurse on staff. Her responsibilities include overseeing the staff, training them in CPR and First Aid, as well as working with doctors to ensure quality patient care, and overseeing the transportation department. **Career Steps:** Director of Nursing, DePaul Adult Care Community (1990–Present); Charge Nurse, Hill Haven Nursing Home (1986–1990); Charge Nurse, Jewish Home (1983–1986). **Education:** Isabella Grahm, L.P.N. (1977). **Personal:** Married to Richard in 1975. Two children: Richard and Shannon. Ms. Olena enjoys bingo, her grandson, crochet, and cross–stitching.

K. J. Page
Chief Executive Officer
Sunnyvale Convalescent Hospital
1291 South Bernardo Avenue
Sunnyvale, CA 94087–2060
(408) 245–8070
Fax: (408) 245–2433

8051

Business Information: Sunnyvale Convalescent Hospital is a 99–bed hospital, providing skilled nursing and full rehabilitative services. With twenty years experience in hospital administration, Ms. Page joined Sunnyvale Convalescent Hospital as Administrator in April 1992. She was then appointed as Executive Director in August 1995. Currently serving as Chief Executive Officer (as of December 1995), she is responsible for all day–to–day operations and financial aspects, as well as profit & loss accountability. **Career Steps:** Sunnyvale Convalescent Hospital: Chief Executive Officer (1995–Present), Executive Director (1995), Administrator (1992); Administrator, Diablo Convalescent Hospital (1989–1991); Administrator, Churchlane Convalescent Hospital (1987–1989); Psychiatric Nurse, Institute of Pennsylvania Hospital (1975–1976). **Associations & Accomplishments:** President, Sunnyvale Chamber of Commerce (1995–1996); Santa Clara Chapter, California Association of Health Facilities (1994–1996); Vice President, American College Health Care Administrators – California Chapter (1994–1996); Board of Directors, American Cancer Society – Sunnyvale Unit (1995–1996); Freelance writer of fiction and professional articles. **Education:** Clayton State University, Doctorate in Naturopathy (1996); Gwynedd Mercy College: B.A. (1975), A.D. (1973).

Lisa M. Parente
Human Resource Director
Leader Nursing and Rehabilitation Center, Manor Health Care Corporation
2125 Elizabeth Avenue
Laureldale, PA 19605–2259
(610) 921–9292
Fax: (610) 921–9561

8051

Business Information: Leader Nursing and Rehabilitation Center specializes in providing inpatient nursing and rehabilitative services to patients who require continuous healthcare. The Center is part of Manor Health Care Corporation, a diversified and integrated company with several services available. As Human Resource Director, Ms. Parente is responsible for all human resource operations of the Facility, including report-

ing to administration, development and training, recruiting, employee benefits, and research. **Career Steps:** Human Resource Director, Leader Nursing and Rehabilitation Center (1994–Present); Human Resources/Operations Manager, The Bon–Ton (1991–1994); Provider Training Specialist, The Computer Company (1989–1991). **Associations & Accomplishments:** Society of Human Resource Managers; Board of Directors, Business Management Association. **Education:** Mansfield University, B.A. in Psychology (1981). **Personal:** Ms. Parente enjoys travel, reading, cooking, and antiquing.

Connie B. Parks, R.N.
Staff Development Coordinator
Bradford County Manor
RR3 Box 322
Troy, PA 16947
(717) 297–4111
Fax: (717) 297–3234

8051

Business Information: Bradford County Manor is a 226–bed long–term care facility offering intermediate and skilled nursing care. Ms. Parks joined Bradford County Manor as an LPN in 1973 and has served in various supervisory positions since, including Staff Development Coordinator LPN, Charge Nurse, and named RN Supervisor upon conferral of her RN Certification in 1990. She presently serves as Staff Development Coordinator, responsible for facility orientation for all staff and conducting the training course for Certified Nursing Assistants. **Career Steps:** Bradford County Manor: Staff Development Coordinator (1994–Present), RN Supervisor (1990–1994), LPN Charge Nurse (1988–1990), Staff Development Coordinator, LPN (1979–1988). **Education:** Corning Community College, RN (1990); Williamsport Area Community College, LPN (1973). **Personal:** Three children: Michael, Stephanie, and Brent. Two grandchildren: Dylan and Kaitlyn. Ms. Parks enjoys crocheting and reading.

Kate Phillips, R.N.C., B.S.N.
Staff Development Coordinator
Life Care Center
P.O. Box 2199
Banner Elk, NC 28604–2199
(704) 898–5136
Fax: (704) 898–8426

8051

Business Information: Life Care Center is a 120–bed skilled nursing facility with centers nationwide. The Center provides nursing services to patients who require long–term care and rehabilitation. As Staff Development Coordinator, Ms. Phillips is responsible for diversified administrative activities, including hiring, training nursing staff, orientation of all employees, employee health, and patient infection control. Concurrently, Ms. Phillips teaches a Nursing course at the local community college and was instrumental in starting the first District Nursing Association in her area. **Career Steps:** Staff Development Coordinator, Life Care Center (1993–Present); Director of Nursing, Evangeline Nursing Home (1992–1993); Director of Nursing, Lotacare Residential Services (1989–1993); Director of Nursing, Heritage Manor Nursing Home (1985–1989). **Associations & Accomplishments:** American Nursing Association; North Carolina Nurses Association: NCNA Strategic Task Force 1992, "92 in 92" – one of 92 nurses recognized by NCNA for Excellence; North Carolina Long Term Care Nurses Association; Board of Directors, Mayland Community College; First President, District 23 North Carolina Nurses Association; Gerontological Certification, American Nurses Association; Board Member, Local Southern States Agricultural Service; Part time Instructor, local community colleges; Hospice Volunteer; Nurse Preceptor for community college RN students; CPR Instructor. **Education:** Winston-Salem State University, B.S.N. (1996); Forsyth Memorial Hospital – School of Nursing, Diploma (1970). **Personal:** One child: Philip Carlton McBrayer. Ms. Phillips enjoys music, singing in the church choir, hiking, reading, and sewing.

Marie R. Plasha, RNC, DON
Director of Nursing
Mifflin Healthcare Center
500 East Philadelphia Avenue
Shillington, PA 19607–2764
(610) 777–7841
Fax: (610) 775–7198

8051

Business Information: Mifflin Healthcare Center is a 136–bed skilled nursing facility specializing in providing higher technical skilled care and ventilator care. All nurses in the Facility are IV Certified. As Director of Nursing, Ms. Plasha is responsible for the overall care provided to residents, infection control, and a large support staff. Additionally, she is certified in infection control and geriatric medicine. **Career Steps:** Mifflin Healthcare Center: Director of Nursing (1992–Present), Assistant Director of Nursing (1987–1992), 7–3 Supervisor (1985–1987). **Associations & Accomplishments:** Sacred Hospital Alumni Association; Association of Practitioners In-

fection Control; Pennsylvania Director of Nurses Association. **Education:** Sacred Heart Hospital, Diploma (1957). **Personal:** Married to Russell in 1963. Three children: Beth, Kay, and John. Ms. Plasha enjoys reading, swimming, and shopping.

Jay E. Plucker
Administrator
Butte Health Care Center
210 Broadway
Butte, NE 68722
(402) 775–2355
Fax: (402) 775–2332

8051

Business Information: Butte Health Care Center is a long term care facility engaged in skilled nursing care of the elderly. Established in 1988, the Center provides occupational, speech, audiology, and rehabilitation services and is comprised of 58 Medicare and Medicaid beds. As Administrator, Mr. Plucker oversees all aspects of the facility. His duties include administration, operations, public relations, ensuring patient quality of care, and strategic planning. **Career Steps:** Administrator, Butte Health Care Center (Present); Administrator, Tealwood Care Centers (1995–Present); Medical Records, Sioux Valley Hospital (1992–1995); Intern, University Physicians (1991). **Associations & Accomplishments:** Board of Directors, South Dakota Chapter of National Candlelighters; Past Vice President, Student Chapter of American College of Health Care Executives; Vice President, Region II, South Dakota Health Care Association. **Education:** University of South Dakota, B.S. (1992); South Dakota State University. **Personal:** Mr. Plucker enjoys hunting, fishing, camping, and jet skiing.

Ronald S. Prince

Administrator
Mariner Health of Port Charlotte
25325 Rampart Boulevard
Punta Gorda, FL 33983–6404
(941) 629–7466
Fax: (941) 629–9053
EMAIL: See Below

8051

Business Information: Mariner Health of Port Charlotte is a 120 bed sub–acute care and 33 bed long–term nursing facility specializing in providing rehabilitation services to residents. As Administrator, Mr. Prince is responsible for all aspects of daily operations, patient services and personnel management. With a U.S. Navy Respiratory Therapist background, Mr. Prince has served as Administrator for Mariner Health since 1995, and intends to remain and grow with the Group. Internet users can reach him via: scorpion@iz.net. **Career Steps:** Administrator, Mariner Health of Port Charlotte (1995–Present); Administrator, Country Park Healthcare (1993–1995); Administrator, Beverly Enterprises (1991–1993); Respiratory Therapist, U.S. Navy (1985–1990). **Associations & Accomplishments:** Port Charlotte Chamber of Commerce. **Education:** Webster University, M.A. in Health Services Management (1989); Western Connecticut State University, Bachelor of Music/Piano (1979). **Personal:** Married to Michele in 1993. Mr. Prince enjoys playing piano, writing music, and exotic birds.

Barbara Quattlebaum
Director of Nursing
St. Vincent de Paul Residence
900 Intervale Avenue
Bronx, NY 10459–4203
(718) 589–6965
Fax: Please mail or call

8051

Business Information: St. Vincent de Paul Residence is a long term care facility. A practicing nurse since 1962 with extensive administrative and long–term care expertise, Barbara Quattlebaum was recruited by St. Vincent's to implement all nursing procedures and protocols upon its opening in 1992. As Director of Nursing, she provides the executive direction for all patient care practices, as well as budgetary management and personnel matters. **Career Steps:** Director of Nursing, St. Vincent de Paul Residence (1992–Present); Assistant Director of Nursing, Kateri Residence (1990–1992); Adjunct Assistant Professor, York College (1988–Present); Assistant Professor, Long Island University (1979–1988 & 1974–1977); Assistant Professor, Hunter College (1977–1979). **Associations & Accomplishments:** Sigma Theta Tau International, Honor Society of Nursing. **Education:** Adelphi University: M.S.N. (1976), B.S.N. (1968); Queens College, A.A.S. (1963). **Personal:** Ms. Quattlebaum enjoys reading, golf, and travel.

Susana Ramos

Comptroller
Portal Del Cielo
P O Box 7887, Suite 133
Guaynabo, Puerto Rico 00970
(787) 783–5103
Fax: (787) 781–2932

8051

Business Information: Portal Del Cielo is a private nursing home for the elderly. Currently the facility has an occupancy of 100 patients. As Comptroller, Ms. Ramos oversees all financial aspects of the residential facility. She handles payroll, financial reports, budgets, and cash management. Ms. Ramos has oversight of all administrative functions including staff recruitment, training, evaluating, and counseling. Other duties include public relations and strategic planning for the future. **Career Steps:** Comptroller, Portal Del Cielo (1995–Present); Banco Cestral Hispano de Puerto Rico: Comptroller Department Supervisor, Banco Cestral Hispano de Puerto Rico (1993–1995), Comptroller Departments Accounts (1990–1993); Comptroller Department Account Clerk, Banco Cestral Corporation (1986–1990). **Education:** University of Sacred Heart, B.B.A. (1985). **Personal:** Married to Ricardo Colon in 1996. Ms. Ramos enjoys the beach, gym, and movies.

Carlos E. Ratliff

Owner and Chief Executive Officer
Ratliff Enterprises
717 North Sprigg Street
Cape Girardeau, MO 63701–4815
(573) 334–9365
Fax: (573) 651–8998

8051

Business Information: Ratliff Enterprises manages three operations: a 46–bed skilled nursing home, a residential care facility, and an accounting & tax service. As Owner and Chief Executive Officer of all three entities, Mr. Ratliff is responsible for corporate management, providing strategic direction, and supervision of executive personnel. **Career Steps:** Owner and Chief Executive Officer, Ratliff Enterprises (1965–Present); Comptroller, Health Facilities Management (1977–1982); Accountant, Schott & Company (1967–1977). **Associations & Accomplishments:** Treasurer and Board of Directors, Mid–America Teen Challenge; Vice President and Treasurer, Bethel Assembly of God Church. **Education:** South East Missouri University, B.S. in Business (1966). **Personal:** Married to Emmagene in 1960. Two children: Carla Jean and Michael Eugene. Mr. Ratliff enjoys flying, hunting, horseback riding, and travel.

James (Jim) J. Schneeberger, CDM, FMP

Food & Beverage Director
Moorings Park
120 Moorings Park Drive
Naples, FL 34105–2122
(941) 261–2415 Ext. 217
Fax: (941) 262–7040

8051

Business Information: Moorings Park provides a total care retirement community comprised of 400 independent living senior citizens and 106 healthcare residents. Mr. Schneeberger is Food & Beverage Director for a three kitchen and six dining room Facility. He supervises 76 employees within these workplaces. **Career Steps:** Food & Beverage Director, Moorings Park (1992–Present); Food & Beverage Director, ACTS, Inc. Indian River Estates E. (1987–1992); Manager, Fast Food Enterprises (1985–1987). **Associations & Accomplishments:** Dietary Managers Association – Certified Dietary Manager; Foodservice Management Professionals; Florida Restaurant Association. **Education:** Genesee Community College, Associate's degree (1982). **Personal:** Married to Debbie in 1983. Two children: Jimmy and Sarah. Mr. Schneeberger enjoys softball, gardening, and bike riding.

Patrice A. Schulz

Administrator
Heritage Manor
307 Royal Avenue
Elroy, WI 53929–0167
(608) 462–8491
Fax: (608) 462–5088

8051

Business Information: Heritage Manor is an 80 bed full–service, skilled nursing home. This establishment accepts Medicare patients, and provides therapy, rehabilitation, and other necessary services. Specialty care is also now available for Alzheimer's patients. As Administrator, Ms. Schulz is responsible for managing the facility, personnel, and all available services. She oversees all day–to–day functions, including finances, budgeting and service quality. Ms. Schulz has been published in "Alzheimer's Care Guide," a national journal, published monthly. She is a frequent speaker at the local high school, and has initiated an extensive inter–generational program at Heritage Manor. **Career Steps:** Administrator, Heritage Manor (1973–Present). **Associations & Accomplishments:** Wisconsin Health Care Association; Pianist for St. Patrick's Church and various school functions; Cub Scout Leader. **Education:** University of Wisconsin at Milwaukee, Bachelor's (1972); Catholic College, Nursing Home Administration. **Personal:** Married to Paul T. in 1971. Five children: Patrick, Abraham, Alexander, Julie and Anthony. Ms. Schulz enjoys music, children, scouts, swimming, snorkeling and exercise.

Dawn A. Shrock

Assistant Manager of Skilled Nursing
Brethren Healthcare Center
RR Rt. 2, Box 97
Flora, IN 46929–9745
(219) 967–4571
Fax: (219) 967–4422

8051

Business Information: The Brethren Healthcare Center is a full–service skilled nursing facility and rehabilitation center for patients between the ages of 40 and 90. With the devoted efforts of the Center's staff, over 70 percent of the rehabilitation patients are able to return to their homes. The Center also operates a skilled care unit. Established in 1923, Brethren Healthcare Center currently employs 100 medical professionals and staff. As Assistant Manager of Skilled Nursing, Ms. Shrock is responsible for admissions and discharges, social services, and is the Resource Professional for skilled patient criteria. Ms. Shrock enjoys people and helping others. She attributes her success to hard work and the challenge of the job. In the future, Ms. Shrock plans to attain her R.N. degree and utilize her knowledge to handle more repsonsibility and supervisory positions. **Career Steps:** Brethren Healthcare Center: Assistant Manager of Skilled Nursing (1995–Present), Social Services (1995), Skilled Nurse Manager (1982–1995); Charge Nurse (1988–1992). **Education:** Kokomo School of Practical Nursing, L.P.N. (1988); Purdue University of Animal Sciences. **Personal:** Two children: Daryn S. and Dustyn. Ms. Shrock enjoys collecting antiques and horseback riding.

Anna L. Simmons

Administrator
Simmons Loving Care Health Facility
P.O. Box 1678
Gary, IN 46407
(219) 882–2563
Fax: (219) 882–1111

8051

Business Information: Simmons Loving Care Facility is a comprehensive intermediate health care center incorporated under Simmons–Miller Investments, Inc., specifically designed to fulfill the physical, emotional, and spiritual needs of their patients. A staff of highly–competent physicians, administrators, nurses, and therapists provide the finest in personal professional health care services in an atmosphere of cleanliness, comfort, and serenity. The Facility provides 24–hour nursing care, daily visiting hours, physical and occupational therapy, activities, recreational areas, and is state licensed and Medicaid approved. As Administrator, Ms. Simmons is responsible for implementing and assuring that policies and procedures are established to protect the overall welfare of geriatric residents. She tries to create an environment that increases the patients' self–esteem and ensures that each patient receives optimal care. **Career Steps:** Administrator, Simmons Loving Care Health Facility (1970–Present). **Associations & Accomplishments:** Indiana Health Care Association; American College of Health Care; Board of Director, Treasurer, Thelma Marshall Children's Home; Life Membership, Golden Heritage, National Association for the Advancement of Colored People; City of Gary; Treasurer, Emergency Referral Board; Better Business Bureau; Chamber of Commerce; Sponsor, East Side Little League Baseball team; Sponsor, Tolleston Community Bowling Team; Former President, Gary City Federation of Colored Women's Club; Methodist Hospital – Gary, IN, Distinguished Service Award; Outstanding Daughter Award, Imperial Court; Daughter of Isis North and South America jurisdiction; Certificate of Achievement, 4th District City of Gary; Distinguished Service and Appreciation Award, Gary City Federation of Colored Womens Club, Inc.; Various other Appreciation and Dedicated Service Awards from various city and civic organizations. **Education:** Attended, Indiana University. **Personal:** One child: Herberta B. Miller. Ms. Simmons enjoys community, fraternal and religious services.

Sister Mary Denise Slocum

Administrator
Saint Elizabeth Home
502 Saint Lawrence Avenue
Janesville, WI 53545
(608) 752–6709
Fax: Please mail or call

8051

Business Information: Saint Elizabeth Home is a 43–bed nursing home facility specializing in providing inpatient nursing and rehabilitation services to patients who require continuous healthcare. As Administrator, Sister Slocum is responsible for all aspects of the Facility's operations, including scheduling, nurse planning, and taking care of patients. **Career Steps:** Saint Elizabeth Home: Administrator (1981–Present), Director of Nursing (1966–1981); Student Nurse, St. Marys Hospital (1963–1965). **Associations & Accomplishments:** Wisconsin Health Care Association. **Education:** St. Marys School of Nursing, Diploma (1965); Administrator License (1972). **Personal:** Sister Slocum enjoys making stuffed animals.

Paul D. Smith

Director of Social Services
Sullivan Park Health Care Center
301 Nantucket Drive
Endicott, NY 13760–2735
(607) 754–2705
Fax: (607) 754–2610
EMAIL: See Below

8051

Business Information: Sullivan Park Health Care Center is a 160–bed nursing home facility specializing in providing inpatient nursing and rehabilitation services to patients who require continuous healthcare. As Director of Social Services, Mr. Smith is responsible for overseeing the mental and social well–being of the residents, and handles the concerns of residents and families. Internet users can reach him via: PSmith4321@Aol.com. **Career Steps:** Director of Social Services, Sullivan Park Health Care Center (1996–Present); Senior Counselor, Broome County Catholic Charities (1994–1995); Case Manager, Salvation Army (1992–1994). **Education:** Binghamton University, B.S. (1991); Monroe Community College, A.A.S. **Personal:** Married to Margaret in 1996. Mr. Smith enjoys spending time with his family and friends, and participating with his church group.

Carol H. Solomon

Director
CHS Geriatric Care & Placement
P.O. Box 1354
Marlton, NJ 08053
(609) 985–1180
Fax: (609) 985–0452

8051

Business Information: CHS Geriatric Care & Placement assists families in placing the elderly in nursing homes when they can no longer live independently. CHS provides resources, strategies, and skills for the elderly and their families. As Director, Ms. Solomon works to meet the needs of the family, as well as the elderly. **Career Steps:** CHS Geriatric Care & Placement: Director (1994–Present), Human Service Consultant (1992–1994); Social Service Coordinator, Kingsbury (1986–1992); Public Relations, Solomon Veterinary (1978–1986). **Associations & Accomplishments:** National Association of Private Geriatric Case Managers; American Society on Aging; Children of Aging Parents; Professional Women Network; Professional Woman Speaker Bureau; Alzheimer Association; National Stroke Association; Professional Rehabilitation; Chamber of Commerce. **Education:** Long Island University, B.A. (1965). **Personal:** Two children: Jason and Jeffrey. Ms. Solomon enjoys travel, exercise, reading, and cooking.

Mary Lou Spence

Director of Nursing Services
Roo Lan Health Care
1505 Carpenter Road, Southeast
Olympia, WA 98503–2906
(360) 491–1765
Fax: (360) 491–4402

8051

Business Information: Roo Lan Health Care is a private, 103–bed, long–term, nursing care facility providing skilled nursing for geriatrics and disability patients. Roo Lan is licensed for Medicare, Medicaid and veterans. Ensuring quality care is provided to patients for the past 25 years, Ms. Mary Lou Spence, as Director of Nursing, is responsible for administration of training and developing policies and procedures. **Career Steps:** Director of Nursing Services, Roo Lan Health Care (1971–Present). **Associations & Accomplishments:** Thurston/Mason Adult Family Home Association; Washington Chapter National Directors of Nursing; Washington Health Care Association; Stephen Ministry, Sacred Heart Church, Lacey, WA. **Education:** Seattle University, M.A.P.S. in progress; City University, B.S.N. (1989). **Personal:** Married to Wayne in 1959. Seven children: Lisa, Jeff, Matt, Jenny, Chris, Patricia, and Melissa. Mrs. Spence enjoys reading, crocheting, and gardening.

Dolores D. Spragg

LNHA/LSW
McGraw Nursing Center
73841 Pleasant Grove
Adena, OH 43901–9506
(614) 546–3013
Fax: (614) 546–4105

8051

Business Information: McGraw Nursing Center is a 43–bed nursing home facility specializing in providing inpatient nursing and rehabilitative services to patients who require continuous healthcare. As LNHA/LSW, Ms. Spragg serves as an Administrator, Nurse, and licensed Social Worker. She is responsible for various administrative duties and the overall operations of the facility. **Career Steps:** McGraw Nursing Center: Administrator (1991–Present), Social Worker (1982–Present), Nursing Supervisor (1966–1982). **Associations & Accomplishments:** Mt. Pleasant First Presbyterian; Mt. Pleasant Historical Society; Board Member, Medi Home Health Care Agency; Volunteer for more than 30 years in 4–H (local, county, and district); Mt. Pleasant Woman's Monday Night Club. **Education:** Ohio University, B.G.S. (1988). **Personal:** Married to Earl in 1952. Three children: Diana Lynn, Dennis William, and Mark Stephen. Four grandsons. Ms. Spragg enjoys music, gardening, and travel.

Gloria N. Stanley

Regional Director
LAP Care Services
6878 NC Highway 150
Reidsville, NC 27320
(704) 258–1272
Fax: (704) 782–6924

8051

Business Information: LAP Care Services manages and oversees the operation of adult care homes which provide health and daily care to elderly citizens in a rest home setting. As Regional Director, Ms. Stanley is responsible for the oversight and management of ten rest homes and five family care homes. **Career Steps:** Regional Director, LAP Care Services (1994–Present); Director, Morgan Enterprises (1985–1994); Supervisor, Danny Tuttle and Associates (1976–1985). **Associations & Accomplishments:** North Carolina Long–Term Care Association; Life Member, Disabled American Veterans; Near Calvary Baptist Church. **Education:** Attended, Carolina Bible College; Central Piedmont Community College, Activity Program (1985). **Personal:** Married to David in 1975. Five children: Jeffrey, Tony, Woody, Angie, and Randy. Ms. Stanley enjoys camping and bible studies.

Ann J. Sullivan, R.N.C.

Corporate Director of Nursing
Country Club Retirement Centers
860 East Iron Avenue
Dover, OH 44622–2031
(330) 343–5568
Fax: (330) 343–0514

8051

Business Information: Country Club Retirement Centers is a group of four long–term care facilities operating under Holland Management. Each of the Centers specializes in providing inpatient nursing and rehabilitative services to patients who require continuous health care. As Corporate Director of Nursing, Ms. Sullivan is responsible for hiring and firing, evaluation of four directors and four assistant directors, a staff of 52 at her site, quarterly meetings for administrators and directors of nursing for nursing homes, mock surveys, and chart reviews. **Career Steps:** Corporate Director of Nursing, Country Club Centers (1996–Present); Director of Nursing, Country Club Retirement Center I (1990–1993); Director of Nursing, Twin City Health Care Center (1980–1982); Supervisor of ICU, Timber Mercy Medical Center. **Associations & Accomplishments:** Ohio Director, Nursing Associations; National Association of Director of Nursing in Long Term Care. **Education:** Ashland University, B.S.N; Kent State University, Associates Degree (1977); Certification for Gerontological Nursing, ANCC (1991); Certification for Directors of Nursing in Long Term Care (1992). **Personal:** Married to James F. in 1953. Five children: Jeanne Eisenhurf, Mary Jo, Beth Nell, David, and Kevin. Ms. Sullivan enjoys cross–stitching, water gardening, and amateur Ornithologist.

Cheryl A. Tibbets

Director of Health Services
Westminister Village
1175 McKee Road
Dover, DE 19904–2268
(302) 674–8030
Fax: (302) 674–8656

8051

Business Information: Westminister Village, established in 1927, is a non–profit Health Care Center and retirement community. As Director of Health Services, Mrs. Tibbets directly oversees the departments of Nursing, Rehabilitation, Quality Assurance, Recruitment, Infectious Control, Medical Records, and Acute Care Medical Services. **Career Steps:** Director of Health Services, Westminister Village (1994–Present); Nursing Coordinator, Delaware Hospice (1992–1994); Nursing Supervisor, Delaware Hospital (1988–1992); Medical Director, Delaware Elwyn (1987–1988); Charge RN Medical–Surgery, Kent General Hospital (1984–1987). **Associations & Accomplishments:** Secretary, Delaware Association Directors of Nursing Administration. **Education:** Delaware State University, BSN (1985). **Personal:** Married to Richard E. Tibbets Jr. in 1989. One child: Lauren.

Marsha F. Trivigno

Executive Director
Woodhouse Inc.
1001 Northeast 3rd Avenue
Pompano Beach, FL 33060
(954) 786–0344
Fax: (954) 785–6635

8051

Business Information: Woodhouse Inc. is a long–term care facility for the mentally and physically disabled. The facility currently employs 80 people to assist the 40 adult residents. As Executive Director, Ms. Trivigno is involved with public relations, budget concerns, staff recruitment, and supervision of the staff. She assists in the development of a viable budget each year and monitors cash management to help plan a budget for the following year. **Career Steps:** Executive Director, Woodhouse Inc. (1979–Present); Program Director, Crisis Line (1977–1979). **Associations & Accomplishments:** City Commissioner, City of Lighthouse Point Florida; Rotary Club of Pompano Beach; Soroptimist International of Pampano Beach; Broward Women's Alliance; Women's Political Caucus; Pompano Beach Board of Trade; Women's Executive Club. **Education:** Nova University: M.S. (1981), B.S. in Psychology; Licensed Nursing Home Administrator. **Personal:** Ms. Trivigno enjoys running, weight training, and antique collecting.

Becky B. Uzzell

Regional Controller
Diversicare
1400 West Markham Street, Suite 330
Little Rock, AR 72201–1846
(501) 372–0707
Fax: (501) 372–7252

8051

Business Information: Diversicare is the management service for a conglomerate of nursing homes located in Arkansas, Texas, Alabama, Tennessee, Florida, West Virginia, Kentucky, Ohio, and Canada. Comprised of 70–142 beds per facility, the centers offer Medicare and Medicaid approved services, as well as Alzheimers care. As Regional Controller, Ms. Uzzell oversees all financial aspects of the Arkansas region. Her duties include taxes, payroll, budgeting, analysis and reports. **Career Steps:** Regional Controller, Diversicare (1995–Present); Senior Associate, Coopers & Lybrand (1991–1995); Senior Associate, Pittman, Casey & Price (1987–1991). **Associations & Accomplishments:** American Institute of Certified Public Accountants (AICPA); Habitat for Humanity. **Education:** Mt. Olive College, B.S.B.A. (1986); Wayne Community College, Associates Degree. **Personal:** Ms. Uzzell enjoys reading, riding, and cooking.

Dr. J.S.R. Van

Chief of Psychiatry
Canandaigua Veterans Affairs Medical Center
400 Fort Hill Avenue
Canandaigua, NY 14424–1159
(716) 396–3622
Fax: (716) 396–3692

8051

Business Information: Canandaigua Veterans Affairs Medical Center is a long–term care facility providing diagnosis, treatment, and long–term care in psychiatry, geriatrics and medicine to veterans. A practicing physician since 1974 and an Internist and Psychiatrist, Dr. Van joined VA Medical Center, North Chicago in 1977, and as Chief of Psychiatry at Canandaigua since 1994. He is responsible for all aspects of operations of the largest bed service (294 beds) at the medical center. He also oversees all administrative functions of the service and supervises 52 employees (doctors, nurses, physician assistants). In this position, Dr. Van has been able to set up new programs, teach medical students, conduct research, and present papers in national, as well as, international meetings. His major areas of interest are in forensic psychiatry and electroconvulsive therapy. **Career Steps:** Chief of Psychiatry, Canandaigua Veterans Affairs Medical Center (1994–Present); Clinical Associate Professor of Psychiatry, University of Rochester (1994–Present); Acting Chief of Psychiatry, North Chicago Veterans Affairs Medical Center (1993); Finch UHS/Chicago Medical School: Associate Professor of Clinical Psychiatry (1992–1994), Assistant Professor of Psychiatry (1982–1992). **Associations & Accomplishments:** Board Certified in Psychiatry, American Board of Psychiatry and Neurology; Fellow, American Psychiatric Association; American Academy of Psychiatry and the Law; Treasurer, Indo American Psychiatric Association; National Association of VA Chiefs of Psychiatry. **Education:** Thanjavur Medical College, India (University of Madras), M.B.B.S. (1974); Madras Medical College (University of Madras), Residency in Internal Medicine (1974–1977); UHS/Chicago Medical School – North Chicago, Residency in Psychiatry (1977–1980). **Personal:** Married to Kanchana in 1987. Two children: Vishnu and Arvind. Dr. Van enjoys travel (has visited 150 countries) and photography.

Rudolf Vela

Administrator
Woodlawn Hills Care Center
3031 West Woodlawn Avenue
San Antonio, TX 78228–5017
(216) 432–2381
Fax: Please mail or call

8051

Business Information: Woodlawn Hills Care Center is a 180 bed licensed nursing home providing health and related services to elderly residents. A historical landmark, the Center is Medicare and Medicaid approved, and offers rehabilitation services, physical, occupational, physical, respiratory, and I.V. therapies. Established in 1897, the Center employs 130 people. As Administrator, Mr. Vela oversees all functions involving the Center. His duties include administration, operations, personnel management, strategic planning, and public relations. **Career Steps:** Administrator, Woodlawn Hills Care Center (1995–Present); Administrator, Texas Health Enterprises (1994–1995); Administrator, Living Centers of America (1992–1994). **Associations & Accomplishments:** Texas Health Care Association; American College of Health Care Executives. **Education:** Our Lady of The Lake University, M.B.A. candidate; University of Texas Health Science Center; Texas State, B.S. Hospital Administration. **Personal:** Married to Olga in 1986. One child: Aristotle Harrison. Mr. Vela enjoys golf and outdoor activities.

Miriam L. Wall

Administrator
Heritage Park
12825 White Bluff Road
Savannah, GA 31419
(912) 927–9416
Fax: (912) 927–9956

8051

Business Information: Heritage Park is a long–term care nursing home offering physical therapy, occupational therapy, speech therapy, and hospice services. As Administrator, Ms. Wall is responsible for overall facility operations, including budgeting, finance, resident care, dietary concerns, housekeeping, and resident activities. **Career Steps:** Administrator, Heritage Park (1995–Present); Nursing Home Administrator, Hillhaven–Savannah Rehabilitation & Nursing Center (1993–1995). **Associations & Accomplishments:** Traveler's Protective Association; American College of Health Care Administrators; Georgia Council of Notaries Public; Sterling Who's Who; Marquis Who's Who. **Education:** Georgia Southern University, M.H.S. (1993); Medical College of Georgia, A.S. (1983); Armstrong Atlantic State University, Certificate in Gerontology (Dec. 1996); Georgia–licensed N.H.A., pursuing certification. **Personal:** One child: Jonathan Reitz and ten pets. Ms. Wall enjoys castle and bear collecting, Olympic pin collecting, baseball, Star Trek, and Star Wars.

Deborah Wickey

Administrator
Cass County Medical Care
23770 Hospital Street
Cassopolis, MI 49031–9644
(616) 445–3801 Ext. 12
Fax: (616) 445–8871

8051

Business Information: Cass County Medical Care is a county–owned, long–term care nursing facility funded by Medicare and Medicaid. As Administrator, Ms. Wickey oversees the day–to–day operations of the Facility. She is responsible for the quality of residential life and care, public relations, and human resource concerns of the staff members. **Career Steps:** Administrator, Cass County Medical Care (1989–Present); Assistant Administrator, Fairview Medical Care Facility (1976–1989). **Associations & Accomplishments:** Cass County Specialized Respite Care Advisory Board Member; Michigan County Medical Care Facilities Council, President 1995–1996; Cass County Health and Human Services Committee; Michigan Association of Counties. **Education:** George Washington University (1981). **Personal:** Married to Leland H. in 1972. Two children: Lisa Anne and Joseph Lee.

Paula Stott Young

A. Director
St. Frances Country House
1412 Landsdowne Avenue
Darby, PA 19023
(610) 461–6510
Fax: (610) 461–3558

8051

Business Information: St. Frances Country House is a 273–bed Catholic nursing home serving the entire community, religious preference notwithstanding, with pride and compassion in a religious environment. The majority of the Facility's residents are wheelchair–bound. As A. Director of Recreation Therapy, Mrs. Young is responsible for coordinating activities for all residents to insure a balance of programs, supervises staff and volunteers of 80 or more. Departments under supervision, include Recreation, Gift Shop, Hairdresser, Pastoral care, and Volunteer Services. She also writes articles for the Facility newsletter, coordinates community interaction, to include recruiting volunteers, and creates programs. **Career Steps:** Director, St. Frances Country House (1995–Present); Assistant Activities Coordinator, Marriott Quadrangle (1994–1995); Recreation Assistant, IHS of Broomall in Pennsylvania (1990–1994). **Associations & Accomplishments:** NAAP; NCAAP; DVA/DVP; PTRS; Pampha Sepampha; PDPR; CMAA; DCAD; NAFE; Working with the Mother's Home in Darby; Published in 2000 Most Notable American Women: To Live Again Organization For Widows; Alzheimer's Association; Received the "Courage To Come Back" award (1996) from Mercy Health and the Phil. '76s and the Philadelphia Tribune; The Marriott Star Performer Award (1995); Most Caring Staff Member (1993). **Education:** Pennsylvania State University, Continuing Education courses; Biscayne College, Bachelor of Arts Degree (1967); Whitman Group, completion of the Advanced Management; The Validation Therapy Institution, Validation; Continual course work in the field of Alzheimer's. **Personal:** Married to William R. in 1965 Widowed in 1976. Three children: Robin Stott–McNulty, Eric R., and Gregory A. Stott. One grandson: Ryan J. McNulty. Mrs. Young enjoys arts & crafts, writing, collecting shells and ocean articles, and photography.

Patricia D. Baccash, M.D.

Medical Director
Philadelphia Protestant Home
600 Glen Echo Road
Philadelphia, PA 19119–2918
(215) 663–0575
Fax: (214) 247–4262

8052

Business Information: Philadelphia Protestant Home is a 550–person, adult day care facility, providing a personalized life care community, offering individual, assisted–living, and home health care services. A practicing physician since 1978, and a Board–Certified Geriatric and Emergency Physician, Dr. Baccash joined the Philadelphia Protestant Home in 1992. Serving as Medical Director, she provides the overall medical and administrative direction of the Home, in addition to her daily patient practice in geriatric and emergency medicine. Concurrent with her executive position, she serves as Attending Emergency Medical Physician at Crozer Chester and Medical Director of Vital Age Jeanes. **Career Steps:** Medical Director, Philadelphia Protestant Home (1992–Present); Attending EM, Crozen Chester (1992–Present); Medical Director, Vital Age Jeanes (1989–Present). **Associations & Accomplishments:** American Academy of Emergency Medicine; American College of Emergency Physicians; American Medical Association; Pennsylvania Medical Society; Philadelphia County Medical Society; American Geriatric Society; National Society of Medical Directors. **Education:** Medical College of Pennsylvania, (1978) M.D.; St. Johns University, B.S. (1972). **Personal:** Married to Michael D. O'Neill in 1985. Dr. Baccash enjoys traveling all over the world, racing, and the Opera.

William E. Bendall

Administrator
Lauderdale Health Care Center
P.O. Box 186
Ripley, TN 38063–0186
(901) 635–5100
Fax: (901) 635–3326

8052

Business Information: Lauderdale Health Care Center specializes in providing long–term, intermediate, and skilled nursing care to the elderly. The Company is a 71–bed facility that also offers occupational, IV, and speech therapy services. As Administrator, Mr. Bendall is responsible for the day–to–day operations of the facility. **Career Steps:** Administrator, Lauderdale Health Care Center (1995–Present); Night Manager, St. Peter Manor (1994–1995); Production Control Manager, Litho Carton Services, Inc. (1985–1994); Production Control Manager, Cleo, Inc. (1984–1985). **Associations & Accomplishments:** Boy Scouts of America; Volunteer, Memphis in May International Festival; St. Paul Presbyterian Church. **Education:** University of Memphis, B.S. (1974). **Personal:** Married to Catherine Marie in 1989. Four children: Billy, Danny, Shelley, and Rachel. One grandson: Avery. Mr. Bendall enjoys recreational boating.

Mary Ellen Breen

Executive Director
Corliss Institute
290 Main Street
Warren, RI 02885–4344
(401) 245–3609
Fax: (401) 245–9565

8052

Business Information: Corliss Institute is a private, not–for–profit, independent living and working services organization, providing apartments, condominiums, and employment opportunities for deaf adults. As Executive Director, Ms. Breen supervises day treatment, coordinates fund–raising and outreach programming, and works closely with the Board of Directors on the development of new projects. **Career Steps:** Executive Director, Corliss Institute (1985–Present). **Associations & Accomplishments:** RID Inc., Certified Interpreter to the Deaf; Gallaudet Alumni Association; Founders Award (1992). **Education:** Gallaudet University – Washington D.C., M.A. (1985). **Personal:** Married in 1985. She has two sons. Ms. Breen enjoys the beach.

Janet L. Davis

Administrator
Clark County Board Mental Retardation / Developmental Disabilities
2535 Kenton Street
Springfield, OH 45505–3352
(513) 328–2685
Fax: (513) 328–4615

8052

Business Information: Clark County Board Mental Retardation/Developmental Disabilities is a non–profit residential facility for persons with mental retardation and developmental disabilities. The Board houses 110 residents in cottage settings, with 14 to 21 people per cottage and in a family setting involving six to eight people. Mostly funded by Medicaid, the Board accepts residents from the ages of 5 to 73 years. As Administrator, Mrs. Davis oversees all day–to–day business functions of the residence. She is responsible for finances, budgeting, personnel, and maintaining quality care for the occupants. **Career Steps:** Clark County Board Mental Retardation / Developmental Disabilities: Administrator (1992–Present); Assistant Director (1991–1992); Supervisor of Unit Coordinators (1989–1991). **Education:** Wright State University: Masters (1986), B.S. **Personal:** Married to Loyd in 1968. Three children: Brent, Steve, and David. Mrs. Davis enjoys reading, sewing, hiking, and photography.

Lucinda Gurst

Director of Nursing
Phoebe Home Inc.
1925 W. Turner Street
Allentown, PA 18104–5551
(610) 794–5255
Fax: (610) 794–5412

8052

Business Information: Phoebe Home Inc. is a geriatric, long–term care facility with a population of 450 residents. Established in 1903, Phoebe Home, Inc. currently employs 450 medical and administrative support staff, 270 of which are in the nursing department. As Director of Nursing, Ms. Gurst is responsible for the care of all residents and direction of employees. **Career Steps:** Phoebe Home, Inc.: Director of Nursing (1987–Present), Assistant Director of Nursing (Aug. 1987–Oct. 1987), Unit Manager (R.N.) (1985–1987). **Associations & Accomplishments:** Pennsylvania Directory of Nursing Association – Long Term Care (PADONA–LTC); Hospital Association of Pennsylvania; Board of Associates, Lehigh Valley Hospital; NEXUS for Geriatric Planning **Education:** Allentown Hospital School of Nursing, Nursing Degree (1975); Coursework taken toward B.S. in Business with a concentration in Healthcare Administration. **Personal:** Two children: Alexis and Joseph. Ms. Gurst enjoys reading, needlework, and collecting antiques.

Linda B. Hagler

Executive Director
Rolla Presbyterian Manor
1200 Homelife Plaza
Rolla, MO 65453
(314) 364–7336
Fax: (314) 364–7336

8052

Business Information: Rolla Presbyterian Manor is a continuing care retirement community, providing independent residential, health, and charitable care for Medicare and Medicaid patients. Rolla Presbyterian Health Manor has incorporated a Share Program with the middle school, in which students assist residents in activities and an Outside Care Program that assists non–residents. Future plans include integrating into hospital computerized medical records, and expanding and building the facility. Rolla Presbyterian Health Manor currently employs 61 people. As Executive Director, Ms. Hagler is responsible for all facets of the day–to–day operations of the facility. **Career Steps:** Executive Director, Rolla Presbyterian Manor (1990–Present); Caseworker, State of Missouri (1989–1990); Administrator, Briarwood Manor, Inc. (1982–1986). **Associations & Accomplishments:** Rolla Kiwanis Club: Member – Board of Directors, Chairman – Kiwanis Social Committee, Member – Kiwanis Fine & Pancake Committee; MOAHA: Member – Board of Directors, Member – Government Relations and Education Committees; Member, NFAC Board of Directors; Member, AAHSA; Member, ACHCA; Certified through ACHCA – Fellowship through ACHCA pending; Member, Phi Theta Kappa; Listed in Who's Who Among Executives & Professionals (1994); Active 4 & 5 year old Sunday school teacher, First Baptist Church, Cuba, Missouri. **Education:** Concordia Lutheran College, B.A. in progress; East Central College, A.A. in Business Administration; University of Missouri – Columbia – Completed AIT Program. **Personal:** Two children: Mallory Nichole and Dylan Carwile Hagler. Ms. Hagler enjoys teaching Sunday school classes.

Timothy J. Leali

Habilitation Director
VOCA Corporation
8200 Traphagen Street NW
Massillon, OH 44646
(330) 830–0050
Fax: (330) 830–0172

8052

Business Information: VOCA Corporation provides private residential services to adults with mental retardation and developmental disabilities. As Habilitation Director, Mr. Leali directs all fiscal and regulatory aspects of operations, contracts occupational and physical therapists, and supervises worksite staff. **Career Steps:** Habilitation Director, VOCA Corporation (1993–Present); Case Manager, Stark County Board of Mental Retardation/Developmental Disabilities (1991–1993); Rehabilitation Specialist, Goodwill Industries of Akron (1989–1991); Case Manager, Community Support Services (1988–1989). **Associations & Accomplishments:** Association for Retarded Citizens of Stark County. **Education:** Malone College, B.A. (1984). **Personal:** One child: Tessa Jordan Leali. Mr. Leali has been a competitive bodybuilder and personal trainer since 1980.

Dorothy M. Marchbanks

Administrator
Colonial Nursing & Retirement Center
105 Washington Street
Pauls Valley, OK 73075
(405) 238–5528
Fax: (405) 238–7989

8052

Business Information: Colonial Nursing & Retirement Center is a 109–bed nursing home and 10–bed retirement center, offering all rehabilitative services including physical, speech, and occupational therapy. The Centers accept Medicare/Medicaid. As Administrator, Mrs. Marchbanks is responsible for all operations, including management services, hiring, and employee relations. **Career Steps:** Administrator, Colonial Nursing & Retirement Center (1995–Present), (1991–1993); Administrator, Cleveland Manor Nursing Home (1993–95). **Education:** University of Oklahoma – Norman, Adm. License (1991); Drumright Vocational Tech, L.P.N. License (1986). **Personal:** Married to Robert in 1991. One child: Shelbi Danielle. Mrs. Marchbanks enjoys biking, swimming, and reading.

Joan C. Mathews

Director of Nursing
North American Healthcare
1008 East Broadway
Astoria, IL 61501
(309) 329–2136
Fax: (307) 329–2569

8052

Business Information: North American Healthcare is a management holding company, owning eleven skilled intermediate care facilities in Indiana, Illinois, Ohio and Missouri. A Registered Nurse with twenty–seven years experience in nursing, Ms. Mathews joined North American Healthcare as Director of Nursing in 1995. She is responsible for the oversight and direction of all nursing staff, schedules, education, budgetary controls, and inventory control, as well as acting as mediator. In addition, she has the overall responsibility for patient care and overall assessment of the Care Plan. **Career Steps:** Director of Nursing, North American Healthcare (1995–Present); Cardiac Surgical Nurse, Methodist Medical Center (1989–1995); Staff Nurse, Graham Hospital (1986–1989). **Education:** Graham School of Nursing, RN (1988); Spoon River College: A.S. in Nursing (1988), A.A.S. (1976). **Personal:** Ms. Mathews enjoys antiques, sewing, refinishing and remodeling.

Wanda H. Matthews

Program Director
Helping Hands Adult Services
633 West Main
Yadkinville, NC 27055
(910) 679–7052
Fax: Please mail or call

8052

Business Information: Helping Hands Adult Services provides residential care for the elderly. In addition to caring for nineteen elderly residents, Helping Hands is also licensed for twelve adult day care clients. Mrs. Matthews was responsible for the initial groundwork that helped with the formation of Helping Hands Adult Services, which was established in 1993. As Program Director, she is also responsible for the management of residential and day care programs, administration, operations, public relations, and strategic planning. **Career Steps:** Program Director, Helping Hands Adult Services (1993–Present); Home Health Aide Coordinator, Yadkin Co. Home Health Agency (1982–1992); Supervisor in Charge, Rosewood Rest Home (1975–1981). **Associations & Accomplishments:** North Carolina Adult Daycare Association; North Carolina Center for Non Profit Associations; Alzheimers Association. **Education:** Surry Community College, Activities Coordinator, Certified Nursing Assistant; Forsythe Tech Homemaker Health Aide. **Personal:** Married to Thomas in 1991. Two children: Keshia and Nicole. Mrs. Matthews enjoys Hospice Volunteering.

Gregory A. Omerzu

Habilitation Director
VOCA Corporation/Alternative Residence III, Inc.
133 Willettsville Pike
Hillsboro, OH 45133
(513) 393–5724
Fax: (513) 393–3577
VM: (800) 837–8622 MB #3

8052

Business Information: Voca Corporation is a professionally managed company committed to providing an increasing range of support services through creative technologies to persons with disabilities. Voca Corporation is governed by a not–for–profit board entitled Alternative Residences III. The company began operations in 1979 in Ohio and currently manages more than 120 group homes in 7 states. As the Habilitation Director, Mr. Omerzu is responsible for directing and monitoring all aspects of the Hillsboro, Ohio area's habilitation services including supervising a staff of over 75 employees. **Career Steps:** Habilitation Director, Alternative Residences III/Voca Corporation (1995–Present); Human Services Administrator/Planner, Miami Valley Regional Planning Commission (1991–1995); Education Specialist, Jewish Vocational Services (1988–1991); Habilitation Specialist and Program Director, Montgomery County Board of MR/DD (1986–1988). **Associations & Accomplishments:** Member of Montgomery County Hunger Coalition; Drug Action Coalition; Member of Montgomery County Homeless Shelter Network; Member of Welfare Reform Task Force of Dayton; Member of American Association of Mental Retardation; Miami Valley Cross Roads to the Future; Criminal Justice Policy Council; Juvenile Justice Advisory Committee; Volunteer experience includes: Planned Parenthood of Miami Valley, United Cerebral Palsy, American Red Cross, Children Have A Potential Camp, Senior Citizens Center and Aids Foundation Dayton. **Education:** Wright State University, Rehabilitation Education (1987). **Personal:** Mr. Omerzu enjoys tennis, swimming, travel, and collecting antiques.

John W. Owens

President
Residential Services, Inc.
204 Frank Street
Easley, SC 29642–1725
(864) 306–8580
Fax: (864) 859–9200

8052

Business Information: Residential Services, Inc., founded in 1986, is an organization of nursing homes and residential care facilities. The Corporation operates two intermediate care facilities, eight community training homes, and one supervised living facility. As President, Mr. Owens oversees all operational aspects, strategic planning and customer relations of the Company. **Career Steps:** President, Residential Services, Inc./West End Retirement Center (1976–Present); President, Village Corporation (1989–1996); Director, Pickens County Board of Disabilities/Special Needs (1982–1996) **Associations & Accomplishments:** American College of Health Care Administrators; South Carolina Association of Residential Care Facilities; National Association of Residential Care; Cattlemens Association; American Quarter Horse Association. **Education:** Spartanburg Methodist College, A.S.S. degree (1974); Attended: University of South Carolina and South Carolina Criminal Justice Academy. **Personal:** Married to Jan in 1976. One child: Lindsey. Mr. Owens enjoys horseback riding and competitions.

Jose G. Santiago

Support Service Director
Jewish Home and Hospital
120 West 106th Street
New York, NY 10025–3712
(212) 870–4830
Fax: (212) 870–4863

8052

Business Information: Jewish Home and Hospital is a 514–bed in–patient nursing home and hospital. As Support Service Director, Mr. Santiago oversees the Housekeeping Department, Resident Services, admissions, labor, purchasing, and elevator maintenance. **Career Steps:** Support Service Director, Jewish Home and Hospital (1990–Present); Director of Housekeeping, Beth Abraham Hospital (1987–1990); Supervisor, Lenox Hill Hospital (1970–1987). **Associations & Accomplishments:** National Executive Housekeepers Association. **Education:** Attended, New York City Community College, Sanitation Management (1976–1978). **Personal:** Three children: Jose, Jr. I, Maritza, and Jose, Jr. II. Mr. Santiago enjoys fishing and working around the house.

Brenda Stiers–Carter

Private Consultant
750 Delray Drive
Indianapolis, IN 46241
(317) 247–1078
Fax: Please mail or call

8052

Business Information: As a Private Consultant, Ms. Stiers–Carter provides behavioral, counseling, and clinical services to mentally retarded and developmentally delayed (MR/DD) individuals living in various community settings. Areas of expertise include behavioral analysis, provision of behavioral management interventions, and assisting families of the MR/DD individual in dealing with problems that arise in the home setting. **Career Steps:** Self–Employed, Private Consultant (1996); Beverly Enterprises dba North Willow Center: Program Director (1994–1996), Director of Social Services (1991–1994); Assistant Director of Rehabilitative Psychology (1989–1991). **Associations & Accomplishments:** Phi Gamma Mu; Administrative Board, Garden City Christian Church; Served on several Human Rights Committees; AAMR. **Education:** Ball State University: M.A. (1987), B.S. (1984). **Personal:** Married to David A. in 1983. Two children: Matthew D. and Allison P. Ms. Stiers–Carter enjoys reading and sports.

Stephanie Teeny

Marketing Director
Regency Park
8300 Barnes Road
Portland, OR 97225
(503) 292–8444
Fax: (503) 292–8409

8052

Business Information: Regency Park, a subsidiary of Regent Assisted Living, Inc. is a privately–held company providing assisted living for older adults. Comprised of 143 apartments, the Facility has three levels of care, Independent, Assisted and Daily Help. Regional in scope, the Company has five locations throughout Washington, California, Oregon and Idaho and is currently expanding to twelve. Established in 1987, the Company employs 125 people. As Marketing Director, Ms. Teeny oversees all admissions, tours and public relations. Additional responsibilities include weekly marketing reports, daily census, discharge planning, and being a coordinator/liaison with other homes. **Career Steps:** Marketing Director, Regency Park (1996–Present); Marketing Director, Franklin Care Center (1995); Director of Social Services and Admissions, Regency at Scenic Pointe (1994–1995). **Associations & Accomplishments:** Chamber of Commerce. **Education:** Christopher Newport University, B.S.W. (1993). **Personal:** Married to Jeff in 1995. Ms. Teeny enjoys mountain biking, hiking, travel and music.

Starla J. Wessels

Director of Nursing Services
Royal Park Care Center
North 7411 Nevada
Spokane, WA 99208
(509) 489–2273
Fax: (509) 489–4509

8052

Business Information: Royal Park Care Center is a 164–bed, long term, skilled health care facility, providing extensive rehabilitation for transition into the community, ongoing counseling and care in their Alzheimer's Unit. Established in 1991, Royal Park Care Center is a part of five Evergreen Living Centers located throughout the Washington and Idaho area and employs 140 people. As Director of Nursing Services, Mrs. Wessels is responsible for the supervision of a nursing staff of 140, ensuring the quality of life for the residents with quality of care, as well as administration, operations, public relations, and strategic planning. **Career Steps:** Director of Nursing Services, Royal Park Care Center (1991–Present); Nursing Service Consultant, Beverly Enterprises (1988–1991); Director of Nursing, Hillcrest Convention Center (1973–1988). **Associations & Accomplishments:** NADONA – National Association for Director of Nurses; Long Term Care Association with Washington State. **Education:** Lewis Clark State, A.S. (1973). **Personal:** Married to Tom in 1973. One child: Stacey. Mrs. Wessels enjoys cross–stitching, country crafts, and home decorating.

Sheila Whitlock

Executive Director
CARES of Northwest Ohio
P.O. Box 521
Bryan, OH 43506
(419) 636–1991
Fax: (419) 636–2799

8052

Business Information: CARES of Northwest Ohio, provides intermediate care for the developmentally disabled. Based in

Northwest Ohio, the company consists of two federally–funded intermediate–care facilities, as well as a state–funded, supported living community. In addition to the operation of their principal facilities, CARES also runs a summer camp program for children. As Executive Director, Ms. Whitlock oversees funds development, manages the budget, and is active in policy development. Additional responsibilities include public speaking, property acquisition and maintenance, and service model. **Career Steps:** CARES of Northwest Ohio: Executive Director (1991–Present), Program Coordinator (1990–1991); Consultant, Whitlock Services (1990–1996). **Associations & Accomplishments:** Ohio Private Residential Association; AAMR; Board Trustee of YWCA; Bryan Chamber of Commerce Leadership Award; JSEC. **Education:** The Defiance College, B.S. (1989). **Personal:** Married to Stanley in 1977. One child: Jennifer. Ms. Whitlock enjoys high school Band Boosters and serves as a Friend of Stryker Library.

Bobbie A. Wilson
Administrator
Garland Convalescent Center
321 North Shiloh Road
Garland, TX 75042
(214) 276–9571
Fax: (214) 272–8660

8052

Business Information: Garland Convalescent Center is a 120–bed Medicare/Medicaid nursing facility with an Alzheimer unit and agressive wound care unit. As Administrator, Ms. Wilson oversees the day–to–day activities of the Facility. Her responsibilities include profit/loss concerns, regulatory compliance, marketing of services to the community, public relations, personnel concerns, and strategic planning. Ms. Wilson counsels family members on dealing with Alzheimer's and works with other members of management at the Facility to ensure patients retain their dignity and are treated with compassion. **Career Steps:** Administrator, Garland Convalescent Center (1994–Present); Administrator, Texas Health Enterprises; Executive Care Options Texas; Personal Care Director, Telesis Corporation. **Associations & Accomplishments:** Texas and American Health Care Association; American College of Health Care Executives; Alzheimer Association; Chamber of Commerce. **Education:** University of Texas, Southwestern Medical School, Post Bac. Licensure (1994); Florida State University, B.S. in Merchandising. **Personal:** Married to Scott in 1994. Two children: Scott and Nick. Ms. Wilson enjoys gourmet cooking, gardening, and making clothes for her grandaughter.

Mary A. Woods
Director/Environmental Services
Towne Centre Retirement Community and Health Care
7250 Arthur Boulevard
Merrillville, IN 46410
(219) 736–2900 Ext.26
Fax: (219) 736–2209

8052

Business Information: Towne Centre Continuing Care Retirement Community is composed of 153 senior living apartments and a 98 bed healthcare facility. As Director of Environmental Services, Ms. Woods is responsible for all aspects of housekeeping, laundry, maintenance, and security. **Career Steps:** Director of Environmental Services, Towne Centre Retirement Community (1987–Present); Director, Housekeeping/Laundry, Lincolnshire Health Care (1984–1987); Director, Housekeeping/Laundry, Breamen Health Care (1981–1982); Director of Housekeeping, The Willows Rehabilitation Center (1974–1982). **Associations & Accomplishments:** National Executive Housekeepers Association: Chapter Recording Secretary (1995–Present), Chapter Treasurer (1993–1995), Chapter Board Member (1978–1993); Certified Lay Speaker. **Education:** Hebron, Indiana High School (1956); Indiana University Northwest Executive Housekeeping School (1976); Methodist Church Lay Speaking School (1990).

Gina M. Greco
Habilitation Director
HLA Healthcare, Inc.
P O Box 2188
Warren, OH 44484–0188
(330) 369–2534
Fax: (330) 369–3573

8051

Business Information: HLA Healthcare, Inc., is a private non–profit corporation. The facility consists of Building One and Building Two. Building One houses a 32–bed Nursing Facility and a 28–bed Intermediate Care Facility for the mentally retarded (ICF/MR). Building Two houses a 32–bed ICF/MR. The ICF/MR provides residential and habilitation services with mental retardation. As Habilitation Director, Ms. Greco develops, organizes and monitors the Individual Habilitation Plans of each of the 28 residents. Ms. Greco also keeps abreast of

current federal and state regulations. In cooperation with other facility directors, Ms. Greco coordinates the Habilitation Department to ensure optimal functioning of each resident. **Career Steps:** Habilitation Director, HLA Healthcare, Inc. (1994–Present). **Education:** Kent State University, B.A. (1994). **Personal:** Ms. Greco enjoys backpacking and camping.

Deborah A. Abelow
Director of Human Resources
Menorah Home and Hospital for the Aged
1516 Oriental Boulevard
Brooklyn, NY 11235–2328
(718) 646–4441
Fax: (718) 769–7542

8059

Business Information: Menorah Home and Hospital for the Aged, established in 1916, is a nursing home providing medical and long–term care to the elderly. As Director of Human Resources, Ms. Abelow is responsible for the oversight of employee and labor relations, as well as various human resource programs. **Career Steps:** Director of Human Resources, Menorah Home and Hospital for the Aged (1995–Present); Director of Human Resources, St. Mary's Hospital for Children (1994–1995); Director of Personnel, Florence Nightingale Nursing Homes (1991–1994). **Associations & Accomplishments:** Association of Healthcare Human Resource Administrators – New York Chapter; Society of Human Resource Managers. **Education:** Hofstra University, M.A. (1990), B.A. **Personal:** Ms. Abelow enjoys scuba diving, softball, and other outdoor activities.

Rosemary Baker
Administrator
Woodlawn Nursing Home
84 Pine Street
Newport, NH 03773–2005
(603) 863–1020
Fax: (603) 863–2250

8059

Business Information: Woodlawn Nursing Home is a private, 53–bed, long–term, intermediate care, nursing facility located in Newport, New Hampshire. As Administrator, Ms. Baker oversees the day–to–day operations of the Facility. She functions as the compliance administrator and makes sure all state, federal and OSHA regulations are met and followed. Other responsibilities include oversight of financial matters, development of strategic plans for the future, and reporting to the Chief Executive Officer on the status of the facility. **Career Steps:** Woodlawn Nursing Home: Administrator (1996–Present), Director of Business Services (1996–1996); Director of Social Services, Westwood Health Care Center (1993–1995). **Associations & Accomplishments:** Kiwanis International; New Hampshire Health Care Association; Delta Mu Delta, Business Honor Society. **Education:** Plymouth State College, M.B.A. Candidate; Keene State College, B.S. (1993). **Personal:** Ms. Baker enjoys outdoor activities and physical fitness.

Tina B. Conner
President and Owner
Birchtree Healthcare, Inc.
106 Padgett Drive
Clinton, KY 42031–9523
(502) 653–2797
Fax: (502) 653–2089

8059

Business Information: Birchtree Healthcare, Inc. is a government–regulated nursing home and rehabilitation facility. A practicing registered nurse, Mrs. Conner founded Birchtree Healthcare, Inc. in 1995 and serves as its President and Owner. She is responsible for all day–to–day operations, with duties including patient care, government regulatory affairs, marketing, and public relations. **Career Steps:** President and Owner, Birchtree Healthcare, Inc. (1995–Present). **Associations & Accomplishments:** American Nursing Association; Kentucky Nurses Association; Sigma Theta Tau International; Rotary; Chamber of Commerce; Hickman County Democratic Chair; Patton–Henry for Kentucky Action Committee Chair; St. Jude Community Awareness Committee Chair; Former Young Farmer Association. **Education:** Murray State University, B.S.N. (1994). **Personal:** Married to Seth in 1990. Three children: Justin, Beth, and Coleman. Mrs. Conner enjoys snow skiing, travel, and cooking.

Akhaya K. Das, M.D.
Chief of Critical Care Unit
Castle Point VA Medical Center
P.O. Box 487 CPVAMC
Castle Point, NY 12511
(914) 831–2000 Ext. 5147
Fax: (914) 896–4545

8059

Business Information: Castle Point VA Medical Center is a full–service, multi–level professional health care facility providing diversified health care for military personnel and their families. As Chief of the Critical Care Unit, Dr. Das is responsible for all aspects of operations in the unit. A Certified Pulmonologist, Dr. Das specializes in the treatment and care of patients with lung disorders, cardiac–related devices (pacemakers) and other thoracic areas. **Career Steps:** Chief of Critical Care Unit, Castle Point, VA Medical Center (1980–Present); Involved in Teaching: Surgery Residents, Dental Residents, Staff Nurses; Instructor, ACLS; Affiliated with the following hospitals: St. Francis, St. Lukes, and Vassar Bros Hospital. **Associations & Accomplishments:** American College of Physicians (Attending Physician); ACCP; Fellow, American College of International Physicians; American Thoracic Society; Pulmonary Fellowship, New York University, Booth Memorial Hospital, Flushing, New York. **Education:** Kasturba Medical College, M.D. (1980). **Personal:** Married to Vaijanti in 1981. Two children: Krishna and Kristina. Dr. Das enjoys photography.

Ruby Lourdes de Guzman–de Venecia, M.D.
Attending Physician
Goldwater Memorial Hospital
Roosevelt Island
New York, NY 10044
(212) 318–8000
Fax: (718) 454–8562

8059

Business Information: Goldwater Memorial Hospital is a long–term care facility specializing in nursing medicine, pediatrics, psychiatry, and elderly care and rehabilitation. As Attending Physician, Dr. de Guzman–de Venecia is responsible for all aspects of patient care. **Career Steps:** Attending Physician, Goldwater Memorial Hospital (1992–Present); Medical Specialist I, Bernard Fineson Developmental Center (1980–1992); Resident Physician, Internal Medicine, Flushing Medical Center (1981–1984); Resident Physician, Pathology, Long Island Jewish Medical Center (1977–1981). **Associations & Accomplishments:** Committee Member, Public Policy, Education and Publication, State Society of Aging of New York; American Medical Association. **Education:** University of St. Thomas, PI, M.D. (1973); University of St. Thomas, Manila, Philippines, B.S. in Psychology (1969). **Personal:** Married to Alex P. in 1976. Three children: Francis Gregory, Dorothy Ann and Carla Alexis. Dr. de Guzman–de Venecia enjoys reading, playing the piano, and dancing.

Gregory C. Hamilton
Assistant to the Chairman
Trinity Healthcare Corporation
2640 Peerless Road
Cleveland, TN 37312
(423) 476–3035
Fax: (423) 339–9711

8059

Business Information: Trinity Healthcare Corporation is a professional management company specializing in long–term health care and senior housing. As Assistant to the Chairman, Mr. Hamilton is responsible for operational management, strategic management, and financial development. **Career Steps:** Assistant to the Chairman, Trinity Healthcare Corporation (1994–Present); Director, Trinity Foundation International (1995–Present); Intern/Clerk, Tennessee State District Attorney (1993–1994). **Associations & Accomplishments:** Sertoma Club; Circle K Club; Assisted Living Facilities Association of America; Cleveland Pachyderm Club; Board of Directors, Trinity Foundation International. **Education:** Lee College, B.S.– Magna Cum Laude (1994); Licensed Nursing Home Administrator (L.N.H.A.). **Personal:** Married to Wendy L. in 1989. One child: Joshua Clark. Mr. Hamilton enjoys his time and energy to causes which benefit the elderly.

Barbara Hostrup
Care Manager
Genesis Health Ventures, Inc.
312 West State Street
Kennett Square, PA 19348–3025
(610) 444–1520
Fax: (610) 444–1560

8059

Business Information: Genesis Health Ventures, Inc. is a regional health care management company, owning and operating skilled, interim and long–term care facilities for the elderly throughout the East Coast states. An experienced BSN with over ten years background in critcal care combined with home care expertise, Barbara Holstrup joined Genesis Health Ventures in 1993 as a nursing supervisor. Appointed to her current role as Care Manager in May of 1995, she provides the overall executive administration for the Community Care Management program of the Managed Care Division at Kennett Square, PA. Her primary duties involve the implementation of program and market development projects, the development and staffing of regionally–based eldercare resource database and referral lines; as well as provides counsel to older clients, their families and caregivers in her role as Director of Clinical Services for the Pennsylvania Home Care operation. **Career Steps:** Genesis Health Ventures, Inc.: Care Manager (1995–Present), Director of Clinical Services (1995), Nursing Supervisor (1993–1995); Staff Nurse – Acute Medical Care Unit, Veteran's Administration Hospital (1992–1993); Staff Nurse – Home Health, Community Visiting Nurse Service (1991–1992); Staff Nurse – Intensive Care Unit, Chester County Hospital (1988–1990); Student Nurse Technician, Veterans Administration Hospital (1985–1987); Research Assistant, Dr. Stephen Wilhite – Widener University (1985–1987); Office Manager, John B. Franklin, M.D. Associates (1976–1983). **Associations & Accomplishments:** Sigma Theta Tau – Eta Beta Chapter – Widener University; National Association of Professional Geriatric Care Managers; "Outstanding Adult Student" Award – Pennsylvania Adult Continuing Education (1987). **Education:** Widener University, B.S.N. (1987); Lehigh Valley Hospital Center, Accelerated Internship Program (1987–1988). **Personal:** One child: Craig Sterling. Mrs. Hostrup enjoys skiing and spending time with family and friends.

Pamela L. Lekas

Senior Vice President of Facility Accounting & Finance
Integrated Health Services
10065 Red Run Boulevard
Owings Mills, MD 21117
(410) 998–8922
Fax: (410) 654–5928

8059

Business Information: Integrated Health Services is a highly diversified health services provider, offering a broad spectrum of subacute and post–acute medical rehabilitative services through its post–acute healthcare system. IHS's post–acute services include subacute care, inpatient and outpatient rehabilitation, respiratory therapy, pharmacy, home healthcare, hospice care, and diagnostic services. The IHS approach to post–acute care is increasingly recognized by insurers and industry experts as an effective, less costly alternative to traditional hospital care. Supporting the full continuum of healthcare needs, IHS currently operates 223 facilities in 30 states throughout the U.S. with more than 28,000 beds. **Career Steps:** Senior Vice President of Facility Accounting & Finance, Integrated Health Services (1994–Present); National Medical Enterprises: Vice President of Finance (1990–1993), Regional Controller (1989–1990), Chief Financial Officer (1986–1989). **Education:** Lycoming College, B.A. (1982). **Personal:** Married to Fotios in 1994. Mrs. Lekas enjoys gardening, bowling, and walking.

Charlotta Smith Niles

Director of Nurses
Plaza Nursing Center
4403 Hospital Road
Pascagoula, MS 39581–5335
(601) 762–8960
Fax: (601) 769–1810

8059

Business Information: Plaza Nursing Center is a 120–bed healthcare facility primarily engaged in providing skilled nursing and rehabilitative services to patients who require continuous health care. As Director of Nurses, Ms. Niles is responsible for policies and procedures, updating materials and standing orders, hiring and training personnel, and accompanying doctors on their rounds. **Career Steps:** RN, Director of Nurses, Plaza Nursing Center (1995–Present); Singing River Hospital: RN, Staff Nurse (1995), LPN, Staff Nurse (1992–1995). **Associations & Accomplishments:** Mississippi Nurses Association. **Education:** Bishop State Community College, A.D.N. (1994); Mississippi Gulf Coast Junior College, Certificate of Nursing (1969). **Personal:** Married to John in 1993. Three children: Wayne Jr. and Misty Linder, and Sissy Kirchharr. Ms. Niles enjoys swimming and working with GA's at Calvary Baptist.

Huu–Trac Pham, M.D.

Director
Charleroi Medical Clinic
4664 Rue Charleroi
Montreal North, Quebec H1H 1T7
(514) 324–1655
Fax: (514) 254–5399

8060

Business Information: Charleroi Medical Clinic is a full–service, general medical clinic, providing diagnosis and treatment to patients. A practicing physician since 1966, Dr. Pham joined Charleroi Medical Clinic as Director in 1981. He is responsible for the direction of all clinical activities and administrative operations for associates and support staff, in addition to his daily patient practice. **Career Steps:** Director, Charleroi Medical Clinic (1981–Present); Staff Physician, Mount Sinai Hospital – Montreal (1978–1981); Resident, University of McGill – Montreal (1976–1978); Manpower and Professional Inspector of the Military Medical Direction in Vietnam (1971–1975); Surgeon, Cong–Hoa General Hospital – Vietnam (1966–1971); Division Surgeon, 1st Infantry Division – Vietnam (1963–1965); Faculty of Medicine, University of Saigon (1957–1963). **Associations & Accomplishments:** President, Association of the Vietnamese Physicians of The Free World (1987–1995); Editor–in Chief, Journal of the Vietnamese Physicians (1986–1995); President, Association of the Vietnamese Physicians of Canada (1989–1992); Recipient, Award from Human Rights Activists (1994); Author and Publisher of five studies: Study of 275 Cases of Cancer of the Uterus Cervix – Stage 1 (1966); Lexicon of Medical Terminology (1969); Amputation Level of the Lower Extremities (1970); Pedicle Graft of the Fracture of Femoral Neck (1971); Editorials in Journal of Vietnamese Physicians for three purposes: 1) to promote solidarity among physicians of Vietnamese origin; to foster and maintain medical ethics; to promote excellence in medical sciences. 2) to promote support for the struggle for freedom, democracy, human rights, and civil rights in Vietnam. 3) to promote the development of the Vietnamese community in different countries of the free world. **Education:** Doctorate in Medicine (1966); Certificate of General Surgery (1965); U.S.A. Federal Licensing Examination (FLEX) (1977); License of Medical Council of Canada (LMCC) (1976); Educational Council for Foreign Medical Graduates Examination (ECFMG) (1976); Certificate of Physics, Chemistry and Biology, Faculty of Science – University of Saigon (1956–1957); College Graduate, Major in Mathematics (1954–1956). **Personal:** Married to Tuyet–Van in 1986. Three children: Caroline, Myriam, and Francois. Dr. Pham enjoys lecturing, movies, and travel.

Paul Abraham, M.D.

Physician and Chief of Nephrology
St. Paul Ramsey Medical Center
640 Jackson Street
St. Paul, MN 55101–2502
(612) 221–3448
Fax: (612) 221–3048

8062

Business Information: St. Paul Ramsey Medical Center is a multi–specialty, primary and acute managed care medical facility. As Physician and Chief of Nephrology, Dr. Abraham is responsible for the care and treatment of renal diseases and dysfunctions, managing a group practice of five associates. Concurrent with his medical practice, Dr. Abraham is also an Associate Professor of Medicine at the University of Minnesota, providing instruction to medical students, and residents, as well as some clinical research. **Career Steps:** Physician and Chief of Nephrology, St. Paul Ramsey Medical Center (1992–Present); Nephrologist, Hennepin County Medical Center (1981–1992). **Associations & Accomplishments:** Chairman of the Medical Advisory Board, National Kidney Foundation of the Upper Midwest; American Society of Nephrology; American Society of Hypertension; Boy Scouts of America; Published over 45 articles and book chapters. **Education:** University of Minnesota, M.D. (1974). **Personal:** Married to Jo–Ellen in 1971. Two children: Peter and Jennifer. Dr. Abraham enjoys running, and cross country skiing.

Minou Absy–Jaghab, M.D., F.A.C.P.

Chairman of Infectious Control
Massapequa General Hospital
750 Hicksville Road
Seaford, NY 11783
(051) 433–8850
Fax: (516) 433–8245

8062

Business Information: Massapequa General Hospital is an acute care medical facility, providing diagnosis and treatment to patients. A practicing physician since 1986, Dr. Absy–Jaghab joined Massapequa General Hospital as Chairman of Infectious Control in 1992. She is responsible for making all decisions on Infection Control policies (isolation, procedures, sterilization) and antibiotics (whether or not prescribed), as well as serving as Infectious Disease Consultant involved with AIDS and HIV patients and lecturing to medical residents. Concurrent with her position at Massapequa General Hospital, she serves as Attending Physician at Nassau County Medical Center. **Career Steps:** Chairman of Infectious Control, Massapequa General Hospital (1992–Present); Attending Physician, Nassau County Medical Center (1986–Present). **Associations & Accomplishments:** American Medical Association. **Education:** University of Uege Medical School – Belgium, M.D. (1986); SUNY at Stony Brook, B.S.; New York University, M.S. **Personal:** Married to Kamil Jaghab, M.D. in 1989.

Joseph J. Abularrage, M.D.

Chairman of the Department of Pediatrics
The New York Hospital Medical Center of Queens
56–45 Main Street
Flushing, NY 11355
(718) 670–1033
Fax: (718) 460–0161

8062

Business Information: The New York Hospital Medical Center of Queens is an acute and critical care hospital, medical research and teaching institution. As Chairman of the Department of Pediatrics, Dr. Abularrage is responsible for administration, teaching, conferences, house staff, and diagnosis & treatment of patients. **Career Steps:** Chairman of the Department of Pediatrics, The New York Hospital Medical Center of Queens (1992–Present). **Associations & Accomplishments:** American Academy of Pediatrics; Has a medical TV show "Dr. J's Health Tips" – New York Mets Diamets – airing through baseball season. **Education:** New York University, M.D. (1975); Fordham University, B.S. (1971); Columbia University, M.P.H. (1975), M.Phil. (1981). **Personal:** Married to Margaret. Three children: Christopher, John, and Margaret. Dr. Abularrage enjoys sailing, golf, and gardening.

Russell A. Acevedo, M.D.

Director of Intensive Care Unit
Crouse–Irving Memorial Hospital
736 Irving Avenue
Syracuse, NY 13210–1690
(315) 470–7186
Fax: (031) 570–2731

8062

Business Information: Crouse–Irving Memorial Hospital is a 600–bed University Hospital with over 450 physicians on staff. Crouse Hospital, one of the oldest hospitals in Syracuse, merged with Irving Memorial Hospital, making Crouse–Irving Memorial Hospital the largest hospital in Syracuse. While serving as Director of the Intensive Care Unit, Dr. Acevedo was elected Chairman of Medical Executive Staff and therefore acts as Chief over all departments. Dr. Acevedo is responsible for defining hospital policies and acts as medical staff representative to the Crouse–Irving Hospital Board of Trustees. **Career Steps:** Crouse–Irving Memorial Hospital, President of Medical Staff (1994–Present), Director of Intensive Care Unit (1990–Present). **Associations & Accomplishments:** Society of Critical Care Medicine; American College of Chest Physicians; American College of Physicians; American Lung Association; American Association for Respiratory Care; Dr. Acevedo lectures to local churches. **Education:** University of Rochester, M.D. (1979); Cornell University, B.A. **Personal:** Married to Anne in 1984. Two children: Daryl and Robin. Dr. Acevedo enjoys skiing, working with his computer, and rollerblading.

A. Lynne Addair

Director of Nurses
Geary Community Hospital
1102 St. Mary's Road
Junction City, KS 66441
(913) 238–4131
Fax: (913) 238–5278

8062

Business Information: Geary Community Hospital is an acute care community hospital, providing quality health care to patients within the Junction City, Kansas area. Starting her nursing career in high school as a volunteer candy striper, Lynne Addair has continued to strive for the utmost in quality and caring patient delivery during her twenty–five years as a nurse and nursing administrator. Appointed as Director of Nursing at Geary Community Hospital in July of 1995 — reporting directly to the Chief Executive Officer — she has full executive charge for all nursing staff and related administrative operations pertaining to patient care practices. **Career Steps:** Director of Nurses, Geary Community Hospital (1995–Present); Irwin Army Community Hospital: Chief Nurse (1994–1995), Assistant Chief Nurse (1992–1994). **Associations & Accomplishments:** Kansas Organization of Nurse Executives. **Education:** University of Southern California, Master's of Science in Education (1979); University of South Carolina, Columbia, Master's in Nursing Administration (1983); Pacific Lutheran University, B.S. in Nursing (1975); Sacred Heart School of Nursing, Nursing Diploma (1964). **Personal:** Married to Dan in 1987. Four children: Dan Jr., Thomas, Lori Smith, and David Smith.

Joel Adler, M.D.

Geriatrics Physician
Bergen Pines Hospital
230 East Ridgewood Avenue
Paramus, NJ 07652
(201) 967–4652
Fax: (201) 967–4118
8062

Business Information: Established in 1994, Bergen Pines Hospital is a full tertiary care teaching hospital, in affiliation with the University of Medicine and Dentistry of New Jersey. Dr. Joel Adler, Board–certified in Geriatrics and Internal Medicine, serves as a staff physician and Director of the Hospital's Geriatric Evaluation and Management Program. Concurrent with his medical practice, he is an Assistant Clinical Professor of Medicine with the University of Medicine and Dentistry–New Jersey, providing Geriatric treatment and clinical research instruction to geriatric fellows, residents and senior medical students. **Career Steps:** Staff Physician and Director of Geriatrics Program, Bergen Pines Hospital (1994–Present); Assistant Clinical Professor, University of Medicine and Dentistry–New Jersey (1994–Present); Director of Long Term Care, VA Medical Center, Buffalo (1991–1994); Director of Long Term Care, VA Medical Center, Batavia (1989–1991) **Associations & Accomplishments:** American College of Physicians; American Geriatrics Society. **Education:** St. George's University, M.D. (1984); City College of New York, B.A. (1980); Fellowship, Geriatric Medicine, SUNY – Buffalo (1987–1989). **Personal:** Married to Liane Fried Adler in 1989. Dr. Adler enjoys music, tropical fish, old cars, bicycle riding, and collecting kaleidoscopes.

Dr. Marc Afilalo

Director of Emergency Department
Jewish General Hospital
3755 Cote–Saint–Catherine, Suite C–015
Montreal, Quebec H3T 1E2
(514) 340–8222
Fax: (514) 340–7519
8062

Business Information: Jewish General Hospital is a 660–bed university hospital established in 1981 and is one of the ten largest medical facilities in Canada. The hospital is an acute and sub–acute care facility with special units for cardiac care, trauma, and emergency services. As Director of Emergency Department, Dr. Afilalo oversees the day–to–day operations of the department. He is responsible for recruiting, training, scheduling, and evaluating staff members, as well as sitting on the Hospital Advisory Committee, acting as liaison between the Emergency Department and other hospital departments, and planning for the future. **Career Steps:** Director of Emergency Department, Jewish General Hospital (1986–Present); Emergency Medicine Expert Consultant, Groupe Tactique D'Intervention (1995–Present); President, Quebec Association of Emergency Physicians (1986). **Associations & Accomplishments:** American Association for Advancement of Science; American College of Emergency Physicians; Quebec Association of Emergency Physicians; Canadian Association of Emergency Physicians; Society of Academic Emergency Medicine; Royal College of Physicians and Surgeons of Canada. **Education:** University of Montreal, M.D. (1979); MCFP(EM) Certificate of Special Competence in Emergency Medicine (1987); FRCP(c), Fellow of the Royal College of Physicians and Surgeons (1988); FACEP, Fellow of the American College of Emergency Physicians (1989); ABEM, Diplomate of the American Board of Emergency Medicine (1989). **Personal:** Married to Marie Elaine Bousquet in 1975. Two children: Jonathan and Stephanie. Dr. Afilalo enjoys ping pong, fishing, and boating.

Dr. Sofia Aksentijevich

Clinical Fellow in Rheumatology
University of Chicago Hospitals
750 North Rush Street, Apt. 2007
Chicago, IL 60611
(312) 702–6800
Fax: (312) 702–5434
8062

Business Information: University of Chicago Hospitals is a full tertiary care, medical research and teaching hospital. As a Fellow in Rheumatology, Dr. Aksentijevich is responsible for providing health care to patients, as well as instructing residents and interns in rheumatology. **Career Steps:** Fellow in Rheumatology, University of Chicago Hospitals (1994–Present); Staff Physician, Clinical Pharmacology, Evanston Hospital Corporation (1993–1994). **Associations & Accomplishments:** Member, American College of Physicians; Diplomate of the Internal Medicine Board. **Education:** A U.S. citizen, Dr. Aksentijevich received her baccalaureate and medical degree education in Belgium, returning to the U.S. to complete her Internship and Residency. Northwestern University, Evanston Hospital, Residency in Internal Medicine (1991–1993); University of Illinois Hospitals, Internship in Internal Medicine (1990–1991). **Personal:** Married to Kenneth Schneider in 1994. Dr. Aksentijevich enjoys traveling to Eastern and Western Europe, tennis, swimming and reading.

Mouhamad O. Al–Daker, M.D., FRCP(c)

Consulting Endocrinologist
Metabolic and Diabetes Education Center, Regina Health District
1440 14th Avenue, Department of Internal Medicine
Regina, Saskatchewan S4P 0W5
(306) 766–4540
Fax: (306) 766–4178
EMAIL: See Below
8062

Business Information: Metabolic and Diabetes Education Center, Regina Health District, is a government–run agency specializing in the treatment of diabetes and metabolic disorders, with special emphasis in the fields of endocrinology and metabolism. Comprised of two endocrinologists, four nurses, three dieticians, and a support staff of four the Center is located at the Regina General Hospital, a full service acute care facility. As Endocrinologist, Dr. Al–Daker consults in the fields of diabetology, lieodology, osteoporosis, and other endocrine diseases, and is responsible for public relations and strategic planning. With a great interest in clinical research for diabetes and osteoporsis, Dr. Al–Daker is a great believer in Synergism, which equals success. Internet users can reach him via: mo.daker@sasknet.sk.ca. **Career Steps:** Consultant Endocrinologist, Metabolic Diabetes Education Center, Regina Health District (1988–Present); Internist, Private Practice, Saudi Arabia (1979–1984). **Associations & Accomplishments:** Endocrine Society; American Diabetes Association; Saskatchewan Medical Association; Ontario Medical Association; Canadian Medical Association; Coordinator/Facilitator, Southern Saskatchewan Diabetes Care Without Compromise; Author of Several articles on medical related subjects. **Education:** University of Damascus, Faculty of Medicine (1965–1972); Rotating Internship, Damascus General Hospital (1971–1972); Rotating Internship, Henrotin Hospital (1973–1974); Residency, General Radiology, Confederate Memorial Medical Center (1974–1975); Residency, Internal Medicine, St. Joseph Hospital, Chicago (1975–1977); Clinical Endocrinology and Metabolism, University of Ottawa, Ottawa Civic Hospital (1985); Clinical Endocrinology and Metabolism, University of Toronto, St. Michael's and Sunnybrook Hospital (1986); Senior Medical Resident, University Hospital, Sakatoon (1988); University of Toronto Hospital; Certified By: American Board of Internal Medicine (1978), The Sub–Specialty Board, Endocrinology and Metabolism (1987), Royal College of Physicians and Surgeons of Canada, Internal Medicine (1988), Certificate of Special Competence in Endocrinology and Metabolism, Royal College of Physicians of Canada (1990). **Personal:** Married to Karema Bokhary in 1972. One child: Souad Farah. Dr. Al–Daker enjoys reading.

Kenneth R. Allen, Ph.D

Senior Administrator/Outpatient Services
Navapache Regional Medical Center
2200 Show Low Lake Road
Show Low, AZ 85901–7831
(520) 537–6395
Fax: (520) 537–8358
8062

Business Information: Navapache Regional Medical Center is a combination of three hospitals in Navaho and Apache Counties of Arizona. The medical center offers hospital/healthcare administration, preventive medicine, community health, outpatient services, acute and subacute health–care. As Senior Administrator/Outpatient Services, Dr. Allen is in charge of outpatient care. He is responsible for recruitment of staff, hiring policies, staff certification, and patient care and satisfaction. Dr. Allen's specialty is in preventive medicine, wherein he works with the local communities to educate residents on healthcare issues. **Career Steps:** Senior Administrator/Outpatient Services, Navapache Regional Medical Center (1995–Present); Director of Protective Medicine, Yavapai Regional Medical Center (1984–1995); Associate Professor, University of Arizona (1985–1987); Director of Cardiopulmonary Rehabilitation, Heart Institute of Tucson (1984–1987). **Associations & Accomplishments:** American College of Sports Medicine; American Association for Cardiovascular and Pulmonary Rehabilitation; American Swim Coaches Association; Promise Keepers. **Education:** University of Arizona: M.S./Ph.D. (1984); University of Southern California, B.S. **Personal:** Married to Patricia A. in 1987. Two children: Jessica and Sarah Elizabeth. Dr. Allen enjoys church, ultra endurance events, marathons, triathalons, and physiology.

Manuela C. Almaguer, M.D.

Pediatric Endocrinologist
St. Joseph's Hospital Medical Center
2 Ivy Court
East Hanover, NJ 07936
(201) 754–2539
Fax: Please mail or call
8062

Business Information: St. Joseph's Hospital Medical Center is a full–service, multi–specialty primary care medical center providing ambulatory surgery, in–patient and out–patient treatment, and tertiary care referral. Working in conjunction with New York's major tertiary teaching hospital — St. Joseph's — the major percentage of patients served are indigents and under–privileged families. As Pediatric Endocrinologist, Dr. Almaguer is responsible for the care and treatment of children with glandular disorders such as diabetes, ricketts, thyroid dysfunctions and obesity. **Career Steps:** Pediatric Endocrinologist, St. Joseph's Hospital Medical Center (1993–Present); Fellow, Montefiore Medical Center (1990–1993); Resident, Flushing Hospital Medical Center (1987–1990). **Education:** University of Malaga, M.D. (1983). **Personal:** Married to Alex Constantinescu in 1990. Two children: Alexandru and Bernard. Dr. Almaguer enjoys spending time with her family.

Angel M. Alvarez

Financial Director
Dr. Susoni Hospital
P.O. Box 145200
Arecibo, Puerto Rico 00614–5200
(809) 879–4750
Fax: (809) 880–4224
8062

Business Information: The Dr. Susoni Hospital is an acute care community hospital, serving the greater Arecibo, Puerto Rico rural populace. Bringing with him an extensive background in health care financial administration, Angel Alvarez serves as Director of Finance and Executive Director Assistant. In this capacity, he is responsible for all financial operations, as well as the administrative oversight of the departments of Budget, Assets, Administration, and Management. **Career Steps:** Financial Director, Dr. Susoni Hospital (1985–Present); Finance Director, Municipality of Arecibo (1981–1985). **Associations & Accomplishments:** Healthcare Financial Management Administration. **Education:** Interamerican University, M.B.A. (1984); University of Puerto Rico, B.B.A. **Personal:** Married to Nelly in 1980. One child: Frances I.

Ron J. Anderson, R.Ph., M.D.

President and Chief Executive Officer
Dallas County Hospital District
5201 Harry Hines Boulevard
Dallas, TX 75235
(214) 590–8076
Fax: (214) 590–8096
8062

Business Information: Dallas County Hospital District is the managing operations office for Dallas County hospital facilities. Established in 1894, Dallas County Hospital District employs 6,000 staff and medical personnel. Dr. Anderson is responsible for all aspects of operations. **Career Steps:** President & Chief Executive Officer, Parkland Memorial Hospital (1982–Present); Professor Internal Medicine, University of Texas Southwestern Medical Center (1986–Present); Division Chief, General Internal Medicine, University of Texas Health Science Center (1976–83); Acting Medical Director, Parkland Memorial Hospital (1981–82); Associate Professor–Internal Medicine, University of Texas Health Science Center (1981–86); Assistant Dean for Clinical Affairs, University of Texas Health Science Center (1979–82); Assistant Professor of Internal Medicine, University of Texas Health Science Center (1976–81); Division Chief Ambulatory Care–Emergency Services, Active Attending, Dallas VA Hospital (1976– 82). **Associations & Accomplishments:** Fellow, American College of Physicians; American Medical Association; American College of Emergency Physicians; Texas Medical Association; Dallas County Medical Society; Society of General Internal Medicine; American Society of Internal Medicine; Association of American Medical Colleges/Council of Teaching Hospitals; American Public Health Association; Executive Committee & Past President, Texas Association of Public & Non–Profit Hospitals; Member, Executive Committee, Chair of Development Committee, (1989–90), Chair (1991), National Public Health & Hospital Institute; Life Member, Texas Public Health Association; Member, National Advisory Committee, Robert Wood Johnson Foundation's 'Healthy Futures: A Program to Improve Maternal and Infant Care in the South,' (1987– Present); Member, Underwriting Committee, Nelson–Tebedo Community Clinic for AIDS Research (1992); Salesmanship Club of Dallas; Salesmanship Program Development & Evaluation Committee; Attorney General's Health Care Committee; Medical Advisory Board, Children's Oncology Services of Texas, Inc.; Board Member, Stemmons Corridor Business Association; Director, Parkland Foundation; AIDS/ARMS Advisory Committee; Deacon, Family Home Ministry; Consultant & Fund– raiser, Greater Dallas Community Council of Churches; Advisory Board Member, Interfaith Housing Coalition; Numerous publications in medical journals; Seminar speaker at civic and public functions; Texas Hospital Association's Earl M. Collier Award. **Education:** Central State University (1964–65); Oklahoma College of Liberal Arts (1965–66); Southwestern University of Oklahoma–Pharmacy School, B.S. in Pharmacy (1969); University of Oklahoma Health Science Center–School of Medicine, M.D. (1973); Residency, UTSW Affiliated Hospitals–Parkland VA Hospital (1974–75); Chief Resident, Internal Medicine–Parkland VA Hospital (1975–76) **Personal:** Married to Sue Ann in 1975. Three children: Sarah Elizabeth, Daniel Jerrod, and John Charles.

Joanna L. Apple
Director of Nursing
Forsyth Memorial Hospital
333 Silas Creek Parkway
Winston–Salem, NC 27103
(910) 718–5978
Fax: Please mail or call

8062

Business Information: Forsyth Memorial Hospital is a 911–bed, nonprofit, acute care hospital providing full service healthcare, diagnosis, treatment, and rehabilitation to patients. As Director of Nursing, Ms. Apple is responsible for coordinating the development of a nursing division budget, providing guidance and consultation to nurse managers regarding unit budgets, formulating proposals for new and improved systems, directing, coordinating, monitoring, and evaluating special projects, coaching and counseling staff on achievements of the nursing role, and participating in the development of the nursing division. **Career Steps:** Forsyth Memorial Hospital: Director of Nursing (1993–Present); Associate Director of Nursing (1983–1987), Value Improvement Coordinator (1985–1987), Clinical Specialist (1972–1983), Assistant Head Nurse for 64–Bed Medical Unit (1970–72); Faculty Member, Forsyth Technical College (1984–86). **Associations & Accomplishments:** Delta Omega, Alpha Chi, and Santa Filomena Honor Societies; Publications: "An Apple A Day", a heart healthy cookbook, "IV Catheter Related Phlebitis", RN Magazine, "Monthly Classification of Medication Errors", Nursing Forms Manual. **Education:** University of North Carolina – Chapel Hill, Masters in Public Health, Health Policy & Administration; Gardner Webb College, B.S. in Business Management summa cum laude; Forsyth Technical Community College, Associate Degree in Business Administration; Funeral Service Director Certificate; Forsyth Hospital School of Nursing, High Honors. **Personal:** Ms. Apple enjoys cooking, gardening, and public speaking.

Debra A. Arendziak
Department Administrator, Department of Pathology
Loyola University Medical Center
2160 S. First Ave.
Maywood, IL 60153
(708) 216–5590
Fax: (708) 216–8482
EMAIL: See Below

8062

Business Information: Loyola University Medical Center is a nationally recognized academic medical center which maintains a world–class reputation for high–caliber specialty health care. Loyola has recently joined with West Suburban Hospital, a leader in community medicine, to form Loyola University Health System. LUHS has 31 primary care offices throughout the region, along with a number of complete outpatient services and diagnostic centers. As Department Administrator, Ms. Arendziak is responsible for all operations management affecting the research and education components of the Department of Pathology. Internet users can reach her via: darendz@wpo.it.luc.ed. **Career Steps:** Department Administrator, Loyola University Medical Center (1991–Present); Baxter Healthcare Corp: Pharmaceutical Analyst/Operations (1986–1991); Research Associate (1982–1986); Research Assistant (1979–1982). **Associations & Accomplishments:** Medical Group Management Association. **Education:** Lewis University, B.A. (1981). **Personal:** Married to Robert in 1981. Two children: Scott, 13 and Elizabeth, 8. Ms. Arendziak enjoys crafts, reading, computing, and spending time with her family.

Nemuel O. Artiles
Executive Director
Bella Vista Hospital
P.O. Box 1750
Mayaguez, Puerto Rico 00681–1750
(787) 834–2350
Fax: (787) 831–6315

8062

Business Information: Bella Vista Hospital is a 157–bed full–service healthcare institution with 200 doctors, several labs, intervention and radiology, imaging, ultra sound, C–scan, MRI, a Cardiac Care Unit, Intensive Care Unit, Emergency Room, and other related services. As Executive Director, Mr. Artiles is responsible for all operations, including management of doctors, nurses, patients, sections, and units. **Career Steps:** Bella Vista Hospital: Executive Director (1985–Present), Assistant Administrator (1984–1985); Administrator, Bella Vista Polyclinic (1980–1984); Administrative Resident, Florida Hospital Medical Center (1979). **Associations & Accomplishments:** President Elect, Puerto Rico Hospital Association; Member, House of Delegate & Regional Policy Board, American Hospital Association; Fellow, Regent Advisory Council, American College of Healthcare Executives; Board Member, Antillian Adventist University; Puerto Rico College of Health Services Administrator; Association of Adventist Healthcare Executives. **Education:** Loma Linda University, M.S.P.H. (1979); University of Puerto Rico, B.B.A. (1977); University of Oregon, B.A.A. (1974). **Personal:** Married to Mayra E. in 1986. Three children: Sharlenne, Cristina, and Mayrel. Mr. Artiles enjoys music and cycling.

Nancy Asay
Director of Nursing
Oneida County Hospital
150 North 200 West
Malad City, ID 83252
(208) 766–2231
Fax: (208) 766–4819

8062

Business Information: Oneida County Hospital is a full–service healthcare institution specializing in the diagnosis, treatment, and rehabilitation of patients. The Hospital has an 11–bed acute care clinic and a 37–bed long–term care unit. As Director of Nursing, Ms. Asay wears many hats at the Hospital, including Acute Care Supervisor, CPR Instructor, and Advanced Cardiac Care Instructor. She is responsible for the schedule arrangements for 35 nurses, yearly evaluations, and policy writing for Acute Care Nursing, Obstetrics, the Operating Room, and the Emergency Room. Ms. Asay has been an RN at Oneida County Hospital for 21 years, so far. **Career Steps:** Oneida County Hospital: Director of Nursing (1994–Present), Acute Care Supervisor (1995–Present), Operating Room Supervisor (1980–1992). **Associations & Accomplishments:** 4–H Leader; Girl Scout Leader; President, Cowbells; Farm Bureau County Womans Board Member; LDS Church: Organist, Chorister, Teacher; CPR Instructor. **Education:** Boise State University, Associate's degree (1975). **Personal:** Married to Bill in 1975. Three children: Buddy, Quincy, and Chanda. Ms. Asay enjoys yard work, gardening, knitting, sewing, playing the piano, walking, teaching CPR, and water tubing.

Adel Antoine Assaf, M.D., FRCPC
Radiologist
Anna–Laberge Hospital Center
200 Brisebois Blvd
Chateauguay, Quebec J6K 4W8
(514) 699–2425
Fax: Please mail or call

8062

Business Information: Anna–Laberge Hospital Center is a full service, healthcare institution specializing in the diagnosis, treatment, and rehabilitation of patients. With 250 beds, the Hospital serves a population of approximately 100,000. As Radiologist, Dr. Assaf is responsible for making diagnosis, based on chest images, ultrasounds, and CT scans and other imaging modalities. He is also an angiographist and interventionist. **Career Steps:** Chief Radiologist, Rouyn–Noranda Hospital Center (1992–1996); Chief Resident, Montreal General Hospital (1991–1992); Emergency Physician, Saint–Laurent Hospital (1988–1992) **Associations & Accomplishments:** College of Physicians and Surgeons of Quebec and of Ontario; College of Physicians and Surgeons of Ontario; Quebec Medical Association; Canada Medical Association; Fellow of the Royal College of Physicians and Surgeons of Canada; Canadian Association of Radiologists; Quebec Association of Radiologists; Radiological Society of North America. **Education:** Laval University, M.D. (1987); McGill University: B.Sc. (1978), M.Sc. (1980), 2 years in the Ph.D. program in Anatomical Sciences, Residency in Radiology

(1988–1992). **Personal:** Married to Chantal in 1992. Dr. Assaf enjoys soccer, volleyball, history, and politics.

Syama Prasad Atluri, M.D., D.D., FACEP, FAAEM
Physician Specialist/Dept. of Emergency Medicine
LAC–King/Drew Medical Center
12021 South Wilmington Avenue
Los Angeles, CA 90059
(310) 668–4404
Fax: Please mail or call

8062

Business Information: Los Angeles County Martin Luther King Jr. General Hospital is one of the nation's busiest trauma and medical emergency centers serving the minority, disadvantaged, and medically underserved population of southwest Los Angeles. Dr. Atluri is a board certified emergency room physician, who is responsible for the diagnosis and treatment of acute trauma and critically ill medical patients and the supervision of residents in the emergency room. Concurrent with his position at King–Drew Medical Center, he serves as an assistant professor in the department of emergency medicine at Charles R. Drew Medical University, teaching emergency medicine to interns, residents, medical students and allied health professionals. He was a passenger on the Pan Am jet that was hijacked in Karachi in 1986 and helped treat the injured passengers. **Career Steps:** Physician Specialist, King–Drew Medical Center, Los Angeles County (1980–Present); Assistant Professor, Department of Emergency Medicine, Charles R. Drew Medical University (1982–Present). **Associations & Accomplishments:** Fellow of American College of Emergency Medicine; Member of Society for Academic Emergency Medicine; Founding Member and Fellow of the American Academic of Emergency Medicine; Life Member, The New York Academy of Sciences; Honored with Faculty Quality Assurance Award by department of emergency medicine at Martin Luther King Jr. Hospital (1992–1993). **Education:** Kakatiya Medical College, Warangal, and Guntur Medical College, Guntur, India, M.D. (1970); Andhra University, Visakhapatnam, India, Diploma in Dermatology, D.D.; Diplomate, American Board of Emergency Medicine; Medical Training: Government General Hospital, Guntur, India; Mount Sinai Medical Center, Chicago; Martin Luther King Jr. General Hospital, Los Angeles. **Personal:** Dr. Atluri enjoys traveling, photography and community service.

Cheryl L. Austin
Director of Human Resources
Lake Pointe Medical Center
P O Box 1550
Rowlett, TX 75030–1550
(214) 412–2273
Fax: (214) 412–3246

8062

Business Information: Lake Pointe Medical Center is a full service medical facility providing health and related services to area residents. Comprised of 100 beds, the Facility is owned by ORNDA and is publicly held and traded on the New York Stock Exchange. Established in 1986, the Hospital employs 420 people. As Director of Human Resources, Ms. Austin oversees recruitment, compensation and benefits, counseling, and ensures compliance with employment laws. She also directly supervises three people and performs personnel evaluations. **Career Steps:** Director of Human Resources, Lake Pointe Medical Center (1996–Present); Legislative Assistant, Congressman John Bryant (1983–1986). **Associations & Accomplishments:** Board of Directors. Rockwall Chamber of Commerce; Board of Directors, CEMCO; Society of Human Resource Managers (SHRM). **Education:** West Texas State University, B.A. (1981); Southern Methodist University, Employment Law (1983). **Personal:** Married to Ron in 1992. Three children: Dani, Barrett and Brittany. Ms. Austin enjoys antiques, travel and research.

Jennifer Bacard–McLaughlin
Director of Rehabilitation Services
IHS Hospital of Houston
5503 Dumfries Drive
Houston, TX 77096–4003
(713) 640–8978
Fax: (713) 640–2935

8062

Business Information: IHS Hospital of Houston is a sub-acute outpatient facility with 54 beds, specializing in the diagnosis, treatment, and rehabilitation of patients. As Director of Rehabilitation Services, Mrs. Bacard–McLaughlin supervises the physical, occupational, and speech and language therapy programs, project development, recruitment, and patient care. Additionally, she handles staffing, billing, budget control, and training. **Career Steps:** Director of Rehabilitation Services, IHS Hospital of Houston (1996–Present); Novacare: Facility Rehabilitation Director (1994–1996), OTR (1992–1994). **Associations & Accomplishments:** National Stroke Association; American Occupational Therapy Association;

Texas Occupational Therapy Association. **Education:** Texas Woman's University, Master of Occupational Therapy (1992); University of Delaware, B.A.L.S. **Personal:** Married to Peter P. Jr. in 1984. Three children: Megan, Katie, and Joey. Mrs. Bacard–McLaughlin enjoys horseback riding, gardening, woodworking, and home improvement.

Martha Bacher

Nurse Manager
Franciscan Hospital Western Hills
3131 Queen City Avenue
Cincinnati, OH 45238–2316
(513) 389–5368
Fax: Please mail or call

8062

Business Information: Franciscan Hospital Western Hills is a full–service health care facility. As Nurse Manager, Ms. Bacher manages the day–to–day operations of an Intensive Care/Coronary Care Unit, consisting of 50 employees. She performs administrative tasks, directs patient care, and coordinates budgeting and training. **Career Steps:** Nurse Manager, Franciscan Hospital Western Hills (1995–Present); Head Nurse, University of Cincinnati (1993–1995); Department Manager, Bethesda, Inc. (1990–1993). **Associations & Accomplishments:** Past President, American Association of Critical Care Nurses; Sigma Theta Tau, International Honor Society for Nurses; Greater Cincinnati Council of Nurse Managers. **Education:** University of Cincinnati: M.S.N. (1991), B.S.N. **Personal:** Married to Ed in 1994. Ms. Bacher enjoys football and other sports, home renovating, and volunteer work at church.

Jon L. Bair

Associate Administrator
Royal Oaks Hospital
307 N. Main Street
Windsor, MO 65360–1449
(800) 456–2631
Fax: Please mail or call

8062

Business Information: Royal Oaks Hospital is a forty bed hospital with a twelve bed partial hospital program. A full service acute care facility, the Hospital offers inpatient care as well as an outpatient clinic. Established in 1992, the Hospital employs 145 people and has estimated annual revenue in excess of $2 million. As Associate Administrator, Mr. Bair is responsible for three main Hospital areas: clinical operations including psychology, rehabilitation, social work, and counseling; information services coordination, billing and administration; and serving as Chief Operations Officer in charge of senior management. Concurrent with his present position, Mr. Bair is an instructor at Central Missouri State University where he will be pursuing his M.B.A. in the Spring. He has also been published in newsletters and has presented a chapter submission to Dr. Hussein of the University of Missouri on the effects of trauma on children. Extremely interested in researching the subject, Mr. Bair has been working with Dr. Hussein, teachers involved in the Oklahoma City bombing, and delegates from Bosnia to further his knowledge on the subject. He plans a trip to Bosnia to confer with professionals on finding an effective means of assisting children traumatized by war and other events. **Career Steps:** Associate Administrator, Royal Oaks Hospital (1992–Present); Director of Rehabilitation Services, Cedar Ridge Hospital (1988–1992); Director of Expressive Therapy, The Kansas Institute (1987–1988); Therapist, The Care Unit Program (1984–1987). **Associations & Accomplishments:** Certified Instructor with Crisis Prevention Institute (CPI); Instructor for Central Missouri State University; Lions Club of Windsor. **Education:** University of Indiana, M.S. (1984); University of Kansas, B.S. (1983). **Personal:** Married to Beth in 1990. Two children: Steven Thomas and Alexis Nicole. Mr. Bair enjoys golf, softball, and computers.

Asad A. Bakir, M.D.

Physician
Cook County Hospital
1835 West Harrison Street
Chicago, IL 60612
(312) 633–8456
Fax: (312) 633–8471

8062

Business Information: Cook County Hospital is a full–service health care facility serving Chicago, Illinois and surrounding community populace. As Senior Physician and Director of the Dialysis Unit, Dr. Bakir is responsible for the care and treatment of patients with kidney diseases. He has been involved in research in the areas of renal disease in Sickle Cell Anemia, Nephrotic Syndrome in African Americans, and Lupus Nephritis. In 1986, he alerted the medical community to the fatal toxicity of aluminum and citrate combinations. Concurrent to his positions with Cook County Hospital, Dr. Bakir is also an Associate Professor of Medicine at the University of Illinois at Chicago. **Career Steps:** Senior Physician, Cook County Hospital (1984–Present); Associate Professor of Medicine, University of Illinois at Chicago (1987–Present). **Associations & Accomplishments:** Fellow of the American College of Physicians; American Society of Nephrology; International Society of Nephrology; Advisory Member, National Kidney Foundation of Illinois; Diplomat of the American Board of Internal Medicine (1975); Diplomat of the American Board of Nephrology (1978). **Education:** University of Bagdad, M.B.Ch.B. (1968). **Personal:** Married to Nadia in 1979. Two children: Ali and May. Dr. Bakir enjoys reading, travel and the theater.

Tejinder S. Bal, M.D.

Chief of Pulmonary Medicine
St. Elizabeth Medical Center
550 Parmalee Avenue
Youngstown, OH 44510–1602
(216) 743–5864
Fax: (216) 743–5847

8062

Business Information: St. Elizabeth Medical Center is a 450–bed tertiary care medical and teaching hospital. A native of India, where he received his medical education, Dr. Bal immigrated to the U.S. in 1970. A practicing physician since 1966 and a Board–certified Thoracic and Chest Surgeon, Dr. Bal has served on the staff of St. Elizabeth Medical Center since 1977. As Chief of Pulmonary Medicine, he oversees all patient care, medical support and residency physicians in the diagnosis, treatment and rehabilitation of patients suffering from lung disorders and diseases. **Career Steps:** Chief of Pulmonary Medicine, St. Elizabeth Medical Center (1977–Present); Assistant Professor of Medicine, Neducom – Rootstown, Ohio (1977); Assistant Professor of Medicine, Temple University School of Medicine (1975–1977). **Associations & Accomplishments:** American College of Physicians; American Thoracic Society; Fellow, American College of Chest Physicians; Fellow, Royal College of Physicians – Canada; Rotary Club. **Education:** Amritsar Medical College – India, M.B.B.S (M.D.) (1966). **Personal:** Married to Surjit in 1969. Three children: Rupinder Singh, Jugdeep Singh, and Anoopdeep Singh. Dr. Bal enjoys travel and hiking.

Angela M. Baldelli

Assistant Professor
Saskatoon City Hospital
701 Queen Street
Saskatoon, Saskatchewan S7K 0M7
(306) 655–8925
Fax: (306) 655–8929

8062

Business Information: Saskatoon City Hospital is a full–service acute and subacute care facility offering in– and outpatient care. The facility is also a teaching hospital. As Assistant Professor, Dr. Baldelli is an instructor of clinical internal medicine and has a background in infectious disease control and geriatrics. **Career Steps:** Associate Professor, Saskatoon City Hospital (1995–Present); Fellowship Infectious Diseases, University of Utah (1994–1995); Internal Medicine Residency, University of Saskatchewan (1991–1994); Internship, St. Paul's Hospital (1990–1991). **Associations & Accomplishments:** Saskatchewan Medical Association; Canadian Medical Association. **Education:** University of Western Ontario, M.D. (1990). **Personal:** Married to Jeff Blushke in 1991. One child: Ryan Jeffrey. Dr. Baldelli enjoys skiing, skating, and cycling.

Ajay K. Bali, M.D.

Staff Cardiologist
Veterans Administration Medical Center
1111 East End Boulevard
Wilkes Barre, PA 18711
(717) 824–3521
Fax: Please mail or call

8062

Business Information: Veterans Administration Medical Center is a medical institute providing diagnosis and treatment of veterans of military forces. The Wilkes–Barre VA Medical Center currently employs 300 people. As Staff Cardiologist, Dr. Bali is responsible for the diagnosis and treatment of patients with cardiovascular diseases, performing and interpreting cardiology tests, as well as the instruction and mentoring of medical interns. **Career Steps:** Staff Cardiologist, Veterans Administration Medical Center (1986–Present); Staff Cardiologist, V.A. Medical Center, Batavia, New York (1984–1986). **Associations & Accomplishments:** Member, American Heart Association; Member, American Diabetic Association; American Medical Association; American College of Physicians; Fellow, American College of Chest Physicians; American College of Cardiology; Fellow, Royal Society of Medicine – United Kingdom; American Geriatics Society; CPR and ACLS Instructor. **Education:** Medical College, Amritsar, India, M.D. (1972); Board Certified by American Board of Medicine in Medicine and Cardiology (ABIMC CV). **Personal:** Dr. Bali enjoys baseball and tennis.

Claudette L. Bardin

Neonatologist
Jewish General Hospital
3755 Cote–Sainte. Catherine
Montreal, Quebec H3T 1E2
(514) 340–8222
Fax: (514) 340–7566

8062

Business Information: Jewish General Hospital is a 700–bed healthcare facility providing diagnosis, treatment, and rehabilitation for patients. As Neonatologist, Dr. Bardin is responsible for providing medical services to newborns. The Neonatal Intensive Care Unit, where Dr. Bardin practices, performs 600–700 admissions per year. Concurrently, she is an Assistant Professor at McGill University. **Career Steps:** Neonatologist, Jewish General Hospital (1988–Present). **Associations & Accomplishments:** FAAP. **Education:** University of Miami Medical School, M.D. (1984); McGill University, Ph.D. in Biochemistry; University de Clermont, France, Maitrise de Chimie, Ingeniueur Chimista. **Personal:** Three children: Lionel, Eric, and Anne. Dr. Bardin enjoys skiing, dancing, knitting, reading, music and outdoor life.

Christopher J. Barlow

Chief Financial Officer
East Montgomery Medical Center
PO Box 241267
Montgomery, AL 36124–1267
(334) 244–8500
Fax: (334) 244–8300

8062

Business Information: East Montgomery Medical Center is a 150–bed acute care facility, providing services in medical, surgical, obstetrics, and psychology. Joining East Montgomery Medical Center as Chief Financial Officer in 1994, Mr. Barlow is responsible for the overall financial operations and the direct supervision of a staff of 50, as well as financial operations for all departments, monitoring revenue enhancement and quality control, negotiating managed care contracts, and approving all expenditures. He also serves on the Admission Process Team and Outpatient Development Committee. **Career Steps:** Chief Financial Officer, East Montgomery Medical Center (1994–Present); Chief Financial Officer, Destin Hospital (1993–1994); Controller, Hamlet Hospital (Apr. 1993 – Aug. 1993). **Education:** Auburn University, B.S. in Accounting (1988). **Personal:** Married to Carol Revans in 1992. Mr. Barlow enjoys golf and tennis in his leisure time.

Kimberly M. Barnes

Director, Rehabilitation Patient Care Services
Providence Hospital and Medical Center
1111 Crater Lake Avenue
Medford, OR 97504
(541) 776–5083
Fax: (541) 770–1350

8062

Business Information: Providence Hospital and Medical Center is a rehabilitation patient care service. The Center has services for acute medical rehabilitation, transitional care, outpatient orthopedic rehabilitation clinic, in–patient neurological/orthopedic rehabilitation services. As Director, Rehabilitation Patient Care Services, Ms. Barnes supervises the Division Managers, is involved in strategic planning for the Center, marketing new and existing services, personnel concerns, financial decisions regarding changes in clinics, and staff recruiting and training. **Career Steps:** Director Rehabilitation Patient Care Services, Providence Hospital and Medical Center (1992–Present); Director Rehabilitation Services, University of Utah Medical Center (1990–1992); Western Rehabilitation Institute: Program Director (1988–1990) and Director Speech Pathology/Audiology (1987–1988). **Associations & Accomplishments:** American College of Healthcare Executives; United Way; Nursing Home Administrators; Northwest Association for Rehabilitation Facilities; Oregon Association for Homes for the Aging. **Education:** California State University at Long Beach, Master's of Arts (1979); University of Utah, BS Communication Disorders. **Personal:** One child: Chelsea Elizabeth. Ms. Barnes enjoys running, weightlifting, swimming, hiking, reading, and cooking.

Margaret Barnes, R.N.C

Director of Education

Keokuk Area Hospital

1600 Morgan Street
Keokuk, IA 52632–3456
(319) 524–7150
Fax: (319) 524–5317

8062

Business Information: Keokuk Area Hospital is a tertiary care hospital, medical research and teaching institution. Currently the hospital employs 450 physicians and medical support staff. As Director of Education and Audio–Visual and Library Services, Ms. Barnes is responsible for all aspects of education for the Nurse's Continuing Education program before degrees and certifications are awarded. She is also responsible for the audio and visual aids used in instruction, including video conferencing. **Career Steps:** Director of Education and Audio–Visual and Library Services, Keokuk Area Hospital (1983–Present); Staff Nurse, Oncology, Burlington Medical Center (1981–1983); Education Director and Assistant Director of Nursing, Ft. Madison Community Hospital (1970–1981). **Associations & Accomplishments:** American Society of Healthcare Educators and Trainers; Iowa Society Healthcare Educators and Trainers; Southeastern Community College Nursing Continuing Education Advisory Committee; Midwest Chapter Medical Library Association; Iowa Library Association; Western Illinois University Advisory Committee For Continuing Education; Recipient, Lewis B. Holloway Mentorship Award, Iowa Society Healthcare Educators and Trainers; Recipient, Governor's Volunteer Award, State of Iowa. **Education:** Western Illinois University, B.A. (1989); Diploma of Nursing, Springfield Memorial Hospital; University of Iowa. **Personal:** Married to Michael in 1961. One child: Peggy Nelson. Ms. Barnes enjoys computer science, satellite communications, gardening, quilting and boating.

Myrlinda V. Barral, M.D.

Staff Psychiatrist

Public General Hospital

106 Emma Street
Chatham, Ontario N7L 1A8
(519) 351–6144
Fax: (519) 351–0450

8062

Business Information: Dr. Barral has been a Staff Psychiatrist at the Mental Health Clinic of Public General Hospital since 1991. She maintains a private office within the facility and is also responsible for an additional caseload at St. Joseph's Hospital. **Career Steps:** Staff Psychiatrist, Public General Hospital (1991–Present). **Education:** University of Santo Thomas, M.D. (1969); Residency in General Psychiatry; Residency in Child and Adolescent Psychiatry. **Personal:** Dr. Barral enjoys stamp collecting, ballroom and line dancing.

Joyce A. Batcheller, R.N.

Senior Vice President/Administrator

Seton Medical Center

1201 West 38th Street
Austin, TX 78705–1006
(512) 323–1957
Fax: (512) 323–1924

8062

Business Information: Seton Medical Center consists of full tertiary care hospitals, in–patient and ambulatory surgical facilities, and emergency medical provision. As Senior Vice President/Administrator, Mrs. Batcheller is in charge of all operational areas of the medical center, and specifically for cardiac, critical care, transplant pulmonary, and emergency room services. In addition, Mrs. Batcheller serves as the Chief Nursing Executive for the Seton Network which includes four acute care hospitals in addition to home care and clinics. **Career Steps:** Seton Medical Center: Senior Vice President (1995–Present), Vice President of Operations (1994–1995); Fairfax Hospital: Patient Care Administrator (1990–1994), Director of Special Projects (1990), Patient Care Coordinator (1988–1990). **Associations & Accomplishments:** AACN; Sigma Theta Tau; Greater Austin Area Chapter of Critical Care Nurses; GWAC–AACN; CV Administrator Organization; Published two chapters of a medical search book and numerous critical care journals; Speaker at National AACN Leadership Conferences and lecturer on various management and critical care topics. **Education:** UTHSCSNSA, M.S.N. (1983). **Personal:** Married to Alan in 1979. Two children: Caitlin and Austin. Mrs. Batcheller enjoys rollerblading, reading, and bike riding.

Charles A. Batt, M.D., F.A.C.I.P.

Medical Director

Seminole Point Hospital

P.O. Box 1995
New London, NH 03257
(603) 526–9655
Fax: (603) 526–9655

8062

Business Information: Seminole Point Hospital is a 71 bed, inpatient, acute care hospital specializing in the treatment of alcohol and drug addiction. Dr. Batt's area of special psychiatric interest is the evaluation and treatment of difficult and/or complex Dual Diagnosis patients, including patients from different language and cultural backgrounds. As Medical Director, Dr. Batt is responsible for coordinating the medical aspects of patient care and for the administration of the Medical Department. **Career Steps:** Medical Director, Seminole Point Hospital (1992–Present); Director of Outpatient Services, Doctors Family Care (1987–1991); Clinical Instructor, Department of Psychiatry, University of Miami (1986); Chief Resident, Jackson Memorial Hospital (1985–1986); Resident in Psychiatry, Jackson Memorial Hospital / University of Miami (1982–1986). **Associations & Accomplishments:** American Medical Association; American Psychiatric Association; American Academy of Addiction Psychiatry; American Society of Addiction Medicine; New Hampshire Medical Association; Fellow, American College of International Physicians; Public Health Trust Outstanding Recognition Award; Veteran's Hospital Special Recognition Award; Dartmouth Book Award; James Goodman Award. **Education:** American University of the Caribbean, M.D. (1981); Bowdoin College, B.A. (1971); Deerfield Academy (1967). **Personal:** Married to Barbara Giusti in 1993. Two children: Veronica and Cristina. Dr. Batt enjoys ornithology, cross–country skiing, swimming, and hiking.

Ruggero Battan, M.D.

Endocrinologist

St. Mary's Health Services

127 Campbell Place Northeast
Grand Rapids, MI 49503
(616) 774–6310
Fax: (616) 732–3029

8062

Business Information: St. Mary's Health Services is a full–service community hospital. A practicing physician since 1981 and a Board–Certified Endocrinologist, Dr. Battan joined St. Mary's Health Services in 1993. He is responsible for providing medical care to patients, specializing in thyroid and hormonal disorders. **Career Steps:** Endocrinologist, St. Mary's Health Services (1993–Present); Fellow in Endocrinology, University of Massachusetts Medical Center (1990–1993); Resident in Medicine, Cabrini Medical Center (1987–1990). **Associations & Accomplishments:** Endocrine Society; American Association of Clinical Endocrinlologists. **Education:** University of Padua Medical School – Italy, M.D. (1981). **Personal:** Married to Donatella in 1986. One child: Enrico. Dr. Battan enjoys music and travel.

Reginald F. Baugh, M.D.

Medical Director

Henry Ford Hospital

2799 West Grand Boulevard, CFP–6
Detroit, MI 48202
(313) 876–2878
Fax: (313) 876–9142

8062

Business Information: Henry Ford Health System, a subsidiary of the Henry Ford Medical Group, is a risk management organization providing support for regional social work. As Medical Director, Dr. Baugh oversees administrative functions of the Organization, in addition to clinical care, and instruction of the residency program. **Career Steps:** Medical Director, Henry Ford Health System (1993–Present); Regional Director, Kaiser Permanente (1990–1993); Assistant Professor, University of Kansas/Veterans Administration Hospital (1988–1990). **Associations & Accomplishments:** American Academy of Otolaryngology; American College of Physician Executives; Barnes Society; National Medical Association. **Education:** University of Michigan Medical School, M.D.

(1981); University of Iowa, Bachelor of Science (1977). **Personal:** Married to Bobbie. Two children: Brandon and Aaron.

Paul Bayardelle, M.D.

Microbiologist and Infectious Disease Specialist

Notre–Dame Hospital

Dept. of Microbiology, 1560 Rue Sherbrooke East
Montreal, Quebec H2L 4M1
(514) 876–5804
Fax: (514) 767–5275

8062

Business Information: Notre–Dame Hospital is a tertiary care facility and university hospital. A Microbiologist and Infectious Disease Specialist, Dr. Bayardelle joined the hospital staff after completing graduate studies at the University of Montreal in 1978. In addition to patient care, laboratory and teaching responsibilities, he also conducts research in the areas of urinary tract and enterobacterial infections. **Career Steps:** Notre Dame Hospital: Microbiologist and Infectious Disease Specialist (1978–Present), Head (Interim) Microbiology Department (1985–1988); Hospital Reseau Sante Richelieu Yamaska: Microbiologist and Infectious Disease Specialist (1982–1996), Head Service of Microbiology (1982–1993). **Associations & Accomplishments:** American Society of Microbiology; Royal College of Physicians (Canada); Association Des Medecins Microbiologist du Quebec; Canadian Society of Infectious Disease. **Education:** Strasbourg – France, M.D. (1972); University of Montreal, Microbiologist (1978). **Personal:** Married to Marie Odile in 1973. Four children: Philippe, Beatrice, Veronique, and Brigitte. Dr. Bayardelle enjoys reading, bicycling, walking, ping–pong, and tennis.

Janice M. Beadleston

Nursing Director

St. John's Regional Health Center

1235 East Cherokee Street
Springfield, MO 65804–2203
(417) 885–2043
Fax: Please mail or call

8062

Business Information: St. John's Regional Health Center is a licensed, 1,041–bed regional medical center serving patients within a 200–mile radius of Springfield. Part of a health system comprised of 43 family practices and a local hospital of 60 beds, St. John's has 400 physicians on staff and employs 5,000 support staff. Rated as one of the Top 100 hospitals in the U.S. in 1994–95 and located in the only large city in southern Missouri, the Hospital also has a cardiovascular unit (open heart surgeries, coronary stents, angioplasty); a formal cardiovascular inpatient education program (20 years); a nutritional unit; an osteoporosis clinic; a psychiatric unit; a long–term care unit; and a 100–bed skilled nursing unit. It also houses the Midwest Orthopedic Sports Outpatient Unit for college athletes, Hammon's Heart Institute, and the Mid–American Cancer Center, which conducts autologous bone marrow transplants. Working at St. John's for the past 34 years in various positions, Ms. Beadleston currently serves as the Nursing Director of one of three Cardiac Intermediate Care units in the Hospital. Concurrently, she serves as a volunteer at the Homeless Shelter serving meals to the homeless. She is also a published author, having co–authored the Patient Education Book by St. John's "Your Heart – Your Life." Additionally, she serves on the Board of the nursing newletter "The Prism" as photographer/writer. **Career Steps:** St. John's Regional Health Center: Nursing Director of the Cardiac Intermediate Care Unit (1973–Present), Supervisor/Coordinator of the Cardiovascular Area (1970–1973), Staff Nurse (1962–1963 and 1969–1970); Nursing Instructor, St. John's School of Nursing (1963–1969). **Associations & Accomplishments:** Charter Member, American Association of Critical Care Nurses; Lay Representative to Annual Meeting, Missouri West United Methodist Church; Volunteer "Partner in Performance", SMSU Performing Arts Center; Certified in Nursingf Administration by the American Nurses Association Credentialing Center. **Education:** Drury College, B.S.N. (1966); St. John's School of Nursing, R.N. (1962). **Personal:** Ms. Beadleston enjoys photography (she has over 100 photos currently on display at the Health Center, and received honorable mention in three categories), volunteering for the Homeless Shelter and the Performing Arts Center, and serving as Church Lay Leader/Teacher.

Toni Beauchamp

Chief Financial Officer

Methodist Hospital

1900 College Avenue
Levelland, TX 79336–6508
(806) 894–4963
Fax: (806) 894–6461

8062

Business Information: Methodist Hospital is a 78–bed acute medical surgical facility. As Chief Financial Officer, Mrs. Beauchamp supervises a staff of five in monitoring and processing payroll, accounts payable and receivable, and accounting activities. **Career Steps:** Chief Financial Officer, Methodist Hospital (1992–Present). **Associations & Accomplishments:** Texas Hospital Association; Texas Association for Healthcare Financial Administration; Healthcare Financial Management Association; Leadership Levelland; American College of Healthcare Executives. **Education:** Abilene Christian University, B.B.A (1981). **Personal:** Married to Kelly in 1995. One child: Hayley Young. Mrs. Beauchamp enjoys reading and yardwork.

Henry Wayne Beneda, M.P.H.

Director of Quality Enhancement
St. Joseph Hospital
1100 West Stewart Drive
Orange, CA 92668–3849
(714) 771–8052
Fax: Please mail or call

8062

Business Information: St. Joseph Hospital is a full service acute care medical facility with 1900 employees and 1000 physicians. Major acute services are cardiac care, oncology, orthopedics, surgical services, psychiatry, and obstetrical services with extensive outpatient surgery and renal dialysis centers. As the Director of Quality Enhancement, Mr. Beneda is responsible for leadership and works directly with the Medical Staff Officers and reports strategic quality and outcomes to the Board. He has developed computer programs to support benchmarking, clinical process models, reappointment, and case management. **Career Steps:** Director of Quality Enhancement, St. Joseph Hospital (1988–Present); Epidemiologist, Daniel Freeman Hospital (1976–1988); Epidemiologist, Mercy Hospital of New Orleans (1975–1976); Senior Research Specialist, Fitzsimmons Medical Center, Denver, Colorado (1970–1972). **Associations & Accomplishments:** Deming Certificate with in–person training by W. Edwards Deming (1993); Publications; Instructor at University of California and California State University. **Education:** Tulane University, M.P.H. (1975); California State University, B.S. and T.Q.M. Certificate; Certification in Infection Control; Registered Medical Technologist (A.S.C.P.). **Personal:** Married in 1978 to Marcia (R.N. and "Buckeye" from Ohio) with two sons actively involved in church and sports.

Karen Benham, R.N., Ph.D.

Director of Nursing
Newport Hospital
714 West Pine Street
Newport, WA 99156
(509) 447–2441
Fax: (509) 447–5527

8062

Business Information: Newport Hospital is a full–service, healthcare institution specializing in the diagnosis, treatment, and rehabilitation of patients. As Director of Nursing, Dr. Benham is responsible for budgeting, staffing, directing patient care, policy review, and procedure writing for the Hospital. **Career Steps:** Director of Nursing, Newport Hospital (1995–Present); Clinical Instructor, Empire Health (1982–1995). **Associations & Accomplishments:** WOCA; WOCN; RNO. **Education:** Gonzaaga University, Ph.D. (1993); Whitworth College: B.S.N., M.H.S. **Personal:** Married to Steven in 1982. Dr. Benham enjoys cooking, gardening, travel, and reading.

Julian Berman, M.D.

Physician
University Hospital
9800 West Sample Road
Coral Springs, FL 33065–4039
(305) 344–8700
Fax: (305) 755–8138

8062

Business Information: The University Hospital is a multi–specialty tertiary hospital, medical research and teaching institution. Affiliated with the hospital, the Coral Springs Cardiology Association specializes in the the care and treatment of patients with heart diseases and disorders. Established in 1974, the Association currently employs 13 people. A Board–certified Cardiologist, Dr. Berman has been a Partner with the Group since 1979. **Career Steps:** Physician, University Hospital, Coral Springs Cardiology Association (1979–Present); Physician, Steve P. Julian, M.D., P.A. (1979); Physician, Harvard University (1976–1979). **Associations & Accomplishments:** American Heart Association; Council for Clinical Cardiology; American College of Cardiology; American College of Physicians; American Medical Association; Board Member (1992–Present), Vice President (1993–1994), Jewish Family Services of Broward County. **Education:** University Pennsylvania, M.D. (1971); Princeton University, B.A. (1967). **Personal:** Married to Anne in 1969. Four children: Benjamin, Alexander, Sara Beth and Marie. Dr. Berman enjoys jogging and basketball.

Dr. Mark L. Bernstein

Physician & Clinical Director
Montreal Children's Hospital
2300 Tupper Ru
Montreal, Quebec H3H 1P3
(514) 934–4400
Fax: (514) 934–4301
Email: See Below

8062

Business Information: The Montreal Children's Hospital is the pediatric teaching hospital of McGill University. It includes an active hematology–oncology service, providing treatment and clinical research for children with blood disorders and cancer, the latter particularly through institutional participation in the Pediatric oncology Group. As Physician & Clinical Director, Dr. Bernstein, who specialized in pediatric hematology and oncology, is responsible for administrative functions, strategic planning, daily operations, clinical research, and enhancing co–worker relations, in addition to his daily patient load. Internet users can reach him via: mberhem@po–box.mch.mcgill.ca. **Career Steps:** Montreal Children's Hospital, Physician and Hematologist (1981–Present); Clinical Director, Hermatology Service (1994–Present). **Associations & Accomplishments:** American Society of Clinical Oncology; Pediatric Oncology Group; American Society of Pediatric Hematology Oncology; Published 30 Articles in Medical Journals; Writer & Co–Writer of Nine Book Chapters. **Education:** A. Einstein College of Medicine, M.D. (1975); B.A. **Personal:** Married to Marie Beland in 1986. Two children: Joshua and Liane.

Debra A. Berntsen

Vice President, Nursing Services
Androscoggin Valley Hospital
59 Page Hill Road
Berlin, NH 03570–3531
(603) 752–2200
Fax: (603) 752–2376

8062

Business Information: Androscoggin Valley Hospital is an acute care medical facility, providing diagnosis and treatment to patients in the Berlin locale. Joining the Androscoggin Valley Hospital in 1987, Ms. Berntsen was appointed as Vice President of Nursing Services in 1995. She directs all activities of the Nursing Division, to establish standards of nursing practices, implement and monitor on–going performance, and overseeing nursing budgets. **Career Steps:** Androscoggin Valley Hospital: Vice President, Nursing Services (1995–Present), Director of Home Health (1993–1995), Assistant Director of Home Health (1990–1993), Supervisor (1987–1989). **Associations & Accomplishments:** New Hampshire Organization of Nurse Executives; Vice President Board of Directors, United Way. **Education:** Attending: College for Lifelong Learning; Concord Hospital School of Nursing, Diploma. **Personal:** Married to Bernard Buzzell in 1990. One child: Danielle Bishop. Ms. Berntsen enjoys volunteering, reading, and crafts.

Janice K. Berry

Education Coordinator
Memorial Hospital of Taylor
135 South Gibson Street
Medford, WI 54451
(715) 748–8100
Fax: (715) 748–8199

8062

Business Information: Memorial Hospital of Taylor is a full–service healthcare institution specializing in the diagnosis, treatment, and rehabilitation of patients (rural hospital and nursing home). As Education Coordinator, Ms. Berry is responsible for community program development, coordinating CPR and First Aid Classes, staff development and competency testing, and coordinating various health screening procedures. **Career Steps:** Education Coordinator, Memorial Hospital of Taylor (1988–Present); Adjunct Faculty, Mount Senario College (1989–1992); Adjunct Faculty, Northcentral Technical College (1987–1990). **Associations & Accomplishments:** Wisconsin Nurses Association – Midstate District: President–Elect, Former Treasurer; American Cancer Society, Wisconsin Division – Taylor Unit: Education Chair, Chaired various cancer screenings, Chair fund raiser "Making Strides Against Cancer"; Board President, Volunteer Award, Stepping Stone Shelter; Deputy Medical Examiner, Taylor County. **Education:** University of Wisconsin – EauClaire: M.S.N. (1988), B.S.N. (1983); St. Joseph's School of Nursing, Nursing Diploma (1970). **Personal:** Three children: Denise, Heather, and Kurt. Ms. Berry enjoys walking, camping, stitchery, and reading.

Manoop S. Bhutani, M.D.

Chief of Endoscopy
Department of Veteran's Affairs Medical Center – Wright State University
P.O. Box 927
Dayton, OH 45401–0927
(513) 268–6511
Fax: (513) 267–3934

8062

Business Information: Department of Veterans' Affairs Medical Center, affiliated with Wright State University, is a government–funded, tertiary care, teaching VA hospital, focusing on providing medical care to military veterans, as well as providing instruction to medical students, residents, and fellows. Dr. Bhutani has been a practicing physician, researcher, and educator since 1992. Appointed as Chief of Endoscopy at the VA Medical Center in 1995, he directs an endoscopy unit, conducts research, and provides patient care in gastroenterology and endoscopy. In addition to his medical practice, he serves as Assistant Professor at the Department of Medicine at Wright State University. Future plans include taking new technology and results of research around the world and developing a laboratory for further research in endoscopy. **Career Steps:** Chief of Endoscopy, Department of Veterans' Affairs Medical Center – Wright State University (1995–Present); Advanced Endoscopy Scholar, Medical University of South Carolina (1994–1995); Fellow in Gastroenterology, Wright State University (1992–1994). **Associations & Accomplishments:** American Society for Gastrointestinal Endoscopy; American College of Gastroenterology; American College of Physicians. **Education:** Wright State University, M.D. (1992); Maharishi Dayanand University – India, M.B.B.S. (1988). **Personal:** Married to Anjali in 1987. One child: Anuj. Dr. Bhutani enjoys music and family activities.

Carrell Blakely

Administrator
Union County General Hospital
301 Harding Street
Clayton, NM 88415
(505) 374–2585
Fax: (505) 374–8146

8062

Business Information: Union County General Hospital is a rural, 30–bed acute care hospital, providing diagnosis and treatment to patients in Clayton, New Mexico and the surrounding area. Services include acute care, subacute care, surgery, and care for infants (four bassinets). Bringing with her twenty–six years of leadership and administrative experience, Ms. Blakely joined Union County General Hospital as Finance Director in 1993. Appointed as Administrator in 1993, she is responsible for all administrative operations, including the oversight of all employees and working with physicians and nurses to ensure the smooth operation of the hospital. **Career Steps:** Union County General Hospital: Administrator (1993–Present), Finance Director (1993); CEO/Owner, Elco Metal Products Corporation (1970–1993). **Associations & Accomplishments:** Rotary Club; New Mexico Cattlewomen; Union County Chamber of Commerce; Economic Development Commission of Union County; Published "True Marriage Vows," a book on her grandfather's life (1974). **Education:** University of New Mexico, B.B.A. (1990); Trinidad Junior College, A.A. (1974). **Personal:** Married to Herbert S. in 1972. Two children: Mickey and Rickey Pugh. Ms. Blakely enjoys oil painting, piloting airplanes, and writing short stories.

Lori L. Blinka

Supervisor of Medical Records
Scott & White Clinic
1600 University Drive East
College Station, TX 77840
(409) 691–3304
Fax: (409) 691–3635

8062

Business Information: Scott & White Clinic is an outpatient health care organization and clinic with thirteen satellites, including several medical specialties, i.e., orthopedic, x–ray, family practice, and laboratory facilities. As Supervisor of Medical Records, Mrs. Blinka is responsible for daily operations of the Medical Records and Release of Information Departments, performing administrative duties, strategic planning, public relations, overseeing employees, supervising medical records, and releasing information to insurance companies. **Career Steps:** Supervisor of Medical Records, Scott & White Clinic (1987–Present); Student Worker, Blinn College Library (1985–1987). **Education:** Blinn College, A.A. (1987). **Personal:** Married to Richard in 1989. Mrs. Blinka enjoys swimming and exercise.

Ruby R. Blois

Director, Partnership Development
I.W.K.–Grace Health Center
5850 University Avenue, P.O. Box 3070
Halifax, Nova Scotia B3J 3G9
(902) 420–3071
Fax: (902) 428–2938

8062

Business Information: I.W.K.–Grace Health Center is a health care facility primarily focused on the treatment of women, children, and the family. Local in scope, the Hospital provides tursary teaching, primary and secondary care to area residents as well as those in the Maritime region. The Hospital's Department of Partnership Development focuses on recognizing mandates and strengthening clinical care partner relations. As Director, Partnership Development, Mrs. Blois is responsible for leading the health care initiative in both the medical and private sector, to focus on clinical care. Additional responsibilities include administration, operations, public relations, and strategic planning. She also oversees a new project which involves providing the Maritime region with a tele–health network comprised of partners linked through technology. **Career Steps:** Director Partnership Development, I.W.K.–Grace Health Center (1995–Present); I.W.K. Children's Hospital: Vice President of Nursing (1985–1995), Director of Nursing Services (1982–1985); Joint Appointment, Dalhousie University School of Nursing (1993–Present); Consultant, Nursing Unit Administration Program, Canadian Hospital Association (1982–1984). **Associations & Accomplishments:** Board Member, Registered Nurses Association of Nova Scotia; Canadian Nurses Association; Pediatric Nurses Association; Pediatric Nurses Interest Group of Nova Scotia; Academy of Chief Nursing Executive Officers of Canada; Past President, Association of Senior Nursing Administrators of Nova; Scotia; Canadian Association of Pediatric Hospitals; Association of the Care of Children's Health; Board Member, I.W.K. Hospital for Children; Member, Standards Committee; Counselor, Nova Scotia Provincial Health Council; Canadian College of Health Service Executives, Executive Category; Honorary Life Membership, I.W.K. Hospital for Children, Board of Governors; Long Service Award, I.W.K. Hospital for Children (1987 and 1992); Staff Recognition Award, I.W.K. Hospital for Children (1983); United Way Canvasser; Member of the Board, Ronald McDonald House; Dartmouth Citizens Against Incineration; Member Alumnae Association, Dalhousie University, Mount Saint Vincent University, and Children's Hospital School of Nursing; Auxiliary, I.W.K. Hospital for Children; Leadership Roles in Children's Miracle Network Telethon in the Maritimes; Participant in Various Workshops and Seminars; Author of Numerous Publications; Vice President of Nursing and Special Services, I.W.K. Hospital for Children; Various RNANS Committees; Provincial Health Council. **Education:** Canadian College Health Services, Education Certification (1986); University of Saskatoon, Certificate in Health Care Organization and Management (1979); Canadian Hospital Association, Certificate, Nursing Unit Administration Program (1975); Mount St. Vincent University, Bachelors of Science in Nursing (1973); Dalhousie University, Diploma, Nursing Unit Administration (1965); Children's Hospital School of Nursing, Diploma in Nursing (1962). **Personal:** Married to Eugene. One child: Jennifer. Mrs. Blois enjoys walking, gardening, reading, and the beach.

Renee A. Bobrowski, M.D.

Perinatologist
Hutzel Hospital/Detroit Medical Center
4707 Saint Antoine Street
Detroit, MI 48201–1427
(313) 745–7269
Fax: (313) 993–2685

8062

Business Information: Hutzel Hospital, a Detroit Medical Center Facility, is an academic institution affiliated with Wayne State University School of Medicine and an acute care medical facility. Dr. Bobrowski joined Hutzel Hospital's Wayne State University School of Medicine Program in 1993 as a Fellow of Maternal–Fetal Medicine and Clinical Instructor in the Department of Obstetrics and Gynecology. In 1995, she moved into Critical Care Obstetrics, specializing in high–risk pregnancy and critical care medicine, and an Assistant Professorship with the University. Dr. Bobrowski is presently responsible for medical student and resident education and patient care. **Career Steps:** Hutzel Hospital/Detroit Medical Center: Perinatologist, (1993–Present), Assistant Professor, Department of Obstetrics and Gynecology, Wayne State University (1995–Present), Fellow, Maternal–Fetal Medicine (1993–1995), Fellow, Critical Care Obstetrics (1995–1996), Clinical Instructor, Department of Obstetrics and Gynecology (1993–1995); Resident, Obstetrics and Gynecology, Indiana University Medical Center (1989–1993). **Associations & Accomplishments:** Junior Fellow, American College of Obstetricians and Gynecologists; Society of Perinatal Obstetricians; Society of Critical Care Medicine; Diplomat, National Board of Medical Examiners; Phi Delta Epsilon Medical Fraternity; Board of Governors, Wayne State University School of Medicine Alumni Association; Alpha Epsilon Delta Pre–Medical Honor Society (1982); Alpha Sigma Nu National Jesuit Honor Society (1984); Scholarship Key Award, University of Detroit (1985); Wayne State University School of Medicine: Distinction in Biomedical Research (1989), Class of 1989 Academic Achievement Award (1989); Alpha Omega Alpha: Alpha Chapter, Indiana School of Medicine (1991); First Prize for Scientific Research Paper, Department of Obstetrics and Gynecology, Indiana University (1992); Various Publications, Presentations, and Lectures. **Education:** Wayne State University, M.D. (1989); University of Detroit, B.S. in Biology, Summa Cum Laude (1985); American Board of Obstetrics and Gynecology: Board Eligible (1993), Division of Maternal–Fetal Medicine, Board Eligible (1995); Certification in Critical Care Obstetrics (1995). **Personal:** Married to Jeffery S. Dzieczkowski, M.D. in 1995. Dr. Bobrowski enjoys golf, skiing, photography, and travel.

Erlinda Bocar–Kantor, M.D.

Laboratory Director
North General Hospital
1879 Madison Avenue
New York, NY 10035–2709
(212) 423–4012
Fax: (212) 423–4282

8062

Business Information: North General Hospital is a private, non–profit, 240–bed hospital providing acute care to patients, as well as providing the services of a recently–acquired nursing home. Future plans include forming a hospital network. Established in 1979, North General Hospital currently employs 1,010 people. As Laboratory Director, Dr. Bocar–Kantor is responsible for all aspects of laboratory operations, including oversight of all laboratory testing. Concurrent with her medical practice at North General, she teaches within the Residency Program at Mt. Sinai Medical Center and is involved in network marketing. **Career Steps:** North General Hospital: Laboratory Director (1992–Present), Associate Pathologist (1979–1992). **Associations & Accomplishments:** New York State Society of Pathologists; New York State County Medical Society; Clinical Laboratory Management Association; American Association for Clinical Chemistry; American Medical Association; College of American Pathologists; Published numerous medical papers. **Education:** UERMMMC Medical Center, Philippines, M.D. (1967). **Personal:** Married to Nathan C. in 1973. Dr. Bocar–Kantor enjoys tennis, photography, painting, travel, ballroom dancing, and playing the piano and electronic keyboards.

Martha H. Bohannon, R.N., C.P.H.Q.

Infection Control Manager
Halifax Regional Hospital
2204 Wilborn Avenue
South Boston, VA 24592
(804) 575–3435
Fax: (805) 575–3683

8062

Business Information: Halifax Regional Hospital is a 142–bed, acute care, rural community hospital. A practicing Registered Nurse since 1976, Ms. Bohannon serves as Infection Control Manager, responsible for medical staff quality improvement, infection control, and employee health. **Career Steps:** Halifax Regional Hospital: Infection Control Manager (1993–Present), Quality Assurance Coordinator (1992–Present), Infection Control Practitioner (1993–Present) Nursing Quality Assurance Coordinator (1990–1992), Nursing Supervisor (1985–1990). **Associations & Accomplishments:** Virginia Nurses Association; Association for Practitioners in Infection Control; Virginia – APIC; National Association for Healthcare Quality; Virginia Association for Healthcare Quality; American Nurses Association; Red Cross Volunteer; Sigma Sigma Sigma Sorority; Chatham Virginia Rescue Squad; Volunteer Fire Department Member. **Education:** The Memorial Hospital School of Nursing, R.N. Diploma (1976); Certified Professional in Healthcare Quality; Attending Old Dominion University, B.S.N. program. **Personal:** Two children: Kelley and Sean. Ms. Bohannon enjoys travel and sewing.

Yvette Bonny, M.D., F.R.C.P. (c)

Pediatric Hematologist
Hopital Maisonneuve–Rosemont
5415 Boulevard de l'Assomption
Montreal, Quebec H1T 2M4
(514) 252–3495
Fax: (514) 254–5094

8062

Business Information: Hospital Maisonneuve–Rosemont is a full service medical/teaching facility providing medical and health related services to the area. Affiliated with the University of Montreal, the Hospital also provides research and training to medical students and residents. As Pediatric Hematologist, Dr. Bonny diagnoses and treats blood and blood–related disorders (i.e. Leukemia, Lymphoma, and Sickle Cell Anemia), in children ages newborn to fifteen. Actively involved in clinical research and development of new treatments, Dr. Bonny is credited with performing the first bone marrow transplant on a child (Quebec, 1980). **Career Steps:** Pediatric Hematologist, Hospital Maisonneuve–Rosemont (1976–Present). **Associations & Accomplishments:** Association of Medical Hematologists of Quebec; American Society of Hematology (ASH); New York Academy of Sciences; Association of Leukemia and Cancer of Children (LEUCAN); Published in "The New England Medical Journal." **Education:** M.D. (1969); Certified Specialist PQ in Pediatrics and Hematology; Fellow, Royal College of Physicians and Surgeons of Canada (FRCP(c)) (1970). **Personal:** Married to Gadbois Pierre in 1973. One child: Natalie Gadbois. Dr. Bonny enjoys helping the Haitian community, reading, classical and popular music, and Scrabble.

Shawn Boshears, R.N.

Director of Nursing
Highland Lakes Medical Center
P.O. Box 840
Burnet, TX 78611
(512) 756–6000
Fax: (512) 756–6405

8062

Business Information: Highland Lakes Medical Center, owned by Quorum Healthcare Services, is an acute care, 48–bed facility, with a 24–hour emergency room, 6–bed Intensive Care Unit, Home Health Center with a Hospice, numerous labs, therapy services, surgery/day surgery, and radiology departments. As Director of Nursing, Mrs. Boshears is responsible for a large support staff of nurses, patient care, labs, therapy, case management, discharge plans, and infection control. She works directly with nine department heads. **Career Steps:** Director of Nursing, Highland Lakes Medical Center (1995–Present); Director of Nurses, Artesia General Hospital (1993–1995); Director of Nursing Support, Presbyterian Hospital (1991–1993). **Associations & Accomplishments:** Texas Organization of Nurse Executives; Partner in Education. **Education:** California State University, B.S. in Nursing (1974); Chapman University, Master in Hospital Administration. **Personal:** Married to Irvin Frank in 1974. One child: Gary. Mrs. Boshears enjoys horseback riding and music.

Lou L. Bottoms, RN, MS, CNOR

Nursing Director of Surgical Services
Georgia Baptist Health Care System
303 Parkway Drive North East
Atlanta, GA 30312–1212
(404) 265–3767
Fax: (404) 265–1737

8062

Business Information: Georgia Baptist Health Care System provides outpatient and ambulatory health care services, and two nursing homes to patients in 22 counties. The System is a full–service, healthcare institution specializing in the diagnosis, treatment, and rehabilitation of patients. As Nursing Director of Surgical Services, Mrs. Bottoms is responsible for all aspects of nursing operations, including overseeing the nursing staff and surgical services staff. **Career Steps:** Nursing Director of Surgical Services, Georgia Baptist Health Care System (1990–Present); Director of Surgical Services, West Paces Ferry Hospital (1980–1990); Education Co–ordinator, Kennestone Hospital (1978–1980). **Associations & Accomplishments:** Association of Operating Room Nurses; American Society of Health Care Executives; Georgia Organization of Nurse Executives; Organization of Nurse Executives; Georgia Hospital Association; Society of Ambulatory Care Professionals. **Education:** Mercer University, M.S. in Health Care Administration (1995); College of St. Francis, B.S. in Health Science (1985); Georgia Baptist School of Nursing, R.N. (1973). **Personal:** Married to William C. in 1973.

Mark Howard Bowles, M.D.

Physician
HCA Wesley Medical Center
1215 North Emporia Street
Wichita, KS 67214–2830
(800) 657–7250
Fax: (316) 688–9183
EMAIL:Drflea.NetSouthwind

8062

Business Information: HCA Wesley Medical Center is a tertiary hospital, medical research and teaching institution. A Board–Certified Cardiologist, Gastroenterologist and Critical Care Intensivist, Dr. Bowles specializes in treatment procedures of angioplasty, atherectomy, stenting, endoscopy, as well as teaching fellows (trainees) and conducting clinical research. Concurrent with his position, he serves as Staff Physician at Galichia Medical Group. **Career Steps:** Physician, HCA Wesley Medical Center (1987–Present); Staff Physician, Galichia Medical Group (1988–Present); Sole Practitioner, Internist and Gastroenterologist (1980–1985); CV Trainee, Mid America Institute (1985–1987). **Associations & Accomplishments:** Metropolitan Baptist Church; Fellow, American College of Cardiology; Member, American College of Gastroenterology; Member of ASCI; AOA Honorary Medical Society; Published 400–page poetry book (1995); Written and recorded 11 songs for gospel, country, and pop album (1995). **Education:** Friends University (1992–1993), Five courses in Marriage & Family Therapy, M.D. (1975), B.S./B.A. in Biology and Psychology (1971), Postgraduate Training (1975–1980) & (1985–1988). **Personal:** Two children: Justin Autumn and Noralee Yvonne.

Michele D. Brown

Director of Finance
Cordelia Martin Health Center
5712 Bannockburn Drive
Toledo, OH 43623
(419) 259–4518
Fax: (419) 255–6438

8062

Business Information: Cordelia Martin Health Center, a non–profit federally–funded and grant–funded organization, is a community health center servicing the under–insured and homeless individuals from six locations in the Inner City of Toledo, Ohio. As Director of Finance, Ms. Brown is responsible for the direction of all financial operations, including financial statements, internal and external reporting, budgeting, cash flow, and forecasting. Additionally, she oversees all information systems operations, ensuring the smooth transition from the manual accounting, medical and dental operation to the newly implemented computer network system. **Career Steps:** Director of Finance, Cordelia Martin Health Care (1994–Present); Accounting Supervisor, Delta USA (1993–1994); Accounting Manager, Flagship Express, Inc. (1991–1992). **Associations & Accomplishments:** Former Member, National Association of Business Women; National Association of Female Executives; Ms. Brown's professional goal is to establish her own consulting business to assist small businesses to get started and to assist in the purchase and setup of computer systems. **Education:** Northwest University, B.S. (1987); Trend Business University, A.A. (1975). **Personal:** One child: Samantha.

Patricia H. Brown, RN, MSN, CNO

Chief Nursing Officer
Mission Hospital, Inc.
900 South Bryan Road
Mission, TX 78572
(210) 280–9105
Fax: (210) 580–9109

8062

Business Information: Mission Hospital, Inc. is an acute care hospital with home health, occupational health, and clinic extensions. As Chief Nursing Officer, Ms. Brown serves as Administrator of Nursing Services, overseeing the nursing staff, respiratory therapists, and grant writing responsibilities. **Career Steps:** Chief Nursing Officer, Mission Hospital, Inc. (1989–Present); Director of Nursing, Merced Medical Center (1989–1993); Manager, Medical University of South Carolina (1988–1989); Manager, Charleston V.A. Medical Center (1983–1988). **Associations & Accomplishments:** American Organization of Nursing Executives; Advisory Council, Regional Trauma; Advisory Council, University of Texas – Pan American; Advisory Council, South Texas Community College. **Education:** Medical University of South Carolina, M.S.N. (1989); St. Louis University, B.S.N. **Personal:** Ms. Brown enjoys golf and travel.

John J. Brownell

Payroll Manager
Illinois Masonic Medical Center
836 West Wellington Avenue
Chicago, IL 60657–5147
(312) 296–5234
Fax: (312) 296–7422
EMail: See Below

8062

Business Information: The Illinois Masonic Medical Center, a member affiliate of the RUSH System for Health, is a full tertiary, 500–bed capacity metropolitan hospital. Celebrating its 75th Anniversary in 1996, IMMC is dedicated to the service of mankind. As Payroll Manager, Mr. Brownell oversees all operations and support staff in the production and maintenance of payroll and benefits dispersal and administration for the Hospital's 3,000+ employees. Internet users can reach him via: JOHNB0526@AOL.COM **Career Steps:** Payroll Manager, Illinois Medical Center (1987–Present); Payroll Manager, Chicago College of Osteopathic Medicine (1980–1987). **Associations & Accomplishments:** American Payroll Association; Aircraft Owners and Pilots Association; Civil Air Patrol; Multi–County Severe Weather Warning System. **Education:** University of Illinois, B.S. in Management (1979). **Personal:** Married to Karen B. Jacobson in 1981. Mr. Brownell enjoys flying and fishing.

Gail Lynn Burkett, R.N.

Director of Medical Services
Midway Hospital Medical Center
2605 Tiden Avenue
Los Angeles, CA 90064
(213) 932–5145
Fax: (213) 932–5194

8062

Business Information: Midway Hospital Medical Center is a full–service, healthcare institution specializing in the diagnosis, treatment, and rehabilitation of patients. As Director of Medical Services, Ms. Burkett is responsible for patient care facilitation, coordination of education for staff, budgeting costs for the nursing unit, and providing leadership to employees. **Career Steps:** Midway Hospital Medical Center: Director of Medical Services (1996–Present), Director of Education (1995–1996), Staff Charge Nurse – R.N. (1991–1995). **Associations & Accomplishments:** ANAC; APLA. **Education:** Mercy School of Nursing, Diploma (1989); University of Toledo. **Personal:** Ms. Burkett enjoys seasonal sports, activities, artistry, and travel.

Christine C. Cameron–Grigun

Director of Continuing Care
Lawrence Memorial Hospital of Medford
40 Holland Street, 4th Floor
Somerville, MA 02144–2705
(617) 625–9490
Fax: (617) 396–4333

8062

Business Information: Lawrence Memorial Hospital of Medford is a small 190–bed acute care community hospital, providing the services of a nursing home, transitional care unit, inpatient geriatric, and medical psychiatric units (first in the area to establish one). As Director of Continuing Care, Ms. Cameron–Grigun oversees the utilization management of the Continuing Care Department, including the provision of skilled nurses, therapists (i.e., speech, occupational, etc.), and home health aides. Concurrently, she serves as the Clinical Director of Home Care with Homecare Connections, a home care agency based in the Lawrence Memorial Hospital. **Career Steps:** Director of Continuing Care, Lawrence Memorial Hospital of Medford (1986–Present); Clinical Director of Home Care, Homecare Connection (1995–Present); Manager of Contracts Unit, Blue Cross/Blue Shield of Massachusetts (1983–1986). **Associations & Accomplishments:** Former President, Boston Regional Continuing Care Nurses Association; Executive Board Member Massachusetts, Boston Regional Contigency Care Nurses Association; Member of the Board of Trustees, Acuity International Corporation. **Education:** St. Joseph's University, B.S. (1987); New England Deaconess Hospital School of Nursing (1970). **Personal:** Married to John Grigun in 1985. One child: Audrie Cameron Grigun. Ms. Cameron–Grigun enjoys skiing, swimming, and coaching a team for "Odyssy of the Mind" for advanced students (her daughter is a member).

Louis D. Camilien, M.D.

Director, Department of Obstetrics and Gynecology
Kings County Hospital Center
233 Crabapple Road
Manhasset, NY 11030–1710
(718) 270–1365
Fax: (718) 245–4766

8062

Business Information: Kings County Hospital Center is an acute health care facility providing diagnosis and treatment of patients residing in Kings County and surrounding areas. A practicing physician for eighteen years, Dr. Camilien joined Kings County Hospital Center in 1995. Serving as Director of the Department of Obstetrics and Gynecology, he is responsible for the direction of all activities in the Ob–Gyn Department. He also provides medical instruction to OB/GYN residents, serving as a Clinical Professor with the S.U.N.Y. Health Science Center in Brooklyn. **Career Steps:** Director, Department of Obstetrics and Gynecology, Kings County Hospital Center (1990–Present); S.U.N.Y. Health Science Center – Brooklyn: Clinical Professor (1995), Associate Professor (1990–1995), Assistant Professor (1986–1990). **Associations & Accomplishments:** Sigma Pi Phi Fraternity. **Education:** State University of Haiti, M.D. (1977); Harvard School of Public Health, Program for Chief of Services. **Personal:** Married to Magalie in 1981. Two children: Garvey and Stanley.

Gregory Y. Campbell

Manager of Technology Development/Security
Akron General Medical Center
400 Wabash Avenue
Akron, OH 44307–2433
(216) 384–1633
Fax: (216) 996–5835

8062

Business Information: Akron General Medical Center is a non–profit 500–bed acute care hospital. With over twenty–five years of information systems technology design expertise, Greg Campbell has held his current position since 1983. As Manager of Technology Development, he evaluates, specifies and recommends all new information technologies for the entire facility, manages security and auditing of enterprise–wide information systems. **Career Steps:** Manager of Technology Development, Akron General Medical Center (1983–Present); Senior Systems Analyst, Picken International (1981–1983); Manager Technical Support, Conflo Manufacturing (1979–1981); Systems Programmer, First National Bank of Akron (1969–1978). **Associations & Accomplishments:** National Honorary and Professional Management Fraternity; National Dean's List. **Education:** University of Akron, B.S in Industrial Management (1995), Minor in Computer Programming Technology. **Personal:** Married to Pamela in 1974. Two children: Christy and Russell. Mr. Campbell enjoys golf, fishing and swimming.

Christina Campos

Chief Financial Officer
Guadalupe County Hospital
P.O. Box A
Santa Rosa, NM 88435–0459
(505) 472–3417
Fax: (505) 472–3417
EMAIL: See Below

8062

Business Information: Guadalupe County Hospital is a 12–bed, full–service, community healthcare institution specializing in the diagnosis, treatment, and rehabilitation of patients. The Hospital also provides a clinic and outreach services. As Chief Financial Officer, Ms. Campos is responsible for diversified administrative activities, including finances, budgets, reports, grants, payroll, and personnel. Internet users can reach her via: ccampos@mozart.umn.edu **Career Steps:** Chief Financial Officer, Guadalupe County Hospital (1994–Present); Owner and Finance Manager, Joseph's Restaurant (1985–Present). **Associations & Accomplishments:** Santa Rosa Chamber of Commerce; International Rotary Club. **Education:** University of New Mexico: B.A. in Economics (1985), B.A. in Latin American Studies (1995). **Personal:** Married to Jose Campos II in 1985. Three children: Analisa, Andrea and Jose III. Ms. Campos enjoys gardening, bike riding, water skiing and reading.

Linda Cannon, M.D.

Chief of the Department of Pediatrics
West End Medical Centers, Inc.
956 Washington Place, SW
Atlanta, GA 30314–2905
(404) 794–3442
Fax: (404) 794–8973

8062

Business Information: West End Medical Centers, Inc. is a community health center providing comprehensive primary health care in six offices in the Atlanta, Georgia area. Established 20 years ago, West End Medical Centers currently employs more than 100 people. As Chief of the Department of Pediatrics, Dr. Cannon is responsible for delivering health care to pediatric patients while coordinating and overseeing the same for three other pediatricians, as well as developing policies and procedures for the Department. Concurrent with her patient practice, she serves as Associate Professor of Pediatrics at Morehouse School of Medicine. **Career Steps:** Chief of the Department of Pediatrics, West End Medical Centers, Inc. (1988–Present); Associate Professor of Pediatrics, Morehouse School of Medicine (1991–Present); Associate Pediatrician, Kidcare Pediatrics (1988–1992). **Associations & Accomplishments:** Rebecca Lee Society of Women in Medicine; Greater Atlanta Pediatric Society; American Academy of Pediatrics. **Education:** Morehouse School of Medicine, M.D. (1985); Emory University, Medical Technology, Clinical Pathology Certificate; Mississippi State University, B.S. in Microbiology. **Personal:** Married to William S. Cannon, V in 1977. One child: William S. Cannon, VI. Dr. Cannon enjoys spending time with her son, jazz, and Broadway musicals.

Sylvia Cannon Wigley, A.R.T.
Director of Health Information Management
Methodist Hospital of Middle Mississippi

Lexington, MS 39095
(601) 834–5165
Fax: (601) 834–5130

8062

Business Information: Methodist Hospital of Middle Mississippi (MHMM) is a regional facility of Methodist Health Systems of Memphis, TN, and provides services to patients in rural Mississippi in Holmes and surrounding counties. This Facility was established as a county hospital in 1916 and provides acute and skilled care as well as emergency room and outpatient services. Mrs. Wigley is responsible for planning, implementing, directing and controlling the activities and operations to provide health information services to physicians, administration, public, patients, and other departments. She is responsible for patient information, transcribing medical reports, coding diagnoses and procedures, abstracting, release of information, birth and death certificates and registers, and tumor registry and filing. She is also responsible for Medical Staff and Allied Health Credentialing and the Knowledge Based Information System. Prior to beginning her career in the medical profession, Mrs. Wigley served as secretary to the President of Holmes Community College, Goodman, MS, from 1964–1966. She began her career in the medical profession in 1967 as office assistant for Drs. Robinson and Rayburn in Bossier City, LA. She returned to Lexington and joined the hospital staff in 1971 as switchboard operator, billing clerk, and patient registration. In 1974, Mrs. Wigley joined the Medical Record Department as transcriptionist and quality assurance coordinator. After obtaining certification as an Accredited Record Technician (A.R.T.) in 1978, she became Director of Medical Records and continues in that capacity. Mrs. Wigley has provided contract medical record services to four physicians since 1974 and has provided consultation services to other hospitals. In October, 1995, Mrs. Wigley conducted a workshop on the medical record profession for the Mississippi Primary Health Care Association's Tenth Annual Conference. She participated on the competition team from MHMM for the Continuous Improvement Award of Excellence, placing runner–up for second place within the Company. **Career Steps:** Director of Health Information Management, Methodist Hospital of Middle Mississippi (1978–Present); Transcriptionist and Quality Assurance Coordinator, MHMM (1974–1978); Clerk, Holmes County Welfare Department (1973); Clerk/Transcriptionist, Holmes County Hospital (1971–1973); Office Assistant, Drs. Robinson and Rayburn (1967–1968); Secretary to the President, Holmes Community College (1964–1966). **Associations & Accomplishments:** American Health Information Management Association; Mississippi Health Information Management Association. **Education:** Holmes Community College, Certificate (1964); American Medical Record Association, Independent Study Program with Certification as Accredited Record Technician (1978). **Personal:** Married to William J. in 1965. Two children: Norma Renee and Alethea Susan. Ms. Cannon Wigley enjoys church, gardening, sewing, reading, and farming.

Charles V. Card
Chief Information Officer
Long Island College Hospital

385 Hicks St.
Brooklyn, NY 11201–5939
(718) 780–1903
Fax: (718) 780–1073

8062

Business Information: Long Island College Hospital is a 602–bed, acute care medical and teaching hospital, providing patient care and instruction to medical students. The Hospital has two satellite locations (clinics) in the Brooklyn area and is in the process of building two more. Long Island College Hospital and satellite locations currently employ 3,000 people. With seven years experience in information systems, Mr. Card joined Long Island College Hospital in 1995. Serving as Chief Information Officer, he oversees the selection, installation, and use of new computer systems being implemented for the Hospital and satellite locations within all departments (i.e., Financial, Payroll, Radiology, Emergency Room, etc.). **Career Steps:** Chief Information Officer, Long Island College Hospital (1995–Present); Assistant Vice President, SUNY Health Science Center–Brooklyn (1993–1995); Assistant Director of IS, New York University Medical Center (1988–1993). **Associations & Accomplishments:** Health Information Management System. **Education:** SUNY–Cortland, B.A. in Sociology (1965). **Personal:** Married to Carol F. in 1990. Mr. Card enjoys golf.

Regina M. Carden
Director of Fiscal & Human Resources
Aleda E. Lutz VA Medical Center

1500 Weiss Street
Saginaw, MI 48602–5251
(517) 793–2340 Ext: 3072
Fax: (517) 791–2221

8062

Business Information: Aleda E. Lutz Veteran's Administration (VA) Medical Center is a medical institute providing diagnosis and treatment to veterans of the military forces. With thirteen years experience in accounting, Ms. Carden joined Aleda E. Lutz VA Medical Center as Director of Fiscal and Human Resources in 1995. She is responsible for the direction of all finances and personnel within the medical center. **Career Steps:** Director of Fiscal and Human Resources, Aleda E. Lutz VA Medical Center (1995–Present); VA Medical Center–Cincinnati, Ohio: Chief Accountant (1991–1995), Budget Analyst (1987–1991). **Associations & Accomplishments:** Former Program Director, Cincinnati Chapter–Association of Governmental Accountants. **Education:** University of Dayton, B.S. in Accounting (1985). **Personal:** Married to Kirkland McDaniel. Three children: Celeste, Michael, and Monique. Ms. Carden enjoys piano, sewing, crafts, and running.

Robbie K. Cartwright
Director of Quality Improvement and Medical Records
American Transitional Heights Hospital

1917 Ashland Street
Houston, TX 77008
(713) 802–8490
Fax: (713) 802–8687

8062

Business Information: American Transitional Heights Hospital is a long–term, acute care hospital with 198 beds. The Hospital is dedicated to providing superior medical services to all patients. As Director of Quality Improvement and Medical Records, Ms. Cartwright ensures that all hospital standards and policies are met by staff members. Her responsibilities as Medical Records Director include performing data collection from records and research. Ms. Cartwright must also produce monthly reports on patient billing information and marketing reports for management upon request. **Career Steps:** Director of Quality Improvement and Medical Records, American Transitional Heights Hospital (1995–Present); Director of Quality Improvement, IHS Hospital of Houston (1994–1995); CQI Specialist, St. Joseph Hospital (1990–1994); Medical Record Specialist, T.I.R.R. (1988–1990). **Associations & Accomplishments:** Texas Gulf Coast Association for Healthcare Quality; Texas Health Information Management Association; American health Information Management Association; Advisory Board and Instructor, Lee College. **Education:** University of Houston at Clear Lake, M.A. (1996); University of Texas at Galveston, B.S.; Wharton County Junior College, A.S. **Personal:** Married to Gary in 1975. Two children: Joshua and Holly. Ms. Cartwright enjoys travel and gardening.

Capt. Micki A. Cavender
Head Nurse
United States Army MEDDAC – Bayne Jones Army Community Hospital

2211 Angus Street
Deridder, LA 70634
(318) 531–3640
Fax: Please mail or call

8062

Business Information: U.S. Army MEDDAC – Bayne Jones Army Community Hospital is a 165–bed, acute health care facility, serving all branches of the military, retirees, and their dependents. Joining the U.S. Army on a nursing scholarship in 1990, Capt. Cavender serves as Head Nurse in the Newborn Nursery at Bayne Jones Army Community Hospital in Deridder, Louisiana. She is responsible for the oversight of the Nursery, in addition to managing the budget, ensuring all staffing requirements are met, attending all committee meetings, and directing the activities of a support staff of 14. **Career Steps:** Head Nurse, U.S. Army MEDDAC – Bayne Jones Army Community Hospital (1995–Present); Charge Nurse – Neonatal ICU, U.S. Army Medical Center (1993–1995). **Associations & Accomplishments:** National Association of Neonatal Nurses (1995–Present); Army Service Ribbon (1990); Army Achievement Medal (1993, 1995); National Defense Service Medal (1991); Overseas Ribbon (1993). **Education:** Masters in Health Administration in progress; Regis University, B.S. in Nursing (1990); Fort Sam Houston, TX: Officer Basic (1990); Armed Forces Combat Casualty Care Course (1996). **Personal:** Married to Michael in 1992. Two children: Elizabeth and Joshua. Capt. Cavender enjoys taking kids to the park, fishing, and camping.

Stuart A. Cayer
Chief of Information Services
Greenbriar Valley Medical Center

P.O. Box 497
Ronceverte, WV 24970
(304) 647–6033
Fax: (304) 647–6059

8062

Business Information: Greenbriar Valley Medical Center is a 122–bed acute care facility providing general surgery, obstetrics/gynecology, and emergency services to area residents. As Chief of Information Services, Mr. Cayer is responsible for ensuring the Hospital's informational needs and future plans coincide with strategic planning. He also oversees and directs operations in the medical records and information departments. **Career Steps:** Chief of Information Services, Greenbriar Valley Medical Center (1995–Present); Director Health Information Services, Breckenridge Hospital (1992–1995); Associate Director Health Information Services, U.T.M.B. (1989–1992). **Education:** U.TM.B., B.S. in Health Information Management (1987); Texas A&M University; Brazosport College. **Personal:** Married to Sharon in 1989. Three children: Kristen, William, and Joe. Mr. Cayer enjoys golf, fishing, hunting, and sporting clays.

Charles Cha, M.D.
Physician
–Independent–

880 The Queensway
Toronto, Ontario M8Z 1P2
(416) 255–1161
Fax: Please mail or call

8062

Business Information: As Physician, Dr. Cha is responsible for teaching medical students and rendering patient care. He began his career in 1989 as staff physician at Moose Factory General Hospital, then went into private practice in 1992. While in private practice, he joined the staffs of Queensway General Hospital and St. Joseph's Health Center in Toronto. Additionally, he is Owner and Chief Executive Officer of an Investment Consulting business. **Career Steps:** Lecturer in the Department of Family and Community Medicine, University of Toronto (1994–Present); Active Staff, Queensway General Hospital (1992–Present); Active Staff, St. Joseph's Health Center (1992–Present); Active Staff, Moose Factory General Hospital (1989–1990). **Associations & Accomplishments:** Boulevard Club; MENSA; Sailing Club; Ski Club; College of Physicians and Surgeons. **Education:** Queen's University, Internal Med. (1989); University of Manitoba, B.Sc. Med (1988); University of Toronto, M.D. (1987); Academic Research and Publication: "Effect of Hippocampal Lesions on Memory and Learning." **Personal:** Dr. Cha enjoys downhill ski racing, competitive tennis, sailing, jujitsu, volleyball, and reading.

Kul Deep Chadda, M.D.
Chief of Electrophysiology Services
South Nassau Communities Hospital

2445 Oceanside Road
Oceanside, NY 11572
(516) 763–3418
Fax: (516) 763–3420

8062

Business Information: South Nassau Communities Hospital is a full–service, multi–specialty medical facility and health service establishment. In his current capacity, Dr. Chadda is responsible for all aspects of operations for the Electrophysiology Laboratory. Concurrent to his position with the hospital, Dr. Chadda is also a Professor of Clinical Medicine at the State University of New York School of Medicine. **Career Steps:** Chief of Electrophysiology, South Nassau Communities Hospital (1993–Present); Long Island Jewish Medical Center: Head of Electrophysiology and Director of the Pacemaker and Arrhythmia Surveillance Center (1983–1988), Section Co–Head, Invasive Cardiology (1979–1981); The Heart Institute: Acting Physician in Charge (1981–1983), Head, Cardiac Catheterization and Electrophysiology (1981–1983); Director of Cardiopulmonary Laboratories and Cardiac Catheterization, Maimonides Medical Center (1976–1979); Mt. Sinai Hospital Services: Chief of Cardiac Laboratories and Catheterization (1974–1976), Associate Director of Cardiac Laboratories (1973–1974); SUNY Downstate Medical Center: Associate Professor of Medicine (1978–1987), Assistant Professor of Medicine (1976–1978); Mt. Sinai School of Medicine of the City University of New York: Assistant Professor of Medicine (1975–1977), Associate in Medicine (1973–1975), Visiting Associate in Medicine (1973). **Associations & Accomplishments:** Fellow, American College of Physicians; Fellow, American College of Cardiology; Fellow, American College of Nutrition; Fellow, American College of Angiology; Fellow, American College of Chest Physicians; Fellow, Council of Clinical Cardiology, American Heart Association; Fellow, Society for Cardiac Angiography; Fellow, New York Cardiology Society; Fellow, International College of Nutrition; Membership Committee, New York Heart Association, Nassau Chapter; American Society of Internal Medicine; American Federation for Clinical Research; Medical Society County of Kings and Academy of Medicine; North American Society of Pacing and Electrophysiology; Certificate of Appreciation, Nassau Chapter of the American Heart Association (1981, 1982); Who's Who in the East; Biography International; Award for Service for Nursing and Paramedical Education, Nassau Chapter of the American Heart Association; Numerous publications; Participated in several programs and seminars. **Education:** Ewing Christian College – Allahabad, India, I.Sc. (PreMed) First Division with Distinction (1961); Maulana Azad Medical College, University of Delhi, India, M.B.B.S. (1966); Board–certified: Internal Medicine and Cardiovascular Disease. **Personal:** Married to Mary. Dr. Chadda enjoys reading and staying current with the latest medical technologies.

Wen–Li Chang, M.D.
Clinical Assistant Professor
Baylor College of Medicine
2642 Trail Creek Drive
Sugarland, TX 77479–1554
(713) 344–0277
Fax: (713) 344–0288

8062

Business Information: The Baylor College of Medicine provides all aspects of post–graduate education to residents and interns, as well as full tertiary care and clinical research hospital facilities. As Clinical Assistant Professor and Physician of Internal Medicine, Dr. Chang directs patient care and resident physician education. An expert in her field, Dr. Chang has published a number of articles and findings in medical journals, including the 1987 article entitled "Thyroxine Transfer and Distribution and Critical Non–thyrodic Illness, Chronic Renal Failure, and Chronic Ethenol Abuse," found in the Journal of Endocrinology and Metabolism. In the near future, she would like to take on a greater patient load as well as continue with her research and writing. **Career Steps:** Baylor College of Medicine: Clinical Assistant Professor and Physician of Internal Medicine (1995–Present), Instructor (1989–1991); Catholic Medical Center of Brooklyn & Queens: Supervising Physician (1994–1995), Administrative teaching attending (1991–1993). **Associations & Accomplishments:** American Medical Association; New York State Medical Society; American College of Physicians. **Education:** University of Texas Health Science Center – Houston, M.D. (1986); Midwestern State University – Wichita Falls, B.S. **Personal:** Married to Bernard C. Yu in 1986. One child: Stanley S. Yu. Dr. Chang enjoys ping pong.

A. Dale Chisum, D.O.
Medical Director – Emergency Services Department
Riverside Health Systems
2622 West Central Avenue
Wichita, KS 67203–4902
(316) 946–8552
Fax: (316) 946–8599

8062

Business Information: Riverside Health Systems is a hospital system with nine clinics providing patients with quality care, treatment, and diagnosis. As Medical Director of the Emergency Services Department, Dr. Chisum oversees the System's operations, public relations, strategic planning, development and implementation of policies and procedures, and patient care quality. **Career Steps:** Medical Director – Emergency Services Department, Riverside Health Systems (1993–Present); Medical Emergency Services Association: Assistant Medical Director/Staff Physician (1990–1993), Staff Physician (1983–1993); Resident Physician, Chicago College of Osteopathic Medicine (1981–1983). **Associations & Accomplishments:** Secretary/Diplomate, American Osteopathic Board of Emergency Medicine; Diplomate, American Board of Emergency Medicine; National Board of Osteopathic Emergency Medicine; Fellow, American College of Emergency Medicine; Fellow, American College of Emergency Physicians; Fellow, American Osteopathic College of Emergency Medicine; American Osteopathic Association. **Education:** Texas College of Osteopathic Medicine, D.O. (1978); University of Houston, B.S.– Pharm.; South West Texas Junior College, A.A. **Personal:** Married to Terry Sue Cavender. Dr. Chisum enjoys golf, hiking, cycling, hunting, and fishing.

Dr. J. Choi

Director of Psychiatry
Oakwood Hospital Heritage Center
10,000 South Telegraph Road
Taylor, MI 48180
(313) 295–5134
Fax: (313) 295–5264

8062

Business Information: Oakwood Hospital Heritage Center is an acute care hospital, providing full surgery, emergency care and outpatient clinic services. A practicing physician since 1968 and a Board–Certified Psychiatrist, Dr. Choi serves as Director of Psychiatry at Oakwood Hospital. He is responsible for coordinating, supervising and maintaining quality of care to patients. His department provides care of mentally–ill patients, private or public, on an in–patient, partial program and out–patient settings. Concurrent with his duties at Oakwood Hospital, he is President and practicing physician of his individual private medical practice and President of Best of Mental Health. **Career Steps:** Director of Psychiatry, Oakwood Hospital Heritage Center (Present); President, J. Choi, M.D., P.C. (Present); President, Best of Mental Health (Present). **Associations & Accomplishments:** American Medical Association; American Psychiatric Association; Michigan Medical Society; Michigan Psychiatric Society; Wayne County Medical Society. **Education:** Seoul National University College of Medicine – Seoul, Korea, M.D. (1968). **Personal:** Married to Kyung–Eun Choi in 1971. Three children: Betty, Susan, and Ronald. Dr. Choi enjoys family activities, oil painting, and golf.

Carlos G. Cigarroa. M.D.
Cardiologist
Mercy Hospital
1420 Logan Street
Laredo, TX 78040–4645
(210) 725–1228
Fax: Please mail or call

8062

Business Information: Mercy Hospital is a multi–specialty, acute care hospital, providing diagnosis and treatment of patients. A practicing physician since 1987, Dr. Cigarroa operates a private practice within Mercy Hospital. He specializes in the diagnosis and treatment of patients suffering from cardiac problems. Concurrent with his private practice, he conducts echo cardio research and publishes his findings. **Career Steps:** Cardiologist, Mercy Hospital **Associations & Accomplishments:** Harvard Medical School Alumni Association **Education:** Harvard University Medical School, M.D. (1987); Notre Dame University, B.S. in Biology **Personal:** Married to Melissa Renteria. Two children: Isabella and Annalis.

Nayda Cintron
Controller
Hospital Damas, Inc.
Ponce By Pass
Ponce, Puerto Rico 00731
(809) 840–8686 Ext. 7070
Fax: (809) 259–0680

8062

Business Information: Hospital Damas, Inc. is a full–service, multi–specialty 355–bed acute care hospital. Established in 1863, Hospital Damas, Inc. reports an operating budget of $35 million and currently employs 850 people. As Controller, Ms. Cintron is responsible for all aspects of finances, including the annual budget, Medicare cost reports, feasibility studies, monthly financial statements and other financially–related matters. **Career Steps:** Hospital Damas, Inc.: Controller (1992–Present), Special Projects Manager (1991–1992); Senior Auditor, Deloitte & Touche (1988–1991). **Associations & Accomplishments:** Puerto Rico Accounting Association; American Institute of Certified Public Accountants (AICPA); Alpha Chi – National Honor Scholarship Society. **Education:** Catholic University of Puerto Rico, B.B.A. (1988); Certified Public Accountant (CPA) (1990). **Personal:** Married to Dr. Ulises R. Rodriguez in 1990. One child: Dania Nicole Rodriguez. Ms. Cintron enjoys movies.

Paul G. Clarke III, M.B.A., R.E.M.T.–P
Director, E.M.S. Institute
The Stamford Hospital
665 Fairfield Avenue No.8
Stamford, CT 06902
(203) 325–7065
Fax: (203) 325–7078
EMAIL: See Below

8062

Business Information: The Stamford Hospital is a 310–bed hospital serving the Stamford, Connecticut area. The hospital was established in 1886 and has approximately 1,900 employees. As Director, E.M.S. Institute, Mr. Clarke is responsible for a variety of management responsibilities. As Hospital Safety Officer, Mr. Clarke must be familiar with JCAHO, OSHA, EPA, and other regulatory and statutory requirements, and ensure Hospital compliance. As Director of Paramedic Education it is his responsibility to be familiar with changes in prehospital and critical care medicine, and to schedule training of his paramedic staff in order to update their credentials. As Department Head, Mr. Clarke manages the personnel in his department. Mr. Clarke feels obtaining each educational credential a milestone in his career and will begin Ph.D. work in Health Policy and management in August of 1996. Internet users can reach him via: E–Mail–paul–clarke@stam-hosp.chime.org. **Career Steps:** Director, E.M.S. Institute, The Stamford Hospital (1995–Present); Director, Paramedic Operations, Eastchester E.M.S. (1994–Present); E.M.S. Coordinator, Hamford Hospital (1992–1995). **Associations & Accomplishments:** Delta Mu Delta, National Business Honor Society; American Public Health Association; American Management Association; National Association of E.M.S. Educators. **Education:** Columbia University, M.P.H. (1997); Sacred Heart University, M.B.A.; Pace University, B.A.; White Plains Hospital Center, New York State Paramedic. **Personal:** Married to Maureen in 1993. One child: Danielle Kathryn. Mr. Clarke enjoys travel and spending time with family.

Kay M. Clayton
Western Regional Director of Quick Cares
University Medical Center – Quick Cares
2760 Lake Sahara Drive, Suite 108
Las Vegas, NV 89117
(702) 254–4900
Fax: (702) 254–4348

8062

Business Information: University Medical Center – Quick Cares have seven satellite locations in Las Vegas. Quick Cares see primary and urgent care patients, do basic lab work, X–rays, and provide ambulatory services. As Western Regional Director of Quick Cares, Ms. Clayton is responsible for the oversight of four clinics, and handles hiring, employee discipline, insurance, education, budget restraints, and working with medical directors. **Career Steps:** Western Regional Director of Quick Cares, University Medical Center – Quick Care (1990–Present); Nurse Surveyor, Illinois Department of Public Health (1987–1989); Assistant Head Nurse of ICU, Riverside Hospital (1984–1987); 3–11 Supervisor, Fairbury Hospital (1983–1984). **Associations & Accomplishments:** Nevada Public Health Association; Board of Directors – Secretary, Bobbie Sox (girls softball). **Education:** St. Louis University, B.S.N. (1982); Joliet Junior College, A.A.S. **Personal:** Two children: Kelli and Kara. Ms. Clayton enjoys being the Secretary of the Bobbie Sox Girls Softball Board of Directors.

Doris L. Cohen, R.N.
Registered Nurse
Morristown Memorial Hospital – Surgical Services
100 Madison Avenue
Morristown, NJ 07960
(201) 971–8861
Fax: Please mail or call

8062

Business Information: Morristown Memorial Hospital – Surgical Services is a full–service medical facility specializing in the diagnosis and treatment of patients. Ms. Cohen was a full–time ER nurse at Morristown until her diagnosis of multiple myeloma, a rare blood cancer, in 1994. With the help of her coworkers, she carries on her duties part–time while undergoing regular treatments of chemotherapy. Ms. Cohen has dedicated her time to educating the African–American and Hispanic populations on the importance of bone marrow testing and donation, cancer diagnosis, and accessing medical systems and resources. She was the Poster Patient for the Morristown Memorial Hospital Bone Marrow Drive, participated in Health Unlimited for Cancer Patients (an organization that sends cancer victims on trips, etc.), and is a recipient of Happiness Unlimited, her experience appearing in their next promotional flyer. Anyone interested in bone marrow donation information can call the Morristown Memorial Hospital Information Hotline at: (800) 447–3337. **Career Steps:** Registered Nurse, Morristown Memorial Hospital – Surgical Services (1991–Present); Registered Nurse, University of Nebraska Medical Center (1985–1989); Registered Nurse, Michigan Osteopathic Medical Center (1980–1985). **Associations & Accomplishments:** American Nurses Association; Nursing Staff Development; Association of Operating Room Nurses; Sigma Theta Tau International; Numerous Certifications of Appreciation Recognition for Outstanding Performance in Clinical and Educational Continuing Education for Nursing and Patient Care; Care and Kind Award for Patient Care; Life Saving Award for Community Services. **Education:** University of Nebraska, M.S.N. (1989); Wayne State University, B.S.N.; Philadelphia Community College, A.D.N. **Personal:** Ms. Cohen enjoys music, reading, and travel.

George Collette Jr.
Clinical Director
Presbyterian Medical Center
39 and Market Street
Philadelphia, PA 19104
(215) 662–9790
Fax: (215) 662–0566

8062

Business Information: Presbyterian Medical Center specializes in providing geropsychiatric services. Aimed towards adults over the age of 55, the Centers assists patients with emotional and behavioral needs. As Clinical Director, Mr. Collette is responsible for program development and design, with hopes of expanding these programs to a national level. He also handles administrative coordination of all clinical services for the Center, coordinating contracts and personnel. **Career Steps:** Presbyterian Medical Center: Clinical Director (1992–Present), Director of Therapies (1989–1992); Director Partial Hospital, Pennsylvania Hospital (1978–1989). **Associations & Accomplishments:** Charter Member, African–American Family Therapy Cooperative; Family Institute of Philadelphia; Association of Mental Health Administrators; American Association for Partial Hospitalization. **Education:** Hahhemann Medical College, MFT (1978); Antioch University, B.A. in Social Welfare. **Personal:** Four children: Melanie, Anika, Njeri, and Murjanie. Mr. Collette enjoys eastern philosophies, jazz, and history of cinema.

Bina Comes, M.D.
• • • ◄———◉———► • • •

Pediatrician
Lil Coll Hospital
6410 Veterans Avenue
Brooklyn, NY 11234–5639
(718) 531–4600
Fax: (718) 531–1628

8062

Business Information: Lil Coll Hospital is a multi–specialty tertiary hospital, medical research and teaching institution. As a Staff Pediatrician, Dr. Comes is responsible for the care and treatment of patients, as well as the instruction of medical students and residents. He also conducts clinical research in the areas of pediatric sinus and urinary tract infections. **Career Steps:** Pediatrician, Lil Coll Hospital (1986–Present). **Associations & Accomplishments:** American Medical Association; Brooklyn Pediatric Society; MSSNY. **Education:** Universidad de Navarra, M.D. (1984). **Personal:** Married to William A. Lois in 1979. Two children: Billy and Christine. Dr. Comes enjoys reading, gardening, gourmet cooking, exercising, and needlepoint.

Caaron Cook, Ph.D., RRT
Director, Respiratory Care & Diagnostics
Detroit Medical Center
4201 St. Antione Street
Detroit, MI 48201–2153
(313) 745–2912
Fax: (313) 993–8928

8062

Business Information: Detroit Medical Center is a seven hospital health care center. With 25 years experience in health care management and administration, Dr. Cook joined Detroit Medical Center in 1991 as Director of the Respiratory Care & Diagnostics Department. She is presently responsible for administration of the EEG/ECG Units, directly supervising a staff of 60 medical and support personnel. **Career Steps:** Director, Respiratory Care & Diagnostics, Detroit Medical Center (1991–Present); Division Chair, Allied Health, Marygrove College (1988–1991); Instructor, Highland Park College (1974–1988). **Associations & Accomplishments:** American Association for Respiratory Care; Michigan Society for Respiratory Care; Marygrove College Allied Health Advisory Board; Sigma Iota Sigma Doctoral Support Group. **Education:** Walden University, Ph.D. (1996); Marygrove College, M.A. in Educational Administration; Siena Heights College, B.A.S. in Allied Health. **Personal:** Married to Ronald in 1967. Four children: Ronda, Terri, Peter, and Cristyn. Dr. Cook enjoys sewing, computers, and spending time with her grandchildren.

Janice A. Cordola, RRA
Director of Medical Information
Northern Westchester Hospital Center
400 East Main Street
Mount Kisco, NY 10549
(914) 666–1866
Fax: Please mail or call

8062

Business Information: Northern Westchester Hospital Center, a 259–bed facility, is a full accredited healthcare institution serving the community and maintaining the highest quality of standards of patient care. As Director of Medical Information, Ms. Cordola is responsible for maintenance of all medical records, preserving confidentiality and meeting all regulatory requirements. She currently supervises a staff of 18. **Career Steps:** Director of Medical Information, Northern Westchester Hospital (1994–Present); Assistant Director of Medical Information, Lawrence Hospital (1992–1994); Consultant/Medical Records, Self–Employed (1990–1992). **Associations & Accomplishments:** American Health Information Management Association; Greater New York Health Information Management Association; New York Health Information Management Association; Parent Teacher Association – Ridgeway School; Co–Leader, Girl Scout Troop #2163. **Education:** University of Bridgeport, B.S. Degree in Medical Record Administration (1980). **Personal:** Married in 1985 and has two children. Ms. Cordola enjoys bicycling, reading books, and exercising.

Becky Sutherland Cornett, Ph.D.
Director of Inpatient Rehabilitation Programs
Ohio State University Medical Center
480 West Ninth Avenue
Columbus, OH 43210
(614) 293–3810
Fax: (614) 293–3125

8062

Business Information: Ohio State University Medical Center, affiliated with Ohio State University is a full–service, tertiary care, teaching and research hospital. Joining Ohio State University Medical Center in 1988, as Director, Speech Pathology Department, Dr. Cornett was appointed as Director of In–patient Rehabilitation Programs in 1994. In this capacity, she administers all inpatient adult rehabilitation programs and services for TBI, SCI, and stroke–related disorders. In addition, Dr. Cornett oversees the admission process of programs and ensures quality improvement. **Career Steps:** Ohio State University Medical Center: Director, In–patient Rehabilitation Programs (1994–Present), Director, Speech Pathology (1988–1994); Assistant Director – Reimbursement Policy Division, American Speech, Language & Hearing Association (1986–1988). **Associations & Accomplishments:** American Speech, Language and Hearing Association; Ohio Speech & Hearing Association. **Education:** University of Pittsburgh, Ph.D. (1988); Northwestern University, M.A. (1976); Western Michigan University: M.A. (1980), B.S., summa cum laude (1975). **Personal:** Married to Rev. Ward L. Cornett in 1981. One child: Andrea. Dr. Cornett enjoys travel, reading, collecting Victorian dolls, and hiking.

Becky B. Crawford, RN, MA
Community Education Coordinator
Caldwell Memorial Hospital
307 Redwood Place
Lenoir, NC 28645
(704) 757–5446
Fax: (704) 757–5521

8062

Business Information: Caldwell Memorial Hospital is a non–profit health care facility specializing in the diagnosis, treatment and rehabilitation of patients. Established in 1954, the Hospital presently employs 700 people. As Community Education Coordinator, Ms. Crawford directs the activities of the Community Education Department. She is involved in planning, developing, and implementing health education programs for businesses, industries, civic clubs, and other organizations in the community. **Career Steps:** Community Education Coordinator, Caldwell Memorial Hospital (1992–Present); Nurse Educator, Caldwell Community College (1983–1992); Staff Nurse, The Women's Center (1978–1983). **Associations & Accomplishments:** Sigma Theta Tau International Nursing Honor Society; County's Council on aging; American Business Women's Association; County's School–to–Work Task Force; North Carolina Association of Community Educators; Continuing Education Board; Northwest Area Educator's Association; Planning and Development Board; Caldwell County Chamber of Commerce Health Care Task Force; Coordinator of County's Scleroderma Support Group. **Education:** Appalachian State University, Master's degree (1987); Pfeiffer College, B.A. in Nursing; Davis hospital School of Nursing, Diploma in Nursing. **Personal:** Married to David in 1978. Ms. Crawford enjoys camping, reading, ACC basketball, and music.

Bruce N. Cronstein, M.D.
Associate Professor of Medicine
New York University Medical Center
550 1st Avenue
New York, NY 10016–6481
(212) 263–6404
Fax: (212) 263–8804
EMail: See Below

8062

Business Information: New York University Medical Center is a tertiary care hospital, medical research and teaching institution in affiliation with the University of New York School of Medicine. Joining New York University in 1980 as a Fellow in Rheumatology, Dr. Cronstein serves as an Associate Professor of Medicine and Principal Investigator. He serves as mentor and clinical educator to medical residents in Rheumatology, as well as conducts research in inflammatory arthritis treatments and procedures. He can also be reached through the Internet as follows: CRONSB01@MCRCR6.MED.NYU.EDU **Career Steps:** New York University Medical Center: Associate Professor of Medicine (1992–Present), Assistant Professor (1985–1992); Fellow in Rheumatology, New York University (1980–1985). **Associations & Accomplishments:** American Society of Clinical Investigation; American Federation of Clinical Research; New York Arthritis Foundation; New York Heart Association; American College of Rheumatology; President (1994), New York Rheumatology Association. **Education:** University of Cincinnati College of Medicine, M.D. (1976); Lake Forest College, B.A. (1972). **Personal:** Married to Susan Goodman in 1975. Two children: Alexander and Jessica. Dr. Cronstein enjoys reading, bicycling and theatre.

Barbara Y. Crooks RN, MSN
Director of Nursing
Howard University Hospital
2041 Georgia Avenue, NW
Washington, DC 20060–0001
(202) 865–6639
Fax: (202) 745–3731

8062

Business Information: Howard University Hospital is a full–service academic medical center specializing in acute and ambulatory care. With twenty–five years of nursing experience, Ms. Crooks joined the Hospital's administrative staff as Director of Nursing in 1993. She is presently responsible for overseeing the Maternal Child Health Psychiatry Unit and Outpatient Services. **Career Steps:** Director of Nursing, Howard University Hospital (1993–Present); District of Columbia General Hospital: Nurse Educator (1990–1993), Nurse Manager (1988–1990). **Associations & Accomplishments:** Sigma Theta Tau International; American Organization of Nurse Educators; AWHONN; Participates through the S.D.A. Church in providing meals to the homeless during the holiday seasons and hospital–sponsored health fairs, as well as coordinates community–based health fairs through the school system of Montgomery County, Maryland. **Education:** Catholic University of America, M.S.N., Administrative Achievement Award (1986); Columbia Union College, B.S.N. (1981); University of The West Indies – Hospital: Midwife Certificate and Diploma in Nursing, Highest Achiever in RN Program (1971). **Personal:** Married to Llewelyn in 1974. Three children: Keith, Collin, and Raymond. Ms. Crooks enjoys swimming and tennis.

Martha Lou Cross, Pharm.D.
Clinical Manager
Methodist Medical Center
990 Oak Ridge Turnpike
Oak Ridge, TN 37830
(423) 481–1315
Fax: (423) 481–1196

8062

Business Information: The Methodist Medical Center, a wholly–owned affiliate of Owen Healthcare, Inc., is a pharmacy service with over 500 independent locations nationwide. Methodist Medical Center of Knoxville, Tennessee, is under contract to OHI to provide pharmaceutical services to its medical staff. The hospital is a 300–bed facility serving five counties in providing intensive care, critical care, and cardiac care, as well as TennCare for Medicare and uninsured patients. As

Clinical Manager, Ms. Cross supervises 28 pharmacists and technicians, manages drug information services, trains technicians, pharmacists, and nurses, participates in various committees, and monitors geriatric patients in prescription intake. **Career Steps:** Owen Healthcare, Inc.: Methodist Medical Center – Clinical Manager (1989–Present), RMG Home Infusion – Pharmacist Manager (1988–1989); Parenteral Supervisor, St. Joseph's Hospital (1985–1987); IV Supervisor, Memorial Mission Hospital (1981–1985); IV Coordinator and Assistant Director, Northside Hospital (1977–1981). **Associations & Accomplishments:** American Society of Parenteral and Enteral Nutrition; American Society of Health System Pharmacists; Tennessee Society of Hospital Pharmacists; Tennessee Pharmaceutical Association; Knoxville Museum of Art. **Education:** University of Tennessee: Pharm.D. (1973), B.S. (1972); City of Memphis Hospitals, Hospital Administration Residency; University of Tennessee Medical Units **Personal:** Ms. Cross enjoys stained glass, hiking, knitting, and house restoration.

Linda S. Cunningham

Director of the Cardiopulmonary Department

Burleson Memorial Hospital

P.O. Drawer 360
Caldwell, TX 77836–0360
(409) 567–3245
Fax: (409) 567–0616

8062

Business Information: Burleson Memorial Hospital is a full tertiary care hospital. With a background in medical technology and administration spanning a twenty–year period, Linda Cunningham was appointed Director of Burleson Memorial's Cardiopulmonary Department in January of 1995. She serves as the executive administrator responsible for the overall administrative and budgetary operations of the Department and its support staff. **Career Steps:** Director of the Cardiopulmonary Department, Burleson Memorial Hospital (1995–Present); Director, Madison County Hospital (1984–1994); Staff Technician, Huntsville Memorial Hospital (1977–1984). **Associations & Accomplishments:** AARC; TSRC; NBRC. **Education:** California College of Health Sciences, CRTT (1987). **Personal:** Married to James W. in 1990. Two children: Lori and Patricia. Ms. Cunningham enjoys crafts and spending time with her four grandchildren.

Ruth Currie

Director of Medical Records

East Texas Medical Center

2000 South Palestine Street
Athens, TX 75751
(903) 676–1140
Fax: (903) 676–4191

8062

Business Information: East Texas Medical Center is a full–service acute care hospital specializing in outpatient procedures. As Director of Medical Records, Ms. Currie manages the medical records department and utilization management functions. She is responsible for the organization of the hospital records and planning for and managing medical records department information systems. Other duties Ms. Currie is responsible for include staff training, evaluations, employment counseling, budgets, and acting as liaison between staff and upper management. **Career Steps:** Director of Medical Records, East Texas Medical Center (1992–Present); Director of Medical Records, Kelsey Memorial Hospital (1990–1992); Director of Medical Records, Trinity Medical Center (1984–1989). **Associations & Accomplishments:** American Health Information Management Association; Advisory Board, Tyler Junior College Medical Record Technology Program; Texas Health Information Management Association. **Education:** Ferris State University, A.A.S. (1981). **Personal:** Married to Melvin in 1995. Two children: Anna and Rachel. Ms. Currie enjoys Christian activities, reading, computers, and spending time with her family.

Pierre D'Amour, M.D.

Director, Parathyroid Glands Physiology Laboratory

Hospital St. Luc – Andre–Viallet Clinical Research Center

264 East Rene–Levesque Blvd.
Montreal, Quebec H2X 1P1
(514) 281–2444 Ext. 5704
Fax: (514) 281–2492

8062

Business Information: Hospital St. Luc is a 600–bed full–service, healthcare facility affiliated with the University of Montreal. The Hospital delivers mainly tertiary care. As Director of a Research Laboratory, Mr. D'Amour is specifically involved in the normal function and in diseases of the parathyroid glands. He studies how the various circulating molecular forms of parathyroid hormone are involved in the biological effects of the hormone in health and in diseases such as primary hyperparathyroidism and renal failure. **Career Steps:** Director of Research Laboratory, Hospital St. Luc (1992–Present); Professor of Medicine, University of Montreal (1992); Endocrinologist (1973–Present). **Associations & Accomplishments:** Canadian Society of Clinical Investigation; Canadian Society of Endocrinology and Metabolism; American Society for Bone and Mineral Research; International Bone and Mineral Society; Endocrine Society; Published articles in major journals including,"Journal of Bone and Mineral Research," Journal of Clinical Endocrinology and Metabolism. **Education:** Harvard Medical School, Post Doctorate (1974–1976); University of Montreal, M.D. (1969); Province of Quebec, CSPQ in Endocrinology (1973). **Personal:** Married to Monique Lefebvre in 1969. One child: Alexandre. Mr. D'Amour enjoys gardening, summer and winter sports and playing with his son.

Jeremy L. D'Morias, M.D.

Chief of Emergency Services

Veterans Administration Medical Center

2615 East Clinton Avenue
Fresno, CA 93703–2223
(209) 228–6918
Fax: (209) 434–3658
E MAIL: See Below

8062

Business Information: V.A. Medical Center is a full–service, 275–300 bed general hospital for veterans of the United States Armed Forces. Affiliated with the University of California at San Francisco, V.A. Medical Center offers residency programs in Surgery, Radiology, OB/GYN, Dental, Internal Medicine, Family Practice, and Pediatrics. The Center provides full acute, ambulatory and long term care for all veterans in Central California. As Chief of Emergency Services, Dr. D'Morias is responsible for the day–to–day running of the emergency room, staffing, and ambulatorye care. Dr. D'Morias also has oversight of the hospital–based, 50 patient, home healthcare unit and its staff (four nurses, a rehabilitation specialist, and a dietician). Internet users can reach him via: jaydeemdee@aol.com. **Career Steps:** Chief of Emergency Services, V.A. Medical Center (1992–Present); U.C.S.F.: Chief Resident (1991–1992), Resident in Internal Medicine (1990–1992). **Associations & Accomplishments:** American College of Physicians; Medical Director, Hospital based home care, California. **Education:** St. John's Medical School, M.D. (1979). **Personal:** Married to Linet in 1983. Three children: Melissa, David, and Samantha. Dr. D'Morias enjoys being a Bridge champion.

Sherry H. Danello

Vice President of Patient Services

St. Joseph's Hospital Healthcare Systems

11705 Mercy Boulevard
Savannah, GA 31406
(912) 927–5416
Fax: (912) 927–5467

8062

Business Information: St. Joseph's Hospital Healthcare Systems, affiliated with nine other hospitals and the Savannah Business Group, is a 305–bed, multi–specialty, acute care hospital, providing cardiac care, orthopaedics, neurology and neuro–surgical centers, a 15–bed rehabilitation center, maternal child care, and pediatrics departments. St. Joseph's recently merged with Blue Cross/Blue Shield of Georgia and also offers an HMO plan. With twelve years experience in the healthcare industry, Mrs. Danello joined St. Joseph's Hospital Healthcare Systems in 1984. Appointed as Vice President of Patient Services in 1993, she is responsible for managing all aspects of patient care services, as well as conducting public speaking and serving as a member of the Executive Management Team. **Career Steps:** St. Joseph's Hospital Healthcare Systems: Vice President of Patient Services (1993–Present), Assistant Vice President (1992–1993), Assistant Director of Nursing (1989–1992), Supervisor of Critical Care (1984–1989). **Associations & Accomplishments:** American Heart Association; Georgia Board of Nurse Executives; American Hospital Association; Council on Patient Care, Sun Health Alliance; Sigma Theta Tau; Board Member, Savannah Swim Team. **Education:** Medical College of Georgia, M.S.N. (1982); Armstrong State College, B.S.N.; University of Florida Hospitals and Clinics, Diploma. **Personal:** Married to Dr. Thomas Danello in 1982. Two children: Stephen and Maria. Mrs. Danello enjoys water sports, swimming, and spending time with her family.

Linda M. Davis

Director of Clinical Services

Westside Urban Health Center, Inc.

115 East York Street
Savannah, GA 31401
(912) 944–6080
Fax: (912) 231–2783

8062

Business Information: Westside Urban Health Center, Inc. was founded as a primary care facility in 1971 to serve the residents of Savannah, Georgia at three sites. Payment plans are on a sliding fee scale as a federally and county funded organization covering the whole range of medical services. As Director of Clinical Services, Ms. Davis serves as the intermediary between providers and health center staff as part of the administrative team. She also provides direct patient care, supervises patient care programs, and coordinates service for eight departments that support patient medical care. **Career Steps:** Westside Urban Health Center, Inc.: Director of Clinical Services (1991–Present), Nurse Practitioner (1974–1989); Nurse Practitioner, Lawrence D. Odom, M.D. (1989–1991). **Associations & Accomplishments:** American Nurses Association; Sigma Theta Tau, International Honor Society of Nursing. **Education:** Armstrong State College, B.S.N. (1981); St. Joseph's Hospital School of Nursing, Diploma; Spartanburg General Hospital, Family Nurse Practitioner Certificate. **Personal:** Married to John in 1965. Three children: Angela, Dana, and John. Ms. Davis enjoys church activities and music.

Donna De Carlo, M.D.

Physician Advisor

Central Florida Regional Hospital

1401 West Seminole Boulevard
Sanford, FL 32771
(407) 321–4500 Ext: 5912
Fax: Please mail or call

8062

Business Information: Central Florida Regional Hospital is a 260–bed acute care medical facility, providing a wide spectrum of health care to patients with the assistance of 160 physicians. A practicing physician since 1987, Dr. De Carlo is a trained and Board–Certified Emergency Medicine Physician. Joining Central Florida Regional Hospital as Physician Advisor in 1995, she offers medical advice to the hospital and case managers, as well as reviewing and suggesting ways for quality utilization. **Career Steps:** Physician Advisor, Central Florida Regional Hospital (1995–Present); Emergency Room Medical Director and Area Medical Director, EmCare, Coastal Emergency Services (1991–1994). **Associations & Accomplishments:** American Medical Association; FMA; DCMA; ACEP; NAEMSP; ABQUARP. **Education:** University of Miami, M.D. (1987). **Personal:** Married to Orville in 1995.

David C. Dean, M.D.

Co–Director of Cardiac Rehabilitation

Buffalo General Hospital

4955 N. Bailey Avenue
Buffalo, NY 14226–1206
(716) 836–0571
Fax: (716) 836–0505

8062

Business Information: Buffalo General Hospital, established in 1961, is a full–service, acute care hospital providing diagnosis and treatment to patients. A Board–Certified Cardiologist, Dr. Dean joined Buffalo General Hospital in 1989. Serving as Co–Director of Cardiac Rehabilitation, he is responsible for providing cardiology rehabilitation and cardiac care to patients, as well as being responsible for administration, operations, and public relations. He also serves as Co–Director of Cardiology Rehabilitation at the Buffalo Veteran's Administration Medical Center and Professor at University of Buffalo Medical Center in the Department of Medicine (consisting of 15–20 professors and 150 medical students). **Career Steps:** Private Practice Cardiologist, (1962–Present); Co–Director of Cardiac Rehabilitation, Buffalo General Hospital (1989–Present); Chief of Cardiology, Buffalo VA Medical Center (1962–1990). **Associations & Accomplishments:** President, Western New York Heart Association; President, Buffalo Academy of Medicine; President, Buffalo Torch Club; President, Veterans Administration Cardiologists; Published more than 35 articles on Cardiology; Frequent lecturer in the medical community. **Education:** The Johns Hopkins University School of Medicine, M.D. (1956); Bowdoin College, B.A. (1952). **Personal:** Married to Jean in 1956. Three children: Bruce, Keith and Laurie. Dr. Dean enjoys travel, tennis, stamp collecting and sports during his leisure time.

Shirley Deems
H.I.M. Director
Berrien County Hospital
1221 McPherson Street
Nashville, GA 31639
(912) 686–7471
Fax: (912) 686–7778

8062

Business Information: Berrien County Hospital is a full–service acute and sub–acute care hospital with 59 beds. The facility accommodates short–term care patients and the attached 108 bed nursing home handles the long–term care patients. Established in 1965 the hospital currently has 80 employees. As H.I.M. Director, Ms. Deems oversees the health information systems, patient billings, patient reimbursements, patient records, and DRG Optimization. She is directly responsible for the activities of her staff of five employees. **Career Steps:** H.I.M. Director, Berrien County Hospital (1978–Present); Coffee Regional Medical Center: Ward Clerk, transferred to Medical Records, became A.R.T., promoted to Assistant (1971–1978). **Associations & Accomplishments:** American Health Information Management Association; South Georgia Health Information Management Association; Georgia Health Information Management Association. **Education:** AMRA Correspondence Course, A.R.T. (1976). **Personal:** Three children: Ricky Deems, Mitchell Deems, and Renee Ogden. Ms. Deems enjoys cross–stitching, reading, walking, and spending time with her grandchild.

Ms. Yvonne Depinet
Director
Medcenter Hospital
1050 Delaware Avenue
Marion, OH 43302–6416
(614) 383–7806
Fax: (614) 383–2414

8062

Business Information: Medcenter Hospital is an acute care hospital, serving Marion, Ohio and surrounding Marion County populace. The hospital also provides an after–discharge continued care services program. As Director of the Continued Care Division, Ms. Depinet is responsible for social services, discharge planning, Home Health Care, Homemakers, and outpatient mental health. **Career Steps:** Director of Continued Care, Medcenter Hospital (1993–Present); Director, S.S.I.D.P., Medcenter Hospital (1989–1993); Director of Nursing, Medical Personnel Pool (1988–1989). **Associations & Accomplishments:** American Association of Continuity of Care; ACCC, certification; Board Member, Reflections Day Care; Sigma Theta Tau. **Education:** California State University, M.A. (1991); Ashland University, Ohio, B.S.L.; Marion Tech, Ohio, A.D. **Personal:** Married to John in 1957. Six children: Donna, Tom, Steve, Andy, Dave and Rod.

James Hugh Devitt, M.D.
Physician
Sunnybrook Health Science Center
2075 Bayview Avenue
Toronto, Ontario M4N 3M5
(416) 480–4794 (416) 480–4864
Fax: (416) 480–6039
EMAIL: See Below

8062

Business Information: Sunnybrook Health Science Center is a healthcare institution specializing in anesthesiology. A practicing physician since 1977, Dr. Devitt is responsible for all anesthesiology and medical research in the Critical Care Unit. Concurrently, he is an Associate Professor at the University of Toronto, teaching medical students and residents. Internet users can reach him via: j.hugh_devitt@mail.magic.ca. **Career Steps:** Physician, Sunnybrook Health Science Center (1984–Present); University of Toronto: Associate Professor (1993–Present), Assistant Professor (1989–1993), Lecturer (1984–1989). **Associations & Accomplishments:** Canadian Medical Association; American Society of Anesthesiologists; Canada Anesthetists Society; Royal College of Physicians & Surgeons of Canada; Canadian Critical Care Society; Society for Critical Care Medicine. **Education:** University of Ottawa, M.D. (1977); University of Alberta, MS.c (1985). **Personal:** Married to Brenda in 1978. Four children: Mark, Janice, Karen, and Kimberly. Dr. Devitt enjoys hiking and skiing.

Anna Dickson
Director of Patient Services
Mary McClellan
One Myrtle Avenue
Cambridge, NY 12816–1003
(518) 677–2611 Ext. 208 or 13
Fax: (518) 677–5145

8062

Business Information: Mary McClellan is a full–service healthcare facility providing treatment, diagnosis, and rehabilitation of patients. As Director of Patient Services, Ms. Dickson is responsible for performing administrative duties, handling duties for the nursing and social services departments, supervising employee benefits, and managing both in– and outpatient records. **Career Steps:** Director of Patient Services, Mary McClellan (1973–Present). **Associations & Accomplishments:** Local Association of Business Women; Northeastern Association of Nurse Executives; Northeastern Association for Healthcare Quality. **Education:** Russell Sage College, B.S.N. **Personal:** Married to James in 1978. Five children: Joseph, Tracey, Paul, David, and Matthew. Ms. Dickson enjoys gardening, needlepoint, and country crafts.

Lourdes M. Dominguez, M.D.
Chief of Psychiatry
Allen Pavilion, Columbia Presbyterian Medical Center
5141 Broadway
New York, NY 10034–1159
(212) 932–4165
Fax: (212) 932–5369

8062

Business Information: Allen Pavilion, a part of Columbia Presbyterian Medical Center system in the City of New York, is a 300–bed community, acute care hospital, providing culturally competent diagnosis and treatment to psychiatric patients on an inpatient unit in Spanish and English, with plans to expand into Russian. This unit also treats dually diagnosed patients with mental illness and substance abuse. A practicing physician since 1986, Dr. Dominguez joined the Columbia Presbyterian Medical Center system in the City of New York in 1990. Serving as Director of Psychiatry Services in the Allen Pavilion since 1995, she is responsible for the direction of all operations, including program planning, supervision of intake, treatment, medical record review, and quality assurance procedures, in addition to staff and program education and performance evaluation. Her duties also include the provision of clinical supervision of multidisciplinary staff treating psychiatric, consult liaison and MICA inpatients. Concurrently, she operates a private practice providing psychotherapy and psychopharmacological treatment of adolescents, adults and geriatric patients – special populations treated have included HIV positive, ethnic and racial minority, and gay patients; Assistant Attending Psychiatrist and Clinical Supervisor at Presbyterian Hospital, providing inpatient consultations for cases with cultural and/or language–related issues impacting on differential diagnosis; and as a teacher of Transcultural Psychiatry and the Introduction to Hispanic Patients at Presbyterian Hospital. **Career Steps:** Director of Psychiatry Services, Allen Pavilion (1995–Present); Presbyterian Hospital: Assistant Attending Psychiatrist (1990–Present), Co–Instructor of Transcultural Psychiatry (1990–Present), Co–Instructor of Introduction to Hispanic Patients (1989–Present), Director of Adult Community Services Psychiatry Clinic (1993–1995), Director of Rafael Tavares Hispanic Mental Health Clinic (1990–1993), Director of Extended Observation Unit for Mentally Ill Chemical Abusers – Psychiatry Emergency Room (July 1990–Nov. 1990). **Associations & Accomplishments:** American Psychiatric Association; Association of Hispanic Mental Health Professionals; American Society of Hispanic Psychiatry; American Board of Psychiatry and Neurology Examiner for Part II of Specialty Boards; Licensures: New State License (D.E.A.), Diplomate in Psychiatry – American Board of Psychiatry and Neurology; NAMI 1993 Exemplary Psychiatrist Award; Sandoz Award for Excellence in Clinical Administration (1990); Premio Dr. Fulgencio Mendez (Award for Achievement) (1987); APA/National Institute of Mental Health Fellowship (1987–1988); Dr. Harry S. Altman Prize in Pediatrics (1986); Lucy B. Moses Award for Service to underserved groups (1981). **Education:** Columbia University College of Physicians & Surgeons, M.D. (1986); Barnard College, B.A. in Psychology and Honors in Psychology, cum laude (1982). **Personal:** Dr. Dominguez enjoys reading, computers, and hiking.

Kwame L. Donkor, M.D., F.R.C.P. (c), F.A.A.P.

Head of Pediatrics/Chief of Department
Niagara Falls General Hospital
6453 Morrison Street, Suite 206
Niagara Falls, Ontario L2E 7H1
(905) 357–4554
Fax: (905) 374–2366

8062

Business Information: Niagara Falls General Hospital is a full–service regional medical facility established in 1958 with one location in Ontario, Canada. As Head of Pediatrics/Chief of Department, Dr. Donkor, is responsible for the administration and strategic planning of his department. Originally from Ghana, West Africa, Dr. Donkor came to Canada in 1966 and has been in private practice for over 20 years, specializing in pediatric consulting, primary care, and pediatric allergies. **Career Steps:** Head of Pediatrics/Chief of Department, Niagara Falls General Hospital (1994–Present). **Associations & Accomplishments:** Canadian Pediatric Society; American Academy of Pediatrics; Ontario Medical Association. **Education:** University of Toronto, M.D. (1972); Trent University, Petersborough, Canada, B.Sc. (1969); Pediatric Training Hospital for Sick Children, Toronto (1974–1976) Primary and High School education in Ghana, West Africa. **Personal:** Two children: Charan and Kwaku. Dr. Donkor enjoys travel, playing squash, reading, and investing in the stock market.

James F. Donohue, M.D.

Professor of Medicine
University of North Carolina School of Medicine
CB # 7020 – UNC School of Medicine
Chapel Hill, NC 27514
(919) 966–2531
Fax: Please mail or call

8062

Business Information: The University of North Carolina School of Medicine provides all aspects of post–graduate medical education to residents and interns, as well as full tertiary care and clinical research hospital facilities. As Professor of Medicine, Dr. Donohue is responsible for the care and treatment of patients, instructing and mentoring medical students and residents, and clinical research. Dr. Donohue is also the Clinical Director of the UNC Pulmonary Division, conducting research in asthma and chronic lung diseases. **Career Steps:** University of North Carolina School of Medicine: Professor of Medicine (1988–Present), Associate Professor of Medicine (1983–1988), Assistant Professor of Medicine (1977–1983). **Associations & Accomplishments:** American Lung Association; American College of Chest Physicians; American College of Physicians; Board of Directors, Glaxo Respiratory Institute; American Thoracic Society; Southern Medical Association; North Carolina State Tuberculosis Medical Advisory Board; Best Doctors in America (1994); Best Doctors in Southeastern Region (1996); Best Medical Specialist in North America, Town and Country Magazine; Section Editor, Yearbook of Pulmonary Disease (1994–1996). **Education:** University of Medicine and Dentistry of New Jersey, M.D. (1969); St. Peter's College, A.B. (1965). **Personal:** Married to Miriam in 1973. Three children: Meghan, Erin Nell and Ann Caitlin. Dr. Donohue enjoys reading, jogging and walking.

Libby Dotson
Director of Community Development
All Saints Health System
1307 8th Ave., Suite 310
Ft. Worth, TX 76104–4140
(817) 922–7701
Fax: (817) 922–7717

8062

Business Information: All Saints Health System is an integrated network of health care services comprised of two hospitals, 11 private physician practices, and one senior health center. As Director of Community Development, Ms. Dotson is responsible for all community relations programs, charitable contributions, and community outreach programs for multi–site health care delivery systems. **Career Steps:** Director of Community Development, All Saints Health System (1993–Present); Assistant Vice–President of Customer Development, Bank One Texas (1990–1992); Corporate Assistant, Texas American Bancshares (1972–1990). **Associations & Accomplishments:** Cancer Care Services; Board (former chair), Executive Committee, Programs Committee (chair); American Red Cross/Tarrant County Chapter: Board, Executive Committee, Special Transportation Committee; Prevent Blindness Texas: Board, Executive Committee, Vice–President of Public Relations, Volunteer of the Year (1995); Board of Directors, Community Health Foundation of Tarrant County. **Education:** Vanderbilt – Peabody College, B.S. (1972). **Personal:** Two children: Jennifer and Christopher. Ms. Dotson enjoys performing arts, reading, and stitchery.

Mr. James F. Downey

Vice President of Finance
United Healthcare System
89 Park Avenue
Newark, NJ 07104
(201) 268–3704
Fax: (201) 483–4729

8062

Business Information: United Healthcare System is an inpatient hospital and ambulatory care center, acute care treatment facility for pediatric cases and a Physician Service. In his current capacity, Mr. Downey is responsible for all financial aspects, as well as the management of information systems. **Career Steps:** Vice President of Finance, United Healthcare System (1994–Present); Chief Financial Officer, Fair Oaks Hospital (1992–1994); Controller, The Regent Hospital (1989–1992). **Associations & Accomplishments:** Hospital Financial Management Association; Sterling Who's Who Executive Club; Indian Guides (YMCA); Brunner School Parent/Teacher Association. **Education:** Drexel University, B.S. (1979); Certified Public Accountant. **Personal:** Married to Toni L. in 1979. One child: Katie. Mr. Downey enjoys golf, woodworking, film and music.

Richard A. Druffner

Chief Operating Officer
Hamilton Health Center
PO Box 5098
Harrisburg, PA 17110–5098
(717) 230–3919
Fax: (717) 232–9326

8062

Business Information: Hamilton Health Center is a primary care community health center. Primarily serving Medicaid patients, the Center also strives to provide the utmost in medical and dental care for the entire community of Harrisburg. Joining Hamilton Health in 1994 following his military career with the U.S. Army, as Chief Operating Officer Mr. Druffner has full executive charge of all administrative operations, as well as the supervision for key management personnel. **Career Steps:** Chief Operating Officer, Hamilton Health Center (1994–Present); U.S. Army: Training Developer (1991–1994), Executive Officer (1991), Logistics Officer (1989–1991). **Education:** Webster University, M.A. (1993); Boston University, M.S. in Business Administration (1982); La Salle College, B.A. in Political Science (1973). **Personal:** Married to Brigitte A. in 1982.

Harold P. Drutz, M.D., FRCS(c)

Division Chief
Mount Sinai Hospital
600 University Avenue
Toronto, Ontario M5G 1X5
(416) 586–4642
Fax: (416) 586–3208

8062

Business Information: Mount Sinai Hospital is affiliated with the University of Toronto, Canada, is a full–service, tertiary teaching hospital, providing healthcare to patients and instruction to medical students. As Division Chief, Dr. Drutz oversees the Urogynecology Section, within the Department of Obstetrics and Gynecology at the University. Concurrently, he supervises the Post Graduate Program. **Career Steps:** Division Chief, Mount Sinai Hospital (1987–Present). **Associations & Accomplishments:** President, International Urogynecological Association; Chairman, Subcommittee on Urogynecology, Society of Obstetricians and Gynecologists of Canada. **Education:** University of Toronto, M.D. (1969); Fellow Royal College of Surgeons (Canada) (1974). **Personal:** Married to Robin. Three children: Corinne, Adam, and Melissa. Dr. Drutz enjoys cooking, golf, tennis, and hockey.

Ernest C. Duerke, M.D.

Doctor of Anesthesia
Western Memorial Regional Hospital
P.O. Box 2005 Station Main, Department of Anesthesiology
Corner Brook, Newfoundla A2H 6J7
(709) 637–5324 (709) 637–5328
Fax: (709) 634–2649

8062

Business Information: Western Memorial Regional Hospital is a 350–bed acute care facility with six operating rooms, which provides medical and related services to area residents. As Doctor of Anesthesiology, Dr. Duerke attends to patients in surgical, outpatient, intensive care, and pre– and post–operative units, providing anesthesia and pain relief. **Career Steps:** Doctor of Anesthesiology, Western Memorial Regional Hospital (1984–Present); Staff Anesthesiologist, County General Hospital, Northern Ireland (1980–1983); Staff Anesthesiologist St. Catherine's Hospital, Ireland (1979–1980); Consultant Anesthesiologist/Wing Commander, Nigerian Air Force Base, Nigeria (1974–1978). **Associations & Accomplishments:** Irish Medical and Anesthetist Association; Danish Medical Association; Critical Committee; Anesthetists Committee; Canadian Anesthesiologists Association; Western Memorial Regional Hospital Corner Brood; CMPA. **Education:** University College, Dublin, Ireland, M.B.B.C.H.B.A.O.(1965); Irish Medical Conjoint Board, D.A.(ROPSI) (1969); M.D. in Anesthesiology; Danish Medical Board, Specialist Degree in Anesthetics (1983). **Personal:** Married to Daphne in 1989. Six children: Ernest, Owen, Ita, Christina, John, and Joanne. Dr. Duerke enjoys gardening, walking, and dancing.

Mary–Louise Dujka, CHE

Director of Operations
Polly Ryon Hospital
1705 Jackson Street
Richmond, TX 77469–3246
(713) 341–4848
Fax: (713) 341–4845

8062

Business Information: Established in 1947, Polly Ryon Hospital is a 185–bed, non–profit primary care community hospital. The hospital is located in one of the fastest growing counties in the United States. As Director of Operations, Ms. Dujka is responsible for hospital operations which includes Professional Services, Support Services, Infection Control, Safety, and hospital–wide JCAHO monitoring. She manages approximately 240 employees in these areas. **Career Steps:** Director of Operations, Polly Ryon Hospital (1991–Present); The Methodist Hospital: Safety Officer (1989–1991), Executive Assistant (1986–1989), Manager of Cardiac Cath Labs (1976–1986), Supervisor Cardiac Cath Labs (1974–1976), Staff Nurse (1970–1974). **Associations & Accomplishments:** American College of Healthcare Executives; Chamber of Commerce; Girl Scouts of America. **Education:** University of Houston – Clear Lake: M.H.A. (1990), B.S. (1984); Stuart Circle Hospital School of Nursing, R.N. (1969). **Personal:** Married to Stephen C. in 1975. Two children: Michael and Kathryn. Ms. Dujka enjoys reading, gardening, snow skiing, and ice skating.

Samer Ellahham, MD, FACC, FCCP

Physician and Director of Cardiac Stress Imaging Laboratory
Washington Hospital Center
110 Irving Street, NW, Washington Heart Suite 1103
Washington, DC 20010
(202) 877–6264
Fax: (202) 877–6168

8062

Business Information: Washington Hospital Center is one of the leading clinical study and research facilities in the world, specializing in cardiovascular treatment and research. A practicing physician since 1988, Board–certified in Cardiology and Internal Medicine, Dr. Ellahham joined Washington Hospital Center as Cardiologist and Director of the Stress Imaging Laboratory in 1993. He is responsible for directing the operations of the Stress Imaging Laboratory, where exercise and drugs are used to stimulate the heart rate in order to study the patient's heart more in depth. He has extenive expertise in using Echo, nuclear imaging and X–ray, for diagnostic cardiovascular purposes. He is currently undergoing research studies involving many protocols for presentation, including: 1) a drug "Arbutamine," which speeds the heart rate of patients unable to exercise, and 2) a second generation contrast agent, in which they inject an agent through a catheter to get a better look at the inside of the heart. In addition, he serves as Assistant Clinical Professor at George Washington Medical Center, instructing attending physicians, fellows, residents, medical students from all over the world. **Career Steps:** President, R&R Series Company, Inc.; Physician and Director of Stress Imaging Laboratory, Washington Hospital Center (1993–Present); Clinical Assistant Professor, George Washington Medical Center (1993–Present); Assistant Professor, Eastern Virginia Medical Schiool (1992–1993); Director of Coronary Care Unit, Hampton Veterans Affairs Medical Center (1992–1993); Clinical Instructor, Medical College of Virginia (1991–1992); Medical House Physician, Henrico Doctors' Hospital and Johnston Willis Hospital (1989–1992). **Associations & Accomplishments:** Founding Member, American Society of Nuclear Cardiology; Fellow, American College of Cardiology; Fellow, American College of Angiology; Fellow, American College of Chest Physicians; American Medical Information Association; American Heart Association; American College of Physicians; American Medical Association; International Society of Heart & Lung Transplantation; American Association for Nuclear Cardiology; Jacobs Institute of Women's Health; The New York Academy of Sciences; Friends of American Medical Women Association; Medical Society of District of Columbia; American Medical Tennis Association; United States Masters Swimming; United States Tennis Association; Peter Burwash International Special Tennis Programs; United States Table Tennis Association; Virginia Happy Trails Running Club; American Running and Fitness Association; Board of Directors, Naim Foundation; President–Elect, Arab American Medical Association – Washington, D.C. Chapter; AWARDS: Finalist, Medical College of Virginia Fellow of the Year 1992; DuPont Pharmaceuticals / ACCP Young Investigator Award – 58th Annual Scientific Assembly; ACCP Alfred Soffer Research Award Finalist (1992); PUBLICATIONS: "Cholesterol Embolism: An Underdiagnosed Clinical Entity"; "Radiation Induced Coronary Heart Disease"; "Management of Cocaine Induced Complications"; "Reversibility of Cocaine Induced Cardiomyopathy"; Cocaine Induced Complications: Possible Relationship to Low Plasma Cholinesterase Enzyme"; Risk of Left Ventricular Hypertrophy in Normotensive Cocaine Users"; RESEARCH INTERESTS: Coronary Artery Disease and Left Ventricular Opacification; Endothelial functions in cardiac & cardiac transplantation; Cardiovascular studies with relation to polycystic kidney disease patients; Licensed to practice in Maryland, Virginia and Washington, D.C.; Fluent in French and Arabic; Epidemilogy of heart disease; Peripheral vascular disease; Sleep apnea; Prevention of cardiovascular disorders; Recently completed a children's coloring book dealing with heart function and prevention of heart disease (In press). **Education:** American University of Beirut School of Medicine, M.D. (1986); The Johns Hopkins University School of Hygiene and Public Health, working towards M.P.H.; American University of Beirut, B.A. in Biology (1982); INTERNSHIP: in Internal Medicine, Good Samaritan Hospital (1986–1987); RESIDENCY: in Internal Medicine, Good Samaritan Hospital (1987–1988), Washington Hospital Center (1988–1989); FELLOWSHIP: Division of Cardiology, Medical College of Virginia (1989–1992); Division of Nuclear Cardiology, Medical College of Virginia (1991–1992); CERTIFICATIONS: ECFMG; Affiliate Faculty, Advanced Cardiac Life Support (ACLS); Nuclear Cardiology; American Board of Internal Medicine; American Board of Cardiovascular Diseases. **Personal:** Dr. Ellahham enjoys writing poetry, running, tennis, volleyball, research, teaching, art and volunteer and community service.

Valena J. Emery

Director, Health Information Management/Performance Improvement
Parkview Community Hospital Medical Center
3865 Jackson Street
Riverside, CA 92503
(909) 352–5434
Fax: (909) 352–5454

8062

Business Information: Parkview Community Hospital Medical Center is a full service medical facility. Selected by the Mercer Group in 1994 as one of the top 100 hospitals in the United States for quality and effectiveness, the Center is comprised of 193 beds, and offers a neonatal intensive care unit, a cancer unit, and a diabetes center. As Director, Health Information Management/Performance Improvement, Ms. Emery oversees all aspects of her Department, is responsible for performance improvement hospital–wide, and handles all case management, cancer registry, and microfilm. **Career Steps:** Director, Health Information Management/Performance Improvement, Parkview Community Hospital Medical Center (1981–Present); Director, Health Information Management, St. Luke's Hospital Medical Center (1974–1981); Consultant, Health Information and Quality Management, Acute Care, Skilled Nursing, Chemical Dependency Facilities (1980–1993). **Associations & Accomplishments:** Professional Services Committee; Hospital Council, Southern California; YMCA Women of Achievement Award (1987); California Health Information Association (Award for Outstanding Performance, 1995); American Health Information Management Association; National Tumor Registrar's Association; Patient Care Assessment Council; Tumor Registrar's Association of California. **Education:** Loma Linda University, B.S. (1994); Registered Record Administrator, RRA (1994); Certified Professional Healthcare Quality,

CPHQ (1986); Certified Tumor Registrar, CTR (1985); Accredited Record Technician, ART (1972); Redlands University, Masters in Quality Management (In Progress). **Personal:** Two children: Brent and Kim. Ms. Emery enjoys having been a Citizen's Ambassador to China in Health Information Management (1995).

Atilla Ertan, M.D.
Physician and Professor of Gastroenterology
Baylor College of Medicine and the Methodist Hospital
6550 Fannin, Suite 1122
Houston, TX 77030
(713) 790–2171
Fax: (713) 790–6216

8062

Business Information: Baylor College of Medicine and the Methodist Hospital, an affiliate of Baylor University, is a multi–specialty, tertiary hospital, medical research and teaching facility. The Baylor Gastroenterology Associates, a division of the hospital, was established in 1990 and currently employs 30 people. As Chief and Medical Director of the department, as well as Physician and Professor of Gastroenterology, Dr. Ertan is responsible for the instruction of students, research, and the care and treatment of patients in the area of Gastroenterology, as well as administrative duties for the department. **Career Steps:** Chief, Medical Director, Physician and Professor of Gastroenterology, Baylor College of Medicine and the Methodist Hospital (1991–Present); Chief of GI Section, Tulane University Medical School (1980–1991); Professor of Medicine, Ankara University Medical School (1974–1980). **Associations & Accomplishments:** American Gastroenterology Association; Organization Mondiale de Gastrenterologia; American Pancreatic Association; Southern Society of Clinical Investigation; American College of Gastroenterology; American Society of Gastrointestinal Endoscopy; Chairman, ACG International GI Training Subcommittee; Distinguished Professor for United Nations for "Transfer of Know–How Through Expatriate Nationals;" Published over 130 times. **Education:** Ankara University Medical School, M.D. (1963); University of Pennsylvannia Hospital, GI Fellowship. **Personal:** Married to Inci Ertan, Ph.D. in 1973. Two children: Basak and Baris R. Dr. Ertan enjoys reading, tennis and outdoor activities.

David A. Esposito

CADD Technician
Brighton Medical Center
335 Brighton Avenue
Portland, ME 04102
(207) 879–8006
Fax: (207) 879–8014

8062

Business Information: Brighton Medical Center is a full–service health care institution specializing in the diagnosis, treatment, and rehabilitation of patients. The Center has just merged with Maine Medical and is under construction, changing from a 150–bed acute care facility to a rehabilitation and outpatient service center. As CADD Technician, Mr. Esposito is responsible for CADD drafting, interior designs, working with blue prints, general maintenance, ADA compliance, asbestos, and working with new architects on design changes. **Career Steps:** Brighton Medical Center: CADD Technician (1996–Present), Engineering (1983–1996). **Associations & Accomplishments:** BOMA. **Education:** PRVTC; Private CADD Tutor, Site License in CADD (1994); South Portland High School graduate (1981). **Personal:** Married to Jean in 1986. One child: Dylan T. Mr. Esposito enjoys painting and the outdoors.

Samuel D. Evans, M.D.
Vice President of Medical Affairs
Blount Memorial Hospital
907 East LaMar Alexander Parkway
Maryville, TN 37804
(423) 981–2155
Fax: (423) 983–8202

8062

Business Information: Blount Memorial Hospital is a 300–bed full–service, healthcare institution specializing in the diagnosis, treatment, and rehabilitation of patients. The Hospital also offers outpatient facilities and is the only hospital in the county. As Vice President of Medical Affairs, Dr. Evans is responsible for quality of medical care provided in the hospital, medical staff issues, and assisting the administration and Board of Directors. He was in private practice between 1978

and 1996, specializing in obstetrics and gynecology. He has held two elected offices at Blount Memorial Hospital (Vice Chief and Chief–of–Staff). **Career Steps:** Vice President of Medical Affairs, Blount Memorial Hospital (Present). **Associations & Accomplishments:** American College of Physician Executives; American College of Obstetricians and Gynecologists; East Tennessee Medical Society; Blount County Medical Society; Committee Founder, Member, Blount County Young Life; Habitat for Humanity – Blount County; AIDS awareness, Red Cross; Family Life Curriculum for School Systems; Vice Chief and Chief of Staff, Blount Memorial Hospital; Deacon of Maryville First Baptist Church; Graduate of Leadership Blount. **Education:** Medical University of South Carolina, M.D. (1972); University of Tennessee, B.S. **Personal:** Married to Sally Vinsant in 1969. Two children: Anna Wade and Vinsant.

Martin Evers, M.D.
Internal Medicine Residency Director
Conemaugh Memorial Medical Center
1086 Franklin Street
Johnstown, PA 15905
(814) 533–9409
Fax: (814) 533–3290

8062

Business Information: Conemaugh Memorial Medical Center is a tertiary care medical hospital, research and teaching institution. As Internal Medicine Residency Director, Dr. Martin Evers is responsible for the instruction of medical residents, as well as clinical research and patient diagnosis and treatment. **Career Steps:** Internal Medicine Residency Director, Conemaugh Memorial Medical Center (1995–Present); Associate Program Director, St. Francis Medical Center (1990–1994); Fellow of Critical Care, Presbyterian University Hospital – Pittsburgh (1989); Internal Medicine Resident, Raritan Bay Medical Center (1986–1989). **Associations & Accomplishments:** Fellow, ACP; Member, American Medical Association; SGIM; SCCM; Played soccer in Belgium for four years; Member, Beth Shalom Choir in Johnstown, PA. **Education:** UMDNJ – Rutgers, M.D. (1985). **Personal:** Married to Rhonda in 1993. Dr. Evers enjoys ice hockey, singing, music, sports, reading, and cooking.

Linda A. Faber
Director of Corporate Health Services
Firelands Community Hospital
2020 Hayes Avenue
Sandusky, OH 44870–8005
(419) 627–5052
Fax: (419) 627–5298

8062

Business Information: Firelands Community Hospital provides all aspects of acute and intermediate health care for the populace of Sandusky, Ohio and outlying counties. An entity of Firelands', the Corporate Health Centre was created in 1981 to provide area businesses a comprehensive package of occupational and safety services tailored to each company's needs. Services provided by the Centre include: physical exams, executive health programs, medical screenings, drug and alcohol screening, injury treatment, rehabilitation for injured workers, work capacity exams, employee assistance programs, and educational programs. As Director of Corporate Health Services, Ms. Faber is accountable for structure, processes and outcomes of Firelands Corporate Health Services, including the Corporate Health Centre and Behavioral Medicine Departments. Serving as the primary liaison with corporate clients and vendors, she designs and implements on–going departmental marketing programs. She also prepares the annual operating and capital budgets, and monitors the operation of each budget account. During her tenure Ms. Faber has been instrumental in the development of occupational health services programs, including: Return–To–Work Program for injured workers; expansion of worksite physical exams and screening programs; addition of Job Analysis, Case Management, and Ergonomic Plant Analysis services; and the expansion of Industrial Education Program with Body Mechanics & Ergonomics Training. **Career Steps:** Director of Corporate Health Services, Firelands Community Hospital (1991–Present); Bowling Green State University, Firelands College: Director of Admissions and Marketing (1991), Associate Director of Admissions (1989–1991); Realtor Associate/Site Consultant, JRW Realty (1986–1988); Executive Director and Project Manager, Downtown Waterfront Development (1985–1986). **Associations & Accomplishments:** Named "1995 Businesswoman of the Year" by Erie County Chamber of Commerce; National Association of Occupational Health Professionals; Society of Ohio Occupational Health Professionals; Board of Trustees, Lead Sandusky Class of 1988; Board of Trustees, Sandusky Volunteer

Centre. **Education:** Bowling Green State University: M.B.A (1985); B.S. magna cum laude in Business Administration (1984). **Personal:** Ms. Faber enjoys community projects, hiking, interior design, travel (especially to historic locations), reading, concerts and plays.

Darrell Ray Fagan, R.N.
Utilization Review Manager
Memorial Hospital Pasadena
906 E. Southmore Avenue
Pasadena, TX 77502–1114
(713) 475–5913
Fax: (713) 475–5942

8062

Business Information: Memorial Hospital Pasadena, part of the Memorial Health Care System, is a non–profit, acute care hospital with 206 licensed beds, over 250 physicians, an intensive care and coronary care unit, and medical and surgical beds. The Hospital provides psychiatric care for adults, children, adolescents, and geriatrics, a skilled nursing facility, CAT scans, MIRs, Mammography scans, and an almost complete service laboratory. As Utilization Review Manager, Mr. Fagan supervises Utilization Review, Social Services, Discharge Planning, and Quality Service Departments. He reviews charts, conditions, treatments, and problems about the patients' stay from the physicians' standpoint. When necessary, he assists in confronting physicians on the reviews and solutions to the problems. **Career Steps:** Utilization Review Manager, Memorial Hospital Pasadena (1996–Present); Southmore Medical Center: Clinical Hospital Educator (1993–1996), Staff Nurse and Relief Supervisor (1991–1993). **Associations & Accomplishments:** American Heart Association: CPR Instructor, CPR Instructor Trainer, ACLS Instructor, ACLS Program Coordinator, ACLS Course Director; Pasadena Chamber of Commerce – Health and Wellness Committee; Case Management Society of America. **Education:** San Jacinto College, A.D.N. (1979). **Personal:** Married to Jackye Lynn in 1983. Five children: Joshua, Chad, Jeremy, Christopher, and Ashlye. Mr. Fagan enjoys fishing, snow skiing, and motor boating.

Peter S. Fail, M.D.
Director of the Catheterization Laboratory
Episcopal Hospital
100 East Lehigh Avenue
Philadelphia, PA 19125
(215) 427–6200
Fax: (215) 427–7358

8062

Business Information: Episcopal Hospital is a full–service, multi–specialty medical facility and health service establishment, as well as a Cardiac Catheterization Laboratory. Established in 1865, the hospital currently employs 1,500 physicians and medical support staff. As Director of the Catheterization Laboratory and Interventional Cardiologist, Dr. Fail is responsible for the care and treatment of patients, the operations of the lab, and clinical research. **Career Steps:** Director of the Catheterization Laboratory and Interventional Cardiologist, Episcopal Hospital (Present). **Associations & Accomplishments:** American College of Cardiology; American College of Chest Physicians; American College of Physicians. **Education:** American University of the Carribean, M.D. (1980). **Personal:** Married to Jean in 1987. One child: Nicholas. Dr. Fail enjoys skiing, sailing and flying.

Charline Falletta
Laboratory Administrator
St. Vincent's Medical Center of Richmond
355 Bard Avenue
Staten Island, NY 10310–1664
(718) 876–3091
Fax: (718) 448–0386

8062

Business Information: St. Vincent's Medical Center of Richmond is a full service health care facility serving the surrounding region. As Laboratory Administrator, Ms. Falletta is responsible for the large labs with millions of lab tests per year. She is also responsible for all operations including budgets, meetings, rare testing, and HIV follow–ups. **Career Steps:** St. Vincent's Medical Center of Richmond: Laboratory Administrator (1988–Present), Section Manager (1975–1988). **Associations & Accomplishments:** Clinical Laboratory Management Association; National Certification Agency for Medical Lab Personnel; College of American Pathologists. **Education:** Wagner College, M.B.A. (1983). **Personal:** Married to Roger Hueckel in 1993. Ms. Falletta enjoys reading, walking, relaxing, and computers.

Mignonette E. Farne

Administrative Director
Center for Primary Care
7411 Lake Street
River Forest, IL 60305–1817
(708) 488–2360
Fax: (708) 488–2370

8062

Business Information: Center for Primary Care is a local healthcare facility associated with West Suburban Hospital. The hospital, located in Oak Park, Illinois, is an acute and sub-acute healthcare facility with 362 beds. As Administrative Director, Ms. Farne is in charge of the daily operations of outpatient care at the Center. Her responsibilities include directing and managing staff, scheduling, recruitment, training, budgets, and CQI. **Career Steps:** Administrative Director, Center for Primary Care (1996–Present); Clinic Manager, West Suburban Hospital (1995); Coordinator, Children's Memorial Hospital (1993–1994). **Associations & Accomplishments:** Medical Group Management Association. **Education:** Loyola University, M.B.A. (1992). **Personal:** Ms. Farne enjoys music, rollerblading, and downhill skiing.

Duncan F. Farquharson, M.D.

Medical Director, Special Care Maternity Care
British Columbia Women's Hospital
4500 Oak Street
Vancouver, British Co V6H 3V5
(604) 875–3174
Fax: (604) 875–3099

8062

Business Information: British Columbia Women's Hospital, located in Vancouver, is a hospital dedicated to the care of women and their medical problems. The Hospital specializes in the care of patients with high–risk pregnancies in the province of British Columbia and is the primary obstetric care facility for the city of Vancouver. As Medical Director, Special Care Maternity Program, Dr. Farquharson has oversight of this program. He handles all administrative duties, assists in staff recruitment, staff review and evaluation, and verification and updating of staff credentials. Dr. Farquharson is a specialist in perinatology and is M.D. qualified in the care of high–risk pregnancy. **Career Steps:** British Columbia Women's Hospital: Medical Director, Special Care Maternity Care, British Columbia Women's Hospital (1994–Present), Director of Post Partum Care (1982–1994). **Associations & Accomplishments:** International Fetal Medicine and Surgery Society. **Education:** University of Toronto, M.D., F.R.C.S. (1980). **Personal:** Married to Valerie in 1977. Two children: Kyle and Julia. Dr. Farquharson enjoys skiing, golf, hiking, and biking.

Bruce Feldman

Administrative Director, Nalitt Cancer Institute
Staten Island University Hospital
256 Mason Avenue
Staten Island, NY 10305–3408
(718) 226–6461
Fax: (718) 226–6467
EMAIL: See Below

8062

Business Information: The Nalitt Cancer Institute is a free–standing ambulatory cancer center located on the campus of Staten Island University Hospital in New York. As Administrative Director of the Institute, Mr. Feldman is responsible for daily operations, medical and support staff supervision, and financial oversight. In addition, he conducts seminars and accepts public speaking engagements within the community. Internet users can reach him via: Nalitt@aol.com **Career Steps:** Administrative Director, Nalitt Cancer Institute, Staten Island University Hospital (1994–Present); Administrator, Department of Medicine, Bronx Lebanon Hospital Center (1993–1994); Administrator, Ambulatory Surgery Center, Montefiore Medical Center (1990–1993); Administrator, Ambulatory Care Department, Kingsbrook Jewish Medical Center (1988–1989). **Associations & Accomplishments:** American College of Oncology Administrators; American College of Healthcare Executives; Association of Cancer Executives; Society for Ambulatory Care Professionals. **Education:** University of Maryland, M.S. (1986); State University of New York at Stony Brook, B.A. (1984). **Personal:** Married to Robin in 1989. Two children: Joshua and Matthew. Mr. Feldman enjoys computers, photography, travel, and spending time with his family.

Dr. Victor John Figurado

Physician
St. Lucia's Medical Center
3461 Dixie Road, Suite 302
Mississauga, Ontario L4Y 3X4
(905) 206–1222
Fax: (905) 206–1966

8062

Business Information: St. Lucia's Medical Center provides family medical care to the community of Mississauga, Ontario. A native of Sri Lanka, Dr. Figurado served as an Interpreter at the Canadian Immigration Services until his acceptance into a family practice residency program in 1988. In August of 1994 he brought his private practice to St. Lucia's Medical Center, supervising an office, laboratory, and two examination rooms with the help of a secretary and lab technician. Dr. Figurado attributes his success to his enjoyment of community service. **Career Steps:** Physician, St. Lucia's Medical Center (1996–Present); Physician, Clinique Familiale Des Pans Val d'Or (1991–1994); Interpreter, Canada Immigration (1982–1988). **Associations & Accomplishments:** Ontario Medical Association; Corporation Professionnelle Des Medecins Du Quebec; Captained the University of Peradeniya Medical Faculty Soccer Team; Elected to the Sri Lankan National Soccer Team Selection Pool (1973). **Education:** University of Peradeniya – Sri Lanka, M.B.B.S. (1979); Attended, Hartley College – Point Pedro, Sri Lanka, and St. Xavier's College – Mannar, Sri Lanka. **Personal:** Married to Mary G. Anthony in 1982. Three children: Priya N., Nila M., and Mathuran M. Dr. Figuarado, son of the late Mr. Emanuel Figurado and Lucia Sabapaty, enjoys soccer, tennis, radio plays, Tamil Literature, and writing medical articles into Tamil language.

Victoria Ann Fincher, RCP, CRTT

Director – Cardiopulmonary Department
Nacogdoches Memorial
1204 North Mound Street
Nacogdoches, TX 75961–4027
(409) 568–8555
Fax: (409) 568–8588

8062

Business Information: Nacogdoches Memorial is 200–bed, non–profit county hospital. Serving the community of Nacogdoches, even though small in size, it provides many specialized treatment facilities, including a hyperbaric chamber, chemotherapy laboratory, hemodialysis, and a state–of–the–art X–ray lab with a self–contained MRI unit. Nacogdoches Memorial was the first facility to implement patient–drive protocols — developed with great support from physicians and administrators. As Director of the Cardiopulmonary Department, Victoria Fincher is responsible for overseeing four branches of the cardiac section: Respiratory Therapy; Cardiac Diagnostics; Neurodiagnostics; and Pulmonary Rehabilitation. These duties entail the coordination and direction for the areas of staff retention, clinical teachings, scheduling and participating in treatments, clinical research and respiratory studies. **Career Steps:** Nacogdoches Memorial: Director Cardiopulmonary Department (1995–Present), Assistant Director (1989–1995); Chairside Assistant and Receptionist, Dr. Larry Sheffield, DDS (1981–1986). **Associations & Accomplishments:** American Association of Respiratory Care; Texas Society of Respiratory Care, Pineywoods District. **Education:** Tyler Junior College, CRTT (1987); Fageling Junior College. **Personal:** Married to William W. in 1971. Two children: Weston and Kelleen. Ms. Fincher enjoys spending time with her granddaughter and her new car.

Mr. Avi Fishman, M.B.A.

Manager, Interventional Cardiology
New York Hospital
525 East 68th Street
New York, NY 10021–4873
(212) 746–4644
Fax: (212) 746–8295

8062

Business Information: New York Hospital was the first hospital in New York City and is the the second oldest hospital in the United States. The facility is one of the world's leading acute care hospitals, with 1,420 beds. It is particularly well known for its specialty care units such as the Helmsley Cardiovascular Center. As Manager of Interventional Cardiology, Mr. Fishman acts as coordinator of business and medical activities for the Invasive Cardiology Department at The New York Hospital. The Interventional Cardiology Section performs approximately 5,000 procedures per year in adult and pediatric cardiac catheterization and cardiac electrophysiology. Internet users can reach Mr. Fishman via: AFishman@NYH.med.edu **Career Steps:** Manager, Interventional Cardiology, New York Hospital (1994–Present); Administrator of Genetics, The Mount Sinai Medical Center (1992–1994); Manager of Cardiology, Long Island Jewish Center (1989–1992); Assistant Director of Admitting, Beth Israel Medical Center (1986–1989). **Associations & Accomplishments:** American Academy of Medical Administrators; American College of Cardiovascular Administrators; American College of Healthcare Executives; American Society of Cardiovascular Professionals; Society for Cardiovascular Management; Society of Invasive Cardiovascular Professionals. **Education:** Baruch College – Mt. Sinai, M.B.A. (1986); Queens College, B.A. (1983). **Personal:** Mr. Fishman enjoys playing softball and going to ballgames.

Todd Neal Fletcher

Director
Touro Infirmary
1401 Foucher Street
New Orleans, LA 70115–3515
(504) 897–8512
Fax: Please mail or call
EMAIL: See Below

8062

Business Information: A non–profit hospital, Touro Infirmary is one of the oldest and most beloved hospitals in New Orleans, working in alliance with eight local hospitals. An expert in health systems management and engineering spanning a period of ten years, Todd Fletcher was appointed to his current position at Touro in September of 1994. As Director of Surgical Services and Intensive Care, he is responsible for the hiring and training of employees, financial aspects and systems improvement. Internet users can also reach him via: JeanLuque@AOL.COM. **Career Steps:** Director, Touro Infirmary (1994–Present); UCSD Medical Center: Business Administrator (1992–1994), Senior Management Engineer (1989–1992); Junior Management Engineer, Georgetown University Hospital (1986–1989). **Associations & Accomplishments:** New Orleans – Youth at Risk. **Education:** University of Wisconsin – Madison, M.S. in Health Systems Engineering (1986); Universitaet Bonn – German Certificate. **Personal:** Mr. Fletcher enjoys skiing, going to the gym, running, rollerblading and photography.

Micheal J. Flinn

Director, Department of Radiology
Herrin Hospital
201 South 14th Street
Herrin, IL 62948–3631
(618) 942–2171
Fax: (618) 942–7892

8062

Business Information: British Columbia Women's Hospital, located in Vancouver, is a hospital dedicated to the care of women and their medical problems. The Hospital specializes in the care of patients with high–risk pregnancies in the province of British Columbia and is the primary obstetric care facility for the city of Vancouver. As Medical Director, Special Care Maternity Program, Dr. Farquharson has oversight of this program. He handles all administrative duties, assists in staff recruitment, staff review and evaluation, and verification and updating of staff credentials. Dr. Farquharson is a specialist in perinatology and is M.D. qualified in the care of high–risk pregnancy. **Career Steps:** British Columbia Women's Hospital: Medical Director, Special Care Maternity Care, British Columbia Women's Hospital (1994–Present), Director of Post Partum Care (1982–1994). **Associations & Accomplishments:** International Fetal Medicine and Surgery Society. **Education:** University of Toronto, M.D., F.R.C.S. (1980). **Personal:** Married to Valerie in 1977. Two children: Kyle and Julia. Mr. Flinn enjoys skiing, golf, hiking, and biking.

Marsha B. Forsyth

Director of Nursing
University of Tennessee Medical Center
294 Summar Drive
Jackson, TN 38301–3906
(901) 423–1932
Fax: (901) 427–2408

8062

Business Information: University of Tennessee Medical Center was established in 1974 as a branch of the University of Tennessee at Memphis, a division of the University of Tennessee. A full service medical/teaching facility, the Center is affiliated with the University of Tennessee's family medicine residency program. As Director of Nursing, Ms. Forsyth left a promising career as a teacher because she felt nursing was what she "wanted in life". In her current capacity, she is responsible for all nursing staff scheduling and supervision, as well as oversight of patient care and medical charts. **Career Steps:** Director of Nursing, University of Tennessee Medical Center (1994–Present); Assistant Director, Medical Center Home Health. **Associations & Accomplishments:**

Association of Family Practice Nurses (AFPRN); American Association of Office Nurses (AAON). **Education:** Union University, A.S.N. (1983). **Personal:** Married to Tom Lewis Forsyth in 1976. Three children: CaRae, Gardner, and Meredith. Ms. Forsyth enjoys Civil War re–enacting, genealogical research, cross–stitch, and sanctuary choir.

Barbara J. Foster

Vice President and Chief Operating Officer
Pacifica Hospital Care Center, Inc.
18800 Delaware Street
Huntington Beach, CA 92648–1959
(714) 842–0611
Fax: (714) 841–8428

8062

Business Information: Pacifica Hospital Care Center, Inc. is a private, free–standing, individually–owned, 100–bed acute care hospital providing services for home care, outpatient, rehabilitation and psychiatrics. Pacifica Hospital Care Center currently employs 275 people. As Vice President and Chief Operating Officer, Ms. Foster is responsible for the administration of daily operations throughout the hospital. **Career Steps:** Vice President and Chief Operating Officer, Pacifica Hospital Care Center, Inc. (1994–Present); Nurse Manager Specialist, Allied Medical Management (1993–1994); Nurse Manager, Indian River Memorial Hospital (1991–1993). **Associations & Accomplishments:** Associate American College of Healthcare Executives; National Association of Nursing; Active in group activities at a youth shelter. **Education:** Barry University, B.S.N. (1992); M. B. Johnson School of Nursing, R.N. (1972); Undergraduate Studies: Akron University and Kent State University. **Personal:** Ms. Foster enjoys walking, reading, and group activities.

Karen A. Francis, CPA

Director of Finance
Sacred Heart Medical Center
P.O. Box 10905
Eugene, OR 97440–2905
(541) 686–7124
Fax: (541) 687–4943

8062

Business Information: Sacred Heart Medical Center is a full tertiary care medical center, providing both in–patient and out–patient services to residents of Eugene, Oregon and surrounding counties. A certified public accountant with twelve years expertise, Karen Francis has served as Sacred Heart's Director of Finance since July of 1991. She oversees all long range and short–term financial planning strategies, budgetary dispersal and management, and financial analysis reporting. **Career Steps:** Director of Finance, Sacred Heart Medical Center (1991–Present); Accounting Manager, Coopers & Lybrand (1984–1991). **Associations & Accomplishments:** Healthcare Financial Management Association; American Society of Certified Public Accountants; Oregon Society of Certified Public Accountants. **Education:** University of Oregon, M.S. (1984); Iowa State University: B.S. in Finance (1979), B.S. in Economics (1979). **Personal:** Married to Russell in 1988. Two children: Ashley and Stephanie. Ms. Francis enjoys camping, biking, and gardening.

Mr. David (Ron) R. Fraser

Radiology Director
Phoebe Putney Memorial Hospital
417 Third Avenue
Albany, GA 31701–1943
(912) 889–4176
Fax: (912) 889–7861

8062

Business Information: Phoebe Putney Memorial Hospital is a regional, non–profit, 450–bed acute care hospital, with eight family practice clinics and three convenient care clinics. As Radiology Director, Ron Fraser oversees five divisions: Radiology, Nuclear Medicine, Ultrasound, MRI and CT departments. His primary duties involve supervision of 64 support staff, budgetary decisions and dispersals, policy and procedures, and materials acquisition. **Career Steps:** Phoebe Putney Memorial Hospital: Radiology Director (1976–Present), Nuclear Medicine Technologist (1974–1976). **Associations & Accomplishments:** Exchange Club of Albany. **Education:** Medical College of Georgia, B.S. (1974); Valdosta Technical School (1971). **Personal:** Married to Anne in 1973. Two children: David and Joseph. Mr. Fraser enjoys gardening and reading.

Aaron L. Friedman, M.D.

Professor of Pediatrics
University of Wisconsin Hospital and Clinics
600 Highland Avenue, #H4/458
Madison, WI 53792–4108
(608) 263–8558
Fax: (608) 263–0440
EMAIL: See Below

8062

Business Information: University of Wisconsin Hospital and Clinics is a full–service medical/teaching facility. Affiliated with the University of Wisconsin, the Hospital offers graduate and undergraduate courses. As Professor of Pediatrics/Chairman, Dr. Friedman oversees administration of all research activities. His own research interest is growth sectors in children with kidney disease. Internet users can reach him via: alfriedm@facstaff.wisc.edu. **Career Steps:** University of Wisconsin Hospital and Clinics: Professor of Pediatrics (1991–Present), Chairman/Pediatrics (1996–Present), Director, Inpatient Clinical Activities (1992–Present). **Associations & Accomplishments:** American Board of Pediatrics; Secretary/Treasurer, American Society of Pediatric Nephrology; International Pediatric Nephrology Association. **Education:** State University of New York, Upstate Medical Center, M.D. (1974); Cornell University, B.S. **Personal:** Married to Sally Jones. Two children: Rebeccah and Robbin.

Rosemary Fritts

Director
Pike Community Memorial Hospital
P.O. Box F
Murfreesboro, AR 71958–1005
(501) 285–3182
Fax: (501) 285–3305

8062

Business Information: Pike Community Memorial Hospital is a 32–bed medical facility providing inpatient and outpatient care to the surrounding rural community. Small in scale, the hospital has no Neo–Natal facilities, but does provide physical therapy and acute care services. As Director, Ms. Fritts oversees administration of human resources and employee relations, handles all finance and strategic planning, and manages the day–to day operations of the facility. **Career Steps:** Director, Pike Community Memorial Hospital (1996–Present). **Associations & Accomplishments:** Chamber of Commerce; Red Cross. **Personal:** Married to Mike in 1970. Two children: Michelle and Micah.

David Fuller

Assistant Administrator and Chief Financial Officer
Lane Memorial Hospital
6300 Main Street
Zachary, LA 70791–4037
(504) 658–4301
Fax: (504) 654–4287

8062

Business Information: Lane Memorial Hospital is a for–profit, 170–bed health care and nursing facility, providing diagnosis and treatment for short– and long–term care patients, in addition to offering rehabilitative and home therapy programs. Joining Lane Memorial Hospital as Assistant Administrator and Chief Financial Officer in 1993, Mr. Fuller is responsible for administrative and financial matters relating to the hospital. **Career Steps:** Assistant Administrator and Chief Financial Officer, Lane Memorial Hospital (1993–Present); Administrator, Yalobusha Hospital and Nursing Home (1992–1993); Administrator, Quitman County Hospital and Nursing Home (1983–1992). **Associations & Accomplishments:** Healthcare Financial Management Association; American College of Healthcare Executives; Certified Fellow, American College of Health Care Administrators; Medical Group Management Association; Rotary International; Who's Who in the South and Southwest; Who's Who in Mississippi. **Education:** Mississippi College: MBA (1985), B.S.B.A. (1980). **Personal:** Married to Cecilia Hubbard in 1978. Four children: Jonathan, Benjamin, Jordan, and Tyler.

Judith A. Furlong, M.D.

Medical Director of Employee Health
Flower Family Physicians
5300 Harroun Road, Suite 304
Sylvania, OH 43560–2189
(419) 882–1100
Fax: Please mail or call

8062

Business Information: Flower Family Physicians is a group family practice medical facility, in affiliation with Flower Hospital. As Medical Director of the Hospital's Employee Health Division and a member of the faculty for the Physician's Group, Dr. Furlong works as an educator with the family practice residency program and a physician. As such, she is responsible for the instruction of students and some research. Dr. Furlong maintains a small medical practice through the residency program and functions as the physician for employee sick call. She is also the Medical Reviews Officer at the Flowers Hospital. **Career Steps:** Faculty Member and Physician, Flower Family Physicians (1994–Present); Medical Director of employee Health, Flower Hospital (1994–Present); Private Practice Physician, Regency Park Physicians (1989–1994). **Associations & Accomplishments:** American Medical Association; Ohio State Medical Association; American Academy of Family Physicians; Academy of Medicine. **Education:** Medical College of Ohio, M.D. (1984); University of Toledo, B.A. in Biology. **Personal:** Married to William D. in 1977. One child: William D. II. Dr. Furlong enjoys Tai Chi and other martial arts, and breeding and training Akitas and Border Collies.

Valentin Fuster, M.D., PhD.

Director of the Cardiovascular Institute
Mount Sinai Medical Center
1 Gustave L. Levy Place, Box 1030
New York, NY 10029–6574
(212) 241–7911
Fax: (212) 423–9488

8062

Business Information: Mount Sinai Medical Center is one of the nation's leading tertiary care medical treatment, surgery, research and teaching facilities; nationally acclaimed for housing the Cardiovascular Institute. Mount Sinai Medical Center currently employs more than 200 medical professional, technical and administrative support staff. A Board–certified Cardiologist, Dr. Fuster is responsible for the administration of the Cardiovascular Institute, as well as the diagnosis and treatment of cardiovascular patients. He also serves as Dean for Academic Affairs for Mt. Sinai Medical Center, responsible for the recruitment, hire and direction of medical faculty and curricula–related decision making. **Career Steps:** Director of the Cardiovascular Institute, Mount Sinai Medical Center (1994–Present); Dean for Academic Affairs, Mt. Sinai Medical Center (1994–Present); Chief of the Cardiac Unit, Massachusetts General Hospital (1991–1994). **Associations & Accomplishments:** American Heart Association (AHA), Commission of Science Advisory Committee; American College of Cardiology (ACC), Co–Chairman 27th Bethesda Conference; President, Spanish Cultural Society (Boston, Massachusetts); Corresponding Member, Cardiac Society of Australia/New Zealand; Founding Member, North American Vascular Biology Organization; AHA Council on Arteriosclerosis, Executive Committee Member; AHA New York City Affiliate, Board of Directors; AHA (National) Board of Directors; Chairman, Scientific Publications (AHA); ACC Board of Trustees; NIH Member of the Council NHLBI. **Education:** Barcelona University, M.D. (1967); Ph.D. **Personal:** Married to Maria Guals. Two children: Silvia and Pablo. Dr. Fuster enjoys bicycling, tennis, and reading.

Jerry H. Futrell

Chief Executive Officer/Administrator
Smith County Memorial Hospital
158 Hospital Drive
Carthage, TN 37030
(615) 735–5150
Fax: (615) 735–5118

8062

Business Information: Smith County Memorial Hospital, an affiliate of the Columbia HCA Corp., is a 63–bed acute care medical facility. As Chief Executive Officer and Administrator, Mr. Futrell provides the overall executive administration for all facets of operations. A successful businessman and politician in Smith County, he has served on the County Commissioners and as Vice Mayor of Carthage, Tennessee; was President of the local bank, and for 20 years owned and managed a full–service drug store. **Career Steps:** Chief Executive Officer/Administrator, Smith County Memorial Hospital (1991–Present); President, Smith County Bank (1985–1990); Owner, Read Brothers Drug Co. (1964–1985). **Associations & Accomplishments:** Vice Mayor, City of Carthage, TN; County Commissioner, Smith County, TN; President, Smith County Housing Authority; Chairman, Smith County Health and Facilities Board. **Education:** University of Mississippi, B.S. Pharm. (1957). **Personal:** Three children: Kenneth, Andrew, and Trent. Mr. Futrell enjoys music and golf.

Juanda Gaines, R.R.A.

Director of Medical Records
Glen Oaks Hospital
P O Box 1885 301 East Division Street
Greenville, TX 75401
(903) 454–6000
Fax: (903) 455–7980

8062

Business Information: Glen Oaks Hospital is a psychiatric and chemical dependency facility. The Hospital has three staff physicians and 50 beds. As Director of Medical Records, Ms. Gaines is responsible for supervising 5 employees as well as administrative duties including budgeting, coding, filing, and insurance. Ms. Gaines is also the facilitator of CQI for Glen Oaks Hospital and has started contract work. Concurrently she is assisting a community clinic in restructuring and automating their medical records department. **Career Steps:** Director of Medical Records, Glen Oaks Hospital (1994–Present); Director of Medical Records, Charter Hospital of Plano (1991–1994). **Associations & Accomplishments:** American Health Information Management Association. **Education:** Texas Woman's University, B.A. (1988); Tyler Junior College, Associates in Science. **Personal:** Married to Gregory in 1985. Three children: Sarah, Zavier, and Gregory II. Ms. Gaines enjoys music and her son's Little League Baseball.

Debra Gallinger

Director of Risk Management

Princess Margaret Hospital

610 University Avenue
Toronto, Ontario M5G 2M9
(416) 946–2171
Fax: (416) 946–6557

8062

Business Information: Princess Margaret Hospital specializes in the treatment and research of cancer and related diseases. Established in 1958, the Hospital employs 1,200 people. As Director of Risk Management, Ms. Gallinger deals with any insurance or accreditation issues that affect Hospital patients, staff, or property, with the intent to reduce and/or eliminate Hospital liability. **Career Steps:** Princess Margaret Hospital: Director of Risk Management (1995–Present), Manager, Radiation Therapy (1990–1995), Supervisor, Radiation Therapy (1988–1990). **Associations & Accomplishments:** Canadian Association of Medical Radiation Technologists; Council Member, College of Medical Radiation Technologists of Ontario; Ontario Association of Medical Radiation Technologists. **Education:** Ontario University/RMH School of Radiation Therapy: M.R.T. (T.) (1976), M.R.T.(T.) A. C. (1983); Canadian Hospital Association, Certificate in Departmental Management (1993); Certification in Joint Occupational Health and Safety (1994). **Personal:** Ms. Gallinger enjoys being a volunteer for the Pleasantview Softball Association.

Jonathan E. Gardner, RCVT

Cardiovascular Coordinator

Hershey Medical Center – Pennsylvania State Cardiovascular Center

500 University Drive, Room H1357
Hershey, PA 17033
(717) 531–6937
Fax: (717) 531–5774
E MAIL: See Below

8062

Business Information: Hershey Medical Center is a full–service, acute care medical facility and teaching hospital with full pediatric and adult cardiovascular care, affiliated with the Pennsylvania State University. As Cardiovascular Labs Coordinator, Mr. Gardner manages the cardiovascular laboratories at Hershey Medical Center. Other responsibilities include: budgetary operations of the center; scheduling of patients, staff, and physicians; staff recruitment, utilization and development; development and implementation of department policies and procedures; selection, installation, and maintenance of equipment; and maintaining communications between management, staff, and physicians. **Career Steps:** Hershey Medical Center: Cardiovascular Coordinator (1986–Present), Senior Cardiovascular Technologist (1983–1986), Cardiovascular Technologist (1980–1983). **Associations & Accomplishments:** American College of Cardiovascular Administrators; Cardiovascular Credentialing International; Bible Baptist Church. "Youth With a Mission" trip to Grenada, West Indies after the invasion, utilizing professional and spiritual skills to assist local residents. Occasional coordination of spiritual/psychological and family values seminars. Occasional coordination and/or assistance with voluntary church–community education. **Education:** La Salle University, B.H.S. (1996); Harrisburg Community College; Pennsylvania State University. **Personal:** Married to Sue in 1979. Five children: Andrea, Cara, Stephen, Joshua, and Laura. Mr. Gardner enjoys family sports, family activities, walking, gardening, electronics, spiritual development, and financial management.

Jason T. Garrison, M.D.

Staff Physician

Riverside Regional Medical Center

100 Muirfield Court
Yorktown, VA 23693
(804) 874–1051
Fax: Please mail or call

8062

Business Information: Riverside Regional Medical Center is a 500–bed acute care hospital with a Level II Trauma Center, providing care to critical patients contracted through the hospital. A practicing physician since 1986 and a Board–Certified Emergency Physician, Dr. Garrison's subspecialty is Hyperbaric Medicine. In 1992, he joined Riverside Regional Medical Center as Staff Physician and is responsible for providing emergency care for the Hospital's Level II Trauma Center, in addition to instructing residents/medical students, and supervising department operations. Concurrently, he serves as Physician at Virginia Emergency Physicians and as an Instructor of Emergency Medicine at Louisiana State University's School of Medicine. **Career Steps:** Staff Physician, Riverside Regional Medical Center (1992–Present); Physician, VA Emergency Physicians (1992–Present); Instructor of Emergency Medicine, Louisiana State University School of Medicine (1990–Present); Physician, James River Emergency Physicians (1990–1992). **Associations & Accomplishments:** Medical Director, Isle of Wight Rescue Squad; Fellow, American College of Emergency Physicians; VA College Emergency Physicians; Southern Medical Association; Undersea and Hyperbaric Medical Society; Newport News Medical Society; Fellow, American Academy Emergency Medicine; 1995 Mosely Award for Teaching. **Education:** Eastern VA Medical School, M.D. (1986); Additional Training in Hyperbaric Medicine. **Personal:** Married to Catherine in 1982. Three children: Jay, Alexandria, and Lindsey. Dr. Garrison enjoys tae kwon do and sailing.

C. Melissa Garza

Director of Business Operations

Health South Surgical Hospital

6818 Austin Center Boulevard, Suite 100
Austin, TX 78731–3100
(512) 346–1994
Fax: (512) 346–2760

8062

Business Information: Health South Surgical Hospital, established in 1995, is a specialized facility with eight private rooms, five operating rooms, and one endoscopy suite. As Director of Business Operations, Ms. Garza is responsible for patient admissions, records, and billing. Other responsibilities include accounts receivable, accounts payable, financial reporting, payroll, and budgetary concerns. Ms. Garza also has oversight of information support and all human resource concerns. **Career Steps:** Director of Business Operations, Health South Surgical Hospital (1995–Present). **Associations & Accomplishments:** Health Care Financial Management Association. **Education:** Southwest Texas State University, B.S. in Heath Care Administration (1993). **Personal:** Married to Garrick D. in 1992. Ms. Garza enjoys mountain biking.

John M. Gaudet

Center Director

Apopka Family Health Center

225 East 7th Street
Apopka, FL 32703
(407) 886–6201
Fax: (407) 886–4282

8062

Business Information: Apopka Family Health Center is a community health care facility providing medical services for residents of the County, particularly catering to the indigent and disadvantaged populace, as well as provides full outreach programs for migrant workers and their families. Established in 1972, the Apopka Family Health Center currently employs 72 physicians and medical professionals. As Center Director, Mr. Gaudet oversees daily clinical and non–clinical activities, and consults with County officials to help provide optimum health care. **Career Steps:** Center Director, Apopka Family Health Center (1994–Present); Specialty Coordinator, Columbia Hospital (1991–1993); Nurse Manager and Co–Director of Education, Mary Lane Hospital (1990–1991). **Associations & Accomplishments:** ENCARE, a program that lectures to school–age children about drugs and alcohol; Milwaukee AIDS Project (MAP). **Education:** Barry University, working towards a B.S. in Health Administration; Springfield Technical Community College, A.D.N.; Youville Hospital School, Practical Nursing degree; Advanced Burn Life Support, Certification. **Personal:** Mr. Gaudet enjoys sailing, history, travel and antiques.

Janusz D. Gawlik

Psychiatrist

Royal Ottawa Hospital

1145 Carling Avenue, Whitney Building
Ottawa, Ontario K1Z 7K4
(613) 722–6521 Ext. 6501
Fax: (613) 722–5048

8062

Business Information: Royal Ottawa Hospital is a psychiatric institution in Eastern Ontario, which provides therapy for patients with a wide spectrum of psychiatric disorders. As a Psychiatrist, Dr. Gawlik works in the general Psychiatry program providing outpatient and inpatient therapy. Dr. Gawlik enjoys his practice particularly because of the recent progress in psycho–pharmacology. Beside his clinical work, Dr. Gawlik, as an Assistant Professor, provides residents' supervision, and participates as a member of the administrative committee. **Career Steps:** Psychiatrist, Royal Ottawa Hospital (1994–Present). **Associations & Accomplishments:** Ontario Medical Association; Canadian Psychiatric Association. **Education:** Queen's University, M.D. (1994) – Psychiatry Residency Program. **Personal:** Married to Barbara in 1971. Two children: Mike and Matthew. Dr. Gawlik enjoys jogging and tennis.

Robert M. Gay Jr.

Associate – Division of Immunology and Rheumatology

University of Alabama at Birmingham Medical Center

1717 6th Avenue South
Birmingham, AL 35294
(205) 934–2130
Fax: (205) 975–6257

8062

Business Information: The University of Alabama at Birmingham Medical Center, an affiliate of the University of Alabama, is a multi–speciality, general practice medical teaching facility and health service establishment. In his current capacity, Dr. Gay is a Physician and Associate in the Division of Immunology and Rheumatology, teaching residents in Clinical Rheumatology as well as conducting research in rheumatoid arthritis. **Career Steps:** Physician and Associate, Division of Immunology and Rheumatology, University of Alabama at Birmingham Medical Center (1993–Present); Internal Medicine President, Medical College of Virginia (1990–1993). **Associations & Accomplishments:** Diplomate, National Board of Medical Examiners; Diplomate, American Board of Internal Medicine; Member, American College of Physicians; Trainee Member, American College of Rheumatology; Member, Southern Medical Association; Co–author, Chapter in textbook: Arthritis and Allied Conditions. **Education:** University of North Carolina: M.D. (1990), B.A. in Chemistry (1986). **Personal:** Married to Kimberly L. in 1991.

Sharyln T. Geerdes

Vice President of Health Services

Carrington Health Center

800 North Fourth Street
Carrington, ND 58421
(701) 652–3141
Fax: (701) 652–3034

8062

Business Information: Carrington Health Center is a full–service healthcare facility providing a hospital, nursing home, home health, and a clinic in a rural setting in North Dakota. As Vice President of Health Services, Ms. Geerdes is responsible for the Nursing within the four functional areas of the facility. **Career Steps:** Vice President of Health Services, Carrington Health Center (1996–Present); Assistant Director of Nursing, Hi–Acres Manor (1990–1996); Assistant Director of Nursing, North Dakota State Hospital (1979–1990); Instructor of Nursing, Jamestown College (1981). **Associations & Accomplishments:** American Nurses Association; North Dakota State Nurses Association; National Association of Directors of Nursing Administration in Long–Term Care: Executive Board Member for the North Dakota Chapter, Founding Member; Eastern North Dakota Chapter of the Alzheimer's Association: Vice President, Development Committee Member; Current Board President, St. John's Academy School Board; Eucharistic Minister, St. James Church. **Education:** University of Mary, M.S.N. (1992); Jamestown College, B.S.N. **Personal:** Married to Terry Geerdes. Three children: Ryan, Grant, and Tara. Ms. Geerdes enjoys travel, candymaking, walking, reading, and crafts.

Vicky L. German–Lemmons

Nurse Manager of the Neuroscience and Spine Center

Sutter Health

2801 L Street
Sacramento, CA 95816–5615
(916) 733–8942
Fax: Please mail or call

8062

Business Information: Established in 1926, Sutter Health is a 355–bed acute care hospital, and is part of a 5,000 bed system, CHS. Having served in various capacities for the hospital since 1982, Ms. German–Lemmons was assigned the position of Nurse Manager of the Neuroscience and Spine Center in 1991. She is responsible for a staff of 77, the budget, standards and protocol, and maintaining the flow of operations. **Career Steps:** Sutter Health: Nurse Manager (1991–Present), Assistant Nurse Manager (1985–1991), Staff RN (1982–1985). **Associations & Accomplishments:** American Association of Neurological Nurses, National and Local; East Sacramento Kiwanis; Multiple Sclerosis Association Walk–a–thon; East Bay Epilepsy League Walk–a–thon and Alzheimers Association. **Education:** University of Phoenix, B.S.N. (1996); Sacramento City College: A.D.N., A.A. in Biological Sciences. **Personal:** One child: Aaron Lee. Ms. German–Lemmons enjoys oil painting, camping, fishing, and water sports (snorkeling, diving, etc.).

Carl C. Gill, M.D.

Chief Executive Officer/Cardiothoracic Surgeon
Cleveland Clinic Facility
3000 West Cypress Creek Road
Ft. Lauderdale, FL 33309–1710
(954) 978–5269
Fax: (954) 978–7416

8062

Business Information: A nonprofit organization comprised of 100 physicians, Cleveland Clinic Facility is a major medical, educational, and research facility. A nonprofit organization, with three clinics in Florida including the 150–bed Ft. Lauderdale facility, the Organization is nonprofit, and has published over 250 articles in trade journals, and has over 150 research programs. Always striving to help the community, the Company is in the process of building a new clinic on the West Coast. As founder of the Florida chapter, Dr. Gill recruited and networked, literally starting the Organization "from the ground up". In his capacity as Chief Executive Officer/Cardiothoracic Surgeon, Dr. Gill is responsible for strategic planning, oversight of administrative and operational duties, and patient care and research. **Career Steps:** Cleveland Clinic Facility: Chief Executive Officer/Cardiothoracic Surgeon (1988–Present), Medical Director (1987–1988); The Cleveland Clinic Foundation: Vice–Chairman, Board of Governors (1987–Present), Member, Board of Governors (1985–1987), Head, Section of Congenital Surgery (1977–1987); University of Oklahoma Health Sciences Center: Assistant Professor of Surgery (1976–1977), Senior Resident, Thoracic Surgery (1974–1975), Senior Resident General Surgery (1973–1974), Assistant Resident, Surgery (1972–1973), Assistant Resident, Surgery (1970–1971), Intern, Surgery (1969–1970); Fellow in Cardiac Surgery, Mayo Clinic (1975–1976); Fellow in Cardiovascular Research, Duke University (1971–1972). **Associations & Accomplishments:** American College of Cardiology; American College of Chest Physicians; American College of Surgeons, Florida Chapter; American Heart Association; American Medical Association; Broward County Medical Association; Cleveland Academy of Medicine; Cleveland Surgical Society; Florida Medical Association; Florida Society of Thoracic and Cardiovascular Surgeons; International Society for Heart Transplantation; Ohio State Medical Association; Oklahoma State Medical Association; Scientific Councils of the American Heart Association: Council on Cardiovascular Disease in the Young, Council on Cardiovascular Surgery; Society of Thoracic Surgeons; Southwestern Surgical Congress. **Education:** University of Oklahoma, M.D. (1969); Westminster College, B.A. (1965); Board of Medical Examiners, Oklahoma (1970); National Board of Medical Examiners (1987); American Board of Surgery (1975); American Board of Thoracic Surgery (1976); Licensed in Oklahoma, Ohio, and Florida; Author/Co–Author of several publications. **Personal:** Married to Diane Ruth Miner in 1965. Three children: Mallory Anne, Erin Elizabeth, and Hudson Carter.

Stephen Glasser, M.D.

Professor of Medicine and Director
Cardiovascular Unit for Research & Education
Univ. So. Florida Medical Ctr, 3500 E. Fletcher Av, #218
Tampa, FL 33613
(813) 971–7272
Fax: (813) 971–7178
EMAIL: See Below

8062

Business Information: University of South Florida Medical Center, associated with the University of South Florida, is a teaching hospital providing diagnosis and treatment of patients and instruction of medical students, as well as conducting medical research. As Professor of Medicine, Dr. Glasser is responsible for the instruction of medical students, as well as serving as Director of the Cardiovascular Unit for Research and Education. His duties consist of administration, teaching, research and patient care. Current research is on the evaluation of blood vessel wall elasticity – the goal is to identify an early marker of blood vessel disease in order to identify people at risk. He can also be reached through the Internet as follows: SGLASSER@COM1.MED.USF.EDU **Career Steps:** University of South Florida: Professor of Medicine and Director of the Cardiovascular Unit for Research and Education (1990–Present), Director of the Division of Cardiology (1978–1990), Director of Cardiac Non–Invasive Laboratory (1976–1989); Visiting Professor of Medicine (Cardiology), University of Minnesota Medical School. **Associations & Accomplishments:** Special Consultant to the Federal Drug Administration; Credentials Committee Humana Health Care Plans; Chairman, Clinical Research Committee, University of South Florida; Editorial Board, American Journal of Cardiology (1992); Member, Research Committee, Council on Geriatric Cardiology; Listed in the Best Doctors in America: Southeast Region; Published over 200 publications. **Education:** University of Miami, M.D. (1964). **Personal:** Married to Donna Arnett, Ph.D. in 1990. Two children: Laurie and Julie. Dr. Glasser enjoys tennis.

Steven W. Gomes, M.Div.

Director and Chaplain
Porter Care Hospital and Porter Care Littleton
2525 South Downing Street, C2K
Denver, CO 80210–5876
(303) 765–3517
Fax: Please mail or call

8062

Business Information: Porter Care Hospital and Porter Care Littleton, a division of Centura Corporation, are regional acute care facilities in the Denver, Colorado area. As Director and Chaplain, Mr. Gomes is on call 24 hours a day for Doctors, grief and crisis management, and general support of patients and staff. Mr. Gomes is in charge of the daily operations and is responsible for all administrative duties of the two hospitals. **Career Steps:** Director and Chaplain, Porter Care Hospital and Porter Care Littleton (1995–Present); Director and Chaplain, Porter Care Littleton (1987–1995); Health Educator, Porter Hospital (1984–1987). **Associations & Accomplishments:** President, Hemophilia Society of Colorado; Governor's Advisory Board on Hemophilia. **Education:** Andrews University, M.Div. (1980). **Personal:** Married to Mary in 1984. Two children: Heather and Joshua. Mr. Gomes enjoys outdoors, camping, four wheeling, skiing, and spending time with his family.

Carlos A. Gomez–Marcial, M.D.

Emergency Room Medical Director/Physician
Auxilio Mutuo Hospital
P.O. Box 191227
San Juan, Puerto Rico 00919–1227
(787) 758–2000
Fax: (787) 758–9876

8062

Business Information: Auxilio Mutuo Hospital is the largest private hospital in Puerto Rico. Comprised of 516 beds, the Hospital offers a cardiac and intensive care unit, pediatrics, surgery, ob–gyn, and internal medicine services. Specializing in renal transplants and related problems, the Hospital also provides a comprehensive dialysis unit. Established in 1883, Auxilio Mutuo Hospital has a staff of over 600 physicians and over 1,400 employees. As Emergency Room Medical Director/Physician, Dr. Gomez–Marcial oversees all the phases of emergency room activities, to include patient care. He is responsible for supervising the performance of staff and physicians, in training, diagnosing and treating patients, coordinating and scheduling staff, and ensuring care of trauma cases are expedited (i.e., sent to surgery, lab work completed, X–rays, etc.). **Career Steps:** Emergency Room Medical Director/Physician, Auxilio Mutuo Hospital (1988–Present); Medical Director, Puerto Rico Base, Aeroambulance International (1992–1995); Emergency Room Medical Director, Puerto Rico Medical Center (1985–1992). **Associations & Accomplishments:** American College of Emergency Physicians; Colegio de Medicos de Puerto Rico. **Education:** University of Puerto Rico Medical School, E.R.M.D. (1985). **Personal:** Married to Nilsa Arroyo in 1975. Dr. Gomez–Marcial enjoys stamps, coins, sports, and travel.

Leisa T. Gonnella

Director of Administration – Department of Anesthesiology
University of Virginia Health Sciences Center
Box 238
Charlottesville, VA 22908
(804) 982–4309
Fax: (804) 982–0019

8062

Business Information: University of Virginia Health Sciences Center, affiliated with the University of Virginia, is a healthcare administration organization. Joining the organization as Director of Administration for the Department of Anesthesiology in 1994, Mrs. Gonnella is financially and administratively responsible for the operations of the department and reports all activities directly to the Chair. **Career Steps:** Director of Administration – Department of Anesthesiology, University of Virginia Health Sciences Center (1994–Present); Managed Care Coordinator, Medical College of Virginia (1993–1994); Administrative Resident, Geisinger Medical Center (1992–1993). **Associations & Accomplishments:** Medical Group Management Association; American College of Medical Practice Executives **Education:** Duke University, M.H.A. (1992); Villanova University, B.S. **Personal:** Married to John in 1993. One child: Joseph Charles. Mrs. Gonnella enjoys running.

Juan A. Gonzalez, M.D.

Emergency Medical Program Director/Chief, Emergency Medical Staff
Carolina University Hospital
Paseo De La Hambra Cordova #15
Carolina, PR 00987
(809) 754–4105
Fax: (809) 754–4105

8062

Business Information: Carolina University Hospital is a full–service medical facility. Affiliated with the University of Puerto Rico Medical School, the Hospital is a basis of teaching and research to medical students, and plans to expand through implementation of new programs such as EMS training, adding a poison control center, and exposing the need for emergency physicians on the island (currently there are 40 out of a needed 300). As Emergency Medical Program Director/Chief, Emergency Medical Staff, Dr. Gonzalez is responsible for instructing three resident programs. He is currently trying to implement an EMS training program, and is striving to bring more emergency physicians to the island. Dr. Gonzalez also works with a geriatric shelter in his spare time. **Career Steps:** Emergency Medical Program Director/Chief, Emergency Medical Staff, Carolina University Hospital (1990–Present); Puerto Rico Medical Center Emergency Department: Attending Physician/PRMCED (1989), Assistant Director (1989–1992); Department and Program Director, University of Puerto Rico Medicine Program (1992–Present). **Associations & Accomplishments:** Director, Egida Posada de la Caudad; Puerto Rico Medical College; American Medical Association; A.C.E.P.; S.A.E.M. **Education:** University of Puerto Rico School of Medicine, M.D. (1986); U.T. Southeastern University, Teaching Fellowship (1996). **Personal:** Married to Nilsat Trenche in 1991. One child: Juan O. Dr. Gonzalez enjoys jogging, weightlifting, softball, and reading.

Vilma G. Gonzalez, M.D.

Director of OB/GYN Department
Centro Medico
410 Carr 2, OB/GYN Department 4th Floor
Mayaguez, Puerto Rico 00680
(809) 265–5090
Fax: (809) 834–3010

8062

Business Information: Centro Medico is a 280–bed, full–service tertiary care medical and teaching hospital, providing diagnosis and treatment to patients and instruction to medical students. A practicing physician since 1984 and a Board–Certified Obstetrician and Gynecologist, Dr. Gonzalez joined Centro Medico as Director of OB/GYN Department in 1990. He is responsible for the direction of the Department, including administration, public relations, and strategic planning, in addition to his daily patient practice. He also provides instruction to medical students in obstetrics and gynecology. **Career Steps:** Director of OB/GYN Department, Centro Medico (1990–Present); Administrator, Obstetrasy Ginecologos Asoc. (1990–1996); Attending Physician, Sociedad Gineco–Obstetrica (1988–1990); Resident OB/GYN, Puerto Rico Health Department (1984–1988). **Associations & Accomplishments:** Mayaguez Medical Center: Faculty President (1993–1994), Accreditation President (1996). **Education:** University of Puerto Rico School of Medicine, M.D. (1984).

Dr. Narasimh Gopalswamy

Attending Physician
Veterans Administration Medical Center
111 4100 West Third Street
Dayton, OH 45428
(513) 268–6511 Ext. 2110
Fax: (513) 267–3934

8062

Business Information: The Veterans Administration Medical Center of Dayton is a full–service, multi–specialty medical facility and health service establishment. Affiliated with Wright State University, the hospital is also a research and instructional institution. Currently the VA Medical Center employs over 1,000 physicians and medical support staff. As Attending Physician, Dr. Gopalswamy specializes in Internal Medicine and Gastroenterology. He is also the Program Director of the Gastroenterology Fellowship. Concurrent to his position with the hospital, Dr. Gopalswamy is also an Associate Professor of Medicine at Wright State University. **Career Steps:** Attending Physician of Internal Medicine and Gastroenterology, Veterans Administration Medical Center (1975–Present). **Associations & Accomplishments:** American Gastroenterology Association; American Society of Physicians; American Society of Gastroenterology; NAVAP. **Education:** University of Mysore, India, M.B.B.S. (1963); M.R.C.P., UK; Board Certified in Gastroenterology, American Physicians Association. **Personal:** Married to Girija in 1966. Two children: Sudhir and Asha. Dr. Gopalswamy enjoys Indian Classical music and travel.

Michael F. Gormley

Manager/Chief Technologist
Carney Hospital
2100 Dorchester Avenue
Dorchester, MA 02124
(617) 296–4000
Fax: (617) 296–4012

8062

Business Information: Carney Hospital is a 231–bed, community–based, acute and sub–acute care hospital serving the South Boston, Massachusetts area. As Manager/Chief Technologist, Mr. Gormley is responsible for all testing results completed by the Neurophysiology and Sleep Disorders Laboratory (i.e. EEG, EMG, and Sleeping Disorder records). Mr. Gormley handles patient billing for tests conducted and payroll for laboratory staff. **Career Steps:** Manager/Chief Technologist, Carney Hospital (1986–Present); EEG Technologist, Bon Secours Hospital (1984–1986); PSG Technologist, New England Medical Center (1982–1984). **Associations & Accomplishments:** Executive Board, New England Society of Electroneurodiagnostic Technologists; Examiner, American Board of Registration of Electroneurodiagnostic Technologists; Elected Town Meeting Member, Braintree; Vice Chairman, East Braintree Civic Association. **Education:** Laboude College A.S. (1983); Northwestern University. **Personal:** Married to Susan in 1985. Two children: Katelyn and Patrick. Mr. Gormley enjoys sports and music.

Dr. Jean Y. Gosselin

Physician/Emeritus Professor of Psychiatry
Ottawa Health Sciences, University of Ottawa
4419–501 Smyth Road
Ottawa, Ontario K1H 8L6
(613) 737–8068
Fax: (613) 739–9980

8062

Business Information: Ottawa Health Sciences, University of Ottawa is a full service medical facility providing health and related services to Ottawa and the surrounding area. As Physician/Emeritus Professor of Psychiatry, Dr. Gosselin, who is semi–retired, treats patients (currently on tinnitus and the emotional components of it), and instructs residents and students. **Career Steps:** Physician/Emeritus Professor of Psychiatry, Ottawa Health Sciences, University of Ottawa (Present); Director, In–Patient Psychiatry, Ottawa General Hospital (1972–1994). **Associations & Accomplishments:** Emeritus Member, Canadian Medical Association; President, Canadian Psychiatric Association; Ontario Medical Association; President, Ontario Psychiatric Association; President, Quebec Psychiatric Association; American Psychiatric Association; American College of Psychiatrists; Royal College of Psychiatrists, U.K.; Pacific Rim College of Psychiatrists; Chairman – Committee to Review the Abuses of Psychiatry for Political Reasons, World Association for Social Psychiatry; Le Cercle Universitaire d' O'Hawa; The National Arts Center; The National Gallery of Canada; Knight of the Military Order of Malta; Knight of the Order of St. Gregory the Great; Emeritus Fellow, American College of Psychiatrists; Honorary Fellow: International Organization of Psychophysiology. **Education:** Laval University, M.D. (1955); The Royal College of Physicians and Surgeons of Canada, Fellowship in Psychiatry. **Personal:** Married to Ghyslaine in 1960. Three children: Dr. Benoit Gosselin, M.D. F.R.C.S., Dr. Anne–Marie Gosselin, M.D., and Francois Gosselin, M.Sc.. Dr. Gosselin enjoys golf, skiing, and music.

Susan P. Graham, M.D.

Director of the Coronary Care Unit
Buffalo General Hospital
100 High Street
Buffalo, NY 14203–1126
(716) 859–5600
Fax: (716) 845–1491

8062

Business Information: Buffalo General Hospital, affiliated with SUNY – University at Buffalo, is a 720–bed, full–service, tertiary care facility, providing diagnosis and treatment of patients, education to medical students, and research. A practicing physician since 1982 and Board–Certified in Cardiology, Dr. Graham joined Buffalo General Hospital in 1989. Serving as Director of the Coronary Care Unit, she is responsible for the direction of all operations, in addition to her daily patient practice. **Career Steps:** Director of the Coronary Care Unit, Buffalo General Hospital (1989–Present). **Associations & Accomplishments:** American College of Physicians; American College of Cardiology; International Heart Lung Transplant Society. **Education:** University of Texas – Houston, M.D. (1982); Vassor College, B.A. **Personal:** Married to Jon Kucera in 1989. Two children: Pete and Alexander. Dr. Graham enjoys outdoor activities.

E. Kay Gray

Administrator
Vencor Hospital
1313 St. Anthony Place
Louisville, KY 40204–1740
(502) 587–7001
Fax: (502) 587–0060

8062

Business Information: Vencor Hospital, a subsidiary of Vencor, Inc., is a 150–bed, acute care hospital, providing diagnosis and treatment to patients in Kentucky, South Indiana, Ohio, and Tennessee. After establishing Vencor Hospital for Vencor, Inc. in 1995, Ms. Gray stayed on as Administrator and is responsible for all aspects of operations for the entire hospital. She also oversees all administration, operations, and financing. Her previous work experience includes working for Vencor, Inc. from 1992 to 1995, during which she directed all start–up facilitation for new hospital affiliations. Vencor, Inc. owns specialty hospitals which provide longer lengths of acute hospital stays for catastrophically ill and injured persons. It presently owns 39 hospitals nationally and during a recent merger acquired 300 nursing homes, pharmaceutical and home health care services. **Career Steps:** Administrator, Vencor Hospital (1995–Present); Vencor, Inc.: Regional Clinical Manager (1993–1995), Regional Quality Manager (1992–1993); Quality Review Manager, St. Luke's Hospital – St. Louis, MO (1989–1992) **Associations & Accomplishments:** Chamber of Commerce; Explorer Scouting Program Advisor **Education:** Webster University, M.B.A. (1996); Tarkio College, B.S. in Health Care Administration; Missouri Baptist School of Nursing, R.N. **Personal:** Married to Edward N. in 1986. Three children: Robert, Brian and Angela Edmiston. Six stepchildren: Scott, Janet, Lynn, Dawn, Eddie and Dana Gray. Ms. Gray enjoys golf.

William B. Green Jr., Ph.D., M.D.

Assistant Professor of Clinical Anesthesiology and Pediatrics
University of Arizona Health Sciences Center
Department of Anesthesiology
Tucson, AZ 85724
(520) 626–7221
Fax: (520) 626–6943
E–mail: see below

8062

Business Information: The University of Arizona Health Sciences Center, an affiliate of the University of Arizona System, is a 500–bed tertiary hospital, multi–specialty medical research and teaching institution. As Assistant Professor of Clinical Anesthesiology and Pediatrics, Dr. Green is responsible for the instruction of medical and resident students, the care and treatment of patients, as well as clinical research in the area of Molecular Genetics. He can also be reached through the Internet as follows: wbg@ccit.arizona.edu **Career Steps:** Assistant Professor of Clinical Anesthesiology and Pediatrics, University of Arizona Health Sciences Center (1993–Present). **Associations & Accomplishments:** Full Fellow, American Academy of Pediatrics; American Society of Anesthesiologists; Society of Pediatric Anesthesiologists; Member, Church of Christ. **Education:** University of Texas Medical School – San Antonio, M.D. (1987); The Ohio State University: Ph.D. in Molecular Genetics (1983), M.S. (1980); Abilene Christian University, B.S. in Biology (1977). **Personal:** Married to Melissa Bennett in 1986. One child: Brent. Dr. Green enjoys camping, hiking, astronomy and Church activites.

Linda B. Griska, M.D.

Chairman – Department of Radiology
Montgomery Hospital
1300 Block Powell St.
Norristown, PA 19404
(610) 270–2266
Fax: (610) 270–2669

8062

Business Information: Montgomery Hospital is an acute care medical facility. A Radiologist and Professor of Radiology since 1976, Dr. Griska joined the Hospital in 1990 as Chairman of the Department of Radiology. Concurrently, she serves as Medical Director of the Women's Center for Diagnostic Imaging and is an attending Radiologist at Valley Forge Medical Center in Norristown, Pennsylvania. **Career Steps:** Chairman of the Department of Radiology, Montgomery Hospital (1990–Present); Medical Director, Women's Center for Diagnostic Imaging (1991–Present); Radiologist, Valley Forge Medical Center (1984–Present); Clinical Associate Professor of Radiology, Medical College of Pennsylvania (1984–1994); Attending Radiologist, Montgomery Hospital (1984–1990); Consultant, Angiography and Diagnostic Radiology, St. Christopher's Hospital for Children (1980–1984); Medical College of Pennsylvania: Associate Professor of Radiology (1981–1984), Director, Section of Angiography and Interventional Radiology (1980–1984), Assistant Professor of Radiology (1977–1981), Instructor in Radiology (1976–1977). **Associations & Accomplishments:** American College of Radiology; Society of Breast Imaging; Pennsylvania Radiologic Society; Philadelphia Roentgen Ray Society; Montgomery Hospital: Medical Executive Committee (1990–Present), Radiation Safety Officer, Chairman Radiation Safety Committee (1990–Present), Bylaws Committee (1989–1994); Director, Fornance Physician Services (1993–1995); Chairman, Board of Directors, Fornance Physician Services (1993–1994); Medical College of Pennsylvania: Medical Student Promotions Committee (Chairman, 1986–1984), Hospital Services Committee (1979–1984), Research Committee – Project Evaluation Subcommittee (1978–1984), Advisory Council to the Dean on Committees (Chairman 1979–1980), Ethics and Credentials Committee (1975–1976); Philadelphia Roentgen Ray Society Committee on Economics (1993–1994); Pennsylvania Medical Society Advisory Committee on Professionalism, Delegate from Philadelphia County Medical Society (1983–1985); Administrative Board, United Methodist Church, Bala Cynwyd, Pennsylvania (1982–Present); Chairman Membership Committee, Medical College of Pennsylvania Alumnae Association (1979–1980); Community Advocacy Board, Northwest Mental Health Center (1979–1980); Executive Board Central Germantown Project Area Committee (Secretary 1974–1975) (1974–1980); Various Publications, Scientific Exhibits, Clinical Research, Abstracts and Presentations. **Education:** Medical College of Pennsylvania – Philadelphia, M.D. (1968–1972); Boston University, B.A. (1964–1968); Medical College of Philadelphia: Fellowship–Angiography (1975–1976), Residency – General Radiology (1973–1975), Internship–Radiology (1972–1973). **Personal:** Married to Joel Adam Griska, M.D. in 1970. Two children: Adam and Jordan.

Nori R. Grossman

Chief Technologist
Guadalupe Valley Hospital
1215 East Court
Seguing, TX 78155
(210) 379–2411
Fax: Please mail or call

8062

Business Information: Guadalupe Valley Hospital is a city and county full–service healthcare institution specializing in the diagnosis, treatment, and rehabilitation of patients. As Chief Technologist, Ms. Grossman supervises all clinical laboratory activities and personnel; with primary duties including schedule coordination, trouble shooting for physicians, and coordinating education for students in college. **Career Steps:** Chief Technologist, Guadalupe Valley Hospital (1993–Present); Hemotology Supervisor, North Central Baptist Hospital (1992–1993); MT Instructor, Baptist Medical Center (1991–1992); MT Generalist, Northeast Baptist Hospital (1990–1991). **Associations & Accomplishments:** Texas Association for Clinical Laboratory Sciences; San Antonio Chapter of Medical Technologists. **Education:** Southwest Texas State University (1995); Tarleton State University, B.S.M.T.; Texas A&M University, Pre–Med Technician Schooling. **Personal:** Married to John A. in 1989. Ms. Grossman enjoys reading, sewing, music, and arts and crafts.

Rochelle Grothaus, R.R.A.
Assistant Director of Information Management
Choctaw Nation Indian Hospital
RR 2, Box 1725
Talihina, OK 74571
(918) 567–2211
Fax: (918) 567–2631

8062

Business Information: Choctaw Nation Indian Hospital is a 52–bed hospital providing medical care services to eligible Native Americans. Services include dental, eye, medical needs, and other certain available outside resources. As Assistant Director of Information Management, Ms. Grothaus is responsible for all aspects of administration, including filing, recordkeeping, keeping track of patients, correspondence, transcription, admissions, and producing the Quarterly Medical Record Review. **Career Steps:** Assistant Director of Information Management, Choctaw Nation Hospital (1994–Present); Health/Handicap Coordinator, Seminole Nation Head Start (1981–1987). **Associations & Accomplishments:** American Health Information Management Association (AHIMA); National Honor Society – High School (1979–1980); High School – Who's Who (1980). **Education:** East Central University, B.S. (1994). **Personal:** Four children: Eric T. Grothaus, Tenetka Madkins, and Joshua and Samson Morgan. Ms. Grothaus enjoys volleyball, softball, and serving as a Church Youth Teacher and Youth Director.

Crystal L. Gue, M.D.

Physician
University of Tennessee Hospital
1928 Alcoa Highway, Suite 127
Knoxville, TN 37920–1506
(423) 925–9020
Fax: (423) 925–9091

8062

Business Information: University of Tennessee Hospital is a full–service, tertiary medical and teaching hospital, providing diagnosis and treatment to patients and instruction to medical students. A practicing physician since 1990, Dr. Gue joined University of Tennessee Hospital as Physician in 1993. She specializes in providing diagnosis and treatment to patients suffering from internal medicine complaints. Having a large female patient load, she is most concerned with women's health issues. She also serves with the Faculty of Medicine at three locations (one of ten physicians): University of Tennessee, North Knoxville, and West Knoxville. Concurrent with her private medical practice, she serves as Professor of Women's Health Issues to residents, as well as teaches family practice and internal medicine residents at University of Tennessee. She also conducts clinical research. **Career Steps:** Physician, University of Tennessee Hospital (1993–Present); Physician, University of Tennessee Medical Center, Internal Medicine Residency (1990–1993). **Associations & Accomplishments:** American College of Physicians; American Medical Association; American Society of Internal Medicine; Author of a chapter in a book on breast cancer and an article on a parasitic disease called, Strongyloides – both publications coming out soon. **Education:** Marshall University – Huntington, WV: M.D. (1990), B.S. **Personal:** Dr. Gue enjoys reading and hiking.

Diana Guerrero Betancourt, M.D.
Physician
Huron Valley Hospital
1601 East Commerce Road
Commerce Township, MI 48382
(810) 360–3300
Fax: Please mail or call

8062

Business Information: Huron Valley Hospital is a 150–bed hospital, providing diagnosis and treatment to patients in all spectrums of medicine. A practicing physician since 1985, and Certified in Critical Care and Chest Medicine, Dr. Guerrero Betancourt provides medical diagnosis and treatment to patients in the intensive care unit (ICU) and telemetry units of the Hospital. **Career Steps:** Physician, Huron Valley Hospital (1992–Present); Physician, Huztel Hospital, Detroit Medical Center (1992–1994). **Associations & Accomplishments:** Society of Critical Care Medicine; American College of Chest Physicians; BBB Biological Honor Society; Native of Puerto Rico. **Education:** UCCEM, Medical School – P.R., M.D. (December 1984). **Personal:** Dr. Guerrero Betancourt enjoys drawing and reading.

James Evbanvban Guobadia
Assistant Chief Occupational Therapy
Kingsbrook Jewish Medical Center
585 Schnectady Avenue
Brooklyn, NY 11203–1854
(718) 604–5924
Fax: (718) 604–5272

8062

Business Information: Kingsbrook Jewish Medical Center, a non–profit, 879–bed facility, has been caring for Brooklyn for more than 70 years. Services include ambulatory surgery center; numerous multi–disciplinary consultant and outpatient clinics; Adult Day Health Care Center; 24–hour emergency services for medical, surgical and pediatric patients; a community outreach program; and a certified home health agency. KJMC is accredited by the New York State Department of Health and by JCAHCO. Mr. Guobadia joined KJMC in 1989 as a Staff Occupational Therapist and was promoted to Assistant Chief of Occupational Therapy in March 1995. He has twenty years of experience in the U.S., Africa, and Europe in psychology, adult rehabilitation, long–term and home care, and management. **Career Steps:** Assistant Chief Occupational Therapy, Kingsbrook Jewish Medical Center (1989–Present); Principal Occupational Therapy, Head of Department, University of Benin Teaching Hospital (1982–1988); Senior Occupational Therapist, Psychiatric Hospital, Benin City, Nigeria (1977–1980). **Associations & Accomplishments:** The American Occupational Therapy Association; The British Association of Occupational Therapists; The Nigerian Association of Occupational Therapists; EDO Club and BINI Unity League, both of Benin City, Nigeria; **Education:** University of Southampton, UK, M.Sc. (1982); London School of Occupational Therapy, DIPCOT (1976). **Personal:** Married to Marie C. Exume–Guobadia in 1990. Three children: Oswald Osaretinmwen, Pierre Eghosasere and Urfine Orobosa. Mr. Guobadia enjoys reading, playing chess and lawn tennis.

Jimmy B. L. Gutman, M.D., F.A.C.E.P.
Consultant & Educational Director in Emergency Medicine
McGill University/Jewish General Hospital
3755 Cote–Sainte–Catherine Rd
Montreal, Quebec H3T 1E2
(514) 340–8222 EXT. 5568
Fax: (514) 685–7392

8062

Business Information: Jewish General Hospital is a teaching facility of McGill University which has one of the world's most renowned medical schools. As Consultant & Educational Director in Emergency Medicine, Dr. Gutman is responsible for strategic planning, administrative duties, teaching, lecturing and overseeing the training of residents and medical students in emergency medicine. **Career Steps:** McGill University: Consultant & Educational Director in Emergency Medicine (1996–Present); Emergency Medicine Residency Director (1995–1996); Board of Directors, Canadian Association of Emergency Physicians, (1993–1995); Emergency Medicine Undergraduate Educational Director, McGill University (1993); Consultant, Jewish General Hospital (1987–1993); Chief Resident, Emergency Medicine, Emory University (1986–1987). **Associations & Accomplishments:** Canadian Association of Emergency Physicians; American College of Emergency Physicians; Society of Academic Emergency Medicine; Canadian Medical Association; Established mandatory undergraduate training in emergency medicine at McGill University. **Education:** Emory University, Emergency Medicine Residency (1987); McGill University, Medical Internship (1983); University of Calgary, M.D. (1982); McGill University, B.Sc. in Botany (1977). **Personal:** Married to Susan Schafer in 1990 with son Evan M. 1993, daughter Bianca J. 1995. Dr. Gutman enjoys artwork, carpentry, playing in a rock band, golf, hockey and multi–level marketing.

Marilyn Guzaski–Kalamaris
Director of Professional Relations
Columbia Olympia Fields Osteopathic Hospital & Medical Center
20201 S. Crawford Avenue
Olympia Fields, IL 60461–1010
(708) 747–4000 Ext. 1680
Fax: (708) 503–3270

8062

Business Information: Columbia Olympia Fields Osteopathic Hospital & Medical Center is a full–service, health care institution specializing in the diagnosis, treatment, and rehabilitation of patients. As Director of Professional Relations, Ms. Guzaski–Kalamaris is responsible for diversified administrative activities, including acting as a physician liaison and recruiter. **Career Steps:** Columbia Olympia Fields Osteopathic Hospital & Medical Center: Director of Professional Relations (1996–Present); Regional Director, Columbia Home Care (1994–1996); Nursing Administrator (1984–1994). **Associations & Accomplishments:** National Association of Female Executives; American Heart Association. **Education:** Lewis University, M.B.A. (1995); Loyola University, B.S.N. (1975). **Personal:** Ms. Guzaski–Kalamaris enjoys aerobics, staying active, and reading.

Loretta C. Gvazdinskas, M.S.
Administrator
Rush–Presbyterian, St. Luke's Medical Center
1653 West Congress Parkway
Chicago, IL 60612
(312) 942–5447
Fax: (312) 942–3355
EMAIL: See Below

8062

Business Information: Rush–Presbyterian, St. Luke's Medical Center is an 800–1000 bed full service medical facility offering obstetrics, gynecology, trauma, surgery, and other medical services to the surrounding community. Established in the 1890's, the Hospital employs 8,000 people. As Administrator, Ms. Gvazdinskas oversees management, administration, and operations related to the perinatal network, obstetrics, gynecology, and the women's and children's hospital. Internet users can reach her via: lgvazdin@rpslmc.edu. **Career Steps:** Rush–Presbyterian, St. Luke's Medical Center: Administrator (1995–Present), Department of Obstetrics/Gynecology Administrator (1994–Present); Women's and Children's Hospital Administrative Manager (1994–Present). **Associations & Accomplishments:** American College of Healthcare Executives; Clinical Laboratory Management Association. **Education:** Benedictine University, M.S. (1996). **Personal:** Married to Paul S. in 1977. Two children: Ingrid and Alex. Ms. Gvazdinskas enjoys reading, gardening, outdoor and volunteer activities.

Wayne Hadley
Director of Physical Therapy
Mid Maine Medical Center
30 Chase Avenue
Waterville, ME 04901–4624
(207) 872–4269
Fax: (207) 872–4034

8062

Business Information: Mid Maine Medical Center is a full service medical facility serving Waterville, Maine and surrounding areas. As Director of Physical Therapy, Mr. Hadley oversees all administrative functions of the department and is responsible for staff scheduling, patient care, and program development. **Career Steps:** Director of Physical Therapy, Mid Maine Medical Center (1995–Present); Therapy Manager, Allied Therapy Services (1994–1995); Clinical Director, Sportsmed (1993–1994). **Associations & Accomplishments:** Council for Professions Allied to Medicine; South African Physiotherapy Asssociation; Chartered Society of Physiotherapists; Sierra Club; Natural Resources Defense Council; Environmental Defense Fund; U.S. Triathlon Federation. **Education:** University of Cape Town, B.Sc. (PT) (1989); University of Pretoria, BMedSci. (1985). **Personal:** Married to Deborah in 1992. Mr. Hadley enjoys being an active triathlete and designing educational software.

Dr. Hassan R. Hakim

Consultant Psychiatrist
Royal Victoria Hospital
49 City View Circle
Barrie, Ontario L4N 7V1
(705) 728–9090 Ext. 4143
Fax: (705) 739–5631

8062

Business Information: Royal Victoria Hospital is a 300–bed full–service regional healthcare facility dedicated to the care and welfare of its patients. As Consultant Psychiatrist, Dr. Hakim sees patients referred from other staff doctors, to evaluate their mental and emotional levels. He also provides an inpatient service for selected patients. **Career Steps:** Consultant / Psychiatrist, Royal Victoria Hospital (1995–Present); Consultant /Psychiatrist, Prince Albert Health Board – Canada (1990–1995); Consultant / Psychiatrist, University of Sains Malaysia (1988–1990); Consultant / Psychiatrist, Monorog Clinic (1987–1988). **Associations & Accomplishments:** Fellow, Royal College of Physicians and Surgeons of Canada; Royal College of Psychiatrists of United Kingdom; Canadian Psychiatric Association; Canadian Medical Association. **Education:** University of Saskatchewan: MRC in Psychiatry (1987), FXCPC (1993); United Kingdom, D.T.M.H.; National University – Ireland, D.C.H.; Royal College of Physicians and Surgeons of Ireland, D.P.M. **Personal:** Married to Salma in

1982. Three children: Shaheed, Hasif, and Aniq. Dr. Hakim enjoys fishing, collecting coins, and travel.

Sandra M. Haley, R.R.A.
Director of Medical Records
Tri–City Community Hospital
P.O. Box 189
Jourdanton, TX 78026
(210) 769–3515 Ext.258
Fax: (210) 769–2322

8062

Business Information: Tri–City Community Hospital serves the medical needs of the approximately 32,000 residents of Jourdanton, Pleasonton, and Patello, Texas. Comprised of 30 inpatient beds and a busy outpatient surgery department and emergency room, the Hospital is currently in the process of implementing managed care and expanding its outpatient surgery services. As Director of Medical Records, Ms. Haley oversees health information, quality assurance, and risk management. Additional duties include finance, accounting, budgetary concerns, strategic planning, and public relations. **Career Steps:** Director of Medical Records, Tri–City Community Hospital (1995–Present); Record Management Officer, County of Atascosa (1991–1995). **Associations & Accomplishments:** American Health Information Management Association (AHIMA); Quality Management Section; Texas Health Information Management Association. **Education:** Incarnate Word College, B.S. (1979). **Personal:** Married to David in 1976. Two children: John David and Ashley. Ms. Haley enjoys riding and showing Arabian horses, counted cross–stitch, and quilting.

Mrs. Kathy J. Hall
Director of Home Health Care and Senior Services
Harrisburg Medical Center, Inc.
17 Country Club Court, P.O. Box 428
Harrisburg, IL 62946
(618) 253–7671 Ext. 489
Fax: (618) 252–0893

8062

Business Information: Harrisburg Medical Center, Inc. is a full–service, multi–specialty medical facility and health service establishment. Located in a rural community, the Hospital offers inpatient psychiatric services and a home health care unit. Established in 1985, Harrisburg Medical Center, Inc. currently employs 60 medical support staff. As Director, Home Health Care and Senior Services, Mrs. Hall is responsible for all aspects of supervision and operations for the home health care services. **Career Steps:** Harrisburg Medical Center, Inc.: Director, Home Health Care and Senior Services (1990–Present), Quality Assurance Specialist (1988–1990); Operating Room and Emergency Room Supervisor, Ferrell Hospital (1981–1988). **Associations & Accomplishments:** American Nurses Association; Illinois Nurses Association; Board Member, Egyptian Area Agency on Aging. **Education:** Bellamire College, M.S.N. (1995); University of Evansville, B.S.N. (1984); Frontier College, A.D.N. (1981); Southeastern Illinois College, L.P.N. (1979). **Personal:** Married to Bert in 1984. Two children: Kailey and Kara. Mrs. Hall enjoys collecting antiques.

Martha A. Hang, R.N.

Vice President for Nursing and Patient Services
St. Elizabeth Medical Center
601 Edwin C. Moses Boulevard
Dayton, OH 45408
(513) 229–6249
Fax: (513) 229–7093

8062

Business Information: St. Elizabeth Medical Center, an affiliate member of the Franciscan Health System of Dayton, Inc., is a 600–bed tertiary hospital. A Certified Nurse Administrator with 20 years expertise, Ms. Hang serves as Vice President for Nursing and Patient Services. She has full executive charge over all nursing care for the hospital and two assisted living facilities and nursing homes, ensuring quality delivered patient care services, as well as budgetary controls. She also serves on several affiliated physician and hospital boards, and is a member of the Hospital's Board of Directors. **Career Steps:** Vice President for Nursing and Patient Services, St. Elizabeth Medical Center (1994–Present); Director of Nursing and Women's Newborn Health, Brigham & Women's Hospital – Boston, MA (1990–1994); Assistant Vice President of Nursing, Elizabeth Blackwell Hospital – Ohio State University's Primary Teaching Facility (1987–1990); Director of Nursing, Borgess Medical Center – Kalamazoo, MI (1975–1987). **Associations & Accomplishments:** American Organization of Nurse Executives; Ohio Organization of Nurse Executives; Dayton Organization of Nurse Executives; Leadership

Dayton; The Commonwealth of Massachusetts Executive Office of Health and Human Services – Department of Public Health: Provides community pro bono care and serves on the Perinatal Advisory Committee; Book review in American Journal of Nursing. **Education:** Western Michigan University, Master's in Public Administration (1983); Nazareth College, Kalamazoo, MI, B.A.; Mercy Hospital School of Nursing, Oklahoma City, OK, Diploma; Certified Nurse Administrator, Recertified (1990 & 1995) – American Nurses Association; Wayne State University College of Nursing– Detroit, MI, Post Graduate Studies in Nursing Administration. **Personal:** Married to Paul in 1966. Two children: Michael C. and Anne E. Mrs. Hang enjoys cooking, reading, and Home Interior Decorating.

Wedad M. Hanna, F.R.C.P.(C)

Pathologist in Chief, Department of Pathology
Women's College Hospital
76 Grenville Street, Department of Pathology
Toronto, Ontario M5S 1B2
(416) 323–6142
Fax: (416) 323–6116

8062

Business Information: Women's College Hospital is a full–service medical/teaching facility. Affiliated with Women's College, the Hospital is located in Toronto, Canada. As Chief Pathologist, Dr. Hanna is responsible for the day–to–day learning activities of the diagnostic, academic, research and publication departments. A skilled electron microscopist in skin disease and breast cancer, Dr. Hana studied in Egypt and has had 65 articles and 150 abstracts published in various journals, including "Modern Pathology", and the "American Journal of Clinical Pathology." **Career Steps:** Women's College Hospital: Chief Pathologist (1993–Present), Staff Pathologist (1977–1993); Associate Professor, University of Toronto (1987–Present). **Associations & Accomplishments:** Chair of the Medical Advisory Committee of the Canadian Far East; Board of Directors,Cancer Foundation; Senior Counselor, Youth Group of St. Mark Orthodox Church. **Education:** Fellow of the Royal College of Physicians and Surgeons of Canada, F.R.C.P (c) (1976); American Board of Pathology (1976). **Personal:** Married to Dr. A.K. Hanna in 1968. Three children: Dr. Sarah Hanna M.D., Mark, and Andrew. Dr. Hanna enjoys reading, gardening, and tennis.

Walid A. Harb, M.D.
Physician
Grace Hospital
27209 Lahser Road #220
Southfield, MI 48034–8403
(810) 353–9860
Fax: (810) 353–6896

8062

Business Information: Grace Hospital, affiliated with Wayne State University School of Medicine, is a full–service, tertiary care research and teaching hospital. A practicing physician since 1986, Dr. Harb is responsible for the direction of the Cardiac Observation and Intermediate Critical Care Units, as well as providing quality medical care to patients suffering from heart problems. He also conducts medical research, instructs medical students, and serves as Coordinator for third year medical students at Wayne State University. **Career Steps:** Grace Hospital: Director of Cardiac Observation Unit (1994–Present), Coordinator of Year III Students – Wayne State University (1994–Present); Director of Intermediate Critical Care Unit (1991–Present), Director of Externship Program (1989–1995), Assistant Director of Intermediate Critical Care Unit (1989–1991); Clinical Assistant Professor of Medicine, Wayne State University (1992–Present); Medical Director of Physician Assistant Training Program, University of Detroit Mercy (1991–Present). **Associations & Accomplishments:** Diplomate, American Board of Internal Medicine – National Board of Examiners, Parts I, II, and III; Licensure, State of Michigan; American College of Physicians; Phi Beta Kappa; Phi Beta Pi; Golden Key National Honor Society; Frequent lecturer and publisher, presenting papers on his research at numerous local and national medical associations and educational institutional symposia and conference proceedings. **Education:** Wayne State University School of Medicine, M.D. (1986); Wayne State University, B.S. (1982); Wayne State University Affiliated Hospitals: Internship in Internal Medicine (1986–1987), Residency in Internal Medicine (1987–1989). **Personal:** Married. Three children. Dr. Harb enjoys tennis and spending time with his children.

Annabeth Hargadine
Executive Assistant
Pershing Memorial Hospital
P.O. Box 408
Brookfield, MO 64628–0408
(816) 258–2222
Fax: Please mail or call

8062

Business Information: Pershing Memorial Hospital, established in 1960, is a 57 bed acute care facility comprised of a rural health clinic, a physicians clinic, in addition to a long term care facility. As Executive Assistant, Ms. Hargadine is responsible for physician recruiting, physician credentialing, coordinating the Out Patient Clinic schedule, and serves as the council recorder. **Career Steps:** Pershing Memorial Hospital: Executive Assistant (1991–Present), Secretary to Director of Human Resources (1989–1990); Secretary to Director of Nurses, St. Frances Hospital (1988–1989). **Associations & Accomplishments:** Beta Sigma Phi; 4–H Club. **Education:** Meadville High School (1955). **Personal:** Married to Robert E. in 1955. Three children: Jim Edwin, Richard Craig, and Loren Dale. Ms. Hargadine enjoys oil painting, travel, and spending time with her grandchildren.

Lance A. Hassell
Administrator
Clearfield Nursing Center
1450 South 1500 East
Clearfield, UT 84015–1633
(801) 779–7700
Fax: (801) 776–2908

8062

Business Information: Clearfield Nursing Center is a rehabilitation center comprised of 112 beds and a staff of 116. Established in 1990, the Center has an estimated annual revenue of $6 million, and is responsible for providing rehabilitative services to clients. As Administrator, Mr. Hassell oversees all aspects of his department, and is responsible for cash flow, patient care, staffing and budget. **Career Steps:** Clearfield Nursing Center: Administrator (1992–Present), Supervisor of CNA's (1991–1992); Owner, Lance Hassell, Inc. (1990–1992); Lead Supervisor, Levelor Blind Company. **Associations & Accomplishments:** Utah Health Care Association; Education Committee for the Utah Health Care Association; Clearfield Chamber of Commerce; Who's Who. **Education:** Weber State University, B.S. (1993). **Personal:** Mr. Hassell enjoys water skiing, raquetball, and stock options.

Carol A. Haumont, RN
Director of Nursing and Long–Term Care
Jennie M. Melham Medical Center
145 Memorial Drive
Broken Bow, NE 68822
(308) 872–5349
Fax: Please mail or call

8062

Business Information: Jennie M. Melham Medical Center provides care in the areas of Acute, Long–Term, Home Health and cardiac rehabilitation. In her current capacity, Ms. Haumont is responsible for management of the nursing staff and Residents of the 77–bed Long–Term Care Unit. **Career Steps:** Jennie M. Melham Medical Center: Director of Nursing (1989–Present), Assistant Director of Nursing (1985–1989), Surgery Staff (1973–1985). **Associations & Accomplishments:** Participate in NHCA through facility membership. **Education:** Mary Lanning School of Nursing, Diploma (1973). **Personal:** Two children: Clancie and Simon. Ms. Haumont enjoys church activities, being a 4–H leader, and activities with her children. She is also an active rancher.

Rosemary J. Havey, D.O.
Chief of Psychiatry
Detroit Riverview Hospital
7733 East Jefferson Avenue
Detroit, MI 48214–3707
(313) 866–2435
Fax: (313) 866–2445

8062

Business Information: Detroit Riverview Hospital is a full–service healthcare institution specializing in the diagnosis, treatment, and rehabilitation of patients. As Chief of Psychiatry, Dr. Havey is responsible for all aspects of Psychiatric operations and administration, including inpatients. **Career Steps:** Chief of Psychiatry, Detroit Riverview Hospital (1992–Present); Chief of Psychiatry, Detroit Osteopathic Hospital (1984–1992). **Associations & Accomplishments:** American Osteopathic Association; Michigan Association of

Osteopathic Physicians and Surgeons; Wayne County Osteopathic Association; Michigan Psychiatric Society. **Education:** Michigan State University College of Osteopathic Medicine, D.O. (1974); Sienna Heights College, Adrian, MI: B.S., M.S. **Personal:** Dr. Havey enjoys jigsaw puzzles, boating, and reading.

Etta Hawkins–Hodge
Director of Surgical Services
St. Joseph's Hospital
1919 LaBranch
Houston, TX 77002
(713) 757–7574
Fax: Please mail or call

8062

Business Information: St. Joseph's Hospital is a full–service, acute care hospital. A member of the St. Joseph team for over 14 years, Mrs. Etta Hawkins–Hodge was appointed Director of Surgical Services in February of 1995. In this capacity, she is responsible for five Cost Centers: OR, PACU, DSU, Anesthesia, and Endoscopy. **Career Steps:** St. Joseph's Hospital: Director of Surgical Services (1995–Present), Associate Director of Operating Room (1991–1995), Nurse Manager (1989–1991), Staff Nurse (1982–1989). **Associations & Accomplishments:** Association of Operating Room Nurses; Management Specialty Assembly. **Education:** Attending: Our Lady of the Lake University, MHA program; Texas Woman's University, B.S. in Nursing (1977). **Personal:** Married to Ralph Eugene in 1981. Two children: Jarvas Dionn and April Latrice. Mrs. Hawkins–Hodge enjoys singing and ministering God's word to others. Contributes her success to God and her parental upbringing.

Edward G. Helm, M.D.
Assistant Dean and Associate Professor of Clinical Surgery
Louisiana State University Medical Center
1542 Tulane Avenue
New Orleans, LA 70112–2825
(504) 568–4779
Fax: (504) 568–4633

8062

Business Information: Louisiana State University Medical Center is a full tertiary care, research and medical teaching hospital, operating in affiliation with Louisiana State University for the training of medical interns and residents. A practicing physician since 1976 and Board–certified in Laparoendoscopic Surgery, Dr. Helm serves as Head of LSUMC's Surgical Endoscopy Section, providing all aspects of administration, as well as surgical practices involving general, vascular and laparoendoscopic procedures. Concurrent with his medical practice, he also serves as an Associate Professor of Clinical Surgery and Assistant Dean with the Louisiana State University School of Medicine. He has the added distinction of being the first Black appointed to a teaching position at LSU. **Career Steps:** Louisiana State University Medical Center: Assistant Dean (1987–Present), Associate Professor of Clinical Surgery (1992–Present), Head Section of Surgical Endoscopy (1990–Present). **Associations & Accomplishments:** Fellow, American Board of Surgery; American Association of Medical Colleges; Society of Laparoendoscopic Surgeons; Society for Surgery of Alimentary Tract. **Education:** Chicago Medical School, M.D. (1976). **Personal:** Married to Jacqueline. Four children: Alesha, Lisa, Eric, and Laura. Dr. Helm enjoys reading, sailing, and sports.

Wilfrid Herard, M.D.
• • • ━━◖◉◗━━ • • •

Chief of Pulmonary Medicine
St. Mary's Hospital
622 Ocean Avenue
Brooklyn, NY 11226
(718) 221–3282
Fax: (718) 693–3724

8062

Business Information: Established in 1993, St. Mary's Hospital is a full–service, multi–specialty medical facility and health service establishment. As Chief of Pulmonary Medicine, Dr. Herard is responsible for the care and treatment of patients, as well as clinical instruction. Concurrent to his position with the hospital, Dr. Herard also has his own private practice, and is an Assistant Professor of Medicine at the Downstate Medical Center. **Career Steps:** Chief of Pulmonary Medicine, St. Mary's Hospital (1992–Present); Attending Physician, Woodhill Hospital (1991–1992). **Associations & Accomplishments:** American Medical Association; American Academy of Chest Physicians; New York State Society of Internal Medicine. **Education:** Universidad Veracruzana, M.D. (1983). **Personal:** Dr. Herard enjoys watching sports on television.

Linda Hercher
Director of Medical Records
Tillamook County General Hospital
1000 3rd Street
Tillamook, OR 97141
(503) 842–5729
Fax: Please mail or call

8062

Business Information: Tillamook County General Hospital is an acute care health facility specializing in the diagnosis, treatment, and rehabilitation of patients. As Director of Medical Records, Ms. Hercher is responsible for acute care medical records and medical transcription. Her daily duties include coding, financial reporting, DRG optimization, budgets, quality review, and various other related activities. **Career Steps:** Director of Medical Records, Tillamook County General Hospital (1977–Present); New Accounts Representative, First Interstate Bank (1972–1977); Assistant Medical Records Manager, Good Samaritan Hospital (1970–1972). **Associations & Accomplishments:** American Health Information Management Association; Oregon Health Information Management Association; Sacred Heart Church – Pastoral Council Secretary. **Education:** AHIMA, Accredited Record Technician (1972). **Personal:** Two children: Jeff and John. Ms. Hercher enjoys music and choir singing.

Christopher M. Hicks, M.D.
Urologist
Bedford County Memorial Hospital
1700B Whitfield Drive
Bedford, VA 24523
(540) 586–6472
Fax: (540) 586–9751

8062

Business Information: Bedford County Memorial Hospital is a full–service acute care hospital located in Bedford, Virginia. As Urology Physician, Dr. Hicks treats patients with urinary tract diseases, kidney ailments, and bladder problems. Concurrently, Dr. Hicks serves as President of Medical Staff for the hospital. He oversees labor problems, scheduling, and recruiting new physicians. **Career Steps:** Urology Physician, Bedford County Memorial Hospital (1990–Present). **Associations & Accomplishments:** American Urology Association; American College of Surgeons; American Medical Association. **Education:** Urology Residency, Walter Reed Army Medical Center (1988); Surgery Internship, Madigan Army Medical Center (1982); Medical College of Virginia, M.D. (1981); Virginia Commonwealth University, B.S. (1976). **Personal:** Married to Susan. Two children: Sarah and David. Dr. Hicks enjoys diving and snow skiing.

Shalom Z. Hirschman, M.D.
• • • ━━◖◉◗━━ • • •

Director of the Division of Infectious Diseases
Mount Sinai Medical Center
1 Gustave Levy Place Box 1090
New York, NY 10029–6504
(212) 241–6741
Fax: (212) 534–3240

8062

Business Information: The Mount Sinai Medical Center, affiliated with Mount Sinai School of Medicine, is a full–service, tertiary care medical facility, providing diagnosis and treatment to patients, education to medical students, and conducting medical research. The School of Medicine is one of the oldest medical schools in the U.S., being the first to discover the Lupus disease, as well as the first to establish a Department of Neurology in the U.S. A practicing physician since 1961 and Board–Certified in Internal Medicine and Clinical Pharmacology, Dr. Hirschman joined The Mount Sinai Hospital in 1971. Serving as Director of the Division of Infectious Diseases, he is responsible for the direction of all Division activities, in addition to his private practice and research activities. Concurrent with his private practice, he serves as Professor of Medicine at The Mount Sinai School of Medicine. Career milestones include founding the DNA that makes up Hepatitis B in 1971. Future plans include continuing to develop the Division of Infectious Diseases and to meet the challenging changes in medicine. **Career Steps:** Director of the Division of Infectious Diseases, The Mount Sinai Hospital (1971–Present); Professor of Medicine, The Mount Sinai School of Medicine (1971–Present); Investigator, National Institutes of Health (1963–1969); Senior Surgeon, United States Public Health Service (1963–1969). **Associations & Accomplishments:** Diplomate, American Board of Internal Medicine, No. 26985 (1968); Alpha Omega Alpha; American Society for Microbiology; Biophysical Society; American Association for the Advancement of Science; American College of Physicians; New York Academy of Sciences: Microbiology Section, Former Vice Chairman, Former Chairman; American Society for the Study of Liver Diseases; American Society for Clinical Investigation; Society for Experimental Biology and Medicine; American Federation for Clinical Research; Association of

American Physicians; The Harvey Society; Fellow, American College of Physicians; Fellow, Infectious Diseases Society of America; Fellow, Royal Society of Tropical Medicine and Hygiene; Fellow, American College of Clinical Pharmacology; Special NIH Fellowship Award (1964); American Men and Women of Science; American Medical Specialists; Who's Who in the East; International Dictionary of Biography; Men of Achievement; Notable Americans of the Bicentennial Era; Community Leaders and Noteworthy Americans; Who's Who In Health Care; Who's Who In America; Who's Who In Society; Who's Who In the World; Who's Who Registry, Platinum Edition; National Advisory Board in Microbiology, American Cancer Society; Society New York Academy of Medicine: Task Force on Tuberculosis, Task Force on Cytokines and Monoclonal Antibodies, Committee on Infectious Diseases; Committee on Therapy with Biologicals; Touro College, New York: Founder, Board of Trustees, Chairman of Academic and Budget Committee; Touro School of Law: Founder, Chairman of Academic Committee; RESEARCH: Infectious Diseases – Chemotherapy; Sexually Transmitted Diseases; Pathogenesis of Infectious Hepatitides; Biochemistry of Hepatitis B Virus; Molecular Biology and Pharmacology of Antimicrobial Agents; Biophysical Studies on Murine Sarcoma and Leukemia Viruses; Molecular Biology of AIDS Virus. **Education:** Albert Einstein College of Medicine, M.D. Summa Cum Laude (1961); Albert Einstein College of Medicine Graduate School of Biochemistry (1958–1960); Yeshiva University, A.B. Summa Cum Laude (1957); Massachusetts General Hospital, Harvard Medical School: Intern in Internal Medicine (1961–1962), First Year Resident Internal Medicine (1962–1963); National Institute Arthritis and Metabole Dis., Lab Molecular Biology, Associate (1963–1965); National Institute Health Graduate School, Ph.D. equivalent (1963–1966); Columbia–Presbyterian Medical Center, Columbia University College of Physicians and Surgeons, NIH Fellow (1966–1967). **Personal:** Married to Fran E. in 1995. Four children: Orin, Raquel, Doritte, and Benjamin. Dr. Hirschman enjoys music and gardening.

Deborah J. Hoadley, M.D., M.P.H., T.M.
Director
Tulane University Travel and Tropical Medicine Clinic
1430 Tulane Avenue
New Orleans, LA 70112
(504) 587–7316
Fax: (504) 584–3644

8062

Business Information: Tulane University Hospital and Clinic, affiliated with Tulane University, is a full tertiary care, research and teaching hospital. A practicing physician since 1983 and Board Certified in Internal Medicine and Infectious Diseases, Dr. Hoadley completed her Masters degree in Public Health and Tropical Medicine at Tulane in 1989, during which time she also served as Chief Resident of Preventive Medicine while completing her fellowship in Infectious Diseases. Appointed as Director of the Tulane University Travel and Tropical Medicine Clinic in 1992, she is responsible for providing specialized clinical care for patients suffering from tropical diseases, as well as supervising the Primary Care physicians who provide pre–travel care to patients who require vaccinations and malaria prophylaxis. Concurrent with her medical practice, she serves as clinical faculty at the Tulane School of Medicine and the Louisiana State University School of Medicine, and is adjunct faculty at the Tulane School of Public Health and Tropical Medicine. She also serves as the Louisiana State Coordinator for Medicine for the federally–funded Delta Region AIDS Education and Training Center. **Career Steps:** Director, Tulane University Travel and Tropical Medicine Clinic (1992–Present); State Coordinator for Medicine, Delta Region AIDS Education and Training Center (1990–Present); Assistant Professor of Clinical Medicine, Tulane University Medical School (1990–Present); Adjunct Assistant Professor of Medicine, Louisiana State University Medical School (1990–Present); Adjunct Assistant Professor of Community Medicine, Tulane University Medical School (1990–Present); Adjunct Assistant Professor of Tropical Medicine, Tulane School of Public Health and Tropical Medicine (1990–Present); Medical Coordinator for Rwanda Airlift Project, Air Care International (1994); Principal Investigator, Health care for the Homeless Program AIDS Risk Behaviors Project (1990–Present); Medical Officer, Ethiopian Border Refugee Camp, Sudan (1986–1987); Outpatient Medical Officer, Phanatnikom Refugee Camp, Thailand (1984–1985); Medical Officer, Albert Schweitzer Hospital, Haiti (1984); Volunteer physician, Chinle Indian Health Services Hospital and Clinic, Arizona (1984); Internal Medicine Residency Program, Dartmouth Hitchcock Medical Center, New Hampshire (1980–1983). **Associations & Accomplishments:** American College of Physicians (1983–Present); American Society of Tropical Medicine and Hygiene (1989–Present); Fellow, Royal Society of Tropical Medicine and Hygiene (1990–Present); National Council for International Health (1983–Present); International Association for Physicians in AIDS Care (1992–Present); International AIDS Society (1993–Present); American Association for Public Health (1989–Present); Women's International Public Health Network (1994–Present); Society for Healthcare Epidemiology of America (SHEA) (1994–Present); Phi Beta Kappa, Smith College Chapter (1974); Sigma Xi Research Society of North America, Smith

College Chapter (1974); Rufus Choate Scholar, Dartmouth College (1974, exchange student); Committee Activities: Delta Region AIDS Education and Training Center Annual Update Planning Committee, Louisiana Community AIDS Research Program Steering Committee; American Committee on Clinical Tropical Medicine and Traveler's Health; NIH/NIAID/Division of AIDS Peer Review Committee for the Women's HIV Interagency Study; Lecturer on local, state, national and international level on AIDS and Tropical Medicine Topics. **Education:** Tulane School of Public Health and Tropical Medicine, New Orleans, LA: M.P.H. and T.M. (1989); McGill University, Faculty of Medicine, Montreal, Canada: M.D., C.M. (1980); Smith College, Northampton, MA: A.B. in Biochemistry, A.B. in Music, Summa Cum Laude (1975); POSTGRADUATE TRAINING IN MEDICINE: Dartmouth–Hitchcock Medical Center, New Hampshire: Internal Medicine Residency Program (1980–1983); Tulane University School of Medicine and School of Public Health and Tropical Medicine: Infectious Diseases Fellowship (1987–1990), Preventive Medicine Residency (1988–1990), Chief Resident of Preventive Medicine (1989–1990), Masters of Public Health and Tropical Medicine (1988–1990). **Personal:** Dr. Hoadley enjoys musical composition, photography, skiing, and hiking.

Mary Lou Hoagland

Deputy Administrator – Integrated Delivery System

Rehoboth McKinley Christian Hospital

1900 Red Rock Drive
Gallup, NM 87301
(505) 863–7200
Fax: Please mail or call

8062

Business Information: Rehoboth McKinley Christian Integrated Delivery System is a medical–surgical clinic, family practice clinic, and acute care hospital. As Deputy Administrator of the Medical–Surgical Clinic, Ms. Hoagland performs a variety of functions, including systems analysis, consolidation of services, human relations, and conflict resolution. **Career Steps:** Deputy Administrator, Rehoboth McKinley Christian Integrated Delivery System at Red Rock (1996–Present); Bethany Village, HHDS, NY: Vice President of Community Services (1995–1996), Vice President of Administration (1994–1995); Employee Assistant Program Specialist, SCT BOCES, HHD, NY (1990–1994). **Associations & Accomplishments:** Pi Alpha Alpha National Honorary Society for Public Affairs and Administration; National Association of Homes and Services for the Aged; N.A.S.W. **Education:** Marywood College: M.P.A. (1992), C.S.W.; Elmira College: M.S in Education, B.S. in Education with Psychology Concentration. **Personal:** Ms. Hoagland enjoys athletics, vocal groups, community theatre, and supporting the local art society.

Vickie A. Hobgood

Director of Rehabilitative Services

Community Methodist Hospital

1305 North Elm Street
Henderson, KY 42420–2783
(502) 827–7593
Fax: (502) 827–7358

8062

Business Information: Community Methodist Hospital is a 197–bed, acute care hospital providing quality care to patients, as well as providing instruction to students in numerous health care areas. Community Methodist Hospital currently employs 900 people. Joining the Hospital as a staff physical therapist in 1982, Ms. Hobgood was appointed as Director of Rehabilitative Services in 1985. She is responsible for the overall rehabilitative operations and supervision of a staff of 23 physical and occupational therapists, and speech pathologists. **Career Steps:** Community Methodist Hospital: Director of Rehabilitative Services (1985–Present), Staff Physical Therapist (1982–1985). **Associations & Accomplishments:** American Physical Therapy Association; Co–Teacher of College and Careers Sunday School Class, Hyland Baptist Church. **Education:** West Virginia University, B.S. in Physical Therapy (1982), B.A. in Psychology (1980). **Personal:** Married to Randy in 1985. Two children: Brian and Moriah. Ms. Hobgood enjoys photography and camping.

Deborah Hopper

Manager, Physician Practice Aquisition/Practice Management

St. Anthony's Medical Center

12700 South Fork Road, Suite 225
St. Louis, MO 63128
(314) 525–4930
Fax: (314) 525–4929

8062

Business Information: St. Anthony's Medical Center is a full service 972–bed tertiary medical center. St. Louis' second largest medical facility, it is reknowned for its Level II Trauma Center. A physician care management executive with ten years expertise, Deborah Hopper was selected by St. Anthony's management team to serve as Manager of its Physician Practice Aquisition/Practice Management unit in November of 1994. She provides the overall management and oversight of all administrative operations, as well as physician recruitment strategies. **Career Steps:** Manager–Physician Practice Aquisition/Practice Management, St. Anthony's Medical Center (1994–Present); Manager–Physician Services, St. John's Mercy Medical Center (1991–1994); Manager – Physician Practice Management, Barnes Hospital (1989–1991). **Associations & Accomplishments:** Medical Group Management Association; Hospital Financial Management Association; ACHE; St. Louis Healthcare Executives; Clinic Managers of Metropolitan St. Louis; Auxiliary of St. Anthony's Medical Center; AHA; Church Healthcare Committee. **Education:** Washington University: M.H.A. (1988), B.A. in Biology (1986). **Personal:** Married to Mark in 1992. Ms. Hopper enjoys golf, step aerobics, art history, music, and theater.

Iffath Abbasi Hoskins, M.D.

Chief of Obstetrics

Bellevue Hospital Center

550 1st Avenue, Room 9, North 28
New York, NY 10016–6481
(212) 263–8122
Fax: (212) 263–8887
EMail: See Below

8062

Business Information: Bellevue Hospital Center is the largest flagship hospital of the Health and Hospital Corporation. This healthcare institution, an arm of New York University Medical Center, is a general care hospital as well as a teaching institute for NYU students. As Chief of Obstetrics, Dr. Hoskins runs all obstetric services, including administrative duties (protocols and policies), clinical duties (managing patients), and research. She is a specialist in high risk Obstetrics and directs the Perinatal Diagnostic Unit. Additionally, she is an Associate Professor at New York University where she teaches residents, medical students, and nurses. Internet users can reach her via: IAHoskins@aol.com. **Career Steps:** Bellevue Hospital Center: Chief of Obstetrics (1995–Present), Director of Labor & Delivery and Testing Center (1992–Present); Attending High Risk Obstetrician, Naval Hospital Bethesda (1985–1987). **Associations & Accomplishments:** Fellow, American College of OB/GYN; Fellow, American College of Surgeons; Society for Perinatal Obstetricians; Society for Gynecologic Investigation; US Navy Rescue: Captain, Reserve Policy Board, Executive Committee Medical Staff. **Education:** Dow Medical College – Karachi, Pakistan, M.D. (1975); Government College for Women – Karachi, Pakistan, Interscience (1967). **Personal:** Married to William John in 1985. Two children: Jamie and Mariya. Dr. Hoskins enjoys reading and music.

Campbell P. Howard, M.D.

Pediatric Endocrinologist and Chief of the Endocrinology Section

Childrens Mercy Hospital

24th and Gillham Road
Kansas City, MO 64108
(816) 234–3070
Fax: (816) 842–0754

8062

Business Information: Affiliated with the University of Missouri, The Children's Mercy Hospital is an acute and critical care Pediatrics research and treatment hospital. Established in 1897, The Children's Mercy Hospital currently employs 1,500 physicians and medical support staff. As Pediatric Endocrinologist and Chief of the Endocrinology Section, Dr. Howard is responsible for the administrative functions within the department and the care and treatment of patients — primarily children with diabetes. Dr. Howard is also responsible for the instruction of medical students and residents, as well as research in the area of diabetes and growth hormones. **Career Steps:** Pediatric Endocrinologist and Chief of the Endocrinology Section, Children's Mercy Hospital (1989–Present); President, Missouri Affiliate, American Diabetes Association (1992–1994); Chairman, University of Missouri at Kansas City Medical School Faculty Council (1990–1992). **Associations & Accomplishments:** Licensed in Minnesota, Missouri, and Kansas; Certified by the American Board of Pediatrics; Certified Diabetes Educator by the American Association of Diabetes Educators; American Academy of Pediatrics; American Medical Association: Section on Medical School (1986–Present); Metropolitan Medical Society of Greater Kansas City/Missouri Medical Association; American Diabetes Association, Heart of America Affiliate: Vice President (1982–1984), President–elect (1984–1985), President (1985–1987), Chairman of the Camp Committee (1982–1985); American Diabetes Association Missouri Affiliate: Board of Directors (1987–Present), Executive Committee (1987–Present); President (1992–1994), Education Committee (1994–Present), Secretary (1988–1990), Vice President (1990–1992), Youth Services Committee Chairman (1987–1989), Chapter Development Committee – Chair (1989–1990); American Diabetes Association – National: Professional Membership (1980–Present), Committee on Youth Services (1985–1988), Education Program Review Panel (1991–Present); Juvenile Diabetes Foundation, Medical Advisory Board of Kansas City Chapter (1984–Present); Human Growth Foundation, Medical Advisor of the Kansas City Chapter (1985–Present); Board of Directors, Human Growth Foundation – National: Member (1986–Present), Vice President (1988–1991), President (1991–1995); International Growth Federation, Executive Committee (1992–1995); American Federation for Clinical Research; Sigma XI Scientific Research Society; Lawson Wilkins Pediatric Endocrine Society; Endocrine Society; Kansas City Roundtable of Endocrinology; American Association of Clinical Endocrinologists; Honors: Who's Who in American Colleges and Universities (1968); History of Medicine Award (1974); Outstanding Contribution to Diabetes and Camping, National American Diabetes Association (1989); Alumni Achievement Award, Simpson College (1992); The Best Doctor's In America (1994); Who's Who in Executives and Professionals (1994); Major National Recognition Service Award, University of Missouri–Kansas City, School of Medicine (1994). **Education:** University of Oklahoma, M.D. (1974); Simpson College – Indianola, IA, B.A. (1969). **Personal:** Married to Anne Marie in 1972. Three children: Bobby, Julie and Mary. Dr. Howard enjoys railroading, reading, and tennis.

Larry E. Howard, D.O.

Staff Emergency Physician

East Texas Medical Center – Pittsburg

414 Quitman Street
Pittsburg, TX 75686–1032
(903) 856–6663
Fax: (903) 856–7825

8062

Business Information: East Texas Medical Center (ETMC) – Pittsburg is a community hospital affiliated with the East Texas Medical Center – Tyler. A practicing physician since 1986, Dr. Howard joined ETMC – Pittsburg as an Emergency Physician in 1993. He provides emergency medical diagnosis and treatment to patients, as well as directs ETMC – Home Health, Theron Grainger Nursing Home, Hughes Springs Volunteer Ambulance Service, and the satellite medical facilities at Daingerfield and Hughes Springs. **Career Steps:** Staff Emergency Physician, East Texas Medical Center (1993–Present); Field Surgeon, U.S. Army Medical Corps (1989–1992); Staff Physician and Medical Director, Rainelle Medical Center – Rainelle, WV (1987–1989); General Medicine Intern, Consortium of Hospitals of the West Virginia School of Osteopathic Medicine (1986–1987). **Associations & Accomplishments:** Association of Emergency Physicians; Council on Cardiopulmonary and Critical Care, American Heart Association; Hughes Springs Volunteer Ambulance Service: Medical Director, Board of Trustees. **Education:** Texas College of Osteopathic Medicine, D.O. (1986); University of Maryland, B.A. (1974); Angelo State University: M.A.T. (1980), B.S. (1979). **Personal:** Married to Debra in 1989. Eight children: Angelina, Matthew, Rebecca, Gail, Aaron, James, Dawn, and Jennifer. Dr. Howard enjoys photography and wood working.

Rolla Hraibeh–Kolf, M.D.

Emergency Physician

Hospital Charles Lemoyne

121 Boul Taschereau
Montreal, Quebec J4V 2H1
(514) 466–5050
Fax: Please mail or call

8062

Business Information: Hospital Charles Lemoyne is a 700–bed, full–service health care institution specializing in the diagnosis, treatment, and rehabilitation of patients. The Hospital is the second largest trauma unit and the second largest emergency hospital in Quebec, housing the largest cardiology unit in Montreal. After finishing her three year residency at the Hospital, Dr. Hraibeh–Kolf is now an Emergency Physician. She supervises emergency room operations and activities. **Career Steps:** Emergency Physician, Hospital Charles Lemoyne (1991–Present). **Associations & Accomplishments:** Association des Medecins Urgentovogue du Canada; Association des Medecins de Langue Francaise. **Education:** Laval University: Surgical Residency, M.D. **Personal:** Married to Olivier in 1993. Two children: Eloise and Elissare. Dr. Hraibeh–Kolf enjoys private piloting, scuba diving, piano playing, historical ship model building, and astronomy.

Joseph M. Hughes

Director of Engineering
Altoona Hospital
620 Howard Avenue
Altoona, PA 16601
(814) 946–2254
Fax: (814) 946–7783

8062

Business Information: Altoona Hospital is a full–service acute care hospital with 350 beds offering such advanced techniques and procedures as a complete heart surgery program and renal dialysis. As Director of Engineering, Mr. Hughes is responsible for facility management, plant operations, construction, supervising 30 people, handling computerized P.M. systems, and managing inspection agencies. **Career Steps:** Director of Engineering, Altoona Hospital (1968–Present); Construction Electrician, Krater Electric – Neff Electic (1961–1968). **Associations & Accomplishments:** American Society of Hospital Engineers; NFPA. **Education:** Master Electrician, NRI Graduate (1972). **Personal:** Married to Patti in 1964. One child: Lori Ann. Mr. Hughes enjoys golf, bowling, fishing, and teaching.

Lt. Cheryl L. Hunt, USN

Division Officer
United States Naval Hospital at Groton, Connecticut
P.O. Box 600
Groton, CT 06349–0600
(860) 449–4846
Fax: (860) 464–1255
EMAIL: See Below

8062

Business Information: The United States Naval Hospital at Groton, Connecticut, provides medical services to active and retired military personnel and dependants. Lt. Hunt joined the Hospital as Division Officer in August of 1995 after serving at the Naval Hospital in Charleston, South Carolina. Her present responsibilities include supervision of the Intensive Care Unit, budget oversight, inventory control, and personnel evaluations and counseling. Internet users may reach her via: CHUNT99@AOL.COM **Career Steps:** Division Officer, United States Naval Hospital – Groton, Connecticut (1995–Present); Naval Hospital – Charleston, SC: Assistant Division Officer (1994–1995), Staff Nurse (1991–1994). **Associations & Accomplishments:** Assistant to the Vice President, Connecticut Post Anesthesia Nurses Association; National Chapter American Society Post Anesthesia Nurses; American Nurses Association; American Association of Critical Care Nurses; Historical Diving Society U.S.A.; Southeast Connecticut Divers Association; 4–H Links Honor Society. **Education:** Rensselaer Polytechnic Institute, Completing M.S. in Management; Immaculata College, B.S.N.; Brandywine Hospital School of Nursing, Diploma. **Personal:** Married to David in 1993. Lt Hunt enjoys scuba diving, skiing, photography (terrestrial and underwater), and learning.

Dr. Richard H. Hunt

Professor
McMaster University Medical Center
Room 4W8A 1200 Main Street West
Hamilton, Ontario L8N 3Z5
(905) 521–2100 Ext.6404
Fax: (905) 521–5072
EMAIL: See Below

8062

Business Information: Founded in Toronto in 1887 through a bequest from the prominent banker and business leader Senator William McMaster, McMaster University is a full–service university offering undergraduate and graduate programs to 13,000 students among its six Faculties – Business, Engineering, Health Sciences, Humanities, Science, and Social Sciences. Approximately 1,000 faculty members and a support staff of more than 2,000 persons contribute to the teaching activities of the University as well as to the diverse variety of research and scholarly programs which have made McMaster one of the top research institutions in the country. McMaster University has achieved an enviable stature in the world as one of the most highly regarded intellectual centers in Canada, perhaps best known for the establishment in 1967 of a completely new kind of medical school. The school sought to train medical doctors through small–group and problem–based learning, rather than through traditional lectures and memory work, and the success of its graduates has inspired institutions all around the world to adopt the "McMaster model." As Professor, Dr. Hunt instructs courses in medicine and gastroenterology, as well as serves as mentor to graduate students' research and student advisor to undergraduate medical majors. Internet users can reach him via: Hunt@fhsicsu.McMaster.ca. **Career Steps:** McMaster University Medical Center: Professor (1982–Present), Intestinal Disease Research Unit (1982–1985), Division of Gastroenterology (1982–1992); Medical Officer, Royal Navy (1963–1982); **Associations & Accomplishments:** Author of over 350 Scientific Publications; Author/Editor of 8 Books; Produced 15 TV Video Films. **Education:** Edinburgh University: M.B., Ch.B (1966), M.R.C.P. (1972), F.R.C.P. (1981), F.R.C.P.C. (1982), F.A.C.G. (1982); F.R.C.P. (1986); Royal College of Physicians Accreditation, (1977). **Personal:** Married to Marlene in 1969. Two children: Annabelle Louise, and Sophie–Jane Victoria.

Steven L. Hunter, FACHE

President
SSM of Oklahoma
P.O. Box 205
Oklahoma City, OK 73101–0205
(405) 272–7280
Fax: (405) 272–6592

8062

Business Information: SSM of Oklahoma is a health care delivery and hospital management firm. Established in 1898, SSM of Oklahoma reports annual revenue of $220 million and currently employs 2,000 people company–wide. As President, Mr. Hunter provides administrative leadership for a 664–bed tertiary care hospital, a 100–bed orthopedic hospital, an 80–bed rural facility and, through a joint operating agreement, a 200–bed osteopathic hospital. Additional administrative leadership responsibilities include an 80–physician group practice at 15 sites, a spine center and rural dialysis centers. He was instrumental in the development of the Community Care HMO, an HMO joint–owned by four hospitals whose enrollment includes the state of Oklahoma, Medicaid, as well as state employees and numerous other businesses throughout the state. A hospital administrator with nineteen years bottom–line experience and accomplishments as CEO, COO, and Vice President of Corporate Planning and Marketing, Mr. Hunter has demonstrated expertise in interdepartment coordination, monitoring quality of service, medical staff interface, physician and healthcare network development, cost containment and revenue enhancement, and mergers and acquisitions. Additional expertise includes managed care contracting, facilities planning, strategic positioning, and development of competitive products and services, as well as development of continuous quality management systems. **Career Steps:** President, SSM of Oklahoma (1993–Present); President and Chief Executive Officer, St. Mary's Health Center & Villa Marie Skilled Nursing Facility (1990–1993); Chief Operating Officer, Incarnate Word Hospital (1987–1990); St. Elizabeth Medical Center: Vice President/Corporate Planning & Marketing, (1981–1987), Assistant Administrator (1978–1981); Staff and Line Management Positions, Cardinal Glennon Hospital and Christian Northeast (1975–1978). **Associations & Accomplishments:** BOARD OF DIRECTORS: Hospital Casualty Company, Health Systems of Oklahoma, St. Anthony Hospital, Allied Arts, Oklahoma Community Health Care Alliance, Community Care HMO, YMCA of Jefferson City (Chairman, Finance Committee), St. Mary's PHO, Missouri River Home Health and Hospice, Mid–Missouri Medical Foundation, Lincoln University Foundation, Jefferson City Chamber of Commerce, Red Cross of Missouri, Oklahoma City Chamber of Commerce; MEMBER: Blue Cross/Blue Shield Claims Committee, Missouri Hospital Association (By–Laws Committee, Finance Committee), Leadership Jefferson City, Rotary Club of Oklahoma City, Faculty Webster University, St. Louis, Missouri (Human Resource Management); Advisor, University of Oklahoma Health Care; Published in Daily Oklahoma and Modern Health Care. **Education:** St. Louis University, M.H.A. (Hospital Administration); Carle Foundation Hospital School of Medical Technology, ASCP, Registry, conferred (1975); Eastern Illinois University, B.S. in Medical Technology and Chemistry, summa cum laude; Fellowship in American College of Health Care Executives. **Personal:** Married to Bobbi in 1981. Three children: Ryan, Jeff, and Victoria. Mr. Hunter enjoys spending time with his family, boating, target shooting, and weightlifting.

Kristi M. Hymel, RRA

Director of Health Information Management
River Parishes Hospital
500 Rue De Sante
La Place, LA 70068
(504) 651–1545
Fax: (504) 651–6366

8062

Business Information: River Parishes Hospital is an acute care multi–specialty healthcare facility offering many clinical services such as cardiopulmonary, ER, ICU, and outpatient surgery. As Director of Health Information Management, Ms. Matherne is responsible for overseeing medical record coding, transcription, supervising the release of information, analysis, and physician relations. **Career Steps:** Director of Health Information Management, River Parishes Hospital (1996–Present); Director of Health Information Management, Orleans Regional Hospital (1993–1995); Medical Record Specialist, Ochsner Foundation Hospital (1992–1993). **Associations & Accomplishments:** President–Elect, Greater New Orleans Health Information Management Association; Louisiana Health Information Management Association; American Health Information Management Association. **Education:** University of SW Louisiana, B.S. (1992); Currently attending College of St. Francis, Health Administration. **Personal:** Ms. Hymel enjoys softball, bicycling, and bowling.

Genia M. Isaacs

Director of Medical Records
Williamson Appalachian Regional Hospital
260 Hospital Drive
South Williamson, KY 41503
(606) 237–1700
Fax: (606) 237–1701

8062

Business Information: Williamson Appalachian Regional Hospital is one of twelve hospitals in remote areas of the Appalachian Mountains (including West Virginia, Virginia, and Kentucky) that provide healthcare in conjunction with multiple local clinics for those who are unable to pay for services rendered. As Director of Medical Records, Ms. Isaacs is responsible for managing all patient health records, this includes handling physician and legal requests for copies of records, filing of all forms and records, and overseeing all departmental administrative duties. **Career Steps:** Director of Medical Records, Williamson Appalachian Regional Hospital (1995–Present); Health Data Analyst, St. Joseph Hospital (1994–1995); Medical Records Clerk, Charter Ridge Hospital (1994). **Associations & Accomplishments:** American Health Information Management Association; Kentucky Health Information Management Association; Bluegrass Health Information Management Association. **Education:** Eastern Kentucky University, B.S. in Health Information Management (1994).

Angel Isidro Carrion, M.D.

Medical Director
Dr. Pila Hospital
P.O. Box 1910
Ponce, Puerto Rico 00733–1910
(809) 848–6915
Fax: (809) 844–6357

8062

Business Information: Dr. Pila Hospital is a 180–bed community health care facility. As Medical Director (Chief of Staff), Dr. Isidro is responsible for all medical–administrative aspects of daily hospital operations, cooperating with medical personnel to ensure patients receive quality health care. Concurrently, he is a Staff Pathologist at Southern Pathology Services and an Assistant Clinical Professor at the Ponce School of Medicine. **Career Steps:** Dr. Pila Hospital: Medical Director (1993–Present), Lab Director (1990–1993); Assistant Clinical Professor, Ponce School of Medicine (1990–Present); Pathologist, Southern Pathology Services (1990–Present). **Associations & Accomplishments:** American Medical Association – Delegate to Medical School Section; College of American Pathologists; State Board of the College of Physicians; Association of Clinical Scientists; American Association of Blood Banks; Chairman of the Board, Caribbean School; Ponce District President and Board Member, Colegio de Medicos Cirujanos de Puerto Rico. **Education:** Yale University, Pathologist (1989); University of Connecticut, Clinical Pathologist. **Personal:** Married to Nilda J. Vega, M.D. in 1978. Two children: Nilda Marie and Raymond Anthony Isidro. Dr. Isidro Carrion enjoys reading Spanish and English literature, history, computers, photography, art, and spending time with his family.

Abraham (Avi) Israeli, M.D.

Physician/Associate Director
Hadassah Medical Organization
Ein Karam, P.O. Box 12000
Jerusalem, Israel 91–120
972–2–677–6089
Fax: 972–2–642–0219

8062

Business Information: Hadassah Medical Organization is an academic medical center with two hospitals and a community center. One hospital is an 800–bed general tertiary care medical center, while the other is a 300–bed community–oriented hospital specializing in the diagnosis, treatment, and rehabilitation of patients. As Physician/Associate Director, Dr. Israeli is responsible for all aspects of the Medical Center's operations, including administration and patient care. **Career Steps:** Hadassah Medical Organization: Physician/ Associate Director (1987–Present), Hospital Director (1985–1987), Assistant Director General (1983–1985), House Physician (1982–1983). **Associations & Accomplishments:** Israel Medical Association; Israel Society of Internal Medicine; Israel Atherosclerosis Society; Association of Hospital Directors in Israel; American College of Physician Executives; International Society of Technology Assessment in Health Care; European Society for Medical Decision Making; International Society of Quality Assurance in Health Care; American College of Healthcare Executives, elected to Associate status; The Israel Society for Quality Healthcare; Scientific and Organizing Committee, International Geriatrics Conference on "Aging in the Mediterranean and the Middle East," Tel Aviv, Israel (1996); Various academic and administrative appointments; Prizes for Excellence in Studies, Medical School – Faculty Prize (1975 and 1976); Dr. Louis H. and Ada Landman Memorial Scholarship (1976); William, Rebecca, and John Lefkowitz Scholarship (1977); Prize in memory of fallen alumni (1977); Molcho Prize, Best thesis of the year (1983); Dean's List for Excellence in Teaching (1994). **Education:** Hebrew University – Hadassah School of Public Health, M.D. (1982); Massachusetts Institute of Technology, Master's degree (1990–1991); Israel License (1982); Foreign Education Certificate (1979); Board Certification as Specialist in Internal Medicine (1987); Board Certification as Specialist in Health Care Management (1992); American Board of Medical Management (1995). **Personal:** Married to Nurit in 1980. Three children: Ayelet, Naama, and Yonathan. Dr. Israeli enjoys chess and hiking.

Rajiv Jain, M.D., F.A.C.P.

Chief of Staff
Veterans Administration Medical Center
Salem, VA 24153
(540) 982–2463
Fax: Please mail or call

8062

Business Information: The Salem Veterans Medical Center is a 500–bed, tertiary and teaching hospital, providing complete medical, surgical and psychological services for veterans of the United States Armed Forces. Currently, the VA Medical Center employs 1,500 medical support staff. As Chief of Staff, Dr. Jain is responsible for all aspects of clinical services, 14 departments, and the management of the medical staff (over 1,000 employees). Concurrent to his position as Chief of Staff, Dr. Jain is also an Associate Professor of Clinical Medicine and Associate Dean of Academic Affairs for the University of Virginia School of Medicine. **Career Steps:** Veterans Medical Center, Salem: Chief of Staff (1993–Present), Acting ACOS for Ambulatory Care (1993–Present), Associate Chief of Staff, Ambulatory Care (1992–1993), Acting Chief of Medical Services (1992), Chief, Hematology and Oncology Section, Head of the Clinical Oncology Program, and Head of the Oncology Center (1979–1992); Veterans Affairs Medical Center, University of Virginia School of Medicine: Associate Dean for Academic Affairs, (1993–Present), Associate Professor of Clinical Medicine (1985–Present), Assistant Professor of Medicine (1979–1985). **Associations & Accomplishments:** American College of Physicians; Roanoke Academy of Medicine; Virginia Society of Hematology; Fellow, American College of Physicians; Gerontology Futures Board of Virginia; Tissue and Transfusion Committee (1980–1992); Co–Chairman, Tumor Board Conference (1979–1992); Quality Assurance Committee (1980–1985); Chairman, Research and Development Committee (1984–1985); Ethics Committee (1991–1992); Chairman, Quality Improvement Board (1992–1993); Chair, Clinical Executive Board (1992–Present); Alternate Chair, Resource Advisory Committee (1992–Present); VA Medical Research Service Award (1982); Member, SE Cancer Study Group (1983–1987); Member, SW Oncology (1987–Present); Member, Community Clinical Oncology Program of Virginia (1983–Present); Member, Board of Directors, American Cancer Society. Virginia Division and Roanoke Valley Unit (1987–1989); Numerous publications, abstracts and presentations. **Education:** Shah Medical College, Jamnager; Saurashtra University: M.B., B.S. (1966–1970); Panjab University, Pre–Medical; S.D. College, Ambala, India (1964–1966); Mount Sinai Hospital, University of Connecticut, Intership (1974–1975), Residency (1975–1977); Fellowship, University of Virginia Health Sciences Center (1978–1979). **Personal:** Married in 1976, Dr. Jain has two children.

Samir Jamil, M.D.

Pediatric Oncologist/Hematologist
William Beaumont Hospital
3601 West 13 Mile Road
Royal Oak, MI 48073–6712
(810) 551–0360
Fax: (810) 551–8865

8062

Business Information: William Beaumont Hospital is a tertiary care hospital, clinical research and teaching institution; working in affiliation with the University of Michigan and Wayne State University. A Board–certified Pediatrician, subspecializing in Hematology/Oncology, Dr. Samir Jamil provides diagnosis, treatment and consultation in the areas of Pediatric Hematology/Oncology. He also serves as mentor and instructor to residents, supervision in their daily rounds, and clinical research. **Career Steps:** Staff Physician, William Beaumont Hospital (1985–Present); Clinical Assistant Professor, Wayne State University, Detroit, MI. **Education:** Mosul University Medical School, M.D. (1971).

Eugene G. Jarrell, M.D.

Physician/Director of Emergency Services
Brantford General Hospital
200 Terrace Hill Street, Department of Emergency
Brantford, Ontario N3R 1G9
(519) 751–5544 Ext.4235
Fax: (519) 752–0098

8062

Business Information: Brantford General Hospital is a secondary and acute care facility located in Brantford, Ontario. As Physician/Director of Emergency Services, Dr. Jarrell is in charge of emergency care services. He recruits medical staff, reviews credentials, schedules training, and acts as liaison between emergency medical staff and hospital administration. Dr. Jarrell is involved in public relations for the hospital with emphasis on emergency services. He coordinates with other hospital directors on budget plans and strategic planning for the future. **Career Steps:** Physician/Director of Emergency Services, Brantford General Hospital (1985–Present); Emergency Physician, Ottawa General Hospital (1984–1985). **Associations & Accomplishments:** Canadian Association of Emergency Physicians (CAEP); Canadian College of Family Practitioners With Specialty Completion in Emergency Medicine (CCFPSEM); American College of Emergency Medicine (FACEP); Canadian Medical Association (CMA); Ontario Medical Association (OMA); Diplomate of American Board of Emergency Medicine (DABEM), **Education:** Queen's College: M.D. (1981), B.Sc. with Honors (1977); Memorial University, Residency in Family Medicine (1981–1983); Ottawa, Residency in Emergency Medicine (1984–1985). **Personal:** Married to Marion Elizabeth in 1977. Three children: Emily, Ian, and Curtis. Dr. Jarrell enjoys playing baseball with his children, squash, and white water canoeing.

Ronald D. Jenkins, M.D.

Director of Cardiology – Boulder Heart Institute
Boulder Medical Center
2750 Broadway
Boulder, CO 80304–3573
(303) 440–3177
Fax: (303) 449–9380

8062

Business Information: Boulder Medical Center is an acute care medical facility, providing diagnosis and treatment of patients. A practicing physician since 1982 and a Board–Certified Cardiologist, Dr. Jenkins joined the Boulder Medical Center as Director of Cardiology in 1993. He serves as an interventional cardiologist, directing all cardiac medicine activities within the Boulder Heart Institute. His duties include conducting invasive cardiac techniques, such as catheterization and placing coronary stents into coronary arteries to fix blocked vessels, thereby avoiding the necessity of actual heart surgery. **Career Steps:** Director of Cardiology – Boulder Heart Institute, Boulder Medical Center (1993–Present); Assistant Professor of Medicine, University of Utah Medical Center (1989–1993); Instructor of Medicine, Harvard University, Beth Israel Hospital (1988–1989). **Associations & Accomplishments:** American Heart Association; President–Elect, Boulder County Heart Association; American College of Cardiology; Boulder County Medical Society; Odyssey of the Mind Coach (1994–Present). **Education:** University of Utah School of Medicine, M.D. (1982); University of Utah, B.S. (1977). **Personal:** Married to Deborah M. in 1980. Three children: Lindsay, Amy, and Michael. Dr. Jenkins enjoys skiing, golf, and windsurfing.

Donna C. Jennings, RRT, MBA

Director of Performance Improvement, Utilization and Risk Managem
Smyth County Community Hospital
700 Park Boulevard, P.O. Box 880
Marion, VA 24354
(540) 782–1188
Fax: (540) 782–9886

8062

Business Information: Smyth County Community Hospital is a rural, 175–bed, acute care facility featuring a broad spectrum of services, including: outpatient and emergency services, general medical/surgical, physical therapy, sleep diagnostic center, home health, cardio–pulmonary, and Francis Marion Manor, a 109–bed long–term care facility. As Director of Performance Improvement and Risk Management, Ms. Jennings is responsible for coordination of Joint Commission (JCAHO) activities throughout the facility, medical staff education, utilization review activities, and Risk Management functions. She is also responsible for budgeting and managerial activities for this department. **Career Steps:** Director of Performance Improvement, Utilization and Risk Management, Smyth County Community Hospital (1994–Present); Strategic Manager, Brett Enterprise (1994); Director of CardioPulmonary, Tazewell Community Hospital (1984–1994). **Associations & Accomplishments:** American Association of Respiratory Care; The Virginia Chapter of American Society of Healthcare Risk Management; National Association of Healthcare Quality; Virginia Association of Healthcare Quality; Virginia Society of Respiratory Care; American Association of Cardiovascular and Pulmonary Rehabilitation; American Lung Association. **Education:** Averett College, M.B.A. (1994); Bluefield State College, B.A.; Southwest Virginia Community College – Richlands, A.A.S.; National Board Certifications: C.R.T.T., R.R.T., C.P.F.T., C.P.H.Q. **Personal:** Married to Donald G. in 1984. Four children: Ashley, Hunter, Whitney, and Caleb. Ms. Jennings enjoys snow skiing, water skiing, hiking, fly fishing, camping, and trout fishing.

Ruby L. Jensen

Nurse Manager
University of Texas Medical Branch
301 University Boulevard
Galveston, TX 77555–0516
(409) 772–1691
Fax: (409) 772–6604

8062

Business Information: Established in 1891, The University of Texas Medical Branch is a full tertiary care, research and teaching hospital. In affiliation with the University of Texas as well as seven other hospitals in the greater Galveston, TX vicinity, UTMB is the largest employer in Galveston. Within the hospital are the school of nursing, school of allied health, and a medical school. Mrs. Jensen began her career with The University of Texas Medical Branch as a Staff Nurse in 1980 and currently holds the position of Nurse Manager. She is responsible for 175 employees and manages 7 units, two of which are intensive care units. **Career Steps:** University of Texas Medical Branch: Nurse Manager (1985–Present), Assistant Nurse Manager (1983–1985), Staff Nurse (1980–1983). **Associations & Accomplishments:** Association of Critical Care Nurses, National and Local Chapters; National Association of Nurse Executives; American Nurses Association. **Education:** University of Texas School of Nursing, B.S.N. (1993); Galveston College, A.D.N. (1980); Certified Nurse Administrator. **Personal:** Married to Terry in 1983. One child: Brenda Kesinger. Mrs. Jensen enjoys arts, crafts, and walking.

Brenda S. Johnson, MSN, RN, CNA

Director of Education
Saint Francis Medical Center
211 Saint Francis Drive
Cape Girardeau, MO 63703–8399
(573) 339–6258 (573) 339–6107
Fax: (573) 339–6940

8062

Business Information: Saint Francis Medical Center is a 264–bed, full–service healthcare institution specializing in the diagnosis, treatment, and rehabilitation of patients. A member of the Franciscan Sisters, the Hospital is a private, not–for–profit center. As Director of Education, Ms. Johnson is responsible for providing and coordinating all education and staff development for employees and regional professionals. **Career Steps:** Director of Education, Saint Francis Medical Center (1982–Present); House Supervisor, Southeast Missouri Hospital (1980–1981); Head Nurse, Presbyterian Hospital (1977–1980). **Associations & Accomplishments:** American Nursing Association; MONA; ASHET; MAHE; SEMAHE; Lamba Theta; Sigma Theta Tau International; Missouri League of Nursing; NMSD. **Education:** Bellarmine College, M.S.N. (1994); SEMO, B.S.N. (1987); TRCC, ADN (1974); Certified Nursing Administrator, American Nursing Association. **Personal:** Two children: Chad and Brandon. Ms. Johnson enjoys church activities and being a Youth Director.

Richard V. Johnson

Chief Financial Officer
Austin State Hospital
4110 Guadalup Street
Austin, TX 78751–4223
(512) 419–2636
Fax: (512) 419–2650

8062

Business Information: Austin State Hospital is a state–affiliated mental health hospital, treating individuals suffering from mental disabilities. With twenty–five years expertise in financial administration, Mr. Johnson joined Austin State Hospital as Chief Financial Officer in 1985. He is responsible for all aspects of financial operations for the hospital. **Career Steps:** Chief Financial Officer, Austin State Hospital (1985–Present); Chief Accountant, Texas Research Institute (1973–1985); Staff Accountant, Daniels, Turnbull & Freeman, CPA's (1970–1973); Hospital Corps, United States Coast Guard (1968–1970). **Education:** Jacksonville University, B.S. (1968) **Personal:** One child: Cheryl. Mr. Johnson enjoys collecting classic cars, Confederate Air Force memorabilia, and model trains.

Royce H. Johnson, M.D., FACP

Professor of Medicine
University of California – Los Angeles
2201 Mount Vernon, Suite 211
Bakersfield, CA 93306
(805) 872–7000
Fax: (805) 872–7156

8062

Business Information: Dr. Royce Johnson, a specialist in Infectious Diseases, serves as a group physician in affiliation with the Kern Medical Center. The Kern Medical Center is a full tertiary care teaching hospital, operating in conjunction with the University of California–Los Angeles. In addition to his patient practice, he also serves as Professor of Medicine at UCLA to interns and residents. He is extensively involved in ongoing clinical research in infectious diseases, currently searching for a vaccine in the cure for "Valley Fever". **Career Steps:** Professor of Medicine, University of California – Los Angeles (1975–Present). **Associations & Accomplishments:** Fellow, American College of Physicians; Fellow, Infectious Disease Society of America; Numerous public seminars and lectures **Education:** University of California – Santa Barbara, B.A. (1966); University of California – Irvine: M.D. (1970), Internal Medicine Residency (1973); Los Angeles County University of Southern California, Internship (1971). **Personal:** Dr. Johnson enjoys travel, and reading spy novels.

Sylvester Johnson

Chief of Infomation Resources Management Service
Dwight D. Eisenhower, Veterans Administration Medical Center
18613 N. Beaman Ave.
Kansas City, MO 64154
(913) 682–2000
Fax: (913) 758–4113
EMail: See Below

8062

Business Information: Dwight D. Eisenhower, Veterans Administration Medical Center is a 445–bed medical facility providing long term psychiatric, ICU, and geriatric care, as well as surgery, podiatry, and prosthetic services for veterans. The facility also conducts geriatric research. As Chief of Information Resources Management Service, Mr. Johnson oversees all computer information software and hardware, performs troubleshooting, and supervises IRM staff. Internet users can reach him via: Johnson.Sylvester@IVA.GOV. **Career Steps:** Chief IRM Service, VA Medical Center (1994–Present); Assistant Chief of IRM Services, Washington D.C. (1990–1994); Assistant Chief of IRM Services, Waco, TX (1986–1990). **Education:** Friend's University: B.S. in Total Quality Management (1996), Associate's Degree in Computer Science (1978). **Personal:** Married to Annie B. in 1986. Five children: John, Carl, Eric, Carlena, and Stephanie. Mr. Johnson enjoys fishing and surfing the Internet.

Catherine M. Jones

Director of Nursing
Emerald Coast Hospital
Washington Square
Apalachicola, FL 32320
(904) 653–8853
Fax: (904) 653–2140

8062

Business Information: Emerald Coast Hospital is an acute care facility. As Director of Nursing, Ms. Jones is responsible for the administrative direction of all nursing care departments. Her responsibility also include standards, compliance, QAI/C coordinator, Risk Management, Staff Development, and acts in the absence of the administrator. **Career Steps:** Director of Nursing, Emerald Coast Hospital (1994–Present); Assistant Director of Nursing, WaKulla Manor (1992–1994); Director of Nursing, Wellsprings Home Health (1991–1992). **Associations & Accomplishments:** Health Professional Representative, 1996 Florida Statewide Education Planning Committee for the Area Health Education Center; Advisory Board, Keiser College; American Heart Association: Advanced Cardiac Life Support Instructor; High Scholastic Achievement Award. **Education:** California College for Health, Masters candidate; Florida State University, graduate studies; State University of New York, B.S.N.; Jefferson Davis Junior College: A.S. and A.A. degrees.

David N. Jones, M.D.

Emergency Medical Physician
Nashville Metropolitan General Hospital
P.O. Box 210149
Nashville, TN 37221
(912) 274–9972
Fax: Please mail or call

8062

Business Information: Nashville Metropolitan General Hospital is an acute care, metropolitan medical facility, providing diagnosis and treatment of patients. A practicing physician since 1969 and a Board–Certified Emergency Physician, Dr. Jones joined the Nashville Metropolitan General Hospital as Emergency Medical Physician in 1992. He is responsible for providing emergency medical care to patients, employee work schedules, and Staff Emergency Departments for four area hospitals, in addition to overseeing the administrative operations for associates and a support staff of eight. Concurrent with his position at Nashville Metropolitan General Hospital, he serves as Emergency Medical Physician at Sumner Regional Medical Center. **Career Steps:** Emergency Medical Physician, Nashville Metropolitan General Hospital (1992–Present); Emergency Medical Physician, Sumner Regional Medical Center (1994–Present); Emergency Physician, Centennial Medical Center (1985–1991). **Associations & Accomplishments:** American Medical Association; Nashville Davidson County Academy of Medicine; Fellow, American College of Emergency Physicians; Fellow, American Academy of Emergency Medicine; Kiwanis; March of Dimes. **Education:** University of Tennessee, M.D. (1969); David Lipscomb College, B.A. **Personal:** Married to Sandra in 1980. Three children: Barbara, Robin, and Ashton. Dr. Jones enjoys golf, hang gliding, sky diving, sailing, and deep sea fishing.

Barbara J. Joswick

Director of Diabetes Center
Florida Hospital
2520 North Orange Avenue, Suite 102
Orlando, FL 32804
(407) 896–6611
Fax: (407) 897–1741

8062

Business Information: Florida Hospital is the fourth most active cardiac procedure and open heart surgery hospital in the United States, and one of the busiest hospitals in the country, serving over 50,000 inpatients, 177,000 outpatients, and 146,000 ER cases per year. Affiliated with the Seventh Day Adventist Church, the hospital boasts a family residency program, a family practice osteopathic residency program, and has won several awards. The Diabetes Care and Education Center focuses on prevention, intervention, and management of diabetes using a team approach of RNs, Dieticians, Exercise Physiologists, and Behavioral Counselors – all nationally certified. The Center has been conducting clinical research since 1993 and boasts an endorcrinology practice within the Center. The Center serviced over 10,000 patients in 1995 and has a 15–bed diabetes dedicated care unit. As the Director of the Diabetes Care Center, Ms. Joswick handles all functions pertaining to the Center, and assures that all programs are being followed. **Career Steps:** Florida Hospital: Director of Diabetes Center (1992–Present), Nurse Instructor/Staff (1989–1992), Nurse Manager (1984–1989). **Associations & Accomplishments:** American Diabetes Association; American Association of Diabetes Educators; Juvenile Diabetes Association; Central Florida Healthcare Executive Group. **Education:** Florida Institute of Technology, M.S. in Health Care Administration (1993); Southern College, B.S. in Nursing (1984). **Personal:** Married to David. One child: Michael. Ms. Joswick enjoys tennis, reading, and volunteer work.

Sayed Jovkar, M.D.

Physician
McGill University Hospital
2 Glendale Avenue
Montreal, Quebec H9W 5P5
(514) 695–3971
Fax: Please mail or call

8062

Business Information: McGill University Hospital, affiliated with McGill University, is a full–service, healthcare institution specializing in the diagnosis, treatment, and rehabilitation of patients. Dr. Jovkar is currently a senior resident (physician in ophthalmology) at McGill University and provides quality care to hospital patients. **Career Steps:** Electrical Engineer, graduate studies in Neurology and Neurosurgery, family physician, specializing in Ophthamology (present). **Associations & Accomplishments:** College of Physicians and Surgeons of Ontario; Association for Research in Visual Sciences and Ophthalmology; American Academy of Ophthalmology; Canadian Society of Cataract and Refractive Surgery; Medical Board of California Physicians and Surgeons; Medical Council of Canada (LMCC). Dr. Jovkar has been the recipient of twelve scholarships and grants, traveling as far as the Max Planck Institute for Neurological Research, West Germany, and the Karolinska Institute, Stockholm, in his research in brain imaging. More than twenty of his articles have appeared in peer–reviewed journals. He has coauthored a book chapter. Education: McGill University, Bachelor of Electrical Engineering, Honors (1984); Montreal Neurological Institute, McGill University, Master of Science in Neurology and Neurosurgery (1986); University of Montreal, Medical Doctor (1991(; McGill University: Internship in Internal Medicine (1992), Specialty training in Ophthalmology (1992–Present). **Personal:** Dr. Jovkar enjoys travel, music, and foreign languages.

Linda L. Kaneer

Administrator
Regional Care Center
300 Portland Street
Columbia, MO 65201
(573) 875–9992
Fax: (573) 449–8422

8062

Business Information: Regional Care Center is a sub–acute medical facility providing health and related services to the area. Comprised of a skilled nursing home, as well as private rooms, the Center offers rehabilitative services including occupational, speech, and I.V. therapy. As Administrator, Mrs. Kaneer oversees admissions and discharges, manages staffing and budgeting, and is responsible for the Center's general operation and compliance with federal regulations. **Career Steps:** Administrator, Regional Care Center (1995–Present); Administrator, Lincoln Manor; Assistant Administrator, Colonial Gardens; Social Service Skilled Coordinator, Keller Memorial Hospital. **Associations & Accomplishments:** Missouri League for Nursing Home Administrators; Regional Hospital Volunteer's Committee; Howard County D.A.R.; ACHCA. **Education:** Central Methodist College, A.D.N. (1993); Moberly Area Community College, Associate Degree of Arts (1990). **Personal:** Married to Clyde Kaneer in 1971. Two children: Jody and Keeley. Mrs. Kaneer enjoys swimming, crochet, cooking, and scuba diving.

Michal Jerzy Kantoch

Physician
Walter C. MacKenzie, H.S.C.
112 Street NW, Room 2c3.88–8440
Edmonton, Alberta T6G 2B7
(403) 492–4011
Fax: (403) 492–9850

8062

Business Information: Walter C. MacKenzie, H.S.C. is a 700–bed full–service healthcare institution specializing in the diagnosis, treatment, and rehabilitation of patients and is affiliated with the Royal Alexandria Hospital and 3 other Edmonton hospitals. Dr. Kantoch works as an Assistant Professor/Physician with the University of Alberta in the Division of Pediatric Cardiology, located within the Walter C. MacKenzie Health Sciences Center. He runs a Arrhythmie Clinic and Electrophysiology Laboratory for children with heart trouble. He spends 25% of his time teaching, 25% doing clinical research, and 50% with clinical care and administration. He provides consultation to community clinics along with five other pediatric candiologists at the University of Alberte. **Career Steps:** Physician, Walter C. MacKenzie, H.S.C. (1987–Present); Assistant Professor, University of Alberta (1994–Present); Assistant Professor, University of Saskatchewan (1992–1994). **Associations & Accomplishments:** Fellow, American College of Cardiology; Fellow, Canadian Cardiovascular Society; Canadian Adult Congenital Heart Disease Network; Fellow, Royal College of Physicians and Surgeons of Canada. **Education:** Medical School of Warsaw, M.D. (1981). **Personal:** Married to Anna in 1983. Three children: Jan, Michal, and Krzysztof. Dr. Kantoch enjoys skiing, sailing, and listening to classical music.

Genia Karnes

Director of Nursing
Transitional Hospital Corporation
898 East Main Street
Greenwood, IN 46143
(317) 888–8155
Fax: (317) 888–7382

8062

Business Information: Transitional Hospital Corporation (T.H.C.) is a 38–bed acute care hospital, providing a variety of services for both in–patient and out–patient services, with its main focus on in–patient services. Current patient facilities capacity consists of thirty–four medical surgical beds, and four intensive care unit beds. T.H.C. also specializes in pulmonary rehabilitation, ventilator and respiratory care, state–of–the–art wound care, and low tolerance rehabilitation programs. With fifteen years experience in nursing, Mrs. Karnes joined T.H.C. as Director of Nursing in 1994. She is responsible for the oversight and leadership of the Nursing Department, as well as providing quality care to patients and clinical coordination for the hospital's projects. **Career Steps:** Director of Nursing, T.H.C. (1994–Present); Director of Nursing, Deltona Healthcare Center (1992–1994); Staff Registered Nurse, HCA Central Florida Regional Hospital (1989–1992); Past experience also includes: Director of Nursing in California in Home Health; Critical Care experience in Louisville, KY; began career in medical field as a Unit Secretary and Nursing Assistant. **Associations & Accomplishments:** Indiana Organization of Nurse Executives. **Education:** Spalding University, B.S. in Nursing (1981). **Personal:** Married to Guy in 1973. Three children: Beth, Meghan, and Matthew. Mrs. Karnes enjoys spending time with her family.

Lorne F. Kastrukoff, M.D.

Physician & Surgeon
Vancouver Hospital & Health Science Center, UBC Site
Department of Medicine, Koerner Pavillion H.S.C., 2211 Wesbrook M
Vancouver, British Co V6T 1Z3
(604) 822–7147
Fax: (604) 822–7897

8062

Business Information: Vancouver Hospital & Health Science Center, UBC Site is a major referral hospital offering full–service medical care, diagnosis, and rehabilitation of patients. As Physician & Surgeon, Dr. Kastrukoff is responsible for teaching, performing neurological research, and handling administrative duties. His primary research focus is on multiple sclerosis. **Career Steps:** Physician & Surgeon, Vancouver Hospital & Health Science Center, UBC Site (1980–Present); Reasearch Associate, University of Pennsylvania (1978–1980); Chief Resident, University of Alberta (1976–1977). **Associations & Accomplishments:** American Academy of Neurology; American Neurological Association; Society of Neuro Sciience; Canadian Neurological Society. **Education:** University of British Columbia, B.Sc., M.D. (1970/1973); University of Alberia (1974–1978). **Personal:** Married to Carol Ann in 1973. Two children: Keely and Ryan. Dr. Kastrukoff enjoys skiing, tennis, golf, and sailing.

Nevin M. Katz, M.D.

Professor of Surgery
Georgetown University Medical Center
3800 Reservoir Road, N.W. – Department of Surgery
Washington, DC 20007
(202) 687–8725
Fax: (202) 687–6498

8062

Business Information: Georgetown University Medical Center is a private, multi–division clinical, research and teaching facility providing hospital and outpatient care, and graduate and postgraduate programs. A board–certified cardiovascular surgeon and Professor of Surgery, Dr. Katz is a full–time faculty member specializing in adult cardiovascular surgery, with special interests in coronary artery surgery, valvular surgery, aortic surgery, cardiac transplantation and cardiac surgery in elderly patients. Additionally, he has been the director of the heart transplantation program at Georgetown since 1987. **Career Steps:** Georgetown University Medical Center, Department of Surgery, Division of Cardiovascular and Thoracic Surgery: Professor of Surgery (1992–Present), Associate Professor of Surgery (1985–1992), Assistant Professor of Surgery (1980–1985); Director of the Cardiac Surgical Program, Veteran's Administration Medical Center, Washington, D.C. (1980–1983); Research Associate in Cardiovascular Surgery and Residency in Thoracic and Cardiovascular Surgery (1980), University of Alabama School of Medicine; Chief Resident in Cardiovascular Surgery, Children's Hospital Medical Center; Internship and Residency in General Surgery, Massachusetts General Hospital. **Associations & Accomplishments:** Alpha Omega Alpha Honor Medical Society; American College of Cardiology; American College of Surgery; American Medical Association; The American Association for Thoracic Surgery; The Society of Thoracic Surgeons; The Washington Academy of Surgery; Washington Regional Transplant Consortium; Chairperson of Heart and Lung Transplant Medical Advisory Committee (1989, 1990); Mended Hearts Surgeon of the Year (1995–1996); Author of over 50 publications. **Education:** Case Western Reserve University, M.D. (1971); Swarthmore College, B.A. in Chemistry (1967) **Personal:** Married to Anne T. Katz in 1974. Three children: Nevin Jr., Paul A., Katherine A. Dr. Katz enjoys tennis, sailing and violin performing.

Kathryn Kelly

Vice President of Patient Services/Chief Nurse Executive
Monmouth Medical Center
300 2nd Avenue
Long Branch, NJ 07740
(908) 870–5212
Fax: (908) 870–5138

8062

Business Information: Monmouth Medical Center is a non–profit medical facility with 525 beds which functions as a teaching center for area schools. As Vice President of Patient Services/Chief Nurse Executive, Ms. Kelly is in charge of all patient care and is responsible for the overall management and coordination of 11 departments with an annual budget of over 36 million dollars. The long range plans Ms. Kelly makes are always changing as advances in the medical fields continue. **Career Steps:** Monmouth Medical Center: Vice President of Patient Services/Chief Nurse Executive (1995–Present), Administrator of Emergency and Patient Access Services (1994–1995), Administrative Director of Emergency (1986–1993). **Associations & Accomplishments:** American Organization of Nurse Executives; Association of Health Care Executives of New Jersey; Central Jersey Visiting Nurse Association; Monmouth University Lambda Delta Chapter of Sigma Theta Tau. **Education:** Farleigh Dickinson, M.A. (1987); Seton Hall University, B.S.N. (1969). **Personal:** Ms. Kelly enjoys travel, outdoors, nature, exercise, and music.

John Martin Kelsch Jr., M.D.

Medical Director of Emergency Medicine
Raleigh Community Hospital
6912 Tanbark Way
Raleigh, NC 27615–5357
(919) 954–3270
Fax: Please mail or call

8062

Business Information: Raleigh Community Hospital is an acute care medical facility, providing diagnosis and treatment to patients. A practicing physician since 1976 and a Board–Certified Emergency Physician, Dr. Kelsch joined Raleigh Community Hospital as Medical Director of Emergency Medicine in 1990. He oversees all administrative operations for associates and a support staff of six, in addition to the medical direction of emergency room activities and practicing emergency medicine. **Career Steps:** Medical Director of Emergency Medicine, Raleigh Community Hospital (1990–Present); Emergency Medicine Physician, Wake Medical Center (1988–1990); Emergency Medicine Physician, Mercy Hospital, Fairfield, Ohio (1986–1988). **Associations & Accomplishments:** Fellow, American College of Emergency Physicians; Member, Powerbilt Golf Tour. **Education:** University of Louisville, M.D. (1976); Morehead State University, B.S. **Personal:** Married to Lesley in 1981. Two children: Betsy and Katie.

Nancy A. Kernan, M.D.

Attending Physician
Memorial Sloan–Kettering Cancer Center
1275 York Avenue
New York, NY 10021–6007
(212) 639–7250
Fax: (212) 744–2245

8062

Business Information: Memorial Sloan–Kettering Cancer Center, a NCI–designated Comprehensive Cancer Center, is a health care institution specializing in the diagnosis, treatment, and research of cancer. As Attending Physician, Dr. Kernan is responsible for providing health care to patients in the areas of pediatric oncology, bone marrow transplants, and patient care of children's cancer and leukemia. **Career Steps:** Associate Attending Physician, Memorial Sloan–Kettering Cancer Center (1984–Present); Associate Professor of Pediatrics, Cornell University Medical College. **Associations & Accomplishments:** Board of Directors, National Marrow Donor Program; Board of Directors, Cornell University Medical College Alumni Association. **Education:** Cornell University Medical College, M.D. (1978).

Kelly K. Kerr

Director of Managed Care
St. Paul Medical Center
2777 Stemmons Freeway, Suite 1055
Dallas, TX 75207
(214) 630–7879
Fax: (214) 630–6677

8062

Business Information: St. Paul Medical Center is a 600–bed, full–service, acute care hospital, providing both in–patient and out–patient surgical and ambulatory surgical care. Currently, the Medical Center has the leading heart transplant success rate, and operates a mental health department and a highly–reputable Cancer Center and Oncology Department. In operation since 1896, the St. Paul Medical Center employs 1,500 physicians and medical support staff. As Director of Managed Care, Ms. Kerr is responsible for all contracted care, as well as the supervision of her 15–member staff. **Career Steps:** Director of Managed Care, St. Paul Medical Center (1995–Present); Regional Manager, Beech Street Corporation (1991–1994); Manager of Physician Relations, St. Paul Medical Center (1989–1991); Provider Relations Representative, Travelers Health Network (1987–1989). **Associations & Accomplishments:** Board Member, Dallas/Fort Worth Managed Healthcare Peer Forum (1993–1995); American Hospital Association (1990–1995); American Association of PPO's (1991–1995); Texas Hospital Association (1990–1995). **Education:** North Texas State University, B.S. (1982). **Personal:** Married to Jerry in 1984. Ms. Kerr enjoys snow skiing, water skiing, swimming, pets, card games, and computers.

Ali Keskiner, M.D.

Chief of Psychiatry Services
Veterans Adminstration Medical Center
10000 Bay Pines Boulevard
Bay Pines, FL 33504
(813) 398–9415
Fax: (813) 398–9515

8062

Business Information: V.A. Medical Center, one of the Nation's busiest VA Hospital, is a full–service general hospital for veterans in the U.S. Affiliated with the University of Florida Medical College, V.A. Medical Center – Bay Pines serves more than 11,000 in–patients and 25,000 out–patients per year. As Chief of Psychiatry Services, Dr. Keskiner is responsible for directing the part of a health delivery system for U.S. veterans, providing a continuum of psychiatric evaluation, treatment and management of the mentally ill and behaviorally dysfunctional. His duties include consulting, teaching, strategic planning, overseeing a staff of professionals, and conducting research. **Career Steps:** V.A. Medical Center – Bay Pines FL: Chief of Psychiatry Services (1983–Present), Staff Psychiatrist (1983–Present); Professor of Clinical Psychiatry, University of South Florida (1984–Present); Staff Psychiatrist and Director of Research, Anclote Manor Hospital (1975–1983); Professor of Psychiatry, University of Missouri Medical School (1964–1975). **Associations & Accomplishments:** Life Fellow, American Psychiatric Association; American Society for the Advancement of Science, New York Academy of Science; Chairman, Fellowship Committee of Florida Psychiatric Society; Former President, Turkish American Neuropsychiatric Association; Strategic Planning and Resource Management Group; Published over 70 scientific papers and book chapters. **Education:** McGill University – Medical Faculty, Diploma in Psychiatry (1962); Istanbul University – Medical Faculty, M.D. (1955); American Board of Psychiatry and Neurology, Board Certified (Diplomate). **Personal:** Two children: Murad Alexander, and Aydin Daniel. Dr. Keskiner enjoys tennis, walking, music and arts.

Satish C. Khaneja, M.D.

Director, Department of Surgery
Mary Immaculate Hospital
15211 89th Avenue
Jamaica, NY 11432
(718) 558–2007
Fax: (718) 558–2053

8062

Business Information: Mary Immaculate Hospital is a 261–bed healthcare facility specializing in the diagnosis, treatment, and rehabilitation of patients. As Director, Department of Surgery, Dr. Khaneja is responsible for overseeing all operations of the surgery department. He specializes in thoracic, vascular, and general surgery. **Career Steps:** Director of Department of Surgery, Mary Immaculate Hospital (1990–Present); Attending Surgeon, Brookdale Hospital (1987–1990); Associate Director of Department of Surgery, Franklin Square Hospital (1977–1987). **Associations & Accomplishments:** Fellow, American College of Surgeons; Society of Critical Care Medicine; Eastern Trauma Society; New York Surgical Society. **Education:** Allms, New Delhi, India: M.B., B.S. (1967). **Personal:** Married to Saroj in 1970. Three children: Neerja, Roopa, and Sandeep. Dr. Khaneja enjoys ballroom dancing, tennis, swimming, and chess.

Albert J. Kirshen, MD, MSc, FRCPC

Program Director
Baycrest Centre for Geriatric Care
3560 Bathurst Street
North York, Ontario M6A 2E1
(416) 785–2500 Ext. 2615
Fax: (416) 785–2491
EMail: See Below

8062

Business Information: Baycrest Centre for Geriatric Care is a health care facility providing health and related programs to the elderly. Offering a variety of day and residential programs as well as specialized services, the Center treats patients on an in– or outpatient basis, as well as in their homes. Providing family support and counseling, education on aging, rehabilitative and recreational facilities, as well as a full range of medical services, the Center treats over 2,000 elderly patients daily, and offers two residential programs, the Baycrest Terrace, an independent living apartment complex for adults over 70, with nursing, medical, and support services, and The Jewish Home for the Aged which provides personalized nursing care. Established in 1926, the Center employs over 1,700 professionals and support staff, in addition to its hundreds of volunteers. As Program Director, Dr. Kirshen is responsible for overseeing all clinical programs and systems and to provide continuing education for the medical staff. Internet users can reach him via: albert.j.kirshen@utoronto.ca. **Career Steps:** Program Director, Baycrest Centre for Geriatric Care (1993–Present); Program Director, Health Sciences Center, Winnipeg (1987–1993); Section Head, Winnipeg Municipal Hospital (1984–1987). **Associations & Accomplishments:** Fellow, Royal College of Physicians and Surgeons of Canada (LCPSC); Fellow, American Geriatrics Society. **Education:** University of Manitoba, M.Sc. (1995); University of Toronto, M.D. (1978); FRCP/RCPSC (1982); Royal College, Certificate of Special Competence in Geriatric Medicine (1983). **Personal:** Married to Janice in 1976. Two children: Chayim and Aliza. Dr. Kirshen enjoys computers and science fiction.

Sharon Kleefield, Ph.D.

Director of Quality Improvement–Department of Quality Measurement
Brigham and Women's Hospital
75 Francis Street
Boston, MA 02115
(617) 732–7096
Fax: (617) 734–9289

8062

Business Information: Brigham and Women's Hospital, an affiliate of the Harvard Medical School and part of Partners Healthcare, Inc., is a not–for–profit, 700–bed, multi–divisional research, teaching, and full–tertiary care medical facility. As Director of Quality Improvement for the Department of Quality Measurement and Improvement, Dr. Kleefield is responsible for developing and monitoring of quality outcomes for the hospital and designs from data opportunities for improvement, as well as oversight of clinical quality measurement and improvement activities. She also teaches physicians, nurses and support staff on clinical quality improvements. Concurrent with her duties for Brigham and Women's Hospital, Dr. Kleefield provides independent consulting to Medical Boards, committees and corporate businesses. **Career Steps:** Director of Quality Improvement–Department of Quality Measurement and Improvement, Brigham and Women's Hospital (1994–Present); Instructor, Harvard Business School, University of Massachusetts (1984–1989); Consultant, Editorial Board, Journal of Quality Improvement, JCAHO (1994–Present); Consultant, Ethics Committee, Brigham and Women's Hospital (1992–Present); Consultant, Editorial Board, Quality Management in Health Care, Aspen Publishers, Inc. (1992–1995); Consultant, Editorial Board, Forum, Harvard Risk Management Foundation, Harvard University (1991–Present); Consultant, Frank Berman, Law Offices (1989–Present); Research Associate, Division of Research, Harvard Business School (1987–Present); **Associations & Accomplishments:** American Association of Bioethics Consultation; Society of Bioethics Consultation; American Society of Quality Control; American Philosophical Association; American Association for the Advancement of Science; Hastings Foundation, Institute for Ethics and Life Sciences; Research conducted in: Clinical research in prolactin and other pituitary hormones (1978–1983) and Research and development of an homologous assay for human prolactin (1971–1977); Milbank Foundation Research Fellowship in Ethics and Sociology of Medicine, Milbank Foundation, New York (1977); Publisher of numerous publications; Conducted numerous seminars and lectures. **Education:** Boston University, Ph.D. in Applied Ethics (1987), M.A. in Philosophy (1977), B.A. in Philosophy, cum laude (1973). **Personal:** Married to Jonathan Kleefield in 1984. One child: Aaron.

Dr. Jan C. Kletter

Chief of Surgery
Montrose General Hospital
3 Grow Avenue
Montrose, PA 18801–1103
(717) 278–3801
Fax: (717) 278–2828

8062

Business Information: Montrose General Hospital is an acute care medical facility, providing services to the rural community of Montrose, Pennsylvania and outlying areas. A practicing physician since 1981 and a Board–Certified Surgeon, Dr. Kletter has served as Chief of Surgery of the Hospital for the past eight years. Additionally, he operates a private surgery practice as a general surgery associate with Medical Arts Clinic. **Career Steps:** Attending Surgeon, Montrose General Hospital (Present); Chief of Surgery, Medical Arts Clinic (Present); Clinical Instructor of Surgery, College of Medicine, Health Science Center at The State University of New York – Syracuse, NY Binghamton Campus (1993–Present). **Associations & Accomplishments:** American College of Surgeons; American Medical Association; Pennsylvania Medical Society **Education:** University of Medicine & Dentistry of New Jersey, M.D. (1981) **Personal:** Married to Marguerite in 1989. One child: Elliott. Dr. Kletter enjoys astronomy, hunting and fishing.

Bello Knoblich, M.S.E.E.

Director of Bio–Engineering
North Central Bronx Hospital
3424 Kossuth Avenue
Bronx, NY 10467–2410
(718) 519–3570
Fax: (718) 519–4738

8062

Business Information: North Central Bronx Hospital is a full–service acute care facility, providing medical care and services to the Bronx and the surrounding community. As Director, Mr. Knoblich oversees medical equipment and instrument control, and is responsible for all operations and administration related to his department. He is actively involved in brain–waves studies. **Career Steps:** Director, Bio–Engineering, North Central Bronx Hospital (1993–Present); Programmer/Analyst, University of Augsburg, Germany (1987–1989); Clinical Engineer, City Industrial – Vranov (1984–1987). **Associations & Accomplishments:** New York City Metropolitan Area Clinical Engineering Directors Group. **Education:** University of Mechanical and Electrical Engineering, M.S.E.E. (1980); Syrit Computer School, Computer Science (1989). **Personal:** Married to Marika in 1980. Two children: Matus and Martha. Mr. Knoblich enjoys spending time with his family.

Trish A. Koebelen

Director of Nurses
Elkview General Hospital
429 West Elm Street
Hobart, OK 73651
(405) 726–3324
Fax: (405) 726–6041

8062

Business Information: Elkview General Hospital is a full–service, healthcare institution specializing in the diagnosis, treatment, and rehabilitation of patients (an acute care facility). As Director of Nurses, Ms. Koebelen oversees 70 nurses in the Hospital, and is responsible for all hiring, scheduling, and policies and procedures. **Career Steps:** Elkview General Hospital: Director of Nurses (1996–Present), Assistant Director of Nurses (1995); Discharge Coordinator (1994), Charge Nurse (1991–1993). **Associations & Accomplishments:** Head of the Volunteer Auxiliary Program at Elkview General Hospital; Little League. **Education:** Western Oklahoma State College: ADN (1991), Associate's degree in Psychology (1978). **Personal:** Married to Joe in 1988. Two children: Heather and Joey. Ms. Koebelen enjoys sewing, cooking, and reading.

Paul Kohn, M.D.

Clinical Research Physician
Mount Sinai Medical Center
1 Mount Sinai Drive
Cleveland, OH 44106
(216) 446–1030
Fax: Please mail or call

8062

Business Information: Mt. Sinai Medical Center is one of the nation's premier tertiary care hospitals, medical research and teaching institutions. An esteemed Internist/Cardiologist, Dr. Paul Kohn, now retired from full–time medical practice, is currently involved in clinical research for the Center. His current focus is in the areas of hypertension and hyperepidemiology. He also provides patient care on a pro bono basis for needy families at Mt. Sinai's out–patient clinic. Serving as a Captain in the United States Army during World War II, Dr. Kohn worked in an evacuation hospital in Europe from 1944–1946. He is very proud of the fact that he was promoted to Captain, and that his promotion orders were signed by General Eisenhower himself. **Career Steps:** Senior Visiting Clinical Research Physician, Mt. Sinai Medical Center (1995–Present); Assistant Clinical Professor, Case Western Reserve University School of Medicine (1980–1995); Private Practice Cardiologist (1947–1995). **Associations & Accomplishments:** American College of Cardiology; American College of Physicians; American Society of Internal Medicine; American Heart Association; American Medical Association; American Society of Echocardiography. **Education:** Case Western Reserve University School of Medicine, M.D. (1942); Adelbert College Case Western Reserve University, B.A. **Personal:** Married to Ruth G. in 1941. Two children: Bruce and Barry. Dr. Kohn enjoys music, golf and travel.

Ala Jo Tester Koonts

Director – Medical Staff Services/Quality Consulting
Bowman Gray/Baptist Hospital Medical Center
200 Happy Hill Court
Lexington, NC 27292
(910) 716–3465 (916) 716–5446
Fax: (910) 716–6415

8062

Business Information: Bowman Gray/Baptist Hospital Medical Center is a full–service healthcare institution. As a Director, Mrs. Koonts is responsible for interacting with the medical staff organization and performing quality consulting. She is directly responsible for 25 medical programs, 500 full–time faculty members, and 500 interns and residents. **Career Steps:** Director – Medical Staff Services/Quality Consulting, Bowman Gray/Baptist Hospital Medical Center (1990–Present); North Carolina Baptist Hospital: Director of Medical Staff/House Staff Services (1984–1990), House Staff Coordinator (1975–1984). **Associations & Accomplishments:** National Association for Female Executives; North Carolina Hospital Association; Association for Quality and Participation. **Education:** Winston–Salem Business College (1968). **Personal:** Married to Jimmy L. in 1970. One child: Shelley Dawn. Mrs. Koonts enjoys reading and antiques.

Thomas Kraven, M.D.

General Surgeon
Presbytarian Hospital of Greenville
4211 Joe Ramsey Boulevard, Suite 203
Greenville, TX 75401
(903) 408–7900
Fax: (903) 408–7909

8062

Business Information: Presbyterian Hospital of Greenville is a 100–bed, acute and subacute care county–supported medical facility. Dr. Kraven has been the Chief of Medical Staff since late 1995. As Chief of Medical Staff, Dr. Kraven is responsible for staff supervision, clinical activities, and providing administrative direction. Other duties include acting as liaison between administrative and medical and nursing staffs. Concurrently, Dr. Kraven, as General Surgeon, has his own private practice in General Surgery. **Career Steps:** Presbyterian Hospital of Greenville: Chief of Medical Staff (1995–Present), General Surgeon (1992–Present); General Surgeon, Trinity Surgical Associates (1984–1992); General Surgeon, Private Practice (1981–1984). **Associations & Accomplishments:** Fellow, American College of Surgeons; Texas Medical Association; Hunt County Medical Society; Board of Directors, Hunt County Hospital District. **Education:** University of Medicine and Dentistry of New Jersey, M.D. (1976); Rutgers University, B.A. in Psychology. **Personal:** Three children: Ryan, Courtney, and Jillian. Dr. Kraven enjoys music, swimming, travel, and cooking.

Judith A. Krupa, R.N., B.S.N.

Director of Primary and Ambulatory Care
Niagara Falls Memorial Medical Center
621 10th Street
Niagara Falls, NY 14301–1813
(716) 278–4542
Fax: (716) 278–4693

8062

Business Information: Niagara Falls Memorial Medical Center is an independent, non–profit, health care facility comprised of 300 beds, a separate but attached nursing home, primary and urgent care centers, and a residency program for private practice physicians, the Hospital is a satellite facility for the city. Offering the only operating room in Niagara County, the Hospital also provides mental health, pediatric, and dental services, in addition to offering one of the few child advocacy programs and collaborated efforts for sexually abused children in the country. Established in 1893, the Hospital employs 1,300 people. As Director of Primary and Ambulatory Care, Mrs. Krupa oversees the emergency and primary care services, as well as the ambulatory clinics. She is also responsible for operation of the pediatric, dental and urgent care centers, and manages the child advocacy program. **Career Steps:** Director of Primary and Ambulatory Care, Niagara Falls Memorial Medical Center (1995–Present); Clinical Manager of Neurology, Wake Forest University Physician's Group/ The Bowman Gray School of Medicine (1993–1995); Nurse Coordinator, Mt. St. Mary's Hospital (1979–1992). **Associations & Accomplishments:** Emergency Nurse Association; American Association of Neurologic Nursing; American Association of Ambulatory Care Nurses; Gamma Chapter, Sigma Theta Tau; New York State Nurse Association; Niagara Falls Domestic Violence Coalition; Western New York Nurse Advisory Committee for Emergency Medical Services; Steering Committee Member, Child Advocacy Center of Niagara; Board Member of Niagara County Rape Victim's Center. **Education:** Niagara University, B.S.N. (1981); SUNY, Buffalo, Certificate in Middle Management in Nursing (1991). **Personal:** Married to Paul A. in 1981. Two children: Kathryn and Julie. Mrs. Krupa enjoys boating, home crafts and gardening.

Jackson Kuan, M.D.

Gastroenterologist
Flushing General Hospital
146 01 45th Avenue, Suite 409
Flushing, NY 11355–2281
(718) 461–0163
Fax: (718) 358–5570
EMail: See Below

8062

Business Information: Established in 1985, Flushing General Hospital is an acute care, multi–specialty hospital. Board–certified in Gastroenterology, Dr. Kuan operates his private practice in affiliation with the Hospital. He can also be reached through the Internet as follows: jKuanmd@tribeca.ios.com **Career Steps:** Physician, Flushing General Hospital (1991–Present); Research Associate, Rockefeller University (1980–1982). **Associations & Accomplishments:** Published in medical journals. **Education:** Albany Medical College, M.D. (1986). **Personal:** Married to Lana Choy in 1987. One child: Kristen.

Elmer L. Kuber, M.H.A., C.H.E., F.A.A.M.A.

Executive Director
Selkirk & District General Hospital
P.O. Box 5000, 100 Easton Drive
Selkirk, Manitoba R1A 2M2
(204) 482–8984 Pager (204) 93
Fax: (204) 785–9113
EMail: See below

8062

Business Information: Selkirk & District General Hospital is a 75–bed, acute care, regional health care facility specializing in the diagnosis, treatment, and rehabilitation of patients. As Executive Director, Mr. Kuber is responsible for reporting to the Board of Trustees, the operation and direction of the hospital, and for Ambulance Service and numerous outreach programs. Internet users can reach him via: ekuber@sirnet.mb.ea. **Career Steps:** Executive Director, Selkirk & District General Hospital (1984–Present); Inter–Regional Executive Director, Beausejour Healthcare Facilities (1996–Present); Executive Director, Northwestern Health and Social Services Board (1982–1984); Administrator and Chief Executive Officer, Miramichi Hospital (1978–1982). **Associations & Accomplishments:** Canadian College of Health Service Executives: Executive, Certified, Former Director for Manitoba; American Academy of Medical Administrators: Fellow, Diplomate, Director for Canada; American College of Health Care Executives; Royal Society of Health, Fellow; Canadian Society for International Health; University of Ottawa Health Administration Alumni Association; Registrant of the Pharmacy Examining Board of Canada; Chairman and Member of numerous professional and advisory boards and committees at international, national, provincial, regional, and local levels; Actively involved in community activities including Community Foundation, Chamber of Commerce, Shrine Circus and Lodge activities; Canadian Who's Who, University of Toronto; '99 Award, Kappa Psi Pharmaceutical Fraternity; International Who's Who of Professionals; Health Executives of the Year Award, American Academy of Medical Administrators; Esprit de Corps Award, Selkirk & District General Hospital; Frequent publisher; Canadian Who's Who; International Who's Who of Top Executives. **Education:** University of Ottawa, Master's in Health Administration (1978); University of Toronto, Postgraduate Residency in Hospital Pharmacy (1973); Temple University, Bachelor of Science in Pharmacy (1972). **Personal:** Married to Linda Irene in 1973. Three children: Emma Lynn, Kathryn Frances, and Magda Mila. Mr. Kuber enjoys Hungarian culture and Jazz music.

Patricia Young Lackey, R.N., C.D.E.

Charge Nurse
Stringfellow Memorial Hospital
P.O. Box 38
Anniston, AL 36202–0038
(205) 235–8939
Fax: Please mail or call

8062

Business Information: Stringfellow Memorial Hospital is an acute care medical facility. A nurse with 21 years of hospital and nursing home experience, Mrs. Lackey joined the Hospital in 1976 as an L.P.N., working in the Med–Surg and Progressive Care Units as well as the Diabetes Treatment Center. She presently serves as Charge Nurse of the Med–Surg Unit and is a Certified Diabetic Educator of both patients and nursing staff. **Career Steps:** Stringfellow Memorial Hospital: Charge Nurse – Medical–Surgical Unit (1993–Present), Case Manager and Nurse Educator – Diabetes Treatment Center (1990–1993), Charge Nurse (1986–1988), L.P.N. – Progressive Care Unit (1983–1986), L.P.N. (1980–1983), Staff Nurse – Medical–Surgical Unit (1976–1980); Office Manager, Forte Internal Medicine (1994–1995); L.P.N., Mary Brandon Nursing Home (1975–1976). **Associations & Accomplishments:** American Diabetic Association; American Association of Diabetic Educators; Phi Theta Kappa National Honor Fraternity; Chairman's Club of the American Diabetes Association; Employee of the Month, Stringfellow Memorial Hospital (1993). **Education:** Gadsden State Junior College, Associate's Degree and Academic Achievement Award in Division of Nursing (1986); Harry M. Ayers State Technical College – Anniston, Alabama, L.P.N. Graduate (1975); C.P.R. Certified; Certified C.P.R. Instructor; Certified Diabetes Educator. **Personal:** Married to Calvin Lackey, Sr. in 1988. Two children: Calvin, Jr. and Elizar. Two granddaughters: Jennie and Katie. Mrs. Lackey enjoys photography, flowers, sewing, collecting antiques, and Alabama football.

Melissa U. LaCour

Director Health Information Management
Columbia Lakeland Medical Center
6000 Bullard Avenue
New Orleans, LA 70128
(504) 243–4200
Fax: (504) 243–4279

8062

Business Information: Columbia Lakeland Medical Center is a full–service medical facility providing health and related services to the New Orleans area. As Director Health Information Management, Ms. LaCour oversees management of three supervisors and a clerical staff of eleven. She is also responsible for coding analysis, abstracting and confidentiality. Other duties include processing of monthly and peer review reports, and marketing information. **Career Steps:** Director Health Information Management, Columbia Lakeland Medical Center (1994–Present); Assistant Director, Health Information Management, Southern Baptist Hospital (1991–1992); Manager, Health Information Management, Health South Rehabilitation Center (1991). **Associations & Accomplishments:** American Health Information Management Association; Greater New Orleans Health Information Management Association. **Education:** Louisiana Technical University, B.S.–M.R.A. (1990). **Personal:** Married to Ricky in 1992. Two children: Brett Thomas and Beth Catherine. Ms. LaCour enjoys family.

Amy M. Simmons–LaFine

Nursing Director — SICU and Respiratory Therapy
St. Mary's Hospital
500 West Court Street
Kankakee, IL 60901–3661
(815) 937–8716 EXT: 2070
Fax: (815) 937–3499

8062

Business Information: Saint Mary's Hospital, a Member of the ServantCor Human Services Family, is a 203–bed, Catholic–affiliated acute care hospital, offering a not–for–profit health care system. Services include the provision of in–house services, a designated trauma center (the first one in the State), three medical units, and in–patient & out–patient, home care, and ambulance services. A practicing nurse since 1978, Amy LaFine joined St. Mary's Hospital in 1989. As Nursing Director of SICU and Respiratory Therapy Units, she is responsible for the quality of the care, as well as the oversight of a support staff of approximately 50 people, hiring, training, counseling, and the implementation of projects. **Career Steps:** Saint Mary's Hospital: Nursing Director — SICU and Respiratory Therapy (1989–Present); Director of Nursing Services (1983–1989), Nursing Supervisor (1980–1983). **Associations & Accomplishments:** Sigma Theta Tau Nursing Honor Society; Illinois Organization of Nurse Executives; American Association of Critical Care Nurses; American Association of Neurosurgical Nurses; Kankakee Historical Society. **Education:** Olivet Nazarene University, B.S.N. (1978); Northwestern University, Kellog Nurse Executive Leadership Program. **Personal:** Married to Alan W. in 1993. One child: Alaina Michelle. Ms. LaFine enjoys renovating her home, gourmet cooking, music, continuing education, and physical fitness.

Douglas K. Laipple, M.D.

Department Chairman – Department of Psychiatry
Floyd Medical Center – Harbin Clinic
330 Turner–McCall Boulevard, Suite 302
Rome, GA 30165–2748
(706) 295–2288
Fax: (706) 802–1023

8062

Business Information: Floyd Medical Center is a tertiary care, teaching and research hospital. A practicing physician since 1977 and a Board–Certified Psychiatrist, Dr. Laipple joined Floyd Medical Center and the Harbin Clinic as Staff Psychiatrist in 1986 and as Chairman of the Department of Psychiatry in 1994. Serving in both capacities, he is a pain specialist, as well as a provider of psychiatric care to patients. Concurrent with his medical duties at Floyd Medical Center, he serves as Associate Staff Psychiatrist at Redmond Regional Medical Center; Staff Psychiatrist and Chairman of the Department of Psychiatry at Windwood Psychiatric Hospital; and as an Associate Clinical Professor of Psychiatry at Uniformed Services University of the Health Sciences. **Career Steps:** Floyd Medical Center: Staff Psychiatrist (1986–Present), Chairman of the Department of Psychiatry (1994–Present); Associate Staff Psychiatrist, Redmond Regional Medical Center (1986–Present); Windwood Psychiatric Hospital: Staff Psychiatrist (1992–Present), Chairman of the Department of Psychiatry (1994–Present); Associate Clinical Professor of Psychiatry, Uniformed Services University of the Health Sciences (1984–Present). **Associations & Accomplishments:** American Medical Association; American Psychiatric Association; American Academy of Clinical Psychiatrists; Licensures: State of Georgia Medical License, American Board of Psychiatry and Neurology, and American Academy of Pain Management; Member of the Pharmacy and Therapeutics Committee, Redmond Regional Medical Center; Medical Association of Georgia; Georgia Psychiatric Physicians Association; American Association of Clinical Psychiatrists; American Medical Association Physician Recognition Award; Military Consultant to the Surgeon General for Psychiatry; Commissioned in the Regular United States Army in 1966 and resigned with Honorable Discharge in 1973; Commissioned in U.S. Air Force in 1973 and retired as a Colonel after more than 20 years of active duty military service in 1986; Military decorations include: Bronze Star Medal for Valor with three oak leaf clusters, Air Medal, Army Commendation Medal for Valor with two oak leaf clusters, Viet Nam Honor Medal, and Viet Nam Gallantry Cross. **Education:** Eisenhower Army Medical Center, Fort Gordon, Georgia, Fellowship in Psychosomatic Medicine (1982); Wilford Hall USAF Medical Center, Lackland Air Force Base, Texas: Residency in General Psychiatry (1981), One Year Internship in Psychiatry (1978); School of Aerospace Medicine, Brooks Air Force Base, Texas, Post Graduate Flight Surgeon (1977); Medical College of Georgia, Augusta, Georgia, M.D. (1977); United States Military Academy, West Point, New York B.S. (1966). **Personal:** Married to Rebecca in 1966. Five children: Julie, Alison, Megan, Kurtiss, and Matthew. Dr. Laipple enjoys playing bridge and baseball.

Danine Lajiness – Polosky
Vice President of Quality Improvement
Six County, Inc.
2927 Bell Street
Zanesville, OH 43701
(614) 455–5754
Fax: (614) 455–5759

8062

Business Information: Six County, Inc. is a community mental health agency servicing six counties in Ohio. The agency offers outpatient counseling, partial hospitalization, group therapy, community support programs, and psychiatric counseling to mentally disabled adults and others. As Vice President of Quality Improvement, Mrs. Lajiness – Polosky oversees the performance of approximately 20 employees. She handles staff training, updating of clinical records, community programs, and client/patient satisfaction. **Career Steps:** Vice President of Quality Improvement, Six County, Inc. (1995–Present); Clinical Coordinator, The Children's Hospital (1993–1995); Float Nurse, The Children's Hospital (1991–1993). **Associations & Accomplishments:** Nursing Honor Society; Who's Who Among Nurses. **Education:** University of Phoenix, MN (1995); University of Detroit – Mercy, BSN & ASASAS (1984). **Personal:** Married to John in 1990. Mrs. Lajiness – Polosky enjoys sewing, reading, running, and spending time with her husband.

Patricia Lake–Blyden
Chief of Medical Records
Roy Lester Schneider Hospital
48 Sugar Estate Road
St. Thomas, Virgin Islands 00802
(809) 776–8311 Ext. 2253
Fax: (809) 776–0610

8062

Business Information: Roy Lester Schneider Hospital, formerly Saint Thomas Hospital, is a 165 bed acute care facility. Local in scope, the Hospital offers ambulatory and inpatient care with skilled care referred out. As Chief of Medical Records, Ms. Lake–Blyden is responsible for the disposition of the Facility's medical records and directing the activities of her department. She also oversees budgeting, committee membership, and is responsible for performance improvement and legal work. Ms. Lake–Blyden also serves as liaison between medical staff and Hospital administration. **Career Steps:** Chief of Medical Records, Roy Lester Schneider Hospital (1993–Present); Manager Custom Services/Claims Processing, GHMSI (1992–1993); Assistant Chief, Medical Records, St. Thomas Hospital (1984–1990). **Associations & Accomplishments:** Alpha Kappa Alpha Sorority, Inc.; Sigma Theta Omega Chapter, St. Thomas/St. John; Founding President, Sima Theta Omega Chapter (1990); Secretary Guardian Angels Youth Group of the Wesley Methodist Church; Gypsy Carnival Troupe. **Education:** University of the Virgin Islands, M.B.A. Program (In Progress); Morris Brown College, B.S. in Health Records Administration; Emory University, Certificate in Health Records Administration; **Personal:** Married to Glenn L. in 1994. Ms. Lake–Blyden enjoys cooking and singing.

Penny L. Lamb, RRA
Director of Medical Records
Roger Mills Memorial Hospital
5th & L.L. Males Avenue
Cheyenne, OK 73628
(405) 497–3336
Fax: (405) 497–2124

8062

Business Information: Roger Mills Memorial Hospital is a fifteen bed acute care emergency services medical facility. Established in 1966, the Hospital is comprised of two staff physicians and one physicians assistant. As Director of Medical Records, Ms. Lamb handles all functions related to medical records and assists the medical care coordinator. **Career Steps:** Director of Medical Records, Roger Mills Memorial Hospital (1995–Present); Medical Coder, Emergency Physician Billing Services (1994–1995); Medical Records Coder, University Hospital. **Associations & Accomplishments:** Oklahoma Hospital Association. **Education:** Southwestern Oklahoma State University, B.S. (1992); Registered Records Administrator. **Personal:** Married to Bill in 1991. One child: Jacob. Ms. Lamb enjoys computers and church.

Philip H. Lander, M.D.
Radiologist
Jewish General Hospital
3755 Cote–Sainte Catherine Road
Montreal, Quebec H3T 1E2
(514) 340–8233 Ext.5350
Fax: (514) 340–7907
EMAIL: See Below

8062

Business Information: Jewish General Hospital, a full service hospital serving the needs of Montreal, Quebec, is a multi–cultural facility for acute and subacute care. As Radiologist, Dr. Lander specializes in musculoskeletal and spine radiology. He does musculoskeletal multi–imaging and interventional studies at the hospital. Internet users can reach him via: P.Lander@Objectpeople.on.ca. **Career Steps:** Radiologist, Jewish General Hospital (1971–Present); Resident, Montreal General Hospital (1968–1970); Resident, Beth Israel Hospital (1967–1968). **Associations & Accomplishments:** Radiologists Society of North America; International Skeletal Society; International Spine Injection Society; American Roentgen Ray Society; Alpha Omega Alpha; Association of Radiologists of Quebec; Canadian Medical Association; Quebec Medical Association; American College of Radiology; New York Academy of Sciences; 54 Publications and Abstracts on Radiology and related subjects; 51 Scientific Presentations on Orthopedics, Arthritis, and other subjects; 20 Scientific Exhibitions and Lectures; Various Awards and Honors; Director of American Men and Women of Science; University Scholar, McGill University; Several Appointments to Specialized Committees and Associations. **Education:** McGill University: M.D.C.M. (1966), B.Sc. with distinction (1964); National Board of Medical Examiners, Diplomate (1967); American Board of Radiology, Diplomate (1972); Royal College of Physicians and Surgeons, Canada, Fellow Diagnostic Radiology (1971); Medical Council of Canada Certification (1966); Corporation of Physicians of Quebec (1971). **Personal:** Married to Freema in 1967. Three children: Anthony, Jonathan, and Michael. Dr. Lander enjoys photography, tennis, sailing, mountain biking, bird watching, skiing, reading, and the relaxation found in music.

Beverly J. Lanigan–Gilmour
Director of Human Resources
Mount Sinai Hospital
600 University Avenue
Toronto, Ontario M5G 1X5
(416) 586–5037
Fax: (416) 586–5045

8062

Business Information: Mount Sinai Hospital is one of the premiere tertiary care hospitals, medical research and teaching institutions in the world. The Toronto location is affiliated with the University of Toronto and has been voted one of the ten best companies for women in Canada. As Director of Human Resources, Ms. Lanigan–Gilmour is responsible for all aspects of human resources, including training and development, counseling, hiring of personnel, as well as administration, operations, finances, public relations, accounting, legal, taxes, and strategic planning. **Career Steps:** Director of Human Resources, Mount Sinai Hospital (1973–Present). **Associations & Accomplishments:** President, Canadian Associates of Health Care Human Resource Management. **Education:** University of Toronto, C.D.N. School of Management **Personal:** Married to Donald Gilmour in 1985. Three children: Kelly, Cathy, and Jim. Ms. Lanigan–Gilmour enjoys swimming, travel, and networking with her peers.

Mollie Larsen
Practice Manager
St. Francis, Inc.
3409 Ludington
Escanaba, MI 49829
(906) 789–4449
Fax: (906) 789–4463

8062

Business Information: St. Francis, Inc. provides healthcare management and consulting to hospital–owned physician practices. As Practice Manager, Ms. Larsen is responsible for managing all phases of operations for twenty–three providers at ten locations, employing 90 people in nine specialties. She is also a Recruiting Specialist, coordinating with client physicians in staff development and training. **Career Steps:** Practice Manager, St. Francis, Inc. (1990–Present); Director of Operations, Partners National Health Plans (1988–1990); Member Services Manager, Wisconsin Health Organization (1985–1988). **Associations & Accomplishments:** Medical Group Management Association; University of Wisconsin – Green Bay Alumni; Optimist Club; City of Escanaba Recreation Board. **Education:** University of Wisconsin – Green Bay, B.A. (1995). **Personal:** Two children: Christopher and Catherine. Ms. Larsen enjoys quilting, singing, and gardening.

Virginia Marie Larson, RN, BSN, MA, CHE, CNAA
Director of Patient Care
Albert Lea Medical Center
404 Fountain Street
Albert Lea, MN 56007
(507) 377–6337
Fax: (507) 377–6327

8062

Business Information: Albert Lea Medical Center is a full–service healthcare institution specializing in the diagnosis, treatment, and rehabilitation of patients. The Hospital provides any type of primary and secondary medical inpatient and outpatient services. As Director of Patient Care, Ms. Larson is responsible for all nursing services, including overseeing and coordinating patient care services in all clinical disciplines. **Career Steps:** Director of Patient Care, Albert Lea Medical Center (1996–Present); Director of Nursing, Naeve Health Care Association (1991); Director of Home Health. **Associations & Accomplishments:** Organization of Leaders in Nursing; College of Health Care Executive; American College of Medical Practice Executives; American Nurses Association. **Education:** St. Mary's, M.A. (1994). **Personal:** Married to Larry. Ms. Larson enjoys spending time with her husband and children.

George H. Latta, III, M.D.
Physician
Methodist Neonatology Associates
Methodist Hospitals of Memphis (Central)
Memphis, TN 38103
(901) 726–7000
Fax: Please mail or call

8062

Business Information: Methodist Neonatology Associates is an in–care hospital Neonatal group practice for the care and treatment of critical and premature infants. Established in 1978, the Group currently employs six people. As Physician, Dr. Latta provides diagnosis and treatment for critically ill infants. **Career Steps:** Physician, Methodist Neonatology Associates (1995–Present); Neonatologist, Southern Mississippi Neonatology (1994–1995); Neonatologist, Colorado Neonatology Associates (1992–1994). **Associations & Accomplishments:** Fellow, American Academy of Pediatrics (during Fellowship, he conducted research on markers for infections in newborns); American Medical Association. **Education:** East Tennessee State University, M.D. (1986); Dartmouth College (1986–1988); Stanford University (1988–1989); Vanderbilt University (1989–1990); University of Tennessee – Memphis (1990–1992). **Personal:** Dr. Latta enjoys camping, hiking, scuba diving, running and restoring an 1890 antique Old Towne canoe made of wood and canvas.

Ms. Beth A. Law
Resources and Solid Waste Manager
National Naval Medical Center
8901 Wisconsin Avenue, Bldg. 14
Bethesda, MD 20889–5600
(301) 295–0725
Fax: (301) 295–6461

8062

Business Information: National Naval Medical Center, funded by the U.S. Navy, is a full–service institution that provides quality medical care (i.e., medical diagnosis, treatment and rehabilitation) to active duty and retired military members and their families. Additionally, research for Navy medicine is conducted and educational services are provided on a 240–acre campus. Established in 1942, National Naval Medical Center currently employs 6,400 people. As Resources and Solid Waste Manager, Ms. Law is responsible for the management of the Solid Waste, Source Reduction, Recycling, Natural Resources and Historical Resources Programs, as well as Cultural Programs in Legacy Fund Grants. She also works with the Volunteer Department coordinators on waste reduction issues. **Career Steps:** Resources and Solid Waste Manager, National Naval Medical Center (1991–Present); Earth Day Coordinator, Open Space Advisory Committee (1990); Environmental Educator, Various locations (1980–1982 and 1987–1991); Assistant for Professional Lecturer, Center for Professional Well–Being (1982–1987). **Associations & Accomplishments:** Sterling Foundation – started first recycling drop–off site in 1990 and is still operated by volunteer staff; Won Governor's Award for Volunteering Excellence and Renew America Outstanding Programs; Published articles in military base paper; 1995 Winner White House Closing the Circle Awards – Environmental Excellence. **Education:** University of Maine at Orono, B.S. (1979). **Personal:** Two children: Robby and Jimmy. Ms. Law enjoys sports, outside activities and volunteer work.

George A. Law Jr.

Chief Financial Officer
South End Community Health Center, Inc.
400 Shawmut Avenue
Boston, MA 02118–2006
(617) 425–2040
Fax: (617) 425–2043

8062

Business Information: South End Community Health Center, Inc. provides health care services including, but not limited to pediatric, adult medicine, OB/GYN, laboratory testing, dentistry, optometry, podiatry, speech/hearing/language, mental health and social services, nutrition counseling, women/infants/children programs, AIDS counseling, and educational services. As Chief Financial Officer, Mr. Law is responsible for coordinating all fiscal activities at four locations, including maintenance of records and developing reports. In addition, he supervises all computer activity: hardware and software acquisition, system development, staff training, and the maintenance and development of a twenty–three workstation LAN. He administers the retirement and savings plan, cafeteria plan, and public transportation program, reporting directly to the Executive Director, Treasurer, and Board of Directors. **Career Steps:** Chief Financial Officer, South End Community Health Center, Inc. (1990–Present); Treasurer/Business Manager, Charmss Collaborative (1987–1990); Controller, Coastal Community Counseling Center (1978–1987). **Associations & Accomplishments:** Institute of Management Accounts; Association of Government Accountants; American Society of Notaries; Nonprofit Financial Managers; Employee Advisory Board for 5 A–Day; Former Auditor, Attleboro Area Council of Churches; Former Member, School Improvement Council. **Education:** Northeastern University, B.S. (1974); University of Massachusetts, A.S. (1963); Stonehill College: Certificates in Management and Computer Science; Pennsylvania State College, Certificate for Economics and Sociology; Military Schools (U.S. Army): Administration, Computer Processing, and Logistics – Superior Student; Attended: Salem College, Bridgewater State College, Boston State College, and Framingham State College. **Personal:** Married to Patricia F. in 1979. Three children: Jennifer Lynne, George Arthur III, and Samuel Edward. Mr. Law enjoys participating in his children's activities, working on his log home, vehicle restoration, coin collecting, stamp collecting, photography, and gardening.

Dr. Jacques E. LeClerc

Physician and Chairman of ENT Department
Center Hospital de L'Universite Laval
2705 Boul Laurier
Sainte–Foy, Quebec G1V 4G2
(418) 654–2118
Fax: (418) 654–2247

8062

Business Information: Center Hospital de L'Universite Laval is a full–service healthcare institution specializing in the diagnosis, treatment, and rehabilitation of patients. Dr. LeClerc chose Otolaryngology as his specialized field because of the variety of procedures that could be performed (between 200–250). Board certified in 1984, Dr. LeClerc is now Department Chairman of the hospital. He is also a practicing Physician, Professor, and Researcher. He handles hands–on teaching and lecturing to ten residents, and, in cooperation with other departments, does research in retrospective studies. **Career Steps:** Physician and Chairman of ENT Department, Center Hospital de L'Universite Laval (1996–Present); Co–Chairman, Royal College of Surgeons ENT Board of Examiners (1996–Present); Director of ENT Department, Jeffery Hale Hospital (1987). **Associations & Accomplishments:** Canadian Medical Association; American College of Surgeons; Royal College of Surgeons; American Board of Otolaryngology; Canadian Society of Otolaryngology and Head and Neck Surgery; Published in numerous papers. **Education:** Post Graduate Training: University of Toronto, Pittsburgh, PA, and Paris, France (1984–1985); Laval University: M.D. (1979), LMCC (1980), NBME (1980); ENT Certifications: Province of Quebec (1984); Royal College of Surgeons, FRCS(c) (1984); American Board of Otolaryngology (1984); American College of Surgeons, FACS (1988). **Personal:** Married to Emmanuelle in 1988. Three children: Jean–Thomas, Antoine, and Louis–David. Dr. LeClerc enjoys snow skiing, tennis, and sailing.

Donna L. Ledbetter

Director of Perioperative Services
Johnson City Medical Center
400 North State of Franklin Road
Johnson City, TN 37604
(423) 461–6502
Fax: (423) 461–6592

8062

Business Information: Johnson City Medical Center is a tertiary care, level I trauma center offering all surgical services, including open heart and renal transplant. Established in 1940, the Center currently employs 1,200 people. As Director of Perioperative Services, Mrs. Ledbetter is responsible for the management of all aspects of surgical services and oversight of a support staff of more than 300 people. **Career Steps:** Johnson City Medical Center: Director of Perioperative Services (1991–Present), Clinical Manager – ASTC (1989–1991), Clinical Manager – PACU (1988–1989). **Associations & Accomplishments:** AONE; TONE; Association of Operating Room Nurses; Tennessee Nurses Association. **Education:** East Tennessee State University, A.S. (1972). **Personal:** Married to Doug in 1984. Three children: Douglas, Jason, and Amber. Mrs. Ledbetter enjoys reading, antiques, and spending time with her children.

Claudia Z. Lee, M.B.A.

President
C Z Lee & Associates
4141 Ball Road, #265
Cypress, CA 90630
(714) 527–7305
Fax: (714) 527–0147
EMAIL: See Below

8062

Business Information: C Z Lee & Associates is a consultation service in comprehensive breast center development, market assessment, and strategic planning. Serving as President, Ms. Lee is responsible for all aspects of operations. In this capacity, she has assisted scores of programs across the country. She has a 20–year history of progressively complex administrative, operational and consultative responsibilities in cancer program development, strategic planning, marketing, education, and research. She also has a broad scope of hands–on, hospital–based experience ranging from an NCI–Designated Comprehensive Cancer Center setting to the private practice–based community hospital oncology and research environment. Concurrently, she serves as Vice President of Oncology Services at United Western Medical Centers at Santa Ana and Anaheim, California, providing leadership direction to the oncology and HIV/AIDS programs. Additionally, she is responsible for business development, marketing, program planning, and oncological research. Internet users can reach her via: CZLEE@UWMC.COM **Career Steps:** President, C Z Lee & Associates (1995–Present); Vice President of Cancer Services, United Western Medical Centers (1995–Present); Vice President, Oncology Associates, Inc. (1994–1995); Senior Manager, Oncology Resource Consultants, Inc. (1994); Director, Oncology Division, Ronning Management Group, Inc. (1991–1994); Vice President, Memorial Cancer Institute, Memorial Health Services (1988–1991); Administrative Director, Hospital Cancer Program, Long Beach Memorial Medical Center (1980–1988); Administrator, Memorial Cancer Research Foundation of Southern California (1978–1980); Cancer Control Administrative Director, Roswell Park Memorial Institute (1976–1978); State University of New York at Buffalo: Research Associate – Preventive Dentistry Program, Department of Behavioral Sciences, School of Dentistry (1974–1976), Lecturer – Learning Center, Oral Communications Department (1972–1973), Teaching and Administrative Assistant, Department of Education Psychology (1971–1973). **Associations & Accomplishments:** Nominating and Education Committees, Association of Cancer Executives (1995–Present); Founding Member, American College of Oncology Administrators (Chapter of American Academy of Medical Administrators); Guest Editor & Co–Editor of two peer–reviewed professional journals (Journal of Oncology Management and Cancer Management); American Cancer Society, Long Beach/Harbor/Southeast Unit (CA); American Cancer Society, California State Division; Community Cancer Control of Los Angeles; General Member, Association of Community Cancer Centers; Co–Founder, President (1983) Cancer Care Network of Greater Long Beach; Health Care Executives of Southern California; Women in Healthcare Administration; Oncology Nursing Society; American Association of Cancer Education; American Cancer Society /Erie County Unit (NY); Soroptimists International of Long Beach (CA); Various Publications, Presentations, Videotapes, Abstracts and Posters. **Education:** La Verne University, M.B.A. (1990); Occidental College, B.A. in Psychology (1962); California State University – Long Beach, Certificate in Executive Mangement Practices (1986). **Personal:** Married to Randy Pesano in 1974. Two children: Phyllis and Pamela. Ms. Lee enjoys gardening and needlework.

Marsha R. Leffel

Director of Nursing Services
OMH Medical Center, Inc.
P.O. Box 1038
Okmulgee, OK 74447–1038
(918) 758–3210
Fax: (918) 756–5968

8062

Business Information: OMH Medical Center, Inc. is a full service acute care hospital and home health agency. Comprised of sixty–six beds, seventeen of which are located in a geriatric/psychiatric unit, the Hospital offers emergency, surgery, labor and delivery services, as well as a home health agency that has so far made over 11,641 visits in 1996. As Director of Nursing Services, Ms. Leffel is responsible for acute care, geripsych unit, and oversight of home health services. She also supervises all aspects of nursing care, schedules, personnel evaluations, and quality of patient care. **Career Steps:** Director of Nursing Services, OMH Medical Center, Inc. (1995–Present); Director of Nursing Services, Community Hospital Lakeview (1994–1995); Francis H. Oliver, M.D. F.A.C.C./The McAlester Clinic, Inc. (1992–1994); Staff Nurse/Surgery, McAlester Regional Health Center (1989–1992); Staff Nurse/Surgery, Arkansas Valley Bone and Joint Clinic (1984–1987). **Associations & Accomplishments:** American Nurses Association; Association of Operating Room Nurses; Past Secretary, OSNA, OR Interest Group; National Bylaws Committee (1971–1973); National Editorial Committee AORN Journal (1973–1974); Former Member, Board of Directors/President Elect, AORN Central OK.; South OK City Junior College Preceptor Faculty; Surgical Technician Program; Served as a consultant to several hospitals and medical affiliates; Author of three publications; DePuy Award for Excellence in Medical Journalism, AORN Congress (1975); Nurse of the Year Award Nominee, Oklahoma State Nurses Association (1972); Charles B. Moore Award Nominee (1969). **Education:** Texas Women's University, B.S. (1967); Central State University, Graduate Level Courses (1972); Harvard Medical School, Intra–Aortic Balloon (1978); AHA: Advanced Cardiac Life Support (1992,1995), Lipid Disorders Training (1993); Acute Care Management of the Cardiovascular Patient; State Registered In: Texas, Oklahoma, and Arkansas. **Personal:** Married to David Lamonte Leffel in 1994. Three children: Larry, Cynthia, and Joseph. Ms. Leffel enjoys being a bronze sculptor, utilizing the lost wax method.

Diane R. Leger

Vice President of Finance
Memorial Health Care Center
645 Osage Street
Sidney, NE 69162–1714
(308) 254–5825
Fax: (308) 254–2300
EMAIL: See Below

8062

Business Information: Memorial Health Center is a general hospital serving the Sidney, Nebraska area, providing a 63–bed acute care unit and a 70–bed long–term care unit. As Vice President of Finance, Ms. Leger is responsible for the management of all financial aspects of the hospital and nursing home, including admissions, patient accounting, information systems, payroll, and accounting. She is also responsible for all medical records and directing the activities of a staff of 25. Internet users can also reach her via: GENLEGER@aol.com **Career Steps:** Vice President of Finance, Memorial Health Center (1994–Present); Chief Finance Officer, Brim Health Care, Inc. (1992–1994); Accounting Manager, Campbell Memorial Hospital (1990–1992). **Associations & Accomplishments:** American Management Association; Hospital Financial Management Association. **Education:** University of South Dakota, M.B.A. (1990); Black Hills State College, B.S. in Accounting. **Personal:** Two children: John and Sarah. Ms. Leger enjoys singing and aerobics.

Sandra Lemiesz

•••━━━◉━━━•••

Assistant Manager of Radiology
United Regional Medical Services
9200 West Wisconsin Avenue
Milwaukee, WI 53226
(414) 777-3784
Fax: (414) 259-9290

8062

Business Information: An entity of Froedtert Hospital, United Regional Medical Services provides in-patient and out-patient services, radiological and diagnostic imaging, and full-line diagnostic laboratory services. A registered radiological technologist, Sandra Lemiesz held various radiologic staff and supervisory positions at Froedtert Hospital since 1980. Transferring to United Regional Medical Services in October of 1993, as Assistant Manager of Radiology she has responsibility for staffing of 95 employees in CT Scanning, Ultrasound and General Diagnostic units. Sandra also assists in the overall management operations of the Radiology Department as whole, as well as the evaluation and monitoring of all support personnel. **Career Steps:** Assistant Manager of Radiology, United Regional Medical Service (1993-Present); Froedtert Hospital: Supervisor of Radiology (1987-1993), Senior Technologist CT Scanning (1983-1987), Staff CT/Diagnostic Radiologic Technology (1980-1982). **Associations & Accomplishments:** American Society of Radiologic Technologists; Wisconsin Society of Radiologic Technologists; Keller Alumni Network Association; General Electric Medical Systems Customer Advisory Board. **Education:** Keller Graduate School of Management, M.B.A. (1994); College of St. Francis, B.S. in Health Arts; St. Luke's Hospital of Milwaukee – School of Radiologic Technology, Registered Radiologic Technologist. **Personal:** Ms. Lemiesz enjoys competitive ballroom dancing, collection of Mattel's Barbie dolls, memorabilia, and travel.

Suzanne Lemire, M.D.
Director
Hopital De L'Enfant–Jesus
1401–18e Rue
Quebec, Quebec G1J 1Z4
(418) 649-5882
Fax: (418) 649-5570

8062

Business Information: Hopital De L'Enfant–Jesus is a full service medical/teaching facility providing medical care and related services to the area, in addition to providing training in medical care and technologies to medical students and residents. As Director, Dr. Lemire oversees all aspects of the hospital's gastroenterology department, and is responsible for ensuring quality patient care, administration, scheduling and personnel management, and strategic planning. Concurrent with her present position, Dr. Lemire is Clinical Professor of Medicine at Laval University, Quebec City. **Career Steps:** Director, Hopital De L'Enfant–Jesus (1968-Present); Clinical Professor of Medicine, Laval University (Present). **Associations & Accomplishments:** Governor of the American College of Gastroenterology for the Province of Quebec; Past President of the Canadian Association of Gastroenterology; American Gastroenterology Association; American Society for Gastroenterology and Endoscopy; Fellow, American College of Gastroenterology. **Education:** John Hopkins Balto, Specialist in Gastroenterology (1967); Laval University Medical School; Licensee of the Medical Council of Canada. **Personal:** Dr. Lemire enjoys camping and cross country skiing.

Kathleen C. Lendosky
Registered Nurse
Saint Mary's Hospital
1183 Lake View Road
West Bend, WI 53095-8201
(414) 291-1220
Fax: Please mail or call

8062

Business Information: Saint Mary's Hospital is a full-service, acute care medical facility, providing diagnosis and treatment of patients. A practicing nurse since 1969, Ms. Lendosky joined Saint Mary's Hospital as a Registered Nurse and Clinician for the Orthopedic Unit in 1986 and transferred to Surgical Intensive Care Unit (SICU) as a Registered Nurse and Clinician in 1989. She is responsible for caring for patients recovering from open heart, vascular, and lung surgeries, in addition to caring for neurosurgical/neurological patients. Other duties and skills include, orthopedic surgical care, pediatric, NICU, telemetry, general medical surgical, angioplasty unit, medical intensive care unit, coronary intensive care unit, and burn care. Concurrently, she floats to area hospitals' ICUs, through an external pool agency. **Career Steps:** Registered Nurse, Saint Mary's Hospital (1986-Present); Registered Nurse Supervisor, Samaritan Extended Care Facility (1983-1986); Licensed Practical Nurse, Pediatric Unit, Saint Alphonsus Hospital (1975-1983); Licensed Practical Nurse, Saint Joseph's

Hospital (1973-1975); Nursing Assistant, Samaritan Extended Care Facility (1969-1973); Dietary (1968-1969). **Associations & Accomplishments:** AACN; American Heart association; VFW Auxiliary Secretary; Chairperson fo Lilian Campbell Scholorship Fund; Archery Club Board Member; Demonstrated CPR to Girl Scout Troop; Showed Visual Aide on Stages of Fetal Development; Chair, Staff and Clinician Meetings; Enviromental Council Member; IVAC Task Force Commitee; Hospital Wide, Length of Stay Commitee; Peer Relations; Outdoor Badger State Games: Archery, Bronze Medal, 1993 – Silver Medal, 1994; Indoor State Archery Champion, 1993. **Education:** Moraine Park Technical College, A.A. (1982); Presently enrolled for B.S.N. at Graceland University, Virginia (Outreach Program). **Personal:** Married to Robert in 1974. Mrs. Lendosky enjoys reading, archery, playing piano, biking, hiking, camping, waterskiing,continuing education through workshops and seminars, and belonging to a book club.

Mila A. Leong, M.D.
Staff Pulmonologist
Atlantic City Medical Center
313 Kelly Drive
Galloway Township, NJ 08201
(609) 441-2148
Fax: (609) 441-2116

8062

Business Information: Atlantic City Medical Center is an acute care hospital, providing multi–specialty physician group practices, emergency and ambulatory care services. As Staff Pulmonologist, Dr. Leong is responsible for providing health care to pediatric patients in pulmonology. Her primary focus is treatment of children with asthma, chronic lung disease, and other pulmonary infections. She has also been involved in the care of critically ill children. Concurrent with her patient practice, she teaches medical students and resident physicians, and conducts research. **Career Steps:** Staff Pulmonologist, Atlantic City Medical Center (1995-Present); Pediatric Pulmonology Fellow, St. Christopher's Hospital for Children (1992-1995); Resident Physician, Rush–Presbyterian – St. Luke's Medical Center (1990-1992). **Associations & Accomplishments:** American Thoracic Society; American Medical Association; American Academy of Pediatrics. **Education:** University of the Philippines, M.D. (1982), B.S. in Zoology (1978). **Personal:** Dr. Leong enjoys interior design, reading, writing, collecting dolls, and traveling.

Michael P. Lewko, M.D.
Chief of Geriatrics
St. Joseph's Hospital and Medical Center
703 Main Street
Paterson, NJ 07053
(201) 754-4152
Fax: (201) 754-4166

8062

Business Information: St. Joseph's Hospital and Medical Center, established in 1867, is a 792-bed, teaching hospital and medical center serving a large urban population of Paterson, Passaic and Clifton, New Jersey. As Chief of Geriatrics, Dr. Lewko is responsible for all administration, clinical care and teaching of medical residents, as well as the supervision of 10–15 people. Concurrent with his position at St. Joseph's Hospital, he operates his own Geriatric–Rheumatology practice providing diagnosis and treatment of patients with arthritic and rheumatic conditions. At St. Joseph's Hospital he is the medical director of a 38–bed Geriatric Special Care Unit. He was also instrumental in setting up a subacute care unit in the hospital. In an outpatient office he runs an inter–disciplinary Geriatric Assessment Program assessing the frail elderly, and serves as Medical Director of a 141–bed nursing home affiliated with St. Joseph's Hospital. Additionally, Dr. Lewko holds faculty appointments at Robert Wood Johnson Medical School and Seton Hall University School of Graduate Medical Education. Dr. Lewko may be reached at his private office as follows: 716 Broad Street; Clifton, NJ 07013; Business Phone: (201) 754-4152; Fax: (201) 754-4166. **Career Steps:** St. Joseph's Hospital and Medical Center: Chief of Geriatrics (1995-Present), Associate Chief of Geriatrics (1991-1995), Office: 703 Main Street, Paterson, NJ, 07053; Faculty Appointment, Robert Wood Johnson Medical School and Seton Hall University School of Graduate Medical Education; Medical Director, St. Vincent's Nursing Home (1991-1995). **Associations & Accomplishments:** American Geriatrics Society; American College of Rheumatology; American Medical Directors Association; Ukrainian Medical Association of North America; Board Member, Robert Wood Johnson Medical School Alumni Association; Interviewed and published in local media; Active in the Ukrainian Scouting Organization "Plast". **Education:** Rutgers University Medical School, M.D. (1985); Robert Wood Johnson University Hospital, Internal Medicine Residency (1985-1988); Roger Williams General Hospital, Geriatric Medicine Fellowship (1988-1989); Brown University, Chief Resident, Veteran's Administration Hospital (1989); Hospital of University of Pennsylvania, Geriatric–Rheumatology Fellowship (1989-1991). **Personal:** Married to Svitlana in 1989. One

child: Marta. Dr. Lewko enjoys playing the piano, tennis and golf.

John Libertino, M.D.

•••━━━◉━━━•••

Chairman, Board of Governors/Hospital President
Lahey–Hitchcock Medical Clinic
41 Mall Road
Burlington, MA 01805
(617) 273-8330
Fax: (617) 273-8999

8062

Business Information: Lahey–Hitchcock Medical Clinic is a full service, 300 bed, medical center and hospital. The second largest facility in the U.S. solely held by physicians, the Hospital provides high–tech tertiary care. Regional in scope, the Hospital has two other facilities throughout three states, and a total staff of 1,000 nationally and internationally known physicians (500 of which are affiliated with Lahey–Hitchcock Medical Clinic). As Chairman, Board of Governors, Dr. Libertino is responsible for all administration and operations involving the Hospital. He serves as president of the Medical Center, and oversees recruitment of physicians, quality of patient care, and strategic planning. **Career Steps:** Lahey–Hitchcock Medical Clinic: Chairman, Board of Governors (Present), Chairman of Surgery, Chairman of Urology. **Associations & Accomplishments:** American Urology Association; Association of G.V. Surgeons; Fellow, American College of Surgery; Society of Clinical Vascular Surgery; International Cardiovasic Society. **Education:** Gerorgetown Medical School, M.D. (1965); N.Y.U., Windham College, B.S. (1961). **Personal:** Married to Mary Jo in 1963. Two children: John and Cristopher. Dr. Libertino enjoys reading.

Jack Liebhart
Chief Operating Officer and Director of Human Resources
Pershing Memorial Hospital
P.O. Box 408
Brookfield, MO 64628-0408
(816) 376-2222
Fax: (816) 376-3521

8062

Business Information: Pershing Memorial Hospital is a 57–bed, rural hospital with two satellite locations, a 44–bed skilled nursing unit and a rural health clinic. As Chief Operating Officer, Mr. Liebhart works with the Chief Executive Officer to plan any changes, agree on management philosophy, and take over in the absence of the CEO. As Director of Human Resources, he is responsible for managing all human resource activities, including employment and benefits. **Career Steps:** Chief Operating Officer and Director of Human Resources, Pershing Memorial Hospital (1991-Present); Director of Economic Development, Brookfield Economic Development Council (1987-1990); Assistant Vice President and Human Resources, Farm Credit Services (1961-1986). **Associations & Accomplishments:** Missouri Society of Human Resources Directors; Rotary International; Elks Lodge. **Education:** Northeastern Missouri State University, B.S. in Business Administration (1961). **Personal:** Married to Schar Lotie in 1962. Mr. Liebhart enjoys golf, hunting, fishing, and computers.

Joseph S. Lim, BS, BRT
Area Manager
Vencor Hospital
Rt. #3, Box 227–B, 1107 Caroline Street
Rusk, TX 75785
(903) 530-7629
Fax: (903) 683-6807

8062

Business Information: Vencor Hospital is a long–term sub-acute setting providing care for the elderly in skilled nursing homes throughout East Texas. As Area Manager, Mr. Lim oversees all daily operations of the Dallas Facility. His responsibilities include marketing, staffing, orientations, and coordinating with clinical therapists. In charge of the Respiratory Rehabilitation Program, Mr. Lim also evaluates therapy programs and serves as a liaison between the Facility and physicians. Dr. Lim wa the first physician to utilize respiratory therapy in the Asian Pacific arena. **Career Steps:** Area Manager, Vencor Hospital (1994-Present); Director, Respiratory Care, East Texas Medical Center (1989-1993); Supervisor–RT, Dharan Health Care, ARAMCO, Saudi Arabia (1983-1988). **Associations & Accomplishments:** American Association of Respiratory Care; Vice President, North East Texas for Respiratory Care; Life Member, Philippine Association for Respiratory Care; Texas Society for Respiratory Care; American Heart Association; American Lung Association; Biology Teachers Association of the Philippines; Past Member of Kiwanis Club; First Founder of Inhalation Therapy in the Philippines (1971). **Education:** University of Chicago, B.S. R.T. (1980); University of San Agustin: B.S. in

Biology, Bachelor of Arts (1970); Tufts University School of Medicine, Respiratory Therapy Program (1975); University of Santo Tomas–Manila, M.S. (1978). **Personal:** Married to Araceli in 1973. Two children: Jocely Lim and Cole Bowman. Mr. Lim enjoys teaching, swimming, and travel.

Rolf Loertscher, M.D.
Director, Transplant Division
Royal Victoria Hospital
687 Des Pine Ave West
Montreal, Quebec PQC H3A 1A
(514) 843–1649
Fax: (514) 843–1708
EMAIL: See Below

8062

Business Information: Royal Victoria Hospital is a full–service, tertiary care and teaching hospital, providing instruction to medical students and diagnosis and treatment to patients. A native of Switzerland, Dr. Loertscher has been a practicing physician since 1975. He joined the Royal Victoria Hospital as Director of the Transplant Division in 1995, specializing in Nephrology research activities. Concurrently, he serves as Associate Professor of Medicine for medical residents. Internet users can reach him via: MCRL@Musica.McGill.CA. **Career Steps:** Director, Transplant Division, Royal Victoria Hospital (1995–Present); Associate Professor, McGill University (1992–Present). **Associations & Accomplishments:** American Society of Transplant Physicians; Transplantation Society; American Society of Nephrology; International Society of Nephrology; Canadian Transplant Society; Canadian Society Clinical Investigation; Swiss Society of Nephrology; Swiss Federation of Physicians. **Education:** University of Zurich, M.D. (1975). **Personal:** Married to Margrit in 1975. Three children: Mathias, Christine and Oliver. Dr. Loertscher enjoys skiing.

Mark D. Lombardi, B.S., R.Ph.

Pharmacy Director
Martin Memorial Health Systems
300 Hospital Drive, P.O. Box 9010
Stuart, FL 34995–9010
(407) 288–5892
Fax: (507) 223–6937

8062

Business Information: Martin Memorial Health Care Systems consists of two hospitals (260–bed and 100–bed, both acute care facilities). Also included are eight medicenters, a surgicenter, numerous physician offices, and a volunteer medicine clinic, which serves the indigent in the community. A healthcare pharmacist with thirteen years experience, Mr. Lombardi joined Martin Memorial Health System as Pharmacy Director in 1995. He provides pharmaceutical services for the entire health care system, as well as management of the pharmacy departments at two hospitals. In addition, he is responsible for hiring and firing procedures, budget establishment for the departments, and overlooks consultant pharmacist services for the surgicenter and volunteer clinic. **Career Steps:** Pharmacy Director, Martin Memorial Health Systems (1995–Present); Diagnostek, Inc.: Pharmacy Director of Bayonet Pt. Medical Center (1993–1995), Assistant Pharmacy Director of Muskegee Regional Medical Center (1991–1993); Pharmacy Director of Gerald Champion Hospital, Owen Healthcare (1989–1991). **Associations & Accomplishments:** Florida Society of Healthcare Pharmacists; American Society of Healthcare Pharmacists; Florida Pharmacy Association; Indian River Pharmacy Association; Palm Beach Regional Society of Hospital Pharmacists. **Education:** University of Iowa, B.S. Pharmacy (1983), Buena Vista College, B.S. in Biology (1980). **Personal:** Married to Cindi in 1990. Mr. Lombardi enjoys golf, fishing and travel.

Concepcion Q. Longo, M.D.

Medical Director
University Pediatric Hospital
P.O. Box 191079
San Juan, Puerto Rico 00919
(809) 754–3700
Fax: (809) 756–8907

8062

Business Information: University Pediatric Hospital, the only children's hospital that the Department of Health has in Puerto Rico, is a 139–bed, tertiary care hospital, providing a full range of medical services. Inpatient services include: pediatric intensive care unit (8 beds), neonatal unit (16 beds), neonatal intensive intermediate care unit (24 beds), general surgery ward (30 beds), pediatric ward (30 beds), oncology ward (13 beds), and an infant ward (14 beds). Other facilities services include pharmacy, pathology, ambulatory care, rehabilitation,

full dental unit for chronic diseases, radiology, and clinical laboratory services. A practicing physician since 1966, Dr. Longo serves as the Medical Director of University Pediatric Hospital, responsible for organizing, coordinating, and supervising all medical services, including serving as a liaison with the medical school, coordinating admissions, directing plans, budgeting, politics, etc. She also assists the CEO in the recruitment of medical staff. **Career Steps:** Medical Director, University Pediatric Hospital (19–Present) **Associations & Accomplishments:** Puerto Rico Medical Association; Head of Medical/Legal Review Board; Member, Governing Board of University Pediatric Hospital; Member, Faculty Executive Committee; Member, Ethics Committee. **Education:** University of Puerto Rico Medical School, M.D. (1966). **Personal:** Married to Dr. Fernando L. Longo in 1964. Four children: Fernando, Luis, Dennise, and Enid. Dr. Longo enjoys reading and gardening.

Lorraine Luciani, LPN
Director of Patient and Volunteer Services
Florida Medical Center
5000 West Oakland Park Boulevard
Ft. Lauderdale, FL 33313
(305) 735–6000 ext 4515
Fax: Please mail or call

8062

Business Information: Florida Medical Center is a 459 bed acute care facility specializing in medical diagnosis, treatment and rehabilitation of primarily elderly patients. Established in 1974, the Medical Center currently employs 10 professionals and has over 150 volunteers. As Director of Patient and Volunteer Services, Mrs. Luciani serves as an administrative liaison between patients, families and volunteers. She is responsible for all administrative aspects regarding the department including recruitment, training and development of volunteer programs. **Career Steps:** Director of Patient and Volunteer Services, Florida Medical Center (1985–Present); LPN, Hollywood Medical Center (1983–1985). **Associations & Accomplishments:** Director, Volunteer Services State of Florida. **Education:** Sheridan Voc–Tech, LPN (1983). **Personal:** Married to Andrew in 1970. Two children: Douglas and Amy. Mrs. Luciani enjoys reading and spending time with family.

Eugene M. Lugano, M.D.
Physician
Pennsylvania Hospital
700 Spruce Street, Suite 500
Philadelphia, PA 19106
(215) 829–5027
Fax: (215) 829–6391

8062

Business Information: Pennsylvania Hospital, affiliated with the University of Pennsylvania and the oldest hospital in North America, is a 480–bed, tertiary medical and teaching hospital. A practicing physician since 1975 and a Pulmonary and Critical Care Specialist, Dr. Lugano joined Pennsylvania Hospital in 1982. Concurrent with his medical practice, he serves as Associate Professor at Thomas Jefferson University, provides consulting services at Wil's Eye Hospital, and conducts clinical research. **Career Steps:** Physician, Pennsylvania Hospital (1982–Present); Assistant Professor of Medicine, Hospital University of Pennsylvania (1981–1982); Associate Professor, Thomas Jefferson University (Present); Consultant, Wil's Eye Hospital (Present). **Associations & Accomplishments:** Fellow, American College of Chest Physicians; American Thoracic Society; Association of Critical Care Medicine. **Education:** University of Pennsylvania Medical College, M.D. (1975); Princeton University, A.B. (1971). **Personal:** Married to Marcia Boraas in 1973. Two children: Elisabeth and Daniel. Dr. Lugano enjoys wine collecting and travel.

Ena A. Lynch

Administrator
Interim Health Care
9654 Brookline Avenue, Suite 110
Baton Rouge, LA 70809
(504) 926–7668 (800) 921–9920
Fax: (504) 926–7768

8062

Business Information: Interim Health Care is a nationwide, home health organization consisting of more than 300 offices in the U.S. and Canada. The Hospital is a 130–bed, primary acute care and psychiatric hospital. As Administrator, Ms. Lynch provides the overall executive administration for all financial, personnel, and day–to–day operations of the Baton Rouge facility. **Career Steps:** Administrator, Interim Health Care (1996–Present); River West Medical Center: Chief Financial Officer (1993–1996), Controller (1990–1993); Controller, Oil and Marine Corporation (1988–1990). **Associations & Accomplishments:** American Institute of Certified Public Accountants; Hospital Financial Management Association; Louisiana Society of Certified Public Accoun-

tants. **Education:** Louisiana State University, B.S. (1988); Certified Public Accountant (1992). **Personal:** Married to William in 1989.

Joseph P. Lynch III, M.D.
Attending Physician and Professor of Medicine
The University of Michigan Medical School
1500 East Medical Center Drive, 3916 TC
Ann Arbor, MI 48109–0360
(313) 936–5040
Fax: (313) 936–5048

8062

Business Information: The University of Michigan Medical School is a tertiary hospital, medical research and instructional institution. Established in 1817 the Center is a University–affiliated academic medical center. As Attending Physician and Professor of Medicine, Dr. Lynch specializes in Pulmonary and Critical Care Medicine, and inpatient and outpatient services. Dr. Lynch is also a Professor of Internal Medicine with the Division of Pulmonary and Critical Care, and the Medical Director for the Lung Transplant Program. **Career Steps:** The University of Michigan Medical School: Attending Physician and Professor of Internal Medicine (1994–Present), Associate Professor of Internal Medicine (1984–1994), Assistant Professor of Internal Medicine (1979–1984). **Associations & Accomplishments:** American Thoracic Society; Fellow and Regent, Board of Governors, American College of Chest Physicians; Written 25 book chapters. **Education:** Harvard Medical School, M.D. (1973); Dartmouth Medical School, B.M.S. (1971); Harvard College, B.A. (1969). **Personal:** Married to Evelyn Shuer. Three children: Michael David, Daniel Patrick and Lindsay Kelly.

Colin S.J. MacColl, M.D.
General Surgeon
Calgary District Hospital Group
Suite 320–401 9 Avenue SW
Calgary, Alberta T2P 3C5
(403) 221–4489
Fax: (403) 221–4406

8062

Business Information: Calgary District Hospital Group is part of the Calgary Regional Health Authority. The Associate Clinic provides general surgery, much of it laparoscopic, to adults and children. Dr. MacColl, a General Surgeon specializing in laparoscopic surgery, is very involved with the laparoscopic programs at the Rockyview Hospital and the Alberta Children's Hospital, and publishes articles related to his field. **Career Steps:** General Surgeon, Calgary District Hospital Group (1994–Present); Laparoscopic Fellowship, McGill University (1993–1994); General Surgery Residency, University of Calgary (1988–1992). **Associations & Accomplishments:** Alberta Association of General Surgeons; Alberta Medical Association; Native Physicians Association in Canada. **Education:** McGill University: Laparoscopic Fellowship (1993), B.Sc., M.D.; Fellow Royal College of Surgeons of Canada. **Personal:** Married to Alice Lee in 1992. Three children: Amy, Amber, and Cailean. Dr. MacColl enjoys biking and antique collecting.

Gordon K. Mahanna, D.D.S.
Director, Section of Maxillofacial Prosthodontics & Dental Oncolo
University of Nebraska Medical Center
600 South 42nd Street
Omaha, NE 68198
(402) 559–7308 (402) 559–9220
Fax: (402) 559–8940

8062

Business Information: University of Nebraska Medical Center provides oral and extra oral prostheses for head and neck Cancer, trauma, and congenital patients, as well as dental oncology support for irradiation and chemotherapy patients. Affiliated with the University of Nebraska, the Center was established in 1991. Dr. Mahanna founded and developed the Section of Maxillofacial Prosthetics and Dental Oncology, and in his current capacity as Director, oversees the program, and is responsible for all research and development. Concurrently an Associate Professor, Dr. Mahanna is also responsible for instructing students and residents in the areas of maxillofacial and dental oncology. **Career Steps:** Director, Section of Maxillofacial Prosthodontics and Dental Oncology, University of Nebraska Medial Center (1989–Present); Fellow, M.D. Anderson Cancer Center (1988–1989); Resident, University of Texas Health Science Center, San Antonio (1986–1988). **Associations & Accomplishments:** American Dental Association; American College of Prosthodontists Fellow, American Academy of Maxillofacial Prosthetics; Fellow, International College of Dentists. **Education:** M.D. Anderson Cancer Center, Certificate, Maxillofacial Prosthodontics (1989); University of Texas Health Science Center, Certificate in Prosthodontics (1986); University of Missouri, D.D.S. with Distinction (1963). **Personal:** Married to Nancy in 1993. Six children: Kent, Thaine, Kimberly, Todd, Tim, and Theresa. Dr. Mahanna enjoys photography and antique bottle collecting.

John J. Maher
President/CEO
Sisters of Charity Hospital
2157 Main Street
Buffalo, NY 14214–2692
(716) 862–2000
Fax: (716) 862–1899

8062

Business Information: Sisters of Charity Hospital is a full–service, multi–specialty regional acute care hospital. As President and Chief Executive Officer, Mr. Maher is responsible for all aspects of operations for the hospital. **Career Steps:** President, Sisters of Charity Hospital (Present); Executive Vice President, St. Vincent Hospitals and Health Services, Indianapolis, IN; Administrator, St. Joseph Hospital, Tacoma, WA; Director, Professional Services, Medical College of Virginia Hospital, Richmond, VA. **Personal:** Mr. Maher enjoys golf, reading, and running.

Jack E. Maidman, M.D.

Chairman of the Department of OB/GYN
Long Island College Hospital
340 Henry Street
Brooklyn, NY 11201–5514
(718) 780–1647
Fax: (718) 780–1392

8062

Business Information: Long Island College Hospital, affiliated with SUNY–Brooklyn, is a full–service, tertiary acute care medical and teaching hospital. The Hospital provides diagnosis and treatment to patients, as well as instruction to students. A practicing physician since 1962 and a Board–Certified Obstetrician and Gynecologist, Dr. Maidman joined Long Island College Hospital as Chairman of the Department of OB/GYN in 1988. He is responsible for the direction of OB/GYN departmental functions and training of residents, in addition to his daily patient practice. **Career Steps:** Chairman of the Department of OB/GYN, Long Island College Hospital (1988–Present). **Associations & Accomplishments:** President (1995–1996), Brooklyn Gynecological Society. **Education:** University of California – San Francisco, M.D. (1962). **Personal:** Married to Ann. Three children: Bret, Ian, and John. Dr. Maidman enjoys reading, gardening, skiing, swimming, and exercising.

Doreen Makos
Director of Utilization Review
Riddle Memorial Hospital
1068 W. Baltimore Pike
Media, PA 19063
(610) 891–3325
Fax: (610) 891–3592

8062

Business Information: Riddle Memorial Hospital is a 251–bed, community hospital specializing in the diagnosis and treatment of patients. As Director of Utilization Review, Ms. Makos handles all record reviews and other administrative duties. **Career Steps:** Riddle Memorial Hospital: Director of Utilization Review (1993–Present), Utilization Review Coordinator (1986–1993), Intensive Care Nurse (1980–1986); NICU, St. Joseph's Hospital (1970–1971). **Associations & Accomplishments:** President, Southeastern Pennsylvania Association Healthcare Quality Professionals; Member Executive Board, Pennsylvania Association of Healthcare Quality; Hospital Association of Pennsylvania; WAWA Civic Association; Welsh Historic Society; Testified before the Pennsylvania House of Representatives Hearing on the Health Plan Accountability Act. **Education:** Neumann College, B.S. (1986); Wilkes Barre General Hospital – School of Nursing, Graduate (1969); Certified Healthcare Quality Professional; Registered Professional Nurse, Licensed in Pennsylvania and New York. **Personal:** Married to Michael J., Jr. in 1970. Two children: Christopher and Russell. Ms. Makos enjoys golf and lighthouses.

Peter E. Makowski

President and Chief Executive Officer
Citrus Valley Health Partners
140 West College Street
Covina, CA 91723
(818) 814–2430
Fax: (818) 814–2524

8062

Business Information: Citrus Valley Health Partners is a health care system management office, overseeing the operations of three acute care hospitals: Queen of the Valley Hospital (260 patients); Citrus Valley Medical Center (175 patients); and Foothill Presbyterian Hospital. Establishing Citrus Valley Health Partners as President and Chief Executive Officer in 1994, Mr. Makowski is responsible for all aspects of operations, including strategic planning, determining financial capabilities, planning, and administering the overall operations for the multi–hospital facilities. **Career Steps:** President and Chief Executive Officer, Citrus Valley Health Partners (1994–Present); President and Chief Executive Officer, Queen of the Valley Health Services (1993–1994); President and Chief Executive Officer, Community Health Corporation (1992–1993). **Associations & Accomplishments:** Board Member, VHA West; Board Member, Healthcare Association of Southern California; University of California – Los Angeles Health Services Management Alumni Association. **Education:** University of California – Los Angeles, M.P.H. (1980); Whittier College, B.A. (1976). **Personal:** Married to Cynthia in 1979. One child: Jacqueline. Mr. Makowski enjoys sports.

Dr. Nazir Malik

Consultant – Psychiatrist
Cape Breton Regional Hospital
1482 George Street
Sydney, Nova Scotia B1P 1P3
(902) 567–7730
Fax: (902) 567–7905

8062

Business Information: Cape Breton Regional Hospital is an acute and subacute care regional hospital located in Nova Scotia. The Hospital, established in 1906, serves approximately 125,000 residents and employs 500 people. As Consultant Psychiatrist, Dr. Malik treats patients with mental diseases and disorders at the hospital and at ALLIED CLINICS. He spends time in London (England), Pakistan and the U.S. consulting with colleagues on new treatments and techniques. **Career Steps:** Consultant Psychiatrist, Cape Breton Regional Hospital (1992–Present); Associate Professor of Psychiatry, King Edward Medical College (1990–1992); Assistant Professor of Psychiatry, F.J. Medical College (1987–1990). **Associations & Accomplishments:** Canadian Psychiatric Association; Nova Scotia Medical Society; Former Member, British Medical Association; International Society of Law and Mental Health; Consultant to Foundain House, Lahore. **Education:** King Edward Medial College, MBBS (1969); Royal College of Physicians – London; Royal College of Surgeons – England; Diplomate Board of Psychiatry (1974); Registered as a Physician, College of Physicians and Surgeons: Nova Scotia, General Medical Council of United Kingdom. **Personal:** Married to Riffett Rehana Malik in 1971. Three children: Ali Jawad, Farah Noushine, Sanaa Anoshey. Dr. Malik enjoys writing, travel, gardening, and cricket.

Alexander J. Malin
Director of Facilities Support Services
Sherman Health Systems
934 Center Street
Elgin, IL 60120
(847) 888–8962
Fax: (847) 742–9585

8062

Business Information: Sherman Health Systems is a management organization, providing medical support services to health care facilities in the Elgin, Illinois community. One of the hospitals it serves includes, Sherman Hospital, a 418–bed, full–service, acute health care facility and the largest providing hospital in the Chicago area suburbs. Sherman Health Systems is the largest provider of cardio–catheterization services, in addition to providing health care services for an excellent trauma center, Level II neonatal unit, and 11 satellite locations; including nursing homes, ambulatory unit, resource center, home health services, and several practicing physicians affiliated with Sherman Hospital. As Director of Facilities Support Services, Mr. Malin administers the facilities departments, as well as corporate oversight for environment of care management. **Career Steps:** Director of Facilities Support Services, Sherman Health Services (1988–Present); Director, Humana Inc. (1984–1988); Director, I.C.H. Inc. (1980–1984). **Associations & Accomplishments:** American Society of Healthcare

---

Environmental Services; International Facility Management Association; Environmental Management Association; N.E.H.A.; National Association of Institutional Linen Management. **Education:** Century University, B.S. H.C.M. (1994); University of New Hampshire, A.A. in Business; University of Southern Maine, B.S.; Certifications: Infection Control, Environmental Management. **Personal:** Married to Christine S. in 1990. Two children: Ian and Paige. Mr. Malin enjoys golf, fishing, and travel.

Marilyn Manco–Johnson, M.D.
Medical Director
Mountain States Regional Hemophilia Center
4200 East 9th Avenue, C220
Denver, CO 80262
(303) 372–1753
Fax: (303) 372–1060

8062

Business Information: The Mountain States Hemophilia Center, operating under the auspices of the University of Colorado Health Science Center, specializes in providing services and on–going treatment research for patients with blood disorders. As Medical Director of the Mountain States Hemophilia Center, Dr. Manco–Johnson is responsible for the care and treatment of children and adults with hemophilia, HIV/AIDS and other blood related diseases. Concurrent to her position with the Medical Center, Dr. Manco–Johnson is a Professor of Pediatrics at the University of Colorado Health Science Center which provides all aspects of post–graduate education to residents and interns, as well as full tertiary care and clinical research hospital facilities. **Career Steps:** Medical Director, Mountain States Regional Hemophilia Center (1988–Present); University of Colorado Health Science Center: Professor of Pediatrics (1995–Present), Associate Professor of Pediatrics (1989–1995). **Associations & Accomplishments:** Society for Pediatric Research; Western Society for Pediatric Research; American Society of Pediatric Hematology and Oncology; Secretary and Treasurer, Hemophilia Research Society (1991–1994); International Society of Thrombosis and Haemostasis; Summer and Wilderness Camp for Children with Hemophilia and HIV+. **Education:** Thomas Jefferson University, M.D. (1974); Pennsylvania State University, B.S. (1972); University of Colorado Health Science Center: Pediatric Internship and Residency (1974–1977), Pediatric Hematology and Oncology Fellowship (1978–1981), Research Fellowship in Pediatric Hematology (1982–1984); Pediatric Clinical Research Center, Clinical Associate Physician (1984–1986). **Personal:** Married to Michael Manco–Johnson in 1984. Five children: Gemma, Jonathan, Brian, Katie and Michael Jr. Dr. Manco–Johnson enjoys hiking and reading.

Myrtle Magdalene (Maggie) Maness
Director
Moore Regional Hospital
P.O. Box 3000
Pinehurst, NC 28374
(910) 215–2056
Fax: (910) 215–2069

8062

Business Information: Moore Regional Hospital is a full service medical facility providing health and related services to the area. Comprised of labor and delivery, post–partum gynecology, nursery, neonatal intensive care units, pediatric and other services, the Hospital was established in 1930, and employs seventy–one people. As Director, Ms. Maness manages the total operation and direction of labor and delivery services. She is responsible for planning, coordinating, controlling and evaluating patient care services, management of personnel, and budgeting. **Career Steps:** Moore Regional Hospital: Director (1990–Present), Nurse Manager (1982–1990), Staff Nurse (1975–1982). **Associations & Accomplishments:** North Carolina Organization of Nurse Executives; Professional Business Women; Who's Who in American Nursing. **Education:** University of North Carolina, Chapel Hill, B.S.N. (1982); Sandhills Community College, A.D.N. (1975). **Personal:** One child: William Jeffrey. Ms. Maness enjoys reading, walking, playing the piano, and shopping.

Pura Manosa
Director of Medical Records
Hospital Pavia
P.O. Box 11137
San Juan, Puerto Rico 00910
(787) 727–6060 Ext.330
Fax: (787) 727–6060 Ext.496

8062

Business Information: Hospital Pavia, established in 1937, is a full–service private hospital comprised of 182 beds. The Hospital offers emergency, acute, ambulatory, and obstetrics/ gynecological care, as well as Cardiovascular surgery. As Director of Medical Records, Ms. Manosa oversees all aspects of the department, including administrative duties, and management of a staff of fourteen. **Career Steps:** Director of Medical Records, Hospital Pavia (1989–Present); Director of Medical Records, Hato Rey Psychiatric Hospital (1982–1994); Director of Medical Records, Hospital Del Maestro (1980–1982). **Associations & Accomplishments:** American Health Management Association; Asociacion de Calidad en Salud de Puerto Rico; Asociacion de Exalumnos de la Universidad del Sagrado Corazon; Asociacion de Manejo de Informacion de Puerto Rico. **Education:** Puerto Rico Health Department, Certification in Medical Records Administration (1989); College of the Sacred Heart, B.A. (1989); **Personal:** Two children: Antonio J. and Maria A. Vasquez. Ms. Manosa enjoys being an artisan in Nativity scene embroidery.

Mary E. Marinaro
Director of Clinical Quality Improvement
Centra State Medical Center
901 West Main Street
Freehold, NJ 07728
(908) 294–2825
Fax: (908) 294–2505

8062

Business Information: Centra State Medical Center, established in 1973, is a 240–bed acute care facility, providing diagnosis and treatment to patients. With nine years experience in the health care industry and a Healthcare Quality Professional, Ms. Marinaro joined the Center in 1994. Serving as Director of Clinical Quality Improvement, she directs the activities of utilization, quality improvement, and social services, as well as overseeing patient representatives and the Infection Control Coordinators Treatment Center, teaching CQI, and answering patient complaints. **Career Steps:** Director of Clinical Quality Improvement, Centra State Medical Center (1994–Present); Director of Nursing, Monmouth Chemical Department Center (1991–1994); Project Manager, MA Resources (1987–1991); Clinical Coordinator of Obstetrical, Monmouth Medical Center (1986–1987). **Associations & Accomplishments:** Healthcare Quality Professional; National Association for Healthcare Quality; Volunteer for a woman's shelter that helps battered women and their children. **Education:** Fairleigh Dickenson, M.P.A. (1994); Brookdale Community College, A.A.S.; Jersey City State, B.A.; Attending: La Salle University. **Personal:** Married to Michael in 1994. Two children: Brian and Amy. Ms. Marinaro enjoys dancing, reading, decorating, and landscaping.

Mina Markazi–Mojdehi
Acting Director, Nurse Anesthesia Program
Kings County Hospital Center
441 Clarkson Avenue
Brooklyn, NY 11203–2012
(718) 245–3259
Fax: (718) 756–1585

8062

Business Information: Kings County Hospital Center is an acute health care facility providing diagnosis and treatment of patients residing in Kings County and surrounding areas. As Acting Director of the Nurse Anesthesia Program, Mrs. Markazi–Mojdehi is a certified registered nurse anesthetist with fourteen years experience. She is responsible for all educational and administrative activities. **Career Steps:** Kings County Hospital Center – Nurse Anesthesia Program: Acting Director (1994–Present), Associate Director (1987–94), Clinical Coordinator – Staff CRNA (1982–87). **Associations & Accomplishments:** American Association of Nurse Anesthesiologists. **Education:** Brooklyn College, M.A. (1992); St. Joseph, B.A.; National Iranian Oil Co., B.S.N. **Personal:** Married to Khosrow Mojdehi, M.D. in 1986. Mrs. Markazi–Mojdehi enjoys dancing, swimming, and sewing.

Anthony P. Markello
Vice–President of Medical Affairs
Mercy Hospital
565 Abbott Road
Buffalo, NY 14220–2039
(716) 828–2053
Fax: (716) 828–2243

8062

Business Information: Mercy Hospital is a 350 bed community hospital affiliated with SUNY at Buffalo School of Medicine. A practicing physician since 1962, Board–certified in Internal Medicine, Dr. Markello was appointed as Vice President of Medical Affairs in 1992. In his current capacity, Dr. Markello is responsible for evaluating and monitoring the performance of medical and dental staff members in regard to the medical care of patients. **Career Steps:** Vice–President of Medical Affairs, Mercy Hospital (1992–Present); Internist, A.P. Markello, M.D., P.C. (1970–92); Attending Physician, Erie County Medical Center (1970–73). **Associations & Accomplishments:** Erie County delegate to the New York State Medical Society (1994–Present); American College of Physicians; American College of Physician Executives. **Education:** State Univeristy of New York – Buffalo, M.D. (1962).

Personal: Married to Nancy in 1955. Three children: Karen, Jeffrey, and Kristin. Dr. Markello enjoys golf, tennis, travel, and sports.

Carol A. Martin
Director
Carondelet St. Joseph's Hospital
350 North Wilmot Road
Tucson, AZ 85711
(520) 821–3803
Fax: Please mail or call

8062

Business Information: Carondelet St. Joseph's Hospital is a full–service acute care medical facility. A member of the Carondelet Health Network, headquartered in St. Louis, Missouri, the Hospital is comprised of 325 beds, with 12 operating rooms, and plans to expand through a sharper focus on out-patient services, consolidation, and an extended recovery plan. As Director of Inpatient and Outpatient Surgery, Mrs. Martin is responsible for oversight of the operating and recovery rooms. Her duties include scheduling, admitting, and support of the heart and eye surgery teams (approximately 25 people). **Career Steps:** Carondelet St. Joseph's Hospital: Director, Inpatient and Outpatient Surgery (1990–Present), Director of Cardiac Services (1980–1990), Director of Critical Care (1975–1980). **Associations & Accomplishments:** Arizona Hospital and Healthcare Association; Manager of the Year (1990); Outstanding Nurse of the Year for Arizona (1985). **Education:** Chadwick University, M.B.A. (1996); R.N. **Personal:** Married to G.B. Bowman in 1981. Two children: John and Jason. Mrs. Martin enjoys spending time with her husband, gardening, being active in Boy Scouts of America, and hiking.

Caroline D. Martin
Director of Practice Management
Macon Northside Hospital
400 Charter Boulevard
Macon, GA 31210
(912) 757–5942
Fax: (912) 757–5941

8062

Business Information: Macon Northside Hospital is an acute care healthcare facility, providing diagnosis and treatment to patients. Established in 1984, Macon Northside Hospital currently employs 415 people. As Director of Practice Management, Ms. Martin is responsible for the management of four physician practices, overseeing the management of three others, and setting up new physician offices for the Hospital. **Career Steps:** Macon Northside Hospital: Director of Practice Management (1995–Present), Administrator (four physician practices) (1991–Present), Client Relations Representative (1990–1991). **Associations & Accomplishments:** Americans for AIDS Research; Patron, Harriet Tubman Museum. **Education:** Mercer University, M.B.A. (1995); Brenau College, B.A. in English and Business Administration. **Personal:** One child: Monty. Ms. Martin enjoys tennis and reading during her leisure time.

Thomas J. Martin, M.D.
Director of Inpatient Pediatrics
Aultman Hospital
2600 6th Street Southwest
Canton, OH 44710
(216) 438–7430
Fax: Please mail or call

8062

Business Information: Aultman Hospital is a tertiary–referral acute care hospital. As Director of Inpatient Pediatrics and Consulting Pediatrician, Dr. Martin is responsible for all aspects of inpatient pediatric operations, including serving as consultant and health care provider for critical care children. Concurrent with his position, he serves as Chairman Emeritus for the Department of Pediatrics at Geisinger Medical Society and Organizer for the Children's Hospital of Geisinger Medical Center, as well as serving as Adjunct Clinical Associate Professor at Jefferson Medical College. **Career Steps:** Director of Inpatient Pediatrics and Consulting Pediatrician, Aultman Hospital (1995–Present); Adjunct Clinical Associate Professor, Jefferson Medical College; Geisinger Medical Center: Chairman of Pediatrics (1975–1995), Founder and Organizer of the Children's Hospital of Geisinger (1990–1995). **Associations & Accomplishments:** American Board of Pediatrics (1968); American Medical Association; Ohio Medical Society; American Academy of Pediatrics (AAP), Ohio Chapter and Pennsylvania Chapter; B.P.O.E. Elks; Accredited Instructor in ATLS (1986–Present), ACLS (1987–Present), PALS (1990–Present), Neonatal Resuscitation (1989–Present), APLS (1990–Present); Various clinical experience and academic appointments; Pennsylvania Medical Society; Montour County Medical Society; Pediatric Society of Northeastern Pennsylvania; Ambulatory Pediatric Association; Association of Pedatric Program Directors; American Medical Society for Sports Medicine; Numerous offices and commit-

tees in Management of Geisinger Medical Center and Jefferson Medical College; Conducted numerous lectures; Pine Street Lutheran Church: Council (1993–Present), Chairman of the Religious Committee (1993–Present), Financial Committee (1994–Present); Author of numerous publications and presentations; Conducted numerous research activities; Recipient of several honors: Mead Johnson Nutritional Group Clinical Scholar Seminar (1987) and National Child Labor Committee Honor Award for Exceptional Service to Children and Youth (1992). **Education:** University of Pittsburgh, Residency (1965–1967), M.D. (1960); The Williamsport Hospital, Internship (1960–1961); Franklin & Marshall College, B.S. (1956). **Personal:** Married to Lois D. in 1992. Five children: Susan L. O'Malley, and Jack T. (M.D.), James S. (M.D.), David S. and Julia E. Martin. Dr. Martin enjoys skiing and athletic events.

Tomas Martinez
Hospital Administrator
Hospital Hermanos Melendez
P.O. Box 306
Bayamon, Puerto Rico 00960–0306
(809) 785–9784
Fax: (809) 269–0085

8062

Business Information: Hospital Hermanos Melendez is a full–service, general hospital. With over twenty–eight years experience in hospital administration, Mr. Martinez was appointed Administrator in 1992. In this capacity, he is responsible for all hospital administration functions, including operations and finances. **Career Steps:** Administrator, Hospital Hermanos Melendez (1992–Present); Administrator, Wilma N. Verquez Medical Center (1989–1992); Administrator, Damas Hospital (1981–1989). **Associations & Accomplishments:** American College of Health Executives; Colegio Administradores de Puerto Rico; Knights of Columbus; American Hospital Association; Puerto Rico Hospital Association. **Education:** University of Puerto Rico: MSHA (1968), BBA (1960). **Personal:** Married to Beatriz in 1959. Four children: Tomas, Beatriz, Astrid, and Ingrid. Mr. Martinez enjoys dominoes, baseball, basketball, classical music, and church activities (catholic).

William F. Mason, M.D.
Interventional Radiologist – QETI Health Sciences Centre
Victoria General Hospital
1278 Tower Road
Halifax, Nova Scotia B3H 2Y9
(902) 428–3770
Fax: (902) 428–3018
EMAIL: See Below

8062

Business Information: A family physician for many years, Dr. Mason began specializing in Interventional Radiology in 1968. He joined a group of twenty–two independent radiologists to form QETI Health Sciences Centre (operating out of Victoria General Hospital) while serving as an Associate Professor at Dalhousie University, a position he presently maintains. Internet users can reach him via: WMason2@dal.ac.ca **Career Steps:** Interventional Radiologist, QETI Health Sciences Centre, Victoria General Hospital (1968–Present); Dalhousie University: Associate Professor (1968–Present), Associate Dean of Postgraduate Medicine (1982–1988). **Associations & Accomplishments:** Founding Director and Chairman, Landmark East School for Children With Learning Disabilities; President, Canadian Association of Radiologists; Former President, Medical Society of Nova Scotia (1976–1977). **Education:** Dalhousie University, M.D. Frcp (1988); Acadia University, B.Sc.; Kings County Academy, Kentville, Nova Scotia. **Personal:** Married to Frances in 1957. Three children: William Thomson, Jennifer L., and Peter A. Dr. Mason enjoys sailing and tennis.

David S. Matheson, M.D.
Vice President of Clinical and Strategic Services
British Columbia's Children's Hospital
4480 Oak Street
Vancouver, British Co V6H 3V4
(604) 875–2494
Fax: (604) 875–3456
E MAIL: See Below

8062

Business Information: British Columbia's Children's Hospital is a 250–bed, full–service, multi–specialty medical facility and health service establishment, as well as a research and instructional institution. The Facility, specializing in acute therapy, performs various transplants (except liver), offers a cardiology and cardiovascular unit, an orthopaedic unit, a 47–bed neonatal nursery, and a 20–bed intensive care unit. BCCH is affiliated with a women's hospital for special high risk deliveries, and with the University of British Columbia. Currently the hospital employs 2,500 staff. As Vice President of Clinical and Strategic Services, Dr. Matheson oversees the medical staff and verifies applicant qualifications and references. Other responsibilities include development of quality assurance programs, quality improvement strategies, clinical practice guideline facilitation, strategic planning for the organization. He can also be reached via the Internet at: DMatheson@WPOG.CHILDHOSP.BC.CA. **Career Steps:** British Columbia's Children's Hospital: Vice President of Strategic Services, (1995–Present), Vice President of Medicine (1989–1995); Associate Professor of Immunology (1987–Present); Head of Division, Immunology, University of British Columbia (1987–1989). **Associations & Accomplishments:** Association of Medical Directors of Canadian Teaching Hospitals; Vancouver Health Board; Chair, British Columbia Reproductive Care Program; Medical Directors and Planning Committees of Council of University Teaching Hospitals. Education: University of Toronto, FRCPC (1979); University of Calgary, B.Sc. (Honors) (1967), M.D. (1974); University of Waterloo, M. Math (1968). **Personal:** Married to Verena in 1968. Two children: Spencer and Allan. Dr. Matheson enjoys tennis and reading."

Beverly A. Maxwell
Vice President of Nursing
Touro Infirmary
1401 Foucher Street
New Orleans, LA 70115
(504) 897–8485
Fax: (504) 897–8447

8062

Business Information: Touro Infirmary is an acute care, teaching hospital providing diagnosis and treatment to patients and education to medical students. One of the first hospitals to perform open heart surgery and having an extensive Cardiology Department, Touro Infirmary is the oldest hospital in New Orleans and one of seven hospitals in the Not–For–Profit Alliance. Established in 1852, Touro Infirmary currently employs 400 people. A practicing nurse practitioner for over six years, Ms. Maxwell joined Touro Informary in 1992. Serving as Vice President of Nursing, she is the senior nursing executive responsible for supervision and coordination of all operational and business aspects of nursing activities, as well as financial management functions and marketing strategies. She also works to ensure top quality patient care by regulating and sustaining the best personnel. **Career Steps:** Vice President of Nursing, Touro Infirmary (1992–Present); Director of Nursing, United Community Hospital (1991–1992); Vice President of Nursing, Suburban General Hospital (1989–1991). **Associations & Accomplishments:** New Orleans Association of Nursing Executives; Louisiana Association of Nursing Executives; American Association of Nursing Executives. **Education:** Loyola College, M.B.A. (1983); Johns Hopkins Hospital School of Healthcare, A.S./Nurse Practitioner; Sinai Hospital School of Nursing **Personal:** One child: John W.. Ms. Maxwell enjoys reading, music and travel.

Shari L. Maxwell, M.D.
Staff Physician
Henry Ford Hospital
131 Kercheval Avenue
Grosse Pointe, MI 48236–3630
(313) 343–5900
Fax: (313) 343–5963

8062

Business Information: Henry Ford Hospital is a full–service, acute–care hospital. A practicing physician since 1988 and Board–Certified in Obstetrics and Gynecology, Dr. Maxwell joined Henry Ford Hospital in 1992 as Staff Physician. She is responsible for providing health care to women, specializing in obstetrics and gynecology, in addition to serving as Clinical Instructor. **Career Steps:** Staff Physician, Henry Ford Hospital (1992–Present). **Associations & Accomplishments:** American College of Obstetrics and Gynecology; NAACP; Wayne County Medical Society; American Medical Association. **Education:** Wayne State Medical School, M.D. (1988); University of Michigan, B.A. (1982). **Personal:** Dr. Maxwell enjoys theater, skiing, and classical piano.

Russell F. Mazda, D.O., F.A.C.E.P.
ER Physician
St. Joseph Hospital
250 College Avenue
Lancaster, PA 17603
(717) 291–8111
Fax: (717) 291–8346

8062

Business Information: St. Joseph Hospital is a 210–bed, tertiary care and teaching hospital, providing acute primary care and instruction to students. A practicing physician since 1980 and a Board Certified Emergency Physician and Osteopathic Physician, Dr. Mazda currently serves in a faculty position at the Osteopathic Medical Center of Philadelphia teaching third and medical students. Concurrently, he serves as the Emergency Room Physician at St. Joseph Hospital, where he is responsible for the treatment of Emergency Room patients, specializing in osteopathic and critical care medicine. **Career Steps:** ER Physician, St. Joseph Hospital (Present); Clinical Instructor, Emergency Medicine Residency (1985–1990). **Associations & Accomplishments:** Fellow, American College of Emergency Physicians; American College of Osteopathic Emergency Physicians; American Osteopathic Association; Aircraft Owners and Pilots Association. **Education:** Philadelphia College of Osteopathic Medicine, D.O. (1980); Muhlenberg College, B.S. (1976). **Personal:** Married to Mary Pat in 1991. Dr. Mazda enjoys flying, scuba diving, windsurfing, bicycling, and travel.

Ron McAnulty
Chief Financial Officer
White County Hospital
400 Plum Street
Carmi, IL 62821
(618) 382–4171 Ext: 226
Fax: (618) 382–3628

8062

Business Information: White County Hospital is a rural, township, acute care hospital licensed for 49 beds for acute care and 98 beds for long term care. Partially funded by the government, eighty percent of White County Hospital's patients are serviced by Medicare. Joining White County Hospital as Chief Financial Officer in 1993, Mr. McAnulty is responsible for all financial aspects for all departments, including Purchasing, Business Office, Environmental Services, Plant Operations, Medical Records, Pharmacy, Re–hab Services, and Dietary departments. In addition, he has the overall supervision of the profit/loss preparation on a monthly basis. **Career Steps:** Chief Financial Officer, White County Hospital (1993–Present); Vice President of Store Development, Martin & Bayley, Inc. (1976–1992). **Associations & Accomplishments:** Hospital Financial Management Association. **Education:** B.A. (1973); Working on Master's Degree in Business Administration. **Personal:** Married to Brenda in 1988. Three children: Mark, Kathi, and Kristi. Mr. McAnulty enjoys golf and yard work.

Janice McDaniel, M.S.N., R.N.
Nurse Administrator
Davie County Hospital
208 Howardtown Road
Mocksville, NC 27028–7237
(704) 634–8328 1–888–507–4658
Fax: (704) 634–8359 (910) 998–8413
Home: (910) 988–4632

8062

Business Information: Davie County Hospital established in 1956, is an 83–bed medical facility located in Mocksville, North Carolina. Part of Carolina Medicorp, Inc. The Hospital provides medical care to a population of approximately 30,000, and plans to continue providing needed services to the community. Beginning her nursing career as a Candy Striper with the Hospital in 1964, Ms. McDaniel is currently one of three Administrators responsible for redesigning hospital monitoring and performance. Additional duties include performance feedback and improvements, and being strategically involved with the community to determine medical and healthcare services needed. Internet users can reach her via: jjmacadee@aol.com. **Career Steps:** Davie County Hospital: Nurse Administrator (1990–Present), Director of Quality Assurance/RM (1984–1990), Educational Coordinator (1978–1984). **Associations & Accomplishments:** Davie County Heart Association; Director, Rexall Showcase International (1996); Certified Nurse Administrator Advanced CNAA (1989); Sigma Theta Tau (1984); Certified Real Estate Investor (1996). **Education:** University of North Carolina, Charlotte: M.S.N. (1988), B.S.N. (1984), N.C.B.H., Diploma in Nursing (1971). **Personal:** Married to Larry in 1971. Two children: Ken and Brian. Ms. McDaniel enjoys singing, music, and networking.

John L. McHargue
Director of Imaging Services
Tri–City Medical Center
4002 Vista Way
Oceanside, CA 92056
(619) 940–3076
Fax: (619) 940–4004

8062

Business Information: Tri–City Medical Center is a district medical center, serving over 500,000 patients throughout north San Diego County. Joining Tri–City Medical Center as Director of Imaging Services in 1993, Mr. McHargue is operationally responsible for a $31 million Radiology Department, including X–ray and cat scanning services. **Career Steps:** Director of Imaging Services, Tri–City Medical Center (1993–Present); Director of Imaging Services, Mercy Healthcare (1990–1993); Director of Imaging, Chandler Regional Hospital (1988–1990). **Associations & Accomplishments:** American Registry of Radiologic Technologists; American Society of Radiologic Technologists; American Healthcare Radiology Administrator; San Diego District Society of Radiologic Technologists. **Education:** Oklahoma State University, B.S.; Cochise College, A.S.; Baylor University/U.S. Army, Diploma in Radiologic Technology. **Personal:** Married to Barbara in 1978. One child: Sean. Mr. McHargue enjoys snow skiing, computing, most sporting activities, reading, and golf.

Deanna McKinney, M.S., B.S.N.
Senior Vice President
Methodist Hospital
3615 19th Street
Lubbock, TX 79410
(806) 793–4301
Fax: (806) 784–5027

8062

Business Information: Methodist Hospital is a full–service acute and subacute care hospital with over 900 beds. Established in 1954 and employing 4,200 people, it is the largest hospital between Dallas, Texas, and the West Coast. As Senior Vice President, Ms. McKinney is in charge of the nursing staff, all 28 operating rooms a 66 bed rehabilitation unit, an Out–patient Rehabilitation Facility and an Endoscopy Center. Responsibilities include accountability for the administration of assigned clinical areas, functioning as a key member of the hospital administrative team and acting as liaison between the nursing staff, medical staff, and administration of Methodist Hospital. **Career Steps:** Methodist Hospital: Senior Vice President (1995–Present), President Texas Organization of Nurse Executives (1994–1995); Vice President (1988–1995); Director of Nursing (1982–1988). **Associations & Accomplishments:** American College of Healthcare Executives; West Texas Chapter of ACHE; American Organization of Nurse Executives; Texas Organization of Nurse Executives; Texas Hospital Association; Sigma Theta Tau International; Member of the Board of Directors, Lubbock Methodist Hospital. **Education:** Trinity University, M.S. (1994); Texas Tech University, B.S. Degree in Nursing; Methodist Hospital School of Nursing. **Personal:** Married to Paul. Two children: Jason and Tonya. Ms. McKinney enjoys gardening and needle work.

Mary Ann McLaughlin, M.D.
Physician
Mount Sinai Medical Center – Cardiovascular Institute
One Gustave L. Levy Place
New York, NY 10029–6574
(212) 241–5581
Fax: Please mail or call
EMAIL:MM374@Columbia.edu

8062

Business Information: Mount Sinai Medical Center – Cardiovascular Institute, a part of Mt. Sinai Hospital and Mount Sinai School of Medicine, is a health care facility specializing in cardiovascular diseases. As Physician, Dr. McLaughlin is responsible for providing diagnosis and treatment of patients in the Cardiology Division. **Career Steps:** Physician, Mount Sinai Medical Center – Cardiovascular Institute (1993–Present); Medical Intern and Resident, New York Hospital/Cornell Medical Center (1990–1993); Research Analyst, Office of Technology Assessment, U.S. Congress (1984–1987). **Associations & Accomplishments:** American College of Cardiology; American Heart Association; Alpha Omega Alpha – Medical Honor Society. **Education:** Columbia School of Public Health, M.P.H., pending 1996; Georgetown University, M.D. (1990); University of Virginia, B.A. (1984).

Mark C. McQuiggan, M.D.
President of Medical Staff
Providence Hospital – Mission Health
22250 Providence Drive, #203
Southfield, MI 48075
(810) 569–0162
Fax: (810) 552–9851

8062

Business Information: Providence Hospital – Mission Health is a 500–bed acute care hospital serving the populace of Southfield, Michigan and surrounding communities. A practicing physician since 1958, Board–certified in Urology, Dr. Mark McQuiggan serves as Providence Hospital's President of Medical Staff. Affiliated with Providence for the last 27 years, Dr. McQuiggan continues to provide full private practice services to patients in the fields of urological disorders and diseases in addition to providing the executive administration for all medical practices, ensuring quality care and patient delivery. **Career Steps:** President of Medical Staff, Providence Hospital – Mission Health (1969–Present). **Associations & Accomplishments:** Past President, Michigan Urological Association; American Medical Association; American Urological Association; American College of Surgeons; Diplomate, American Board of Urology. **Education:** University of Michigan, M.D. (1958). **Personal:** Married to Carolyn in 1961. Dr. McQuiggan enjoys bridge and tennis.

Allen G. Meek, M.D.
Professor & Chairman, Department of Radiation Oncology
Stony Brook University Hospital
SUNY at Stony Brook
Stony Brook, NY 11794–7028
(516) 444–2200
Fax: (516) 689–8801
EMAIL: See Below

8062

Business Information: The Stony Brook University Hospital is a full service hospital and medical school specializing in the diagnosis, treatment, and rehabilitation of patients. Dr. Meek currently serves as Professor and Chairman for the Department of Radiation Oncology. He may be reached through the Internet via: AMEEK@RADONC.SOM.SUNYSB.EDU **Career Steps:** Internship: The Johns Hopkins Hospital, MD – Medicine (1975); Residences: The Johns Hopkins Hospital – Medicine (1976,1978) – Radiation Oncology (1980–82); Fellowships: The Johns Hopkins Hospital – Medical Oncology (1979); Professional Boards & Licenses: FLEX (1974), Internal Medicine (1979), Therapeutic Radiology (1983); Medical Licensure: State of Maryland – D#17064 (1974), State of New York – #155889 (1983), National Cancer Institute – Investigator #11596; Academic Appointments: Assistant in Oncology, Johns Hopkins University (1979–1982); Assistant in Radiological Sciences, The Johns Hopkins University (1980–1982); Assistant Professor of Oncology, The Johns Hopkins University (1983–1984); Assistant Professor of Medicine, Johns Hopkins Hospital (1983–1984); Assistant Professor of Radiology, Johns Hopkins Hospital (1983–1984); Assistant Professor and Chairman of Radiation Oncology, SUNY Stony Brook (1983–1985); Associate Professor and Chairman of Radiation Oncology, SUNY Stony Brook (1985–1993); Professor & Chairman of Radiation Oncology, SUNY Stony Brook (1993–Present). **Associations & Accomplishments:** Phi Beta Kappa (1970); Member, Breast Cancer Treatment Quality Advisory Board for New York State (1993–Present); American College of Physicians; American Society of Clinical Oncology; American College of Radiology; N.Y. Roentgen Society; Radiation Research Society; International Society for Neutron Capture Therapy; American Radium Society; American Society of Therapeutic Radiology and Oncology; Numerous articles published in professional journals. **Education:** Amherst College – Massachusetts, B.A. Degree in Chemistry (1970); The Johns Hopkins University – Maryland, M.D. (1974).

Julian Ramsey Mellette Jr., M.D.
Professor of Dermatology and Director of Cutaneous Surgery
University of Colorado Health Sciences Center
Campus Box E153, 4200 East Ninth Avenue
Denver, CO 80262
(303) 372–1111
Fax: (303) 372–1159

8062

Business Information: University of Colorado Health Sciences Center is a full tertiary–care hospital, in affiliation with the University of Colorado providing research and medical education to residents. A Board–certified in Dermatology in 1978 and in Dermatopathology in 1984, Dr. Mellette serves as Professor of Dermatology and Director of Cutaneous Surgery. He focuses his practice in the medical and surgical treatment of skin disorders, as well as performs and teaches Mohs surgery — a highly sucessful method of surgical treatment of skin cancer. **Career Steps:** University of Colorado Health Sciences Center: Professor of Dermatology and Director of Cutaneous Surgery (1995–Present), Associate Professor of Dermatology (1990–1995); Chief of Dermatology, Fitzsimons Army Medical Center (1982–1990); Colonel, United States Army. **Associations & Accomplishments:** American Academy of Dermatology; American College of Mohs Micrographic Surgery and Cutaneous Surgery; American Society of Dermatologic Surgery; International Society of Dermatologic Surgery; Colorado Dermatologic Surgery; Noah Worchester Society; American Society of Dermatologic Pathology; Association of Military Dermatologists; Board Member, American College of Mohs Micrographic Surgery and Cutaneous Surgery; Best Doctors of America (1994). **Education:** Medical University of South Carolina, M.D. (1969); Wofford College, A.B. (1961). **Personal:** Married to Betty in 1991. Three children: Beth Ritland, Ramsey, and Brad. Dr. Mellette enjoys snow skiing, flying, and golf.

David C. Mendelssohn
Nephrologist
Toronto Hospital – General Division
200 Elizabeth St. Room 239, 13th Floor Eaton North
Toronto, Ontario M5G 2C4
(416) 340–4418
Fax: (416) 340–0029
EMail: See Below

8062

Business Information: Toronto Hospital – General Division is a full-service healthcare institution specializing in the diagnosis, treatment, and rehabilitation of patients. As Nephrologist, Dr. Mendelssohn is responsible for clinical teaching (for interns and residents), research in resource constraints, dialysis, and kidney biopsies. Internet users can reach him via: david.mendelssohn@utoronto.ca. **Career Steps:** Nephrologist, Toronto Hospital – General Division (1989–Present). **Associations & Accomplishments:** Board of Directors, Kidney Foundation; Frequent publisher. **Education:** Dalhousie University, M.D. (1983); McGill University, B.S.C. (1979). **Personal:** Married to Krisanne in 1982. Two children: Jamie and Joshua. Dr. Mendelssohn enjoys hockey.

Vicki L. Mentele
Vice President of Patient Services
Box Butte General Hospital
2101 Box Butte Avenue
Alliance, NC 69301
(308) 762–6660
Fax: (308) 762–1923

8062

Business Information: Box Butte General Hospital is a full–service acute care facility. A "stand alone" facility (not supported by county funds), the Hospital is comprised of 44 beds, and a staff of five doctors, two physician assistants, and one nurse practitioner. Established in 1976, the Hospital offers respiratory therapy, orthopedics, cardiovascular, dermatology, opthamology, podiatry, plastic surgery, and ear, nose, and throat care. As Vice President of Patient Services, Ms. Mentele supervises and directs all clinical services, and acts as a member of the administrative team. She is also responsible for attending board meetings, and acting as liaison between the employees and the Hospital. **Career Steps:** Box Butte General Hospital: Vice President of Patient Services (1994–Present), Medial/Surgical Nurse Manager (1990–1994); Director of Nursing, Ottumwa Manor (1974–1976). **Associations & Accomplishments:** Nebraska Organization of Nurse Executives; Box Butte General Hospital Auxiliary Advisory Board. **Education:** Methodist School of Nursing, Diploma; St. Joseph College, B.S.N. (In Progress). **Personal:** Married to Louis S. in 1974. Two children: Jaime and Justin. Ms. Mentele enjoys bowling and golf.

Susan R. Merryfield, MHCA, HFA, OTR
Administrator
Ball Memorial Hospital
2401 W. University Avenue
Muncie, IN 47303
(317) 747–4416
Fax: (317) 741–1562

8062

Business Information: Ball Memorial Hospital is an acute care, 460–bed hospital specializing in the diagnosis, treatment, and rehabilitation of patients. As Administrator, Mrs. Merryfield is responsible for the management of the sub–acute care unit, and the entire Hospital's compliance with state and federal regulations. She also coordinates and supervises care for patients aged 18 to over 100 years. **Career Steps:** Administrator, Ball Memorial Hospital (1994–Present); Director of Occupational Therapy, St. Francis Hospital (1992–1994); Director of Rehabilitation Services, University of Kansas Medical Center (1987–1992); Pediatric Rehabilitation Coordinator, Research Hospital (1976–1992). **Associations & Accomplishments:** Academy of Health Care Administrators; American Occupational Therapy Association; Board Member, Noblesville Soccer Club. **Education:** University of Kansas: MHCA (1992), B.S. in Occupational Therapy (1975). **Personal:** Married to David in 1974. Two children: Jessica and Alex. Mrs. Merryfield enjoys cross–stitch and bridge.

Susan M. Miles
Director of Communications
Carolinas Medical Center
1000 Blythe Boulevard
Charlotte, NC 28203–5812
(704) 355–2712
Fax: (704) 355–7239
E MAIL: See Below

8062

Business Information: Carolinas Medical Center is an acute and sub–acute medical facility serving the residents of Charlotte, North Carolina and surrounding areas. As Director of Communications, Ms. Miles manages the telecommunications support system for the Medical Center. Other responsibilities include staff recruitment, training, scheduling, and evaluating. Ms. Miles is involved in developing and implementing departmental budgets, and strategic planning for the future. Internet users can reach her via: miles@interpath.com. **Career Steps:** Director of Communications, Carolinas Medical Center (1986–Present); Charlotte Institute of Rehabilitation: Assistant Administrator (1981–1986), Director/Dietetics (1980–1981). **Associations & Accomplishments:** American Dietetic Association; HIMSS. Recipient of Outstanding Telecommunication Person of the Year award from HIMSS (1995). **Education:** Virginia Polytechnic Institute, B.S. (1975). **Personal:** Married to Paul in 1988. Ms. Miles enjoys scuba diving and dog obedience training.

Chuck L. Millburg
Chief Executive Officer
Shenandoah Memorial Hospital
300 Pershing Avenue
Shenandoah, IA 51601–2355
(712) 246–1230
Fax: Please mail or call

8062

Business Information: Shenandoah Memorial Hospital is a 110–bed, acute care and long term care hospital, providing diagnosis and treatment to patients. The Hospital provides 62 beds for long term patients and 48 beds for acute care patients. With nine years experience in hospital administration, Mr. Millburg joined Shenandoah Memorial Hospital in 1995. Serving as Chief Executive Officer, he is responsible for strategic planning, ensuring the hospital follows the Board of Directors direction, as well as overseeing all operations. Career milestones include the development of a Physician Hospital Organization, that has been used as a model throughout the State of Iowa. **Career Steps:** Chief Executive Officer, Shenandoah Memorial Hospital (1995–Present); Chief Executive Officer, EME Healthcare Consulting (1993–1995); Chief Executive Officer, Myrtug Memorial Hospital (1988–1993); Associate Administrator, Doctors Regional Medical Center (1986–1988). **Associations & Accomplishments:** Nu Pi – Nurses Honor Society; American College of Healthcare Executives; Board of Directors, Midwest Blood Services; American Red Cross. **Education:** Sangamon State University: M.B.A. (1982), B.N. **Personal:** Mr. Millburg enjoys sailing.

Martha J. Millett
Director of Admissions/Central Scheduling
St. Elizabeth Hospital
2209 Genesee Street
Utica, NY 13501–5930
(315) 798–8355
Fax: (315) 734–3461

8062

Business Information: St. Elizabeth Hospital is a 217–bed, healthcare facility providing acute and psychiatric care to patients. Future plans include offering cardiac surgery services in the Spring of 1997. As Director of Admissions/Central Scheduling, Ms. Millett is responsible for managing all admissions and registration activities, as well as planning, organizing, managing, and scheduling. **Career Steps:** St. Elizabeth Hospital: Director of Admissions/Central Scheduling (1995–Present), Patient Financial Representative (1993–1995). **Associations & Accomplishments:** Fingerlake Health Access Association; National Association Hospital Access Managers. **Education:** New School of Social Research: Masters in Healthcare (1995), Bachelor's.

Renee Mills, Ph.D.
Administrative Director of Integrated Services
St. Mary's Hospital
5801 Bremo Road
Richmond, VA 23226–1907
(804) 285–2011
Fax: (804) 285–1639

8062

Business Information: St. Mary's Hospital is a 391–bed, full–service, acute care medical facility, providing the diagnosis and treatment of patients through in–patient and out–patient services. As Administrative Director of Integrated Services,

Dr. Mills oversees support services, including Biomedical Engineering, Environmental Services, and Food and Nutrition Services. Concurrently, she operates a balloon decorating business, in which she shares ownership with her sister. **Career Steps:** Administrative Director of Integrated Services, St. Mary's Hospital (1993–Present); State of Virginia: Employee Relations Counselor (1989–1993), State EEO Specialist (1984–1989); Assistant Director of Career Planning and Placement, University of Virginia (1981–1984). **Associations & Accomplishments:** Outstanding Woman of America (1981), (1987); Honor Society of Phi Kappa Phi. **Education:** Recipient of Ph.D. in Human Resource Management and Adult Education, with Honors. **Personal:** Dr. Mills enjoys travel, church activities, and designing jewelry.

Abigail (Gayle) Mina
Administrative Clinical Coordinator
South Shore Hospital
55 Fogg Road
Weymouth, MA 02189
(617) 340–8328
Fax: (617) 340–8699

8062

Business Information: South Shore Hospital is a 350–bed hospital providing the diagnosis and treatment of patients, and offering progressive DNA Outreach services. As Administrative Clinical Coordinator, Ms. Mina is responsible for the administrative direction of 1,700 nurses, including medical and surgical nurses. Concurrently, she serves as a Clinical Instructor of Medical–Surgical Nursing at the Quincy College School of Nursing, teaching undergraduates in the Nursing Program. **Career Steps:** Administrative Clinical Coordinator, South Shore Hospital (Present); Clinical Instructor, Quincy College (Present). **Associations & Accomplishments:** Massachusetts Nurses Association; Sigma Theta Tau Gamma Epsilon; South Shore Nurses; Civic Lyons Club; Eye Research Fund raisers; Critical Care Association; Authored article entitled "1995 Managed Care, published in American Association of Nursing Newspaper. **Education:** Northeastern University: M.N.S. (1991), B.S.N.; Quincy College, A.S.; Critical Care Certified (CCRN). **Personal:** Married to Vincent J. in 1962. Three children: Diane Marie Manchester, and Vincent J. II and Deborah Lee. Ms. Mina enjoys reading and spending time with her grandchildren.

Kathryn Minnix
Director of Home Care
Indiana University Medical Center
575 West Dr., Rm. 040
Indianapolis, IN 46202–5272
(317) 274–8264
Fax: (317) 274–6639

8062

Business Information: Indiana University Medical Center is a full tertiary care, research and teaching hospital. Serving in various nursing administrative roles for IUMC since 1978, Kathryn Minnix was appointed Director of the Home Care unit in 1988. In this capacity, she is responsible for the overall operation of several home care services, including infusion, nursing agency, RT/DME, and hemophilia. **Career Steps:** Indiana University Medical Center: Director (1988–Present), Continuity of Care Coordinator (1984–1988); Unit Director (1978–1984). **Associations & Accomplishments:** Indiana University Alumni; Indiana Continuity of Care Association; American Association for Continuity of Care; American Academy of Home Care Physicians. **Education:** Indiana University: M.S.N. (1983), B.S.N.; Currently working towards doctorate in Community Health & Policy Making. **Personal:** Two children: Eric and Rachael Marie. Ms. Minnix enjoys singing, gardening, and coaching girls basketball.

Elaine H. Mischler, M.D.
•••➤━◄●●━◄•••

Professor of Pediatrics
Medical College of Wisconsin and Childrens Hospital of Wisconsin
9000 West Wisconsin Avenue, P.O. Box 1997, MS 211
Milwaukee, WI 53201
(414) 266–6730
Fax: (414) 266–2653

8062

Business Information: The Medical College of Wisconsin is a full–service, multi–specialty medical facility and health service establishment, as well as a research and instructional institution. As Pediatrician and Professor of Pediatrics, Dr. Mischler specializes in Pediatric Pulmonary Medicine. As such, she is responsible for the care and treatment of patients, the instruction of medical students, residents, and fellows in pulmonology, and clinical research in the areas of cystic fibrosis and asthma. **Career Steps:** Pediatrician and Professor of

Pediatrics, The Medical College of Wisconsin (1995–Present); Professor of Pediatrics and Associate Dean, University of Wisconsin Medical School (1976–1995). **Associations & Accomplishments:** American Academy of Pediatrics; American College of Chest Physicians; American Thoracic Society; American Association of Medical Colleges; American Medical Womens Association. **Education:** University of Pennsylvania, M.D. (1970); Pennsylvania State University, B.S. in Pre–Med (1966). **Personal:** Married to Nicholas E. in 1969. Three children: Curtis, Craig, and Elizabeth. Dr. Mischler enjoys hiking and music. She plays the pipe organ, the piano and the clarinet.

Loretta M. Mitchell
Chief, Health Information Management
VA Medical Center

Mountain Home, TN 37684
(423) 926–1171 Ext. 7465
Fax: (423) 461–7919
E MAIL: See Below

8062

Business Information: Veteran's Administration (VA) Medical Center is an acute care, long–term care, and domiciliary, medical institute providing diagnosis and treatment to veterans of military forces. Affiliated with James Quillen College of Medicine, the Medical Center also serves as a teaching facility. As Chief, Health Information Management, Ms. Mitchell is responsible for the release of information, filing, coding, and computerizing medical records, and teaching information law and statistical information to employees. Concurrently, she also serves on various committees. **Career Steps:** Chief, Health Information Management, VA Medical Center (1991–Present); Chief, Medical Information, VA Medical Center, Perry Point, MD (1989–1991); DRG Coordinator, VA Medical Center, Shreveport, LA (1986–1989); Data Manager, Louisiana Medical Review Foundation (1982–1986). **Associations & Accomplishments:** American Health Information Management Association; Tennessee Health Information Management Association. **Education:** Central Michigan University, M.S.A. (1992); Louisiana Technical University, B.S. (1981). **Personal:** Married to Aubrey in 1968. Six children: Terri Carter, Donna Mills, Cindy Walter, Roger Bozeman, Rhonda Bunting, and Denise Moss. Ms. Mitchell enjoys reading, bowling, and sewing.

Frances M. Moffett
Director of Environmental Services
Methodist Medical Center
1850 Chadwick Drive
Jackson, MS 39204
(601) 376–1109
Fax: (601) 376–2814

8062

Business Information: Methodist Medical Center — one of 19 affiliate institutions owned by Methodist Health Systems, is a 500–bed acute care hospital serving patients throughout Jackson, Mississippi. With over twenty years experience in housekeeping operations and a Registered Executive Housekeeper, Mrs. Moffett joined the Methodist Medical Center in 1976. Serving as Director of the Environmental Services Department, she is in charge of all aspects of housekeeping operations for the hospital and the oversight of a staff of 60 employees. **Career Steps:** Director of Environmental Services Department, Methodist Medical Center (1976–Present); Executive Housekeeper, Sun Sand Motel (1971–1976); Supervisor, Jackson Park Hospital (1967–1971). **Associations & Accomplishments:** National Executive Housekeeper Association; Recipient of an award from the hospital administrator for her public relations efforts. **Education:** Hinds Junior College, B.A. (1994). **Personal:** Married to Jimmie in 1955. Three children: Jacqueline, Gregory, and Sharon. Mrs. Moffett enjoys reading, collecting antiques, and refinishing old furniture.

David L. Moody
Director of Human Resources
St. Catherine Hospital
410 East Walnut Street
Garden City, KS 67846
(316) 272–2532
Fax: (316) 272–2566

8062

Business Information: St. Catherine Hospital, privately owned and operated by Catholic Health Initiatives, is a 132–bed acute care medical facility with a Level 2 neonatal unit. The hospital is also the regional referral center and focal point of a 22 hospital network. As Director of Human Resources, Mr. Moody is responsible for staff performance evaluation, counsel, and training, monitoring hospital productivity, benchmarking, and development of strategic initiatives. **Career Steps:** Director of Human Resources, St. Catherine Hospital (1995–Present); Director of Support Services, United

Memorial Hospital (1990–1995); Assistant Personnel Manager, St. Mary's Health Services (1984–1990). **Associations & Accomplishments:** American Society for Healthcare Human Resource Administration; Society for Human Resource Management, SPHR Certification; American Cancer Society; Garden City YMCA. **Education:** Alma College, B.S. (1971); Grand Valley State University, M.B.A. Candidate. **Personal:** Mr. Moody enjoys jogging, golf, and, rollerblading. He is also a private pilot.

Ron Moore
Corporate Director of Vascular Services
Charleston Area Medical Center
3200 MacCorkle Avenue, SE
Charleston, WV 25304–1200
(304) 348–4255
Fax: Please mail or call
EMAIL: MQGH94A

8062

Business Information: Charleston Area Medical Center is a 900–bed tertiary hospital, medical research and teaching institution serving the surrounding areas of Charleston, West Virginia. The Center currently employs more than 5,000 people. As Corporate Director of Vascular Services, Mr. Moore is responsible for all aspects of healthcare administration and clinical research in vascular work. **Career Steps:** Charleston Area Medical Center: Corporate Director of Vascular Services (1995–Present), Assistant Administrator (1992–1995), Nurse Manager (1987–1992). **Associations & Accomplishments:** American Association of Critical Care Nurses; West Virginia Nurses Association. **Education:** Bellarmine College, M.S. in Nursing (1992); Marshall University, B.S. in Nursing (1985); Southern West Virginia Community College, A.S. in Nursing (1978). **Personal:** Mr. Moore enjoys landscaping, gardening, boating, and bowling.

Tammy L. Moore
Director of Patient Care Redesign
Mount Carmel Medical Center
793 West State Street
Columbus, OH 43222–1551
(614) 234–2633
Fax: Please mail or call

8062

Business Information: Mount Carmel Medical Center is part of a regional organization consisting of three public hospitals. The Medical Center is a not–for–profit teaching hospital offering instruction in a variety of fields. As Director of Patient Care Redesign, Ms. Moore plans, implements, and evaluates the organization–wide care delivery system focused on enhancing quality and decreasing patient costs. She is involved in the redesign of patient services such as bedside registration, decentralization of lab and EKG services, and improving overall patient care delivery. **Career Steps:** Mount Carmel Medical Center: Director of Patient Care Redesign (1995–Present), Unit Director (1992–1995), Staff Nurse (1985–1992). **Associations & Accomplishments:** AACN; C.O.C.A.A.C.N., CCRN **Education:** Ohio State University, M.S. (1994); Franklin University, B.S.N. **Personal:** Ms. Moore enjoys travel, golf, and spending time with family and friends.

Joan E. Moran
Interim Director, Office of Diversity and Affirmative Action
University of Connecticut Health Center
263 Farmington Avenue
Farmington, CT 06030
(860) 679–3563
Fax: (860) 679–3805

8062

Business Information: The University of Connecticut Health Center provides all aspects of post–graduate education to residents and interns, as well as full–tertiary care and clinical research facilities. Established in 1961, the University of Connecticut Health Center currently employs 2,900 medical and educational professionals. As Interim Director – Office of Diversity and Affirmative Action, Ms. Moran is responsible for all aspects of the civil rights programs, the affirmative action programs, and assuring that the Health Center complies with all State and Federally mandated laws. **Career Steps:** University of Connecticut Health Center: Interim Director, Office of Diversity and Affirmative Action (1995–Present), Assistant Director (1988–1995), Project Coordinator (1985–1988). **Associations & Accomplishments:** Rotary Club of New Britain; American Association of Affirmative Action; Connecticut Association of Affirmative Action Professionals. **Education:** St. Joseph College, working towards degree in Social Work. **Personal:** Married to Daniel in 1966. Two children: Kathleen and Brendan. Ms. Moran enjoys antique collecting, aerobics, and photography.

Maj. Marie C. Morency

Head Nurse of Psychiatry

Tripler Army Medical Center

Ward 3B1
Tripler AMC, HI 96859
(808) 433–2610
Fax: (808) 433–2907

8062

Business Information: Tripler Army Medical Center is a full–service medical facility serving the Army, Navy, and Air Force, as well as providing support services to Japan and Korea. As Head Nurse of Psychiatry, Maj. Morency is responsible for departmental leadership, coordination of patient care, and supervises a staff of 24. **Career Steps:** Head Nurse of Psychiatry, Tripler Army Medical Center (1995–Present); 98th General Hospital – Nuernberg, GE: Evening/Night Supervision (1992), Head Nurse of Psychiatry (1989–92). **Associations & Accomplishments:** American Nurses Association; American Psychiatric Nurses Association; Arizona Nurses Association; Women In Military Service For America Memorial. **Education:** Arizona State University, M.S.N. (1994); New York City College, B.S.N. (1984). **Personal:** Maj. Morency enjoys reading, exercise, needlepoint, and movies.

Mark V. Morgenstern

Staff Pharmacist

Veterans Administration Medical Center – Outpatient Pharmacy –119

1670 Clairmont Road
Decatur, GA 30333
(404) 728–7690
Fax: Please mail or call
EMail: See Below

8062

Business Information: V.A. Medical Center – Outpatient Pharmacy –119 is a full–service, healthcare facility specializing in the diagnosis, treatment, and rehabilitation of the veterans of the community. As Staff Pharmacist, Mr. Morgenstern is responsible for counseling with patients and families regarding prescribed medication. **Career Steps:** Staff Pharmacist, V.A. Medical Center – Outpatient Pharmacy –119 (1985–Present); Staff Pharmacist, Lee Memorial Hospital (1976–1985). **Associations & Accomplishments:** American Association of Pharmacist; Georgia Association of Pharmacist; NDPA. **Education:** St. John's University, B.S. (1976). **Personal:** Mr. Morgenstern enjoys reading, bowling, and travel.

Tom Neal Morris

Assistant Clinical Manager

Medical Center of Central Georgia

777 Hemlock Street
Macon, GA 31201–2102
(912) 633–1163
Fax: (912) 633–1627
EMAIL: See Below

8062

Business Information: Operating as a hospital, medical and surgical center, Medical Center of Central Georgia is a part of the Central Georgia Health System. Joining the Medical Center of Central Georgia upon conferral of his bachelors in nursing in 1991, Tom Morris serves as Assistant Clinical Manager. His primary role is the supervision and administration of nurses, technicians and aides in an 18 room surgery center. He also serves as a liaison with physicians, coordinating the schedules of the operating room staff, which includes assigning operating rooms and procedure start times to surgeons and their patient procedures. Internet users can also reach Tom via: TNeal545@ix.netcom.com **Career Steps:** Medical Center of Central Georgia: Assistant Clinical Manager (1992–Present), Clinical Nurse I (1991–1992). **Associations & Accomplishments:** Sigma Theta Tau – Nursing Honor Society; Association of Operating Room Nurses; Gamma Beta Phi. **Education:** Georgia College, B.S.N. (1991). **Personal:** Mr. Morris enjoys acting for the community theatre, computers, singing and working out. Mr. Morris has also acted in commercials on local television programs.

Annette C. Morrison, A.R.T., C.C.S.

Director of Medical Records

Presbyterian Hospital in Matthews

P O Box 3310
Matthews, NC 28106
(704) 384–6741
Fax: (704) 384–6523

8062

Business Information: Presbyterian Hospital in Matthews is a full–service, 102 bed, acute care medical facility. A new satellite Hospital of the Presbyterian Hospital Network, the Facility takes pride in the new high tech services offered, i.e., new technology in prostate surgery. As Director of Medical Records, Ms. Morrison oversees all administrative operations for a support staff of 17, in addition to the overall administrative operations of the Medical Records Division. **Career Steps:** Director of Medical Records, Presbyterian Hospital in Matthews (1984–Present); Consultant–Coding, Health Information Associates, (1994); Coding/QA Analyst and Tumor Registrar, Presbyterian Orthopedic Hospital (1993–1994). **Associations & Accomplishments:** American Health Information Management Association; North Carolina Health Information Management Association: Publication Chair, Program Committee, Education Committee, Shaper/HOSA Committee, and Editor of Footprints (NCHIMA Newsletter); Region VI–NCHIMA Coordinator and Nominating Committee Chair. **Education:** Marshall University: A.A.S. in Medical Records Technology (1988), A.A.S. Medical Secretarial Studies (1984); Stephens College. **Personal:** Married to Craig Allen in 1986. Two children: Brad Allen and Madeline Ann. Ms. Morrison enjoys being a T–ball and PTA Mom, camping, and coed softball.

Mary Ann Morrison, RN

• • • ◄━━━ ◎ ━━━► • • •

Vice–President — Clinical Services

St. Francis Medical Center

3036 E. Imperial Highway
Lynwood, CA 90260
(310) 603–6832
Fax: Please mail or call

8062

Business Information: St. Francis Medical Center, sponsored by the Daughters of Charity, is one of the 22 CHW system Medical Centers. c. The 478–bed acute care facility and trauma center provides treatment to all, including the homeless and indigent, and assists in approximately 6,000 births a year. Living by core values, including respect, dignity, and inventiveness to infinity, St. Francis Medical Center is an advocate for the poor, providing quality service, simplicity, and serving the underprivileged. operations of patient care services in an acute care facility, including the direction of all inpatient units, surgical, children's center, social services, and The Leavey Educational Center. In addition, she conducts research on noise reduction in a health environment, works for grants and charity balls, and is active in promoting Healthier Communities. **Career Steps:** Vice–President of Clinical Services, St. Francis Medical Center (1992–Present); Chief Operations Officer, Health Trust Inc. Chino Community Hospital (1990–1992); Associate Administrator, Los Alamitos Hospital (1985–1990). **Associations & Accomplishments:** AONNE; ONE–C; ACHE; Chairperson, Board of Directors, Home Health Agency; Health Trust Western Region Nurse Executive of the Year 1992; Johnson–Johnson Wharton Fellowship; Interviewed on television and Los Angeles Times on the "Abandoned Baby Program." **Education:** California State University – Los Angeles, MSN (1982); California State University – Long Beach, B.S.N; Golden West College, A.A.; Queens Hospital School of Nursing, Diploma in Nursing. **Personal:** Married to Roger in 1982. Ms. Morrison enjoys travel, gourmet cooking, Scrabble, bridge, listening to books on tapes, and reading.

Alice Jean Morrow

Administrative Director

Citizens Memorial Hospital

1500 North Oakland
Bolivar, MO 65613–3011
(417) 326–0432
Fax: (417) 326–0338

8062

Business Information: Citizens Memorial Hospital is a 74–bed, acute care hospital. Established in 1982, Citizens Memorial Hospital currently employs 550 people. As Administrative Director for the Non–Clinical Hospital Departments, Ms. Morrow is responsible for all administrative matters, including total management of the business office. **Career Steps:** Administrative Director for the Non–Clinical Hospital Departments, Citizens Memorial Hospital (1982–Present); Book Store Purchasing Clerk, Southwest Baptist University (1978–1982); Homemaker and Seamstress (1972–1978). **Associations & Accomplishments:** Rotary Member, International Committee Chairman & Board Member; P.E.O. Member, Recording Secretary; Member of First Baptist Church – Member of Finance Committee; Member of Bolivar R–I School Board. **Education:** Southwest Baptist University, M.A. in Healthcare Administration (1992), B.A. in Business Administration. **Personal:** Married to Stephen C.. Two children: Matthew S. and Melissa J.. Ms. Morrow enjoys spending time with her family, reading, cross–stitch, sewing, and gardening.

Michael A. Moss, M.D.

Head/Department of Pathology & Laboratory Medicine

Queen Elizabeth II Health Sciences Centre

5788 University Avenue
Halifax, Nova Scotia B3H 1V8
(902) 428–3867
Fax: (902) 428–2123
EMAIL: See Below

8062

Business Information: Queen Elizabeth II Health Sciences Centre is a full service medical facility located in Nova Scotia, Canada. Dr. Moss was one of three principals involved in the formation of one of Dalhousie University's first technology transfer companies, Path Scientific Research, which was formed to facilitate the application of novel analytical approaches, and computerized data processing in the chemical analysis of environmental samples. Formed in conjunction with the Hospital, its Foundation, and Dalhousie University, their goal was to harness new technologies in order to reduce sample volumes, processing time, labor and cost. **Career Steps:** Head/Department of Pathology & Laboratory Medicine, Queen Elizabeth II Health Sciences Centre (1995–Present); Dalhousie University: Head, Department of Pathology (1992–Present), Director, Division of Clinical Chemistry, Department of Pathology (1983–Present); Medical Examiner, Halifax County, Nova Scotia (1983–Present). **Associations & Accomplishments:** Honors: Co–Recipient, Med Chem Award (1984+1989); Fellow, Royal College of Physicians and Surgeons of Canada; Canadian Association of Medical Biochemists; Canadian Society of Clinical Chemists; Founding Member, Canadian Academy of Clinical Biochemistry; Nova Scotia Medical Society; Nova Scotia Society of Clinical Chemists; Numerous Invited Presentations on various medical subjects; Various Publications and Research Articles; Several Committee and Administrative Appointments; Management Program for Clinical Leaders, Henson College; Executive Development Seminar for Associate Deans and Department Chairs, Association of American Medical Colleges; Dalhousie University: Lecturer, Department of Pathology (1982–1985), Assistant Professor, Department of Pathology (1985–1988), Associate Professor, Department of Pathology (1988–1993), Full Professor, Department of Pathology (1993–Present). **Education:** Dalhousie University: F.R.C.P.(C) (1982), M.Sc.; University of London: M.B., B.S. **Personal:** Married to Margaret in 1976. Two children: Andrea and Alison. Dr. Moss enjoys motion pictures and literature.

Kathleen I. Moulton

Director of Managed Care

Weiner Memorial Medical Center

300 South Bruce Street
Marshall, MN 56258–1934
(507) 532–9661
Fax: (507) 537–9259

8062

Business Information: Weiner Memorial Medical Center is a 49–bed hospital, offering a full line of services to a rural population, including but not limited to rehabilitation services and general care. A long–term 76–bed care unit, is also a part of the facility, as well as a rehabilitation center. As Director of Managed Care, Ms. Moulton is responsible for all aspects of managed care operations, including administration, quality and risk management, peer review, patient rights and ethics, and supervision of all personnel. **Career Steps:** Director of Managed Care, Weiner Memorial Medical Center (Present). **Associations & Accomplishments:** Sigma Theta Tau; American Nurses Association; National Association for Healthcare Quality. **Education:** University of South Dakota, M.P.A. (1992); Augustana College, B.S. Nursing. **Personal:** Ms. Moulton enjoys reading, music, walking, vacationing and hiking in the Rockies.

Martha Mulvihill–Martinez Sr. OTR

Senior Occupational Therapy Rehabilitator

Columbia Rehabilitation Hospital

2690 Boldt Street
Las Cruces, NM 88005–3874
(915) 577–2623
Fax: Please mail or call

8062

Business Information: Columbia Rehabilitation Hospital is an inpatient rehabilitative hospital for patients diagnosed with CVA, SCI, CHI, and orthopedic disorders. As Senior Occupational Therapy Rehabilitator, Mrs. Mulvihill–Martinez supervises the Occupational Therapy Department, Recreational Therapy Department, clinical technician staff, and provides hands–on patient care. **Career Steps:** Senior Occupational Therapy Rehabilitator, Columbia Rehabilitation Hospital (1995–Present); Occupational Therapy Rehabilitator, C.O.R.E. (1992–1995); Occupational Therapy Rehabilitator, Santa Rosa Rehabilitation Hospital (1990–1992). **Associations & Accomplishments:** New Mexico Occupational

Therapy Association; Texas Occupational Therapy Association; American Occupational Therapy Association; National Spinal Cord Association; Las Cruces Closed Head Injury Association. **Education:** UTHSCSA, B.S. in Occupational Therapy (1990). **Personal:** Married to Edward Martinez. Two children: Mauricia and Gabrielle. Mrs. Mulvihill–Martinez enjoys crafts, horseback riding, water skiing, and painting.

M. Luther Musselman, M.D.
Physician
Millard Fillmore Hospital
3 Gates Circle
Buffalo, NY 14209–1120
(716) 887–4663
Fax: (716) 887–4298

8062

Business Information: Established in 1872, Millard Fillmore Hospital is a tertiary care hospital, medical research and teaching institution. As Physician and Director of Medical Education, Dr. Musselman is responsible for the administration and instruction of 120 resident physicians, as well as the care and treatment of patients. **Career Steps:** Physician and Director of Medical Education, Millard Fillmore Hospital (1980–Present); Assistant Dean and Director of Health Services, State University of New York – Buffalo (1964–1980); Physician, Private Practice (1946–1964); Major, United States Army (1942–1945). **Associations & Accomplishments:** Board of Directors, North West Buffalo Health Center; Coordinated Care Management Corporation; Former President, Erie County Medical Society; Former President, New York State College Health Association; Former President, Buffalo Academy of Medicine; Visiting Nurses Association. **Education:** State University of New York – Buffalo, M.D. (1937); Fellow, Gastroenterology, Lohey Clinic, Boston, MA (1942). **Personal:** Married to Rita M. in 1980. Two children: David and Ann Collins. Dr. Musselman enjoys gardening.

David L. Myers
Superintendent, Medical Logistics Office
United States Air Force Hospital – Fairchild AFB
701 Hospital Loop, Suite 40
Fairchild Air Force Base, WA 99011
(509) 247–7464
Fax: (509) 247–3255
EMAIL: See Below

8062

Business Information: The United States Air Force Hospital at Fairchild Air Force Base in Washington is an acute care medical facility, serving Air Force personnel and their dependents. An experienced Air Force Officer, Sgt. Myers has served in various managerial capacities with the USAF, most recently assigned to Fairchild AFB as Superintendent of the Medical Logistics Office in 1993. He is responsible for staff supervision, various administrative activities, and supervision of daily operations. Internet users can reach him via: UncleDavey@aol.com **Career Steps:** United States Air Force: Superintendent, Medical Logistics Office – USAF Hospital, Fairchild Air Force Base, Washington (1993–Present); Manager, Major Construction – USAF Hospital, Lakenheath, United Kingdom (1988–1993); Manager, Medical Supply Office – USAF Clinic, San Vito, Italy (1984–1988); Manager, Medical Equipment Office – USAF Hospital, Hill Air Force Base, Utah (1982–1984). **Associations & Accomplishments:** Secretary for the Harrington School District, Learning Improvement Team; Fairchild Air Force Base, Speakers Bureau. **Education:** Community College of the Air Force, Associates in Applied Science; Attended: University of Maryland and Chapman College – Orange County, California. **Personal:** Married to Kim in 1983. Three children: Amy, Patricia, and Chelsea. Sgt. Myers enjoys computers, gardening, and coaching youth sports.

Rosie Myrick
Director of the Health Information Management Department
Montevista Hospital
5900 West Rochelle Avenue
Las Vegas, NV 89103
(702) 251–1256
Fax: (702) 364–8183

8062

Business Information: Montevista Hospital is an acute psychiatric facility providing healthcare to patients in the Las Vegas locale. As Director of the Health Information Management Department, Ms. Myrick is responsible for managing a staff of three, in addition to directing all coding analysis of health information. **Career Steps:** Director of the Health Information Management Department, Montevista Hospital (1989–Present); Transcription Supervisor, McKay Dee Hospital (1985–1989); Office Manager, J. Richard Rees, M.D. (1981–1985); Director, Mark E. Reed Hospital (1971–1980). **Associations & Accomplishments:** Nevada Health Information Management Association; American Health Information Management Association. **Education:** St. Bene-

dict Medical Rec., ART (1965). **Personal:** Married to Jim in 1967. Three children: Trisha Ann, Christopher James, and Jennifer Jo. Ms. Myrick enjoys travel, reading and cooking.

Pradeep K. Narotam
Physician
Health Sciences Centre
820 Sherbrook Street
Winnipeg, Manitoba R3A 1R9
(204) 987–1400
Fax: (204) 787–1424

8062

Business Information: Health Sciences Centre is a local, 600–bed medical facility with a major trauma unit providing health care services to residents of the Province of Manitoba. As Physician, Dr. Narotam specializes in neurosurgery, tumors, spine, vascular, and trauma care. Dr. Narotam sees patients on a private basis and conducts surgery at the Health Sciences Centre. Concurrently he is an Assistant Professor and Researcher at the University of Manitoba. Dr. Narotam is responsible for the accuracy and quality of his research findings and the reporting of said results to the University administration. It is his obligation to assist in raising funds for the research conducted. **Career Steps:** Physician, Health Sciences Centre (1995–Present); Assistant Professor, University of Manitoba (1995–Present); Wentworth Hospital: Consultant (1993–1994) and Principal Medical Officer (1992–1993). **Associations & Accomplishments:** Manitoba Medical Association; Canadian Medical Association; College of Medicine of South Africa. **Education:** University of Arizona, M.D.; University of Natal, M.MED(NS) and M.B.Ch.B. (1984); College of Medicine of South Africa F.C.S.(SA). **Personal:** Married to Nalini in 1984. Two children: Annika and Bhavishya. Dr. Narotam enjoys swimming, surfing, automobiles, and computers.

Joanne E. Nathem, RN, MSN
Patient Care Services Director
Battle Creek Health Systems
300 North Avenue
Battle Creek, MI 49016
(616) 966–8095
Fax: (616) 966–8590

8062

Business Information: Battle Creek Health Systems is a 410–bed, acute care hospital affiliated with Mercy Hospital Systems. Specialized services offered include: substance abuse, widowed persons, Alzheimer's disease, teaching disabled children, Life Line, Health Network, and women's services. With 19 years expertise in the medical profession, Ms. Nathem joined the Battle Creek Health System in 1994. Currently serving as Patient Care Services Director, she directs four areas of patient care units, including Critical Care, Cardio–Pulmonary, Cath Lab Recovery, and Nursing Supervisors. **Career Steps:** Patient Care Services Director, Battle Creek Health Systems (1994–Present); Manager, Montana Deaconess Medical Center (1990–1994); Manager, Allen Memorial Hospital (1976–1990). **Associations & Accomplishments:** Sigma Theta Tau; Board Member, American Heart Association; Rotary; American Nurse Association; American Association Critical Care Nurses. **Education:** Western Michigan University, M.B.A. – in progress; University of Dubuque, M.S.N. (1994); B.S.N. (1989). **Personal:** Married to Wayne in 1970. Three children: Sara, Hazel, and Wayne M. Ms. Nathem enjoys piloting aircraft, motorcycling (owner – Honda Gold Wing), reading, and traveling.

Harry E. Needham III
Director of Public Safety
Norwich Hospital Police
P.O. Box 508
Norwich, CT 06360
(203) 823–5256 (203) 287–0571
Fax: (203) 823–5327 (203) 287–0108

8062

Business Information: Norwich Hospital, is a state–supported tertiary care hospital. As Director of Public Safety, Mr. Needham has full executive administration over all police, fire, and EMS departments in the hospital. **Career Steps:** Director of Public Safety, Norwich Hospital Police (1993–Present); Director of Public Safety, State of Connecticut – Mental Health Center Police (1984–1993); Police Sergeant, Southern Connecticut State University Police (1978–1984). **Associations & Accomplishments:** American Society of Law Enforcement Trainers; Connecticut Police Chiefs Association; American Society of Industrial Security; Who's Who in Police; Who's Who in Security; Defensive Tactics Police Instructor (since 1982); Martial Arts Instructor (30 years). **Education:** University of New Haven, New Haven, CT, M.B.A., executive program (1990). **Personal:** Married to Anne in 1982. Three children: Kristina, Harry IV, and Darcy. Mr. Needham enjoys collecting baseball cards and martial arts (6th degree Master Black belt in Tang Soo Do).

Ann L. Neikam
Director of Medical Records
Speare Memorial Hospital
2 Hospital Road
Plymouth, NH 03264
(603) 536–1120
Fax: (603) 536–2017

8062

Business Information: Speare Memorial Hospital is a full–service acute care facility. Comprised of 47 beds, and an ambulatory unit, the Hospital was founded in 1951, and employs 175 people. As Director of Medical Records, Ms. Neikam is responsible for all functions of her department. Her duties include coding records, answering insurance questions, transcriptions, analyzing charts, filing procedures, and supervision of five people. **Career Steps:** Speare Memorial Hospital: Director of Medical Records (1989–Present), Director of Utility Review (1974–1989); Pulmonary Lab, Hahnemann Hospital, Philadelphia, Pennsylvania (1961–1963). **Associations & Accomplishments:** State of New Hampshire Quality and Accountability Committee; Permigewasset Choral Society; New Hampshire Health Information Management Association (NHHIMA). **Education:** Presbyterian Hospital, Pittsburgh, Pennsylvania, R.N. (1954); Correspondence Study–AMRA, Art (1992). **Personal:** Married to William C. in 1962. Three children: Diane, Christopher, and Derrick.

Marcia K. Nelsen, M.D.
Orthopaedic Surgeon
Yankton Medical Clinic
1104 W 8th Street
Yankton, SD 57078–3306
(605) 665–8910
Fax: (605) 665–0546

8062

Business Information: Yankton Medical Clinic, established in 1926, is a multi–disciplinary clinic with over 40 physicians on staff. The clinic offers orthopaedic and general surgery, urology, cardiology, and internal medicine services to patients. As Orthopaedic Surgeon, Dr. Nelsen treats patients with musculoskeletal problems, operates on broken bones, and performs joint replacement procedures. **Career Steps:** Orthopaedic Surgeon, Yankton Medical Clinic (1987–Present). **Associations & Accomplishments:** American Medical Association; American Association of Orthopaedic Surgeons; ABIME. **Education:** University of Nebraska Medical Center, Orthopedic training (1987); University of South Dakota School of Medicine, B.S.; Certified Independent Medical Examiner; University of California – San Diego, Orthopaedic Research. **Personal:** Married to Jerry in 1989. Dr. Nelsen enjoys gardening and playing the piano.

Lewis Geoffrey New, ART, HIA
Health Information Administrator
Whitesburg Appalachian Regional Hospital
550 Jenkins Road
Whitesburg, KY 41585
(606) 633–3522
Fax: (606) 633–3667

8062

Business Information: Whitesburg Appalachian Regional Hospital is a full–service, 90–bed healthcare institution specializing in the diagnosis, treatment, and rehabilitation of patients. As Health Information Administrator, Mr. New administers the Health Information for the facility as well as manages the Health Information Management Department. **Career Steps:** Health Information Administrator, Whitesburg Appalachian Regional Hospital (1995–Present); Coding Specialist, Humana Hospital Lexington (1992–1995); Medical Records Clerk, Central Baptist Hospital (1991–1992). **Associations & Accomplishments:** American Health Information Management Association; Southeast Kentucky Health Information Management Association; Kentucky Health Information Management Association. **Education:** Eastern Kentucky University, Bachelor of Science (1991). **Personal:** Mr. New enjoys reading, biking, hiking, and camping.

Clayton Lee Newman
Director of Engineering Services
Baptist Regional Medical Center
1 Trillium Way
Corbin, KY 40701
(606) 523–8578
Fax: (606) 528–3233

8062

Business Information: Baptist Regional Medical Center is a non–profit, 263–bed acute and subacute care hospital offering healthcare services to 15 counties in Kentucky. As Director of Engineering Services, Mr. Newman is responsible for coordinating engineering services, biomedical engineering, housekeeping, renovations, and construction. He lays out the plans, reviews contracts, recruits, and trains new employees on policy matters and procedures. Due to Mr. Newman's superior quality services in codes, regulations, and ethics, he received an accommodation from the joint commission for a perfect program. **Career Steps:** Director of Engineering Services, Baptist Regional Medical Center (1994–Present); ServiceMaster: Director of Engineering Services (1994–Present), Director of Environmental Services (1991–1994); Systems Engineer, Emerson Electric Company (1989–1991); Active Duty, U.S. Navy Reserves (1978–1986); Served with Naval Seals and 2nd Force Recon during Desert Storm. **Associations & Accomplishments:** NFPA; ASHE. **Education:** Cumbler Land College; State University of New York: A.S. in Electronics, B.S. in Physics. **Personal:** Married to Cindy in 1990. One child: Nicole. Mr. Newman enjoys boating, fishing, and hiking.

Cam Nguyen, M.D., C.M.

Attending Physician, Department of Radiation Oncology
Rush–Presbyterian, St. Luke's Medical Center
1653 West Congress Parkway
Chicago, IL 60612
(312) 942–5751
Fax: (312) 942–2339

8062

Business Information: Rush–Presbyterian, St. Luke's Medical Center is a 1,000–bed full–service hospital with an extensive residency program. Dr. Nguyen has been an Attending Physician in the Department of Radiation Oncology at Rush–Presbyterian since early 1996. **Career Steps:** Attending Physician, Department of Radiation Oncology, Rush–Presbyterian, St. Luke's Medical Center (1996–Present). **Associations & Accomplishments:** Canadian Medical Association; American Society for Therapeutic Radiology & Oncology. **Education:** McGill University, M.D., C.M. (1989); Fellow, Royal College of Physicians and Surgeons of Canada – F.R.C.P. (C). **Personal:** Married to Tam in 1990. One child: My–Anh. Dr. Nguyen enjoys classical guitar.

Abraham Ninan, M.D.

Associate Professor, Department of Pediatrics
Royal University Hospital
103 Hospital Drive
Saskatoon, Saskatchewan S7N 0W8
(306) 966–8118
Fax: (306) 975–3767

8062

Business Information: Royal University Hospital is an acute care medical facility affiliated with the University of Saskatchewan School of Medicine. Dr. Ninan has been instructing undergraduate and post–graduate students at the Hospital as an Associate Professor with the Department of Pediatrics since 1977, teaching courses and seminars in neonatology and pediatric political science. He also serves as the Director of Education for Pediatrics. In addition to his academic duties, he supervises patient care in the neonatal and pediatric intensive care units. Dr. Ninan also travels periodically to his native India to teach post–graduate interns and physicians. **Career Steps:** Associate Professor, Department of Pediatrics, Royal University Hospital (1977–Present). **Associations & Accomplishments:** Canadian Pediatric Society; Canadian Medical Association; Royal College of Physicians and Surgeons. **Education:** University of Saskatchewan, F.R.C.P.C. (1977); Christian Medical College – Vellore, India, M.B.B.S. (1966); Bishopi School – Pune, India. **Personal:** Married to Leela in 1969. Three children: Santosh, Asha and Dilip. Dr. Ninan enjoys working in the international health field.

John Nkansah, M.D., F.R.C.P.(C)

Chief of Psychiatry
Scarborough Grace Hospital
220 Duncan Mill Road, Suite 318
Don Mills, Ontario M3B 3J5
(416) 391–5304
Fax: (416) 391–5305

8062

Business Information: Scarborough Grace Hospital is a full–service, healthcare institution specializing in the diagnosis, treatment, and rehabilitation of patients. As Chief of Psychiatry, Dr. Nkansah is responsible for all aspects of the Psychiatric Department of the Hospital. Concurrent with his duties at the hospital, Dr. Nkansah also owns a private psychiatry practice and is a consultant with the Toronto East General Hospital. **Career Steps:** Chief of Psychiatry, Scarborough Grace Hospital (1990–Present); Chief of Psychiatry, Toronto East General Hospital (1977–1990); Staff Psychiatrist, Toronto Western Hospital (1974–1978). **Associations & Accomplishments:** President, Association of General Hospital Psychiatric Services; Board of Directors, Toronto Home Care Program; Vice President, Ghanadian International Society; Canadian Psychiatric Association; Ontario Psychiatric Association; Assistant Professor, Dept. of Psychiatry, University of Toronto; Member of the Canadian Medical Association and the Ontario Medical Association. **Education:** University of Toronto: D.Psych (1967), M.D. (1964), B.A. (1960); Royal College of Physicians and Surgeons of Canada, F.R.C.P.(c) (1969). **Personal:** Married to Avis in 1963. Two children: Dr. Peter, and Susan. Dr. Nkansah enjoys golf, swimming, travel, and reading.

Eileen Mary O'Connell–Goodfellow

Director of Rehabilitation Services
Maine Coast Memorial Hospital
50 Union Street
Ellsworth, ME 04605–1534
(207) 667–5311 Ext.132
Fax: (207) 667–1843

8062

Business Information: Maine Coast Memorial Hospital is a 40–bed full service, acute care facility specializing in the diagnosis, treatment, and rehabilitation of patients. As Director of Rehabilitation Services, Ms. O'Connell–Goodfellow is responsible for all physical, occupational, massage, and speech therapy services. **Career Steps:** Director of Rehabilitation Services, Maine Coast Memorial Hospital (1995–Present); Rehabilitation Manager, Mount Auburn Hospital Home Care (1992–1995); Clinical Coordinator, Nova Care. **Associations & Accomplishments:** American Speech, Language, and Hearing Association. **Education:** Boston University, M.S. (1983); University of Oregon (1981). **Personal:** Married to N. Kim in 1979. One child: Amelia Kay. Ms. O'Connell–Goodfellow enjoys biking, hiking, and skiing.

Shelagh T. O'Connor, RN, MNA

Director, Emergency Services
Flagstaff Medical Center
1200 North Beaver Street
Flagstaff, AZ 86001–3118
(520) 773–2202
Fax: (520) 773–2296

8062

Business Information: Flagstaff Medical Center is a 135–bed general care facility providing a trauma center, emergency services, cardiac, OB/GYN, and pediatric care. Ms. O'Connor joined the Center in 1979, serving in the Emergency Department as a Staff RN until her promotion to Clinical Coordinator in 1984. Named to her present position as Director of Emergency Services in 1988, she is responsible for the management of 40 employees in the Emergency Department, Trauma Services, and Pre Hospital Department. Instrumental in the development of the Trauma Center, Ms. O'Connor is also heavily involved in the design of the new Emergency Service Center, set to open in the Fall of 1997. Concurrently, she sits on the State Trauma Advisory Board and its Systems Committee and Task Force subcommittee. **Career Steps:** Flagstaff Medical Center: Director, Emergency Services (1988–Present), Clinical Coordinator, Emergency Services (1984–1988), Staff RN, Emergency Services (1979–1984). **Associations & Accomplishments:** Emergency Nurses Association, National Managers Committee. **Education:** University of Phoenix, M.N.A. (1992); Northern Arizona University, B.S. in Education; Diploma in Nursing–London, England. **Personal:** Married to Randy Hale in 1984. Ms. O'Connor enjoys running, skiing, mountain biking, hiking.

Virginia Denise O'Dell

Associate Chief Nurse Acute Care
Martinsburg Veterans Affairs Medical Center
Route 9
Martinsburg, WV 25401
(304) 263–0811 Ext. 3651
Fax: (304) 263–4150
EMail: See Below

8062

Business Information: Martinsburg Veterans Affairs Medical Center is an 706–bed health care facility which provides a continuum of care from emergency care to nursing home care for veterans. As Associate Chief Nurse Acute Care, Ms. O'Dell manages the nursing programs in primary care, emergency, critical care, medical/surgical, psychiatry, and drug/alcohol rehabilitation. Internet users can reach her via: VIRODELL@aol.com. **Career Steps:** Martinsburg Veterans Affairs Medical Center: Associate Chief Nurse Acute Care (1995–Present), Chief Nursing Home Care Unit (1990–1995); Nursing Home Supervisor, Saginaw Veterans Affairs Medical Center (1989–1990); Nursing Home Supervisor Trainee, Veteran Affair Medical Center – Richmond, VA (1988–1989). **Associations & Accomplishments:** National Association of Female Executives; Choice in Dying; Excellence in Nursing Award (1996);; Federal Employee of the Year in Manager Catagory (1995). **Education:** Central Michigan, M.S.A. (1987); College of Notre Dame, B.S.N. (1982); Harford Community College, A.A. in Nursing (1975). **Personal:** Married to Charles S. in 1974. Two children: Cassandra Dawn and Brandon Lee. Ms. O'Dell enjoys needlework, flower arranging, fishing, and her family pets.

LTC David T. Orman, M.D.

Chief of Psychiatry and Psychology
Darnall Army Community Hospital
MCXI–PSY, USA MEDDAC, DACH
Ft. Hood, TX 76544–5063
(817) 288–8725 (817) 288–8893
Fax: (817) 288–8743
EMAIL: See Below

8062

Business Information: Darnall Army Community Hospital (DACH) is an acute care medical and teaching community hospital, providing diagnosis and treatment to members of the uniformed services (active and retired) and their dependents in the local area, as well as providing instruction to medical students. A practicing physician since 1982, a Board–Certified Psychiatrist, and a Lt. Colonel in the U.S. Army Medical Corps, Dr. Orman was appointed as Chief of Psychiatry and Psychology at Darnall Army Community Hospital in 1988. He is responsible for providing managerial, clinical, and teaching services in an academic hospital setting. Concurrently, Dr. Orman serves as Chief of Psychiatry at Rumbaugh Health Science Center; as Psychiatry Consultant at DOD Region 6, TRICARE Program; and as Associate Professor of Psychiatry and Assistant Director of Residency Training at Texas A&M. Internet users can also reach Dr. Orman via: dorman@uvm.com **Career Steps:** Chief of Psychiatry and Psychology, Darnall Army Community Hospital (1988–Present); Chief of Psychiatry, Rumbaugh Health Science Center (includes both Brooke Army Medical Center & DACH) (1995–Present); Psychiatry Consultant, DOD Region 6 – TRICARE Program (1994–Present); Texas A&M Health Science Center, College of Medicine, Department of Psychiatry & Behavior Science: Assistant Director of Residency Training in Psychiatry (1992–Present), Associate Professor of Psychiatry (1989–Present); Division Psychiatrist, 1st Cavalry Division, Fort Hood Army Base (1986–1988). **Associations & Accomplishments:** American Psychiatric Association; Professional licensure and certification: Diplomate – National Board of Medical Examiners (1983), Certified in Psychiatry – American Board of Psychiatry and Neurology (1988), Medical Licensure in Texas; Co–author of numerous publications. **Education:** Uniformed Services University School of Medicine, M.D. (1982); Midwestern State University, B.S., summa cum laude (1977). **Personal:** Married to Carrie Carson, R.N. in 1991. Four children: Jason, Ellena, Ben, and Karli. Dr. Orman enjoys houseboating on the lake, and jet and water skiing.

Teri L. Osterkamp, RN, BSN

Director of Nursing, Safety/Risk Manager
Hawarden Community Hospital
1111 11th Street
Hawarden, IA 51023
(712) 552–3100
Fax: (712) 552–1547

8062

Business Information: Hawarden Community Hospital is a community owned, 27–bed, acute care facility. As Director of Nursing, Safety/Risk Manager, Ms. Osterkamp is responsible for the oversight and leadership of the Nursing Department, as well as providing quality care to patients and clinical coordination for the hospital's projects. **Career Steps:** Hawarden Community Hospital: Safety/Risk Manager, (1994–Present), Director of Nursing (1990–Present), RN (1983–1990). **Associations & Accomplishments:** Sigma Theta Tau Nursing Society; Northwest Iowa Health Assessment Coalition; Area 4 Nursing Network; Ethics Consortium. **Education:** Briarcliff College, B.S.N. (1995); Western Iowa Technical Community College, A.D.N. (1983). **Personal:** Married to Steve in 1979. Three children: Shelly, Tyler, and Savana. Ms. Osterkamp enjoys farm work and antiques.

Twyman R. Owens, M.D.

Pediatric Cardiologist
Harbor UCLA Medical Center
28009 Calzada Drive
Rancho Palos Verde, CA 90275–5847
(310) 222–4007
Fax: (310) 320–2271

8062

Business Information: Affiliated with the University of California – Los Angeles, Harbor UCLA Medical Center is a multi–specialty tertiary care, clinical research and medical teaching hospital. Board–certified in Pediatrics with a subspecialty in Cardiology, Dr. Owens is responsible for the care and treatment of pediatric patients suffering from heart disease and disorders. He is also engaged in research in the areas of coronary blood flow and congestive heart failure. **Career Steps:** Pediatric Cardiologist, Harbor UCLA Medical Center (1993–Present); Physician, University of California – San Francisco (1990–1993); Physician, Children's Hospital of Michigan (1987–1990). **Associations & Accomplishments:** American College of Cardiology; American Heart Association; Association of Black Cardiologists; Fellow, American Academy of Pediatrics. **Education:** Michigan State University, M.D. (1987); Morehouse College, B.S. in Biochemistry and Chemistry; University of California – San Francisco, Clinical Pediatric Cardiology Fellow. **Personal:** Married to C. Renee Bryant, M.D. in 1987. One child: Ashley Renee. Dr. Owens enjoys basketball.

Gregory F. Oxenkrug, M.D., Ph.D.

Chairman — Department of Psychiatry
St. Elizabeth's Medical Center
736 Cambridge Street
Boston, MA 02135
(617) 789–2109
Fax: (617) 789–2066

8062

Business Information: St. Elizabeth's Medical Center is a 450–bed tertiary care medical and teaching hospital. A practicing physician since 1965 and a Board–Certified Neuropsychopharmarologist, Dr. Oxenkrub joined St. Elizabeth's Medical Center as Chairman of the Department of Psychiatry in 1994. He is responsible for all aspects of operations for the department, including administration, supervision, and clinical activities, in addition to overseeing a 50–bed hospital ward. His duties include providing care to patients with psychological problems, conducting research in the area of melatonin (aging, jet–lag, rhythms–biological), teaching medical residents, and providing services to outpatient clinics and crisis hot–lines. **Career Steps:** Chairman of the Department of Psychiatry, St. Elizabeth's Medical Center (1994–Present); Chief of Psychiatry Service, Veteran's Administration Hospital – Providence, Rhode Island (1988–1994); Chief of Psychiatry In–Patient, Lafayette Clinic – Detroit (1982–1988); Staff Psychiatrist, Medfield State Hospital – Massachusetts (1980–1982); Professor, Tufts University School of Medicine; Director, Pineal Research Laboratory. **Associations & Accomplishments:** Fellow, American College of Neuropsychopharmarology (1995). **Education:** Pavlov Medical School – Petersburg, Russia, M.D. (1965); Bekhterev Psychoneurological Research Institute, Ph.D. (1970); Brown University – Providence, Rhode Island, M.A. **Personal:** Two children: Alexander and David. Dr. Oxenkrug enjoys studying English history.

Henry F. Pabst, M.D., F.R.C.P. (c)

Professor/Physician
University of Alberta Hospital
8440 112 Street, NW
Edmonton, Alberta T6G 2R7
(403) 492–4023
Fax: (403) 492–7136

8062

Business Information: University of Alberta Hospital is a full service medical/teaching facility, providing health and related services to area residents. As Professor/Physician, Dr. Pabst is responsible for instructing medical students and residents in general pediatrics and immunology. Also a practicing physician, he treats patients on a daily basis, specializing in handicapped children and pediatric immune deficiencies. He is also involved in joint and independent research in pediatric immunology, ontogeny of immune response, immunomodulation by breast feeding, immunodeficiencies, infant vaccine responses, active in international health, and is responsible for various administrative duties. **Career Steps:** University of Alberta Hospital: Professor/Physician (1980–Present), Associate Professor (1973–1980), Assistant Professor (1970–1973). **Associations & Accomplishments:** Canadian Society of Clinical Investigation; Canadian Pediatric Society; Western Society for Pediatric Research; Royal College of Physicians and Surgeons; Canadian Society of Immunology; American Society of Immunology; National Scientist Award for Research in Immunology (1978). **Education:** University of Alberta, M.D. (1962); Fellow of the Royal College of Physicians, F.R.C.P.(C) (1967). **Personal:** Married. Dr. Pabst enjoys kayaking, and spending time with his grandchildren.

Deanna L. Page

Director of Health Information Management
Canton Potsdam Hospital
50 Leroy Street
Potsdam, NY 13676
(315) 265–3300
Fax: (315) 265–0562

8062

Business Information: Canton Potsdam Hospital is an acute care hospital with alcohol rehabilitation and neuro–rehabilitation services. As Director of Health Information Management, Ms. Page is responsible for the supervision of the Health Information Management Department, as well as Patient Registration, Centralized Scheduling, and Communication Operators. Career milestones include serving as a Board Member to Executive 3M National Board and attending a three–day conference in Utah for the first User Group in April 1995. **Career Steps:** Canton Potsdam Hospital: Director of Health Information Management (1986–Present), Utilization Review Coordinator (1985–1986), L.P.N. – Surgical & Pediatric Unit (1981–1985); L.P.N. Obstetrics Unit, Wuerzburg Army Hospital – Wuerzburg, Germany (1978–1980). **Associations & Accomplishments:** Northern New York Health Information Management Association: positions held include, President, Vice President, and Secretary; St. Lawrence Central School Board (6 years). **Education:** AHIMA: Accredited Record Technician – Independent Study; Seaway Area Technology Center, Licensed Practical Nurse. **Personal:** Married to Randel in 1977. Three children: Rebecca, Angela, and Corey. Ms. Page enjoys family activities, camping at Cranberry Lake in New York, snowmobiling, and crafts.

Pierre Page, M.D.

Physician
Hopital du Sacre – Coeur de Montreal
5400 Gouin Boulevard West
Montreal, Quebec H4J 1C5
(514) 338–3246
Fax: (514) 338–2694
EMail: See Below

8062

Business Information: Hopital du Sacre – Coeur de Montreal is a full–service healthcare institution specializing in the diagnosis, treatment, and rehabilitation of patients. A practicing surgeon since 1981, Dr. Page joined the Hospital in 1982 as a Cardiovascular and Thoracic Surgeon. He conducts extensive research on cardio–vascular ailments, with emphasis on arrhythmia. Grant–in–aid: Medical Research Council of Canada, Heart and Stroke Foundation of Quebec. **Career Steps:** Staff Cardiac Surgeon, Hopital du Sacre – Coeur de Montreal (1982–Present); Scholar, Fouds de la Recherche en Sante de Quebec (1987–1996); Research Associate, Department of Surgery, University of Montreal; Staff Cardiac Surgeon, Montreal Heart Institute (1996–Present); Member, Research Center, Hopital du Sacre – Coeur de Montreal (1983–Present); Member, Research Center, Montreal heart Institute (1996–Present); Universite de Montreal: Assistant Professor (1984–1989), Associate Professor (1990–1998). **Associations & Accomplishments:** Fellow, Royal College of Physicians and Surgeons of Canada; Fellow, American College of Surgeons; Fellow, American College of Cardiology; Canadian Medical Association; Association des medecins de langue francaise du Canada; North American Society of Pacing and Electrophysiology; Canadian Cardiovascular Society; American Heart Association, Council on Cardiovascular Surgery; Society of Thoracic Surgeon; Canadian Cardiac Electrophysiology Society; Canadian Association of Clinical Surgeons; Club de recherches cliniques du Quebec; Canadian Society of Clinical Investigation; Association canadienne francaise pour l'avancement des sciences; Cardiac Electrophysiology Society; Former Vice President and President, Montreal Cardiac Society; Canadian Society of Cardiovascular and Thoracic Surgeons. **Education:** Universite de Montreal: Cardiovascular & Thoracic Surgery (1981), M.D. (1975). **Personal:** Married to Josee Corbeil. Two children: Maude and Luc. Dr Page enjoys Alpine skiing.

Christine Palitti

Administrative Assistant – Department of Obstetrics & Gynecology
Hutzel Hospital/Detroit Medical Center
4707 Saint Antoine Street
Detroit, MI 48201
(313) 993–8331
Fax: (313) 745–7037

8062

Business Information: Hutzel Hospital/Detroit Medical Center is a medical hospital and academic teaching center, which is affiliated with Wayne State University. As Administrative Assistant in the Department of Obstetrics and Gynecology of the Reproductive Endocrinology and Infertility Division, Ms. Palitti is responsible for all administrative work for the department. Concurrently, she spends her spare time building a home business, "3 Keys Marketing" (keys to success – focus, dedication, and discipline), conducting retail marketing of health care products (vitamins, skin care, perfumes, supplements, etc.) for continued success. **Career Steps:** Hutzel Hospital/Detroit Medical Center: Administrative Assistant (1994–Present), Administrative Medical Secretary (1986–1994), Secretary II (1984–1986). **Associations & Accomplishments:** Professional Secretaries International; Elected Director, White Birch Lakes Recreation Association Board of Directors; National Association for Female Executives; Honorary Board of Advisors, American Biographical Institute, Inc.; "2000 Notable American Women" 8th Edition (1996). **Education:** Detroit College of Business (1984–1986). **Personal:** Married to Peter John in 1966. Three children: Peter John, Tracine Rebecca, and Anthony James. Ms. Palitti enjoys outdoor activities (i.e., camping, bird watching, nature and trail hiking).

Prakash N. Pande, M.D., FACC, FACP

Chief – Cardiology Unit
Rochester General Hospital
1415 Portland Avenue, Suite 210
Rochester, NY 14621–3095
(716) 338–3310
Fax: (716) 338–3416

8062

Business Information: Rochester General Hospital is a tertiary care, research and teaching hospital, affiliated with the University of Rochester School of Medicine and Dentistry. A practicing physician since 1964, Board–certified in Cardiology, Dr. Prakash Pande has served in various clinical cardiology roles for Rochester General Hospital since 1975. Appointed Chief of the Cardiology Unit in July of 1991, Dr. Pande oversees all invasive, non–invasive and interventional cardiac surgeries and staff affiliates. He also instructs and mentors residents and cardiology interns by serving as a Clinical Professor of Medicine with the University of Rochester School of Medicine. **Career Steps:** Rochester General Hospital: Chief of Cardiology Unit (1991–Present), Director, Cath Lab (1982–1991), Cardiac Consultant (1975–Present). **Associations & Accomplishments:** Fellow, American College of Cardiology; Fellow, American College of Physicians; Fellow, Council on Clinical Cardiology, American Heart Association; Senior Fellow, Society for Cardiac Angiography and Interventions. **Education:** University of Lucknow – India: M.D. (1968), B.S., Bachelor of Medicine, Bachelor of Surgery; University of the State of New York, M.D. **Personal:** Married to Lora J. in 1974. Two children: Jennifer and Robby. Dr. Pande enjoys hiking, travel, tourism, and nature.

Sumanchandra Pandya, M.D., FACEP

Emergency Physician
St. Cloud Hospital
2906 17th Street
St. Cloud, FL 34769
(407) 892–2135
Fax: (407) 892–6128

8062

Business Information: St. Cloud Hospital is a full–service acute care community hospital. Board–certified in Emergency Medicine and a practicing physician since 1952, Dr. Pandya provides medical care for the Emergency Division at St. Clouds. A native of India, he has devoted extensive time and financial support to the betterment of educational and health care in his homeland of Gujarat, India. **Career Steps:** Emergency Physician, St. Cloud Hospital (1995–Present); EM Dept. Physician, Florida Hospital (Apr. 1995–Jul 1995); EM Dept. Physician, Heart of Florida Hospital (1994–1995); Medical Director – Emergency Department, St. Francis Hospital Regional Heart Institute – Columbus, GA (1992–1994); Director of Emergency Medical Services, Phoenix Medical Park Hospital (1984–1992); Emergency Dept. Physician, Spectrum Emergency Care (1978–1983); Emergency Department Physician, Emergency Consultants, Inc. (1977–1978); Emergency Department Physician, Good Samaritan Hospital (1976–1977); Surgical Resident including Chief Resident in Surgery, New York Infirmary – New York, NY (1972–1976); Chief Medical Officer, Gujarat State Civil Services, India (1954–1971); House Surgeon, S.S.G. Hospital, – Baroda, India (1954); House Physician and Registar, V.S. General Hospital – Ahmedabad, India (1953–1954); Casualty Medical Officer, V.S. General Hospital (1952). **Associations & Accomplishments:** American Board of Emergency Medicine; Fellow, American College of Medicine; Life Member, Society of Critical Care Medicine. **Education:** Gujarat University, India, M.B.B.S. (1952) **Personal:** Married to Subhadra in 1950. Two children: Janak and Rekha.

Marilyn R. Pankey

Director of Medical Information Systems
Sierra View District Hospital
465 West Putnam Avenue
Porterville, CA 93257
(209) 784–5398
Fax: (209) 784–9240
8062

Business Information: Sierra View District Hospital is a full–service healthcare institution specializing in the diagnosis, treatment, and rehabilitation of patients. As Director of Medical Information Systems, Ms. Pankey is responsible for the management of medical information systems, including medical records, medical transcription, utilization and quality management, and cancer registry. **Career Steps:** Sierra View District Hospital: Director of Medical Information Systems (1994–Present), Medical Staff Coordinator (1970–1996), Quality Assurance Coordinator (1966–1980), Director of Medical Records (1962–Present). **Associations & Accomplishments:** American Health Information Management Association; California Health Information Association; Sierra Health Information Association; National Association Medical Staff Services; Delegate to Prople's Republic of China (1995) (People to People Citizen Ambassador Program). **Education:** Stephens College, B.A. (1986). **Personal:** Married to James in 1953. Two children: Leslie Hill and Julie Mattern. Ms. Pankey enjoys travel, reading, writing, and needlecraft.

John A. Paraskos, M.D.

Cardiologist
University of Massachusetts Medical Center
55 Lake Avenue North
Worcester, MA 01655–0214
(508) 856–3905
Fax: (508) 856–4571
8062

Business Information: University of Massachusetts Medical Center is a 350–bed, full–service, tertiary care and teaching hospital affiliated with the University of Massachusetts. A practicing physician since 1964 and a Board–Certified Cardiologist, Dr. Paraskos joined the University of Massachusetts Medical Center in 1975 as Director of Diagnostic Cardiology. He is currently Medical Director of the Cardiovascular Center and Ambulatory Cardiology in January 1995. He is responsible for the direction of all cardiac medicine and emergency cardiology activities, as well as the oversight of all administrative operations for associates and support staff, in addition to his daily patient practice. He also serves as a Clinical Faculty member and is involved with research in critical cardiac care, cardiopulmonary resuscitation, stress echocardiography, and the history of medicine. Concurrent with his medical profession, he serves as Professor of Medicine at the University of Massachusetts Medical School. **Career Steps:** Cardiologist, Medical Director of the Cardiovascular Center and Ambulatory Cardiology, University of Massachusetts Medical Center (1995–Present); Professor of Medicine, University of Massachusetts Medical School (1975–Present); Chief of Cardiology, Veterans Administration Medical Center – Boston (1971–1975). **Associations & Accomplishments:** Fellow, American College of Physicians; Fellow, American College of Cardiologists; Fellow, American College of Chest Physicians; Fellow, Laennec Society – American Heart Association; Massachusetts Medical Society; American Federation for Clinical Research; American Institute of Ultrasound Medicine; American Society of Echocardiography; Author of 50 peer–review articles and book chapters. **Education:** Tufts University School of Medicine, M.D. (1964). **Personal:** Married to Sophia M. Georgian in 1966. Two children: Alexander John and Gregory James. Dr. Paraskos enjoys mountain biking and skiing.

Mark Anthony Parrish

Administrator
Cook County Hospital
1835 West Harrison Street
Chicago, IL 60612–3701
(312) 633–6721
Fax: (312) 572–3792
8062

Business Information: Cook County Hospital is a full–service health care facility serving Chicago, Illinois, and the surrounding community. The Hospital is one of the largest and busiest in the country. As Administrator of Adult Emergency Services (AES), Mr. Parrish makes sure everything is operating smoothly, correctly, and in a sound financial manner. He oversees the activities of 150 nurses, 60 medical staff members, and 100 students, interns, and residents working in AES. Mr. Parrish has oversight of the AES laboratory also. **Career Steps:** Cook County Hospital: Administrator (1991–Present), Quality Assurance Coordinator (1990–1991), Patient Services Coordinator (1989–1990). **Associations & Accomplishments:** National Association of Health Care Executives; Metropolitan Council on Health Care; Chairman of Health Services for United Negro College Fund. **Education:** Roosevelt University, M.P.A. (In Progress); Tennessee State University, B.S. in Psychology (1984). **Personal:** Married to Gwendolyn in 1990. Two children: Janae and Aliyah. Mr. Parrish enjoys chess, basketball, political fund raisers, and reading.

Candace L. Partee

Director, Cardiovascular and Pulmonary Services
University Medical Center
1411 West Baddour
Lebanon, TN 37087
(615) 443–3016
Fax: (615) 443–6021
EMAIL: See Below
8062

Business Information: University Medical Center provides clinical services for cardiac, pulmonary, EEG and sleep diagnostics. As Director, Mrs. Partee manages all clinical services, and is responsible for all administrative duties, public relations, and strategic planning. She is also directly responsible for 58 employees. Internet users can reach her via: cpartee890@aol.com. **Career Steps:** Director, Cardiovascular and Pulmonary Services, University Medical Center (1974–Present). **Associations & Accomplishments:** American Association for Respiratory Care; American Academy of Medical Administrators; American Society of Cardiovascular Professionals/Society of Cardiovascular Management; Rotary International. **Education:** Cumberland University. **Personal:** Married to Al L. Jr. in 1978. Mrs. Partee enjoys travel.

Dr. Yogesh C. Patel, M.D., Ph.D., F.R.S.C.

Director, Division of Endocrinology and Metabolism, McGill UHC
Royal Victoria Hospital
687 Pine Avenue West
Montreal, Quebec H3A 1A1
(514) 842–1231 Ext. 5042
Fax: (514) 849–3681
EMAIL: See Below
8062

Business Information: McGill University Health Center is a full service tertiary care and teaching hospital complex providing instruction to medical students and diagnosis and treatment to patients. As Senior Physician, Research Director and Head of Endocrinology at McGill University, Dr. Patel specializes in endocrine disorders (i.e. diabetes, thyroid, fertility). He also conducts research into hormones, specifically somatostatin, (a hormone which may play a key role in diseases such as diabetes, cancer, and neurodegenerative disorders). Additional duties include preparing for future research into molecular cloning, compounds acting on one receptor, selective treatments in cancers, and widespread clinical trials in the U.S., Canada, and Europe dealing with new treatments for breast cancer. Internet users can reach him via: Patel@RVH.lan.McGill.CA. **Career Steps:** Senior Physician/Director, Fraser Labs for Diabetes Research, Royal Victoria Hospital (1977–Present); Professor of Medicine, Neurology & Neurosurgery (1981–Present); McGill University: Pharmacology & Therapeutics (1996–Present), Professor of Medicine, Neurology, and Neurosurgery, McGill University (1981–Present). **Associations & Accomplishments:** Fellow, Royal Society of Canada; Distinguished Scientist, Canadian Medical Research Council; Member, Association of American Physicians; American Society for Clinical Investigation; Canadian Institute of Academic Medicine. **Education:** Otago, New Zealand, M.D. (1965); Monash, Australia, Ph.D. (1974); Felow, Royal Australasian College of Physicians and of the Royal College of Physicians and Surgeons of Canada; C.J. Martin Post–Doctoral Fellow at Tufts New England Medical Center, Boston; Visiting Professor, Geneva Medical School. **Personal:** Married to Vimla L. in 1966. Two children: Sunil and Camille. Dr. Patel enjoys music, photography, and travel.

David E. Patterson, M.D.

Physician and Associate Professor of Urology
Mayo Foundation and Mayo Graduate School of Medicine
200 First Street SW, Department of Urology
Rochester, MN 55905
(507) 284–4015
Fax: (507) 284–4987
8062

Business Information: The Mayo Foundation and Mayo Graduate School of Medicine is a full–service medical facility and health service establishment, as well as an instructional institution. The Mayo foundation operates the largest Urology Department in the world. As Physician and Associate Professor of Urology, Dr. Patterson is responsible for the care and treatment of patients in the area of clinical Urology, as well as the instruction of medical students and residents. **Career Steps:** Physician and Associate Professor of Urology, Mayo Foundation and Mayo Graduate School of Medicine (1981–Present). **Associations & Accomplishments:** Minnesota Urological Society; American Urological Association. **Education:** University of Colorado, M.D. (1976); University of South Dakota, B.S. in Medicine; Ohio State University, Surgical Internship; Mayo Graduate School of Medicine, Residency and Fellowship Training. **Personal:** Married to Valere. Two children: Lauren and Cole. Dr. Patterson enjoys hunting and fishing.

John W. Patterson, M.D.

Department Chair and Physician
St. Luke's Hospital
801 Ostrum Street
Bethlehem, PA 18015
(610) 954–4531
Fax: Please mail or call
8062

Business Information: St. Luke's Hospital is a full–service, acute care community hospital, providing diagnosis and treatment of patients. A practicing physician since 1978, Board–certified in Internal and Emergency Medicine, Dr. John Patterson has served as Department Chair and Emergency Medical Physician at St. Luke's Hospital since 1981. Dr. Patterson is responsible for the overall administration for medical and clerical support staff, including planning, unit functions and quality improvement, in addition to his daily patient duties. **Career Steps:** St. Luke's Hospital: Department Chair (1983–Present), Physician (1981–Present). **Associations & Accomplishments:** American Medical Association; Northampton County Medical Society; ACEP, Research and Ultrasound Section; SAEM; Medical Advisor, Bethlehem ALS; Medical Advisor, Bethlehem Township ALS; St. Lukes Hospital, Executive Committee; Diplomate, American Board Internal Medicine; Diplomate, American Board Emergency Medicine. **Education:** Jefferson Medical College, M.D. (1978); Rudgers, B.A. (1974). **Personal:** Married to Margaret Ann in 1978. Four children: Brian, Joseph, Nicole, and Kevin. Dr. Patterson enjoys music, woodworking, and wine–making.

Gerald E. Payne

Health Systems Administrator
Federal Medical Center
3301 Leestown
Lexington, KY 40511–8702
(606) 255–6812
Fax: (606) 253–8835
8062

Business Information: The Federal Medical Center — operating under the U.S. Department of Justice – Federal Bureau of Prisons — is a 20–bed hospital with a 31–bed psychiatric ward, providing medical care to prisoners incarcerated in Kentucky correctional institutions. An administrative agent with the U.S. Department of Justice–Federal Bureau of Prisons since 1991 serving in various Federal healthcare institutions throughout the U.S., Gerald Payne was transferred to the Federal Medical Center in Lexington, Kentucky in 1995. As Administrator, he is responsible for all aspects of administration, including budgetary operations for the Center and supervising a staff of two assistants. **Career Steps:** U.S. Department of Justice – Federal Bureau of Prisons, Health Administrator in following facilities: Federal Medical Center – Lexington, KY (1995–Present); Federal Care Institute – Manchester, KY (1992–1995); Medical Care Center – Miami, Florida (1991–1992). **Education:** University of Kentucky, B.H.S. (1986); Eastern Kentucky University, B.S. (1973). **Personal:** Married to Beatriz B. in 1982. Two children: Zachary and Christian. Mr. Payne enjoys raquetball, golf, reading and computers.

Rolanda Pearson, A.R.T.

Medical Records Supervisor
Memorial Health Center
645 Osage Street
Sidney, NE 69162
(308) 254–5825
Fax: (308) 254–0396
8062

Business Information: Memorial Health Center is a full–service acute care facility and outpatient clinic comprised of 63 beds, (49 of which are certified), providing health and medical services to the community. As Medical Records Supervisor, Mrs. Pearson develops and implements all policies and procedures directly related to the medical records department. She is responsible for coding all records per diagnosis and procedure, keeping physicians updated on all HIM issues, and directly supervising a staff of five. **Career Steps:** Medical Records Supervisor, Memorial Health Center (1995–Present); Office Manager, Hospice of the Prairie, Dodge City, Kansas (1994–1995). **Associations & Accomplishments:** American Health Information Management Association (AHIMA); Nebraska Health Information Association (NHIMA); Author of Several Published Poems. **Education:** Dodge City Community College, Associates in Health Information Management (1995). **Personal:** Married to James B. in 1981. Four children: Amy, Jacob, Tyson, and Kristin. Mrs. Pearson enjoys being a free–lance writer and family.

Paul M.J. Peloso, M.D.

Doctor & Professor
Royal University Hospital
103 Hospital Drive, Rdu 3rd Floor – Ellis Hall
Saskatoon, Saskatchewan S7N 0W8
(306) 966–8262
Fax: (306) 966–8381
EMail: See Below

8062

Business Information: Royal University Hospital is a multi–specialty tertiary hospital, medical research and teaching facility, specializing in the diagnosis, treatment, and rehabilitation of patients. As Doctor & Professor, Dr. Peloso conducts research into arthritis and passes his findings on to new interns. Internet users can reach him via: pelosop@duke.usask.ca. **Career Steps:** Doctor & Professor, Royal University Hospital (1994–Present); Assistant Professor, University of Saskatchewan (1994–Present); Research Assistant, Wellesley Hospital, Toronto (1991–1994). **Associations & Accomplishments:** Canadian Medical Association; American College of Rheumatology; Canadian Rheumatology Association. **Education:** University of Toronto, M.Sc. (1994); University of Calgary, M.D.; McMaster University: B.A., B.Sc. **Personal:** Married to Lise in 1989. Two children: Nicholas and Oliver. Dr. Peloso enjoys photography, bicycling, and skiing.

Patricia J. Peterson

Laboratory Director
Mercy Hospital
821 Burke
Ft. Scott, KS 66701
(316) 223–7084
Fax: (316) 223–3265

8062

Business Information: Mercy Hospital is a full service tertiary hospital, serving the populace of Fort Scott, Kansas and the surrounding area. Joining Mercy Hospital in 1960 as a medical technologist, Patricia Peterson was appointed to her current position as Laboratory Director in 1992. Her primary role is to direct and supervise laboratory personnel and it's overall operation. **Career Steps:** Mercy Hospital: Laboratory Director (1992–Present), Assistant Lab Director (1980–1992), Medical Technologist (1960–1980). **Associations & Accomplishments:** American Society for Clinical Laboratory Science; Kansas Society for Clinical Laboratory Science; Clinical Laboratory Managers Association; Mission trip for 1 week to Mexico with Campus Christians, PSU, Pittsburg, KS. **Education:** Pittsburgh State University, M.S. (1991); Kansas State University, B.S.; KU Medical Center, MT Certificate. **Personal:** Married to Gary W. in 1959. Two children: Kristin Peterson–Girard and Gary D. Peterson. Mrs. Peterson enjoys quilting, sewing, reading, and church activities.

Judy C. Philo, A.R.T.

Supervisor of Psychiatric Records
Lewis Gale Medical Center
1902 Braeburn Drive
Salem, VA 24153
(540) 772–2825
Fax: (540) 772–2893

8062

Business Information: Lewis Gale Medical Center is a psychiatric hospital which also deals with substance abuse and adolescent problems. The Center has five satellite clinics throughout Virginia as well as outpatient programs and evening programs. As Supervisor of Psychiatric Records, Mrs. Philo is responsible for three employees and the complete operation of the medical center psychiatric records division. **Career Steps:** Supervisor of Psychiatric Records, Lewis Gale Medical Center (1979–Present); Assistant Director of Medical Records, Bedford Memorial Hospital (1970–1979). **Associations & Accomplishments:** Virginia Association of Quality Assurance Professionals; National Association of Quality Assurance Professionals: Southwest Virginia Association of Quality Assurance Professionals; Roanoke Area Medical Record Association; Association of Health Information Professionals; Totera Womans Club; Mental Health Association of Roanoke Valley. **Education:** Phillips Business College, American Medical Record Association, A.R.T. (1979). **Personal:** Married to Steven in 1995. Two children: Karen Johnson Hughes and Melanie Vilinda Johnson. Mrs. Philo enjoys flea markets, miniature golf, reading, movies, gardening, and her grandchild.

Sharon E. Polite–Baxter

Executive Director
New York Methodist Hospital Family Health Center
210 Flatbush Avenue
Brooklyn, NY 11217
(718) 783–0070
Fax: (718) 783–6799

8062

Business Information: New York Methodist Hospital Family Health Center is a community medical health center offering primary health care. One of three off–site centers, it was opened in 1992 and treats over 10,000 patients a year. Comprised of six examination rooms and a staff of fifteen (including physicians, nurses, social workers and support staff), the Facility provides health education, HIV counseling and testing, and various special services. As Executive Director, Mrs. Polite–Baxter oversees all administrative duties, medical, and clerical functions. Instrumental in the development of the Center, she is also responsible for grants, proposals, and strategic planning. **Career Steps:** Executive Director, New York Methodist Hospital Family Health Center (1992–Present); Nursing Supervisor, Brownsville Multi–Service Family Health Center (1988–1992); Staff Nurse, New York Hospital, Cornell Medical Center (1985–1987). **Associations & Accomplishments:** American College of Healthcare Executives; CHCANYS; NYAAC; CDN; Sigma Theta Tau. **Education:** SUNY at Stony Brook, B.S. (1985); Registered Nurse (1985); Certified Phlebotomy Technician (1988); Certified in Community Health (1996). **Personal:** Married to George in 1985. Two children: Jarrett and Harrison. Mrs. Polite–Baxter enjoys shopping, travel, time with her kids, bus trips with friends, running a small gift basket business from home, and being an Amway distributor.

Michael Porte, M.D.

Director of Neonatal ICU & Neonatologist
Freeman Hospital
1102 West 32nd Street
Joplin, MO 64804
(419) 625–3740
Fax: Please mail or call

8062

Business Information: Freeman Hospital is a tertiary care hospital. A Board–certified Neonatologist, Dr. Michael Porte established Freeman Hospital's Neonatal ICU in 1993. He has been instrumental in implementing a transport network for critical care infants across portions of four states. The ICU provides tertiary care for these infants as well as a developmental follow up program. **Career Steps:** Director of Neonatal ICU & Neonatologist, Freeman Hospital. **Associations & Accomplishments:** American Academy of Pediatrics. **Education:** Loyola University Medical Center, M.D. (1981); University of Pennsylvania, B.A. (1974); Loyola University, Residency in Pediatrics (1984), Fellowship in Neonatology (1986). **Personal:** Married to Karen L. Porte, M.D.. Four children: Joshua, Rebecca, Matthew, and Talia.

Ian H. Porter, M.D.

Medical Director & Vice President of Medical Affairs
Albany Medical Center Hospital
43 New Scotland Avenue
Albany, NY 12208
(518) 262–3589
Fax: (518) 262–3398

8062

Business Information: Albany Medical Center Hospital is a full–service, tertiary medical care and teaching hospital, providing health care to patients and instruction to medical students. As Medical Director and Vice President of Medical Affairs, Dr. Porter is responsible for the medical direction and medical affairs of the hospital, in addition to his patient practice. Concurrently, he conducts research through various grants and contracts with the New York State Office of Mental Retardation and Developmental Disabilities, and Albany County Department of Mental Health – Preschool Early Development & Screening Service; New York State Department of Health – Genetic Services Grant; and the New York State Department of Health, Health Care Development Grant – Northeastern New York Academic Health System Consortium. **Career Steps:** Albany Medical Center Hospital: Medical Director & Vice President of Medical Affairs (1986–Present); Albany Medical College: Professor of Pediatrics and Attending Pediatrician (1968–Present); Expert for the Office of Professional Medical Conduct (1994–Present); Consultant, Glens Falls Hospital – Glens Falls, New York (1990–Present); Consultant, Vassar Brother's Hospital – Poughkeepsie, New York (1968–Present); Consultant, St. Peter's Hospital – Albany, New York (1967–Present); **Associations & Accomplishments:** American Board of Pediatrics; Central New York Pediatric Club (1993–Present); Fellow, American Academy of Pediatrics; The American College of Physician Executives; The American Federation of Clinical Research; The American Society of Human Genetics; The Society of Pediatric Research (Emeritus); The Society of Health and Human Values; Alpha Omega Alpha; Who's Who in the East (1993–Present); Who's Who in the World (1993–Present); Who's Who in Medicine and Healthcare (1995–Present); International Who's Who of Professionals (1995–Present). **Education:** St. Thomas' Hospital – London University, M.D. (1956); St. Thomas' Hospital – London, England: Clinical Assistant in Cardiology (1958), House Physician in Pediatrics (1957–1958), House Physician in the Medical Unit (1957), House Surgeon in the Casualty Department (1956–1957); Hammersmith Hospital and Royal Postgraduate Medical School – London, England: Medical Registrar in Rheumatology (1962–1963), Research Fellow in Rheumatology (1959), House Physician in Neurology (1958–1959), House Physician in Rheumatology (1958); The Johns Hopkins University School of Medicine – Baltimore, MD: Fellow in Medicine in Medical Genetics (1960–1962); **Personal:** Two children: Julian and Robert. Dr. Porter enjoys art (17th Century Dutch and 19th Century USA) and racquet sports.

Maria Guillen Portilla, M.D.

Pediatrician
Arkansas Children's Hospital
800 Marshall Street
Little Rock, AR 72202–3510
(501) 320–1849
Fax: (501) 320–1564

8062

Business Information: Arkansas Children's Hospital is a full–service pediatric hospital affiliated with the University of Arkansas for Medical Sciences. A practicing physician since 1980 and a Board–Certified Pediatrician, Dr. Portilla joined Arkansas Children's Hospital as Pediatrician in 1991. She is responsible for providing quality medical care to infants, children, and adolescents, as well as instructing medical students in pediatric medicine. **Career Steps:** Pediatrician, Arkansas Children's Hospital (1991–Present); Pediatrician, University of North Carolina – Chapel Hill (1988–1991); Pediatrician, St. Louis University School of Medicine. **Associations & Accomplishments:** Society for Adolescent Medicine; American Academy of Pediatrics; Ambulatory Pediatric Association; Bilingual – Spanish/English. **Education:** St. Louis University School of Medicine, Pediatric Residency (1984); Universidad del Valle Medical School – Colombia, M.D. (1980). **Personal:** Married to Didier in 1981. Two children: Ricardo and Diana. Dr. Portilla enjoys travel and dancing.

Rodolfo V. Punzalan, M.D.

President and Chairman of the Board
Covina Valley Community Hospital (SGVMI)
1630 Puente Avenue
Baldwin Park, CA 91706
(818) 339–5451
Fax: (818) 814–2156

8062

Business Information: Covina Valley Community Hospital (SGVMI) is a 76–bed, acute care hospital providing diagnosis and treatment of patients in the local community of Baldwin Park. A partial outpatient psychiatric satellite is also provided. As President and Chairman of the Board, Dr. Punzalan is responsible for all aspects of operations, including administration. Concurrent with his administrative role, he serves as President and Staff Physician for the Convenience Surgical Medical Clinic. **Career Steps:** President and Chairman of the Board, Covina Valley Community Hospital (SGVMI) (1986–Present); President and Physician, Convenience Surgical Medical Clinic (1980–Present); Commander, U.S. Navy (1972–1980). **Associations & Accomplishments:** American Academy of Family Practice; Physicians & Surgeons; Association of Military Surgeons; Board of Governors and Secretary, Association of Philippine Physicians in America; Vice President, Philippine Medical Society of Southern California; Philippine American Association of Southern California; Past President, Philippine Association of North San Diego County; Past President, Philippine Association of El Paso, Texas; Member, Catholic Ministry. **Education:** Texas Technological School of Medicine, Family Practice Residency (1979); LaVerne University, Business Administration and Management (1987); Great Lakes Naval Hospital, Internship (1973); Oakland Naval Hospital, Internship (1974); Manila Central University, Manila Philippines, M.D. (1965) **Personal:** Married to Angelita M. Punzalan in 1967. Five children: Anthony, Rodolfo Jr., Roderick, Gail Roy, and Justin. Dr. Punzalan enjoys bowling, singing, farming, raising poultry and goats, and yearly medical missions to disadvantaged communities in the Philippines.

Peter S. Rahko, M.D.

Associate Professor of Medicine
The University of Wisconsin Medical School
H6/334 CSC, 600 Highland Avenue
Madison, WI 53792–3248
(608) 263–1531
Fax: (608) 263–0405

8062

Business Information: The University of Wisconsin Hospital and clinics is a 470–bed tertiary referral center as well as a clinical research and instructional institution. In his current capacity, Dr. Rahko is an Associate Professor of Medicine, Director of the Adult Echocardiography Lab, and Director of the Cardiology Clinic. As such, he divides his time between patient care, clinical research and instruction of medical students, residents and fellows. **Career Steps:** Associate Professor of Medicine, The University of Wisconsin Medical School (Present). **Associations & Accomplishments:** Fellow, American College of Physicians; Fellow, American College of Cardiology; American Society of Echocardiography; American Heart Association. **Education:** University of Minnesota, M.D. (1979); Saint Olaf College, B.A. in Chemistry (1975). **Personal:** Married to Beth in 1982.

Rama Raju, M.D.

Chief of Medical Staff
Hempstead General Hospital
815 Front Street
Hempstead, NY 11550–4600
(516) 481–2232
Fax: (516) 481–2368

8062

Business Information: Hempstead General Hospital is a full service acute care community facility comprised of 220 beds. Providing health and related services to the community, the Hospital offers obstetrics and gynecological care, as well as emergency and pediatric services. As Chief of Medical Staff, Dr. Raju oversees all aspects of the Hospital, and is responsible for all levels of patient care. His duties include supervision of 200 doctors and their functions, development and implementation of policies and procedures, administration, operations and strategic planning. A certified medical director, Dr. Raja also oversees operations in two nursing homes (one with 200 beds, the other with 135) and consults in internal medicine. Concurrent with the above positions, he has his own practice, Rama Raju, M.D., specializing in internal medicine (i.e. CAT scans, etc.). **Career Steps:** Chief of Medical Staff, Hempstead General Hospital (1995–Present); Medical Staff, Wedgewood Nursing Home (Present); Medical Director, South Shore Nursing Home (1994–1995); Medical Director, Woodmere Nursing Home (1994). **Associations & Accomplishments:** American Medical Directors Association; American College of Physicians; New York State Medical Society. **Education:** Calcutta Medical College, M.B.B.S. (1974); D.M.R. College, India, B.Sc. (1968). **Personal:** Married to Parvati in 1972. Two children: Sujani and Shanti. Dr. Raju enjoys skiing.

Dr. Rajam S. Ramamurthy

Physician and Professor of Pediatrics
University of Texas Health Science Center – San Antonio
7703 Floyd Curl Drive
San Antonio, TX 78284–6200
(210) 567–5228
Fax: (210) 567–5169

8062

Business Information: University of Texas Health Science Center – San Antonio is a tertiary medical care and teaching facility providing diagnosis and treatment to patients and instruction to medical students. Established in 1966, the Center currently employs 4,040 people. As Physician and Professor of Pediatrics, Dr. Ramamurthy is responsible for providing health care to patients and instruction of medical students in neonatology. **Career Steps:** University of Texas Health Science Center – San Antonio: Physician and Professor of Pediatrics (1990–Present), Associate Professor (1983–1990), Assistant Professor (1977–1983). **Associations & Accomplishments:** American Pediatric Society (1992); American Association of Physicians from India (1988); Texas Indian Physicians Society (1987); Texas Medical Association (1987); American Medical Women's Association (1984); Perinatal Section (1981); American Academy of Pediatrics; Southern Society of Pediatric Research (1977); American Academy of Pediatrics (1974); Elected to San Antonio Women's Hall of Fame (1984); Advisory Board of Texas Commission on the Arts (1993–1995); Board of Directors for Arathi School of Indian Dance, San Antonio (1993–Present); Carver Development Board (1988–Present); Chairman, Board of Trustees, India Asia Association of San Antonio (198l5–1987); Mayor's Commission on Women – Women's Fair Forum (1980–1986); Published 100 publications and 60+ articles; Substitute teacher in Indian classical dance. **Education:** University of Mysore, The Bangalore Medical College, India, M.B.B.S. (1965). **Personal:** Married to Somayaji Ramamurthy in 1972. Two children: Sujatha & Sendhil. Dr. Ramamurthy enjoys classical dancing and tennis.

Robert D. Ramsey Jr., FHFMA, CPA, CIA

Vice President/Chief Financial Officer
Doctors Hospital
5230 South 6th Street
Springfield, IL 62703–5194
(217) 529–7151 Ext. 2690
Fax: (217) 529–9472
EMAIL: See Below

8062

Business Information: Doctors Hospital is a 177–bed, full–service, healthcare institution specializing in the diagnosis, treatment, and rehabilitation of patients. As Vice President/Chief Financial Officer, Mr. Ramsey is responsible for all aspects of the Hospital's financial operations, including accounting and budgeting. Internet users can reach him via: ramet@cencom.net. **Career Steps:** Vice President/Chief Financial Officer, Doctors Hospital (1995–Present); Director of Reimbursement, St. Johns Mercy Health System (1993–1995); Director of Reimbursement, ASC Health System (1990–1993). **Associations & Accomplishments:** Healthcare Financial Management Association; American Institute of Certified Public Accountants; Institute of Internal Auditors; Elks Lodge #158; Ancient Accepted Scottish Rite; AF & AM #635. **Education:** University of Illinois – Springfield, M.A. in Accounting (In Progress); Southern Illinois University, B.S. in Business, Major, Accountancy. **Personal:** Married to Gayle in 1987. One child: Chelsey R. Bonnett. Mr. Ramsey enjoys golf, fishing, wine, and travel.

Kakarala J. Rao, M.D.

Physician
VA Medical Center
State Route 104
Chillicothe, OH 45601
(614) 773–1141
Fax: (614) 772–7023

8062

Business Information: Veteran's Administration (VA) Medical Center is a medical institute providing diagnosis and treatment to veterans of military forces. Educated and receiving his medical doctorate in India in 1970, Dr. Rao joined the VA Medical Service as Physician in 1972. Previously a Flight Surgeon in the U.S. Air Force, he currently provides diagnosis and treatment to patients, specializing in Internal Medicine, Endrocrinology, and aviation medicine. **Career Steps:** Physician, VA Medical Center (1972–Present); Retired, Air Force Reserves. **Associations & Accomplishments:** American Medical Association; Aerospace Medical Society; Association of Military Surgeons of United States; National Geography Society; Sierra Club. **Education:** Guntur Medical College A.P. – India, M.D. (1970); University of Kansas School of Medicine, M.S. (1992); Chingleput Medical College – India, M.B.B.S. (1966); Kilpauic Medical College Madras – India, G.C.I.M. (1960). **Personal:** Married to K. L. V. Devi in 1962. Three children: Sivaram Krishna, K. U. Geethavani, and Hema Meenakshi. Dr. Rao enjoys physical fitness and health promotion.

Kaushik J. Raval, M.D.

Medical Director of Mental Health Clinic
Aleda E. Lutz VA Medical Center
1500 Weiss Street
Saginaw, MI 48602–5251
(517) 793–2340
Fax: (517) 791–2274

8062

Business Information: Aleda E. Lutz VA Medical Center is a 120–bed acute care hospital with a 120 bed nursing home care unit, a primary care ambulatory unit, and a mental health clinic, servicing Northern Lower Michigan and part of the Upper Peninsula. As Medical Director of Mental Health Clinic, Dr. Raval is responsible for the oversight of all programs and supervision of staff and administrative duties of the Mental Health Clinic, in addition to his daily patient practice. He also serves as Clinical Instructor in Psychiatry at Michigan State University. **Career Steps:** Medical Director of Mental Health Clinic, Aleda E. Lutz VA Medical Center (1994–Present); Residency in Psychiatry, Wayne State University (1990–1994); Reseacher in Psychiatry, Royal Ottawa Hospital (1986–1989); Clinical Instructor, Michigan State University. **Associations & Accomplishments:** American Psychiatric Association; Michigan Psychiatric Society. **Education:** Wayne State University, M.D. in Psychiatry (1994); Grant Medical College – Bombay, India, M.B.B.S. (1984). **Personal:** Married to Pratibha in 1983. Three children: Sons: Kunil and Nilesh. Daughter: Kavita. Dr. Raval enjoys golf, swimming, reading philosophical books, and foreign travel.

Gregory J. Redding, M.D.

Professor of Pediatrics
University of Washington School of Medicine
Box C5371, Pulmonary Division Ch–68 Childrens Hospital
Seattle, WA 98105
(206) 526–2174
Fax: (206) 528–2639

8062

Business Information: The University of Washington School of Medicine provides all aspects of post–graduate education to residents and interns, as well as full tertiary care and clinical research hospital facilities. Dr. Redding is the Pediatric Respiratory Specialist for the University, the Children's Hospital and the Medical Center, as well as regional clinics throughout the Pacific Northwest. He is also a lecturer, an instructor, and conducts clinical research in the areas of asthma, respiratory failure in children, and new treatments for pediatric lung diseases. Board–certified in Pediatrics with a sub–specialty in Pediatric Pulmonology, Dr. Redding has published over 50 articles and chapters in research journals. **Career Steps:** University of Washington School of Medicine: Professor of Pediatrics (1994–Present), Associate Professor of Pediatrics (1986–1994), Assistant Professor of Pediatrics (1980–1986). **Associations & Accomplishments:** Society for Pediatric Research; American Thoracic Society; American College of Chest Physicians; American Physiologic Society; Best Doctors in America (1992–1993, 1994–1995); American Heart Association; American Board of Pediatrics; Society of Critical Care Medicine. **Education:** Stanford University School of Medicine, M.D. (1974); University of California – San Diego, B.A. in Biology (1970); University of Colorado School of Medicine, Pediatric Pulmonary Fellowship Training. **Personal:** Married to Joyce Jacobs in 1993. One child: Joshua Lehman. Dr. Redding enjoys photography, sports, and travel.

Helga M. Redmond, R.N.

Nursing Program Director
Elkins Park Hospital
60 East Township Line Road
Elkins Park, PA 19027–2220
(215) 663–6155
Fax: Please mail or call

8062

Business Information: Elkins Park Hospital, affiliated with AHARF organization, is a 220–bed, full–service community hospital. As Nursing Program Director for the Acute Care Units, Mrs. Redmond is responsible for sixty acute care medical and surgical beds, as well as a staff of 85 employees. She also conducts lectures to nurses on health issues. **Career Steps:** Elkins Park Hospital: Nursing Program Director (1994–Present), QA Coordinator (1993–1994), Clinical Educator (1989–1992), Staff RN (1984–1989). **Education:** Holy Family College, B.S. in Nursing (1984). **Personal:** Married to Joseph in 1986. Two children: Nicole and Ryan. Mrs. Redmond enjoys spending time with her family, sports, and travel.

Catherine Orr Reed, RNC, MS, MSN

Director
Southwest Mississippi Regional Medical Center
215 Marion Avenue, P.O. Box 1307
McComb, MS 39648–1307
(601) 249–1445
Fax: (601) 249–1704

8062

Business Information: Southwest Mississippi Regional Medical Center is a public hospital, providing health care services for a large community in Southwest Mississippi, consisting of seven Mississippi counties and two Louisiana parishes. A practicing nurse since 1974, Ms. Reed joined Southwest Mississippi Regional Medical Center as Director. She is responsible for directing all personnel, staffing, and budgeting for three nursing units within Perinatal and Maternal/Child Nursing, in addition to serving as Nurse Administrator. **Career Steps:** Director, Southwest Mississippi Regional Medical Center (1995–Present); Clinical Nurse Specialist, Promina Cobb Hopsital – Austell, GA (1993–1994); Instructor, Auburn University – School of Nursing (1991–1993). **Associations & Accomplishments:** Sigma Theta Tau; Mississippi March of Dimes Health Professional Advisory Council; Phi Kappa Phi; Epsilon Sigma Alpha; American Nurses Association; Community Chorale; Association of Women's Health, Obstetric & Neonatal Nursing; Pike County Little Theater. **Education:** University of Texas – Austin, M.S.N. (1984); American Technological University, M.S. (1981); University of Maryland, B.S.N. (1974); Nursing Certifications: Inpatient Obstetrics,

Nursing Administration. **Personal:** Three children: Christopher, Jonathan, and Elizabeth. Ms. Reed enjoys reading, crafts, cross–stitching, theater, acting, and singing.

Michael Reese
Director of Environmental Services
The Christ Hospital
2139 Auburn Avenue
Cincinnati, OH 45240
(513) 369–2995
Fax: (513) 369–2989

8062

Business Information: The Christ Hospital is a tertiary teaching hospital, providing instruction to student nurses and health care to patients. As Director of Environmental Services, Mr. Reese is responsible for the direction of all operations and personnel within the department, as well as overseeing operations of the health care facilities' inside and outside environment, such as the garages, grounds, and transportation facilities. **Career Steps:** Director of Environmental Services, The Christ Hospital (1974–Present); Life Underwriter, Western Southern Life Insurance Company (1973–1974). **Associations & Accomplishments:** Black Achiever, YMCA; American Society for Healthcare Environmental Service; T.C.H. Management Association; Environmental Management Association. **Education:** Cincinnati Technical College, Associates in Business (1978); Xavier University, Supervisory Training. **Personal:** Mr. Reese enjoys painting, music, basketball, and travel.

Kyle V. Reeves, R.N., A.T.C.
Director Orthopedics, Rehabilitation, and Therapy Services
Columbia Alaska Regional Hospital
2807 DeBarr Road
Anchorage, AK 99508
(907) 264–1759
Fax: (907) 264–1143

8062

Business Information: Columbia Alaska Regional Hospital is a regional acute care hospital serving the surrounding areas of Anchorage, Alaska. The Hospital currently employs more than 45 people. As Director Orthopedics, Rehabilitation, and Therapy Services, Mr. Reeves oversees the daily operations of the services. He is responsible for budgetary concerns, scheduling, and strategic planning for the three units/services. **Career Steps:** Director Orthopedics, Rehabilitation, and Therapy Services, Columbia Alaska Regional Hospital (1995–Present); Staff Nurse, Sunnyside Hospital (1993–1995); Clinical Coordinator of Sports Medicine, University Orthopedics (1991–1993). **Associations & Accomplishments:** National Association Orthopedic Nurses; National Athletic Trainers Association; Phi Alpha Theta; Golden Key Honors Society. **Education:** United States Sports Academy, Masters in Sports Science (1990); University of Alaska, Bachelors in Education; Anchorage Community College, Associate Degree in Nursing. **Personal:** Married to Nikka in 1989. Mr. Reeves enjoys photography, biking, and mountain climbing.

Ann–Marie Regan, BSN, RN, CIC
Education and Infection Control Coordinator
Fairview Hospital
29 Lewis Avenue
Great Barrington, MA 01230
(413) 528–0790
Fax: (413) 528–0290

8062

Business Information: Fairview Hospital, a part of Berkshire Health Systems, is a full–service, 38–bed acute care hospital, providing emergency room, obstetrics, acute in–patient, surgical, and outpatient services. Located in a highly tourist industry area, Fairview Hospital serves the New York, Connecticut and South Massachusetts borders. Berkshire Health Systems also includes Berkshire Medical Center, a sister hospital to Fairview Hospital, which is a full–service, 150–bed acute care hospital located in Pittsfield, Massachusetts. With seventeen years in health care and a Certified Infection Control Practitioner, Ms. Regan joined Fairview Hospital 1991. Appointed as Education and Infection Control Coordinator in 1992, she is responsible for the coordination of staff education and competency, and infection control procedures. She also serves as the Coordinator of cardiopulmonary resuscitation (CPR). **Career Steps:** Fairview Hospital: Education and Infection Control Coordinator (1992–Present), Director of Total Quality (1994–1996), Coordinator of CPR (1992–Present); RN Coordinator, Fairview Manor (1991–1992); Staff Development Coordinator, Hill Haven Great Barrington Healthcare (1981–1991). **Associations & Accomplishments:** Intructor/Trainer, American Heart Association; Association of Infection Control Prevention; American Cancer Society; Association for Professional in Infection Control; Girl Scout Leader.

Education: Oral Roberts University, B.S. in Nursing (1979); CIC, Certified in Infection Control by CBIC (1995). **Personal:** Married to Peter in 1996. Three children: Ellen, Shanna, and Gordon Hamm. Ms. Regan enjoys painting wall and ceiling murals.

Mary H. Reid, RN
Department Manager
Dominican Hospital
1555 Soquel Drive
Santa Cruz, CA 95065–1705
(408) 462–7633
Fax: Please mail or call

8062

Business Information: Dominican Hospital is a 250–bed, full–service acute care hospital consisting of three units and an Education Department. A practicing nurse since 1974, Mrs. Reid joined the Dominican Hospital as Staff Nurse in 1977. Promoted to Charge Nurse in 1979, she was then appointed as Department Manager in 1990, responsible for the management of two units (Medical, Surgical) of the Hospital. She is also responsible for all strategic planning, financing, day–to–day operations, and oversight of Human Resources activities for both units. **Career Steps:** Dominican Hospital: Department Manager (1990–Present), Charge Nurse (1979–1990), Staff Nurse (1977–1979). **Associations & Accomplishments:** Academy of Medical Surgical Nurses. **Education:** University of Nevada – Reno, B.S.N. (1974). **Personal:** Married to Michael P. in 1977. Two children: Nicholas and Courtney. Mrs. Reid enjoys soccer and reading mysteries.

Nancy J. Rethman
Director of Health Information Services
Upper Valley Medical Centers
624 Park Avenue
Piqua, OH 45356
(513) 332–8650
Fax: (513) 778–6658

8062

Business Information: Upper Valley Medical Centers are acute care hospitals. The hospitals also provide an after–discharge continued care services program. As Director of Health Information Services, Mrs. Rethman supervises and maintains the Medical Records Department, providing health information management and research information for three area medical centers. Other duties include coding records and submitting bills for payment to insurance plans or individuals. **Career Steps:** Director of Health Information Services, Upper Valley Medical Centers (1995–Present); Manager of Health Information Services, P.M.M.C. (1987–1995). **Associations & Accomplishments:** Miami Valley Health Information Management Association; Ohio Health Information Association; Advisory Board for JVS, Edison College. **Education:** Bowling Green State University, B.S. (1987). **Personal:** Married to Michael in 1990. Four children: Kayla, Morgan, Wesley, and Kacie. Mrs. Rethman enjoys spending time with her family.

F. Carlene Reuscher
Senior Vice President
Torrance Memorial Medical Center
3330 Lomita Boulevard
Torrance, CA 90505–5002
(310) 517–4657
Fax: (310) 784–4801

8062

Business Information: Torrance Memorial Medical Center is a free standing, non–profit community hospital providing inpatient/outpatient services, as well as health education. As Senior Vice President, Ms. Reuscher is responsible for inpatient/outpatient care services, including admitting, human resources, nursing, and operational and strategic planning. **Career Steps:** Senior Vice President, Torrance Memorial Medical Center (1982–Present); Director of Nursing – Miller Children's Hospital, Long Beach Memorial Medical Center (1977–1982); Assistant Professor, California State University – Long Beach (1971–1976). **Associations & Accomplishments:** World Future Society; Organization of Nurse Executives. **Education:** University of California – Los Angeles, M.S. (1964); Hospital of Good Samaritan – Bishop Johnson College of Nursing, R.N.; California State University – Los Angeles, B.S. **Personal:** Married to Edward Joseph in 1978. Three children: Gretchen Corkrean, Ian Campbell, and Heidi Campbell. Ms. Reuscher enjoys music and church activities.

Luis A. Rivera–Colon
Human Resources Director
Hospital I Gonzalez Martinez
P.O. Box 191811
San Juan, Puerto Rico 00919–1811
(787) 763–4149 Ext.246
Fax: (787) 751–7940

8062

Business Information: Hospital I Gonzalez Martinez is a nonprofit 144–bed medical facility, offering oncology service and medical care to San Juan and surrounding areas. As Human Resources Director, Mr. Rivera–Colon handles all administrative duties related to his department, including accounting and public relations. Additionally, he is part of the labor union, and supervises a small support staff. **Career Steps:** Human Resources Director, Hospital I Gonzalez Martinez (1990–Present); Human Resources Director, Eugenio Fernandez Garcia, Clinic (1984–1990); Human Resources Director, Copey Hospital and Nursing Home (1983–1984); Administrative Assistant to Human Resources Director, Municipal of San Juan Department of Health (1970–1983). **Associations & Accomplishments:** Founder, Human Resources Association of Health Organization of Puerto Rico; Labor Practitioner Association of Puerto Rico. **Education:** Sacred Heart University, B.B.A. in Business Administration (1983). **Personal:** Married to Maria S. Figueroa in 1972. Four children: Carlos, Alexis, Luis, and Gerardo. Mr. Rivera–Colon enjoys being a musician (guitar).

Jeremy K. Roberts, M.D.
Clinical Physician/Associate Professor
Calgary General Hospital, University of Calgary
Room 92–039–841 Centre Avenue East
Calgary, Alberta T2E 0A1
(403) 261–0070
Fax: (403) 268–9240

8062

Business Information: Calgary General Hospital/University of Calgary is a full service acute care facility providing medical and related services to the area. Affiliated with the University of Calgary, a secondary educational establishment specializing in graduate and under–graduate medical programs, the Hospital offers hands–on training to medical students and residents in all fields. As Clinical Physician/Associate Professor, Dr. Roberts specializes in Neurology research, specifically Huntington's Disease, about which he plans to publish a book. Additional responsibilities include instruction of students and residents in neurology/clinical psychiatry, as well as management of his private medical practice, where he treats patients with psychiatric and neurological disorders. **Career Steps:** Clinical Physician/Associate Professor, Calgary General Hospital/University of Calgary (1993–Present). **Associations & Accomplishments:** Canadian Medical Association; Alberta Psychiatric Association; Author of a Book on Neurology (1984); Active Volunteer, Homeless Shelters and the Community. **Education:** Medical Degree. **Personal:** Dr. Roberts enjoys photographic reproduction and art collecting.

John M. Roberts, M.D.
Chief of Staff
Shriner's Hospital
516 Carew Street
Springfield, MA 01104
(413) 787–2047
Fax: (413) 787–2054
EMAIL:Taylar W@aol.com

8062

Business Information: Shriners Hospital in Springfield is an endowed hospital providing free services to crippled children. A practicing physician since 1957, a Pediatric Orthopaedic Surgeon and an Educator, Dr. Roberts serves as Chief of Staff, overseeing the functions of the medical staff and the hospital, in addition to his daily patient practice. Concurrently, he serves as Professor of Orthopaedic Surgery at Boston University, Clinical Professor of Orthopaedic Surgery at Albany Medical College, and Lecturer in Orthopaedics at Columbia University. **Career Steps:** Chief of Staff, Pediatric Orthopaedic Surgeon, and Educator, Shriner's Hospital (1989–Present); Professor of Orthopaedic Surgery, Boston University (1989–Present); Clinical Professor of Orthopaedic Surgery, Albany Medical College (1989–Present); Lecturer in Orthopaedic, Columbia University (1989–Present); Acting Chairman – Department of Orthopaedic Surgery, Brown University and Rhode Island Hospital (1986–1989); Professor of Orthopaedics & Pediatrics, Brown University (1986–1989); Professor of Orthopaedics Surgery, Louisiana State University (1975–1986); Clinical Professor of Orthopaedic Surgery, Tulane University, (1975–1986) Chairman, Orthopaedic Department, Children's Hospital, New Orleans, Louisiana (1975–1986). **Associations & Accomplishments:** American Orthopaedic Association; American Academy of Orthopaedic Surgeons; American Medical Association; Pediatric Orthopaedic Society of North America, President (1982–1983); Scoliosis Research Society; International Society of Childrens' Orthopaedics and Traumatology. **Education:** Columbia University, M.D. (1957); Brown University, M.A., Ad. Eundem (1987); Yale University, B.A. (1953); Phillips Exeter Academy (1949). **Personal:** Married to Edith N. in 1977. Two children: Manley Woolfolk and Carter Street. Dr. Roberts enjoys sailing "True North," a 30–foot Vindo, on the coast of Maine.

Lois May Roberts, M.D.
Physician
Sunrise Valley Hospital
741 N. Main Street
Cedarville, CA 91604
(916) 279–6111
Fax: (916) 279–2680

8062

Business Information: Sunrise Valley Hospital is the smallest hospital in California. Comprised of four beds and located in an agricultural area, it is predominantly an emergency hospital with life flight services. As Physician, Dr. Roberts oversees all aspects of the Hospital. The sole practitioner, she is responsible for all emergencies including OB/GYN. Formerly in charge of a bush hospital in Africa, Dr. Roberts also oversees all patient care and diagnosis. **Career Steps:** Physician, Sunrise Valley Hospital (1986–Present); Physician, Mayers Memorial Hospital (1990–Present); Physician, Sonoma Valley Hospital (1979–1986). **Associations & Accomplishments:** Alumnae, Woman's Medical College of Pennsylvania; Wilderness Medical Society; Commonwealth Club of California. **Education:** Woman's Medical College of Pennsylvania, M.D. (1950); University of California, Berkeley: A.B., M.S. **Personal:** Dr. Roberts enjoys birding, river rafting and fishing.

Marcy Roberts, RN
Chief Utilization Management
Womack Army Medical Center
Managed Care Division
Ft. Bragg, NC 28307
(910) 432–9359
Fax: (910) 432–4083
EMAIL: See Below

8062

Business Information: Womack Army Medical Center is an acute care medical facility, providing medical care to active duty military members, retirees, and their family members. A former Army operating nurse and a practicing nurse since 1974, Mrs. Roberts joined Womack in 1990. Serving as Chief Utilization Management in 1993, she supervises utilization review, discharge planning, and case management, as well as participating in the guide development of new utilization management initiatives. Internet users can reach her via: marcy_roberts@smtplink.bragg_amedd.army.mil **Career Steps:** Womack Army Medical Center: Chief Utilization Management (1993–Present), Staff Nurse of Operating Room (1992–1993), Chief of OR/CMS Nursing Service (1990–1991). **Associations & Accomplishments:** Association of Operating Room Nurses; American Association of Utilization Management Nurses; Quality Utilization Management of North Carolina. **Education:** Northeast Missouri State University: M.A. in Human Resource Management (1981), B.S. in Nursing (1974); Certifications: CNOR and CPUR. **Personal:** Married to Don in 1992. Mrs. Roberts enjoys counted cross–stitching, hunting, and computers.

Dale F. Robertson, M.D.C.M.
Pediatrician/Pulmonologist
Summit Health Centre
P.O. Box 3420
Canmore, Alberta TOL OMO
(403) 678–9822
Fax: (403) 678–9938

8062

Business Information: Summit Health Centre is a health care office with two physicians, a pediatrician/pulmonologist, and a cardiologist, as well as a nutritionist and an exercise therapist. A Former Lecturer at McGill University and Visiting Assistant Professor at the University of Utah, Dr. Robertson joined Summit Health Centre in 1996, consulting in pediatrics and pulmonology. **Career Steps:** Pediatrician/Pulmonologist, Summit Health Centre (1996–Present); Visiting Assistant Professor, University of Utah (1994–1995); Lecturer, McGill University (1992–1993). **Associations & Accomplishments:** Canadian Pediatric Society; Canadian Thoracic Society; American Thoracic Society; Canadian Medical Association. **Education:** McGill University, M.D.C.M. (1987).

Personal: Married to Thomas Sinclair in 1990. Dr. Robertson enjoys sewing, reading, and skiing.

Evelyn C. Robertson Jr.
Vice President
West Tennessee Health Care Inc.
238 Summar Drive
Jackson, TN 38301–3901
(901) 935–8320
Fax: (901) 935–8327

8062

Business Information: West Tennessee Healthcare, Inc. serves as the umbrella organization for six rural hospitals in West Tennessee which includes Jackson Madison General Hospital. West Tennessee Healthcare, Inc. serves 17 counties offering emergency, home health, skilled nursing and behavioral health. Joining West Tennessee Healthcare, Inc. in 1994, Mr. Robertson serves as Vice president of Behavioral Health. He is also Executive Director of Pathways, Inc. of Tennessee, a comprehensive mental health center serving 8 of the 17 counties and an affiliate of Jackson Madison General Hospital. Pathways was formed by a merger in March 1995. Career milestones include implementation of the merger and the adaptation to managed care. **Career Steps:** Vice President of Behavioral Health, West Tennessee Healthcare, Inc. (1994–Present); Executive Director, Pathways (1994–Present); Commissioner, Tennessee Department of Mental Health & Mental Retardation (1991–1994); Superintendent, Western Mental Health Institute (1983–1991); Superintendent, National T. Winston Developmental Center (1979–1983). **Associations & Accomplishments:** President (1994), National Association of State Mental Health Program Directors; Center for Mental Health Services National Advisory Council; American Association on Mental Deficiency; Tennessee Hospital Association. **Education:** Tennessee State University: M.A. in Administration and Supervision (1969), B.S. in Political Science and History; Southwest Missouri State University – N.D.E.A. Institute, Certificate. **Personal:** Married to Hugholene. Mr. Robertson enjoys reading, music, spectator sports, and community relations.

Minnie P. Roddy
Intensive Care Unit Manager
Hereford Regional Medical Center
801 E. 3rd Street
Hereford, TX 79045
(806) 364–2141
Fax: Please mail or call

8062

Business Information: Hereford Regional Medical Center is a 41 bed full service medical facility providing medical and nursing care to the sick and injured and educating the community on health–related issues. As Intensive Care Unit Manager, Ms. Roddy supervises all R.N.'s, L.V.N.'s, and N.T.'s on specific nursing care procedures. She also acts as a nurse advocate, manages all aspects of the Intensive Care Unit, and provides in–service training. Additional responsibilities include direct supervision of seventy–five people, handles problems as they arise and ensures quality of patient care. **Career Steps:** Intensive Care Unit Manager, Hereford Regional Medical Center (1973–Present); Staffing Nurse–General, Palo Duro Hospital (184–1986); Staff Nurse–Critical Care, Northwest Texas Hospital (1990). **Associations & Accomplishments:** Panhandle Trauma Forum Educational Sector; American Heart Association; National ENA Trauma Nursing Care Course; Captain, United States Army Reserves AMED Core. **Education:** West Texas A&M University, B.S.N. (1993); American Technical Institute, Certified Administrative Assistant. **Personal:** Four children: Sherald, Angelina, Daphne and April. Ms. Roddy enjoys being a host mentor at an elementary school and home care nursing.

Marcella Renee Rogers, R.N., B.S.N.
Director of Human Resources
Devereux Hospital and Children's Center
8000 Devereux Drive
Viera, FL 32940–7907
(407) 242–9100 Ext. 162
Fax: (407) 259–0786

8062

Business Information: Devereux Hospital and Children's Center, is a pediatric behavioral and psychiatric children's facility that provides healthcare and related services to emotionally disturbed children. Established in 1912, the center is located in Melbourne, Florida. As Director of Human

Resources, Ms. Rogers is responsible for diversified managerial duties, including recruitment, discipline, internal grievances, employment support, and consulting with managed care physicians for quality improvement. With 11 years of nursing experience, Ms. Rogers looks forward to completing her M.B.A., and continuing her work as an administrator. **Career Steps:** Director of Human Resources, Devereux Hospital and Children's Center (1995–Present); Dialysis Nurse, Holmes Regional (1990–1995); Nurse Manager, Florida Keys Memorial (1987–1990). **Associations & Accomplishments:** Space Coast Human Resources; Florida Organization of Nurse Executives; American Heart Association; American Nephrology Nurses Association; Florida Nurses Association; American Association of Critical Care Nurses; United Way; Dialysis Spirit Representative; U.S. Power Squadron Member; HRMC Ball Supporter. **Education:** Florida Tech, M.B.A. (In Progress); University of Central Florida, B.S.N. (193); Florida Key Community College, A.A. (1989); Vincennes University, A.S. (1985). **Personal:** Married to Robert in 1991. Three children: Amber, Kim, and Kristi. Ms. Rogers enjoys diving, boating, and school.

Ruben Norat Roig
Chief Financial Officer
Hospital Menonita de Aibonito
P.O. Box 1379
Aibonito, Puerto Rico 00705
(787) 735–8001
Fax: (787) 735–2961

8062

Business Information: Hospital Menonita de Aibonito is one of two affiliated full–service community hospitals in the Aibonito area of Puerto Rico. As Chief Financial Officer, Mr. Roig is responsible for a staff of 70 in conducting all financial and accounting activities for the Hospital and its sister facility in Cayey. **Career Steps:** Chief Financial Officer, Hospital Menonita de Aibonito (1995–Present). **Associations & Accomplishments:** Eta Delta Alpha Fraternity; Healthcare Financial Management Association. **Education:** University of Puerto Rico, B.A. (1987). **Personal:** Married to Iris Y. Rosario in 1988. Three children: Ruben, Yolian, and Yoliana. Mr. Roig plays trumpet, piano, and guitar.

James E. Ross
Administrator
West Tennessee Surgery Center
637 Skyline Drive
Jackson, TN 38301–3922
(901) 935–8859
Fax: (901) 935–8861

8062

Business Information: West Tennessee Surgery Center, an affiliate of West Tennessee Healthcare, Inc., is a hospital–based, ambulatory surgery center consisting of eight operating rooms and a pain clinic. With fifteen physicians on staff, the Center conducts 4,300 procedures annually. As Administrator, Mr. Ross is responsible for the administration of eight operating room suites, which conduct 5,000 surgeries and 20,000 surgical–related procedures. Additional duties include: coordination of optimetric network management of the faculty, development of nursing and surgical suites, managed care negotiation for facilities, FDA Toy Program, budgeting processes, and strategic plans for the organization. **Career Steps:** Administrator, West Tennessee Surgery Center (1995–Present); Jackson General Hospital: Director of Cardiac Intensive Care (1991–1995), Manager Cardiology Services (1989–1991), Coordinator Critical Care (1987–1989). **Associations & Accomplishments:** Executive Board Member, Boy Scouts of America; Emergency Cardiac Care Division of America; Tennessee Organization of Nurse Executives; American College of Cardiovascular Administrators; National Association of Health Services Executives; Officiate Faculty Member, Heart Association; Promise Keepers; Sigma Theta Tha. **Education:** University of Alabama–Birmingham, M.S.H.A. (1993); Union University: B.S.N.(1987), A.S.N. (1985); Nursing Home Administration License (1995); Jackson State Community College, A.S. (1982). **Personal:** Married to Cynthia in 1993. Two children: Ashley and Kelsey. Mr. Ross enjoys outdoors, water sports and electronics.

Brian H. Rowe, M.D.

Physician/Researcher
Sudbury General Hospital
700 Paris Street
Sudbury, Ontario P3E 3B5
(705) 688–0200
Fax: (705) 671–1688
E MAIL: See Below

8062

Business Information: Sudbury General Hospital is a full–service acute and subacute care hospital providing health care to citizens of Sudbury, Ontario. As Physician/Researcher, Dr. Rowe is an emergency care and family medicine physician. As Research Director, Dr. Rowe is concerned with medical problems and injuries affecting the elderly. He oversees the research done by hospital residents and other departments and develops educational programs based on their findings. Concurrently, Dr. Rowe is an instructor at the University of Ottawa teaching critical appraisal. Internet users may contact Dr. Rowe via: roweb@nolm.laurentiar.com. **Career Steps:** Physician/Researcher, Sudbury General Hospital (1991–Present); Research Director, Northeastern Ontario Family Medical Program (1991–Present); Research Director, Sudbury General Hospital Trauma Program (1991–Present); Instructor, University of Ottawa (1991–Present). **Associations & Accomplishments:** Canadian Association of Emergency Physicians; College of Family Physicians of Canada; Society of Academic Emergency Medicine; Safe Kids of Canada Section of Teachers (CFPC); Cochran Collaboration; Canadian Medical Association. **Education:** McMaster University, M.Sc. (1991); University of Ottawa: M.D. and CCFP(EM); Queen's University, B.A. **Personal:** Married to Katharyn Webb in 1991. Two children: Bradley and Stewart. Dr. Rowe enjoys biking, swimming, and cross country skiing.

Roger N. Ruckman, M.D.

Professor of Pediatrics
George Washington University Medical Center
Children's National Medical Center, 111 Michigan Avenue, N.W.
Washington, DC 20010
(202) 884–3911
Fax: (202) 884–3914

8062

Business Information: George Washington University Medical Center is a full–service health care institution specializing in the diagnosis, treatment and rehabilitation of patients. Established in 1870, the Hospital currently employs 2,000 medical professionals. As Professor of Pediatrics at George Washington University Medical Center, Dr. Ruckman is a pediatric cardiologist whose duties include teaching, patient care, administration and research in his area of expertise. He also serves as Medical Director for the Consultative Centers at Children's National Medical Center, the pediatric hospital of George Washington University Medical Center, and has provided each with sixteen years of combined service. **Career Steps:** Medical Director, Children's Consultative Centers, Children's National Medical Center (1993–Present); Professor of Pediatrics, George Washington University Medical Center (1990–Present); Senior Attending, Cardiology, Children's National Medical Center (1980–Present). **Associations & Accomplishments:** American Medical Association; American Heart Association; Fellow, American Academy of Pediatrics; Fellow, American College of Cardiology; Society for Pediatric Research; Society for Pediatric Echocardiography. **Education:** University of Virginia, M.D. (1970); Williams College, B.A. in Chemistry (1966). **Personal:** Married to Kathleen Smith in 1969. Four children: Robert Elliott, Karen Beth, Stephen Merrill and Jonathan Roger. Dr. Ruckman enjoys music, tennis, squash and golf.

Kenneth W. Ryder, M.D., Ph.D.

Chief of Pathology
Wishard Memorial Hospital
1001 West 10th Street
Indianapolis, IN 46202
(317) 630–7208
Fax: (317) 630–7913

8062

Business Information: Wishard Memorial Hospital is a multi–specialty, acute care hospital affilliated with Indiana University School of Medicine. The Department of Pathology at Wishard Hospital employs over 160 physicians and medical support staff. Board–certified in Clinical and Radioisotopic Pathology by the American Board of Pathology, Dr. Ryder is the Chief of Pathology at Wishard Memorial Hospital. As such, he is responsible for all aspects of laboratory functions, research, and results. Concurrent to his position with the hospital, Dr. Ryder is also the Associate Chair of the Deparment of Pathology at Indiana University. A widely acknowledged expert in his field, he has published eight books and numerous articles. **Career Steps:** Wishard Memorial Hospital: Chief of Pathology (1986–Present), Assistant Pathologist (1978–1986). **Associations & Accomplishments:** American Medical Association; American Society of Clinical Pathologists; Academy of Clinical Laboratory Physicians and Scientists; American Association for Clinical Chemistry; Fellow, College of American Pathologists; Fellow, National Academy of Clinical Biochemistry; Joseph A. Kleiner Award (1986); Outstanding Teacher Award (1990). **Education:** University of Illinois School of Medicine, M.D. (1975); Indiana University Graduate School, Ph.D. in Chemistry (1972); Knox College, B.A. in Chemistry (1967).

Ms. Susan K. Sabas

Director of Resident Services
Bonell Good Samaritan Center
708 22nd Street
Greeley, CO 80631–7041
(970) 352–6082
Fax: (970) 356–7970

8062

Business Information: The Bonell Good Samaritan Center provides complete long and short term health care to individuals in Greeley and surrounding communities. The Center is a multi–level care facility offering apartments, assisted living and total care options. At present, the Center has 261 beds, 41 assisted living facilities and 121 apartments. Established in 1937, Bonell Good Samaritan Center currently employs 360. As Director of Resident Services, Ms. Sabas is the Social Worker for the apartments and assisted living facilities. She supports and directs all the social services staff, activity staff, admissions, transportation, and all of the volunteer programs. **Career Steps:** Director of Resident Services, Bonell Good Samaritan Center (1987–Present); Social Worker, Hospice of Northern Colorado (1995–Present); Social Worker, Northeast Home Health (1986–1987). **Associations & Accomplishments:** National Association of Social Workers; Weld County AIDS Coalition; Co–Chair, Colorado Health Care Association Social Services Committee; Academy of Certified Social Workers; Colorado AIDS in Long Term Care Committee. **Education:** University of Denver, M.S.W. (1986); Quincy College, B.A. in Crisis Intervention (1982). **Personal:** Ms. Sabas enjoys yard work, bicycling, hiking, softball, music, and hot air balloons.

Ramesh C. Sachdeva, M.D.

Assistant Professor of Pediatrics and Medical Ethics
Baylor College of Medicine
6621 Fannin Street, MC 2–3450, Critical Care Section
Houston, TX 77030–2399
(713) 770–6231
Fax: (713) 770–6229

8062

Business Information: The Baylor College of Medicine is a post–graduate medical education institution, working in affiliation with the Texas Children's Hospital for the training of resident specialists and interns. As Assistant Professor of Pediatrics and Medical Ethics, Dr. Sachdeva is responsible for the care and treatment of patients, research in the areas of Epidemiology and Outcome Analysis, as well as the instruction of fellows, residents and medical students. Dr. Sachdeva is also the attending physician in the Pediatric Intensive Care Unit. **Career Steps:** Assistant Professor of Pediatrics and Medical Ethics, Baylor College of Medicine (1993–Present); Critical Care Fellow, Children's Hospital of Wisconsin (1990–1993); Pediatric Resident, Wayne Oakland Child & Adolescent Medicine Program (1987–1990). **Associations & Accomplishments:** American Medical Association; American Academy of Pediatrics; Society of Critical Care Medicine; American Public Health Associaton; Society of Medical Decision Making. **Education:** University of Texas School of Public Health, Ph.D. in progress; Armed Forces Medical College – India, M.D. (1984); American Board of Pediatrics, F.A.A.P. (1992); Medical College of Wisconsin – Milwaukee, M.S. (1993). **Personal:** Married to Sue in 1986. Dr. Sachdeva enjoys computers, statistical software and databases, skiing and travel.

Issac Sachmechi, M.D.

Physician
Queens Hospital Center/Long Island Jewish Hospital
82–68 164th Street
Jamaica, NY 11432
(718) 883–4061
Fax: (718) 470–0827

8062

Business Information: Queens Hospital Center is a tertiary care hospital. A Board–certified Endocrinologist, Dr. Sachmechi administers all aspects of patient treatment and medical staff supervision for the Department of Endocrinology. Concurrent to his position with the hospital, Dr. Sachmechi is also an Assistant Professor of Medicine at the Mount Sinai School of Medicine. Responsible for the instruction of medical students as well as research, he is presently working on two projects: the effects of anti–lipid drugs, and mechanisms of hyperfiltration in high protein diets. **Career Steps:** Physician, Queens Hospital Center (1990–Present); The Brooklyn–Caledonian Hospital: Chief of Endocrinology (1988–1992), Assistant Director of Medicine (1987–1989). **Associations & Accomplishments:** Endocrine Society; American Diabetes Association; American Medical Association; American College of Medicine; American Association for the Advancement of Science; Published in Kidney International, European Journal of Endocrinology, Journal of Clinical Endocrinology, GYN–Oncology Journal of American Medicine; Active in Queens Hospital Center and Long Island Jewish Hospital; Fellow of American College of Endocrinology (May 1996); Fellow of American College of Physicians (July 1996). **Education:** Technion Medical School, Israel, M.D. (1979); Residency in Medicine, The Brooklyn Hospital; Fellowship in Endocrinology, SUNY – Downstate. **Personal:** Married to Farah in 1981. Three children: Amanda, Alon and Ariel. Dr. Sachmechi enjoys swimming, tennis, fishing and gardening.

Nader Sadoughi, M.D., F.A.C.S.

President of the Medical Staff
Good Samaritan Hospital
3825 Highland Avenue, Suite 2A
Downers Grove, IL 60515–1500
(708) 852–9220
Fax: (708) 852–9931

8062

Business Information: Good Samaritan Hospital is a full–service acute care hospital providing medical diagnosis and treatment to patients in the Downers Grove area and outlying communities. A practicing physician since 1962 and Board–certified in 1971, Dr. Sadoughi joined Good Samaritan Hospital as Chairman of Surgery in 1990 and later was appointed President of the Medical Staff. In 1995, he was appointed as Chief of the Medical Staff, responsible for the oversight of all related administrative operations. Specializing in the clinical urology, Dr. Sadoughi also conducts urologic surgeries and research, and instructs medical students and physicians in his specialty. **Career Steps:** Good Samaritan Hospital: Chief of the Medical Staff (1995–Present), President of the Medical Staff (1994–1995), Chairman of Surgery (1990–1992); Chairman of Urology, Mt. Sinai Medical Center (1972–1983). **Associations & Accomplishments:** American Urological Association; American College of Surgeons; American Medical Association; Du Page Medical Society; Illinois State Medical Society; Illinois Urological Society; American Urological Association – North Carolina Section; Chicago Urologic Society; Recipient of a special award, E.L. Thirlby for a special procedure designed by him. **Education:** Shiraz Medical School, M.D. (1962). **Personal:** Married to Wanda in 1964. Two children: Dina and Armand. Dr. Sadoughi enjoys writing articles, golf, and bicycling.

Carey L. Sager, R.R.A.

North Regional Director of Health Information Services
DePaul Health Center
12303 DePaul Drive
Bridgeton, MO 63044
(314) 344–7020
Fax: (314) 344–7367

8062

Business Information: DePaul Health Center is a full service acute care facility providing medical and related services to area residents. Part of a medical network comprised of four other hospitals, the Network has locations throughout Missouri. As North Regional Director of Health Information Services, Ms. Sager oversees three of the Company's five hospitals (DePaul – 3 days per week, St. Joseph– 1 day per week, and Hospital West – 1 day per week). Her duties include developing and implementing new programs, streamlining efficiency, and overseeing budgetary concerns, to include improving cost effectiveness. She is also responsible for software implementation, developing and participating on committees, and system integration. Additionally, Ms. Sanger conducts training for various programs, sets up contracts, and does some public relations work. **Career Steps:** North Regional Director of Health Information Services, DePaul Health Center (1995–Present); Director, St. Christopher's Hospital for Children (1993–1995); Assistant Director, Bayonne Hospital (Mar.1992–Dec.1992). **Associations & Accomplishments:** University of Kansas Alumni; American Health Information Management (AHIMA); Missouri Health Information Management (MHIMA); Pennsylvania Health Information Management (PAIMA); Executive Female Corporate Association. **Education:** University of Kansas Medical Center, B.S. Degree, Registered Record Administrator (1988). **Personal:** Married to John D. in 1989. Two children: Crystal Powelson and Courtney Sager. Ms. Sager enjoys aerobics and spending time with family.

Paul T. Salo, M.D.
Surgeon/Assistant Professor
Toronto Hospital, Western Division
399 Bathurst Street
Toronto, Ontario M5T 2S8
(416) 603–5851
Fax: (416) 603–3437

8062

Business Information: Toronto Hospital, Western Division is a 700–1000 bed acute care facility located on two sites. Affiliated with the University of Toronto, it is considered the largest hospital in Toronto, and one of eight teaching hospitals in the city. Offering the largest medical school surgical training program in North America, the Hospital is also affiliated with five physicians in the spine program, two neurologists, and three orthopedics. As Surgeon/Assistant Professor, Dr. Salo instructs medical students and residents in spinal surgery and general orthopedics. Active in research, Dr. Salo is sponsored by the Orthopedic Research and Educational Foundation, and Medical Research of Canada. **Career Steps:** Surgeon/Assistant Professor, Toronto Hospital, Western Division (1993–Present). **Associations & Accomplishments:** Canadian Orthopedic Association; Canadian Orthopedic Research Society; Society of Neuroscience; New York Academy of Sciences; Associate Investigator at Playfair Neuroscience Unit. **Education:** University of Toronto, M.D. (1982); Fellow, Royal College of Physicians and Surgeons of Canada (1987). **Personal:** Married to Karen Ashbee in 1995.

Col. Armando G. San Diego
••• ◉ •••

President of Medical Staff
United States Air Force Hospital
149 Hart Street, Suite 1
Sheppard AFB, TX 76311–3477
(817) 676–6194
Fax: (817) 676–7064

8062

Business Information: United States Air Force Hospital is a full–service, health care institution specializing in the diagnosis, treatment, and rehabilitation of military personnel and their dependents. As President of Medical Staff, Col. San Diego is responsible for the quality of medical services, quality improvement, continuing medical education, and insurance compliance with joint commission requirements. **Career Steps:** President of Medical Staff, United States Air Force Hospital (1994–Present); Vice President of Medical Staff, 82nd Medical Group (1992–1994); Chairman of Department of Pathology, Sheppard Hospital (1985–1992). **Associations & Accomplishments:** Association of Military Surgeons of the United States; Society of Medical Consultants to the Armed Forces; American Society of Clinical Pathologist; The Retired Officers Association; American Board of Forensic Medicine Certified. **Education:** School of Aerospace Medicine, Flight Surgeon (1988); St. Tomas University, Doctor of Medicine. **Personal:** Married to LoLita in 1959. Three children: Eric Joseph, Eileen Marie, and Jerry William. Col. San Diego enjoys scuba diving, hunting, and fishing.

Ginger Anne Sandell, C.P.A.
••• ◉ •••

Chief Financial Officer
Kona Community Hospital
P.O. Box 69
Kealakekua, HI 96745
(808) 322–4433
Fax: (808) 322–4488

8062

Business Information: Kona Community Hospital is an acute and long–term health care facility located on the West side of the Big Island of Hawaii. With 75 beds (53 acute and 22 long term), the Hospital has become a public benefit corporation as of July 1, 1996. This means that the Hospital will no longer receive special or general funds from the State of Hawaii. Affiliated with twelve other state hospitals, Kona Community Hospital plans to expand their level of patient care by providing new services. A capital construction project is expected to begin in September 1996. New services that will be provided include: the addition of 10 psychiatric beds, nuclear medicine, radiation oncology, magnetic resonance imaging, nephrology and cardiology to name a few. As Chief Financial Officer, Ms. Sandell is responsible for information systems and financial management of the Hospital. She supervises the admitting, medical records, storeroom, security, business office and data processing departments. Additionally, she is an integral part of the Financial Management and Information Systems Task Force Implementation Team. This Task Force

Team has members from serveral of the 13 State Hospitals. The group oversees contract negotiations, budgeting, revenue enhancement, materials management and information systems evaluation and development. **Career Steps:** Chief Financial Officer, Kona Community Hospital (1996–Present); Fiscal Officer, Family Crisis Shelter (1994–1995); Audit Manager, Jennifer Gossert, C.P.A. (1993–1994); Senior Accountant, Taketa, Iwata, Hara & Associates (1989–1993). **Associations & Accomplishments:** Finance Committee for Hawaii Island United Way; American Institute of Certified Public Accountants; Hawaii Society of Certified Public Accountants. **Education:** University of Hawaii, Hilo, B.A. (1989); University of California, Los Angeles. **Personal:** Four children: Dylan Berg, Jason, Lonnie, and Paul Martin. Ms. Sandell enjoys swimming, hiking and weight lifting.

Delilah A. Sanderson
Laboratory Administrative Section Chief
Mercy Health Center
4300 West Memorial Road
Oklahoma City, OK 73120–8304
(405) 752–3675
Fax: Please mail or call

8062

Business Information: Mercy Health Center is a tertiary care hospital system, consisting of the main 363–bed capacity Health Center, Neuroscience Institute for medical research and teaching affiliations, nine Mercy Clinics and three acute care community hospitals (Fairview, O'Keene, Seiling). As Laboratory Administrative Section Chief, Ms. Sanderson's primary role is to direct and supervize laboratory personnel and it's overall operation. This includes such services as specimen processing, CAI, education, and LIS coordination. **Career Steps:** Laboratory Administrative Section Chief, Mercy Health Center (1989–Present); Lab Manager, Satanta District Hospital (1987–1989). **Associations & Accomplishments:** A.S.C.P.; Alpha Chi; Toastmaster. **Education:** O.U.H.S.C., M.P.H. (1992). **Personal:** Two children: Elanna and Erin. Ms. Sanderson enjoys camping, travel, and movies.

Maria J. Santana
Section Chief – Pathology
Memorial Regional Hospital
3501 Johnson Street
Hollywood, FL 33021
(954) 985–5921
Fax: (954) 985–3471

8062

Business Information: Memorial Regional Hospital was established in 1953 and has three locations in the district with over 1,000 beds. Memorial Regional Hospital also includes 22 medical facilities in the district. As Section Chief – Pathology, Ms. Santana oversees medical transcriptions, surgical reports, and consult letters. Ms. Santana's duties also consist of the scheduling of 11 physicians and the troubleshooting of all office equipment and updates on computer data base. **Career Steps:** Memorial Regional Hospital: Section Chief – Pathology (1987–Present), Medical Secretary I and Medical Secretary II (1975–1986). **Associations & Accomplishments:** National Notary Association. **Education:** Broward Community College, A.S. (1980). **Personal:** Married to Joseph in 1990. One child: Matthew. Ms. Santana enjoys swimming, bowling, and bicycling.

Luis A. Santos
MIS/Finance Officer
Morovis Community Health Center
P.O. Box 518
Morovis, Puerto Rico 00687
(787) 862–3225
Fax: (787) 862–3070

8062

Business Information: Morovis Community Health Center, a non–profit organization, is a primary healthcare facility funded by the federal government. The Center services outpatient clients with six doctors, one obstetrician, and one pediatrician. As MIS/Finance Officer, Mr. Santos manages the cash flow, keeps track of accounting functions, budgeting, finance, and payroll. **Career Steps:** Morovis Community Health Center: MIS/Finance Officer (1994–Present); Sub Director of Finance (1992–1994); Accounts Payable Clerk, Air Master Awning (1990–1992). **Education:** American University of Puerto Rico, B.B.A. (1990). **Personal:** Married to Jury S. in 1986. One child: Sherry M. Mr. Santos enjoys amateur radio, computers, and reading.

Laura S. Scales
Nurse Manager
Moses H. Cone Hospital
1200 North Elm Street
Greensboro, NC 27401–1004
(910) 574–8188
Fax: Please mail or call

8062

Business Information: Moses H. Cone Hospital is a Level II trauma, acute care center, providing diagnosis and treatment to patients. A practicing nurse since 1982, Ms. Scales joined Moses H. Cone Hospital as Nurse Manager in 1990. Ms. Scales manages all activities of a 40–bed medical surgical unit, focusing on the brain, spinal cord, and nerves. She also manages all patient services and patient population. **Career Steps:** Nurse Manager, Moses H. Cone Hospital (1990–Present); Patient Care Coordinator, Wesley L. Hospital (1988–1990); Nurse Manager, Alamance Memorial Hospital (1986–1988). **Associations & Accomplishments:** Sigma Theta Tau (1982); American Nurses Association (1982); American Association Neuroscience Nurses (1990); North Carolina Nurses Association (1982). **Education:** University of North Carolina – Greensboro: M.S.N. (1995), B.S.N. (1982); Rockingham Community College, A.A.S. in Business Administration (1970). **Personal:** One child: Ashley Lauren. Ms. Scales enjoys classical music, movies, plays, and reading.

Hyman Morris Schipper
Clinician Scientist
Jewish General Hospital
3755 Cote–Catherine Road
Montreal, Quebec H3T 1E2
(514) 340–8260
Fax: (514) 340–7502
EMAIL: czhs@Musica.McGil

8062

Business Information: Jewish General Hospital is a full–service, health care institution specializing in the diagnosis, treatment, and rehabilitation of patients. Affiliation: McGill University. As Clinician Scientist, Dr. Schipper is responsible for diversified administrative activities, including clinical neurology staffing. Additionally, he is a consultant at St. Mary's Hospital and also does research in brain aging and neurodegenerative disorders. **Career Steps:** Jewish General Hospital: Clinician–Scientist (1988–Present), Staff Neurologist (1988–Present). **Associations & Accomplishments:** Royal College of Physicians and Surgeons of Canada; American Academy of Neurology; Society for Neuroscience; International Brain Research Organization; Canadian Medical Association; New York Academy of Sciences; The Histochemical Society; International Federal Society of Histochemistry and Cytochemistry; Canadian Movement and Disorder Group. **Education:** McGill University, M.D., Ph.D. (1982); Columbia University, Neurology Residency; Tufts University, Endocrinology Fellowship. **Personal:** Married to Dr. Rachel Rubinstein in 1994. One child: Joshua Nathan.

Jim L. Schlenker
Assistant Chief Financial Officer
Sunnyside Community Hospital
10th and Tacoma St.
Sunnyside, WA 98944
(509) 837–1641
Fax: (509) 837–1512
EMAIL: See Below

8062

Business Information: Sunnyside Community Hospital is a 38–bed, small rural hospital located in a community population of more than 12,000 people. Employing 250 employees (178 full–time), Sunnyside Community Hospital serves approximately 1,100–1,200 patients in its Emergency Room. A Certified Public Accountant, Mr. Schlenker joined Sunnyside Community Hospital upon the conferral of his bachelor's in Accounting in 1987. As Assistant Chief Financial Officer and Accounting Manager, he is responsible for assisting the Chief Financial Officer in all day–to–day operations of accounting and financial matters, including budgets, analysis, accounts payable, accounts receivable, and internal and external auditing. Concurrently, he serves as MIS Manager and Manager of the Microfilming Archives Department. Internet users can reach Mr. Schlenker via: jimmylee@televar.com **Career Steps:** Assistant Chief Financial Officer, Sunnyside Community Hospital (1987–Present). **Associations & Accomplishments:** American Institute of Certified Public Accountants; Washington Society of Certified Public Accountants; Healthcare Financial Management Association; College Alumni; Future Business Leaders of America. **Education:** Central Washington State University, B.S. in Accounting (1987); Yakima Valley Community College, B.A. **Personal:** Married to Mary in 1989. Mr. Schlenker enjoys bowling, basketball, computers, and video game systems.

George E.P. Schloicka

Director of Educational Services
Union Hospital
1000 Galloping Hill Rd.
Union, NJ 07083
(908) 851-7267
Fax: (908) 687-8274

8062

Business Information: Union Hospital — an affiliate of the Saint Barnabas Health Care System — is an acute health care provider. Established in 1944, Union Hospital currently employs 1,000 physicians and medical support staff. As Director of Educational Services, Mr. Schloicka is responsible for all aspects of training and quality improvements for supervisory management development, as well as customer care training. Concurrent to his position with the Hospital, he is the owner of a private consulting firm, Organizational Management Associates. **Career Steps:** Director of Educational Services, Union Hospital, An Affiliate of the Saint Barnabas Health Care System (1990–Present); Director of Human Resources and Development, Cosmair, Inc. (1982–1987); Senior Manager of Human Resources Development, Nabisco Brands, Inc. (1978–1982). **Associations & Accomplishments:** Society of Human Resource Management; Free and Accepted Masons of the State of New Jersey. **Education:** Nova Southeastern, D.B.A. Candidate (expected completion 1997); Fairleigh–Dickinson University, M.A. (1977); Rutgers University, B.A. (1971). **Personal:** Married to Nancy in 1970. One child: Jeffrey. Mr. Schloicka enjoys writing, amateur radio, and computers.

Brian Schneider

Director of Financial Planning
Montgomery Hospital
1301 Powell Street
Norristown, PA 19401
(610) 270-2454
Fax: (610) 270-2540

8062

Business Information: Montgomery Hospital is a full service, 275–bed acute care hospital, having programs in hospice, out–patient, homecare, psychology and surgery. As Director of Financial Planning, Brian Schneider is responsible for contracting, cost accounting, product line management, budgeting and revenue enhancement. In addition to his services at the hospital, Mr. Schneider is a consultant around the county for medical management. **Career Steps:** Montgomery Hospital: Director of Financial Planning (1993–Present), Director of Budget and Reimbursement (1991–1993); Audit Senior, Aenta Life (Medicare Interm) (1987–1991); Home Office Coordinator, Universal Health Services, Inc. (1985–1987). **Associations & Accomplishments:** Hospital Financial Management Association; Lansdale Jaycees; NTPS. **Education:** La Salle University, M.B.A. in Health Care (1991); Drexel University, B.S. in Accounting (1983). **Personal:** Married to Kelly in 1985. Mr. Schneider enjoys baseball, hunting, and bowling.

Susan L. Schultz

Director of Nursing/Acute Care
Lincoln County Hospital
10 Nichols Street
Davenport, WA 99122-9729
(509) 725-7101
Fax: (509) 725-2112

8062

Business Information: Lincoln County Hospital is a full service rural hospital with 24 acute care beds and 71 long–term care beds. The facility offers assisted living, medical, surgical, obstetric, pediatric and emergency room services to patients. As Director of Nursing/Acute Care, Ms. Schultz is responsible for administration of training and developing policies and procedures. Other duties include management of the acute care services. **Career Steps:** Lincoln County Hospital: Director of Nursing/Acute Care (1992–Present), Staff Nurse (1986–1992); Home Health Care Nurse (1983–1986); Staff Nurse, SHMC (1978–1983). **Associations & Accomplishments:** WONE; Columbia Basin Council of Nurse Executives; Rural Nurse Organization. **Education:** Whitworth College, M.S. (1992); Intercollegiate Nursing Education B.S.N. **Personal:** Married to Gary. Two children: Jacob and Megan. Ms. Schultz enjoys reading and mountain biking.

S. Charles Schulz, M.D.

Chief of Psychiatry
University Hospitals – Cleveland
11100 Euclid Avenue
Cleveland, OH 44106-1736
(216) 844-3883
Fax: (216) 844-3851

8062

Business Information: University Hospitals – Cleveland is a 50–bed, large ambulatory practice with over 5,000 registered ambulatory patients. They also offer a residency training program. A practicing physician since 1973 and a Psychiatrist, Dr. Schulz joined University Hospitals – Cleveland as Chief of Psychiatry in 1989. He is responsible for the direction of all administrative functions of the Psychiatric Department, including overseeing all administrative operations for faculty and students. He also teaches (medical students, residents, post resident fellows), conducts lecture classes, and provides clinical supervision. In addition, he conducts research, with a current focus on medication treatment therapies to teenagers diagnosed with schizophrenic disorders. Concurrent with his academic and medical practice, he serves as Chairman of the Psychiatric Department for Case Western Reserve University. **Career Steps:** Chief of Psychiatry, University Hospitals – Cleveland (1989–Present); Chairman of the Psychiatric Department, Case Western Reserve University (1989–Present); Branch Chief, NIMH (1986–1989); Medical Director, University of Pittsburgh (1983–1986) **Associations & Accomplishments:** Cleveland Psychiatric Association; American Psychiatric Association; Society of Biological Psychiatry. **Education:** University of California–Los Angeles, M.D. (1973); University of South Carolina, B.A. (1968) **Personal:** Married to Shannon in 1992. Two children: Lindsey and William.

Dr. Michael Schumacher

Chief of Allergy & Immunology
University of Arizona Health Sciences Center
Department of Pediatrics, P.O. Box 245073
Tucson, AZ 85724-5073
(520) 626-6055
Fax: (520) 626-3636

8062

Business Information: University of Arizona Health Sciences Center is a full–service, tertiary facility and Medical School. As Chief of Allergy & Immunology, Dr. Schumacher is responsible for consultative services for patients in this specialty, and conducts research in Allergy and Clinical Immunology. Concurrent with his Departmental position, he serves as instructor to medical students, is active in postgraduate education in allergy and immunology, and serves on the Medical School Curriculum Committee. **Career Steps:** Chief of Allergy & Immunology, University of Arizona Health Sciences Center (1969–Present); First Assistant Physician of Clinical Research Unit, Walter and Eliza Hall Institute of Medical Research, Melbourne, Australia (1977–1979); Associate Physician, Royal Prince Alfred Hospital, Sidney, Australia (1973–1976). **Associations & Accomplishments:** American Academy of Allergy and Immunology; Pediatric Research Society; American Thoracic Society; Past President, Arizona Allergy Society; Past President, Tucson Allergy Society; Listed in Western Edition of The Best Doctors in America; Numerous publications, including the articles: Lethality of Killer Bee Stings ("Nature" magazine) and Recognition of Particulate Aeroantigens by Immunoblot Microscopy. **Education:** University of Melbourne, M.B.B.S. (1960); Fellow, Royal Australasian College of Physicians; Allergy training program, National Jewish Center, Denver. **Personal:** Dr. Schumacher enjoys playing the violin in a semiprofessional chamber orchestra.

Aileen Sedman, M.D.

Pediatric Nephrologist/Instructor
University of Michigan Medical Center
1500 East Medical Center Drive
Ann Arbor, MI 48109
(313) 936-4210
Fax: (313) 763-6997

8062

Business Information: University of Michigan Medical Center is a full–tertiary health care facility providing diagnosis and treatment of patients and instruction of medical students. A Board–Certified Pediatrician and Pediatric Nephrologist, Dr. Sedman joined the College in 1984 and currently serves as a tenured faculty member. She is responsible for the instruction of medical students in pediatrics and pediatric nephrology. **Career Steps:** Tenured Faculty, University of Michigan Medical Center (1984–Present). **Associations & Accomplishments:** Council Member, Society of Pediatric Nephrology; American Society of Nephrologists; Fellow, American Academy of Pediatrics; Awarded FDA Commissioners Special Citation (1992) for drug use warning to pregnant women (petitioned the FDA to use this warning); Published literature in Pediatric Nephrology Journal and the New England Journal of Medicine. **Education:** University of Michigan Medical School, M.D. (1978); Board–Certified in Pediatrics (1981) and Pediatric Nephrology (1984).

Lynda Serfass

Senior Human Resource Representative
Scott & White Hospital
2401 South 31st Street
Temple, TX 76508
(817) 724-7925
Fax: (817) 724-5591

8062

Business Information: Scott & White Hospital is the ninth largest hospital and clinic in the United States with 500 licensed beds and 17 regional clinics. The Hospital specializes in oncology care and research, has rehabilitation programs, cardiology, pediatric services, dialysis, and currently is putting together a transplant team for liver and kidneys. The Hospital provides its own HMO and currently has over 119,000 insured lives. As Senior Human Resource Representative, Ms. Serfass provides management training to the Hospital, Clinic, and Health Plan managers. He is responsible for training of new employees, orientation, employee law, special projects, OSHA compliance, and policies and procedures. **Career Steps:** Scott & White Hospital: Senior Human Resource Representative (1995–Present), Compensation Analyst (1992–1995); Training Coordinator, Smith International, Inc. (1989–1991). **Associations & Accomplishments:** American Society for Hospital Human Resource Association; Society for Human Resource Management; Austin Human Resource Management Association; Central Texas Compensation Association. **Education:** University of Houston: M.S. in Occupational Education (1992), B.S. in Psychology (1989). **Personal:** Married to Kenneth in 1990. Ms. Serfass enjoys gardening, sewing, and arts and crafts.

Louise M. Serpico

Administrative Director of Radiology Imaging
Community Medical Center
1800 Mulberry Street
Scranton, PA 18510
(717) 969-8151
Fax: (717) 969-7416

8062

Business Information: Community Medical Center is a full service acute care facility comprised of 325 beds. The Hospital provides trauma, maternity, cardiology, intensive care, skilled nursing, neo–natal, and mental health services to the community. Regional in scope, the Hospital has several satellite locations throughout the area with the Imaging department employing sixty people. As Administrative Director of Radiology Imaging, Ms. Serpico oversees all aspects of the department including diagnostic radiology, ultra sound, nuclear medicine, computerized tomography, mammography, interventional radiology, and the School of Radiologic Technology. Instrumental in developing the Department into what it has become today, she is responsible for implementing all modalities except basic radiology, and handles all budgetary concerns, purchasing, supplies, and re–engineering due to managed care. **Career Steps:** Administrative Director of Radiology Imaging, Community Medical Center (1961–Present). **Associations & Accomplishments:** Pennsylvania Society of Radiologic Technology; American Society of Radiologic Technology; American Hospital Radiology Administrators. **Education:** University of Scranton; School of Rad–Technology, Graduate of Radiological Group. **Personal:** Married to Dominick J. in 1987. Two children: Dominick R. and William E.. Ms. Serpico enjoys antique collecting, and travel to significant U.S. historical sites such as the Grand Canyon.

D. Tony Sethuram, M.D., CCFP

Physician
South Shore Regional Hospital
150 Aberdeen Road
Bridgewater, Nova Scotia B4V 258
(902) 543-2733 (902) 543-2733
Fax: Please mail or call

8062

Business Information: South Shore Regional Hospital is a 60–bed, regional acute and subacute care medical facility in Nova Scotia. The Hospital has physicians on staff or on call to handle general medical problems, family medicine, emergency medicine and obstetrics. As Physician, Dr. Sethuram offers medical care to residents of Bridgewater, Nova Scotia. His services include family medicine, preventative medicine, emergency medicine, and obstetrics. **Career Steps:** Physician: Ottawa Civic Hospital, South Shore Regional Hospital, Fisherman's Memorial Hospital. **Associations & Accom-**

plishments: Medical Society of Nova Scotia; Ontario Medical Association; Davis Cup Regional Champions in Tennis (1984); Continuing Medical Education Director; Medical Services Advisory Committee (Acting Chairman). **Education:** Ottawa University, CCFP (1994); Dalhousie University, M.D., B.Sc. Honors. **Personal:** Dr. Sethuram enjoys tennis and being a concert pianist and violinist.

Bradley L. Sexauer

Vice President of Planning & Marketing
Danville Regional Medical Center
142 South Main Street
Danville, VA 24541–2922
(804) 799–2240
Fax: (804) 799–4446

8062

Business Information: Danville Regional Medical Center is a full–service healthcare institution specializing in the diagnosis, treatment, and rehabilitation of patients in the community. As Vice President of Planning & Marketing, Mr. Sexauer directs business development activities. **Career Steps:** Vice President of Planning & Marketing, Danville Regional Medical Center (1993–Present); Corporate Vice President, Ingalls Health Systems (1987–1992); Field Vice President, National Medical Enterprises (1984–1987); Regional Planning Director, Humana, Inc. (1981–1984). **Associations & Accomplishments:** American College of Healthcare Executives; Virginia Institute for Political Leadership at the University of Virginia; Society for Healthcare Planning & Marketing – AHA; Board of Directors, Danville/Pittsylvania Co. United Way; Rotary Club. **Education:** University of South Dakota, M.B.A. (1980); Tulane University, M.H.A. (1976); DePauw University, B.A. (1973). **Personal:** Mr. Sexauer enjoys running, whitewater rafting, and travel.

Lynn E. T. Shaffer

Senior Manager – Research Department
Riverside Methodist Hospital
3535 Olentangy River Rd.
Columbus, OH 43214–3925
(614) 566–4344
Fax: (614) 265–2464

8062

Business Information: Riverside Methodist Hospital is a full–service acute care hospital. In 1990, Ms. Shaffer joined Riverside as Epidemiologist and was appointed to Senior Manager of the Research Department in 1994. In her current capacity, she assures all FDA and HHS regulations are followed by the Hospital, as well as helps investigators with protocol design. **Career Steps:** Riverside Methodist Hospital: Senior Manager of Research Department (1995–Present), Technical Advisor (1994–1995), Epidemiologist (1990–1994); Epidemiologist, Ohio Department of Health (1988–1990). **Education:** Ohio State University, M.S. (1990); Kenyon College: B.A. in Economics and Music, M.S. in Preventive Medicine. **Personal:** Married to Scott in 1995. Ms. Shaffer enjoys weightlifting.

Dr. Malavika K. Shah

Staff Physician
Tuscaloosa VA Medical Center
4912 Lakeview Estate
Northport, AL 35476
(205) 554–2000
Fax: Please mail or call

8062

Business Information: Tuscaloosa VA Medical Center is a medical institute providing diagnosis and treatment to veterans of the military forces. A practicing physician since 1972, Dr. Shah joined the Tuscaloosa VA Medical Center in 1993 as Staff Physician. Dr. Shah also serves as an Associate Professor at Tuscaloosa School of Medicine. **Career Steps:** Staff Physician, Tuscaloosa VA Medical Center (1993–Present); Staff Physician, Montgomery VA Medical Center (1991–1993); Staff Physician, Bonham, TX VA Medical Center (1989–1991). **Associations & Accomplishments:** American College of Physicians; American Women's Medical Association; American Geriatric Medical Society. **Education:** Basoda Medical School, M.B.B.S. (1972). **Personal:** Four children: Amit, Preeti, Masumi and Neil. Dr. Shah enjoys fitness exercise, music, meditation and interior decorating during her spare time.

Diane W. Sharpe

Chief Executive Officer
Pine Grove Hospital
7011 Shoup Avenue
Canoga Park, CA 91307
(818) 348–0500
Fax: (818) 595–3712

8062

Business Information: Pine Grove Hospital is an 82–bed, private, psychiatric hospital with an outpatient department, providing diagnosis and treatment to patients suffering from mental disorders. Established in 1995, Pine Grove Hospital currently employs 86 people. With twenty–five years in healthcare administration, Ms. Sharpe joined Pine Grove Hospital in 1995. Serving as Chief Executive Officer, she is responsible for all aspects of operations, including administration and supervision of staff. **Career Steps:** Chief Executive Officer, Pine Grove Hospital (1995–Present); Administrator, Ventura County Mental Health (1994–1995); Chief Operating Officer, Regent Hospital (1989–1994); Nurse Administrator, Memorial Sloane Kettering (1984–1989). **Associations & Accomplishments:** American College of Health Care Executives; Consolidated Association of Nurses in Substance Abuse **Education:** Alfred University, B.S. (1963). **Personal:** Miss Sharpe enjoys golf during her leisure time.

Susan C. Shauer

Controller
Valley Hospital Association, Inc.
P.O. Box 1356
Palmer, AK 99645
(907) 352–2837
Fax: (907) 325–2869

8062

Business Information: Valley Hospital, operated by Valley Hospital Association, Inc., is a 36–bed acute care hospital with 36 active physicians and 60 on–call physicians, located 50 miles north of Anchorage, Alaska. Valley Hospital Association, Inc. is a healthcare organization consisting of hospitals, clinics, pharmacies, homecare and hospice facilities. As Controller, Mrs. Shauer is responsible for all financial aspects of the Hospital, including arranging insurance benefits, establishing Medicare & Medicaid rates, serving as part of the administrative staff (Steering Committee for Information Services and the Steering Committee for TQM), monitoring budgets, and conducting year–end audits, in addition to supervising a staff of five. **Career Steps:** Controller, Valley Hospital – Valley Hospital Association, Inc. (1985–Present); Controller, Empire Sand & Gravel (1981–1984); Accounting Manager, Yellowstone Valley Chemicals (1978–1981). **Associations & Accomplishments:** Healthcare Financial Managers Association; Alaska State Hospital Association; Medicaid Rate Setting Subcommittee; American Cancer Society; Optimist. **Education:** University of Wyoming, B.B.S. in Business Administration (1974). **Personal:** Married to Kenneth in 1984. Three children: Richard, Steven, and Nicole.

St. Luke's
HOSPITAL

Daniel J. Shea, M.D., FACEP

Associate Director of Emergency Services
St. Luke's Hospital
101 Page Street
New Bedford, MA 02740–3464
(508) 997–1515 Ext: 2183
Fax: (508) 990–1411

8062

Business Information: St. Luke's Hospital is a full–service, acute care community hospital, providing diagnosis and treatment of patients. A practicing physician since 1981 and a Board Certified Emergency Physician, Dr. Shea joined St. Luke's Hospital in 1988 as Associate Director of Emergency Services. He is responsible for both administrative and clinical activities of emergency services in his daily practice, in addition to overseeing administrative operations for associates and a support staff of 150. **Career Steps:** St. Luke's Hospital (1988–Present): Associate Director of Emergency Services, Vice Chairman for Department of Emergency Medicine, Associate Medical Director of Paramedic Services; The Cheshire Medical Center (1986–1988): Medical Director of Emergency Center, Chairman of Department of Emergency Medicine; Medical Director of Special Services Center, Medical Director for Advanced Life Support; New Hampshire Emergency Medical Services (1986–1988): Chairman, Protocol Committee, Region II EMS Council, District B2 EMS Board, Medical Advisor for Keen Fire Department; Burbank Hospital (1981–1986): Staff Emergency Physician, Coordinator for Emergency Medicine Education Program, Medical Attending for Family Practice Residency Program; University of Massachusetts Medical Center (1981–1985): Emergency Department Attending, Flight Physician for New England Life-flight; Staff Emergency Physician, Holden Hospital (1983–1986). **Associations & Accomplishments:** American Board of Emergency Medicine (1986); American Board of Internal Medicine (1981); Fellow, American College of Emergency Physicians (1987–Present); American College of Emergency Physicians; President (1993–1994), Massachusetts College of Emergency Physicians; American College of Physician Executives; Massachusetts Medical Society; Bristol South District Medical Society; Numerous publications regarding emergency medical care; AWARDS: The Vanguard Award and The Past President's Award by Massachusetts College of Emergency Physicians. **Education:** University of Massachusetts Medical Center, Internship and Residency (1981); Georgetown University School of Medicine, M.D. (1978); Saint Anselm College, B.A. in Biology magna cum laude (1974). **Personal:** Married to Monica Ann in 1977. Two children: Daniel and Ryan. Dr. Shea enjoys scuba diving, skiing, sailing, camping, and hiking.

Barbara Sheets Olson, M.D.

Chief of Staff
Community Memorial Hospital
P O Box 353
Lisbon, ND 58054–0353
(701) 683–4134
Fax: (701) 683–4094

8062

Business Information: Community Memorial Hospital is small community medical facility comprised of seventeen beds, an emergency, operating and birthing room, a two bed critical care unit, and physical and occupational therapy services. As Chief of Staff, Dr. Sheets Olson oversees all aspects of medical and patient care related to the Hospital. Active in women's health issues, she has been instrumental in bringing mammographies, ultrasound, and fetal monitoring to the area. Concurrent to her present position, Dr. Sheets Olson instructs a yearly medical class for 3rd and 4th year students, and has done medical research through the University of Minnesota on cholesterol in rural communities. **Career Steps:** Chief of Staff, Community Memorial Hospital (1987–Present); Physician, Dakota Clinic Lisbon (1987–Present); Physician, Lisbon Clinic (1986–1987); Physician, Sheyenne Clinic (1983–1986). **Associations & Accomplishments:** American Medical Association; North Dakota Medical Society; North Dakota OB/GYN Society; American Association of Family Physicians; AMWA; Great Plains Organization; Trinity Lutheran Church; Presented a paper at the American College of Surgeons. **Education:** Hahnemann Medical College, M.D. (1982); Ohio Northern University, B.A. Chemistry. **Personal:** Married to Lyle Olson in 1985. Three children: Melissa, Andrea, and Patrick. Dr. Sheets Olson enjoys rollerblading, swimming, biking, walking, reading, and needlepoint.

Andrew T. Shennan, M.D.

Neonatal Pediatric Physician
Women's College Hospital
76 Grenville Street
Toronto, Ontario M5S 1B2
(416) 323–6265
Fax: (416) 323–6274

8062

Business Information: Women's College Hospital is a full–service medical/teaching facility specializing in the health concerns of women. Established in 1911, the Hospital is affiliated with the University of Toronto. As Chief of the Neonatal Department, Dr. Shennan utilizes his twenty–one years of experience in the field of Neonatal Pediatrics, to provide quality intensive care for premature and full–term newborns. **Career Steps:** Chief of the Neonatal Department, Women's College Hospital (1975–Present); Clinical Fellow (Neonatal), Hospital For Sick Children (1974–1975); Registrar (Pediatrics), Royal Aberdeen Children's Hospital (1970–1974). **Associations & Accomplishments:** Canadian Medical Association; Canadian Pediatric Society; Associate Member, Society of Obstetricians and Gynecologists of Canada; Canadian Health Executives. **Education:** Aberdeen University: M.B. Ch.B (1967), M.R.C.P. (UK) (1972), FRCP(C) (1976). **Personal:** Married to Anne Stewart in 1968. Three children: Michael, Catriona, and Graeme. Dr. Shennan enjoys golf and travel.

Walter Shepperd, Ph.D.

Director of Behavioral Health Services
Carson–Tahoe Hospital
775 Fleischmann Way
Carson City, NV 89702–2158
(702) 885–4460
Fax: (702) 885–4563

8062

Business Information: Carson–Tahoe Hospital is a state–supported psychiatric hospital. As Director of Behavioral Health Services, Dr. Shepperd is responsible for all aspects of clinical and administrative functions of the Department, in addition to a 28–bed psychiatric ward. **Career Steps:** Director of Behavioral Health Services, Carson–Tahoe Hospital (1992–Present); Director, Family Renewal Centers (1990–1992); Director, Family & Adolescent Chemical Treatment System (1987–1990); Clinical Psychologist, U.S. Air Force (1978–1987). **Associations & Accomplishments:** Retired – U.S. Air Force; NAADAC; AAPH; NIDA Resource Specialist; Co–author "Criterion – Referenced Testing: Review, Evaluation, and Extension," August 1979, AFHRL, Air Force Systems Command, Brooks AFB, TX. **Education:** University of Sussex, Sussex College of Technology, Ph.D. (1973). **Personal:** Two children: daughter, N. Tatjana and son, Gordon. Dr. Shepperd enjoys computing, flying, and spending time at his country home.

Jacob Shnayder

Director of Biomedical Engineering
Beth Israel Medical Center
1st Avenue at 16th Street
New York, NY 10003
(212) 420–2610
Fax: (212) 420–2678

8062

Business Information: Beth Israel Medical Center is a multi–hospital health care system. As Director of Biomedical Engineering, Mr. Shnayder manages a group of sixteen technicians, engineers, and specialists in medical equipment technology management and consulting, including evaluation, lifecycle cost analysis, maintenance, and regulatory compliance. **Career Steps:** Director of Biomedical Engineering, Beth Israel Medical Center (1988–Present); Director of Biomedical Engineering, Raritan Bay Health Care System (1982–1988); Senior Clinical Engineer, Interfaith Medical Center (1980–1982); Field Engineer, General Electric Company – Medical Division (1979–1980). **Associations & Accomplishments:** Consultant for Project Hope (Virginia) – Establishing the Biomedical Engineering Laboratory of the Moscow Children's Hospital #9, Burn Unit; Consultant for Armenian Benevolent Association – Establishing the Biomedical Engineering Laboratory at the Erevan, Armenia, Plastic Surgery Center; Institute of Electronics and Electrical Engineers; A.A.M.I.; A.S.H.E. **Education:** Tulsa Polytechnical Institute, M.S.E.E. (1970); Numerous Certified Programs and Seminars in the Medical Equipment Technology Field. **Personal:** Married to Inna in 1980. Two children: Julia and Alex. Mr. Shnayder enjoys crafts, travel, and tennis.

Muhammad Siddigi, M.D.

Director of Cardiac Catheterization Laboratory
Michael Reese Hospital and Medical Center
2929 South Ellis Avenue
Chicago, IL 60616–3302
(312) 791–3712
Fax: (312) 791–3641

8062

Business Information: Michael Reese Hospital and Medical Center, affiliated with the University of Illinois, is a full–service, tertiary care medical and teaching hospital. A practicing physician since 1981 and a Board–Certified Cardiologist, Dr. Siddigi joined Michael Reese Hospital and Medical Center as Associate Director of Cardiology in 1994. Appointed as Director of Cardiac Cath Lab in 1995, he directs all laboratory activities, in addition to his daily patient practice. **Career Steps:** Michael Reese Hospital and Medical Center: Director of Cardiac Catheterization Lab (1995–Present), Associate Director of Cardiology (1994–1995). **Associations & Accomplishments:** American College of Cardiology. **Education:** C.O.M. University of Lagos: M.D., B.S. (1981). **Personal:** Married to Shehla in 1984. Dr. Siddigi enjoys golf.

Neal T. Silverstein, M.D.

Pediatrician
Florida Hospital
661 E. Altamonte Drive, Suite 116
Altamonte Springs, FL 32701
(407) 830–2694
Fax: (407) 830–2692

8062

Business Information: The Florida Hospital is a full–service, multi–specialty tertiary hospital, medical research and teaching institution. As a Staff Pediatrician, Dr. Silverstein is responsible for clinical instruction of resident students, as well as the care and treatment of patients. Dr. Silverstein concentrates his practice in the areas of bedwetting, pediatric psychological problems, and general pediatrics. **Career Steps:** Pediatrician, Florida Hospital – CIGNA Healthcare (1984–1995); Attending Physician, Cook County Hospital. **Associations & Accomplishments:** Juvenile Diabetes Foundation; President, Central Florida Pediatric Society; Seminole County Special Olympics; Chairman Florida Hospital Perinatal–Pediatrics Ethics Committee. **Education:** University of Illinois, M.D. (1974); University of Illinois – Chicago Circle, B.S. **Personal:** Married to Rosa in 1972. Three children: Leonard, Brian and Mitchell. Dr. Silverstein enjoys horseback riding.

Karlene E. Sinclair, M.D.

Associate Director of Trauma
Atlantic City Medical Center
1925 Pacific Avenue
Atlantic City, NJ 08401
(609) 441–8023
Fax: (609) 441–8178

8062

Business Information: Atlantic City Medical Center is a regional, 500–bed hospital with two divisions located in Atlantic City, New Jersey. As Associate Director of Trauma, Dr. Sinclair is involved in the administrative duties of the department. She is also a general and trauma surgeon and handles surgical critical care patients for the Center. Other medical responsibilities include flu shots, auto accidents, and clinical research. **Career Steps:** Associate Director of Trauma, Atlantic City Medical Center (1993–Present). **Associations & Accomplishments:** American Trauma Society; National Association for the Advancement of Colored People; National Medical Association; Society of Critical Care Medicine; Atlantic County Medical Society. **Education:** Loma Linda University, M.D. (1987); Andrews University, B.S. **Personal:** Dr. Sinclair enjoys Tae Kwon Do, sewing, and baking.

Sara J. Sirna, M.D., F.A.C.C.

Staff Intervention Cardiologist
Mercy Hospital
45621 South Summit Street
Iowa City, IA 52240
(319) 339–0300
Fax: (319) 337–8788

8062

Business Information: Mercy Hospital is an acute care hospital, providing full surgical, emergency and ambulatory services. As Staff Intervention Cardiologist, Dr. Sirna is responsible for inpatient and outpatient care in cardiology, including cardiac catheterizations, angioplasty, making hospital rounds, and intervention MI. Concurrent with her staff position, she operates a private medical practice. **Career Steps:** Staff Intervention Cardiologist, Mercy Hospital (1989–Present); Chief Resident and Cardiology Fellow, University of Iowa Medical Center (1988–1989). **Associations & Accomplishments:** American College of Cardiology – Iowa Chapter and National Organization; Clinical Coordinator for Iowa Foundation for Medical Care; Radio speaking; Public speaking; Published in medical journals. **Education:** State University of New York – Downstate, M.D., F.A.C.C. (1980); Molloy College, B.S. in Nursing (1974). **Personal:** Married to Christopher Loftus in 1979. Four children: Christopher, Matthew, Mark, and Mary. Dr. Sirna enjoys tennis, reading, and having fun with her children.

Sharon Hampton Sizemore

Director
Jewish Hospital Health Care Services, Inc.
217 East Chestnut Street
Louisville, KY 40202–1821
(502) 587–4121
Fax: (502) 587–4864
E MAIL: See Below

8062

Business Information: Jewish Hospital is the flagship of Jewish Healthcare Services, Inc. a multi–service health care network based in Louisville, Kentucky. The Rudd Heart & Lung Institute is a free standing center involved in the care and research of heart and lung disease. Over 2,000 open hearts surgeries are performed here each year ranking it the 8th largest heart institute in the United States. The Invasive Cardiology Department performs complex cardiac interventions, cardiac caths and electrophysiology studies. Pacemaker and internal defibrilator implants are also a part of this service arena. The Invasive Cardiology Department serves 47 invasive cardiologists, and performs approximately 5,000 cardiac catherizations each year. Additionally, over 2,000 interventions and electrophysiology studies are completed. As Director, Ms. Sizemore oversees all daily operations of Invasive Cardiology. This includes administration, personnel management and strategic planning. Internet users can reach her via: ssizemore @aol. **Career Steps:** Jewish Hospital Health Care Services, Inc.: Director (1994–Present), Quality Improvement Director (1990–1994), Executive Director Long Term Care (1984–1990). **Associations & Accomplishments:** Board Member, Heart Association; Malcolm Baldridge Health Care Pilot Examiner; American College of Cardiology Administrators; Recipient: Award for advancing Quality in Employee Assistance; Department of Commerce Award (1995). Publications: "The Role of the Director of Nursing in Long Term Care", Journal of Long Term Care (1985); "Falls of the Elderly in a Nursing Home Environment", Masters Thesis (1990); Payne Leadership Award, Spalding University; Ms. Sizemore has presented papers at numerous workshops, seminars, and training programs on a number of topics. **Education:** Bellarmine College, M.S.N. (1990); Spalding University, B.S.N. (1979). **Personal:** Married to Ray Sr in 1965. Three children: Ray, Jr., Richard, and Rebecca.

Kay Skaggs

Personnel Director
Benewah Community Hospital
229 South 7th Street
St. Maries, ID 83861–1803
(208) 245–5551 (208) 245–8603
Fax: (208) 245–4879

8062

Business Information: Benewah Community Hospital is a 25–bed, acute care county–owned hospital and family practice clinic. The facility began operation in 1957 and currently employs 130 physicians and support staff. As Personnel Director, Ms. Skaggs is responsible for all human resource concerns for the facility staff. She is responsible for payroll, employee benefits, retirement plans, employee grievances, and acts as liaison between management and staff. **Career Steps:** Personnel Director, Benewah Community Hospital (1995–Present); Human Resources Administrator, NRx–Merck and Company (1990–1995); Officer Manager/Personnel, Dexter Clinic (1982–1990). **Associations & Accomplishments:** National Association of Female Executives; Board of Directors, Benewah Community Hospital. **Education:** Eastern Oregon State, A.A. (1981). **Personal:** Four children: Jessica, Alison, Kembr, and Zachary. Ms. Skaggs enjoys volleyball, organic gardening, and training wellness programs.

Princess R. Skaggs, R.R.A.

Director of Medical Records
Muenster Memorial Hospital
605 North Maple, Box 370
Muenster, TX 76252
(817) 759–2271 Ext. 40
Fax: (817) 759–5080

8062

Business Information: Muenster Memorial Hospital, established by a nun in 1964, is an 18–bed, acute care and long–term care facility. As Director of Medical Records, Miss Skaggs is responsible for all aspects of operations within the Medical Records Department, including coding of physical therapy, training home health nurses for coding, dictation, procedure appeals, Medicare, Medicaid appeals, insurance reviews, filing, and organizing, DRG Analysis, OB coding, birth certificates, and hospital statistics. She also serves as the Utilization Review Director, as well as oversees medical staff credentialing. **Career Steps:** Muenster Memorial Hospital: Director of Medical Records (1993–Present), Utilization Review Director (1993–Present); Medical Records Director, Clay County Memorial Hospital (1991–1993). **Associations & Accomplishments:** American Information Management Association; Texas Health Information Management Association; Certified Professional Utilization Review Specialist – InterQual; Board of Advisors, North Central Texas College. **Education:** Southwestern Oklahoma State University, Medical Records Administration with minor in Allied Health (1991). **Personal:** One child: BillyBob Skaggs–Duerr. Miss Skaggs enjoys horses, reading, caring for plants, and playing with her son, dog, and cats.

Myra L. Skluth

Chief of General Internal Medicine
Norwalk Hospital
Stevens Street
Norwalk, CT 06856
(203) 852–2375
Fax: (203) 866–9113

8062

Business Information: Norwalk Hospital is a 325–bed, full–service, acute care medical facility, providing diagnosis and treatment to patients. Norwalk Hospital currently employs of a staff of 600 physicians. A practicing physician since 1986 and Board–Certified in Internal Medicine and Geriatrics, Dr. Skluth joined Norwalk Hospital in 1994. Serving as Chief of General Internal Medicine, she is responsible for the administration of the Internal Medicine Department, in addition to providing health care to patients and instructing medical residents on internal medicine. **Career Steps:** Chief of General Internal Medicine, Norwalk Hospital (1994–Present). **Associations & Accomplishments:** American Medical Women's Association; American College of Physicians; Society of General Internal Medicine; American Geriatrics Society; American Medical Association; Connecticut State Medical Association; Fairfield County Medical Society. **Education:** Albert Einstein College of Medicine, M.D. (1986); Bryn Mawr College, B.A.; Columbia University – Graduate School of Arts and Sciences, M.A., Ph.D. **Personal:** One child: Elisabeth. Dr. Skluth enjoys working out with personal trainer, tennis, piano, and movies.

Craig A. Skoglund, M.D.
Physician
Oakfield Medical
Suite 102–1021 Court Avenue
Winnipeg, Manitoba R2P 1V7
(204) 338–3062
Fax: (204) 338–7660

8062

Business Information: Oakfield Medical, affiliated with the Seven Oaks General Hospital, is a private medical practice specializing in family medical care. A practicing physician since 1977 and a Board Certified Family Physician, Dr. Skoglund oversees all administrative operations for associates and a support staff of four, in addition to his daily patient practice. He also is responsible for business management. **Career Steps:** Physician, Oakfield Medical (1987–Present); Emergency Medical Officer, Health Services Center (1977–1987). **Associations & Accomplishments:** Canadian College of Family Physicians; Canadian Medical Association; Manitoba Medical Association; Canadian Medical Protective Association. **Education:** University of Manitoba, M.D. (1977); Brandon University, B.S. (1973). **Personal:** Dr. Skoglund enjoys golf, reading, curling and classical music.

Connie L. Small, ART
Director of Medical Records
Yale Hospital and Clinic
510 West Tidwell Road
Houston, TX 77091
(713) 691–1111 EXT. 207
Fax: (713) 691–2930

8062

Business Information: Yale Hospital and Clinic is a full–service 99–bed healthcare facility offering inpatient/outpatient, acute care, emergency room, rehabilitation, and pediatric services with the exception of heart surgery and birthing operations. As Director of Medical Records, Ms. Small is reponsible for supervising three employees, handling emergency room coding, registration, statistics, quality assurance, and assessments. **Career Steps:** Director of Medical Records, Yale Hospital and Clinic (1996–Present); St. Joseph Hospital: Quality Assessment Specialist (1993–1995), Medical Record Technician (1991–1993). **Associations & Accomplishments:** National Association of Female Executives; American Health Information Management Association; Texas Gulf Coast for Healthcare Quality; Houston Area Health Information Management Association. **Education:** University of Houston, Associate of Applied Science – Medical Record Technology. **Personal:** One child: Vanessa M. Ms. Small enjoys in–line skating, bowling, swimming, and dancing.

Barbara J. Smith, R.N., B.S.N., C.C.R.N.
Registered Nurse
Bristol Regional Medical Center
1 Medical Park Boulevard
Bristol, TN 37620–7434
(423) 844–2400
Fax: Please mail or call

8062

Business Information: Bristol Regional Medical Center is a tertiary care teaching hospital, providing diagnosis and treatment of patients. A practicing nurse since 1975, Mrs. Smith joined the Bristol Regional Medical Center in 1982. Currently serving as Registered Nurse for the Cardiac Intensive Care Unit, she is responsible for rotating charge nursing duties and directing bedside care to critically–ill patients. Additionally, she serves as RN Preceptor for students and new employees, as well as teaching critical care and advanced cardiac life support classes at Genetech, Inc. **Career Steps:** Registered Nurse, Bristol Regional Medical Center (1982–Present); Registered Nurse Preceptor, Genentech, Inc. (1993–Present); Nurse and Deputy, Bristol, Virginia Sheriff's Office (1975–1980). **Associations & Accomplishments:** Board of Directors, American Heart Association; American Association of Critical Care Nurses; National College of Nurse Practitioners; Local and National Chapters, Nurse Practitioners. **Education:** East Tennessee State University: M.S.N./F.N.P.

(1996), B.S.N. (1992). **Personal:** Married to Carl in 1982. One child: Nicole T. Adams. Mrs. Smith enjoys weight training, racquetball, and reading.

David Lee Smith, M.D.
Medical Director
Riverview Regional Medical Center
600 South 3rd Street
Gadsden, AL 35901–5304
(205) 543–5390
Fax: (205) 543–5393
EMAIL: See Below

8062

Business Information: Riverview Regional Medical Center is a full service acute care facility providing medical and related health care services to the area. Comprised of 220 beds, the Hospital is regional in scope, and is affiliated with String Fellow Hospital in Anniston, Alabama. As Medical Director, Dr. Smith oversees the emergency medical department, and is responsible for physician management, quality assurance, scheduling, and patient care. Internet users can reach him via: 73137,31452@Compuserve.com. **Career Steps:** Medical Director, Riverview Regional Medical Center (1994–Present); Emergency Physician, Spectrum (1994–Present); Emergency Physician, EMSA (1992–1994); Emergency Physician, Southern Medical Group (1988–1992). **Associations & Accomplishments:** American Medical Association; ACEP; SMA. **Education:** UMKC Medical School, M.D. (1976). **Personal:** Married to Donna in 1980. Dr. Smith enjoys photography, computers, database programming, fishing and the Internet.

Deborah L. Smith, Ph.D.
••• ━━◖◉◗━━ •••

Director of Medical Imaging
Charleston Area Medical Center
800 Pennsylvania Avenue
Charleston, WV 25302
(304) 348–2419
Fax: (304) 348–2425

8062

Business Information: Charleston Area Medical Center, affiliated with the University of Charleston, is a 752–bed, tertiary care teaching facility with three campuses and five medical centers. The medical centers provide services to residents in the Charleston, West Virginia locale and vicinity. As Director of Medical Imaging Services, Dr. Smith is responsible for all radiology, mammography, CT diagnostic ultrasounds, OB ultrasounds, strategic planning, and coordination of Medical Imaging Services. Concurrent with her radiology duties, she heads up a consolidation and restructuring task force for the Medical Center. **Career Steps:** Charleston Area Medical Center: Director of Medical Imaging Services – Women & Children (1992–Present), Assistant Director of Medical Imaging – Memorial (1991–1992), Clinical Instructor – University of Charleston (1988–1992). **Associations & Accomplishments:** Capitol Area Society of Radiologic Technology; West Virginia Society of Radiologic Technology; American Society of Radiologic Technology; West Virginia Association of Licensure Boards; Board of Examiners, West Virginia Radiologic Technology. **Education:** LaSalle University, Ph.D. in Health Administration (1995); University of Charleston, Masters in Human Resource Management (1991); Bluefield State College; Bachelors Board of Regents (1986); Morris Harvey College, Associates in Radiological Sciences. **Personal:** Married to David M. in 1974. Two children: Heather and Heidi. Dr. Smith enjoys camping, reading, tennis and church activities.

Jon F. Smith
Chief Financial Officer
Harms Memorial Hospital
510 Roosevelt Street, P.O. Box 420
American Falls, ID 83211–0420
(208) 226–2327
Fax: (208) 226–2653

8062

Business Information: Harms Memorial Hospital is a long– and short–term skilled care medical facility, consisting of 31 long–term and 10 acute care beds. As Chief Financial Officer, Mr. Smith is responsible for all accounts payable and payroll, as well as the supervision of the business office. In addition, he serves as Human Resource Director and Head of the Business Office. **Career Steps:** Chief Financial Officer, Harms Memorial Hospital (1995–Present); Ward Clerk, Pocatello Medical Center (1991–1995). **Associations & Accomplishments:** Healthcare Financial Managers Association. **Education:** Idaho State University, B.B.A. in Finance (1995). **Personal:** Mr. Smith enjoys running, sports, and travel.

Gregory E. Sneep, M.D.
Medical Director of Emergency Medicine
Edgewater Medical Center –
Emergency Department
5700 North Ashland Avenue
Chicago, IL 60660
(312) 878–6000
Fax: (312) 878–5587

8062

Business Information: Edgewater Medical Center – Emergency Department provides emergency medical treatment to patients in the greater Chicago–metro community. As Attending Physician, Dr. Sneep is responsible for all aspects of diagnosis and treatment of patients in emergency medicine, working with a group of physicians that staff seven emergency facilities. Concurrent with his position at Edgewater Medical Center, Dr. Sneep serves as Staff Physician at a satellite clinic through Christ Hospital, Occupational Health Clinic, providing occupational medicine for corporate participants. **Career Steps:** Attending Physician, Edgewater Medical Center – Emergency Department (1992–Present); Staff Physician, Trinity Occupational Health Clinic (1993–1996); Clinic Preceptor of Department of Internal Medicine, Christ Hospital (1993–1994). **Associations & Accomplishments:** American College of Emergency Physicians; Association of Emergency Physicians; Illinois College of Emergency Physicians; American College of Occupational & Environmental Medicine; AMA; Physician's Recognition Award for continuing medical education (1996); Served as a Paramedic while attending college; Who's Who in High School; Attended school in the Carribean. **Education:** Ross University, School of Medicine, M.D. (1990); University of California – Davis, B.S. (1985). **Personal:** Married to Britta in 1991. Dr. Sneep enjoys scuba diving, nature photography and hiking.

Clarence E. Snyder, M.D.
••• ━━◖◉◗━━ •••

Chairman of Emergency Medicine Department
Jennie Stuart Medical Center
320 West 18th Street
Hopkinsville, KY 42240
(502) 887–0125
Fax: Please mail or call

8062

Business Information: Jennie Stuart Medical Center is a regional, 200–bed acute and sub acute care medical facility located in Hopkinsville, Kentucky. As Chairman of Emergency Medicine Department, Dr. Snyder, who has been practicing medicine in the Jennie Stuart Emergency Room (ER) for 20 years, oversees all aspects of the ER. His responsibilities include overall supervision of ER operations, staffing and training of ER personnel, and public relations. Concurrently Dr. Snyder is an Assistant Professor of Emergency Medicine at the University of Kentucky School of Medicine. **Career Steps:** Chairman of Emergency Medicine Department, Jennie Stuart Medical Center; Assistant Professor, University of Kentucky School of Medicine. **Education:** Indiana School of Medicine, M.D. (1962).· **Personal:** Married to Cheryl in 1973. Dr. Snyder enjoys motorcycling.

Lynn L. Soderlund
Vice President of Support Operations
Lutheran General Hospital
1775 Dempster Road
Park Ridge, IL 60068–1270
(847) 723–7441
Fax: (847) 723–2285

8062

Business Information: Lutheran General Hospital is a full service, licensed, acute care facility. Comprised of 642 beds, Lutheran General provides emergency, OB/GYN, and related health and medical services to patients. Established in 1959, the Hospital has a staff of 800 physicians, in addition to 3,200 full–time employees. Regional in scope, Lutheran General is also part of an eight hospital health system, advocate health care. As Vice President of Support Operations, Ms. Soderlund oversees all non–clinical and non–financial services. She is responsible for volunteers, food and nutrition, parking garages, and construction. **Career Steps:** Lutheran General Hospital: Vice President of Support Operations (1992–Present), Administrator, Support Services (1982–1992), Director of Respiratory Care (1979–1982). **Associations & Accomplishments:** Hospital Laundry Services: Finance Committee Chair, Executive Committee; Recording Secretary, Shanton Point Subdivision; Kiwanis. **Education:** University of Minnesota, Three Year Post Graduate Studies (1985); Northeastern University, B.A.; Triton College, Respiratory Care. **Personal:** Ms. Soderlund enjoys golf, boating, and woodwork.

Barbara A. Soltes, M.D.

Physician & Surgeon

Rush–Presbyterian–St. Luke's Medical Center, Department of Ob/Gyn

1653 Congress Parkway
Chicago, IL 60612
(312) 563–9389
Fax: (312) 829–3431

8062

Business Information: Rush–Presbyterian–St. Luke's Medical Center is a major medical center in Chicago. Dr. Soltes is an Assistant Professor in the Department of Ob/Gyn; She is the Clinical Director of the Women's Health Research Center within the Department. She also has a private practice, Center for Women's Care, at the University. Dr. Soltes is a Reproductive Endocrinologist who specializes in the care of women with hormonal disorders. Specialty areas include: Infertility, Endometriosis, and Menopause. **Career Steps:** Surgeon & Physician, Rush Medical Center–Department of Ob/Gyn (1992–Present); Clinical Director, Women's Health Research Center (1992–Present); Junior Fellow Chairman, American College Ob/Gyn (1994–1996); Treasurer, Chicago Association of Reproductive Endocrinologists (1994–1996). **Associations & Accomplishments:** American College of Ob/Gyn; American Society for Reproducing Medicine; North American Menopause Society; American Medical Association; Illinois Medical Society; Society for Gynecologic Investigation; Society for Study of Reproduction; Chicago Medical Society; American College of Surgeons. **Education:** Mt. Sinai School of Medicine, M.D. (1995); SUNY, Specialty Board in Ob/Gyn; Rush Medical Center, Reproductive Endocrinology Fellowship. **Personal:** Dr. Soltes enjoys foreign travel, imported wines, and art collecting.

Dr. Gautam R. Soparkar

Physician/Associate Professor

Royal University Hospital – Department of Medicine

103 Hospital Drive
Saskatoon, Saskatchewan S7N 0W8
(306) 966–7947
Fax: (306) 966–8021

8062

Business Information: Royal University Hospital is a full–service, healthcare institution specializing in the diagnosis, treatment, and rehabilitation of patients. Affiliated with the University of Saskatchewan, the Hospital serves as a teaching facility for the Medical Department. As Physician/Associate Professor, Dr. Soparkar is responsible for patient care, supervising trainee physicians, research, and serves as Director of the Internal Medicine Residency Training Program. **Career Steps:** Physician, Royal University Hospital – Department of Medicine (1996–Present); University of Saskatchewan: Associate Professor of Medicine (1996–Present), Assistant Professor of Medicine (1994–1996), Assistant Professor of Medicine with term (1993–1994). **Associations & Accomplishments:** Canadian Association of Internal Medicine Program Directors; Royal College Specialty Training Committee in Internal Medicine; Corresponding Member, Royal College Test Committee In Internal Medicine; Canadian Thoracic Society. **Education:** University of Delhi, India: M.B.B.S. (1981), D.T.C.D. (1983), M.D. (1985); Royal College of Physicians of London, England, MRCP (UK) (1987); Royal College of Physicians and Surgeons, of CANADA FRCPC(c) (1993). **Personal:** Married to Arati in 1986. Two children: Mihir and Samira. Dr. Soparkar enjoys badminton and music.

Daniel J. Sprague, M.D.

Physician

St. Joseph's Hospital

300 West Clarendin Avenue, Suite 375
Phoenix, AZ 85013
(602) 277–4161
Fax: (602) 274–3394

8062

Business Information: St. Joseph's Hospital is a full–service, acute care medical hospital, providing diagnosis and treatment to patients. Established in 1972, St. Joseph's Hospital currently employs 37 people. A practicing physician since 1979 and a Board–Certified Neonatologist, Dr. Sprague joined St. Joseph's Hospital and Medical Center in 1986 as Associate Medical Director of the Newborn Nurseries, a position he still holds. Additionally, he was appointed as Co–Director of the Newborn Follow–up Program in 1987, in which he provides quality healthcare to newborns, in addition to co–directing Program activities. Concurrent with his hospital activities, he serves as Co–Director at Arizona State Newborn Intensive Care Program and as Faculty Advisory at Grand Canyon College in Phoenix, Arizona. **Career Steps:** Co–Director and Neonatologist, St. Joseph's Hospital (1987–Present); Co–Director, Arizona State Newborn Intensive Care Program (1985–Present); Faculty Advisor, Grand Canyon College (1988–Present); Staff Neonatologist, CIGNA Healthplan of America (1984–1985). **Associations & Accomplishments:** American Medical Association; Arizona Medical Association; Maricopa County Medical Society; Phoenix Pediatric Society; Presentation on Paper: Total Body Plethysmographic Demonstration of Bronchodilatory Response to Inhaled Isoetharine in Preterm Infants with Hyaline Membrane Disease presented at 52nd Annual Scientific Assemby, Atlanta 1987. **Education:** University of South Dakota: M.D. (1979), B.S. (1976); Maricopa County General Hospital: Pediatric Internship (1979–1980), Pediatric Residency (1980–1982); Good Samaritan Medical Center, Neonatology Fellowship (1982–1984); Diplomate, American Board of Pediatrics (1989); Diplomate, American Board of Pediatrics, Subspecialty Board in Neonatal–Perinatal Medicine (1991). **Personal:** Dr. Sprague enjoys reading, running, and travel.

Judith Spunaugle

Associate Director

Parkland Memorial Hospital

6303 Forest Park Road, Suite 250B
Dallas, TX 75235–5401
(214) 590–4906
Fax: (214) 590–4190

8062

Business Information: Parkland Memorial Hospital is a 1,025–bed county hospital providing quality health care to patients. As Associate Director for Parkland's Exchange Park Business Services, Ms. Spunaugle is responsible for the supervision and management of all Medicare and Medicaid billing and collection activities. The division currently employs 92 support staff. **Career Steps:** Parkland Memorial Hospital: Associate Director (1994–Present), Reconciliation Manager (1992–1994), Billing Supervisor (1990–1992). **Associations & Accomplishments:** Past President, Dallas, TX and Claremore, OK, Credit Professionals International; Past President, Pilot Club, International; International Credit Association; Chamber of Commerce Health and Education Committee; Actively attend seminars at the hospital. **Education:** Eastfield College; Oklahoma University; Oklahoma City University; Rogers State College. **Personal:** Two children: Douglas and Shirley Spunaugle. Ms. Spunaugle enjoys dancing, listening to music, painting, and having fun with her church group and other friends.

Jeane Stegall

Director of Medical Records

Okolona Community Hospital

P.O. Box 420
Okolona, MS 38860
(601) 447–3311
Fax: (601) 447–3856

8062

Business Information: Okolona Community Hospital is a Medicaid/Medicare skilled nursing and rehabilitation center with 61 nursing home beds and 10 acute care beds. As Director of Medical Records, Ms. Stegall is responsible for supervising employees, managing medical records department functions including: transcription, discharges, admissions, indexing, correspondence, filing, and statistics. **Career Steps:** Director of Medical Records, Okolona Community Hospital (1980–Present); Tumor Registrar/PRO Review Coordinator, NMMC – Tupelo (1973–1980); Dental Assistant, Dr. J.W. McCollister (1962–1972). **Associations & Accomplishments:** American Health Information Management Association; Northeast Mississippi Medical Record Council; Consultant for Shearer – Richardson Nursing Home; Swing Bed Committee. **Education:** Itawamba Community College (1992); Accredited Record Technician (1975). **Personal:** Married to Joe Samuel in 1953. Three children: Richard Wayne, Charles Larry, and Terri Kay. Ms. Stegall enjoys church, reading, crocheting, and swimming.

Dennis L. Stevens, M.D., Ph.D.

Chief of Infectious Diseases

Veterans Affairs Medical Center

500 West Fort Street
Boise, ID 83702
(208) 422–1364
Fax: (208) 422–1365

8062

Business Information: Veterans Affairs Medical Center, affiliated with the University of Washington, is a 160–bed, full–service health care facility serving veterans in Boise and surrounding communities, as well as an instructional and research institution. As Chief of Infectious Diseases, Dr. Stevens is responsible for instruction and research within the Department, and the care and treatment of patients. Dr. Stevens is primarily engaged in the research of Group A Streptococcal infections, and runs the AIDS Center for the hospital. Concurrent to his position with the Veterans Affairs Medical Center, Dr. Stevens is also a Professor of Medicine at the University of Washington. **Career Steps:** Chief of Infectious Diseases, Veterans Affairs Medical Center (1979–Present); Brooks Army Medical Center: Assistant Chief of Infectious Diseases (1977–1979), Fellow, Infectious Diseases (1975–1977). **Associations & Accomplishments:** President, Lancefield Society; American Society of Microbiology; Fellow, American College of Physicians; Fellow, Infectious Diseases Society of America; American Federation for Clinical Research; University of Minnesota Lectureship Award (1992). **Education:** University of Utah, M.D. (1971); Montana State University, Ph.D. in Microbiology (1967); University of Montana, B.A. in Microbiology (1964); University of Utah, Residency in Internal Medicine (1971–1974). **Personal:** Two children: Karsten and Marisa. Dr. Stevens enjoys tennis, skiing, camping and photography.

Noel W. Stevenson, A.M., M.D.

Director of Emergency Room

Ferry County Memorial Hospital

470 Thorton Drive
Republic, WA 99166–9701
(509) 775–3153
Fax: (509) 773–2078
E MAIL: See Below

8062

Business Information: Ferry County Memorial Hospital, established in 1973, is a 25–bed non–profit hospital. The Hospital has a 10–bed nursing unit, a 15–bed acute care unit, and a family practice clinic on the grounds, with visiting specialists in the fields of surgery, cardiology, orthopedics, and podiatry. Affiliated with the University of Washington, the Hospital accepts 1st and 4th year medical students for training. As Director of Emergency Room, Dr. Stevenson works in the Emergency Room on rotating weeks. Other responsibilities include instructing 1st and 4th year students from the University of Washington and working as a family physician. Internet users can reach him via: drstevetelevar.com. **Career Steps:** Director of Emergency Room, Ferry County Memorial Hospital (1993–Present); Director Emergency Department, Princess Alexandra Hospital, Brisbane Australia (1976–1993). **Associations & Accomplishments:** Member, Order of Australia, an honor given by the Prime Minister and Governor General of Australia for work in Emergency Medicine; Honorary Member, Institute of Ambulance Officers of Australia; F.A.C.E.M. (Specialist in Emergency Medicine); Co–recipient of Australia's award for top journal article of the year (1995). **Education:** Old University, M.B., B.S. (1959); Washington State University, M.D. (1967); Australia, F.A.C.E.M. (1984); St. John, OB (Honorary) (1990). **Personal:** Married to Roslyn in 1959. Four children: Kay, Ian, Andrew, and Lindsey.

James L. Stewart Jr., M.D.

Vice President for Medical Affairs

Lakewood Hospital

14519 Detroit Avenue
Lakewood, OH 44107
(216) 521–4200
Fax: None, please m

8062

Business Information: Lakewood Hospital is an acute health care facility specializing in the diagnosis, treatment and rehabilitation of patients (full–service community hospital). As Vice President for Medical Affairs, Dr. Stewart serves as the liaison between independent medical staff and administration. He also provides physician direction and implements the practice of quality improvement throughout the hospital. Established in 1907, Lakewood Hospital presently employs 1,100 people. **Career Steps:** Vice President for Medical Affairs, Lakewood Hospital (1987–Present); Commanding Officer, Ft. Belvoir Hospital – U.S. Army (1984–1987); Deputy Commander, Army Medical Center – U.S. Army (1979–1984); Chairman of Department Pediatrics, Army Medical Center – U.S. Army (1969–197 9). **Associations & Accomplishments:** American Medical Association; American Academy of Pediatrics; American Society of Hematology; American Public Health Association; American College of Physician Executives; Member of the Baptist Church. **Education:** Medical University of South Carolina, M.D. (1958); Furman University, M.S. Degree in Health Care Administration (1978), B.S. Degree in Chemistry (1954).

Mary Ann Stiefvater

Director of Medical Information

Conway Regional Medical Center

2302 College Avenue
Conway, AR 72032
(501) 450–2132
Fax: (501) 450–2103

8062

Business Information: Conway Regional Medical Center is an acute care regional, nonprofit medical facility located in Conway, Arkansas. Ms. Stiefvater serves as Director of Medical Information and manages all functions related to Medical Records. **Career Steps:** Previously served as Instructor Hospital Utilization Project, teaching ICD–9–CM Coding Seminars, Consultants, Arkansas Utilization Program, Arkansas

Blue Cross Blue Shield and fifteen hospitals, nursing homes and related facilities in Arkansas. Has conducted numerous ICD–9–CM Coding Seminars in Arkansas and surrounding states. **Associations & Accomplishments:** American & Ark; American Health Information Management Association; President, Arkansas Health Information Management Association (1975–1977) (1962–1963); Recipient of first Distinguished Member Award (1981). **Education:** University of Central Arkansas, B.S. (1967); St. Joseph Hospital School, Medical Records, Houston, Texas (1957); Attended University of St. Thomas, University of Houston, serving affiliations with MD Anderson Hospital and several hospitals in Houston; Registration American Health Information Management Association (1958). **Personal:** Ms. Stiefvater enjoys travel, playing bridge, and snow skiing.

R. E. "Ed" Stone, Jr., Ph.D.

Director of Speaking Arts and Sciences/Associate Professor
Vanderbilt Voice Center
1500 21st Avenue South, Suite 2700
Nashville, TN 37212–3102
(615) 343–SING
Fax: (615) 343–0872
EMAIL: See Below

8062

Business Information: Vanderbilt Voice Center, a division of Vanderbilt University School of Medicine, specializes in treatment of the voice and related disorders. Developed in 1992, the Center treats such disorders as spasmodic dysphonia and provides treatment and rehabilitation for patients who have undergone larynx surgeries and removal, as well as patients needing vocal care and behavioral management of the voice. Dr. Stone was first a Junior High Teacher and then a public school speech–language pathologist before earning his Doctorate from the University of Michigan in Speech Pathology/Speech Science in 1971. During his training he worked in the Department of Otolaryngology as a voice clinician, then as an Instructor and later as an Assistant Instructor of Speech Pathology in Otolaryngology. There he developed a treatment approach for functional voice disorders that has received international recognition. His research interests involved development of an implanted nerve stimulating electrode that permitted induced voice production in canines. In 1978 he became an Assistant Professor of Otolaryngology at Indiana University Medical Center and was instrumental in developing 17 videotaped programs on laryngectomy rehabilitation. He was appointed Associate Professor of Otolaryngology before receiving a similar academic appointment at Vanderbilt University Medical Center in 1987. Dr. Stone is a practicing clinician at the Vanderbilt Voice Center, which sees over 20 professional voice users weekly. Research interests focus on acoustic and aerodynamic assessment of dysphonia and on spasmodic dysphonia. He is a fellow of the American Speech–Language Association and serves on the Scientific Advisory Board of The Voice Foundation. He has served as an editorial consultant for the "Journal of Speech and Hearing Disorders" and as an Associate Editor for the "American Journal of Speech Pathology." He is serving his 13th year as Director of Education for the Florida Laryngectomee Association Voice Institute. A fully certified member of the Professional Ski Instructors of America for over 25 years, an Elder in the Presbyterian Church, a singer with the Bohemians, he has also sung on the Grand Ole Opry. Dr. Stone also holds memberships in many professional associations including the Acoustical Society of America, International Association of Logopedics and Phoniatrics, and others. Internet users can reach him via: ed.stone@mcmail.vanderbilt.edu. **Career Steps:** Director of Speaking Arts and Sciences/Associate Professor, Vanderbilt Voice Center (1987–Present); Associate Professor, Indiana University Medical Center (1979–1987); Assistant Professor, University of Michigan Medical Center (1968–1978). **Associations & Accomplishments:** Sertoma; American Speech and Hearing Association; Acoustical Society of America; International Association of Logopedicas and Phoniatrics; Elder, Presbyterian Church; Professional Ski Instructors; National Association of Teachers of Singing. **Education:** University of Michigan, Ph.D. (1971); University of Oregon, M.Ed.; Whitworth College, B.S. **Personal:** Married to Dee Ann in 1962. Three children: Kimberly, Julie, and Robert. Dr. Stone enjoys skiing, golf, and photography.

Sharon V. Stormer

Director of Inpatient Nursing
Shriner's Hospital
2001 South Lindbergh Boulevard
St. Louis, MO 63131
(314) 432–3600
Fax: (314) 432–2930

8062

Business Information: Shriner's Hospital can be found in 22 locations across North America. The hospitals include 19 pediatric/orthopaedic hospitals and 3 burn care centers. The Shriner's Hospital offers pediatric–orthopaedic care to all at no cost to patients and their families. As Director of Inpatient Nursing, Ms. Stormer has administrative responsibility for inpatient nursing, clinical and research laboratories, and infection control/employee health. She is involved in recruitment of the nursing staff, and is responsible for planning, coordinating, administering policies and delivering services which are efficient and cost effective relating to departments listed above and acts as liaison between nursing and medical staffs and other health care disciplines. **Career Steps:** Shriner's Hospital – St. Louis, Director, Inpatient Nursing (1986–Present), Nursing Supervisor (1981–1986); Community Liaison, Bellevue Hospital – Bellevue, OH (1979–1980). **Associations & Accomplishments:** United States Coast Guard Auxiliary; National Association of Orthopedic Nurses; Sigma Theta Tau; Orthopaedic Nurse, Certified (ONC). **Education:** St. Joseph College – Maine, B.S.P.A. (1980); DePaul School of Nursing – St. Louis, (1968). **Personal:** Married to Robert in 1968. Two children: Sean and Amy. Ms. Stormer enjoys Coast Guard Auxiliary and boating.

Richard J. Streck, M.D.

Director of the Department of Medicine
Good Samaritan Hospital
375 Dixmyth Avenue
Cincinnati, OH 45220
(513) 872–3306
Fax: (513) 221–5865

8062

Business Information: Good Samaritan Hospital is a full–service acute care hospital providing medical diagnosis and treatment to patients in the greater Cincinnati–metro and outlying communities. A Board–Certified Medical Examiner and Board–Certified in Internal Medicine, Dr. Streck has been a practicing physician for fifteen years. Completing his residency in Internal Medicine in 1980 at Good Samaritan Hospital, he was appointed to his present position in 1992. He is responsible for directing all clinical functions within the Department of Medicine. Concurrent with his clinical duties, he operates a limited private practice one day a week, providing diagnosis and treatment of patients in Internal Medicine. **Career Steps:** Practicing General Internist, Private Practice (1994–Present); Good Samaritan Hospital: Director of the Department of Medicine (1992–Present), Program Director of Internal Medicine Residency (1993–Present), Associate Program Director of Internal Medicine Residency (1991–1993), Coordinator of the Junior Medical Clerkship Program (1988–1993), Outpatient Clinical Preceptor (1988–1993), Emergency Department Physician (1983–1987); Faculty Attending – Department of Medicine; Assistant Clinical Professor, Department of Medicine, University of Cincinnati School of Medicine; **Associations & Accomplishments:** Diplomate, National Board of Medical Examiners (1982); Diplomate, American Board of Internal Medicine (1987); Association of Program Directors in Internal Medicine; Cincinnati Academy of Medicine; Cincinnati Society of Internal Medicine; Ohio Society of Internal Medicine; Ohio State Medical Association; The American College of Physicians; Member, Educational Coordinating Committee, University of Cincinnati School of Medicine; Chairman and Member of numerous committees, Good Samaritan Hospital; The American College of Physician Executives; The American Medical Association; Co–author: "Moyamoya Phenomenon Due to Recklinghausen's Neurofibromatosis: A Case Report and Review of the Literature"; Presentations: "Anterior Spinal Artery Syndrome"; "Ethical Considerations and Living Wills"; "Internal Medicine Review." **Education:** Xavier University: M.B.A. in Management (1989–1991), B.S. in Natural Sciences (1971–1975); Good Samaritan Hospital, Internal Medicine Residency (1980–1983); University of Miami School of Medicine, M.D. (1976–1980). **Personal:** Married to Joan in 1976. Three children: Patricia, Philip, and Joseph. Dr. Streck enjoys swimming, photography, and computers.

Jean Hall Streppa

Wellness Director
Nicholas Noyes Memorial Hospital
111 Clara Barton Street
Dansville, NY 14437–9503
(716) 335–4218
Fax: (716) 335–5881

8062

Business Information: Nicholas Noyes Memorial Hospital is an acute care hospital, providing diagnosis and treatment of patients in a rural part of Western New York State. With twenty–six years experience in nursing and a Registered Professional Nurse in New York, Ms. Streppa joined Nicholas Noyes Memorial Hospital as Wellness Director in 1994. She is responsible for designing and implementing a comprehensive and preventative health care program for the employees and for the community at large. **Career Steps:** Wellness Director, Nicholas Noyes Memorial Hospital (1994–Present); Adjunct Clinical Instructor in Nursing, Keuka College (1992–1994); Discharge Planner, Monroe Community Hospital (1992–1993); Sales Associate, Cohoes, Inc. (1991–1993); Trained Mediator, Mediation Center of Rochester (1987–1990); Executive Director, Epilepsy Association of Rochester (1979–1988); Acting Assistant Director and Public Health Nurse Consultant, Rochester Society for the Prevention of Cruelty to Children, Homemaker/Health Aide Service (1973–1976); Executive Director, Epilepsy Association of Greater Rochester (1979–1988); Director of Temporary Care Program, Mary Cariola Children's Center (1968–1973); Guest Lecturer/Consultant, University of Rochester Department of Preventive Medicine (1972); Staff Nurse, Cornell University (Gannett Medical Clinic), University of Rochester (Strong Memorial Hospital and Columbia Presbyterian Hospital) (1962–1964). **Associations & Accomplishments:** Advisory Board, Keuka College Division of Nursing Professional; New York State Council of Mediation; National Council of Family Mediators; Rochester Area Council of Family Mediator; Epilepsy Association Professional Advisory Board; Council and Strategic Planning Committee Chair, Rochester Friendly Home; Greater Rochester Area Partnership for the Elderly; Head Injury Advisory Board Monroe County Community Services Board: Mental Health Retardation and Developmental Disabilities Subcommittee. **Education:** University of Rochester, M.S. (1978); Keuka College, B.S. in Nursing (1962); Degree in Community Health and Preventive Medicine. **Personal:** Two children: Michael Scott and Karen Lynn. Ms. Streppa enjoys travel (works abroad in Scotland).

Narayana Subramany, M.D.

Surgeon
Dr. Joseph–Subramany, Inc.
615 Dewey Street
Ridgeway, PA 15853
(814) 772–2485
Fax: (814) 772–2702

8062

Business Information: Dr. Joseph–Subramany, Inc. is a private general and vascular surgery practice affiliated with St. Mary's Regional Medical Center. In addition to patient care and administrative duties at his private practice, Dr. Subramany also serves as the Chief of Staff at St. Mary's Regional Medical Center and the Chief of Surgery at Elk County Regional Medical Center. **Career Steps:** Surgeon, Dr. Joseph–Subramany, Inc. (1979–Present); Chief of Staff, St. Mary's Regional Medical Center (1995–Present); Chief of Surgery, Elk County Regional Medical Center (1986–Present). **Associations & Accomplishments:** American Medical Association; Pennsylvania Medical Society; Fellow of American College of Surgeons; Fellow of International College of Surgeons; **Education:** Hahnemann Medical University, D.A.B.S. (1983); Arizona Heart Institute, Fellow in Cardiovascular Surgery (1984). **Personal:** Married to Bhani in 1981. Two children: Vivek and Kartik. Dr. Subramany enjoys tennis and jogging.

Jamie Sullivan

Director of Ancillary Services
Bryan Whitfield Memorial Hospital
1117 Philps Drive
Demopolis, AL 36732
(334) 289–0334
Fax: (334) 287–2679

8062

Business Information: Bryan Whitfield Memorial Hospital is a not–for–profit community hospital, providing surgical, emergency, and pharmaceutical services. Mr. Sullivan joined the Hospital in 1982 as Staff Pharmacist and was promoted to Director of Ancillary Services in 1985. His current responsibilities include managing the Departments of Pharmacy, Purchasing, Central Supply, Dietary, Laboratory, and Print Shop. He is responsible for diversified administrative activities and personnel supervision. **Career Steps:** Bryan Whitfield Memorial Hospital: Director of Ancillary Services (1985–Present); Pharmacist (1982–1985); Pharmacist, Bryce Hospital (1981–1982). **Associations & Accomplishments:** ASHP; AISHP; APA; ASHMM; Founder and President, Demopolis Dixie Youth Girls Fastpitch Softball League. **Education:** Auburn University: Pharmacy (1981), B.S. in Biological Sciences. **Personal:** Married to Rebecca in 1972. One child: Blythe. Mr. Sullivan enjoys writing, public speaking, and turkey hunting.

Winston V. Sullivan

Director of Information Services/Chief Information Officer
St. Joseph's Health Centre
30 The Queensway
Toronto, Ontario M6R 1B5
(416) 530–6841
Fax: Please mail or call
EMAIL: See Below

8062

Business Information: St. Joseph's Health Centre is a health care center providing diagnosis, treatment, and rehabilitation to patients. As Director of Information Services/Chief Information Officer, Mr. Sullivan is responsible for all aspects of information services for the Centre. Internet users can reach him via: Sullivan@STJOE.ON.CA. **Career Steps:** Director of Information Services/CIO, St. Joseph's Health Centre (1993–Present); Systems Architect, University Hospital London (1991–1993); Systems Architect, Toronto Stock Exchange (1988–1991); Systems Architect, Toronto Stock Exchange (1988–1991); Systems Architect, Canadian Imperial Bank of Canada (1985–1988). **Associations & Accomplish-**

ments: C.O.A.C.H.; H.I.M.S.S.; C.H.I.M.E. **Education:** Attended Ryprson University (1969). **Personal:** Mr. Sullivan enjoys cycling and gardening.

Aurelia K. Summerlin

Director of Nursing
Alabama Oncology Hematology Association
4145 Carmichael Road
Montgomery, AL 36106
(334) 260–2000
Fax: (334) 260–2010

8062

Business Information: Alabama Oncology Hematology Associates, P.C., located at the Montgomery Cancer Center, is a full–service medical office, providing care to patients suffering from oncological and hematological disorders, as well as providing diagnosis and treatment to cancer patients. As Director of Nursing, Ms. Summerlin is responsible for all nursing functions for the Hemotology Oncology Department. She oversees 25 nurses and a total staff of 45. **Career Steps:** Director of Nursing, Alabama Oncology Hematology Association (1992–Present); Baptist Medical Center: Director of Medical Nursing (1988–1992), Assistant Director of Nursing Service (1987–1988). **Associations & Accomplishments:** American Heart Association; American Cancer Society; Delta Sigma Theta Sorority Nu Theta Chapter; Southeast Alabama Oncology Nursing Society; National Oncology Nursing Society. **Education:** Troy State University: Montgomery, M.S.N. (1988), Troy, B.S.N. (1980). **Personal:** Married to Nelson L. Jr. in 1981. Two children: Nelson III and Kayla. Ms. Summerlin enjoys walking, reading, and playing soccer.

Ann M. Summers

Clinical Geneticist
North York General Hospital – Genetics Programme
4001 Leslie Street
North York, Ontario M2K 1E1
(416) 756–6345
Fax: (416) 756–6727

8062

Business Information: North York General Hospital – Genetics Programme is a full–service, healthcare institution specializing in the diagnosis, treatment, and rehabilitation of patients. As Clinical Geneticist, Dr. Summers sees patients for genetic testing, counsels patients in genetics, and does research related to genetics. **Career Steps:** Clinical Geneticist, North York General Hospital – Genetics Programme (1988–Present). **Associations & Accomplishments:** Ontario Medical Association; Canadian Medical Association; American Society of Human Genetics; Canadian Bioethics Society; American Society of Law, Medicine, and Ethics; Associate Member, Kennedy Institute of Ethics. **Education:** University of Toronto: M.D. (1982), B.Sc., FRCPC, FCCMC; Hospital for Sick Children, Residency and Fellowship in Genetics. **Personal:** Married to Peter Karalis in 1983. Two children: John Michael and Kate. Dr. Summers enjoys reading, cooking, and gardening.

I. Marlene Summers

Nurse Educator
McKay Dee Hospital
3939 Harrison Boulevard
Ogden, UT 84403–2386
(801) 625–2757
Fax: (801) 629–5452

8062

Business Information: McKay Dee Hospital is a full–service healthcare institution specializing in the diagnosis, treatment, and rehabilitation of patients. As Nurse Educator, Miss Summers is responsible for all aspects of nursing operations, including strategic planning, patient care, teaching LPN's and RN's, orientation, and teaching IV certification classes. **Career Steps:** Nurse Educator, McKay Dee Hospital (1994–Present); Staff Nurse, Ogden Regional Medical Center (1994–Present); Executive Officer, U.S. Army Reserves (1975–Present). **Associations & Accomplishments:** American Nurses Association; American Association of Critical Care Nurses; National Association for Female Executives; National Nursing Staff Development Organization; Nightingale Society; Rogeian Society; Reserve Officers Association; Army Reserve Association; 91st Division League. **Education:** Weber State University: B.S.N. (1992), A.D.N. (1988), B.S. (1980), B.S. (1974); Utah State University, M.Ed. (1982); Ricks College, A.D. (1972). **Personal:** Miss Summers enjoys water skiing, marathon running, meditation, and myotherapy.

Doris Sutton

Director of Medical Records
Clara Barton Hospital
250 West 9th Street
Hoisington, KS 67544
(316) 653–2114 EXT. 274
Fax: (316) 653–2738

8062

Business Information: Clara Barton Hospital was established in 1950. It is an acute care medical facility, hospital has 48 beds, six physicians, and 20 nurses on–staff. As Director of Medical Records, Ms. Sutton is in charge of all patient medical records. She is responsible for making sure each record is updated and filed properly. Ms. Sutton is responsible for the activities of her staff and is involved in developing a budget for the department. She is employed as a coder at CKMC. Concurrently, Ms. Sutton serves as a transcriptionist for Robert L. Frayser, D.O. and Robin Durrett, D.O. and is Medical Staff secretary. **Career Steps:** Director of Medical Records, Clara Barton Hospital (1983–Present); Coder, CKMC (1996–Present); Office Clerk, WKRA (1981–1983). **Associations & Accomplishments:** AHIMA; KHIMA; Hospital Auxiliary; Employee of the year (1990); QA/RM Committee. **Education:** University of Kansas, B.S. (1994); AHIMA Certification as Art (1979); RRA Certification (1994). **Personal:** Married to Jerry in 1969. One child: Brian. Ms. Sutton enjoys reading and gardening.

Richard D. Sutton

Manager of Construction and Engineering
Indiana University Medical Center
550 University Boulevard
Indianapolis, IN 46202–5270
(317) 274–0304
Fax: (317) 274–7335

8062

Business Information: Indiana University Medical Center is a major tertiary care, research and teaching hospital. As Manager of Construction and Engineering, Mr. Sutton is responsible for all construction and engineering planning, in addition to supervising all Hospital construction and maintenance activities. **Career Steps:** Manager of Construction and Engineering, Indiana University Medical Center (1981–Present); Assistant Director of the Physical Plant, Indiana University at Indianapolis (1978–1981); Project Management, Indiana University (1965–1978). **Associations & Accomplishments:** American Society of Hospital Engineers; National Fire Protection Association – Health Care Section; Construction Specification Institute; Former President/Charter Member, Greenwood Little League (15 years); President, National Sojourners, Inc. – Indianapolis–Ft. Harrison, Chapter #66; Former President, Central Nine Vocational School; Former President, Board of Education – Greenwood, Indiana; Former coach for his sons' baseball team; Designed a softball field and started a girls softball league; Disabled Veteran – U.S. Army – Korean Campaign. **Education:** Purdue University, Construction Engineer (1980). **Personal:** Married to Mary Jane in 1963. Eight children: Sherri, Steve, Vicki, Charles, Randy, Patsy, Stephen, and Timothy (deceased). Mr. Sutton enjoys woodworking, hunting, fishing, and travel.

Ms. Mathilda Tatem

Director of Surgery
Mary Shiels Hospital
3515 Howell Street
Dallas, TX 75204–2825
(214) 443–3050
Fax: (214) 443–3049

8062

Business Information: Mary Shiels Hospital is a small, privately–owned, 15–bed hospital, providing operating rooms and outpatient services (10 chairs). Surgeries performed include plastic surgery, face lifts, breast reduction, laparascopic procedures, hysterectomies, D&C's, and hand surgeries. With thirty–three years in the health care field, Ms. Tatem joined Mary Shiels Hospital in 1986. As Director of Surgery, she provides the overall day–to–day operations for the units of Surgery, Recovery and Anesthesia. Her primary duties involve purchasing all capital equipment and supplies, assurance of quality patient care, payroll and personnel matters, equipment and supplies procurement and maintenance, departmental policies and procedures, as well as working closely with the CPA in financial reports closures. During her tenure with Mary Shiels Hospital, she has been involved in the opening of two new hospitals, the closure of one, as well as equipment and supplies implementation needed for the start–up of OR units. **Career Steps:** Director of Surgery, Mary Shiels Hospital (1986–Present); Gaston Episcopal Hospital: Director of Surgery (1986), Staff Nurse (1980–1986); Assistant Supervisor Orthopedic, Baylor Hospital (1988). **Associations & Accomplishments:** AORN; American Heart Association; Texas Hospital Association. **Education:** St. Elizabeth Hospital Nursing School – N.S. Canada (1963); ACLS Certified; BLS Instructor; C.N.O.R. Certification. **Personal:** Married to James A. in 1965. Two children: James A. III and Nicole. Ms. Tatem enjoys swimming, reading, and gardening.

William Robert Templeton, M.D.

Chief, Department of Geriatric Services
Victoria General Hospital Society
35 Helmcken Road
Victoria, British Co V8Z 6R5
(604) 370–8591
Fax: (604) 370–8285
EMAIL: See Below

8062

Business Information: Victoria General Hospital Society is an acute care facility providing health and related services to area residents. Comprised of 1,300 beds, the Hospital is the largest multi–site facility in Canada. As Chief, Department of Geriatric Services, Dr. Templeton consults with private physicians on geriatric patients, as well as instructs medical students and residents. His duties consist of clinical responsibilities and administrative functions. Internet users can reach him via: rtempleton@gvhs.gov.bc.ca. **Career Steps:** Chief, Department of Geriatric Services, Victoria General Hospital Society (Present). **Associations & Accomplishments:** American Geriatric Society; Canadian Society of Geriatric Medicine. **Education:** Queen's University, Belfast: B.Sc. With Honors, M.B., B.Ch., B.A.O.; C.C.F., Canada. **Personal:** Married to Marion in 1964. Two children: Lesley and Glenn. Dr. Templeton enjoys sailing, reading, and woodworking.

Daniel Teres, M.D., FCCM

Clinical Research Associate
Baystate Medical Center
759 Chestnut Street
Springfield, MA 01199–1001
(413) 784–5439
Fax: (413) 784–5940
E–mail: see below

8062

Business Information: Baystate Medical Center is a full–service, multi–specialty tertiary hospital, medical research and teaching institution. Baystate Health Systems is the western campus of the Tufts University School of Medicine, located in Boston. As Director of the Adult Critical Care Division, Dr. Teres is responsible for the care and treatment of patients, as well as clinical research in the areas of probabilities and prognosis. Dr. Teres has developed a computer program that works with probabilities. This work has been done in conjunction with the school of Public Health at the University of Massachusetts, located in Amherst. The models are called Mortality Probability Model (MPM II) and the simplified Acute Physiology Model (SAPS II). Dr. Teres is an active member of Critical Care Analytics, Inc., an inter–active database company. He is currently doing outcomes research. He also lectures on the strengths and weaknesses of probability models. Dr. Teres can also be reached through the Internet as follows: dteres@library.bhs.org **Career Steps:** Director, Adult Critical Care Division, Baystate Medical Center (1973–Present); Associate Professor of Medicine and Surgery, Tufts University School of Medicine; Section Editor, 3rd Edition Rippe's Textbook, Intensive Care Medicine. **Education:** New Jersey College of Medicine, M.D. (1966); Tufts College (1962); Beth Israel Hospital – Boston (1973); Boston City Hospital (1970). **Personal:** Married to Evelyne H. in 1967. Four children: Rishona, Ilana, Jeremy and Lorin. Dr. Teres enjoys riding bicycles.

Lorrie E. Thibeault, MSN

Director of Nursing & Assistant Administrator
Good Samaritan Hospital
P.O. Box 85002, 901 Olive Dr.
Bakersfield, CA 93380–5002
(805) 399–4461
Fax: (805) 399–4224

8062

Business Information: Good Samaritan Hospital is a full–service, healthcare institution specializing in medical surgery, intensive care, urgent care, and general healthcare. The Hospital has a psychiatric unit, nine feeder clinics, and an urgent care center (no emergency room). As Director of Nursing and Assistant Administrator, Miss Thibeault is responsible for all aspects of nursing operations, including staffing, budgeting, quality of care, patient outcomes, risk management, and multi–disciplinary issues. Miss Thibeault is also responsible for laboratory and surgery services. **Career Steps:** Director of Nursing & Assistant Administrator, Good Samaritan Hospital (1996–Present); Director of Nursing, Bear Valley Community Hospital (1993–96); Department Supervisor, Hunt Memorial Hospital (1982–85); Instructor, St. Anselm's College (1975–82). **Associations & Accomplishments:** Association of Nurse Executives; NACOAG. **Education:** Boston University, M.S. in Nursing (1985); Boston College, B.S. in Nursing (1967). **Personal:** Two children: Michelle and Marc. Miss Thibeault enjoys exercising, walking, swimming, cross-stitch, crochet, playing cards, the arts, and time spent with friends.

Muthayipalayam Thirumoorthi, M.D.

Physician
Saint John Hospital
22251 Moross Road, #270
Detroit, MI 48236-2148
(313) 343-4785
Fax: (313) 343-7937
E-mail: see below

8062

Business Information: Saint John Hospital is a multi-specialty tertiary hospital, medical research and teaching institution. As Physician, Dr. Thirumoorthi is responsible for the care and treatment of patients, the instruction of resident students, and some administrative work. Dr. Thirumoorthi specializes in the area of Pediatric Infectious Diseases, and conducts limited clinical research. He can also be reached through the Internet as follows: TMOORTHI@AOL.COM **Career Steps:** Physician, Saint John Hospital (1976–Present); Associate Professor of Pediatrics, Wayne State University School of Medicine (1976–Present). **Associations & Accomplishments:** American Academy of Pediatrics; Infectious Diseases Society of America; Pediatric Infectious Diseases Society; American Association of Physicians From India; Published his own bibliography; Appeared in numerous peer review articles, local papers, and on television. **Education:** Madras University – India, M.D. (1970). **Personal:** Married to Vani in 1974. Three children: Arul, Ilango and Vidya. Dr. Thirumoorthi enjoys photography and travel.

Deborah L. Thorne

Director of Human Resources
Delaware Valley Hospital
1 Titus Place
Walton, NY 13856
(607) 865-2160
Fax: (607) 865-8482

8062

Business Information: Delaware Valley Hospital is a 42-bed, full-service, healthcare institution specializing in the diagnosis, treatment, and rehabilitation of patients. As Director of Human Resources, Ms. Thorne is responsible for recruitment of staff, handling compensation, benefits, an employee relations program, acting as an advisor on state and federal legal issues, monitoring employee performance programs, evaluating disciplines, employee recognition, and special events programs, and the training and education of employees. **Career Steps:** Director of Human Resources, Delaware Valley Hospital (1995–Present); District Human Resources Manager, Lowes Home Improvement (1992–1995). **Associations & Accomplishments:** New York Healthcare Human Resource Association; Society of Human Resource Management. **Education:** State University of New York – Oneonta, B.S. (1992). **Personal:** Ms. Thorne enjoys scuba diving and vacationing.

Genaro I. Tiongson, M.D.

Medical Director
Rehabilitation Hospital, United Hospital
1300 S. Columbia Road
Grand Forks, ND 58201-4012
(701) 780-2473
Fax: (701) 780-2599

8062

Business Information: Rehabilitation Hospital is a full-service rehabilitation facility providing physical, occupational, and speech therapy services to patients. The Rehabilitation Division became part of the United Hospital in 1995. Previously, it was under the University of North Dakota. As Medical Director, Dr. Tiongson directs patient care, consultations, electrical studies (diagnosis of nerve problems), and administration. A specialist in physical medicine and rehabilitation, he is also involved with several Hospital committees. **Career Steps:** Medical Director, Rehabilitation Hospital – part of United Hospital (1989–Present); Chief of Physical Medicine Services, Fitzsimmons Army Medical Center – Denver, CO (1970–1976); Assistant Chief of Physical Medicine Services, Walter Reed Medical Center – Washington, DC (1969–1970). **Associations & Accomplishments:** American Medical Association; Diplomate, American Board of Physical Medicine and Rehabilitation; North Dakota Medical Association; 3rd District Medical Society; American Academy of Physical Medicine and Rehabilitation. **Education:** Far Eastern University – Manila, Philippines, M.D. (1963). **Personal:** Married to Kathryn in 1966. Four children: Christopher, Jeffrey, Amy, and Gregory. Dr. Tiongson enjoys tennis, fishing, and oil painting.

Donna M. Tozer

Administrative Director of Laboratory
Indiana Hospital
Hospital Road
Indiana, PA 15701
(412) 357-7165
Fax: Please mail or call

8062

Business Information: Indiana Hospital is a full service acute care facility comprised of 150 beds, as well as a 20 bed skilled nursing unit for patients needing long-term care. The Facility, established in 1920, is the only hospital in Indiana County. As Administrative Director of Laboratory, Ms. Tozer oversees all functions related to the twenty-four hour, seven day-a-week operation of the Laboratory. She is responsible for human resources including personnel management and scheduling, budget, and ensuring the needs of patients and physicians are met quickly and well. Additional duties include implementing and monitoring quality control, complying with licensure and accreditation standards and developing laboratory policies. **Career Steps:** Administrative Director of Laboratory, Indiana Hospital (1992–Present); Assistant Administrative Director, Lancaster General Hospital (1975–1992); Medical Technologist, Hershey Medical Center (1972–1974). **Associations & Accomplishments:** American Society of Clinical Pathologists; Clinical Laboratory Management Association; Penn State Alumni Association. **Education:** College of St. Francis, M.S. (1990); Penn State University, B.S. **Personal:** Ms. Tozer enjoys riding horses and working on her house.

Joseph K.C. Tsui, M.D.

Associate Professor
Vancouver Hospital & Health Sciences Center, UBC Site
Room M32, Purdy Pavilion, 221 Wes Brook Mall
Vancouver, British Co V6T 2B5
(604) 822-7660
Fax: (604) 822-7866
EMAIL: See Below

8062

Business Information: Vancouver Hospital & Health Sciences Center, UBC Site is a medical/teaching facility specializing in clinical research on movement disorders such as Parkinson's disease. Affiliated with the University of British Columbia, the Hospital plans to expand through continued research. As Associate Professor, Dr. Tsui is also a practicing neurologist. Recruited from private practice, he is responsible for providing patient services, researching activities in movement disorders, and teaching medical students and graduates. **Career Steps:** University of British Columbia: Associate Professor (1994–Present), Assistant Professor (1989–1994), Research Associate (1985–1989). **Education:** University of Hong Kong Medical School: M.D., B.S. (1974); Member, Royal College of Physicians, London (MRCP(UK)); Fellow, Royal College of Physicians of Canada (Neurology) (FRCPC). **Personal:** Married to Gigi in 1981. Four children: Telan, Derek, Shaolin, and Shaopin. Dr. Tsui enjoys music and swimming.

Maureen McElroy Ulizio

Nursing Manager – CCU/Telemetry
VA Connecticut – West Haven Campus
950 Campbell Avenue
West Haven, CT 06516
(203) 932-5711 Ext.: 3977
Fax: Please mail or call

8062

Business Information: VA Connecticut – West Haven Campus is a 500-bed, acute care VA hospital, providing health care to veterans of the Armed Forces. A high percentage of their population consists of men over the age of 45, including some Desert Storm patients. Primarily involved in Cardiology, the Hospital performs approximately 150 open heart surgeries per year. A massive reorganization is in process, resulting in the Hospital focusing more on outpatient care and decreasing the amount of time each patient spends in their facility. At the same time, they will be increasing the quality of care to patients to compensate for time spent. With more computerized operations, they will also be adding more responsibilities to the staff and referring more patients to their satellite clinic – two more clinics will be established in the area to fulfill their needs. A practicing nurse since 1970, Ms. Ulizio joined VA Connecticut – West Haven Campus as Nursing Manager of CCU/Telemetry in 1993. She is responsible for the management of a 16-bed acute care unit, assuring quality patient care, in addition to overseeing a staff of 22, including three research data collectors. She also will be responsible for the implementation of new plans resulting from the reorganization. **Career Steps:** Nursing Manager of CCU/Telemetry, VA Connecticut – West Haven Campus (1993–Present); Clinical Specialist, Yale – New Haven Hospital (1992–Present); Clinical Specialist, Town of Cheshire (1985–1993); Assistant to Ed McMann, NBC; Consultant, Yale University. **Associations & Accomplishments:** American Association Critical Core Nurses; American Nurses Association; Cheshire Democratic Town Committee **Education:** Catholic University, M.S.N. (1970); Salve Regina College, B.S.. **Personal:** Married to David in 1972. Three children: Kara, Ryan and David. Ms. Ulizio enjoys family and politics.

Dr. Filemon J. Umali

Physician
–Independent–
130 West Alosta Avenue, Suite 210
Glendora, CA 91740-0395
(818) 963-8597
Fax: (818) 852-0223

8062

Business Information: Intercommunity Medical Center is a regional obstetrics and gynecology practice affiliated with four regional hospitals. As Physician, Dr. Umali specializing in women's medical problems. He is sole practitioner, and so is responsible for all concerns of his medical practice. Dr. Umali deals with insurance claims, counseling of patients, financial matters of the practice, and staffing concerns. **Career Steps:** Physician, Intercommunity Medical Center (1988–Present); Obstetrician/Gynecologist, Huntington East Valley Hospital (1985–Present); Obstetrician/Gynecologist, Covina Valley Community Hospital (1985–Present); Obstetrician/Gynecologist, Doctors Hospital of West Covina (1985–Present). **Associations & Accomplishments:** American Society of Abdominal Surgeons; Society of Philippine Surgeons of America; American Association of Gynecological Laparoscopists; American Association of Sex Educators, Counselors, and Therapists. **Education:** Manila Central University, M.D. (1956); Cosmopolitan College, Manila, B.S. **Personal:** Widow to Nancy Jane Criswell in 1961. Three children: Glenda Umali-Matsumura, M.D., Erica Umali, M.D., Donna Ruth Umali, B.S., and a stepdaughter Holli Vandeman. Dr. Umali enjoys music, piano, violin, cello, and coin collecting.

Joanna M. Valentine

Nurse Manager
Methodist North Hospital
3960 New Covington Pike
Memphis, TN 38128-2504
(901) 384-5403
Fax: (901) 384-5397

8062

Business Information: Methodist North Hospital is a full-service, 175-bed acute care hospital, providing diagnosis and treatment to patients — best known for its cardiac units. With fourteen years of experience in nursing, Ms. Valentine joined Methodist North Hospital as Nurse Manager in 1992. She is responsible for the management of the Telemetry and ICU Stepdown Units, as well as the development of a second stepdown unit — Intermediate Cardiac Care. **Career Steps:** Nurse Manager, Methodist North Hospital (1992–Present); Nurse Manager, Denver General Hospital (1991–1992); Administrative Supervisor, Porter Memorial Hospital (1989–1991). **Associations & Accomplishments:** Association of Acute Care Nurses (AACN); American Nursing Association. **Education:** Wayne State Univesity, B.S.N. (1982); Macomb Community College, A.A. (1975); University of Phoenix, working towards M.B.A.; Certifications: Nursing Administration (1994); ACLS (1978); Critical Care Nurse. **Personal:** Married to Larry J. in 1973. Three children: Michael, Daniel, and Robert. Ms. Valentine enjoys golf and gardening.

Anthony M. Valeri, M.D.

Director of Hemodialysis
Columbia-Presbyterian Medical Center
622 West 168th Street
New York, NY 10032-3784
(212) 305-3273
Fax: (212) 305-6692

8062

Business Information: Columbia-Presbyterian Medical Center, associated with Columbia University, is a 1,000-bed teaching hospital providing diagnosis and treatment of patients and instruction of medical students. A Board-certified Nephrologist, Dr. Valeri serves as Director of the Acute Hemodialysis Unit, responsible for the oversight of all acute and chronic treatments. **Career Steps:** Director of the Acute Hemodialysis Unit, Columbia-Presbyterian Medical Center

(1991–Present); Assistant Attending, Bellevue Hospital Center (1986–1991). **Associations & Accomplishments:** International Society of Nephrology; American Society of Nephrology; New York Society of Nephrology; Published in medical journals: American Journal of Kidney Diseases, Kidney International, Clinical Nephrology; Teaches twice a year, for a period of a month, at Columbia–Presbyterian Medical Center. Areas of Research Interest: Glomerular Diseases, Hemodialysis, Acute Renal Failure. **Education:** State University of New York–Health Science Center at Brooklyn, M.D., magna cum laude (1981); Polytechnic University, B.S. in Life Sciences, Summa Cum Laude and Salutorian (1977). **Personal:** Married to Florence R. Dacanay, R.N. in 1990. Dr. Valeri enjoys walking, travelling, dancing, and computers.

Johannes (John) D. Van Schalkwyk, M.D.
Staff Anesthesiologist
Western Memorial Regional Hospital
P.O. Box 2005 Station Main, West Valley Road
Corner Brook, Newfoundla A2H 6J7
(709) 637–5324
Fax: Please mail or call

8062

Business Information: Western Memorial Regional Hospital is a full–service, health care institution specializing in the diagnosis, treatment, and rehabilitation of patients. Western Memorial Regional Hospital is the only general healthcare facility that serves a town of 25,000. The Hospital provides the public with four general internists, four neurologists, four gynecologists, eight internists, and six anesthesiologists. As Staff Anesthesiologist, Dr. Van Schalkwyk is responsible for providing all anesthesia and pain control procedures for surgeries within the hospital. **Career Steps:** Staff Anesthesiologist, Western Memorial Regional Hospital (1987–Present); Private Anesthesiologist Practice, Dr. Johannes Van Schalkwyk (1986–1987); Staff Anesthesiologist, Johannesburg Hospital (1979–1985). **Associations & Accomplishments:** Canadian Anesthesiologists Society; American Society of Regional Anesthesia; Newfoundland Medical Association; Church Board Member; The American Society of Regional Anesthesia; Forever Young Fitness Centre. **Education:** University of Pretoria, M.B.Ch.B. (1970); University of South Africa, B.Sc. (1963); Mount Sinai Hospital; University Hospital of Wales; Pretoria University, Post Graduate Training in Anesthesia. **Personal:** Married to Maria Catharina in 1970. One child: Emile Theunis. Dr. Van Schalkwyk enjoys playing trumpet (cornet) in a brass band, collecting classical brass band recordings, gardening, building a varied library, automobiles, and fitness training.

William F. Vanaskie

President and Chief Executive Officer
Via Christi Regional Medical Center
929 North St. Francis Avenue
Wichita, KS 67214–3821
(316) 268–5106
Fax: (316) 291–7363

8062

Business Information: Via Christi Regional Medical Center, a result of a merger between St. Francis Regional Medical Center and CSJ Organization and part of Via Christi Health System, is a health care facility, licensed for a 1,500 bed capacity, providing diagnosis and treatment to patients. The Via Christi Health System owns three hospitals in Kansas, eight senior facilities, a home health care program, MRI, etc. Via Christie Health System is also a major owner in an HMO. Joining Via Christi Regional Medical Center as President in 1995, Mr. Vanaskie is responsible for overseeing all administrative and operational functions of the Center. Concurrent with his position at Via Christi Regional Medical Center, he serves as Executive Vice President of Via Christi Health System. Career milestones include being responsible for the creation of a physician organization within St. Frances Regional Medical Center. **Career Steps:** President, Via Christi Regional Medical Center (1995–Present); Executive Vice President, Via Christi Health System (1995–Present); Professor, West Point U.S. Military Academy; Adjunct Professor, Bucknell University. **Associations & Accomplishments:** Colonel, U.S. Army of Corps of Engineers (12 1/2 years). **Education:** Bucknell University, M.B.A. (1992); United States Military Academy; University of Colorado; Licensed Structural Engineer. **Personal:** Four children: Matthew, Christopher, Ann Marie, and Stephen. Mr. Vanaskie enjoys running.

Billie H. Vaughn
Regional Laboratory Operations Manager
Bon Secours – St. Mary's Hospital
5801 Bremo Road
Richmond, VA 23226–1907
(804) 287–7324
Fax: (804) 285–7419

8062

Business Information: Bon Secours – St. Mary's Hospital, a regional laboratory affiliated with the Central Virginia Health Network, is a full–service, hospital–based laboratory (core) servicing four rapid–response hospital labs, plus 150 physicians' office accounts and several nursing homes. As Regional Operations Manager for Bon Secours–Richmond System, Ms. Vaughn is responsible for the compliance of state and federal regulations for all lab operations, including providing the best for the least amount, meeting the needs of all strategic planning, ensuring that goals are being met, and overseeing the budget and other administrative functions. **Career Steps:** Regional Operations Manager, Bon Secours – St. Mary's Hospital (1995–Present); Lab Manager, Bon Secours – Stuart Circle Hospital (1987–1995); Supervisor B – Laboratory, Medical College of Virginia Hospital (1979–1987). **Associations & Accomplishments:** President, Central Virginia Chapter of Clinical Laboratory Management Association; Board of Directors, Alumni Association of the Medical College of Virginia (1990–1996). **Education:** Medical College of Virginia of Virginia Commonwealth University, B.S. (1977) **Personal:** Married to Larry in 1977. Two children: Sarah Ashley and Jennifer Lauren. Ms. Vaughn enjoys rock gardening, animals, and family activities.

Salvador Vazquez – Balaguer, M.D.
Assistant Manager of Legal Division
Hospital Interamericano Medicina Avanzada
P.O. Box 4980
Caguas, Puerto Rico 00726
(809) 743–3434
Fax: Please mail or call

8062

Business Information: Hospital Interamericano Medicina Avanzada is a community hospital serving the Caguas, Puerto Rico area. A practicing physician since 1977, Dr. Vazquez–Balaguer joined the hospital in 1993. Currently serving as Assistant Manager of the Legal Division since 1995, he serves as the legal advisor to the hospital legal counselor, assisting in the evaluation of medical malpractice claims, in addition to his daily patient practice. **Career Steps:** Hospital Interamericano Medicina Avanzada: Assistant Manager of Legal Division (1995–Present), Director of Quality Assurance (1993–1995); Medical Director, Health Plus Insurance Plan (1987–1992). **Associations & Accomplishments:** Phi Sigma Alpha Fraternity; Torrimar Basketball Association: Coach, Instructor; Boy Scout Movement; Organizer, Tennis Tournaments for professionals in the Medical Field. **Education:** Santiago De Compostela – Spain, M.D. (1977). **Personal:** Married to Magda Morell in 1967. Three children: Lourves Marie, William Manuel, and Eric Salvador. Dr. Vazquez – Balaguer enjoys basketball and tennis.

Carolyn J. Vizzard
Vice President
Jeanes Hospital
7600 Central Avenue
Philadelphia, PA 19111
(215) 728–2313
Fax: Please mail or call

8062

Business Information: Jeanes Hospital is an acute care hospital located in Philadelphia, Pennsylvania. The hospital has 220 beds and approximately 1,200 employees. As Vice President of Quality Management Services, Ms. Vizzard is responsible for quality management, utilization management, infection control, health information management, and social work. Included under Ms. Vizzard's oversight are pharmacy and medical staff services and employee and staff education. **Career Steps:** Jeanes Hospital: Vice President (1993–Present), Director Education /Quality Management (1980–1993); Assistant Professor, Thomas Jefferson University (1972–1980). **Associations & Accomplishments:** American Association for Healthcare Education and Training; Board of Directors, Community College of Philadelphia School of Nursing; National League of Nursing; SEPASHET; SPONE; DVEA. **Education:** Thomas Jefferson University, RN (1961). **Personal:** Married to Joseph in 1964. Two children: Joseph and Margaret Ann. Ms. Vizzard enjoys gardening.

Carol L. Wagner, M.D.
Attending Neonatologist
Medical University of South Carolina
171 Ashley Avenue
Charleston, SC 29425–0001
(803) 792–2112
Fax: (803) 792–8801
E–mail: see below

8062

Business Information: The Medical University of South Carolina is a full–service, multi–specialty medical facility and health service establishment, as well as an instructional institution. As Attending Neonatologist, Dr. Wagner is responsible for the care and treatment of newborn patients. Concurrent to her clinical position, Dr. Wagner is also an Assistant Professor, responsible for the instruction of medical students, residents and fellows in the Department of Pediatrics, Division of Neonatology, as well as clinical research in the areas of human milk growth factors. Dr. Wagner is a large promoter of breast–feeding. Dr. Wagner can also be reached through the Internet as follows: WagnerCL@MUSC.edu **Career Steps:** Attending Neonatologist and Assistant Professor, Medical University of South Carolina (1992–Present); Instructor, University of Rochester (1989–1992). **Associations & Accomplishments:** American Academy of Pediatrics, Perinatal Section; American Medical Women's Association; American Academy of Physicians for Breast–feeding Medicine; Massachusetts Medical Society; South Carolina Medical Society; International Society for Research on Human Milk and Lactation; William B. Bradford Award (1991). **Education:** Boston University, M.D. (1986); Brown University, A.B., magna cum laude, Phi Beta Kappa (1981).

Phillip Walker
Director of Environmental Services
Mississippi State Hospital
Whitfield, MS 39193
(601) 351–8000
Fax: Please mail or call

8062

Business Information: Mississippi State Hospital, part of the Mississippi Department of Mental Health, is a 2,000–bed mental health institute located in Whitfield, Mississippi. As Director of Environmental Services, Mr. Walker is responsible for all support services, including laundry, sewing, and staff housing. **Career Steps:** Director of Environmental Services, Mississippi State Hospital (1989–Present). **Education:** University of Mississippi: M.S. in Social Science, B.S. in Social Science.

Yvette L. Walker, M.D., M.P.H.
Director, AIDS Center
Catholic Medical Center
90 23 Vanderveer Street
Queens Village, NY 11428–1220
(718) 558–7291
Fax: (718) 558–6165

8062

Business Information: The Catholic Medical Center is a full–service, multi–specialty medical facility and health service establishment. A division of the hospital, the AIDS Center provides inpatient and outpatient services for HIV–positive individuals, as well as research in the areas of treatment and prevention of the AIDS disease. Established in 1994, the Hospital currently employs 60 physicians and medical support staff. As Director of the AIDS Center, Dr. Walker is responsible for the care and treatment of patients, administrative functions, and clinical reserach. **Career Steps:** Director, AIDS Center, Catholic Medical Center (1994–Present); Montefiore Medical Center: Director, Montefiore Rikers Island (1993–1994), Medical Director (1990–1993). **Associations & Accomplishments:** American College of Physicians; American College of Physician Executives; Board Member, New York City Health Association; American Public Health Association; New York City HIV Planning Council. **Education:** Columbia University, M.P.H. (1994); SUNY – Downstate Medical Center, M.D.; Syracuse University, B.S. **Personal:** Married. Dr. Walker enjoys reading Stephen King novels and working out at the gym.

James S. Ward, M.D.
Director of Clinical Services
Naval Hospital
6500 Navy Road
Millington, TN 38053–2789
(901) 873–7062
Fax: (901) 873–5928

8062

Business Information: Naval Hospital at Millington Air Station is a full–service, healthcare institution specializing in the diagnosis, treatment, and rehabilitation of military personnel and their dependents. As Director of Clinical Services, Dr. Ward serves as the intermediary between staff and hospital administration. He also provides direct patient care and supervises patient care programs. **Career Steps:** Naval Hospital: Director/Clinical Services – Millington, TN (1992–Present), Director/Medial Services – Pensacola, FL (1991–1992), Family Practice Residency Chairman – Pensacola, FL (1986–1991), Assistant Residency Chairman/Family Practice Dept – Charleston, SC (1983–1986). **Associations & Accomplishments:** American Medical Association; Uniform Services Chapter, American Academy of Family Physicians; Association of Military Surgeons of the United States; Taught on the Staff of Bowman Gray, Medical University of South Carolina, University of South Alabama, Mobile, and Uniformed Services University of Health, Lecturer at the University of Tennessee on Medical Ethics. **Education:** University of Rochester, M.D. (1970); Hamilton College – Clinton, NY, A.B. (1965); Highland Hospital, Rochester, NY, Residency in Family Practice (1973); American Board of Family Practice: Diplomate (1973–Present), Certificate of Added Qualification in Geriatric Medicine (1990–Present). **Personal:** Married to Linda Ann in 1968. Two children: Lynne Marie and Sarah Elizabeth. Dr. Ward enjoys camping, hiking, and auto and home repair.

Susan B. Ward, M.D.

Associate Director of the Jefferson Osteoporosis Center
Thomas Jefferson University Hospital
1015 Walnut Street, Room 613
Philadelphia, PA 19107
(215) 955–6942
Fax: (215) 923–7885

8062

Business Information: Thomas Jefferson University Hospital, affiliated with Jefferson Medical College, is a tertiary care teaching hospital and medical research institution. As Associate Director of the Jefferson Osteoporosis Center, Dr. Ward is responsible for direction of the Center, treating patients, consultations, and conducting clinical research in osteoporosis. Concurrent with her administrative and research at the Center, she serves as a practicing rheumatologist in a university setting with a large clinical practice and as Assistant Professor of Medicine at Jefferson Medical College. **Career Steps:** Associate Director of the Jefferson Osteoporosis Center, Thomas Jefferson University Hospital (1992–Present); Assistant Professor of Medicine, Jefferson Medical College (1992–Present). **Associations & Accomplishments:** American Medical Association; American College of Rheumatology; National Osteoporosis Foundation; Clinical Densitometry Association; Philadelphia Rheumatism Society; Author of articles and chapters in books; Lectures nationally. **Education:** Jefferson Medical College, M.D. (1985); Delaware Valley College, B.S. **Personal:** Dr. Ward enjoys tennis, golf, sailing, windsurfing, playing the guitar, and reading.

Earl Washington Jr., M.D.

Medical Director
Saint Berndan Rehabilitation
P.O. Box 4027
Lafayette, LA 70502–4027
(318) 289–2240
Fax: (318) 235–5450

8062

Business Information: Saint Berndan Rehabilitation is a 25–bed acute care unit within Our Lady of Lourdes Regional Medical Center. As Medical Director, Dr. Washington supervises the medical staff, performs various administrative functions, and reports to the Committee Director. Concurrently, he has maintained a private gastroenterology practice since 1987. **Career Steps:** Medical Director, Saint Berndan Rehabilitation (Present); Owner, The Office of Earl Washington, Jr., M.D. (1987–Present). **Associations & Accomplishments:** Published in "Newsweek," November 1995. **Education:** Tulane University, M.D. (1978); Dillard University, B.A. in Chemistry (1974). **Personal:** Married to Dianna Jane in 1975. One child: Joshua. Dr. Washington is a Lt. Colonel in the U.S. Army Reserve.

Marjorie A. Wasseen

Director Clinical Support Services
Sheltering Arms Hospital
1311 Palmyra Avenue
Richmond, VA 23227–4418
(804) 342–4194
Fax: Please mail or call

8062

Business Information: Established in 1887, Sheltering Arms Hospital is an acute care medical facility, specializing in the diagnosis, care, and treatment of patients. Serving Sheltering Arms as a dedicated nurse and administrator for the past ten years, Marjorie Wasseen was promoted to her current position in 1994. As Director of Clinical Support Services, she oversees all materials management and contract services for inpatient services. **Career Steps:** Sheltering Arms Hospital: Director Clinical Support Services (1994–Present), Nurse Manager (1990–1994), Head Nurse (1988–1990), Primary Nurse (1986–1988). **Associations & Accomplishments:** Association of Rehabilitation Nurses; Association of Nurse Executives; Farrington Fire Department Ladies Auxiliary. **Education:** York Hospital School of Nursing (1966); Certified Rehabilitation Nurse. **Personal:** Married to James A. in 1966. Three children: Melissa Anne, James Andrew II, and Julie Anne. Ms. Wasseen enjoys sketching the outdoors, needlework, and refinishing old furniture.

Kim D. Waters

Quality Improvement Analyst
Providence Medical Center
8929 Parallel Parkway
Kansas City, KS 66112
(913) 596–4640
Fax: Please mail or call

8062

Business Information: Providence Medical Center is a 400–bed, acute care medical facility providing pediatric, OB/GYN, and general health care to patients in the Kansas City area . As Quality Improvement Analyst, Mrs. Waters is responsible for reviewing medical records using set criteria to help ensure patients receive quality care. Established in 1920, Providence Medical Center employs 1,050 professionals, to include 300 physicians people. **Career Steps:** Quality Improvement Analyst, Providence Medical Center (1996–Present); Director of Medical Records, Charter Behavior Health Systems – Overland Park, KS (1994–1996); Data Collection Supervisor, Villa Christi Medical Center – Wichita, KS (1991–1993); Medical Review Coordinator, Missouri Patient Care Review Foundation – Jefferson City, MO (1990–1991). **Associations & Accomplishments:** American Health Information Management Association; American Health Information Management Association Professional Performance Committee (1993–1994). **Education:** University of Kansas, B.S. in Medical Record Administration (1990); Wichita State University, A.A. in Sociology. **Personal:** Married to Brian in 1993. One child: Kole Waters. Mrs. Waters enjoys crocheting, golf, bowling, and spending time with her family.

Dana Mark Weber, M.D.

Chairman, Department of Emergency Medicine
Lower Bucks Hospital
501 Bath Road
Bristol, PA 19007
(215) 785–9212
Fax: Please mail or call

8062

Business Information: Lower Bucks Hospital is a 350–licensed bed, acute care community hospital, serving Bucks County. A practicing physician since 1980 and a Board certified specialist in Emergency Medicine, Dr. Weber joined the Lower Bucks Hospital in 1988. Serving as Chairman of the Department of Emergency Medicine, he is responsible for the direction of all activities of the emergency room, in addition to his daily patient practice. His department serves approximately 34,000 patients yearly, with 5,000 patients admitted to the hospital. Concurrent with his hospital duties, he has been a Regional EMS Medical Director of Pennsylvania since 1991, serving Bucks County. He also serves as a Regional Medical Director for Coordinated Health Services, providing contracted services with physicians for Emergency Departments in the Middle Atlantic states area through a network of 35 hospitals and 200 physicians. **Career Steps:** Chairman, Department of Emergency Medicine, Lower Bucks Hospital (1988–Present); Assistant Director of Emergency Medicine, Mercy Catholic Medical Center (1986–1988); Director of Emergency Medical Services, Heritage Hospital (1983–1986). **Associations & Accomplishments:** American College of Emergency Physicians; National Association of Emergency Medical Service Physicians; Public Health Service (1983–1986). **Education:** Medical College of Pennsylvania, M.D. (1980); Villanova University, B.S. (1976); Emergency Medicine Residency, Medical College of Pennsylvania (1980–1983). **Personal:** Married to Pamela in 1982. Three children: Kara, Devin, and Kent. Dr. Weber enjoys sports, photography, wildlife, and spending time with family.

Nadine Weems

Administrator
Perry Hospital
1120 Morningside Drive
Perry, GA 31069–2906
(912) 987–3605
Fax: (912) 987–0012

8062

Business Information: Perry Hospital is a forty–five bed primary care facility providing medical and related services to the community. A county Facility, the Hospital is part of a larger organization and is affiliated with a sister hospital. As Administrator, Ms. Weems oversees all operations. Her duties include administration, operations, public relations, and strategic planning. She also serves as liaison for the hospital and Chief Executive Officer, manages the staff, and meets with the Board of Directors. **Career Steps:** Perry Hospital: Administrator (1994–Present), Business Office Manager (1977–1994), Assistant Administrator (1977–1994). **Associations & Accomplishments:** Kiwanis; Chamber of Commerce; Georgia Hospital Association; American Hospital Association. **Personal:** Married to Horace Eugene in 1993. Four children: Jo Anne, Beth, Hew, and Gale. Ms. Weems enjoys playing piano, art, fishing, travel, baseball, and football.

Jodene J. Weeter, LCSW

Coordinator – Post Traumatic Stress Disorder (PTSD) Clinic
Veterans Administration Medical Center
5500 East Kellogg
Wichita, KS 67218–1607
(316) 651–3677
Fax: (316) 651–3666

8062

Business Information: The Veterans Administration Medical Center is a Department of Wichita provides 125–beds for inpatient and outpatient services and health care services for American veterans. A Licensed Clinical Social Worker with twenty–eight years of experience, and a Certified Group Psycho–Therapist, Ms. Weeter joined the VA Medical Center as Coordinator of the Post Traumatic Stress Disorder (PTSD) Clinic in 1993. She is responsible for providing counseling to both veterans and their family members for PTSD, as well as helping to set up new programs. **Career Steps:** Coordinator – Post Traumatic Stress Disorder (PTSD) Clinic, Veterans Administration Medical Center (1992–Present); Director of Social Work Services, Hospice of St. John's, Lakewood, Colorado (1992–1993); Social Worker/Qualified Mental Retardation Professional (QMRP), State of Colorado (1986–1992);Social worker, Jefferson County, Colorado (1973–1986) **Associations & Accomplishments:** National Association of Social Work (NASW); National Episcopal AIDS Task Force – Witchita; Episcopal Church of America; Licensed Clinical Social Worker (LCSW); Certified Group Psycho–Therapist (CGPT). **Education:** Denver University, MSW (1982); Adams State University, B.A. in Social Anthropology & Psychology (1965). **Personal:** One child: Giles Scott Weeter. Ms. Weeter enjoys volunteering, reading, travel, bird watching, and church activities.

Barry M. Weinberger, D.O.

Physician and Director of Electrophysiology and Cardiology
Episcopal Hospital
1006 Lehigh Avenue, MAB #305
Philadelphia, PA 19125
(215) 427–7578
Fax: (215) 427–7258

8062

Business Information: Episcopal Hospital is a multi–specialty tertiary hospital, medical research and teaching institution. As Physician and Director of Electrophysiology and Cardiology, Dr. Weinberger is responsible for the care and treatment of patients (i.e., arrhythmia management, pacemaker and defibrillator insertion, patient follow–up), as well as clinical research and instructor and mentor to resident Fellows. **Career Steps:** Physician and Director of Electrophysiology and Cardiology, Episcopal Hospital (1994–Present); Associate Cardiologist, Central Ohio Cardiovascular Consultants (1993–1994). **Associations & Accomplishments:** American College of Cardiology; North American Society of Pacing and Electrophysiology; American College of Physicians. **Education:** New York College, D.O. (1985); New York University, B.A. **Personal:** Married to Sharon in 1980. Three children: Jason, Ariella and Aliza. Dr. Weinberger enjoys music, reading and planting.

Gary S. Weiner
Director of Management Information Systems
Windham Memorial Hospital
112 Mansfield Avenue
Willimantic, CT 06226
(203) 456–6728
Fax: (203) 456–6838

8062

Business Information: Windham Memorial Hospital is a 120–bed, acute care community hospital, employing 650 people, including 100 physicians. As Director of Management Information Systems, Mr. Weiner is responsible for directing information technology, data flow processes and computer systems. **Career Steps:** Director of Management Information Systems, Windham Community Memorial Hospital (1993–Present); Vice President, Penrich (1992–1993); Programmer Analyst, New Britain Hospital (1989–1991). **Associations & Accomplishments:** Vice Chairman, Central Connecticut Health Care Credit Union. **Education:** Central Connecticut State University, B.S. in Marketing (1985). **Personal:** Married to Judith in 1990. Two children: Jared and Daniel. Mr. Weiner enjoys spending time with his family, hiking, photography, skiing, and canoeing.

Gail Kuhn Weissman, EdD, RN, FAAN
Corporate Vice President for Patient Care & Chief Nurse Executive
The Massachusetts General Hospital
Bulfinch Building, Room 230–B, Fruit Street
Boston, MA 02114
(617) 726–3100
Fax: (617) 724–3486
EMAIL: See Below

8062

Business Information: The Massachusetts General Hospital (MGH) provides integrated delivery systems, primary care, and acute care services. Joining The Massachusetts General Hospital as Corporate Vice President for Patient Care and Chief Nurse Executive in 1994, Dr. Weissman provides executive management of the Department of Patient Care Services, which includes: nursing, physical therapy, occupational therapy, respiratory care, reading disabilities, orthotics & prosthetics and speech/language pathology, and patient care representatives. She also oversees corporate liaisons with McLean Hospital, Spaulding Rehabilitation Hospital, MGH/Spaulding Home Care, and the MGH Institute of Health Professions. Internet users can reach Dr. Weissman via: weissmang@a1.mgh.harvard.edu **Career Steps:** Corporate Vice President for Patient Care and Chief Nurse Executive, The Massachusetts General Hospital (1994–Present); Vice President for Nursing, The Mount Sinai Medical Center (1972–1994). **Associations & Accomplishments:** American Academy of Nursing; American Nurses Association; American Organization of Nurse Executives; National League for Nursing; New York State Nurses Association; Sigma Theta Tau; Co–Director, Massachusetts General Hospital/Timilty School Science Connection Program. **Education:** Columbia University – Teacher's College, Ed.D. (1988); Harvard College, Certificate in Program for Health Systems Management; Columbia University, M.S. in Nursing; Vanderbilt University, B.S. in Nursing. **Personal:** Dr. Weissman enjoys family, sports and fine art.

Jo Ellen Welborn, MS, RN, CS
Education Director
Palo Pinto General Hospital
400 South West 25th Avenue
Mineral Wells, TX 76067–9600
(817) 328–6254
Fax: (817) 325–9362

8062

Business Information: Palo Pinto General Hospital, a county–owned hospital, is the largest health care facility in Texas. As Education Director, Ms. Welborn is responsible for nursing and staff orientation, in–service programs, continuing education for employees, support groups, and public CPR/ First Aid courses. She interacts with all departments of the hospital and helps with the rural and home health care network. **Career Steps:** Education Director, Palo Pinto General Hospital (1993–Present); Nursing Faculty, East Central University (1990–1993); Nursing Manager – Surgical Unit, Valley View Hospital (1989–1990); Nursing Faculty, Baylor University – College of Nursing (1988–1989). **Associations & Accomplishments:** Business and Professional Women's Association; Texas Society of Healthcare Educators; Texas Nursing Association; American Nurses Association; Board Member, American Cancer Society; Board Member, American Heart Association; Sigma Theta Tau, National Honor Society; Varsity Member, St. Lukes Episcopal Church. **Education:** University of Oklahoma, M.S.N. (1982); East Central University, B.S.N. (1974); Attended, William Woods College.

Personal: Four children: Christopher, Michael, Nikolaus, and Stephen. Ms. Welborn enjoys quilting and gardening.

Alan M. Werner, M.D.
General Surgeon
Mercy Hospital of Pittsburgh
Locust Street
Pittsburgh, PA 15219
(412) 232–8112
Fax: Please mail or

8062

Business Information: Mercy Hospital of Pittsburgh is the world's first operating hospital of the Mercy Health System. Affiliated with the University of Pittsburgh, the 550–bed hospital has the only combined trauma and burn center in the Pittsburgh region A Resident Physician, Dr. Werner is a General Surgeon and plans to specialize in cardiothoracic surgery. **Career Steps:** General Surgery, Mercy Hospital of Pittsburgh (1991–1996). **Associations & Accomplishments:** Pennsylvania Medical Society; Allegheny County Medical Society; Candidate, American College of Surgeons; Who's Who in American Colleges and Universities; Hadassah Jewish Organization; Authored numerous publications and textbook chapters in General and Cardiothoracic Surgery. **Education:** University of Pittsburgh School of Medicine, M.D. (1991); Geneva College, B.S. in Chemistry (1987).

Linton A. Whitaker, M.D.
Professor and Chairman of Plastic Surgery
University of Pennsylvania Medical Center
10 Penn Tower, 3400 Spruce Street
Philadelphia, PA 19104
(215) 662–2048
Fax: (215) 349–5895

8062

Business Information: University of Pennsylvania Medical Center, the oldest medical teaching center in the country provides full scale medical services in a 1,100 bed facility. The Center has the largest children's medical complex in the world. In addition to his full–time plastic surgery practice, specializing in reconstructive and aesthetic plastic surgery of the face, Dr. Whitaker is the Chief of Plastic Surgery in the Children's Hospital in Philadelphia and Director of Research for the Center for Human Appearance. An internationally renowned expert on Cranial Facial Reconstruction, Dr. Whitaker has published numerous articles and written five books on the subject and his research work. He also currently teaches Residents at the University's medical school. **Career Steps:** Professor and Chairman of Plastic Surgery, University of Pennsylvania Medical Center (1975–Present); Partner, John Rhea Barton Surgical Associates (1975– Present); Partner, Children's Hospital of Philadelphia, Department of Surgery (1974–Present). **Associations & Accomplishments:** American Association of Plastic Surgeons; American Society of Plastic and Reconstructive Surgeons; American Society for Aesthetic Plastic Surgery; International Society of Plastic and Reconstructive Surgery; International Society of Craniofacial Surgery; American Surgical Association. **Education:** Tulane University, M.D. (1962); University of Texas–Austin, B.A. (1958); Dartmouth Affiliated Hospital, Resident in Plastic Surgery; University of Pennsylvania Medical Center, Resident in Plastic Surgery. **Personal:** Married to Renata G. in 1963. Two children: Ingrid Marlena and Brandon Andrew. Whitaker enjoys mountaineering, snow skiing, wine, renaissance art and antiques.

Ian W. White, M.D.
Head of the Section of Neuroanaesthesia
St. Boniface General Hospital
409 Tache Avenue
Winnepeg, Manitoba R2H 2A6
(204) 237–2580
Fax: (204) 231–0425
EMAIL: See Below

8062

Business Information: St. Boniface General Hospital is a full–service medical facility, primarily engaged in delivering tertiary medical and related services to area residents. As head of the Section of Neuroanaesthesia, Dr. White is responsible for providing quality comprehensive anaesthesia care to pateints. Internet users can reach him via: iwhite@pangea.ca. **Career Steps:** Associate Professor and Head Neuroanaesthesia, St. Boniface General Hospital (1982–Present); Clinical Fellow, Neuroanaesthesia and Intensive Care, University of Western Ontario (1981–1982); Staff, Groote Schuur Hospital, University of Cape Town, South Africa (1979–1981). **Associations & Accomplishments:** AFROX Gold Medal (1977); Co–chair, Provincial Physician Resource Committee, Manitoba (1995–1996); President, Canadian Anaesthetists' Society (1996–1997); President Elect, Manitoba Medical Association (1996–1997); Chair, Committee of Affiliated Societies, Canadian Medical Association. **Education:**

St. Thomas' Hospital, University of London, M.B.B.S. (1973); University of Cape Town, FCA (CMSA); University of Manitoba, FRCP. **Personal:** Married to Erica in 1974. Three children: Philippa, Catherine, and Alexander (Ziggy). Dr. White enjoys skiing, sailing, canoeing, backpacking, and wine making.

Patience H. White, M.D.
••• ▬▬◉▬ •••

Professor of Medicine and Pediatrics
George Washington University Medical Center
2150 Pennsylvania Avenue, NW
Washington, DC 20037–2396
(202) 994–4416
Fax: (202) 994–3949

8062

Business Information: George Washington University Medical Center is a full tertiary hospital, medical research and teaching institution — in affiliation with George Washington University. Board–Certified in Internal Medicine and Rheumatology, Dr. White serves as Professor of Medicine. She is responsible for the instruction of medical professionals in pediatric and adult rheumatology, as well as providing health care to patients. Dr. White also serves as Professor of Pediatrics and Director of Pediatric Rheumatology at Children's National Medical Center. She directs an internationally known program of Employment readiness for children with disabilities. **Career Steps:** Professor of Medicine, George Washington University Medical Center (1989–Present); Professor of Pediatrics, Children's National Medical Center (1990–Present); Executive Director of Adolescent Employment Medicine Center, Children's National Medical Center (1985–Present). **Associations & Accomplishments:** American College of Rheumatology; American Society of Adolescent Medicine; American Academy of Pediatrics; Business for Social Responsiblity; Recipient of awards for national and international work. She has been published in many journals, including The New England Journal of Medicine. **Education:** Harvard Medical School, M.D. (1974), Training in Adult Rheumatology (1976–1978), Training in Pediatric Rheumatology (1980–1981); Board Certified in Internal Medicine (1978); Board Certified in Rheumatology (1982). **Personal:** Dr. White enjoys growing orchids, riding, sailing, spending time with her family (her husband and two children).

M. Christo Wiggins
General Surgeon
Prince Rupert Regional Hospital
1305 Summit Avenue
Prince Rupert, British Co V8J 2A6
(604) 624–0299
Fax: (604) 624–0291
EMAIL: cwiggins@citytel.

8062

Business Information: Prince Rupert Regional Hospital serves the needs of the residents of Prince Rupert, British Columbia. The Hospital is an acute and subacute care facility. As General Surgeon, Dr. Wiggins is a member of the surgical staff at Prince Rupert Regional Hospital. He performs general surgery and does follow up consultations with patients. Dr. Wiggins worked as a General Surgeon in South Africa from 1988 through 1993. **Career Steps:** General Surgeon, Prince Rupert Regional Hospital (1993–Present); General Surgeon, South Africa (1988–1993). **Associations & Accomplishments:** B.C.M.A.; M.A.S.A. **Education:** University of Cape Town, F.C.S.(S.A.) (1993); University of Stellnbosch, M. Family Medicine (1989); University of Pretoria, M.B.Ch.B. (1979). **Personal:** Married to Sonja in 1978. Two children: Henry and Alexis. Dr. Wiggins enjoys golf, squash, and jogging.

Mary B. Williams
Clinical Coordinator
Aiken Regional Medical Center
1007 Edisto Avenue
Aiken, SC 29801–3005
(803) 641–5100
Fax: (803) 641–5080

8062

Business Information: Aiken Regional Medical Center is a full–service healthcare institute specializing in the diagnosis, treatment, and rehabilitation of patients. As Clinical Coordinator, Ms. Williams is responsible for all aspects of the Emergency Department operations, including administration and strategic planning. **Career Steps:** Aiken Regional Medical Center: Clinical Coordinator (1993–Present), Staff Nurse – Emergency Department (1992–1993), Charge Nurse (1991–1992). **Associations & Accomplishments:** American Nurses Association; Emergency Nurses Association. **Education:** University of South Carolina – Aiken: B.S.N. (1992), A.D.N. (1981). **Personal:** Married to Robert W. in

1971. Three children: Autumn, Rachel, and Winter. Ms. Williams enjoys sewing, needle crafts, and reading.

Charles Edward Wilson

Director of Medical Records
Wellington Regional Medical Center
10101 Forest Hill Boulevard
West Palm Beach, FL 33414–6103
(407) 798–8510
Fax: (407) 798–8578

8062

Business Information: Wellington Regional Medical Center is an acute care hospital, providing diagnosis and treatment to patients in the West Palm Beach locale. As Director of Medical Records, Mr. Wilson supervises and maintains the Medical Records Department, providing health information management and research information. **Career Steps:** Director of Medical Records, Wellington Regional Medical Center (1995–Present); Director of Medical Records, Fawcett Memorial Hospital (1991–1995); Director of Medical Records, Holy Cross Hospital (1976–1991). **Associations & Accomplishments:** American Health Information Management Association; Florida Health Information Management Association; Palm Beach Health Information Management Association; American Association for Advancement of Science. **Education:** Nova University, M.S. in Health Care Administration (1981); Oklahoma State University, B.S. in Zoology (1966); University of Tulsa, B.S. in Medical Records Administration (1976). **Personal:** Married to Susan in 1983. Two children: James E. and Charles E. Jr. Mr. Wilson enjoys amateur radio and golf.

CPT David W. Wilson

Chief of Operations & Staff Development
United States Army Medical Department Activity – Fort George G. Meade
2690–D Buckner Avenue
Ft. Meade, MD 20755–2106
(301) 677–8608 (301) 677–8453
Fax: (301) 677–8980
EMAIL: See Below

8062

Business Information: USA MEDDAC – Fort George G. Meade is a full–service community hospital serving military personnel and their families. Established in 1961, the hospital has 86 beds and specializes in same day surgery. As Chief of Operations and Staff Development, Mr. Wilson is responsible for nursing education issues, training, security, and disaster planning. Internet users can reach him via: WILSON_CPT_DAVID@SMTPLINK.MEADE–AMEDD.ARMY.MIL. **Career Steps:** Chief of Operations and Staff Development, USA MEDDAC, Fort George G. Meade (1995–Present); Medical Plans and Operations Officer, 3rd Infantry Division, Germany (1993–1994); Company Commander, Main Support Medical Company (1992–1993); Logistics, Forward Support Battalion, Fort Stewart, Georgia (1990–1991). **Associations & Accomplishments:** Who's Who Among Students in American Junior Colleges. **Education:** Fairmont State College, B.A. in Education (1987); Army Medical Department Officer Courses, Basic (1987), Advanced (1991). **Personal:** Married to Diane in 1984. Two children: Jennifer and Christopher. David enjoys hunting and particularly activities involving his family.

William L. Winters Jr., M.D.

Deputy Chief of Medicine and Director of Clinical Cardiology
Baylor College of Medicine
6550 Fannin, Suite 1025
Houston, TX 77030
(713) 798–8770
Fax: (713) 798–8744

8062

Business Information: The Baylor College of Medicine provides all aspects of post–graduate education to residents and interns, as well as full tertiary care and clinical research hospital facilities. As Deputy Chief of Medicine, Dr. Winters is responsible for the care and treatment of patients, the instruction of medical students, and clinical research. Board Certified in Cardiovascular Diseases and Internal Medicine, Dr. Winters has had many professional appointments including those to Temple University School of Medicine, Baylor College of Medicine, Methodist Hospital, Hermann Hospital, St. Luke's Episcopal Hospital, San Jacinto Methodist Hospital and the Diagnostic Center Hospital. **Career Steps:** Deputy Chief of Medicine, Baylor College of Medicine (1995–Present); President, Houston Cardiovascular Associates (1968–1994); President, American College of Cardiology (1990–1991). **Associations & Accomplishments:** American Association for the Advancement of Sciences; American College of Cardiology; American College of Physicians; American Federation for Clinical Research; American Heart Association; American Heart Association, Southeastern Pennsylvania Chapter; American Institute of Ultrasound in Medicine; American Medical Association; American Society of Echocardiography; Cardionics, Inc.; Doctor's Club, Houston; New York Academy of Sciences; Pennsylvania Medical Society; Philadelphia County Medical society; The Royal Society of Medicine; Sigma Xi, Temple University Medical Center Branch; Texas Medical Association; Museum of Health and Medical Sciences, Houston; Alpha Omega Alpha; Pi Kappa Epsilon; Paul V. Lodbottor Award, American Heart Association (1987), Paul D. White Award; American Heart Association (1984); Honorary Chairman, American Heart Association Heart Ball (1987); Numerous publications and abstracts. **Education:** Princeton University (1946–1949); Northwestern University Medical School: M.D. (1953), B.S. (1950); Temple University, M.A. in Science (1967); Intern, Philadelphia General Hospital (1953–1954); Residency in Internal Medicine, Temple University Hospital (1954–1957). **Personal:** Married to Barbara in 1953. Three children: Christopher, William and Scott. Dr. Winters enjoys tennis, fly fishing and hunting.

Paul R. Wolfgang

Senior Software Specialist
Mount Sinai Medical Center
210–50 41st Avenue, Apt. 6H
Bayside, NY 11361–1917
(212) 824–7252
Fax: (212) 876–3476
EMAIL: See Below

8062

Business Information: Mount Sinai Medical Center is a full service acute care facility comprised of 1,100 beds and employing 13,000 people. As Senior Software Specialist, Mr. Wolfgang is directly involved with systems design and development, interacts with user departments, and assists in training. Internet users can reach him via: Paul_Wolfgang@smtplink.mssm.edu. **Career Steps:** Senior Software Specialist, Mount Sinai Medical Center (1996–Present); Senior Systems Analyst, Interfaith Medical Center (1994–1996); Training Manager, Columbia–Presbyterian Medical Center (1990–1994). **Associations & Accomplishments:** Healthcare Financial Management Association; Healthcare Information Management and Systems Society. **Education:** New York University Graduate School of Public Administration, M.P.A. (1982); Herbert H. Lehman College of the City University of New York, B.A. (1979). **Personal:** Married to Naomi in 1995. One child: Ezra. Mr. Wolfgang enjoys surfing the Internet and spending time doing things with his family.

Teresa Ann Wollo

Director of Respiratory Therapy
Bartlett Memorial Medical Center
P.O. Box 1368
Sapulpa, OK 74067–1368
(918) 224–4280
Fax: (918) 224–6290

8062

Business Information: The Bartlett Memorial Medical Center is a 120–bed tertitary care facility. Established in 1957, the Medical Center currently employs 250 physicians and medical suport staff. As Director of Respiratory Therapy and a Certified Therapist, Mrs. Wollo oversees the Department and is responsible for the care and treatment of respiratory patients. The Department is staffed with seven employees and treats children and adults. The Respiratory Therapy Department is equipped to see over 20 patients a week. In addition to her management position at the Medical Center, Mrs. Wollo also provides home health care services. She plans to return to school to become a registered respiratory therapist and a Pulmonary Physicians Assistant. She spends a lot of her time involved in community education programs and political speaking engagements answering health care and medical reform questions. **Career Steps:** Director of Respiratory Therapy, Bartlett Memorial Medical Center (1987–Present); Home Care Therapist, Fields Respiratory Services (1989–Present); Respiratory Therapy Technician, St. Francis Hospital (1986–1987). **Associations & Accomplishments:** National Board for Respiratory Care. **Education:** South West Virginia Community College, Respiratory Therapy Program (1980); Certified by the National Board for Respiratory Care (1985). **Personal:** Married to Ralph K. in 1995. Three children: Corey, Carrie and Christopher. Mrs. Wollo enjoys listening to music, reading, and dancing.

Dr. Andrew L. Wong

Pediatric General Surgeon
Alberta Children's General Hospital
1820 Richmond Road, South West
Calgary, Alberta T2T 5C7
(403) 229–7253
Fax: (403) 228–9453
EMAIL: See Below

8062

Business Information: Alberta Children's General Hospital is a 143–bed hospital. The hospital specializes in the surgical and non–surgical care of children in and around Alberta. As Director of Pediatric General Surgery, Dr. Wong performs minimal access and Surgical Oncology surgery on children. He also has a private practice with two area physicians. Internet users can reach him via: Wong@acs.ucalgary.ca. **Career Steps:** Director of Pediatric General Surgery, Alberta Children's General Hospital (1994–Present); Clinical Assistant Professor, University of Calgary (1994); President, Calgary Medical Society. **Associations & Accomplishments:** Canadian Association of Pediatric Surgeons; British Association of Pediatric Surgeons; Canadian Association of General Surgeons; Royal College of Physicians and Surgeons of Glasgow; Royal College of Physicians and Surgeons of Canada; Canadian Medical Association; Alberta Medical Association; Alberta Association of General Surgeons; Calgary Society of Surgeons; Calgary Medical Society; Pediatric Oncology Group. **Education:** University of Glasgow: M.B., Ch.B (1971), F.R.C.S. (1978), M.Sc. (1981); F.R.C.S., Canada (1986); Certification of Special Competence in Pediatric Surgery, Canada (1988). **Personal:** Married to Maureen in 1972. Four children: Jonathan, Rachael, Rebecca, and Sarah.

Dr. Peter C. Wozniak

Medical Doctor
CAMBRIDGE FAMILY MEDICAL CENTRE
101B Holiday Inn Drive
Cambridge, Ontario N3C 1Z3
(519) 654–2260
Fax: (519) 654–2231

8062

Business Information: Cambridge Family Medical Centre is a full–service general family practice health care facility, providing diagnosis, treatment, psychotherapy and family therapy. Concurrently, Dr. Wozniak is also a licenced Veterinarian. **Career Steps:** Certified in the College of Family Physicians (1990); Chief Resident–Family Practice, St. Joseph's Hospital (1989–90); Medical Doctor, University of Ottawa (magna cum laude–1988); Doctor of Veterinary Medicine, University of Guelph (honours with distinction–1983). **Associations & Accomplishments:** Certified College of Family Physicians; Ontario Medical Association; College of Physicians and Surgeons of Ontario; Ontario Veterinary Medical Association; Hospital Affiliations; Cambridge Memorial Hospital; St. Joseph's Hospital; Guelph General Hospital; Gold Medalist; Merck Sharp Domme Award; Academic Excellence; Miles–Ames Award, Medical Biochemistry; CWMA Award for Academic Standing; McArthur Humphries Scholarship; Internal Medicine Medal; Excellence in Internal Medicine; Community Medicine Award; First Class Standing (1985–1988); University of Ottawa Scholarship (1985–1987); Lang Award (1985–1988); Upjohn Award: L. Belager Award; Park Davis Award; University of Ottawa Gold Medal for Highest Standing; Jean–Jacques Lussier Gold Metal for Highest Standing throughout Medical Training; Dr. Arthur Richard Award; Sandoz Prize for Highest Standing in Clinical Medicine; Association Del Medecine De Langue Francaise Du Canada Award; Lange Book Award; Rhone–Poulenc Pharma Inc. Award; Upjohn Placque Medal for Highest Standing; Obstetrics and Gynecology Award; Owner of Cambridge Family Medical Centre; Author, Cadmium Toxicity; Research Grant, Ontario Ministry of Agriculture & Food; National Research Council Fellowship (1979–1981); Ivan Smith Fellowship (med. & radiation oncology) (1985); Ottawa Faculty of Medicine Fellowship in Pathology (1986); Presentations–International Conference Laboratory Research, Immune Therapy for Feline Leukemia, Hyperlipidemia and Hypertension, etc. **Education:** University of Western Ontario, CCFP (1990); University of Ottawa, M.D. (magna cum laude–1988); University of Guelph, Onatrio: DVM (1983–honours with distinction). **Personal:** Married to Kimberly in 1985. Three children: Nicole, Jason, and Lucas. Dr. Wozniak enjoys the investigation and treatment of infertility, oncology and cutting edge technology. Dr. Wozniak practices both Human and Veterinary Medicine and treats all living, non–botanical patients without restrictions. Dr. Wozniak's current interests lie in computer technological innovations in the treatment in learning disabilities.

Laban Joseph Wright
Administrator
Limestone Medical Center
900 North Ellis Street
Groesbeck, TX 76642
(817) 729-3281
Fax: (817) 729-3080

8062

Business Information: Limestone Medical Center is a 38–bed, primary care rural medical facility. With thirteen years in hospital administration, Mr. Wright joined Limestone Medical Center as Administrator in 1994. He is responsible for all aspects of operations, including guiding the delivery of health services to the rural Texas community. In addition, he oversees all administrative operations for associates and a support staff of 102. **Career Steps:** Administrator, Limestone Medical Center (1994–Present); Chief Financial Officer, Burleson Memorial Hospital (1991–1994); Administrator, Parkside Medical Services (1986–1991). **Associations & Accomplishments:** Texas Hospital Association; Texas Organization of Rural and Community Hospitals; Lions Club; Director, Groesbeck Chamber of Commerce; First United Methodist Church: Volunteer, Youth Leader. **Education:** Webster University, M.A. in HSRV Management (1983); George Washington University, B.S. in HC Administration (1978). **Personal:** Married to Elizabeth in 1990. Two children: Laban Joseph Jr. and Tiffany Lynn. Two stepsons: Nicky and Joshua Briggs. Mr. Wright enjoys collecting antiques and reading.

LaVerne Wright
Patient Accounts Director
Greenville Memorial Hospital
214 Weaver Avenue
Emporia, VA 23847
(804) 348-2095
Fax: (804) 348-2158

8062

Business Information: Greenville Memorial Hospital is a small, community, acute care medical facility, providing health and related services to area residents. Established in 1969, the Hospital is comprised of 117 beds, and employs 370 people. As Patient Accounts Director, Ms. Wright oversees all monetary functions of the Hospital, and is responsible for patient registration, managing the business office, and handling all collections, including insurance billings. **Career Steps:** Manager, Finance Department, Greenville Memorial Hospital (1980–Present). **Associations & Accomplishments:** American Guild of Patient Accounts Managers; National Association of Hospital Admissions Managers; Healthcare Financial Managers Association; National Association of Female Executives; Trustee for local library; Medical Community Federal Credit Union. **Education:** Southside Virginia Community College. **Personal:** One child: Clifton. Ms. Wright enjoys reading, travel, and volunteer youth work.

Clifford A. Yeager
Chief Executive Officer
Twin Rivers Regional Medical Center
1301 1st Street
Kennett, MO 638577525
(573) 888-8420
Fax: (573) 888-5525

8062

Business Information: Twin Rivers Regional Medical Center is a 650–bed comprehensive medical center, providing diagnosis and treatment of patients. With a medical background in nursing, Mr. Yeager serves as Chief Executive Officer, responsible for all aspects of operations, including administration, strategic planning, and ensuring the quality of the services provided. **Career Steps:** Chief Executive Officer, Twin Rivers Regional Medical Center (1994–Present); Chief Operating Officer, Columbia Regional Medical Center (1993–1994); Chief Operating Officer, Lucy Lee Hospital (1987–1993). **Education:** Southern Illinois University: M.B.A. (1988), B.S. in Nursing (1979). **Personal:** Married to Cheryl D. in 1979. Two children: Jason and Christopher. Mr. Yeager enjoys golf and woodworking.

Mr. Yun Yen
Physician and Assistant Professor
City of Hope, National Medical Center
369 West Norman Avenue
Arcadia, CA 91007–8042
(818) 359–8111
Fax: (818) 574–9751

8062

Business Information: City of Hope, National Medical Center is a full–service, tertiary hospital with an oncology research laboratory. As Physician and Assistant Professor, Mr. Yen is responsible for providing health care to patients, as well as patient management, conducting basic research and clinical teaching. He is also involved in Drug Resistance Chemotherapy Resistance in cancer patients (trying to define the mechanism for this resistance) and the development of new cancer drugs. Concurrent with his position, he serves as a volunteer physician at his local community free clinic, seeing cancer patients who do not have the means to get appropriate care. **Career Steps:** Physician and Assistant Professor, City of Hope, National Medical Center (1993–Present); Physician, Yale University (1990–1993); Physician, Temple University (1987–1990). **Associations & Accomplishments:** American Medical Association; American Association of Cancer Research; American College of Physicians; American Society of Clinical Oncology; American Society of Bone Marrow Transplantation; Sigma Xi Association; Numerous publications in cancer research and oncology. **Education:** Thomas Jefferson University, Ph.D. in Cellular Biology (1988); Taipei Medical Oncology, M.D. **Personal:** Married to Sophie Yen in 1986. Two children: Alexandria and Christina. Mr. Yen enjoys volunteering and playing the piano.

Linda Marie Young
Director of Health Information Systems
Saints Memorial Medical Center
1 Hospital Drive
Lowell, MA 01852
(508) 934–8254
Fax: (508) 934–8205
EMail: See Below

8062

Business Information: Saints Memorial Medical Center is a 227–bed healthcare facility specializing in the diagnosis, treatment, and rehabilitation of patients (acute care facility). As Director of Health Information Systems, Mrs. Young is responsible for diversified administrative activities, including improving the quality of patient care. Internet users can reach him via: Tyoung@tiac.net. **Career Steps:** Saints Memorial Medical Center: Director of Health Information Systems (1994–Present), Manager of Clinical Data (1993–1994), Senior Analyst – Patient Care (1993). **Associations & Accomplishments:** American Health Information Management Association. **Education:** Attending, Northwestern University, Health Information Program (expected graduation June 1996); Worcester State College, B.S. in Computer Science. **Personal:** Married to Timothy in 1991. Two children: Danae Lindsey and Joshua Robert. Mrs. Young enjoys spending time with her family, hiking, surfing the Internet, and skiing.

Andrew W. Yung
Director of Medical Records
Lawrence Memorial Hospital
Lawrence, KS 66044
(913) 749–6353
Fax: (913) 749–0983

8062

Business Information: Lawrence Memorial Hospital is a full service medical facility. Comprised of 149 beds, the Hospital offers skilled nursing and outpatient services. As Director of Medical Records, Mr. Yung plans, directs, and organizes the overall functions of the patient record system. Utilizing paper file methods at present, he hopes to implement an electronic file environment in the near future. **Career Steps:** Lawrence Memorial Hospital: Director of Medical Records (1995–Present), Assistant Director Medical Records (1992–1995); Healthcare Planning Consultant, Kansas Department of Health and Environment (1994). **Associations & Accomplishments:** Kansas Health Information Management Association; American Health Information Management Association. **Education:** University of Kansas: M.A. (1987), B.S. (1985). **Personal:** Married to Judy in 1984. Three children: Steven, Daniel, and Amy. Mr. Yung enjoys bicycling, photography, car care, and going to church.

Maratha L. Zachary
Personnel Director
Mangum City Hospital
1 Wickersham Drive
Mangum, OK 73554
(405) 782–3353
Fax: (405) 782–5944

8662

Business Information: Mangum City Hospital is a local hospital with 40 beds, 6 resident physicians, and approximately 80 employees. The hospital is located in Mangum, Oklahoma and services approximately 3,500 people. As Personnel Director, Ms. Zachary is responsible for all personnel and payroll issues, and public relations. Due to the size of the hospital, Ms. Zachary wears many different hats and performs a variety of duties not associated with her position. **Career Steps:** Personnel Director, Mangum City Hospital (1993–Present); Bookkeeper, David O. Tate, CPA (1991–1993); Office Manager, OU Health Sciences Center (1987–1992). **Associations & Accomplishments:** Epsilon Sigma Alpha; Future Farmers of America. **Personal:** Three children: Rod, Scout and Zack. Ms. Zachary enjoys watching her children participate in sports.

Noe Zamel, M.D.
Physician
Mount Sinai Hospital
600 University Avenue, Room 656
Toronto, Ontario M5G 1X5
(416) 586–4473
Fax: (416) 586–8558
EMAIL: noe@io.org

8062

Business Information: Mount Sinai Hospital, affiliated with the University of Toronto, Canada, is a full–service, tertiary teaching hospital, providing healthcare to patients and instruction to medical students. A practicing physician since 1958, Dr. Zamel joined Mount Sinai Hospital in 1972. Currently serving as Physician, his practice concentrates on the treatment of patients suffering from lung disease and asthma. Concurrently, he is a Professor of Medicine at the University of Toronto. **Career Steps:** Physician, Mount Sinai Hospital (1972–Present); Professor of Medicine, University of Toronto (1972–Present); Professor, University of Nebraska (1970–1972). **Associations & Accomplishments:** American Thoracic Society; European Respiratory Society; American College of Chest Physicians; Canadian Thoracic Society; American Physiologic Society. **Education:** University of Rio Grande do Sul, Brazil: M.D., Faculty of Medicine (1958). **Personal:** Married to Regina in 1959. Three children: Denis, Andre, and Ricardo. Dr. Zamel enjoys travel.

Maria Znamirowski, PHR, CCP
Human Resources Director
Richland Memorial Hospital
5 Medical Park Drive
Columbia, SC 29203
(803) 434–2587
Fax: (803) 434–3945

8062

Business Information: Richland Memorial Hospital is a 649–bed, full–service, healthcare institution specializing in the diagnosis, treatment, and rehabilitation of patients. The Hospital serves as a teaching facility affiliated with the University of South Carolina, and its Cancer Center, Women & Children services and a psychiatric hospital serves as its centers of excellence. As Human Resources Director, Ms. Znamirowski is responsible for all aspects of human resources and education for the hospital. **Career Steps:** Richland Memorial Hospital: Human Resources Director (1992–Present), Assistant Director/Human Resources, Personnel Analyst, Personnel Specialist (1986–1992). **Associations & Accomplishments:** South Carolina Healthcare Human Resources Association; American Hospital Association; Certified PHR, Society for Human Resource Management; Certified CCP, American Compensation Association. **Education:** Webster University, M.A. (1995); Bowling Green State University, B.S. in Business Administration. **Personal:** Married to Skip in 1977. One child: Katie. Ms. Znamirowski enjoys reading, water skiing, going to the movies, and boating.

Gary N. Zook
Vice President of Rehabilitation Services
Southwest Medical Center, Oklahoma Health System
4401 Southwestern
Oklahoma City, OK 73109
(405) 636–7670
Fax: (405) 636–7702

8062

Business Information: Southwest Medical Center, in affiliation with the Oklahoma Health System is a major tertiary care, research and teaching hospital. OHS is the managerial arm for major medical facility units, currently consisting of: Jim Thorpe Rehabilitation Hospital, Southwest Medical Center, and Baptist Medical Center. As Vice President of Rehabilitation Services for Oklahoma Health System, Mr. Zook is responsible for the efficient and effective operations of five units and full integration of the program into the OHS, local community, state, and regional market, the development of marketing plans based on the analysis of community needs and referral potential; the state peer review organization criteria and implications for patient admission; working closely with rehabilitation teams and medical directors to implement cost effective treatment strategies; allocating staffing resources; implementing all clinical, administrative, and personnel policies and procedures. The Units supervised consist of: The Jim Thorpe Rehabilitation Hospital, Jim Thorpe Comprehensive Outpatient Center at Southwest Medical Center and Baptist Medical Center, Hand Rehabilitation Center at Baptist Medical Center; Occupational Health Center; and Meridian–Priority Care Industrial Medicine Clinics at Southwest Medical Center and Baptist Medical Center. **Career Steps:** Vice President of Rehabilitation Services, Southwest Medical Center, Oklahoma Health System (1988–Present); Administrator, Radiology Associates (1986–1988); Assistant Executive Director, Kansas Foundation for Medical Care, Inc. (1982–1986); Chief Lobbyist and Division Director, Kansas Association of Commerce and Industry (1972–1982). **Associations & Accomplishments:** Former Member: Consumer Credit Commission of the State of Kansas, American Society of Association Executives; American Psychiatric Association; Kiwanis Club of Oklahoma City; National Association of Rehabilitation Professionals; American Hospital Association. **Education:** Washburn University, B.A. in Music; Indiana University, M.B.A.; American Society of Association Executives, Certified Association Executive; Oklahoma University, Masters in Education and Community Counseling. **Personal:** Married to Janey in 1956. Two children: Lynda and Benjamin.

David S. Zorub, M.D.
Chairman, Department of Surgery
Shadyside Hospital
5230 Centre Avenue
Pittsburgh, PA 15232–1304
(412) 623–2211
Fax: (412) 623–2754

8062

Business Information: Shadyside Hospital is a 474–bed, acute care hospital with primary and specialty care units. The regional center for Cardio Neuro Orthopedics, and serving the areas in and around Pittsburgh,PA, Shadyside has the largest volume of cardiac surgeries in the region. Also containing a modern and intensive Neuro Surgery Department, the hospital has approximately 180 surgeons on staff who perform 13,000 surgeries a year and produce 20% of the $400 million budget. Having a cost effective care plan with managed care, Shadyside expects to maintain a positively–managed institution, with excellant care over patients. Board–Certified in Neurological Surgery and practicing physician since 1970, as Chairman of the Department of Surgery, Dr. David Zorub oversees all surgical patient care practices and staff surgery associates. He also provides instruction and mentoring to residents, as well as continuing clinical education to staff physicians and surgery support staff. Concurrent with his administrative and surgery practices, Dr. Zorub continues with his clinical research studies. Past and current studies have included: Computerized stereotactic surgery procedures, Gonadotrophic secretion mechanisms, Hypothalmic roles in cerebral vasospasm, FSH hormonal studies, and Pituitary studies. **Career Steps:** Shadyside Hospital: Chairman, Department of Surgery (1993–Present), Director, Surgical Administrqative Services (1993–Present), Staff Physician/ Surgeon (1979–Present), Chief, Division of Neurological Surgery (1979–Present); University of Pittsburgh School of Medicine: Clinical Assistant Professor – Department of Neurological Surgery (1979–Present), Director of Neurosurgery – Intensive Care Unit (1976–1979), Assistant Professor (1976–1979), Faculty Cooirdinator of Undergraduate Teaching (1976–1979), Acting Chief – Presbyterian Hospital (1978–1979); Director, University Health Center of Pittsburgyh – Stereotactgic and Functional Neurosurgery (1978–1979); HOSPITAL AFFILIATIONS: Presbyterian–University Hospital, Department of Neurosurgery; Children's Hospital of Pittsburgh – Dept. of Neurosurgery; Montefiore Hospital – Dept. of Neurosurgery; Shadyside Hospital – Dept. of Surgery; South Hills Health System / Jefferson Hospital; Allegheny General Hospital; Braddock General Hospital; McKeesport Hospital; Forbves Health System; Greater Pittsburgh Rehabilitation; South Side Hospital; St. Francis Hospital; MILITARY: Reserve Officer, U.S. Air Force (1978). **Associations & Accomplishments:** Diplomate, American Board of Neurological Surgery; American College of Surgeons; American Association of Neurological Surgeons; International Association for the Study of Pain; Mid–Atlantic Neurosurgical Society; Pennsylvania Neurosurgical Society; Congress of Neurological Surgeons; Allegheny Medical Society; Pittsburgh Neuroscience Society; Sigma XI; Alpha Omega Alpha; Phi Beta Kappa; Eta Sigma Phi; Phi Eta Sigma; Frequent publisher and lecturer at international, national, state and local conferences and institutional symposia and proceedings in the following fields of expertise: Facial Disorders, Cultural Disorders, Pituitary Disorders, Neurosurgical technological procedures. **Education:** Tulane University

School of Medicine, M.D. cum laude (1970); Tulane University: M.S. in Anatomy (1970), B.A. summa cum laude in History (1966); Duke University, Specialty in Neurosurgical Procedures; INTERNSHIP: Duke University Medical Center in Surgery (1970–1971); RESIDENCY: Duke University Medical Center, Neurological Surgery (1971–1976) and Fellowship in Basic Neurosciences (1971–1974); Postdoctoral Fellowship, Institute of Physiology – University of Pisa, Italy (1974). **Personal:** Married to Carla in 1971. Three children: David, Grazia, and Alexander. Dr. Zorub enjoys hunting, fishing, travel and golf.

William Bernet, M.D.
Medical Director
The Psychiatric Hospital at Vanderbilt
1601 23rd Avenue South
Nashville, TN 37212–3133
(615) 327–7130
Fax: (615) 327–7114

8063

Business Information: The Psychiatric Hospital at Vanderbilt, jointly–owned by Vanderbilt University and Columbia/ HCA, is a full–service, freestanding, psychiatric hospital and teaching facility consisting of 88–beds, providing a full range of psychiatric services. As Medical Director, Dr. Bernet is responsible for supervising and organizing treatment, providing clinical treatment for patients, and conducting administrative functions. Concurrently, he directs Vanderbilt Forensic Psychiatry, a component of the Department of Psychiatry, Vanderbilt University Medical Center. **Career Steps:** Medical Director, The Psychiatric Hospital at Vanderbilt (1992–Present); Clinical Director of Outpatient Services, Charter Lakeside Hospital (1990–1992); Medical Director, The MidSouth Hospital (1988–1990); Director, Family Counseling Centers (1980–1988). **Associations & Accomplishments:** Fellow of American Psychiatric Association; Fellow of American Academy of Child and Adolescent Psychiatry; American Academy of Psychiatry and the Law; Author of "Children of Divorce" and co–author of "The Fragile Alliance." **Education:** Harvard Medical School, M.D. (1967); Holy Cross College, A.B. (1963). **Personal:** Married to Susan S. in 1978. Two children: Alice Caroline and Henry Gardner. Dr. Bernet enjoys spending time with his family, movies, and antiques.

Robert E. Cosgray
Director of Nursing
Logansport State Hospital
1098 South State Road 25
Logansport, IN 46947–6723
(219) 722–4141
Fax: (219) 735–3414
EMail: See Below

8063

Business Information: Logansport State Hospital is a 496–bed, state hospital providing long term psychiatric care. As Director of Nursing, Mr. Cosgray is responsible for setting standards, supervision of Nursing Department, and a large support staff. Internet users can reach him via: rcosgray@netusal.net. **Career Steps:** Director of Nursing, Logansport State Hospital (Present). **Associations & Accomplishments:** Indiana Association of Healthcare Quality: State Legislative Committee, State Credentialing Committee; Sigma Theta Tau International – Nu Omicron Chapter. **Education:** Ball State University: M.A. in Geronotology (1988), B.S. in Nursing (1978). **Personal:** Mr. Cosgray enjoys writing for publications.

Dana F. Echols (R.R.A.)
Director of Health Information Management and Quality Improvement
Charter Savannah B.H.S.
P O Box 13817
Savannah, GA 31416
(912) 692–4243
Fax: (912) 354–0352

8063

Business Information: Charter Savannah B.H.S. is a psychiatric and chemical dependency hospital serving the Savannah, Georgia area. As Director of Health Information Management and Quality Improvement, Ms. Echols is responsible for the administration and operation of the medical records department. Her department is in charge of making sure patient records are organized and accessible to the medical staff at the hospital. Ms. Echols works closely with other department heads in the development of a quality improvement program for the hospital. **Career Steps:** Director of Health Information Management and Quality Improvement, Charter Savannah B.H.S. (1994–Present); Health Information Analyst, Memorial Medical Center (1991–1994). **Associations & Accomplishments:** President Elect, Southeast Georgia Health Information Management Association. **Education:** Medical College of Georgia, B.S. in Health Information Management (1991).

Personal: Married to Barry in 1995. Ms. Echols enjoys reading, going to the beach, and spending time with her husband.

Emily C. Erickson, RRA
Director of Health Information Management
CPC College Meadows Hospital
14425 College Boulevard
Lenexa, KS 66215
(913) 469–1100 Ext. 203
Fax: (913) 469–4261
EMail: See Below

8063

Business Information: CPC College Meadows Hospital is a mental health and substance abuse treatment hospital for children and adults. The Center provides an outpatient program, inpatient residential program, and partial hospitalization program. With 106–beds, the Hospital services the Midwest. As Director of Health Information Management, Ms. Erickson is responsible for a large support staff, patient records, processing patient information, distribution of patient information to authorized personnel, and processing of records. Internet users can reach her via: Emily18@AOL.COM. **Career Steps:** Director of Health Information Management, CPC College Meadows Hospital (1996–Present); Area Service Manager, Smart Corporation (1995–1996). **Associations & Accomplishments:** American Health Information Management Association; Kansas Health Information Management Association; Kansas City Health Information Management Association; Alpha Sigma Tau Sorority Alumna. **Education:** St. Louis University, B.S. in Health Information Management (1995). **Personal:** Ms. Erickson enjoys church activities, sports, and being a member of Alpha Sigma Tau Sorority.

Bernice Fidelia–Morris, R.R.A.
Director of Medical Records
Health South Larkin Hospital
7031 S W 62nd Avenue
South Miami, FL 33143
(305) 284–7644 (305) 758–1906
Fax: (305) 284–7649

8063

Business Information: Health South Larkin Hospital is a full–service medical facility which specializes in psychiatrics. National in scope, the Hospital services people all over the United States and is affiliated with over 200 rehabilitation centers. As Director of Medical Records, Ms. Fidelia–Morris oversees all aspects of her Department. She is responsible for personnel management, budgeting, tumor registry, and direct supervision of a staff of eight. Acting as a liaison between the "Professional Regulator Organization", (which oversees quality of care), and the Hospital, Ms. Morris also handles the "Utilization Review Function", which reviews concurrent records of the Hospital to ascertain justification of resource allocation. She is also fluent in Spanish and French. **Career Steps:** Director of Medical Records, Health South Larkin Hospital (1993–Present); Director, Medical Records Department, Little Neck Community Hospital, New York (1992); Associate Director, Medical Records, Long Island College Hospital, New York (1991); Patient Care Evaluation Coordinator of Quality Assurance, Kingsbrook Jewish Medical Center, New York (1989); Utilization Review/DRG Coordinator/Assist. Director, Medical Record, Larkin Hospital (1988). **Associations & Accomplishments:** South Florida Hospital Association; South Florida Health Information Management Association; American Health Information Management Association. **Education:** Downstate Medical Center in New York: B.S., R.R.A. (1987); Brooklyn College. **Personal:** Married to Jolyon W. in 1987. Two children: Trendt Dexile and Rashad Emile. Ms. Fidelia–Morris enjoys tennis, strength training, gardening, and reading.

M. Kathryn Fiero
Director of Information Services
Wichita Falls State Hospital
P.O. Box 300/6515 Lake Road
Wichita Falls, TX 76307–0300
(817) 689–5510
Fax: (817) 689–5737
EMAIL: See Below

8063

Business Information: Wichita Falls State Hospital is a specialized psychiatric hospital providing diagnosis and treatment of patients with psychiatric disorders. Established in 1909, Wichita Falls State Hospital currently employs 1,250 people. As Director of Information Services, Ms. Fiero is responsible for all aspects of computer operations and information services. While a programmer analyst with PPG Industries, she designed and wrote the Company's data interchange system; resulting in its patent and national market distribution. Concurrent with her position as Director of Information Services, she serves as Vice President of Systems at Insurance Filing Service, Inc. and is the owner of a ranch where she raises ostriches and horses. She can also be reached through the Internet via: Katie.fiero@mhmr.state.tx.us **Career Steps:** Director of Information Services, Wichita Falls State Hospital (1991–Present); Vice President of Systems, Insurance Filing Service, Inc. (1986–Present); Programmer Analyst II, PPG Industries, Inc. (1974–1984). **Education:** Midwestern State University, M.S. in Computer Science (1986), B.S. (1970); University of Texas Southwestern Medical School, M.A. in Biochemistry (1973). **Personal:** Ms. Fiero enjoys consulting, ranching, and raising horses & ostriches.

Andre Gagnon, M.D., FRCP(C)

Clinical Director of Adopsychiatry
Centre Hospitalier Pierre–Janet
20 Rue Pharand
Hull, Quebec J9A 1K7
(819) 776–8085
Fax: (819) 771–4727

8063

Business Information: Centre Hospitalier Pierre–Janet is a 120–bed, specialty hospital providing treatment and rehabilitation to patients of all ages suffering from psychiatric disorders. First serving as the Chief of the Department of Psychiatry, Dr. Gagnon decided to focus on the Adopsychiatry program to have more time to research adolescent psychiatry disorders. As a Clinical Director, he researches psychosis, suicide, and depression problems, and how to assist in the rehabilitation of children suffering from those disorders. **Career Steps:** Centre Hospitalier Pierre–Janet: Clinical Director (1994–Present), Chief of Department of Psychiatry (1983–1992); University of Ottawa: Associate Professor – Department of Psychiatry (1996–), Assistant Professor – Department of Psychiatry, (1985–1995); Assistant Professor, McGill University (1985–Present). **Associations & Accomplishments:** Association Medecins Psychiatres du Quebec; Canadian Psychiatric Association; American Society of Adolescent Psychiatry; International Society of Adolescent Psychiatry; Canadian Association of Adolescent Health; Canadian Society of PsychoAnalysis; International Society of PsychoAnalysis. **Education:** Universite of Ottawa, FRCP(C) (1980); University of Laval, M.D. (1975); Canadian Institute of PsychoAnalysis, PsychoAnalyst (1984). **Personal:** Married to Suzanne St. Jacques in 1982. Three children: Thierry, Louis–Philippe, and Arnaud. Dr. Gagnon enjoys team handball, hockey, movies, and gardening.

David T. George

Administrator
Comprehensive Community Development Corporation d.b.a. Soundview Health Center
731 White Plains Road
Bronx, NY 10473
(718) 589–2232
Fax: (718) 801–9762
EMAIL: See Below

8063

Business Information: Mr. George was appointed as the Administrator for a major managed health care coproation located in Bronx, New York on Jun 5, 1996. Whith over 18 years of administrative health care experience, Mr. George provides overall executive leadership for the Clinical, Professional, Operational, and Support Services at the Center. Internet users can reach him via: Trinity4@AOL.Com. **Career Steps:** Administrator, Soundview Heath Center (1996–Present); Associate Director of Human Resources, Kingsboro Psychiatric Center (1990–1996); Vice President of Distributions, Fenem Inc. (1988–1990); AVP Materials Management, Bronx Lebanon Hospital (1986–1988); Assistant Administrator, Flushing Hospital and Medical Center (1980–1986). **Associations & Accomplishments:** Fellow, American Hospital Associations; Board of Directors, CHCANYS; International Society for Hospital Materials Management – CPHM; Published, AHA. **Education:** St. Joseph's College, M.S.H.A. (April, 1997); SUNY, B.P.S. (1992); St. John's University, A.A.S. **Personal:** Mr. George enjoys reading, writing, computers, intra–internet, rollerblading, football, and swimming.

James R. Hess

Director of Rehabilitation
Villa Fairmont Mental Health Center – Telecare Corporation
15200 Foothill Boulevard
San Leandro, CA 94578
(510) 352–9690
Fax: (510) 352–9564

8063

Business Information: Villa Fairmont Mental Health Center – Telecare Corporation provides psychiatric services to individuals suffering from chronic mental illness. The Facility is a licensed, 16 bed skilled nursing facility providing sub–acute psychiatric services. The Center is inspected regularly by appropriate agencies of both federal and state governments, including health departments. Telecare Corporation has 16 facilities in California and over 22 programs at various locations throughout the community. Mr. Hess has been with the Villa Fairmont Telecare Facility for 4 1/2 years. He supervises a large support staff, and oversees treatments, all plans for care, policies, and procedures, and aids communities in dealing with patients' re–entry into the community. **Career Steps:** Villa Fairmont Mental Health Center – Telecare Corporation: Director of Rehabilitation (1996–Present), Program Director (1992–1996); Program Director, Beverly Enterprises (1989–1992). **Associations & Accomplishments:** American Psychological Association; Association for the Advancement of Applied Sport Psychology; California Association of Special Treatment Program Directors; Youth Empowered to Succeed; Athletes United for Peace. **Education:** John F. Kennedy University, Master of Arts (1991); Brigham Young University, B.S. **Personal:** Married to Cynthia D. in 1982. Four children: Brandon, Brady, Britney, and Ashley. Mr. Hess enjoys writing, music, sports, and spending time with his family.

Perry W. Kaplan, M.S.

Director, Quality Assurance and Program Development
Post Graduate Center for Mental Health
344 West 36th Street
New York, NY 10018–6402
(212) 560–6759
Fax: (212) 576–4198

8063

Business Information: Post Graduate Center for Mental Health is a non–profit, community–based mental health service providing treatment and postgraduate psychotherapy training. As Director of Quality Assurance and Program Development, Mr. Kaplan is responsible for grant writing, new program development, quality assurance, and utilization review. **Career Steps:** Director, Quality Assurance and Program Development, Post Graduate Center for Mental Health (1992–Present); Consultant, MICA Training and Support Services (1992–Present); Director of Community Residence Program, The New York Hospital (1988–1993); Director of MICA, Fordham–Tremont CMAC (1991–1993). **Associations & Accomplishments:** Advisory Council, New York City Department of Mental Health; Association for Community Living; Coalition of Westside Human Service Agencies. **Education:** Teachers College – Columbia University, M.S. (1987); State University of New York – Empire State College. **Personal:** Married to Wendy Weingart in 1994. Mr. Kaplan enjoys woodworking.

Evelyn–Elizabeth Keller, M.D.

Chief of Geriatric Psychiatry
Clinique Roy–Rousseau
2579 Ch de la Canardiere
Beaupat, Quebec G1J 2G2
(418) 663–5721
Fax: (418) 663–0494
EMAIL: See Below

8063

Business Information: Clinique Roy–Rousseau is a psychiatric hospital serving Quebec City, Quebec. As Chief of Geriatric Psychiatry, Dr. Keller provides clinical services to geriatric patients, instructs medical students and residents, and conducts various administrative duties. Dr. Keller will be involved in collaborative research in geriatric psychiatry in the near future. Internet users may reach her via: evkeller@quebectel.com **Career Steps:** Chief of Geriatric Psychiatry, Clinique Roy–Rousseau (1995–Present); Fellow in Geriatric Psychiatry, McGill–Sandoz Fellowship (1994–1995); Resident in Psychiatry/Geriatric Psychiatry, Universite Laval (1989–1994). **Associations & Accomplishments:** Canadian Academy of Geriatric Psychiatry; American Association for Geriatric Psychiatry; Canadian Psychiatric Association; American Psychiatric Association; Canadian/Quebec Medical Association; Societe Quebecoise de Psychogeriatrie; Delta Society (American–based organization concerned with human–animal interactions). **Education:** McGill University, M.Sc. (1995); Laval University: M.D. (1989), B.A. in Music (1984). **Personal:** Dr. Keller enjoys travel and cinema. She is also a classical pianist, exercise enthusiast, animal lover, and an avid reader.

Marian E. Kellogg

Marketing Director
Horsham Clinic
722 East Butler Pike
Ambler, PA 19002–2310
(215) 643–7800
Fax: (215) 643–5384

8063

Business Information: Horsham Clinic is a 138–bed, free–standing psychiatric hospital, employing 200 people. As Marketing Director, Miss Kellogg is responsible for directing and coordinating all sales, marketing, and public relations activities. **Career Steps:** Marketing Director, Horsham Clinic (1994–Present); Combined Plans Officer, United States Air Force Reserve (1987–Present); Marketing Director, Fairmount Professional Association (1993–1994); Public Relations Assistant, Freedom Valley Girl Scout Council (1992–1993). **Associations & Accomplishments:** American Business Women's Association; American Marketing Association; Delaware Valley Healthcare Marketing and Public Relations Association; Reserve Officer's Association; Physicians Relations Professionals Group; Published in local papers. **Education:** Ursinus College, B.A. in Communications (1992). **Personal:** One child: Rachael. Miss Kellogg enjoys travel.

Anthony J. Maffia

Vice President of Psychiatry and Mental Health
Jamaica Hospital Medical Center
8900 Van Wyck Expressway
Jamaica, NY 11418–2897
(718) 206–7160
Fax: Please mail or call

8063

Business Information: Jamaica Hospital Medical Center is a health care facility providing diagnosis and treatment to patients. A Board–Certified Diplomate in Clinical Social Work in the state of New York, Mr. Maffia joined Jamaica Hospital Medical Center as Vice President of Psychiatry and Mental Health in 1995. He is responsible for the administration of a 50–bed inpatient psychiatric unit, a psychiatric emergency room, and a large mental health care clinic. Concurrently, he serves as Evening Administrator at Jamaica Hospital and operates a private practice in Psychotherapy at Briarwood Family Physicians. **Career Steps:** Jamaica Hospital Medical Center: Vice President Psychiatry and Mental Health (1995–Present), Director of Social Work (1986–1995); Assistant Director of Social Work, Winthrop University Hospital (1985–1986). **Associations & Accomplishments:** National Association of Social Workers; College of Health Care Executives; American Hospital Association; numerous publications, speaking engagements, and presentations upon request. **Education:** Adelphi University, M.S.W. (1977): Iowa College, B.A. in Leisure Arts; Board Certified Diploma in Clinical Social Work.

Wendy S. Mamoon

Associate Administrator/Chief Financial Officer
Rock Creek Center
40 Timberline Drive
Lemont, IL 60439–3848
(708) 257–3636
Fax: (708) 257–8846

8063

Business Information: Rock Creek Center is a private, full–service psychiatric hospital, providing diagnosis and treatment to patients through in–patient services and six out–patient facilities. Established in 1989, Rock Creek Center is also affiliated with seven other facilities. As Associate Administrator/Chief Financial Officer, Mrs. Mamoon is responsible for the total financial control of the hospital operations, in addition to assisting the Chief Executive Officer in managing the administrative operations of the hospital. **Career Steps:** Associate Administrator/Chief Financial Officer, Rock Creek Center (1993–Present); Controller, Z Management, Inc. (1977–1986). **Associations & Accomplishments:** Healthcare Financial Management Association. **Education:** University of Wisconsin – Milwaukee, M.B.A. (1978). **Personal:** Married to Sam in 1988. Five children: Troy, Jordan, Jaraad, Hanna and Yousuf. Mrs. Mamoon enjoys reading and activities with her children.

Anita Mattingly

Director of Medical Records
Children's Psychiatric Hospital of Northern Kentucky
P.O. Box 2680
Covington, KY 41012
(606) 578–3200
Fax: (606) 578–3251

8063

Business Information: Children's Psychiatric Hospital of Northern Kentucky provides inpatient, outpatient, and partial hospitalization services to children ages 5–18. As Director of Medical Records, Ms. Mattingly directly supervises nursing and medical records staff. She is also responsible for performing Utilization Review with third party payers to ensure patients have necessary/adequate time for treatment. **Career Steps:** Children's Psychiatric Hospital of Northern Kentucky; Director of Medical Records, (1992–Present); Registered Nurse/Staff Nurse (1986–1992); Registered Nurse/Staff Nurse, Pulmonary Specialty Unit, Good Samaritan Hospital, Cincinnati, Ohio (1981–1986). **Associations & Accomplishments:** Greater Cincinnati Children's Choir; Volunteer Grandparent, Villa Madonna Academy; National Diabetes Association; National Ski Patrol. **Education:** Regents College, B.S.N. (In Progress); Northern Kentucky University, Associates Degree in Nursing (1981). **Personal:** Married to William in 1964. Two children: Susan Marie and Theresa Kay and one granddaughter Amanda. Ms. Mattingly enjoys golf, camping, skiing, and taking care of her family and granddaughter.

Miss Susan D. McCoy
President
AGI and AGE
182 North Waverly Street
Orange, CA 92866
(714) 997-2544
Fax: (714) 997-2544

8063

Business Information: Advanced Geriatric Interventions (AGI) and Advanced Geropsychiatric Education (AGE) is a mental health consultation and education provider in long-term care facilities. As President and Founder, Miss McCoy coordinated consultation and education services for the long-term facilities, and designs and implements new programs. Established in 1993, Advanced Geriatric Interventions (AGI) and Advanced Geropsychiatric Education (AGE) employs a professional staff of 15. **Career Steps:** President, Advanced Geriatric Interventions (AGI) and Advanced Geropsychiatric Education (AGE) (1993–Present); Program Director, Gerontology Services, Lakeview Medical Group (1985–1993); Counselor/Liaison, Adult Learning Disability Program, California State University (1986–1988); Consultant, San Clemente Seniors (1986). **Associations & Accomplishments:** Kappa Delta Pi Education Honor Society; Chi Sigma Iota Counseling Honor Society; Phi Kappa Phi Academic Honor Society; National Association of Female Executives. **Education:** California State University, M.S. in Counseling (1989); Mount Union College, B.S. in Elementary Education (1966).

Nell R. McGee
Director of Human Resources
Central Louisiana State Hospital
P O Box 5031
Pineville, LA 71361
(318) 484-6319
Fax: (318) 484-6345

8063

Business Information: Central Louisiana State Hospital is a specialized psychiatric hospital providing diagnosis and treatment of patients with psychiatric disorders. Established in 1902, Louisiana State Hospital currently employs 550 people. As Director of Human Resources, Ms. McGee is responsible for all aspects of human resource activities, including recruiting, retention, salary administration, benefits management, employee relations and safety. **Career Steps:** Director of Human Resources, Central Louisiana State Hospital (1990–Present); Human Resource Program Director, Pinecrest Developmental Center (1989–1990); Human Resource Director, Columbia State School (1970–1989). **Associations & Accomplishments:** Louisiana State Personnel; State Human Resource Managers' Association; Central Louisiana Personnel Association. **Education:** Northeast Louisiana State University. **Personal:** Married to Wayne in 1956. One child: Carol McGee Sparrow. Ms. McGee enjoys travel, camping, and reading."

Michael MonDoux
Director of Plant Operations and Safety Manager
Jackson Brook Institute
175 Running Hill Road
South Portland, ME 04106-3220
(207) 761-2341
Fax: (207) 761-2108

8063

Business Information: Established in 1984, Jackson Brook Institute is a privately-owned psychiatric hospital with 104 beds. Reengineering plans are now in place for the consolidation with sister satellite subsidiaries in Massachusetts to become one managed care facility. As Director of Plant Operations and Safety Manager, Mr. MonDoux is responsible for 23 employees, maintenance, housekeeping, laundry, security, and is a safety officer and materials manager. **Career Steps:** Director of Plant Operations and Safety Manager, Jackson Brook Institute (1993–Present); Facilities Manager, Seacoast

Mental Health Company (1990–1993); Electrical Manager, German Electric Company (1985–1990); Maintenance Manager, B.C.P. Realty (1978–1985). **Associations & Accomplishments:** Maine Hospital Engineers Association; N.F.P.A. Hospital Section; Maine Safety Association; New England Healthcare Association. **Education:** Leslie College, B.S. in Management in progress; Plymouth State College; New Hampshire Vocational and Technical Institute. **Personal:** Married to Bari in 1995. Five children: Jeany, Bret, Mindy, Kyle and Wade. Mr. MonDoux enjoys baseball, boating, and skiing.

Edward J. Murray, Ph.D.
Therapist
Murray's Psychological Services
1710 Warrick Drive
Ashtabula, OH 44004-2255
(216) 964-3322
Fax: Please mail or call

8063

Business Information: Murray's Psychological Services is a private psychology practice, providing family counseling in the areas of depression, anxiety, learning disabilities, and anti-social behavioral disorders. Founding his private practice in 1978, Dr. Murray is a clinical psychologist responsible for all aspects of company operations and administrative activities for a support staff, as well as his daily patient practice. In addition, he is an academic research professor of psychology at Kent State University. **Career Steps:** Therapist, Murray's Psychological Services (1978–Present); Professor of Psychology, Kent State University (1970–Present); Priest, Diocese of Cleveland (1963–1973). **Associations & Accomplishments:** American Association of University Professors; Phi Delta Kappa. **Education:** Universidad INCA Guci/ASO De La Vega, Ph.D. (1993); Kent State University, M.A. (1972); St. Mary Seminary, M.Div. (1963); Borrom Seminary, Ph.B. (1959); Athenaeum of Ohio (1955–1957). **Personal:** Married to Carol Ann in 1973. Two children: Michelle Marie and Meghan Patrice. Dr. Murray enjoys physical recreation, swimming, and boating.

Cecil F. Mynatt, M.D.
Chief of Medical Staff
Rolling Hills Hospital
1000 Rolling Hills Lane
Ada, OK 74820
(405) 436-3600
Fax: (405) 436-6024

8063

Business Information: Rolling Hills Hospital is a private psychiatric hospital with special inpatient programs for children, adolescents, and adults. Three satellite outpatient facilities in Oklahoma offer partial hospitalization. a practicing Psychiatrist since 1951, Dr. Cecil Mynatt joined the staff at Rolling Hills in 1990. As Chief of Medical Staff, he is responsible for staff supervision, clinical activities, and providing administrative direction. An experienced publisher, he is also President of Sun Enterprises, Inc., the holding company for his practice and two medical newsletters — "The Voice of Experience," a geriatric health and recreation publication with subscribers in 28 states. His new publication for private psychiatrists will be made available to all practicing psychiatrists in the United States. **Career Steps:** Private Psychiatric Practice & Chief of Medical Staff, Rolling Hills Hospital – Ada, Oklahoma (1990–Present); Private Practice: Lawton, Oklahoma (1985–1990), Las Vegas, Nevada (1969–1985). **Associations & Accomplishments:** American Medical Association; Oklahoma State Medical Association; Royal Society Heath; Who's Who In Southwest. **Education:** Menniger School of Psychiatry, Psychiatry (1961); University of Tennessee Medical School, M.D. (1951); University of Tennessee, B.A. (1949). **Personal:** Married to Yong Cha in 1989. Seven children: Matthew, Cecilia, Martha, Melissa, Richard, Katherine and John. Dr. Mynatt enjoys tennis, motorcycling, boating, writing fiction and poetry, and collecting antiques (Old Korean and Victorian).

Timothy D. Nolt
Director of Administrative Services
Sioux Trails Mental Health
1407 South State
New Ulm, MN 56073
(507) 354-3181
Fax: (507) 354-3183

8063

Business Information: Sioux Trails Mental Health is a private, non–profit, community mental health center providing all types of psychiatric outpatient services. As Director of Administrative Services, Mr. Nolt handles all business related functions of the Organization, including accounts receivable/payable, all human resources activities, strategic planning, marketing, and budgeting. **Career Steps:** Director of Adminis-

trative Services, Sioux Trails Mental Health (1994–Present); Administrator, Family Health Center (1986–1994). **Associations & Accomplishments:** Former Member, President, Slayton Area Chamber of Commerce. **Education:** St. Cloud State University, B.S. (1982). **Personal:** Married to Machelle in 1980. Three children: Travis, Jacob, and Cody. Mr. Nolt enjoys golf, softball, and working with the ambulance service.

Richard B. Oni
Director
Team Concept Community Resources
567 Livingston Avenue
St. Paul, MN 55107
(612) 290-0905
Fax: Please mail or call

8063

Business Information: Team Concept Community Resources, established in 1991, is a community based residential facility for people who have Mental Retardation. Services include but not limited to counseling for anger management and daily living skill. As Director, Dr. Oni is responsible for daily operations, strategic planning, public relations, supervising services, overseeing programming and staffing, managing 50 people, and training the employees. **Career Steps:** Director, Team Concept Community Resources (1993–Present); Program Consultant, Dakota Children, Inc. (1987–1993); Program Manager, New Concept Foundations (1984–1986). **Associations & Accomplishments:** American Association on Mental Retardation; American Correctional Association; Minnesota Governors Council on Developmental Disability. **Education:** Union Institute, Ph.D. (1994); Mankato State University; Viterbo College, BLS. **Personal:** Married to Tracy Hanson–Oni in 1984. Two children: Ashley and Nicole. Dr. Oni enjoys pin pong, racquetball, running, and soccer.

Dr. L. Kola Oyewumi
Associate Professor of Psychiatry
University of Western Ontario
P. O. Box 2532 Station B
London, Ontario N6A 4H1
(519) 455-5110
Fax: (519) 455-2355
EMAIL: See Below

8063

Business Information: A Fellow of the Royal College of Physicians and Surgeons of Canada, Dr. Oyewumi joined the London Psychiatric Hospital in 1989, establishing the Clinical Evaluation Unit with his focus on the treatment of clinically resistant patients. As Director of the Unit, his responsibilities include patient care – concentrating on the treatment of schizophrenia – in addition to various administrative activities. Concurrently, he maintains an Associate Professorship at the University of Western Ontario. Internet users can reach him via: Loyewumi@julian.uwo.ca. **Career Steps:** Director – Clinical Evaluation Unit, London Psychiatric Hospital (1989–Present); Associate Professor, University of Western Ontario (1989–Present); Associate Professor, University of Saskatchewan (1986–1989); Chief of Psychiatry, Saskatoon City Hospital (1986–1989); Reader, University of Ilorin (1983–1986); Head of Department of Behavioral Sciences, The University of Ilorin Teaching Hospital (1983–1986). **Associations & Accomplishments:** Royal College of Physicians and Surgeons of Canada; Canadian and Ontario Medical Association; Canadian and Ontario Psychiatric Associations; Canadian College of NeuroPyscho Pharmacology; Nigerian Medical Association; Canadian Mental Health Association; Lions Club; Exclusive Club. **Education:** University of Ottawa, Canada: Diploma in Psychiatry, Fellow – Royal College of Physicians and Surgeons (1979); Diplomate, American Board of Psychiatry and Neurology; Fellow, West African College of Physicians; Fellow Postgraduate Medical, Medical College of Nigeria; University of Ibadan Medical School, Nigeria: B.Sc., M.B., B.S. (1973). **Personal:** Married to Cecilia Adeola in 1976. Four children: Lamide, Kikelomo, Oluseyi, and Modupe. Dr. Oyewumi enjoys swimming, travel, walking, table tennis, music and billiards.

Ronald L. Parson, RRA,BS
Health Information Management Technician
Norristown State Hospital
1001 Sterigere Street
Norristown, PA 19401
(610) 270-1074
Fax: (610) 270-1666

8063

Business Information: Norristown State Hospital, established in 1867, is the sole state–supported psychiatric mental hospital in Pennsylvania. The hospital serves adolescents and adults with emotional and mental health disorders. As Health Information Management Technician, Mr. Parson supervises the operations of the Health Information Management Department. Other responsibilities include quality assurance of the department for state accreditation. **Career Steps:** Health Information Management Technician, Norristown State Hospital (1996–Present); Medical Records Director, Eastern State School and Hospital (1980–1996); Medical Records Coding Clerk, Suburban General Hospital (1979–1980). **Associations & Accomplishments:** American Health Information Management Association; Delaware Valley Health Information Management System Society; Southeastern Pennsylvania Health Information Management Association. **Education:** Temple University, Health Care Administration (1980); Cheyney State University, B.S. (1975). **Personal:** Married to Ann L. Maitz–Parson in 1993. Mr. Parson enjoys football, hockey, reading, and tennis.

David G. Pierce, LCSW/BCD
Outpatient Director
Billings Mental Health Center
1245 North 29th
Billings, MT 59103
(406) 252–5658
Fax: (406) 252–4641

8063

Business Information: Billings Mental Health Center is a team of over 125 qualified professionals offering comprehensive mental health evaluations and treatment services in a eleven county area of South Central Montana. As Outpatient Director, Mr. Pierce is responsible for the following treatment programs: Outpatient Chemical Dependent Program, School based Day Treatment Program, Youth Managed Care Program, Seven Satellite Offices, Billings Outpatient Clinical Staff, and Clinical Programming at the Women's State Prison . As the Outpatient Director, Mr. Pierce is the acting MHC Executive Director in the absence of the Executive Director. **Career Steps:** Outpatient Director, Billings Mental Health Center (1974–Present); Director of Community Action Programs, Northern Cheyenne Reservation, Lame Deer, MT (1971–1973). **Associations & Accomplishments:** State of Montana Licensed Clinical Social Worker; National Board of Examiners in Clinical Social Work; Rotary Club; President, Mental Health Center Professional Staff Organization; First Chairperson, Children's Managed Care Regional Ad Board, South Central Montana. **Education:** University of Arkansas, Masters in Social Work (1974); Montana State University, B.S. **Personal:** Married to Julia in 1971. Two children: Derek and Justin. Mr. Pierce enjoys running competitively and raising registered longhorn cattle.

Jess Preciphs, Ph.D.
Director of Clinical Services
Dartmouth Hospital – Behavioral Health System
5350 Lamme Road
Dayton, OH 45439–3215
(513) 296–7552
Fax: Please mail or call

8063

Business Information: Dartmouth Hospital is a private psychiatric behavioral health care system, offering a 60–bed residential treatment for ages 11–18 and a 30–bed, fully-functional outpatient clinic. A practicing psychologist since 1978, Dr. Preciphs joined Dartmouth Hospital – Behavioral Health System as Director of Clinical Services in 1995. He is responsible for directing all clinical services, including training young therapists, supervising the staff, developing programming, providing direct treatment services, teaching parenting skills classes, and conducting research. **Career Steps:** Director of Clinical Services, Dartmouth Hospital – Behavioral Health System (1995–Present); Consultant, Dayton Urban League (1991–1995); Private Practice, Gordon Harris and Associates (1990–Present); Psychologist, Institute for Juvenile Research – Chicago, IL (1977–1985). **Associations & Accomplishments:** American Orthophsychiatric Association; President (1983–1985), Near West Side Council – Chicago. **Education:** University of Texas – Austin: Ph.D. (1978), B.S. in Psychology. **Personal:** Two children: Jason Christopher and Joseph Cameron. Dr. Preciphs enjoys piano, vocal performing, and gourmet cooking.

Lourdes Ramos
Human Resources Manager
LifeStream Behavioral Center
P.O. Box 491000
Leesburg, FL 34749–1000
(352) 360–6575
Fax: (352) 360–6595

8063

Business Information: Established in 1970, LifeStream Behavioral Center is a mental health hospital and out–patient facility, also offering a full geriatric residential program. As Human Resources Manager, Mrs. Ramos is responsible for diversified managerial duties, including recruitment, disci-

pline, internal grievances, employment support services, wellness programs, health insurance, payroll, and all benefits and compensation. **Career Steps:** Human Resources Manager, LifeStream Behavioral Center (1994–Present); Coordinator of Diversity Programs, New York State Office of Mental Retardation and Developmental Disabilities (1983–1993). **Associations & Accomplishments:** First Vice President, Lake Sumter Society for Human Resource Management; Society for Human Resource Management; Recording Secretary, Greenwood Lakes, MS – Parent Teacher Association. **Education:** City College of New York, M.A. in Bilingual Education (1978); Certified Senior Professional in Human Resource Management. **Personal:** Married to Cesar in 1981. One child: Celina. Mrs. Ramos enjoys calligraphy, aerobic weight training, and latin dancing.

Edna M. Ruffin
Assistant Director of Nursing and Section Chief
Ancora Hospital
5 Marcia Ct.
Sicklerville, NJ 08081
(609) 567–7208
Fax: (609) 567–7292

8063

Business Information: Established in 1954, Ancora Hospital is a 600–bed, state mental health facility. A Registered Nurse with over ten years expertise in psychiatric administration, Mrs. Ruffin joined Ancora Hospital in 1965 and worked in several nursing and nursing management positions to her present position. Currently serving as Assistant Director of Nursing and Section Chief, she ensures all safety, physical, and mental needs are met for a 150–bed unit. In addition to her daily duties, Mrs. Ruffin oversees physicians, nurses, aides, and quality assurance. **Career Steps:** Assistant Director of Nursing and Section Chief, Ancora Hospital (1990–Present); Director of Nurses, Kingsboro Psychiatric Hospital. **Associations & Accomplishments:** Eastern Star, Prince Hall Affiliate; Reserve Officers Association; Ancora Volunteer Fire Company. **Education:** Antioch University: M.A. (1989), B.A. (1987); Atlantic Community College, A.S. **Personal:** Married to Robert D. in 1986. Mrs. Ruffin enjoys collecting tea pots, craft making (latch hook rugs) and horseback riding.

Larry L. Rutledge, Ph.D.
• • • ━━◉━━ • • •

Director of Psychology and Neuro Rehab Services
HealthSouth Southern Hills Regional Rehabilitation Hospital
120 12th Street
Princeton, WV 24740–2312
(304) 487–8127
Fax: (304) 425–4137

8063

Business Information: HealthSouth Southern Hills Regional Rehabilitation Hospital is a full service, rehabilitation hospital, providing specialized treatment to patients suffering from psychological and neuropsychological problems. A practicing psychologist since 1987, Dr. Rutledge joined HealthSouth Southern Hills Regional Rehabilitation Hospital as Director of Psychology and Neuro Rehab Services in 1992. He is responsible for the direction of all departmental operations, including oversight of staff and clinical functions. **Career Steps:** Director of Psychology and Neuro Rehab Services, HealthSouth Southern Hills Regional Rehabilitation Hospital (1992–Present); Neuropsychology Supervisor, Renaissance Rehabilitation Services (1990–1992); Assistant Clinical Professor, Medical College of Georgia (1989–1990); Clinical Neuropsychologist, Walton Rehabilitation Hospital (1988–1990). **Associations & Accomplishments:** American Psychological Association; International Neuropsychological Society; National Head Injury Foundation; Commander, United States Naval Reserve. **Education:** University of South Carolina, Ph.D. (1987); California State University – Long Beach, M.A. (1981); University of Central Arkansas, B.A. (1975). **Personal:** One child: Laura Noel. Dr. Rutledge leads a traumatic brain injury support group.

Pamela Rhodes Segel
Director of Education, Superintendent, and Principal
Childrens Psychiatric Hospital
1001 Yale Boulevard North East
Albuquerque, NM 87131–5631
(505) 843–2878
Fax: (505) 843–0052

8063

Business Information: Childrens Psychiatric Hospital is a 78–bed (18 acute care, 36 residential treatment, 20 partial hospital, and a 1–15 adolescent unit) public health agency that serves emotionally disturbed children between the ages of 4–16. As Director of Education, Ms. Segel is responsible for diversified administrative activities, including working with Di-

rectors, setting guidelines, and assisting in the direction of the Hospital. As Superintendent, she sets policy and procedures at district and state level and makes sure all federal guidelines and mandates are met. As Principal, she sets goals and plans direction, policy, procedure, supervises a staff of nine teachers, and prepares curriculum. **Career Steps:** Director of Education, Superintendent, and Principal, Childrens Psychiatric Hospital (1996–Present); Program Director, University of New Mexico (1992–1996); Director of Education, Desert Hills R.T.C. (1990–1992); Assistant Principal, Albuquerque Public Schools (1989–1990). **Associations & Accomplishments:** Council for Exceptional Children; Division of Behavior Disorders; Division of Learning Disabilities; Division of Early Childhood. **Education:** University of New Mexico, Ed.S. (1989); Jersey City State College, M.A. (1973); St. Peters College, B.A. (1972). **Personal:** Married to Norm in 1982. Two children: Tallie and Alexis. Ms. Segel enjoys weaving, quilting, and reading.

Dr. Vinodbala Shah
Psychiatrist
Community Mental Healthcare, Inc.
201 Hospital Drive
Dover, OH 44622
(216) 343–6631
Fax: (216) 343–6631

8063

Business Information: Community Mental Healthcare, Inc. is a Community Mental Health Care Center with a staff of more than 35 professionals. A practicing physician since 1968, Dr. Shah joined CMH, Inc. as a Psychiatrist in 1982. She provides quality mental health care to individuals. Concurrent with her position at CMH, Inc., she is the Chief of Psychiatric Services at Union Hospital. **Career Steps:** Psychiatrist, Community Mental Healthcare, Inc. (1982–Present); Chief of Psychiatric Services, Union Hospital. **Associations & Accomplishments:** Ohio State Medical Association. **Education:** B.J. Medical College, India, M.B.B.S. (equivalent to M.D.) (1968) and M.S. (Board Certified Surgeon) (1971); Residency Training, Akron City Hospital, Akron, Ohio; Board Certified by American College of Psychiatry and Neurology (1988). **Personal:** Married to Dr. Sanjay Shah in 1972. Three children: Shailaja, Seema, and Sapna. Dr. Shah enjoys singing, playing an harmonium (accordian–like instrument) and Bridge.

Sherry L. Spicer
Director of Human Resources
St. Joseph State Hospital
3400 Frederick Avenue
St. Joseph, MO 64506
(816) 387–2300
Fax: (816) 387–2329

8063

Business Information: St. Joseph State Hospital is a 108 bed state–supported facility which provides forensic and rehabilitative care. Established in 1874, St. Joseph State Hospital currently employs 404 people. As Director of Human Resources, Ms. Spicer is responsible for all aspects of human resources, counseling, hiring personnel, as well as administration, operations, public relations, legal, and strategic planning. **Career Steps:** St. Joseph State Hospital: Director of Human Resources (1993–Present), Personnel Analyst II (1992–1993), Personnel Analyst I (1989–1992), Personnel Clerk (1975–1989). **Associations & Accomplishments:** Board of Directors, Travelers Protective Association. **Education:** Lafayette High School (1966). **Personal:** Married to Gale in 1970. Three children: Stacy, Darin, and Cory. Ms. Spicer enjoys beach combing, swimming, and travel.

Robert W. Spiegel
President
Community Care Systems, Inc.
15 Walnut Street
Wellesley Hills, MA 02181–0001
(617) 431–3000
Fax: (617) 431–3040

8063

Business Information: Community Care Systems, Inc. are privately–owned and managed behavioral health care facilities located in New England. The corporation owns three facilities in Maine and Massachusetts, many outpatient clinics, and ten managed–care systems with Charles River Health Management. As President, Mr. Spiegel has oversight of all corporate operations. He handles public relations, personnel concerns, financial concerns, marketing of services, and long–term strategic planning. **Career Steps:** Community Care Systems, Inc.: President (1994–Present), Vice President (1981–1986); Director of Operations, New Medico Associates, Inc. (1986–1994); Administrator, Hahnemann Hospital (1981–1983). **Associations & Accomplishments:** Massachusetts Financial Management Association; Massachusetts Hospital Association; Former President, Med Beaver Brook Social Club; American Hospital Association – Psychiatric Section; National Association of Private Psychiatric

Hospitals. **Education:** George Washington University, MHA (1973); Boston University, B.A. (1971). **Personal:** Married to Betsy. Mr. Spiegel enjoys meteorology, Marine Aquatics, music, and cycling.

Naomi W. Spiller
Administrator
Spiller's Personal Care
10323 Mayberry Street
Houston, TX 77078
(713) 635-1231
Fax: (713) 635-1231

8063

Business Information: Spiller's Personal Care is a private (medical) facility providing personal care to mentally ill individuals in a residential setting. As Administrator, Ms. Spiller is responsible for all aspects of the Facility, including administration, operations, payroll, strategic planning, and public relations. **Career Steps:** Administrator, Spiller's Personal Care (1985–Present); Process Operator, ARCO Refinery (1977–1985); Sales and Public Relations, Foleys (1972–1985). **Education:** Associate (1964). **Personal:** Married to Terry in 1952. Four children: Hal, Charlene, Terry, and Darlene. Ms. Spiller enjoys cooking and reading.

William B. Tollefson, Ph.D.
President
Inner Values, Inc.
1627 SW 30th Street
Cape Coral, FL 33914
(941) 549-3060
Fax: (941) 549-6060
EMail: See Below

8063

Business Information: Inner Values, Inc., called the Women's Institute for Incorporation Therapy, offers treatment for women suffering from psychological trauma (dissociative disorders). The Center is housed in a psychiatric hospital unit, but also contracts their services out to individuals and clinics. Dr. Tollefson developed the Incorporation therapy process. He serves as President and Director of Inner Values, responsible for all operations, business strategies, and patient treatment. Internet users can reach him via: WIIT@Palmnet.Net. **Career Steps:** President, Inner Values, Inc. (1995–Present); Director of Specialty Programs, CareGroup (1994–1995); Clinical Director of Women's Center for Positive Growth, Medfield Hospital (1993–1994), Director of Therapeutic Programs, Horizon Hospital (1987–1993). **Associations & Accomplishments:** American Association for Trauma Professionals; South Florida Society for Trauma Base Disorders; National Association of Alcoholism and Drug Abuse Counselors; American Association of Professional Hypnotherapists; National Association of Psychotherapists; American Counseling Association; Association for Specialists in Group Work; Who's Who in Universities and Colleges (1972); Who's Who in America (1990); Frequent lecturer at international, national, state, and local conferences and institutional symposia and proceedings. **Education:** Roosevelt University, Post Master's Studies (1978–1979); Forest Institute of Professional Psychology, Doctoral Training (1981–1982); University of Humanistic Studies, Ph.D. in Clinical Psychology (1984); Governor's State University, M.A. in Counseling (1978); Georgia Southern University, B.A. in Psychology and Sociology (1972) **Personal:** Married to Melody L. in 1982. One child: Tammy. Dr. Tollefson enjoys gardening, golf, and tennis.

Steve Embree
Chief Financial Officer
Planned Behavioral Health Care
9535 Forest Lane, Suite 110
Dallas, TX 75243-5958
(214) 680-0400 Ext: 272
Fax: (214) 238-9492

8064

Business Information: Planned Behavioral Health Care is an international managed health care organization, specializing in providing behavioral health services such as substance abuse, learning disabled, mentally challenged and emotionally disturbed rehabilitation programs. Serving as a point-of-service HMO staff model, PBHC has locations in all 50 states, as well as Mexico and Australia. As Chief Financial Officer, Mr. Embree oversees all financial reporting, administration operations, Human Resources and MIS divisions from the Dallas headquarters. **Career Steps:** Chief Financial Officer, Planned Behavioral Health Care (1990–Present); Senior Manager, Grant Thonton (1985–1990); Manager, Peat Marwick (1979–1985). **Education:** Northeast Louisiana University, MBA (1978); Michigan State University, B.S. in Mathematics **Personal:** Married to Carolyn in 1973. Two children: Angela and Stephanie.

Claude N. Adkins Jr.
Chief Executive Officer/Chairman of the Board
Northeast Tennessee Rehabilitation Hospital
2511 Wesley Street
Johnson City, TN 37601-1723
(423) 283-0700
Fax: (423) 283-0356

8069

Business Information: Northeast Tennessee Rehabilitation Hospital is a 60–bed free–standing physical rehabilitation hospital for patients suffering from strokes, brain trauma, and other injuries. As Chief Executive Officer/Chairman of the Board, Mr. Adkins oversees the day–to–day operations of the Hospital, including strategic planning, administration, and setting future goals. **Career Steps:** Chief Executive Officer/Chairman of the Board, Northeast Tennessee Rehabilitation Hospital (1995–Present); Vice President of Outreach Services, Glenwood Regional Medical Center (1986–1995); Owner/Director, Respiratory Therapy Counseling Services (1982–86); Director Cardio–Pulmonary Department, Rapides General Hospital (1978–82). **Associations & Accomplishments:** Johnson City Rotary; American Association for Respiratory Care; United Way Board Member; YMCA Board Member. **Education:** University of Southern Mississippi: M.S. in Business Education (1977), B.S.; Hinds Junior College, A.S. **Personal:** Married to Dianne in 1977. Two children: Nathan and Blaire. Mr. Adkins enjoys reading, fishing, golf, and antiques.

Thomas F. Allred, M.D.
Neonatologist
Neonatal Associates, P.A.
100 Willow Lane
Spartanburg, SC 29307-1343
(803) 573-9917
Fax: (803) 591-0559
EMAIL: See Below

8069

Business Information: Neonatal Associates, P.A. is a private Physician's Association specializing in providing health care to critically ill newborns. Board–certified in Pediatrics, Dr. Allred is an associate with the practice, providing administrative direction in addition to his primary duties as physician for the diagnosis and treatment of infants with acute and critical illnesses. In concurrence with his medical practice, he also conducts private consultations in computer systems. Dr. Allred can be reached through the Internet at: allred@interpath.com **Career Steps:** Neonatologist, Neonatal Associates, P.A. (1993–Present); Fellow (Post–Doctoral), Duke University Medical Center (1990–1993); Physician (per diem), Carolina Permanente (1992–1993); Resident Physician, Greenville Memorial Hospital (1987–1990). **Associations & Accomplishments:** South Carolina Perinatal Association; Board of Directors, Institute for Sustainable Tropical Resource Management; 13–year Black Belt in martial arts. **Education:** Medical University of South Carolina, M.D. (1987); University of Virginia, B.A. **Personal:** Married to Jeanne–Marie in 1987. One child: Criosanna. Dr. Allred enjoys martial arts, photography and providing care and handling of large cats.

Gilbert P. August, M.D.
Chairman of Pediatric Endocrinology
Children's National Medical Center
111 Michigan Avenue NW
Washington, DC 20010
(202) 884-2121
Fax: (202) 884-4095

8069

Business Information: The Children's National Medical Center is a 240–bed tertiary care academic medical center providing high–level acute care, critical care and a trauma care center for patients in inner city Washington D.C. With over 200 physicians, the Center serves as the regional medical center for cardiac surgery. In operation since 1870, the Children's National Medical Center currently employs 2,000 medical support staff. As Chairman of Pediatric Endocrinology, Dr. August is responsible for the care and treatment of patients with diabetes, growth hormone disorders, and thyroid deficiencies. Other responsibilities include on–call scheduling, finance, and administrative functions. Concurrent to his position at the Medical Center, Dr. August is also a Professor of Pediatric Medicine at George Washington University Medical School. **Career Steps:** Children's National Medical Center: Chairman of Pediatric Endocrinology (1992–Present), Pediatric Endocrinologist (1969–1992). **Associations & Accomplishments:** President, Lawson Wilkins Pediatric Endocrine Society (1993–1994); Endocrine Society; Society for Pediatric Research; American Pediatric Society; American Academy of Pediatrics; American Association for the Advancement of Science; Published peer review articles and co–authored "Pediatric Endocrinology." **Education:** New York University, M.D. (1962); CCNY, B.S. (1958). **Personal:** Married to Bernice in 1960. Two children: Sharon and Lauren. Dr. August enjoys cooking, travel and photography.

Shirley Bassler
Director of Critical Care and Respiratory Care
University of Southern California, Kenneth Norris, Jr. Cancer Hospital
1441 Eastlake Avenue
Los Angeles, CA 90033-1048
(213) 764-3470
Fax: (213) 764-0085

8069

Business Information: University of Southern California, Kenneth Norris, Jr. Cancer Hospital is one of eight Comprehensive Cancer Centers devoted to treatment of only cancer patients both inpatient and outpatient. The Comprehensive Cancer Center has two floors dedicated to inpatient care and the remaining floors for research and development. As Director of Critical Care and Respiratory Care, Mrs. Bassler is responsible for the Intensive Care Unit (ICU), the Bone Marrow Transplant Unit (BMTU), and the Respiratory Therapy Department. She is responsible for providing direction and development for her staff. Other duties include coordination of staffing, preparing and administering budgets, providing leadership and vision for staff. Ms. Bassler is also responsible for maintaining quality patient care and program development. **Career Steps:** Director of Critical Care and Respiratory Care, University of Southern California, Norris Cancer Hospital (1995–Present); Good Samaritan Hospital: Director of Intensive Care Unit (ICU), Cardiac Surgery Unit (CSU), and Post Procedure Recovery Unit (PPRU), (1993–1995); Nurse Manager of BMT Unit, UCLA Medical Center, Pediatric Observation Unit (POBU), (1985–1991). **Associations & Accomplishments:** Oncology Nursing Society; American Association of Critical Care Nurses; Certified Nurse Administrator; American Organization of Nurse Executives. **Education:** California State University, M.S.N. (1993); University of New York, B.S.N. (1988). **Personal:** Married to Richard in 1971. Two children: Tanya Hughes and Jeanne Bassler. Mrs. Bassler enjoys gourmet cooking and camping.

Rob S.B. Beanlands, M.D.
Director of Cardiac PET Centre
University of Ottawa Heart Institute
1053 Carling Avenue, Room H1-149
Ottawa, Ontario K1Y 4E9
(613) 761-5296
Fax: (613) 761-4690

8069

Business Information: University of Ottawa Heart Institute, an affiliate of the University of Ottawa, is a cardiac hospital emphasizing teaching, research, and tertiary care. In his current capacity as Director of the Cardiac PET Centre, Dr. Beanlands is a cardiologist with an interest in Nuclear Cardiology and PET (Positron Emission Tomography) imaging. The PET Centre at the University of Ottawa Heart Institute was started by Dr. Beanlands in 1995 and was the first of its kind in Canada. Concurrently Dr. Beanlands is a visiting scholar at the Department of Medicine of McMaster University Medical Centre. **Career Steps:** Director of Cardiac PET Centre, University of Ottawa Heart Institute (1992–Present); Visiting Scholar, Department of Medicine McMaster University Medical Centre (1993–Present); Fellow of Nuclear Cardiology, University of Michigan (1990–1992). **Associations & Accomplishments:** Executive Director, Canadian Nuclear Cardiology Society; Fellow Royal College of Physicians of Canada; OCPS; OMA; CMA; CCS; SNM; ASNC; AHA; Alpha Omega, Alpha Honors Medical Society. **Awards:** Young Investigators SNM 94; Canadian Cardiovascular Society 1994. **Education:** University of Ottawa, M.D. (1983); Fellow Royal College of Physicians of Canada (1988). **Personal:** Married to Genevieve in 1982. Three children: Angela, Nolan, and Rachelle. Dr. Beanlands enjoys swimming, hockey, soccer, and music.

Edward D. Blackburn, M.D.
Medical Director
Mount Vernon Developmental Center
1250 Vernonview Drive
Mount Vernon, OH 43050
(614) 393-6355
Fax: (614) 393-2908
EMAIL: See Below

8069

Business Information: Mount Vernon Development Center is the largest center of its kind in Ohio. A state facility, the Center provides a laboratory, occupational and physical therapy, pharmacy, dental, x–ray, dietetic, and related medical services to the area. As Medical Director, Dr. Blackburn supervises all aspects of the Center, and is responsible for supervision of all medical services. A practicing physician Dr. Blackburn specializes in epilepsy and emergency room procedures. Internet users can reach him via: Mv_Mr_Edb@a1@mrvax. **Career Steps:** Medical Director, Mount Vernon Development Center (1991–Present); Physician/Owner, Private Practice (1974–1991). **Associations & Accomplishments:** American Epilepsy Association; Academy of Family Physicians; Society of Teachers of Family Medicine; American Medical

Association; Ohio State Medical Association; Ohio State Coroner's Association; Fellow, American College of Angiology. **Education:** Ohio State University, M.D. (1973), Ph.D. (1973), M.Sc. (1969); Miami University, B.A. (1967). **Personal:** Two children: Christopher and Alison. Dr. Blackburn enjoys travel.

Suzanne–Therese Boussin
Psychiatrist
–Independent–
180 Rue Valleyfield
Salaberry–de–Valleyfield, Quebec J6T 1A7
(514) 373–5705
Fax: Please mail or call

8069

Business Information: Rouyn–Noranda is an acute care medical facility serving Montreal and surrounding areas. Dr. Boussin, whose public practice was associated with Rouyn–Noranda from 1988–1993, was originally a pharmacist and biologist. Upon further study, she realized that was the field where her talents were most–needed. Upon conferral of her degree in 1980, Dr. Boussin opened a practice in France. While practicing, she continued to study and specialized in 1982 in child/adolescent psychiatry. She moved from France to practice in Canada, working in conjunction with Valleyfield Hospital until 1988, when she once again moved her practice, this time to Montreal and Rouyn Noranda. She continues to practice in the Montreal area, and has been recently published. **Career Steps:** Psychiatrist, Rouyn–Noranda (1988–Present). **Education:** Child and Adolescent Psychiatry (1982); Doctorate (1980). **Personal:** Dr. Boussin enjoys theology, music and working with children.

Benjamin Carcamo, M.D.
••• ◉ •••

Physician
St. Joseph Children's Hospital
P.O. Box 4227
Tampa, FL 33677–4227
(813) 870–4252
Fax: Please mail or call

8069

Business Information: St. Joseph Children's Hospital is a full–service, multi–speciality pediatric hospital. As Physician, Dr. Carcamo concentrates his practice in the areas of Pediatric Hematology and Oncology. As such, he is responsible for the care and treatment of patients, as well as clinical research. **Career Steps:** Physician, St. Joseph Children's Hospital (1995–Present); Pediatric Hematology and Oncology Fellow, Baylor College of Medicine, Texas Children's Cancer Center; Pediatric Resident, Texas Tech University Health Science Center (1988–1991); Physicians Assistant, Texas Nephrology Associates (1986–1988). **Associations & Accomplishments:** American Medical Association; American Academy of Pediatrics; Published in Journal of Neurochemistry. **Education:** University de San Carlos – Guatemala, M.D. (1980); Board Certified in Pediatrics, Texas Tech University; Subspeciality Board Certified in Hematology and Oncology, Baylor College of Medicine. **Personal:** Married to Eileen in 1983. Two children: Ricardo and Benjamin. Dr. Carcamo enjoys tennis, swimming, playing chess, and computers.

JeMe Cioppa–Mosca
Director of Rehabilitation
Hospital for Special Surgery
535 East 70th Street, 2nd Floor Rehab
New York, NY 10021–4892
(212) 606–1357
Fax: (212) 535–0612

8069

Business Information: Hospital for Special Surgery, the first orthopedic hospital in the Nation, is a 140–bed, acute care hospital, providing physical, occupational, and speech therapy, as well as clinical psychology, and prosthetic and orthotic services. As Director of Rehabilitation, Ms. Cioppa–Mosca is responsible for the oversight and coordination of operations, including administration and strategic planning. In addition, the department interacts with 100,000 patient visits annually. **Career Steps:** Hospital for Special Surgery: Director of Rehabilitation (1992–Present), Assistant Director of Rehabilitation (1988–1992); Outpatient Supervisor, Lawrence Hospital (1987–1988). **Associations & Accomplishments:** American Physical Therapy Association; American College of Rheumatology/Allied Health Professional Association; American College of Healthcare Executives. **Education:** Pace University, M.B.A. (1987); Russell Sage College, B.S. in Physical Therapy (1982).

William M. Corbett Jr.
Director of Research Administration
Dana–Farber Cancer Institute
44 Binney Street
Boston, MA 02115–6013
(617) 632–3489
Fax: (617) 632–4452
EMAIL: See Below

8069

Business Information: Dana–Farber Cancer Institute is an acute care cancer center and a world recognized cancer research institution. A licensed facility, the Center is comprised of fifty–two outpatient beds, a research center, and a pediatric care facility. Established in 1947, the Institute employs 1,700 people and has estimated annual funding of $90 million. As Director of Research Administration, Mr. Corbett provides operational and administrative direction for the research component, which represents approximately $90 million a year. Internet users can reach him via: william_corbett@dfci.harvard.edu. **Career Steps:** Dana–Farber Cancer Institute: Director of Research Administration (1988–Present), Associate Director, Research Administration (1983–1988), Manager, Grants and Contracts (1979–1983). **Associations & Accomplishments:** Secretary, Region I, National Council of University Research Administrators; Society of Research Administrators; Association of University Technology Managers; Cancer Centers Administrative Forum. **Education:** Northeastern University, B.S. in Accounting (1977); University of Maine, Undergraduate work toward a Teaching Certificate. **Personal:** Mr. Corbett enjoys skiing, landscaping, gourmet cooking, and travel.

Ann N. Crews
Administrator
Meadow View
2815 Medlin Drive
Arlington, TX 76015–2329
(817) 465–9596
Fax: (817) 465–4026

8069

Business Information: Meadow View, a program of Family Service, Inc., a non–profit agency, provides a secure environment, private accommodations, and a landscaped view in a loving, home–like environment. Meadow View is an alternative to nursing homes and offers residential care for the elderly or handicapped adults who are not able to live at home. The Facility has 80 beds and provides 24 hour supervision, on–site medical services, meals, recreation areas and programs, and beauty shop services. As Administrator, Ms. Crews is the only nurse and is available 24 hours a day. She runs the facility, supervises, makes financial decisions, troubleshooting, and purchases. **Career Steps:** Administrator, Meadow View (1983–Present); Nurse/Insurance Clerk, Coastal Family Clinic (1970–1981); Nurse, Onslow Memorial Hospital (1981–1983). **Associations & Accomplishments:** American Association of Medical Assistants; Onslow County Chapter American Academy of Medical Assistants: President, Education Chairman, Seminar Chairman, Immediate Past President; North Carolina State Chapter American Academy of Medical Assistants: Education Committee, NCSS Convention Exhibit Chairman, Executive Council, First Vice President, President, Immediate Past President; Service Award from Onslow Chapter AAMA; Three State Program Awards; Eleanor Richards Award. **Education:** St. Peter Hospital – Olympia, Washington (1959); Alma–Mt. Pleasant Practical Nurse Center (1967–1968); Coastal Carolina Community College, Terminology (1975); Licensed Practical Nurse: Michigan (1968), North Carolina (1969), Washington (1973); Certified Medical Assistant (1977); Clinical Specialty (1977); Administrative Specialty (1979); Pediatric Specialty (1980); Licensed Vocational Nurse, Texas (1982); Certified Residential Care Administrator (1992). **Personal:** Two children: Ronald Lee Jr. and Douglas Edward. Ms. Crews enjoys computers, travel, and the beach.

Abdalleh Dallal, MD, MSc, FRCP
Clinical Medical Researcher
Hotel Dieu De St. Jerome
290 Rue Montigny
St. Jerome, Quebec J7Z 5T3
(514) 431–8200
Fax: Please mail or call

8069

Business Information: Hotel Dieu De St. Jerome is a community hospital providing health care to the citizens of St. Jerome. As Clinical Medical Researcher, Dr. Dallal conducts research in psychopharmacolo medications at the hospital. Concurrently, he spends time at the hospital working in the clinic, acting as a medical educator, and working with the Correctional Service as a medical psychiatrist. **Career Steps:** Hotel Dieu De St. Jerome: Clinical Medical Researcher (1995–Present), Medical Educator (1995–Present); Legal Medical Psychiatrist, Federal Canadian Correctional Service

(1994–Present) **Associations & Accomplishments:** APA; QPA; CMA; CPA; AFPQ; and waiting for ALP. Dr. Dallal has been a featured speaker at numerous medical conferences in Canada and the United States. **Education:** McGill University, M.D., FRCP(c) (1993); University of Montreal, Master of Science; University of Alexandria, Bachelor of Science. **Personal:** Married to Sonia Calouche in 1989. Dr. Dallal enjoys reading and travel.

H. Dele Davies, M.D., M.Sc., FRCPC
Consultant Pediatrician and Epidemiologist
Alberta Children's General Hospital
1820 Richmond Road Southwest
Calgary, Alberta T2T 5C7
(403) 229–7815
Fax: (403) 541–7508
EMAIL: See Below

8069

Business Information: Alberta Children's Hospital is a referral hospital for the provinces of Alberta, Saskatchewan, and British Columbia. This multi–disciplinary hospital provides service for approximately 1.3 million people in the area and has 143 beds of which 21% are intensive care units. As an epidemiologist, infectious disease consultant, and pediatrician, Dr. Davies does clinical research in the area of Group A Streptococcus, spends time teaching as an assistant professor at the University of Calgary, and treats private patients. Internet users can also reach him via: dele.davies@crha-health.ab.ca. **Career Steps:** Consultant Pediatrician, Alberta Children's Hospital (1994–Present); Staff, Division of Infectious Disease, Hospital for Sick Children – Toronto (1993–1994). **Associations & Accomplishments:** American Society for Microbiology; Royal College of Physicians and Surgeons of Canada; Infectious Disease Society of America; Pediatric Investigator Collaborative Network on Infections in Canada; Canadian Infectious Disease Society Fellowship Award (1991–1992); Ontario Ministry of Health Research Personnel Development Award (1992–1993); Alberta Children's Hospital Teacher of the Year (1994–1995); Hospital For Sick Children Humanitarian Award (1992); Alberta Heritage Foundation for Medical Research, Clinical Investigator Award at University of Calgary (1995). **Education:** University of Toronto: M.D. (1985), M.Sc. (1993), Fellow of the Royal College of Physicians and Surgeons, Canada (1989). **Personal:** Dr. Davies enjoys travel, reading, hiking, and skiing.

Juan Luis Dominguez
Finance Director
Hospital De Ninos San Jorge (Saint Jorge Children's Hospital)
258 San Jorge Avenue
Santurce, Puerto Rico 00912–3310
(809) 727–7390
Fax: (809) 727–2529

8069

Business Information: Hospital De Ninos San Jorge (Saint Jorge Children's Hospital), the only privately–owned pediatrics hospital in Puerto Rico, is a 91–bed, full–service and for–profit health care facility, specializing in the diagnosis and treatment of children. As Finance Director, Mr. Dominguez is responsible for the direction of overall financial activities, including operations, accounting departments, MIS, billing and collections, and third party negotiations. **Career Steps:** Finance Director, Hospital De Ninos San Jorge (Saint Jorge Children's Hospital) (1993–Present); Financial Analyst, Hospital Povia (1992–1993); Senior Associate, Coopers and Lybrand (1988–1992). **Associations & Accomplishments:** Healthcare Financial Management Association. **Education:** Bentley College, B.S. in Accounting (1988). **Personal:** Married to Nirvana in 1990. One child: JC. Mr. Dominguez enjoys rappelling and cave exploration.

Daniel E. Furst, M.D.
Director of Arthritis Clinical Research
Virginia Mason Research and Medical Center
1000 Seneca Street
Seattle, WA 98101
(206) 223–6836
Fax: (206) 223–7554
EMAIL: See Below

8069

Business Information: Virginia Mason Research and Medical Center (VMR&MC) is a non–profit institute with 270 specialists and 300–hospital beds, involved in the research of medical problems, such as diabetes, sclerederma, and rheumatology. A practicing physician since 1970, Dr. Furst joined VMR&MC as Director of Arthritis Clinical Research Unit in 1992. He is responsible for the functions of the Board, research personnel, and the research unit consisting of a laboratory and clinical pharmacology of drugs. Internet users can reach him via: CRGDEF@VMMC.ORG. **Career Steps:** Director of Arthritis Clinical Research, Virginia Mason Research and Medical Center (1992–Present); Professor, University of Washington (Present); Director of Anti–Inflammatory and Pulmonary Research, CIBA–GEIGY Pharmaceuticals (1987–1992); Associate Professor of Medicine, University of Iowa (1982–1987); Assistant Professor of Medicine, University of California – Los Angeles (1977–1982). **Associations & Accomplishments:** American Society of Clinical Pharmaceutical and Therapeutics; American College of Rheumatology; United Scleroderma Foundation; Author of over 200 articles about rheumatic conditions and drugs; Edited five books. **Education:** University of California – San Francisco, Fellow (1975); University of California – Los Angeles, Fellow (1973); Johns Hopkins University: M.D., B.A. (1962–1970). **Personal:** Married to Elaine in 1966. Two children: Marc and Shawn. Dr. Furst enjoys sailing, reading, tennis, and travel.

Ms. Joyce W. Green

Senior Vice President of Public Affairs & Development
John Wayne Cancer Institute
2200 Santa Monica Boulevard
Santa Monica, CA 90404
(310) 315–6111
Fax: (310) 315–6195

8069

Business Information: The John Wayne Cancer Institute specializes in cancer research and patient care (melanoma, breast cancer, colon cancer, lung cancer, tumor). Established since 1981, John Wayne Cancer Institute presently employs 135 people, and has an $11 million annual budget. Ms. Green currently serves as Senior Vice President of Public Affairs and Development. **Career Steps:** Senior Vice President, Public Affairs & Development, John Wayne Cancer Institute (1981–Present); Administrative Assistant, Division of Surgery/Oncology – UCLA (1972– 1981); Founder/Owner, Medi Sec, Inc. (1971–1991). **Education:** Stanford University, B.A. Degree (1948). **Personal:** Married since 1949 to John R. – widowed. One child: Neal Green.

Jessie R. Groothuis, M.D.

Pediatrician
The Children's Hospital of Denver
1056 East 19th Avenue, Box 070
Denver, CO 80218–1007
(303) 861–6877
Fax: (303) 764–8117

8069

Business Information: The Children's Hospital of Denver, affiliated with the University of Colorado School of Medicine, is a specialized 200–bed tertiary hospital providing all areas of acute care and medical research for critical needs children; widely–acclaimed for its Neonatal Clinic. Serving as Staff Physician and Head of the Neonatal follow–up program, Dr. Groothuis concentrates her practice in the diagnosis and treatment of premature or high–risk infants with chronic lung disorders. She directs all operations for the Neonatal Referral Center, coordinating with pediatric professionals and medical centers throughout Colorado and surrounding states. In concurrence with her daily patient practice, Dr. Groothuis also serves as a Professor with the Department of Pediatrics at University of Colorado's School of Medicine. She serves as instructor and mentor to pediatric residents and interns, as well as conducts research in the field of viral respiratory infections and neonatal lung disorders. Her research is currently being funded by the National Institute of Health and major pharmaceutical companies. **Career Steps:** Pediatrician, The Childrens Hospital of Denver (1982–Present); University of Colorado School of Medicine – Department of Pediatrics: Professor (1995–Present), Associate Professor (1988–Present), Assistant Professor (1982–1988); Associate Clinical Professor, Medical School of Ohio (1980–1982). **Associations & Accomplishments:** Society for Pediatric Research; Western Society for Pediatric Research; Editor, Pediatric Diagnosis (1990–1995). **Education:** University of Chicago, Pritzker School of Medicine, M.D. (1972); Stanford University, B.S. (1968); Fellowship: Vanderbilt University (1975–1977). **Personal:** Three children: Derek, Leah, and Melissa. Dr. Groothuis enjoys reading, exercising, playing the guitar and piano, and singing.

Dr. E. Lyle Gross

Founder/President
Gross Rehabilitation Institute
11010 101 Street Northwest
Edmonton, Alberta T5H 4B9
(403) 429–4761
Fax: (403) 425–4274

8069

Business Information: Gross Rehabilitation Institute, headquartered in Edmonton, Alberta, has satellite offices in Lucerne, Switzerland and Riyadh, Saudi Arabia. The Institute, a leader in providing comprehensive interdisciplinary rehabilitation for government and third party–funded injured or ill, was one of the first facilities in Canada funded by government and third party, given that Canada strives to provide healthcare equally for all, irrespective of coverage. Dr. Gross is the President of ELGHN, which is an interdisciplinary managed care group whose current international work includes Europe and the middle east. Dr. Gross is a leader in medical/legal ethics and has served as an expert throughout Canada, the United States and Europe. Dr. Gross has a special interest in counseling professionals with various forms of disability in guiding them in career change. Additional business interests include serving as founder of Health Spa International, which is a medical health spa in which clinicians from around the world provide comprehensive care in this exportable product. Dr. Gross is also majority owner of Team of the Century, a registered trademark in the United States and Canada. **Career Steps:** Founder/Physician/Medical Legal Ethicist, Gross Rehabilitation Institute (1991–Present); Director, Workers Compensation Board of Alberta (1988–1990); Consultant, Mayo Clinic, Rochester, Minnesota (1984–1986). **Associations & Accomplishments:** Advisory Committee, Canadian Bar Association Task Force on Health Care Reform; Chairperson, Chronic Nonmalignant Pain, Province of Alberta; National Ethics and Legislation Committee, Canadian Association of Rehabilitation Personnel; member of: American College of Legal Medicine; American Society of Forensic Obstetricians and Gynecologists; Canadian and American Associations of Physical Medicine and Rehabilitation; Royal College of Physicians and Surgeons of Canada; Advisor to the Canadian Bar Association (Saskatchewan) on no fault insurance; numerous Corporate appointments; Author of "Injury Evaluation: Medical/Legal Principles" Butterworths (Toronto, 1991). **Education:** University of Alberta: B.Sc. in Honors Physiology (1974), M.Sc. in Physiology (1975); University of Calgary: M.D. (1979), specialty training Universities of Alberta, British Columbia and Washington, FRCP(C) in Physical Medicine and Rehabilitation (1983); Fellowship, Department of Orthopedics: University of Alberta (1994); University of Calgary first year law (1994); Licenses: Province of Alberta, State of Minnesota, State of Washington. **Personal:** Married to Daune. Two children: Carly and Rebecca. Dr. Gross has completed a nonfiction book entitled "Subject to the Rules" currently in print. He enjoys fly fishing, hiking, and as a photographer, he has published a fashion magazine and has had photographs published in a variety of magazines. He also enjoys painting and drawing.

John C. Haley

Chief Operating Officer
Seafield Center, Inc.
7 Seafield Lane
West Hampton Beach, NY 11978–2714
(516) 288–1122
Fax: (516) 288–1638

8069

Business Information: Seafield Center, Inc. is a for–profit, alcoholic rehabilitation treatment facility comprised of one 80–bed inpatient rehabilitative center and seven outpatient facilities. The facilities serve patients residing in the New York Metropolitan area, from Manhattan to West Hampton Beach. As Chief Operating Officer, Mr. Haley is responsible for the operations and management of all levels of care offered, including detox, intensive outpatient care, sober living homes, and inpatient treatment. He finds it most rewarding to be involved with an alumni which sponsors annual non–alcoholic parties, and the promotion of intact families and individuals leading productive lives (sober, holding jobs, driver's licenses, etc.). **Career Steps:** Seafield Center, Inc.: Chief Operating Officer (1995–Present), Executive Director (1992–1995), Director of Support Services (1988–1992), Administrative Assistant (1986–1988). **Associations & Accomplishments:** American Management Association; Suffolk Coalition; Advancement for Commerce and Industry. **Education:** New York State University at Cortland, B.A. (1995); Completed American Management Association Courses for Young Executives. **Personal:** Mr. Haley enjoys volleyball, softball, gardening, and swimming.

Margaret A. Hamill, MHS, RN, C.

Director of Nursing
Beech Hill Hospital
P.O. Box 254
Dublin, NH 03444–0254
(603) 563–7353
Fax: Please mail or call

8069

Business Information: Established in 1948, Beech Hill Hospital is a 130–bed rehabilitation care hospital, focusing primarily on dual diagnosis patients. Services include counseling, substance abuse education, and rehabilitation. Having worked her way up at Beech Hill Hospital from Charge Nurse in 1987, Ms. Hamill currently serves as Director of Nursing. In this capacity, she is responsible for a 25 member staff team, as well as oversees staff scheduling, budgeting, presenting lectures, seminars, and workshops to patients, and to nurses on an outreach basis. **Career Steps:** Beech Hill Hospital: Director of Nursing (1995–Present), Nurse Manager (1992–1995), Charge Nurse (1987–1992). **Associations & Accomplishments:** Massachusetts Mental Health Nurses Association; National Consortium of Chemical Dependency Nurses; Vermont, New Hampshire Network. **Education:** Keene State College, Masters in Human Services (1991); University of New Hampshire, Bachelors in Human Services; New Rochelle Hospital School of Nursing, R.N.; Certification: Substance Abuse – National Consortium of Chemical Dependency Nurses, American Credentialing Nurses Center, Psychiatric and Mental Health Nurses. **Personal:** Two children: Christoper William and Meghan Aindrea. Ms. Hamill enjoys kayaking, canoeing, backpacking, camping, travel, photography, reading, gardening, and nature.

Nancy A. Harrington

Center Director
Boston Regional Center for Reproductive Medicine
3 Woodland Road, Suite 321
Stoneham, MA 02180
(617) 979–7599
Fax: (617) 665–9386

8069

Business Information: Boston Regional Center for Reproductive Medicine is part of the Boston Regional Hospital. The Center is a full reproductive service from basic infertility to highly technological procedures. As Center Director, Mrs. Harrington coordinates all facets of operation for the Center's employees. She oversees staffing, billing, financial reporting, and personnel policies and procedures. **Career Steps:** Center Director, Boston Regional Center for Reproductive Medicine (1993–Present); Administration and Clinical Director, Boston Regional Medical Center (1990–1993); Nursing Coordinator, New England Memorial Hospital (1989–1990); Nursing Coordinator, Atlantic Care Medical (1988–1989). **Associations & Accomplishments:** Coordinator, New England Nurses for Reproductive Medicine; Executive Secretary, Boston Fertility Society (1994); Parent Coordinating Committee, St. Pius School (1994–1996); Ms. Harrington was a speaker at the the 1996 National Nurses Conference. **Education:** LaBoure College, A.S. (1978); Attended, Regis College, Biology major. **Personal:** Married to Kevin in 1978. Two children: Katie and Martin. Mrs. Harrington enjoys reading and gardening.

John W. Hawley

Finance Director
Northwoods Children's Home
714 West College Street
Duluth, MN 55811–4906
(218) 724–8815
Fax: (218) 724–0251

8069

Business Information: Northwoods Children's Home is a private, non–profit corporation, providing residential and day treatment services to troubled children (aged 2 to 18 years old) and their families. A psychiatrist serves on staff, providing consulting services to help change the behavior patterns in emotionally–disturbed children. As Finance Director, Mr. Hawley is responsible for the direction of all financial activities, including budgeting, financial reporting, and employee benefits, as well as coordinating business services. **Career Steps:** Finance Director, Northwood's Childrens Home (1990–Present); Executive Director, North Star Community Development Corporation (1985–1987); Executive Director, Central Hillside

United Ministry (1972–1980). **Associations & Accomplishments:** Chairperson, Minnesota Nonprofit Employers Workers Compensation Fund; Duluth School Board (1980–1992), Chair, (1984,1986); Board Chair, Association for Retarted Citizens (3 years); United Way, Various Roles, (1974–1996); Founding Chair, Duluth Democratic Farmer Labor Party (1975–1979). **Education:** University of Minnesota: M.B.A. (1991), B.A. Political Science (1969). **Personal:** Married to Louise Ann Hawley, Ph.D. in 1970. Two children: Amanda and Kathryn. Mr. Hawley enjoys politics, and reading about history and culture.

David Hodges

Chief Information Officer
Cancer Treatment Centers
3150 Salt Creek Lane, Suite 122
Arlington Heights, IL 60005
(847) 342–7459
Fax: (847) 342–7382

8069

Business Information: Cancer Treatment Centers manage/own hospitals, physician practices, and home care services related to and supporting the care of cancer patients. The Centers provide traditional and non traditional treatments for patients. As Chief Information Officer, Mr. Hodges is responsible for the supervision and development of an Information Technology Department supporting a network of companies providing oncology services. This network of oncology services includes two hospitals, nationwide physician practice management, and home infusion services. Strategic development of the department includes management of a $6 million annual expense budget, a $3 million capital budget, and a staff of 33 support personnel. Other responsibilities include technical support of systems that include wide and local area networks, client server technology, DEC VAX and Alpha systems, an HP–9000, VMS, Unix, Novell, Oracle, Powerhouse as well as Northern Telcom PBX's. Additional strategic functions include CPI and TQM process implementation, corporate reengineering processes, project management, and cost benefit analysis of all corporate technology. **Career Steps:** Chief Information Officer, Cancer Treatment Centers (1995–Present); Vice President of Strategic Information Technology, APAC Teleservices, Inc. (1993–1995); Vice President of Operations, Global Communications (1992–1993); President, Advance Computer and Communications Concepts, Inc. (1987–1993); MIS Director, Hemmeter Corporation (1987–1988); Marketing Manager/Computer Sales, AT&T Information Systems (1985–1987); Systems Marketing Strategist, AT&T Bell Laboratories (1979–1985). **Associations & Accomplishments:** Data Processing Management Association; Executive Club of Chicago. While with the Cancer Treatment Centers, Mr. Hodges has implemented a Healthcare Information System in eight months, that was ten months ahead of schedule and $1.2 million under budget, reduced the corporate long distance network expense by 44%, designed and implemented a corporate training/university program for all aspects and divisions of the corporation, implemented a goal tracking system for corporate management, designed an executive information system (i.e. financials, hospital census, management goals, oncology outcomes, and Human Resource information) allowing corporate executives to be provided on–line data to make real time decisions, and implemented a corporate data base warehouse and web site for the Internet. **Education:** Roosevelt University, B.S.B.A. (1985). **Personal:** Mr. Hodges enjoys golf, water skiing, and fund raising for charitable concerns.

F. Gordon Jones, Jr

Director of Development
FPA Medical Management, Inc.
400 Arbor Lake Drive, Suite B–700
Columbia, SC 29223
(803) 786–9588
Fax: (803) 786–9557

8069

Business Information: FPA Medical Management is a physician practice management company in the managed care arena. As Director, Mr. Jones is responsible for the development of new and existing business for the Southeast region. **Career Steps:** Director, FPA Medical Management (1996–Present); Account Executive, James L. Dooley and Associates; Assistant Administrator, Children's Hospital. **Associations & Accomplishments:** Healthcare Financial Managers Association; Foreign Policy Association. Mr. Jones has been published in "Health Care Journal". **Education:** Medical University of South Carolina, M.H.S.A. (1993); University of South Carolina, B.A. in International Studies (1991); The Citadel, B.S. in Business Administration (1984). **Personal:** Mr. Jones enjoys soccer, tennis, golf, reading the Classics, and studying career and personal development techniques.

Martin Juneau, M.D.

Chief – Division of Cardiology
Institut De Cardiologie De Montreal
5000 Belanger Rue
Montreal, Quebec H1T 1C8
(514) 376–3330 Ext. 3444
Fax: (514) 376–5241

8069

Business Information: Institut De Cardiologie De Montreal is a 170–bed hospital dedicated to the treatment and research of heart diseases. The Institute has four catheter labs (which provides diagnostic/therapeutic treatments for approximately 6,000 patients), four operating rooms (for approximately 15,500 patients), 21 coronary care centers, and a 21–bed non–coronary ICU. The Institute also has a full–service ER which sees over 10,000 patients per year and the Hospital treats over 30,000 people annually on an outpatient basis. As Chief of the Division of Cardiology, Dr. Juneau's responsibilities include clinical activities, scheduling, appointment of chiefs to sections, budgeting, recruiting new fellows, training, and lobbying for funding and research grants. In addition to his administrative duties, Dr. Juneau maintains his daily patient care and treatment. **Career Steps:** Institut De Cardiologie De Montreal: Chief – Division of Cardiology (1994–Present), Chief – Cardiac Prevention and Rehabilitation Center (1988–Present); Associate Professor – Faculty of Medicine, University of Montreal (1986–Present). **Associations & Accomplishments:** President, Cardiology Examination Board; Royal College of Physicians and Surgeons of Canada; Executive Board Member, Canadian Association of Cardiac Rehabilitation; Canadian Cardiovascular Society; American College of Cardiology. **Education:** University of Stanford, Fellow (1985); University of Montreal: Master in Psychology, Cardiology; University of Shebrooke., M.D. **Personal:** Married to Dr. Sylvie Marillette in 1989. Dr. Juneau enjoys snowboarding, windsurfing, tennis, and running.

Praveen Khilnani, M.D., F.A.A.P.

Director and Owner
Children's Intensive Care Inc.
1602 Skipwith Road, Suite 210
Richmond, VA 23229–5205
(804) 289–4627
Fax: (804) 287–4309

8069

Business Information: Children's Intensive Care Inc. is a specialized healthcare agency, providing the transport and treatment of children suffering from critical, life threatening conditions such as multiple injuries, shock, heart failure or respiratory failure including children requiring heart, kidney, or liver transplants. Services are provided through a Critical Transport Team consisting of a staff of three – a physician, a clinical nurse, and a respiratory technician. Operating from two locations in the Richmond area, the Agency is affiliated with two hospitals owned by Columbia Health Care: Henrico Doctors Hospital (with an 8–bed intensive pediatric unit) and Johnston Willis Hospital (with a 4–bed intensive pediatric unit). Bringing with him more than fifteen years of experience in pediatric specialties, including anesthesiology and intensive care, Dr. Khilnani established Children's Intensive Care, Inc. in 1990. He oversees all administrative operations for associates and support staff, in addition to his daily patient practice. Dr. Khilnani practices at both locations with two other physicians to provide pediatric intensive care to sick children. Career milestones include implementing a practice of Pediatric Critical Care Transport Programs in Richmond and being able to touch children–in–need on a national level by helping other health care centers set up units in other states. At national level under the auspices of American Academy of Pediatrics, a training program has recently been developed by him that is currently being used by many health care facilities. He is currently a member of the State of Virginia Critical Care Task Force and the Committee for Pediatric Emergency Services in Virginia. His contribution to pediatric intensive care extends to countries like India, as well as conducting research on stress in children during surgery, hormonal changes in children, the effect of calcium and magnesium in critically ill children, and complications related to intravenous central line placed in children. Concurrently, he appears weekly (Saturdays) on an Asian India News TV syndicated progam — Sangam. **Career Steps:** Director and Owner, Childrens Intensive Care Inc. (1990–Present). **Associations & Accomplishments:** Former President: India Association of Virginia and Virginia Commonwealth University, an Indian Aassociation of Richmond Tri–City Area; Cultural Director: Hindu Center of Virginia, an organization which promotes the Indian culture and Hindu religion. **Education:** Harvard Medical School – Boston, MA, Fellowship in Pediatric Intensive Care (1988–1990); Cardinal Glennon Childrens Hospital, St. Louis, MO, Pediatrics; All India Institute of Medical Sciences; University of Delhi, India, Anesthesiology. **Personal:** Married to Sheela in 1984. Two children: Tara and Akash. Dr. Khilnani enjoys singing, music, playing the keyboard, flute, has recently cut a compact disc of his own songs, and received many awards for community service.

Miriam P. Lowi

President/Chief Executive Officer
St. John's Rehabilitation Hospital
285 Cummer Avenue
North York, Ontario M2M 2G1
(416) 226–6780
Fax: (416) 226–0104
EMAIL: See Below

8069

Business Information: St. John's Rehabilitation Hospital provides tertiary specialty rehabilitation services to patients. A teaching and research facility as well, the Hospital is the largest free–standing rehabilitation center in Ontario, and is affiliated with the Anglican Order. Established in 1937, the Hospital employs 230 people. Accountable to the Board of Directors, Ms. Lowi is responsible for the entire operation of the Hospital. Ms. Lowi is the first lay woman to be placed in charge of a medical facility. Her duties include administration, operations, finance, public relations, and strategic planning. Internet users can reach her via: mplowi@istar.ca. **Career Steps:** President/Chief Executive Officer, St. John's Rehabilitation Hospital (1996–Present); Associate Executive Director, The Perley Rideau Veterans' Health Centre (1990–1996); the Queensway Carleton Hospital: Director of Planning (1986–1990), Director of Rehabilitation Services (1982–1986). **Associations & Accomplishments:** Regent's Advisory Council of American College of Health Services Executives; Board of Canadian College of Health Service Executives; Major Sub–Committee of Joint Priority and Planning, Committee of Ministry of Health; Ontario Hospital Association. Ms. Lowi has received the Chairman's "Award for Distinguished Service" with the Canadian College of Health Service Executives. Author of two articles for the "Canadian Hospital Association Journal" and a presenter at major international and national conferences. **Education:** University of Ottawa: Diploma in Business Administration (1988), Masters in Health Administration (1981); McGill University, B.Sc. in Physical Therapy (1975). **Personal:** Ms. Lowi enjoys the theater, arts, and sports.

Dr. James L. McEwen

Executive Director
Greenery Neurologic Rehabilitation at Slidell
1400 Lindberg Drive
Slidell, LA 70458
(504) 641–4985
Fax: (504) 646–0793

8069

Business Information: Greenery Neurologic Rehabilitation at Slidell is a 118–bed rehabilitation facility, providing physical, cognitive, and behavioral rehabilitation for children and adults. The facility provides skilled nursing services, treating acute and sub–acute individuals with brain injuries, specializing in pediatric neural behavior. Joining Greenery Neurologic Rehabilitation at Slidell as Program Director for Rehabilitative Services in 1992, Dr. McEwen was appointed as Executive Director in 1994. He oversees all marketing, operations, and clinical activities for the $12 million facility and its 250–member support staff. **Career Steps:** Greenery Neurologic Rehabilitation at Slidell: Executive Director (1994–Present), Program Director (Rehab. Services) (1992–1994); Program Director (Rehab. Services), New Medico Head Injury Systems (1989–1992). **Associations & Accomplishments:** Board Member, Brain Injury Association of Mississippi; Vice President and Surveyor, Commission on Accreditation of Rehabilitation Facilities (CARF) **Education:** University of Southern Mississippi: Ph.D. (1984), M.S. (1982); William Carey College, B.S. in Psychology and B.A. in Music Therapy **Personal:** Married to Dorothy Roberts in 1978. Two children: Jessica D. and Lauren E. Dr. McEwen enjoys chess, distance running, personal empowerment through self–improvement.

Donna M. Mertens, RN, BSN

Nurse Manager
Shriner's Hospital
3229 Burnet Avenue
Cincinnati, OH 45229–3018
(513) 872–6217
Fax: Please mail or call

8069

Business Information: Shriner's Hospital is a full–service, healthcare institution specializing in the treatment of pediatric burn patients. The hospital offers 9 physicians and 30 beds. As Nurse Manager, Ms. Mertens manages the Outpatient Department and all outpatient functions. **Career Steps:** Shriner's Hospital: Nurse Manager (1984–Present), Staff Nurse (1979–1983). **Associations & Accomplishments:** American Burn Association; Boy Scouts of America; Everybody Counts. **Education:** University of Cincinnati, B.S.N. (1979). **Personal:** Married to Richard in 1981. Two children: Timothy and Krista. Ms. Mertens enjoys swimming, activities with her family, Boy Scouts, travel, and water sports.

James Moore
Vice President of Finance & Business Development
Sinai Samaritan Medical Center
950 North 12th Street
Milwaukee, WI 53233
(414) 283–7263
Fax: (414) 283–7402

8069

Business Information: Sinai Samaritan Medical Center, a part of the Aurora Healthcare System, is a licensed 588–bed, acute care hospital with two campuses, admitting 20,000 patients and 300,000 outpatients annually. With over twenty years of experience in the health care industry, Mr. Moore joined Sinai Samaritan Medical Center as Vice President of Finance & Business Development in 1990. He is responsible for all financial and business development activities, including managed care contracts, development of marketing products lines, physician integration, and all other related financial responsibilities. **Career Steps:** Vice President of Finance & Business Development, Sinai Samaritan Medical Center (1990–Present); Vice President/Finance Controller, St. Mary's Hospital, (1983–1990). **Associations & Accomplishments:** Healthcare Financial Management Association (HFMA); WCYHA; City Finance Committee Member; Public and Private School Boards; Consulting Professor, Marquette University for two years. **Education:** University of Michigan, Masters of Finance (1973); Oakland University. **Personal:** Married in 1975. Mr. Moore enjoys both playing and coaching hockey.

Dr. Jean–Marc A. Nabholtz

Senior Medical Oncologist
Cross Cancer Institute
11560 University Avenue North West
Edmonton, Alberta T6G 1Z2
(403) 432–8514
Fax: (403) 432–8888
EMAIL: See Below

8069

Business Information: Cross Cancer Institute is a cancer institute servicing all of Northern Alberta. As Senior Medical Oncologist, Dr. Nabholtz is responsible for research into oncology. He also serves as Chairman of the Northern Alberta Breast Cancer Program. Internet users can reach him via: jmarkn@cancerboard.ab.ca. **Career Steps:** Senior Medical Oncologist, Cross Cancer Institute (1990–Present); Associate Professor of Medicine, University of Alberta – School of Medicine (1990–Present). **Associations & Accomplishments:** American Society of Clinical Oncology; European Society for Medical Oncology. **Education:** Dijon University – France, M.D. (1980); University of Burgundy – France, Ph.D.; University of Paris, M.S in Human Biology. **Personal:** Married to Zdena in 1996. Two children: Gregory and Valery. Dr. Nabholtz enjoys sports and spending time with his family.

Kenneth L. Parker
Director of Material Management
Hospital For Sick Children
1731 Bunker Hill Road, NE
Washington, DC 20017
(202) 635–6153
Fax: (202) 636–5393

8069

Business Information: Hospital For Sick Children, established in 1883, is a transitional care and rehabilitation hospital for children dealing with trauma recovery, recovery from nerve damage, physical disabilities, premature birth complications, and AIDS adjustment. The Hospital has 130 beds and 350 employees to see to patient comfort, care, and satisfaction. As Director of Material Management, Mr. Parker is involved in the purchase of goods and services to enhance the quality of patient care. He coordinates with departmental management in order to stay within established budgets and maintains inventory control and management to avoid shortages and overstocking. Mr. Parker reviews contracts with service providers for hospital compliance. **Career Steps:** Hospital for Sick Children, Washington, DC, Director of Materials Management (1993–Present); Information Network Systems, Inc., Program Analyst (1991–1993); Bethesda Naval Hospital, Supply Director (1990–1991); Office of United States Navy Surgeon General, Logistics Director; Office of Secretary of Navy, Assistant Director for Acquisition & Contract Policy; Retired for United States Navy after serving 22 years as Senior Logistics Manager. **Associations & Accomplishments:** American College of Healthcare Executives; National Contract Management Association; American Society for Healthcare Materials Management. **Education:** Cornell University, B.S. (1969). **Personal:** Mr. Parker enjoys golf, boating, and gardening.

Eric S. Quivers, M.D.
Physician
Children's National Medical Center
111 Michigan Avenue, N.W.
Washington, DC 20010–2970
(202) 884–2020
Fax: (202) 884–5700

8069

Business Information: Children's National Medical Center (CNMC) is a full–service, multi–specialty children's medical hospital and research institution. A Board–Certified Pediatrician and Pediatric Cardiologist, Dr. Quivers joined CNMC in 1991. Serving as Pediatric Cardiologist, he is responsible for providing specialized patient care to children suffering from heart disorders. **Career Steps:** Physician, Children's National Medical Center (1991–Present); Pediatrician, Park West Medical Center (1986–1988). **Associations & Accomplishments:** Fellow, American College of Cardiology; American College of Sports Medicine. **Education:** Howard University Medical School, M.D. (1983); Morehouse College, B.S. **Personal:** Married to Mara in 1985. Two children: Micah and Lucas. Dr. Quivers enjoys fishing, camping, and sports.

J. Dean Reed
Director of Marketing
THC Hospital
700 High Street
Albuquerque, NM 87102
(505) 842–5611 Ext. 102
Fax: (505) 244–1852

8069

Business Information: THC Hospital is a 61–bed long–term acute care hospital. As Director of Marketing, Mr. Reed is responsible for data and statistical market analysis, adherence to patient eligibility regulations, quality assurance, and various administrative functions. **Career Steps:** Director of Marketing, THC Hospital (1992–Present); District Sales Manager, Nellcor Medical (1986–1992); District Sales Manager, Olympus Medical (1984–1986). **Associations & Accomplishments:** Albuquerque Chamber of Commerce; Lions Club. **Education:** Western New Mexico University: M.B.A. (1984), B.A. (1983). **Personal:** Married to Vicki R. in 1990. Three children: Stephanie, Sam, and Tyler. Mr. Reed enjoys all sports, boating, golf, and horse racing.

Laura Reider–Novakowski
Administrator
Mercy Health Care Center
147 Newport Street
Nanticoke, PA 19634
(717) 735–7300
Fax: (717) 735–8810

8069

Business Information: Mercy Health Care Center, established in 1972, is a non–profit, free standing, 110–bed skilled nursing facility specializing in respiratory and ventilator management and sub–acute care. The Facility presently employs 118 people. As Administrator, Ms. Reider–Novakowski oversees the daily operations of the Center. She is responsible for budgetary concerns, program development, contract negotiations, development of marketing techniques for new and existing services, and public relations. Other duties include general oversight of patient care, compliance to state and federal regulations, and strategic planning for the future. **Career Steps:** Mercy Health Care Center: Administrator (1994–Present), Director of Nursing (1991–1993); Director of Aging Services,Mercy Special Care (1993–1994); Information Specialist, Wilkes–Barre General (1987–1989). **Associations & Accomplishments:** Nursing Advisory Board, Luzerne County Community College; American College of Health Care Administration;; Sigma Theta Tau, Nursing Honor Society; Assistant Cheerleading Coach, Elementary grade level; Co–Editor of Nursing Care Planning Manual. **Education:** Wilkes University, M.B.A. (1992); College Misericordia, B.S. in Nursing; Wilkes–Barre General Hospital, Diploma in Nursing. **Personal:** Married to Edward in 1973. One child: Karyn. Ms. Reider–Novakowski enjoys creative writing, public speaking, and computers.

Dennis Roccaforte
Controller
Horizon West Headquarters, Inc.
4020 Sierra College Boulevard, Suite 190
Rocklin, CA 95677
(916) 624–6230
Fax: (916) 624–6249

8069

Business Information: Horizon West Headquarters, Inc. owns and operates forty convalescent hospitals and retirement facilities throughout California and Utah. The Company is privately funded by patients, Medicare, and Medicaid. As

Controller, Mr. Roccaforte is responsible for budgeting, cost reporting, and audit scheduling for all forty facilities. **Career Steps:** Controller, Horizon West Headquarters, Inc. (1986–Present); Controller, Palco International (1982–1986). **Education:** San Francisco State University, B.A. in Business Administration (1978). **Personal:** Married to Lynne C. in 1991. Two children: Darren and Ryan.

Vickie Rodden
Director of Nursing, Ambulatory Care
Children's Hospital of Oklahoma
940 NE 13th Street
Oklahoma City, OK 73104–5008
(405) 271–5151
Fax: (405) 271–7200

8069

Business Information: Children's Hospital of Oklahoma, the only children's hospital in Oklahoma, is a regional, tertiary, multi–trauma children's hospital. With twenty–seven years of experience in nursing and a Certified Pediatric Nurse, Ms. Rodden joined Children's Hospital of Oklahoma as a Staff Nurse in 1970, progressing to Supervisor in 1971 to Head Nurse of the Burn Center in 1977, with a promotion to Ambulatory Care Coordinator in 1987 and Assistant Director of Nursing in 1992. Appointed as Director of Nursing in 1994, she is responsible for directing all nursing activities in the ambulatory care (outpatient) units, including the direction of programs in 41 specialty clinics and 4 primary care clinics serving 90,000 outpatient visits per year; coordinating and implementing new clinic services/programs; responsible for a $4 million budget; and serving as administrative liaison to physicians, nursing staff and families. **Career Steps:** Children's Hospital of Oklahoma: Director of Nursing (1994–Present), Assistant Director of Nursing (1992–1994), Ambulatory Care Coordinator (1987–1992), Head Nurse – Burn Center (1977–1981), Burn Nurse Coordinator (1975–1977), Nursing Supervisor (1974–1975), Week–End Nursing Supervisor (1971–1974). **Associations & Accomplishments:** American Academy of Ambulatory Care Nurses, Member for 8 years; Chairperson (1993–1995), Oklahoma County Immunization Coalition; State of Oklahoma Immunization Advisory Board; "Sooner Sensations" Chapter of Sweet Adelines International – Chorus Member, Historian, and 1993 Member of the Year; Member of Grace Lutheran Church and Member of Church Choir; Member of a Registered Quartet with Sweet Adelines International. **Education:** Oklahoma Baptist University, B.S. in Nursing (1969); C.P.N. Certified Pediatric Nurse (1990–1996) (obtained through National Certification and annual CEUS). **Personal:** Married to Thomas in 1986. Three children: Lynna, Clark and Heather. Ms. Rodden enjoys singing, dancing, reading, snow skiing, collecting antiques, civil war enthusiast and geneaology.

Vidya Sagar, M.D.
Chief of Department of Nuclear Medicine
Christiana Nuclear Medicine
16 Stone Tower Lane
Wilmington, DE 19803–4536
(302) 733–1530
Fax: (302) 733–1518

8069

Business Information: Christiana Nuclear Medicine is a research and development organization specializing in the study and practice of nuclear medicine. Dr. Sagar joined CNM in 1976. Promoted to Chief of the Department of Nuclear Medicine in 1990, he is currently responsible for daily operations, supervises a medical staff of fifteen, and performs diversified administrative activities. **Career Steps:** Christiana Nuclear Medicine: Department Head (1990–Present), Associate Head (1973–1990). **Associations & Accomplishments:** Fellow, American College of Physicians; Fellow, American College of Nuclear Physicians; American Medical Association; A.C.R.; Who's Who of the East (1973). **Education:** State University of New York at Buffalo, M.S. (1975); Kerala University, India: Calicut Medical College, M.D., Christ College, B.Sc. **Personal:** Married to Deborah in 1988. Three children: Anita, Jina, and Jay. Dr. Sagar enjoys tennis and travel.

Richard A. Schreiber
Director of Pediatric Liver Transplantation Program
Montreal Children's Hospital – Division of Gastroenterology
2300 Tupper Street
Montreal, Quebec H3H 1P3
(514) 934–4474 ext. 2494
Fax: (514) 934–4392
EMAIL: See Below

8069

Business Information: Montreal Children's Hospital is a full–service healthcare institution specializing in the diagnosis, treatment, and rehabilitation of children. As Director of Pediatric Liver Transplantation Program, Dr. Schreiber is responsible for all aspects of the transplant program and the patient. Internet users can reach him via: MCRS@musica.mcgill.ca.

Career Steps: Director of Pediatric Liver Transplantation Program, Montreal Children's Hospital – Division of Gastroenterology (Present). Education: Harvard University; McGill University, M.D.C.M.; Faculty of the Royal College of Canada.

Stuart E. Siegel, M.D.

Head of the Division of Hematology and Oncology
Childrens Hospital Los Angeles
4650 Sunset Boulevard
Los Angeles, CA 90027
(213) 669–2205
Fax: (213) 660–7128
8069

Business Information: Childrens Hospital Los Angeles is a 312–bed, full–service, multi–specialty medical facility and health service establishment, as well as a research and instructional institution. Currently the hospital employs 200 physicians and medical support staff. As Head of the Division of Hematology and Oncology, Dr. Siegel is responsible for the care and treatment of patients, as well as instruction and research. Concurrent to his position with the hospital, Dr. Siegel is also a Professor of Pediatrics at the University of Southern California School of Medicine. **Career Steps:** Head of the Division of Hematology and Oncology, Childrens Hospital Los Angeles (1976–Present); Deputy Physician–In–Chief, Childrens Hospital Los Angeles (1987–1991); Coordinator for Pediatric Oncology, University of Southern California School of Medicine (1976–Present); Associate Hematologist, Attending Physician and Consultant to the Clinical Laboratories, Childrens Hospital Los Angeles (1972–1976); Associate Director for Pediatric Oncology, Kenneth Norris Jr. Comprehensive Cancer Center (1989–Present); Associate Chair, Department of Pediatrics, Childrens Hospital Los Angeles (1994–Present); Vice Chairman, Department of Pediatrics, University of Southern California School of Medicine (1994–Present). **Associations & Accomplishments:** Los Angeles County Medical Association; Los Angeles Pediatric Society; Western Society for Pediatric Research; Fellow, American Academy of Pediatrics; American Medical Association; American Association for the Advancement of Science; American Association for Cancer research; American Society of Hematology; American Society of Microbiology; American Society for Clinical Oncology; American Society of Pediatric Hematology and Oncology; American Association for Cancer Education; Society for Pediatric Research; American Pediatric Society; Societe Internationale d'Oncologie Pediatrique; Israel Cancer Research Fund Honoree (1994); President, Southern California Childrens Cancer Services, Inc. (1978–Present); Medical Director, Camp Ronald McDonald for Good Times (1982–Present); Member, Board of Directors, Ronald McDonald Children's Charities (1988–Present); Chairman, Grant Review Committee, Children's Cancer Research Fund (1990–Present). **Education:** Boston University: M.D., magna cum laude (1967), B.A., summa cum laude (1967); University of Minnesota Hospitals, Department of Pediatrics: Intern (1967–1968), Residency (1968–1969); Clinical Associate, National Cancer Institute, National Institutes of Health (1962–1972). **Personal:** One child: Joshua David. Dr. Siegel enjoys the opera, hockey, reading and travel.

Leigh M. Simpson

Chief Financial Officer
Washington County Infirmary
P.O. Box 597, St. Stephens Avenue
Chatom, AL 36518–0597
(334) 847–2223
Fax: (334) 847–3808
8069

Business Information: Washington County Infirmary is a 30–bed hospital, 73–bed nursing home facility and physicians' clinic. As Chief Financial Officer, Mr. Simpson is responsible for all financial activity and planning for the hospital, nursing home, and affiliated doctors' clinics. **Career Steps:** Chief Financial Officer, Washington County Infirmary (1995–Present); Accountant, Infirmary Health System, Inc. (1992–1995). **Associations & Accomplishments:** Healthcare Financial Management Association; National Association of Female Executives. **Education:** Troy State University, B.S. in Accounting (1991). **Personal:** Married to Gregory J. in 1994.

Susan R. Slocum

Treasury Director
Children's Health Care
2525 Chicago Avenue
Minneapolis, MN 55404–4578
(612) 813–6040
Fax: (612) 813–5972
8069

Business Information: Children's Health Care is a specialty and tertiary care hospital, providing health care services to children residing in eleven counties surrounding the St. Paul area. A hi–tech financial expert with ten years of experience, Ms. Slocum joined Children's Health Care as Treasury Director in 1995. She is responsible for the management of all investments, as well as pension assets, corporate cash management, and debt management. **Career Steps:** Treasury Director, Children's Health Care (1995–Present); Senior Portfolio Manager, Wallace Investment Management (193–1995); Investment Manager, Health Span Health Systems (1988–1993); Commodity Trader, Western Commodities Inc. (1986–1988). **Associations & Accomplishments:** Women's Bond Club of New York; Board Member, MNA Pension Board; Investment Committee, MN Women's Fund. **Education:** University of Minnesota, M.B.A. (1986); Carleton College, B.A. **Personal:** Married to Stephen Holloway in 1996. One child: Edith Elizabeth Lee. Ms. Slocum enjoys horseback riding, dog training, tennis and golf.

Bill Spindler, C.P.A., M.B.A.

Manager
M.D. Anderson Cancer Center
1515 Holcombe Boulevard
Houston, TX 77030–3911
(713) 792–7371
Fax: (713) 794–1352
EMAIL: See Below
8069

Business Information: M.D. Anderson Cancer Center, an entity of the University of Texas System, is a specialty hospital dedicated to cancer treatment, research and education. A Certified Public Accountant, Bill Spindler has held various accounting managerial positions with M.D. Anderson since 1988. In his current capacity, he coordinates and supervises information systems support, involving executive and managerial information systems; group systems; programming and designated information support staff. Internet users can reach him via: bspindler@utmdacc.mda.uth.tmc.edu **Career Steps:** M.D. Anderson: Manager (1993–Present), Coordinator of Information Systems (1991–1993), Administrative Manager (1991–1990), Manager of Accounting (1988–1990). **Associations & Accomplishments:** Texas Society of Certified Public Accountants; Volunteer, Leadership Houston. **Education:** University of Houston, M.B.A. (1977); Certified Public Accountant (1994). **Personal:** Married to Christy in 1977. One child: Ian. Mr. Spindler enjoys karate and Judo.

Jagannathan Srinivasaraghavan, M.D.

Chief of Psychiatry
Veterans Affairs Medical Center
400 Fort Hill Avenue
Canandaigua, NY 14424–1159
(716) 396–3622
Fax: (716) 396–4737
8069

Business Information: Veterans Affairs Medical Center is a medical institute providing diagnosis and treatment to veterans of military forces. A practicing physician since 1974, and an Internist and Psychiatrist, Dr. Srinivasaraghavan joined VA Medical Center as Chief of Psychiatry in 1993. He is responsible for all aspects of operations for the largest bed department (330–340 beds) at the Center. He also oversees all administrative operations for associates and a support staff of 52 (doctors, nurses, physician assistants), in addition to his daily patient practice. In this position, Dr. Srinivasaraghavan has been able to set up new programs, as well as conduct conferences and seminars nationally and internationally on electro–convulsive therapy and restraints used on patients. **Career Steps:** Chief of Psychiatry, Veterans Affairs Medical Center (1993–Present); Clinical Associate Professor of Psychiatry, University of Rochester (1994–Present); Acting Chief of Psychiatry, North Chicago Veteran Affairs Medical Center (1993); Associate Professor of Clinical Psychiatry, Finch UHS/Chicago Medical School (1992–1994). **Associations & Accomplishments:** American Psychiatric Association; American Academy of Psychiatry and The Law; Treasurer, Indo–American Psychiatric Association. **Education:** Thanjavur Medical College, India (University of Madras), M.B.B.S. (1974); Madras Medical College (University of Madras), Residency in Internal Medicine (1974–1977); UHS/Chicago Medical School – North Chicago, Residency in Psychiatry (1977–1980). **Personal:** Married to Kanchana in 1987. Two children: Vishnu and Arvind. Dr. Srinivasaraghavan enjoys travel (has visited 150 countries) and photography.

Philomena Thomas, M.D.

Attending Pediatrician
Schneider Childrens Hospital
New Hyde Park, NY 11040
(718) 470–7640
Fax: Please mail or call
8069

Business Information: Schneider Childrens Hospital is a multi–specialty childrens hospital, teaching institution and research center. Dr. Thomas is an Attending Pediatrician in the Pediatric Emergency Room. As such, she is responsible for the care and treatment of sick children as well as the supervision and instruction of Pediatric residents, fellows and medical students. **Career Steps:** Attending Pediatrician, Schneider Childrens Hospital (1989–Present); Director, Ambulatory Pediatrics, St. Johns Episcopal Hospital, Far Rockaway (1988–1989); Fellow Ambulatory Pediatrics, Schneider Childrens Hospital and North Shore University Hospital (1986–1987 & 1987–1988); Residency – North Shore University Hospital (1984–1986); Worked as a Pediatrician in the U.K. (1980–1984); Senior and Junio Resident in Pediatrics at Jawaharlal Institute Pondicherry, India (1974–1979). **Associations & Accomplishments:** Fellow, American Academy of Pediatrics; Member, Royal College of Physicians of U.K.; Member, Jipmer Alumni Association of North America. **Education:** Jawaharlal Institute, M.D. in Pediatrics (1977); M.B.B.S. (1974), Diploma in Child Health (1976), Madras, India; Membership Royal College of Physicians (1982); Diploma in Child Health, London (1981); Fellow, American Academy of Pediatrics (1987); Diplomat American Board of Pediatric (1995). **Personal:** Married to Thomas Mulakkan, M.D. in 1979. One child: Lisa Ann. Dr. Thomas enjoys sewing, gardening, and cooking.

Alan H. Wilde, M.D.

Vice President
Cleveland Center for Joint Reconstruction
2322 E. 22nd Street
Cleveland, OH 44115–3176
(216) 736–7980
Fax: (216) 736–7969
8069

Business Information: Cleveland Center for Joint Reconstruction, a part of Cleveland Clinic, is a full–service, medical facility, specializing in orthopedic surgery for joint reconstruction. A practicing physician since 1959 and a Board–Certified Orthopaedic Surgeon, Dr. Wilde joined Cleveland Center for Joint Reconstruction as Vice President in 1992. He is responsible for all administrative operations for associates and a support staff, in addition to his daily patient surgery practice. **Career Steps:** Vice President, Cleveland Center for Joint Reconstruction (1992–Present) **Associations & Accomplishments:** American Orthopaedic Association; American Academy of Orthopaedic Surgeons; MidAmerica Orthopaedic Association; American Shoulder and Elbow Surgeons **Education:** Hahnemann University, M.D. (1959); University of Pennsylvania, A.B. (1955) **Personal:** Married to Marilyn in 1958. Three children: Alan Jr., Douglas and Laurie. Dr. Wilde enjoys gardening and tennis.

Hyungkoo Yun, M.D.

Founder and Executive Medical Director
New Margaret Hague Women's Health Institute
3540 Kennedy Boulevard
Jersey City, NJ 07306
(201) 915–2468
Fax: (201) 915–2481
8069

Business Information: A Board–Certified Gynecologic Laparoscopist and Laparascopic Surgeon, Dr. Yun founded the New Margaret Hague Women's Health Institute in 1995, providing specialty health care for women, education to Ob–Gyn physicians, residents, and medical students, and conducting Ob–Gyn research. Serving as Executive Medical Director, he is responsible for the management of the Institute, as well as providing health care to patients. Concurrent with his position at the Institute, he is the founder and President at Hudson Ob & Gyn Associates, Inc. and Vice President and Clinical Director of the Department of Gynecology at Jersey City Medical Center. Strategic plans include conducting more research on preventing premature birth and labor. **Career Steps:** Executive Medical Director and Founder, New Margaret Hague Womens Health Institute (1995–Present); President and Founder, Hudson Ob–Gyn Associates, Inc. (1986–Present); Vice President and Clinical Director, Department Ob–Gyn Jersey City Medical Center (1990–Present). **Associations & Accom-**

plishments: American Medical Association; American Association of Gynecologic Laparoscopists; Society of Laparoscopic Surgeons; Korean American Medical Association; Published in Lady's Journal on women's health care. **Education:** Seoul National University Medical School, M.D. (1973). **Personal:** Married to InSook in 1973. Three children: Grace, David, and Joshua. Dr. Yun enjoys skiing, golf, mountain climbing, and travel.

Javier Cruz, M.D., Ph.D.

Physician
Clinique Medicale Nova
3755 Saint – Laurent Boulevard
Montreal, Quebec H2W 1X8
(514) 987–0080
Fax: Please mail or call

8071

Business Information: Clinique Medicale Nova, comprised of five pediatricians, four General Doctors, and ten Specialists, is a medical facility providing treatment, diagnosis, and rehabilitation to patients. As Physician, Dr. Cruz, one of four General Practitioners, is responsible for general health and rehabilitation of patients, and psychotherapy. **Career Steps:** Physician, Clinique Medicale Nova (1992–Present). **Education:** McGill University, Ph.D. (1990), M.D. (1979); Contributed to discovery of link between endocytic and exocytic pathway in mammalian cells. **Personal:** Married to Denise Camara in 1994. Dr. Cruz enjoys oil painting and spending time with his family.

Sharon E. Ercoliani

Operations Manager
Townley Laboratories, Inc.
1750 West Front Street
Plainfield, NJ 07063–1022
(908) 757–1137 Ext.26
Fax: (908) 757–0335

8071

Business Information: Townley Laboratories, Inc. is an international environmental testing laboratory established in 1961 in New Jersey. The corporation has approximately 40 employees. As Operations Manager, Ms. Ercoliani is responsible for 36 employees and is in charge of all aspects of the daily operations of the laboratory. Ms. Ercoliani is currently training to become President of the corporation and hopes to assume the position within the next two years. **Career Steps:** Townley Laboratories, Inc Operations Manager (1992–Present), Laboratory Manager (1989–1992), Technical Director (1988–1989). **Associations & Accomplishments:** Current Chairperson, Environmental Laboratory Advisory Committee to New Jersey Department of Environmental Protection. **Education:** Kean College, B.S. (1985). **Personal:** Married to David in 1992. Two children: Cindy and Susan. Ms. Ercoliani enjoys being head coach Dukes Pop Warner Cheerleaders.

Lucrecia Fernandez

Senior Manager and General Counsel
Hato Rey Pathology & Associates
570 J.J. Jimenez St.
Hato Rey, Puerto Rico 00918
(809) 765–7320
Fax: (809) 753–7656

8071

Business Information: Hato Rey Pathology & Associates, established in 1989, is an anatomical, surgical and cytopathological laboratory providing pathological testing. Ms. Fernandez, working with her husband who is co–founder of the Lab, serves as Senior Manager. She oversees all lab testing operations (with the exception of highly–specialized cell testing), as well as provides all administrative and operational management for a support staff of 40. A practicing attorney since 1982, she also represents the Lab in all legal matters. **Career Steps:** Senior Manager and General Counsel, Hato Rey Pathology & Associates (1989–Present); Manager and Lawyer, Domenech Pathology Association (1983–1989). **Associations & Accomplishments:** Colegio de Abogados de Puerto Rico; Phi Delta Phi International Legal Fraternity. **Education:** University of Puerto Rico School of Law, J.D. (1982), B.A. in Humanities. **Personal:** Married to Guillermo Villarmarzo, M.D. in 1969. Two children: Guillermo A. and Gabriela Villarmarzo Fernandez. Mrs. Fernandez enjoys snorkeling, reading, travel, and spending time with family.

Janett Gray

Quality Assurance Director
Lifeblood
1040 Madison Avenue
Memphis, TN 38104–2106
(901) 529–6379
Fax: (901) 529–6388
EMAIL: See Below

8071

Business Information: Lifeblood is the second largest bone marrow donor blood bank in the world with facilities in Arkansas, Mississippi, and Tennessee. As Quality Assurance Director, Ms. Gray is responsible for ensuring the safety of the facility and the blood supply, by requiring accuracy of medical forms and records, securing the quality assurance of medical control elements, and troubleshooting. Internet users can reach her via: Jangray@aol.com **Career Steps:** Quality Assurance Director, Lifeblood (1993–Present); Quality Assurance Technologist/Analyst, Coors (1991–1993); Quality Assurance Microbiologist/Analyst, Stroh/Schlitz (1981–1991). **Associations & Accomplishments:** American Sociey for Quality Control; National Society of Black Engineers; Society of Manufacturing Engineers; American Association of Blood Banks; Optimist Club; Community Council of Blood Centers. **Education:** University of Memphis, M.S. in Engineering (1989); Arkansas Technical University, B.S. **Personal:** Ms. Gray enjoys tennis and reading.

John R. Hadden

Associate Vice President of Sales and Marketing
Labcorp
5610 W. La Salle Street
Tampa, FL 33607–1770
(813) 289–5227
Fax: (813) 286–7431

8071

Business Information: Concentrating on research in AIDS, DNA, PCR technology, cancer drug testing, and other health diseases, Labcorp is the nations largest clinical reference laboratory. Labcorp has 16 main labs in the U.S., with the Florida division operating from two main facilities and 110 satellite sites. Working in various managerial roles with Labcorp since 1989, John Hadden was appointed as Associate Vice President in 1995. In this capacity, he provides the direction and motivation for growth development strategies, as well as overall customer relations. Concurrent to his executive duties with Labcorp, Mr. Hadden is Vice President of a private investment and leasing firm, which he founded in 1991. **Career Steps:** Labcorp: Associate Vice President (1995–Present), Regional Director (1992–1995), Director of Sales and Marketing (1989–1992); Senior Sales Representative (1985–1989); Vice President, J. Hadden and Investments (1991–Present). **Associations & Accomplishments:** National Spokesperson, March of Dimes; Tampa, Florida Committee of 100 Top Business Leaders; Former Director of Marketing Republican Party; Florida Healthcare Professionals; Former Vice President, Make–A–Wish Foundation. **Personal:** Married to Susie in 1989. Two children: Lindsey Kaye and Victoria Christian. Mr. Hadden enjoys exercising, reading, golf and spending time with his family.

William K. Hofer

Director of Sales & Marketing
Clinical Laboratories of the Midwest
1100 South Euclid Avenue
Sioux Falls, SD 57105–0411
(605) 333–5258
Fax: (605) 333–5253

8071

Business Information: Clinical Laboratories of the Midwest, affiliated with Sioux Valley Hospital in Sioux Falls, South Dakota, provides all aspects of clinical laboratory analysis and reference source information. As Director of Sales, Marketing, and Client Support, Bill Hofer provides the supervision and overall administration for client support staff, ensuring quality client relationships and product output as well as directs all sales, pricing, budget and strategic marketing areas. **Career Steps:** Director of Sales, Marketing, and Client Support, Clinical Laboratories of the Midwest (1994–Present); Nichols Institute: District Manager (1991–1994), Director of Sales (1990–1991). **Associations & Accomplishments:** Medical Group Managers Association; Clinical Laboratory Managers Association; Volunteer Coach, YMCA; Booster Club; Band Parents. **Education:** University of South Dakota, B.S. (1977); Medical Technology Certification (ASCP) (1977). **Personal:** Married to Holly in 1974. Four children: Rachel, Jordan, Thomas and Jaime. Mr. Hofer enjoys reading, hunting, fishing, camping, and his children.

Steven D. Jones

Associate Vice President
Lab Corporation
6370 Wilcox Road
Dublin, OH 43016–1269
(614) 889–1061
Fax: (614) 761–2603

8071

Business Information: Lab Corporation is a medical laboratory providing testing services to physicians, hospitals, veterinarians and other healthcare professions. As Associate Vice President, Mr. Jones is responsible for managing laboratory operations for the Great Lakes Division, as well as performing administrative duties. Additionally, he is the National Director for Chemistry, Hematology, Coagulation, and Urinalysis. Established in 1995, Lab Corporation employs 23,000 people with annual sales of $1.7 billion. **Career Steps:** Associate Vice President, Lab Corporation (1995–Present); ROCHE Biomedical Labs: Assistant Vice President of Operations (1990–1995), General Manager (1987–1989). **Associations & Accomplishments:** American Association for Clinical Chemistry; Ohio State University Alumni Association; Golden Endings of Central Ohio. **Education:** Ohio State University, B.S. (1972). **Personal:** Married to Diane in 1973. Mr. Jones enjoys golf, dogs, Ohio, and U.S. History.

Soverin Karmiol, Ph.D

Director of Research and Development
Clonetics Corporation
9620 Chesapeake Drive
San Diego, CA 92123
(619) 541–0086 Ext.149
Fax: (619) 541–0823
EMAIL: See Below

8071

Business Information: Clonetics Corporation focuses on the design and manufacture of human cell culture systems for research purposes. The corporation specializes in isolation, purification and identification of the human cell. After the systems are manufactured, they are distributed to academic, government, and industrial laboratories for research purposes. As Director of Research and Development, Dr. Karmiol manages a department of research assistants and works with them on the development of new products. He is responsible for maintaining the quality of existing Clonetics products and assists in establishing the quality standards for new products. Internet users can reach him via: Sov@Clonetics.com. **Career Steps:** Director of Research and Development, Clonetics Corporation (1993–Present); Post Doctoral Fellow, Department of Pathology, University of Michigan Medical School (1989–1993). **Associations & Accomplishments:** American Association for Cancer Research; The American Chemical Society; The American Association for the Advancement of Science; New York Academy of Sciences; American Heart Association; Cell Transplantation Society; The American Society for Cell Biology. **Education:** University of Guelph, Canada, Ph.D. (1989); University of Windsor, M.Sc. (1981); University of Toronto, B.Sc. (1969). **Personal:** Married to Erika K. Gentsch in 1980. Two children: Benjamin and Zachary. Dr. Karmiol enjoys martial arts.

Jean M. Katz, RN, BSN, PHN

Co–Founder/Director
Univ. of California San Francisco Medical Center Donor Lab & Platelet Aphresis
500 Parnassus, Box 0100, Room L–131 – Donor Center
San Francisco, CA 94131–0100
(415) 476–6989
Fax: (415) 476–6374

8071

Business Information: University of California San Francisco Medical Center/Mount Zion Blood Donor Center and Platelet Aphresis Unit is a clinical laboratory and donor center. The Blood Donor Center is a revenue generator for the non–profit Medical Center. Ms. Katz started the Blood Donor center in 1987 with only a $50,000 grant and has since created millions in revenue for the Blood Donor Center. She provides clinical direction, as well as administration and operational direction. **Career Steps:** Co–Founder/Director, University of California San Francisco Medical Center/Mount Zion Blood Donor Center and Platelet Aphresis Unit (1987–Present), First Blood Donor Center in USA with all staff to successfully complete the American Association for Blood Banks Phlebotomy Program with certification. **Associations & Accomplishments:** American Association for Blood Banks; California Blood Bank Society; San Mateo Junior Auxiliary; Chairperson for Campership grants for less fortunate children; Who's Who in American Colleges and Universities (1979–80). **Education:** Bachelor of Science in Nursing (1983); Public Health Nursing

Certificate (1984); American Association for Blood Banks Phlebotomy Instructor. **Personal:** Ms. Katz enjoys hiking, biking, skiing, and golf.

Erik T. Larsen, M.D.

President
E.T. Larsen Professional Corporation
6730 Legare Drive SW
Calgary, Alberta T3E 6H2
(403) 541–3387
Fax: (403) 541–3333

8071

Business Information: E.T. Larsen Professional Corporation is a contract health facility providing medical laboratory services to all of Canada. Dr. Larsen established the facility in 1989; he serves as President and oversees all aspects of operations, including support staff supervision and client interface. **Career Steps:** President, E.T. Larsen Professional Corporation (1989–Present). **Associations & Accomplishments:** American Society of Pathologists; College of American Pathologists. **Education:** University of Alberta, M.D. (1988); University of Calgary, B.Sc. (1984). **Personal:** Married. Dr. Larsen enjoys golf, hiking, and skiing.

Carlos A. Malaga–Somerford, D.V.M.

Director, Animal Resources Center
University of Puerto Rico
P.O. Box 365067
San Juan, Puerto Rico 00936
(787) 756–6540
Fax: (787) 758–2452
EMAIL: See Below

8071

Business Information: The University of Puerto Rico Animal Resources Center conducts animal testing and research using animals as models of human disease with a special interest in vaccinology. Research focuses on standard animal care (feeding and grooming), contract disease testing for the National Institute of Health (AIDS vaccines), and private research for Puerto Rican industries (rabies vaccines). As Director of the Center, Dr. Malaga–Somerford is responsible for supervising all aspects of animal care and testing, grants and funds dispersal, and research analysis. Internet users can reach him via: c_malaga@rcmad.upr.clu.edu **Career Steps:** Director, Animal Resources Center, University of Puerto Rico (1990–Present); Research Veterinarian, Battelle PNW Laboratories (1988–1990); Long Term Consultant, Pan American Health Organization (1979–1987). **Associations & Accomplishments:** American Veterinary Medical Association; Association of Primate Veterinarians; ASLAP; AALAS; AALAS, Caribbean Branch; Society for Tropical Veterinary Medicine; Peruvian Veterinary Association. **Education:** University of California at Davis, M.P.V.M. (1977); University of San Marcos, Peru, D.V.M. (1974); AALAS–ILAM, Mississippi, RILAM (1994). **Personal:** Married to Carmen in 1975. One child: Carol Windy. Dr. Malaga–Somerford enjoys golf, handiwork, and community activities.

Julia Maldonado Lopez

Owner/Director
Laboratorio Clinico Sabana Del Palm
P.O. Box 1134
Comerio, Puerto Rico 00782–1134
(787) 875–8335
Fax: (787) 875–7707

8071

Business Information: Laboratorio Clinico Sabana Del Palm is a clinical laboratory working with 150 physicians. The laboratory tests body fluids and relays the results to the physicians. As Director, Ms. Maldonado Lopez handles the day–to–day operations of the laboratory. She is responsible for marketing, financial duties, personnel concerns, and maintaining the quality of laboratory services. **Career Steps:** Owner/Director, Laboratorio Clinico Sabana Del Palm (1977–Present); Director, CDT Corozal, Puerto Rico (1975–1977); Technologist, Hospital Matildes Brenes (1974–1975). **Associations & Accomplishments:** Laboratories Owners Association of Puerto Rico; College of Medical Technologists of Puerto Rico. **Education:** Post Graduate, Masters (1994); Medical Technologist; Data Entry. **Personal:** Married to Benjamin Nieves in 1993. Three children: Benjamin, Julibeth, and Joe B. Nieves. Ms. Maldonado Lopez enjoys reading, studying for her Ph.D., and learning about other cultures.

Michael A. Moss

Head of the Department of Pathology
QE II Health Sciences Centre – Department of Pathology & Laboratory
5788 University Avenue
Halifax, Nova Scotia B3H 1V8
(902) 428–3867
Fax: (902) 428–2123

8071

Business Information: Queen Elizabeth II Health Sciences Centre is a full–service medical facility located in Nova Scotia, Canada. Dr. Moss was one of three principals involved in the formation of one of Dalhousie University's first technology transfer companies, Path Scientific Research, which was formed to facilitate the application of novel analytical approaches, and computerized data processing in the chemical analysis of environmental supplies. Formed in conjunction with the Hospital, its Foundation, and Dalhousie University, their goal was to harness new technologies in order to reduce sample volumes, processing time, labor, and cost. **Career Steps:** Head/Department of Pathology & Laboratory Medicine, Queen Elizabeth Ili Health Sciences Centre (1995–Present); Dalhousie University: Head, Department of Pathology (1992–Present), Director, Division of Clinical Chemistry, Department of Pathology (1983–Present); Medical Examiner, Halifax County, Nova Scotia (1983–Present). **Associations & Accomplishments:** Honors: Co–Recipient, Med Chem Award (1984 and 1989); Fellow, Royal College of Physicians and Surgeons of Canada; Canadian Association of Medical Biochemists; Canadian Society of Clinical Chemists; Founding Member, Canadian Academy of Clinical Biochemistry; Nova Scotia Medical Society; Nova Scotia Society of Clinical Chemists; Numerous Invited Presentations on various medical subjects; Several Committee and Administrative Appointments; Management Program for Clinical Leaders, Henson College; Executive Development Seminar for Associate Deans and Department Chairs; Association of American Medical Colleges; Dalhousie University: Lecturer, Department of Pathology (1982–1985), Assistant Professor, Department of Pathology (1985–1988), Associate Professor, Department of Pathology (1988–1993), Full Professor, Department of Pathology (1993–Present). **Education:** Dalhousie University: F.R.C.P.(C) (1982), M.Sc.; University of London: M.B., B.S. **Personal:** Married to Margaret in 1976. Two children: Andrea and Alison. Dr. Moss enjoys motion pictures and literature.

Anil V. Narayan

Account Manager
Northern California Cancer Center
32960 Alvarado Nils Road, Suite 600
Union City, CA 94587
(510) 429–2506
Fax: (510) 429–2550
EMAIL: See Below

8071

Business Information: Northern California Cancer Center is a non–profit medical facility specializing in analysis and research into all forms of cancer. Established in 1974, the Facility employs 145 people and estimates annual revenue in excess of $8.5 million. As Account Manager, Mr. Narayan oversees the management of cash flow, budgeting for projects and organization, and is responsible for all accounts payable and receivable. Internet users can reach him via: Anarayan.nccc.org. **Career Steps:** Account Manager, Northern California Cancer Center (1991–Present); Chief Accountant, Burns Philip (SS) Company Limited, Suva, Fiji (1982–1990); Senior Auditor, Price Waterhouse (1977–1981). **Associations & Accomplishments:** Past Treasurer, Fiji Football Association (National Soccer Team); Past Treasurer Fiji Amateur Athletics Association (National Athletic Team); Past Accountant, Fiji Basketball Association. **Education:** University of West Australia, Bachelor in Communications (1978). **Personal:** Married to Madhu Lata in 1977. Three children: Praneal, Sandika, and Neal. Mr. Narayan enjoys fishing.

Patricia A. Nelson, Ph.D.

Director of the Immunology Department
AutoImmune Inc.
128 Spring Street
Lexington, MA 02173–7800
(617) 860–0710
Fax: (617) 860–0705
EMAIL: See Below

8071

Business Information: Established in 1988, AutoImmune Inc. is an institute primarily engaged in the development of oral tolerance immunotherapy for the treatment of autoimmune diseases such as multiple sclerosis, rheumatoid arthritis, and diabetes. As Director of the Immunology Department, Dr. Nelson coordinates the scientific research of the Preclinical Pharmacology, Animal Science Research, Immunoassay Development, and Clinical Trial Support Group. Internet users can also reach her via: AIMM@WORLD.STD.COM. **Career Steps:** Director of the Immunology Department, AutoImmune Inc. (1993–Present); Staff Scientist, Immunology, Vertex Phamaceuticals (1990–1993); Senior Scientist, Head of Cell Biology, GeneLabs Inc. (1987–1990). **Associations & Accomplishments:** American Association of Immunologists; American Association for the Advancement of Science; New York Academy of Sciences; Society for Mucosal Immunology. **Education:** University of California – San Diego, Ph.D. in Biology (1981); Postdoctoral Studies in Medicine, Stanford University (1982–1983); Montana State University: M.S. in Microbiology (1976), B.S. in Microbiology (1974). **Personal:** Married to Dr. Scott S. Zamvil in 1985. Three children: Christopher and Melissa Rampy, and Samuel Zamvil. Dr. Nelson enjoys singing in the Temple choir, sewing, cooking, and raising Shetland Sheepdogs.

Susan W. O'Reilly

Laboratory Director
Columbia Southern Hills Medical Center
391 Wallace Road
Nashville, TN 37211
(615) 781–3530
Fax: Please mail or call

8071

Business Information: Columbia Southern Hills Medical Center is a general acute care hospital serving the Nashville, Tennessee region. As Laboratory Director, Mrs. O'Reilly is responsible for directing and coordinating the activities of the laboratory department to ensure accurate, efficient and timely test results for the diagnosis and treatment of disease. Other operational responsibilities include staff recruitment, staff training and employment counseling. Technical responsibilities include compliance with state and national inspections, environmental concerns, and compliance with state and national laboratory safety regulations. **Career Steps:** Laboratory Director, Columbia Southern Hills Medical Center (1995–Present); National Reference Laboratory/National Health Laboratory/LabCorp: Acting Director of Operations (1995), Supervisor, Special Chemistry Department (1992–1995), Medical Technologist, Special Chemistry (1989–1992), Medical Technologist, Infectious Disease (1989); Medical Technologist, Immunology Department, Center for Clinical Science/International Clinical Laboratory (1987–1989); Medical Technologist, Hematology Department, Vanderbilt Hospital (1973–1975); Medical Technologist, Mercy Hospital (1970–1971); Office Manager, Office of Dr. Leroy Howell (1969). **Associations & Accomplishments:** American Society of Clinical Pathologists; Chemical Laboratory Management Association; Awards: Outstanding Young Women of America (1977), Certificate of Appreciation, NHL (1994). **Education:** Mercy Hospital, M.T. (1971); Mississippi University for Women, B.S. (1969). **Personal:** Married to Robert in 1968. Two children: Eric and Leigh. Mrs. O'Reilly enjoys walking, travel, and reading.

Libo Qiu, M.D.

Postdoctoral Research Associate
Walt Disney Memorial Cancer Institute at Florida Hospital
12722 Research Parkway
Orlando, FL 32826–3227
(407) 380–9977
Fax: (407) 380–9978
EMAIL: See Below

8071

Business Information: Walt Disney Memorial Cancer Institute at Florida Hospital is a not–for–profit hospital providing patient care and cancer research facilities. A Postdoctoral Research Associate at the Institute since 1994, Dr. Qiu previously taught students in China and pursued research in hematology and cardiology. He is presently conducting hematopoietic growth factor and monoclonal antibody production research projects through an independent study program at the Institute. In addition to his own research, Dr. Qiu also supervises both graduate and undergraduate student research and studies. Internet users can reach him at LBQ@libo.fhis.net **Career Steps:** Postdoctoral Research Associate, Walt Disney Memorial Cancer Institute at Florida Hospital (1994–Present); Visiting Scientist, IMM – University of Oxford (1992–1994); Instructor, Hengyang Medical College, China (1988–1992). **Associations & Accomplishments:** International Society for Hematotherapy & Graft Engineering; International Society for Analytical Cytology; American Society of Hematology; Chinese Association of Physiological Science. **Education:** Hengyang Medical College, M.D. (1985); Hunan Medical University, M.S.c (1988). **Personal:** Married to Huiling Li in 1991. One child: Qi Qiu. Dr. Qiu enjoys tennis and watching NBA Basketball.

Josef C. Schoell

Chief Financial Officer
American Biogenetic Sciences, Inc.
1375 Akron Street
Copiague, NY 11726
(516) 789–2600
Fax: Please mail or call

8071

Business Information: American Biogenetic Sciences, Inc. provides research and development in the biotech area, focusing on cardiovascular disease and neuroprotective disorders through research on antigens used to produce antibodies. Headquartered in New York, the Company has consulting and research locations in Indiana, Ireland, Moscow, Tel Aviv, and Peking. Specializing in assisting the health field in diagnosis and therapeutic medicine, the Company will, within the next six months, be releasing a new product called TPP which will assist in identifying clots in the blood stream. Established in 1983, the Company employs 30 people, and is publicly traded on the NASDAQ. As Chief Financial Officer, Mr. Schoell oversees all monetary functions of the Company, to include accounting, taxes. marketing, budgetary concerns, and marketing. **Career Steps:** Chief Financial Officer, American Biogenetic Sciences, Inc. (1992–Present); Assistant Controller, J.P. Stevens & Company, Inc. (1979–1988); Senior Auditor, Ernst & Young (1975–1979). **Associations & Accomplishments:** Financial Executive Institution; American Institute of Certified Public Accountants; New York State Certified Public Accountants. **Education:** New York University, B.S. in Accounting (1975). **Personal:** Married to Vicki in 1978. Two children: Carrie and Ashley. Mr. Schoell enjoys skiing and building anything.

Jennifer M. Scott

Vice President of Special Projects
Fabre Research Clinics, Inc.
5503 Crawford
Houston, TX 77004
(713) 526–2328
Fax: (713) 526–2453

8071

Business Information: Fabre Research Clinics, Inc. is a pharmaceutical inpatient/outpatient research clinic, specializing in the area of pyschotropic drugs (i.e., Prozac, Valium). Jennifer Scott pursued an Accounting Degree in 1986 while serving as Bookkeeper at Fabre. Promoted to Comptroller in 1987, she has steadily moved up the corporate structure to her current status as Vice President of Special Projects. In this role, she is responsible for seeing all special projects through from start to finish. In addition, Ms. Scott serves as Managing Human Resource Specialist. **Career Steps:** Fabre Research Clinics, Inc.: Vice President of Special Projects (1995–Present), Vice President/Project Manager (1995), Vice President Administration (1989–1995), Comptroller (1987–1989). **Associations & Accomplishments:** American Business Women's Association; National Association of Female Executives; Family Life Committee Representative; Class President, United Methodist Couples; Campaigned for and attended the Texas Gubernatorial Inauguration and Ball (1991); Volunteer, March of Dimes. **Education:** Northwood University, Bachelor's of Business Management, magna cum laude (1996). **Personal:** Married to William J. in 1987. Two children: Jason Garrett McNeese and Jessica Ann Scott. Ms. Scott enjoys politics, computers, gourmet cooking, and travel. She is also a flutist.

Jim M. Urtz

Laboratory Manager
Centrex Clinical Laboratories, Inc.
6700 Kirkville Road, Suite 202
East Syracuse, NY 13057–9373
(315) 434–9821
Fax: (315) 434–9825
EMAIL:JUrtz@aol.com

8071

Business Information: Centrex Clinical Laboratories, Inc. is a regional clinical reference laboratory, performing diagnostic patient testing on humans and animals. With headquarters located in Utica, New York, the Laboratory serves the Onondaga County, running three hospital laboratories, nursing homes, and outpatient laboratories, as well as an animal hospital. Established in 1969, Centrex Clinical Laboratories, Inc. reports annual budget of $2.5 million and currently employs 31 people. As Laboratory Manager, Mr. Urtz serves as the operational manager of all Syracuse locations under the direction of the Chief Executive Officer. **Career Steps:** Laboratory Manager, Centrex Clinical Laboratories, Inc. (1990–Present); Medical Technologist, Drs. Robert Parker & Lewis Robinson (1984–1990); Director, Stratford Schools (1980–1984).

Associations & Accomplishments: Associate Member, American Society of Clinical Pathologist; Clinical Laboratory Managers Association; Committee Member, Onondaga County and Dewitt Democratic Party; Worked with Nicaraguan and Salvadorian refugees for six months. **Education:** Albany College of Pharmacy, B.S. in Medical Technology (1969); St. Peter's School of Medical Technology, M.T. (ASCP); Lemoyne College, Post Graduate work in Religion and Philosophy. **Personal:** Mr. Urtz enjoys canoeing, camping, hiking, travel, and reading.

Dr. Barry S. Wagner, D.O.

Medical Director
Cumberland Medical Center
7715 Asherton Avenue
Chattanooga, TN 37421–1848
(615) 456–7125
Fax: (615) 456–7107

8071

Business Information: Cumberland Medical Center is a local acute and subacute medical center located in Chattanooga, Tennessee. The Center offers a wide variety of medical services and will soon be starting the first Physician's Assistant Residency program in Tennessee. The Hospital was established in 1953 and currently has over 700 employees. As Medical Director, Dr. Wagner serves as President of the medical staff and as Director of the Emergency Medical Department. He oversees the Industrial Medicine Department and employee health and wellness centers. Concurrently, Dr. Wagner owns four non–medicine related companies – a musical jingle company, two publishing companies, and a management company. **Career Steps:** Medical Director, Cumberland Medical Center (1992–Present); Staff Physician, Hutcheson Medical Center (1984–1992); Staff Physician, Fayette County Memorial Hospital (1982–1984). **Associations & Accomplishments:** American Medical Association; American College of Emergency Physicians; Tennessee Osteopathic Medical Association; American Osteopathic Association; Country Music Association. **Education:** Kinksville College of Osteopathic; Tennessee State University, B.S. **Personal:** Married to Amy in 1988. Two children: Lyndsay and Seth. Dr. Wagner enjoys producing music, writing songs, and running.

Ernest L. York, M.D.

Doctor
Wetaskiwin Lung Lab
5006 51 Street
Wetaskiwin, Alberta T9A 1L3
(403) 352–7085
Fax: (403) 352–7870

8071

Business Information: Wetaskiwin Lung Lab is a private practice, within a hospital, specializing in diagnosis and treatment of patients in internal medicine. The Lab also serves as a lung function laboratory. As Doctor and Medical Director, Dr. York provides medical care to his patients as sole practitioner, as well as performing tests and experiments in the Laboratory to further research the abilities and weaknesses of the lungs. **Career Steps:** Doctor, Wetaskiwin Lung Lab (1991–Present); Respirologist, University Alberta Hospital (1984–1991); Respirologist, Plains Health Centre. **Education:** M.B.B.Ch.; F.R.C.P.C; M.R.C.P; F.A.C.P. **Personal:** Married to Lily in 1975. Four children: Jennifer, Keith, Christopher, and Richard. Dr. York enjoys fishing, gardening, tennis, and ballroom dancing.

Z. Jenny Zhang, M.D., Ph.D.

Medical Assistant and Consultant
Cytogen Corporation
600 College Road, CN 5308
Princeton, NJ 08540
(617) 332–2500 Ext. 416
Fax: Please mail or call

8071

Business Information: Cytogen Corporation, merged with Cellcor in 1995, is a biotechnology company engaged in the development of autolymphocyte therapy for cancer and infectious diseases. As Medical Assistant and Consultant in the Clinical Research Department, Dr. Zhang is responsible for dealing with ALT and related clinical issues. She assists in the coordination of clinical trial, design, protocols, and activities for Cytogen and Cellcor. **Career Steps:** Medical Assistant/Consultant, Cytogen Corporation (1996–Present); Senior Scientist, Cellcor/Cytogen (1992–1996); Post–Doctorate, Brigham & Women's Hospital, Harvard Medical School (1989–1992). **Associations & Accomplishments:** American Association of Immunologists. **Education:** University of Cincinnati, Ph.D. (1988); Beijing Second Medical College, M.D. (1982). **Personal:** Married to Xiaotao Guo in 1982. Two children: Orie and Alex Ming Guo. Dr. Zhang enjoys reading, tennis, hiking, and skiing.

Dee A. Anderson, BSN,, PHN

Director of Nursing
Comfort Home Health Care
321 Hoffman Drive
Owatonna, MN 55060–2352
(507) 455–1077
Fax: (507) 455–0051

8082

Business Information: Comfort Home Health Care is a private home health agency that provides skilled nursing and personal care to patients. Headquartered in Rochester, Minnesota, the Agency has approximately 100 clients ages three weeks to 96 years, and services nine counties in South Central and South Eastern Minnesota. As Director of Nursing, Ms. Anderson manages the nursing department, and oversees training and supervision of the staff. She is also responsible for personnel recruitment and patient services. **Career Steps:** Director of Nursing, Comfort Home Health Care (1990–Present); Head Nurse, Obstetrics, St. Francis Regional Medical Center (1986–1988); Assistant Head Nurse, Obstetrics, University of Minnesota Hospitals (1981–1986). **Associations & Accomplishments:** Minnesota Home Care Association; Healthy Owatonna 2000 Task Force; Adult Leader for Church Youth Group. **Education:** University of Minnesota School of Nursing: B.S.N., P.H.N. (1972). **Personal:** Married to Lee G. in 1972. Two children: Joshua and Joanna. Ms. Anderson enjoys sailing, cross country skiing, and reading."

Marvin E. Armstrong

Vice President/CFO
United Home Care Services, Inc.
5255 N. W. 87th Avenue, Suite 400
Miami, FL 33178–2100
(305) 716–0767
Fax: (305) 716–0288

8082

Business Information: United Home Care Services is a Health and Human Services facility, as well as a licensed Home Health Agency. The Company provides in–home care to elderly and disabled adults in South Florida, so as to prevent institutionalization. As Vice President of Corporate Development, Mr. Armstrong is charged with the task of managing budgeting, finances, and strategic planning for the Company. He is also responsible for planning, general services, operations, and contract management for the 12 different agencies that interact with the Company. Mr. Armstrong was instrumental in Company's evolution into a financially stable non–profit organization. **Career Steps:** Vice President/CFO, United Home Care Services (1990–Present); Deputy Director, Health Crisis Network (1988–1990); Director of Finance, United Way of Dade County (1981–1988). **Associations & Accomplishments:** National Association of Black Accountants; Florida Association of Service Providers; Dade–Monroe Coalition of Aging; State of Florida/DOEA; FEMA Allocation Committee; City of Miami Audit Committee; Volunteer, Youth Mentor and Substance Counselor; Substance Abuse Counselor, Leadership Miami Graduate 1986, Big Brothers & Big Sisters. **Education:** Barry University, M.B.A. (1991); University of Florida, B.S.B.A. (1974); Miami–Dade Community College. **Personal:** Mr. Armstrong enjoys sports, theater, movies, reading, church activities, and travel.

Shirley A. Bardell, R.N.

Regional Manager
Housecall Home Healthcare
10012 North Dale Mabry, Suite 107
Tampa, FL 33618
(813) 968–9344
Fax: (813) 969–0296

8082

Business Information: Housecall Home Healthcare provides a full spectrum of home health services in Indiana, Tennessee, Virginia, Kentucky, and Florida. The Company is JCAHO–accredited and Medicare/Medicaid–certified. The parent company is Housecall Medical Resources, Inc. Its five divisions include Housecall Home Healthcare, Housecall Hospice, Housecall Infusion Services, Housecall Management Services, and Housecall Medical Equipment. Housecall Medical Resources has projected an annual gross revenue of approximately $275 million for 1995. Ms. Bardell is the Regional Manager for the Central Florida Region, responsible for all aspects of daily operations for fourteen offices in the Central Florida area. **Career Steps:** Housecall Home Healthcare: Regional Manager (1996–Present), District Manager (1994–1996), Administrator (1992–1994); Adjunct Professor, College of St. Francis – Florida Campus (Present). **Associations & Accomplishments:** Co–Chair Economic Development Committee, Brandon Chamber of Commerce; Regulatory and Legislative Committee, Association Home Health Industries; Board of Directors, American Heart Association. **Education:** Webster University, Master's in Healthcare Administration (1990); University of Toledo, Toledo, Ohio, B.S. in Health Administration; City University, Los Angeles, California, B.S. in Nursing; Toledo Hospital, Toledo, Ohio, R.N. Diploma. **Personal:** Married to Michael W. Bardell. Five children: Shawn, Travis, Matt, Sarah, and Megan.

Mrs. Myrna P. Barinaga
Vice President
L&M Home Health Corporation/d.b.a. Bethany Home Health Care
301 North Lake Avenue, Suite 200
Pasadena, CA 91101
(818) 683–0415
Fax: (818) 449–3060

8082

Business Information: L&M Home Health Corporation is a health service provider of Nurses, Medical Social Services, Rehabilitation Services such as Physical, Speech and Occupational therapy, Respiratory therapy and Dietary Service to homebound patients. L & M Home Health Corporation employs a professional staff of 78. **Career Steps:** Vice President, L&M Home Health Corporation (1991–Present); Director of Nurses, Nursing Care Provider (1990–1991); Director of Nurses, Bethany Home Health Care (1991–Present); Director of Education, Angeles Home Health (1989–1990). **Associations & Accomplishments:** Sillman University Alumni Association in Southern California; University of Southern California in Los Angeles Alumni Association; The National Association for Female Executives, Organization of Nurse Executives in California. **Education:** University of Southern California, M.S. in Education (1985); B.S. in Nursing (1959).

Eva Marie Beisner
Director of Finance
Visiting Nurse Association
P.O. Box 908
Claremont, CA 91711
(909) 624–3574
Fax: (909) 624–3574
EMail: See Below

8082

Business Information: Visiting Nurse Association is a home health care agency providing quality home health care to homebound patients, thereby making it possible for them to remain at home. As Director of Finance, Ms. Beisner is responsible for financial statements and all financial reports to the President and Board of Directors of the Company. She handles a large support staff, including billing clerks, an accountant, an accounts payable clerk, and data entry personnel. Internet users can reach her via: OWENSE@aol.com. **Career Steps:** Director of Finance, Visiting Nurse Association (1989–Present); Assistant Manager, Sunny Hills Racquet Club (1985–1989); Credit Manager, Coleman Systems (1980–1985); Cost Accounting, Locke Products (1978–1980). **Associations & Accomplishments:** Lions Club. **Education:** University of Phoenix, Bachelor of Science in Business Administration (1996). **Personal:** Two children: Patrick–Thomas Fairfield Owens and Michael Scott Owens. Ms. Beisner enjoys computers, horses, and travel.

Kristine Bennett Bradsher
Director of Managed Care
Interim Health Care
300 University Ridge, Suite 103
Greenville, SC 29601
(864) 233–1644
Fax: (864) 235–7597

8082

Business Information: Interim Health Care is a nationwide home health organization consisting of more than 927 offices in the U.S. and Canada. As Director of Managed Care, Ms. Bennett Bradsher directs reimbursement and utilization functions from the private insurance side of the business for one of Interim Healthcare's largest franchise operations. Additionally, she acts as a liaison between Interim and the clinical program in order to regulate program costs. She also handles marketing, oversees contract negotiation, case management, and internal processes. **Career Steps:** Director of Managed Care, Interim Health Care (1994–Present); Policy Analyst – Health, Partnership for Prevention (1992–1993); Consultant, Advanced Performance Solutions (1992); Manager/Nutritionist, Marriott Corporation (1986–1990). **Associations & Accomplishments:** American Dietetic Association; Sports Cardiovascular Nutritionists; U.S. Navy Reserves Medical Service Corps; Junior League; Delta Gamma Fraternity; Republican Women. **Education:** University of South Carolina, M.B.A. (1992); University of Wisconsin – Madison, B.S. **Personal:** Married to Charles in 1996. Ms. Bennett Bradsher enjoys running, piano, and travel.

Margaret S. Benton
Executive Director
Regional Visiting Nurse Agency Inc.
1100 Sherman Avenue
Hamden, CT 06514
(203) 288–1623
Fax: (203) 248–9215

8082

Business Information: Regional Visiting Nurse Agency Inc., an affiliate of Connecticut–based Saint Raphael Health Care System, is a voluntary non–profit health care organization providing home healthcare services within the greater Hamden, Connecticut area. Skilled professional services are provided in the areas of physical therapy, skilled nursing, speech therapy, well child conferences, medical social work, and preventive programs. Reporting directly to the Board of Directors, Margaret Benton was appointed as Executive Director in 1974. In this capacity, she provides the overall executive administration for the Agency, ensuring quality patient care, as well as supervises all care givers. **Career Steps:** Executive Director, Regional Visiting Nurse Agency Inc. (1974–Present); **Associations & Accomplishments:** President (1991–1995), Connecticut Home Care; National Association of Home Care; American Nursing Association; National League for Nursing. **Education:** Yale University, MSN (1955); Wheaton College, Psychology.

Ralph R. Bertrand
Program Director
Gentle Home Health Care, Inc.
2360 Calder Suite 114
Beaumont, TX 77702
(409) 838–4145
Fax: (409) 839–8704

8082

Business Information: Gentle Home Health Care, Inc. provides care for home bound geriatric clients, working within the atmosphere of the home. Established in 1995, the Company provides IV therapy, diabetic treatment, and other services. As Program Director, Mr. Bertrand is responsible for training, personnel management, implementing policy and procedures, and all community research and health awareness. He also oversees the Medicare program, and ensures compliance with all guidelines. **Career Steps:** Program Director, Gentle Home Health Care, Inc. (1996–Present); Program Director, Managed HHC (1994–1995); Store Manager, Modica Brothers Tire and Wheel (1988–1994). **Associations & Accomplishments:** Apostolic Church Youth Director; Licensed Minister, United Pentecostal Church, Inc. **Education:** Lamar University; Local 195 Pipefitters Apprentice School (1978). **Personal:** Married to Linda Marie in 1973. Two children: Holly and Jami.

Janis M. Betz
Nursing Administrator
Tri–County Healthcare, Inc.
310 West Linn Street
Bellefonte, PA 16823
(814) 355–0571
Fax: (814) 355–5918

8082

Business Information: Tri–County Healthcare, Inc.'s mission is to provide quality, safe, and cost–effective delivery of home health care services to individuals in Center, Clinton, and Clearfield counties, including private–duty nursing, supplemental staffing, ventilator, hospice, and respite care, 24–hour companion or nursing service, and homemaker/companion service. As Nursing Administrator, Ms. Betz is responsible for overseeing the Nursing Department, as well as ensuring compliance with state regulations to operate as a home health care agency. In addition, she is co–owner of Tri–County Healthcare, Inc., and is involved in all company operations. **Career Steps:** Nursing Administrator, Tri–County Healthcare, Inc. (1996–Present); Director of Nursing, Tri–County Nurses, Inc. (1995); Community Health Nurse, State Health Center (1994–1995); Admissions Nurse/Supervisor, University Park Nursing Center (1993–1994); Relief Shift Coordinator, Healthsouth Rehabilitation Hospital of Altoona (1993–1994); Visiting Nurse, Home Nursing Agency (1993–1994); Rehabilitation Nurse, Reading Rehabilitation Hospital (1986–1992); Medical/Surgical Nurse, Reading Hospital Medical Center (1984–1986). **Associations & Accomplishments:** CPR Instructor, American Heart Association; Sigma Theta Tau International Honor Society of Nursing. **Education:** Indiana University of Pennsylvania, Master's of Nursing Program (1992–1993); Kutztown University, B.S.N. (1991); Reading Hospital School of Nursing (1984). **Personal:** Married to Thomas in 1996. Ms. Betz has also been known as Holzman (1962–1987) and Wiggins (1987–1996). She enjoys gardening and caring for her fish.

Kenneth M. Bires
Division Controller
Olsten Kimberly Quality Care
17905 Singwood Pl.
Lutz, FL 33549
(813) 264–3000 Ext. 3022
Fax: (813) 264–3117

8082

Business Information: Olsten Kimberly Quality Care is the largest home health care provider in the United States. The Company provides skilled nursing or medical care in the home, under the supervision of a physician. As Division Controller, Mr. Bires is responsible for a team of twenty people, handling finance, budget, network, and other duties. **Career Steps:** Division Controller, Olsten Kimberly Quality Care (1995–Present); Controller, Lix Corporation (1984–1993); Senior Tax Manager, Arthur Andersen & Company (1975–1984). **Education:** Wharton Graduate, M.B.A. (1975); Xavier University, B.S. in Mathematics. **Personal:** Married to Cindy in 1993. Two children: Matthew and Taylor. Mr. Bires enjoys sports, reading, and cooking.

Karen A. Boudreaux
Corporate Executive Director
Home Health Concepts, Inc.
8901 E.F. Lowry Expressway
Texas City, TX 77591
(409) 935–1234
Fax: Please mail or call

8082

Business Information: Home Health Concepts, Inc. is the largest independently owned for–profit home health company in Texas. The Corporation provides local managed care contracts for hospitals and has 15 locations throughout Texas. Services are provided from five different companies; DME provides home medical equipment, Coastal Therapy provides occupational, physical, and speech therapy, Home Health Infusion provides insurance and third–party payer home infusion therapy, Hospice of The GulfCoast provides in–home hospice care, and Home Health Providers staffing, providers, self–pay, and medicaid services. As Corporate Executive Director over four of the five companies, Ms. Boudreaux is responsible for management of contracts, policy procedure, compliance with policy and procedure, state & federal licensure, and JCAHO accreditation. Established in 1989, Home Health Concepts, Inc. employs 700 people. **Career Steps:** Corporate Executive Director, Home Health Concepts, Inc. (1992–Present); Director of Homecare, Lexus Homecare (1990–1992). **Associations & Accomplishments:** American Cancer Society; Intravenous Nurses Society; Nicholls State University Alumni; American Heart Association; GCCA; TAHC; BACC. **Education:** Nicholls State University, Thibodaux, Louisiana, R.N. (1981). **Personal:** Ms. Boudreaux enjoys saltwater surf and wade fishing.

Jean Brian
Branch Director
American Home Health and Hospice
25814–B Business Center Drive
Redlands, CA 92374
(909) 799–8488
Fax: (909) 799–8495

8082

Business Information: American Home Health and Hospice, one of four branches, is a state–wide, in–home skilled health care provider. With twenty–five years experience of all branch activities, Ms. Brian joined American Home Health and Hospice in 1993. Serving as Branch Director, she is responsible for ensuring quality care through personalized service. **Career Steps:** Branch Director, American Home Health and Hospice (1993–Present); Director of Nurses, Community Care Center of Riverside (1990–1993); Case Manager, Desnt Hospital (1988–1990); Director of Nurses, Care Enterprises (1979–1988). **Associations & Accomplishments:** California Association for Health Services at Home; California Association of Health Facilities; Council of Long Term Care Nurses; Inland Association of Continuity of Care; Inland Home Care Council. **Education:** U of R, Gerintology Certificate; UCSB, Human Resource Management; CAHSAH, Home Care Management Certificate; UCI, Wound Care Certificate; Newport University; College of Desert, A.A. **Personal:** Two children: John Jacob Martin and Steven William Dombroski. Ms. Brian enjoys camping, rafting, and golf.

Christine A. Brogan
Controller
Coordinated Care Services
3505 East Royalton Road, Suite 165
Broadview Heights, OH 44147
(216) 526–7383
Fax: (216) 526–7267

8082

Business Information: Coordinated Care Services is a home health care agency. Joining Coordinated Care as Controller,

Ms. Brogan is responsible for all financial activities, including payroll, accounts receivable & payable, monthly closings, journal entries, payroll taxes, and tax matters. Concurrent with her position at Coordinated Care Services, she operates her own distributorship in Mary Kay Cosmetics: (216) 556–1833. **Career Steps:** Controller, Coordinated Care Services (1994–Present); Assistant Controller, Wilcox Transfer (1993); Accounts Receivable, Central Petroleum (1989–1992). **Associations & Accomplishments:** Volunteer, St. Margaret of Hungary's church functions; Published in Hungarian newsletter. **Education:** Bryant & Stratton, Associates in Accounting (1994). **Personal:** One child: Thomas. Ms. Brogan enjoys golf, camping, crafts, and selling Mary Kay cosmetics.

Doris J. Brown, R.N.

Director of Nursing
Carolina Hospital Systems
121 East Cedar Street
Florence, SC 29501
(803) 661–3000
Fax: Please mail or call

8082

Business Information: Carolina Hospital Systems is a network for home health care affiliations (two hospitals merged together with four different branches). A practicing registered nurse for nine years, Mrs. Brown joined Superior Home Health Care in 1994. Serving as Director of Nursing, she oversees all administrative operations for associates and a support staff of 90, in addition to directing all nursing and facility operations for the Kingsport and Gate City offices (covering a five county area). **Career Steps:** Director of Nursing, Carolina Hospital Systems (1995–Present); Director of Nursing, Superior Home Health Care (1994–1995); Operating Room Coordinator, Bristol Regional Medical Center (1990–1994); RN First Assistant, Bristol Plastic Surgery Center (1987–1990). **Associations & Accomplishments:** Kingsport Chamber of Commerce; National Association of Home Care; Tennessee Association of Home Care; Virginia Association of Home Care; Board of Directors, American Heart Association. **Education:** St. Joseph's College, B.S. P.A. (1995); Southwest Virginia Community College, A.D.N.; Currently working towards M.S. in Health Administration – St. Joseph's College. **Personal:** Married to Russell in 1975. Three children: Rus, Autumn and Jessica. Mrs. Brown enjoys stained glass crafting and reading.

Gina G. Burk

Director of Clinical Operations and Service
Olsten Kimberly Quality Care
2319 West 7th Place
Stillwater, OK 74074
(405) 377–1191
Fax: Please mail or call

8082

Business Information: Olsten Kimberly Quality Care is an integrated home health care system and management corporation providing complete in–home skilled nursing, physical therapy, and infusion therapy. The Stillwell, Oklahoma office currently staffs between 30 and 40 employees. Established in 1993, Olsten Kimberly Quality Care currently has 675 offices nationwide. As Director of Clinical Operations and Service, Ms. Burk oversees the administrative operations and services for her region. Occasionally, when needed, Ms. Burk fills in for the nursing staff but has been doing administrative functions for the past three years. **Career Steps:** Director of Clinical Operations and Service, Olsten Kimberly Quality Care (1994–Present); Director of Nursing, Westhaven Nursing Home (1992–1994); R.N., Mercy Hospital (1987–1992). **Education:** Langston University, B.S.N. (1990). **Personal:** Married to Bill in 1991. Four children: Brian, Jason, William, and Trina. Ms. Burk enjoys riding horses, fishing, and softball.

Shirley A. Byrd

Vice President of Education
APC Home Health Services, Inc.
2730 South 77 Sunshine Strip
Harlingen, TX 78550–8317
(210) 428–8301
Fax: (210) 428–5291

8082

Business Information: APC Home Health Services, Inc. is a home heath care organization, providing nursing services in the home from ten offices in Texas. With over twenty years experience in nursing and nursing management, Ms. Byrd joined APC Home Health Services as Vice President of the Insurance Division in 1995. Recently promoted to Vice President of Education for the Medicare Division, she oversees all Medicare operations for the ten Texas locations. **Career Steps:** APC Home Health Services, Inc.: Vice President of Education – Medicare Division (1996–Present), Vice President of the Insurance Division (1995–1996); Director of Medical & Surgical, Pediatrics, Valley Regional Hospital (1992–1995); Director of Nurses, South Texas Hospital (1987–1991); Director of Nurses, Golden Palms Helath Care (1986–1987). **Associations & Accomplishments:** Texas Nursing Association; American Nursing Association. **Education:** UTHSC – SA, currently attending; VTSAHC for a Masters in Nursing (1996); St. Joseph's University, B.S.; Blinn Junior College, B.A.A.; Breckenridge Hospital School of Nursing, Nursing Diploma. **Personal:** Married to Donald in 1982. Two children: Kevin and Dawn. Ms. Byrd enjoys arts and crafts, swimming, and fishing.

Kim L. Causey, RN

Director of Nursing
Health Systems Home Care, Inc.
702 South Wheeler Street
Jasper, TX 75951–4544
(409) 383–0244
Fax: Please mail or call

8082

Business Information: Health Systems Home Care, Inc. delivers nursing and personal care to the homes of elderly and disabled clients. As Director of Nursing, Ms. Causey supervises the nursing staff, including staff RN's, LVN's, and Certified Nursing Assistants. **Career Steps:** Director of Nursing, Health Systems Home Care, Inc. (1995–Present); Staff RN, Labor & Delivery, Jasper Memorial Hospital (1994–1995); Staff RN, Labor & Delivery, Southwest Medical Center (1989–1994). **Education:** Louisiana State University, ADN (1987). **Personal:** Married to Gerald in 1988. Two children: Jordan and Chelsey. Ms. Causey enjoys reading and antiques.

Jessica C. Corley

Director of Continuous Care
Heritage Health Care Services, Inc.
3737 Princeton, Suite 110
Albuquerque, NM 87107
(505) 884–3311
Fax: (505) 884–0082

8082

Business Information: Heritage Health Care Services, Inc. is a home health care agency, serving the greater Albuquerque–metro and surrounding five county area of New Mexico. The Agency provides a full range of medical services, including personal home visits by certified home health care professionals (i.e., physical therapists). A psychological rehabilitative counselor and Certified AIDS Trainer since 1989, Jessica Corley joined Heritage Health Care Services, Inc. as Director of Continuous Care in 1994. She is responsible for the direction of the division responsible for providing non–skilled medical care to patients in their homes. Duties include scheduling and other administrative responsibilities, as well as training individuals to work with HIV patients. **Career Steps:** Director of Continuous Care, Heritage Health Care Services, Inc. (1994–Present); Unit Director, Desert Hills Center for Youths and Families (1993–1994); IEP Coordinator, George Junior Republic Union Free School District (1991–1993); Director of Psychological Rehabilitation, North Central Connecticut Mental Health Department (1989–1991). **Associations & Accomplishments:** New Mexico Association of Home Care; New Mexico Association for Continuity of Care; Certified AIDS Trainer; Basketball Coach for high school students. **Education:** Cambridge College, M.Ed. (1989). **Personal:** Ms. Corley enjoys coaching basketball.

John L. Costello Jr.

Vice President of Finance and Chief Financial Officer
Visiting Nurse and Health Service
354 Union Avenue, P.O. Box 170
Elizabeth, NJ 07207–0170
(908) 352–5694 Ext: 281
Fax: (908) 352–1692

8082

Business Information: Visiting Nurse and Health Service is the parent company of three home care agencies located in New Jersey. One in Elizabeth (serving Union County) and one in Plainfield (serving Union, Somerset, and Middlesex counties) – both Medicaid–Certified home health agencies. The third agency is in Cranford, supplying home health aids throughout New Jersey. The Agencies offer skilled nursing; physical, occupational, and speech therapy; social workers; and home health aides. They also have psychiatric outreach programs, pediatrics, early maternity discharges, IV therapy, and cardiology programs. Visiting Nurse and Health Services also runs a Hospice and Acute Medical Infant Day Care in Elizabeth. Established in 1911, the Company reports annual revenue of $19.5 million and currently employs 445 people. As Vice President of Finance and Chief Financial Officer, Mr. Costello is responsible for direction of the General Ledger and Accounting departments, as well as the oversight of data processing and MIS departments. He is also the Company's representative for the local and regional coalitions. **Career Steps:** Vice President of Finance and Chief Financial Officer, Visiting Nurse and Health Service (1994–Present); Consultant, Actuarial Sciences Associates, Inc. (1994); Corporate Controller, Cathedral Healthcare System, Inc. (1992–1994), Corporate Assistant Controller, Franciscan Health System of New Jersey, Inc. (1987–1992). **Associations & Accomplishments:** New Jersey Hospital Financial Management Association; Friendly Sons of St. Patrick; Volunteer, Morristown Soup Kitchen; Home Health Assembly. **Education:** Seton Hall University, M.B.A. (1982); University of Scranton, B.S. in Biology. **Personal:** Married to Linda in 1982. Two children: Colleen E. and James B. Mr. Costello enjoys triathlons.

Cyndee Kelley Cromer

Director of Nursing and Administrator
Advanced Home Care
P.O. Box 18049
Greensboro, NC 27419–8049
(910) 852–3033
Fax: (910) 632–1750

8082

Business Information: Advanced Home Care is a home health care agency providing nursing, social work, and rehabilitation services to homebound patients throughout the Guilford County, NC area. Owned and operated by three area hospitals, Advanced Home Care can handle over 12,000 home visits a month. Established in 1985, Advanced Home Care currently employs 300 people. As Director of Nursing and Administrator, Mrs. Cromer is responsible for the management of the nursing staff, administrative and financial functions, public relations and strategic planning. **Career Steps:** Director of Nursing and Administrator, Advanced Home Care (1985–Present); HomeCare of Central Carolina: Clinical Nurse Manager (1992–1993), Clinical Team Leader (1991–1992), Registered Nurse (1986–1991). **Associations & Accomplishments:** American Nurses Association; North Carolina Nurses Association; Who's Who of Rising Young Professionals; Sigma Theta Tau. **Education:** University of North Carolina – Charlotte, B.S.N. (1981); University of North Carolina – Greensboro, Masters of Nursing Administration, in progress. **Personal:** Married to Randy Cromer in 1986. Four children: Phillip, Mark, Erin and Chip. Mrs. Cromer enjoys collecting and camping.

Robert G. Cunningham

President/Chief Executive Officer
Senex, Inc.
400 Crown Colony Drive
Quincy, MA 02169–0930
(617) 472–5594
Fax: (617) 472–0169

8082

Business Information: Senex, Inc. is unique in the United States. The Company specializes in the use of compression pumps to assist patients suffering from swelling of the limbs due to radiation treatments and traumatic injuries. Senex, Inc. was established in 1992 and currently has 12 locations nationwide. As President/CEO, Mr. Cunningham oversees the operation of the Company. He is responsible for decisions regarding financial concerns, strategic planning, and budgets. Other responsibilities include public relations and marketing of services. **Career Steps:** President/CEO, Senex, Inc. (1992–Present); President, Continuing Case Associates (1982–1990); Vice President of Marketing, Johnson Rents, Inc. (1976–1982). **Associations & Accomplishments:** National Association of Medical Equipment Suppliers; Former Board Member, MACHA and VNAMI; Active in local and state politics. Mr. Cunningham built Continuing Case Associates into a $30 million in annual revenues and became #31 on Inc. 100 list in 1988. **Education:** Brown University, M.A. (1981); Harvard University, B.A. in Political Science and Government. **Personal:** Married to Katherine in 1995. One child: Sean. Mr. Cunningham enjoys being a professional film writer (with credits), rollerblading, tennis, and scuba diving.

Joseph F. Danner

General Counsel
Saad's Healthcare Services
P.O. Box 16368
Mobile, AL 36616
(334) 343–9600
Fax: (334) 380–3328

8082

Business Information: The largest home health agency in Mobile, Saad's Healthcare Services provides all facets of home health services, including nurses, aides, therapists, social workers, and medical supplies and equipment. A practicing attorney in Alabama state and federal courts since 1981, Joseph Danner serves as General Counsel for the Agency. He provides all in–house counsel for labor and employment issues, which includes administrative and judicial litigation, coordinates all patient complaints and insurance claims, prepares, reviews and finalizes contracts, leases and other corporate instruments, as well as serves as compliance officer in matters pertaining to governmental regulatory affairs. **Career**

Steps: General Counsel, Saad's Healthcare Services (1995–Present); Of Counsel, McRight, Jackson, Dorman, Myrick & Moore (1989–1995); Shareholder and Director, Darby & Danner (1978–1989); Law Clerk and Associate, Darby & Myrick (1978–1995). **Associations & Accomplishments:** Alabama State Bar Association; American Bar Association; Order of the Coif / Farrah Law Society; Mobile Area Chamber of Commerce. **Education:** University of Alabama School of Law, J.D. (1981); University of Virginia, Graduate School of Arts & Sciences, M.A. in Latin American History (1972); Springhill College, A.B. in History (1970). **Personal:** Mr. Danner enjoys breeding and showing horses.

Sharon M. Durfee, R.Ph., BCNSP

Pharmacy Coordinator
Poudre Care Connection
1235 Riverside Avenue
Ft. Collins, CO 80524–3218
(970) 493–3444
Fax: (970) 493–0628
EMAIL: See Below

8082

Business Information: Poudre Care Connection is a home care nursing and pharmacy agency, providing care to patients in their home. They administer intravenous, chemo, and antibiotic therapy; as well as provide ostomy products and supplies, nursing services, pharmaceuticals, health care aids and the training of patients to administer self–medication. Poudre Care Connection also has a pharmaceutical and medical supply home delivery service. Joining Poudre Care Connection as Pharmacy Coordinator in 1995, Ms. Durfee coordinates and manages the day–to–day activities of the home care pharmacy, including IV therapy, total parenteral nutrition, enteral therapy, ostomy and wound care products. She also is responsible for administration, public relations, marketing, and strategic planning functions, as well as mixing pharmaceuticals, monitoring clients and deliveries, maintaining client accounts, and monitoring supplies. For Internet users, Ms. Durfee can be reached at the following address: smd@gemini.pvh.org **Career Steps:** Pharmacy Coordinator, Poudre Care Connection (1995–Present); Nutritional Support Pharmacist, Poudre Valley Hospital (1977–1995); Adjunct Clinical Faculty, University of Wyoming School of Pharmacy (1991–Present). **Associations & Accomplishments:** Licensure: State of Colorado, California, and Arizona; American Society for Parenteral and Enteral Nutrition – Chapters Committee, Liaison Region 2; Board of Directors, Colorado Society for Parenteral and Enteral Nutrition; American Society of Hospital Pharmacists (ASHP); Colorado Society of Hospital Pharmacists (CSHP); Junior League of Ft. Collins: Community Projects Vice President (1996) and multiple projects; Kappa Kappa Gamma Advisory Board (1983–1993); Kappa Kappa Gamma House Board (1983–1993); Participant in Ross Forum for Pharmacy Leadership, Ross Laboratories; Board of Pharmaceutical Specialties, Proctor, Nutrition Support Pharmacy Practice Specialty; National Multiple Sclerosis Society – Fort Collins Branch; Frequent lecturer on nutrition and other related areas. **Education:** University of Wyoming College of Pharmacy, B.S. in Pharmacy (1976); Board Certification in Nutrition Support Pharmacy Practice. **Personal:** Ms. Durfee enjoys travel and the Arts.

Ms. Cynthia Eitnier

President and Chief Executive Officer
Ross Ventures
166 Lancelot Way
Lawrenceville, GA 30245–4756
(404) 439–9199
Fax: Please mail or call

8082

Business Information: Ross Ventures is a provider of personal care and assisted living care for the elderly. They currently have a management contract for two (14– and 24–bed) care centers. Future plans include expanding into South Carolina. Established in 1994, Ross Ventures currently employs eight people. As President and Chief Executive Officer, Ms. Eitnier is responsible for all aspects of operations. Concurrent with her position, she serves as Director of Nursing at Brian Center Corporation. **Career Steps:** President and Chief Executive Officer, Ross Ventures (1994–Present); Director of Nursing, Brian Center Corporation (1994–Present); Assistant President, Atrium (1992–1994). **Associations & Accomplishments:** National Association of Directors of Nursing Long–Term Care (NADONNA); National Association of Executive Females (NAFNE); American Nursing Association (ANA); Georgia Nursing Home Association; Listed in Who's Who in American Women and Who's Who of Professional Nursing. **Education:** Kennesaw State University, M.B.A. (1994); University of South Carolina, M.S. in Nursing (1988); Millersville University, B.S. in Nursing (1984); Harrisburg Area Community College, A.S. in Nursing. **Personal:** Ms. Eitnier enjoys reading and Tae Kwon Do.

CHALMETTE HEALTH CARE D B A
Qualified Health Services
A privately owned propriety Health Care agency

Sonia Falcon

Chief Executive Officer and Owner
Qualified Health Services
8809 West Judge Perez Drive
Chalmette, LA 70043
(800) 390–0095
Fax: (504) 277–1114

8082

Business Information: Qualified Health Services is a fast growing home health agency which provides nursing, HCA, and therapy services in the Metropolitan New Orleans area and surrounding service areas. Additional services include: consulting, staffing, organizing for other health agencies, and developing specialty programs in psychology, OB chemotherapy, IV therapy, and AIDS cases. Establishing Qualified Health Services as Chief Executive Officer in 1993, Ms. Falcon is responsible for the oversight of the daily operations, as well as having full legal authority to operate the Agency. She is also conducting consulting and strategic planning, as well as contracting with other health agencies. Concurrent with her position at QHS, she is Owner of Falcon Home Care Consultants. **Career Steps:** Qualified Health Services: Chief Executive Officer (1993), Owner (1995); Owner, Falcon Home Care Consultants (1988–Present); Systems Manager, Egan Health Care Services (1991–1992); Director of Private Duty Division, American Nursing Services (1990–1991). **Associations & Accomplishments:** American Marketing Association; National Association of Female Executives; American Management Association; National Home Care Association of Louisiana; Hubbard Dianetics Foundation; Professional Business Women Association; Women Business Owners Association; St. Bernard Athletic Association. **Personal:** Two children: Summer and Robert III. Ms. Falcon enjoys jazz music, athletics, and travel.

Diana L. Farmer

Chief Operating Officer
North Central Texas Home Care
5608 Malvey, Suite 300
Ft. Worth, TX 76107
(817) 377–0880
Fax: (817) 377–0948

8082

Business Information: North Central Texas Home Care provides home health care services. Joining the Company as co–owner after the death of her mother's partner in 1980, Mrs. Farmer serves as Chief Operating Officer. She oversees all administrative operations for associates and a support staff of 100, in addition to all administrative functions, legislative issues, employee relations, traveling on behalf of the Company throughout Texas and the U.S. (regarding home care), and budgeting. **Career Steps:** North Central Texas Home Care: Chief Operations Officer (1995–Present), Chief Administrative Officer (1985–1995); Apartment Manager, Woodland Oaks (1984–1985); National Computer Dispatch, Harris Corp. (1982–1984). **Associations & Accomplishments:** Texas Association for Home Care; National Association for Home Care. **Education:** TCJC, working towards Business and Home Care Law. **Personal:** Married to Rick in 1990. Two children: Shirley (first year of college) and Summer Nicole (born on February 8, 1996). Mrs. Farmer enjoys cooking, reading, boating, and deer hunting.

Becky Fortner

Administrator
Extendicare Home Health
7375 Mount Carmel Road
Covington, TN 38019
(901) 476–7107
Fax: (901) 368–0155

8082

Business Information: Extendicare Home Health is a Medicare–Certified home health care and private duty nursing services agency. Certified in Home Health Nursing and a practicing nurse since 1974, Ms. Fortner joined Extendicare Home Health as Administrator in 1994. She serves as the execuitve administrator responsible for the overall day–to–day functioning, ensuring quality patient care is administered as well as the supervision of all nursing and administrative support staff. **Career Steps:** Administrator, Extendicare Home Health (1994–Present); Owner and Consultant, Associates In Care (1987–Present); Reg. Director of Nursing, Home–Bound Medical Care (1980–1987). **Associations & Accomplishments:** President, Memphis Chapter – Home Health Nurses Association; International Who's Who of Professionals (1996); Mid–South Health Care Executives. **Education:** University of Memphis, B.S. in Nursing (1990); Certified in Home Health Nursing by ANCC. **Personal:** Married to Chris in 1967. Two children: Kim and Todd.

Linda C. Foust

Program Director
River Mountain Services
P.O. Box 2864
Sparks, NV 89432
(702) 331–0654
Fax: (702) 331–7156

8082

Business Information: River Mountain Services, established in 1982, is a residential training center for adults with developmental disabilities. This is a nonprofit organization located in Nevada with approximately 90 employees. As Program Director, Ms. Foust is responsible for the supervision of all programs and program coordinators. Ms. Foust is also responsible for coordinating all programmatic issues for clients. The long range plans of Ms. Foust include becoming Managing Director or perhaps Chief Executive Officer of River Mountain Services. **Career Steps:** Program Director, River Mountain Services (1993–Present); Vocational Specialists Supervisor, Eastern Montana Industries (1992–1993); Vice President/Program Director, Ravalli Services (1988–1993). **Associations & Accomplishments:** United Way; Chamber of Commerce; American Association on Mental Retardation; Past Member and Officer, Beta Sigma Phi Sorority Jayceens; Citizens Advocacy; Eagles Auxiliary Association on Mental Retardation. **Education:** Carroll College, B.A. (1974). **Personal:** Two children: Stephani and Edward. Ms. Foust enjoys reading, camping, hiking, and bowling.

Nolberto (J.R.) Frausto III

Chief Operations Officer
Visiting Nurses of Del Rio
712 North Bedell
Del Rio, TX 78840–4111
(210) 774–4651
Fax: (210) 775–0493

8082

Business Information: Visiting Nurses of Del Rio is a home health care service company, providing two types of services: Professional and skilled nursing; and Homemaker and non–professional services from five offices throughout fifty–eight counties in West Texas. As Chief Operations Officer, Mr. Frausto is responsible for maintaining satellite offices, including supervising the MIS Department, personnel files, budgeting, and all daily operations and computer network. He also serves as Assistant Administrator and Secretary on the Board of Directors. **Career Steps:** Visiting Nurses of Del Rio: Chief Operations Officer (1995–Present), Full–Time (1991–1995), Part–Time (1989–1991). **Associations & Accomplishments:** Lions Club International. **Education:** Southwest Texas State University, B.A. (1991). **Personal:** Married to Vicki in 1993.

Joby Fussell

Information Systems Manager
Nurses Unlimited
700 North Grant Avenue
Odessa, TX 79761–4561
(915) 580–0181
Fax: (915) 580–2042
EMAIL: See Below

8082

Business Information: Nurses Unlimited is a skilled nursing home health care agency. The Agency provides medical equipment, medicare, and physical, occupational, and IV therapy. Nurses Unlimited offers a hospice center and also works with the Department of Health. As Information Systems Manager, Mr. Fussell deals mainly with computer networks and the telephone systems. He manages all aspects of the Information Systems Department and takes on special projects. Internet users can reach him via: Jfussel@marshill.com. **Career Steps:** Information Systems Manager, Nurses Unlimited (1994–Present); Programmer/Analyst, Wagner & Brown (1987–1994); Programmer, ClayDosta (1985–1987). **Personal:** Married to Kim in 1987. Two children: Ashli and Jaycee. Mr. Fussell enjoys guitar and music.

Gianfranco Galluzzo

Chief Financial Officer/Senior Vice President
OMNI Home Health Services, Inc.
8 Research Parkway
Wallingford, CT 06492–1929
(203) 294–6664
Fax: (203) 294–6711

8082

Business Information: OMNI Home Health Services, Inc. is a full service home care agency providing skilled nursing, physical therapy, occupational therapy, speech therapy, medical social workers, home health aides, homemakers, and a variety of clinical specialty programs. OMNI has grown from one office with seven employees to five offices (Wallingford, New Haven, Shelton, Farmington, and Waterbury) with over 950 employees. Last year OMNI Home Health Services reported an annual revenue of $16 million. Serving as Chief Financial Officer/Senior Vice President, Mr. Galluzzo is responsible for the oversight of business operations and finances. **Career Steps:** Chief Financial Officer/Senior Vice President, OMNI Home Health Services, Inc. (1990–Present); Private Practice Attorney (1978–1990). **Associations & Accomplishments:** National Association for Home Care – Fraud and Abuse Task Force; National Policy Forum – Medicare, Medicaid, and Long Term Care Reform. **Education:** Suffolk Law School, J.D. (1977); Fairfield University, B.A. (1974); Liverpool University (1972–1973). **Personal:** Married to Donna in 1985. Four children: Stephanie, Rachel, Gianfranco, and Justin. Mr. Galluzzo enjoys travel and music.

Serafin M. Garcia, M.D.

President
Glendale Home Health Care
1236 South Glendale, Suite D
Glendale, CA 91205
(818) 242–4966
Fax: (818) 502–2124

8082

Business Information: Glendale Home Health Care provides home health care services to individuals in the Los Angeles area. Services offered include physical, occupational, and speech therapy as well as nursing care, provided by a staff of trained professionals. As President, Dr. Garcia oversees every aspect of the Company, including operations, marketing, public relations and planning. Co–founder of Covina Valley Hospital, Dr. Garcia also has a private practice in pulmonary and internal medicine. **Career Steps:** President, Glendale Home Health Care (1988–Present); Chairman of the Board, Covina Valley Hospital (1978–1988); Chairman of the Board, Thompson Memorial Hospital (1992–1994); President, Home Related Services, Inc. (1988–Present). **Associations & Accomplishments:** American College of Physicians. **Education:** Loma Linda University, M.D. (1973). **Personal:** Married to Zanaida E. in 1966. Three children: John Richard, Linda Joyce, and Kimberly Jill. Dr. Garcia enjoys tennis, skiing, bicycling, and fishing.

Irma P. Garza

Chief Executive Officer
First Rate Home Health
1100 West Sam Houston Street
Pharr, TX 78577–5104
(512) 256–4401
Fax: Please mail or call

8082

Business Information: First Rate Home Health is a home health care agency offering the services, to include general home health care, speech therapy, and physical therapy, of fifteen registered nurses and two medical directors. Regional in scope, the Agency operates from four branch locations, and accepts Medicare, Medicaid, and/or private insurance. As Chief Executive Officer, Mrs. Garza is responsible for exercising due care and diligence in her role as Chief Agent/Leader of the Organization. Her duties include monitoring, evaluating, and implementing the Organization's mission statement, overseeing all operations, ensuring compliance of all state, local, and federal regulations, and promoting education and training of staff. **Career Steps:** Chief Executive Officer, First Rate Home Health (1994–Present); Benovides Elementary ISD: Librarian (1989–1995), Teacher (1976–1989). **Associations & Accomplishments:** Texas Association of Home Care; Pharr Chamber of Commerce; Falfurias Chamber of Commerce; Benovides PTA; Alice Chamber of Commerce. **Education:** Sam Houston State University, Library Sciences (1993); Texas A&I: B.A. in Education, Masters Degree in Bilingual Education, Diagnostician. **Personal:** Married to Nestor in 1949. Five children: Rene, Nestor III, Louis Roberto, Priscilla, and David. Mrs. Garza enjoys travel, decorating, dancing, socializing, and politics (state and local).

Joella J. Gettinger

Administrative Director
Hospice of East San Gabriel Valley
820 North Phillips Avenue
West Covina, CA 91791–1121
(818) 859–2266
Fax: (818) 859–2272

8082

Business Information: Hospice of East San Gabriel Valley is the management company for diversified home health services as follows: Home Care Advantage – a non–profit home health agency providing high–tech services, including chemotherapy and intravenous infusion therapy; Home Hospice Care; and In–patient Unit – an acute level care for hospice patients. Hospice of East San Gabriel Valley serves a 30–mile radius in Los Angeles County and Southern California. With ten years in health care, Ms. Gettinger joined Hospice of East San Gabriel Valley in 1995. Serving as Administrative Director, she is responsible for all clinical functions of the three companies, as well as ensuring the quality of nursing care and the profit and loss of corporation. In addition, she practices as an RN at Glendale Adventist Hospital. **Career Steps:** Administrative Director, Hospice of East San Gabriel Valley (1995–Present); Home Care Advantage: Director (1994–1995); Nursing Supervisor (1991–1995); U. Healthcare (1986–1991); Registered Nurse (1982–1986). **Associations & Accomplishments:** LIGA Flying Doctors of Mercy; New Hospice Organization; Nursing Honor Society. **Education:** Pacific Union College: B.S.N. (1986), A.S.; California State – Los Angeles, Enrolled in M.S.N Program. **Personal:** One child: Jordan. Ms. Gettinger enjoys golf.

Judy M. Gossett, R.N.

Nursing Support Services Coordinator
Hospice, Inc.
313 South Market Street
Wichita, KS 67202–3267
(316) 265–9441 (800) 767–4965
Fax: (316) 265–6066

8082

Business Information: Hospice, Inc. is a non–profit agency serving the terminally ill, which offers a comprehensive, coordinated program of services to patients and their families in both home and inpatient settings by a medically–directed inter–disciplinary team. As Nursing Support Services Coordinator, Ms. Gossett coordinates inventory control of medical supplies and equipment maintenance, staffing and supervising of Health Care Aides and Contracting Agency staff relief, infection control, and Clinical Skills Lab. **Career Steps:** Nursing Support Services Coordinator, Hospice, Inc. (1990–Present); Nursing Field Supervisor, Professional Care Associates, Inc. (1986–1991); Oncology R.N., St. Joseph Medical Center (1981–1987). **Associations & Accomplishments:** Council of Hospice Professionals of the National Hospice Organization; Hospice Nurses Association; Kansas Hospice Nurses Association; Associate Member, Association of Kansas Hospices. **Education:** Friends University, B.S. HRM (1995); St. Mary of the Plains College, A.D. Nursing for RN (1985); Wichita State University, course work (1982–1984). **Personal:** Married to Robert W. in 1971. Two children: Micky and Robin. Four grandchildren. Ms. Gossett enjoys family genealogy, reading, crocheting, stamping, and sewing.

Johnny J. Grice

Director of Operations
Jordan Health Services
P.O. Box 1387
Mt. Vernon, TX 75457
(903) 537–2376
Fax: (903) 537–7089

8082

Business Information: Jordan Health Services is a home health care corporation with four companies providing services to patients in 43 east Texas counties. Jordan health Services has been providing quality home health care since 1975. As Director of Operations, Mr. Grice serves as Chief Operations Officer and is responsible for overseeing and managing daily operations of the Corporation. Mr. Grice is also a retired Army Major with 24 years of service. **Career Steps:** Director of Operations, Jordan Health Services (1993–Present); Vice President of Operations, Riverside Lure Company (1991–1992); Owner, Toledo Bend Guide Service, Inc. (1986–1991). **Associations & Accomplishments:** American Management Association; National Institute of Business Management; Vietnam Helicopter Pilots Association. **Education:** Coker College, BS (1974); BA, Social Sciences; Command and General Staff College, US Army. **Personal:** Married to Catherine in 1985. Two children: Jessica and Caitlin. Mr. Grice enjoys hunting, flying, and participating in professional fishing tournaments.

Bobby Dean Hamner, R.N.

Chief Financial Officer
Town and Country Home Health
502 East First Street
Heavener, OK 74937–3204
(918) 653–7676
Fax: (918) 653–2772

8082

Business Information: Town and Country Home Health provides medical health care service to patients in their homes, serving patients from three locations based throughout Oklahoma. Services include nursing, respiratory therapy, physical therapy, outpatient rehabilitation and social services. As Chief Financial Officer and Assistant Administrator, Mr. Hamner is responsible for all aspects of financial and accounting functions, as well as the overall administrative operation and supervision of the nursing staff. **Career Steps:** Town and Country Home Health: Chief Financial Officer (1992–Present), Branch Supervisor (1991–1992); Head Nurse, Harbor View Mercy Hospital (1989–1992); Senior Clinical Nurse, Oklahoma Department of Corrections (1984–1989). **Associations & Accomplishments:** Education Committee, Oklahoma Association of Home Care; Volunteer, Boy Scouts of America. **Education:** Carl Albert State College, A.A.S. (1984); Poteau Community College, A.A. in Education; Attended: Park College; Baylor University. **Personal:** Married to Margaret Ann in 1962. Mr. Hamner enjoys basketball, reading, and taking his granddaughter to the park.

Marwan Hanania

Associate Director
Indiana University Medical Center (IUMC) Homecare
575 West Drive, XE040
Indianapolis, IN 46202–5272
(317) 274–8264
Fax: (317) 274–6639
EMAIL: See Below

8082

Business Information: IUMC Homecare is a comprehensive home care company providing infusion services, durable medical equipment, home health, RT, and oxygen to homebound persons. As Associate Director, Mr. Hanania is responsible for accounting, billing, information systems, and operations. Internet users can reach him via: Mhanania@indymed.iupui.edu. **Career Steps:** Associate Director, University of Indiana Medical Center Homecare (1992–Present); Assistant Director, Indiana Medical Center Hospitals (1990–1992); Finance Officer, United Nations Development Program (1988–1990); In 1985, Mr. Hanania opened a two–story gift and clothing store; From 1982 – 1985, he was employed by Catholic Relief Services, as a Rural Developer, designing and supporting programs to bring businesses and basic essentials to communities; Co–Owner and Manager, Gemco World Trading Company – promoted international trade between U.S. and West Bank (1988–1992) **Associations & Accomplishments:** Health Care Financial Management; Indiana Association of Homecare; Beta Gamma Sigma highest scholastic honor Indiana University MBA program. **Education:** Indiana University, M.B.A. (1987); Birzeit University – Israel, B.A. in Business Administration; Certified Public Accountant. **Personal:** Married to Denisa in 1994. One child: Daniel. Mr. Hanania enjoys swimming, travel, and coaching and watching soccer.

Anita Colleen Hastings Pyle

Executive Director
Visiting Nurse Service, Inc.
128 East Olin Avenue, Suite 200
Madison, WI 53713–1466
(608) 257–6710
Fax: (608) 257–8700

8082

Business Information: Visiting Nurse Service, Inc. (VNS), an 87–year old community–based home health care agency, is a state–licensed Medicare and Medicaid certified home health care agency, providing a full range of clinical and supportive services and home delivered meals. Services include: nursing; psychiatric nursing; physical, speech, and occupational therapies; medical social work; home health aide; personal care workers; case management; occupational health and community wellness programs and mobile meals. Joining VNS as Executive Director in 1992, Ms. Hastings Pyle is responsible to the Board of Directors for all administrative and management functions of agency operations, in addition to overseeing all operations for associates and a support staff of 96. Her responsibilities include budget development, community relations development and implementation, strategic planning, and general administration. She also provides clinical supervision to agency social workers, as well as incorporating her special skills in the areas of policy development, planning, grant–writing, and quality assurance. **Ca-**

reer Steps: Executive Director, Visiting Nurse Service, Inc. (1992–Present); Social Work Instructor, Saint Mary – of – The – Woods College (1988–1994); Consultant, University of Colorado Health Sciences Center for Home Care Quality Study (1988–1994); Vice President and Chief Operating Officer, Visiting Nurse Association of the Wabash Valley, Inc. (1983–1992); Field Instructor, BSW and MSW social work students from six universities (1968–1992); Instructor – Sociology/Social Work Department, Indiana State University (Jan 1988–May 1988); Various Consulting and Practicum Placement assignments: Bedford Medical Center Home Care, In–Home Services of Hoosier Uplands Economic Development Corporation, The Center for Mental Health – Anderson, IN (Periods 1982–1983); Madison County Department of Public Welfare – Child Welfare, Intake, Food Stamps, ADC and Adult Programs: Supervisor (1968–1981), Caseworker (1966–1968); Library Assistant, Anderson Carnegie Public Library (1961–1965). **Associations & Accomplishments:** Board of Directors, Wisconsin HomeCare Organization; Chair, Board of Directors, Wisconsin HomeCare PAC; Chair, Legislative Committee, Wisconsin HomeCare Organization; Chair (1993–1995), Region 1, Wisconsin HomeCare Organization; Vice President, Wisconsin Coalition of VNA's Inc.; Government Affairs Committee, Visiting Nurse Associations of America; United Way's Management Assistance Committee; Steering Committee, Support People Now; Purchase of Service Advisory Committee, Dane County Executive; Member, Community Services and Music Committees, Rotary Club of Madison; Agency Executives Council; Technical Advisory Committee, JCAHO Homecare Professional, Technical; National Association for Home Care Accreditation Program Board: Region V Director (1987–1991), Chair Quality Assurance Committee (1991); Indiana Association of Home Health Agencies: Southern Region Representative, Past President, Treasurer; Class XII Leadership Terre Haute; Academy of Certified Social Workers; National Association of Social Workers; Alpha Delta Mu; Governor's Human Service Initiative, Health Care Task Force for State of Indiana; Advisory Committee, McMillan Adult Day Care Center; Past officer and member of numerous boards, service and professional organizations. Frequent speaker on local, state and national level for workshops, community organizatins and media. SPECIAL AWARDS: Wisconsin HomeCare Organization Annual Regional Award (1995); Helping Hands Award (1991, 1992, 1990) by McMillan Adult Day Care Center; Nominee, Sister Mary Joseph Pomeroy Faculty Excellence Award (1990) – St. Mary of the Woods College; Robah Kellogg Award (1989) – Region V Home Care Association; Social Worker fo the Year (1987) – by both the NASW Region VII and Indiana Chapter's. **Education:** Indiana University, M.S.W. emphasis in Planning & Management/Health, with high distinction (1983); Anderson College, B.A. in Sociology/Social Work; Numerous continuing education workshops and seminars in management, health care and human services. **Personal:** Four children: Roxanne, Douglas, Russell and Raymond. Ms. Hastings Pyle enjoys reading, gardening, music, nature walks, needlework, quilting, symphonies and the theatre during her leisure time.

Kathryn F. Henry

Owner and Chief Executive Officer
Providers Home Health Service Inc.
8301 West Judge Perez, Suite 300
Chalmette, LA 70043
(504) 279–9005
Fax: (504) 279–8001

8082

Business Information: Providers Home Health Service Inc. provides a wide–range of nursing and social services to individuals who are otherwise homebound. Established in 1994, Providers Home Health Services currently employs 40 people. As Owner and Chief Executive Officer, Mrs. Henry is responsible for all aspects of operations. **Career Steps:** Owner and Chief Executive Officer, Providers Home Health Service Inc. (1994–Present); Practice Administrator, Salvador Velazquez (1985–1995). **Associations & Accomplishments:** President–Elect, St. Bernard Business and Professional Women's Club; Health Site Chair and Board Member, American Heart Association; Support Group Leader, Alzheimers Association; Louisiana Medical Group Manager Associaton. **Education:** Elaine P. Nunez, Associates in Business Administration, in progress; St. Bernard School of Practical Nursing, L.P.N. **Personal:** Married to Anthony Sr. in 1987. One child: Jason. Mrs. Henry enjoys reading, camping and hiking.

Elizabeth A Hessburg

Nursing Director
Progressive Home Care Inc.
1801 Carol Sue Avenue
Gretna, LA 70056–4113
(504) 368–3626
Fax: (504) 368–2708

8082

Business Information: Progressive Home Care Inc. provides home care service for patients within a 50 mile radius of Gretna, LA. To qualify for assistance the patients must be on Medicare/Medicaid or have been referred by their attending physician. The service began in 1994 and currently employs approximately 120 people. As Nursing Director, Ms. Hessburg directs the operations of approximately 20 nurses. She is responsible for making sure everything runs smoothly and her nurses follow proper medical procedures. It is also within her realm of responsibility to research problems when they occur and to make the proper recommendations to correct them. **Career Steps:** Nursing Director, Progressive Home Care Inc. (1995–Present); IV Nurse, HIV Case Manager, TPN, Inc. Las Vegas (1993–1994); Home Care Case Manager, Nathan Adelson Hospice (1990–1993); Inpatient Staff RN, Connecticut Hospice (1988–1989). **Associations & Accomplishments:** Sigma Theta Tau Nursing Honor Society; Intravenous Nurses Society; PICC and Midline Certified. **Education:** Louisiana State University Medical College, B.S.N. (1987). **Personal:** Two children: Joseph and Katie Sudderth.

Kathleen Heuertz

Director of Nurses
Allen Home Health Agency
P.O. Box 39
Maple Park, IL 60151
(815) 827–3210
Fax: (815) 827–3701

8082

Business Information: Allen Home Health Agency provides nurses offering healthcare and rehabilitation services to home bound patients. As Director of Nurses, Ms. Heuertz is responsible for scheduling, training, performing administrative duties, handling daily operations, providing in–service education, and documentation. **Career Steps:** Allen Home Health Agency: Director of Nurses (1993–Present), Nursing Supervisor (1989–1993), Staff Nurse (1980–1989). **Associations & Accomplishments:** Continuity of Care, State of Illinois and American Association; Illinois Council of Home Health Services. **Education:** College of St. Francis, M.S. (1995); Waubonsee Community College, ADN (1978); Aurora University, BSN (1985). **Personal:** Married to Curtis in 1981. One child: Diana. Ms. Heuertz enjoys sewing, quilting, reading, gardening, and cooking.

Valerie Lynn Hobbs

Clinical Director
North West Personal Support System, Inc.
1444 East Church Street
Jasper, GA 30143
(706) 692–3770
Fax: (706) 692–5461

8082

Business Information: North West Personal Support System, Inc., in conjunction with North West Home Health, provides support to homebound patients including homemaker and sitter services, respite care for Alzheimers patients, and geriatric case management. Funded through medicaid and private grants, the Company was established in 1994 and employs seventy–six people. As Clinical Director, Ms. Hobbs oversees personnel management and staffing in eight counties, and is responsible for ensuring completion of life insurance physicals, performance and evaluation reviews, handling new admissions, and managing schedules of 186–200 clients. Additional duties include serving as Educational Director of the Company and handling all training, education, and certification of nursing assistants in compliance with state regulations. **Career Steps:** Clinical Director, North West Personal Support System, Inc. (1995–Present); Charge Nurse, Day Surgery Unit, Baylor University Hospital (1991–1995); Perinatal Nurse/Women's Center Instructor, Northside Hospital (1982–1991); Charge Nurse, OB/GYN Office (1989–1991). **Associations & Accomplishments:** Director of Children's Activities Committee; American Cancer Society. **Education:** Ohio Valley School of Nursing, Diploma (1981). **Personal:** One child: Tyler. Ms. Hobbs enjoys tennis, children's activities and travel.

Mark Hodgson

Administrator
Visiting Nurse Association/Hospice of Monroe County
RR 5 Box 5169, Suite 101
East Stroudsburg, PA 18301–9208
(717) 421–5390
Fax: (717) 421–7423

8082

Business Information: Visiting Nurse Association/Hospice of Monroe County is a certified home health agency with 100 employees, serving East Stroudsburg, PA and surrounding areas. Established in 1950, services include skilled nursing, home health aides, physical, speech and occupational therapy along with medical, social and nutritional counseling. With ten years of health care experience, as Administrator, Mr. Hodgson is responsible for all aspects of operations for the Association. **Career Steps:** Administrator, Visiting Nurse Association/Hospice of Monroe County (1992–Present); Assistant Administrator, Laurel Manor Nursing Home (1989–1992). **Associations & Accomplishments:** Former President, Optimist Club of the Stroudsburgs; Former President, Monroe County Interagency Council; Chairman, Non–Profit Committee, Pocono Mountain Chamber of Commerce; Chairman, Northeast Support Group. **Personal:** Married to Sally in 1995. Mr. Hodgson enjoys golf, skiing, soccer, and fishing.

Richard Hogan

Chief Executive Officer
SpectraCare, Inc.
500 S. Hurstbourne Parkway
Louisville, KY 40222
(502) 429–5500
Fax: (502) 426–0666

8082

Business Information: SpectraCare, Inc. is a home health care company providing nursing services; occupational, speech, and physical therapies; infusion pharmacy services; and dialysis. Regional in scope, the Company is comprised of eight offices within Indiana, Kentucky, Ohio, and Georgia. Established in 1988, the Company employs 350 full–time people and has estimated annual revenue of $35 million. As Chief Executive Officer, Mr. Hogan oversees all operations and strategic planning. He is responsible for new business development and handles all financial aspects of the Company. **Career Steps:** CEO, SpectraCare, Inc. (1993–Present); Area Vice President, Home Intensive Care, Inc. (1991–1993); Vice President/Chief Operating Officer, Curaflex Infusion Services (1988–1991). **Education:** St. Louis University: M.A. in Finance (1981), B.S.B.A. (1973). **Personal:** Married to Marilyn in 1973. Four children: Erin, Kelly, Patrick, and Michael. Mr. Hogan enjoys golf, antique reproduction woodworking, and fishing.

Lynn A. Howes, R.N.

Professional Services Coordinator
Heartland Home Health Care
401 Center Avenue
Bay City, MI 48708
(517) 723–7177
Fax: (517) 895–9093

8082

Business Information: Heartland Home Health Care is a home health care organization, providing skilled and non–skilled services (i.e., RNs, LPNs, physical therapists, occupational therapists, speech therapists, MSWs, RDs, HHAs, CNAs) to nursing homes, for home health care, and hospices from 36 functioning offices. With ten years of experience in nursing, Mrs. Howes joined Heartland Home Health Care as Nursing Supervisor in 1992. Appointed as Professional Services Coordinator in 1995, she is responsible for the coordination of all professional services, as well as coordinating quality assurance matters. **Career Steps:** Heartland Home Health Care: Professional Services Coordinator (1995–Present), Nursing Supervisor (1992–1995); Oncology Unit RN, Memorial Hospital, NJ (1986–1992). **Associations & Accomplishments:** Oncology Nursing Society; Mid–Michigan Hospice Organization. **Education:** Mercer County College, A.A.S. (1986). **Personal:** Married to Troy in 1994. Mrs. Howes enjoys bowling, golf, working, crafts and gardening.

Bonnie M. Hudon

Director of Education
Quality Home Health Care
102 West 5th Street, Ste. B
Long Beach, MS 39560
(601) 865–0029
Fax: (601)864–5090
EMAIL: See Below

8082

Business Information: Quality Home Health Care provides home nursing services to the community of Long Beach, Mississippi, and surrounding areas including the counties of Hancock, Harrison, Jackson, Pearl River, Stone, and George. As Director of Education, Ms. Hudon is responsible for developing teaching materials for medical staff, providing up–to–date educational assistance, and conducting various administrative activities. Internet users can reach her via: bmh@datasync.com **Career Steps:** Director of Education, Quality Home Health Care (1996–Present); Educator, InterHealth, Inc. (1994–1995); Patient Care Coordinator, Alexander's Home Health (1991–1994). **Associations & Accomplishments:** Beta Sigma Phi. **Education:** University of the State of New York, A.S.N. (1983); R.N.C. in Med–Surg Nursing (1993). **Personal:** Four children: Susan, Scott, Cindy, and Lisa. Ms. Hudon enjoys skydiving and computers.

Jack F. Hull
Owner/Administrator
Loving Care and More
603 West Mullen
Osburn, ID 83849
(208) 752–8411
Fax: (208) 752–5221

8082

Business Information: Loving Care and More is a home health agency providing skilled nursing care to patients in their homes. Established in 1993, Loving Care & More employs 62 people with annual revenue in excess of $952,000. As Owner/Administrator, Mr. Hull's responsibilities consists of filing government reports, acting as a patient advocate, and purchasing medical equipment. Additionally, he handles all incoming donations of equipment and performs 60+ hours of in–house training per month. **Career Steps:** Owner/Administrator, Loving Care and More (1993–Present); President, Hun Construction Company (1988); President, Moll B. Dam Motel (1978); First Sergeant, 321st Engineers, United States Army Reserves (12 Years). **Associations & Accomplishments:** Wallace Elks Lodge #331, Exalted Ruler (1992–1993); President, Silver Valley Snow Cat Association; Vice President, Osburn Business Association; CLDM Temple, Shainsu. **Education:** University of Idaho. **Personal:** Married to Marianne in 1960. Three children: Mary, John, and Mike.

Hillary R. Jevtic, RN, BSN
Administrator
House Call Home Health Care, Inc.
2739 U.S. 19 North, 5th Floor
Holiday, FL 34691
(813) 938–2841
Fax: Please mail or call

8082

Business Information: House Call Home Health Care, Inc., a nationwide health care company, is a state certified home–health agency providing comprehensive services which include occupational, respiratory and physical therapy, combined with home infusion, speech therapy, chemo therapy, outpatient rehabilitation and social services. Located in Holiday, Florida this company has been serving others in it's community since 1987. With extensive medical services experience in skilled and managed care administration, Ms. Jevtic was appointed Administrator in January of 1991. In this capacity she is responsible for all aspects of clinical and financial operations. **Career Steps:** Administrator, House Call Home Health Care, Inc. (19–Present); Administrator, Paragon Home Health Care (1989–1990); Charge Nurse, North Florida Regional Medical Center (1986–1988). **Associations & Accomplishments:** Pasco County Community Service Council; New Port Richey Chamber of Commerce; Chi Omega Sorority Alumni: Sustaining Member, Former President. **Education:** University of South Florida, B.S. (1986).

Libby Jones

Administrator
Succor Health Systems
PO Box 307
Hutto, TX 78634
(512) 244–3600
Fax: (512) 244–5993

8082

Business Information: Succor Health Systems is a home health care system, providing nursing care, nurse's aides, physical therapy, speech therapy, and medical social work services. Established in 1991, Succor Health Systems serves Travis City and the surrounding six–county area. Joining Succor Health Systems as Administrator in 1991, Ms. Jones manages all business operations and finances, as well as assisting in the hiring of personnel. **Career Steps:** Administrator, Succor Health Systems (1991–Present); Medicare Coordinator, Williamson County Health (1989–1991); Administrator, Mobile Nurses, Inc. (1978–1988). **Associations & Accomplishments:** Texas Association of Home Care; Chamber of Commerce; 4–H Sponsor and Member **Personal:** Three children: Deanna Jeffrey; David R. Jones and Renda Napolitano. Ms. Jones enjoys deer hunting, traveling throughout the U.S., music, cooking, reading, football and gardening.

Diane L. Hunter
Nursing Director
Interim Healthcare
1509 Main Street
Wheeling, WV 26003
(304) 233–7800
Fax: (304) 233–7855

8082

Business Information: Interim Healthcare is a home health care facility/service located in Wheeling, West Virginia. As Nursing Director, Ms. Hunter oversees two health care locations. Her duties include staff recruitment, qualification verification, hiring, evaluating, and employment counseling. Ms. Hunter assists in the development of training programs and makes sure all nursing staff members are in compliance with state regulations. **Career Steps:** Nursing Director, Interim Healthcare (1993–Present); Director of Professional Services, Brookside Home Health Care (1991–1992); Director of Professional Services, Williamsburg Community Home Health (1988–1991). **Associations & Accomplishments:** Board Member, American Heart Association; Chamber of Commerce. **Education:** Thomas Nelson Community College, Associates in Nursing (1980). **Personal:** Married to Bradford in 1977. Two children: Brent and Brandon. Ms. Hunter enjoys reading, travel, 4–H, and fishing.

Edward C. Jewett
Director of State Programs
Outreach Health Services
1111 Babcock Road
San Antonio, TX 78201–6905
(210) 736–1812
Fax: (210) 736–2866

8082

Business Information: Established in 1978, Outreach Health Services is a state–certified home–health agency. Comprehensive services provided include skilled–care nursing, respiratory therapy, physical therapy, outpatient rehabilitation and social services. Located in San Antonio, Texas, this company has been serving others in it's community since 1978. An eleven year veteran of medical administration, Mr. Jewett was appointed Director of State Programs in 1990. In this capacity he has full executive administration, directing all programs funded through the State of Texas. **Career Steps:** Outreach Health Services: Director of State Programs (1990–Present), Administrator (1989–1990); Manager, Concepts of Care (1984–1989). **Associations & Accomplishments:** Texas Association of Home Care. **Education:** Trinity University, B.A. (1976). **Personal:** Married to Doris in 1983. One child: Isabel. Mr. Jewett enjoys hunting and fishing.

Jackie M. Kastner
Chief Financial Officer/Owner
Qualified Health Services
8809 West Judge Perez Drive
Chalmette, LA 70043
(504) 277–1109
Fax: (504) 277–1114

8082

Business Information: Qualified Health Services is a home health care services provider, serving a 50–mile radius surrounding Chalmette, Louisiana. As Chief Financial Officer/Owner, Ms. Kastner shares the responsiblities of overall operations, in addition to the oversight of all aspects of financial matters. **Career Steps:** Chief Financial Officer/Owner, Qualified Health Services (1992–Present); Administrator, Drs. Iteld & Samuels (1981–1995). **Associations & Accomplishments:** The National Association for Home Care; Home Care Association of Louisiana; Medical Group Management Association. **Personal:** Married to Robert in 1968. One child: Tanya. Ms. Kastner enjoys snorkeling, reading, and going to the movies.

Dennis H. Jardine, Ph.D.

President/CEO
Lyndon B. Johnson Health Complex
276 Nostrand Avenue
Brooklyn, NY 11205–4927
(718) 636–2261
Fax: (718) 398–3450

8082

Business Information: Lyndon B. Johnson Health Complex is a regional health care facility offering home care for immobile individuals. The Complex supplies non–technical domestic attendants and offers ambulatory health diagnostics and treatments for clients/patients. As President/CEO, Dr. Jardine, who started in 1968 as a Consultant with the Complex, oversees daily operations. He is involved in marketing strategies, cash management, product quality, and human resource management. **Career Steps:** President/CEO, Lyndon B. Johnson Health Complex (1968–Present). **Associations & Accomplishments:** Chairman–Board of Directors, Central Brooklyn Coordination Council; Chairman–Board of Directors, Brooklyn Primary Hear Care Network; Vice Chairman–Advisory Board, Kings County Hospital; Chairman–Credit Committee, Spc Brooklyn National Federal Credit Union. **Education:** Columbia University, M.P.H.; University of London, B.A., D.D.S, M.D., D.HyC. **Personal:** One child: Denice. Dr. Jardine enjoys antique cars, specifically Jaguars.

Gregory D. Jones
Administrator
Lake Country Home Care, Inc.
1019 15th Avenue Northwest
Ardmore, OK 73401–1810
(405) 226–5253
Fax: (405) 226–5258

8082

Business Information: Lake Country Home Care, Inc. is a Oklahoma–state certified home health agency, providing skilled, high–tech medical care to a service populace area of over 350,000. A successful health care administrator for the past ten years, Gregory Jones established Lake Country Home Care in May of 1992. As Administrator, he designs and implements all company policies, as well as provides backup support to high–level management staff. **Career Steps:** Administrator, Lake Country Home Care, Inc. (1992–Present); Business Manager, Pilot Point Home Health, Inc. (1991–1992); Business Manager, Marshall County Home Health, Inc. (1990–1991). **Associations & Accomplishments:** ProCare Home Health Care Alliance (a multi–state alliance organization): Chairman of Main Street Economic Restructuring Committee, Chairman of Benefits Committee; Health Care Association of America; Oklahoma Association of Home Care; National Association of Home Care; Southern Oklahoma Association of Life Underwriters; International Texas Longhorn Association; American Quarter and Paint Horse Association; Oklahoma Cattlemen's Association. **Education:** Columbia College, B.A. in Business Administration (1985). **Personal:** Married to Kimberly R. in 1986. One child: Joshua David. Mr. Jones enjoys raising registered Paint and Quarter Horses and Longhorn cattle.

Orael M. Keenan, RN, MSN

Executive Director/Chief Executive Officer
Visiting Nurse Association of L.I. Inc.
100 Garden City Plaza, Suite 100
Garden City, NY 11530–3201
(516) 739–1270
Fax: (516) 739–3864

8082

Business Information: Visiting Nurse Association of L.I. Inc., in Garden City, N.Y., provides a variety of home healthcare services to patients. Concentrating primarily in the Nassau County area, the Association offers registered nurses, physical, speech, and language therapy, as well as basic home health services. Established in 1914, the Company is comprised of seventy five nurses, who have made over 108,000 visits so far this year. Plans for the future include expanding to cover a wider geographic area, enabling them to provide care to a larger portion of the population. As Executive Director/Chief Executive Officer, Ms. Keenan oversees all finance, personnel, and administrative duties, as well as patient care and meetings with the board of directors. **Career Steps:** Executive Director/Chief Executive Officer, Visiting Nurse Association of L.I. Inc. (1994–Present); Director of Patient Services, Mary Immaculate Hospital (1992–1994); St. Mary's Hospital of Brooklyn – CHHA: Director of Patient Services (1990–1992), Director – Long Term Home Health Care Program (1988–1990). **Associations & Accomplishments:** Nurses Association of the Counties of Long Island; Sigma Theta Tau; Home Heathcare Nurses Association. **Education:** Hunter College, M.S.N. (1988); City College of City University of New York, B.S.N. **Personal:** Married to James in 1978. Ms. Keenan enjoys spending time with her husband.

Kathy Keeton

Chief Financial Officer/Vice President
Housecalls Home Health Services, Inc.
120 North 24th Street
Muskogee, OK 74401–5152
(918) 683–5900
Fax: Please mail or call

8082

Business Information: Housecalls Home Health Services, Inc. was established in 1991 and provides health care (i.e. housekeepers, skilled nurse, home health aide, physical therapy, social work visits) to homebound individuals. As Chief Financial Officer/Vice President, Ms. Keeton manages the Muskogee branch office and handles all financial responsibilities. Other duties include payroll, accounts receivable, accounts payable, and cash management. Ms. Keeton is also in charge of medicare updates for the corporation. **Career Steps:** Chief Financial Officer/Vice President, Housecalls Home Health Services, Inc. (1992–Present); Executive Vice President, Commercial Financial Services (1986–1992); Executive Vice President, Bartmann Enterprises (1982–1986). **Associations & Accomplishments:** National Association of Female Executives. **Education:** Attended, Northeastern State University. **Personal:** Ms. Keeton enjoys travel and reading.

Rebecca A. Kittell
Director of Human Resources
Professional In–Home Health Care, Inc.
975 Interstate 10 North
Beaumont, TX 77706–4815
(409) 898–1366
Fax: (409) 898–4383

8082

Business Information: Professional In–Home Health Care, Inc. is an intermittent home health care agency for Medicare, Medicaid, and private insurance patients. Ms. Kittell joined the Agency in April of 1995 as an Administrative Assistant, moving into her present position as Director of Human Resources in July of the same year. She is responsible for the planning, development, and supervision of the Agency's Human Resources policies and procedures. In addition, she holds a position on the Agency's governing body, Performance Improvement Committee, and the Agency Utilization Review Board. **Career Steps:** Professional In–Home Health Care, Inc: Director of Human Resources (1995–Present), Administrative Assistant (Apr.1995–Jul.1995); Human Resource Secretary, Managed Home Health Care, Inc. (1993–1994). **Personal:** Married to Wylie Charles in 1970. Two children: Janet Marie Kittell Dugas and David Ryan Kittell. One grandchild: Kourtney Nichole Dugas. Ms. Kittell enjoys home decoration and design, and church activities (choir member).

Sherry M. Knight, R.N.
Director
Home Health Care
1100 South Main Street
Bluffton, IN 46714
(219) 824–7406
Fax: Please mail or call

8082

Business Information: Home Health Care provides home health care services, including infusion therapy, post partum visits, and rehabilitation, occupational, and recreational therapy. Home Health Care is affiliated with Wells Community Hospital, providing physical therapy care for Medicare patients. As Director, Mrs. Knight directly supervises all staff, staff education and certification, billing, budgeting, and working with clinical coordinators to assure that patients are receiving the appropriate care. She reports directly to the CEO, and assures that regulations are followed. **Career Steps:** Director, Home Health Care (1996–Present); Wells Community Hospital: Assistant Nurse Manager (1995–1996), OB Nurse Educator (1988–1995). **Associations & Accomplishments:** ICEA. **Education:** Indiana Wesleyan University, Bachelor's degree (1988). **Personal:** Married to Terry in 1984. Five children: Kristen, Shannon, Megan, Erin, and Matthew. Mrs. Knight enjoys sewing, reading, and distance walking.

Judy G. Lewis, RN, BSN, RNC
Director of Professional Services
TLC Home Health
1195 Main Street
Mullins, SC 29574
(800) 774–0010
Fax: (803) 464–0010

8082

Business Information: TLC Home Health is a provider of personal care and assisted–living care for the elderly. As Director of Professional Services, Ms. Lewis is responsible for the specialty selections of the facility's nurses, overseeing Medicare and Medicaid follow–ups, and the education and training of the nurses. **Career Steps:** Director of Professional Services, TLC Home Health (1990–Present); Administrator, VNS (1990–1993); NICU Transport Nurse, McLeod Regional Medical Center (1984–1989); Head Nurse of Obstetrics and Nursery, Marion Memorial Hospital (1980–1984). **Associations & Accomplishments:** National Home Health Nurses Association; National Home Care Association. **Education:** M.U.S.C., B.S.N. (1986). **Personal:** Three children: Becky, Mary, and Andy Simmons. Ms. Lewis enjoys gardening and reading.

Michael J. Licari

Chief Financial Officer
Hospitals Home Health Care, Inc.
59 South First Street
Fulton, NY 13069–2903
(315) 598–6867
Fax: (315) 598–6868

8082

Business Information: Hospitals Home Health Care, Inc. is a managed care organization, providing professional medical personnel staffing (Aides, RNs, LPNs, CNAs) services to hospitals and physicians for patients discharged to home care. As Chief Financial Officer, Mr. Licari is responsible for the financial prosperity and growth within the home care marketplace. **Career Steps:** Chief Financial Officer, Hospitals Home Health Care (1995–Present); Senior Accountant, Oneida City Hospitals (1985–1995). **Associations & Accomplishments:** National Association of Certified Public Accountants. **Education:** State University of New York, B.S. in Accounting (1995). **Personal:** Married to Theresa A. in 1983. One child: Deanna. Mr. Licari enjoys golf and spending time with family.

Mary E. Lindquist
President and Chief Executive Officer
Arbor Hospice Homecare & Care–ousel
3810 Packard Street, Suite 200
Ann Arbor, MI 48108–2054
(313) 677–0500
Fax: (313) 677–2014

8082

Business Information: Arbor Hospice Homecare & Care–ousel is a hospice agency, providing care and support for terminally ill adults and children at home and in facilities throughout South East Michigan and surrounding areas. Specializing in anticipatory grief and bereavement programs, the Agency developed a specialty program for children two years ago which provides art therapy and child life specialists to comfort dying children and their families. With thirty–six years experience in the medical field, Ms. Lindquist began her professional career as a nurse in 1960. As President and Chief Operating Officer of Arbor Hospice Homecare & Care–ousel, she is responsible for all aspects of operations for the agency she started in 1984 and oversees a staff of 120 medical professionals. **Career Steps:** President and Chief Executive Officer, Arbor Hospice Homecare & Care–ousel (1984–Present). **Associations & Accomplishments:** International Hospice Institute; National Association of Home Care; Hospice Association of America; Michigan Hospice Organization. **Education:** University of Michigan, BSN (1960). **Personal:** Married to George in 1961. Three children: Meg, Lisa, and Trina. Ms. Lindquist enjoys quilting and gardening.

James L. Mantooth

Chief Executive Officer and Administrator
Mantooth Home Health Care
2525 South Shore Boulevard, Suite 405
League City, TX 77573–2990
(713) 334–6263
Fax: (713) 334–5307

8082

Business Information: Mantooth Home Health Care provides health care services in the home, nursing homes, hospitals, and foster homes. They offer the services of skilled nurses, chemotherapy, speech and occupational therapy, X–rays, laboratory tests, medical equipment, and respiratory therapy to the regional area of League City, Texas. Establishing Mantooth Home Health Care in 1992, Mr. Mantooth serves as Chief Executive Officer and Administrator, overseeing all administrative operations for associates and a support staff of 94. He also manages and directs all aspects of the Company, including the oversight of a $3 million operating budget. **Career Steps:** Chief Executive Officer and Administrator, Mantooth Home Health Care (1992–Present); Deputy Administrator, Texas Emergency Physicians (1983–1992). **Associations & Accomplishments:** Texas Association for Home Care; Fraternal Order of Eagles; Sons of the American Legion; Flaming Arrows S.O.S. **Education:** Lamar University, B.S. (1987); Attended: Southwest Texas State University.

Tina M. Martenson
Director
Home Health Services – McCamey Hospital District
2500 Highway 305 South
McCamey, TX 79752
(915) 452–8626
Fax: (915) 652–3465

8082

Business Information: Home Health Services is a hospital–based home health agency, providing skilled nursing care to patients in their homes throughout the McCamey Hospital District. Established in 1992, the Agency currently employs 22 people. With fourteen years expertise in skilled care nursing, Ms. Martenson founded Home Health Services in 1992. Serving as Director, she is responsible for the oversight of all functions, as well as the development of policy and procedures, management of nursing staff schedules, and serving as a "buffer" liaison in confrontations between staff and patients. Established in 1992, Home Health Services – McCamey Hospital District employs 22 people. **Career Steps:** Director, Home Health Services – McCamey Hospital District (1992–Present); Charge Nurse, Rankin Hospital (1991–1993); Case Manager, Kimberly Quality Care (1991–1993). **Associations & Accomplishments:** McCamey Hospital Auxillary; Texas Hospital Home Health Association. **Education:** Texas Tech University, working toward Bachelor of Science in Nursing; Odessa College, Associate Degree (1981); Sul Ross State University, Licensed Vocational Nurse (1981). **Personal:** Married to Christopher in 1982. One child: Michelle Ann Martenson. Ms. Martenson enjoys going to the beach and spending time with her family.

Cynthia K. Martin, B.S.R.N.
Director of Nursing
Country Care Private Nursing Services
100 Irwin Herminie Road
Rillton, PA 15678
(412) 446–2408
Fax: (412) 446–2435

8082

Business Information: Country Care Private Nursing Services provides personal services to individuals, primarily the elderly, in the community. The Company offers services to assist seniors in their independence, possibly eliminating the need for nursing home placement. With approximately 350 clients currently, the Company offers visiting nurses, shopping, and cleaning assistance. As Director of Nursing, Ms. Martin oversees all scheduling and administrative duties of the Company. She is directly responsible for a staff of fifty, and handles strategic planning and customer relations. **Career Steps:** Director of Nursing, Country Care Private Nursing Services (1995–Present); Inservice Director, Hempfield Manor (1989–1995); Owner and Instructor of Nurses Aides, Social Dimension Institute (1984–1989). **Associations & Accomplishments:** American Red Cross; Eastern Star; Board of Directors, Country Care. **Education:** California State College, B.S. in Nursing Education (1972); Management Training Institute; Homestead Hospital School of Nursing, R.N. (1963). **Personal:** Two children: Robert A. II and Kelly C.. Ms. Martin enjoys reading, games of chance, and crafts.

Ellen L. Martin, RN

Director of Clinical Services
Utah Senior Service Home Care
2180 E. 4500 So. #165
Salt Lake City, UT 84117
(801) 268–6262
Fax: (801) 268–4989
8082

Business Information: Utah Senior Service Home Care is a home health care agency, providing nurses, nurse's aides, and therapists services in the patient's home. A registered nurse with over twenty years in home health and long–term care administration, Ms. Martin serves as Director of Clinical Services for the Salt Lake City Office of the Utah Senior Service Home Care Agency. She leads a team of more than thirty health care professionals in the provision of quality health care, as well as oversees budgeting and marketing activities. **Career Steps:** Director of Clinical Services, Utah Senior Service Home Care (1993–Present); Director of Nursing, London Springs Care Center (1991–1993); Area Administrator, Creekside Home Health (1988–1990); Nursing Supervisor/Consultant, Idaho State Department of Health and Welfare (1984–1987). **Associations & Accomplishments:** Education Chair (1995–1997), Utah Association of Home Health Agencies; Club Secretary (1994–Present), Toastmasters International; Swiss Chorus of Midway, Utah; Outstanding Young Women of America (1991). **Education:** American Institute Wholistic, M.S. (1996); Weber State University, R.N. (1976). **Personal:** Two children: Jacob Campbell Martin and Katie Lee Gassett. Ms. Martin enjoys sewing.

Angelina Martinez, MSW, CSW

Secretary and Treasurer
Utopia Home Care, Inc.
60 East Main Street
Kings Park, NY 11754
(516) 666–4804
Fax: (516) 544–5141
8082

Business Information: Utopia Home Care, Inc. provides R.N.'s, L.P.N.'s, Home Health and Personal Care Aides, and live–in personnel to patients in hospitals and private homes. As Secretary and Treasurer, Mrs. Martinez is responsible for the supervision of the Quality Assurance Committees, and is a member of the Executive Board. Her primary duties involve the training of employees on how to work with the sick and how to cope with the familiy members and their feelings. **Career Steps:** Secretary and Treasurer, Utopia Home Care, Inc. (1982–Present); Part–time Bereavement Counselor, Hospice of the South Shore (1992–Present); Bereavement Counselor, Cancer Care (1991–1992); Case Worker, Child Protective Services (1982–1991). **Associations & Accomplishments:** National Association of Social Workers; National Association of Puerto Rican and Hispanic Social Workers; National Association of Hispanic Professional Women; New York State Association of Health Care Providers; Member of the Advisory Board, St. John's Episcopal Hospital; Board Member, Child Care Council, Suffolk Inc. **Education:** Adelphi University: M.S.W. (1992), B.S. (1990); Cornell University, 2 week intensive training in child abuse. **Personal:** Married to Manuel F. in 1959. Four children: Manuel Jr., David, Diane and Paul. Mrs. Martinez enjoys gardening, walking, and exercising.

Ipe Mathai

President/CEO
Mathai, Inc.
1313 Holland Avenue
Houston, TX 77029
(800) MATHAIJ (713) 450–4646
Fax: (713) 450–1844
8082

Business Information: With over 35 years of clinical and administrative experiences in hospitals and domiciliary care, Mr. Mathai had the great desire to start an independent health care entity to serve the needy. In 1987, Tender Loving Care Health Services of Texas was established specializing in home health care. In 1991, it was incorporated to Mathai Inc. to establish this service into many different cities. At present, it has four branches. Shortly thereafter, EJS Medical was started to provide a complete line of respiratory and medical equipment for home care with a retail medical supply store. In 1994, after having extensive training in Great Britain, Mr. Mathai started East Harris County Hospice Services Inc. to care for the terminally ill. His desire to have a full–service, "one–stop" shop for home care. He believes that health care should be accessible to the sick in the comfort of their own homes. **Career Steps:** President/CEO, Mathai, Inc. (1991–Present); Executive Director, East Harris County Hospice Services (1994–Present); Administrator, Tender Loving Care Health Services (1987–1991). **Associations & Accomplishments:** National Association for Home Care; Texas Hospice Organization; Swiss Emmaus Leprosy Relief Association; National Treasurer – Maranatha Full Gospel Churches General Home Missions; President/Founder – Mathai Outreach Ministries; Golf & Travel Club; Who's Who Among Outstanding Business Executives; Financial Decisions for the Successful Entrepreneur Conference. **Education:** University of Houston – Clear Lake, B.S. in Health Services Administration (1985); Catherine Booth School of Nursing, India, Registered Professional Nurse (1971); Swiss Emmaus Association, PMW (1963). **Personal:** Married to Susie in 1972. Three children: Elizabeth, Jacob, and Sarah Ann. Mr. Mathai enjoys golf, gardening, travel and charitable community activities.

Sharon Maurice

Administrator
United Home Health
936 South 59th
Belleville, IL 62223
(618) 277–8899
Fax: (618) 277–8628
8082

Business Information: United Home Health provides home health services, including rehabilitation and nursing services. As Administrator, Mrs. Maurice manages over 150 patients, over 50 staff members, and all aspects of daily operations for the local home care office. **Career Steps:** Administrator, United Home Health (1995–Present); Case Manager, Blue-Cross BlueShield (1995); Clinical Supervisor, Deaconess Home Care (1993–1995). **Education:** Sanford Brown, A.D.N. (1993); McKendree College, currently enrolled. **Personal:** Married to Rick in 1984. Two children: Jacob Andrew and Rochelle Elizabeth. Mrs. Maurice enjoys outdoor activities, boating, fishing, and reading.

Lola Mays

Administrator
Mays Housecall Home Health
801 SW "C" Street
Antlers, OK 74523
(405) 298–6447
Fax: (405) 298–5979
8082

Business Information: Mays Housecall Home Health provides home health care services to the infirmed in the rural communities of Southeastern Oklahoma. Services include in–home nursing; physical therapy, speech therapy, and medical social work. A registered nurse with over ten years in home health management and care, Ms. Mays founded the agency in 1991. As Administrator, she oversees all aspects of operation, ranging from patient care to administrative supervision. **Career Steps:** Owner and Administrator, Mays Housecall Home Health (1991–Present); Owner and Administrator, Community Rehab Medical Equipment, Inc. (1988–Present); Director, Request Care Inc. (1987–1988); Coordinator, Muskogee Home Health (1982–1987). **Associations & Accomplishments:** Oklahoma Home Health Association; National Association for Home Care; Chairperson, Healthcare Association of America. **Education:** Century College, M.B.A. (1995); Nursing Degree. **Personal:** Married to Dwaine in 1966. One child: Ronald. Ms. Mays enjoys gardening during her spare time.

John (Jack) F. McCarthy

Vice President of Finance
National Medical Care – Home Care Division
1601 Trapelo Road
Waltham, MA 02154
(617) 466–9850
Fax: (617) 890–8953
8082

Business Information: National Medical Care – Home Care Division is a national home health care service provider, providing intraveneous therapy, respiratory therapy and home nursing care. There are 120 locations, throughout the U.S., in major metropolitan and suburb areas. Established in 1982, National Medical Care reports annual revenue of $350 million and currently employs 2,500 people. As Vice President of Finance, Mr. McCarthy is responsible for all aspects of finances, including billings & collections, maintaining and preparing statements, annual forecasts, systems development, long– and short–term financial planning. **Career Steps:** Vice President of Finance, National Medical Care – Home Care Division (1988–Present); National Medical Care Dialysis Division: Director of Finance (1986–1988), Manager of Operations Analysis (1985–1986). **Associations & Accomplishments:** Financial Executives Institute; Health Care Financial Management Association; Sudbury Youth Hockey Board of Directors. **Education:** Babson College, M.B.A. (1982); University of Massachusetts at Amherst, B.A. (1979); Boston Latin School (1975). **Personal:** Married to Catherine Hawke in 1978. Two children: Katherine (Kate) and Andrew. Mr. McCarthy enjoys coaching youth hockey and Little League baseball.

Aggie McDonald

Vice President – Clinical Services
Mid–Delta Home Health Inc.
PO Box 373
Belzoni, MS 39038
(601) 247–1254
Fax: (601) 247–4111
8082

Business Information: Mid–Delta Home Health Inc., a CHAP and JCAHO accredited home health service provider, provides service to the homebound in need of healthcare throughout the rural mid–section of Mississippi. A registered nurse with over twenty years in home health and skilled care nursing administration, Ms. McDonald serves as Vice President of Clinical Services. She has full executive administration over all nursing, therapy and clinical services staff, ensuring quality patient care is provided. **Career Steps:** Vice President – Clinical Services, Mid–Delta Home Health Inc. (1994–Present); CHAP Survey Peer Nurse (1995); Director of CQI, Sta Home Health Agency, Inc. (1992–1994); Director of QM, Mississippi Methodist Rehabilitation Center (1988–1992); Director of QM, Central Mississippi HHA, Inc. (1985–1988). **Associations & Accomplishments:** Mississippi Nurses Association; Home Health Nursing Association; American Nurses Association; Calvary Baptist Church; Sigma Theta Tau; Baptist Nursing Fellowship. **Education:** University of Southern Mississippi, M.S.N. (1993); Mississippi College, B.S.N. (1975); Gilfoy School of Nursing (1962). **Personal:** Married to John A. McDonald, Sr. in 1962. Three children: John Jr., James and Angela. Ms. McDonald enjoys crafts, sewing, and reading.

Kevin P. McDonough, R.T.(R)

Service Director
Mobile X–Ray Specialists, Inc.
P.O. Box 151412
Altamonte Springs, FL 32715–1412
(407) 339–7744
Fax: (407) 339–7686
EMAIL: See Below
8082

Business Information: Mobile X–Ray Specialists, Inc. is a Medicare–certified, portable x–ray and EKG provider, serving 75 nursing homes in a six county radius, as well as private residences and major sporting events (NBA Orlando Magic, NCAA Basketball, World Cup Soccer, Arena Football, Florida State University, and University of Central Florida). Mobile X–Ray and its sister company in Georgia both hold the #2 position among providers in their respective states. Mr. McDonough established the company in 1983, serving eight states and opening a second office in Georgia in 1994. His duties as Service Director and Chief Executive Officer entail supervision of daily operations, financial and budgetary oversight, personnel management, and corporate leadership. He is also the Editor of the company's newsletter, "Looking Inside." Internet users can reach him via: MobileXRay@aol.com **Career Steps:** Service Director, Mobile X–Ray Specialists, Inc. (1983–Present); Chief Technologist, Central Florida X–Ray (1981–1983). **Associations & Accomplishments:** Vice President and Membership Chairman, National Association of Portable X–Ray Providers; Membership Chairman, First Presbyterian Church of Maitland, Florida; Ordained Elder, Presbyterian Church U.S.A. **Education:** Attended: University of Central Florida (1978–1981), Stetson University (1975–1978). **Personal:** Married to Debbie in 1983. Two children: Amy Lauryn and Megan Pamela. Mr. McDonough enjoys guitar, bicycling, mountain climbing, and fishing.

Ruth L. McGirl

Director of IV Therapy
NSI Home Health Care
55 Madison Street, Suite 200
Denver, CO 80206
(303) 333–2255
Fax: (303) 333–2290
8082

Business Information: NSI Home Health Care is a provider of home health care services and short–term intermittent care for Medicare and private insurance patients, as well as for managed care contracts. Services include nursing, aide, physical, occupational and speech therapy and medical social worker. With the main office located in Gardena, California, NSI serves the metropolitan Denver area (a 65–mile radius), providing services to 300 patients a day (about 1600–1800 people every week), from eleven branch locations. Future plans include the expansion of their service to the north and south and along the Wyoming border, in order to have state-wide coverage in Colorado. Established in 1982, NSI currently employs 60 people, including 25 nurses, 16 physical therapists, 5 occupational therapists, 2 speech therapists, and 3 social workers. With thirty–eight years experience in nursing, Ms. McGirl joined NSI in 1992. Serving as Director of IV Therapy, she oversees all aspects of the IV Program for home health care clientele, as well as serves as Clinical Supervisor. **Career Steps:** Director of IV Therapy, NSI Home Health Care (1992–Present); Clinical Supervisor, Lutheran Home Health Services (1989–1992); Administrator, ComCare Home Health Services (1985–1992); Clinical Supervisor, Partner's Home Health (1982–1985). **Associations & Accomplishments:** Intravenous Nurses Society (1987–1995); Case Management Society of America (1994–1995). **Education:** St. Joseph's College, M.S. in Health Care Management Candidate; Mercy Hospital School of Nursing, R.N. (1957); Metro State College, B.S.N. (1979); Webster College, classes toward M.S. in Health Care Management (1989). **Personal:** Two children: Roy Michael and James Allen. Ms. McGirl enjoys needlepoint, crochet, reading, travel, and doing crafts.

Brandon Migliore

Chief Operating Officer
Qualified Health Services
809 West Judge Perez Drive
Chalmette, LA 70043
(504) 277–1109
Fax: (504) 277–1114

8082

Business Information: Qualified Health Services is a health care agency providing health and related services to clients in their homes. More cost–effective than hospital care, the Agency is fully accredited, and offers such services as: skilled nursing care, speech, occupational, and physical therapy, medical social services, and home aid. The Agency also has a consultant on staff to assist other health care agencies in handling managed care. As Chief Operating Officer, Mr. Migliore is responsible for positioning the organization to compete within a managed care environment. His duties include: administration, strategic planning, and updating of patient care and programs. He is also responsible for budgeting and finance, overseeing the profit/loss ratio of the Company, and ensuring its continued growth and cost effectiveness. **Career Steps:** Chief Operating Officer, Qualified Health Services (1995–Present); Director of Employee/Patient Affairs, River Region Home Health (1994–1995); Regional Marketing Manager, Omni Medical Systems (1993–1994). **Associations & Accomplishments:** National Association for Home Care; Louisiana Home Care Association; Louisiana Medical Group Managers Association. **Education:** Loyola University, M.B.A. (1996); Nicholls State University, B.S. in Business Administration. **Personal:** Mr. Migliore enjoys volleyball and water sports.

Holly J. Minder

Director of Total Quality Management
NR HomeHealth, Infusion & Inc.
101 Venture Court
Lexington, KY 40510
(606) 254–1605
Fax: (606) 231–7470

8082

Business Information: NR HomeHealth, Infusion & Inc. is a home care organization providing nutritional support, personal care and support services. As Director Total Quality Management, Ms. Minder is responsible for developing programs, workman's compensation, overseeing risk management, infection control, and staff development. **Career Steps:** Director Total Quality Management, NR HomeHealth, Infusion & Inc. (1996–Present); Director of Operations, NR Home Infusion (1995–1996); Divisional Manager, UK Med Center (1989–1995). **Associations & Accomplishments:** Kentucky HomeHealth Association; Bluegrass Continuity Care; Bluegrass Health Care Quality; Pioneer Instructor, First Alliance Church. **Education:** Timken Mercy Sen. Nursing, Diploma (1983). **Personal:** Two children: Kayla and Amanda. Ms. Minder enjoys gardening and reading.

Jim Monroe

Chief Financial Officer
Century Health Services, Inc.
1023 North Highland Avenue
Murfreesboro, TN 37130–2450
(615) 848–9060
Fax: (615) 849–3916

8082

Business Information: Established in 1993, Century Health Services, Inc. is a large holding company that operates 11 home health care facilities. The base company reports an annual revenue of $50 million and employs over 700 people. As Chief Financial Officer, Vice President, Secretary and Treasurer, Mr. Monroe was instrumental in rescuing the corporation from bankruptcy with his expertise in finance and accounting. He is also involved in Amedico, a medical equipment, and comprehensive therapy company that employs 150 people and has an estimated annual revenue of $8 million. **Career Steps:** Chief Financial Officer, Vice President, Secretary and Treasurer, Century Health Services, Inc. (1993–Present); Partner, Amick & Company, C.P.A.s (1979–1993). **Associations & Accomplishments:** Kentucky Society of Certified Public Accountants; Indiana Certified Public Accountants Society; American Institute of Certified Public Accountants; Former Member, Board of Directors, United Way of New Albany, Indiana; Executive Committee Member, Chamber of Commerce; Shriner. **Education:** Western Kentucky University, B.S. in Accounting and Personnel and Production Management (1964); Post–Graduate Work in Science and Pre–Med. **Personal:** Married to Vickie in 1971. One child: Brent. Mr. Monroe enjoys golf.

July Mora

Owner, Vice President and Chief Financial Officer
International Health Care
4051 Veterans Blvd., Suite 312
Metairie, LA 70002
(504) 885–7145
Fax: (504) 885–7127

8082

Business Information: International Health Care is a unique home health care agency, providing quality home care services including nursing, home health aides, family care, medical social services, homemakers and rehabilitative care. All of IHC's medical support staff are bi– or multi–lingual, due to the majority of patients served in the greater New Orleans metropolitan area being of Spanish and Vietnamese origin. As Owner, Vice President and Chief Financial Officer, Ms. Mora provides the overall executive administration for a support staff of 70, ensuring quality patient care as well as oversight of all budgetary allocations. **Career Steps:** Owner, Vice President and Chief Financial Officer, International Health Care (1992–Present); Emergency Medical Technician, East Jefferson General Hospital (1981–1992) **Associations & Accomplishments:** Hispanic Chamber of Commerce; Spanish American Business Association; National Association of Home Care. **Education:** College of St. Francis, courses toward M.S. in Health Administration; William Carey College, B.S. in Nursing (1991). **Personal:** Ms. Mora enjoys travel, movies, horseback riding and scuba diving in her leisure time.

Cynthia R. Morgan, M.S.N.

Regional Director
St. Joseph of the Pines, Inc.
95 Aviemore Drive
Pinehurst, NC 28374
(910) 295–3920
Fax: (910) 295–4789

8082

Business Information: St. Joseph of the Pines, Inc. is a provider of home health care services, serving a fourteen county area in the State of North Carolina. Starting her career in nursing more than ten years ago, Ms. Morgan directed her career towards the home health industry upon the conferral of her Masters in Nursing in 1992. She joined St. Joseph of the Pines, Inc. as Director of Education in 1993 and was appointed as Regional Director two years later. In this position, she is responsible for the direction of five of fourteen county areas, including operations, personnel, training, and administration. **Career Steps:** St. Joseph of the Pines, Inc.: Regional Director (1995–Present), Director of Education (1993–1994); Director of Biofeedback, Moore Regional Hospital (1986–1988). **Associations & Accomplishments:** Government Affairs Committee, North Carolina Home Care Association; Board of Directors, North Carolina Assisted Living Association; Chair–Board of Directors, Sandhills Mental Health Center; Board of Directors, North Carolina Center for Nursing; Pinehurst Kiwanis. **Education:** University of North Carolina – Greensboro, M.S. in Nursing (1992); University of North Carolina – Chapel Hill, B.S. in Nursing; Sandshill Community College, A.S. in Nursing; Louisburg College, A.A. **Personal:** Married to Richard in 1988. Ms. Morgan enjoys politics, reading, needlework, and cattle farming.

Richard C. Mossor, R.Ph., M.B.A.

Pharmacy Director
Apria Healthcare
780–D Primos Avenue, Unit D
Folcroft, PA 19032
(800) 637–9539
Fax: (800) 283–7364

8082

Business Information: Apria Healthcare is a Durable Medical Equipment and Pharmacy provider, servicing homebound patients with I.V. and respiratory drugs and other pharmaceutical products. Comprised of 360 offices, the Company receives prescription/equipment orders that are processed according to physician directions. The orders are then distributed to homebound clients, thereby eliminating the trip to a pharmacy. Established in 1991, the Pharmacy serves a clientele of approximately ten thousand active patients. Employing thirty people, this division has an estimated annual revenue of $24 million. As Director, Mr. Mossor oversees all operations east of the Mississippi. He is responsible for providing home care medications to patients in 300 field locations. Additional duties include administration, operations, marketing, public relations, and strategic planning. **Career Steps:** Pharmacy Director, Apria Healthcare (1991–Present); Pharmacy Director, MEDIQ (1987–1991); Pharmacy Manager, Mercy Catholic Medical Center (1987); Pharmacy Manager, Thrift Drug Company (1980–1987). **Associations & Accomplishments:** National Association of Retail Druggist (NARD); American Pharmaceutical Association (APHA); Served on committees for DMERCS and HCFA in Washington, DC. Several articles published in various home care journals. **Education:** St. Joseph's University, M.B.A. (1994); Temple University, B.S. in Pharmacy (1980). **Personal:** Mr. Mossor enjoys sports, music, and the outdoors.

Ted Diep Nguyen

President/CEO
ComQuest Holding Corporation
1585 Blair Avenue
St. Paul, MN 55104
(612) 642–9540
Fax: (612) 642–9548

8082

Business Information: ComQuest Holding Corporation, established in 1993, is the parent company of four home health care facilities. The subsidiaries are: Asian American Health Care, Inc., which was established in 1990, and employs three nurses; Right At Home Corporation, established in 1992; International Interpretation Services, established in 1996, is an international consulting company which trains people to be successful on the international market; and Universal Home Health Care, established in 1996, is a medicare certification company. As President/CEO, Mr. Nguyen oversees the operations of three health care companies, one consulting company and the parent holding company. He is responsible for long–term strategic planning, final decisions regarding fiscal matters, public relations, and recruitment of senior management staff. **Career Steps:** President/CEO: ComQuest Holding Corporation (1990–Present); Asian American Health Care, Inc. (1990–Present); Right At Home Corporation (1992–Present); International Interpretation Services (1996–Present); Universal Home Health Care (1996–Present). **Associations & Accomplishments:** Vietnamese Communities of the United States of America; Vietnamese Minnesotan Association. **Education:** Attended, University of Minnesota **Personal:** Married to Thuy N. Nguyen in 1994. One child: Vincent. Mr. Nguyen enjoys computers and being with his son.

F. Edward Nicolas Jr., CPA

Vice President and Chief Financial Officer
Visiting Nurse Services of Connecticut, Inc.
765 Fairfield Avenue
Bridgeport, CT 06604–3702
(203) 366–3821
Fax: (203) 334–0543

8082

Business Information: Visiting Nurse Services of Connecticut, Inc. is a home health agency, consisting of 600 health care givers and 5,500 subscribers per year. Established in 1909, the Agency reports annual revenue of $24 million and currently employs 600 people. With seven years of experience in the accounting industry and a Connecticut Certified Public Accountant, Mr. Nicolas joined the Agency in 1992. Serving as

Vice President and Chief Financial Officer, he is responsible for coordinating financial planning, all accounting, and the supervision of accounting support staff. **Career Steps:** Vice President and Chief Financial Officer, Visiting Nurse Services of Connecticut, Inc. (1992–Present); Senior Auditor, Grant Thornton (1991–1992); Senior Auditor, Dworken, Hillman, LaMorte & Sterczala (1988–1991). **Associations & Accomplishments:** American Institute of Certified Public Accountants; Connecticut Society of Certified Public Accountants. **Education:** Suffolk University, B.S.B.A. in Accounting (1988); Certified Public Accountant (1992). **Personal:** Married to Janice M. Freddino in 1990. Mr. Nicolas enjoys running, music, and woodworking.

Faith B. Noles, B.S.N.
Administrator
First American Home Care
333 West Main Street
Lakeland, GA 31635–1417
(912) 482–2811
Fax: Please mail or call

8082

Business Information: First American Home Care provides home health care and services to home bound patients. Services offered include CNA's, nurses, physical therapists, occupational therapists, speech therapists, and social workers. Established in 1975, the Association currently employs over 150 persons. As Administrator, Ms. Noles manages the Lakeland, Georgia location. She is responsible for all administrative duties, the day–to–day operations, staffing concerns, and strategic planning for the future. **Career Steps:** Administrator, First American Home Care (1993–Present); Quality Assurance Coordinator, ABC Home Health (1990–1993); Staff Nurse, Berrien County Hospital (1990–1991); Establishment of own business in September 1995, "Faith Productions," which is involved in the publication and marketing of beginning songwriters. **Associations & Accomplishments:** American Cancer Association; Muscular Dystrophy Association; Listed in: Who's Who Among American Business Women (1993); Who's Who Among Creative Writers (1994). Ms. Noles is a published poet and has just completed her first gospel album, "Songs of Faith". **Education:** Valdosta State College, B.S.N. (1989); Lee College. **Personal:** Married to Dean in 1996. Five children: Angelique, Elana, and Tiffany Harper, Elijah Roberts, and Jason Noles. Ms. Noles enjoys being a songwriter and playing the guitar and the piano.

Mary E. Nolfo, R.N./ADMN
Owner/Administrator
Sunrise Home Health Services, Inc.
14700 Farmington Road, Suite 103
Livonia, MI 48154–5434
(313) 522–2909
Fax: (313) 522–0055

8082

Business Information: Sunrise Home Health Services, Inc., a Medicare–certified facility, provides skilled nursing or medical care, under the supervision of a physician. As Owner/Administrator, Mrs. Nolfo is responsible for all aspects of Company operations, including educational, networking, billing, and administrative function, as well as community speaking engagements. **Career Steps:** Owner/Administrator, Sunrise Home Health Services, Inc. (1993–Present); Director of Education/QA, Prime Care Services, Inc. (1989–1994); Oncology Nurse, Dr. R. Mohindra, M.D. (1987–1988); Oncology Nurse, Mt. Carmel Mercy Hospital (1984–1990). **Associations & Accomplishments:** Michigan Home Health Association; Home Care Association of America; Michigan League of Nursing; Past Member Oncology Nurses Society; Certifications: OCN, ACLS, PADI. **Education:** Wayne County Community College, A.S.N. (1984); Frequent Ongoing Education Through Conferences. **Personal:** Married to Gene Michael in 1986. One child: Christopher Thomas. Mrs. Nolfo enjoys scuba diving and wildlife conservation.

Beverly C. Norwood–Matheney
Administrator
Care Net Health Services
4948 Chef Menteur Highway, Suite 621
New Orleans, LA 70126
(504) 947–2273
Fax: (504) 943–4911

8082

Business Information: Care Net Health Services provides home health care (physical, speech and respiratory services) for patients, both young and old, to eliminate the need for hospital stays. Comprised of over forty employees, the Company was established in 1993 and has an estimated annual gross of $2.0 million. As Administrator, Mrs. Norwood–Matheney su-pervises all aspects of the Company and is responsible for all financial and clinical functions. Additional duties include administration, operations, public relations and strategic planning. Concurrent to her present position, Mrs. Norwood–Matheney is a partner of "Home Care Production" which produces a medical talk show that focuses on health maintenance and related issues. Additionally, the Company promotes seminars, trade shows, and speeches on medical and related issues nationally. **Career Steps:** Care Net Health Services: Administrator (1996–Present), Director of Nursing (1993–1994); Clinical Coordinator, Mercy Hospital (1990–1992); Assistant Director of Nursing, Reliable Home Health (1992–1993). **Associations & Accomplishments:** American Heart Association; Home Care of Louisiana Association; National Association of Home Care; Home Care Association of America, Inc. **Education:** University of Arkansas, Little Rock, A.D.N. (1989). **Personal:** Married to Robert Matheney, M.D. in 1983. One child: Robert Aaron. Mrs. Norwood–Matheney enjoys jogging, her responsibilities as wife, mother, and businesswoman.

Patricia E. O'Neill
Vice President
Home X–Ray & Medical Services
7461 NW 4th Street
Plantation, FL 33317
(954) 791–6146
Fax: (954) 584–9778

8082

Business Information: Home X–Ray & Medical Services provides portable x–ray, electrocardiogram, and related medical diagnostic services. As Vice President, Ms. O'Neill serves as Manager and Administrator, coordinating all business aspects of Company operations. **Career Steps:** Vice President, Home X–Ray & Medical Services (1969–Present); Vice President/Administrator, American Home Health Care (1975–1986); Vice President/Administrator, American Health & Rehabilitation Center (1970–1979); Administrator, Para-Medical Nursing Centers (1967–1970). **Associations & Accomplishments:** Secretary, National Association of Portable X–Ray Providers; National Association of Women Business Owners; Ft. Lauderdale Chapter Membership Committee; Greater Plantation Chamber of Commerce, Chair – Health Services Commission; Former President, Board of Directors, The Lifeline for Children, Inc. **Education:** Michigan State, B.S. (1967). **Personal:** Two children: Maria and Mariela. Ms. O'Neill is active in Church, serves on S.I.T. Sunset School, and is a Community Advisor for Sunset School.

Romy T. Pangilinan
President and Administrator
MEDCARE PLUS Home Health Services, a Division of Primedicare, Inc.
568 East Foothill Boulevard, Suite 123
Azusa, CA 91702–2527
(818) 812–4533
Fax: (818) 815–8967

8082

Business Information: MEDCARE PLUS Home Health Services, a Division of Primedicare, Inc. is a non–profit, state–licensed and Medicare–certified home healthcare provider. Services include visiting patients in their home by nurses, therapists, and social workers. As President and Administrator, Mr. Pangilinan is responsible for overseeing all operations on a daily basis, including budgeting, administration, and ensuring the innovative delivery of good quality services to patients, as well as taking steps to improve Medicare and Medicaid programs. **Career Steps:** President and Administrator, MEDCARE PLUS Home Health Services, a Division of Primedicare, Inc. (1994–Present); Administrator, UNICARE Home Health Professional (1993); Director, Northshore Community Hospital (1982). **Associations & Accomplishments:** Vice President, California Coalition of Filipino American Chamber of Commerce; President, FACC, San Gabriel Valley, CA; Member and serves on the Public Relations Committee, California Association For Health Services at Home (CAH-SAH); Azusa and West Covina Chamber of Commerce; Vice President for Governmental Affairs, Federation of Philippine–American Chamber of Commerce of U.S.A.; President, FACC, San Gabriel Valley; Recipient, 1996 PANAMA Awards for Outstanding Civic/Community Accomplishments. **Education:** Aurora University, B.S.N. (1990); Cuyamaca College, Associate in Respiratory Therapy; Northwestern University, Hospital Administration Course; Creighton University, Management in Respiratory Therapy; B.S. in Criminology in Manila. **Personal:** Married to Julie D. in 1980. Five children: Richard, Sharon Ann, Romy II (Jon), Romy III (Jo), and Sara Ann. Mr. Pangilinan enjoys reading, basketball, baseball, and politics.

Cherryl Phillips
Director
Highland Lakes Home Health/Hospice
P O Box 840
Burnet, TX 78611
(512) 756–7511
Fax: (512) 756–8046

8082

Business Information: Highland Lakes Home Health/Hospice is a rural home health care operation for patients within a 60–mile radius of Burnet, Texas. Established in 1989, Highland Lakes employs 30 people. As Director, Ms. Phillips oversees the daily operations of the home health and hospice programs. She is responsible for all billing operations, insurance claims, and as a practicing RN, conducts home visits to patients. Other responsibilities include recruiting, training, scheduling, and evaluating staff. **Career Steps:** Director, Highland Lakes Home Health/Hospice (1995–Present); Community Education Coordinator, highland Lakes Home Health (1993–1995); Director of Nurses, Northwood Health Care (1992–1993). **Associations & Accomplishments:** Active at State level of School to Work Consortium; Habitat for Humanity 1993–1995; Past Director, Volunteer Burnet Emergency Medical Service; Chairperson Burnet High School Tech Prep Stakeholders Group 1994–1995; **Education:** Central Texas College, Associates Degree in Nursing (1988). **Personal:** Married to Jack in 1988. Four children: Scott Garrett, Jeff Phillips, Amanda Ware, and Beth Cravey. Ms. Phillips enjoys arts and crafts.

Marvin Pierce
Chief Financial Officer
N.S.I. Home Care Plus, Inc.
2981 Highway 28 East
Pineville, LA 71360–5716
(318) 484–3869
Fax: (318) 442–0709

8082

Business Information: N.S.I. Home Care Plus, Inc. is a provider of home health care services, including skilled nursing, certified nursing assistants, speech therapy, physical and occupational therapy, and medical social services. N.S.I. Home Care Plus, Inc. serves residents of Pineville and a 50–mile radius. A forty percent owner and partner with two registered nurses, Mr. Pierce purchased N.S.I. Home Care Plus as Director of Marketing in January 1993 and was appointed as Chief Financial Officer in November 1993. He is responsible for planning overall development of the Company, including reviewing and evaluating policies, preparing budgets, handling all contact agreements, financial activities, billing of Medicare, and ensuring compliance of regulatory guidelines. **Career Steps:** N.S.I. Home Care Plus, Inc.: Chief Financial Officer (Nov. 1993–Present), Director of Marketing (Jan. – Nov. 1993). **Associations & Accomplishments:** Southern University Executive and Marketing Club; Eastend 209 Masonic Lodge; Epsilon Chi Chapter, Omega Psi Phi; Central Louisiana Business League; Cenla Chamber of Commerce; Federal and State Commissioned Officer, U.S. Army Reserves; First Lieutenant, U.S. National Guard. **Education:** Southern University (A&M College), B.S. in Management (1994). **Personal:** One child: Jazmin Pierce. Mr. Pierce enjoys supporting local community services and the boys league of Cenla, church, basketball, baseball, and weight lifting.

Kem K. Pinegar, Ph.D.
Chief Executive Officer
The Resource Team, Inc.
2 Metroplex, Suite 111
Birmingham, AL 35209
(205) 999–8142
Fax: Please mail or call

8082

Business Information: The Resource Team, Inc. provides therapy and rehabilitation services in nursing homes, home health care, and on an outpatient basis. As Chief Executive Officer, Dr. Pinegar is responsible for the development of the business, as well as administration, finance, public relations, accounting, and strategic planning. Concurrent with her position at The Resource Team, Inc., she is the Owner and Consultant of Results Group. **Career Steps:** Chief Executive Officer, The Resource Team, Inc. (1995–Present); Owner/Consultant, Results Group (1994–Present); Management Professor, Birmingham–Southern College (1987–1992). **Associations & Accomplishments:** Academy of Management; Alabama Nursing Home Association; Network Birmingham; Women's Business Ownership Council; American Society for Training and Development; American Lung Association of Alabama; Founding Member, Discovery United Methodist Church. **Education:** University of Alabama, Ph.D. (1994); University of Alabama, Ed.S.; East Tennesse State University, MBA; Mississippi State University, BBA. **Personal:** Married to Jeff in 1986. Two children: Tyler and Connor.

Tracy L. Polaski, RN, BSN
Service Director
Caregivers Home Health
P.O. Box 436
Marinette, WI 54143–0436
(715) 735–6490
Fax: (715) 735–6461

8082

Business Information: Caregivers Home Health provides skilled nursing and medical care in the home, under the supervision of a physician, as well as administrative and financial functions of the Marinette Office. Caregivers Home Health currently has several offices in Wisconsin and Illinois. Providing services to over 700 clients. Servicing clients with Medicare, Medicaid, and private insurance. As Service Director, Ms. Polaski is responsible for all aspects of the Agency's operations, to include customer and staff concerns. **Career Steps:** Service Director, Caregivers Home Health (1992–Present); Director of Nursing, Menominee Care Center (1991–1992); RN – Lead Nurse, Bayshore Home Health (1992–1993). **Associations & Accomplishments:** President, Marinette/Menominee County Youth Suicide Prevention; Instructor HIV/AIDS, American Red Cross; Therapy Dogs, Inc. **Education:** Marian College of Fondulac, BSN (1984); Currently working on Masters Degree in Health and Wellness Promotion. **Personal:** Married to Jeff in 1990. Ms. Polaski enjoys dog training, crochet, gardening, and hiking.

Susan Porter, RN
Director of Health Services
Interim Health Care
1625 West 4th Avenue
Spokane, WA 99204
(509) 456–5665
Fax: (509) 456–7703

8082

Business Information: Interim Health Care is a home healthcare agency that provides staff relief in skilled nursing facilities. Established in 1988, the Company employs 100 people. As Director of Health Services, Ms. Porter, who is semi–retired, is responsible for supervision of employees and clients, case management, administration, and patient care. **Career Steps:** Director of Health Services, Interim Health Care (1994–Present); Director of Nursing, Olston Kimberly Quality Care (1988–1994); ICU/CCU RN, Kootenai Medical Center (1983–1988). **Education:** North Idaho Community College, Ass. Degree RN (1983); University of Eugene. **Personal:** Married to Billy Ray in 1976. Two children: Angela and John. Ms. Porter enjoys motorcycle riding.

Suzanne L. Purdy
Vice President
West Healthcare Home Care Services
180 Otay Lakes Road, Suite 100
Bonita, CA 91902
(619) 472–7500
Fax: (619) 472–0886

8082

Business Information: West Healthcare Home Care Services, an affiliate of Paradise Valley Hospital, is a fully integrated homecare server organization for the regional area of San Diego County, providing Medicare Home Health Services, private duty and extended care services, as well as hospice, home infusion therapy, and home medical equipment. Services are provided by registered nurses, licensed practical nurses, private nurses, and therapists. With twelve years experience in home care administration management, Ms. Purdy joined West Healthcare Home Care Services in 1990. As Vice President, she is responsible for management, business growth and development. **Career Steps:** West Healthcare Home Care Services: Vice President (1995–Present), Executive Director (1990–1995); Administrator, Mercy Home Health Services (1986–1990); Administrator, Bay View Home Health (1983–1986). **Associations & Accomplishments:** Greater San Diego Chamber of Commerce; National City Chamber of Commerce; San Diego Regional Home Care Council; California Association for Health Services at Home; National Association for Home Care; American Hospital Association. **Education:** Loma Linda University, B.S. in Nursing (1964). **Personal:** Four children: Michael, Dennis, Lance, and Jon Shetler. Ms. Purdy enjoys reading, water sports, and her grandchildren.

Lois M. Quinn
Administrator
Tenet Healthcare Corporation
420 North Center Street
Hickory, NC 28601–5033
(704) 324–3025
Fax: (704) 324–1930

8082

Business Information: Tenet Healthcare Corporation is a home health care service providing medical nursing, psychiatric nursing, home infusion therapy, DME, personal care, physical therapy, speech therapy, occupational therapy, and medical social work. As Administrator, Ms. Quinn is responsible for diversified administrative activities, including direction, development, and expansion of services, medical operations, public relations, and strategic planning. **Career Steps:** Administrator, Tenet Healthcare Corporation (1994–Present); Administrator, Frye Regional Medical Center (1990–1994); Administrator, Thomas Memorial Hospital (1988–1990). **Associations & Accomplishments:** American Nurse Association; Certifications in Nursing Administration and Gerontological Nursing; National Gerontological Nurses Association; Community Education on local radio stations; Live health education program host on WVMR (1982–1985). **Education:** West Virginia State College, Regents B.A. (1989); West Virginia Institute of Technology; University of Charleston – Morris Harvey College, A.A. in Nursing. **Personal:** Married to Nathan A. in 1976. One child: Brandon. Ms. Quinn enjoys piano, singing, fishing, and boating.

Lillian V. Quintanilla, R.N.
Director of Professional Services & Director of Nurses
Home Health Concepts, Inc.
8901 Emmett Lowry Expressway
Texas City, TX 77591
(800) 324–4442
Fax: (409) 935–8501

8082

Business Information: Home Health Concepts, Inc. is one of the largest home health agencies in Texas. It has seventeen offices throughout the state, with corporate headquarters in Texas City. The Agency provides home health equipment, hospice, home provider services, physical, occupational, and speech therapy services, and social services. As Director of Professional Services and Director of Nurses, Ms. Quintanilla is responsible for the overall operation of the facility. She oversees nurses, clerical and case managers, aides, and all aspects of client care services. **Career Steps:** Director of Professional Services and Director of Nurses, Home Health Concepts, Inc. (1994–Present); Associate Director, Mainland Home Health Concepts (1993–1994); Supervisor of Ambulatory Care, AMI (1986–1989). **Associations & Accomplishments:** Bay Area Continuity of Care; Graduated from college and high school with honors. **Education:** Galveston Community College, Associate's degree (1972). **Personal:** Married to Antonio in 1973. Two children: Abel and Angela. Ms. Quintanilla enjoys reading and crafts.

A. Rabie
Chief Executive Officer, Administrator, and Owner
Napp Medical Services, Inc.
2646 South Loop West, Suite 335
Houston, TX 77054–2640
(713) 668–2744
Fax: (713) 668–4410

8082

Business Information: Napp Medical Services, Inc., one of the fastest growing agencies in Houston, is a home health care agency, providing services to over 100 patients residing in Houston, Texas and the surrounding suburbs. Future plans include opening their first branch in 1996 and expanding throughout the rest of the state. Establishing Napp Medical Services, Inc. in 1993, Mr. Rabie serves as Chief Executive Officer, Administrator, and Owner, overseeing all administrative operations for associates and a staff of 53. **Career Steps:** Chief Executive Officer, Administrator, and Owner, Napp Medical Services, Inc. (1993–Present); President, Lone Star Ventures (1978–1993); Operations Director, International Property Management (1978–1978); General Manager, Al Gosabi Hotel (1974–1976). **Associations & Accomplishments:** Former First Vice President, The Lions Club; Delta Sigma Phi; Arab American Anti–Discrimination Committee; Arab American Cultural & Community Center; Founding Member, Vice President. **Education:** University of Houston, B.S. in Hotel and Restaurant Management (1971); American University, M.B.A. in Management (1973); California State University, P.G.D. Program. **Personal:** Married to Sana in 1975. Four children: Abby, Naveen, Nader, and Summer. Mr. Rabie enjoys reading, fishing, hunting, sports, and soccer.

Kevin Rath
Executive Director
Manos Home Care
2869 38th Avenue
Oakland, CA 94619
(510) 533–0665
Fax: (510) 534–0446

8082

Business Information: Manos Home Care specializes in the care of elderly, sick adults, and disabled children in their homes. Focusing primarily on personal as opposed to medical care, the Company provides services such as cooking, cleaning, and assistance with personal hygiene. A non–profit organization, the Company operates on a fee for service basis, and also offers counseling to families of disabled children. As Executive Director, Mr. Rath co–founded the Facility. He is responsible for sales, management of administrative staff, development of operations, and information systems. Concurrent with his present position, Mr. Rath owns a consulting business which assists clients in establishing their own non–profit organization. **Career Steps:** Executive Director, Manos Home Care (1989–Present); Executive Director, Manos Referral Project (1987–1989). **Associations & Accomplishments:** Summit Hospital Community Health Education Advisory Board; California Association for Health Care at Home, Legislative Committee; Co–Founder, In Home Support Services Task Force of Alameda County; Published in: Wall Street Journal, San Francisco Chronicle, and Oakland Tribune. **Education:** University of California, Berkeley, B.S. (1981); Pacific Theological Seminary, Masters of Divinity. **Personal:** Married to Karen in 1981. One child: Lauren E.. Mr. Rath enjoys bike riding, reading novels, family, and micro brewing.

Amanda W. Reeves
Executive Director
Hospice of Laurens County
16 Peachtree Street
Clinton, SC 29325
(864) 833–6287
Fax: (864) 833–0556

8082

Business Information: Hospice of Laurens County is a non–profit home care agency for the terminally ill (with a life expectancy of six months or less). The Hospice usually cares for 15 patients at any one time. As Executive Director, Mrs. Reeves oversees the entire Agency operation, including business relations, public relations, employee relations, policies and procedures, and reporting to the Board of Directors. **Career Steps:** Executive Director, Hospice of Laurens County (1995–Present); Administrator, NHC Healthcare North Augusta (1994–1995); Administrator, Fountain Inn Convalescent Home (1994–1994). **Associations & Accomplishments:** Rotary – Clinton, SC; South Carolina Health Care Association; Hospice for the Carolinas. **Education:** Presbyterian College, B.S. (1981); University of South Carolina, 32 hours toward M.S.W. **Personal:** Married to M.E. III in 1987. Two children: Brad and Jacob. Mrs. Reeves enjoys gardening and spending time with her family.

Carolyn A. Reser
President
Senior Services Unlimited
64 Taylor Avenue
Manasquan, NJ 08736
(800) 251–0977
Fax: (908) 528–4337

8082

Business Information: Privately–owned, Senior Services Unlimited provides home health care services and specializes in live–in care for those individuals who are otherwise homebound. Established in 1983, Senior Services Unlimited currently employs 90 health care professionals. As President and Founder, Ms. Reser is responsible for the organization and direction of all agency functions. **Career Steps:** President, Senior Services Unlimited (1983–Present); Buyer, B. Altman & Company (1965–through the 1970's). **Associations & Accomplishments:** Vice President and Board of Directors, The Ocean County Center for the Arts; Juvenile Intervention Commission of Monmouth County; Lab VI Member, New Jersey Governor's Long Term Task Force on Aging. **Education:** Rutgers University, majored in Sociology. **Personal:** Two children: David Steele and Greg Lewis Glassberg.

Norma A. Rios
CQI Director
Columbia Health Services
15600 San Pedro, Suite 100
San Antonio, TX 78232–3730
(210) 490–8888
Fax: (210) 490–8922

8082

Business Information: Columbia Health Services, established in 1988, is a company providing management services for home health care agencies. As CQI Director, Ms. Rios is in charge of maintaining quality care in the three facilities managed by Columbia Health Services. She is responsible for personnel concerns, scheduling, budget compliance, staff training, and certification of medical staff. **Career Steps:** CQI Director, Columbia Health Services (1995–Present); Interim Cardiopulmonary Director, Valley Regional Medical Center (1995); Office Manager, Lazer Import and Export (1992). **Associations & Accomplishments:** Texas Society Respiratory Care; American Association Respiratory Care; Texas Home Care Association. **Education:** Associate in Applied Science.

Debra Roberts
Administrator
Home Care Services of Dothan
430 West Main Street
Dothan, AL 36301–1616
(334) 793–6854
Fax: (334) 347–4790

8082

Business Information: Home Health Care Services of Dothan is a home health care agency, providing nursing care and personal care to persons who are homebound. Serving patients from nineteen different offices in South Alabama, Home Care Services also has three offices in Florida. The Dothan location is the second largest facility within the company. As Administrator, Mrs. Roberts is responsible for the administration of the Agency, including operations, and supervision of a staff of more than 50 consisting of CNA's, RN's, and other supervisors. **Career Steps:** Administrator, Home Care Services of Dothan (1992–Present). **Associations & Accomplishments:** National Association of Home Health Agencies; Alabama Association of Home Health Agencies. **Education:** George C. Wallace Community College, Associates (1989). **Personal:** Married to William in 1978. Two children: Jeri and Melanie. Mrs. Roberts enjoys reading, crafts, and boating.

Michael E. Rochford, RN
Clinical Director
Medical Services of North West Florida
99 Elgin Parkway #34A
Ft. Walton Beach, FL 32548
(904) 243–9390
Fax: (904) 243–3821

8082

Business Information: Medical Services of North West Florida provides medical health care service to patients in their homes. Services include nursing, respiratory therapy, physical therapy, outpatient rehabilitation and social services; operating from three locations (Ft. Walton Beach, Pensacola, Panama City Beach). A Registered Nurse with over twenty years expertise in medical administration, Mr. Rochford was appointed as Clinical Director in 1994. He is responsible for the administrative oversight of staff and clients at the Ft. Walton Beach facility. **Career Steps:** Clinical Director, Medical Services of North West Florida (1994–Present); Home Health Case Manager, Olsten (1993–1994); Various Positions, West Florida Regional Medical Center and Pensacola Developmental Center (1989–1993); Rehab, Flagstaff Regional Medical Center (1988–1989); Adolescent Health Care for Vision Quest (1987–1988); Rehab, Home Health and Hospice, and Geriatric Care, Baldwin County, Alabama Area (1980–1986); Various Positions, Mobile Area Hospitals (1970's). **Education:** University of Nebraska (1966–1967); University of South Alabama (1967–1968); Providence School of Nursing – Springhill College (1968–1971). **Personal:** One child: Conar Michael. Mr. Rochford enjoys astronomy, carving, and sculpting.

Tamara L. Royse, B.S., R.N., C.P.H.Q.
Performance Improvement Director
Columbia Homecare
1084 Bradford Hicks Drive
Livingston, TN 38570–2302
(615) 823–2050
Fax: (615) 823–1338
EMAIL: TRoyse@infoave.net

8082

Business Information: Columbia Homecare is a home health care provider, offering a wide range of services from Skilled Nursing Care, Personal Care, Medical Social Worker, Physical, Occupational, and Speech Therapy. As Performance Improvement Director, Ms. Royce evaluates the systems in place within the agency and works with teams to improve the current processes. **Career Steps:** Performance Improvement Director, Columbia Homecare (1993–Present); Quality Assurance Manager, Jackson County Hospital

(1991–1993); Skilled Nurse, PHC Home Health (1988–1991). **Associations & Accomplishments:** National Association for Healthcare Quality; Middle Tennessee Association for Healthcare Quality; Certified Professional Healthcare Quality; Second Vice Regent, Daughters of the American Revolution, Roaring River Chapter. **Education:** Tennessee Technical University, B.S. in Education (1990); University of State of New York, A.D. in Nursing, working toward M.A. in Humanities. **Personal:** Ms. Royse enjoys her involvement in local theater, watching plays, riding motorcycles and wave runners, writing short stories, "surfing the net", playing the piano, playing golf and softball, and watching professional basketball and football games.

Rebecca C. Santana, R.N.
Regional Director
Consolidated Care Crew Home Health Agency, Inc.
1995 Main Street
Eagle Pass, TX 78852
(210) 757–0073
Fax: (210) 757–9087

8082

Business Information: Consolidated Care Crew Home Health Agency, Inc. provides medical care and supplies for patients at home throughout Texas. Branch locations are in Eagle Pass, Carrizo Springs, Uvalde and Del Rio. As Regional Director and a Registered Nurse, Mrs. Santana directs all operational activities for the Eagle Pass office, including administration and training of a staff of 45. She also directed the openings of the Carrizo Springs and El Paso branches. **Career Steps:** Regional Director, Consolidated Care Crew Home Health Agency, Inc. (1995–Present); Assistant Director of Nursing, Fort Duncan Medical Center (1991–1995); Combat Field Nurse, Persian Gulf War, U.S. Army Reserves (1990–1991); Administrator, Eagle Pass Surgi–Center (1985–1990); Lieutenant, U.S. Army Reserve (1987–1996). **Associations & Accomplishments:** Board of Directors (1985–1989), Fort Duncan Medical Center; Veterans of Foreign Wars (1991–1996); AWARDS: Army Achievement Medal, Army Commendation Medal; Kuwaiti Liberation Medal; U.S. Army Reserves as Captain. **Education:** San Antonio College, A.A. in Nursing (1980); Registered Nurse in Texas (1980–1996); Job Corps Graduate in Clerical Skills (1966); Licensed Vocational Nurse (1975). **Personal:** Married to Major James Santana, USMC in 1992. Three children: Erika Yvette, Saul Xavier, and Kristal Ann. Mrs. Santana enjoys encouraging migrant children to pursue an education.

Denise S. Schlegel
Executive Director/Chief Executive Administrator
Pennsylvania Hospice Network
128 State Street
Harrisburg, PA 17106–0636
(717) 230–9993
Fax: (717) 230–9997

8082

Business Information: Pennsylvania Hospice Network is a statewide, non–profit association for hospice organizations, professionals and persons who support the hospice philosophy. The PHN's mission is to define and foster quality hospice programs and promote the hospice concept of providing compassionate, comprehensive care to terminally–ill patients and their families. As Executive Director/Chief Executive Administrator, Ms. Schlegel represents the association at the state and national level, manages all aspects of the association including correspondence, public relations and marketing, educational programs, financial management and program and policy development. **Career Steps:** Executive Director/Chief Executive Administrator, Pennsylvania Hospice Network (1995–Present); Director of Programs, Pennsylvania Association of Resources for People with Mental Retardation (1992–1995); Facility Director, Developmental Enterprises Corporation (1990–1992); President, Lanel Consulting (1991–1996). **Associations & Accomplishments:** Legislative Committee, Council of States, Shoer Group, National Hospice Organization; Pennsylvania Society of Association Executives; National Association of Regulatory Administration; National Rehabilitation Association; Charter Member, American Association of People with Disabilities; Board of Director & Annual Conference Committee, Governor's Committee on Employment of People with Disabilities New Directions for Progress Foundation, the ARC of Schuykill County; St. Andrews United Methodist Church, Pastor/Parish Relations, Choir, Vision Team; Tri–Valley School District, Valley View, PA, Strategic Planning Council, School to Work Advisory Board. **Education:** University of Delaware, B.A.A.S. (1978). **Personal:** Married to Lanier H.. Two children: Andrew David and Rebecca Amelia.

Renee J. Schwermer
Administrator and Registered Nurse
First American Home Care
117 East Broadway
Sedalia, MO 65301–5801
(816) 817–3121
Fax: (816) 827–5190

8082

Business Information: First American Home Care is a home health care agency, providing health care services to people in their home versus an "institutional" setting. The agency provides the services of nurses, aides, and therapists. First American Home Care is a corporation nation wide. Established in 1977, First American Home Care is currently in 23 states. A practicing nurse since 1988, Ms. Schwermer joined First American Home Care as an administrator in 1994. Serving as Administrator and a Registered Nurse for two agencies, she directs and coordinates overall department and administration of the home health agency. Ms. Schwermer ensures the vision of the agency by promoting a healthy attitude. **Career Steps:** Administrator and Registered Nurse, First American Home Care (1994–Present); Real Estate Sales person, Kaysinger Real Estate (1987–Present); Clinical Nurse Supervisor, ABC Home Health (1993–1994); Case Manager and Registered Nurse, Ozark Prairie Home Health (1992–1993). **Associations & Accomplishments:** C.H.A.R.T.; Sedalia Chamber of Commerce; Legislative Health Care Committee. **Education:** Central Missouri State University, B.S.N. with emphasis in Accounting (1995); State Fair Community College, L.P.N. (1988), R.N. (1993). **Personal:** Married to Cris in 1992. Three children: Nichole, Paul, and Joey. Ms. Schwermer enjoys sewing and crafts, and the outdoors.

Dawn L. Scott
Administrator
Hospitals Home Health Care
59 South First Street
Fulton, NY 13069–2903
(315) 598–4442
Fax: (315) 598–6868
EMAIL: See Below

8082

Business Information: Hospitals Home Health Care provides certified (Medicare) home health care services to home care patients, including skilled nurses, physical therapy, occupational therapy, speech therapy, respiratory therapy, medical social workers, and home health aids. With twenty–one years in the health care industry, Mrs. Scott joined Hospitals Home Health Care as Administrator and Director of Patient Services in 1995. She reports to the Board of Directors and is responsible for administering and directing all patient services, as well as managing a staff of 100. Internet users can reach her via: dscot02@mailbox.syr.edu. **Career Steps:** Administrator, Hospitals Home Health Care (1995–Present); Custom Case Manager, Olsten Kimberly Quality Care (1990–1994); Critical Care Staff Nurse, Albany – Syracuse (1975–1986). **Associations & Accomplishments:** DPS/CNY; HCP; HANYS. **Education:** Syracuse University; SUNY – Utica, B.S.N. **Personal:** Married to Gregory in 1982. Two children: Victor and Rob. Mrs. Scott enjoys water and snow skiing.

Ronald A. Shecut
Director of Video and Broadcasting
First American Health Care
777 Gloucester Street, Suite 300
Brunswick, GA 31520–7068
(912) 261–3191
Fax: (912) 261–3198

8082

Business Information: First American Health Care is the largest privately–owned health care services company in the U.S., located in 22 states. Established in 1982, First American Health Care currently employs 17,000 people. With twenty–two years expertise in the film and video communications industry, Mr. Shecut joined First American Health Care in 1993. Serving as Director of Video and Broadcasting, he is responsible for corporate film and video communications, as well as production activities, such as promotional and training films. **Career Steps:** Director of Video and Broadcasting, First American Health Care, A Corporation (1993–Present); Independent Corporate Producer (1991–1993); Producer, Vision 2 Predictions (1986–1991); Senior Producer, Instructional Services USC Television (1973–1985). **Associations & Accomplishments:** International Television Association; American Society for Training and Development; Recipient of Silver Screen award with U.S. Industrial Film Festival; Interviewed by newspapers and newsletters. **Education:** University of South Carolina, B.A. in Broadcast Journalism (1973). **Personal:** Married to Carrie Moore. One child: Ronald Chantel. Mr. Shecut enjoys photography, camping, and riding motorcycles.

Judith A. Shue

Branch Manager and Director of Professional Services

Staff Builders Home Health

15 North Fifth Street, Suite 500
Grand Junction, CO 81501–2679
(970) 245–4852
Fax: (970) 245–0772

8082

Business Information: Staff Builders Home Health is a national home care corporation, offering skilled nursing, physical, speech, and occupational therapies, home health aides, and medical social services. Staff Builders Home Health serves clientele in four counties from the Grand Junction locale. Joining Staff Builders Home Health as Branch Manager and Director of Professional Services in 1992, Ms. Shue has the dual role of acting as Director of Nursing, as well as overseeing all professional development, staff development, and education. She also ensures compliance of quality care in accordance with state and federal regulations. As Director, she is responsible for strategic planning, growth and budget management for the business. **Career Steps:** Branch Manager and Director of Professional Services, Staff Builders Home Health (1992–Present); Nurse Manager (interim)–Critical Care, St. Vincent Hospital Santa Fe, NM (1990–1991); Staff Relief, Metro ICU's, Med–Pro, Phoenix, AZ (1988–1992). **Associations & Accomplishments:** Fundraising Chair, Western Colorado AIDS Memorial Quilt Display Project; Nominee, (3 times) Nightingale Award – Colorado; AIDS activist and fundraising program coordination; Pro Bono services at annual free flu vaccinations for the homeless clinics. **Education:** Mesa College, A.D.N. (1984); Certified Trauma Nurse. **Personal:** Ms. Shue enjoys skiing, biking, public speaking, and photography. She is also an avid civil rights and AIDS support activist.

Melda L. Skinner

President/Owner

Rayburn Health

614 West Houston
Jasper, TX 75951
(409) 384–2399
Fax: (409) 423–6444

8082

Business Information: Established in 1994, Texas Medical Enterprise, Inc. is a home health care organization, providing RN's, LPN's, and HHA's to private Medicare and Medicaid patients. As President/Owner, Mrs. Skinner oversees all aspects of management and daily operations. Rayburn Health, her new 265 acre health spa, will open in 1997, complete with staff psychologists, nutritionists, and cardiologists. The new facility will focus on the international market. **Career Steps:** President/Owner, Texas Medical Enterprise, Inc. (1994–Present); Administrator/Owner/CEO, Jefferson County Home (1993–1994); Administrator/Owner/CEO, Superior Home Health (1990–1993). **Associations & Accomplishments:** Texas Association of Home Care; National Association of Home Health Care; Executive Female Association; Jasper Chamber of Commerce. **Education:** Lamar University: B.B.A. (1986), Associates in Property Tax Administration. **Personal:** Married to Robert in 1994. Five children: Kim, James, Brad, Elizabeth, and Michael. Mrs. Skinner enjoys golf, tennis, reading, teaching, and setting up her own business.

Denise C. Smith

Director

Continue Care Home Health

P O Box 432
Cleveland, MS 38732
(601) 843–3537
Fax: (601) 846–5736

8082

Business Information: Continue Care Home Health offers advanced technological healthcare services in the comfort and convenience of the home setting. Comprised of seventeen offices in four states, the Company has 825 employees, fourteen of whom are medial educators who coordinate with phusicians and other members of the medical community on new policies, program updates, and services. As Director, Ms. Smith is responsible for the development of all educational materials, co–ordination of managed care activities, public relations, and demographic market research/analysis. **Career Steps:** Director, Continue Care Home Health (1994–Present); Social Worker, Mississippi Regional Home Health (1990–1994); Counselor, Bolivar County Compulsory School (1985–1990). **Associations & Accomplishments:** Chamber of Commerce; Multiple sclerosis Leadership Class of 1996; Volunteer for American Cancer Society; American Heart Association Volunteer; Licensed Social Worker; Phi Alpha Theta; Pi Gamma Mu. **Education:** Delta State University, B.A. (1985). **Personal:** Three children: Jade Elizabeth,

Joshua Cade, and Jacob Niles Chambers. Ms. Smith enjoys tennis and reading.

Janet L. Smith

Administrator and Chief Executive Officer

First American Home Care

1415 Hillyer Robinson Ind. Parkway
Anniston, AL 36207–6707
(205) 835–9531
Fax: (205) 835–9539

8082

Business Information: First American Home Care is the largest privately–owned medical care provider of home health care services in the U.S. With 475 locations in the U.S and in Mexico, they provide the services of skilled, specialty, psychiatric, obstetric, and pediatric nurses, physical and speech therapists, and medical social workers. Buying into the Company in 1993, she established the Anniston, Alabama location and formed it into the fastest growing office in the First American Home Care network. Serving as Administrator and Chief Executive Officer, she is responsible for all day–to–day operations of the office, including the direction of hiring, nursing orientations, programs, public relations, and financial issues. In addition, she oversees all administrative operations for associates and a support staff of 70. **Career Steps:** Administrator and Chief Executive Officer, First American Home Care (1993–Present); Cardiology Specialty Case Manager, University of Alabama Hospital (1989–93); Vital Care Home in Fusion Director, Consolidated Health Care and Healthsouth Rehab. Systems Intensive Care Unit (1989–1993); Assistant Director of Nursing, Beckwood Manor Health Systems (1983–1985); Nurse Manager and Head Nurse, Jacksonville Hospital (1981–1983). **Associations & Accomplishments:** Chamber of Commerce; Business After Hours; President, County Health Council; Seniors Committee; Advisory Board, State of Alabama First American Home Care; National Organization for Women; Episcopal for Women. **Education:** Wallace Community College, A.S. (1977); Ayers Technical College, LPN; George C. Wallace School of Nursing, RN; Attending: Jacksonville State University, Junior Level in Pre–Medical Program. **Personal:** One child: Natalie Brooke. Ms. Smith enjoys sports, gardening, horseback riding, golf, reading, science, astronomy, and psychology.

Celina Barsamian Staley

Vice President of Operations

Lifeline Homecare – Kangaroo Kids

10330 Pioneer Boulevard #150
Santa Fe Springs, CA 90670
(310) 906–0996
Fax: (310) 906–0772

8082

Business Information: Mrs. Staley serves as Vice President of Operations of Lifeline Homecare – Kangaroo Kids, a home care company that delivers infusion therapy and general home health care services for pediatric and adult patients throughout Southern California. She is responsible for pharmaceutical services providing the most up–to–date high tech infusion therapies available in home care, Medicare–Certified Home Health Agencies, and centralized Case Management services. The Home Health Agencies provide intermittent visits by RNs, LVNs, CHHAs, physical, occupational, speech, and ET therapists, and medical social workers, as well as hourly extended care services by RNs, LPNs, CNAs, Homemakers, and Live–ins. **Career Steps:** Vice President of Operations, Lifeline Homecare – Kangaroo Kids (1993–Present); Regional Director, Unihealth America – Clinishare (1987–1993); Resident Care Coordinator, Hebrew Rehabilitation Center (1982–1987). **Associations & Accomplishments:** CAHSAH Private Home Care Committee; Rehabilitation Nurse's Society; Former Member, California Nurses Association; Fluent in Armenian. **Education:** Brigham Young University, B.S. in Nursing (1979); University of Massachusetts – Amherst. **Personal:** Married to Grant in 1982. Mrs. Staley enjoys gardening, reading, and travel.

Elina Veksler

Nurse Manager

Innovative Home Health

3525 West Peterson
Chicago, IL 60659
(312) 267–3232
Fax: (312) 267–9401

8082

Business Information: Innovative Home Health is a home health care agency, serving geriatric and AIDS patients. The Agency monitors the care of patients, as well as conducts IV therapy and physical therapy throughout three counties in the Chicago area. With ten years experience in nursing, Ms. Veksler joined Innovative Home Health as Nurse Manager at its

conception in 1993. She is responsible for hiring, firing, training, and orienting nursing staff. In addition, she manages physical therapists and nurses and supervises all CNA's and the home health care agency. **Career Steps:** Nurse Manager, Innovative Home Health (1993–Present); RN–ICU, St. Francis Hospital of Evanston (1988–1993); Staff RN of Oncology, Evanson Hospital (1986–1988). **Associations & Accomplishments:** American Nurses Association. **Education:** Kharkov State University – Russia, B.S.N. (1986); School of Nursing – Kharkov, Russia, A.S.N. **Personal:** Married to Simon in 1984. Two children: Maggie and Matthew. Ms. Veksler enjoys spending time with her family, playing the guitar, fitness activities, and reading.

John T. Viola

Chief Financial Officer

Island Home Care Agency, Inc.

30 Central Avenue
Hauppauge, NY 11788–4734
(516) 232–1800
Fax: (516) 232–1870

8082

Business Information: Island Home Care Agency, Inc. provides home health care services and in–patient pharmacy operations. Established in 1985, Island Home Care Agency, Inc. reports annual revenue of $12 million and currently employs 200 people. With nine years expertise in the accounting industry, Mr. Viola joined Island Home Care Agency, Inc. as Chief Financial Officer in 1994. He is responsible for the management of all aspects of financial functions. **Career Steps:** Chief Financial Officer, Island Home Care Agency, Inc. (1994–Present); Controller, Home Mortgage Corporation (1992–1994); Senior Accountant, New Brunswick Development Corporation (1988–1992); Accountant, Sunlight Pictures Corporation (1986–1988). **Education:** SUNY – Old Westbury, B.S. (1986); Nassau Community College, A.A.S. (1984). **Personal:** Married to Donna J. in 1987. Two children: Heather and Matthew. Mr. Viola enjoys golf and bowling.

Beth Walker

Administrative Director

Massillon Community Hospital – Home Health Agency

875 8th Street, Northeast
Massillon, OH 44646–8503
(330) 837–6873
Fax: (330) 837–6829

8082

Business Information: Massillon Community Hospital – Home Health Agency is a professional home healthcare facility offering full services to six counties. As Administrative Director, Ms. Walker is responsible for administrative duties and public relations. **Career Steps:** Administrative Director, Massillon Community Hospital – Home Health Agency (1995–Present); Administrator, St. Johns Home Care (1985–1995); Administrator, Riverways Home Health (1979–1985); Administrator, Central Neb. Family Plan (1975–1979). **Associations & Accomplishments:** National Association for Home Care – SMSU West Plains Campus; Board Member, Ohio Council for Home Care; Who's Who Worldwide (1992–1993). **Education:** Washington University, M.S. (1956). **Personal:** Two children: Mary King and Chuck. Ms. Walker enjoys golf, bowling, fishing, and painting.

Sue J. Watson

Clinical Services Director

Care Connection VNA

25 Prim Road
Colchester, VT 05446
(802) 860–4491
Fax: (802) 860–4454
EMAIL: See Below

8082

Business Information: Care Connection VNA is a non–profit home health care agency providing Medicare certified, CHAP accredited nursing services to area residents. Established in 1986, the Agency employs 300 people, and has an estimated annual budget of $3 million. As Clinical Services Director, Ms. Watson is responsible for day–to–day operations of the Agency. Her responsibilities include, administrative duties, public relations, strategic planning, and accounting. Internet users can reach her via: Watson@VNA–Vermont.org. **Career Steps:** Care Connection VNA: Clinical Services Director (1995–Present), Associate Director of Home Care (1994–1995), Clinical Specialist (1986–1994). **Associations & Accomplishments:** Sigma Theta Tau; Committee Member of Practice Committee for Vermont Board of Nursing; INS. **Education:** University of Vermont, B.S.N. (1975). **Personal:** Married to Richard Dickhaut in 1995. Three children: Alison, Ainsley, and Michael. Ms. Watson enjoys volleyball, sewing, and gardening.

Nancy B. Wheeler
Nursing Director
NMC Homecare
5025A West Wt Harris Boulevard
Charlotte, NC 28269–1861
(704) 597–4100
Fax: (704) 597–4122

8082

Business Information: Wheeler Technologies, Inc. established in 1990, specializes in data communications, systems consulting, outsourcing, and software development. The Corporation currently employs over 500 people and has a client base of Fortune 100 companies. As President/CEO, Mr. Wheeler oversees all aspects of the business. He coordinates reports from all departments/division, detailing Corporate operations and reports to the Board of Directors on the status of the Corporation. He represents the Corporation at various public functions. Mr. Wheeler is closely involved in the strategic planning for controlled growth of the Corporation in order to maintain excellent customer service and quality products. **Career Steps:** President/CEO, Wheeler Technologies, Inc. (1990–Present). **Associations & Accomplishments:** I.E.E.E.; Chamber of Commerce; Gator Alumni. **Education:** University of Florida, B.S.E.E. (1990). **Personal:** Ms. Wheeler enjoys boating, working out, running, and golf.

Frances E. Whisman
Case Manager
Columbia Homecare Oklahoma
405 S. Main
Sapulpa, OK 74066
(918) 224–2244
Fax: (918) 367–3825

8082

Business Information: Columbia Homecare Oklahoma is a major homecare organization in Northeastern Oklahoma providing medical, surgical, specialty IV therapy, psychiatry, and pre–op/post op services to clients. As Case Manager, Ms. Whisman oversees all aspects of the Company, monitoring both the quality of patient care and the scheduling and supervision of four to six LPN's. She is also active in the field, and handles all administrative duties. **Career Steps:** Case Manager, Columbia Homecare Oklahoma (1994–Present); Director of Nursing, Bristow Hospital (1991–1993); CDU Nurse/Infection Control, Wetumka Hospital (1989–1991); Assistant Director of Transplantation/Retrievals, American Red Cross (1989); Director of Surgical Technology, Tulsa County Vo–Tech (1981–1989). **Associations & Accomplishments:** National Association of Orthopedic Nurses; Association of Operating Room Nurses; Operating Room Certifications; Northeastern Oklahoma Infection Control/Employee Health Association; International Director, La Sertoma International. **Education:** Graceland College, B.S.N. (In Progress); William Newton Memorial School of Nursing, Nursing Diploma; Several Colleges for Pre–Requisites. **Personal:** Married to Jim in 1981. Four children: Toni Zweigart, Gay Asbell, Jenny Watts, and Beth Whisman. Ms. Whisman enjoys reading, needlework, crochet, and working with La Sertoma activities.

Thomas J. Wiese
Director of Social Work
Comprehensive Home Health Care
P.O. Box 200
Supply, NC 28462
(910) 251–8111
Fax: (910) 343–1218

8082

Business Information: Comprehensive Home Health Care is an industry leader in providing skilled and therapeutic home health care throughout North and South Carolina. Established in 1982, Comprehensive Home Health Care currently employs 837 people. As Director, Mr. Wiese is responsible for the direction of social work activities, comprehensive home health and hospice care, as well as providing clinical supervision, administrative support and field instructing for graduate and undergraduate students of social work. **Career Steps:** Director, Comprehensive Home Health Care (1987–Present); Medical Social Worker, Bayley – Seton Hospital, New York, NY (1982–1986); School Social Worker, Aero Special Education – Burbank, IL (1980–1982). **Associations & Accomplishments:** Member, St. Mark Catholic Church – Wilmington, NC; Member, National Association of Social Workers; Member, North Carolina Association of Home Health and Hospice Social Workers. **Education:** Marywood College, M.S.W. (1980); Lock Haven State College, B.S.W. (1978). **Personal:** Married to Rita L. in 1980. One child: Brian. Mr. Wiese enjoys sports, reading, and travel.

June Wilson, R.N, B.S.N., L.N.H.A.
Owner
Big Country Home Health
4717 40th Street
Lubbock, TX 79414
(619) 538–8638
Fax: Please mail or call

8082

Business Information: Big Country Home Health is a small home health agency providing all health services to area residents in a home based setting. As Owner, Ms. Wilson manages the total operation of licensed staff. As Administrator of Lubbock Health Care, a Beverly Enterprise long term care facility, she manages all aspects of the facility day–to–day operation. The facility is a 120–bed licensed facility employing 110 staff members. **Career Steps:** Owner, Big Country Home Health (1995–Present); Administrator, Beverly Enterprises (1990–Present); Consultant R.N., ARA Living Centers (1983–1988); RN Inservice, Proctor & Gamble (1980–1981). **Associations & Accomplishments:** American Business Women's Association; Harris College Alumni; Texas Christian University Alumni; Wayland Baptist College Alumni. **Education:** Wayland Baptist College, Licensed Administrator (1988); Harris College Nursing and Texas Christian University, R.N., B.S.N. **Personal:** Four children: Carla Norton, Jeff Wilson, Susan Tucker, Laura Etie. Ms. Wilson enjoys golf, reading, U.S. travel, gardening, volunteer work and refinishing antique furniture.

M. Allene Winfree
Nurse Supervisor
Home Touch Health Care (NPMC)
1250 Central
Hot Springs National Park, AR 71901–9567
(501) 321–0708
Fax: (501) 321–9567

8082

Business Information: Home Touch Health Care (NPMC) is a home care agency based from National Park Medical Center, which also offers a hospice program and personal care. There are specialty nurses to care for pediatric, obstetric, cardiovascular, and psychiatric patients, in addition to the many challenging needs of home care patients. Ms. Winfree supervises approximately 80 nurses, in addition to organizing the efficiency of nursing care, and providing leadership, instruction, problem–solving, and future goals for the Agency. **Career Steps:** Nurse Supervisor, Home Touch Health Care (NPMC) (1994–Present); Case Manager, St. Johns (1990–1994); Staff RN, Brookside Home Care (1989–1990); ICU/CCU, Open Heart Staff RN, St. Charles Medical Center (1987–1988). **Associations & Accomplishments:** Member, Home Care Association of Arkansas; Past Member, SCAN; Volunteer, Red Cross Disaster Team; Past Chairman, Commercial Ducks Unlimited – Stuttgart, Arkansas. **Education:** Jeff. Regional Medical Center, Nursing (1985); Baptist Medical Center, Coronary Care Certificate; University of Arkansas for Medical Science, Nursing; Arkansas State University, Secondary Education (1973); University of Arkansas at Pine Bluff, Nursing (1984). **Personal:** Married to Terry R. Sr. in 1987.

Brinda C. Woodall, B.S.N., R.N.
Director
Home Touch Health Care
1250 Central Avenue
Hot Springs Natural Park, AR 71901
(501) 321–0708
Fax: (501) 321–9567

8082

Business Information: Home Touch Health Care is an NPMC home health care agency, providing skilled nursing services (CNA's, LPN's, RN's) to people who need medical help. Services include following physician's orders from changing dressings to physical therapy, as well as speech therapy and social working. A practicing nurse since 1993, Ms. Woodall joined Home Touch Health in 1994. She is responsible for directing the agency, personal care, and hospice, as well as overseeing the budget, staffing, policies and procedures, and federal and state regulations compliance. **Career Steps:** Director, Home Touch Health Care (NPMC) (1995–Present); Branch Supervisor at Glenwood for NPMC Hometouch Health care (1994–1995); Staff RN, St. Joseph Home Health (1992–1994). **Associations & Accomplishments:** National Home Health Association; Arkansas Home Health Association: Program Committee, Legislative Committee; Volunteer Fire Fighter (12 years); Who's Who in Universities. **Education:** Henderson State University, B.S.N. in Nursing (1993); GCCC, A.S. (1989). **Personal:** Married to Steven Woodall in 1974. Two children: Johnny Woodall and Jennifer Floyd. Ms. Woodall enjoys reading, snow skiing, and camping.

Joseph S. Zangrilli
Director of Clinical Services
Nahatan Medical Services
129 Lenox Street
Norwood, MA 02062–3438
(617) 769–2449
Fax: (617) 769–6981
E MAIL: See Below

8082

Business Information: Nahatan Medical Services specializes in providing health care and medical equipment (i.e. oxygen, ventilators, apnea monitors) to patients in their homes. Established in 1963, the Company employs 70 people, and has an estimated annual revenue of $10 million. As Director of Clinical Services, Mr. Zangrilli is responsible for the day–to–day operations of the Company to include staffing, payroll, managed care contracts, and statistics. He is also responsible for personnel management, and the direct supervision of 35 employees, including respiratory therapists. Internet users can reach him via: Nmso2@aol.com. **Career Steps:** Director of Clinical Services, Nahatan Medical Services (1996–Present); Manager, Amcare Medical Service (1991–1994); Respiratory Therapist, Rhode Island Hospital (1988–1991); Respiratory Therapist, Landmark Medical Center. **Associations & Accomplishments:** American Association of Respiratory Care; Massachusetts Society of Respiratory Care; Rhode Island Society of Respiratory Care; Several Awards in Respiratory Therapy and Disease Management. **Education:** Newbury College, B.S. (1983). **Personal:** Married to Cheryl in 1985. Four children: Heather, Amanda, Joseph III, and Marissa. Mr. Zangrilli enjoys playing the guitar, music, and football.

Denise Zoeterman
Executive Vice President
HHS, Inc.
5363 44th Street Southeast
Grand Rapids, MI 49512–4001
(616) 956–9440
Fax: (616) 956–6843

8082

Business Information: HHS, Inc. is a non–profit organization, providing health management to over 300 self insured employer groups. Established in 1980, HHS, Inc. worked to provide services for the frail elderly and disabled population of Western Michigan. This Care Management program still exists and has expanded to include the Medicaid waiver, a state program to assist the Medicaid population by assessing their medical/psychiatric needs, cost containment and quality services are monitored by HHS, Inc. staff. As Vice President/Chief Operating Officer, Ms. Zoeterman is responsible for the day–to–day operations of the Company. **Career Steps:** Vice President/Chief Operating Officer, Home Health Services Inc. (1993–Present); Pine Rest Mental Health Services (1977–1993); Director of Contact Center, Director of Admissions, Coordinator of EAP. **Associations & Accomplishments:** Sponsor, Leadership Grand Rapids; Sponsor, YWCA Run Jane Run. **Education:** Western Michigan University, M.A. (1988); Calvin College, B.A. (1977). **Personal:** Ms. Zoeterman enjoys tennis, golf, and working around the house.

Neal D. Barnes
MIS Director
National Healthcare Alliance
770 South Post Oak Lane, Suite 445
Houston, TX 77056–1913
(713) 888–1911
Fax: Please mail or call

8090

Business Information: National Healthcare Alliance is a PPO, HMO, EPO medical provider, coordinating claims and third party insurance. As MIS Director, Mr. Barnes is responsible for the oversight, maintenance, and troubleshooting of all computer operations, importing and exporting of data. **Career Steps:** MIS Director, National Healthcare Alliance (1994–Present); System Analyst, CAE–Link (1993–1994); System Technician, International Computer Service (1991–1993); Service Technician, Computer Quick (1985–1990). **Education:** Attended, Houston Community College. **Personal:** Mr. Barnes enjoys Japanese Anime.

Richanda A. Bears Ghost
Administrative Officer/Contracting Specialist
Acoma–Canoncito–Laguna Hospital
P.O. Box 130
San Fidel, NM 87049–0130
(505) 552–6634 Ext.400
Fax: (505) 552–7363

8090

Business Information: Acoma–Canoncito–Laguna Hospital is a health care delivery system and part of the United States Public Health Service, Indian Health Service. An Administrative Officer and Contracting Specialist at the Hospital since

1995, Ms. Bears Ghost is responsible for contracting, personnel supervision, financial oversight, property and supply management, and serves as an Assistant to the Service Unit Director. **Career Steps:** Administrative Officer/Contracting Specialist, Acoma–Canoncito–Laguna Hospital (1995–Present); Administrative Officer, New Sunrise Regional Treatment Center (1992–1994); Personnel Management Specialist, IHS–Headquarters, Rockville, Maryland (1988–1992). **Associations & Accomplishments:** Volunteer, Democratic Party; Albuquerque Urban Indian Center; Montgomery County School Board – Rockville, Maryland; American Indian Tutoring Program – Montgomery County, Rockville, Maryland; Native American Indian Women Association. **Education:** Attended: Montgomery College, University of New Mexico, University of Santiago de Compostela – Spain, Portland State University, Mount Hood Community College. **Personal:** Three children: Anutira, Palani, and Celina Dawn. Ms. Bears Ghost enjoys horses, hiking, mountain climbing, and skiing.

Ms. Pascale C. Gousseland
Vice President and Founder
Service Express, Inc.
135 East 71st
New York, NY 10021
(212) 472–6881
Fax: (212) 535–3683

8091

Business Information: Service Express, Inc., established in 1988, is an information company specializing in the provision of marketing and direct mail services. Ms. Gousseland is also a psychotherapist and hypnotherapist in private practice, as well as an accomplished writer of published screenplays, poetry, and novels. Ms. Gousseland is a frequent Feature Poet at live venues and on cable TV in the New York City area. She received the Gradiva Award for Best Poetry from the National Association for the Advancement of Psychoanalysts. **Career Steps:** Vice President and Founder, Service Express, Inc. (1988–Present); Psychotherapist, Self– employed (1991–Present); Importer, Gousseland Cognac (1985–1991); Securities Executive, E.F. Hutton (1980–1985); Fashion Import and Export, Takano, Inc. Tokyo (1975–1980); Marketing Trainee, Creusot Loire, Paris (1974–1975) . **Associations & Accomplishments:** Member, National League of American Pen Women; Member, C.G. Jung Foundation for Analytic Psychology; Associate Member, National Association for the Advancement of Psychoanalysis; The American Boards of Accreditation and Certification; Associate Member, National Association for the Advancement of Psychoanalysts; The American Board of Accreditation and Certification; International Association of Counselors and Therapists. **Education:** C. G. Jung Foundation, Continuing Studies in Jungian Analysis (1994); Mid Manhattan Institute for Psychoanalysis, Continuing Studies (1994); Sorbonne, Paris, Masters of English (1974); Assas, Paris, Masters of Science of Information and Law (1973); New School, New York, Certificate of English, German, Spanish, Literature, and Philosophy (1972); Paris, France, Baccalaureat of Philosophy (1968).

Mr. Kevin A. Adams
Assistant Director
NorthStar AMHC
34 South Chalfonte Avenue
Atlantic City, NJ 08401
(609) 348–0001
Fax: (609) 344–0001

8093

Business Information: NorthStar AMHC (Atlantic Mental Health Center), a member of the AtlantiCare Health System, is an intensive outpatient drug and alcohol treatment facility. Established in 1944, Northstar AMHC currently employs 21 people. As Assistant Director, Mr. Adams is responsible for assisting the Director in staffing issues (i.e., hiring, firing, and discipline), as well as budgeting, day–to–day operations, and strategic planning. **Career Steps:** Assistant Director, North-Star AMHC (1990–Present); Systems Consultant, AT&T (1979–1990). **Associations & Accomplishments:** President of Foster Parent Association of Atlantic County; Member of Division of Youth and Family Services Advisory Board; Deacon, Commandment Prayer Band Church in Washington, D.C.; Past Class President, 1995 Class for Atlantic City Tomorrow (Leadership organization). **Education:** Pierce Junior College, A.S. (1978); Chemical Dependent Associate (CDA); Certified Social Worker (CSW). **Personal:** Married to Kim R. Adams in 1984. Four children: Kevin Jr., Dawn, Andrew, and Stephanie Adams.

Robert J. Barry
Director of Human Resources
Roosevelt Warm Springs Institute for Rehabilitation
P O Box 1000 Oak Road
Warm Springs, GA 31830
(706) 655–5171
Fax: (706) 655–5187

8093

Business Information: Roosevelt Warm Springs Institute for Rehabilitation was founded in 1927 by Franklin D. Roosevelt. The Institute was developed primarily for the rehabilitation of post–polio patients, but now has clinics for glaucoma, dialysis, and diabetic foot problems. The facility also has educational programs to assist the physically challenged in becoming independent. As Director of Human Resources, Mr. Barry is concerned with all aspects of human resource and personnel development within the Roosevelt Warm Springs Institute. He develops, implements, and monitors budgets for his department, and recruits, verifies, evaluates, and counsels employees. He works closely with other members of the management staff in the development of benefit packages and retirement and pension plans. **Career Steps:** Director of Human Resources, Roosevelt Warm Springs Institute for Rehabilitation (1994–Present); Personnel Analyst, Georgia Department of Corrections (1994); Lt. Col., Personnel Officer, US Army (1980–1990). **Associations & Accomplishments:** Certified Public Managers Society; Military Order of the Purple Heart. **Education:** Pepperdine University, M.A. in Human Resource Management (1980); Coker College, B.S. (1975). **Personal:** Four children: Tom, Debi, John, and Robert Jr.. Mr. Barry enjoys collecting eagle and lighthouse memorabilia.

Sherry Lynn Beatty
Director of Operations
Symphony Mobilex
11441 Beach Street
Cerritos, CA 90703–1726
(310) 860–4146
Fax: (310) 860–5499

8093

Business Information: Symphony Mobilex is recognized leader in providing mobile diagnostic imaging services. As Director of Operations, Miss Beatty oversees all operations, including transcription, dispatch, technologists, radiologist–assistants, quality assurance and customer service. **Career Steps:** Director of Operations, Symphony Mobilex (1994–Present); Assistant Director of Operations, Chase Mobilex Diagnostic Services (1991–1994); Co – Owner, "Hi" On The Hog Creations (1980–1983). **Associations & Accomplishments:** The American Registry of Radiologic Technologists; The American Society of Radiologic Technologists; California Certified Radiologic Technologist. **Education:** Orange Coast College, A.A., Certificate of Achievement, Radiologic Technology; Orange County Medical Center School of Radiologic Technology, Internship; Attended, California State Polytechnic University – Pomona (1980); Los Angeles College of Chiropractic (1976–1977). **Personal:** Miss Beatty enjoys bicycling, hiking, and gardening, and reading biographies.

Mary Jo Bridenstine Chapman
Clinical Services Manager
Inland Empire Physical Therapy
1303 West Sixth Street
Corona, CA 91720–3196
(909) 273–7742
Fax: (909) 273–7747

8093

Business Information: Inland Empire Physical Therapy is an outpatient clinic, providing full–service outpatient physical therapy services. The Clinic is part of a California health maintenance alliance, which assists in the management of its managed care contracts, and in turn upgrades the quality of care provided to their patients, as well as encourages the development of new programs. A Certified Physical Therapist, Ms. Chapman joined Inland Empire Physical Therapy as Clinical Services Manager in 1993. She is responsible for the supervision of a support staff of 19, in addition to providing patient care. **Career Steps:** Clinical Services Manager, Inland Empire Physical Therapy (1993–Present); Physical Therapist and Owner, Mid–County Physical Therapy (1987–1993); Physical Therapist, Physicians Physical Therapy (1975–1987). **Associations & Accomplishments:** American Physical Therapy Association; Feldenkrais Guild. **Education:** University of Iowa, B.S. in Biology (1975); Certification: Physical Therapy, Feldenkrais Training Program. **Personal:** Married to Gary in 1976. Two children: Kris and Brady. Ms. Bridenstine Chapman enjoys hiking, backpacking, music, piano, bells, church and drama.

Elizabeth T. Broussard, RRA
Office Manager
Whitney Atchetee Physical Therapy Clinic
317 Odea Street
Abbeville, LA 70510–4052
(318) 893–3258
Fax: (318) 898–0495

8093

Business Information: Whitney Atchetee Physical Therapy Clinic employs two physical therapists and a support staff of four. As Office Manager, Ms. Broussard is responsible for all office duties, personnel and payroll oversight, billing procedures, and transcription of all medical reports. Concurrently, she owns and serves as Assistant Administrator and Travel Agent for Travel Quest, a travel agency specializing in airline ticket packages. **Career Steps:** Office Manager, Whitney Atchetee Physical Therapy Clinic (1993–Present); Assistant Administrator, Travel Agent/Owner, Travel Quest (1990–Present); Director of Medical Records, Women's & Children's Hospital (1991–1992); Bookkeeper/Vice President, Toups Propeller Service (1983–1991); Director of Quality Assurance, Erath General Hospital (1980–1983). **Associations & Accomplishments:** American Health Information Management Association; Louisiana Health Information Management Association; South West Louisiana Health Information Management Association; Confrerie d' Abbeville (promoting French Culture and International relations with other French–speaking nations). **Education:** University of Southwestern Louisiana: B.S. (1975), B.A. (1990). **Personal:** Married to Clayton J. in 1993. Three children: Mark, Trent, and Zachary. Ms. Broussard enjoys movies, working out, and Judo.

Kirstin E. Brunner, D.O.
Department Head of Psychiatry
Integra Health Family Development Center (Iowa Health System)
855 A Avenue
Cedar Rapids, IA 52402
(319) 638–5684
Fax: (319) 368–5682

8093

Business Information: Established in 1994, Integra Health Family Development Center, an affiliate of Iowa Health Systems, is a full–service psychiatric outpatient center (40 physician group). A Child Psychiatrist, Dr. Brunner is responsible for all aspects of operations for the Department of Psychiatry. **Career Steps:** Department Head of Psychiatry, Integra Health Family Development Center (Iowa Health System) (1992–Present). **Associations & Accomplishments:** American Academy of Child and Adolescent Psychiatry; American Academy of Pediatrics; American Psychiatric Association; American Medical Association; American Osteopathic Association. **Education:** Philadelphia College of Osteopathic Medicine, D.O. (1986); Muhlenberg College, B.S. **Personal:** Dr. Brunner enjoys canoeing, hiking, and reading.

Jess B. Caderao, M.D.
(Radiation Oncologist)

Partner
Arlington Cancer Center
906 W. Randol Mill Road
Arlington, TX 76012–6509
(817) 261–4906
Fax: (817) 261–5837

8093

Business Information: Arlington Cancer Center is a full–service medical facility, specializing in the diagnosis, treatment, and research of cancer. A practicing physician since 1957 and Board–Certified in Radiotherapy and Oncology, Radiology, and Clinical Oncology, Dr. Caderao joined Arlington Cancer Center as Partner and Radiation Oncologist in 1989. He is responsible for providing quality medical care to patients suffering from cancer diseases, as well as conducting clinical research in radioactive implants and hyperthermia – using direct heat on cancer cells to kill and make them more sensitive to radiation. **Career Steps:** Partner and Radiation Oncologist, Arlington Cancer Center (1989–Present); Solo Practitioner (1977–1988); Assistant Professor, University Texas – MD Anderson Hospital (1973–1976) **Associations & Accomplishments:** American College of Radiology; American Society of Radiotherapy and Oncology; American Society of Clinical Oncology; American Radium Society **Education:** University of the Phillipines, M.D. (1957) **Personal:** Three children: Jessica, Jon and Travis.

James Campbell
Chief Executive Officer
Laurel Fork Clear Fork Health Center
107 Main Street South
Jellico, TN 37762
(423) 784–8492
Fax: (423) 784–8358

8093

Business Information: Laurel Fork Clear Fork Health Center, a community health center, is partially funded by the Federal government and serves the underprivileged in eastern Tennessee and Kentucky. Regional in scope, the Center has three full–time and one part–time operation. Established in 1976, the Center employs 43 people and has an estimated annual revenue of $2.6 million. As Chief Executive Officer, Mr. Campbell oversees every aspect of the organization, focusing heavily on strategic planning (i.e. changes in managed care). He also coordinates with the county Chamber of Commerce,and the State Primary Care Association. **Career Steps:** Chief Executive Officer, Laurel Fork Clear Fork Health Center (1994–Present); United States Air Force: Chief, Medical Information Systems, Air Mobility Command (1991–1994), Administrator, 305 Medical Group (1990–1992), Chief, Medical Information System (1986–1990). **Associations & Accomplishments:** American College of Healthcare Executives; Kiwanis International; Rotary International; Habitat for Humanity; President, Appalachia Health Partnership; Board of Directors, Tennessee Primary Care Association. **Education:** Central Michigan University; Park College, B.S. (1977); Squadron Officer School (1986); Air Command and Staff College (1987). **Personal:** Married to Marilyn in 1970. Mr. Campbell enjoys trapping, hunting, fishing, and camping.

Lon W. Castle, M.D.

Cardiologist and Electrophysiologist
North Ohio Heart Center
Lakewood Professional Building, 14601 Detroit Avenue, Suite 650
Lakewood, OH 44107
(216) 228–9955
Fax: (216) 228–9957

8093

Business Information: North Ohio Heart Center is a large medical care facility specializing in cardiology and electrophysiology. Established in 1976, North Ohio Heart Center has six offices located in northeastern Ohio and currently employs 150 people. As Cardiologist and Electrophysiologist, Dr. Castle is responsible for cardiac electrophysiology and pacing. **Career Steps:** Cardiologist and Electrophysiologist, North Ohio Heart Center (1994–Present); Cardiologist, Cleveland Clinic (1971–1994); Internist, U.S. Air Force, Little Rock, Arkansas (1969–1971). **Associations & Accomplishments:** Associate Team Physician, Cleveland Browns (1978–1994); Past President, NFL Physicians Association (1992–1994). **Education:** Temple University, M.D. (1965). **Personal:** Married to Terri in 1983. Eight children: Lon, Lynn, Laura, Lisa, Lee, Lance, Brittany, and Melany. Dr. Castle enjoys sports medicine and jogging.

Felix A. Colon, M.D.

Medical Director
Damas Hospital, Inc.
Ponce By Pass
Ponce, Puerto Rico 00731
(787) 840–2395 (787) 840–6615
Fax: Please mail or call

8093

Business Information: Damas Hospital, Inc. is a 350–bed, full–service healthcare institution specializing in the diagnosis, treatment, and rehabilitation of patients. The Hospital has several specialty doctors on staff, including gastroenterologists, pulmonologists, and a cardiologist. As Medical Director, Dr. Colon oversees the entire medical facility, including doctors, nurses, and all operations. Concurrently, Dr. Colon is a Professor at the Ponce School of Medicine. As a Sub specialist in the field of Pediatric Pulmonary Disease, he also serves as Consultant to the major hospital in the area. **Career Steps:** Medical Director, Damas Hospital, Inc. (1993–Present). **Associations & Accomplishments:** American Academy of Pediatrics; Puerto Rico Medical Association; Board of Directors, Ponce School of Medicine; Past President, Southern Medical Association (1993); Delegate to the Puerto Rican Medical Association (1992). **Education:** University of Puerto Rico – School of Medicine, M.D. (1978); Specialist degree in Pediatrics, San Juan Municipal Hospital (1980); Sub Specialist in Pulmonary Disease, Centro Medico Hospital San Juan, Puerto Rico (1983). **Personal:** Married to Nereida in 1971.

One child: Luis Antonio. Dr. Colon enjoys tennis, jogging, physical fitness, and sports.

J. Carlene Cox
Administrative Director
Bethesda Company Care
945 Bethesda Drive
Zanesville, OH 43701
(614) 454–4010
Fax: (614) 454–4008

8093

Business Information: Affiliated with the larger Bethesda Care System, Bethesda Company Care provides occupational health care, therapy, rehabilitation, and urgent care services to company and corporate employees who have work–related injuries. Established in 1991, Bethesda Company Care currently employs 28 medical professionals and staff. As Administrative Director, Ms. Cox is responsible for all aspects of company administration and operations. **Career Steps:** Administration Director, Bethesda Company Care (1991–Present); Bethesda Hospital: Service Representative (1984–1991), Clinical Lab Technician (1982–1984). **Associations & Accomplishments:** Rotary International; Muskingum County Community Foundation Council; Duncan Falls Presbyterian Church; Ohio Hospital Association; National Association of Occupational Health Professionals; Friends of Philo High School. **Education:** Bethesda Hospital School of Laboratory, C.L.A./A.S.C.P. (1977). **Personal:** Two children: Danielle Cox McDonald and DeAnn. Ms. Cox enjoys travel, football, movies, and being involved in her teennage daughter's school activities.

Michael W. De La Garza

Chief Operating Officer
Medical Synergies, Inc.
122 West Colorado Boulevard, Suite 100
Dallas, TX 75208
(214) 780–7831
Fax: (214) 780–8633

8093

Business Information: Medical Synergies, Inc. was formed to acquire diagnostic imaging systems throughout the southern United States. The Company currently has seven sites and 93 managed care contracts in Texas, New Mexico, and Louisiana . As COO, Mr. De La Garza has oversight of the day–to–day operations of the corporation. His responsibilities include personnel and financial concerns, budgetary matters, marketing of new and existing services, and public relations. Concurrently, Mr. De La Garza is the COO of Dallas Medical and Injury, a group of physical therapy and chiropractic clinics. **Career Steps:** COO, Medical Synergies, Inc. (1991–Present); COO, Dallas Medical and Injury (1991–Present); Production Manager, Union Carbide (1979–1991). **Associations & Accomplishments:** Radiological Society of North America; Hispanic Chamber of Dallas; Hispanic Chamber of Tarrant County. **Education:** University of Houston; University of Texas; Southwest State University. **Personal:** Married to Robin in 1995. Two children: Olivia and Courtney. Mr. De La Garza enjoys weightlifting, fishing, and golf.

Mr. Glenn J. Decker
Physical Therapist and Owner
Physical Therapy Clinic of Danville
473 West Walnut Street
Danville, KY 40422
(606) 238–7650
Fax: (606) 238–4160

8093

Business Information: Physical Therapy Clinic of Danville is an outpatient physical therapy clinic, serving patients in the Danville, Kentucky and surrounding counties. As Owner of the Clinic, Mr. Decker oversees all administrative functions. He is a licensed Physical Therapist, responsible for the treatment and evaluation of patients, performs job analysis and functional capacity evaluations. Established in 1983, Physical Therapy Clinic of Danville employs two Licensed Physical Therapists and a Licensed Physical Therapy Assistant, and has a total staff of seven. Operational budget for the Clinic is in excess of $250K. **Career Steps:** Physical Therapist and Owner, Physical Therapy Clinic of Danville (1991–1993); Musculoskeletal Coordinator, Lexington Physical Therapy (1990–1991); Director of Physical Therapy, Progressive Physical Therapy (1988–1990); Directed and Developed Sports Medicine Clinic, Central Baptist Hospital, Lexington, KY (1986–1988). **Associations & Accomplishments:** American Physical Therapy Association (APTA), Orthopedic Section and Private Practice Section; Kentucky Physical Therapy Association; Medical Corpsman, United States Navy Reserves; Volunteer Faculty, University of Kentucky; Certified Manual Therapist, American Academy of Orthopedic Manual Physical Therapists. **Education:** University of Pitts-

---

burgh, B.S. (1983); Trenton State College, B.S. in Health and Physical Education (1975).

Reza Feiz, M.D.
Unit Director
Upper Shore Community Mental Health
P.O. Box 229
Chestertown, MD 21620
(410) 778–6800
Fax: Please mail or call

8093

Business Information: Upper Shore Community Mental Health Center (USCMHC) is a mental health facility, providing treatment to individuals 18 years of age and older. A practicing psychiatrist for the past twenty years, Dr. Feiz joined Upper Shore Community Mental Health as Unit Director in 1985. He is responsible for the treatment of emotionally–disturbed individuals through individual, group, and activity therapy, as well as Team meetings. Concurrent with his private practice, he evaluates children and adolescents for any disorder and provides recommendations for treatment at Kent County Mental Health Clinic. He also serves as a consultant for Kent & Queen Anne's Mobile Treatment Team for these Eastern Shore counties. **Career Steps:** Unit Director, Upper Shore Community Mental Health (1985–Present); Psychiatric Consultant, Kent County Mental Health Clinic (1990–Present); Psychiatric Consultant, Kent County Mental Health Clinic (1990–Present); Director Asolescnet Treatment Program, Taylor Manor Psychiatric Hospital; Treatment Director Adolescent Treatment Center; Assistant Professor of Psychiatry, Medical College of Wisconsin. **Associations & Accomplishments:** American Psychiatric Association; National Center for Infant Clinical Programs; International Association for Infant Psychiatry; Society of Iranian Psychiatrist in North America; Co–Authored "Platlet Monoamine–Oxidase Activity in Children and Adolescents with Psychiatric Disorders" in the bulletin of Schizophrenzia, Vol.6No.2 and "Catecholamine–Thyroid Hormone Interaction and MAO Activity in Psychiatrically Disturbed Children Vol.8, No.2. **Education:** Child Study Center – Yale University (1974–1976); Temple University, Psychiatric Department (1970–1973); and Community Psychiatry Training (1973–1974), Board Certified in General Psychiatry (1979), Board Certified in Child and Adolescent Psychiatry (1986). **Personal:** Dr. Feiz enjoys herbal gardening and bird watching.

Samantha S. Girton
Director of Clinical Operations
RehabWorks, Inc.
521 South Greenwood Avenue
Clearwater, FL 34616
(813) 441–8954 Ext. 3057
Fax: (813) 449–1173
EMAIL: See Below

8093

Business Information: RehabWorks, Inc., a subsidiary of Horizon/CMS Health Care Corporation, is a health care organization, specializing in physical, occupational, and speech rehabilitation. As Regional Director of Clinical Operations, Ms. Girton is responsible for the direction of fifteen outpatient facilities located in Florida, including the oversight of all marketing, development, and operations. Internet users can reach her via: SGirton@AOL.COM. **Career Steps:** RehabWorks, Inc.: Regional Director of Clinical Operations (1994–Present), Program Development Coordinator (1991–1994). **Associations & Accomplishments:** American Management Association; American Marketing Association; Published article on clinical programs for Community Outreach. **Education:** Eckerd College, B.A. (1991); LaSalle University, Masters in Healthcare Marketing in progress. **Personal:** Ms. Girton enjoys competitive volleyball and attending motivational speaking seminars.

Patricia Guidry–Pannell
Adminstrator
Sunrise Healthcare
1310 West 7th Street
Kaplan, LA 70548
(318) 643–6743
Fax: (318) 643–5246

8093

Business Information: Sunrise Healthcare is a geriatric psychiatric behavioral health facility dedicated to assisting elderly patients cope with problems and stresses that they may encounter in their daily lives. The facility began operations in 1993 and currently employs 60 people. As Administrator, Ms. Guidry–Pannell oversees the daily operations of the facility. Other responsibilities include oversight of all nursing personnel concerns such as recruiting, training, scheduling, and counseling. Ms. Guidry–Pannell is also in charge of quality control, patient satisfaction, and patient billing. **Career Steps:** Administrator, Sunrise Healthcare (1994–Present); Director of Nursing, JRJ Services (1993–94); Director of Nursing, Acadian Oaks Hospital (1992–1993); Regional Director of Nursing, A.M.E. (1990–1992). **Education:** Louisiana State University, A.D. (1985); Attending, Graceland College. **Personal:** Married to Richard Pannell in 1990. Two children: Kylie and Kyrick Pannell. Ms. Guidry–Pannell enjoys gardening, reading, and cooking.

Bobbi M. Harman–Pemberton

Director of Nursing
Peninsula Blood Bank
1791 El Camino Real
Burlingame, CA 94010
(415) 697–4034
Fax: (415) 697–4332
8093

Business Information: Peninsula Blood Bank is a not–for–profit community health blood bank. As Director of Nursing, Ms. Harman–Pemberton is responsible for supervising employees, patient relations, and administrative duties. **Career Steps:** Director of Nursing, Peninsula Blood Bank (1995–Present); Director of Nursing, Blood Bank of Hawaii (1993–1995); Director of Donor Services, Hunter Blood Center (1990–1993); Coordinator, St. Anthony's Hospital Blood Bank (1989–1990); Assistant Director Blood Services, American Red Cross (1988–1989); Operating Room Staff Nurse, University of California – Davis (1987–1988); Air Force Reserve Flight Nurse, 65th Aeromedical Evacuation Squadron, Travis AFB (1983–1988). **Associations & Accomplishments:** American Association of Blood Banks; Air Force Association; Air Force Reserve Officers Association; National Association for Female Executives; American Business Women's Association; California Blood Bank Society; Clinical Educator, Irwin Memorial Blood Bank (1978–1987); Who's Who of American Women. **Education:** University of San Francisco, BSN; University of San Francisco, PHN; Registered Nurse License: Indiana, California, and Hawaii; Certified Flight Nurse, US Air Force; Certified Operating Room Nurse; Blood Donor Phlebotomist Instructor, American Association of Blood Banks; Certification Quality Management; Various Lectures; Published "Keeping Staff Current" in The American Association of Blood Banks. **Personal:** Ms. Harman–Pemberton enjoys swimming, horseback riding, and research into civil war history.

Shakeela F. Hussain, M.D.

Physician
Buena Ventura Medical Clinic
86 Daily Drive
Camarillo, CA 93010
(805) 383–2100
Fax: Please mail or call
8093

Business Information: Buena Ventura Medical Clinic is a full–service health care institution specializing in the diagnosis, treatment and rehabilitation of patients. Specializing in internal medicine, Dr. Hussain specifically works in the area of geriatrics. **Career Steps:** Physician, Buena Ventura Medical Clinic (1991–Present); Intern/Resident, Henry Ford Hospital (1988–1991). **Associations & Accomplishments:** American College of Physicians; American Medical Association. **Education:** Wayne State University School of Medicine, M.D. (1988); University of California – Los Angeles, B.S. in Biochemistry (1982). **Personal:** Married to Mukarram Hussain, M.D. in 1981. Two children: Jamal and Jameel. Dr. Hussain enjoys writing poems and short stories. Dr. Hussain thanks God, her husband and her parents for her success.

Dr. Kabirudeen Jivraj

Anesthesiologist/Intensive Care Physician
Foothills Hospital/Outpatient Anesthesia Clinic
739 Hillcrest Avenue, Southwest
Calgary, Alberta T2S 0N3
(403) 228–4823
Fax: (403) 245–6651
8093

Business Information: Outpatient Anesthesia Clinic is a private medical practice providing outpatient anesthesia and full–service operating room facilities for ambulatory surgical patients. With three locations in Canada, the Clinic employs 10 people. As Anesthesiologist / Intensive Care Physician, Dr. Jivraj oversees admission and care of critical patients, and is responsible for administering general anesthesia, post operative pain service, and labor pain management to patients. He is also responsible for administration, operations, public relations, and strategic planning. Currently the President – Elect (until September 20, 1996, then President from September 20 until September 20, 1997) of the Alberta Medical Association, Dr. Jivraj has been interviewed several times on related operations. **Career Steps:** Anesthesiologist/Intensive Care Physician, Foothills Hospital/Outpatient Anesthesia Clinic (1994–Present); Calgary General Hospital: Vice President, Medical Services (1993–1994), Chair, Department of Anesthesia (1991–1993), Assistant Director, Department of Intensive Care (1988–1991). **Associations & Accomplishments:** Society of Critical Care Medicine; Canadian Critical Care Society; Alberta Society of Critical Care Medicine; Canadian and Alberta Society of Anesthesia; Canadian and Alberta Medical Association. **Education:** University of British Columbia, F.R.C.P. in Anesthesia (1985); University of London, M.B.B.S.; University of Alberta, Subspecialty Training, Critical Care Medicine (1986). **Personal:** Married to Munira in 1985. Two children: Ashiana and Naheed. Dr. Jivraj enjoys squash, golf, and downhill/water skiing.

Glenn W. Jones, M.D.

Physician
Hamilton Regional Cancer Center/Ontario Cancer Foundation
699 Concession Street
Hamilton, Ontario L8V 5C2
(905) 387–9495
Fax: (905) 575–6326
EMAIL: See Below
8093

Business Information: Hamilton Regional Cancer Center/ Ontario Cancer Foundation is comprised of eight medical facilities specializing in the treatment of cancer and related illnesses. As Physician, Dr. Jones, a radiation oncologist, is considered one of the world's foremost experts on Mycosis Fungoides, a type of skin lymphoma. Concentrating mainly in gastrointestinal malignancies, he also specializes in "total body irradiation" for bone marrow transplants. Author of several papers and publications in medical journals, and two chapters of a book, he is very active in research. Internet users can reach him via: gjones@octrf.on.ca. **Career Steps:** Physician, Hamilton Regional Cancer Center/Ontario Cancer Foundation (1989–Present). **Associations & Accomplishments:** Canadian and Ontario Medical Association; Tariff Committee Member; Royal College of Physicians and Surgeons of Canada; Canadian Association of Radiation Oncologists; Society for the Advancement of Socio–Economics; Medical Dental Society Ethics Commission; National Evangelical Fellowship of Canada; Social Action Commission; Sub–Committee on Poverty and Related Issues, Including Health Care. **Education:** McMaster University: M.Sc. in Clinical Epidemiology and Biostatistics (1996), B.Sc. in Biochemistry and Chemistry (1980); Queen's University, M.D. (1984). **Personal:** Married to Eeva Riitta Kastikainen in 1987. Three children: Nathan, Sharaya, and Kai. Dr. Jones enjoys philosophy, decision science, conflict simulations, classical music, and medical ethics.

Patricia L. Kalinowski

Territory Director
Intracorp
8600 LaSalle Road
Baltimore, MD 21286
(410) 828–6750
Fax: (410) 828–6216
Email: See Below
8093

Business Information: Intracorp is a private rehabilitation center providing medical management and cost containment services. Clients consist of workers' compensation and personal injury patients. Service is provided to persons on worker's compensation, personal injury, accident and health, and other disability groups. As Territory Director, Ms. Kalinowski is responsible for managing disability services, handling daily operations, and strategic planning for Maryland, Washington, D.C., and Northern Virginia. AT&T email users can reach her via: PRALINOWSKI. **Career Steps:** Intracorp: Territory Director (1996–Present), Field Service Manager (1990–1995), Field Specialist (1986–1990); Vocational Evaluator, Maryland Rehabilitation Center (1984–1985). **Associations & Accomplishments:** NARPPS; Chesapeake Association of Rehabilitation Professionals – Private Sector; National Rehab Association; Maryland Rehab Association; VEWAA; MDVEWAA; Job Placement Development Association. **Education:** Syracuse University, M.S. (1982), B.S. (1981). **Personal:** Two children: Christopher and Jessica. Ms. Kalinowski enjoys embroidery, reading, and gardening.

Herbert Jay Kaplan

Financial Manager
Genesee Health Service
220 Alexander Street, Suite 608
Rochester, NY 14607–4004
(716) 263–5963
Fax: (716) 263–2693
8093

Business Information: Genesee Health Service, a division of Genesee Hospital, is an outpatient center specializing in the diagnosis and treatment of patients. A financial accounting management expert with over twenty–five years expertise, Mr. Kaplan was appointed Financial Manager in 1985. In this capacity, he oversees all financial analysis and reporting and related accounting support staff. **Career Steps:** Financial Manager, Genesee Health Service (1985–Present); Divisional Controller, Glassrock Home Health Care (1982–1985); Senior Accountant, Greece Central School District (1968–1982). **Education:** Clarkson University, B.B.A. (1963) **Personal:** Married to Barbara in 1964. Two children: Deborah and Diane. Mr. Kaplan enjoys collecting coins and stamps.

Laura J. Kasperski

Director of Medical Records
Suburban Cook County Tuberculosis Sanitarium District
7556 West Jackson Boulevard
Forest Park, IL 60130–1854
(708) 366–5000
Fax: (708) 366–3756
8093

Business Information: The Suburban Cook County Tuberculosis Sanitarium District administers all operational functions for three non–profit tuberculosis outpatient clinics located in Cook County, Illinois' suburban communities. Entities include: Piszczek Tuberculosis Clinic, Des Plaines Clinic, and Harvey Clinic. As Director of Medical Records — operating from the Piszczek Tuberculosis Clinic — Ms. Kasperski oversees all administrative operations for a support staff of 25, in addition to the overall administrative operations of the Medical Records Division. **Career Steps:** Director of Medical Records, Suburban Cook County Tuberculosis Sanitarium District (1994–Present); Medical Records Supervisor, Olympia Fields Osteopathic Hospital and Medical Center (1993–1994); Medical Record Coordinator, Hinsdale Hospital – Bolingbrook Medical Center (1990–1992); Cancer Registrar, Elmhurst Hospital (1989–1990). **Associations & Accomplishments:** American Health Information Management Association; Illinois Health Information Management Association; Chicago Area Health Information Management Association. **Education:** Illinois State University, B.S. in Medical Record Administration (1989); Attending: Lewis University, working towards M.B.A. **Personal:** Ms. Kasperski enjoys travel and reading.

Marilyn A. LaCelle, ACSW

Chief Executive Officer
Valley Cities Counseling and Consultation
2704 I Street, NE
Auburn, WA 98002–2411
(206) 833–7444 Ext. 3104
Fax: (206) 833–0480
EMAIL: See Below
8093

Business Information: Valley Cities Counseling and Consultation provides a continuum of behavioral health outpatient services for all age groups. Operating from five Washington satellite office sites in Auburn (2), Federal Way (2), and Renton, some of VCCC's programs include: outpatient, school and in–home services, short–term residential services, partial hospitalization, inter–agency coordination and business consultation services. As Chief Executive Officer, Marilyn LaCelle oversees the administration for all operations. Reporting to the Board of Directors, she provides leadership in strategic planning, community relations, fiscal, personnel, and clinical management. Internet users can reach her via: Lacellem@pie.org **Career Steps:** Chief executive Officer, Valley Cities Couseling and Consultation (1989–Present); Seattle Mental Health: Associate Director and Acting Executive Director (1984–1989). **Associations & Accomplishments:** Board of Directors, Spectrum Health of Washington, Inc. Federal Region X Representative to National Community Mental Healthcare Council; Mental Health Corporations of America; Chair, King County Children and Family Commission; Past President, Washington Community Mental Health Council. **Education:** University of Denver, M.S.W. (1975). **Personal:** Married to LeRoy. One child: Denise. Ms. LaCelle enjoys spending quality time with her family.

Theresa A. Langdon

Program Director
North Baltimore Center, Inc.
2225 North Charles Street
Baltimore, MD 21218–5730
(410) 366–4360
Fax: (410) 467–8024
8093

Business Information: North Baltimore Center, Inc. is a privately–owned, not–for–profit, comprehensive community mental health facility, providing psychiatric treatment and rehabilitation services for treatment of substance abuse and mental disorders in adults and children on an outpatient basis. Joining North Baltimore Center in 1984, Ms. Langdon currently serves as Program Director for Rehabilitative Services since 1990. She directs all rehabilitation programs for seriously mentally ill adults. **Career Steps:** North Baltimore Center, Inc.: Program Director (1990–Present), Residential Director (1987–1990); Residential Director, Project PLASE (1984–1987). **Associations & Accomplishments:** Maryland Association of Psychiatric Support Services: Secretary, Board of Directors; Alliance for the Mentally Ill. **Education:** State University of New York, M.S. in Counseling (1980); Keuka College, B.A. in Psychology (1975). **Personal:** Ms. Langdon enjoys writing, hiking, and travel.

Virginia Lohr Ortis
Regional President
Rehab Works
80A Commerce Street
Glastonbury, CT 06033
(800) 564–5330
Fax: (860) 871–1552

8093

Business Information: Rehab Works, a division of Horizon Health, provides rehabilitation services to patients wherever necessary, i.e. homes, nursing homes, hospitals, etc. Services provided include physical therapy, occupational therapy and speech therapy. As Regional President, Ms. Lohr Ortis oversees the activities of Rehab Works' northeast region. Her responsibilities include maintaining quality assurance of care, human resource concerns, marketing of services, financial and budgetary concerns, and supervision of state directors. **Career Steps:** Regional President, Rehab Works (1994–Present); Executive Director, Hillhaven Corporation (1978–1993). **Associations & Accomplishments:** Volunteer work: Community Services; Soup Kitchens; Homeless Shelters. **Education:** Emmanuel College, B.S. (1985). **Personal:** Married to Carlos in 1982. One child: Loree Jean. Ms. Lohr Ortis enjoys international travel, gardening, and photography.

Charlotte L. Mooradian

Administrator
Jupiter Medical Center – Pavilion
1230 S. Old Dixie Highway
Jupiter, FL 33458–7205
(561) 744–4444
Fax: (561) 745–5730

8093

Business Information: Jupiter Medical Center – Pavilion is a health care and rehabilitative services facility. The Center offers general hospital services, a skilled nursing center, cancer research center, dialysis, diabetes center, and a womens clinic that will be completed by October 1996. As Administrator, Ms. Mooradian heads the 120–bed skilled nursing facility and 30–bed certified sub–acute unit. She oversees the entire Facility's staff of nurses, administrative staff, records, restorative, rehabilitation, technical, and dietary staff. **Career Steps:** Administrator, Jupiter Medical Center – Pavilion (1995–Present); Administrator/R.N., Ridge Terrace N.H. (1993–1995); Administrator/R.N., Jupiter Care Center (1990–1994); Administrator/R.N., Beverly Enterprises (1992–1993). **Associations & Accomplishments:** Florida Department of Professional Regulation – Board of Nursing Home Administrators; Florida Department of Business and Professional Regulation – Board of Nursing Home Administrators; State of Alabama – Board of Nursing Home Administrators; Florida Health Care; Advisor of Practical Nursing Program. **Education:** Lynn University, N.H.A. Preceptor (1992); Licensed Nursing Home Administrator: Alabama (1979), Florida (1980); Sylacauga Hospital School of Nursing; University of Alabama; Alabama A&M University. **Personal:** Married to Harry. Two children: Jeffrey Billingsley and Dawn Dickerson; and four grandchildren. Ms. Mooradian enjoys reading, boating, and art appreciation.

Mrs. Adalia Moreno
Chief Executive Officer
Life Improvement Center
1017 NW 10th
Oklahoma City, OK 73106
(405) 528–4357
Fax: (405) 239–2637

8093

Business Information: Life Improvement Center is a medical facility specializing in oral narcotic substitution treatment for opioid dependent persons on an outpatient basis. Established in 1979, the Center currently employs 40 medical support staff members. As Chief Executive Officer, Mrs. Moreno oversees all aspects of operations of both the Tulsa and Oklahoma City facilities, including control, utilization and conservation of physical and financial assets as well as recruitment and direction of staff. **Career Steps:** Life Improvement Center: Chief Executive Officer (1993–Present), Administrator (1990–1993); Bi–Lingual Administrator, MAPS, Inc.

(1988–1990). **Personal:** Married to Angel. Three children: Nathaniel, Natasha and Eli. Mrs. Moreno enjoys gardening, singing and living life to its fullest.

Zach O. Oyefesobi
Administrator
Complete Rehab, Inc.
303 George Street, Building G7
New Brunswick, NJ 08901
(908) 828–3100
Fax: (908) 828–3288

8093

Business Information: Complete Rehab, Inc., established in 1991, provides a wide range of rehabilitation services to patients in various settings (i.e. homes, nursing homes, hospitals). Services provided include physical therapy, occupational therapy and speech therapy. As Administrator, Mr. Oyefesobi is responsible for maintaining quality assurance of care, human resource concerns, marketing of services, financial and budgetary concerns. **Career Steps:** Administrator, Complete Rehab, Inc. (1993–Present); CEO, Interstate Rehab, Inc. (1990–1992). **Associations & Accomplishments:** American Management Association; American College of Healthcare Executives; Society for Human Resource Management. **Education:** Greenwich University, Ph.D. candidate; New Jersey Institute of Technology, M.S.; Kean College of New Jersey, B.A. (1987). **Personal:** Married to Stella in 1994. Four children: Abimbola, Tomi, Antoinette, and Tokunbo. Mr. Oyefesobi enjoys travel, tennis, and ping pong.

T. Angelina Pabon, ICS, Ph.D.

President and Owner
La Derma Gallery
3180 West Sahara Avenue Ste. C–13
Las Vegas, NV 89102
(702) 871–0505
Fax: (702) 871–3840

8093

Business Information: La Derma Gallery provides reconstructive surgery to cancer patients. Also available are less–invasive procedures: permanent make–up; skin care; manicures; and pedicures, all in a metaphysical environment. As Owner, Miss Pabon is responsible for all aspects of administration, as well as performing reconstructions to clients through pedicures, manicures, and permanent make–up. **Career Steps:** Owner, La Derma Gallery (1992–Present); Owner, Dermagraphic Institute (1996–Present); Owner, The Oasis (1988–1990). **Associations & Accomplishments:** Las Vegas Chamber of Commerce; Las Vegas Better Business Bureau; Nevada State Board of Cosmetology; Mediphysical Institute. **Education:** Mediphysical Institute, Ph.D. (1993); University of San Francisco, B.A. in Business; Cosmetological Degree in California, New York, Nevada, Chicago; Cosmetological Degree from Christian Dior – Paris, France.

Patty A. Paisley
Regional Director of Operations
Golden Care
8451 Pearl Street
Thorton, CO 80229–4804
(303) 286–5104
Fax: (303) 286–5113

8093

Business Information: Golden Care, a subsidiary of Sun Health, provides acute and subacute respiratory therapy. The Company has fourteen facilities throughout Colorado, Montana, Wyoming, Idaho, and Utah. As Regional Director of Operations, Mrs. Paisley is responsible for all operations for the fourteen facility region. Her duties include annual budgeting, marketing, employee recruitment, and directing a staff of area managers and staff therapists. **Career Steps:** Regional Director of Operations, Golden Care (1995–Present); Subacute Manager, Health–One/Columbia (1994–1995); Program Director – Respiratory Therapy Department, Pima Medical Institute (1990–1994). **Associations & Accomplishments:** American Association for Respiratory Care; Colorado Society for Respiratory Care. **Education:** Attending, Western Michigan University (1994–Present); Biosystems, Inc. **Personal:** Married to Jerold in 1966. One child: Melissa. Mrs. Paisley enjoys crewel work, bicycling, and skiing.

Ms. Suzanne M. Schunk
Executive Director and CEO
Family Services of Cecil County, Inc.
718 Bridge Street
Elkton, MD 21921
(410) 398–4060
Fax: (410) 398–8893

8093

Business Information: Family Services of Cecil County, Inc. provides outpatient mental health counseling, parenting education, stress management, counceling for men with a history of domestic violence, personnel management, employee assistance and community and professional training. As Executive Director and CEO, Ms. Schunk oversees all aspects of the business including management, budget, personnel, clinical program development and implementation, and clinical consultation. She expects to expand the business throughout the county over the next three to five years. Established in 1982, Family Services of Cecil County, Inc. employs 200 people with annual sales of $4.5 million. **Career Steps:** Executive Director and CEO, Family Services of Cecil County, Inc. (1986–Present); Potomac Valley Nursing Home (1984–1986); Alexandria Community Mental Health Center (1980–1984). **Associations & Accomplishments:** Member, National Association of Social Workers; Member, Cecil County Criminal Justice Advisory Board; Member, National Network of Social Work Managers; President, Mental Health Support Services; Vice President, Family Resource Board of Cecil County; Treasurer, Core Service/Mental Health Advisory Council; Former Board Member, Cecil County Chamber of Commerce. The Chamber gave Ms. Schunk a Business and Education Training Award in 1994. Ms. Schunk is a supporter of the United Way. **Education:** Catholic University, M.S.W. (1978); Fordham University, B.A. **Personal:** Married to Don S. Wilson in 1989. Six children: 4 adopted, 1 biological, 1 stepchild. Ms. Schunk enjoys playing the piano and guitar. He also is an accomplished public speaker, having given over 200 professional and community seminars.

Shirley B. Shands
Admission & Marketing Director
Huntingdon Health & Rehabilitation Center
635 High Street
Huntington, TN 38344
(901) 986–8943
Fax: (901) 986–3881

8093

Business Information: Huntingdon Health & Rehabilitation Center, formerly named Hillhaven Convalescent Center, is a 196–bed nursing home, handling all nursing home needs except respiratory care. The Center currently has a new rehabilitation center and all types of therapy programs. As Admission & Marketing Director, Ms. Shands is responsible for admissions, keeping the 196 beds filled in the nursing home, and all marketing for the Center. She does all public relations work, advertising, and public speaking about the Center, its programs, and new projects. **Career Steps:** Admission & Marketing Director, Huntingdon Health & Rehabilitation Center (1988–Present); Owner, Shand's Men Shop (1971–1988); Secretary, Bank of Huntingdon–President (1965–1971). **Associations & Accomplishments:** Huntingdon Ruritan Club; County Commissioner, Carroll County – 7th Mag. District; Board Member, Baptist Home Health Association; Lay Leader, Palmer Shelter Church; Parent Representative, Parent Teacher Organization High School. **Personal:** Three children: Jeffery Bennet, Timothy Lynn, and Amanda Nicole. Ms. Shands enjoys helping people, working with the elderly and children, swimming, and reading.

Dr. Ronald Garth Smith
Pediatric Consultant
Office of Ronald Garth Smith, M.D.
107–20 Emma Street
Chatham, Ontario N7L 5K5
(519) 351–9175
Fax: (519) 351–7307

8093

Business Information: A Pediatric Consultant with special interest in developmental/behavioral pediatrics and Attention Deficit Hyperactivity Disorder, Dr. Smith attends patients referred to him with special pediatric developmental/behavioral problems. He will also begin an Assistant Professorship at the Child Development Clinic of Hoteu Dieu Hospital at Queen's University in Kingston, Ontario, in September of 1996. **Career Steps:** Pediatric Consultant (1987–Present); Assistant Professor – Child Development Clinic, Hoteu Dieu Hospital at Queen's University in Kingston, Ontario (Sept. 1996–Present); Chief Pediatric Resident, The Hospital for Sick Children, Toronto, Ontario (1985–1986); Fellow in Neonatology, Women's College Hospital, Toronto, Ontario (1986–1987). **Associations & Accomplishments:** Professional Advisor, Children & Adults With Attention Deficit Disorder; Ontario Medical Association; Canadian Medical Association; Canadian Pediatric Society – Developmental/Behavioral Division; American Academy of Pediatrics. **Education:** University of the West Indies: M.B., B.S. (1981); Fellowship in Pediatrics – F.R.C.P (C), Ontario, Canada (1986). **Personal:** Married to Gail Eaton–Smith in 1976. Three children: Alyna, Brendon, and Craig. Dr. Smith enjoys table tennis, watching ice hockey & baseball, and speaking to parent support groups on subjects of special interest (e.g. behavioral problems, etc.).

Jan Stokosa, C.P.
President/Chief Prosthetist
Stokosa Prosthetic Clinic
2414 Pine Hollow Place
East Lansing, MI 48823–9742
(517) 349–3130
Fax: (517) 349–8887

8093

Business Information: Stokosa Prosthetic Clinic is a full-service healthcare facility specializing in lower limb prosthetics and prosthesis. As President/Chief Prosthestist, Mr. Stokosa is responsible for all aspects of company operations, including amputation and replacement of limbs. **Career Steps:** President/Chief Prosthestist, Stokosa Prosthetic Clinic (1989–Present); Director, Institute for the Advancement of Prosthetics (1978–1989); Jan Stokosa, C.P. (1966–1978). **Associations & Accomplishments:** All National and State Prosthetics Associations; ABC Certified Prosthetist. **Personal:** Married to Norean in 1985. Two children: Amber and Melody.

Paul Sumrow

Regional Director
Sundance Rehabilitation Corporation
15851 Dallas Parkway, Suite 240
Dallas, TX 75248–3330
(214) 770–7955
Fax: (214) 770–7931

8093

Business Information: A subsidiary of the Sun Health Group, Sundance Rehabilitation Corporation is a nursing home rehabilitation management organization providing services on a contract basis. Established in 1989, Sundance Rehabilitation currently employs 110 professionals. As Regional Director, Mr. Sumrow is responsible for the overall direction of rehabilitation contracts in Northern Texas, including the profit and loss margins for revenues exceeding $11 million. Mr. Sumrow sees kindness as the key to success, and hopes to utilize his skills to some day start his own enterprise. **Career Steps:** Regional Director, Sundance Rehabilitation Corporation (1992–Present); Vice President of Operations, HealthTech, Inc. (1994); Area Vice President, Nova Care Inc. (1991–1994); Staffing Manager, Convex Computers (1989–1990). **Education:** Stephen F. Austin State University, B.B.A. (1982). **Personal:** Married to Allison in 1991. Mr. Sumrow enjoys golf, reading, animals, Harley Cruisers and spending time with his wife.

Edna B. Swartzlander
Practice Manager
Rehabilitation Associates
8202 Clear Vista Parkway, Suite 8E
Indianapolis, IN 46256
(317) 588–7130
Fax: (317) 588–7133

8093

Business Information: Rehabilitation Associates is a rehabilitative medical practice specializing in physical medicine and rehabilitation. As Practice Manager, Ms. Swartzlander is responsible for various administrative activities, ensuring quality patient care, personnel management, and oversight of day–to–day operations. **Career Steps:** Practice Manager, Rehabilitation Associates (1994–Present); Department Head – Radiology, Gadsden Memorial Hospital (1993); Department Head – Radiology, Bainbridge Memorial Hospital (1980–1993). **Associations & Accomplishments:** Mayor – Climax, Georgia; City Council – Climax, Georgia; Florida Society of Radiology Technologist; Georgia Society of Radiologist Technologist; Georgia Emergency Medical Technician. **Education:** Attended, Bainbridge Jr. College. **Personal:** Married to USAF TSgt Darryle E. Swartzlander in 1990. Two children: Sean and Logan. Ms. Swartzlander enjoys sewing and baseball.

Christopher G. Thomas
Special Project Coordinator
Toronto Rehabilitation Centre
347 Rumsey Road
Toronto, Ontario M4G 1R7
(416) 425–1117
Fax: (416) 425–0301

8093

Business Information: Toronto Rehabilitation Centre is a medical facility specializing in the outpatient rehabilitative treatment of cardiac patients, tracking patients for years post-treatment. As Special Project Coordinator, Mr. Thomas oversees all administrative duties, manages record–keeping, and handles fund raising events. He is also responsible for contracting through the network, and internal communications. **Career Steps:** Special Project Coordinator, Toronto Rehabilitation Centre (1995–Present); Public Relations Assistant, Metro Toronto Zoo (Apr. 1994–Oct. 1994); Account Manager, Ethno Promo Agency (1994–1995). **Associations & Accomplishments:** Board Member and Chair of Communications Committee of the North West Unit, Canadian Cancer Society. **Education:** Humber College, Post Graduate Studies in Public Relations Certificate, With Honors (1994); McMaster University, B.A. with Honors. **Personal:** Mr. Thomas enjoys painting, tennis, fishing, and reading.

Sharon L. Tolhurst
Director
Cape Surgery Center
1941 Waldemere Street
Sarasota, FL 34239–2922
(941) 917–1900
Fax: Please mail or call

8093

Business Information: Cape Surgery Center is an outpatient freestanding ambulatory surgery center providing same–day surgical procedures, from the simple to complex. Established in 1985, Cape Surgery Center currently employs 45 people. As Director, Ms. Tolhurst is responsible for all administrative matters of the Center, answering directly to the Vice President and Board of Directors. **Career Steps:** Cape Surgery Center: Director (1995–Present), Nurse Manager (1990–1995). **Associations & Accomplishments:** American Organization of Registered Nurses (AORN); Florida Hospital Association; Society for Ambulatory Care Professionals; Former Red Cross Nurse; Corporate Volunteer, United Way. **Education:** University of Sarasota, M.B.A. (1995); St. Leo College, B.S. in Healthcare Administration. **Personal:** Married to Charles in 1965. One child: Sandra Saxon. Ms. Tolhurst enjoys showing horses and swimming.

Lorie A. Untch

President and Chief Executive Officer
Easter Seal Rehabilitation Center
1305 National Road
Wheeling, WV 26003–5705
(304) 242–1390
Fax: (304) 243–5880

8093

Business Information: Established in 1937, Easter Seal Rehabilitation Center is a non–profit pediatric rehabilitation outpatient clinic and early intervention/preschool development program. As President and Chief Executive Officer, Ms. Untch is responsible for both strategic visioning and day–to–day operational management. **Career Steps:** Easter Seal Rehabilitation Center: President and Chief Executive Officer (1995–Present), Vice President of Administration (1995); Senior Consultant, Deloitte & Touche (1992–1995); Academic Advisor, Ohio State University (1990–1992). **Associations & Accomplishments:** E.S. Management Association; HHSA Alumni; Life Member, Ohio State Alumni Association. **Education:** Ohio State University: M.H.A. (1992), B.S. in Business Administration and Human Resources. **Personal:** Married to Eric. Ms. Untch enjoys travel and family activities.

Cheryl Veldhuis
Clinical Director
Sportsmed
235 Lake Street Apt. F
East Weymouth, MA 02189–1232
(617) 770–1696
Fax: (617) 770–0335

8093

Business Information: Sportsmed is a privately–owned organization providing outpatient physical therapy and related training to athletes. As Clinical Director, Miss Veldhuis oversees all patient treatment and provides consultation and evaluation. She is also responsible for athletic training, personnel management, and marketing. **Career Steps:** Clinical Director, Sportsmed (1995–Present); Physical Therapist, Caremark Physical Therapy (1992–1994). **Education:** University of Connecticut, B.S. in Physical Therapy (1992). **Personal:** Miss Veldhuis enjoys mountain biking, kayaking, hiking, and physical fitness.

Karen E. Wagner
Medical Physicist
St. Joseph Medical Center
450 West High Street
Womelsdorf, PA 19567–1414
(610) 378–2117
Fax: (610) 378–2803

8093

Business Information: St. Joseph Medical Center, affiliated with Catholic Health Initiatives, is a community hospital offering a full scope of medical services to the residents of Reading and Berks counties. As a Therapeutic Radiological Physicist, Certified in 1990 by the American Board of Radiology, Ms. Wagner is responsible for radiation dosimetry, radiation safety, equipment (linear accelerator, co–60 unit, simulator), and quality assurance activities associated with cancer patient treatment. She also provides radiation safety and radiation biology training for hospital staff and radiologic technology students. Concurrently, she serves as a Clinical Assistant Professor of Nuclear Medicine at Cedar Crest College, providing didactic instruction regarding the physics of Nuclear Medicine to college seniors. Additionally, she provides consulting medical physics services regarding high dose rate (HDR) brachy therapy, mammography, radiation shielding design, and quality assurance. **Career Steps:** Medical Physicist, St. Joseph Medical Center (1987–Present); Clinical Assistant Professor of Nuclear Medicine, Cedar Crest College, Allentown, PA (1991–Present); Consulting Medical Physicist, Therapeutic Radiological Physics (1988–Present); Consulting Medical Physicist (1987–Present); Medical Physics Clinic Intern, Emory University Clinic, DeKalb General Hospital (Jun.–Dec. 1986); Graduate Research Assistant and Graduate Teaching Assistant, Georgia Institute of Technology (1985–1986); Staff Nuclear Medicine Technologist, Lehigh Valley Hospital Center (1983–1985). **Associations & Accomplishments:** American Association of Physicists in Medicine; Health Physics Society; American College of Radiology; Pennsylvania Radiological Society; American Association of Medical Dosimetrists; Susquehanna Valley Chapter of the HPS; Delaware Valley Chapter of the AAPM; Central Pennsylvania Medical Physics Group; Cedar Crest College Alumnae Association; American Board of Radiology; Therapeutic Radiological Physics (1990); Certified Nuclear Medicine Technologist (CNMT) (1983); American Registry of Radiologic Technologists (Nuclear) (1983); Appointed St. Joseph Medical Center representative to the Franciscan Health System Technology Assessment Task Force Committee and Technology Steering Committee; Listed in Who's Who in American Colleges and Universities; Cedar Crest College Presidential Scholar (1979–1983); Elected to Delphi Honor Society, Beta Beta Beta National Biology Honor Society, and the National Honor Society. **Education:** Georgia Institute of Technology, M.S. in Health Physics (Medical Option) (1986); Cedar Crest College, B.S. in Nuclear Medicine Technology, magna cum laude (1983). **Personal:** Married to Michael S. in 1987. Ms. Wagner enjoys skiing, rollerblading, mountain biking, walking, and music.

Debra L. Warner
Chief Financial Officer
Charter Behavioral Health System of Toledo
1725 Timber Line Road
Maumee, OH 43537
(419) 891–9333
Fax: (419) 891–9330

8093

Business Information: Charter Behavioral Health System of Toledo is an international mental health care agency, providing inpatient and outpatient care through 104 hospitals around the world. With eleven years of experience in accounting, Ms. Warner joined the Charter Behavioral Health System of Toledo as Chief Financial Officer in 1995. She is responsible for all aspects of financial matters, including the management of Business Office finances and the production of financial statements for the Toledo location. **Career Steps:** Chief Financial Officer, Charter Behavioral Health System of Toledo (1995–Present); Controller, Charter Midwest Service Center (1994–1995); Accountant, Caretenders Health Corporation (1985–1994). **Education:** University of Louisville, B.S. in Accounting (1985). **Personal:** Three children: Travis, Traci, and Troy Meadows.

LaVerl Wilhelm, Ph.D.
Chief Executive Officer
Little Colorado Behavioral Centers
470 West Cleveland
St. Johns, AZ 85936
(520) 337–4301
Fax: (520) 337–2269

8093

Business Information: Little Colorado Behavioral Centers is a rural community outpatient behavioral health counseling facility, providing counseling in all spectrums from "birth to death," including nursing homes, marriage reconciliation, drug, alcohol, entire families and more. Joining Little Colorado Behavioral Centers in 1971, Dr. Wilhelm serves as Chief Executive Officer, Clinical Director, and Psychologist. Reporting all activities to the Board of Directors, he is responsible for all aspects of operations, including administration, finances, public relations, and strategic planning. **Career Steps:** Chief Executive Officer, Little Colorado Behavioral Centers (1971–Present); Religion Instructor, LDS Seminaries and Institutes of Religion (1966–1971). **Associations & Accomplishments:** American Society of Clinical Hypnosis; American Association of Mormon Counselors and Psychotherapists; Recipient: District Award of Merit; Silver Beaver Award for volunteer service to the Boy Scouts of America. **Education:** Brigham Young University, Ph.D. (1978); Arizona State University: M.Ed. in Counseling (1969), B.A. in Education (1968). **Personal:** Married to Linda Gore Wilhelm in 1964. Nine children: Sonia, Vaughn, Kurt, Shanie, Kathi, Diane, Todd, Mark, and Craig. Dr. Wilhelm enjoys cattle ranching and religious instruction.

Diana L. Williams
Clinical Director
Tara Treatment Center
6231 South U.S. Highway 31
Franklin, IN 46131
(812) 526–2611
Fax: (812) 526–8527

8093

Business Information: Tara Treatment Center is a chemical dependency treatment center which includes residential, transitional residential, detox, outpatient, and aftercare programs. The primary focus of the Clinic is on women, women with children, and pregnant women. As Clinical Director, Ms. Williams is responsible for the day–to–day activities, including the supervision of all programs and staff, development of new programs, and networking with outside referrals. **Career Steps:** Clinical Director, Tara Treatment Center (1993–Present); Koala Hospital: Outpatient Supervisor, (1992–1993), Clinical Supervisor for Adolescent Dual–Diagnosis Unit (1990–1992). **Associations & Accomplishments:** Certified Social Worker in Indiana; Certified Alcohol and Drug Abuse Counselor in Indiana; National Certification for Addiction Counselor, Level 1. **Education:** Marian College, B.A. in Psychology (1987); Indiana University, Purdue University Incorp., Master's Program in Social Work (In Progress). **Personal:** Ms. Williams enjoys singing, playing piano, and fishing.

Elizabeth Williams
Operations Manager
Dynamic Rehabilitation Services
8080 Old York Road, Suite 208
Elkins Park, PA 19027–1426
(215) 782–8761
Fax: (215) 635–7130

8093

Business Information: Dynamic Rehabilitation Services is a physical therapy rehabilitation center. Services provided include treatment of collision trauma and sports injuries, as well as offering cancer therapy and rehabilitation, and services for congenitally–disabled individuals. With seventeen years experience in the health care field and a Certified Medical Assistant, Ms. Williams joined Dynamic Rehabilitation Services as Operations Manager in 1986. She is responsible for all aspects of operations, including administration, auditing, scheduling, hiring, inventory, training, implementing new programs & protocols, management functions, evaluating, etc. **Career Steps:** Operations Manager, Dynamic Rehabilitation Services (1986–Present); Medical Assistant, Dr. George Bonafino (1979–1983); Coordinator, Civic Center Museum (1975–1977). **Associations & Accomplishments:** Advisory Board, Thompson Institute; Fundraising Committee, Cardeza

Sickle Cell Center – Thomas Jefferson University Hospital. **Education:** LaSalle University, Psychology; Community College of Pennsylvania, Liberal Arts and Science; National School of Health Technology, Medical Assistant. **Personal:** Married to Clayton Lee in 1983. Two children: Daniel Lee and Justin Stephen. Ms. Williams enjoys writing.

Roy L. Alexander
Psychotherapist
Managed Care Center
700 Austin Street, Suite 101
Levelland, TX 79336
(806) 894–4750
Fax: Please mail or call

8099

Business Information: Managed Care Center provides individual, couple, and family counseling. A Practicing Psychotherapist since 1972, Mr. Alexander founded the Managed Care Center (formerly known as the Family Institute of the South Plains) in 1995, specializing in adolescent psychotherapy and chemical addictions. **Career Steps:** Psychotherapist, Managed Care Center/Family Institute of the South Plains (1995–Present); Executive Director, Hockley County Senior Citizens (1993–1995); Psychotherapist, Tri County Mental Health – Conroe, Texas (1983–1992) **Associations & Accomplishments:** American Association Marriage & Family Therapy; Toastmasters: Area Governor/Club President; President Elect, Rotary Club; Board Vice President, Chamber of Commerce; Board Member, Family Outreach; Licensed Chemical Dependent Counselor. **Education:** Eastern New Mexico University, M.Ed. (1972); Attended: Texas A&M University and Sul Ross State University. **Personal:** Married to Judy in 1968. One child: Bryan. Mr. Alexander enjoys reading, public speaking, racquetball, playing guitar and singing.

Christopher L. Anderson
Corporate Director of Compliance
HMRI
1000 Abernathy Road
Atlanta, GA 30528
(502) 394–3100
Fax: (502) 394–3145

8099

Business Information: Housecall Medical Resources, Inc. (HMRI) specializes in the operation and management of over 200 professional nurse, aide, infusion, and medical equipment locations. HMRI is a publically–held company with headquarters in Atlanta, Georgia. As Corporate Director of Compliance, Mr. Anderson is responsible for internal oversight and management of the Company's compliance programs. He is responsible for ensuring all operations to comply with federal and state rules and regulations. Mr. Anderson also serves as national consultant for establishing compliance programs through HMRI. **Career Steps:** Corporate Director of Compliance, HMRI (1994–Present); Specialty Sales, Selig Chemical Corporation (1993–1994); Director of Audit, Flag Inn, Inc. (1992–1993). **Associations & Accomplishments:** Association of Certified Fraud Examiners. **Education:** Georgetown College, B.A. (1994). **Personal:** Married to Karen in 1994. Mr. Anderson enjoys golf and historical research.

Robert A. Anselmo
Director
West Jersey Health System
101 Carnie Boulevard
Voorhees, NJ 08043
(609) 772–5529
Fax: (609) 772–5550

8099

Business Information: West Jersey Health System is a health management system for four community hospitals. As Director, Mr. Anselmo handles all personnel aspects of the company. He has oversight of the day–to–day operation and is responsible for the smooth operation of the laboratories. **Career Steps:** Director, West Jersey Health System (19–Present) **Associations & Accomplishments:** Clinical Lab Management Association; American College of Healthcare Executives; American Society of Clinical Pathologists. **Personal:** Mr. Anselmo enjoys fitness, reading, and biking.

Abasse Asgaraly
President
International SOS Assistance
PO Box 11568
Philadelphia, PA 19116–0568
(215) 244–1500
Fax: (215) 245–1963
EMAIL: See Below

8099

Business Information: International SOS Assistance provides emergency and non–emergency assistance to American and foreign travelers worldwide. Future plans include reaching $40 million in revenue and improving their operations margin from 5.5% to 8%. Established in 1974, International SOS Assistance reports annual revenue of $19 million and currently employs 65 people. With fourteen years experience in providing assistance to travelers, Mr. Asgaraly joined International SOS Assistance in 1994. Serving as President, he is responsible for all aspects of operations, with primary focus on corporate strategies, business development in the U.S., and sales and marketing development in Asia Pacific/Central and Latin America. He can also be reached through the Internet via: Abasse.AOL.COM **Career Steps:** President, International SOS Assistance (1994–Present); Managing Director, Europe Assistance Japan (1987–1994); Worldwide Marketing, Europe Assistance France (1981–1987). **Associations & Accomplishments:** American Society of Association Executives **Education:** University of Paris–Sorbonne, Masters in Marketing (1973) **Personal:** Married to Kalocsay Olga in 1972. Two children: Sharmila and Adeline. Mr. Asgaraly enjoys swimming, jogging and stamp collecting during his leisure time.

Ann Avino
Director
Children At Play, Inc.
40 Merrill Avenue
Staten Island, NY 10314–3312
(718) 370–7529
Fax: (718) 370–7551

8099

Business Information: Children At Play, Inc. provides therapeutic and support services to developmentally delayed infants, toddlers, and their families. As Director of Children At Play's Early Intervention Program, Ms. Avino oversees program development and various administrative functions. She is also responsible for monitoring the overall functioning of Children At Play's preschool and community services program. **Career Steps:** Director, Children At Play (1991–Present); Psychotherapist, Private Practice (1992–1995); Psychotherapist, St. Vincent's Hospital (1989–1991); Social Work Intern, Staten Island University Hospital/Outpatient Mental Health Clinic (1987–1988). **Associations & Accomplishments:** National Association of Social Workers; Richmond County Business and Professional Women's Organization. **Education:** New York University: M.S.W. (1990), C.S.W. (1990), Masters in Community Psychology (1988); Pace University, B.S. in Pre–Med. (1981). **Personal:** Married to Rick Rivers in 1991.

Sanford E. Avner, M.D.
President
Colorado Allergy
1450 South Havana Street, Suite 500
Aurora, CO 80012–4030
(303) 696–7331
Fax: Please mail or call

8099

Business Information: Colorado Allergy is a medical care clinic specializing in high quality care of people afflicted with allergies and asthma. Colorado Allergy has 8 offices and 5 affiliates and currently employs five Allergy Specialists and four physicians in the regional area. As President and Chairman of Care Centers, Dr. Avner is responsible for all aspects of operations, including providing health care to patients. **Career Steps:** President and Chairman of Care Centers, Colorado Allergy; Physician, U.S. Air Force. **Associations & Accomplishments:** Published in several periodicals. **Education:** Yale University; State University of New York. **Personal:** Two grown sons.

Marjorie M. Babcock
Director of Education
Woman Care
355 W. Northwest Hwy
Palatine, IL 60067
(708) 202–1306
Fax: Please mail or call

8099

Business Information: Woman Care is an alliance of health care professionals, specializing in the care of women. Services include obstetrics, gynecology, nutrition, massage, mammography, ultrasound, in–office surgery, and education. Established in 1985, Woman Care currently employs 50 people and accepts approximately 150 new patients per month. As Director of Education, Mrs. Babcock is responsible for coordinating public relations, patient education, and staff development. She is also responsible for the supervision of various disciplines within Woman Care and initial assessment of new obstetric patients. **Career Steps:** Director of Education, Woman Care (1975–Present); Perinatal Educator, Hoffman Estates Medical Center (1987–Present); Independent Perinatal Educator/Consultant (1978–1987); OB/GYN Staff Nurse, University Hospitals – Madison, WI (1969–1975). **Associations & Accomplishments:** American Nurses Association; International Childbirth Education Association; Treasurer, Local Chapter – Women's Club; Frequent speaker at community seminars on breast cancer. **Education:** Medical College of Wisconsin, R.N. (1969); Certification: International Childbirth Education Association, Certified Instructor **Personal:** Married to William in 1969. Three children: Rebecca, Nicholas and Zachary. Mrs. Babcock enjoys lecturing for community programs, civic organizations and schools, as well as playing the piano during her leisure time.

Carolyn M. Bacon

Organization Development Consultant – Corporate Services
Allina Health System
5601 Smetana Drive P O Box 9310
Minnetonka, MN 55440–9310
(612) 992–3007
Fax: (612) 992–3014

8099

Business Information: Allina Health System is a vertical integrated regional healthcare delivery system providing physicians and general staff to clinics and hospitals. As Organization Development Consultant – Corporate Services, Ms. Bacon is positioned at a strategic level to provide large–scale organizational change, including design, implementation, and evaluation of health care systems for corporate clients. Ms. Bacon works with the Company's top leaders to bring about these changes, and she also does process consultation, strategic planning, and helps create an organizational culture. **Career Steps:** Organization Development Consultant, Allina Health System (1993–Present); Manager of Organization Development and Quality, Minnesota Department of Transportation (1990–1993); Service Excellence Coordinator, Fairview Riverside Hospital (1989–1990). **Associations & Accomplishments:** American Management Association; Twin City Personnel Association; Minnesota Facilitators Network; American Society for Training and Development; National Organization Development Network; Executive Committee, Board of Directors of the YWCA of St. Paul. **Education:** University of Minnesota, M.Ed. (1990); Augsburg College, Bachelor of Arts (1977). **Personal:** Ms. Bacon enjoys working in the garden, skiing, and travel.

Lodovico Balducci, M.D.

Program Leader – Senior Adult Oncology Program
H. Lee Moffitt Cancer Center and Research Institute
12902 Magnolia Drive
Tampa, FL 33612
(813) 979–3822
Fax: (813) 972–8468

8099

Business Information: H. Lee Moffitt Cancer Center and Research Institute, established in 1986, is a cancer treatment facility providing diagnosis and treatment of cancer in patients, as well as researching causes and treatments of cancer. As Program Leader of the Senior Adult Oncology Program, Dr. Balducci is responsible for leading all programs and activity in adult oncology. His research programs include effective individual cancer treatments, correlation of cancer to AIDS, and geriatric oncology studies. **Career Steps:** Program Leader and Senior Adult Oncology Program, H. Lee Moffitt Cancer Center and Research Institute (1994–Present); Chief Oncology, Tampa Veterans Administration (1989–1994); Chief Hematologist and Oncologist, Bay Pines Veteran (1987–1989); Staff Oncologist, Jackson Veterans Administration. **Associations & Accomplishments:** Southern Society for Clinical Investigations; American Association for Cancer Research; American Society of Hematology; American Society for Clinical Oncology; American Geriatrics Society; American College of Physicians; Edited first book in 1992 as Senior Editor, (Lippincott) "Geriatric Oncology" and working on 2nd edition; Publisher of 100 papers; Published American poetry, "Poetry & Pros." **Education:** Catholic University – Rome, M.D. (1968). **Personal:** Married to Claudia in 1971. One child: Marco. Dr. Balducci enjoys writing poetry, mountain climbing, and Biblical archaeology studies.

Billie A. Bales, MSW

Clinical Director
Copper Mountain Behavioral Health Services
247 South Hill Street
Globe, AZ 85501–2226
(520) 425–9054
Fax: (520) 425–3222

8099

Business Information: Copper Mountain Behavioral Health Services is a not–for–profit community outpatient counseling center with an 11–bed unit for the seriously mentally ill, a day–services unit, shelter services for victims of domestic violence. An experienced public social worker, Ms. Bales joined Copper Mountain Behavioral Health Services as Clinician in 1992. In addition to counseling children, adults, and families of the mentally ill, she also facilitates group therapy sessions, pre-petitions patients to local hospitals, and is on–call for crisis intervention. **Career Steps:** Clinical Director, Copper Mountain Behavioral Health Services (1992–Present); Clinician I, Superstition Mountain Mental Health (1987–1991); Case Manager, Arizona State Department of Child Services. **Associations & Accomplishments:** Domestic Violence Task Force; Elks Club; National Association of Female Executives; National Association of Social Workers. **Education:** Arizona State University: M.S.W. (1991); Arizona State University, B.S.W. (1989); Gila Pueblo College: A.A.S., A.A. **Personal:** Married to Everett in 1991. Nine children: Doug, Deb, James, Lawrence, Ron, Tamara, Kimberley, Trunion, and Jamie. Twenty-six grandchildren and one great–granddaughter. Ms. Bales enjoys gardening, reading, taking college classes, and building on to her home.

John P. Balko

Owner
John Balko and Associates
60 Strawbridge Avenue
Sharon, PA 16146–3234
(412) 347–4327
Fax: (412) 347–3930

8099

Business Information: John Balko and Associates is a hearing health care organization comprised of three divisions. Hearing HealthCare Associates provides diagnostic testing for hearing and balance problems and rehabilitative services. The second division, Industrial Audiological Services provides industrial hearing conversation to over 500 clients in four states. The third division, Senior HealthCare Associates services 208 nursing homes in Eastern Ohio and Western Pennsylvania offering, Audiology, Cerumen Management, Podiatry, Optometry, and Dentistry to residential care patients. The organization has five offices in two states. Established in 1971, the Company employs 21 people with an estimated annual revenue of $2 million. As Owner, Mr. Balko oversees all operations and is responsible for strategic planning, new business development, and public relations. **Career Steps:** Owner, John Balko and Associates (1971–Present). **Associations & Accomplishments:** American Speech, Language, and Hearing Association; Academy of Dispensing Audiologists; National Hearing Conservation Association; Rotary International; Fellow, Academy of Audiology; Author of Two Books; National Reining Organization 1985 World Champion. **Education:** Kent State University, M.A., CCC/A (1973). **Personal:** Married to Marsha in 1978. Mr. Balko enjoys showing reining horses.

Mark A. Barnes

Executive Director
Canadian Play Therapy Institute
P.O. Box 2153
Kingston, Ontario K7L 5J9
(613) 384–2795
Fax: (613) 634–2581
Email/Internet: see below

8099

Business Information: Canadian Play Therapy Institute is a child psychology training institute. Canadian Play Therapy Institute runs 50–60 training programs each year with a variety of presenters in many regions of North America and the Pacific. In addition, the Institute provides training and in–service education in a number of mental health topics, including child psychotherapy and play therapy, as well as child abuse and other mental health issues for staff and the public at the request of agencies, institutions and facilities throughout the world with programs geared specifically to the requirements of the host institution. With twelve years post–graduate experience in children's services and certified in Child Psychotherapy and Play Therapy, Mr. Barnes joined the Canadian Play Therapy Institute as Executive Director in 1990. He is responsible for directing all activities of the Institute, including overseeing the budget. In addition, he oversees all administrative operations for associates and a support staff of nine. Mr. Barnes may also be reached by Email: cplayti@limestone.kosone.com or the Internet: www.kosone.com/play/ **Career Steps:** Executive Director, Canadian Play Therapy Institute (1990–Present); Director of Non–Residential Services, Sunnyside Children's Centre (1987–1990); Clinical Coordinator of Children's Services, Family Counseling Centre (1985–1987); Clinical Therapist, Post–Trauma Unit, Toronto Hospital (1981–1985); Mental Health Consultant, Ontario Provincial Government (1978–1981). **Associations & Accomplishments:** Certified Child Psychotherapist and Play Therapist, The Canadian Association for Child and Play Therapy; Received International Play Therapy Association Award for "Outstanding Career Contribution to the Field of Child Psychology and Play Therapy" (1996); President, The Canadian Association for Child and Play Therapy (1986–1990); Registered Play Therapist–Supervisor, The Association for Play Therapy in the United States; Author of "The Healing Path with Children" (1995); Co–author of "Self Discovery Through Inner Play" (1995); Pilot. **Education:** Ph.D.; M.S.W.; B.A. in Psychology; B.Sc. in Wildlife Biology. **Personal:** Mr. Barnes enjoys playing with his family, flying, being a musician, herbal gardening, collecting rocks and minerals, and studying cross–cultural healing methods.

Olivia R. Benitez–Rivas

Facility Manager
Burton Health Center
4051 Chamberlain SE
Grand Rapids, MI 49508–2615
(616) 247–3638
Fax: (216) 247–0780

8099

Business Information: Burton Health Center provides medical and counseling services to students. An MSW graduate of Grand Valley State University, Ms. Benitez serves as Facility Manager, responsible for client counsel, daily operations of the clinic, support staff management, and office administration. Concurrently, she has counseled clients at Steelcase since 1994. **Career Steps:** Facility Manager, Burton Health Center (1994–Present); Counselor, Steelcase (1994–Present); Faculty Therapist, Project Rehab (1990–1995); Resource Developer, State of Michigan (1994–1995). **Associations & Accomplishments:** President, Mexican Cultural Patriotic Corporation; Michigan T– Girl Scouts. **Education:** Grand Valley State University: M.S.W. (1994), B.S. (1992). **Personal:** Three children: Elizabeth, Angela, and Amanda Rivas. Ms. Benitez–Rivas enjoys exercising, tennis, and walking.

Warren D. Benson

Consultant/Partner
Torrey Pines Group
500 West Harbour Drive, Suite 116
San Diego, CA 92101
Fax: (619) 531–0059

8099

Business Information: Torrey Pines Group is a management consulting firm for the health care industry, whose primary mission is to assist executives in the health care field nationwide to deal with managed care organizations. As Consultant/Founding Partner, Mr. Benson is responsible for supervising daily operations, managing contract negotiations with HMO's, and financial planning. **Career Steps:** Consultant/Founding Partner, Torrey Pines Group (1996–Present); Director, Government Contracts, Aetna, San Diego (1993–1996); Manager, PPO, Sanus/New York Life – Houston (1991–1993); President/Owner, DCCI, Hilton Head, SC (1988–1991); Senior Vice President/COO, Mt. Washington Pediatric Hospital – Baltimore (1985–1988). **Associations & Accomplishments:** Healthcare Financial Management Association; Certified Managed Care Professional (CMCP); American College of Healthcare Executives; Retired Officers Association; Retired Army Colonel. **Education:** University of South Dakota, M.B.A. (1971); Iowa State University, B.S. **Personal:** Married to Peggy in 1994. Two children: W. David and Lynda. Mr. Benson enjoys golf, travel and swimming.

Juergen H. Bertram, M.D.

Physician
Southern Indiana Cancer Center
1302 Wall Street
Jeffersonville, IN 47130
(812) 285–5665
Fax: Please mail or call

8099

Business Information: Southern Indiana Cancer Center is a 15–bed treatment facility with an office building, specializing in the treatment of cancer and blood disorders. Established in 1991, Southern Indiana Cancer Center currently employs 33 people, including four physicians. As Physician, Dr. Bertram is responsible for providing clinical health care to patients, as well as conducting extensive research on cancer and publishing his research. **Career Steps:** Physician, Southern Indiana Cancer Center (1995–Present); Medical Director, Kootenai Medical Center (1987–1995); Associate Professor, University of Southern California (1981–1987); Assistant, The Johns Hopkins Oncology Center (1979–1981). **Associations & Accomplishments:** American Association for Cancer Research (AACR); American Society for Clinical Oncology (ASCO); American Society for Hematology (ASH). **Education:** University of Giessen, M.D. (1970); Max Planck Society, Max Planck Institute for Experimental Medicine, Goettingen, Germany, Ph.D. in Immunochemistry. **Personal:** Dr. Bertram enjoys photography.

Harry Blair
Principal & Chief Financial Officer
Gallico and Associates
P.O. Box 751764
Dayton, OH 45475–1764
(513) 435–2137
Fax: (513) 435–0991

8099

Business Information: Gallico and Associates is a multi–function firm offering consulting, foundation management, internet services, and eating disorder counseling. As Principal & Chief Financial Officer, Mr. Blair handles all financial aspects of Gallico and Associates. He is responsible for cash management, accounting functions, personnel concerns, public relations, and marketing of offered services. **Career Steps:** Principal & Chief Financial Officer, Gallico and Associates (1995–Present); Director – Telefony Services, AT&T GIS (1966–1995); Senior Analyst, ASA/NSA (1963–1966); Senior Laboratory Technician, T.K. Duncan Research Laboratory (1961–1963). **Associations & Accomplishments:** MENSA, Ltd.; American Academy of Sciences; New York Academy of Science; World Futures Society; Trustee, Henrietta's House; Trustee, Gallico – Blair Memorial Foundation; Judge, Odyssey of the Mind. **Education:** Wright State University, M.S. Degree in Economics (1994); Capital University, B.A. Degree in Business Administration; University of Colorado, B.S. Degree in Mathematics; Criminal Attorney. **Personal:** Married to Margaret in 1986. Mr. Blair enjoys mathematical equations, golf, and reading.

Patricia Bobermin
Clinical Director
Health Association Employee Assistance Program
1 Mount Hope Avenue
Rochester, NY 14620–1014
(716) 423–9490
Fax: (716) 423–9056

8099

Business Information: Health Association Employee Assistance Program offers short–term, solution–focused counseling to more than 140 employees in the Rochester and Greater Finger Lakes area of New York State. In addition to individual counseling/assessment, services include leadership training, critical incident management, and a variety of seminars and training. As Clinical Director, Ms. Bobermin supervises 22 counselors and monitors their activities and client progress. She handles public relations and the marketing of services offered by Health Association. Ms. Bobermin works with alcoholism counselors and survivors of substance, mental, and physical abuse. **Career Steps:** Clinical Director, Health Association Employee Assistance Program (1993–Present); Adjunct Faculty, University of Rochester School of Medicine (1989–Present); Director of Addiction, Recovery Center, Clifton Springs Hospital (1982–1993); Executive Director, Huther – Dayle Institute (1978–1982). **Associations & Accomplishments:** Numerous training/workshops; Council on Alcoholism; Addiction Providers Consortium; Employee Assistance Professionals; Chairman of Women's Committee, Association on Rochester; Advisory Panel, Addiction Statewide. **Education:** New York University, M.A. (1969); Russell Sage College (1966); Certified Employee Assistance Professional; National Credentialed Addiction Counselor – Level II **Personal:** Married to Charles Corbett in 1980. Two children: Christopher and Jeffrey Corbett. Ms. Bobermin maintains a private practice, specializing in clinical supervision for addiction counselors. She enjoys sailing, gardening, and collecting antique Christmas ornaments..

C. Angela Bontempo

Chief Operating Officer
Roswell Park Cancer Institute
Elm & Carlton Streets
Buffalo, NY 14263
(716) 845–3385
Fax: Please mail or call

8099

Business Information: Roswell Park Cancer Institute is an institute for large cancer research endeavors, education, and treatment. With over 500 scientists, the Institute is involved in major fundraising efforts. The Institute receives over $30 million in grants and other government grants, and is designated as a comprehensive cancer center by the National Cancer Institute. As Chief Operating Officer, Ms. Bontempo is responsible for all aspects of the Institute's operations. She ensures that the thousands of patients that pass through the Institute are taken care of properly. **Career Steps:** Chief Operating Officer, Roswell Park Cancer Institute (1993–Present); President/CEO, Sisters Hospital (1986–1993); President/CEO, St. Mary's Hospital (1981–1986); Senior Vice President, Lourdes Hospital (1977–1981). **Education:** St. Louis University, M.H.A. (1977); Yale University.

Christopher S. Bordnick
Regional Marketing Director
OccuSystems
6244 Washington Boulevard
Elkridge, MD 21227
(410) 796–4470 Ext. 104
Fax: (410) 379–2013

8099

Business Information: Established in 1979, OccuSystems is a national occupational healthcare provider. As Regional Marketing Director, Mr. Bordnick handles marketing plans, major accounts, market budgets, sales, advertising, and promotions for the region of the eastern United States. He also handles new account service and service centers, and federal government bids for the states of Pennsylvania, Delaware, Maryland, and Washington, D.C. Though employed by Occusystems, Mr. Bordnick works from an affiliate office under the auspices of Concentra Medical Centers. **Career Steps:** Regional Marketing Director, OccuSystems (1996–Present). **Associations & Accomplishments:** Baltimore–Washington D.C. Chamber of Commerce; Maryland Motor Truck Association; Associated Builders and Contractors, Inc. **Education:** Madonna University, B.A. in Journalism/Public Relations (1988). **Personal:** Mr. Bordnick enjoys hockey, fishing, and reading.

Barbara T. Bowden
Assistant Vice President
Lifeguard, Inc.
2840 Junction Avenue
San Jose, CA 95134–1922
(408) 432–3660
Fax: (408) 383–4289

8099

Business Information: Lifeguard, Inc. is a twenty year old, non–profit, fee–for–service company started by physicians to handle all managed care in their HMO network. Functioning in 25 counties in California, the Company is data rich, and shares information freely with their participating providers. Voted one of the top three performers in the Hedis Commission for providing preventative services to clients (1995), the Company plans to expand state–wide, along with their Medicare network. As Assistant Vice President, Ms. Bowden plans and executes the provider network, overseeing maintenance and development for all contracted counties, which encompasses over 200,000 HMO members. **Career Steps:** Assistant Vice President, Lifeguard, Inc. (1994–Present); Regional Vice President, BPS (1985–1994). **Associations & Accomplishments:** Association for Senior Day Health, American Association of University Women; Hospital Finance Management Association. **Education:** Pepperdine University, M.B.A. (1982); College of Notre Dame, B.S. **Personal:** Married to Bert Laurence in 1985. Four children: JoAnn, John, Todd, and Pamela. Ms. Bowden enjoys travel, family, and photography.

Fred L. Brown

President
BJC Health System
4444 Forest Park Avenue, Suite 500
St. Louis, MO 63108
(314) 286–2024
Fax: (314) 286–2060
E MAIL: See Below

8099

Business Information: BJC Health System, a not–for–profit organization, is a combination of health care services including 13 hospitals, six nursing homes, numerous in home care programs, and is affiliated with 32 additional hospitals. The System is unique as it has combined a tertiary care center with urban, rural, and university ties. As President, Mr. Brown manages all aspects of Company operations, concentrating on sales, marketing, and staff training and development. Internet users can reach him via: flb9212@bjc.carenet.org. **Career Steps:** President, BJC Health System (1993–Present); President and CEO, Christian Hospital NE/NW (1992–1993); President and CEO, Christian Health Services (1986–1993). **Associations & Accomplishments:** Board of Trustees, Executive Committee, Tools of Change Committee, AHA; Governor, ACHE. **Education:** George Washington University, Masters degree; Northwestern University, B.A. **Personal:** Two children: Michael and Greg. Mr. Brown enjoys golf and sailing.

Deanna L. Bush
Director – Account Management
Merck–Medco Managed Care, Inc.
8111 Royal Ridge Parkway
Irving, TX 75063
(214) 915–6638
Fax: (214) 915–6630
EMail: See Below

8099

Business Information: Merck–Medco Managed Care, Inc. is a third party prescription drug benefits manager. The Company is a subsidiary of Merck & Company, a large pharmaceutical corporation. As Director – Account Management, Ms. Bush is responsible for the Western region client and staff, including sales presentations, the implementation process, problem/escalation resolution, and staffing issues. Additionally, she handles all client relations and reports directly to the Vice President of her division. Internet users can reach her via: DEANNA_BUSH@MERCK.COM. **Career Steps:** Director – Account Management, Merck–Medco Managed Care, Inc. (1995–Present); Healthcare Consultant, Met–Life & Walgreens Healthcare (1993–1994); Supervisor – Operations, PCS Health Systems (1987–1993). **Associations & Accomplishments:** Merck–Pac Leadership Circle. **Education:** Northern Illinois University, B.A. (1986). **Personal:** Married to Kevin in 1984. Two children: David and Breanna. Ms. Bush enjoys reading, boating, and spending time with her family.

Dr. Osvaldo D. Calvani

Vice President
Assurance Medicale
Pringles 788 Bernal 1876
Buenos Aires, Argentina
(54) 1784–8448
Fax: (54) 1788–8585

8099

Business Information: Assurance Medicale provides medical and health insurance to Argentinians who travel to other countries on business. The Company serves all of Argentina, Chile, Paraguay, and Uruguay. As Vice President, Dr. Calvani is responsible for all aspects of Company operations, including all day–to–day operations, including administration, finance, public relations, and marketing. **Career Steps:** Vice President, Assurance Medicale (1992–Present). **Associations & Accomplishments:** Coris–Paris Insurance Company; Medical Assistant of the Argentine Senator, Mr. Miranda Julio. **Education:** La Plata University, M.D. (1973); First English Certificate. **Personal:** Married to Maria Cristina Marcenaro in 1974. Five children: Alejandro, Pablo, Cecilia, Marina, and Andrea. Dr. Calvani enjoys tennis, soccer, and computers.

Mark Caron
Vice President of Information Systems
HealthSource, Inc.
2 College Drive
Manchester, NH 03106
(603) 268–7460
Fax: Please mail or call

8099

Business Information: HealthSource, Inc. is an integrated health care system and management corporation providing complete medical, surgical and psychiatric services to its members. Established in 1985, Healthsource Inc. currently employs 5,100 people and has an estimated annual revenue of $1.4 billion. As Vice President of Information Systems, Mr. Caron is responsible for telecommunications, desktop computing and distributed systems, as well as all networking functions. **Career Steps:** Vice President of Information Systems, HealthSource, Inc. (1994–Present); Regional Manager, Digital Equipment Corporation (1986–1994); Senior Systems Engineer, Sun Micro Systems, Inc. (1983–1986). **Associations & Accomplishments:** College of Healthcare Information Management Executives; Healthcare Information and Management Systems Society; Elks Lodge Cancer Fund Raiser. **Education:** New Hampshire College: M.S. in Computer Information Systems (1995), M.B.A. (1987); Franklin Pierce College, B.S. in Computer Science (1984). **Personal:** Married to Debra Jean in 1981. Two children: Tony and Stacy. Mr. Caron enjoys golf, skiing, reading, teaching and spending time with friends.

Kath M. Carter

Director of Mergers & Acquisitions
American Medical Response
12020 Intraplex Parkway
Gulfport, MS 39503–4602
(601) 897–6665
Fax: (601) 897–1198

8099

Business Information: American Medical Response is a commercial industry providing emergency medical services to the nation. As Director of Mergers & Acquisitions, Ms. Carter is responsible for conducting and coordinating merger and acquisition activity for the South Region (nine states). She handles contracts, analysis of finances, terms negotiation, presentations, follow through on business deals, and leasing. **Career Steps:** Director of Mergers & Acquisitions, American Medical Response (1995–Present); Moore & Powell, CPAs: Audit Manager (1994–1995), Audit Senior (1992–1994), Staff Accountant (1990–1992). **Associations & Accomplishments:** Mississippi Society of Certified Public Accountants; American Institute of Certified Public Accountants; Former Officer, Biloxi Rotary Club; Former Officer, American Heart Association; Leadership Gulf Coast; Gayfer Career Club. **Education:** Auburn University – Montgomery, B.S.B.A. (1990). **Personal:** Married to Billy W. in 1988. Ms. Carter enjoys running, golf, swimming, tennis, and reading.

Robin Castle

Human Resources Director
Quality Life Concepts
600 6th Street NW
Great Falls, MT 59404
(406) 452–9532
Fax: (406) 453–5930

8099

Business Information: Quality Life Concepts, established in 1977, is a private, non–profit facility serving people with developmental disabilities, i.e., children with Downs Syndrome. As Human Resources Director, Mrs. Castle is responsible for recruitment, hiring, counseling, and retention of employees, compliance with all laws, management consulting, and authors policies, procedures, training documents, etc. **Career Steps:** Quality Life Concepts: Human Resources Director (1989–Present), Office Manager/Administrative Support Director/Acting Personnel Director (1984–1989); Construction, Safety Officer (1982–1983). **Associations & Accomplishments:** Secretary/Treasurer, Montana Association of Independent Disability Services Insurance Trustee; Crimestoppers, President (1995); President, Society for Human Resource Management of Great Falls; Bluecoats Committee, Chamber of Commerce; Military Affairs Committee, Chamber of Commerce; Statewide Abuse Prevention Task Force; University of Montana Alumni; College of Great Falls Alumni; Leadership Great Falls Alumni. **Education:** University of Montana, MA in Administrative Science/Public Administration; College of Great Falls, B.S. in Elementary Education (K–8), with a minor in Special Education (K–12). **Personal:** Married to Trevor Mikkelsen in 1995. One child: Lexi Jo Jacobson. Mrs. Castle enjoys golf, cross–country skiing, and relaxing with her daughter.

Raymond E. Cecora, M.D.

Medical Director
Boro Park Primary Care Center
4915 10th Avenue, Room 422
Brooklyn, NY 11219
(718) 851–5920
Fax: (718) 921–1499

8099

Business Information: Boro Park Primary Care Center specializes in health care delivery services, providing treatment to patients for short– or long–term illnesses, such as AIDS, Alzheimer's Disease, etc. National in scope, Boro Park is one of three health care delivery services in New York (Boro Park Primary Care Center, Elderplan, Inc., Metropolitan Jewish Geriatric Center). As Medical Director, Dr. Cecora oversees the administrative operations of associates and a support staff of 20, in addition to coordinating and overseeing medical activities, directing patient care, and providing consultations and employee health services. Concurrent with his position at Boro Park, he serves as Medical Director of two affiliates – Elderplan, Inc. and Metropolitan Jewish Geriatric Enterprises. **Career Steps:** Medical Director, Boro Park Primary Care Center (1995–Present); Medical Director, Elderplan, Inc. (1986–Present); Medical Director, Metropolitan Jewish Geriatric Center (1985–Present). **Associations & Accomplishments:** Kings County Medical Society; Gerontological Society of America; American Geriatric Society; American Medical Directors Association; Publish health care articles on topics of prevention and primary care; Lecture to community groups and civic clubs on health care insurance. **Education:** University of Bologna School of Medicine, M.D. (1975); St. John's University, B.S. (1968). **Personal:** Married to Jennifer in 1979. Three children: Raymond, Christopher, and Peter. Dr. Cecora enjoys swimming, boating, sports, and computers.

Harriet Character, M.D.

Pediatrician
CIGNA Health Care of Phoenix
1717 West Chandler Boulevard
Chandler, AZ 85224–6145
(602) 821–7565
Fax: (602) 821–4371

8099

Business Information: CIGNA Health Care of Phoenix, a health maintenance organization, is a health care facility providing diagnosis and treatment of patients. As Pediatrician, Dr. Character is responsible for providing health care to pediatric patients. **Career Steps:** Pediatrician, CIGNA Health Care of Phoenix (1984–Present); Pediatrician, Pediatric Consultants of Houston (1983–1984). **Associations & Accomplishments:** Board Member, American Cancer Society (ACS) (8 yrs); Board Member, Advisory Board, Unlimited Potential; Volunteer, Homeless Shelter and Phoenix Foundation of Homeless Children; Publishes annual "10 Commandments to a Healthy Baby" and articles concerning preventative medicine for minority communities health care safety. **Education:** Hahnemann University, M.D. (1980). **Personal:** Dr. Character enjoys snow skiing, bicycling, and aerobics.

Neeoo W. Chin, M.D.

Co–Director
Greater Cincinnati Institute for Reproductive Health
2123 Auburn Avenue, #44
Cincinnati, OH 45219–2971
(513) 629–4400
Fax: (513) 629–4595

8099

Business Information: Greater Cincinnati Institute for Reproductive Health is a private research and health facility specializing in reproductive endocrinology and infertility. A practicing physician since 1981, Dr. Chin Co–Founded the Institute in 1992, specializing in obstetrics and gynecology with a sub-specialization in infertility. He has performed various clinical studies in in–vitro fertilization, succeeding in producing the first test tube baby gorilla at the Cincinnati Zoo in 1995 for the Cincinnati Zoo CREW (Center for Reproduction of Endangered Wildlife). **Career Steps:** Co–Director, Greater Cincinnati Institute for Reproductive Health (1992–Present); Director, Bethesda Hospital Fertility Center (1987–1992). **Education:** Ohio State University Hospitals, Fellow (1987); Duke University Medical Center, Resident (1985); Ohio State University College of Medicine, M.D. (1981); University of Cincinnati, B.A. (1977). **Personal:** Married to Shelly in 1977. Two children: Jason and Taryn. Dr. Chin enjoys ballroom dancing, lacrosse, and karate.

Lareen Chonzena

Regional Vice President
Learning Services Corporation
10855 DeBruin Way
Gilroy, CA 95020
(408) 848–4379
Fax: (408) 848–6509

8099

Business Information: Learning Services Corporation is a 24–bed, post acute rehabilitation facility and supported living program for individuals with acquired brain injury. LSC serves patients nationally from nine locations nationally, and three locations in California. As Regional Vice President, Ms. Chonzena is responsible for all business functions, including financial services and administrative operations, as well as and oversight of a staff of 80. She also serves as the Clinical Supervisor for the rehabilitative portion of the Clinic. Concurrently, she is a public speaker for insurance companies regarding brain injuries. **Career Steps:** Vice President, Learning Services Corporation (1994–Present); Private Practice Owner, Communication Specialist of Roseville (1993–1994); Case Manager/Speech Pathologist and Assistant Manager, Sierra Gates Rehabilitation (1991–1994). **Associations & Accomplishments:** Case Management Society: CMSA/South Bay Chapter; Case Management Society of American: Northern California Chapter/Secretary; American Speech, Language & Hearing Association (ASHA); National Head Injury Association; California Rehabilitation Association. **Education:** Colorado State University, M.S. (1983); San Jose State University, B.S.; Chabot Junior College, A.A. **Personal:** One child: Tyler S. Ms. Chonzena enjoys legislative activities, research, and serving as Support Group Facilitator.

Leighton Clark

Partner
Perspectives Ltd.
17W733 Butterfield Road, Suite A
Oakbrook Terrace, IL 60181
(708) 932–8008
Fax: (708) 932–2315

8099

Business Information: Perspectives Ltd. is an employee assistance program, providing managed mental health care program development and psychotherapy consulting. Perspectives Ltd. has twelve locations in Chicago and serves clientele throughout the U.S. Co–founding Perspectives Ltd. in 1986, Mr. Clark serves as Executive Vice President and Partner. He is responsible for the development and implementation of all programs for corporations and organizations, as well as providing consultations. **Career Steps:** Executive Vice President and Partner, Perspectives Ltd. (1986–Present); Regional Manager, Parkside Medical Services Corporation (1984–1986); Employee Assistance Representative, United Airlines (1981–1984); United States Navy (1969–1973). **Associations & Accomplishments:** Board of Trustees, Institute of Clinical Social Work (Ph.D. Program); Employee Assistance Professionals Association: Chair of Ethics Committee (1991–Present), Board of Directors (1992–1995); Chair, Task Force on Colleague Assistance – National Association of Social Workers; American Legion. **Education:** George Williams College, M.S.W. (1982), B.S. **Personal:** Married to Mary Lindsey in 1975. Mr. Clark enjoys photography, travel, sailing, movies, and theatre.

Lisa R. Cobet

Chief Executive Officer and Founder
Speciman Specialists, Inc.
37481 Maple Street, Suite K
Fremont, CA 94536
(510) 713–2140
Fax: (510) 713–8712

8099

Business Information: Speciman Specialists, Inc., the only company of its kind in the U.S., is an international company, providing phlebotomy services (drawing blood) for paternity (DNA) testing, bone marrow drives, urine collection for drug screenings, and breath alcohol testing. There are 400 independent contractors throughout the nation, serving clientele nationally and internationally. Founding Speciman Specialists, Inc. in 1991, Ms. Cobet serves as Chief Executive Officer. She is responsible for all aspects of operations, including administration, upper management, financing, sales, public relations, and traveling on behalf of the Company to seek new qualified personnel. **Career Steps:** Chief Executive Officer and Founder, Speciman Specialists, Inc. (1991–Present); State Coordinator, Genetic Design, Inc. (1988–1991); Phlebotomist, Washington Hospital (1980–1988); Lab Technician, Pulmonary Associates (1976–1980). **Associations & Accomplishments:** American Society of Phlebotomy Technicians; Substance of Abuse Program Administrators Association. **Education:** Brumans Nursing School, CMA (1975); Certified: Phlebotomist and Breath Alcohol Technician. **Personal:** Single parent of four children: Chrystie, Ashley, Jennifer, and Andrea. Ms. Cobet enjoys water skiing, scuba diving, sewing, cooking, exercising, church activities, and reading.

Lisa Collings, Ph.D.

Director, OD & Education
Harris Methodist Health System
601 N. Ryan Plaza Dr. #140
Arlington, TX 76011
(817) 462-6188
Fax: (817) 462-6166

8099

Business Information: Harris Methodist Health System is an integrated financing, management, and delivery healthcare system providing services to hospitals and health plans. As Director, OD & Education, Dr. Collings develops and implements all training and education of employees and oversees all management of organization and team interventions. **Career Steps:** Harris Methodist Health System: Director (1995–Present), O.D. Specialist (Apr.1995–Nov.1995); Hughes Aircraft (HTI): Training Specialist (Jan.1995–Mar.1995), Research Specialist (1992–1994). **Associations & Accomplishments:** Organization Development Network; American Society for Training and Development (ASTD); Society for Industrial/Organizational Psychology (SIOP); Member of SIOP Workshop Committee. **Education:** California School of Professional Psychology: Ph.D. (1993), Master of Science in Organizational Psychology (1991), Bachelor of Arts in Psychology (1989). **Personal:** Married to Dr. Michael Herron in 1994. Dr. Collings enjoys dance, aerobics, and rollerblading.

Evelyn Cook, R.N.

Director of Nurses
UTMB/TDCJ Managed Health Care
301 University Boulevard
Gatesville, TX 76528
(817) 865-6663
Fax: (817) 865-6663 Ext.316

8099

Business Information: UTMB/TDCJ Managed Health Care is a correctional health care setting in a maximum security male prison. The inmates, approximately 2,900 currently, are provided with both inpatient and outpatient care. As Director of Nurses, Ms. Cook is responsible for supervising the nursing staff and the day-to-day medical needs of the inmates. She handles public relations, marketing, and often does recruiting for the medical branch. **Career Steps:** Director of Nurses, UTMB/TDCT Managed Health Care (1994–Present); Charge Nurse, TDCJ ID Hughes Unit (1993–1994); Training Coordinator, Clifton Lutheran Sunset Home (1990). **Education:** University of Maryland, B.S.N. (1985). **Personal:** Ms. Cook enjoys antiques, gardening, and travel.

Mitchell Cordover, M.D.

Vice President of Medical Affairs and Director of Risk Management
Spectrum Emergency Care
12647 Olive Boulevard, P.O. Box 419052
St. Louis, MO 63141-1752
(314) 919-9077
Fax: Please mail or call

8099

Business Information: Spectrum Emergency Care is a contract health care service, providing health care in emergency medicine and multiple other areas. A practicing physician since 1982, Dr. Cordover joined Spectrum Emergency Care as Vice President of Medical Affairs and Director of Risk Management. He is responsible for the development of physician education and policies, as well as helping to develop scientific defense for malpractice cases, and development of policies and programs in all different lines of businesses, 500 emergency departments, correctional facilities, and primary care clinics nationwide. **Career Steps:** Vice President of Medical Affairs and Director of Risk Management, Spectrum Emergency Care (Present); Emergency Physician, Synergon Emergency Care; Clinical Instructor, Washington University – Barnes Hospital. **Associations & Accomplishments:** American College of Emergency Physicians; American College of Physician Executives; So. Medical Association; St. Louis Physician Executives; American Medical Association; Extensive oversees experience. **Education:** University of Arizona, M.D. (1982); University of Cincinnati, M.S. in Epidemiology, Health Planning. **Personal:** Dr. Cordover enjoys biking and woodworking.

Leslie De La Paz Cortina

Comptroller
Southwestern Health Management Associates, Inc.
600 West 20th Street
Hialeah, FL 33010
(305) 863-8860
Fax: (305) 863-8668

8099

Business Information: Southwestern Health Management Associates, Inc. is a provider of medical services to home health care agencies, diagnostic centers, medical practices, mental health practices, and hospitals. As Comptroller, Ms. Cortina serves as the Chief Financial Officer responsible for all aspects of the Accounting, Billing and Collections departments. Responsibilities include the preparation of financial statements and tax reports, establishing internal controls, and writing procedures manuals, in addition to overseeing a staff of 30 in the Accounting Department. **Career Steps:** Comptroller, Southwestern Health Management Association, Inc. (1995–Present); Audit Manager, Grainger & Company, P.A. (1991–1995); Senior Manager, BDO Seidman (1988–1991); Sole Practitioner (1985–1988); Audit Manager, KMG Main Hurdman (1978–1984). **Associations & Accomplishments:** Board of Directors of Florida Education Fund (Since 1993); Board of Directors, Health and Human Services Board – Dade County (Since 1996); Past President, Latin Business and Professional Women's Club (1987); American Institute of Certified Public Accountants; Florida Institute of Certified Public Accounts; Cuban-American Certified Public Accounts; Coalition of Hispanic American Women: (Served as Director 1989); Greater Miami Chamber of Commerce – Hispanic Affairs Committee; Dade County Commission on the Status of Women; Paella Circle, Miami Dade Community College; Barbara Plager Award, Latin Business and Professional Women's Club; Certificate of Appreciation, Camara De Comercio Latina (CAMACOL); Certificate of Appreciation, Dade County Commission; Bilingual – English and Spanish. **Education:** Florida International University, B.B.A. in Accounting (1978); Certified Public Accountant (1980–Present). **Personal:** Married to Humberto in 1992. Two children: Ericka and Rafael De La Paz. Ms. Cortina enjoys playing the piano and spending time with her family.

Mr. John V. Crisan

Chief Financial Officer and Senior Vice President
Access Health Marketing, Inc.
11020 White Rock Road
Rancho Cordova, CA 95670
(916) 851-4100
Fax: (916) 852-3890

8099

Business Information: Access Health Marketing, Inc. provides consumers a healthcare information services. In his capacity as Chief Financial Officer and Senior Vice President, Mr. Crisan is responsible for overseeing management of finance and operations, including regulatory reporting, treasury, pricing, legal, and human resources. Established in 1986, Access Health Marketing, Inc. employs a staff of 250 and reports annual revenue of $20 million. **Career Steps:** Chief Financial Officer and Senior Vice President, Access Health Marketing, Inc. (1994–Present); Chief Financial Officer and Chief Operating Officer, American Psychological Management, Inc. (1991–1994); Vice President of Health Affairs, Blue Cross Blue Shield of Ohio (1990–1991). **Associations & Accomplishments:** American Institute of Certified Public Accountants; Ohio Society of Certified Public Accountants; FEI. **Education:** Cleveland State University, B.A. (1967).

Mike J. Cummings

Loss Prevention Manager
Horizon Healthcare Corporation
P.O. Box 30650
Albuquerque, NM 87190-0650
(505) 878-6482
Fax: (505) 822-8201

8099

Business Information: Horizon Healthcare Corporation is the leading provider of post-acute health care services, including specialty health care and long term care services nationally. Services are currently offered throughout 42 states. As Loss Prevention Manager, Mr. Cummings is responsible for risk managment and loss prevention through on-going evaluation of potential liability, training program development, and prevention programs to reduce risk (liability) losses. **Career Steps:** Loss Prevention Manager, Horizon Healthcare Corporation (1995–Present); Vocational Consultant, Genex, Inc. (1993–1995); Director of Vocational Services, Greater Bridgeport Mental Health Center (1989–1993). **Associations & Accomplishments:** Workers Compensation Association of New Mexico; Board Member, Construction Advisory Management Committee – Albuquerque Technical Vocational Institute; New Mexico Rehabilitation Association. **Education:** University of California – Los Angeles, B.S. (1979); University of Bridgeport, post graduate work in Clinical Psychology; New School of Social Research, New York, NY – Organizational, Clinical and Experimental Psychology. **Personal:** Married to Lauren in 1989. Six children: Jennifer, Katie and Megan Stobie; and Alisa, Nina and Ryan Cummings. Mr. Cummings enjoys woodworking, carpentry, basketball, surfing, reading, and most importantly — family activities.

James Rudy Darling

President and Chief Executive Officer
Carroll Health Systems
P.O. Box 387
Berryville, AR 72616-0387
(501) 423-5230
Fax: (501) 425-5268
EMAIL: See Below

8099

Business Information: Carroll Health Systems is the administrative parent company, owning and operating health care facilities throughout the Berryville, Arkansas vicinity. Facility entities include: Carroll Medical Center, d.b.a. Carroll Regional Medical Center — a not-for-profit, 50-bed acute care, 4-bed Intensive Care Unit, Emergency Room, and a Paramedic Unit Service; Carroll Home Health Services — a not-for-profit home health care service; Carroll Hospice Care — a not-for-profit hospice care service; and Durable Medical Equipment — a not-for-profit medical equipment retail distributor. As President and Chief Executive Officer, Mr. Darling is responsible for all aspects of operations for all four corporations, in addition to overseeing the administrative operations for associates and a support staff of 205. **Career Steps:** President and Chief Executive Officer, Carroll Health Systems (1991–Present); Carroll Regional Medical Center: Associate Administrator (1991), Director of Pharmacy (1983–1991); Director of Pharmacy, Howard Memorial (1975–1983). **Associations & Accomplishments:** Kiwanis Club; Diplomate, ACHE; President, Arkansas Hospital Association of Administrators; President, Northwest District of Arkansas Hospital Association. **Education:** Northeast Louisiana University, B.S. in Pharmacy (1972). **Personal:** Married to Carolyn in 1969. Three children: Blake, Annie, and Jessica. Mr. Darling enjoys hunting and fly fishing.

Davis M. Dayhoff

Clinical Supervisor
ACHD Addictions
11007 Cash Valley Road, NW
Lavale, MD 21502
(301) 777-2285
Fax: (301) 777-5832

8099

Business Information: ACHD Addictions is an alcohol and drug residential treatment facility treating addicted clients and their families. Established in 1979, ACHD Addiction currently employs 27 people. As Clinical Supervisor, Mr. Dayhoff is responsible for overseeing clinical operations and staff functions, as well as providing direct therapy to clinics. Concurrent with his position as Clinical Director, he serves as Professional Counselor to eight year olds in his private practice and as Consultant at the Veteran's Administration Hospital for Vietnam veterans. Future plans include writing a book with his brother, a psychologist from New York. **Career Steps:** Clinical Supervisor, ACHD Addictions (1980–Present); Professional Counselor, Self-Employed (1989–Present); Readjustment Specialist, Re-entry Counseling Associates (1985–1995). **Associations & Accomplishments:** Member, National Association of Alcoholism & Drug Abuse Counselors; Member, Cash Valley PTA; Member, Certified Addictions Counselor of Maryland; Member, Bethel Church of the Nazarene; Member, International Association of Trauma Counselors; Member, Frostburg State University Social Work Advisory Board. **Education:** Frostburg State University, M.S. in Counseling Psychology (1983), B.S.; Alleghany Community College, A.A. **Personal:** Married to Wilma L. in 1981. Two children: Tasha L. and David C. Mr. Dayhoff enjoys photography, directing church music, conducting geneological research, and concerts.

Angela Lynn Diaz

President
Beacon Rehabilitation Center
6043 NW 167th Street, Suite #21-A
Miami, FL 33015
(305) 821-0502
Fax: (305) 362-5209

8099

Business Information: Beacon Rehabilitation Center is a rehabilitation center providing outpatient and home health physical, occupational, and speech therapy. As President, Ms. Diaz, a Florida-registered Physical Therapist, is responsible for all aspects of Company operations, including physical therapy, administration, marketing, and business development. **Career Steps:** President, Beacon Rehabilitation Center (1994–Present); Self Employed, Angela Diaz, P.T., P.A. (1992–1994); Staff Physical Therapist, Mercy Hospital (1990–1992); Physical Therapy Aide, Green Briar Nursing Center (1987–1990); Children's Counselor, YMCA (1985–1987). **Associations & Accomplishments:** Women in Healthcare Network; Associate Member, Dade Association of Rehabilitation Nurses; Coral Gables Chamber of Commerce/Women in Business; Board Member, Florida International University Alumni; National Multiple Sclerosis Society; American Physical Therapy Association; Florida Physical Therapy Association; Council Person At Large, Southeast District Florida Physical Therapy Association; Rehab Provider Network in Florida; Professional Review Network in Florida; Numerous certificates. **Education:** Florida International University, B.S. in Physical Therapy (1990); Miami–Dade Community College, Associate in Art (1988); Miami–Dade Medical Campus, Physical Therapy Procedures (1987); Registered Physical Therapist in the State of Florida. **Personal:** Ms. Diaz enjoys travel, reading, biking, and swimming.

Irene L. Dieterich

Director of Client Services
Medicus Systems, Inc.
6 Vicksburg Station
St. Charles, MO 63303–6143
(314) 441–0444
Fax: (314) 441–6546

8099

Business Information: Medicus Systems, Inc. develops financial analysis software for hospitals; Executive Information Systems (EIS), Decision Support Systems (DSS), Contract Management, and Managed Care. Medicus Systems, Inc. currently employs approximately 250 people within three software divisions. As Director of Client Services, Ms. Dieterich is reponsible for the management of the financial and computer analysts who install software, as well as manage the finances, monthly bills, revenues, and client relations. **Career Steps:** Director of Client Services, Medicus Systems, Inc. (1994–Present); Manager of Nursing Systems, Barnes Hospital (1992–1994); Sales Manager, Source Data Systems (1990–1992); Senior Clinical Technical Consultant, GTE Health Systems (1987–1990); Mercy Health Systems: Order Communications Coordinator (1983–1987), Nursing Administration Staffing Coordinator (1966–1983). **Education:** University of Dubuque, B.S. in Computer Science (1987); University of Missouri – St. Louis Campus, additional micro computer classes. **Personal:** Married to Russell B. Dieterich, M.D. in 1992. Six children: Jonathan, Katie, Kristen, Patrick, Pamela, and Paula. Ms. Dieterich enjoys skiing, hiking, big band music, and gardening.

Keith A. Dines

Vice President of Strategic Development
Sun Health Corporation
P.O. Box 1278
Sun City, AZ 85373
(602) 815–7620
Fax: (602) 815–6654

8099

Business Information: Sun Health Corporation is a health care and integrated delivery system, providing health care services through physicians, hospitals, skilled nurses, and HMO licenses. Established in 1969, Sun Health Corporation reports annual revenue of $130 million and currently employs 2,300 people corporate–wide. With twelve years of experience in health care administration, Mr. Dines joined Sun Health Corporation in 1992. Serving as Vice President of Strategic Development, he is responsible for business development, strategic planning, marketing, and managed care administration. **Career Steps:** Vice President of Strategic Development, Sun Health Corporation (1992–Present); Administrator, Maui Dental Center (1983–1990). **Associations & Accomplishments:** American College of Healthcare Executives; Health Administrators Forum; Healthcare Financial Management Association; Medical Group Management Association; Dental Group Management Association. **Education:** Arizona State University, M.H.S.A. (1993); Geneva College, B.S.B.A. **Personal:** Married to Shirley in 1985. Two children: Nicole and Krissi. Mr. Dines enjoys golf, photography, and fishing.

Maria Ilona Dittrich

LTC Pharmacy Director
Compupharm – LTC
3006 South Michigan Street
South Bend, IN 46614
(219) 291–9974
Fax: (800) 745–1980

8099

Business Information: Compupharm – LTC provides pharmaceutical services to long–term care facilities. Services provided include: medication, wound care, IV's, medical records, enteral therapy, Med/Surg products, and consulting services. As LTC Pharmacy Director and a licensed pharmacist, Ms. Dittrich provides the overall development procedures for the pharmacy, which includes the training and supervision of In–service staff, quality assurance, evaluations, scheduling and overall business strategies. **Career Steps:** LTC Pharmacy Director, Compupharm – LTC (1994–Present); Pharmacist, Merjer Thrifty Acres (1993–1994). **Associations & Accomplishments:** American Society Consultant Pharmacists. **Education:** Ferris State University, B.S. in Pharmacy (1993). **Personal:** Married to Eric in 1995. Ms. Dittrich enjoys sewing and spending time with her dogs (English Mastiff).

Eileen Lavin Dohmann

Executive Director
VNA Community Hospice
2775 South Quincy Street, Suite 260
Arlington, VA 22206–2236
(703) 824–5200
Fax: (703) 824–5228

8099

Business Information: VNA Community Hospice is a community–based, free–standing Medicare–certified hospice program, specializing in the care of those individuals with a life expectancy of less than six months. With fourteen years of experience in health care and a Certified Home Health Nurse since 1980, Mrs. Dohmann joined VNA Community Hospice as Clinical Director in 1993. Appointed as Executive Director in 1994, she is responsible for the overall management and administration of the Program, including finances, staffing, and recruiting. **Career Steps:** VNA Community Hospice: Executive Director (1994–Present), Clinical Director (1993–1994); Weekend Nurse Manager, VNA of Northern Virginia (1989–1993); Nursing Supervisor, Kent County VNA (1983–1988). **Associations & Accomplishments:** Hospice Nurses Association; Oncology Nurses Society; Sigma Theta Tau; American Cancer Society. **Education:** Averett College, M.B.A. (1991); Fairfield University, B.S.N. (1980). **Personal:** Married to Herman A. Dohmann Jr. in 1981. Three children: Jeffrey, Gregory, and Patrick. Mrs. Dohmann enjoys cooking, crafts, and reading.

Robert Donnelly

Vice President
Medcon Financial Services
301 Route 17N, P.O. Box 464
Rutherford, NJ 07070–0464
(201) 804–2800
Fax: (201) 804–8883

8099

Business Information: Medcon Financial Services is a national healthcare management office, providing physician healthcare management services to healthcare facitilies in eleven states, including all practice types and financial services (i.e., billing, collecting). As Vice President and Co–Founder, Mr. Donnelly is responsible for all operational and marketing issues within the Company. **Career Steps:** Vice President, Medcon Financial Services (1990–Present); Client Representative, Advacare, Inc. (1986–1990). **Associations & Accomplishments:** Medical Group Management Association; American Management Association; International Billing Association; Published in trade journals and newspapers. **Education:** Rutgers University, B.S. (1989). **Personal:** Married to Katherine Donnelly in 1988. One child: Geanna Marie. Mr. Donnelly enjoys golf and family activities.

Edward M. Duke III

Director of Managed Care–Nevada/Managed Care Executive
Universal Health Services, Inc.
2300 West Sahara Avenue, Suite 1030, Box 35
Las Vegas, NV 89102–4352
(702) 367–1713
Fax: (702) 367–0713

8099

Business Information: Universal Health Services, Inc. is a national hospital and healthcare corporation. The Corporation owns 32 hospitals which are located throughout the U.S., ranging from psychiatric to acute care facilities. As Director of Managed Care–Nevada, Mr. Duke directs managed healthcare strategies and contracting, including integrated delivery systems development. **Career Steps:** Director of Managed Care, Universal Health Services, Inc. (1994–Present); Director of Corporate Provider Services, Sierra Health Services, Inc. – Nevada (1985–1994); Director of Medical Delivery Systems, Health Plan of America – California (1983–1985); Executive Director, Lane County Medical Society – Eugene, Oregon (1976–1982). **Associations & Accomplishments:** Healthcare Financial Management Association; Society for Healthcare Planning and Marketing of the American Hospital Association; American Management Association; Served as Adjunct Faculty at three universities; Guest lecturer at American Medical Association; Presenter at Group Health Association of America. **Education:** University of Oregon, Master's Degree in Planning and Administration (1974); San Diego State University, A.B. in Social Science. **Personal:** Married to Sharon P. Mr. Duke enjoys backpacking, biking, woodworking, and automobile restoration.

C. Shelby Durham

Founder, President and Chief Executive Officer
Rehab Options, Inc.
111 Presidential Boulevard, Suite 101
Bala Cynwyd, PA 19004
(610) 617–8775
Fax: (610) 617–8785

8099

Business Information: Rehab Options, Inc. is a health care management company, providing physical, occupational, and speech therapy to patients in skilled nursing facilities and is expanding to include freestanding outpatient clinics. Beginning as a home–based operation, with $5,000 of Ms. Durham's personal savings, a handful of employees, and one contract in 1992, Rehab Options currently services 10 contracts with 53 employees serving a patient base of about 3,000. Its staff consists of a world–wide base of employees, including professionals from Kenya, Bermuda, Philippines, and the U.S., providing a level of diversity that enriches the staff and enables them to serve a diverse group of clientele. Through its work, Rehab Options helps elderly patients to enjoy a better quality of life and, in most cases, benefit from clinical and emotional support that its staff provides. Health care and supportive services include: screenings to determine therapeutic need, if any; department survey and program development; interdisciplinary communication; in–service programs; skilled and routine rehabilitation services; restorative care services; productivity projects; billing consultation; and other services. In addition to its services, the Corporation has contributed time and money to charitable organizations, including the contribution of fans to senior citizens at Philadelphia Senior Center; providing free care to Medicaid recipients (generally low–income skilled nursing home residents who could not otherwise afford care, with the realization that Medicare, not Medicaid, covers rehabilitation services); providing scholarship programs to promising area high school students; working with an area long–term care facility to develop a Philadelphia–based two–year education program for minority students (training students to be Certified Occupational Therapist Assistants); to name a few. Granted state certification in 1993 from the Commonwealth of Pennsylvania's Department of Health & Human Services, Rehab Options is able to participate as an outpatient physical, occupational, and speech therapy provider under the Health Insurance for the Aged Program (Title XVIII of the Social Security Act). With an administrative office in Bala Cynwyd, Pennsylvania and with an employee base that expands almost daily, the Corporation is the only African–American–owned health care company, providing therapy and management services to nursing homes and other care providers throughout the Delaware Valley. A veteran speech therapist and manager of thirteen years, Ms. Durham founded Rehab Options in 1992 with her husband, Melvin Jackson — (serves as Vice President of Strategic Planning). As President and Chief Executive Officer, she is responsible for all aspects of operations and subsidiary corporations, including coordinating therapy for each patient, administration of therapy programs, establishing goals and objectives, overseeing financial affairs, and maintaining a personal relationship with her employees. Concurrent with her position at Re-

hab Options, Ms. Durham volunteers her time in schools (by speaking to area youth about career opportunities in health care and encouraging them to stay in school), hospitals, and nursing homes, in addition to conducting presentations at professional speaking engagements, such as the American Speech and Hearing Association Conference. **Career Steps:** President and Chief Executive Officer, Rehab Options, Inc. (1992–Present); Keystone Rehabilitation Systems: District Director (1987–1992), Speech Pathologist (1986–1987). **Associations & Accomplishments:** National Association of Women Business Owners; National Association for Female Executives; National Council of Negro Women, Inc.; American Speech–Language Hearing Association; Who's Who in Leading American Executives; World Who's Who of Women. **Education:** Howard University, M.S. (1983); North Carolina Agricultural and Technical State University, B.A. **Personal:** Married to Melvin T. Jackson in 1994.

Maureen K. Dwyer

Vice President
North Shore Health System
150 Community Drive
Great Neck, NY 11021
(516) 465–8007
Fax: (516) 465–8396

8099

Business Information: North Shore University Hospital was established in 1953 but has evolved into an integrated health system comprised of nine hospitals, two nursing homes, and over fifty ambulatory sites in the counties of Queens, Nassau, Suffolk, and Staten Island. The Health System currently employs over 11,000 people. As Vice President, Ms, Dwyer is a member of the Board of Trustees of the sponsored institutions, and as such has a general involvement with all facets of the North Shore Health System. Ms. Dwyer functions as liaison among the parent Board of Trustees, facilities, trade unions, community residents, community government and research. **Career Steps:** Vice President, North Shore Health System – Corporate Office (1995–Present); Vice President Administration, North Shore University Hospital (1993–1995); Administrator, NSUH/Manhasset/Glen Cove (1990–1993). **Associations & Accomplishments:** American Association of Hospital Administrators; Board of Economic Opportunity Commission; Queens Chamber of Commerce; St Mary's Children & Family Services; Mill Neck Manor School for the Deaf: elected as Woman–of–the–Year, and elected to Phi Alpha Alpha. **Education:** Long Island University–Roth School of Business, M.P.H. (1978); Hofstra University, Masters (1968); Marymount Manhattan College, B.A. (1964). **Personal:** Married to James D. Robertson in 1990. One step–child: Kerry O'Brien. Ms Dwyer enjoys swimming, gardening, securing historical landmark status for neighborhood, ice skating, and taking on the role as a Eucharistic Minister.

Elizabeth Brown Egan

Director of Human Resources
Team Rehab
123 Saint Joseph Avenue, Suite B
Long Beach, CA 90803
(310) 434–4992
Fax: (310) 434–4964

8099

Business Information: Serving over 40 facilities in Central and Southern California, Team Rehab is a provider of rehabilitation services for skilled nursing facilities, hospitals, outpatient clinics, and home health agencies. As Director of Human Resources, Ms. Egan oversees all human resource functions, including recruitment, benefits, compensation, and employee relations. **Career Steps:** Director of Human Resources, Team Rehab (1994–Present); Recruitment Manager, PACE Therapy (1992–1994); Staffing Officer, Bank of America (1990–1992); Human Resource Representative, American Savings Bank (1989–1990). **Associations & Accomplishments:** Orange County Employment Managers Association. **Education:** University of California – Irvine, B.A. in Psychology (1989). **Personal:** Married to Richard in 1995. Ms. Egan enjoys travel, going to the beach, and outdoor sports.

Mr. Louis A. Falligant

Physician Assistant Supervisor
Dean Medical Center
1313 Fish Hatchery Road
Madison, WI 53715
(608) 252–8328
Fax: (608) 252–8245

8099

Business Information: Dean Medical Center is an outpatient medical clinic providing a wide variety of family health care services to residents of Madison, Wisconsin. As Physician Assistant Supervisor, Mr. Falligant supervises the physician assistant staff and works in family practice as a physician assistant. Dean Medical Center presently employs 340 physicians, 45 physician assistants, and over 1,000 support staff. **Career Steps:** Physician Assistant Supervisor, Dean Medical Center (1993–Present); Diagnostics Representative, Squibb Diagnostics (1991–1993); Cardiology Manager, Meriter Hospital (1982–1991); Family Practice Physician Assistant, Buffalo Medical Center (1975–1981). **Associations & Accomplishments:** Director–at–Large, Consortium for Primary Care in Wisconsin (1994–1995); Member, Medicare Carrier Advisory Committee, WPS (1994–1995); Member, Rural Health Clinic Task Force, State of Wisconsin Office of Rural Health (1994–1995); Member, Committee for Promotion of Non–Physician Health Care Providers, Office of Rural Health (1994–1995); House of Delegates, American Academy of Physician Assistants; Wisconsin Academy of Physician Assistants: Current Member and Former Chair of Legislative Committee (1976–81), President–Elect (1978–79 and 1993–94), President (1979–80 and 1994–95), Board of Directors (1977–78 and 1980–81), Third Party Reimbursement Chair (1993–95); Medical Examining Board (1976–1980); Physician Assistant Advisory Council. **Education:** Central Michigan University, M.S. in Health Services Administration Candidate (1995); Yale University Medical School, Physician Assistant Program (1975); University of Wisconsin, B.S. in Zoology (1968). **Personal:** Married to Marilee in 1986. Five children: Tera, Erin, Louis, Katie and Kelsey. Mr. Falligant enjoys woodworking, playing golf, hiking and cycling.

Frederick A. Flatow, M.D.

Medical Director
The Connecticut Hospice, Inc.
61 Burban Drive
Branford, CT 06405–4003
(203) 481–6231 Ext: 290
Fax: (203) 483–9539

8099

Business Information: The Connecticut Hospice, Inc., built in 1975, was the first facility of its kind built in the United States. Headquartered in Branford, Connecticut and equipped with a fifty–two bed facility, with three other clinics across the state, it provides compassionate and dignified care for terminally ill patients and their families. Seventy–five percent of the patients in the Hospice are ill with cancer. In addition they offer care for patients with AIDS, heart and kidney disease. Serving the greater New Haven area, the Hospice provides outpatient services as well as grief counseling to those in need, with an experienced and empathetic staff. A practicing physician since 1960, Dr. Flatow was appointed as Medical Director in 1991. In this capacity he evaluates, coordinates and provides patient care. Dr. Flatow also teaches and lectures on pain control and management. **Career Steps:** Medical Director, The Connecticut Hospice, Inc. (1991–Present); Practicing Physician, The Springfield Medical Association (1967–1991). **Associations & Accomplishments:** Fellow, American College of Physicians; Academy of Hospice Physicians; The New England Cancer Society; Yale Cancer Center. **Education:** Cornell University Medical College, M.D. (1960); Yale University, B.S. in Engineering. **Personal:** Married to Sandra in 1959.

Susan Foreman

Director of Network Design and Development
Ultramedix Healthcare Systems, Inc.
4201 Tampico Trail
Springhill, FL 34607
(352) 597–2846 (800) 293–8235
Fax: (813) 930–2751

8099

Business Information: Ultramedix Healthcare Systems, Inc. is a commercial and Medicaid health management organization. Joining Ultramedix as its first employee in 1993, Mr. Foreman currently serves as Director of Network Development, in charge of networking for the state of Florida for physicians, hospitals, and ancillary providers. Duties include marketing, strategic planning, policies and procedures, and administration. **Career Steps:** Vice President and Director of Network Design and Development, Ultramedix Healthcare Systems, Inc. (1993–Present); Director of Physician Relations, Regional Healthcare, Inc. (1990–1993); Director of Provider Services, Humana Healthcare Systems (1988–1990); Humana (1979–1990). **Associations & Accomplishments:** Hernando County Healthcare Advisory Board; Juvenile Justice Council; Board of Directors, Central Healthy Start Coalition; Board of Trustees, Temple Beth David, Advisory Council Head Start. **Education:** Broward Community College, A.S. (1980); Registered Nurse; Licensed Health Insurance Agent. **Personal:** Married to Robert in 1982. Three children: Matthew, Patrick, and Darrin. Mrs. Foreman enjoys reading, needlepoint, golf, and soccer.

Nelson J. Fowlkes

Director of Marketing Sales
St. Francis Medical Center
3680 East Imperial Highway, Suite 400
Lynwood, CA 90262
(310) 603–1826
Fax: (909) 737–7851

8099

Business Information: St. Francis Medical Center, a member of Daughters of Charity National System, is a multi–specialty managed community health services system for the greater Lynwood, California area. A health care executive administrator with over fourteen years expertise, Nelson Fowlkes has served in administrative roles for St. Francis Medical Center since 1992. Appointed as Director of Marketing and Clinic Manager in 1994, he is responsible for diversified marketing activities, including contacting clients and off–site management. In addition, he supervises three clinics, establishes new sites, and administers the Medi–Cal Marketing Program. **Career Steps:** St. Francis Medical Center: Director of Marketing and Clinic Manager (1994–Present), Director of Marketing and Industrial Medicine (1992–1994); Executive Director, St. Jude Medical Center – Fullerton (1990–1992). **Associations & Accomplishments:** National Association of Occupational Health Professionals. **Education:** California State University–Fresno, M.P.A. (1982); University of Tennessee, M.S. in Biochemistry; Central State University, B.S. in Chemistry; Professional Certificate in Gerontology. **Personal:** Married to Peggy in 1957. Three children: Errol Allen, Janet Lynn and Nelson Joseph. Mr. Fowlkes enjoys bicycling and golf.

Natalie Garcia

Home Director
Sunrise Community, Inc.
9040 Sunset Drive
Miami, FL 33173
(305) 829–5010
Fax: (305) 829–5004

8099

Business Information: Sunrise Community, Inc. is comprised of approximately 22 group homes in the Miami area and is expanding to other locations in Florida, Tennessee and Virginia. The group homes serve individuals who are developmentally disabled. Staff members assist with the rehabilitation of individuals who function within the mild, moderate, or profound level of mental retardation. As Home Director, Ms. Garcia directs a staff of 10 employees. Ms. Garcia is responsible for rehabilitation planning and development for the disabled, staff training, employment policies and procedures, and providing new and existing services for the staff and residents. Ms. Garcia's long range plans include helping the organization expand and grow and to expand her supervisory role. **Career Steps:** Home Director, Sunrise Community, Inc. (1995–Present); Secondary Marketing, Bank United (1990–1995). **Associations & Accomplishments:** Student Affiliate of the American Psychological Association; National Honor Society in Psychology; Southern Bell Future Business Leader of America Award; 1995 Sunrise Group 3 Employee of the Year Award. **Education:** Florida International University, B.A. (1993); Certified Associate Behavior Analyst. **Personal:** Ms. Garcia enjoys community and volunteer work, reading and travel.

Alan K. Gardner

Director of Operations
Pharmacy Associates, Inc.
P.O. Box 23007
Little Rock, AR 72221–3007
(501) 221–2330
Fax: (501) 221–2611

8099

Business Information: Established in 1989, Pharmacy Associates, Inc. provides pharmacy benefits management services. Serving insurance companies and self–insured employers throughout the U.S., PAI processes prescription claims for client member. With extensive experience in systems technology management, Alan Gardner serves as Director of Operations. In this capacity, he oversees information systems, plan configuration, eligibility, customer service, and reception. **Career Steps:** Director of Operations, Pharmacy Associates, Inc. (1995–Present); University of Arkansas – Medical Sciences: Manager of Academic Computer Support Center (1993–1995), Systems Analyst (1991–1993); Business Analyst, Cleveland Clinic Foundation (1989–1991). **Education:** University of North Carolina – Chapel Hill, B.S. in Math/Science (1986); Attending: University of Arkansas – Little Rock, M.B.A. candidate. **Personal:** Married to Stephanie F. in 1983. Two children: David and Erica. Mr. Gardner enjoys volleyball and snow skiing.

Daryl L. Gohl

Director of Human Resources
Tuality Healthcare
335 South East 8th Avenue
Hillsboro, OR 97123–4246
(503) 681–1664
Fax: (503) 681–1695
EMAIL: See Below

8099

Business Information: Tuality Healthcare is a local hospital system with two acute care hospitals, clinics, and also a durable medical equipment and supply business, as well as a home health care program. Established in 1918, the Company is headquartered in Hillsboro, Oregon. As Director of Human Resources, Mr. Gohl oversees volunteers and auxiliaries, in addition to managing organizational development and Chaplain services. Internet users can reach him via: dgohl@teleport.com. **Career Steps:** Director of Human Resources, Tuality Healthcare (1988–Present); Assistant Director of Human Resources, Adventist Health (1983–1988); Director of Human Resources, Hialeah Hospital (1981–1983). **Associations & Accomplishments:** Society for Human Resource Management; American Society for Healthcare Human Resources Administration; Board Member, SHRM Oregon State Council; Board Member, NHRMA Portland Chapter; Board Member, PIC Mult/Wash Counties; Board Member, Bus/Ed Compact of WA County; Outstanding President Award, (1992); OSHHRA; NHRMA. **Education:** Walla Walla College, B.S.B.A. (1975). **Personal:** Married to Ruthie in 1989. Five children: James, Michael, Melissa, Padraic, and Heather. Mr. Gohl enjoys golf, boating, hiking, photography, and gardening.

Robert O. Gramling

Director of Security
North Philadelphia Health System
8th Street and Girard Avenue
Philadelphia, PA 19122
(215) 787–2099
Fax: (609) 871–2758

8099

Business Information: North Philadelphia Health System is the administrative management parent company for acute, chronic and addiction treatment facilities located in the greater Philadelphia–metro area. With twenty–six years experience in security operations, Mr. Gramling joined the North Philadelphia Health System in 1994. Serving as Director of Security, he is responsible for the direction of all aspects of security systems, as well as transportation functions for two hospitals, Gerard Medical Center and St. Joseph's Hospital. He also oversees administrative operations for associates and a support staff of 70, in addition to providing public relations, strategic planning, and employee training. **Career Steps:** Director of Security, North Philadelphia Health System (1994–Present); Director of Security, Presbyterian Medical Center (1993); Deputy Director of the Campus Police, Temple University (1969–1992). **Associations & Accomplishments:** International Association of Healthcare Security and Safety, Delaware Valley Chapter; Visually–Impaired Co–Partners/School Climate Committee, Willingsboro Schools; Pastor, Mount Calvary Baptist Church, Mullica Hill, New Jersey. **Education:** Temple University, A.S. (1977); International Seminary, Plymouth, Florida, Bachelor and Master in Bible Theology (1984 and 1985). **Personal:** Married to Patricia. Five children: Lucile, Timothy, Jonathan, Elizabeth, and Rebecca. Mr. Gramling enjoys reading, playing Scrabble, and yard work.

Mark T. Grant

Director of Pulmonary Services
Bromenn Healthcare
Virginia at Franklin
Normal, IL 61702
(309) 454–0736
Fax: (309) 454–0786

8099

Business Information: Bromenn Healthcare is a multi–disciplinary health care system based from a non–profit hospital that provides primary care to all age groups. As Director of Pulmonary Services, Mr. Grant oversees every aspect of critical care services, respiratory sleep medicine, and neurodiagnostics areas. **Career Steps:** Bromenn Healthcare: Director of Pulmonary Services (1994–Present), Manager, Respiratory Care (1988–1994); Director, Respiratory Care, St. John's Hospital (1985–1988). **Associations & Accomplishments:** President, Jaycees; Allied Member, College of Chest Physicians; American Legion; American Association of Respiratory Care; Illinois Society for Respiratory Care; Veterans Administration. **Education:** University of Illinois, B.A. (1990); Lincoln College, A.A.; St. Johns Hospital, Respiratory Therapy School; U.S. Military Schools. **Personal:** Married to Michelle in 1988. Three children: Sean, Jason, and Robert. Mr. Grant enjoys building, remodeling, softball, and racquetball.

Beverley Jean Gudex

President and Secretary
Adult Care Consultants, Inc.
68 East 9th Street
Fond Du Lac, WI 54935–5009
(414) 921–7723
Fax: (414) 921–7986

8099

Business Information: Adult Care Consultants specializes in care management for the elderly and mentally ill, and teaching independent living and parenting skills. As Co–Director, Ms. Gudex directs all services and administration. **Career Steps:** President, Adult Care Consultants (1992–Present); Co–Owner, Community Alternatives of Fond du Lac County (1989–1992); Support Services Director, Visiting Nurse Association (1987–1988); Director Social Work Services, Waugun Memorial Hospital (1980–1986). **Associations & Accomplishments:** National Association of Social Workers; National Association of Professional Geriatric Care Managers; Current Secretary, Fond du Lac County Genealogical Society. **Education:** University of Wisconsin: Milwaukee, M.S.W (1989), Madison, B.S.W. (1975). **Personal:** Married to Ron Cross in 1979. One child: David Gudex–Cross. Ms. Gudex enjoys genealogy, travel, and gardening.

Stephen D. Haid

Executive Director
Southwest Organ Bank
3500 Maple Avenue, Suite 800
Dallas, TX 75219–3931
(214) 821–1931
Fax: (214) 827–8352
EMAIL: See Below

8099

Business Information: Southwest Organ Bank is an organ procurement organization. The Company covers 1/3rd of the state of Texas and is connected through a network of computers to other organ centers throughout the country. Since opening in Dallas in 1974, the Company has surpassed its 5000th transplant. As Executive Director, Mr. Haid is responsible for all aspects of Company operations, including administration, strategic planning, and public relations. Internet users can reach him via: sdhaid@ix.netcom.com. **Career Steps:** Southwest Organ Bank: Executive Director (1987–Present), Manager of Recovery Services (1982–1987); Executive Director, Organ Recovery Systems, Inc. (1987–Present). **Associations & Accomplishments:** Former President, Association of Organ Procurement Organizations; Former President, North American Transplant Coordinators Organizations; Former Member of Board of Directors, United Network for Organ Sharing; Rotary Club of Dallas. **Education:** Texas Women's University, M.S. (1992); University of Missouri – St. Louis, B.A. **Personal:** Married to Jamie in 1985. Two children: Cristin and Michael. Mr. Haid enjoys woodworking, running, fly fishing, and fly tying.

Michael D. Hallock

Materials Manager
Suburban Heights Medical Center
333 Dixie Highway
Chicago Heights, IL 60411
(708) 756–0100
Fax: (708) 756–9954

8099

Business Information: Suburban Heights Medical Center is a full–service healthcare institute specializing in group medical practice and outpatient surgery, with four satellite facilities in the Chicago area. Established in 1973, the Center currently employs 420 people, including 64 physicians. As Materials Manager, Mr. Hallock is responsible for directing purchasing, inventory control, and distribution. **Career Steps:** Materials Manager, Suburban Heights Medical Center (1991–Present); Purchasing Manager, Suburban Heights Medical Center (1990–91); Director of Purchasing, Garst Seed Company Research Department Division ICI (1987–90); Director of Materials Management, Kewanee Hospital (1980–86). **Associations & Accomplishments:** American Society of Healthcare Materials Management; First Baptist Church of Park Forest; Illini Society for Hospital Material Management. **Education:** Blackburn University, B.A. (1976). **Personal:** Married to Katherine in 1976. Two children: Amanda and Michelle. Mr. Hallock enjoys woodworking.

Michael A. Hamilton, M.D.

Director and Physician
Duke University Diet and Fitness Center
804 West Trinity Avenue
Durham, NC 27701–1826
(919) 684–6331
Fax: (919) 688–8022

8099

Business Information: Duke University Diet and Fitness Center, affiliated with Duke University Medical Center, is a full–service, obesity treatment center, providing residental diet and fitness facilities. Services provided include educating individuals on nutrition and fitness, providing emotional help, and group therapy. Serving about 100 people at a time, the Center receives patients from around the world on a doctor's referral or self–enrollment, working with individuals that are slightly overweight to obese (10 pounds and up). Cost of services for a four–week session is approximately $5,000. The majority of the Center's patients include celebrities. Established in 1972, Duke University Diet and Fitness Center reports annual operating budget of $4 million and currently employs 30 people. A practicing physician for thirty–one years, Dr. Hamilton joined the Duke University Diet and Fitness Center in 1985. Serving as Director and Physician, he is responsible for all aspects of operations, including writing and developing new programs and policies, and overseeing the budget. Fifty percent of his time is spent working directly with the patients. **Career Steps:** Director and Physician, Duke University Diet and Fitness Center (1985–Present); Director, Duke PA Program (1975–1985); Medical Director, Lincoln Community Health Center (1971–1975). **Associations & Accomplishments:** North American Society for the Study of Obesity. **Education:** University of Rochester, M.D. (1964); Eastman School of Music, B.M. (1955). **Personal:** Two children: Sebastian and Sunita. Dr. Hamilton enjoys classical music and gardening.

Marie Ryan Hansbarger

Nurse Manager
Carilion Health Systems Trauma Center
P.O. Box 13727
Roanoke, VA 24036–3727
(540) 981–7454
Fax: Please mail or call

8099

Business Information: Carilion Health Systems Trauma Center provides acute in–patient care personnel for a Level–3 Trauma Center (the highest level for trauma patients) located at Roanoke Memorial Hospital. A practicing nurse since 1984, Mr. Hansbarger joined Carilion Health Systems as Nurse Manager in 1992. She is responsible for the management of all aspects of human resources (i.e., hiring, firing, training, scheduling, a $2 million budget), as well as overseeing a 25–bed PCU and supervising a support staff of 37. **Career Steps:** Nurse Manager, Carilion Health Systems Trauma Center (1992–Present); Staff Nurse, Roanoke Memorial Hospital (1984–1992). **Associations & Accomplishments:** Virginia Organization of Nurse Executives; American Association of Critical Care Nurses. **Education:** Roanoke College, B.B.A. (1992); RMH School of Professional Nursing, R.N. (1984). **Personal:** Married to Orran O., Jr. in 1987. Two children: Ryan Oakey and Dylan Thomas. Mrs. Hansbarger enjoys singing in the church choir.

Edward M. Hanton, M.D., MBA

Medical Director
Harris Methodist Health System
611 Ryan Plaza Suite 900
Arlington, TX 76011–4008
(817) 462–6830
Fax: (817) 462–7235
EMAIL: See Below

8099

Business Information: Harris Methodist Health System is a managed delivery health care organization. Consisting of 270,000 HMO members, HMHS owns seven (7) hospitals, and is also contracted through 53 hospitals, home health and medical supplies services. A practicing physician specializing in Internal Medicine and OB/Gyn practices since 1970, Dr. Hanton joined HMHS in 1993. As Medical Director he provides the overall executive administration for the Arlington, Texas facility, ensuring quality patient care and delivery. **Career Steps:** Medical Director, Harris Methodist Health System (1993–Present); Physician in Chief, Kaiser–Permanente (1985–1993); Chief Executive Officer, Women's Health (1984–1985); Partner and Vice President, St. Paul OB/Gyn Ltd. (1970–1984). **Education:** Loyola College of Maryland, MBA (1991); University of Minnesota, B.S., M.D. **Personal:** Married to Mary in 1981. Eight children: Jim, Michael, Mary,

Cathy, Margaret, Susan, MJ and Lisa. 10 grandchildren. Dr. Hanton enjoys golf, computers, fishing, and running.

Sally L. Hein, Ph.D.
Executive Director
Southern Human Resource Development Consortium for Mental Health
2414 Bull Street
Columbia, SC 29202–0485
(803) 734–7893
Fax: (803) 734–7897

8099

Business Information: The Southern Human Resource Development Consortium for Mental Health is a 13 state federally-funded financial and resource sharing arrangement. The Consortium serves State Departments/Divisions of Mental Health, providing Human Resources programs and financial support. Appointed Executive Director in 1989, Dr. Hein is responsible for the development of marketing products (i.e., training materials and technical assistance reports), as well as the overall administrative operations of the Agency. **Career Steps:** Executive Director, Southern Human Resource Development Consortium for Mental Health (1989–Present); Director of Educational Services, Parkland Memorial Hospital (1984–1989); Assistant Professor, North Texas State University (1980–1984); Clinical Supervisor, Memphis State University (1977–1980). **Associations & Accomplishments:** American Society for Training and Development; Vice President, Tree of Life Congregation; Vice President, Hadassan (Columbia Chapter). **Education:** Memphis State University, Ph.D. (1980); Vanderbuilt University, M.A. (1974); University of Cincinnati, B.S. (1973). **Personal:** Dr. Hein enjoys acting in Community theater productions, volunteer work, travel, and walking.

Dave Hekel
Director of Quality Management
Pikes Peak Mental Health Center
220 Ruskin Drive
Colorado Springs, CO 80910
(719) 572–6100 (719) 572–6144
Fax: (719) 572–6199

8099

Business Information: Pikes Peak Mental Health Center is a mental health care facility, providing a variety of mental health services to a mixed population of clientele. Established in 1972, Pikes Peak Mental Health Center currently employs 450 people. As Director of Quality Management and Staff Development, Mr. Hekel guides the organization's movement into total quality, as well as serving as Chief Trainer, coordinating staff development activities and wellness programs. Mr. Hekel also owns and operates his own training business, High Expectations. **Career Steps:** Director of Quality Management and Staff Development, Pikes Peak Mental Health Center (1992–Present); Director of Quality Improvement, Century Healthcare Corporation (1990–1992); Associate Administrator, Cheyenne Mesa Adolescent Residential Treatment Center (1985–1990). **Associations & Accomplishments:** National Association of Social Workers; Pikes Peak Movement for Children. **Education:** University of Denver, Master of Social Work (1978); Northwestern Oklahoma State University, Bachelor of Social Work (1971). **Personal:** Three children: David, Jennifer, and Chris. Mr. Hekel enjoys hiking, weightlifting, and travel.

Jim E. Henry
Director of Environmental Services
Irving Health Care System
1901 North MacArthur Boulevard
Irving, TX 75061
(214) 579–8746
Fax: (214) 579–4428

8099

Business Information: Irving Healthcare System is a contract service for the management of hazardous materials, biohazardous waste, general cleanliness, linen distribution, and recycling program for two local hospitals. The Company was established in 1964 and currently has 75 employees providing and maintaining a clean and safe hospital environment for all patients, employees, visitors, and the community. As Director of Environmental Services, Mr. Henry oversees the activities of all employees. It is his responsibility to develop and maintain safe conditions for the disposal of hazardous and biohazardous waste materials and to be current on EPA and OSHA regulations regarding waste disposal. **Career Steps:** Director of Environmental Services, Irving Health Care System (1989–Present); Regional Operations Director, Hospital Housekeeping System (1986–1989); General Manager, U–Haul Corporation (1981–1986) **Associations & Accomplishments:** American Society for Healthcare Environmental Services; National Executive Housekeepers Association;

American Cancer Society; Center for Healthcare Environmental Management; Volunteer of the Year (1994–1995) for Partners in Education; Chairman, United Way Campaign for Irving Healthcare System (1992). **Education:** Variety of trade related courses. **Personal:** Married to Pat in 1978. Two children: Joshua and Jacob (Twins). Mr. Henry enjoys golf, family outings, snorkling, and scuba diving.

Carmen L. Hernando Clark, N.H.A.
Director of Team Development
Angel Care Health Corporation
300 71st Street, Suite 610
Miami, FL 33141
(305) 868–7080
Fax: (305) 868–3020

8099

Business Information: Angel Care Health Corporation is a rehabilitation company providing physical, occupational, and speech therapy. As Director of Team Development, Ms. Clark is responsible for over 100 employee files, maintains and updates changes in regulatory issues, develops employee evaluation systems, and handles all human resource issues. **Career Steps:** Director of Team Development, Angel Care Health Corporation (1994–Present); Southpoint Manor: Assistant Administrator (1993–1994), Admission Director (1992–1993); Outreach Coordinator, Chicago Department on Aging (1992). **Associations & Accomplishments:** South Florida Healthcare Executive Forum; Licensed Nursing Home Administrator. **Education:** Slippery Rock University, B.S. (1992). **Personal:** Married to Douglas in 1996. Ms. Hernando Clark enjoys church activities.

Michael Hertz
Treasurer
Hospice Provider Group, Inc.
220 Lenox Avenue
Westfield, NJ 07090
(908) 233–4688
Fax: (908) 352–5621

8099

Business Information: Hospice Provider Group, Inc. provides group purchasing for 400 pharmacies and hospices around the U.S., encompassing 43 states. Initiating the idea of Hospice Provider Group in 1992, Mr. Hertz formed the partnership with his wife Sandra and Ron Silber, the attorney who drew up the papers for the Group. Serving as Co–Owner and Treasurer, he is responsible for coordinating contracts and overseeing finances. A registered pharmacist since 1975, Mr. Hertz also owns and operates Elmora Pharmacy, Inc., an established retail pharmacy since 1934 which he acquired in 1981. **Career Steps:** Treasurer, Hospice Provider Group, Inc. (1992–Present); Pharmacist and Owner, Elmora Pharmacy, Inc. (1979–Present); Pharmacist, Roxy Drugs (1978–1979). **Associations & Accomplishments:** Board of Trustees, Center for Hope Hospice, Inc.; Board of Trustees, Elizabeth Development Company. **Education:** Northeastern University, B.S. in Pharmacy (1975). **Personal:** Married to Sandra L. in 1976. Two children: Benjamin and Daniel. Mr. Hertz enjoys automobiles and art.

Gladys T. Hollingsead
•••━━◉━━•••
Chief Executive Officer
Pacific Health Education Center
7600 Delight Avenue
Lamond, CA 93241
(805) 633–5300
Fax: (805) 633–5302

8099

Business Information: Pacific Health Education Center is a non–profit foundation dedicated to helping people live healthier, happier, more successful lives. The foundation seeks to contribute to the preservation and restoration of physical, emotional, and mental qualities of life through classes, seminars, workshops, and in–house services. Programs offered include weight control, positive solutions for negative emotions, vegetarian cooking, and a smoking cessation program. As Chief Executive Officer and Chairperson of the Board of Directors, Ms. Hollingsead oversees the operation of the Pacific Health Education Center. She coordinates with the other members of the Board in regards to developing, implementing, and marketing new and existing services to perspective clients. Other responsibilities include coordination of family life, preventative care, nutrition, and bilingual departments. Ms. Hollingsead works closely with other members of management in the development of an annual budget and in complying with the accepted budget. **Career Steps:** Chief Executive Officer, Pacific Health Education Center (1992–Present); Medical Office Manager, M.C. Hollingsead, M.D. (1960–1992); Head Nurse, Bereins Hospital. **Associations & Accomplish-**

ments: Bakersfield Chamber of Commerce; President of ASI Pacific Union Conference (since 1993); Woman of the Year (1995); Vice President of Communications, Pacific Union A.S.I.; Board of Directors, Pan African Development Corporation; Hewitt Foundation; House of Manna; San Joaquin Community Hospital; Loma Linda Women's Auxiliary; Hillcrest Seventh–day Adventist Church; Board of Regents Member, American College of Health Care Executives. Listed in Who's Who in Executives and Professionals since 1995; Who's Who among Outstanding Americans since 1995; Member of the executive committee of LA VOZ (since 1996); Singer/Composer – Selection of her composition by the OTI Composers Association in 1996. **Education:** Loma Linda University School of Nursing, B.S. and P.H.N.; **Personal:** Married to Marshall C. Hollingsead, M.D. in 1958. Two children: John and Marshall II. Ms. Hollingsead enjoys composing music, performing her own compositions, and interior decorating.

Daniel E. Hoodin
Vice President of Managed Care
VHA Tri–State
8900 Keystone Crossing, Suite 480
Indianapolis, IN 46240
(317) 574–7182
Fax: (317) 574–7173

8099

Business Information: VHA Tri–State, established in 1977, is a national healthcare alliance consisting of 59 hospitals and 5,200 medical providers. VHA Tri–State provides state–wide preferred provider services to customers and providers on contract who reside in the states of Indiana and Kentucky. As Vice President of Managed Care, Mr. Hoodin is responsible for the operations of state–wide preferred provider services, including marketing and strategic planning. **Career Steps:** Vice President of Managed Care, VHA Tri–State (1993–Present); Assistant Administrator and General Counsel, Schumpert Medical Center (1987–1993); Resident, Providence Hospital (1985–1987). **Associations & Accomplishments:** American Bar Association; Ohio Bar Association; National Healthcare Lawyers Association; American Academy of Healthcare Attorneys; Louisiana Bar Association. **Education:** Xavier University, MHHA (1986); University of Dayton School of Law, J.D. (1982); Marietta College, B.A. in Political Science (1979). **Personal:** Married to Heather in 1985. Two children: Aaron Leland and Derek Ryan Hoodin. Mr. Hoodin enjoys rugby and historic miniature wargaming.

Kathy E. Horn–Dalton, Ph.D.
President
Southwest Wyoming Rehabilitation Center
2632 Foothill Boulevard, Suite 107
Rock Springs, WY 82901
(307) 382–3842
Fax: (307) 362–4615

8099

Business Information: Southwest Wyoming Rehabilitation Center is a non–profit rehabilitation center for the developmentally disabled, providing employment opportunities, residential facilities, testing, and case management. As President, Ms. Horn–Dalton is responsible for all aspects of operations, with complete budgetary and administrative authority over twelve departments and 52 professional staff members. Affiliated with SWRC since 1975, other duties involved budget development, grant writing, program design and development, shop contract bidding and procurement, and client supervision. **Career Steps:** Southwest Wyoming Rehabilitation Center: President (1981–Present), Executive Director (1976–1981), Shop Foreman (1975–1976); President, Desert Winds Inc.(HUD Project) (1987–Present); Consultant: Sage View Care Center (1986–Present), Park Manor (1991–Present), and Fremont Manor (1986–1988); Grants Administrator, Sweetwater County, Wyoming Community Development (1981–1982); Group Home Counselor, Somerset/ Bedford Mental Health Center (1974); Psychiatric Aide, Torrence State Hospital (1974); Organizer and Counselor, Women's Information Center – Morgantown, WV (1973); Counselor, West Virginia Black Lung Association (1972); Counselor, Kennedy Youth Center (1971). **Associations & Accomplishments:** Special Education & Rehabilitative Peer Reviewer, U.S. Department of Education (1991); Women of the Year, International Biographical Centre, Cambridge, England (1992); Distinguished Leadership Award, American Biographical Institute, Released in 1994 (1993); Honored Member, Who's Who Among Outstanding Business Executives (1995); Numerous funded grants and proposals; Numerous publications and presentations; Member, Sweetwater Association of Retarded Citizens (1975–Present); Member, Wyoming Human Resources Confederation (1976–Present); Member, Wyoming Association of Rehabilitation Facilities (1976–Present); Member, Rock Springs Chamber of Commerce (1976–Present); Member, Young Women Christian Association (1976–Present); Member, National Council of Community Mental Health Centers (1977–Present); Member, Rock Springs Energy Conservation Board (1978–Present); Member, Advisory Committee of the University of Northern Colorado (1978–Present); Member, Sweetwater Human Resource Council (1979–Present); Member, Wyoming Association for Retarded Citizens (1981–Present); Member, Executive Female (1982–Present); Member, Task Force on Aging and Developmental Disabilities (Since 1989). **Education:** Columbia Pacific University, Ph.D. in Administration (1983); West Virginia University, M.S.W. in Social Work (1975), B.S.W. in Social Work (1974); Numerous other educational experiences. **Personal:** Married to Randy Richards in 1995. She is an avid walker.

J. Deborah Hughes

Manager
HCIA
462 South 4th Avenue, Suite 405
Louisville, KY 40202–3469
(502) 560–1322
Fax: (502) 560–1330
EMail: See Below

8099

Business Information: HCIA is a health care information content company that develops and markets clinical and financial decision support systems used by hospitals, integrated networks, managed– care organizations, employers, and pharmaceutical companies. As Manager, Ms. Hughes is responsible for accreditation services and performance improvement, and provides analysis and on–site delivery of the Company's products. Internet users can reach her via: dhugh@HCIA.com. **Career Steps:** Manager, HCIA (1995–Present) Manager, Accrediation Services/Performance Improvement; Senior Consultant, MetriCor (1993–1995); Regional Director, Humana (1990–1993); Director of Medical Staff Services, Monongahela Valley Hospital (1987–1990). **Associations & Accomplishments:** International Society for Quality Assurance; National Association for Healthcare Quality; Kentucky Association for Healthcare Quality; Sigma Theta Tau, International Honor Nursing Society. **Education:** Carnegie Mellon University, MPM (1988); La Roche College, B.S. in Nursing (1987); Certified Professional in Healthcare Quality; Certified Medical Staff Services Coordinator.

Patricia C. Jacobson

Corporate Director of Executive Staffing
Pacificare Health Systems, Inc.
5995 Plaza Drive, Mail Stop 1111
Cypress, CA 90630–5028
(714) 220–3620
Fax: (619) 757–8176

8099

Business Information: Pacificare Health Systems, Inc. is a national managed health care plan, providing contracted health care services. Joining Pacificare Health Systems, Inc. as Manager of Human Resources in 1986, Mrs. Jacobson was appointed as Corporate Director of Executive Staffing and Staffing Systems in 1993. She is responsible for all activities relating to personnel. **Career Steps:** Pacificare Health Systems, Inc. Corporate Director of Executive Staffing (1993–Present), Regional Manager of Human Resources (1989–1993), Manager of Human Resources (1986–1989). **Associations & Accomplishments:** Society of Human Resource Management; National Association of Female Executives. **Education:** University of Southern California, working towards M.B.A. (expected completion – 1998); California State University – Long Beach, B.S. **Personal:** Married to Alan in 1983. Two children: Ryan Alan and Samuel Martin. Ms. Jacobson enjoys the cultivation of Bonsai trees and volunteering at the Children's Hospital Cancer Unit.

Mrs. Jayne Johns Progar

Corporate Officer
The Invictus Group, Ltd.
Box 520
Canonsburg, PA 15317
(412) 746–6512
Fax: (412) 746–6515

8099

Business Information: The Invictus Group, Ltd. is a health care consulting firm co–founded in 1988 by Mrs. Progar and her husband, David. The organization provides clinical and business continuing education seminars, case management services to the elderly and disabled and reviews the impact of pending health care legislation. As a Legal Nurse Consultant, Mrs. Progar provides assistance to attorneys with the medical aspects of their cases. The firm is currently administering a Medicare Advocacy program for the Commonwealth of Pennsylvania. PAMAP (PA. Medicare Advocacy Program) will challenge denied Medicare claims on behalf of the Commonwealth's dual eligible population enrolled in both the Medicare and Medicaid programs. The program is unique in that it will utilize nurses experienced in Medicare claims review and medical necessity criteria to review and challenge denials. An educational component will also attempt to keep Pennsylvania's health care providers abreast of changes in Medicare billing requirements and reimbursement issues. **Career Steps:** Partner, The Invictus Group (1988–Present). **Associations & Accomplishments:** Who's Who in American Nursing (1993–1994); American Association of Legal Nurse Consultants; National Association of Female Executives; Pennsylvania Licensed Registered Nurse. **Education:** Pennsylvania State University (1983–1984); California University of Pennsylvania, B.S. in Nursing (expected graduation date – 1996); Allegheny Valley Hospital, School of Nursing, Diploma R.N. **Personal:** Married to David in 1991. Mrs. Johns Progar enjoys music (piano), travel and interior design and decorating.

Benjamin A. Jones

Executive Vice President
National Council on Alcoholism and Drug Dependence/Greater Detroit Area
18954 James Couzens Freeway
Detroit, MI 48235–2516
(313) 345–9400
Fax: (313) 345–9017

8099

Business Information: National Council on Alcoholism and Drug Dependence/Greater Detroit Area (NCADD/GDA) is a substance abuse treatment and prevention facility, providing outpatient treatment for adults and adolescents on substance abuse. Additional services include providing presentations and workshops to schools and churches on substance abuse. Established in 1947, the Agency has three local facilities in Detroit, Michigan and currently employs 15 people. As Executive Vice President, Mr. Jones is in charge of all programs, budgets, planning, staffing, and meeting contractual obligations. In February 1996, he was appointed as President and Chief Executive Officer. **Career Steps:** National Council on Alcoholism and Drug Dependence/Greater Detroit Area: Executive Vice President (1995–Present), Program Director (1993–1995). **Associations & Accomplishments:** Kappa Alpha Psi Fraternity; National Association of Social Workers; American Association of Christian Counselors; Pentacostal Churches of the Apostolic Faith; Golden Key National Honor Society; National Association of Black Social Workers; Board Member, Detroit Red Ribbon Campaign. **Education:** University of Michigan, M.S.W. (1995); Wayne State University, B.A. **Personal:** Married to Shayla in 1980. Four children: Joseph, Benjamin, Shaylin, and Dontia. Mr. Jones enjoys bowhunting, archery, and coaching softball & basketball.

Richard E. Jones

Vice President
MedBuy Corporation
1325 Corley Drive
London, Ontario N6G 4L4
Fax: (519) 685–8184
EMAIL: See Below

8099

Business Information: MedBuy Corporation Specializes in group contracting for institutional health care. As Vice President, Mr. Jones manages all aspects of the Company's pharmacy program. Mr. Jones has more than 7 years of progressive management experience in the institutional healthcare industry. He has negotiated and managed mutually beneficial supply agreements for all pharmaceutical contrast media, imaging film and opthalmic procurement needs of 46 hospitals across Canada with a total value of $125 million annually. Internet users can reach him via: RICHARD.JONES@RESO-NET.COM. **Career Steps:** Medbury Corporation: Vice President (1996–Present); Vice President of Pharmacy (1993–1995); Saskatoon City Hospital: Department Head, Pharmacy (1992–1993), Assistant Director, Pharmacy (1989–1992); Staff Pharmacist – Psychiatry, Victoria Hospital Corporation (1988–1989); Pharmacy Resident, Saskatoon City Hospital (1987–1988); Research Biochemist, University of Virginia – Department of Physiology (1983–1984); Research Biochemist, University of Guelph – Department of Chemistry & Biochemistry (1981–1983). **Associations & Accomplishments:** Canadian Pharmaceutical Association; Canadian College of Health Service Executives; Canadian Society of Hospital Pharmacists; Ontario College of Pharmacy; American Society of Health–System Pharmacists; Rotary Club of London; Caseload Committee, Easter Seals Society of London; Co–Chair, Weldon Park Academy Parents and Friends Association; Strategic Planning Committee of the Board of Governors, Weldon Park Academy; Awarded, Wyeth Award of Excellence for University of Saskatchewan College of Pharmacy Class of 1987; Awarded, Smith, Kline and French Scholarship, University of Sasktchewan College of Pharmacy; Divers Alert Network; London and District Pharmacist Association; National Association for Photographic Art; Undersea Hyperbaric Medical Society. **Education:** University of Saskatchewan, Bachelor of Science in Pharmacy (1987); University of Western Ontario, B.Sc. with Honours, in Biochemistry (1981). **Personal:** Mr. Jones enjoys photography, scuba diving, boating, golf, camping and assisting with the "cub" group of Scouts Canada.

Shirley Jones

Senior Vice President
United Methodist Homes
1605 Davis Avenue
Endwell, NY 13760
(607) 785–7770
Fax: (607) 785–7774

8099

Business Information: United Methodist Homes is the management office for fifteen regional locations, including retirement homes, nursing homes, and day care facilities. The non-profit corporation is funded through Medicaid, Medicare, and donations. In addition, United Methodist Homes subcontracts dietary services. As Senior Vice President, Ms. Jones is responsible for the Financial Department activities, including billing, collections, and computerization. **Career Steps:** Senior Vice President, United Methodist Homes (1980–Present); Director of Computer Services, United Health Services (1968–1980); Computer Analysis, Endicott Johnson Corporation (1960–1968). **Associations & Accomplishments:** Woman's International Bowling Conference. **Education:** SUNY–Canton, Associates Degree (1954). **Personal:** Ms. Jones enjoys bowling, computers, spending time at her cabin, and participating in outdoor activities (fishing, hiking, etc.) and other sports.

Ronald L. Jordison

Regional Vice President – Midwest
Prison Health Services, Inc.
112 SW Sixth, Suite 311
Topeka, KS 66603
(913) 234–5100
Fax: (913) 234–2549

8099

Business Information: Prison Health Services, Inc. is a contract healthcare service, providing contracted healthcare (i.e., inpatient/outpatient, physicians) to prison and jail inmates. Established in 1978, Prison Health Services, Inc. operates nation wide. As Regional Vice President, Mr. Jordison is responsible for all midwest contract services. Prison Health Services, Inc. employs approximately 2000 employees, of which approximately 300 are in the midwest region. **Career Steps:** Regional Vice President – Midwest, Prison Health Services, Inc. (1995–Present), Regional Manager (1991–1995); Project Manager, PHP Healthcare (1987–1991); Project Manager, Health Management Association (1982–1987). **Associations & Accomplishments:** American Correctional Health Services Association (11 years); American Correctional Association (11 years); National Commission Correction Health Care; American Legion. **Education:** Allen County Community College; Certified Correctional Health Professional – Advanced. **Personal:** Four children: Sean, Linda, Loni, and Lorie. Mr. Jordison enjoys dining out, reading and travel.

Lynda D. Justus–Galbreath

Director
Riverview Behavioral Healthcare Services, Inc.
500 East Court Street
Sidney, OH 45365–2316
(513) 492–4178
Fax: (513) 492–3128

8099

Business Information: Riverview Behavioral Healthcare Services, Inc. is a private, not–for–profit mental health and substance abuse agency. Established in 1967, Riverview Behavior Healthcare Services, Inc. reports an operating budget of $3 million and currently employs 61 people. Joining Riverview Behavioral Health in 1991 as Coordinator of Intake Service, Ms. Justus–Galbreath was appointed as Director in December of 1995. She oversees all administrative operations for associates and a support staff of 61, in addition to directing all non–clinical operations and management of facilities. **Career Steps:** Riverview Behavioral Healthcare Services, Inc.: Director (1995–Present), Vice President of Management Services (1995), Director of Services for Children (1994–1995), Coordinator of Intake Services (1991–1994). **Associations & Accomplishments:** Association for Mental Health Administrators; Ohio Council of Mental Health Agencies Youth and Family Services; MENSA; Youth Cluster Chairperson, Family and Children First Council; Red Cross Board; Chairman, New Choices Board of Directors; Administrative Board, Mountain Dulcimer Society of Dayton. **Education:** Wright State University, M.S. (1979); University of Dayton, Courses toward M.P.A.; Ohio Northern University, B.A. in Education (1971); Attending: Kennedy – Western University, Courses toward Ph.D. **Personal:** Married to David B. in 1981. Two children: Kelli and Ginger. Ms. Justus–Galbreath enjoys vocal and instrumental music performances (using a traditional mountain dulcimer) for area organizations and special events.

Eric Kawaoka, M.D.

Pediatric Hematologist and Oncologist
Southern California Permanente Medical Group
9449 East Imperial Highway
Downey, CA 90242–2814
(310) 803–2354 (310) 803–2360
Fax: (310) 803–2743

8099

Business Information: Southern California Permanente Medical Group is a wholly–owned entity of Kaiser Permanente, the leading health maintenance organization (HMO) in the U.S. Established in 1945, SCPMG (with headquarters in Oakland, California) serves members in the Northern and Southern California sectors. Dr. Eric Kawaoka serves as a Physician Associate in SPMG's Downey, Calfornia offices, specializing in Pediatric Hematology/Oncology. **Career Steps:** Pediatric Hematologist and Oncologist, Southern California Permanente Medical Group (1984–Present); Assistant Professor, University of California–Davis (1982–1984); Research Fellow, University of California–Los Angeles School of Medicine (1979–1982). **Associations & Accomplishments:** American Society of Hematology; Athletic Booster Club; American Cancer Society. **Education:** Cornell University, M.D. (1974); University of Hawaii, B.A. **Personal:** Married to Esta Kawaoka in 1973. One child: John. Dr. Kawaoka enjoys jogging and golf.

Thomas Keenan

Executive Vice President/Chief Operating Officer
Harris Methodist Health System
611 Ryan Plaza Dr, Suite 900
Arlington, TX 76011
(817) 462–7802
Fax: (817) 462–7235

8099

Business Information: Harris Methodist Health System is the largest, fully–integrated health care system in north central Texas, and is one of the few health care organizations to successfully make the transition to financing, managing and delivering health care. Harris Methodist leads the Fort Worth managed care market with more than 240,000 members and more than 900 clients. As Executive Vice President and Chief Operating Officer for Harris Methodist Health System, Thomas Keenan has overall responsibility for management and oversight of managed care operations for Harris Methodist Health Plan, the System's health maintenance organization (HMO). His responsibilities include business and product development. During his three years with Harris Methodist, Mr. Keenan has been the instrumental leader in implementing and developing a Medicare Risk HMO, PPO, insurance company and CHAMPUS Reform Initiative contract arrangement. He also services on the System's Leadership Council to provide guidance and recommendations regarding strategic development and direction. **Career Steps:** Executive Vice President and Chief Operating Officer, Harris Methodist Health System (1992–Present); Regional Vice President, Travelers Health Network (1990–1992); Director of Network Development and Chief Operating Officer, Metlife Healthcare Network (1985–1990). **Associations & Accomplishments:** Managed Care Advisory Committee, American Healthcare Systems; North Texas Healthcare Network Operations Committee and Professional Affairs Committee; Health Industry Council – Dallas/Ft. Worth Region; Committee Member, Congressman Joe Barton's Health Care Advisory Committee; Elected Officer of the Year 1993 – Harris Methodist. **Education:** Indiana University, B.S. in Business Administration (1969). **Personal:** Married to Deborah in 1969. Two children: David and Kevin. Mr. Keenan enjoys hunting and fishing during his leisure time.

Bradley J. Keller

Director of Medical Records
90th Medical Group
6900 Alden Drive
Cheyenne, WY 82005
(307) 775–2732
Fax: (307) 775–3809

8099

Business Information: 90th Medical Group manages all aspects of medical disaster planning activities. As Director of Medical Records for the 90th Medical Group, Mr. Keller provides direct oversight for over 25,000 medical records, ensuring that accuracy and security of these records are uncompromised. While serving as Chief, Personnel & Administration, Mr. Keller managed all administrative and personnel actions for a 25–bed medical facility while reporting directly to the CEO. He directed and advised on all placement decisions, job rotations, and training opportunities for 21 administrative support personnel. Mr. Keller developed and instituted an inservice training program, which was sought after and implemented at 6 other hospitals. As Chief of Medical Plans, he developed disaster plans for medical resources in a tri–state area with multiple small, rural medical facilities. Mr. Keller initiated agreements between medical facilities at local, state, and federal level with disaster response agencies to provide optimal support during disaster operations. He directed the federal response to an oil refinery disaster in Cheyenne which included air and land evacuation of patients, preparation for emergency medical treatment operations, and patient decontamination operations. **Career Steps:** 90th Medical Group: Director of Medical Records (1995–Present), Chief of Personnel and Administration (1992–1995), Chief of Medical Plans (1990–1992). **Associations & Accomplishments:** Awards: Air Force Meritorious Service Medal with 1 oak leaf cluster and Air Force Commendation Medal with three oak leaf clusters. **Personal:** Married to Laura Lee in 1975. Two children: Jennifer Walker and Jessica. Mr. Keller enjoys golf, computers, softball, and fantasy baseball.

Marc W. Kelley

Executive Director
Greystone Programs Inc.
20 Delavergne Avenue
Wappingers Falls, NY 12590–1202
(914) 471–1918 /297–8800
Fax: (914) 297–6323
EMAIL: See Below

8099

Business Information: Greystone Programs Inc. is a mental health service provider, specializing in Mental Retardation and Autism. Established in 1979, Greystone Programs, Inc., which has five locations throughout New York, treats patients on a residential and outpatient basis. The Agency also provides employment and a therapeutic riding stable. As Executive Director and Founder, Mr. Kelley, oversees the daily operation of all services and operations, as well as the administrative and planning elements. His long–term goal is to radically change the residential services to provide more normal environments. Internet users can also reach him via: AOL.COM MWK – 49 **Career Steps:** Executive Director and Founder, Greystone Programs Inc. (1979–Present). **Associations & Accomplishments:** New York State Association of Community Residential Alternatives; American Horse Show Association; North American Handicaps Riding Association; Indian Harbor Yacht Club; Board Member, Watson Industries. **Education:** Columbia University: M.A. (1978); Antioch College at Antioch University, B.A. in Music (1976). **Personal:** Mr. Kelley enjoys horseback riding and sailing the Caribbean.

Glenn E. Kempka

Area Account Manager
ABBOTT Diagnostic Laboratories
805 McCasten Street
Milwaukee, WI 53202
(414) 339–9664
Fax: (414) 339–9668
EMAIL: thekempkas@msn.co

8099

Business Information: ABBOTT Diagnostic Laboratories, the leading medical diagnostics company in the world, is one of the world's leading research manufacturers and distributors of healthcare products. Products marketed include pharmaceutical, antibiotics, diagnostic and agricultural/veterinary. Global in scope, Abbott has offices and facilities in over 130 countries. As Area Account Manager of the Diagnostics Division, Mr. Kempka serves as the sales representative to area hospitals (totally 50) and government offices in the Wisconsin Region, with his main focus on equipment for testing and the products used for testing. Concurrently, he conducts state and local presentations, lectures, and seminars. **Career Steps:** ABBOTT Diagnostic Laboratories: Area Account Manager (1994–Present), Technical Marketing Representative (1991–1994); Medical Microbiologist, Franciscan Shared Laboratories (1981–1991); Medical Microbiologist, VA Hospital, Madison WI (1979–1981). **Associations & Accomplishments:** American Society for Clinical Lab Scientists; Brookfield Jaycees; National Autism Society. **Education:** University of Wisconsin, B.S. (1979); U.S. Army Field Service School – Medical Technologist; U.S.N. Chelsea Naval Hospital, Histology. **Personal:** Married to Carol in 1985. Four children: Libby, Daniel, Madeline, and John. Mr. Kempka enjoys golf and computers.

Mary A. Kossakoski

Regional Director of Operations
South Coast Rehabilitation Services
311 East Washington
Berrien Spings, MI 49103–1032
(616) 473–3226
Fax: (616) 471–5068

8099

Business Information: South Coast Rehabilitation Services, established in 1988, provides rehabilitation in the form of speech, occupational, and physical therapy to residents at long term care facilities located throughout the U.S. As Regional Director of Operations, Ms. Kossakoski manages the operations for three states (Indiana, Michigan, and part Florida), as well as being responsible for maintaining profit margins, budget, and generally overseeing the total operation. **Career Steps:** Regional Director of Operations, South Coast Rehabilitation Services (1992–Present); Audiologist, Nova-Care, Inc. (1989–1992); Audiologist, Berrien County Day Program for Hearing Impaired Children (1987–1989); Teacher of Hearing Impaired Children, C.O.P.I.S.D. (1980–1985). **Associations & Accomplishments:** American Speech–Language–Hearing Association. **Education:** Central Michigan University, M.A. (1988); Eastern Michigan University, B.S. (1971). **Personal:** Married to Michael in 1985. Four children: Kellie, George, David, and Michael Grix. Ms. Kossakoski enjoys mountain biking, dancing, reading, music, and sailing.

Ms. Catherine E. Kowal

Director of Quality Management
Blue Cross/Blue Shield of Massachusetts (HMO Blue)
360 Birnie Avenue
Springfield, MA 01107
(413) 747–1269
Fax: (413) 747–1244

8099

Business Information: Blue Cross/Blue Shield of Massachusetts (HMO Blue) is a mutual insurance company whose primary business is health insurance and health benefits management. They also have HMO managed health care programs, providing complete medical, dental, surgical, and pharmacy services to its members. As Director of Quality Management, Ms. Kowal is responsible for the management of various educational and training programs and clinical improvement teams. Her plans include starting a consulting business in the near future. **Career Steps:** Director of Quality Management, Blue Cross/Blue Shield of Massachusetts (HMO Blue) (1993–Present); Staff Nurse (R.N.), Baystate Medical Center (1989–1993). **Associations & Accomplishments:** Massachusetts Nurses Association; National Association for Healthcare Quality; Recipient of two awards of Outstanding Clinical Practice in College: Florence Henderson Award and Lavinia Dock Award; National Association for Female Executives; Article to be published in the Journal of Nursing Staff Development about the educational program she developed called, "An Educational Model to Educate Staff Nurses about CQI/TQM"; Member, Sigma Theta Tau International. **Education:** Keuka College, B.S. in Nursing (1988); Western New England College, Graduate School, M.B.A. in Healthcare – in process.

Doris E. Kraemer

Vice President
Commonwealth Care, Inc.
246 Walnut Street
Newton, MA 02160–1639
(617) 332–9554
Fax: (617) 332–9757

8099

Business Information: Commonwealth Care, Inc. is an international, Medicare–certified, managed health care agency, providing health care services to patients with the help of HMO's and self–insured groups. Established in 1990, Commonwealth Care, Inc. reports annual revenue of $6 million and currently employs 22 people. As Vice President, Mrs. Kraemer serves as a professional advisor for the Agency and is responsible for account management, business development, and quality assurance. **Career Steps:** Commonwealth Care, Inc.: Vice President (1994–Present), General Manager (1993–1994); Director of Patient Services, Home Care PRN – Technical Aid Corporation (1983–1989); Owner and Operator, Private Family Daycare (1983–1989). **Associations & Accomplishments:** Membership Committee, Home and Health Care Association of Massachusetts (1992–1995); Legislative and Lobbying Committee, Boston Regional Continuing Care Association (1990–1993); Member, Brockton Chamber of Commerce (1992–1993); Vestry Member, Trinity Episcopal Church (1994–1996); St. Paul's Cathedral Soup Kitchen – provides meals for the homeless. **Education:** Fitchburg State College, B.S. in Nursing (1978); Boston University School of Gerontology; American Nurses Credentialing Center, Certified in Community Health (1992). **Personal:** Married to Joseph P. in 1979. Three children: Leah, Erik, and Keith. Mrs. Kraemer enjoys gourmet cooking, holiday craft-making, boating, and fishing.

John Kurvink

Administrator
West Side Care Center
3324 Old Okanagan Hwy.
West Bank, British Co V4T 1N3
(604) 768–0488
Fax: (604) 768–4777

8099

Business Information: West Side Care Center is an 85–bed, long–term care facility providing multi–level care services including a special care unit and adult day care program. As Administrator, Mr. Kurvink is responsible for all aspects of operations for the Center including administrative support for a staff of 90. He is currently working towards attaining a Masters in Hospital Administration from the University of Minnesota. **Career Steps:** Administrator, West Side Care Center (1995–Present); Director of Finance, Mount St. Mary Hospital (1993–1995); Senior Internal Auditor, Ministry of Finance, Province of B.C. (1992–1993); Senior Auditor, Arthur Andersen & Co. (1988–1992). **Associations & Accomplishments:** Canadian College of Health Service Executives; Canadian Institute of Chartered Accountants; Canadian Society of Medical Technologists; Published in local newspapers. **Education:** Ottawa University, B.Comm. (1991); University of Minnesota, working towards Masters Degree in Health Administration. **Personal:** Married to Caroline in 1982. Mr. Kurvink enjoys reading, skiing, and swimming.

Cleve W. Laird, Ph.D.
President
Drial Consultants
3341 Southwest 15th Street
Pompano Beach, FL 33069–4808
(305) 971–7595
Fax: (305) 975–6803

8099

Business Information: Drial Consultants is a consulting firm, providing consultations on medical regulatory affairs. Sixty–seven consultants, brought out of retirement or recruited from other businesses, run the gamut of biological endeavors, conducting clinical trials and providing submissions for drug compounds. Joining the Company as President and Chief Executive Officer in 1989, Dr. Laird is responsible for all aspects of operations, as well as serving as Senior Consultant. He also oversees all administrative operations for associates and a support staff of 67. Concurrent with his executive position with Drial Consultants, he is the Executive Vice President at Technical Chemicals and Products, Inc. **Career Steps:** President, Drial Consultants (1989–Present); Executive Vice President, Technical Chemicals & Products, Inc. (1994–Present); Director of Research, International Remote Imaging (1981–1988). **Associations & Accomplishments:** Staff of Mammalian Genetics Course Jackson Laboratory; Adjunct Associate Professor, Baylor College of Medicine; Adjunct Assistant Professor, Boston University; Instructor, Harvard Medical School. **Education:** Rutgers University, Ph.D. (1968); Gettysburg College, B.A.; University of Nebraska, M.S. **Personal:** Married to Elizabeth Cortelyou in 1965. Two children: Brian C. and Kevin W.. Dr. Laird enjoys woodworking and model ship building.

Georgetta D. Lake
Executive Director – Founder
Passage Homes
823 East Long Street
Columbus, OH 43203
(614) 258–5555
Fax: (614) 258–6598

8099

Business Information: Passage Homes is a nonprofit corporation which operates community–based foster care "networks" of many families of different life styles and communities. They use a unique "Extended Family" approach in reaching out to children and natural family members who need help and support to become healthy contributing members of society. Passage provides adjunct therapies, i.e. group, individual and family counseling, therapeutic enrichment activities, respite and short–term crisis care. As Founder and Executive Director, Ms. Lake serves as chief administrative officer of the organization. She oversees new program development, financial stability and case management and treatment services offered by the organization. She reports regularly to the Board of Trustees on the progress of the organization. **Career Steps:** Executive Director – Founder, Passage Homes (1991–Present); Co–Director / Founder / Advocate, Parenthesis Family Advocates (1984–1991); Co–Director / Founder / Advocate, Youth Advocate Services (1976–1984). **Associations & Accomplishments:** Ohio Family Care Association; Ohio Association Child Care Agencies; National Black Child Institute; National Association Black Social Workers. **Education:** Attending, Ohio Diocese School of Biblical Theology; Licensed Social Worker (1990). **Personal:** Three children: Dale Bridges, Maleehah Bridges–McDowell, Atiba W.S. Jones. Ms. Lake enjoys teaching Sunday school and sewing.

Psychological Associates, Inc.®
The Dimensional Training System:®
results through people-skills

Joseph J. LaMantia
Regional Vice President – Eastern Region
Psychological Associates, Inc.
8201 Maryland Avenue
St. Louis, MO 63105
(314) 862–9300
Fax: (314) 862–0477

8099

Business Information: Psychological Associates is a full–service human resource development firm with a 35–year history of helping organizations become more effective and productive. Serving clients large and small, public and private, national and international, Psychological Associates is an international leader in its industry — with regional offices and affiliates across the U.S. and abroad. As Regional Vice President – Eastern Region, Mr. LaMantia oversees all Sales and administration of this division. **Career Steps:** Regional Vice President – Eastern Region, Psychological Associates, Inc. (1990–Present); President, American Reading Consultants, Inc. (1985–1990); National Director of Instruction, Evelyn Wood Reading Dynamics (1975–1985). **Associations & Accomplishments:** Speaker on Learning Styles and Leadership Development at association meetings and workshops; Facilitator and consultant to many Fortune 500 companies; Rotary #11, St. Louis, Missouri; American Association of Training and Development; Sales and Marketing Executives of St. Louis. **Education:** University of Missouri – St. Louis, B.A. (1971); University of Illinois, Carbondale, Illinois, Graduate; Maryville University – Washington University, St. Louis, Certificate in Education. **Personal:** Five children: Angela Mers, Elizabeth, Christopher, Jason, and Dominic.

Kenneth P. Leasure
Human Resources Systems Manager
Group Health Cooperative
521 Wall Street
Seattle, WA 98121–1524
(206) 448–2734
Fax: (206) 448–5963
EMAIL: See Below

8099

Business Information: Group Health Cooperative is a health maintenance organization, consisting of two hospitals and over 30 clinics. Holding various management positions with GHC since 1986, Ken Leasure was appointed to his current position as Human Resources Systems Manager in 1993. In this capacity he is responsible for the overall development and implementation for all personnel processes and training programs. Internet users can reach him via: KLEASURE@ACC.GHC.ORG **Career Steps:** Group Health Cooperative: Human Resources Systems Manager (1993–Present), Senior Systems Analyst (1990–1993), Payroll Manager (1986–1990). **Associations & Accomplishments:** Human Resource Systems Professionals; International Human Resource Systems Professionals **Education:** Milligan College, M.S. (1976). **Personal:** Mr. Leasure enjoys writing poetry, camping and hiking in his leisure time.

Sharon Legge
Administrator
Professional Therapy Services
5314 George Washington Memorial Highway
Yorktown, VA 23692
(804) 898–4325
Fax: (804) 890–3117

8099

Business Information: Professional Therapy Services is a certified rehabilitation agency that contracts with five school systems, seven nursing homes, three home health agencies, and two hospitals. The Center provides physical therapy, occupational therapy, speech therapy, counseling, massage therapy, and consulting services. As Administrator, Ms. Legge is responsible for all aspects of the Center's operations, including contracting professional services and all management operations. **Career Steps:** Administrator, Professional Therapy Services (1991–Present); Staff Physical Therapist, Commonwealth Health Care (1990–1991); Director of Outpatient Services, NDC Medical Center (1984–1985); Senior Physical Therapist, Williamsburg Community Hospital (1979–1984). **Associations & Accomplishments:** American Physical Therapy Association. **Education:** Duquesne: M.A. in Psychology (1989), B.S. in Physical Therapy. **Personal:** Married to David L. in 1985. Ms. Legge enjoys reading, nutrition, and attending success seminars.

Alan M. Lesselroth, M.D.
Founder, President, and Chief Executive Officer
Mountain Diagnostics
800 Shadow Lane
Las Vegas, NV 89106–4123
(702) 366–9700
Fax: Please mail or call

8099

Business Information: Mountain Diagnostics is an international medical diagnostic imaging firm. Starting out as a joint venture with local hospitals, Mountain Diagnostics is not currently associated with a hospital, but in the near future will be affiliating with two area hospitals. Established in 1988, Mountain Diagnostics currently employs 105 people. A practicing physician since 1970 and Board–Certified in Radiology, Dr. Lesselroth founded Mountain Diagnostics in 1988. Serving as President and Chief Executive Officer, he is responsible for all aspects of operations. Future plans include establishing an advertising agency and a separate maintenance corporation. Established in 1988, Mountain Diagnostics employs 105 people. **Career Steps:** President/Chief Executive Officer/Founder, Mountain Diagnostics (19–Present); Staff Diagnostic Radiologist, Steinberg Diagnostic Imaging (1981–1988); Diagnostic Radiologist, Community Radiology Oncology Medical (1974–1981); Consulting Radiologist, Uniform Health Services Administration (1975–Present); Douglas Aircraft, Missile and Space Division, St. Monica (1964); General Dynamics, San Diego, CA (1963). **Associations & Accomplishments:** RSNA; American College of Radiology. **Education:** New York Medical College, M.D. (1970); University of California – Los Angeles, M.S. in Physics/Engineering; City University of New York, Brooklyn Polytechnic Institute, B.Sc. in Physics. **Personal:** Married to Lynn in 1964. Two children: Blake Justin and Lori Anne. Dr. Lesselroth enjoys scuba diving, flying, auto racing, exotic cars, music, art, cartooning, and writing.

Laura Lewis
Senior Director
Southwest Community Health Systems
18697 Bagley Road
Middleburg Heights, OH 44130
(216) 816–6710
Fax: (216) 816–6716

8099

Business Information: Southwest Community Health Systems is comprised of a full–service community hospital and its subsidiaries. As Senior Director, Ms. Lewis is operationally responsible for home health, hospice, home infusion therapy, Emergency Room, Urgicare, occupational health, geriatric assessment programs, and the Retail Pharmacy. **Career Steps:** Southwest Community Health Systems: Senior Director (1994–Present), Care Center Leader (Present), Assistant to the President (1990–1994), Administrative Fellow (1989–1990). **Associations & Accomplishments:** American College of Healthcare Administrators; Healthcare Administrators of Northeast Ohio; University of Pittsburgh Alumni. **Education:** University of Pittsburgh: M.B.A. (1989), M.H.A. (1989), B.S. (1986). **Personal:** Married to Joseph in 1994. Ms. Lewis enjoys skiing, golf, and reading.

Marc R. Linzer
Director of Organizational Development
Contact
1400 E. Southern, Suite 301
Tempe, AZ 85282–5679
(602) 831–3930
Fax: Please mail or call

8099

Business Information: Contact is a behavioral health organization providing mental health services for businesses, as well as employee wellness programs and systems. Currently, Contact holds 95 contracts with Fortune 500 companies in which they have set up in–house wellness programs. Contact pioneered the Traumatic Events Counseling Program ten years ago, specializing in CISD training for fire departments, rescue personnel, police officers, and anyone directly involved in a crisis situation. Contact is the largest behavioral health system in Arizona and is owned by Samarian Health Care. Established in 1979, they have over 100 employees and over 365,000 covered lives (persons eligible for service). As Director of Organizational Development, Dr. Linzer is responsible for the managing of the systems, assuring that the services are properly and effectively delivered and also delivering services himself as well. He is also the director of Outcome Research and Traumatic Events coordinator, arranging the CISD programs during crisis situations. **Career Steps:** Contact (1995–Present): Director of Organizational Development (1995–Present), Regional Manager (1992–95); Psychologist, Offices of Marc Linzer (1987–96). **Associations & Accomplishments:** American Psychological Association; Board

Member, Southwest Critical Incident Rebriefing Association; Advisory Board Member, Free Arts for Abused Children. **Education:** University of Arizona, Ph.D. (1986), State University of New York – New Paltz, M.S. in Education; University of Arizona, B.S. **Personal:** Married to Adrienne in 1969. Two children: Janine Danielle and Sage Maxwell. Dr. Linzer enjoys art, antiques, playing piano, rose gardening, meditation, yoga, and swimming.

Adonna Lowe

Vice President – Patient Care/Nursing
St. Joseph Healthcare System
601 E. Martin Luther King Jr. Blvd.
Albuquerque, NM 87102
(505) 244–8107
Fax: (505) 244–8162
8099

Business Information: St. Joseph Healthcare System is the management office overseeing a group of four hospitals in the Albuquerque, New Mexico area. Owned by Sisters of Charities, the St. Joseph Healthcare System is responsible for 560–beds and rehabilitative and home care services, in addition to surgical, emergency, and outpatient activities. Established in 1903, the System reports annual revenue of $130 million and currently employs 2,200 professionals. With twenty–five years experience in nursing, Ms. Lowe joined the St. Joseph Healthcare System as Vice President – Patient Care/Nursing in 1991. She is the senior nursing executive for the multi–hospital system, responsible for all patient care and nursing activities. **Career Steps:** Vice President – Patient Care/Nursing, St. Joseph Healthcare System (1991–Present); Assistant Administrator, Baptist Regional Health Center (1987–1991); Assistant Vice President, Baylor Healthcare System (1983–1987); Regional Administrator, Wesley Medical Center (1970–1993). **Associations & Accomplishments:** New Mexico Organization of Nurse Executives; American Organization of Nurse Executives; American College of Healthcare Executives; Licensed Pilot. **Education:** Wichita State University, M.A. (1975); Kansas Newman College, B.A. (1973); Wesley School of Nursing, Nursing Diploma (1970). **Personal:** Married to Rod. Two children: Steve and Kelsey. Ms. Lowe enjoys flying, skiing, and reading.

Nick Macchione

Chief Executive Officer
Newark EMA HIV Health Services Planning Council
315 North Sixth Street, 2nd Floor, P.O. Box 7007
Newark, NJ 07107
(201) 485–5220
Fax: (201) 485–5085
8099

Business Information: Newark EMA HIV Health Services Planning Council is a federally–funded health services planning organization. An executive staff member with the Newark Health Department since 1992, Nick Macchione was appointed as Chief Executive Officer for the HIV Council in 1993. The Council prioritizes care and treatment services for a $12 million budget in Northern New Jersey. **Career Steps:** Chief Executive Officer, Newark EMA HIV Health Services Planning Council (1993–Present); Program Director, Newark Health Department (1992–1993). **Associations & Accomplishments:** American College of Healthcare Executives; American Hospital Association; American Public Health Association; New Jersey AIDS Partnership of the Community Foundation of New Jersey; American Management Association. **Education:** Columbia University, Studies in Progress — M.S. in Executive Health Policy; New York University, M.S. in Health Services Management; Rutgers State University, B.A. in Biology.

Charles P. Magal, M.D.

Partner
Centre Radiology, P.A.
600 Memorial Avenue
Cumberland, MD 21502
(301) 334–2155 Ext. 230
Fax: (301) 724–7429
8099

Business Information: Centre Radiology, P.A. is a medical–diagnostic radiology practice specializing in performing and interpreting X–rays to assist the health care field in medical diagnosis. Established in 1974, Centre Radiology, P.A. currently employs 16 people. As Partner, Dr. Magal is responsible for the interpretation of X–rays. Concurrent with his position, he serves as Radiologist at Memorial Hospital & Medical Center and Meyersdale Medical Center and as Radiology Chairman at Garrett County Memorial Hospital. **Career Steps:** Partner, Centre Radiology, P.A. (1989–Present); Radiologist, Meyersdale Medical Center (1993–Present); Radiologist, Memorial Hospital and Medical Center (1989–Present); Radiology Chairman, Garrett County Memorial Hospital (1989–Present); Associate, Groover, Cristie & Merit, P.C. (1988–1989). **Associations & Accomplishments:** American College of Radiology; American Medical Association; Society of Cardiovascular & Interventional Radiology. **Education:** George Washington School of Medicine, M.D. (1982); Goshen College, B.S.; George Washington University Medical Center, M.S., Clinical Instructor in Radiology (1987–1989), Fellowship in Cross–Section Imaging (1987–1988); M.D. Anderson Hospital & Tumor Institute, Fellowship in Interventional Radiology (1986–1987). **Personal:** Married to Helen in 1989. One child: Angelina. Dr. Magal enjoys studying Greek and restoring historic houses.

Sandra K. Mahkorn, MD, MPH, MS

President
SKM Health Matters, Inc.
3050 South Superior Street
Milwaukee, WI 53207
(414) 482–0225
Fax: (414) 482–0225
8099

Business Information: SKM Health Matters, Inc. is a private consulting concern located in Milwaukee, Wisconsin. The corporation consults on health care, health policy administration, cost–effective approaches to health care delivery for high risk patients, provider network development, staff management, containment strategies, and risk management. As President, Dr. Mahkorn does all of the consulting on health care and health policies contracted by SKM Health Matters. She helps clients design health care systems, develop quality and utilization management programs, cost containment strategies, MIS systems, and risk management. Due to her extensive career in health care policy, administration, academics and medical practice, Dr. Mahkorn is able to advise clients on provider network development, grant proposals, presentations to potential investors, and the development of innovative and cost–effective approaches to health care delivery for high risk patients. After working with the U.S. Department of Health, the U.S. Public Health Service, and with members of Congress, Dr. Mahkorn has the knowledge needed to assist a diverse client base in the administration of their health care policies and practices. **Career Steps:** President, SKM Health Matters, Inc. (1995–Present); Chief Medical Officer, FHC Managed Health Systems; Associate Director Presidents' Council on Competitiveness, The White House – Washington, D.C. (1992–1993); Deputy Assistant Secretary for Public Health Policy, Department of Health /Human Services (1991–1992). **Associations & Accomplishments:** American College of Physician Executives; Wisconsin Medical Examining Board; American College of Preventive Medicine; Dr. Mahkorn has been appointed to numerous national committees such as: National Policy Forum, Policy Council on Health Care Reform and Heritage Foundation Physicians Council; Articles have appeared in a variety of publications; Media presentations and appearances to many health care organizations. **Education:** Tulane University, MPH (1990); University of Wisconsin – Milwaukee: M.D. (1981), M.S. in Urban Affairs; M.S. in Educational Psychology, B.A. **Personal:** One child: Gretchen Patricia. Dr. Mahkorn enjoys spending time with her daughter.

Lesa Malott

Controller
Nacogdoches Medical Center
4920 Northeast Stallings
Nacogdoches, TX 75961
(409) 568–3177
Fax: Please mail or call
8099

Business Information: Nacogdoches Medical Center is a 150–bed, full–service healthcare facility, providing diagnosis and treatment of patients. As Controller, Ms. Malott is responsible for all financial activities, including payroll, taxes, accounts receivable, and accounts payable. **Career Steps:** Controller, Nacogdoches Medical Center (1995–Present); Assistant Manager, Allied Finance (1993–1995); Accountant, Taylor Service Company (Feb. 1993 – Oct. 1993). **Associations & Accomplishments:** United Way. **Education:** Steven F. Austin State University, B.B.A. in Accounting (1992). **Personal:** Married to Mitch in 1994. Ms. Malott enjoys skiing (water & snow), reading, dancing, and exercise.

Kenneth L. Manning, PharmD

Corporate Director
Apria Pharmacy Network
350 North Lantana Street
Camarillo, CA 93010
(805) 388–2811
Fax: (805) 987–9952
8099

Business Information: Apria Pharmacy Network, a subsidiary of Apria Healthcare, provides respiratory medications via nebulizers that are delivered directly to the patient at home. As Corporate Director, Dr. Manning is responsible for the operational and sales related activities for two pharmacies with a national scope. He locates and develops new medication lines, creates tools for selling, communication, and marketing efforts to organizations outside the network and other clients. **Career Steps:** Corporate Director, Apria Pharmacy Network (1994–Present); Caremark, Inc: Zone Operations Manager (1991–1992), General Manager (1989–1991). **Associations & Accomplishments:** National Association of Retail Druggists; National Association of Medical Equipment Suppliers. **Education:** University of California at San Francisco, PharmD (1983). **Personal:** Married to Janette in 1994. Five children: Tyler, Raymond, Lauren, Mark, and Camille. Dr. Manning enjoys hiking, cycling, and reading.

Ms. Patricia A. Markle

Director of Patient and Family Services
Fletcher Allen Health Care
30 West Oak Hill Road
Williston, VT 05495
(802) 656–3553
Fax: Please mail or call
8099

Business Information: Fletcher Allen Health Care is a healthcare system network, providing outpatient clinic hospitals and physician group practices. In her current role, Patricia Markle oversees all administrative staff and operations activities for the Departments of Patient and Family Services and Social Work Services. **Career Steps:** Fletcher Allen Health Care, Patient and Family Services: Director (1993–Present), Supervisor (1980–1993), Social Worker (1973–1980). **Associations & Accomplishments:** Vermont/New Hampshire Hospital Social Work Directors; Chittenden County Adult Assessment Team; Chittenden County Child Protection Network. **Education:** Trinity College, B.A. (1961). **Personal:** Two children: Joshua and Seth. Ms. Markle enjoys cross country skiing, horseback riding and reading.

Antonio Martins Cortada

International Affairs Manager
Unimed do Brasil
Alameda Santos 1827–9 Andar
Sao Paulo, SP, Brazil 01419–909
55–11–245–9787
Fax: 55–11–245–9880
Email: See Below
8099

Business Information: Unimed do Brasil is a cooperative organization providing healthcare for over 10 million users. The Organization offers the services of 77,000 doctors and manages a complex of 31 hospitals in addition to several companies like insurance, medical transportation and medical supplies. Unimed does business in Brazil, Paraguay and Colombia. As Internal Affairs Manager, Mr. Martins Cortada is responsible for supervising all international business, establishing commercial and institutional contacts and handling strategic planning. Established in 1987, Unimed employs in Brazil 28,000 people with annual sales of over $2.2 billion. Established in 1967, Unimed do Brasil employs 26,000 people with annual sales of $2.2 billion. **Career Steps:** Internal Affairs Manager, Unimed Do Brasil (1994–Present); Economics Teacher, Mackenzie University (1989–94); Business Consulting Manager, Trevisan Auditing & Consulting (1988–93); Economics Teacher, University of Sao Paulo – USP (1986–87). **Education:** University of Sao Paulo, Master (1987); University of Sao Paulo – USP, Bachelor of Economics. **Personal:** Married to Beatriz Maria Luchetti in 1989. One child: Guido Luchetti. Mr. Martins Cortada enjoys ceramics and soaring.

Valerie B. McCaleb

Vice President of Training and Development
Total Rehab
1411 Sherwood Forest Drive
West Carrollton, OH 45449–2306
(800) 998–8900
Fax: (513) 866–9857
8099

Business Information: Total Rehab is a contract Rehab company providing occupational, physical, and speech therapy services to hospitals, nursing homes, schools, and clinics. As Vice President of Training and Development, Mrs. McCaleb develops programs, orientates and trains employees, negotiates therapy contracts, and assists with marketing, promoting intraprofessional and interprofessional exchange of information, techniques, new theories, and treatment procedures.She is also the Vice President of Operations for West Texas Rehab Management, a subsidiary of Total Rehab. **Career Steps:** Total Rehab: Vice President of Training and Development (1995–Present), Regional Director (1993–1995); Staff Occupational Therapist, St. Elizabeth Hospital. **Associations & Accomplishments:** American Occupational Therapy Association; Ohio Half Arabian Horse Association; Advisory Committee for Sinclair College; International Arabian Horse Association. **Education:** Northeast Louisiana University, B.S (1991). **Personal:** Married to Marty in 1979. Three children: Shawn, Kamilah, and Joey. Mrs. McCaleb enjoys English horseback riding, running, and weightlifting.

Barbara A. McCann
Health Outcomes and Managed Care Consultant
–Independent–
1508 Oakwood Avenue
Highland Park, IL 60035
(847) 266–0125
Fax: Please mail or call

8099

Business Information: Combining several years of national experience in home care and other outpatient services, Ms. McCann is currently a consultant in the development of measures of health outcomes, cost, and utilization. Other duties include reporting and monitoring programs for use by a variety of providers of health care, as well as purchasers of care to demonstrate value for health care expenditure. Ms. McCann also works with manufacturers, and professional associations to develop national standards of care, and monitoring processes. Prior to becoming an independent consultant, Ms. McCann was the Vice President of Outcomes Management and Analytic Services at Caremark, Inc., a $2 billion international health care company, providing home care, orthopedic clinic, renal dialysis, home infusion, physician practice management, PPO, and disease state management services. Ms. McCann's national experience began at the Joint Commission on the Accreditation of Healthcare, where she was the director of the Home Care and Hospice Accreditation Programs, developing the first national standards and survey processes for both industries. Addressing national and international audiences, Ms. McCann has made over 300 presentations focused on health care quality and measurement of patient outcomes. She regularly publishes results of clinical research and articles addressing changes in the health industry's accountability for patient care. **Career Steps:** Independent Health Care Consultant (1996); Vice President, Outcomes Management & Analytic Services, Caremark, Inc. (1990–1996); Director – Home Care and Hospice Accreditation Programs, Joint Commission on the Accreditation of Healthcare (1981–1990). **Associations & Accomplishments:** Member of national task forces working with government and research organizations developing national standardized measures of home care, clinical patient outcomes, and patient satisfaction; Recipient of awards from the National Hospice Organization, the National Home Care Association, and the Health Care Financing Administration for exemplary work in the field of ensuring quality Hospice Care in the U.S. **Education:** University of New Mexico–Albuquerque, M.A. (1981); University of California–Berkeley, B.A., Phi Beta Kappa (1974). **Personal:** Married to Eugene Scanzera in 1983. Two children: Alexander and Evan. Ms. McCann enjoys attending sporting events and travel.

Pate L. McCartney, D.S.W.
Executive Director
First Mental Health, Inc.
501 Great Circle Road, Suite 300
Nashville, TN 37228
(615) 256–3400
Fax: (615) 256–8071
EMAIL: See Below

8099

Business Information: First Mental Health, Inc. provides managed health care services, including utilization management, quality review, information systems and claims processing for medical, behavioral and long–term care customers. First Mental Health is a subsidiary of FIRST HEALTH the largest Third Part Administrator of health benefits in the country. FIRST HEALTH is a subsidiary of First Data Corporation, a health care, merchant and financial services company spanning 100 countries. As Executive Director, Dr. McCartney is responsible for the overall budgetary, clinical, and administrative operation of the national managed–care firm. Additional responsibilities include supervision of more than 100 staff and 1,000 subcontractors, and administering the Company's contracts in 14 states. Internet users can reach him via: 74507,2300@compuserve.com. **Career Steps:** First Mental Health, Inc: Executive Director (1993–Present), Director of Development (1993–1995); Massachusetts Department of Mental Health: Director of Policy and Planning (1990–1993), Director of Mental Health (1982–1990); Mental Health Coordinator, Berkshire Community Action Council (1980–1982); Tennessee Department of Mental Health (1975–1977). **Associations & Accomplishments:** Faculty, and Thesis Advisor, Smith College School of Social Work; Adjunct Faculty, Adelphi University School of Social Work; Author of Five Publications on Mental Health related subjects; National Association of Social Workers; National Alliance for Mental Illness; Middle Tennessee Health Care Executives Association; Academy of Certified Social Workers; Frequently presents at national and state conferences on managed health care. **Education:** Columbia University: Doctorate in Social Welfare (1988); Masters of Science in Social Work (1979); Rhodes College, B.A. in Psychology (1975). **Personal:** Dr. McCartney enjoys golf, downhill skiing, biking, tennis, and camping.

Preston Thomas McClain III
Center Director
Southeast Raleigh Center for Community Health & Development
P.O. Box 28716
Raleigh, NC 27611
(919) 856–5270
Fax: (919) 856–6575

8099

Business Information: Southeast Raleigh Center for Community Health & Development provides a variety of programs and services aimed at improving the overall health and wellness of the community. Joining the Agency as Center Director in 1992, Mr. McClain is responsible for the day–to–day activities of the Center, particularly focusing on quality patient services delivery and care. **Career Steps:** Center Director, Southeast Raleigh Center for Community Health & Development (1992–Present). **Associations & Accomplishments:** University of North Carolina General Alumni Association; Martin Street Baptist Church. **Education:** North Carolina Central University, M.P.A. (1993); University of North Carolina – Chapel Hill, B.A. in History. **Personal:** Mr. McClain enjoys sports (i.e. basketball, tennis, swimming).

James H. McNierney
Director of Information Technologies
Value Behavioral Health
433 River Street
Troy, NY 12180–2250
(518) 271–2822
Fax: (518) 266–3299
EMAIL: See Below

8099

Business Information: Value Behavioral Health is a managed health care firm, specializing in managing substance abuse and psychiatric claims. As Director of Information Technologies, Mr. McNierney is responsible for the management, design, and implementation of advancing technologies to solve business problems or support existing business processes. **Career Steps:** Value Behavioral Health: Director of Information Technologies (1995–Present), Director of Information Systems (1994–1995); American Psych Management: Manager of I.S. (1992–1994), Data Analyst, (1992). **Education:** Dutchess Community College (1991); SUNY – Stoney Brook (1977). **Personal:** One child: James Kenneth. Mr. McNierney enjoys playing music, reading, writing, and baseball.

Ms. Sherrie Messer

Administrative Manager
Norman Peterson Associates
287 4th Street, Suite 4
Ashland, OR 97520–2091
(541) 488–0162
Fax: (503) 488–5408

8099

Business Information: Norman Peterson Associates provides an early return–to–work program for workers injured on the job, working with companies to design and oversee implementation of the OUR System. NPA currently operates in fifteen states, including Hawaii, and has implemented over 200 OUR Systems in those states. Established in 1988, Norman Peterson Associates reports annual revenue of $2.5 million and currently employs 13 people. As Administrative Manager, Ms. Messer is responsible for the management of the overall daily functioning, coordination of various areas of the Company, project development, and long range planning. **Career Steps:** Administrative Manager, Norman Peterson Associates (1995–Present); Senior Programs Director, ACCESS, Inc. (1989–1995); Operations and Sales Director, Southern Oregon Goodwill Industries (1982–1985); Executive Director, Rogue Council Camp Fire (1978–1983). **Associations & Accomplishments:** Soroptimist International; National Association of Meals Programs; Advisor, Venture Club of Medford; Previously nine years on School District Budget Committee, three years as Chair. **Education:** Northwest Christian College, B.S. (1993). **Personal:** Married to Marvin L. Messer in 1961. Three children: Trasi (Messer) Fugate, Mara and Korby Messer. Ms. Messer enjoys community service projects and reading.

Paul Meyer

Executive Director
Western Montana Mental Health Center
T9 Fort Missoula
Missoula, MT 59801
(406) 728–6870
Fax: (406) 728–6819

8099

Business Information: Western Montana Mental Health Center is a regional mental health care facility serving seven counties within Montana. The Center provides mental health and substance abuse services, as well as offering programs for children (i.e., group homes, foster care, adolescent alcohol and drug treatment) and outpatient services for adults. Supportive living, emergency care, and medical support are also readily available. As Executive Director, Mr. Meyer serves as the chief operating officer reporting to the Board of Directors. His duties include dealing with all aspects of the office, including administration and oversight of supportive living, emergency care, medical support, and outpatient programs. He also manages the business office, finances, and the Purchasing Department. **Career Steps:** Executive Director, Western Montana Mental Health Center (1990–Present); Mental Health Center Director, Central South Dakota, Pierre (1978–1980); Mental Health Director, Dane County, WI (1980–1990). **Associations & Accomplishments:** Treasurer, State Council of Mental Health Centers (1991–Current); President, Garden City Community Housing Development Corporation (1994–Current); Chair, Missoula Correctional Services (1994–Current). **Education:** University of Chicago, M.A. (1972); Fordham University, B.A. (1969). **Personal:** Married to Peg Shea in 1991. Five children: Suzie, Adam, Patrick, Paul, and James. Mr. Meyer enjoys hiking rafting, fishing, and gardening.

Bessy C. Miller, M.S., P.T.
Vice President and Co–Owner
Therapy Network Resources, P.C.
9575 West Higgins, Suite 300
Rosemont, IL 60018
(847) 318–8814
Fax: (847) 318–8821

8099

Business Information: Therapy Network Resources, P.C. provides contract therapists and social workers to homes, hospitals, nursing homes, schools, and out–patient clinics. Mrs. Miller co–founded TNR in 1988, serving as Vice President and performing various administrative and marketing functions, overseeing daily operations, and providing executive leadership. In 1993 she established Therapy Network Home Care, P.C., a Certified Medicare Home Health Agency, providing nursing, therapy, and social work services to home–bound patients. She is also the President and Co–Owner of Fox Physical Therapy, offering out–patient physical therapy services, and Therapy Network International, recruiting therapists from abroad for permanent placement in American health care facilities. **Career Steps:** Vice President and Co–Owner, Therapy Network Resources, P.C. (1988–Present); President and Co–Owner, Therapy Network Home Care, P.C. (1993–Present); President and Co–Owner, Fox Physical Therapy (1995–Present); Vice President and Co–Owner, Therapy Network International (1995–Present); Physical Therapy Consultant, Allied Health Services (1987–1988); Chief of Physical Therapy, Northwest Orthopedic Rehabilitation Center (1982–1987); Staff Physical Therapist, St. Mary's Hospital – Chicago (1981–1982); Director of Physical Therapy, Therapeutic Consultants (1979–1981); Physical Therapist, Learning Center (1977–1979). **Associations & Accomplishments:** American Management Association. **Education:** DePaul University – Chicago, M.S. in Rehabilitation Management (1993); University of the Philippines, B.S. in Physical Therapy (1977). **Personal:** Married to Charles D. in 1990. One child: Jay Robert. Mrs. Miller enjoys reading, theater, movies, bowling.

Robert C. Miner

Chief Executive Officer
Space Coast Orthopaedic Center
270 North Sykes Creek Parkway
Merrit Island, FL 32953–3427
(407) 459–1446
Fax: (407) 452–1261

8099

Business Information: Space Coast Orthopaedic Center is a full–service medical facility specializing in orthopaedic treatment, surgery, care, and rehabilitation. As Chief Executive Officer, Mr. Miner is responsible for diversified administrative activities, including finance, accounting, and strategic planning. **Career Steps:** Chief Executive Officer, Space Coast Orthopaedic Center (1995–Present); Chief Executive Officer, R&D Innovations Corporation (1986–1995); Chairman of the Board, Mountain Crest Marketing (1989–1991); United States Air Force (1979–1986). **Associations & Accomplishments:** American Heart Association; Local Small Business Volunteer; Recognized in numerous Who's Who publications from around the world. **Education:** Florida State University, B.S.; Herott Watt University, Edinburg, Scotland, Pursuing M.B.A.; Community College of the Air Force, A.S. in Nursing and Emergency Medicine. **Personal:** Married to Pamela. Mr. Miner enjoys music, writing and gardening.

Mr. Mark B. Moody

Vice President
O'Pin Systemems
7900 International Drive, Suite 635
Bloomington, MN 55435
(612) 854–3360 (612) 883–2868
Fax: (612) 854–3072

8099

Business Information: O'Pin Systemems is a managed care information services firm, providing data anaylsis, physician profiting, decision support and executive information services for the managed health care industry. Established in 1985, O'Pin Systemems currently employs 60 people. As Vice President, Mr. Moody is responsible for business development including business partnerships and alliances, distributor channels and new market entry strategy. **Career Steps:** Vice President, O'Pin Systemems (1995–Present); Vice President of Business Development, Aetna International in New Zealand (1993–1995); Assistant Vice President, Aetna Health Plans (1991–1993); Executive Director, Aetna Health Plan of Northern Ohio (1989–1991). **Associations & Accomplishments:** Beta Gamma Sigma – Business Honors Fraternity. **Education:** University of Wisconsin – Madison (1989); University of California – Santa Cruz, B.A. in Economics with Honors. **Personal:** Married to Candace Moody. Two children: Jonathan and Matthew. Mr. Moody enjoys coaching, camping, and travel.

Ed G. Mury

Vice President of Contract Services
Acadian Ambulance Services
P.O. Box 98000
Lafayette, LA 70509–8000
(318) 267–3333
Fax: (318) 267–1594
EMail: See Below

8099

Business Information: Acadian Ambulance Services is a private emergency medical service company. The Company provides ground and air ambulance transportation to roughly 2 million residents in Southern Louisiana. As Vice President of Contract Services, Mr. Mury handles all corporate development and contracting of medical staff for oil and gas, industrial construction, and movie companies. Additionally, he handles internal development and the credential process. Internet users can reach him via: EGMury@aol.com. **Career Steps:** Acadian Ambulance Services: Vice President of Contract Services (1991–Present), Community Relations Supervisor (1990–1991), Flight Paramedic (1989–1990). **Associations & Accomplishments:** National Registry of Emergency Medical Technicians; Commission on Accreditation of Ambulance Services; Chamber of Commerce President's Club. **Education:** University of Alabama – Birmingham, B.S. in Health Services Administration (1987).

Blue Dolphin
Health Care

Micheline Nader

President
Blue Dolphin Health Care
6800 College Boulevard, Suite 440
Overland Park, KS 66211
(913) 344–0744
Fax: (913) 344–0745

8099

Business Information: Blue Dolphin Health Care is a health care management consultancy, serving physicians, therapists and health care institutions throughout the U.S. As President, Micheline Nader oversees all facets of the Firm, including serving major clients with management strategies. Concurrent with her private consulting practice, Ms. Nader serves as the Chief Operations Officer for Carewell Corporation, a major client of Blue Dolphin Health Care. Carewell Corporation owns and manages long–term and skilled–care health facilities throughout the U.S. and Canada. As Chief Operations Officer, she provides the overall executive administration for all Carewell facilities located in Oklahoma (currently nine), with primary duties involving quality care assurance, cost control, regulatory compliance, program development, and Human Resources administration. **Career Steps:** President, Blue Dolphin Health Care (1994–Present); Vice President of Operations, Carex – Canada (1990–1994); President, IMEC Sante – France (1985–1989); Assistant Director, American University Hospital (1978–1981). **Education:** Universite Dauphine – Paris, DESS in Health Services Management (1989); New York State University: M.P.H. (1978), B.S. in Nursing. **Personal:** Married to Francois Nader, M.D. in 1979. Two children: Ralph and Jessica.

Gerry Nevill

Director of the Respiratory Care Department
Fox Subacute Center
2644 Bristol Road
Warrington, PA 18976–1404
(215) 343–2700 (800) 424–7220
Fax: (215) 343–8023

8099

Business Information: Fox Subacute Center is a subacute rehabilitation center specializing in patients requiring ventilators and/or pulmonary care. As Director of the Respiratory Care Department, Mr. Nevill is responsible for admissions, assessments, marketing, hiring, counseling, and policies and procedures. Mr. Nevill also lectures at hospitals and state shows. He is a clinical coordinator for Gwynedd Mercy College and lectures nursing students regarding the proper procedures for dealing with ventilated patients. **Career Steps:** Director of Respiratory Care Department, Fox Subacute Center (1994–Present); Sacred Heart Hospital: Director (1990–1994), Supervisor (1988–1990). **Associations & Accomplishments:** American Association of Respiratory Care; Pennsylvania Society of Respiratory Care; National Board of Respiratory Care; National Safety Council; Tri–State Society for Cardiovascular and Pulmonary Rehabilitation. **Education:** Thomas A. Edison State College: B.S. (1995), A.A. (1992); Gwynedd Mercy College, Respiratory Certification (1986); Registered Respiratory Therapist (1990); CRTT (1986). **Personal:** One child: Carl Andrew. Mr. Nevill enjoys karate and soccer.

Joseph I.M. Njamfa, Pharm.D.

Clinical Pharmacist
Dameron Hospital
3067 Burl Hollow Drive
Stockton, CA 95209
(209) 472–1632
Fax: Please mail or call

8099

Business Information: Dameron Hospital is a medical facility providing tertiary care and an in–house pharmacy. As a Clinical Pharmacist, Dr. Njamfa is responsible for the distribution of pharmaceuticals and recommending cost–effective pharmaceutical therapy to physicians. Concurrent with his duties at Dameron Hospital, Joseph Njamfa serves as an adjunct professor at the University of the Pacific, teaching clinical Pharmacy; Director at Rexall Showcase International, teaching preventive health and market natural preventive health products for prevention and reversal of heart disease without surgery, weight–loss without dieting, cholesterol reduction, stabilization of blood sugar in diabetics, colds, allergy, stress, insomnia, fatigue, gum disease, indigestion and skin care. He is also an executive director at Excel Telecommunications (the fastest growing long distance company in the world), marketing discount long–distance telephone service. **Career Steps:** Clinical Pharmacist, Dameron Hospital; Director, Rexall Showcase International; Executive Director, Excel Telecommunications. **Associations & Accomplishments:** California Society of Hospital Pharmacists; Central Valley Society of Hospital Pharmacists. Education: University of California – San Francisco, Pharm.D. (1989); University of California – Los Angeles, B.S. in Biology (1985). **Personal:** Married to Dr. Lydia Njamfa, M.D. One child: Nyla. Dr. Njamta enjoys tennis and network marketing (multi–level marketing).

Janet Ann Norton

Administrative Director of Pyschiatric Services
Clean Start
919 West Wellington Street
Chicago, IL 60657–4421
(312) 477–2000
Fax: (312) 477–2002

8099

Business Information: Clean Start, affiliated with the Illinois Medical Center, is a chemical dependency treatment center, providing inpatient and outpatient psychiatric services for individuals with drug and alcohol problems. Established in 1990, Clean Start currently employs 11 people. As Administrative Director of Psychiatric Services, Ms. Norton coordinates the hiring, training, and supervision of personnel, as well as planning and implementation of the budget for Clean Start, ensuring compliance of regulatory and compensation work. **Career Steps:** Clean Start: Administrative Director of Psychiatric Services (1995–Present), Program Director (1990–1995); Director of In Patient Services, Martha Washington Hospital (1983–1989); Nurse/Counselor, Hines V.A. Hospital (1972–1983). **Associations & Accomplishments:** State Treasurer and Member of the Board of Directors, Illinois Alcohol and Other Drug Abuse Professional Certification Association, Inc. (1981–Present); NAADAC National Certification Commission; The International Certification Consortium/Alcohol and Other Drug Abuse, Inc.; Illinois Nurses Association; Paper published in the proceedings of the 31st International Institute on Prevention and Treatment of Alcoholism in Rome (1985). **Education:** National Lewis University, B.A. (1993); Northeastern University, B.A. in Sociology (1988); Triton College, A.D. in Nursing (1972). **Personal:** Two children: Julie and James Gilmour. Ms. Norton enjoys cooking, travel, and being with my grandchildren.

Robert M. Notkin, M.D., C.M., F.R.C.P. (C)

Self–Employed Professional and Consultant
Mental Health Disability Management
Suite 100–5, Fairview Mall Drive
North York, Ontario M2J 2Z1
(416) 490–8347
Fax: (419) 499–1707

8099

Business Information: Mental Health Disability Management provides occupational psychiatry and disability management consultations to self–insure and insurance companies. The Company conducts disability management and insurer's examinations for various companies in the Greater Toronto area. As Self–Employed Professional and Consultant, Dr. Notkin provides consultation to companies in regards to disability management, mental health, and independent psychiatric examinations. He has also developed and is in the process of introducing a tool which will benefit insurance companies. It will help them reduce claims costs and enable employees to return to work quicker. **Career Steps:** Self–Employed Professional and Consultant, Mental Health Disability Management (1986–Present). **Associations & Accomplishments:** Member, American Psychiatric Association; Canadian Psychiatric Association; Ontario Medical Association; Canadian Society of Medical Evaluators. **Education:** McGill University: M.D., C.M. (1982), B.Sc., F.R.C.P. (C) in Psychiatry (1986). **Personal:** Married to Heather in 1984. Three children: Harrison, Benjamin, and Hilary. Dr. Notkin enjoys skiing.

Cecelia I. O'Donnell

Vice President of Client Services
CareSYS
15 River Road
Wilton, CT 06897–4025
(954) 796–8737
Fax: (954) 796–8727

8099

Business Information: Established in 1987, CareSYS, a subsidiary of Value Health, is a provider of managed care for workers' compensation for large companies and government agencies. As Vice President of Client Services, Mrs. O'Donnell is responsible for network development and maintenance, sales, marketing, new account implementation, and training. **Career Steps:** Vice President of Client Services, CareSYS (1995–Present); Director Provider Systems, Preferred Works, Inc. (1992–1995); Director RM/QA, Danbury Hospital (1983–1991); Head Nurse, Ortho, Lake Charles Memorial Hospital (1975–1983). **Associations & Accomplishments:** Who's Who in American Nursing (1990–1991). **Education:** Olney Central College, A.S.N. (1975); MacNeese State University; Western Connecticut University. **Personal:** Married to Terrance in 1992. Mrs. O'Donnell enjoys skiing, reading, and travel.

Kim D. Osterhoudt
Director of Healthcare Access Management
United Healthcare System
15 South Ninth Street
Newark, NJ 07107
(201) 268–8144
Fax: (201) 484–9741

8099

Business Information: United Healthcare System is a network including an adult hospital – United Medical Center, the Children's Hospital of New Jersey, and five Family Health Centers. United Healthcare System currently employs more than 1,700 people. Ms. Osterhoudt is responsible for the management of admissions, registration, and financial counseling. She directs staff in the Ambulatory Care sites, Emergency Department, and inpatient areas. **Career Steps:** Director of Healthcare Access Management, United Healthcare System (1994–Present); Director of Customer Service, United Hospitals Medical Center (1991–1994); Director of Business Services and Contract Performance, University of Medicine and Dentistry of New Jersey (1988–1991). **Associations & Accomplishments:** Trustee, Rutgers Graduate School of Business/Management Alumni Association; National Association Healthcare Access Management; Director, Rutgers Minority Investment Company; Toastmasters International; Troop Leader, Washington Rock Girl Scout Council Troop #391; New Jersey Association Healthcare Access Management; Healthcare Financial Management Association. **Education:** Rutgers Graduate School of Management, M.B.A. (1978); College of the Holy Cross, B.A. (1977). **Personal:** One child: Sara Elizabeth Osterhoudt Brown.

Javan P. Owens
Director of Operations
Professional Network Group
1511 K Street NW, Suite 949
Washington, DC 20005–1401
(202) 628–0303
Fax: (202) 628–1919

8099

Business Information: Professional Network Group is a full–service, mental health agency. Established in 1988, Professional Network Group reports annual revenue of $2 million and currently employs 30 people. A Certified Social Worker since 1993, Mr. Owens joined Professional Network Group in 1995. Serving as Director of Operations, he is responsible for providing oversight and management for all non–clinical functions of the Agency. **Career Steps:** Director of Operations, Professional Network Group (1995–Present); Admissions Coordinator, PFP KOBA Associates (1994–1995); Social Worker, Child and Family Service Division (1993–1994). **Associations & Accomplishments:** National Association of Social Workers; National Association of Black Social Workers. **Education:** Loyola University, Chicago, MSW (1993). **Personal:** Mr. Owens enjoys racquetball, reading, movies, and going to the gym.

Sherry–Anne A. Pajari–Joseph
Director of Clinical Operations
Roxbury Comprehensive Community Health Center, Inc.
435 Warren Street
Boston, MA 02119
(617) 442–7400
Fax: (617) 442–1409
EMail: See Below

8099

Business Information: Roxbury Comprehensive Community Health Center, Inc. is a non–profit community health center providing various types of care, including ambulatory. As Director of Clinical Operations, Ms. Pajari–Joseph oversees all clinical operations for the six–site organization, including leadership support, administrative duties, report filing, and nursing staff supervision. Internet users can reach her via: SAPajari@AOL.com. **Career Steps:** Roxbury Comprehensive Community Health Center, Inc.: Director of Clinical Operations (1994–Present), Director of Utilization Management (1993–1994); Utilization Management Nurse, FHP of New Mexico (1990–1993); Vice President, Pajari Instruments, Ltd. (Present). **Associations & Accomplishments:** American College of Healthcare Executives; Secretary, Association of Community/Migrant Healthcare Nurses of New England. **Education:** Chapman University, Master's of Science (summa cum laude) in Healthcare Administration (1993); University of Toronto, Bachelor's of Science in Nursing. **Personal:** Married to Louis L. Joseph in 1987.

Todd R. Palmieri

Managing Director
MIM Holdings, L.L.C.
PO Box 3689
Peace Dale, RI 02883–0394
(401) 782–0778
Fax: (401) 783–3557
EMAIL: See Below

8099

Business Information: MIM Holdings, L.L.C., a wholly–owned subsidiary of Pro–Mark Holdings, Inc., is a health care management and strategies firm. Originally created to assist start–up health care professionals and companies, the Firm's focus is now in the management of retail pharmacy operations. Serving as Chief Financial Officer with the parent company (Pro–Mark) since 1994, and bringing with him an extensive background in pharmaceutical industry management, Mr. Palmieri was appointed as Managing Director for MIM in September of 1995. In this capacity, he is responsible for the overall day–to–day operations and strategies needed to keep the company a viable presence in the ever–changing pharmaceutical management marketplace. **Career Steps:** Managing Director, MIM Holdings, L.L.C. (1995–Present); Chief Financial Officer, Pro–Mark Holdings, Inc. (1994–1995); Vice President of Operations, Payer Prescribing Information, Inc. (1992–1993); Manager of Business Planning, Rhone–Poulenc Rorer (1988–1991). **Education:** Drexel University, B.S. (1988) **Personal:** Married to Stephanie in 1994. One child: John.

Nancy C. Paskin

Director of Rehabilitation Teaching
The Lighthouse, Inc.
3771 Valley View Street
Mohegan Lake, NY 10547
(212) 821–9250
Fax: (212) 821–9708

8099

Business Information: Operating as the largest rehab center for the blind in the world, Lighthouse, Inc. serves in three areas of expertise: Education – training professional workers, writing books and pamphlets and producing videos; Research – social vision research on family and individual structure; and direct services to the blind and visually impaired in the greater New York City area. As Director of Rehabilitation Teaching, Nancy Paskin is supervisor over a rehabilitation teaching staff of twenty and a therapeutic recreation staff of five, serving all seven Lighthouse facilities. **Career Steps:** Director of Rehabilitation Teaching, The Lighthouse, Inc. (1989–Present); Adjunct Professor RT, Hunter College (1989–96); Director of Rehabilitation Services, Westchester Lighthouse (1980–1990); Adjunct Instructor RT, Dominican College (1980–1990). **Associations & Accomplishments:** Association for the Education and Rehabilitation of the Blind and Visually Impaired; National Certification Chairperson, New York State American Educational Research Association; Board Member, Western Michigan University – New York Chapter; Advisory Board Member – New York State CBVH; Board Member, Mid American Conference of Rehabilitation Teachers; Advisory Board Member, AWARE; Author (1979), Sensory Development, An Instructors Manual; Co–Author (1994), Whatever Works. **Education:** Western Michigan University: M.A. (1971), B.A. (1970). **Personal:** Married to Samuel M. in 1973.

Shashikant S. Patel, M.D.
Medical Director and Psychiatrist
Hamilton Center
620 Eighth Avenue
Terre Haute, IN 47804–2744
(812) 231–8254
Fax: (812) 232–8228

8099

Business Information: Hamilton Center is a free–standing, non–profit comprehensive mental health services center, providing in– and out–patient services to chronically ill children and adults from five locations. Special programs include offering mental health services and halfway houses. A practicing physician since 1968, Dr. Patel joined Hamilton Center as Psychiatrist in 1980. Still serving in the capacity of Psychiatrist, he was appointed as Medical Director in 1992, responsible for all patient care services, including individual and family counseling. In addition to his daily psychiatric practice, he is affiliated with the local hospital, providing specialized psychiatric services and counseling. **Career Steps:** Hamilton Center: Medical Director (1992–Present), Psychiatrist (1980–1992); Psychiatrist, Creedmoor Psychiatric Center (1978–1980). **Associations & Accomplishments:** American Psychiatric Association; Indiana Psychiatric Association; Diplomate, American Board Psychiatry and Neurology. **Education:** University of Poona, India, M.D. (1968). **Personal:** Married to Mradula in 1977. Two children: Neesha and Neil. Dr. Patel enjoys reading and music.

John F. Peddle
Executive Director
Newfoundland and Labrador Health Care Association
1118 Topsail Road
St. John's, Newfoundla A1B 3N4
(709) 364–7701
Fax: (709) 364–6460

8099

Business Information: Newfoundland and Labrador Health Care Association is a provincial health care association consisting of all acute care, long term care, and community based organizations in Newfoundland and Labrador. As Executive Director, Mr. Peddle is the CEO of this organization which provides consultative services to member organizations on administrative issues, group purchasing, labour relations, and educational services. Mr. Peddle is actively involved with the Newfoundland and Labrador Employer's Council as an executive member dealing with all major issues affecting employers in Newfoundland and Labrador. **Career Steps:** Graduated from Memorial University of Newfoundland in 1971 with a Bachelor of Commerce Degree. Employment record: General Manager of the Newfoundland Association of Public Employees from 1971 to 1975, serving as CEO of the largest public sector union in Newfoundland; Director of Labour Relations with the Newfoundland and Labrador Health Care Association from 1976 to 1995, having responsibility for all major labour relations' issues in the health care sector; Executive Director of the Newfoundland and Labrador Health Care Association from 1995 to present). **Personal:** Married. One child: Beth. Mr. Peddle enjoys gardening, and coin and stamp collecting.

Sandra A. Pelton

President
RCSA, Inc.
1000 Austin Street
Richmond, TX 77469
(713) 239–0213
Fax: (713) 239–0413

8099

Business Information: RCSA, Inc. (Rehabilitative Care Systems of America) is a physical and occupational therapy management company, providing therapy and rehabilitative services to hospitals and clinics throughout Texas. Future plans include expanding their services into New Mexico. Established in 1985, RCSA, Inc. currently employs 91 people. A Licensed Physical Therapist since 1977, Ms. Pelton co–founded RCSA, Inc. in 1985. Serving as President, Ms. Pelton shares ownership with her husband. She is responsible for overseeing the development and operation of all therapy services. **Career Steps:** President, RCSA, Inc. (1985–Present); TPT, Inc.: President (1984–1985), Vice President (1982–1984). **Associations & Accomplishments:** Private Practice Section, American Physical Therapy Association; Texas Physical Therapy Associaton; American Management Association; American Academy of Medical Administrators; Speaker on Health Care Reform and Managed Care at association meetings and universities statewide; Advisory Committee, Houston Community College P.T.A. Program; Private Pilot. **Education:** University of Texas Medical Branch – Galveston, B.S. in Physical Therapy (1977); Trinity University – San Antonio, TX, Major: Pre–Physical Therapy. **Personal:** Married to Richard. One child: Tiffany. Ms. Pelton enjoys riding wave runners, the beach, shooting (sporting clay & birds), flying, riding motorcycles, skiing, and hiking.

Tim Pezold

President and Chief Executive Officer
Harrington Southwest, Inc.
2660 East 32nd Street, Suite 100
Joplin, MO 64804–4361
(800) 826–6912
Fax: (417) 623–1943

8099

Business Information: Harrington Southwest, Inc. is a managed health care organization administrator. As President and Chief Executive Officer, Mr. Pezold directs all operations for the regional office. **Career Steps:** President and Chief Executive Officer, Harrington Southwest, Inc. (1995–Present); Vice President of Marketing and Sales, Healthsource (1993–1995); National Director of Marketing and Sales, The Grant Nelson Group (1990–1993); Sales Account Executive, Sanus/New York Life (1987–1990). **Associations & Accomplishments:** Springfield/Joplin Missouri Chamber of Commerce; American Cancer Society. **Education:** California State University, Microbiology (1976); Shasta College. **Personal:** Two children: Sarah Jean and Joshua Michael. Mr. Pezold enjoys tennis and snow skiing.

Barbara A. Phillips–Carey

Director of Special Projects
The Village – Virgin Islands Partners In Recovery
2212 Queen Street, Suite 38
Christiansted, Virgin Islands 00820
(305) 573–3784
Fax: (809) 773–2900

8099

Business Information: The Village – Virgin Islands Partners in Recovery is a not–for–profit comprehensive addiction treatment facility. Serving individuals throughout the Virgin Islands, programs offered include drug treatment, juvenile justice, HIV, and runaway halfway houses. As Director of Special Projects, Ms. Phillips–Carey coordinates all treatment modules, such as residential, outpatient, halfway houses, and aftercare which includes the development of outreach programs and overall fundraising efforts. **Career Steps:** The Village – Virgin Islands Partners in Recovery: Director of Special Projects (1996–Present), Director of Treatment Services (1990–1996), Director of Community Services/Director of Admissions (1988–1990), Primary Therapist (1987–1988); National Marketing Representative, Lieba, Inc. (1981–1987); Food Service Manager, Walgreens (1979–1981); Director – Pupil Personnel Services, Minister of Education, Bahamas (1973–1977). **Associations & Accomplishments:** Chairperson, State Juvenile Justice Delinquency Prevention Advisory Group; Co–Chair, Terr. HIV Prevention Advisory Group; Victim–Witness Task Force; Child Abuse & Neglect Task Force; Drug Demand Reduction Subcommittee; Former Chairperson, Terr. Family Planning Advisory Board; Founding Member, Coalition of Non–Profit Directors; Advisory Board, Women with Children Task Force. **Education:** LaSalle University, Ph.D. Candidate (exp. comp. 1996); Stockton State College, B.A.; Atlantic Community College, A.A.; Secondary Education Certificate. **Personal:** One child: Melissa Rae Phillips and two grandchildren, Jewels and Justina. Ms. Phillips–Carey enjoys music, chorale, piano and reading.

Marcia A. Potter

Education Specialist
OSF Saint Frances Medical Center
530 N.E. Glen Oak Avenue
Peoria, IL 61637–0001
(309) 655–3230
Fax: Please mail or call

8099

Business Information: Saint Frances Medical Center is a 600–bed community trauma center, specializing in the care of neonates to geriatrics, including rehabilitation. As Education Specialist, Ms. Potter is a member of the Education and Development Department, and is responsible for staff in–service education, teaching CNA courses, PCT training, and diversified administrative activities. **Career Steps:** Education Specialist, Saint Francis Medical Center (1995–Present); Assistant Nursing Care Manager/Clinical Nurse Educator, Saint Francis Medical Center (1992–1995); Instructor/Health Occupations, Illinois Central College (1989–Present). **Associations & Accomplishments:** Women in Management;

Association of Rehabilitation Nurses; American Heart Association; CPR Coordinating Committee; Tri County Stroke Rehabilitation Committee; Alzheimer's Education Committee. **Education:** College of Saint Francis: M.S. in Health Care Services Administration (1991), B.S. in Health Arts (1983); Saint Francis Hospital School of Nursing, Diploma (1974) and CRRN, Certified Rehabilitation RN (1992). **Personal:** Married to Raymond Larry in 1974. Three children: Brian, Michael and David. Ms. Potter enjoys reading, walking and music.

Sherry Poulin

President
Pacific Medical Management, Inc.
7 Waterfront Plaza, Suite 421, 500 Ala Moana Boulevard
Honolulu, HI 96813–4920
(808) 599–6394
Fax: (808) 521–0784

8099

Business Information: Pacific Medical Management, Inc. is an independent medical evaluation firm, providing management of industrial and no–fault medical claims through insurance companies and lawyers. Established in 1991, Pacific Medical Management, Inc. reports annual revenue of $1.5 million. As President, Mrs. Poulin is responsible for hands–on administration of all phases of the Corporation, as well as producing marketing reports. **Career Steps:** President, Pacific Medical Management, Inc. (1991–Present); Litigation Manager, Hawaiian Insurance Group (1989–1991); Litigation Manager, Golub Insurance (1986–1989); Litigation Manager, Nova Insurance (1980–1986). **Associations & Accomplishments:** National Association of Women Executives; Hawaii Women's Insurance Association. **Education:** Boston School of Nursing, Nursing (1960). **Personal:** Married to Luke. Three children: Lorraine Lewis, Amy Carrell, and Rick Noone. Mrs. Poulin enjoys bike riding and swimming.

Wayne Powers

Director of Operations
Medtrans of Illinois
5640 Howard Street
Skokie, IL 60077
(847) 933–0299
Fax: (847) 933–0288
EMAIL: badmedic7@aol.com

8099

Business Information: Medtrans of Illinois began operations in 1992 and currently has 300 employees. The Company provides medical transport to hospitals, clinics and physicians offices in the Chicago area. As Director of Operations, Mr. Powers is responsible for everything with field employees, ambulance maintenance, operation budget and scheduling. He has an administrative assistant, seven supervisors and over 250 field employees. Internet users can reach him via: badmedic7@aol.com. **Career Steps:** Director of Operations, Medtrans of Illinois (1995–Present); Operations Supervisor, Tidewater Ambulance Service (1990–1995); Paramedic, City of Chesapeake, Virginia (1994); hospital Corpsman, US Navy (1984–1988). **Associations & Accomplishments:** National Registry of Emergency Medical Technicians (Paramedic). **Education:** Attended, Tidewater Community College at Virginia Beach (1992); Attended, New River Community College (1989). **Personal:** Married to Cheryl in 1992. Two children: Chris and Brian. Mr. Powers enjoys softball, camping, outdoor activities, and family activities.

Mr. Jean–Michel Quinot

President
Roussel Uclaf Holdings Corporation
95 Chestnut Ridge Road
Montvale, NJ 07645
(201) 307–3282
Fax: (201) 302–3279

8099

Business Information: Roussel Uclaf Holdings Corporation (RUHC) is a holding company having three subsidiaries in the U.S. in the manufacturing and distribution of environmental health, pharmaceutical bulk, animal health and crop protection. The parent company of RUHC is Roussel Uclaf, the third largest pharmaceutical company in France. Roussel Uclaf Holdings Corporation, located in New Jersey employs 160 persons and reported 1993 sales in excess of $200 million. Mr. Quinot started working with Roussel Uclaf in 1982 in the Parisian headquarters. He moved to the U.S. to serve as President for the Corporation's U.S operations. He is a member of the Board responsible for all subsidiaries of RUHC, in charge of all business management, represents shareholders in the U.S. and acts as liaison for Roussel Uclaf–France. **Career Steps:** President, Roussel Uclaf Holdings Corporation and Uclaf Corporation (subsidiary) (1993–Present); Vice Presi-

dent, Roussel Uclaf Eastern Europe (1991–1993); Chief Financial Officer, Roussel Uclaf Southern Europe (1989–1991); Chief Financial Officer, Roussel Uclaf Ivory Coast (1984–1988). **Education:** ISA, French MBA (1981) and Electro–Chemical Engineer (1979). **Personal:** Mr. Quinot enjoys tennis and is fluent in five languages (French, English, German, Spanish, Italian).

Brendan T. Rhatigan

Vice President
National Prescription Administrators (NPA), Inc.
3 Van Wyk Road
Lake Hiawatha, NJ 07034–1239
(201) 503–1035
Fax: (201) 503–1083
EMAIL: See Below

8099

Business Information: National Prescription Administrators (NPA), Inc. is a prescription benefits administrator, providing the management and processing of prescription claims for corporations, unions, etc. NPA has three data centers across the U.S. and over 50,000 pharmacies hooked up to those centers, enabling them to check eligibility and benefits of their members, as well as to ensure that no counteractive drugs are prescribed. As Vice President, Mr. Rhatigan is responsible for the oversight and management of all data services for three data centers, including operations, production control, technical services, systems programs, new technology, and communications. In addition, he oversees a support staff of 35. Internet users can also reach Brendan via: doc@btr.com **Career Steps:** Vice President, National Prescription Administrators, Inc. (1993–Present); Director of Data Processing, Spicer & Oppenheim (1974–1990); Supervisor, Smith Barney (1969–1974). **Associations & Accomplishments:** Saint John's Mentor Program; Vietnam Veteran's Association; Who's Who in College and Universities; Featured in Technical Journal regarding third party maintenance; Guest Lecturer, St. Francis College; President, Evening Student Association; Dun's Scotus Honor Society; Franciscan Spirit Award Magna Cum Laude. **Education:** St. John's University, M.B.A. (1994); St. Francis College, B.S.; Kennedy Western University, Currently working toward a Ph.D. in Business Administration. **Personal:** Married to Carolyn in 1968. Two children: Brendan Jr. and Jennifer. Two Grandchildren: Christopher and Samantha. Mr. Rhatigan enjoys golf and researching his family history.

cooperative
physician services, inc.

Sandra L. Rice

President
Cooperative Physician Services
4400 West 109th Street, Suite 110
Overland Park, KS 66211
(913) 469–0440
Fax: (913) 469–1611

8099

Business Information: Cooperative Physician Services, Inc. is a consulting and physicians' practice management firm. The service provides administrative services to 30 primary care physician and specialists affiliated with St. Josephs Hospital. By having Cooperative Physican Service, Inc. supply these services, the physicians are able to concentrate on the practice of medicine rather than the day–to–day operation of their offices. As President, Ms. Rice is responsible for overseeing operations, strategic planning, public relations, marketing of services, and consulting to hospitals and large physician groups. **Career Steps:** President, Cooperative Physicians Services, Inc. (1991–Present); Vice President of Finance, Research Medical Center (1990–1991); Chief Financial Officer, Swedish American Hospital (1984–1989); Controller, Mary Thompson Hospital (1982–1984). **Associations & Accomplishments:** Healthcare Financial Management Association; Medical Management Group Association; Past President, Newhouse Shelter for Battered Women and Children; Heart to Heart, donates and delivers medical supplies world wide; Treasurer, Louisburg Rotary Club. **Education:** University of Wisconsin, M.S. (1989); Eastern Kentucky University, B.B.A. **Personal:** Ms. Rice enjoys showing horses and downhill skiing.

Mr. Winthrop S. Risk, M.D., Ph.D.

President
Cedar Rapids Neurologists
811 5th Avenue, SE
Cedar Rapids, IA 52403
(319) 362–7924
Fax: (319) 362–1435

8099

Business Information: Cedar Rapids Neurologists and Neurodiagnostic Center PC is a provider of neurology consultative and diagnostic services. Established in 1980, the Center serves patients (both in and outpatient) throughout Eastern Iowa and in Beirut Lebanon. As President, Dr. Risk is responsible for all aspects of operations for the Center. He also serves as President of Cedar Rapids Enterprises PC. Established in 1995, Cedar Rapids Enterprises, PC provides unique investment and venture capital management in relation to neuroscience and health care concerns throughout the world. **Career Steps:** President, Cedar Rapids Neurologists and Neurodiagnostic Center PC (1980–Present); President, Cedar Rapids Enterprises PC (1995–Present); Assistant Professor of Physics, University of Maryland (1967–1972). **Associations & Accomplishments:** American Academy of Neurology; American Physical Society; American Medical Association; American Academy of Neurological and Orthopedic Surgeons; American Society of Neuroimaging; Cedar Rapids Chamber of Commerce; American Sleep Disorder Association. **Education:** American University of Beirut School of Medicine, M.D. (1977); Princeton University, Ph.D. (1965); Massachusetts Institute of Technology, B.S. (1960). **Personal:** Married to Alice. Two children: David and Winthrop II.

Mrs. Ellen C. Rittenhouse

Mental Health Therapist
St. Francis Medical Center/Home
415 Oak Street
Breckenridge, MN 56520
(218) 643–7223
Fax: (218) 643–7502

8099

Business Information: St. Francis Medical Center/Home provides inpatient and outpatient medical services and nursing home care. Services included are drug rehabilitation and other forms of addiction, such as gambling. Established in 1899, St. Francis Medical Center/Home currently employs 400 people. As Mental Health Therapist, Mrs. Rittenhouse is responsible for providing mental health therapy through outpatient service and consultation to general medical services. **Career Steps:** Mental Health Therapist, St. Francis Medical Center/Home (1991–Present); Clinical Social Worker, Lakeland Mental Health Center, Inc. (1982–1991); Aging Services Coordinator, Lakeland Mental Health Center, Inc. (1978–1981). **Education:** University of Missouri, M.S. in Social Work (1965); Dana College, B.S. **Personal:** Married to Don Rittenhouse in 1970. Three children: Karen J., Kristi J. and Kalli J. Mrs. Rittenhouse enjoys cooking, reading, and spending time with her family.

Mr. Anthony Rizzato

Director
Central States Institute of Addiction
120 West Huron Street, 2nd Floor
Chicago, IL 60610–3706
(312) 655–7530
Fax: (312) 266–9027

8099

Business Information: Central States Institute of Addiction is a non–profit charity organization affiliated with the Catholic Church providing supervision and services for individuals with drug and alcohol addictions, and victims of domestic violence. Established in 1963, Central States Institute currently employs 90 people. As Director, Mr. Rizzato is responsible for all aspects of administration. **Career Steps:** Director, Central States Institute, Central States of Addiction (1989–Present); Mercy Hospital: Medical Social Worker (1989), Floor Supervisor (1989). **Associations & Accomplishments:** National Association of Social Workers; Illinois Alcohol and Other Drug Abuse Professional Certification Association; Cook County Citizens Advisory Group on Law Enforcement and Corrections; Three published works. **Education:** Loyola University – Chicago: M.S.W. (1989), B.S. **Personal:** Married to Susan in 1991. Mr. Rizzato enjoys jogging and bicycling.

Nancy L. Roberts

Director of Pharmacy
South–East Health Care Corporation
135 MacBeath Avenue
Moncton, New Brunswick E1C 6Z8
(506) 857–5342
Fax: (506) 857–5540

8099

Business Information: South–East Health Care Corporation provides health care services to three health care centers, two hospitals, and home health care. Established in 1992, The Corporation employs over 2,000 people. As Director of Pharmacy, Ms. Roberts oversees services at two hospitals and three health care centers. Internet users can reach her via: robertsn@nbnet.nb.ca. **Career Steps:** Director of Pharmacy, South–East Health Care Corporation (1994–Present); The Moncton Hospital: Assistant Director of Pharmacy (1988–1994), Regional Coordinator of Pharmacy (1984–1988), Staff Pharmacist (1982–1984). **Associations & Accomplishments:** Past President, Canadian Society of Hospital Pharmacies; Member of the Canadian Pharmaceutical Association; New Brunswick Pharmaceutical Society; New Brunswick Pharmaceutical Association; American Society of Health Systems Pharmacists. **Education:** Dalhousie University, B.Sc. in Pharmacy (1982). **Personal:** Married to Thomas Landry in 1984. Three children: Alina, Oliver, and Ana. Ms. Roberts enjoys curling and travel.

Scott Robinson

Supervisory Engineer
National Institute of Health
Building 13 Room 201
Bethesda, MD 20892
(301) 496–7943
Fax: (301) 496–7172

8099

Business Information: National Institute of Health (NIH) is an independent grant–making federal government agency for support, research and public programs in health and science–related ventures. As Supervisory Engineer, Mr. Robinson is responsible for diversified administrative activities, including public relations, marketing, and strategic planning. In addition, he is in charge of the design and construction for the National Institute of Healthcare and Research. **Career Steps:** Supervisory Engineer, National Institute of Health (1992–Present); Naval Architect/Hydrodynamics, National Sea Systems Command (1989–1992); Marine Engineer, M. Rosenblatt and Son (1988–1989); U.S. Naval Engineer/Corp. Officer, U.S. Navy (1982–1988). **Education:** University of Michigan, B.S.E. (1982). **Personal:** Married to Lauri in 1988. Two children: Chelsea and Hunter. Mr. Robinson enjoys boating, woodworking, antique autos, skiing, and water skiing.

Abigail Roddie–Hamlin, MPH, CHES

Los Angeles Region Cancer Control Director
American Cancer Society
3255 Wilshire Boulevard, Suite 701
Los Angeles, CA 90010
(213) 386–7660
Fax: (213) 380–6286

8099

Business Information: The American Cancer Society is the largest voluntary, not–for–profit organization dedicated to eliminating cancer as a major health problem through research, education, and services. Headquartered in Atlanta, Georgia, the American Cancer Society has location sites in almost every city throughout the United States, plus 57 chartered divisions. The Los Angeles Region consists of nine offices within Los Angeles County and serving over 10 million people. As Los Angeles Region Cancer Control Director, Ms. Roddie–Hamlin is responsible for the direction of Cancer Control activities, including administration, planning, management, and supervising the development of cancer control programs for schools, businesses, medical, and treatment facilities throughout Los Angeles County. **Career Steps:** American Cancer Society: Director, Los Angeles Region, Cancer Control (1995–Present), Executive Director (1993–1995), Associate Executive Director (1985–1993). **Associations & Accomplishments:** American Public Health Association; Trainer, American Cancer Society, California Division; Treasurer, Alpha Kappa Alpha Sorority, Inc.; Jack and Jill of America; Choir, Loreland Church, Rancho Cucamonga. **Education:** California State University – Long Beach: M.P.H. (1988), B.S. in Health Science (1980); Certified Health Education Specialist (Chest) Credential (1990). **Personal:** Married to Vincent in 1992. One child: Alisha. Ms. Roddie–Hamlin enjoys singing, writing, reading, event planning, public speaking, and playing softball.

Mr. George Andrew Rose

Director, Software Development and Information Services
United Seniors Health Cooperative
1331 H Street, NW, Suite 500
Washington, DC 20005–4706
(202) 393–6222
Fax: (202) 783–0588

8099

Business Information: United Seniors Health Cooperative is a charitable 501 (C)(3) organization founded in 1985. USHC's mission is to enable older persons and low–income children, families and individuals of all ages to remain healthy, independent and financially secure. USHC is led by a distinguished Board of Directors consisting of twenty–six national and community leaders. The Chair of the Board is Arthur Flemming, former Secretary of the U.S. Department of Health, Education and Welfare. The Vice Chair is Esther Peterson, Consumer Advisor to three U.S. Presidents. Since 1986, USHC has been in the forefront of harnessing the power of new computer and telecommunications technologies to develop innovative and practical solutions to problems faced by low–income older persons, children, and families and is the national leader in developing software specifically for community–based agencies. As an independent consumer advocacy organization, USHC is committed to fostering a culture of health and independence through increased access to unbiased, affordable, quality consumer information and community services and resources. USHC reports annual revenue of $1.2 million and currently employs 15 people. Serving as a strong advocate of an effective social service safety–net for those in our society who are in critical need of assistance, Mr. Rose is responsible for providing project management and strategic planning, directing the design, development, testing, and implementation of all software and network systems, directing the research on the eligibility criteria for public and private benefits programs, and the training for the local community project personnel. Early in his career, as a clinical social worker, he focused on providing direct social services to substance abusers within the criminal justice system and designing and developing substance abuse treatment programs. More recently, he has focused his financial, technical and computer skills on increasing access to benefits for those in need of assistance and increasing the efficiency and reducing the cost of human services delivery systems. Mr. Rose is a strong advocate of closing the widening gap between information "haves" and "have nots" and believes that basic computer and telecommunications technologies should be affordable and available to all, regardless of geographical location, race, income or special needs. He designed and directed the development of the Community Services Gateway (CSG), a complete on–line interactive electronic bulletin board service that assists communities to organize and broker its services, resources and information in a manner that is relevant to the special needs and problems of the local community and its unique culture. Mr. Rose also designed and directed the development of the Benefits Outreach & Screening Software (BOSS) Version 4.0 and 5.0, the BOSS Distributor Network and is the chief architect of several major computer software and network projects across the country. **Career Steps:** Director – Software Development and Information Services, United Seniors Health Cooperative (1993–Present); Project Manager, UMWA (1987–1993); Clinical Social Worker, DISC, Inc. (1984–1987); Social Worker, Bureau of Rehabilitation (1979–1984). **Education:** George Washington University, M.B.A.; Eastern Michigan University. **Personal:** Mr. Rose enjoys rock climbing, hiking, and running.

Alfred R. Rowlett

Director of Program Services
Turning Point Residential Treatment Program
3440 Viking Drive
Sacramento, CA 95827
(916) 364–8395
Fax: (916) 364–5051

8099

Business Information: Turning Point Residential Treatment Program is a residential mental health agency, providing support for people with psychiatric,physical and developmental disabilities. Established in 1975, Turning Point Residential Treatment program reports annual operating budget of $4 million and currently employs a staff of 150 including nurses, psychologists, psychiatrists, and social workers, etc. Serving as Director of Program Services, Mr. Rowlett is responsible for all aspects of administrative functions and programs for the Agency. **Career Steps:** Director of Program Services, Turning Point Residential Treatment Program (1991–Present). **Associations & Accomplishments:** National Association of Social Workers; Autism Society of America; Little League soccer; Church activities; Chamber of Commerce. **Education:** California State University, M.S.W. (1997); Golden Gate University, M.B.A. (1989); Ottawa University – Kansas, B.S. **Personal:** Married to Yvette in 1981.

Eli Roza, M.D.

President

Meadow Dialysis Facility

12931 Oak Hill Avenue
Hagerstown, MD 21742
(301) 797–2311 (301) 797–9600
Fax: (301) 797–3854

8099

Business Information: Meadow Dialysis Facility is a medical facility specializing in the treatment of kidney disease by dialysis (the process by which waste products are removed from circulating blood by means of a dialyzer). Meadow Dialysis Facility currently employs 23 people. As President, Dr. Roza serves as Chief Executive Officer and Physician and is responsible for all aspects of operations, including working with people who have kidney disorders, high blood pressure, require kidney dialysis or kidney transplants. **Career Steps:** President, Meadow Dialysis Facility (1980–Present); Physician and Partner, Otto Roza, M.D., P.A. (1980–Present); Washington County Hospital – Hagerstown, MD: Vice Chief of Staff (1995–Present), Chairman of Medicine (1985–1987). **Associations & Accomplishments:** American Medical Association; American College of Physicians; Renal Physicians Association; American Society of Nephrology. **Education:** State University of New York – Buffalo, M.D. (1975); Case Western Reserve University, B.A. **Personal:** Married to Susan in 1979. Four children: Caroline, Katie, David, and Danny. Dr. Roza enjoys sports, exercise, and travel.

Paul Ruchames

Management Consultant

Counseling Service EDNY

186 Montague Street
Brooklyn, NY 11201
(718) 858–6631
Fax: (718) 243–2715

8099

Business Information: Counseling Service is a multi–site, nonprofit organization providing substance abuse counseling on an inpatient and outpatient basis. As Management Consultant, Mr. Ruchames is responsible for all fiscal, programmatic, and personnel functions. **Career Steps:** Management Consultant, Counseling Service (1986–Present); Program Director, Staten Island University Hospital (1983–1986); Family Program Director, South Beach Alcohol Treatment Center (1980–1983); Aftercare Director, Brunswick Hospital (1978–1980). **Associations & Accomplishments:** Advisory Council; Irondale Theater Group; Certified Biofeedback Operator; Numerous appearance on public service T.V. and radio; Speaker, various conferences regarding substance abuse and administration of substance abuse agencies. **Education:** Washington University, M.S.W. (1978); Certified Social Worker (1978); Certified Substance Abuse Specialist (1995). **Personal:** Married to Michelle Benjamin–Ruchames in 1980. Three children: Jeremy, Rebecca, and Adena. Mr. Ruchames enjoys spending time with his family, sports, travel, and reading.

Joseph S. Saffles

President

Little Drugs

202 North High Street
Sweetwater, TN 37874–2800
(423) 337–7933
Fax: (423) 337–7016

8099

Business Information: Little Drugs, established in 1958, is a professional pharmacy practice, providing specialized pharmaceutical care to patients. Services include custom compounding, diabetes training, home infusion, and durable medical equipment. With sixteen years experience in pharmaceutical applications and a Computerized Systems Specialist and Pharmacist, Mr. Saffles joined Little Drugs in 1979. Serving as President, he oversees the administrative operations of a staff of eight, in addition to providing all pharmaceutical and drug prescription dispensal. **Career Steps:** President, Little Drugs (1979–Present); Director of Pharmacy, Sweetwater Hospital (1986–1988). **Associations & Accomplishments:** Kiwanis: Sustained Member, Former President; District 4 Pharmacist Association: Sustained Member, Former President; Fellow, American Society of Consulting Pharmacists; Certified Diabetes Educator; NARD; Tennessee Pharmacist Association; American Diabetes Association; American Society of Diabetes Educators. **Education:** Samford University, B.S. (1977). **Personal:** Married to Tammy in 1979. Two children: Bo and Mandy. Mr. Saffles enjoys sailing and snow skiing.

Kenneth B. Safft

Director of Human Resources – Connecticut Region

Horizon/CMS Healthcare Corporation

177 Whitewood Road
Waterbury, CT 06708–1545
(203) 757–9491
Fax: (203) 575–1714

8099

Business Information: Horizon/CMS Healthcare Corporation is a national provider of various healthcare services. As Director of Human Resources – Connecticut Region, Mr. Safft develops, coordinates, and oversees all of the Human Resource functions for 3 convalescent homes. **Career Steps:** Director of Human Resources – Connecticut Region, Horizon/CMS Healthcare Corporation (1995–Present); Assistant Business Manager, St. Francis Home for Children (1994–1995). **Associations & Accomplishments:** Division of Industrial/Organizational Psychology, American Psychological Association. **Education:** University of Hartford: M.A. (1994), B.A. **Personal:** Mr. Safft enjoys tennis, travel, camping, and reading.

Rein Saral, M.D.

President

Emory University System of Health Care, Inc.

1365 Clifton Road
Atlanta, GA 30322
(404) 778–3774
Fax: (404) 778–5020

8099

Business Information: Emory University System of Health Care, Inc., is the management and administrative organization for Emory University's health care components, which include Emory University Hospital, Crawford Long Hospital of Emory University, Emory Adventist Hospital, and The Emory Clinic, a multi specialty, medical facility that employs approximately 800 physicians. As President and Director of the Emory Clinic, Dr. Saral oversees all aspects of operations for the Health Care System, as well as the care and treatment of patients. Concurrent to his position with the Emory University System of Health Care, Inc., Dr. Saral is also a Professor of Medicine and the Associate Dean for Clinical Service at the Emory University School of Medicine. **Career Steps:** President, Emory University System of Health Care, Inc. (1991–Present); Director, The Emory Clinic, Inc. (1991–Present); Professor of Medicine and Associate Dean for Clinical Service, Emory University School of Medicine (1991–Present); Director, Bone Marrow Transplant Program, The Emory Clinic (Present); Johns Hopkins Hospital and University: Clinical Director – Bone Marrow Transplantation Unity Oncology Center (1985–1991); Associate Professor of Medicine and Oncology (1983–1991) Active Staff Member of Hospital and Oncology Staff (1976–1991), Assistant Professor of Medicine and Oncology (1976–1983), Fellow, Department of Oncology School of Medicine (1974–1976); Research Associate, Laboratory of Molecular Biology, National Institute of Arthritis, Metabolic and Digestive Diseases, Bethesda, MD (1971–1974). **Associations & Accomplishments:** Phi Beta Kappa; Alpha Omega Alpha; American Society of Clinical Oncology; International Society of Experimental Hematology; Medical Association of Georgia; Medical Association of Atlanta; Georgia Society of Clinical Oncology; American Medical Association; Membership Chair, American Society for Blood and Marrow Transplantation (1993–1994); Johns Hopkins University School of Medicine, Hospital and Oncology Center: Committee on Admissions, Staff Conference Committee, Medical School Council, Intern Selection Committee, Medical Services Committee, Pharmacy and Therapeutics Committee, Clinical Fellowship Committee, Antibiotic Subcommittee, Clinical Research Oncology Committee, Task Force on Admissions, Committee on Infection Control, Cancer Center Grants Review Committee, Advisory Council, Clinical Research Center; Consultant, Hoffman–LaRoche, Inc.; Clinical Cancer Program Project Review Committee, National Cancer Institute, National Institutes of Health; Advisory Board, International Interdisciplinary AIDS Foundation; Consultant, Arizona Disease Control Research Commisssion; Advisory Committee, International Bone Marrow Transplant Registry; Editorial Board, Marrow Transplantation Reviews; Autologous Bone Marrow Tranplantation Panel; Patient Advocacy Committee, Georgia Society of Clinical Oncology; Public Relations Committee, American Society of Clinical Oncology; Pacific Rim Study Group; Numerous publications, book chapters and journal entries. **Education:** Johns Hopkins University School of Medicine, M.D. (1969), Grinnell College, B.A. (1965); Intern, Internal Medicine, Osler Medical Service, Johns Hopkins Hospital (1970); Resident, Internal Medicine, Osler Medical Service, Johns Hopkins Hospital (1971). **Personal:** Married to Jane McCleary in 1970. Two children: Alexandra McCleary and Katherine Robinson. Dr. Saral enjoys gardening, tennis and reading history and fiction.

Mr. James M. Schlaman

Manager

New Horizons Physical Rehabilitation Center

1960 South 11th Street
Niles, MI 49120
(616) 683–6800
Fax: (616) 683–6888

8099

Business Information: New Horizons Physical Rehabilitation Center is a rehabilitation facility providing treatment for the physically disabled. Established in 1988, New Horizons Physical Rehabilitation Center currently employs 31 people. As Manager, Mr. Schlaman is responsible for the management of physical, occupational, and speech therapy for the Center. Concurrent with his position as Manager, he serves as Chief of Occupational Therapy throughout the Lakeland Regional Health System. **Career Steps:** Manager of Rehabilitation, New Horizons Physical Rehabilitation Center (1993–Present); Lakeland Regional Health System: Chief of Occupational Therapy (1993–Present), Staff Occupational Therapist (1990–1993); Staff Occupational Therapist, Ballard Rehabilitation (1988–1990). **Associations & Accomplishments:** American Occupational Therapy Association; Michigan Occupational Therapy Association; YMCA, "Y–Uncles" Program – similar to Big Brothers of America. **Education:** Western Michigan University, M.Sc. (1995); Loma Linda University, B.S. in Occupational Therapy. **Personal:** Married to Erin in 1994. Mr. Schlaman enjoys sports, rollerblading, and golf.

George H. Schmitt, D.Sc.

Senior Vice President and Chief Financial Officer

California Healthcare System

1 California Street, Floor 15
San Francisco, CA 94111–5401
(415) 296–1844
Fax: (415) 296–1812

8099

Business Information: California Healthcare System serves as owner and manager of hospitals and health systems throughout the state. Established in 1986, California Healthcare System reports annual revenue of $1 billion and currently employs 9,000 people. As Senior Vice President and Chief Financial Officer, Mr. Schmitt is responsible for multiple administration and financial matters. **Career Steps:** Senior Vice President and Chief Financial Officer, California Healthcare System (1991–Present); President and Chief Executive Officer, Main Line Health, Inc. (1988–1991); President and Chief Executive Officer, Forbes Health System (1974–1988); St. Joseph Infirmary, Louisville: Executive Director (1970–1974), Associate Administrative Director of Planning & Development (19678–1970); Assistant Director, Stanford Medical Center – Palo Alto (1966–1968); General Accountant, Ameron Corporation – St. Louis (1965–1966). **Associations & Accomplishments:** Former Board Member, Chairman Region 2 – New York, New Jersey and Pennsylvania, American Hospital Association; Board of Directors – Pennsylvania, Hospital Association; Board of Directors, Hospital Council Western Pennsylvania; Published in numerous magazines; Listed in several Who's Who publications. **Education:** Maryville College, Sc.D. (1978); University of Minnesota, M.H.A. (1967); Kenrick Seminary–St. Louis, Post-graduate studies (1961–1963); Cardinal Glennon College – St. Louis, A.B. (1961). **Personal:** Married to Sue in 1966. Six children: Ruit, G. Michael, Kristin S. (deceased), Joseph C., Nichole Suzanne, and Elizabeth Teresa. Mr. Schmitt enjoys sailing, reading, music, biking, and fishing.

Humana®

Michael A. Seltzer

Director of Texas Operations

Humana Health Care Plan

8431 Fredericksburg Road, Suite 570
San Antonio, TX 78229
(210) 617–1708
Fax: (210) 617–1704

8099

Business Information: Humana Health Care Plans of Texas is a 125,000 member mixed model managed care plan offering HMO, PPO, POS, and Medicare HMO products in Houston, Dallas, Corpus Christi, San Antonio, Austin and Laredo. As Director of Texas Operations, Mr. Seltzer overs the operational activities, planning, marketing and sales of of a 125,000 member mixed model managed care plan offering HMO, PPO, POS and Medicare HMO products in Houston, Dallas, Corpus Christi, San Antonio, Austin and Laredo. As Director of Texas Operations, Mr. Seltzer oversees the operational activities, planning, marketing and sales of Humana's Texas markets which have more than 625 employees. Mr. Seltzer previously served as Executive Director of Humana Health Care Plans –

San Antonio. **Career Steps:** Director of Texas Operations, Humana Health Care Plans (1993–Present); Executive Director, Humana Health Care Plans – San Antonio (1993–1996): Executive Director, Humana Health Care Plans – Phoenix (1988–1993); Director of Operations, Cigna health Plan of Florida (1986–1988). **Associations & Accomplishments:** Delegate, American Association of Health Plans; member, American College of Health Care Executives, Medical Group Management Association, the American Association of Health Plans, Texas HMO Association; Board Member, Juvenile Diabetes Foundation, American Lung Association; Greater San Antonio Chamber of Commerce. **Education:** Rutgers University, M.P.A. (1978); New Jersey Institute of Technology, M.S. (1975); Newark College of Engineering, B. S. (1972). **Personal:** Married to Lynn in 1978. Three children: David, Danny, and Jennifer. Mr. Seltzer enjoys reading and photography.

Deborah Leach Shahan

Geriatric Program Director
The Guidance Center
2126 N. Thompson Lane
Murfreesboro, TN 37129–6025
(615) 898–0771
Fax: (615) 849–2333

8099

Business Information: The Guidance Center is a non–profit community mental health center, providing a place for anyone in the community (covering a three–county area) to obtain counseling through outpatient services. Working in various geriatric services and administrative roles with the Center since 1988, Deborah Shahan was appointed to her current position as Director of the Geriatric Program in 1993. In this capacity, she is responsible for providing outpatient therapy to geriatric clients and supervising the Nursing Home and Geriatric Day Treatment programs. Duties include home and office visits to mentally–ill clients, intensive outpatient therapy through Day Treatment Program to clients living independently, and supervision of therapists in contracted nursing homes. **Career Steps:** The Guidance Center: Geriatric Program Director (1993–Present), Nursing Home Program Coordinator (1990–1993), Nursing Home Program Therapist (1988–1990). **Associations & Accomplishments:** Chairperson, Cannon County Foster Care Review Board; Auburn Baptist Church: Pianist, Youth Discipleship Training Teacher, Youth Leader, Support Group Leader; Tennessee Association Gerontology/Geriatrics Education; Published article in Gerontology & Geriatrics Education Volume 15, Number 3 1995. **Education:** Middle Tennessee State University: M.A. in Sociology (1992), B.S.W. (1988), Gerontology Certification (1992). **Personal:** Married to Tommy in 1993. Mrs. Shahan enjoys travel, sports, church related activities, yardwork, and home decorating.

Maria R. Sheetz

Director of Mental Health Agency
Central Plains Center for Mental Health, Mental Retardation, & Substance Abuse
3302 Grandview Street
Plainview, TX 79072–6620
(806) 296–2726
Fax: (806) 296–7170

8099

Business Information: Central Plains Center for Mental Health, Mental Retardation, and Substance Abuse, established in 1966, is a community mental health agency. Joining the Agency as Coordinator of C.S.P. in 1986, Mrs. Sheetz was appointed as Director of the Mental Health Agency in 1994. She is responsible for the direction of all administration, operations, public relations, and strategic planning activities, as well as working directly with patients. **Career Steps:** Central Plains Center for Mental Health, Mental Retardation, and Substance Abuse: Director of Mental Health Agency (1994–Present), Coordinator of Rehabilitation Services (1992–1995), Coordinator of C.S.P. (1986–1992). **Associations & Accomplishments:** Advocacy, Inc. (mandated by federal government to insure services provided to the mental health); Former President, International Association of Psychological and Social Rehabilitative Services; Texas Mental Health Directors Consortium. **Education:** Boston University, M.S. (1990); Wayland Baptist University, B.A. (1985). **Personal:** Married to Richard in 1974. Two children: Deborah and Sebastian. Mrs. Sheetz enjoys walking, reading, and gardening.

Morris L. Sherman

Regional Director of Human Resources
Beverly Health and Rehabilitation Services
600 Six Flags Drive, Suite 226
Arlington, TX 76011–6328
(817) 640–2393
Fax: (817) 640–5229

8099

Business Information: Beverly Health and Rehabilitation Services is a provider of long term health care services. With sixteen years experience in management, an authority in Human Resources and trained in Labor Relations, Mr. Sherman joined Beverly Health and Rehabilitation Services as Human Resources Manager in 1983. He was promoted to Regional Director of Human Resources in 1991 and is responsible for the entire operations of the Human Resources Department. **Career Steps:** Beverly Health and Rehabilitation Services: Regional Director of Human Resources (1991–Present), Human Resources Manager (1983–1991); Corporate Director of Personnel, DataPlex, Inc. (1982–1983); Personnel Manager, Mississippi Hospital Association (1980–1982); Assistant Personnel Manager, Mississippi Baptist Medical Center (1977–1980). **Education:** Mississippi State University, B.S. in Business Management (1976). **Personal:** Mr. Sherman enjoys reading and attending Dallas Cowboy home games.

Carol Shively Mizes

Director of Recreation Therapy
Judson Retirement Community
2181 Ambleside Road
Cleveland, OH 44106–4621
(216) 791–2277
Fax: (216) 721–2607

8099

Business Information: Judson Retirement Community is a continuum of care facility located in the hub of University Circle of Cleveland. With two locations in the Cleveland area, the majority of the residents are retired professionals that have lived and worked in the Cleveland and surrounding areas and have re–located to the Judson Retirement Community, by choice, in order to stay in the area. According to a publication by Reader's Digest called New Choices, Judson Retirement Community is in the Top 20 (for four years running) of approximately 1200–1400 retirement communities nationwide. Established in 1906, Judson Retirement Community currently employs 420 people. As Director of Recreation Therapy and a Registered, Board Certified Music Therapist of the Bruening Health Center, Mrs. Shively Mizes is responsible for the direction of recreation therapeutic activities, including music therapy and therapeutic art. All activities are geared to prevent depression and regression of disease and promote health and wellness. **Career Steps:** Director of Recreation Therapy, Judson Retirement Community (1993–Present); Music Therapy Consultant, Meadowview Care Center (1995–1996); Music Therapist and Recreation Assistant, Metro Health Center for Skilled Nursing Care (1988–1993); Consultant, Villa Sancta Anna (1992); Music Therapist and Recreation Assistant, Menorah Park Center for Aging (1982–1987); Consultant, Heather Hill, Inc. (1986). **Associations & Accomplishments:** Regional Representative on Gerontology Subcommittee (1985–1987), National Association for Music Therapy; Regional Association for Music Therapy; Government Relations Committee, Ohio Association for Music Therapy; National Association for Activity Personnel; Cleveland Alzheimer Association and Related Disorders (1984–1987); Speakers' Bureau (1994–Present); Outstanding Young Women Award of America (1986); Innovation of the Year Award for creating a music and movement experience group with Alzheimer residents from Association of Ohio Philanthropic Homes and Housing for the Aging (1985); Extensive lectures and seminars given at National, Regional, and State Conferences and at numerous facilities on the topic of Music Therapy; Numerous interviews on radio and in professional newsletters on various topics re: Long Term Care. **Education:** Cleveland State University, B.A. in Music cum laude (1982); Department of Music Therapy Cleveland Music School Settlement, Music Therapy Intern (1981–1982); Registered Music Therapist by National Association for Music Therapy (1982); Board Certification by Certification Board for Music Therapy (1987). **Personal:** Married to Dr. J. Scott Mizes in 1992. Two children: Jeremy J. Shively and J. Christopher Mizes. Mrs. Shively Mizes enjoys singing in church, weddings, and at work.

Michael E. Showers

Controller
Adult Care Services, Inc.
826 Sunset Avenue
Prescott, AZ 86301–1824
(520) 445-6384
Fax: (520) 445–2847

8099

Business Information: Adult Care Services, Inc. is an adult day care facility. The facility is an alternative to full residential care for adults who must not be left alone to care for themselves. Adult Care offers recreational programs, educational programs, and nursing care to clients. As Controller, Mr. Showers handles all financial and accounting responsibilities of Adult Care Services. He compiles financial reports and tax returns for the facility. Mr. Showers works closely with management in the establishment of workable budgets and monitors departments for budget compliance. **Career Steps:** Controller, Adult Care Services (1995–Present); Controller, Rainbow Acres, Inc. (1994–1995); Assistant Controller, ARI, Inc. (1991–1992). **Education:** Arizona State University, B.S. (1991). **Personal:** Married to Robin in 1989. Two children: Emily and Madeline. Mr. Showers enjoys skiing and being a youth pastor.

Barbara L. Smith, M.D.

Pediatrician
Health Partners of Southern Arizona
6565 East Carondelet
Tucson, AZ 85710
(510) 721–5350
Fax: (510) 721–5319

8099

Business Information: Health Partners of Southern Arizona is an integrated health system, medical group, and management corporation (HMO) providing complete medical, surgical, and psychiatric service to its members in Southern Arizona. Currently the Group employs 70 physicians and includes the operation of two hospitals and clinics. As a Pediatrics Associate, Dr. Smith is one of eight Pediatricians with the Group. As such, she is responsible for the care and treatment of patients. **Career Steps:** Physician, Health Partners of Southern Arizona (1979–Present). **Associations & Accomplishments:** Fellow and Member of the Committee on Injury and Poison Prevention, American Academy of Pediatrics; Board of Trustees, Health Partners of Southern Arizona; Medical Director, Tucson Safe Kids. **Education:** University of Iowa, M.D. (1976); Grinnell College, B.A. (1972); University of Arizona: Pediatric Internship (1977), Pediatric Residency (1979). **Personal:** Married to Craig Gordon in 1974. Two children: Shelley and Lisa. Dr. Smith enjoys biking, fishing, and hiking.

Cynthia A. Smith

Executive Vice President
Bon Secours Health Systems – Southeastern Region
901 Venetia Bay Boulevard, Suite 250
Venice, FL 34292
(941) 486–6903
Fax: (941) 486–6905
EMAIL: See Below

8099

Business Information: Bon Secours Health Systems – Southeastern Region is a health care system affiliated with the Roman Catholic Church. The System acquires acute care hospitals, nursing homes, home health services, and ambulatory care centers throughout the region, then supervises the daily operations and general management of these health care facilities. As Executive Vice President, Ms. Smith is responsible for the Southeastern Region. She oversees the non–acute care services which include nursing homes, home health care, ambulatory care, and rehabilitation services. She directs day–to–day operations, develops budgets, and assists with financial concerns. Internet users can also reach her via: CINDY_SMITH@BSHSI.com. **Career Steps:** Executive Vice President, Bon Secours Health Systems – Southeastern Region (1996–Present); Venice Hospital: Chief Nursing Officer (1994–1996), Executive Director (1993–1994), Director Surgical Services (1986–1993). **Associations & Accomplishments:** Sertoma Club of Venice; American Society of Post Anesthesia Nurses; American College of Health Care Executives. **Education:** University of South Florida: M.B.A. (1993), B.S. in Nursing. **Personal:** Married to Bill in 1984. Ms. Smith enjoys reading, aerobics, and boating.

Winston C. Smith

Special Projects & Community Relations Director
Morris Heights Health Center
85 West Burnside Avenue
Bronx, NY 10453–4015
(718) 716–4400
Fax: (718) 294–6912

8099

Business Information: Morris Heights Health Center provides primary comprehensive healthcare to Bronx, New York, residents. As Special Projects & Community Relations Director, Mr. Smith is responsible for strategic planning of organizational goals and objectives, developing community outreach programs and networking services. **Career Steps:** Special Projects & Community Relations Director, Morris Heights Health Center (1994–Present); Area Financial Executive,

General Board of Global Ministries, The United Methodist Church (1992–1994); Field Treasurer, Conference Treasurer and Business Manager, General Board of Global Ministries, United Methodist Church West African Region (1982–1991). **Associations & Accomplishments:** Independent Order of Foresters; American Museum of Natural History; Cambria Heights Civic Association; American Society of Notaries. **Education:** Century University, California, M.B.A. (1958); Baruch College of the City University of New York, B.B.A.; Manhattan College of the City University of New York, A.A.S.; University of the West Indies, Certificate in Social Work. **Personal:** Married to Margaret in 1962. Four children: Michael Augustin, Christopher William, Nancy Hilda, and Linda Judith. Mr. Smith enjoys classical religious music, singing, language study, and travel.

Mark I. Solomon, Ph.D.

Vice President
Optimum Health Institute of San Diego
6970 Central Avenue
Lemon Grove, CA 91945–2110
(619) 464–3346
Fax: (619) 589–4098

8099

Business Information: Optimum Health Institute of San Diego is a non–medical teaching institute, and health care establishment. As Vice President, Dr. Solomon is responsible for all aspects of the Institute's program, the primary underlying assumption of which is that the body and mind heals and balances itself, if given the proper tools. Concurrent with his duties as Vice President, Dr. Solomon is Dean of Education. **Career Steps:** Optimum Health Institute of San Diego: Vice President (1990–Present), Dean of Education (1988–Present), Providence Suicidologist, Alberta, Canada (1979–1984). **Associations & Accomplishments:** Past Member, American Association of Suicide Prevention; International Association of Suicide Prevention; Canadian Association of Suicide Prevention. **Education:** University of Oregon, Ph.D. (1975); San Diego State University: M.A., B.A. **Personal:** Dr. Solomon enjoys writing (published books and articles).

Ludwig Spinelli

Executive Director
Bridgeport Community Health Center
471 Barnum Avenue
Bridgeport, CT 06608–2409
(203) 333–6846
Fax: (203) 332–0376

8099

Business Information: Bridgeport Community Health Center is a non–profit ambulatory care organization providing primary care for those most in need. As Executive Director, Mr. Spinelli is responsible for all aspects of Health Center operations and administrative activities, including hiring and directing staff. Under his tenure the Center grew from a $300,000 yearly budget in 1983 to $6.2 million in 1996. **Career Steps:** Executive Director, Bridgeport Community Health Center (1983–Present); Deputy Director, City of Bridgeport – Human Resource Development (1976–1983); Planning Director, Community Progress Inc. (1974–1976). **Associations & Accomplishments:** Named Outstanding Executive Director by the New England Community Health Center Association (May 1994); American and Connecticut Public Health Association; Vice–President, Connecticut Primary Care Association; Treasurer, Community Health Network; Board Member, East Main Street Revitalization Association; Former Member, Shelton Board of Alderman; Shelton High Fathers Club; Shelton Democrat Town Committee; Board Member, Babe Ruth Sports League. **Education:** South Connecticut State University: M.S.(1978), B.S. (1971). **Personal:** Married to Christina Grandison in 1972. Three children: Matthew, Geoffrey and Justin.

Laurie K. Spirek

Product Development Analyst
Compucare
12110 Sunset Hills
Reston, VA 20190
(703) 742–5328
Fax: (703) 709–2390
EMAIL: See Below

8099

Business Information: The Compucare Company serves the healthcare industry with integrated information systems and technology solutions for the entire healthcare enterprise including multi–facility organizations, Hospitals, HMO/PPO/ Managed Care, Long term Care, Clinincs/Group practices, Home Health, Physicians, and Insurance Companies. Products include affinity, a GUI–based patient centered dat repository with comprehensive, clinical, patient, business, and departmental information systems; HSII managed care and practice management systems; and answers multi–site hospital laboratory systems. Scope includes National, Canada, and Mexico market with over 100 systems installed. As Product Development Analyst, Ms. Spirek oversees product development, database design, and is responsible for functional requirements definition of software enhancements to Health Information Systems applications. Additional duties include technical coordination with software programmers, strategic planning, and active participation in the products evaluation committee, which addresses software enhancement based on client needs and requests. Internet users can reach her via: lspirek@msmail.affinity.ccare.com. **Career Steps:** Product Development Analyst, Compucare (1995–Present); Senior Business Analyst, Healthtrust, Inc. (1990–1995); Assistant Director, Medical Records, Seton Medical Center (1986–1990); Director of Medical Records, Willbarger General Hospital (1984–1986). **Associations & Accomplishments:** American Health Information Management Association; Healthcare Information and Management Systems Society. **Education:** S.W.T.S.U., San Marcos, B.S. in M.R.A. (1983). **Personal:** Ms. Spirek enjoys reading, Jazzercise, silk flower arrangements, gardening, and skiing.

Peggy M. Stanley, LPN

Corporate Safety Director
Americare Systems, Inc.
10983 Granada Lane #102
Overland Park, KS 66211
(913) 661–1731
Fax: (913) 661–1798

8099

Business Information: Americare Systems, Inc. is a management firm operating 45 long–term care facilities in Kansas and Missouri (eventually branching out to Tennessee, creating 6 more facilities). The Company philosophy states that as a company their first responsibility is to provide a safe living environment to their residents, their second responsibility is to offer a safe working environment with continued training to their employees, and their third responsibility is to be a good neighbor in the community. As Corporate Safety Director, Ms. Stanley provides three corporate training seminars yearly as well as guest speaking engagements, supervises loss control visits to reduce the risk of injury, works with injured employees, the facility administrator, physicians, and attorneys, and has written her own worker's compensation program. **Career Steps:** Corporate Safety Director, Americare Systems, Inc. (1993–Present); Education Staff Development, Timberlake Care Center (1992–1993); Education/Staff Development, Carondelet Manor (1989–1992). **Associations & Accomplishments:** Board Member, Health Care Facilities of Missouri Trust; Board Member, Kansas Health Care Association Trust; HIV/AIDS Instructor; CPR Instructor. **Education:** Johnson Cty; KCK Community College; College of Ozarks, Springfield; SMS – (Spfld.); Drury – (Spfld.) **Personal:** Two children: Caleb and Joshua. Ms. Stanley enjoys softball, rollerblading, running, and weightlifting.

Thomas R. Steele

Program Director
Park Ridge Health Connection
125 Indigo Creek Drive, Suite 25
Rochester, NY 14626
(716) 723–5227
Fax: (716) 723–6733

8099

Business Information: Park Ridge Health Connection specializes in occupational health programs and employee assistance programs. As Program Director, Mr. Steele manages and directs clinical, administrative, and all financial aspects of programs. **Career Steps:** Program Director, Park Ridge Health Connection (1994–Present); Consultant, Self–Employed (1993–1994); Product/Sales Manager, Paychex, Inc. (1985–1993); Sales/Sales Management, New York Life Insurance Company (1972–1985). **Education:** Rochester Institute of Technology, B.S. (1972); Fellowship Life Management Institute. **Personal:** Married to Karen in 1972. Two children: Kelly and Matthew. Mr. Steele enjoys golf, basketball, and reading.

Janet M. Stiles

President and Treasurer
A Way to Better Living, Inc.
P.O. Box 1721
Manchester, NH 03105–174
(603) 623–4523
Fax: Please mail or call

8099

Business Information: A Way to Better Living, Inc. is a non–profit, self–help agency for the mentally–ill, providing employment for only those diagnosed as having a mental illness, as well as assisting many to become employed in the community. As President and Treasurer, Ms. Stiles is responsible for all aspects of operations, including administration and finances, as well as signing contracts, officiating at Board of Directors meetings, transferring funds, and preparing proposals for funding. **Career Steps:** President and Treasurer, A Way to Better Living, Inc. (1987–Present); Friendly Visitor for Mentally Ill Clients, Office of Public Guardian (1987–Present); Technical Assistant Level 1, AMICA Mutual Insurance Co. (1973–1986); Office Manager, President Nixon Campaign, Committee to Re–Elect the President (1972). **Associations & Accomplishments:** First Baptist Church, Manchester NH; Prison Ministry, Church Choir; American Bible Society Volunteer; New Hampshire Hospital Consumer Council; New Hampshire Hospital Volunteer; Elliot Hospital Hospice Volunteer; Tutor, New Hampshire State Prison Secure Psychiatric Unit; Republican National Committee; Republican Senatorial Committee; Republican Task Force; Outstanding Young Women (1965). **Education:** University of New Hampshire, B.A. in Psychology (1952); Business courses in typing, clerical, and management. **Personal:** Married to Walter in 1952. Three children: William, Carolyn and Thomas. Ms. Stiles enjoys history, genealogy, politics, family, music and travel.

Michael G. Strother

Director
CHA Provider Network, Inc.
P.O. Box 22171
Lexington, KY 40522–2171
(606) 257–2369
Fax: (606) 257–7848

8099

Business Information: CHA Provider Network, Inc. (formerly Commonwealth Healthcare Alliance) is a regional integrated health care delivery network, serving HMOs, PPOs, and third–party administrators. The Organization covers the eastern half of the state of Kentucky, with future plans of expansion. As Executive Director, Mr. Strother is responsible for developing and managing all contracts with Physicians, Hospitals, and other health care providers, as well as marketing the network to insurance companies, third–party administrators, self–insured companies, and national managed care networks (over 25,000 members). **Career Steps:** Director, CHA Provider Network, Inc. (1992–Present); Manager of Network Development, Humana (1988–1991); Manager of Administrative Services, Community Mutual Blue Cross/Blue Shield (1985–1988). **Associations & Accomplishments:** Certified Health Consultant; Club President, Rotary International; Silver Beaver Recipient, Boy Scouts of America; Kentucky Colonel; Editor, International Philatelic Publication; Interviewed in local medical news articles on health care industry, and has written articles for several philatelic publications. **Education:** Xavier University, M.B.A. (1979); Purdue University, B.A. (1969). **Personal:** Married to Margot in 1969. Two children: Christopher and Scott. Mr. Strother enjoys collecting stamps, caving, and being involved in Boy Scout activities.

Thomas J. Sullivan

General Manager
NABHL
199 South Black Horse Pike
Blackwood, NJ 08012
(609) 228–0300
Fax: (609) 228–9667

8099

Business Information: NABHL is a national association for better health and living, providing health benefits consulting to large companies nationwide on trust law. Joining NABHL as General Manager in 1995, Mr. Sullivan is responsible for the oversight of all operations, as well as the oversight of all sales managers, administration, and management. **Career Steps:** General Manager, NABHL (1995–Present); Owner/Operator, Carden St. Benefit Company (1987–1995); Director of Personnel, Infotron Systems (1975–1987). **Associations & Accomplishments:** Cherry Hill Chamber of Commerce; South Jersey Business Owners. **Education:** Rutgers University, B.S.B.A. (1959). **Personal:** Four children: Gary, Glenn, Tracy, and Cheryl. Mr. Sullivan enjoys golf.

Roy L. Swank, M.D., Ph.D.

Director and Chief of Clinical Research
Swank Multiple Sclerosis Clinic
13655 SW Jenkins Road
Beaverton, OR 97005
(503) 520–1050
Fax: (503) 520–1223

8099

Business Information: Swank Multiple Sclerosis Clinic specializes in the care and treatment of patients with Multiple Sclerosis, as well as research of the disease in an attempt to find more productive methods of treatment. Established in 1994, the Swank MS Clinic currently employs five people. As Director and Chief of Clinical Research, Dr. Swank is responsible for all aspects of operations. In his 35 years of studying Multiple Sclerosis, Dr. Swank's studies show that a low–fat diet can slow progress of the disease. He was instrumental in discovering a protein key to treatment. **Career Steps:** Director and Chief of Clinical Research, Swank Multiple Sclerosis Clinic (1994–Present); Professor Emeritus, Oregon Health and Science University (1976–Present); Professor of Neurology, University of Oregon Medical School (1954–1976); Instructor, Harvard University Medical School; Assistant Professor, McGill University (1948–1954). **Associations & Accomplishments:** Annals of Neurology; Who's Who of America; Who's Who of the World; Numerous Publications. **Education:** Northwestern University Medical School, M.D., Ph.D. (1935); Harvard Medical School (1935–1948). **Personal:** Married to Betty in 1987. Two children: Robert and Susan. Dr. Swank enjoys music and research.

TENET℠

Sarah E. Swindall

Manager of Records Management Department
Tenet HealthSystem
14001 Dallas Parkway, Suite 200
Dallas, TX 75240–4346
(214) 789–2329
Fax: (214) 789–2359

8099

Business Information: Tenet HealthSystem is a health care organization that provides financial and legal services to 75 hospitals and other associated facilities nationally. As Manager of the Records Management Department, Ms. Swindall oversees the retention and destruction of all corporate records and financial and medical records for hospitals that have been either sold or closed down. She maintains the retention schedule, as well as oversees the Record Center, microfilming, and vital records. **Career Steps:** Manager of Records Management Department, Tenet HealthSystem (1993–Present); Records Management Officer, Superconducting Super Collider Lab (1990–1993); Records Administrator, Dallas Fort Worth Airport Bd. (1984–1990). **Associations & Accomplishments:** Association of Records Managers and Administrators; American Health Information Management Association; Institute of Certified Records Managers; Winners Circle Investment Club; Dallas Genealogy Society; Van Zandt County Genealogy Society; First United Methodist Church, Canton, TX: Member, Choir and Missions Committee. **Education:** University of North Texas, M.S. (1990); University of North Central Oklahoma, B.A. in Education (1966); Institute of Certified Records Managers, Certified Records Manager (1985). **Personal:** Married to Donald W. in 1980. Four children: Earl A. and William D. Garrison, and Bradley W. and Terry J. Swindall. Ms. Swindall enjoys genealogy, and church activities.

Roger S. Taylor, M.D., M.P.A.

President and Chief Executive Officer
Connecticut Health Enterprises
401 Monroe Turnpike
Monroe, CT 06468
(203) 452–6900
Fax: (203) 452–2200

8099

Business Information: Connecticut Health Enterprises develops and operates Integrated Systems of Care. Beginning operations in 1996, Connecticut Health Enterprises is a joint venture between The Daughters of Charity National Health Care System, St. Vincent's Hospital, and PHP Healthcare Corporation – which serves as managing partner of the enterprise. Connecticut Health Enterprise contracts with HMOs and other payors and is expanding to include other physicians and hospitals throughout the area. Dr. Taylor has nearly two decades of healthcare management experience, including executive responsibility for every form of health insurance and managed care delivery product available today. Until joining Connecticut Health Enterprise in July, 1996, Dr. Taylor was executive Vice President and Chief Medical Officer of Pacifi-Care Health Systems, a multi–regional managed care company serving 2 million people in six states, over 250,000 of which are seniors. In that role, he was also responsible for many of PacifiCares non–HMO subsidiaries. Prior to joining Pacifi-Care Health Systems, he served as National Leader in the health care industry for The Wyatt Company, one of the world's leading employee benefits consulting companies. Dr. Taylor is a well–known speaker on U.S. healthcare issues and has consulted internationally on health reform. **Career Steps:** Executive Vice President and Chief Medical Officer, PacifiCare Health Systems (CA) (1993–1996); Senior Vice President, PacifiCare Health Systems (CA) (1992–1993); National Leader in Health Consulting, The Wyatt Company (DC) (1990–1992); Senior Vice President, Equicor, Inc. (TN) (1988–1990); Vice President, Health Care Systems, Equicor, Inc.(TN) (1986–1988); General Manager, United Medical Plan of Richmond and Director of Development, Mid–Atlantic Region, Hospital Corporation of America, Health Plans (VA) (1985–1986); Senior Vice President and Corporate Medical Director, United Medical Plan, Inc. (VA) (1983–1985); Regional Medical Director, Cigna Health Plans (CA) (1983); Director of Emergency Medical Services Authority, State of California (CA) (1981–1983); Founding Partner and Director of Emergency Medical Services, California Emergency Physicians (CA) (1973–1982); Systems Analyst, Univac, Division of Sperry Rand Corp (CA) (1967–1968). **Associations & Accomplishments:** Physician Payment Review Commission; Group Health Association of America, Committee on Quality Health Care; Integrated Health Systems, Inc., Managed Care Advisory Board; Managing Employee Health Benefits, Editorial Board; Multiple boards and committees of Pacifi–Care Health Systems; American College of Emergency Physicians; American College of Physicians Executives; American Medical Association; Group Health Association of America, Medical Directors Division; Various presentations and publications; President and Co–Founder, Utilization Review Accreditation Commission; Commissioner, California Health Facilities Commission; Director, California's Emergency Medical Services Authority. **Education:** American Board of Emergency Medicine, Diplomat (1983–1993); California State University at Los Angeles, B.S. in Zoology (1967); University of Southern California, School of Public Administration, M.P.A. in Health Administration (1981); University of Southern California, School of Medicine, M.D. (1972). **Personal:** Married to Marian in 1984. Two children: Lisa and Laura.

Alain J. Thibault, M.D.

Assistant Professor
University of Virginia Health Sciences Center
Jordan Annex Box 513, Room 2229
Charlottesville, VA 22908
(804) 243–6356
Fax: (804) 243–6746

8099

Business Information: University of Virginia Health Sciences Center, an affiliate of the University of Virginia, is a multi–speciality medical research and teaching institution. A Board–certified Oncologist/Hematologist, Dr. Thibault serves as an Assistant Professor with the University's Cancer Center. He provides clinical research in conjunction with the Experimental Therapeutics Program for the development of cancer therapy and drug treatments. **Career Steps:** Assistant Professor, University of Virginia Health Sciences Center (1995–Present); Visiting Associate, National Cancer Institute (1991–1995); Resident, McGill University (1986–1991). **Associations & Accomplishments:** American Association of Cancer Research; European Association of Neuro–Oncology. **Education:** McGill University, M.D. C.M. (1986). **Personal:** Married to Mireille Lapeyre in 1987. Three children: Charlotte, Segolene, and Athenais. Dr. Thibault enjoys studies in Philosophy and Medical History.

Laurie A. Thinel

President
Care Managers Inc.
4435 West Saginaw Highway, Suite 204
Lansing, MI 48917–2757
(517) 886–9444
Fax: (517) 321–9520

8099

Business Information: Care Managers Inc. is a medical case management corporation, consisting of three major departments: medical case management, life care planning, and vocational rehabilitation services. Care Managers, Inc. provides services statewide. With more than thirteen years experience in nursing, Mrs. Thinel joined Care Managers, Inc. as President in 1994. She is responsible for all aspects for operations, including business management, personnel, case management, and overseeing a staff of 17. She also serves as Senior Rehabilitation Consultant Supervisor for West Michigan. **Career Steps:** President, Care Managers Inc. (1994–Present) Rehabilitation Nurse, Thinel Rehabilitation Inc. (1989–1994); Nursing Supervisor, United Memorial Hospital (1983–1989). **Associations & Accomplishments:** Independent Care Management Association; Rehabilitation Insurance Nurse Council; Lansing Chamber of Commerce. **Education:** University of Florida, Catistrophic Case Management (1995); University of Michigan, B.S.N. Studies; Lansing Community College, A.D. in Nursing; Certified Case Manager. **Personal:** Married to Dudley in 1989. Mrs. Thinel enjoys travel, antiques, and water sports.

Demetrio R. Timban, M.D.

Physician
Lakeshore Services
4455 Tallman
Troy, MI 48098
(810) 524–9166
Fax: (810) 524–9001

8099

Business Information: Lakeshore Services is a health maintenance medical facility, providing its members with all aspects of medical treatment and care. A native of Manila, where he obtained his medical degree, as well as was a practicing general surgeon, Dr. Demetrio Timban joined Lakeshore Services in 1995. Dr. Timban also serves as Director of Surgery at Harbor Beach Hospital. Aside from his medical practice, he also owns an ethnic restaurant — Taste of Manila, providing patrons with authentic oriental food store and carry–out restaurant. **Career Steps:** Physician, Lakeshore Services (1995–Present); Owner, Taste of Manila (Present); Director of Surgery, Harbor Beach Hospital (1995–Present); Chief of Surgery, Saratoga Hospital (1988–1995); Chief of Surgery, Holy Cross Hospital (1990–1992). **Associations & Accomplishments:** Michigan Board of Medicine; Past President, Philippines Medical Association of Michigan; Past President, Circulo Pampagueno of Michigan; Past President and Executive Director, Manila Central University Medical Alumni Association; Past President, Medical Staff Holy Cross Hospital. **Education:** Manila Center University – College of Medicine (1962). **Personal:** Married to Teresita S. Timban, M.D. (a psychiatrist) in 1964. Three children: Marinita, Demetrio S. Jr., and Emersita. Dr. Timban enjoys reading, fishing, and hunting.

G. A. Valero

Administrative Director, Finance
Facey Medical Foundation
11165 Sepulveda Boulevard
Mission Hills, CA 91345
(818) 837–5705
Fax: (818) 837–5718

8099

Business Information: Facey Medical Foundation is a non–profit charitable organization licensed under 50l(C3) of the IRS code. The Foundation provides contracted medical and surgical services. It is a community–based Facility with 110 doctors onboard and 300 doctors contracted from outside the Facility. As Administrative Director, Finance, Mr. Valero handles all Facility financial operations, including collections, setting up managed care contracts, and finding quality care for the best price. **Career Steps:** Facey Medical Foundation: Director of Finance (1991–Present), Assistant Administrator (1985–1991); Service Technician, University of California – Los Angeles (1979–1985); Petty Officer 2nd Class, U.S. Navy (1973–1979). **Associations & Accomplishments:** Healthcare Finance and Management Association. **Education:** California State University – Los Angeles: Ms.B.A.in Financial Management (1988), B.S.B.A. in Finance (1984); Los Angeles City College, A.A. in Finance/Law (1982). **Personal:** Married to Zenaida in 1976. Three children: Jenny, Dennis, and Michael. Mr. Valero enjoys fishing and sport shooting.

Nelly T. Velasco

Nursing Supervisor
Camden County Health Services
P.O. Box 1639
Blackwood, NJ 08012
(609) 227–3000 Ext. 3141
Fax: (609) 232–7783

8099

Business Information: Camden County Health Services is the administrative office overseeing the quality care and development of community health care facilities throughout Camden County, New Jersey. Facilities provided include a full mental health division, long–term care facilities, home health operations, and a 500–bed acute care hospital. A nursing administrator with over twenty–five years expertise, Nelly Velasco was appointed as Nursing Supervisor for the Mental Health Division in 1976. She oversees all patient–care and nursing staff for 150–bed in–patient and over 200 out–patient capacity services. This also includes budgetary management, scheduling and coordination with all outside satellite facilities. **Career Steps:** Nursing Supervisor, Camden County Health Services (1976–Present); Charge Nurse, John F. Kennedy Hospital (1976–1987); Charge Nurse, Hohneman Hospital (1970–1976). **Associations & Accomplishments:** Philadelphia Nurses Association; Filitipino American Society of South Jersey. **Education:** Central Philadelphia University, B.S.N. (1967); Rutgers University. **Personal:** Married to Dick in 1971. Two children: Dheranie and Dinelle. Mrs. Velasco enjoys movies, social dancing, and being a volunteer for geriatrics.

Thomas G. Veres
Executive Director
Leukemia Society of America, Upstate New York Chapter
85 Watervliet Avenue
Albany, NY 12206–2023
(518) 438–3583
Fax: (518) 438–6431

8099

Business Information: Leukemia Society of America is a national voluntary health agency. Its mission is to cure leukemia and its related cancers–lymphoma, multiple myeloma and Hodgkin's desease, and to improve the quality of life of patients and their families. The Leukemia Society supports five major programs: research, patient aid, public and professional education, and community service. As Executive Director, Mr. Veres is responsible for all aspects of the Organization's operations, including managing the above activities for 20 counties in upstate New York and Vermont. **Career Steps:** Executive Director, Leukemia Society of America (1994–Present); Leukemia Society, New York City Chapter: Associate Executive Director (1993–94), Assistant Executive Director (1989–93). **Education:** Ithaca College, B.A., Communication, Speech (1982) **Personal:** Married to Cheryl in 1983. Two children: Jennifer and Tommy. Mr. Veres enjoys hockey, golf, running, and being a father.

Silvia Gabriele von Hanna, M.D.
Medical Consultant
Turtle House Enterprises
16 Park Drive
Stouffville, Ontario L4A 1G1
(905) 642–0970
Fax: (905) 642–0681
EMAIL: See Below

8099

Business Information: Turtle House Enterprises is a provider of lifestyle and nutritional counseling for health maintenance, weight loss, anti–aging, sports psychology, and nutrition for athletes. As Medical Consultant, Dr. von Hanna is responsible for providing personal and individual counseling, including community education and networking with other people in the health care area. A general practice physician since 1972 and a Board–certified Psychotherapist, Dr. von Hanna also maintains her private patient practice. **Career Steps:** Medical Consultant, Turtle House Enterprises; Private General Practice Physician and Psychotherapist (1976–Present). **Associations & Accomplishments:** College of Physicians & Surgeons of Ontario; Ontario Trail Riding Association; Ontario Competitive Trail Riding Association. **Education:** McMaster University, M.D. (1972), B.Sc. in Medicine. **Personal:** Dr. von Hanna enjoys horseback riding, power lifting, dancing, and acting.

Larry Von Kuster, M.D.
President and Pathologist
ZIRRM Pathology, Inc.
715 South Teft
Freemont, OH 43420
(419) 483–4040
Fax: (419) 483–3260

8099

Business Information: ZIRRM Pathology, Inc. is a private pathology group providing pathology services to Bellevue Hospital and Fremont Memorial Hospital. A practicing physician since 1977 and a Board–Certified Anatomic Pathologist, Clinical Pathologist, and Dermatopathologist, Dr. Von Kuster joined ZIRRM Pathology, Inc. as President and Pathologist in 1989. He is responsible for the management and administration of all aspects of the practice, in addition to his daily patient practice and oversight of all administrative operations for a support staff of five. **Career Steps:** President and Pathologist, ZIRRM Pathology, Inc. (1989–Present); Assistant Professor, University of Cincinnati (1983–1989); Pathologist, Cincinnati Veteran's Administration Medical Center (1983–1989). **Associations & Accomplishments:** American Society of Dermatopathology; United States and Canadian Academy of Pathology; College of American Pathologists; American Association of Blood Banks. **Education:** Loma Linda University, M.D. (1977), Walla Walla College, B.A.; Board–Certified in Anatomic Pathology, Clinical Pathology, and Dermatopathology. **Personal:** Married to Paula Revolinski in 1969. Two children: Jeremiah and Joshua. Dr. Von Kuster enjoys bicycling, dancing, and reading.

W. Douglas Wagner
Program Director
Cancer Information Service, Region 9
Markey Cancer Center, MRISC Room 305, 800 Rose Street
Lexington, KY 40536–0098
(606) 257–4447
Fax: (606) 323–1902

8099

Business Information: A division of the National Cancer Institute and its 1–800–4 CANCER network, the Cancer Information Service, Region 9 provides state–of–the–art cancer treatment information to the public and professionals, and outreach education programs in the region. Established in 1978, the Cancer Information Service currently employs 17 people. As Program Director, Mr. Wagner is responsible for all aspects of operations. **Career Steps:** Program Director, Cancer Information Service, Region 9 (1990–Present); Social Work Consultant, Hospice of the Bluegrass (1985–1990); Private Practice Social Work (1985–1992); Medical Social Worker, University of Kentucky Hospital (1978–1985). **Associations & Accomplishments:** National Association of Social Workers; Kentucky Licensed Clinical Social Worker; American Public Health Association; Academy of Certified Social Workers. **Education:** University of Kentucky College of Social Work, M.S.W. (1978). **Personal:** Married to Esther C. in 1985. Mr. Wagner enjoys photography and growing antique roses.

Thomas Enoch Watson
Director
Hampton County EMS
201 Jackson Street West
Hampton, SC 29924
(803) 943–7523
Fax: (803) 943–7524

8099

Business Information: Hampton County EMS is a provider of emergency medical services for Hampton County. With the use of six ambulances and a staff of 21 full–time and 20 part–time emergency medical technicians, Hampton County EMS answers an average of 10 calls per day throughout the county. As Director, Mr. Watson is responsible for the direction of all EMS activities, including administration, operations, and training. **Career Steps:** Director, Hampton County EMS (1992–Present); Deputy Director, Richland County Emergency Services (1990–1992); Director of EMS, Laurens County EMS (1987–1990). **Associations & Accomplishments:** Rotary International; Kiwanis International; South Carolina EMS Association; Low Country Regional EMS Council; Recognized as 1993 EMS Director of the Year and recipient of the 1988 Douglas McArthur Leadership Award and 1995 Rotarian of the Year Award. **Education:** Attended Newberry College (1970) and Palmetto Military Academy: CAS3 School, Officer Basic (MSC), and Officer Advanced (MSC). **Personal:** Two children: Thomas Albert and Tammie Elaine. Mr. Watson enjoys reading, sports, and outdoor activities.

Michael Weaver
Vice President of Corporate Development
Sheridan Health Corporation
4651 Sheridan Street, Suite 200
Hollywood, FL 33021–3430
(305) 986–7561
Fax: (305) 964–5461

8099

Business Information: Sheridan Health Corporation is a physician practice management organization, providing hospital–based and primary care services. As Vice President of Corporate Development, Michael Weaver is responsible for contract negotiations for hospital–based contracts, mergers & acquisitions for primary care practices and new business development. **Career Steps:** Vice President Corporate Development, Sheridan Health Corporation (1994–Present); Vice President Marketing, N.E.S. (1993–1994); Director of Marketing, Premier Anesthesia (1992–1993); Associate Vice President, Medicus Medical Group (1988–1992). **Associations & Accomplishments:** American Marketing Association; ACHE; United Way; Rotary International; Ducks Unlimited; Trout Unlimited; FFS. **Education:** Virginia Polytechnical Institute and State University; M.B.A. (1988), B.S. in Business (1986). **Personal:** Married to Jamie C. in 1996. Mr. Weaver enjoys fly fishing and duck hunting.

Dr. Alvin G. Wee
Prosthodontic Resident (Graduate Student)
Department of Prosthodontics of The University of Iowa
39 Sian Tuan Avenue
Singapore, Republic o 588313
(065) 466–0736
Fax: Please mail or call

8099

Business Information: The University of Iowa is a public, four–year, co–educational, liberal arts institute with graduate programs. The Department of Prosthodontics offers all aspects of Prosthodontic instruction (Prosthodontics is the branch of dentistry that deals with the restoration and maintenance of oral function by the replacement of missing teeth and other oral structures by artificial devices). Dr. Wee is currently a Teaching Assistant for the University's Department of Prosthodontics. He is also a Posthodontic Resident (Graduate Student) pursuing his Masters and Certificate in Prosthodontics. **Career Steps:** Prosthodontic Resident (Graduate Student), Department of Prosthodontics of The University of Iowa (1994–Present); Teaching Assistant, Department of Prosthodontics of The University of Iowa (1994–Present); Dental Surgeon, Private Practice at Singapore (1993–1994); Dental Officer, Ministry of Health at Singapore (1992–1993). **Associations & Accomplishments:** Singapore Dental Association; Singapore Dental Health Foundation; Guild of Dental Graduates at Singapore; Prosthodontic Society at Singapore; Student Member, Association of Osteointegration; American Prosthodontic Society; Peoples Action Party at Singapore; Mensa at Singapore; Immediate Past President, NUS Alumni Toastmasters Club; Past President, National University of Singapore Student's Union; Past President, National University of Singapore Dental Society; Singapore Asian Japan Friendship Association; Featured in publications and television. **Education:** University of Iowa, M.S. (1996); National University of Singapore, (B.D.S.) Bachelor of Dental Surgery (1992), NUS Dental Society Silver Jubilee Award (1991); Rotary Ambassadorial Scholar (1994 and 1995). **Personal:** Dr. Wee enjoys scuba diving, trekking, traveling, ballroom dancing and public speaking.

Allan J. Weiland, M.D.
•••———◖◉◗———•••

President and Chief Executive Officer
Northwest Permanente, P.C.
500 Northeast Multnomah Street, Suite 100
Portland, OR 97232–2099
(503) 813–3870
Fax: (503) 813–3889

8099

Business Information: Northwest Permanente, P.C. is a wholly–owned entity of Kaiser Permanente, the leading health maintenance organization (HMO) in the U.S. Kaiser Permanente is in 16 states and the District of Columbia, with over six million members. Established in 1945, Northwest Permanente serves 390,000 members in the Portland metropolitan area. As President and Chief Executive Officer, Dr. Weiland is responsible for overall administrative operations for Northwest Permanente, as well as serving as Regional Medical Director for Kaiser Permanente. **Career Steps:** Northwest Permanente, P.C.: President and Chief Executive Officer (1993–Present); Vice President of Operations (1988–1993), Assistant Medical Director and Bess Kaiser Area and Director Quality Assurance (1984–1988). **Associations & Accomplishments:** American Medical Association; Oregon Medical Association; Multnomah City Medical Society; Oregon OB/GYN Society; Urogynecological Society; Board Member, Northwest Center for Physician–Patient Communication; Board Member, Community Choices 2010. **Education:** Northwestern University Medical School, M.D. (1973); Harvard University Business School, Advanced Management Program (1992); University of Washington, B.S. with honors (1969). **Personal:** Married to Deidre in 1980. Three children: Eric, Laurie, and Alexis. Dr. Weiland enjoys gardening, tennis, and raquetball.

W. DeWayne Wells, CPA
•••———◖◉◗———•••

Vice President of Finance and Administration
Mercy Information Systems
34605 West 12 Mile Road
Farmington Hills, MI 48331–3263
(810) 489–6601
Fax: Please mail or call

8099

Business Information: Mercy Information Systems is an information systems division of Mercy Health Services, a catholic healthcare system with 14 hospitals that provide information systems to Michigan and Ohio. As Vice President of Finance and Administration, Mr. Wells is responsible for all aspects of financial and administrative activities, including accounting, budget, system searching, contract administration, client information hotline, human resources, and risk management. **Career Steps:** Mercy Information Systems: Vice President of Finance and Administration (1991–Present), Financial Reporting and Controls Specialist (1989–1991); Audit Supervisor, Coopers & Lybrand (1983–1989). **Associations & Accomplishments:** Michigan Association of Certified Public Accountants; National Association of Black Accountants; Healthcare Financial Management Association; United Way Campaign Coordinator. **Education:** Wayne State University, M.B.A. (1991); Western Michigan University, B.B.A. (1983). **Personal:** Married to Audrey M. in 1991. Mr. Wells enjoys travel, gardening, and music.

Mr. William Hardy Wickwar

President

Public Service Associates, Inc.

P.O. Box 12151
Columbia, SC 29211
Fax: Please mail or call

8099

Business Information: Public Service Associates, Inc. specializes in the consulting and advising on health and social administration issues, particularly in the area of aging. As President, Mr. Wickwar concentrates his activities on consulting to non–profit and public agencies. An esteemed expert on social issues, Mr. Wickwar was a member of the United Nations for over 20 years. While there he served as consultant and liaison on health concerns, primarily in the Middle Eastern block countries. Public Service Associates, Inc was established in 1975. **Career Steps:** President, Public Service Associates, Inc., (1975–Present); Chief Executive Officer, Council on Aging (1991–1994); Planning Consultant, Richland Memorial Hospital (1975–1990); Planning Director, Richland Memorial Hospital (1971–1975); Various Civil Servant Positions which include: Deputy Director of Middle East Office; Liaison Director for World Food Program; Consultant in Lebanon; Advisor on Community Development in Africa – United Nations (1944–1965) **Associations & Accomplishments:** Member of Boards on Hospital Foundation and all State and Local Aging Organizations; Charter Member, American Society for Public Administration; Chapter President, South Carolina Chapter of American Society for Public Administration; Author of over 10 books, cited in the U.S. Supreme Court. **Education:** Kings College, London, M.A. (1927); University of Paris, Rockefeller Foundation Fellow (1927–1930). **Personal:** Widower in 1987. One child: Vincent B. Wickwar, Professor of Physics at Utah State University.

Yvonne Ann Wood

Regional Director

Telecare Corporation

1100 Marina Village Parkway
Alameda Island, CA 94501
(510) 337–7950
Fax: (510) 337–7969

8099

Business Information: Telecare Corporation was solely developed to service the needs of states and countries in providing care to the mentally ill. As Regional Director, Ms. Wood is responsible for five Sub–Acute hospitals and one day treatment center covering 460 beds in Northern California. **Career Steps:** Telecare Corporation: Regional Director (1994–Present), Project Administrator (1989–1994); Executive Director, Mission Sub–Acute (1987–1989). **Associations & Accomplishments:** California Association of Health Facilities: President (1986–1989), Secretary (1995–1996); Consultant, Telecare (1989); Consultant, American Health Centers (1979); Speaker and Presenter: American Psychiatric Association (1995), International Association of Psychiatric Rehabilitation Programs (1995), Process Outcome Consultation and Systems Hawaiian Seminars (1994–1995), Quality Training Institute (1995). **Education:** University of San Francisco, M.P.A. (1993); University of California Polytechnic State College. **Personal:** Ms. Wood enjoys boating and international travel.

Catherine L. Yadamec

Director of Residential Services

Aaron Psychology Centers

P.O. Box 2182
Maryland Heights, MO 63043
(314) 275–7600
Fax: Please mail or call

8099

Business Information: Aaron Psychology Centers is a provider of direct intervention and instruction to persons to improve the quality of their life. The Center also provides necessary support to facilitate independence for persons with disabilities. As Director of Residential Services, Ms. Yadamec provides direct intervention and instruction support to individuals, their families, and/or other people involved in their lives. She is also responsible for therapy services, strategic planning, teaching of special and family skills, and budgeting. **Career Steps:** Director of Residential Services, Aaron Psychology Centers (1982–Present); Director of Residential Services, Emmaus Homes (1991–1995); Director of Developmental Programs, Community Living (1980–1989). **Associations & Accomplishments:** Communtiy Membership Training Committee. **Education:** Lindenwood College, Masters in Education (1982); University of Missouri – Columbia, Bachelor of Education (1977). **Personal:** Ms. Yadamec enjoys camping, hiking, fishing, sailing, and cross country skiing.

Thomas F. Yeargin

Regional Sales Manager

Eckerd Health Services

2761 Interlaken Drive
Marietta, GA 30062
(770) 518–0582
Fax: (770) 645–2423

8099

Business Information: Eckerd Health Services is a pharmacy benefit management service specializing in designing Rx benefit plans for managed care organizations and self–insured employers. As Regional Sales Manager, Mr. Yeargin is responsible for consulting and designing Rx plans for clients. In addition, he is responsible for diversified operational aspects, including administration, sales, public relations, accounting, and strategic planning. **Career Steps:** Regional Sales Manager, Eckerd Health Services (1993–Present); Manager, Training and Development, Glaxo Pharmaceuticals (1990–1993); District Manager, Hospital, Glaxo Pharmaceuticals (1987–1990); Sales Representative, Hospital, Glaxo Pharmaceuticals (1986–1987). **Associations & Accomplishments:** Georgia Health Decisions; Atlanta Board of Directors; Rowell Recreation Department. **Education:** Medical University of South Carolina, BS (1975). **Personal:** Married to Tina W. in 1985. Three children: Lindsay Catherine, Erin Jennifer and Samuel Thomas. Mr. Yeargin enjoys golf and reading.

Nick Z. Young

Regional Director of Operations

Sundance Rehabilitation Corporation

120 East Sheridan, Suite 211
Oklahoma City, OK 73104
(405) 235–0747
Fax: (405) 235–0749

8099

Business Information: Sundance Rehabilitation Corporation is a health care management firm, contracting with health facilities to provide the rehabilitation services of physical, occupational, and speech therapists in Central and Western Oklahoma. There are 50 regions in the U.S. Sundance Rehabilitation Corporation, established in the Oklahoma Region in 1994, reports annual revenue of $10 million and currently employs 98 people. With thirteen years expertise in the health care industry, Mr. Young joined Sundance in 1994 as Regional Director of Operations. He is responsible for the overall operations and management of three areas of services (physical, speech, occupational), with the directors of each department reporting to him. **Career Steps:** Regional Director of Operations, Sundance Rehabilitation Corporation (1994–Present); Director of Physical Therapy, Rebound Oklahoma (1992–1994); Director of Physical Therapy, Southwest Medical Center of Oklahoma (1989–1992); Physical Medicine Manager, Phoenix Baptist Hospital & Medical Center (1986–1989). **Associations & Accomplishments:** National Physical Therapy Association; Oklahoma Physical Therapy Association; Member, First Baptist Church, Yukon, Oklahoma. **Education:** University of Oklahoma Health Sciences Center, B.S. (1982). **Personal:** Married to Cheryl Young in 1980. Three children: Andrea, Kyra, and Dana. Mr. Young enjoys all sports, especially golf, and music.

Darlene Zase

Administrative Director

Bridgeport Radiology Associates, P.C.

15 Corporate Drive
Trumbull, CT 06611
(203) 261–1441
Fax: (203) 452–1832

8099

Business Information: Bridgeport Radiology Associates, P.C. offers diagnostic and therapeutic imaging services. With over fifteen years expertise in the medical management field, ranging from the nursing services and home health care profession to a large anesthesiology practice, Ms. Zase joined Bridgeport Radiology Associates — a significant and growing comprehensive imaging services company — in 1995. Currently serving as Administrative Director, Ms. Zase is responsible for overseeing all the business aspects of the organization. **Career Steps:** Administrative Director, Bridgeport Radiology Associates (1995–Present); Senior Administrator, Hartford Anesthesiology (1989–1995); Director of Business Operations, Johnson Healthcare (1987–1989). **Associations & Accomplishments:** President, Connecticut Medical Group Management Association; Member, Radiology Business Managers Association; Medical Group Mangement Association; Radiology Assembly; Managed Care Assembly. **Education:** Quinnipiac College, B.S.; Certified Medical Practice Executive. **Personal:** Married to Richard Molenaar in 1995. One child: Nicole Rioux. Ms. Zase enjoys skiing, scuba diving, cooking, and reading.

8100 Legal Services

8111 Legal services

Michael C. Ablan, Esq.

Attorney

Michael Ablan Law Office

205 5th Ave A., Ste 411
La Crosse, WI 54601
Fax: (608) 785–1976

8111

Business Information: Michael Ablan Law Office is a full–service, general practice law firm concentrating on real estate property and construction law for large and small business owners. The Firm has offices in California, Minnesota, Iowa, and Wisconsin. A practicing attorney in Wisconsin and Minnesota state and federal courts, Mr. Ablan founded the Firm in 1974. He oversees all administrative operations for associates and support staff, in addition to his daily client service. **Career Steps:** Attorney, Michael Ablan Law Office (1974–Present); Law Educator, Viterbo College (1978–Present); Law Educator, University of Wisconsin – La Crosse. **Associations & Accomplishments:** State Bar of Wisconsin: Business Law Section, Entrepreneurial Law Committee, Business Assistance Program, Lawyer Referral and Information Service; State Bar of Minnesota; Local Bar Association; U.S. Tax Court; U.S. Court of Appeals; Eastern District of Federal Court; Western District of Federal Court; Counsel for Small Business Development Center; Coalition of Wisconsin Aging Groups; La Crosse Area Estate Planning Council; Wisconsin Realtors Association Affiliate; Title Insurance Licensee – Wisconsin; Certified Arbitrator, American Arbitration Association; Tri–State Quality Improvement Network; Small Business Council, Greater La Crosse Chamber of Commerce; Winona Area Chamber of Commerce; La Crescent Area Chamber of Commerce; Caledonia Area Chamber of Commerce; Adjunct Professor, Viterbo College: Faculty of Health Care Administration, Faculty of Business Law; Faculty University of Wisconsin – La Crosse: Business Outreach, Graduate Program, Undergraduate Program; Faculty of Business Law, Western Wisconsin Technical College; Valley View Fitness & Racquet Club; The Wilderness Society; Friends of Hixon Forest Nature Center; Greenpeace; National Parks & Conservation Association; La Crosse Nordic Ski Club; La Crosse Symphony Orchestra; Friends of the Symphony; Pump House Regional Center for the Arts; Big Brothers/Big Sisters: Big Brother, Member of Advisory Board; United Temple Association; Loyal Order of the Moose; United Masonic Board for DeMolay in Wisconsin, Inc.; Founder, St. Elias Church; Grand Lodge Free and Accepted Masons of Wisconsin; Wisconsin Bow Hunters; La Crosse Community Foundation; La Crosse County Historical Foundation; Downtown Main Street, Inc.; National Trust for Historic Preservation; Native American Rights Fund; American Task Force for Lebanon; La Crosse Riding Club; U.S. Tennis Association. **Education:** Marquette University Law School, J.D.; Gustavus Adolphus College, B.B.A. **Personal:** Three children: Alyssa, John, and Antony.

Joseph E. Abodeely

Sole Practitioner

Joseph E. Abodeely Law Office

1345 W. Monroe Street
Phoenix, AZ 85007
(602) 253–2378
Fax: (602) 253–3342

8111

Business Information: The Law Office of Joseph E. Abodeely is a full–service, general practice law firm. A practicing attorney in Arizona city, state, and federal courts since 1971, Mr. Abodeely established his sole practice in 1986. His practice concentrates on all aspects of criminal defense, military law, domestic relations, and litigation matters. **Career Steps:** Sole Practitioner, Joseph E. Abodeely Law Office (1986–Present); Colonel, U.S. Army Reserve (1965–1995); Deputy County Attorney, Maricopa County Attorney's Office – Phoenix, AZ (1971–1985). **Associations & Accomplishments:** President, Arizona National Guard Historical Society; Arab–American Cultural Association; National Association of Criminal Defense Lawyers; Arizona Attorneys for Criminal Justice; State Bar of Arizona – "World Peace Through Law" Section. **Education:** University of Arizona College of Law, J.D. (1971); University of Arizona, B.A. in English (1965); Air War College (Non–Resident 1992); Judge Advocate General's School – Legal Aspects of Terrorism (Resident 1980); Naval Amphibious School – Amphibious Orientation Training (Resident 1993); National Defense University, National Security Management Course (Non–Resident 1980). **Personal:** Married to Donna in 1974. Mr. Abodeely enjoys hiking, camping, and historical studies.

Martin J. Abramson
Attorney
The Law Offices of Martin J. Abramson
29 South Broad Street
Woodbury, NJ 08096–7312
(609) 845–1400
Fax: (609) 384–8868

8111

Business Information: Establishing his private law firm in 1990, Mr. Abramson concentrates his practice in the area of family law, from marriage to custody. A trial attorney admitted to practice in both State and Federal courts, Mr. Abramson is the First Assistant on the County Council. Since the conferral of his law degree in 1976, he has been a member of a legal partnership and in practice for himself, and for the past ten years he has concentrated his focus on family law. As Attorney and the Owner of his own law practice, Mr. Abramson attributes his success to his wife and her never–ending support. **Career Steps:** Attorney, The Law Offices of Martin J. Abramson (1992–Present, 1982–1990); Partner, Abramson & Rand (1990–1992); Partner, Abramson & Hickey (1978–1982). **Associations & Accomplishments:** Fellow and Board of Managers of the New Jersey Chapter, American Academy of Matrimonial Lawyers; President, Deptford Rotary. **Education:** Temple University School of Law, J.D. (1976); Temple University, B.S. in Business (1969). **Personal:** Married to Z. Marcia in 1969. Two children: Robert T. and Jennifer Leigh. Mr. Abramson enjoys studying the Civil War.

Luis F. Abreu Elias, Esq.

Attorney
Abreu Law Offices
70 Calle Mayaguez Office 2B
Hato Rey, Puerto Rico 00917
(787) 751–4941
Fax: (787) 250–7268

8111

Business Information: Abreu Law Offices is a general practice law firm. The Firm concentrates on such legal matters as civil and criminal litigation. The Firm has three attorneys working in one office. Although the attorneys also appear in Circuit, Superior, and Supreme Courts, sixty percent of the cases that are handled by Abreu Law Offices are in federal courts. A practicing attorney since 1968, Mr. Abreu Elias founded the Firm in 1969. **Career Steps:** Attorney, Abreu Law Offices (1969–Present). **Associations & Accomplishments:** Puerto Rico Bar Association. **Education:** University of Puerto Rico: J.D. (1968), Chemist. **Personal:** Married to Zenaida Arias in 1971. One child: Fernando Luis Abreu Arias. Mr. Abreu Elias enjoys stamp and art collecting, swimming, sports, theatre, music, and gardening.

Rolando Machado Acevedo, Esq.

Lawyer
Rolando Machado Law Offices
4429 Avenida Militar, Suite 1
Isabela, Puerto Rico 00662
(787) 830–1227
Fax: Please mail or call

8111

Business Information: The Law Office of Rolando Machado Acevedo located in Isabela, Puerto Rico, is a general practice law firm working with both civil and criminal litigation. The firm also handles fraud detection and persecution cases. As an attorney, Mr. Machado practices both civil and criminal law. He works with fraud detection and persecution cases, and with the courts handling pro bono cases. **Career Steps:** Lawyer, Rolando Machado Law Offices (1996–Present); Legal Counselor, Office of the Controller of Puerto Rico (1994–1996); Management Analysis Tech, General Court of Justice (1987–1990); Management Analysis Tech, Department of

Health of Puerto Rico (1984–1987). **Associations & Accomplishments:** Colegio de Abogados de Puerto Rico; Director, Board of Directors of Cooperative de Ahorro y Credito de Isabela (1985–1988). **Education:** University of Puerto Rico: School of Law, J.D (1993), Mayaguez, B.A. (1982). **Personal:** Mr. Acevedo enjoys beach sports.

Alberto Acevedo–Colom, Esq.
Attorney
Ramos & Ramos–Camara
1479 Ashford
San Juan, Puerto Rico 00907–1583
(809) 721–6666
Fax: (809) 724–5446

8111

Business Information: Ramos & Ramos–Camara, established in 1963, is an international, full–service, general practice law firm with offices located in Puerto Rico, Spain, and the U.S. (Florida). The Practice offers legal services throughout Puerto Rico and the U.S. (New York, Connecticut, and Massachusetts). A practicing attorney since 1977, Mr. Acevedo–Colom joined the Firm in 1994. His practice concentrates on providing legal counseling and litigation. Concurrent with his legal practice, he is a Labor Law Instructor at the University of Puerto Rico. **Career Steps:** Attorney, Ramos & Ramos–Camara (1994–Present); Labor Law Teacher, University of Puerto Rico (1993–Present); Adm. Law Judge, Labor Relations Board of Puerto Rico (1990–1994). **Associations & Accomplishments:** Author of Legislacion Protectora del Trabajo Comentada which received law work Award for the Year 1988 by Puerto Rico Bar Association. **Education:** Interamerican University, J.D. (1977); University of Puerto Rico, B.B.A. (1974). **Personal:** Married to Norah Sanchez in 1992. Two children: Edgardo and Maria Alejandra. Mr. Acevedo–Colom enjoys jogging, scuba diving, writing, and reading.

Hugh W. Adamson, Esq.
Attorney
Adamson & Associates
3630 Brentwood Road Northwest Suite 247
Calgary, Alberta T2L 1K8
(403) 289–6240
Fax: (403) 289–6301

8111

Business Information: Adamson & Associates is a general practice law firm comprised of four attorneys who represent several closely–held corporations and companies. A practicing attorney in Canadian courts since obtaining his degree in 1989, Mr. Adamson founded the Firm in 1990. As Attorney and President, he is responsible for handling business, estate, and real estate cases as well as a large support staff. **Career Steps:** Attorney, Adamson & Associates (1990–Present); Student, Burnet, Duckworth & Palmer (1989–1990). **Associations & Accomplishments:** Treasurer, Rotary Club; Master Masonic Lodge; Chamber of Commerce. **Education:** University of Calgary, LL.B. (1987). **Personal:** Married to Rosemary in 1984. Two children: Craig Richard and Blake MacKenzie. Mr. Adamson enjoys skiing and golf.

Ms. Marilyn Biggs Adkins
Owner/Attorney
Adkins & Associates, P.C.
1410 High Street
Denver, CO 80218
(303) 832–8396
Fax: (303) 321–4005

8111

Business Information: Adkins & Associates is a full–service, general practice law firm with emphasis in civil litigation for small business and estate planning. Established in 1982, the Firm currently employs more than eight attorneys, legal and administrative support staff. Founder of the Firm in 1982, Ms. Adkins is responsible for all aspects of operations. Admitted to Colorado state and federal courts, she concentrates her practice in the representation of plaintiffs in personal injury and domestic relations. **Career Steps:** Owner/Attorney, Adkins & Associates (1982–Present); Legislative Director, Colorado Trial Lawyers Association (1982–1987); Owner, Bookkeeping Business (1978–1982); Owner, Texaco Service Station & Truck Rentals (1971–1978). **Associations & Accomplishments:** Member, Colorado Supreme Court Public Education Committee (1982–1994); Member, American, Colorado, Denver and First District Bar Associations; Member, Association of Trial Lawyers of America; Colorado Trial Lawyers Association; Trial Lawyers for Public Justice; Advisor, U.S. Senate Committee of Petroleum Marketing Practicing Act 1978; Member District Attorney Arbitration Panel (1976); Member, Board of Directors of Temple Sinai, Denver, CO (1983–1989); Published in "Trial Talk"; Lecturer at University of Denver Law School, Colorado Bar Association, Colorado Trial Lawyers Association and local women's groups; Who's Who Among American Women. **Education:** University of Denver Law School, J.D. (1982); University of Denver, B.A. (1967). **Personal:** Married to Charles T. Wood in 1989. Two children:

Christopher Adkins and Shawneen Morrison. Ms. Adkins enjoys music, gardening and cooking.

Job Ola Agboola

President
CALEB International Services
43 Gibbs Street
New Haven, CT 06511–1807
(203) 562–9656
Fax: (203) 562–6131

8111

Business Information: CALEB International Services provides exporting and importing legal consultation to corporations worldwide. Former Vice President of Concord Newspaper, the largest national newspaper in Nigeria, Mr. Agboola founded CALEB in 1992. He serves as President and Chief Executive Officer in the day–to–day management of corporate operations, business growth, and administration. **Career Steps:** President, CALEB International Services (1992–Present); Assistant Managing Director, King's Square Supermarket (1981–1984); Vice President, Concord Newspaper, Nigeria (1980–1981). **Associations & Accomplishments:** Nigeria Bar Association; Chairman and Trustee of Nigeria Historical Association. **Education:** University of Bemin, Nigeria: M.S. (1990), L.L.B., B.A. **Personal:** Married to Sharnell L. in 1994. Mr. Agboola enjoys reading, soccer, and politics.

Luis A. Aguila–Lopez, Esq.

Attorney
Law Offices of Luis A. Aguila–Lopez
73 Calle M. J. Cabrero
San Sebastian, Puerto Rico 00685–2243
(809) 896–4113
Fax: (809) 896–4113

8111

Business Information: The Law Office of Luis A. Aguila–Lopez is a private, full–service law firm specializing in professional services in civil and criminal matters. A practicing attorney since 1986 in Puerto Rico state courts, Mr. Aguila–Lopez established his private law practice in 1987. He is responsible for diversified law practices, including labor law and local contracts. **Career Steps:** Sole Practitioner, Law Offices of Luis A. Aguila–Lopez (1987–Present); Region Director, Puerto Rico Federation of Teachers (1978–1983); Teacher, Education Department (1976–1978). **Associations & Accomplishments:** Secretary of Organization, Education Workers, National Committee; President, National Association of Law Students; Law School Review; President Comite Pepiniano de Defensa de la Cultura; Member of Centro Cultural de San Sebastian. **Education:** University of Puerto Rico School of Law, J.D., magnum cum laude (1986); University of Puerto Rico, B.A., magna cum laude. **Personal:** Married to Maria Aviles–Soto in 1974. 3 children: Mayte, Luis E., and Luis F. Mr. Aguila–Lopez enjoys playing basketball, movies, and reading.

Reema I. Ali
Manager of International Practice
Ali & Partners
700 13th Street NW, Suite 950
Washington, DC 20005–3960
(202) 347–2400
Fax: (202) 347–2229

8111

Business Information: Ali & Partners is an international corporate law firm, representing major U.S and European companies and law firms in the Middle East in international corporate matters. The Firm's headquarters are located in the Middle East in international corporate matters. The Firm's headquarters are located in Kuwait with offices throughout the Middle–East. Admitted to practice in U.S. and International courts, Ms. Ali joined the Firm in 1989 and serves as Manager of International Practices and Resident Partner of the D.C. office. She is responsible for providing legal counsel to U.S. companies and firms on Middle East regional law matters. An Arab American born in Denver, raised in the West Bank of Jordan, she received her post–secondary education in England and then returned to the U.S. to obtain her law doctorate. Based on her varied background, Ms. Ali attributes her success on the ability to understand both U.S. and Middle Eastern views. **Career Steps:** Manager of International Practice and Managing Partner of the D.C. Office, Ali & Partners (1994–Present); Manager of Middle East Law Practice, Al–Ayoub, Shea & Gould (1992–1994); Manager of Middle East Law Practice, Al–Ayoub, Donovan Leisure (1990–1992); Counselor – Kuwait, Graham & James (1984–1989). **Associations & Accomplishments:** Chairperson, Palestine Legal Committee on the Palestine American Congress; Vice President, Legal Affairs, Kuwait American Business Council. **Education:** S.M.U., J.D. (1983); Leeds Polytechnic University, LL.B. (1981). **Person-

al: Married to Munzer Al–Qaneh in 1984. Two children: Khaled and Basil. Ms. Ali enjoys reading, gardening, swimming and walking.

Mark H. Allen
Attorney/President
Johnson, Allen, Jones & Dornblaser
601 South Boulder Avenue, Suite 900
Tulsa, OK 74119
(918) 584–6644
Fax: (918) 584–6645

8111

Business Information: Johnson, Allen, Jones & Dornblaser established in 1994, is a law firm comprised of eight attorneys and a support staff of eighteen. As Attorney/President, Mr. Allen was instrumental in forming the Firm with seven associate attorneys two years ago. The Partners elected him President of the Firm, despite the fact that several other partners are senior to Mr. Allen in experience and age. Receiving an "AV" rating in the largest attorney rating service, Martindale–Hubbell, Mr. Allen is one of only fifteen attorneys in Oklahoma listed in the Best Lawyers in America publication. Concentrating in Taxation and Business law, he is a Certified Public Accountant, and has served as Lead Counsel to Whirlpool Corporation regarding site selection and governmental incentive negotiations, which led to Whirlpool locating in Tulsa. An alumnae of Southern Methodist University School of Law, Mr. Allen attained membership in the Order of the Coif, served as editor of the Journal of Air Law & Commerce, was selected as a Hatton W. Summers Scholar, and recognized as an Outstanding Future Tax Practitioner. **Career Steps:** Attorney/President, Johnson, Allen, Jones & Dornblaser (1994–Present); Gable & Gotwals, Inc: Member/Board of Directors/Treasurer (1991–1994), Shareholder (1988–1994), Associate (1982–1987); Member, Board of Directors, XRS Technologies, Inc. (1996–Present). **Associations & Accomplishments:** Oklahoma/Tulsa County Society of Certified Public Accountants; Oklahoma Bar Association, Taxation Section/Past Chairman; Tulsa County Bar Association, Taxation Section; Tulsa Tax Club; Tulsa Tax Lawyers Group; National Health Lawyers Association; American Bar Association: Section of Corporation, Banking and Business Law, Section on Taxation, Former member of Affiliated and Related Corporations Committee, Corporate Tax Committee, Adjunct Member of Natural Resources, Real Estate Tax and Partnership Committees; Ten Outstanding Young Tulsans (1996); Board of Directors, Youth Services of Tulsa; Board of Directors, American Heart Association; Board of Directors, Leadership Tulsa; Hillcrest Associates; Downtown Kiwanis Club; Tulsa Metropolitan Chamber of Commerce; Tulsa Area United Way. **Education:** University of Oklahoma, B.B.A. in Accounting with special distinction (1978); Southern Methodist University School of Law, J.D. (1982). **Personal:** Married to Cindy in 1978. Three children: Kelly, Kyle, and Corey. Mr. Allen enjoys golf, running, and travel.

Ivan Alonso
President
Law Office of Ivan Alonso
59 San Jose Street
Aibonito, Puerto Rico 00705–0107
(809) 735–8550
Fax: (809) 735–8550

8111

Business Information: The Law Office of Ivan Alonso is a full–service, general practice law firm, concentrating on criminal and civil law. Establishing the Firm as a sole practice upon conferral of his law degree in 1985, Mr. Alonso now serves as President for the growing practice. He oversees all administrative operations for associates and support staff of 30, in addition to his private law practice. He also serves as Chairman of the San Jose Cooperative Board of the San Jose Cooperative Bank. **Career Steps:** Law Office of Ivan Alonso: President (1986–Present), Sole Practitioner (1985–1986). **Associations & Accomplishments:** San Jose Cooperative Board; Chairman, Instructor, International Tae Kwon Do Center; President, Puerto Rican Independence Party, Municipality of Aibonito. **Education:** University of Puerto Rico, J.D. (1985). **Personal:** Married to Mildred Gonzalez in 1985. Two children: Alfredo Jose and Rocio. Mr. Alonso enjoys martial arts.

Thomas John Alworth
Partner
Shanley & Fisher, P.C.
131 Madison Avenue
Morristown, NJ 07960–6086
(201) 285–1000
Fax: (201) 538–5960

8111

Business Information: Shanley & Fisher, P.C. is a full–service, general practice law firm. Established in 1944, the Firm currently employs 110 attorneys. A practicing attorney since 1966 and a Certified Trial Lawyer in New Jersey, Mr. Alworth joined the Firm as Partner in 1970. Serving as a Trial Attorney, his practice concentrates on products liability, personal injury, and construction matters. **Career Steps:** Partner, Shanley & Fisher, P.C. (1970–Present); Assistant U.S. Attorney, U.S. Attorney's Office, Newark, New Jersey (1967–1970); Law Clerk, Hon. Robert Shaw, Judge, U.S. District Court (1966–1967). **Associations & Accomplishments:** Fellow, American College of Trial Lawyers; Member, American Board of Trial Advocates; Certified Civil Trial Lawyer, State of New Jersey; Former President, Richard J. Hughes Inn of Court; American Bar Association; New Jersey State Bar Association; Morris & Essex County Bar Association; Member, Essex County Judicial Selection Committee. **Education:** George Washington University School of Law, J.D. (1966); Duke University, A.B. (1963). **Personal:** Married to Linda in 1995. Mr. Alworth enjoys fund raising for Duke University and golf.

Susan D'Alonzo Ament
Attorney
Ament Lynch & Carr
6 Stone Hill Road – Augustine Hills
Wilmington, DE 19899
(302) 655–8808
Fax: (302) 655–8831

8111

Business Information: Ament Lynch & Carr is a general service law firm with a focus on personal injury litigation. The Firm is licensed in Pennsylvania and Delaware and practices in both states. Mrs. Ament is a Director of the Firm and works with other directors in the establishment of policies and procedures. **Career Steps:** Attorney, Ament Lynch & Carr. **Associations & Accomplishments:** Board of Governors, State of Delaware; State of Delaware Board of Bar Examiners; Delaware Superior Court Mediator; Chairperson, The Fee Dispute Mediation and Conciliation Committee of the Delaware Bar Association (1991–1995); Nominating Committee, Delaware State Bar Association (1993); Former Co–Chair, Medical/Legal Committee of the Delaware State Bar Association; New Castle County Member at Large of the Board of governors, Delaware Trial Lawyers Association (1993–1994); State of Delaware Industrial Accident Board Rules Committee; American Immigration Lawyers Association; National Health Lawyers Association, Association of Trial Lawyers of America; President, St. Thomas More Society (1994–1995); Past President, Board of Directors of Bayard House (1989–1993); Appointed counsellor of the Due Process Commission of the Catholic Diocese of Wilmington (1995); St. Joseph on the Brandywine Church; Volunteer, Mary Campbell Center; Honorary Member Philippino–American Association of Delaware; Human Relations Committee, University and Whist Club. **Education:** Widner University School of Law, J.D. (1982); University of Delaware, B.S. (1979). **Personal:** Mrs. Ament enjoys spending quality time with her three children ages 17, 14, and 12.

David Robert Amerine, Esq.
Partner and Attorney
Manatt Phelps & Phillips
1501 M Street NW, Suite 700
Washington, DC 20005–1700
(202) 463–4300 Ext. 335
Fax: (301) 229–5618
E–mail: see below

8111

Business Information: Manatt, Phelps & Phillips is a full–service international law firm. Established in 1965, the Firm currently employs 250 attorneys and legal support staff. A trial attorney admitted to both State and Federal courts, David Amerine concentrates his practice in the area of international trade. Mr. Amerine investigates U.S. unfair trade practices, and can take administrative action through the Department of Commerce and the U.S. Department of Trade. Mr. Amerine has been a Partner with Manatt, Phelps & Phillips since 1993. He can be reached through the Internet as follows: DAMERINE@MANATT.COM **Career Steps:** Partner and Attorney,

Manatt, Phelps & Phillips (1993–Present); Partner, Brownstein, Zeivman & Sclomers (1984–1993); Employee, Treasury Department and Commerce Department (until 1981); Associate, Stein, Shostack & Ottero (until 1984). **Associations & Accomplishments:** American Bar Association, Interior Law Section; District of Columbia Bar Association, International Trade Section. **Education:** Georgetown University, LL.M (1981); Catholic University, J.D. (1978); Marietta College, B.A. **Personal:** Married to Mary Louise in 1984. One child: Mary Catherine. Mr. Amerine enjoys tennis, sailing and travel.

Eric A. Andujar–Vargas, Esq.
Junior Partner
Luis E. Andujar–Moreno Law Offices
1697 Calle Diamela
San Juan, Puerto Rico 00927
(809) 763–2232
Fax: (809) 763–3472

8111

Business Information: Luis E. Andujar–Moreno Law Offices is a full–service, general law practice. Established in 1965, the Firm currently employs 7 attorneys, legal aide and administrative support staff. Mr. Andujar–Vargas, an associate with the Firm upon conferral of his law degree in 1990, and appointed Junior Partner in 1994, serves as Closing Attorney for a major bank. He also practices civil litigation, as well as limited criminal cases. **Career Steps:** Luis E. Andujar–Moreno Law Offices: Junior Partner (1994–Present), Associate Attorney (1991–1994), Law Clerk (1985–1991). **Associations & Accomplishments:** Board of Governors, Puerto Rico Bar Association (Colegio de Abogados de Puerto Rico); Puerto Rico Notary Public Association (Asociacion de Notarios de Puerto Rico); Phi Alpa Delta Law Fraternity International; American Bar Association; Lifetime Alumnus, American Mensa; Presidential Classroom for Young Americans. **Education:** University of Puerto Rico: J.D. (1990), B.A. in Political Sciences (1986). **Personal:** Married to Milva E. Dordal–Andujar in 1988. Two children: Astrid L. and Monica I. Mr. Andujar–Vargas enjoys reading, walking, playing the guitar, and water sports.

Michael Antin
Attorney–at–Law
Antin & Taylor
1875 Century Park East, Suite 700
Los Angeles, CA 90067–2508
(310) 788–2733
Fax: (310) 788–0754
EMAIL: See Below

8111

Business Information: Antin & Taylor is a full–service tax law firm. A certified Taxation Law specialist admitted to the Bar in 1964, Mr. Antin focuses his practice on wealth planning. Co–founding Antin & Taylor in 1993, as Senior Partner he shares responsibility of supervising a legal staff of five, in addition to representing major clientele. Internet users can reach him via: mantin@ix.netcom.com **Career Steps:** Senior Partner and Attorney, Antin & Taylor (1993–Present); Tax Partner, Gold, Marks, Ring, & Pepper (1991–1992); Tax Lawyer and President, Antin, Litz, & Gilbert (1963–1991). **Associations & Accomplishments:** Fellow, American College of Tax Counsel; Fellow, American College of Trust and Estate Counsel; Director, Small Business Counsel of America; Director, The Group, Inc.; Director, Ventura County National Bancorp; American Bar Association; State Bar of California; Los Angeles County Bar Association; Beverly Hills Bar Association; Beverly Hills Estate Planning Council; Director, Frontier Bank, N.A. **Education:** University of California – Berkeley School of Law, J.D. (1963); University of California – Los Angeles School of Business, B.S. in Accounting (1960). **Personal:** Married to Evelyne in 1960. Three children: Stephanie, Bryan, and Randy. Mr. Antin enjoys tennis, bowling, jogging, birding, and marine fish.

Marlene Aponte–Cabrera, Esquire
Attorney
Law Office of Marlene Aponte–Cabrera
Edif Bco Coop Plaza Suite 404B, 623 Ponce De Leon
San Juan, Puerto Rico 00917
(809) 764–4342
Fax: (809) 763–6684

8111

Business Information: The Law Office of Marlene Aponte–Cabrera is a full–service, federal and state criminal practice law firm. A practicing attorney since 1988, Ms. Aponte–Cabrera is admitted to practice in the states of Puerto Rico, Florida, Virginia, and the United States Supreme Court. Establishing her private legal practice in 1993, she oversees the administrative operations for associates and a support staff of seven. Her practice concentrates on civil rights and criminal law in federal courts and strictly criminal law in state courts, focusing on bank fraud and narcotic cases. **Career Steps:** Attorney, Law Office of Marlene Aponte–Cabrera (1993–Present); Family Law Task Force Trial Attorney, Legal Services Northern Virginia (1993); Assistant General Counsel, U.S. Department of Justice (1989–1993); Legislative Counsel for Hon. Jaime B. Fuster, U.S. House of Representatives (1988–1989). **Associations & Accomplishments:** Puerto Rico Bar Association; Virginia Bar Association; Florida Bar Association; National Hispanic Bar Association; National Association of Criminal Defense Lawyers. **Education:** University of Puerto Rico Law School, J.D. (1988); University of Puerto Rico – College of Humanities, Major in English, Minor in Foreign Languages; Attended: Houston Baptist University. **Personal:** One child: Candice M. Ms. Aponte–Cabrera enjoys gourmet cooking, sewing, and classic literature.

Jose E. Aquino–Nunaz
Sole Practitioner
Law Offices of Jose E. Aquino–Nunez
P.O. Box 967
Quebradillas, Puerto Rico 00678
(809) 895–3413
Fax: (809) 895–1124

8111

Business Information: The Law Office of Jose E. Aquino–Nunez is a full–service, general practice law firm, engaged in civil constitutional corporations, labor, property and torts law cases. Establishing the firm upon the conferral of his law degree in 1980, Mr. Aquino–Nunez oversees the administrative operations for associates and a support staff of four, in addition to his daily legal practice. His practice concentrates on labor (60%), civil, property, and family law. Concurrent with his legal practice, he serves as an Adjunct Instructor, teaching classes on Criminal and Juvenile Law. **Career Steps:** Attorney, Jose E. Aquino–Nunaz (1980–Present); Professor, Catholic University of Puerto Rico, J.D. (1981–1989); Personnel Manager, Daniel Construction Company International (1970–1979). **Associations & Accomplishments:** Colegio de Abogados de Puerto Rico; Asociacion de Notarios de Puerto Rico. **Education:** Interamerica University of Puerto Rico, J.D. (1980); University of Puerto Rico, B.A. **Personal:** Married to Irazema Gonzalez in 1977. Two children: Laura and Lydia. Mr. Aquino–Nunez enjoys reading, and writing poems.

Sanford Astor
Attorney
Stall, Astor, & Goldstein
10507 West Pico Boulevard, Suite 200
Los Angeles, CA 90064–2319
(310) 470–6852
Fax: (310) 470–3673
EMAIL: See Below

8111

Business Information: Stall, Astor, & Goldstein is an international, general practice law firm, comprised of three partners and two associates. As Attorney, Mr. Astor concentrates in the areas of patents, trademarks, copyrights, and intellectual property law. He specializes in representation of smaller businesses and individual clients. Internet users can reach him via: STASGO@MSN.COM. **Career Steps:** Attorney, Stall, Astor, & Goldstein (1994–Present); Attorney/Partner, Thaler & Astor (1987–1994); Attorney, Self Employed, Sanford Astor (1984–1987); Attorney/Partner, Astor & Merdler (1980–1984). **Associations & Accomplishments:** State Bar of California; Los Angeles County Bar Association; Beverly Hills Bar Association; American Bar Association; Outstanding Young Men in America (1969); Chairman, Intellectual Property Committee of Torts and Insurance Practice (TIPS) Section of American Bar Association. **Education:** George Washington University, J.D. (1962); Purdue University, B.S. in Chemical Engineering (1958). **Personal:** Married to Bonny Dore in 1987. Three children: Shelley, Scot, and Stacy. Mr. Astor enjoys tennis and golf.

Dr. Paul G. Atkinson, Ed.D., J.D.
Owner
Law Office of Paul G. Atkinson
703 West 23rd Street
Merced, CA 95340–3609
(209) 726–1636
Fax: (209) 726–1689

8111

Business Information: The Law Office of Paul G. Atkinson is a general practice law firm. As Owner and Sole Practitioner, Dr. Atkinson handles all aspects of the practice. Prior to his law career, Dr. Atkinson held numerous educational administrative and teaching positions, primarily with the Atwater Public School District. Established in 1991, the Law Office of Paul G. Atkinson employs 2 people. **Career Steps:** Owner, Law Office of Paul G. Atkinson (1991–Present); School Administrator, Atwater School District (1970–1980); School Teacher, Atwater School District (1957–1991). **Associations & Accomplishments:** Member, ExComm General/Solo Practice Section, State Bar of California; American Bar Association; Delta Theta Phi, International Law Fraternity; Phi Delta Kappa; University of the Pacific Education Alumni Executive Committee; Association of California School Administrators; American Association of School Business Officials; National Organization for Legal Problems in Education; California Teachers Association; National Education Association; California Farm Bureau Federation; Alpha Zeta; Gamma Pi Delta; Listed in : "Who's Who Among American Teachers" 1990; Licensed to practice: California and the U.S. District Courts. **Education:** Humphries School of Law, J.D. (1989); University of the Pacific, Ed.D. (1981); Chapman University, M.A. (1970); California State University, Polytechnic, B.S. (1960). **Personal:** Married to Ellen E. Bauer in 1966. Two children: Rosalie M. and Paul Alexander.

Fanny Auz Patino, Esq.
Attorney at Law and Notary Public
In house counsel for McDonald's Corporation for the Caribe and Central America
156 Fortaleza Street
Old San Juan, Puerto Rico 00902
(787) 722–6397
Fax: (787) 722–6340

8111

Business Information: A practicing attorney in Puerto Rico courts since 1982, also admitted to practice in Washington, D.C. and New York. Ms. Auz founded the firm in 1995. **Career Steps:** Senior Partner/Owner, Auz–Patino Law Office (1995–Present); Partner, Martinez, Odell & Calabria (1990–1995); Senior Associate, Goldman & Antonetti (1983–1989). **Associations & Accomplishments:** Member of the Finance Committee, Casa Protegida Julia de Burgos – a shelter for battered women and their children; Civil Rights Commission of Puerto Rico (1995). **Education:** University of Puerto Rico, J.D. (1982); Interamerican University, magna cum laude (1978).

Edward Gomes Avila
Attorney
Roberts, Carroll, Feldstein & Peirce
10 Weybosset Street
Providence, RI 02903
(401) 521–7000
Fax: (401) 521–1328

8111

Business Information: Roberts, Carroll, Feldstein & Pierce is a general practice law firm. Established in 1970, the Firm currently employs 50 attorneys and legal support staff. Joining the Firm upon the conferral of his law degree in 1987, Mr. Avila concentrates his practice in the areas of business, corporate, banking and real estate law. Admitted to both State and federal courts, Mr. Avila has been with Roberts Caroll Et Al for eight years. **Career Steps:** Attorney, Roberts, Carroll, Feldstein & Pierce (1987–Present). **Associations & Accomplishments:** Finance Committee, Saint Francis Xavier Church; American Bar Association; Rhode Island Bar Association; Massachusetts Bar Association; Published chapter in construction handbook. **Education:** Boston College Law School, J.D. (1987); Providence College, B.A. in Economics. **Personal:** Married to Nancy Ann in 1990. Two children: Benjamin and Bethany. Mr. Avila enjoys sports.

Jose A. Axtmayer
Attorney/Partner
Axtmayer Adsuar Muniz Goyco
Suite 1400 Hato Rey Towers
Hato Rey, Puerto Rico 00918
(787) 756–9000 (787) 281–1800
Fax: (787) 756–9010
EMAIL: axtmayer@aamg.org

8111

Business Information: Axtmayer Adsuar Muniz Goyco is a full service, private practice law firm employing approximately 50 people. The firm is located in Puerto Rico and practices in the Caribbean area, Latin America, New York, and Puerto Rico. As Attorney/Partner, Mr. Axtmayer heads up the corporate banking and securities division and is licensed to practice in Puerto Rico and New York. He is involved in the recruiting of new legal staff members, decisions regarding expansion of the practice, investments, and general operations of the partnership. **Career Steps:** Attorney/Partner, Axtmayer Adsuar Muniz Goyco (1994–Present); Partner, Goldman Antonetti Cordova & Axtmeyer (1990–1994); Partner,Ferraiuoli Axtmayer & Hertell (1982–1990); Associate, Hughes Hubbard & Reed (1977–1981). **Associations & Accomplishments:** American Bar Association; New York State Bar Association; Colegio De Abogados de Puerto Rico; Federal Bar Association. **Education:** Yale Law School, JD (1975); Yale University, MA (1974) and BA (1971). **Personal:** One child: Sofia Maria. Mr. Axtmayer enjoys golf and being an arbitrator to the World Court for Sports Arbitration.

Sidney K. Ayabe
Managing Partner
Ayabe, Chong, Nishimoto, Sia & Nakamura
1001 Bishop Street
Honolulu, HI 96813–3429
(808) 537–6119
Fax: (808) 526–3491

8111

Business Information: Ayabe, Chong, Nishimoto, Sia & Nakamura is a full–service, general practice law firm, concentrating on insurance issues, serving clients throughout the Hawaiian islands, as well as limited mainland U.S. clientele. A practicing attorney since 1970, Mr. Ayabe co–founded the firm in 1972. As Managing Partner, he oversees all administrative areas and junior associates, in addition to his daily legal practice. His practice concentrates in the areas of insurance defense litigation("fender benders", slip & fall, wrongful discharge, malpractice), as well as estate planning, plaintiff work, legal, dental, and product liability cases. **Career Steps:** Managing Partner, Ayabe, Chong, Nishimoto, Sia & Nakamura (1972–Present); Deputy Attorney General, Attorney General's Office (1970–1972). **Associations & Accomplishments:** President (1995), Hawaii State Bar Association; American Bar Association; State Chair (1993–1995), American College of Trial Lawyers; International Association of Defense Counsel; American Board of Trial Advocates. **Education:** University of Iowa, J.D. (1970); Lawrence University, B.A. (1967). **Personal:** Married to Gloria in 1977. Three children: Lisa, Sara, and Marie. Mr. Ayabe enjoys golf and skiing.

Julien P. Ayotte, Ph.D.
Chief Operating Officer
Mirick, O'Connell, DeMallie & Lougee
1700 Bank of Boston Tower – 100 Front St.
Worcester, MA 01608
(508) 799–0541
Fax: (508) 752–7305
EMAIL: See Below

8111

Business Information: Mirick, O'Connell, DeMallie & Lougee, established in 1916, is a private, corporate practice law firm, consisting of 50 associate attorneys and over 120 legal and administrative support personnel. As Chief Operating Officer, Dr. Ayotte is responsible for the overall day–to–day administrative operations of the firm. Primary duties involve banking relationships, risk management, insurance matters and overall strategies. Concurrent with his duties for the Firm, he is also a Professor of Finance with Assumption and Anna Marie Colleges. He can also be reached through the Internet via: jpayotte@MODL.COM. **Career Steps:** Chief Operating Officer, Mirick, O'Connell, DeMallie & Lougee (1989–Present); Director of Finance & Administration, Partridge, Snow & Hahn (1988–1989); Treasurer & Chief Financial Officer, Concept Industries, Inc (1985–1986); Assistant Corporate Controller, Textron, Inc. (1977–1985). **Associations & Accomplishments:** Association of Legal Administrators; Financial Executives Institute; American Bar Association; Central Massachusetts Financial Executives Organization. **Education:** Columbia Pacific University, Ph.D. (1992); University of Rhode Island: M.B.A., B.S.; Harvard Business School, Management Development Program. **Personal:** Married to Pauline A. in 1963. Three children: Barbara, David and Julie. Dr. Ayotte enjoys tennis, golf, stock market trading and investment ventures.

D. Gregory Baker

Attorney at Law
Kilgore & Baker
*126 Cedar Avenue
Gate City, VA 24251–3610
(540) 386–7701
Fax: (540) 386–2377*

8111

Business Information: Kilgore & Baker is a general law firm. Established in 1994, the Firm currently employs three attorneys and legal support staff. A trial attorney since 1985, Mr. Baker is admitted to both State and Federal courts. **Career Steps:** Attorney at Law and Partner, Kilgore & Baker (1994–Present); Chairman of the Board, Dickenson–Buchanan Bank (1985–1994). **Education:** Samford University Cumberland School of Law, J.D. (1985); Clinch Valley College of the University of Virginia, B.A. (1982). **Personal:** Married to Joye Thomas in 1986. One child: Emily Ann. Mr. Baker enjoys sports and travel.

Cecil J. Banks, Esq.

Managing Partner
Banks Erlanger
*One Gateway Center
Newark, NJ 07102
(201) 648–0800
Fax: (201) 648–0700*

8111

Business Information: Banks Erlanger is a full–service, general practice law firm. A practicing attorney in New Jersey state courts since 1976, Mr. Banks co–established the Firm in 1995. A practicing litigator, he is responsible for the management of the Firm, as well as his daily legal practice. **Career Steps:** Managing Partner, Banks Erlanger (1995–Present); Partner, Sills Cummis (1984–1995); Associate, McCarter & English (1976–1978); General Counsel, Newark Board of Education (1978–1982). **Associations & Accomplishments:** Presidential Appointment with U.S. Senate Approval – Board of Directors, African Development Foundation; African American Summit; U.S. Business Executive Club. **Education:** Rutgers Law School, J.D. (1976); University of Pittsburgh Graduate School, M.P.A. in Public and International Affairs (1974); DuQuesne University, B.A. (1970); Sophia University (1966). **Personal:** Married to Dr. Margot Banks in 1972. Three children: Kimberly, Imani, and Jamaal. Mr. Banks enjoys tennis.

Phillip D. Barber

Lawyer
Dufford & Brown, P.C.
*1700 Broadway, Suite 1700
Denver, CO 80290–1701
(303) 861–8013
Fax: (303) 832–3804*

8111

Business Information: Dufford & Brown, P.C. is a full–service, general practice law firm with special concentrations in the areas of environmental law, commercial litigation, business transactions, utilities and natural resources work. Additional areas of concentration include trusts and estates, employment and Worker's Compensation defense. A practicing attorney since 1975, Mr. Barber joined the Firm as Attorney in 1979. His practice focuses on commercial litigation and natural resources law, as well as contract disputes and securities litigation. **Career Steps:** Lawyer, Dufford & Brown, P.C. (1979–Present). **Associations & Accomplishments:** President, Capital Hill Community Services; Colorado Bar Association; American Bar Association; Denver Bar Association. **Education:** University of Colorado – School of Law, J.D. (1975); Dartmouth College, A.B., magna cum laude (1975). **Personal:** Two children: Lucy and Madeleine. Mr. Barber enjoys outdoor activities and piano in his leisure time.

Mr. Stanley A. Barg Esq.

Partner
Sherr, Joffe & Zuckerman, P.C.
*P.O. Box 800, 200 Four Falls Corporate Center, Suite 400
West Conshohocken, PA 19428–0800
(610) 941–2348
Fax: (610) 941–0711*

8111

Business Information: Sherr, Joffe & Zuckerman, P.C. is a full–service, international practice law firm. The Firm currently has 22 attorneys representing an international client base, particularly in Switzerland (Zurich and Geneva). A practicing attorney since 1975, Stanley Barg joined as partner with the Firm in 1988. Specializing in international tax law, he represents both individual and international corporate clients in estate planning and tax matters. **Career Steps:** Partner, Sherr, Joffe & Zuckerman, P.C. (1988–Present); Partner, Reed, Smith, Shaw & McClay (1985–1988); Partner, Baskin and Sears (1978–1984). **Associations & Accomplishments:** American Bar Association – Tax Section; Pennsylvania Bar Association; Philadelphia Bar Association – Tax Section; Chairman – Probate & Tax Section, Montgomery County Bar Association (1994 & 1995); Chairman – Tax Section, Allegheny County Bar Association (1981–1982); Tax Supper Club – Philadelphia; President, Allegheny Tax Society (1988) ; Advisory Board, Philadelphia Tax Conference; Board of Directors, Har Zion Temple. **Education:** New York University School of Law, L.L.M. Degree in Taxation (1975); George Washington University – National Law Center, Juris Doctor with honors (1974); George Washington University, B.A. (Phi Beta Kappa, Dean's List) (1971). **Personal:** Married to Frances in 1973. Two children: Mallory and Jeffrey.

Joseph N. Barker

Senior Partner
Farris Warfield & Kanaday
*424 Church Street, Suite 1900
Nashville, TN 37219–2308
(615) 782–2333
Fax: Please mail or call*

8111

Business Information: Farris Warfield & Kanaday is a full–service, commercial practice law firm, with emphasis on financial institutions and consisting of 45 attorneys. A practicing attorney since 1969 and a Certified Real Estate Attorney, Mr. Barker joined the Firm as Senior Partner in the Corporate Real Estate Section in 1992. His practice focuses on finance, corporate, and international transactions, in addition to overseeing administrative operations for associates and the support staff in his section. **Career Steps:** Senior Partner, Farris Warfield & Kanaday (1992–Present); Partner, Dearborn & Ewing (1972–1992); Captain, U.S. Marine Corps (1969–1972). **Associations & Accomplishments:** American College of Real Estate Lawyers; Board of Directors, Local American Diabetes Association; American Cancer Society; Published articles for law journals and association trade journals. **Education:** Vanderbilt University, J.D. (1969); Dartmouth College, A.B. (1966); Attended Stanford University and Universite Laval, Quebec, Canada. **Personal:** Married to Patricia in 1988. Four children: Leah, Nate, Teri, and Michelle. Mr. Barker enjoys fishing and farming.

Pamela Ellen Barker, Esq.

Shareholder
Godfrey & Kahn, S.C.
*780 N. Water Street
Milwaukee, WI 53202–3512
(414) 273–3500
Fax: (414) 273–5198*

8111

Business Information: Godfrey & Kahn, S.C. is a full–service, environmental law firm, consisting of five offices located in Milwaukee, Green Bay, Madison, Oshkosh, and Sheboygan, Wisconsin. The Firm currently employs 124 attorneys, and more than 26 legal and administrative support staff. A practicing attorney in Wisconsin state and federal courts since 1979, Ms. Barker joined the Firm in 1981. Serving as Shareholder, her practice concentrates on federal and state environmental law, focusing primarily on issues arising out of real estate transactions and corporate acquisitions, including environmental audits and due diligence, contract negotiations and sales, lender liability, and site contamination. **Career Steps:** Shareholder, Godfrey & Kahn, S.C. (1981–Present); Associate Attorney, Cook & Franke (1979–1981). **Associations & Accomplishments:** American Bar Association: Litigation Section, Real Estate Section, Natural Resources, Energy, and Environmental Law Section – Solid and Hazardous Waste Committee (1994–Present), Lender Liability Committee (1994–Present), Planning Committee for Programs for Environmental Quality (1994–Present), House of Delegates (1990–Present), Executive Council of Young Lawyer Division; State Bar of Wisconsin: President (1993–1994), Vice Chair, Commission on Delivery of Legal Services (1994–1995), Chairperson, Non–Lawyer Delivery Subcommittee (1994–1995), Subcommittee Chair, Environmental Law of the Construction and Public Contract Law Committee, Chairperson, Personnel Subcommittee (1994–Present), Executive Committee, Environmental Law Section – Board of Governors, Government Lawyers Committee (1994–1995), Chairperson, Board of Governors, Affiliate/Associate Task Force, Subcommittee on Sections and Divisions, Executive Committee, Finance Committee, Post–Graduate Education Comittee, Convention and Entertainment Committee; Judicial Selection Committee (1989–Present), Milwaukee Bar Association; Milwaukee Young Lawyers Association: President, Board of Directors, Chairperson, Law and You Committee, Dispute Resolution Committee (1983–Present); Board of Directors (1993–1994), Wisconsin Law Foundation; Moderator of The Law and You television program for WTMJ; University of Wisconsin: Community Law Office, Legal Assistance to Inmates, Board of Directors, School Alumni Association (1994–Present), Board of Visitors (1994–Present); Participated in Joint Civilian Orientation Conference 57 – sponsored by the Department of Defense (1994); TEMPO (1984–Present); BOMA (1985–Present); Frequent speaker at Bar conference proceedings and other civic and corporate gatherings. AWARDS: Martindale–Hubbell Rating – AV; Outstanding Young Women of America; Outstanding Young Lawyer Award presented by the Milwaukee Jaycees (1985); Board of Directors Award and Special Service Award presented by the Milwaukee Young Lawyers Association; Award of Achievement by Young Lawyers Division, American Bar Association; Appointed by Wisconsin Senators Herbert Kohl and Russ Feingold to Serve on the Wisconsin Federal Nominating Commission to Advise Senators on Federal Judicial and U.S. Attorney nominations (1994). **Education:** University of Wisconsin – Madison, J.D. (1979); University of Wisconsin – Beloit, B.A. (1976). **Personal:** Married to Jeffrey Phillips in 1980. One child: Jeffrey Phillips. Ms. Barker enjoys golf.

Richard M.H. Baron

Director of Human Resources
Brown, Clark, and Walters
*1819 Main Street
Sarasota, FL 34236
(941) 957–3800
Fax: (941) 957–3888*

8111

Business Information: Brown, Clark, and Walters, a full–service law firm established in 1991, employs 55 people. As Director of Human Resources, Mr. Baron oversees recruitment, benefits, human resources information systems, employee relations, facility management, and security. **Career Steps:** Director of Human Resources, Brown, Clark, and Walters (1995–Present); Legal Assistant, Kirk Pinkerton, P.A. (1993–1995); Psychiatric Technician, Sarasota Memorial Hospital (1992–1993); Police Officer, Sarasota Police Department (1991–1992). **Associations & Accomplishments:** Society for Human Resources Management; Sarasota Human Resources Association; National Association of Legal Assistants; American Legion. **Education:** Center For Degree Studies; Paralegal Institute, Certificate in Paralegal Studies. **Personal:** Married to Susan Lynn in 1991. One child: Rebecca Marie. Mr. Baron enjoys golf, music, cooking, and travel.

Eileen J. Barresi–Ramos

Attorney
Law Office of Eileen J. Barresi–Ramos
*Cond. Montecillo II, Apartado 2402, Encantada
Trujillo Alto, Puerto Rico 00976
(809) 760–0345
Fax: Please mail or call*

8111

Business Information: Law Office of Eileen J. Barresi–Ramos is a full–service, general practice law firm. A practicing attorney in Puerto Rico since 1990, Ms. Barresi–Ramos established her sole practice law office in 1995. Her practice focuses on civil cases, family law, custody and child support cases, and divorce law. In her spare time, she gives lectures to high school and elementary school students on Juvenile Justice. **Career Steps:** Attorney, Law Office of Eileen J. Barresi–Ramos (1995–Present); Deputy Advisor Governor, La Fortaleza (1995); Legal Advisor, Adm. Juvenile Institutions (1993–1995); Attorney, Women's Affairs Office San Juan (1991–1993). **Associations & Accomplishments:** American Correctional Association; Community Anti–Drug Coalitions; National Drug Court Professionals. **Education:** University of Puerto Rico, J.D. (1990). **Personal:** Married to Miguel A. Rivera in 1995.

Renato Barrios Maldonado

Attorney
Law Offices of Renato Barrios Maldonado
Cond El Centro I Apt. 220, 500 Avenue Munoz Rivera
San Juan, Puerto Rico 00918
(809) 753–1815
Fax: (809) 753–1915

8111

Business Information: Law Offices of Renato Barrios Maldonado is a full–service, general practice law firm, concentrating on litigations. A practicing trial and labor attorney in Puerto Rico since 1980, Mr. Barrios Maldonado established his sole practice law office in 1981. He oversees all administrative operations for associates and of a support staff of ten, in addition to his private law practice in the areas of litigation law. **Career Steps:** Attorney, Law Offices of Renato Barrios Maldonado (1981–Present); Adjunct Professor, John Jay College CUNY (1994–1995). **Associations & Accomplishments:** Rotary Club; Puerto Rico Bar Association; American Bar Association. **Education:** UIA University, J.D. (1980).

Susan L. Barry

Attorney and Of Counsel
Orrick, Herrington & Sutcliffe
666 Fifth Avenue
New York, NY 10019
(212) 326–8800
Fax: (212) 506–5151

8111

Business Information: Orrick, Herrington & Sutcliffe is a full–service, general practice law firm concentrating on securities and municipals. Established in the 1890's, the Firm currently employs 500 attorneys, legal and administrative support staff. Admitted to practice law in 1979, Ms. Barry serves in an Of Counsel capacity, concentrating on public and project finance. **Career Steps:** Attorney and Of Counsel, Orrick, Herrington & Sutcliffe (1990–Present); Vice President, Bond Investors Allegheny County (1987–1990); Associate, Brown & Wood (1979–1987). **Associations & Accomplishments:** American Bar Association. **Education:** George Washington University, J.D. (1979); University of Virginia (1971); Barnard College, A.B. (1970). **Personal:** One child: Karen. Ms. Barry enjoys spending time with her daughter.

Jacqueline Rose Bart

Senior Business Immigration Counsel
White, Sosa, & Bart
181 University Avenue, Suite 2200
Toronto, Ontario M5H 3M7
(416) 601–1346
Fax: (416) 601–1357

8111

Business Information: White, Sosa, & Bart is a general practice law firm. Jacqueline R. Bart, B.A., LL.B, J.D., Barrister and Solicitor, obtained her undergraduate and law degrees in Canada, and her Juris Doctor in the U.S. Her professional affiliations include Barristers Chamber in London, England, the UK High Court of Justice, United Nations (International Immigration Law), Osler, Hoskin & Harcourt (one of Canada's largest firms), and her current position as Senior Business Immigration Counsel, White, Sosa & Bart. Co–author of a Canadian Practice Guide, "Work Permits and Visas", Ms. Bart has spoken at various seminars and conferences including the Canadian Bar Association, The Law Society of Upper Canada, the Centre D'Etudes en Administration Internationale, and numerous others. She has also contributed various articles to national and international publications, newspapers and magazines, including the Canadian Immigration Handbook, and a current work in progress, "Permanent Residence" a Practice Guide. Possessing a substantial amount of practical experience in the area of cross border transfers, Ms. Bart has also acted for a significant number of multinational and international companies assisting their human resource departments in transferring foreign workers to Canada. **Career Steps:** Senior Business Immigration Counsel, White, Sosa, & Bart (Present); Attorney, Stewart, Roper & Associates (Three Years); Attorney, Osler, Hoskin, & Harcourt. **Associations & Accomplishments:** Canadian Bar Association, Immigration Section; American Immigration Lawyer's Association. **Education:** York University: B.A., J.D., LL.B.; University of Michigan, Detroit, J.D.

Morgan La Veeda Battle

Partner
Gorham & Waldrep, P.C.
2101 6th Avenue, North, Suite 700
Birmingham, AL 35203–2749
(205) 254–3216
Fax: (205) 324–3802

8111

Business Information: Gorham & Waldrep, P.C. is a full–service, general practice law firm, concentrating in general, family, municipal, government, corporate, tax, and estate planning law, as well as cases on federal crimes and military issues. The Firm has two regional offices employing 20 attorneys. A practicing attorney in Alabama state and federal courts since 1978, Ms. Battle joined the Firm as Partner in 1985. Serving as Chair of the Labor Department, she is responsible for providing employment defense to state and local government agencies, and private, corporate and utility clients. Career milestones include representing AT&T's request for a rate increase, and a Supreme Court case representing firefighters. **Career Steps:** Partner, Gorham & Waldrep, P.C. (1985–Present); General Counsel, Governor's Public Staff (1983–1985); Administrative Judge, U.S. EEOC (1981–1983); Managing Attorney, Birmingham Area Legal Services (1979–1980). **Associations & Accomplishments:** Board of Directors, Legal Services Corporation – appointed by President Clinton and confirmed by the U.S. Senate; Board Member, Museum of Art; Board Member, Girls, Inc. – serving Kindergarten through junior high school–aged girls; Member, United Methodist Church. **Education:** University of California – Davis, J.D. (1978); Howard University, B.S. (1974). **Personal:** Married to Lynn in 1983. Three children: Heather, Aisha, and Jessica. Ms. Battle enjoys spending time with her children.

Kathleen F. Bay

Attorney At Law
Hilgers & Watkins, PC
98 San Jacinto Boulevard, Suite 1300
Austin, TX 78701–4039
(512) 476–4716
Fax: (512) 476–5139
Email: See Below

8111

Business Information: Hilgers & Watkins, PC is a law firm specializing in estate and disability planning. As Attorney at Law, Ms. Bay is responsible for litigation and concentration in two areas of her practice: estate and disability planning. Internet users can reach her via: Hilgers@hwlaw.com. **Career Steps:** Attorney At Law, Hilgers & Watkins, PC (1979–Present); Attorney, Small, Craig & Werkenthin, P.C. (1987–1991); Attorney, Milbank, Tweed, Hadley & McCloy (1982–1987); Attorney, Sullivan & Cromwell (1979–1981). **Associations & Accomplishments:** Austin Symphony; New York & Texas Bars; Admitted to Practice Before U.S. Tax Court, U.S. District Court, and Southern District of New York; Board Certified in Estate Planning and Probate; Texas Board of Legal Specialization; Mediator; American College of Trust and Estate Counsel (1993–Present); Advisory Commission, Texas State Bar, Board of Legal Specialization, Estate Planning and Probate (1993–Present); College Board Committee, State Bar of Texas (1995–Present); Council, Real Property, Probate and Trust Law Section of the American Bar Association (1991–1995); Chair, ABA Committee; Federal Death Tax Problems of Estates & Trusts (1987–1991); Vice Chair, ABA Committee, Estate Planning and Drafting: Marital Deduction (1982–1987); ABA AIDS Coordinating Committee, Liaison from Section of Real Property, Probate and Trust Law (1990–1992); District Director, The University of Texas at Austin (fundraising) (1986–1990); New York Bar, Charitable Organizations Committee (1986–1987); Board, Austin Groups for the Elderly; Advisory Board (1992); Rotary Club of Austin (1988–Present); Board, Lone Star Girl Scout Council (1988–1991); Monitor, Recording for the Blind (1987–1989); Speaker for Non–Profit Organizations, Capital Area Volunteer Center (1991–Present); Endowment Committee and Speaker on Non–Profit Issues, United Way – Capital Area (1994–Present); Rotary International Paul Harris Fellow (1994); Leadership Austin (1994–1995); Austin Symphony Orchestra Board (1995–Present); Publications & Speeches: Co–Authored, "Estate Planning for Persons With Aids" (1989), "Curing Defective QTIP Elections" (1989), "Repercussions of Gifts Under Powers of Attorney — The Ripple Effect" (1989), "Community Property With Right of Survivorship" (1990), Recent Developments in Estate, Gift and Generation–Skipping Developments (1991), Board Training for Non–Profit Organizations (1990), Non–Profit Corporations Speech Regarding Law Issues, Living Wills/Planning for the Terminally Ill (1990), Selected Marital Deduction Issues in Pre–Death Planning and Audits (1990), Estate Planning for Persons with AIDS (1990), Curing Defective QTIP Elections (1990), Estate Planning for Owners of Small Businesses (1990), Recent Developments in Estate, Gift, and GST Taxation (1990); Life Insurance Trusts and QTIP Elections (1992); Update and Planning Ideas for Defective QTIP Elections (1992), Handling Tax Controversy (1992), Reformation of Trusts in Texas (1992), Liabilities, Pleasures, and Duties (1992), Advanced Estate Planning and Probate Course (1993), Artists' Legal & Accounting Assistance of Austin (1994); Guest Editorial, "Austin American–Statesman, How a Living Will Works" (1994). **Education:** Rice University, B.A. English (1974). **Personal:** Married to Austin in 1975. Two children: Annabelle and Christiana. Ms. Bay enjoys reading her husband's books, including his new book, entitled "Prism".

Franklin D. Beahm

Partner
Chehardy, Sherman, Ellis, Breslin & Murray
One Galleria Boulevard, Suite 1100
Metairie, LA 70001
(504) 833–5600
Fax: (504) 833–8080

8111

Business Information: Chehardy, Sherman is a multi–faceted law firm, providing legal services in the areas of tax law, estate planning, bankruptcy, health care, commercial litigation, casualty defense, personal injury, domestic relations and white collar criminal defense. Operating from two offices in Louisiana, the Firm consists of fourteen attorneys. Admitted to Louisiana in 1988 and Colorado in 1993 to practice law, Franklin Beahm joined as a Partner with the Firm in November of 1995. He focuses his practice on health care law, representing physicans and hospitals in matters pertaining to malpractice, Medicaid/Medicare fraud, reimbursements, medical staff, credentialing, and contracts. **Career Steps:** Partner, Chehardy, Sherman (1995–Present); Partner, Thomas, Hayes & Beahm (1985–1995); Hammett, Leake & Hammett: Partner (1983–1985), Associate (1980–1983). **Associations & Accomplishments:** National Health Lawyers Association; Louisiana State Bar Association; American Bar Association Forum Committee in Health Law (1985–1992); Louisiana Society of Hospital Attorneys of the Louisiana Hospital Association; International Association of Defense Counsel – Defense Research Institute. **Education:** Tulane – School of Law, J.D. (1977); Southern Methodist University, B.B.A. (1975). **Personal:** Married to Tawny M. in 1994. Mr. Beahm enjoys golf and snow skiing.

Mr. Stuart D. Bear

Attorney and Shareholder
Zeldes, Needle & Cooper
1000 Lafayette Boulevard, Fifth Floor
Bridgeport, CT 06604
(203) 333–9441
Fax: (203) 333–1489

8111

Business Information: Zeldes, Needle & Cooper is a general practice law firm. A practicing attorney since 1968, Mr. Bear specializes in the areas of civil litigation, commercial litigation, and bankruptcy for individuals and corporations. Established in 1971, Zeldes, Needle & Cooper employs 62 legal professional and administrative support staff. **Career Steps:** Attorney and Shareholder, Zeldes, Needle & Cooper (1973–Present); Attorney, New Haven Legal Assistance Association (1968–1973). **Associations & Accomplishments:** Branford Land Trust; Ethics Committee, Lawyer to Lawyer Mediation/Arbitration Committee, Federal Practice, Commercial Law and Bankruptcy Sections, Connecticut Bar Association. **Education:** Harvard University Law School, LL.B. (1968); Harvard College, A.B. (1965); Hamden High School (1961).

W. Gregory Beard

Attorney
Beard & Beard
P.O. Box 12982
Alexandria, LA 71315–2982
(318) 445–5648
Fax: (318) 445–5648

8111

Business Information: Beard & Beard is a full service general practice law firm. A practicing attorney since 1991, Mr. Beard co–founded the Firm with his brother in 1993. As a trial attorney in Louisiana state courts, his areas of practice are in personal injury and debt collection. **Career Steps:** Attorney, Beard & Beard (1993–Present); Law Clerk and Attorney, Cave & McKay (1989–1993); Senatorial Aide, Lousiana State Senate (1987–1991). **Associations & Accomplishments:** America Trial Lawyers Association; Louisiana Trial Lawyers Association; Alexandria Kiwanis Club; Louisiana State University Alumni Association. **Education:** Southern Law Center, J.D. (1991); Louisiana State University, Bachelors in General Studies (1987). **Personal:** Married to Lisa in 1994. Mr. Beard enjoys snow skiing, golf, and church.

Maury D. Beaulier
Partner
Crosby & Associates
25 Empire Drive
St. Paul, MN 55103
(612) 298-9462
Fax: (612) 298-9237

8111

Business Information: Crosby & Associates is a full–service, general practice law firm, concentrating on commercial, family, banking, and appellate law. A practicing attorney in Minnesota and Wisconsin state courts since 1991, Mr. Beaulier joined the Firm as Partner in 1995. His practice concentrates on commercial, family and Indian law issues. He also served as an Assistant Adjunct Professor with Normandale Community College teaching a course entitled Business and the Legal Environment. **Career Steps:** Partner, Crosby & Associates (1995–Present); Associate Attorney, Williams Peterson and Associates (1992–1995); District Court Judicial Clerk, Kanabee County (1991–1992); Partner, B & B Legal Services (1991). **Associations & Accomplishments:** Wisconsin Bar Association; Minnesota State Bar Association; American Bar Association; Ramsey County Bar Association; Human Rights Committee of Ramsey Bar Association; Prairie Island Tribal Court. **Education:** Hamline University Law School, J.D. (1991); University of Wisconsin – LaCrosse, B.A. (1987). **Personal:** Mr. Beaulier enjoys being active in skiing, running, triathalons, swimming, and writing poetry and short stories.

Robert S. Beehm
Partner
Cahill & Beehm
P.O. Box 119, 145 Washington Avenue
Endicott, NY 13761
(607) 748-7481
Fax: (607) 748-4831

8111

Business Information: Cahill & Beehm is a full–service, general practice law firm. A practicing attorney in New York courts since 1990, Mr. Beehm co–founded the Firm in 1995. His practice concentrates on civil litigation trial work and breach of construction contracts litigation. **Career Steps:** Partner, Cahill & Beehm (1995–Present); Associate Attorney, Cahill Law Office (1990–1995). **Associations & Accomplishments:** American Bar Association; New York State Bar Association; Broome County Bar Association. **Education:** Albany Law School, J.D. (1989); State University of New York – Binghamton, B.A. (1986). **Personal:** Married to Angelina C.

Sean P. Beiter
Attorney at Law
Jaeckle Fleischmann et al.
Fleet Bank Building 12 Fountain Plaza
Buffalo, NY 14202
(716) 856-0600
Fax: (716) 856-0432

8111

Business Information: Jaeckle Fleischmann et al. is a full–service, general practice law firm, providing management representation in collective bargaining, grievance arbitrations, NLRB & PERB proceedings, and in employment discrimination matters. Joining the Firm upon the conferral of his law degree in 1991, Mr. Beiter focuses his practice in the areas of labor and employment law, representing employers. **Career Steps:** Attorney at Law, Jaeckle Fleischmann et al. (1991–Present); Blue Cross of WNY, Inc.: Informatiion Systems Specialist (1987–1991), Employment Specialist (1985–1987). **Associations & Accomplishments:** American Bar Association; Erie County Bar Association; Organization of Public Employment Negotiators; Industrial Relations Research Association. **Education:** SUNY – Buffalo, J.D. cum laude (1991); Canisius College, B.A. in Economics and Political Science magna cum laude. **Personal:** Married to Angeline in 1988. Two children: Patrick and Andrew. Mr. Beiter enjoys golf.

C. Denise Benoit
Attorney
Bryan, Ames, Willis & Benoit
44 West Alisal Street, P.O. Box 2155
Salinas, CA 93901
(408) 424-0844
Fax: (408) 424-9625

8111

Business Information: Bryan, Ames, Willis & Benoit is a general practice law firm with focus on personal injury, criminal law, family law and probate. Ms. Benoit, a Certified Family Law Specialist with the California Board of Legal Specialization and a practicing attorney since 1986, joined the firm in 1990 as an Associate and was appointed Partner in 1994. She represents individuals in divorces, custody, paternity suits, adoptions and other related family law matters. **Career Steps:** Attorney, Bryan, Ames, Willis & Benoit (1990–Present); Private Practice (1988–1990); Attorney, Trucha, Inc. (1987–1988); Contract Attorney, Women's Crisis Center (1986–1987). **Associations & Accomplishments:** Monterey County Bar Association; California Bar Association; American Bar Association; California Board of Legal Specialization; Monterey County Women Lawyer's Association. **Education:** Monterey College of Law, J.D. (1986); University of Florida. **Personal:** Ms. Benoit enjoys horseback riding, aerobics, rollerblading, swimming, and reading.

Robert E. Benson
Partner
Holland & Hart
555 17th Street, Suite 3200
Denver, CO 80202
(303) 295-8000
Fax: (303) 295-8261
EMAIL: See Below

8111

Business Information: Holland & Hart is a full–service, general practice law firm, concentrating on white collar criminal law. The Firm consists of eleven offices and employs 225 attorneys, some of which practice law internationally. Joining the Firm as Associate upon the conferral of his law degree in 1965, Mr. Benson was appointed as Partner in 1971. Admitted to practice in Colorado state courts, his practice concentrates on civil litigation. He can also be reached through the Internet via: RBenson@HollandHart.com **Career Steps:** Holland & Hart: Partner (1971–Present), Associate (1965–1971). **Associations & Accomplishments:** American Bar Association; Colorado Bar Association; Denver Bar Association; Advisory Council, American Arbitration Association. **Education:** University of Pennsylvania, Ll.B. (1965); University of Iowa, B.A. (1962). **Personal:** Married to Ann M. in 1968. Three children: Steven, Robert, and Katherine. Mr. Benson enjoys golf, skiing, and biking.

Gregory M. Bentz
Director
Shughart, Thomson & Kilroy, P.C.
120 West 12th Street, Suite 1800
Kansas City, MO 64105
(816) 421-3355
Fax: (816) 374-0509

8111

Business Information: Shughart, Thomson & Kilroy, P.C. is a premier, general practice law firm. Established in 1942, the Firm consists of 300 attorneys, legal and administrative support staff. Joining the Firm as an associate upon conferral of his law degree in 1983 and appointed as Director in 1989, Gregory Bentz oversees all associates for the Litigation Section. Admitted to all Missouri and Nebraska state and federal courts, he concentrates his practice on business litigation and transactional law disputes. **Career Steps:** Shughart, Thomson & Kilroy, P.C.: Director (1989–Present), Associate (1983–1989). **Associations & Accomplishments:** Kansas City Metropolitan Bar Association; Missouri Bar Association; Nebraska Bar Association; American Bar Association; Kansas City Chamber of Commerce – Centurions Program. **Education:** University of Nebraska: J.D. (1983), B.S. in Business Administration (1980). **Personal:** Married to Nancy in 1981. Two children: Elizabeth and Jeffrey. Mr. Bentz enjoys golf and scuba diving.

Michael M. Bercier, Esq.
Sole Practitioner
The Law Office of Michael M. Bercier
P.O. Box 1158, 132 Cedar Lane
Cameron, LA 70631
(318) 775-5192
Fax: (318) 775-7131

8111

Business Information: The Law Office of Michael M. Bercier is a full–service, general practice law firm, specializing in personal injury and insurance policy issues nationally and internationally. Establishing his sole practice law firm upon the conferral of his law degree, Mr. Bercier specializes in handling only personal injury and insurance policy cases, as well as providing consultation to other firms or providing them with referrals. **Career Steps:** Attorney at Law, The Law Office of Michael M. Bercier (1981–Present); Assistant District Attorney, Calcosieu Parish District Attorneys Office (1980–1981). **Associations & Accomplishments:** Louisiana Trial Lawyers Association; American Bar Association. **Education:** Louisiana State University, J.D. (1981); McNesse University (1978). **Personal:** Two children: Michael Frederick and Baret Bercier. Mr. Bercier enjoys boat & car racing, scuba diving, cattle–farming, raising horses & registered chow–chows, hunting, and snow skiing.

John Torrey Berger Jr.
Partner and Attorney
Lewis, Rice & Fingersh, L.C.
500 North Broadway
St. Louis, MO 63102
(314) 444-7600
Fax: (314) 444-7788

8111

Business Information: Established in 1903, Lewis, Rice & Fingersh, L.C. is a full–service law firm. Joining the Firm upon the conferral of his law degree in 1963, Mr. Berger concentrates his practice in the areas of real estate, mergers, and acquisitions, including negotiations, and contract preparation reviews. Mr. Berger also gives direction to the younger attorneys in the Firm and adds his support as a Partner. **Career Steps:** Attorney and Partner, Lewis, Rice & Fingersh, L.C. (1963–Present). **Associations & Accomplishments:** Real Estate Section, Missouri Bar Association; Real Estate Section, American Bar Association; St. Louis Bar Association; International Conference of Shopping Centers; Board of Directors, Logos High School; Presbyterian Childrens Services. **Education:** Washington University – St. Louis, J.D. (1963). **Personal:** Married to Helen Lee Thompson in 1962. Two children: John T., III and Helen E. Mr. Berger enjoys sports, writing poetry, and woodcarving.

Stuart Berlin
Director of Computer Systems
The EMMES Corporation
11325 Seven Locks Road, Suite 214
Potomac, MD 20854-3205
(301) 299-8655
Fax: (301) 299-3991
EMAIL: See Below

8111

Business Information: The EMMES Corporation is a Coordinating Center for clinical trials and medical research studies. A principal activity of the Company is the collection and analysis of data for these efforts. As Director of Computer Systems, Mr. Berlin oversees the computer–related activities, including internal operations as well as the management and administration of the data collection process. Internet users can reach him via: SBERLIN@EMMES.COM **Career Steps:** The EMMES Corporation: Director of Computer Systems (1995–Present), Senior Programmer (1988–1995); EDP Manager, Friedman & Fuller, PC (1984–1988). **Education:** University of Maryland, B.S. in Computer Science (1983). **Personal:** Married to Joy Esterlitz in 1993. One child: Deborah Eve. Mr. Berlin enjoys fishing, hiking, and running.

Pamela J. Bertram
Attorney
Pamela J. Bertram, Attorney at Law
480 South High Street
Columbus, OH 43215
(614) 221-0725
Fax: (614) 221-2055

8111

Business Information: Pamela J. Bertram, Attorney at Law is a full–service, general practice law firm. A practicing attorney in Ohio state courts since 1982, Ms. Bertram established her sole practice law firm in 1993. Her practice concentrates on all aspects of domestic law. **Career Steps:** Attorney, Pamela J. Bertram, Attorney at Law (1993–Present); Attorney, Bertram, Hudson & Gill (1992–1993); Attorney, Luper, Wolinetz, Sheriff & Neidenthal (1986–1992); Attorney, Law Firm of Gary Paul Price (1980–1986). **Associations & Accomplishments:** Junior League of Columbus; Family Law Committee, Columbus Bar Association; Ohio State Bar Association; American Bar Association. **Education:** Ohio State University College of Law, J.D. (1982); Miami University: B.A. International Studies, B.A. Modern Foreign Languages (1978). **Personal:** Married to David A. Laing in 1984. One child: Jay A. Ms. Bertram enjoys gardening and sports.

Fernando E. Betancourt–Medina, Esq.

Owner and Partner
Law Offices of Betancourt & Iguina
P.O. Box 935, Ave. Rotarios #525, P.O. Box 935
Arecibo, Puerto Rico 00613–0935
(809) 878–2642
Fax: (809) 878–2642

8111

Business Information: Established in 1985, Betancourt & Iguina is a full–service, general practice law firm. A practicing trial attorney in Puerto Rico courts since 1982, Mr. Betancourt–Medina joined the Firm in January of 1994. Serving as Senior Partner, he oversees all administrative operations of the practice, in addition to his legal practice. He concentrates his practice in the areas of Constitutional Law, Personal Injury, and Medical Malpractice Defense. **Career Steps:** Owner and Partner, Law Offices of Betancourt & Iguina (1994–Present); Partner, Morell & Betancourt (1991–1994); Attorney, Governor's Advisory Council on Labor Policy. **Associations & Accomplishments:** Board of Directors, Arecibo–Capitanes; House of Hope, Inc.; Eagle Scout, Boy Scouts of America; District Vice–Governor Area E Coordinator, Leo Club; Fideicomiso para la conservacion de los Estuarios del Atlantico Norte; Secretary of Board of Directors, Surfing Federation of Puerto Rico. **Education:** University of Puerto Rico School of Law, J.D. (1982). **Personal:** Mr. Betancourt–Medina enjoys high adventure activities, water sports, and horseback riding.

Kirk Howard Betts, Esq.

Partner
Betts & Holt
815 Connecticut Avenue, NW, Suite 1201
Washington, DC 20006
(202) 530–3380
Fax: (202) 452–7074
EMAIL: See Below

8111

Business Information: Betts & Holt, a law firm, is engaged in the practice of law on behalf of large purchasers and consumers of electricity, producers of natural gas–consuming industries. Mr. Betts, a Partner in the Firm, develops and implements negotiating strategies for municipal electric utilities, rural electric cooperatives, and energy–dependent industries to obtain the lowest cost electricity while competitively positioning his clients to exploit opportunities that will arise as the electric utility industry evolves from being a regulated to a predominantly transactional industry. Internet users can reach him via: 102653.3064@CompuServe.com. **Career Steps:** Partner, Betts & Holt (1996–Present); Partner, Dickinson, Wright, Moon, VanDusen & Freeman (1988–1996) (Administrative and Managing Partner of the Washington Office, 1992–1995); Of Counsel, Dickinson, Wright, et al (1986–1987); Partner, Ely, Ritts, Brickfield & Betts (1982–1986); Associate, Law Offices of Northcutt Ely (1979–1982); Legislative Counsel, U.S. Senate Subcommittee on Intergovernmental Relations of the Government Operations Committee (1974–1976); Legislative Aide to U.S. Senator William V. Roth (1973–1974). **Associations & Accomplishments:** American Bar Association; Federal Energy Bar Association; District of Columbia Bar; Maryland State Bar Association; admitted before U.S. Supreme Court, U.S. Court of Appeals for the District of Columbia, Fifth, Sixth, and Eleventh Circuits; service on a variety of non–profit boards. **Education:** Washington College of Law of The American University, J.D. (1979); George Washington University, B.A. (1973). **Personal:** Married to Christine Sheridan in 1976. One child: Abigail. Mr. Betts enjoys sailing, tennis and piano.

Deborah H. Biggers

Sole Practitioner
Deborah Hill Biggers, Attorney at Law
113 East Northside
Tuskegee, AL 36083
(334) 727–0092
Fax: (334) 727–7117

8111

Business Information: Deborah Hill Biggers, Attorney at Law is a full–service, general practice law firm. A practicing attorney in Alabama state courts since 1979, Ms. Biggers established the sole practice law office in 1983. She oversees the administrative operations of a support staff of two, in addition to her law practice. In conjunction with her private legal practice, Ms. Biggers serves as Counsel for the Macon County Board of Education and Macon County Racing Commission. **Career Steps:** Sole Practitioner, Deborah Hill Biggers, Attorney at Law (1983–Present); Attorney, Alabama Public Service Commission (1982–1983); Assistant Attorney General, State of Alabama (1981–1982); Attorney, Department of Energy Inspector General (1979–1980). **Associations & Accomplishments:** Alabama State Bar; National Bar Association; Macon County Bar Association; Kiwanis Club of Macon County; Board, Macon County YMCA; Federal Defender Program; Coalition of 100 Black Women; Macon County Education Support Systems, Inc.; Macon County Role Model Association; President, Beta Xi Omega of Alpha Kappa Alpha Sorority, Inc.; Alabama Lawyers Association. **Education:** Vanderbilt Law School, J.D. (1978); Fisk University, B.A. (1975). **Personal:** Two children: Calvin David Jr. and Alneada Denise. Ms. Biggers enjoys reading, travel, shopping, and working with youth.

David J. Bilinsky

Partner and Attorney
Lakes, Straith & Bilinsky
145 15th Street West, Suite 301
North Vancouver, British Co V7M 1R9
(604) 984–3646
Fax: (604) 984–8573
EMAIL: See Below

8111

Business Information: Lakes, Straith & Bilinsky, established in 1986, is a full–service, general practice law firm, concentrating on criminal prosecutions for the Department of Justice in commercial law, real estate, business and civil litigations. A practicing attorney since 1980, Mr. Bilinsky joined the Firm in 1991. Serving as Partner and Attorney, his practice focuses on civil litigation, primarily in personal injury and contested estate litigations. **Career Steps:** Partner and Attorney, Lakes, Straith & Bilinsky (1991–Present; Sole Practitioner, David J. Bilinsky (1982–1991); Goldman Company (1980–1981). **Associations & Accomplishments:** Canadian Bar Association: National Membership Committee, Member Services Committee, Various other Committees; American Bar Association: Law Practice Management Section, Newsletter Board, Leadership Activities Board; Trial Lawyers Association of British Columbia; Editorial Board Member, Co–Editor, and Contributing Author, "Law Office Management Practice Manual", "Litigations Applications"; Co–Faculty for courses on 2–10 and 2–15 law firm management; Author, "Practice Talk" — monthly column on law practice management; Frequent lecturer and presenter at Bar Association proceedings and symposia. **Education:** University of British Columbia, M.B.A. (1991); University of Manitoba: LL.B. (1980), B.S. (1977). **Personal:** Married to Jo Anne in 1981. One child: Lauren Louise. Mr. Bilinsky enjoys writing, technology, and skiing.

Tom H. Billiris, Esq.

Attorney
Tom H. Billiris, P.A., Attorney at Law
733 Charlotte Avenue
Tarpon Springs, FL 34689–2106
(813) 943–9466
Fax: (813) 937–9280

8111

Business Information: Tom H. Billiris, P.A., Attorney at Law, established in 1993, is a full–service, general practice law firm, concentrating on business law, immigration, and personal injury. Admitted to practice in Florida state courts, Mr. Billiris established his solo practice upon the conferral of his law degree in 1993. **Career Steps:** Attorney, Tom H. Billiris, P.A., Attorney at Law (1993–Present). **Associations & Accomplishments:** American Bar Association; Rotary Club; Phi Alpha Delta Legal Fraternity. **Education:** Mercer University, J.D. (1992); University of South Florida, B.S. in Finance; St. Petersburg Junior College, A.A. in Business and Engineering. **Personal:** Mr. Billiris enjoys scuba diving, boating, wave running, weightlifting, and biking.

Parker Bond Binion

Attorney
Baker & Botts, L.L.P.
3000 One Shell Plaza
Houston, TX 77002
(713) 229–1714
Fax: (713) 229–1522

8111

Business Information: Baker & Botts, L.L.P. is a premier, international civil litigation law firm. Consisting of 400 attorneys, the Firm has offices in New York, Washington, D.C., Texas and Moscow. Joining Baker & Botts' Houston office upon the conferral of his law degree in 1991, Parker Binion concentrates his practice in the areas of commercial law and personal injury litigation. **Career Steps:** Attorney, Baker & Botts, L.L.P. (1991–Present). **Associations & Accomplishments:** American Bar Association; Fellow, Houston Bar Association. **Education:** University of Texas Law School, J.D. (1991); Duke University, A.B. (1988). **Personal:** Mr. Binion enjoys golf.

Steven R. Bird

Attorney and Partner
Newcomer, Shaffer, Bird, & Spangler
117 West Maple Street
Bryan, OH 43506
(419) 636–3196
Fax: (419) 636–0867

8111

Business Information: Newcomer, Shaffer, Bird, & Spangler is a full–service, general practice law firm. In existence since the Civil War, the Firm currently employs 13 attorneys and legal support staff from two offices (Bryan, Ohio; Montpelier, Ohio) As Attorney and Partner, Mr. Bird concentrates his practice in the areas of probate estate planning, real estate law, general criminal law (including traffic and some felony), personal injury, wrongful death, and worker's compensation. A trial attorney since 1984, Mr. Bird is admitted to both State and Federal courts, and primarily represents individual clientele regarding income tax law. **Career Steps:** Attorney and Partner, Newcomer, Shaffer, Bird, & Spangler (1984–Present); Law Clerk, United States Air Force – WPAFB in Dayton, OH (1982–1984); Teacher, Mad River Township Schools (1979–1980). **Associations & Accomplishments:** Federal Taxation Committee, Ohio State Bar Association; American Bar Association; Northwest Ohio Bar Association; Courthouse Security Advisory Committee; Williams County Bar Association; Bryan Historic Home Association; Williams County Historical Society; Culture Explosion Steering Committee; Williams County Community Concert Association; Williams County Courthouse Centennial Committee; Pheasants Forever; Society National Bank Advisory Board; Children's Trust Fund Board, Ohio Department of Human Services; Candidate for Probate Judge. **Education:** University of Dayton Law School, J.D. (1984); Beloit College: M.A. in Education, B.A. in History. **Personal:** Married to Lora L. in 1977. Three children: Lindsey, Michael, and Emily. Mr. Bird enjoys historic preservation, travel, church choir, cooking, hunting, and clay shooting.

James Dodson Bishop, Esq.

Department Director–The Archdiocesan Legal Network
Catholic Charities of Washington, D.C., Inc.
1221 Massachusetts Avenue Northwest
Washington, DC 20005
(202) 628–4265
Fax: (202) 737–3421

8111

Business Information: Catholic Charities of Washington, D.C., Inc. – The Archdiocesan Legal Network provides $600,000 of free legal services to low income and indigent clients within the District of Columbia and neighboring counties in Maryland. The Network has 46 major law firms participating, and an additional 150 volunteer individual attorneys. A practicing attorney in District of Columbia and Pennsylvania courts since 1982, Mr. Bishop joined Catholic Charities of Washington, D.C., Inc. as Department Director of The Archdiocesan Legal Network in 1993. He is responsible for the direction of the Network, as well as serving as liaison between clients in need of legal assistance and participating law firms. **Career Steps:** Department Director of The Archdiocesan Legal Network, Catholic Charities of Washington, D.C., Inc. (1993–Present); Director, Attorney of Client Arbitration Board, District of Columbia Bar (1987–1993). **Associations & Accomplishments:** Mediator, DC Superior Court; District of Columbia Bar Association; Pennsylvania Bar Association; Philadephia Bar Association; Washington Bar Association;

Vice Chair, American Bar Association – State & Local Bar Dispute Resolution Committee; Lincoln University: Dean's List, Alpha Chi Honor Society; St. George's Church. **Education:** Howard University Law School, J.D. (1982); Lincoln University, B.A. magna cum laude (1979). **Personal:** Mr. Bishop enjoys attending church.

Carlos Bobonis–Gonzales, Esq.
Partner
Bobonis, Bobonis & Rodriquez Poventud
129 Avenue De Diego
San Juan, Puerto Rico 00911–1928
(809) 725–7941
Fax: (809) 725–4245

8111

Business Information: Bobonis, Bobonis & Rodriquez Poventud is a full–service corporate law firm, serving businesses throughout the Carribean with litigation and other general practices. Established in 1980, the Firm consists of 15 attorneys, legal and administrative support staff. Some of the major corporate clientele include: AT&T, Emerson Electric, and Trans–America Financial. A practicing attorney admitted to state and federal courts in Puerto Rico since 1975, Mr. Bobonis–Gonzales joined the Firm in 1981. Serving as Partner, he directs all activities of the Labor and Employment Law division. **Career Steps:** Partner, Bobonis, Bobonis & Rodriquez Poventud (1981–Present); Associate, O'Neill & Borges (1977–1981). **Associations & Accomplishments:** American Bar Association; Puerto Rico Bar Association; Admitted to: Supreme Court of Puerto Rico, U.S. District Court of Puerto Rico, Court of Appeals – First Circuit (Labor Law) **Education:** New York Universt, LL.M. (1976); University of Puerto Rico: J.D. (1975), B.B.A. in Economics **Personal:** Married to Gloria Colorado in 1975. Three children: Carlos Juan, Antonio Luis and Miguel Angel. Mr. Bobonis–Gonzales enjoys horse riding, sailing and reading.

Jeffrey H. Boiler
President, Shareholder and Managing Attorney
Boiler & Cartwright, P.C.
927 Country Club Rd., Suite 175
Eugene, OR 97401
(541) 683–1901
Fax: (541) 683–2774

8111

Business Information: Boiler & Cartwright is a private, general practice law firm and business consulting service. Establishing the Firm in 1986, as President, Shareholder and Managing Attorney, Mr. Boiler is responsible for all aspects of operations. A trial attorney since 1982, he is admitted to both State and Federal courts, primarily representing law enforcement individuals and Federal government concerns. Future plans involve evolving the Firm into non–profit organization series sites, serving law enforcement personnel and governmental agencies. **Career Steps:** President, Shareholder and Managing Attorney, Boiler & Cartwright, P.C. (1986–Present); Attorney, Jaqua & Wheatley, P.C. (1980–1985); Police Officer, City of Springfield (1977–1978); Military Court Reporter, U.S. Marine Corps (1973–1975). **Associations & Accomplishments:** Oregon State Bar Association; American Bar Association; Admitted to Federal Bar U.S. District Court (1983); Admitted to Federal Appellate Bar, 9th U.S. Court of Appeals (1993); Co–Chair, Oregon Bar Real Estate and Land Use Section and Education Committee (1987). **Education:** University of Oregon: J.D. (1982), B.S. Political Science (1979); University of Oregon School of Law, Certificate of Background Specialty, Ocean and Coastal Resources Law (1982). **Personal:** Married to Margaret in 1975. Mr. Boiler enjoys weight training and pro bono and non–profit service to local, state and federal enforcement officers and substance abuse programs.

Michael J. Bordy
Managing Partner
Jacobson, Runes & Bordy
9777 Wilshire Boulevard, Suite 718
Beverly Hills, CA 90212
(310) 777–7488
Fax: (310) 777–7492

8111

Business Information: Jacobson, Runes & Bordy is a full–service, general practice law firm. Established in 1994, the Firm reports annual revenue of $1.5 million. A practicing attorney in California state courts, Mr. Bordy joined the Firm in 1993. Serving as Managing Partner, he shares responsibility of the management of the Firm, as well as serves as a transaction attorney for real estate and business transactions. **Career Steps:** Managing Partner, Jacobson, Runes & Bordy

(1993–Present); Attorney, Cooper, Epstein & Hurewitz (1989–1993); Attorney, Wood, Lucksinger & Epstein (1988–1989); Attorney, Thelen, Marrin, Johnson & Bridges (1986–1988). **Associations & Accomplishments:** Beverly Hills Bar Association; Barristers Board of Governors (1989–1992); Board of Governors, Cedars–Sinai Medical Center; Cabinet Member – Real Estate and Construction Division, United Jewish Fund; Board of Governors, Lawyers Against Hunger; Author of legal aspects of heart transplant articles in "Cogitations" and several others. **Education:** University of Southern California, J.D. (1986); Hamilton College, B.A. (1974); University of Kansas, Ph.D. in Biology (1980). **Personal:** Married to Melissa Anne Held in 1987. Two children: Shayna Robyn and Jenna Alexis. Mr. Bordy enjoys coaching his daughter's soccer team, participating in civic activities, and is an avid runner.

Mr. Timothy H. Bosler
Owner
Law Offices of Timothy H. Bosler
5440 North Oak Trafficway
Kansas City, MO 64118
(816) 454–5444
Fax: (816) 454–7789

8111

Business Information: Law Offices of Timothy H. Bosler is a private practice law firm. As Owner and Sole Practitioner, Timothy Bosler handles all matters pertaining to the firm as well as practice law. Areas of concentration are in civil litigation including professional malpractice, product liability, employment discrimination and personal injury matters. **Career Steps:** Owner, Law Offices of Timothy H. Bosler (1973–Present); Owner, Weatherford Flight School (1967–1969); Flight Instructor, Hickman Aero Club (1966–1968). **Associations & Accomplishments:** American Bar Association; Kansas City Metropolitan Bar Association; Diplomat, Court Practices Institute; Trustee, Christian Church of Liberty, MO; Wood Badge Staff, Boy Scouts of America; District Leadership Staff, Troop Committee Chairman, Boy Scouts of America **Education:** University of Missouri–Kansas City, J.D. (1972); Weatherby College, A.A. (1969); University of Missouri–Kansas City, B.A. in Economics (1971). **Personal:** Married to Hazel in 1976. One child: Timothy H. Bosler, Jr. Mr. Bosler enjoys tennis and the breeding and field training of Pointers.

Paul A. Braden
Managing Partner
Delgado, Acosta & Braden
221 North Kansas, Suite 1400
El Paso, TX 79901
(915) 544–9997
Fax: (915) 544–8544

8111

Business Information: Delgado, Acosta & Braden is a full–service, general practice law firm in El Paso, Texas. A practicing attorney in Texas state courts since 1989, Paul Braden joined the Firm as Partner in 1994. Appointed as Managing Partner in 1995, his practice concentrates on corporate, international and securities work. **Career Steps:** Delgado, Acosta & Braden: Managing Partner (1995–Present), Partner (1994–1995); Associate, Kemp, Smith, Duncan & Hammond (1989–1994). **Associations & Accomplishments:** Texas–Mexico Bar Association; El Paso Young Lawyers Association; American Bar Association; El Paso Bar Association; State Bar of Texas; Texas Society to Prevent Blindness: Director, Executive Vice President. **Education:** University of Texas – School of Law, J.D. with honors (1989); University of Dallas, B.A. cum laude (1986). **Personal:** Married to Virginia in 1996. Mr. Braden enjoys running and hiking.

Roger N. Braden
Managing Partner
Wasson, Braden, Heeter & King
1 River Front Place, Suite 950B
Newport, KY 41071
(606) 491–5297
Fax: (606) 292–7790

8111

Business Information: Wasson, Braden, Heeter & King is a boutique law firm concentrating in litigation and taxation. It's lawyers are licensed in Kentucky, Ohio, and Indiana federal courts. Mr. Braden joined the Firm as Managing Partner in 1994, concentrating his practice on litigation. **Career Steps:** Managing Partner, Wasson, Braden, Heeter & King (1994–Present); Partner, Greenebaum Doll & McDonald (1993); Associate Attorney, Robert E. Sanders & Associates (1986–1990); Adjunct Professor, Salmond P. Chase College of Law (1995). **Associations & Accomplishments:** Former Chairperson, Northern Kentucky Bar Association – Health Law Section (1994); Co–Chairperson, Northern Kentucky University – Parents Advisory Council (1995); Alumni Board of Directors, Chase College of Law. **Education:** Salmon P.

Chase College of Law, J.D. (1984); Northern Kentucky University, B.A. (1979); Henderson Community College, R.N. (1977). **Personal:** Married to Caroline in 1987. Five children: Chris, Amy, Rebecca, Ben, and Katie. Mr. Braden enjoys chess, sports, and music.

Thomas R. Breeden, Esq.
Sole Practitioner
Thomas R. Breeden, P.C.
7900 Sudley Road, Suite 301
Manassas, VA 22110–2806
(703) 361–9277
Fax: (703) 368–9280

8111

Business Information: Thomas R. Breeden, P.C. is a sole practice general law firm. A practicing attorney since 1991, Thomas Breeden established his private practice in 1993. **Career Steps:** Attorney, Thomas R. Breeden, P.C. (1993–Present); Attorney, Vanderpool, Frostick & Massey, P.C. (1991–1993). **Associations & Accomplishments:** Business Network International; Democratic Committee; Prince William NARAL; Greater Manassas Jaycees. **Education:** Washington & Lee School of Law, J.D., cum laude (1991); Cornell University, B.A. (1988); The Lawrenceville School. **Personal:** Married to Lori Jane Blankenship in 1994.

Marcia L. Brehmer
Executive Director
Legal Aide Society of Columbus
40 West Gay Street
Columbus, OH 43215
(614) 224–8374 Ext: 135
Fax: (614) 224–4514

8111

Business Information: Legal Aide Society of Columbus provides legal aide services to indigent and needy persons residing in Columbus, Ohio and a surrounding five county area. Funding for the Agency comes from a variety of governmental agencies (i.e., United Way) and private source grants. There are currently 25 associate attorneys and over 55 legal aide and administrative support staff employed at the Columbus headquarters. As Executive Director, Ms. Brehmer has full budgetary and supervisory authority over a $2.75 million budget, staff personnel, as well as the implementation of organizational policies, grant writing, and community relations. **Career Steps:** The Legal Aide Society of Columbus: Executive Director (1982–Present); Supervising Attorney (1978–1982); Staff Attorney (1976–1978). **Associations & Accomplishments:** American Bar Association; Columbus Bar Association; Ohio State Bar Association; Women Lawyers of Franklin County; Board Member, St. Mark's Community Health Center; Former Committee Member, Franklin County Public Defenders Office; Former Board Member, Ohio State Legal Services Associates **Education:** Boston University School of Law, J.D. (1976); Miami University, B.A. in Sociology (1971). **Personal:** Ms. Brehmer enjoys biking, canoeing, bird watching, golf, hiking and gardening.

William F. Bresee
Principal
Law Offices of William F. Bresee
305 Whispering Oaks Drive
Glendora, CA 91741–3993
(818) 963–7880
Fax: (818) 963–7507

8111

Business Information: Law Offices of William F. Bresee is a full–service, general practice law firm concentrating in domestic and international business and commercial transactional law. A practicing attorney in California state courts since 1981, Mr. Bresee established his law firm in 1992. Currently serving as Principal, he is involved in all aspects of operations, including administration, finances, public relations, accounting, legal representation, strategic planning, and overseeing a staff of two attorneys. **Career Steps:** Principal, Law Offices of William F. Bresee (1992–Present); Vice President and General Counsel, Luz Engineering Corporation (1988–1992); Senior Counsel, Bechtel Corporation (1980–1988); Naval Officer, U.S. Navy (1974–1978). **Associations & Accomplishments:** Captain, U.S. Naval Reserve; Forum on Construction Law, International Construction Committee, American Bar Association; Governing Council, Board of Trustees, Foothill Hospital Foundation; Knights Templar, Sovereign Military Order of the Temple of Jerusalem; Life Member, Deputy Judge Advocate, Department of California, Reserve Officers Association **Education:** University of San Francisco, J.D., with honors (1981); University of California – Los Angeles, B.A. in Economics (1974). **Personal:** Married to Josephine in 1991. Three children: Daniel, Caroline, and Joseph. Mr. Bresee enjoys woodworking, photography, and travel.

Ms. Elvira Madden Breslin
Attorney
Madden Breslin, P.C.
2655 Oakton Glen Drive
Vienna, VA 22181
(703) 281–5590
Fax: Please mail or call

8111

Business Information: Madden Breslin, P.C. is a full–service, general practice law firm not limited to taxation, estates, and education. Admitted to practice in both state and federal courts in Pennsylvania and District of Columbia, Ms. Breslin is responsible for administration and legal representation for the Firm's clientele. **Career Steps:** Attorney/Independent Contractor, Madden Breslin, P.C. (1990–Present); Research Associate, Villanova University LL.M. Graduate Taxation Program; Law Clerk, Beins, Axelrod, Osborne & Mooney and Federation of Tax Administrators, Washington DC (1989–1990); Research Associate, Akin, Gump, Strauss, Hauer & Feld, Washington DC and Meade & Associates, Fairfax, VA (1988); Computer/Paralegal Specialist, Personnel Pool, Washington DC (1987); Educator/Legal Intern, Specialist/Administrator/Teacher, Fairfax County Public Schools, Fairfax, VA (1979–1994); Teacher, Baldwin–Whitehall Public Schools, Pittsburgh, PA (1971–1975); Teacher, Cheltenham Public Schools, Cheltenham, PA (1965–1971). **Associations & Accomplishments:** U.S. Court of Appeals, 3rd Circuit (1994); U.S. District Court, Pennsylvania (1994) and Washington D.C. (1992); District of Columbia Bar (1992); Pennsylvania Bar (1991); Virginia State Department of Education High School Principal Certification (1985); High School English Certification (1983); Pennsylvania Department of Public Instruction High School English Certification (1965). American Bar Association; State and Local Bar Associations; Served at the White House, Office Of First Lady Correspondence, OEOB, with legal/computer skills (Clinton–English); Served as legal resource/research specialist to the Director of Testing and Evaluation at Walnut Hill Center, consulting and writing memos of educational issues/law (educational research). **Education:** Villanova University, LL.M. in in Taxation Law (1996); The Catholic University of America, Columbus School of Law, J.D. (1990); Villanova University, M.A. in High School Educational Administration (1968); Chestnut College, B.A. in English and in Secondary Education (1965). **Personal:** Married to John A. Breslin in 1971. Two children: Kristen and John. Ms. Breslin enjoys genealogy, reading, swimming, biking and gardening.

William P. Bresnahan, J.D.
Managing Shareholder and Attorney
Hollinshead, Mendelson, Bresnahan & Nixon, P.C.
820 Grant Building
Pittsburgh, PA 15219
(412) 355–7070
Fax: (412) 281–6099

8111

Business Information: Hollinshead, Mendelson, Bresnahan & Nixon, P.C. is a full–service, general practice law firm concentrating on real estate trial law. Established in 1973, the Firm currently employs 13 attorneys, legal and administrative support staff. Admitted to practice in both state and federal courts in Pennsylvania and the Tri–State area, Mr. Bresnahan is responsible for all aspects of operations and management as well as serving as a trial lawyer. **Career Steps:** Managing Shareholder and Trial Attorney, Hollinshead, Mendelson, Bresnahan & Nixon, P.C. (1990–Present); Litigation Department Head and Trial Attorney, Rothman, Gordon, Foreman & Groudine (1984–1990); Managing Shareholder and Trial Attorney, William P. Bresnahan, P.C. (1982–1984). **Associations & Accomplishments:** Member, American Bar Association, Pennsylvania Bar Association, Allegheny County Bar Association; Academy of Trial Lawyers of Alleghany County; School Director, Fox Chapel Area School District; School Director, Northern Area Special Purpose Schools; The Best Lawyers in America. **Education:** Duquesne University School of Law, J.D. (1967); Wheeling Jesuit College, B.A. (1964). **Personal:** Married to Margaret in 1969. Three children: Susan Ann, William Preston II and Jeffrey Walter. Mr. Bresnahan enjoys playing golf, managing baseball and coaching basketball for children.

Howard A. Brick
Attorney
Burns & Levinson
125 Summer Street
Boston, MA 02110–1616
(617) 345–3562
Fax: (617) 345–3299

8111

Business Information: Burns & Levinson is a general law practice concentrating on business law, white–collar criminal, healthcare and litigation. Admitted to practice in Massachusetts state and federal courts since 1987, Howard Brick joined the Firm in 1994. A litigation attorney, he focuses his practice in the areas of business litigation, intellectual property, health care, and white collar criminal defense. **Career Steps:** Attorney, Burns & Levinson (1994–Present); Assistant Attorney General, Massachusetts Attorney General's Office (1991–1994); Associate, Hale and Dorr (1987–1991). **Associations & Accomplishments:** Massachusetts Bar Association; Boston Bar Association; Anti–Defamation League; Combined Jewish Philanthropies. **Education:** Columbia University Law School, J.D. (1987); Dartmouth College, B.A. (1983). **Personal:** Married to Jill A. Smilow in 1990. Two children: Jeremy L. and Elijah M. Mr. Brick enjoys tennis, skiing, hiking, music, politics, reading, and travel.

Victoria E. Brieant
Partner
Coudert Brothers
4 Embarcadero Center, Suite 3300
San Francisco, CA 94111–4106
(415) 986–1300
Fax: (415) 986–0320

8111

Business Information: Coudert Brothers is a premier, international full–service law firm. Established in 1856, the Firm is the oldest continuing practice of its kind in the U.S. International in scope, the Firm has presence in 17 countries. A practicing attorney since 1983, Ms. Brieant joined the Firm as Associate in 1990. Appointed as Partner in 1995, her practice involves primarily companies experiencing antitrust and intellectual property litigations. She also is responsible for computer–related consumer issues. **Career Steps:** Coudert Brothers: Partner (1995–Present), Associate (1990–1994); Associate, Wilson, Sonsini, Goodrich & Rosati (1989–1990); Associate, LeBoeuf, Lamb, Leiby & MacRae (1984–1989). **Associations & Accomplishments:** American Bar Association; California Women's Bar Association; Bar Association of San Francisco. **Education:** State University of New York at Buffalo, Faculty of Law & Jurisprudence, J.D. (1983); St. Lawrence University, B.A., magna cum laude, Phi Beta Kappa. **Personal:** Married to Malcolm A. Miswaca in 1989. Ms. Brieant enjoys reading, travel, and sailing.

Christopher Charles Brockman
Real Estate Attorney
Maguire, Voorhis & Wells, P.A.
P.O. Box 633, 2 South Orange Avenue
Orlando, FL 32802–0633
(407) 244–1123
Fax: (407) 423–8796

8111

Business Information: Maguire, Voorhis & Wells, P.A. is a full–service, general practice law firm, specializing in bankruptcy cases. Established in 1918, the Firm currently employs more than 115 attorneys, legal, and administrative support staff. Joining the Firm upon the conferral of his law degree in 1985, Mr. Brockman is admitted to practice in Florida state courts. Serving as a Real Estate Attorney, his practice concentrates on civil cases. **Career Steps:** Real Estate Attorney, Maguire, Voorhis & Wells, P.A. (1985–Present). **Associations & Accomplishments:** Center for Community Involvement (formerly, Volunteer Center of Central Florida); Catholic Social Services; United Way Board Member; Downtown Orlando Partnership Board Member; Leadership Orlando Graduate. **Education:** Florida State College of Law, J.D. (1985); Florida State University, B.A. Magna Cum Laude (1981). **Personal:** Married to Maureen in 1983. Four children: Shannon, Christopher, Daniel, and Benjamin. Mr. Brockman enjoys spending time with his family and golf.

Thomas Willcox Brooke
• • • ━━━◉━━━ • • •

Attorney at Law
Gadsby & Hannah
1747 Pennsylvania Ave., N.W. 800
Washington, DC 20006–4604
(202) 429–9600
Fax: (202) 419–9894

8111

Business Information: Gadsby & Hannah is a general, civil practice law firm. A practicing attorney since 1990, Thomas Brooke joined the Firm in 1993. Admitted to practice in Washington, DC and Virginia courts, he concentrates his practice on intellectual property law. Active in politics and civic affairs, he served as a legislative and administrative aid for members of Congress prior to pursuing his legal career and continues to serve as a volunteer for candidates for Local, State and Federal office. **Career Steps:** Attorney at Law, Gadsby & Hannah (1993–Present); Attorney – Mason, Fenwick & Lawrence (1989–1993); Legislative Assistant, Senator John McCain (1983–1987); Staff Assistant, Congressman Frank Wolf

(1983). **Associations & Accomplishments:** International Trademark Association: Chairman, International Roundtables Subcommittee, Forums Committee; American Bar Association: Intellectual Property Section, Unfair Competition Committee. **Education:** Marshall–Wythe School of Law, J.D. (1990); College of William and Mary, B.A. (1982). **Personal:** Married to Kim in 1992.

Maria Magdalena Brown, J.D.
Attorney
Law Office of Maria Magdalena Brown, J.D.
67 Fort Royal Avenue
Charleston, SC 29407
(803) 766–7478
Fax: (803) 755–3079

8111

Business Information: Maria Magdalena Brown, J.D. is an independent attorney in Charleston, South Carolina, concentrating in probate and estate planning. Career highlights include the writing of two Appellate briefs for the South Carolina Supreme Court in the year 1995–1996. **Career Steps:** Attorney (1993–Present); Office Manager, Carolina Sound Communications (1992); Legal Research Analyst, Legislative Research Division (1990–1992); Assistant Library Technician, University of Nebraska College of Law Library (1990); Law Clerk, Burns and Associates (1990); Paralegal, D. Dusty Rhoades, Esq. (1987–1988); Data Manager/Research Analyst, Medical University of South Carolina (1984–1986); Legal Secretary/Paralegal, Drose and Rhoades, Attorneys at Law (1983–1984); Psychiatric Learning System Coordinator, Medical University of South Carolina (1979–1980); Research Assistant, Medical University of South Carolina (1978–1979); Resident Counselor, Carolina Youth Development Center; Assistant Manager, Marine Enlisted Club, Charleston Naval Base; Manager, Dress Shop, Ann Arbor, MI. **Associations & Accomplishments:** American Chemical Society; American Association for the Advancement of Science; Dean and Vice Dean, Delta Theta Phi Law Fraternity; National Association of Elder Law Attorneys; South Carolina Bar Association; American Bar Association; Charleston County Bar Association; Volunteer, American Red Cross; Performer, Notre Dame and Saint Mary's Theatre; Natural Resources Law Society; Nebraska Student Bar Association (1988–1991); Multi–Cultural Legal Society; Freshman Winner, Freshman Group Coordinator, and Chairman of the Board, Client Counseling Competition; Group Leader, SPICE; Chairman, Big Brother/Big Sister; Latino Translator, Legal Clinic; Student Board Member; President, Psychology Club; Internship on Drug Abuse; Student Teacher, Psychology; Chemistry Tutor; Implemented two new theatre companies in the Charleston Area; Assistant Director, Choreographer, and Dancer, American Cancer Society's "Step 'n' Time" Show; Member, Corps de Ballet – Charleston Civic Ballet; Theater Actor, Footlight Players; Fluent in Spanish; Publications: Assistant Editor and Coordinator, Department of Psychiatry, Medical University of South Carolina, Medical Textbook in accordance with DSM III (1980), Co–Author, "The Incidence and Frequency of Alcohol Use in Diabetics", Diabetic Medical Journal (1985); Research Assistant, "Training Family Practice Residents to Recognize Psychiatric Disturbances", Lancet (1979); Independent Research: Eating Disorders (1979); Informed Consent (1991); An analysis of 26 U.S.C. (1992); The South Carolina Tort Claims Act (1993); Member of the National Network of Estate Planning Attorneys; Book Reviewer for the Post & Courier Newspaper in Charleston, South Carolina. **Education:** University of Nebraska, J.D. (1991); Saint Mary's College at Notre Dame, B.A., Dean's List (1978); Bishop England High School, Charleston, SC, Honors (1974). **Personal:** Miss Brown enjoys fine art, literature, sports, outdoor activities, fine cuisine, nature, music (plays piano), drawing, and traveling.

Michael L. Brown
Partner
Brown, Adkins & Jowers, L.L.P.
712 Main Street, Suite 2120
Houston, TX 77002–3206
(713) 546–2444
Fax: (713) 546–2440

8111

Business Information: Brown, Adkins & Jowers, L.L.P., founded in 1986, is a full–service, civil practice law firm, concentrating on gas, natural resources, real estate, trust, and tort law. A practicing attorney in Texas state courts in 1975, Mr. Brown is one of the founders of the Firm and serves as one of three partners. His practice specializes in oil, gas, and mineral oil issues. **Career Steps:** Partner, Brown, Adkins & Jowers, L.L.P. (1986–Present); Partner, Dohoney & Collier (1981–1986); Staff Attorney of Law Department, Getty Oil Company (1979–1981); Staff Attorney of Land Department, Coastal Corporation (1979). **Associations & Accomplishments:** Texas Bar Association; Louisiana Bar Association; American Bar Association; American Association of Professional Landmen; Executive Vice President, Boy's & Girl's Harbor, Inc. Children's Home; Former President, Optimist Club of Downtown Houston; Sustaining Member, United Phi Beta Kappa Chapters. **Education:** University of Texas – Austin: J.D. (1975), B.A. with honors (1972). **Personal:** Married to

Nela Laura Thomas in 1971. One child: Robert Allen. Mr. Brown enjoys antique autos, hunting, and coin collecting.

Francisco G. Bruno

Partner/Attorney
McConnell Valdes
P. O. Box 364225
San Juan, Puerto Rico 00936–4225
(787) 250–5608
Fax: (787) 759–9225
EMAIL: See Below

8111

Business Information: McConnell Valdes, the largest law firm in Puerto Rico and the Caribbean, is a full–service, general practice law firm. The Firm provides legal services in four areas, including corporate law, taxes, labor law, and litigations in Puerto Rico. Established in 1946, the Firm currently employs 110 attorneys and 85 legal and administrative support staff. Mr. Bruno currently serves as one of forty–two partners. His practice focuses on litigation in commercial, environmental, and admiralty law, in addition to conducting pro bono work. Internet users can reach him via: FGB@MCPR.COM. **Career Steps:** Partner, McConnell Valdes. **Associations & Accomplishments:** American College of Trial Lawyers; American Bar Association; U.S. Maritime Law Association. **Education:** University of Puerto Rico Law School, L.L.B. (1970). **Personal:** Married with three children. Mr. Bruno enjoys sailing and fishing.

John C. Brzustowicz, J.D.

Shareholder/Officer
Day & Brzustowicz, P.C.
3821 Washington Road
McMurray, PA 15317–2946
(412) 942–3789
Fax: (412) 942–3791

8111

Business Information: Day & Brzustowicz, P.C. is a full–service, general practice law firm, concentrating in corporate, construction, and real estate law, and civil litigation. Established in 1958, the Firm currently employs 10 attorneys, legal and administrative support staff. Admitted to practice in Pennsylvania and Washington state courts, Mr. Brzustowicz joined the Firm as Partner in 1995. Previously operating a private practice, he currently serves as Shareholder and Officer and is responsible for all aspects of operations, including providing legal representation of the Firm's clientele. **Career Steps:** Shareholder/Officer, Day & Brzustowicz, P.C. (1995–Present); Senior Partner, Brzustowicz Law Offices (1992–1994); Attorney, Sable Markroff & Libemim (1989–1992). **Associations & Accomplishments:** Member, Board of Trustees of Institute of American Music, Eastman School of Music, Rochester, New York (1979–Present); Assistant to Director, Institute of American Music (1977–Present); American Bar Association; Pennsylvania Bar Association; Allegheny Bar Association; Washington Bar Association. **Education:** Case Western Reserve University, J.D. (1985); Cornell University School of Labor Relations (1980–1981); College of Wooster, B.A. (1979). **Personal:** Married to Diane in 1982. Three children: Richard Reed, Megan Day, and Emily Anne Hanson. Mr. Brzustowicz enjoys woodworking, boating, and being a bibliophile.

Eileen E. Buholtz

Partner
Connors & Corcoran L.L.P.
400 Times Square Building, 45 Exchange Street
Rochester, NY 14614
(716) 232–5885
Fax: (716) 546–3631

8111

Business Information: Connors & Corcoran L.L.P. is a general civil practice law firm, with practice emphasis in the areas of personal injury and commercial litigation for both plaintiff and defense matters. Joining the Firm as an associate in 1982, Ms. Buholtz was appointed Partner in 1991. She focuses her legal counsel and representation as a defense attorney in tort litigation and as plaintiff and defense attorney in commercial litigation. **Career Steps:** Connors & Corcoran LLP: Partner (1991–Present); Associate (1982–1990) **Associations & Accomplishments:** New York State Bar Association; American Bar Association; Monroe County Bar Association; Greater Rochester Association of Women Attorneys; Women's Bar Association of the State of New York; Officer/Board Member, Volunteer Legal Services Project and other organizations providing legal services to the poor; Counsel to Penfield Symphony Orchestra. **Education:** Syracuse Uni-

versity, J.D.; Eastman School of Music, Bachelor of Music. **Personal:** Married to Joseph W. Blackburn in 1973.

Dale A. Burket

Partner
Lowndes, Drosdick, Doster, Kantor & Reed, PA
215 North Eola Drive
Orlando, FL 32802
(407) 843–4600 Ext: 363
Fax: (407) 423–4495
EMail: See Below

8111

Business Information: Lowndes, Drosdick, Doster, Kantor & Reed, PA is a full–service, business practice law firm. Joining the Firm upon the conferral of his law degree in 1981, Mr. Burket concentrates his practice on real estate issues, primarily representing institutional investors in national restaurants and retail stores. Internet users can reach him via: dburket@ix.netcom.com. **Career Steps:** Partner, Lowndes, Drosdick, Doster, Kantor & Reed, PA (Present). **Associations & Accomplishments:** Board Certified Real Estate Lawyer; Florida Bar Board of Legal Specialization and Education; Chairperson of Board of Zoning Adjustment (1994–Present), City of Maitland; International Council of Shopping Centers; American Bar Association (1981–Present). **Education:** Florida State University: J.D. (1981) with honors; B.A. in Music Education (1976); Florida Jr. College – Jacksonville, A.A. (1974). **Personal:** Married to Patricia in 1976. Three children: Charles Allen, Ryan Harrison, and Austin Taylor.

Robert Lee Byington

Partner
Depot Law Offices
P.O. Box 248
Hastings, MI 49058–0248
(616) 945–9557
Fax: (616) 945–2555

8111

Business Information: Depot Law Offices is a full–service, general practice law firm. Joining Depot Law Offices as Associate Attorney upon the conferral of his law degree in 1977, Mr. Byington was appointed as Partner in 1983. Admitted to practice law in Michigan state courts, his practice concentrates on real estate and probate law. **Career Steps:** Depot Law Offices: Partner (1983–Present), Associate Attorney (1977–1982). **Associations & Accomplishments:** Former Chair–Juvenile Law Section, State Bar of Michigan; Fellow, American Bar Association; Judicature Society. **Education:** Cooley Law School, J.D. (1977); Michigan State University, B.A. (1973) **Personal:** Married to Martha in 1971. Two children: Sarah and Eric. Mr. Byington enjoys Classic cars and music.

Olivia S. Byrne

Partner
Weinberg & Jacobs
11300 Rockville Pike, Suite 1200
Rockville, MD 20852
(301) 468–5500
Fax: (301) 468–5504

8111

Business Information: Weinberg & Jacobs is a full–service, general practice law firm, concentrating on corporate, tax and tax exemption, real estate planning, and business law. Future plans include expanding the practice in the area of tax exemption on a national level. A practicing attorney in Maryland state courts since 1982, Ms. Byrne joined the Firm as Partner in 1990. Her practice's main focus is on non–profit estate planning and business law. **Career Steps:** Partner, Weinberg & Jacobs (1990–Present); Attorney, Linowes & Blocher (1987–1990); Associate, Whiteford, Taylor & Preston (1984–1987). **Associations & Accomplishments:** Tax Council for State of Maryland; Exempt Organization Committee, American Bar Association; Council Taxation Section, Maryland Bar Association; Chairman Speakers Bur. Young Lawyers Section, Baltimore City Bar Association; Lawyers for Arts of Washington; Commercial Real Estate for Women: Board of Directors, President; Professionals for Strathmore Hall; Rotary Club; President, D.C. Bowdoin College Alumni Association. **Education:** Georgetown University, Ll.M. in Taxation (1987); University of Toledo, J.D. (1982); Bowdoin College, B.A. (1979); Vanderbilt University (1975–1976). **Personal:** Ms. Byrne enjoys tennis, swimming, paddle tennis, and ice skating.

Mildred Caban

Associate
Goldman, Antonetti & Cordova
P.O. Box 70364
San Juan, Puerto Rico 00936–8364
(809) 759–4213
Fax: (809) 767–9177

8111

Business Information: Goldman, Antonetti & Cordova, one of Puerto Rico's leading law firms, provides corporate and individual clients throughout Puerto Rico and the United States with legal services in the areas of litigation, environmental, tax, corporate and labor law. A practicing attorney since 1986, Ms. Caban joined the Firm in 1993. As an associate with the Litigation Department, she concentrates her practice on bankruptcy law matters, as well as litigation. A civic–minded person, she also volunteers extensive time to the youth within her church, organizing a youth camp by sponsoring, fund–raising, and developing activities for teens ages 13 and up. **Career Steps:** Associate, Goldman, Antonetti & Cordova (1993–Present); Associate, Brown, Newsom & Cordova (1990–1993); Law Clerk, Hon. Hector Laffitte, USDC (1987–1990). **Associations & Accomplishments:** American Bar Association; National Hispanic Bar Association; Puerto Rico Bar Association; Federal Bar Association; Youth Leader; Youth Camp Counselor; Sunday School Teacher, Deaconess. **Education:** New York University School of Law, J.D. (1986); Barnard College, B.A. (1983). **Personal:** Ms. Caban enjoys reading and walking.

Roberto L. Cabanas

Partner
McConnell Valdes
P.O. Box 364225
San Juan, Puerto Rico 00936–4225
(787) 250–5611
Fax: (787) 759–9225
EMAIL: See Below

8111

Business Information: McConnell Valdes is a full–service, general practice law firm concentrating on general corporate, work, labor, and tax law. The largest Hispanic law firm in the world, the Firm employs 120 attorneys and 300 support personnel. A practicing attorney in Puerto Rico courts since 1978, Mr. Cabanas joined the Firm in 1986. He is a Partner in the Tax Division concentrating his practice on tax planning, structuring real estate, tourism, and mortgage–backed securities transactions. Internet users can reach him via: RLC@MCVPR.COM. **Career Steps:** Partner, McConnell Valdes (1986–Present); Tax Manager, Arthur Andersen & Company (1980–1986). **Associations & Accomplishments:** American Institute of Certified Public Accountants; Board of Directors, Puerto Rico Society of Certified Public Accountants; American Bar Association; Puerto Rico Bar Association; Board of Directors, Amigos de San Juan Cinema Fest, Inc. **Education:** University of Massachusetts, M.S. in Accounting (1980); Georgetown University: Law Center, J.D. (1978), B.S.F.S. (1975). **Personal:** Mr. Cabanas enjoys travel and boating.

Joyce Annette Caesar, Esq.

Sole Practitioner
Joyce Annette Caesar – Attorney–at–Law
67 Quabeck Avenue
Irvington, NJ 07111
(201) 372–6136
Fax: Please mail or call

8111

Business Information: After conferral of her law degree in 1986, Joyce A. Caesar passed the bar and established her private practice in 1987. She is admitted to practice in New Jersey and Pennsylvania in both state and federal courts. She concentrates her practice in all areas of civil law, with a particular focus on entertainment law and real estate. **Career Steps:** Sole Practitioner, Joyce Annette Caesar – Attorney–at–Law (1987–Present). **Associations & Accomplishments:** American Bar Association; Executive Board Member, African American Heritage Parade Committee; Concerned Citizens, Inc. **Education:** Rutgers University Law School, J.D. (1986); Rutgers University Graduate School of Management, M.B.A. (1986). **Personal:** Three children: Jameisha, JaMeil and Jacquel Carter. Ms. Caesar enjoys bowling, music and exercise.

Charles Kevin Cahill, Esq.

Shareholder/Director
Clanahan, Tanner, Downing & Knowlton, P.C.
1600 Broadway Street, Suite 2400
Denver, CO 80202–4924
(303) 830–9111
Fax: (303) 830–0299

8111

Business Information: Clanahan, Tanner, Downing & Knowlton, P.C. is a full–service, general practice law firm. Established in 1950, the Firm currently employs 50 attorneys, legal and administrative support staff. Attaining his law degree in 1978, Mr. Cahill has been with Clanahan, Tanner, Downing & Knowlton, P.C. for over five years. As Shareholder/Director, he is responsible for all aspects of the Firm's operation. Admitted to practice in state and federal courts throughout Colorado and Denver, he is a trial lawyer specializing in civil litigation. **Career Steps:** Shareholder/Director, Clanahan, Tanner, Downing & Knowlton, P.C. (1990–Present); Shareholder/Director, Cogswell & Wehale (1986–1990); Shareholder/Director, Shafroth & Toll (1980–1986). **Associations & Accomplishments:** American Bar Association; Colorado Bar Association; Denver Bar Association; Defense Research Institute; NRA. **Education:** Lewis University College of Law, J.D. (1978); University of California, B.A. **Personal:** Married to Karen L. in 1984. Two children: Molly Burke and Kathleen Gard.

Juan Orlando Calderon Lithgow
Attorney
Law Office of Juan Orlando Calderon Lithgow
P.O. Box 4524
Vega Baja, Puerto Rico 00694
(787) 858–5476
Fax: Please mail or call

8111

Business Information: Law Office of Juan Orlando Calderon Lithgow is a law firm concentrating on bankruptcy law. Established in 1995, the Firm is regional in scope, and employs two attorneys. As Attorney, Mr. Calderon Lithgow specializes in the area of bankruptcy law. Active in pro–bono cases, he represents several non–profit organizations in the area, in addition to advising callers on local radio station WZOL on general law questions. Concurrent with his position as attorney, Mr. Calderon Lithgow is a public speaking instructor. **Career Steps:** Attorney, Law Office of Juan Orlando Calderon Lithgow (1995–Present); Deputy Ombudsman, Office of the Ombudsman (1989–1992); Attorney, Legal Services Office (1992–1995). **Associations & Accomplishments:** Colegio de Abogados (Puerto Rico Bar Association); Federal Bar Association. **Education:** Puerto Rico Law School, J.D. (1988); University of Puerto Rico, M.A.; World University, B.S. **Personal:** Mr. Calderon Lithgow enjoys piano playing and computer programming.

Mr. John L. Capone
Attorney
Pitts & Brittian, P.C.
P.O. Box 51295 1116 Weisgarber Road
Knoxville, TN 37950–1295
(423) 584–0105
Fax: (423) 584–0104

8111

Business Information: Pitts & Brittian, P.C. is a law firm. Mr. Capone is an associate attorney with the firm, where he specializes in intellectual property law and patent litigation. He is licensed to practice in both state and federal courts. Mr. Capone is also Adjunct Professor of Law at the University of Tennessee College of Law, where he instructs on the principles of legal pretrial litigation, research, writing and oral advocacy. **Career Steps:** Attorney, Pitts & Brittian, P.C. (1994–Present); Adjunct Associate Professor of Law, University of Tennessee College of Law (1993–Present); Senior Litigation Associate, Higgins, Cavanaugh & Cooney (1986–1993); Law Clerk, U.S. Magistrate Frederick R. DeCesaris, U.S. District Court for the State of Rhode Island (1985–1986). **Associations & Accomplishments:** American Bar Association; Tennessee Bar Association; Rhode Island Bar Association; American Intellectual Property Association; Past Member, United Way; Past Board Member, The Music School; Published in the Case Western Reserve Law Review, "Bartling vs. Glendale Adventist Medical Center: The Final Transgression of a Patient's Right to Die?". **Education:** University of Tennessee, B.S. in Biochemistry (1996); Case Western Reserve University School of Law, J.D. (1985); Tufts University, B.A. (1982). **Personal:** Married to Linda Tobiasz in 1994.

Magdalena Caratini
Partner
Diaz Law Firm
Urb. Delgado – 0–13
Caguas, Puerto Rico 00725
(809) 743–1474
Fax: (809) 746–3565

8111

Business Information: Diaz Law Firm is a full–service, general practice law firm. The Firm currently employs three legal specialists. As Partner, Ms. Caratini is responsible for all aspects of the Firm's operation and specializes in civil, criminal and administrative litigation. Attaining her Master's of Law in 1994, she aspires one day to become a superior court judge. **Career Steps:** Partner, Diaz Law Firm (1994–Present); Municipal Judge, Judicial System (1989–1994); Lawyer, Justice Department (1987–1988). **Associations & Accomplishments:** Phi Alpha Delta Law Fraternity, Former President Jose D. Diego Charter (1983); Women's Civic Club Puerto Rico Chapter (1995–Present). **Education:** Pontificie Catholic University, LL.M. (1994), J.D., B.S. **Personal:** Married to Jose J. Davila in 1987. Ms. Caratini enjoys water sports, chess, and reading.

Jorge Carazo–Quetglas
Partner
Toledo, Toledo & Carazo–Quetglas
Royal Bank Center Suite 508, 255 Ponce De Leon Avenue
San Juan, Puerto Rico 00917
(809) 751–0520
Fax: (809) 763–5961

8111

Business Information: Toledo, Toledo & Carazo–Quetglas is a full–service, general practice law firm, concentrating on general civil litigation (15%) – plaintiff claims for personal injuries – in local and federal courts, medical malpractice, torts, construction law (70%), and maritime law (15%). A practicing attorney in Puerto Rico courts since 1982, Mr. Carazo–Quetglas joined the Firm in 1994. His practice concentrates on litigation and consultations, as well as the administration of personnel and supervision of associate attorneys. **Career Steps:** Partner, Toledo, Toledo & Carazo–Quetglas (1994–Present); Attorney, Sole Practitioner (1991–1994); Partner, Sweeting, Gonzalez & Cestero (1985–1991). **Associations & Accomplishments:** Puerto Rico Bar Association; Federal Bar Association; University of Puerto Rico Law School Alumni Association; Puerto Rico Public Notary Association; Georgetown University Alumni Association. **Education:** University of Puerto Rico Law School, J.D. (1982); Georgetown University, B.A. in Business Administration. **Personal:** Married to Carmen Gonzalez–Badillo in 1980. Two children: Jorge Miguel and Carmen Elena. Mr. Carazo–Quetglas enjoys tae kwon do and church charities.

Brad Carey
Partner
Hardy & Carey
111 Veterans Memorial Boulevard, Suite 255
Metairie, LA 70005
(504) 830–4646
Fax: (504) 830–4659

8111

Business Information: Hardy & Carey is a national and international telecommunications law firm. Customers include radio, television stations, communities, and cellular phone companies. As Partner, Mr. Carey is responsible for advising clients on a broad range of telecommunications law issues and representing them before the FCC. **Career Steps:** Partner, Hardy & Carey (1984–Present). **Associations & Accomplishments:** Federal Communications Bar Association; Association of Federal Communications Consulting Engineers; Coxswain, United States Coast Guard Auxiliary. **Education:** University of Louisville, J.D. (1983); University of Kentucky, B.B.A. (1975).

Deborah A. Carman
Founding Partner
Law Offices of Carman and Smith, P.A.
165 East Palmetto Park Road
Boca Raton, FL 33432
(407) 392–7031
Fax: (407) 750–3896

8111

Business Information: The Law Offices of Carman and Smith, P.A. is a full–service, general practice law firm. A practicing attorney in Florida state courts since 1983, Ms. Carman co–founded the Firm in 1988. Her practice concentrates on Worker's Compensation, real estate, trusts, wills, probate, commercial, business law, and personal injury, as well as pro–bono work. Concurrent with her private law practice, she teaches at F.A.U. and the Board of Realtors. **Career Steps:** Founding Partner, Law Offices of Carman and Smith, P.A. (1988–Present); Attorney, Law Offices of Deborah A. Carman, Esq. (1984–1988). **Associations & Accomplishments:** Chair, Community Relations Board; Board of Trustees, Florida Philharmonic; Florida Bar Association; Marketing Chair, Women's Council of Realtors; National Association of Women Business Owners; Boca Raton Chamber of Commerce; South Palm Beach County Association of Realtors. **Education:** Tulane University, J.D. (1983); Newcomb Collogo at Tulane, B.A. (1900). **Personal:** Married to Jack Berger. Three children: Amy Michelle, Julia Nicole, and Laura Allyson. Ms. Carman enjoys spending time with her children, music, and art.

Dale Sanford Carpenter III
President/Attorney
Carpenter & Henderson
143 Union Boulevard, Suite 900
Lakewood, CO 80228–1829
(303) 988–9100
Fax: (303) 988–9103
EMAIL: dsc@lawyernet.com

8111

Business Information: Carpenter & Henderson is a general practice law firm with two partners. In addition to maintaining his private practice since 1980, Mr. Carpenter also co–founded Carpenter & Henderson in 1995, focusing his practice in civil litigation and compensation. Concurrently, he serves as the Director of Membership and Development for LawyerNet, an internet access provider established in 1995. Internet users can reach him via: dsc@lawyernet.com **Career Steps:** President/Attorney, Carpenter & Henderson (1995–Present); Membership and Development, LawyerNet (1995–Present); President, Dale S. Carpenter, III P.C. (1980–Present). **Associations & Accomplishments:** Board Member, Juvenile Diabetes Foundation; Former Board Member, St. Joseph Hospital Foundation; Troop Chaplain, Boy Scouts of America; Jefferson Board of Realtors. **Education:** University of Denver, J.D. (1974); Cornell University, M.B.A. (1969); University of Rochester, B.A. (1967). **Personal:** Married to Diane E. in 1981.

Paul V. Carty, Esq.
Associate Attorney
Farren & King
20 Swampscott Street
West Haven, CT 06516–1424
(203) 562–9813
Fax: (203) 562–3248

8111

Business Information: Farren & King is a general practice law firm. Currently the Firm employs 5 attorneys. As Associate Attorney, Mr. Carty concentrates his practice in the areas of criminal litigation, personal injury, family law, worker's compensation, and landlord/tenant disputes. A trial attorney since the conferral of his law degree in 1985, Mr. Carty is admitted to both State and Federal courts. **Career Steps:** Associate Attorney, Farren & King (1985–Present); Senior Claims Representative, Cigna Insurance Company (1980–1988); Claims Representatives, Liberty Mutual Insurance Company (1977–1980). **Associations & Accomplishments:** New Haven Bar Association; Connecticut Bar Association; West Haven Bar Association; American Bar Association; Connecticut Criminal Defense Lawyers Association; Prince Hall Masons; West Haven Black Coalition. **Education:** University of Connecticut School of Law, J.D. (1985); Wesleyan University, B.A. (1977). **Personal:** Married to Kimberly A. in 1982. Three children: Rachel Lee, Paul Vernon, Jr. and Trevor Dudley. Mr. Carty enjoys Karate and photography.

Roberto Casas Sanchez
•••─◉─•••
President
Roberto Casas Abogados A.C.
Durango No. 81–301
Col. Roma, Mexico 06700
(525) 533–0912
Fax: (525) 533–4307

8111

Business Information: Roberto Casas Abogados is an independent law firm with a focus on corporate law. Established in 1979, the Firm is comprised of six partners, 14 attorneys and a support staff of ten. As President, Mr. Casas Sanchez oversees tax and corporate matters in the Republic of Mexico. Other responsibilities include tax planning, tax law cases, and insuring new client satisfaction. **Career Steps:** Roberto Casas Abogados: President (1992–Present), Partner (1982–1992). **Associations & Accomplishments:** Barra Mexicana Colegio De Abogados; Board Member, Associacion Nacional de Abogados de Empresa; University Club of Mexico; International Fiscal Association; Interpacific Bar Association; Boy Scouts. **Education:** UNAM, Law (1981). **Personal:** Married to Ana Rosa U. de Casas in 1976. Three children: Anna Cristina, Adriana, and Andrea. Mr. Casas Sanchez enjoys camping, scuba diving, and photography.

Mr. James H. Case
Partner
Carlsmith, Ball, Wichman, Case & Ichiki
P.O. Box 656
Honolulu, HI 96809
(808) 523–2500
Fax: (808) 523–0842

8111

Business Information: Carlsmith, Ball, Wichman, Case & Ichiki is a full–service law firm specializing in Business and Corporate Law (Nationally and Internationally). Established in 1857, Carlsmith, Ball, Wichman, Case & Ichiki presently employs 400 people and has an estimated annual revenue in excess of $40 million. In his current capacity, Mr. Case concentrates his practice in business and corporate law. **Career Steps:** Partner, Carlsmith, Ball, Wichman, Case & Ichiki (1959–Present); Associate, Carlsmith, Ball, Wichman, Murray, Case & Ichiki (1951–1959). **Associations & Accomplishments:** Director, Mauna Loa Resources; Member, Pacific Club; Member, Kaneohe Yacht Club; Member, Central Union Church (congregational); 3rd Generation Lawyer; Interviewed in business magazines and local newspapers. **Education:** Harvard LAW, J.D. (1949); Williams College, A.B. (1941). **Personal:** Married to Suzanne E. in 1948. Six children: Edward E., John H., Suzanne D., Russell L., Elizabeth D., and Bradford. Mr. Case enjoys sailing and tennis in his leisure time.

Robert R. Casey
Partner
Jones, Walker, Waechter, Poitevent, Correre & Denegre
One American Place, Suite 1700
Baton Rouge, LA 70825
(504) 377–8910
Fax: (504) 377–8933

8111

Business Information: Jones, Walker, Waechter, Poitevent, Correre & Denegre is a full–service, general practice law firm consisting of 150 attorneys in four offices. A practicing attorney for twenty–four years in Louisiana state courts, Mr. Casey joined the Firm in 1971. Appointed as Partner in 1976, he is a tax attorney, focusing his practice on tax issues. **Career Steps:** Partner, Jones, Walker, Waechter, Poitevent, Correre & Denegre (1971–Present). **Associations & Accomplishments:** Tax Section, American Bar Association; Tax Section, Louisiana Bar Association; Louisiana State Law Institute; American College of Tax Counsel; Board of Editors, Journal of Taxation and Journal of S Corporation Taxation; Author of over six articles published in law reviews; Frequent speaker at legal seminars. **Education:** New York University, LL.M. (1973); Tulane University, J.D. (1971); University of Notre Dame, B.B.A. (1968)

Lourdes Castillo – Garcia
Associate
Keenan Powers & Andrews, P.A.
220 Sunrise Avenue
Palm Beach, FL 33480
(561) 832–8799
Fax: (561) 659–7634

8111

Business Information: Keenan Powers & Andrews, P.A. is a law firm with offices in New York, New Jersey, Florida, and Connecticut. The law firm handles estates & trusts, bankruptcy, real estate law, and foreclosure. As Associate, Mrs. Castillo–Garcia handles real estate law, CitiBank closings, and foreclosures. She also has a personal business purchasing, refurbishing, and selling foreclosed homes. **Career Steps:** Associate, Keenan Powers & Andrews, P.A. (1993–Present); Assistant Prosecutor, Hudson County Prosecutor's Office (1988–1992); Law Clerk, Judge John J. Grossi Jr. (1987–1988). **Education:** New York Law School, J.D. (1987).

Keith Michael Casto

Partner
Bronson, Bronson & McKinnon
Ten Almaden Boulevard, Suite 600
San Jose, CA 95113
(408) 293–0599
Fax: (408) 999–6553
EMAIL: See Below

8111

Business Information: Bronson, Bronson & McKinnon is an international general practice law firm. Established in 1912, the Firm serves clientele worldwide from three offices in California (San Jose, San Francisco, Los Angeles) and currently employs 161 attorneys. A practicing attorney since 1973, Mr. Casto joined the Firm as Partner and Head of the Environmental Department in 1995. His practice concentrates on environmental, toxic tort, criminal prosecution, criminal defense, government, and litigation cases. Internet users can reach him via: KCasto@bronson.com. **Career Steps:** Partner, Bronson, Bronson & McKinnon (1995–Present); Partner, Pettit & Martin (1992–1995); Partner, Hoge, Fenton, Jones & Appel (1988–1992); Associate, Troutman, Sanders, Lockerman & Ashmore (1985–1988). **Associations & Accomplishments:** American Bar Association; Florida Bar Association; Georgia Bar Association; California Bar Association; San Jose Chamber of Commerce; Peninsula Industry and Business Association; Santa Clara County Bar Association; Semiconductor Industry Association. **Education:** Stetson University: J.D. (1973), B.A. (1969). **Personal:** Two children: Kristopher Michael and Timothy Lucas. Mr. Casto enjoys tennis, skiing, backpacking, running, and bicycling.

Tanja H. Castro
Principal and Attorney
Amram & Hahn
815 Connecticut Avenue NW, Suite 601
Washington, DC 20006
(202) 833–3344
Fax: (202) 785–2337

8111

Business Information: Established in 1959, Amram & Hahn is a general practice law firm. Currently the Firm employs 8 attorneys and legal support staff. Ms. Castro joined the firm in 1985 and became a Principal in 1992. She concentrates her practice in the areas of litigation and real assessment appeals, as well as conservatorship, general guardianships and decedents estates in the District of Columbia and Northern Virginia. **Career Steps:** Amram & Hahn: Principal and Attorney (1992–Present), Associate Attorney (1985–1992). **Associations & Accomplishments:** Executive Committee, Commercial Real Estate Women (1993–Present); District of Columbia Building Industry Association. **Education:** American University Washington College of Law, J.D. (1985); Vassar College, A.B. (1981). **Personal:** Married to Ernesto D. in 1986. Ms. Castro enjoys golf, gardening, gourmet cooking, and collecting wine.

Mark E. Cedrone
Partner
Carroll & Cedrone Law Firm
Independence Square West 750 Curtis Center
Philadelphia, PA 19106
(215) 925–2500
Fax: (215) 925–6471

8111

Business Information: Carroll & Cedrone Law Firm is a law firm, focusing on criminal and civil fraud litigation. A practicing attorney in Pennsylvania state and federal courts since 1985, Mark Cedrone established the Firm in 1993. Mr. Cedrone handles some court–appointed work, pro bono work, and much of the Firm's white collar criminal work in federal courts. He also performs some appellate work. **Career Steps:** Shareholder, Carroll & Cedrone Law Firm (1993–Present); Attorney, Mark E. Cedrone Esq. (1992–1993); Attorney, Duane, Morris, Heckschen (1986–1992); Attorney Advisor, Judge Helen Buckley, U.S.Tax Court (1985–1986). **Associations & Accomplishments:** Philadelphia Bar Association; American Bar Association; Federal Bar Association; Pennsylvania Bar Association; National Association of Criminal Defense Lawyers; Pennsylvania Association of Criminal Defense Lawyers. **Education:** Temple Law School, J.D. (1985); La Salle University, B.S. in Accounting (1982). **Personal:** Married to Marianne in 1979. Three children: Aubrey, Amy, and Allyson. Mr. Cedrone enjoys coaching girls softball.

Jeffrey K. Chambers, Esq.
Partner
Chambers, Salzman & Bannon, P.A.
P.O. Box 1191 520 4th Street North
St. Petersburg, FL 33731
(813) 896–2167
Fax: (813) 822–8981

8111

Business Information: Chambers, Salzman & Bannon, P.A. is a law firm, established in 1964 and specializing solely in personal injury and workers compensation, practicing in both state and federal courts. As Partner, Mr. Chambers is responsible for establishing policy and decision making for long–term expansion. In 1994, at 29 years of age, he was one of the youngest attorneys in the country to ever obtain a multi–million dollar verdict. He plans to expand his practice more into medical negligence. **Career Steps:** Partner, Chambers, Salzman & Bannon, P.A. (1990–Present); President, Jeff Chambers Enterprises, Inc. (1987–1988). **Associations & Accomplishments:** Academy of Florida Trial Lawyers; American Bar Association; Florida Bar; One of the Youngest Lawyers in America Obtaining Multi–Million Dollar Verdict; Former Professional Tennis Player. **Education:** Stetson College of Law, Doctorate (1990); University of North Carolina, Psychology (1987). **Personal:** One child: Austin. Mr. Chambers enjoys travel, working out, and spending time with his son.

James P. Chandler, Sr., Esq.
Chairman
Chandler Law Firm
1815 Pennsylvania Avenue, NW, Suite 800
Washington, DC 20035
(202) 842–4800
Fax: (202) 296–4098
EMAIL: See Below

8111

Business Information: Chandler Law Firm is a chartered legal practice concentrating on the area of intellectual property law for companies and large corporations. Established in 1992, the Firm employs 22 people. As Chairman, Mr. Chandler oversees all aspects of the Firm. His responsibilities include client consultation, trial preparation, public relations and strategic planning. Concurrent with his present position, Mr. Chandler is President of the National Intellectual Property Law Institute. Internet users can reach him via: Nipwind@aol.com. **Career Steps:** Chairman, Chandler Law Firm (1992–Present); Professor of Law, George Washington University (1976–1994). **Associations & Accomplishments:** American Bar Association; American Society of International Law; American Intellectual Property Law Association; Consultant to Comptroller General of the U.S.; Consultant to Congressional Committees. **Education:** Harvard Law School, LL.M. (1971); University of California, Davis, J.D.; University of California, Berkeley, B.A. **Personal:** Married to Elizabeth Thompson in 1962. Seven children: Elizabeth Lynn, James P. Jr., Isaac, Dennis A., David M., Ruth R. and Aaron D.. Mr. Chandler enjoys reading biographies and auto–biographies, travel, and symphonies.

Margaret–Mary Ann Chaplinsky

Partner
Brown, Winick, Graves, Gross, Baskerville, Schoenebaum & Walker, P.L.C.
Suite 1100 Two Ruan Center, 601 Locust Street
Des Moines, IA 50309–3765
(515) 242–2472
Fax: (515) 242–2461

8111

Business Information: Brown, Winick, Graves, Gross, Baskerville, Schoenebaum & Walker, P.L.C. is a full–service, general law practice. Serving clients throughout Iowa from two locations (Des Moines and Pella), the Firm currently consists of 30 attorneys, and employs over 50 legal aide and administrative support staff. A practicing attorney since 1983, Ms. Chaplinsky joined the Firm as Partner in 1991. She concentrates her practice in the areas of civil and commercial litigation, as well as health care products liability. **Career Steps:** Partner, Brown, Winick, Graves, Gross, Baskerville, Schoenebaum & Walker, P.L.C. (1991–Present); Attorney and Partner, Davis, Hockenberg, Wine, Brown, Koehn & Shors, P.C. (1988–1990); Attorney, Mesirov, Gelman, Jaffe, Cromer & Jamieson (1983–1986). **Education:** Delaware Law School of Widener University, J.D. (1983); Villanova University, B.A. (1980). **Personal:** Married to Charles J. Kalinoski, Esq. in 1988. Ms. Chaplinsky enjoys wines and gourmet cooking.

Scott Bruce Chapman
Attorney at Law
Scott B. Chapman, Attorney at Law
7900 Glades Road, Suite 330
Boca Raton, FL 33434
(407) 361–9109
Fax: (407) 483–0200

8111

Business Information: Scott B. Chapman, Attorney at Law is a full–service, general practice law firm, concentrating on civil litigation cases. Establishing his individual practice upon conferral of his law degree in 1991, Mr. Chapman oversees all administrative operations for associates and support staff, in addition to his daily client base representation. **Career Steps:** Attorney at Law, Scott B. Chapman, Attorney at Law (1993–Present); Attorney, Aronson & Saltzer (1991–1993). **Associations & Accomplishments:** Litigation Section, American Bar Association; Florida Bar Association. **Education:** Cleveland State University, Cleveland–Marshall College of Law, J.D. (1991); Ohio State University, B.S.B.A. **Personal:** Married to Laura in 1994.

Thomas V. Chema
••• ◄██◉██► •••

Partner
Arter & Hadden
925 Euclid Avenue, Huntington Bldg. #1100
Cleveland, OH 44115
(216) 696–2564
Fax: (216) 696–2645

8111

Business Information: Arter & Hadden is a premier, general practice law firm with offices in Ohio, Washington, D.C., Texas, and California. A practicing attorney since 1971, Mr. Chema has served the Firm in various periods since 1972. Admitted to all Ohio courts, he now concentrates in the areas of energy and telecommunications law with emphasis on regulatory aspects of electric utility and local exchange carrier business. Prior to rejoining the Firm in 1989, his practice was devoted to litigation, particularly personal injury and medical malpractice cases; later evolving into commercial litigation with emphasis on complex manufacturing issues and intra–corporate disputes. Concurrent to his private legal practice, he is the Founder and President of Gateway Consultants, Inc., providing consulting services to sport franchises, government entities and developers involved in the development of new venues for sports teams and related entertainment. He is responsible for administrative activities, overseeing the development of public sector consensus to support construction of new venues, funding and finance plans, and negotiation of leases and management agreements. **Career Steps:** Partner, Arter & Hadden (1989–Present); President, Gateway Consultants, Inc. (1994–Present); Executive Director, Gateway Economic Development Corporation of Greater Cleveland (1990–1995); Chairman, Public Utilities Commission of Ohio (1985–1989); Executive Director, Ohio Lottery Commission (1983–1985); Attorney, Arter & Hadden (1972–1983); Intelligence and Legal Officer, United States Air Force (1971–1972); Hearing Officer, Cambridge Rent Control Administration (1970–1971). **Associations & Accomplishments:** Chairman, Ohio Building Authority – Columbus, Ohio; Ohio Bar Association; Bar Association of Greater Cleveland; National Association of Regulatory Utility Commissioners; Director, Transtechnology Corporation; Director, NuMed HomeHealth Systems, Inc.; Trustee, Roulston Family of Funds; Chairman and Director, Interactive MultiMedia Network, Inc.; Trustee, Hiram College; Trustee, St. Ignatius High School; Trustee, Sister's of Charity of St. Augustine Health System, Inc.; Trustee, City Club of Cleveland; Trustee, Historic Gateway Neighborhood Economic Development Corporation; Trustee, Cleveland Works; Trustee, Cleveland Foundation for Architecture; Trustee, Ohio Legal Assistance Foundation; Downtown Development Partners; Task Force Member, Birthday Celebration, Cleveland Bicentennial Commission; Garfield Society Award – Hiram College (1995); Downtown Development Award – Growth Association of Greater Cleveland (1994); Public Administrator of the Year – American Society for Public Administration (1989); Various Publications. **Education:** University of Notre Dame, A.B. in History, magna cum laude, Phi Beta Kappa (1968); Harvard Law School, J.D. cum laude (1971). **Personal:** Married to Barbara Burke Orr Chema. Two children: Christine M. Beall and Stephen T. Chema.

Frank J. Chiara Jr.
Sole Practitioner
Law Offices of Frank J. Chiara, Jr.
637 Massachusetts Avenue
Arlington, MA 02174
(617) 646–5050
Fax: (617) 646–5050

8111

Business Information: The Law Offices of Frank J. Chiara, Jr. is a full–service, private practice law firm. Establishing his sole practice firm in 1968, Mr. Chiara concentrates in the areas of probate, real estate and taxation law. Mr. Chiara has a masters of law degree in taxation. **Career Steps:** Sole Practitioner, Law Offices of Frank J. Chiara, Jr. **Personal:** Mr. Chiara enjoys working on the computer with his grandchildren, golf, and snow skiing.

Mr. Mark James Christman
Partner
Robert N. Hackett & Associates
1105 Boyce Road, Boyce House
Pittsburgh, PA 15241–3908
(412) 941–3331
Fax: (412) 941–6785

8111

Business Information: Robert N. Hackett & Associates is a full–service, general practice law firm. Established in 1989, the Firm currently employs five legal, administration and support staff. Admitted to practice in Pennsylvania and West Virginia state courts, Mr. Christman joined the firm as an associate upon the conferral of his law degree in 1986, attaining partnership in 1990. He concentrates his practice in landuse litigation for principalities and zone planning. **Career Steps:** Robert N. Hackett & Associates: Partner (1990–Present), Associate (1986–1989); Law Clerk, Disciplinary Board of the Supreme Court of Pennsylvania (1985–1986). **Associations & Accomplishments:** Allegheny County, Pennsylvania, West Virginia and American Bar Associations; Cloverleaf Area YMCA Board of Management; Rotary Club; YMCA "Indian Princesses" – a father/daughter program providing monthly meetings and three camping trips a year; Elder, Whitehall Presbyterian Church; He has presented a brief to the Supreme Court. **Education:** Dickinson School of Law, J.D. (1986). **Personal:** Married to Renee M. Christman in 1985. Three children: Rachel Lynn, Leah Elizabeth, and Zachary Paul Christman. Mr. Christman enjoys his children and reading.

Mrs. Milena C. Christopher
President and Managing Attorney
Law Offices of Milena C. Christopher
500 Southeast 6th Street, Suite 100
Ft. Lauderdale, FL 33301
(305) 462–5297
Fax: (305) 764–0077

8111

Business Information: The Law Offices of Milena Christopher is a full–service, general practice law firm with emphasis on family law, criminal law, wills, trusts and guardianship, and family mediation. The Firm currently consists of seven attorneys, and employs 12 legal and administrative support staff. Admitted to practice in Florida state courts in 1987, Mrs. Christopher established the firm in 1993. Her practice concentrates in family law, criminal law and pro bono work. **Career Steps:** President and Managing Attorney (1993–Present); Assistant State Attorney, Broward County State Attorney's Office (1988–1993). **Associations & Accomplishments:** Florida Bar Association; American Bar Association; Broward County Bar Association; H.A.N.D.Y. (Helping Abused Needy & Dependent Youth); Broward International Women's Club; Published numerous articles, primarily in child support issues. **Education:** Nova University Law Center, J.D. (1987); University of West Florida, M.S. in Psychology; Furman University, B.S. in Psychology. **Personal:** Married to Kenneth W. Christopher in 1983. Two children: Christina and Jacquelyn. Mrs. Christopher enjoys travel, photography, and writing.

Jimmy Torres Cintron
Sole Practitioner
Law Office of Jimmy Torres
34 S. Calle Pasarell
Yauco, Puerto Rico 00698–4961
(809) 856–7129
Fax: Please mail or call

8111

Business Information: The Law Office of Jimmy Torres is a full–service, general practice law firm, concentrating on civil cases. Establishing his sole practice firm upon conferral of his law degree in 1980, Mr. Torres–Cintron provides legal representation in civil cases for private individuals throughout Puerto Rico. A Notary Public, he also provides public and legal document notarization for individuals and law firms. **Career Steps:** Sole Practitioner, Law Office of Jimmy Torres (1980–Present). **Associations & Accomplishments:** Puerto Rico Bar Association. **Education:** Catholic Universitu, J.D. (1979), Bachelor in Business Administration. **Personal:** Married to Nydia Rodriguez in 1987. Four children: Mariel, Jaime G., Billy, and Maria V. Torres. Mr. Cintron enjoys travel in the Caribbean, and playing Dominoes.

Diane Elizabeth Cleaveland
Attorney at Law
Jonap & Assoc.
330 Woodchuck Court
Roswell, GA 30076–3633
(404) 329–2000
Fax: (404) 633–3300

8111

Business Information: Jonap & Associates, P.C. is a general practice law firm. Joining the Firm upon the conferral of her law degree in 1990, Diane Cleaveland is now the Senior Associate. Admitted to all Georgia courts, she focuses her practice in the areas of workers' compensation, personal injury, mass tort and medical malpractice law. **Career Steps:** Attorney, Jonap & Associates, P.C. (1990–Present). **Associations & Accomplishments:** Phi Alpha Delta; Georgia Bar Association; American Bar Association; Atlanta Bar Association; Georgia Trial Lawyers Association; American Trial Lawyers Association. **Education:** Georgia State University, J.D. (1989); Florida State University, B.S. in Criminology (1982). **Personal:** Ms. Cleaveland enjoys international travel.

Thomas J. Code
Attorney
Reichard & Escalera
Urb Bucare, 2057 Topacio Street
Guaynabo, Puerto Rico 00969
(809) 758–8888 EXT: 308
Fax: Please mail or call

8111

Business Information: Reichard & Escalera is a general practice law firm. A practicing attorney in Puerto Rico state and federal courts since 1992, Mr. Code joined the Firm in 1995. He concentrates his practice in all areas of litigation. **Career Steps:** Attorney, Reichard & Escalera (1995–Present); Associate Attorney, Rivera, Tulla & Ferrer (1993–1995). **Associations & Accomplishments:** Federal Bar Association; American Bar Association; Phi Alpha Delta; Puerto Rico Bar Association. **Education:** Univeristy of Puerto Rico, J.D. (1992); Tulane University, B.S.M. (1989). **Personal:** Married to Mariee in 1995. Mr. Code enjoys travel, fishing and just relaxing at home.

Avram N. Cohen, Esq.
President
Law Offices of Avram N. Cohen
311 Angell Street
Providence, RI 02906
(401) 521–1525
Fax: (401) 621–8885

8111

Business Information: Law Offices of Avram N. Cohen is a full–service, general practice law firm primarily concentrating on commercial and business litigation, bankruptcy, and criminal defense work. The firm represents closely held and large public companies and civil matters. Mr. Cohen is responsble for all aspects of operations for the firm. He practices in both state and federal courts as well as handling criminal and business litigations. **Career Steps:** President, Law Offices of Avram N. Cohen (1972–Present); General Counsel, Rhode Island Division of Taxation (1969–1972); Law Clerk to the Chief Justice, Rhode Island Supreme Court (1964–1966). **Associations & Accomplishments:** Rhode Island Bar Association; American Bar Association; Commercial Law League of America; Chairman, Unauthorized Practice of Law

Committee – Rhode Island Supreme Court; Licensed Racing Official, U.S. Ski Association. **Education:** Boston University Law School, J.D. (1963); Babson College, B.S. Degree in Business Administration (1954). **Personal:** Married to Maxine E. in 1970. One child: Brenna E. Cohen. Mr. Cohen enjoys skiing.

Charles C. Cohen, Esq.

Director
Cohen & Grigsby
625 Liberty Avenue
Pittsburgh, PA 15222–3115
(412) 394–4900
Fax: (412) 391–3382
EMAIL:ccohen@cohenlaw.com

8111

Business Information: Cohen & Grigsby is a full–service, general practice law firm. Established in 1981, the Firm currently employs 124 attorneys, legal and administrative support staff. A practicing attorney for 30 years in Pennsylvania state courts, Mr. Cohen co–founded the Firm in 1981. Currently serving as Director, his private practice concentrates in corporate and securities law — practicing exclusively in this area for the past 25 years. Concurrent with his private law practice, he serves as an Adjunct Professor of Securities Regulation at the University of Pittsburgh School of Law. **Career Steps:** Director, Cohen & Grigsby (1981–Present); Reed Smith Shaw & McClay: Partner (1975–1981), Associate (1965–1974). **Associations & Accomplishments:** American Law Institute; Director, Institute for Transfusion Medicine; Director, Riverview Center for Jewish Seniors; Director, The Pressley Ridge Schools Foundation; Director, Jewish Healthcare Foundation; Director, Arbitrator for American Arbitration Association; Director, New York Stock Exchange. **Education:** University of Michigan School of Law, J.D. with Distinction (1965); Dartmouth College, A.B. with Distinction (1962). **Personal:** Three children: Andrew, Jared, and Sari. Mr. Cohen enjoys golf, squash, and Talmudic study.

Ms. Terri E. Cohn, J.D.

Principal
Terri E. Cohn, A Professional Corporation
1801 Century Park East, 23rd Floor
Los Angeles, CA 90067
(310) 553–8333
Fax: (310) 553–8337

8111

Business Information: Terri E. Cohn, A Professional Corporation is a full service, general practice law firm with emphasis in corporate and business law, business litigation, international and domestic transactions and telecommunications. Founding the Firm, Ms. Cohn concentrates her practice in telecommunications, business law and international and domestic transactional law. Her primary areas of practice include assisting clients in the formation, upkeep, governance and daily legal concerns of corporations and other businesses, advising, negotiating and carrying out the legal aspects of business transactions including: mergers, acquisitions, divestitures, joint ventures, strategic partnerships and other business alliances, both domestic and international. She has assisted clients in participating in multinational ventures including joint ventures, financing arrangements and general business exploits. Ms. Cohn has represented individuals and businesses across the country and around the world. **Career Steps:** Principal, Terri E. Cohn, A Professional Corporation. **Associations & Accomplishments:** Proudian Interdisciplinary Honors Society; State Bar of California: Member, Resolutions Committee Conference of Delegates; American Bar Association; Beverly Hills Bar Association: Member, Board of Governors; Chairman, Resolutions Committee, (Distinguished Service Award); Chairman, Business Law Section, (Executive Director Award); Chairman, Business Law School Committee; Chairman, Bylaws Committee; Co–Chairman, Judge ProTempore Committee; Los Angeles County Bar Association: Member, Business and Corporate Law Section; Member, Subcommittee on Federal Regulation of Securities, and Director, Barristers; Languages: French, German and Russian; Speaker in corporate structure, authority, maintenance and governance; articles published. Education: McGeorge School of the Law, J.D. (1986); University of Redlands, Bachelor in Political Philosophy (1983). **Personal:** Ms. Cohn enjoys skiing, theatre, golf, tennis, travel and literature.

Anthony J. Colleluori

Partner and Trial Lawyer
Kirk, Medina, Miello and Colleluori, L.L.P.
43 Conklin Street
Farmingdale, NY 11735
(516) 249–6020
Fax: (516) 249–3237

8111

Business Information: Kirk, Medina, Miello and Colleluor, L.L.P. is a full–service, general practice law firm. Established in 1995, the Firm currently employs 12 people. Admitted to practice in New York state and federal courts since 1994, Mr. Colleluori joined the Firm as Partner and Trial Lawyer in 1995. He concentrates his practice in the areas of personal injury, auto accidents and litigations. **Career Steps:** Partner and Trial Lawyer, Kirk, Medina, Miello and Colleluori, L.L.P. (1995–Present); Partner, Breen, Medino, Mielo and Kirk (1993–1995); Associate, Liotti & Skelos (1992–1993). **Associations & Accomplishments:** President, Nassau County Criminal Court Bar Association; New York State Bar; New York State Association of Criminal Defense Lawyer; National Association of Criminal Defense Lawyers; National Nassau County Republican Committee; Syossett New York PTA. **Education:** Hofstra University School of Law, J.D. (1984); Tufts University, B.A. **Personal:** Mr. Colleluori enjoys chess, music, and writing.

Mr. Bart J. Colli

Partner
McCarter & English
Four Gateway Center, 100 Mulberry Street
Newark, NJ 07102
(201) 622–4444
Fax: (201) 624–7070

8111

Business Information: McCarter & English, celebrating its 150th Anniversary, is New Jersey's oldest and largest corporate banking and securities law firm providing a full range of services to include, mergers, acquisitions, public offerings, reporting and more. Mr. Colli is a Partner in the Corporate and Securities Department. His experience is in private and public offerings, SEC filings, reorganizations, recapitalization, mergers and acquisitions, financing, banking and defense of securities class actions and derivative actions. In addition to his duties with McCarter & English he is also an Adjunct Professor with Seton Hall Law School teaching 'Corporate Litigation, Mergers and Acquisitions'. Mr. Colli is a frequent lecturer on corporate law issues and has served as an expert witness in litigation on securities matters. McCarter & English, established in 1854, employs over 230 legal assistants, administrative, clerical staff and attorneys. **Career Steps:** Partner, McCarter & English (1985–Present); Partner, Hughes & Luce (1976–1985); Associate, White & Case (1971–1975). **Associations & Accomplishments:** New Jersey Bar Association: Director, Corporate and Business Law Section, Member, Securities Law Committee, Chairman, Business Organizations Committee of the Corporate and Business Law Section; American Bar Association: Member, Section of Corporation, Banking and Business Law, Federal Regulation of Securities Committee; Member, International Bar Association; Leukemia Society of America, Inc., Northern New Jersey Chapter – Board Member; American Cancer Society, Morris County Unit – Board Member; Member of Board of Trustees, Tri– County Scholarship Fund; Council Member, Lincoln Center Business Council of the Consolidated Corporate Fund; Listed in Who's Who in American Law, The Best Lawyers in America; Author of numerous books and articles in media and law journals some of which include: '10 Points of Light on Limited Liability Companies' published in the New Jersey Law Journal (Nov. 1993), 'Fiduciaries Duties of Directors of Nonprofit Organizations' published in The Corporate Governance Advisory (Jan./Feb. 1995), 'Lending Against Securities Under Proposed UCC Revisions' published in New Jersey Lawyer (April 1995), and 'New Wrinkles in Capital Formation: Traps for the Unwary' published in the Supplement to the New Jersey Law Journal (Nov. 1995). **Education:** Harvard Law School, J.D. (1971) Cum laude, Board of Student Advisors; Fordham College, B.A. (1968) Summa cum laude, Phi Beta Kappa; Fordham Preparatory School, Advanced Program (1965), graduated with honors, 30 advanced placement credits; Admitted to practice in New Jersey, New York and Texas. **Personal:** Married for 23 years to Mary Ellen Colli. One child: Michael.

James P. Collins Jr., Esq.

Partner
Cotkin & Collins
P.O. Box 22005
Santa Ana, CA 92702–2005
(714) 835–2330
Fax: (214) 835–2209

8111

Business Information: Cotkin & Collins is a full–service, general practice law firm. With locations in Santa Ana and Los Angeles, California, the Firm currently consists of 22 lawyers and 50 legal and administrative support staff. Co–founding the Firm in 1978, Mr. Collins administers all litigation areas from the Santa Ana office. A practicing attorney since 1970, he concentrates his practice in the areas of civil litigation, contractual disputes, professional liability, hospital and insurance coverage representation. **Career Steps:** Partner, Cotkin & Collins (1978–Present). **Associations & Accomplishments:** President Elect, Southern California Defense Counsel; Past President, Orange County Federal Bar Association. **Education:** Harvard Law School, J.D. (1970); Johns Hopkins University, Masters in International Studies (1967); Occidental College, B.A., magna cum laude, Phi Beta Kappa (1965). **Personal:** Married to Patricia Ann in 1977. One child: Elizabeth Cooper; and four stepchildren: Mitchell, Matthew, Michael, and Kimberly. Mr. Collins enjoys tennis, golf, fly fishing, and gardening.

Mr. Richard T. Colman

Senior Partner
Howrey & Simon
1299 Pennsylvania Avenue, N.W.
Washington, DC 20004
(202) 783–0800
Fax: (202) 383–6610

8111

Business Information: Howrey & Simon is a law firm practicing in the areas of white collar criminal law, intellectual property, insurance coverage, government contracts, antitrust, commercial, environmental and international trade law. The Firm also has offices in Los Angeles and Palo Alto, California. As Senior Partner, Mr. Colman handles counseling, civil litigation and appellate work. He practices in both state and federal courts, and also deals with the Department of Justice and the Federal Trade Commission. Established in 1956, Howrey & Simon employs 806 people. **Career Steps:** Associate ... Senior Partner, Howrey & Simon (1966–Present); Trial Attorney, United States Department of Justice (1962–1966); Lieutenant, United States Marine Corps Reserve (1957–1959). **Associations & Accomplishments:** Trustee, Indian Mountain School, Lakeville, CT (1992–Present); Regional Delegate, Boston College Law School Alumni Association (1992–Present); Massachusetts and District of Columbia Bar. **Education:** Boston College Law School, L.L.B. cum laude (1962); University of Notre Dame, A.B. magna cum laude (1957). **Personal:** Married to Marilyn in 1962. Four children: Elizabeth, Catherine, Richard Jr. and Patrick.

David M. Cook

Principal
Manley, Burke, Lipton & Cook
225 West Court Street
Cincinnati, OH 45202
(513) 721–5525
Fax: (513) 721–4268

8111

Business Information: Manley, Burke, Lipton & Cook is a 16 attorney law firm which focuses on several specialized areas of the law. A practicing attorney in Ohio state courts since 1978, Mr. Cook joined the Firm in 1994 as Principal. His practice concentrates on labor and employee benefits law, as well as representing the Firm's clientele in court cases. **Career Steps:** Principal, Manley, Burke, Lipton & Cook (1994–Present); Principal, Kircher, Robinson, Cook, Newman & Welch (1991–1994); Kircher & Phalen: Partner (1984–1991), Associate (1979–1993). **Associations & Accomplishments:** American Bar Association: Labor & Employment Law Section, Union Co–Chair – Employee Benefits Committee; Board of Trustees, Minorities in Math, Science & Engineering – Cincinnati; Board of Trustees, Hamilton County Democratic Forum. **Education:** University of Cincinnati College of Law, J.D. (1978); Indiana University, A.B. in Political Science (1975). **Personal:** Married to Ann Maris Bernard Cook in 1978. Two children: Elizabeth Steele and Forrest Dean Cook.

Timothy P. Coon

Partner
Bleakley, Platt & Schmidt
1 North Lexington Avenue
White Plains, NY 10601–1712
(914) 949–2700
Fax: (914) 683–6956

8111

Business Information: Bleakley, Platt & Schmidt is a full–service, general practice law firm consisting of 51 lawyers in two offices (New York and Connecticut). Areas of concentration include trusts, wills, estates, banking, real estate, tax CRA, labor, and commercial litigation nationwide. A practicing attorney in New York state courts since 1980, Mr. Coon joined the Firm and was named a partner in January, 1993. His practice concentrates on commercial litigation, representing Fortune 500 companies and significant local businesses. Mr. Coon has sucessfully represented municipalities in civil rights cases. His experience encompasses cases involving major life insurance companies, civil fraud, bank issues, breech of contract, and arbitration. He also serves as the Co–Chairman in the Litigation Department, overseeing 14 other lawyers. **Career Steps:** Partner, Bleakley, Platt & Schmidt (1989–Present); Associate, Mead, Dore & Voute (1986–1989); Associate, Clark, Gagliardi & Miller (1984–1986); Associate, Mead, Dore & Voute (1981–1984). **Associations & Accomplishments:** Vice Chairman, Tarrytowns YMCA; Board Member, John Jay Legal Services Corporation; American Bar Association; New York State Bar Association. **Education:** Pace University School of Law, J.D. (1980); Manhattan College, B.A. (1974). **Personal:** Married to Phyllis M. in 1976. Two children: Taylor and Shelby. Mr. Coon enjoys golf and other sports.

Gary A. Cooper

Partner
Fleissner, Cooper, Marcus & Quinn
800 Vine Street
Chattanooga, TN 37403–2317
(423) 756–3595
Fax: (423) 266–5455

8111

Business Information: Fleissner, Cooper, Marcus & Quinn is a full–service, general practice law firm, with emphasis on civil litigation. A practicing attorney in Tennessee state courts since 1972, Mr. Cooper joined the Firm as Partner in 1981. Serving as a civil trial attorney, his practice concentrates on civil litigation, personal injury, professional negligence, and Worker's Compensation issues. **Career Steps:** Partner, Fleissner, Cooper, Marcus & Quinn (1981–Present); Partner, Anderson, Cleary & Cooper (1974–1980); Associate Attorney, Luther, Anderson & Roth (1972–1974). **Associations & Accomplishments:** American Bar Association; Tennessee Bar Association; Chattanooga Bar Association; The Florida Bar; Tennessee Defense Lawyers Association. **Education:** University of Tennessee College of Law, J.D. (1972); University of Tennessee, B.S. in Journalism (1969). **Personal:** Married to Lynn W. in 1973. Two children: Drew K. and Gavin M. Mr. Cooper enjoys golf and reading.

John F. X. Costello

Partner
McCarthy, Bacon, & Costello
4640 Forbes Blvd., Suite 300
Lanham, MD 20706–4323
(301) 306–1900
Fax: (301) 306–1988

8111

Business Information: McCarthy, Bacon, & Costello is a general practice law firm with thirteen attorneys. A practicing attorney since 1977, Mr. Costello co–founded the Firm in 1987. He now concentrates his practice in personal injury litigation, insurance defense, and commercial law. In addition, he performs pro bono work in criminal, estate, and personal injury litigation. **Career Steps:** Partner, McCarthy, Bacon, & Costello (1987–Present); Partner, O'Malley, Maurs, Farrington, & McCarthy (1978–1987); Law Clerk, Judge John F. McAuffline (1977–1978). **Associations & Accomplishments:** St. John's Men's Club; American Bar Association; Maryland State Bar Association. **Education:** Catholic University, L.L.B/J.D. (1977). **Personal:** Married to Elizabeth in 1975. Four children: Mary, Lauren, John, and Sara. Mr. Costello enjoys gardening.

Francis Aitkens Courtenay Jr.

Attorney
Courtenay, Forstall
1621 Leon C. Simon Drive
New Orleans, LA 70122
(504) 566–1801
Fax: (504) 565–5626
EMAIL: See Below

8111

Business Information: Representing clients worldwide, Courtenay, Forstall is a six partner law firm, concentrating on international law, maritime law, insurance law, and transportation law in New Orleans. Establishing the Firm in 1975, as Senior Partner and Attorney Francis Courtenay focuses his work on the international level, representing maritime and transportation entities in New York, London, France and Germany. He can also be reached through the Internet via: FCOURTENAY@AOL.COM **Career Steps:** Senior Partner and Attorney, Courtenay, Forstall (1975–Present); Partner, Leach, Grossez, Rossi & Payne (1971–1975); Associate, Deutsch, Kerrigan & Stiles (1966–1971). **Associations & Accomplishments:** International President, The Propellor Club of the United States; Maritime Law Association of the United States; Transportation Lawyers Association; Board of Directors, Mount Carmel Academy – New Orleans; Founder, and Member of Management Committee, The Courtenay Society – Devon, England. **Education:** Tulane University, LL.B. (1964); Louisiana State University, B.S. in Business Administration (1961). **Personal:** Married to Janet in 1972. Six children: Kristine, Lauren, Stephanie, Francis, III, William and James. Mr. Courtenay enjoys golf, gardening, hunting and fishing.

J. Craig Cowgill

President
J. Craig Cowgill and Associates, P.C.
2919 Allen Parkway, Suite 202 Liberty Tower
Houston, TX 77019–2122
(713) 523–0995
Fax: (713) 529–5988

8111

Business Information: J. Craig Cowgill and Associates, P.C. is a full–service, general practice law firm, concentrating on bankruptcy cases. A practicing attorney in Texas state courts since 1970, Mr. Cowgill established his sole practice law office in 1975. Serving as President, he oversees all administrative operations for associates and a support staff of six, in addition to his daily law practice. **Career Steps:** President, J. Craig Cowgill and Associates, P.C. (1975–Present) **Associations & Accomplishments:** Director, Houston Livestock Show & Rodeo; Director, Farm & Ranch Club; Director, Green Trails M.U.D. (public office, municipal utility district) **Education:** South Texas College of Law, J.D. (1970); University of Houston, B.B.A. **Personal:** Married to Carol in 1979. Two children: Kate Elaine and John Clay. Mr. Cowgill enjoys hunting during his leisure time.

Donna L. Crary, Esq.

Owner
Law Offices of Donna L. Crary
639 Main Street, Patuxent Place
Laurel, MD 20902
(301) 470–1331
Fax: (301) 490–5567

8111

Business Information: Donna L. Crary operates a full–service law office representing clients in collections, family, criminal, and personal injury areas of law. Handling all facets of litigation, negotiation, and arbitration, she is admitted to practice in Maryland and U.S. federal courts. Ms. Crary has tried cases in federal courts, as well as Maryland state courts. **Career Steps:** Owner, Law Offices of Donna L. Crary (1995–Present); Attorney, Joel A. Skirble & Associates (1993–1995); Law Clerk, Piper & Marbury (1992–1993); Law Clerk, Richard P. Shapiro, P.A. (1991–1993); Law Intern, Harry Fox, Esq. (1991); Law Library Assistant, University of Baltimore (1990–1991); Law Intern, State's Attorney's Office (1990); Law Intern, District Attorney's Office (1989). **Associations & Accomplishments:** Montgomery County Bar Association; Prince George's County Bar Association; Maryland State Bar Association; Admitted to practice in State of Maryland and U.S. District Court – District of Maryland; Maryland Trial Lawyers Association; Published poetry: "Room of Our Own"; Public speaking at state universities; Outstanding Performance Award in Spanish (1989); Merit Award Poetry (1987–1989); Who's Who in American Universities and Colleges (1989); National Collegiate English Award (1988); United States Scholar (1988); National Dean's List (1985–1987); Vice President, Spanish Club – Bowie State University; Student Bar Association and Moot Court at University of Baltimore (1992). **Education:** University of Baltimore School of Law, J.D. (1992); Bowie State University, B.A. in English, magna cum laude (1989). **Personal:** One child: Joel N. Crary. Ms. Crary was raised in Windsor, Vermont and enjoys writing poetry and swimming.

Douglas Crichlow

Administrator
Clarke & Co.
Hincks Prince Alfred Street, Beckwith House
Bridgetown, Barbados
(809) 436–6287
Fax: (809) 436–9812
EMAIL: See Below

8111

Business Information: Clarke & Company is an international, general practice law firm. Serving clients throughout the island of Barbados, the Firm consists of five attorneys and eleven legal and administrative support staff. As Administrator, Douglas Crichlow is responsible for all administrative direction for the Firm, to include full financial accountability and reporting. **Career Steps:** Administrator, Clarke & Company (1991–Present); Accountant, Barbados Steel Works Ltd. (1989–1991); Accountant and Financial Controller, Canada House & Chemical Industries, Ltd. (1983–1988). **Associations & Accomplishments:** Institute of Chartered Accountants of Barbados; Association of Legal Administrators; Fellow, Chartered Association of Certified Accountants (UK). **Education:** Distance Learning, ICSA (1995). **Personal:** Married to Patricia in 1982. Mr. Crichlow enjoys lawn tennis and reading.

Terrence Lee Croft

Attorney
King & Croft
191 Peachtree Street, NE, 20th Floor
Atlanta, GA 30303–1741
(404) 577–8400
Fax: (404) 577–8401
E–mail: see below

8111

Business Information: King & Croft is a law firm with special emphasis on the resolution of disputes through negotiation, mediation, arbitration, and litigation in state and federal courts. Established in 1994, King & Croft currently employs seven legal and administrative support staff. A practicing trial attorney since 1965, Mr. Croft is admitted to both State and Federal Courts, and has been an advocate and neutral in mediation and arbitration for over 25 years. Mr. Croft can be reached through the Internet as follows: tcroftnn@counsel.com **Career Steps:** Senior Partner, King & Croft (1993–Present); Senior Share Holder, Griffin, Cochrane and Marshall (1983–1993); Senior Partner, Kutak, Rock and Huie (1973–1983); Associate Attorney, Hansell and Post (1969–1973); Associate Attorney, Coburn, Croft & Putzel (1965–1969). **Associations & Accomplishments:** President, Atlanta Bar Association (1993–1994); American Bar Association, House of Delegates (1994–Present); State Bar of Georgia; Florida Bar Association; ATLA; GTLA; Lawyers Club of Atlanta; Board of Trustees of Fulton County ADR Program; AAA Arbitrator; Registered Mediator of the State of Georgia. **Education:** University of Michigan Law School, J.D. with distinction (1965); Yale University, A.B. (1962). **Personal:** Married to Merry Croft in 1977. Six children: Michael Regas, Kimberly Sabonis–Chafee, Shannon, Kristin, Bethann and Kate. Mr. Croft enjoys hiking, shooting, reading, and riding motorcycles and ATV's.

Debra Kristine Crumb

Attorney at Law
–Independent–
316 Drive C, Strathmont Park
Elmira, NY 14905
(607) 737–0159
Fax: Please mail or call

8111

Business Information: A practicing attorney since 1990 in North Carolina and Illinois state and federal courts, Debra Crumb is currently on furlough from full–time legal practice. Now residing in New York, prior to transferring to the State, she worked as Attorney at Law in private practice and at O'Callaghan & Associates, P.C. in Chicago, Illinois. Her practice expertise focuses on civil litigation. Upon completion of the New York Bar Exam, Ms. Crumb will resume her private legal practice. **Career Steps:** Attorney at Law, O'Callaghan & Associates, P.C. (1993–1995); Attorney at Law, The Law Office of Debra Kristine Crumb – NC (1990–1992); Registered Nurse, Duke University Medical Center (1981–1992). **Associations & Accomplishments:** American Bar Association; Illinois Bar Association; Chicago Area Nurse Attorneys; North Carolina Bar Association. **Education:** North Carolina Central University, J.D. (1990). **Personal:** Married to Robert L. Quigley, M.D., Ph.D. in 1993. Ms. Crumb enjoys sports.

Josefina Cruz–Melendez
Associate Attorney
Goldman, Antonetti & Cordova
Urb University Garden, 266 Calle Fordham
San Juan, Puerto Rico 00927–4115
(809) 759–4225
Fax: (809) 767–9333

8111

Business Information: Goldman, Antonetti & Cordova is a full–service, general practice law firm, concentrating on labor and employment relations issues. The Firm handles five major areas, the largest being Labor and Employment Relations throughout the U.S. and Puerto Rico. Joining the Firm upon the conferral of his law degree in 1992, Ms. Cruz–Melendez's practice concentrates on labor and employment law, pro bono immigration disability, and alien issues. Career milestones include establishing a program to provide legal services to aliens in the U.S. who have been detained. **Career Steps:** Associate Attorney, Goldman, Antonetti & Cordova (1992–Present); Adjunct Professor, University of Puerto Rico Law School (1994–Present); Staff Attorney, University of Puerto Rico Law School (1990–1992). **Associations & Accomplishments:** Labor Practitioners Association of Puerto Rico; American Bar Association; Inter–American Federation of Attorneys; Puerto Rico Bar Association. **Education:** Harvard Law School, Ll.M. (1994); University of Puerto Rico Law School, J.D.; Trinity University, B.A. **Personal:** Married to Christopher Stuzin in 1994.

Jose A. Cuevas–Segarra, S.J.D.

Attorney
Cuevas–Segarra Law Firm
Apartado Num. 191735
Hato Rey, Puerto Rico 00919–1735
(809) 763–1418
Fax: (809) 756–7905

8111

Business Information: Cuevas–Segarra Law Firm is a full–service, general practice law firm. Establishing the Firm in 1981, Mr. Cuevas–Segarra is the Senior Partner responsible for all administrative operations, support staff and two associates. He also represents major corporate clientele in civil litigation and arbitration. Concurrent to his legal practice, he also serves as a Professor of Law with several major universities throughout Puerto Rico. **Career Steps:** Attorney/Owner, Cuevas–Segarra Law Firm; Lecturer and Professor of Law, Interamerican University, Pontificia Catholic University – Ponce, and Centro de Estudios Juridicos Avanzados; Member, Civil Procedure Committee designated by the Puerto Rico Supreme Court; Member, Continuing Legal Education Committee designated by the Puerto Rico Supreme Court; Member, Alternative Disputes Resolution Committee designated by the Puerto Rico Supreme Court; Professor, U.I.A Law Fundacion – Facultad de Derecho Eugenio Maria de Hostos; President Board of Trustees, Fundacion – Facultad de Derecho Eugenio Maria de Hostos; Law Clerk, Chief Justice of Puerto Rico Supreme Court, Honorable Jose Trias Monge (1979–1981); Law Clerk, Migrant Division Puerto Rico Legal Services (Summer 1978). **Associations & Accomplishments:** Member: Puerto Rico Bar Association; Blanco Lugo Inn; AWARDS and HONORS: Puerto Rico Bar Association: Award for highest average in University of Puerto Rico Law School class of 1978–1979; Award for Book of the Year (1993); Honor mention for book (1995); Award for Continuance and Fruitful Law Books (1995); West Publishing Company Award for Highest Average in Anglo American Studies; University of Puerto Rico Award for highest average in Civil Law; Certificate of Recognition Province V as Graduate of the Year (Florida and Puerto Rico); 1979 of the International Legal Fraternity Phi Delta Legal Phi; Blanco Lugo Inn, Award for Graduate of the Year, University of Puerto Rico (1979); University of Puerto Rico Law Review Merit Certificate (1978); Nu Eta Phi Graduate of the Year (1975); Honor Certificate, Recinto Universitario de Mayaguez (1972–1973); Outstanding Young Men of America, Jaycees (1984); Award from Pontificia Universidad Catolica de Puerto Rico y el Centro de Estudios Juridicos Avanzados for Doctoral Degree (1992); Award from Mayaguez City Hall as Preferred Son of the City (1993); Award from Tony's Restaurant and Hotel for Book of the Year (1993); Who's Who in Hispanic America (1993); Award from Puerto Rico Judge Association (1989); Honor Mention, Interamerican Bar Association for the book Aprobacion e Interpretacion de Las Leyes (1989); Numerous publications in law journals and at various conference proceedings. **Education:** University of Puerto Rico, Recinto de Rio Piedras, J.D., magna cum laude, class valedictorian (1979); Valladolid University – Spain, S.J.D. in Civil Law, apto cum laude (1992); Centro de Estudios Juridicos Avanzados, LL.M. studies; University of Puerto Rico, Recinto Universitario de Mayaguez, B.A. Ciencias Sociales y Cultura (1975); Harvard Law School – Cambridge, MA, National Institute for Trial Advocacy, Teacher Training Trial Advocacy Workshop, Diploma (1986). **Personal:** Mr. Cuevas–Segarra enjoys swimming and farming.

Stephen E. Cupples
Partner
Thompson & Mitchell
One Mercantile Center
St. Louis, MO 63101–1643
(314) 231–7676
Fax: Please mail or call

8111

Business Information: Thompson & Mitchell is a full–service, civil practice law firm consisting of 180 lawyers and concentrating on estate planning. The Firm has offices in the District of Columbia, Missouri (St. Louis and St. Charles), and Illinois (Belleville). A practicing attorney in Missouri state courts since 1979, Mr. Cupples joined the Firm as a Partner in the Estate Planning Department in 1995. His practice concentrates on estate planning, tax planning, gifts, wills, trusts, probate, and compliance, as well as general corporate work. **Career Steps:** Partner, Thompson & Mitchell (1995–Present); Partner, Lashly & Baer, P.C. (1987–1995); Partner, Cupples, Edwards, Cooper, & Singer (1985–1986). **Associations & Accomplishments:** American College of Trust & Estate Counsel (ACTEC); National Association of Elder Law Attorneys (NAELA); American Bar Association; Missouri Bar Association; Bar Association of Metropolitan St. Louis: Former Chairman, Tax Section; Published six articles in law journals. **Education:** University of Missouri – Columbia School of Law, J.D. (1979); University of Missouri – Columbia, A.B. in Mathematics, summa cum laude. **Personal:** Mr. Cupples enjoys model trains, boating, and golf.

Lawrence N. Curtis
President
Curtis & Lambert
201 Rue Iberville, Suite 300
Lafayette, LA 70508
(318) 235–1825
Fax: (318) 237–0241

8111

Business Information: Curtis & Lambert is a full–service, general practice law firm, concentrating on maritime and personal injury cases. Established in 1991, the Firm currently employs fifteen attorneys, legal, and administrative support staff. A practicing attorney in Louisiana state courts since 1977, Mr. Curtis co–founded the Firm in 1991. Serving as President and sharing overall administrative and business responsibilities with his partner, his practice concentrates on maritime personal injury, railroad crossing accidents, products liability, and medical malpractice cases. **Career Steps:** President, Curtis & Lambert (1991–Present); Partner, J. Minos Simon (1983–1991); Associate/Partner, Adler, Barish, et at. (1982). **Associations & Accomplishments:** Insurance, Negligence, and Compensation Section, Louisiana State Bar Association; Federal Bar Association; American Bar Association; The Association of Trial Lawyers of America; Louisiana Trial Lawyers Association: Board of Governors (1989–1991), President's Advisory Council (1987–1989); Lafayette Trial Lawyers Association; Southeastern Admiralty Law Institute. **Education:** Loyola University, J.D. (1977); St. John's University, B.A. (1974). **Personal:** Married to Lynn Sorola in 1987. One child: Lauren.

Michael G. Curtis, Esq.
Sole Practitioner
Law Office of Michael G. Curtis, Esq.
65 Main Street, The Winslow Warren Building
Plymouth, MA 02360
(508) 746–1199
Fax: (508) 746–6763
EMAIL: See Below

8111

Business Information: The Law Office of Michael G. Curtis, Esq. is a full–service, general practice law firm. Admitted to practice law in Massachusetts, Pennsylvania, and New Jersey state courts, Mr. Curtis has been a practicing attorney since 1989. He established his sole practice law firm in 1995, responsible for all aspects of operations, in addition to his daily law practice. His practice emphasizes on corporate litigation. Internet users can also reach him via: AttyCurtis@aol.clm **Career Steps:** Sole Practitioner, Law Office of Michael G. Curtis, Esq. (1995–Present); Attorney, Gillis & Angley (1994–1995); Attorney, Harvey, Pennington, Herting & Renneisen (1993–1994); Attorney, Liberty Mutual Insurance Company (1990–1993). **Associations & Accomplishments:** Lieutenant, U.S. Naval Reserves (Cryptology); Wareham Kiwanis; Plymouth AF&AM; Wareham Planning Board; Southeastern Massachusetts Economic and Planning Council. **Education:** Villanova University, J.D. (1989); Boston University, B.A. (1986). **Personal:** Married to Jeanette in 1978.

Lawrence T. D'Aloise Jr., Esq.

Attorney/Partner
Clark, Gagliardi & Miller, P.C.
The Inns of Court, 99 Court Street
White Plains, NY 10601–4220
(914) 946–8900
Fax: (914) 946–8960

8111

Business Information: Clark, Gagliardi & Miller P.C. is a law firm concentrating on civil litigation, primarily in the personal injury field. Established in 1907, Clark, Gagliardi & Miller P.C. is the oldest law firm in Westchester County. The Firm currently employs 8 attorneys and 25 legal support staff. Admitted to practice in both State and Federal courts, and the U.S. Supreme Court, Mr. D'Aloise concentrates his practice in the areas of civil litigation and appeals. A widely–acknowledged appellate practice expert, he lectures on the subject. **Career Steps:** Attorney, Clark, Gagliardi & Miller P.C. (1969–Present). **Associations & Accomplishments:** American Bar Association; New York Bar Association; Westchester County Bar Association; Member, Appellate Advocacy Committee, American Bar Association; Former Member, Tort Committee, Association of the Bar of the City of New York. **Education:** Villanova Law School, J.D. (1969); Holy Cross College, B.S. (1966). **Personal:** Mr. D'Aloise enjoys collecting and showing cars. He owns 6 classic cars, ranging from a 1920's model T Ford to a 1994 Corvette ZR1.

Joao Afonso da Silveira de Assis

Partner
Xavier, Bernardes, & Braganca, Soc. Adv.
Rio Branco 01–14 Ala A
Rio De Janeiro, Brazil 20090–003
55–21–516–1069
Fax: 55–21–283–0023

8111

Business Information: Xavier, Bernardes, & Braganca, Soc. Adv. is a general practice law firm concentrating in business law. Consisting of seven partners and four attorneys, the Firm is a spin off of Castro, Barros, Sobral, & Xavier, Adv. International in scope, the Firm has four locations, two in Brazil, and two in Portugal. Plans for the future include further international expansion, with plans to open offices in New York, London, and Paris. As Partner, Mr. da Silveira de Assis is responsible for advising clients and preparing cases for trial, as well as for daily administrative duties and Firm operations. **Career Steps:** Partner, Xavier, Bernardes, & Braganca, Soc. Adv. (1995–Present); Partner, Castro, Barros, Sobral, and Xavier, Adv. (1990–1995). **Associations & Accomplishments:** SBL Committee on Banking Law at the International Bar Association; Legislation Committee of The American Chamber of Commerce for Rio De Janeiro; Admitted to the Brazilian Bar Association, Rio De Janeiro Chapter (1982), Santa Catarina Chapter (1983); Telecommunications Information Association; International Fiscal Association. **Education:** Catholic University of Rio De Janeiro, L.L.B. (1981); IBMEC (Brazilian Stock Market Institute), M.B.A. in Finance; Institute for Economic Law Studies, Post Graduate in Economic Law; Professor of Commercial Law, "IAG Master on Business Law", Catholic University of Rio de Janeiro. **Personal:** Married to Cristane Maria Pereira. Two children: Joao Manoel and Joao Vicente Pereira de Assis. Mr. da Silveira de Assis enjoys tennis.

William S. Daniel
President
Daniel & Fleming, L.C.
7711 Carondelet Avenue, Suite 400
St. Louis, MO 63105–3313
(314) 725–5150
Fax: (314) 725–5190

8111

Business Information: Daniel & Fleming, L.C. is a private practice law firm, with emphasis on the representation of insurance companies in alternative dispute resolution. Other areas of practice include appraisal; arbitration; mediation; settlement negotiation; civil litigation of insurance coverage disputes against fraudulent claims for arson fires, explosions, theft, property damage, business interruption, products liability, negligence, casualty, subrogation, personal injury and wrongful death defense in all Illinois and Missouri courts. As President, Mr. Daniel is responsible for all aspects of the Firm's operation. Having attained his law degree in 1975, Mr. Daniel has been senior trial and appellate legal counsel with the Firm for 11 years serving over 40 client companies. **Career Steps:** President, Daniel & Fleming, L.C. (1994–Present); Senior Partner, Daniel Law Offices (1985–1994). **Associa-**

tions & Accomplishments: Vice Chair, Property Insurance Law Committee, American Bar Association; Director, International Association of Arson Investigators Educational Foundation, Inc.; Former Director (1991–1994), International Association of Arson Investigators; Habitat for Humanity. **Education:** Washington University, J.D. (1975); Monmouth College, B.A. cum laude with honors in Government (1972). **Personal:** Married to Mary Ellen Daniel in 1993. Four children: Emily, Joe, Lauren, and Diana. Mr. Daniel enjoys travel, coaching his children's sports, gardening, and landscaping.

Richard S. Daniels Jr.
President and Chief Executive Officer
Daniels Law Offices
18 Tremont Street
Boston, MA 02108–2301
(617) 227-7300
Fax: (617) 227-9643

8111

Business Information: Daniels Law Offices is an international retail collection law firm, consisting of a support staff of 37, including five attorneys. The Firm has been able to obtain approximately $6 million in collections for their clients. Clientele include a variety of businesses and organizations, such as Sears–Roebuck, Harvard University, numerous banks, etc. A practicing attorney in Massachusetts since 1969, Mr. Daniels established Daniels Law Offices in 1971. Serving as its President and Chief Executive Officer, he is responsible for all aspects of operations, in addition to his daily law practice. **Career Steps:** President and Chief Executive Officer, Daniels Law Offices (1971–Present). **Associations & Accomplishments:** Published, Healthcare Financial Management Journal (1987–1988); Religious Educator, St. Theresa's Parish – West Roxbury, MA. **Education:** Boston College Law School, J.D. (1969); Boston College, B.S. in Business Administration (1966); Boston Latin School, Diploma (1962). **Personal:** Married to Martha in 1969. Six children: Richard S. III, Timothy F., Gregory P., Elizabeth A., Christine M., and Meghan T. Mr. Daniels enjoys pistol shooting and fishing.

Jeffrey A. Darling
Partner/Attorney/Shareholder
Darling and Reynolds
171 N. Upper Street
Lexington, KY 40507
(606) 254–3302
Fax: (606) 252–2917

8111

Business Information: Darling and Reynolds is a full service law firm which concentrates on criminal law. Established in 1989, the Firm presently employs 10 people. A practicing criminal attorney since 1983, Mr. Darling became a Partner/Shareholder in the Firm of Darling and Reynolds in 1992. The focus of the Firm is on criminal and personal law, with Mr. Darling concentrating on litigation for clients. **Career Steps:** Partner, Darling and Reynolds (1989–Present); Attorney, Landrum and Shouse (1989–1992); Assistant Commonwealth Attorney, Fayette Commonwealth Attorney's Office (1986–1989); Public Advocate, Department of of Public Advocacy (1983–1986). **Education:** University of Kentucky, J.D. (1983); Morehead State University, B.A. (1979). **Personal:** Married to Allene. Two children: Jason and Jared. Mr. Darling enjoys golf, bicycling, and scuba diving.

Eric Bliss Darnell

Attorney and Counselor at Law
Law Offices of Michael Cohen
310 North Mesa Street, Suite 515
El Paso, TX 79901–1301
(915) 577–0757
Fax: (915) 577–9918

8111

Business Information: Law Offices of Michael Cohen is a full–service, general practice law firm concentrating in complex commercial litigation for the Plaintiff (i.e., consumer, medical malpractice, etc.). Established in 1995, the Firm currently employs five attorneys, legal and administrative support staff. Admitted to practice in Texas and New Mexico state courts since 1992, Mr. Darnell serves as Attorney and Counselor at Law, providing legal representation and management consultations. **Career Steps:** Attorney and Counselor at Law, Law Offices of Michael Cohen (1995–Present); Attorney, Grambling/Darnell (1992–1995). **Associations & Accomplishments:** State Bar of Texas; State Bar of New Mexico; American Bar Association; Texas Trial Lawyers Association; New Mexico Trial Lawyers Association; American Trial Lawyers Association; Board of Directors, El Paso Zoological Society; As a Management Consultant, conducted quality management lectures and author of articles; Boy Scouts of America. **Education:** Southern Methodist University/Tulsa

University, J.D. (1992); University of Dallas, M.B.A.; Springfield College; Dartmouth College, B.S. **Personal:** Married to Ann in 1981. Three children: two sons, Ryan and Eric, and one daughter, Erin.

Yolanda DaSilveira Neves

Associate
Lespier & Munoz Noya
P.O. Box 364428
San Juan, Puerto Rico 00936–4428
(787) 721–6166
Fax: (787) 725–8645

8111

Business Information: Lespier & Munoz Noya is a labor and employment law firm representing employees. The Firm has two locations, one in Puerto Rico and one in New York, with a total of 90 employees. After obtaining his degree in 1990, Mrs. DaSilveira Neves represents the Firm's clients before both federal and local courts, and in arbitration proceedings. **Career Steps:** Associate, Lespier & Munoz Noya (1991–Present). **Associations & Accomplishments:** American Bar Association – Labor and Employment Section; Catholic Daughters of America; Puerto Rico Bar Association. **Education:** University of Puerto Rico: J.D. (1990) Major in Labor Relations. **Personal:** Married to Raul Mendez in 1990. One child: Raul Guillermo Mendez. Mrs. DaSilveira Neves enjoys golf, swimming, and reading.

Angela E. Davis
Sole Practitioner
Office of Angela E. Davis
2206 Hardy Street
Hattiesburg, MS 39403–1553
(601) 545–3127
Fax: (601) 582–7388
EMAIL: See Below

8111

Business Information: Office of Angela E. Davis is a full–service, general practice law firm, specializing in various areas of law. Establishing her private practice upon the conferral of her law degree in 1992, Ms. Davis oversees all administrative operations for associates and support staff, in addition to her daily law practice. Her practice concentrates on DUI, Social Security issues, and general criminal and domestic law. She may be reached through the Internet via: AEDJD@AOL.COM **Career Steps:** Sole Practitioner, Office of Angela E. Davis (1992–Present); Law Clerk, Hickman, Goza & Gore, Attorneys (1990–1992); Paralegal, Al Shiyou, Attorney at Law (1988–1989). **Associations & Accomplishments:** Mississippi Bar Association; American Bar Association; National Organization of Social Security Claimants Representatives; South Central Mississippi Bar Association; Co–Editor, Kiwanis–Newsletter; University of Southern Mississippi Alumni Association; Phi Delta Phi; Participant, Mississippi Pro–Bono Project. **Education:** University of Mississippi, J.D. (1992); University of Southern Mississippi, B.S. in Paralegal Studies and Minor in English. **Personal:** Ms. Davis enjoys target shooting, musical performances (flutist), volleyball, travel, and reading.

Howard J. Davis, Esq.
Partner
Kleinbard, Bell & Brecker
1900 Market Street, Suite 700
Philadelphia, PA 19103
(215) 568–2000
Fax: (215) 568–0140

8111

Business Information: Kleinbard, Bell & Brecker is a full–service, general practice law firm concentrating in commercial law. Two locations: Pennsylvania and New Jersey. As Partner, Mr. Davis is involved in all activities of the Firm; concentrating his practice in the areas of business law. He counsels clients with sales of $5 million to $1 billion annually (mergers and acquisitions and corporate finance matters). **Career Steps:** Partner, Kleinbard, Bell & Brecker (1983–Present); Associate, Schnader, Harrison, Segal & Lewis (1980–1983). **Associations & Accomplishments:** American Bar Association – Business Law Section; Philadelphia Bar Association; Trustee of the Federation of Jewish Agencies of Philadelphia; Pennsylvania Special Olympics. **Education:** University of Chicago, J.D. (1980); Princeton University, B.A. (1977). **Personal:** Married to Barbara in 1980. Three children: Sara, Amanda, and Eliza. Mr. Davis enjoys tennis, golf, sports and philanthropy.

Kirk Stuart Davis
Attorney
Annis, Mitchell, Cockey, Edwards, and Roehn, P.A.
P.O. Box 3433
Tampa, FL 33601
(813) 229–3321
Fax: (813) 223–9067

8111

Business Information: Annis, Mitchell, Cockey, Edwards, and Roehn, P.A. is a full–service, general practice law firm. Established in 1982, the Firm currently employs 115 attorneys, legal and administrative support staff. A Florida Board–Certified Health Law Attorney, Mr. Davis joined the Firm as Attorney in 1994. He concentrates his practice in the areas of health law legal representation to hospitals and health care providers in general health care matters, malpractice, IPA's, HMO's, risk management, termination of life support systems, AIDS, litigation and transactional law in Florida State courts.. **Career Steps:** Attorney, Annis, Mitchell, Cockey, Edwards, and Roehn, P.A. (1994–Present); Partner, Elias & Davis, P.A. (1991–1994); Partner, Greene & Mastry, P.A. (1983–1991). **Associations & Accomplishments:** Saint Anthony's Health Care Foundation Fundraisers; Appointed to the Innovational Board of Health Care Law Committee; Frequent speaker at AIDS Foundation. **Education:** Stetson University, J.D. (1982), B.S. in Biology, magna cum laude (1979). **Personal:** Married to Aileen Davis in 1982. Mr. Davis enjoys golf.

Cristina De Jesus Marquez

Senior Attorney
De Jesus Marquez & Associates
Calle Munoz Rivera #30
Aguas Buenas, Puerto Rico 00703–1394
(787) 732–2769
Fax: (787) 732–0379

8111

Business Information: De Jesus Marquez & Associates is a general practice law firm concentrating on civil and criminal cases, including Bankruptcy and Business law. A practicing attorney in Puerto Rico state and federal courts since obtaining her degree in 1980, Ms. De Jesus Marquez founded the Firm in 1994. As Senior Attorney, she manages the general operations of the Firm as well as her daily client services. **Career Steps:** Senior Attorney, De Jesus Marquez & Associates (1994–Present); Puerto Rico Higher Education Assistance Corp: Director of Legal Department (1989–1994), Acting Executive Director (1992–1993). **Associations & Accomplishments:** Association of Trial Lawyers of America; Association of Female Executives; Association of Bankruptcy Lawyers of Puerto Rico; Federal Bar Association. **Education:** University of Puerto Rico Law School, J.D. (1980); Montclair University, B.A. (1976); Licensed Private Detective in New Jersey and Puerto Rico. **Personal:** Three children: Maribel, Jose Miguel, and Marcelino Perez.. Ms. De Jesus Marquez enjoys being a Licensed private detective in New Jersey and Puerto Rico.

Mr. David P. De Stefano
Attorney
Offices of David P. De Stefano
875 Centerville Road 4C
Warwick, RI 02886–4381
(401) 822–1300
Fax: (401) 821–4188

8111

Business Information: Offices of David P. De Stefano, established in 1988, is a full–service, general practice law firm with offices in Rhode Island and Massachusetts. Future plans include moving towards international banking law. Admitted to practice in Rhode Island and Massachusetts state courts, Mr. De Stefano established his private practice in 1988. He is responsible for all aspects of operations, including providing legal representation, concentrating in business law, litigation, commercial, real estate, transactional litigation (state court), small business consultation, and construction law. Concurrent with his position, he is attending Boston University finishing LL.M. studies in International Banking Law. **Career Steps:** Attorney, Offices of David P. De Stefano (1988–Present). **Associations & Accomplishments:** American Bar Association; Rhode Island Bar Association; Massachusetts Bar Association; American Trial Lawyer Association; Rhode Island Trial Lawyers Association; Aircraft Owner & Pilots Association; Rhode Island Pilots Association; Finance Committee, Town of East Greenwich, Rhode Island; Alumni Golf Tournament, University of Rhode Island. **Education:** Boston University, LL.M. in International Banking Law (In Progress, expected 1997); New England School of Law, J.D. (1981); University of Rhode Island, B.S. in Mechanical Engineering (1970). **Personal:** Married to Diane Angelini in 1986. Mr. De Stefano enjoys flying, golf, and travel.

Michael J. DeBlasi
Systems Administrator
ABC Legal Messengers, Inc.
601 Third Avenue
Seattle, WA 98104–1806
(206) 623–8771
Fax: (206) 340–0452
EMAIL: See below

8111

Business Information: ABC Legal Messengers, Inc. provides legal processing services for attorneys and law firms. Established in 1945, ABC Legal Messengers Inc. currently employs 100 people. As Systems Administrator, Mr. DeBlasi is responsible for all aspects of systems administration, including the LAN and the database. He can be reached through the Internet via: 102634,1602.compuserv **Career Steps:** Systems Administrator, ABC Legal Messengers, Inc. (1993–Present); Test Engineer, Baxter Healthcare (1987–1992). **Associations & Accomplishments:** Seattle Luncheon Club; Microsoft Certified Professional. **Education:** California State University – Hayward, B.S. in Physics (1986); Don Bosco Technical Institute, A.S. in Manufacturing Technology (1979).

Ronald O. Dederick, Esq.
Partner
Day, Berry & Howard
One Canterbury Green, 7th Floor
Stamford, CT 06901
(203) 977–7300
Fax: (203) 977–7301

8111

Business Information: Day, Berry & Howard, the largest law firm in Connecticut, provides all types of law and litigation, serving both domestic and international clients in offices located in Stamford, Hartford, Connecticut, and Boston, MA. Established in 1919, Day, Berry & Howard has 210 lawyers with the Firm, and employs over 500 legal assistant and administrative clerical staff personnel. A Partner with the Firm, Mr. Dederick specializes in international and domestic estate planning, trust administration and fiduciary litigation representation. **Career Steps:** Partner, Day, Berry & Howard (1979–Present); Partner, Durey & Pierson (1969– 1979); Associate, Sullivan and Cromwell (1962–1969). **Associations & Accomplishments:** Former Chairman Estates & Probate Section, Connecticut Bar Association (1988– 1990); Fellow, ACTEC; Former Chairman, Committee on Special Problems of Multi– Jurisdictional Clients, American Bar Association; Director, Guardianship Advocacy Resource Program, Inc.; Former Chairman–Board of Trustees, Greenwich Arts Council; Member, International Academy of Estate & Trust Law; Director and Secretary, Western Connecticut Chapter of Multiple Sclerosis Society. **Education:** University of Virginia School of Law, LL.B. (1962); University of Virginia, B.A (1957). **Personal:** Married since 1959 to Dorothy S. Two children: Kenneth S. Dederick and Cynthia R. Stroili; and one granddaughter, Caitlin Rae Stroili. Dederick enjoys enjoys golf and fishing in his leisure time.

Francis X. Dee
Senior Partner
Carpenter Bennett & Morrissey
Three Gateway Center, 100 Mulberry Street
Newark, NJ 07102
(201) 622–7711
Fax: (201) 622–5314
EMAIL: See below

8111

Business Information: Carpenter Bennett & Morrissey is a general practice law firm. One of Newark, New Jersey's oldest and most respected firms (est. 1898), the Firm consists of 90 attorneys and over 170 legal and administrative support staff. A practicing attorney since 1969, Francis X. Dee has served as Senior Partner of the Firm since 1985. He joined the Firm in 1976, and was elected to partnership in 1978. He heads the Labor & Employment Law Group, in addition to representing major clients in labor and employment law matters. Internet users can reach him via: FXD@CARPBEN.COM. **Career Steps:** Carpenter Bennett & Morrissey (1976–Present – currently Senior Partner); Labor Counsel, Litton Industries, Inc. (1972–1976); Trial Attorney, National Labor Relations Board (1969–1972). **Associations & Accomplishments:** American Bar Association: Labor & Employment Section, Administrative Law & Litigation Section; New Jersey State Bar Association, Labor & Employment Law Sections – Former Chair; New Jersey Supreme Court Committee on Sexual Harassment. **Education:** New York University, LL.M. (1975); Catholic University School of Law, J.D. (1969); Manhattan College, B.A. in Psychology (1966). **Personal:** Married to Jane E. in 1971. Three children: Alicia, Stephen, and Michael. Mr. Dee enjoys sport fishing and golf.

Ms. Edna L. Deeb
Attorney at Law and Certified Mediator
Law Firm of Edna L. Deeb/ELD Mediation Services
20929–47 Venture Blvd., Suite 334
Woodland Hills, CA 91364–2380
(818) 340–0448
Fax: (818) 340–0412
E/M: ELDMEDIATE@aol.com

8111

Business Information: Edna L. Deeb is in private practice law, specializing in transactional work in real estate, corporate and entertainment matters. As Attorney at Law and Certified Mediator, Ms. Deeb oversees all aspects of the Firm. She also is the owner of ELD Mediation Services and volunteers for the Los Angeles County Bar Association serving as a Settlement Officer in Municipal and Superior Court cases. She practices in state courts, however has international clients from the Sudan, Lebanon, and the MIddle East. Ms. Deeb attributes her success to ethics, morals and values; never sacrificing these when dealing with clients. **Career Steps:** Attorney at Law, Law Firm of Edna L. Deeb (1984–Present); Certified Mediator, ELD Mediator Services (1992–Present). **Associations & Accomplishments:** California Copyright Conference; Speaks English and Spanish fluently, has knowledge of French and Arabic; Frequent lecturer at civic and educational institutions concerning mediation, also gives seminars and workshops on same. **Education:** Southwestern University, J.D. (1982); California State University–Northridge, B.A. in Political Science; California Real Estate Brokerage License; Municipal and Superior Court Officer; Certified Mediator.

Lcda. Sonia M. Del Valle–Rivera
Sole Practitioner
Law Offices of Sonia M. Del Valle–Rivera
P.O. Box 1438
Isabela, Puerto Rico 00662–1438
(809) 872–0070
Fax: (809) 872–0070

8111

Business Information: The Law Office of Sonia M. Del Valle– Rivera is a full–service, general practice law firm. Establishing her sole practice law office upon the conferral of her law degree in 1969, Ms. Del Valle–Rivera is responsible for all aspects of operations, in addition to her daily law practice and notary responsibilities. Concurrent to her private law practice, she has owned and operated two dairy farms since 1985, consisting of a total of 1,000 acres. **Career Steps:** Owner, Law Offices of Sonia M. Del Valle–Rivera (1969–Present); Owner, Dairywoman (1985–Present). **Associations & Accomplishments:** Capitan de la Guardia Estatal de PR; Outstanding Young Women of America; Prominent Distinction of the National Register of Prominent Americans; Miembro de la Comision de Investigacion; Procesamiento y Apelacion; Miembro de la Comision para el Mejoramiento de los derechos de la Mujer; Directors of Puerto Rico Farm Credit; AG First Farm Credit Bank; Commisions for Womens Rights; Commissioner of Police Department; Captain, Puerto Rico National Guard; Board of Directors, Association of Milk Producer of Isabela; Delegate, Democratic National Convention Party (1980); Puerto Rico Woman–Civic's Association; "Altrusas" Club of Puerto Rico. **Education:** Catholic University of Puerto Rico – Law School (1959); Escuela de Derecho–Bachillerato en Leyes; College of the Sacred Heart Degree, B.B.L. **Personal:** Married. Three children: Sonia M., Calixto Javier, and Juan Antonio. Ms. Del Valle–Rivera enjoys riding her motorcycle, and traveling around the world.

Steven Michael Delaney, Esq.

• • • ━━━◉━━━ • • •

Partner
Hascall, Jungers, Garvey & Delaney
101 West Mission Avenue
Bellevue, NE 68005–5236
(402) 291–8900
Fax: (402) 291–6023

8111

Business Information: Hascall, Jungers, Garvey & Delaney is a full–service, general practice law firm. Established in 1966, the Firm consists of six associate attorneys and employs four legal and administrative support staff. A practicing attorney since 1988, Mr. Delaney joined the Firm as an associate in 1990, appointed Partner in 1993. As Partner, he heads the Litigation Section, overseeing all associates, as well as representing major clients in defense litigation. **Career Steps:** Partner, Hascall, Jungers, Garvey & Delaney (1993–Present); Associate, Hascall, Jungars & Garvey

(1990–1993); Associate, O'Hanlon Law Offices (1988–1990). **Associations & Accomplishments:** Sarpy County Bar Association: Secretary (1995), Vice President (1996); Nebraska State Bar Association; Association of Trial Lawyers of America; Attorney Coach, Bellevue East High School Mock Trial Team; Bellevue Volunteer Fire Department. **Education:** Creighton University, J.D. (1988); Gonzaga University, B.A. in Political Science (1985). **Personal:** Married to Sheryl in 1990. Two children: Matthew and Julia. Mr. Delaney enjoys sports and spending time with family.

Timothy Q. Delaney
Shareholder and Attorney
Brinks, Hofer, Gilson and Lione
455 N. Cityfront Plaza Drive, 3600 NBC Tower
Chicago, IL 60611
(312) 321–4200
Fax: (312) 321–4299
EMAIL: See Below

8111

Business Information: Established in 1917, Brinks, Hofer, Gilson and Lione is a general practice law firm with 100 partners, concentrating on Intellectual Property Law (e.g., trademarks and patents). Joining the Firm upon the conferral of his law degree in 1988, Mr. Delaney is now a Shareholder, focusing his practice on patent litigation law. Internet users may reach him via: QUINDEL@AOL.COM **Career Steps:** Brinks, Hofer, Gilson and Lione: Shareholder and Attorney (1996–Present), Associate Attorney (1988–1995); Engineer, Portion Packaging (1983–1985). **Associations & Accomplishments:** American Bar Association; American Intellectual Property Association; Intellectual Property Law Association of Chicago; Chairman, Writing Competition, Federal Circuit Bar Association. **Education:** George Washington University, National Law Center, J.D., with honors (1988); University of Illinois – Urbana–Champaign, B.S. in General Engineering. **Personal:** Married to Marjorie Lee in 1981. Three children: Quinn, Mark and Stephen. Mr. Delaney enjoys literature, golf and baseball.

Mr. Renato S. DeLuca

• • • ━━━◉━━━ • • •

Principal
Law Offices of Renato S. DeLuca
445 Middle Holland Road
Holland, PA 18966–2763
(215) 968–9054
Fax: (215) 968–9054

8111

Business Information: Law Offices of Renato S. DeLuca, established in 1994, is an international, full–service, general practice law firm, concentrating in international law. The Practice assists international clientele moving businesses into the U.S. and/or expanding business in the U.S. with financing and investments. Admitted to practice in Pennsylvania and New Jersey state courts, Mr. DeLuca established the Firm in 1976. As Principal, Mr. DeLuca is responsible for all aspects of operations, including providing legal representation to the Firm's clientele, concentrating in international law, litigation, and mediation. **Career Steps:** Principal, Law Offices of Renato S. DeLuca (1994–Present); Litigator, The Home Insurance Company (1990–1994); Litigator and Counselor, Kubert & Associates, P.C. (1982–1990); Litigator, Mattioni, Mattioni, Mattioni, Ltd. (1978–1982). **Associations & Accomplishments:** American Bar Association; Inter–American Bar Association; Pennsylvania Bar Association; New Jersey Bar Association; Philadelphia Bar Association; Pennsylvania Trial Lawyers Association; Justinians; 4th Degree Knights of Columbus; Certified Mediator in U.S. District Court; Author on International Law/Financial Investor. **Education:** Temple University Law School, J.D. (1976); Pennsylvania State University, B.A. in Political Science, B.S. in Secondary Education. **Personal:** Mr. DeLuca enjoys fishing, reading, and writing.

Jill L. DeStefano, Esq.
Attorney
Akman & Associates, P.C.
247 Smokey Wood Drive
Pittsburgh, PA 15218
(412) 281–3588
Fax: (412) 281–2252

8111

Business Information: Akman & Associates, P.C. is a full– service, general practice law firm with branch offices in Washington, D.C., Maryland, Pennsylvania, and Massachusetts. Joining the Firm upon the conferral of her law degree in 1992, Ms. DeStefano's practice includes litigations and domestic law issues in Pennsylvania state courts. She also serves as a fund attorney for Prepaid Legal Benefits with the Food & Commercial Workers' Union Local 25. **Career Steps:** Attorney, Akman & Associates, P.C. (1992–Present). **Associations & Accomplishments:** Allegheny County Bar Association;

Pennsylvania Bar Association. **Education:** University of Pittsburgh School of Law, J.D. (1992); Catholic University – Washington, D.C. **Personal:** Married to John Smelko in 1995. Ms. DeStefano enjoys reading.

Mr. Mathew J. Dew

Partner
Dew & Blaney
437 South Yellowstone Drive, Suite 101
Madison, WI 53719
(608) 278–9600
Fax: (608) 278–9672

8111

Business Information: Dew & Blaney is a general practice law firm emphasizing the collection of student loans. The Firm also provides legal services in the areas of estate planning and real estate law. Established in 1979, Dew & Blaney currently employs three legal support staff. A trial attorney since the conferral of his law degree in 1977, Mr. Dew is admitted to both State and Federal courts. Concurrent to his position with the Firm, Mr. Dew is also a JAG Officer with the Wisconsin National Guard. **Career Steps:** Partner, Dew & Blaney (1979–Present); Trust Officer, American Exchange Bank (1977–1979). **Associations & Accomplishments:** Chair, Long Range Planning Committee, Dane County Bar Association; Wisconsin Bar Association; American Bar Association; Director and Chair of the Investment Committee, Wisconsin National Guard Association. **Education:** University of Wisconsin – Madison, J.D. (1977); Harvard University, B.A. (1971). **Personal:** Married to Karla in 1976. Two children: Michael and Steven. Mr. Dew enjoys soccer, basketball, hockey, computers and military history.

Elizabeth Diaz Calderon, Esq.

Attorney
Verner, Liipfert, Bernhard, McPherson, and Hand
901 15th Street, N.W.
Washington, DC 20005
(202) 371–6143
Fax: Please mail or call

8111

Business Information: Verner, Liipfert, Bernhard, McPherson, and Hand is a full–service, general practice law firm. A practicing attorney since 1993, Ms. Diaz joined the Firm as Associate in 1995. Her practice concentrates on assessing and analyzing various Latin American, Caribbean and other international legal issues, as well as conducting legal research and writing primarily in the legislative area. She also serves as an advocate on behalf of the Firm's clients before federal agencies and the U.S. Congress. **Career Steps:** Attorney, Verner, Liipfert, Bernhard, McPherson, and Hand (1995–Present); Assistant Legal Advisor for the Governor on Federal Affairs, Office of the Governor of Puerto Rico (1993–1995); Bilingual Caseworker, Inquilinos Boricuas en Accion (1985–1988). **Associations & Accomplishments:** United States Court of Appeals for the 1st Circuit; United States District Court for the District of Puerto Rico; Federal Bar Association; Puerto Rico Bar Association; American Bar Association; Vice President of the Young Lawyers Section for the North American Region, InterAmerican Bar Association; Special Assistant to the General Secretary, InterAmerican Bar Association; U.S. Chamber of Commerce Jaycees; Board of Directors, Development Evaluation and Adjustment Facilitites; WIBA Channel 6 CATV, Boston. **Education:** InterAmerican University of Puerto Rico – School of Law, J.D. (1992); Boston University, B.A. in International Relations with honors (1985). **Personal:** Ms. Diaz Calderon enjoys dancing, jogging, bicycling, swimming, hiking, travel, reading and the theater. She is also fluent in English, Spanish and Portuguese.

Virginia Diaz Sanchez

Assistant Director
Institute of Judicial Studies
P.O. Box 22381
San Juan, Puerto Rico 00931–2381
(787) 751–8806
Fax: (787) 763–0380

8111

Business Information: The Institute of Judicial Studies is attached to the Office of Courts Administration. It functions as a service and support unit to expedite judicial proceedings and promote the professional advancement of judges. As Assistant Director, Ms. Diaz Sanchez takes part in the organization and development of such services. **Career Steps:** Assistant Director, Institute of Judicial Studies (1992–Present); Legal Advisor, Supreme Court of Puerto Rico (1990–1992); Legal Advisor, Justice Department (1986–1990); Dean of Student Affairs, Interamerican University (1985–1986). **Associations & Accomplishments:** Phi Delta Phi; Asociacion Seminaristas Pentecostales; American Bar Association; Colegio de Abogados de Puerto Rico; Abogados y Abogadas Evangelicos de Puerto Rico. **Education:** University of Puerto Rico: J.D. (1984), M.A. (1978), D.Ed. (in progress); Evangelical Seminary of Puerto Rico, M.Div. (in progress). **Personal:** Married to Melvin L. Torres in 1970. One child: Melvin Raul. Ms. Diaz Sanchez enjoys travel, walking, and watching Chicago Bulls games.

Nicholas Anthony DiCerbo, Esq.

Senior Partner
DiCerbo & Palumbo Law Firm
410 Community Bank Building, 201 North Union Street
Olean, NY 14760–2738
(716) 373–2165
Fax: (716) 373–5180

8111

Business Information: DiCerbo & Palumbo Law Firm is a full–service, general practice law firm, concentrating in banking and financial law. One of the Firm's larger clients, Community Bank, N.A. has 52 branches. The Firm currently employs six attorneys, legal and administrative support staff. Admitted to practice in New York and Nebraska state courts, Mr. DiCerbo established the Firm with his partner in 1972. He currently serves as Senior Partner and is responsible for providing all aspects of legal representation to the Firm's clientele. His practice concentrates on banking matters, title searches, mergers, acquisitions. Concurrent with his private legal practice, he serves as Associate Attorney for Cattaraugus County and serves on the Board of Directors of Community Bank, N.A. Additionally, he and his sons own a several hundred–acre cattle farm, raising thoroughbred Semmental cattle. **Career Steps:** Senior Partner, DiCerbo & Palumbo Law Firm (1972–Present); Associate Attorney, Cattaraugus County (1974–Present); Board of Directors, Community Bank, N.A. (1984–Present). **Associations & Accomplishments:** American Bar Association; New York Bar Association; Nebraska Bar Association; American Banking Association; American Association of Bank Directors; National Cattlemen's Association; Vice President, New York Semmental Association; Archbishop Walsh School Board; St. Mary's Parish–Olean; Olean Lions Club; Olean Chamber of Commerce; Board of Directors of Community Bank; Chairman of Personnel Committee, National Association. **Education:** Creighton University, J.D. (1972); St. Leo College, B.A. **Personal:** Married to Ann E. DiCerbo in 1969. Four children: Nick Jr., Angela, Anthony, and Christopher. Mr. DiCerbo enjoys hunting, fishing, and horseback riding.

Bradford Clay Dodds

Associate Attorney
Law Offices of Funderburk, Day and Lane
P.O. Box 388
Columbus, GA 31902–0388
(706) 324–2531
Fax: (706) 324–2737
EMAIL:brdodds@aol.com

8111

Business Information: Law Offices of Funderburk, Day and Lane is a full–service, general practice law firm. The Firm has two offices located in Alabama and Georgia and currently employs 15 attorneys, legal and administrative support staff. Admitted to practice in Georgia State courts since 1988, Mr. Dodds joined the Firm in 1995. His area of practice concentration is in plaintiff civil litigation, as well as business law and litigation matters. **Career Steps:** Associate Attorney, Law Offices of Funderburk, Day and Lane (1995–Present); Associate Attorney, Denney, Pease, Allison and Kirk (1988–1995). **Associations & Accomplishments:** Columbus Bar Association, Inc.; Kiwanis Club of Columbus, Inc. **Education:** University of Georgia, J.D. (1988), B.B.A. (1985). **Personal:** Mr. Dodds enjoys music, computers, and University of Georgia athletics.

Ian Donaldson

Attorney/Partner
Oliver & Company
777 Hornby Street
Vancouver, British Co V6Z 2L1
(604) 681–5232
Fax: (604) 681–1331

8111

Business Information: Oliver & Company is a general practice law firm concentrating on criminal defense. A practicing attorney in Canadian courts since obtaining his degree in 1983, Mr. Donaldson joined the Firm in 1984. In addition to his daily client load, he handles administrative operations and support staff. **Career Steps:** Attorney/Partner, Oliver & Company (1984–Present). **Associations & Accomplishments:** Chairman, Criminal Justice Section, Canadian Bar Association; Former Chair, Trial Lawyers Association of British Columbia; National Association of Criminal Defense Lawyers; American Trial Lawyers Association. **Education:** Queens University, LL.B. (1983); University of British Columbia, B.A. with honors in Economics (1979). **Personal:** Mr. Donaldson enjoys sailing.

Mariemma Dorna–Llompart

Attorney
Totti, Rodriguez, Diaz & Fuentes
Garden Valley Club Box 37
San Juan, Puerto Rico 00926
(809) 753–7910
Fax: (809) 764–7980

8111

Business Information: Totti, Rodriguez, Diaz & Fuentes is a full–service, general practice law firm. A practicing attorney in Puerto Rico courts since 1994, Mrs. Dorna–Llompart joined the Firm in 1995. Serving as Attorney in the Labor Law Department, her practice concentrates on the legal representation of clientele in the areas of labor law cases, arbitration, sexual harassment, and libel. **Career Steps:** Attorney, Totti, Rodriguez, Diaz & Fuentes (1995–Present); Attorney, Montavez & Alicia Law Offices (1994–1995); Special Assistant to Former Puerto Rico Resident Commissioner – Washington. **Associations & Accomplishments:** American Bar Association; National Deans List (1985–1994); Puerto Rico Bar Association; Felisa Riocor Medal (1991) by University of Puerto Rico. **Education:** Interamerican University, J.D. (1994); University of Puerto Rico, M.P.A. (1991). **Personal:** Married to Alex Reyes–Gilestra. Mrs. Dorna–Llompart enjoys foreign movies.

Jose Dorta Lucca

Sole Practitioner
Law Office of Jose Dorta Lucca
P.O. Box 41202
San Juan, Puerto Rico 00940
(809) 754–7200
Fax: (809) 754–7200

8111

Business Information: Law Office of Jose Dorta Lucca is a full–service, general practice law firm. Establishing the sole practice law office upon the conferral of his law degree in 1970, Mr. Dorta Lucca is responsible for all aspects of operations, in addition to his daily law practice, concentrating in the areas of civil and criminal law. **Career Steps:** Sole Practitioner, Law Office of Jose Dorta Lucca (1970–Present). **Education:** University Catolica de Puerto Rico, J.D. (1970); University Inter-Americana de Puerto Rico, B.A. in Arts (1966). **Personal:** Married to Carmen L. Martinez in 1971. Two children: Emilio J. Dorta Martinez and Jose Dorta Martinez. Mr. Dorta Lucca enjoys fishing.

Mr. Frank Douglass

Partner
Scott, Douglas, Luton & McConnico, L.L.P.
901 Main Street, Suite 2800
Dallas, TX 75202–3776
(214) 651–5300
Fax: (214) 651–5399

8111

Business Information: Scott, Douglas, Luton & McConnico, L.L.P. is a specialty law firm, concentrating on civil litigation for oil, gas and mineral concerns. Serving international clientele, the firm has locations in Dallas and Austin, Texas. Founding Partner of the Firm, Frank Douglas oversees all administrative functions, as well as practicing law. He is a specialist in the area of commercial energy law, as well as business property and estate planning. He serves as an arbitrator and mediator in energy–related litigation representing major oil and gas companies. A successful entrepreneur, he is the Founding Director and Board Chairman for seven corporations, including four (4) oil and gas concerns, two (2) banks and one (1) real estate development firm. Established in 1976, Scott, Douglas, Luton & McConnico, L.L.P. employs 165 attorneys, legal aide professional and administratvie support staff people. **Career Steps:** Founding Partner, Scott, Douglas, Luton & McConnico, L.L.P. (1976–Present); Partner, McGinnis, Lockridge & Kilgore (1957–1976); Enlisted, U.S. Air Force. **Associations & Accomplishments:** American Bar Association; Texas State Bar Association; American Aribtration Association; Advisory Board Member, Southwest Legal Foundation; Trustee, Southwestern University; Fellow, American College of Trial Lawyers; Numerous law review and journal publications. **Education:** University of Texas Law School, LL.B. (1958); Southwestern University, Georgetown, Texas, B.A. in Business Administration (1953). **Personal:** Married to Betty in 1983. Six children: Russel, Tom, Andrew, Cathy Douglass, Rick and Mike McKinney.

Charles M. Driggs, Esq.
Partner
Driggs & Vynalek
7864 Mayfield Road
Chesterland, OH 44026
(216) 729–4446
Fax: (216) 729–4447

8111

Business Information: Driggs & Vynalek is a full–service, general practice law firm with a broad civil practice, including corporate work, zoning matters, general litigation, estate planning and intellectual property & patent law. Established in 1995, the Firm currently employs five professionals, including two partners and two associates. Retired from a large firm in 1991, Mr. Driggs went into private practice as Sole Practitioner for four years. His case load expanded from a two–day to a five–day operation, therefore in order for Mr. Driggs to spend more time with his extensive organization activities, he added a business partner to his practice. During the Second World War, while attending his junior year in college, he became an officer on a Naval ship in the Pacific Fleet. His Commanding Officer was a lawyer and under his influence, changed his major from Electronic Engineering to Industrial Administration, entering law school after the war's end. **Career Steps:** Partner, Driggs & Vynalek (1995–Present); Attorney, Charles M. Driggs & Assoc. (1991–1995); Attorney, General Partner & Administrator of Estates & Trust Division, Squire, Sanders & Dempsey (1950–1991). **Associations & Accomplishments:** Estate Planning, Trust & Probate Law Sections of American Bar Association; Ohio State Bar Association & Cleveland Bar Association; Geauga Bar Association; The American College of Trust & Estate Counsel; Member of Court of Nisi Prius (a 90 year old organization made up of 100 lawyers in the Cleveland area – they hold mock court sessions and do skits for clients, all in fun during the first two weeks of April); Past Trustee of Cleveland Law Library; Past Director of The City Club of Cleveland, Ohio; Biography can be found in Who's Who in America, Who's Who in American Law, and Who's Who Best Lawyers in America; Lecturer on Lecture Circuit at Bar Association functions. **Education:** Yale University Law School, J.D. (1950); Yale University, B.S. in Industrial Administration, Graduated with honors (1947). **Personal:** Married to Ann Eileen Driggs, a paralegal R.N. in 1991. Five children: Ruth Ellen Driggs, Rachel K. Love, Carrie E. Driggs, Karl H. Driggs and C. Matthew Driggs. Mr. Driggs enjoys boating, classic cars, skiing and a patron of performing arts.

Patrick J. Ducharme
Counsel to Firm Management and Partner
Gignac Sutts Law Firm
251 Goyeau Street # 600
Windsor, Ontario N9A 6V4
(519) 258–9333
Fax: (519) 258–9527

8111

Business Information: Gignac Sutts Law Firm is an international organization of attorneys focusing on criminal and civil law. The Firm currently has 23 attorneys and over 70 support staff members. As Counsel to Firm Management and Partner, Mr. Ducharme concentrates on the defense of individuals charged with criminal violations, mainly in the province of Ontario, but has been granted the special privilege of appearing for and making presentations on behalf of clients in the United States. Mr. Ducharme counsels other members of the law firm with problem cases. His colleagues in the profession have recognized his innovative courtroom techniques and strategies by honoring him with prestigious designation of Criminal Law Specialist, an honor given only to those who have displayed excellence over many years. Concurrently, Mr. Ducharme is an instructor in the areas of Criminal Trial Advocacy and Criminal Procedures and Evidence at the University of Windsor. **Career Steps:** Gignac, Sutts Law Firm: Counsel to Firm Management and Partner (1985–Present), Attorney, Associate (1982–1985); Attorney, Self Employed (1977–1982). **Associations & Accomplishments:** Past President Essex County Criminal Lawyers Association; Lecturer & Demonstrator for Law Society of Upper Canada; Ontario Criminal Lawyers Association; Canadian Bar Association; Ontario Advocates Society; Canadian Law Professors Association; Board of Directors, New Beginnings; Board Member, Brentwood Recovery Home; Windsor Chamber of Commerce; Counsel and Advisor, Capital theatre of Windsor. **Education:** University of Windsor, L.L.B. (1975); University of Western Ontario, Bar Admission **Personal:** Married. Two children: Stephen and Michael. Mr. Ducharme enjoys hockey, squash, and golf.

Mr. Richard A. Earle
Attorney at Law
Patton Boggs, L.L.P.
2550 M Street NW
Washington, DC 20037–1301
(202) 457–6430
Fax: (202) 338–2625

8111

Business Information: Patton Boggs, L.L.P. is a full–service corporate and commercial law firm. Established in 1961, Patton Boggs, L.L.P. currently employs 300 Attorneys and legal support staff, and has an estimated annual revenue of $60 million. Joining the Firm upon the conferral of his law degree in 1968, Richard Earle concentrates his practice in the areas of international law and finance. He is admitted to practice in both State and Federal courts, as well as the international arena. **Career Steps:** Partner and Attorney at Law, Patton Boggs, L.L.P. (1968–Present); Lieutenant, United States Navy (1964–1966). **Associations & Accomplishments:** American Bar Association; Washington Bar Association; Washington Society of International Law; Association of Foreign Law. **Education:** University of Michigan: J.D. (1968), M.B.S. (1964), B.B.A. (1963). **Personal:** Married to Dr. Nancy Earle, M.D. in 1991. Three children: Jonathan, Karen, Geoffrey. Mr. Earle enjoys sailing and fishing.

Morris L. Eckhart
• • ◄ ━━━●━━━ ► • •
Lawyer
Milroy and Eckhart
218 West Fourth Street
Vinton, IA 52349
(319) 472–4711
Fax: (319) 472–4523

8111

Business Information: Milroy and Eckhart, established in 1974, is a full–service, general practice law firm, concentrating on family law, real estate law and litigation in both state and federal courts. Admitted to practice in Iowa state and federal courts (Northern District), Mr. Eckhart's practice focuses on providing legal representation in legal, architectural, engineering, medical malpractice, product liability and personal injury cases. Career milestones include participating in a prominent case – State vs. Veader, an appellate court decision (1978), giving the individual the right to contact an attorney before taking a breath analysis test. Concurrent with his law practice, he owns and operates a Christmas Tree farm. **Career Steps:** Lawyer, Milroy and Eckhart (1974–Present). **Associations & Accomplishments:** American Bar Association; Association of Trial Lawyers of America; Iowa State Bar Association, Member of the Dissolution of Marriage Committee; Benton County Bar Association; Vinton Unlimited; Former Councilman–at–Large, City Council of Vinton, Iowa; Active Member, Presbyterian Church of Vinton; Published in various newspapers, such as Des Moines Register and the Dubque Telegraph Herald; Former Instructor, Kirkwood Community College. **Education:** Drake University, J.D. with Honors (1973); University of Northern Iowa, B.A. (1971). **Personal:** Married to Martha in 1969. Two children: Peter and Ann. Mr. Eckhart enjoys growing Christmas trees, boating, and sports.

Michael D. Edelson
Senior Partner
Edelson & Associates
85 Albert Street, 9th Floor
Ottawa, Ontario K1P 6A4
(613) 237–2290
Fax: (613) 237–0071
EMail: See Below

8111

Business Information: Edelson & Associates is a full–service, criminal defense law firm. The Firm is one of the busiest in Ottawa with two associates and one counsel. A practicing attorney in the provincial courts of Ottawa since obtaining his degree in 1975, Mr. Edelson founded the Firm in 1996. As Senior Partner, he is a specialist in criminal litigation as certified by the Law Society. Internet users can reach him via: edel@ican.ca. **Career Steps:** Senior Partner, Edelson & Associates (1996–Present); Senior Partner, Addelman, Edelson & Meagher (1980–1996). **Associations & Accomplishments:** President, Defense Counsel Association of Ottawa – Carleton; American Trial Lawyers Association; National Association of Criminal Defense Lawyers; Criminal Lawyers Association. **Education:** University of Ottawa, LL.B. (1975); Bar of Ottawa (1977). **Personal:** Mr. Edelson enjoys travel, golf, and weight training.

Laurel Olson Eggers
Sole Practitioner
The Law Office of Laurel Olson Eggers, P.C.
101 South Main Avenue, Suite 210
Sioux Falls, SD 57102–1124
(605) 338–9143
Fax: (605) 338–2382

8111

Business Information: The Law Office of Laurel Olson Eggers, P.C. is a full–service, general law practice. Establishing her private practice in 1988, Mrs. Eggers ia a trial attorney admitted to both State and Federal courts. A practicing attorney since 1979, Ms. Eggers spent eight years with the Deputy State's Attorney's Office in South Dakota. **Career Steps:** Sole Practitioner, The Law Office of Laurel Olson Eggers, P.C. (1988–Present); Deputy State's Attorney, Minnehaha County, South Dakota (1980–1988). **Associations & Accomplishments:** South Dakota State Bar Association; Second Circuit Bar Association; American Bar Association. **Education:** University of South Dakota, J.D. (1979); South Dakota State University, B.A. (1973). **Personal:** Four children: Rob, Ross, Bethany, and Maren. Mrs. Eggers enjoys reading and travel.

Michael Scott Eisenbaum
Attorney
Gray, York, Duffy & Rattet
15760 Ventural Boulevard, 16th Floor
Encino, CA 91436
(818) 907–4000
Fax: (818) 783–4551

8111

Business Information: Gray, York, Duffy & Rattet is a full–service, general practice law firm, concentrating on general/civil litigation, construction defects, employment law, and business law. A practicing attorney in California state courts since 1990, Mr. Eisenbaum joined the Firm as Attorney in 1993. His practice concentrates on general/civil litigation and construction defects. **Career Steps:** Attorney, Gray, York, Duffy & Rattet (1973–Present); Attorney, Wilson, Elser, Moskowitz, et al (1990–1993). **Associations & Accomplishments:** California Bar Association; San Fernando Valley Bar Association. **Education:** Pepperdine University Law School, J.D. (1990); Colorado State University, B.A. (1987). **Personal:** Mr. Eisenbaum enjoys basketball, skiing, creative writing, and ceramics.

Shelley A. Elder
Partner
Carpenter, Woodward & Elder, P.L.C.
10173 Grandbury Circle
Mechanicsville, VA 23111–4703
(804) 643–1003
Fax: (804) 788–4823
EMail: See Below

8111

Business Information: Carpenter, Woodward & Elder, P.L.C., a woman–owned business, is a unique full–service, general practice law firm, specializing in providing female–oriented legal work (i.e., commercial, sexual discrimination, employee relations, domestic relations, etc.) from a relaxed and comfortable, home–like environment. A practicing attorney in Virginia state courts since 1988, Ms. Elder merged her practice with Carpenter and Woodward in 1994. Her area of focus is in business and estate planning. She also conducts monthly seminars and offers legal advice on an appointment basis. Internet users can reach her via: 52Elderlaw@AOL.com **Career Steps:** Partner, Carpenter, Woodward & Elder, P.L.C. (1994–Present); Attorney, Elder Law Firm, P.C. (1993–1995). **Associations & Accomplishments:** Virginia Women's Attorneys Association; Metropolitan Richmond Women's Bar Association; Virginia Planned Giving Study Group. **Education:** Widener University School of Law, J.D. (1988); University of Delaware, B.A. (1978). **Personal:** Married to William A. in 1987. Four children: Stephen, Charles, Caitlin, and Lisa. Ms. Elder enjoys gardening, carpentry, reading, and fishing.

Patricia L. Engels

Sole Practitioner
Patricia L. Engels – Attorney–at–Law
112 Washington Street
Lowell, IN 46356
(219) 696–1000
Fax: Please mail or call

8111

Business Information: Established in 1979, The Office of Patricia L. Engels is a general practice law firm, specializing in estates, real estate, and bankruptcy. With 17 years experience, Mrs. Engels focuses on explaining to her clients how the legal system works, making them feel like more than just a number. She also provides services pro bono if needed. **Career Steps:** Attorney, The Office of Patricia L. Engels (1979–Present); Instructor, Kankakee Community College (1975); Teacher, Bourbonnais Illinois Unit School (1970–1976). **Associations & Accomplishments:** Newton Bar Association; Kankakee County Bar Association; Lake County Bar Association; American Bar Association; Indiana Bar Association; Illinois Bar Association; Public Defender Bar Association; Family Law and Estate Sections; Theta Chi Sigma; Kappa Delta Pi. **Education:** John Marshal Law School, J.D. (1979); University of Illinois, Advanced Education (1972); Olivet Nazarene College: M.Ed. (1971), B.E. (1970); Certified to teach elementary school, high school and college, and education administration, Illinois; Real Estate Broker's License, Illinois (1979). **Personal:** Married to Henry William in 1947. Three children: Patrick Henry, Michael Bruce, and Timothy William. Mrs. Engels enjoys line dancing, swimming, walking, reading, gardening, sewing, and crafts.

Jeffrey A. Ernico

Attorney/Shareholder
Buchanan Ingersoll, P.C.
8th Floor 30 North 3rd Street
Harrisburg, PA 17101
(717) 237–4851
Fax: (717) 233–0852

8111

Business Information: Buchanan Ingersoll, P.C. is a full–service, general practice law firm concentrating on the business industry and tax planning. A practicing attorney in Pennsylvania state and federal courts, Mr. Ernico joined the Firm in 1994. Mr. Ernico focuses mainly on tax planning, real estate, and real estate planning. **Career Steps:** Attorney/Shareholder, Buchanan Ingersoll, P.C. (1994–Present); Attorney/Shareholder, Hetrick Zaleski Ernico & Fenicle (1986–1994); Attorney/Shareholder, Ernico & Fenicle, P.C. (1976–1986). **Associations & Accomplishments:** American Bar Association; Pennsylvania Bar Association; President, Dauphin County Bar Association (1992–1993); Christian Legal Society; NAIOP: Pennsylvania Alliance, Central Pennsylvania Board Member; Board Member, Teen Challenge Training Center; Jacob Eagle Foundation; Pennsylvania Legal Services, Inc.; Central Pennsylvania Legal Services: Secretary President. **Education:** Temple University – School of Law, J.D. (1970); University of Pittsburgh, B.A. (1967). **Personal:** Married to Barbara B. in 1971. Two children: Jennifer A. and Jared J. Mr. Ernico enjoys writing, skiing, tennis, golf, and reading.

Petra M. Espada–Hernandez, J.D.

Mayoral Legal Counselor
Lcda. Petra M. Espada–Hernandez
330 Calle Victoria
Ponce, Puerto Rico 00731–2859
Fax: (809) 848–4494

8111

Business Information: A practicing attorney in Puerto Rico state courts since 1977, Ms. Espada–Hernandez currently focuses her practice as a mayoral legal counselor. She provides legal advice to the Mayors of Orocovis, Salinas, Arroyo, and Maunabo, Puerto Rico. **Career Steps:** Mayoral Legal Counselor (1984–Present); Municipal and District Judge, (1979–1983); Fine Arts Teacher, Department of Education, (1970–1978). **Associations & Accomplishments:** Puerto Rico Teachers Association (1960–1978); Colegio Abogados De Puerto Rico; Legal Advisor to Puerto Rico Presidents of Neighborhood Committees Against Crime (Volunteer) **Education:** Law School, J.D. (1977); Catholic University, B.A. in Elementary Education. **Personal:** Married to Carlos D. Flores, Police Sergeant. Two children: Jasmin A. and Ivelisse. Two grandchildren: Amber and Stany. Ms. Espada–Hernandez enjoys oil painting and providing pro bono legal assistance to the poor.

Lora J. Espada–Medina, Esq.

Associate Attorney
Goldman, Antonetti & Cordova
P.O. Box 70364
San Juan, Puerto Rico 00936
(809) 789–8036
Fax: (809) 767–8660

8111

Business Information: Goldman, Antonetti & Cordova is a full service, general practice law firm, providing legal services in five departments: litigation, corporate, taxes, environmental, and labor law. Established in 1960, the Firm currently employs 100 attorneys, legal and administrative support staff. A practicing attorney in Puerto Rico courts since 1989, Ms. Espada–Medina joined the Firm 1994. As Associate Attorney in the Labor Department, her practice concentrates on litigation in Puerto Rico courts and in front of Administrative Law Judges. **Career Steps:** Associate Attorney, Goldman, Antonetti & Cordova (1994–Present); Auxiliary Secretary of Legal Affairs in the Consumer Department (DACO) (1991–1992); Associate Lawyer, Ramirez & Ramirez (law firm) (1989–1991). **Associations & Accomplishments:** American Bar Association; Puerto Rico Lawyers Bar; National Labor Relations Practitioners; Phi Alpha Delta Law Fraternity, Jose De Diego Chapter; General Student Council, First woman been President. **Education:** Catholic University of Puerto Rico, J.D. (1989); University of Puerto Rico, Mayaguez Campus, B.A. **Personal:** Ms. Espada–Medina enjoys racquetball and going on expeditions to rivers, lagoons, and mountains in Puerto Rico.

Barry L. Evans

Attorney
Barry L. Evans Barrister, Solicitor
419 King Street, West, Suite 208
Oshawa, Ontario L1J 2K5
(905) 433–1200
Fax: (905) 433–2555

8111

Business Information: Barry L. Evans Barrister, Solicitor is a private practice law firm concentrating on litigation for civil, criminal, and family suits. A practicing attorney in Canadian courts since obtaining his degree in 1975, Mr. Evans founded the Firm in 1977. As Sole Practitioner, Mr. Evans oversees all administrative operation for support staff, in addition in his daily client load. **Career Steps:** Attorney, Barry L. Evans Barrister, Solicitor (1977–Present). **Associations & Accomplishments:** Canadian Bar Association; Ontario Trial Lawyer Association; MENSA; Volunteer at various high schools. **Education:** York University: LL.B. (1975), B.A. **Personal:** Married in 1970. Mr. Evans enjoys golf, the Internet, and attending children's sporting activities.

Mr. Patrick J. Falvey

General Counsel
Port Authority of New York and New Jersey
81 Pond Field Rd. 358
Bronxville, NY 10708
(718) 325–7847
Fax: (914) 779–0161

8111

Business Information: Port Authority of New York and New Jersey is a government transportation and trade agency. Mr. Falvey was formerly supervising counsel of the Port Authority in charge of eighty lawyers and a support staff of one hundred twenty. He also serves as an arbitrator and mediator in complex commercial cases and as a consultant on trade and transportation matters. After forty years at the company, he retired, but was immediately rehired as Special Counsel. Mr. Falvey advises the General Counsel on specified legal matters: for example, now he is advising on the World Trade Center bombing cases. Mr. Falvey also has a private law practice, where he specializes in transportation and trade law, and advises consulting firms. Established in 1921, Port Authority of New York and New Jersey employs 9,000 people with annual sales of $2 billion. **Career Steps:** Port Authority of New York and New Jersey: General Counsel (1996–Present), Special Counsel (1991–1996); First Deputy Executive Director, Port Authority of New York and New Jersey (1989–1991); General Counsel, Port Authority of New York and New Jersey (1972–1991); Deputy Director, Port Authority of New York and New Jersey (1985–1989). **Associations & Accomplishments:** Member, American Bar Association, Chairman, Urban, State, and Local Government Law Section (1984–1985); Member, International Association of Ports and Harbors, Chairman, Legal Counselors (1978); Advisor, United States Delegation to U.N. Diplomatic Convention on Liability of Terminal Operators (1990). Mr. Falvey has also had various articles published in professional journals, and he has been a guest lecturer at The Iona Graduate School of Business and at international seminars on trade law, construction and procurement law and at Bar Association programs; Member, U.S. State Department's Private Advisory Committee on International Trade Law. **Education:** St. John's Law, J.D. cum laude (1950); Iona College Pre–Law. **Personal:** Married to Eileen in 1963. One child: Patrick. Mr. Falvey enjoys reading, golf, and music.

Miss Lisa Jo Fanelli

Assistant Counsel
Commonwealth of Pennsylvania, Department of Labor & Industry
1620 Labor & Industry Building, Seventh & Forster Streets
Harrisburg, PA 17121
(717) 783–5829
Fax: (717) 787–1303

8111

Business Information: Commonwealth of Pennsylvania, Department of Labor & Industry is a state regulatory agency for the State of Pennsylvania. Commonwealth of Pennsylvania, Department of Labor & Industry employs a staff of over 1,000. As Assistant Counsel, Miss Fanelli specializes in labor, employment, and unemployment compensation law. Miss Fanelli also handles appellate litigation. **Career Steps:** Assistant Counsel, Commonwealth of Pennsylvania, Department of Labor & Industry (1990– Present); Attorney, Friedman & Friedman (1989); Law Clerk, Peoples Gas (1988–1989). **Associations & Accomplishments:** Member, Pennsylvania Bar; Admitted to Practice: Federal District Court for the Eastern, Middle, and Western Districts of Pennsylvania, United States Supreme Court; American Bar Association; Ethics and Professionalism Committee; Labor and Employment Law Committee; CLE Instructor; Dickinson School of Law Alumni Reunion Committee; Judge for Regional Client Counseling Competition; Who's Who Among American Law Students; 1989: Outstanding Young Women of America; 1987: The National Dean's List, Who's Who Among Students in American Universities and Colleges, Dean's List, Mortar Board, Omicron Delta Kappa, Lambda Iota Tau, Phi Sigma Tau, Society of Collegiate Journalists, Junior League of Harrisburg; Public Policy Chair (1994–1995), Strategic Planning Committee; Project Liaison (1993–1994). **Education:** Dickinson School of Law, J.D. (1989); Duquesne University School of Law, Visiting Student (1988–1989); Westminster College, B.A. in English, cum laude, honors in English (1986); University of Chicago, NEH Fellow in English (Summer 1985). **Personal:** Miss Fanelli enjoys interpretive dance, drama, and songwriting in her leisure time.

Joseph Anthony Fanone

Partner
Piper & Marbury, L.L.P.
1200 19th Street, NW
Washington, DC 20036
(202) 861–3929
Fax: (202) 223–2085

8111

Business Information: Piper & Marbury, L.L.P. is a full–service, general practice law firm concentrating in municipal finances. With five offices located in Baltimore (MD), New York City (NY), Philadelphia (PA), Washington (DC), and London, England, the Firm currently employs 90 attorneys in the District of Columbia office and more than 300 attorneys firm wide. Admitted to practice in the District of Columbia state courts, Mr. Fanone joined the Firm as Partner in 1994. He concentrates his practice in the areas of municipal finance, corporate trust and banking, representing underwriters and banks in the District of Columbia, Maryland, and Virginia. **Career Steps:** Partner, Piper & Marbury, L.L.P. (1994–Present); Partner, Ballard, Spahr, Andrews & Ingersoll (1981–1994); Associate, Squire Sanders & Dempsey (1978–1981). **Associations & Accomplishments:** American Bar Association; District of Columbia Bar Association; National Association of Bond Lawyers. **Education:** Georgetown University, J.D. (1974), A.B. in Government (1971). **Personal:** Married to Joyce Gorman. Three children: Michael, Kathleen, and Peter.

E. Lambert Farmer Jr.

Partner
Brown, Todd & Heyburn, P.L.L.C.
2700 Lexington Financial Center, 27th Floor
Lexington, KY 40507
(606) 231–0000
Fax: (606) 231–0011

8111

Business Information: Brown, Todd & Heyburn, the second largest law firm in Kentucky, is a full–service, general practice law firm. Established in 1972, the Firm operates four offices and currently employs more than 300 attorneys, legal and administrative support staff. Admitted to practice in Kentucky state and federal courts since 1972, Mr. Farmer joined the Firm as Partner in 1984. He concentrates his practice in the areas of litigation and trial work, product liability, fire, and disasters, as well as directs the Firm's Litigation Department and its 15 representative attorney associates. **Career Steps:**

Partner, Brown, Todd & Heyburn (1984–Present); Partner, King, Deep, Brananam & Farmer (1972–1984). **Associations & Accomplishments:** American Trial Lawyers Association (ATLA); Defense Research Institute (DRI); Past President, Kentucky Defense Counsel, Inc. (1994–1995); Kentucky Academy of Trial Lawyers (KATL); American Bar Association – Litigation Section; Federal Bar Association; Kentucky Bar Association – Litigation – Civil Section; Past Club President, Rotary International; Fellowship of Christian Athletes, Kentucky State Board; Past Treasurer, Fayette County Bar Association. **Education:** University of Kentucky, J.D. (1972); Indiana University, B.S. in Business (1968). **Personal:** Married to Deloris Hughes Farmer in 1987. Two children: Elliott C. and Annette E. Farmer. Mr. Farmer enjoys running and tennis.

Scot J. Farrell
Director of Finance/Chief Financial Officer
Fulbright & Jaworski L.L.P.
1301 McKinney Street, Suite 5100
Houston, TX 77010
(713) 651–5157
Fax: (713) 667–6760
E–mail: See below

8111

Business Information: Fulbright & Jaworski L.L.P., a full-service law firm, is an international partnership with 625 attorneys, seven domestic offices, two international offices and annual cash receipts in excess of $225 million. As Chief Financial Officer, Mr. Farrell serves as a liaison to the Executive and Policy Committees and ex–officio member of the Finance Committee. He reports to the Administrative Partner, assists in the development and implementation of national and international policies and procedures regarding administrative and financially related matters involved in increasing profit, improving staff efficiency, and reduction of the administrative duties of staff attorneys. In 1989, Mr. Farrell was extensively involved in one of the largest law firm mergers in U.S. history. In 1990, he directly participated in the establishment of the Firm's Pacific Rim office. Mr. Farrell is a certified public accountant and is certified in the states of Texas and Pennsylvania. Internet users can reach him via: SFarrell@Fulbright.com. **Career Steps:** Chief Financial Officer, Fulbright & Jaworski L.L.P. (1985–Present); Senior Supervision Accountant, Coopers & Lybrand L.L.P. (1981–1985). **Associations & Accomplishments:** Association of Legal Administrators; American Institute of Certified Public Accountants; Texas Society of Certified Public Accountants; Financial Executive's Institute; Houston Pension Association. **Education:** Lehigh University, B.S. (1981). **Personal:** Married to Sherri in 1985. Three children: Ariana, Lauren, and Matthew. Mr. Farrell enjoys cooking, bicycling, and gardening.

Timothy M. Farris
Attorney at Law
The Law Office of Timothy M. Farris, J.D.
P.O. Box 1190
Hattiesburg, MS 39403–1190
(601) 544–7661
Fax: (601) 584–0434

8111

Business Information: The Farris Law Office is a full-service, general law firm concentrating in personal injury, criminal defense, domestic relations, wills, real estate, titles and corporate law. A member of this family firm, in practice with his father and brother for four years, Timothy Farris concentrates his practice in the areas of corporate law, criminal defense and personal injury. **Career Steps:** Attorney at Law, Farris Law Offices (1991–Present). **Associations & Accomplishments:** American Trial Lawyers Association; Mississippi Trial Lawyers Association; National Association of Criminal Defense Lawyers. **Education:** Mississippi College School of Law, J.D. (1991); University of Southern Mississippi, B.S. (1988). **Personal:** Married to Kimberly Bates in 1993. Mr. Farris enjoys horseback riding, tennis, boating and golf.

David J. Federbush

Partner
Mark A. Cohen & Associates, PC
1501 M Street, NW, Suite 1150
Washington, DC 20005
(202) 835–3800
Fax: (202) 331–9253

8111

Business Information: Mark A. Cohen & Associates, PC is a full–service law firm concentrating in commercial and business litigation, with two offices located in Miami, Florida and Washington, D.C. The firm's offices are integrated through

computer networking and video conferencing. Established in 1989, the Firm currently employs 14 attorneys, legal and administrative support staff. Admitted to practice in Florida, plus District of Columbia and Maryland state and federal courts since 1977, Mr. Federbush joined the Firm in 1994. Serving as Partner, his practice concentrates on commercial litigation. **Career Steps:** Partner, Mark A. Cohen & Associates, PC (1994–Present); Partner, Williams & Eoannon, P.A. – Bethesda, MD (1993–1994); Associate, Greer, Homer & Bonner, P.A., Miami; Senior Trial Attorney, Bureau of Consumer Protection, Federal Trade Commission (1976–1988). **Associations & Accomplishments:** American Bar Association; Vice President, Yale Club of Miami (1992–1993); Board of Directors, Alliance Francaise of Miami (1992–1993); Awards for Meritorious Service and for Superior Service for sustained excellence in the prosecution of investment fraud at the Federal Trade Commission; Phi Beta Kappa (while at Yale University). **Education:** Stanford University Law School, J.D. (1976); Yale University, B.A. summa cum laude (1971). **Personal:** Mr. Federbush enjoys tennis in his leisure time.

Roberto Feliberti–Cintron
Associate Attorney
Cancio, Nadal, Rivera & Diaz
P.O. Box 10971
San Juan, Puerto Rico 00922–0971
(809) 767–9625
Fax: (809) 764–4430

8111

Business Information: Cancio, Nadal, Rivera & Diaz As Associate Attorney, Mr. Feliberti–Cintron **Career Steps:** Associate Attorney, Cancio, Nadal, Rivera & Diaz (1993–Present); Judicial Law Clerk, U.S. District Court, P.R. (1990–1993); Commissioned Officer, U.S. Navy (1985–1989). **Associations & Accomplishments:** American Bar Association; Federal Bar Association; Puerto Rico Bar Association; Board of Directors, Caribe Federal Credit Union (1995–Present). **Education:** University of Puerto Rico School of Law, J.D. (1991); Purdue University, Bachelor of Science (1985). **Personal:** Married to Lizette Torres in 1994. Mr. Feliberti–Cintron enjoys basketball, fishing, reading, and spending time with his wife.

Sherman Gene Fendler
Partner
Liskow & Lewis
1 Shell Square Building, 50th Floor
New Orleans, LA 70139
(504) 581–7979
Fax: (504) 556–5108

8111

Business Information: Liskow & Lewis is a general practice law firm with 80 attorneys. Mr. Fendler joined the firm upon conferral of his law degree in 1973. Now a Partner and trial lawyer, he concentrates his practice in the areas of maritime law, toxic tort, and aviation. **Career Steps:** Partner, Liskow & Lewis (1974–Present). **Associations & Accomplishments:** American Bar Association; Maritime Law Association; Lawyer–Pilots Bar Association; Board of Directors, Congregation Temple Sinai. **Education:** Louisiana State University, J.D. (1973); University of Virginia, B.A. (1969). **Personal:** Married to Linda D. in 1976. Three children: Julia, Abigail, and Benjamin. Mr. Fendler enjoys flying and golf.

Orlando Fernandez

Partner
Garcia & Fernandez
117 Avenue Eleanor Roosevelt, 3rd Floor
San Juan, Puerto Rico 00918
(787) 764–1932
Fax: (787) 766–2132

8111

Business Information: Garcia & Fernandez is a general practice law firm with six attorneys. A practicing attorney since 1979, Mr. Fernandez established the Firm with his partner in 1988. The Practice focuses on commercial litigation with an emphasis placed on bankruptcy and construction law. Admitted to practice in both state and federal courts, Mr. Fernandez handles many of the business aspects of the Practice. **Career Steps:** Partner, Garcia & Fernandez (1988–Present); Associate, John M. Garcia Law Offices (1984–1988); Associate, Falcon & Fernandez (1979–1983). **Associations & Accomplishments:** Secretary, Rio Mar Golf Association; Colegio San Jose School Council; American Bar Association; Federal Bar Association; Puerto Rico Bankruptcy Bar Association; Roosevelt Neighborhood Council; Former President, Subdivision Neighborhood Council. **Education:** Louisiana State University, J.D. (1979); Tulane University, B.A. (1975). **Personal:** Married to Peggy in 1984. Two children:

Priscilla Marie and Eric O. Mr. Fernandez enjoys golf and fishing.

LCBO Pedro J. Fernandez–Barreto

Broker and Of Counsel
–Independent–
P.O. Box 8194
San Juan, Puerto Rico 00910–0194
(809) 764–3801
Fax: (809) 764–3801

8111

Business Information: Obtaining his law degree in 1980 and a Certified Insurance Broker, Pedro Fernandez–Baretto provides clients throughout the greater San Juan metro with a full scope of insurance products, as well as legal counsel in the areas of torts and personal injury matters. **Career Steps:** Broker and Of Counsel, (1977–Present). **Associations & Accomplishments:** Colegio de Ahogados de Puerto Rico **Education:** Inter–American University, J.D. (1980) **Personal:** Four children: Yanira, Sigrid, Pedro, and Esther Fernandez Cobberg. Mr. Fernandez–Barreto enjoys restoring and collecting Volkswagens, reading and church activities.

Roberto A. Fernandez–Quiles
Associate Attorney
Goldman, Antonetti & Cordova
P.O. Box 70364
San Juan, Puerto Rico 00936–0364
(809) 759–4217
Fax: (809) 767–9333

8111

Business Information: Goldman, Antonetti & Cordova is a full–service, multi–specialty law practice, consisting of sixty attorneys throughout five departments. Established in 1959, the Firm currently employs 130 attorneys, legal, and administrative support staff. A practicing attorney in Puerto Rico state courts since 1989, Mr. Fernandez–Quiles joined the Firm in 1993. Serving as Associate Attorney in the Department of Labor and Employment Law, he provides legal representation to the Firm's clientele on labor and employment law issues. **Career Steps:** Associate Attorney, Goldman, Antonetti & Cordova (1993–Present); Associate Attorney, Ramirez & Ramirez (1990–1993). **Associations & Accomplishments:** Puerto Rico Bar Association; Defenders of Wildlife; UNICEF; Cystic Fibrosis Association. **Education:** University of Puerto Rico: J.D. (1989), B.S. (1986); Diploma de Estudios Hispanicos, Latinoamericanos y Europeos; Jose Ortega y Gasset Foundation, Toledo, Spain (1986). **Personal:** Married to Vivea M. Mejias in 1991. Mr. Fernandez–Quiles enjoys the saxophone, sports, and reading.

Rafael Fernandez–Suarez

Partner
McConnell Valdes
270 Munoz Rivera Avenue
Hato Rey, Puerto Rico 00919
(809) 250–5629
Fax: (809) 759–9225

8111

Business Information: McConnell Valdes, the leading law firm in Puerto Rico and the Caribbean, is a full–service, general practice law firm. The Firm provides legal services in four areas, including corporate law, taxes, labor law, and litigations. Future plans include expanding the Firm into other areas of the Caribbean and into Latin America. Established in 1946, the Firm currently employs 115 attorneys and 85 legal and administrative support staff. A practicing attorney in Puerto Rico and U.S. District of Columbia courts, Mr. Fernandez–Suarez joined the Firm in 1977. He serves as Partner in the Firm's Tax Department, responsible for legal opinions, litigation, and providing representation before the Puerto Rico Treasury Department and its municipalities. **Career Steps:** Partner, McConnell Valdes (1977–Present); Director of Intelligence Officer, Puerto Rico Treasury Department (1971–1976) **Associations & Accomplishments:** American Bar Association; Puerto Rico Bar Association; District of Columbia Bar Association; Puerto Rico Manufacturer's Association; Frequent speaker at seminars and meetings. **Education:** Georgetown University, LL.M. in Taxation (1977); University of Puerto Rico: B.A. in Business Administration, and LL.B. from Law School **Personal:** Married to Minette I. in 1986. Three children: Sandra, Vivian and Rafael. Mr. Fernandez–Suarez enjoys rasing and riding Apaloosa horses.

Richard J. Fildes

Partner
Lowndes, Drosdick, Doster, Kantor & Reed, PA
215 North Eola Drive
Orlando, FL 32802
(407) 843–4600
Fax: (407) 423–4495

8111

Business Information: Lowndes, Drosdick, Doster, Kantor & Reed, PA, the leading law firm in Orlando, is a full–service, general practice law firm consisting of more than 70 attorneys. Part of the Commercial Law Affiliates — an international law group — the Firm concentrates on real estate, litigation, tax, estate planning, environmental, securities, land use planning, and labor practice law. Joining the Firm as an associate upon the conferral of his law degree in 1977, Mr. Fildes was appointed as Partner in 1981. His practice concentrates on real estate law, representing developers, lenders, hotel owners and landlords, as well as sports law. The majority of his practice focuses on large commercial real estate transactions. Mr. Fildes also often acts as local counsel to out–of–state law firms with clients in Florida. **Career Steps:** Partner, Lowndes, Drosdick, Doster, Kantor & Reed, PA (1977–Present). **Associations & Accomplishments:** Chairman, Florida Citrus Sports Association; Downtown Athletic Club of Orlando; Lake Nona Golf Committee; Florida Citrus Sports Foundation; Published in trade and law journals. **Education:** University of Florida, J.D. (1977); Duke University, B.A. in Economics and Psychology (1974). **Personal:** Married to Deborah in 1979. Two children: Melissa and Heather. Mr. Fildes enjoys golf, fishing, jogging, boating, swimming, tennis, and reading.

Richard Isaac Fine, Ph.D.

President
Law Offices of Richard I. Fine and Associates
10100 Santa Monica Boulevard, Suite 1000
Los Angeles, CA 90067–4101
(310) 277–5833
Fax: (310) 277–1543

8111

Business Information: Law Offices of Richard I. Fine and Associates is a general practice law firm concentrating on international anti trust, complex litigation, and unique cases pertaining to society impact. Additionally, the Firm does public interest work on behalf of the people against the Government. A practicing attorney since 1964 and admitted to practice law in California state courts, Mr. Fine established the Firm in 1974 and serves as its President. He is responsible for all aspects of the Firm's operations, including administration, legal, marketing, and strategic planning. **Career Steps:** President, Law Offices of Richard I. Fine and Associates (1974–Present); Swerdlow, Glikbarg, and Shimer, Los Angeles (1972–1973); Coudert Brothers, London Office (1968); U.S. Department of Justice: Antitrust Division (1968–1972), Founder and Chief of the Antitrust Division for the City of Los Angeles (1973–1974); The First Municipal Antitrust Division in the United States, Special Counsel Governmental Efficiency Committee, Los Angeles City Council (1973). **Associations & Accomplishments:** BNA Antitrust Advisory Board (1980–Present); Executive Council (1984–1987), Budget Committee (1992–Present), American Society of International Law; Regional Coordinator (1994–Present), International Legal Materials Corresponding Editor; American Bar Association, International Law Section, Chairman Committee on International Economic Organizations (1977–1981); Founder and Chairman of Antitrust Trade Regulation Law Committee (1987), State Bar of California; Founder and Chairman of Antitrust Section, Los Angeles County Bar (1977–1978), Executive Committee International Law Section (1993–Present); Board of Directors, Lake Havasu City, Arizona, Citizens Island Bridge Company, Ltd.; Los Angeles World Affairs Council–International Circle (1991–Present); Founders, Los Angeles County Music Center (1984–Present); Board of Directors (1994–Present), Missing Children's Data Center; Retinitis Pigmentosa International Board of Directors (1985–1990) White House Conference on NAFTA October 21,1993 Participant; University of Chicago Law School Visiting Committee (1992–1994); Board of Directors (1984–Present), American Friends of the London School of Economics; (University of London); Southern California Chapter (1984–Present); Los Angeles Advisory Committee, London School of Economics. **Education:** University of Chicago, J.D. (1964); University of London, London School of Economics and Political Science, Ph.D. in International Law (1967); Hague Academy of International Law: Certificate (1965,1966), Certificate of Comparative Law; International University of Comparative Science, Luxembourg (1966); Diploma d'Etudes Superieures du Droit Compare (Faculte Internationale pour L'Enseignment du Droit Compare) Strasbourg (1967); University of Wisconsin, B.S. (1961). **Personal:** Married to Maryellen Olman. One child: Victoria.

Joseph M. Finley

Attorney
Leonard, Street and Deinard
150 South 5th Street, Suite 2300
Minneapolis, MN 55402
(612) 335–1970
Fax: (612) 335–1657
E MAIL: See Below

8111

Business Information: Leonard, Street and Deinard is a full–service law firm with 135 general practice attorneys. The Firm concentrates on commercial litigation, corporate practice, and financial law. Established in 1922, the Firm has 350 employees and projects revenues for 1996 to exceed $40 million. As a Partner, Mr. Finley is the Chairman of the Firm's Business Division, which comprises approximately 50% of the firm. Other responsibilities include real estate and corporate transactions, and land use matters. Mr. Finley is on the Board of Directors, the Compensation Committee, and the Operations Committee. He works closely with other members of management on planning for future expansion. Internet users can reach him via: JMF1970@email.leonard.com. **Career Steps:** Leonard, Street and Deinard: Attorney (1980–Present), Chairman of Real Estate Department (1990–1995), Chairman of Business Division (1996–Present) **Associations & Accomplishments:** American Bar Association; Minnesota Bar Association; American Planning Association; Urban Land Institute; Sensible Land Use Coalition; Chairman of Schools and Scholarships Committee, Harvard Club of Minnesota; Edgcumbe Hockey Club; Numerous expert panels regarding civic affairs. **Education:** University of Minnesota, J.D. (1980); Harvard University, B.A. (1974) and M.C.P. (1977). **Personal:** Married to Mary in 1983. Three children: Bridget, William, and Brenna. Mr. Finley enjoys golf, coaching youth hockey and baseball, and collecting old maps and atlases.

Joseph G. Finnerty Jr.

Partner
Piper & Marbury, L.L.P.
53 Wall Street
New York, NY 10005–2899
(212) 858–8989
Fax: (212) 858–5301

8111

Business Information: Piper & Marbury, L.L.P. is a full–service, general practice law firm. Established in 1952, the Firm currently employs 706 people company–wide. Admitted to practice law in New York, Maryland, and District of Columbia courts, Mr. Finnerty joined the Firm in 1972 as Partner. He is responsible for managing the New York office, and provides legal representation in trial and litigation law. He also serves as a member of the Executive Committee. **Career Steps:** Partner, Piper & Marbury, L.L.P. (1972–Present); Partner, Gallagher, Evelius & Finnerty (1966–1972); Associate, Piper & Marbury (1963–1966). **Associations & Accomplishments:** American Bar Association; New York Bar Association; Maryland Bar Association; District of Columbia Bar Association; American College of Trial Lawyers; American Bar Foundation; Published numerous articles in legal journals. **Education:** University of Maryland, J.D. (1963); Loyola College, B.S. (1958); Cornell University (attended 1958–1959). **Personal:** Married to Deborah B. in 1990. Seven children: Sara F. Kelly; Alice Ann Martin; Kathleen F. Curtis; Joseph G. III, Thomas P., Mary Eileen and Bridget Porter Finnerty. Mr. Finnerty enjoys managing his family farm.

Merrick B. Firestone, P.C.

Attorney at Law
Kimerer & LaVelle
100 West Clarendon Avenue, Suite 2100
Phoenix, AZ 85013–3515
(602) 279–5900
Fax: (602) 264–5566

8111

Business Information: Kimerer & LaVelle is a full–service, general practice law firm, concentrating on commercial and securities litigation. Mr. Firestone has been a practicing trial attorney in Arizona and all federal courts since 1988. Mr. Firestone joined the firm as Attorney at Law in 1993. As a trial lawyer, his practice concentrates on complicated commercial litigation and personal injury litigation. Mr. Firestone has had extensive trial practice and has represented major corporations involving the Central Arizona Water Project, land fraud and federal racketeering. **Career Steps:** Attorney at Law, Kimerer & LaVelle (1993–Present); Trial Lawyer, Allen, Kimerer & LaVelle (1988–1993). **Associations & Accomplishments:** Admitted to Practice – Ninth Circuit Court of Appeals; United States District Court for the District of Arizona, State of Arizona; Arizona State Bar Association; Maricopa County Bar Association; Treasurer for the Non–Profit Amateur Athletic Association and P.O.B.R.F.C. **Education:** University of Arizona College of Law, J.D. (1988); University of Arizona, B.A. in Political Science and Psychology (1985). **Personal:** Married to Monica in 1990. Two children: Dillan N. and Camille J. Mr. Firestone enjoys rugby, hunting, running, and bicycling.

Dr. Domingo O. Flores

President SAP, S.A.
The Office of Domingo O. Flores
Corrientes 4416, piso 5 Dpto F.
Buenos Aires, Argentina 1195
(541) 371–4117
Fax: (541) 374–2482
EMAIL: See Below

8111

Business Information: The Office of Domingo O. Flores is a full–service Criminal and Labor Union Law firm located in Buenos Aires, Argentina. Dr. Flores acts as Head Attorney for the Firm. Concurrently, he is the President of Servicios Asistenciales Patagonicos (SAP, S.A.), a Company that manages Health Care Systems. As Head Attorney within the Law Firm, Mr. Flores has multiple responsibilities, to include recruitment of legal staff, plans for the Firm's expansion, and assisting in the daily management of the Office. As President of SAP, S.A., he is responsible for managing health care facilities, to include maintaining the quality of medical treatment, recruiting staff, and handling daily operations of the Company. Additionally, he is the President of Centro de Estudios de Etica Medica Aplicada a los Recursos, and editor of "Cemar," a health care bi–monthly magazine. Internet users can reach him via: apsa@century.com.ar. **Career Steps:** Head Lawyer, Office of Domingo Flores (1955–Present); President, SAP, S.A. (1993–Present); President, Cemar (1995–Present). **Associations & Accomplishments:** Vice President, Fundacion Servicios Asistenciales Patagonicos (Fundacion SAP). **Education:** Universidad Nacional de Litoral: Doctor at Law (1957), Lawyer (1955). **Personal:** Married to Amalia Berta Salzman in 1976. Dr. Flores enjoys lecturing and conducting country wide seminars in sociological problems.

Mr. Thomas P. Flynn

Attorney
Legler & Flynn
2027 Manatee Avenue, West
Bradenton, FL 34205
(813) 748–5599
Fax: (813) 747–2371

8111

Business Information: Legler & Flynn is a law firm limiting its practice to personal injury plaintiff representation. An Attorney and Partner with the Firm, Mr. Flynn handles all aspects of administrative direction as well as serving as trial attorney. Established in 1989, Legler & Flynn employs 7 legal aide professionals and administrative support staff people. **Career Steps:** Attorney, Legler & Flynn (1989–Present); Partner, Bohman, Flynn & Stump (1978–1989). **Associations & Accomplishments:** President, St. Joseph Church Parish Council; Founder and Past President, Dayton Chapter of Juvenile Diabetes Foundation; Sponsor and Manager, Little League and Babe Ruth baseball; Youth Soccer Coach; Coach, High School Moot Court. **Education:** University of Dayton School of Law, J.D. (1978); Miami University, M.A. (1975); Miami University, B.A. (1974). **Personal:** Married to Gayle in 1972. Three children: Danny, Sean and Kelly. Mr. Flynn enjoys baseball, soccer, basketball, fishing, archery, boating and tennis.

Ronald J. Frappier

Shareholder Attorney
Jenkins & Gilchrist
1445 Ross Avenue, Suite 3200
Dallas, TX 75202
(214) 855–4743
Fax: (214) 855–4300

8111

Business Information: Jenkins & Gilchrist is a full–service, general practice law firm. Joining the Firm as Associate Attorney upon the conferral of his law degree in 1984, Mr. Frappier was appointed as Shareholder Attorney in 1992. His practice concentrates on corporate and securities law. **Career Steps:** Jenkins & Gilchrist: Shareholder Attorney (1992–Present), Associate Attorney (1984–1991). **Associations & Accomplishments:** Dallas Business Association; Dallas Bar Association; American Bar Association; Conducts public seminars to introduce new companies into the limelight. **Education:** University of Virginia, J.D. (1984); George Mason University, B.S. in Psychology (1979). **Personal:** Married to Janice in 1980. Two children: Jason and Meagan. Mr. Frappier enjoys cars and music.

William H. Freedman

Partner
McCutchen, Doyle, Brown & Enersen
355 South Grand Avenue, Suite 4400
Los Angeles, CA 90071–1560
(213) 680–6426
Fax: (213) 680–6499
EMAIL: See Below

8111

Business Information: McCutchen, Doyle, Brown & Enersen is a full–service, multi–national law firm practicing in all areas relevant to commercial activities. International in scope, the Firm has offices located in California (San Francisco, Los Angeles, San Jose, Walnut Creek, Menlo Park), Washington, D.C., and Taipei, Taiwan. Affiliated offices are located in Bangkok, Beijing, and Shanghai. Established in 1883, the Firm currently employs 500 attorneys, legal and administrative support staff. A practicing attorney in California state and international law, Mr. Freedman joined the Firm in 1992. Serving as Partner in the Environmental Group, his practice specializes in all environmental media and international environmental issues (both policy–related and due diligence). **Career Steps:** Partner, McCutchen, Doyle, Brown & Enersen (1992–Present); Office Counsel, Kaye, Scholer, Fierman, Hays & Handler (1990–1992); Senior Environmental Counsel, Northrop Corporation (1986–1990); Senior Prosecutor, South Coast Air Quality Management District (1983–1986). **Associations & Accomplishments:** Southern California Chinese Lawyers Association; Asia – Pacific Bar Association; International Section, Air and Waste Management Association; Environmental and International Sections, Los Angeles County Bar Association; California – Southeast Asia Business Council; Asian American Bar Association; Environmental and International Sections, California Bar Association; Environmental and International Sections, American Bar Association. **Education:** Emory University, J.D. (1981); Washington University, B.S. in English (1979). **Personal:** Mr. Freedman enjoys tennis, golf, skiing, basketball, music, photography, and international travel.

Paul D. Friedman

Attorney
Goldman & Kaplan, Ltd.
2930 North Seventh Street
Phoenix, AZ 85014
(602) 264–9323
Fax: (602) 274–7006

8111

Business Information: Goldman & Kaplan, Ltd. is a full–service, general practice law firm. Established in 1971, Goldman & Kaplan currently employs four attorneys and nine support personnel. A practicing trial attorney in Arizona since 1989 and Colorado since 1992, Mr. Friedman concentrates his practice in the areas of claimant and defense personal injury and wrongful death as well as claimant product liability and significant malpractice cases. He is licensed to practice in Arizona, Colorado, Ninth Circuit District Court and Ninth Circuit Court of Appeals. **Career Steps:** Trial Attorney, Goldman & Kaplan, Ltd. (1995–Present); Trial Attorney, James F. Brook & Associates (1991–1994); Litigation Associate Attorney, Teilborg, Sanders & Parks (1989–1991); Licensed Real Estate Sales, Friedman Sanders Associates (1986–Present). **Associations & Accomplishments:** Board of Directors, Boys and Girls Clubs of Phoenix; Regional Board of Directors, B'Nai B'rith Youth Organization; American Bar Association, Torts and Litigation Subcommittee Member; Arizona Trial Lawyers Association; Maricopa County Bar Association; Editor and Staff–Writer, California Western Law Review–International Law Journal; Phi Beta Kappa. **Education:** California Western School of Law, Juris Doctorate (1989); University of Arizona, B.A. in Political Science (1985). **Personal:** Mr. Friedman enjoys racquetball and competes in Olympic distance triathlon events (run, bike, swim).

Eva M. Fromm

Attorney at Law
Fulbright & Jaworski L.L.P.
1301 McKinney Street, Suite 5100
Houston, TX 77010–3029
(713) 651–5321
Fax: (713) 651–5246

8111

Business Information: Fulbright & Jaworski L.L.P. is a full–service, general practice law firm. A practicing attorney in Texas state courts since 1985, Ms. Fromm joined the Firm as Associate in 1986. Currently serving as Partner, her practice concentrates on environmental law, including advising clients on environmental regulations, enforcement matters, contested permit matters, environmental aspects of business transactions, and environmental property damage and toxic tort actions. Prior to entering the legal profession, Ms. Fromm had extensive experience as an environmental consultant and a process engineer. **Career Steps:** Attorney at Law, Fulbright & Jaworski L.L.P. (1986–Present); Attorney, Hill, Parker, Franklin, Cardwell & Jones (1985–1986); Chemical Engineer, NUS Corporation (1982–1984). **Associations & Accomplishments:** State Bar of Texas; Environmental Law Section, Houston Bar Association; American Bar Association. **Education:** University of Houston, J.D. (1985); Syracuse University, B.S. in Chemical Engineering – Minor in Environmental Engineering (1978). **Personal:** Married to Jerry McGonigal in 1988. Ms. Fromm enjoys gardening.

Ms. Sharla J. Frost

Managing Partner
Powers & Frost, L.L.P.
24 Greenway Plaza, Suite 2020
Houston, TX 77046
(713) 961–2800
Fax: (713) 961–5090

8111

Business Information: Powers & Frost, L.L.P. is a full–service, general practice law firm, concentrating on litigation and defense in the areas of tort and business law. Established in 1994, the Firm currently employs five attorneys, plus legal and administrative support staff. Admitted to practice in Texas state courts since 1987, Ms. Frost co–founded the Firm in 1994. Currently serving as Managing Partner, she is responsible for the management of daily activities, as well as focusing her practice on product liability and tort law. **Career Steps:** Managing Partner, Powers & Frost, L.L.P. (1994–Present); Associate, Roberts, Markel, Folger & Powers (1993–1994); Associate, Holtzman & Urquhart (1989–1992); Associate, Fulbright & Jaworski (1987–1989). **Associations & Accomplishments:** British American Business Association; Rice Design Alliance; American Bar Association; Texas State Bar; Houston Bar Association; Houston Young Lawyers Association; Defense Research Institute; Volunteer at Houston public schools. **Education:** Baylor University Law School, J.D. (1987); Southeastern Oklahoma State University, B.A. (1984). **Personal:** Ms. Frost enjoys reading and bicycling.

Loula M. Fuller

Partner
Adams, Quinton & Fuller
402A North Office Plaza Drive
Tallahassee, FL 32301
(904) 878–7415
Fax: (904) 878–0438

8111

Business Information: Adams, Quinton & Fuller is a general practice law firm. With offices located in Miami, Boca Raton, and Tallahassee, Florida, the Firm handles litigation and administrative work in federal and circuit courts; employing six attorneys, legal and administrative support staff. Admitted to practice in Florida state courts since 1985, Ms. Fuller joined the Firm in 1993 as Partner. Her practice is focused on auto franchise legislation and environmental law, representing franchise dealers and corporate consumers. **Career Steps:** Partner, Adams, Quinton & Fuller (1993–Present); Associate, Carlton, Fields, Ward, Emmanuel, Smith & Cutler, P.A. (1990–1993); Trial Attorney, Frost & Purcell (1987–1989); Clerk, Honorable Judge Ann Booth (1985–1987). **Associations & Accomplishments:** American Bar Association; Tallahassee Bar Association; Guardian Ad Litem Program; Florida Bar Association. **Education:** Florida State University, J.D. (1985); Florida State University, B.S. (1973). **Personal:** Married to Daniel E. Myers in 1990. Two children: Michelle and David Fuller. Ms. Fuller enjoys snow skiing, water skiing, and white water rafting.

William E. Gahwyler, Esq.

Sole Practitioner
Law Offices of W. Gahwyler
88 Yale Avenue
Wyckoff, NJ 07481–3167
(201) 342–0154
Fax: (201) 343–8089

8111

Business Information: Law Offices of W. Gahwyler is a specialized law practice, concentrating on real estate law issues, as well as serves as a brokerage for mortgage, real estate and real property investment planning. Establishing his sole practice law firm upon the conferral of his law degree in 1990, Mr. Gahwyler is responsible for all aspects of operations, including the buying and selling of distressed real estate and brokering hard money real estate loans and accounts receivables. **Career Steps:** Sole Practitioner, Law Offices of W. Gahwyler (1990–Present); Partner, First Equity Funding (1994–Present); Partner, Commercial Equities (1994–Present). **Associations & Accomplishments:** New Jersey State Bar Association; New York State Bar Association; Florida Bar; American Bar Association; Volunteer, Tomorrows Childrens Fund – Children with terminal diseases. **Education:** U. M. Law School, J.D. (1990). **Personal:** Married to Jacklyn Collins in 1989. Mr. Gahwyler enjoys home improvements, running, and skiing.

Francisco A. Galiano–Toro

Sole Practitioner
LCDO. Francisco A. Galiano–Toro
HC–01 Box 3590
Hormigueros, Puerto Rico 00660–9701
(809) 849–3315
Fax: (809) 831–2229

8111

Business Information: LCDO. Francisco A. Galiano–Toro, is a full–service, general practice law firm with concentration on civil law cases. A practicing attorney in Puerto Rico since 1964, Mr. Galiano–Toro established his sole practice law firm in 1964. His practice concentrates on providing legal representation for the protection of minors in civil law. Concurrent with his private legal practice, he is a free–lance writer, writing poetry, legal papers, and other literary works. **Career Steps:** Attorney, LCDO. Francisco A. Galiano–Toro (1964–Present); Attorney for Child Protection, Department of Social Services (1984–1992); Professor, Fundacion Ana G. Mendez (1973–1976); Vacacional Rehabilitation Counselor, Government of Puerto Rico (1951–1953). **Associations & Accomplishments:** Optiminst Club; Board of Directors, Mayaguez Geriatric Center; Board of Directors, Puerto Rico Bar Association; Caquas Writers Association; Vice President, Mayaguez Bar Association. **Education:** Catholic University – Puerto Rico, J.D. (1964); Polytechnic Institute of Puerto Rico, B.A. (1951). **Personal:** Married to Luisa A. Perea in 1952. Three children: Maristella, Francisco A., and Rosa Miriam. Mr. Galiano–Toro enjoys reading and writing.

Michele G. Gangnes

Sole Practitioner
Law Offices of Michele G. Gangnes
PO Box 6366, 1602 East Cesar Chavez
Austin, TX 78762–6366
(512) 479–6862
Fax: (512) 479–0882

8111

Business Information: Law Offices of Michele G. Gangnes, established in 1995, is a full–service, general practice law firm serving clients in Texas and the Pacific Northwest. Admitted to practice law in Washington in 1978 and Texas in 1975, Ms. Gangnes established her sole practice law office in 1995. Her practice concentrates on municipal finance, corporate fiduciary law, and business transactions. **Career Steps:** Sole Practitioner, Law Offices of Michele G. Gangnes (1995–Present); Partner, Riddell, Williams, Bullitt & Walkinshaw (1988–1995); Partner, Karr Tuttle Campbell (1978–1988). **Associations & Accomplishments:** American Bar Association; State Bar of Texas; Washington State Bar Association; National Association of Bond Lawyers; Public speaker to consumer groups, banks, and the National Association of Bond Lawyers. **Education:** University of Texas, J.D. (1975); Rice University, B.A. (1972). **Personal:** Ms. Gangnes enjoys outdoor activities, cooking, and reading.

Deborah E. Ganjavi

Personnel Director
Andrews & Kurth, L.L.P.
600 Travis Street, Suite 4200
Houston, TX 77002
(713) 220–4174
Fax: (713) 220–3655

8111

Business Information: Andrews and Kurth is a law firm, providing services indomestic and international law practice including: Energy and natural resources, project and structured finance, mergers and acquisitions, private placements, and general corporate and commerical law. As Personnel Director, Ms. Ganjavi handles all human resource concerns for the law firm. She is responsible for recruitment, hiring, training and employment counseling for the support staff. Currently the firm is revamping policies and procedures, training and developmental systems, retirement and benefit plans, and a long–term consolidation of payroll and the human resources database, all of which is under Ms. Ganjavi's purview. **Career Steps:** Andrews and Kurth: Personnel Director (1994–Present), Network Systems Manager (1989–1994), Training Coordinator (1986–1989), Legal Assistant, Secretary (1979–1986). **Associations & Accomplishments:** Association of Legal Administrators, National and Local; Society for Human Resource Management. **Education:** University of Houston, B.S. candidate in Industrial and organizational psychology. **Personal:** Married to Vahid in 1980. Two children: Joshua and Lauren. Ms. Ganjavi enjoys music, reading, biking, swimming, and crafts.

Elfren Garcia Munoz
Attorney/Owner
Elfren Garcia Munoz
Calle Santiago Iglesias #74
Coamo, Puerto Rico 00769–2433
(787) 825–6983
Fax: (787) 825 6083

8111

Business Information: A practicing attorney since 1990 and licensed in Puerto Rico and Boston, Massachusetts, Mr. Garcia Munoz established his private practice in 1994, concentrating in civil law. **Career Steps:** Attorney/Owner, Law Office of Elfren Garcia Munoz (1994–Present); Child Support Judge, Superior Court (1990–1994); Law Clerk, Puerto Rico Superior Court (1988–1990). **Associations & Accomplishments:** Puerto Rico Lawyers Bar Association; American Lawyers Bar Association; Rotary Club. **Education:** Inter–American University, J.D. (1992); Catholic University of Puerto Rico, Arts and Humanities. **Personal:** Married to Edna Nolasco in 1982. Three children: Elfren J., Daniel J., and Ana N. Mr. Garcia Munoz enjoys diving.

Gene W. Gardner
Attorney at Law
Gardner & Cyrus
P.O. Box 2144
Huntington, WV 25722
(304) 522–9593
Fax: (304) 522–9596

8111

Business Information: Gardner & Cyrus is a full–service law firm concentrating in the areas of personal injury, medical malpractice and divorce law. Established in 1985, the Firm currently employs three attorneys and legal support staff. A trial attorney admitted to practice in 1981, Mr. Gardner is the Senior Partner. **Career Steps:** Senior Partner and Attorney at Law, Gardner & Cyrus (1985–Present); Associate Attorney, Barrett & Chafin (1981–1985). **Associations & Accomplishments:** American Trial Lawyers Association; West Virginia State Bar Association; American Bar Association; West Virginia Trial Lawyers Association; West Virginia Law Review; Order of the Coif; Published law review article, "Speeding Away from the Fourth Amendment," West Virginia Law Review (1981); Life long member of his community. **Education:** West Virginia University, J.D. (1981); Marshall University, B.A. (1975). **Personal:** Married to Kim in 1977, they have three children. In his leisure time, Mr. Gardner enjoys playing golf.

Kevin William Gaughen, Esq.
Managing Partner
Gaughen, Gaughen, & Gaughen
528 Broad Street
Weymouth, MA 02189–1303
(617) 335–0374
Fax: (617) 340–6315

8111

Business Information: Gaughen, Gaughen, & Gaughen is a full–service, general practice law firm concentrating in litigation, primarily civil, banking and real estate transactions. Established in 1954, the Firm currently employs nine attorneys, legal and administration support staff. Admitted to practice in Massachusetts state and federal courts and licensed for the U.S. Supreme Court, Kevin Gaughen joined the Firm in 1988 as Managing Partner. He concentrates his practice in the areas of litigation and banking issues. One of his landmark cases was the $150 million proxy contest case he represented and won on behalf of Hingham Institute for Savings. **Career Steps:** Managing Partner, Gaughen, Gaughen, & Gaughen (1988–Present); Vice President and General Counsel, East Weymouth Savings Bank (1980–1988); Assistant District Attorney, Norfolk County District Attorney's Office (1979–1980). **Associations & Accomplishments:** Director, Hingham Institution for Savings; American Bar Association; Massachusetts Bar Association; Massachusetts Trial Lawyers' Association; Massachusetts Academy of Trial Attorneys; Hingham Yacht Club; Weymouth Sportsman's Club. **Education:** Suffolk University Law School, J.D. (1979); Georgetown University, A.B. (1976). **Personal:** Married to Eileen in 1980. Three children: Kevin Jr., Anne C., and Michael W.. Mr. Gaughen enjoys Bluewater Yacht racing and pistol match competition.

Melisa W. Gay
Sole Practitioner
Melisa W. Gay, P.C.
15 Broad Street
Charleston, SC 29401
(803) 937–0611
Fax: (803) 853–6872

8111

Business Information: Melisa W. Gay, P.C. is a full–service, general practice law firm, concentrating on criminal, family, and civil practice of law. A practicing attorney in South Carolina state courts since 1990, Mrs. Gay established her private law practice in 1995. Her practice concentrates on criminal matters both in civil and criminal courts, as well as conducting pro bono work in criminal cases. **Career Steps:** Sole Practitioner, Melisa W. Gay, P.C. (1995–Present); Attorney, Charleston County Public Defender (1991–1995); Attorney, State of South Carolina (1990); Student, University of South Carolina Law School (1987–1990). **Associations & Accomplishments:** Charleston Bar Association; South Carolina Bar Association; American Bar Association. **Education:** University of South Carolina, J.D. (1990); Furman University, B.A. **Personal:** Married to David T. Gay in 1990. One child: Sophia Belle.

Ms. Gaylynn Gee
Sole Practitioner
Law Office of Gaylynn Gee
P.O. Box 271558
Dallas, TX 75227
(214) 329–1201
Fax: (214) 288–0509

8111

Business Information: Law Office of Gaylynn Gee is a privately owned, general practice law office specializing in healthcare, hospital collections, personal injury, probate and family law. A practicing attorney since 1992, Gaylynn Gee established her individual practice in 1994. As Sole Practitioner, she is responsible for all aspects of operations and serves as an officer of the court representing her clients. **Career Steps:** Law Office of Gaylynn Gee (1994–Present); Attorney, Law Office of George T. Harris, P.C. (1992–1994). **Associations & Accomplishments:** American Bar Association; Texas Bar Association; Healthcare Financial Management Association. **Education:** Wake Forest University School of Law, J.D. (1990); University of Texas at Dallas, B.A. in Government. **Personal:** Ms. Gee enjoys church and golf.

Molly L. George
Director of Marketing
Quorum Group
3105 East 80th Street, Suite A2000
Minneapolis, MN 55425
(612) 858–6585
Fax: (612) 858–6656

8111

Business Information: Quorum Group provides diversified legal services to businesses, including automated document management and legal staffing. Concentrating primarily on litigation, the Company is headquartered in Minneapolis but has nine other locations, two of which are overseas. As Director of Marketing, Ms. George is responsible for all marketing communications, data research, strategic planning, publicity and public relations, in addition to supervision of a small support staff. **Career Steps:** Director of Marketing, Quorum Group (1991–Present); Director of Marketing, Access Management Corporation (1989–1991); Vice President, Associate Paralegal Cons. (1984–1989); Owner, George Litigation Services (1976–1984). **Associations & Accomplishments:** Phi Betta Kappa; Inland Lakes Yachting Association. **Education:** University of St. Thomas, M.B.A. (1990); University of Minnesota, B.A. in American Studies, Magna cum Laude. **Personal:** Married to Timothy M. Burke in 1972. One child: Kate Eileen Burke. Ms. George enjoys being a yacht racing judge for Inland Lakes Yachting Association.

Richard F. Gerry
Partner
Casey Gerry Reed & Schenk
110 Laurel Street
San Diego, CA 92101
(619) 238–1811
Fax: (907) 276–0288

8111

Business Information: Casey Gerry Reed & Schenk is a national, full–service, general practice law firm concentrating in personal injury and environmental law. Established in 1974, the Firm currently employs 40 attorneys, legal and administrative support staff. An esteemed attorney and acknowledged expert in environmental law since 1956, Richard Gerry is a Senior Partner with the Firm. He has been the representative in landmark cases for commercial fishermen's behalf in the Exxon Valdese and Prince Edward Sound destructions. Soon to retire from active practice, he will continue to serve in an Of Counsel capacity from his home in Anchorage, Alaska. **Career Steps:** Partner, Casey Gerry Reed & Schenk (1973–Present); Sole Practitioner (1967–1973); Partner, Behli Ashr & Gerry (1958–1967); Associate, Melvin M. Behli (1956–1958). **Associations & Accomplishments:** Association of Trial Lawyers of America: President (1981–1982), President Elect (1980–1981), Vice President–Secretary (1978–1980); Western Trial Lawyers Association: President (1970); American Board of Trial Advocates: President (1964); California Trial Lawyers; Published articles and interview on radio and television. **Education:** Columbia University School of Law, J.D. (1956); Columbia University School of General Studies, B.S. (1954). **Personal:** Married to Charlotte in 1962. Three children: Evelyn Adams, Lisa Whittaker, and David Gerry. Mr. Gerry enjoys fishing, hunting, sailing, flying, and golf.

Jeffrey Gery
Attorney
Coons, Maddox, & Koeller
9233 Aintree Drive
Indianapolis, IN 46250
(317) 574–2048
Fax: (317) 574–2050

8111

Business Information: Coons, Maddox, & Koeller, established in 1993, is a full–service, general practice law firm, concentrating on securities arbitration and litigation areas. Admitted to practice in Indiana state courts, Mr. Gery joined the Firm in 1994 upon the conferrral of his law degree. With his extensive background in risk management and insurance marketing, he focuses on securities and exchanges internationally, as well as mediation; particularly for the representation of investors against brokerage agencies. **Career Steps:** Attorney, Coons, Maddox, & Koeller (1994–Present). **Associations & Accomplishments:** American Bar Association; Indiana Bar Association; Public Investors Arbitration Bar Association; American Cancer Society – Golf Tournament; Indianapolis Entrepreneurs Academy; Frequent speaker to small groups. **Education:** Indiana University School of Law, J.D. (1994); Indiana University, B.A. in Economics and Political Science. **Personal:** Mr. Gery enjoys golf, gourmet cooking, and wine collecting.

Francis D. Gibson III
• • • ⬤ • • •

Sole Practitioner
Francis D. Gibson,
Attorney–at–Law
116 East Harper
Maryville, TN 37804
(423) 983–5642
Fax: (423) 681–3523

8111

Business Information: The Law Office of Francis D. Gibson, Attorney at Law is a general practice law firm concentrating on family law, personal injury and social security disability. As Sole Practitioner, Mr. Gibson is responsible for all aspects of legal operations. He also operates an evening walk–in clinic for his new and existing clients, a service unique to the legal profession. A trial attorney since 1966, he is admitted to both State and Federal courts. **Career Steps:** Sole Practitioner, Francis D. Gibson, Attorney–at–Law (1975–Present); Claims Adjuster, State Farm Insurance Company (1966–1975). **Associations & Accomplishments:** American Bar Association; Tennessee Bar Association; American Legion Post 123; Civitan Club of Maryville – Alcoa; Tennessee Association of Criminal Defense Lawyers. **Education:** University of Tennessee, J.D. (1966); United States Naval Academy (1961–1964). **Personal:** Married to Doris in 1969. Mr. Gibson enjoys golf, fishing, sporting events and attending University of Tennessee football games.

Elaine V. Giddens, C.C.P.
Director of Information Systems & Telecommunications
Powell, Goldstein, Frazer & Murphy
191 Peachtree Street
Atlanta, GA 30303–1740
(404) 572–4539
Fax: (404) 572–5950
EMAIL: See Below

8111

Business Information: Powell, Goldstein, Frazer & Murphy is a full–service, general practice law firm, providing legal representation in all aspects of law, with the exception of criminal law, from two locations in Georgia (Atlanta and Washington). With eighteen years of experience in computer applications, Ms. Giddens joined the Firm as Director of Information Systems & Telecommunications in 1988. She is responsible for the evaluation and recommendation of technology for use in all legal applications. Internet users can reach her via: egiddens%PGFM@MCIMAIL.COM **Career Steps:** Director of Information Systems & Telecommunications, Powell, Goldstein, Frazer & Murphy (1988–Present); Data Processing Manager, Trimline Sales Company (1983–1988); Systems Design Manager, System Dynamics, Inc. (1978–1983). **Associations & Accomplishments:** National Chairperson, Large Firm Advisory Counsel; Association of Legal Administrators; Information Managers of Atlanta; Computer Managers of Atlanta Law Firms; Institute for Certification of Computer Professionals; Volunteer, Hands on Atlanta; Volunteer, Habitat for Humanity. **Education:** University of Georgia, B.S. (1971). **Personal:** Ms. Giddens enjoys camping, bowling, theatre, and travel.

R. Marcus Givhan
Attorney at Law
Johnston, Barton, Proctor & Powell
1901 6th Avenue, North
Birmingham, AL 35203–2618
(205) 458–9400
Fax: (205) 458–9500

8111

Business Information: Johnston, Barton, Proctor & Powell, established in 1920, is a full–service, general practice law firm, concentrating in media law, commercial litigation, lender liability, health care, products liability, antitrust, securities law, and general litigation. Admitted to practice in Alabama and District of Columbia state and federal courts, Mr. Givhan joined the Firm as Counsel in 1995. He concentrates his practice in the areas of litigation, antitrust, administrative law and health care law. **Career Steps:** Counsel, Johnston, Barton, Proctor, Swedlaw & Naff (1995–Present); Deputy Attorney General, Office of the Alabama Attorney General (1991–1995); Deputy District Attorney, Office of Montgomery County District Attorney (1988–1991); Associate, Perry & Russell (1987–1988). **Associations & Accomplishments:** Alabama State Bar; Washington, D.C. Bar; Fellow, American College of Prosecuting Attorneys; Vice Chairman of the Antitrust, Competition and Trade Regulation Committee of the Administrative Practice Section of the American Bar Association; Admitted to: U.S. Supreme Court; U.S. Court of Appeals–District of Columbia Circuit; U.S. Court of Appeals – 11th Circuit. **Education:** Cumberland School of Law, J.D. (1986); The University of Alabama, B.A. (1981). **Personal:** Married to Janet Dothard Givhan in 1989. Two children: Vivian Lee and Charlotte Ann Givhan. Mr. Givhan enjoys hiking, music and book collecting.

Gary A. Godard, Esq.
President
Godard, West & Adelman, P.C.
3975 University Drive, Suite #220, P. O. Box 1287
Fairfax, VA 22030
(703) 273–4800
Fax: (703) 691–0804

8111

Business Information: Godard, West & Adelman, P.C. is a full–service law firm specializing in medical malpractice defense and personal injury (primarily dealing with hospitals and physicians). As President, Mr. Godard is responsible for all aspects of operations for the practice as well as serving as a Trial Attorney. Established in 1985, Godard, West & Adelman, P.C. employs 24 people with annual sales of $3 million. **Career Steps:** President, Godard, West & Adelman, P.C., (1985–Present); Partner, Donahue, Erhmentrast & Montedorio (1976–1985); Claims Manager, St. Paul Insurance Company (1990–1976). **Associations & Accomplishments:** American Bar Association; Virginia Trial Lawyers Association; Defense Research Institute; Best Lawyers in America (1993–1994 and 1994–1995). **Education:** American University, J.D. (1974); University of Oklahoma, B.A. Degree in Political Science (1962). **Personal:** Married to Virginia Godard in 1982. Mr. Godard enjoys golf and flying.

Mr. David O. Godwin, Jr.
Treasurer
Montedonico, Hamilton & Altman
220 North Market Street
Frederick, MD 21701
(301) 695–7004
Fax: (301) 695–0055

8111

Business Information: Montedonico, Hamilton & Altman is a multi–operational law firm with offices in Virginia, Maryland and the District of Columbia. Established in 1959, Montedonico, Hamilton & Altman with 40 attorneys representing the Firm, currently employs over 100 legal assistant and administrative clerical staff personnel. In addition to being a full trial lawyer with the Firm, Mr. Godwin is responsible for the management of offices in Maryland, Virginia and District of Columbia. **Career Steps:** Treasurer, Montedonico, Hamilton & Altman (1992–Present); Attorney and Partner, Montedonico,

Hamilton & Altman (1986–Present); Legal Counsel, Royal Insurance Company of America (1982–1985); Claim Representative, CNA Insurance Company (1978–1982). **Associations & Accomplishments:** American Bar Association; Maryland Bar Association; District of Columbia Bar Association; Montgomery County Bar Association; Frederick County Bar Association; Maryland Association of Defense Trial Counsel; National Association of Municipal Law Officers; Republican National Lawyers Association; Mens Republican Club of Frederick County; Lions Club. **Education:** Antioch–Potomac Law School, J.D. (1982); American University, B.A. (1977). **Personal:** Married since 1979 to Teresa. Three children: Julia, Kyle and Jennifer.

Rosemary G. Gold, Esq.

Principal/Attorney
Buckley King & Bluso Co. L.P.A.
Suite 1400, 600 Superior Avenue E
Cleveland, OH 44114–2652
(216) 363–1400
Fax: (216) 579–7156

8111

Business Information: Buckley King & Bluso Co. L.P.A. is a general practice law firm. With office locations in Akron, Columbus and Cleveland, Ohio, the Firm consists of 65 attorneys, legal and administrative support staff. A civil litigation attorney admitted to Ohio state and federal courts since 1982, Ms. Gold joined the Firm's Cleveland office in 1986 as a Principal and Attorney. A member of the Litigation Section and also serving on its Management Committee, she concentrates her practice in the representation and counsel for clients in civil defense, business litigation and family law. Other limited practice areas include insurance defense, personal injury, sexual and racial discrimination, and computer litigation. **Career Steps:** Principal/Attorney, Buckley King & Bluso Co. L.P.A. (1986–Present); Attorney/Associate, Parks, Eisele, Bates & Wilsman (1982–1986). **Associations & Accomplishments:** American Bar Association; Ohio State Bar Association; Cleveland Bar Association; Ohio Association of Civil Trial Attorneys; Cleveland–Marshall College of Law Alumni Association; Inn of Court No. 85; Board Member and Officer, Transitional Housing Inc. – (Housing facility for homeless women); Defense Research Institute; Speaker at National Business Institute Seminar and Cleveland Bar Association on family law matters. **Education:** Cleveland–Marshall College of Law, J.D. cum laude (1982); Notre Dame College of Ohio, B.A. magna cum laude (1979). **Personal:** Married to Gerald S. in 1994. Mrs. Gold enjoys tennis.

Michael Golden
Owner
Law Office of Michael Golden
710 Kingsway, Suite 718
Burnaby, British Co V5H 4M2
(604) 439–2420
Fax: (604) 435–2059

8111

Business Information: Law Office of Michael Golden is a full–service, general practice law firm, located in the greater Vancouver area, providing legal services to clientele in the Vancouver area, throughout British Columbia, China and Vietnam. A practicing attorney since 1985 in British Columbia courts, Mr. Golden established his private law practice in 1985. He oversees all administrative operations for associates and a support staff, in addition to his daily law practice. **Career Steps:** Owner, Law Office of Michael Golden (1985–Present) **Education:** University of British Columbia, L.L.B. (1984); Simon Fraser University, B.A. (1982). **Personal:** Married. Mr. Golden enjoys spending time with family and travel.

Mr. Richard A. Gollhofer
Partner
Staas & Halsey
700 Eleventh Street NW
Washington, DC 20001
(202) 434–1500
Fax: (202) 434–1501

8111

Business Information: Staas & Halsey is a general practice law firm specializing in the area of intellectual property. A practicing attorney since 1981, Richard Gollhofer joined the Firm as an associate in 1983, later to become Partner in 1990. Admitted to practice in state and federal courts, he specializes in patent preparations, prosecution and counseling, and firm management. **Career Steps:** Partner, Staas & Halsey (1990–Present); Associate, Staas & Halsey (1983–1989); Programmer/Systems Analyst, Chicago Public Works (1977–1983). **Associations & Accomplishments:** American Bar Association; American Intellectual Property Law

Association; District of Columbia Bar; Association for Computing Machinery; Adult Leader, Boy Scouts of America; Referee and Coach, Hernon Youth Soccer; Published in the Software Law Journal. **Education:** IIT/ Chicago – Kent, J.D. (1981). Rose – Hulman Institute of Technology, B.S. in Computer Science. **Personal:** Married to M. Theresa in 1977. Two children: Richard and Meghan.

Nydia Gonzales–Ortiz, Esq.
Associate Attorney
Santiago & Gonzales
Ponce de Leon Bldg., 42 Mattei Lluvreas Street, Suite 4
Yauco, Puerto Rico 00698
(809) 267–2205
Fax: (809) 856–7005

8111

Business Information: Santiago & Gonzales is a general practice law firm. A practicing attorney in Puerto Rico and U.S. state and federal courts since 1977, Ms. Ortiz joined the Firm in 1995. As Associate, she concentrates in the counsel and representation for matters pertaining to federal litigation and employment law. Growing up in the Bronx burroughs of New York City, she attributes her drive and success to the inspiration of her mother who told her she could be anything she wanted and could overcome the discrimination surrounding her. **Career Steps:** Associate Attorney, Santiago & Gonzales (1995–Present); Regional Supervisor, Puerto Rico Legal Services (1990–1995). **Associations & Accomplishments:** American Bar Association; Puerto Rico Bar Association **Education:** Catholic University Law School, J.D. (1977). **Personal:** Married to Adolfo Santiago, Esq. in 1982. Four children: Peter, Gustavo, Mario and Carolyn.

Dalia Stella Gonzalez Diaz

Principal Partner
Stella & Colon Perez
P.O. Box 960
Guayama, Puerto Rico 00785
(787) 864–5030
Fax: (787) 864–5069

8111

Business Information: Stella & Colon Perez is a general practice law firm which concentrates on municipal corporations, environmental law, and family law. A practicing attorney in Puerto Rican courts since obtaining her degree in 1987, Ms. Gonzalez Diaz founded the Firm in 1993. As Principal Partner, she is a trial lawyer and executive law firm coordinator. **Career Steps:** Principal Partner, Stella & Colon Perez (1993–Present); Vice President Legal, American Tire–System PR (1994). **Associations & Accomplishments:** Youngest Appointed to the Governor Office, Women Rights Commission (1983–1988); Caribbean Environmental Group; Script Advisor, Julie Mayoral's Theater Ballet Company. **Education:** Valladolid University Law School, Ph.D., J.D. (1996); Puerto Rico University: J.D. (1987), B.A. (1984). **Personal:** Ms. Gonzalez Diaz enjoys short story writing, composing music, and playing guitar.

Carmen M. Gonzalez–Gorritz, J.D.

Attorney
The Law Office of Carmen Gonzalez–Gorritz, J.D.
Box 852
Narajito, Puerto Rico 00719
(787) 869–4042
Fax: Please mail or call

8111

Business Information: The Law Office of Carmen Gonzalez–Gorritz, J.D. is a general practice law firm focusing on civil and criminal matters. The two member law firm also accepts some local pro–bono cases. As Attorney, Ms. Gonzalez–Gorritz works with clients in civil and criminal cases, with her primary focus on labor law. **Career Steps:** Attorney, The Law Office of Carmen Gonzalez–Gorritz, J.D. (1996–Present); Puerto Rico Legal Service Corporation: Director, Corozal Office (1988–1996), Lawyer III (1979–1985); Lawyer IV, Puerto Rico Labor Department (1985–1988). **Associations & Accomplishments:** Colegio de Abogados de Puerto Rico; Puerto Rico Bar Association. **Education:** University of Puerto Rico, J.D. (1975). **Personal:** Ms. Gonzalez–Gorritz enjoys reading and video taping scenery.

J. A. Gonzalez–Lecaroz

Sole Practitioner

The Law Office of J.A. Gonzalez, Attorney and Counselor at Law

6006 Bellaire Boulevard, Suite 206
Houston, TX 77081
(713) 665–4686
Fax: Please mail or call

8111

Business Information: A practicing attorney admitted to all Texas state courts and federal court since 1990, J.A. Gonzalez–Lecaroz established his private firm in 1992. As Sole Practitioner, he oversees all administrative support staff, in addition to his client base, concentrating in all areas of personal injury representation. **Career Steps:** Attorney, The Law Offices of J.A. Gonzalez (1992–Present); Claims Negotiator and Attorney, Makris, Warren & Brockway (1988–1992); Claims Representative and Senior Claims Examiner, Ranger Insurance Company (1984–1988). **Associations & Accomplishments:** State Bar of Texas; Houston Bar Association; American Bar Association; Association of Trial Lawyers of America; American Translators Association. **Education:** University of Houston, LL.M. (International Economic Law) (1994); University of Puerto Rico: A.A. (1975), B.B.A. (1977), J.D (1980). **Personal:** Married to Iris E. Guzman in 1980. One child: Alanna. Mr. Gonzalez–Lecaroz enjoys reading about American film history, travel, writing, bookstores and motion pictures. His LL.M. Masters degree paper dealt with film, censorship and international law, fields he seeks to get more involved in professionally.

Arturo Gonzalez–Martin, Esq.

Attorney

Law Offices of Arturo Gonzalez–Martin, Esq.

P.O. Box 193377
San Juan, Puerto Rico 00919–3377
(809) 250–8982
Fax: (809) 250–0118

8111

Business Information: The Law Offices of Auturo Gonzalez–Martin, Esq., established in 1981, is a full–service, general practice law firm, concentrating on bankruptcy cases and criminal work. Clientele include financial institutions, the Chamber of Commerce, Coca Cola and Pepsi. A practicing attorney in Puerto Rico state courts since 1981, Mr. Gonzalez–Martin established his sole practice legal office in 1981. He is responsible for all aspects of operations, including providing legal representation, overseeing a support staff of four, and serving as a Notary Public. **Career Steps:** Sole Practitioner, Law Offices of Arturo Gonzalez–Martin, Esq. (1980–Present); Advisor, Senate Commonwealth of Puerto Rico (1995–Present); United States Bankruptcy Court District of Puerto Rico: Trustee (1983–1985), Estate Administrator (1981–1983). **Associations & Accomplishments:** Published in Puerto Rico newspapers; Lecturer in Puerto Rico Bar Association; Interviewed on talk and radio shows; Guest speaker at law schools. **Education:** InterAmerican University, J.D. (1981). **Personal:** Married to Bernice Marrero in 1975. Four children: Daniel, Annette, Jose, and Karina. Mr. Gonzalez–Martin enjoys breeding Paso Fino horses.

Noel S. Gonzalez–Miranda

Partner

Gonzalez & Cestero

P.O. Box 364251
San Juan, Puerto Rico 00936–4251
(787) 767–9494
Fax: (787) 281–6585

8111

Business Information: Gonzalez & Cestero is a full–service general practice law firm. They engage in such legal matters as civil and commercial law. A practicing attorney in Puerto Rico courts since 1967, Mr. Gonzalez–Miranda co–founded the Firm in 1994. **Career Steps:** Partner, Gonzalez & Cestero (1994–Present); Partner, McConnell Valdes (1993–1994); Managing Partner, Sweeting Gonzalez & Cestero (1972–1993). **Associations & Accomplishments:** Fellow, American Bar Foundation; American Bar Association. **Education:** Harvard Law School, LL.M. (1968); University of Puerto Rico: B.B.A. (1964), LL.B. (1967). **Personal:** Married to Celeste in 1970. Three children: Noel, Beatriz, and Carlos Ivan.

Ann Paton Goodman

Partner

McCullough, Campbell & Lane

401 N. Michigan Avenue, Suite 1300
Chicago, IL 60611–4277
(312) 923–4000
Fax: (312) 923–4329

8111

Business Information: McCullough, Campbell & Lane is a full–service, general practice law firm, specializing in defense work (insurance, aviation, and product liability). Joining the Firm as an Associate in 1987, Ms. Goodman was appointed as Partner in 1993. Serving as the Firm's senior female partner, her practice concentrates on commercial and aviation litigation, as well as conducting appellate work in state and federal courts. **Career Steps:** McCullough, Campbell & Lane: Partner (1993–Present), Associate (1987–1992); Associate, Peterson, Ross, Schloerb & Seidel (1984–1987). **Associations & Accomplishments:** International Association of Women in Aviation; Bar of the U.S. Supreme Court. **Education:** Vanderbilt University Law School, J.D. (1984); Wellesley College, A.B. (1979). **Personal:** Ms. Goodman enjoys cycling, skiing, golf and foreign travel.

Pamela L. Gordon

Lawyer and Operations Manager

Robinson & Dixon Attorneys

1259 Metropolitan Avenue
Atlanta, GA 30316–1901
(404) 688–0254
Fax: (404) 688–0717

8111

Business Information: Robinson & Dixon Attorneys, established in 1988, is a general civil law firm. Consisting of eight attorneys, the Firm's main focus is on personal injury matters, however it also provides limited domestic law and criminal defense representation. As Lawyer and Operations Manager, Pamela Gordon is responsible for the supervision of 12 employees, making sure the files are correct and calls are made on time. She reports settlement proposals to the Senior Attorney, Mr. Robinson. Ms. Gordon hopes to run for a legislative office in the future. **Career Steps:** Lawyer and Operations Manager, Robinson & Dixon Attorneys (1990–Present); Legal Assistant, Charels B. Pekier Jr., Attorney (1985–1988); Legal Assistant, Jim White Attorney Office (1984–1985). **Associations & Accomplishments:** Dekalb City Zoning Community Council; Georgia Trial Lawyer Association; Sigma Delta Kappa Law Fraternity; Who's Who American Colleges and University. **Education:** Woodrow Wilson College of Law, J.D. (1986); Clark Atlanta University, B.A. (1983). **Personal:** Ms. Gordon enjoys being with her dog, shopping, and working with animals.

Kathryn S. Grant Belleau, Esq.

Owner

Future Endeavors

5830 Dogwood Drive, Suite 200
Lincoln, NE 68516
(402) 486–4117
Fax: (402) 486–4117

8111

Business Information: Future Endeavors is an intellectual property legal consulting firm, specializing in new product development for small– to mid–sized companies. The firm is also able to search trademarks and apply for formal protection on a global basis. Recently establishing her own business, Mrs. Grant Belleau is the Principal Attorney responsible for all legal consulting activities. **Career Steps:** Owner and Principal Attorney, Future Endeavors (1995–Present); Corporate Counsel, American Tool Companies, Inc. (1992–1995); Senior Associate, Lackenbach Seigel et al (1987–1992); Paralegal, The Law Office of Karl F. Ross, P.C. (1975–1987). **Associations & Accomplishments:** American Bar Association: Business Law Section, IPR Section, Tort and Insurance Law Section; International Trademark Association; New York State Bar Association. **Education:** Brooklyn Law School, J.D. (1983); McGill University – Montreal, B.A. **Personal:** Married to John in 1988. One child: Sean. Mrs. Grant Belleau enjoys foreign languages, gardening, travel, and spending time with her family.

Stephen J. Grifferty

Founding Partner

Tobin–Grifferty, P.C.

1 Executive Centre Drive
Albany, NY 12203
(518) 452–2552
Fax: (518) 452–0175

8111

Business Information: Tobin–Grifferty, P.C. is a full–service, four–attorney general practice law firm, with focus on health, non–profit, and corporate law. The Firm also represents numerous religious orders. A practicing attorney in New York state courts since 1987, Mr. Grifferty founded the Firm in 1992. Serving as Founding Partner, he manages all aspects of operations for the Firm, as well as representing clients in not–for–profit and business environments in health care, real estate, and elder law, as well as charitable giving and title insurance defense. Career milestones include being the first in New York State to develop an offering plan for the retirement community. He also set the precedence in New York State law. **Career Steps:** Founding Partner, Tobin–Grifferty, P.C. (1992–Present); Associate Attorney, Tobin and Dempf (1988–1992); Title Examiner, Gifford Abstract Corporation (1981–1988); Special Counsel, Town of Cambridge. **Associations & Accomplishments:** New York State Bar Association; Albany & Schonoctady County Bar Associations; National Health Lawyers Association; New York State Association of Homes and Services for the Aged; American Association of Homes and Services for the Aged; General Counsel – Medical Society of Albany County; General Counsel – Northeast Health; Chair of Planned Giving Committee and Finance Committee Member, St. John the Evangelist Church, Schenectady, NY. **Education:** Union University Albany Law School, J.D. (1987); University of the State of New York at Albany, B.S. in Accounting. **Personal:** Married to Katherine Riker in 1988. Two children: Matthew and Sarah. Mr. Grifferty enjoys home renovations, antique collector, and is a Bing Crosby enthusiast.

Benjamin E. Griffith

Attorney at Law

Griffith & Griffith

P.O. Box 1680
Cleveland, MS 38732–1680
(601) 843–6100
Fax: (601) 843–8153

8111

Business Information: Griffith & Griffith is a general practice law firm. Established in 1975, the Firm currently employs three attorneys and legal support staff. A trial attorney since 1975, Mr. Griffith concentrates his practice in the areas of federal and state civil litigation. Admitted to both State and Federal courts, Mr. Griffith is also a Board Attorney with the Bolivar County Board of Supervisors and the YMD Joint Water Management District. **Career Steps:** Attorney at Law, Griffith & Griffith (1975–Present); Board Attorney: Bolivar County Board of Supervisors (1983–Present), YMD Joint Water Management District (1986–Present). **Associations & Accomplishments:** President, National Association of County Civil Attorneys (1992–1993); National Institute of Municipal Law Officers, Recorder, Litigation and Risk Management Section; Chairman, Mississippi Bar Association, Government Law Section (1992–1993); President, Mississippi Association of County Board Attorneys (1989–1990); President, Cleveland Noon Lions Club (1981–1982); National Board of Trial Advocacy Certification in Civil Trial Advocacy; Defense Research Institute, Governmental Liability Committee; Mississippi Defense Lawyers Association; American Bar Association: State and Local Government Section, Law Government Operations Committee Member, Torts and Insurance Practice Section, and Litigation Section; Professional Liability Committee of the Mississippi Bar; Mississippi Law Journal Association. **Education:** University of Mississippi Law Center, J.D. (1975); University of Mississippi, B.A. in English and German (1973). **Personal:** Married to Kathy Orr in 1974. Two children: Benjamin Clark and Julie Faulkner. Mr. Griffith enjoys downhill skiing, youth work, travel.

John P. Griffith

Director

Hamblett & Kerrigan P.A.

One Indian Head Plaza, 7th Floor
Nashua, NH 03060–3467
(603) 883–5501
Fax: (603) 880–0458

8111

Business Information: Hamblett & Kerrigan P.A. is a full–service, general practice law firm. A practicing attorney in New Hampshire state and federal courts since 1966, Mr. Griffith joined the Firm in 1971 as an associate and served as President of the firm from 1987 through 1991 overseeing the operations for lawyers and support staff of more than 40. He now serves as a Director and maintains a law practice concentrated in the areas of commercial litigation, products liability, and family law. **Career Steps:** Hamblett & Kerrigan P.A.: Attorney/Director (1991–Present), Attorney/President (1987–1991), Attorney/Director (1972–1986); Associate, McLane, Carleton, Graf, Greene & Brown (1966–1971). **Associations & Accomplishments:** New Hampshire Trial Lawyers Association: President (1985–1986), Board of Governors Award (1990); Association of Trial Lawyers of America; Board of Governors (1986–1990), Recipient – Weidman–Wysocki Citation of Excellence (1990); President (1986–1987), Nashua Bar Associaton; Board of Governors (1978–1980), New Hampshire Bar Association; American Bar Association, Litigation Section and Family Law Section; American Board of Trial Advocates; Fellow, International Society of Barristers;

Board of Trustees (1993–Present), New Hampshire Bar Foundation; Master: American Inns of Court, Daniel Webster Chapter, Counselor (1994–1995); Certified Civil Trial Advocate; National Board of Trial Advocacy (1990–Present); Trained Divorce Arbitrator, Divorce Arbitration Institute (1995). **Education:** Boston University School of Law, LL.B. (1966); University of New Hampshire, B.S. (1961). **Personal:** Married to Joan H. in 1965. Three children: Robert W., Joel C. and James H. Griffith. Mr. Griffith enjoys golf, tennis, hiking, and reading.

J. Ernesto Grijalva
Sole Practitioner
Law Offices of J. Ernesto Gritlolva
550 West B. Street, Suite 340
San Diego, CA 92101
(619) 234–1776
Fax: (619) 235–6749

8111

Business Information: The Law Office of J. Ernesto Grijalva is an international law firm. Establishing his practice in 1987, Mr. Grijlava is admitted to both State and Federal courts, as well as the international law arena. A trial attorney since 1984, he concentrates his practice in the areas of business litigation. **Career Steps:** Sole Practitioner, The Law Office of J. Ernesto Grijalva (1987–Present); Associate Attorney, Hollywood & Neil (1986–1987); Recruitment Coordinator, University of San Diego School of Law (1984–1985); United Sttes International University: Adjunct Faculty – Legal Environment of International Business, Member – College of Business Advisory Board; Consultant, Southwestern Colleges Small Business Development and International Trade Center. **Associations & Accomplishments:** American Bar Association; San Diego County Bar Association: Member and Co-Chair (1989–1992) Mexican Bar Liaison Committee; Inter – American Bar Association; Hispanic National Bar Association; California Bar Association; San Diego La Raza Lawyers; International Lawyers; Co–Chair – International Trade Development Committee, San Diego County Board of Supervisors Economic Advisory Board; Greater San Diego Chamber of Commerce: Board of Directors, Co–Chair – San Diego NAFTA Coalition (1993), Chair – International Trade Development Coalition, Business Advisor – Small Business Development Center; American Arbitration Association: Panel of Neutrals, Asia/Pacific Center for the Resolution of International Business Disputes; University of San Diego School of Law Board of Visitors; University of San Diego School of Law Alumni Association: Board of Directors (1988–1994), President (1992–1993); San Diego/Tijuana Sister Cities Society (Since 1993): Board of Directors, Vice–President Community and Municipal Relations; Founding Member and Secretary (1991–1994), Border Region Action Group; Board Member, Miramar Community College International Business Advisory Board; Foreign Observer to Mexico's 1994 Presidential Elections. **Education:** University of San Diego School of law, J.D. (1984); University of California at San Diego, B.A. in Political Science (1981). **Personal:** Married to Rebecca in 1976. Two children: Lauren Theresa and Julian David.

Gregory H. Guillot
Managing Partner
Guillot & Gazala, L.L.P.
1660 L Street, Suite 316
Washington, DC 20036
(202) 955–1100
Fax: (202) 955–1100
EMAIL: See Below

8111

Business Information: Guillot & Gazala, L.L.P. is an international full–service, general practice law firm, specializing in trademark law. A practicing attorney in Louisiana state courts since 1986, Mr. Guillot co–established the Firm in 1995. Serving as Managing Partner, he oversees all administrative operations for associates and a support staff, in addition to his daily law practice. He can also be reached through the Internet as follows: ggmark@radix.net **Career Steps:** Managing Partner, Guillot & Gazala, L.L.P. (1995–Present); Partner, Midlen & Guillot, Chartered (1989–1995). **Associations & Accomplishments:** American Bar Association; Louisiana State Bar Association; American Intellectual Property Law Association; International Trademark Association; Inter–American Industrial Property Association; Federal Communications Bar Association **Education:** Tulane University School of Law, J.D. (1986); Vanderbilt University, B.A. in Philosophy (1983). **Personal:** Mr. Guillot enjoys anything to do with computers.

Michael T. Gunner
Sole Practitioner
Michael T. Gunner Law Offices
3455 Mill Run Drive, Suite 101
Hilliard, OH 43026–9080
(614) 777–1203
Fax: (614) 771–7078

8111

Business Information: A practicing attorney since 1973 in Ohio state and federal courts, Michael Gunner concentrates his private practice in the areas of bankruptcy and litigation. A widely acknowledged expert in this area of law, he also serves as a Trustee in Bankruptcy for Ohio's U.S. Bankruptcy Court, as well as serving as Hearing Officer for the State of Ohio's Department of Health. **Career Steps:** Michael T. Gunner Law Offices, Sole Practitioner (1973–Present); Trustee in Bankruptcy, U.S. Bankruptcy Court (1988–Present); Hearing Officer, State of Ohio – Dept. of Public Health (1978–Present). **Associations & Accomplishments:** American Bar Association; Ohio State Bar Association; Columbus Bar Association; Dayton Bar Association; National Association of Bankruptcy Trustees; American Bankruptcy Institute; American Trial Lawyers Association; National Association of Consumer Bankruptcy Counsel; Knights of Columbus; Thomas More Society. **Education:** Capital University, LL.M. (1988); University of Toledo: J.D. cum laude (1973), B.A. (1970); University of Detroit (1966–1968). **Personal:** Married to Barbara in 1974. Two children: Lora P. and Michelle N. Mr. Gunner enjoys reading and numismatics.

Santiago Gutierrez–Armstrong, Esq.
Attorney
Law Office of Santiago Gutierrez–Armstrong, Esq.
Plaza San Francisco, Suite 210, 201 De Diego Ave.
San Juan, Puerto Rico 00927–5817
(809) 250–8002
Fax: (809) 250–6857

8111

Business Information: The Law Office of Santiago Gutierrez–Armstrong, Esq. is a general practice law firm, serving corporate clientele throughout Puerto Rico in the areas of worker's compensation and employers' liability statutes representation. A practicing attorney since 1981, Mr. Gutierrez–Armstrong established his private legal practice following a successful corporate career with some of the leading insurance consulting groups in the country. As Sole Practitioner, he oversees all areas of the Firm, assisting employers in reducing their work–related accidents and costs of insurance programs, as well as extensive arbitration and mediation in legislative appeals. **Career Steps:** Attorney, Law Office of Santiago Gutierrez–Armstrong, Esq. (1995–Present); President and Chief Executive Officer, Allied Advisory Group (1991–1995); Practice Leader, The Wyatt Company (1985–1990); Director of Insurance, State Insurance Fund (1979–1985). **Associations & Accomplishments:** American Bar Association; Puerto Rico Bar Association. **Education:** Inter American University of Puerto Rico, J.D. (1981). **Personal:** Married to Neysa in 1965. Two children: Santiago Agustin and Jorge Alberto. One grandson: Jorge Alberto, Jr. Mr. Gutierrez–Armstrong enjoys boating.

Jennifer Haltom–Doan
Partner
Patton, Haltom, Roberts, McWilliams & Greer, L.L.P.
P.O. Box 1928
Texarkana, TX 45504
(903) 794–3341
Fax: (903) 792–6542

8111

Business Information: Patton, Haltom, Roberts, McWilliams & Greer, L.L.P. is a full–service, general practice law firm, serving clients nationwide from one location in Texarkana, Texas. A practicing attorney since 1989, Ms. Haltom–Doan joined the Firm as Partner in 1995. Her practice concentrates on commercial litigation, defense and prosecution, and insurance disputes. **Career Steps:** Partner, Patton, Haltom, Roberts, McWilliams & Greer, L.L.P. (1995–Present); Attorney, Figari & Davenport (1989–1995). **Education:** University of Texas – School of Law, J.D. (1989); Abilene Christian University, B.B.A. (1986). **Personal:** Married to Darby in 1991. Ms. Haltom–Doan enjoys tennis and golf.

Ms. Deborah R. Hambleton
Partner
Rexon, Freedman, et al.
12100 Wilshire Boulevard, Suite 730
Los Angeles, CA 90025–7107
(310) 826–8300
Fax: (310) 826–0333

8111

Business Information: Established in 1985, Rexon, Freedman, et al. is a full–service law firm. A practicing attorney since 1983, Ms. Hambleton joined The Firm in 1987 and now concentrates in labor relations law, specifically in the resolution of management disputes. **Career Steps:** Partner, Rexon, Freedman, et al. (1987–Present); Attorney, Calif. Edison Co. (1983–1987). **Associations & Accomplishments:** American Bar Association – Los Angeles County Chapter; California Bar Association; Los Angeles Bar Association; County Bar Labor and Employment Law Section; Women of Achievement Award, Los Angeles (1992 & 1993). **Education:** Pepperdine Law School, J.D. (1984); University of Nevada – Reno, B.A. **Personal:** Married to Wendell L. McClenton in 1993. Ms. Hambleton enjoys sports events and reading novels.

Cary Hammond
Attorney
Diekemper, Hammond, Shinners, Turcotte & Larrew, P.C.
7730 Carondelet, Suite 200
Clayton, MO 63105
(314) 727–1015
Fax: (314) 727–6804

8111

Business Information: Diekemper, Hammond, Shinners, Turcotte & Larrew, P.C. is a general civil practice law firm specializing in labor and employee benefits law. Established in 1979, the Firm consists of 17 attorneys. Cary Hammond serves as Managing Principal. He focuses his practice in the areas of labor and employee benefits law. **Career Steps:** Principal, Diekemper, Hammond, Shinners, Turcotte & Larrew, P.C. (1979–Present); Associate, Bartley, Goffstein, Bollato & Lange (1976–1979); Associate, Hearnes, Paberg, McSweeney & Slater (1975). **Associations & Accomplishments:** Missouri Bar Association; Bar Association of Metropolitan St. Louis; Lawyers Association of St. Louis. **Education:** St. Louis University Law School, J.D. (1975); University of Missouri – St. Louis, B.A. (1970). **Personal:** Married to Leigh in 1976. One child: Clayton. Mr. Hammond enjoys travel and tennis.

Mr. Herbert J. Hammond
Shareholder
Thompson & Knight, P.C.
1700 Pacific Avenue, Suite 3300
Dallas, TX 75201
(214) 969–1607
Fax: (214) 969–1751

8111

Business Information: Thompson & Knight, P.C. is an international full–service, general practice law firm. The Firm, with four offices located in Texas (Dallas, Houston, Austin and Ft. Worth) and one in Monterey, Mexico, currently employs 500 people, including 200 attorneys. A practicing attorney since 1976, Herbert Hammond joined the Firm as partner and senior shareholder in 1994. He specializes in the counsel and representation for individual and international corporate clientele in matters pertaining to intellectual property, computer and entertainment law. **Career Steps:** Shareholder, Thompson & Knight, P.C. (1994–Present); Partner, Gardere & Wynne (1984–1994); Associate, Gardere & Wynne (1983–1984); Associate, Richards, Harris & Mellock (1976–1983). **Associations & Accomplishments:** American Bar Association; American Intellectual Property Law Association; Phi Beta Kappa. **Education:** New York University, J.D. (1976); University of New Mexico, B.S. in Mathematics and Physics. **Personal:** Married to Myra in 1980. Two children: Ariel and Herbert J. Hammond V.

James W. Han
Attorney–at–Law
Cates & Han, L.L.P.
19800 MacArthur Boulevard, Suite 1450
Irvine, CA 92715–2442
(714) 757–4104
Fax: (714) 757–4107
E-mail: see below

8111

Business Information: A trial attorney since 1983, Mr. Han concentrates his practice in the areas of business litigation, with an emphasis on franchising and unfair competition and business practices. In practice since 1990 with two other attorneys who also concentrate in corporate law, Mr. Han is admitted to both State and Federal courts. With the aid of the six legal staff members, the Firm plans to expand to a premier franchise law practice for the state of California. Concurrent to his legal practice, Mr. Han is also an Instructor of Franchise and Business Opportunity Laws at the University of California – Irvine Extension. **Career Steps:** Partner and Attorney, Cates & Han, L.L.P. (1990–Present); Sole Practitioner Attorney (1984–1990).. **Associations & Accomplishments:** Business Law Section and Chairman of Franchise Law Committee, California State Bar Association; Forum on Franchising, American Bar Association; Steering Committee, American Association of Franchisees and Dealers; Orange County Asian American Bar Association. **Education:** University of California – Hastings College of the Law, J.D. (1983); University of California – Berkeley, A.B. **Personal:** Married to Tami Joycelyn in 1987. Five children: Justin, Julianna, Jenna, Joshua, and Joseph.

Nathan E. Hardwick, IV
Partner

Jackson and Hardwick Law Firm
1707 Mount Vernon Road
Dunwoody, GA 30338
(770) 392–0500
Fax: (770) 392–0479

8111

Business Information: Jackson and Hardwick Law Firm is a full–service, general practice law firm specializing in real estate law, with concentration in closings, land negotiations, corporate transactions, wills and trusts. Established in 1994, the Firm currently employs 35 legal professionals. Mr. Hardwick established the Firm with his partner, Mr. Jackson in 1994. As Partner he is responsible for day–to–day activities of the multi–office Firm, and represents clients in real estate and corporate law. **Career Steps:** Partner, Jackson and Hardwick Law Firm (1994–Present); Senior Associate, Jackson, Feagin and Tanner (1990–1993); Law Clerk, South Carolina Senate Judiciary Committee (1987–1989); Graduate Advisor, Tau Kappa Epsilon Fraternity (1986–1987). **Associations & Accomplishments:** Tau Kappa Epsilon Fraternity; Founding Member and Board of Trustees, Scroll #1; American Bar Association; Georgia Bar Association; Member of Dunwoody, Beech Mountain, Melrose, and the University Country Clubs. **Education:** University of South Carolina, J.D. (1990); University of South Carolina, B.S. in Business Administration. **Personal:** Married to Terri in 1994. Mr. Hardwick enjoys being a civil war buff and entrepreneur, playing golf and sports.

Lance August Harke
Attorney

Steel, Hector & Davis, L.L.P.
200 South Biscayne Boulevard, Suite 4000
Miami, FL 33131–2398
(305) 577–2951
Fax: (305) 577–7001
EMAIL: See Below

8111

Business Information: Established in the Roaring '20s, Steel, Hector & Davis, L.L.P. is a full–service law firm. Mr. Harke joined The Firm in 1990 after attaining his J.D., cum laude, from the University of Miami. Currently, he specializes in product liability cases, accountant malpractice, environmental disputes, and general commercial litigation. Internet users can reach him via: LHarke@counsel.com. **Career Steps:** Attorney, Steel, Hector & Davis, L.L.P.(1990–Present). **Associations & Accomplishments:** Advisory Committee, Village of Miami Shores; Board Member, Friends of Fellowship House. **Education:** University of Miami, J.D. cum laude (1990); University of Florida, B.A. in Philosophy, with honors (1987). **Personal:** Married to Alison in 1990. Two children: Jacob and Erik.

Roger L. Haskell, Esq.

Attorney

Law Offices of Roger L. Haskell
4897 Cass Street
San Diego, CA 92109
(619) 273–2140
Fax: (619) 273–2140

8111

Business Information: A practicing attorney since 1985, Roger L. Haskell established his private practice in 1996, concentrating in traumatic brain injury law. Mr. Haskell and the Firm's two other attorneys represent clients on a national basis and advise clients internationally. In addition, Mr. Haskell is also a researcher and inventor at Rowlstone International in Canada, a family–owned development firm. **Career Steps:** Attorney, Law Offices of Roger L. Haskell (1996–Present);

Researcher/Inventor, Rowlstone International (1994–Present); Partner, Brown & Haskell, APLC (1991–1995); Attorney, Aguirre & Eckman (1991). **Associations & Accomplishments:** International Brain Injury Association; National Brain Injury Association; American Trial Lawyers Association; Disabilities Awareness Week Network; San Diego County Bar Association; California State Bar Association; American Bar Association. **Education:** Western Sierra School of Law, J.D. (1985); Bucknell University, B.A. (1980). **Personal:** Mr. Haskell is an inventor and enjoys surfing and the restoration of vintage automobiles.

Samuel C. Hasler
Senior Attorney

Law Office of Samuel C. Hasler
334 West 8th Street
Anderson, IN 46016
(317) 644–6606
Fax: (317) 640–9348

8111

Business Information: A practicing attorney in Indiana state and federal courts since 1987, Mr. Hasler established his private practice law firm in 1993. Serving as Senior Attorney, he is responsible for all aspects of operations, in addition to his daily law practice. His practice concentrates on bankruptcy, criminal defense and consumer protection law. **Career Steps:** Senior Partner, Law Office of Samuel C. Hasler (1993–Present); Sole Practitioner (1980–1992). **Associations & Accomplishments:** American Bar Association; Indiana Bar Association; Madison County Bar Association; East Central Legal Services; Published in Valparaiso Law Review. **Education:** Valparaiso University School of Law, J.D. (1987); Ball State University, B.S.

John D. Hastie

President

The Hastie Law Firm
3000 Oklahoma Tower, 210 Park Avenue
Oklahoma City, OK 73102
(405) 239–6404
Fax: (405) 239–6403

8111

Business Information: The Hastie Law Firm is a full–service, general practice law firm consisting of 20 attorneys. The Firm concentrates on commercial law, litigation, environmental law, bankruptcy, banking, energy and real estate. A practicing attorney in Oklahoma and New York state courts since 1964, Mr. Hastie established his private law practice in 1974. Serving as President and Sole Shareholder, he oversees all administrative operations for associates and a support staff of 16, in addition to his daily law practice. His focus is on banking, bankruptcy, corporate, and real estate law. **Career Steps:** President, The Hastie Law Firm (1974–Present); Adjunct Professor, University of Oklahoma College of Law (1982–1990); Captain, US Army (1964–1966) **Associations & Accomplishments:** American Bar Association; Oklahoma Bar Association; Oklahoma County Bar Association; Association of the Bar of the City of New York; American College of Mortgage Attorneys; American College of Real Estate Lawyers; Governor (1990–1994), Executive Committee (1992–1993), Secretary (1994–1995); Anglo American Real Property Institute; American Law Institute; Phi Delta Phi Law Fraternity; Hawes Award (1964); Frequent lecturer at international, national, state and local conferences and institutional symposia and proceedings. **Education:** University of Oklahoma: LL.B. (1964), B.A. (1961) **Personal:** Married to Nita G. in 1980. Mr. Hastie enjoys fishing.

Mr. John J. Hay
Partner

Feldman & Hay
100 Park Avenue, 35th Floor
New York, NY 10017–5516
(212) 808–9500
Fax: (212) 808–9506

8111

Business Information: Feldman & Hay is a full–service, general practice law firm concentrating on commercial litigation, transactional corporate work, commercial arbitration, trust & estate, and personal injury cases. Established in 1988, the Firm currently employs 13 attorneys, legal and administrative support staff. Admitted to practice in New York and Connecticut state and federal courts since 1980, Mr. Hay joined the Firm in 1988 as Partner. He concentrates his practice in the areas of commercial litigation and limited trial cases. **Career Steps:** Partner, Feldman & Hay (1988–Present); Associate and Partner, Wood Lucksinger & Epstein (1986–1987); Associate, Traub & Lesser (1984–1986); Associate, Walsh & Frisch (1980–1984). **Associations & Accomplishments:** American Red Cross; American Bar Association; New York Bar Association; Connecticut Bar Association; Federal Bar

Council; Corporate Volunteers in Action (Connecticut). **Education:** George Washington University, J.D. (1980); State University of New York, B.A. (1977). **Personal:** Married to Loretta A. Lacci in 1986. Three children: John Christopher, Jacquelyn Michele, and Alexandra Nicole. Mr. Hay enjoys golf and tennis.

Chantal M. Healey
Litigation Attorney

Peabody and Arnold
50 Rowes Wharf
Boston, MA 02110–3328
(617) 951–2041
Fax: (617) 951–2125

8111

Business Information: Peabody and Arnold is a general practice law firm. Headquartered in Boston, Massachusetts with a satellite office in Providence, Rhode Island, the Firm consists of 62 partners and 43 associate attorneys. Joining the Firm upon conferral of her law degree in 1990, Ms. Healey serves as an associate with the Litigation Section. She concentrates her practice in the areas of commercial business law, environmental law, personal injury, and employment law. **Career Steps:** Litigation Attorney, Peabody and Arnold (1990–Present). **Associations & Accomplishments:** Massachusetts Bar Association: Individual Rights and Responsibilities Section, Labor and Employment Law Section; American Bar Association: International Law Litigation Section, Health Law Forum Litigation Section, Tort and Insurance Practice Section, Litigation Section; United Nations Association of Greater Boston; Volunteer Lawyers Project. **Education:** Boston College School of Law, J.D. (1990); Boston College, B.A. (1987). **Personal:** Married to Tim Healey in 1990.

Alan R. Hecht
Attorney and Certified Public Accountant

Law Office of Alan R. Hecht
2670 NE 215th Street
Miami, FL 33180–1127
(305) 933–1441
Fax: (305) 935–2041

8111

Business Information: Alan R. Hecht has been a member of the Florida Bar since 1974, and is admitted to both State and Federal Courts. He concentrates his practice representing individuals, professionals, businesses, and corporations in all aspects of tax planning, tax matters before the Internal Revenue Service including tax audits, Offers in Compromise, and tax litigation before the U.S. Tax Court, trusts and estates, acquisition and leasing transactions, general corporate matters, real estate and commercial litigation. **Career Steps:** Attorney, Law Office of Alan R. Hecht (1983–Present); Tax Partner, Fine, Jacobson & Block (1981–1983); Senior Tax Associate, Paul & Thomson (1979–1980); Senior Tax Manager, Coopers & Lybrand, CPA's (1974–1979). **Associations & Accomplishments:** American Bar Association; Florida Bar Association; New York State Bar Association; American Institute of Certified Public Accountants; Florida Institute of Certified Public Accountants; New York Institute of Certified Public Accountants; American Association of Attorneys – Certified Public Accountants; Greater Miami Tax Institute; Published in Florida Trend and other journals. **Education:** St. John's University School of Law, J.D. (1974); Pennsylvania State University, B.S. in Accounting; Certified Public Accountant. **Personal:** Married to Marsha in 1972. Two children: Rachel and Alana. Mr. Hecht enjoys reading, fishing and computers.

John R. Heitkamp Jr.
Partner

Foley & Lardner
777 East Wisconsin Avenue
Milwaukee, WI 53202–5367
(414) 297–5842
Fax: (414) 297–4900

8111

Business Information: Foley & Lardner, established in 1842, is an international, general practice law firm with 14 offices in Florida, California, Illinois, Wisconsin, and the District of Columbia. A practicing attorney since 1985, Mr. Heitkamp joined the Firm in 1989. Now a Partner, he concentrates in corporate insurance regulatory law, insurance coverage, and risk management. **Career Steps:** Foley and Lardner: Partner (1994–Present); Attorney (1989–1994); Attorney, Whyte & Hirschboeck, S.C. (1985–1989). **Associations & Accomplishments:** American Bar Association; State Bar Association of Wisconsin; Milwaukee Bar Association; Minnesota Bar Association; Hennepin County Bar Association; National Health Lawyers Association. **Education:** Notre Dame Law School, J.D. (1985); University of Notre Dame, M.M.S. (1982); College of St. Thomas, B.A.; L'Universite de Fribourg, Switzerland (1977–1978). **Personal:** Married to Kathleen M. in 1977. Six children: Marie–Therese, Rachel, Thomas, Margaret, Michael and Robert. Mr. Heitkamp enjoys golf, racquetball, softball, reading, bicycling and kids' activities.

Stanley Heller

Attorney/Partner
Thomas R. Cirignani and Associates
200 West Madison Street, Suite 3660
Chicago, IL 60606
(312) 346–8700
Fax: (312) 346–5180

8111

Business Information: Thomas R. Cirignani and Associates is a full service law firm concentrating on personal injury and medical malpractice law. Comprised of five partners, the Firm was established in 1988 and has six branch offices in Georgia, Arizona, Iowa, Michigan, and Indiana. As Attorney/Partner, Mr. Heller, who was formerly a physican, is responsible for overseeing all administrative functions, as well as practicing law. He is a specialist in the area of medical malpractice law, and serves as an arbitrator and mediator in health–related litigation. **Career Steps:** Attorney/Partner, Thomas R. Cirignani and Associates (1988–Present); President, Northside Cardiology Group Limited (1971–1985). **Associations & Accomplishments:** Illinois Trial Lawyers Association. **Education:** Northwestern University School of Law, J.D. (1988); Johns Hopkins University: M.D. (1965), B.A. (1962). **Personal:** Married to Brenda Anita West in 1990. Three children: Stephanie Gail, Michael Lawrence, and Deborah Arlene. Mr. Heller enjoys hiking, fishing, and collecting wines.

Dorothy L. Helling

Attorney at law
The Law Office of Dorothy L. Helling
29 East State Street
Montpelier, VT 05602–3011
(802) 223–1555
Fax: (802) 223–4208

8111

Business Information: The Law Office of Dorothy L. Helling is a general law practice concentrating in the areas of general civil law, civil litigation, landlord/tenant law, probate matters and simple wills/estates, real estate, personal injury and contracts. Admitted to both State and Federal courts, Mrs. Helling established her solo practice in 1989, but has been in private practice since 1984. She is also an Acting Judge of the Washington County Small Claims District Court, as well as an Adjunct Faculty member with Woodbury College. **Career Steps:** Attorney at Law, The Law Office of Dorothy L. Helling (1989–Present); Attorney, Theriault & Joslin, P.C. (1984–1989); Trial Court Law Clerk, State of Vermont (1981–1982; 1983–1984); Associate, Spokes, Foley & Stitzel (1983); Volunteer/Paralegal, Vista/Action, Cattaraugus Community Action (1975–1976). **Associations & Accomplishments:** Past President, Washington County Bar Association; Vermont Trial Lawyers Association; Vermont Volunteers Lawyers Project; Vermont Bar Association; American Bar Association; Lawyers Title Insurance Corporation; Vermont Attorneys Title; Who's Who in Practicing Attorneys; 1994 and 1993 Nominating Committee for VBF Board of Directors; Bench/Bar Committee of the Washington County Family Court; Honorary Member, Vermont Sheriffs Association; VBA Special Committee Judicial Confirmation and Retention of Judges; Criminal Defense Counsel; Recipient, Vermont Bar Association Public Service Award (1994); Member, Board of Bar Managus, Vermont Bar Association. **Education:** Vermont Law School, J.D. (1981); Quinnipiac College, B.A. in Psychology with honors (1974); University of Vermont, Masters program (1976–1978).

Sally J. Herald, Esq.

Attorney
Tranter & Meier
33 North Fort Thomas Avenue
Ft. Thomas, KY 41075
(606) 781–5700
Fax: (606) 781–6309

8111

Business Information: Tranter & Meier, established in 1985, is a full–service, general practice law firm. Admitted to practice in Kentucky state and federal courts, Mrs. Herald joined the Firm in 1984 as a paralegal and joined as an attorney in 1989. Her practice specializes in the areas of bankruptcy, real estate, domestic relations, probate, and personal injury law. **Career Steps:** Tranter & Meier: Attorney (1989–Present), Paralegal (1984–1989); Secretary/Paralegal, Portia F. Schaeter (1962–1984). **Associations & Accomplishments:** Kentucky Bar Association; Northern Kentucky Bar Association; American Bar Association; American Association of Trial Lawyers; New Macedonia Regular Baptist Church. **Education:** Salmon P. Chase College of Law, J.D. (1988); Northern Kentucky University (1985). **Personal:** Married to Mitchel in 1962. Four children: Stephen, Jeffrey, Mitchel, and Jennifer. Mrs. Herald enjoys reading and sewing.

Pedro Hernandez Alvarado

Principal Attorney
Pedro Hernandez Alvarado Law Offices
P.O. Box 7499
Caguas, Puerto Rico 00726–7499
(809) 746–0554
Fax: Please mail or call

8111

Business Information: The Law Offices of Pedro H. Alvarado is a general practice law firm, focusing primarily on Criminal Law. Establishing the Firm upon the conferral of his law degree in 1994, Mr. Alvardo is the Principal Attorney, overseeing all associates and related legal and administrative support staff, in addition to his client base. **Career Steps:** Attorney, Pedro Hernandez Alvarado Law Offices (1974–Present); Sales & Marketing Executive, San Juan Gas Company (1969–1973); Teacher, Puerto Rico Educational Department (1967–1969). **Associations & Accomplishments:** Colegio de Abogados de Puerto Rico; American Bar Association; Lion's Club; Logia Masonica Union y Amparo #44; Federacion Caballos de Paso Fino de Puerto Rico. **Education:** Interamerican University Law School, J.D. (1973); Catholic University of Puerto Rico, B.A. **Personal:** Married to Mildred Del Valle in 1986. Three children: Debra–Angie, Pedro C., and Monica M. Hernandez. Mr. Hernandez Alvarado enjoys riding Paso Fino horses and nature.

Manuel D. Herrero

Owner and Partner
Herrero & Herrero Law Firm
623 Ponce de Leon Avenue, Suite 205B
San Juan, Puerto Rico 00917
(809) 751–2045
Fax: (809) 764–5645

8111

Business Information: Herrero & Herrero Law Firm is as full–service, general practice law firm, concentrating on municipal and criminal cases. Co–founding the Firm upon conferral of his law degree in 1981, Manuel Herrero serves as Managing Partner. He oversees all administrative operations for associates and a staff of six, in addition to his client base representation. **Career Steps:** Owner and Partner, Herrero & Herrero Law Firm (1981–Present); President, Municipality of San Juan Municipal Counsil (1993–1995); Sub–Electoral Commissioner, Puerto Rico Electoral Board (1980–1984). **Associations & Accomplishments:** American Bar Association; Puerto Rico Bar Association; President, Municipality of San Juan Municipal Counsil. **Education:** University of Puerto Rico: J.D. cum laude (1980), B.B.A. magna cum laude. **Personal:** Married to Adalisa Rodriguez in 1986. Two children: Liana Esther and Natalia Isabel Herrero Rodriguez. Mr. Herrero enjoys yachting, horseback riding, and water sports.

Raymond Scott Heyman

Principal Partner
Roshka Heyman & DeWulf
400 North 5th Street, Suite 1000
Phoenix, AZ 85004–3902
(602) 256–6100
Fax: (602) 256–6800

8111

Business Information: Roshka Heyman & DeWulf concentrates in the area of commercial litigation, securities litigation and the representation of regulated industries. Mr. Heyman has represented regulated industries such as electric and telecommunications companies since 1983. Mr. Heyman also represents foreign companies who do business in the United States and domestic corporations doing business abroad. Mr. Heyman is fluent in Spanish. **Career Steps:** Principal Partner, Roshka Heyman & DeWulf (1995–Present); Senior Partner, O'Connor, Cavanagh Law Firm (1987–1995); Attorney, Arizona Public Service Company (1983–1987); Law Clerk, Ralph Gano Miller, P.C. (1981–1983). **Associations & Accomplishments:** American Bar Association; Arizona Bar Association; Maricopa County Bar Association; Boy Scouts of America – Arizona Legal Counsel (1993–Present); Fiesta Bowl Hot Air Balloon Race Committee (1985–Present); Phoenix Children's Hospital Children Cancer Center Christmas Card Committee (1990–1993). **Education:** California Western School of Law, J.D., cum laude (1983); Brigham Young University, B.A. in Political Science. **Personal:** Married to Diane in 1979. Five children: Curtis, Christopher, Jennifer, Allison, and Taylor.

Tim J. Hilborn

Owner
Hillborn and Konduros
P.O. Box 25008/39 Queen Street West
Cambridge, Ontario N3C 1G2
(519) 658–6341
Fax: (519) 654–9127

8111

Business Information: Hillborn and Konduros is a general practice law firm located in Cambridge, Ontario. Established in 1980, the Firm consists of 3 attorneys who concentrate on Criminal, Civil, Corporate and Business Law, as well as Estate and Tax Planning. As Owner and Attorney, Mr. Hilborn oversees the daily operation and strategic planning of the Firm. Additionally, he is responsible for preparing cases for trial, performing legal research, writing briefs, and meeting with clients. **Career Steps:** Owner, Hillborn and Konduros (1980–Present). **Associations & Accomplishments:** Canadian Bar Association; Law Society of Upper Canada; Shades Min Law Association; Waterloo County Law Association; Hespeler Village Business Association; Big Brothers of Cambridge. **Education:** Windsor Law School, L.L.B. (1977); Western University, B.A. (1973). **Personal:** Mr. Hilborn enjoys travel and hiking.

Dave Hill

Partner
Hill & Abra
360 Main Street, Suite 2670
Winnipeg, Manitoba R3C 3Z3
(204) 943–6740
Fax: (204) 943–3934

8111

Business Information: Hill & Abra is a general practice, litigation counsel law firm with seven lawyers, concentrating in commerce, mediation, administration, and insurance defense work. A practicing attorney in Canadian courts since obtaining his degree in 1974, Mr. Hill founded the Firm in 1988. As Partner, Mr Hill is responsible for managing his support staff as well as his daily client load. **Career Steps:** Partner, Hill & Abra (1988–Present); Aikins MacAulay Thorvaldson: Self–Employed Partner (1979–1988), Employed Lawyer (1974–1979). **Associations & Accomplishments:** Director, Manitoba Heart & Stroke Foundation; Board of Governors, St. Charles Country Club; Board of Directors, St. John's–Ravenscourt School; Elected Bencher, Manitoba Law Society; Director, Winnipeg Blue Bombers Football Club. **Education:** University of Manitoba Law School, LL.B. (1974); Dartmouth College, B.A. (1971). **Personal:** Married to Kathleen in 1975. Two children: David and Deborah. Mr. Hill enjoys recreational activities such as golf and old–timers hockey.

Ms. Adria S. Hillman

Senior Partner
Law Offices of Adria S. Hillman
41 East 57th Street, 15th Floor
New York, NY 10022
(212) 593–5223
Fax: (212) 593–4633

8111

Business Information: Law Offices of Adria S. Hillman is a full–service, general practice law firm, concentrating in the areas of civil, international and business law and litigation. A practicing attorney since 1970, Adria Hillman established the Firm in 1993. As Senior Partner she oversees all administrative aspects of the Firm. Admitted to both state and federal courts, she concentrates in the areas of literary, publishing and entertainment law, employment law and civil rights, estates and trusts, matrimonial and family law. **Career Steps:** Senior Partner, Law Offices of Adria S. Hillman (1993–Present); Partner, Green & Hillman (1976–1993); Associate, Richard C. Green (1971–1976). **Associations & Accomplishments:** Bar Association of the City of New York – Matrimonial Committee; Women's Bar Association of the City of New York – Judiciary Committee; New York State Bar Association – Children and the Law Committee; Editor, "Women and the Law" – Clark Boardman; Volunteer, Special Master New York County; Director, New York Women's Foundation; Institute for Child Adolescent and Family Studies; Mentor, Network for Women's Services, Inc.; Founder and Co–Chair, New York State Coalition on Women's Legal Issues; Member, Coalition for Choice – NY State coalition analyzing legislation and public policy issues concerning reproductive choice; United Federation of Teachers; Diocese of Rockville Center, NY; Legal Awareness for Women (LAW); numerous lectures and seminar presentations; Author: "Separation Agreements" Chapter in Family Law Manual; Co–Author with Harriet N. Cohen of 96–page "Analysis of Equitable Distribution in Divorce in New York" and other articles in recognized magazines. COMMISSIONS AND APPOINTMENTS: New York State Legislative Advisory Committee to study The Estates Powers and Trusts Law (1990–Present); Special Master, New York County Supreme Court (1989–Present); American Arbitration Association Arbitrator, Commercial Arbitrations (1991–Present). **Education:** New York University School of Law, J.D. (1970); Bennington College, B.A. (1967); Admitted to Practice: U.S. District Court Southern District (1973); First Department (1971); U.S. Court of Appeals 2nd Circuit (1975); U.S. Supreme Court (1979). **Personal:** Married to Donald in 1968. Two children: Jethro and Charlotte.

Mr. John W. Hinchey

Partner
King & Spalding
191 Peachtree Street, NE
Atlanta, GA 30303
(404) 572–4600
Fax: (404) 572–5144

8111

Business Information: King & Spalding, one of the largest and oldest law firms in Atlanta and among the top 30 firms nationwide, is a full–service, general practice law firm. Mr. Hinchey concentrates his practice in construction law, suretyship, government contracts and procurement law, and bank insurance law, with particular emphasis upon the drafting and negotiation of contracts for major construction projects, and litigation and alternative dispute resolution of complex cases. The Firm has four offices located in Atlanta, Houston, New York and Washington, D.C. Admitted to practice before the United States Supreme Court and Georgia state and federal courts, Mr. Hinchey joined the Firm in 1992 as Partner. He is responsible for the legal representation of the Firm's clientele, including negotiating and drafting construction agreements for the Atlanta Committee on the Olympic Games, design and build operations and management of waste–to–energy plant contracts, and a broad variety of construction agreements, agreement guarantees and payment and performance bonds; the litigation and arbitration of major construction disputes, and multi–state construction project disputes between contractors, their sureties and other parties. Other matters include complex disputes among financial institution bond insurers, major banks and the Federal Deposit Insurance Corporation. Representing a broad variety of clients in his fields of expertise, including national and multi–national companies, Mr. Hinchey has also represented private and public schools, and universities; state, city and county governments; public authorities; medical institutions; public utilities; private developers and owners; as well as architects and contractors. His expertise includes a number of years in public law, having served as Assistant Attorney General for the State of Georgia, and as special counsel to two Governor's Commissions to study and propose reforms to the judiciary of the State of Georgia. **Career Steps:** Partner, King & Spalding (1992–Present); Assistant Attorney General, State of Georgia (1968–1972); Fellowship, Ford Foundation, Assigned to Chief Justice, Supreme Court of Pakistan (1966–1967). **Associations & Accomplishments:** Active Member and has served on the Administrative Board, Glenn Memorial United Methodist Church in Atlanta; American Bar Association; Fellow, American College of Construction Lawyers (1992–Present); Member, The London Court of International Arbitration (1991–Present); American Arbitration Association: Construction Advisory Council, Atlanta Region (1990–Present), Panel of Arbitrators, Panel of Mediators; American Bar Association: General Practice Section: Vice Chair of ADR Committee (1989), Litigation Section, Fidelity and Surety Law Committee: Vice Chair of the Tort and Insurance Practice Section (1988–1990), Public Law Section, Forum on the Construction Industry: Chair of Dispute Avoidance and Resolution Division (1988–1990), Special Achievement Award (for service as Chair, Task Force on Special ADR Procedures for Complex Construction Cases); State Bar of Georgia; Atlanta Bar Association; Admitted to practice before: Supreme Court of the United States (1970), United States Court of Appeals for the Eleventh Circuit, United States District Court of Georgia (1968), and the Supreme Court of Georgia (1965); Who's Who in American Law (1983–Present); Speaker and lecturer in numerous seminars and workshops on construction law, alternative dispute resolution, suretyship, fidelity insurance law, and bank insurance law topics; Counsel to the Governor's Commission on Court Organization and Structure (1975–1976), a special commission appointed by former Governor, George Busbee of Georgia, to make proposals to implement a unified court structure in Georgia; President, Decature–DeKalb County, Younger Lawyer's Section (1973–1974); Appointed as Special Hearing Examiner for contested cases of alleged professional licensing violations, State of Georgia (1972–1976); Chairman, Administrative Law Section, State Bar of Georgia (1972–1973); Counsel to the Govenor's Commission on Judicial Processes (1971–1972), a special commission appointed by former Governor, Jimmy Carter of Georgia, to study and make recommendations for the improvement of judicial processes in the State of Georgia. **Education:** Oxford University, Oxford, England, M.Lit. (1976); Harvard Law School, LL.M. (1966); Emory University School of Law, J.D. (1965); Emory University, A.B. (1964). **Personal:** Married to Paulette Hinchey. Mr. Hinchey enjoys time with his family, reading history, theology and scientific books, fly fishing, hiking and cross–country skiing.

Judith A. Hoggan

Special Counsel
Friedlander, Misler, Friedlander, Sloan & Herz
1101 17th Street NW, Suite 700
Washington, DC 20036
(202) 872–0800
Fax: (202) 857–8343 (301) 972–4027

8111

Business Information: Friedlander, Misler, Friedlander, Sloan & Herz is a general law firm serving the Maryland, Virginia, and District of Columbia areas. As Special Counsel, Ms. Hoggan is a Senior litigator with over fourteen years of experience in general practice of law with a focus in general litigation, commercial litigation, collections, landlord and tenant law and litigation, and family law. **Career Steps:** Special Counsel, Friedlander, Misler, Friedlander, Sloan & Herz (1996–Present); Keck, Mahin & Cate: Partner/Senior Litagator (1995–1996), Senior Assocate Litigation; Senior Associate Litigation, Casson, Harkins & Greenberg, P.C. (1990–1991); Senior Associate/Litigation, Deso & Greenberg, P.C. (1988–1991); Associate/General Practice and Litigation, Moran & Pilger, P.C. (1982–1988). **Associations & Accomplishments:** American Bar Association; Maryland Bar Association; Virginia Bar Association; District of Columbia Bar Association; Montgomery County, Maryland Bar Association. Co–chair, Legislative Subcommittee, Family Division of the District of Columbia Bar Association; Speaker, Career Real Estate Women; Guest Speaker American Association of Marriage and Family Therapists; Guest Speaker, Center for the Study of Children with Troubling Behavior; Panel member, Montgomery County Bar Association Fee Arbitration Committee; Mediator, Montgomery County Circuit Court, Maryland; PRO BONA AND CIVIC ACTIVITIES: Alternatives to Violence (Maryland Prisons) (1985); Legal Counsel for the Elderly (1983–Current); Parents Supporting Parents (1994–95); Legal Advocate, Crisis Center Abused Persons Program (1981–82); Foster Parent (1991–96). **Education:** Georgetown University Law Center, Juris Doctor, (1982); University of Maryland, B. S. in Psychology and Personnel Management, summa cum laude (1977). **Personal:** Married to James E. Brown in 1981. Ms. Hoggan enjoys reading, movies, gems and minerals, music, dogs, and working out with her personal trainer.

Robert H. Hood, Esq.

Senior Partner
Hood Law Firm
P.O. Box 1508
Charleston, SC 29402–1508
(803) 577–4435
Fax: (803) 722–1630

8111

Business Information: Hood Law Firm is a full–service, general practice law firm, emphasizing civil litigation in the areas of medical malpractice and product liability. The Firm consists of 18 attorney associates, and employs 35 legal support and administrative staff. Admitted to practice in South Carolina State and Federal courts since 1969, Mr. Hood established the Firm in 1985 and currently serves as Senior Partner. He is responsible for all aspects of operations, including the provision of legal representation. **Career Steps:** Senior Partner, Hood Law Firm (1985–Present); Attorney and Partner, Sinkler, Gibbs & Simons, P.A. (1970–1985); Assistant Attorney General, State of South Carolina (1969–1970). **Associations & Accomplishments:** President (1980–1981), South Carolina Defense Trial Attorneys Association; Chairman of the Ethics Advisory Committee (1983–1990), South Carolina Bar Association; Charleston County Bar Association; Board of Directors (1987–1990), Defense Research and Trial Institute; President (1985–1986), Association of Defense Trial Attorneys; American Board of Trial Advocates; International Association of Defense Counsel. **Education:** University of South Carolina Law School, J.D. (1969); University of the South, B.A. in Political Science (1966). **Personal:** Married to Mary Agnes Hood in 1967. Four children: Molly, Elizabeth, Bobby Jr., and Jamie. Mr. Hood enjoys fishing and hunting.

Kimberly Hill Hoover

Head – China Transactional Practice
Dichstein Shapiro & Morin
4106 Aspen Street
Chevy Chase, MD 20815–5059
(202) 775–4760
Fax: (202) 887–0689
EMAIL: See Below

8111

Business Information: Dichstein Shapiro & Morin is a premier, international law firm. A practicing attorney since 1983, Kimberly Hoover joined the Firm in 1991. As Head of China Transactional Practices, she oversees all transactional work for clients in the Republic of China. In addition, she is responsible for all telecommunications. Internet users can reach her via: girlswrk@ix.netcom.com. **Career Steps:** Head of China Transactional Practice, Dichstein Shapiro & Morin (1991–Present); Adjunct Professor, Washington College of Law at American University (1990–Present); Partner, Ross & Hardies (1990–1991); Associate Attorney, Foley Hoag & Eliot (1988–1990). **Associations & Accomplishments:** American Bar Association; Board of Directors, Chevy Chase United Methodist Preschool; Director, Treasury Bank – Washington, DC (1990–1992). **Education:** Duke University, J.D. (1983); Baylor University, B.A., magna cum laude (1980). **Personal:** Married to Craig A. in 1986. Two children: Stephanie Claire and Lauren Michelle. Ms. Hoover enjoys golf and computers.

Don Lee Horn

Partner
Gallwey, Gillman, Curtis, Vento & Horn
200 Southeast First Street, Suite 1100
Miami, FL 33131
(305) 358–1313
Fax: (305) 371–5826

8111

Business Information: Gallwey, Gillman, Curtis, Vento & Horn is a full–service, general practice law firm concentrating in commercial litigation, insurance defense and banking. Established in 1995, the Firm currently employs 22 people, including 9 attorneys, and 3 paralegals. A practicing attorney since 1982, Mr. Horn co–founded the Firm in 1995. Currently serving as Partner, he is responsible for the legal representation of franchisors, focusing on franchise litigation in Florida state and federal courts. **Career Steps:** Partner, Gallwey, Gillman, Curtis, Vento & Horn (1995–Present); Partner, Shutts & Bowen (1990–1995); Dade County State Attorney's Office: Assistant State Attorney (1982–1990), Major Crimes Division (1989–1990). **Associations & Accomplishments:** President of the Board, Legal Services of Greater Miami, Inc.; The Florida Bar Association; American Bar Association; National Bar Association; U.S. District Court; Judicial Nominating Committee for 11th Circuit Court of Florida; Southern District of Florida; Black Lawyers Association; Dade County Bar Association; Faculty Member, National Institute for Trial Advocacy; Member, Greater Miami Chamber of Commerce; Black Economic Development Group; Member, Dade Partners for Safe Neighborhoods, Juvenile Task Force; Church deacon, trustee, member of 3 choirs, adult Sunday school teacher. **Education:** University of Miami School of Law, J.D. (1982); University of Texas at El Paso, B.S. in Criminal Justice; Miami–Dade Community College, A.A., Dean's List. **Personal:** Married to Rita in 1986. Two children: Adrienne and Don Avery. Mr. Horn enjoys church activities.

Darryl J. Horowitt

Attorney/Partner
Coleman & Horowitt
499 West Shaw Avenue, Suite 116
Fresno, CA 93704–2516
(209) 248–4820
Fax: (209) 248–4830
EMAIL: See Below

8111

Business Information: Established in 1994, Coleman & Horowitt is a full service general law practice. A practicing trial attorney in California state and federal courts since 1981, Darryl Horowitt joined the Firm in 1994. As Partner with the Fresno office, he oversees all litigation areas. Internet users can reach him via: DJHLAW@AOL.COM **Career Steps:** Attorney/Partner, Coleman & Horowitt (1994–Present); Partner, Lerrigo, Niblar, Berryman, Coleman & Bennett (1991–1994); Owner, Law Offices of Darryl J. Harowitt (1987–1989). **Associations & Accomplishments:** American Bar Association; Consumer Attorneys of California; Fresno Bar Association; Fresno Trial Lawyers Association; Board Member, Cinco De Mayo Charity Golf Tournament. **Education:** Western State University, J.D. (1981); California State University – Long Beach, B.A. in History (1978). **Personal:** Married to Erika in 1987. Two children: Andrea and Aaron. Mr. Horowitt enjoys tennis and golf.

Michael J. Horvitz

Partner
Jones, Day, Reavis & Pogue
901 Lakeside Avenue
Cleveland, OH 44114
(216) 586–7170
Fax: (216) 579–0212

8111

Business Information: Jones, Day, Reavis & Pogue, one of the nation's leading law firms, is an international full–service, general practice law firm consisting of nineteen offices worldwide. Established in 1894, the Firm currently employs 900 attorneys, legal and administrative support staff company–wide. A practicing attorney for the past fifteen years, Mr. Horvitz joined the Firm in 1980 as one of more than 350 partners. Serving as Tax Attorney, he concentrates his practice in the areas of tax law, private business investments, charitable endowments, business divorces, and family business. **Career Steps:** Partner, Jones, Day, Reavis & Pogue (1980–Present). **Associations & Accomplishments:** Chairman, H.R.H. Family Trust; Chairman of the Board, Parkland Management Company; Vice Chairman, Horvitz Newspapers, Inc.; Member of the Advisory Board, Kirtland Capital Partners, L.P.; Trustee, Case Western Reserve University; The Cleveland Museum of Art; Musical Arts Association; The Jewish Community Federation of Cleveland; The Mt. Sinai Medical Center; Active member of various committees for United Way Services; Former Trustee, Health Hill Hospital for Children; Chairman, Health Hill's Board of Trustees. **Education:** New York University Law School, LL.M. in Taxation; University of Virginia Law School, J.D.; University of Pennsylvania's Wharton School, B.S. in Economics. **Personal:** Married to Jane Rosenthal in 1979. Two children: Katherine R. and Elizabeth R.. Mr. Horvitz enjoys golf.

Rod J. Howard

Attorney
Gray, Cary, Ware & Freidenrich
400 Hamilton Avenue
Palo Alto, CA 94301–1825
(415) 833–2496
Fax: (415) 327–3699

8111

Business Information: Gray, Cary, Ware & Freidenrich is a full–service commercial law firm providing business, corporate, securities, litigation, banking, intellectual property, patent, real estate, employment, tax, trust and estate planning services with an industry focus on emerging technologies, as well as initial public offerings of privately–owned corporations. Established in 1994 and comprised of 270 attorneys, the Firm has two principal California locations, one in Palo Alto, and the other in San Diego. Mr. Howard specializes in mergers and acquisitions, practicing in the Firm's Corporate and Securities Group. Mr. Howard, joined the Firm in June, 1996. He is also chairman of the Firm's Public Utilities Group. **Career Steps:** Attorney, Gray, Cary, Ware & Freidenrich (1996–Present); Milbank, Tweed, Hadley & McCloy: Of Counsel (1994–1996), Associate (1989–1994); Associate, Watchell, Lipton, Rosen & Katz (1984–1989); Law Clerk, U.S. Court of Appeals, First Circuit (1982–1983). **Associations & Accomplishments:** American Bar Association. **Education:** University of Chicago, J.D. (1982); University of Arizona, B.A. **Personal:** Married to Emiko Higashi in 1992.

Helen Hsu, Esq.

Attorney
Law Offices of Benton Musslewhite
440 Louisiana Avenue, 1520 Lyric Centre
Houston, TX 77002
(713) 222–2288
Fax: (713) 222–0319

8111

Business Information: The Law Offices of Benton Musslewhite is a full–service, general practice law firm, specializing in toxic tort litigation and personal injury cases. Admitted to practice in Louisiana state and federal courts since 1990 and in Texas state and federal courts since 1995, Miss Hsu joined the Firm as Attorney in 1995. She serves as the Firm's only associate, representing clientele as a trial attorney, particularly focusing on personal injury matters. **Career Steps:** Attorney, Law Offices of Benton Musslewhite (1995–Present); Staff Attorney, Louisiana House of Representatives (1992–1995); Trial Attorney, Michael Roy Fugler & Associates (1990–1992). **Associations & Accomplishments:** American Bar Association; American Trial Lawyers Association; Dallas Bar Association; Houston Bar Association; State of Texas Bar Association; Louisiana State Bar Association; Baton Rouge Bar Association. **Education:** Louisiana State University – Paul M. Hebert Law Center, J.D. (1990); Louisiana State University – Baton Rouge & Louisiana State University Medical Center – New Orleans School of Allied Health, B.S. in Medical Technology.

Bruce L. Hudson, Esq.

President
Law Offices of Bruce L. Hudson
300 Delaware Avenue, Suite 1130
Wilmington, DE 19801
(302) 656–9850
Fax: (302) 656–9836

8111

Business Information: Established in 1993, the Law Office of Bruce L. Hudson is a full–service, general practice, law firm, specializing in plaintiff representation in the areas of personal injury, medical and civil law. A practicing attorney since 1978, Bruce Hudson established his individual practice firm in 1993. As President, Mr. Hudson is responsible for all aspects of the Firm. **Career Steps:** Attorney, Law Office of Bruce L. Hudson (1993–Present); Law Partner, Daley Erisman Van OgTrop & Hudson (1989–1993); Law Partner, Marin & Hudson (1979–1988). **Associations & Accomplishments:** President (1992–1993), Delaware Trial Lawyers Association; Association of Trial Lawyers of America; Delaware Bar Association; American Bar Association; Certified in 1994 by the National Board of Trial Advocacy as Civil Trial Advocate. **Education:** Delaware Law School, J.D. (1978); University of Delaware, M.S and B.S. **Personal:** Two children: Tyler and Spencer. Mr. Hudson enjoys photography.

Richard Alan Hudson, J.D., C.P.A.

Attorney at Law
Spilman, Thomas & Battle
417 Grand Park Drive, Suite 203
Parkersburg, WV 26101
(304) 422–6700
Fax: (304) 422–6733

8111

Business Information: Spilman, Thomas & Battle, established in 1840, is a full–service, general practice law firm with four offices located in West Virginia. Admitted to practice in West Virginia state courts, Mr. Hudson joined the Firm in 1992. He concentrates his practice in the areas of health care law, estate planning and administration, and trusts. **Career Steps:** Lawyer, Spilman, Thomas & Battle (1992–Present); Lawyer, Bayley, Zimmerman & Hudson (1986–1992); Certified Public Accountant, Harman, Thompson & Mallory (1982–1986). **Associations & Accomplishments:** Vice President, Parkersburg YMCA; Board Director, Good Samaritan Clinic; Assistant Scoutmaster, Boy Scouts of America; Treasurer, Parkersburg Catholic School Foundation; Knights of Columbus, 4th Degree; American Bar Association; Virginia Bar Association; West Virginia State Bar; National Health Lawyers Association; American Association Hospital Attorneys; American Institute of Certified Public Accountants; West Virginia Society of Certified Public Accountants; Active in St. Margaret Mary Parish; Who's Who Among Rising Young Men of America (1992). **Education:** Georgetown University, J.D. (1976); Bethany College, B.A. (1973). **Personal:** Married to Judith D. Hudson in 1976. Three children: Kathleen, Richard, Jr., and J. Charles. Mr. Hudson enjoys astronomy and collecting baseball cards.

James D. Hughes, Esq.

Tax Attorney
Armbrecht, Jackson, DeMouy, Crowe, Holmes & Reeves, L.L.C.
1300 Amsouth Center
Mobile, AL 36602
(334) 432–6751 Ext: 219
Fax: (334) 432–6843

8111

Business Information: Armbrecht, Jackson, DeMouy, Crowe, Holmes & Reeves, L.L.C. is a full–service, general practice law firm, concentrating on civil law cases. A practicing attorney in Texas and Alabama state courts since 1976, Mr. Hughes joined the Firm as Tax Attorney in 1978. His practice concentrates on tax law, handling estate planning, employee benefits, corporate financing, taxation, and real estate issues. **Career Steps:** Tax Attorney, Armbrecht, Jackson, DeMouy, Crowe, Holmes & Reeves, L.L.C. (1978–Present); Attorney, O. N. Baker, Inc. (1977); Shipping and Receiving Manager, Plico–Flex, Inc. (1969). **Associations & Accomplishments:** American Bar Association; Mobile County Bar Association; Texas State Bar Association; Alabama State Bar Association; Mobile Estate Planning Council; Mobile Employee Benefits Council; Small Business Council of America. **Education:** New York University, Ll.M. in Taxation (1978); University of Texas, J.D. (1976); Stanford University, B.S. (1973). **Personal:** Married to Sheryl in 1992. Mr. Hughes enjoys sports, stained glass, and history.

Frederick E. Hulser, Esq.

Partner
McConnell Valdes
P.O. Box 364225
San Juan, Puerto Rico 00936
(787) 250–5645
Fax: (787) 759–9225
EMAIL: See Below
8111

Business Information: McConnell Valdes is the largest law firm in Puerto Rico, with 110 attorneys and 46 partners. Mr. Hulser joined the Firm as a Partner upon conferral of his law degree in 1973. He now concentrates his practice in corporate debt, venture capital, mergers and acquisitions, finance, estate and tax planning, and securities. Internet users can reach him via: FEH@mcvpr.com **Career Steps:** Partner, McConnell Valdes (1973–Present). **Associations & Accomplishments:** UNICEF; President, Columbia University Alumni Club; American Bar Association; Federal Bar Association; Interamerican Bar Association; Holland Club. **Education:** Columbia University Law School, J.D. (1973); Columbia College, B.A. (1969); Columbia Business School, M.B.A. (1973). **Personal:** Two children: Andrea and Eric. Mr. Hulser enjoys sailing, sculpture, skiing, tennis, and golf.

Donna L. Hwalek, Esq.

Sole Practitioner
The Law Offices of Donna L. Hwalek, Esq.
7217 Wareham Drive
Tampa, FL 33647–1167
(813) 971–0027
Fax: (813) 977–7484
8111

Business Information: The Law Offices of Donna L. Hwalek, Esq. is a full–service, general practice law firm concentrating on medical malpractice. Admitted to practice law in Florida state courts in 1990, Ms. Hwalek established her private practice firm in 1994. Prior to entering the legal world, Ms. Hwalek was a registered nurse for over 18 years. This background enables her to provide the utmost representation in medical issue cases. **Career Steps:** Sole Practitioner, The Law Offices of Donna L. Hwalek, Esq. (1994–Present). **Associations & Accomplishments:** American Bar Association; Florida Bar Association; Hillsborough County Bar Association; Registered Nurse with the State of Florida. **Education:** Florida State University, J.D. (1990); University of South Florida, B.S. in Nursing, graduated magna cum laude (1987), A.S. in Nursing with Honors (1984), A.A. in Liberal Arts with Honors (1983).

Terrill A. Hyde

Partner
Wilmer, Cutler & Pickering
2445 M Street, NW
Washington, DC 20037–1420
(202) 663–6238
Fax: (202) 663–6363
8111

Business Information: Wilmer, Cutler & Pickering is an international full–service, general practice law firm with offices in the District of Columbia, England (London), Belgium (Brussels), and Germany (Berlin). Employing more than 200 attorneys, the Firm's practice concentrates on business law and federal regulations. A practicing attorney in the District of Columbia since 1979, Ms. Hyde previously joined the Firm as Partner in 1987. Leaving the practice in 1989 to serve with the U.S. Department of Treasury, she returned in 1992 to resume the same position. Her practice concentrates on tax and business law. **Career Steps:** Partner, Wilmer, Cutler & Pickering (1992–Present and 1987–1989); U.S. Department of Treasury: Tax Legislative Counsel (1991–1992), Deputy Tax Legislative Counsel (1989–1991). **Associations & Accomplishments:** American Bar Association: Chair, Committee on Affiliated and Related Corporations, Section of Taxation; District of Columbia Bar Association: Vice–Chair, Exempt Organizations Committee, Taxation Section; Published in Tax Management Portfolio; Fellow, American Bar Foundation (1993). **Education:** University of Nebraska School of Law, J.D. (1979); South Dakota State University, M.A. (1976); Dakota State College, B.S., summa cum laude (1973). **Personal:** Two children: Laura and Tanya.

Yvonne M. Imbert–Garraton

Lawyer
Curbelo & Nunez
Nogal A–1 Apt. 903
Guaynabo, Puerto Rico 00968
(809) 781–9189
Fax: Please mail or call
8111

Business Information: Curbelo & Nunez is a full–service, general practice law firm, concentrating on civil law throughout

Puerto Rico. Established in 1982, the Firm currently employs eight attorneys, legal and administrative support staff. A practicing attorney in Puerto Rico state courts since 1990, Miss Imbert–Garraton joined the Firm in 1995. Serving as one of three lawyers, her practice concentrates on civil law court cases and contracts. **Career Steps:** Lawyer, Curbelo & Nunez (1995–Present); Associate Lawyer, Alex Gonzalez Law Office (1991–1995); Law Clerk, Pedro Gavilla, Esq. (1990–1991). **Associations & Accomplishments:** American Bar Association; Puerto Rico Bar Association; Phi Alpha Delta Law Fraternity. **Education:** Universidad de Puerto Rico, J.D. (1990); Loyola University, B.A.B.S. **Personal:** Miss Imbert–Garraton enjoys snow skiing, volleyball, tennis, and paddleball.

John Jacob Ing
Sole Practitioner
John Jacob Ing, Attorney at Law
1314 South King Street, Apt. 1063
Honolulu, HI 96814–1945
(808) 593–2299
Fax: (808) 593–2240

8111

Business Information: John Jacob Ing, Attorney at Law is a full–service, general practice law firm. A practicing attorney in Hawaii state courts since 1982, Mr. Ing established his private practice in 1984. He oversees the administrative operations of a support staff of one full– and one part–time, in addition to his private legal practice. Concurrent with his private legal practice, he serves as Principal Broker and Realtor of Ing Realty. **Career Steps:** Sole Practitioner, John Jacob Ing, Attorney at Law (1984–Present); Principal Broker and Realtor, Ing Realty, Inc. (1989–Present). **Associations & Accomplishments:** State Board of Health; Needle Exchange Oversight Committee; Hawaii Lawyers Care. **Education:** University of Hawaii, J.D. (1982); Occidental College, A.B. **Personal:** Mr. Ing enjoys foreign languages, cooking, and lifting weights.

Osvaldo A. Izquierdo–Capella
Sole Practitioner
Law Offices of Osualdo A. Izquierdo–Capella
Box 51077, Levittown Station
Toa Baja, Puerto Rico 00950–1077
(809) 784–0515
Fax: (809) 784–0515

8111

Business Information: The Law Offices of Osvaldo A. Izquierdo–Capella is a private general practice law firm, serving corporate and private clientele throughout Puerto Rico. A practicing attorney in state and federal courts since 1982, Mr. Izquierdo–Capella established his individual practice firm in 1995. As Sole Practitioner he is involved in all areas of its operation, focusing his legal practice in the areas of civil litigation, federal tort and malpractice law. A retired Lieutenant Colonel in the Army, he served as a General Counsel and other prior clerical roles for the Veterans Administration for almost 20 years before establishing his private legal practice. **Career Steps:** Sole Practitioner, Law Offices of Osvaldo A. Izquierdo–Capella (1995–Present); Department of Veterans Affairs – Puerto Rico: General Attorney (1982–1995), Personnel Specialist (1976–1982); Marketing Manager, American Optical Company–Caribbean (1974–1976). **Associations & Accomplishments:** Panama Consistory (Masons); Association of Retired Federal Personnel. **Education:** InterAmerican University: LL.B. (1982), M.B.A. (1973), B.B.A. (1964). **Personal:** Married to Sonia Cesareo Bermudez in 1987. Three children: Osvaldo Antonio, Ada Ligia and Antonio Osvaldo. Mr. Izquierdo–Capella enjoys bowling, golf and karate.

John J. Jawor
Managing Partner
Jawor Law Firm
2602 Flossmoor Road
Flossmoor, IL 60422
(708) 799–7300
Fax: (708) 799–7377

8111

Business Information: Jawor Law Firm is a private law firm, concentrating on the areas of environment, employment and labor law, and commercial litigation. A practicing attorney in Illinois state and federal courts since 1981, Mr. Jawor founded the firm in 1994. As Managing Partner he oversees all administrative operations, as well as serves as counsel to major international corporate clientele. **Career Steps:** Managing Partner, Jawor Law Firm (1994–Present); Partner, Abramson & Fox (1990–1994); Partner, Ruberry, Palmer & Phares (1989–1990); Partner, McDermott, Will & Emery (1988–1989). **Associations & Accomplishments:** American Bar Association; Illinois Trial Lawyers Association; Chicago Bar Association; Southwest Suburban Bar Association; Illinois Defense Lawyers; Chicago Chamber of Commerce; Czech/U.S. Business Association; Polish/American Chamber of Commerce; Romanian Business Association; Illinois

Municipal League **Education:** Northwestern University, J.D. magna cum laude (1981); Georgetown University, B.A. magna cum laude (1978). **Personal:** Married to Susan in 1988. One child: Justin. Mr. Jawor enjoys dance, martial arts and soccer.

Jeffrey M. Jayson
Attorney and President
J.M. Jayson, Esq. & Associates, PC
2350 North Forest Road, Suite 12A
Getzville, NY 14068–1598
(716) 636–0273
Fax: (716) 636–0466

8111

Business Information: Jeffrey M. Jayson began his career as one of the youngest licensed stock brokers in New York. Establishing his private practice upon the conferral of his law degree in 1990, he now focuses on estate planning, international asset planning, collection, and personal injury. **Career Steps:** Attorney and President, J.M. Jayson, Esq. & Associates, PC (1990–Present); Stockbroker, Westmoreland Capital Corporation (1983–1992); International Corporate Finance Division, Securities & Exchange Commodities (1989). **Associations & Accomplishments:** National Network of Estate Planning Attorneys; American Academy of Estate Planning Attorneys; Commercial Bar League. **Education:** Catholic University of America: J.D. (1990), International Law Degree (1990); Indiana University, B.S. in Business Management (1982); New York State Insurance License. **Personal:** Mr. Jayson enjoys snow skiing, sailing and chess. His family also trains horses for teams in the U.S. and Canada.

Mr. Robert L. Jennings
Officer, Director, Shareholder
Jennings, Valancy & Edwards, P.A.
633 South Andrews Avenue, Suite 202
Ft. Lauderdale, FL 33301
(305) 463–1600
Fax: (305) 463–1222

8111

Business Information: Jennings, Valancy & Edwards, P.A. is a law firm specializing in commercial litigation. As Officer, Director, Shareholder, Mr. Jennings manages the firm's operations, and is a practicing attorney. Established in 1992, Jennings, Valancy & Edwards, P.A. employs 6 people. **Career Steps:** Officer, Director, Shareholder, Jennings, Valancy & Edwards, P.A., (1992–Present); Partner, Holland & Knight (1989–1992); Associate, Holland & Knight (1985–1989); Associate, Schwartz & Wilson (1982–1985). **Associations & Accomplishments:** National Institute of Trial Advocacy; Broward County Bar Association; Broward Lawyers Care; American Bar Association; Leadership Broward Alumni, Harvard Club of Broward County; Bankruptcy Bar Association, Southern District of Florida; Ft. Lauderdale Rugby Club; Co–Author, "Indemnification of Corporate Officers and Directors", NOVA Law Journal, (Spring 1991). **Education:** University of Florida Law School, J.D. with Honors (1982); Harvard College, A.B. cum laude (1979). **Personal:** Married to Rita in 1986. One child: Sean. Mr. Jennings enjoys boating, reading, and rugby.

Frankie Jimenez Santoni
• • • ━━━●━━━ • • •

Senior Partner
Jimenez & Santoni Law Offices
Coll & Toste Tower, 3rd Floor, 650 Penuelas
San Juan, Puerto Rico 00918
(787) 763–0070
Fax: (787) 763–0848

8111

Business Information: Jimenez & Santoni Law Offices is a full–service, general practice law firm concentrating on insurance law. A practicing attorney in Puerto Rico courts since 1975, Mr. Jimenez Santoni co–founded the Firm in 1980. His greatest accomplishment as a lawyer was when he was defender in the case of the biggest Dupont fire in a casino in San Juan in 1986. The case lasted until 1996 and had the largest number of documents filed and largest number of plaintiffs and attorneys. Mr. Jimenez Santoni represented one person who died in the fire and one man who broke a window for victims to escape. **Career Steps:** Senior Partner, Jimenez & Santoni Law Offices (1980–Present); Lawyer, Corporacion Insular de Seguros (1978–1980); Lawyer, Insurance Commissioner's Office (1975–1977). **Associations & Accomplishments:** Colegio de Abogados de Puerto Rico. **Education:** University of Puerto Rico – Law School, J.D. (1975); Villanova University, B.S. in Business Administration. **Personal:** Married to Sally Riley in 1979. Two children: Marissa and Nicolas. Mr. Jimenez Santoni enjoys golf, basketball, swimming, and walking.

Charles T. Johnson, Esq.
Attorney at Law
–Independent–
Church Hill Road, P.O. Box 6
South Woodstock, VT 05071
Fax: Please mail or call

8111

Business Information: Mr. Johnson is a full service general law practitioner, specializing in real estate and litigation. Upon conferral of his law degree in 1991, Mr. Johnson handles simple and complex commercial and residential real estate matters, corporate law, trusts & estates, trial & appellate civil litigation. **Career Steps:** Sole Practitioner (1995–Present); Attorney at Law, Johnson & Associates (1991–1995); Intern/Clerk, State of Connecticut, Juvenile Advocates Division (1991); Clerk/Paralegal, Johnson & Associates (1988–1991). **Associations & Accomplishments:** American Bar Association; Vermont Bar Association; Theta Delta Chi Fraternity. **Education:** Vermont Law School, J.D. (1991); Bowdoin College, B.A. in Political Science (1986); Brooks School (1982). **Personal:** Mr. Johnson enjoys tennis, golf, skiing, cooking, reading, domestic and international travel, and hiking.

Will D. Johnson
Attorney–at–Law
Law Offices of Will D. Johnson & Associates
3500 South Figueroa Street, Suite 217
Los Angeles, CA 90007–4363
(213) 749–1186
Fax: (213) 749–0413

8111

Business Information: Law Offices of Will D. Johnson & Associates is a general practice law firm, concentrating in personal injury and civil litigation. A trial Attorney since 1977, Mr. Johnson established his practice in 1978 and shares the responsibilities of directing a legal staff of 15 and practicing law with his fellow associates. **Career Steps:** Owner, Law Offices of Will D. Johnson & Associates (1978–Present). **Associations & Accomplishments:** Consumer Attorneys Association of Los Angeles; Consumer Attorneys Associatin of California; Los Angeles County Bar Association; American Bar Association; American Trial Lawyers Association. **Education:** University of California – Los Angeles: J.D. (1977), B.A. in Political Science (1973). **Personal:** Married to Marilyn Ann in 1967. Three children: Renita Annette, Jomaal Curtis, and Courtnay Erin. Mr. Johnson enjoys music and staying physically fit.

Michael P. Joyce
Shareholder
Wyrsch Atwell Mirakian Lee & Hobbs, P.C.
1101 Walnut, Suite 1300
Kansas City, MO 64106
(816) 221–0080
Fax: (816) 221–3280

8111

Business Information: Wyrsch Atwell Mirakian Lee & Hobbs, P.C. is a full–service, litigation law firm. The Firm currently employs 11 attorneys, legal and administrative support staff. Admitted to practice in Missouri and Kansas state and federal courts, Mr. Joyce joined the Firm in 1988 as Associate. Currently serving as Shareholder, he is responsible for providing legal representation, concentrating his practice in litigation in civil and criminal trial and appellate courts. Mr. Joyce's practice emphasizes white collar criminal defense, healthcare fraud and abuse litigation and corporate internal investigation. **Career Steps:** Shareholder, Wyrsch Atwell Mirakian Lee & Hobbs, P.C. (1988–Present); Briefing Clerk, Bracewell & Patterson (1986–1987); Research Assistant, Professor Richard M. Alderman, University of Houston (1986); Associate Manager, Avco Financial Services International (1983–1985). **Associations & Accomplishments:** President, Kansas City Alumni Club, Creighton University (1992–1994); Director – Region IV, National Alumni Board of Directors, Creighton University Alumni Association (1993–1996); The Missouri Bar Association; Kansas Bar Association; Kansas City Metropolitan Bar Association; Johnson County Bar Association; American Bar Association; Missouri Association of Trial Attorneys; The Association of Trial Lawyers of America; Missouri Association of Criminal Defense Lawyers; National Association of Criminal Defense Lawyers; Who's Who in the World (1995); Who's Who in American Law (1992–1993, 1994–1995); Outstanding Young Man of America (1988); Citation's Who's Who Registry of Rising Young Americans (1992–1993); American Biographical Institute's Man of the Year (1993); Assistant Editor, Caveat Vendor, Newsletter of State Bar of Texas for the Consumer Law Section; Admissions to Bar: U.S. Supreme Court (1994), Supreme Court of Missouri (1988), Supreme Court of Kansas (1989), U.S. District Court, Western District of Missouri (1988), U.S. District Court, Kansas (1989), U.S. Court of Appeals, Eighth Circuit (1988), U.S. Court of Appeals, Tenth Circuit (1988); President, Student Bar Association (1987–1988); Secretary–Treasurer, National Student Bar Association (1987–1988); 2d Vice President, Student Bar Association (1986–1987); Civil Trial Advocacy Course Completed – Course conducted by National Institute of Trial Advocacy (NITA); Moot Court Competition – Quarterfinalist; Who's Who Among American Law Students (1987 & 1988); Omicron Delta Kappa; Pi Kappa Alpha Fraternity; Tutor–Upward Bound Program, Creighton University. **Education:** University of Houston Law Center, J.D. (1988); Creighton University, B.S. and B.A. (1982); Miami University, Oxford, Ohio (1978–1979); Graduate, Mid–American Region, NITA Trial Course (1992). **Personal:** Married to Rebecca in 1991. One child: Thomas. Mr. Joyce enjoys golf, basketball, skiing, and doing community service.

Michael L. Judy

Partner
Johnson, Judy, True & Guarnieri, L.L.P.
326 West Main Street
Frankfort, KY 40601
(502) 875–6000
Fax: Please mail or call

8111

Business Information: Johnson, Judy, True & Guarnieri, L.L.P. is a full–service, general practice law firm. Admitted to practice law in the U.S. Supreme Court, U.S. 6th Circuit Court of Appeals, U.S. District Courts for the Eastern and Western Districts of Kentucky, Supreme Court of Kentucky, Kentucky Court of Appeals, and all circuit courts for the State of Kentucky, Mr. Judy joined the Firm as Partner in 1995. He provides legal representation to the Firm's clientele. **Career Steps:** Partner, Johnson, Judy, True & Guarnieri, L.L.P. (1995–Present); Partner, Stoll, Keenon & Park (1982–1995); Partner, Johnson & Judy, P.S.C. (1974–1981); Associate, Johnson & Burton (1971–1974); Clerk, Johnson, Burton & Emberton (1969–1971); Intern, Northern Virginia Regional Planning Center (1968); Staff Assistant, Kentucky Department of Personnel (1963–1964); Clerk, Kentucky Department of Public Safety (1962); E–6/Infantry, United States Army Reserves – 100th Division. **Associations & Accomplishments:** American Bar Association; Kentucky Bar Association; Association of Trial Lawyers of America; Kentucky Academy of Trial Lawyers; Franklin County Bar Association; Kentucky Home Builders; National College of Trial Advocacy; Founder, Franklin County Public Defender's Program; Who's Who in American Law; Best Lawyers in America; Recognized as an Outstanding Trial Lawyer in Kentucky; United States Jaycees' President's Award; Kentucky Jaycees: Outstanding Speaker Award, State General Counsel (Six years); Distinguished Service Award, Kentucky Press Association; YMCA: Service to Youth Award, President, Board of Directors (Since 1986); Outstanding Young Man of America; University of Kentucky Fellow; Board of Directors, Frankfort Chamber of Commerce; Board of Directors, United Way; President, Franklin County Young Democrats; Kentucky Young Democrats: Board of Directors, General Counsel; Recipient of Emerson "Doc" Beauchamp Award; Kentucky Colonel; Phi Delta Phi Honorary Society, University of Kentucky. **Education:** University of Kentucky, J.D. with honors; George Washington University. **Personal:** Married to Marilyn Barrett Judy in 1968. Two children: Michelle Judy Harnsberger and M. David Judy.

Gregory T. Juge

Sole Practitioner
Gregory T. Juge, Attorney At Law, N.O., LA
3636 S. I–10 Service Road, Suite 220
Metairie, CA 70001
(504) 837–2838
Fax: (504) 837–4220

8111

Business Information: Gregory T. Juge, Attorney At Law, N.O., LA is a full–service law firm that serves national and international clientele. The Firm represents corporate and individual interests in employment matters. As Sole Practitioner and Attorney At Law, Mr. Juge handles issues of Employment Law, such as sexual harassment, race discrimination, disability discrimination, breach of contract, and retaliatory discharge claims. He also handles Unfair Trade Practices, Intellectual Property cases, and Commercial Contract Disputes. Mr. Juge is admitted to practice before the Supreme Court of Louisiana, all three United States District Courts of Louisiana, and the Fifth Circuit Court of Appeals. **Career Steps:** Attorney At Law, Gregory T. Juge, Attorney At Law, N.O. L.A. (1993–Present); Associate, McCalla, Thompson, Pyburn & Ridley, N.O., LA (1992–1993); Associate, Jones, Walker, Waechter, Poitevent, Carrere & Denegre, N.O., LA (1991–1992). **Associations & Accomplishments:** American Bar Association (Section of Labor and Employment Law); Federal Bar Association; Phi Beta Kappa; 1988 Rhodes Scholarship semi–finalist; Columbia International Law Society; Columbia Advocates for the Arts; Omicron Delta Kappa; National Collegiate Economics Award Winner; Treasurer, Executive Committee, Tulane Scholars Organization. **Education:** Columbia University School of Law, NY, J.D. (1991); Tulane University, N.O., LA, B.A. Degree in Economics (1988) summa cum laude; The Outstanding Scholar in Economics; 1988 Japan–Tulane Friendship Award for Honors Thesis on Bilateral Trade Imbalance. **Personal:** Mr. Juge enjoys weight training, music, sports, reading, and painting.

Gloria M. Justiniano–Irizarry, J.D.

Sole Practitioner
Lcda. Gloria M. Justiniano
14 Sur Calle Martinez Nadal
Mayaguez, Puerto Rico 00680
(809) 831–2577
Fax: (809) 831–2577

8111

Business Information: Lcda. Gloria M. Justiniano is a private, full–service general practice law office. A practicing attorney since 1986, Ms. Justiniano–Irizarry established her sole practice law office in 1992, concentrating on litigation cases. **Career Steps:** Sole Practitioner, Lcda. Gloria M. Justiniano (1992–Present); In–House Attorney, SOTEL Corporation (1991–1992); Judicial Law Clerk, Superior Court (1988–1989); Attorney, Department of Justice (1986–1988). **Associations & Accomplishments:** Puerto Rico Bankruptcy Bar Assocation; Colegio de Abogados de Puerto Rico. **Education:** Inter–American University Law School, J.D. (1986); Universidad de Puerto Rico, B.A. **Personal:** Three children: Gloriam and Homel Mercado, and Priscilla Soto. Ms. Justiniano–Irizarry enjoys martial arts, jogging, and writing.

Gerald F. Kandestin

Senior Partner
Kugler Kandestin
1 Place Ville Marie, Suite 2101
Montreal, Quebec H3B 2C6
(514) 878–2861
Fax: (514) 875–8424

8111

Business Information: Kugler Kandestin is a full–service law firm, a sector of which is heavily focused on loan and security transactions, security realizations, loan restructurings and insolvency. The Firm acts regularly for several major banks, including The Bank of Nova Scotia, Bank of Montreal, Bank of Boston Canada, Swiss Bank Corporation (Canada), and BNY Financial Corporation–Canada. The Firm is active in the representation of, and has acted for, various high level bankruptcy trustees and receivers. Mr. Kandestin has been a practicing attorney in Canadian courts since obtaining his degree in 1974. He now serves as a Senior Partner in the law firm of Kugler Kandestin. As a Senior Partner, he sits on the Firm's Executive Committee, as well as practicing banking and secured lending, bankruptcy, creditors rights, and insolvency law. **Career Steps:** Associate, Partner, and Senior Partner, Kugler Kandestin (1976–Present); Associate Attorney, Gameroff, Fenster, Kandestin, Gelfand & Kugler; Associate Attorney, Stikeman, Elliott, Tamaki, Mercier & Robb (1974–1976). **Associations & Accomplishments:** Canadian Bar Association; Quebec Bar Association – Bankruptcy Liaison Committee, The Insolvency Institute of Canada, Insol International; Founding Member and Director, Canadian Turnaround Management Association; Former President, The Lord Reading Law Society; Active in various charitable organizations; President, Montefiore Club of Montreal. **Education:** McGill University, Bachelor of Civil Law (1974); University Scholar, Carswell Prize for High Standing. **Personal:** Married to Janice in 1978. Three children: Cory, Carly, and Dale. Mr. Kandestin enjoys skiing, golf, and is an avid wine collector and amateur musician.

Mr. Charles J. Kane

Senior Partner
Greenspan and Kane
301 Yamato Road, Suite 3160
Boca Raton, FL 33431–4917
(407) 995–8180
Fax: (407) 995–8188

8111

Business Information: Greenspan and Kane, established in 1993, is a full–service, general practice law firm. The partnership includes Charles Kane, Leon Greenspan, Michael Greenspan, Harley Kane and Glenn Jett. The Firm has regional offices in New York, New Jersey, and Florida. Admitted to practice in Florida state and federal courts since 1965, Mr. Kane joined the Firm in 1993 as Senior Partner. He concentrates his practice in the areas of real estate and transactional law, personal injury and family law, as well as issuing insurance policies. Concurrent with his corporate law practice, he serves as President of Charles J. Kane, P.A. and conducts lectures annually for the Florida State Bar on attorney fees and contracts representation. **Career Steps:** Senior Partner, Greenspan and Kane (1993–Present); President, Charles J. Kane, P.A. (1977–Present); Partner, Green and Kane, P.A. (1972–1977); Associate, Broad & Cassel (1971–1972). **Associations & Accomplishments:** Million Dollar Advocates Forum; Member, Executive Council, General Practice Section, Florida Bar; Member, American Bar Association; Member, Association of Trial Lawyers of America (ATLA); Licensed in Florida State Courts, Federal Court – 5th District, U.S. Court of Claims, and Circuit Court in Districts 11 & 5; Published in 1977 Prentice Hall on U.S. Tax Information for International Operators. **Education:** New York University, LL.M. in Tax (1966); University of Miami, J.D. (1965); University of Pennsylvania Wharton School of Finance and Commerce, B.S. in Economics (1962). **Personal:** Two children: Harley N., Esq. and Scott R. Kane. Mr. Kane enjoys scuba diving.

Mr. Yukio Kashiba

Counsel
Rogers & Wells
200 Park Avenue
New York, NY 10166
(212) 878–3144
Fax: (212) 878–8375

8111

Business Information: Rogers & Wells is a major international law firm with offices in New York, Los Angeles, Washington, D.C., London, Paris, and Frankfurt. Mr. Kashiba specializes in Japanese business practice. Established in 1871, Rogers & Wells employs a legal professional and administrative support staff of over 900. **Career Steps:** Counsel, Rogers & Wells (1994–Present); Counsel, Shea & Gould (1993–1994); Associate, Morgan & Finnegan (1990–1993); Patent Manager, Sharp Corporation, Japan (1981–1989). **Associations & Accomplishments:** New York State Bar Association; American Bar Association; New York County Lawyers' Association; New York Intellectual Property Law Association; American Intellectual Property Law Association; International Intellectual Property Association; Senri Club of New York, Chairman. **Education:** Georgetown Law School, LL.M. (1990); Kansai University, Japan, LL.M. (1970).

Cherol B. Katz

Attorney
Law Office of Cherol B. Katz
6122 Lincoln Avenue, Suite 107
Cypress, CA 90630
(714) 952–7868
Fax: (714) 995–6325

8111

Business Information: A practicing attorney for a number of years, Ms. Katz opened the Law Offices of Cherol B. Katz in 1989. Her focus is on entertainment law and intellectual property law. Concurrently Ms. Katz is an instructor at Western State University College of Law and at the American Bar Association approved Paralegal College of Southern California College of Business and Law. Ms. Katz teaches classes in Tortes, Ethics, Contracts Legal Writing and Research, and Civil Procedure. Ms. Katz was just chosen by the North Orange County Regional Occupational Programs to teach the course "Careers in Law". The Pilot Program being taught by Ms. Katz is the first of its kind being offered to High School students and adults in Orange County seeking careers in Law. **Career Steps:** Attorney, Law Office of Cherol B. Katz (1989–Present); Vice President Business and Legal Affairs, Tele–Seminars, Inc. (1994); Assistant Vice President Business and Legal Affairs, Concorde New Horizons Corporation (1993–1994); Deputy City Attorney, City of Garden Grove (1991–1992); Attorney, Mitchell, Sizberberg & Knupp. **Associations & Accomplishments:** American Bar Association, Entertainment and Sports Law; American Bar Association, Lawyers and the Arts, Education Committees, Young Lawyers Division; Intellectual Property Section, State Bar of California; California Elected Women's Association for Education and Research; Docent for "Anne Frank in the World" Exhibit. **Education:** Western State University College of Law, Juris Doctor (1987); University of California at Los Angeles, B.A. in English Literature (1983); Cypress College, A.S. in Biology (1981); California Community Colleges Instructor Lifetime Credential in Law. **Personal:** Ms. Katz enjoys swimming and treadmill walking.

Robert D. Kawamura
Partner
Kawamura & Lobdell, Attorneys at Law
1221 Kapiolani Boulevard, Penthouse
Honolulu, HI 96814–3503
(808) 523–3777
Fax: (808) 591–9000

8111

Business Information: Kawamura & Lobdell is a full–service law practice specializing in general civil litigation. Established in 1990, the Firm currently employs 6 people. As Partner, Mr. Kawamura is responsible for all aspects of company operations, and emphasizes personal injury, product liability, business litigation, and litigation coordination. **Career Steps:** Partner, Kawamura & Lobdell (1990–Present); Attorney, Carlsmith Ball Et al. (1988–1990); Attorney, Somers Hall Verrastro & Kern (1986–1988). **Associations & Accomplishments:** American Bar Association; Hawaii State Bar Association; State Bar of California; Consumer Lawyers of Hawaii; American Trial Lawyers of Hawaii. **Education:** Whittier College School of Law, J.D. (1986); University of Hawaii, B.F.A. (1982). **Personal:** Married to Lisa in 1988. Two children: Jenna and Kayla. Mr. Kawamura enjoys spending time with his family.

Mr. John Murray Keefe, Attorney
–Independent–
10620 NE 26th Street
Bellevue, WA 98004–2222
(206) 827–7068
Fax: (206) 827–7849

8111

Business Information: John M. Keefe is an attorney in solo practice. Mr. Keefe's area of expertise is securities and commercial litigation, and pro bono representation. Established in 1990. **Career Steps:** Owner, John M. Keefe, Attorney, (1990–Present); President, Sequoia Systems (1986–1992). **Associations & Accomplishments:** YMCA; Washington State Trial Lawyers Association; Eastside Legal Assistance Program. **Education:** Southwestern University, J.D. (1984); Cal–State University, B.A. in Political Science (1980). **Personal:** Married to Afkenine de Jong–Keefe in 1987. Mr. Keefe's interests include skiing and fly–fishing.

Charles R. Keeton
Attorney
Brown, Todd & Heyburn, PLLC
3200 Providian Center
Louisville, KY 40202–3363
(502) 589–5400
Fax: (502) 581–1087

8111

Business Information: Brown, Todd & Heyburn, PLLC is a law firm concentrating in commercial transactions and finance. A trial Attorney since 1975, Mr. Keeton is a Partner with the Firm and the Coordinator of the Commercial Transaction and Finance Group. Mr. Keeton is admitted to both State and Federal courts. **Career Steps:** Attorney, Brown, Todd & Heyburn, PLLC (1980–Present). **Associations & Accomplishments:** Kentucky Bar Association Committee on Uniform Commercial Code; Louisville Bar Association Bankruptcy Section and Court; Board of Directors, Louisville Youth Orchestra; Board of Directors, Neighborhood House; Chairman, Board of Deacons, St. Matthews Baptist Church; Coach, Atherton High School Mock Trial Team; American Bar Association; Kentucky Bar Association; Louisville Bar Association. **Education:** University of Kentucky Law School, J.D. (1975); Marshall University, B.A. **Personal:** Married to Mary Alice McGlone in 1969. Three children: Charles R., Jr., Benjamin Curtis, Mary Afton. Mr. Keeton enjoys flying, fishing and spending time with his family. Mr. Keeton has his private pilot's license.

Norman A. Keith, B.A., L.L.B.
Senior Litigation Partner
Mathews, Dinsdale & Clark
1 Queen Street East, Suite 2500
Toronto, Ontario M5C 2Z1
(416) 869–8545 (416) 862–8280
Fax: (416) 862–8247

8111

Business Information: Mathews, Dinsdale & Clark is a full–service employment law firm. A practicing lawyer in Canadian courts since receiving his degree in 1981, Mr. Keith joined the Firm in 1981. He is responsible for the development, practice, and supervision of the employment litigation group at the Firm. He also handles employment litigation for occupational safety and environmental practices, including drafting health and safety policies; drafting health and safety liability indemnity language; drafting employment contracts; drafting sexual harrassment policies; employment standard hearings; labour arbitration hearings; illegal picketing injunctions; wrongful resignation cases; wrongful dismissal cases; human rights complaints; health and safety prosecutions; appeal of Ministry of Labour Orders; environmental prosecutions; appeals of environmental Orders; Coroner's Inquests; safety related discipline arbitration and Ontario Labour Relations Board cases; fiduciary duty lawsuits; firefighter risk management training, Municipal and Fire Department liability cases; trade mark injunctions; and judicial review of various tribunal decisions, applications and appeals in Freedom of Information and Protection of Privacy Act matters. **Career Steps:** Senior Litigation Partner, Mathews, Dinsdale & Clark (1988–Present); Associate of Norman A. Keith (1983–1988). **Associations & Accomplishments:** Canadian Bar Association; Human Resources Professional Association of Ontario; General Council of Reference, Canadian Council of Christian Chanties; Canadian Society of Safety Engineers; Christian Legal Fellowship; Frequent publisher /lecturer at international, national, state, and local conferences and institutional symposia and proceedings; Authored "Ontario Health and Safety Law" and other books and articles regarding employment law. **Education:** Osgoode Law School: Bachelor of Laws (1981), Intensive Trail Advocacy Course; York University, B.A. (1979); Articles of Clerkship, Matthews, Dinsdale, and Clark (1981–1982); Bar Admission Course (1982–1983); Call to the Ontario Bar (1983); Numerous Continuing Education Programs. **Personal:** Mr. Keith enjoys youth soccer coaching, recreational skiing, and cycling.

Mr. George M. Kelakos
Partner
Cohn & Kelakos
265 Franklin Street
Boston, MA 02110
(617) 951–2505
Fax: (617) 951–0679

8111

Business Information: Cohn & Kelakos, established in 1990, is a law firm specializing in bankruptcy law and business litigation. The Firm's practice focuses on representation of substantial businesses undergoing a restructuring of liabilities, including Chapter 11 reorganizations, federal and state court receiverships, and out–of–court workouts. The Firm also represents lenders, suppliers, creditors' committees, stockholders and potential acquirers of troubled companies and assets, as well as the representation of plaintiffs and defendants in civil litigation. The Firm currently has five attorney members, all of which have appeared in courts throughout New England, as well as elsewhere. Clients and case involvements include: Shape, Inc.; New Hampshire Electric Cooperative, Inc.; Kendall Square Research Corporation; P.J. Keating Company; A.J. Lane & Co., Inc.; Stadium Management Corporation; Cape Cod Broadcasting, L.P., et al; Westra Plastics, Inc.; Wang Laboratories, Inc.; Mars Stores, Inc.; and Healthco International, Inc. A practicing attorney since 1982, George Kelakos established the Firm in 1990. As the Partner responsible for Firm management, he oversees the administrative operations in addition to representing major clients. Mr. Kelakos focuses his practice on providing counsel to foreign investors and professionals in his field of expertise. **Career Steps:** Partner, Cohn & Kelakos (1990–Present); Associate, Fine & Ambrogne's Reorganization and Bankruptcy Group (1989–1990); Associate, Riemer & Braunstein (1985–1989); Associate, Sterling & Miller, P.C. (1984–1985); Associate, Inman & Flynn (1982–1984). **Associations & Accomplishments:** American Bankruptcy Institute; Boston Bar Association; Kuntao Silat Association (Martial Arts); Mr. Kelakos lectures on bankruptcy and related topics for Massachusetts Continuing Legal Education as well as for private trade and creditor groups. **Education:** University of Denver – College of Law, J.D. (1982) – also served as a developments editor of the Denver Journal of International Law and Policy; Brandeis University, B.A. Degree in Politics, cum laude (1979) **Personal:** Mr. Kelakos enjoys martial arts (26 years experience), music (musician – guitar player and singer), motorcycle racing, touring and traveling. He also speaks French, Italian, conversational Hebrew, and some Greek.

Joseph R. Kelly
Shareholder and Corporate Secretary
Westman, Champlin, & Kelly, P.A.
Suite 720, TCF Tower, 121 S. 8th Street
Minneapolis, MN 55402
(612) 334–3222
Fax: (612) 334–3312

8111

Business Information: Westman, Champlin, & Kelly, P.A. is a general practice law firm concentrating in Intellectual Property Law. Established in 1993, the firm currently employs 7 attorneys and 14 legal support staff. A practicing attorney since 1989, Mr. Kelly has been with the Firm for two years. In his current position as a Shareholder and the Corporate Secretary, Mr. Kelly is admitted to both State and Federal courts and is responsible for the administrative functions of the Firm. As a Partner, he shares the responsibility of the direction of the staff as well as the continued growth and success of the Firm. Previous to attending law school and graduating Valedictorian, Mr. Kelly was an Electrical Design Engineer. **Career Steps:** Shareholder, Corporate Secretary and Attorney, Westman, Champlin, & Kelly, P.A. (1993–Present); Attorney, Kinney & Lange, P.A. (1987–1993); Design Engineer, Micro Control Company (1984–1986). **Associations & Accomplishments:** Minnesota State Bar Association; American Bar Association; American Intellectual Property Lawyers Association; Minnesota Intellectual Property Lawyers Association; Advisory Committee for Intellectual Property Law Studies, William Mitchell College of Law. **Education:** William Mitchell College of Law, J.D. (1989); Iowa State University, B.S. in Electrical Engineering. **Personal:** Married to Julie L. Sprau in 1985. One child: Lauren S. Mr. Kelly enjoys running, biking, swimming, and golf.

Mr. Keenan K. Kelly
Associate Attorney
Kelly, Townsend & Thomas
137 St. Denis Street
Natchitoches, LA 71458
(318) 352–2353
Fax: (318) 352–8918

8111

Business Information: Kelly, Townsend & Thomas is a full–service, general practice law firm specializing in maritime and personal injury law. Established in 1990, the Firm currently employs five attorneys, three partners and two associates. Joining the Firm (co–founded by his father) upon the conferral of his law degree in 1993, Keenan Kelly specializes in personal injury law, as well as serves as defense attorney in limited criminal matters. **Career Steps:** Associate Attorney, Kelly, Townsend & Thomas (1993–Present); Law Clerk, Martzell & Bickford (1991–1993); Technicians Helper, Southwest Engineers (1989–1990); Self employed, Hunting Guide (1986–1990). **Associations & Accomplishments:** Member, Louisiana Trial Lawyers Association; Member, Louisiana Bar Association; Member, State Bar of Texas; Member, American Bar Association; Member, Jaycees of Natchitoches Parish. **Education:** Loyola University School of Law, J.D. (1993); Northwestern State University, B.S. **Personal:** Married to Melissa C. Kelly in 1991. One child: Brandon Kyle. Mr. Kelly enjoys hunting, fishing and water skiing.

Richard R. Kennedy
Attorney
The Law Offices of Richard R. Kennedy
P.O. Box 3243
Lafayette, LA 70502–3243
(318) 232–1934
Fax: (318) 232–9720

8111

Business Information: The Law Offices of Richard R. Kennedy is a full–service, general practice law firm, specializing in maritime law and personal injury cases. Establishing the Firm upon the conferral of his law degree in 1965, Mr. Kennedy oversees all administrative operations for associates and a support staff of four, in addition to his daily private law practice. Admitted to practice in state and federal courts, he serves as a trial attorney, serving clientele located throughout the U.S. **Career Steps:** Attorney, The Law Offices of Richard R. Kennedy (1965–Present). **Education:** Tulane University School of Law, J.D. (1965); University of Southwestern Louisiana, B.A. **Personal:** Married to Judith in 1974. One child: Richard R. III. Mr. Kennedy enjoys reading, travel, riding his Harley Davidson motorcycle.

Mr. Joseph Francis Kessler
• • •━━◉━━• • •

Partner
Dilworth Paxson Kalesh & Kauffman
3200 Mellon Bank Center, 1735 Market Street
Philadelphia, PA 19103–7501
(215) 575–7198
Fax: (215) 575–7200

8111

Business Information: Dilworth Paxson Kalesh & Kauffman is a full–service, general practice law firm concentrating in civil law. Established in 1930, the Firm currently consists of 80 attorneys and employs 70 legal and administrative support staff. Admitted to practice law in 1982, Mr. Kessler joined the Firm as Partner in 1983. His practice concentrates in corporate real estate transactions. **Career Steps:** Partner, Dilworth Paxson Kalesh & Kauffman (1983–Present). **Associations & Accomplishments:** Pro bono work for local activities for church. **Education:** Villanova University, J.D. (1982); St. Joseph's University, B.A. (1979). **Personal:** Mr. Kessler enjoys travel, college basketball, sportsman, golf, theatre, and orchestras.

Mr. Mitchell S. Kessler

Attorney
Law Office of Mitch Kessler
286 Fair Street
Kingston, NY 12401
(914) 331–5380
Fax: (914) 331–5024

8111

Business Information: The Law Office of Mitch Kessler is a full–service, general practice law office with emphasis in family law and criminal law at the trial and appellate levels. Admitted to practice in state courts in New York and Massachusetts and federal district courts in the Northern and Southern Districts of New York, Mr. Kessler established this solo practice in 1995. **Career Steps:** Mr. Kessler was previously employed as a trial attorney in the Bronx, New York office of the Legal Aid Society, Juvenile Rights Divisions (1989–1994), and prior to pursuing a career in law, as a professional musician. **Associations & Accomplishments:** Mr. Kessler is a member of the National Ski Patrol, Nordic Division; a volunteer firefighter with the Centerville Fire Company in Saugerties, New York; and a member of the American, New York State and Ulster County Bar Association and the American Society of Notaries. In addition, Mr. Kessler was included in Outstanding Young Men of America in 1985. **Education:** Boston College Law School, J.D. (1989); New England Conservatory, Bachelor of Music (1982), Masters in Music (1984). **Personal:** Mr. Kessler enjoys hiking, nordic skiing, and jazz.

Jeffery A. Key, Esq.

Partner
Martindale, Brzytwa, & Quick
900 Skylight Office Tower, 1660 West 2nd Street
Cleveland, OH 44113–1411
(216) 664–6900
Fax: (216) 664–6901

8111

Business Information: Martindale, Brzytwa, & Quick, established in 1994, is a full–service, general practice law firm, focusing on litigation. A practicing attorney in Ohio and Florida state and federal courts since 1982, Mr. Key joined the Firm in 1994. Serving as Partner, he is responsible for providing legal representation to the Firm's clientele, focusing on construction, contract, business, and injury litigation. **Career Steps:** Partner, Martindale, Brzytwa, & Quick (1994–Present); Sole Practitioner, Melamed, Friedman & Key; Partner, Benesch, Friedlander & Coplan (1987–1993); Associate, Thompson, Hine & Flory (1983–1987). **Associations & Accomplishments:** Board Member, Ohio Human Rights Bar Association; Ohio Bar Association, Legal Ethics and Professional Conduct Committee; Florida Bar Association; Federal Bar Association; American Bar Association; ACLU. **Education:** Cleveland–Marshall College of Law, J.D. summa cum laude (1982); Cleveland State University, B.A., cum laude (1979). **Personal:** Mr. Key enjoys scuba diving, water and snow skiing, and racquetball.

Kurt L. Kicklighter

Partner
Higgs, Fletcher & Mack
401 West A Street, Suite 2000
San Diego, CA 92101
(619) 236–1551
Fax: (619) 696–1410

8111

Business Information: Higgs, Fletcher & Mack is a full–service general practice law firm. A practicing attorney since 1981, Mr. Kicklighter joined the Firm in 1988. As Partner he heads the Firm's banking section, focusing his practice in the areas of corporate law, securities, mergers and acquisitions matters. **Career Steps:** Partner, Higgs, Fletcher & Mack (1988–Present); Associate, Stroock and Stroock and Lavan (1986–1988); Associate, Leff & Jensen (1985–1986). **Associations & Accomplishments:** American Bar Association; California State Bar Association: Business Law Section, Financial Institutions Committee, Ad Hoc Committee on Professional Liability; San Diego County Bar Association; Board of Directors, San Diego Financial Managers; California League of Savings Institutions, Attorneys Committee; Board of Directors, Columbia University Alumni Club of San Diego; KidzArtz; Old Mission Rotary Club. **Education:** Columbia University School of Law, J.D. (1981); University of California–Berkeley, B.A. in Economics and Sociology (1978). **Personal:** Married to Carol in 1984. Mr. Kicklighter enjoys golf.

Karen Smith Kienbaum

Of Counsel
Abbott, Nicholsen, Quilten, Essacki and Youngblood
One Woodward Drive, 19th Floor
Detroit, MI 48230
(313) 963–2500
Fax: Please mail or call

8111

Business Information: Abbott, Nicholsen, Quilten, Essacki and Youngblood is a full–service, general practice law firm. Established in 1975, the Firm currently employs 40 people. A practicing attorney in Michigan state courts since 1975, Ms. Kienbaum joined the Firm as Of Counsel in 1993. Her practice specializes in labor and employment counsel and litigation. **Career Steps:** Of Counsel, Abbott, Nicholsen, Quilten, Essacki and Youngblood (1993–Present); Of Counsel, Varnum Riddering (1993); Senior Counsel, Ford Motor Company (1989–1993); Assistant General Counsel, Blue Cross/Blue Shield (1979–1993). **Associations & Accomplishments:** Former President, Detroit Bar Association; Former President, American Corporate Counsel Association; American Bar Association: Member and Member of House of Delegates; Michigan State Bar Association: Chair – Judge Magistrate Selection Committee, Committtee on Professionalism; Martindale–Hubbell rating: AV. **Education:** University of Detroit School of Law, J.D. (1975); University of Michigan – Ann Arbor, B.A. in History and Education (1965). **Personal:** One child: Ursula. Ms. Kienbaum enjoys downhill and cross–country skiing, water sports, hiking and reading during her leisure time.

Thomas J. Killeen

Partner
Farrell Fritz
EAB Plaza
Uniondale, NY 11556–0120
(516) 227–0631
Fax: (516) 227–0777
EMAIL: See Below

8111

Business Information: Established in 1967, Farrell, Fritz is a general civil practice law firm of approximately 50 attorneys, including 15 partners. A practicing attorney since 1973, Thomas Killeen has been a Partner with the Firm since 1983. Admitted to the New York state and federal courts, including the Tax Court, he concentrates his practice in the areas of corporate, securities, banking, and real estate law on behalf of public and private corporations, banks, insurance companies and other financial institutions. Internet users can reach him via: TKILLEEN@COUNSEL.COM. **Career Steps:** Partner, Farrell, Fritz (1983–Present); Fulton, Duncombe & Rowe (1973–1983). **Associations & Accomplishments:** American Bar Association; New York State Bar Association: Banking, Corporation and Business Law Section, Real Property Law Section; Nassau County Bar Association; Chair, Banking Law Committee (1994–Present), Speaker's Bureau, Corporate Law Committee; American Inns of Court; Munsey Park Civic Association; Manhasset Athletic Advisory Committee. **Education:** St. John's University School of Law, J.D. (1972) (Managing Editor, St. John's Law Review); St. Francis College, B.A. in English cum laude (1969).

John H. Kim

Attorney
Fisher, Gallagher & Lewis
1000 Louisianna 70th Floor
Houston, TX 77002
(713) 654–4433
Fax: (713) 654–5070

8111

Business Information: Fisher, Gallagher & Lewis is a full–service, general practice law firm. Based in Houston, Texas, with an additional office in Austin/Beaumont, Texas, the Firm currently employs 85 attorneys, legal, and administrative support staff. Admitted to state and federal Texas courts, Mr. Kim represents clients in the areas of product liability, personal injury, medical and pharmaceutical litigation, and other appellate and arbitration matters. Concurrent with his legal practice, he also serves as an Adjunct Professor of Appellate Advocacy at the South Texas College of Law. **Career Steps:** Attorney, Fisher, Gallagher & Lewis **Associations & Accomplishments:** American Bar Association; State Bar of Texas; Texas Young Lawyers Association – Star Mentor Program; American Trial Lawyers Association; Board of Directors (1994–1995), Texas Trial Lawyers Association: Vice Chair of Political Section, Fund–raising Committee Member, Legislative Lobbyist at 1995 Tort Reform, Board of Director (1994–95); Houston Trial Lawyers Association; Houston Bar Association; South Texas College of Law: Alumni Association, Law Review – Budget Committee Member, Moot Court Varsity Coach, Center for Legal Responsibility Planning Committee, Phi Delta Phi, Order of Lytae, Order of Barristers, ABA National Moot Court Champion; Various Publications and Lectures. **Education:** South Texas College of Law, J.D. with honors; University of Texas, B.B.A. in International Business and Marketing (1983). **Personal:** Mr. Kim enjoys golf, reading, and travel.

Mr. James Coyne King

President
Hanify & King, Professional Corporation
One Federal Street
Boston, MA 02110
(617) 423–0400
Fax: (617) 423–0498

8111

Business Information: Hanify & King, Professional Corporation is a general practice law firm, specializing in commercial law and litigation including international trade, fraud claims, transactional law, and bankruptcy. As President, Mr. King acts as Chief Operating Officer, overseeing management of the Firm's operations, and directs the antitrust and international trade regulation practice. Established in 1980, Hanify & King, Professional Corporation employs 29 attorneys and an administrative support staff of approximately 30. **Career Steps:** President, Hanify & King, Professional Corporation (1980–Present); Special Assistant, U.S. Attorneys Office, (MA & CO), U.S. Department of Justice (1979–1980); Administrative Assistant, National Commission to Review Anti–Trust Laws (1978–1979); Trial Attorney, Anti– Trust Department, U.S. Department of Justice (1973–1978). **Associations & Accomplishments:** Chairman, Georgetown University Law Alumni Board; Director, Catholic Charities of Boston Advisory Board; Fellow, Massachusetts Bar Foundation; Member, World Affairs Council of Boston. **Education:** Georgetown University Law Center, LL.M. (Tax) (1978); Georgetown University Law Center, J.D. (1973); University de Fribourg, Switzerland; Georgetown University, A.B. (1970).

William B. Kingman

Sole Practitioner
Law Offices of William B. Kingman
106 South Saint Marys Street, Suite 800
San Antonio, TX 78205–3603
(210) 224–0223
Fax: (210) 226–0521

8111

Business Information: The Law Office of William B. Kingman is a general practice law firm concentrating in the areas of corporate real estate and bankruptcy law. Establishing his private practice in 1994, Mr. Kingman has been a trial attorney since 1986 and is admitted to both State and Federal courts. His areas of expertise include bankruptcy and creditors rights; real estate law; corporate, commercial and general business law; and mediations. Involved with several entrepreneurial enterprises, he is also founder and President of Shoulder to Shoulder, Inc. – a wholesale craft distribution operation. **Career Steps:** Sole Practitioner, The Law Office of William B. Kingman (1994–Present); President, Shoulder to Shoulder, Inc. (1994–Present); Law Firm of Foster, Lewis, Langley, Gardner & Banack, Inc.: Attorney and Shareholder (1986–1994), Head of Bankruptcy and Creditors Rights Section, Chairman of Charitable Contribution Committee (1993–1994), Marketing Committee (1993–1994); Teacher of Fifth Grade Religious Education, St. Anthony of Padua Catholic Church. **Associations & Accomplishments:** Young Lawyers Division, American Bar Association; State Bar of Texas; College of The State Bar of Texas; San Antonio Bar Association: Community Relations Committee (1993–Present), Medical/Legal Liaison Committee (1988–Present); Young Lawyers Division, American Bankruptcy Institute; Secretary (1993–Present), San Antonio Bankruptcy Bar Association; San Antonio Young Lawyers Association; Young Lawyers Division, Federal Bar Association; San Antonio Defense Counsel; Texas Young Lawyers Association; Association of Attorney Mediators; Who's Who in American Law; Greater San Antonio Chamber of Commerce (Since 1993): Governmental Affairs Council, Education Committee, Small Business Council, International Affairs Committee; Participant – Leadership San Antonio XX – 1994–1995 Sponsored By Greater San Antonio Chamber and San Antonio Hispanic Chamber; San Antonio Texas Exes: Director (Since 1994), Liaison for 1994 Habitat for Humanity Project, Assistant Vice President for Scholarship (1995–1996); Alamo Kiwanis Club (Since 1993); Chairman – International Relations Committee (1994–1995), Chairman – Programs (1995–1996); Chairman, Alamo Heights Independent School District Legislative Committee; Alamo Heights I.S.D. Technology Committee; Alamo Heights I.S.D. Elementary School Task Force Curriculum Committee; Alamo Heights High School Site Based Management Committee; Woodridge Elementary School: PTO (Mentorship Coordinator), Curriculum Enrichment and Technonogy Committees; Director (Since 1983), Kingman Foundation; Mentor, Edgewood and Alamo Heights High Schools and Woodridge Elementary School; Alamo Heights Little League: Director (Since 1994), Secretary (1994–1995), Treasurer (1995–1996); Licensed to Practice: Texas State Courts;

United States District Court, Eastern, Northern, Southern and Western Districts of Texas; United States Court of Appeals, Fifth Circuit; United States Supreme Court; Speaker and Author: Advanced Collections and Bankruptcy Process in Texas (1994); Seminar sponsored by the National Business Institute. **Education:** University of Texas: J.D. (1986), B.B.A. in Finance (1983); Texas Board of Legal Specializations, Certification in Business Bankruptcy Law. **Personal:** Married to Kate in 1983. Four children: Katherine, Will, Libby, and Jack. Mr. Kingman enjoys mentoring, coaching youth sports, golf, hunting, and fishing.

Mr. Richard A. Kissel
Partner
Nicoletti, Kissel and Pesce, L.L.P.
805 Third Avenue
New York, NY 10021
(212) 317-1200
Fax: (212) 317-0704

8111

Business Information: Nicoletti, Kissel and Pesce, L.L.P. handles all aspects of legal problems facing the insurance industry. Mr. Kissel, together with Frank Nicoletti and Randy Pesce, is one of the Firm's founding partners. **Career Steps:** Partner, Nicoletti, Kissel and Pesce, L.L.P. (1995–Present); Partner, Ober, Kaler, Grimes & Shriver (1991–1995); Partner, Sheft & Sheft (1986–1991); Associate, Mendes & Mount (1980–1986). **Associations & Accomplishments:** American Bar Association; Professional Liability Underwriting Society; Defense Research Institute. **Education:** Syracuse University, College of Law, J.D. (1979); Boston University, School of Law, B.S. in Business Administration (1976). **Personal:** Married to Michelle Simon (Associate Professor of Law, Pace University College of Law). Three children: Amanda, Margaret and Robert. Mr. Kissel enjoys sports, theater and American History.

Ms. Joyce E. Kitchens
Attorney
Joyce E. Kitchen, Attorney at Law
3166 Mathieson Drive NE
Atlanta, GA 30305
(404) 266-9895
Fax: (404) 364-0031
EMAIL:JEK@AOL.Com

8111

Business Information: Joyce E. Kitchens, Attorney at Law, established in 1991, is a full-service, general practice law firm. Admitted to practice in Georgia state and federal courts, Ms. Kitchens founded this solo-practice in 1991. She is responsible for all aspects of operations, including providing legal representation. **Career Steps:** Attorney, Joyce E. Kitchens, Attorney at Law (1991–Present); Department of Veteran Affairs: Assistant District Counsel (1989–1991), Staff Attorney (1982–1989). **Associations & Accomplishments:** Vice President of Eleventh Circuit, Federal Bar Association; Atlanta Bar Association; Lawyer Club of Atlanta; American Bar Association; Past President, Kiwanis Club. **Education:** Emory University School of Law, J.D. (1982); Purdue University, M.A. in English Literature. **Personal:** Married to Jerry B. Barnes in 1980. Two children: Suzanne Cynthia and Craig Kendall Barnes. Ms. Kitchens enjoys travel and reading.

Edward D. Kleinbard
Partner
Cleary, Gottlieb, Steen & Hamilton
1 Liberty Plaza 38th Floor
New York, NY 10006
(212) 225-2480
Fax: (212) 225-3999

8111

Business Information: Cleary, Gottlieb, Steen & Hamilton is one of the leading and best-known U.S.–based international law firms. The Firm currently consists of approximately 400 attorneys, operating from eight locations. A practicing attorney in New York state courts since 1976, Mr. Kleinbard joined the Firm in 1977 and was appointed as Partner in 1984. His practice focuses on federal income tax matters, including specialties in the taxation of new financial products, financial institutions and international mergers and acquisitions. A highly esteemed attorney in his field, he was named as one of New York's finest lawyers by "New York" magazine, and one of America's leading lawyers under the age of 45 by "American Lawyer" magazine in 1995. **Career Steps:** Cleary, Gottlieb, Steen & Hamilton: Partner (1984–Present), Associate (1977–1984). **Associations & Accomplishments:** American College of Tax Counsel; Board of Advisors, American Association of Financial Engineers; American Bar Association; Association of the Bar of the City of New York; New York Bar Association: Sustained Member, Former Member of Executive Committee of the Tax Section, Former Co–Chairman of New Financial Products Subcommittee. He has published numerous articles pertaining to taxation in various law journals, as well as lectures regularly at local, staet, and na-

tional law association and educational conference and symposia proceedings. **Education:** Yale Law School, J.D. (1976); Brown University: M.A. in History (1973), B.A. in Medieval and Renaissance Studies (1973). **Personal:** Married to Norma F. Cirincione in 1985. One child: Martin.

John A. Klobasa
Partner
Kohn, Shands, Elbert, Gianoulakis & Giljum
One Mercantile Center, 24th Floor
St. Louis, MO 63101
(314) 241-3963
Fax: (314) 241-2509

8111

Business Information: Kohn, Shands, Elbert, Gianoulakis & Giljum is a full-service, general practice law firm. Joining the Firm as Associate upon the conferral of his law degree from Washington University in 1975, Mr. Klobasa was appointed as Partner in 1981. His practice concentrates on litigation and probate law. Litigation experience includes participating as lead trial counsel or assistant trial counsel in a wide variety of federal and state court actions in Missouri, Illinois, California and Maine, including school law, contract, UCC, will contests, trust and probate matters, securities, anti–trust, real estate, negligence, domestic relations, and various equitable actions. He also has argued appellate cases in various fields of law in state and federal courts, as well as representing numerous corporations and public entities as plaintiff and defendant. **Career Steps:** Kohn, Shands, Elbert, Gianoulakis & Giljum: Partner (1981–Present), Associate (1975–1980). **Associations & Accomplishments:** Phi Beta Kappa; Order of the Coif, Washington University School of Law; Who's Who in America; Who's Who of American Law; Who's Who Among Practicing Attorneys; Who's Who of Emerging Leaders; Bar Association of Metropolitan St. Louis; Missouri Bar Association; American Bar Association; Phi Delta Phi; City of Des Peres: Alderman (1989–1991), Special Counsel (1987), Board of Adjustment (1986–1989), Aldermanic Member (1990), Aldermanic Representative – Parks & Recreation Commission (1989); Special Counsel, City of Town & Country (1987). **Education:** Washington University School of Law, J.D. (1975); Emory University, B.A. in Economics (1972). **Personal:** Married to Kathleen in 1979. Two children: Jennifer and Christine. Mr. Klobasa enjoys fishing, jogging, travel, and reading.

Mr. Christopher S. Knopik
Shareholder
Yerrid, Knopik & Mudano, P.A.
Barnett Plaza, Suite 2160, 101 East Kennedy Boulevard
Tampa, FL 33602
(813) 222-8222
Fax: (813) 222-8224

8111

Business Information: Yerrid, Knopik & Mudano, P.A. is a law firm specializing in civil litigation: personal injury; wrongful death; premises liability; maritime; medical and legal negligence; and products liability. As Shareholder, Mr. Knopik is a Board Certified Trial Lawyer who has practiced in both state and federal courts and has been recognized as a "Leading Florida Attorney." **Career Steps:** Shareholder, Yerrid, Knopik and Mudano, P.A. (1996–Present); Shareholder, Yerrid, Knopik & Valenzuela, P.A. (1990–1996); Shareholder, Stagg, Hardy & Yerrid, P.A. (1986–1989); Attorney, Holland & Knight (1985–1986). **Associations & Accomplishments:** Member, American Bar Association (Tort and Insurance Practice, Litigation and Public Utilities); Member, The Florida Bar (Fee Arbitration Program, 13th Judicial Circuit and Trial Lawyers Section); Member, Hillsborough County Bar Association (Director, Trial Lawyers Section, Co–Chairman, Mock Trial Committee and Young Lawyers Division); Member, Federal Bar Association; Member, American Judicature Society; Member, The Defense Research Institute; Member, The Association of Trial Lawyers of America; Member, Southeastern Admiralty Law Institute; Member, Maritime Law Association of the United States; Member, Bay Area Volunteer Lawyers Program; Member, Ferguson–White Inn of Court; Mr. Knopik has also presented seminars on legal matters. **Education:** University of Virginia, J.D. (1983); Florida State University, B.S. (1980). **Personal:** Married to Andrea Cheney Knopik in 1988. One child: Christopher Kyle and Ora Rae. Mr. Knopik enjoys physical fitness and sports.

Peter John Kok
Attorney/Partner
Miller, Johnson, Snell, & Cummiskey, P.L.C.
800 Calder Plaza Building, 250 Monroe Avenue, Northwest
Grand Rapids, MI 49503
(616) 459-8311
Fax: (616) 459-6708

8111

Business Information: Miller, Johnson, Snell, & Cummiskey, P.L.C. is a full-service, general practice law firm. A practicing attorney in Michigan state and federal courts since receiving his degree in 1970, Mr. Kok joined the Firm in 1970. His areas of practice include employment counseling and litigation in federal courts, state courts, and administrative agencies, involving labor, employment, civil rights matters, discrimination, wrongful discharge claims, arbitration, union avoidance, unemployment, NLRB, ERISA, OSHA/MIOSHA, and wage-hour and collective bargaining matters. **Career Steps:** Attorney/Partner, Miller, Johnson, Snell, & Cummiskey, P.L.C. (1976–Present). **Associations & Accomplishments:** Administrative Management Society of Western Michigan; Alliance of Commerce and Industry; American Bar Association; American Society of Personnel Administrators; Michigan and National Chapters, Associated Builders and Contractors; Associated General Contractors of America; Association of Human Resource Management; Cadillac Area Personnel Association; Calvin College; Clearinghouse for Training Resources; Construction Financial Management Association; East Central Region Construction Users Council; Forest Products Research Association; Grand Haven: Personnel Association, Committee for Economic Development; Grand Rapids: Bar Association, Chamber of Commerce, Personnel Association, Plumbing and Heating Contractors, Press Club; Greater Elkhart Personnel Association; Holland–Zeeland Personnel Association; Hope College; Lakeshore Retirement Planning Committee; Lansing Area Joint Labor Management Committee, Inc.; Lansing Chamber of Commerce; Michigan: Association of School Personnel Administrators, Construction Users Council, Federation of Private Child and Family Agencies, Manufacturers Association, Public Employer Labor Relations Association, Restaurant Association, Road Builders Association, Safety Council; Mid–Michigan Personnel Association; National Tooling & Machinery Association; Nursing Home Association; Personnel Association of South Haven; Restaurant Association of Western Michigan; South West Michigan Personnel Roundtable; State Bar of Michigan Business Section; Surety Association of West Michigan; The Employer's Association Board; The Employer's Association Human Resources Group; Underground Contractors Association; United Way; Washtenaw Contractors Association; West Michigan: Health Systems Agency, Personnel Association, Association of Occupational Health Nurses; YMCA Industrial & Business Council. **Education:** University of Michigan, J.D. cum laude (1970); Calvin College, B.A. (1967). **Personal:** Married to Evonne A. in 1968. Four children: Michelle, Jonathan, Alisa, and Christian. Mr. Kok enjoys racquetball, sailing, and tennis.

Richard A. Kraemer, Esq.
Partner
Marshall Dennehey et al
1845 Walnut Street
Philadelphia, PA 19103
(215) 575-2812
Fax: Please mail or call

8111

Business Information: Marshall Dennehey, et al is a premier litigation law firm. Established in 1960, the Firm consists of 215 attorneys and 600 legal and administrative support staff. A practicing attorney since 1969, Mr. Kraemer joined the Firm as Partner in 1992. He serves as a trial attorney, providing legal counsel and litigation representation throughout three states (New York, New Jersey, Pennsylvania). **Career Steps:** Partner, Marshall Dennehey, et al (1992–Present); Partner, Margolis Edelsfern, Siberts & Kraemer (1976–1992). **Associations & Accomplishments:** American Bar Association; National Association of Railroad Trial Counsel; Pennsylvania Bar Association; Philadelphia Bar Association; Defense Research Institute; Philadelphia Association of Defense Counsel. **Education:** University of Pennsylvania Law School, J.D. (1969); Williams College, A.B. (1966). **Personal:** Married to Barbara in 1977. Mr. Kraemer enjoys golf and coaching Little League.

Ralph J. Kreitzman, Esq.
Partner
Hughes Hubbard & Reed, L.L.P.
One Battery Park Plaza
New York, NY 10004
(212) 837-6740
Fax: (212) 422-4726

8111

Business Information: Hughes Hubbard & Reed L.L.P., which traces its history to 1871, is an international law firm, specializing in litigation, tax, real estate, corporate, trust and estates, banking and financial services, environmental, government affairs, employee benefits, executive compensation, employment litigation, insurance, intellectual property, international, mergers and acquisitions, Pacific Basin, securities, bankruptcy and corporate reorganization matters for public and private corporations, governments and individuals. The Firm has over 230 attorneys practicing out of its offices in New York City, NY, Washington, D.C., Los Angeles, CA, Miami, FL, Paris, France, Newark, NJ, and Berlin, Germany. Mr. Kreitzman, with the Firm for over 25 years specializing in real estate, hotel and international law, is Co–Chair of the Firm-wide Real Estate Group, which consists of over 25 attorneys. **Career Steps:** Partner (1980–Present), Associate (1970–1980), Hughes Hubbard & Reed L.L.P. **Associations & Accomplishments:** Admitted to practice in New York State and before U.S. Supreme Court; U.S. District Courts for Southern and Eastern Districts of New York; U. S. Court of Appeals for the Second Circuit; and N.Y. State Courts; Member of Real Property Law Section and Committee on Foreign Investment in U.S. Real Estate of the American Bar Association; Member of the Real Property Law Section and Committees on Commercial Leasing and Financing of the New York State Bar Association; Member of the Committee on Real Property Law of the Association of the Bar of the City of New York. Member (1968–1970), Articles Editor (1969–1970), and published in Brooklyn Law Review. **Education:** Brooklyn Law School, J.D. with honors (1970); Rider University, B.S. in Accounting (1967).

Bruce Anthony Kunz

Partner

Cannon, Kunz & Fischer

310 North Main Street, P.O. Box 480
Mahnomen, MN 56557
(218) 935–5322
Fax: (318) 935–2482

8111

Business Information: Cannon, Kunz & Fischer is a general practice law firm. A practicing attorney since 1991, Mr. Kunz became a partner in 1992. He heads the criminal defense section of their firm which also has a primary focus in the area of Native American Law, and represents a tribal government and its various entities. **Career Steps:** Partner, Cannon, Kunz & Fischer (1991–Present); Law Clerk, 7th Judicial District of Minnesota (1987–1988); Law Clerk, Becker County Law Library – Detroit Lakes, MN (1986–1987); Law Clerk, Schroeder & Schroeder Law Office – Detroit Lakes, MN (1984–1985). **Associations & Accomplishments:** Minnesota State Bar Association; National Association of Criminal Defense Lawyers; Legal Aid Association; American Bar Association; Delta Theta Phi. **Education:** University of North Dakota, J.D. (1988); Moorhead State University, B.A. (1985–1987). **Personal:** Married to Jane in 1987. Two children: Benjamin and Andrew. Mr. Kunz enjoys hunting, fishing, and trap shooting.

Joseph A. La Bella

Partner and Litigator

Cooney, Scully, & Dowling

10 Columbus Blvd.
Hartford, CT 06106–1944
(760) 527–1141
Fax: (860) 247–5215

8111

Business Information: Cooney, Scully, & Dowling is a full-service, general practice law firm. Established in 1929, the Firm currently employs 46 people. A practicing attorney in Connecticut state courts, Mr. La Bella joined the Firm in 1986 as Partner and Litigator upon the conferral of his law degree. His practice concentrates in trial law, professional liability defense (physicians, attorneys), and criminal cases. **Career Steps:** Attorney, Cooney, Scully, & Dowling (1986–Present). **Associations & Accomplishments:** American Bar Association; Connecticut Bar Association; Hartford County Bar Association; Published article in the American Criminal Law Review on securities fraud. **Education:** Georgetown University Law Center, J.D. (1986); University of Notre Dame, B.A. (1983). **Personal:** Mr. La Bella enjoys athletics, running, and local politics.

Kenneth A. Lakin, Esq.

Managing Partner

Broadhurst, Lakin & Lakin

One Elm Square
Andover, MA 01810–364
(508) 470–3545
Fax: (508) 470–3464

8111

Business Information: Broadhurst, Lakin & Lakin is a full-service, general practice law firm, providing legal services in the areas of environmental, toxic tort, real estate, criminal, corporate, health, finance, and reinsurance law. The Firm serves clientele from two locations in Massachusetts (Andover and Boston). A practicing attorney in Massachusetts state courts since 1991, Kenneth Lakin joined the Firm as Managing Partner in 1992. He oversees all administrative staff and associates at the Andover location, in addition to his legal practice. Mr. Lakin concentrates his practice in the areas of environmental, toxic tort, insurance, health law, and litigation. **Career Steps:** Managing Partner, Broadhurst, Lakin & Lakin (1992–Present); Environmental Claims Manager, Lexington Insurance Company – Boston (1987–1992); Liability Supervisor, Liberty Mutual Insurance Company (1983–1987). **Associations & Accomplishments:** American Bar Association; Essex County Bar Association; Massachusetts Bar Association; Boston Bar Association; Defense Research Institute. **Education:** Massachusetts School of Law, J.D. (1991); Boston College, A.B. (1983). **Personal:** Married to Elizabeth in 1989. Three children: Kyle, Kara, and Kasey. Mr. Lakin enjoys golf and fishing.

Robert S. Lamar Jr.

President

Lamar, Nelson, and Miller, P.C.

505 20th Street North
Birmingham, AL 35203–2605
(205) 326–0000
Fax: (205) 323–2945
EMAIL: See Below

8111

Business Information: Established in 1989, Lamar, Nelson, and Miller, P.C. is a full–service law firm specializing in insurance work. The Firm works closely with national insurance companies in property and casualty law. As President, Mr. Lamar is responsible for all aspects of company operations, including administration, legal, and strategic planning. Internet users can reach him via: blamar@snsnet.net. **Career Steps:** President, Lamar, Nelson, and Miller, P.C. (1989–Present). **Associations & Accomplishments:** Alabama Bar Association; Alabama Defense Lawyers Association; Defense Research Institute; International Association of Defense Counsel. **Education:** University of Alabama: J.D. (1966), B.A. (1963). **Personal:** Married to Ellen in 1980. Two children: Catherine and Elizabeth. Mr. Lamar enjoys photography, spectator sports, and travel.

Nicole Y. Lamb–Hale

Associate

Dykema Gossett, P.L.L.C.

400 Renaissance Center
Detroit, MI 48243
(313) 568–6513
Fax: (313) 568–6915

8111

Business Information: Dykema Gossett, P.L.L.C. is a full-service, general practice law firm consisting of 140 partners and six offices in the Michigan and Illinois region and one office in Washington, D.C. Established in the 1920's, the Firm currently employs 230 attorneys, legal, and administrative support staff. A practicing attorney in Michigan state and federal courts, including the U.S. Court of Appeals for the Sixth Circuit, Ms. Lamb–Hale joined the Firm in 1991 upon conferral of her law degree. Serving as an Associate, her practice concentrates on commercial, transactional, bankruptcy, and creditor's rights law. Career milestones include serving as legal advisor to the City of Detroit in connection with its successful quest for designation as a Federal empowerment zone — a HUD–sponsored program involving tax benefits to businesses and the infusion of Federal capital funds to be used for social services programs. **Career Steps:** Associate, Dykema Gossett, P.L.L.C. (1991–Present); Intern, Brown, Rudrick, Freed and Gesmer (1989); Intern, General Motors Corporation (1988); Intern, Saturn Corporaton (1986–1987). **Associations & Accomplishments:** Detroit Housing Commission; Delta Sigma Theta Sorority, Inc.; Advisory Board, Detroit Association of Black Storytellers; Crain's Detroit Business, 40 professionals under the age of 40 (1995). **Education:** Harvard Law School, J.D. (1991); University of Michigan – Ann Arbor, A.B. with high honors. **Personal:** Married to John H. Hale III in 1991. Ms. Lamb–Hale enjoys community service, politics and reading.

Sally Hardin Lambert

Managing Partner

Conliffe, Sandmann & Sullivan

621 West Main Street
Louisville, KY 40202
(502) 587–7711
Fax: (502) 587–7756

8111

Business Information: Conliffe, Sandmann & Sullivan, a private law firm with 50 employees, has offices in Kentucky and Indiana. Because Mr. Conliffe is the County Attorney, the Firm concentrates on business, bankruptcy, and environmental law rather than criminal defense. As Managing Partner, Ms. Lambert handles daily operation of the Firm. She assists in the recruitment of legal staff, office administration, marketing of services, public relations, and planning for expansion. Ms. Lambert works with clients regarding employment law, workers' compensation, personal injury, and property law. **Career Steps:** Managing Partner, Conliffe, Sandmann & Sullivan (1993–Present); Partner, Keats, Schwietz & O'Donnell (1992–1993); Partner, Keats, Hibbs & O'Donnell (1991–1992); Partner, Nicolas, Welsh & Brooks (1988–1991). **Associations & Accomplishments:** Louisville Astronomical Society; Kentuckiana Chinese School, Inc.; Louisville Ballet. **Education:** University of Louisville, J.D. With Honors (1974); Indiana University, M.B.A. (1989); Denison University, B.A. With Honors (1970). **Personal:** One child: Josiah Lambert Keats. Ms. Lambert enjoys reading, astronomy, studying Chinese language and culture, ballet, and travel.

Mr. Richard L. Lancione

President

Lancione, Davis & Lloyd Law Office Company, L.P.A.

3800 Jefferson Street
Bellaire, OH 43906
(614) 676–2034
Fax: (614) 676–3931

8111

Business Information: Lancione, Davis & Lloyd Law Office Company, L.P.A. is a full service law firm. In the practice of law since 1966, starting as an associate in his father's firm, Richard Lancione is the President and Chief Litigator for Lancione, Davis & Lloyd. In addition to his administrative duties with the Firm he is also a trial lawyer, concentrating in the areas of personal injury and general civil litigation. Established in 1929, Lancione, Davis & Lloyd Law Office Company, L.P.A. employs 7 attorneys, legal aide professionals and administrative support staff people. **Career Steps:** President, Lancione, Davis & Lloyd Law Office Company, L.P.A. (1968–Present); Associate, Nelson Lancione Law Office (1966–1968). **Associations & Accomplishments:** Association of Trial Lawyers of America; Ohio Academy of Trial Lawyers; American Bar Association; Ohio State Bar Association; Belmont County Bar Association; Salvation Army Advisory Council; Ohio University Eastern Regional Coordinating Council; National Imperial Glass Collectors Society Board; National Association of Burger King Franchisees. **Education:** Ohio State University School of Law, J.D. (1966); Wittenberg University; Ohio State University College of Business, B.S. in Economics (1963). **Personal:** Married to Joyce in 1963. Two children: Tracey and Brant. Mr. Lancione enjoys the collecting of Imperial glass.

Edward A. Landry, Esq.

Senior Partner

Musick, Peeler & Garrett

1 Wilshire Boulevard
Los Angeles, CA 90017–3806
(213) 629–7657
Fax: (213) 624–1376

8111

Business Information: Musick, Peeler & Garrett is a full–service, general practice law firm. With offices in San Francisco, Los Angeles, San Diego and Sacramento, the Firm concentrates primarily on civil litigation and the professional defense of lawyers, doctors, and engineers. Joining the Firm upon the conferral of his law degree in 1962, Mr. Landry currently serves as one of five senior partners. His practice concentrates exclusively on estate and tax planning issues. **Career Steps:** Senior Partner, Musick, Peeler & Garrett (1962–Present). **Associations & Accomplishments:** State Bar of California; Los Angeles County Bar Association; American Bar Associaton; Chancery Club; The American College of Trust and Estate Counsel; Trustee, Harvey Mudd College; Director, Music Center Opera Association; Trustee, Rancho Santa Ana Botanic Gardens; Trustee, Dan Murphy Foundation; Trustee, Museum of Natural History; Director, Estelle Doheny Eye Institute; Trustee, Jaquelin Hume Foundation; Trustee, Walter Lantz Foundation; Trustee, Flora Thornton Foundation; Director, Foundation for Teaching Economics; Director, Calmat Company; The California Club; Wine and Food Society of Southern California; Breakfast Panel; California Vintage Wine Society; Chevalier's Du Tastevin; Bordeaux Society; Beta Gamma Sigma; Order of the Coif; University of California Los Angeles Law Review; Who's Who in California; Best Lawyer's in America; Kappa Alpha Order; Phi Delta Phi; Lecturer: U.C.L.A. Law School, California Continuing Education of the Bar, Practicing Law Institute, U.C.L.A.–C.E.B. Estate Planning Institute, The American College of Trust and Estate Counsel, and Various other programs and institutions; Author of various articles in Continuing Education Legal publications relating to estate planning and taxation. **Education:** University of California – Los Angeles, Ll.B. (1964); Louisiana State University, B.A. in Business Administration with honors (1961) **Personal:** Married to Madeleine in 1962. Two children: Monique and Lucette. Mr. Landry enjoys theatre, art, food, and wine.

Charles A. Lanford Jr., Esq.

Senior Partner
Lanford, Smith and Kapiloff
3266 Pio Nono Avenue
Macon, GA 31206–3030
(912) 788–7236
Fax: (912) 788–0999

8111

Business Information: Lanford, Smith and Kapiloff, established in 1991, is a full–service, general practice law firm specializing in probate law and guardianships. Admitted to practice in Georgia and Mississippi state courts, Mr. Lanford co–founded the Firm in 1991 and currently serves as Senior Partner. **Career Steps:** Senior Partner, Lanford, Smith and Kapiloff (1991–Present); General Partner and Attorney, Anderson and Lanford (1987–1990); Associate Attorney, Benton and Boyer (1986–1987); First Lieutenant and Finance Officer, U.S. Army (1980–1983). **Associations & Accomplishments:** State Bar of Georgia; American Bar Association; Macon Bar Association; Mississippi State Bar; Georgia Trial Lawyers Association; Benevolent and Protective Order of Elks; Kappa Alpha Alumni Association; American Legion; Phi Alpha Delta Legal Fraternity; Sons of Confederate Veterans. **Education:** Georgia State University College of Law, J.D. (1986); Central Michigan University, M.A.; University of Georgia, B.B.A. **Personal:** Married to Sherri G. Lanford in 1992. One child: David. Mr. Lanford enjoys hunting, fishing, public speaking, Civil War History, and downhill skiing in Colorado.

Donald H. Lapowich, Q.C.

Partner/Attorney
Koskie Minsky
20 Queen Street, West, Suite 900
Toronto, Ontario M5H 3R3
(416) 977–8353
Fax: (416) 977–3316
EMail: See Below

8111

Business Information: Koskie Minsky is a boutique practice law firm concentrating on civil litigation, employee litigation, pension, and trusts. With 27 attorneys, the Firm does some international work in England and across Canada. A practicing attorney in the Courts of Ontario since obtaining his degree in 1967, Mr. Lapowich became a Partner of the Firm in 1985. As a Partner and Attorney, he handles civil litigation, insurance, defense, malpractice, and general commercial litigation, as well as heads the Litigation Department and is a member of the Executive Committee. Mr. Lapowich enjoys working with professional people and helping colleagues in legal matters. Internet users can reach him via: DLapowich@Koskie-Minsky.com. **Career Steps:** Partner, Koskie Minsky (1985–Present); Partner, Altwerger Lapowich (1973–1985); Associate, Thomson Rogers (1969–1973). **Associations & Accomplishments:** Canadian Bar Association; Insurance Institute of Ontario; Advocacy Association; Chairman, Family Advisory Baycrest Geriatric Hospital; County of York Law Association; Certified in Civil Litigation; Law Society of Upper Canada lecturer in Risk Management, as well as other Professional Lectures; Speaker at various seminars for Law Society and Dental Associations, Insurance Appraisers, and other Professional Groups; Published in a number of papers for the Law Journal of Upper Canada and Canadian Bar Association; Publishes a monthly newsletter on current affairs to his clients; Publishes bi–monthly tips and reminders to 2,500 lawyers in Canada; Lecturer to the Canadian Real Estate Institute and Insurance Institute of Ontario, Board of Trade, and local Real Estate Boards; and publishes monthly articles in Real Estate Magazine. **Education:** Osgoode Hall Law School, LL.B. (1967), prize for First Standing and various awards of merit; Called to the Bar in 1967, awarded Treasurer's Medal of Upper Canada; University of Western Ontario, B.A. with honors (1962), Dean's Honour Roll; Certified as a Specialist in Civil Litigation by the Law Society of Upper Canada; Received Queen's Counsel appointment in 1982, as certified by Mr. Justice White of Supreme Court of Ontario. **Personal:** Married to Arlene in 1969. Two children: Hyla and Stuart. Mr. Lapowich enjoys art and community work, and is a supporter and participant with the Heart and Stroke Foundation, Baycrest Hospital, community colleges (professional courses), and a past youth group director.

Therese M. Lawless

Partner
Lawless, Harowitz & Lawless
600 Montgomery Street, Transamerica Pyramid – 33rd Floor
San Francisco, CA 94111
(415) 391–7555
Fax: (415) 391–4228

8111

Business Information: Lawless, Harowitz & Lawless is a full–service, general practice law firm concentrating on employment and discrimination law, consisting of three partners and two associates. A practicing attorney in California state and federal courts since 1986, Ms. Lawless joined the Firm in 1988 as an associate attorney. Appointed as Partner in 1994, her practice focuses on employment law, sexual harassment, and sexual and age discrimination. **Career Steps:** Lawless, Harowitz & Lawless: Partner (1994–Present), Associate (1988–1994); Associate, Gastan & Snow (1987–1988); Law Clerk, Ninth Circuit Court of Appeals (1986–1987). **Associations & Accomplishments:** San Francisco Trial Lawyers Association; Edition of Quarterly Newsletter; Consumer Attorneys of California; San Francisco Bar Association; Lawyers Club. **Education:** George Washington University, J.D. (1986); Cornell University, B.S. (1982).

Dolores Y. Leal

Partner
Allred, Maroko & Goldberg
6300 Wilshire Boulevard, Suite 1500
Los Angeles, CA 90048
(213) 653–6530
Fax: (213) 653–1660

8111

Business Information: Allred, Maroko & Goldberg is a full–service, general practice law firm, concentrating on civil matters. A practicing attorney in California state and federal courts since 1987, Ms. Leal joined the Firm as Associate in 1991. Appointed as a Partner of the Firm in 1994, her practice concentrates on employment litigation, including sexual harassment cases (forming 65% of her cases) and the remainder on wrongful termination and discrimination on the basis of age, race, religion, color, sex, national origin, physical disability and medical condition. Prior to joining the Firm, Ms. Leal was employed by the U.S. Equal Employment Opportunity Commission. Holding various positions with EEOC, her last position was that of Senior Trial Attorney. During her tenure there she was initially responsible for investigating hundreds of charges of employment discrimination under Title VII and ADEA. Ms. Leal has appeared as a speaker in the area of employment discrimination and sexual harrassment before several attorney continuation education seminars, business groups, radio and television programs. She has also taught torts, employment discrimination and critical studies at Peoples College of Law. **Career Steps:** Allred, Maroko & Goldberg: Partner (1994–Present), Associate (1991–1994); Senior Trial Attorney, U.S. Equal Employment Opportunity Commission (1987–1991). **Associations & Accomplishments:** Board Member, California Employment Lawyers Association; Board Member, Peoples College of Law; Mexican American Bar Association; Los Angeles County Bar Association; Federal Bar Association. **Education:** Western State College of Law, J.D. (1987).

Mr. Brian W. LeClair

Shareholder and Attorney
Fordham & Starrett, P.C.
260 Franklin Street
Boston, MA 02109
(617) 439–0300
Fax: (617) 439–0320
EMail: See below

8111

Business Information: Fordham & Starrett, P.C. is a full–service, general practice law firm. Established in 1985, the Firm currently employs 16 attorneys, legal and administrative support staff. Admitted to practice law in Massachusetts state courts since 1973, Mr. LeClair joined the Firm as Shareholder and Attorney in 1985. He is responsible for legal representation, as well as serves as Officer and Director. He can also be reached through the Internet as follows: blc@triple–i.com **Career Steps:** Shareholder and Attorney, Fordham & Starrett, P.C. (1985–Present); Associate, Foley, Hoag & Eliot (1974–1985); Law Clerk, Hon. W. Arthur Garrity, U.S.D.C. (1973–1974); Law Clerk, Hon. James Jeffords (Summer–1972). **Associations & Accomplishments:** President (1985–1986), Director (1980–1992), Cambridge Civic Association; American Bar Association; Massachusetts Bar Association; Boston Bar Association. **Education:** Boston University Law School, J.D. (1973); University of Vermont, B.S. (1970). **Personal:** Married to Linda Kane LeClair in 1988. Two children: Michael and Lindsey. Mr. LeClair enjoys sailing and cross country skiing.

David Woon Lee

Founder and Partner
David & Ramond
108 North Ynez Avenue, Suite 118
Monterey Park, CA 91770
(818) 571–9812
Fax: (818) 287–9564

8111

Business Information: David & Raymond is a full service private patent law firm. As Founder and Partner, Mr. Lee is responsible for the daily patent law practice within the firm. Concurrent to his duties as Founder and Partner with David & Raymond, he is the sole practitioner of the Law Offices of David W. Lee. **Career Steps:** Founder and Partner, David & Raymond (1994–Present); Legal and Patent Law Consultant for American Chinese Inventor Association (1995–Present); Sole Practitioner, Law Offices of David W. Lee (1992–Present); Supervisor, Chalk River Nuclear Laboratories (1970–1987). **Associations & Accomplishments:** State Bar of California; Registered Patent Attorney to practice before the U.S. Patent & Trademark Office since 1993; People to People International, Citizen Ambassador Program; Who's Who in the World; Who's Who in the West; Who's Who in Science & Engineering; Delegate, Citizen Ambassador Program, Nuclear Waste Management, U.S.S.R.; Delegate, Citizen Ambassador Program, Mission to Asia for International Understanding; Atomic Energy of Canadian Professional Employees Association; Judge, Pembroke Regional Science Fair; American Nuclear Society; Numerous articles in professional journals; Speaker on Patent Cooperation Treaty Application Procedures to International School of Innovative Technologies for Cleaning the Environment in Italy in 1995. **Education:** Glendale University – College of Law, J.D. (1991); University of Waterloo, Canada, B.S. with honors (1979); University of Winnipeg, Canada, B.S. (1970). **Personal:** Married to Helen in 1970. Two children: Victor and Malinda. Mr. Lee enjoys travel, fishing, writing, music, reading, and teaching.

Paul P. Lee, M.D.

Associate Professor
University of Southern California School of Medicine
1450 San Pablo Street
Los Angeles, CA 90033
(213) 342–6413
Fax: (213) 342–6460

8111

Business Information: University of Southern California School of Medicine is a medical school, health care delivery, and health services research institution. As Associate Professor in the Department of Ophthalmology, Dr. Lee establishes the school's overall approach for improving the quality of health care, focusing on patient care, residency, and research. Dr. Lee is also a consultant for the Rand Corporation, on the issues of quality health care and the impact of managed care. Established in 1880, University of Southern California is a private, co–ed university in Los Angeles, with over 30,000 students. **Career Steps:** University of Southern California School of Medicine: Associate Professor (1995–Present), Assistant Professor (1991–1995). **Associations & Accomplishments:** American Bar Association; American Bar Association; ARVO; AAO. **Education:** University of Michigan Medical School, M.D. (1986); Columbia Law School, J.D. (1986).

Paul W. Lee, Esq.

Partner
Goodwin, Procter & Hoar
Exchange Place
Boston, MA 02109
(617) 570–1590
Fax: (617) 523–1231

8111

Business Information: Goodwin, Procter & Hoar is a full–service, general practice law firm concentrating in the representation of business clients, including corporations, institutional investors and other parties to business transactions. With offices located in Boston, Massachusetts, District of Columbia, and Albany, New York, the Firm currently employs over 300 attorneys. Admitted to practice in New York state courts in 1976 and Massachusetts state courts in 1981, Mr. Lee joined the Firm as an Associate in 1981 and was elected partner in 1984. He is Chairman of the Firm's Corporate Practice Group, which consists of approximately 150 attorneys. In his practice, he acts as counsel to international corporate entities, both established public international corporations as well as private corporations, including high technology companies, in public and private offerings, venture capital financing, mergers, acquisitions and other business transactions. **Career Steps:** Goodwin, Procter & Hoar: Partner (1984–Present), Associate (1981–1984); Associate, Donovan, Leisure Newton & Irvine (1976–1981). **Associations & Accomplishments:** President, National Asian Pacific–American Bar Association; Member, American Bar Association Commission on Opportunities for Minorities in the Profession; Past President, Asian American Lawyers of Massachusetts; Board Member, Asian Community Development Center; Lead Boston (1994–1995). **Education:** Cornell Law School, J.D. (1976). **Personal:** Married to Dr. Mary Y. Lee in 1980. Two children: Gregory and Samantha.

Gerald A. Lefebvre

Owner and Attorney
Law Office of Gerald Lefebvre, Attorney At Law
414 Northwest Third Street
Okeechobee, FL 34972–4129
(941) 763–3333
Fax: (941) 763–9561

8111

Business Information: Law Office of Gerald Lefebvre, Attorney At Law is a full–service, specialized practice law firm, limited to personal injury and wrongful death. A Board Certified Civil Trial Lawyer and Civil Trial Advocate, Mr. Lefebvre was admitted to practice in Florida state courts in 1976. Establishing his sole practice in 1983, his legal practice provides legal representation and litigation to the firm's clientele. His jury trial expertise includes automobile accidents, wrongful death, product liability, murder, slip & fall, eminent domain, professional negligence, capital sexual battery and others. **Career Steps:** Owner and Attorney, Law Office of Gerald Lefebvre, Attorney At Law (1983–Present); Attorney, Conlon & Tooker (1981–1983); Prosecutor, State's Attorney Office, 19th Judicial Circuit, State of Florida (1977–1981); Public Defender, Public Defender's Office, 16th Judicial Circuit, State of Florida (1977). **Associations & Accomplishments:** The Florida Bar; American Bar Association; The Association of Trial Lawyers of America; The Academy of Florida Trial Lawyers; Who's Who in Practicing Attorneys; Marquis Who's Who in American Law; Board of Directors, Childrens' Home Society, Treasure Coast Division (1989–1990); Chairman, Childrens' Service Council of Okeechobee County, Florida; 19th Judicial Circuit Civil Trial Bar Association; Florida Lawyers Action Group; Juvenile Arbitrator, 19th Judicial Circuit, Okeechobee County, Florida (1992–1993); Florida Association of State Troopers, Inc.; Advisory Committee for the Tri–County Healthy Kids Corporation; Recognized as one of Florida's Leading Attorneys in Personal Injury Law by the American Research Corporation (1995–1996); Florida Bar Board Certified Civil Trial Lawyer (1989); Board Certified in Civil Trial Advocacy by the National Institute of Trial Advocacy (1989); State and Federal Court Admissions: United States Supreme Court (1991), United States District Court, Southern District of Florida (1983), Trial Bar United States District Court, Southern District of Florida (1983), United States District Court, Middle District of Florida (1981), United States Court of Appeals, Eleventh Circuit (1981), all Florida Courts (1976). **Education:** Stetson University College of Law, J.D. (1976); Bethany College, B.A. in Philosophy (1972). **Personal:** Married to Brenda in 1981. One child: Timothy Adam McCann Lefebvre. Mr. Lefebvre enjoys racquetball, softball, jogging, skiing, and weightlifting.

Lewis E. Leibowitz

Partner
Hogan & Hartson, L.L.P.
555 13th Street NW
Washington, DC 20004–1109
(202) 637–5638
Fax: (202) 637–5910
EMAIL: See Below

8111

Business Information: Hogan & Hartson, L.L.P., Washington, D.C.'s oldest and largest law firm, is a premier international litigation law firm. Hogan & Hartson has offices located throughout the U.S. (Baltimore & Bethesda, Maryland; Colorado Springs & Denver, Colorado; McLean, Virginia) and internationally (Brussels, London, Paris, Prague, Warsaw, Moscow). Established in 1904, the Firm currently employs over 400 attorneys company–wide. A practicing attorney for the past twenty years in Washington, D.C. and international courts, Mr. Leibowitz joined the Firm in 1988 as Partner. His practice specializes in international trade law, representing clientele from offices located in Washington, D.C. and in the former Soviet Union. He can also be reached through the Internet via: LEL@DC2.HHLAW.COM **Career Steps:** Partner, Hogan & Hartson, L.L.P. (1988–Present); Adjunct Professor, University of Maryland School of Law (1995–Present); Arent, Fox, Kintner, Plotkin & Kahn: Partner (1983–1988), Associate (1976–1982); Law Clerk, Hon. Roszel C. Thomson – District Judge (1975–1976). **Associations & Accomplishments:** American Bar Association; National Foreign Trade Council; National Association of Foreign Trade Zones; German American Business Council; Washington Foreign Law Society; Supreme Court Historical Society. **Education:** University of Maryland School of Law, J.D. (1975); University of Maryland, B.A. (1970). **Personal:** Married to Patricia Anne in 1971. Three children: Amy, Susan, and Daniel.

Jacques LeMay

Senior Partner
Flynn, Rivard
70 Dalhousie Street, Suite 500
Quebec, Quebec G1K 7A6
(418) 692–3751
Fax: (418) 692–2887

8111

Business Information: Flynn, Rivard is a general practice law firm, with 45 attorneys concentrating in all areas of law (i.e., commercial, litigation, worker's compensation, liability, and insurance). The Firm currently operates out of three locations in Quebec. A practicing attorney in Canadian courts since 1962, Mr. LeMay joined the Firm that year. He gained the title of Senior Partner in 1976. Mr. LeMay concentrates his practices on litigation, liability, and insurance law. **Career Steps:** Senior Partner, Flynn, Rivard (1966–Present); Attorney, Prevost, Gagne, Flynn, Chouinard & Jacques (1963–1966). **Associations & Accomplishments:** Quebec Bar Association: Disciplinary Committee, Arbitration Committee, Equivalence Committee; Canadian Bar Association: Member of Council, Secretary Quebec Division, Committee for Judges' Appointments; Societe des Etudes Juridiques (Quebec Bar); Societe des Experts en Sinistres Ltee (Legal Adviser); Societe de Medecine et de Droit of Quebec; Defence Research Institute; Law Education Institute; Union Internationale des Avocats; Inter Pacific Bar Association; La St–Maurice Compagnie d' Assurance – Quebec; Canadian 88 Energy Corporation. **Education:** Laval University: D.E.S. (1965), LL.L. (1962); University of Toronto Law School (1964); Seminaire de Quebec, B.A. (1959). **Personal:** Married to Denise Cardinal in 1991. Two children: Diane and Chantal. Mr. LeMay enjoys skiing, tennis, biking, and travel.

Theodore T. Lemberis

Partner
Arnstein & Lehr
120 South Riverside Plaza, Suite 1200
Chicago, IL 60606–3913
(312) 876–7124
Fax: (312) 876–0298

8111

Business Information: Arnstein & Lehr is a general practice law firm, concentrating on business law, specifically contracts and agreements. Established 100 years ago, the Firm is comprised of 75 attorneys, with offices in West Palm Beach, Florida, Chicago, Illinois, and Milwaukee, Wisconsin. As Partner, Mr. Lemberis specializes in commercial transaction law, i.e., international business transactions, securities, and letters of credit. Concurrently, he is an Adjunct Professor at Chicago Kent Law School. **Career Steps:** Partner, Arnstein & Lehr (1996–Present); Professor of Law, Chicago Kent Law School (1994–1995); Partner, Kerck, Mahin & Cate (1987–1991). **Associations & Accomplishments:** American Bar Association; Illinois State Bar Association. **Education:** John Marshall, J.D. (1982); Roosevelt University, M.P.A.; Purdue University, B.A. **Personal:** Married to Renna in 1978. Two children: Eleni and Stephanie. Mr. Lemberis enjoys tennis, horseback riding, and golf.

Christine Lepera

Member
Gold, Farrell & Marks
41 Madison Avenue
New York, NY 10010
(212) 481–1700
Fax: (212) 481–1722

8111

Business Information: Gold, Farrell & Marks is a general practice law firm, concentrating in litigation representation for commercial and entertainment clientele. A practicing attorney since 1982, Ms. Lepera concentrates in the areas of civil litigation, specializing in intellectual property disputes. Ms. Lepera represents large and small companies, as well as individuals. **Career Steps:** Member, Gold, Farrell & Marks (1991–Present); Associate, Gold, Farrell & Marks (1986–1991); Associate, Cahill, Gordon & Reindel Law Firm (1982–1986). **Associations & Accomplishments:** American Bar Association; American Arbitration Association; New York State Bar Association; New York City Bar Association. **Education:** New York Law School, J.D. (1982); Drew University, B.S. (1979).

Mr. Gary B. Leuchtman

Attorney at Law and Partner
Beggs & Lane
P.O. Box 12950
Pensacola, FL 32576–2950
(904) 432–2451
Fax: (904) 469–3331

8111

Business Information: Beggs & Lane is a full–service, general practice law firm, currently consisting of 20 attorney associates. Admitted to practice in Florida state courts, Mr. Leuchtman joined the Firm as Attorney at Law and Partner in 1983. He concentrates his practice in the areas of wills, trusts and estates law. **Career Steps:** Attorney at Law and Partner, Beggs & Lane (1983–Present). **Associations & Accomplishments:** Estate Planning Council of Northwest Florida, Leadership Pensacola, Probate Rules Committee of Florida Bar, Committee of 100 – Pensacola Area Chamber of Commerce; Board Certified Wills, Trusts & Estates Specialist by Board of Legal Specialization of Florida Bar. **Education:** LL.M in Taxes (1982), J.D. (1981), Undergraduate in Accounting.

Cheryl J. Levin, Esq.

President and Partner
Cheryl J. Levin, P.A.
10226 NW 47th Street
Sunrise, FL 33351
(305) 742–9034
Fax: (305) 746–0387

8111

Business Information: Cheryl J. Levin, P.A., established in 1994, is a full–service, general practice law firm, concentrating on condominium and homeowner law. As President and Partner, Miss Levin is responsible for all aspects of operations, as well as serving in a pro bono capacity for Habitat for Humanity. Taking over full responsiblity for the Firm (previously Garfield & Levin) in 1994, she turned the small, struggling firm into a flourishing and growing practice. **Career Steps:** President and Partner, Cheryl J. Levin, P.A. (1994–Present); Partner, Garfield & Levin, P.A. (1992–1994); Associate, Garfield & Associates, P.A. (1990–1992). **Associations & Accomplishments:** Florida Bar Association; McGraw Hill Construction & Contracting – 90; Matthew Bender for Fair Housing Act (1992–1993); Matthew Bender, Published Two Chapters in Practice Manuals on Fair Housing. **Education:** Nova University Law Center, J.D. (1981); Brandeis University, B.A. in Political Science and History (1978). **Personal:** Miss Levin enjoys photography; won a National Award in 1991 by Parade Magazine & Eastman Kodak.

Mr. Richard L. Levine

Partner and Attorney
Weil, Gotshal & Manges
767 5th Avenue, 27th Floor
New York, NY 10153–0002
(212) 310–8286
Fax: (212) 833–3928

8111

Business Information: Weil, Gotshal & Manges is an international general practice law firm. Established in 1931, the firm currently employs 1,600 people. As Partner and Attorney, Mr. Levine concentrates his practice in the areas of business and securities litigation. He became a Partner with the Firm in 1990 after spending 7 years as an Associate. A trial attorney since the conferral of his law degree in 1983, Mr. Levine is admitted to both State and Federal courts. **Career Steps:** Attorney, Weil, Gotshal & Manges (1983–Present). **Associations & Accomplishments:** American Bar Association; New York State Bar Association. **Education:** New York University School of Law, J.D. (1983); Wesleyan University, B.A. (1980). **Personal:** Married to Sarah B. Biser in 1984. Three children: Danielle, David and Jamie.

Russell E. Levine

Partner
Kirkland & Ellis
200 East Randolph Street, Suite 6100
Chicago, IL 60601–6436
(312) 861–2466
Fax: (312) 861–3481
EMAIL: See Below

8111

Business Information: Kirkland & Ellis is a leading international, full–service, general practice law firm. With the main office located in Chicago, Illinois, the Firm spans throughout the U.S. with offices located in Colorado (Denver), California (Los Angeles), New York, and District of Columbia, as well as an international office located in London, England. A Registered Patent Attorney and admitted to practice law in Illinois, New York, numerous Federal District Courts, The Court of Appeals for the Federal Circuit and the United States Supreme Court, Mr. Levine joined the Firm upon the conferral of his law degree in 1986. Currently serving as one of the Firm's partners, he concentrates his practice on trial cases involving intellectual property matters. Additionally, he provides legal services to clientele throughout the U.S. and participates in the coordination of international cases. Mr. Levine can also be reached through the Internet via: Russell_levine@Kirkland.com **Career Steps:** Partner, Kirkland & Ellis (1992–Present). **Associations & Accomplishments:** American Intellectual Property Association; Licensing Executives Society; American Bar Association; Federal Circuit Bar Association; Frequent lecturer for various Bar Association conferences; Author of "Legal Protection for Computer Software" which was presented to the International Computer Graphics Conference; Instructor of "Patent Trademark & Copyright Law for Engineers." **Education:** University of Chicago Law School, J.D. (1986); University of Michigan: B.S. in Interdisciplinary Engineering (1982), B.S. in Economics (1982). **Personal:** Married to Anne Marie in 1992. One child: David.

Morgan, Lewis & Bockius LLP
COUNSELORS AT LAW

John H. Lewis Jr.
Partner/Chairman of Litigation Section
Morgan, Lewis & Bockius
One Logan Square, Suite 2000
Philadelphia, PA 19103–6993
(215) 963–5409
Fax: (215) 963–5299

8111

Business Information: Morgan, Lewis & Bockius is an international full–service, general practice law firm consisting of more than 600 lawyers. Admitted to practice in Pennsylvania state and federal courts, Mr. Lewis joined the Firm in 1969 as Partner and has been Chairman of the Litigation Section since 1994. He is responsible for legal representation of the Firm's clientele and serves as Trial Attorney, concentrating in securities, fraud, civil litigation, patents, libel, and criminal law. Career milestones include the FOF v. Vesco case, in which he won a $90 settlement for the shareholders. **Career Steps:** Partner/Chairman of Litigation Section, Morgan, Lewis & Bockius (1969–Present). **Associations & Accomplishments:** Fellow, American College of Trial Lawyers; Rector's Warden at All Saints' Church – Wynnewood, PA; Board of Trustees, Blair Academy. **Education:** Harvard Law School, J.D. (1961); Princeton University, A.B. (1958). **Personal:** Married to Mary Ann in 1960. Three children: Peter, David, and Mark.

Irwin I. Liebman

Owner/Attorney
Liebman and Associates
1 Westmount Square, Suite 1800
Montreal, Quebec H3Z 2P9
(514) 846–0666
Fax: (514) 935–2380

8111

Business Information: Liebman and Associates is a law firm concentrating on commercial, insurance, and family law. Currently the firm has seven attorneys on staff. As Owner, Mr. Liebman oversees the daily operations of the Firm and litigates cases involving commercial, family, and insurance law. Other administrative and operational concerns include marketing of services, public relations, planning for firm expansion, and budgetary concerns. **Career Steps:** Owner/Attorney, Liebman and Associates (1980–Present). **Associations & Accomplishments:** Quebec Bar Association; Canadian Bar Association. **Education:** McGill University, J.D. (1972), B.A. (1969). **Personal:** Married to Anne in 1975. Mr. Liebman enjoys basketball, golf, swimming, football, working out, and weightlifting.

Lois A. Lindstrom

Partner/Attorney
Ericksen, Arbuthnot, Kilduff, Day & Lindstrom
329 Paraiso Drive
Danville, CA 94526–5001
(510) 832–7770
Fax: (510) 832–0102

8111

Business Information: Ericksen, Arbuthnot, Kilduff, Day & Lindstrom is a general law practice concentrating in defense litigation, civil law, and administrative law. As Partner in the Law Firm, Ms. Lindstrom serves as Managing Partner, and Chairperson of the Board. Ms. Linstrom's concentration is defense litigation. **Career Steps:** Ericksen, Arbuthnot, Kilduff, Day & Lindstrom: Partner (1987–Present), Associate (1984–1987); Claims Manager, General Accident (1982–1984). **Associations & Accomplishments:** American Bar Association; California Bar Association; Alameda County Bar Association; Contra Costa County Bar Association; Defense Counsel, Northern California; Smithsonian Member; Golden Gate University School of Law Alumni; World Wildlife Association; Marine Mammal Center; KQED; United States Humane Society; Lindsey Museum. **Education:** Golden Gate University, J.D. (1983); University of Wisconsin at Madison, B.A. (1970). **Personal:** Married to Harry in 1972. Ms. Lindstrom enjoys golf, photography, and being a naturalist.

Thomas E. Littler
Managing Partner
Warnicke & Littler
2020 N. Central Avenue, Floor 5
Phoenix, AZ 85004–4501
(602) 256–0400
Fax: Please mail or call

8111

Business Information: Warnicke & Littler is a full–service, general practice law firm, concentrating on business litigation and bankruptcy cases. A practicing attorney in Arizona state courts since 1981, Mr. Littler joined the Firm as Managing Partner in 1989. He is responsible for the management of the Firm, in addition to his daily law practice. **Career Steps:** Managing Partner, Warnicke & Littler (1989–Present); Attorney, Littler & Miller (1987–1989); Attorney, Treon, Warnilke & Roush (1979–1987). **Associations & Accomplishments:** American Bar Association **Education:** Arizona State University: J.D. (1981), B.S. (1978). **Personal:** Married to Debra in 1973. Two children: Courtney and Christopher.

Linda S. Lodenkamper, Esq.
Sole Practitioner
Law Office of Linda S. Lodenkamper
143 Union Boulevard, Suite 900
Lakewood, CO 80228
(303) 642–3078
Fax: (303) 642–3577

8111

Business Information: The Law Office of Linda S. Lodenkamper specializes in franchise law but also provides general legal services for businesses, particularly in the areas of trademarks and copyrights. A practicing attorney since 1978, Ms. Lodenkamper established her solo practice in 1985. She concentrates her practice on general business law, franchise law, trademarks, and copyrights. **Career Steps:** Sole Practitioner, Law Offices of Linda S. Lodenkamper, Esq. (1985–Present); Attorney, New Jersey Public Advocate's Office (1980–1984); Attorney, Federal Trade Commission (1978–1979). **Associations & Accomplishments:** President, National Association of Women Business Owners, Colorado Chapter (1991–1992); Colorado Bar Association; Colorado Women's Bar Association; 1st Judicial District Bar Association; Franchising Forum, American Bar Association; Alliance of Professional Women; Denver City Club; Author: Legislative statute on alternative sentencing, now passed and incorporated as a law; Published by C.R.S. 17–27.9–101 et seq. **Education:** Rutgers University Law School, J.D. (1978); Beloit College/Purdue University, B.A. (1961). **Personal:** Married to John in 1960. Two children: Lisa and Robert. Ms. Lodenkamper enjoys music and politics.

Ellen R. Lokker
Partner
Hogan & Hartson, L.L.P.
555 13th Street, NW
Washington, DC 20004
(202) 637–5653
Fax: (202) 637–5910

8111

Business Information: Hogan & Hartson, L.L.P. is a large, Mid–Atlantic, full–service, general practice law firm. With extensive experience in all aspects of civil and appellate work in state and federal courts, Ms. Lokker has been a practicing attorney since 1987. She joined the Firm's Franchise Group at the Washington, D.C. office as Partner in 1995, serving as a Trial Attorney. She specializes in commercial litigation and regularly represents parties in arbitration and mediation of business disputes. She also represents franchisors in state and federal court litigation throughout the U.S., as well as serving as counsel to franchisors on all aspects of franchise relationships. Her experience also includes the defense of franchisors in suits brought by franchisees, including enterprise–threatening class actions. In addition, she has represented franchisors in courts across the country in suits for injunctive relief against trademark infringement and breaches of covenants against competition. **Career Steps:** Partner, Hogan & Hartson, L.L.P. (1995–Present); Attorney, Reed, Smith, Shaw and McClay (1987–1995). **Associations & Accomplishments:** District of Columbia Bar; Virginia Bar; Active in the American Bar Association and the ABA Forum on Franchising; The Barristers, an association of trial lawyers; Author of articles on franchising and civil procedure issues; Speaker at programs on franchising – focusing on topics including judicial developments in franchise cases and mediation, and litigation of franchise disputes. **Education:** University of Virginia, School of Law: J.D. (1987), B.A., with Distinction (1981). **Personal:** Married to Mark E. Baker in 1986. One child: Claire Julia. Ms. Lokker enjoys hiking, skiing, canoeing, and gardening.

Edward Long Jr., J.D.
Senior Staff Attorney
East Texas Legal Service, Inc.
1425 College Drive
Texarkana, TX 75503–3533
(903) 793–7661
Fax: (903) 792–2150

8111

Business Information: East Texas Legal Service, Inc., the only legal service that crosses two states, is a private, non–profit organization providing free legal services for the under–served and indigent populace of Texas and Arkansas. A practicing attorney in Texas and Mississippi state courts since 1973, Mr. Long joined East Texas Legal Service, Inc. as Senior Staff Attorney in 1983. His practice includes performing impact litigation and various other services, such as deeds, wills, public housing problems, conducting community legal information seminars, planning legal programs, and training young attorneys. **Career Steps:** Senior Staff Attorney, East Texas Legal Service, Inc. (1983–Present); Managing Attorney, North Mississippi Rural Legal Services (1977–1983); Practicing Attorney, Funchess, Charles, Long & Fain (1975–1977). **Associations & Accomplishments:** American Bar Association; Texas State Bar Association; Mississippi Bar Association. **Education:** Texas Southern University, J.D. (1973); Rust College, B.A. **Personal:** Mr. Long enjoys fishing, reading, and gardening.

Charles Lynn Lowder

Partner
Bullaro, Carton & Stone
100 N. Riverside Plaza, Suite 2100
Chicago, IL 60606–1518
(312) 831–1000
Fax: (312) 831–0647

8111

Business Information: Bullaro, Carton & Stone is a full–service, general practice law firm, concentrating on personal injury defense law. A practicing attorney in Illinois state courts since 1980 and a Trial Attorney, Mr. Lowder joined the Firm as Partner in 1986. His practice specializes in medical, dental, veterinary, chiropractic and sexual molestation defense. **Career Steps:** Partner, Bullaro, Carton & Stone (1986–Present); Associate, Pretzel & Stouffer (1984–1986); Officer, U.S. Marine Corps (1968–1983) **Associations & Accomplishments:** American Bar Association; American Trial Lawyers Association; Vice Chairman – Non–Profit Organizations Committee, Illinois Bar Association; Tort and Insurance Practice Section, American Bar Association; Professional Liability

Underwriting Society; Frequent Speaker at Civic, Legal Associations and Corporate proceedings and symposia; Published: "Good Medical Records Make a Good Defense", American Veterinary Medical Association Trust Report (July 1987); "Proving Veterinary Malpractice in a Court of Law", American Veterinary Medical Association Trust Report (December 1987); Chairman of the Board, Goad Ministries International; Boy Scouts of America – Chicago Area Council: Sponsor/Advisor, Insurance Committee Member; President and Board Member, Dad's Club – Benet Academy (1988–1993); American Legion; Veterans of Foreign Wars; U.S. Marine Corps Force Recon Association; MILITARY: U.S. Marine Corps (1967–1983) – Rose from rank of Private to Major. Served ten years in the Infantry and six years as Judge Advocate (criminal prosecution and defense). Combat service in Vietnam (1969) with First Force Recon Company as long–range reconnaissance platoon/patrol leader. Awarded Silver Star Medal for Valor, Bronze Star with Combat "V", Vietnamese Cross of Gallantry and Purple Heart, also a member of the All–Marine Football Team (intercollegiate) – Quantico, Virginia (1970). **Education:** DePaul University College of Law, J.D. with honors (1980); University of Illinois–Champaign–Urbana, B.A. with honors (1976) **Personal:** Married to Sandra Earl in 1968. Three children: Kathleen, Lisa and Danny. Mr. Lowder enjoys physical fitness, reading and travel during his leisure time.

Jacqueline H. Lower
Partner
Sheehan & Lower
6 Spring Street
Cary, IL 60013
(847) 516–3200
Fax: (847) 516–3443
EMail: See Below

8111

Business Information: The firm of Sheehan & Lower P.C. concentrates in employment law and product liability defense, including the defense of amusement ride manufacturers and the leisure industry. The Firm currently employs four lawyers. A practicing attorney in Illinois state and federal courts since obtaining her degree in 1982, Ms. Lower co–founded the Firm in 1995. Ms. Lower practices litigation in the area of employment law. Internet users can reach her via: ridelaw@aol.com. **Career Steps:** Partner, Sheehan & Lower (1995–Present); Attorney, Abrahamson; Attorney, Fox & Grove; Attorney, Cherry & Flynn. **Associations & Accomplishments:** National Employment Liability Association; Chicago Bar Association; Illinois State Bar Association. **Education:** Loyola University – School of Law, J.D. (1982); University of Chicago, M.A. in English; DePaul University, B.A. in English. **Personal:** Married to Thomas Sheehan in 1985. Two children: Stephanie and Ryan Sheehan. Ms. Lower enjoys reading and spending time with her family.

Maria E. Luccese
Director, Technology and Operations
Epstein, Becker & Green, P.C.
250 Park Avenue, Suite 1200
New York, NY 10177–0077
(212) 351–4547
Fax: (212) 661–0989
EMAIL: See Below

8111

Business Information: Epstein, Becker & Green, P.C. is a national law firm specializing in labor and health concerns, and corporate law. The law firm employs approximately 200 attorneys and was established in 1973. As Director, Technology and Operations, Ms. Luccese manages a staff of 12. She is responsible for strategic planning, budget analysis, and the establishing policies and procedures. Continuing her education and receiving a Doctorate in Management are Ms. Luccese's goals. Internet users can also reach her via: MELuccese@aol.com **Career Steps:** Epstein, Becker & Green, P.C. Director, Technology and Operations (1995–Present), Director of Operations (1990–1995), Manager of Operations (1987–1990), Assistant to Controller (1984–1987). **Associations & Accomplishments:** American Management Association; Association of Legal Administrators; Board of Directors, Girl Scouts of Westchester / Putnam Counties. **Education:** Attending Pace University, Post Graduate Certificate in Strategic Management (May 1997); Iona College: M.B.A. in Management Information Systems (1990), B.B.A. in Finance (1994). **Personal:** Married to Laurence I. Bradley in 1995. Ms. Luccese enjoys English horseback riding, golf, and tennis.

Allen H. Lynde
Sole Practitioner
Big Apple Hawaii Productions
1655 Makaloa Street, Suite 2311
Honolulu, HI 96814–3937
(808) 941–2320
Fax: (808) 941–2320

8111

Business Information: Big Apple Hawaii Productions is a commerical transaction law firm, concentrating on entertainment law – emphasizing film, theatre and music. A practicing attorney since 1978, Mr. Lynde established his private law practice in 1990. As Sole Practitioner he represents clients in negotiations and provides advice on all aspects of entertainment production. **Career Steps:** Sole Practitioner, Big Apple Hawaii Productions (1990–Present); Actor, Regional Theatre & SAG (1985–Present); Senior Associate Attorney, Kiefer, Oshima, Chun & Webb (1980–1985). **Associations & Accomplishments:** American Bar Association; New York Bar Association; Hawaii Bar Association: Entertainment and Intellectual Property Sections; Screen Actors Guild; Film & Video Association of Hawaii; Honolulu Neighborhood Board **Education:** New York University: J.D. (1978); M.A. in Political Science; University of Hawaii, B.A. summa cum laude in Liberal Studies; NYU Film SCE; CUNY Performing Arts Management; Hastings Law Center/Trial Advocacy **Personal:** Mr. Lynde enjoys acting (professional & stock); teaching (UH Law School, Director/Assistant Professor of Affirmative Action); singing.

J. Henry Lyons III
Sole Practitioner
The Office of J. Henry Lyons III, Attorney at Law
178 Middle Street, Suite 504
Portland, ME 04101
(207) 773–3600
Fax: (207) 772–0577
E–mail: see below

8111

Business Information: The Office of J. Henry Lyons III is a private, general practice law firm, focusing on domestic issues. Establishing his individual practice firm in 1991, Mr. Lyons represents plaintiff appeals before the Department of Human Services, such as unwed parents appeals and other related matters. His practice also includes child protective custody and post–divorce amendments. Concurrent with his legal practice, Mr. Lyons is also an independent computer and Internet consultant. Internet users can reach him via: corbeau@q.sdi.agate.net and also the World Wide Web: http://www.agate.net/~corbeau/lyons.html **Career Steps:** Attorney, The Office of J. Henry Lyons, III, Attorney at Law (1991–Present); Seasonal Employee, L.L. Bean, Inc. (1989–1990); Chairman, Bright Ideas, Inc. (1986–1989); Legal Clerk, Dyer & Goodall (1987). **Associations & Accomplishments:** Maine State Bar Association; Federal Bar Association; Maine Trial Lawyers Association; American Bar Association; American Trial Lawyers Association; State Sections: Family Law, Young Lawyers, Law Practice Management Committee; Chair, South Portland Democratic City Committee (1993–1994); Cumberland Bar Association. **Education:** University of Maine School of Law, J.D. (1988); Bates College, B.A.(1985); Hebron Academy Preparatory School (1981); Sorbonne, Paris, Certificat Moyen (1984). **Personal:** Mr. Lyons enjoys computers and surfing the Internet.

Ms. Pamela S. Mac'Kie
Sole Practitioner
The Law Office of Pamela S. Mac'Kie, P.A.
5551 Ridgewood Drive, Suite 201
Naples, FL 33963–2718
(813) 597–4339
Fax: (813) 597–1414

8111

Business Information: The Law Office of Pamela S. Mac'Kie, P.A. is a full–service law firm. Admitted to the Bar in 1984, Ms. Mac'Kie established her sole practice firm in 1993. She concentrates her practice in real estate law and transactions. Active in local politics, she is currently serving as an elected member of the Collier County Commissioners. **Career Steps:** Attorney, The Law Office of Pamela S. Mac'Kie, P.A. (1993–Present); Attorney, Cummings & Lockwood (1986–1992). **Associations & Accomplishments:** Founding Member, Women's Political Caucus of Collier County; Leadership Southwest Florida; Leadership Collier; Florida Bar Pro Bono Award; Published with Bar Association. **Education:** University of Mississippi, J.D. (1984); University of Ten-

nessee; Delta State University. **Personal:** Two children: Ann and Jack.

Carolyn L. MacDonald, LLB, BA
Carolyn L. MacDonald, Barrister and Solicitor
17070 Yonge Street, Suite 209
Newmarket, Ontario L3Y 4V8
(905) 898–0445
Fax: (905) 898–0824

8111

Business Information: Law Office of Carolyn L. MacDonald, Barrister and Solicitor, practices in the criminal courts only. Ms. MacDonald, as sole practitioner, represents accused persons in all levels of criminal court, as a defense counsel. **Career Steps:** Law Office of Carolyn L. MacDonald, LLB, BA (1989–Present); Defense Counsel, Articling Student, Gold & Fuerst, Barristers & Solicitors (1985–1988). **Associations & Accomplishments:** Criminal Lawyers Association; York Region Law Association. **Education:** Osgoode Hall Law School, LL.B. (1988); York University, Bachelor of Arts Degree. **Personal:** Spouse of Timothy Breen, of Fleming, Breen, Barristers & Solicitors, since 1990. Ms. MacDonald enjoys outdoor activities, hiking, skiing, swimming, horse racing, sports, animals, and gardening.

Richard Barry MacDonald, J.D.
Sole Practitioner
Richard B. MacDonald – Attorney at Law
312 West Orange Street
Lancaster, PA 17603–3749
(717) 394–1508
Fax: Please mail or call

8111

Business Information: The Law Offices of Richard B. MacDonald, is a general practice law firm. Admitted to the Bar in 1979, Mr. MacDonald established his private practice firm in 1984. As Sole Practitioner he is involved in all areas of its operation, concentrating his legal representation in the areas of criminal defense. He also serves in a pro bono capacity for court–appointed defense cases. **Career Steps:** Sole Practitioner, The Law Offices of Richard B. MacDonald (1984–Present); Attorney, Krank, Gross & Kasper (1980–1984). **Associations & Accomplishments:** American Bar Association; Pennsylvania Bar Association; Lancaster Bar Association; West Hensel Brown Inn of Court No. 169; Republican Committeeman, East Hempfield Township; Covenant United Methodist Church; United States Air Force, Vietnam Veteran; Chairman of the Board of Directors, Covenant UMC Child Care Center. **Education:** Williamette University College of Law, J.D. (1979); Colorado College, B.A. (1976); Manchester Community College, A.A. (1974). **Personal:** Married to Barbara in 1979. Two children: Miles and Morgan. Mr. MacDonald enjoys computers, chess, motorcycles and reading.

G. Thomas MacIntosh II
Attorney & Member of Board of Governors
Mackall, Crounse & Moore, P.L.C.
1400 AT&T Tower, 901 Marquette Avenue
Minneapolis, MN 55402–2859
(612) 305–1400
Fax: (612) 305–1414
EMAIL: See Below

8111

Business Information: Mackall, Crounse & Moore, P.L.C. is a general practice law firm. A practicing attorney since 1965, Mr. MacIntosh joined the Firm in 1993. Now a Member of the Board of Governors, he concentrates his practice in business, antitrust, and franchise legislation and regulation. Internet users can reach him via: tmacintosh@mcmlaw.com **Career Steps:** Attorney & Member of Board of Governors, Mackall, Crounse & Moore, P.L.C. (1993–Present); Attorney, O'Connor & Hannan (1986–1993); Attorney, MacIntosh & Commers (1968–1986). **Associations & Accomplishments:** Legal/Legislative Committee, International Franchise Association; Advisory Board, University of St. Thomas Franchising Institute; Best Lawyers in America (1994, 1995); Minnesota Law and Leading Attorneys (1994, 1995); International Franchising Committee, International Bar Association; American Bar Association: Antitrust Law Section, Task Force on Franchise Legislation and Regulation, Forum Committee on Franchising; Minnesota Bar Association: Business Law Section, Ad Hoc Committee on Franchising, Corporate/Banking/Business Law Section, Former Chairman–Subcommittee on Franchising Regulations, Antitrust Section, Former Chairman–Unfair

Trade Practices and Franchise Law Committee. **Education:** University of Minnesota Law School, L.L.B. (1965); DePaul University, B.S. in Commerce (1962). **Personal:** Married to Elaine in 1972. Three children: Lee, Brian, and Joel.

Sarah MacLeod

Partner
The Law Firm of Obadaland MacLeod, P.C.
121 North Henry Street
Alexandria, VA 22314–2903
(703) 739–9485
Fax: (703) 739–9488

8111

Business Information: Obadal and MacLeod Law Firm, is a full–service, general practice law firm, providing general counsel in legislative, manufacturer/distributor contracts and aviation law. The Firm serves national and international clientele from its location in Alexandria, Virginia. Ms. MacLeod started her career as Office Manager of the Firm, formerly known as Obadal & O'Leary, in 1985. Upon the conferral of her law degree in 1992, she was given the duties of Attorney and was appointed as Partner in 1993. Her practice covers the regulatory aspects of aviation Law. She serves as the Aeronautical Repair Station Association Executive Director. **Career Steps:** Partner, Obadal and MacLeod (1993–Present); Obadal & O'Leary: Attorney (1992–1993), Office Manager (1985–1992). **Associations & Accomplishments:** Aeronautical Repair Station Association; Aviation Rulemaking Advisory Committee: Chair (1995–1996), Former Vice President (1994–1995); Published in guest editorials in trade magazines; Publishes a monthly newsletter for trade association (started ten years ago); The Catholic University, Columbus, School of Law. **Education:** Law Degree (1992). **Personal:** Ms. MacLeod enjoys cooking, gardening, and travel.

Marsha Gerre Madorsky

Attorney
The Law Office of Marsha Gerre Madorsky
2665 South Bayshore Drive
Miami, FL 33133–5401
(305) 856–0879
Fax: (305) 854–6093

8111

Business Information: The Law Office of Marsha Gerre Madorsky is a full–service, general business practice law firm, concentrating on estate planning, probate, probate litigation, and business planning. A practicing attorney in Florida state courts since 1983 and a Board–Certified Tax Attorney, Ms. Madorsky established her solo law practice in 1984. Overseeing all administrative operations for associates and a support staff of six, her practice concentrates on estate planning and elder law in Florida. **Career Steps:** Attorney, The Law Office of Marsha Gerre Madorsky (1984–Present); State Attorney's Office: Assistant State Attorney (1982–1983), Attorney: Florida Auditor Medical Fraud (1981–1982), Assistant Florida Attorney General (1975–1977). **Associations & Accomplishments:** National Academy Elder Law Attorneys; Greater Miami Jewish Federation; Florida Association for Women Lawyers; Elected Coconut Grove Village Council; Florida Bar Association. **Education:** University of Miami, LL.M. in Taxation (1983); Board Certified in Tax. **Personal:** Married to Dr. Jeffrey Rothstein in 1985. Two children: Amy and Whitney Rothstein. Ms. Madorsky enjoys horseback riding and travel.

Jeffrey A. Maidenberg, Esq.

Attorney & Counselor at Law
Law Office of Jeffrey A. Maidenberg
6300 S. Syracuse Way, Suite 210
Englewood, CO 80111
(303) 689–9865
Fax: (303) 694–1188

8111

Business Information: The Law Office of Jeffrey A. Maidenberg is a private law firm specializing in personal injury, employment law, civil litigation and criminal defense. Establishing the Firm in 1992, Mr. Maidenberg is reponsible for all aspects of its growth and development. **Career Steps:** Attorney, The Law Office of Jeffrey A. Maidenberg (1992–Present); Mergers & Acquisitions Coordinator, Sherman & Sterling (1986–1987). **Associations & Accomplishments:** Colorado Bar Association; First Judicial Bar Association; American Bar Association; American Inns of Court; Vice President, Riva Ridge Board of Directors; Board Member, Castle Pines North; Vice President, Union Square Community Association; Leadership Lakewood; Beta Gamma Sigma Honor Society; Admitted to U.S. District Court (1992); Published in Iowa Law Review Vol.75:1, Associate Editor Iowa Law Review (1989 &1990). **Education:** University of Iowa, J.D. (1990); University of Iowa, M.B.A. (1991); University of Texas at Austin, B.A. (1983).

James John Maiwurm

Partner
Crowell & Moring
1001 Pennsylvania Avenue, NW
Washington, DC 20004
(202) 624–2903
Fax: (202) 628–5116

8111

Business Information: Crowell & Moring is a full–service, general practice law firm. Established in 1979, the Firm currently employs more than 230 attorneys. A financially–oriented and versatile business lawyer with a twenty–year track record of creatively assisting clients, Mr. Maiwurm joined the Firm in 1990 as Partner and Head of the Corporate Practice Group. He is responsible for providing legal assistance to the Firm's clientele, such as: assisting clients in capital formation and securities transactions, including public offerings and private placements of equity and debt securities; merger, acquisition and divesture transactions involving North American, European and Pacific Rim interests and operations, including leveraged buyouts and tender offers; domestic and international joint ventures and strategic alliances; commercial lending and financial workouts, including debt restructurings and recapitalizations; general corporate and securities counseling, review of disclosure issues, proxy contests, development of acquisition strategies, dealing with financing sources, and advising boards of directors. Career milestones include: organizing and negotiating public offering of $125 million of high yield debt; structuring $65 million sale of international medical products business with operations in the United States and Europe to Canadian purchasers; coordinated a diverse group of complex transactions to a simultaneous closing to recapitalize a publicly–held client; saved a troubled publicly–held client from probable bankruptcy by creatively restructuring under extreme adverse circumstances; managed and negotiated a $450 million leveraged buyout acquisition of a semiconductor business with operations in the United States, Europe and Asia, including resolution of complex intellectual property, environmental and employee benefits issues; created an innovative multi–class preferred stock structure with unique voting rights and detachable warrants; established the structure for and closed a multi–layer $100 million non–recourse industrial project financing with limited partnership equity investment vehicles; negotiated a complex $225 million leveraged buy–out of chemical and related business units from a major oil company, including the resolution of environmental risk issues and the use of shared facilities; developed a plan for U.S. registration of equity offering to United Kingdom investors; and originated and implemented the strategy and structure for obtaining shareholder approval and consents from holders of $200 million of multiple series of debentures, including the preparation of related proxy/consent solicitation/tender offer materials, in connection with a $500 million disposition. **Career Steps:** Partner and Head of Corporate Practice Group, Crowell & Moring (1990–Present); Partner, Squire, Sanders & Dempsey (1974–1990). **Associations & Accomplishments:** Selected, Leadership Washington, Class of 1993–94; Member, Economic Club of Washington; Member, Federal City Council; The George Mason University Century Club: Member of Board of Directors, Chair of Grubstake Breakfast Venture Capital Forum and Chair of GMU Technology Business Alliance; Listed in Who's Who in America and other Who's Who directories; Chair of Board of Governors, Corporate Counsel Section, Ohio State Bar Association; Numerous publications and speaking: "Begin Now to Get Ready for New Executive Pay Rules," Washington Business Journal (1992), "Annual Disclosure in a Declining Economy – Some Year–End Reminders," 5 Insights – The Corporate and Securities Law Advisor (1991), and "Beachhead Acquisitions: Creating Waves in the Marketplace and Uncertainty in the Regulatory Framework," 53 Business Lawyer (1983); Speaker on topics involving capital formation, domestic and international joint ventures and strategic alliances, financial disclosure, securities law developments, and mergers and acquisitions. **Education:** University of Michigan Law School, J.D. (1974); College of Wooster, Ohio, B.A., Phi Beta Kappa (1971); National Institute for Trial Advocacy. **Personal:** Married to Wendy S. in 1974. Two children: James G. and Michelle K.. Mr. Maiwurm enjoys water sports, boating, and scuba diving.

Marianne O. Maloney

Controller
Burke and Casserly, P.C.
255 Washinton Avenue Extension
Albany, NY 12205–5504
(518) 452–1961
Fax: (518) 452–4230
E MAIL: See Below

8111

Business Information: Burke and Casserly, P.C. is a general practice law firm concentrating on estate planning, real estate law, wills, trusts, and investments. Established in 1988, the Firm has eight attorneys and 13 support personnel on staff. As Controller, Ms. Maloney oversees all financial reporting and activities. Other responsibilities include accounts receivable and payable departments, sales tax filings, treasury and investments, as well as insurance for the Company and its employees. Internet users can reach her via: burcas@crisny.org. **Career Steps:** Controller, Burke and Casserly, P.C. (1996–Present); Intern, New York City Division for Criminal Justice Services (1994); Registered Nurse, Hospitals, Nursing Home, Visiting Nurse (1973–1984). **Associations & Accomplishments:** Religious Education Teacher; Applied to Institute of Management Accountants. **Education:** Siena College (1995); Hudson Valley Community College, Associates degree in Nursing. **Personal:** Married to Jeffrey in 1975. Two children: Tara Christina and Lani Patricia. Ms. Maloney enjoys aerobics, swimming, movies, needlepoint, and bridge.

James H. Manahan

Trial Attorney
Manahan & Bluth Law Office, Chartered
416 South Front Street
Mankato, MN 56002–0287
(507) 387–5661
Fax: (507) 387–2111

8111

Business Information: Manahan & Bluth Law Office, Chartered is a general practice law firm concentrating in the areas of divorce, criminal law and personal injury law. Established in 1972, the Firm currently employs 2 attorneys and legal support staff. As Trial Attorney and President of the Firm, Mr. Manahan is responsible for all aspects of operations, as well as practicing law. A trial attorney since 1961, he is admitted to both State and Federal courts in Minnesota, Hawaii and Colorado. **Career Steps:** Trial Attorney, Manahan & Bluth Law Office Chartered (1972–Present); Public Defender, Blue Earth County (1980–Present); Assistant Professor, Mankato State University (1970–1982); Trial Attorney, Farrish, Zimmerman, Johnson & Manahan (1962–1972); Law Clerk, Minnesota Supreme Court (1961–1962). **Associations & Accomplishments:** American Civil Liberties Union; Minnesota Civil Liberties Union; DFL Feminist Caucus; NOW; League of Women Voters; President, Mankato Kiwanis Club (1969–1970); Association of Trail Lawyers of America; Minnesota Association of Criminal Defense Lawyers; Lawyers Alliance for Nuclear Arms Control; Minnesota Lawyers International; Human Rights Committee; Amnesty International Lawyers Network: American Arbitration Association; Academy of Certified Trial Lawyers of Minnesota; Board of Governors, Minnesota Trial Lawyers Association; Diplomate and Founding Member, The American College of Family Trial Lawyers; Life Fellow, American Bar Foundation; Life Fellow, American Academy of Matrimonial Lawyers Foundation; Who's Who in American Law; The Best Lawyers in America (1993–1996); Minnesota Consumer Guidebook to Law and Leading Attorneys (1994–1995); Various Committees, American Bar Association; Various Committees, Minnesota State Bar Association; Chair, Common Cause in Minnesota (1974–1975); Secretary, Mankato Police Civil Service Commission (1971–1976). **Education:** Harvard University Law School, J.D. (1961); Harvard College, A.B. (1958). **Personal:** Married to Vanda in 1989. Mr. Manahan enjoys playing volleyball, skiing and reading law–related novels.

Mr. David E. Manoogian

Partner
Epstein, Becker & Green, P.C.
1227 25th NW, Suite 700
Washington, DC 20037–1156
(202) 861–1848
Fax: (202) 296–2882

8111

Business Information: Epstein, Becker & Green, P.C. is a major national law firm, concentrating in the practice of health and labor law for both civil and criminal matters. As a Partner with the Firm, Mr. Manoogian specializes in medical malpractice and health litigation issues. He is an active voice in managed care issues and lectures extensively to associations and health care providers. Established in 1974, Epstein, Becker & Green, P.C. is the 106th largest law firm in the U.S, with 232 attorneys in 11 locations nationally. **Career Steps:** Partner, Epstein, Becker & Green, P.C. (1992–Present); Partner, Frank, Bernstein, Conaway & Goldman (1976–1992); Partner, Macdonald & Manoogian (1971–1976); Law Clerk, Appellate Judge, Maryland (1969–1971). **Associations & Accomplishments:** Member of the Bar: United States Supreme Court, United States Court of Appeals (4th Circuit), United States District Court for the District of Maryland, United States District Court for the District of Columbia, Court of Appeals of Maryland; American Bar Association; Maryland State Bar Association; Montgomery County (Maryland) Bar Association; Maryland Society for Health Care Risk Management; Maryland Association of Defense Trial Counsel; Author of numerous publications regarding health care–related legal subjects. **Education:** George Washington University, J.D. (1969); Dickinson College, B.A. (1966).

Richard M. Marano
Partner and Attorney
Marano & Diamond
P.O. Box 765
Waterbury, CT 06720
(203) 757–6313
Fax: (203) 754–9883

8111

Business Information: Marano & Diamond is a general practice law firm. Establishing his Partnership in 1987, Mr. Marano is a trial attorney concentrating on personal injury. Admitted to both State and Federal courts since 1985, Mr. Marano is also a Justice of the Peace for the State of Connecticut. **Career Steps:** Partner and Attorney, Marano & Diamond (1987–Present); Associate Attorney, Moynahan & Ruskin (1985–1987); Justice of the Peace, State of Connecticut (1989–Present). **Associations & Accomplishments:** Former President, Connecticut Italian American Bar Association (1993–1995); Board of Directors, Waterbury Bar Association (1993–Present); Secretary, Connecticut Criminal Defense Lawyers Association (1994–Present); Board of Directors, Anderson Boys Club (1989–Present); Board of Directors, Central Naugatuck Valley HELP, Inc. (1992–Present); Board of Directors, Waterbury Crimestoppers (1994–Present); Who's Who in American Law; Who's Who in the East; Published in the Connecticut Bar Association Journal and the Connecticut Criminal Defense Lawyers Association Journal; President, Sons of Italy. **Education:** Seton Hall Law School, J.D. (1985); Fairfield University, B.A. (1982). **Personal:** Married to Eileen in 1988. Three children: Michelle, Richard Jr. and Christine. Mr. Marano enjoys studying genealogy and American politics.

Benjamin Marcano–Roman, Esq.
•••◄██►◎◄██►•••

Managing Partner
Marcano & Gonzales Law Firm
P.O. Box 2781
Orlando, FL 32802
(407) 649–8389 (809) 783–1884
Fax: (809) 783–7990

8111

Business Information: Marcano & Gonzales Law Firm is a full–service, general practice firm with offices in Orlando, Florida and San Juan, Puerto Rico. The Firm concentrates on personal injury, Worker's Compensation, and Social Security claim cases. Future plans include opening a second office in Florida and one in Texas. A practicing attorney in New York, District of Columbia, and Puerto Rico state and federal courts since 1976, Benjamin Marcano–Roman joined the Firm as Managing Partner in 1978. He is responsible for the management of office activities, in addition to his daily law practice. Winning 95% of his cases, he focuses on Social Security claims, as well as conducting pro bono work for individuals with little or no money in Social Security claim cases. **Career Steps:** Managing Partner, Marcano & Gonzales Law Firm (1978–Present). **Associations & Accomplishments:** New York Bar Association; District of Columbia Bar Association; Puerto Rico Bar Association; Federal Bar Association; American Bar Association; Notary Association of Puerto Rico. **Education:** University of Puerto Rico, J.D. (1976). **Personal:** Married to Carmen J. Frau in 1975. Four children: Benjamin, Jr., Enid Lig, Liliana, and Carlos. Mr. Marcano–Roman enjoys golf, tennis, travel, and spending time with his children.

Mr. Stephen M. Marcusa
Partner
Bigham Englar Jones & Houston
14 Wall Street
New York, NY 10005–2140
(212) 732–4646
Fax: (212) 227–9491

8111

Business Information: Bigham Englar Jones & Houston is a law firm, specializing in insurance and maritime law and litigation. As a Partner, Mr. Marcusa participates in management of the Firm's operations, and specializes in insurance litigation, counsel, and commercial litigation. He is licensed in Massachusetts and New York. Established in 1909, Bigham Englar Jones & Houston employs 80 people. **Career Steps:** Partner, Bigham Englar Jones & Houston (1981–Present); Associate, Bigham Englar Jones & Houston (1973–1980). **Associations & Accomplishments:** American Bar Association, Tort and Insurance Practice and Litigation Sections; Loss Executives Association; Defense Association of New York; Maritime Law Association of the United States; Panel of Arbitrators, American Arbitration Association; Coach–Ridgewood, NJ Soccer Association and Baseball Association. **Education:** Boston University Law School, J.D. (1972); Rutgers College, A.B.(1969). **Personal:** Married to Laura in 1982. Two children: Aysa and Seth. Mr. Marcusa enjoys Ham Radio (KB2 SDC), reading tennis, and fishing.

Michael J. Margosian
Partner
Tatarian & Margosian, Attorneys at Law
1221 Van Ness, Suite 550
Fresno, CA 93721
(209) 486–1761
Fax: (209) 486–1524

8111

Business Information: Tatarian & Margosian, Attorneys at Law, established in 1988, is a full–service, general practice law firm emphasizing on family law, including dissolution, child support, custody, property division, and juvenile law. Admitted to practice in California state courts, Mr. Margosian co-founded the Firm in 1988 with his partner. A practicing attorney since 1978, he concentrates his practice on adoption cases. **Career Steps:** Partner, Tatarian & Margosian, Attorneys at Law (1988–Present); Attorney, Gerald Lee Tuhajian, Inc. (1981–1988); Lecturer, San Joaquin Law School (1989–1994). **Associations & Accomplishments:** Past President, Exchange Club of Fresno; YMCA Board of Directors; Vice President, Clovis West Band Boosters; Longhouse Chief, Indian Guides. **Education:** McGeorge Law School, J.D. (1978); California State University – Fresno, B.S. (1975). **Personal:** Married to Carla in 1975. Three children: Amanda, Nikki, and Ted. Mr. Margosian enjoys woodworking, collecting sports cards and antiques.

Sonia Maria Giannini Marques Dobler
•••◄██►◎◄██►•••

Founder/Partner
Sonia Marques Dobler Advogados
R. Maria Paula 123 – 19 andar
Sao Paulo – SP–, Brazil 01319–001
55–11–605–7823 55–11–605–9764
Fax: 55–11–605–5540

8111

Business Information: Sonia Marques Dobler Advogados is a general practice law firm with eight attorneys and two partners. A practicing attorney in Brazilian courts since obtaining her degree in 1970, by the University of Sao Paulo. Ms. Marques Dobler established the Firm in 1996. Presently, she is the Senior and majority Partner and an attorney concentrating on corporate and antitrust–law. **Career Steps:** Founder/Partner, Sonia Marques Dobler Advogados (1996–Present); Hoechst do Brasil S.A.: General Counsel (1984–1995), Manager of Legal Department (1981–1984), Lawyer (1972–1980). **Associations & Accomplishments:** American Chamber of Commerce; Brazilian Bar Association (OAB–SP); Brazil–Germany Law Studies Association (Sejubra); Brazil–Germany Chamber of Commerce and Industry of Sao Paulo. **Education:** University of Sao Paulo: Law School (1970), Specialization in Competition Law (USP). **Personal:** Ms. Marques Dobler enjoys walking and reading.

Mr. Francis J. Martin
Shareholder
Berry & Martin
The Widener Building, One South Penn Square
Philadelphia, PA 19107
(215) 977–1100
Fax: (215) 557–9670

8111

Business Information: Berry & Martin is a full service law firm specializing in banking law, corporate finance, real estate, asset recovery, bankruptcy, insurance and reinsurance law, and commercial litigation, both on a national and international basis. As a founding shareholder, Mr. Martin oversees all client matters involving banking law and corporate finance. Established in 1993, Berry & Martin maintains offices in Philadelphia and New Jersey and has an estimated annual revenue in excess of $1.5 million. **Career Steps:** Shareholder, Berry & Martin (1993–Present); Shareholder, Bray Berry Martin & Reardon (1992–1993); Shareholder, Elliott Bray & Riley (1990–1992); Associate, Drinker, Biddle & Reath (1986–1990); Law Clerk to the Honorable Jacob C. Kalish (deceased), Commonwealth Court of Pennsylvania (1985–1986). **Associations & Accomplishments:** Board Member, Justinian Society (1992–Present); Executive Committee, Philadelphia Bar Association – Young Lawyers Division (1988–1991); Treasurer, Young Lawyers Division, Philadelphia Bar Association (1989–1991); Philadelphia Bar Foundation Board Member (1988– 1990); Business Leadership Forum,Democratic National Committee (1993–Present). **Education:** Suffolk University Law School, J.D. with honors (1985); Winner Justice Tom C. Clark Moot Court Competition (1984); Boston University, B.S. Degree, with honors (1981).

Mr. James C. Martin
Managing Director – Los Angeles Office
Crosby, Heafey, Roach & May, P.C.
700 South Flower Street, Suite 2200
Los Angeles, CA 90017
(213) 896–8000
Fax: (213) 896–8080

8111

Business Information: Crosby, Heafey, Roach & May, P.C. is a full–service, general practice law firm specializing in civil litigation, legal transactions, trial court and civil appeals. As Managing Director of the Los Angeles Office, Mr. Martin is responsible for the management of staff, including attorneys in the Los Angeles branch office, as well as legal representation of the Firm's clientele in appellate and civil courts. **Career Steps:** Managing Director – Los Angeles Office, Crosby, Heafey, Roach & May, P.C. **Associations & Accomplishments:** California Academy of Appellate Lawyers; State Bar of California; American Bar Association. **Education:** Santa Clara University, J.D., summa cum laude (1978); Colorado College, B.A. in History, Phi Beta Kappa (1974). **Personal:** Married to Jennifer in 1976. Three children: Carie, Leslie and Christopher. Mr. Martin enjoys running and golf.

Joseph A. Materna, Esq.
Partner and Head of Trusts & Estates Department
Shapiro, Beilly, Rosenberg, Albert & Fox
225 Broadway
New York, NY 10007
(212) 267–9020
Fax: (212) 608–2072

8111

Business Information: Shapiro, Beilly, Rosenberg, Albert & Fox is a full–service law firm. Established in 1927, Shapiro, Beilly, Rosenberg, Albert & Fox presently employs 50 people. Mr. Materna currently serves as Partner and Head of Trusts & Estates Department for the general law practice. He also draws up Q–DOT Documents (Qualified Domestic Trust) – an estate planning document for foreign citizens working in this country or married to American citizens (especially important for estate tax and inheritance purposes). **Career Steps:** Partner and Head of Trusts & Estates Department, Shapiro, Beilly, Rosenberg, Albert & Fox (1990–Present); Partner, Newman, Tannenbaum, Helpern, Syracuse & Hirschtritt (1985–1990); Senior Associate, Finley, Kumble, Wagner, Heine, Underberg and Carey (1980–1985). **Associations & Accomplishments:** New York State Bar Association; The Association of the Bar of the City of New York; Richmond County Bar Association; Queens County Bar Association; New York County Lawyers' Association; The Florida Bar; American Judges Association; Estate Planning Council of the City of New York; President, Columbia College Alumni Association of Columbia University; Member of the Board of Governors and the Planned Giving Committee of the Arthritis Foundation – New York Chapter; Member of the Board of Directors of the Catholic Interracial Council; Member of the Bequests and Planned Gifts Committee of the Archdiocese of New York; Member of the Society of Columbia Graduates; Author of numerous publications in the Trusts and Estates field; Frequent lecturer and guest speaker in the Trusts and Estates area of Law and in all aspects of Trusts and Estates Planning and Administration. **Education:** Columbia Law School, J.D. (1973); Columbia College of Columbia University, B.A. (1969). **Personal:** Married to Dolores in 1975. Three children: Jodi, Jennifer, and Janine.

Nina B. Matis
•••◄██►◎◄██►•••

Partner and Attorney
Katten, Muchin & Zavis
525 West Monroe Street
Chicago, IL 60661–3629
(312) 902–5560
Fax: (312) 902–1061

8111

Business Information: Katten, Muchin & Zavis is a full–service law firm. A practicing attorney in Illinois state and federal courts since 1972, Ms. Matis joined the Firm in 1986. She serves on the Firm's Board of Directors and Executive Committee. Additionally, she has a national practice and is considered one of the premier real estate lawyers in Chicago. She has handled the acquisition and financing of major downtown properties and also has extensive experience in structured and rated financings and workouts and restructuring of loans and partnerships. She also has extensive experience in the organization and investment activities of debt and equity funds, comprised of pension funds, and of domestic and foreign investors. **Career Steps:** Partner and Attorney, Katten, Muchin & Zavis (1986–Present); Attorney, Greenberger and Kaufman (1976–1986); Attorney, Arnstein & Lehr (1973–1976). **Associations & Accomplishments:** American College of Real Estate Lawyers; Ely Chapter of Lambda

Alpha International; Chicago Finance Exchange; Urban Land Institute; REFF; Chicago Real Estate Executive Women; The Chicago Network; Economic Club of Chicago; Listed in: Best Lawyers in America, Guide to the World Leading Real Estate Lawyers, Sterling's Who's Who. **Education:** New York University – School of Law, J.D. (1972); Smith College, B.A. with honors (1968). **Personal:** One child: Garson Steven Fischer.

Michael D. McArthur

··· —————◉————— ···

Partner/Attorney
Cline, Backus, Nightingale and McArthur
28 Colborne Street North
Simcoe, Ontario N3Y 4N5
(519) 426–6763
Fax: (519) 426–2055
EMAIL: See Below

8111

Business Information: Cline, Backus, Nightingale and McArthur is a general practice law firm with six attorneys. A practicing attorney since 1984, Mr. McArthur joined the Firm in 1987 as an Associate Lawyer. Now a Partner, he concentrates his practice in criminal defense and prosecution as well as civil litigation matters. Mr. McArthur has been designated by the Canadian federal government to prosecute federal narcotics cases. He is also highly involved in the assessing and defending of civil and criminal cases involving false accusations of abuse, and AIDWYC, reviewing wrongful conviction cases. Internet users may reach Mr. McArthur via: mdmcart@nor-net.on.ca **Career Steps:** Cline, Backus, Nightingale and McArthur: Partner/Attorney (1992–Present), Associate Lawyer (1987–1992); Associate Lawyer, MacKay, Artindale, Wunder (1984–1987). **Associations & Accomplishments:** Criminal Lawyers Association (Canada); Canadian Bar Association; Ontario Trial Lawyer's Association; Simcoe Lions Club. **Education:** Osgood Hall Law School, L.L.B. (1984); University of Western Ontario – London, B.A. in English (1981). **Personal:** Married to Carol Ann in 1985. Four children: Mark, Heather, Rebecca, and Alison. Mr. McArthur enjoys hockey, reading, and theatre.

Lee B. McClain

Partner
Wildman, Harrold, Allen & Dixon
225 West Wacker Drive, 27th Floor
Chicago, IL 60606–1229
(312) 201–2542
Fax: (312) 201–2555

8111

Business Information: Wildman, Harrold, Allen & Dixon is a full–service law firm concentrating in strategic business problem solving, including litigation, transactional, and sophisticated defense law. A practicing insurance and corporate attorney since 1975, Lee McClain joined the Firm in 1991. As Partner, he directs all corporate business consultants, as well as represents major corporate clientele in matters pertaining to mergers, acquisitions, restructuring, legislative and regulatory affairs. **Career Steps:** Partner, Wildman, Harrold, Allen & Dixon (1991–Present); Kemper: General Counsel and Manager of Governmental Affairs (1986–1991), Director–Employee Relations (1978–1982); Director–Corporate Planning, Spiegel, Inc. (1972–1976). **Associations & Accomplishments:** Director, Arbella Insurance Group – Massachusetts; Director, Preferred Risk Insurance Group – Des Moines, Iowa. **Education:** Loyola University: J.D. (1975), M.B.A in Finance (1968); Purdue University, B.S.I.E. (1966); Duke University, Senior Executive Program (1986). **Personal:** Mr. McClain enjoys tennis, theater, and opera.

Patricia Polis McCrory

Managing Partner
Harrison & Moberly
2100 First Indiana Plaza, 135 North Pennsylvania Street
Indianapolis, IN 46204
(317) 639–4511
Fax: (317) 639–9565

8111

Business Information: Harrison & Moberly, founded in 1950 by James D. Harrison and Warren C. Moberly is a general civil practice law firm. Proud of its heritage and reputation for providing quality legal services to its individual and corporate clientele, the Firm consists of 10 partners, 6 associates, Of Counsel and legal support consultants providing legal representation in the following areas: Apellate Practice (State and Federal), Arson and Fraud Law, Business and Commercial Litigation, Construction Law and Litigation, Corporate Law and Business Transactions, Environmental Law, Employment Law, Health Law, Insurance Defense and Policyholder Law, Medical Malpractice Law, Municipal Liability, Police Misconduct Law, Estate Planning, Probate Litigation, Products Liabil-

ity Law, Real Estate Law, Taxation (State, Federal, Estate, Gift), and Workers Compensation Law. A practicing attorney in all state and federal Indiana courts since 1980, Patricia McCrory joined the Firm in 1985 as an associate, later named as Managing Partner in December of 1994. Ms. McCrory's election as managing partner marked the first time in the Firm's 45–year history that a woman was chosen to assume this top leadership role. Though honored to be the first woman elected to run Harrison & Moberly, Patricia feels her gender had absolutely no bearing on the selection process, this was unanimously voiced by one of the senior partners as well. It is McCrory's work ethic — her dedication to the Firm, willingness to put in the extra hours and organization skills — that made her the unanimous choice for managing partner. Ms. McCrory believes her background in business and litigation was also a significant factor in the selection process. Her areas of legal concentration include commercial and civil litigation, banking, construction and employment law. She also heads the Firm's Business Services Group. **Career Steps:** Harrison & Moberly: Managing Partner (1994–Present), Partner (1991–Present), Associate (1983–1991), Federal Law Clerk (1980–1983). **Associations & Accomplishments:** National Institute for Trial Advocacy Advanced Litigation Series; Distinguished Fellow (1995), Indianapolis Bar Foundation – Litigation Section; Indiana State Bar Association: Business Law Section, Labor and Employment Law Section, Litigation Section; 7th Federal Circuit Bar Association; Indiana Defense Lawyers Association; President, Catholic Social Services; Board Member, St. Thomas More Society; Indianapolis Zoological Guild; Kiwanis Club of Downtown Indianapolis; Legal Aid Society; Trustee, University of Indianapolis. **Education:** Indiana University, J.D. (1979); University of Indianapolis, B.S. cum laude (1976). **Personal:** Married to Michael in 1981. Mrs. McCrory enjoys scuba diving, photography, walking, and running.

Keith W. McFatridge Jr.

Of Counsel and Attorney–at–Law
Maxwell and Walker, L.L.P.
17625 El Camino Real, Suite 310
Houston, TX 77058–3052
(713) 286–1040
Fax: (713) 286–1043

8111

Business Information: Maxwell and Walker, L.L.P. is a full–service, general practice law firm. As Attorney and Of Counsel, Mr. McFatridge concentrates his practice in the areas of federal and state tax law, real estate law, estate planning, and corporate and business law. Prior to pursuing his legal career (law doctorate conferred in 1991), Mr. McFatridge held various executive positions in the corporate banking and financial industry. **Career Steps:** Attorney–at–Law and Of Counsel, Maxwell & Walker, L.L.P. (1989–Present); Chief Operating Officer, United States National Bank (1975–1993); Treasury and Secretary to the Board, Woods Tucker Leasing Sales (1972–1975); Credit Manager and Officer, First National Bank of Atlanta (1971–1972); Credit Manager and Officer, Citizens National Bank (1971–1972). **Associations & Accomplishments:** Rotary; Texas Bar Association, Real Estate and Tax Division; American Bar Association Tax and Corporate Division; Board of Director, Moody Gardens. **Education:** University of Houston, L.L.M. in Tax Law (1995); South Texas College of Law, J.D. (1991); Southern Methodist University, M.B.A. (1969); Southern Methodist University, B.S. (1968). **Personal:** Married to Marilyn in 1979. Five children: Keith, Eric, Kyle, Michael, and Jeffrey. Mr. McFatridge enjoys golf and travel.

Patrick C. McGarrigle

Attorney
Gernsbacher and McGarrigle
9100 Wilshire Boulevard, Suite 710 East
Beverly Hills, CA 90212
(310) 281–0100
Fax: (310) 281–0755

8111

Business Information: Gernsbacher and McGarrigle is a full–service law firm. Established in 1993, the Firm currently has locations in California and New York. Mr. McGarrigle is one of two managing partners with the Firm. As Attorney, he specializes in real estate and business litigation as well as handles legal transactions for clients. He is licensed to serve in California. **Career Steps:** Attorney, Gernsbacher and McGarrigle (1993–Present). **Associations & Accomplishments:** Los Angeles County Bar Association; Beverly Hills Bar Association; California State Bar. **Education:** Southwestern University School of Law, J.D. (1990); Columbia College, Columbia University, B.A. (1986).

Dan L. McGookey

Partner and Attorney
Lucal & McGookey
P.O. Box 357
Sandusky, OH 44871–0357
(419) 625–0515
Fax: (419) 625–0170

8111

Business Information: Lucal & McGookey is a general practice law firm. The Firm currently employs 4 attorneys and a legal support staff, and is continuing to grow. Joining the original Firm as an Associate upon conferral of his law degree in 1979, Mr. McGookey was elected Partner in 1988. He concentrates his practice in the fields of personal injury and domestic law. **Career Steps:** Partner and Attorney, Lucal & McGookey (1988–Present); Associate, Lucal, Pfefferle & McGookey (1979–1988). **Associations & Accomplishments:** American Bar Association: Litigation Section Consumer and Personal Rights Committee, Section of Litigation Committee on Insurance Coverage Litigation, Section of Litigation Committee on Domestic Relations and Family Law Litigation; Ohio State Bar Association; Erie County Bar Association; U.S. District Court, Northern District of Ohio, and the U.S. Court of Appeals, Sixth Circut; Association of Trial Lawyers of America; Member, Motor Vehicle Collision, Highway and Premises Liability Section; Ohio Academy of Trial Lawyers; **Education:** University of Toledo College of Law, J.D. (1979); Universtiy of Notre Dame, B.B.A. (1975). **Personal:** Married to Beverly K. in 1974. Three children: Lauren, Beth and Michael. Mr. McGookey enjoys golf and boating.

James J. McGraw Jr.

Senior Partner
The Suddes Group
441 Vine Street
Cincinnati, OH 45202–3001
(513) 579–1414
Fax: (513) 579–1418

8111

Business Information: The Suddes Group is a full–service consulting firm, providing services to the economic development industry, related not–for–profit organizations, and for–profit organizations and their executives. A practicing attorney in Ohio state courts and federal courts since 1974, Mr. McGraw joined the Firm as Senior Partner in 1984. He provides management consulting, strategic planning, business and capital formation, leadership consensus building, program design and implementation. He also is responsible for working with community leaders and senior corporate executives. Concurrent with his consulting services, he is a practicing attorney at a private law firm, Schwartz, Manes & Ruby. **Career Steps:** Senior Partner, The Suddes Group (1984–Present); Attorney, Schwartz, Manes & Ruby (1984–Present); Attorney, Cincinnati Gas & Electric (1980–1984); Attorney, U.S. Air Force (1975–1979). **Associations & Accomplishments:** National Council of Urban Economic Development; California Association of Local Economic Developers; Florida Economic Development Council; American Chamber of Commerce Executives; Association of Health Care Philanthropy; American Bar Association; Ohio State Bar Association; Cincinnati Bar Association; Kentucky Bar Association. **Education:** University of Akron School of Law, J.D. (1974); University of Notre Dame, B.B.A. in Accounting (1971). **Personal:** Married to Anne in 1974. Four children: Carey, Lauren, Jennifer and Courtney. Mr. McGraw enjoys golf, tennis and skiing.

Thomas J. McKay

Firm Manager
McQueen & Brown, L.C.
P.O. Box 1831
Charleston, WV 25327–1831
(304) 342–4200
Fax: (304) 342–4277

8111

Business Information: McQueen & Brown, L.C. is a general practice law firm. Established in 1987, the Firm currently employs 25 attorneys and legal support staff. As Firm Manager, Mr. McKay is responsible for all aspects of operations. **Career Steps:** Firm Manager, McQueen & Brown, L.C. (1993–Present); Marketing Manager, AT&T (1991–1993); Marketing Manager, NCR (1981–1991); Production Planner, Corning Glass Works (1977–1981). **Education:** George Washington University, M.B.A. (1971); United States Naval Academy, B.S. in Engineering (1965); East Tennessee State University, M.A. in History (1980). **Personal:** Married to Erline in 1982. Four children: James, Thomas, Chris and Jason. Mr. McKay enjoys travel and the theatre.

Mr. John F. McKenzie

Partner
Baker & McKenzie
Two Embarcadero Center, Suite 2400
San Francisco, CA 94111
(415) 576–3000
Fax: (415) 576–3099

8111

Business Information: Baker & McKenzie is a major international law firm. Established in 1949, the firm employs over 4,000 legal professional, administrative and translation support staff in their worldwide locations (51 as of this date). With the firm since his law degree conferral in 1976, Mr. McKenzie specializes in the areas of import/export law, finance, sales and contractual review, trade counseling and some litigation representation for major corporate accounts. **Career Steps:** Partner, Baker & McKenzie (1976–Present). **Associations & Accomplishments:** California Council on International Trade; Professional Association of Importers and Exporters; Santa Clara Valley World Trade Association; American Electronics Association; Northern California District Export Council; Northern California Association of Customs Brokers & Freight Forwarders. **Education:** Harvard University, J.D. (1976); Williams College, B.A. (1969).

Patrick J. McNamara

Attorney
Scarinci & Hollenbeck
500 Plaza Drive
Secaucus, NJ 07096–3819
(201) 392–8900
Fax: (201) 348–3877

8111

Business Information: Scarinci & Hollenbeck, located in Secaucus, New Jersey, is a law firm comprised of 24 attorneys. The Firm is mainly involved in Environmental Law Planning and Zoning, Public Sector Law, Government Relations, Land Use & Development, Utility Authority, Commercial and Corporate Transactions, as well as Labor, Bankruptcy, Worker's Compensation, Civil, Litigation, and Criminal Law. Mr. McNamara is Senior Associate in the Environmental Law Department, and focuses primarily on issues involving the Environmental Law, Municipal Law, and Utility Law. Related duties include overseeing the cleanup of contaminated property, regulatory compliance, Superfund litigation, due diligence on transfer of real property, preparation of pleadings, motions, briefs, and memoranda on various issues of law, as well as assisting in negotiations with the New Jersey Department of Environmental Protection, and the U.S. Environmental Protection Agency. Mr. McNamara also served as Municipal Counsel to Aberdeen Township, N.J. (1992–1995), and General Counsel to the National Association of Fruits, Flavors & Syrups, Inc., since 1994. **Career Steps:** Attorney, Scarinci & Hollenbeck (1994–Present); Associate, Carpenter, Bennett & Morrissey (1991–1994); Associate, Giordano, Halleran & Ciesla (1988–1991); Law Secretary, Honorable Neil F. Deighan Jr., Appellate Division, Superior Court (1987–1988). **Associations & Accomplishments:** American Bar Association; New Jersey State Bar Association; New Jersey Institute of Municipal Attorneys; Environmental Law Institute; Author/Co–Author of 10 publications on Environmental and Land Use Law and related subjects; Selected for inclusion in Who's Who Among Rising Young Americans (1992 & 1993); Board of Directors, Rutgers Alumni Association. **Education:** Rutgers University School of Law: J.D. (1987); Rutgers University: B.A. in History (1981); Eagleton Institute of Politics, M.A. in Political Science (1985); Trinity College School of Law, Dublin, Ireland (1985). **Personal:** Married to Kim in 1991. One child: James Patrick. Mr. McNamara enjoys golf, softball, and politics.

William J. McNichol Jr.

Lawyer
Stoel Rives, L.L.P.
Suite 3600, 1 Union Square 600 University Street
Seattle, WA 98101–3197
(206) 386–7581
Fax: (206) 386–7500
EMAIL: See Below

8111

Business Information: Stoel Rives, L.L.P. is a general practice law firm with offices in Oregon, Utah, Washington, Idaho, and Washington D.C.. Currently employing over 635 attorneys, the Firm was established in 1901. As Lawyer and Partner, Mr. McNichol specializes in Intellectual Property Law. This includes such subfields as patents, trademarks, copyrights, and trade secrets. He assists with office operations for the Seattle office and serves on the Board of Trustees. Internet users can also reach him via: wjmcnichol@stoel.com **Career Steps:** Lawyer, Stoel Rives, L.L.P. (1992–Present). **Associations & Accomplishments:** Washington State Bar Association; New York State Bar Association; King County Bar Association; Registered with USPTO; Trustee, Washington Biotechnology Foundation; Junior Achievement of Puget Sound. **Education:** Villanova University School of Law, J.D. (1983); Villanova University: M.S. (1979), B.S. (1977). **Personal:** Mr. McNichol enjoys triathalons, marathons, and swimming.

Micheline McNicoll

Attorney
Protecteur Du Citoyen
2875 Laurier Boulevard
Quebec, Quebec G1V 2M2
(418) 643–2688
Fax: (418) 643–8759

8111

Business Information: Protecteur Du Citoyen is a public institution general practice law firm, providing legal counsel and arbitration services to clients. As an Attorney, Ms. McNicoll councils and advises citizens corporations on Canadian laws and serves as a delegate with the powers of an Ombudsman. She is also a lecturer on privacy and technology. **Career Steps:** Attorney, Protecteur De Citoyen (1992–Present); Counselor, Department of Communications (1989–1992); General Manager, Quebec Press Council (1988–1989); Teacher, Public School (1972–1974). **Associations & Accomplishments:** Quebec Bar Association; Association de Securite Informantique Region de Quebec; Ligue des Droits et Libertes; Amis du Quebec. **Education:** Universite Laval, Master in Law (1984); Etu des cours du communication; **Personal:** Ms. McNicoll enjoys outdoor activities, hiking, reading, and fine arts.

Douglas Lawrence McSwain

Partner and Attorney at Law
Sturgill, Turner & Truitt
155 East Main Street
Lexington, KY 40507–1300
(606) 255–8581
Fax: (606) 231–0851

8111

Business Information: Sturgill, Turner & Truitt is a full–service law firm concentrating in corporate litigation and business law. Established in 1957, Sturgill, Turner & Truitt currently employs 38 attorneys and legal support staff. Admitted to practice in both State and Federal courts since 1985, Mr. McSwain joined the Firm as Partner in 1989. **Career Steps:** Partner and Attorney at Law, Sturgill, Turner & Truitt (1989–Present); Attorney, Gordon & Gordon, P.S.C. (1985–1989); Judicial Law Clerk, U.S. District Court, Eastern District of Kentucky (1983–1985). **Associations & Accomplishments:** Association of Trial Lawyers of America; Kentucky Academy of Trial Lawyers; Kentucky Bar Association; American Bar Association; Secretaty and Treasurer, Kentucky Bar Foundation; President, Kentucky Young Lawyers Association (1989); Chairman, Joint Local Rules Commission, Federal District Courts in Kentucky; Life Member, Sixth Circuit Judicial Conference; Federal Bar Association: Sports and Entertainment Law Section, Employment Law Section, Civil Litigation Section; Published in Legal Times. **Education:** University of Kentucky College of Law, J.D. with distinction (1983); Vanderbilt University, B.A. cum laude (1979). **Personal:** Married to Nan Gabbert in 1977. Two children: Lauren T. and Kathryn Jeanne. Mr. McSwain enjoys being involved with his Church.

Rosa M. Mendez Santoni

Junior Partner
Fiddler Gonzalez & Rodriguez
P.O. Box 363507
San Juan, Puerto Rico 00936–3507
(787) 759–3140
Fax: (787) 250–7555
EMail: See Below

8111

Business Information: Fiddler Gonzalez & Rodriguez is a full–service law firm with well–established practices in Corporate, Litigation, Banking and Financial Institutions, Labor and Employment Law, Real Estate, Environmental, Tax, Securities, Bankruptcy, and Business Reorganizations, Insurance, Financing, and Intellectual Property. With 75 attorneys, Fiddler Gonzalez & Rodriguez is the second–largest firm in Puerto Rico. A practicing attorney in Puerto Rico courts since 1987, Ms. Mendez Santoni joined the Firm in 1985 as a Law Clerk. As Attorney/Junior Partner, she specializes in such legal matters as Labor and Employment Law, representing the employers in state and federal courts. Internet users can reach her via: RMENDEZ@FGRLAW.COM. **Career Steps:** Fiddler Gonzalez & Rodriguez: Junior Partner (1994–Present), Senior Associate (1992–1994), Associate (1988–1992), Law Clerk (1985–1987). **Associations & Accomplishments:** Puerto Rico Bar Association; American Bar Association; Federal Bar Association; Association of Labor Relations Practitioners; Society for Human Resource Management; Legal Advisor, Puerto Rico Manufacturing Association; Offered numerous conferences by the PRMA and Puerto Rico Bar Association. **Education:** Interamerican University: B.A. cum laude (1984), School of Law, J.D. summa cum laude (1987). **Personal:** Married to Benny F. Figueroa–Lugo, Esq. in 1989.

Gretchen M. Mendez Vilella, Esq.

Attorney
Goldman, Antonetti & Cordova
P O Box 70364
San Juan, Puerto Rico 00936–0364
(787) 759–4207
Fax: (787) 767–9325
E MAIL: See Below

8111

Business Information: Goldman, Antonetti & Cordova is a general practice law firm with 60 attorneys on staff concentrating on business/corporate law. Established in 1964, the Firm currently has over 70 employees. As Attorney, Mrs. Mendez Vilella concentrates on environmental law and represents clients in administrative and civil cases as well as counseling. Internet users can reach her via: gmendez@gaclaw.com. **Career Steps:** Attorney, Goldman, Antonetti & Cordova (1993–Present); Public Interest Attorney, Environmental Quality Board of Puerto Rico (1992–1993); Counsel's Aide, Christopher Columbus Quincentennary Commission. **Associations & Accomplishments:** Centro Ecuestre de Puerto Rico; Federacion Ecuestre de Puerto Rico; Federal Bar Association; American Bar Association; Colegio de Abogados de Puerto Rico. **Education:** Vermont Law School, M.S.L. (1994); Interamerican University of Puerto Rico, J.D. (1991); Catholic University of America, B.A. (1988). **Personal:** Married to Carlos Grovas–Porrata in 1993. One child: Mariano Jose Grovas. Mrs. Mendez Vilella enjoys equestrian sports, sailing, aerobics, and snowboarding.

Nestor Mendez–Gomez, LL.M.

Founding Partner
Pietrantoni, Mendez & Alvarez
209 Munoz Rivera, Banco Popular Center, Suite 1901
San Juan, Puerto Rico 00918–1000
(809) 274–1212
Fax: (809) 274–1470

8111

Business Information: Pietrantoni, Mendez & Alvarez is a full–service, general practice law firm (no criminal cases). Headquartered in Puerto Rico, the international firm represents both large public and closely–held corporations throughout the U.S., South America, and the Caribbean. A practicing attorney since 1973 and a Founding Partner of the Firm (est. 1992), Mr. Mendez–Gomez directs the activities of the Litigation Group. His practice concentrates on commercial litigation, anti–trust, intellectual property and security law, in addition to conducting pro bono work in commercial litigation. **Career Steps:** Founding Partner, Pietrantoni, Mendez & Alvarez (1992–Present); Partner, McConnell Valdes (1976–1992); Chairman and Board of Directors, Doctors Hospital (1981–1982, 1989–1991). **Associations & Accomplishments:** Puerto Rico Community Foundation: Vice Chairman, Board of Directors; University of the Sacred Heart: Trustee, Board of Trustees; Trustee, Enrique Marti Coll Foundation; Professor, University of Puerto Rico Law School. **Education:** Harvard Law School, Ll.M. (1976); University of Pennsylvania Wharton School, B.S. in Economics (1970); University of Puerto Rico Law School, J.D. (1973). **Personal:** Married to Nellie Marti in 1972. Four children: Carla, Camelia, Claudia, and Carolina. Mr. Mendez–Gomez enjoys scuba diving, reading, tennis, and providing pro bono services to the needy and non–profit charitable organizations.

Jose E. Mendoza–Vidal

Partner
Mendoza & Baco
P.O. Box 190–0404
San Juan, Puerto Rico 00919–404
(787) 754–6700
Fax: (787) 754–7079

8111

Business Information: Mendoza & Baco is a general practice law firm with three partners, four attorneys, and two legal assistants. A practicing attorney since 1974 and a Retired District Judge for the Commonwealth of Puerto Rico, Mr. Mendoza–Vidal established the Firm in 1992. He now concentrates his practice in civil, corporate, and commercial litigation, collections, labor and estate planning. **Career Steps:** Partner, Mendoza & Baco (1990–Present); District Judge (Ret.), Commonwealth of Puerto Rico (1979–1990); Sole Practitioner, Law Office of Jose E. Mendoza–Vidal (1975–1979). **Associations & Accomplishments:** Former President, Exchange

Club, Rio Piedras Chapter (1960–1961); A.B.X. University Fraternity: Former Great Chancellor (1961–1962), Editor – "El Frate" (1995–1996). **Education:** University of Puerto Rico: J.D. (1974), B.B.A. (1950); Fort Benning Associates Officers Training Course (1952). **Personal:** Married to Carmen in 1950. Three children: Carmen, Enrique, and Marie Jossie. Mr. Mendoza–Vidal enjoys travel, aerobics, baseball, and basketball.

Mr. Benjamin E. Meredith

Attorney at Law

Law Offices of Benjamin E. Meredith

163 West Main Street, Suite 301
Dothan, AL 36301–1625
(334) 671–0289
Fax: (334) 671–0290

8111

Business Information: Law Offices of Benjamin E. Meredith is a full–service, general practice law firm. Admitted to practice law in California (1986), Illinois (1991), and Alabama (1992) state and federal courts, Benjamin E. Meredith began his private practice firm in Alabama in 1993. He is responsible for all aspects of operations and legal representation, concentrating in the areas of personal injury and workmen's compensation cases. **Career Steps:** Attorney at Law, Law Offices of Benjamin E. Meredith (1993–Present); Office Manager, Veigas & Cox, P.C. (1992–1993); Colonel, U.S. Army Reserves – Retired (27 years). **Associations & Accomplishments:** Lion's Club; Veterans of Foreign Wars; Retired Officer's Association; Houston County Bar Association; American Bar Association; Alabama State Bar; California State Bar; Illinois State Bar; Psychological Association; Alabama Trial Lawyers Association; National Federation of Independent Businesses; National Civil Affairs Association. **Education:** University of Santa Clara, B.S. (1978); University of Santa Clara, School of Law, J.D. (1981); U.S. Army War College (1990). **Personal:** Married to Carol Ann Meredith in 1992. Five children: Anne Maria, Frank, Michael, John, and Joe. Mr. Meredith enjoys hunting, boating, skeet shooting, and tennis.

Tanya R. Meyers, Esq.

Attorney

Law Office of Tanya R. Meyers

2101 Webster Street, Suite 1500
Oakland, CA 94612
(510) 446–7777
Fax: (510) 293–0177

8111

Business Information: Law Office of Tanya R. Meyers, established in 1995, is a full–service, general practice law firm, concentrating on commercial litigation, family law, employment law, personal injury, and mass torts. A practicing attorney in California state courts since 1990, Ms. Meyers established her sole practice law office in 1995. Her practice concentrates on employment law and commercial litigation. Future expansion goals include general and family law practices and adding up to four attorneys. Extensively involved in youth offenders programs, Ms. Meyers serves as a mentor to those youths on parole programs. She is also the Editor of a California State Bar Association–supported newsletter which recruits attorneys to serve as mentors for these parole program youths. The Firm may also be reached at P.O. Box 291, Mount Eden, CA 94557. **Career Steps:** Attorney, Law Office of Tanya R. Meyers (1995–Present); General Counsel, Elegant Entertainment, Inc. (1994–1995); Associate Attorney, Wilson, Sonsini, Goodrich & Rosati (1990–1994). **Associations & Accomplishments:** Infraction Review Committee, Santa Clara Bar Association; American Inns of Court; Board of Governors, Volunteers In Parade. **Education:** University of California – Los Angeles, J.D. (1990); University of San Francisco, B.S. in Management; Los Angeles Trade Technical College, A.A. **Personal:** Ms. Meyers enjoys reading, hiking, snorkeling, and skiing.

Richard H. Middleton Jr.

Founder and Senior Trial Attorney

Middleton, Mixson, Orr & Adams, P.C.

P.O. Box 10006
Savannah, GA 31412–0206
(912) 234–1133
Fax: (912) 234–8818

8111

Business Information: Middleton, Mixson, Orr & Adams, P.C. is a full–service, civil trial practice law firm, providing legal representation in all state and federal courts. The Firm serves clientele from two locations in Georgia (Savannah and Atlanta). A practicing attorney in Georgia state courts since 1976, Mr. Middleton founded the Firm in 1980 and currently serves as Lead Trial Counsel. His practice concentrates on products liability, ERISA, antitrust, and catastrophic personal injury cases. **Career Steps:** Founder and Senior Trial Attorney, Middleton, Mixson, Orr & Adams, P.C. (1980–Present); Associate, Portman, et al (1977–1979). **Associations & Accomplishments:** Treasurer, Association of Trial Lawyers of America; Former President, Savannah Trial Lawyers Association; Former President of Georgia Chapter, American Board of Trial Advocates; Trustee, Civil Justice Foundation; Lifetime Trustee, American Jury Trial Foundation; National Board of Directors, Trial Lawyers for Public Justice; Former National Board Member, American Board of Trial Advocates; Diplomate, American Board of Professional Liability Attorneys; SCRIBES; National Board of Directors, Southern Trial Lawyers Association. **Education:** Washington and Lee University: J.D. (1976), B.A. **Personal:** Married to Nancy Gibson Middleton in 1995. Two children: Christopher Townsend and Elizabeth Logan. Mr. Middleton enjoys collecting antiques & fine art and raising golden retrievers.

Cesar Millan Nicolet

Senior Partner

Corssen, Millan & Stone

Morande 322 Oficina 215
Santiago, Chile
562–698–8098
Fax: 562–696–2678

8111

Business Information: Corssen, Millan & Stone is a law firm with 6 partners and 10 attorneys who specialize in all legal fields to give individuals and enterprises a complete and global service. The Firm is mainly specialized in the commercial field including Foreign Investments, Exchange Control, and specific advice to the client on all legal aspects of domestic and International Transactions, Corporate Finance, Banking Mergers and Acquisitions, Leveraged Buy Outs, Securities, Stock exchange, Advertising Agencies, Litigation and Arbitration, Bankruptcy, Taxation and Customs Duties, Labor/Workers Redundancy Procedures, Intellectual Property (Patents, Trademarks and Copyrights). Of counsel International Affairs. As Senior Partner, Mr. Millan Nicolet is responsible for directing exports in foreign investments and implementing new business. **Career Steps:** Senior Partner, Corssen, Millan & Stone (1986–Present). **Associations & Accomplishments:** Presidential Delegate for Chile of International Association of Young Lawyers (AIJA); Member of Chilean Bar Association; Official Chilean – Spanish Chamber of Commerce. **Education:** Lawyer of Gabricla Misress University; Salaitanca University (19984–1988); Lawyer of Salamanca University, Salamanca Spain (1990); special courses in Environmental law (Universidad de Chile, 1996); World Trade Organization (Foreign Studies Institute, 1996, Santiago Chile). **Personal:** Mr. Millan Nicolet enjoys skiing.

James R. Miller

Attorney and Shareholder

Dickie, McCamey & Chilcote

2PPG Place, Suite 400
Pittsburgh, PA 15222–5402
(412) 392–5238
Fax: (412) 392–5367

8111

Business Information: Dickie, McCamey & Chilcote is a full–service, general corporate practice law firm, with emphasis on civil litigation. Headquartered in Pittsburgh, Pennsylvania, the Firm has a satellite office in Wheeling, West Virginia. A practicing attorney in Pennsylvania state courts since 1972, Mr. Miller joined the Firm as Attorney in 1974. Appointed as Shareholder in 1978, his practice is 100% civil trial work, focusing on medical malpractice defense and toxic tort litigation. He also serves as the National Trial Attorney for PPG Industries' Paint and Chemical Division, in which he coordinates the cases and either tries them himself or directs the lawyer appointed in other states. **Career Steps:** Dickie, McCamey & Chilcote: Shareholder (1978–Present), Attorney (1974–1978); Law Clerk, Commonwealth Court of Pennsylvania (1972–1974). **Associations & Accomplishments:** American Bar Association; American College of Trial Lawyers; Academy of Trial Lawyers. **Education:** Duquesne University School of Law, J.D. (1972); New York University, B.S. (1969). **Personal:** Married to Kate in 1975. Two children: Jesse J. and Cassidy A. Mr. Miller enjoys sports.

Michael T. Mills

President and Owner

Michael T. Mills, Chartered

111 East Marlin, P.O. Box 276
McPherson, KS 67460
(316) 241–7007
Fax: (316) 241–7016

8111

Business Information: Michael T. Mills, Chartered, established in 1963, is a full–service, general practice law firm, representing corporations and individuals in Kansas and surrounding areas. A practicing attorney in Kansas state courts since 1962, Mr. Mills established his sole practice firm in 1980. His practice concentrates on Worker's Compensation, estate planning, probate & trusts, personal injury, business law, and domestic relations. Concurrent with his legal practice, he is Owner and Director of LAMCO, a property development and management company, mainly involved with residental properties in and around McPherson County. **Career Steps:** President and Owner, Michael T. Mills, Chartered (1980–Present); Partner, Mills & Prather (1978–1980); Attorney, Mills & Mills (1962–1978); Captain, United States Navy Reserves – Retired. **Associations & Accomplishments:** Director/Owner, LAMCO; Director, Home State Bank and Trust; President, McPherson County Small Business Development Association; Director, Chrome Plus International, Inc.; American Bar Association; American Trial Lawyers Association; Kansas Bar Association; Kansas Trial Lawyers Association; Veterans of Foreign Wars; Reserve Officers Association; NRA; U. S. Chamber of Commerce; Rotary Clubs of America. **Education:** University of Kansas, J.D. (1962); University of Kansas, B.A. (1958). **Personal:** Married to Leonor D. C. in 1963. Mr. Mills enjoys community economic development.

Ana T. Miranda

Associate Attorney

McConnell Valdes

P.O. Box 364225
San Juan, Puerto Rico 00936–4225
(809) 250–5675
Fax: (809) 759–9225
EMAIL: See Below

8111

Business Information: McConnell Valdes, the leading law firm in Puerto Rico, is a full–service, general practice law firm, concentrating on litigation, tax law, corporate, and labor law. Established in 1949, the Firm currently employs 120 attorneys and 230 legal and administrative support staff. Joining the firm upon the conferral of her law degree in 1993, Ms. Miranda concentrates her practice in all areas of litigation. **Career Steps:** Associate Attorney, McConnell Valdes (1993–Present). **Associations & Accomplishments:** Harvard Club of Puerto Rico; Hasty Pudding Club; World Association of Former United Nations Interns & Fellows. **Education:** Stanford University, J.D. (1993); Harvard University, B.A. cum laude (1990). **Personal:** Ms. Miranda enjoys reading, camping, and movies.

Mr. Roy S. Mitchell

Partner

Morgan, Lewis & Bockius

1800 M Street, N.W.
Washington, DC 20036–5869
(202) 467–7170
Fax: (202) 467–7176 (703) 759–6963

8111

Business Information: Morgan, Lewis & Bockius is a full–service international law firm with offices in Washington D.C., New York, Philadelphia, Miami, Los Angeles, Brussels, Frankfurt, London, Singapore, Jakarta and Tokyo. As a Partner, Mr. Mitchell specializes in the field of Construction and International Government Contract Law. He has handled cases in more than forty states and thirty foreign countries. Established in 1873, Morgan, Lewis & Bockius employs 1,500 people. **Career Steps:** Partner, Morgan, Lewis & Bockius (1987–Present); Vice Chairman, Ameribanc Savings Bank (1980–Present); Chairman, Audit Committee, Ameribanc Investors Group (1984–Present). **Associations & Accomplishments:** Member, American Bar Association: Fellow and former National Chairman (1976–1977) – Public Contract Law Section Member, Chairman (1974–1975) – Committee on Environmental and Ecology Law, Chairman (1973–1974) – Committee on Current Federal Procurement Statutes, Regulations and Forms, and Chairman (1969–1972) – Bids and Protests Committee; Member, Virginia Bar Association; Member, D.C. Bar Association; Member, International Bar Association; Life Elder, Lewinsville Presbyterian Church. In addition, Mr. Mitchell has served on various special projects such as the Model Procurement Code, was a contributor to the Government Procurement Commission Study, served as a faculty member at Stanford University and Texas A&M, University Construction Executive Programs and is a member of the National Panel of Arbitrators for Construction Contract Disputes. Mr. Mitchell is internationally known for his knowledge of international contract and construction law: he has spoken at professional forums and has many books and articles published in these fields. **Education:** George Washington University Law School, J.D. (1959); Cornell University, B.S. in Industrial and Labor Relations (1957). **Personal:** Married to Nancy B. Mitchell in 1959. Three children: Mark E. Mitchell, Jeffrey B. Mitchell and Jennifer Mitchell–Copeland. Mr. Mitchell enjoys boating.

Ms. Holly Mitten
Partner
Law Office of Mitten & Farrell
P.O. Box 999
Half Moon Bay, CA 94019
(415) 728–0787
Fax: (415) 728–0785

8111

Business Information: Law Office of Mitten & Farrell is a full–service, general practice law firm concentrating in workers' compensation defense, representing insurance carriers and self–employed employers. As Partner, Ms. Mitten is responsible for all aspects of operations for the Half Moon Bay, CA office. Established in 1993, Law Offices of Mitten & Farrell currently employs five professionals. **Career Steps:** Sole Practitioner, Law Office of Holly Mitten (1995–Present); Partner, Law Offices of Mitten & Farrell (1993–Present); Associate/Client Relations, Law Offices of Liebman Reiner & McNeil (1990–1993); Managing Partner, San Francisco Office, Law Offices of Crymes, Hardie & Heer (1986–1990); Partner, Law Offices of Mullen & Filippi (1981–1986). **Associations & Accomplishments:** Advisor and Past Chairperson for Workers' Compensation Section of the State Bar of California; Docent for National Park Service – Golden Gate National Rec. Area; Faculty for Multiple Educational Seminars through the State Bar of California, the Insurance Claims Association and National Business Institute; Articles in Various Industry Publications, particularly relating to Workers' Compensation Industry. **Education:** Case Western Reserve University, J.D. (1978); Ohio University, B.A. in Philosophy. **Personal:** Married to Richard Loebick in 1978. Ms. Mitten enjoys travel, outdoor activities, including hiking and backpacking.

Mr. Paul M. Moldenhauer
President
Paul M. Moldenhauer, S.C.
1215 Belknap Street
Superior, WI 54880
(715) 394–7783
Fax: (715) 394–7786

8111

Business Information: Paul M. Moldenhauer, S.C. is a trial practice handling matters of divorce, custody, criminal defense, personal injury, and worker's compensation. The firm also handles wills, real estate, and contracts. As President, Mr. Moldenhauer manages the firm's operations. Established in 1990, Paul M. Moldenhauer, S.C. employs 3 people. **Career Steps:** President, Paul M. Moldenhauer, S.C. (1990–Present); Trial Lawyer, Paul M. Moldenhauer (1982–1990); Interim & Supply Pastor, Evangelical Lutheran Church in America (1979–Present). **Associations & Accomplishments:** Order of the Coif; Senior Editor, University of North Dakota Law Review; Delta Theta Phi International Law Fraternity; Wisconsin & Minnesota Supreme Courts; U.S. District Court for Western & Eastern Districts of Wisconsin and of Minnesota; U.S. Court of Appeals for 7th Circuit; U.S. Claims Court; Ordained Pastor of the former American Lutheran Church (currently known as Evangelical Lutheran Church in America); Elks Club; Who's Who in American Universities and Colleges (1982); Young Leaders of America (1968). **Education:** University of North Dakota School of Law, J.D. with distinction (1982); Luther Theological Seminary, M.Div. (1976); University of Wisconsin, B.S. in Education (1972). **Personal:** Mr. Moldenhauer enjoys writing, public speaking, carpentry, lead glass work, carving and boating.

Ismael Molina–Serrano
Registrar of the Property
Justice Department of Puerto Rico
Calle 6 K–6 Prado Alto
Guaynabo, Puerto Rico 00966
(809) 743–5003 (809) 749–9287
Fax: (809) 751–1038

8111

Business Information: The Justice Department of Puerto Rico is responsible for the enforcement of the laws in the Commonwealth of Puerto Rico. A practicing attorney in Puerto Rico since 1987, Mr. Molina–Serrano joined the Justice Department in November 1995. Appointed as Registrar of the Property (one of 27 sections in the Puerto Rican government) by the Governor of Puerto Rico, he is serving a twelve–year term. His primary duties include study, review, and recording of legal transactions involving real property. **Career Steps:**

Registrar of the Property, Justice Department of Puerto Rico (1995–Present); Attorney, Notary Public, Vazquez, Vizcarrondo & Angelet (1993–1995); Attorney, Notary Public, Fiddler, Gonzalez & Rodriquez (1989–1993); Attorney, Notary Public, Franco, Quiles–Mariani & Godinez (1987–1989). **Associations & Accomplishments:** Notaries Association of Puerto Rico; American Bar Association: Real and Probate Property Section, Young Lawyers Division; Phi Alpha Delta; Puerto Rico Bar Association; Air Force Museum Foundation. **Education:** University of Puerto Rico School of Law, J.D. (1986); University of Puerto Rico – Rio Piedras Campus, B.A. (1982). **Personal:** Married to Esther Villarino in 1988. Two children: Ismael Antonio Molina–Villarino and Andres Molina–Villarino. Mr. Molina–Serrano enjoys jogging, running, music collecting and fountain pen collecting.

Brian M. Monahan
Partner
Lauer & Monahan, P.C.
704 Washington Street
Easton, PA 18042
(610) 258–5329
Fax: (610) 258–0155

8111

Business Information: Lauer & Monahan, P.C. is a full–service, general practice law firm. Serving clients throughout Easton, PA and surrounding communities, the Firm focuses on civil and criminal law matters. A practicing attorney since 1982, Mr. Monahan became a Partner of the Firm in 1986. His areas of concentration include criminal and civil litigation, administrative law, municipal law, and real estate and family law. Concurrently, he serves as the Chief Public Defender for Northampton County, Pennsylvania. **Career Steps:** Partner, Lauer & Monahan, P.C. (1986–Present); Chief Public Defender, Northampton County, Pennsylvania (1994–Present); Associate, Philip D. Lauer, P.C. (1987–1992); Associate, William P. Coffin, Esq. (1983–1987). **Education:** Franklin Pierce Law Center, J.D. (1982); Villanova University, B.A., cum laude (1978).

Ronald E. Monard
Law Clerk
Law Office of Crystal Sluyter
44 Fairlane Road
Laguna Niguel, CA 92677
(714) 374–3515
Fax: (714) 374–3518

8111

Business Information: Law Office of Crystal Sluyter is a full service law firm providing legal advice and related services to clients. Established in 1994, the Firm employs eight people. As Law Clerk, Mr. Monard is responsible for office management, and the negotiation of all settlement negotiations. He is also responsible for assisting attorneys in all phases of trial preparation, and handles personnel management and scheduling. Mr. Monard is currently in the process of incorporating a business which will produce a new kitchen appliance. **Career Steps:** Law Clerk, Law Office of Crystal Sluyter (1995–Present); Arbitrator, Better Business Bureau (1992–Present); Political Coordinator, Kate Squires for Senate (1993–1994); Law Librarian, Western State University (1991–1993). **Associations & Accomplishments:** Western Society of Criminology; Golden Key National Honor Society Member; American Jurisprudence Award for Federal Appellate Writing; 1990 National Dean's List. **Education:** Washington State University School of Law, J.D. (1994); University of California, Irvine, B.A. in Social Ecology (1990). **Personal:** Mr. Monard enjoys being a musician.

Ms. Julie–April Montgomery
Assistant Corporation Counsel – Tax Division
City of Chicago, Department of Law
121 North LaSalle, Room 610
Chicago, IL 60602
(312) 744–6921
Fax: (312) 744–3932

8111

Business Information: City of Chicago, Department of Law handles all legal functions for City administration. As Assistant Corporation Counsel – Tax Division, Ms. Montgomery handles negotiations, drafts and reviews tax settlements/payment contracts, issues opinion letters, litigates in court and administratively, drafts laws and rulings, and administers the City's voluntary disclosure program. Established in 1836, City of Chicago, Department of Law employs a staff of over 300. **Career Steps:** Assistant Corporation Counsel – Tax Division, City of Chicago, Department of Law (1986– Present); Private Practice (1985–1986); Legal Advisor & Legislative Assistant, State Senator Charles Chew, Jr. (1983–1984); Legal Researcher, United Nations Institute for Training & Research (1981–1983). **Associations & Accomplishments:** American, New York State, Illinois, and Chicago Bar Associations; Chair, Chicago Bar Association, State and Local Tax Committee; Phi Alpha Delta Law Fraternity International, Current Mar-

shall of the Chicago Alumni Chapter; M.L.E.R., Inc. (Illinois supplemental bar review course) Past Board Chairman and CEO, Current Advisor to Board; Lecturer and speaker on State & Local Tax; Co–Author, Illinois Institute for Continuing Legal Education. **Education:** New York University, LL.M. in Taxation (1985); New York University, J.D. (1983); Roosevelt University, M.B.A. (1979); University of San Francisco, B.S. (1978).

Edward O. Moody, P.A.
Owner/Attorney
Edward O. Moody, P.A.
801 West 4th Street
Little Rock, AR 72201–2107
(501) 376–0000
Fax: (501) 376–0546

8111

Business Information: Licensed to practice law in Texas and Arkansas, Mr. Moody established his private practice upon conferral of his law degree in 1978, concentrating in asbestos injury law. The Firm presently employs two attorneys focusing in plaintiff's civil litigation. As Owner and Attorney, he is responsible for the administrative operations for associates and support staff, in addition to his daily law practice. **Career Steps:** Owner, Edward O. Moody, P.A. (1978–Present). **Education:** University of Arkansas – Little Rock, J.D. (1978), B.A. (1971); University of Arkansas – Fayetteville, M.P.A. (1974). **Personal:** Married to Vicki Reed Moody in 1972. They have three sons. Mr. Moody enjoys flying, skiing, and fishing.

Dawn Enoch Moore
President
TICOR Land Title Company
8115 Preston Road, Suite 100
Dallas, TX 75225
(214) 373–3500
Fax: (214) 368–7520

8111

Business Information: TICOR Land Title Company is a title insurance agency consisting of four offices located in Texas. Established in 1995, TICOR reports annual revenue of $5 million and currently employs 37 people. As President, Ms. Moore is responsible for all aspects of operations, including administration, finances, public relations, accounting, legal matters, and strategic planning. Concurrent with her position at TICOR, she is Co–Founder and Partner of Seal, Lawrence & Moore, PLLC – a full–service, general practice law firm, with concentration on real estate law. **Career Steps:** President, TICOR Land Title Company (1995–Present); Founder and Partner, Seal, Lawrence & Moore, PLLC (1995–Present); President, Dawn Enoch Moore, P.C. (1987–1995); Partner, Settle & Pou (1984–1987); Associate, Passman & Jones (1981–1983). **Associations & Accomplishments:** Board of Directors, Chairman of Forms and Contracts Committee, Greater Dallas Association of Realtors; Board Member, Dallas Area Habitat for Humanity, Inc.; Board Member, Exploring, Circle Ten, Boy Scouts; Building Committee, Sunday School Teacher, University Park United Methodist Church; Dallas Bar Association; Texas Bar Association; Commercial Real Estate Women; The Real Estate Council. **Education:** Southern Methodist University: J.D. (1981), B.S. in Economics; Attended: Wellesley College. **Personal:** Married to Steve in 1980. Three children: Brett, Blair, and Brooke. Ms. Moore enjoys playing the harp, walking, swimming, and entertaining.

Mr. James R. Moore
Partner and Chair of Environmental & Natural Resources Practice
Perkins Coie
1201 Third Avenue, Suite 4100
Seattle, WA 98101
(206) 583–8888
Fax: (206) 583–8500

8111

Business Information: Perkins Coie is a full–service, general practice law firm specializing in environmental law. The Firm has thirteen locations (ten in the U.S. and three international – England, Hong Kong and Taiwan). Established in 1912, the Practice currently employs 900 professionals worldwide. As Partner and Chair of Environmental & Natural Resources Practice Group, Mr. Moore is responsible for all aspects of environmental law. Practicing in this field since 1970, he was one of the first attorneys to specialize in this area. **Career Steps:** Partner and Chair of Environmental & Natural Resources Practice Group, Perkins Coie (1989–Present); Associate, Perkins Coie (1987–1989); Regional Counsel, U.S. EPA, Region 10 (1982–1987); Assistant U.S. Attorney, U.S. Attorney's Office, Western District of Washington (1974–1982); Trial Attorney, U.S. Department of Justice, Pollution Control (1970–1974). **Associations & Accom-**

plishments: Board of Directors, Environmental Law Institute, Washington, D.C.; Special District Counsel, Washington State Bar Association; Chair, Audit Committee, Whitman College; Member, American Bar Association. **Education:** Duke University Law School, J.D. (1969); Whitman College, B.A. (1966). **Personal:** Married to Katherine Lindquist in 1996. Four children: Amy & John McKenna (stepchildren), Katherine Keehn (daughter) and Zia Sunseri (foster daughter). Mr. Moore enjoys softball, jogging, skiing, sailing and model railroading.

Peggy Braden Moore
Attorney
Peggy Braden Moore, Attorney at Law
P.O. Box 3454
Stamford, CT 06905
(203) 353-1811
Fax: (203) 975-7736

8111

Business Information: A practicing attorney since 1968, Mrs. Moore established her private practice in 1986, concentrating in labor and employee benefits issues for large and small businesses. She also accepts juvenile court cases and serves as a Magistrate in the Motor Vehicle Court. **Career Steps:** Peggy Braden Moore, Attorney at Law (1986-Present); Senior Corporate Counsel, The Singer Company (1979-1986); Attorney/Partner, Jackson, Lewis, Schnitzler (1971-1979). **Associations & Accomplishments:** Board Member, Boys and Girls Club of Stamford, Connecticut. **Education:** University of Denver, College of Law, J.D. (1968); University of the Pacific, Raymond College, B.A. (1965). **Personal:** Married to Frank in 1981. Two children: Charles and Douglas. Mrs. Moore enjoys family and church.

Karen Morales-Ramirez, Esq.

Attorney
Law Offices of Benjamin Acosta, Jr.
P. O. Box 1677
Guaynabo, Puerto Rico 00970
(787) 722-2363
Fax: (787) 724-5970

8111

Business Information: Law Offices of Benjamin Acosta, Jr. is a full-service, general practice law firm concentrating on mainly civil cases, insurance, and tort law. A practicing attorney in Puerto Rico courts since 1993, Mrs. Morales-Ramirez joined the Firm in 1993. She handles torts law, insurance, and civil cases. **Career Steps:** Attorney, Law Offices of Benjamin Acosta Jr. (1995-Present); Law Clerk, Special Unit of Judges of Appeals (1993). **Associations & Accomplishments:** Puerto Rico Bar Association; Phi Alpha Delta. **Education:** Interamerican University of Puerto Rico, J.D. (1993); University of Puerto Rico, B.A. in Psychology. **Personal:** Married to Angel Ortiz-Guzman in 1995. Mrs. Morales-Ramirez enjoys reading and the beach.

Margaret C. Morasca
Director, Human Resources and Recruitment
Archer & Greiner
P.O. Box 3000
Haddonfield, NJ 08033-0968
(609) 354-3112
Fax: (609) 795-0574
EMAIL: See Below

8111

Business Information: Archer & Greiner is a full-service law firm with 75 attorneys in various departments, including matrimonial, labor, litigation, real estate, corporate, trust and estate, and land use. As Director of Human Resources and Recruitment, Ms. Morasca is responsible for policy development, hiring and firing, benefits administration, lateral recruitment and campus interviews. Internet users can reach her via: MMorasca@archerlaw.com **Career Steps:** Director, Human Resources and Recruitment, Archer & Greiner (1992-Present); Director, Human Resources, Reed, Smith, Shan & McClay (1983-1992). **Associations & Accomplishments:** Society of Human Resource Management; Association of Legal Administrators; National Association of Law Placement; Philadelphia Bar Association. **Education:** Ohio University, B.A. (1971); Attended, Yale University. **Personal:** One child: Jessica Leigh Bruno. Ms. Morasca enjoys swimming and travel.

John L. Morel

Attorney-at-Law
The Law Office of John L. Morel, P. C.
235 East Front Street, P.O. Box 1471
Bloomington, IL 61702-1471
(309) 829-1614
Fax: (309) 828-5623

0111

Business Information: The Law Office of John L. Morel, PC is a private practice law firm concentrating in the area of civil trial law, appellate practice, personal injury, commercial litigation and insurance law. Establishing his private practice in 1993, Mr. Morel is admitted to both State and Federal courts, and has been a trial attorney since 1965. Concurrent to his legal responsibilities, he has been a contributing editor for the Illinois Defense Counsel Quarterly for the past two years. **Career Steps:** Attorney-at-Law, John L. Morel, PC (1993-Present); Attorney, Dunn Law Firm (1966-1993); Legal Counsel, Board of higher Education, State of Illinois (1969-1975); Legal Counsel, Board of Governors of State Colle-ges (Western Illinois, Eastern Illinois and Chicago State Universities) (1968-1985); Legal Counsel, Gridley, Odell and Cornell School Districts; Military Service, United States Marine Corps Reserves (1956-1962); Legislative Assistant, Speaker of the House John W. Lewis – Illinois (1962). **Associations & Accomplishments:** American Bar Association; Illinois State Bar Association; McLean County Bar Association; Illinois Association of Defense Trial Counsel; Federation of Insurance and Corporate Counsel; Defense Research Institute; National Association of College and University Attorneys; Illinois Appellate Lawyers Association; McLean County Heart Association; McLean County Mental Health Association; McLean County Public Building Commission; Board of Directors, County Young Representatives; National Advisory Council of Small Business Administration; Ford Foundation Fellow; Who's Who in the Midwest; Phi Delta Phi; Pi Gamma Mu; Martindale-Hubbell Rating: AV; Numerous publications in Illinois law journals. **Education:** Univertsity of Illinois, J.D. (1965); Western Illinois University, B.A. with honors (1963).

James E. Morreau Jr.
Chief Litigation Attorney
Kruger, Schwartz & Morreau
Two Paragon Centre, 6040 Dutchman's Lane, Ste 220
Louisville, KY 40205-3305
(502) 485-9200
Fax: (502) 485-9220

8111

Business Information: Kruger, Schwartz & Morreau is a full-service, private practice law firm. Established in 1992, the Firm currently employs 10 legal and administrative support staff. Admitted to practice law in Kentucky state courts, Mr. Morreau established the Firm in 1992. He serves as Chief Litigation Attorney and is responsible for all aspects of operations, including legal representation, litigation, and commercial cases representing closely-held corporations and companies. He also provides limited pro bono representation. **Career Steps:** Chief Litigation Attorney, Kruger, Schwartz & Morreau (1992-Present); Co-Owner, Investment Properties Associates (1984-Present); Attorney and General Counsel, MKS Enterprises (1985-1992); Attorney and Associate, Taustine, Post, et al (1980-1987). **Associations & Accomplishments:** American Trial Lawyers Association; Kentucky Bar Association; American Bar Association. **Education:** University of Louisville, J.D. (1980), B.A. (1977). **Personal:** Married to Jane C. Morreau in 1981. Two children: Jacqueline and Gregory. Mr. Morreau enjoys computers and real estate investing.

Frank C. Morris Jr., Esq.

Senior Partner
Epstein, Becker & Green, P.C.
1227 25th Street, NW Suite 700
Washington, DC 20037-1156
(202) 861-0900
Fax: (202) 296-2882

8111

Business Information: Epstein Becker & Green, P.C. is a general practice law firm, concentrating in labor, employee, and healthcare law. National in scope, the firm has 11 offices located throughout the U.S. Future plans include establishing more locations and expanding at the international level. A practicing attorney in District of Columbia and Pennsylvania state and federal courts since 1973, Mr. Morris joined the Firm as an Associate Attorney in 1978, attaining partnership in 1981. Appointed Senior Partner in 1988, he is responsible for the management of the Labor Department at the Washington,

---

DC office. **Career Steps:** Epstein Becker & Green, P.C.: Senior Partner (1988-Present), Partner (1981-1988), Associate Attorney (1978-1980). **Associations & Accomplishments:** American Bar Association; Pennsylvania Bar Association; D.C. Bar Association; Federal Bar Association; D.C. Road Runners Club. **Education:** University of Virginia, J.D. (1973); Northwestern University, B.S. with distinction (1970). **Personal:** Married to Kathleen Williams. Two children: Frank Charles III and Alexander Greg. Mr. Morris enjoys McLean youth basketball and soccer.

Steven Moyer
Partner
Haight, Brown & Bonestel
1620 26th Street, Suite 4000N
Santa Monica, CA 90404
(310) 449-6000
Fax: Please mail or call

8111

Business Information: Haight, Brown & Bonestel is a full-service law firm concentrating in liability defense and general tort litigation. Established in 1940, the Firm has locations in Santa Monica, San Francisco, Santa Anna, and Riverside, California. As Partner, Mr. Moyer, who practices in both state and federal courts, is responsible for trying civil cases, specifically those dealing with professional/product liability, and commercial litigation. **Career Steps:** Partner, Haight, Brown & Bonestel (1986-Present); Proprietor, Law Offices of Steven E. Moyer (Jan.1985-Dec.1985); Attorney, Los Angeles County Public Defender's Office (1970-1984). **Associations & Accomplishments:** American Bar Association; California State Bar Association; Los Angeles County Bar Association; Southern California Defense Counsel. **Education:** University of California, Los Angeles: Law School J.D. (1969), B.A. (1966). **Personal:** Married to Joan D. in 1972. Two children: Alexander D. and David M.. Mr. Moyer enjoys bicycling, skiing, hiking, and music.

T. Aladdin Mozingo, Esq.
Sole Practitioner
Mozingo Law Offices, P.C.
720 South Coit Street, Suite 2
Florence, SC 29501-5113
(803) 673-0102
Fax: (803) 673-0251

8111

Business Information: Mozingo Law Offices, P.A., established in 1995, is a full-service, general practice law firm, concentrating on medical malpractice, product liability, worker's compensation and catastrophic bodily injury. Admitted to practice in all Federal and State Courts in South Carolina since 1988, Mr. Mozingo established his sole practice firm in April 1995. **Career Steps:** Sole Practitioner, Mozingo Law Offices, P.A. (1995-Present); Associate, A. Parker Barnes, Jr., P.A. & Associates; Associate, King & Vernon, P.A. **Associations & Accomplishments:** Medical University Heart Institute; Help in the promotion of literacy; Tort Reform Committee; Employee Benefits Committee; Medicine and Law Committee; Worker's Compensation Law Committee; Automobile Law Committee; American Trial Lawyers Association; South Carolina Trial Lawyers Association. **Education:** University of South Carolina Law School, J.D. (1988). **Personal:** Mr. Mozingo enjoys water sports and tennis.

J. Marvin Mullis Jr.
Attorney
The Law Office of J. Marvin Mullis Jr.
P.O. Box 7757
Columbia, SC 29202-7757
(803) 799-9577
Fax: (803) 254-8956

8111

Business Information: The Law Office of J. Marvin Mullis Jr. is a full-service law firm, concentrating on workers compensation cases. A practicing trial attorney since 1965, Mr. Mullis founded the Firm in 1971 and is permitted to practice in state and federal courts. **Career Steps:** Attorney, The Law Office of J. Marvin Mullis Jr. (1971-Present). **Associations & Accomplishments:** Former President, South Carolina Trial Lawyers Association; Continuing Legal Education Chairman; State

Delegate, Association of Trial Lawyers of America; Former President, Columbia Jaycees; Former Member, Columbia Chamber of Commerce Board; Founding Member, Palmetto Place. **Education:** University of South Carolina: LL.B. (1965), Degree in Business Economics. **Personal:** Married to Bonita Brewer in 1989. Three children: James Marvin III, Pamela Ricey, and Ashley Wilson. Mr. Mullis enjoys flying, golf, and woodworking.

David H. Murphree, Esquire

Member
Brown, Rudnick, Freed & Gesmer
One Financial Center
Boston, MA 02111
(617) 856–8362
Fax: (617) 856–8201

8111

Business Information: Brown, Rudnick, Freed & Gesmer is a general practice law firm, with an emphasis on corporate law for small to medium companies. Mr. Murphree is a corporate and securities lawyer, and a member in the Corporate Practice Group. Established in 1947, Brown, Rudnick, Freed & Gesmer employs 120 attorneys, and an administrative support staff of over 280 people. **Career Steps:** Attorney, Brown, Rudnick, Freed & Gesmer (1985–Present); Associate, Brown, Rudnick, Freed & Gesmer (1982–1984); Associate, Goodwin, Procter & Hoar (1978–1982). **Associations & Accomplishments:** President and Director, Concord–Carlisle Community Chest, Inc.; Vice–Chair Boston Bar Association Securities Law Committee; Contributing Author, International Business Transactions, Business Law Instructor, Babson College. Education: Boston University, LL.M. (1977); Harvard Law School, J.D. (1973); Duke University, B.A. (1970). **Personal:** Married to Carol in 1979. One child: Caroline Marie. Mr. Murphree enjoys tennis and travel."

Yvette T. Murray

Attorney
Lytal & Reiter
515 North Flagler Drive, Floor 10
West Palm Beach, FL 33401–4321
(407) 655–1990
Fax: (407) 832–2932

8111

Business Information: Lytal & Reiter is a law firm of 14 attorneys and a support staff of 70 based in West Palm Beach, Florida. Established in 1985, the Firm focuses in personal injury, product liability, and medical malpractice law. As Attorney and Associate, Ms. Murray has been with Lytal & Reiter since 1992 and concentrates on personal injury cases. **Career Steps:** Attorney, Lytal & Reiter (1992–Present). **Associations & Accomplishments:** Chairperson, Law Week; President, Hispanic Bar Association of Palm Beach County; Vice President, Hispanic Cultural Arts Board; Chair, Young Lawyers of the Academy of Florida Trial Lawyers; Board Member, Young Lawyers of Palm Beach County; Catholic Lawyer's Guild. **Education:** University of Florida, J.D. (1991), B.S.B.A. **Personal:** Married to Scott C. in 1992. Ms. Murray enjoys boating and outdoor activities.

Mr. Neil Myers

President
Neil Myers Co., L.P.A.
26111 Brush Avenue
Euclid, OH 44132
(216) 289–9500
Fax: (216) 289–6416

8111

Business Information: Neil Myers Co., L.P.A. is a legal service. In his capacity as Assistant Director of Law for the City of Euclid, Ohio, he handles citizens' complaints, issues warrants for arrests, handles zoning and other legal matters common to a municipal corporation. He is also assigned to represent subcommittees of the city, and from time to time trial and appeal proceedings. The Firm also handles matters in the general practice of law. As President, Mr. Myers is an attorney and serves as the Assistant Law Director for the City of Euclid, Ohio. The Firm is a sole–proprietorship. Mr. Myers enjoys table tennis, and is a two–time Gold Medalist and two–time Bronze Medalist in U.S. Senior Olympics Table Tennis Tournaments. **Career Steps:** President, Neil Myers Co., L.P.A., (1965–Present); Assistant Law Director, City of Euclid, Ohio (1971–Present). **Associations & Accomplishments:** American Bar Association; Cuyahoga County Bar Association; U.S. Table Tennis Association. **Education:** Cleveland Marshall Law; J.D. (1965); Kent State University, B.S. & B.A.; Real Estate License, State of Ohio. **Personal:** Married to Sondra in 1961. Three children: Howard, Marcia, and Andrew. Mr. Myers enjoys participating in State and National Table Tennis Tournaments and Senior Olympics.

Richard D. Myers

Shareholder/Director
Schmid, Mooney & Frederick, P.C.
11404 West Dodge Road, Suite 700 First National Plaza
Omaha, NE 68154–2576
(402) 493–7700
Fax: (404) 493–7005
EMAIL: See Below

8111

Business Information: Schmid, Mooney & Frederick, P.C. is a full–service, general practice business law firm. The Company presently has 18 attorneys, many of whom are licensed to practice in more than one state for federal and state cases. A practicing attorney in Nebraska state and federal courts since 1971, Mr. Myers joined the Firm in 1980. His area of concentration is banking, real estate, bankruptcy, and commercial law. Internet users can reach him via: rmyers@radiks.net. **Career Steps:** Shareholder/Director, Schmid, Mooney & Frederick, P.C. (1980–Present); Bankruptcy Trustee, United States Bankruptcy Court for Nebraska (1978–Present). **Associations & Accomplishments:** Omaha Bar Association; Nebraska Bar Association – Bankruptcy Section; Commercial Law League of America; Commercial Arbitrator, American Arbitration Association; Former President, Nebraska Association of Bank Attorneys (1990–1991); Director, Radio Talking Book Services, Inc.; Chairman, Nebraska Lions Foundation (1997–1998). **Education:** Creighton University College of Law, J.D. (1971); Midland College, B.A. (1968); Licensed to Practice Law, Nebraska (1971). **Personal:** Married to Marsha in 1974. Mr. Myers enjoys golf and travel.

Kenneth B. Myklebust

Partner/Attorney
Irwin, Myklebust, Savage & Brown, P.S.
SE 1230 Bishop Boulevard
Pullman, WA 99163
(509) 332–3502
Fax: (509) 332–6565

8111

Business Information: Irwin, Myklebust, Savage & Brown, P.S. is a law firm concentrating on estate planning, probate, trust, real estate, and tax law. Established in 1945 and incorporated in 1971, the firm currently employs 15 people. In 1964, Mr. Myklebust joined the Firm and in 1965 was made a Partner. As a Partner, he is involved in all management decisions affecting the policies and procedures established by the Firm. As an Attorney, his focus is on estate planning, trust, and tax law. A member of the Washington State Bar, Mr. Myklebust has also been admitted to practice before the United States Supreme Court, the U.S. Tax Court, and the U.S. District Court. **Career Steps:** Partner, Irwin, Myklebust, Savage & Brown, P.S. (1984–Present); Lecturer/Instructor, Washington State University (1964–1994). **Associations & Accomplishments:** Admitted to practice before the United States Supreme Court, United States Tax Court, and United States District Court. Fellow, American College of Trust and Estate Counsel; Washington State Bar Association: Tax Section and Real Property, Probate and Trust Section; American Bar Association: Tax Section and Real Property, Probate, and Trust Section; Founding Trustee and Secretary, Washington State University Foundation; Past President, Pullman United Way; Pullman Chamber of Commerce, Outstanding Member Award. **Education:** University of Washington: J.D. (1962) and B.A. (1959). **Personal:** Married to Suzanne in 1959. Four children: K. Richard, James K., Krystal D., and Karin A.. Mr. Myklebust enjoys snow skiing, water skiing, golf, gardening, and sailing.

Mr. David Nadler

President
Ballon, Stoll, Bader and Nadler, P.C.
1450 Broadway
New York, NY 10018
(212) 575–7900
Fax: (212) 764–5060

8111

Business Information: Ballon, Stoll, Bader and Nadler, P.C. is a general practice law firm, with offices in New York, and Hackensack, New Jersey. In his capacity as President, Mr. Nadler oversees the Firm's management, and is in charge of the Real Estate and Corporate Departments. Established in 1930, Ballon, Stoll, Bader and Nadler, P.C. employs a full–time staff of 30. **Career Steps:** President, Ballon, Stoll, Bader and Nadler, P.C. (1966–Present). **Associations & Accomplishments:** New York State and American Bar Association; Who's Who Among Practicing Attorneys; Board of Directors, 200 East Tenant's Corporation; Board of Directors, Colonial Arms Condominium. **Education:** St. John's University, LL.B. (1966); Boston University, B.S.

Amilcar Velazquez Nazario, Esquire

Trial Lawyer/Notary Public
Law Office of Amilcar Velazquez–Nazario, Esquire
Urb Town Park, D27 Calle Trevi
San Juan, Puerto Rico 00924
(787) 752–4570
Fax: (787) 768–2325

8111

Business Information: Law Office of Amilcar Velazquez–Nazario, Esquire is a general practice law firm. Established in 1992, and located in San Juan, Puerto Rico, the Firm concentrates in criminal and civil cases. As Trial Lawyer/Notary Public, Mr. Nazario oversees the daily operation of the Firm, prepares cases for trial, writes briefs, and conducts legal research. A former trial judge with over 20 years experience, Mr. Nazario looks forward to the continued growth of the Firm and expanding his practice. **Career Steps:** Trial Lawyer/ Notary Public, Law Office of Amilcar Velazquez–Nazario, Esquire (1990–Present); Judicial System of Puerto Rico: Superior Court Judge (1978–1990), District Court Judge (1970–1978); Attorney, Legal Aid Society of Puerto Rico (1968–1970). **Associations & Accomplishments:** Commissioner of the Municipal Hearing Commission of Puerto Rico; Commissioner of Special Commission to Advise the Governor in Relation to Use of Public Funds in Advertising of Government Agencies. **Education:** University of Puerto Rico: L.L.B. (1966), B.B.A. (1958), B.A. in Education (1954), ROTC Second Lieutenant (1954). **Personal:** Three children: Vilma, Marirosa, and Patsy Velazquez Dei Valle. Mr. Nazario enjoys baseball games.

Jose J. Nazario

Senior Partner
Nazario & Santiago
867 Calle Domingo Cabrera
San Juan, Puerto Rico 00925–2412
(809) 758–0315
Fax: (809) 756–0315
EMAIL: See Below

8111

Business Information: Nazario & Santiago is a full–service, general practice law firm, concentrating on constitutional law and civil rights law. A practicing attorney in Puerto Rico state courts since 1985, Mr. Nazario co–established the Firm in 1987. Serving as Senior Partner, he is responsible for all administrative operations for associates and a support staff of five, in addition to his daily law practice. Internet users can reach him via: JJN23@lgc. apc. org. **Career Steps:** Senior Partner, Nazario & Santiago (1987–Present); Supreme Court of Puerto Rico: Director, Central Staff (1985–1986), Law Clerk (1982–1984). **Associations & Accomplishments:** Colegio de Abogados de Puerto Rico. **Education:** Harvard Law School, Ll.M. (1985). **Personal:** Mr. Nazario enjoys reading and travel.

Vivian Nazario Cancel

Attorney
Puerto Rico Legal Aids
P.O. Box 588
Hormigueros, Puerto Rico 00660
(809) 832–7620
Fax: Please mail or call

8111

Business Information: Puerto Rico Legal Aids is a state–funded legal service, providing legal services to poverty–level income clients in Puerto Rico. Services provided include: legal representation on civil matters, landlord/tenant disputes, consumer protection, and public benefits. A practicing attorney in Puerto Rico since 1983, Mrs. Nazario Cancel joined the Puerto Rico Legal Aids in 1986. She is responsible for providing the legal service given to the Agency's clientele, as well as providing legal services study and receiving knowledge, analysis and understanding of the legal problems, laws and needs of the poor. She also prepares cases, conducts legal research, analysis pleading, legislations, laws to appear before the courts and administrative bodies, redact legal documents, assess local community and people's needs, and making radio and television programs to advise the people about their rights and new laws. **Career Steps:** Attorney, Puerto Rico Legal Aids (1986–Present); Medical Center: Personnel Manager (1979–1980), Auxiliar Administrator (1978–1979). **Associations & Accomplishments:** Fraternidad Legal Phi Alpha Delta, Jose De Diego Chapter; American Bar Association; The National Dean's List; Federacion de Deportes de caballos de Paso Fino; Vice President Law School (1983). **Education:** Catholic University, J.D. (1983); Interamerican University, B.A. Summa Cum Laude (1979). **Personal:** Married to Jose A. Flores Morales in 1990. Two children: Luis G. and Vivian I. Mrs. Nazario Cancel enjoys reading, painting, and raising Paso Fino horses.

David Lawrence Neale

Partner
Levene, Neale & Bender
1801 Avenue of the Stars, Suite 1120
Los Angeles, CA 90067
(310) 229–1234
Fax: (310) 229–1244

8111

Business Information: Levene, Neale & Bender is a law firm specializing in bankruptcy, solvency work, commercial law, reorganization and workouts. Established in 1995, the Firm currently employs seven attorneys, legal and administrative support staff. Admitted to practice in California state and federal courts since 1988, Mr. Neale joined the Firm as Partner in 1995 and is responsible for providing legal representation to the Firm's major clientele. **Career Steps:** Partner, Levene, Neale & Bender (1995–Present); Shareholder, Levene & Eisenberg, P.C. (1989–1995); Associate, Kramer, Levin, Nessen, Kamin & Frankel (1987–1989). **Associations & Accomplishments:** Beverly Hills Bar Association; Century City Bar Association; American Bar Association; Financial Lawyers Conference; American Bankruptcy Institute; Federal Bar Association; Published two articles in "Entertainment Publishing & Arts Handbook" on Bankruptcy. **Education:** Columbia University Law School, J.D. (1987); Princeton University, B.A., summa cum laude (1984). **Personal:** Married to Mary H. Neale in 1988. Two children: Ethan and Henry.

Robert C. Neff Jr.

Attorney
Budd, Larner & Gross
Two Gateway Center 12th Floor
Newark, NJ 07102
(201) 624–0800
Fax: (201) 624–0808

8111

Business Information: Budd, Larner & Gross is a full–service law firm. As Attorney, Mr. Neff is responsible for litigation, and often represents companies in the engineering, construction, and manufacturing industries. **Career Steps:** Attorney, Budd, Larner & Gross (1994–Present); Judicial Clerk, U.S. District Court (1991–1992). **Associations & Accomplishments:** Appointed by NJ Governor Christine Whitman to the Tidelands Resource Council. **Education:** Seton Hall Law School, J.D. (1991); Middlebury College, B.A. (1984) departmental honors. **Personal:** Married to Cynthia Spera in 1991. One child: Robert Carey. Mr. Neff enjoys tennis.

Todd M. Nelson

Partner
Oles Morrison & Rinker
3300 Columbia Center, 701 5th Avenue
Seattle, WA 98104–7082
(206) 623–3427
Fax: (206) 682–6234

8111

Business Information: The law firm of Oles Morrison & Rinker, concentrates primarily on complex litigation in Construction, Contracts, Commercial and Insurance Defense, and Real Estate. Comprised of 18 partners and 14 associates, the Firm, established in 1893, is located in Seattle, Washington. As Partner, Mr. Nelson is responsible for resolving and litigating various complex construction and commercial disputes on behalf of clients in Federal and State courts or alternative dispute forums. **Career Steps:** Partner, Oles Morrison & Rinker (Present). **Associations & Accomplishments:** American Bar Association Forum Committee on the Construction Industry; Seattle – King County Bar Association; Washington State Bar Association; American Bar Association Litigation and Public Procurement and Construction Law Sections; Association of General Contractors; Associated Builders And Contractors. **Education:** University of Notre Dame, J.D. (1988); Whitman College, B.A. Degree in Economics and History (1984). **Personal:** Married to Tara Marie in 1991. One child: Conner Michael. Mr. Nelson enjoys sports, public speaking, international relations, and travel.

Susan K. Neuman

Attorney
Offices of Susan K. Neuman
618 Forrest Avenue
Larchmont, NY 10538
(914) 834–1309
Fax: Please mail or call

8111

Business Information: Offices of Susan K. Neuman is a private environmental and contracts attorney's office. Admitted to practice in New York state courts in 1983, Ms. Neuman established her private practice in 1995. Her previous experience includes serving as Senior Counsel with Home Insurance and as Counsel with Crur & Forstor. **Career Steps:** Attorney, Offices of Susan K. Neuman (1995–Present); Senior Counsel, Home Insurance (1992–1995); Counsel; Crur & Forstor (1991–1992); Associate, Lord Day & Lord, Barrett Sreth (1987–1991). **Associations & Accomplishments:** American Society of Testing and Materials; American Bar Association; New York Bar Association; Published numerous pollution papers and policies; Conducted numerous speeches at Air and Waste Management Association. **Education:** Yale University, J.D. (1983); New York University, Ph.D.; Columbia University, M.A.; Smith College, B.A. **Personal:** Married to Fredric Neuman in 1958. Three children: Eve, James, and Michael. Ms. Neuman enjoys being involved in Toastmasters, opera, ballet, and reading.

Mr. Francis Patrick Newell

Partner and Attorney
Montgomery, McCracken, Walker & Rhoads
3 Benjamin Franklin Parkway
Philadelphia, PA 19102–1321
(215) 665–7310
Fax: (215) 636–9373

8111

Business Information: Montgomery, McCracken, Walker & Rhoads is a general practice law firm. Established in 1912, the Firm currently employs 300 attorneys and legal support staff. As Partner and Attorney in the Litigation Department, Mr. Newell concentrates his practice in the areas of complex and class–action litigation, including antitrust, securities, products, intellectual property, regulatory and criminal matters. A trial attorney since the conferral of his law degree in 1975, Mr. Newell is admitted to both State and Federal courts. **Career Steps:** Partner and Attorney, Litigation Department, Montgomery, McCracken, Walker & Rhoads (1978–Present); Trial Attorney, Honors Program, Antitrust Division, United States Department of Justice. **Associations & Accomplishments:** Philadelphia Bar Association: Chairman, Federal Courts Committee, Nominating Committee, Special Antitrust Counsel to the Board of Governors; International Litigation and Antitrust Sections, American Bar Association; Antitrust, Trade Regulation and Litigation Sections, District of Columbia Bar Association; Litigation Section, Pennsylvania Bar Association; Board of Directors, Historical Society of the United States District Court for the Eastern District of Pennsylvania; Membership Chairman, Historical Society of the United States Court of Appeals for the Third Circuit; Reporter of the Local Rules Advisory Committee and Mediator in the Mediation Program, United States District Court for the Eastern District of Pennsylvania; National Scholastic Honor Society; Beta Gamma Sigma; Villanova Law Review: Casenote and Comment Editor, Member of the Board of Editors; Union League of Philadelphia; The Art Alliance; Philadelphia Museum of Art; Porsche Club of America. **Education:** Pennsylvania State University, B.S. with honors (1972); Villanova University School of Law, J.D. (1975). **Personal:** Married to Katherine A. in 1978.

Luis M. Nolla–Villa

Attorney
Dubon & Dubon
255 Ponce de Leon Avenue
San Juan, Puerto Rico 00936–6123
(809) 758–2526
Fax: (809) 754–6698

8111

Business Information: Dubon & Dubon is a full–service, general civil practice law firm, consisting of six attorneys and three partners, concentrating on general law issues. A practicing attorney in Puerto Rico state and federal courts, Mr. Nolla–Villa joined the Firm upon conferral of his law degree in 1991. Serving as Associate Attorney, his practice concentrates in the areas of real estate, mortgage, banking, commercial financing, foreclosures, and general civil law. **Career Steps:** Attorney, Dubon & Dubon (1991–Present) **Associations & Accomplishments:** American Bar Association; Federal Bar Association; Hispanic Bar Association; Puerto Rico Bar Association; Puerto Rico Notary Public Association; Phi Delta Alpha; Phi Kappa Theta; Board of Directors, Jose Jaime Pierluisi Foundation. **Education:** InterAmerican University, J.D. (1990); St. Louis University, B.A. (1987). **Personal:** Married to Mari Carmen Schell in 1993. One child: Luis M. III. Mr. Nolla–Villa enjoys golf, music and spectator sports.

Gregory R. Noonan, J.D., C.P.A., LL.M. (TAX)

Shareholder and Equity Partner
DeYoung, Walfish & Noonan, P.C.
144 East DeKalb Oike, Ste. 200
King of Prussia, PA 19406
(610) 265–4600
Fax: (610) 265–4814

8111

Business Information: DeYoung, Walfish & Noonan, P.C. is a full–service, general practice law firm concentrating on tax, business, and financial law. The Firm also does business consulting and forensic accounting. As a practicing attorney in New Jersey, North Carolina, and Pennsylvania state and federal courts since 1985, Mr. Noonan's overall concentration is on tax, bankruptcy, tax exempt organizations, corporate, business and commercial law, commercial litigation, collections, debtor/creditor law, administration, forensic accounting and fraud examinations, and general business. **Career Steps:** Shareholder and Equity Partner, DeYoung, Walfish & Noonan, P.C. (1980–Present); Instructor, Pierce Junior College (1991–1992). **Associations & Accomplishments:** Certified Public Accountant; Certified Fraud Examiner (pending); New Jersey, North Carolina and Pennsylvania Bar Associations; Montgomery County, Pennsylvania and Camden County, New Jersey Bar Associations; American Bar Association: Sections on Tax and Real Estate, Property and Probate; Director, Norristown Jaycees; Vice President, American Businessman's Club; Board of Directors: Mainline Mortgage Corporation, Southeast Healthcare, The Growing Tree; Advisory Board, American Credit Counseling Institute. **Education:** Villanova University – School of Law, L.L.M. in Taxation (1990); Wake Forest University – School of Law, J.D. (1985); North Carolina State University, B.A. in Accounting – cum laude (1982). **Personal:** Mr. Noonan enjoys golf, tennis, racquetball, skiing, reading, chess, and Division 1, NCAA college basketball (Big East and ACC conferences).

Adalberto Nunez Lopez, Esq.

Attorney
Adalberto Nunez Lopez Law Office
P.O. Box 6400, Suite 200
Cayey, Puerto Rico 00737
(78) 265–2900 (787) 263–4982
Fax: (787) 263–4982

8111

Business Information: Adalberto Nunez Lopez Law Office is a full–service, general practice law firm handling both civil and criminal cases. A practicing attorney since 1989, Mr. Nunez Lopez established the Firm in 1994. He concentrates his practice on torts, insurance, trial law, and litigation. **Career Steps:** Attorney, Adalberto Nunez Lopez Law Office (1994–Present); Attorney, Puerto Rico Legal Services (1991–1994); Attorney, Gonzalez and Gonzalez Law Office (1989–1991). **Associations & Accomplishments:** Former President, American Red Cross Youth Division; Muscular Dystrophy Association; Former Treasurer, Puerto Rico's National Law Student Association; Former President, University of Puerto Rico – Rio Piedras Student Council; Puerto Rico Bar Association; Puerto Rican Parliamentary Procedure Liceum; American Institute of Parliamentarians. **Education:** University of Puerto Rico – Law School, J.D. (1989). **Personal:** Married to Astrid Pinero in 1989. Two children: Atabey and Nanishi. Mr. Nunez Lopez enjoys writing poems and short stories.

Donal C. O'Brien Jr

Partner
Milbank, Tweed, Hadley & McCloy
1 Chase Manhattan Plaza
New York, NY 10005–1401
(212) 530–5813
Fax: (212) 530–0158
E MAIL: See Below

8111

Business Information: Milbank, Tweed, Hadley & McCloy is a full–service law firm with over 1,000 employees. As Partner, Mr. O'Brien represents clients in legal and fiduciary capacities. Other responsibilities to the Firm include staff recruitment, public relations, and setting firm policies and procedures. Concurrently, Mr. O'Brien serves as Chief Legal Counsel for the Rockefeller Trust Company and the Rockefeller family. Internet users may contact him via: dobrien@Milbank.com. **Career Steps:** Milbank, Tweed, Hadley & McCloy: Partner (1991–Present), Attorney (1967–1983); Chief Legal Counsel, Rockefeller Family and Associates (1966–1968); President and CEO, Rockefeller Trust Company (1986–1991). **Associations & Accomplishments:** Connecticut Council on Environmental Quality (By Appointment); Chairman, Board of Directors, Atlantic Salmon Federation; Board of Directors, Bird Conservation Alliance; Trustee, Greenacre Foundation; Trustee, The JDR 3rd Fund, Inc.; Trustee, LSR Fund; Trustee, Jackson Hole Preserve, Inc.; Chairman,

Board of Directors. National Audubon Society; The Rockefeller University Council; Save–The–Redwoods League; Advisory Committee Member, The Trustees of the Reservations; Trustee, Waterfowl Research Foundation; Trustee, Wendell Gilley Museum; Board of Directors, Rockefeller Trust Company. Past Associations: Commissioner of State of Connecticut Board of Fisheries and Game (1971–1972); Connecticut Council on Environmental Quality (1971–1976), (1991–1995). **Education:** University of Virginia Law School, L.L.B. (1959); Williams College, B.A. (1956). **Personal:** Married to Katharine in 1956. Four children: Donal III, Constance, Katharine, and Caroline. Mr. O'Brien enjoys hunting, fishing, bird watching, dog training, photography, and art.

Steven M. O'Connor

Attorney
O'Connor & O'Connor
200 Mamaroneck Avenue
White Plains, NY 10601
(914) 686–1700
Fax: (914) 328–3184

8111

Business Information: O'Connor & O'Connor is an eight attorney, general practice law firm concentrating on insurance coverage and construction litigation. A practicing attorney in New York state and federal courts since obtaining his degree in 1985, Mr. O'Connor co–founded the Firm in 1993. As a Senior Partner, he is responsible for supervising all Firm activities and litigation. Mr. O'Connor has been a guest speaker with the New York State Bar Association on complex production liability litigation, and with other groups on various law topics. **Career Steps:** Attorney, O'Connor & O'Connor (1993–Present); Senior Associate, Worby, P.C. (1990–1993); Associate, Wilson, Elser, Moskowitz, Edelman & Dicker (1989–1990); Associate, Bower & Gardener (1986–1989). **Associations & Accomplishments:** Professional Member, American Society of Safety Engineers; Defense Research Institute; New York State Bar Association; New York State Trial Lawyers Association; American Bar Association; American Juris Prudence Award. **Education:** Pace University – School of Law, J.D. (1985); Northwestern University, B.A. **Personal:** Married to Denise in 1987. Two children: Cameron and Tom. Mr. O'Connor enjoys diving.

Michael L. O'Donnell

Director and Shareholder
Parcel, Mauro, Hultin & Spaanstra, P.C.
1801 California Street, Suite 3600
Denver, CO 80202–2636
(303) 297–4577
Fax: (303) 295–3040

8111

Business Information: Parcel, Mauro, Hultin & Spaanstra, P.C. is a general practice law firm. Established in 1985, the Firm currently employs 200 attorneys and legal support staff. As Director and Shareholder, Mr. O'Donnell concentrates his practice in litigation. A trial attorney since the conferral of his law degree in 1979, Mr. O'Donnell is admitted to both State and Federal courts. **Career Steps:** Director and Shareholder, Parcel, Mauro, Hultin & Spaanstra, P.C. (1993–Present); Director and Shareholder, White & Steele, P.C. (1980–1993). **Associations & Accomplishments:** Vice President and Board of Trustees, Denver Bar Association; Chairman of the Board, American Heart Association of Colorado; Board of Governors, Colorado Bar Association. **Education:** University of Denver, J.D. (1979); University of Notre Dame, B.A. in English (1976). **Personal:** Married to Ann Brett in 1979. Three children: Conor, Devon and Daniel. Mr. O'Donnell enjoys reading, golf, tennis, travel and coaching his childrens' athletic teams.

James T. O'Hara

Attorney
Jones, Day, Reavis & Pogue
1450 G Street Northwest
Washington, DC 20005–2001
(202) 879–3910
Fax: (202) 879–3807

8111

Business Information: Jones, Day, Reavis & Pogue is a full–service, general practice law firm, concentrating on commercial law. A practicing attorney in the District of Columbia since 1962, Mr. O'Hara joined the Firm as Attorney in 1973. Currently serving as Partner, his practice concentrates on corporate taxation issues. **Career Steps:** Attorney, Jones, Day, Reavis & Pogue (1973–Present); Adjunct Professor, Georgetown University Law Center. **Associations & Accomplishments:** Fellow, American Bar Association; Fellow, American College of Tax Counsel. **Education:** Georgetown University, Ll.M. in

Tax (1966); Catholic University, Ll.B. (1962); Kings College, B.S. (1958). **Personal:** Married to Kathleen in 1963. Three children: Colleen, Michael, and Brian. Mr. O'Hara enjoys skiing, boating, running, and reading.

Brian D. O'Keefe

Attorney and Shareholder
Hyman and Lippitt, P.C.
185 Oakland Avenue, Suite 300
Birmingham, MI 48009
(810) 646–8292
Fax: (810) 646–8375

8111

Business Information: Hyman and Lippitt, P.C. is a general practice law firm specializing in corporate, real estate, securities international and business law and litigation. Currently the Firm employs 14 attorneys and 15 legal staff members. An Attorney and Shareholder with the Firm since 1991, Mr. O'Keefe is admitted in both State and Federal courts and heads the Firm's Business and Real Estate Law Department. Mr. O'Keefe speaks and writes in his areas of specialty; and is actively involved in the Michigan Republican Party. **Career Steps:** Attorney and Shareholder, Hyman and Lippitt, P.C. (1991–Present); Attorney, Carson, Fischer, & Potts (1988–1991); Attorney, Marco, Eagan, Kennedy, and Timmis (1986–1988); Account Executive, Ross Roy, Inc. (1981–1983). **Associations & Accomplishments:** American Bar Association; Michigan State Bar Association; Oakland County Bar Association; Gold Key Honor Society. **Education:** Catholic University, J.D. (1986); Michigan State University, B.A. with honors (1981). **Personal:** Married to Robyn in 1993. Two children: Cullen Christopher and Kieran August. Mr. O'Keefe enjoys golf, tennis, and sailing.

Mr. Henry Oechler Jr.

Partner
Chadbourne and Parke
30 Rockefeller Plaza
New York, NY 10112–0002
(212) 408–5100
Fax: (212) 541–5369

8111

Business Information: Chadbourne & Parke LLP is a premier domestic and international practice law firm of approximately 300 lawyers. Besides New York, offices are located in the District of Columbia, Los Angeles, Moscow, London, New Delhi and Hong Kong. Established in the early 1900's, the Firm currently reports annual revenue of approximately $125 million and currently employs 800 legal and administrative support staff. Mr. Oechler joined the Firm in 1971 as an associate and became a Partner in 1980. He concentrates on aviation and product liability law and is admitted to practice in New York state and federal courts, various Federal appellate courts and the United States Supreme Court. His most prominent cases have included arguing a case in the United States Supreme Court on mandatory retirement of airline pilots. **Career Steps:** Partner, Chadbourne & Parke LLP (1980–Present); Associate, Chadbourne & Parke (1971–1980). **Associations & Accomplishments:** Conducted television interviews on the Fox Network, NBC (The Today Show and Dateline) and on CNBC in connection with the airline industry. **Education:** Duke University, J.D. (1971); Princeton University, A.B. (1968). **Personal:** Mr. Oechler enjoys his work in law and aviation.

Judge Wilson Ogg

Lawyer/Owner
Law Offices of Wilson Ogg
1104 Keith Avenue
Berkeley, CA 94708
(510) 845–1607
Fax: (510) 841–9663

8111

Business Information: Judge Ogg is an arbitrator, mediator, lawyer, real estate broker, retired judge, poet, lyricist, graphic illustrator, publisher, and curator in residence. As a poet, Judge Ogg has been following his muse since 1988. He also serves as an independent representative and area coordinator for Excel Telecommunications Inc. **Career Steps:** Poet, Pinebrook at Bret Harte Way (1988–Present); Curator, Pinebrook (1964–Present); Administrative Law Judge (1974–1993); Attorney at Law (1955–Present); Independent Representative and Area Coordinator, Excel Telecommunications Inc. (1996–Present). **Associations & Accomplishments:** American Bar Association; State Bar of California; San Francisco Bar Association; Berkeley City Commons Club; Commonwealth Club of California; Town Hall of California; American Association for Advancement of Science; National Library of Poetry; Faculty Club, University of California at Berkeley; American Legion; Veterans of Foreign Wars; American Veterans, Oakland, Durant, Rockridge Lodge No.

188, F.&A.M.; Aahmes Temple. **Education:** University of California at Berkeley, Boalt Hall School of Law, J.D. (1952); University of California at Berkeley, B.A. (1949). **Personal:** Judge Ogg enjoys architectural and landscape design.

German Ojeda–Bracero, Esq., CPA

Senior Associate
Fiddler Gonzalez & Rodriguez
P.O. Box 363507
San Juan, Puerto Rico 00936–3507
(809) 759–3218
Fax: (809) 754–7539

8111

Business Information: Fiddler Gonzalez & Rodriguez is an international corporate law firm, serving clientele throughout Latin America. Established in 1933, the Firm consists of over 150 attorneys, legal and adminstrative support staff. Joining the Firm in 1994 upon conferral of his law degree in 1993, as a senior associate Mr. Ojeda–Bracero represents corporate clientele in all tax matters, as well as serves as counsel in the areas of corporate reorganizations, financial institution transactions, and Section 936 Code transactions. His background in public accounting, serving as a tax manager with the leading accounting firm in the nation (Ernst & Young), gives him the edge necessary to keep abreast of the ever–changing taxation regulations and the corporate market as a whole. **Career Steps:** Senior Associate, Fiddler Gonzalez & Rodriguez (1994–Present); Tax Manager, Ernst & Young (1987–1994). **Associations & Accomplishments:** Puerto Rico Society of Certified Public Accountants; American Institute of Certified Public Accountants; Puerto Rico Bar Association; American Bar Association; Puerto Rico Manufacturers Association. **Education:** University of Puerto Rico: J.D. (1993), B.B.A. in Finance & Accounting (1985); Certified Public Accountant (1986). **Personal:** Married to Arlivon C. Vega in 1988. Two children: Glenn and Gregory. Mr. Ojeda–Bracero enjoys reading and spending time with his family.

Thomas M. Olejniczak

Partner
Liebmann, Conway, Olejniczak and Jerry, S.C.
P.O. Box 23200
Green Bay, WI 54305–3200
(414) 437–0476
Fax: (414) 437–2868

8111

Business Information: Liebmann, Conway, Olejniczak and Jerry, S.C. is a full–service, general practice law firm, concentrating on civil law issues. A practicing attorney in Wisconsin state courts since 1974, Mr. Olejniczak co–founded the Firm with three partners in 1976. Serving as Partner, his practice concentrates on corporate, real estate, and trust law issues. **Career Steps:** Attorney, Liebmann, Conway, Olejniczak and Jerry, S.C. (1976–Present). **Associations & Accomplishments:** American Bar Association; Wisconsin State Bar; Brown County Bar Association; United Way of Brown County; Trustee, St. Norbert College; Director, Green Bay Packers; Director, M & I Bank, Northeast; President, Oneida Golf & Riding Club. **Education:** Marquette University, J.D. (1974); St. Norbert College, B.A. (1971). **Personal:** Married to Dawn in 1971. Two children: Aaron Thomas and Ann Marie. Mr. Olejniczak enjoys hunting, fishing, and golf.

Charles M. Oliver

Partner
Cohn and Marks
1333 New Hampshire Ave, NW, Suite 600
Washington, DC 20036–1511
(202) 293–3860
Fax: (202) 293–4827
EMail: See Below

8111

Business Information: Cohn and Marks is a boutique law firm concentrating on telecommunications and related fields. Clientele include Intelsat, Internet service providers, long distance resellers, mass media, and health informatics clients. A practicing attorney since 1978, Mr. Oliver joined the Firm as Partner in 1993. He concentrates on telecommunications issues and is currently representing the largest provider of international satellite services and the largest provider of Internet services to businesses and institutions. Internet users can reach him via: cmo@cohnmarks.com **Career Steps:** Partner, Cohn and Marks (1993–Present); Senior Policy Advisor, Office of Assistant Secretary of Commerce for Communications and Information (1989–1993); Attorney Advisor, FCC Common Carrier Bureau (1987–1989); Senior Vice President, National Association of Broadcasters (1986–1987). **Associations & Accomplishments:** American Bar Association;

Federal Communications Bar Association; District of Columbia Bar Association; Executive Council, International Engineering Consortium; Edited and Co–Authored: "Communications Revolution and Public Policy," a white paper issued by the Executive Office of the President of the United States; "New Technologies Affecting Radio and Television Broadcasting", a book published by the National Association of Broadcasters; "The Telecommunications Act of 1996," published as an article in "Washington Telecom Week" and to be published as a chapter in the International Engineering Consortium (IEC) "Annual Review of Communications" (1996–1997); Appeared on "KMB Video Journal" telecast, "What Will the Current Plans for the Information Superhighway Contribute to the World of Health and Medicine?"; "Regulation of Domestic Radio Spectrum," chapter in the IEC's book, "Worldwide Wireless Communications"; Also a frequent publisher and speaker at international, national, and state and local conferences and institutional symposia and proceedings. **Education:** University of Virginia, J.D. (1978); University of Pennsylvania – Annenburg School of Communications, M.A. (1976); Yale University, B.A. (1971). **Personal:** Married to Claudia Pabo in 1980. Two children: Victor and Christina. Mr. Oliver enjoys sailing, jogging, canoeing, computer programming, and reading.

David W. Olsen
Attorney
Migliore & Infranco, P.C.
353 Veterans Memorial Highway
Commack, NY 11725–4325
(516) 543–3663
Fax: (516) 543–3682

8111

Business Information: Migliore & Infranco, P.C. is a general practice law firm serving New York City, and Nassau and Suffolk counties. Mr. Olsen joined the Firm as a Law Clerk in 1988, becoming an Attorney with the Firm upon the conferral of his Law Degree in 1990. He now focuses his practice in the areas of estate planning and administration, trusts, wills, and taxation. **Career Steps:** Migliore & Infranco, P.C.: Attorney (1990–Present), Law Clerk (1988–1990). **Associations & Accomplishments:** American Bar Association; New York Bar Association; Suffolk County Bar Association; Editor–in–Chief, Journal of Suffolk Academy of Law; Tax Committee; Surrogate's Court Committee of Suffolk Bar Association; Published two articles on Grantor Retained Trusts in Volumes 6 and 7 of the Journal of the Suffolk Academy of Law. **Education:** Georgetown University Law Center, LL.M. (1991); Touro College, Jacob D. Fuchsberg Law Center, J.D. (1990); State University of New York at Stonybrook, B.S. (1985). **Personal:** Married to Pamela J. in 1986. One child: Kimberly Jean. Mr. Olsen enjoys spending time with his family, skiing, golf, fishing, classical music, and target shooting.

Ralph Oman

Counsel
Dechert, Price & Rhoads
Suite 500, 1500 K Street North West
Washington, DC 20005–1208
(202) 626–3339
Fax: (202) 626–3334

8111

Business Information: Dechert, Price & Rhoads is a full–service law firm concentrating on general practice cases. Multinational in scope, the Firm is headquartered in Philadelphia, Pennsylvania, and has offices throughout the U.S. Established in 1874, the Firm is comprised of 350 attorneys. As Counsel, Mr. Oman works with international clients on property matters. **Career Steps:** Counsel, Dechert, Price & Rhoads (1995–Present); Of Counsel, Mudge, Rose, Guthrie, Alexander & Ferndon, LLP (1994–1995); Register of Copyrights, U. S. Copyrights Office (1985–1993); Chief Counsel, U.S. Senate Subcommittee on Patents, Copyrights, and Trademarks (1983–1985). **Associations & Accomplishments:** Master of the Court, Giles S. Rich Inn of Court; Court of Appeals for the Federal Circuit (1990–Present); Member, Editorial Advisory Board, Fordham Intellectual Property Media and Entertainment Journal (1993–Present); Trustee, Copyright Society of the U.S.A.; President, Capitol Hill Chapter of the Federal Bar Association (1993–1994); Chair, Committee 302, Intellectual Property Section, ABA (1995–Present); Counsel, Asian Pacific Exchange Foundation (1994–Present). **Education:** George Washington Law School, J.D. (1973); Hamilton College, A.B. in History (1962). **Personal:** Married to Anne in 1967. Three children: Tabitha, Caroline, and Charlotte. Mr. Oman enjoys racquet sports, skiing, boating, and woodworking.

Rhonda D. Orin
Attorney/Partner
Anderson, Kill, Olick and Oshinsky, L.L.P.
2000 Pennsylvania Avenue, NW
Washington, DC 20006–1812
(202) 728–3100 Ext. 270
Fax: (202) 728–3199

8111

Business Information: Anderson, Kill, Olick and Oshinsky, L.L.P. is an International law firm concentrating on policy holder coverage/insurance and product liability law. Primarily focused on corporate clientele, the Firm has offices in the U.S. and London. As Attorney/Partner, Ms. Orin is responsible for litigation involving insurance claim subsidies. She is probably best known for the case of W.S. Kirkpatrick vs. Environmental Tectonics Corporation, a U.S. Supreme Court case which ruled on the theory of the "Act of State" Doctrine in 1988. Other prestigious cases include Hercules, Inc. vs. United Sates of America, and Maryland Casualty Company vs. W.R. Grace and Company. **Career Steps:** Attorney/Partner, Anderson, Kill, Olick and Oshinsky, L.L.P. (1988–Present). **Associations & Accomplishments:** Published "The Wrong War, The Wrong Time, The Wrong Enemy", in the "Tort and Insurance Law Journal" (1996). **Education:** New York University Law School, J.D. (1984); University of Pennsylvania, B.A. Communications, Summa Cum Laude (1978). **Personal:** Married to Harry Eisenstein. Two children: Eric and Ethan. Ms. Orin enjoys skiing, public speaking, and spending time with her family.

Simeon J. Osborn

Senior Partner
Simeon J. Osborn, P.S.
7201 Columbia Center, 701 Fifth Avenue
Seattle, WA 98104–7016
(206) 386–5505
Fax: (206) 233–2809
EMAIL: See Below

8111

Business Information: Simeon J. Osborn, P.S. is a private law practice concentrating in personal injury and products liability. A practicing attorney since 1984, Mr. Osborn established his private practice in 1995. As Senior Partner, Mr. Osborn is responsible for all aspects of office and administrative operations as well as practicing civil litigation law. Internet users can reach him via: SIM@1stop.com. **Career Steps:** Senior Partner, Simeon J. Osborn, P.S. (1995–Present); Senior Partner, Kargianis, Osborn, Watkins (1992–1995); Senior Partner, Kargianis & Osborn (1990–1992). **Associations & Accomplishments:** Seattle–King County Bar Association; Washington State Bar Association; Washington State Trial Lawyers Association; Association of Trial Lawyers of America; American Bar Association; Board Member, Make–A–Wish Foundation; He has the highest personal injury jury verdict in the State of Washington at $16.35 million. **Education:** University of Puget Sound, J.D. (1984); Whitman College, B.A. in History (1984). **Personal:** Married to Monica in 1992. One child: Courtland. Mr. Osborn enjoys golf (Inglewood Country Club).

Stephen H. Osborne
Attorney
Osborne Law Office
555 South Center Street
Reno, NV 89501–2205
(702) 323–8676
Fax: (702) 786–6631

8111

Business Information: Osborne Law Office is a full–service civil practice law firm. The Firm was founded in 1949 and has the highest rating possible by Martindale–Hubbell Law Directory for legal ability, ethical standards and professional diligence. Admitted to both Nevada state and U.S. Federal courts, Stephen Osborne concentrates his practice in the areas of insurance, products liability, and medical malpractice litigation. He also provides limited practices in California. **Career Steps:** Osborne Law Office (1992–Present); Law Clerk, Mallery, Stern & Halperin (1990–1992). **Associations & Accomplishments:** American Bar Association; Nevada State Bar; Washoe County Bar Association; Nevada Trial Lawyers Association; Association of Trial Lawyers of America; American Inns of Court. **Education:** Southwestern School of Law, J.D. (1992); Southern Methodist University, B.A. (1987). **Personal:** Married to Elizabeth in 1995.

Gerard L. Oskam
Attorney
McDonald Carano Wilson McCune, et al
241 Ridge Street, 4th Floor
Reno, NV 89501
(702) 322–0635
Fax: (702) 786–9532

8111

Business Information: McDonald Carano Wilson McCune Bergin Frankovich & Hicks is a private, full service, general practice law firm. A practicing attorney in Nevada and California state courts since 1990, Mr. Oskam joined the Firm as Attorney in 1993. His practice concentrates on corporate law, mergers & acquisitions, finance, and securities law. **Career Steps:** Attorney, McDonald Carano Wilson McCune Bergin Frankovich & Hicks (1993–Present); Attorney, Stradling, Yocca, Carlson & Rauth – Newport Beach, CA (1991–1993); Attorney, Sheppard Mullin Richter & Hampton – Newport Beach, CA (1990–1991). **Associations & Accomplishments:** American Bar Association – Business Law Section; Nevada Bar Association – Business Law Section; California Bar Association – Business Law Section; Los Angeles County Bar Association; Washoe County Bar Association. **Education:** Harvard University Law School, J.D. (1990); University of Southern California: B.S.B.A. in Finance (1987), A.B. in Philosophy (1987); Orange Coast College, A.A. in Business Administration **Personal:** Married to Denise L. in 1980. Three children: Monique, Michael and Johnny.

Barry R. Ostrager
Partner
Simpson Thacher & Bartlett
425 Lexington Avenue
New York, NY 10017
(212) 455–2655
Fax: (212) 455–2502

8111

Business Information: Simpson Thacher & Bartlett is an international, full–service, general practice law firm. Established in 1855, the Firm currently employs 425 lawyers in three offices located in New York, London, and Hong Kong. A practicing attorney for 25 years in New York trial and appellate courts, Mr. Ostrager joined the Firm as Associate in 1973. Currently serving as Partner, he is a senior partner primarily responsible for insurance coverage issues and specializing in trial and appellate law. **Career Steps:** Partner, Simpson Thacher & Bartlett (1973–Present). **Associations & Accomplishments:** American Bar Association; City of New York Bar Association; American Law Institute; Co–Author, Modern Reinsurance Law & Practice Book, a Glasser Legal Publication; Co–Author, Handbook on Insurance Coverage Dispute, published by Aspen; Published numerous articles in Wall Street Journal, American Lawyer, American Bar Association, National Law Journal, and The New York Times; Listed in Who's Who in America. **Education:** New York University, J.D. (1973). **Personal:** Married to Pamela in 1972. Three children: Anne, Katie, and Jane.

Mr. Nehad S. Othman
Partner
Foley & Lardner
One IBM Plaza, Suite 3300, 330 North Wabash Ave.
Chicago, IL 60611–3608
(312) 755–1900
Fax: (312) 755–1925

8111

Business Information: Nehad (Ned) S. Othman, a partner in Foley & Lardner's Chicago office, is a member of the firm's Business Law Group. Foley & Lardner is a general practice law firm, with offices in fourteen U.S. cities and membership in the GlobaLex association of independent international law firms. Mr. Othman's practice includes representation of banking and other financial institutions, secured financing, asset–based lending, mergers and acquisitions, public finance, corporate structuring, international transactions and commercial law. His clients include domestic and international commercial banks, asset–based lenders, finance companies, financial affiliates of commercial and industrial concerns, and other financial and investment institutions. Mr. Othman has also represented numerous corporations in general business matters. Mr. Othman is also involved in firm management, recruiting and administration. He has spoken and written extensively on banking and commercial law matters. **Career Steps:** Partner, Foley & Lardner (1993–Present); Attorney, Jones Day Reavis & Pogue (1991–1993); Attorney, Winston & Strawn (1986–1991); Dearborn Financial, Inc. (1982–1986); Amoco Corporation (1977–1982). **Associations & Accomplishments:** American Bar Association; Illinois State Bar Association; Chicago Bar Association; American Society of International Law; Admitted to practice: Illinois Supreme Court, U.S. District Court – Northern District of Illinois, U.S. Court of Appeals – Seventh Circuit. **Education:** The University of Michigan Law School, Juris Doctor (1977); The University of Michigan, A.B. in Economics with Honors and High Distinction (1974).

Keith F. Overholt
Managing Partner
Shimmel, Hill, Bishop & Gruender, P.C.
3700 North 24th Street
Phoenix, AZ 85016
(602) 224–9500
Fax: (602) 955–6176

8111

Business Information: Shimmel, Hill, Bishop & Gruender, P.C. is a full–service, general practice law firm. Established in 1947, the Firm reports annual revenue of $3 million and currently employs 40 people. A practicing attorney since 1982 in Arizona state courts, Mr. Overholt joined the Firm as Attorney in 1983. Currently serving as Managing Partner, Mr. Overholt is responsible for all business operations of the Firm, as well as directing operations of the Employee Benefits Department. **Career Steps:** Managing Partner, Shimmel, Hill, Bishop & Gruender, P.C. (1983–Present). **Education:** John Marshall Law School, J.D. (1982); University of Arizona, B.A. (1978). **Personal:** Married to Elizabeth in 1981. Two children: Katherine Clare and Emily Ann. Mr. Overholt enjoys spending time with his children.

John A. Owens
Attorney and Senior Partner
Owens and Carver
P.O. Box 031707
Tuscaloosa, AL 35403–5707
(205) 750–0750
Fax: (205) 750–0355

8111

Business Information: Owens & Carver, Attorneys at Law is a full–service general practice law firm representing individuals, small businesses and some insurers. As a Partner, Mr. Owens oversees the Firm's management and devotes substantial time to civil litigation including medical malpractice defense. A trial attorney, he is admitted to practice in both state and federal courts. Established in 1994, Owens & Carver, Attorneys at Law employs 12 people. **Career Steps:** Partner, Owens & Carver, Attorneys at Law (1994–Present); Senior Partner, Phelps, Owens, Jenkins, Gibson & Fowler (1969–1994). **Associations & Accomplishments:** Alabama State Bar Association: President (1995–1996), Board of Bar Commissioners (1987–1994); President, Rotary Club of Tuscaloosa (1983–1986); Three Time President, Arts Council of Tuscaloosa County; Board of Trustees, First United Methodist Church of Tuscaloosa; Vice President of Tuscaloosa Academy Board of Trustees (1984–1986); Tuscaloosa Symphony Board of Directors; President, Rotary Club of Tuscaloosa (1983–1984); Arts Council of Tuscaloosa Patron of the Arts (1985). **Education:** University of Alabama: LL.B. (1967), B.S. in Business Administration and Accounting (1961). **Personal:** Married to Dorothy in 1962. Two children: Apsilah Geer Owens and Terry Owens Hurt. Mr. Owens enjoys sailing, reading, fishing and playing golf.

Mr. Albert F. Pagni, Esquire
President
Vargas & Bartlett
201 West Liberty Street
Reno, NV 89502
(702) 786–5000
Fax: (702) 786–1177

8111

Business Information: Vargas & Bartlett is a professional law practice generally specializing in the commercial field of banking, natural resources, litigation in insurance defense, corporate defense, and public utilities. Established since 1971, Vargas & Bartlett presently employs 75 people. Mr. Pagni currently serves as Managing Partner, President and Attorney. **Career Steps:** President and Managing Partner, Vargas & Bartlett (1972–Present); Associate Attorney, Vargas & Bartlett (1964–1972). **Associations & Accomplishments:** Fellow American College of Trial Lawyers; Nevada State Bar Association; American Bar Association; National Board and American Board of Trial Advocates; Trustee, Nevada Law Foundation; Past President and Governor of the Nevada State Bar Association; Past Director, Better Business Bureau; Past President, Italian Benevolent Society; Past Treasurer, President, Awards Chair, Outstanding Alumni; University of Nevada Alumni Council; Appeals Officer, Selective Service. **Education:** Hastings College Law, J.D. (1964); University of Nevada, B.A. Degree (1961). **Personal:** Married to Nancy T in 1961. Four children: Elisa Kelley, Michelle Pagni, Melissa

Bernard, and Michael Pagni. Mr. Pagni enjoys biking, outdoor camping, and hunting in his leisure time.

Stephen C. Paine
Attorney–at–Law
Schlanger, Mills, Mayer, Grossberg, L.L.P.
5847 San Felipe, Suite 1700
Houston, TX 77057
(713) 785–1700
Fax: (713) 785–2091

8111

Business Information: Schlanger, Mills, Mayer, Grossberg, L.L.P. is a premier full–service general practice law firm. Established in 1965, the Firm currently employs 24 attorneys and 50 legal support staff. As Attorney, Mr. Paine concentrates his practice in the areas of estate planning and probate and commercial real estate. Mr. Paine is admitted to practice in both State and Federal courts **Career Steps:** Attorney, Schlanger, Mills, Mayer, Grossberg, L.L.P. (1969–Present). **Associations & Accomplishments:** American Bar Association; State Bar of Texas; Houston Bar Association; Houston Estate and Financial Forum; Houston Business and Estate Planning Council; Committee on Lawyers' Opinion; Letters in Mortgage Loan Transactions of the State Bar of Texas. **Education:** University of Texas, LL.B. (1967); Rice University, Bachelor's Degree (1964). **Personal:** Married to Linda in 1975. Two children: Jonathan and Marc. Mr. Paine enjoys hiking, snow skiing, reading, and computers.

Emily A. Parker
Senior Tax Counsel
Thompson & Knight, P.C.
1700 Pacific Avenue, Suite 3300
Dallas, TX 75201–7322
(214) 969–1502
Fax: (214) 969–1473

8111

Business Information: Thompson & Knight, P.C. is a full–service, general practice law firm. A practicing attorney in Texas state courts since 1973, Emily Parker joined the Firm in 1973. As Senior Tax Counsel, Ms. Parker is responsible for tax advising and litigation for her clients, mainly people in the petroleum industry. **Career Steps:** Senior Tax Counsel, Thompson & Knight, P.C. (1973–Present). **Associations & Accomplishments:** American Bar Association; Tax Section, Dallas Bar Association; Taxation Section of State Bar of Texas; American College of Tax Counsel; Board Certified in Tax Law; Board of Directors, Easter Seals Society of Dallas; Former Board of Directors, Child Care Dallas; Royal Oaks Country Club; Marquis Who's Who. **Education:** S.M.U. Law School, J.D. (1973); Stephen F. Austin, B.A. (1970). **Personal:** Ms. Parker enjoys golf.

Lee S. Parks, J.D.
Partner
Fried, Frank, Harris, Shriver & Jacobson
One New York Plaza, Suite 2500
New York, NY 10004
(212) 859–8142
Fax: (212) 820–8586

8111

Business Information: Fried, Frank, Harris, Shriver & Jacobson is a full–service, general practice law firm specializing primarily in criminal defense issues, corporate law, mergers and acquisitions. As Partner, Mr. Parks is responsible for all aspects of operations for the firm. Fried, Frank, Harris, Shriver & Jacobson was established in the 1930's and employs over 1,000 people. **Career Steps:** Partner, Fried, Frank, Harris, Shriver & Jacobson; Associate, Fried, Frank, Harris, Shriver & Jacobson; Research Staff, IBM. **Associations & Accomplishments:** Sigma XI; American Bar Association; New York State Bar Association; New York Academy of Science; U.J.A. Federation. **Education:** Columbia Law School, J.D. (1984); MIT, S.B. in Math (1979), S.B. in Physics (1979). **Personal:** Married to Lori in 1993. One child: Andrew. Mr. Parks enjoys family activities.

Scott R. Paulsen
Associate Attorney
Quinn, Johnston, Henderson & Pretorius
227 Northeast Jefferson Street
Peoria, IL 61602–1211
(309) 674–1133
Fax: (309) 674–6503

8111

Business Information: Quinn, Johnston, Henderson & Pretorius is a full–service, general practice law firm consisting of 30 attorneys, concentrating on civil defense litigation. Headquartered in Peoria, Illinois, the Firm also serves clientele from Springfield. A practicing attorney in Illinois state courts since 1990, Mr. Paulsen joined the Firm as Associate Attorney in 1992. His practice concentrates on civil and appellate litigation. **Career Steps:** Associate Attorney, Quinn, Johnston, Henderson & Pretorius (1992–Present); Law Clerk, Hon. Robert J. Stergmann, Appellate Court of Illinois, Fourth District (1990–1992). **Associations & Accomplishments:** Iowa Bar Association; Illinois Bar Association; Appellate Lawyers Association; Defense Research Institute; American Inns of Court; Peoria County Bar Association; Greater Peorin Claims Association; Illinois Association of Defense Trial Counsel; Coach, Bradley University Intercollegiate Mock Trial Team. **Education:** University of Iowa: J.D., M.B.A. (1990); Illinois State University, B.S. (1986); Lancaster University U.K. **Personal:** Mr. Paulsen enjoys music and sports.

L. Howard Payne
•••—◉—•••

President
Kirk Pinkerton
720 S. Orange Avenue
Sarasota, FL 34236
(941) 364–2480
Fax: (941) 364–2490

8111

Business Information: Kirk Pinkerton is a full–service law firm concentrating in five different areas: Real Estate (purchase, sale, and development), Litigation (not criminal), Administrative, Tax (both transactional and transfer), and Probate. Mr. Payne has been a practicing attorney since obtaining his degree in 1959. Currently, he is the President of the law firm, Kirk Pinkerton P.A. He is responsible for all aspects of the Firm's operations, including running internal meetings, Attorney/Shareholder/supervision of client development, and attorney training. **Career Steps:** Attorney/Shareholder/President, Kirk Pinkerton (1993–Present); Attorney/Shareholder/Vice President, Isphording Korp Payne (1988–1993); Attorney/Shareholder/President, Payne Wheeler Hric & Lee (1984–1987); Lawyer/Shareholder/Vice President, Isphording Payne Korp, et al. (1974–1984). **Associations & Accomplishments:** Board of Directors, Boys and Girls Club Foundation; Board of Directors, Sarasota County Chapter, American Red Cross; Board of Directors, Wellness Community of Sarasota; Planned Giving Committee, Sarasota Chapter, American Cancer Society; Fellow, American College of Trust and Estate Counsel; Board Certified by the Florida Bar in both Taxation and Wills, Trusts and Estates; Chairman, Estate and Trust Tax Planning Committee, Real Property, Probate and Trust Law Section of the Florida Bar; Member of The Florida and New York Bars and the U.S. Tax Court; Chartered Life Underwriter, American Society of Chartered Life Underwriters. **Education:** Cornell Law School, LL.B. (1959); Yale University, B.A. (1956); Phillips Academy (1952). **Personal:** Married to Bendel Tracy in 1959. Two children: Candace and David. Mr. Payne enjoys sailboat racing and snow skiing, and is active in his church.

Loree G. Peacock LeBoeuf
Associate Attorney
Lugenbuhl, Burke, Wheaton, Peck, Rankin & Hubbard
601 Poydras Street, Suite 2775 Pan American Life Center
New Orleans, LA 70130–6027
(504) 568–1990
Fax: (504) 529–7418

8111

Business Information: Lugenbuhl, Burke, Wheaton, Peck, Rankin & Hubbard is a full–service, general practice law firm, concentrating on maritime, insurance defense, commercial literature, bankruptcy, and estate planning. A practicing attorney in Louisiana state and federal courts since 1992, Mrs. Peacock LeBoeuf joined the Firm as Associate Attorney in 1994. Serving as one of 14 attorneys, her main area of concentration is on insurance defense. **Career Steps:** Associate Attorney, Lugenbuhl, Burke, Wheaton, Peck, Rankin & Hubbard (1994–Present); Associate, Nesser, King & LeBlanc (1992–1994). **Associations & Accomplishments:** New Orleans Bar Association; Louisiana State Bar Association; Federal Bar Associaton; American Bar Association; Lakeview Civic Association. **Education:** Loyola University School of Law, J.D. (1992); Millsaps College, B.S. cum laude (1988). **Personal:** Married to Carl J. LeBoeuf in 1995. Mrs. Peacock LeBoeuf enjoys golf, bicycling, walking, and reading.

David H. Pearlman

Attorney
McDivitt Law Firm, PC
90 South Cascade, Suite 1490
Colorado Springs, CO 80903–1680
(719) 471–3700
Fax: (719) 471–9782

8111

Business Information: McDivitt Law Firm is a full–service, general practice law firm with concentration on personal injury litigation. A practicing attorney in Colorado state courts and a Certified Civil Trial Specialist, NBTA, since 1981, Mr. Pearlman joined the Firm in 1994 after being in private practice for twenty–seven years. Serving as Attorney, he provides legal services to the Firm's clientele, focusing on litigation cases. **Career Steps:** Attorney, McDivitt Law Firm (1994–Present); Attorney, David H. Pealman, P.A. (1969–1994). **Associations & Accomplishments:** National Board of Trial Advocacy; Certified Civil Trial Specialist Since (1981); Licensed in New Mexico and Colorado. **Education:** University of New Mexico, J.D. (1969); University of Minnesota, B.A. (1965). **Personal:** Married to Carol in 1971. Three children: David, Gavin, and Adam. Mr. Pearlman enjoys golf, swimming, and walking.

Gordon O. Pehrson Jr.

Partner
Sutherland, Asbill & Brennan
1275 Pennsylvania Avenue Northwest
Washington, DC 20004–2404
(202) 383–0169
Fax: (202) 637–3593
EMAIL: See Below

8111

Business Information: Sutherland, Asbill & Brennan is a premier, general practice law firm. Established in 1924, the Firm consists of over 475 attorneys, legal and administrative support staff. A practicing attorney since 1968, Mr. Pehrson joined the Firm in 1970. He leads the insurance practice of the Firm as well as representing insurance corporate clients in matters pertaining to taxation, legislation, and mergers and acquisitions. He can also be reached on the Internet via: GPEHRSON@SABLAW.COM **Career Steps:** Partner, Sutherland, Asbill & Brennan (1970–Present); Lt. USNR JAGC (1968–1970). **Associations & Accomplishments:** Advisory Council, Hartford Institute on Insurance Taxation; Advisory Board, The Insurance Tax Review; American Bar Association: Section of Torts and Insurance Practice, Section of Administrative Law and Regulatory Practice, Section of Taxation. **Education:** University of Michigan School of Law, J.D. (1967); College of William and Mary, A.B. (1964). **Personal:** Two children: Christopher Wells and Ashley Stewart.

Mr. Gerald J. Pels

Partner
Liddell, Sapp, Zivley, Hill & LaBoon L.L.P.
3400 Texas Commerce Tower
Houston, TX 77002
(713) 226–1402
Fax: (713) 223–3717

8111

Business Information: Liddell, Sapp, Zivley, Hill & LaBoon L.L.P., established in 1916, is a general practice law firm with offices located throughout Texas (Houston, Austin and Dallas). A member of the Firm since the conferral of his law degree in 1983, he attained partnership in 1990. As an environmental attorney, Mr. Pels represents corporate clientele in the areas of environmental regulatory compliance, administrative hearings, and enforcement actions and litigation, as well as counsels clients in business transactions (mergers and acquisitions). **Career Steps:** Partner, Liddell, Sapp, Zivley, Hill & LaBoon L.L.P. (1990–Present); Associate, Liddell, Sapp, Zivley, Hill & La Boon, L.L.P. (1983–1990). **Associations & Accomplishments:** Greater Houston Partnership; Texas Hazardous Waste Management Society; Hazardous Materials Control Resources Institute; The Texas Registry for Environmental Professionals. **Education:** Vanderbilt University, J.D. (1983), Order of the Coif; St. Joseph's University, A.B. (Summa Cum Laude) (1980). **Personal:** Married to Karen in 1981. Two children: Danielle and Devyn. Mr. Pels enjoys restoring sports cars, collecting baseball cards and internet navigating.

Amado A. Pereira–Santiago, Esq.

Attorney/Owner
Amado Pereira Law Office
Constancia 607 8th St.
Ponce, Puerto Rico 00731
(787) 843–8406 (787) 848–6586
Fax: (787) 843–8406
EMAIL: See Below

8111

Business Information: Amado Pereira Law Office is a full–service law firm, specializing in Personal Bankruptcy, Social Security, Inheritance, and Civil Cases. A practicing attorney in Puerto Rico state courts since 1976, Mr. Pereira–Santiago established the Firm in 1977. As Owner of the Firm, he oversees all administrative operations for associates and support staff, in addition to his daily law practice. He is also admitted to practice before the First Circuit Court of Appeals, U.S. Supreme Court, U.S. District Court for the Eastern of New York, U.S. District Court for the Southern District of Manhattan, and State Court of New York. He may be reached through Internet via: licpereira@aol.com **Career Steps:** Attorney/Owner, Amado Pereira Law Office (1977–Present); Professor of Political Science, Catholic University of Puerto Rico (1981–1986); Professor of History & Political Science, Inter American University of Puerto Rico (1970–1980) **Associations & Accomplishments:** Puerto Rico Bar Association; New York State Bar Association; Ponce Bar Delegation – President, 1983; Federal Bar Association; National Association of Chapter 13 Trustees; National Association of Consumer Bankruptcy Attorneys; Puerto Rico Bankruptcy Bar; National Education Association; National Organization of Social Security Claimant's Representatives; Puerto Rico Teacher's Association; Nominated as an Outstanding Young Man of America (1982). **Education:** Catholic University of Puerto Rico: Ll.M. (1985); J.D. (1976); M.Ed. (1972); Inter American University of Puerto Rico, B.A. (1970) – Magna Cum Laude; Harvard Law School, Summer Program for Lawyers (1978); Center for Advanced Studies of Puerto Rico and the Caribbean, M.A. – Puerto Rican Studies (Candidate – 1983). **Personal:** Married to Ruth Zilkya Diaz in 1984. Four children: Katherine A. and Arnaldo E. Pereira–Diaz, and Marian and Amado E. Pereira–Rangel. Mr. Pereira–Santiago enjoys traveling, reading, and writing poems. He is a lecturer in Bankruptcy to various groups and institutions.

Hector H. Perez Villanueva, Esq.

Attorney
Perez Villanueva Law Offices
BCO. Cooperative Plaza Ponce de Leon Avenue 623, Suite 301A
San Juan, Puerto Rico 00927
(787) 281–8220
Fax: (787) 754–4285

8111

Business Information: Perez Villanueva Law Offices is a general practice law firm specializing in civil law. The firm, which handles torts, insurance, contracts, labor relations, and commercial law, was established in 1994 and has two attorneys on staff. As Attorney, Mr. Perez Villanueva handles civil cases only. These include torts, insurance, commercial, and labor relations. Mr. Villanueva is also responsible for overseeing the day–to–day operations of the office. **Career Steps:** Attorney, Perez Villanueva Law Offices (1994–Present); Attorney, Hernadez and Vidal (1992–1994); 1st Lieutenant, Signal Corps, U.S. Army (1989–1992). **Education:** InterAmerican University, J.D. (1992); University of Puerto Rico, B.A. in Social Sciences; U.S. Army, Signal Officer Course (1989). **Personal:** Mr. Perez Villanueva enjoys reading and boating.

Edward A. Peterson

Shareholder and Attorney
Winstead, Sechrest, & Minick P.C.
5400 Renaissance Tower, 1201 Elm Street
Dallas, TX 75270
(214) 745–5642
Fax: (214) 745–5131

8111

Business Information: Winstead, Sechrest, & Minick P.C. is an international, full–service, general practice law firm with offices in Texas (Dallas, Houston, Austin) and Mexico (Mexico City). Established in 1972, the Firm currently employs 500 attorneys, legal and administrative support staff. With 29 years expertise in the legal field, Mr. Peterson joined the Firm in 1989 as Shareholder. His practice includes the representation of financial institutions, including life insurance companies, banks and savings and loans, in relation to acquisitions and dispositions of financial institutions, regulatory representation (filing and prosecution of applications for change of control), and representation before state and federal regulatory agencies. Additional areas of expertise include real estate and asset–based lending for life insurance companies, banks, savings & loans associations, and credit unions; workouts of troubled assets for lenders and borrowers involving restructuring of debt, lender liability issues, litigation, and reorganization strategies; sale and leaseback and master lease transactions; and real estate syndications, both private and public. **Career Steps:** Shareholder and Attorney, Winstead, Sechrest, & Minick, P.C. (1989–Present); Shareholder, Moore & Peterson, P.C. (1972–1989). **Associations & Accomplishments:** American College of Real Estate Lawyers: Member, Chairman of Professionalism and Practice Committee; Texas College of Real Estate Lawyers; College of the State Bar of Texas; Life Fellow, Texas Bar Foundation; State Bar of Texas: Member, Real Estate, Trust and Probate and Business Law Sections; American Bar Association: Member, Real Estate, Trust and Probate (and Committee on Foreclosure and Related Remedies) and Corporate, Banking and Business Law Sections; Listed in "Best Lawyers in America"; Member, Board of Directors, North Texas Commission; Member, Our Redeemer Lutheran Church; Dallas Bar Association (formerly a member of the Unauthorized Practice of Law and Fee Disputes Committees; Former Director, Southern Methodist University School of Law Alumni Association; Author of numerous speeches and publications. **Education:** Southern Methodist University School of Law, LL.B. (1966); Washington University – St. Louis, B.S.B.A. (1963). **Personal:** Married to Catherine Y. Peterson in 1960. Two children: Kristin Baltus and Kendra Lindholm. Mr. Peterson enjoys snow skiing, classical music, and water sports.

B. Buck Pettitt

Partner/Attorney
Flores, Casso, Romero & Pettitt
321 South 12th St.
McAllen, TX 78505–2128
(210) 686–9591
Fax: (210) 686–9478

8111

Business Information: Flores, Casso, Romero & Pettitt is a full–service, general practice law firm concentrating on mainly civil cases. A practicing attorney in Texas state and federal courts since 1970, Mr. Pettitt co–founded the Firm in 1994. Mr. Pettitt handles personal injury and other civil cases. **Career Steps:** Partner, Flores, Casso, Romero & Pettitt (1994–Present); Partner, Lewis & Pettitt (1990–1994); Partner, Lewis, Pettitt & Hinojosa (1980–1990). **Associations & Accomplishments:** Former President, McAllen Rotary North; Former President, Hidalgo County Bar Assn.; Texas Trial Lawyers Association; Association of Trial Lawyers of America. **Education:** University of Houston: J.D. (1970), B.B.A. (1977).; Vanderbilt University. **Personal:** Married to Penny in 1966. Two children: Anthony and Alexander. Mr. Pettitt enjoys spending quality time with family..

Pamela Kim Phillips

Partner
LeBoeuf, Lamb, Greene & MacRae, L.L.P.
50 North Laura Street, Suite 2800
Jacksonville, FL 32202–3656
(904) 354–8000
Fax: (904) 353–1673

8111

Business Information: LeBoeuf, Lamb, Greene & MacRae, L.L.P. is a premier, general practice law firm. Established in the 1950's, the Firm has 16 offices and currently employs 1,500 people, including 500 lawyers. Admitted to practice in New York and Florida state courts in 1982, Ms. Phillips joined the Firm as Associate in 1984, attaining Partnership in 1991. She concentrates her practice in the areas of corporate finance, serving in an advisory and transactional capacity. **Career Steps:** LeBoeuf, Lamb, Greene & MacRae, L.L.P.: Partner (1991–Present); Associate (1984–1990); Associate, Curtis, Mallet–Prevost, Colt & Mosle (1982–1984). **Associations & Accomplishments:** Association of the Bar of the City of New York: Chair, Young Lawyers Committee (1990–1991), Member, Banking Law Committee, Member, Second Century Committee; American Bar Association; Jacksonville (Florida) Bar Association. **Education:** Georgetown University, J.D. (1982); The American University, B.A., cum laude. **Personal:** Married to Richard Zanghetti in 1989. One child: Marianna Kimiko. Ms. Phillips enjoys travel.

Stephen S. Phillips, Esquire

Partner
Pepper, Hamilton & Scheetz
3000 Two Logan Square
Philadelphia, PA 19103
(215) 981–4464
Fax: (215) 981–4750

8111

Business Information: Pepper, Hamilton & Scheetz is a full–service, general practice law firm. Established in 1890, the Firm currently employs more than 800 attorneys, legal and administrative support staff. Admitted to practice in Pennsylvania and the United States Supreme Court, Mr. Phillips joined the Firm in 1973. He became a partner in 1979. He specializes in multi–party product liability, "toxic tort," insurance and commercial litigation. He is currently Defense Liaison Counsel in "In re: Orthopedic Bone Screw Product Liability Litigation" (MDL 1014), pending in the U.S. District Court for the Eastern District of Pennsylvania. **Career Steps:** Pepper, Hamilton & Scheetz: Partner (1979–Present), Associate (1973–1979); Law Clerk with Hon. John B. Hannum, U.S. District Court, E.D. Pennsylvania (1971–1973). **Associations & Accomplishments:** International, American, Pennsylvania, and Philadelphia Bar Associations; National Moot Court; President, Order of Barristers (1971–1972); Member of the Board of Directors: Schindler Enterprises, Inc., Franke Holding USA, Inc., Pepper International Associates; Member: Union League of Philadelphia (1973–1990), Philadelphia Country Club. **Education:** Dickinson School of Law, J.D. (1971); Wesleyan University, B.A. (1968). **Personal:** Married to Mary Ann in 1983. One child: William Douglas. Mr. Phillips enjoys business development in Asia.

Kay Marie Philon

Attorney at Law
Law Office of Kay Marie Philon
P O Box 1047
Waukegan, IL 60085
(847) 599–0023
Fax: Please mail or call

8111

Business Information: Law Office of Kay Marie Philon specializes in Family Law, i.e., wills, real estate, and traffic. As Attorney at Law, Ms. Philon represents a variety of clients. She handles cases dealing with family matters and her specialty is Employment Discrimination cases. **Career Steps:** Attorney at Law, Law Office of Kay Marie Philon (1996–Present); Attorney at Law, Kanter and MacHenson, Ltd. (1995–1996); Assistant States Attorney, Cook County State's Attorney's Office (1992–1995). **Associations & Accomplishments:** Hellenic Bar Association; Illinois State Bar Association; American Bar Association; Chicago Bar Association; Lake County Bar Association. **Education:** John Marshall Law School, J.D. (1991); Augustina College, B.A. **Personal:** Ms. Philon enjoys mountain biking, rollerblading, walking, and music.

Domingo Pillot Resto, Esq.

Sole Practitioner
Law Office of Domingo Pillot Resto
Urb Ciudad Universitaria, Y18 Calle 27
Trujillo Alto, Puerto Rico 00976–2115
(809) 751–0488
Fax:

8111

Business Information: The Law Offices of Domingo Pillot Resto is a general practice law firm. A practicing attorney in Puerto Rico courts since 1972, Domingo Resto founded his private law practice in 1985. As Sole Practitioner, he oversees all administrative support staff, in addition to representing clients in the areas of inheritance, marriage dissolution, and commercial property law. **Career Steps:** Sole Practitioner, Law Offices of Domingo Pillot Resto (1985–Present); School Supervisor, Department of Instruction (1966–1984); College Center Director, Inter–American University–Peurto Rico (1962–1966). **Associations & Accomplishments:** President, Guayama Absent–Citizens; Colegio Abogadis de Puerto Rico. **Education :** Interamerican University, J.D. (1972); New York University, M.A. (1962); University of Puerto Rico, B.A. (1954). **Personal:** Married to Carmen Lopez Notal in 1954. Two children: Carmen and Dominick Pillot. Mr. Pillot Resto enjoys sports, track and field athletics.

Paul Pineo Jr.

Attorney at Law
Harris Beach
130 East Main
Rochester, NY 14604–1620
(716) 232–4440
Fax: Please mail or call

8111

Business Information: Harris Beach is a full–service corporate law firm, concentrating in the fields of Federal and State Tax Law, Corporate Law, and Real Estate Financing. Established in 1856, the Firm currently employs 215 attorneys and legal support staff. A trial attorney admitted to practice in both State and Federal courts since 1967, Mr. Pineo joined the Firm in 1994. He concentrates his practice in the area of Tax Law. **Career Steps:** Attorney at Law, Harris Beach (1994–Present); Partner, Hallenbeck, Lascell & Pineo (1991–1994); General Counselor and Executive Vice President, Home Leasing Corporation (1987–1991); Partner, Nixon Hargrave Devans & Doyle (1971–1986). **Associations & Accomplishments:** Board Member, Park Ridge Hospital, Rochester, NY. **Education :** George Washington University, LL.M. (1970); Georgetown University, J.D. (1967); Colby College, A.B. (1963). **Personal:** Married to Susan in 1963. One child: Paul F. Mr. Pineo enjoys biking.

Will Jay Pirkey

Attorney and Shareholder
Spray, Gould & Bowers
3530 Wilshire Boulevard, #1500
Los Angeles, CA 90010
(213) 385–3402
Fax: (213) 385–2014

8111

Business Information: Spray, Gould & Bowers is a full–service, general practice law firm, concentrating on general civil litigation cases. Established in the 1920's, the Firm currently employs 50 attorneys, legal, and administrative support staff. A practicing attorney in California state and federal courts and international law for the past eighteen years, Mr. Pirkey joined the Firm in 1987. Serving as Attorney and Shareholder, his practice emphasizes civil and commercial litigation, as well as professional negligence, business, products, and entertainment law. **Career Steps:** Attorney and Shareholder, Spray, Gould & Bowers (1987–Present). **Associations & Accomplishments:** American Board of Trial Advocates; American Bar Association; State Bar of California; Association of Southern California Defense Counsel; Federal Bar Association; Los Angeles Library Foundation; Los Angeles County Museum of Art; Author of numerous articles for legal newsletters; He has lectured at legal conferences; Served as Judge for American Bar Association Appellate contests; Fluent in English, Spanish and French. **Education:** California Western School of Law, J.D. (1977); University of the Americas, B.A. (1973). **Personal:** Married to Annie Sabroux in 1992. Mr. Pirkey enjoys music, writing, reading, skiing, and hiking.

Regina M. Pisa, P.C.

Partner
Goodwin, Procter & Hoar
Exchange Place
Boston, MA 02109
(617) 570–1525
Fax: (617) 523–1231

8111

Business Information: Goodwin, Procter & Hoar is a full–service, general practice law firm, specializing in corporate securities and banking law. The Firm currently employs more than 300 lawyers and more than 400 legal and administrative support staff. A practicing attorney for 13 years in Massachusetts state courts, Ms. Pisa joined the Firm in 1982 as Partner, responsible for providing legal representation to the Firm's clientele. She also is member of a nine lawyer Executive Committee and a three person Management Committee. **Career Steps:** Partner, Goodwin, Procter & Hoar (1982–Present). **Associations & Accomplishments:** President, Somerville Museum; American Bar Association; Massachusetts Bar Association; Boston Bar Association; Executive Committee, Harvard Association of Class Secretaries; Executive Committee, American Friends of St. Hilda's College. **Education:** Harvard University, A.B. (1977); Georgetown University Law Center, J.D. (1982); St. Hilda's College – Oxford University, England, M.A. (1983). **Personal:** Ms. Pisa enjoys gardening.

Laura A. Pitta

Attorney
Law Offices of Rafael Chodos
P.O. Box 134
Pacific Palisades, CA 90272–0134
(310) 393–9811
Fax: (310) 451–2851
EMAIL: See Below

8111

Business Information: Law Offices of Rafael Chodos is a full–service corporate litigation law firm. Joining the Firm following the completion of her post–graduate degree in international business law from the University of London in February of 1995, Laura Pitta concentrates her practice in the areas of national and international copyright, patent and contract issues; business litigation; international business law; contracts review and drafting. Prior to entering her full–time law practice, Ms. Pitta served as the manager of a 280–acre family vineyard, as well as has extensive expertise in operations and industrial engineering. Her fluency in French, German and Spanish, as well as graduating with honors from some of the world's foremost universities has given Laura the necessary edge to provide her international business clients with the utmost in legal representation. Internet users can also reach her via: 73524.1450@compuserve.com **Career Steps:** Attorney, Law Offices of Rafael Chodos (1995–Present); Manager, Rancho De Vino (1991–1993); Summer Associate, Keck, Mahin & Cate (1991); Summer Associate, Hughes Aircraft Company (1990). **Associations & Accomplishments:** International Bar Association; Licensing Executives Society; International Society of Author's Rights; State Bar of California (1992); Federal Court, Northern District of California (1992); Patent Bar, U.S. Patent and Trademark (1989); Association Juridique Francaise Pour la Protection Internationale Du Droit d'Auteur (ALAI–USA); American Bar Association; Los Angeles Bar Association. **Education:** University of London, King's College – London, England, LL.M. with Merit in International Business (1994); Hague Academy of International Law, The Netherlands, Certificate of Attendence in Private International Law (1993); Santa Clara University, J.D. with honors, Concentration in Intellectual Property Law (1992); University of Chicago, M.A. in Public Policy Studies (1988); Cornell University, B.S. in Operations Research and Industrial Engineering (1986). **Personal:** Miss Pitta enjoys golf, theatre, gourmet foods, and ballroom dancing.

Normand F. Pizza

Partner
Brook, Morial, Pizza & Van Loon, L.L.P.
400 Poydras Street, Suite 2500
New Orleans, LA 70130
(504) 566–0600
Fax: (504) 595–8715

8111

Business Information: Brook, Morial, Pizza & Van Loon, L.L.P. is a full–service, general practice law firm consisting of fifteen attorneys in three Louisiana offices. A practicing attorney in Louisiana state and federal courts since 1974, Mr. Pizza co–found the Firm in 1987. Serving as Partner, his practice concentrates on medical practice law. Career milestones include setting the precedent for national laws, winning cases for 49 hospitals in Louisiana for Medicaid reimbursement. **Career Steps:** Partner, Brook, Morial, Pizza & Van Loon, L.L.P. (1987–Present); Partner, Broadhurst, Brook, Mangham & Hardy (Mar. 1987–Jun. 1987); Partner, Reuter, Reuter, Reuter & Pizza (1979–1987); General Counsel, Slidell Memorial Hospital (1983–1993); Principal Counsel, Louisiana Hospital Association (1993). **Associations & Accomplishments:** Beta Lamba Chi; American Bar Association – Forum on the Construction Industry; Construction Industry Association; Associated Builders and Contractors, Inc.; Louisiana Association of Defense Counsel; Defense Research Institute; Federation of Insurance and Corporate Counsel, Inc.; International Association of Defense Counsel; Louisiana Association of Self–Insured Employers; World Trade Center of New Orleans; Slidell Chamber of Commerce; National Bar Association; Louisiana Bar Association; New Orleans Bar Association; St. Tammany Bar Association; Slidell Bar Association; The Maritime Law Association: Proctor Member (since 1988), Member of River & Ocean Towing Committee (1992); Defense Research Institute; Federation of Insurance and Corporate Counsel, Inc.; International Association of Defense Counsel; Louisiana Association of Defense Counsel; New Orleans Health Care Managers Association: Member, Seminar Chair (1994), Treasurer (1995); Advisory Council, American College of Healthcare Executives; New Orleans Health Lawyers Association; Founding Member and Former Director, Louisiana Society of Hospital Attorneys for Louisiana Hospital Association; Articles published in Health Law Journals; A frequent lecturer, the topics of his speeches and articles include among others: EMTALA, Outcome Measurement and Practice Parameters, Medicaid Records, Employment of Physicians, Hospital Acquisitions, Stark II, Fraud and Abuse, and the special legal problems related to HIV infection; Admitted to: Louisiana Supreme Court; U.S. District Courts in

Eastern, Middle and Western Districts of Louisiana; U.S. Fifth Circuit Court of Appeals; U.S. Supreme Court. **Education:** Louisiana State University, J.D. (1974); University of New Orleans, B.S. in Business Management (1970). **Personal:** Married to Diane C. in 1972. Eight children: Anna Marie, Alice Diane, Amy Louise, Andrew Joseph, Amanda Frances, Adrienne Theresa, Andrea Ruth and Anthony Norman. Mr. Pizza enjoys fishing and golf during his leisure time.

Donna J. Platt

Of Counsel
Burch & Cracchiolo, P.A.
702 East Osborn Road, Suite 200
Phoenix, AZ 85014–5241
(602) 274–7611
Fax: (602) 234–0341

8111

Business Information: Burch & Cracchiolo, P.A. is a full–service, general practice law firm, serving clientele on a national level. A practicing attorney since 1988, Ms. Platt joined the Firm as Of Counsel in 1994. Serving as a Trial Attorney, her practice specializes in plaintiff's personal injury, medical malpractice, and product liability issues. **Career Steps:** Of Counsel, Burch & Cracchiolo, P.A. (1994–Present); Attorney, K.L. Tucker & Associates, P.C. (1991–1994); Attorney, Treon Strick (1988–1991). **Associations & Accomplishments:** State County & American Bar Association; American Trial Lawyers Association; Arizona Trial Lawyers Association; Women Lawyers Association; Valley Big Brothers & Sisters; Arizona Historical Foundation; Who's Who in Law Schools. **Education:** University of Arizona, J.D. (1988); Arizona State University; Phoenix Community College, Undergraduate courses. **Personal:** Two children: John and Michael. Ms. Platt enjoys skiing, golf, involvement in political issues, and spending time with her children.

James E. Pocius

Attorney at Law
Marshall, Dennehey, Warner, Coleman and Goggin
507 London Street
Scranton, PA 18501
(717) 342–1999
Fax: (717) 342–4999

8111

Business Information: Marshall, Dennehey, Warner, Coleman and Goggin is a premier defense law firm concentrating on civil litigation, worker's compensation and civil rights defense. A trial attorney since 1978, James Pocius joined the Firm in 1991. A Shareholder, he oversees five regional offices, in addition to his trial practice. **Career Steps:** Attorney at Law and Shareholder, Marshall, Dennehey, Warner, Coleman and Goggin (1992–Present). **Associations & Accomplishments:** Scranton Chamber of Commerce; Lacka Bar Association; American Bar Association; Pennsylvania Bar Association; Pennsylvania Defense Institute; Frequent speaker on the subject of worker's compensation; Published article: "The Relationship of Pennsylvania Worker's Compensation Act with the Heart and Lung Act in Pennsylvania" (1995). **Education:** Duquesne Law School, J.D. (1978); Pennsylvania State University. **Personal:** Married to Kristine in 1978. One child: Victoria. Mr. Pocius enjoys travel.

Eric S. Pommer

Partner
Nobel & Pommer, PLC
1001 Partridge Drive, Suite 300
Ventura, CA 93003–5562
(805) 658–6266
Fax: Please mail or call
EMAIL: See Below

8111

Business Information: Nobel & Pommer, PLC is a general practice law firm with four attorneys. A practicing attorney since 1977, Mr. Pommer founded the Partnership in 1992, concentrating on business start–up, commercial and governmental contracts and assets. Internet users can reach him via: 74663.3232@compuserve.com **Career Steps:** Partner, Nobel & Pommer, PLC (1992–Present); Abex Aerospace: Manager, Manufacturing Systems (1989–1990), Manager, Contracts (1985–1989); Contracts Specialist, Martin Marietta Aerospace (1981–1985). **Associations & Accomplishments:** Fellow, National Contract Management Association; American Bar Association: Public Contract Law Section, Published in Public Contract Law Journal; California Bar Association; Ventura Beach Lions Club; Gold Coast Concert Chorus. **Education:** University of Southern California, M.S. (1989); Thomas Jefferson School of Law, J.D. (1977); Pomona College, B.A. (1973). **Personal:** Married to Amy Jane in 1986. One child: Pete. Mr. Pommer enjoys fencing, golf, and tennis.

Lisa Lee Poole

Tax Attorney
Hogan & Hartson, L.L.P.
555 13th Street NW
Washington, DC 20004–1109
(202) 637–5708
Fax: (202) 637–5910
EMAIL: See Below

8111

Business Information: Hogan & Hartson, L.L.P. is a full–service, general practice law firm, providing legal services to clientele from twelve national and international locations. A practicing attorney since 1988, Ms. Poole joined the Firm as Tax Attorney in 1993. She specializes in tax planning for international and domestic business transactions. She can be reached through the Internet via: LP1@DC1.HHLAW.COM **Career Steps:** Tax Attorney, Hogan & Hartson L.L.P. (1993–Present); Attorney, Gibson, Dunn & Crutcher (1988–93). **Associations & Accomplishments:** American Bar Association. **Education:** Duke Law School, J.D. (1988); University of Michigan, A.B. (1982). **Personal:** Ms. Poole enjoys cross–country skiing, hiking, running, and the arts.

Daniel James Pope, Esq.

Partner
Seyfarth Shaw, et al
55 East Monroe Street, Suite 4300
Chicago, IL 60603–5702
(312) 269–8510
Fax: (312) 269–8869

8111

Business Information: Seyfarth, Shaw, et al, is a full–service, general practice law firm. Established in 1945, the Firm reports annual revenue of $110 million and currently employs 1,000 attorneys, legal and administrative support staff. Admitted to practice in Illinois state courts, Mr. Pope joined the Firm as an attorney in 1990. Currently serving as Partner and Trial Lawyer, he is responsible for litigation and providing legal representation to the Firm's major clientele. **Career Steps:** Partner, Seyfarth Shaw, et al (1990–Present). **Associations & Accomplishments:** Director, Pro Bono Advocates; Legal Association for Women; Author of numerous publications and articles; Author of "Trial Objections" book (1995); Regular contributor of annual articles to the International Association of Defense Lawyers. **Education:** University of Chicago (1977–1978); The John Marshall Law School, J.D., cum laude; Loyola University, B.A. **Personal:** Married to Helen in 1994. Two children: Laura Jeane and Caitlin. Mr. Pope enjoys golf and running.

Renee M. Porter

Attorney and Partner
Porter, Porter & Kittrell
915 Main Street
Columbia, MS 39429
(601) 731–1886
Fax: (601) 731–1887

8111

Business Information: Porter, Porter & Kittrell, established in 1989, is a full–service, general practice law firm, concentrating on civil litigation dealing most specifically with domestic relations. A practicing attorney in Mississippi state courts since 1988, Mrs. Porter was a beginning partner with the Firm when it was established in 1989. Her practice concentrates on domestic relations cases as the Firm's lead trial attorney. **Career Steps:** Attorney and Partner, Porter, Porter & Kittrell (1989–Present) **Associations & Accomplishments:** Columbia and Mississippi Business and Professional Women's Association (currently serving Mississippi as Alternate Young Careerist); Kiwanis Club of Columbia: Member, Chairperson – Priority One; Mississippi State Bar Association: Nominations Chair, Young Lawyer's Division; Member and Music Director, Edna Baptist Church; Prayer Coordinator, Marion County Baptist Association. **Education:** University of Mississippi, J.D. (1988); University of Southern Mississippi, B.S. (1985). **Personal:** Married to H. Thomas in 1987. Two children: Julia and Javan. Mrs. Porter enjoys reading.

Mr. David D. Powell

Attorney
Hammerle & Couch, P.L.C.
1660 South Stemmeons at Corporate, Suite 330 Lock Box 10
Lewisville, TX 75067
(214) 436–9300
Fax: (214) 436–9000

8111

Business Information: Hammerle & Couch, P.L.C. is a specialty law firm concentrating in the areas of taxation (bankruptcy), criminal, and family law. Established in 1985, the Firm currently employs 30 professionals. A practicing trial attorney since 1977, David Powell joined the Firm in 1985. Admitted to practice in state and federal courts, he specializes in family law. **Career Steps:** Senior Litigation Attorney, Hammerle & Couch, P.L.C. (1993–Present); Solo Litigator, David D. Powell, P.C. (1990–1993); Partner, Dalton, Sorenson & Powell (1988–1990). **Associations & Accomplishments:** Board of Directors, Flower Mound Chamber of Commerce, Flower Mound, TX (1993); Ambassador, Lewisville Chamber of Commerce, Lewisville, TX (1993); Family Law Section, American Bar Association; Texas Bar Association; North Texas Specialist Association; Founding Member, Alliance Bar Association; Soccer Coach. **Education:** Southern Methodist University, J.D. (1977); The American University, B.S. (1974). **Personal:** Married to Sherry Lynn Ethridge in 1985. Four children: Scott, Chad, Kathryn and Brett. Mr. Powell enjoys soccer.

Florence Annette Powell

Attorney
Freeman Associates
121 North Church Street
Marion, VA 24354–2745
(540) 783–8197
Fax: (540) 783–1888

8111

Business Information: Freeman Associates is a full–service, general practice law firm consisting of three attorneys and concentrating on family, personal injury cases, and business law. A practicing attorney since 1983 in Virginia state courts, Ms. Powell joined the Firm in 1991. Serving as Attorney, she is responsible for legal representation of the Firm's clientele. Concurrent with her private practice, she was appointed Assistant Commonwealth Attorney for Smith County, Virginia in 1991. **Career Steps:** Attorney, Freeman Associates (Present); Assistant Com. Attorney, Smyth County, VA (1991–Present); Associate, Mullins Thomason & Harris (1984–1991); Law Clerk, The Honorable Glen M. Williams, U.S. District Court Judge (1983–1984). **Associations & Accomplishments:** Marion Junior Women's Club: President (1995), Treasurer (1993 & 1994); Oak Hill FCE; Washington County Chamber of Commerce; Smyth County Bar Association; American Bar Association; Virginia State Bar; Virginia Trial Lawyers Association; Smyth County Community Choir; Virginia Polled Hereford Associaton; American Polled Hereford Association; Washington County Farm Bureau; Washington County Farmers Cooperative; Washington County Extension Leadership Council. **Education:** University of Memphis, J.D. (1983); Sweet Briar College, A.B. (1980). **Personal:** Ms. Powell enjoys singing, crafts, gardening, hiking, and swimming.

Daniel M. Preminger, Esq.

Sole Practitioner
Daniel M. Preminger, P.C.
1050 Robinson Building
Philadelphia, PA 19102
(215) 564–1227
Fax: (215) 564–0396

8111

Business Information: Daniel M. Preminger, P.C. is a full–service, general practice law firm, concentrating on criminal defense and personal injury cases. A practicing attorney in Pennsylvania state courts since 1971, Mr. Preminger established his sole practice law firm in 1976. His practice concentrates on trial and appellate litigations. **Career Steps:** Sole Practitioner, Daniel M. Preminger, P.C. (1976–Present). **Associations & Accomplishments:** Member of the Board of Trustees, Mid Atlantic Center for the Arts (MAC) – Cape May, New Jersey. **Education:** George Washington University School of Law, J.D. (1971); Hunter College in the Bronx, B.A. (1967). **Personal:** Married to Barbara in 1979. Mr. Preminger enjoys exercise and collecting antiques.

Wendy L. Press Sweeny

Sole Practitioner
Law Offices of Wendy Press Sweeny
1121 Big Horn Avenue
Worland, WY 82401
(307) 347–2979
Fax: (307) 347–4124

8111

Business Information: Law Offices of Wendy Press Sweeny is a full service, general practice law firm specializing in family and domestic relations and criminal law, including probate wills and trusts and title searches. A practicing attorney since 1987, Ms. Press Sweeny established her individual practice firm in 1995. As Sole Practitioner she is responsible for all aspects of operations. **Career Steps:** Sole Practitioner, Law Offices of Wendy Press Sweeny (1995–Present); County and Prosecuting Attorney, Washakie County, Worland WY (1991–1994); Associate, Messenger & Jurovich, Thermopolis, Wyoming (1987–1990). **Associations & Accomplish-**

ments: Chairman, Human Resource Council; Business and Professional Women's Club; Girl Scouts, U.S.A.; Wyoming State Bar Association; Florida Bar Association; American Bar Association, Family Law Section; Wyoming Trial Lawyers Association; Child Protection Team; Board for Mental Health facilities; Published in Law Review at Nova Southeastern University; Recognized for Outstanding Volunteer in the community. **Education:** Nova University, J.D. (1989); University of South Florida, B.A. in Business (1983); Broward Community College, A.A. in Business (1981). **Personal:** Married to Kermit P. in 1989. Four children: Richard, Michael, Nicholas and Briana. Ms. Press Sweeny enjoys body building, hiking, needlepoint, reading, and going to the mountains.

John H. Price

Sole Practitioner
The Law Offices of John H. Price
1504 Taylor Avenue
Baltimore, MD 21234–5237
(410) 789–0510
Fax: (410) 789–1057

8111

Business Information: The Law Offices of John H. Price is a full–service law practice. Currently the office employs 3 legal support staff. As Sole Practitioner, Mr. Price established his private practice in 1973 after the conferral of his law degree. A trial attorney admitted to both State and Federal courts, Mr. Price concentrates his practice in the areas of worker's compensation, domestic law, personal injury and labor law. **Career Steps:** Sole Practitioner, The Law Offices of John H. Price (1973–Present). **Associations & Accomplishments:** Chairman, Judicare Committee, Maryland State Bar Association; Executive Board and Chairman, Lawyer Referral Committee, Baltimore City Bar Association; President, Community Association. **Education:** University of Baltimore, J.D. (1973); University of Scranton, B.S. in Accounting and Economics. **Personal:** Married to Gail Mary in 1967. Two children: John H., III and Deedra Price Earl. Mr. Price enjoys fishing, crabbing, walking, going to the ocean and spending time with his grandchildren.

Mario A. Prieto Batista, Esq.

Attorney
Mario A. Prieto Batista Law Offices
268 Ponce de Leon, Suite 1113
Hato Rey, Puerto Rico 00918
(787) 751–2671
Fax: (787) 274–8509

8111

Business Information: Mario A. Prieto Batista Law Offices is a full–service, general practice law firm, concentrating in corporate and labor law, litigation, and pro–bono work for non–profit organizations in Puerto Rico. A practicing attorney since 1980, Mr. Prieto Batista established his private practice in 1989. He is responsible for overseeing all administrative operations for associates and support staff, in addition to his daily law practice. **Career Steps:** Attorney, Mario A. Prieto Batista Law Offices (1989–Present); President and General Manager, Metro Bus Authority (1984–1989); Inter–American University: Associate Vice President (1982–1983), Personnel Director (1981–1982), Assistant Dean (1977–1981). **Associations & Accomplishments:** Colegio de Abogadas de Puerto Rico. **Education:** Inter–American University, J.D. (1980); University of Puerto Rico, B.S. **Personal:** Married to Xiomara in 1979. Two children: Marco and Pablo. Mr. Prieto Batista enjoys spending time with family and golf.

Michael R. Pritchard

Vice President, Chief Operating Officer, and Co–Founder
LSI
7951 Beaver Lake Drive
San Diego, CA 92119
(619) 497–5044 (800) 557–9208
Fax: (619) 697–3504
EMAIL: See Below

8111

Business Information: LSI is a litigation and investigation support firm for plaintiffs vs. major corporations. Services are provided for alleged consumer wrongdoing, healthcare fraud and product liability, mental health advocacy, and criminal and civil investigation cases. As Vice President, Chief Operating Officer, and Co–Founder, Mr. Pritchard is responsible for the oversight of all investigations and witness ID/interviews, and the procurement of documentary evidence. In addition, he serves as a medical/government agency liaison. He also may be reached through Internet via: MRPLSI@ix.netcom.com. **Career Steps:** Vice President, Chief Operating Officer, and Co–Founder, LSI (1989–Present); Litigation Property & Construction Title Searcher, Fidelity National Title (1988–1989); Land & Property Title Searcher, Chicago National Title (1987–1988); Land & Property Title Searcher, Westland and Land Title (1983–1987). **Associations & Accomplishments:** San Diego Alliance for the Mentally Ill; San Diego County Mediation Board; People for the American Way; Doctors Without Borders; Amnesty International; Habitat for Humanity; American Civil Liberties Union. **Education:** Southwestern College, A.A. in Legal Administration (1989). **Personal:** Mr. Pritchard enjoys dog training, skiing, snowmobiling, virtual reality games, and acting with the community theater.

Steven E. Psarellis

Principal
Steven E. Psarellis, P.L.C.
501 World Trade Center
New Orleans, LA 70130
(504) 596–6777
Fax: Please mail or call

8111

Business Information: The Law Office of Steven E. Psarellis is an international general law practice, concentrating on Maritime and Commercial Law. As Principal and Founding Attorney, Mr. Psarellis is responsible for all aspects of the Law Firm. Licensed in Texas, Louisiana, Mississippi and Alabama state and federal courts, he primarily focuses on Maritime Law, but he also represents clients in International Commercial Law and Offshore Financial Transactions. He performs extensive pro bono work, providing legislative lobbying on behalf of maritime trade with Greece. **Career Steps:** Principal, Steven E. Psarellis, P.L.C. (1994–Present). **Associations & Accomplishments:** Has published articles in various journals. **Personal:** Mr. Psarellis enjoys Soccor (co–sponsor of local team). Active in local Church..

Richard D. Pullman

Partner/Attorney
Vial, Hamilton, Koch & Knox
1717 Main Street, Suite 4400
Dallas, TX 75201–7388
(214) 712–4564
Fax: (214) 712–4402

8111

Business Information: Vial, Hamilton, Koch & Knox is a general practice law firm. A practicing attorney since 1971, Mr. Pullman joined the Firm as a Partner in 1989 and became a Member of the Management Committee in 1995. Concentrating his practice in business litigation and some pro bono work. **Career Steps:** Partner, Vial, Hamilton, Koch & Knox (1989–Present); Partner, Pullman & Schendle (1976–1989); Associate, Stroud & Smith (1971–1976). **Associations & Accomplishments:** American Board of Trial Advocates; Board of Directors, Jewish Welfare Federation; United Way – Dallas, Texas; Editor, Southwestern Law Journal; American Bar Association; Texas Bar Association; Dallas Bar Association; Member and Member of the Board of Governors, Columbian Country Club. **Education:** Southern Methodist University, J.D. (1971); Trinity College – Connecticut, B.A. (1968). **Personal:** Married to Janice in 1968. Two children: Michael Alan and Rebecca Diane. Mr. Pullman enjoys golf and travel.

Manuel A. Quilichini

Partner
Totti, Rodriguez, Diaz & Fuentes
416 Ponce de Leon Avenue, Suite 1200
San Juan, Puerto Rico 00918
(787) 753–7910
Fax: (787) 764–9480
EMAIL: See Below

8111

Business Information: Totti, Rodriguez, Diaz & Fuentes is an international, full–service, general practice law firm providing representation in civil (95–98%) and criminal (2–5%) cases, as well as conducting pro bono work. The Firm has a total of 21 attorneys, which includes nine partners. A practicing attorney in Puerto Rico state and federal courts since 1982, Mr. Quilichini joined the Firm as Partner in the Labor, Employment Law Division. He provides counseling and representation to clients in all labor and employment matters, insurance coverage disputes, and general litigation. He may also be reached through the Internet via: ManualQ.@Caribe.Net **Career Steps:** Partner, Totti, Rodriguez, Diaz & Fuentes (Present); Partner, Quilichini & Silva Ayala; Partner, Lasa, Escalera & Reichard; Associate, Lespier, Munoz Noya & Ramirez. **Associations & Accomplishments:** American Bar Association; Puerto Rico Association; Federal Bar Association; Special Consultant to Puerto Rico Bar Association on Automation; Member, Presidential Classroom Advisory Committee of Puerto Rico; National Hispanic Bar Association. **Education:** University of Puerto Rico Law School, J.D. (1982); University of Puerto Rico, B.S. in Business Administration, majored in Finance (1975–1979). **Personal:** Married to Maria del P. Martinez in 1985. Two children: Christine Marie and Jean Manuel. Mr. Quilichini enjoys flying, computers, and tennis.

Jonathan Stuart Quinn

Partner
Sachnoff & Weaver, Ltd.
30 South Wacker Drive, Suite 2900
Chicago, IL 60606
(312) 207–6443
Fax: (312) 207–6400

8111

Business Information: Sachnoff & Weaver, Ltd. is a Chicago–based law firm with approximately 90 professionals providing legal services in two primary areas of law: Business and Litigation. Admitted to practice in New York and Illinois state courts, Mr. Quinn joined the Firm as Partner in 1992. He represents clients in a wide variety of commercial litigation matters in state and federal courts throughout the U.S. **Career Steps:** Partner, Sachnoff & Weaver, Ltd. (1992–Present); Associate, Mayer, Brown & Platt (1988–1992); Assistant District Attorney, New York County District Attorney's Office (1985–1988). **Associations & Accomplishments:** Delegate, Democratic National Convention (1992); American Bar Association; Chicago Bar Association; Chicago Council of Lawyers; Civil Rights Committee – Midwest Region, Anti–Defamation League; Adjunct Professor of Trial Advocacy, Northwestern University School of Law; Faculty, National Institute of Trial Advocacy (NITA). **Education:** Northwestern University School of Law, J.D. (1985); Haverford College, B.A. (1981). **Personal:** Married to Jennifer Lebold in 1989. Two children: Lily and Noah. Mr. Quinn enjoys all sports, movies, travel, and reading.

Rafael Quinones Cruz

District Judge (Retired)
–Independent–
Urb Country Club, Gk 14 Calle 201
Carolina, Puerto Rico 00982
Fax: Please mail or call

8111

Business Information: Mr. Quinones Cruz retired in 1988 as a District Judge for the Puerto Rican general justice court. He also served as a representative of the House of Puerto Rico and worked for the Department of the Treasury as an accountant specializing in tax accounting matters. **Career Steps:** District Judge (Retired), General Justice Court, Puerto Rico (1979–1988); Staff Attorney for The Legal Service Corporation of San Juan (1974–1978); Representative of the House, House of Representatives, Puerto Rico (1969–1972); Income Tax Accountant, Department of the Treasury (1960–1968); Statitian for The Office of the Commissioner of Insurances of Puerto Rico (1960); Veteran of The Korean War (1951–1952). **Associations & Accomplishments:** Colegio de Abogados de Puerto Rico. **Education:** School of Law, J.D. (1965). **Personal:** Born in Penuelas, Puerto Rico. Married to Angelina Irizarry in 1955. Eight children: Heydee, Sahily, Rafael, Iulmer, Exel, Bailey, Joselyn, and Elliot. Mr. Quinones Cruz enjoys chess and dominoes.

Gustavo A. Quinones–Pinto, Esq.

Attorney
Gustavo A. Quinones–Pinto Law Firm
Santiago I. Pantin #502
Fajardo, Puerto Rico 00738
(787) 860–4041
Fax: Please mail or call

8111

Business Information: A practicing attorney since 1986, Mr. Quinones–Pinto established the Firm in 1989 after teaching part–time at Interamerican University and the University of Puerto Rico. He now concentrates his practice in general civil law, as well as criminal law, corporate business law, tort, and pro bono work. **Career Steps:** Attorney, Gustavo A. Quinones–Pinto Law Firm (1986–Present); Part–time Professor, Interamerican University (1985–1989); Part–time Professor, University of Puerto Rico (1987). **Associations & Accomplishments:** Board of Directors, Fajardo Culture Center; Master Mason, Antonio Valero Lodge; Former President, Political Science Students Association – University of Puerto Rico Rio Piedras Campus; Puerto Rico Bar Association. **Education:** University of Puerto Rico: J.D. (1985), Bachelor of Arts, Magna Cum Laude (1980). **Personal:** Three children: Gustavo A., Nairely M., and Gustavo E. Mr. Quinones–

Pinto enjoys fishing, reading, writing, singing, playing bass and guitar.

Mr. Fred R. Radolovich

Sole Practitioner
The Law Office of Fred R. Radolovich
429 West Muhammad Ali Boulevard
Louisville, KY 40202–2348
(502) 589–2775
Fax: (502) 589–2776

8111

Business Information: The Law Office of Fred R. Radolovich is a full–service law office A trial attorney since 1974, Mr. Radolovich established his sole practice in 1987. Admitted to both State and Federal courts, he concentrates his practice in the areas of litigation, personal injury and criminal law. **Career Steps:** Sole Practitioner, The Law Office of Fred R. Radolovich (1987–Present). **Associations & Accomplishments:** American Bar Association; Kentucky Bar Association; Louisville Bar Association; Kentucky Academy of Justice; National Academy of Criminal Defense Lawyers; Kentucky Academy of Criminal Defense Lawyers; American Trial Lawyers Association; Kentucky Academy of Trial Attorneys; International Bar Association; Named as an Honorary Barrister in London; Published frequently in Louisville Courier Journal; Who's Who in American Law; Guest Lecturer at conferences and seminars. **Education:** University of Louisville, J.D. (1974); Fordham College/Fordham University, M.A., B.A. **Personal:** Married to Linda in 1992. Mr. Radolovich enjoys diving, golf and travel.

Susan J. Radom, Esq.

Attorney and Founding Partner
DiFazio, Radom, Wetter & Bennett
3121 Route 22 East
Somerville, NJ 08876
(908) 707–1500
Fax: (908) 707–4181

8111

Business Information: DiFazio, Radom, Wetter & Bennett is a full–service, general practice law firm consisting of five practicing attorneys. Areas of practice include: Community Association Law, Construction Litigation, Business Law, Commercial Transactions, Real Property Law, and Collections. A practicing attorney in New Jersey state courts since 1988, Ms. Radom is one of four attorneys who founded the Firm in 1995. Her practice areas include: Community Association Law, Construction Litigation, Business Law, Commercial Transactions, Real Property Law, Collections, Officer and Director Liability, Employer/Employee Disputes, General Litigation, Construction Litigation, Landlord/Tenant Disputes, Administrative Claims, Arbitration, Premises Liability, and Personal Injury Litigation Liability. **Career Steps:** Attorney and Founding Partner, DiFazio, Radom, Wetter & Bennett (1995–Present); Attorney, Golden, Rothschild, et al (1988–1995). **Associations & Accomplishments:** Warren County Bar Association; Common Interest Ownership Committee, New Jersey State Bar Association; American Bar Association; Community Association Institute: Board of Directors (1995), Legislative Action Committee (1993–Present), Chair – Educational Subcommittee for Legislative Committee (1995), Chair – FRT Task Force (1994); New Jersey Apartment Association; Phi Beta Kappa. **Education:** Rutgers University: J.D. (1988), B.A. (1980). **Personal:** Ms. Radom enjoys water skiing, horseback riding, and parasailing.

Barbara Louise Raimondi, Esq.

Partner
Trafton & Matzen
P.O. Box 470
Auburn, ME 04212–0470
(207) 784–4531
Fax: (207) 784–8738

8111

Business Information: Trafton & Matzen is a full–service, general practice law firm. The Firm consists of three practicing partners, four attorneys, and six legal support staff. Admitted to practice in Maine state courts since 1980, Mrs. Raimondi joined the Firm as an Associate in 1985, attaining partnership in 1990. She concentrates her practice in the areas of civil litigation, personal injury and domestic law. **Career Steps:** Trafton & Matzen: Partner (1990–Present), Associate (1985–1990); Attorney, Lipman & Katz (1980–1985). **Associations & Accomplishments:** President, Pine Tree Legal, Inc. (1991–1993); Auburn Public Library: Trustee (1993–Present), Treasurer (1994–Present); Diamond Island

Association: Director (1993–Present), Vice President (1995–Present); Member, Maine State Bar Association; Maine Trial Lawyers Association; American Trial Lawyers Association; American Bar Association. **Education:** Boston University, J.D. (1980) **Personal:** Married to William Robitzek in 1973. One child: Laura. Mrs. Raimondi enjoys sailing, swimming, skiing, hiking, biking, and aerobics.

Alberto L. Ramos–Perez

Owner/Lawyer
Alberto L. Ramos Law Offices
P.O. Box 1271
Penuelas, Puerto Rico 00624–1290
(787) 835–4207
Fax: (787) 835–4207

8111

Business Information: Alberto L. Ramos Law Offices is a private practice law firm, concentrating on environmental law matters. A practicing attorney since 1991, Mr. Ramos–Perez established his private practice in 1993. As Owner/Attorney, he is responsible for all aspects of Company operations, including engineering and legal counsel in the areas of environmental and OSHA regulations. Concurrent with his private legal practice, he is also an adjunct professor at Pontificia Universidad Catolica de Puerto Rico. **Career Steps:** Owner/Lawyer, Alberto L. Ramos Law Offices (1993–Present); Managing Partner, Caban, Martinez, Ramos & Ramon (1991–1993); Regional Manager, Pedro Pazardi & Associates (1987–1991). **Associations & Accomplishments:** American Bar Association; Colegio de Abogados de Puerto Rico; American Institute of Chemical Engineers; Colegio de Ingenieros de Puerto Rico. **Education:** Catholic University of Puerto Rico, J.D. (1991); University of Puerto Rico, B.S. in Chemical Engineering (1986). **Personal:** Married to Ana M. in 1986. Three children: Jorge Alberto, Annelisse, and Paola Marie. Mr. Ramos–Perez enjoys spending time with his family.

Mr. Halbert B. Rasmussen

Partner
Manning, Leaver, et al.
5750 Wilshire Boulevard, Suite 655
Los Angeles, CA 90036
(213) 937–4730
Fax: (213) 937–6727

8111

Business Information: Manning, Leaver, et al. is a full service law firm with a civil practice. They focus on all legal concerns of the motor vehicle dealer and finance industries and do estate and tax planning. They represent both individual dealerships and large corporations. As a Partner, Mr. Rasmussen handles important cases, some of which have resulted in new law. Established in 1923, Manning, Leaver, et al. employs 25 people. **Career Steps:** Associate and later Partner, Manning, Leaver, et al. (1984–Present); Associate General Counsel, Syncor International Corporation (1983–1984). **Associations & Accomplishments:** Member, American Bar Association; Member, California Bar Association. Mr. Rasmussen has also had articles published in professional journals. **Education:** Loyola Law School, J.D. (1982); UCLA, B.A. (1980).

P. Donald Rasmussen

Partner
Rasmussen Starr Ruddy
55 Metcalf Street, Suite 500
Ottawa, Ontario K1P 6L5
(613) 232–1830
Fax: (613) 232–2499

8111

Business Information: Rasmussen Starr Ruddy is a general practice law firm with an emphasis on civil litigation. The Firm works with businesses and individuals in Canada, and Canadian individuals living in the United States. A practicing attorney in Canadian courts since obtaining his degree in 1965, Mr. Rasmussen founded the Firm in 1987. As a Partner, he handles administration of the office and its support staff, as well as his daily client load. **Career Steps:** Partner, Rasmussen Starr Ruddy (1987–Present); Partner, Hewitt Hewitt Nesbitt Reid (1974–1987). **Education:** Queen's University, LL.B. (1965). **Personal:** Married to Kersti in 1965. Two children: Erika and Derek. Mr. Rasmussen enjoys cabinet making.

Frederick Ratzburg II, Esq.

Attorney
The Law Office of Frederick Ratzburg, II, Esq.
400 Travis Street, Suite 1404
Shreveport, LA 71101–3113
(318) 424–1059
Fax: (318) 227–9762

0111

Business Information: A Sole Practitioner since 1989, Frederick Ratzburg concentrates his practice in the areas of criminal and civil litigation, and some worker's compensation. A trial lawyer since 1982, he is admitted to both State and Federal courts. **Career Steps:** Sole Practitioner, The Law Office of Frederick Ratzburg, II, Esq. (1989–Present); Attorney, Graves, Daye, Bowie, Beresko and Flowers (1988–1989); Assistant District Attorney, Caddo Parish District Attorney's Office (1984–1988); Law Clerk, Judge William Polk, Rapides Parish, Alexandria (1983–1984). **Associations & Accomplishments:** Downtown Rotary Club of Shreveport; Shreveport Bar Association; Vice President, Gideons; City Attorney for Town of Blanchard; Shreveport Chamber of Commerce. **Education:** Southern University, J.D. (1982); Northwestern State University, B.A. **Personal:** Married to Karen in 1979. Three children: Sonya, Heather and Carl II. Mr. Ratzburg enjoys jogging, hunting and fishing.

A. Peter Rausch Jr.

Owner/Attorney
Law Offices of A. Peter Rausch Jr.
2800 West March Lane, Suite 220
Stockton, CA 95219
(209) 952–5000
Fax: (209) 952–5009

8111

Business Information: Law Offices of A. Peter Rausch Jr. is a full–service, general practice law firm. The Firm provides legal counsel and representation to individual, business and corporate clients in a wide variety of areas. Focusing primarily on complex commercial and business litigation, it also provides general business and personal matters, including business transactions, entity formation, operation and dissolution, asset protection, and the development of strategies for avoiding disputes. Clients, served from two offices in California (San Francisco, Stockton), are represented in State and Federal Courts throughout California, and the Firm has appeared in association with local counsel in State and Federal Courts located outside California, including, New York, Florida, Texas, Iowa and New Jersey. A practicing attorney in California State and Federal courts since 1986, Mr. Rausch established the Firm in 1991. His areas of expertise include: Complex Commercial and Business Litigation; Corporate and Business Entity Formation, Governance and Dissolution; Commercial and Business Transactions; Trademarks, Trade Secrets and Related Unfair Competition Disputes; Copyright Registration and Infringement Litigation; Community Association Representation and Assessment Lien Foreclosures; and Intellectual Property matters, including issues relating to the use of the Internet. Utilizing the latest in computer technology to better serve his clients, Mr. Rausch shares his expertise by speaking to attorney groups on the use of computers in the legal profession. **Career Steps:** Senior Named Partner, Law Offices of A. Peter Rausch Jr. (1991–Present). **Associations & Accomplishments:** ADMITTED: California State Courts (1987), U.S. District Court – Eastern & Northern Districts of California (1987), U.S. District Court – Central District of California (1990), U.S. Court of Appeals – Ninth Circuit (1990), U.S. District Court – Southern District of California (1992), U.S. Supreme Court (1992); American Bar Association; California State Bar Association; Los Angeles County Bar Association; San Francisco County Bar Association; San Joaquin County Bar Association; Executive Committee, Computer Users Section of San Joaquin County Bar Association; Stockton Good Guys; Pacific Athletic Foundation; Martindale–Hubbel rating: BV **Education:** McGeorge School of Law, J.D. (1986); University of the Pacific, B.A. in Philosophy (1981).

Carol M. Reahard

Attorney
Office of Carol M. Reahard
6715 Ossington Dr.
Indianapolis, IN 46254–4875
(317) 387–9998
Fax: (317) 387–9998

8111

Business Information: Office of Carol M. Reahard is a full–service, general practice law firm, specializing in the investigation of riverboat applicants and gaming suppliers. A practicing attorney in Indiana and New Mexico state and federal courts since 1989, Ms. Reahard founded the Firm in 1990. **Career Steps:** Attorney, Office of Carol M. Reahard (1990–Present); State of Indiana: Supervisor Tax Appeals, Tax Analyst.

Associations & Accomplishments: American Bar Association; Indiana Bar Association; New Mexico State Bar Association. **Education:** Indiana University – Indianapolis: J.D. (1989), B.S. **Personal:** One child: Rhod J. Fitzpatrick.

Adam Regenbogen

Senior Attorney
Worker's Compensation Board
44 Hawley Street
Binghamton, NY 13901–4440
(607) 721–8331
Fax: (607) 723–5786
EMAIL: See Below

8111

Business Information: The Worker's Compensation Board provides legal services and support for employees who are unable to perform their jobs because of a work–related injury. As Senior Attorney, Mr. Regenbogen is responsible for aspects of legal support. Concurrent to his position with the Board, Mr. Regenbogen is also a part–time attorney. He concentrates his private practice in the areas of divorce mediation and criminal law. Mr. Regenbogen established his practice in 1983 and is admitted to practice in State courts. He can also be reached through the Internet as follows: ARCATTY@aol.com **Career Steps:** Senior Attorney, Worker's Compensation Board (1992–Present); Director of Quality Assurance, New York State Office of Mental Health (1987–1991); Director of Internal Affairs, U.S. Veterans Administration (1980–1987). **Associations & Accomplishments:** Broome County Bar Association; Tompkins County Bar Association; Suffolk County Bar Association; American Bar Association; Ithaca Reform Temple; Child of Survivors of the Holocaust. **Education:** Temple University, J.D. (1980); University of Pennsylvania, Masters of Social Work; Temple University, B.A. **Personal:** Two children: Stacy and Candice. Mr. Regenbogen enjoys spending time with his family.

Robert L. Rehberger

Attorney
Robert L. Rehberger and Associates
5025 North Henry Boulevard
Stockbridge, GA 30281
(770) 389–8134
Fax: (770) 389–5493

8111

Business Information: Robert L. Rehberger and Associates is a private full–service law firm concentrating in workers' compensation law, criminal bankruptcy, and divorce law. A practicing attorney since 1980, Mr. Rehberger established his private practice in 1988. He oversees all administrative activities, providing counseling for associates and a support staff, as well as providing legal direction for clients. Mr. Rehberger is licensed in the States of Georgia, Florida, Illinois, Missouri, Oklahoma, and the District of Columbia. Concurrent to his legal practice, Mr. Rehberger also serves as an Adjunct Professor, teaching civil law at Clayton State College. **Career Steps:** Attorney at Law, Robert L. Rehberger and Associates (1988–Present); Adjunct Professor, Clayton State College (1991–Present); Corporate Consultant, Olympia Produce (1988–1990); Professor, Southwestern Oklahoma State University (1982–1986); Instructor, University of Missouri (1982); Assistant States Attorney, Madison County (1981–1982); Law Clerk, Presiding Justice (1981); Computer Circuit Controller, Madison County (1976–1977). **Associations & Accomplishments:** American Bar Association; Oklahoma Bar Association; Association of Trial Lawyers of America; Illinois Bar Association; Metropolitan Bar Association of St. Louis; Metropolitan Bar Association of Kansas City; Washington D.C. Bar Association; Alpha Kappa Psi; Delta Phi, Moose Lodge, Masonic Lodge, Optimists Club. **Education:** University of Missouri, J.D. (1980); University of Puget Sound, M.B.A. (1971); Benedictine College, B.S. (1971). **Personal:** Mr. Rehberger enjoys water skiing, snow skiing, and horseback riding during his leisure time.

William Z. Reich

Senior Partner
Serotte, Reich, Scipp & Kenmore
300 Delaware Avenue
Buffalo, NY 14202–1807
(716) 854–7525
Fax: (716) 854–0294

8111

Business Information: Serotte, Reich, Scipp & Kenmore is a full–service, general practice law firm, specializing in immigration and nationality law. The Firm serves the bordering region of Canada (America's #1 trade partner for commercial businesses) and has offices located close to the American Consulate Office in Toronto. Joining the Firm upon the conferral of his law degree in 1974, Mr. Reich currently serves as Senior Partner. Admitted to practice in New York state courts, his practice concentrates on immigration law issues. **Career Steps:** Senior Partner, Serotte, Reich, Scipp & Kenmore (1974–Present). **Associations & Accomplishments:** American Bar Association; American Immigration Lawyers Association (AILA); Erie County Bar Association; New York State Bar Association; Nominated in Best Lawyers in America (1993). **Education:** State University of New York – Buffalo, J.D. (1974); City University of New York – Queens College, B.A. **Personal:** Married to Catharine Venzon in 1985. Four children: Eric, Justin, Zabrina, Aviva. Mr. Reich enjoys skiing, hiking, and reading.

M. Therese Reilly

Attorney
Independent
110 Garden Avenue
Richmond Hill, Ontario L4C 6M1
Fax: Please mail or call
EMAIL: See Below

8111

Business Information: Called to the Bar of Ontario, Ms. Reilly has eight years of experience in a broad and diverse range of legal issues, including extensive litigation experience with emphasis on transportation, contract, property, employment and environmental issues and as a corporate lawyer providing legal support services involving corporate, commercial, securities, and environmental law. Experienced in handling corporate secretarial responsibilities with a private sector public corporation, she is a motivated, ambitious, hardworking, and conscientious professional with a proven track record and strong analytical, organizational, negotiating, and oral and written communication skills. Ms. Reilly is an effective troubleshooter and advocate, as well. Her strengths lie in leadership, administration, negotiating, effecting settlements, and managing. She is fluently bilingual in French and English, and is computer proficient. **Career Steps:** Attorney, Independent (1996–Present); Corporate Secretary/Counsel, QUNO Corporation (1993–1996); Solicitor, Canadian Pacific (1990–1993); Law Clerk to the Justices of the High Court of Ontario, Ministry of the Attorney General (1988–1989). **Associations & Accomplishments:** Law Society of Upper Canada; Member, Environmental, Young Lawyers, and Business Law Sections of the Canadian Bar Association; Lincoln County Law Association; County of York Law Association; Council Member, Ontario Branch of the Institute of Chartered Secretaries and Administrators in Canada. **Education:** University of Alberta: L.L.B. (1986), B.A. (1983). **Personal:** Married to Brian in 1983. One child: Brennan. Ms. Reilly enjoys golf and refinishing antiques.

S. Scott Reynolds, Esq.

President
Reynolds & Forthun
300 East State Street, Suite 450
Redlands, CA 92373–5235
(909) 798–3190
Fax: (909) 798–3092

8111

Business Information: Reynolds & Forthun is a full–service, general practice law firm. A practicing attorney in California courts since 1976 and a Certified Specialist in Estate Planning, Mr. Reynolds co–founded the Firm in 1982 and currently serves as President. He oversees the administrative operations for associates (five attorneys) and a support staff of nine, in addition to his legal practice in which he specializes in estate planning (wills, trusts, probate) and tax and corporate law. A civic–minded individual, Mr. Reynolds has tirelessly contributed his services in various community projects, providing pro bono legal advice to such organizations as: Food for All, Inc.; Redlands Terrier Benchwarmers; Cassie's Friends; Mentone United Church of Christ; D.A.S.H. and Chemical People Task Force to name a few. **Career Steps:** President, Reynolds & Forthun (1982–Present); Attorney, Welebir & Brunick (1979–1982); Attorney, Arthur Anderson & Company (1976–1979). **Associations & Accomplishments:** California State Bar; American Bar Association; San Bernardino County Bar Association; United States District Court: Northern and Central Districts; United States Tax Court; National Academy of Elder Law Attorneys; 1972 Journey for Perspective; Redlands Jaycees Distinguished Service Award (1982); Who's Who in California; Who's Who in Society; Participant, Thirty–Third Annual National Security Forum; Redlands Chamber of Commerce: Director (1980–1986, 1994–Present), President (1985, 1988); United Way of Redlands Area: Director (1980–1988), President (1985), Campaign Chairman (1988); Redlands Community Hospital: Member, Corporate Body (1982–1986), Director, RCH, Inc. (1986–1990), Director (1990–1991); Redlands Rotary Club: Member (1982–Present), President (1986–1987); Redlands Planning Commission: Commissioner (1982–1986), Chairman (1984–1986); Redlands Chili Cookoff and Fireman's Muster: Member (1982–Present), Chairman (1985–Present); Director (1984–Present), Redlands 4th of July Committee; Redlands Bicycle Classic: Chairman, Prime Committee (1985–1988), Director (1987–Present), President (1992–Present); Redlands YMCA: Director (1994–Present), Chairman, Sustaining Membership Campaign (1994–Present), Chairman, Building and Grounds (1995–Present); Director (1987–1989), Redlands Town Center Corporation; Director (1980–1986), Redlands Economic Development Corporation; Trustee (1979–1982), Redlands United Church of Christ; Member (1982–1985), Bank of Redlands Advisory Board; Director (1984–1990), Inland Action, Inc.; Redlands Dive Club: Founder (1988), President (1988–1993). **Education:** McGeorge School of Law University of the Pacific, J.D. (1976); University of California – Berkeley, M.B.A. in Real Estate and Finance (1973); Stanford University, B.A. in History and Biology (1971). **Personal:** Married to Cathy L. in 1990. Five children: Amy, Travis, Stephanie, Jessica, and Scott. Mr. Reynolds enjoys water skiing, tennis, racquetball, golf, swimming, jogging, scuba diving, and weightlifting.

Jesse J. Richardson Jr.

President and Attorney
Jesse J. Richardson, Jr., P.C.
115 South Kent Street
Winchester, VA 22601–5051
(540) 722–0325
Fax: (540) 722–0327

8111

Business Information: Jesse J. Richardson, Jr., P.C., established in 1993, is a full–service, general practice law firm, concentrating in civil law, environmental law and litigation. Admitted to practice in state and federal courts, Mr. Richardson serves as sole owner of this two–attorney law firm. He is responsible for all aspects of operations, concentrating in business planning (land use and local taxation), environmental law, real estate, estate planning, employment law, federal and state courts litigation, and local government law. Concurrent with his legal practice, he serves as Visiting Adjunct Lecturer of Agricultural and Environmental Law at Virginia Polytechnic Institute and State University in the Department of Agricultural and Applied Economics. **Career Steps:** President and Attorney, Jesse J. Richardson, Jr., P.C. (1993–Present); Virginia Polytechnic Institute and State University, Department of Agricultural and Applied Economics: Visiting Adjunct Lecturer of Agricultural and Environmental Law (1994–Present), Graduate Research Assistant (1991–1993); Law Clerk, City of Winchester, Virginia, City Attorney's Office (1991–1993); Hazel & Thomas, P.C.: Summer Law Clerk (Summer 1986), Associate Attorney (1987–1991). **Associations & Accomplishments:** American Bar Association; American Agricultural Law Association; Virginia Bar Association–Young Lawyer's Committee, Special Project–Agricultural Law; Winchester–Frederick County Bar Association; University of Virginia School of Law Alumni Association–Young Lawyers Committee; University of Virginia School of Law First Year Oral Arguments–Chief Justice; Lawyers v. Doctors Softball (to benefit The March of Dimes and The Shelter for Abused Women); Lawyer v. Doctors Basketball (March of Dimes); Outstanding Chapter Officer, Virginia Tech Alumni Association (1994); Named to Outstanding Young Men in America (1992); Frederick County FFA Parents and Alumni Association–President (1989–1991), Vice President; Shenandoah Chapter, Virginia Tech Alumni Association–President (1993), President–Elect, Vice President, Secretary; Virginia Tech College of Agriculture Alumni Association–County Coordinator; Winchester–Frederick County Chamber of Commerce–President's Club; Shenandoah Apple Blossom Festival: In–Town Membership Committee, Judge for Out–of–Town Honorary Fire Chief Contest; First Night Winchester–Solicitor, Volunteer; James Wood High School Class of 1980–Reunion Committee; Doo Dah Day Parade (to benefit abused children); Shenandoah University Athletic Association Advisory Board; The Great American Duck Race (Winchester, Virginia)–Duck Marshall; Shenandoah University Athletic Association Board; Frederick County–Winchester Boy Scout Law Enforcement Camporee; Recipient of a full four year scholarship; Graduate of an Urban Affairs Scholarship; Collegiate Future Farmers of American: President, Vice President; Agricultural Club Council; College of Agriculture Newsletter–Business Editor, Staff Writer; Phi Kappa Pi Honor Society; Gamma Sigma Delta Agricultural Honor Society; National Dean's List; Who's Who Among Students at American Colleges and Universities; Numerous publications, seminars and presentations. **Education:** University of Virginia School of Law, J.D. (1987); Virginia Polytechnic Institute and State University, M.S. in Agricultural and Applied Economics (1995); B.S. in Agricultural Economics (1984), magna cum laude. **Personal:** Mr. Richardson enjoys running, biking, and college basketball.

Michael P. Richman

Attorney and Partner
Mayer Brown Et Al
1675 Broadway
New York, NY 10019–5820
(212) 506–2505
Fax: (212) 262–1910

8111

Business Information: One of the ten largest Firms in the U.S., Mayer Brown, et al is an international premier law firm. Established in 1881 with headquarters in New York City, the

Firm currently employs over 1,000 attorneys and legal support staff in satellite offices in London, Brussels, Berlin and Mexico City. As Attorney and Partner, Mr. Richman concentrates his practice in the areas of bankruptcy litigation and creditor's rights. A practicing attorney since 1979, he is admitted to both State and Federal courts. One of his landmark cases was serving as counsel to ten foreign banks in a bankruptcy case versus a major international holding company. He was able to arbitrate and return over 80% of assets to the Banks. **Career Steps:** Attorney and Partner, Mayer Brown et al (1989–Present); Associate: Rosenman & Colin (1986–1989), Schocman, Marsh et al (1984–1986), Covington & Burling (1979–1984). **Associations & Accomplishments:** American Bar Association; Association of the Bar of the City of New York; American Bankruptcy Institute; New York State Bar Association. **Education:** Columbia Law School, J.D. (1979); Vassar College, A.B. cum laude (1975). **Personal:** Married to Elizabeth Fried in 1977. Two children: Joseph and Peter. Mr. Richman enjoys music, running and tennis.

Michael S. Richmond
Senior Partner
Richmond, Hochron & Burns
209 North Center Drive
North Brunswick, NJ 08902
(908) 821–0200
Fax: (908) 422–9444

8111

Business Information: Richmond, Hochron & Burns is a law firm concentrating in health law, matrimonial, criminal and municipal court practice, business planning, personal financial planning, bankruptcy and collections, real estate, and litigation. A practicing attorney in New Jersey since 1974, Mr. Richmond co–founded the Firm with Keith J. Burns and Stuart M. Hochron, M.D. in 1994. He is responsible for the bankruptcy and collection, real estate, personal financial planning, and criminal and municipal court areas of the Firm. He serves as the Municipal Prosecutor for South Brunswick Township and Milltown Borough. He has served as the Municipal Prosecutor for Franklin Township, Somerset County, Millstone Borough, and as Public Defender for Plainsboro Township. **Career Steps:** Senior Partner, Richmond, Hochron & Burns (1994–Present); Attorney, Michael S. Richmond, Esq. (1986–1994); Partner, Golden, Shore, Zahn & Richmond (1977–1986). **Associations & Accomplishments:** Co–author with Keith Burns of "Municipal Court Practice in New Jersey"; Candidate for State Senate (1987); American Bar Association, Section Business Law; New Jersey State Bar Association; Middlesex County Bar Association; Vice President, Middlesex County Municipal Prosecutors Association (1986–Present); Middlesex County Chairman for the candidacies of Jim Courter for Governor; Dick Zimmer for Congress; Jim Courter for Congress and Pete Inverso for State Senate, Paul Kramer and Barbara Wright for Assembly; Republican Committeeman, Middlesex County; Counsel to Local Boards of Health Association of New Jersey; Former counsel to Fire Districts 1 & 2 South Brunswick Township; Former counsel to the South Brunswick Fire Prevention Bureau; Former Assistant Township Attorney for South Brunswick; Counsel to the Spotswood Senior Citizens Housing Corporation and the Older American Housing Corporation in Spotswood. **Education:** University of Kansas – Law School, J.D. (1973); Lafayette College, A.B. (1970). **Personal:** Married to Marguerite E. "Cookie" in 1979. One child: Lori–Ann Richmond, born 11/14/80. Four step–children: Dalton D., David K., Michael B., and Theresa L. Featherston. Mr. Richmond enjoys computers, history, games, and genealogy.

Mr. William Campbell Ries
Partner
Dickie, McCamey & Chilcote
Two PPG Place, Suite 400
Pittsburgh, PA 15222
(412) 392–5477
Fax: (412) 392–5367

8111

Business Information: Dickie, McCamey & Chilcote is a full–service law firm. Its practice includes financial affairs and investment law. As Partner and Attorney, Mr. Ries is responsible for all aspects of this practice. In addition to his duties with the Firm, he is an Adjunct Professor of Law at Duquesne University School of Law. Established in the 1900's, Dickie, McCamey & Chilcote presently employs 300 professionals. **Career Steps:** Partner, Dickie, McCamey & Chilcote (1990–Present); Managing Counsel–Trust and Investment Services, Mellon Bank (1971–1990). **Associations & Accomplishments:** Chairman of the Trust and Investment Services Committee, American Bar Association; Pennsylvania Joint State Government Commission Advisory Committee; Former Co–Chair, National Conference of Lawyers and Corporate Fiduciaries; Former Chair, American Bankers Association – Trust Counsel Committee; Fellow of the American Bar Foundation; Councilman, McCandless Town Council; Frequent speaker and author. **Education:** Carnegie–Mellon University Graduate School of Industrial Administration – Executive Program

(1980); Duquesne University School of Law, J.D. (1974); the Catholic University of America, A.B. (1970).

Dr. Richard L. Rikard
Attorney
The Law Office of Richard L. Rikard
6055 Privacy Parkway, Suite 115
Memphis, TN 38119
(901) 685–8600
Fax: (901) 685–8616

8111

Business Information: The Law Office of Richard L. Rikard is a general practice law firm providing legal services to the community. Establishing the firm in 1992, Mr. Rikard is trial Attorney admitted to both State and Federal courts. He concentrates his practice in the areas of litigation and trial work, providing all forms of legal consultation, with the exception of felony and real estate law. Mr. Rikard serves clients within a 200 mile radius, and looks forward to the day that he is able to practice before the United States Supreme Court. **Career Steps:** Attorney, The Law Office of Richard L. Rikard (1992–Present); Quality Control, Kroger (up to 1989). **Associations & Accomplishments:** Tennessee Trial Lawyer's Association; Association of Trial Lawyer's of America. **Education:** University of Memphis: J.D. (1992), B.S. (1989). **Personal:** Two children: Danielle and Michael. Dr. Rikard enjoys being with his family and working on his computer.

Jerome L. Ringler
Partner
Fogel, Feldman, Ostrov, Ringler & Klevens
1620 26th Street, Suite 100–S
Santa Monica, CA 90404–4013
(310) 453–6711
Fax: (210) 828–2191

8111

Business Information: Fogel, Feldman, Ostrov, Ringler & Klevens is a full–service, general practice law firm specializing in civil litigation matters. A practicing attorney since 1974, Mr. Ringler joined the Firm as an associate in 1976, later to become a Partner in 1982. Admitted to practice in state and federal courts, he specializes in personal injury trial work, product liability, medical malpractice, FELA, and construction cases. **Career Steps:** Partner, Fogel, Feldman, Ostrov, Ringler & Klevens (1976–Present). **Associations & Accomplishments:** American Board of Trial Advocates (ABOTA); Associate (1988), Advocate (1991); Master, American Inns of Court (1991 & 1992); Los Angeles County Bar Association; California Bar Association (1974); American Bar Association; American Trial Lawyers Association; California Trial Lawyers Association; Los Angeles Trial Lawyers Association; Board of Governors (1980–1987) and Executive Board (1988–Present), Trial Lawyer of the Year (1987), Treasurer (1988), Secretary (1989), Vice President (1990), President–Elect (1991), and President (1992); California Bar (1974); California U.S. Court of Appeals, 9th Circuit, and U.S. District Court, Northern District of California (1974); U.S. District Court, Central District Court of California (1975); U.S. District Court, Southern District of California (1981); Arbitrator, Los Angeles Superior Court Arbitration Program (1980–1985); Practice Areas: civil litigation, tort litigation, railroad law, construction law, products liability law, medical negligence actions, and business torts. Listed In: The Best Lawyers in America, Marquis Who's Who in American Law. **Education:** University of San Francisco, J.D. (1974); Michigan State University, B.A. (1970). **Personal:** Married to Bonnie Mass in 1987. Mr. Ringler enjoys skiing and tennis.

Andrew Rinker Jr.
Partner
Chaffe, McCall, Phillips, Toler & Sarpy
2300 Energy Centre, 1100 Poydras Street
New Orleans, LA 70163–2300
(504) 585–7000
Fax: (504) 585–7075

8111

Business Information: Chaffe, McCall, Phillips, Toler & Sarpy is a full–service law firm. Established in 1826, the Firm presently employs 200 people. As Partner, Mr. Rinker handles mergers, acquisitions, financings, and valuations. He also serves as Managing Partner for Legacy Capital, Inc. – an investment banking company handling sales and financing of companies, mergers and acquisitions, and consulting for entities seeking to go public. **Career Steps:** Partner, Chaffe, McCall, Phillips, Toler & Sarpy (1982–Present); Managing Director, Legacy Capital, Inc. (1993–Present). **Associations & Accomplishments:** Board Member and Major Gifts Chair-

man, New Orleans Educational Television Foundation; Founding Director, Young Leadership Council; Council Member, Louisiana State Law Institute; Board Member, Bureau of Government Research; Order of the Coif; Editor–in–Chief, Tulane Law Review; Omicron Delta Kappa; Mortar Board; American, Louisiana, and New Orleans Bar Associations. **Education:** Tulane University, J.D. (1982); Louisiana State University: B.S. in Finance (1978), M.B.A. (1981).

Brenda F. Rioles, J.D.

Owner and Attorney
Rioles Law Office
426 Broadway
Providence, RI 02909
(401) 831–8077
Fax: (401) 273–1371

8111

Business Information: Rioles Law Office, established in 1986, is a full–service, general practice law firm concentrating in trial litigation, contested divorce litigation, and criminal litigation. Admitted to practice in Rhode Island state courts, Ms. Rioles serves as Owner and Attorney. She is responsible for all aspects of operations, concentrating in trial litigations. **Career Steps:** Owner and Attorney, Rioles Law Office (1986–Present); Owner and Proprietor, Little Brown Derby Restaurant (1983–1986). **Associations & Accomplishments:** American Bar Association; Rhode Island Family Court Bench/Bar Committee; American Family Law Inn of Court – Barrister. **Education:** New England School of Law, J.D., summa cum laude (1986). **Personal:** Ms. Rioles enjoys sports cars, motorcycles, and her dogs.

Elizabeth A. Ritter, Esq.
Senior Partner
Ponce & Ritter
14369 Park Avenue, Suite 200
Victorville, CA 92392–2300
(619) 241–4577
Fax: (619) 241–6474

8111

Business Information: Ponce & Ritter is a general, civil practice law firm, serving clients from two locations within the San Bernardino County, California area. A practicing attorney in California state and federal courts since 1983, Elizabeth Ritter serves as Senior Partner, founding the Firm in 1992. Sharing administrative supervision of both locations with her partner for a legal and administrative support staff of twelve, Ms. Ritter concentrates her practice in the areas of family law. **Career Steps:** Senior Partner, Ponce & Ritter (1992–Present); Managing Partner, Hirschi, Clark, Mederos, Ponce & Ritter (1990–1992); Associate, Hirschi & Clark (1989–1990). **Associations & Accomplishments:** American Bar Association; San Bernardino County Bar Association; High Desert Bar Association; Delta Theta Phi; Republican Women's Club. **Education:** Southwestern University School of Law, J.D. (1983); Lafayette College, B.A. (1977). **Personal:** Married to Edward J. LeClere in 1985. Two children: Andrew Charles and Matthew Edward Ritter LeClere. Ms. Ritter enjoys photography, needlepoint, gardening and politics.

Jose Juan Belen Rivera, Esq.

President
Belen–Rivera & Associates
50 Acuamarina Street, Villa Blanca
Caguas, Puerto Rico 00725
(787) 258–1336
Fax: (787) 258–1337

8111

Business Information: Belen–Rivera & Associates is a general practice law firm concentrating on corporate, financial, and credit union law. A practicing attorney in Puerto Rico state and federal courts since obtaining his degree in 1988, Mr. Belen–Rivera founded the Firm in 1992. As the Firm Administrator, he is responsible for counseling and litigation. **Career Steps:** President, Belen–Rivera & Associates (1989–Present); Chairman, Coop. de Seguros Multiples (1993). **Associations & Accomplishments:** Colegio de Abogados de Puerto Rico; Federal Bar Association; Hispanic Bar Association; APACEDO, Handicapped Children Parents Association. **Education:** University of Puerto Rico: J.D. (1988), B.A. **Personal:** Married to Carmen Concepcion. Two children: Sahira Vanessa and Laura Josel Belen Concepcion. Mr. Rivera enjoys boating.

Rafael Angulo Rivera

Sole Practitioner

Law Office of Rafael Angulo Rivera

Laguna Gardens Shopping Center, Suite 201, Isle Verde
Carolina, Puerto Rico 00979
(787) 791–4400
Fax: (787) 253–7302

8111

Business Information: Law Office of Rafael Angulo Rivera is a full service, general practice law firm specializing in civil law issues. A practicing attorney in Puerto Rico state courts since 1967, Mr. Rivera established his sole practice law office in 1968. He is responsible for all administrative operations for associates and support staff, in addition to his daily law practice. **Career Steps:** Sole Practitioner, Law Office of Rafael Angulo Rivera (1968–Present). **Associations & Accomplishments:** Puerto Rico Bar Association. **Education:** Catholic University, J.D. (1967). **Personal:** Three children: Leslia D., Rafael, and Sarika J. Mr. Rivera enjoys writing, playing tennis, and reading.

Julian R. Rivera–Aspinall

Attorney

Otero Suro Law Firm

Urb Mayorca R–11 Calle Nebraska
Guaynabo, Puerto Rico 00969–3907
(809) 753–9154
Fax: (809) 765–7347

8111

Business Information: Otero Suro Law Firm, established in 1942, is a full–service, general practice law firm, concentrating on bankruptcy and civil litigation. Joining the firm upon conferral of his law degree in 1991, Mr. Rivera–Aspinall focuses his practice on commercial litgation and tort law. **Career Steps:** Attorney, Otero Suro Law Firm (1991–Present); Captain, United States Army (1982–1988). **Associations & Accomplishments:** American Bar Association; Federal Bar Association; Association of the United States Army. **Education:** Inter–American University, J.D. (1991); High Point College, B.A. **Personal:** Married to Pia in 1986. Three children: Maria, Isabel, and Julian. Mr. Rivera–Aspinall enjoys golf and scuba diving.

Melba N. Rivera–Camacho

Partner

Rivera, Requena & Associates

3K S1 Avenue Fragoso
Carolina, Puerto Rico 00983
(809) 276–5348
Fax: (809) 750–2545

8111

Business Information: Rivera, Requena & Associates is a full–service, general practice law firm, concentrating on Social Security, Worker's Compensation, state insurance fund, civil, family relation, and tort law issues. A practicing attorney in Puerto Rico Federal and State courts since 1986, Ms. Rivera–Camacho joined the Firm as Partner in 1994. Her areas of concentration focus on medical and legal malpractice cases, Social Security issues, and tort law. **Career Steps:** Partner, Rivera, Requena & Associates (1994–Present); Attorney, Juan A. Hernandez & Associates (1989–1994). **Associations & Accomplishments:** Puerto Rico Bar Association; Public Notary Association; Admitted to practice in Puerto Rico Federal District Court/Circuit Court – 1st Circuit Court/Circuit Court for the Federal Circuit/Court of Veterans Appeals. **Education:** Interamerican University, J.D. (1986); University of Puerto Rico: B.S. (1984), currently working toward a Master's Degree. **Personal:** Ms. Rivera–Camacho enjoys singing, tennis, concerts, theater, and attending Broadway musicals.

Ana I. Rivera–Lassen

Senior Partner

Rivera–Lassen & Associates

131 Eleanor Roosevelt
San Juan, Puerto Rico 00918–3106
(809) 753–6430
Fax: (809) 753–6430
EMAIL: See Below

8111

Business Information: Rivera–Lassen & Associates is a full–service, private practice law firm, concentrating on civil litigation, family law, and corporate law. A practicing attorney in Puerto Rico state courts since 1977, Ms. Rivera–Lassen established her sole practice law firm in 1987. Currently serving as Senior Partner, she oversees all aspects of operations, in addition to her daily law practice. Internet users can reach her via: ANARLPEM@IGC.APC.ORG. **Career Steps:** Senior Partner, Rivera–Lassen & Associates (1987–Present); Senior Partner, Rivera, Mendez & Viverito (1983–1987); Partner, Cruz, Martinez & Rivera (1978–1983); Part–time Professor of Social Sciences Department, Interamerican University of Puerto Rico (1992–Present); Curriculum Designer and Script Writer for Television Program Social Sciences 101, Metropolitan University of Puerto Rico; Curriculum Designer, Script Writer, and Producer of Educational Programs, Social Sciences 101–102, Puerto Rico Junior College, Center of Education Television (1978–1980); Law Clerk, Torres Peralt's Law Office (1977–1978); Librarian Assistant, Zenobia and Juan Ramon Jimenez Section of the General Library University of Puerto Rico (1974–1977); Teacher Assistant, Dos Pinos Cooperative School (1973–1974); Research Assistant, Center for Environmental and Consumer Justice (1973). **Associations & Accomplishments:** Vice President of Commission for Women's Rights, Puerto Rico Bar Association (1981); Advisor on Women's Issues, President of the Senate of Puerto Rico (1984–1988); Women and the Law Steering Committee, 12th National Conference (1980); Youth Representative, Commission for the Betterment of Women's Rights (1974–1995); Speaker, Feministas en Marcha (F.E.M.); Latin American Solidarity Network; Caribbean Association for Feminist Research and Action; Latina: Partners for Health; Latin American Studies Association. **Education:** University of Puerto Rico – Rio Piedras Campus: J.D. (1977), B.A. in Humanities cum laude (1974). **Personal:** Ms. Rivera–Lassen enjoys being active in feminist organizations.

Annette Rivero–Marin, Esq.

Associate

Enrique Umpierre Suarez Law Firm

Esquire Building, Suite 700
Hato Rey, Puerto Rico 00918
(787) 753–1039
Fax: (787) 765–3101

8111

Business Information: Enrique Umpierre Suarez Law Firm is a full–service, general practice law firm. A practicing attorney in Puerto Rican courts since 1994, Ms. Rivero–Marin joined the Firm in 1995. As an Associate, she practices civil litigation and construction law. She also serves as the Office Manager, in charge of supervising employees and any employee–related matters. Additionally, she is a notary public for Puerto Rico. **Career Steps:** Associate, Enrique Umpierre Suarez Law Firm (1995–Present); Associate and Notary Public, Del Toro & Santana Law Firm (1994–1995); Law Clerk, Bufete Santiago Guzman, Esquilin (1993). **Associations & Accomplishments:** American Bar Association; Colegio de Abogados de Puerto Rico; Editor, Carta Noticiosa del Butete Enrique Umpierre Suarez; All American Scholar Award (1993); High School Class Valedictorian (1982); Member of Who's Who Among American High School Students; Society of Distinguished American High School Students; The National Honor Society (Historian). **Education:** University of Puerto Rico, J.D., magna cum laude and Law Review (1994); Yale University, Bachelor of Arts in Comparative Literature (1986). **Personal:** Married to Gilberto Colon in 1996. Five children: Annelise & Gabriella Rivera Rivero, and Gilberto, Luis, & Gloria Colon. Ms. Rivero–Marin enjoys reading, cooking, travel, and writing poetry and children's stories.

Mr. Randal W. Roahrig

Senior Attorney

Randal W. Roahrig & Associates, Attorneys at Law

1512 Princeton Avenue
Princeton, WV 24740–2732
(304) 425–2116
Fax: Please mail or call

8111

Business Information: Randal W. Roahrig & Associates, Attorneys at Law is a full–service, general law firm. Established in 1992, the Firm currently employs two full–time attorneys. As Senior Attorney, Mr. Roahrig concentrates his practice in the areas of personal injury and bankruptcy. A trial attorney since 1978, Mr. Roahrig is admitted to both State and Federal courts. **Career Steps:** Senior Attorney, Randal W. Roahrig & Associates, Attorneys at Law (1992–Present); Attorney, Princeton Rescue Squad; City Attorney, City of Hinton, WV (1980's). **Associations & Accomplishments:** American Bar Association; American Trial Lawyers Association; West Virginia Bar Association; West Virginia Trial Lawyers Association; Board of Directors and Officer, Southern Highland Community Mental Health Center (1980's). **Education:** Washington Lee University, J.D. (1978); Ball State University, B.S. magna cum laude (1975). **Personal:** Married to Mary B. in 1991. One child: Travis Wade. Mr. Roahrig enjoys skiing and the outdoors.

James T. Robertson

Attorney

The Law Office of James T. Robertson

922 Kentucky Home Life Buidling
Louisville, KY 40202
(502) 583–6521
Fax: (502) 583–6522

8111

Business Information: The Law Office of James T. Robertson is a Legal Office specializing in torts, Constitutional Law, Income Tax and Estate cases. As a Trial Attorney, Mr. Robertson has litigated cases for Churchill Downs (The Kentucky Derby) to close another race track in Louisville, and has represented H.L. Hunt and Colonel Curtis B. Dall (President Roosevelt's son–in–law) in Constitutional matters. Mr. Robertson is in charge of public relations, administrative concerns, daily operations, and strategic planning for the Office. **Career Steps:** Attorney, The Law Office of James T. Robertson. **Associations & Accomplishments:** American Trial Lawyers Association; Kentucky Association of Trial Lawyers; Kentucky Bar Association; Louisville Bar Association; Kiwanis Club of Louisville; Executive Club; Filson Club; Sons of the American Revolution; Civil War Round Table; Board of Directors, L Club (University of Louisville Hall of Fame). Education: University of Virginia School of Law, Doctor of Law and B.L.; University of Louisville, B.A. **Personal:** Married to Laverne. Two children: James T. Jr. and Beverly Ann Robertson Clark.

John Marion Robinson

Attorney and Municipal Judge

John Marion Robinson, Attorney at Law

206 Butler Street
Springhill, LA 71075–2732
(318) 539–2557
Fax: (318) 539–2557

8111

Business Information: A practicing attorney in Louisiana state courts since 1974, Mr. Robinson established his sole practice, general law office in 1988. His practice concentrates on civil law cases, providing legal representation to the Firm's clientele and conducting pro bono work. Concurrent with his private law practice, he serves as an elected Municipal Judge (first elected in 1986 to fill an unexpired term, then reelected in 1990). **Career Steps:** Sole Practitioner, John Marion Robinson: Attorney at Law (1988–Present), Municipal Judge (1986–Present); Partner, Fish, Montgomery & Robinson (1977–1988). **Associations & Accomplishments:** Louisiana Council of Juvenile and Family Law Judges: Former President, Sustained Member; Webster Parish Bar Association: Former President, Sustained Member; Springhill Lions Club: Former President, Sustained Member; Springhill Shrine Club: Former President, Sustained Member. **Education:** Louisiana State University Law School, J.D. (1974); Louisiana State University, B.S. (1971). **Personal:** Married to Cindy in 1973. Two children: Eric and Kyle. Mr. Robinson enjoys hunting and golf.

Michael R.L. Robinson

Controller

Barclay Law Corporation

5000 Birch Street, Suite 2900
Newport Beach, CA 92660–2139
(714) 476–2672
Fax: (714) 476–2383
EMAIL: See Below

8111

Business Information: Barclay Law Corporation is a law office specializing in civil, real estate, estate planning, and corporate banking law. The firm, with five attorneys on staff, has clients throughout the United States and some international clients as well. As Controller, Mr. Robinson is responsible for maintaining the financial records of the firm. Mr. Robinson is in charge of human resource management also. His long range plans are to become more involved with, and eventually maintain complete control of all financial aspects of the firm. Internet users can also reach him via: RayRobin@aol.com **Career Steps:** Barclay Law Corporation: Controller (1994–Present), A/R, Assistant Controller (1991–1994); Office Assistant, Banner, Birch, McKie and Beckett (1990–1991); Bookkeeper, Martin Lawernce Galleries (1990). **Associations & Accomplishments:** Chair, Elections Committee of the County of Orange; Committee to Elect Libby Cowan – Costa Mesa City Council; Delegate, L.I.F.E./AIDS Lobby; Log Cabin Republican. **Education:** University of California – Irvine, B.A. (1995); Attended, John Hopkins University, general course work in Political Science. **Personal:** Mr. Robinson enjoys running, hiking, sky diving, and tennis.

Arlene Rochelle
Marketing Manager
Cox Castle & Nicholson
2049 Century Park East, Floor 28
Los Angeles, CA 90067
(310) 284–2222
Fax: (310) 277–7889
arochel@primenet.com

8111

Business Information: Cox Castle & Nicholson specializes in providing real estate–associated legal services. As Marketing Manager, Ms. Rochelle is responsible for managing the marketing department in all marketing and client development activities, including marketing and client development. Internet users can reach her via: arochel@primenet.com **Career Steps:** Marketing Manager, Cox Castle & Nicholson (1995–Present); CB Commercial Real Estate Group, Inc.: Manager of Market Research and Technology (1994–1995), Assistant Account Officer (1992–1994), Marketing Coordinator (1990–1992). **Associations & Accomplishments:** American Marketing Association; National Law Firm Marketing Association; Public Relations Society; Notary Public; California Real Estate Salesperson License. **Education:** Azusa Pacific University, M.B.A. (1994); Ambassador University, B.A. (1987). **Personal:** Married to Michael in 1991. Ms. Rochelle enjoys golf, tennis, and dance.

Luis Guillermo Leon Rodriguez
Lawyer
The Law Office of Luis Guillermo Leon Rodriguez
Urb Morell Campos Street #2 Figaro
Ponce, Puerto Rico 00731–2764
(809) 840–5471
Fax: (809) 840–5471

8111

Business Information: The Law Office of Luis Guillermo Leon Rodriguez is a full–service, general practice law firm, specializing in criminal law. A practicing attorney in Puerto Rico courts since 1992, Mr. Rodriguez established his sole practice law firm in 1995. He is responsible for all aspects of operations, including overseeing all administrative operations of two associates, in addition to his private law practice. **Career Steps:** Lawyer, The Law Office of Luis Guillermo Leon Rodriguez (1995–Present); Lawyer, Senate of Puerto Rico (1992). **Associations & Accomplishments:** American Bar Association; Colegio de Abogados de Puerto Rico. **Education:** P.U.C.P.R., J.D. (1992). **Personal:** Married to Lizette M. Alvarado in 1986. Two children: Luis G. Leon and Helen Marie Leon.

Milagros Alicea Rodriguez
Attorney/Owner
Milagros Alicea Rodriguez
DW 429 Marg Rambla 301
Ponce, Puerto Rico 00731
(787) 843–5369
Fax: (787) 843–5369

8111

Business Information: An attorney since 1992, Mrs. Alicea Rodriguez established her private law firm in 1995, concentrating in civil law. In addition, she writes weekly articles for the local newspaper – "La Perla del Sur" – regarding legal issues, the rights of the public, and general law. **Career Steps:** Attorney/Owner, Milagros Alicea Rodriguez (1995–Present); Professor, Candido Martinez School of Real Estates (1996); Administrative Judge, Department of Consumer Affairs (1992–1994). **Associations & Accomplishments:** Notary Association of Puerto Rico; Legal Fraternity of Puerto Rico; Lawyers Association of Puerto Rico. **Education:** Pontifical Catholic University of Puerto Rico: J.D. (1992), B.A. (1988). **Personal:** Married to Felix E. Negron in 1978. One child: Angelica M. Negron Rodriguez. Mrs. Rodriguez enjoys writing articles.

Juan Ramon Rodriguez Lopez, Esquire
Attorney/Managing Partner
Rodriguez Lopez Law Office
P.O. Box 41236
San Juan, Puerto Rico 00940–1236
(787) 792–2482
Fax: (787) 273–9033

8111

Business Information: Rodriguez Lopez Law Office is a general practice law firm focusing on civil cases, especially tort claims. Consisting of 2 attorneys, the Firm serves clients throughout Puerto Rico. As Attorney/Managing Partner, Mr. Rodriguez Lopez works with his brother, who is the other attorney in the Firm. Mr. Rodriguez Lopez handles pro bono work with the state courts and provides legal services for corporations that are assigned to him. **Career Steps:** Attorney/Managing Partner, Rodriguez Lopez Law Office (1995–Present); Executive Vice President, Marketing Industry and Food Distribution Association (1994–1995); Assistant Secretary, Department of Consumer Affairs (1993–1994); Associate, Matta & Matta Law Office (1992–1993). **Associations & Accomplishments:** Chamber of Commerce of Puerto Rico; U.S. Army National Guard; Phi Alpha Delta International; Colegio De Abogados De Puerto Rico; National Conference on Weights and Measures; Food Marketing Institute. **Education:** Interamerican University, M.A. in Labor Relations (In Progress); Catholic University of Puerto Rico Law School: D.A. in Science, Associate Degree in Natural Sciences. **Personal:** Mr. Rodriguez Lopez enjoys water sports, scuba diving, and sailing.

Carmen T. Rodriguez–Alicia
Attorney
Law Office of Carmen T. Rodriguez–Alicia
P.O. Box 312
Gurabo, Puerto Rico 00778–0312
(809) 737–3743
Fax: Please mail or call

8111

Business Information: Law Office of Carmen T. Rodriguez–Alicia is a full–service, general practice law firm. A practicing attorney in Puerto Rico courts since 1985, Ms. Rodriguez–Alicia established this Practice in 1987. Her practice concentrates on criminal and general law issues. **Career Steps:** Attorney, Law Office of Carmen T. Rodriguez–Alicia (1987–Present); Attorney, Legal Services of Puerto Rico (1986–1987); Manager Carmera– Mundi, Inc. (1981–1985). **Associations & Accomplishments:** Colegio de Abogados de Puerto Rico; Asociacion de Notarios de Puerto Rico. **Education:** Interamerican University, J.D. (1985); University of Puerto Rico, B.A. **Personal:** One child: Mara T. Acevedo Rodriguez. Ms. Rodriguez–Alicia enjoys reading.

Lilia R. Rodriguez–Ruiz
Partner
McConnell Valdes
P.O. Box 364225
San Juan, Puerto Rico 00936–4225
(809) 250–5651
Fax: (809) 759–9225
EMAIL: See Below

8111

Business Information: McConnell Valde's, the biggest law firm in Puerto Rico and the Caribbean, is a full–service firm. The Firm provides legal services in four major areas: corporate, taxes, labor and employment, and litigations. Future plans include expanding the Firm into other areas of the Caribbean and into Latin America. Established in 1946, the Firm currently employs 115 attorneys and over 85 legal and administrative support staff. A practicing attorney in Puerto Rico since 1990, Mrs. Rodriguez–Ruiz joined the Firm as a law clerk in 1988. At present, serving as Partner in the Litigation Department, her practice concentrates in general civil and commercial litigation in various administrative agencies and in both Federal and State courts. She can also be reached through the Internet via: LR@MCVPR.COM or LR+aMV%McConnell_Valdes@MCIMAIL.COM **Career Steps:** Partner, McConnell Valdes (1995–Present); Park Ranger, U.S. Department of Interior (1988 and 1989); Law Clerk, McConnell Valdes (1988–1989). **Associations & Accomplishments:** American Bar Association; Federal Bar Association; Hispanic National Bar Association; Puerto Rico Bar Association; "Asociacion de Notarios"; Lecturer at U.P.R. Law School; and Speaks at seminars. **Education:** University of Puerto Rico Law School, J.D., magna cum laude (1990); University of Puerto Rico, Bachelor's Degree in Science, major in Biology, magna cum laude (1987). **Personal:** Married to Luis A. Gierbolini in 1995. Mrs. Rodriguez–Ruiz enjoys scuba diving, volleyball, music, and the arts.

Lawrence D. Rohlfing
Owner and Proprietor
Law Offices of Lawrence D. Rohlfing
12631 East Imperial Highway, Suite C–115
Santa Fe Springs, CA 90670–4710
(310) 868–5886
Fax: Please mail or call

8111

Business Information: Law Offices of Lawrence D. Rohlfing, established in 1989, is a full–service, general practice law firm. A practicing attorney in California and Arizona state and federal courts since 1985, Mr. Rohlfing established his private law firm in 1989. As owner and proprietor of this two–attorney firm, he oversees all administrative functions and support staff, as well as his daily client representation. He concentrates his legal practice primarily on social security disability and ERISA disability claims. **Career Steps:** Sole Proprietor, Law Offices of Lawrence D. Rohlfing (1989–Present); Partner, Rohlfing & Donnelly (1987–1989); Partner, Williams & Rohlfing (1985–1987). **Associations & Accomplishments:** National Organization of Social Security Claimants' Representatives; Treasurer, Los Angeles County Bar Association and Social Security Section; Association of Trial Lawyers of America; California Trial Lawyers Association; Los Angeles Trial Lawyers Association; American Bar Association. **Education:** Whittier College School of Law, J.D. cum laude (1985); Whittier College, B.A. (1982). **Personal:** Three children: Eric, Jessica, and Maureen. Mr. Rohlfing enjoys scuba diving, hunting, fishing, and coaching his son's Little League team.

Fabio A. Roman Garcia
Sole Practitioner
Fabio A. Roman Garcia
P.O. Box 1121
Arecibo, Puerto Rico 00613–1121
(787) 880–7677
Fax: (787) 880–1270

8111

Business Information: Fabio A. Roman Garcia is a full–service general practice law firm providing legal and notarial services. The Firm specializes in the representation of claimants for disability benefits before the Social Security Administration. A practicing attorney in Puerto Rico state courts since 1971, Mr. Roman Garcia is responsible for all administrative operations for support staff, in addition to his daily law practice. **Career Steps:** Sole Practitioner, Fabio A. Roman Garcia (1995–Present); Partner, Cordero, Gonzalez & Roman (1990–1995); Hearing Examiner, Superior Court – Arecibo, PR (1987–1990); Attorney, Private Practice (1979–1987). **Associations & Accomplishments:** Puerto Rico Bar Association; National Organization of Social Security Claimants' Representatives; National Guard Association of the U.S.; National Guard Association of Puerto Rico; Alumni Association of the Judge Advocate General School; Zeta Phi Beta Fraternity; Lieutenant Colonel, US Army Reserve (Retired). **Education:** University of Puerto Rico Law School, LL.B. (1971); University of Puerto Rico, B.B.A. (1968); Attended U.S. Army Command and General Staff School; U.S. Army Judge Advocate General's School, graduate of Basic and Advanced Courses **Personal:** Married to Miriam in 1982. Four children: Wanda, Yolanda, Fabienne, and Barbara. Mr. Roman Garcia enjoys playing the guitar and the "cuatro," a Puerto Rican folk instrument.

Laurie Romana Rivera Aviks
Esquire
Law Offices of Castillo & Rivera
P.O. Box 34462
Ft. Buchanon, Puerto Rico 00934
(787) 250–0650
Fax: (787) 747–0758

8111

Business Information: Law Offices of Castillo & Rivera is a general practice law firm, comprised of two attorneys, who specialize in federal and state court litigation. As Esquire, Ms. Rivera, Partner and Attorney, specializes in family and tort law, defending the rights of families. **Career Steps:** Esquire, Law Offices of Castillo & Rivera (1994–Present); Esquire, Sole Practitioner (1993); Esquire, Escudelo & Bonilla Law Office (1992); Spanish Teacher, Louisiana–Vernon Parish Leesville (1990–1992). **Associations & Accomplishments:** LDS; Puerto Rico Bar Association. **Education:** Inter–American University, J.D. (1985); University of Puerto Rico, B.A. in Political Science. **Personal:** Married to Graham A. in 1981. Three children: Paola Emelina, Paloma Eduvi, and Pamela Estefania. Ms. Romana Rivera Aviks enjoys kayaking, tennis, dance, and golf.

Mr. Victor K. Rones
Principal and Attorney
Margulies and Rones, P.A.
16105 NE 18th Avenue
Miami, FL 33162–4749
(305) 945–6522
Fax: Please mail or call

8111

Business Information: Margulies and Rones, P.A. is a general practice law firm. Established in 1983, the Firm currently employs 2 attorneys and legal support staff. As Principal and Attorney, Mr. Rones concentrates his practice in the areas of commercial, probate and personal injury law. A trial attorney since the conferral of his law degree in 1977, Mr. Rones is admitted to both State and Federal courts. **Career Steps:** Principal and Attorney, Margulies and Rones, P.A. (1983–Present). **Associations & Accomplishments:** Florida Bar Association; American Bar Association; American Trial Lawyers Association; Federal Trial Bar; Tax Court Bar; 11th Circuit Bar; 5th Circuit Bar. **Education:** University of Miami, LL.M. (1978); University of Florida: J.D., B.A. in Finance. **Personal:** Married to Ellen in 1977. Two children: Marshal and Jeremy.

Christian James Root
Senior Staff Attorney
Legal Aid for Broome and Chenango, Inc.
30 Fayette St.
Binghamton, NY 13901–3609
(607) 723–7966
Fax: (607) 724–7211

8111

Business Information: Legal Aid for Broome and Chenango, Inc. is a civil legal aid office, providing consumer litigation and family court services. The office has 6 attorneys on staff and employs 3 full–time paralegals. As Senior Staff Attorney, Mr. Root is responsible for litigation, computer technology, and phone systems. In addition, he is responsible for the supervision of the attorney and paralegal staff. **Career Steps:** Senior Staff Attorney, Legal Aid for Broome and Chenango, Inc. (1994–Present); Partner, Hartjen, Hudarich, and Root (1994); Staff Attorney, Broome Legal Assistance Corporation (1991–1993). **Associations & Accomplishments:** New York State Bar Association; Broome County Bar Association; American Bar Association; Pennsylvania Commonwealth Bar Association; Georgia Bar Association. **Education:** Vermont Law School, J.D. cum laude (1991); Rochester Institute of Technology, B.S. with honors; Broome Community College, A.A.S. **Personal:** Married to Stacy in 1992. Mr. Root enjoys computers, hockey, reading, and bodybuilding.

Engadi Rosario
Legal Counsel
The Law Office of Engadi Rosario
P.O. Box 38083
San Juan, Puerto Rico 00937–8083
(809) 282–6158
Fax: (809) 766–0609
Call Before Faxing

8111

Business Information: The Law Office of Engadi Rosario is a private full–service, civil and criminal practice law firm, specializing in all aspects of case litigation at local and federal courts and administrative forums. The Firm concentrates on medical malpractice, contracts, domestic relations, and administrative law. A practicing attorney in Puerto Rico courts since 1988, Ms. Rosario established her sole practice law firm in 1995. She operates a general litigation practice, as well as providing legal counsel to government agencies and private institutions. **Career Steps:** Legal Counsel, The Law Office of Engadi Rosario (1995–Present); Senate Health Commission, Legislature of Puerto Rico (1995); Legal Counsel, Puerto Rico Department of Health (1991–1994); Legal Counsel, Puerto Rico Department of Justice (1989–1991). **Associations & Accomplishments:** Colegio de Abogados; Pro–Bono, Inc.; Hogar El Buen Pastor; Invited speaker to University of Puerto Rico, School of Medicine in topics such as Legal and ethical aspects of Aids patience in the Odonthologist profession, PR laws and protection on reproductive issues and PR law on sex discrimination. **Education:** University of Valladolid – Spain, Currently attending for Doctoral Degree; Pontifical Catholic University of Puerto Rico: J.D. (1984), B.A. in Political Science (1980). **Personal:** Married to Ivan Rosario, M.D. in 1994. Ms. Rosario enjoys aerobics, camping, and rappelling.

Mr. Frederick W. (Bud) Rose
Partner
Cooper, Rose & English
480 Morris Avenue
Summit, NJ 07901–1583
(908) 273–1212
Fax: Please mail or call

8111

Business Information: Cooper, Rose & English is a national, full–service, general practice law firm, concentrating in corporate litigation, environmental law, estate & tax law, and some municipal pro–bono work. Merging from two enterprises in 1994, the Firm operates an interstate practice in federal courts in Massachusetts, New York, Alaska, and New Jersey. Future plans include expanding to other states. The Firm currently employs 28 lawyers within two offices. A practicing attorney for 35 years, Mr. Rose has been with the Firm since it merged in 1994 and serves as Partner and Trial Attorney. He is re-

sponsible for the legal representation of corporate CEO's, professionals and business owners in state and federal courts. He has defended Corning University in federal court suits and many other significant cases. **Career Steps:** Partner, Cooper, Rose & English (1994–Present) **Associations & Accomplishments:** Board of Directors, Fairbanks Daily News; Former Trustee, Rutgers University and Blair Academy; Former two year Alumni, Cornell University; Published law books discussing outcome of cases. **Personal:** Married. Six children. Mr. Rose enjoys camping and gardening.

Mr. Harold I. Rosen
Managing Principal
Seltzer & Rosen, P.C.
1301 K Street, N.W., Suite 310 East
Washington, DC 20005
(202) 682–4585
Fax: (202) 682–4599

8111

Business Information: Seltzer & Rosen, P.C. is a full–service, civil practice law firm concentrating in construction contract law for government, private and commercial construction projects, including military and international clients. Established in 1992, Seltzer & Rosen, P.C. currently employs six people. Admitted to practice in 1967, Mr. Rosen joined the Firm in 1992 as Managing Principal. He is responsible for the representation of clients world–wide in the Construction and Engineering fields. **Career Steps:** Managing Principal, Seltzer & Rosen, P.C. (1992–Present); Managing Partner, Rissetto, Weaver & Rosen (1989–1992); Member, King & King Chartered (1975–1987). **Associations & Accomplishments:** Member, Board of Directors, Lightning Group, Inc. and Chariton Transportation Company; Fellow and Life Member, Society of American Military Engineers (currently Vice–Chairman of Academy of Fellows). **Education:** George Washington University, LL.M. (1973), J.D. (1967), B.B.A. (1964). **Personal:** Two children: Allison Beth and Arthur Jay. Mr. Rosen enjoys art and photography.

Daniel W. Roslokken, Esquire

Attorney
Law Office of Daniel W. Roslokken
42 Canterbury Drive
Midland Park, NJ 07432
(201) 447–5328
Fax: (201) 447–9338

8111

Business Information: The Law Office of Daniel W. Roslokken is a full–service law firm that handles both civil and criminal cases. As Attorney, Mr. Roslokken specializes in health care law. He also deals and consults regularly with corporate professionals and Fortune 500 companies. He has worked on cases dealing with sexual harassment, corporate funds, insurance and personal injury. Reported Cases: R.T.C. v. Lanzaro, 140 N.J. 244, 658 A.2d 282 (1995). He consults on the Federal Paper Board, and has some international clients. Established in 1993, Law Office of Daniel W. Roslokken employs 1 person. **Career Steps:** Attorney, Law Office of Daniel W. Roslokken (1993–Present); Consultant/Government Relations, International Brotherhood of Teamsters (1993); General Counsel, Preventive Plus (1990–1992); Judicial Intern, The Honorable Andrew P. Napolitano (1989–1990). **Associations & Accomplishments:** Member, American Bar Association, Health and Hospital Law Section; Member, New Jersey Bar Association; Member, Pennsylvania Bar Association; Member, Philadelphia Bar Association; Member, American Society of Association Executives; Author of "Court Invalidates Sheriff's Fee As A Burdensome Tax," 142 N.J.L.J. Supp.15(10/3/95), "Is There A Right To Health Care?" 143 N.J.L.J. 1159 (3/25/96). **Education:** Seton Hall Law School, J.D. Cum Laude (1991); Columbia University, graduate studies in Psychology, Neuro–physiology, Psych–pharmacology; Northeastern Bible College, B.A. 1985. **Personal:** Mr. Roslokken enjoys skiing, swimming, photography, and art.

Margaret A. Ross
Partner
Gowling, Strathy, & Henderson
160 Elgin Street, Suite 2600
Ottawa, Ontario K1P 1C3
(613) 786–0130 (613) 233–1781
Fax: (613) 563–9869
EMAIL: See Below

8111

Business Information: Gowling, Strathy, & Henderson is one of the largest law firms in Canada and one of the top ten in Ontario. The Firm's practice has a high concentration of intellectual property law, including patents, trademarks, copyright,

and trade secrets. Established in the 1800's, the Firm is comprised of almost 300 attorneys and has six locations throughout Canada and the world, including Ottawa, Toronto, Hamilton, the Waterloo region, Vancouver, and Moscow. As Partner, Mrs. Ross specializes in the area of professional liability, specifically medical malpractice cases. Her duties include research and litigation of cases, advising clients, and serving as liaison between them and other attorneys. She is also fluent in English and French. Internet users can reach her via: rossm@gowlings.com. **Career Steps:** Gowling, Strathy, & Henderson: Partner (1983–Present), Associate (1976–1983). **Associations & Accomplishments:** Past President, County of Carleton Law Association; Past President, Medical–Legal Society of Ottawa–Carleton; President, Advocates' Society; Awarded Law Society Medal (1992); Former Commissioner, Ontario Law Reform Commission; Former Chair, Canadian Bar Association, National Editorial Board; Director, Thomas More Lawyers' Guild of Ottawa; Civil Litigation Specialty Committee, Law Society of Upper Canada Certification Board; Author of Numerous Publications; Speaker/Lecturer at Various Seminars and Lectures. **Education:** Ottawa University, LL.B. (1974); Loyola College, B.A. With Honors; Admitted to the Bar of Ontario (1976); Harvard Law School, Mediation Workshop (June 1994). **Personal:** Married to Kenneth J. in 1977. Three children: Adam, Gregory, and David. Mrs. Ross enjoys travel, skiing, tennis, reading, and wine sampling.

James P. Rowles
Attorney at Law
Bingham, Dana & Gould
150 Federal Street
Boston, MA 02110
(617) 951–8138
Fax: (617) 951–8736

8111

Business Information: Bingham, Dana & Gould is a full–service, general practice law firm. A practicing attorney in Massachusetts state courts since 1993, Mr. Rowles joined the Firm as Attorney at Law in 1994. His practice specializes in corporate international transactions, particularly in Latin America. **Career Steps:** Attorney at Law, Bingham, Dana & Gould (1994–Present); Consultant, Self–Employed (1990–1994); Adjunct Professor, Branders University (1990–1992); Lecturer on Law, Harvard Law School (1987–1989). **Associations & Accomplishments:** Chair, Committee on Public International Law; Boston Bar Association; French–American Chamber of Commerce; German American Business Club of Boston; Director, New England – Latin American Business Council; Fellow and Associate Director for International Programs (1986–1989), Center for Criminal Justice at Harvard Law School; Attorney, Inter–American Commission on Human Rights (1977–1978); Fluent in French, German, Portuguese, and Spanish. **Education:** Harvard Law School, S.J.D. (1993); Stanford Law School: J.S.M. (1976), J.D. (1972); Stanford University, A.B. (1967). **Personal:** Mr. Rowles enjoys tennis.

Lori S. Rubenstein, Esq.
Regional Director and Attorney
Oregon Legal Services
735 SE Cass Avenue
Roseburg, OR 97470–0039
(503) 673–1182
Fax: (503) 673–1183

8111

Business Information: Oregon Legal Services, established in 1978, is a private, non–profit organization consisting of five attorneys plus support staff, providing pro bono legal assistance in civil cases to low–income individuals who cannot afford to hire an attorney. Cases handled generally involve administrative law, civil rights, domestic violence cases, etc. Admitted to practice in Oregon state and federal courts in 1985, Mrs. Rubenstein joined the staff of Oregon Legal Services in 1990. As Regional Director and Attorney, she handles divorce, custody, domestic violence and guardianship cases, being responsible for all aspects of legal representation and direction of the regional office. **Career Steps:** Regional Director and Attorney, Oregon Legal Services (1990–Present); Staff Attorney, Central Pennsylvania Legal Services (1987–1990); Intern, Washoe County Public Defenders (1985–1986). **Associations & Accomplishments:** Statewide Young Careerist and Local Board, Business and Professional Women; Board of Advisors, Confidence Clinic – consisting of 16–75 teen parents obtaining their GEDs in 16–week sessions; President, Douglas County Bar Association (1993–1994); Statewide Court Protocols Committee for Domestic Violence; President, Jewish Community Center. **Education:** Antioch School of Law, J.D. (1985); University of Nevada – Reno, B.A. in Social Services (1982). **Personal:** Married to Hanan Bowman in 1986. Two children: Landan and Tamar. Mrs. Rubenstein enjoys the support of her family and aerobics.

Michael D. Rudolph

Attorney

Barrs, Williamson, Stolberg & Townsend, P.A.

601 North Franklin Street, 4th Floor
Tampa, FL 33602
(813) 228–9819
Fax: (813) 221–8388

8111

Business Information: Barrs, Williamson, Stolberg & Townsend, P.A. is a full–service, general practice law firm, specializing in personal injury cases, Worker's Compensation, and Social Security actions locally and throughout the state. The Firm also handles plaintiff work and some longshore work for the harbor, which is a federal Worker's Compensation for longshoreman, dock personnel, etc. A practicing attorney in Florida state courts since 1991, Mr. Rudolph joined the Firm as Attorney in 1993. His practice concentrates in all three areas of the Firm, having over 300 active files. **Career Steps:** Attorney, Barrs, Williamson, Stolberg & Townsend, P.A. (1993–Present); Attorney, Katman & Eshelman, P.A. (1992–1993). **Associations & Accomplishments:** American Bar Association; Florida Bar Association; Hillsborough County Bar Association; Florida Workers Advocates; Academy of Florida Trial Lawyers; Association of Trial Lawyers of America; Speaker for Speaker Bureau Program – Hillsborough County School Board; Editor, Case Law Monitor – News and 440 Report. **Education:** Stetson University College of Law, J.D. (1991); SUNY – Buffalo, B.A. **Personal:** Mr. Rudolph enjoys all types of athletic and fitness activities.

E. Thom Rumberger Jr.

Attorney at Law

Ballard Spahr Andrews & Ingersoll

1735 Market Street, 51st Floor
Philadelphia, PA 19103
(215) 864–8723
Fax: (215) 864–8999

8111

Business Information: Ballard Spahr Andrews & Ingersoll is a premier, international practice law firm, concentrating on corporate law and specializing in corporate finance and project finance in Russia and Eastern Europe. Established in the 1880's, the Firm currently employs 280 attorneys. A practicing attorney in Florida and Pennsylvania courts since 1993, Mr. Rumberger joined the Firm in 1995 as Associate responsible for representing the Firm's clientele in corporate law matters. **Career Steps:** Attorney at Law, Ballard Spahr Andrews & Ingersoll (1995–Present); Partner, Rumberger, Cote, Meyers & Markovich (1993–1994); Law Clerk, The Honorable Patricia Fawsett and The Honorable Kendall Sharp, U.S. District Court Judges (1989–1991). **Associations & Accomplishments:** The Florida Bar; The American Bar Association; LSE Club; Fluent in Russian. **Education:** London School of Economics (1993); University of Florida, J.D.; Wake University, B.A. in History. **Personal:** Married to Julie Cote Rumberger in 1995. Mr. Rumberger enjoys running, mountain biking, and basketball.

Ronald Rus

President and Shareholder

Rus, Miliband, Williams, Smith

2600 Michelson Drive
Irvine, CA 92715–1550
(714) 752–7100
Fax: (714) 252–1514

8111

Business Information: Rus, Miliband, Williams, Smith is a full–service, general practice law firm, specializing in litigation and bankruptcy cases. A practicing attorney in California state and federal courts since 1975, Mr. Rus co–established the Firm in 1976. Currently serving as President and Shareholder, he oversees all administrative operations for associates and a support staff of 25, in addition to his daily legal practice. His practice concentrates on complex litigation cases in all forums. **Career Steps:** President and Shareholder, Rus, Miliband, Williams, Smith (1976–Present) **Associations & Accomplishments:** American Bar Association; State Bar of California; Founding Member, Federal Bar Association – Orange County Chapter; Orange County Bar Association; National Bankruptcy Conference; American Bankruptcy Institute; Panel member with Continuing Education and other Bar Association panels relating to complex litigation and bankruptcy; Co–author, 1990 CEB Trial Practice Institute's manual on Complex Civil Litigation in bankruptcy cases; Panelist, State Bar Litigation in bankruptcy cases; Panelist, State Bar Litigation sections 1993 symposium on dispute resolutions in the 90's; Visiting Lecturer on complex litigation, Stanford University School of Law; Frequent speaker for various continuing legal education programs in his area of emphasis; Founding Director, Orange County Bankruptcy Forum (served as President 1989–1990); Board of Directors, California Bankruptcy Forum (selected as Chairman of annual conference 1994); Master of the Bench, American Inns of Court, Peter M. Elliott Chapter; Board of Directors: Santa Ana Zoo, the Saint Joseph Hospital Foundation of Orange County, and the Orange County Council of the Boy Scouts of America. **Education:** Pepperdine University School of Law, J.D. (1975); University of Southern California, B.A. in International Relations (1972). **Personal:** Married to Tamera in 1991. Two children: Garret and Brandon.

Ms. Laurie Rush–Masuret

Attorney

Laurie Rush–Masuret, P.A.

200 Executive Drive, Suite 220
West Orange, NJ 07052
(201) 325–1221
Fax: (201) 325–0290

8111

Business Information: Laurie Rush–Masuret, P.A., established in 1995, is a full–service, general practice law firm. Admitted to practice in New Jersey state courts, Ms. Rush–Masuret established this solo–practice in 1995. She is responsible for all aspects of operations, including providing legal representation to the Firm's clientele. **Career Steps:** Attorney, Laurie Rush–Masuret, P.A. (1995–Present); Attorney and Partner, Rush–Masuret & Conoshenti, P.A. (1987–1995); Attorney, John J. Rush, P.A. (1986–1987). **Associations & Accomplishments:** American Bar Association: Torts & Insurance Practice Section; New Jersey Bar Association: Past Chair of Fidelity & Surety Law Committee; Bernardsville Business & Professional Women's Association; Somerset County Federation of Republican Women. **Education:** Seton Hall Law School, J.D. (1986); College of the Holy Cross, B.A. (1983). **Personal:** Married to Michael in 1986. Two children: Christopher and Megan. Ms. Rush–Masuret enjoys ice dancing.

Mr. Albert B. Russ

Retired Attorney

CSX

500 Water Street
Jacksonville, FL 32207
(904) 645–0688
Fax: Please mail or call

8111

Business Information: CSX Transportation grew out of the merger of Seaboard Coast Line Railroad and the Chesapeake and Ohio Railroad companies. Mr. Russ was an Attorney with the firm for over thirty years. He dealt with cases involving competitive rates and commodity identifications. A high point of his career was when he successfully argued before the North Carolina Supreme Court an important trade rate case. **Career Steps:** Chief Commerce Counsel, Atlantic Coast Line Railroad; Assistant General Attorney, Seaboard Coast Line Railroad; General Attorney, CSX. **Associations & Accomplishments:** Lieutenant Governor, Kiwanis Florida District; Member, Masonic Lodge (also lecturer); Trustee, Florida Foundation; Chairman of the Board, All Saints Early Learning Center; Lay Reader, All Saints Episcopal Church; Trustee, Scottish Rite Foundation. Mr. Russ has lectured on railroad law and commodity rates at the Railroad Transportation Institute and other professional venues. Education: Wake Forest University, L.L.B. (1955); Wake Forest University, B.S. **Personal:** Married to Gerry Russ. Three children: Deborah Lynne, Kelly and Albert. Mr. Russ enjoys tennis, and his Jacksonville USTA Tennis teams have been to the Nationals twice.

James B. Rylander

Partner

Vinson & Elkins, L.L.P.

1001 Fannin, Suite 2300
Houston, TX 77002
(713) 758–2428
Fax: (713) 615–5234

8111

Business Information: Vinson & Elkins, L.L.P. is a premier, international law firm. International in scope, the Firm has offices in the U.S. (Houston, Dallas & Austin, Texas and Washington, D.C.), England (London), Moscow, Singapore, and Mexico City, Mexico. Established in 1919, the Firm currently employs 600 attorneys and 900 legal and administrative support staff. Joining the Houston affiliate as Associate upon conferral of his law degree in 1969, and appointed Partner in 1976, Mr. Rylander represents small and closely–held corporations in business and financial transactions. His current focus is in Latin American financing with energy–related companies. **Career Steps:** Vinson & Elkins: Partner (1976–Present), Associate (1969–1976). **Associations & Accomplishments:** Member, Southern Regional Advisory Board for the Institute of International Education; Member, Board of Directors, YMCA; Advisory Director, Trees for Houston; Fluent in Spanish. **Education:** The University of Texas: J.D. (1969), B.A. (1966); Facultad de Derecho Universidad de Chile (1966). **Personal:** Married to Deborah in 1969. Three children: Reagan, Emily, and Karen.

Hans J. Saamen

Partner

Stiver Vale

195 Main Street, South
Newmarket, Ontario L3Y 4X4
(905) 895–4571
Fax: (905) 895–6030

8111

Business Information: Stiver Vale, is a full–service law firm consisting of 8 attorneys. The Firm, which was established in 1937, has one location in Ontario, Canada. As Partner, Mr. Saamen concentrates in Civil and Criminal Litigation, with emphasis on debtor/creditor rights and construction law. Licensed to practice in the Federal Court of Canada, as well as all levels of Ontario courts, Mr. Saamen has set several precedents in construction law cases. **Career Steps:** Stiver Vale: Partner (1990–Present), Employee (1983–1990). **Associations & Accomplishments:** Canadian Bar Association; Law Society of Upper Canada; Secretary, Board of Directors, York Legion Law Association; Legal Aid Area Committee; Vice President, of Newmarket German Canadian Business and Professional Association. **Education:** York University: L.L.B. (1983), B.A. (1980). **Personal:** Married to Karen in 1989. Two children: Marie and Brian. Mr. Saamen enjoys fishing, golf, skiing, and bowling.

Michael Arthur Sabian

Of Counsel

Freeborn & Peters

950 17th Street, Suite 2600
Denver, CO 80202
(303) 628–4200
Fax: (303) 628–4250

8111

Business Information: Freeborn & Peters is a full–service, commercial law firm. Based in Chicago, Illinois, the Firm has two offices (Chicago, Illinois and Denver, Colorado), serving clientele internationally. Established in 1982, the Firm currently employs 140 attorneys, legal and administrative support staff. A practicing attorney in Colorado state courts since 1968, Mr. Sabian joined the Firm in 1995. Currently serving as Of Counsel, Mr. Sabian provides legal advice to clients in business transactions, including corporate, securities, healthcare, and franchise law. **Career Steps:** Of Counsel, Freeborn & Peters (1995–Present); Founding Shareholder, Pendleton & Sabian, P.C. (1970–1995). **Associations & Accomplishments:** American Bar Association; Denver Bar Association; Colorado Bar Association: Board of Governors Member, Business Law and Judiciary Sections, Chair and Council Member; Colorado Secretary of State Advisory Council; Past Member of Colorado Supreme Court Judicial Planning Council. **Education:** Harvard University Law School, LL.B. (1968); University of Rochester, A.B. (1963). **Personal:** Married to Fern Sabian in 1968. One child: Lori. Mr. Sabian enjoys traveling to Russia and China to participate in people–to–people goodwill tours.

Emilio J. Sahurie, Esq.

Partner/Attorney

Estudio & Carvallo, S.A.

Ahumada 179, 4th Floor
Santiago, Chile
(562) 698–0969
Fax: (562) 699–0762

8111

Business Information: Estudio & Carvallo, S.A. is a full–service international law firm concentrating on maritime, aviation, and insurance law. Established in 1885, the Firm presently has seven offices with 25 attorneys on staff, and a support staff of over 80 people. As Attorney, Mr. Sahurie concentrates on maritime and international insurance cases. As Partner, he is involved in developing and implementing policies and procedures for the Firm, public relations, and strategic planning. **Career Steps:** Partner/Attorney, Estudio & Carvallo, S.A. (1988–Present); Legal Adviser, Empremar (1986–1988); Professor of Law, Universidad Catolica (1986–1988). **Associations & Accomplishments:** American Society of International Law; Santiago Bar Association. **Education:** Yale University: L.L.M. (1983), J.S.D. (1987); Universidad Catolica de Valparaiso L.L.B. **Personal:** Mr. Sahurie enjoys mountain biking, snow boarding, travel, skiing, and scuba diving.

Allen H. Sakai

President

Allen H. Sakai, Attorney–at–Law, A Law Corporation

32 Merchant Street, Suite 201
Honolulu, HI 96813
(808) 532–7217
Fax: (808) 532–7214

8111

Business Information: Allen H. Sakai, Attorney–at–Law, A Law Corporation, is an international, full–service, general practice law firm, providing legal representation to corporations. A practicing attorney since 1983 in Hawaii state courts, Mr. Sakai established his sole practice firm in 1995. Serving as Owner and President, his practice concentrates in the areas of corporate securities with national and international corporations. He is also working internationally with various Philipine and Japanese companies, as well as provides pro bono work for the Hawaiian Bar Association. **Career Steps:** President, Allen H. Sakai, Attorney–at–Law, A Law Corporation (1995–Present); Director and Shareholder, Torkildson, Katz, Jossem, Fonseca, Jaffe, Moore & Hetherington (1989–1995); Associate and Partner, Cades, Schutte, Fleming & Wright (1983–1989). **Associations & Accomplishments:** American Bar Association; American Management Association; Hawaii State Bar Association: Chair, Corporations & Securities Section. **Education:** University of Oregon, J.D. (1983); University of Hawaii–Manoa: M.B.A. in Finance, B.A. in Economics. **Personal:** Married to Susan Cachero in 1990. Four children: Kristy, Eric, Amanda and Andrew. Mr. Sakai is an avid sport fisher and surfer during his leisure time.

Carlos A. Samour, Esq.

Associate Attorney

Holland & Hart

555 17th Street, Suite 3200
Denver, CO 80202
(303) 295–8000
Fax: (303) 295–8261

8111

Business Information: Holland & Hart is a premier general practice law firm, primarily concentrating in corporate commercial law. Established in 1945, Holland & Hart currently employs over 500 attorneys and legal support staff. An Associate Attorney since 1991 and originally from El Salvador, Mr. Samour concentrates his practice in the areas of personal injury and product liability. A trial attorney since 1990, Mr. Samour is admitted to both State and Federal courts. **Career Steps:** Attorney, Holland & Hart (1991–Present); Clerk, Tenth Circuit Court of Appeals (1990–1991); Teaching Assistant, University of Denver College of Law (1988–1990). **Associations & Accomplishments:** Colorado Bar Association; Denver Bar Association; Hispanic Bar Association; Colorado Trial Lawyers Association; Colorado Board of Law Examiners; Minority Caucus of the Colorado Trial Lawyers Association; Association of Trial Lawyers of America. **Education:** University of Denver College of Law, J.D. (1990); University of Colorado, B.A. in Psychology (1987). **Personal:** Mr. Samour enjoys sports and public speaking, particulary debate and argument.

M. Dee Samuels

Attorney

Samuels, Shawn, Marx & Duffy, P.C.

1388 Sutter Street, Suite 1210
San Francisco, CA 94109
(415) 567–7000
Fax: (415) 567–6116

8111

Business Information: Samuels, Shawn, Marx & Duffy, P.C. is a full–service, family practice law firm consisting of five attorneys. Admitted to practice in California state courts in 1977 and a Certified Family Law Specialist since 1981, Ms. Samuels joined the Firm in 1994. Serving as Attorney, her practice concentrates on family law. Concurrent with her private law practice, she serves as Editor for the "Family Advocate", as well as serves as Judge Pro Tem for San Francisco and Marin County Superior Courts. **Career Steps:** Attorney, Samuels, Shawn, Marx & Duffy, P.C. (1994–Present); Serves as Judge Pro Tem: Motion Calendar for San Francisco Superior Court, Settlement Conferences for San Francisco and Marin County Superior Court; Samuels & Shawn, P.C. (1991–1994); Sole Practitioner, Law Offices of M. Dee Samuels (1988–1991); Partner, Stotter, Samuels & Chamberlin (1981–1988); Associate, Law Offices of Lawrence H. Stotter (1977–1981). **Associations & Accomplishments:** American Bar Association – Family Law Section: Council Member (1988–1994), Committee Chairperson for Marital Property (1986–87) / Divorce Laws & Procedures (1985–86) / Adoption Committee (1983–84, 1984–85, 1992–93) / Economics of Practice Committee (1982–83) / Stepfamilies (1992–93) and Adoption Act Drafting Committee (1989–91), Liaison to ABA National Conference of Commissioners on Uniform State Laws; Association of Family and Conciliation Courts; Treasurer (1979), Queen's Bench; Member and Chairperson (1981, 1982), San Francisco Bar Association – Family Law Section; State Bar of California: Property Committee (1982), San Francisco Delegate to Conference of Delegates at State Bar Convention (1981, 1982); Frequent lecturer, instructor and author on Family Law; Editor, 'Family Advocate', Editorial Board (1990–Present). **Education:** University of San Francisco, J.D. (1977); Whittier College, B.A. (1962); Certified Family Law Specialist (1981)

Diana Santa Maria, P.A.

Owner/Attorney

Law Offices of Diana Santa Maria, P.A.

4801 South University Drive
Ft. Lauderdale, FL 33328–3839
(954) 434–1077
Fax: (954) 434–4462

8111

Business Information: An attorney since 1985, Ms. Santa Maria formed her own law firm in 1991, dedicating herself to representing plaintiffs in personal injury cases such as defective highway construction, medical negligence, product defect, automobile accident, and unsafe building cases. The Firm has handled high–profile cases against major insurance companies, hospitals, airlines, grocery and department stores, state agencies, car rental firms, and large Fortune 500 corporations. A number of damage awards have exceeded $1 million and all cases are accepted on a contingency fee basis. **Career Steps:** Owner/Attorney, Law Offices of Diana Santa Maria, P.A. (1991–Present); Attorney/Associate, Law Office of Sheldon J. Schlesinger, P.A. (1985–1990). **Associations & Accomplishments:** American Bar Association; Association of Trial Lawyers of America; Academy of Florida Trial Lawyers; Florida Bar Association; Broward County Trial Lawyers Association; Broward County Bar Association; Better Business Bureau; Who's Who Among American Law Students; Young Community Leaders of America; and Order of Barristers. **Education:** University of Miami: School of Law, J.D. (1984), B.A. in English with honors (1981). **Personal:** Married to Brian K. Sidella in 1984. Two children: Nickolas and Alexander. Ms. Santa Maria enjoys snow skiing, piano playing, reading, and writing.

Mr. William J. Sapone

Partner

McAulay, Fisher, Nissen, Goldberg & Kiel

261 Madison Avenue
New York, NY 10016
(212) 986–4090
Fax: (212) 818–9479

8111

Business Information: McAulay, Fisher, Nissen, Goldberg & Kiel is a law firm specializing in patent, trademark, copyright, unfair competition, all aspects of intellectual property law. A Partner with the Firm since 1990, Mr. Sapone oversees the functions and supervises associates involved with patent and trademark matters. A practicing attorney since 1984, he specializes in patent and trademark registrations, litigation and counsels clients on intellectual property issues. Established in 1970, McAulay, Fisher, Nissen, Goldberg & Kiel employs 45 legal professionals and administrative support staff. **Career Steps:** Partner, McAulay, Fisher, Nissen, Goldberg & Kiel, (1990–Present); Attorney, Darby & Darby, P.C. (1988–1990); Attorney, United Technologies Corporation (1985–1988). **Associations & Accomplishments:** Connecticut Patent Law Association; Connecticut Bar Association; New York Bar Association; AIPPI; IPPI; International Trademark Association; American Intellectual Property Law Association; American Bar Association **Education:** Pace University, J.D. (1984); University of Lowell, B.S. in Chemical Engineering (1977) **Personal:** Married to Mary A. Guerrera in 1982. One child: Max.

C. Forbes Sargent III

Attorney and Partner

Mahoney, Hawkes & Goldings

The Heritage on the Garden, 75 Park Plaza
Boston, MA 02116
(617) 457–3100
Fax: (617) 457–3125

8111

Business Information: Mahoney, Hawkes & Goldings is a full–service, general practice law firm. Established in 1961, the Firm currently employs 50 people. Admitted to practice in Massachusetts state courts since 1985, Mr. Sargent joined the firm in 1987. Serving as Partner in the Transactional Group, his practice concentrates on general business and real estate law for small family–owned businesses, closely–held companies, private high–tech companies, and non–profit organizations. Additional practice areas include commercial real estate, leasing, banking, advertising law, copyright, and trademark law. **Career Steps:** Mahoney, Hawkes & Goldings: Partner (1994–Present), Associate (1987–1994); Associate, Warner & Stackpole (1985–1987). **Associations & Accomplishments:** American Bar Association; Massachusetts Bar Association; Boston Bar Association; American Cancer Society – Massachusetts Division: Director (1991–1995), Chairperson for Fund–raising Committee (1992–1994). **Education:** Duke University School of Law, J.D. (1985); Vassar College, A.B. (1982); St. Mark's School, Southborough, MA (1978). **Personal:** Married to Maura Walsh in 1989. One child: Katherine Elizabeth. Mr. Sargent enjoys gardening and golf during his leisure time.

James Alton Satcher Jr.

Trial Lawyer

Law Offices of James Alton Satcher Jr., P.A.

520 Broad Street
Rome, GA 30161–3010
(706) 291–4019
Fax: (706) 291–4336

8111

Business Information: Law Offices of James Alton Satcher Jr., P.A. is a full–service, general practice law firm, concentrating on litigation. Admitted to practice in Georgia state courts, Mr. Satcher established his sole practice firm upon conferral of his law degree in 1975. He is responsible for all aspects of operations, specializing in civil rights cases for plaintiffs and medical malpractice. His most publicized winning case involves an individual who drew a pocketknife on five police officers and was shot by the officers, blowing his leg away. **Career Steps:** Trial Lawyer, Law Offices of James Alton Satcher Jr., P.A. (1975–Present). **Associations & Accomplishments:** Georgia Trial Lawyers Association; American Trial Lawyers Association; Rome Bar Association. **Education:** University of Georgia, J.D. (1975); Berry College, B.A. (1971). **Personal:** Four children: Kimberly, Jaimie, Jason, and Thomas. Mr. Satcher enjoys collecting classic cars.

Carl D. Savely

Director

Lionel, Sawyer & Collins

300 South 4th Street, Suite 1700
Las Vegas, NV 89101–6014
(702) 383–8874
Fax: (702) 383–8845

8111

Business Information: Lionel, Sawyer & Collins is a general practice law firm with 22 partners and 70 attorneys located in Reno and Las Vegas, Nevada, concentrating in commercial litigation and bankruptcy. Mr. Savely joined the Firm as an Associate Attorney in 1988. Promoted to Director in 1995, he presently focuses his practice in natural resources, environmental law, public land, and real estate. **Career Steps:** Lionel, Sawyer & Collins: Director (1995–Present), Associate Attorney (1988–1994); Mine Geologist, Homestake Mining Company (1977–1985). **Associations & Accomplishments:** American Association of Petroleum Geologists; Geological Society of America; American Institute of Professional Geologists; State Bar of Nevada; State Bar of Colorado; Clark County Bar Association. **Education:** California Western School of Law, J.D. (1966); Adams State College, B.A. **Personal:** Married to Jill in 1978. Two children: Byron and Nadine. Mr. Savely enjoys hunting, fishing, model railroading, and mining history.

SAYRE & SAYRE ATTORNEYS AT LAW

Richard L. Sayre

Managing Partner

Sayre & Sayre, P.S.

111 West Cataldo, Suite 210
Spokane, WA 99201–3204
(509) 325–7330
Fax: (509) 325–7334

8111

Business Information: Sayre & Sayre, P.S. is a client–centered firm emphasizing developing areas of law. The Firm concentrates in the areas of estate planning, asset preservation, Medicaid and Medicare eligibility and benefit issues, estate tax and administration, guardianship, sexual discrimination, harassment and abuse. The Firm also emphasizes employment law, environmental regulation, public health law, public disclose and open meetings issues, and health care law. A practicing attorney in Washington state and federal courts since 1979, Mr. Sayre co–founded the Firm in 1992 and serves as Managing Partner. He is responsible for overseeing all administrative operations in addition to his daily law practice. His practice focuses in the areas of estate and disability planning and the taxation aspects thereof. Other areas include disability law and related medical program entitlement law, estate administration, geriatric law, health care law, and environmental law, as well as litigation related to those areas. **Career Steps:** Managing Partner, Sayre & Sayre, P.S. (1992–Present); Shareholder and Vice President, Underwood, Campbell, Brock & Cerutti (1984–1992); Deputy Prosecuting Attorney, Spokane County Prosecuting Attorney (1979–1984). **Associations & Accomplishments:** Washington State Bar Association; American Bar Association; Spokane County Bar Association; National Academy of Elder Law Attorneys (1995–1996); President, Washington Chapter National Academy of Elder Law Attorneys; Spokane Estate Planning Council; Chair, Spokane County Superior Court Guardianship Training Committee; Phi Alpha Delta Legal Fraternity; Certified as an Elder Law Attorney by the National Elder Law Foundation; Board of Governors, Spokane Shriners Hospital, will serve as Potentate of El Katif Shrine in 1997. **Education:** Gonzaga University School of Law, J.D (1979); University of Washington, B.A. in Psychology (1976). **Personal:** Married to Karen L. in 1979. Two children: Wendi and Tracey. Mr. Sayre enjoys sailing, skiing, motorcycling, and spending time with family.

Richard G. Scheib
· · · ◄━━◉━━► · · ·

Senior Associate
Ernst & Young
RR 1 Box 96A
Dornsife, PA 17823
(215) 448–5340
Fax: Please mail or call

8111

Business Information: Ernst & Young, one of the Big Six accounting firms, is the second largest accounting firm in the United States and the third in the world. Representing major international corporate clientele, services provided include financial accounting, auditing, tax and management consulting services, investment, stocks, bonds and securities, group financing and administration. A practicing tax law attorney in Pennsylvania courts since 1993, Richard Scheib joined Ernst & Young's Dornsife, PA branch in January of 1995. As the Senior Associate in the Legal Department, he formulates and compiles all petitions in appellate matters. **Career Steps:** Senior Associate, Ernst & Young (1995–Present); Associate, Price Waterhouse (1993–1994). **Associations & Accomplishments:** American Bar Association – Tax Section; Pennsylvania Bar Association – Tax Section; Philadelphia Bar Association – Tax Section. **Education:** Georgetown University, LL.M. (1993); Widener University School of Law, J.D.; Bloomsburg University, B.S. **Personal:** Mr. Scheib enjoys coin collecting, weightlifting, and wrestling.

Steven C. Scheinfeldt
President
Steven C. Scheinfeldt, P.A.
4801 South University Drive, Atrium Centre, Suite 258
Davie, FL 33328
(954) 434–3410
Fax: (954) 434–9422

8111

Business Information: Steven C. Scheinfeldt, P.A. is a full–service, general practice law firm. A practicing attorney in Florida state courts since 1992, Mr. Scheinfeldt established his private practice in 1995. He oversees all administrative operations, in addition to his daily law practice and strategic planning. Areas of practice involve wills, trusts, family law, real estate law, personal injury, general litigation, collections, and corporate law. **Career Steps:** Attorney/President, Steven C. Scheinfeldt, P.A. (1995–Present); General Counsel, Global Environmental Management Resources, Inc. (1995); Associate Attorney, Law Offices of Bernard F. Siegel (1993–1995); American Jurisprudence Book Award, Appellate Practice and Procedure; Who's Who Among American Law Students (1990, 1991, 1992); Phi Alpha Delta Law Fraternity International; Phi Beta Kappa; Golden Key National Honor Society; Criminal Justice Honor Society; Phi Kappa Phi; Engineered Leadership Award from Delta Sigma Phi Fraternity. **Associations & Accomplishments:** Florida Bar Association: Real Property, Probate and Trust Law Section, Family Law Section; American Bar Association: Real Property, Probate and Trust Law Section, Family Law Section, Business Law Section; Listed in Who's Who of Law Students (3 years), graduated Cum Laude University of Miami School of Law; graduated Cum Laude and with highest honors, University of Florida. **Education:** University of Miami – School of Law, J.D. Cum Laude (1992); University of Florida, B.A. in Lib-

eral Arts and Sciences Highest Honors (1989); Florida Atlantic University (1985–1986).

Matthew W. Schlegel, Esq.
· · · ◄━━◉━━► · · ·

Attorney and Shareholder
Kupelian Ormond & Magy, P.C.
25800 Northwestern Hwy., Suite 950
Southfield, MI 48075–8403
(810) 357–0000
Fax: (810) 357–7488

8111

Business Information: Kupelian Ormond & Magy, P.C., f/k/a Tucker & Rolf, P.C., established in 1987, is a full–service, civil law firm. As Attorney and Shareholder, Mr. Schlegel is responsible for all aspects of legal representation, placing emphasis on commercial litigation. **Career Steps:** Attorney and Shareholder, Kupelian Ormond & Magy, P.C. (1987–Present); Associate Attorney, Simon, Deitch, Tucker & Friedman (1984–1987); Teacher/Coach, Detroit County Day School (1978–1981); Assistant Editor, Building Design and Construction Magazine (1976–1978). **Associations & Accomplishments:** American Bar Association; American Arbitration Association (approved arbitrator); National Association of Securities Dealers (approved arbitrator); Oakland County Bar Association (approved mediator); Wayne County Mediation Tribunal (approved mediator). **Education:** Wayne State University Law School, J.D., cum laude (1984); St. Lawrence University, B.A. in English, honors (1976). **Personal:** Married to Nancy Dewan in 1992. Two children: Hannah and Allison. Mr. Schlegel enjoys squash, reading, movies, and travel.

Karen B. Schleimer
Principal Attorney
Karen B. Shleimer
250 West 57th Street
New York, NY 10107–2099
(212) 245–0798
Fax: (212) 245–2480
EMail: See Below

8111

Business Information: Law Offices of Karen B. Shleimer is a national full–service, private practice law firm, focusing on real estate and finance issues with major corporations. A practicing attorney for more than sixteen years, Ms. Schleimer established her private practice in 1984 and serves as its Owner, President, and Principal Attorney. She oversees all administrative operations for associates and support staff, in addition to her daily law practice. She also conducts local pro bono work. Internet users can reach her via: Redfriz@AOL.Com. **Career Steps:** Principal Attorney, Karen B. Shleimer (1984–Present); Associate Attorney, Weil Gotshal & Manges (1980–1984); Associate Attorney, Finley Kumble Wagner (1979–1980); Associate Attorney, Carter Ledyard & Milburn (1978–1979). **Associations & Accomplishments:** American Bar Association; Zoning Board of Appeals. **Education:** University of Pennsylvania, B.A. (1970). **Personal:** One child: Kimberly. Ms. Schleimer enjoys canoeing, skiing, and photography.

Stephen R. Schmidt
Member
Brown, Todd & Heyburn, PLLC
3200 Providian Center
Louisville, KY 40202
(502) 589–5400
Fax: (502) 581–1087
EMail: See Below

8111

Business Information: Brown, Todd & Heyburn, PLLC, is an international, full–service, general practice law firm, concentrating in the fields of litigation, estate, and international corporate law. Established in 1972, the Firm currently employs 200 attorneys, legal and administrative support staff. Admitted to practice in Kentucky state courts, Mr. Schmidt joined the Firm as an Associate upon the conferral of his law degree in 1974, and was appointed as Director of the Litigation Section in 1979. He is a trial attorney, serving in both a defense and prosecuting role. He can also be reached through the Internet as follows: SSchmidt@counsel.com **Career Steps:** Member, Brown, Todd & Heyburn, P.L.L.C. (1979–Present); Associate, Brown, Todd & Heyburn (1974–1979). **Associations & Accomplishments:** Fulbright Association, Ohio State University; President (1983 & 1988), Alumni Club of Louisville. **Education:** Ohio State University College of Law, J.D. (1974); Ohio State University, M.A. (1971); St. Louis University, A.B. (1969); University of Hamburg (Germany), Fulbright Scholar (1969–1970). **Personal:** Married to Wanda Owen. Two children: Johannes and Kathryn. Mr. Schmidt enjoys photography, collecting playing cards, and golf.

Robert J. Sciglimpaglia Jr., Esq.
Attorney
The Law Office of Robert J. Sciglimpaglia Jr., Esq.
1200 Summer Street
Stamford, CT 06905
(203) 359–9515
Fax: (203) 359–0346
E–mail: see below

8111

Business Information: The Office of Robert J. Sciglimpaglia Jr., Esq. is a general practice law firm concentrating in real estate law. Mr. Sciglimpaglia established his private practice in 1992. He recently hired an Associate, and attributes the success of his practice to hard work and being at the right place at the right time. A trial attorney since 1991, Mr. Sciglimpaglia is admitted to both State and Federal courts. He can also be reached through the Internet as follows: robscig@AOL.COM. **Career Steps:** Attorney, The Office of Robert J. Sciglimpaglia Jr., Esq. (1992–Present); Attorney, Eveleigh & McCabe (1991–1992); Law Clerk, Danforth & Clery (1989–1991). **Associations & Accomplishments:** American Bar Association; Connecticut Bar Association; New York Bar Association; Executive Committee, Young Lawyers Division, Lower Fairfield County Bar Association; Admitted to Practice in the following states: Connecticut, New York, Pennsylvania, District of Columbia, and the Federal District Court of Connecticut. **Education:** Pace Law School, J.D. (1991); University of Connecticut, B.A. (1988). **Personal:** Married to Jennifer in 1989. Two children: Mary and Patricia. Mr. Sciglimpaglia enjoys sports, music, and working with electronics and computers.

Christian Dietrich Searcy
President and Chief Executive Officer
Searcy Denney Scarola Barnhart & Shipley, P.A.
Post Office Drawer 3626, 2139 Palm Beach Lakes Boulevard
West Palm Beach, FL 33402–3626
(407) 686–6300
Fax: (407) 684–5707

8111

Business Information: Searcy Denney Scarola Barnhart & Shipley, P.A. is a law firm specializing primarily in personal injury, wrongful death litigation and commercial litigation (80% individual plaintiffs and 20% companies). Searcy Denney Scarola Barnhart & Shipley, P.A. presently employs 132 people, and has been established for 16 years. In his current capacity Mr. Searcy oversees all aspects of operations, as well as practicing law for the firm. **Career Steps:** President and Chief Executive Officer, Searcy Denney Scarola Barnhart & Shipley, P.A. (1989–Present); Partner, Montgomery, Searcy, and Denney, P.A. (1985–1989); Partner, Montgomery, Lytal, Reiter, Denney and Searcy, P.A. (1976–1985); Associate, Howell, Kirby, Montgomery, D'Aiuto and Dean, P.A. (1974–1976); Associate, Frates, Floyd, Pearson & Stewart, P.A. (1973–1974). **Associations & Accomplishments:** President, Academy of Florida Trial Lawyers (1986–1987); President–Elect, Academy of Florida Trial Lawyers (1985–1986); Board of Directors, Academy of Florida Trial Lawyers (1979–Present); Florida Bar Association; American Bar Association; Palm Beach County Bar Association; Academy of Florida Trial Lawyers; Association of Trial Lawyers of America; American Board of Trial Advocates (Advocate); National Board of Trial Advocates; Trial Lawyers for Public Justice; International Academy of Trial Lawyers; Trial Bar of U.S. District Court, Southern District of Florida; Trial Bar of U.S. District Court, Middle District of Florida; Supreme Court of the United States; Board of Overseers, Stetson Law School; Board of Directors, Seminole Landing Association; Board of Directors, United Cerebral Palsy; Advisory Board of Horses and the Handicapped of South Florida, Inc.; Board of Directors, The Benjamin School; Contributor to civic and charitable organizations; Continuing Legal Education Committee of Florida Bar Association and Palm Beach County Bar Association; Rules of Civil Procedure Committee of Florida Bar Association; Key Man Committee of Academy of Florida Trial Lawyers; Medical Jurisprudence Committee of Academy of Florida Trial Lawyers; Who's Who in American Law; Selected as one of the best lawyers in America, The Best Lawyers in America; Outstanding Trial Lawyer in the United States, Trial Advocacy Society of Stetson University Law School (1983); Youngest Lawyer in the U.S. to achieve a verdict of one million dollars for a single personal injury, which was in the case of, Bernard v. Florida East Coast Railway, March 1978 at age 30; Many articles published. **Education:** University of Virginia, Bachelor of Arts with Distinction (1970); Stetson University Law School, Juris Doctor Degree (1973). **Personal:** Married to Priscilla for 23 years. Four children: Wil, Angela, Christian, and Henry.

Randall W. Segatto

Partner/Attorney
Barber, Segatto, Hoffee and Hines
831 East Monroe
Springfield, IL 62701
(217) 544–4868
Fax: (217) 544–5225

8111

Business Information: Barber, Segatto, Hoffee and Hines is a general practice law firm. As Partner, Mr. Segatto concentrates on real estate law and estate planning. He offers consultation both nationally and internationally. **Career Steps:** Barber, Segatto, Hoffee and Hines: Partner (1996–Present), Staff Member (1986–1996). **Associations & Accomplishments:** American Bar Association; Sangamon County Bar Association; American Business Club; Springfield Arts Association; Listed in Who's Who in Young Americans (1992). **Education:** Southern Illinois University, J.D. (1986); Beloit College, B.A. (1983). **Personal:** Married to Suzann in 1991. One child: Matthew. Mr. Segatto enjoys golf and spending time with his son.

Harry H. Selph II

President
Fellers, Snider, Blankenship, Bailey & Tippens, P.C.
First National Center, 120 North Robinson, Suite 2400
Oklahoma City, OK 73102–7875
(405) 232–0621
Fax: (405) 232–9659

8111

Business Information: Fellers, Snider, et al. is a full–service, premier practice law firm, with emphasis on business law. The Firm has law offices in Oklahoma City and Tulsa, Oklahoma. The Firm handles real estate transactions, acquisitions, and disposition of assets and businesses and due diligence examination projects throughout the United States. Well–known for major litigation cases, the Firm has international clientele, primarily in Europe and Asia, and represents domestic corporations and partnerships which own companies and businesses throughout the world. A practicing attorney in Oklahoma state and federal courts since 1970, Mr. Selph joined the Firm as Vice President and Director in 1980. He serves as a member of the three–person Executive Committee, in addition to serving as a general business lawyer with specialties in oil and gas and real estate law. Career milestones include participating in oil and gas litigation which established the legal precedent of fraudulent drainage; defending natural gas pipelines in take–or–pay contract disputes involving damages exposure exceeding $1 billion dollars; assisting in the transaction of the sale of Wilson's Foods Poultry Division to Tyson Foods which then became the largest producer and marketer of poultry products in the world. **Career Steps:** Fellers, Snider, Blankenship, Bailey & Tippens, P.C.: President and Director (1996–Present), Vice President and Director (1980–1995); Partner, Baker, Baker, Wilson & Selph (1978–1980); Partner, Thompson, Selph & Ford (1975–1978). **Associations & Accomplishments:** Chairman, Oklahoma State University College of Business Administration Associates – an organization comprised of 175 business executives and professionals (1995–1996); Editor–in–Chief, Oklahoma Law Review (1969–1970). **Education:** University of Oklahoma, J.D. (1970); Oklahoma State University, B.S. in Business Administration (1965). **Personal:** Married to Sheralyn in 1974. Two children: Lindsey Elizabeth and Ashley Dawn. Mr. Selph enjoys golf, snow skiing, and dancing.

Fernando L. Sepulveda–Silva

Attorney
The Law Office of Fernando L. Sepulveda–Silva
P.O. Box 202
Cabo Rojo, Puerto Rico 00623–0202
(809) 851–2708
Fax: (809) 851–1111

8111

Business Information: The Law Office of Fernando L. Sepulveda–Silva is a full–service, general practice law office. Attaining his law degree in 1989, Mr. Sepulveda–Silva established his individual practice in 1994. He concentrates his practice in the area of litigation and serves as a Notary Public. **Career Steps:** Attorney, The Law Office of Fernando L. Sepulveda–Silva (1994–Present); Attorney, Agustin Silva Montalvo (1991–1994). **Associations & Accomplishments:** Rotary International; Delta Theta Phi; Puerto Rico Bar Associaion; National Audubon Society; American Bar Association; Sierra Club; National Wildlife Federation; Fraternidad Phi Eta Mu. **Education:** Catholic University of Puerto Rico, J.D. (1989); University of Puerto Rico – Mayaguez Campus, B.A. (1986). **Personal:** Mr. Sepulveda–Silva enjoys cooking, hiking, and conservation of nature.

Nidtza I. Serrano–Roman

Administrator and Human Resources Director
Cancio, Nadal, Rivera & Diaz
Munoz Rivera Avenue
Hato Rey, Puerto Rico 00918–3345
(809) 767–9625
Fax: (809) 767–4140

8111

Business Information: Cancio, Nadal, Rivera & Diaz, the third largest law firm in Puerto Rico, is a full–service, general practice law firm. Established in 1975, the Firm reports annual revenue of $6 million and currently employs 80 people. With sixteen years expertise in administration, Ms. Serrano–Roman joined the Firm in 1977. Serving as Administrator and Human Resources Director, she is responsible for overall administration matters, including the implementation and update of office system procedures (hiring, firing, training, scheduling and supervising personnel), delegating responsibilities assuring compliance with regulations and company policies, personnel administration, finances, budgeting, purchasing, credit and collections, and organizing all activities and meetings. **Career Steps:** Administrator and Human Resources Director, Cancio, Nadal, Rivera & Diaz (1977–Present). **Associations & Accomplishments:** Assistant Regional Director, Puerto Rico Manufacturers Association; Fluent in Spanish, English & French. **Education:** Kennedy–Western University, Master's Degree in progress (1995); University of Puerto Rico, B.B.A.; Has attended a variety of seminars **Personal:** Ms. Serrano–Roman enjoys reading and writing poems.

Henry F. Siedzikowski, Esq.

Managing Partner
Elliot, Reihner, Siedzikowski, & Egan, P.C.
925 Harvest Dr.
Blue Bell, PA 19422–1956
(215) 977–1038
Fax: (215) 977–1099

8111

Business Information: Elliot, Reihner, Siedzikowski, & Egan, P.C. is an international, full–service, general practice law firm, concentrating on labor law, general representation, intellectual property, health law, insurance issues, and government contract law. The Firm has 35 attorneys, including 17 shareholders; serving clients regionally, nationally, and internationally from three offices in Pennsylvania (Scranton & Blue Bell) and New Jersey. A practicing attorney in Pennsylvania state and federal courts since 1979, Mr. Siedzikowski joined the Firm as Managing Partner in 1990. His expertise lies in commercial litigation, intellectual property, and health care law. **Career Steps:** Managing Partner, Elliot, Reihner, Siedzikowski, & Egan, P.C. (1990–Present), Baskin Flaherty Elliot & Mannino (1986–1990), Dilworth Paxson Kalish & Kauffman (1979–1986). **Associations & Accomplishments:** Order of the Coif; Pennsylvania Bar Institute: Sustaining Member (Since 1985), Chair (1986–89) – Disciplinary Board Hearing Committee; Montgomery County Bar Association: Sustaining Member, Co–Chair – Health Law Committee; Philadelphia Bar Association: Sustaining Member, Chair – Sub–Committee on Rules of Disciplinary Enforcement, Professional Responsibility Committee; Pennsylvania Bar Association; American Bar Association: Sustaining Member, Antitrust Section Franchise Committee, Litigation Section, Rotating Editor – "Of Interest" Newsletter, Business Torts Committee, Chair – Lanham Act Subcommittee; Associate Editor, Villanova Law Review (1977–79). **Education:** Villanova Law School, J.D. magna cum laude (1979); Juniata College, B.A. cum laude (1975) **Personal:** Married to Mary Rita in 1991. Mr. Siedzikowski enjoys nature hikes, relaxing, and spending time with his family.

Mr. Neil Y. Siegel

Associate and Attorney
Pullman & Comley, L.L.C.
850 Main Street, P.O. Box 7006
Bridgeport, CT 06601–7006
(203) 330–2204
Fax: (203) 576–8888

8111

Business Information: Pullman & Comley, L.L.C. is a general practice law firm. Established in 1919, the Firm concentrates primarily in civil law. As Associate Attorney, Mr. Siegel is a full–time bankruptcy and workout attorney. A trial attorney since the conferral of his law degree in 1979, Mr. Siegel is admitted to both State and Federal courts, and is board–certified in business bankruptcy law. **Career Steps:** Associate and Attorney, Pullman & Comley, L.L.C. (1991–Present); Junior Partner, Bernstein & Bernstein, P.C. (1985–1991); Managing Attorney, Hyatt Legal Services (1980–1985). **Associations & Accomplishments:** American Bankruptcy Institute; Commercial Law League of America; Secretary, Men's Club of the Jewish Home for the Elderly of Fairfield County; Academic Excellence Committee, Tashua School; President and Baritone Soloist, Mendelssohn Choir of Connecticut; Member of Connecticut Grand Opera and Orchestra, selected performances. **Education:** Boston College: J.D. (1979), A.B. (1976); Certified Business Bankruptcy Attorney, American Board of Bankruptcy Certification (1995). **Personal:** Married to Debra H. in 1978. Two children: Ann and Sarah. Mr. Siegel enjoys singing.

Lewis R. Sifford, Esq.

Attorney
Sifford & Anderson, L.L.P.
901 Main Street, Suite 6300
Dallas, TX 75202–3714
(214) 742–1200
Fax: (214) 220–0206

8111

Business Information: Sifford & Anderson, L.L.P. is a full–service, general practice law firm. A practicing attorney in Texas state courts since 1972, Mr. Sifford co–founded the Firm upon the conferral of his law degree in 1973. As Managing Partner and Trial Attorney, he oversees all administrative operations for associates and a support staff of 14, in addition to his daily law practice. Concurrent with his private law practice, Mr. Sifford is an adjunct lecturer at Southern Methodist University School of Law. **Career Steps:** Attorney, Sifford & Anderson, L.L.P. (1973–Present). **Associations & Accomplishments:** American Bar Association; Advocate, American Board of Trial Advocates; College of the State Bar of Texas; Dallas Association of Defense Counsel; Fellow, Texas Bar Foundation; Fifth Circuit Bar Association; International Association of Defense Counsel; National Institute of Municipal Law Officers; NITA Advocates Association; National Institute of Trial Advocacy; State Bar of Texas; Texas Association of Defense Counsel; Texas City Attorneys Association; Charter Member, Texas Supreme Court Historical Society; The Defense Research and Trial Lawyers Association. **Education:** Baylor University School of Law, J.D. (1972); Baylor University, B.A. **Personal:** Married to Teresa in 1995. Mr. Sifford enjoys reading and writing.

Vincent A. Signorile

Partner
Signorile & Saminski
309 Baldwin Avenue
Jersey City, NJ 07306
(201) 795–5566
Fax: (201) 795–2836

8111

Business Information: Signorile & Saminski is a full–service, general practice law firm concentrating in civil and criminal law. Established in 1989, the Firm currently employs a staff of 15 employees including attorneys, legal and administrative support staff. Admitted to practice in New Jersey state courts since 1985, Mr. Signorile established the Firm with his partner in 1989. Serving as Partner, he is responsible for providing legal representation for the Firm's clientele, including real estate, bankruptcy and some corporate and criminal law. **Career Steps:** Partner, Signorile & Saminski (1989–Present); Councilperson, City of Jersey City (1989–1993); Council Aide, City of Jersey City (1980–1981). **Associations & Accomplishments:** Jersey City Planning Board Commissioner; Jersey City Environmental Commissioner; Jersey City Insurance Fund Commissioner; Jersey City Zoning Board. **Education:** Seton Hall Law School, J.D. (1985); St. Peter's College, B.S. **Personal:** Mr. Signorile enjoys sports, softball, and baseball.

Rolando A. Silva

President
Consultores Legales Asociados, C.S.P.
61 De Diego Avenue – Santurce, Ste. 2A
San Juan, Puerto Rico 00911
(787) 726–1919
Fax: (787) 726–1975

8111

Business Information: Consultores Legales Asociados, C.S.P. is a professional legal service. As President, Mr. Silva is responsible for real estate and business law and litigation. **Career Steps:** President, Consultores Legales Asociados, C.S.P. (1996–Present); Senator, Senate of PR (1981–1996); Deputy Attorney General, Department of Justice (1977–1978); Private Law Practice (1979–1980). **Associa-**

tions & Accomplishments: Puerto Rico Bar Association; American Bar Association; Federal Bar Association; American Legion; International J.C.'s, Outstanding Young Man of the Year (1980) **Education:** University of Puerto Rico, J.D. (1969), Bachelors in Business Administration cum laude (1966). **Personal:** Married to Ana M. in 1985. Three children: Rolando, Antonio, and Natalia. Mr. Silva enjoys scuba diving, riding horses, skiing, and travel.

Ms. Marsha E. Simms
Attorney and Partner
Weil, Gotshal & Manges
767 Fifth Avenue
New York, NY 10153–0002
(212) 310–8116
Fax: (212) 310–8007
E–mail: see below

8111

Business Information: Weil, Gotshal & Manges is a general practice law firm. The Firm currently employs 1,800 attorneys and legal support staff. As Attorney and Partner, Ms. Simms concentrates her practice in the areas of debt financing and re-structuring. Ms. Simms can also be reached through the Internet as follows: marsha.simms@weil.com **Career Steps:** Weil, Gotshal & Manges: Partner (1987–Present); Associate (1985–1987); Associate, Shearman & Sterling (1977–1985). **Associations & Accomplishments:** American Bar Association: Vice Chair, Secured Transactions Subcommittee, UCC Committee of the Business Law Section; National Bar Association; New York State Bar Association: Member of the Banking Law Committee, Committee on Minorities in the Profession; Association of the Bar of the City of New York: Secretary, Committee to Enhance Diversity in the Profession; Metropolitan Black Bar Association; Board of Trustees, Educational Broadcasting Corporation. **Education:** Stanford Law School, J.D. (1977); Barnard College, B.A. **Personal:** Ms. Simms enjoys travel and reading mysteries.

Ms. Pamela Huessy Simon
Partner
Pope, McMillian, Kutten & Simon, P.A.
P.O. Box 1776
Statesville, NC 28687–1776
(704) 873–2131
Fax: (704) 872–7629

8111

Business Information: Pope, McMillian, Kutten & Simon, P.A. is a general practice law firm. Established in 1920, the Firm currently employs 4 principal attorneys, one associate and 10 legal support staff. As Partner in the Firm, Ms. Simon concentrates her practice in the areas of domestic relations. She also practices some real estate and corporate contract law. Admitted to both State and Federal courts, Ms. Simon has been a trial attorney since the conferral of her law degree in 1984. **Career Steps:** Partner, Pope, McMillian, Kutten & Simon, P.A. (1992–Present); Attorney and Partner, Mattox, Mallory & Simon (1986–1992); Associate, Tucker, Hicks, Moon, Hodge & Crawford (1985–1986). **Associations & Accomplishments:** North Carolina Bar Association; American Academy of Matrimonial Lawyers; Chair, Fifth Street Shelter Ministries; Board Certified Specialist in Family Law; Chair, North Carolina Bar Association Family Law Curriculum Committee. **Education:** University of North Carolina – Chapel Hill, J.D. (1984); University of California – Berkeley, B.A. (1968). **Personal:** Married to L. P. Hazel, Jr. in 1979. Two children: Thomas Alexander Hazel and Alice Lyle Hazel. Ms. Simon enjoys snow skiing, singing and playing the piano and the guitar.

Mr. Robert S. Simon
Corporate Counsel
Westland Development Company, Inc.
401 Coors N.W.
Albuquerque, NM 87121
(505) 831–9600
Fax: (505) 831–4865 (505) 242–4366

8111

Business Information: Westland Development Company, Inc. specializes in corporate, securities, real estate, and business law. Mr. Simon splits his time 50/50 between being business counsel for a small public company and his small business clients. He especially likes to represent new start–ups such as one developing 3D Sonograms; a revolutionary wall mounting systems business; and he is also founder and counsel for the Wildlife West Nature Park. **Career Steps:** Corporate Counsel, Westland Development Company, Inc. (1989–Present); Corporate Counsel, Pier 1 Imports, Inc. (1972–1982). **Associations & Accomplishments:** Founder, United Yoga Institute; Director, La Motinda Food Coop; Member, Neighborhood Association, Albuquerque school system parent activities. Mr. Simon has also published restau-

rant reviews. **Education:** Texas Christian University, M.B.A. (1976); University of Texas, Austin, J.D. (1970); University of Texas, Austin, B.B.A. with honors (1967). **Personal:** Married to Amy in 1975. Two children: Luke and William. Mr. Simon enjoys collecting cowry shells, helping start–up businesses, and school/parent activities.

Stephen L. Simonton
Attorney
Simonton and Simonton
1092 Sheridan Avenue
Cody, WY 82414
(307) 587–5575
Fax: (307) 587–2746

8111

Business Information: Simonton and Simonton is a full–service, general practice law firm, specifically concentrating on personal injury cases. A practicing attorney in Wyoming states courts since 1967, Mr. Simonton co–founded the Firm with his brother in 1975. Serving as a trial attorney, his practice focuses on personal injury and environmental law cases. **Career Steps:** Attorney, Simonton and Simonton (1975–Present); Park County, Wyoming: Public Defender, Deputy County Attorney. **Associations & Accomplishments:** Wyoming Trial Lawyers Association: President, Treasurer; Board of Directors, Cody Medical Foundation; Board of Trustees, West Park Hospital; National Council of Hospital Governing Boards; Cody Volunteer Fire Department (1974–1989); American Bar Association; Park County Travel Council; Big Brothers Program; Professional Trial Lawyers Association. **Education:** University of Wyoming College of Law, J.D. (1967); Allegheny College, B.A. (1964). **Personal:** Two children: Shelley Marie and Michael J. Mr. Simonton enjoys fly fishing, hiking, scuba diving, camping, and public service.

Mr. Arthur Skibell
Vice President
Bird & Skibell, P.C.
Comerica Tower, Suite 600
Dallas, TX 75225
(214) 750–6300
Fax: (214) 363–0719

8111

Business Information: Bird & Skibell, P.C. is a general practice law firm. As Vice President, Mr. Skibell is responsible for overseeing management of the Firm's operations, as well as practicing business and real estate law and major commercial litigation. Established in 1988, Bird & Skibell, P.C. employs a professional legal and administrative support staff of 14 and reports annual revenue in excess of $1 million. **Career Steps:** Attorney, Bird & Skibell, P.C. (1988–Present); Municipal Judge, City of Farmersbranch (1984– 1990); Vice President and General Counsel, Rodeway Inns of America (1972–1980); Assistant Attorney General, State of Texas (1967–1968). **Associations & Accomplishments:** American Bar Association; Texas Bar Association; Dallas Bar Association. **Education:** University of Texas Law School, J.D. (1966); University of Texas at Austin, B.A. (1964).

Michelle Bendien Skole
Attorney
Law Office of Michelle Skole
3036 Alden Court
Bensalem, PA 19020
(215) 752–2524
Fax: (215) 752–2527

8111

Business Information: The Law Office of Michelle Skole is a private practice law firm concentrating on immigration law. Mrs. Skole established her private practice in 1991. She was admitted to the state and federal courts in New Jersey and Pennsylvania. An attorney since 1990, Mrs. Skole is also employed by the State of New Jersey, Department of Labor as a supervisor in the Office of Alien Labor Certification. **Career Steps:** Attorney, The Law Office of Michelle Skole (1991–Present); State of New Jersey Labor Department (1965–Present). **Education:** Temple Law School, J.D. (1990); Syracuse University, B.A. (1964). **Personal:** Two children: Nicole and Danielle and a grandson Stephen. Mrs. Skole enjoys painting and doing artwork.

Marilyn Sloane
Attorney
Marilyn Sloane, Esq.
8 Shawnee Trail
Harrison, NY 10528
(914) 835–2722
Fax: (914) 835–0378

8111

Business Information: A practicing attorney since 1968, Ms. Sloane established her own law firm in 1994, concentrating on employee benefits and insurance (e.g., pensions, 401K and 403b plans, distribution planning, cafeteria plans, IRS documentation) in the Greater New York area. **Career Steps:** Sole Proprietor, Marilyn Sloane, Esq. (1994–Present); Associate, Weil, Gotshal & Manges (1995); Chief Counsel, Schloss & Co./ Shore & Reich (1990–1995); Senior Vice President, Mutual of America (1974–1990). **Associations & Accomplishments:** President, New York Chapter, Chartered Life Underwriters; American Bar Association; New York State Bar Association; Association of the Bar of the City of New York. **Education:** Columbia Law School, J.D. (1968); University of Vermont, B.A. (1965). **Personal:** Married to Stanley Lisman in 1990. One child: Craig. Ms. Sloane enjoys skiing, bicycling and gardening.

Brian R. Smith
Partner
Robinson & Cole
212 Sunset Drive
Glastonbury, CT 06033–4145
(860) 275–8200
Fax: (860) 275–8299
E–mail: bsmith@rc.com

8111

Business Information: Robinson & Cole is a general practice law firm. Established in 1845, the Firm currently employs 350 attorneys and legal support staff. As Partner, Mr. Smith concentrates his practice in the areas of land use, real estate law and real estate–related litigation. Mr. Smith is also responsible for the training of new associates. A trial attorney since the conferral of his law degree in 1985, Mr. Smith is admitted to both State and Federal courts. **Career Steps:** Robinson & Cole: Partner (1993–Present), Associate (1985–1992); Legislative Associate, New York State Assembly (1982). **Associations & Accomplishments:** Connecticut State Coordinator and President of the Hartford Sister Cities Organization, Sister Cities International; American Bar Association; Member, Executive Committee for Planning and Zoning, Connecticut Bar Association; Hartford County Bar Association; Director, Patrons of the John F. Kennedy Trust of New Ross Ireland, Inc.; Published article concerning land use law. **Education:** Cornell Law School, J.D. (1985); Colgate University, B.A. cum laude with Honors in history (1977). **Personal:** Married to Kim K.V. McClain in 1985. Mr. Smith enjoys fencing, gardening, music, writing Haikus, and studying the Japanese language.

Claude R. Smith, J.D.
Attorney
The Law Office of Claude R. Smith
2817 Harvard Avenue, Suite 103
Metairie, LA 70006
(504) 455–4283
Fax: (504) 455–3686

8111

Business Information: The Law Office of Claude R. Smith is a private general practice law firm concentrating in bankruptcy law. As Attorney, Mr. Smith established his private practice in 1981 and since 1982 he has been a Trustee in Bankruptcy for the East District of Louisiana concurrent to running his own legal practice. A trial attorney since 1967, Mr. Smith is admitted to both State and Federal courts. **Career Steps:** Attorney, Law Office of Claude R. Smith (1981–Present); Trustee in Bankruptcy, East District Louisiana (1982–Present); General Counsel, Federal Inter. Credit Bank (1978–1981); Senior Attorney, Federal Land Bank (1969–1978). **Associations & Accomplishments:** Jefferson Bar Association; East Jefferson Business Association; Alabama State Bar Association; Louisiana State Bar Association; American Bar Association. **Education:** Cumberland School of Law, J.D. (1967); University of Alabama, A.B. (1964); Loyola Law School (1970–1972). **Personal:** Married to Mary A. Shadix in 1968. Two children: Paul Steven and Mark Richard. Mr. Smith enjoys being a University of Alabama football fan.

Jerry M. Smith, Esq.
Attorney at Law
Sigler & Smith Law Office
2020 East D Street
Torrington, WY 82240–2934
(307) 532–2121
Fax: (307) 532–2122

8111

Business Information: Sigler & Smith Law Office, formerly Bob C. Sigler Law Office, is a full–service, general practice law firm with office space for three attorneys. The Firm is the only practice in Torrington that regularly handles Social Security disability and bankruptcy cases. A practicing attorney in Wyoming state and federal courts, Mr. Smith bought the Firm from Bob C. Sigler in 1992. Serving as Owner, with Mr. Sigler still practicing with the Firm, his main areas of concentration are agricultural and small business financial issues, estate planning and litigation. **Career Steps:** Attorney at Law, Sigler & Smith Law Office (1992–Present); Attorney at Law, Bob C. Sigler Law Office (1983–1992). **Associations & Accomplishments:** American Bar Association; Wyoming Bar Association; Goshen County Bar Association; Wyoming Trial Lawyers Association; Torrington Lions Club. **Education:** University of Wyoming – College of Law, J.D. (1983); University of Wyoming, B.A. (1966). **Personal:** Three children: Corey Mack, Sheila A. and Amanda L. Mr. Smith enjoys hunting, fishing, and farming.

Todd A. Smith

Partner
Power Rogers & Smith, P.C.
35 West Wacker Drive, Suite 3700
Chicago, IL 60601–1614
(312) 236–9381
Fax: (312) 236–0920

8111

Business Information: Power Rogers & Smith, P.C. is a law firm representing plaintiffs in all types of personal injury litigation, including Wrongful Death, Product Liability, Aviation, Structural Work Act, Medical Malpractice, and Automobile Negligence. As a Partner, Mr. Smith oversees the Firm's management, and is a trial attorney admitted to practice in the State of Illinois; U.S. Court of Appeals, Seventh Circuit; U.S. District Court, Northern District of Illinois; and U.S. Supreme Court. **Career Steps:** Partner, Power Rogers & Smith, P.C., (1976–Present). **Associations & Accomplishments:** American Bar Association: Litigation Section; Tort and Insurance Practice Section; Space and Aviation Section; Editorial Board, "The Brief" (1990–1992); American Inn of Court, Markey Wigmore Chapter; Appellate Lawyers Association; Association of Trial Lawyers: Sustaining Member, Amicus Curiae Committee (1988–Present), Fellow – Roscoe Pound Foundation, Member – Board of Governors; Chicago Bar Association; Illinois State Bar Association; Illinois Trial Lawyers Association; "Law Journal", Loyola University School of Law; National College of Advocacy; The Society of Trial Lawyers; Trial Lawyers for Public Justice; Trial Lawyers Club of Chicago; Active Teacher and Lecturer on legal issues; Author of numerous articles on legal issues for trade journals. **Education:** Loyola University School of Law, J.D. (1976); Northwestern University Graduate School of Business, M.B.A. (1973); Kansas University, B.S.B. (1971). **Personal:** Married to Marcia Friedl Smith in 1989. Two children: Benjamin and Grace Marie. Mr. Smith enjoys writing and lecturing.

William P. Smith

Partner
Chapman and Cutler
111 West Monroe Street
Chicago, IL 60603
(312) 845–3877
Fax: (312) 701–2361

8111

Business Information: Chapman and Cutler is an international, full–service, boutique law firm, representing lenders and issuers of various capital markets in financial matters. The Firm's main focus is the consolidation of hospitals. Established in 1913, the Firm reports annual revenue of $80 million and currently employs 500 people, including 200 attorneys. A practicing attorney since 1977, Mr. Smith joined the Firm in 1983. Currently serving as Partner, he is responsible for the restructuring of defaulted securities in the U.S. (60% in Florida, 5% in Connecticut, and the rest in North & South Dakota, Colorado, Arizona, California) and Canada. **Career Steps:** Partner, Chapman and Cutler (1983–Present); Estabrook, Finn & McKee: Partner (1982–1983), Associate (1977–1982). **Associations & Accomplishments:** Member: Chicago, Illinois, and American Bar Associations; Speaker at the annual conference on National Association of Educational Facilities Authorities and various other professional conferences. **Education:** University of Cincinnati, J.D. (1977); Cornell University, B.A. (1974). **Personal:** Married to Kiki K. in 1978. Four children: Hilary Coe, Duncan Pfeiffer, Lydia Cadaret, and Beatrice Carr. Mr. Smith enjoys spending time with his family.

Laverne Lair Sochats

Owner and Attorney
Laverne Lair Sochats, Esq.
4106 Butler Street
Pittsburgh, PA 15201
(412) 621–3305
Fax: (412) 621–3424

8111

Business Information: The Law Office of Laverne Lair Sochats is a sole practice general law firm. Admitted to practice in 1990, Ms. Sochats established her private law firm in 1993. **Career Steps:** Sole Practitioner, Laverne Lair Sochats, Esq. (1993–Present); Morton B. DeBroff, P.C.: Attorney (1990–1993), Office Manager (1979–1993). **Associations & Accomplishments:** Lawrenceville Rotary Club; Lawrenceville Business Association; Delta Sigma Pi. **Education:** University of Pittsburgh, J.D. (1990), M.B.A., B.S. **Personal:** Married to Kenneth M. Sochats in 1982. Ms. Sochats enjoys reading and gardening.

Iris K. Socolofsky–Linder

Attorney
Fraser Trebilcock Davis & Foster, P.C.
1000 Michigan National Tower
Lansing, MI 48933
(517) 482–5800
Fax: (517) 482–0887

8111

Business Information: Fraser Trebilcock Davis & Foster, P.C. is a full–service, general practice law firm, concentrating on corporate, business, and securities law issues. Joining the Firm upon the conferral of her law degree in 1980, Ms. Socolofsky–Linder serves as Attorney and Shareholder. Admitted to practice in Michigan state courts, she concentrates her practice in the areas of securities law, business and corporate planning, intellectual property law, administrative law, franchise law, and non–profit corporation law. **Career Steps:** Attorney, Fraser Trebilcock Davis & Foster, P.C. (Current). **Associations & Accomplishments:** Lansing Regional Chamber of Commerce: Board Member (1987–1992), Government Affairs Division Director (1991–1992); Capital Enterprise Forum: Secretary (1989–1990), Vice President of Investor Development (1991), Vice President (1992), President (1993); City of Lansing Mayor's Parking Advisory Committee (1990–1994), LRC PAC (1990–Present), Chair (1995–Present); Michigan Corporation and Securities Bureau Advisory Committee (1991–Present); American Bar Association; State Bar of Michigan, Blue Sky Law Subcommittee and Transportation Law Committee; Ingham County Bar Association; Board Member, Capital Area United Way (1994–Present); Capital Area Girl Scouts Council; Board Member, National Association of Career Women, Lansing Chapter; Treasurer, Congregation Kehillat Israel (1995–Present); Director, The Venture Center, Inc. (1996–Present). **Education:** University of Michigan Law School, J.D., cum laude (1980); University of Kansas; Michigan State University, B.S., High Honors. **Personal:** Married to Stephen J. in 1992. One child: Eric. Mrs. Socolofsky–Linder enjoys tennis.

Mark J. Sommaruga

Associate Attorney
Sullivan, Schoen, Campane & Connon, L.L.C.
646 Prospect Avenue
Hartford, CT 06105–4203
(860) 233–2141
Fax: (860) 233–0516

8111

Business Information: Sullivan, Schoen, Campane & Connon, L.L.C. is a full–service, general practice law firm concentrating on educational issues, labor and employment issues, constitutional issues, and special education. The Firm represents 65 school boards in Connecticut and several municipalities. Established in 1975, the Firm currently employs 10 attorneys and legal and administrative support staff. Admitted to practice in Connecticut state courts and the federal courts, Mr. Sommaruga joined the Firm upon conferral of his law degree in 1991. He focuses his practice on special education litigation, administration appeals, practice before the appellate courts, and advising clients on various issues. **Career Steps:** Associate Attorney, Sullivan, Schoen, Campane & Connon, L.L.C. (1991–Present). **Associations & Accomplishments:** American Bar Association; Connecticut Bar Association: Education Law Committee, Labor & Employment Section, Young Lawyers Section; Hartford County Bar Association; National School Boards Association; Council of School Attorneys; Trinity Club of Hartford; Season ticket holder for the New England Patriots; Phi Beta Kappa; Authored several articles on education/school law issues. **Education:** University of Connecticut School of Law, J.D., with High Honors (1991); Trinity College, B.A. (1988). **Personal:** Mr. Sommaruga enjoys reading and music.

Dennis A. Sommese

Sole Practitioner
Law Offices of Dennis A. Sommese
3000 Ardenway, Suite 1
Sacramento, CA 95825
(916) 485–6396
Fax: (916) 485–8073
EMAIL: See Below

8111

Business Information: Law Offices of Dennis A. Sommese is a private, full–service, general practice law firm, concentrating on on– and off–the–job disability cases. A practicing attorney since 1984, Mr. Sommese established his private law practice in 1991. He oversees all administrative operations for associates and a support staff of four, in addition to his daily legal practice. His practice concentrates on litigation in Worker's Compensation, Social Security, Social Security Disability, Personal Injury, and Labor Employment law. Internet users can reach him via: sommese@aol.com. **Career Steps:** Attorney at Law, Law Offices of Dennis A. Sommese (1991–Present); Military: Retired Major, serving as Attorney U.S. Army Reserves – Judge Advocate General Corps (1984–1992), Active Commission Major – Attorney – JAG U.S. Army Reserves (1967–1984). **Associations & Accomplishments:** Counselor, Billy Graham Crusade; Phi Alpha Delta International Law Fraternity; Sacramento County Bar Association; American Bar Association; Public Sector Labor Law Committee (1986–1987), State Bar of California; The Association of Trial Lawyers of America; California Trial Lawyers Association; Best Brief Finalist, Moot Court Award, Author of "How to Handle Military Clauses in a Lease" Fort Riley Post, (1986) **Education:** University of Pacific, McGeorge School of Law, J.D. (1984); University of Southern California, M.S. (1976); Seton Hall University, B.A. in Pre Law (1971); University of Virginia, U.S. Army Judge Advocate General's School (1985). **Personal:** Married to Jeri Ann in 1989. Two children: Jeremy and Nicole Beard. Mr. Sommese enjoys boating and fund raising.

Steven P. Sonnenberg

Partner
Sonnenberg & Anderson
200 S. Wacker Drive, 33rd Floor
Chicago, IL 60606
(312) 441–1700
Fax: Please mail or call

8111

Business Information: Sonnenberg & Anderson is a full–service, general practice law firm concentrating on customs and international trade law for exporters and importers. The Firm deals with the classification and value of goods through customs, agencies, and the International Trade Association (ITA). Established in 1981, the Firm has two locations (Chicago and New York City) and currently employs 7 attorneys (5 in Chicago, 2 in New York City) and 20 legal and administrative support staff. A practicing attorney in Illinois state courts since 1974, Mr. Sonnenberg co–founded the Firm in 1981. Serving as Senior Partner, he is responsible for the financial management of the Firm, as well as trying lawsuits and arguing appeals in a full administrative practice. **Career Steps:** Partner, Sonnenberg & Anderson (1981–Present) **Associations & Accomplishments:** Director, International Trade Association of Greater Chicago; Director, American Association of Exporters & Importers; Chairman, International Affairs Subcommittee Union; League Club of Chicago; Author of more than 20 published articles. **Education:** Illinois Institute of Technology–Chicago Kent College of Law, J.D. (1974); Elmhurst College, B.A. in Psychology. **Personal:** Married to Janis in 1985. One child: Sarah Catherine. Mr. Sonnenberg enjoys scuba diving, tennis, golf, swimming and competing in triathlon events.

Jorge O. Sosa Ramirez

Partner
Sosa and Sosa
P.O. Box 1389
Mayaguez, Puerto Rico 00681–1389
(809) 833–6981
Fax: (809) 833–2548

8111

Business Information: Sosa and Sosa is a full–service, general practice law firm, concentrating on civil and criminal cases in Puerto Rico. Additionally, the Puerto Rico District Court uses the Firm as "masters" to solve inventory and cessation problems. Co–establishing the Firm upon the conferral of his law degree in 1988, Mr. Sosa Ramirez serves as one of two partners of the Firm. He shares his daily law practice with his brother (the other partner), and one associate. His practice concentrates on civil, estate, and banking law, as well as providing counsel for corporations in charge of administration and parking lots. Concurrent with his private practice, he serves as Legal Assistant of the Municipal Assembly for the Puerto Rico government. **Career Steps:** Partner, Sosa and Sosa (1988–Present). **Associations & Accomplishments:** Puerto Rico Lawyer's Bar; Phi Alpha Delta; Social and Civic Lions International; Sports President, Puerto Rico Shooting Federation; Delegate, Puerto Rico Olympic Committee. **Education:** Catholic University Law School, J.D. (1988); Puerto Rico State University, B.A. (1985). **Personal:** Married to Angela I. Natavio in 1990. Two children: Relin Sosa and Thalia M. Sosa. Mr. Sosa Ramirez enjoys target shooting, hunting, and fishing.

Cesar H. Soto–Cintron, Esq., CPA
Associate Attorney
Totti, Rodriguez, Diaz & Fuentes
P.O. Box 10723
San Juan, Puerto Rico 00922–0723
(809) 753–7910
Fax: (809) 764–9480

8111

Business Information: Totti, Rodriguez, Diaz & Fuentes is a full–service, general practice law firm. As Associate, Mr. Soto–Cintron specializes in corporate, bankruptcy, and tax law. Mr. Soto–Cintron has litigation experience in both, federal and state courts. He has also participated in labor arbitrations, and collective bargaining negotiations. Finally, Mr. Soto–Cintron is part of the Mergers and Acquisitions team of his firm. **Career Steps:** Associate Attorney, Totti, Rodriguez, Diaz & Fuentes (1995–Present); Law Clerk, Dominguez & Totti (1993–1994). **Associations & Accomplishments:** Puerto Rico Bar Association; American Bar Association; Federal Bar Association; Puerto Rico State Board of Accountancy; American Institute of Certified Public Accountants (AICPA); Member, Tax Section, AICPA; San Juan Board of Realtors; Puerto Rico Board of Realtors; Admitted to the United States Tax Court. **Education:** University of Puerto Rico School of Law, J.D. magna cum laude (1994); University of the Sacred Heart, B.B.A. cum laude in Accounting (1990).

Miss Jonna M. Spilbor
Attorney at Law
Law Office of Jonna M. Spilbor
852 Fifth Avenue Suite 306
San Diego, CA 92101
(619) 233–9787 1–888–4CRIMDEF
Fax: (619) 233–9788

8111

Business Information: Law Office of Jonna M. Spilbor is a general practice law firm, concentrating in the fields of criminal defense, and selected civil law matters and litigation. An individual law practice firm, Miss Spilbor oversees all administrative aspects in addition to her client representation. Established in 1994, Law Office of Jonna M. Spilbor has two associate attorneys and three legal and administrative support staff. **Career Steps:** Attorney at Law, Law Office of Jonna M. Spilbor (1994–Present); Attorney, Law Office of Robert C. Anderson (1993–1994); Law Clerk, United States Attorney Office (6/1992–12/1992); Law Clerk, San Diego City Attorneys Office (1991–1992). **Associations & Accomplishments:** President, Western State University Alumni Association; California Young Lawyers Association; American Bar Association; Los Angeles Lawyers Club; Law Review Author (WSU); President, Thomas Jefferson School of Law Alumni Association (1994–1995). **Education:** WSU–San Diego, J.D. (1992); Marist College; Thomas Jefferson School of Law (1987).

Mr. John W. Spire
Chief Financial Officer & Deputy Director of Administration
Vinson & Elkins, L.L.P.
1001 Fannin
Houston, TX 77002–6760
(713) 758–2697
Fax: (713) 615–5450

8111

Business Information: Vinson & Elkins, L.L.P. is a full–service, premier practice law firm. Established in 1917, the Firm has an estimated annual revenue of $230 million and currently employs 1,420 employees at seven locations (four in the U.S. and three internationally). As Chief Financial Officer & Deputy Director of Administration, Mr. Spire supports the Executive Director in all administrative services, as well as being responsible for all financial matters for the law firm. **Career Steps:** Chief Financial Officer & Deputy Director of Administration, Vinson & Elkins, L.L.P. (1986–Present); Chief Financial Officer, Enterprise Technologies, Inc. (1984–1986); Controller, Armco, Inc. – Tubular Division (1977–1981); Manager, Arm-

co, Inc. – Metal Products Division (1970–1975). **Associations & Accomplishments:** American Institute of Certified Public Accountants (CPA); Texas Society of CPAs; Financial Executive Institute; Association of Legal Administrators and the Planning Forum; Member, Treasurer and Board of Directors, Houston Dare Corporation. **Education:** Kansas State College, B.S. in Business Administration (1963). CPA Certification (1986). **Personal:** Married to Sheila in 1966. Two children: Amy Alise and Gregory Scott. Mr. Spire enjoys saltwater fishing, sports and reading.

Mr. Jack F. St. Clair
Owner and Attorney
Jack F. St. Clair, Attorney at Law
2 Mattoon Street
Springfield, MA 01105
(913) 737–3549
Fax: (913) 737–3382

8111

Business Information: Jack F. St. Clair, Attorney at Law, is a private, full–service, general practice law firm. Admitted to practice in Massachusetts State courts, Mr. St. Clair established his private practice in 1990. He is responsible for all aspects of operations, including providing legal representation and litigation. **Career Steps:** Owner and Attorney, Jack F. St. Clair, Attorney at Law (1990–Present); Partner, Murphy, McCoubrey (1985–1990); Commonwealth of Massachusetts: First Assistant District Attorney (1983–1985), Assistant District Attorney (1979–1983). **Associations & Accomplishments:** Massachusetts Bar Association; American Bar Association; Hampden County Bar Association; Massachusetts Association of Criminal Defense Lawyers; National Association of Criminal Defense Lawyers; Western Massachusetts Chief of Police Association; The Association of Trial Lawyers of America; Massachusetts Academy of Trial Attorneys; Martindale – Hubbell – AV Rating; Listed in Best Lawyers in America by Naifeh & Smith for Criminal Defense; Community Teachers Partnership Program, Advisory Committee to The Learning Tree and Springfield College (1994–Present); Board of Directors, Springfield Metropolitan YMCA (1992–Present); Board Member, New England Board of Higher Education (1990–Present); Board Member, Springfield Technical Community College Foundation (1990–Present). **Education:** Western New England College – School of Law, J.D. (1976); University of Massachusetts, M.S. in Labor Studies (1972); American International College, B.A. in Economics (1969). **Personal:** Married to Anita. Three children: Michael, Kerry, and Darren. Mr. St. Clair enjoys golf, skiing, and reading.

Richard T. Stabnick, Esq.

Senior Partner
Pomeranz, Drayton & Stabnick
95 Glastonbury Boulevard
Glastonbury, CT 06033–4412
(860) 657–8000 Ext: 106
Fax: (860) 657–9838

8111

Business Information: Pomeranz, Drayton & Stabnick is a general practice law firm, currently consisting of fifty attorneys, legal and administrative support staff. A practicing attorney since 1970, as Senior Partner Mr. Stabnick oversees all adminstrative operations of the practice, in addition to his daily client base. He concentrates his practice on worker's compensation litigation. **Career Steps:** Senior Partner, Pomeranz, Drayton & Stabnick (1979–Present); Partner, Lynch, Riscassi & Stabnick (1970–1979). **Associations & Accomplishments:** American Bar Association; Connecticut Bar Association; Hartford County Bar Association; Best Lawyers in America (1995–1996); Alternate West Hartford Town Council; Chairman, Senior Parents Committee, St. Lawrence University. **Education:** University of Conecticut, J.D. (1970); Wesleyan University, B.A. (1966). **Personal:** Married to Cheryl J. in 1968. Two children: Jennifer and Courtney. Mr. Stabnick enjoys reading and golf.

G. Michael Stakias, Esquire
Partner
Blank, Rome, Comisky & McCauley
1200 Four Penn Center Plaza
Philadelphia, PA 19103
(215) 569–5547
Fax: (215) 569–5555

8111

Business Information: Blank, Rome, Comisky & McCauley is a large full–service law firm that handles both domestic and international legal matters. Besides the headquarters in Philadelphia, the Firm has locations in Washington, D.C., Wilmington, DE, West Palm Beach, FL, Cherry Hill, NJ, Allentown, PA and Media, PA. As Partner, Mr. Stakias specializes in corporate transactional work, securities, mergers, acquisitions and is Chairman of the Business and Corporate Department. Established in 1946, Blank, Rome, Comisky & McCauley employs 600 people. **Career Steps:** Partner, Blank, Rome, Comisky & McCauley (1980–Present); Attorney, United States Securities & Exchange Commission (1977–1980). **Associations & Accomplishments:** Member, American Bar Association and Subcommittee Chairman; Board of Trustees, Thomas M. Cooley Law School; Mr. Stakias has also had articles published in various professional journals. He belongs to the Patrons Foundation, which is a charitable organization that consists of 100 well–known Philadelphia business people. **Education:** New York University School of Law, L.L.M. (1977); Thomas M. Cooley Law School, J.D.; College of William & Mary, B.A. in Government. **Personal:** Married. Two children: . Mr. Stakias enjoys tennis.

Ms. Patricia A. Stamler
Partner
Sommers, Schwartz, Silver & Schwartz, P.C.
2000 Town Center, Suite 900
Southfield, MI 48075
(810) 355–0300
Fax: (810) 746–4001

8111

Business Information: Sommers, Schwartz, Silver & Schwartz, P.C. is a law firm which handles all aspects of personal injury and corporate law. A practicing attorney since 1983, Ms. Stamler has been an associate with the Firm since 1989. She became a Partner in December, 1994. As a litigator for the Firm, Ms. Stamler handles all aspects of pre–trial and trial work. Her areas of practice are focused on civil rights, employment discrimination, clergy sexual abuse and incest cases, disability rights, special education and sports law. The Firm employs 75 attorneys. **Career Steps:** Partner, Sommers, Schwartz, Silver & Schwartz, P.C., (1994–Present); Associate Attorney, Sommers, Schwartz, Silver & Schwartz, P.C. (1989–1994); Supervising and Staff Attorney, Michigan Protection & Advocacy Service (1985–1989); Staff Attorney, Law Offices of Joseph A. Golden (1983–1985); Student Attorney, Free Legal Aid Clinic (1981–1983). **Associations & Accomplishments:** Board Member, National Lawyers Guild; Board Member, JARC; Board Member, Mid–Michigan Youth & Family; Member and Committee Member, Committee on Mental Disabilities, Michigan State Bar Association; Michigan Trial Lawyers Association; American Trial Lawyers Association; Womens Justice Center; Detroit Founders Society; Oakland County ARC; American Bar Association. **Education:** Wayne State University Law School, J.D. (1983); Graduated with Honors from Michigan State University with a dual major in English and Anthropology (B.A. 1980); Law Day Award for Best Brief in 1982 for Moot Court. **Personal:** Married to Joel Jonas in 1991. Ms. Stamler enjoys hiking, canoeing, camping and other outdoor recreational activities.

Sally Fite Stanfield
Sole Practitioner
The Law Office of Sally Fite Stanfield
2829 Offutt Road
Randallstown, MD 21133
(410) 922–6523
Fax: Please mail or call

8111

Business Information: The Law Office of Sally Fite Stanfield is a full–service, general practice law firm. A practicing attorney in Washington and Maryland state courts since 1981, Ms. Stanfield established her private practice firm in 1991. Responsible for all aspects of operations, she serves as a Play Agent, representing LPGA golfers and marketing players for sponsorships and product or service endorsement, as well as conducting contract negotiations. Concurrent with her private law practice, she breeds and shows Arabian horses. **Career Steps:** Sole Practitioner, The Law Office of Sally Fite Stanfield

(1991–Present); Associate Lawyer, Weiss, Jensen, Ellis & Howard (1989–1991); Independent Contractor/Attorney (1988–1989); Deputy Prosecutor, King County Prosecutor – Seattle, WA (1984–88); **Associations & Accomplishments:** Maryland State Bar Association; Washington State Bar Association; Northwest Heritage Arabian Horse Club; International Arabian Horse Association. **Education:** Washington and Lee University School of Law, J.D. (1981); Western Maryland College, B.A. **Personal:** Ms. Stanfield enjoys golf, hiking, exercising, equestrian events, and reading.

Ms. Roberta G. Stanley

President, Administrator and Attorney
The Law Office of Roberta G. Stanley, P.A.
1 East Broward Boulevard, Suite 1501
Ft. Lauderdale, FL 33301–1865
(305) 523–1515
Fax: (305) 523–1614

8111

Business Information: The Law Office of Roberta G. Stanley, P.A. is a general practice family law firm, concentrating in the areas of adoption, divorce, and custody. Established in 1993, the Office currently employs three legal support staff. As President, Administrator and Attorney, Ms. Stanley is responsible for all aspects of operations. A trial attorney since the conferral of her law degree in 1983, Ms. Stanley is admitted to both State and Federal courts. **Career Steps:** President, Administrator and Attorney, Offices of Roberta G. Stanley (1993–Present); Attorney, Bruno, Digiulian & Associates (1988–1992); Attorney and Partner, Dingwall & Stanley (1983–1988). **Associations & Accomplishments:** Broward County Bar Association; Palm Beach County Bar Association; American Bar Association; Florida Bar Association; Broward County Women Lawyers Association. **Education:** Nova University, J.D. (1983); University of Pittsburgh, B.A. **Personal:** Married to James Welzien in 1990. Ms. Stanley enjoys skiing, jogging and reading.

Lawrence S. Starkopf

Partner
Grund & Starkopf
111 East Wacker Drive, Suite 28
Chicago, IL 60601–4208
(312) 616–6600
Fax: (312) 616–6606

8111

Business Information: Grund & Starkopf is a full–service, matrimonial boutique law firm specializing in all aspects of family law including prenuptial agreements, divorce and child custody. Grund & Starkopf currently employs 7 attorneys and 2 paralegals. Attaining his law degree in 1975, Mr. Starkopf began his legal career as a litigation associate for the Public Defenders Office. As Partner, he is responsible for all aspects of the Firm's operation. Licensed to practice in state and federal courts, he represents top executives of "Carriage Trade" in Chicago, IL. **Career Steps:** Partner, Grund & Starkopf (1993–Present); Associate, Feiwell, Galper, Ltd (1980–1993); Associate, Edward Vrdolyak (1976–1980); Litigation Associate, Public Defenders Office (1975–1976). **Associations & Accomplishments:** Chicago Bar Association; Illinois State Bar Association; American Bar Association; American Academy of Matrimonial Lawyers. **Education:** University of Baltimore School of Law, J.D. (1975); University of Arizona, B.A. (1971).

David John Stefany

Attorney and Shareholder
Hogg, Allen, Norton & Blue, P.A.
324 South Hyde Park Avenue, Suite 350
Tampa, FL 33606–2234
(813) 251–1210
Fax: (813) 253–2006

8111

Business Information: Hogg, Allen, Norton & Blue, P.A. is a full–service, general practice law firm, specializing in the representation of employers (management) in labor and employment law issues. Offices are located in Coral Gables, Tampa, Orlando, and Tallahassee, Florida. Joining the Firm upon the conferral of his law degree in 1984, Mr. Stefany currently serves as a Shareholder of the Firm, providing legal representation to the Firm's clientele. His practice focuses in the area of litigations in Florida state and federal courts. **Career Steps:** Attorney and Shareholder, Hogg, Allen, Norton & Blue, P.A. (1984–Present). **Associations & Accomplishments:** American Bar Association; Florida Bar Association; Hillsborough County Bar; Leadership Tampa 1995; Wake Forest

University Alumni Council (1989–1996); President, Wake Forest University Alumni Association (1995–1996); President, Tampa Bay Little League (1996); Regional Chair, Wake Forest's Presidential Scholarship for Distinguished Achievement; United Way Sectional Chair; United Way Keel Club (1994–1996); Centre Club; Harbour Island Athletic Club. **Education:** Stetson University College of Law, J.D. (1984); Wake Forest University, B.S. (1980). **Personal:** Married to E. Carol in 1980. Two children: Matthew David and Daniel Robert. Mr. Stefany enjoys music, golf, tennis, and fishing.

Mr. Sanford M. Stein

Partner
Wildman, Harrold, Allen & Dixon
225 West Wacker Drive
Chicago, IL 60606
(312) 201–2617
Fax: (312) 201–2555

8111

Business Information: Wildman, Harrold, Allen & Dixon is a full–service law firm, specializing in civil business with some criminal law. They represent both large public corporations and closely held corporations, and also practice international law. As Partner, Mr. Stein specializes in environmental law, such as land use and zoning cases. Established in 1967, Wildman, Harrold, Allen & Dixon employs 600 people. **Career Steps:** Partner, Wildman, Harrold, Allen & Dixon (1992–Present); Partner, Gordon & Glickson, P.C. (1985–1992); Owner, Law Office of Sanford M. Stein (1981–1985); Associate, Ancel, Glink, Diamond & Cope (1978–1981). **Associations & Accomplishments:** Member, American Bar Association; Member, Illinois State Bar Association; Member, Chicago Bar Association (Former Chairman, Environmental Law Committee); Editor, Illinois Environmental Law Letter; Moderator, Counsel Connect Illinois Environmental Law Forum; Former Member, Lake County Regional Planning Commission; Former Member, District III, Illinois, Board of Education. Mr. Stein has also had many articles published in professional journals. **Education:** George Washington University, J.D. (1974); University of Illinois, B.A. (1970). **Personal:** Married to Linda Barbera–Stein in 1978. Two children: Marilyn and Bradford. Mr. Stein enjoys politics and hockey.

Mrs. Lea Ann Sterling

Social Justice Attorney and Organizer
Legal Aid Society of Columbus
40 West Gay Street
Columbus, OH 43215
(614) 224–8374 Ext. 131
Fax: (614) 224–4514

8111

Business Information: Admitted to practice in Ohio state and federal courts in 1981, Mrs. Sterling joined the staff of The Legal Aid Society of Columbus in 1986. The agency is a non-profit corporation employing 26 attorneys plus support staff in five counties whose mission it is "to secure equal access to the justice system for and protect the legal rights of indigent individuals unable to retain private counsel, and to educate and inform the poor as to their rights and obligations under existing law". As a member of the domestic relations unit, Mrs. Sterling handles divorce, custody, domestic violence, and guardianship cases, being responsible for all aspects of legal representation. **Career Steps:** Attorney, Legal Aid Society of Columbus (1986–Present); Attorney, Spater, Gittes, Schulte & Kolman (1981–1986); Community Needs Assessment Survey Director, Marion County, Ohio Welfare Department (1977); Field Interviewer, Westat, Inc. (1976). **Associations & Accomplishments:** Ohio American Civil Liberties Union, Civil Liberties Award (1996); Dresden, Germany–Columbus, Ohio Study Tour host family (1996); Women Lawyers of Franklin County, Inc., board member, chair, community service committee (1990–1991); National Lawyers Guild; Academy of Family Mediators; Columbus Bar Association; Olde Towne East Neighborhood Association (1987–Present), OTENA Home Tour (1994). Mrs. Sterling successfully represented plaintiffs in civil rights litigation, including police misconduct actions, sexual harassment claims, and employment discrimination cases, one being a major federal race discrimination class action (1981–1985). She also represented alternative medical practitioners, including certified nurse midwives, achieving wider community acceptance of such alternatives. Mrs. Sterling was an organizer of the Federation of Ohio River Cooperatives (1976–1980), served as its corporate president, (1981–1982) and on its World Food Hunger Committee (1977–1981) and was legal counsel (1982–1985); Infant Formula Action Coalition (INFACT) Central Ohio Coordinator (1978–1981); Marion Ohio National Organization for Women (1976–1979), legislative coordinator (1977); Organized Marion Good Foods Cooperative (1977); Planned Parenthood of East Central Indiana, board member (1975); Ball State University London Centre, London England (1975); U.N. World Population Conference, Bucharest, Romania (1974). **Education:** Ohio State University, J.D. (1980); Ball State University, B.S. summa cum laude (1976). **Personal:** Married to Lanny Sterling in 1987. Three children. Mrs. Sterling enjoys camping, gardening, bicycling, hiking, gourmet cooking, travel, history, genealogy, and the sand dunes of Leelanau County, Michigan.

Mr. Walter R. Stewart

Attorney
Stewart Law Office
330 East Wilson, Suite 100
Madison, WI 53703
(608) 256–7902
Fax: (608) 256–7909

8111

Business Information: Stewart Law Office is a general practice law firm, specializing in business law and transactions, tax law, family law, real estate law and credit collections. Founding the Firm in 1984, as Sole Practitioner Mr. Stewart oversees the overall administrative functioning, as well as practices law. He prides himself on being a fourth generation family attorney. **Career Steps:** Attorney, Stewart Law Office (1984–Present); Legislative Aide, Wisconsin State Assembly (1978–1984). **Associations & Accomplishments:** Public Member, University of Wisconsin–Whitewater Institutional Review Board; President, Madison Classic Guitar Society; Director, Attorney's Title Guaranty (Wisconsin); Member, Village of Maple Bluff Parks and Recreation Committee. **Education:** University of Wisconsin, J.D. (1982); Beloit College, B.A. **Personal:** Married to Pamela Hanson Stewart in 1989. Mr. Stewart enjoys music, yachting and golf.

Robert D. Storey, Esq.

Partner
Thompson, Hine & Flory P.L.L.
3900 Society Center, 127 Public Square
Cleveland, OH 44114
(216) 566–5870
Fax: (216) 566–5800

8111

Business Information: Thompson, Hine & Flory P.L.L. is a premier international law firm. Established in 1911, it has offices in major Ohio cities, Washington D.C., Palm Beach, Florida, and Brussels, Belgium. The Firm currently employs more than 350 legal professionals. Mr. Storey, who received his Juris Doctor degree in 1964, has over 30 years of legal experience. He practices in the Firm's corporate and securities group which provides general corporate counsel to numerous businesses, represents many Fortune 500 companies, and provides services to smaller domestic and foreign businesses in the manufacturing, service, finance, and retail fields. **Career Steps:** Partner, Thompson, Hine & Flory (1993–Present). **Associations & Accomplishments:** Director, GTE Corporation; May Department Stores Company; Procter & Gamble Co.; Bank One, Cleveland, NA; Overseer, Harvard University (1978–1984); Trustee, Phillips Exeter Academy (1969–1983); Trustee, The Kresge Foundation; Case Western Reserve University; Great Lakes Science Center; Cleveland Council on World Affairs; Federal Reserve Bank of Cleveland (1987–1990). **Education:** Harvard University, A.B. (1958); Case Western Reserve University, J.D. (1964). **Personal:** Married to Juanita in 1959. Three children: Charles, Christopher, and Rebecca.

Mr. Dan Stormer

Partner
Hadsell & Stormer, A Law Corporation
128 North Fair Oaks Avenue, Suite 204
Pasadena, CA 91103
(818) 585–9600
Fax: (818) 577–7079

8111

Business Information: Hadsell & Stormer, A Law Corporation is a law firm concentrating in civil rights, constitutional law and public interest litigation. Established in 1991, the Firm currently employs 14 attorneys, legal and administrative support staff. A practicing attorney since 1974, Mr. Stormer co-founded the Firm in 1991. Admitted to practice in state and federal courts in the states of Colorado, Washington and California, Mr. Stormer has argued cases in all levels, including in the U.S. Supreme Court. He is a Civil Rights lawyer who for the past 20 years has specialized in Civil Rights and Constitutional Law litigation and appellate practice. **Career Steps:** Co–Founder, Partner, Hadsell & Stormer, A Law Corporation (1991–Present); Partner, Law Offices of Litt & Stormer (1984–1991); Attorney, Western Center on Law and Poverty (1981–1984); Project Director, Farmworker Project, Evergreen Legal Services (1980); Litigation Director, Spokane Legal Services Center (1978–1980); Directing Attorney, Institutional Legal Services Project, Prison Component (1976–1978); Staff Attorney, Colorado Rural Legal Services, Inc. (1974–1976); Military Service, United States Army, Honorable Discharge (1968–1970). **Associations & Accomplishments:** Bar Membership: State – Colorado, Washington and California. Federal – District of Colorado, Eastern District of Washington, Western District of Washington, Central District of California, Eastern District of California, Ninth Circuit Court of Appeals, Tenth Circuit Court of Appeals, Court of Claims, Federal Circuit Court of Appeals, United States Supreme Court; Member, Board of Directors, Western Center for the Handicapped; Member, Board of Directors, Mental Health Advocacy Services; Executive Committee, Los Angeles County Board Association Committee on Individual Rights; Member, Los Angeles County Bar Association; Member, Los Angeles Trial Lawyers Association; Member, American Bar Association; Member, State Bar of California; Consumer Attorneys Association of Los Angeles; Consumer Attorneys Association of California; Involved in 46 published appellate decisions; Profiled repeatedly in various local and national publications; Named as one of the 10 top plaintiff–side employment lawyers in California by "The Daily Journal", and has been profiled repeatedly by various legal periodicals; Member, Million Dollar Advocates; Lead counsel in several cases (i.e., Martin v. Texaco, Zinzun v. City of Los Angeles, Bonsangue v. ADP and Troffer v. United States); Lecturer and Publisher; Adjunct Professor: Evidence–Advocacy and Pretrial Criminal Procedure at Hastings College of Law, Sentencing and the Correctional Process at Loyola University School of Law, Political Trials at Southwestern University School of Law, Trial Advocacy at San Fernando/La Verne College of Law; Profiled in: Daily Journal, Los Angeles Lawyer, California Lawyer and Legal Exchange; Various publications. **Education:** New York University School of Law, J.D. (1974); Wagner College, B.A. in European History (1968). **Personal:** Married to Jan Breidenbach. Three children: Stephen Stormer and Jesse and Jacob Stormer–Breidenbach. Mr. Stormer enjoys coaching Little League baseball and soccer, skiing and ski-racing.

Thomas L. Story

Vice President and Shareholder
Greensfelder, Hemker & Gale, P.C.
10 South Broadway, Suite 2000
St. Louis, MO 63102
(314) 241–9090
Fax: (314) 241–8624

8111

Business Information: Greensfelder, Hemker & Gale, P.C. is a full–service, general practice law firm concentrating in real estate law. Established in 1895, the Firm currently employs 200 attorneys, legal and administrative support staff. Admitted to practice in Oregon and Missouri state courts since 1972, Mr. Storey joined the Firm in 1975 as Associate. Currently serving as Vice President, Shareholder, and Chairperson of the Real Estate Practice Group, his practice concentrates in real estate law with emphasis on commercial real estate development. **Career Steps:** Greensfelder, Hemker & Gale, P.C.: Vice President, Shareholder, and Chairperson of the Real Estate Practice Group (1981–Present), Associate (1975–1981); Partner, Conn, Lynch & Story, Lakeview, OR (1973–1975). **Associations & Accomplishments:** Missouri Bar – Property Law Committee; Oregon State Bar; Metropolitan St. Louis Bar Association – Business Law Section; American Bar Association – Real Property, Probate and Trust Section; Past President, Phi Delta Theta Alumni Club, St. Louis, MO. **Education:** Washington University, J.D. (1972); Miami University, Oxford, Ohio, B.S. in Business Administration (1969). **Personal:** Married to Brenda H. in 1968. Three children: Braden, Matthew, and Susan. Mr. Story enjoys forestry, woodworking, fishing, and hunting.

William E. Strickland Jr.

Attorney, Vice President & Shareholder
Strickland & Strickland, P.C.
4400 E. Broadway Boulevard, Suite 700
Tucson, AZ 85711
(520) 795–8727
Fax: (520) 795–5649

8111

Business Information: Mr. Strickland is Vice President of and Shareholder in the Strickland & Strickland law firm which concentrates its practice in the areas of Indian Affairs/Gaming Law, Water Law, Personal Injury and Medical Malpractice. Mr. Strickland, who is licensed to practice in Arizona state and federal courts, is responsible for certain legal aspects of the corporation, including negotiating and drafting contracts, counseling clients and litigation. Mr. Strickland and his father, William E. Strickland, Sr., have practiced law together since 1984. **Career Steps:** Attorney, Vice President & Shareholder, Strickland & Strickland (1995–Present); Attorney, Vice President & Shareholder, Strickland & O'Hair, P.C. (1992–1995); Attorney & Treasurer, Strickland & Altaffer, P.C. (1984–1992). **Associations & Accomplishments:** American Bar Association; Pima County Bar Association; State Bar of Arizona; Association of Trial Lawyers of America; Admitted to Bar – Arizona; U.S. District Court, District of Arizona; U.S. Court of Appeals, Ninth Circuit; U.S. Supreme Court; Mayor's Award of Outstanding Citizen of Tucson; Law Firm Listed in Martindale – Hubbell Bar Register of Preeminent Lawyers. **Education:** California Western School of Law, J.D. (1982); University of Arizona, B.S., B.A. (1979). **Personal:** Married to Tammy "Branam" in 1991. Two children: Sean William and Stephanie Lynn. Mr. Strickland enjoys music (drummer), softball, basketball, football, tennis, fishing, and other sports.

Richard L. Strohm, Esq.

Attorney
Law Offices of Richard L. Strohm, Esq., P.C.
1136 East Campbell
Phoenix, AZ 85014–3913
(602) 279–6316
Fax: (602) 279–7102

8111

Business Information: Law Offices of Richard L. Strohm, Esq., P.C. is a litigation firm consisting of full and part–time attorneys who specialize in different areas. With twenty years experience as a trial lawyer, Mr. Strohm has been a practicing attorney in Arizona state and federal courts since 1976. Establishing his sole practice law firm in 1977, his practice concentrates on civil trials in all courts, including criminal defense, professional malpractice (plaintiff and defense), and complex litigation (Antitrust, Employment Law, Entertainment and Sports Law. Mr. Strohm's legal experience includes over 50 jury trials as lead counsel in Arizona Superior and Federal District courts, including murder, fraud and political crimes, and defense of multimillion dollar personal injury and medical malpractice claims. He has also made numerous appearances in Arizona Supreme Court and Arizona Courts of Appeals. Some of his significant reported Apellate cases which he served as Lead Counsel include as follows: U.S. Fidelity & Guaranty vs. Advance Roofing (Ariz. App. 1989); Dodge vs. Fidelity & Deposit Co. of Maryland (Ariz. App. 1986); State vs. Grounds (Ariz. 1981); State vs. Love (Ariz. 1978); State vs. 1969 Volkswagen Bus, Etc. (Ariz. 1978); State vs. Diffenderfer (Ariz. 1978); and, State vs. Arnold (Ariz. 1977). **Career Steps:** Attorney, Law Offices of Richard L. Strohm, Esq., P.C. (1977–Present); Special Assistant Attorney General Appointed January 1995 – Statewide Antitrust Investigation. **Associations & Accomplishments:** AV Rated Attorney, Appointed Commissioner, Arizona State Lottery by Governor Fife Symington, confirmed by the Arizona State Senate (1991); Chairman, Arizona State Bar Trial Practice Section (1993); Board Member, Southwest Funding Corporation (1995); Who's Who in Arizona (1991); Who's Who in Practicing Attorneys (1992); Who's Who in American Law (1994); Arizona Association of Defense Attorneys; Arizona Trial Lawyers Association; Association of Trial Lawyers of America; American Bar Association Forum on the Entertianment and Sports Industries; NBAPA, NHLPA and JFLPA Contract Advisor; Published articles on family and domestic legal matters as well as a frequent lecturer at educational institutions and bar association symposia. **Education:** University of Arizona, J.D. (1976). Northern Illinois University, B.A. in History with honors (1971). **Personal:** Married to Marie Vivian in 1991. One child: Christian Edward.

Jeffrey A. Strother

Attorney at Law
Lojek & Strother Chartered
P.O. Box 1712
Boise, ID 83702–1712
(208) 343–7733
Fax: (208) 389–1294

8111

Business Information: Lojek & Strother Chartered is a full–service, general practice law firm, with concentration on construction law and general business, commercial and personal injury litigation, and employment law. A practicing attorney in Idaho state and federal courts since 1975, Mr. Strother co–founded the Firm in 1992. As a Trial Attorney, his practice concentrates on construction law and general business, commercial and personal injury litigation. Additional experience includes class actions and related procedures in the Federal courts. Career milestones include being designated as Rechtsanwalt to the West German Consulate for Idaho (out of Seattle), as well as conducting work for the German government and German banks. **Career Steps:** Attorney at Law, Lojek & Strother Chartered (1992–Present); Attorney at Law, Meuleman, Miller, Strother, & Cummings (1988–1992); Attorney at Law, Moffett, Thomas, Barrett & Blanton (1976–1988); Clerk, Colorado Court of Appeals (1975–1976). **Associations & Accomplishments:** American Bar Association; Idaho Association of Defense Counsel; Rotary Club. **Education:** University of Colorado School of Law, J.D. (1975); Yale University, B.A. (1972). **Personal:** Married to Margaret in 1977. Three children: Luke, Matt, and Katherine.

Robert A. Stuart, Jr.

Partner
Brown, Hay & Stephens
700 1st National Bank Building
Springfield, IL 62702
(217) 544–8491
Fax: (217) 544–9609

8111

Business Information: Brown, Hay & Stephens is a full–service, general practice law firm. A fifth generation family firm, Brown, Hay & Stephens employs 22 attorneys and legal support staff. Joining his family firm upon the attainment of his law degree in 1973, Mr. Stuart concentrates his practice in the areas of estate planning, probate and trust law. **Career Steps:** Partner, Brown, Hay & Stephens (1973–Present). **Associations & Accomplishments:** Past Chairman, Illinois State Bar Association; Section Council on Estate Planning Probate & Trust (1986); Elder, First Presbyterian Church; Past President, A. Lincoln Council; Silver Beaver, Boy Scouts of America; Past District Governor, Rotary International; 33rd Degree Mason; Board Member, National Recreation Foundation; United Way of Sanganion County; A. Lincoln Association; School of Medicine Advisory Board, Southern Illinois University; Illinois State Museum Society Trustees. **Education:** University of Illinois College of Law, J.D. (1973); Bowdoin College, B.A.; University of Edinburgh. **Personal:** Married to Margie in 1977. One child: Corinne. Mr. Stuart enjoys golf.

Daniel S. Sullivan

Partner
Best, Sharp, Holden, Sheridan, Best & Sullivan
100 West 5th Street, Suite 808
Tulsa, OK 74103–4291
(918) 582–1234
Fax: (918) 585–9447

8111

Business Information: Best, Sharp, Holden, Sheridan, Best & Sullivan is a full–service civil defense and trial practice. Mr. Sullivan joined the firm in 1988, concentrating in the defense of medical and other professionals in malpractice, premises liability, and product liability suits. **Career Steps:** Partner, Best, Sharp, Holden, Sheridan, Best & Sullivan (1988–Present). **Associations & Accomplishments:** Tulsa County Bar Association: Secretary (1994–1995), Treasurer (1995–1996); International Association of Defense Counsel; Defense Research Institute. **Education:** University of Tulsa, J.D. (1988); Northeastern State University, B.A. in Business Administration (1985). **Personal:** Married to Janet K. in 1983. Mr. Sullivan enjoys golf and fly–fishing.

Jack Neil Swickard, J.D.

Sole Practitioner
Law Offices of Jack Neil Swickard
4630 Campus Drive
Newport Beach, CA 92660
(714) 261–0694
Fax: (714) 261–0784

8111

Business Information: Jack Neil Swickard, Attorney at Law is a sole proprietorship law practice, representing clientele on all aspects of international law, concentrating on international arbitration in construction laws (i.e., delay claims, unpaid contracts). Primary business activities are in Rijadh, Saudi Arabia. A practicing attorney in international legal affairs since 1986, Mr. Swickard established his sole practice law office in 1988. He engages in the representation of clientele with international construction legal matters, such as unpaid contractors, construction delays, etc. and preparing and presenting court cases and arbitrations. **Career Steps:** Sole Practitioner, Jack Neil Swickard, Attorney at Law (1988–Present); Senior Subcontract Manager, Kuwait Santa Fe Braun, Mina Abdullah – Kuwait (1986–1987); Senior Facilities Planner, Sysorey, Rijadh – Saudia Arabia (1983–1984); Senior Contract Supervisor, Bechtel, Jubayl – Saudi Arabia (1981–1982). **Associations & Accomplishments:** American Arbitration Association – International Construction Panel; Chartered Institute of Arbitrators – London, United Kingdom; International Bar Association; U.S. Supreme Court Bar Association; Calyoria Bar Association; Cairo Regional Centre for Dispute Resolution; International Platform Association. **Education:** University of LaVerne, J.D. (1986); Whittier College, B.A. (1968). **Personal:** Mr. Swickard enjoys photography, public speaking, and the study of the Arabic language and Islamic culture and law.

WEIR & FOULDS

Lynda C. E. Tanaka
Barrister and Solicitor
Weir & Foulds
Suite 1600 Exchange Tower, P O Box 480 Station 1st Canadian Place
Toronto, Ontario M5X 1J5
(416) 947–5036
Fax: (416) 365–1876

8111

Business Information: Weir & Foulds is a general service law firm located in Toronto, Canada. The Firm has 66 attorneys and a support staff of approximately 124 employees. As Barrister and Solicitor, Ms. Tanaka is a partner in the firm and practices civil litigation, land law, and administrative law including alternative dispute resolution. **Career Steps:** Weir & Foulds: Partner (1980–Present), Litigation Associate (1975–1980), Articling Student (1973–1975). **Associations & Accomplishments:** Vice Chair, Ontario Racing Commission; Arbitration and Mediation Institute of Ontario; International Right of Way Society; Canadian Bar Association; Women's Law Association of Ontario; Chartered Institute of Arbitrators, London. Ms. Tanaka is the recipient of the President's Award from the Women's Law Association – Ontario and the Distinguished Service Award by the Canadian Bar Association – Ontario. **Education:** University of Toronto: L.L.B. (1973), Bachelor of Arts; Called to the Bar of Ontario (1975). **Personal:** Married to Minoru in 1982. Two children: Cornell and Kevin.

Marshall H. Tanick
Partner
Mansfield & Tanick
900 2nd Avenue South, International Center
Minneapolis, MN 55402
(612) 339–4295
Fax: (612) 339–3161

8111

Business Information: Mansfield & Tanick is a full–service, general practice law firm, concentrating on employment, constitutional, class action, and media law. The Firm also provides legal representation in high–profile cases. A practicing attorney in Minnesota state and federal courts since 1973 and a Certified Civil Trial Specialist, Mr. Tanick joined the Firm as Partner in 1989. His practice concentrates on employment (representing both the employer and employee), constitutional, employment, and media law in both civil and criminal courts. **Career Steps:** Partner, Mansfield & Tanick (1989–Present); Tanick & Heins (1976–1989); Robins, Downs & Lyons (1974–1976); Law Clerk, U.S. District Court – Minnesota (1973–1974). **Associations & Accomplishments:** American Bar Association; Minnesota State Bar; Hennepin County Bar Association; Member, First Amendment Lawyers Association; Chairman, First Amendment Fund. **Education:** Stanford University Law School, J.D. (1973); University of Minnesota, B.A. (1969); Certified Civil Trial Specialist. **Personal:** Married to Cathy in 1984. Two children: Lauren and Ross. Mr. Tanick enjoys reading, writing, and bicycling.

Gwyn Ann Taylor
Attorney
McKenna & Cuneo, L.L.P.
1575 Eye Street, N.W.
Washington, DC 20005–1105
(202) 789–7705
Fax: (202) 789–7594

8111

Business Information: McKenna & Cuneo, L.L.P. is a large private law firm with a national and international practice, concentrating on a wide range of government contracts and international specialties. The Firm currently employs more than 500 attorneys, legal, and administrative support staff. A practicing attorney in state and federal courts in the Washington, D.C. area since 1985, Ms. Taylor joined the Firm in 1995. Serving as an Attorney in the Government Contracts Department, she is responsible for handling a wide range of government and construction contract issues, practicing before the U.S. District Court for the District of Columbia and the boards of contract appeals. She also serves as the team coordinator on assignments to advise newly independent and developing

countries in strengthening their Ministry of Justice and Judicial Systems, as well as advising state and local governments regarding procurement for services. **Career Steps:** Attorney, McKenna & Cuneo (1995–Present); Attorney, Morgan, Lewis & Bockius (1993–1995); Attorney, Bastianelli, Brown & Touhey, Chartered (1988–1993); Trial Attorney, U.S. Department of Defense: Office of General Counsel–Arlington Virginia (1987–1988), Department Counsel, Directorate for Industrial Security Clearance Review (1987–1988), Attorney (1986–1987); Law Clerk, Oregon State Department of Justice – General Counsel Division, Salem, Oregon (1984–1985). **Associations & Accomplishments:** Admitted to Practice: U.S. Supreme Court and Court of Appeals for Federal, District of Columbia, and Fourth Circuits, U.S. Court of Federal Claims, U.S. District Court for the District of Columbia; District of Columbia Bar Association; Washington State Bar Association; Federal Bar Association – District of Columbia Chapter: President (1995–1996), Editor of "The Forum" (1992–1994), Recipient of President's Award (1991), Member of Continuing Legal Education Board (1993–1994), Chair, 1996 U.S.–South African Trade & Economic Summit; American Bar Association: Section of Public Contract Law (Commercial Products and Services Committee), Forum Committee for the Construction Industry (Mideast Coordinator for Division I Dispute Avoidance & Resolution Project); National Contract Management Association; Junior League of Washington, District of Columbia; Frequent lecturer and presentations on Outsourcing Government Services and Alternative Dispute Resolution for: National Council for Public–Private Partnerships Ninth Annual Conference (Oct. 1995), Attorney Admissions Ceremony (September 1994). **Education:** Willamette College of Law, J.D. (1985); Washington State University, B.A. in English (1982); University Honors Program (1978–1982); SPECIAL TRAINING: National Institute of Trial Advocacy, Washington, D.C., intensive thirteen–day trial practice seminar and workshop. **Personal:** Ms. Taylor enjoys outdoor sports, triathlons, music, skiing, and equestrian competition.

Sundee M. Teeple
Managing Attorney
Law Offices of Robert G. Winterbotham
1901 East 4th Street, Suite 312
Santa Ana, CA 92705
(714) 543–7717
Fax: (714) 836–5030

8111

Business Information: The Law Offices of Robert G. Winterbotham is Orange County's largest consumer bankruptcy law firm. Clientele include individuals, small businesses and corporations. Established in 1978, the Firm currently employs 48 attorneys, legal and administrative support staff. A practicing attorney in California state courts and the U.S. Federal courts since 1992, Ms. Teeple joined the Firm in 1994. She is involved in all areas of bankruptcy litigation and filings. **Career Steps:** Attorney, Law Offices of Robert G. Winterbotham (1994–Present); Law Offices of John A. Bodney: Attorney (1992–1994), Law Clerk (1990–1992). **Associations & Accomplishments:** Women Lawyers of Sacramento; State Bar of California; American Bar Association; Orange County Bankruptcy Forum; Young Lawyer's Association; UOP McGeorge School of Law Alumni Association. **Education:** McGeorge School of Law, J.D. (1992); University of Nevada – Reno, B.A.; Reno Business College, A.A. **Personal:** Ms. Teeple enjoys aerobics, weight training, and rollerblading.

Michael J. Terhar
Partner
Kern and Wooley
10900 Wilshire Boulevard 11th Floor
Los Angeles, CA 90024
(310) 824–1777
Fax: (310) 824–0892

8111

Business Information: Kern and Wooley is a law firm specializing in aviation litigation, products liability defense litigation, and insurance coverage, with offices in Arizona, Texas, and California. As a Partner and Management Committee member, Mr. Terhar oversees the day–to–day operations of the firm. **Career Steps:** Partner, Kern and Wooley (1985–Present). **Associations & Accomplishments:** American Bar Association; Defense Research Institute; Association of Southern California Defense Counsel; State Bar of California; U.S. District Court, Central, South, Eastern, and Northern Districts of California; U.S. Supreme Court. **Education:** Loyola Law School, J.D. (1979); University of Washington, B.A. in Political Science (1975). **Personal:** married to Susan. Three children: Jeffrey, Riley, and Kyle.

J. Kevin Thompson
Attorney
E. Thomas Bishop, P.C.
5910 North Central Expressway, Suite 1600
Dallas, TX 75206
(214) 987–8181
Fax: (214) 987–8180

8111

Business Information: E. Thomas Bishop, P.C. is a full–service, general practice law firm specializing in insurance defense litigation. Established in 1989, the Firm currently employs 13 attorneys and 19 legal and administrative support staff. Admitted to practice in Texas state courts since 1987, Mr. Thompson joined the Firm in 1991 as Attorney and Equity Participant. He concentrates his practice in the areas of personal injury, construction, and insurance coverage litigation. **Career Steps:** Attorney, E. Thomas Bishop, P.C. (1991–Present); Attorney, Cowles & Thompson (1987–1991). **Associations & Accomplishments:** American Bar Association; Texas Bar Association; Fifth Circuit Bar Association; Dallas Bar Association; Texas Association of Defense Counsel; Dallas Association of Young Lawyers. **Education:** Southern Methodist University Law School, J.D. (1987); Trinity University, B.A. **Personal:** Married to Patti in 1990. One child: Meghan. Mr. Thompson enjoys golf and volleyball.

Mr. Michael J. Thompson
Attorney
Wright & Talisman, P.C.
1200 G. Street, N.W., Suite 600
Washington, DC 20005
(202) 393–1200
Fax: (202) 393–1240

8111

Business Information: Wright & Talisman, P.C. is a law firm that specializes in civil matters such as energy, environment and commercial litigation. As Attorney, Mr. Thompson represents clients in state and federal agency proceedings and other transactions. He is also a member of the firm's Board of Directors. Established in 1948, Wright & Talisman, P.C. employs 55 people. **Career Steps:** Attorney, Wright & Talisman, P.C. (1985–Present); Attorney, Wheatley & Wolleson (1981–1985); Attorney–Advisor, United States Environmental Protection Agency (1980–1981). **Associations & Accomplishments:** American Bar Association (Sections on Natural Resources, Environment, Litigation and Public Utilities); California Conference of Public Utility Counsel & Section on Antitrust Law; District of Columbia Bar; Virginia State Bar; Federal Energy Bar Association. **Education:** George Washington University, J.D. (1981); Ohio State University, B.S., B.A. (1977). **Personal:** Married in 1980. Mr. Thompson enjoys bicycling, racquetball, golf and computers.

Arthur H. Thorn, Esq.

Managing Litigation Partner
Thorn & Gershon
P.O. Box 15054
Albany, NY 12212–5054
(518) 464–6770
Fax: (518) 464–6778

8111

Business Information: Thorn & Gershon is a full–service, general practice law firm specializing in civil litigation, trials and appeals. Established in 1988, the Firm currently employs 39 professionals. Attaining his law degree in 1969, Mr. Thorn is a Litigation and Managing Partner responsible for all aspects of the Firm's operations. A career milestone was achieved when he won the case of Kramer vs Harley Davidson, which established new guidelines on product liability. **Career Steps:** Managing Litagation Partner, Thorn & Gershon (1988–Present); Attorney, Carter, Conboy, Bardwell & Case (1973–1988); Attorney, Don Gulling, Jr. (1969–1973). **Associations & Accomplishments:** Product Liability Advisory Council; Association for Advancement of Automotive Medicine; Trial Attorneys of America; Defense Research Institute; American Trial Lawyers Association; American Bar Association; New York Bar Association. **Education:** Syracuse University – College of Law, J.D. (1969); New York University, A.B. **Personal:** Married to Marianne in 1968. Two children: Michael and Jessica. Mr. Thorn enjoys hiking, mountain climbing, and photography.

Roger K. Timm
Attorney
Dykema Gossett, P.L.L.C.
400 Renaissance Center
Detroit, MI 48243–1668
(313) 568–6597
Fax: (313) 568–6594

8111

Business Information: Dykema Gossett, P.L.L.C. is a private, general practice law firm, providing legal representation to clientele from seven offices located throughout the U.S. Established in 1923, the Firm currently consists of 250 attorney associates, and employs 600 legal and administrative support staff. Joining the Firm upon the conferral of his law degree as an associate in 1972, Mr. Timm was appointed Partner in 1980. Admitted to practice in Michigan state and federal, Supreme Courts, and 5th, 6th, 7th, 9th, and 11th Circuit courts, his practice concentrates in the areas of complex commercial litigation, as well as providing representation in antitrust securities, insurance coverage actions, and class action law suits. **Career Steps:** Dykema Gossett, P.L.L.C.: Partner/Member (1980–Present), Associate (1972–1980). **Education:** Harvard University, J.D. (1972); University of Michigan, B.S. in Chemistry with Honors (1969). **Personal:** Married to Barbara C. in 1969. Mr. Timm enjoys travel, biking, and reading.

David A. Tornetta
Partner
Lynch, Tornetta & Mirabile
617 Swede Street
Norristown, PA 19401
(610) 275–2600
Fax: (610) 277–2043

8111

Business Information: Lynch, Tornetta & Mirabile is a full–service, general practice law firm, concentrating on personal injury and medical malpractice law. Consisting of two offices, the Firm reports annual revenue of $1.2 million and currently employs 10 attorneys, legal, and administrative support staff. A practicing attorney in Pennsylvania state and federal courts since 1984, Mr. Tornetta joined the Firm in 1992 as Partner, responsible for co–managing all business affairs. He also serves as Chief of Litigations. **Career Steps:** Partner, Lynch, Tornetta & Mirabile (1994–Present); Partner & Chief of Litigation, Gultanoff, Lynch & Tornetta (1992–1994); Chief Litigator, Gultanoff & Lynch (1991–1992); Associate, Marshall, Dennehey & Warner (1984–1991). **Associations & Accomplishments:** Pennsylvania Bar Association; American Bar Association; Pennsylvania Trial Lawyer's Association; Montgomery Trial Lawyer's Association; United States District Court for the Eastern District of Pennsylvania; Board of Directors, American Red Cross; M.S.S. Club (Societa' Di M.S. Maria S.S. Del Soccorso Di Sciacca). **Education:** Delaware University Law School, J.D. (1984); Ursinus College, B.A. **Personal:** Two children: Cecilee and David. Mr. Tornetta enjoys reading, golf, hunting, raising reptiles, baseball card collecting, biking and cooking.

Mary T. Torres
Attorney at Law
Law Office of T. A. Sandenaw
2951A Roadrunner Parkway
Las Cruces, NM 88011
(505) 522–7500
Fax: (505) 522–5544

8111

Business Information: Law Office of T. A. Sandenaw is a full–service legal office concentrating in civil defense work. Establishing her private practice upon conferral of her law degree in 1992, Ms. Torres is a trial attorney concentrating in employment law, civil rights, and governmental entities law. Admitted to both State and Federal courts, Ms. Torres became interested in law while sponsoring the Mock Trial Team at the high school where she was a teacher. **Career Steps:** Attorney at Law, Law Office of T. A. Sandenaw (1992–Present); Educator, Socorro High School, New Mexico (1983–1989). **Associations & Accomplishments:** American Bar Association; New Mexico State Bar Association; New Mexico Defense Lawyer's Association; American Inn of Court; Chairman, Young Lawyers Association. **Education:** University of New Mexico, J.D. (1992); New Mexico Institute of Mining and Technology, B.S. in General Studies (1983). **Personal:** Ms. Torres enjoys needlework.

Gloria A. Torres–Roman, Esq.

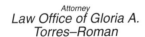

Attorney
Law Office of Gloria A. Torres–Roman
12 Calle Betances
San Sebastian, Puerto Rico 00685–2320
(809) 896–4583
Fax: (809) 896–4583
EMAIL: See Below

8111

Business Information: Law Office of Gloria A. Torres–Roman is a full–service, general practice law firm. A practicing

attorney in Puerto Rico since 1991, Ms. Torres–Roman established her sole practice law firm in 1995. Her practice concentrates on civil and family law, and civil rights issues. Concurrent with her private law practice, she serves as Adjunct Law Professor at Eugenio Maria de Hostos Law School. She can also be reached through the Internet via: gtorres@fddemdh.edu **Career Steps:** Attorney, Law Office of Gloria A. Torres–Roman (1993–Present); Administrative Judge, Consumer Affairs Department (1991–1993); Regional Director, PRO BONO, Inc. (1993–1995); Adjunct Law Professor, Eugenio Maria de Hostos Law School (1995–Present). **Associations & Accomplishments:** Hispanic Lawyers Bar; American Bar Association; Puerto Rico Bar Association; Civil Rights Institute; L.A.M.B.D.A.; National Institute for Dispute Resolution. **Education:** Catholic University School of Law, J.D. (1991); Certifications: Disputes Resolution Methos, Buenos Aires University; San Diego School of Law, Poverty Law; Music Conservatory. **Personal:** Ms. Torres–Roman enjoys reading, lectures, music – piano & saxophone, swimming, travel, tennis, and bowling.

Mark G. Tratos
Partner
Quirk & Tratos, Chtd
550 East Charleston Boulevard, Suite D
Las Vegas, NV 89104
(702) 386–1778
Fax: (702) 386–1934

8111

Business Information: Quirk & Tratos, Chtd. is an international full–service, general practice law firm, concentrating on intellectual property and entertainment law litigation. A practicing attorney in Nevada and California state courts since 1979, Mr. Tratos joined the Firm as Partner in 1983. He represents clientele in gaming and resort entertainment law issues worldwide, servicing major resort communities. He also teaches entertainment law. **Career Steps:** Partner, Quirk & Tratos, CHTD (1983–Present); Partner, Galliher & Tratos (1980–1983); Associate, Mills, Galliher, Lukens, Gibson, et al (1979–1980). **Associations & Accomplishments:** American Bar Association; Nevada Bar Association; Clark County Bar Association; California Bar Association; Officer, Nevada Intellectual Property Law Association. **Education:** Northwestern School of Law, J.D. (1979); University of Nevada – Las Vegas: M.A. (A.B.D.) in Political Science, B.A. in Political Science (1974). **Personal:** Mr. Tratos enjoys exercising, swimming, and cross–training.

W. Stacy Trotter
Attorney
Shafer Law Firm
700 North Grant, Suite 201
Odessa, TX 79760
(915) 332–0893 Ext. 7
Fax: (915) 335–3289

8111

Business Information: Shafer Law Firm, established over sixty years ago, is a general practice law firm that handles all aspects of law. A practicing attorney since 1984, Mr. Trotter handles trial work for insurance and unemployment. He also does some pro bono work. **Career Steps:** Attorney, Shafer Law Firm (1984–Present). **Associations & Accomplishments:** District Director, Texas Association Civil Defense Counsel; Board Member, Jim Parker Little League. **Education:** Texas Technical Law School, J.D. (1984); Texas Tech University, B.A. with honors (1981). **Personal:** Married to Teresa in 1984. Two children: Sean and Noelle. Mr. Trotter enjoys golf, coaching, and family.

Dr. Estelle J. Tsevdos, Esquire
Partner
Kenyon and Kenyon
One Broadway
New York, NY 10004
(212) 425–7200
Fax: (212) 425–5288

8111

Business Information: Kenyon and Kenyon is an intellectual law firm concentrating on patent, trade secret, and license law. The Firm was established in 1879 and currently employs 125 people. As Partner, Dr. Tsevdos focuses on litigation, prosecutions, and transactional agreements dealing with license, trade secret, and patent concerns for clients. **Career Steps:** Partner, Kenyon and Kenyon (1995–Present); American Cyanamid: Section Manager (1988–1995), Patent Council (1983–1988). **Associations & Accomplishments:** Board of Directors, Biotechnology Institute. **Education:** Case Western Reserve University, J.D. (1981); Ohio State University, Ph.D. in Pharmacology (1978); Ohio Wesleyan University, B.A. (1973). **Personal:** Dr. Tsevdos enjoys music and gardening.

Thomas G. Tucker
Attorney
Sutherland, Asbill & Brennan
111 Congress Avenue, 23rd Floor
Austin, TX 78701–4043
(512) 469–3350
Fax: (512) 469–3351

8111

Business Information: Sutherland, Asbill & Brennan is an international, full–service, general practice law firm. A practicing attorney in Texas state and federal courts since 1989, Mr. Tucker joined the Firm as Attorney in 1994. Serving as International Litigation Attorney, his practice specializes in commercial litigation of international business disputes for banks, corporations, and individuals in the Americas, Europe, and Asia. **Career Steps:** Attorney, Sutherland, Asbill & Brennan (1994–Present); Attorney, Brown, Parker & Leahy (1991–1994); Judicial Law Clerk, U.S. District Court for the District of Hawaii (1990–1991). **Associations & Accomplishments:** Federal Bar Association; American Bar Association; State Bar of Texas; Travis County Bar Association; Austin Young Lawyers Association; Houston Bar Association; Houston Young Lawyers Associaton; Frequent participant of bar–related, community activities, including mentoring of underprivileged youths. **Education:** University of Texas, B.B.A. in Real Estate and Finance (1985); University of Houston Law Center, J.D. (1989). **Personal:** Married to Nanci N. F. in 1993. Mr. Tucker enjoys golf, scuba diving, travel, and community service.

Mr. Hurshal C. Tummelson
Partner
Tummelson Bryan & Knox
115 North Broadway
Urbana, IL 61801
(217) 367–2500
Fax: (217) 367–2555

8111

Business Information: Tummelson Bryan & Knox is a full–service, general practice law firm specializing in civil litigation, including estate planning. Attaining his law degree in 1949, Mr. Tummelson began his legal career as a partner with Phebus, Tummelson, Bryan & Knox and served the Firm for 43 years. In 1993, he founded Tummelson Bryan & Knox and as partner, Mr. Tummelson is responsible for all aspects of the Firm's operation. **Career Steps:** Partner, Tummelson Bryan & Knox (1993–Present); Partner, Phebus, Tummelson, Bryan & Knox (1950–1993). **Associations & Accomplishments:** Fellow, American College of Trial Lawyers; Champaign County Bar Association; Illinois State Bar Association; American College of International Society of Barristers; Association of Insurance Attorneys; Delta Phi Fraternity; First Presbyterian Church; Kiwanis Club; Boy Scouts; American Cancer Association; Navigator, 8th Air Force, World War II. **Education:** University of Illinois, LL.B. – J.D. (1949). **Personal:** Married to Jo Elaine in 1946. Four children: Gary Lee Tummelson, Gwen Ann Roughton, Jo Ellen Bloch and Nancy Sue Karr. Mr. Tummelson enjoys golf, music and gardening.

Mr. Bobby C. Underwood

Partner and Attorney at Law
Bradley, Arant, Rose & White
2001 Park Place, Suite 1400
Birmingham, AL 35203
(205) 521–8331
Fax: (205) 521–8714

8111

Business Information: Bradley, Arant, Rose & White is a full–service law firm. Established in 1900, the Firm currently employs 365 attorneys and legal support staff. Joining the Firm upon conferral of his law degree in 1981, Bobby Underwood is a Partner involved in administrative direction as well as legal representation to major corporate clientele. **Career Steps:** Partner and Attorney at Law, Bradley, Arant, Rose & White (1981–Present); Procurement Contracting and Staff Officer, United States Air Force (1967–1978). **Associations & Accomplishments:** American Bar Association; Alabama Bar Association; Birmingham Bar Association. **Education:** University of Michigan Law School, J.D. cum laude (1980); George Washington University, M.B.A. (1972); Ohio State University, B.S. in Business Administration and Industrial Management, summa cum laude (1966). **Personal:** Married to Masako T. in 1958. Mr. Underwood enjoys swimming and designing houses.

Jane Van Valkenburg

Attorney
Arnold, Anderson & Dove, P.L.L.P.
5881 Cedar Lake Road
St. Louis Park, MN 55416
(612) 545–9000
Fax: (612) 545–1793
8111

Business Information: Arnold, Anderson & Dove, P.L.L.P. is a general practice law firm. Located in Saint Louis Missouri, the office currently employs 10 professionals. An Attorney since 1983, Ms. Van Valkenburg, a fourth generation attorney, is responsible for all aspects of legal representation placing emphasis on matrimonial law. **Career Steps:** Attorney, Arnold, Anderson & Dove, P.L.L.P. (1994–Present); Attorney/ Owner, Van Valkenburg Law Office (1988–1994). **Education:** Wm. Mitchell College of Law, J.D. (1983). **Personal:** Married to David Psyhos in 1992. Three children: Nickolas A., Andrew D., and Christopher D. Psyhos. Ms. Van Valkenburg enjoys needlepoint and spending time with her three step–children.

Rafael V. Vassallo Collazo

Associate
Totti, Rodriquez, Diaz & Fuentes
416 Ponce de Leon Ave., Suite 1200
San Juan, Puerto Rico 00918
(809) 753–7910
Fax: (809) 764–9480
8111

Business Information: Totti, Rodriquez, Diaz & Fuentes is a full–service, general practice law firm. Established in 1994, the Firm currently employs 20 attorneys, legal, and administrative support staff. A corporate manufacturing executive prior to pursuing his legal career, Mr. Vassallo–Collazo joined the firm upon conferral of his law degree in 1993. Serving as Associate, he concentrates his practice in the areas of civil litigation, business law, tax law, trademarks and copyrights, contracts, and collections. **Career Steps:** Associate, Totti, Rodriquez, Diaz & Fuentes (1993–Present); Vice President and General Manager, Cristalia, Inc. (1986–1989). **Associations & Accomplishments:** Puerto Rico Bar Association; American Bar Association. **Education:** Catholic University of Puerto Rico, J.D. (1992); Boston University, Bachelor in Arts (1992). **Personal:** Married to Oreli Rafols Mendez in 1994. Mr. Vassallo Collazo enjoys horseback riding, boating, and outdoor sports.

Mr. Robert R. Veach, Jr.

Attorney at Law – Senior Shareholder
Locke Purnell Rain Harrell (A Professional Corporation)
2200 Ross Avenue, Suite 2200
Dallas, TX 75201
(214) 740–8706
Fax: (214) 740–8800
8111

Business Information: Locke Purnell Rain Harrell (A Professional Corporation) is a full–service law firm. Established since 1892, Locke Purnell Rain Harrell (A Professional Corporation) presently employs 500 people. In his current capacity, Mr. Veach is responsible for corporate securities and finance. **Career Steps:** Attorney at Law – Senior Shareholder, Locke Purnell Rain Harrell (1987–Present); President, RPR Mortgage Finance Corporation (1985–1987); Vice President, Rauscher Pierce Refsnes, Inc. (1983–1987). **Associations & Accomplishments:** Texas State Bar Association; Nebraska State Bar Association; Dallas Bar Association; Federal Bar Association; American Bar Association; Former Board Member, American Diabetes Association – North Texas Affiliate; Board Member of private companies; Speaker at professional seminars and conferences; Author, legal articles. **Education:** Southern Methodist University, Juris Doctor (1975); Arizona State University, Bachelor of Science. **Personal:** Married to Lori Sue in 1989. Mr. Veach enjoys golf and collecting antique American firearms in his leisure time.

Xenia Velez–Silva

Partner
McConnell Valdes
P.O. Box 364225
San Juan, Puerto Rico 00936–4225
(809) 250–5685
Fax: (809) 759–9225
8111

Business Information: McConnell Valdes is a full–service, premier law firm with offices in San Juan, Puerto Rico. Established in 1946, the Firm currently employs 240 attorneys, legal and administrative support staff. A practicing attorney in Puerto Rico courts since 1983, Miss Velez–Silva joined the Firm in 1984. Serving as Partner in the Law Department, her practice focuses on international law issues, representing individuals and corporations in the U.S. and Puerto Rico with international operations. **Career Steps:** Partner, McConnell Valdes (1984–Present); Tax Manager, Price Waterhouse (1979–1984); Upjohn Manufacturing Company (1976–1979). **Associations & Accomplishments:** Puerto Rico Bar Association; Puerto Rico Society of Certified Public Accountants; National Association of Bond Lawyers; Tax Committee, Puerto Rico Manufacturers Association. **Education:** University of Puerto Rico: J.D. (1983), B.B.A. in Accounting and Marketing. **Personal:** Miss Velez–Silva enjoys reading, travel, and decorating.

Annette Verdesco

Attorney
Pope, Bergrin & Toscano, P.A.
893 Franklin Avenue
Newark, NJ 07107
(201) 482–7766
Fax: (201) 484–7555
8111

Business Information: Pope, Bergrin & Toscano, P.A. is a full–service, general practice law firm concentrating in real estate, matrimonial, and personal injuries. Established in 1991, the Firm currently employs 13 attorneys, legal and administrative support staff. Admitted to practice in New Jersey state courts since 1990, Mrs. Verdesco joined the Firm as Attorney in 1991. She is responsible for the legal representation of the Firm's corporate clientele, as well as public relations. **Career Steps:** Attorney, Pope, Bergrin & Toscano, P.A. (1991–Present); Piro, Zinna, Cifelli & Paris: Attorney (1990–1991), Law Clerk (1989–1990). **Associations & Accomplishments:** American Bar Association. **Education:** Seton Hall Law School, J.D. (1990); Seton Hall University, B.A. & B.S. **Personal:** Married to Stephen Cafiero in 1992. Mrs. Verdesco enjoys collecting toys and dolls, drawing, reading True Crime novels, and writing articles for True Crime magazines.

Carlos J. Villafane–Real

Tax Attorney
Pietrantoni, Mendez & Alvarez
Banco Popular Center, Suite 1901, 209 Munoz Rivera Avenue
San Juan, Puerto Rico 00979
(809) 274–1212
Fax: (809) 274–1470
8111

Business Information: Pietrantoni, Mendez & Alvarez, one of the top law firms in Puerto Rico, concentrates in areas such as corporate and commercial law, corporate and public finance, tax and employee benefits. Joining the firm upon conferral of his L.L.M. degree in 1993, Mr. Villafane–Real represents clients in the areas of tax law, as well as counsels in commercial and financial transactions. **Career Steps:** Pietrantoni, Mendez & Alvarez: Tax Attorney (1993–Present); Summer Associate, Martinez O'Dell & Calabria (1992); Spring Clerkship, McConnell & Valdes (1991). **Associations & Accomplishments:** American Bar Association (1991–Present); La Alianza del Derecho (1992–1993); Phi Alpa Delta Law Fraternity (1991–1993); Delta Mu Delta (1986–1988); International Student Association (1985–1988). **Education:** Georgetown University, L.L.M. in Tax (1993); University of Puerto Rico School of Law, J.D. cum laude; State University of New York – Oswego, B.S. in Accounting, magna cum laude; Certified Public Accountant (1994).

Ismael Vincenty–Medina

Associate Attorney
Pellot–Gonzalez Law Office
P.O. Box 87
St. Just, Puerto Rico 00978–0087
(787) 250–6300
Fax: (787) 250–6330
8111

Business Information: Pellot–Gonzalez Law Office is a general law office that specializes in tax law. As Associate Attorney, Mr. Vincenty–Medina is responsible for diversified law practices, including accounting and taxes. **Career Steps:** Associate Attorney, Pellot–Gonzalez Law Office (1995–Present). **Associations & Accomplishments:** Puerto Rico Law Bar Association; Puerto Rico Society of Certified Public Accountants. **Education:** Georgetown University Law Center, Master of Laws in Taxation; University of Puerto Rico: J.D., Bachelor in Business Administration.

James W. Vititoe

Attorney
Masser & Vititoe, Attorneys at Law
18050 Riverside Drive, Suite 605
Taluko, CA 91610
(818) 755–4888
Fax: Please mail or call
8111

Business Information: Masser & Vititoe, Attorneys at Law is a full–service, general practice law firm concentrating on toxic tort, civil, and malpractice law. A practicing attorney in state and federal courts since 1977, Mr.Vititoe joined founded the Firm in 1977. **Career Steps:** Attorney, Masser & Vititoe, Attorneys at Law (1977–Present). **Associations & Accomplishments:** Lawyer of the Year (1991–1992); Dean's List and Presidential Scholarship; Freddie Graff Award; President, Student Bar; Has been interviewed on several news documentaries, the most recent being ABC PrimeTime, regarding the largest toxic tort law suit in California history. He was also involved in the Landmark Discrimination Case "Sherin Jones vs. Los Angeles Community College." **Education:** University of Los Angeles, J.D. (1976).

Charles A. Viviano

Attorney
Viviano & Clark
110 West C # 1300
San Diego, CA 92101
(619) 688–9751
Fax: (619) 688–9783
8111

Business Information: Viviano & Clark is a trial and civil litigation law firm. A practicing attorney licensed in California and Hawaii courts since 1974, Charles Viviano co–founded the Firm in 1995. Prior to this, he founded and managed the insurance law firm of Viviano & Bradley — a 20–attorney San Diego based firm. Concurrent with his law practice, he teaches continuing education courses to attorneys who are preparing for State Bar exams, as well as practicing attorneys. **Career Steps:** Attorney, Viviano & Clark (1995–Present); Senior Partner, Viviano & Bradley (1985–1994); Senior Trial Counsel, County of San Diego (1979–1984). **Associations & Accomplishments:** American Bar Association; Hawaii Bar Association; California Bar Association; Republican National Committee–President's Council; Outrigger Canoe Club; San Diego Tennis & Racquet Club; Who's Who in American Law; Who's Who in America. **Education:** Gonzaga University, J.D. (1974); University of San Diego, B.A. (1970). **Personal:** One child: Charles Anthony Jr. Mr. Viviano enjoys golf, swimming, tennis, and history.

Timothy Wayne Volpe

Partner
Smith Hulsey & Busey
225 Water Street, Suite 1800
Jacksonville, FL 32202–3315
(904) 359–7700
Fax: (904) 359–7708
8111

Business Information: Smith Hulsey & Busey is a full–service, general practice law firm concentrating in complex commercial litigation. Established in 1935, the Firm reports annual revenue in excess of $10 million and currently employs 120 attorneys, legal and administrative support staff. Admitted to practice before state courts in Florida, the United States District Court, Middle District of Florida, and Eleventh Circuit Court of Appeals, Mr. Volpe joined the Firm as an associate in 1982. Appointed as Partner in 1987, he provides legal representation for the Firm's major clientele, concentrating in complex commercial and civil litigation. **Career Steps:** Smith Hulsey & Busey: Partner (1987–Present), Lawyer (1982–1987). **Associations & Accomplishments:** American Bar Association; The Florida Bar Association; Jacksonville Bar Association; American Branch of the International Law Association; American Trial Lawyers Association; The Florida Academy of Trial Lawyers; American Judicature Society; The American Society of Law and Medicine; President–Elect and President, Northeast Florida Medical Malpractice Claims Council, Inc.; Who's Who in American Law; University of Florida Law Review; Editor–In–Chief (1982); Associate Editor (1981); Florida Blue Key Leadership Honorary; Omicron Delta Kappa Leadership/Scholarship Honorary; Outstanding Young Men in America; Selected for Who's Who in American Universities and Colleges (1979); Florida Blue Key Citation for Chapter Service (1979); Phi Kappa Phi; Numerous presentations. **Education:** University of Florida, J.D. with Honors (1982), M.A. in Political Science in Public Administration Program with High Honors (1982), B.A. with High Honors in Interdisciplinary Studies, Certified in Eastern European Area Studies (1979). **Personal:** Married to Roslyn in 1993. Four children: Joshua Volpe, Roslyn, Kaye, and Leigh Henderson. Mr. Volpe enjoys boating, jogging, biking, racquetball, and tennis.

Ms. Katrina A. Von Hedemann

Attorney
Katrina A. Von Hedemann, Attorney at Law
6524 San Felipe, #393
Houston, TX 77057
(713) 785–9471
Fax: Please mail or

8111

Business Information: Katrina A. Von Hedemann, Attorney at Law is a general practice legal service, specializing in litigation. Ms. Von Hedemann is in private practice, and contracts her services with legal firms. **Career Steps:** Attorney, Katrina A. Von Hedemann, Attorney at Law (1992–Present); Contract Attorney, Fleming, Hovenkamp & Grayson (1994–Present); Attorney, James H. Elder (1992–1993). **Associations & Accomplishments:** Texas State Bar Association; Houston Bar Association; Houston Young Lawyers Association; American Bar Association; Junior League of Houston; Houston Museum of Fine Arts. **Education:** South Texas College of Law, J.D. (1992); University of Texas, B.A. (1987).

Robert B. Walker

Partner
Shawn, Mann & Niedermayer, L.L.P.
1850 M. Street NW, Suite 280
Washington, DC 20036–5803
(202) 331–7900 (202) 331–2306
Fax: (202) 331–0726

8111

Business Information: Shawn, Mann & Niedermayer, L.L.P. is a law firm, providing services in international law, bankruptcy, general corporate law, private placements, trade association representation, civil litigation, international transportation. As a Partner, Mr. Walker oversees the Firm's operations, and specializes in transportation, litigation and general corporate law. Shawn, Mann & Niedermayer, L.L.P. employs 21 people. **Career Steps:** Partner, Shawn, Mann & Niedermayer, L.L.P. **Associations & Accomplishments:** American Bar Association; Transportation Lawyer's Association, Distinguished Lawyers Award 1989; Board of Directors, Local High School. **Education:** Memphis State University, J.D. (1975); University of Tennessee, M.S.; Arkansas State University, B.S. **Personal:** Married to Peggy J. Walker in 1968. Two children: Robert B. Walker, Jr. and Robin E. Walker.

Denise Wallace

Attorney
Steel, Hector & Davis, LLP
200 South Biscayne Boulevard
Miami, FL 33131–2310
(305) 577–7023
Fax: (305) 577–7001

8111

Business Information: Steel, Hector & Davis, LLP is a general practice law firm concentrating on commerce and corporations. The Firm is comprised of approximately 170 attorneys. A practicing attorney since 1990, Ms. Wallace serves as a litigation attorney. **Career Steps:** Attorney, Steel, Hector & Davis, LLP (1992–Present); Attorney, Adorno & Zeder (1990–1992); Law Clerk, Brooks, Morial, Et. al (1990–1992); Law Clerk, Adams & Reese (1989–1990). **Education:** Southern University, J.D. (1990); School for International Training, M.A. (1987); University of Massachusetts (1978). **Personal:** Two children: Nichelle and Shante. Ms. Wallace enjoys travel and creative writing.

Robert P. Walsh

Attorney
Law Office of Robert P. Walsh
P.O. Box 1132
Battle Creek, MI 49016–1132
(616) 963–4682
Fax: (616) 963–3716

8111

Business Information: Law Office of Robert P. Walsh is an international law firm. In the practice of law since 1989, Mr. Walsh handles all operational aspects of his individual practice. **Career Steps:** Attorney, Law Office of Robert P. Walsh (1989–Present); Of Counsel, Dixon & Dixon, D.C. (1993–1994); Manager of Telecommunications, DynCorp International (1992–1994); Communications Analyst, Arabian American Oil Company (1980–1986). **Associations & Accomplishments:** Senior Life Member, Radio Club of America; Member, American Bar Association; State Bar of Michigan; District of Columbia Bar Association; Federal Communications Bar Association; Federal Bar Association; American Radio Relay League; Amateur Radio call sign – WA8MOA since 1964. International operations from: Mellish Reef (UK9ZR, 1978), Saudi Arabia (HZ1AB, 1980–1986), Heard Island (VK0JS, 1983), and Kuwait (9K2ZR, 9KZUSA, 1992–1994); 101st Airborne Division, Republic of Vietnam (1971–1972); 101st Airborne Division Association. **Education:** Thomas M. Cooley Law School, J.D. (1989); Western Michigan University, B.A. in Business Administration (1978). **Personal:** Married to Santan Florina D'Souza in 1994. One child: Katlin Elizabeth.

Mr. Lu Wang

Attorney
Lu Wang, Attorney at Law
3490 Shallowford Road, Suite 302
Chamblee, GA 30341
(770) 458–2809
Fax: (770) 458–6631

8111

Business Information: The Law Office of Lu Wang, Attorney at Law is a full–service, civil practice law firm specializing in the areas of international, corporate, and immigration law. Beginning his legal career in 1984 as an Attorney with the Economic Enhancement Law Firm, Mr. Wang established his individual practice firm in 1993 after the conferral of his law doctorate in 1992. As President and Owner he is responsible for all aspects of operations and legal representation. **Career Steps:** Attorney, Lu Wang, Attorney at Law (1993–Present); International Law Advisor, Long, Aldridge & Norman (1988–1991); Attorney, Economic Enhancement Law Firm (1984–1986). **Associations & Accomplishments:** American Bar Association; American Immigration Lawyer's Association; Atlanta Chinese Business Association; National American Chinese Association; Pro Bono work for minorities; Published in local papers; First Chinese Attorney in the City of Atlanta, Georgia. **Education:** University of Georgia School of Law, J.D. (1992); University of Georgia School of Law, LL.M. (1988); Shanghai Maritime Institute, Master of International Commercial Law (1986); Shanghai Teacher's University, B.A. in English Literature (1982). **Personal:** Married to Jessie Liu in 1994. Mr. Wang enjoys singing, swimming, and reading.

Lloyd E. Ward, Esquire

Head Litigator
Lloyd Ward & Associates P.C.
13760 Noel Road, Suite 210
Dallas, TX 75240
(214) 385–8498
Fax: (214) 701–8759

8111

Business Information: Lloyd Ward & Associates P.C. is a law firm specializing in general business and property litigation. As Founder and Head Litigator, Mr. Ward oversees all aspects of the firm including administration, operations, finance and strategic planning. Mr. Ward has specialized for six years in real estate litigation. Established in 1991, Lloyd Ward & Associates P.C. employs four people. **Career Steps:** Head Litigator, Lloyd Ward & Associates P.C. (1991–Present); Litigator, Friedman & Kaplan P.C. (1989–1991); Litigator, Simpson, Dowd, Kaplan & Moon P.C. (1987–1989). **Associations & Accomplishments:** Member, College of the State Bar of Texas; Member, Texas Bar Association; Member, Arkansas Bar Association; Member, Trial Lawyers Association of America. Mr. Ward has had two cases published where he was head attorney. **Education:** University of Arkansas, J.D. (1985); University of Arkansas, B.S.B.A. **Personal:** One child: Alexander James Ward.

Michael W. Ward

Partner
O'Keefe, Ashenden, Lyons & Ward
30 North LaSalle, Suite 4100
Chicago, IL 60602
(312) 621–0400
Fax: (312) 621–0297

8111

Business Information: O'Keefe, Ashenden, Lyons & Ward is a full–service, general practice law firm, with emphasis on real estate, tax, telecommunications, and auto trade association law. A practicing attorney in Illinois courts since 1976, Mr. Ward joined the Firm as Partner in 1986. His practice concentrates in the areas of telecommunications, and state and local taxes, as well as litigation and regulatory matters. **Career Steps:** O'Keefe, Ashenden, Lyons & Ward: Partner (1986–Present), Associate (1980–1985); Assistant State's Attorney, Cook County, IL (1976–1980). **Associations & Accomplishments:** Board of Advisors, Chicago Catholic Charities; Chairman, St. Nicholas Church Finance Council; New Horizons Youth Group Director; Board of Directors, Pele Stars Soccer Club; AYSO Coach; Midwest Chapter Coordinating Committee, Federal Communications Bar Association; Chicago Bar Association; Illinois Bar Association; American Public Communications Council; Illinois Public Telecommunications Associaton. **Education:** Illinois Institute of Technology – Chicago/Kent College of Law, J.D. (1976); Notre Dame, B.A. **Personal:** Married to Amy in 1974. Two children: Daniel and Jamie. Mr. Ward enjoys soccer, skiing, and music.

Sara Beth Watson, J.D.

Of Counsel
Steptoe & Johnson, L.L.P.
1330 Connecticut Avenue Northwest
Washington, DC 20036–1704
(202) 429–6460
Fax: (202) 429–3902
EMAIL: See Below

8111

Business Information: Steptoe & Johnson, L.L.P. is an international litigation law firm. With offices in Washington, D.C.; Phoenix, AZ; and Moscow, the Firm's areas of concentration include environmental law, worker's safety, and food and drug compliance matters. Admitted to all State and Federal courts in the District of Columbia, Sara Beth Watson joined the Firm upon conferral of her law doctorate in 1986 as an Associate. Appointed as an Of Counsel in 1994, she focuses her practice in the representation of U.S. companies with international holdings, as well as international companies doing business in the U.S. in matters pertaining to FDA and OSHA litigation. She also contributes substantial pro bono services on a local level to non–profit environmental organizations, as well as serving the homeless and indigent throughout greater Washington, D.C.–metro. Internet users can reach her via: SWATSONSteptoe.Con **Career Steps:** Steptoe & Johnson, L.L.P.: Of Counsel (1994–Present), Associate (1986–1993); Clerk, The Honorable Will Garwood, US Court of Appeal Fifth Circuit (1985–1986). **Associations & Accomplishments:** American Bar Association: Section of Natural Resources, Energy and Environmental Law, Environmental Quality Committee, Solid and Hazardous Waste Committee, Pesticide Subcommittee; Section on Energy and the Environment, Washington, D.C. Bar Association; Texas State Society; Texas Breakfast Club. **Education:** Southern Methodist University, J.D. cum laude (1985); Texas Christian University, B.S. magna cum laude (1979).

Merl H. Wayman

Attorney/Manager of Workers' Compensation
Barkon & Neff Company, LPA
P.O. Box 1989
Columbus, OH 43216
(614) 221–4221
Fax: (614) 221–5423

8111

Business Information: Barkon & Neff Company, LPA is a full–service, general practice consumer law firm concentrating on workers' compensation, social security and personal injury. As Manager of Workers' Compensation, Mr. Wayman handles workers' compensation for the Firm. His area covers central and southeast Ohio. **Career Steps:** Manager of Workers' Compensation, Barkon & Neff Company, LPA (1993–Present); Ohio Attorney Generals Office: Assistant Chief (1989–1993), Assistant Attorney General (1984–1989). **Associations & Accomplishments:** Ohio State Bar Association; Columbus Bar Association; Ohio Academy of Trial Lawyers; Volunteer Mediator; Volunteer Judge; Seminar Speaker; Appellate Cases successfully argued: 36 cases in Ohio Supreme Court, Over 200 in other Appellate Courts, South Ridge Baptist Church vs. Indus. Comm. (1987), State Ex Rel. Burley vs. Coal Packing, Inc. (1987), Woodrum vs. Premier Auto Glass Co. (1995). **Education:** Cleveland Marshall College of Law, J.D. (1982); Kent State University, M.Ed.; Ohio University, B.A. **Personal:** Mr. Wayman enjoys Bar Associations, computers, and entertainment.

Laurie K. Weatherford

Of Counsel/Associate
Maguire, Voorhis & Wells, P.A.
2 South Orange Avenue
Orlando, FL 32801–2606
(407) 244–1141
Fax: (407) 426–7313

8111

Business Information: Maguire, Voorhis & Wells, P.A. is a full–service, general practice law firm, specializing in bankruptcy cases. Established in 1918, the Firm currently employs more than 140 attorneys, legal, and administrative support staff. A practicing attorney since 1986, Mrs. Weatherford joined the Firm in 1987 as Of Counsel/Associate. Licensed in Florida and serving as a Bankruptcy Attorney, she practices in mostly federal courts on bankruptcy cases, in addition to conducting pro–bono work. **Career Steps:** Of Counsel/Associate, Maguire, Voorhis & Wells, P.A. (1987–Present); Student Coordinator, Southeastern Academy (1979–1983). **Education:** Cumberland School of Law, J.D. (1986); University of Florida, B.S. **Personal:** Married to A. Harry Ducker in 1988. Two children: Carolyn Elizabeth and James Riley. Mrs. Weatherford enjoys spending time with her family and being a Florida Gator football fan.

Mrs. Dianne J. Weaver
Attorney
Weaver & Weaver, P.A. and Of
Counsel to: Krupnick Campbell
Malone Roselli, et al
700 S.E. 3rd Ave., Suite 100
Ft. Lauderdale, FL 33316
(954) 763–8181
Fax: (954) 763–8292

8111

Business Information: Weaver & Weaver, P.A. has been a general practice law firm, specializing in complex litigation. Founding the firm in 1977 with her husband Ben, Mrs. Weaver shared the overall administrative functions of the practice with him. A Board–certified trial attorney, she is licensed to practice in the states of Indiana, Florida and Colorado. A nationally recognized arbitrator and lobbyist, she has testified at the following: U.S. Senate Judiciary Committee on Confidentiality Orders, Florida Legislature on Confidentiality Orders and Conference on Courtroom Secrecy at Washington, D.C in April 1990. She also spearheaded the passage of legislation in Florida outlawing sealing orders with reference to dangerous products. Established in 1977, Weaver & Weaver, P.A. and Of Counsel to: Krupnick Campbell Malone Roselli Buser Slama & Hancock employs 20 associates, legal aide professional and administrative people. **Career Steps:** Attorney, Weaver & Weaver, P.A. (1977–Present); and of counsel to Krupnick Campbell Malone Roselli Buser Slama & Hancock (May 1996–Present). **Associations & Accomplishments:** Association of Trial Lawyers of America: Board of Governors, Past Parliamentarian, Present Treasurer, Reorganization Committee, Chair, Pre–Trial and Discovery Abuse Committee, Federal Rules, Jurisdiction and Venue Committee, Products Liability Advisory Committee, Chair, Secrecy Task Force; Board of Directors and Legislative Contact, Academy of Florida Trial Lawyers; Board of Governors, Southern Trial Lawyers' Association; Lifetime Fellow, Roscoe Pound Foundation; Sustaining Founder and Board of Directors, Trial Lawyers for Public Justice; Board of Trustees, Civil Justice Foundation; American Board of Trial Advocates; The Florida Bar Bench/Bar Commission; Listed in [The Best Lawyers in America]; Named: One of the "Top 10" trial lawyers in the U.S. by the [National Law Journal]; Founding Member, National Committee on Litigation of Head Injuries; Florida 500, National Head Injury Foundation; Chairperson, Seventeenth Judicial Circuit Judicial Nominating Commission; Board of Directors, Broward County Trial Lawyers; American Bar Association; Federal Bar Association; American Judicature Society; Southeastern Admiralty Law Institute; Florida Bar Association; Indiana Bar Association; Panel Member, Columbia University in conjunction with Public Television on Medical Malpractice, Moderated by Ted Koppel with Supreme Court Justice Blackman, Surgeon General Koop and National recognized trial attorneys attending; Former Special Prosecutor, The Florida Bar Grievance Committee; Numerous invited speaking engagements throughout the North America on behalf of State and Provincial Trial Lawyers Associations; Author of over 11 publications on various trial and injury advocacy cases in law journals and convention proceedings; HONORARIUMS: Award for educational contribution to the Justice League by B'Nai B'rith; Marine Industries Association; Broward County Bar Association – Legal Aid Society; Charlee House of Florida; Board of Directors of Covenant House of Florida; Board of Governors, 21st Century Democrats; Child Advocate of the Year (1990–91); Woman of the Year in Broward County, Florida. **Personal:** Married to Ben in 1971. Four children: Jay, Jenny, Scott and Elizabeth. Mrs. Weaver enjoys pro–bono legal work for children.

Kathleen M. Weinheimer
Sole Practitioner
Kathleen M. Weinheimer, Attorney
at Law
1020 Calle Malaga
Santa Barbara, CA 93109–1136
(805) 965–2777
Fax: (805) 965–6388

8111

Business Information: A practicing attorney in California state courts since 1979, Ms. Weinheimer established her solo law practice in 1993. Her practice provides legal representation, with emphasis on land use, municipal law, and administrative law matters. **Career Steps:** Attorney at Law, Kathleen M. Weinheimer, Attorney at Law (1993–Present); Attorney at Law, Schramm & Raddue (1991–1993); Pismo Beach: City Attorney (1993–1995), Assistant City Attorney (1991–1993); Assistant City Attorney, City of Solvang (1991–1993); Assistant City Attorney, City of Santa Barbara (1985–1991). **Associations & Accomplishments:** Santa Barbara Choral Society; Land Trust for Santa Barbara. **Education:** University of the Pacific, J.D. (1979); Santa Clara University, B.S. in Economics (1974). **Personal:** Married to Peter K. Wilson in 1992. Ms. Weinheimer enjoys choral singing and yachting.

Jordan H. Weinstein
Managing Partner
Weinstein, Bernstein & Burwick,
P.C.
10 Mechanic Street, Suite 300
Worcester, MA 01608
(508) 756–4393
Fax: (508) 755–2347

8111

Business Information: Weinstein, Bernstein, & Burwick, P.C., established in 1932, is a general practice law firm concentrating in civil litigation, and commercial, corporate, and real estate transactions. Presently employing between seven to ten lawyers, the Firm is considered to be among the top firms in Massachusetts. A practicing attorney in Massachusetts state and federal courts. Mr. Weinstein joined the Firm in 1979. He concentrates his practice in civil litigation. **Career Steps:** Managing Partner, Weinstein, Bernstein, & Burwick, P.C. (1991–Present). **Associations & Accomplishments:** Worcester County Bar Association; Massachusetts Bar Association; American Bar Association; Association of Trial Lawyers of America; Massachusetts Academy of Trial Lawyers; Massachusetts Bar Foundation; Vice President and Executive Committee member, Maccabi, USA/Sports for Israel; National Co–Chairman of Sports and Executive Committee member; United States Maccabiah Organizing Committee, U.S. Maccabiah Team; U.S. Delegate to International Maccabiah Committee in Israel. **Education:** Osgoode Hall Law School, LL.B. (1978); University of Michigan, B.A. (1974). **Personal:** Married to Deborah in 1982. Four children: Jennifer, David, Allison, and Melissa. Mr. Weinstein enjoys coaching rugby and soccer, and working to send U.S. Maccabi teams to international athletic events.

Mr. Leon A. Weiss
Secretary
Reminger & Reminger Co., L.P.A.
The 113 St. Clair Bldg., Ste. 700
Cleveland, OH 44114
(216) 687–1311
Fax: (216) 687–1311

8111

Business Information: Reminger & Reminger Co., L.P.A. is a full–service general law practice. Attaining his law degree in 1966, Mr. Weiss joined Reminger & Reminger in 1979. As Secretary he is responsible for certain administrative and financial aspects for the practice. Mr. Weiss is licensed to practice in Ohio and in Federal Courts specializing in estate and trust litigation for individuals and financial institutions. **Career Steps:** Secretary and Attorney, Reminger & Reminger Co., L.P.A. (1979–Present); Attorney, Leon Weiss Co., L.P.A. (1970–1979); Attorney, Rippner, Schwartz & Carlin (1966–1970). **Associations & Accomplishments:** American College of Trust and Estate Counsel; American Bar Association; Ohio State Bar Association; Cleveland Bar Association; Public Speaker concerning continuing education; Published in Legal Publications. **Education:** Case Western Reserve, J.D. (1966); Bucknell University, B.S. in Business Administration (1963). **Personal:** Two children: Michael and Daniel. Mr. Weiss enjoys problem solving and helping others.

Mr. Christopher P. Wesierski
Managing Partner
Wesierski & Zurek
5 Park Plaza, Suite 1500
Irvine, CA 92714
(714) 975–1000
Fax: None, please m

8111

Business Information: Wesierski & Zurek is a full–service, general practice law firm specializing in Civil Litigation. In his current capacity, Mr. Wesierski is responsible for all aspects of operations for the practice to include client development, and administrative management. He also serves as trial attorney. His areas of specialty include: Sexual Harassment, Product Liability, and Bad Faith. Established in 1987, Wesierski & Zurek presently employs 90 people and has an estimated annual revenue in excess of $7 million. **Career Steps:** Managing Partner, Wesierski & Zurek (1987–Present); Partner and Member of the Executive Committee, Knapp, Petersen, & Clarke (1983–1987); Associate, Spray, Gould & Bowers (1980– 1983); Associate, Frank Moore (1979–1980). **Associations & Accomplishments:** American Board of Trial Advocates; YMCA; American Bar Association; Orange County Bar Association; Outstanding Young Man in America; Who's Who in California Law; Who's Who Among Emerging Leaders. **Education:** University of San Diego, J.D. (1978), CSULB, B.A. (1975).

James P. White Jr.
Attorney and Partner
Pullman & Comley, LLC
850 Main Street, 8th Floor
Bridgeport, CT 06604
(203) 330–2132
Fax: (203) 330–2288

8111

Business Information: Pullman & Comley, LLC is a full–service law firm with 70 attorneys and 5 offices in the State of Connecticut. A practicing attorney since 1967, Mr. White joined the Firm in 1983 and is now a Managing Partner. He focuses his practice in the areas of real estate, land use and environmental law, including representation of property owners, developers and lenders. He is also involved in the formation of business enterprises for start up and middle market companies. **Career Steps:** Attorney and Partner, Pullman & Comley, LLC (1983–Present); Partner, Flynn, White & Ambrose (1978–1982). **Associations & Accomplishments:** Vice Chairman and Chairman of Human Services Planning Committee, United Way of Eastern Fairfield County; Board Member, Food Bank of Fairfield County; Membership Co–Chairman, Monroe Rotary Club; Fairfield University Alumni Board of Directors; Monroe Republican Town Committee; Executive Committee of Connecticut Bar Association, P&Z Section; Published in "National Association of Industrial and Office Parks." **Education:** Fordham University School of Law, L.L.B. (1967); Fairfield University, A.B. (1964). **Personal:** Married to Patricia in 1966. Two children: Kristin and Devin. Mr. White enjoys golf, tennis and photography.

Raymond C. Whiteaker
Managing Partner
Adams & Whiteaker, P.C.
444 James Robertson Pkwy #201
Nashville, TN 37219
(615) 726–0900
Fax: (615) 256–3634

8111

Business Information: Adams & Whiteaker, P.C. is a full–service, general corporate, partnership law practice, concentrating on corporate law, family law, collection law, and litigation. The Firm's major client, Bell South (located in nine states) is represented by them in collection cases. A practicing attorney in Tennessee courts since 1953, Mr. Whiteaker co–established the Firm in 1991. Serving as Managing Partner and Chief Financial Officer, he oversees all aspects of operations, as well as all legal and financial functions. His practice specializes on public utility rate–making and collection law. **Career Steps:** Managing Partner, Adams & Whiteaker, P.C. (1991–Present); General Counsel, South Central Bell Telephone Co. (1968–1991); General Attorney, Southern Bell Telephone & Telephone Co. (1959–1968). **Associations & Accomplishments:** Tennessee Bar Association; Nashville Bar Association; Federal Bar Association. **Education:** New York University, L.L.M. (1954); Vanderbilt University Law School, J.D. (1953); Vanderbilt University, B.A. (1951). **Personal:** Married to Janice M. in 1957. Three children: Dorothy Maloy, Kent D., and Lon N.

Mrs. Vivianne A. Wicker
Partner and Trial Litigator
–Independent–
6900 Granada Boulevard
Coral Gables, FL 33146
(305) 448–3939
Fax: Please mail or call

8111

Business Information: Admitted to practice in Florida state courts, Mrs. Wicker joined the Firm in 1981 as Partner and Trial Litigator. She is responsible for providing legal representation to the Firm's clientele, concentrating in civil litigation and general negligence. **Career Steps:** Partner and Trial Litigation (1981–Present). **Associations & Accomplishments:** Vice President, Planning Junior League of Miami, Inc. – helping families at risk. **Education:** Samford University Cumberland Law School, J.D. (1981); Samford University, B.S. in Business and Accounting (1978). **Personal:** Married to John Strausburgh in 1994. Mrs. Wicker enjoys boating, travel, and cooking.

Harry E. Wigner Jr.
Attorney
Lathrop & Gage
9401 Indian Creek Parkway, Suite 1050
Overland Park, KS 66210
(913) 451–0820
Fax: (913) 451–0875

8111

Business Information: Lathrop & Gage is a full–service, general practice law firm consisting of 175 attorneys, concentrating on general civil cases. Joining the Firm as Attorney upon the conferral of his law degree in 1980, Mr. Wigner's practice concentrates on general business, real estate, and secured lending law. **Career Steps:** Attorney, Lathrop & Gage (1980–Present). **Associations & Accomplishments:** American Bar Association; Kansas Bar Association; Prairie Village Planning Commission; GOP Club, Inc.; Former Head of the Republican Party. **Education:** University of Michigan, J.D. (1980); University of Kansas, B.A. 1977. **Personal:** Married to Beth in 1979. Mr. Wigner enjoys family activities, gardening and collegiate sports.

Craig L. Wildey, Esq.

Managing Attorney
Richardson, Bambrick, Cermak & Bennett
2843 South Diamond Bar Boulevard
Diamond Bar, CA 91765–3417
(909) 444–6900
Fax: (909) 598–9724

8111

Business Information: Richardson, Bambrick, Cermak & Bennett is a full–service general practice law firm concentrating on insurance defense litigation. The Firm acts as staff counsel to the Automobile Club of Southern California. The Firm, with one main office and 11 satellite offices, employs 58 attorneys. A practicing attorney since obtaining his degree in 1987, Mr. Wildey joined Richardson, Bambrick, Cermak & Bennett in 1990. Besides practicing law, he is responsible for the day–to–day operations of three satellite offices. **Career Steps:** Richardson, Bambrick, Cermak & Bennett: Managing Attorney (1996–Present), Lead Attorney (1992–1996), Trial Attorney (1990–1992); Trial Attorney, Wilson, Becks & Pyfrom (1988–1990). **Associations & Accomplishments:** American Bar Association; Orange County Bar Association; Association of Southern California Defense Counsel; Association of California House Counsel; Licensed to practice law in all courts of the State of California; U.S. District Court for the Central District of California; U.S. Court of Appeals for the 9th Circuit; U.S. Supreme Court & United States Tax Court. **Education:** Western State University – School of Law, J.D. (1987); Murray State University, B.S. (1983). **Personal:** Married to Kimberly E. in 1989. One child: Zachary A. Mr. Wildey enjoys bicycling, travel, and spending time with his family.

Derek H. Wilson

Attorney at Law
Morrison & Foerster
555 West Fifth Street, Suite 3500
Los Angeles, CA 90013–1024
(213) 892–5745
Fax: (213) 892–5454
EMAIL: See Below

8111

Business Information: Morrison & Foerster is a premier, international corporate law firm. Admitted to practice in California and Washington, D.C., Derek Wilson joined the Firm in 1993. His practice concentrates on corporate finance, technology, and corporate partnering. **Career Steps:** Attorney at Law, Morrison & Foerster (1993–Present); Vice President and General Counsel, Thomas Bros. Maps (1992–1993); Foreign Legal Consultant, Yanagida, Nomura & Akai – Tokyo (1987–1988); Associate, Pillsbury Madison & Sutro (1986–1991). **Associations & Accomplishments:** Voting Member, Memorial Union Building Association – University of Wisconsin. **Education:** Harvard University, J.D. (1986); University of Wisconsin – Madison, B.A. (1982). **Personal:** Mr. Wilson enjoys reading, sports, and the arts.

Frank M. Wilson, J.D.

Litigation Attorney
Beasley, Wilson, Allen, Main & Crow, P.C.
218 Commerce Street
Montgomery, AL 36103–4160
(334) 269–2343
Fax: (334) 241–4336

8111

Business Information: Beasley, Wilson, Allen, Main & Crow, P.C. is a full–service, general practice law firm of trial attorneys, concentrating in business litigation. Established in 1979, the Firm currently employs 85 attorneys, legal and administrative support staff. Admitted to practice law in Alabama state courts, Mr. Wilson joined the Firm as Litigation and Trial

Attorney in 1979. **Career Steps:** Litigation and Trial Attorney, Beasley, Wilson, Allen, Main & Crow, P.C. (1979–Present). **Associations & Accomplishments:** Alabama State Bar Association; Association of Trial Lawyers of America; Alabama Trial Lawyers Association; Montgomery County Trial Lawyers Association; Board of Directors, Alabama Head Injury Foundation. **Personal:** Married to Barbara Grant in 1982. Three children: Eli, F. Booth, and Francis Wilson. Mr. Wilson enjoys travel, reading, and spending time with his family.

Pamela J. Wilson

Senior Partner
Hale and Dorr
60 State Street
Boston, MA 02109–1803
(617) 526–6371
Fax: (617) 526–5000
E–mail: see below

8111

Business Information: The third largest firm in Boston, Hale and Dorr is a premier law firm with a diverse practice. The lawyers in Hale and Dorr's investment company and advisory group represent, among others, the Eaton Vance, Goldman Sachs, John Hancock, Pioneer and Standish mutual fund complexes. Established in 1918, the firm currently employs over 250 attorneys. Admitted to the bar in 1980, Ms. Wilson joined the firm as a senior partner in 1991. She concentrates her practice on the representation of mutual funds and investment advisers, including advice about securities regulation. She can also be reached at the following Internet address: pamela.wilson@haledorr.com. **Career Steps:** Senior Partner, Hale and Dorr (1991–Present); Associate and Partner, Gaston & Snow (1980–1991). **Associations & Accomplishments:** American Bar Association; Federal Bar Association; Massachusetts Bar Association; Boston Bar Association; Frequent speaker; Published articles. **Education:** Boston University Law School, J.D. (1980); Harvard College, B.A. (1977). **Personal:** Married to Jeffery in 1977. Ms. Wilson enjoys reading, sewing and gardening.

Bruce Winaker

Financial Services Manager
Dewey Ballantine Law Firm
333 S. Hope Street, 30th Floor
Los Angeles, CA 90071
(213) 617–6554
Fax: (213) 617–0796

8111

Business Information: Dewey Ballantine Law Firm is an international general practice law firm comprised of 400 attorneys corporate–wide (40 in the Los Angeles office). The Firm is headquartered in New York City, and has eight other locations worldwide. As Financial Services Manager, Mr. Winaker serves as the Firms Financial Analyst, Manager of the Accounting Department, and oversees all accounting functions related to the Los Angeles office. **Career Steps:** Financial Services Manager, Dewey Ballantine Law Firm (1994–Present); Financial Analyst, Weil, Gotshal & Manges (1983–1994). **Education:** SUNY, Buffalo, B.A. (1982); CUNY, Baruch College, Paralegal Certification (1983). **Personal:** Mr. Winaker enjoys baseball, skiing, going to concerts, travel, swimming, and fitness.

Steven B. Witman, Esq.

Attorney/President/Owner
Law Offices of Steven B. Witman
3900 North Causeway Boulevard, Suite 600
Metairie, LA 70002
(504) 836–2200
Fax: (504) 836–2001
EMAIL: See Below

8111

Business Information: Law Offices of Steven B. Witman is a general practice law firm, focusing on corporate and insurance defense, business law, property and casualty insurance, and some international work. A practicing attorney since 1974, Mr. Witman acts as an attorney for corporations and businesses. Internet users can reach him via: Sbarth@access.com. **Career Steps:** Attorney/President/Owner, Law Offices of Steven B. Witman (1996–Present); Partner, Duplass, Witman, Zwain and Williams (1987–1996). **Associations & Accomplishments:** International Bar Association; American Bar Association; President, Archbishop Rummel High School Parent's Board; Former President and Treasurer, Beverly Knoll Civic Association. **Education:** Tulane University: J.D.

(1974), B.A. (1970). **Personal:** Married to Nell Laborde in 1971. Two children: Matthew and Jonathan. Mr. Witman enjoys collecting wine, travel and computers.

Lynn B. Witte

Partner
Reish & Luftman
11755 Wilshire Boulevard, 10th Floor
Los Angeles, CA 90025–1516
(310) 478–5656
Fax: (310) 478–5831

8111

Business Information: Reish & Luftman is a full–service, general practice law firm, concentrating on employee benefits consulting and litigation. A practicing attorney since 1979, Ms. Witte joined the Firm as Partner in 1987. Her practice concentrates on litigation and providing consulting for employee's benefits, as well as working with ARISA. **Career Steps:** Partner, Reish & Luftman (1987–Present); Associate, Grebe, Gross, Peer, Osborne & Dagle (1985–1987); Pension Attorney, Standard Insurance Company (1981–1985). **Associations & Accomplishments:** Oregan State Bar (1979–Present); State Bar of California (1988–Present); American Bar Association; Los Angeles County Bar Association; Secretary, Employee Benefits Committee – Tax Section; Beverly Hills Bar Association: Tax Section, Employee Benefits Section; U.S. Holocaust Museum; Museum of Tolerance (L.A.); First Church of Christ – Scientist, Boston; Published in California Bankruptcy Journal, ARISA Journals, Journal of Medical Economics, and RIA. **Education:** Lewis & Clark University Law School, J.D. (1979); Principia College, B.A. **Personal:** Ms. Witte enjoys tennis, movies, and reading novels.

Mr. R. Bradley Wolfe

Partner
Gordon, Muir and Foley
10 Columbus Boulevard, 3rd Floor
Hartford, CT 06106–1976
(860) 525–5361 Ext. 4625
Fax: (860) 525–4849

8111

Business Information: Gordon, Muir and Foley is a full–service, general practice law firm, concentrating in commercial & construction law, insurance defense, and personal representation law. Established in 1953, the Firm currently employs 50 attorneys, legal and administrative support staff. Admitted to practice in Connecticut state courts, Mr. Wolfe joined the Firm as Partner upon the conferral of his law degree. He is responsible for providing legal presentation, concentrating in commercial and construction law, litigation, defense claims, security industry law, and payment & recovery bonds. **Career Steps:** Partner, Gordon, Muir and Foley (1973–Present). **Associations & Accomplishments:** American Bar Association; Democratic Town Committee; Building and Town Committees; Forum Committee on Construction Industry; TIPS Construction Law Section; Association of General Contractors. **Education:** University of Connecticut, J.D. (1973); Haverford College, B.A. (1970). **Personal:** Mr. Wolfe enjoys golf, skiing, and watching soccer.

James A. Woods

Senior Partner
Woods and Partners
2000 McGill College Avenue
Montreal, Quebec H3A 3H3
(514) 982–4503
Fax: (514) 284–2046

8111

Business Information: Woods and Partners is a full–service litigation law firm. With a staff of eight attorneys, the Firm specializes in commercial and corporation litigation cases. As Senior Partner, Mr. Woods oversees all day–to–day operations of the Firm, including budgeting, finances, and personnel. In addition to his administrative duties, Mr. Woods also tends to his current clients and their cases. **Career Steps:** Senior Partner, Woods and Partners (1992–Present); Senior Partner, Clark, Woods, Rochefort, Fortier (1982–1992); Member of Montreal And Toronto Offices, Stikeman Elliott (1976–1982). **Associations & Accomplishments:** Quebec Bar Association; Canadian Bar Association; Law Society of Upper Canada; Association of Trial Lawyers of America; American Bar Association; American Arbitration Association; Fellow, Chartered Institute of Arbitrators **Education:** McGill University: L.L.B. (1974), B.C.L. (1973), B.A. (1970). **Personal:** Married to Solange Laferte in 1971. Three children: Sarah, James, and Alexander. Mr. Woods enjoys reading, sports, theatre, and ballet.

Phyllis B. Worley

Sole Practitioner
Phyllis B. Worley, Attorney at Law
606–A West Arch Avenue
Searcy, AR 72143–5206
(501) 268–1722
Fax: (501) 268–3533

8111

Business Information: A trial attorney admitted to all Arkansas state and federal courts since 1988, Phyllis Worley established her sole practice law office in 1990. Her practice concentrates on providing defense to White County residents in criminal and juvenile cases, primarily focusing on helping children in child abuse cases. Concurrent with her law practice, she travels throughout the U.S. conducting seminars on child abuse in the church environment. **Career Steps:** Sole Practitioner, Phyllis B. Worley, Attorney at Law (1990–Present); Clerk, 1st Division, 6th Judicial District Court (1989–1990); Attorney, Public Defender, 6th Judicial District Court (1988–1989). **Associations & Accomplishments:** American, Arkansas, White County Bar Associations; Trial Lawyers Association; National Association of Criminal Defense Lawyers; Commissioner, Arkansas Sentencing Commission; Director, Arkansas Sheriff's Boys & Girls Ranches, Inc.; Chair, Program Services Committee; Secretary, Domestic Violence Board; Instructor, Child Abuse in Church Environment seminars. **Education:** University of Arkansas at Little Rock, J.D. (1988); University of Central Arkansas, B.S. in Public Administration (1985). **Personal:** Married to Tom in 1972. Two children: Brad and Brent.

J. Stephen Wright

Attorney
Frascogna, Courtney, Wright et al
P.O. Box 23126
Jackson, MS 39225–3126
(601) 969–1737
Fax: (601) 969–1739

8111

Business Information: Frascogna, Courtney, Wright et al is a full–service, general practice law firm. Established in 1990, the Firm consists of nine attorneys, legal, and administrative support staff. A practicing attorney in Mississippi state courts since 1976, Mr. Wright co–founded the Firm in 1990. Serving as Principal and Partner, he provides all aspects of legal representation to the Firm's major clientele. Concurrent with his private legal practice, he serves as Judge and Attorney for the City of Madison, Mississippi. **Career Steps:** Attorney, Frascogna, Courtney, Wright et al (1990–Present); Attorney and Judge, City of Madison (1986–Present); Attorney, Stennett, Wilkinson & Ward (1984–1990). **Associations & Accomplishments:** President (1982–1983), National Association of Extradition Officials **Education:** University of Mississippi, J.D. (1975); Florida State University, B.A. (1972). **Personal:** Married to Jane Ann in 1992. Four children: Daniel, Michael, Nathan and Judson.

E. Robert Yoches

Partner
Finnegan, Henderson, Farbow, Garrett & Dunner, L.L.P.
1300 I Street Northwest, Suite 700
Washington, DC 20005–3314
(202) 408–4000 Ext: 4039
Fax: (202) 408–4400

8111

Business Information: Finnegan, Henderson, Farbow, Garrett & Dunner, L.L.P. is the largest intellectual law firm in the country consisting of 155 attorneys. International in scope, the Firm spans the U.S. (District of Columbia), Belgium (Brussels), and Japan (Tokyo). A practicing attorney in the District of Columbia state and federal courts since 1980, Mr. Yoches joined the Firm as Partner in 1988. His practice specializes in the relationship of intellectual property law to computer technology patents, as well as providing opinions on the patentability, infringement, and validity of patents and copyrights relating to computer technology and the licensing of intellectual property rights in computer technology. With extensive litigation experience in prosecuting patents in the ever changing software technology arena, he advises clients on strategies to protect their intellectual property rights and to avoid violating others' rights. His legal background includes litigation, licensing, opinion, and prosecution work for several large hardware and software companies and has been selected as an expert witness to testify on patents for software technology. Other duties include pre–filing investigations to discovery, trial, and appeal; serving as lead counsel and second chair on cases involving patents, copyrights, and trade secrets; and drafting patent applications for computer–related technology. Prior to

his legal career, he worked for NASA at the Goddard Space Flight Center in Greenbelt, Maryland as an engineer. His duties included involvement in computerized testing of spacecraft and Space Shuttle operations, in which he gained his initial working knowledge in the area of computer technology. **Career Steps:** Partner, Finnegan, Henderson, Farbow, Garrett & Dunner, L.L.P. (1988–Present); Engineer, NASA (1974–1977). **Associations & Accomplishments:** American Bar Association; Licensing Executive Society; Co-Founder, Computer Law Section, Washington, DC Bar Association; Washington DC Computer Law Forum; International Bar Association; American Intellectual Property Law Association. **Education:** University of Pennsylvania, J.D. (1980); University of Colorado, B.S. in Electrical Enginering and Computer Science, with highest honors, Tau Beta Pi (1974). **Personal:** Married to Karen in 1978. Two children: Aaron and Meryl. Mr. Yoches enjoys tennis.

Bennett G. Young

Partner
LeBoeuf, Lamb, Greene & MacRae, LLP
One Embarcadero Center
San Francisco, CA 94111
(415) 951–1100
Fax: (415) 951–1180

8111

Business Information: LeBoeuf, Lamb, Greene & MacRae, LLP is a premier corporate law firm. Established in 1929, the Firm currently employs over 500 attorneys worldwide. A practicing attorney in California state courts since 1982, Mr. Young joined the Firm in 1991. Serving as Partner, his practice concentrates in all areas of bankruptcy law. **Career Steps:** Partner, LeBoeuf, Lamb, Greene & MacRae, LLP (1991–Present). **Associations & Accomplishments:** Association for Corporate Growth; Turnaround Management Association; Interviewed by local legal San Francisco paper. **Education:** Hastings College of Law, J.D. (1982); University of California–San Diego, B.A. in Mathematics (1979). **Personal:** Married to Molly L. in 1982. Two children: Nathan and William. Mr. Young enjoys fly fishing and reading.

Mark Travis Young

Sole Proprietor
Mark Young & Associates
5211 Highway 153, Suite B, P.O. Box 909
Hixson, TN 37343–0909
(423) 870–5225
Fax: (423) 877–0363

8111

Business Information: Mark Young & Associates is a full–service, general practice law firm, specializing in consumer bankruptcy. The Firm consists of five full–time and two part–time staff, including Associate, Sandra Benton, who concentrates on Worker's Compensation and personal injury cases. A practicing attorney since 1976 and a Certified Bankruptcy Specialist, Mr. Young established the Firm in 1991. He oversees all administrative operations for associates and a support team of eight, in addition to his daily law practice. He also conducts pro bono work primarily on bankruptcy referrals for cases. **Career Steps:** Sole Proprietor, Mark Young & Associates (1991–Present). **Associations & Accomplishments:** Tennessee Bar Association; American Bar Association; National Association of Chapter 13 Trustees; American Bankruptcy Institute; National Association of Consumer Bankruptcy Attorneys. **Education:** University of Tennessee, J.D. (1976); Tennessee Technological University, B.S. in History (1974). **Personal:** One child: Bonnie. Mr. Young enjoys spending time with his daughter, canoeing, sailing, and hiking.

Craig A. Zanot

Partner and Attorney
Davidson, Breen & Doud, P.C.
1121 North Michigan Avenue
Saginaw, MI 48602
(517) 752–9595
Fax: (517) 752–0531

8111

Business Information: Davidson, Breen & Doud, P.C. is a full–service law firm concentrating in civil litigation, liability and personal injury. Established in 1971, Davidson, Breen &

Doud, P.C. currently employs 10 attorneys and 15 legal support staff. A trial attorney admitted to both State and Federal courts, Mr. Zanot concentrates his practice in the areas of litigation and administration. He has been with the Firm since 1981, following a year of clerkship and the conferral of his law degree. **Career Steps:** Partner and Attorney, Davidson, Breen & Doud, P.C. (1981–Present). **Associations & Accomplishments:** Saginaw Country Club; State Bar of Michigan; Indiana State Bar Association; Chi Phi Fraternity; Saginaw County Bar Association; Genesee County Bar Association. **Education:** Indiana University, J.D. (1980); University of Michigan, A.B. (1977). **Personal:** Mr. Zanot enjoys golf and water sports.

Scott Zegeer

Tax/Corporate Lawyer
Sable, Makoroff & Gusky
7th Floor, Frick Building
Pittsburgh, PA 15219
(412) 471–4996
Fax: (412) 281–2859

8111

Business Information: Established in 1987, Sable, Makoroff & Gusky is a full–service law firm specializing in tax practice, bankruptcy, corporate law, and litigation. Having been with the firm for three years, and practicing law for eleven years, Mr. Zegeer's specialty is tax and corporate law. His pro bono work is primarily with tax exempt organizations. **Career Steps:** Tax/Corporate Lawyer, Sable, Makoroff & Gusky (1993–Present). **Associations & Accomplishments:** Pennslvania Bar Association; Washington Bar Association; West Virginia Bar Association; Pennsylvania Institute of C.P.A.'s; West Virginia Institute of C.P.A.'s. **Education:** George Washington University, J.D. (1985); West Virginia University, B.S. in Accounting. **Personal:** Married to Mary A. in 1995. One child: Melissa Marie. Mr. Zegeer enjoys skiing, golf, and tennis.

Robert T. Zielinski

Partner
Ross & Hardies
150 North Michigan Avenue, Suite 2500
Chicago, IL 60601
(312) 558–1000
Fax: (312) 750–8600

8111

Business Information: Ross & Hardies is an international, full–service premier law firm, concentrating on labor, employment law, and customs cases. Established in 1890, the Firm consists of 400 attorneys within four offices located in Illinois (Chicago), District of Columbia, New Jersey, and New York. A practicing attorney in Illinois state courts since 1982, Mr. Zielinski joined the Firm as Attorney in 1986. Currently serving as Partner of the Firm, his practice focuses on labor and employment law, consumer products, educational institutions, company transactions, age and racial discriminations. He also provides legal advice and participates in Union campaigns and litigations. **Career Steps:** Partner, Ross & Hardies (1986–Present). **Associations & Accomplishments:** Frequent public speaker on employee relations; Author and producer of a training video for employers – now being marketed. **Education:** New York University, J.D. (1982); Harvard College, B.A., cum laude (1979). **Personal:** Married to Maggie in 1988. One child: Daniel. Mr. Zielinski enjoys tennis and raising his son.

Gregory R. Yates

Associate Vice President
Frederic R. Harris, Inc.
260 South Broad Street, Suite 1500
Philadelphia, PA 19102
(215) 735–0832
Fax: (215) 735–0883

8177

Business Information: Frederic R. Harris, Inc. is a transportation engineering consulting firm specializing in mass transit systems. As Associate Vice President, Mr. Yates is responsible for directing the Mass Transit Systems, including traction power, signals, and communications. **Career Steps:** Associate Vice President, Frederic R. Harris, Inc. (1995–Present); Manager of Systems Engineering, Urban Engineers, Inc. (1990–1995); Project Manager, Morrison–Knudsen Engineers (1985–1990); Project Engineer, Tel–Stock, Inc. (1980–1985). **Associations & Accomplishments:** American Society of Civil Engineers – Philadelphia Section; American Public Transportation Association – Electric Trolley Bus Subcommittee. **Education:** Drexel University: B.S.C.E. (1981), coursework toward Master's degree in Engineering

Management. **Personal:** Married to Debra in 1981. Two children: Jennifer and Lindsay. Mr. Yates enjoys sports and golf.

8200 Educational Services

8211 Elementary and secondary schools
8221 Colleges and universities
8222 Junior colleges
8231 Libraries
8243 Data processing schools
8244 Business and secretarial schools
8249 Vocational schools, NEC
8299 Schools and educational services, NEC

Catherine Augustine, Ph.D.

Director
Center for Advanced Technologies
1415 Sixth Avenue
Altoona, PA 16602–2427
(814) 946–8524
Fax: (814) 946–8526
EMAIL: See Below

8211

Business Information: Center for Advanced Technologies provides multimedia and technology training, multimedia instructional programs and interactive computer–based training. As Director, Dr. Augustine manages project and educational development, curricular planning, and attends various conferences regarding training techniques. Concurrently, she serves as President of Moondance Multimedia. Internet users can reach her via: augustine@techcenter.altoona.k12.pa.us **Career Steps:** Director, Center for Advanced Technologies (1995–Present); President, Moondance Multimedia (1995–Present); Assistant Professor, Lock Haven University (1992–1994); Instructor, Pennsylvania State University (1988–1994). **Associations & Accomplishments:** Pennsylvania Association of Educational Communications & Technology; Association of Educational Communications & Technology; Association of Supervision & Curriculum Development. **Education:** Pennsylvania State University, Ph.D. (1992); Rutgers University, Ed.M. in Creative Arts in Education; Livingston College, Rutgers University, B.A. in Anthropology. **Personal:** Married to Kyle L. Peck in 1992. Four children: Kyla, K.C., Erin, and Jamie. Dr. Augustine enjoys gardening, travel, and spending time with family.

Everardo R. Avila

Teacher – Val Verde Juvenile Detention Center
San Felipe Del Rio Consolidated Independent School District
200 Griner Street
Del Rio, TX 78840
(210) 774–7553
Fax: Please mail or call

8211

Business Information: San Felipe Del Rio Consolidated Independent School District is the municipal governmental office responsible for the administration of all public elementary and secondary educational facilities and activities within its jurisdiction. The Agency's mission is to establish partnerships between community businesses and individuals which promote collaborative and mutually beneficial results, to enhance student achievement through these partnerships, and to provide learning opportunities for the community. With more than eighteen years of experience in education, Mr. Avila was assigned to the Val Verde Juvenile Detention Center in the San Felipe Del Rio Consolidated Independent School District in 1994. He is responsible for the development of an educational and counseling program for the Center. His duties include teaching students in a variety of areas, including: TAAS skills in all areas and grade levels; content area via the use of dialectical notetaking and review via oral examination of same; study skills; and the method of inquiry; in addition to providing vocational, career, and personal social adjustment skills counseling. **Career Steps:** Teacher, Val Verde Juvenile Detention Center (1994–Present); Program Facilitator, Retention Action Program–Developmental Education, El Paso Community College (1981–1994); Vocational Rehabilitation Counselor, Texas Rehabilitation Commission (1977–1981); Interviewer/Job Corp Recruiter/Counselor, Texas Employment Commission (1976–1977); Counselor/Coordinator of Manpower Programs, Brazos Valley Development Council (1975–1976); Counselor/Coordinator of Manpower Programs Pre–vocational Remedial Education Instructor, Webb County Commissioners Court Out of School Neighborhood Yourth Corps (1968–1972); Supervisor, Neighborhood Youth Corp Program Zavala County, Winter Garden Tri–County Community Action Programs (1966–1968); Label Machine Operator, Libby McNiel Libby (1961); Medical Specialist, U.S. Army Medical Corp 250th General Hospital (1964–1966). **Associations & Accomplishments:** French Horn Player, El Paso Community College Civic Orchestra & Symphony (1982–1994); Texas Jr. College Association; Texas Association for Bilingual Education, "Excellence in Writing" (October 23, 1987); National Association for Bilingual Education; Life Time Member, Full Gospel Business Men International, El Paso Downtown Chapter; The National Institute for Staff and Organizational Development (NISOD), Department of Educational Administration, College of Education, The University of Texas, "Master Teacher Award"; The University of Texas at El Paso for "Contribution to Excellence in Bilingual Education," at the Third Annual bilingual Education/ESL Conference for Teacher (October 15, 1983); Letter of Recognition for Honorable Military Service, and Service to the State of Texas. Governor William P. Clements, Jr. (Dated May 29, 1979); Numerous presentations and publications at international, national, state, and local conference and institutional symposia proceedings, some recent ones to include: "A comparative analysis of leadership traits and traits that exemplify good teaching qualities."; "The new retention action program operations manual and guide". **Education:** Webster University – Fort Bliss, Texas Site, M.A. in Human Resource Development (1990); Texas A&M University – College Station, Texas, B.S. in Sociology/Educational Psychology (1973); Southwest Texas Jr. College – Uvalde, Texas, A.A. (1972). **Personal:** Married to Dora Elia in 1972. Mr. Avila enjoys being an artist, writer, musician, and poet.

Minner J. Baldwin

Assistant Principal
Cook Middle School
310 N. Martin Luther King Jr. Street
Adel, GA 31620
(912) 896–4541
Fax: (912) 892–5034

8211

Business Information: Cook Middle School, originally established as the Cook County Training School for Blacks, has the distinction of being the first ethnically–integrated as well as the first ever implemented Middle School in the South. The School educates students in grades six through eight residing in the community of Adel, Georgia. Working as a teacher and administrator for Cook County area schools as well as the Board of Education since 1971, Minner Baldwin was appointed as Assistant Principal to Cook Middle School in 1992. Providing the leadership and overall efficient operation of the School, her primary functions entail enforcement of student disciplinary guidelines, coordination of parent/student conferences, presiding at all disciplinary hearings, promotion of public relations on a continual basis, evaluation of staff members, and other duties as assigned by the Principal. **Career Steps:** Assistant Principal, Cook Middle School (1992–Present); Director of Personnel, Cook County Board of Education (1988–1992); Lowndes High School: Teacher (1971–1988), Part–time Administrator (1981–1985); Evening Instructor– Troy State University satellite site, Moody Air Force Base, Valdosta, GA (1985). **Associations & Accomplishments:** National Middle School Association; Georgia Middle School Association; Georgia Association of Educators; National Association of Educators: Sustaining Member, Congressional Contact Team Member, Official Representative at National Conventions, Liaison to NEA Educational Legislation Representative Charles Hatcher; Cook County Association of Educators; Georgia Association of Educational Leaders; Georgia Association of Assistant Principals; Cook County Association of Reading; National Reading Association; 1990 Leadership Lowndes; Board of Directors, Valdosta State College Alumni Association; Advisory Committee, Langdale Park; Lowndes County Public Facility Assembly; Valdosta/Lowndes County Education Committee; Board of Directors, E–9 Zoning Project; Lowndes/Valdosta Chapter, Albany State College Alumni; Valdosta Alumnus Chapter, Delta Sigma Theta Sorority; Black Voters League; Democratic Party; Official Delegate, 1988 National Democratic Convention; HONORS: Nominated "Administrator of the Year" (1991) – by Georgia Association of Educators; Nominated "Outstanding Young Woman of America" – Professional Women's Club; "Outstanding Woman of the Year" (1991–92) and "Outstanding Black American" (1992) – Lowndes County, Georgia. **Education:** Valdosta State College: Ed.Sp. in Educational Administration–Supervision (1991), M.Ed. in Educational Administration–Supervision (1980), M.Ed. in History (1977); Albany State College, B.A. in Sociology/History (1971). **Personal:** Married to Rufus in 1977. Two children: Rufus II and Aesha. Ms. Baldwin enjoys reading, traveling, meeting people, community work and listening to music.

Barbara G. Bell

Administrator
Eton School
2701 Bel – Red Road
Bellevue, WA 98008
(206) 881–4230
Fax: (206) 861–8011

8211

Business Information: Eton School is a Montessori School (private) established in 1978 with approximately 60 employees. Eton School has classes through 8th grade and also offers a day care curriculum. As Administrator, Ms. Bell is responsible for grades 4 through 8. This responsibility includes organization of field trips, testing of incoming students, arranging tours of the school, speaking with parents, and discipline of the students. Concurrently, Ms. Bell is also responsible for the ordering of course materials, coordinating courses for the school, supervising the music and foreign language instructors, and attending career related workshops. Long range plans for Ms. Bell include continuing in her current position and refining the curriculum. **Career Steps:** Eton School: Administrator (1993–Present), Upper Level Director (1993–Present), Curriculum Director (1991–Present), Specialist Supervisor (1995–1996). **Associations & Accomplishments:** Former President, Treasurer, Pacific Northwest Montessori Society. **Education:** Seattle University, Master in Curriculum and Supervision; University of Washington, B.Edu.; American Montessori Society, Montessori (3–6); Spring Valley Montessori (6–12); Attended, University of Puget Sound. **Personal:** Married to Frank in 1961. Three children: Jeffrey Dean Bell, Bambi Lynne Meehan, and Robyn Bell – Bangerter. Ms. Bell enjoys reading.

Patt Bergeron

Principal
Woodland Elementary School
2000 Pyle Drive
Kingsford, MI 49802–4382
(906) 779–2685
Fax: (906) 779–7701

8211

Business Information: Woodland Elementary School is a regional elementary school serving 1,100 students in grades Kindergarten through 5th grade. The School has a staff of 100 and is actually five small schools in one. As Principal, Ms. Bergeron is responsible for the supervision of all educational activities and support staff, as well as establishing the mission and vision for continued growth. **Career Steps:** Principal, Woodland Elementary School (1995–Present); Brietung Township Schools: Assistant Principle (1990–1995) and Teacher, Grades 1–6 (1972–1990). **Associations & Accomplishments:** Phi Delta Kappa; Board Member, Northern Michigan University Alumni. **Education:** Northern Michigan University, MA (1988) and Administrator Certification (1991). **Personal:** Married to Adrian in 1975. One child: Cameron Tellis. Ms. Bergeron enjoys downhill skiing, swimming, and reading.

Juneria P. Berges, Ed.D.

Principal
Grapevine Middle School
730 East Worth
Grapevine, TX 76051
(817) 488–9592
Fax: (817) 424–1626

8211

Business Information: Grapevine Middle School is a secondary educational institution for 6th, 7th, and 8th graders, promoting caring, nuturing and development of our country's and the world's tomorrow. Grapevine Middle School is within the Colleyville Independent School District and currently employs a staff of 90. As Principal, Ms. Berges is responsible for effectively communicating the vision; faciliating & stimulating creative thought; and motivating, supporting, and enabling master teachers to effectively meet the diverse needs of all students in order to appropriately educate, cultivate, inspire, and prepare the leaders of tomorrow. Her vast experience includes teaching 3 year olds through high school seniors (choir, science, self–contained fourth graders, language arts, and general music) to administrative duties. **Career Steps:** Principal, Grapevine Middle School (1992–Present); Grapevine High School: Assistant Principal (1988–1992), Choir Director (1983–1988). **Associations & Accomplishments:** President of the Women's Division, Grapevine Chamber of Commerce (1994); Charter Member, Dallas/Fort Worth Rotary Club; President, The Texas Council of Women School Executives; President of the Colleyville Lions Club; 1 of 57 Texas Middle School Mentor Principals; Member, Delta Kappa Gamma; Texas Branch, Association for Supervision & Curriculum Development; Texas Association of School Administrators;

Texas Branch, National Association of Secondary School Principals; Texas Women's Alliance. **Education:** East Texas State University, Ed.D. (1993); Texas Women's University, M.Ed., Mid–Management and Supervision Certification (1988), Superintendent Certification (1990); University of Southern Mississippi, B.M.Ed. **Personal:** One child: Ashley Nicole Berges. Ms. Berges enjoys singing, playing the piano, reading, travel, fine dining, community involvement & services, learning, conducting research and being with people.

Brian David Billstein

Special Education Director
Cuero School District
405 Park Heights Drive
Cuero, TX 7954
(512) 275–6911
Fax: (512) 275–8597
EMAIL: See Below
8211

Business Information: Cuero School District provides special education services to over one thousand students with special handicaps and needs, developing specific programs to benefit the students educationally. Established in 1982, the District serves students from thirteen school districts that belong to the DeWitt Lavaca Special Education Cooperation. As Special Education Director, Mr. Billstein is responsible for managing the thirteen participating school districts. With twenty years experience in the field, he oversees all testing that is used to determine the eligibility of students for the special education. Mr. Billstein also determines appropriate program placement for all children. Internet users can reach him via: briab@tenet.edu. **Career Steps:** Special Education Director, Cuero School District (1993–Present); Administrator, Gulf Bard MH/MR (1993–1994); Region III Consultant, Education Service Center, Region III ESC (1991–1993); Education Diagnostician, Victoria Independent School District (190–1993). **Associations & Accomplishments:** Board Vice President, Child Surgery Clinic; Board Member: Juvenile Probation Department, Tender Loving Care, Child Care Management Advisory Group for Department of Human Services. **Education:** Master of Education; Mid Management Artification; Certified in Special Education. **Personal:** Three children: Shelly, Briana, and Michelle. Mr. Billstein enjoys fishing, hunting, gardening, and playing the guitar.

Vicki Jones Brooks

Senior Director
Orange County Public Schools
445 West Amelia Avenue
Orlando, FL 32801
(407) 849–3340
Fax: (407) 849–3345
8211

Business Information: Orange County Public Schools, established in 1965, is the municipal office responsible for the administration of all secondary education facilities and activities within the County jurisdiction. With fourteen years experience in education, Ms. Brooks joined the Orange County Public School System as Administrator of Zoning in 1980. She served as an Elementary School Principal from 1982 to 1994, before being appointed to her present position as Senior Director in 1994. She is responsible for the direction of all program activities, as well as all implementation decisions of the $15 million federal program to design reading and math programs for "at risk" students. **Career Steps:** Orange County Public Schools: Senior Director – Title I (1994–Present), Elementary School Principal (1982–1994), Administrator of Zoning (1980–1982). **Associations & Accomplishments:** National Association for School Administrators; International Reading Association; Alpha Kappa Alpha Sorority, Inc.; National Association of Federal School Administrators; Interviewed by professional advocants, local newspapers, and by school board members. **Education:** University of Central Florida, Administration (1980); University of Kentucky, M.S.L.S.; Clark Atlanta University, B.A. **Personal:** One child: Michael. Ms. Brooks enjoys sports, reading, travel, and jazz music.

Julia R. Bryant, Ph.D.

Assistant Food Service Director
Hampton City Schools
1819 Nickerson Blvd.
Hampton, VA 23663–1026
(804) 850–5252
Fax: (804) 850–5257
8211

Business Information: Hampton City Schools – Food and Nutrition Services Department provides nutrition education and food service, performs custodial duties, and purchases food, supplies, and chemicals for the District. As Assistant Food Service Director, Dr. Bryant assists the Food Service Director in the administration of the school lunch program, serves as the purchasing agent for all food and disposable items, tracks inventory and accounting, and performs various bookkeeping and clerical duties. Additionally, she supervises warehouse operations, evaluates cafeteria operating efficiency and makes necessary recommendations, and plans and conducts in–service training programs for managers and employees. **Career Steps:** Assistant Food Service Director, Hampton City Schools (1993–Present); Assistant Professor, Hampton University (1987–1993); Assistant Professor, Norfolk State University (1987). **Associations & Accomplishments:** Dietetic Association: American and Virginia Chapters; Home Economic Association: American and Virginia Chapters; Faculty Advisor, Kappa Omicron Phi Home Economics Honor Society; American School Foodservice Association; Program Chair and Former President, Peninsula Nutrition Council; Tidewater District Dietetic Association; Tidewater Nutrition Council. **Education:** University of Maryland, Ph.D. (1988); Kansas State University, M.S.; Bennett College, B.S. **Personal:** Married to James in 1969. One child: James II. Dr. Bryant enjoys refinishing furniture, quilting, reading, writing, sewing, and cooking.

Mr. Tommie L. Burton

Principal
Winship Middle School
14717 Curtis Street
Detroit, MI 48235–2773
(313) 270–0293
Fax: Please mail or call
8211

Business Information: Winship Middle School is a public school providing quality education to middle school students in the Detroit, Michigan area. As Principal, Mr. Burton is responsible for the supervision of all educational activities and support staff, as well as establishing the mission and vision for continued growth. **Career Steps:** Principal, Winship Middle School (1985–Present). **Associations & Accomplishments:** Active in church; NAACP; ASCD; Black Educators of Detroit; NABSE; Phi Delta Kappa; Alumni Association Board of Governors, WSU; Board of Directors, Northwestern YMCA; Omega Psi Phi Fraternity; League of Cooperating Principal; O.S.A.S. Executive Board. **Personal:** Mr. Burton enjoys people, bowling, and photography.

Sister Mary Clare Buthod, O.S.B.

Director
Monte Cassino School, Inc.
2206 South Lewis Avenue
Tulsa, OK 74114–3117
(918) 742–3364
Fax: (918) 744–1374
8211

Business Information: Monte Cassino School, Inc. is a private, Catholic school with an enrollment of 1,190 students, providing quality Christian education to elementary school students (K–8 grades) in the Tulsa, Oklahoma area. Some of its acclaimed educational programs include: Schools Attuned, Advanced Placement in Math and Foreign Language, Rainbows, Mission Awareness, Positive Action, Quest, and Operation Aware. The School was the recipient of the National Drug Free School Award in 1989–1990. Established in 1926, Monte Cassino School, Inc. currently employs 149 people. Sister Mary Clare serves as Director and is responsible for all administrative aspects, including supervision of all educational activities and support staff (4 principals), as well as establishing the mission and vision for continued growth. **Career Steps:** Monte Cassino School, Inc.: Director (1986–Present), Principal (1979–1986), Teacher (1968–1979). **Associations & Accomplishments:** Director, Rainbows Program in Northeast Oklahoma; 1993–1994 Recipient, U.S. Department of Education Plaque for Excellence in Education. **Education:** Creighton University, M.A. (1987); Tulsa University, M.A. in Teaching Arts (1976).

Robert F. Castellano

President of General Partnership
Educational Development Resources Association, Ltd.
12420 Telecom Drive
Temple Terrace, FL 33637–0911
(813) 979–0002
Fax: (813) 621–2666
8211

Business Information: Educational Development Resources Association, Ltd., dba Aberdeen Preparatory is a private school, providing education for preschoolers through the ninth grades. Established in 1992, the School currently employs 25 faculty. With twenty–seven years in education, Mr. Castellano joined the Educational Development Resources Association in 1992. As President of General Partnership, he serves as Principal of Aberdeen Preparatory School, responsible for the supervision of all educational activities and support staff, as well as establishing the mission and vision for continued growth. **Career Steps:** President of General Partnership, Educational Develoment Resources Association, Ltd. DBA Aberdeen Preparatory (1992–Present); Principal/Owner, Soffner Hills Academy (1981–1992); Manalapan–Englishtown Regional School: Assistant to the Superintendent of Schools (1981), Elementary School Principal (1968–1981). **Associations & Accomplishments:** Temple Terrace Chamber of Commerce; National Association of Elementary School Principals. **Education:** Keane University, M.A. (1968); Newark State College, B.A. (1963). **Personal:** Married to Sandra L. in 1962. Three children: Nicci D., Anthony R., and Maria C. Mr. Castellano enjoys computer programming.

Sherry G. Clark

Principal
Early Primary
P O Box 3315
Early, TX 76803
(915) 643–9622
Fax: (915) 646–5469
EMAIL: See Below
8211

Business Information: Early Primary provides early childhood education to children in grades K–2. Local in scope, the School was established in 1993 and employs 45 people. As Principal, Ms. Clark oversees all aspects of the School. She is responsible for development and implementation of policies, personnel management, and curriculum oversight. Internet users can reach her via: sclark@tenet.edu. **Career Steps:** Principal, Early Primary (1993–Present); Early I.S.D: Technical Coordinator (1989–1993), G/T Coordinator (1988–1993), K Lead Teacher (1979–1988). **Associations & Accomplishments:** Association of Supervision/Curriculum Development; Texas Elementary Principals and Supervisors Association; Delta Kappa Gamma; Phi Delta Kappa; Texas Association of the Gifted and Talented. **Education:** Tarleton State University, Masters of Education (1986); Three Advanced Certificates. **Personal:** Married to Douglas in 1965. Three children: Kimberley, Matt and Quentin. Ms. Clark enjoys reading, learning, crafts and travel.

Mary–Lou Cleveland

Principal
Edmonton Public Schools
14607 59th Street
Edmonton, Alberta T5A 1Y3
(403) 478–5319
Fax: (403) 473–7755
8211

Business Information: Steele Heights School is a full service educational facility providing scholastic and related services to students in grades seven through nine. Employing 35 educational professionals and support staff, and with a student population of approximately 560, the school has a strict discipline behaviour and contact policy that is based on accountability and responsibility. Although consequences can include suspension and expulsion, it does not include physical punishment. The School works to help students develop strategies for appropriate behaviour though the SAFEroom (Student Attitudes for Excellence) a unique program that is school specific. As Principal, Ms. Cleveland oversees all aspects of the School and is responsible for ensuring implementation of provincially mandated curriculum. Additional duties include the safety and welfare of students and maintaining positive relations with the surrounding community. **Career Steps:** Principal, Edmonton Public Schools/Steele Heights Jr. High (1993–Present); Principal at Large, Edmonton Public Schools (1992–1993); Principal, Sifton Elementary (1989–1992). **Associations & Accomplishments:** Public School Administrators Association (PSAA); United Way; Public School

Committee. **Education:** University of Alberta: P.S.A.D. (1971), Bachelor of Music (1970). **Personal:** Married. Ms. Cleveland enjoys running, weight training, reading, and music.

Rev. Lawrence Cole

School Administrator
First Baptist School
140 East Seventh Street
Hialeah, FL 33010
(305) 888–9776
Fax: (305) 888–9783

8211

Business Information: First Baptist School is a private Christian school providing quality education to preschool, elementary and secondary students (nursery–aged children to 12th graders). Established in 1971, First Baptist School reports an operating budget of $1.5 million and currently employs 51 people. As School Administrator, Rev. Cole serves as Head Principal and Director of the School Operations. He is responsible for budget policies, personnel hiring and firing, disciplinary measures, public relations, working closely with the church, and the supervision of all educational activities and support staff, as well as establishing the mission and vision for continued growth. **Career Steps:** School Administrator, First Baptist School (1993–Present); Minister of Education, First Baptist Church of Hialeah (1991–1993); Minister of Education, College Avenue Baptist Church (1988–1990); Foreign Missionary, Foreign Mission Board, Southern Baptist Convention (1984–1986). **Associations & Accomplishments:** Southern Baptist Association of Christian Schools. **Education:** Southwestern Baptist Theological Seminary, Master of Divinity and M.A. in Religious Education (1990); Samford University, B.A. **Personal:** Married to Rhonda S. Cole in 1988. Two children: Clinton and Sarah Cole. Rev. Cole enjoys spending time with his children, jogging, soccer, reading, and church activities.

Mary C. Connolly

Director of Special Education
Newport School Department
437 Broadway
Newport, RI 02840–1739
(401) 847–2100
Fax: (401) 849–0170

8211

Business Information: Newport School Department is the municipal office responsible for the administration of all public elementary and secondary education programs within the City of Newport, RI jurisdiction. A special educations educator for the past twenty–five years, Mary Connolly was appointed as Director of Special Education for Newport Schools in 1987. She provides the overall coordination and supervisory direction of support programs for children with special disabilities. Concurrent with her duties at Newport Schools, Ms. Connolly is an Adjunct Professor in the Special Education Department at Salve Regina University. **Career Steps:** Newport School Department: Director of Special Education (1987–Present), Special Education Teacher (1970–1987); Adjunct Professor – Special Education Department, Salve Regina University (1993–1996). **Associations & Accomplishments:** President, Association of Rhode Island Administrators of Special Education; President (1978–1981), St. Joseph Parish Council (1975–1987); Board Member (1976–1978), Newport County Chapter Retarded Citizens (1970–Present). **Education:** Rhode Island College, M.Ed. (1973); College of Our Lady of the Elms, B.A. (1965). **Personal:** Ms. Connolly enjoys walking and sailing.

Ellen L. Cooper

Director of Special Programs
Alvarado Independent School District
P.O. Box 387
Alvarado, TX 76009
(817) 783–6812
Fax: (817) 783–6811

8211

Business Information: Alvarado Independent School District (ISD) is the municipal governmental office responsible for the administration of all secondary education facilities and activities within its county jurisdiction. The Alvarado ISD's mission is to establish partnerships between community businesses and individuals which promote collaborative and mutually beneficial results, to enhance student achievement through these partnerships, and to provide learning opportunities for the community. Alvarado ISD currently employs 330 people. With eighteen years of experience in education, Mrs. Cooper joined the Alvarado ISD in 1992. Serving as Director of Special Programs, she directs and coordinates special programs throughout the District. **Career Steps:** Director of Special Programs, Alvarado ISD (1992–Present); Director of Special Education, Refugio ISD (1988–1992); Educational Diagnostician, Goliad Special Education Coop. (1980–1987); Math Teacher, Goliad ISD (1977–1980). **Associations & Accomplishments:** TASA; Delta Kappa Gamma; TACLD; CEC; ASCD; Association of Professional Women. **Education:** University of Houston, M.S. (1984); Southwest Texas State University, B.S. in Education. **Personal:** Married to M. L. in 1968. Two children: John and Bryan. Mrs. Cooper enjoys aerobic exercise, reading, crafts, swimming, and travel.

Thomas Costanzo

Director of Development
Mater Dei High School
1202 West Edinger Avenue
Santa Ana, CA 92707
(714) 850–9532
Fax: Please mail or call

8211

Business Information: Mater Dei High School is the largest private high school west of Chicago. Located in Santa Ana, California, the school offers instruction to students in grades 9 through 12. Students are accepted on a recommendation only basis and must have an excellent academic record from their primary schools. Approximately 97% of their graduates enroll in college. Established in 1950, the school presently employs 200 faculty and support staff. As Director of Development, Mr. Costanzo is responsible for marketing of school services, recruiting and retaining students, developing a donor network, and obtaining finances for scholarship programs. Other responsibilities include public relations, preparation of publications, and strategic planning for the future. **Career Steps:** Director of Development, Mater Dei High School (1992–Present); Regional Manager, Seaboard Life Insurance Company (1990–1992); Regional Manager, Travelers Insurance Company (1977–1990). **Associations & Accomplishments:** Planned Giving Roundtable; National Society of CLU/CHFC; Chamber of Commerce; Yale Alumni Association; Crespi High School Alumni Association: Beer Drinkers of America. **Education:** American College, CHFC (1983), CLU (1981); Yale University, B.A. (1973). **Personal:** Two children: Erica and Brian. Mr. Costanzo enjoys computers, volleyball, literature, and marine biology.

Steven J. Danenberg

Director of Admissions
Pomfret School
Pomfret School
Pomfret, CT 06258
(860) 963–6120
Fax: (860) 963–2042

8211

Business Information: Pomfret School is a 102–year old boarding/day school with 300 students (210 boarders & 90 day students) from 28 states and 14 countries, providing college preparation courses for grades 9–12. With more than twenty–six years of experience as an educator, Mr. Danenberg currently serves as Director of Admissions. He is responsible for all aspects of student admissions, including recruiting and evaluating students. He is currently involved in the production of a promotional video for Pomfret School, as well as traveling extensively worldwide on behalf of the school's $300,000 budget for the recruitment of students. **Career Steps:** Director of Admissions, Pomfret School (1994–Present); Headmaster, Williams School – New London, CT (1978–1994); Acting Headmaster, Cambridge School – Weston, MA (1974–1978); History Teacher, Pomfret School (1970–1974). **Associations & Accomplishments:** Former Director, CAIS; Corporator, Lawrence & Memorial Hospitals; Board Member, County School of Madison, CT; Peace Corps Volunteer in Venezuela (1965–1967). **Education:** Teachers College – Columbia University, M.A. (1969); Columbia College – Columbia University, B.A. (1965). **Personal:** Married to Mary A. in 1969. Two children: Michael and Amy. Mr. Danenberg enjoys running, reading, and travel.

Ms. Virginia Daugherty

Vocational Director
Hertford County Public Schools
P.O. Box 158
Winton, NC 27986–0158
(919) 358–1761
Fax: (919) 358–4745

8211

Business Information: Hertford County Public Schools is the municipal governmental office responsible for the administration of all elementary and secondary educational facilities and activities within its jurisdiction. As Vocational Director, Ms. Daugherty is responsible for the supervision of the vocational and technical education programs in a public high school and middle school. **Career Steps:** Vocational Director, Hertford County Public Schools (1994–Present); Workforce Development Director (1990–1992); Vocational Assessment Coordinator, Lenoir County Schools (1990–1992); Community Service Director, Department of Human Resources (1978–1980). **Associations & Accomplishments:** Governors Volunteer Awards (1984, 1991, 1993); Scoutmaster, (1990–Present); Volunteer Administrator and Board Member, Lenoir County Teens Program; Board Member, Middle School Alternative Program; Board Member, Lenior County Youth Community Based Alternative Progam; Board Member, United Way Budget Committee; Hawaiian Algebra Project; North Carolina Writing Project Level II – London, England; Nominated for Coastal Plains Writing Project Level I, East Carolina University; Nominated for North Carolina Teacher Academy, East Carolina Academy; Nominated for Dropout Prevention Outstanding State Service Award (1988). **Education:** East Carolina University, M.A.Ed. in Educational Administration and Supervision (1988); Long Island University, M.B.A. (1979); Elizabeth City State University, B.S. (1967). **Personal:** Two children: Leamon S., III and Kimmika M. Ms. Daugherty enjoys reading, bowling, tennis and travel.

Charles V. Demeter

Director of Facilities
La Joya I.S.D.
P.O. Box J
La Joya, TX 78560
(210) 580–6060
Fax: (210) 785–6054

8211

Business Information: La Joya I.S.D. is the municipal office responsible for the administration of all secondary education Facilities and activities within the County jurisdiction. As Director of Facilities, Mr. Demeter is responsible for the maintenance and oversight of all facilities, construction, custodial activities, grounds, and security for the District. **Career Steps:** Director of Facilities, La Joya I.S.D. (1985–Present); Construction Superintendent, Holzem Construction (1972–1985); Furniture Designer, Crawford Furniture (1967–1969). **Associations & Accomplishments:** Council of Educational Facility Planners, International/Rio Grande Valley; Lions Club. **Education:** Pan American University, B.S. (1966). **Personal:** Mr. Demeter enjoys fishing, hunting, art work, and woodworking.

Dr. Gwendolyn Dixon–Coe

Director of Title I Programs
Marlboro County School District
100 Matheson Street
Bennettsville, SC 29512
(803) 479–5926
Fax: (803) 479–5922

8211

Business Information: Title I is Marlboro County Schools' largest federally funded program which assists in the academic achievement of students and improvement of schools. Title I assists school districts who are economically disadvantaged, providing them with funds towards educational advancement. Serving MCSD in various executive roles since 1977, Dr. Dixon–Coe was appointed Director of Title I Programs in 1993. In this role, she is responsible for implementing programs and administering Schoolwide activities. Additional duties involve acting as liasion for all interagency collaboration and home/school/community relations. **Career Steps:** Marlboro County School District: Director for Title I Programs (1993–Present), Evaluator/Parent Coordinator (1977–1993); Senior Consultant, The Home and School Institute, Washington D.C. (1989–Present); Parent Associate, American Friends Service Committee – Columbia, SC. **Associations & Accomplishments:** National Education Association; South Carolina Association of School Administrators; South Carolina Network for Women Administrators; National Coalition for Title I/Chapter I Parents; South Carolina ESEA Administrators;

Chapel Board, Evans Correctional Institution; Marlboro Civic Center Board; Healthy Start Project; Co–founder and President, UJAMA Drama Club. **Education:** South Carolina State University: Ed.D. (1995), B.S. in Biology (1976), M.Ed. in Guidance (1980). **Personal:** Married to Ernest Lee Coe in 1995. One child: Ryan Ernest Lee Coe. Dr. Dixon–Coe enjoys arts, church, community theater (UJAMA) and public speaking.

Dr. Emery Dosdall

Superintendent of Schools
Edmonton Public Schools
Centre for Education, One Kingsway
Edmonton, Alberta T5H 4G9
(403) 429–8080
Fax: (403) 429–8383

8211

Business Information: Edmonton Public Schools is a district of schools specializing in public education (kindergarten through 12th grade – 76,000 students). As Superintendent of Schools, Dr. Dosdall is responsible for the overall administration and operation of the entire district of public schools in Edmonton. He also maintains the mission and vision for continued growth. **Career Steps:** Superintendent of Schools, Edmonton Public Schools, (1995–Present); Superintendent of Schools, Langley School District No. 35 (1982–1994); Associate Superintendent, Edmonton Public Schools (1980–1982). **Associations & Accomplishments:** Former President of the B.C. School Superintendent's Association; Former Director of the Langley Lodge; Director of the Rotary Club; Lecturer at the University of Victoria; United Way Cabinet Member; P.D.K. **Education:** Nova Southeastern University, Florida Educational Doctorate (1996); University of Oregon, Masters (1974); University of Alberta, Educational Administration – Diploma (1969); University of Alberta, Bachelor of Education (1965). **Personal:** Married to Hilda.

Evelyn L. Drury

Director of Education
Tupelo Christian Academy
1801 East Main Street, P.O. Box 167
Tupelo, MS 38802–0167
(601) 791–7731
Fax: (601) 791–7715

8211

Business Information: Tupelo Christian Academy is a Christian–based educational facility, providing education to the orphaned children residing at the Tupelo Children's Mansion and to children with special needs, such as Attention Deficit Disorder (ADD) in grades K–12. The Academy facilitates the Beka System of learning and offers remedial reading classes and computer programs. Joining Tupelo Christian Academy as Director of Education in 1991, Ms. Drury is responsible for directing the overall educational operations, focusing on the emotional and educational development of the children. Concurrent with her academic position, she and her husband, Stephen, operate a non–profit adoption agency, called "New Beginnings" (for more information, call 601–842–6752) — because of it being a 'new beginning' for the unwed mother, the child, and the adoptive parents. She also serves as Corporate Assistant Secretary at Tupelo Children's Mansion, in which her husband serves as Director. **Career Steps:** Director of Education, Tupelo Christian Academy (1991–Present); Corporate Assistant Secretary, Tupelo Children's Mansion (1975–Present). **Associations & Accomplishments:** International Fellowship of Christian School Administrators; Member, Abundant Life Tabernacle; Handed out 10,000 Bibles to children and adults (100,000 people showed up). **Education:** Apostolic Bible Institute, Th.B. (1970). **Personal:** Married to Stephen in 1972. Three children: James, Stephanie, and Mendy.

Terry Eason
Principal
Terrell Middle School
701 Town North Drive
Terrell, TX 75160–5137
(214) 563–7501
Fax: (214) 563–5721

8211

Business Information: Terrell Middle School provides 7th and 8th grade education to 610 students in Terrell, Texas, and surrounding areas. With fourteen years of experience in the field of education as a middle school teacher and coach, high school teacher and coach, and middle school and high school building level administrator, Mr. Eason joined Terrell Middle School as Assistant Principal in 1991. Promoted to Head Principal during the summer of 1995, he is presently responsible

for providing academic leadership to school faculty, staff, and students, coordinating all parent/teacher/student relations, community outreach programs and curriculum development. **Career Steps:** Terrell Middle School: Head Principal (1996–Present), Assistant Principal (1991–1996); Head Boy's Basketball Coach: Terrell High School, Terrell I.S.D. (1993–1995); Head Boys Basketball Coach/High School Social Studies Teacher, Athens I.S.D. (1983–1991); High School Teacher/Coach, Mt. Pleasant I.S.D. (1981–1983). **Associations & Accomplishments:** National Association for Secondary School Principals; Texas Association of Secondary School Principals; Phi Delta Kappa; The National Alliance of Black School Educators; Texas High School Coaches Association; Association for Supervision and Curriculum Development; Member and Former Vice President, Alpha Phi Alpha; Basketball Coach of the Year – Terrell High School (1994–1995); Basketball Coach of the Year – Athens High School (1988–1989); Nominated Outstanding Young Man of America (1981). **Education:** East Texas State University: Superintendent Certification (in progress), Master's in Education (1992), The Meadows Principal's Improvement Program – Selected as a Meadows Fellow, The Meadows Foundation of Texas (1992); Henderson State University, B.S. in Education (1981). **Personal:** Married to Donna in 1983. One child: Torrey. Mr. Eason enjoys sports and fishing.

Ms. Pamela A. Foster

Teacher of Developmental/Adapted Physical Education
St. Paul Public Schools, Como Park Elementary School
780 West Wheelock Parkway
St. Paul, MN 55117
(612) 293–8823
Fax: (612) 293–8828

8211

Business Information: St. Paul Public Schools, Como Park Elementary School is a public school providing quality education to elementary school students in the St. Paul Public School system. Como Park Elementary School currently employs 200 people. As Teacher of Developmental and Adapted Physical Education, Ms. Foster teaches Adapted Physical Education and Aquatics to special education students with learning disabilities, hearing impaired, physically disabled and autistic children. **Career Steps:** Teacher of Developmental/Adapted Physical Education, St. Paul Public Schools, Como Park Elementary School (1965–Present); Instructor of Physical Education, Northwestern College, Minneapolis, Minnesota (1963–1965); Camp and Conference Director, YWCA, Minneapolis, Minnesota (1962–1963). **Associations & Accomplishments:** Courage Center (Volunteer, Team Leader and Coach for three Junior National Wheelchair Games – 1988, 1989, and 1990); Advisory Council, Ramsey County Lung Association, St. Paul, MN (1977–1992); Faculty Representative, Minnesota Education Association; National Education Association; American Association Health, Physical Education, Recreation and Dance; Minnesota Association of Health, Physical Education, Recreation & Dance; National Wheelchair Athletic Association; Minnesota Aquatic Education; The Box Project, Inc., Plainville, CT: Volunteer helper in the Mississippi Delta (1990–Present), Board of Directors (1994–Present); People to People International (Member of Fitness Delegation to China), Citizen's Ambassador Program, Seattle Chapter (1991). **Education:** Indiana University, M.S. (1962); Boston University Sargent College, B.S. (1959); Logos Bible College, Florida, Certificate of Biblical Studies (1986). **Personal:** Ms. Foster enjoys traveling, photography, fishing, teaching crafts, sailing, camping, gardening, volunteering and bargain hunting.

Dagmar C. Franke

Principal
Epping Elementary School
17 Prospect Street
Epping, NH 03042–2907
(603) 679–8018
Fax: Please mail or call

8211

Business Information: Epping Elementary School is an integrated school from grades Pre–K to 5th. The School has 405 students, 31 certified staff, and numerous support staff and aides. As Principal, Mrs. Franke is responsible for all aspects of school operations, including building administration, supervision of teachers and students, evaluation of curriculum, coordination of programs with parents, and writing grants. **Career Steps:** Principal, Epping Elementary School (1994–Present); Program Director/Teacher, S.A.U.#19 – Goffstown, N.H. (1988–1994); Elementary School Principal, Rowley School District – Rowley, MA (1979–1982). **Associations & Accomplishments:** New Hampshire Association of School Principals; National Association of Elementary School

Principals. **Education:** Keene State College: Master of Education (1976), Bachelor of Education (1971). **Personal:** Married to George E. Gosselin in 1980. One child: Christopher. Mrs. Franke enjoys tennis, photography, antiques, Native American crafts, collecting Hopi Kachina dolls, gardening, reading, and travel.

Lise Frenette

Public Relations Officer
CECLF
4000 Labelle Street
Gloucester, Ontario K1J 1A1
(613) 746–3066
Fax: (613) 746–3081
E MAIL: See Below

8211

Business Information: CECLF is a French Catholic School Board that was established in 1989. Currently the organization includes 45 schools and over 14,500 students from junior Kindergarten to grade 13 (pre–university). As Public Relations Officer, Ms. Frenette handles all public relations for CECLF including advertising, promotions, and general communications. Concurrently Ms. Frenette is a counselor for media strategy and teaches classes at the local credit union in public relations and contracts. Internet users may contact her via: http://www.ceclf.edu.on.ca. **Career Steps:** Public Relations Officer, CECLF (1989–Present); Director of Communications, C.P. St. Raymond (1987–1989); Promotion and Communications Director, C.P. Cyrville Rockland (1983–1987). **Associations & Accomplishments:** Ms. Frenette has been published in local business magazines. **Education:** Ottawa University, BAC (1983). **Personal:** Ms. Frenette enjoys golf and walking.

Mariluz Garcia

Secretary to the Headmaster
Saint John's School
1454–66 Ashford Avenue
San Juan, Puerto Rico 00907
(787) 728–5343
Fax: (787) 268–1454

8211

Business Information: Saint John's School, the most prominent school in Puerto Rico, is a private school specializing in the education of Pre–K through 12th grade students. As Secretary to the Headmaster, Ms. Garcia is responsible for diversified secretarial activities, including preparing mail, answering questions to faculty and parents. **Career Steps:** Secretary to the Headmaster, Saint John's School (1995–Present); Secretary of Human Resources Department, McConnell Valdes (Recognized as the biggest law firm in the Caribbean)(1989–1994). **Education:** Interamerican University, B.S. (1990). **Personal:** Married to Rafael Del Valle in 1996. Ms. Garcia enjoys music, aerobics, and dancing.

Willie Roy Gentry
Executive Director
Houston Independent School District
3830 Richmond Avenue
Houston, TX 77027–5864
(713) 892–6100
Fax: (713) 892–6109

8211

Business Information: Houston Independent School District is responsible for the administration of all public education within its boundary in Houston, Texas. As Executive Director, Mr. Gentry is responsible for supervising alternative schools and programs within the district, as well as working with children with special needs (children with drug problems, pregnancy, etc.). **Career Steps:** Houston Independent School District: Executive Director (1995–Present), Principal – Worthing High School (1982–1992), Principal – Woodson Middle School (1980–1982), Principal – numerous elementary schools (1968–1980). **Associations & Accomplishments:** Member, Teachers' Professional Practices Commission of Texas – appointed by the Governor; Astrodome Rotary Club; Century Club Member of YMCA; Recipient: Silver Beaver Award from Boy Scouts of America; Spaulding for Children; Houston Association of School Administrators; Woodshire Civic Club; National Association of Secondary School Principals. **Education:** Texas Southern University, M.Ed. (1962); University of Houston, Administrative Certification; Texas A&M University, Superintendent Certification (1982). **Personal:** Married to Shirley Session in 1961. One child: Dr. Hilda A. Gentry. Mr. Gentry enjoys music and youth involvement.

Rita M. Georgeon
Principal
Henry Wilson School
401 Wilson Street
Manchester, NH 03103
(603) 624–6350
Fax: Please mail or call

8211

Business Information: Henry Wilson School is a public school providing quality education to elementary school students in the Hampton, New Hampshire area. Henry Wilson School serves about 375 children from kindergarten through third grades with school–based programs and was nominated for national recognition for the Title 1 Program. The School operates a totally–networked system of technology, including developmental teacher strategy, inclusionary model Title 1 Special Education Programs, multi–disciplinary approach (thematic unit), and a reading program (literature–based strategy). With twenty–two years of experience in education, Ms. Georgeon joined Henry Wilson School as Principal in 1987. She is responsible for the supervision of all educational activities and support staff of 55 (teachers, professionals, paraprofessionals), as well as establishing the mission and vision for continued growth. Currently she employs a full–time Parent Coordinator and program volunteer facilitator. **Career Steps:** Principal, Henry Wilson School (1987–Present); Assistant Principal, Jewett School (1985–1987); Teacher, Webster School (1974–1985). **Associations & Accomplishments:** National Reading Association; New Hampshire Reading Association; National Association of Elementary School Principals; Association of Manchester Principals; National Association of University Women; ADK Sorority of Women Educators (GAMMA Chapter). **Education:** University of New Hampshire, C.A.G,S, (1987); River College, Masters in Education; Notre Dame College, B.A. in Elementary Education. **Personal:** Married to Alexander in 1959. Three children: Lisa, Devine, and Diana. Ms. Georgeon enjoys reading, dancing, travel, tennis, walking, home decorating, and piano.

Barbara G. Gilbert

Director
Dekalb County School Nutrition/Food Service
3770 North Decatur Road
Decatur, GA 30032
(404) 297–2326
Fax: (404) 297–2385

8211

Business Information: Dekalb County School Nutrition/Food Service provides food and nutritional services to the Dekalb County School system. Self–supported from the general school budget, the Company purchases and warehouses some of their own supplies. Responsible for 114 public schools, (K–12), some private and outward feeding, the Company provides daily breakfast, lunch, and after school menus, special diet, and catering services. Established in the 1930's, the Company employs 850 people, and has an estimated annual budget of $25 million. As Director, Ms. Gilbert is responsible for budgeting, oversight of all programs, and supervision of all employees. She is also responsible for interfacing and coordinating with personnel, ensuring they comply with all state and federal guidelines. Since becoming Director she has developed employee training, implemented programs to promote quality and helped bring state and national recognition to the program. **Career Steps:** Dekalb County School Nutrition/Food Service: Director (1993–Present), Coordinator (1984–1992), Manager (1972–1984). **Associations & Accomplishments:** American Dietetic Association; American School Food and Nutrition Association; Georgia School Food Service Association; District and Local Food Service Association; DAR. She has held offices in all of the above mentioned associations, as well as served as committee chairman many times. **Education:** University of Georgia, Masters (1984); University of Florida, B.S. **Personal:** Married to James in 1967. Two children: Scott and Leslie. Ms. Gilbert enjoys reading, rock collecting, and walking.

Lek Gittisriboongul
Chief Financial Officer
Planada School District
9525 East Brodrick Street, P.O. Box 236
Planada, CA 95365
(209) 382–0666
Fax: (209) 382–1750

8211

Business Information: Planada School District is a local agency responsible for the administration and operation of local elementary schools (grades K–8) in the Planada, California area. As Chief Financial Officer, Mr. Gittisriboongul is responsible for school financial affairs, preparation of the annual budget, cash flow, and strategic planning. **Career Steps:**
Chief Financial Officer, Planada School District (1994–Present); Chief Accountant, Menifer Union School District (1984–1994); Regional Accounting Manager, Thai Airways International (1974–1983); Chief Accountant, Amoco Oil (Thailand) (1971–1974). **Associations & Accomplishments:** Accounting and Development Eastern Section; CASBO; Fluent in Chinese and the dialects of Mandarin, Chinese Hakka, Chochew, as well as Cantonese. **Education:** Woodbury University, Bachelor of Science in Business Administration; University of Chulalongkorn, Thailand, M.B.A. in Middle Management. **Personal:** Married to Krissara in 1965. One child: Alvin Sr., Esquire.

Tresea (Teri) M. Goff
Elementary Principal
Mona Shores Schools, Lincoln Park Elementary
2951 Leon
Norton Shores, MI 49441
(616) 755–1257
Fax: Please mail or call

8211

Business Information: Mona Shores Schools, Lincoln Park Elementary provides instruction to 567 students in kindergarten through 5th grade. Currently Lincoln Park Elementary employs 48 people. As Elementary Principal, Ms. Goff is responsible for all aspects of personnel, budget, and operations for her school. Ms. Goff is also the District Math Co–Chair. **Career Steps:** Elementary Principal, Mona Shores Schools, Lincoln Park Elementary (1987–Present); Elementary Principal and Director of K–8 Alternative Education, Ann Arbor Schools (1984–1987); Elementary Principal, Westwood Heights Schools (1979–1984); Elementary Principal and Director of Special Education, Hanover – Horton Schools (1977–1979). **Associations & Accomplishments:** Executive Board and President–Elect, Michigan Elementary and Middle School Principals Association; Treasurer, Michigan State University College of Education Alumni Board; Former President, Jackson County Principals Association; Former President, Phi Delta Kappa Chapter; Former President, MUS Region Area Principals Association; Regional Principal of the Year, Michigan Elementary and Middle Schools Principals Association (1992); Member, Cherry Guild Volunteers, Hackley Hospital **Education:** Michigan State University: M.A. and all Ph.D. coursework (1972), B.A. (1970). **Personal:** One child: Aimee. Ms. Goff enjoys arts and crafts, singing and being a gymnastics scorekeeper.

David F. Grace
Chief Financial Officer
Champaign Community Unit School District #4
703 South New Street
Champaign, IL 61820–5818
(217) 351–3825
Fax: Please mail or call
EMAIL: see below

8211

Business Information: Champaign Community Unit School District #4 is the public school system directing educational programs for children in pre–kindergarten through twelfth grades residing in or around the Champaign community. Joining the Champaign Community Unit School District #4 as Chief Financial Officer in 1993, Mr. Grace is responsible for all aspects of financial functions for the school system. Duties include directing all accounting, payroll, accounts payable and receivable activities. In addition, Mr. Grace manages all risk management for the district and food service operations. He also directs all maintenance activities for seventeen buildings in the District. **Career Steps:** Chief Financial Officer, Champaign Community Unit School District #4 (1993–Present); Business Manager/Treasurer, Lombard School District #44 (1987–1993); Manager of Business Services & Computers, Sheboygan Area School District (1983–1987); Teacher, middle and high schools (1973–1983). **Associations & Accomplishments:** Association of School Business Officials (Research Committee); Illinois Association of School Business Officials; Lions Club (Treasurer and Director); Kiwanis Club; East Central Illinois Association of School Business Officials (Chairman). **Education:** Indiana State University, M.B.A. (1983); Eastern Illinois University, M.S. in Zoology (1977), B.S. in Education (1973); University of Illinois, Doctorate Degree in process. **Personal:** Married to Mary Lou in 1972. Five children: Ryan, Camille, Devin, Laura, and Kathryn. Mr. Grace enjoys golf, gardening, reading, and playing games and sports with his children.

Bryan T. Green
Director of Admissions
Tallulah Falls School
P.O. Box 10
Tallulah Falls, GA 30573
(706) 754–3171
Fax: (706) 754–3595

8211

Business Information: Tallulah Falls School is an independent boarding school with 168 students. The School is owned by the Georgia Womens Club. As Director of Admissions, Mr. Green is responsible for marketing, admission, candidate interviews, and reviewing academic reports. **Career Steps:** Director of Admissions, Tallulah Falls School (1995–Present); Director of Admissions, Hoosac School (1990–1995); Legal Assistant, Carroll, Lehman & Colter (1988–1990). **Associations & Accomplishments:** NAIS; SSATB; ICCA; SBSA. **Education:** Southeastern (NOVA) University, Legal Studies (1990). **Personal:** One child: Brittany. Mr. Green enjoys hiking, water sports, and travel.

Edward J. Harris Jr.

Principal
Edwardsville High School
145 West Street
Edwardsville, IL 62025
(618) 656–7100
Fax: (217) 228–7149

8211

Business Information: Edwardsville High School is a public school providing quality education to high school students in the Edwardsville, Illinois area. As Principal, Mr. Harris is responsible for the supervision of all educational activities and support staff, as well as establishing the mission and vision for continued growth. **Career Steps:** Principal, Edwardsville High School (1995–Present); Principal, Quincy High School (1992–1995); Assistant Principal, Ladue High School (1989–1992); Assistant Principal, Parkway Central (1988–1989); Assistant Principal, Parkway South (1986–1988). **Associations & Accomplishments:** Rotary; Board of Directors, American Heart Association; National Association of Secondary School Principal; National Council School Desegregation; Illinois Association of Secondary School Principals; A World of Difference. **Education:** Northeast Missouri State University, Specialist Education (1990); Maryville University, St. Louis, MO, Masters in Education; University of Missouri, St. Louis, Bachelors Degree in Education. **Personal:** One child: Kai Jarrett Harris. Mr. Harris enjoys tennis, weight lifting, chess, and writing.

Rev. William J. Harry, O. Carm.

President/Chief Executive Officer
Carmel High School
One Carmel Parkway
Mundelein, IL 60060–2499
(847) 566–3000
Fax: (847) 566–8465
EMAIL: See Below

8211

Business Information: Carmel High School is a private Catholic high school providing educational services to students grades 9–12. Located on a 50–acre campus, the School provides its services to over 1,300 families. As President/Chief Executive Officer, Rev. Harry works with the School Board and public to educate them on the school's activities. He oversees all aspects of the School's operations, including a preschool for the public and the development, and business offices. Internet users can reach him via: president@carmel.k12.il.us. **Career Steps:** President/Chief Executive Officer, Carmel High School (1988–Present). **Associations & Accomplishments:** Rotary International; Libertyville/Mundelein/Vernon Hill Chamber of Commerce; Southern Lake County Regional Action Planning Project; Chaplain, Mundelein Fire Department; Lake County Learns; Critical Incident Stress Debriefing Team at Northern Illinois; President, The Leadership Foundation. **Education:** Pontifical Gregorian University, S.T.L. (1986); University of Arizona, Masters in Education; Marquette University, B.A. **Personal:** Rev. Harry enjoys geneology and history.

James L. Hayden
Principal
New York City Board of Education,
Intermediate School 223
4200 16th Avenue
Brooklyn, NY 11204
(718) 438–0155
Fax: (718) 871–7477

8211

Business Information: New York City Board of Education is the municipal governmental office responsible for the administration of all education facilities and activities within the jurisdiction of the city. The Intermediate School 223 provides public education to students in grade 6 through 9. Currently the school employs 90 faculty. As Principal of the Intermediate School 223, Mr. Hayden is responsible for all aspects of education for the school, including personnel, programs and student affairs. Prior to becoming Principal, Mr. Hayden was a teacher and Assistant Principal with the New York City Schools. **Career Steps:** New York City Board of Education, Intermediate School 223: Principal (1991–Present), Assistant Principal (1982–1991), Teacher (1966–1982). **Associations & Accomplishments:** Council of Supervisory Associations; National Associaiton of Secondary School Principals; Junior High School Principal's Association. **Education:** Baruch College, M.S. (1977); Long Island University, M.S. (1970); St. John's University, B.A. (1966). **Personal:** Married to Lydia in 1979. Two children: Douglas and Joseph. Mr. Hayden enjoys reading, sports and the theatre.

Thecla Helmbrecht–Trost, Ed.S.
Education Director/Principal
St. Croix Camp
RR 2 Box 220
Sandstone, MN 55072–9563
(302) 245–5219
Fax: (612) 245–5153

8211

Business Information: St. Croix Camp is a correctional facility for adjudicated juveniles ages 12 thru 18. Established in 1976, St. Croix Camp currently employs 106 people. Students, 350–400 per year, are taught academic as well as survival skills. An adventure based program is utilized with positive and negative consequences for behaviors using a realty therapy approach. Yearly scholarships are given to one boy and one girl who have been successful in the post residential phase in home, school, and community. As Education Director, Mrs. Helmbrecht–Trost's day–to–day functions include supervision of staff and students curriculum development, program integration, public relations, and staff developments. **Career Steps:** Education Director, St. Croix Camp (1993–Present); Department Head, Special Education, Webster Schools (1983–1987); Rehab. Coordinator, Tomah Rehab. (1980–1983); Special Education Supervisor, Cooperative Service Agency (1978–1980). **Associations & Accomplishments:** Curriculum & Supervision Association; Phi Delta Kappa Fraternity; Minnesota Corrections Association; National Association of Secondary School Principals (NASSP); Council of Administrators of Special Education (CASE). **Education:** University of Wisconsin: Superior, Ed.S. (1991), LaCrosse, M.S. (1978); Marquette University B.S. (1971). **Personal:** Married to Thomas E. in 1981. Six children and seven step children: Tania, Tarra, Trisha, Charlie, Andrew, and Chirstina; Toni, Tim, Julie, Dan, Ron, Paul, and Lorena. Ms. Helmbrecht–Trost enjoys music, camping, and endurance riding.

Patricia A. Hennessey
Superintendent of Schools
Southold Union Free School District
420 Oaklawn Avenue, P.O. Box 470
Southold, NY 11971–0470
(516) 765–5400
Fax: (516) 765–5086

8211

Business Information: Southold Union Free School District is the municipal governmental office responsible for the administration of all public elementary educational facilities and activities within jurisdiction of Southold, New York. Joining Southold Union Free School District as Superintendent of Schools in 1991, Mrs. Hennessey is responsible for the administrative direction of all aspects of the Agency, as well as serve as community and governmental spokesperson on behalf of the School District and its mission objectives as a whole. **Career Steps:** Superintendent of Schools, Southold Union Free School District (1991–Present); Assistant Superintendent, Patchogue–Medford (1983–1991). **Associations & Accomplishments:** Southold Historical Society; Nassau–Suffolk Council of Women in Administration. **Education:** New York University, Ph.D. candidate; Long Island University, M.S.; Catholic University of America, B.A. **Personal:** Married to Stephen. Three children: Keith, Logan, and Moira.

Reinilda Henning de Davila
German Teacher/Librarian
Colegio Aleman
Diagonal 21, 19–20 Zona 11
Guatemala City, Guatemala
(502) 474–5115
Fax: (502) 473–1825

8211

Business Information: Colegio Aleman is a private, trilingual elementary and high school. Sponsored by the German government, the School combines the Spanish and German curricula. As German Teacher/Librarian, Ms. Henning de Davila teaches German and runs the trilingual School and German community library. **Career Steps:** German Teacher/Librarian, Colegio Aleman (1986–Present); ESL Teacher/Librarian, International American School – Guatemala (1963–1986); 11th and 12th grade Teacher for the Dutch language and literature, Gemeetelijke HBS – Nijmegen, Holland (1961). **Associations & Accomplishments:** NGO for street children in Guatemala. **Education:** Francisco Marroquin University – Guatemala, H.S. teacher Spanish, Social Studies (Magna Cum Laude) (1983); Roman Catholic University – Nijmegen, Holland, Dutch Language and Literature, General Linguistics. **Personal:** Married to Enrique Davila in 1962. Four children: Gerlach, Hadewych, Albrik, and Ludger. Ms. Henning de Davila enjoys volunteering for NGO's.

Sally M. Hershberger
•••═══◉═══•••

Director of Research & Development
Huntsville City Schools
200 White Street
Huntsville, AL 35801
(205) 532–4847
Fax: (205) 532–4630

8211

Business Information: Huntsville City School System, Division of Research and Development oversees all mandatory testing, within their district, for students in grades K–12. As Director of Research & Development, Ms. Hershberger is responsible for supervising all program evaluations, directing employees, and coordinating testing services for 43 schools. **Career Steps:** Huntsville City Schools: Director of Research & Development (1995–Present), Attendance Specialist (1992–1995), Special Education Coordinator (1989–1992), Teacher (1987–1989). **Associations & Accomplishments:** Huntsville Education Association; Alabama Education Association; National Education Association; Association for Supervising and Curriculum Development; Delta Kappa Gamma Society; American Association of School Administrators; Alabama Council for School Administration; Association of School Administrators; Alabama Council for School Administration and Supervision; ARC, Madison County. **Education:** University of Alabama, Ed.S. (1995); University of Arizona, B.S., MEd. **Personal:** Married to Robert in 1968. Two children: John Robert and Sarah Marie. Ms. Hershberger enjoys reading, knitting, and skiing.

Kathyrene Hughes
Curriculum Director
Fairbanks North Star Borough
School District
520 5th Avenue
Fairbanks, AK 99701–4756
(907) 452–2000
Fax: (907) 451–6160
EMAIL: See Below

8211

Business Information: Fairbanks North Star Borough School District As Curriculum Director, Mrs. Hughes **Career Steps:** Fairbanks North Star Borough School District: Curriculum Director (1992–Present), High School English Teacher (1986–1992), Middle School Language Arts Teacher (1983–1986). **Associations & Accomplishments:** ASCD. **Education:** University of Alaska – Fairbanks, M.Ed. (1996); University of San Francisco, B.A. (1981). **Personal:** Married to Brian J. in 1981. Three children: Jacob, James, and Joseph.

Lloyd C. Humphrey
Principal
Riverton Elementary School
2615 Winchester Road
Huntsville, AL 35811
(205) 852–7187
Fax: (205) 852–0039

8211

Business Information: Riverton Elementary School is a public school serving students in grades Kindergarten through

fourth, residing in the city jurisdiction of Huntsville, Alabama. Currently, the school employs 90 people. As Principal, Mr. Humphrey is responsible for all aspects of administration for the entire school, with duties involving faculty and staff administration, faculty/student/parent relations, community outreach programs, curriculum and special events programs, and budgetary oversight. **Career Steps:** Principal, Riverton Elementary School (1980–Present); Principal, Big Cove School (1973–1980); Principal, Brownshord School (1971–1973); Assistant Principal, Riverto Junior High School (1970–1971); Assistant Principal, West Madison Junior High School (1969–1970); Principal, Mt. Fork Junior High School (1967–1968). **Associations & Accomplishments:** Madison County Education Association; Alabama Education Association; National Association of Educators; National Association of Elementary Principals; Alabama Association of Elementary Principals; Alabama Council for School Administrators and Supervisors; Madison County Administrators Association; Principal of the Year (1987); Omega Psi Phi Fraternity; Elks Lodge #977; Vice President, Booster Club of Huntsville, AL; First Missionary Baptist Church, Huntsville, AL: Deacon, Senior Usher, Board of Directors President. **Education:** Masters, Bachelors and Associate degrees in Education. **Personal:** Married to Charman in 1965. One child: Lloyd Lemoyne. Mr. Humphrey enjoys golf.

Pamela E. Ingram
Director of Special Education
Joshua Independent School District
720 South Broadway
Joshua, TX 76058–3147
(817) 645–7722
Fax: (817) 641–2738

8211

Business Information: Joshua Independent School District is the municipal governmental office responsible for the administration of all public elementary and secondary educational facilities and activities within its jurisdiction. Joshua Independent School District's mission is to establish partnerships between community businesses and individuals which promote collaborative and mutually beneficial results, to enhance student achievement through these partnerships, and to provide learning opportunities for the community. With seventeen years of experience in education as an educator, Ms. Ingram joined Joshua Independent School District as Director of Special Education in 1990. She is responsible for the direction of the Special Education Department, including overseeing the compliance of Federal and State laws regarding the education of students with disabilities, planning and implementing educational programs, ensuring that district personnel are informed of any legal changes, coordinating services with other area agencies, developing classes building projects, and hiring and training of personnel. She also trains staff in behavioral, instructional techniques, and child development, working on enhancing and broadening the message used for teaching, reading, and language development. **Career Steps:** Director of Special Education, Joshua Independent School District (1990–Present); Teacher, Amarillo Independent School District (1987–1990); Teacher, Joshua Independent School District (1983–1987); Teacher/Coordinator, Edison School (1979–1983); Teacher, Oklahoma City Public Schools (1971–1979); Assistant, University of Oklahoma (1974–1975). **Associations & Accomplishments:** Area Coordinator, Special Olympics; Association For Retarded Citizens; Council For Exceptional Children: Local Chairperson – State Convention, Chairperson – State Committee for Awards and Honors; Phi Delta Kappa; Texas Council of Administrators of Special Education; Association For Supervision and Curriculum Development; Metropolitan President–Elect, state and national committees, Kappa Kappa Iota; Lion of the Year, President, Lions Club International; Sunday School teacher, department director, childrens choir director, First Baptist Church. **Education:** University of Oklahoma, M.Ed. (1975); Oklahoma Baptist University; Central State College; Panhandle State University; West Texas State University; Texas Women's University. **Personal:** Married to Stephen Michael. Four children: Gregory, Demetri, William, and Valkyrie. Grandaughter: Miranda. Ms. Ingram enjoys attending children's sports and fine arts events.

Greg L. King
Director of Transportation
Ionia Public Schools
709 North Jefferson
Ionia, MI 48846
(616) 866–1856
Fax: (616) 866–7115

8211

Business Information: Ionia Public Schools is comprised of a 120–square mile school district in a rural community. With an approximate student population of 3,800, the District consists of one secondary, one middle, and five elementary schools. As Director of Transportation, Mr. King oversees all aspects of transportation involving the bussing of approximately 2,000 of the district's students. He is responsible for personnel management, training of drivers, budget, maintenance, purchasing, and supervision of a staff of 71. He also develops the routes, and has had an article published regarding his computerized scheduling methods. **Career Steps:** Director of Transportation, Ionia Public Schools (1996–Present); Director of Transportation, Rockford Public Schools (1994–1996); Supervisor of Transportation, Ionia Public Schools (1988–1994); Head Mechanic, Central Montcalm Public Schools (1974–1988). **Associations & Accomplishments:** Michigan Association for Pupil Transportation; Regional Representative MAPT; National Association for Pupil Transportation; Pupil Transportation Director, National Committee for Motor Fleet. **Education:** Michigan Motor Vehicle Mechanic Certification, Master H.D. Truck. **Personal:** Three children: Charity, Faith, and Lance. Mr. King enjoys sports, watching his children, and biking.

Beverly M. O. Kirk

Administrator
Eagle River Christian Academy
10336 East Eagle River Loop Road
Eagle River, AK 99577–8301
(907) 694–4602
Fax: (907) 694–4141

8211

Business Information: Eagle River Christian Academy is a non–denominational private elementary and secondary school funded by donations and tuition. Established in 1988, the school provides education to 105 students. An educator in Alaskan systems for the past ten years, Beverly Kirk was appointed as ERCA's Administrator in 1993. She provides the overall executive administration for all day–to–day operations, with primary duties including faculty and staff supervision, budgetary oversight and dispersal, curriculum development, parent / student / teacher relations, and community outreach programs. **Career Steps:** School Administrator, Eagle River Christian Academy (1993–Present); English Instructor, Alaska Pacific University (1989–1993); English Tutor, University of Alaska – Anchorage (1988–1989). **Associations & Accomplishments:** Boy Scout Merit Badge Counselor; State Representative, National Tuberous Sclerosis Association; Leader, La Leche League; Alaska Alliance for the Mentally Ill; Alaska Pacific Alumni Association; frequent publisher; Who's Who Among Students in American Colleges and Universities (1991). **Education:** Alaska Pacific University: M.A. in Liberal Arts, with emphasis on Alaskan Native Cultures (1991), B.A. in Humanities and Communication (1989). **Personal:** Married to William L. in 1965. Five children: Frank, Sara, Kirsten, James, and Shane. Mrs. Kirk enjoys fishing, kayaking, camping, skiing, hiking, spelunking, music, writing, reading, and chess.

Fransene Krause Nagle

Director of Guidance and Counseling
Roeper School
2190 N. Woodward
Bloomfield Hills, MI 48304
(810) 642–1500
Fax: (810) 642–8619

8211

Business Information: Roeper School is a coeducational day school for gifted students and is an internationally known leader in the field of gifted education. Conceptual and experiential learning are the norm. Critical and divergent thinking are encouraged in all disciplines. All courses and sequences are geared to the gifted learner and the School offers 14 AP courses. Serving the Detroit metropolitan area, the School is comprised of 100 teachers and approximately 600 students. As Director of Guidance and Counseling, Ms. Nagle oversees all counseling–related matters with students, teachers, and parents for grades 6–12. **Career Steps:** Director of Guidance and Counseling, The Roeper School (1993–Present); Guardianship, Evergreen Children Services (Apr.1993–Nov.1993). **Associations & Accomplishments:** American Counselors Association; Michigan Counselors Association; National Association of Cognitive Behavioral Therapists; Certified Chemical Dependency Counselor; ASCA; ACES; NCDA; IAMFC; AMHCA; IAAOC; NACAC. Ms. Nagle has written three publications for the Roeper school: The Roeper School College Counseling Guide; Financial Aid for College Students; and The Roeper Upper School Crisis Plan. **Education:** Wayne State University: M.Ed. (1993), B.S. (1973). **Personal:** Four children: Ericka Beletskiy, Beth, Lisa, and Jennifer Nagle. Ms. Krause Nagle enjoys ballroom dancing, movies, the theater and her children.

Dr. Napoleon B. Lewis Jr.

Principal/Chief Executive Officer
Dallas Public Schools
2826 Hatcher
Dallas, TX 75232
(214) 565–6730
Fax: (214) 565–6545

8211

Business Information: Lincoln Humanities/Communications High School – part of the Dallas Public School System – instructs 1,300–1,400 students from all areas of Dallas, Texas. With a staff of approximately 100 teachers, administrators, and support personnel, the School has access to the most modern teaching laboratories in Biology, Chemistry, and Physics. An Administrator with more than twenty–four years of experience, Dr. Lewis was named Principal of Lincoln Humanities/Communications High School in March of 1980. As such, he serves as Chief Executive Officer, supervising and evaluating School staff, providing academic leadership, and consulting with schools and executive academic personnel across the United States. **Career Steps:** Principal, Lincoln Humanities/Communications High School, Dallas Public Schools (1980–Present); Superintendent, Wilmer Hutchins Independent Schools (1987–1989); District of Columbia Public Schools: Regional Superintendent (1974–1977), Principal, Woodson Senior High School (1972–1974). **Associations & Accomplishments:** National Education Association; National Alliance of Black School Educators; Dallas School Administrators Association; Association for Supervision and Curriculum Development; Phi Delta Kappa; Omega Psi Phi Fraternity. **Education:** Virginia Polytechnic Institute and State University, Ed.D. (1983); Morgan State University, B.S.; New York University, M.A.; Graduate Studies at: University of Texas at Dallas, East Texas State University, University of Maryland, American University. **Personal:** Married to Nellie R. in 1966. Three children: Michael C., Napoleon B., Jr., and Roderick A. Dr. Lewis enjoys farming (breeding Beefmaster cows), bridge, poker, fishing, and sports.

Jean G. Litterer, Ph.D.

Executive Principal
Hillsboro Comprehensive High School
3812 Hillsboro Rd.
Nashville, TN 37215
(615) 298–8400
Fax: (615) 298–8402

8211

Business Information: Hillsboro Comprehensive High School is a U.S. "School of Excellence" recognized by the College Board for leadership and service in the pursuit of excellence in education. As Executive Principal, Dr. Litterer is responsible for providing administration, leadership, and management to 1,450 high school students, grades 9–12. **Career Steps:** Executive Principal, Hillsboro Comprehensive High School (1979–Present); Principal, West End Junior High School (1975–1979). **Associations & Accomplishments:** Chamber of Commerce; Leadership Nashville; Ladies Hermitage Association; TSSAA Athletic Conucil; Former President, Tennessee Principals' Association; Chairman, Metro Public Schools Insurance Trust; National Association of Secondary School Principals; Recognized as the Educational Administrator of the Year; Advisory Board of the Junior League; Phi Delta Kappa. **Education:** Vanderbilt University, Ph.D. (1981); George Peabody College for Teachers: M.A., Ed.S.; University of Tennessee – Knoxville, B.A. **Personal:** Dr. Litterer enjoys playing bridge, reading, antiques, and flower arranging.

Rita R. Lorio

Director of Guidance
New Summerfield Independent School District
Highway 79 and 110
New Summerfield, TX 75780
(903) 726–3306
Fax: (903) 726–3402

8211

Business Information: New Summerfield Independent School District is the management organization for public education facilities of Pre–Kindergarten through 12th grade, serving the populace of New Summerfield, Texas. With twenty–seven years of experience in education, Ms. Lorio joined New Summerfield Independent School District as Director of Guidance in 1991. A Pro–active Counselor, she is responsible for curriculum direction for the district, including guiding students career–wise and socially, as well as personally counseling the students with the involvement of their parents. She also serves as a Drug Education and At–Risk Coordinator for the District. Prior to accepting the position as Director of Guidance at New Summerfield ISD, she taught elementary, middle and high school in Houston, New Orleans, and several other independent school districts from 1970 to 1985. **Career Steps:** Director of Guidance, New Summerfield Independent School District (1991–Present); Counselor K–8 and Drug Education Coordinator, Huntington Independent School District (1989–1991); Education Specialist, Region VII Education Service Center (1987–1989). **Associations & Accomplishments:** American School Counselors Association; Texas School Counselors Association; Texas Counseling Association; Pineywoods Counseling Association; Parent Teacher Organization; Association of Texas Professional Educators. **Education:** Sam Houston State University, M.Ed. (1979); University of Houston, B.S. in Education (1970). **Personal:** Married to Ed in 1967. Two children: Rischa Irwin and Alisha. Ms. Lorio enjoys metaphysics, counted cross–stitching; watching her husband's softball team, and enjoying time with her children and grandchildren.

David W. Lyon

Director of Business
King George County Schools
10459 Court House Drive
King George, VA 22485–0021
(540) 775–5833
Fax: (540) 775–2165

8211

Business Information: King George County Schools is the municipal government office responsible for the administration of all elementary and secondary education facilities and activities within the King George County, Virginia jurisdiction. As Director of Business, David Lyon provides the overall direction and management for all business operational departments, which include: Purchasing, Payroll, Risk Management, Accounting and Employee Compensation. He is also responsible for the oversight and development of budgetary guidelines and dispersals, as well as vendor contract negotiations. **Career Steps:** Director of Business, King George County Schools (1993–Present); Manager of Consulting, KPMG Peat Marwick (1987–1993); Captain/Combat Development, US Army (1983–1987). **Associations & Accomplishments:** Virginia Association of School Business Officials; Institute for Certification of Computer Professionals; Order of the Engineer; Fredericksburg Chamber of Commerce; Former Member, Church Finance Committee; Open Plan Users Group. **Education:** Averett College, M.B.A. (1991); Rose–Hulman Institute of Technology, B.S. in Electrical Engineering (1983). **Personal:** Married to Debra in 1985. Three children: Whitney, Nicholas and Lucas. Mr. Lyon enjoys sponsoring and coaching children's sports in conjunction with local Parks and Recreation Department and Cub Scouts.

Linda E. Matlock, Ed.D.

Administrator of Special Services
Centralia School District
6625 La Palma
Buena Park, CA 90620
(714) 228–3141
Fax: Please mail or call

8211

Business Information: Established in 1875, Centralia School District is the municipal governmental office responsible for the administration of all elementary (preschool through grade six) education facilities and activities within its county jurisdiction. As Administrator of Special Services, Dr. Matlock is responsible for the coordination of the Gate Program, the Title One Program, the Special Education Programs, State and Federally funded programs, and numerous activities for the District. **Career Steps:** Administrator of Special Services (K–6), Centralia School District (1993–Present); Principal (K–6), Lucia Mar Unified School District, Branch Elementary School (Jul. – Oct. 1993); Shandon Unified School District: Director of Student Services (K–12) and Principal (K–6) (1989–1993), Principal/Resource Specialist Teacher (K–6) (1988–1989); Adjunct Professor (Part–Time), University of La Verne (1991–1993); Adjunct Professor, Center for Teacher Education, California Polytechnic University (1987–1993); Adjunct Professor, Department of Education, California State University (1982–1985). **Associations & Accomplishments:** Council for Exceptional Children (CEC); American Association of University Women (AAUW); Phi Delta Kappa; Association of California School Administrators (ACSA): Exemplary Performance (1991–1992); CAG; Association for Supervision and Curriculum Development (ASCD); CSLA: Regional Merit Award (1990); National Council for Self–Esteem; SLO–CAP Council: Child Abuse Prevention; National Association of Elementary School Principals; University of La Verne Alumni Association. **Education:** University of La Verna, California: Doctorate Degree (1995), A.B.D. (1993); California State University – Chico: M.A. (1982), B.A. (1970); Credentials earned: Administrative Services – Second Tier (1993) and Administrative Services – First Tier (1989), Resource Specialist Certificate (1980), Learning Handicapped (1979), Standard Elementary (1974). **Personal:** Two children: Eric and Brian. Dr. Matlock enjoys sports, travel, volunteering with the Special Olympics, and Church activities.

Sharon L. McGaffie

Executive Director
Shelton's Primary Educational Center
3339 Martin Luther King Jr. Way
Berkeley, CA 94703–2720
(510) 652–6132
Fax: (510) 652–5676

8211

Business Information: Shelton's Primary Educational Center is a private elementary school, catering primarily to ethnic minority children in Preschool through Fourth grade levels residing in the greater Berkeley, California metro area. An elementary educator and education consultant for the past twenty years, Sharon McGaffie was appointed as Executive Director in September of 1974. She provides the overall executive direction for all administrative functions of the institution, overseeing a staff of 20, as well as serves as spokesperson on behalf of all public and compliance matters. **Career Steps:** Executive Director, Shelton's Primary Educational Center (1974–Present); School Teacher, Atlanta Public Schools (1973–1974); Consultant, County Child Care Programs (1976–1981). **Associations & Accomplishments:** Professional Association for Childhood Education; Oakland Chamber of Commerce; Institute for Independent Schools. **Education:** Atlanta University, M.A. (1973); University of California – Berkeley, B.A. (1972). **Personal:** Married to John in 1975. Two children: Saniyyah and Mika.

Mr. Dan J. McPherson
Principal
Lubbock Independent School District, Preston Smith Elementary School
8707 Dover Avenue
Lubbock, TX 79424
(806) 766–2022
Fax: (806) 766–2042

8211

Business Information: Lubbock Independent School District has 54 schools (40 elementary schools), and 31,000 students. Preston Smith Elementary School is a public educational facility for grades K–6, with 820 students. The School has a gifted/talented program and an accelerated reading program. As Principal, Mr. McPherson is responsible for administration of all aspects of school operations. Lubbock Independent School District, Preston Smith Elementary School employs a staff of 73 . **Career Steps:** Principal, Lubbock Independent School District, Preston Smith Elementary School (1987–Present); Principal, Mahon School (1983–1987); Principal, Bayless School (1979–1983); Consultant, LISD (1977–1979). **Associations & Accomplishments:** President (1982–1983), Lubbock Elementary Principals' Association; Texas Elementary Principals' Association; Texas PTA; Phi Delta Kappa; Lubbock Chamber of Commerce Beautification Committee; National Elementary Principal Association. **Education:** Texas Tech, M.E. (1973); Abilene Christian University, B.S. (1962).

Patricia M. Monson, Ed.D.
Principal
St. James the Less Catholic School
4635 Dunsmore Avenue
La Crescenta, CA 91214–1812
(818) 248–7778
Fax: (818) 248–7778

8211

Business Information: St. James the Less Catholic School is a private educational facility providing scholastic and related services to students in grades K–8th. Focusing on moral values and high academic standards, the School is non–profit and comprised of twelve teachers and three assistants. Established in 1956, the School has an estimated student population of 280. As Principal, Dr. Monson provides moral leadership and is responsible for curriculum development and updates, serving as a community liaison, and maintaining a high level of academia. Additional duties include administration, operations, finance, and strategic planning. **Career Steps:** Principal, St. James the Less Catholic School (1992–Present); Los Angeles Unified School District: Graduate Instructor (1992–Present) Bilingual Coordinator (1985–1992); Bilingual (Spanish/English) teacher (1971–1985); Instructor, Bilingual Methods and English as a Second Language, California State University. **Associations & Accomplishments:** Phi Delta Kappa (PDK); National Catholic Education Association (NCEA); Presentations to the Department of Catholic Schools of Los Angeles Archdiocese and other Educators. **Education:** University of La Verne, Ed.D. (1991); Southampton University, UK, B.A.; California State University, Los Angeles, M.A. **Personal:** One child: Grayling C.. Dr. Monson enjoys writing, reading, ceramics, and painting.

E. Ann Moore
Director of Resource Development
St. Peter Claver Catholic School
1401 Governor Street
Tampa, FL 33602
(813) 223–1982
Fax: (813) 223–1982

8211

Business Information: St. Peter Claver Catholic School, established in 1894, is a predominantly African–American Catholic school providing education for students in Kindergarten through fifth grades. Future plans include expanding the school to include seventh and eight grades. As Director of Resource Development, Ms. Moore is responsible for raising money for expansion (goal of $2 million) and acquiring equipment for the school. She also is developing an Outreach Program for the children and their parents in two public housing developments. **Career Steps:** Director of Resource Development, St. Peter Claver Catholic School (1995–Present); Johnson & Johnson, Inc.: Finance/Accountant (1990–1994), Senior Finance Accounting Support (1988–1990). **Associations & Accomplishments:** National Association of Female Executives; National Society of Fundraising Executives; Mayor's Beautification Board. **Education:** Certified Network Administration. **Personal:** Two children: Carlton and Chachere. Ms. Moore enjoys tennis, reading, and exercise.

Olvin Moreland Jr., ED.D.
••• ◆━◉━◆ •••

Director of Special Programs
Seattle Public Schools
815 Fourth Avenue North
Seattle, WA 98109–9985
(206) 281–6687
Fax: (206) 281–6685
E–mail: see below

8211

Business Information: The Seattle Public Schools is the municipal government office responsible for the administration of all public educational facilities and activities for students in grades kindergarten through twelfth within the city jurisdiction. Currently the school system employs 4,000 people. As Director of Special Programs, Dr. Moreland is responsible for the administration for several programs, including Homeless Education, Magnet Programs, Indian Education, and drug and alcohol services. He can be reached through the Internet via: OMORELAND **Career Steps:** Seattle Public Schools: Director of Special Programs (1992–Present); Supervisor of the Drug and Alcohol Services (1989–1992); Bureau Chief for School of Improvement and Planning, New York State Department of Education (1987–1989). **Associations & Accomplishments:** Black Professional Educators of Puget Sound; Join Together Fellow, Boston University School of Public Health. **Education:** Harvard University: ED.D. (1981), M.Ed.; Oregon State University, B.S. **Personal:** Two children: Kim Marie and Derron Olvin. Dr. Moreland enjoys sports, jazz, jogging, bowling, reading, and travel.

Barbara A. Mori, Ed.D.
Director of Student Services
Rialto Unified School District
182 East Walnut Avenue
Rialto, CA 92376–3530
(909) 820–7750
Fax: (909) 421–3471

8211

Business Information: Rialto Unified School District provides education to 24,000 students in Rialto, California, and surrounding areas. As Director of Student Services, Dr. Mori supervises 98 special education programs, overseeing a staff of special education teachers, instructional aids, speech therapists, adapted physical education teachers, and psychologists. She is responsible for coordinating staff and program development, staff recruitment and training, speech services, adapted physical education, and psychological services. **Career Steps:** Director of Student Services, Rialto Unified School District (1994–Present); Director, Escalon Nonpublic School (1993–1994); Supervisor of Student Services, Santa Monica–Malibu Unified School District (1991–1993). **Associations & Accomplishments:** Association of California School Administrators; Council for Exceptional Children, (Divisions: CASE, DCD, DEC, TED); Phi Delta Kappa; American Contract Bridge League; Published Author. **Education:** University of LaVerne, Ed.D. (1991); University of Nevada, Las Vegas, M.A. (1977); Bloomsburg State University, M.Ed. (1971); Pennsylvania State University, B.S. (1965). **Personal:** Married to Allen in 1971. One child: Kirsten. Dr. Mori enjoys aerobics, bridge, travel, and tennis.

Timothy P. Mulvany
President
Bishop Ward High School
708 North 18th Street
Kansas City, KS 66102
(913) 262–2700
Fax: (913) 371–2145

8211

Business Information: Bishop Ward High School is a Catholic High School serving 375 students in Kansas City, Kansas. As President, Mr. Mulvany is responsible for marketing, supervision of operations, and the development of academic funding. **Career Steps:** President, Bishop Ward High School (1996–Present); Bishop Miege High School: Director of Development (1992–1996), Teacher/Coach (1984–1996). **Associations & Accomplishments:** Mid American Planned Giving Council; Greater Kansas City Council on Philanthropy. **Education:** Benedictine College, B.A. (1981). **Personal:** Married to Sandra K. in 1983. Three children: Megan, Timmy, and Colin. Mr. Mulvany enjoys golf, reading, and coaching Little League.

Karen Y. Murphy
Principal
Abundant Life Christian Academy
1494 Banks Road
Margate, FL 33063
Fax: (954) 979–1983

8211

Business Information: Abundant Life Christian Academy is an elementary school that provides academic excellence along with spiritual vitality. The Academy presently teaches through grade six, with 215 students in attendance and 25 faculty members. The Academy's students are an average of two years ahead of the students in corresponding state schools. As Principal, Mrs. Murphy is responsible for budgetary concerns, financial aspects, short–range and long–term planning, and supervising faculty. Her other responsibilities include student recruitment, public relations, fund raising, and attending student needs as Chaplain. Mrs. Murphy is also the Director of the Pre–School and serves on the School Board. **Career Steps:** Principal, Abundant Life Christian Academy (1993–Present); Teacher, Broward County Schools (1986–1993); Teacher, American Heritage School (1983–1985). **Associations & Accomplishments:** Foundation for American Christian Education (FACE); International Fellowship Christian School Administration (IFCSA); Oral Roberts Educational Fellowship (ORUEF); Association for Christian Schools International (ACSI). **Education:** Oral Roberts University: M.Ed. (1995), B.S. in Elementary/Special Education. **Personal:** Married to Craven in 1983. Three children: Peter, Patrick, and Phillip. Mrs. Murphy enjoys helping the needy, arts and crafts, painting, and athletics.

Mark A. Murray
Principal
Paintsville City Schools
832 Fm Stafford Avenue
Paintsville, KY 41240–1252
(606) 789–2656
Fax: Please mail or call

8211

Business Information: Paintsville City Schools is the administration system for public elementary and secondary schools lying within the jurisdiction of Paintsville County. As Principal, Mr. Murray serves as the head of the Paintsville Junior High and High School. In addition to administrative duties, he is the Athletic Director and is responsible for scheduling all extra–curricular activities and civic functions. **Career Steps:** Principal, Paintsville City Schools (1994–Present); Teacher, Johnson Central High School (1993–1994); Teacher, FlatGap Elementary School (1989–1993). **Associations & Accomplishments:** National Association of Secondary School Principals; Kentucky Association of Secondary School Principals; Kentucky Association of School Administrators; Board of Directors From Region 15, Kentucky Association of Secondary School Principals; President, 15th Region Principals Association of KASSP; Board of Directors, Mayo Technical School, Kentucky Tech. **Education:** Attending, Eastern Kentucky University (1996); Morehead State University, Master's Degree in Middle School Education Area Curriculum Design; Clinch Valley College, Teaching Certification in Middle Grades; University of Virginia, B.S. in Mining, Reclamation, and Energy Studies with an Area in Energy Industry Administration; Wyoming Technology, A.A.S. **Personal:** Married to Marsha in 1993. Two children: Allitha Jo and Alex. Mr. Murray enjoys fox, coyote, and deer hunting, and training hounds for field trials.

Stephen A. Nagy
Campus Director
Lake Grove School
1 Farley Road, P.O. Box 767
Wendell, MA 01379–0767
(508) 544–6913
Fax: (508) 544–8672

8211

Business Information: Lake Grove School is a private, not–for–profit residential school serving children with special needs. The School can accommodate 36 students per year, who range from 13 to 22 years of age. Lake Grove accepts children from many states with a variety of emotional and learning disabilities. As Campus Director, Mr. Nagy must wear many hats. He directs emotional, clinical, and residential care of the students and 80 staff members. Mr. Nagy handles general administrative duties, maintenance of the physical plant, and foodservices. He is very involved, as well, in public relations for the School and oversees the development of new methods of assisting the children to learn and increase their self–esteem. **Career Steps:** Lake Grove School: Campus Director (1993–Present), Business Manager (1987–1993); Senior Accountant, Hampshire College (1985–1987); Graduate Assistant, University of Massachusetts (1982–1984).

Associations & Accomplishments: Massachusetts Associations of Approved Private Schools; Capital Planning Committee, Towns of Leverett, Massachusetts. **Education:** University of Massachusetts: M.B.A. (1984), B.S. in Hotel Management; Park Management – Stockridge School of Agriculture, A.S. **Personal:** Married to Susan in 1989. Two children: Gabrielle and Timothy.

Mr. Larry Noonan

Member
Metro Separate School Board
1007 Amberlea Road
Pickering, Ontario L1V 6P4
(416) 393–5308
Fax: (416) 397–6013

8211

Business Information: Larry Noonan serves as a member of the Metro Separate School Board which is responsible for the administrative functions and the education of children from Kindergarten to OAC (grade 13) in the Toronto, Ontario jurisdiction. He formerly served as a Coordinator of Computers in Education, responsible for establishing the Computer Department and placing between 15,000 – 20,000 computers in Canada's largest school district consisting of 237 schools. His duties included directing software evaluations and acquisitions for over 100,000 students and provide in–services for the teachers in the board with computers. He was appointed Principal of St. Nicholas Elementary School in 1995, responsible for establishing a communication technology–oriented school, where students from grades one through eight can use computers for WP, DB, etc, but also for advanced animation techniques by using 30 Pentium computers and a variety of other equipment. **Career Steps:** Metro Separate School Board: Member (1994–Present), Coordinator of Computers (1993–1995), Supervisor of Computers (1982–1993), Resource Teacher (1979–1982); Principal, St. Nicholas Elementary School (1995–Present). **Associations & Accomplishments:** Ontario English Catholic Teachers Association; Ontario Genealogical Society; Historical Committee for Pickering Village; St. Francis de Sales Church; Publisher of four books (3 computer books, one administrative educational index) and a TV documentary on the Fenian Raids of 1866. **Education:** University of Toronto, Masters (1982); York University: B.A., Computer Specialist (1987). **Personal:** Married to Janice in 1993. Three children: Meaghan, Michael, and Kristyl. Mr. Noonan enjoys writing.

Peggy C. O'Keeffe

Curriculum Director
Mount Morris Schools
12356 Walter Street
Mount Morris, MI 48458
(810) 686–8760
Fax: (810) 686–7470

8211

Business Information: Mount Morris Schools are the local public education centers in Mount Morris, Michigan. The schools offer classes from Kindergarten to 12th grade for approximately 3,150 students. As Curriculum Director, Mrs. O'Keeffe is in charge of directing programs with emphasis on what children are taught and the methods used to teach them. She assists in the development and design of the curriculum being offered to each grade level in the Mount Morris Schools. Mrs. O'Keeffe recruits instructors, assists in the verification of teacher credentials, and helps with the scheduling of professional developmental opportunities for faculty and staff members. **Career Steps:** MT Morris Schools: Curriculum Director (1995–Present), Principal (1985–1995), Reading Consultant (1979–1985), Teacher (1976–1979). **Associations & Accomplishments:** Professional Development Chair, Michigan Elementary and Middle School Principals Association; Phi Delta Kappa; Michigan Association of State and Federal Program Specialists. **Education:** Wayne State University, Ed.S. (1995); University of Michigan: M.A., B.A. **Personal:** Married to Dr. Vincent in 1982. Mrs. O'Keeffe enjoys equestrian sports.

Roderick R. Paige

Superintendent of Schools
Houston Independent School District
3830 Richmond Avenue
Houston, TX 77027–5864
(713) 892–6300
Fax: (713) 892–6061

8211

Business Information: Houston Independent School District, the fifth largest school district in the U.S., is the municipal governmental office responsible for the administration of all public elementary and secondary educational facilities and activities within jurisdiction of Houston, Texas. Joining Houston ISD as Superintendent of Schools in 1994, Dr. Paige is responsible for the oversight and direction of all school district activities, including administration, operations, finances, public relations, accounting, and strategic planning. **Career Steps:** Superintendent of Schools, Houston Independent School District (1994–Present); Texas Southern University: Dean of College of Education, Athletic Director. **Associations & Accomplishments:** AASA; ASCD; Coalition of Essential Schools Board; Rice University Center for Education Board; National Association for the Advancement of Colored People; National Commission for Employment Policy; Boy Scouts of America. **Education:** Indiana University; Ed.D.; Jackson State University; University of Indiana. **Personal:** Dr. Paige enjoys playing tennis and reading during his spare time."

Stephen J. Perepeluk

Principal
Elementary Magnet School
305 May Road
East Hartford, CT 06118–3434
(860) 282–3396
Fax: (860) 282–3372

8211

Business Information: Elementary Magnet School is a primary educational facility educating kindergarten through sixth grade students teaching Japanese at the kindergarten level. The School enhances its population by accepting children on a lottery–based system offering technology and science programs. As Principal, Mr. Perepeluk is responsible for performing administrative duties, supervising faculty and staff, and coordinating all parent/teacher/student relations. **Career Steps:** Principal, Elementary Magnet School (1995–Present); Principal Intern, NYC Public Schools (1994–1995); Teacher, P.S. 124 Manhanttan (1989–1994). **Associations & Accomplishments:** Association for Supervisory and Curriculum Development; National Association of Elementary School Principals. **Education:** New York University School of Education, M.A. (1995); Teachers College, Columbia University, M.A. (1989); Hamilton College, B.A. (1986). **Personal:** Mr. Perepeluk enjoys antiques, theatre, travel, and reading.

Patty C. Rice, Ph.D.

Educational Consultant/Author
Macomb Intermediate School District
44001 Garfield Road
Clinton Township, MI 48038–1100
(810) 228–3841
Fax: (810) 286–2523

8211

Business Information: Macomb Intermediate School District is the regional educational service center which acts as liaison between the State Department of Education and the local K–12 School Districts in Macomb County, Michigan. As a Curriculum Consultant for the district, Dr. Rice's work experience includes consultation for Macomb County Schools in developing language arts, reading, arts education, and coordination of ESL/Bilingual Multicultural Education Programs for the past thirty years. During this time, she has directed the MISD Folk Artist in the Schools Project for three years and the Chinese Arts in Education Project for three years. She was the Coordinator of the MISD Regional Arts Education Service Center which provided Teacher Development in Comprehensive Arts Education following the MDE New Essential Goals and Objectives for Arts K–12 and provided awareness programs, model development workshops and skill development training sessions for Macomb County teachers. Dr. Rice has made presentations at four International Reading Association Conferences and two World Congresses on Reading on her innovative approaches for teaching reading, visual imagery, and creativity through the arts. She is also an internationally known author and published photographer. Her comprehensive study on the gemstone Amber was published as a definitive work titled "Amber: The Golden Gem of the Ages" by Van Nostrand Reinhold originally in 1980. Revisions were published by Kosciuszko Foundation in 1987, with a second revision in 1993. She has lectured at Gem and Mineral Shows throughout the United States, Canada, and Poland. She was invited to present her "Artistry in Amber Exhibition" materials at the World Conference on Amber at the Museum Zeimi, Warsaw, Poland, in 1988, and to consult on amber in Italy in 1996. **Career Steps:** Macomb Intermediate School District: Bilingual/ESL Coordinator (1985–Present), Educational Consultant (1965–Present); Fine Arts Coordinator, Michigan Department of Education Region C, Northeast Metro Arts Education Support Center (1988–1991); Arts Education Consultant (1980–1994); Birmingham Public Schools (1960–1965); Waterford Public Schools (1958–1960); Delta Kappa Gamma Carolyn Guss International Scholarship Recipient (1969–1970). **Associations & Accomplishments:** Vice President, Warren Symphony Orchestra Society; Former President OMEGA, Delta Kappa Gamma; Michigan Mineralogical Society; Mt. Clemens Gem and Mineral Club former Editor, Newsletter: Crystal Gazer; International Reading Association, former President SIG Gifted and Talented; National Association for Bilingual Education; Michigan Association for Bilingual Education; Michigan Reading Association, Former President, Macomb Reading Council; Detroit Women Writers; Board Member, Friends of Polish Art; Honorary Member, American Polish Engineers Association and Engineer Illustrators; Board of Directors, Former President, Macomb Arts Council; Michigan Art Education Association; Michigan Alliance for the Arts in Education; Women's Division of Project Hope; Midwest Faceter's Guild; National Art Education Association; E/K//N/E Association: Former State President, Conference Chairperson (1975), Journal Editor (1973–1977); Author, "Amber, the Golden Gem of the Ages" (Van Nostrand Reinhold, 1980; Kosciuszko Foundation 1987,1993). **Education:** Wayne State University, Bilingual Endorsement (1992); Michigan State University: Ph.D. (1971), Ed. Sp. (1968), M.A. (1964), B.S. (1960) with Honors; University of Michigan, Asian Studies Program (1994–1996). **Personal:** One child: Diana Lyn Calomeni Odenwalder. Dr. Rice enjoys concerts and the arts, travel (has traveled extensively throughout Europe, Eastern Europe, China, Australia, and the Dominican Republic).

Rodrigo Solis Romero

Chief Executive Officer
Esuvela Comercial Edmara de Comercio
Queretaro #34, Col Roma
Mexico City, Mexico 06700
(525) 584–1641
Fax: (525) 584–6741

8211

Business Information: Esuvela Comercial Edmara de Comercio is a school with programs for students from Kindegarten through College. Established in 1923, the school currently has seven campuses and over 4,000 students with placement programs from middle school through college. As Chief Executive Officer, Mr. Romero sets the course the school will be taking each year. He is responsible for new program direction, marketing of services, financial concerns, budgetary matters, public relations, and strategic planning. **Career Steps:** Chief Executive Officer, Esuvela Comercial Edmara de Comercio (1991–Present). **Associations & Accomplishments:** Mexican Astronomical Society; various Fitness Clubs. **Education:** University of the Americas, M.B.A., (1996), L.A.E. (1991). **Personal:** Mr. Romero enjoys photography, fitness, nature, sky watching, and travel.

Barry E. Rowe

Director of Educational Technology
Champaign Schools
703 South New Street
Champaign, IL 61820–5818
(217) 351–1907
Fax: (217) 351–3871
EMAIL: See Below

8211

Business Information: Champaign Schools District has 16 schools (2 high schools, 3 middle schools, and 11 elementary schools) located in Central Illinois. As Director of Educational Technology, Mr. Rowe is responsible for working on the Internet and networking with other teachers. He trains teachers on how to use assets and equipment. Mr. Rowe is also responsible for writing grants and proposals. Internet users can reach him via: roweba@cmi.k12.il.us. **Career Steps:** Director of Educational Technology, Champaign Schools (1993–Present); Teacher, Champaign Unit 4 Schools (1979–1993); Teacher, Urbana Adult Education (1978–1979); Teacher Danville Schools (1975–1977). **Associations & Accomplishments:** ISTE. **Education:** Illinois State University: M.S.Ed. (1986), B.S.Ed. (1970). **Personal:** Two children: David and Morgan. Mr. Rowe enjoys sports cars and TVR sports cars.

Mr. Raymond J. Roy Jr.

Director of Computer Operations
Groton School
Farmers Row
Groton, MA 01450
(508) 448–3363
Fax: (508) 448–3100

8211

Business Information: Groton School is a private educational institution for individuals in programs Kindergarten through 12th grade. In his current capacity, Mr. Roy directs all administrative computer operations, including telecommunications and cabling, WAN and INTERNET access network administration. Established in 1884, Groton School has a faculty and administrative support staff of 200. **Career Steps:** Director of Computer Operations, Groton School (1989–Present); Vice President of Operations, R–R Jewelry & Gift Distributors (1982–1989); Data Processing Manager, Godroy Wholesale Company (1976–1982). **Associations & Accomplishments:** The Association for Corporate Computing Technical Professionals (NASPA); The Association of Network Computing Professionals Association (NCPA); Common, IBM User's

Group; Institute of Electronic and Electrical Engineers. **Education:** Holy Cross College, B.A. (1969).

Richard D. Saddlemire, Ph.D.

Superintendent
Antilles Consolidated School System
Superintendent Office, Building 19
Ft. Buchanan, Puerto Rico 00934
(809) 792–7555
Fax: (809) 273–0573
8211

Business Information: Antilles Consolidated School System is responsible for the oversight of elementary and secondary schools (seven total) aboard Ft. Buchanan Army Base, Puerto Rico. Sanctioned by the U.S. Department of Defense, the District manages all education and curriculum for dependents of active duty members stationed aboard the base. Employing 520 people, the District oversees a student population of approximately 3,800. As Superintendent, Dr. Saddlemire oversees all administration and operations involving district curriculum and staff. A National Distinguished Principal by the Department of Defense, Dr. Saddlemire's duties include public relations, budgeting and strategic planning. **Career Steps:** Superintendent, Antilles Consolidated School System (1993–Present); Department of Defense Dependent Schools: Assistant Superintendent of Coordination (1993–1994), School Improvement, Principal. **Associations & Accomplishments:** Phi Delta Kappa; Department of Defense and NAESP National Distinguished Principal (1987); Author of three articles, " Tips for Principals", "How to Improve Media Centers" and "How to Decrease Vandalism". **Education:** Manila University, Ph.D. (1983); Michigan State, Education Specialist; Rochester: B.A., M.A. **Personal:** Married to Dr. Patricia M in 1971. Three children: Christina, Carlyn and Catherine. Dr. Saddlemire enjoys writing.

Katherine K. Schloemer

Principal
St. Francis of Assisi School
1938 Alfresco Place
Louisville, KY 40205–1810
(502) 459–3088 (502) 548–2855
Fax: (502) 456–9462
8211

Business Information: St. Francis of Assisi School is a parochial elementary school affiliated with the Roman Catholic Church. As Principal, Ms. Schloemer is responsible for all aspects of the School's operations, including administration of students, strategic planning, and other related activities. **Career Steps:** Principal, St. Francis of Assisi School (1990–Present); Teacher, St. Joseph School (1976–1990); Teacher, St. Leonard School (1974–1975). **Associations & Accomplishments:** NCEA; ASCD; NCTE. **Education:** Spalding University: Ed.Spec. (1997), M.Ed.; University of Louisville, Bachelors Degree in English. **Personal:** Married to Lewis Fred in 1972. Two children: Alexis and Max. Ms. Schloemer enjoys farming, horses, gardening, and dogs.

Nancy G. Schnabel

Transportation Manager
Summit School District RE–I
P.O. Box 07
Frisco, CO 80443–0007
(970) 668–3015
Fax: (970) 668–8347
8211

Business Information: Summit School District RE–I is the municipal governmental office responsible for the administration of all education facilities, activities, and transportation within its county jurisdiction. As Transportation Manager, Mrs. Schnabel is responsible for the supervision of 25 employees, routing and scheduling for a fleet of 26 vehicles, and supervision of the mechanics shop. **Career Steps:** Transportation Manager, Summit School District RE–I (Present). **Education:** Northwest Community College, A.S. (1972). **Personal:** Married to Alan in 1973. Two children: Eric and Kurt. Mrs. Schnabel enjoys golf, camping, and tennis.

Mrs. Jacqueline B. Sears

School Finance Officer
Gates County Public Schools
P. O. Box 125, Main Street
Gatesville, NC 27938
(919) 357–1113
Fax: (919) 357–0207
8211

Business Information: Gates County Public Schools is the municipal office responsible for the administration of all secondary education facilities and activities within the County jurisdiction. The school district includes six schools (two Pre–K through 3rd grades; two elementary – 4th through 6th grades; one middle – 7th through 9th grades; and one high school – 10th through 12th Grades). Gates County Public Schools reports annual operating budget of $10 million and currently employs 365 people. As School Finance Officer, Mrs. Sears is responsible for all aspects of financial matters, including all payrolls for the school system, all funds dealing with the schools (local, state and federal funding), purchasing and in charge of reports for state and federal offices and local governing board. **Career Steps:** School Finance Officer, Gates County Public Schools (1985–Present); Local Schools Bookkeeper, Gates County Public Schools (1984–1985); Federal Bookkeeper/Payroll, Gates County Public Schools (1965–1984); School Secretary, Amanda Cherry Elementary School (1961–1965). **Associations & Accomplishments:** Gates County NAACP Branch, Gates County; Citizens Improvement League; Board Member, State Employees' Credit Union – Ahoskie Branch; Local, State and National Member of Educational Office Personnel Organizations; The North Carolina Association Professional School Finance Officers; Southeastern Association of School Business Officials; State Employees Association of North Carolina; North Carolina Association for School Administrators; Girl Scout Council of Colonial Coast. **Education:** Elizabeth City State University; Roanoke Chowan Community College; College of the Albermarle; University of North Carolina – Charlotte – Course work related to her job as School Finance Officer – received the North Carolina State Board of Education Professional Certification for North Carolina School Finance Officers (1986). **Personal:** Married to James in 1965. Two children: Malcolm Anthony and Teresa Gail Sears. Mrs. Sears enjoys cooking, bowling, gospel music, sewing and helping others.

Joan Semedo, Ed.D.

Instruction Specialist in Art and Art History/Certified Educator
Boston Public Schools
42 Menlo Street
Brockton, MA 02401
(508) 580–0718
Fax: Please mail or call
8211

Business Information: Boston Public Schools is a public school providing quality education to elementary school students in the City of Boston and surrounding locale. With seventeen years of educational training, Dr. Semedo joined Boston Public Schools as Instruction Specialist in Art and Art History and a Certified Educator in 1979. She is responsible for instructing elementary and secondary students in art and art history. Concurrent with her position with the Boston Public School System, she serves as Adjunct Professor of Art at Lesley College. **Career Steps:** Instruction Specialist in Art and Art History/Certified Educator, Boston Public Schools (1979–Present); Adjunct Professor of Art, Lesley College (1994–Present); Federal Internship, Headstart and Cambridge Welfare Department (1968–1970). **Associations & Accomplishments:** Governors Commission Member (1993), African Advisory Commission – Commonwealth of Massachusetts, State House; National Association of Colored Womens Club, Inc.; Representative, Boston Teachers Union; Board of Directors (1993–Present), City of Brockton Health Department; Board of Directors (1988–1989), Jefferson Park Reading and Writing Center; Advocate, K–1 Art Program representing the Charles Sumner K–1 Program Parent Conference (1989); Visiting Artist, Jefferson Park Reading and Writing Center (1988–1989); Kiwanis Club (1995); Several professional art exhibits; Founder of the late "Josephine Baker Award," in Paris, France – presented to community women who have worked unselfishly for or with children of Brockton, Massachusetts; Author of "African–American Art," "Whatever Happened To Sam," "Runaway Slave, Stoughton, Massachusetts," and "Memorial Statutes On The Boston Common"; Numerous honors, awards, and recognitions, including being recognized by HEADSTART as crucial to the development of their Cambridge, MA program and to the progress of the reading and writing center for high school drop outs and adult illiterates at Jefferson Park, Cambridge (1985–1986). **Education:** University of Massachusetts: Ed.D. (1994), M.Ed. (1987), B.S. in Education (1979); Teacher Certified in the Commonwealth of Massachusetts; Wheelock College, Early Childhood; Harvard University, Certification in Interior Design. **Personal:** Married to John Semedo in 1976. Three children: Claire, Elizabeth, and SaraAnn. Dr. Semedo enjoys reading, writing, and painting.

Sandra Silver, Ph.D

Director, Curriculum, Instruction and Evaluation
Windham Public Schools
355 High Street, Room 100A
Willimantic, CT 06226
(860) 465–2526
Fax: (860) 465–2509
EMAIL: See Below
8211

Business Information: Windham Public Schools is a local agency responsible for the oversight of public education in the Willimantic, Connecticut area. As Director, Curriculum, Instruction and Evaluation, Dr. Silver is responsible for overseeing the curriculum and professional development of the school system, as well as being responsible for multi–cultural programming, teacher evaluations, and mentoring programs. Internet users can reach her via: ssilver@neca.com. **Career Steps:** Director, Curriculum, Instruction and Evaluation, Windham Public Schools (1995–Present); Bemidji Area Schools: Elementary Principal (1989–1994), Assistant Professor, State University (1985–1989); Instructor, College of South Alameda (1983–1985). **Associations & Accomplishments:** Northeast Coalition of Education Leaders; Kappa Delta Pi; Pi Lambda Theta; Phi Delta Kappa; ASCD; CEC; AASA. **Education:** University of California, Berkeley/San Francisco State, Ph.D (1986); Northeastern, C.A.G.S.; Fitchburg State, M.Ed.; Boston University, B.S. **Personal:** Ms. Silver enjoys folk dancing, needlework, gardening, hiking, and reading.

Steven G. Stafford

Director of Special Education & Psychological Services
Tulare City School District
600 North Cherry
Tulare, CA 93274
(209) 685–7232
Fax: (209) 685–7248
8211

Business Information: Tulare City School District is the management organization for public education facilities of Pre–Kindergarten through 8th grade, serving the populace of Tulare, California. Holding various administrative educational positions within Tulare City School District since 1984, Steven Stafford was appointed as Director of Special Education in r1994. He is responsible for the administration of special education classes, teachers, and other staff. Additional duties involve directing school psychologists and social workers; overseeing training for teachers; administer all Federal, State, and local mandates and laws; administer all norm–referenced tests and scores. **Career Steps:** Tulare City School District: Director – Special Education and Psychological Services (1994–Present); Principal, Garden Elementary (1987–1993); Vice Principal, Mulcahy Junior High School (1984–1987). **Associations & Accomplishments:** Kiwanis; Volunteer Bureau Board of Directors; Board of Directors, YMCA Camp Committee; Advisory Board, Tulare Pro–Youth; Encore Theatre. **Education:** California State University–Bakersfield, M.A. (1987); California State University–Fresno, B.A. (1976); University of Southern California; Notre Dame College; Fresno Pacific College. **Personal:** Married to Lynn in 1980. Three children: Devin, Jenna, and Krista. Mr. Stafford enjoys bicycling, sailing, travel, and all sports.

Gena Stanley

Principal
Rocky Ford High School
100 West Washington Avenue
Rocky Ford, CO 81067
(719) 254–7431
Fax: (719) 254–7436
8211

Business Information: Rocky Ford High School provides educational services to students grades 9–12. The School has 350 students participating in ESL, art, and computer graphics classes. As Principal, Mrs. Stanley oversees all learning instruction, personnel, curriculum, budget, student concerns, disciplinary actions, and program planning. **Career Steps:** Principal, Rocky Ford High School (1995–Present); Alternative School Principal, Garden City School District #457 (1991–1995); Director of Grants Center, St. Mary of the Plains College (1989–1991); Teacher, Dodge City School District #443 (1984–1989). **Associations & Accomplishments:** Phi Delta Kappa; Colorado Association of School Executives; National Association of Secondary School Principals. **Education:** Ft. Hayes State University, M.S. (1991); St. Mary of the Plains College, B.S.; Dodge City Community College, A.A. **Personal:** Married to Sean Davis in 1994. Four children: Chris, Bridget, Dion Stanley, and Shannon Crocker. Mrs. Stanley enjoys reading.

Mrs. Audrey I. Sullivan

Principal
Brevard County School System
2601 Fountainhead Boulevard
Melbourne, FL 32935
(407) 242–6450
Fax: (407) 242–6453
8211

Business Information: Brevard County School System is the public school administration system for institutions lying within the jurisdiction of Brevard County, Florida. As Principal of Roy Allen Elementary School, Mrs. Sullivan is the administrator in charge of all operations for an elementary educational facility serving grades Pre–Kindergarten through 6th grade. As such she supervises faculty and staff, coordinates all parent/teacher/student relations, community outreach programs and curriculum development. The school currently enrolls 560 students residing in the Melbourne, Florida vicinity. Roy Allen Elementary School employs 60 faculty and administrative support staff. **Career Steps:** Principal, Brevard County School System (1986–Present); Assistant Principal, Brevard County School System (1980–1985); Media Specialist, Brevard County School System (1968–1979). **Associations & Accomplishments:** Brevard Reading Council; Brevard Association of School Administrators; Florida Association of School Administrators; National Association of Elementary School Principals; Delta Kappa Gamma (Womens Educational Honor Society). **Education:** University of Central Florida, M.S. (1973); Florida State University, B.A. **Personal:** Married to C.J. in 1964. One child: Christopher. Mrs. Sullivan enjoys sports (avid Florida State University fan) and reading.

Faith Szambelanczyk, OSF

President/Chief Executive Officer
Joliet Catholic Academy
1200 North Larkin Avenue
Joliet, IL 60435–3777
(815) 741–0500
Fax: (815) 741–8825

8211

Business Information: Joliet Catholic Academy is a regional, coed, not–for–profit academy for children in grades 9 through 12. As President/CEO, Sister Szambelanczyk is responsible for all administrative duties associated with the School. She is also responsible for institutional advancement, development and implementation of curricula, staff recruitment and evaluation, and Academy budgetary concerns. **Career Steps:** President/CEO, Joliet Catholic Academy (1993–Present); Director of Development, Our Lady of Angels Retirement Home (1992–1994); Administrator, Sisters of Saint Francis (1984–1992); Teacher, Bishop Ready High School (1976–1984). **Associations & Accomplishments:** Rotary International; Joliet/Will County Project Pride; National Association of Boards of Catholic Education; Lions. **Education:** Saint Mary University of Minnesota, M.S. (1970); Illinois Institute of Technology; DePaul University. **Personal:** Sister Szambelanczyk enjoys reading, music, sports, and organizing events.

Dr. Carol A. Theodorou

Director
Polaris School for Individual Education
4625 West 107th Street
Oak Lawn, IL 60453–5293
(708) 424–2000
Fax: (708) 636–5700

8211

Business Information: Polaris School for Individual Education is a small school educating children in grades 9–12 using the four R's: respect, responsibility, resourcefulness, and responsiveness. As Director, Dr. Theodorou is responsible for handling administrative duties, fiscal matters, daily operations, marketing, sales, and public relations. Additionally, she teaches, performs evaluations and observations, and oversees a new curriculum and inter disciplinary program. **Career Steps:** Director, Polaris School for Individual Education (1993–Present); Assistant Principal, H.L. Richards H.S.–CHSD 218 (1982–1993); Social Studies Teacher, AB Shepard H.S.–CHSD 218 (1980–1982). **Associations & Accomplishments:** Association of Curriculum & Instructional Development (ASCD); Illinois Association of Curriculum & Instructional Development (IASCD); Association of Administrators and Superintendents (AASA); National Association of Secondary School Principals (NASSP). **Education:** University of Illinois – Champaign, Ed.D. (1993), M.E.; Governors State University, B.A. in SocioCultural Processes; Moraine Valley Community College, A.A. **Personal:** Married to Dr. Phillip C. in 1957. Three children: Stefanie Anastasia, B.S., M.S., CCC; Suzanne Meersman, B.A.; and Kevin Theodorou, M.D. Dr. Theodorou enjoys reading, travel, and her grandchildren.

Susan A. VanLandingham

Director of Admissions
The Seven Hills School
975 N. San Carlos Drive
Walnut Creek, CA 94598
(510) 933–0666
Fax: (510) 933–6271

8211

Business Information: The Seven Hills School, funded through tuitions and fundraising, is an independent, private elementary school, providing education for children from grades, Pre–Kindergarten through Eighth. Established in 1962, Seven Hills School has a current enrollment of 310 students, expecting 330 by 1997, with an ultimate goal of 350. As Director of Admissions, Mrs. VanLandingham is responsible for all student admissions, as well as public relations, review and selection of qualified candidates, and conducting tours of the school. Her background includes social work and child development. **Career Steps:** Director of Admissions, The Seven Hills School (Present). **Education:** California State University – Sacramento, B.A. (1979). **Personal:** Married to John in 1980. One child: Joshua. Mrs. VanLandingham enjoys sewing, antiques, and travel.

Haroldeen U. Wakida

Principal
Ali'iolani Elementary School
1240 Seventh Avenue
Honolulu, HI 96816
(808) 733–4750
Fax: (808) 733–4758

8211

Business Information: Ali'iolani Elementary School, State of Hawaii – Department of Education, is a public school providing quality education to elementary school students (kindergarten through fifth grades). Established in 1925, Ali'iolani Elementary School currently employs 45 faculty. As Principal, Mrs. Wakida is responsible for the administration and supervision of all educational activities and support staff, as well as facilitating the establishment of the mission and vision of the school for continued growth. **Career Steps:** Principal, Ali'iolani Elementary School (1986–Present); Vice Principal, Kalani High School (1984–1986); State President, Hawaii State Teachers Association (1982–1984); Teacher, Jefferson Elementary School (1974–1982); Teacher, Red Hill Elementary (1967–1974). **Associations & Accomplishments:** Hawaii Government Employees Association; Hawaii State Teachers Association–National Education Association; Hawaii Association of Middle Schools; Hawaii Community Education Association. **Education:** University of Hawaii–Manoa, M.Ed.A., B.Ed. in Elementary Education. **Personal:** Married to Donald Yukio Wakida in 1967. Two children: Traci Kei and Todd Tetsuji Wakida. Mrs. Wakida enjoys reading, sewing, and organizational work.

Richard Warren, Ph.D.

Superintendent of Schools
Ayer Public Schools
141 Washington Street
Ayer, MA 01432–1150
(508) 772–8602
Fax: (508) 772–7444

8211

Business Information: Ayer Public Schools is the municipal governmental office responsible for the administration of all public elementary and secondary educational facilities and activities within its jurisdiction. Ayer Public School's mission is to establish partnerships between community businesses and individuals which promote collaborative and mutually beneficial results, to enhance student achievement through these partnerships, and to provide learning opportunities for the community. With twenty–five years experience in educational administration, Dr. Warren joined Ayer Public Schools as Superintendent of Schools in 1993. He oversees all aspects of operations and management of all schools within the Ayer Public School District. **Career Steps:** Superintendent of Schools, Ayer Public Schools, Ayer, MA (1993–Present); Superintendent of Schools, Mansfield, MA (1990–1993); Superintendent of Schools, Dartmouth, MA (1987–1990); Assistant Superintendent of Schools, Bourn, MA (1985–1987). **Associations & Accomplishments:** American Association of School Administrators; Massachusetts Association of School Superintendents; Association for Supervision and Curriculum Development; Massachusetts Association of Supervision and Curriculum Development; Chairman, Commission on Public Elementary Schools, New England Association of Schools and Colleges; Chair, Society for Human Advancement Through Rehabilitative Engineering (SHARE). **Education:** University of Connecticut, Ph.D. (1980); University of Connecticut, Certificate of Advanced Graduate Study; Rhode Island College, M.Ed.; Bryant College, B.S. in Business Administration. **Personal:** Married to Linda in 1960. Two children: Lisa and Barbara. Dr. Warren enjoys travel, photography, walking (competitively), and athletic activities.

Lt. Cmdr. Matthew G. Williams, USCG (Ret.)

Coordinator–Naval Junior Reserve Officers Training Corps
South Tahoe High School
P.O. Box 8876
South Lake Tahoe, CA 96158–1876
(916) 542–4221
Fax: (916) 541–4157

8211

Business Information: South Tahoe High School is a public secondary school, offering general instructional programs for high school students. After serving twenty years in the U.S. Coast Guard as a Ship Deck Watch Officer, attorney, and maritime casualty investigator, Mr. Williams decided to pursue the joy of developing young minds by joining South Tahoe High School as Coordinator of the Naval Junior Reserve Officers Training Corps in 1995. He is responsible for the coordination and training of the R.O.T.C. program, with less of an emphasis on military functions and more of an emphasis on a strong drive to develop strong leaders for tomorrow. He takes an active hand in curriculum modification from traditional Navy textbooks and guidelines to managing a five–class teaching load. **Career Steps:** Coordinator of the Naval Junior Reserve Officers Training Corps, South Tahoe High School (1995–Present); U.S. Coast Guard: Chief of Investigations (1991–1995), Staff Attorney (1990–1991); Chief Prosecutor, U.S. Navy (1989–1990). **Associations & Accomplishments:** MENSA; National Eagle Scout Association; Association of Trial Lawyers of America; Washington State Bar Association; Coast Guard Auxiliary; Skipper–Sea Explorers; Assistant Scoutmaster, Boy Scouts; Youth Baseball Coach. **Education:** University of Washington School of Law, J.D. (1987); Seattle University, MPA (1983); U.S. Coast Guard Academy, B.S. (1975). **Personal:** Married to Erma H. in 1979. Four children: Matthew, Justin, Brianna and Michael. Lt. Cmdr. Williams enjoys photography, reading, boating, racquetball and running.

Deborah A. Wilson–Imhulse

Treasurer
Urbana City Schools – Ohio
711 Wood Street
Urbana, OH 43078
(513) 653–6022
Fax: (513) 652–3845

8211

Business Information: Urbana City Schools – Ohio is the management office for State of Ohio public schools (K–12) for the Urbana City District. The District consists of six schools. Joining Urbana City Schools – Ohio as Treasurer in 1986, Ms. Wilson–Imhulse is responsible for the administrative and financial functions of the school district. **Career Steps:** Chief Fiscal Officer and Treasurer, Urbana City Schools – Ohio (1986–Present); Chief Fiscal Officer, Mad–River Green Local Schools (1982–1986); Chief Fiscal Officer, Southeastern Local Schools (1975–1982). **Associations & Accomplishments:** Ohio School Business Officials – Ohio affililate of National organization; Miami School Business Officials. **Education:** Attending: Capital University. **Personal:** Married to Dr. Stanley Imhulse, Ph.D. in 1992. Five children: Craig, Kris, Deb, Kurt, and Jenny. Ms. Wilson–Imhulse enjoys golf, geneaology, music, volunteer work, boating, travel, and art.

Patricia P. Woodruff, Ed.D.

Administrator
Collier County Public Schools, Vineyards Elementary School
6225 Arbor Boulevard West
Naples, FL 33999
(941) 455–3600
Fax: (941) 455–7143

8211

Business Information: Collier County Public Schools is the municipal governmental office responsible for the administration of all elementary and secondary education facilities and activities within its county jurisdiction. An affiliate of Collier County Public Schools, Vineyards Elementary School is charged with the mission to provide an educational environment for 1,100 students, pre–kindergarten through fifth grade. Established in 1990, Vineyards Elementary School currently employs 138 faculty and administrative support staff. As Administrator, Dr. Woodruff is responsible for all aspects of administration for Vineyards Elementary School, including personnel, finance and facility management. **Career Steps:** Administrator, Collier County Public Schools, Vineyards Elementary School (1990–Present); Principal, Sea Gate Elementary School (1982–1990); Director of Elementary Schools, Collier County Schools (1979–1982); Assistant Principal, East Naples Middle School (1977–1979). **Associations & Accomplishments:** National Association of Elementary School Principals; Florida Association of School Administrators; Collier Association of School Administrators; Phi Delta

Kappa; Board of Directors, YMCA; Elder, First Presbyterian Church. **Education:** University of Miami, Ed.D. (1982); State University of New york at Oswego: M.S. (1968), B.S. (1964). **Personal:** Two children: Mark Ashley and Eric Jonah. Dr. Woodruff enjoys golf, traveling and scuba diving.

Karen Victoria Dahlberg Wynn, Ph.D.

Director
Tucson Unified School District
1010 East 10th Street
Tucson, AZ 85719
(520) 617–7365
Fax: Please mail or call

8211

Business Information: Tucson Unified School District is an educational institution, with a large Native American population, which teaches alternate studies. As Director, Dr. Wynn is responsible for managing daily operations and programs for 2,400 Native American students and providing academic support. **Career Steps:** Tucson Unified School District: Director (1994–Present), Resource Teacher (1993–1994), Classroom Teacher (1987–1993); Director of Consulting Firm, AIEC. **Associations & Accomplishments:** NAEYC; NIEA; NEA; TEA; OCR Committee; United Way Allocation Comm.; Board of Directors, Ed. Enrichment Foundation; Tlanatinime Award for Challenging Minority Students to Fulfill Their Potential; Leadership Academy; Literacy Award from IRA; Superintendent's Honor Roll Award. **Education:** University of Arizona, Ph.D. (1995), M.Ed., B.A. **Personal:** Married to Paul in 1969. Four children: Dyann, Wesley, Michael, and Joshua. Dr. Wynn enjoys softball.

Audrea Isaac Anderson

Director of Institutional Advancement
Edison Community College
8099 College Parkway
Ft. Myers, FL 33919–5566
(941) 489–9492
Fax: (941) 433–8035

8220

Business Information: Edison Community College is a state–supported, coed school founded in 1962 that awards associate transfer and terminal degrees. The school has an enrollment of 9,800 students. As Director of Institutional Advancement, Ms. Anderson directs the internal and external relations of the College. She handles public relations, newsletter releases, and deals with the media. Ms. Anderson was recently appointed by the Governor to the Florida Board of Regents. **Career Steps:** Edison Community College: Director of Institutional Advancement (1995–Present), Director of Learning Assistance and English Professor (1980–1995), and English Professor (1976–1980). **Associations & Accomplishments:** Florida Board of Regents; State Electrical Contractors Licensing Board; Dunbar Improvement Association; Public School Enrichment Program Board; Lee County Library Board; Florida A & M University Foundation Board; Southern Association of Colleges & Schools; Family Health Centers Capital Improvement Board. **Education:** Miami University at Oxford, MA (1970); Allen University, BA (1968). **Personal:** Married to Judge Isaac Anderson in 1969. Three children: Isaac, Christopher, and Justin. Ms. Anderson enjoys reading and collecting antiques.

Harold E. Nolte, Jr., Ed.D.

Vice President for Student Services
Edison Community College
8099 College Parkway
Ft. Myers, FL 33919
(941) 489–9221
Fax: (941) 489–9084

8220

Business Information: Edison Community College is a coed facility, established in 1962, awarding associate transfer and terminal degrees. As Vice President for Student Services, Dr. Nolte serves as Chief Administrator for admissions, records, advising, counseling, student development and activities, and student support services. Concurrently, he is also responsible for articulation, enrollment management and athletics. **Career Steps:** Vice President for Student Services, Edison Community College (1991–Present); Navarro College, Corsicano, TX: Vice President for Student Services (1987–91), Dean of Student Services (1986–87), Assistant Dean of Student Services (1985–86); Panhellenic Advisor, Mississippi State University (1982–85); Director of Student Activities, South Plain College (1980–82). **Associations & Accomplishments:** Administrative support and financial accountability, Student Life Program; Leadership in setting challenging goals and objectives within Student Services; Facilitate the process which includes services to minority, disabled, disadvantaged, and special populations students; Coalition for a Drug–Free Lee County; Council of Student Affairs. **Education:** Mississippi State University, Ed.D. (1985); Baylor University: M.S. in Counseling (1980), B.S. in Sociology (1978); McLennan Community College, A.A. (1976). **Personal:** Dr. Nolte enjoys water sports, rollerblading, golf, tennis, and providing leadership in facilitating an open climate for communication.

Masood Ahmad, M.D.

Professor of Medicine
University of Texas Medical Branch – Galveston
301 University Boulevard
Galveston, TX 77555–0533
(409) 772–1533
Fax: (409) 772–4982

8221

Business Information: University of Texas Medical Branch at Galveston is a public, upper division, coed, specialized university with graduate programs. Department of Medicine at University of Texas Medical Branch at Galveston currently employs 105 full–time and 13 part–time faculty. As Professor of Medicine in the Department of Internal Medicine, Dr. Ahmad is responsible for teaching, research and patient care. Concurrent with his present academic position, he serves as Director of the Echocardiography Laboratory, as well as being affiliated with John Sealy Hospital. Most of his research is in echocardiography (ultrasound) – scanning of the heart for heart disease. **Career Steps:** University of Texas Medical Branch at Galveston: Professor of Medicine, Department of Medicine (1990–Present), Director of Echocardiography Laboratory (1981–Present); Chief of Cardiology, V.A. Hospital, Columbia, Missouri (1978–1981). **Associations & Accomplishments:** Fellow, American College of Physicians; Fellow, American College of Cardiology; Fellow, Clinic Council, American Heart Association; Senior Member, American Federation of Clinical Research; Fellow, Royal College of Physicians and Surgeons of Canada. **Education:** Kashmir University Medical School, M.B.B.S. (1967); F.R.C.P.C.; Diplomate American Board of Internal Medicine and Cardiovascular Disease. **Personal:** Married to Gulshan Ara. One child: Yembur Ahmad. Dr. Ahmad enjoys spending time with his daughter.

Brad Albers, Ph.D.

Director of Institutional Technology
Ringling School of Art and Design
2700 North Tamiami Trail
Sarasota, FL 34234
(941) 359–7625
Fax: (941) 359–7517
EMAIL: See Below

8221

Business Information: Ringling School of Art and Design is a private, four–year, coed, specialized college. Established in 1931 on a 30–acre campus in Sarasota, the College currently employs 73 full–time and 8 part–time faculty members. Majors with the largest enrollment are graphic design, illustration, and interior design. As Director of Institutional Technology, Dr. Albers is responsible for technology related contract negotiation, budget management, strategic planning, and recapitalization. He heads special projects management. In addition, Dr. Albers is reponsible for the operation, support and integration of administrative and academic technologies and related environments, including engineering staff management. He is the project manager for the Disney, GTE ANSI – ATM pipeline between Sarasota and Orlando, and designs and implements facilities. Internet users can reach him via: balbers@rsad.edu **Career Steps:** Director of Institutional Technology, Ringling School of Art and Design (1994–Present); Associate Director of Graduate Conservatory of Motion Picture, Television and Recording Arts, Florida State University (1989–1994); Director of Systems Complex, University of South Florida (1978–1989). **Associations & Accomplishments:** Association of Computing Machinery; SIGGRAPH; Society of Motion Picture and Television Engineers; Institute of Electronics and Electrical Engineers; BMI; Board of Directors, Pine View School for the Gifted; Who's Who in MIS Management; International Who's Who; International Biography of Contemporary Achievement; Who's Who in American Music; International Who's Who in Music; Who's Who in the South and Southwest, Marquis Who's Who; Musical Compositions Published by ACA: "Exegeses" for B–flat Clarinet and computer–generated tape; "Martial Cadenza" for male Voice, Bassoon and Percussion and computer–generated tape; "Aggregate" for Symphonic Band; "Shards" for flute, alto flute and computer–generated tape (pending final inking of score); "Nexus" for oboe and computer–generated tape (pending final inking of score). **Education:** University of Illinois: Ph.D. (1978), M.M. (1976); Sam Houston State University, B.M. summa cum laude with honors in Music History (1975); Read and Write in German. **Personal:** Dr. Albers enjoys lapidary arts and painting.

Terrence A. Alexis

Human Resource Director
University of California – San Diego
8950 La Jolla Village Drive, Suite 2222C
La Jolla, CA 92093
(619) 622–5717
Fax: (619) 546–9328
Email: See Below

8221

Business Information: University of California – San Diego is one of the largest and most acclaimed institutions of higher education dedicated to excellence in teaching, research, and public service, and with 17,000 employees UCSD is the second largest employer in the San Diego area. As Human Resource Director Mr. Alexis is responsible for providing overall management and direction for the Human Resources Division, developing and implementing strategic planning objectives, overall support for departmental planning and organizational development, creating human resource–related programs to include career development, professional assessment and training, advising management on progressive disciplinary procedures in compliance with policy, mediating disputes, representing the department, developing financial goals, forecasting expenditures, and authorizing the budget. Additionally, he is the Affirmative Action Officer advocating, educating, and directing activities of all department staff. Internet users can reach him via: talexis@ucsd.edu. **Career Steps:** Human Resource Director, University of California – San Diego (1995–Present); Personnel Manager, UCSD School of Medicine – Neurosciences (1995); Administrative Assistant to the Unit Head, UCSD Academic Personnel (1990–1991); Administrative Assistant, UCSD Human Resources (1989–1990). **Associations & Accomplishments:** American Management Association; Society for Human Resource Management; San Diego Urban League; Chancellor's Affirmative Action Advisory Committee (1996); Staff Affirmative Action Training Program Committee (1996); Chair, ESPP Incentive Award Committee (1996); Sustaining Excellence Award (1995); Staff Employee of the Year – Nominee (1995); Staff Education Internship Program Award (1994); Environmental Health & Safety Award (1994); Summer Youth Employment Program (1993 & 1994); Virgin Islands Territorial Scholarship (1982); Student of the Year (1982). **Education:** University of California – San Diego, B.A. – Revelle College (1989). **Personal:** Married to Cherette M. in 1993. One child: Tyler Nicholas. Mr. Alexis enjoys reading and travel.

Ilona H. Anderson, Ed.D.

Acting Dean for Faculty Relations
The City College
Convent Avenue at 138th Street
New York, NY 10031
(212) 650–7444
Fax: (212) 650–8277
EMAIL: See Below

8221

Business Information: City College (CUNY) is a public, four–year college with graduate programs. Majors with the largest enrollment include Electrical Engineering, Architecture, and Nursing. Preprofessional programs are in Law and Medicine. As Acting Dean for Faculty Relations, Dr. Anderson provides oversight to ensure compliance within regulated guidelines set forth by its own Governance Charter, the Bylaws of the Board of Trustees of the The CUNY, the collective bargaining agreements and the Ethics Commission of the State of New York. She serves as the President's Designee for labor relations, acting as Hearing Officer at Step I grievances and representing the College at Step II hearings, and assisting legal counsel with arbitrations and outside grievances. She also serves as the College's Legal Affairs Designee, Records Access Officer and Ethics Officer. Internet users can reach her via: ihacc@cunyvm.cuny.edu. **Career Steps:** City College (CUNY): Acting Dean for Faculty Relations (1993–Present), Associate Dean for Special Programs and SEEK Director (1988–1993), Tenured Full Professor (1990–Present), Affirmative Action Director (1980–1983); Chairperson, Department of Special Programs; Chairperson, Middle States Self–Study Team; Project Coordinator, Resource Center for Science and Engineering; Coordinator, College Skills Laboratory; Bronx Community College (CUNY): Adjunct Lecturer, Department of Special Education Services; Westchester Community College (SUNY); Adjunct Lecturer, College Adapter Program; Harvard University, Instructor, MA–5 Training Program; New York Police Academy, Basic Education Instructor, Manpower Act–Teacher Training Program. **Associations & Accomplishments:** New York Coalition of 100 Black Women: Board of Directors (1990–1994, 1996–Present), Political Action Committee (1988–Present); Advisory Board, National Association for the Advancement of Colored People; ACT–SO (1996–Present); Manhattan Branch of New York Urban League (1983–1993); Delta Sigma Theta Sorority, Inc.: Golden Life Member, Westchester Alumni Chapter. **Education:** Teachers College – Columbia University: Ed.D. (1979), Ed.M. in Communications (1976); Harvard University, M.A.T. Teacher of Reading; New York University, B.S. in English (1968). **Personal:** Married to R. John in 1991.

Three children: Damien J., Nyree D., and Rahmah–Ann. Dr. Anderson enjoys reading, travel, tennis, and computers.

S. Eric Anderson, Ph.D.

• • • ◆━━◉━━◆ • • •

Assistant Professor
Loma Linda University
26234 Windsor Drive
Loma Linda, CA 92354–4142
(909) 824–4573
Fax: (909) 824–4087

8221

Business Information: As Assistant Professor of Health Administration, Dr. Anderson instructs courses in Health Systems Operations, Strategic Planning, Internal Environment, Research, Investment and Portfolio Issues, and Health Care Organizational Behavior. Concurrent with his academic duties, he serves as Financial Officer and Associate Director in the Center for Health Promotion at the University. Career milestones include the establishment of numerous development programs and scholarships, such as the S. Eric Anderson Scholarship in 1992 and the S. Eric Anderson Community Development Program (1994) at Southwestern Adventist College, Adventist College Community Development Program (1995), Southwestern Union Academy Community Development Program (1995), S. Eric Anderson School of Public Health Scholarship at Loma Linda University (1995), and the Chisolm Trail Academy Community Development Program (1995). **Career Steps:** Assistant Professor of Health Administration and Associate Director of Health Promotion, Loma Linda University (1992–Present); Part–time Instructor, Southwestern Adventist College (1991–1992); Grocery Supervisor and Assistant Manager, La Loma Foods (1981–1990). **Associations & Accomplishments:** American Public Health Association; Business and Health Administration Association (1995); Committee of 100, Southwestern Adventist College (1995); Far West Popular and American Culture Association (1995); Society Human Resources and Industrial Relations (1994); Management Society (1994); Tarleton State University Century Club (1995); Best Paper Award – Business and Health Administration Association Conference (1995); Several athletic organizations and awards; Outstanding Young Men of America (1989); Sandefur Business Scholarship (1987, 1988); Business Certificate of Merit (1988, 1989); Who's Who in American Colleges and Universities (1988, 1989); Numerous research publications for peer review and non–peer review, such as: An Evaluation on the Effectiveness of Injury Prevention Programs (1995), A Critical Examination of a Newly Implemented Performance Evaluation System in a Health Service Organization (1995), Comparative Advertising: The Use of Market–Share Differential to Determine a Brand's Usage of Comparative Advertising (1995), Characteristics Associated with Retention in Health Care Organizations, Regional Economic Activity and Its Impact on the Music Industry (1995), Why Males Are More Romantic Than Females (1995), and an article: When Will Health Plans Start Taking Prevention Seriously? (1995); School of Public Health committees: Admissions Committee (1992–Present), Administration Departmental Committee (1992–Present), Marketing Committee (Chair) (1994–Present), Computer Director Search Committee (1995), CEPH Reaccreditation Governance Task Force Committee (1995), CEPH Reaccreditation Facility Development Task Force Committee (1995), Office of Extended Program Site Committee (1995); Loma Linda University and Medical Center: numerous committees, including Center for Health Research Operating Committee (1995), Center for Health Promotion Executive Committee (1992–Present); Numerous consultations, technical presentations, non–technical presentations, and establishment of numerous development programs. **Education:** University of North Texas, Ph.D. (1992); Tarleton State University, M.B.A.; Southwestern Adventist College, B.B.A. **Personal:** Dr. Anderson enjoys travel, reading, and athletics.

Richard M. Artz

Brigadier General
Valley Forge Military Academy & College
2335 Turnberry Drive
Oviedo, FL 32765
(407) 359–7276
Fax: Please mail or call

8221

Business Information: Richard M. Artz was promoted from Colonel to Brigadier General of Valley Forge Military Academy & College on May 17, 1993. Colonel Artz has spent much of his life at the Academy, first as a cadet and then as a record–breaking career officer. His connection with Valley Forge has been a great association, meeting and speaking with Gen. Dwight D. Eisenhower, Richard Nixon, Ronald Reagan, George Bush, and fellow Academy graduate Gen. H. Norman Schwarzkopf. Mr. Artz graduated from the Academy in 1946, going on to Ohio University where he earned his Bachelor's degree in Commerce. THe Colonel served in the U.S. Army as a Forward and Aerial Observer with the 29th Infantry Regi-

ment, Ryukus Command on Okinawa from 1950 unit 1952. In 1953, he returned to Valley Forge as a Tactical Officer, responsible for the residential life and military training of cadets. He was also Deputy Commandant of Cadets, Director of Summer Camps, and Admissions Director in addition to serving on the Academy's Executive Policy Board. He is proud of his cadets, many of them doctors, lawyers, and businessmen. Upon Mr. Artz's retirement and promotion to Brigadier General, the Academy celebrated the occasion with a parade. He now lives with his wife, Barbara, in Oviedo, Florida, where he has recently been appointed to the Board of Directors of the University Club of Winter Park, Florida, using his Academy experience to aid membership and development. He has also become a member of the English Speaking Union of Winter Park. **Career Steps:** Valley Forge Military Academy & College: Brigadior General (1996–Present), Director of Admissions (1990–1993), Registrar (1968–1990), Deputy Commandant (1960–1963), Adjutant, Tactical Officer (1953–1960); Director of Summer Camps (1959–1963), Commandant of Summer Camps (1953–1959); Director, Lost Trail Camps – Montana (1964–1968); Active Duty – Infantry Leader's Course, U.S. Army (1950). **Associations & Accomplishments:** Rotary International: Marion, Ohio, and Wayne, Pennsylvania; Masonic Lodge #70 – Marion, Ohio; Presbyterian Church; Pennsylvania Guard; Former Chairman, Troop 23 BSA (1972–1984); Director, University Club of Winter Park, Florida; American Legion; English Speaking Union; Consultant, Development and Enrollment Management – Schools. Camps (1993–Present). **Education:** Ohio University, B.S. in Commerce (1953); Valley Forge Military Academy & College, A.A.; Attended Ohio Northern University. **Personal:** Married to Barbara Louise in 1955. Two children: Scott Mattox and Richard Craig.

Darryl C. Aubrey, Sc.D.

Chairman of the Management Faculty
Sacred Heart University
5151 Park Avenue
Fairfield, CT 06432–1000
(203) 371–7855
Fax: (203) 834–2996

8221

Business Information: Sacred Heart University, affiliated with the Roman Catholic Church, is a private, four–year, coed, liberal arts university with graduate programs. Majors with the largest enrollment include Business Administration, Accounting, and Psychology. Preprofessional programs are in Law, Medicine, Veterinary Science, Pharmacy, Dentistry, Theology, and Optometry. Established in 1963 on a 53–acre campus in Fairfield, the University currently employs 500 faculty. As Chairman of the Management Faculty, Dr. Aubrey oversees all faculty associates and the related recruitment and hiring of faculty for the Department of Management (offering Business Administration and International Business undergraduate and MBA degrees of seven concentrations). Overseeing all administrative operations of a faculty of 16, he is additionally responsible for curriculum and programs. He also teaches one management course per semester, as well as providing consultation in Chemistry Business in his spare time. **Career Steps:** Chairman of the Management Faculty, Sacred Heart University (1986–Present); Exxon Chemical: Director of Purchasing (1979–1986), Product Executive (1977–1979), Plant Manager (1974–1977). **Associations & Accomplishments:** American Association of University Professors; American Institute of Chemical Engineers; The Racemics. **Education:** University of New Haven, Sc.D. (1993); Adelphi University, M.B.A. (1980); Georgia Tech, B.S. in Chemical Engineering (1955). **Personal:** Married to Dr. Joan Vogt Aubrey in 1957. Three children: Debra, Morton, and David.

Mr. James C. Auckland

Director of Facilities Management
James Madison University
Wellington Hall, 967 South Main Street
Harrisonburg, VA 22807
(540) 568–6181
Fax: (540) 568–3547

8221

Business Information: James Madison University is a comprehensive, private, four–year, co–ed, liberal arts university with graduate programs. Established in 1908, the University has 12,500 students and a 472–acre campus located in Harrisonburg, 120 miles from Washington, D.C. and Richmond, Virginia. In his capacity as Director of Facilities Management, Mr. Auckland is responsible for directing daily maintenance activities, and overseeing building and renovation projects for 130 buildings (3 million square feet) and the University power plant. **Career Steps:** Director of Facilities Management, James Madison University (1992–Present); Chief Engineer, James Madison University (1979–1992); Project Engineer, Riddleberger Brothers, Inc. (1978–1979); General Engineer, Newport News Shipbuilding (1974–1978); Nuclear Engineer, Norfolk Naval Shipyard (1970–1974). **Associations & Accomplishments:** Association of Physical Plant Administrators; American Institute of Plant Engineers; Association of Energy Engineers; American Society of Heating, Refrigeration, and Air Conditioning Engineers; Advisor and Charter Mem-

ber, James Madison University Jaycees. **Education:** Clarkson University, B.S. in Mechanical Engineering (1970).

Dwight L. Ausbrooks

• • • ◆━━◉━━◆ • • •

Assistant Coordinator
Virginia Polytechnic Institute and State University
400 Green Street, Apartment 25B
Blacksburg, VA 24060
(703) 231–9094
Fax: Please mail or call

8221

Business Information: Virginia Polytechnic Institute and State University is a private, four–year, coed, specialized institute. As Assistant Coordinator, Mr. Ausbrooks is responsible for monitoring and advising athletes on academic matters, interacting with professors, and coaches. He also recruits and monitors tutors, institutes study hall programs, and advises student–athletes regarding NCAA, University, and Department policies and regulations. **Career Steps:** Assistant Coordinator, Virginia Polytechnic Institute and State University (1994–Present); Executive Director, Indianapolis Challenge (1992–1994); Regional Coordinating Officer, Governor's Commission for a Drug–Free Indiana (1992); Prevention/Intervention Coordinator, Office of Substance Abuse Prevention Education (1991–1992); Program Coordinator, Youth Leadership Institute (1988–1991). **Associations & Accomplishments:** Coordinator, Best of Friends; Coordinator, Virginia Tech Peer Educators, Athletics (1994–); Founder/Chair of the Local Coordinator's Network of Indiana (1992–1994); Black Coaches Association (1988–); Marion County Traffic Safety Partnership (1994); Certified Speaker for National Collegiate Athletic Association (1993). **Education:** Virginia Polytechnic Institute and State University, Candidate for Ph.D., M.S. in Community Health (1992), B.S. in Community Health Education (1986).

Denise Ann Baca

Director of Education
Fashion Institute of Design and Merchandising
1010 2nd Avenue
San Diego, CA 92101–4912
(619) 235–4515
Fax: (619) 232–4322

8221

Business Information: Fashion Institute of Design and Merchandising is a two–year, private college awarding Associate of Arts Degrees with a specialized major in the fashion or interior design industry. The College has four branch campus sites located throughout California. An administrative director, as well as instructor with the Fashion Institute of Design and Merchandising since 1990, Ms. Baca was appointed as Director of Education in 1993. She is responsible for the direction of all aspects of the Education Department, including departmental faculty recruitment and supervision, acting as the San Diego campus Registrar, academic counseling, and organization of any duties related to the Education Department. **Career Steps:** Fashion Institute of Design and Merchandising: Director of Education (1993–Present), Education Coordinator (1991–1993); Placement Advisor (1990–1991); Student Manager, UCSD Science & Engineering Library (1988–1990). **Associations & Accomplishments:** San Diego High School Advisory Board; Member, Roller Hockey League. **Education:** University of California – San Diego, B.A. in Sociology (1989). **Personal:** Ms. Baca enjoys roller hockey, yoga, biking, and tennis.

William K. Back, J.D.

Director of Planned Giving
Ohio Northern University
525 S. Main Street
Ada, OH 45810–1555
(419) 772–2008
Fax: (419) 772–1932
EMAIL: See Below

8221

Business Information: Ohio Northern University, a private institution affiliated with the United Methodist Church, enrolls more than 2,900 students in the Colleges of Arts and Sciences, Business Administration, Engineering, Pharmacy, and Law. The University, which is recognized as a premier institution in the midwest and the country, offers the intimacy of a small university and the breadth and depth of five colleges. As Director of Planned Giving, Mr. Back introduces prospective donors to methods of making appropriate significant contributions through deferred giving; focusing on protecting the donor's assets, increasing their income and reducing tax liability. Dr. Back provides instruction and guidance to donors throughout the entire deferred giving process. Additionally, he conducts seminars to educate professionals in selecting and using appropriate Planned Giving vehicles, including wills, trusts, and estate planning techniques, for assisting their clients in achieving their financial goals. Internet users can reach him via: w–back@onu.edu. **Career Steps:** Director of Planned Giving, Ohio Northern University (1994–Present); Commissioned Officer, Department of Defense, United States Army (1979–1994). **Associations & Accomplishments:** American Bar Association; National Committee on Planned Giving; Trustee of Local United Way; Corporate Trustee, Lima Memorial Hospital; Kiwanis International; Grand Lodge of Free and Accepted Masons of Ohio; 32nd degree Scottish Rite Mason, Southern Jursidiction; Chapter, Council, Commandery, York Rite Mason, Heidelberg, Germany; Odenwald Chapter #12, Order of Eastern Star, Mainz, Germany; Member, Antioch Shrine Temple, Dayton, Ohio; Veterans of Foreign Wars; Honorable Order of Kentucky Colonels; Aircraft and Pilots Association; National Quarter Horse Association. **Education:** Ohio Northern University College of Law, Juris Doctor (1994); Eastern Kentucky University, Masters Degree Study; University of Dayton, B.S. **Personal:** Married to Debra in 1990. Two children: Christina Joy and Sarah Madison. Mr. Back enjoys military history, flying, and horseback riding.

Amanda Sirmon Baker, Ph.D.
Dean – College of Nursing
University of South Alabama – College of Nursing
Springhill Campus
Mobile, AL 36688
(334) 434–3415
Fax: (334) 434–3413

8221

Business Information: University of South Alabama – College of Nursing is an educational institution preparing professional nurses at the baccalaureate or master's levels. The College of Nursing has a current enrollment of 1,200 students. With twenty–two years of experience as a Dean of Nursing and a Registered Nurse since 1955, Dr. Baker joined the University of Southern Alabama – College of Nursing as Dean and Chief Executive Officer in 1989. She is responsible for all aspects of operations for the College and nursing activities, as well as reporting all academic activities to the Senior Vice President of Academic Affairs. **Career Steps:** Dean, University of South Alabama – College of Nursing (1989–Present); Dean, Troy State University School of Nursing (1985–1989); University of Florida College of Nursing: Associate Dean (1980–1985), Acting Dean (1978–1980). **Associations & Accomplishments:** American Nurses Association; Alabama State Nurses Association; American Association of Colleges of Nursing; Sigma Theta Tau International Honor Society of Nursing; Phi Kappa Phi, Honorary. **Education:** University of Florida: Ph.D. (1974), Masters in Nursing; University of Alabama, B.S. in Nursing; Bryn Mawr College, Certificate, Summer Seminar (1983). **Personal:** Married to Malcolm D. in 1957. Two children: Leonard Eric and Michael Davis Baker. Dr. Baker enjoys physical fitness, sewing, and reading.

Eliseo R. Baraan
Vice President of Business & Finance
Napa College
2277 Napa Vallejo Highway
Napa, CA 94558–6236
(707) 253–3311
Fax: (707) 259–8010
Email: See Below

8221

Business Information: Napa College, established in 1942, is a community college offering a variety of public educational courses, leading to a transferrable Associate of Arts degree. The College also offers vocational, non–credit, and continuing education courses, as well as several community service classes, i.e. sports, dance, etc. As Vice President of Business & Finance, Mr. Baraan is responsible for administrative duties such as payroll, budgeting, accounting, auditing, supervising the bookstore, and food service. Last year's audit of the College's finances reflected "Perfect – No Recommendations," which is an increasingly rare occurence. Internet users can reach him via: ebaraan@admin.nvc.cc.ca.us. **Career Steps:** Napa College: Vice President of Business & Finance (1992–Present), Director of Fiscal Services (1988–1992), Controller (1986–1988). **Associations & Accomplishments:** Association of Chief Business Officials – California Community Colleges; Vallejo FILAM Lions Club; National Association of Auxiliary Services. **Education:** University of the East, B.B.A. in Accounting (1961). **Personal:** Married to the former Erlinda Basconcillo in 1970. Three children: Edmund Ray, Eloise Anne, and Emily Jane. Mr. Baraan enjoys bowling, movies, and golf.

Mohamed E. Bayou, Ph.D.
• • • ⬤ • • •

Assistant Professor
University of Michigan – Dearborn
4901 Evergreen Road
Dearborn, MI 48128–2406
(313) 593–9962
Fax: (313) 593–5636
EMAIL: See Below

8221

Business Information: The University of Michigan – Dearborn is a public, four–year, coed, liberal arts university with a graduate program. Established in 1959, UM–Dearborn consists of 203 full–time and 182 part–time faculty. Majors with the largest enrollment are psychology, mechanical engineering, and electrical engineering. Preprofessional programs are offered in law, medicine, and dentistry. As Assistant Professor, Dr. Bayou instructs and mentors graduate and undergraduate students, specializing in the studies of cost, international, and managerial accounting. Internet users can reach him via: mbayou@fob–fl.umd.umich.edu **Career Steps:** Assistant Professor of Accounting, University of Michigan at Dearborn (1990–Present); Assistant Professor of Accounting, University of Detroit (1987–1990); Assistant Professor of Accounting, Xavier University (1984–1987). **Associations & Accomplishments:** American Accounting Association: General Membership, Management Accounting Section, International Accounting Section, Behavioral Accounting Section; Institute of Management Accountants; Board Member, Institute of Management Accountants – Oakland County Chapter; Director of Education, Institute of Management Accountants – Michigan Council. **Education:** University of Cincinnati: Ph.D. (1983), M.B.A. in Accounting and Finance; University of Wisconsin–Madison, M.S. in Accounting; University of Libya, B.A. in Accounting. **Personal:** One child: Hana. Dr. Bayou enjoys reading and travel.

Jann–Douglass Bell
Director of Multicultural Student Services
Bryant College
1150 Douglas Pike
Smithfield, RI 02917
(401) 232–6946
Fax: (401) 232–6362
EMAIL: See Below

8221

Business Information: Bryant College is a private, four–year, coed, specialized college with graduate programs. Established in 1863, the College is located on a 287–acre campus in Smithfield, 12 miles from Providence. Majors include: Accounting, Applied Actuarial Mathematics, Business Communications, Computer Information Systems, Economics, English, Finance, History, International Studies, Management, and Marketing. As Director of Multicultural Student Services, Ms. Bell concentrates on minority and international student services. Internet users can reach her at JBell@ACAD.Bryant.EDU. **Career Steps:** Director of Multicultural Student Services, Bryant College (1992–Present); President/Chief Executive Officer, JDB Associates, Inc. (Present); Assistant Professor, Johnson & Wales University (1986–1994); Assistant Director, Cornell University Council (1984–1986). **Associations & Accomplishments:** Urban League of Rhode Island; American Association of University Women; N.A.F.S.A. **Education:** Rhode Island College, M.A. (1980); Boston University, A.B.; Cornell University, Certification. **Personal:** Two children: David Douglass and Andrea Victoria Lisbon.

Mr. Donald L. Belles
Assistant Professor & Department Head of HVAC Tech.
Pennsylvania College of Technology
One College Avenue
Williamsport, PA 17701
(717) 326–3761
Fax: (717) 327–4503

8221

Business Information: Pennsylvania College of Technology is Pennsylvania's premier technical college. An affiliate of Penn State, Penn College has a national reputation for the quality and diversity of instruction in traditional and advanced technologies and for its hands–on approach to learning. Baccalaureate, associate degree, and certificate programs range from business, computer, and industrial technologies to health sciences, construction, transportation, and natural resources management. Programs for transfer students are offered as well. New facilities opened since 1993 include a $6 million Aviation Center, $11 million Community Arts Center, and $12 million Campus Center. A new Diesel Center is scheduled to open in 1994. As Assistant Professor and Department Head of HVAC Technology, Mr. Belles instructs 2–4 year degree students in HVAC/R installation, service and design, as well as develops all curriculum courses for the Department. **Career Steps:** Assistant Professor & Department Head of HVAC Technology, Pennsylvania College of Technology (1983–Present); Service Manager, Dixon AC&R (1975–1983). **Associations & Accomplishments:** Refrigeration Service Engineers Society (RSES); Air Conditioning Contractors of America (ACCA); Association for Supervision and Curriculum Development (ASCD); Original Little League, Inc. **Education:** Penn College, A.A.S. (1985); Commercial Trade Institute, Certificate, HVAC/R; Attended many trade related schools. **Personal:** Married to Alice. One child: Justin. Mr. Belles enjoys model railroading.

Stephen G. Berry
Director – Print and Mail Operations
Columbia University
2950 Broadway Room 106
New York, NY 10027–7004
(212) 854–3233
Fax: (212) 665–3257
EMAIL: See Below

8221

Business Information: Columbia University is a private, four–year, coed liberal arts university. Established in 1754, the main campus is located in Manhattan, New York. Currently there are 478 faculty instructing undergraduate students. Major course studies with the largest enrollment include English, History and Political Science. Starting with Columbia University's Print Operations in 1979 as a manager, Stephen Berry has steadily worked his way up through management promotions to his current position as Director for Print and Mail Operations. His primary role is to provide the overall executive administration of support staff and operations involved in the timely production of internal, digital and traditional offset printing services to the campus community. Additionally, he oversees all campus mail processes and distribution. **Career Steps:** Columbia University: Associate Director (1987–1992), Assistant Director (1983–1987), Manager (1979–1983). **Associations & Accomplishments:** NCUMS; IPMA. **Education:** Columbia University: M. Philosophy (1976), M.A. (1974), B.A. (1973). **Personal:** Married to Mary in 1977. Mr. Berry enjoys photography, hiking and travel.

Charles L. Bertrand, Ph.D.
Vice Rector of Services
Concordia University
1455 De Maisonneuve Boulevard West
Montreal, Quebec H3G 1M8
(514) 848–4819
Fax: (514) 848–2821

8221

Business Information: Established in 1974, Concordia University is a public, four–year, coed, specialized university with graduate programs. The University has about 26,000 students and 1,800 faculty members. As Vice Rector of Services, Dr. Bertrand is responsible for diversified administrative activities, including the libraries, computing services, physical resources, student services, mail services, etc. Additionally, he teaches at least one class each year. **Career Steps:** Concordia University: Vice Rector of Services (1994–Present), Interim Rector and Vice Chancellor (1994–1995), Dean of Arts and Science (1985–1992). **Associations & Accomplishments:** American Historical Association; Canadian Historical Association; Montreal Amateur Athletic Association; Board of Directors, YMCA; Canadian Who's Who. **Education:** University of Wisconsin – Madison, Ph.D. (1969); University of Oregon, M.A.; Western Washington University, B.A. **Personal:** One child: Rachel. Dr. Bertrand enjoys golf, squash, and tennis.

Shobha K. Bhatia, Ph.D.
Professor/Researcher
Syracuse University
233 Hinds Hall
Syracuse, NY 13224
(315) 443–3352
Fax: (315) 443–1243
EMail: See Below

8221

Business Information: Syracuse University is a private, four–year, coed, liberal arts university located in urban Syracuse. Established in 1870, the University offers undergraduate and graduate programs. As Professor, Dr. Bhatia is responsible for teaching programs in the civil and environmental engineering fields. He also advises students, does consulting work, and is heavily involved in research for the governmental and science industries. Research studies include arenas of the geo–technical field, such as the use of polymer materials in civil engineering structures, the use and removal of contaminents, earthquake engineering dealing with dams and embankments. Internet users can reach him via: skbhatia@summon.syr.edu. **Career Steps:** Professor/Researcher, Syracuse University (1986–Present). **Associations & Accomplishments:** American Society of Civil Engineers; North

American Society of Geosynthetics; American Standard of Testing Materials. **Education:** University of British Columbia, Ph.D. (1981); University of Roorkee – India, Master of Engineering. **Personal:** Married to Dr. Tej K. in 1976. Two children: Kanika and Aukit. Dr. Bhatia enjoys reading, gardening, painting, and cooking.

LaVerne Bishop
Director of Hospital Admissions
University of Illinois Hospital
1740 West Taylor Street Room 1100
Chicago. IL 60612–7232
(312) 996–0333
Fax: (312) 996–0334

8221

Business Information: University of Illinois Hospital is a university healthcare facility providing diagnosis and treatment for patients. As Director of Hospital Admissions, Ms. Bishop is responsible for planning, directing, controlling, monitoring, and evaluating departmental activities to promote and ensure effective operation. She also obtains and verifies financial and personal data from persons being admitted. **Career Steps:** University of Illinois Hospital : Director of Hospital Admissions (1995–Present), Director of Material Management (1993–1995), Associate Director of Material Management (1988–1992), Accountant of Hospital Finance (1981–1987), Account Technician of Patient Accounts (1973–1991); Counselor for Thornton Township Youth Committee (1996–Present); Foster Parent (Bobby and Bennie) (1995–Present); Riverdale Park District Girl Club, Volunteer (1994–1995); **Associations & Accomplishments:** National Association for Female Executives; Chicago Black Women Association; American Association for Counselors; Illinois Foster Parent Association. **Education:** Currently attending Governor's State University; Chicago State University, B.A. in Accounting; Illinois State University; University of Illinois. **Personal:** Married to Ernest. Four children: Ricky, Tamara, Bobbie, and Bennie. Ms. Bishop enjoys working with youth in the community.

H. Scott Bjerke, M.D.
Associate Professor
University of Nevada School of Medicine
2040 Charleston Boulevard, Suite 601
Las Vegas, NV 89102
(702) 385–3775 Ext. 12
Fax: (702) 384–7506

8221

Business Information: University of Nevada School of Medicine is a state–affiliated, multi–specialty research and teaching facility providing graduate and post–graduate programs in medicine and health care to patients at a 325–bed hospital which has an ICU with 14 beds. As Associate Professor, Dr. Bjerke is responsible for providing education to paramedics and surgery students in trauma and critical care surgery, in addition to caring for trauma patients. Concurrently, he serves as Medical Director at both the Clark County Fire Department and the Trauma Intensive Care Unit. Internet users can reach him via: TraumaDoc@aol.com. **Career Steps:** Associate Professor, University of Nevada School of Medicine (1991–Present); Medical Director, Clark County Fire Department (1993–Present); Medical Director, Trauma Intensive Care Unit (1993–Present). **Associations & Accomplishments:** National Association of EMS Physicians; American College of Surgeons; American Association for the Surgery of Trauma; Association for Academic Surgery; Society of Critical Care Medicine; Association for Surgical Education; FEMA Physician at Oklahoma Bombing Site; Medical Director, UMC Paramedic Training Program; Recipient, Frank McDowell Excellence in Surgery Award (1983). **Education:** University of Hawaii, M.D. (1983); University of Michigan, B.S. with Honors (1979); New England Medical Center, General Surgery Residency (1983–1988); Cedars Sinai Medical Center, Critical Care Fellow (1990–1991). **Personal:** Married to Janet in 1995. Dr. Bjerke enjoys spending time with his wife and scuba diving.

Jerry C. Black Sr.
Director of Facilities Management
Duke University
200 Facilities Center, P.O. Box 90144
Durham, NC 27708
(919) 660–4252
Fax: (919) 684–6083
EMAIL: See Below

8221

Business Information: Duke University is a private, four–year, coed, liberal arts university, affiliated with the United Methodist Church. Established in 1838, Duke offers bachelors, masters and doctoral degrees. Majors with the highest enrollment include: political science, psychology, and history. As Director of the Facilities Management Department, Jerry Black is responsible for overseeing all construction, maintenance and repairs operations on the Duke campus. He is also in charge of budgetary disbursements, human resources, business accounting, and complete supervision for the high pressure steam/gas station and high voltage distribution substations. Internet users can reach him via: Jerry_Black@mail101.adm.duke.edu. **Career Steps:** Director – Facilities Management Department, Duke University (1994–Present); The University of Arizona–Tucson: Director – Facilities Management Division (1989–1994), Facilitator – College of Career Counseling, Dept. of Counseling & Guidance (1990–1991); Executive Director – Facilities Management Division, Virginia Commonwealth University (1987–1989); U.S. Marine Corps: Head – U.S. Marine Corps Facilities Branch, Washington, DC (1985–1987); Director – Base Maintenance Division, Quantico, VA (1980–1985); Adjunct Faculty positions: Virginia Community and Germanna Community Colleges (1983–1987), Arizona Community and Pima Community Colleges (1989–1994); Instructor, Department of the Navy Personnel Department – Sexual Harassment and Discrimination (1980–1983). **Associations & Accomplishments:** Association of Higher Education Facilities Officer; International Facilities Management Association; American Institute of Plant Engineers; MILITARY HONORS: Legion of Merit (2); Bronze Star with Combat "V" (2); Navy Commendation Medal (2); Combat Action Ribbon; Presidential Unit Citation; Navy Unit Commendation Medal with Bronze Star (2); Meritorious Unit Citation with Bronze Star (2); Good Conduct Medal with three stars; National Defense Service Medal with Bronze Star; Armed Forces Expeditionary Medal; Vietnamese Campaign Medal with five stars; Sea Service Deployment Award; Vietnamese Presidential Unit Citation with palm and bar; Cross of Gallantry with gold star; Vietnamese Honor Medal (1st Class); Vietnamese Technical Service Medal (1st Class); Vietnamese Civic–Action Medal with palm and bar; Vietnam Service Medal.; PUBLICATIONS: U.S. Army War College Professional Writing Publication (1984), U.S. Marine Corps Command & Staff Publication on Landmine Warfare Countermeasures; Frequent presenter at APPA convention and symposia proceedings. **Education:** Central Michigan University, M.A. in Management and Supervision (1980); Radford College, B.S. in Business Management (1978); University of Arizona–Tucson, Post–graduate studies (1994); MILITARY TRAINING: U.S. Marine Corps — Command and Staff College, Amphibious Warfare School, Utilities Engineer Course, Combat Engineer Course, Refrigeration Course; U.S. Army — U.S. Army War College, Facilities Engineer Course; U.S. Navy Public Works Course. **Personal:** Married to Jo Ann in 1963. Two children: Jerry Jr. and James. Mr. Black enjoys golf, volleyball, boxing, basketball and is a volunteer for church.

Dr. David P. Bodycombe
Director of Research and Information Management
American College of Cardiologists
9111 Old Geogetown Road
Bethesda, MD 20814–1616
(301) 897–5400
Fax: (301) 897–9745

8221

Business Information: American College of Cardiologists, located on the NIH campus, in Bethesda, Maryland, and established in 1949, is the worldwide educational association for approximately 23,000 members. As Director of Research and Information Management, Dr. Bodycombe, manages the operations of the college's clinical databases, supervises survey research, and evaluates activities while providing methodologic support for practice guidelines. Internet users can reach him via: dbodycom@acc.org. **Career Steps:** Director of Research / Information Management, American College of Cardiologists (1993–Present); Principal, Birch and Davis Associates, Inc. (1986–1993); Executive Vice President, La Jollo Management Corporation (1978–1985); Research Associate, Information Sciences Research Institute (1977–1978). **Associations & Accomplishments:** American Statistical Association; American Public Health Association; Association for Health Services Research; American Medical Informatics Association; American Society of Association Executives; International Society of Technology; Assessment in Health Care; Delta Omega Public Health Honorary Society. **Education:** Johns Hopkins University: Science Doctorate (1993), B.A. (1971); Georgetown University, M.Sc. (1977). **Personal:** Dr. Bodycombe enjoys singing is a semi–professional Choral Society. During May 1996, he sang the lead in a Society performance of Annie Get Your Gun for the NIH, and plans to be on tour with the Society in England for 10 days in July 1996..

William G. Boggess, Ph.D.
Professor and Department Head
Oregon State University – Department of Agriculture & Resource Economics
213 Ballard Extension Hall
Corvallis, OR 97331
(541) 737–1395
Fax: (541) 737–1441
EMail: See Below

8221

Business Information: Oregon State University is a public, four–year, coed, land grant University. Established in 1868, the University is located on a 422–acre campus in Willamette Valley. Majors with the largest enrollment are Business Administration, Elementary Education, and Speech Communications. Preprofessional programs are offered in Medicine, Veterinary Science, Dentistry, Optometry, and Agriculture. The Agriculture and Resource Economics department has 150 undergraduate and 40 graduate majors. The undergraduate offers two degrees, one in Agricultural Business Management and the other in Agricultural and Resource Economics. The graduate offers a Masters or a Ph.D. with two options, Natural Resource and Environmental Economics and Markets and International Trade focused on the Pacific Rim. As Professor and Department Head, Dr. Boggess handles all administrative duties, including personnel, annual reviews, coordinating, hiring new faculty, graduate and undergraduate programs, curriculum review, thesis and dissertation research and review, budgeting, and grants and funds. He oversees 25 faculty members and 190 students. Dr. Boggess also teaches a sophomore level course in Introduction to Natural Resources and Environmental Economics once a year. Internet users can reach him via: boggessb@ccmail.orst.edu. **Career Steps:** Professor and Department Head, Oregon State University – Department of Agriculture & Resource Economics (1995–Present); Professor, University of Florida (1979–1995). **Associations & Accomplishments:** American Agricultural Economics Association; Southern Agricultural Economics Association; Western Agricultural Economics Association; Presbyterian Church; Phi Kappa Phi; Gamma Sigma Delta. **Education:** Iowa State University: Ph.D. (1979), B.S. **Personal:** Married to Carolyn in 1989. Three children: Anthony, Matthew, and Michael. Dr. Boggess enjoys mountain biking, backpacking, and hiking.